1990, 1991, 1992, 1993, 1994, 1995, 1996, 1997, 1998, 1999, 2000, 2001, 2002, 2003, 2004, 2005, , 2010, 2011, 2012, 2013, 2014, 2015 by

anies

788-0489

a

alog Card Number 96-656029

/edited by James M. Wiggins, Ph.D.

ndex.

es.  2. Celebrities - United States - Directories.  3. Social registers.  4. United States - Social

933-  .  II. Title: VIP Address Book. CT120.V15

i 96-656029 (ISBN 1043-0261)

ook Number 978-0-938731-60-3

ited States of America

Associated Media Co
PO Box 489
Gleneden Beach, OR
United States of Ame

Library of Congress

(ISSN 1043-0261)

The V.I.P. Address B

Biography: p. Includ

1. Celebrities - Direc
registers.

I. Wiggins, James M

1990i 920'.0025'73

International Standa

Manufactured in the

AD

# TABLE OF CONTENTS

# INTRODUCTION

The purpose of the **V.I.P. ADDRESS BOOK** is to provide readers with a means of reaching Very Important People — Celebrities, Government Officials, Business Leaders, Entertainers, Sports Stars, Scientists and Artists.

It is genuinely hoped that people will use this volume to write for information about an entrant's work or to express encouragement. Compliments and praise for one's efforts are always appreciated. Being at the top of one's chosen profession is no exception. And for those who are no longer active in a field, it is especially flattering to be contacted about one's past accomplishments.

## Methodology

The determination of candidates for inclusion in this reference work is an on-going process. Committees of prominent and knowledgeable people review those included in the nine major areas (listed in **bold** below).

**Public Service** includes World Leaders, Government Officials (both U.S. and International), Law Enforcement Officials and Members of the Legal and Judicial Fields.

**Adventure** includes Military Leaders (both U.S. and International), Astronauts and Cosmonauts, Heroes and Explorers.

**Business, Religion and Education** includes Financial and Labor Leaders as well as Businesspeople and Nobel Prize Winners in Economics and Peace.

**Life and Leisure** includes Fashion Design, Modeling, Beauty and Health Care and Social Activists.

**Communications** includes Columnists, Commentators, Editors and Publishers, along with Editorial and Comic Book Cartoonists.

**Fine Arts** includes Architects, Artists, Opera, Ballet and Dance Performers, Conductors, Concert Artists, Composers (both classical and popular), Writers, Photographers and Nobel Literature Laureates.

**Science** covers Nobel Prize winners in Chemistry, Medicine and Physics, Engineers, Inventors, Earth, Space and Computer Scientists, Psychologists and Psychiatrists, Medical and Research Scientists.

**Entertainment** includes stars of Radio, Stage, Screen and Television, Musicians, Cinematographers, Producers and Directors.

**Sports** includes all major spectator and participatory sports.

The committees define the parameters of the people included and prepare a list of additions and deletions to the candidate list. The research staff checks and updates information daily.

## Occupations and Titles

The category listed after an entrant's name is selected to best describe his/her most noteworthy accomplishment. No distinction is made as to whether the person still holds that position. It is felt that a person who made a name for herself or himself still retains that identity even if it was accomplished in the past.

## How Addresses Are Obtained

The editors of the **V.I.P. ADDRESS BOOK** have made every effort possible to insure that the addresses listed are accurate and current. Once it is determined a person is eligible for inclusion in the book, that person is contacted to determine which address he or she prefers. If a person prefers a home address, it is included. If a person prefers a business address or one in care of an agent or representative, that address is included. If a person specifically asks that their name not be included, his/her name is omitted. Once an address is listed, we continue efforts to verify that the address has not changed. These efforts include random sampling of the entire database and follow-up on all returned mailings received including those received from users of the book.

Users of the book should realize that people's addresses are in a state of constant change. The U.S. Bureau of Statistics says that almost 20 percent of people move each year. Not only do people change places of residence, they may also change business affiliations. Businesses move their headquarters as well as downsizing, merging or selling portions of their companies. Athletes get traded or retire. Entertainers change agents or personal managers and television shows get canceled. Politicians leave office or run for new positions. In addition, there are deaths almost daily which affect the address listings.

## National Change of Address Program

Our staff notes changes on a daily basis by watching television news shows and reading newspapers around the world. But we also take an extra step which few other directory or address book attempts. We match addresses of all U.S. listees with the U.S. Postal Service's National Change of Address program. The National Change of Address match is a process that compares mailing lists with more than 100 million address change cards filed by postal customers over the past three years. Address change information is provided for mailing list records that match with information from address change cards.

If a person/family/business moves, there are several factors which determine whether the National Change of Address program is effective. These include whether the mover filed an address change with the Postal Service, when the change was filed, whether the mover lived in an area covered by the automated address change systems (which includes more than 90 percent of the United States) and whether the name and address information in our files matches the information provided by the mover.

## Bad Addresses/Corrections

We keep track of not only current addresses but outdated ones as well. Our files list more than 250,000 people and we have up to 40 addresses for some of the people in the book. We continually update our data base and you can help. While we no longer provide address corrections, we do welcome information about bad addresses from users of the book.

## Envelope Markings

On your outgoing letters, you should always write "Address Correction Requested" beneath your return address in a clear and noticeable manner. If you do this, postal workers are supposed to send the forwarding address for a nominal fee.

## V.I.P. Address Book Update

Realizing the ever-changing aspect of addresses, we also publish the **V.I.P. ADDRESS BOOK UPDATE** which is available in late August for an additional fee. The UPDATE lists several thousand address changes and new addresses as well as informing users of the names of celebrities who pass away.

## Recommendations for the Book

If you are interested in people who are not listed in the book, send us a letter or email with their name, address and biographical information. If these people are deemed worthy for inclusion, they may be listed in a future edition.

Until people stop moving or changing jobs, there are going to be address changes. We want to provide the best service possible and we know we have the highest percentage of accuracy of any directory or address book.

If you have suggestions for improving accuracy beyond random follow-ups, following daily news events, checking on all bad address notifications and using the Postal Service's National Change of Address service, let us know your ideas.

## Forms of Address

An important part of writing to people - regardless of their positions - is to properly address envelopes and to use the correct salutations in the letters. Although the titles and positions of people listed in this directory are too numerous to cover, there are a number of people whose forms of address are worth noting. The table below is a guide to enhance the likelihood your letter will be received in a favorable light.

| POSITION | ENVELOPE/ADDRESS | SALUTATION |
|---|---|---|
| Presidents | The President of Countries | Dear Mr/Madam President - - - |
| Vice Presidents | The Vice President of Countries | Dear Mr/Madam Vice President - - - |
| Cabinet Officers | The Honorable John/Jane Doe Secretary of --- | Dear Mr/Madam Secretary of - - - |
| Senators | The Honorable John/Jane Doe US Senator from - - - | Dear Mr/Ms Senator - - - |
| Representatives | The Honorable John/Jane Doe US Representative from - - - | Dear Mr/Ms Representative - - - |
| Judges | The Honorable John/Jane Doe, Judge, US - - - Court | Dear Judge - - - |
| US Ambassadors | The Honorable John/Jane Doe US Ambassador to (Country) | Dear Mr/Ms Ambassador - - - |

# TABLE OF ABBREVIATIONS

**A**

| | |
|---|---|
| AB | Alberta |
| ACT | Australian Capital Territory |
| AFB | Air Force Base |
| AK | Alaska |
| AL | Alabama |
| APO | Army Post Office |
| AR | Arkansas |
| Arc | Arcade |
| AS | American Samoa |
| Assn | Association |
| Assoc | Associates |
| Ave | Avenue |
| AZ | Arizona |

**B**

| | |
|---|---|
| BC | British Columbia |
| Bd | Board |
| Beds | Bedfordshire |
| Berks | Berkshire |
| Bldg | Building |
| Blvd | Boulevard |
| Br | Branch |
| Bros | Brothers |
| Bucks | Buckinghamshire |
| BWI | British West Indies |
| Byp | Bypass |

**C**

| | |
|---|---|
| CA | California |
| Cambs | Cambridgeshire |
| Cir | Circle |
| CM | Mariana Islands |
| CMH | Congressional Medal of Honor |
| CO | Colorado |
| Co | Company |
| Corp | Corporation |
| Cres | Crescent |
| Cswy | Causeway |
| CT | Connecticut |
| Ct | Court |
| Ctr | Center |
| Ctrl | Central |
| Cts | Courts |
| CZ | Canal Zone |

**D**

| | |
|---|---|
| DC | District of Columbia |
| DE | Delaware |
| Dept | Department |
| Dis | District |
| Div | Division |
| Dr | Drive |
| Drwy | Driveway |

**E**

| | |
|---|---|
| E | East |
| Edin | Edinburgh |
| Ent | Entertainment |
| Expy | Expressway |
| Ext | Extended, Extension |

**F**

| | |
|---|---|
| Fedn | Federation |
| FL | Florida |
| FPO | Fleet Post Office |
| Ft | Fort |
| Fwy | Freeway |

**G**

| | |
|---|---|
| GA | Georgia |
| Gdns | Gardens |
| Glos | Gloucestershire |
| Grp | Group |
| Grv | Grove |
| Gt | Great |
| GU | Guam |

**H**

| | |
|---|---|
| Hants | Hampshire |
| Herts | Hertfordshire |
| HI | Hawaii |
| HOF | Hall of Fame |
| Hq | Headquarters |
| Hts | Heights |
| Hwy | Highway |

**I**

| | |
|---|---|
| IA | Iowa |
| ID | Idaho |
| IL | Illinois |
| IN | Indiana |
| Inc | Incorporated |
| Inst | Institute |
| Int'l | International |
| Intercoll | Intercollegiate |

**J**

| | |
|---|---|
| Jr | Junior |

**K**

| | |
|---|---|
| KS | Kansas |
| KY | Kentucky |

**L**

| | |
|---|---|
| LA | Louisiana |
| Lab | Laboratory |
| Lancs | Lancashire |
| Lincs | Lincolnshire |
| Ln | Lane |
| Ltd | Limited |

# 2015 Edition

# V.I.P. ADDRESS BOOK

**PUBLISHER AND EDITOR**
James M Wiggins, PhD

**PRESIDENT AND MANAGING EDITOR**
Adele M Cooke

**VICE PRESIDENT OF TECHNICAL AFFAIRS**
Mike K Maloy

**DESIGN DIRECTOR**
LeeAnn Nelson

**WEBSITE DESIGNERS &**
Rawn Rhoades
Ernie Brown

**SOCIAL MEDIA CONSULTANT**
Verin Lewis

**PUBLISHER**
Associated Media Companies
PO Box 489
Gleneden Beach, OR 97388-0489
United States of America
Phone/Fax - 1-541-764-4233
Email – info@vipaddress.com
Website - www.vipaddress.com

**M**

| | |
|---|---|
| MA | Massachusetts |
| MB | Manitoba |
| MD | Maryland |
| Mddx | Middlesex |
| ME | Maine |
| Med | Medical |
| Mgmt | Management |
| MI | Michigan |
| MN | Minnesota |
| MO | Missouri |
| Mon | Monmouthshire |
| MS | Mississippi |
| MT | Montana |
| Mt | Mount |

**N**

| | |
|---|---|
| N | North |
| NB | New Brunswick |
| NC | North Carolina |
| ND | North Dakota |
| NE | Northeast, Nebraska |
| NH | New Hampshire |
| NJ | New Jersey |
| NL | Newfoundland |
| NM | New Mexico |
| Northants | Northamptonshire |
| Notts | Nottinghamshire |
| NS | Nova Scotia |
| NSW | New South Wales |
| NT | Northwest Territories, Northern Territory |
| NV | Nevada |
| NW | Northwest |
| NY | New York |

**O**

| | |
|---|---|
| OH | Ohio |
| OK | Oklahoma |
| ON | Ontario |
| OR | Oregon |
| Oxon | Oxfordshire |

**P**

| | |
|---|---|
| PA | Pennsylvania |
| PE | Prince Edward Island |
| Pkwy | Parkway |
| Pl | Place |
| Plz | Plaza |
| PO | Post Office |
| PR | Puerto Rico |
| Prof | Professional |
| Pt | Point |

**Q**

| | |
|---|---|
| QC | Quebec |
| QLD | Queensland |

**R**

| | |
|---|---|
| RD | Rural Delivery |
| Rd | Road |
| Rep | Republic |
| RI | Rhode Island |
| RR | Rural Route |

**S**

| | |
|---|---|
| S | South |
| SA | South Australia |
| SC | South Carolina |
| Sci | Science |
| SD | South Dakota |
| SE | Southeast |
| SK | Saskatchewan |
| Spdwy | Speedway |
| Sq | Square |
| St | Saint, Street |
| SW | Southwest |

**T**

| | |
|---|---|
| Tas | Tasmania |
| Ter | Territory |
| Terr | Terrace |
| TN | Tennessee |
| Tpke | Turnpike |
| Trl | Trail |
| TX | Texas |

**U**

| | |
|---|---|
| Univ | University |
| USA | United States of America |
| UT | Utah |

**V**

| | |
|---|---|
| VA | Virginia |
| VC | Victoria Cross |
| VI | Virgin Islands |
| VIC | Victoria |
| VT | Vermont |

**W**

| | |
|---|---|
| W | West |
| WA | Washington, Western Australia |
| WI | Wisconsin |
| Worcs | Worcestershire |
| WV | West Virginia |
| WY | Wyoming |

**X-Y-Z**

| | |
|---|---|
| YT | Yukon Territory |
| Yorks | Yorkshire |

| | | |
|---|---|---|
| Foreign Ambassadors | His/Her Excellency John/Jane Doe | Dear Mr/MsAmbassador - - - |
| Kings/Queens | His/Her Royal Highness --- King/Queen of --- | Your Royal Highness --- |
| Military Leaders (Attention should be given to the actual rank) | General/Admiral John/Jane Doe | Dear General/Admiral - - - |
| Governors | The Honorable John/Jane Doe Governor of - - - | Dear Governor - - - |
| Mayors | The Honorable John/Jane Doe Mayor of - - - | Dear Mayor - - - |

The Clergy

Catholic

| | | |
|---|---|---|
| The Pope | His Eminence the Pope - - - | Your Holiness - - - |
| Cardinals | His Eminence John Cardinal Doe | Dear Your Eminence Cardinal |
| Episcopalian | The Rt Rev John Doe | Dear Bishop - - - |
| Protestant | The Rev John Doe | Dear Mr/Mrs - - - |
| Eastern Orthodox Patriarch | His Holiness, the Patriarch - - - | Your Holiness - - - |
| Jewish | Rabbi John Doe | Dear Rabbi - - - |

Forms of addresses can vary to almost impossible proportions. If you are a real stickler for proper protocol, you will need to obtain one of the many excellent reference books on etiquette or consult your local reference librarian for assistance.

Times are less formal so if you are polite and spell names correctly, your letter should be favorable received.

### ACKNOWLEDGEMENTS

The Editors would like to thank the following people for their generous assistance in maintaining the accuracy of this publication:

Robert Allen, Jr., Florence Bagdasian, Ed Bielucke, III, Jake Bommer, John Gracen Brown, William Butts, Gloria & Len Bytnar, Thomas Burford, Bill Clogston, David Coston, James A. Cox, Charlie Dixon, Jimmy Dodson, Jr., Douglas Files, John T. Gillin, Brian Graybill, Tom Hall, Harold Hamel, Jack Hilton, Steve Koroknay, Dewey Linze, Helen Mangani, Wayne McDonald, Massee McKinley, Larry Miller, Pacer Center's Jan Flora, Mark J. Quilling, Ed Sammels, Ira Sabin, Juergen Schwarz, Eric Shuman, Jay F. Smith, Christopher Snowden, Darryl Spurlock, Kim Tangye, Jim Thomson, Anders Tvegard, Joe Wagner, Deanna Ward, Jim & Judy Watt, Marci Yates.

THE
DIRECTORY
OF
ADDRESS
LISTINGS

Although we have made every effort to provide
current addresses, we assume no responsibility for
address that become outdated.

Neither do we guarantee that people listed in the book
will personally answer their mail or that they will
respond to correspondence.

**A$AP Rocky** — Rap Artist
Polo Grounds Music, 243 W 30th St, #302, New York NY 10001, USA

**Aaker, Lee W** — Actor
PO Box 1386, Mammoth Lakes CA 93546, USA

**Aaltonen, Juhamatti T** — Ice Hockey Player
Karpat Oulu, Lekatie 6, 90150 Oulu, Finland

**Aames, Willie** — Actor
Jeff Ballard Public Relations, 4814 N Lemona Ave, Sherman Oaks CA 91403, USA

**Aamodt, Kjetil Andre** — Alpine Skier
8 Quai Jean Charles Rey, 98000 Monte Carlo, Monaco

**Aardsma, David A** — Baseball Player
6009 E Turquoise Ave, Paradise Valley AZ 85253, USA

**Aaron, Caroline** — Actress
Abrams Artists, 9200 W Sunset Blvd, #1125, West Hollywood CA 90069 USA

**Aaron, Chester** — Writer
PO Box 388, Occidental CA 95465, USA

**Aaron, Henry J** — Economist
Brookings Institute, 1775 Massachusetts Ave NW, Washington DC 20036 USA

**Aaron, Henry L (Hank)** — Baseball Player, Executive
1611 Adams Dr SW, Atlanta GA 30311, USA

**Aaron, Jeffrey** — Actor
Johnson & Laird Mgmt, PO Box 78340, Grey Lynn, Auckland 1245, New Zealand

**Aaron, Lee** — Singer, Songwriter
Paquin Entertainment Agency, 219 Dufferin St, #206B, Toronto ON M6K 3J1, Canada

**Aaron, Paul** — Director
Suntaur/Elsboy Entertainment, 1581 N Crescent Heights Blvd, Los Angeles CA 90046, USA

**Aaron, Thomas D (Tommy)** — Golfer
440 E Lake Dr, Gainesville GA 30506, USA

**Aase, Donald W (Don)** — Baseball Player
5055 Via Ricardo, Yorba Linda CA 92886, USA

**Abadi, Haidar al-** — Prime Minister, Iraq
Prime Minister's Office, Karradat Mariam, Baghdad, Iraq

**Abagnale, Frank W, Jr** — Businessman
Abagnale Assoc, PO Box 701290, Tulsa OK 74170, USA

**Abair, Mindi** — Singer, Jazz Saxophonist
Chapman Company Mgmt, 14011 Ventura Blvd, #405, Sherman Oaks CA 91423, USA

**Abakanowicz, Magdalena** — Artist
Ul Bzowa 1, 02 708 Warsaw, Poland

**Abalakin, Victor K** — Astronomer
Main Observatory, Pulkovskoye Shosse 65, 196140 Saint Petersburg, Russia

**Abbado, Roberto** — Conductor
Opus 3 Artists, 470 Park Ave S, #900N, New York NY 10016 USA

**Abbas, Mahmoud** — President, Palestine
President's Office, Gaza City, Gaza Strip, Palestine, Israel

**Abbass, Hiam** — Actress
Untitled Entertainment, 350 S Beverly Dr, #200, Beverly Hills CA 90212 USA

**Abbatiello, Carmine** — Harness Racing Driver
7 Whirlaway Road, Manalapan NJ 07726, USA

**Abbe, Elfriede M** — Artist
Applewood, Manchester Center VT 05255, USA

**Abbot, Charles S** — Navy Admiral, Government Official
Navy-Marine Corps Relief Society, 875 N Randolph St, #225, Arlington VA 22203, USA

**Abbot, Russ** — Actor, Comedian
Harvey Voices, 58 Woodlands Road, London N9 8RT, England

**Abbott, Anthony J (Tony)** — Prime Minister, Australia
Prime Minister's Office, Parliament House, Canberra ACT 2600, Australia

**Abbott, Bruce** — Actor
29500 Heathercliff Road, Malibu CA 90265, USA

**Abbott, Christie** — Actress
Kim Dawson Agency, 1645 Stemmons Freeway, #B, Dallas TX 75207, USA

**Abbott, Christopher** — Actor
Gersh Agency, 9465 Wilshire Blvd, #600, Beverly Hills CA 90212 USA

**Abbott, Diahnne** — Actress
460 W Ave 46, Los Angeles CA 90065, USA

**Abbott, James A (Jim)** — Baseball Player
Lilly Walters Schermerhorn, 740 W Purdue Dr, Claremont CA 91711, USA

**Abbott, James W** — Educator
University of South Dakota, President's Office, Vermillion SD 57069, USA

**Abbott, Jeff** — Writer
Hachette/Grand Central Publishing, 3 Center Plaza, Boston MA 02108, USA

**Abbott, Jeffrey W (Jeff)** — Baseball Player
119 Little John Lane, Murrayville GA 30564, USA

**Abbott, Jeremy** — Figure Skater
19603 W 12 Milve Road, Southfield MI 48076, USA

**Abbott, Jude** — Singer (Chumbawamba)
Doug Smith Assoc, PO Box 1151, London W3 8ZJ, England

**Abbott, Karen** — Writer
Random House, 1745 Broadway, #1800, New York NY 10019 USA

**Abbott, Kurt T** — Baseball Player
1704 NW Spruce Ridge Dr, Stuart FL 34994, USA

**Abbott, Paul** — Producer, Writer
The Agency, 24 Pottery Lane, Holland Park, London W11 4LZ, England

**Abbott, Paul D** — Baseball Player
1809 Yermo Place, Fullerton CA 92833, USA

**Abbott, Reg** — Ice Hockey Player
5239 Hanover Place, Victoria BC V8Y 2C7, Canada

**Abbott, Vinnie Paul** — Drummer (Pantera, Damageplan)
Clubhouse, 2250 Manana Dr, Dallas TX 75220, USA

**Abbott, W Glenn** — Baseball Player
4413 Dawson Dr, North Little Rock AR 72116, USA

**Abboud, A Robert** — Businessman
209 Braeburn Road, Barrington Hills IL 60010, USA

**Abboud, Francois M** — Internist, Physician
24 Kennedy Parkway, Iowa City IA 52246, USA

**Abboud, Joseph M** — Fashion Designer
650 5th Ave, #2700, New York NY 10019, USA

**Abd, Rodrigo** — Photojournalist
Associated Press, Editorial Dept, 450 W 33rd St, #1500, New York NY 10001 USA

**Abdalla, Nick** — Artist
Western Graphics Workshop, PO Box 375, Corona NM 88318, USA

**Abdallah Mohamed Sambi, Ahmed** — President, Comoros
President's Office, Palais de Beit Salam, BP 421, Moroni, Grand Comoro, Comoros

**Abdel Aziz, Mohamed Ould** — Head of State Council, Mauritania
President's Office, BP 184, Nouakchott, Mauritania

**Abdi, Barkhad** — Actor
S M S Talent, 8383 Wilshire Blvd, #230, Beverly Hills CA 90211 USA

**Abdoo, Rose** — Actress
Innovative Artists, 1505 10th St, Santa Monica CA 90401 USA

**Abdrashitov, Vadim Y** — Director
3D Frunzenskaya 8, #211, 119270 Moscow, Russia

**Abdrazakov, Ildar** — Opera Singer
Mariinsky Theater, Theater Square, 1 Pl Iskusstr, 190000 Saint Petersburg, Russia

**Abdul Ahad Mohmand** — Cosmonaut, Afghanistan
Cosmonaut Training Center, Star City, 141160 Zvezdny Gorodok, Moscow Oblast, Russia

**Abdul, Paula J** — Singer, Dancer
Tudor Management Group, 1610 Oak St, #2, Santa Monica CA 90405, USA

**Abdul-Aziz, Zaid** — Basketball Player
11355 3rd Ave NE, #A207, Seattle WA 98125, USA

**Abdul-Ghani, Abdul Aziz** — Prime Minister, Yemen
Haddah St, San'a, Yemen

**Abdul-Jabbar, Kareem** — Basketball Player
Amsel Eisenstadt Frazier, 5055 Wilshire Blvd, #865, Los Angeles CA 90036 USA

**Abdul-Jabbar, Karim** — Football Player
17044 Downing St, Gaithersburg MD 20877, USA

**Abdullah Ibn Abdul al-Aziz** — King, Saudi Arabia
Council of Ministers, Murabba, Riyadh 11121, Saudi Arabia

**Abdullah II** — King, Jordan; Army General
Royal Palace, Royal Hashemite Court, Amman, Jordan

**Abdullah, Rabíh F** — Football Player
12810 Wallingford Dr, Tampa FL 33624, USA

**Abduraimov, Behzod** — Concert Pianist
Harrison/Parrott, 5-6 Albion Court, London W6 0QT, England

**Abdur-Rahim, Shareef** — Basketball Player
9890 Wexford Circle, Granite Bay CA 95746, USA

**Abe, Shana** — Writer
303 S Broadway St, #200-124, Denver CO 80209, USA

**Abe, Shinzo** — Prime Minister, Japan
Prime Minister's Office, 1-6-1 Nagatoicho, Chiyodaku, Tokyo 100 8968, Japan

**Abel, Dominique** — Actress, Director, Writer
Courage Mon Amour, 9 Rue Ruysdael, 1070 Brussels, Belgium

**Abel, Gerald (Gerry)** — Ice Hockey Player
23570 Samoset Trail, Southfield MI 48033, USA

**Abel, Jennifer** — Diver
C A M O Diving Club, 1000 Ave Emile-Journault, Montreal QC H2M 2E7, Canada

**Abel, Jessica** — Cartoonist
Fantagraphics Books, 7563 Lake City Way NE, Seattle WA 98115, USA

**Abel, Joy** — Bowler
PO Box 296, Lansing IL 60438, USA

**Abel, Yves** — Conductor
Askonas Holt, Lincoln House, 300 High Holborn, London WC1V 7JH, England

**Abela, George** — President, Malta
President's Office, Palace, Valletta, Malta

**Abele, Jim** — Actor
S M S Talent, 8383 Wilshire Blvd, #230, Beverly Hills CA 90211 USA

**Abell, Timothy S (Tim)** — Actor, Producer
Tactical Media Productions, 578 Washington Blvd, #346, Marina del Rey CA 90292, USA

**Abelson, John N** — Biologist
112 Laidley St, San Francisco CA 94131, USA

**Abendroth, John K** — Golfer
Hooked on Golf, 1620 McDonald Way, Burlingame CA 94010, USA

**Abercrombie, John L** — Jazz Guitarist
iGuitar Workshop, 290 Main St, Building #3, Cold Spring NY 10516, USA

**Abercrombie, Walter A** — Football Player
217 Westlane Circle, Woodway TX 76712, USA

**Abernathy, Frederick H** — Mechanical Engineer
43 Islington Road, Auburndale MA 02466, USA

**Abernathy, M Brent** — Baseball Player
5920 Buxton Dr, Columbus GA 31907, USA

**Abernethy, Robert** — Commentator
Public Broadcasting System, 1320 Braddock Place, Alexandria VA 22314, USA

**Abernethy, Thomas C (Tom)** — Basketball Player
5268 Woodfield Dr N, Carmel IN 46033, USA

**Abeyta, Tony** — Artist
1127 W Madison St, Chicago IL 60607, USA

**Abgrall, Dennis** — Ice Hockey Player
16607 S 12th Place, Phoenix AZ 85048, USA

**Abidine, Dhafer** — Actor
Hamilton Hodell, 20 Golden Square, London W1F 9JL, England

**Abigail** — Singer
T-Best Talent Agency, 508 Honey Lake Court, Danville CA 94506 USA

**Abil, Iolu Johnson** — President, Vanuatu
President's Office, Port Vila, Vanuatu

**Abiodun, Oyewole** — Rap Artist (Last Poets)
Rykodisc, 3 Broadway, #E, Beverly MA 01915, USA

**Abiola-Muller, Joy Lee** — Actress
Grundy U F A TV Productions, Coloneum, Geb B-S, Butzweiler Str 255, 50829 Cologne, Germany

**Abizaid, John P** — Army General
Stanford University, Hoover Institution, Stanford CA 94305, USA

**Abkarian, Simon** — Actor
Cineart, 28 Rue Mogador, 75009 Paris, France

**Able, Forest E** — Basketball Player
11102 Mitchell Hill Road, Fairdale KY 40118, USA

**Ablon, Ralph E** — Businessman
Ogden Corp, PO Box 2615, Fairfield NJ 07004, USA
**Abner, Shawn W** — Baseball Player
1443 Olde Oak Court, Mechanicsburg PA 17050, USA
**Aboud, John** — Writer
Principato-Young, 9465 Wilshire Blvd, #880, Beverly Hills CA 90212 USA
**Aboulela, Amir** — Actor
Grace Talent Organization, 8370 Wilshire Blvd, #210, Beverly Hills CA 90211, USA
**Aboulela, Leila** — Writer
Polygon Books, 22 George Square, Edinburgh EH8 9IF, Scotland
**Abourezk, James G** — Senator, SD
21 Dupont Circle NW, #400, Washington DC 20036, USA
**Abraham, Arthur** — Boxer
Boxsport Gmbh, Hanns-Braun-Str, 14053 Berlin, Germany
**Abraham, E Spencer** — Secretary of Energy; Senator, MI
Abraham Group, 600 14th St NW, #500, Washington DC 20005, USA
**Abraham, F Murray** — Actor
Innovative Artists, 1505 10th St, Santa Monica CA 90401 USA
**Abraham, John A** — Football Player
101 Irongate Dr, Columbia SC 29223, USA
**Abraham, Marc** — Producer
Strike Entertainment, 3000 W Olympic Blvd, Building 5, Santa Monica CA 90404, USA
**Abraham, Phil** — Director
Skouras Agency, 1149 3rd St, #300, Santa Monica CA 90403 USA
**Abraham, Robert E** — Football Player
831 Canal St, Myrtle Beach SC 29577, USA
**Abraham, Vader** — Singer
Uitgeverij bv, PO Box 4758, 4803 Breda ET, Netherlands
**Abrahamian, Emil** — Cartoonist (Stumpy Stumbler)
147 Woodleaf Dr, Winter Springs FL 32708, USA
**Abrahams, Elihu** — Physicist
Rutgers University, Physics/Astronomy Dept, 136 Frelinghuysen Road, Piscataway NJ 08854, USA
**Abrahams, Ivor** — Sculptor
Royal Arts Academy, Burlington House, Piccadilly, London W1V 0DS, England
**Abrahams, Jim S** — Director
Ziffren Brittenham Branca, 1801 Century Park W, #700, Los Angeles CA 90067 USA
**Abrahams, Michael T (Mick)** — Guitarist (Jethro Tull)
Primary Talent International, 2-12 Pentonville Road, London N1 9PL, England
**Abrahamson, James A** — Air Force General, Businessman
StratCom International, 20112 Marble Quarry Road, Keedysville MD 21756, USA
**Abrahamson, Lenny** — Director
Casorotto Ramsay, Waverley House, 7-12 Noel St, London W1F 8GQ, England
**Abrahamyan, Hovik A** — Prime Minister, Armenia
Prime Minister's Office, Ul Nalbandyyrna 32, 375010 Yerevan, Armenia
**Abramovic, Marina** — Performance Artist, Photographer
Sean Kelly Gallery, 528 W 29th St, New York, NY 10001, USA
**Abramowicz, Daniel S (Danny)** — Football Player
143 Parkdale Road, Steubenville OH 43952, USA
**Abrams, Aaron** — Actor, Producer, Writer
Characters Talent Mgmt, 8 Elm St, Toronto ON M5G 1G7, Canada
**Abrams, Bobby E** — Football Player
1470 Pampas Dr, Montgomery AL 36117, USA
**Abrams, Dan** — Actor
MSNBC, 30 Rockefeller Plaza, New York NY 10112, USA
**Abrams, Elliott** — Government Official
10607 Dogwood Farm Lane, Great Falls VA 22066, USA
**Abrams, Herbert L** — Radiologist
620 Sand Hill Road, #109G, Palo Alto CA 94304, USA
**Abrams, Jeffrey J (J J)** — Director, Producer, Writer
Bad Robot, 1221 Olympic Blvd, Santa Monica CA 90404, USA
**Abrams, John N** — Army General
Abrams Learning/Information Systems, 2800 Shirlington Road, #1100, Arlington VA 22206, USA
**Abramson, Leslie** — Attorney
4929 Wilshire Blvd, #490, Los Angeles CA 90010, USA
**Abramson, Neil** — Director, Writer
United Talent Agency, U T A Plaza, 9336 Civic Center Dr, Beverly Hills CA 90210 USA
**Abreu, Dilip J** — Economist
Princeton University, Economics Dept, Princeton NJ 08544, USA
**Abreu, Irina** — Actress
Televisa, Blvd A Lopez Mateos 232, Colonia San Angel, Mexico City DF 01060 CP, Mexico
**Abrigo, Megan** — Model
Jet Set Models, 2160 Avenida de la Playa, La Jolla CA 92037, USA
**Abrikosov, Alexei A** — Nobel Physics Laureate
804 Houston St, Lemont IL 60439, USA
**Abril Y Castello, Santos Cardinal** — Religious Leader
Saint Mary Major Basilica, Via Liberiana 27, 00185 Rome, Italy
**Abril, Victoria** — Actress
Stephanie Zitzermann, Rue du Louvre 1, 75001 Paris, France
**Abroms, Edward M** — Director
E M A Enterprises, 1866 Marlowe St, Thousand Oaks CA 91360, USA
**Abrosimova, Svetlana I** — Basketball Player
Seattle Storm, Key Arena, 351 Elliott Ave W, #500, Seattle WA 98119 USA
**Abruzzo, Ray** — Actor
Bret Adams Agency, 448 W 44th St, New York NY 10036, USA
**Absher, Richard A (Dick), Jr** — Football Player
353 Tavistock Dr, Saint Augustine FL 32095, USA
**Abtahi, Omid** — Actor
Greene Assoc, 1901 Ave of Stars, #130, Los Angeles CA 90067 USA
**Abts, Tomma** — Artist
Kunsthalle Basel, Steinenberg 7, 4051 Basel, Switzerland
**Abu-Assad, Hany** — Director
Creative Artists Agency, 2000 Ave of Stars, #100, Los Angeles CA 90067 USA
**Abu-Jaber, Diana** — Writer
W W Norton, 500 5th Ave, #600, New York NY 10110 USA
**Abusahmain, Nouri** — President, Libya
President's Office, Bab el Asiziya Barracks, Tripoli, Libya

Ablon - Abusahmain

**A**

**Acaba, Joseph M (Joe)** — Astronaut
N A S A, Johnson Space Center, 2101 NASA Road, Houston TX 77058 USA
**Accambray, William** — Handball Player
Montpellier Agglomeration H B, 1000 Ave du val de Montferrand, 34090 Montpellier, France
**Accardo, Salvatore** — Concert Violinist
Agenzia Resia Srl Rappresentanze, Via Manzoni 31, 20121 Milan, Italy
**Accola, Candice** — Actress
A P A Talent & Literary Agency, 405 S Beverly Dr, #300, Beverly Hills CA 90212 USA
**Accola, Paul** — Alpine Skier
Bolgenstr 17, 7270 Davos Platz, Switzerland
**Acconci, Vito** — Conceptual Artist
39 Pearl St, Brooklyn NY 11201, USA
**Ace** — Guitarist (Skunk Anansie)
13 Artists, 11-14 Kensington St, Brighton BN1 4AJ, England
**Ace Hood** — Rap Artist
Def Soul Records, 825 8th Ave, #2700, New York NY 10019 USA
**Acero-Sanchez, Hector** — Boxer
Shelly Finkel Mgmt, 110 Greene St, #403, New York NY 10012 USA
**Aceto, Raymond** — Opera Singer
I M G Artists, Hogarth Business Park, Chiswick, London W4 2TH, England
**Acevedo, Juan C** — Baseball Player
143 Madera Circle, Mesa AZ 85204, USA
**Acevedo, Kirk** — Actor
Abrams Artists, 9200 W Sunset Blvd, #1125, West Hollywood CA 90069 USA
**Achatz, Grant** — Chef, Restaurateur
Alinea Restaurant, 1723 N Halsted, Chicago IL 60614, USA
**Achen, Christopher H** — Social Scientist
Princeton University, Politics Dept, Robertson Hall, Princeton NJ 08544, USA
**Acheson, James** — Costume Designer
I C M Partners, 10250 Constellation Blvd, #900, Los Angeles CA 90067 USA
**Achica, George** — Football Player
3165 Lone Bluff Way, San Jose CA 95111, USA
**Achterberg, Chantal** — Rowing Athlete
D S R Proteus-Ereyes, Rotterdamseweg 362A, 2628 AT Delft, Netherlands
**Achtymichuk, Gene** — Ice Hockey Player
305-9985 93rd Ave, Fort Saskatchewan AB T8L 1N5, Canada
**Acker, Amy** — Actress
A P A Talent & Literary Agency, 405 S Beverly Dr, #300, Beverly Hills CA 90212 USA
**Acker, James J (Jim)** — Baseball Player
PO Box 214, Freer TX 78357, USA
**Acker, Sharon** — Actress
2530 Alister Ave, Tustin CA 92782, USA
**Acker, William B (Bill), Jr** — Football Player
1809 Walker Dr, Alice TX 78332, USA
**Ackeren, Robert V** — Director, Producer, Writer
Kurfurstendamm 132A, 10711 Berlin, Germany
**Acker-Macosko, Anna** — Golfer
304 Earl Dr, Kerrville TX 78028, USA
**Ackerman, Bruce A** — Attorney, Educator
Yale University, Law School, 127 Wall St, New Haven CT 06511, USA
**Ackerman, Diane** — Writer
W W Norton, 500 5th Ave, #600, New York NY 10110 USA
**Ackerman, R Andrew (Andy)** — Director
W M E Entertainment, 9601 Wilshire Blvd, #300, Beverly Hills CA 90210 USA
**Ackerman, Richard C (Rick)** — Football Player
995 N US Highway 30, Laramie WY 82072, USA
**Ackerman, Robert Allan** — Director
I C M Partners, 10250 Constellation Blvd, #900, Los Angeles CA 90067 USA
**Ackerman, Thomas E** — Cinematographer
280 Halcyon Ave, Winston Salem NC 27104, USA
**Ackerman, Thomas M (Tom)** — Football Player
17511 N Greenbluff Road, Colbert WA 99005, USA
**Ackerman, William** — Composer, Guitarist
Drake Assoc, 177 Woodland Ave, Westwood NJ 07675, USA
**Ackermann, Rosemarie** — Track Athlete
Yuri-Gagarin Str 14, 03046 Cottbus, Germany
**Ackland, Joss** — Actor
London Theatrical, 18 Leamore St, London W6 0JZ, England , USA
**Ackland, Oliver** — Actor
United Talent Agency, U T A Plaza, 9336 Civic Center Dr, Beverly Hills CA 90210 USA
**Ackles, Danneel** — Actress
Gersh Agency, 9465 Wilshire Blvd, #600, Beverly Hills CA 90212 USA
**Ackles, Jensen** — Actor, Director
Gersh Agency, 9465 Wilshire Blvd, #600, Beverly Hills CA 90212 USA
**Ackman, William A (Bill)** — Financier
Pershing Square Capital Mgmt, 888 7th Ave, New York NY 10001, USA
**Ackroyd, Barry** — Cinematographer
United Agents, 12-26 Lexington St, London W1F 0LE, England
**Ackroyd, David** — Actor
PO Box 9041, Kalispell MT 59904, USA
**Ackroyd, Norman** — Artist
Royal Academy of Arts, Picadilly, London W1V 0DS, England
**Ackroyd, Peter** — Writer
Anthony Sheil Assoc, 43 Doughty St, London WC1N 2LF, England
**Acks, Ronald W (Ron)** — Football Player
563 Licklog Ridge, Hayesville NC 28904, USA
**Acler, Rarika** — Model
Ten Model Mgmt, Rua Iquatemi 448, CEP 01451 010 Sao Paulo SP, Brazil
**Acogny, Germaine** — Dancer, Choreographer
Jant-Bi, BP 22626, 15523 Dakar, Senegal
**Acohido, Byron** — Journalist
Seattle Times, Editorial Dept, 1000 Denny Way, Seattle WA 98109 USA
**Acord, Lance** — Cinematographer
Creative Artists Agency, 2000 Ave of Stars, #100, Los Angeles CA 90067 USA
**Acosta, Carlos** — Ballet Dancer
Royal Opera House, Covent Garden, London WC2E 9DD, England

**Acaba - Acosta**

| | |
|---|---|
| **Acosta, George** | Producer (Planet Soul) |
| Richard Walters, PO Box 2789, Toluca Lake CA 91610 USA | |
| **Acra, Reem** | Fashion Designer |
| 730 5th Ave, #205, New York NY 10019, USA | |
| **Acres, Mark R** | Basketball Player |
| 233 6th St, Manhattan Beach CA 90266, USA | |
| **Acrivos, Andreas** | Chemical Engineer |
| 788 Cedro Way, Stanford CA 94305, USA | |
| **Acta, Manuel E (Manny)** | Baseball Manager |
| 6427 Shoreline Dr, Saint Cloud FL 34771, USA | |
| **Acton, Charles R (Bud)** | Basketball Player |
| PO Box 87, Empire MI 49630, USA | |
| **Acton, Keith** | Ice Hockey Player |
| 14 Cornell Place, Rye NY 10580, USA | |
| **Acton, Loren W** | Astronaut |
| PO Box 1857, Bozeman MT 59771, USA | |
| **Acuff, Carl, Jr** | Singer |
| PO Box 2367, Harrison AR 72602, USA | |
| **Aczel, Janos D** | Mathematician |
| University of Waterloo, Pure Mathematics Dept, Waterloo ON N2L 3G1, Canada | |
| **Adair, Deborah** | Actress |
| 2530 J St, #330, Sacramento CA 95816, USA | |
| **Adair, Robert K** | Physicist |
| Harvard University, Belfer Science Center, Cambridge MA 02138, USA | |
| **Adam, Ken** | Designer |
| Mirisch Agency, 1025 Colorado Ave, #B, Santa Monica CA 90211 USA | |
| **Adam, Mike** | Curling Athlete |
| Curling Association, 1660 Vimont Court, Cumberland ON K4A 4J4, Canada | |
| **Adam, Robert** | Architect |
| Winchester Design, 9 Upper High St, Winchester, Hants SO23 8UT, England | |
| **Adam, Russ** | Ice Hockey Player |
| 69 Old Petty Harbour Road, Saint Johns NL A1G 1H5, Canada | |
| **Adam, Theo** | Opera Singer |
| Schillerstr 14, 01326 Dresden, Germany | |
| **Adamek, Donna** | Bowler |
| 29834 Webster Place, Stevenson Ranch CA 91381, USA | |
| **Adamek, Tomasz** | Boxer |
| Ul Viantykowka 6, 34-322 Gilowice, Poland | |
| **Adami, Franco** | Sculptor |
| Via del Vicinato, Pontestrada, 55045 Piatrasanta, Italy | |
| **Adamle, Michael D (Mike)** | Football Player, Sportscaster |
| 826 Lincoln St, Evanston IL 60201, USA | |
| **Adams Beckham, Victoria** | Singer (Spice Girls) |
| 19 Entertainment, 32/33 Ransomes Dock, 35-37 Parkgate Road, London SW11 4NP, England | |
| **Adams, Alvan L** | Basketball Player |
| 5617 N Palo Cristi Road, Paradise Valley AZ 85253, USA | |
| **Adams, Amy** | Actress |
| Brillstein Entertainment Partners, 9150 Wilshire Blvd, #350, Beverly Hills CA 90212 USA | |
| **Adams, Anthony L (Tony)** | Football Player |
| 14012 Juniper St, Overland Park KS 66224, USA | |
| **Adams, Brooke** | Actress |
| C E S D, 10635 Santa Monica Blvd, #130, Los Angeles CA 90025 USA | |
| **Adams, Bryan** | Singer, Guitarist, Songwriter |
| Jillie Bushell Associates, Chichester House, #100 1-3 Brixton Road, London SW9 6DE, England | |
| **Adams, Bryan** | Singer (Color Me Badd) |
| J Bird Entertainment, 4905 S Atlantic Ave, Ponce Inlet FL 32127, USA | |
| **Adams, Christine** | Actress |
| Innovative Artists, 1505 10th St, Santa Monica CA 90401 USA | |
| **Adams, Craig** | Ice Hockey Player |
| 8030 Sherwood Dr, Presto PA 15142, USA | |
| **Adams, Flozell J** | Football Player |
| 5201 Reflection Court, Flower Mound TX 75022, USA | |
| **Adams, Fred** | Astrophysicist |
| University of Michigan, Astrophysics Dept, Ann Arbor MI 48109, USA | |
| **Adams, George** | Basketball Player |
| 508 Watergate Circle, Gastonia NC 28052, USA | |
| **Adams, George W** | Football Player |
| 2410 Damsel Katie Dr, Lewisville TX 75056, USA | |
| **Adams, Gerard (Gerry)** | Political Leader, Northern Ireland |
| Sinn Fein/I R A, 51/55 Falls Road, Belfast BT12 4PD, Northern Ireland | |
| **Adams, Glenn C** | Baseball Player |
| 2108 S Santa Fe Ave, #103, Moore OK 73160, USA | |
| **Adams, Greg** | Ice Hockey Player |
| Cowichan Valley Capitals, 2687 James St, Duncan BC V9L 2X5, Canada | |
| **Adams, Greg** | Singer, Trumpeter (Tower of Power) |
| A L M Management Group, PO Box 16608, Encino CA 91416, USA | |
| **Adams, Hunter Patch** | Physician |
| 122 Franklin St, Urbana IL 61801, USA | |
| **Adams, Jane** | Actress |
| Framework Entertainment, 9057 Nemo St, #C, West Hollywood CA 90069 USA | |
| **Adams, Joey Lauren** | Actress |
| Paradigm Agency, 360 N Crescent Dr, North Building, Beverly Hills CA 90210 USA | |
| **Adams, John** | Ice Hockey Player |
| 109 Nottingham Crescent, Thunder Bay ON P7G 1B4, Canada | |
| **Adams, John C** | Composer, Conductor |
| I M G Artists, Carnegie Hall Tower, 152 W 57th St, #500, New York NY 10019 USA | |
| **Adams, John G** | Golfer |
| 4610 County Road 42200, Paris TX 75462, USA | |
| **Adams, John Luther** | Composer |
| Taiga Press, PO Box 81382, Fairbanks AK 99708, USA | |
| **Adams, Jordan** | Basketball Player |
| Memphis Grizzlies, 191 Beale St, Memphis TN 38103 USA | |
| **Adams, Julie** | Actress |
| 5915 Corbin Ave, Tarzana CA 91356, USA | |
| **Adams, Julius T** | Football Player, Coach |
| 2135 Jefferson Davis St, Macon GA 31201, USA | |

**Adams, Katie** — Actress
Hollander Talent Group, 14011 Ventura Blvd, #202, Sherman Oaks CA 91423, USA
**Adams, Keith A** — Football Player
9 N 9th St, #712, Philadelphia PA 19107, USA
**Adams, Kevyn** — Ice Hockey Player
Arizona Coyotes, 6751 N Sunset Blvd, #200, Glendale AZ 85305 USA
**Adams, Lindsey** — Auto Racing Driver
819 W Arapho, #24B-188, Richardson TX 75080, USA
**Adams, Lorraine** — Journalist
Washington Post, Editorial Dept, 1150 15th St, Washington DC 20071, USA
**Adams, Lynn** — Golfer
2445 Bryant St, #207, San Diego CA 92101, USA
**Adams, Mary Kay** — Actress
Ingber Assoc, 1140 Broadway, #907, New York NY 10001, USA
**Adams, Maud** — Actress
PO Box 10838, Beverly Hills CA 90213, USA
**Adams, Michael** — Basketball Player
WWRC-Radio, Sports Dept, 8121 Georgia Ave, Silver Spring MD 20910, USA
**Adams, Michael C (Mike)** — Football Player
70 Graham Ave, Paterson NJ 07524, USA
**Adams, Neal** — Cartoonist
W M E Entertainment, 9601 Wilshire Blvd, #300, Beverly Hills CA 90210 USA
**Adams, Nicola V** — Boxer
Haringey Amateur Boxing Club, 701 High Road, Tottenham Greater London N17 8AD, England
**Adams, Noah** — Commentator
National Public Radio, 635 Massachusetts Ave NW, #1, Washington DC 20001, USA
**Adams, Norman** — Artist
6 Gainsborough Road, London W4 1NJ, England
**Adams, Oleta** — Singer
Tom Estey Publicity, 144 E 22nd St, #1B, New York NY 10010, USA
**Adams, Patrick J** — Actor
Gersh Agency, 9465 Wilshire Blvd, #600, Beverly Hills CA 90212 USA
**Adams, Paul L** — WW II Army Air Corps Hero
6800 A St, #139, Lincoln NE 68510, USA
**Adams, Phillip A** — Humanist, Social Commentator
Radio National, GPO Box 9994, Sydney NSW 2001, Australia
**Adams, R Michael (Mike)** — Baseball Player
13205 Jo Lane NE, Albuquerque NM 87111, USA
**Adams, Ranald T, Jr** — Air Force General
1002 Emerald Dr, Alexandria VA 22308, USA
**Adams, Rhonda** — Model
Playboy Promotions, 9346 Civic Center Dr, #200, Beverly Hills CA 90210 USA
**Adams, Richard G** — Writer
Benwell's, 26 Church St, Whitchurch, Hantshire RG28 7AR, England
**Adams, Robert B (Bob)** — Football Player
16422 SE 17th St, Bellevue WA 98008, USA
**Adams, Robert H** — Photographer
306 Lincoln St, Longmont CO 80501, USA
**Adams, Robert M, Jr** — Anthropologist
PO Box ZZ, Basalt CO 81621, USA
**Adams, Ryan** — Singer, Songwriter
S A M, 722 Seward St, Los Angeles CA 90038, USA
**Adams, Sam A** — Football Player
218 Main St, #514, Kirkland WA 98033, USA
**Adams, Sam E** — Football Player
12010 Holly Stone Dr, Houston TX 77070, USA
**Adams, Scott** — Cartoonist (Dilbert)
Harper Business Publishers, 10 E 53rd St, New York NY 10022, USA
**Adams, Seth** — Actor
Mark Robert, PO Box 1549, Studio City CA 91614, USA
**Adams, Stefon L** — Football Player
937 Bingham Lane, Stone Mountain GA 30083, USA
**Adams, Steven** — Basketball Player
Oklahoma City Thunder, 211 N Robinson Ave, #300, Oklahoma City OK 73102 USA
**Adams, Terry** — Pianist, Clarinet Player (NRBQ)
Skyline Music, 2270 Maiden Lane SW, Roanoke VA 24015, USA
**Adams, Terry W** — Baseball Player
PO Box 1035, Mobile AL 36633, USA
**Adams, Tom** — Actor
Langford, 17 Westfields Ave, London SW19 0AT, England
**Adams, Tony (T-Bone)** — Boxer
1209 56th Court, Northport AL 35473, USA
**Adams, Valerie Vili** — Track Athlete
1155 Union Circle, Denton TX 76201, USA
**Adams, Vicki** — Curling Athlete
Stanraer Ice Rink, North West Castle, Royal Crescent, Stanraer, Wigtownshire DG9 8EH, England
**Adams, Willis D** — Football Player
7831 Quail Meadow Dr, Houston TX 77071, USA
**Adams, Yolanda** — Singer
Grand Gospel Bookings, 3933 Harrison St, #103, Oakland CA 94611, USA
**Adams-Geller, Paige** — Model, Fashion Designer
Paige Premium Denim, 10119 Jefferson Blvd, Culver City CA 90232, USA
**Adamski, Filip K** — Rowing Athlete
U 1, #9, 67161 Mannheim, Germany
**Adamson, Andrew** — Director, Producer
United Talent Agency, U T A Plaza, 9336 Civic Center Dr, Beverly Hills CA 90210 USA
**Adamson, Andrew** — Director, Writer, Animator
Strange Weather Films, 4205 Santa Monica Blvd, Santa Monica CA 90029, USA
**Adamson, James C** — Astronaut
25 Tradewind Circle, Fishersville VA 22939, USA
**Adamson, Robert E, Jr** — Navy Admiral
1709 Bohnhoff Court, Virginia Beach VA 23454, USA
**Adams-Sassoon, Beverly** — Model
1800 The Strand, Manhattan Beach CA 90266, USA
**Addai, Joseph** — Football Player
6710 Rosedale Path Court, Sugar Land TX 77479, USA

**Addario, Lisa** — Writer
United Talent Agency, U T A Plaza, 9336 Civic Center Dr, Beverly Hills CA 90210 USA

**Addazio, Steve** — Football Coach
Boston College, Athletic Dept, Chestnut Hill MA 02467, USA

**Adderley, Herbert A (Herb)** — Football Player
1058 Tristram Circle, Mantua NJ 08051, USA

**Addington, Crandell** — Poker Player
Phoenix Biotechnology, 8626 Tesoro Dr, #801, San Antonio TX 78217, USA

**Addison, Adele** — Concert Singer
98 Riverside Dr, New York NY 10024, USA

**Addison, Chris** — Actor, Comedian, Writer, Director
Avalon Mgmt, 4A Exmoor St, London W10 6BD, England

**Addison, Rafael** — Basketball Player
6 Bernadette Court, East Hanover NH 07936, USA

**Adduci, James D (Jim)** — Baseball Player
16314 Crescent Lake Dr, Crest Hill IL 60403, USA

**Adduono, Rick** — Ice Hockey Player
153 Donald St W, Thunder Bay ON P7E 5X8, Canada

**Addy, Mark** — Actor
Independent Talent Group, 40 Whitfield St, London W1T 2RH, England

**Ade, King Sunny** — Singer
Monterey International, 200 W Superior St, #202, Chicago IL 60654 USA

**Adebimpe, Tunde** — Singer (TV on the Radio)
D G C/Interscope Records, 2220 Colorado Ave, Santa Monica CA 90404, USA

**Adel, Marwa** — Photographer
Safar Khan Art Gallery, 6 Brazil St, Zamalek, Cairo 11211, Egypt

**Adele** — Singer, Songwriter
September Mgmt, 80/82 Chiswick High Road, London W4 1SY, England

**Adelin, Jean-Claude** — Actor
Artmedia, 20 Ave Rapp, 75007 Paris, France

**Adell, Traci** — Actress, Model
Playboy Promotions, 9346 Civic Center Dr, #200, Beverly Hills CA 90210 USA

**Adelman, Kenneth L** — Government Official
1601 Clarendon Blvd, #1501, Arlington VA 22209, USA

**Adelman, Richard L (Rick)** — Basketball Player, Coach
5109 Tangle Lane, Houston TX 77056, USA

**Adelson, Sheldon G** — Businessman
Las Vegas Sands Corp, 3355 Las Vegas Blvd S, Las Vegas NV 89109, USA

**Adelstein, Paul** — Actor
Abrams Artists, 9200 W Sunset Blvd, #1125, West Hollywood CA 90069 USA

**Ader, Tammy** — Producer, Writer
Creative Artists Agency, 2000 Ave of Stars, #100, Los Angeles CA 90067 USA

**Ades, Thomas J E** — Composer, Pianist, Conductor
I M G Artists, Hogarth Business Park, Chiswick, London W4 2TH, England

**Adey, Christopher** — Conductor
Richard Haigh Performing Arts, 6 Windmill St, London W1P 1HF, England

**Adey, William R** — Physician
20 Sunrise Hill Road, Orinda CA 94563, USA

**Adichie, Chimamanda N** — Writer
Wylie Agency, 17 Bedford Square, London WC1B 3JA, England

**Adickes, David P** — Sculptor
2500 Summer St, Houston TX 77007, USA

**Adickes, Mark S** — Football Player
6146 Bordley Dr, Houston TX 77057, USA

**Adiga, Aravind** — Writer
Simon & Schuster, 1230 Ave of Americas, Concourse 1, New York NY 10020 USA

**Adisa, Lawrence B** — Actor
Synergy Pictures, PO Box 16772, North Hollywood CA 91615, USA

**Adjani, Isabelle** — Actress
Orbis Media, 27 Rue Cardinet, 75017 Paris, France

**Adkins, Bennie G** — Army Vietnam War Hero (CMH)
2205 Heritage, Opelika AL 36804, USA

**Adkins, Derrick** — Track Athlete
909 Derrick Adkins Lane, West Hempstead NY 11552, USA

**Adkins, Jim** — Singer, Guitarist (Jimmy Eat World)
S A M, 722 Seward St, Los Angeles CA 90038, USA

**Adkins, Jonathan S (Jon)** — Baseball Player
RR 3 Box 2306, Wayne WV 25570, USA

**Adkins, Samuel A (Sam)** — Football Player
15912 NE 160th St, Woodinville WA 98072, USA

**Adkins, Seth** — Actor
Paradigm Agency, 360 N Crescent Dr, North Building, Beverly Hills CA 90210 USA

**Adkins, Trace** — Singer
1607 17th Ave S, Nashville TN 37212, USA

**Adkisson, Perry L** — Etomologist, Educator
3805 Park Village Court, Bryan TX 77802, USA

**Adleman, Leonard M** — Computer Scientist
University of Southern California, Computer Mathematics Dept, Los Angeles CA 90089, USA

**Adler, Brian** — Composer
Evolution Music Partners, 1680 Vine St, #500, Los Angeles CA 90028 USA

**Adler, Charles** — Actor
Innovative Artists, 1505 10th St, Santa Monica CA 90401 USA

**Adler, Chris** — Drummer (Lamb of God)
Entertainment Services, 1000 Main Street Plaza, #303, Voorhees NJ 08043, USA

**Adler, Jerry** — Actor
Paradigm Agency, 360 N Crescent Dr, North Building, Beverly Hills CA 90210 USA

**Adler, Joanna** — Actress
Innovative Artists, 235 Park Ave S, #1000, New York NY 10003 USA

**Adler, Julius** — Biologist, Biochemist
1234 Wellesley Road, Madison WI 53705, USA

**Adler, Lee** — Artist
Lime Kiln Farm, Climax NY 12042, USA

**Adler, Lou** — Director, Producer, Actor
Ode Sounds & Visuals, 3969 Villa Costera, Malibu CA 90265, USA

**Adler, Max** — Actor
C E S D, 10635 Santa Monica Blvd, #130, Los Angeles CA 90025 USA

**A**

**Adler, Renata** — Writer, Journalist
198 Hattertown Road, Newtown CT 06470, USA

**Adler, Stephen J** — Editor
Business Week, Editor's Office, 1221 Ave of Americas, New York NY 10020, USA

**Adler, Steven** — Drummer (Guns N' Roses)
Artists Worldwide, 3921 Wilshire Blvd, #619, Los Angeles CA 90010, USA

**Adler, Willie** — Guitarist (Lamb of God)
Entertainment Services, 1000 Main Street Plaza, #303, Voorhees NJ 08043, USA

**Adlington, Rebecca (Becky)** — Swimmer
Nova Centurion S C, Beechdale Road, Bilborough, Nottingham NG8 3LL, England

**Adlon, Pamela S** — Actress
C E S D, 10635 Santa Monica Blvd, #130, Los Angeles CA 90025 USA

**Adly-Guirgis, Stephen** — Actor
W M E Entertainment, 9601 Wilshire Blvd, #300, Beverly Hills CA 90210 USA

**Adonis** — Writer
College de France, 11 Marchelin Berthelot, 75231 Paris Cedux O5, France

**Adoor, Gopalakrishnan** — Director
Darsanam, Trivandrum, 695017 Kerala, India

**Adoti, Razaaq** — Actor
Abrams Artists, 9200 W Sunset Blvd, #1125, West Hollywood CA 90069 USA

**Adria Acosta, Albert** — Chef
Tickets Restaurant, Av Paralel 164, 08015 Barcelona, Spain

**Adria, Ferran** — Chef
El Bulli, Portaferrisa 7, Pral 2A, 08002 Barcelona, Spain

**Adrian, Nathan G** — Swimmer
University of California, Athletic Dept, Dwinelle Hall, Berkeley CA 94720, USA

**Adriana** — Model
Luna Presse, Villa Grande Armee, 8 Rue des Acacias, 75017 Paris, France

**Adsit, Scott** — Actor
A P A Talent & Literary Agency, 405 S Beverly Dr, #300, Beverly Hills CA 90212 USA

**Adu, Freddie** — Soccer Player
Philadelphia Union, Union Field, Seaport Dr, Chester PA 19013 USA

**Aduba, Uzo** — Actress, Singer
A P A Talent & Literary Agency, 405 S Beverly Dr, #300, Beverly Hills CA 90212 USA

**Adubato, Richie** — Basketball Coach
290 Chiswell Place, Lake Mary FL 32746, USA

**Adway, Dwayne** — Actor
Arch Talent Group, 117 N Robertson Blvd, Los Angeles CA 90048, USA

**Adyrkhayeva, Svetlana D** — Ballerina
1 Smolensky Pereulor 9, #74, 121099 Moscow, Russia

**Aesop Rock** — Rap Artist
Kork Agency, 1880 Century Park E, #711, Los Angeles CA 90067 USA

**Afanasenkov, Dmitry** — Ice Hockey Player
HC Moscow Dynamo, Leningradsky Prospect 36, 125167 Moscow, Russia

**Afanasyev, Viktor M** — Cosmonaut
Cosmonaut Training Center, Star City, 141160 Zvezdny Gorodok, Moscow Oblast, Russia

**Aferiat, Paul** — Interior Designer
Stamberg Aferiat Assoc, 126 5th Ave, #13ANew York NY 10011, USA

**Afewerki, Issaias** — President, Eritrea
President's Office, PO Box 257, Gejeret, Asmara, Eritrea

**Affeldt, Jeremy D** — Baseball Player
6211 E Mandalay Lane, Spokane WA 99217, USA

**Afflalo, Arron A** — Basketball Player
Denver Nuggets, Pepsi Center, 1000 Chopper Circle, Denver CO 80204 USA

**Affleck, Benjamin G (Ben)** — Actor, Director, Writer
W M E Entertainment, 9601 Wilshire Blvd, #300, Beverly Hills CA 90210 USA

**Affleck, Bruce** — Ice Hockey Player
1847 Oxborough Court, Chesterfield MO 63017, USA

**Affleck, Casey** — Actor
I/D Public Relations, 7060 Hollywood Blvd, #800, Los Angeles CA 90028 USA

**Affleck, James G** — Businessman
American Cyanamid, 5 Giralda Farms, Madison NJ 07940, USA

**Afinogenov, Maxim S** — Ice Hockey Player
3700 S Ocean Blvd, #1502, Highland Beach FL 33487, USA

**Afrika Bambaataa** — Rap Artist, DJ Musician
K L B Productions, 302A W 12th St, PH A #26, New York NY 10014, USA

**Afroman** — Rap Artist
Crescent Moon Talent, 20 Music Square W, Nashville TN 37203, USA

**Aga Khan IV, Prince Karim** — Spiritual Leader
Aiglemont, 60270 Gouvieux, France

**Agajanian, Benjamin J (Ben)** — Football Player
27950 Avenida Terrazo, Cathedral City CA 92234, USA

**Agam, Yaacov** — Artist
26 Rue Boulard, 75014 Paris, France

**Agassi, Andre** — Tennis Player
9804 Caden Hills Ave, Las Vegas NV 89145, USA

**Agatston, Arthur S** — Cardiologist, Writer
1633 N View Dr, Miami Beach FL 33140, USA

**Agbayani, Benny P, Jr** — Baseball Player
66-948 Kolu Place, Waialua HI 96791, USA

**Agee, Tommie L** — Football Player
1505 Blackhawk Dr, Opelika AL 36801, USA

**Aghdashloo, Shohreh** — Actress
Creative Artists Agency, 2000 Ave of Stars, #100, Los Angeles CA 90067 USA

**Agischewa, Marijam** — Actress
Doells, Rosenheimer Stra 38, 10781 Berlin, Germany

**Agler, Brian** — Basketball Coach
Seattle Storm, Key Arena, 351 Elliott Ave W, #500, Seattle WA 98119 USA

**Agliotti, Marilyn** — Field Hockey Player
Oranje-Zwart M H C, Charles Roelslaan 13, 5644 Eindhoven HX, Netherlands

**Aglukark, Susan** — Singer, Songwriter
Agency Group Ltd, 142 W 57th St, #600, New York NY 10019 USA

**Agnel, Yannick** — Swimmer
30 Boul General Louis Delfino, 06300 Nice, France

**Agnelo, Geraldo Majella Cardinal** — Religious Leader
Curia Metropolitana, Av Leovigildo Filgueiras 270, Garcia, 40100 000 Salvador BA, Brazil

**Agnes, Emily** — Model
Playboy Promotions, 9346 Civic Center Dr, #200, Beverly Hills CA 90210 USA
**Agnew, Chloe** — Singer (Celtic Woman)
W M E Entertainment, 9601 Wilshire Blvd, #300, Beverly Hills CA 90210 USA
**Agnew, Jim** — Ice Hockey Player
10080 Equestrian Way, Missoula MT 59808, USA
**Agnew, Paul** — Conductor
Theatre de Caen, 135 Boul du Marechal Leclerc, 14000 Caen, France
**Agnew, Ray M, Jr** — Football Player
2215 Cline St, Winston Salem NC 27107, USA
**Agnew, Rudolph I J** — Businessman
7 Eccleston St, London SW1X 9LX, England
**Agoos, Jeff** — Soccer Player, Executive
235 Pascack Road, Park Ridge NJ 07656, USA
**Agosta-Marciano, Meghan** — Ice Hockey Player
Team Canada, 2424 University Dr NW, Calgary AB T2N 3Y9, Canada
**Agosto Gonzalez, Juan R** — Baseball Player
4748 Sweetmeadow Circle, Sarasota FL 34238, USA
**Agosto, Benjamin A (Ben)** — Ice Dancer
31284 Huntley Square E, #1124, Beverly Hills MI 48025, USA
**Agranoff, Bernard W** — Biochemist
University of Michigan, Biological Chemistry Dept, 1150 W Medical Center Dr, Ann Arbor MI 48109, USA
**Agre, Peter** — Nobel Chemistry Laureate
7033 Lenleigh Road, Baltimore MD 21212, USA
**Agrelo, Marilyn** — Director
Gersh Agency, 9465 Wilshire Blvd, #600, Beverly Hills CA 90212 USA
**Agresta, Maria** — Opera Singer
I M G Artists, Hogarth Business Park, Chiswick, London W4 2TH, England
**Agria, John J** — Educator
5626 S Doubloon Court, #E, Tempe AZ 85283, USA
**Agron, Dianna** — Actress
Creative Artists Agency, 2000 Ave of Stars, #100, Los Angeles CA 90067 USA
**Agt, Andries A M Van** — Prime Minister, Netherlands
6564 Heilig Landstichting AG, Netherlands
**Aguayo Muriel, Luis** — Baseball Player
PO Box 1427, Vega Baja PR 00694, USA
**Aguayo, Albert J** — Neurophysiologist
648 Ave Belmont, Westmount QC H3Y 2W2, Canada
**Aguayo, Roberto** — Football Player
Florida State University, Athletic Dept, Tallahassee FL 32306, USA
**Aguerre, Gustavo** — Photographer, Artist
FA+, Drottninggatan 71A, 111 36 Stockholm, Sweden
**Aguilar Diaz, Macarena** — Handball Player
Randers H K, Sjaellandsgade 57, 8900 Randers, Denmark
**Aguilar, Fernando Sebastian Cardinal** — Religious Leader
Archdioces of Pamplona y Tudela, Plaza de Santa Maria la Real 1, 31001 Pamplona, Navarra, Spain
**Aguilar, George** — Actor
Artists First, PO Box 7217, Beverly Hills CA 90212, USA
**Aguilar, Louis R (Louie)** — Football Player
1411 Palmer Creek Dr, Columbia IL 62236, USA
**Aguilar, Pepe** — Singer
J E P Entertainment Group, 16207 Ventura Blvd, #510, Encino CA 91436, USA
**Aguilera, Christina** — Singer, Songwriter, Actress
Creative Artists Agency, 2000 Ave of Stars, #100, Los Angeles CA 90067 USA
**Aguilera, Marian** — Actress
Kuranda Mgmt, Santo Angel 84, 28043 Madrid, Spain
**Aguilera, Richard W (Rick)** — Baseball Player
PO Box 174, Rancho Santa Fe CA 92067, USA
**Aguirre, Mark A** — Basketball Player, Executive
10281 Highland Court, Frisco TX 75034, USA
**Agurcia, Ricardo** — Archaeologist
Copan Assn, Casa Yax Na, Avenida Los Jaguares, Copan Runinas, Honduras
**Agustoni, Gilberto Cardinal** — Religious Leader
Apostolic Signatura, Palazzo della Cancelleria, 00186 Rome, Italy
**Agutter, Jenny** — Actress
Artists Partnership, 101 Finsbury Pavement, London EC2A 1RS, England
**Agyeman, Freema** — Actress
Independent Talent Group, 40 Whitfield St, London W1T 2RH, England
**Ahanotu, Chidi O** — Football Player
1000 S Harbour Island Blvd, #2611, Tampa FL 33602, USA
**Ahdout, Jonathan** — Actor
Paradigm Agency, 360 N Crescent Dr, North Building, Beverly Hills CA 90210 USA
**Ahearn, Kevin J** — Ice Hockey Player
174 Marlborough St, Boston MA 02116, USA
**A'Hern, Basia** — Actress
Nickelodeon U K, PO Box 6425, London W1A 6UR, England
**Ahern, Fred** — Ice Hockey Player
21 Crescent St, Plympton MA 02367, USA
**Ahern, Jim** — Golfer
130 E Glendale Ave, Phoenix AZ 85020, USA
**Ahern, Neal, Jr** — Producer
Paradigm Agency, 360 N Crescent Dr, North Building, Beverly Hills CA 90210 USA
**Ahern, P Batholomew (Bertie)** — Prime Minister, Ireland
Saint Luke's, 161 Lower Drumcondra, Dublin 9, Ireland
**Ahlberg, Dennis A** — Educator
Trinity University, President's Office, 1 Trinity Place, San Antonio TX 78212, USA
**Ahlund, Joakim** — Guitarist, Singer (Caesars)
Paradigm Agency, 360 Park Ave, #1600, New York NY 10022 USA
**Ahmadzai, Ashraf Ghani** — President, Afghanistan
President's Office, Shar Rahi Sedarat, Kabul, Afghanistan
**Ahmed, Akbar** — Political Scientist
American University, International Relations Dept, Washington DC 20006, USA
**Ahmed, Fakhruddin** — Prime Minister, Bangladesh
Sere-e Bangla Nagar, Gono, Bhaban, Sher-e-Banglanagar, Dhakar 1207, Bangladesh
**Ahmed, Kazi Zafar** — Prime Minister, Bangladesh
National Parliament, Jatiya Sangsad, Dhaka 1801, Bangladesh

**A**

**Ahmed, Rafi** — Immunologist
Emory University Medical Center, 954 Gatewood Road, Atlanta GA 30329, USA

**Ahmed, Riz** — Actor, Writer, Director
Gordon & French, 12-13 Poland St, London W1F 8QB, England

**Ahn, Priscilla** — Singer, Songwriter
Blue Note Records, 6920 W Sunset Blvd, Los Angeles CA 90028 USA

**Ahn, Viktor** — Speed Skater
All-Russian Skating Union, Luzhnetskaia Nab 8, 119992 Moscow, Russia

**Aho, Esko T** — Prime Minister, Finland
Finnish Centre Party, Apollonkatu 11A, 00100 Helsinki, Finland

**Ahoussou-Kouadio, Jeannot** — Prime Minister, Cote d'Ivoire
Prime Minister's Office, Blvd Angoulvant Plateau, 01 BP 1533 Abidjan 01, Cote d'Ivoire

**Ahrends, Peter** — Architect
16 Rochester Road, London NW1 9JH, England

**Ahrens, David I** — Football Player
5864 Manchester Court, Pittsboro IN 46167, USA

**Ahrens, Lynn** — Lyricist
W M E Entertainment, 1325 Ave of Americas, New York NY 10019 USA

**Ahtisaari, Martti** — President, Finland; Nobel Peace Laureate
Erottajankatu 11A, #400, 00130 Helsinki, Finland

**Aibel, Howard J** — Businessman
183 Steep Hill Road, Weston CT 06883, USA

**Aicardi, Matteo** — Water Polo Player
A S D Pro Recco, Via Biagio Assereto 10/A, 16036 Recco (GE), Italy

**Aida, Takefumi** — Architect
1-3-2 Okubo, Shinjukuku, Tokyo 169 0072, Japan

**Aiello, Danny** — Actor
Artists Agency, 9430 Olympic Blvd, Beverly Hills CA 90212 USA

**Aigner, Hannes** — Canoeing Athlete
Augsburger Kajak Verein E V, Am Eiskanal 49, 86161 Augsburg, Germany

**Aigrain, Pierre R** — Physicist
56 Rue de Boulainvilliers, 75016 Paris, France

**Aiken, Clay** — Singer
Strategic Artist Mgmt, 1100 Glendon Ave, #1000, Los Angeles CA 90024, USA

**Aiken, John (Johnny)** — Ice Hockey Player
18 Pinetree Road, Billerica MA 01821, USA

**Aiken, Liam** — Actor
Brillstein Entertainment Partners, 9150 Wilshire Blvd, #350, Beverly Hills CA 90212 USA

**Aiken, Linda H** — Sociologist
2209 Lombard St, Philadelphia PA 19146, USA

**Aiken, Sam** — Football Player
104 Winter Ridge Dr, Holly Springs NC 27540, USA

**Aikens, Curtis** — Chef
PO Box 575, Conyers GA 30012, USA

**Aikens, Willie M** — Baseball Player
10206 Locust St, Kansas City MO 64131, USA

**Aikin, Laura** — Opera Singer
Ingpen & Williams, 131 Putney Bridge Road, London SW15 2PA, England

**Aikman, Troy K** — Football Player, Sportscaster
3801 Normandy Ave, Dallas TX 75205, USA

**Aiko** — Princess, Japan
Imperial Palace, 1-1 Chiyoda, Chiyodaku, Tokyo 100 0001, Japan

**Ailes, Roger E** — Businessman
218 Truman Dr, Cresskill NJ 07626, USA

**Aimard, Pierre-Laurent** — Concert Pianist
Harrison/Parrott, 5-6 Albion Court, London W6 0QT, England

**Aimee, Anouk** — Actress
Artmedia, 20 Ave Rapp, 75007 Paris, France

**Ainge, Daniel R (Danny)** — Basketball Player, Coach
140 Wellesley Ave, Wellesley Hills MA 02481, USA

**Ainsleigh, H Gordon** — Ultra Marathon Athlete
17119 Placer Hills Road, Meadow Vista CA 95722, USA

**Ainslie, C Benedict (Ben)** — Yachtsman
Royal Lymington Yacht Club, Bath Road, Lymington, Hampshire S041 3SE, England

**Ainsworth, Kacey** — Actress
United Agents, 12-26 Lexington St, London W1F 0LE, England

**Ainsworth, Kurt** — Baseball Player
15220 Memorial Tower Dr, Baton Rouge LA 70810, USA

**Airiana** — Circus Aerialist
Ringling Bros Barnum & Bailey, 8607 Westwood Circle Dr, Vienna VA 22182 USA

**Airlie, Andrew** — Actor
Noble/Caplan/Abrams, 1260 Yonge St, #200, Toronto ON MT4 1W6, Canada

**Aislin** — Editorial Cartoonist
Gazette, 1010 Sainte Catherine Street W, Montreal QC H3B 5L1, Canada

**Aitay, Victor** — Concert Violinist
800 Deerfield Road, #203, Highland Park IL 60035, USA

**Aitcheson, Joe, Jr** — Steeplechase Racing Jockey
15404 Riding Stable Road, Laurel MD 20707, USA

**Aitken, Brad** — Ice Hockey Player
825 Royal Orchard Dr, Oshawa ON L1K 1Z8, Canada

**Aitken, Doug** — Artist
2437 Via Sonoma, Palos Verdes Estates CA 90274, USA

**Aivazoff, Micah** — Ice Hockey Player
6916 Hammond St, Powell River BC V8A 1R4, Canada

**Aizenberg Selove, Fay** — Physicist
259 N Radnor Chester Road, #160, Wayne PA 19087, USA

**Aja, Alexandre** — Director
W M E Entertainment, 9601 Wilshire Blvd, #300, Beverly Hills CA 90210 USA

**Ajayan, Pulickel M** — Materials Engineer
Rice University, Materials Science Dept, Houston TX 77005, USA

**Ajodhia, Jules R** — Prime Minister, Suriname
Prime Minister's Office, Paramaribo, Suriname

**Akalaitis, JoAnne** — Director, Writer, Actress
Mabon Mimes, 150 1st Ave, New York NY 10009, USA

**Akasaki, Isamu** — Nobel Physics Laureate
Nagoya University, Asasaki Institute, Furo-cho, Chikusaku, Nagoya 464-8601, Japan

**Ahmed - Akasaki**

**Akbar, Taufik** — Astronaut, Indonesia
Jalan Simp, Pahlawan III/24, Bandung 40124, Indonesia
**Akebono** — Sumo Wrestler
Azumazeki Stable, 4-6-4 Higashi Komagata, Ryogoku, Sumidaku, Tokyo 130 0005, Japan
**Akel, Mike** — Director, Producer, Writer
United Talent Agency, U T A Plaza, 9336 Civic Center Dr, Beverly Hills CA 90210 USA
**Aker, Jack D** — Baseball Player
5911 E Bloomfield Road, Scottsdale AZ 85254, USA
**Akerlof, George A** — Nobel Economics Laureate
University of California, Economics Dept, Evans Hall, Berkeley CA 94720, USA
**Akerlund, Jonas** — Director
I C M Partners, 10250 Constellation Blvd, #900, Los Angeles CA 90067 USA
**Akerman, Malin** — Actress, Singer
Sanders Armstrong Caserta, 2120 Colorado Ave, #120, Santa Monica CA 90404, USA
**Akers, Angie** — Volleyball Player
Gaylord Sports Mgmt, 13845 N Northsight Blvd, #200, Scottsdale AZ 85260 USA
**Akers, David R** — Football Player
2509 Belle Brook Dr, Franklin TN 37067, USA
**Akers, Michelle A** — Soccer Player
1690 Tallapoosa Dr, Geneva FL 32732, USA
**Akers, Thomas D (Tom)** — Astronaut
HC 3 Box 35, Eminence MO 65466, USA
**Akey, Lisa** — Actress
Metropolitan Talent Agency, 5405 Wilshire Blvd, #218, Los Angeles CA 90036 USA
**Akhmedow, Han A** — Prime Minister, Turkmenistan
Presidential Administration, Karl Marx 24, 744017 Ashgabat, Turkmenistan
**Akhurst, Lucy** — Actress
Emptage Hallett, 14 Rathbone Place, London W1T 1HT, England
**Akihito** — Emperor, Japan
Imperial Palace, 1-1 Chiyoda, Chiyodaku, Tokyo 100 0001, Japan
**Akil** — Rap Artist (Jurassic 5)
Vision Entertainment Group, 1100 Glendon Ave, #1100, Los Angeles CA 90024, USA
**Akilov, Akil G** — Prime Minister, Tajikistan
Prime Minister's Office, Rudaki Prospect 42, 743051 Dushaube, Tajikistan
**Akin, Fatih** — Director, Producer, Actor
Corazon International, Ditmar-Koel-Str 26, 20459 Hamburg, Germany
**Akinnagbe, Gbenga** — Actor
Stone Manners Salners, 6100 Wilshire Blvd, #1500, Los Angeles CA 90035 USA
**Akinnuoye-Agbaje, Adewale** — Actor
A P A Talent/Literary Agency, 250 W 57th St, #1701, New York NY 10107 USA
**Akinradewo, Foluke A** — Volleyball Player
1181 NW 101st Way, Plantation FL 33322, USA
**Akins, Christopher D (Chris)** — Football Player
60 Gold Mine Springs Road, Conway AR 72032, USA
**Akins, Rhett** — Singer
R P M Mgmt, 209 10th Ave S, #229, Nashville TN 37203, USA
**Akishino** — Prince, Japan
Imperial Palace, 1-1 Chiyoda, Chiyodaku, Tokyo 100 0001, Japan
**Akiyama, Kazuyoshi** — Conductor
Columbia Artists Mgmt Inc, 5 Columbus Circle, 1790 Broadway, #1600, New York NY 10019 USA
**Akiyoshi, Toshiko** — Jazz Pianist, Composer
38 W 94th St, New York NY 10025, USA
**Akon** — Singer, Songwriter
H G X Marketing, 307 W 38th St, #807, New York NY 10018, USA
**Akpan, Uwem** — Writer
Little Brown, 3 Center Plaza, #100, Boston MA 02108 USA
**Akram, Omar** — Singer
Real Music, 85 Liberty Ship Way, #207, Sausalito CA 94965, USA
**Akre, Carrie** — Singer
Good-Ink Records, 203 Underhill Ave, #3D, Brooklyn NY 11238, USA
**Aksyonov, Vladimir V** — Cosmonaut
Astrakhansky Per 5, Kv 100, 129010 Moscow, Russia
**Al Hussein** — Crown Prince, Jordan
Royal Palace, Royal Hashemite Court, Amman, Jordan
**Alabau Neira, Marina** — Yachtswoman
Real Federacion Espanola de Vela, Luis de Salazar 9, 28002 Madrid, Spain
**Aladag, Feo** — Director, Writer, Actress
Wasted Mgmt, Dieffenbachstr 33, 10967 Berlin, Germany
**Aladjem, Silvio** — Obstetrician, Gynecologist
1655 W State Road, Hastings MI 49058, USA
**Alagna, Roberto** — Opera Singer
Askonas Holt, Lincoln House, 300 High Holborn, London WC1V 7JH, England
**Alaia, Azzeddine** — Fashion Designer
7 Rue de Moussy, 75002 Paris, France
**Alaimo, Simone** — Opera Singer
Stage Door, Via S Giorgio 4, 40121 Bologna, Italy
**Alarcon, Arthur L** — Judge
US Court of Appeals, 312 N Spring St, #G33, Los Angeles CA 90012, USA
**Alarie, Mark S** — Basketball Player, Coach
8514 Country Club Dr, Bethesda MD 20817, USA
**Alas, Mert** — Photographer
Art Partner, 155 6th Ave, #1500, New York NY 10013, USA
**Alaskey, Joe** — Actor
Vox Inc, 6420 Wilshire Blvd, #1080, Los Angeles CA 90048 USA
**Alazzqui, Carlos** — Actor, Writer
Sovereign Talent Group, 8421 Wilshire Blvd, #200, Beverly Hills CA 90211 USA
**Alba, Jessica** — Actress
3 Arts Entertainment, 9460 Wilshire Blvd, #700, Beverly Hills CA 90212 USA
**Alban, Carlo** — Actor
Don Buchwald Talent Agency, 6500 Wilshire Blvd, #2200, Los Angeles CA 90048 USA
**Alban, Richard H (Dick)** — Football Player
306 Belpaire Court, Newtown Square PA 19073, USA
**Albarn, Damon** — Singer (Blur, Gorillaz); Songwriter
C M O Mgmt, Shepherds East, Richmond Way, London W14 0DQ, England
**Albeck, C Stanley (Stan)** — Basketball Coach
130 Tall Oak Dr, San Antonio TX 78232, USA

| | |
|---|---|
| **Albee, Arden L** | Space Scientist, Geologist |
| 2040 Midlothian Dr, Altadena CA 91001, USA | |
| **Albee, Edward F** | Writer |
| 14 Harrison St, New York NY 10013, USA | |
| **Albelin, Tommy** | Ice Hockey Player |
| 23 Fellswood Dr, Verona NJ 07044, USA | |
| **Alberghetti, Anna Maria** | Singer, Actress |
| 10755 Massachusetts Ave, #204, Los Angeles CA 90024, USA | |
| **Albers, Kristi** | Golfer |
| 5872 Via Cuesta Dr, El Paso TX 79912, USA | |
| **Alberstein, Chava** | Singer |
| Aviv Productions, 10418 E Meadowhill Dr, Scottsdale AZ 85255, USA | |
| **Albert II** | Prince, Monaco |
| Palais de Monaco, BP 518, 98015 Monaco Cedex, Monaco | |
| **Albert II** | King, Belgium |
| Koninklijk Palais, Rue de Brederode, 1000 Brussels, Belgium | |
| **Albert, Arthur** | Cinematographer |
| 707 Haverford Ave, Pacific Palisades CA 90272, USA | |
| **Albert, Jason** | Singer (Heartland) |
| Country Thunder Records, 1016 17th Ave S, Nashville TN 37212, USA | |
| **Albert, Jodie** | Actress, Singer |
| Susan Angel & Kevin Francis, 12 D'Arblay St, London W1F 8DU, England | |
| **Albert, John** | Writer |
| Simon & Schuster, 1230 Ave of Americas, Concourse 1, New York NY 10020, USA | |
| **Albert, John G** | Air Force General |
| Albert Farms, RR 2, Monroe VA 24574, USA | |
| **Albert, Kenny** | Sportscaster |
| Fox-TV, Sports Dept, 205 W 67th St, New York NY 10065 USA | |
| **Albert, Marv** | Sportscaster |
| TNT-TV, Sports Dept, 1050 Techwood Dr, Atlanta GA 30318 USA | |
| **Alberti, Maryse** | Cinematographer |
| Dattner Dispoto, 10635 Santa Monica Blvd, #165, Los Angeles CA 90025, USA | |
| **Alberti, Micah** | Actor |
| Innovative Artists, 1505 10th St, Santa Monica CA 90401 USA | |
| **Alberts, Andrew J** | Ice Hockey Player |
| 4265 Cottonwood Lane, Excelsior MN 55331, USA | |
| **Alberts, Bruce M** | Foundation Executive, Biochemist |
| National Academy of Sciences, 500 5th St NW, #1, Washington DC 20001, USA | |
| **Alberts, Trev K** | Football Player |
| University of Nebraska, Athletic Dept, Omaha, NE 68106, USA | |
| **Albertsen, Jordan** | Director, Writer |
| Paradigm Agency, 360 N Crescent Dr, North Building, Beverly Hills CA 90210 USA | |
| **Albita** | Singer, Songwriter |
| Albita Rodriguez Enterprises, 5825 SW 8th St, #200, Miami FL 33144, USA | |
| **Albom, Mitch** | Writer |
| Hyperion Books, 114 5th Ave, New York NY 10011 USA | |
| **Alborn, Alan** | Ski Jumper |
| PO Box 109, Willow AK 99688, USA | |
| **Albrecht, A Chim** | Body Builder |
| Physique Promotions, 9668 Moss Glen Ave, Fountain Valley CA 92708, USA | |
| **Albrecht, Marc** | Conductor |
| I M G Artists, Hogarth Business Park, Chiswick, London W4 2TH, England | |
| **Albrecht, Stan L** | Educator |
| Utah State University, President's Office, Logan UT 84322, USA | |
| **Albrecht, Theodore C (Ted)** | Football Player |
| 1205 Cherry St, Winnetka IL 60093, USA | |
| **Albright, Christopher J (Chris)** | Soccer Player |
| Philadelphia Union, Union Field, Seaport Dr, Chester PA 19013 USA | |
| **Albright, Gerald** | Jazz Saxophonist, Singer |
| Chapman & Co Mgmt, PO Box 55246, Sherman Oaks CA 91413, USA | |
| **Albright, Jack L** | Animal Scientist |
| 839 E Village Dr, Carmel IN 46032, USA | |
| **Albright, L Ethan** | Football Player |
| 19181 Ferry Field Terrace, Leesburg VA 20176, USA | |
| **Albright, Lola** | Actress |
| PO Box 6067, Glendale CA 91225, USA | |
| **Albright, Madeleine K** | Secretary, State |
| Albright Stonebridge Group, 1101 New York Ave NW, #900, Washington DC 20005, USA | |
| **Albright, Tenley E** | Figure Skater |
| 70 Suffolk Road, Chestnut Hill MA 02467, USA | |
| **Albuquerque, Lita** | Artist |
| Art Center College of Design, 1700 Lida St, Pasadena CA 91103, USA | |
| **Albus, Jim** | Golfer |
| 3972 Somerset Dr, #1, Sarasota FL 34242, USA | |
| **Alcaraz, Lalo** | Editorial Cartoonist |
| PO Box 63052, Los Angeles CA 90063, USA | |
| **Alcock, Charles** | Theoretical Physicist |
| Lawrence Livermore Laboratory, 7000 East St, Livermore CA 94550, USA | |
| **Alcott, Amy S** | Golfer |
| 323 Amalfi Dr, Santa Monica CA 90402, USA | |
| **Alda, Alan** | Actor |
| I C M Partners, 10250 Constellation Blvd, #900, Los Angeles CA 90067 USA | |
| **Alda, Rutanya** | Actress |
| Shallon Star Mgmt, 14320 Ventura Blvd, #624, Sherman Oaks CA 91423, USA | |
| **Aldaco, Marco** | Architect |
| Paseo de la Canada 3872, Guadalajara 45129 Jalisco, Mexico | |
| **Aldean, Jason** | Singer, Guitarist |
| Spalding Entertainment, 54 Music Square E, #200, Nashville TN 37203, USA | |
| **Alden, Ginger** | Model, Actress, Singer |
| Ron Leyser, 25 Rolling Hill Court W, Sag Harbor NY 11963, USA | |
| **Alden, Howard** | Jazz Guitarist |
| Hot Jazz Mgmt, 116 E 27th St, New York NY 10016, USA | |
| **Alder, Berni J** | Theoretical Physicist |
| 1245 Contra Costa Dr, El Cerrito CA 94530, USA | |
| **Alder, Janine** | Ice Hockey Player |
| E H C Winterthur, Postfach 1729, 8401 Winterthur, Switzerland | |

**Alderete, Loretta** — Golfer
80194 Delphi Court, Indio CA 92201, USA

**Alderfer-Benner, Gertrude** — Baseball Player
2191 County Line Road, East Greenville PA 18041, USA

**Alderman, Daniel** — Drag Racing Driver
6730 Flemingsburg Road, Morehead KY 40351, USA

**Alderman, Darrell** — Auto Racing Driver
D A Construction, 8145 Flemingsburg Road, Morehead KY 40351, USA

**Alderman, Grady C** — Football Player
62 Elk Valley Way, Evergreen CO 80439, USA

**Aldisert, Ruggero J** — Judge
120 Cremona Dr, #D, Santa Barbara CA 93117, USA

**Aldiss, Brian W** — Writer
Hambledon, 39 Saint Andrews Road, Old Headington, Oxford OX3 9DL, England

**Aldred, Scott W** — Baseball Player
13435 Lakebrook Dr, Fenton MI 48430, USA

**Aldred, Sophie** — Actress
1 Duchess St, #1, London S1N 3EE, England

**Aldrete, Michael P (Mike)** — Baseball Player
22160 Toro Hills Dr, Salinas CA 93908, USA

**Aldrich, Lance** — Cartoonist (Real Life Adventures)
Universal Press Syndicate, 4520 Main St, #700, Kansas City MO 64111 USA

**Aldrich, Richard** — Artist
Bortolami Gallery, 520 W 20th St, New York NY 10011, USA

**Aldridge, Allen R, Jr** — Football Player
2111 Hammerwood Dr, Missouri City TX 77489, USA

**Aldridge, Donald O** — Air Force General
1004 Lincoln Road, #168, Bellevue NE 68005, USA

**Aldridge, Edward C (Pete), Jr** — Government Official, Businessman
4308 Lorcom Lane, Arlington VA 22207, USA

**Aldridge, LaMarcus** — Basketball Player
01819 SW Radcliffe Road, Portland OR 97219, USA

**Aldridge, Lily** — Model
I M G Models, 304 Park Ave S, #1200, New York NY 10010 USA

**Aldrin, Edwin E (Buzz), Jr** — Astronaut
10380 Wilshire Blvd, #703, Los Angeles CA 90024, USA

**Aleandro, Norma** — Actress
Blanco Encalada 1150, 1428 Buenos Aires, Argentina

**Alechinsky, Pierre** — Artist
2 Bis Rue Henri Barbusse, 78380 Bougival, France

**Alejandro, Kevin** — Actor
Gersh Agency, 9465 Wilshire Blvd, #600, Beverly Hills CA 90212 USA

**Alekna, Virgilijus** — Track Athlete
Prime Minister's Office, Tumo-Vaizganto 2, 01511 Vilnius, Lithuania

**Aleksander, Grant** — Actor
Abrams Artists, 9200 W Sunset Blvd, #1125, West Hollywood CA 90069 USA

**Aleksandrov, Aleksandr P** — Cosmonaut
Space Research Institute, 6 Moskovska St, 1000 Sofia, Bulgaria

**Aleksinas, Charles (Chuck)** — Basketball Player
16 Litchfield Road, Morris CT 06763, USA

**Aleksiy II** — Religious Leader
Moscow Patriarchate, Chisty Per 5, 119034 Moscow, Russia

**Alencherry, George Cardinal** — Religious Leader
Syro-Malabar Archiepiscopal Curia, Mount Saint Thomas, PO Box 3110, Kerala 682030, India

**Alerlof, George** — Nobel Economics Laureate
University of California, Economics Dept, Berkeley CA 94720, USA

**Alesi, Jean** — Auto Racing Driver
A F Corse Srl, Via Farnesiana 242/B, 29100 Piacenza, Italy

**Alesi, Tommy** — Percussionist (BeauSoleil)
Rosebud Agency, PO Box 170429, San Francisco CA 94117 USA

**Alessi, Raquel** — Actress
Vincent Cirrincione Assoc, 1516 N Fairfax Ave, Los Angeles CA 90046 USA

**Alessio, Josephine** — Actress
Giuseppino Alessio, Via Aquara 75, 84020 Bellosguardo, Italy

**Alexakis, Art** — Singer, Guitarist (Everclear)
Pinnacle Entertainment, 30 Glenn St, White Plains NY 10603, USA

**Alexander** — Crown Prince, Yugoslavia
Royal Palace, Dedinje, 11040 Belgrade, Serbia

**Alexander, A J** — Model, Actress
Playboy Promotions, 9346 Civic Center Dr, #200, Beverly Hills CA 90210 USA

**Alexander, Brooke** — Actress, Model
Abrams Artists, 9200 W Sunset Blvd, #1125, West Hollywood CA 90069 USA

**Alexander, Bruce E** — Football Player
508 Englewood Dr, Lufkin TX 75901, USA

**Alexander, Charles F, Jr** — Football Player
3711 Heritage Colony Dr, Missouri City TX 77459, USA

**Alexander, Christopher W J** — Architect
2701 Shasta Road, Berkeley CA 94708, USA

**Alexander, Claire** — Ice Hockey Player
11 Tammy Circle, Saint Catherines ON L2N 1R2, Canada

**Alexander, Claudia** — Space Scientist
Jet Propulsion Laboratory, 4800 Oak Grove Dr, Pasadena CA 91109 USA

**Alexander, Clifford L, Jr** — Government Official
Alexander Assoc, 400 C St NE, Washington DC 20002, USA

**Alexander, Dan L** — Football Player
58520 Saint Clement Ave, Plaquemine LA 70764, USA

**Alexander, Derrick** — Football Player
5301 Gulf Blvd, #E303, Saint Pete Beach FL 33706, USA

**Alexander, Derrick S** — Football Player
25381 W 149th Court, Olathe KS 66061, USA

**Alexander, Doyle L** — Baseball Player
5416 Hunter Park Court, Arlington TX 76017, USA

**Alexander, Eliana** — Actress
TalentWorks, 3500 W Olive Ave, #1400, Burbank CA 91505 USA

**Alexander, Elizabeth** — Writer
Yale University, English Dept, New Haven CT 06520, USA

**Alexander, Emily** — Model, Actress
Playboy Promotions, 9346 Civic Center Dr, #200, Beverly Hills CA 90210 USA
**Alexander, Eric** — Jazz Saxophonist
Joel Chriss Co, 300 Mercer St, #3J, New York NY 10003 USA
**Alexander, Erika** — Actress
Untitled Entertainment, 350 S Beverly Dr, #200, Beverly Hills CA 90212 USA
**Alexander, Flex** — Actor
Global Artists Agency, 6253 Hollywood Blvd, #508, Los Angeles CA 90028 USA
**Alexander, Gary W** — Baseball Player
5420 Senford Ave, Los Angeles CA 90056, USA
**Alexander, Jaimie** — Actress
W M E Entertainment, 9601 Wilshire Blvd, #300, Beverly Hills CA 90210 USA
**Alexander, James** — Bassist (Bar-Kays)
Entertainment Artists, 2409 21st Ave S, #100, Nashville TN 10019 USA
**Alexander, Jane** — Actress, Government Official
W M E Entertainment, 9601 Wilshire Blvd, #300, Beverly Hills CA 90210 USA
**Alexander, Jason** — Actor, Comedian
Innovative Artists, 1505 10th St, Santa Monica CA 90401 USA
**Alexander, Jesse** — Producer, Writer
Creative Artists Agency, 2000 Ave of Stars, #100, Los Angeles CA 90067 USA
**Alexander, Jessica (Jessi)** — Singer, Songwriter
W M E Entertainment, 1600 Division St, #300, Nashville TN 37203 USA
**Alexander, Jim** — Actor
Associated International Mgmt, 7 Hatton Garden, #400, London EC1N 8AD, England
**Alexander, Joe A** — Basketball Player
Chicago Bulls, United Center, 1901 W Madison St, Chicago IL 60612 USA
**Alexander, John E** — Artist
University of Houston, Art Dept, 4800 Calhoun, Houston TX 77004, USA
**Alexander, Jules** — Musician (Association)
Variety Artists, 1924 Spring St, Paso Robles CA 93446 USA
**Alexander, Kala** — Actor, Surfer
Innovative Artists, 235 Park Ave S, #1000, New York NY 10003 USA
**Alexander, Kermit J** — Football Player
16651 Stallion Place, Riverside CA 92504, USA
**Alexander, Khandi** — Actress
Resolution, 1801 Century Park E, #2300, Los Angeles CA 90067 USA
**Alexander, Manuel D (Manny)** — Baseball Player
3660 N Lake Dr, #2664, Chicago IL 60613, USA
**Alexander, Matthew (Matt)** — Baseball Player
2419 Stonewall St, Shreveport LA 71103, USA
**Alexander, Monty** — Jazz Pianist
Abby Hoffer, 223 1/2 E 48th St, New York NY 10017, USA
**Alexander, Peter** — Sculptor
1811 16th St, Santa Monica CA 90404, USA
**Alexander, R Brent** — Football Player
349 Remington Ave, Gallatin TN 37066, USA
**Alexander, R Minter** — Air Force General
824 Eden Court, Alexandria VA 22308, USA
**Alexander, Sarah** — Actress
Independent Talent Group, 40 Whitfield St, London W1T 2RH, England
**Alexander, Sasha** — Actress
United Talent Agency, U T A Plaza, 9336 Civic Center Dr, Beverly Hills CA 90210 USA
**Alexander, Shaun** — Football Player
13655 NE 36th Place, Bellevue WA 98005, USA
**Alexander, Stephen T** — Football Player
30677 Santa Fe Ave, Norman OK 73072, USA
**Alexander, V Raymond (Ray)** — Football Player
1631 Royal Palm Dr, Edgewater FL 32132, USA
**Alexander, Willie** — Bassist, Guitarist (Velvet Underground)
Tourmaline Music Group, 894 Mayville Road, Bethel PA 19507, USA
**Alexander, Willie J** — Football Player
7219 Holder Forest Circle, Houston TX 77088, USA
**Alexandre, Maxime** — Cinematographer
Partos Co, 227 Broadway, #204, Santa Monica CA 90401, USA
**Alexeev, Dmitri K** — Concert Pianist
I M G Artists, Hogarth Business Park, Chiswick, London W4 2TH, England
**Alexeev, Nikita** — Ice Hockey Player
PO Box 3342, Riverview FL 33568, USA
**Alexeev, Nikolai G** — Conductor
Estonian National Symphony, Estonia Ave 4, 10148 Tallinn, Estonia
**Alexeyeva, Lyudmila M** — Social Activist, Historian
Moscow Prison Reform Center, Luchnikov Lane 4, Entrance 3, 101000 Moscow, Russia
**Alexie, Sherman** — Writer
PO Box 376, Wellpinit WA 99040, USA
**Alexi-Malle, Adam** — Actor
Innovative Artists, 1505 10th St, Santa Monica CA 90401 USA
**Alexis, Kim** — Model
Axiom Sports & Entertainment, 28 W 44th St, #1600, New York NY 10036, USA
**Alexrod, Albert** — Fencer
798 Heritage Hills, #A, Somers NY 10589, USA
**Alfaro, Andreu** — Sculptor
Urbanizacion Sta Barbara 138R, 46111 Rocafort, Valencia, Spain
**Alfaro, Victor** — Fashion Designer
130 Barrow St, New York NY 10014, USA
**Alferov, Zhores** — Nobel Physics Laureate
Zhakia Duclo Str 8/3-82, 194223 Saint Petersburg, Russia
**Alfieri, Janet** — Cartoonist (Suburban Cowgirls)
15 Bumpus Road, Plymouth MA 02360, USA
**Alfieri, Victor** — Actor
Metropolitan Talent Agency, 5405 Wilshire Blvd, #218, Los Angeles CA 90036 USA
**Alfonseca, Antonio** — Baseball Player
3020 SW 169th Terrace, Miramar FL 33029, USA
**Alfonso, Kristian** — Actress
I C M Partners, 10250 Constellation Blvd, #900, Los Angeles CA 90067 USA
**Alfonzo, Edgardo A** — Baseball Player
3745 Marietta Way, Saint Cloud FL 34772, USA

**Alford, Steve** — Basketball Player, Coach
5425 Collingwood Circle, Calabasas CA 91302, USA
**Alford, William P** — Attorney, Writer
Harvard University, International Legal Studies, Cambridge MA 02138, USA
**Alfredson, Tomas** — Director
Cinetic Mgmt, 555 W 25th St, #400, New York NY 10001, USA
**Alfredsson, H Daniel** — Ice Hockey Player
Hamravagen 124, 429 44 Saro, Sweden
**Alfredsson, Helen** — Golfer
9034 Crichton Woods Dr, Orlando FL 32819, USA
**Algabid, Hamid** — Prime Minister, Niger
National Assembly, Vice President's Office, Niamey, Niger
**Alger, Pat** — Singer, Guitarist, Songwriter
A S C A P, 1 Lincoln Plaza, New York NY 10023, USA
**Algotsson Ostholt, Sara** — Equestrian
Vohren 31, 482 31 Warendorf, Sweden
**Ali, Aires B B** — Prime Minister, Mozambique
Prime Minister's Office, Avenida Julius Nyerere 1780, Maputo, Mozambique
**Ali, Laila** — Boxer
She Bee Stingin Inc, 20929 Ventura Blvd, #47-432, Woodland Hills CA 91364, USA
**Ali, Monica** — Writer
Charles Scribner's Sons, 866 3rd Ave, New York NY 10022 USA
**Ali, Muhammad** — Boxer
PO Box 160, Berrien Springs MI 49103, USA
**Ali, Robin** — Ophthalmologist
Moorfields Eye Hospital, 162 City Road, London EC1V 2PD, England
**Ali, Tatyana** — Singer, Actress
Innovative Artists, 1505 10th St, Santa Monica CA 90401 USA
**Alibar, Lucy** — Writer
Gersh Agency, 9465 Wilshire Blvd, #600, Beverly Hills CA 90212 USA
**Alicea de Jesus, Luis R** — Baseball Player
2140 C Road, Loxahatchee FL 33470, USA
**Alis, Robert** — Cinematographer
13920 72nd Road, Flushing NY 11367, USA
**Alisha** — Singer, Songwriter
International Artists, PO Box 32, 5360 Grave AA, Netherlands
**Alison, Jane** — Writer
Farrar Straus Giroux, 18 W 18th St, #700, New York NY 10011 USA
**Alito, Samuel A, Jr** — Supreme Court Justice
US Supreme Court, 1 1st St NE, Washington DC 20543 USA
**Alivisatos, A Paul** — Chemist
Lawrence Berkeley National Laboratory, 1 Cycloton Road, Berkeley CA 94720 USA
**Aliyev, Ilham** — President, Azerbaijan
President's Office, Istiglaliyyat St 19, 371066 Baku, Azerbaijan
**Allan, Gabrielle** — Producer, Writer
United Talent Agency, U T A Plaza, 9336 Civic Center Dr, Beverly Hills CA 90210 USA
**Allan, Gary** — Singer, Guitarist
H B Public Relations & Mgmt, 4611 Dakota Ave, Nashville TN 37209, USA
**Allan, James** — Singer, Guitarist (Glasvegas)
Sony Music, 9 Derry St, London W8 5HY, England
**Allan, Jed** — Actor
477 White Horse Trail, Palm Desert CA 92211, USA
**Allan, Jennifer** — Model
Playboy Promotions, 9346 Civic Center Dr, #200, Beverly Hills CA 90210 USA
**Allan, Mitch** — Singer, Guitarist (SR-71); Songwriter
Supreme Entertainment Artists, PO Box 15601, Boston MA 02215, USA
**Allan, Rab** — Singer, Guitarist (Glasvegas)
Sony Music, 9 Derry St, London W8 5HY, England
**Allan, William G** — Artist
73 Ranch Road, San Rafael CA 94903, USA
**Allard, Beatrice (Bea)** — Baseball Player
1040 Ridgewood Dr, Lillian AL 36549, USA
**Allard, Linda M** — Fashion Designer
Ellen Tracy Corp, 575 Fashion Ave, #300, New York NY 10018, USA
**Allbaugh, Joseph** — Government Official
Federal Emergency Management Agency, 500 C St SW, Washington DC 20472, USA
**Allegre, Claude J** — Geochemist
Institut de France, 23 Quai Conti, 75006 Paris, France
**Allegre, Raul E** — Football Player
6500 Rain Creek Parkway, Austin TX 78759, USA
**Allem, Fulton P** — Golfer
6786 Hidden Glade Place, Sanford FL 32771, USA
**Allen, Amy** — Actress
PO Box 8081, Calabasas CA 91372, USA
**Allen, Andrew M** — Astronaut
205 Highland Woods Dr, Safety Harbor FL 34695, USA
**Allen, Anthony (Tony)** — Basketball Player
70 Kodiak Way, #2638, Waltham MA 02451, USA
**Allen, Anthony D** — Football Player
956 20th Ave, Seattle WA 98122, USA
**Allen, Ashley** — Model
Playboy Promotions, 9346 Civic Center Dr, #200, Beverly Hills CA 90210 USA
**Allen, Bernard K (Bernie)** — Baseball Player
3725 Coventry Way, Carmel IN 46033, USA
**Allen, Bruce** — Auto Racing Driver
Reher-Morrison Racing Engines, 1120 Enterprise Place, Arlington TX 76001, USA
**Allen, Bryan** — Ice Hockey Player
6635 NW 122nd Ave, Parkland FL 33076, USA
**Allen, C Keith (Bingo)** — Ice Hockey Coach, Executive
20011 Sanibel View Circle, #201, Fort Myers FL 33908, USA
**Allen, Chad** — Actor
Kazarian/Measures/Ruskin, 11969 Ventura Blvd, #300, Studio City CA 91604 USA
**Allen, Charles R (Chuck)** — Football Player
192 Victoria Loop, Port Townsend WA 98368, USA
**Allen, Chris** — Guitarist, Singer (Neon Trees)
Creative Artists Agency, 2000 Ave of Stars, #100, Los Angeles CA 90067 USA

**Allen, Christa B** — Actress
Maydew & Golenberg, 8383 Wilshire Blvd, #1050, Beverly Hills CA 90211, USA
**Allen, Dalva R** — Football Player
411 County Road 1925, Mount Pleasant TX 75455, USA
**Allen, Davis** — Interior Designer
Skidmore Owings Merrill, 14 Wall St, #2500, New York NY 10005, USA
**Allen, Debbie** — Dancer, Singer, Actress
Red Bird Productions, 3623 Hayden Ave, Culver City CA 90232, USA
**Allen, Deborah** — Singer
104 Broadley Court, Franklin TN 37069, USA
**Allen, Dion** — Singer (Az Yet)
Richard Walters, PO Box 2789, Toluca Lake CA 91610 USA
**Allen, Doug** — Artist
Fantagraphics Books, 7563 Lake City Way NE, Seattle WA 98115, USA
**Allen, Duane D** — Singer (Oak Ridge Boys)
88 New Shackle Island Road, Hendersonville TN 37075, USA
**Allen, Elizabeth Anne** — Actress
Boutique, 3034 Havrone Way, Lawrence KS 66047, USA
**Allen, Eric A** — Football Player
484 San Elijo St, San Diego CA 92106, USA
**Allen, George F** — Senator, Governor, VA
4296 Neitzey Place, Alexandria VA 22309, USA
**Allen, Geri** — Jazz Pianist, Composer
Clayton Ross Productions, 508 Shoreline Highway, Mill Valley CA 94941, USA
**Allen, Ginger Lynn** — Actress
Schiowitz Connor, 1680 N Vine St, #1016, Los Angeles CA 90028 USA
**Allen, Giselle** — Opera Singer
Hazard Chase, 25 City Road, Cambridge CB1 1DP, England
**Allen, Harold A (Hank)** — Baseball Player
PO Box 4612, Upper Marlboro MD 20775, USA
**Allen, Henry** — Critic
Washington Post, Editorial Dept, 1150 15th St NW, Washington DC 20071 USA
**Allen, India** — Actress, Model
Playboy Promotions, 9346 Civic Center Dr, #200, Beverly Hills CA 90210 USA
**Allen, J Carl** — Football Player
1614 Hornsby Ave, Saint Louis MO 63147, USA
**Allen, J Randall (Randy)** — Basketball Player
10185 Nichols Lake Road, Milton FL 32583, USA
**Allen, Jackie** — Singer
Dan Cleary Mgmt, 6399 Wilshire Blvd, #1019, Los Angeles CA 90048, USA
**Allen, Jared S** — Football Player
2303 Silver Breeze Court, San Jose CA 95138, USA
**Allen, Jason J** — Football Player
Cincinnati Bengals, 1 Paul Brown Stadium, Cincinnati OH 45202 USA
**Allen, Jennifer** — Sportscaster
N F L Network, 10950 Washington Blvd, #100, Culver City CA 90232 USA
**Allen, Joan** — Actress
I C M Partners, 10250 Constellation Blvd, #900, Los Angeles CA 90067 USA
**Allen, Joseph P, IV** — Astronaut
N A S A, Johnson Space Center, 2101 NASA Road, Houston TX 77058 USA
**Allen, Karen** — Actress
Hyler Mgmt, 20 Ocean Park Blvd, #25, Santa Monica CA 90405 USA
**Allen, Keegan** — Actor
A P A Talent & Literary Agency, 405 S Beverly Dr, #300, Beverly Hills CA 90212 USA
**Allen, Keith** — Actor, Comedian
Independent Talent Group, 40 Whitfield St, London W1T 2RH, England
**Allen, Kevin** — Director, Actor
United Talent Agency, U T A Plaza, 9336 Civic Center Dr, Beverly Hills CA 90210 USA
**Allen, Kevin** — Singer, Guitarist (And You Will Know Us)
Kork Agency, 1880 Century Park E, #711, Los Angeles CA 90067 USA
**Allen, Kris** — Singer
Sony Records, 550 Madison Ave, #600, New York NY 10022 USA
**Allen, Krista** — Actress, Model
A K A Talent, 6310 San Vicente Blvd, #200, Los Angeles CA 90048 USA
**Allen, L Patrick** — Football Player
20801 32nd Lane S, #A, Seatac WA 98198, USA
**Allen, Larry C** — Football Player
7 Shelby Hill Lane, Danville CA 94526, USA
**Allen, Laura** — Actress
Gersh Agency, 9465 Wilshire Blvd, #600, Beverly Hills CA 90212 USA
**Allen, Leopold R (Leo)** — Actor, Comedian, Writer
Generate, 1545 26th St, #200, Santa Monica CA 90404, USA
**Allen, Lily R B** — Singer, Songwriter
Brillstein Entertainment Partners, 9150 Wilshire Blvd, #350, Beverly Hills CA 90212 USA
**Allen, Lloyd C** — Baseball Player
2340 Castlewood Dr, Toledo OH 43613, USA
**Allen, Loy, Jr** — Auto Racing Driver
323 Lochside Dr, Cary NC 27518, USA
**Allen, Lucas G (Luke)** — Baseball Player
282 Cooper Road, Social Circle GA 30025, USA
**Allen, Lucius O** — Basketball Player
1915 Buckingham Road, Los Angeles CA 90016, USA
**Allen, Malik** — Basketball Player
Detroit Pistons, Palace, 4 Championship Dr, Auburn Hills MI 48326 USA
**Allen, Marcus L** — Football Player, Sportscaster
9536 Wilshire Blvd, #300, Beverly Hills CA 90212, USA
**Allen, Marty** — Actor, Comedian
3847 Tropical Vine St, Las Vegas NV 89147, USA
**Allen, Maryon P** — Senator, AL
1551 Creekstone Circle, Birmingham AL 35243, USA
**Allen, Michael L** — Golfer
5827 E Anderson Dr, Scottsdale AZ 85254, USA
**Allen, Nancy** — Actress
Bauman Redanty Shaul Agency, 5757 Wilshire Blvd, #473, Los Angeles CA 90036 USA
**Allen, Neil P** — Baseball Player
3619 Torrey Pines Blvd, Sarasota FL 34238, USA

**Allen, Patrick L** — Governor General, Jamaica
Governor General's Office, King's House, Hope Road, Kingston 10, Jamaica

**Allen, Paul G** — Co-Developer (PC Language)
6451 W Mercer Way, Mercer Island WA 98040, USA

**Allen, Rae** — Actress
Kyle Fritz Mgmt, 6325 Heather Dr, Los Angeles CA 90068 USA

**Allen, Rex, Jr** — Singer
Leroy Van Dyke Enterprises, 29000 Highway V, Smithton MO 65350, USA

**Allen, Richard** — Actor
89 Saltergate, Chesterfield S40 lUS, England

**Allen, Richard A (Richie)** — Baseball Player
PO Box 254, Wampum PA 16157, USA

**Allen, Richard J (Rick)** — Drummer (Def Leppard)
Front Line Mgmt, 1100 Glendon Ave, #2000, Los Angeles CA 90024 USA

**Allen, Richard V** — Government Official
1615 L St NW, #900, Washington DC 20036, USA

**Allen, Robert E** — Businessman
11 Country Road W, Boynton Beach FL 33436, USA

**Allen, Robert G (Bob)** — Baseball Player
PO Box 667, Tatum TX 75691, USA

**Allen, Robert J (Bob)** — Basketball Player
117 Quarter Mile Way, Nicholasville KY 40356, USA

**Allen, Rosalind** — Actress
A K A Talent Agency, 6310 San Vicente Blvd, #200, Los Angeles CA 90048, USA

**Allen, Scott E** — Figure Skater
2109 Broadway, #15109, New York NY 10023, USA

**Allen, Sian Barbara** — Actress
1411 NE 16th Ave, #219, Portland OR 97232, USA

**Allen, Taje L** — Football Player
1209 Valorie Court, Cedar Park TX 78613, USA

**Allen, Ted** — Entertainer
W M E Entertainment, 1325 Ave of Americas, New York NY 10019 USA

**Allen, Teddy G** — Army General
6900 Shackle Place, Burke VA 22015, USA

**Allen, Terry** — Artist, Songwriter
Route 10 Box 88N, Santa Fe NM 87501, USA

**Allen, Terry** — Singer (Stamps Quartet)
PO Box 1471, Brentwood TN 37024, USA

**Allen, Terry T, Jr** — Football Player
3176 Sable Ridge Dr, Buford GA 30519, USA

**Allen, Tessa** — Actress
Abrams Artists, 9200 W Sunset Blvd, #1125, West Hollywood CA 90069 USA

**Allen, Thad W** — Coast Guard Admiral
Booz Allen Hamilton, 8283 Greensboro Drive, McLean VA 22102, USA

**Allen, Thomas B** — Opera Singer
Askonas Holt, Lincoln House, 300 High Holborn, London WC1V 7JH, England

**Allen, Tim** — Actor, Comedian
Boxing Cat Productions, 11500 Hart St, North Hollywood CA 91605, USA

**Allen, W Ray** — Basketball Player, Actor
10185 Nichols Lake Road, Milton FL 32583, USA

**Allen, Will** — Football Player
Pittsburgh Steelers, 3400 S Water St, Pittsburgh PA 15203 USA

**Allen, Will D** — Football Player
2325 SW 105th Terrace, Davie FL 33324, USA

**Allen, Woody** — Actor, Comedian, Director
118 E 70th St, New York NY 10021, USA

**Allenby, Robert** — Golfer
4901 Pacifico Court, Palm Beach Gardens FL 33418, USA

**Allende, Fernando** — Actor, Singer
El Dorado Productions, PM Box 888, 425 Carr 693, Dorado PR 06646, USA

**Allende, Isabel** — Writer
92 Fernwood Dr, San Rafael CA 94901, USA

**Allen-Dutton, Jordan** — Writer
Gersh Agency, 9465 Wilshire Blvd, #600, Beverly Hills CA 90212 USA

**Allen-Meares, Paula** — Educator
University of Illinois, Chancellor's Office, 840 S Wood St, Chicago IL 60612, USA

**Allenson, Gary M** — Baseball Player, Manager
711 SE 34th St, Cape Coral FL 33904, USA

**Allerman, Kurt D** — Football Player
68 Cache Cay Dr, Vero Beach FL 32963, USA

**Allert, Ty H** — Football Player
1504 County Road 308, Lexington TX 78947, USA

**Alley, Kirstie** — Actress
United Talent Agency, U T A Plaza, 9336 Civic Center Dr, Beverly Hills CA 90210 USA

**Alley, L Eugene (Gene)** — Baseball Player
10236 Steuben Dr, Glen Allen VA 23060, USA

**Alley, Steve** — Ice Hockey Player
545 College Road, Lake Forest IL 60045, USA

**Allford, Simon** — Architect
232 Bickenhall Mansions, Bickenhall St, London W1V 6BW, England

**Allison, Brooke** — Singer, Songwriter
2 K/E M I America Records, 6920 Sunset Blvd, Los Angeles CA 90028, USA

**Allison, David B (Dave)** — Ice Hockey Player, Coach
Iowa Stars, 833 5th Ave, Des Moines IA 50309, USA

**Allison, Dorothy** — Writer
Penguin Putnam, 375 Hudson St, New York NY 10014, USA

**Allison, Dunkiny (Donnie)** — Auto Racing Driver
355 Quail Dr, Salisbury NC 28147, USA

**Allison, Glenn** — Bowler
1844 S Haster St, #138, Anaheim CA 92802, USA

**Allison, Graham T, Jr** — Educator
69 Pinhurst Road, Belmont MA 02478, USA

**Allison, Henry H (Hank)** — Football Player
458 W Ellis Ave, Inglewood CA 90302, USA

**Allison, Jerry** — Drummer (Crickets), Songwriter
8455 New Bethal Road, Lyles TN 37098, USA

**A**

**Allison, John A, IV** — Financier
B B & T Corp, 200 W 2nd St, #260, Winston Salem NC 27101, USA
**Allison, John V** — Vietnam War Air Force Hero
6606 Britt St, Navarre FL 32566, USA
**Allison, Margaret** — Singer
I B A Productions, 3 Av Florimont, 1829 Montreux, Switzerland
**Allison, Mike** — Ice Hockey Player
7204 Birchmont Court NE, Bemidji MN 56601, USA
**Allison, Mose J, Jr** — Jazz Pianist, Composer, Singer
82 Ballad Court, Eastport NY 11941, USA
**Allison, Odis** — Basketball Player
3162 Majestic Shadows Ave, Henderson NV 89052, USA
**Allison, Ray** — Ice Hockey Player
106 N Valleybrook Road, Cherry Hill NJ 08034, USA
**Allison, Richard C** — Judge
224 Circle Dr, Manhasset NY 11030, USA
**Allison, Robert A (Bobby)** — Auto Racing Driver
PO Box 3696, Mooresville NC 28117, USA
**Allison, Robert J, Jr** — Businessman
Anadarko Petroleum Corp, 1201 Lake Robbins Dr, Spring TX 77380, USA
**Allison, Stacy** — Mountaineer
6633 SE 29th Ave, Portland OR 97202, USA
**Allison, Verne** — Singer (Dells)
Associated Booking Corp, 501 Madison Ave, #501, New York NY 10022 USA
**Alliss, Peter** — Sportscaster
Peter Alliss Golf Ltd, PO Box 224, Surrey GU26 6WQ, England
**Allman, Gregory L (Gregg)** — Singer, Musician, Songwriter
Allman Brothers Band Inc, 18 Tamworth Road, Waban MA 02468, USA
**Allman, Jamie Anne** — Actress
Greene Assoc, 1901 Ave of Stars, #130, Los Angeles CA 90067 USA
**Allman, Marshall** — Actor
Gersh Agency, 9465 Wilshire Blvd, #600, Beverly Hills CA 90212 USA
**Allnutt, Robert** — Space Scientist, Biochemist
5400 Edgemoor Lane, Bethesda MD 20814, USA
**Allouache, Merzak** — Director
Cite des Asphodeles, Bt D15, 183 Ben Aknoun, Algiers, Algeria
**Allred, Corbin M** — Actor
Aquarius Public Relations, 5320 Sylmar Ave, Sherman Oaks CA 91401, USA
**Allred, Gloria R** — Attorney
Allred Maroko Goldberg, 6300 Wilshire Blvd, #1500, Los Angeles CA 90048, USA
**Allred, Jason** — Golfer
10239 E Salt Bush Dr, Scottsdale AZ 85255, USA
**Allred, John** — Football Player
PO Box 748, Del Mar CA 92014, USA
**Allyn, Daniel B** — Army General
Vice Chief of Staff, HqUSA, Pentagon, Washington DC 20310 USA
**Allyson, Karrin** — Singer, Pianist
Stilleto Entertainment, 5200 W 83rd St, #G, Los Angeles CA 90045, USA
**Al-Mansour, Haifaa** — Director
Anonymous Content, 3532 Hayden Ave, Culver City CA 90232 USA
**Almanza, Armando N** — Baseball Player
2024 Paseo Del Prado Dr, El Paso TX 79936, USA
**Almers, Wolfhard** — Biochemist
Oregon Health & Science University, Vollum Institute, Portland OR 97239, USA
**Almirola, Aric** — Auto Racing Driver
Aric Almirola Inc, 215 Overhill Dr, #A, Mooresville NC 28117, USA
**Almodovar, Pedro** — Director
El Deseo SA, Francisco Navacerrada 24, 28028 Madrid, Spain
**Almon, William F (Billy)** — Baseball Player
42 Channel View, #4, Warwick RI 02889, USA
**Almond, Lincoln C** — Governor, RI
82 Smith St, #222, Providence RI 02903, USA
**Almond, Marc** — Singer (Soft Cell), Songwriter
Take Out Productions, 630 9th Ave, #603, New York NY 10036, USA
**Almond, Morris** — Basketball Player
Red Star Belgrade, Obilicev Wreath 24, Belgrade, Serbia
**Almquist, John O** — Physiologist
300 Lions Hill Road, #W502, State College PA 16803, USA
**Almunia Amann, Joaquin** — Government Official, Spain
Carrera de San Jeronimo S/N 28014 Madrid, Spain
**Alois** — Prince, Liechtenstein
Schloss Vaduz, 9490 Vaduz, Liechtenstein
**Alomar, Roberto V (Robbie)** — Baseball Player
Urbana Monserrate B-56, PO Box 367, Salinas PR 00751, USA
**Alomar, Santos C (Sandy), Jr** — Baseball Player
1906 W Cortland St, Chicago IL 60622, USA
**Alomar, Santos C (Sandy), Sr** — Baseball Player
PO Box 367, Salinas PR 00751, USA
**Alonso Bernardo, Jessica** — Handball Player
R K Zajecar, Dositejeva 11, 19000 Zajecar, Serbia
**Alonso, Adrian** — Actor
Featured Artists Agency, 6210 Wilshire Blvd, #311, Los Angeles CA 90048, USA
**Alonso, Alicia** — Ballerina
National Ballet of Cuba, Calzada 510 Entre D & E, El Vedado, Havana, Cuba
**Alonso, Anabel** — Actress
Ramon Pilaces, C/Hortaleza 20, #1 Izqda, 28004 Madrid, Spain
**Alonso, Daniella** — Actress, Model
Gersh Agency, 9465 Wilshire Blvd, #600, Beverly Hills CA 90212 USA
**Alonso, Fernando** — Auto Racing Driver
Riera La 6, 33100 Riera, Spain
**Alonso, Laz** — Actor
I C M Partners, 10250 Constellation Blvd, #900, Los Angeles CA 90067 USA
**Alonso, Maria Conchita** — Actress, Singer
Don Buchwald Talent Agency, 6500 Wilshire Blvd, #2200, Los Angeles CA 90048 USA
**Alou, Felipe R** — Baseball Player, Manager
6891 Cobia Circle, Boynton Beach FL 33437, USA

*Allison - Alou*

**Alou, Jesus M R** — Baseball Player
Apartado Postal 539/2 Lafaria, Santo Domingo, Dominican Republic
**Alou, Moises R** — Baseball Player
13095 NW 13th St, Pembroke Pines FL 33028, USA
**Alpay, David** — Actor
A P A Talent & Literary Agency, 405 S Beverly Dr, #300, Beverly Hills CA 90212 USA
**Alpert, Herb** — Musician
31930 Pacific Coast Highway, Malibu CA 90265, USA
**Alpert, Joseph S** — Physician
3440 E Cathedral Rock Circle, Tucson AZ 85718, USA
**Alphand, Luc** — Alpine Skier
Chalet Le Balme, Chantemerie, 05330 Sierre Chavalier, France
**Alphin, W Kenneth (Big Kenny)** — Singer, Songwriter
Morris Management Group, 818 19th Ave S, Nashville TN 37203, USA
**Al-Saud, Abdullah** — Equestrian
Haras de Wisbecq, Rue de Bierghes 4, 1430 Rebecq, Belgium
**Al-Sebesi, Al-Baji** — Prime Minister, Tunisia
Prime Minister's Office, Place du Gouvernement, La Kasbah, 1008 Tunis, Tunisia
**Alsgaard, Thomas** — Cross Country Skier
Alpina Sports, Strojarska Ulica 2, 4226 Ziri, Slovenia
**Alsop, Marin** — Conductor
Baltimore Symphony Orchestra, 1212 Cathedral St, #1, Baltimore MD 21201, USA
**Alsop, William A** — Architect
72 Pembroke Road, London W8 6NX, England
**Alston Reeves, Shirley** — Singer (Shirelles)
G H R Entertainment, 6014 N Pointe Place, Woodland Hills CA 91367, USA
**Alston, Barbara** — Singer (Crystals)
Tingrassia Entertainment, PO Box 314, Holden MA 01520, USA
**Alston, Gerald** — Singer (Manhattans)
Wenig-LaMonica Associates, 580 White Plains Road, #130, Tarrytown NY 10591 USA
**Alston, Mack, Jr** — Football Player
5421 Echols Ave, Alexandria VA 22311, USA
**Alston, Rafer J** — Basketball Player
9002 Legends Lane, Missouri City TX 77459, USA
**Alstott, Michael J (Mike)** — Football Player
7800 9th Ave S, Saint Petersburg FL 33707, USA
**Alt, Carol** — Model, Actress
Scott Hart Mgmt, 14622 Ventura Blvd, #746, Sherman Oaks CA 91403, USA
**Alt, John M** — Football Player
21 Crescent Lane, Saint Paul MN 55127, USA
**Altbach, Philip G** — Sociologist
Boston College, Campion Hall, Chestnut Hill MA 02467, USA
**Altea, Rosemary** — Writer, Medium
PO Box 1390, Venice FL 34284, USA
**Alter, Harvey J** — Hematologist
National Institutes of Health, Magnuson Center, 10 Center Dr, Bethesda MD 20892, USA
**Alterman, Kent** — Director
Creative Artists Agency, 2000 Ave of Stars, #100, Los Angeles CA 90067 USA
**Al-Thani, Abdullah** — Prime Minister, Libya
Prime Minister's Office, Ghabat Al Nasr Convention Centre, Tripoli, Libya
**Alther, Lisa** — Writer
1086 Silver St, Hinesburg VT 05461, USA
**Althoff, Kai** — Artist
Christian Nagel Gallery, Richard-Wagner-Str 28, 50674 Cologne, Germany
**Altice, Summer** — Model, Actress
Elite Model Mgmt, 404 Park Ave S, #900, New York NY 10016 USA
**Altman, Bruce** — Actor
Don Buchwald Talent Agency, 6500 Wilshire Blvd, #2200, Los Angeles CA 90048 USA
**Altman, Chelsea** — Actress
Liebman Entertainment, 25 E 21st St, #PH, New York NY 10010, USA
**Altman, Jeff** — Actor, Comedian
Agency S G H, 6525 Sunset Blvd, #PH9, Los Angeles CA 90028, USA
**Altman, Scott** — Opera Singer
Columbia Artists Mgmt Inc, 5 Columbus Circle, 1790 Broadway, #1600, New York NY 10019 USA
**Altman, Scott D** — Astronaut
PO Box 25053, Washington DC 20027, USA
**Altman, Sidney** — Nobel Chemistry Laureate
71 Blake Road, Hamden CT 06517, USA
**Altman, Stuart H** — Educator
11 Bakers Hill Road, Weston MA 02493, USA
**Altmann, Livia** — Ice Hockey Player
Jory-Jenny-Str, 7050 Arosa/GR, Switzerland
**Altmeyer, Jeannine T** — Opera Singer
Im Muhlader, 8709 Herrliberg, Switzerland
**Altobelli, Joseph (Joe)** — Baseball Player, Manager
10 Stowell Dr, #3, Rochester NY 14616, USA
**Alton, Kevin B** — Chemist
Schering-Plough Research, 2000 Galloping Hill Road, Kenilworth NJ 07033, USA
**Altschul, Serena** — Commentator
MTV, News Dept, 1515 Broadway, New York NY 10036, USA
**Altshuler, Alan A** — Political Scientist
Harvard University, Kennedy Government School, Cambridge MA 02138, USA
**Altwegg, Jeanette E** — Figure Skater
British Olympic Assn, 60 Charlotte St, London W1T 2NU, England
**Alusik, George J** — Baseball Player
PO Box 454, Woodbridge NJ 07095, USA
**Alvarado, Natividad (Naty)** — Handball Player
Equitable of Iowa, 2700 N Main St, Santa Ana CA 92705, USA
**Alvarez, Al** — Writer
Gillon Atkin, 18-21 Caraye Place, London SW10 9PT, England
**Alvarez, Barry** — Football Coach, Sportscaster
Fox-TV, Sports Dept, 205 W 67th St, New York NY 10065 USA
**Alvarez, George** — Actor
Michael Bruno Group, 13576 Cheltenham Dr, Sherman Oaks CA 91423, USA
**Alvarez, Isabel** — Baseball Player
2416 Monmouth Ave, Fort Wayne IN 46809, USA

**Alvarez, Julia** — Writer
Susan Bergholz Literary Agency, 17 W 10th St, #5N, New York NY 10011, USA
**Alvarez, Kyle Patrick** — Writer, Director
United Talent Agency, U T A Plaza, 9336 Civic Center Dr, Beverly Hills CA 90210 USA
**Alvarez, Marcelo** — Opera Singer
Zemsky/Greene Artists Mgmt, 104 W 73rd St, #1, New York NY 10023, USA
**Alvarez, Rigoberto** — Boxer
Golden Boy Promotions, 626 Wilshire Blvd, #350, Los Angeles CA 90017 USA
**Alvarez, Saul (Canelo)** — Boxer
Canelo Promotions, D Rodriguez 1667, Sec Libertad CP 44730, Guadalajara Jalisco, Mexico
**Alvarez, Wilson E** — Baseball Player
6927 Westchester Circle, Bradenton FL 34202, USA
**Alvarez-Buylla, Arturo** — Biologist
Rockefeller University Medical Center, 1230 York Ave, New York NY 10065 USA
**Alvart, Christian** — Director
Paradigm Agency, 360 N Crescent Dr, North Building, Beverly Hills CA 90210 USA
**Alverson, Tommy** — Singer, Songwriter
Ken-Ran Entertainment, 418 S Barton St, Grapevine TX 76051, USA
**Alves, Joe** — Director
Gersh Agency, 9465 Wilshire Blvd, #600, Beverly Hills CA 90212 USA
**Alves, Rick** — Musician (Pirates of the Mississippi)
Third Coast Talent, PO Box 110225, Nashville TN 37222, USA
**Alvin, Dave** — Guitarist (Blasters); Songwriter
Mongrel Music, 743 Center Blvd, Fairfax CA 94930, USA
**Alvis, R Maxwell (Max)** — Baseball Player
806 Hunterwood Dr, Jasper TX 75951, USA
**Alwaleed Bin Talal Bin Abdulaziz Alsaud** — Prince, Saudi Arabia; Businessman
Kingdom Holdings, Kingdom Centre, Al-Urubah Road, Riyadh, Saudi Arabia
**Alworth, Lance D** — Football Player
Del Mar Corporate Center, 990 Highland Dr, #300, Solana Beach CA 92075, USA
**Alyea, Garrabrant R (Brant)** — Baseball Player
125 Dobbs Place, Goldsboro NC 27534, USA
**Alys, Francis** — Artist
David Zwirner Gallery, 537 W 20th St, New York NY 10011, USA
**Alyse, Alice** — Actress, Ballerina, Model
Mademoiselle Talent Agency, 24328 Vermont Ave, #309, Harbor City CA 90710, USA
**Ama, Shola** — Singer
Concorde International, 101 Shepherds Bush Road, London W6 7LP, England
**Amadou, Hama** — Prime Minister, Niger
Prime Minister's Office, State House, BP 353, Abuja, Niger
**Amaechi, John E** — Basketball Player
5747 E Aire Libre Ave, Scottsdale AZ 85254, USA
**Amaker, H Tommy** — Basketball Player, Coach
Harvard University, Athletic Dept, Cambridge MA 02138, USA
**Amalfitano, J Joseph (Joe)** — Baseball Player, Manager
60 Sheath Dr, Sedona AZ 86336, USA
**Amalric, Mathieu** — Actor, Diector
Zelig Films, 57 Rue Reamur, 75002 Paris, France
**Aman, Zeenat** — Actress
Neelam Apts, Mount Mary Road, #300, Bandra, Mumbai MS 400050, India
**Amandes, Tom** — Actor
Paul Kohner, 9300 Wilshire Blvd, #555, Beverly Hills CA 90212 USA
**Amano, Eugene P** — Football Player
495 Jones Parkway, Brentwood TN 37027, USA
**Amano, Hiroshi** — Nobel Physics Laureate
Nagoya University, Electrical Engineering Dept, Furo-cho, Chikusaku, Nagoya 464-8601, Japan
**Amanpour, Christiane** — Commentator
Cable News Network, 2 Stephen St, #100, London W1P 1PL, England
**Amante, Michael** — Singer
Dera Roslan Campion, 132 Nassau St, New York NY 10038, USA
**Amara, Lucine** — Opera Singer
260 W End Ave, #7A, New York NY 10023, USA
**Amaral, Richard L (Rich)** — Baseball Player
3122 Country Club Dr, Costa Mesa CA 92626, USA
**Amaro, Ruben M, Sr** — Baseball Player
4098 Cinnamon Way, Weston FL 33331, USA
**Amato, Angelo Cardinal** — Religious Leader
Santa Maria in Aquiro, Piazza Capranica, 00186 Rome, Lazio, Italy
**Amato, Giuliano** — Prime Minister, Italy
Carmera dei Deputati, Piazza di Montecitorio, 00186 Rome, Italy
**Amato, Joe** — Auto Racing Driver
PO Box 615, Wilkes Barre PA 18703, USA
**Amato, Kenneth C (Ken)** — Football Player
641 Old Hickory Blvd, #305, Brentwood TN 37027, USA
**Amaury, Jean-Etienne** — Businessman, Sports Executive
Amaury Sports, 2 Rue de Lisle, 92137 Issy-le-Mounlineaux, France
**Amavia Lunkewitz, Daniela** — Actress
Global Artists Agency, 6253 Hollywood Blvd, #508, Los Angeles CA 90028 USA
**Amaya, Armando** — Sculptor
Cuauh Temoc, 168 Col Deo Carmen, Coyoacan DF 04100, Mexico
**Ambani, Mukesh** — Businessman
Reliance Industries, Makers Chambers IV, Nariman Point, 400021 Mumbai, India
**Ambasz, Emilio** — Architect
43 E 63rd St, New York NY 10065, USA
**Amber** — Singer, Songwriter
Central Entertainment Group, 166 5th Ave, #400, New York NY 10010, USA
**Ambramovich, Roman A** — Businessman
Chelsea F C, Stamford Bridge, Fulham Road, London SW6 1HS, England
**Ambro, Thomas L** — Judge
US Court of Appeals, Federal Building, 844 N King St, Wilmington DE 19801, USA
**Ambros, Victor R** — Geneticist
University of Massachusetts Medical School, 55 Lake Ave N, Worcester MA 01655, USA
**Ambrose, Ashley A** — Football Player
2726 Eudora Trail, Duluth GA 30097, USA
**Ambrose, Lauren** — Actress, Singer
United Talent Agency, U T A Plaza, 9336 Civic Center Dr, Beverly Hills CA 90210 USA

**Ambrose, Marcus** — Auto Racing Driver
Richard Petty Racing, 7065 Zephyr Place, Concord NC 28027, USA

**Ambrose, Richard J (Dick)** — Football Player
24049 Stonehedge Dr, Westlake OH 44145, USA

**Ambrosio, Alessandra** — Model, Actress
Ulla Models, Lijnbaansgracht 338-339, 1017 Amsterdam XA, Netherlands

**Ambrosius, Marsha** — Singer (Floetry), Songwriter
I C M Partners, 10250 Constellation Blvd, #900, Los Angeles CA 90067 USA

**Ambuehl, Cindy** — Actress
28343 Ave Crocker, #1, Valencia CA 91355, USA

**Amdahl, Gene M** — Computer Engineer, Businessman
620 Sand Hill Road, #212G, Palo Alto CA 94304, USA

**Amedori, John Patrick** — Actor
Gersh Agency, 9465 Wilshire Blvd, #600, Beverly Hills CA 90212 USA

**Ameling, Elly** — Concert Singer
Hubstein Artist Services, 65 W 90th St, #13F, New York NY 10024, USA

**Amelio, Gilbert F** — Businessman
13416 Middle Fork Lane, Los Altos CA 94022, USA

**Amell, Robert P (Robbie)** — Actor
Protege Entertainment, 710 E Angeleno Ave, Burbank CA 91501, USA

**Amell, Stephen** — Actor
Leverage Mgmt, 3030 Pennsylvania Ave, Santa Monica CA 90404 USA

**Amelung, Edward V (Ed)** — Baseball Player
16681 Cedar Circle, Fountain Valley CA 92708, USA

**Amen, Irving** — Artist
PO Box 812365, Boca Raton FL 33481, USA

**Amend, Bill** — Cartoonist (FoxTrot)
Universal Press Syndicate, 4520 Main St, #700, Kansas City MO 64111 USA

**Amendola, Tony** — Actor
Marc Bass Agency, 9255 W Sunset Blvd, #727, West Hollywood CA 90069, USA

**Ament, Jeff** — Bassist (Green River, Pearl Jam)
Curtis Mgmt, 1900 S Corgiat Dr, Seattle WA 98108, USA

**Amentler, James (Jim)** — Photographer
8117 Manchester Ave, #573, Playa del Rey CA 90293, USA

**Amer, Ghada** — Artist
Cheim & Read Gallery, 547 W 25th St, New York NY 10001, USA

**Amer, Nicholas** — Actor
14 Great Russell St, London WC18 3NH, England

**Amerie** — Singer, Songwriter, Actress
Feenix Entertainment, 1360 Clifton Ave, #318, Clifton NJ 07012, USA

**Ames, Bruce N** — Biochemist
1324 Spruce St, Berkeley CA 94709, USA

**Ames, Denise** — Actress
Coralie Junior Theatrical Agency, 907 S Victory Blvd, Burbank CA 91502, USA

**Ames, Ed** — Singer, Actor
Paradise Artists, PO Box 1821, Ojai CA 93024 USA

**Ames, Rachel** — Actress
1156 Corte Riviera, Camarillo CA 93010, USA

**Ames, Stephen M** — Golfer
Professional Golfers Association, 100 Ave of Champions, Palm Beach Gardens FL 33418 USA

**Amick, Madchen** — Actress
Gersh Agency, 9465 Wilshire Blvd, #600, Beverly Hills CA 90212 USA

**Amiel, Jon** — Director, Producer, Writer
Resolution, 1801 Century Park E, #2300, Los Angeles CA 90067, USA

**Amigo Vallejo, Carlos Cardinal** — Religious Leader
Archdiocese of Seville, Plaza Virgen de los Reyes S/N, 41004 Seville, Spain

**Amis, Martin L** — Writer, Journalist
Wylie Agency, 17 Bedford Square, London WC1B 3JA, England

**Amis, Suzy** — Actress, Model
I C M Partners, 10250 Constellation Blvd, #900, Los Angeles CA 90067 USA

**Amlee, Jessica** — Actress
Real 2 Real Talent, 20475 Lougheed Highway, Maple Ridge BC V2X 9B6, Canada

**Amlong, Joseph** — Rowing Athlete
2445 4th Lane, Vero Beach FL 32962, USA

**Amlong, Thomas** — Rowing Athlete
166 Four Mile River Road, Old Lyme CT 06371, USA

**Ammaccapane, Danielle** — Golfer
13214 N 13th St, Phoenix AZ 85022, USA

**Ammaccapane, Dina** — Golfer
4407 E Blanche Dr, Phoenix AZ 85032, USA

**Ammachi** — Religious Leader
Amrita Institutions, Ettimadai, Coimbatore, Tamil Nadu 641105, India

**Ammann, Simon** — Ski Jumper
W W P Weirather-Wenzel, Lustenauer Str 64, 6850 Dornbirn, Austria

**Amodeo, Mike** — Ice Hockey Player
556 Fralicks Beach Road, RR 5, Port Perry ON L9L 1B6, Canada

**Amoia, Charlene** — Actress
House of Representatives, 1434 6th St, #1, Santa Monica CA 90401 USA

**Amonte, Tony** — Ice Hockey Player
PO Box 771, Humarock MA 02047, USA

**Amorello, Matthew J** — Government Administrator
Massachusettes Turnpike Authority, 10 Park Plaza, #4160, Boston MA 02116, USA

**Amorosi, Vanessa** — Singer, Songwriter
Harbour Agency, 135 Forbes Road, Woolloomooloo NSW 2011, Australia

**Amory, Misha** — Concert Violist
David Rowe Artists, 24 Bessom St, #2, Marblehead MA 01945, USA

**Amos, Daniel P (Dan)** — Businessman
A F L A C Inc, A F L A C Center, 1932 Wynnton Road, Columbus GA 31999, USA

**Amos, James F** — Marine Corps General
Commandant, HqUSMC, 2 Navy Annex, Washington DC 20380 USA

**Amos, Tori** — Singer, Pianist, Songwriter
Creative Artists Agency, 2000 Ave of Stars, #100, Los Angeles CA 90067 USA

**Amos, Wally (Famous)** — Businessman
PO Box 88323, Honolulu HI 96830, USA

**Amoyal, Pierre A W** — Concert Violinist
Jacques Thelen, 15 Ave Montaigne, 75008 Paris, France

**Amram, David W, III**  Jazz, Classical Composer, Conductor
Ed Keane Assoc, 573 Pleasant St, Winthrop MA 02152, USA
**Amrapurkar, Sadashiv**  Actor, Comedian
A/201 Panchdhara Off Yari Road, Versova Andheri, Mumbai MS 400058, India
**Amritraj, Ashok**  Actor, Producer, Writer
Hyde Park Entertainment, 16555 Sherman Way, #A1, Van Nuys CA 91406, USA
**Amritraj, Vijay**  Tennis Player
First Serve, 10/5A 13th Ave, Harrington Road, Chetpet, Chennai 600031, India
**Amsden, Ben C**  WW II Navy Air Force Hero
514 C St, Farmington MO 63640, USA
**Amsellem, Norah**  Opera Singer
Columbia Artists Mgmt Inc, 5 Columbus Circle, 1790 Broadway, #1600, New York NY 10019 USA
**Amsterdam, Anthony G**  Attorney, Educator
68 Middle Lane Highway, Southampton NY 11968, USA
**Amuka-Bird, Nikki**  Actress
Greene Assoc, 1901 Ave of Stars, #130, Los Angeles CA 90067 USA
**Amy, Susie**  Actress
Curtis Brown Group, 28-29 Haymarket St, #500, London SW1Y 4SP, England
**An Sang-Mi**  Speed Skater
Skating Union, 88 Bangyee-Dong, Songpaku, Seoul 138 749, South Korea
**An Yulong**  Speed Skater
Skating Association, 56 Zhonguancun South St, Beijing 100044, China
**Ana Alicia**  Actress
S D B Partners, 315 S Beverly Dr, #411, Beverly Hills CA 90067 USA
**Anagnostopoulos, Constantine E**  Heart Surgeon
435 Dockside Dr, #902, Naples FL 34110, USA
**Anahi**  Actress, Singer, Model
E M I Music, Rio Tigris 33, Col Cuahtemoc CP 06500, Mexico
**Anand, Vijay**  Actor, Director
Ketnav 17 Union Park Pali Hill, Khar, Mumbai MS 400052, India
**Anand, Viswanathan (Vishy)**  Chess Player
F I D E, 9 Ave de Beaumont, 1012 Lausanne, Switzerland
**Ananiashvili, Nina G**  Ballerina
Frunzenskaya Nab 46, #79, 119270 Moscow, Russia
**Anappau, Kristina**  Actress
Untitled Entertainment, 350 S Beverly Dr, #200, Beverly Hills CA 90212 USA
**Anastacia**  Singer
Braude Mgmt, PO Box 7249, San Diego CA 92167, USA
**Anastasio, Trey**  Guitarist (Phish, Oysterhead)
Red Light Mgmt, 44 Wall St, #2200, New York NY 10005, USA
**Anatsui, El**  Sculptor
University of Nigeria, Art Dept, Nsukka, Nigeria
**Anaya, Elena**  Actress
Kuranda Mgmt, Santo Angel 84, 28043 Madrid, Spain
**Anaya, Rudolfo**  Writer
5324 Canada Vista NW, Albuquerque NM 87120, USA
**Anaya, Toney**  Governor, NM
711 E May Ave, Las Cruces NM 88001, USA
**Ancelotti, Carlo**  Soccer Player, Coach
F C Milan, Via Filippo Turati 3, 20121 Milan, Italy
**Anchultz Thoms, Daniela**  Speed Skater
Eissportclub Erfurt, Arnstaedter Str 53, 99096 Erfurt, Germany
**Ancona, Bill**  Drag Racing Driver
260 Nelson Wyatt Road, Mansfield TX 76063, USA
**Anconina, Richard**  Actor
Artmedia, 20 Ave Rapp, 75007 Paris, France
**Anden, Mini**  Model, Actress
More/Medavoy Mgmt, 10203 Santa Monica Blvd, #400, Los Angeles CA 90067 USA
**Anderegg, Robert H (Bob)**  Basketball Player
11708 E Onyx Ave, Scottsdale AZ 85259, USA
**Anders, Allison**  Director, Writer
A P A Talent & Literary Agency, 405 S Beverly Dr, #300, Beverly Hills CA 90212 USA
**Anders, Andrea**  Actress
Abrams Artists, 9200 W Sunset Blvd, #1125, West Hollywood CA 90069 USA
**Anders, David**  Actor
Liberman-Zerman Mgmt, 252 N Larchmont Blvd, #200, Los Angeles CA 90004 USA
**Anders, Kimble L**  Football Player
Running Back Giving Back Foundation, 4435 Prospect Ave, Kansas City MO 64130, USA
**Anders, Sean**  Director, Producer, Writer, Actor
Mosiac Media Group, 9200 W Sunset Blvd, #1000, Los Angeles CA 90069 USA
**Anders, William A**  Astronaut, Air Force General
1 Aeroview Lane, Eastsound WA 98245, USA
**Andersen, Anthony L**  Businessman
H B Fuller Co, PO Box 64683, Saint Paul MN 55164, USA
**Andersen, Christopher P**  Writer
Hyperion Books, 114 5th Ave, New York NY 10011 USA
**Andersen, Eric**  Singer, Songwriter
Charles Rothschild Productions, 330 E 48th St, #2D, New York NY 10017, USA
**Andersen, Greta**  Swimmer
16222 Monterey Lane, #264, Huntington Beach CA 92649, USA
**Andersen, Kurt**  Writer
Random House, 1745 Broadway, #1800, New York NY 10019 USA
**Andersen, Ladell**  Basketball Coach
41 W Cedar Dr, Hermiston OR 97838, USA
**Andersen, Larry E**  Baseball Player
2043 Sunray Circle, West Linn OR 97068, USA
**Andersen, Linda**  Yachtswoman
Aroysund, 3135 Torod, Norway
**Andersen, Lisa**  Surfer
5008 Camino Escollo, San Clemente CA 92673, USA
**Andersen, May**  Model
2 P M Model Mgmt, Norregade 2, 1165 Copenhagen K, Denmark
**Andersen, Morten**  Football Player
6501 Old Shadburn Ferry Road, Buford GA 30518, USA
**Andersen, Susan**  Writer
Jane Rotrosen Agency, 318 E 51st St, New York NY 10022, USA

**Anderson, Al** — Singer, Guitarist (NRBQ)
Skyline Music, 2270 Maiden Lane SW, Roanoke VA 24015, USA
**Anderson, Alfa** — Singer (Chic)
Lustig Talent, PO Box 770850, Orlando FL 32877 USA
**Anderson, Alfred A** — Football Player
2805 Chesterwood Court, Mansfield TX 76063, USA
**Anderson, Anthony A** — Actor, Comedian, Writer
United Talent Agency, U T A Plaza, 9336 Civic Center Dr, Beverly Hills CA 90210 USA
**Anderson, Audrey Marie** — Actress
I C M Partners, 10250 Constellation Blvd, #900, Los Angeles CA 90067 USA
**Anderson, Billy** — Professional Wrestler, Actor
7120 S 7th Lane, Phoenix AZ 85041, USA
**Anderson, Blake** — Actor, Writer
United Talent Agency, U T A Plaza, 9336 Civic Center Dr, Beverly Hills CA 90210 USA
**Anderson, Brad** — Drag Racing Driver
Brad Anderson Enterprises, 1240 S Cucamonga Ave, Ontario CA 91761, USA
**Anderson, Brad** — Director
422 Santa Monica Court, Escondido CA 92029, USA
**Anderson, Bradbury H** — Businessman
Best Buy Co, 7601 Penn Ave S, Minneapolis MN 55423, USA
**Anderson, Bradford** — Actor
Michael Enfield Mgmt, 10630 Moorpark, #101, Toluca Lake CA 91602, USA
**Anderson, Bradley J (Brad)** — Cartoonist (Marmaduke)
13022 Wood Harbour Dr, Montgomery TX 77356, USA
**Anderson, Brady K** — Baseball Player
2205 Warwick Way, #200, Marriottsville MD 21104, USA
**Anderson, Brett** — Singer (Suede)
Lookout Records, PO Box 40828, San Francisco CA 94140, USA
**Anderson, Brett F** — Baseball Player
Colorado Rockies, Coors Field, 2001 Blake St, #A, Denver CO 80205 USA
**Anderson, Brian J** — Baseball Player
3571 N Meyers Road, Geneva OH 44041, USA
**Anderson, Brian N** — Baseball Player
3750 E Via Palomita, #16202, Tucson AZ 85718, USA
**Anderson, Bruce A** — Football Player
910 NE Parkview Court, Roseburg OR 97470, USA
**Anderson, C Neal** — Football Player
10626 SW 41st Place, Gainesville FL 32608, USA
**Anderson, Camille** — Actress, Model
A C Talent, 8447 Wilshire Blvd, #PH, Beverly Hills CA 90211, USA
**Anderson, Christine** — Singer, Pianist, Songwriter
Brian Lewis Presents, 781 Herman Ave, Medford OR 97501, USA
**Anderson, Clarence E (Bud)** — WW II Army Air Corps Hero
1060 Southridge Dr, Auburn CA 95603, USA
**Anderson, Clayton C** — Astronaut
N A S A, Johnson Space Center, 2101 NASA Road, Houston TX 77058 USA
**Anderson, Craig** — Guitarist (Heartland)
Country Thunder Records, 1016 17th Ave S, Nashville TN 37212, USA
**Anderson, Dale** — Ice Hockey Player
2217 Ave Haultain, Saskatoon SK S7J 1PT, Canada
**Anderson, Daniel E (Dan)** — Basketball Player
19000 NW Squirrel Tail Loop, Bend OR 97701, USA
**Anderson, Daniel W (Dan)** — Basketball Player
100 3rd Ave S, #2002, Minneapolis MN 55401, USA
**Anderson, Darren H** — Football Player
7328 Overland Park Court, West Chester OH 45069, USA
**Anderson, Daryl** — Actor
House of Representatives, 1434 6th St, #1, Santa Monica CA 90401 USA
**Anderson, David C (Dave)** — Baseball Player
421 Lockett St, Monticello KY 42633, USA
**Anderson, David J** — Biologist
California Institute of Technology, Biology Division, Pasadena CA 91125, USA
**Anderson, David P (Dave)** — Sportswriter
8 Inness Road, Tenafly NJ 07670, USA
**Anderson, Derek L** — Basketball Player
Legendary Liquids, 500 Bishop St, Building B2, Atlanta GA 30318, USA
**Anderson, Derek M** — Football Player
Carolina Panthers, Ericsson Stadium, 800 S Mint St, Charlotte NC 28202 USA
**Anderson, Dion** — Actor
S D B Partners, 315 S Beverly Dr, #411, Beverly Hills CA 90067 USA
**Anderson, Don** — Sculptor
3711 Cabrant Road, Everson WA 98247, USA
**Anderson, Don L** — Geophysicist
PO Box 1417, Cambria CA 93428, USA
**Anderson, Duwayne M** — Polar Scientist
6119 139th Place SE, Bellevue WA 98006, USA
**Anderson, Earl** — Ice Hockey Player
602 3rd Ave NE, Roseau MN 56751, USA
**Anderson, Earl E** — Marine Corps General
West Virginia University, Morgantown WV 26506 USA
**Anderson, Eddie Lee, Jr** — Football Player
PO Box 6363, Warner Robins GA 31095, USA
**Anderson, Eric W** — Basketball Player
12284 Whirlaway Dr, Noblesville IN 46060, USA
**Anderson, Erich** — Actor
Paradigm Agency, 360 N Crescent Dr, North Building, Beverly Hills CA 90210 USA
**Anderson, Erika** — Actress, Model
Click Model Mgmt, 9057 Nemo St, West Hollywood CA 90069, USA
**Anderson, Ernestine I** — Singer
Thomas Cassidy, PO Box 1311, Tucson AZ 85702 USA
**Anderson, Fredell L (Fred)** — Football Player
11810 NE 48th Place, Kirkland WA 98033, USA
**Anderson, G Don (Donny)** — Football Player
4516 Lovers Lane, #133, Dallas TX 75225, USA
**Anderson, Garret J** — Baseball Player
34 Vernal Spring, Irvine CA 92603, USA

| | |
|---|---|
| **Anderson, Gary A** | Football Player |
| 265 Miskow Close, Cannmore AB T1W 3G7, Canada | |
| **Anderson, Gary L** | Marksman |
| National Rifle Association, 11250 Waples Mill Road, Fairfax VA 22030, USA | |
| **Anderson, Gary W** | Football Player |
| 1 Ridgefield Court, Little Rock AR 72223, USA | |
| **Anderson, Gillian** | Actress |
| Independent Talent Group, 40 Whitfield St, London W1T 2RH, England | |
| **Anderson, Glenn** | Ice Hockey Player |
| 42 W 69th St, #2A, New York NY 10023, USA | |
| **Anderson, Harry L** | Actor |
| 204 Pearson Dr, Asheville NC 28801, USA | |
| **Anderson, Howard A, Jr** | Cinematographer |
| Howard A Anderson Co, 5161 Lankershim Blvd, North Hollywood CA 91601, USA | |
| **Anderson, Ian** | Singer (Jethro Tull), Songwriter |
| W M E Entertainment, 9601 Wilshire Blvd, #300, Beverly Hills CA 90210 USA | |
| **Anderson, J C** | Golfer |
| 232 Fairway Green Dr, O Fallon MO 63368, USA | |
| **Anderson, J William (Bill)** | Singer, Guitarist, Songwriter |
| Tessier-Marsh Talent, 2825 Blue Book Dr, Nashville TN 37214 USA | |
| **Anderson, Jade** | Singer |
| Evolution Entertainment, 901 N Highland Ave, Los Angeles CA 90038 USA | |
| **Anderson, Jamal S** | Football Player |
| 10540 Montclair Way, Duluth GA 30097, USA | |
| **Anderson, James L (Jim)** | Baseball Player |
| 2111 Bennington Court, Thousand Oaks CA 91360, USA | |
| **Anderson, James M (Jamie)** | Cinematographer |
| 19 Hanson St, Portland ME 04103, USA | |
| **Anderson, James W** | Endocrinologist |
| University of Kentucky Medical Center, Endocrinology Dept, Lexington KY 40506, USA | |
| **Anderson, Jamie** | Actress, Writer, Producer |
| Rage Talent Agency, 23501 Park Sorrento, Calabasas CA 91302, USA | |
| **Anderson, Jamie L** | Snowboarding Athlete |
| 1148 Navahoe Dr, South Lake Tahoe CA 96150, USA | |
| **Anderson, Janet** | Golfer |
| 4311 W Ardmore Road, Laveen AZ 85339, USA | |
| **Anderson, Janina** | Actress |
| Ominiquest Entertainment, 1416 N La Brea Ave, Los Angeles CA 90028, USA | |
| **Anderson, Jasey-Jay** | Snowboarding Athlete |
| 728 Rue Mattie, Mont-Tremblant QC J8E 1P3, Canada | |
| **Anderson, Joel** | Director, Writer |
| Bloom Hergott Diemer, 150 S Rodeo Dr, #300, Beverly Hills CA 90212 USA | |
| **Anderson, John B** | Representative, Presidential Candidate |
| 4120 48th St NW, Washington DC 20016, USA | |
| **Anderson, John D** | Singer, Songwriter |
| Pathfinder Mgmt, PO Box 159006, Nashville TN 37215, USA | |
| **Anderson, John M** | Ice Hockey Player, Coach |
| 260 Sunset Ave, Glen Ellyn IL 60137, USA | |
| **Anderson, Jon** | Singer (Yes) |
| Agency Group Ltd, 142 W 57th St, #600, New York NY 10019 USA | |
| **Anderson, Joseph (Joe)** | Actor |
| United Agents, 12-26 Lexington St, London W1F 0LE, England | |
| **Anderson, June** | Opera Singer |
| Bettina Brentano, 44 Rue Barbet de Jouy, 75007 Paris, France | |
| **Anderson, Kenneth (Kenny)** | Basketball Player |
| 270 N Canon Dr, #1289, Beverly Hills CA 90210, USA | |
| **Anderson, Kenneth A (Ken)** | Football Player, Coach |
| 41 Sedge Fern Dr, Hilton Head SC 29926, USA | |
| **Anderson, Kerrii** | Businesswoman |
| P F Chang's, 7676 E Pinnacle Peak Road, Scottsdale AZ 85255, USA | |
| **Anderson, Kevin** | Actor |
| 1575 Spinnaker Dr, #105B, Ventura CA 93001, USA | |
| **Anderson, Kevin J** | Writer |
| AnderZone, PO Box 767, Monument CO 80132, USA | |
| **Anderson, Kim S** | Football Player |
| 6709 La Tijera Blvd, #222, Los Angeles CA 90045, USA | |
| **Anderson, Kyle F** | Basketball Player |
| San Antonio Spurs, Alamodome, 1 AT&T Center Parkway, San Antonio TX 78219 USA | |
| **Anderson, Lauren** | Model |
| 5200 NW 43rd St, #102-304, Gainesville FL 32606, USA | |
| **Anderson, Laurie** | Performance Artist, Singer |
| Pomgranate Arts, 1140 Broadway, #305, New York NY 10001, USA | |
| **Anderson, Lawrence A (Larry)** | Football Player |
| 3170 Blanchard Road, Shreveport LA 71103, USA | |
| **Anderson, Layke** | Actor |
| Artists Partnership, 101 Finsbury Pavement, London EC2A 1RS, England | |
| **Anderson, Loni** | Actress |
| Innovative Artists, 1505 10th St, Santa Monica CA 90401 USA | |
| **Anderson, Louie** | Actor, Comedian |
| A P A Talent & Literary Agency, 405 S Beverly Dr, #300, Beverly Hills CA 90212 USA | |
| **Anderson, Lynn** | Singer |
| P L A Media, 1303 16th Ave S, Nashville TN 37212, USA | |
| **Anderson, Mark** | Football Player |
| PO Box 27551, Tulsa OK 74149, USA | |
| **Anderson, Marlon O** | Baseball Player |
| 780 Glenleigh Lane, Duluth GA 30097, USA | |
| **Anderson, Melissa Sue** | Actress |
| Globe Pequot Press, 246 Goose Lane, PO Box 480, Guilford CT 06437, USA | |
| **Anderson, Melody** | Actress |
| PO Box 24483, Los Angeles CA 90024, USA | |
| **Anderson, Michael** | Singer, Songwriter |
| A&M Records, 70 Universal City Plaza, Universal City CA 91608 USA | |
| **Anderson, Michael A (Mike)** | Baseball Player, Coach |
| 4112 Westbrook Dr, Florence SC 29501, USA | |
| **Anderson, Michael H** | Physicist |
| University of Colorado, Physics Dept, Boulder CO 80309, USA | |

**Anderson, Michael J** — Director
Paul Burford, 52 Yorkminster Road, North York ON M2P 1M3, Canada
**Anderson, Michael J** — Actor
C R Mgmt, 23852 Pacific Coast Highway, #627, Malibu CA 90265, USA
**Anderson, Michael M (Mike)** — Football Player
PO Box 12753, Chandler AZ 85248, USA
**Anderson, Miles** — Actor
Cassie Mayer, 5 Old Garden House, Lanterns, Bridge Lane, London SW11 3AD, England
**Anderson, Murray** — Ice Hockey Player
38 Head Ave, PO Box 38 Station Main, Pas MB R9A 1K3, Canada
**Anderson, Nathan** — Actor
Geddes Agency, 8430 Santa Monica Blvd, #201, West Hollywood CA 90069 USA
**Anderson, Nelison (Nick)** — Basketball Player
163 Harbor Isle Circle N, Memphis TN 38103, USA
**Anderson, Nick** — Editorial Cartoonist
Houston Chronicle, Editorial Dept, PO Box 4260, Houston TX 77210, USA
**Anderson, Nicole G** — Actress, Model
3035 Oldfield Way, San Jose CA 95135, USA
**Anderson, Ottis J (O J)** — Football Player
9636 Guehring Dr, Saint Louis MO 63123, USA
**Anderson, Pamela** — Model, Actress
I C M Partners, 10250 Constellation Blvd, #900, Los Angeles CA 90067 USA
**Anderson, Paul Thomas** — Director, Writer
Creative Artists Agency, 2000 Ave of Stars, #100, Los Angeles CA 90067 USA
**Anderson, Paul W S** — Director
Key Creatives, 1800 N Highland Ave, Los Angeles CA 90028, USA
**Anderson, Perry** — Ice Hockey Player
3516 E Meadowbrook Ave, Phoenix AZ 85018, USA
**Anderson, Pete** — Guitarist
Little Dog Records, 2219 W Olive Ave, #150, Burbank CA 91506, USA
**Anderson, Philip W** — Nobel Physics Laureate
Princeton University, Physics Dept, Princeton NJ 08544, USA
**Anderson, R John** — Football Player
14739 Crestwood Court, Sewickley PA 15143, USA
**Anderson, R Lanier, III** — Judge
US Court of Appeals, PO Box 977, Macon GA 31202, USA
**Anderson, Randy** — Auto Racing Driver
Anderson Racing, 1240 S Cucamonga Ave, Ontario CA 91761, USA
**Anderson, Ray** — Jazz Trombonist, Trumpeter
Ellicott Talent Group, 2503 Marilyn Circle, Petaluma CA 94954, USA
**Anderson, Rebecca Moesta** — Writer
Word Fire, PO Box 1840, Monument CO 80132, USA
**Anderson, Reid B** — Ballet Dancer, Artistic Director
Stuttgart Ballet, Ober Schlossgarten 6, 70173 Stuttgart, Germany
**Anderson, Richard** — Actor
10120 Cielo Dr, Beverly Hills CA 90210, USA
**Anderson, Richard** — Businessman
Delta Air Lines, Hartsfield International Airport, Atlanta GA 30320, USA
**Anderson, Richard D (Richie)** — Football Player
6311 Meandering Woods Court, Frederick MD 21701, USA
**Anderson, Richard Dean** — Actor
I C M Partners, 10250 Constellation Blvd, #900, Los Angeles CA 90067 USA
**Anderson, Richard P (Dick)** — Football Player
4603 Santa Maria St, Miami FL 33146, USA
**Anderson, Robert C (Bob)** — Baseball Player
3140 E 89th St, Tulsa OK 74137, USA
**Anderson, Robert C (Bobby)** — Football Player
79125 Big Horn Trail, La Quinta CA 92253, USA
**Anderson, Robert G W** — Museum Executive
British Museum, Great Russell St, London WC1B 3DG, England
**Anderson, Robert P (Bob)** — Football Player
244 Carmel Dr, Melbourne FL 32940, USA
**Anderson, Ronald C (Ron)** — Ice Hockey Player
72 Woodside Close, Airdie AB T4B 2C7, Canada
**Anderson, Ross** — Journalist
Seattle Times, Editorial Dept, 1000 Denny Way, Seattle WA 98109 USA
**Anderson, Russ** — Ice Hockey Player
76 Fern Dr, Plantsville CT 06479, USA
**Anderson, Ryan J** — Basketball Player
New Orleans Pelicans, 3500 Poydras St, #101, New Orleans LA 70113 USA
**Anderson, Samuel (Sam)** — Actor
TalentWorks, 3500 W Olive Ave, #1400, Burbank CA 91505 USA
**Anderson, Scott E** — Director
I C M Partners, 10250 Constellation Blvd, #900, Los Angeles CA 90067 USA
**Anderson, Shandon R** — Basketball Player
63 Mangum St SW, #6, Atlanta GA 30313, USA
**Anderson, Shawn** — Ice Hockey Player
Hockey S T, 19 51st Ave, Notre Dame de L'ile Perrot QC J7V 7L8, Canada
**Anderson, Shelly** — Drag Racing Driver
Brad Anderson Racing, 1240 S Cucamonga Ave, Ontario CA 91761, USA
**Anderson, Stephen H** — Judge
US Court of Appeals, Federal Building, 125 S State St, Salt Lake City UT 84138, USA
**Anderson, Sunshine** — Singer
Music World Entertainment, 1505 Hadley St, Houston TX 77002, USA
**Anderson, Tai** — Bassist (Third Day)
Creative Trust, 5141 Virginia Way, #320, Brentwood TN 37027, USA
**Anderson, Tazwell L (Taz), Jr** — Football Player
Taz Anderson Realty, 2931 Paces Ferry Road SE, #150, Atlanta GA 30339, USA
**Anderson, Terence (Terry)** — Journalist, Iran Hostage
17 Sunlight Hill, Yonkers NY 10704, USA
**Anderson, Thomas (Tom)** — Businessman
MySpace, 1333 2nd St, Santa Monica CA 90401, USA
**Anderson, Tim** — Actor
Herb Tannen, 10801 National Blvd, #101, Los Angeles CA 90064 USA
**Anderson, Todd** — Drummer (Heartland)
Country Thunder Records, 1016 17th Ave S, Nashville TN 37212, USA

**Anderson, Tom**                                                                 Actor
Feast Mgmt, 34 Upper St, London N1 0PN, England
**Anderson, Tyrone L (Bennie)**                                    Football Player
6450 Virginia Ave, Saint Louis MO 63111, USA
**Anderson, W French**                                          Biochemist, Geneticist
University of Southern California Medical School, 1510 San Pablo St, Los Angeles CA 90033, USA
**Anderson, W William (Bill)**                                      Football Player
6924 Lark Lane, Knoxville TN 37919, USA
**Anderson, Walter**                                                            Publisher
Parade Publications, Publisher's Office, 711 3rd Ave, New York NY 10017, USA
**Anderson, Wendell**                                            Ice Hockey Player
PO Box 49097, Minneapolis MN 55449, USA
**Anderson, Wendell R**                                      Governor, Senator, MN
Baker Building, 706 2nd Ave S, #720, Minneapolis MN 55402, USA
**Anderson, Wes**                                                  Director, Writer
American Empirical Pictures, 405 E 13th St, #6R, New York NY 10009, USA
**Anderson, Wessell**                                          Jazz Saxophonist
Fat City Artists, 1906 Chet Atkins Place, #502, Nashville TN 37212 USA
**Anderson, Wilford C**                                          WW II Army Hero
3585 Round Barn Blvd, Santa Rosa CA 95403, USA
**Anderson, Willie A**                                            Football Player
1490 Meadowcreek Court, Atlanta GA 30338, USA
**Anderson, Willie L**                                          Basketball Player
Toronto Raptors, Air Canada Center, 20 Bay St, Toronto ON M5J 2N8, Canada
**Anderson, Willie L (Flipper)**                                  Football Player
190 Abbey Hill Road, Suwanee GA 30024, USA
**Anderson, Winslow**                                                            Artist
PO Box 1700, Huntington WV 25717, USA
**Andersson, Benny**                                    Singer (ABBA), Composer
Mono Music, Sodra Brobaeken 41A, 111 49 Stockholm, Sweden
**Andersson, Bibi**                                                              Actress
Agents Associes, 201 Faubourg Saint Honore, 75008 Paris, France
**Andersson, Harriet**                                                          Actress
Agentfirman Planthaber/Kildén, Drottninggatan 55, 111 21 Stockholm, Sweden
**Andersson, Kim**                                                Handball Player
K I F Kolding, Ambolten 2-6, 6000 Kolding, Denmark
**Andersson, Lina M**                                          Cross Country Skier
Skiforbundet, Riksskistadion, 791 19 Falun, Sweden
**Andersson, Mattias**                                            Handball Player
S G Flensburg-Handewitt, Schiffbrucke 66, 24939 Flensburg, Germany
**Anderszewski, Piotr**                                   Concert Pianist, Conductor
I M G Artists, Hogarth Business Park, Chiswick, London W4 2TH, England
**Andes, Karen**                                                        Body Builder
G P Putnam's Sons, 375 Hudson St, New York NY 10014 USA
**Andino, Robert L**                                              Baseball Player
2250 NW 2nd St, Miami FL 33125, USA
**Andion Gonzalez, Patxi**                              Singer, Songwriter, Actor
Calle Pavia N 2, 28013 Madrid, Spain
**Ando, Kozue**                                                    Soccer Player
F C R 2001 Duisburg, Mundelheimer Str 123-125, 47259 Duisburg, Germany
**Ando, Miki**                                                      Figure Skater
International Mangement Group, 1 Erieview Plaza, 1360 E 9th St, #100, Cleveland OH 44114 USA
**Ando, Tadao**                                      Pritzker Architectural Laureate
Tadao Ando Architect, 5-23-2 Toyosaki, Kitaku, Osaka 531 0072, Japan
**Andrade, William T (Billy)**                                              Golfer
4429 E Brookhaven Dr NE, Atlanta GA 30319, USA
**Andrascik, Steve**                                            Ice Hockey Player
32 Early Lane, Annville PA 17003, USA
**Andre 3000**                                            Rap Artist (Outkast), Actor
4016 Elizabeth Terrace, Rex GA 30273, USA
**Andre, Annette**                                                              Actress
Infinite Artists, Pinewood Studios, Iver Heath, Buckinghamshire SLO ONH, England
**Andre, Carl**                                                              Sculptor
689 Crown St, Brooklyn NY 11213, USA
**Andrea, Pat**                                                                  Artist
18 Rue Henri Regnault, 75014 Paris, France
**Andrea, Paul**                                                  Ice Hockey Player
136 Regent St, North Sydney NS B2A 2G5, Canada
**Andreas, G Allen**                                                    Businessman
Archer Daniels Midland Co, 4666 E Faries Parkway, Decatur IL 62526, USA
**Andreasen, Nancy C**                                                    Psychiatrist
200 Hawkings Dr, Iowa City IA 52242, USA
**Andreason, Larry**                                                              Diver
10874 Kyle St, Los Alamitos CA 90720, USA
**Andree, Ingrid**                                                              Actress
Freie Akademie der Kunste, Klosterwall 23, 20095 Hamburg, Germany
**Andreeff, Starr**                                                            Actress
C N A Assoc, 1875 Century Park East, #2250, Los Angeles CA 90067 USA
**Andreessen, Marc**                                  Computer Software Designer
Opsware, 19420 Homestead Road, Cupertino CA 95014, USA
**Andreoli, Severino**                                                          Cyclist
Via Carolucci 19, 37060 Lugagnamo, Italy
**Andreone, Leah**                                            Singer, Songwriter
Metropolitan Entertainment Group, 2 Penn Plaza, #1500, New York NY 10121, USA
**Andres Puerta, Jose R**                                      Chef, Restauranteur
ThinkFoodGroup, 717 D St NW, #600, Washington DC 20004, USA
**Andres, Dominic**                                              Curling Athlete
Curling Association, PO Box 606, 3000 Bern, Switzerland
**Andresen, Frode**                                                          Biathlete
Borgergt 3, 3514 Honefoss, Norway
**Andress, Tuck**                                    Jazz Guitarist (Tuck & Patti)
T & P Productions, PO Box 1363, Menlo Park CA 94026, USA
**Andress, Ursula**                                                            Actress
Via Francesco Siacci 38, 00186 Rome, Italy
**Andretti, John**                                            Auto Racing Driver
Andretti Autosport, 7615 Zionsville Road, Indianapolis IN 46268, USA

| | |
|---|---|
| **Andretti, Mario** | Auto Racing Driver |
| 457 Rose Inn Ave, Nazareth PA 18064, USA | |
| **Andretti, Michael M** | Auto Racing Driver, Executive |
| Andretti Autosport, 7615 Zionsville Road, Indianapolis IN 46268, USA | |
| **Andrew** | Prince, England |
| Buckingham Palace, London SW1A 1AA, England | |
| **Andrew, Philip** | Actor |
| Bohemia Entertainment, 8170 Beverly Blvd, #102, Los Angeles CA 90048, USA | |
| **Andrew, Samuel H (Sam), III** | Guitarist (Big Brother Holding Company) |
| Gen-X Entertainment, PO Box 128164, Nashville TN 37212, USA | |
| **Andrews, Amy Leigh** | Model |
| Playboy Promotions, 9346 Civic Center Dr, #200, Beverly Hills CA 90210 USA | |
| **Andrews, Andy** | Actor, Comedian |
| PO Box 17321, Nashville TN 37217, USA | |
| **Andrews, Anthony** | Actor |
| Paradigm Agency, 360 N Crescent Dr, North Building, Beverly Hills CA 90210 USA | |
| **Andrews, Brittany** | Exotic Dancer, Model, Actress |
| Look North Promotions, 7-9 Clifford St, York, Yorkshire YO1 9RA, England | |
| **Andrews, Christopher F (Chris)** | Singer, Songwriter |
| Alexandra Andrews, Postfach 1139, 59369 Selm-Ternsche, Germany | |
| **Andrews, D Shane** | Baseball Player |
| 807 Dennis Way, Carlsbad NM 88220, USA | |
| **Andrews, Donna** | Golfer |
| 2301 Hawthorne Road, Lynchburg VA 24503, USA | |
| **Andrews, Erin** | Sportscaster |
| Fox-TV, Sports Dept, 205 W 67th St, New York NY 10065 USA | |
| **Andrews, George E** | Mathematician |
| 119 Meadow Lane, Centre Hall PA 16828, USA | |
| **Andrews, George E, II** | Football Player |
| 10195 Overhill Dr, Santa Ana CA 92705, USA | |
| **Andrews, Giuseppe** | Actor, Director, Writer |
| 1221 S Congress Ave, #612, Austin TX 78704, USA | |
| **Andrews, Jessica** | Singer |
| Creative Artists Agency, 2000 Ave of Stars, #100, Los Angeles CA 90067 USA | |
| **Andrews, John H** | Architect |
| Colleton, Cargo Road, Orange NSW 2800, Australia | |
| **Andrews, John R** | Baseball Player |
| 9292 Gordon Ave, La Habra CA 90631, USA | |
| **Andrews, Julie E** | Actress, Singer |
| PO Box 491668, Los Angeles CA 90049, USA | |
| **Andrews, Lee** | Singer |
| Mars Talent, 27 L'Ambiance Court, Nanuet NY 10954, USA | |
| **Andrews, Mark** | Senator, ND |
| 3354 165th Ave SE, Mapleton ND 58059, USA | |
| **Andrews, Michael J (Mike)** | Baseball Player |
| Jimmy Fund, 10 Brookline Place W, #600, Brookline MA 02445, USA | |
| **Andrews, Naveen** | Actor |
| Gersh Agency, 9465 Wilshire Blvd, #600, Beverly Hills CA 90212 USA | |
| **Andrews, Real** | Actor |
| Abrams Artists, 275 7th Ave, #2600, New York NY 10001 USA | |
| **Andrews, Robert** | Writer |
| G P Putnam's Sons, 375 Hudson St, New York NY 10014 USA | |
| **Andrews, Robert E (Rob)** | Representative, NJ |
| Dilworth Paxson LLP, 1500 Market St, #3500E, Philadelphia PA 19102, USA | |
| **Andrews, Robert F** | Religious Leader |
| 5404 Sharon Trail, Lakeland FL 33810, USA | |
| **Andrews, Robert P (Rob)** | Baseball Player |
| 1280 Mountbatten Court, Concord CA 94518, USA | |
| **Andrews, Scott** | Curling Athlete |
| Curl Aberdeen, Eday Walk off Lang Stracht, Summerhill, Aberdeen AB15 6LN, Scotland | |
| **Andrews, Shawn** | Football Player |
| 8 Sezanne Cove, Little Rock AR 72223, USA | |
| **Andrews, Theresa** | Swimmer |
| 2004 Homewood Road, Annapolis MD 21402, USA | |
| **Andrews, Tina** | Actress, Producer, Writer |
| Sharp Assoc, 1516 N Fairfax Ave, Los Angeles CA 90046, USA | |
| **Andrews, V C** | Writer |
| Pocket Books, 1230 Ave of Americas, New York NY 10020 USA | |
| **Andrews, William D (Billy), Jr** | Football Player |
| PO Box 703, Clinton LA 70722, USA | |
| **Andreychuck, Dave** | Ice Hockey Player |
| 18130 Longwater Run Dr, Tampa FL 33647, USA | |
| **Andrie, George J** | Football Player |
| 26356 E Zeerip, Drummond Island MI 49726, USA | |
| **Andriessen, Louis** | Composer |
| Nonesuch Records, 75 Rockefeller Plaza, #800, New York NY 10019 USA | |
| **Androsky, Carol** | Actress |
| Henderson/Hogan, 850 7th Ave, #1003, New York NY 10019 USA | |
| **Andruff, Ron** | Ice Hockey Player |
| 71 1/2 Irving Place, #1F, New York NY 10003, USA | |
| **Andrus, Cecil D** | Secretary, Interior; Governor, ID |
| PO Box 852, Boise ID 83701, USA | |
| **Andrusak, Greg** | Ice Hockey Player |
| 5240 Highway 3A, Nelson BC V1L 6N6, Canada | |
| **Andruzzi, Joseph D (Joe)** | Football Player |
| 682 Bellmore Ave, East Meadow NY 11554, USA | |
| **Andsnes, Leif Ove** | Concert Pianist |
| I M G Artists, Hogarth Business Park, Chiswick, London W4 2TH, England | |
| **Andujar, Joaquin** | Baseball Player |
| Ave L Amiama Tio #47, San Pedro de Macoris, Dominican Republic | |
| **Andy, Horace** | Singer, Songwriter |
| Agency Group Ltd, 1880 Century Park E, #711, Los Angeles CA 90067 USA | |
| **Ane, Charles T (Charlie), III** | Football Player |
| Punahou School, 1601 Punahou St, Honolulu HI 96822, USA | |
| **Anemone** | Actress |
| 82 Rue Bonaparte, 75006 Paris, France | |

**A**

**Andretti - Anemone**

**Angarano, Michael** — Actor
United Talent Agency, U T A Plaza, 9336 Civic Center Dr, Beverly Hills CA 90210 USA
**Angel Arango, Juan Pablo** — Soccer Player
Chivas U S A, Home Depot Center, 18400 S Avalon Blvd, Carson CA 90746, USA
**Angel, Ashley Parker** — Singer (O-Town)
Mavrick Artists Agency, 6100 Wilshire Blvd, #550, Los Angeles CA 90048, USA
**Angel, Criss** — Illusionist
Renaissance Literary & Talent, PO Box 17379, Beverly Hills CA 90209, USA
**Angel, Heather H** — Photographer
Highways, 6 Vicarage Hill, Farnham, Surrey GU9 8HJ, England
**Angel, J Roger P** — Astronomer
University of Arizona, Stewart Observatory, 933 N Cherry Ave, Tucson AZ 85721, USA
**Angel, Marie** — Opera Singer
Allied Artists, 42 Montpelier Square, London SW7 1JZ, England
**Angel, Vanessa** — Actress, Model
Media Artists Group, 8255 Sunset Blvd, Los Angeles CA 90046, USA
**Angela, Sharon** — Actress
C E S D, 257 Park Ave S, #950, New York NY 10010 USA
**Angelil, Rene** — Actress, Writer
United Talent Agency, U T A Plaza, 9336 Civic Center Dr, Beverly Hills CA 90210 USA
**Angell, Wayne D** — Financier, Government Official
1600 N Oak St, Arlington VA 22209, USA
**Angeloni, Umberto** — Fashion Executive
Brioni's Srl, Via Barberini 79, 00187 Rome, Italy
**Angelyne** — Actress, Artist, Model
Angelyne Mgmt, 5670 Wilshire Blvd, #2200, Los Angeles CA 90036, USA
**Angerer, Paul** — Composer
Esteplatz 3/26, 1030 Vienna, Austria
**Angerer, Peter** — Biathlete
Gampermuhlstr 2, 83313 Siegsdorf, Germany
**Angerer, Tobias** — Cross Country Skier
Hubertusstr 4, 83278 Traunstein, Germany
**Angier, Natalie M** — Journalist
New York Times, Editorial Dept, 229 W 43rd St, New York NY 10036, USA
**Anglade, Jean-Hughes** — Actor
Intertalent, 16 Rue Henri Barbusse, 75005 Paris, France
**Angle, Kurt S** — Freestyle Wrestler
5032 Stags Leap Lane, Coraopolis PA 15108, USA
**Anglim, Philip** — Actor
2404 Grand Canal, Venice CA 90291, USA
**Angula, Nahas** — Prime Minister, Namibia
Premier's Office, South Parliament Building, Windhoek 9000, Namibia
**Angulo, Richard** — Football Player
4801 W Libby St, Glendale AZ 85308, USA
**Anholt, Darrell** — Ice Hockey Player
4935 49th St, Hughenden, AL T0B 2E0, Canada
**Anikulap-Kuti, Femi** — Singer, Songwriter
M C A Records, 70 Universal City Plaza, Universal City CA 91608 USA
**Anissina, Marina V** — Figure Skater
Sports de Glace Federation, 35 Rue Felicien David, 75016 Paris, France
**Aniston, Jennifer** — Actress
Brillstein Entertainment Partners, 9150 Wilshire Blvd, #350, Beverly Hills CA 90212 USA
**Aniston, John** — Actor
Geddes Agency, 8430 Santa Monica Blvd, #201, West Hollywood CA 90069 USA
**Anjou, Danielle** — Sculptor
Voila Gallery, 518 N La Brea Ave, Los Angeles CA 90036, USA
**Anka, Paul** — Singer, Songwriter, Actor
2674 Stafford Road, Thousand Oaks CA 91361, USA
**Ankiel, Richard A (Rick)** — Baseball Player
126 Sandpiper Circle, Jupiter FL 33477, USA
**Ankvab, Alexander Z** — Prime Minister, Abkhazia
Prime Minister's Office, People's Assembly, Sukhumi, Abkhazia, Georgia
**Anlyan, William G** — Surgeon
Duke University Medical Center, Seeley Mudd Building, #109, Durham NC 27710, USA
**Annable, Dave** — Actor
Creative Artists Agency, 2000 Ave of Stars, #100, Los Angeles CA 90067 USA
**Annable, Odette** — Actress
United Talent Agency, U T A Plaza, 9336 Civic Center Dr, Beverly Hills CA 90210 USA
**Annan, Kofi A** — Secretary-General, United Nations
799 United Nations Plaza, New York NY 10017, USA
**Annaud, Jean-Jacques** — Director
9 Rue Guenegard, 75006 Paris, France
**Anne** — Princess, England
Buckingham Palace, London SW1 1AA, England
**Anne of Bourbon-Palma** — Queen, Romania
Villa Serena, 77 Chemin Louis-Degallier, 1290 Versoix-Geneva, Switzerland
**Annenberg, Wallis** — Publisher
10273 Century Woods Dr, Los Angeles CA 90067, USA
**Annett, Chloe** — Actress
Spotlight, 7 Leicester Place, London WC2H 7RJ, England
**Annis, Francesca** — Actress
Independent Talent Group, 40 Whitfield St, London W1T 2RH, England
**Ann-Margret** — Actress, Singer, Dancer
2707 Benedict Canyon Road, Beverly Hills CA 90210, USA
**Anno, Sam S** — Football Player
12934 Ferndale Ave, Los Angeles CA 90066, USA
**Anosike, Nkolika N (Nicky)** — Basketball Player
Los Angeles Sparks, 888 S Figueroa St, #2010, Los Angeles CA 90017 USA
**Anouk** — Singer
Artmedia, 20 Ave Rapp, 75007 Paris, France
**Anozie, Nonso** — Actor
Garricks, Angel House, 76 Mallinson Road, London SW11 1BN, England
**Ansa, Tina McElroy** — Writer
Jonee Ansa, 422 Sea Breeze Dr, PO Box 20602, Saint Simons Island GA 31522, USA
**Ansari, Anousheh** — Tourist Cosmonaut
Prodea Systems, 6101 W Plano Parkway, #210, Plano TX 75093, USA

**A**

**Ansari, Aziz** — Actor, Comedian
3 Arts Entertainment, 9460 Wilshire Blvd, #700, Beverly Hills CA 90212 USA

**Anschutz, Philip F** — Businessman, Sports Executive
Qwest Communications, 1801 California St, #5200, Denver CO 80202, USA

**Ansell, Jonathan** — Singer
Agency Group Ltd, 142 W 57th St, #600, New York NY 10019 USA

**Anselmo, Philip H** — Singer (Pantera)
5869 Colbert St, New Orleans LA 70124, USA

**Ansip, Andrus** — Prime Minister, Estonia
Prime Minister's Office, Stenbocki Maja, Rahukothu 3, 15161 Tallinn, Estonia

**Anspach, Susan** — Actress
11734 Wilshire Blvd, #207, Los Angeles CA 90025, USA

**Anspaugh, David** — Director
I C M Partners, 10250 Constellation Blvd, #900, Los Angeles CA 90067 USA

**Ant** — Actor, Comedian
Mavrick Artists Agency, 1680 N Vine St, #802, Hollywood CA 90028, USA

**Ant, Adam** — Singer, Guitarist
Tony Denton Promotions, PO Box 2839, London W1K 5LE, England

**Antal, Nimrod** — Director, Actor, Writer
Creative Artists Agency, 2000 Ave of Stars, #100, Los Angeles CA 90067 USA

**Antes, Horst** — Artist
Hohenbergstr 11, 76228 Karlsruhe (Wolfartsweier), Germany

**Anthamatten, Sophie** — Ice Hockey Player
E H C Saastal Sportzentrum, Wichel Kunsteisbahn, 3910 Saas-Grund, Switzerland

**Anthony, Carl** — Environmentalist
Harvard University, Kennedy Government School, Cambridge MA 02138, USA

**Anthony, Carmelo F** — Basketball Player
New York Knicks, Madison Square Garden, 2 Penn Plaza, New York, NY 10121 USA

**Anthony, Eric T** — Baseball Player
42 Fosters Court, Sugar Land TX 77479, USA

**Anthony, Gregory C (Greg)** — Basketball Player
63 Corso Italia, Freehold NJ 07728, USA

**Anthony, Lysette** — Actress
Belfield & Ward, 80-81 Saint Martin's Lane, London WC2N 4AA, England

**Anthony, Marc** — Singer, Actor, Songwriter
Marc Anthony Productions, 146 W 57th St, #38C, New York NY 10019, USA

**Anthony, Piers** — Writer
PO Box 2289, Inverness FL 34451, USA

**Anthony, Ray** — Orchestra Leader, Trumpeter
9288 Kinglet Dr, Los Angeles CA 90069, USA

**Anthony, Reidel C** — Football Player
PO Box 23, South Bay FL 33493, USA

**Anti, Michael (Mike)** — Marksman
13383 Honey Run Way, Colorado Springs CO 80921, USA

**Antin, Steve** — Actor, Writer
United Talent Agency, U T A Plaza, 9336 Civic Center Dr, Beverly Hills CA 90210 USA

**Antioco, John** — Businessman
Blockbuster Inc, 3704 Stratford Ave, Dallas TX 75205, USA

**Antoine, Lionel S** — Football Player
1455 Glencliff Dr, Dallas TX 75217, USA

**Antoine, Marc** — Jazz Guitarist
Variety Artists, 1924 Spring St, Paso Robles CA 93446 USA

**Antoine, Matthew** — Skeleton Athlete
316 N Beaumont Road, Prairie du Chien WI 53821, USA

**Anton, Alan** — Bassist (Cowboy Junkies)
S L Feldman Mgmt, 1505 W 2nd Ave, #200, Vancouver BC V6H 3Y4, Canada

**Anton, Susan** — Actress, Singer
10300 W Charleston Blvd, #13, Las Vegas NV 89135, USA

**Antonakakis, Dimitris** — Architect
Atelier 66, Emm Benaki 118, Athens 11473, Greece

**Antonakakis, Suzana M** — Architect
Atelier 66, Emm Benaki 118, Athens 11473, Greece

**Antonelli, Dominic A (Tony)** — Astronaut
4106 Oak Blossom Court, Houston TX 77059, USA

**Antonelli, Ennio Cardinal** — Religious Leader
Pontifical Council for the Family, Piazza S Calisto 16, 00153 Rome, Italy

**Antonelli, Laura** — Actress
Pietrovalle, Via B Buozzi 51, 00197 Rome, Italy

**Antonicheva, Anna** — Ballerina
Bolshoi Theater, Teatralnaya Pl 1, 103009 Moscow, Russia

**Antonio, James D (Jim)** — Actor
Epstein-Wyckoff, 280 S Beverly Dr, #400, Beverly Hills CA 90212 USA

**Antonio, Lou** — Actor
Actor's Studio, 8341 DeLongpre Ave, West Hollywood CA 90069, USA

**Antonoff, Jack M** — Guitarist (Fun)
Nettwerk Management Group, 1650 W 2nd Ave, Vancouver BC V6J 4R3, Canada

**Antonov, Vladislav N** — Luge Athlete
All-Russian Luge Federation, Luzhnetskaja Nab 11, 119992 Moscow, Russia

**Antonova, Lana** — Actress
Creative Artists Agency, 2000 Ave of Stars, #100, Los Angeles CA 90067 USA

**Antonovich, Mike** — Ice Hockey Player
4701 Desmond Beach, Fort Gratiot MI 48059, USA

**Antrim, Donald** — Writer
Wylie Agency, 250 W 57th St, #2114, New York NY 10107 USA

**Antunes, Arnaldo** — Singer, Songwriter
Monte Criacao Producao, Tra Santa Leocadia 40, Rio de Janiero 22061 050 Brazil

**Antuofermo, Vito** — Boxer, Actor
16452 98th St, Howard Beach NY 11414, USA

**Anu, Christine** — Singer
Robert Barnham Mgmt, 432 Tyagarah Road, Myocum NSW 2481, Australia

**Anuszkiewicz, Richard J** — Artist
76 Chestnut St, Englewood NJ 07631, USA

**Anwar, Gabrielle** — Actress
Innovative Artists, 1505 10th St, Santa Monica CA 90401 USA

**Aoi, Sora** — Actress
Prime Agency, 2-14-17-5F Shibuya, Shibuya, Tokyo 150 0002, Japan

*Ansari - Aoi*

# A

**Aoki, Chieko N** — Businesswoman
Westin Hotels, Westin Building, 777 Westchester Ave, West Harrison NY 10604, USA
**Aoki, Devon E** — Actress, Model
Schiff Co, 9220 Sunset Blvd, #106, West Hollywood CA 90069 USA
**Aoki, Isao** — Golfer
International Mangement Group, 1 Erieview Plaza, 1360 E 9th St, #100, Cleveland OH 44114 USA
**Aoki, Jun** — Architect, Interior Designer
Jun Aoki Assoc, 3-38-11 Jingumae, Shibuyaku, Tokyo 150 0001, Japan
**Aoki, Satoshi** — Businessman
Honda Motor Co, 2-1-1 Minami-Aoyama, Minatoku, Tokyo 107 8556, Japan
**Aoki, Steve** — DJ Musician
Ministry of Sound, 103 Gaunt St, London SE1 6DP, England
**Aouita, Said** — Track Athlete
Abdejil Bencheikh, 9 Rue Soivissi, Loubira, Rabat, Morocco
**Aoun, Michel N** — Prime Minister, Lebanon; Army General
Assemble Nationale, Place de L'Etoile, Beirut, Lebanon
**Apache Indian** — DJ Musician
Mission Control, City Business Center, Lower Road, London SE16 2XB, England
**Apap, Gilles** — Concert Violinist
Columbia Artists Mgmt Inc, 5 Columbus Circle, 1790 Broadway, #1600, New York NY 10019 USA
**Aparicio, Luis E** — Baseball Player
Calle 67, #26-82, Maracaibo, Venezuela
**Apatow, Judd** — Director, Producer, Writer
Apatow Productions, 11788 W Pico Blvd, Los Angeles CA 90064, USA
**Apel, Katrin** — Biathlete
Suedlung 9, 99330 Grafenroda, Germany
**Apiata, Bill H (Willie)** — Afghanistan War Army Hero (VC)
Victoria Cross Assn, Old Admiralty Building, London SW1A 2BL, England
**Apicella, Lorenzo F** — Architect
Pentagram, 11 Needham Road, London W11 2RP, England
**Apking, Stephen A** — Interior Designer
Skidmore Owings Merrill, 14 Wall St, #2500, New York NY 10005, USA
**Apl.De.Ap** — Rap Artist (Elephunk, Black Eyed Peas)
Paradigm Agency, 404 W Franklin St, Monterey CA 93940 USA
**Apodaca, Raymond S (Jerry)** — Governor, NM
6223 Utah Ave NW, Washington DC 20015, USA
**Apodaca, Robert J (Bob)** — Baseball Player
2999 SW Van Buren Terrace, Port Saint Lucie FL 34953, USA
**Apollonia** — Model, Actress, Singer
M G A Talent, 269 S Beverly Dr, #1088, Beverly Hills CA 90212, USA
**Appadurai, Arjun** — Anthropologist
New York University, Steinhardt School, New York, NY 10012, USA
**Appel, Deena** — Costume Designer
Montana Artists Agency, 7715 W Sunset Blvd, #300, Los Angeles CA 90046, USA
**Appel, Jayne** — Basketball Player
San Antonio Silver Stars, 1 AT&T Center, San Antonio TX 78219 USA
**Appel, Peter** — Actor
Hartig-Hilepo Agency, 54 W 21st St, #610, New York NY 10010 USA
**Appel, Richard** — Producer, Writer
W M E Entertainment, 9601 Wilshire Blvd, #300, Beverly Hills CA 90210 USA
**Appelbaum, Ralph** — Museum Designer
Ralph Appelbaum Assoc, 88 Pine St, #2900, New York NY 10005, USA
**Appelfeld, Aharon** — Writer
Wylie Agency, 17 Bedford Square, London WC1B 3JA, England
**Appice, Carmine** — Drummer (Vanilla Fudge, Cactus)
Worldsound, 17837 1st Ave S, #3, Seattle WA 98148, USA
**Appier, R Kevin** — Baseball Player
30743 Victory Road, Paola KS 66071, USA
**Apple, Fiona** — Singer, Songwriter
Front Line Mgmt, 1100 Glendon Ave, #2000, Los Angeles CA 90024 USA
**Applebaum, Anne** — Writer
Doubleday Press, 1745 Broadway, New York NY 10019 USA
**Appleberry, James B** — Educator
1400 Willow Ave, #605, Louisville KY 40204, USA
**Appleby, Malcolm A** — Artist
Aultberg, Grandtully by Aberfeldy, Perthshire PH15 2QU, England
**Appleby, Shiri** — Actress
United Talent Agency, U T A Plaza, 9336 Civic Center Dr, Beverly Hills CA 90210 USA
**Appleby, Steven** — Cartoonist, Writer
Bloomsbury Publishing, 50 Bedford Square, London WC1B 3DP, England
**Appleby, Stuart** — Golfer
9724 Chestnut Ridge Dr, Windermere FL 34786, USA
**Applegate, Christina** — Actress
Management 360, 9111 Wilshire Blvd, Beverly Hills CA 90210 USA
**Applegate, Debby** — Writer
125 Lawrence St, New Haven CT 06511, USA
**Applegate, Eddie** — Actor
PO Box 55592, Valencia CA 91385, USA
**Applegate, Jodi** — Commentator
News 12 Long Island, 1 Media Crossways, Woodbury NY 11797, USA
**Applegate, K A** — Writer
Scholastic Press, 555 Broadway, New York NY 10012 USA
**Applegate, Kendall** — Actress
Greene Assoc, 1901 Ave of Stars, #130, Los Angeles CA 90067 USA
**Appleton, Marc** — Architect
Appleton Assoc, 1556 17th St, Santa Monica CA 90404, USA
**Appleton, Steve** — Singer, Songwriter
Agency Group Ltd, 142 W 57th St, #600, New York NY 10019 USA
**Apps, Gillian M** — Ice Hockey Player
Hockey Canada, 151 Canada Olympic Road SW, #201, Calgary AB T3B 6B7, Canada
**Apps, Sylvanus M (Syl), Jr** — Ice Hockey Player
36 Pennock Crescent, Markham ON L3R 3M4, Canada
**Aprea, John** — Actor
Mavrick Artists Agency, 6100 Wilshire Blvd, #550, Los Angeles CA 90048, USA
**April, Renee** — Costume Designer
Sandra Marsh Assoc, 9150 Wilshire Blvd, #220, Beverly Hills CA 90212 USA

Aoki - April

**Apt, Jerome (Jay)** — Astronaut
4 Shadycourt Dr, Pittsburgh PA 15232, USA
**Apted, Michael D** — Director
1126 Indiana Ave, Venice CA 90291, USA
**Aqualung** — Singer, Songwriter
First Column Mgmt, 60 Compton Road, Brighton BN1 5AN, England
**Aqueduct** — Singer, Keyboardist, Guitarist
Aero Booking, 8008 Greenwood Ave N, #3, Seattle WA 98103, USA
**Aquilino, Thomas J, Jr** — Judge
US Court of International Trade, 1 Federal Plaza, New York NY 10278, USA
**Aquino Carmona, Javier I** — Soccer Player
Cruz Azul C D, San Pablo 100, C La Noria Xochimilco, Mexico City DF 16030, Mexico
**Aquino, Amy** — Actress
TalentWorks, 3500 W Olive Ave, #1400, Burbank CA 91505 USA
**Aquino, Luis A C** — Baseball Player
17201 Collins Ave, #606, Sunny Isles Beach FL 33160, USA
**Arabo, Claude** — Fencer
9 Rue Franquet, 75015 Paris, France
**Arad, Michael** — Architect
Handel Architects, 150 Varick St, #800, New York NY 10013, USA
**Arad, Ron** — Architect
Arad Assoc, 62 Chalk Farm Road, London NW1 8AN, England
**Aragall Garriga, Giacomo** — Opera Singer
Stafford Law Assoc, 6 Barham Close, Weybridge, Surrey KT1 9PR, England
**Aragones, Sergio** — Cartoonist (Mad Comics)
PO Box 696, Ojai CA 93024, USA
**Araguz, Leo J** — Football Player
3201 Araguz St, Harlingen TX 78552, USA
**Araiza Herrera, Armando** — Actor
Televisa, Blvd A Lopez Mateos 232, Colonia San Angel, Mexico City DF 01060 CP, Mexico
**Araiza, Francisco** — Opera Singer
Kuntsler Mgmt, M Kursidem, Tal 15, 80331 Munich, Germany
**Arakawa, Shizuka** — Figure Skater
International Skating Center, 1375 Hopemeadow St, Simsbury CT 06070, USA
**Araki, Gregg** — Director, Writer
I C M Partners, 10250 Constellation Blvd, #900, Los Angeles CA 90067 USA
**Arana, Tomas** — Actor
Affirmative Entertainment, 425 N Robertson Blvd, Los Angeles CA 90048, USA
**Aranauskas, Leonas S** — Architect
Glavmozarchitectura, Mayakovsky Square 1, 103001 Moscow, Russia
**Ararktsyan, Babken G** — Supreme Council Chairman, Armenia
3 Tamanian St, #35, 375009 Yerevan, Armenia
**Araskog, Rand V** — Businessman
I T T Corp, 1330 Ave of Americas, New York NY 10019, USA
**Arasmith, Lester L** — WW II Army Air Corps Hero
6601 Flint Ridge Road, Lincoln NE 68506, USA
**Arau, Alfonso** — Director
Glick Agency, 347 5th Ave, #1404, New York NY 10016 USA
**Araujo Razo, Nestor A** — Soccer Player
Cruz Azul C D, San Pablo 100, C La Noria Xochimilco, Mexico City DF 16030, Mexico
**Araujo, Ana Paula** — Model
Next Model Mgmt, 188 Rue de Rivoli, 75001 Paris, France
**Araya, Tomas E (Tom)** — Singer, Bassist (Slayer)
Work Hard Public Relations, 190 Pinfold Road, London SW16 2SL, England
**Arbanas, Frederick V (Fred)** — Football Player
3350 SW Hook Road, Lees Summit MO 64082, USA
**Arbatt, Alexandre** — Actor
Artmedia, 20 Ave Rapp, 75007 Paris, France
**Arber, Werner** — Nobel Medicine Laureate
Klingelbergstr 70, 4056 Basel, Switzerland
**Arbour, Alan (Al)** — Ice Hockey Player, Coach, Executive
2071 Harbour Links Dr, Longboat Key FL 34228, USA
**Arbour, Louise** — Government Official, Canada; Judge
130 Queen St W, Toronto ON M5H 2N5, Canada
**Arbulu Galliani, Guillermo** — Prime Minister, Peru; Army General
Prime Minister's Office, Urb Corpac, Calle 1 Oeste S/N, Lima 27, Peru
**Arcand, Denys** — Director
Agence Goodwin, 839 E Sherbrooke St, #200, Montreal QC H2L 1K6, Canada
**Arce, Alyssa** — Model
Playboy Promotions, 9346 Civic Center Dr, #200, Beverly Hills CA 90210 USA
**Arce, Jorge A** — Boxer
Top Rank, 3908 Howard Hughes Highway, #580, Las Vegas NV 89169, USA
**Archambault, Lee J** — Astronaut
4318 Sweet Cicely Court, Houston TX 77059, USA
**Archambeau, Lester M** — Football Player
10520 Montclair Way, Duluth GA 30097, USA
**Archer of Weston-Super-Mare, Jeffrey H** — Government Official, England; Writer
Peninsula Heights, 93 Albert Embankment, London SE1 7TY, England
**Archer, Anne** — Actress
L I N K Entertainment, 11872 La Grange Ave, Los Angeles CA 90025 USA
**Archer, Dave** — Artist
1541 Buckhorn Road, Roseburg OR 97470, USA
**Archer, David** — Football Player
3831 Upland Dr, Marietta GA 30066, USA
**Archer, Glenn L, Jr** — Judge
US Court of Appeals, 717 Madison Place NW, Washington DC 20439, USA
**Archer, Jeffrey** — Writer
Curtis Brown Group, 28-29 Haymarket St, #500, London SW1Y 4SP, England
**Archer, Robyn** — Actress, Songwriter, Director
Rick Raftos Mgmt, Box 445, Paddington NSW 2021, Australia
**Archibald, David (Dave)** — Ice Hockey Player
PO Box 2108, Saint Sardis Main, Chilliwack BC V2R 1A6, Canada
**Archibald, Jane** — Opera Singer
I M G Artists, Hogarth Business Park, Chiswick, London W4 2TH, England
**Archibald, Nathaniel (Nate)** — Basketball Player
2720 Grand Concourse, #218, Bronx NY 10458, USA

**Archibald, Nolan D** — Businessman
Black & Decker Corp, 701 E Joppa Road, Towson MD 21286, USA
**Archipowski, Ken** — Singer (Randy & the Rainbows)
Brothers Management Assoc, 141 Dunbar Ave, Fords NJ 08863 USA
**Architzel, David** — Navy Admiral
Old Dominion University, Military Affairs Office, Koch Hall, Norfolk VA 23529, USA
**Archuleta, Adam J** — Football Player
1237 W Galveston St, Chandler AZ 85224, USA
**Archuleta, David J** — Singer, Keyboardist, Guitarist
Arch Consulting Group, 340 W Whitney Ave, Salt Lake City UT 84115, USA
**Arcia Orta, Jose R** — Baseball Player
7325 NW 3rd St, Miami FL 33126, USA
**Arcieri, Leila** — Actress
Luber Rocklin Entertainment, 5815 Sunset Blvd, #206, Los Angeles CA 90028 USA
**Arciero, Frank** — Auto Racing Executive
Arciero Racing, 1901 Nancita Circle, Placentia CA 92870, USA
**Arcuri, Manuela** — Actress, Model
Condominio L'Orologio, Via Isonzo Int 25, 04100 Latina, Italy
**Arcuri, Robin** — Model
17128 Colima Road, #411, Hacienda Heights CA 91745, USA
**Ard, William D (Bill)** — Football Player
41 Vail Lane, Watchung NJ 07069, USA
**Ardant, Fanny** — Actress
Les Visiteurs du Soir, 40 Rue de la Folie Regnault, 75011 Paris, France
**Arden, Jann** — Singer, Songwriter
S L Feldman Mgmt, 1505 W 2nd Ave, #200, Vancouver BC V6H 3Y4, Canada
**Arden, Toni** — Singer
3434 75th St, Jackson Heights NY 11372, USA
**Arditi, Pierre** — Actor
Voyez Mon Agent, 20 Ave Rapp, 75007 Paris, France
**Ardito Barletta Vallarino, Nicolas** — President, Panama
PO Box 7737, Panama City 9, Panama
**Arditti, Irvine** — Concert Violinist
Latitude Arts, 109 Boul Saint-Joseph Quest, Montreal PA H2T 2P7, Canada
**Ardoin, Daniel W (Danny)** — Baseball Player
1524 Lee St, Ville Platte LA 70586, USA
**Arena, Bruce** — Soccer Player, Coach
Los Angeles Galaxy, Home Depot Center, 18400 Avalon Blvd, Carson CA 90746 USA
**Arena, Tina** — Singer
Harbour Agency, 135 Forbes St, Wooloomooloo NSW 2011, Australia
**Arenas, Gilbert J** — Basketball Player
4550 Gable Dr, Encino CA 91316, USA
**Arenas, L Joseph (Joe)** — Football Player
780 W Bay Area Blvd, #1215, Webster TX 77598, USA
**Arend, Geoffrey** — Actor
United Talent Agency, U T A Plaza, 9336 Civic Center Dr, Beverly Hills CA 90210 USA
**Arend, Jeff** — Drag Racing Driver, Owner
Arend/Smith Racing, 2 Mallingham Court, Toronto ON M2N 6C4, Canada
**Arens, Moshe** — Government Official, Israel
49 Hagderot, Savyon 56526, Israel
**Aresco, Joey** — Actor
Carrier Talent Mgmt, 705-1080 Howe St, Vancouver BC V6Z 2T1, Canada
**Areshenkoff, Ron** — Ice Hockey Player
1701 1st St, Estevan SK S4A 0H5, Canada
**Arestrup, Niels** — Actor
Voyez Mon Agent, 20 Ave Rapp, 75007 Paris, France
**Arfin, Lesley** — Actress
W M E Entertainment, 9601 Wilshire Blvd, #300, Beverly Hills CA 90210 USA
**Argent, Rod** — Keyboardist (Zombies)
Gen-X Entertainment, PO Box 140, Cedar MN 55011, USA
**Argento, Asia** — Actress, Director
Cineart, 28 Rue Mogador, 78009 Paris, France
**Argento, Dario** — Director
A D C, Via Balamonti 2, Rome, Italy
**Argento, Dominick** — Composer
University of Minnesota, Music Dept, Ferguson Hall, Minneapolis MN 55455, USA
**Argerich, Martha** — Concert Pianist
Jacques Thelen Agence, 15 Ave Montaigne, 75008 Paris, France
**Argos, Eddie** — Singer (Art Brut)
Coda Agency, 229 Shoreditch High St, London E1 6PJ, England
**Argott, Don** — Director, Producer, Cinematogapher
9.14 Pictures, 1804 Chestnut St, #2, Philadelphia PA 19104, USA
**Ariail, Robert** — Editorial Cartoonist
The State, Editorial Dept, PO Box 1333, Columbia SC 29202, USA
**Arianda, Nina** — Actress
I C M Partners, 10250 Constellation Blvd, #900, Los Angeles CA 90067 USA
**Arias Sanchez, Oscar** — Nobel Laureate; President, Costa Rica
Arias Foundation for Peace, Apdo 8-6410-1000, San Jose, Costa Rica
**Arias, Alejandro (Alex)** — Baseball Player
37 Edmund Road, West Park FL 33023, USA
**Arias, Moises** — Actor
Greene Assoc, 1901 Ave of Stars, #130, Los Angeles CA 90067 USA
**Arias, Yancey** — Actor
Global Artists Agency, 6253 Hollywood Blvd, #508, Los Angeles CA 90028 USA
**Arienti, Luigi** — Cyclist
Via Trincea delle Frasche 80, 20832 Desio (MB), Italy
**Arigoni, Dulio** — Chemist
Im Glockenacker 42, 8053 Zurich, Switzerland
**Arii, Takendo** — Architect
1117 W Arbor Dr, San Diego CA 92103, USA
**Arima, Akito** — Physicist
Physical Research Institute, Hirosawa 2-1, Wakoshi, Saitama 351 01, Japan
**Arinze, Francis Cardinal** — Religious Leader
Congregation for Divine Worship, Palazzo delle Congregazioni, 00193 Rome, Italy
**Arison, M Micky** — Businessman, Basketball Executive
Carnival Corp, 3655 NW 87th Ave, Doral FL 33178, USA

**Ariyoshi, George R**
745 Fort St, #500, Honolulu HI 96813, USA — Governor, HI

**Ariza, Trevor A**
1111 S Grand Ave, #PH 2, Los Angeles CA 90015, USA — Basketball Player

**Arizmendi, Yareli**
C E S D, 10635 Santa Monica Blvd, #130, Los Angeles CA 90025 USA — Actress

**Arkhipov, Denis**
716 Sweet Cherry Court, Nashville TN 37215, USA — Ice Hockey Player

**Arkin, Adam**
3531 Coldwater Canyon Ave, Studio City CA 91604, USA — Actor

**Arkin, Adam**
University of California, Physical Chemistry Dept, Berkeley CA 94720, USA — Physical Chemist

**Arkin, Alan W**
Principal Entertainment, 9255 Sunset Blvd, #500, Los Angeles CA 90069 USA — Actor

**Arkin, Jordana**
W M E Entertainment, 9601 Wilshire Blvd, #300, Beverly Hills CA 90210 USA — Producer

**Arkush, Allan**
Paradigm Agency, 360 N Crescent Dr, North Building, Beverly Hills CA 90210 USA — Director, Producer

**Arlauckas, Joseph (Joe)**
917 Night Heron Dr, Mount Pleasant SC 29464, USA — Basketball Player

**Arlen, Michael J**
New Yorker, Editorial Dept, 4 Times Square, Basement C1B, New York NY 10036 USA — Writer

**Arlin, Stephen R (Steve)**
6819 Claremore Ave, San Diego CA 92120, USA — Baseball Player

**Arlt, Tobias**
Oberschonauer Str 105, 83471 Schonau, Germany — Luge Athlete

**Armacost, Michael H**
9425 Tarnberry Dr, Potomac MD 20854, USA — Government Official, Diplomat

**Armadroff, Taft**
W M Keck Observatory, 65-1120 Mamalahoa Highway, Kamuela HI 96743, USA — Astronomer

**Armani, Giorgio**
Via Borgonuovo 11, 20121 Milan, Italy — Fashion Designer

**Armano, Mario**
Olympic Committee, Foro Italico, Largo Lauro de Bosis 15, 00135 Rome, Italy — Bobsled Athlete

**Armant, Ivonne**
Tayrona Entertainment Group, 9663 Santa Monica Blvd, #623, Beverly Hills CA 90210, USA — Model, Actress

**Armaou, Lindsay**
Clintons, 55 Drury Lane, Covent Garden, London WC2B 5SQ, England — Singer (B*Witched)

**Armas, Antonio R (Tony)**
Calle Las Mercedes 37, Puerto Piritu, Venezuela — Baseball Player

**Armas, Chris**
Chicago Fire, Toyota Park, 7000 S Harlem Ave, Bridgeview IL 60455 USA — Soccer Player

**Armatrading, Joan**
Entourage Talent Assoc, 236 W 27th St, #800, New York NY 10001, USA — Singer, Songwriter

**Armbrister, Edison R (Ed)**
McQuay St, Box 2003, Nassau, Bahamas, West Indies — Baseball Player

**Armedariz, Pedro, Jr**
Diamond Artists, 9200 W Sunset Blvd, #701, West Hollywood CA 90069 USA — Actor

**Armenante, Jillian**
Framework Entertainment, 9057 Nemo St, #C, West Hollywood CA 90069 USA — Actress

**Armerding, Hudson T**
780 Schick Road, #29W, Bartlett IL 60103, USA — Educator

**Armesto, Sebastian**
Curtis Brown Group, 28-29 Haymarket St, #500, London SW1Y 4SP, England — Actor

**Armey, Richard K**
Citizens for a Sound Economy, 1775 Pennsylvania Ave NW, Washington DC 20006, USA — Representative, TX

**Armfield, Diana M**
10 High Park, Kew, Richmond, Surrey TW9 4BH, England — Artist

**Armiliato, Marco**
I M G Artists, Hogarth Business Park, Chiswick, London W4 2TH, England — Conductor

**Armisen, Fred**
W M E Entertainment, 9601 Wilshire Blvd, #300, Beverly Hills CA 90210 USA — Actor, Comedian

**Armitage, Alison**
9220 W Sunset Blvd, #305, West Hollywood CA 90069, USA — Actress, Model

**Armitage, George**
Gersh Agency, 9465 Wilshire Blvd, #600, Beverly Hills CA 90212 USA — Director, Producer, Writer

**Armitage, Karole**
350 W 21st St, New York NY 10011, USA — Choreographer, Dancer

**Armitage, Richard**
W M E Entertainment, 9601 Wilshire Blvd, #300, Beverly Hills CA 90210 USA — Actor

**Armitstead, Elizabeth M (Lizzie)**
M T C (UK) Ltd, 71 Gloucester Place, London W1U 8JW, England — Cyclist

**Armleder, John**
Simon Lee Gallery, 12 Berkeley St, London W1J 8DT, England — Artist

**Armour, Justin H**
8 Crystal Park Place, #B, Manitou Springs CO 80829, USA — Football Player

**Armour, Thomas D (Tommy), III**
4211 Saint Andrews Blvd, Irving TX 75038, USA — Golfer

**Armstead, Jessie W**
1316 Mill Stream Dr, Dallas TX 75232, USA — Football Player

**Armstead, Ray**
7953 Bloom Dr, Saint Louis MO 63133, USA — Track Athlete

**Armstrong Savola, Kristin**
Joe Savola, 455 E Cave Court, Boise ID 83702, USA — Cyclist

**Armstrong, A James**
Broadway Methodist Church, 1100 W 42nd St, #210, Indianapolis IN 46208, USA — Religious Leader

**Armstrong, Adger, Jr**
6403 Paddington St, Houston TX 77085, USA — Football Player

**Armstrong, Alex**
Rights House, Drury Lane, 34-43 Russell St, London WC2B 5HA, England — Actor, Comedian

**Armstrong, Alun**
Markham Froggatt Irwin, Julian House, 4 Windmill St, London W1P 1HF, England — Actor

**Armstrong, Ami**
United Talent Agency, U T A Plaza, 9336 Civic Center Dr, Beverly Hills CA 90210 USA — Producer, Director, Writer

**Armstrong, Anthony**
Paradigm Agency, 404 W Franklin St, Monterey CA 93940 USA — Guitarist (Red)

A

Ariyoshi - Armstrong

# A

**Armstrong, Benjamin R (B J)** — Basketball Player, Executive
1550 Hawthorne Lane, Highland Park IL 60035, USA
**Armstrong, Bess** — Actress
Vox Inc, 6420 Wilshire Blvd, #1080, Los Angeles CA 90048 USA
**Armstrong, Billie Joe** — Singer, Guitarist (Green Day)
5652 Florence Terrace, Oakland CA 94611, USA
**Armstrong, Brandon S** — Basketball Player
New Jersey Nets, 390 Murray Hill Parkway, East Rutherford NJ 07073 USA
**Armstrong, Bruce C** — Football Player
12543 Brookwood Court, Davie FL 33330, USA
**Armstrong, Clay M** — Physiologist
University of Pennsylvania Medical School, 3400 Spruce, Philadelphia PA 19104, USA
**Armstrong, Craig** — Composer
First Artists Mgmt, 4764 Park Granada, #210, Calabasas CA 91302 USA
**Armstrong, Curtis** — Actor
Marshak/Zachary/Mills, 8840 Wilshire Blvd, #100, Beverly Hills CA 90211 USA
**Armstrong, Darrell E** — Basketball Player
337 Broadmoor Way, McDonough GA 30253, USA
**Armstrong, Deborah (Debbie)** — Alpine Skier
PO Box 770925, Steamboat Springs CO 80477, USA
**Armstrong, Derek** — Ice Hockey Player
873 8th St, Manhattan Beach CA 90266, USA
**Armstrong, George E** — Ice Hockey Player
22 Saint Cuthbert's Road, East York ON M4G 1V1, Canada
**Armstrong, Gillian** — Director
Creative Artists Agency, 2000 Ave of Stars, #100, Los Angeles CA 90067 USA
**Armstrong, Hilton A, Jr** — Basketball Player
Golden State Warriors, 1011 Broadway, Oakland CA 94605 USA
**Armstrong, Jack W** — Baseball Player
272 E River Park Dr, Jupiter FL 33477, USA
**Armstrong, Jonas** — Actor
I C M Partners, 10250 Constellation Blvd, #900, Los Angeles CA 90067 USA
**Armstrong, Kerry** — Actress
Mike Morrissey Assoc, 16 Princess Ave, Rosebery, Sydney NSW 2018, Australia
**Armstrong, Kit** — Concert Pianist, Composer
June Artists Mgmt, Charlottenstra 43, 10117 Berlin, Germany
**Armstrong, Lance** — Cyclist
901 Rio Grande St, #100, Austin TX 78701, USA
**Armstrong, Linda** — Actress
Associated International Mgmt, 7 Hatton Garden, #400, London EC1N 8AD, England
**Armstrong, M Tate** — Basketball Player
14704 Westbury Road, Rockville MD 20853, USA
**Armstrong, Matthew John** — Actor
Don Buchwald Talent Agency, 6500 Wilshire Blvd, #2200, Los Angeles CA 90048 USA
**Armstrong, Michael D (Mike)** — Baseball Player
525 Ashbrook Court, Athens GA 30605, USA
**Armstrong, Neil** — Ice Hockey Referee
1169 Sherwood Trail, Sarnia ON N7V 2H3, Canada
**Armstrong, Neil F** — Football Player, Coach
312 Lakewood Dr, Roanoke TX 76262, USA
**Armstrong, Otis** — Football Player
7183 S Newport St, Denver CO 80220, USA
**Armstrong, Randy** — Bassist (Red)
Paradigm Agency, 404 W Franklin St, Monterey CA 93940 USA
**Armstrong, Raymond L (Trace)** — Football Player
422 SW 88th Terrace, Gainesville FL 32607, USA
**Armstrong, Rob** — Singer, Cittern Player (Tarras)
Rounder Records, 1 Rounder Way, Burlington MA 01803 USA
**Armstrong, Robb** — Cartoonist (Jump Start)
United Feature Syndicate, PO Box 5610, Cincinnati OH 45201 USA
**Armstrong, Robin L** — Physicist
383 Ellis Park Road, #383-303, Toronto ON M6S 5B2, Canada
**Armstrong, Rowland C O (Rolle)** — Musician (Faithless)
Helter Skelter, 347-353 Chiswick High Road, London W4 4HS, England
**Armstrong, Russell P** — Vietnam War Marine Corps Hero
425 Bench Road, Fallon NV 89406, USA
**Armstrong, Sheila A** — Opera, Concert Singer
Harvesters, Tilford Road, Hindhead, Surrey GU26 6SQ, England
**Armstrong, Spence M** — Air Force General
9120 Belvoir Woods Parkway, #117, Fort Belvoir VA 22060, USA
**Armstrong, T Robert (Bob)** — Basketball Player
6802 Packer Dr NE, Belmont MI 49306, USA
**Armstrong, Thomas** — Auto Racing Driver
PacWest Racing Group, PO Box 1717, Bellevue WA 98009, USA
**Armstrong, Thomas H W** — Concert Organist
1 East St, Olney, Bucks MK46 4AP, England
**Armstrong, Timothy L (Tim)** — Guitarist (Rancid)
Leave Home Booking, 10 W Broadway, #608, Salt Lake City UT 84101, USA
**Armstrong, Tom** — Cartoonist (Marvin)
North American Syndicate, 235 E 45th St, New York NY 10017 USA
**Armstrong, Ty** — Golfer
11529 Kensington Dr, Eden Prairie MN 55347, USA
**Armstrong, Valorie** — Actress
Contemporary Artists, 610 Santa Monica Blvd, #202, Santa Monica CA 90401 USA
**Armstrong, Vaughn** — Actor
1903 Apex Ave, Los Angeles CA 90039, USA
**Armstrong, Victor M (Vic)** — Actor, Stuntman
Gersh Agency, 9465 Wilshire Blvd, #600, Beverly Hills CA 90212 USA
**Armstrong, William L** — Senator, CO
Colorado Christian University, President's Office, Lakewood CO 80226, USA
**Arnason, Chuck** — Ice Hockey Player
39 Grimston Road, Winnipeg MB R3T 3T2, Canada
**Arnaud, Jean-Loup** — Government Official, France
55 Ave du Maine, 75014 Paris, France
**Arnault, Bernard** — Businessman
Moet Hennessy Louis Vuitton, 30 Ave Hoche, 75008 Paris, France

**Arnaz, Desi, Jr** — Actor
516 Avenue M, Boulder City NV 89005, USA
**Arnaz, Lucie** — Actress, Singer
3 Big Shop Lane, Ridgefield CT 06877, USA
**Arndt, Denis** — Actor, Writer, Producer
Innovative Artists, 1505 10th St, Santa Monica CA 90401 USA
**Arndt, Judith** — Cyclist
Wermsdorder Str 28, 94277 Leipzig, Germany
**Arndt, Michael** — Writer
Verve Talent & Literary Agency, 96310 San Vicente Blvd, #100, Los Angeles CA 90048 USA
**Arndt, Stefan** — Producer
X-Filme Creative Pool, Kurfuerstenstr 57, 10785 Berlin, Germany
**Arnelle, Jesse** — Basketball Player
400 Urbano Dr, San Francisco CA 94127, USA
**Arnesen, Liv** — Polar Skier
16560 220th St N, Scandia MN 55073, USA
**Arnett, Jon D** — Football Player
200 Greenridge Dr, #715, Lake Oswego OR 97035, USA
**Arnett, Peter** — Commentator, Journalist
ForeignTV.com, 162 5th Ave, #105A, New York NY 10010, USA
**Arnett, Will** — Actor
W M E Entertainment, 9601 Wilshire Blvd, #300, Beverly Hills CA 90210 USA
**Arnette, Jay H** — Basketball Player
2 Hillside Court, Austin TX 78746, USA
**Arnette, Jeannetta** — Actress
Connor Ankrum Assoc, 1680 Vine St, #1016, Los Angeles CA 90028, USA
**Arnez, J** — Actor, Comedian
I C M Partners, 10250 Constellation Blvd, #900, Los Angeles CA 90067 USA
**Arngrim, Alison** — Actress
PO Box 98, Tujunga CA 91043, USA
**Arnhold, Henry H** — Financier
Arnhold & S Bleichroeder, 1345 Ave of Americas, #4300, New York NY 10105, USA
**Arniel, Scott** — Ice Hockey Player
6 Edmond Muys Place, Winnipeg MB R3P 2R1, Canada
**Arning, Lisa** — Actress
Chasen Agency, 8899 Beverly Blvd, #405, Los Angeles CA 90048 USA
**Arnold, Andrea** — Director
Sayle Screen, 11 Jubilee Place, London SW3 3TD, England
**Arnold, Andrew** — Geneticist
Massachusetts General Hospital, Genetics Dept, Boston MA 02114, USA
**Arnold, Anna Bing** — Philanthropist
Anna Bing Arnold Foundation, 9700 W Pico Blvd, Los Angeles CA 90035, USA
**Arnold, Christopher P (Chris)** — Baseball Player
2219 El Capitan Ave, Arcadia CA 91006, USA
**Arnold, David** — Composer
Coalition Mgmt, 12 Barley Mow Passage, London W4 4PH, England
**Arnold, Frances H** — Engineer
California Institute of Technology, Spalding Building, Pasadena CA 91125, USA
**Arnold, Gary H** — Film Critic
5133 N 1st St, Arlington VA 22203, USA
**Arnold, James E (Jim)** — Football Player
223 Boxwood Dr, Franklin TN 37069, USA
**Arnold, Kristine** — Singer (Sweethearts of the Rodeo)
2803 Bransford Ave, Nashville TN 37204, USA
**Arnold, Morris S** — Judge
US Court of Appeals, 600 W Capitol Ave, #224, Little Rock AR 72201, USA
**Arnold, Richard R (Ricky), II** — Astronaut
N A S A, Johnson Space Center, 2101 NASA Road, Houston TX 77058 USA
**Arnold, Thomas D (Tom)** — Actor, Comedian
9958 Kip Dr, Beverly Hills CA 90210, USA
**Arnold, Tichina** — Actress, Singer
A P A Talent & Literary Agency, 405 S Beverly Dr, #300, Beverly Hills CA 90212 USA
**Arnold, Walt** — Football Player
8503 La Sala Grande NE, Albuquerque NM 87111, USA
**Arnold, Walter (Walt)** — Rodeo Steer Roper
PO Box 713, Silverton TX 79257, USA
**Arnoldi, Charles A** — Artist
721 Hampton Dr, Venice CA 90291, USA
**Arnott, Jason** — Ice Hockey Player
155 Carondelet Plaza, #302, Saint Louis MO 63105, USA
**Arnoul, Francoise** — Actress
53 Rue Censier, 75005 Paris, France
**Arns, Paulo E Cardinal** — Religious Leader
Curia Metropolitana, Avenida Higienopolis 890, Sao Paulo 01238 000 SP, Brazil
**Arnsberg, Bradley J (Brad)** — Baseball Player
4610 E Thunder Hawk Road, Cave Creek AZ 85331, USA
**Arnsparger, Bill** — Football Coach, Administrator
1574 Pine Needles Lane, Lexington KY 40513, USA
**Arnstein, Holly** — Singer (Dream)
Bad Boy Entertainment, 1540 Broadway, #3000, New York NY 10036, USA
**Arnzen, Robert L (Bob)** — Basketball Player
8 Grand Lake Dr, Fort Thomas KY 41075, USA
**Aronofsky, Darren** — Director
Creative Artists Agency, 2000 Ave of Stars, #100, Los Angeles CA 90067 USA
**Arons, Arnold B** — Physicist
10313 Lake Shore Blvd NE, Seattle WA 98125, USA
**Aronsohn, Lee** — Producer, Writer
Paradigm Agency, 360 N Crescent Dr, North Building, Beverly Hills CA 90210 USA
**Aronson, David** — Artist
137 Brimstone Lane, Sudbury MA 01776, USA
**Aronson, Eliot** — Psychologist
University of California, Psychology Dept, Santa Cruz CA 95064, USA
**Aronson, Judie** — Actress
A T M Mgmt, 292 5th Ave, #400, New York NY 10001, USA
**Arpaia, Donatella** — Restaurateur
Anthos Restaurant, 36 W 52nd St, New York NY 10019, USA

**Arpaio, Joseph M (Joe)** — Law Enforcement Official
102 W Madison St, Phoenix AZ 85003, USA

**Arpel, Adrien** — Businesswoman
Adrien Arpel Cosmetics, 400 Hackensack Ave, Hackensack NJ 07601, USA

**Arpey, Gerard J** — Businessman
A M R Corp, 4333 Amon Carter Blvd, Fort Worth TX 76155, USA

**Arquette, Alexis** — Actress
Innovative Artists, 1505 10th St, Santa Monica CA 90401 USA

**Arquette, David** — Actor
A P A Talent & Literary Agency, 405 S Beverly Dr, #300, Beverly Hills CA 90212 USA

**Arquette, Patricia** — Actress
Gersh Agency, 9465 Wilshire Blvd, #600, Beverly Hills CA 90212 USA

**Arquette, Rosanna** — Actress
Lovett Mgmt, 1327 Brinkley Ave, Los Angeles CA 90049, USA

**Arquez, Gaelle** — Opera Singer
I M G Artists, Hogarth Business Park, Chiswick, London W4 2TH, England

**Arraras, Maria Celeste** — Commentator
Telemundo Network Group, News Dept, 2470 W 8th Ave, Hialeah FL 33010, USA

**Arredondo, Rosa** — Actress
TalentWorks, 3500 W Olive Ave, #1400, Burbank CA 91505 USA

**Arriaga, Guillermo** — Director, Writer
United Talent Agency, U T A Plaza, 9336 Civic Center Dr, Beverly Hills CA 90210 USA

**Arriale, Lynne** — Singer, Pianist
347 Clearwater Dr, Ponte Vedra Beach FL 32082, USA

**Arrigo, Gerald W (Jerry)** — Baseball Player
3740 Red Thorne Dr, Amelia OH 45102, USA

**Arrington, Jill** — Sportscaster
ESPN-TV, Sports Dept, ESPN Plaza, 935 Middle St, Bristol CT 06010 USA

**Arrington, LaVar R** — Football Player
1514 Cedar Lane Farm Road, Annapolis MD 21409, USA

**Arrow, Kenneth J** — Nobel Economics Laureate
620 Sand Hill Road, #406C, Palo Alto CA 94304, USA

**Arroyo, Bronson A** — Baseball Player
23315 Frontier Way, Brooksville FL 34601, USA

**Arroyo, Carlos** — Basketball Player
1115 NW 126th Court, Miami FL 33182, USA

**Arroyo, Fernando** — Baseball Player
702 Hampton Woods Lane SW, Vero Beach FL 32962, USA

**Arroyo, Harry** — Boxer
726 S Salem Road, North Jackson OH 44451, USA

**Arroyo, Luis E** — Baseball Player
PO Box 1452, Yauco PR 00698, USA

**Arroyo, Martina** — Opera Singer
Berkshire Concert Artists, 20 Alfred Dr, Pittsfield MA 01201, USA

**Artemas, Cole** — Cartoonist
1050 Colonial St, Rutland VT 05701, USA

**Artemov, Vladimir N** — Gymnast
Artemov Gymnastics, 21750 Hardy Oak Blvd, San Aontonio TX 78258, USA

**Artemyev, Oleg G** — Cosmonaut
Cosmonaut Training Center, Star City, 141160 Zvezdny Gorodok, Moscow Oblast, Russia

**Arter, Robert** — Army General
C G S C Foundation, Lewis & Clark Center, 100 Stimson Ave, #1149, Fort Leavenworth KS

**Arterton, Gemma** — Actress
Independent Talent Group, 40 Whitfield St, London W1T 2RH, England

**Arteta, Miguel** — Director, Producer
W M E Entertainment, 9601 Wilshire Blvd, #300, Beverly Hills CA 90210 USA

**Arthur, Darrell** — Basketball Player
Memphis Grizzlies, 191 Beale St, Memphis TN 38103 USA

**Arthur, Elizabeth** — Writer
Bloomsbury LLC, 36 Soho Square, London W1D 3Q4, England

**Arthur, Fred** — Ice Hockey Player
203-1408 Ernest Ave, London ON N6E 3B2, Canada

**Arthur, James A** — Singer, Musician, Songwriter
S Y C O Music, Redford House, 69-79 Fulham High St, London SW6 3JW, England

**Arthur, Michael S (Mike)** — Football Player
11271 Terwilligers Vallet Lane, Cincinnati OH 45249, USA

**Arthur, Perry** — Golfer
7513 Zurich Dr, Plano TX 75025, USA

**Arthur, Rebeca** — Actress
Momentum Talent Mgmt, 13935 Burbank Blvd, #102, Valley Glen CA 91401, USA

**Arthur, Stacy Leigh** — Model
Playboy Promotions, 9346 Civic Center Dr, #200, Beverly Hills CA 90210 USA

**Arthurs, Paul (Bonehead)** — Guitarist (Oasis)
Ignition Mgmt, 54 Linhope St, London NW1 6HL, England

**Arthus-Bertrand, Yann M** — Photographer
Altitude, 30 Rue des Favorites, 75015 Paris, France

**Artist, Jacob** — Actor
A P A Talent & Literary Agency, 405 S Beverly Dr, #300, Beverly Hills CA 90212 USA

**Artsebarsky, Anatoli P** — Cosmonaut
Cosmonaut Training Center, Star City, 141160 Zvezdny Gorodok, Moscow Oblast, Russia

**Artson, Bradley Shavit** — Religious Leader, Rabbi, Educator
American Jewish University, 15600 Mulholland Dr, Los Angeles CA 90077, USA

**Artur, Sophie** — Actress
Agence Laurence Bagoe, 11 Rue Delambre, 75014 Paris, France

**Artzt, Alice J** — Concert Guitarist
51 Hawthorne Ave, Princeton NJ 08540, USA

**Artzt, Edwin L** — Businessman
3849 Hedgewood Dr, Lawrenceburg IN 47025, USA

**Arum, Robert (Bob)** — Boxing Promoter
36 Gulf Stream Court, Las Vegas NV 89113, USA

**Arutyunyan, Gagik G** — Prime Minister, Armenia
Prime Minister's Office, Republic Square, Government House 1, 0010 Yerevan, Armenia

**Arvesen, Nina** — Actress
20315 Lanark St, Winnetka CA 91306, USA

**Arvidsson, Margareta** — Beauty Queen, Model
Miss Universe Organization, 1370 Ave of Americas, #1600, New York NY 10019 USA

**Arvizu, Reginald (Fieldy)** — Bassist (Korn)
Mitch Schneider Organization, 14724 Ventura Blvd, #500, Sherman Oaks CA 91403 USA
**Arwady, Meredith** — Opera Singer
Columbia Artists Mgmt Inc, 5 Columbus Circle, 1790 Broadway, #1600, New York NY 10019 USA
**Arzu Irigoyen, Álvaro E** — President, Guatemala
Partida de Avanzada Nacional, 7A Avda 10-38, Guatemala City, Guatemala
**Asada, Mao** — Figure Skater
Kishi Kinen Taiikukan 1-1-1, Jinnan Shibuyahku, Tokyo 150 8050, Japan
**Asano, Tadanobu** — Actor
Anore, Ochial Building, 6-17-15 Jingumae Shibuyuku, #9F, Tokyo 150 0001, Japan
**Asante, Amma** — Director, Writer
United Agents, 12-26 Lexington St, London W1F 0LE, England
**Asawa, Brian** — Opera Singer
Askonas Holt, Lincoln House, 300 High Holborn, London WC1V 7JH, England
**Asay, Chuck** — Cartoonist
Colorado Springs Gazette, 303 S Prospect St, Colorado Springs CO 80903, USA
**Asbaek, Pilou** — Actor
Lindberg Mgmt, Lavendelstraad 5-7, 1462 Copenhagen K, Denmark
**Asbaty, Diandra** — Bowler
Kaizen, 100 E 14th St, #1005, Chicago IL 60605, USA
**Asbury, Kelly** — Animator, Director, Writer
United Talent Agency, U T A Plaza, 9336 Civic Center Dr, Beverly Hills CA 90210 USA
**Asbury, Martin** — Cartoonist (Garth)
Stoneworld, Pitch Green, Princes Risborough, Buckinghamshire HP27 9QG, England
**Asbury, Richard** — WWII Army Air Corps Hero
2499 E Dale Court, Bettendorf IA 52722, USA
**Ascaride, Ariane** — Actress
Zelig, 57 Rue Reaumur, 75002 Paris, France
**Asch, Peter** — Water Polo Player
1946 Green St, San Francisco CA 94123, USA
**Aselton, Kathryn (Katie)** — Actress, Director, Producer
I C M Partners, 10250 Constellation Blvd, #900, Los Angeles CA 90067 USA
**Asencio, Henry** — Artist
Crown Thorn Publishing, 2375 Northside Dr, #200, San Diego CA 92108, USA
**Asfaw, Ingida** — Physician, Social Activist
2278 W Philadelphia St, Detroit MI 48206, USA
**Ash, Daniel** — Guitarist (Bauhaus, Love & Rockets)
Agency Group Ltd, 142 W 57th St, #600, New York NY 10019 USA
**Ash, Nadine** — Golfer
Quantum Sports Mgmt, 5625 E Wethersfield Road, Scottsdale AZ 85254, USA
**Ashanti** — Singer, Songwriter, Actress
Media Artists Group, 8222 Melrose Ave, #203, Los Angeles CA 90048 USA
**Ashbery, John L** — Writer
326 Belmont Ave, Buffalo NY 14223, USA
**Ashbrook, Dana** — Actor
B R S / Gage Talent Agency, 5757 Wilshire Blvd, #659, Los Angeles CA 90036 USA
**Ashbrook, Daphne** — Actress
Defining Artists, 10 Universal City Plaza, #2000, Universal City CA 91608, USA
**Ashby, Alan D** — Baseball Player
12011 Cypress Creek Lakes Dr, Cypress TX 77433, USA
**Ashby, Andrew J (Andy)** — Baseball Player
2 Osborne Dr, Pittston PA 18640, USA
**Ashby, Jeffrey S** — Astronaut
N A S A, Johnson Space Center, 2101 NASA Road, Houston TX 77058 USA
**Ashby, Linden** — Actor
639 N Larchmont Blvd, #207, Los Angeles CA 90004, USA
**Ashcroft, John D** — Attorney General; Senator, Governor, MO
5603 W Farm Road 54, Willard MO 65781, USA
**Ashcroft, Richard** — Singer (Verve), Songwriter
Fresh & Clean Media, 12701 Venice Blvd, Los Angeles CA 90066, USA
**Ashdown, J J D (Paddy)** — Government Official, England
Vane Cottage, Norton Sub Hamdon, Somerset TA14 6SG, England
**Ashenfelter, Horace, III** — Track Athlete
100 Hawthorne Ave, Glen Ridge NJ 07028, USA
**Asher, Barry** — Bowler
Professional Bowlers Association, 719 2nd Ave, #701, Seattle WA 98104 USA
**Asher, Jane** — Actress
Jane Asher Cakes & Sugarcraft, 22-24 Cole St, London SW3 3QU, England
**Asher, Peter** — Singer (Peter & Gordon), Businessman
Santuary Artist Mgmt, 45-53 Sinclair Road, London W14 0NS, England
**Asher, Robert D (Bob)** — Football Player
4800 S Chicago Beach Dr, #612, Chicago IL 60615, USA
**Ashfield, Kate** — Actress
Independent Talent Group, 40 Whitfield St, London W1T 2RH, England
**Ashford, Annaleigh** — Actress
A P A Talent & Literary Agency, 405 S Beverly Dr, #300, Beverly Hills CA 90212 USA
**Ashford, Matthew** — Actor
260 S Beverly Dr, #208, Beverly Hills CA 90212, USA
**Ashford, Rob** — Choreographer
Creative Artists Agency, 2000 Ave of Stars, #100, Los Angeles CA 90067 USA
**Ashford, Roslyn** — Singer (Martha & Vandellas)
Soundedge Personal Mgmt, 332 Southdown Road, Huntington NY 11743, USA
**Ashford, Thomas S (Tucker)** — Baseball Player
502 S Maple St, Covington TX 76636, USA
**Ashida, Jun** — Fashion Designer
1-3-3 Aobadai, Meguroku, Tokyo 153 8521, Japan
**Ashihara, Yoshinobu** — Architect
47-10 Nishihara 3, Shibuyaku, Tokyo 151 0066, Japan
**Ashitey, Clare-Hope** — Actress
United Agents, 12-26 Lexington St, London W1F 0LE, England
**Ashkar, Saleem Abboud** — Concert Pianist
I M G Artists, Hogarth Business Park, Chiswick, London W4 2TH, England
**Ashkenasi, Shmuel** — Concert Violinist
Caecilia, 5 Place de la Fustene, 1204 Geneva, Switzerland
**Ashkenazy, Dimitri** — Concert Clarinetist
Harrison/Parrott, 5-6 Albion Court, London W6 0QT, England

# A

| | |
|---|---|
| **Ashkenazy, Vladimir D** | Concert Pianist, Conductor |
| Savinka, Kappelistr 15, 6045 Meggen, Switzerland | |
| **Ashley, Adryenn** | Actress, Writer, Filmmaker |
| 925 Lakeville St, #304, Petaluma CA 94952, USA | |
| **Ashley, Billy M** | Baseball Player |
| 2787 Autumn Ridge Dr, Thousand Oaks CA 91362, USA | |
| **Ashley, Christopher** | Director |
| I C M Partners, 730 5th Ave, New York NY 10019 USA | |
| **Ashley, David** | Educator |
| University of Nevada Las Vegas, President's Office, Las Vegas NV 89154, USA | |
| **Ashley, Elizabeth** | Actress |
| 1223 N Ogden Dr, West Hollywood CA 90046, USA | |
| **Ashley, Jennifer** | Actress |
| Morgan Agency, 1200 N Doheny Dr, Los Angeles CA 90069, USA | |
| **Ashley, Jessica** | Model |
| Playboy Promotions, 9346 Civic Center Dr, #200, Beverly Hills CA 90210 USA | |
| **Ashley, Merrill** | Ballerina |
| New York City Ballet, Lincoln Center Plaza, New York NY 10023 USA | |
| **Ashman, Duane A** | Football Player |
| 2625 Antler Court, Silver Spring MD 20904, USA | |
| **Ashmore, Aaron** | Actor |
| K G Talent, 55A Sumach St, Toronto ON M5A 3J6, Canada | |
| **Ashmore, Darryl A** | Football Player |
| 8695 Thornbrook Terrace Point, Boynton Beach FL 33473, USA | |
| **Ashmore, Edward B** | Navy Admiral, England |
| Naval Secretary, Victory Building, H M Naval Base, Portsmouth, Hampshire PO1 3LJ, England | |
| **Ashmore, Shawn** | Actor |
| Gersh Agency, 9465 Wilshire Blvd, #600, Beverly Hills CA 90212 USA | |
| **Ashrawi, Hanan** | Political Leader, Palestine |
| Arab League, PO Box 11642, Tahrir Square, Cairo, Egypt | |
| **Ashton, Brent** | Ice Hockey Player |
| 311 Brabent Crescent, Saskatoon SK S7J 4Y9, Canada | |
| **Ashton, Dean** | Actor |
| Laine Mgmt, Laine House, 131 Laine Road, Salford M6 8LF, England | |
| **Ashton, John** | Actor |
| Beddingfield Co, 13600 Ventura Blvd, #B, Sherman Oaks CA 91423, USA | |
| **Ashton, Joseph** | Actor |
| Don Buchwald Talent Agency, 6500 Wilshire Blvd, #2200, Los Angeles CA 90048 USA | |
| **Ashton, Susan** | Singer |
| Sparrow Communications, 101 Winners Circle, Brentwood TN 37027, USA | |
| **Ashton-Griffiths, Roger** | Actor |
| 16 Chelmsford Road, London E11 1BS, England | |
| **Ashworth, Frank** | Ice Hockey Player |
| 5110 Hot Springs, Fairmont Hot Springs BC V0B 1L0, Canada | |
| **Ashworth, Gerald (Gerry)** | Track Athlete |
| PO Box 2, Ogunquit ME 03907, USA | |
| **Ashworth, Jeanne C** | Speed Skater |
| Whiteface Highway, Wilmington NY 12997, USA | |
| **Askew, Bobby D (B J), Jr** | Football Player |
| 4216 Lantana Dr, Lebanon OH 45036, USA | |
| **Askew, Desmond** | Actor |
| Paul Kohner, 9300 Wilshire Blvd, #555, Beverly Hills CA 90212 USA | |
| **Askey, Tom** | Ice Hockey Player |
| 5732 S 6th St, Kalamazoo MI 49009, USA | |
| **Askson, Bert** | Football Player |
| 7713 Charlesmont St, Houston TX 77016, USA | |
| **Asman, David** | Commentator |
| Fox-TV, News Dept, 205 E 67th St, New York NY 10065 USA | |
| **Asmussen, Cash** | Thoroughbred Racing Jockey |
| 111 Devonshire Court, Laredo TX 78041, USA | |
| **Asner, Edward** | Actor |
| Greene Assoc, 1901 Ave of Stars, #130, Los Angeles CA 90067 USA | |
| **Asomugha, Nnamdi** | Football Player, Actor |
| 1050 Armitage St, Alameda CA 94502, USA | |
| **Asplin, Edward W** | Businessman |
| 601 Carlson Parkway, #1050, Hopkins MN 55305, USA | |
| **Aspromonte, Kenneth J (Ken)** | Baseball Player, Manager |
| 2 Derham Park St, Houston TX 77024, USA | |
| **Aspromonte, Robert T (Bob)** | Baseball Player |
| 1000 Uptown Park Blvd, #241, Houston TX 77056, USA | |
| **Assad, Badi** | Singer, Guitarist, Pianist |
| Aviv Productions, 10418 E Meadowhill Dr, Scottsdale AZ 85255, USA | |
| **Assad, Bashar al-** | President, Syria; Army General |
| Presidential Palace, Muharreem Abu Rumanch, Al-Rashid St, Damascas, Syria | |
| **Assad, Odair** | Concert Guitarist |
| Opus 3 Artists, 470 Park Ave S, #900N, New York NY 10016 USA | |
| **Assad, Sergio** | Concert Guitarist |
| Opus 3 Artists, 470 Park Ave S, #900N, New York NY 10016 USA | |
| **Assange, Julian P** | Businessman, Editor, Activist |
| Wikileaks, PO Box 4080, University of Melbourne, Melbourne VIC 3052, Australia | |
| **Assante, Armand** | Actor |
| A P A Talent & Literary Agency, 405 S Beverly Dr, #300, Beverly Hills CA 90212 USA | |
| **Assayas, Olivier** | Director, Writer |
| Creative Artists Agency, 2000 Ave of Stars, #100, Los Angeles CA 90067 USA | |
| **Asseltine, Brian H** | Baseball Player |
| 1488 Country Court, Santa Ynez CA 93460, USA | |
| **Assenmacher, Paul A** | Baseball Player |
| 500 Covington Cove, Alpharetta GA 30022, USA | |
| **Assia, Lys** | Singer |
| Cariblue Music, Laubenheimer Str 5, 14197 Berlin, Germany | |
| **Assim** | Rap Artist |
| Bad Boy Entertainment, 1440 Broadway, #16, New York NY 10018 USA | |
| **Assinger, Armin** | Skier |
| Kuhweg 23, 9620 Hermagor, Austria | |
| **Assis, Raymundo D Cardinal** | Religious Leader |
| Curia Metropolitana, Rua Barao do Rio Branco 412, CP 82, 12570 000 Aparecida, SP, Brazil | |

*Ashkenazy - Assis*

**Astacio Pura, Pedro J** — Baseball Player
2695 E Long Lane, Littleton CO 80121, USA
**Astar, Shay** — Actress
Franchot Mgmt, PO Box 48890A, Los Angeles CA 90048, USA
**Astbury, Ian R** — Singer (Cult)
Tom Vitorino Mgmt, 11606 Viny Road, Granada Hills CA 91344, USA
**Astin, Allen V** — Physicist
5008 Battery Lane, Bethesda MD 20814, USA
**Astin, John** — Actor, Director
3801 Canterbury Road, #505, Baltimore MD 21218, USA
**Astin, Mackenzie** — Actor
Sovereign Talent Group, 8421 Wilshire Blvd, #200, Beverly Hills CA 90211, USA
**Astin, Sean** — Actor
A C M Talent, 2 W 45th St, #1201, New York NY 10036, USA
**Astin, Skylar** — Actor
United Talent Agency, U T A Plaza, 9336 Civic Center Dr, Beverly Hills CA 90210 USA
**Astley, Rick** — Singer
Barry Collings Entertainment, PO Box 2112, Essex Hockley SS5 4WD, England
**Astrid** — Queen, Belgium
Royal Palace, Rue Brederode, 1000 Brussels, Belgium
**Asylmuratova, Altynai** — Ballerina
Mariinsky Ballet, Teatralnaya Square 1, 190000 Saint Petersburg, Russia
**Atala, Anthony** — Surgeon
Wake Forest University, Regenerative Medical Institute, Winston-Salem NC 27109, USA
**Atambayev, Almazbek S** — Prime Minister, Kyrgyzstan
President's Office, Government House, 720003 Bishkek, Kyrgyzstan
**Ataneli, Lado** — Opera Singer
I M G Artists, Hogarth Business Park, Chiswick, London W4 2TH, England
**Atchison, Doug** — Director, Writer
United Talent Agency, U T A Plaza, 9336 Civic Center Dr, Beverly Hills CA 90210 USA
**Atchison, Michael** — Editorial Cartoonist
Associated Press, Editorial Dept, 450 W 33rd St, #1500, New York NY 10001 USA
**Atchison, Scott B** — Baseball Player
1820 Barrington Dr, Keller TX 76262, USA
**Atelian, Taylor** — Actress
Abrams Artists, 9200 W Sunset Blvd, #1125, West Hollywood CA 90069 USA
**Athas, Peter G (Pete)** — Football Player
1125 NW 130th St, Miami FL 33168, USA
**Atherton, David** — Conductor
Askonas Holt, Lincoln House, 300 High Holborn, London WC1V 7JH, England
**Atherton, Keith R** — Baseball Player
1014 Cobbs Creek Lane, Cobbs Creek VA 23035, USA
**Atherton, Michael A** — Cricketer
Lancashire County Cricket Club, Old Trafford, Manchester M16 0PX, England
**Atherton, William** — Actor
Stone Manners Salners, 6100 Wilshire Blvd, #1500, Los Angeles CA 90035 USA
**Atias, Moran** — Actress
A D D Agency, 2 Raoul Wallenberg St, Ramat Hachayal, Tel Aviv 69719, Israel
**Atigha, Giuma Ahmed** — President, Libya
President's Office, Bab el Asiziya Barracks, Tripoli, Libya
**Atika, Aure** — Actress
Agence Artiste Adequat, 108 Rue Reaumur, 75002 Paris, France
**Atkin, Harvey** — Actor
527 S Curson St, Los Angeles CA 90036, USA
**Atkins, Christopher** — Actor
6934 Bevis Ave, Van Nuys CA 91405, USA
**Atkins, Douglas L (Doug)** — Football Player
8005 Clapps Chapel Road, Knoxville TN 37902, USA
**Atkins, Eileen** — Actress
Independent Talent Group, 40 Whitfield St, London W1T 2RH, England
**Atkins, Erica** — Singer (Mary Mary), Songwriter
Paradigm Agency, 404 W Franklin St, Monterey CA 93940 USA
**Atkins, Essence** — Actress
Don Buchwald Talent Agency, 6500 Wilshire Blvd, #2200, Los Angeles CA 90048 USA
**Atkins, Garrett B** — Baseball Player
Colorado Rockies Foundation, 2001 Blake St, #A, Denver CO 80205, USA
**Atkins, Gene R** — Football Player
3515 Sunnyside Dr, Tallahassee FL 32305, USA
**Atkins, Kenneth L (Chucky)** — Basketball Player
229 S Ortman Dr, Orlando FL 32811, USA
**Atkins, Pervis** — Football Player
8040 Ventura Canyon Ave, Springfield PA 19064, USA
**Atkins, Rodney** — Singer
McGhee Entertainment, 8730 Sunset Blvd, #200, West Hollywood CA 90069, USA
**Atkins, Sharif** — Actor
Christopher Wright Mgmt, 3207 Winnie Dr, Los Angeles CA 90068, USA
**Atkins, Tina** — Singer (Mary Mary), Songwriter
Paradigm Agency, 404 W Franklin St, Monterey CA 93940 USA
**Atkins, Tom** — Actor
106 Forestwood Dr, Venetia PA 15367, USA
**Atkinson, Allen E (Al)** — Football Player
218 Wells Lane, Springfield PA 19064, USA
**Atkinson, Conrad** — Artist
172 Erlanger Road, London SE14 5TJ, England
**Atkinson, George H (Butch)** — Football Player
6331 Fairmount Ave, El Cerrito CA 94530, USA
**Atkinson, Jayne** — Actress
S M S Talent, 8383 Wilshire Blvd, #230, Beverly Hills CA 90211 USA
**Atkinson, Kate** — Writer
Transworld Publishing, 61-63 Uxbridge Road, London W5 5SA, England
**Atkinson, Rick** — Journalist, Writer
Kansas City Times, Editorial Dept, 1729 Grand Ave, Kansas City MO 64108, USA
**Atkinson, Rowan S** — Actor, Comedian
P B J Mgmt, 22 Rathbone St, London W1T 1LA, England
**Atkov, Oleg Y** — Cosmonaut
Cosmonaut Training Center, Star City, 141160 Zvezdny Gorodok, Moscow Oblast, Russia

**Atlantov, Vladimir A** — Opera Singer
Vienna State Opera, Opernring 2, 1015 Vienna, Austria
**Atogwe, Oshiomogho I (O J)** — Football Player
496 Speyer Place, Saint Charles MO 63303, USA
**Attai, Kader** — Artist
Saatachi Gallery, Duke of York's H Q, King's Road, London SW3 4RY, England
**Attal, Yvan** — Actor, Director
Voyez Mon Agent, 20 Ave Rapp, 75007 Paris, France
**Attell, Dave** — Actor, Comedian
Creative Artists Agency, 2000 Ave of Stars, #100, Los Angeles CA 90067 USA
**Attenborough, David F** — Entertainer, Writer, Naturist
5 Park Road, Richmond, Surrey TW10 6NS, England
**Attersee, Christian** — Artist
Vienna University of Applied Arts, Oskar Kokoschka-Platz 2, #3, 1010 Vienna, Austria
**Atterton, Edward** — Actor
I C M Partners, 10250 Constellation Blvd, #900, Los Angeles CA 90067 USA
**Attias, Daniel** — Director, Producer
Principato-Young, 9465 Wilshire Blvd, #880, Beverly Hills CA 90212 USA
**Attig, Rick** — Journalist
Portland Oregonian, Editorial Dept, 1320 SW Broadway, Portland OR 97201, USA
**Attkisson, Sharyl** — Commentator
CNN-TV, News Dept, 190 Marietta Ave SW, Atlanta GA 30303 USA
**Attlee, Frank, III** — Businessman
Monsanto Co, 800 N Lindbergh Blvd, Saint Louis MO 63167, USA
**Attles, Alvin A (Al)** — Basketball Player, Coach
195 Villanova Dr, Oakland CA 94611, USA
**Atwal, Arjun** — Golfer
International Mgmt Group, Burlington Lane, London W4 2TH, England
**Atwater, H Brewster, Jr** — Businessman
I D S Center, 80 S 8th St, Minneapolis MN 55402, USA
**Atwater, Stephen D (Steve)** — Football Player
2510 Sugarloaf Club Dr, Duluth GA 30097, USA
**Atwell, Hayley** — Actress
Hamilton Hodell, 66-68 Margaret St, #500, London, W1W 8SR, England
**Atwood, Casey L** — Auto Racing Driver
Day Enterprises, 107 Flat Ridge Road, Goodlettsville TN 37072, USA
**Atwood, Colleen C** — Costume Designer
232 Aderno Way, Pacific Palisades CA 90272, USA
**Atwood, Harold L** — Zoologist
602 Castlefield Ave, Toronto ON M5N 1L8, Canada
**Atwood, Margaret E** — Writer
Curtis Brown, Haymarket House, 28-29 Haymarket, London SW14 4SP, England
**Atwood, Susie (Sue)** — Swimmer
5624 E 2nd St, Long Beach CA 90803, USA
**Atzmon, Moshe** — Conductor
P M G, 59 Lansdowne Place, Hove, East Sussex BN3 1FL, England
**Auber, Brigitte** — Actress
Agence A Berthomme, 72 Rue Notre Dame des Champs, 75006 Paris, France
**Auberjonois, Rene** — Actor
448 S Arden Blvd, Los Angeles CA 90020, USA
**Aubert, Brian** — Singer, Guitarist (Silversun Pickups)
Ink Tank Public Relations, 1824 W Sunset Blvd, #102, Los Angeles CA 90026, USA
**Aubert, Karen D (K D)** — Actress
Sovereign Talent, 8421 Wilshire Blvd, #200, Beverly Hills CA 90211, USA
**Aubin, Normand** — Ice Hockey Player
1287 Rue des Berges, Sorel-Tracy QC J3P 7X5, Canada
**Aubret, Isabelle** — Singer
Gerard Mays Productions, 110 Rue Saint Martin, 75001 Paris, France
**Aubrey, Juliet** — Actress
Artists Partnership, 101 Finsbury Pavement, London EC2A 1RS, England
**Aubry, Eugene E** — Architect
Morris/Aubry Architects, 3465 W Alabama St, Houston TX 77027, USA
**Aubry, Pierre** — Ice Hockey Player
110 Rue Buisson, Cap-de-la-Madelain, QC G8V 1K4, Canada
**Auburn, David** — Writer, Director
97 W Elmwood Ave, Clawson MI 48017, USA
**Aucoin, Adrian M** — Ice Hockey Player
421 N Grant St, Hinsdale IL 60521, USA
**AuCoin, Les** — Representative, OR
Bogle & Gates, 601 13th St NW, #370, Washington DC 20005, USA
**Aucoin, Rich** — Singer
Agency Group Ltd, 142 W 57th St, #600, New York NY 10019 USA
**Audette, Donald (Don)** — Ice Hockey Player
15 Rue de Chinon, Blainville QB J7B 1Y2, Canada
**Audiard, Jacques** — Director, Writer
Voyez Mon Agent, 20 Ave Rapp, 75007 Paris, France
**Audick, Daniel J B (Dan)** — Football Player
13253 Sparren Ave, San Diego CA 92129, USA
**Audran, Stephane** — Actress
Artmedia, 20 Ave Rapp, 75007 Paris, France
**Auel, Jean M** — Writer
PO Box 8278, Portland OR 97207, USA
**Auer, Jonathon (Jon)** — Musician, Songwriter (Posies)
Entourage Talent Assoc, 236 W 27th St, #800, New York NY 10001, USA
**Auer, Joseph (Joe)** — Football Player
1138 Washington Ave, Winter Park FL 32789, USA
**Auer, Peter L** — Plasma Physicist
220 Devon Road, Ithaca NY 14850, USA
**Auer, Victor** — Marksman
8 Dellbrook Ave, San Francisco CA 94131, USA
**Auerbach, Daniel Q (Dan)** — Singer, Guitarist (Black Keys)
Q-Prime South, 131 S 11th St, Nashville TN 37206 USA
**Auerbach, Frank** — Artist
Marlborough Fine Art Gallery, 6 Albermarle St, London W1X 4BY, England
**Auerbach, Frederick S (Rick)** — Baseball Player
2139 Stunt Road, Calabasas CA 91302, USA

**Auerbach, Stanley I** — Ecologist
3314 W End Ave, #202, Nashville TN 37203, USA

**Auermann, Nadja** — Model, Actress
D N A Model Mgmt, 555 W 25th St, #600, New York NY 10001 USA

**Auger, Brian** — Jazz Pianist
Earthtone, 8306 Wilshire Blvd, #981, Beverly Hills CA 90211, USA

**Auger, Claudine** — Actress
Steve Kenis Co, 95 Barkston Gardens, London SW5 0EU, England

**Augmon, Stacey** — Basketball Player
1412 European Dr, Henderson NV 89052, USA

**Auguin, Philippe** — Conductor
I M G Artists, Hogarth Business Park, Chiswick, London W4 2TH, England

**August, Bille** — Director
Creative Artists Agency, 2000 Ave of Stars, #100, Los Angeles CA 90067 USA

**August, John** — Writer
United Talent Agency, U T A Plaza, 9336 Civic Center Dr, Beverly Hills CA 90210 USA

**August, Pernilla** — Actress, Director
Agentfirman Planthaber/Kilden, Drottninggatan 55, 111 21 Stockholm, Sweden

**August, Steve P** — Football Player
7704 E 86th St, Tulsa OK 74133, USA

**Augusta, Kim** — Golfer
16 Rachella Court, East Providence RI 02914, USA

**Augusta, Patrik** — Ice Hockey Player
H C Dukla Jihlava, Tolsteno 23, 58601 Jihlava, Czech Republic

**Augustain, Ira** — Actor
4715 Fauna St, Montclair CA 91763, USA

**Augustin, Darrel J (D J), Jr** — Basketball Player
Toronto Raptors, Air Canada Center, 20 Bay St, Toronto ON M5J 2N8, Canada

**Augustine, Gerald L (Jerry)** — Baseball Player
S74W13490 Courtland Lane, Muskego WI 53150, USA

**Augustine, Norman R** — Businessman
24131 Doreen Dr, Gaithersburg MD 20882, USA

**Augustnyiak, Jerry** — Drummer (10000 Maniacs)
Paradise Artists, PO Box 1821, Ojai CA 93024 USA

**Augustus, Seimone** — Basketball Player
9315 Pettit Road, Baker LA 70714, USA

**Aulby, Michael (Mike)** — Bowler
2331 Brothers Dr, Lafayette IN 47909, USA

**Auld, Alexander (Alex)** — Ice Hockey Player
2005 Swallow Crescent, Thunder Bay ON P7C 4T9, Canada

**Ault, Chris** — Football Coach
University of Nevada, Athletic Dept, Reno NV 89557, USA

**Aumann, Robert J** — Nobel Economics Laureate
Hebrew University, Economics Dept, Mount Scopus, 91904 Jerusalem, Israel

**Aumont, Michel** — Actor
8 Rue Herold, 75001 Paris, France

**Aung San Suu Kyi** — Nobel Peace Laureate
National League for Democracy, 97B W Shwegondine Road, Yangon, Myanmar

**Auriemma, Geno** — Basketball Coach
185 Garth Road, Manchester CT 06040, USA

**Aurilla, Richard S (Rich)** — Baseball Player
5448 E Mariposa St, Phoenix AZ 85018, USA

**Ausbie, Hubert E (Geese)** — Basketball Player
902 Arthur Dr, Little Rock AR 72204, USA

**Ausmus, Bradley D (Brad)** — Baseball Player, Manager
1644 Stratford Way, Del Mar CA 92014, USA

**Auster, Paul** — Writer, Director
I C M Partners, 10250 Constellation Blvd, #900, Los Angeles CA 90067 USA

**Austin, A Woody** — Golfer
10906 W Havenhurst St, Maize KS 67101, USA

**Austin, Charles** — Track Athlete
514 Duncan Dr, San Marcos TX 78666, USA

**Austin, Cliff** — Football Player
5410 Maltdie Court, Sugar Hill GA 30518, USA

**Austin, Dallas** — Actor
J M G Mgmt, 18000 Coastline Dr, #8, Malibu CA 90265, USA

**Austin, Debbie** — Golfer
6733 Bittersweet Lane, Orlando FL 32819, USA

**Austin, Denise** — Physical Fitness Expert
PrimeCare Systems, 610 Thimble Shoals Blvd, #402A, Newport News VA 23606, USA

**Austin, Issac E (Ike)** — Basketball Player
1221 S 800 E, Salt Lake City UT 84105, USA

**Austin, Jake T** — Actor
Paradigm Agency, 360 N Crescent Dr, North Building, Beverly Hills CA 90210 USA

**Austin, John** — Basketball Player
1330 Riggs St NW, Washington DC 20009, USA

**Austin, Julie** — Actress
Abrams Artists, 9200 W Sunset Blvd, #1125, West Hollywood CA 90069 USA

**Austin, K Darrell** — Football Player
268 Austin Road, Union SC 29379, USA

**Austin, Karen** — Actress
A M T Artists, 15260 Ventura Blvd, #1200, Sherman Oaks CA 91403, USA

**Austin, Lloyd J, III** — Army General
Commander, Central Command, 7115 S Boundary, MacDill Air Force Base FL 33621 USA

**Austin, Lynne** — Model
Playboy Promotions, 9346 Civic Center Dr, #200, Beverly Hills CA 90210 USA

**Austin, Miles J, III** — Football Player
Cleveland Browns, 76 Lou Groza Blvd, Berea OH 44017 USA

**Austin, Patti** — Singer
Tom Estey Publicity, 144 E 22nd St, #1B, New York NY 10010, USA

**Austin, Steve (Stone Cold)** — Professional Wrestler
Caliber Media, 9229 W Sunset Blvd, #720, West Hollywood CA 90069, USA

**Austin, Teri** — Actress
4245 Laurel Grove, Studio City CA 91604, USA

**Austin, Timothy (Tim)** — Boxer
9261 Calista Dr, North Ridgeville OH 44039, USA

**A**

| | |
|---|---|
| **Austin, Tracy** | Tennis Player |
| Octagon Worldwide, 1751 Pinnacle Dr, #1500, McLean VA 22102 USA | |
| **Auteuil, Daniel** | Actor |
| Artmedia, 20 Ave Rapp, 75007 Paris, France | |
| **Autry, Alan** | Actor |
| David Shapira Assoc, 193 N Robertson Blvd, Beverly Hills CA 90211 USA | |
| **Auzenne, Troy A** | Football Player |
| 1501 Bluff Court, Diamond Bar CA 91765, USA | |
| **Avalon, Frankie** | Singer, Actor |
| 4303 Spring Forest Lane, Westlake Village CA 91362, USA | |
| **Avant** | Singer |
| Paradigm Agency, 360 N Crescent Dr, North Building, Beverly Hills CA 90210 USA | |
| **Avant, Jason** | Football Player |
| 112 Villas Court, Clementon NJ 08021, USA | |
| **Avari, Erick** | Actor |
| Greene Assoc, 1901 Ave of Stars, #130, Los Angeles CA 90067 USA | |
| **Avary, Roger** | Director, Writer |
| I C M Partners, 10250 Constellation Blvd, #900, Los Angeles CA 90067 USA | |
| **Avati, Pupi** | Director |
| Via del Babuino 135, 00187 Rome, Italy | |
| **Avdeeva, Yulianna** | Concert Pianist |
| Harrison/Parrott, 5-6 Albion Court, London W6 0QT, England | |
| **Avdeyev, Sergei V** | Cosmonaut |
| Cosmonaut Training Center, Star City, 141160 Zvezdny Gorodok, Moscow Oblast, Russia | |
| **Avellini, Robert H (Bob)** | Football Player |
| 1085 Flamingo Dr, Roselle IL 60172, USA | |
| **Averbukh, Ilia** | Ice Dancer |
| Skating Assn, Luchneksia Nab 8, 119871 Moscow, Russia | |
| **Averill, Earl D** | Baseball Player |
| 1806 19th Dr NE, Auburn WA 98002, USA | |
| **Averitt, William R (Bird)** | Basketball Player |
| Kim Averitt, 103 N O'Neal Ave, Hopkinsville KY 42240, USA | |
| **Averno, Sisto J** | Football Player |
| 4759 Bonnie Brae Road, Pikesville MD 21208, USA | |
| **Averre, Berton** | Guitarist (Knack) |
| 17510 Posetano Road, Pacific Palisades CA 90272, USA | |
| **Avery, Brad** | Guitarist (Third Day) |
| Creative Trust, 5141 Virginia Way, #320, Brentwood TN 37027, USA | |
| **Avery, Bryan R** | Architect |
| Avery Architects, 270 Vauxhall Bridge Road, London SW1V 1BB, England | |
| **Avery, Eric A** | Bassist (Jane's Addiction) |
| DeMann Entertainment, 9465 Wilshire Blvd, #426, Beverly Hills CA 90212, USA | |
| **Avery, John E, Jr** | Football Player |
| 12 Ballantree Circle, Asheville NC 28803, USA | |
| **Avery, Kenneth W (Ken)** | Football Player |
| 625 Indian Ridge Dr, Nashville TN 37221, USA | |
| **Avery, Margaret** | Actress |
| TalentWorks, 3500 W Olive Ave, #1400, Burbank CA 91505 USA | |
| **Avery, Sean** | Ice Hockey Player |
| I C M Partners, 10250 Constellation Blvd, #900, Los Angeles CA 90067 USA | |
| **Avery, Steven T (Steve)** | Baseball Player |
| 2 Glenagles Court, Dearborn MI 48120, USA | |
| **Avi** | Writer |
| 859 S York St, Denver CO 80209, USA | |
| **Avila Cordeiro de Melo, Artur** | Mathematician |
| C N R S, Mathematics Institute, Building Sophie Germain, Box 7012, 75205 Paris Cedex 13, France | |
| **Avila, Jim** | Commentator |
| ABC-TV, News Dept, 77 W 66th St, New York NY 10023 USA | |
| **Avildsen, John G** | Director |
| 2423 Briarcrest Road, Beverly Hills CA 90210, USA | |
| **Avise, John C** | Geneticist |
| University of Georgia, Genetics Dept, Athens GA 30602, USA | |
| **Avital, Mili** | Actress |
| Liebman Entertainment, 25 E 21st St, #PH, New York NY 10010, USA | |
| **Avnet, Jonathan M (Jon)** | Director, Producer |
| Creative Artists Agency, 2000 Ave of Stars, #100, Los Angeles CA 90067 USA | |
| **Avni, Aki** | Actor |
| Sovereign Talent Group, 8421 Wilshire Blvd, #200, Beverly Hills CA 90211 USA | |
| **Avola, Giorgio** | Fencer |
| Federazione Fechten, Viale Tiziano 74, 00196 Rome, Italy | |
| **Avory, Mike** | Drummer (Rolling Stones, Kinks) |
| Larry Page, 29 Rushton Mews, London W11 1RB, England | |
| **Avril, Clifford S (Cliff)** | Football Player |
| Seattle Seahawks, 12 Seahawks Way, Renton WA 98056 USA | |
| **Awalt, Robert M (Rob)** | Football Player |
| 5011 Highgrove Court, Granite Bay CA 95746, USA | |
| **Awrey, Donald W (Don)** | Ice Hockey Player |
| 1015 Alaska Ave, Lehigh Acres FL 33971, USA | |
| **Awtrey, Dennis W** | Basketball Player |
| 38245 James Road, Nehalem OR 97131, USA | |
| **Ax, Emmanuel** | Concert Pianist |
| Opus 3 Artists, 470 Park Ave S, #900N, New York NY 10016, USA | |
| **Axel, Ian** | Singer, Composer (Great Big World) |
| Epic Records, 9830 Wilshire Blvd, Beverly Hills CA 90212 USA | |
| **Axel, Richard** | Nobel Medicine Laureate |
| 435 Riverside Dr, #62, New York NY 10025, USA | |
| **Axelrod, Jonathan H** | Molecular Biologist |
| Goldyne Savad Institute of Gene Therapy, PO Box 12000, Jerusalem 91120, Israel | |
| **Axelsson, A Per Johan (P J)** | Ice Hockey Player |
| 50 Fleet St, #301, Boston MA 02109, USA | |
| **Axen, K Martin** | Guitarist (The Ark) |
| Live Nation, Linnegatan 89, Box 21451, 10451 Stockholm, Sweden | |
| **Axley, Eric** | Golfer |
| 4708 Calumet Dr, Knoxville TN 37919, USA | |
| **Axwell** | DJ Musician |
| Mission Control, City Business Center, Lower Road, London SE16 2XB, England | |

**Austin - Axwell**

**Ayadi, Naidra** — Actress
Josiane Stoh, 3 Allee Marie Laurent, 75020 Paris, France
**Ayala Gonzales, Robert J (Bobby)** — Baseball Player
11011 W Cottonwood Lane, Avondale AZ 85392, USA
**Ayala, Benigno (Benny)** — Baseball Player
PO Box 222, Dorado PR 00646, USA
**Ayala, Francisco J** — Geneticist, Molecular Biologist
2 Locke Court, Irvine CA 92617, USA
**Ayala, Luis I** — Baseball Player
Atlanta Braves, Turner Field, 755 Hank Aaron Dr, Atlanta GA 30315 USA
**Ayala, Paulie** — Boxer
3817 Southwest Blvd, Fort Worth TX 76116, USA
**Ayanbadejo, O Brendan** — Football Player
1636 S Beverly Glen Blvd, #102, Los Angeles CA 90024, USA
**Ayanbadejo, Obafemi** — Football Player
707 President St, #438, Baltimore MD 21202, USA
**Ayanna, Charlotte** — Actress
Bohemia Group, 8170 Beverly Blvd, #102, Los Angeles CA 90048, USA
**Aybar, Erick J** — Baseball Player
773 W Raven Dr, Chandler AZ 85286, USA
**Ayckbourn, Alan** — Writer, Director
Casorotto Ramsay, Waverley House, 7-12 Noel St, London W1F 8GQ, England
**Aycock, Alice** — Sculptor
62 Green St, #4, New York NY 10012, USA
**Aycox, Nicki** — Actress
Innovative Artists, 1505 10th St, Santa Monica CA 90401 USA
**Ayer, David** — Director, Writer
Creative Artists Agency, 2000 Ave of Stars, #100, Los Angeles CA 90067 USA
**Ayer, William S (Bill)** — Businessman
Alaska Airlines, 19300 International Blvd, Seattle WA 98188, USA
**Ayers, Chuck** — Cartoonist (Crankshaft)
Universal Press Syndicate, 4520 Main St, #700, Kansas City MO 64111 USA
**Ayers, Dick** — Cartoonist (Sgt Fury)
64 Beech St W, White Plains NY 10604, USA
**Ayers, Sam** — Actor
Bobby Ball Talent Agency, 4116 W Magnolia Blvd, #205, Burbank CA 91505, USA
**Aykroyd, Dan** — Actor, Comedian
Creative Artists Agency, 2000 Ave of Stars, #100, Los Angeles CA 90067 USA
**Aylesworth, Reiko** — Actress
Gersh Agency, 9465 Wilshire Blvd, #600, Beverly Hills CA 90212 USA
**Ayling, Robert J** — Businessman
Dwr Cymru Welsh Water, PO Box 690, Cardiff, CF3 5WL, Wales
**Aylward, John J** — Actor
Mitchell K Stubbs Assoc, 8695 Washington Blvd, #204, Culver City CA 90232, USA
**Aylwin Azocar, Patricio** — President, Chile
Teresa Salas 786, Providencia, Santiago, Chile
**Ayoade, Richard** — Director
W M E Entertainment, 9601 Wilshire Blvd, #300, Beverly Hills CA 90210 USA
**Ayodele, Akinnola J (Akin)** — Football Player
7105 David Lane, Colleyville TX 76034, USA
**Ayres, Gillian** — Artist
Alan Cristea Gallery, 31-34 Cork St, London W1S 3NU, England
**Ayres, Rosalind** — Actress
Lou Coulson Assoc, 37 Berwick St, London W1V 8RS, England
**Aytes, Rochelle** — Actress, Producer
Innovative Artists, 1505 10th St, Santa Monica CA 90401 USA
**Ayton, Sarah L** — Yachtswoman
Lynx Sports Mgmt, Lymington Road, Lymington, Hampshire SO41 5S5, England
**AZ** — Rap Artist
Celebrity Talent Agency, 111 E 14th St, #249, New York NY 10003, USA
**Azalea, Iggy** — Rap Artist, Songwriter, Model
Turn First Artists, 7080 Hollywood Blvd, Los Angeles CA 90028, USA
**Azarenka, Victoria** — Tennis Player
Best, 303 E Main St, #200, Louisville KY 40202 USA
**Azaria, Hank** — Actor, Singer
W M E Entertainment, 9601 Wilshire Blvd, #300, Beverly Hills CA 90210 USA
**Azevedo, Anthony L (Tony)** — Water Polo Player
U S A Water Polo, 2124 Main St, #240, Huntington Beach CA 92648, USA
**Azinger, Paul W** — Golfer
6410 21st Ave W, Bradenton FL 34209, USA
**Aznavour, Charles** — Singer, Actor, Songwriter
Melodium Music, 5 Rue Faucigny, 1700 Fribourg, Germany
**Azria, Max** — Fashion Designer
B C B G/Max Azria, 1450 Broadway, #1700, New York NY 10018, USA
**Azuma, Norio** — Artist
4530 Broadway, #4F, New York NY 10040, USA
**Azuma, Takamitsu** — Architect
Azuma Architects, 3-6-1 Minami-Aoyama Minatoku, Tokyo 107 0016, Japan
**Azumah, Jerry** — Football Player
462 W Superior St, Chicago IL 60654, USA
**Azzara, Candice** — Actress
Maverick Entertainment, 6100 Wilshire Blvd, #550, Los Angeles CA 90048, USA
**Azzi, Jennifer L** — Basketball Player, Coach
Azzi Training, 8589 S Mardi Gras Lane, West Jordan UT 84088, USA

# B

**Baab, Michael J (Mike)** — Football Player
PO Box 1808, Euless TX 76039, USA
**Babashoff, Jack** — Swimmer
17254 Santa Clara St, Fountain Valley CA 92708, USA
**Babashoff, Shirley** — Swimmer
17254 Santa Clara St, Fountain Valley CA 92708, USA
**Babbitt, Bruce E** — Secretary, Interior; Governor, AZ
World Wildlife Fund,1250 24th St NW, Washington DC 20090, USA
**Babb-Sprague, Kristen** — Synchronized Swimmer
4677 Pine Valley Dr, Stockton CA 95219, USA
**Babcock, Barbara** — Actress
Paradigm Agency, 360 N Crescent Dr, North Building, Beverly Hills CA 90210 USA
**Babcock, Michael (Mike), Jr** — Ice Hockey Coach
17891 Stonebrook Circle, Northville MI 48168, USA
**Babcock, Tim M** — Governor, MT
Ox Bow Ranch, PO Box 877, Helena MT 59624, USA
**Babenco, Hector E** — Director
I C M Partners, 10250 Constellation Blvd, #900, Los Angeles CA 90067 USA
**Babey, Pamela** — Interior Designer
Babey Moulton Jue Booth, 510 3rd St, #110, San Francisco CA 94107, USA
**Babich, Robert (Bob)** — Football Player
4994 Mount Ashmun Dr, San Diego CA 92111, USA
**Babilonia, Tai R** — Figure Skater
Diverse Talent Group, 1900 Ave of Stars, #2840, Los Angeles CA 90067, USA
**Babineaux, Jonathan J** — Football Player
5659 Legends Club Circle, Braselton GA 30517, USA
**Babka, Richard (Rink)** — Track Athlete
1080 Silver Hill Road, Redwood City CA 94061, USA
**Baby Bash** — Rap Artist
J L Entertainment, 18653 Ventura Blvd, #340, Los Angeles CA 91356 USA
**Baby Oje** — Rap Artist (Arrested Development)
Agency Group Ltd, 142 W 57th St, #600, New York NY 10019 USA
**Baby Peggy** — Actress
1279 Southport Way, Gustine CA 95322, USA
**Babych, Dave** — Ice Hockey Player
1315 Wellington Crescent, Winnipeg MB R3N 0A9, Canada
**Baca, David** — Drag Racing Driver
529 Garcia Ave, #C, Pittsburg CA 94565, USA
**Baca, John P** — Vietnam War Army Hero (CMH)
PO Box 154, Julian CA 92036, USA
**Baca, Susana** — Singer
Luaka Bop, 195 Chrystie St, #901, New York NY 10002, USA
**Bacall, Michael** — Actor, Writer
Timaeus Group, PO Box 1432, Pacific Palisades CA 90272, USA
**Baccarin, Morena** — Actress
United Talent Agency, U T A Plaza, 9336 Civic Center Dr, Beverly Hills CA 90210 USA
**Bach Nunez, Jaume** — Architect
Avenida Diagonal 335, 08037 Barcelona, Spain
**Bach, Barbara** — Actress
2 Glynde Mews, London SW3 1SB, England
**Bach, Catherine** — Actress
Ziffren Brittenham Branca, 1801 Century Park W, #700, Los Angeles CA 90067 USA
**Bach, David** — Writer
W M E Entertainment, 9601 Wilshire Blvd, #300, Beverly Hills CA 90210 USA
**Bach, Jillian** — Actress
A K A Talent, 6310 San Vicente Blvd, #200, Los Angeles CA 90048 USA
**Bach, John W (Johnny)** — Basketball Player, Coach
2300 Clarendon Blvd, #306, Arlington VA 22201, USA
**Bach, Richard** — Writer
Dell Publishing, 1540 Broadway, New York NY 10036, USA
**Bach, Thomas** — Sports Executive
International Olympic Committee, Chateau de Vidy, 1007 Lausanne, Switzerland
**Bacham, Aishwarya Rai** — Actress, Beauty Queen
A B Corp, 13 North South Road, Juhu, Mumbai 400049, India
**Bachar, Carmit** — Singer (Pussycat Dolls), Dancer, Actress
R S S Mgmt, 137 N Larchmont Blvd, #213, Los Angeles CA 90004, USA
**Bacharach, Burt** — Composer, Musician
681 Amalfi Dr, Pacific Palisades CA 90272, USA
**Bachardy, Don** — Artist
145 Adelaide Dr, Santa Monica CA 90402, USA
**Bachchan, Amitabh** — Actor
A B Corp, 13 North South Road, Juhu, Mumbai 400049, India
**Bacher, Aron (Ali)** — Cricketer, Cricket Executive
17 Romajador Ave, Sandhurst #4, Sandton, South Africa
**Bachfeld, Jochem** — Boxer
Wandrumer Str 19, 19073 Wittenssorde, Germany
**Bachleda, Alicja** — Actress
Berwick & Kovacik, 6300 Wilshire Blvd, #1410, Los Angeles CA 90048, USA
**Bachleda-Curus, Katarzyna** — Speed Skater
Piotr Wyszynski, Ul Matarewicza 4D, 05 230 Kobylka, Ossow, Poland
**Bachman, Randy** — Singer, Songwriter, Guitarist
Paquin Entertainment, 468 Stradbrooke Ave, Winnipeg MB R3L 0J9, Canada
**Bachtadze, Michael** — Opera Singer
I M G Artists, Hogarth Business Park, Chiswick, London W4 2TH, England
**Baciocco, Albert J, Jr** — Navy Admiral
747 Pitt St, Mount Pleasant SC 29464, USA
**Backe, John D** — Businessman
399 Park Ave, #1900, New York NY 10022, USA
**Backhaus, Robin** — Swimmer
PO Box 6271, Ocean View HI 96737, USA
**Backis, Audrys Juozas Cardinal** — Religious Leader
Archdiocese of Vilnius, Sventaragio 4, 01122 Vilnius, Lithuania
**Backley, Stephen (Steve)** — Track Athlete
Cambridge Harriers, 56A-60 Glenhurst Ave, Bexley, Kent DA5 3QN, England
**Backlinie, Susan** — Actress
PO Box 24262, Ventura CA 93002, USA

**Backman, R Christian** — Ice Hockey Player
784 Bellerive Manor Dr, Saint Louis MO 63141, USA
**Backman, Walter W (Wally)** — Baseball Player, Manager
241 SE Mercury Lane, Prineville OR 97754, USA
**Backstrom, Niklas O** — Ice Hockey Player
3534 N Somerset St, Arlington VA 22213, USA
**Backstrom, Ralph G** — Ice Hockey Player
1625 Pelican Lakes Point, Windsor CO 80550, USA
**Backus, Christopher** — Actor
Don Buchwald Talent Agency, 6500 Wilshire Blvd, #2200, Los Angeles CA 90048 USA
**Backus, George E** — Geophysicist
9362 La Jolla Farms Road, La Jolla CA 92037, USA
**Backus, Gus** — Singer (Del Vikings)
Lustig Talent, PO Box 770850, Orlando FL 32877 USA
**Backus, Jeffrey C (Jeff)** — Football Player
48075 Bellagio Court, Northville MI 48167, USA
**Backus, Sharon** — Softball Player, Coach
University of California, Athletic Dept, Los Angeles CA 90024, USA
**Bacon, Kevin N** — Actor
W M E Entertainment, 9601 Wilshire Blvd, #300, Beverly Hills CA 90210 USA
**Bacon, Richard P** — Producer, Actor, Writer
Rights House, Drury House, 34-43 Russell St, London WC2B 5HA, England
**Bacon, Roger F** — Navy Admiral
1980 Silverleaf Circle, #122, Carlsbad CA 92009, USA
**Bacquier, Gabriel** — Opera Singer
141 Rue de Rome, 75017 Paris, France
**Bacri, Jean-Pierre** — Actor
Anne Alvares Correa, 34 Rue Jouffroy d'Abbans, 75017 Paris, France
**Bacs, Ludovic** — Conductor, Composer
31 D Golescu, Sc III, E7 V Ap 87, Bucharest 1, Romania
**Bacsik, Michael Joseph (Mike)** — Baseball Player
4014 Falcon Lake Dr, Arlington TX 76016, USA
**Bacsinszky, Timea** — Tennis Player
Case Postale 22, 1092 Belmont-sur-Lausanne, Switzerland
**Badalamenti, Angelo** — Composer
11 Fidelian Way, Lincoln Park NJ 07035, USA
**Badalucco, Michael** — Actor
Stone Manners Salners, 6100 Wilshire Blvd, #1500, Los Angeles CA 90035 USA
**Badami, Anita Rau** — Writer
Carlisle Co, 121 E 17th St, New York NY 10003, USA
**Baddeley, Aaron** — Golfer
8606 E Via del Sol Dr, Scottsdale AZ 85255, USA
**Baddour, Raymond F** — Chemical Engineer
6495 SW 122nd St, Miami FL 33156, USA
**Bade, Lance** — Marksman
9491 Berrey Lane, Colorado Springs CO 80925, USA
**Badenhop, Burke H** — Baseball Player
1421 Rivercrest Dr, Perrysburg OH 43551, USA
**Bader, Larry** — Ice Hockey Player
1413 Westwood Dr SW, Faribault MN 55021, USA
**Badger, Brad** — Football Player
3553 Milleford Court, Pleasanton CA 94588, USA
**Badgley, Mark** — Fashion Designer
Badgley Mischka, 215 W 40th St, New York NY 10018, USA
**Badgley, William S** — Financier
505 E Waters Edge Dr, Belleville IL 62221, USA
**Badham, John M** — Director, Producer
23622 Calabasas Road, #107, Calabasas CA 91302, USA
**Badian, Ernst** — Historian
Harvard University, History Dept, Robinson Hall, Cambridge MA 02138, USA
**Badler, Jane** — Actress
PO Box 43, South Yarra VIC 3141, Australia
**Badly Drawn Boy** — Singer, Songwriter
Big Life Mgmt, 67-69 Charlton St, London NW11 1HY, England
**Badrov, Sergei** — Director
Arlook Group, 205 S Beverly Dr, #209, Beverly Hills CA 90212, USA
**Badu, Erykah** — Singer, Songwriter
Five Burroughs Entertainment, 2503 Main St, #201, Santa Monica CA 90405, USA
**Badura-Skoda, Paul** — Concert Pianist, Composer
Hochschule Musik, Lothringerstr 18, 1037 Vienna, Austria
**Baechtold, James E (Jim)** — Basketball Player
225 W Irvine St, Richmond KY 40475, USA
**Baek Sung-Dong** — Soccer Player
Football Association, 1-131 Sinmunno, 2-Ga Jongno-Gu, Seoul 110 062, South Korea
**Baeling, Rebecca D (Becky)** — Singer, Actress
Abrams Artists, 9200 W Sunset Blvd, #1125, West Hollywood CA 90069 USA
**Baena, Marisa** — Golfer
3605 Dandelion Dr, Plano TX 75093, USA
**Baer, Gordy** — Bowler
8577 Tullamore Dr, Tinley Park IL 60487, USA
**Baer, Max, Jr** — Producer, Director, Actor
10433 Wilshire Blvd, #104, Los Angeles CA 90024, USA
**Baer, Olaf** — Opera Singer
Olbersdorferstr 7, 01324 Dresden, Germany
**Baer, Ralph H** — Inventor (Video Game Console)
134 Mayflower Dr, Manchester NH 03104, USA
**Baer, Robert** — Writer
Crown Publishing Group, 1745 Broadway, #1300, New York NY 10019 USA
**Baer, Robert J (Jacob)** — Army General
6213 Militia Court, Fairfax Station VA 22039, USA
**Baer, William** — Attorney, Government Official
Arnold & Porter, 555 12th St NW, Washington DC 20004, USA
**Baerga, Carlos O** — Baseball Player
PO Box 1667, Bayamon PR 00960, USA
**Baez, Joan** — Singer, Songwriter
Mark Spector Co, 100 5th Ave, #1100, New York NY 10011, USA

**Baeza, Braulio** — Thoroughbred Racing Jockey
1588 Rosalind Ave, Elmont NY 11003, USA

**Baffert, Robert A (Bob)** — Thoroughbred Racing Trainer
705 Carriage House Dr, Arcadia CA 91006, USA

**Bagayoko, Amadou** — Singer, Guitarist (Amadou & Mariam)
Partisan Arts, PO Box 5085, Larkspur CA 94977, USA

**Baggetta, Vincent** — Actor
4812 Ranchito Ave, Sherman Oaks CA 91423, USA

**Baggio, Roberto** — Soccer Player
Brescia F C, Via Bazoli 10, 27127 Brescia, Italy

**Baggott, Julianna** — Writer
Pocket Books, 1230 Ave of Americas, New York NY 10020 USA

**Bagian, James P** — Astronaut
21537 Holmbury Road, Northville MI 48167, USA

**Baginsky, Gaby** — Singer, Actress
Industriestr 11, 48455 Bad Bentheim, Germany

**Bagley, John E** — Basketball Player
31W450 Circle Dr, Elgin IL 60120, USA

**Bagley, Lorri** — Actress
Cinetic Mgmt, 555 W 25th St, #400, New York NY 10001 USA

**Bagley, Patrick (Pat)** — Editorial Cartoonist
Salt Lake Tribune, Editorial Dept, 1435 Main St, Salt Lake City UT 84115, USA

**Bagnal, Charles W** — Army General
Ratchford Assoc, 221 W Springs Road, Columbia SC 29223, USA

**Bagnasco, Angelo Cardinal** — Religious Leader
Arcivescovado, Piazza Matteotti 4, 16123 Genoa, Italy

**Bagshawe, Tilly** — Writer
Warner Books, 1271 Ave of Americas, New York NY 10020 USA

**Bagwell, Jeffrey R (Jeff)** — Baseball Player
405 Timberwilde Lane, Houston TX 77024, USA

**Bahah, Khaled** — Prime Minister, Yemen
Premier's Office, Street of 26th September, Sana'a, Yemen Arab Republic

**Bahns, Maxine L** — Actress, Model
Vincent Cirrincione Assoc, 1516 N Fairfax Ave, Los Angeles CA 90046 USA

**Bahnsen, Stanley R (Stan)** — Baseball Player
3500 Blue Lake Dr, #402, Pompano Beach FL 33064, USA

**Bahouth, Peter** — Association Executive
Greenpeace, 702 H St NW, #300, Washington DC 20001, USA

**Bahr, Chris** — Football Player
122 Kaywood Dr, Boalsburg PA 16827, USA

**Bahr, Iris** — Actress
Abrams Artists, 9200 W Sunset Blvd, #1125, West Hollywood CA 90069 USA

**Bahr, Matthew D (Matt)** — Football Player
53 Parkridge Lane, Pittsburgh PA 15228, USA

**Bahr, Walter A** — Soccer Player
250 Elks Road, Boalsburg PA 16827, USA

**Bahrke, Shannon** — Freestyle Skier
Q Sports Marketing, 534 W Evergreen St, Wheaton IL 60187 USA

**Bai Ling** — Actress, Model
Global Artists Agency, 6253 Hollywood Blvd, #508, Los Angeles CA 90028 USA

**Bailar, Benjamin F** — Government Official, Educator
410 Walnut Road, Lake Forest IL 60045, USA

**Bailes, Scott A** — Baseball Player
2920 S Ranch Dr, Springfield MO 65809, USA

**Bailey, Christina (Chris)** — Ice Hockey Player
3902 N Main St, Marion NY 14505, USA

**Bailey, Christopher** — Fashion Designer
Burberry Prorsum, 18-22 Haymarket St, London SW1Y 4DQ, England

**Bailey, David** — Photographer
Robert Montgomery, 3 Junction Mews, Sale Place, London W2, England

**Bailey, Donovan** — Track Athlete
625 Hales Chapel Road, Johnson City TN 37615, USA

**Bailey, F Lee** — Attorney
38 Blueberry Cove, Yarmouth ME 04096, USA

**Bailey, G W** — Actor
Essential Talent Management, 7958 Beverly Blvd, Los Angeles CA 90048, USA

**Bailey, Harold** — Football Player
22502 Prince George Lane, Katy TX 77449, USA

**Bailey, J Mark** — Baseball Player
32703 Waltham Crossing, Fulshear TX 77441, USA

**Bailey, James R (Jim)** — Football Player
5219 Stone Creek Court, Lawrence KS 66049, USA

**Bailey, Jerry D** — Thoroughbred Racing Jockey
105 Nurmi Dr, Fort Lauderdale FL 33301, USA

**Bailey, Jim** — Actor, Singer, Female Impersonator
Stephen Campbell Management, 350 N Crescent Dr, #105, Beverly Hills CA 90210, USA

**Bailey, Keith E** — Businessman
Williams Companies, 1 Williams Center, Tulsa OK 74172, USA

**Bailey, Maxwell C** — Air Force General
4704 W Pearl Ave, Tampa FL 33611, USA

**Bailey, Mike** — Actor
University of Teesside, Performing Arts Dept, Middlesbrough Tees Valley, TS1 3BA, England

**Bailey, Norman S** — Opera Singer
84 Warham Road, South Croydon, Surrey CR2 6LB, England

**Bailey, Paul** — Writer
79 Davisville Road, London W12 9SH, England

**Bailey, Philip** — Singer, Musician (Earth Wind & Fire)
Performers of the World, 5657 Wilshire Blvd, #280, Los Angeles CA 90036 USA

**Bailey, Razzy** — Singer, Songwriter
Doc Sedelmeier, PO Box 62, Geneva NE 68361, USA

**Bailey, Robert M L** — Football Player
15325 SW 99th Ave, Miami FL 33157, USA

**Bailey, Robert S (Bob)** — Baseball Player
3181 Lido Isle Court, Las Vegas NV 89117, USA

**Bailey, Ronal (Champ), III** — Football Player
5744 Aspen Leaf Dr, Littleton CO 80125, USA

**Bailey, Scott** — Actor
Prestige Talent Agency, 9250 Wilshire Blvd, #208, Beverly Hills CA 90212, USA
**Bailey, T Wayne** — Political Scientist, Social Activist
Stetson University, Political Science Dept, Deland FL 32720, USA
**Bailey, Thurl L** — Basketball Player
10265 N 6960 W, Highland UT 84003, USA
**Bailey, W Donald (Don)** — Football Player
14831 NW 7th Ave, North Miami FL 33168, USA
**Baillie, Kathy** — Singer (Baillie & the Boys)
1703 Old Hillsboro Road, Franklin TN 37063, USA
**Baillie, Victoria** — Singer, Songwriter
17 Coalville Road, Moe VIC 3825, Australia
**Bailly, Sandrine** — Biathlete
Residence Saint-Laurent, 10 Rue Jacques Cartier, 25300 Pontarlier, France
**Bailon, Adrienne E** — Singer (Cheetah Girls), Actress
Creative Artists Agency, 2000 Ave of Stars, #100, Los Angeles CA 90067 USA
**Bailor, Robert M (Bob)** — Baseball Player
1950 Swan Lane, Palm Harbor FL 34683, USA
**Baily, Martin N** — Government Official, Economist
McKinsey Global Institute, 1101 Pennsylvania Ave NW, Washington DC 20004, USA
**Bailyn, Bernard** — Historian
170 Clifton St, Belmont MA 02478, USA
**Bain, Barbara** — Actress
Barry Krost Management, 838 N Doheny Dr, #501, Los Angeles CA 90069, USA
**Bain, Michael** — Actor
W M E Entertainment, 9601 Wilshire Blvd, #300, Beverly Hills CA 90210 USA
**Baines, Harold D** — Baseball Player
PO Box 10, Saint Michaels MD 21663, USA
**Baines, Nicholas M (Peanut)** — Keyboardist (Kaiser Chiefs)
Red Light Mgmt, 8439 Sunset Blvd, West Hollywood CA 90069, USA
**Bainimarama, Josaia Voreqe (Frank)** — Prime Minister, Fiji
Prime Minister's Office, New Government Buildings, 6 Berkeley Crescent, Suva, Viti Levu, Fiji
**Baio, Christopher** — Bassist (Vampire Weekend)
L B I Entertainment, 2000 Ave of Stars, Los Angeles CA 90067, USA
**Baio, Scott** — Actor
TalentWorks, 3500 W Olive Ave, #1400, Burbank CA 91505 USA
**Baiocchi, Hugh** — Golfer
142 Royal Saint Georges Way, Rancho Mirage CA 92270, USA
**Bair, C Douglas (Doug)** — Baseball Player
11545 Kemper Woods Dr, Cincinnati OH 45249, USA
**Bair, Sheila C** — Government Official
Federal Deposit Insurance Corp, 550 17th St NW, Washington DC 20429, USA
**Baird, Briny** — Golfer
3340 SW Rivers End Way, Palm City FL 34990, USA
**Baird, Diora** — Model, Actress
Don Buchwald Talent Agency, 6500 Wilshire Blvd, #2200, Los Angeles CA 90048 USA
**Baird, Fred (Butch)** — Golfer
PO Box 2633, Carefree AZ 85377, USA
**Baird, Janice** — Opera Singer
Opera et Concert, 37 Rue de la Chaussee d'Antin, 75009 Paris, France
**Baird, Jenni** — Actress
Levine Mgmt, 9028 W Sunset Blvd, #PH-1, West Hollywood CA 90069, USA
**Baird, Scott** — Curling Athlete
5835 Tall Pines Road, Bemidji MN 56601, USA
**Baird, Stuart** — Director
Mirisch Agency, 1025 Colorado Ave, #B, Santa Monica CA 90211 USA
**Baird, William A (Bill)** — Football Player
6050 E Heaton Ave, Fresno CA 93727, USA
**Baird, Zoe** — Attorney
Aetna Life & Casualty, 151 Farmington Ave, Hartford CT 06156, USA
**Bairstow, Cameron D** — Basketball Player
Chicago Bulls, United Center, 1901 W Madison St, Chicago IL 60612 USA
**Baitz, Jon Robin** — Writer
Creative Artists Agency, 2000 Ave of Stars, #100, Los Angeles CA 90067 USA
**Baiul, Oksana** — Figure Skater
Bob Young, PO Box 988, Niantic CT 06357, USA
**Bajcsy, Ruzena** — Electrical Engineer
University of California, Electrical Engineering Dept, Berkeley CA 94720, USA
**Bajema, Billy** — Football Player
2605 SW 120th St, Oklahoma City OK 73170, USA
**Bakatin, Vadim V** — Government Official, Russia
Reforma, Kotelnicheskaya Nab 17, 103240 Moscow, Russia
**Bakay, Nick** — Actor, Producer
A P A Talent & Literary Agency, 405 S Beverly Dr, #300, Beverly Hills CA 90212 USA
**Bakels, Kees** — Conductor
I M G Artists, Hogarth Business Park, Chiswick, London W4 2TH, England
**Baker, Alan** — Mathematician
Mathematical Science Center, Wilberforce Road, Cambridge CB3 0WB, England
**Baker, Anita** — Singer
W M E Entertainment, 9601 Wilshire Blvd, #300, Beverly Hills CA 90210 USA
**Baker, Annie** — Playwright
State University of New York Stony Brook, Creative Writing Dept, Southampton NY 11968, USA
**Baker, Betsy** — Actress
C E S D, 10635 Santa Monica Blvd, #130, Los Angeles CA 90025 USA
**Baker, Blanche** — Actress
Abrams Artists, 9200 W Sunset Blvd, #1125, West Hollywood CA 90069 USA
**Baker, Brian** — Guitarist (Bad Religion)
Goldstar Public Relations, PO Box 130, Ross on Wye HR9 6WY, England
**Baker, Carroll** — Actress
Abrams Artists, 9200 W Sunset Blvd, #1125, West Hollywood CA 90069 USA
**Baker, Charles** — Actor
Greene Assoc, 1901 Ave of Stars, #130, Los Angeles CA 90067 USA
**Baker, Charles E (Charlie)** — Football Player
PO Box 112593, Carrollton TX 75011, USA
**Baker, Colin** — Actor
Evans & Reiss, 100 Fawe Park Road, London SW15 2EA, England

**Baker, Dale** — Drummer (Sixpence None the Richer)
Nettwerk Mgmt, 1201 Villa Place, #206, Nashville TN 37212 USA
**Baker, Deanna** — Model
Playboy Promotions, 9346 Civic Center Dr, #200, Beverly Hills CA 90210 USA
**Baker, Diane** — Actress
Blake Agency, 23441 Malibu Colony Road, Malibu CA 90265 USA
**Baker, Donald K** — Cinematographer
11789 Lakeshore N, Auburn CA 95602, USA
**Baker, Douglas L (Doug)** — Baseball Player
116 Woodthrush Lane, Fallbrook CA 92028, USA
**Baker, Dwight A** — Multi-Instrumentalist (Wind + Wave)
Triple 8 Mgmt, 5524 W Highway 290, Austin TX 78735, USA
**Baker, Dylan** — Actor
Paradigm Agency, 360 N Crescent Dr, North Building, Beverly Hills CA 90210 USA
**Baker, Earl P, Jr** — WW II Navy Hero (CMH)
10100 Cypress Cove Dr, #320, Fort Myers FL 33908, USA
**Baker, Ellen Shulman** — Astronaut
2207 Garden Stream Court, Houston TX 77062, USA
**Baker, Elzie W (Buddy), Jr** — Auto Racing Driver
4860 Moonlite Bay Dr, Sherrills Ford NC 28673, USA
**Baker, Ginger** — Drummer (Cream, Masters of Reality)
Twist Mgmt, 4230 Del Rey Ave, #621, Marina del Rey CA 90292, USA
**Baker, Graham** — Director
United Agents, 12-26 Lexington St, London W1F 0LE, England
**Baker, Homer** — WW II Army Air Corps Hero
8112 S Los Feliz Dr, Tempe AZ 85284, USA
**Baker, J Albert L (Bubba)** — Football Player
2784 Trinity Court, Avon OH 44011, USA
**Baker, Jaime** — Ice Hockey Player
210 Highland Oaks Dr, Los Gatos CA 95032, USA
**Baker, James A, III** — Secretary, State
Baker & Botts, 1299 Pennsylvania Ave NW, #1200, Washington DC 20004, USA
**Baker, James P (Jamie)** — Ice Hockey Player
18590 Farragut Lane, Los Gatos CA 95030, USA
**Baker, Janet A** — Opera, Concert Singer
Transart Ltd, 8 Bristol Gardens, London W9 2JG, England
**Baker, Jason M** — Football Player
435 S Tryon St, #906, Charlotte NC 28202, USA
**Baker, Joe Don** — Actor
23339 Hatteras St, Woodland Hills CA 91367, USA
**Baker, John** — Dog Sled Racer
General Delivery, Kotzebue AK 99752, USA
**Baker, Johnnie B (Dusty), Jr** — Baseball Player, Manager
40 Livingston Terrace Dr, San Bruno CA 94066, USA
**Baker, Jordan** — Actress
Douglas Gorman Rothacker, 1501 Broadway, #703, New York NY 10036, USA
**Baker, Kathy** — Actress
Abrams Artists, 9200 W Sunset Blvd, #1125, West Hollywood CA 90069 USA
**Baker, Kenneth (Kenny)** — Actor
51 Mulgrave Ave, Aston upon Ribble, Preston, Lancashire PR2 1HJ, England
**Baker, Kitana** — Model, Actress
PO Box 452, 231 E Alessandro Blvd, #A, Riverside CA 92502, USA
**Baker, Laurie** — Ice Hockey Player
67 Prairie St, Concord MA 01742, USA
**Baker, Leigh-Allyn** — Actress
Stone Manners Salners, 6100 Wilshire Blvd, #1500, Los Angeles CA 90035 USA
**Baker, Leslie David** — Actor
Innovative Artists, 1505 10th St, Santa Monica CA 90401 USA
**Baker, Lewis** — Singer (Danny & the Juniors)
Joe Terry Mgmt, PO Box 279, Williamstown NJ 08094, USA
**Baker, Mark** — Bowler
665 Park Dr, #20, Costa Mesa CA 92627, USA
**Baker, Mark-Linn** — Actor
2625 6th St, #2, Santa Monica CA 90405, USA
**Baker, Melissa** — Model
Click Model Mgmt, 881 7th Ave, New York NY 10019 USA
**Baker, Michael A (Mike)** — Astronaut
N A S A, Johnson Space Center, 2101 NASA Road, Houston TX 77058 USA
**Baker, Myron T** — Football Player
297 Pearl Road, Alexandria LA 71302, USA
**Baker, Paul T** — Anthropologist
337 Upton Pyne Dr, Brentwood CA 94513, USA
**Baker, Penny** — Model, Actress
PO Box 1116, Orchard Park NY 14127, USA
**Baker, Peter** — Golfer
Int'l Mgmt Group, Hogarth Business Park, Chiswick, London W4 2TH, England
**Baker, Phil** — Producer, Writer
I C M Partners, 10250 Constellation Blvd, #900, Los Angeles CA 90067 USA
**Baker, Ralph R** — Football Player
36 Sunshine Circle, Lewistown PA 17044, USA
**Baker, Raymond (Ray)** — Actor
Abrams Artists, 9200 W Sunset Blvd, #1125, West Hollywood CA 90069 USA
**Baker, Richard H** — Representative, LA
Managed Funds Assn, 2025 M St NW, #610, Washington DC 20036, USA
**Baker, Rick** — Makeup Artist
Cinovation Studios, 6527 San Fernando Road, Glendale CA 91201, USA
**Baker, Robby** — Guitarist (Tragically Hip)
Bobby Breen Mgmt, 13 Blackburn St, #300, Toronto ON M4M 2B3, Canada
**Baker, Robert** — Actor
Paul Kohner, 9300 Wilshire Blvd, #555, Beverly Hills CA 90212 USA
**Baker, Russell W** — Columnist
New York Times, Editorial Dept, 229 W 43rd St, New York NY 10036, USA
**Baker, Scott Thompson** — Actor, Director
11661 San Vicente Blvd, #307, Los Angeles CA 90049, USA
**Baker, Sean S** — Director, Producer, Writer
Gersh Agency, 9465 Wilshire Blvd, #600, Beverly Hills CA 90212 USA

**Baker, Simon** — Actor
Untitled Entertainment, 350 S Beverly Dr, #200, Beverly Hills CA 90212 USA
**Baker, Stephen B** — Football Player
358 Rector St, #601, Perth Amboy NJ 08861, USA
**Baker, Steve** — Ice Hockey Player
2929 N 70th St, #3087, Scottsdale AZ 85251, USA
**Baker, T Scott** — Baseball Player
327 Lingering Lane, Henderson NV 89012, USA
**Baker, Terry W** — Football Player
3208 SW Fairmount Blvd, Portland OR 97239, USA
**Baker, Tony F** — Football Player
3847 Eagleston Court, High Point NC 27265, USA
**Baker, Vincent L (Vin)** — Basketball Player
PO Box 179, Old Saybrook CT 06475, USA
**Baker, W Thane** — Track Athlete
6704 Saint John Court, Granbury TX 76049, USA
**Baker, William (Bill)** — Ice Hockey Player
5638 Ojibwa Road, Brainerd MN 56401, USA
**Baker-Finch, Ian M** — Golfer
11309 Caladium Lane, Palm Beach Gardens FL 33418, USA
**Baker-Guadagnino, Kathy** — Golfer
1535 SW 4th Circle, Boca Raton FL 33486, USA
**Bakhit, Marouf al-** — Prime Minister, Jordan
Prime Minister's Office, PO Box 80, 35216 Amman, Jordan
**Bakhtair, Rudi** — Commentator
CNN-TV, News Dept, 190 Marietta Ave SW, Atlanta GA 30303 USA
**Bakke, Brenda** — Actress
5805 Oak Bend Lane, #203, Oak Park CA 91377, USA
**Bakkedahl, Dan** — Actor
Paradigm Agency, 360 N Crescent Dr, North Building, Beverly Hills CA 90210 USA
**Bakken, Earl** — Heart Surgeon, Inventor
Medtronic Inc, PO Box 38460, Waikoloa HI 96738, USA
**Bakken, James L (Jim)** — Football Player
4801 Holiday Dr, Madison WI 53711, USA
**Bakken, Jill** — Bobsled Athlete
23701 3rd Place W, Bothell WA 98021, USA
**Bakker, Billy** — Field Hockey Player
Amsterdamsche Hockey Club, Postbus 7843, 1008 Amsterdam AA, Netherlands
**Bakker, James O (Jim)** — Religious Leader
180 Grace Chapel Road, #201, Blue Eye MO 65611, USA
**Bako, Brigitte** — Actress
Hartig-Hilepo Agency, 54 W 21st St, #610, New York NY 10010 USA
**Bako, G Paul, II** — Baseball Player
500 Princeton Woods Loop, Lafayette LA 70508, USA
**Bakovic, Peter (Pete)** — Ice Hockey Player
7991 S 47th St, Franklin WI 53132, USA
**Bakshi, Ralph** — Animator
PO Box 4322, Los Angeles CA 90076, USA
**Bakula, Scott** — Actor
Anonymous Content, 3532 Hayden Ave, Culver City CA 90232 USA
**Bala, Chris** — Ice Hockey Player
271 Beacon Dr, Phoenixville PA 19460, USA
**Balaban, Bob** — Actor, Director
Paradigm Agency, 360 N Crescent Dr, North Building, Beverly Hills CA 90210 USA
**Baladi, Patrick** — Actor
United Agents, 12-26 Lexington St, London W1F 0LE, England
**Baladmenti, Angelo** — Composer
4146 Lankershim Blvd, #401, North Hollywood CA 91602, USA
**Balan, Vidya** — Actress
Bling Entertainment Solutions, Off Dr E Moses Road, Worli, Mumbai 400018, India
**Balandin, Aleksandr N** — Cosmonaut
Cosmonaut Training Center, Star City, 141160 Zvezdny Gorodok, Moscow Oblast, Russia
**Balanzino, Sergio S** — Government Official
Loyola University, Rome Center, 6339 N Sheridan Road, Chicago IL 60660, USA
**Balaski, Belinda** — Actress
731 N Laurel Ave, Los Angeles CA 90046, USA
**Balassa, Sandor** — Composer
18 Sumegvar Str, 1118 Budapest, Hungary
**Balasubramanian, Shankar** — Chemist
University of Cambridge, Chemistry Dept, Old Schools, Trinity Lane, Cambridge CB2 1TN, England
**Balasubramanyam, Rajeev** — Writer
Bloomsbury Publishing, 50 Bedford Square, London WC1B 3DP, England
**Balaz, John L** — Baseball Player
2916 Worden St, San Diego CA 92110, USA
**Balbi, Raul H (Pepe)** — Boxer
Edgardo Rosani Morresi, Cortina 2057, Buenos Aires 1408, Argentina
**Balboa, Marcelo** — Soccer Player
13139 Hedda Dr, Cerritos CA 90703, USA
**Balboni, Stephen C (Steve)** — Baseball Player
117 Burlington Road, New Providence NJ 07974, USA
**Baldacci, David** — Writer
10509 Braddock Road, #2D, Fairfax VA 22032, USA
**Baldacci, John E** — Governor, ME; Government Official
Pierce Atwood L L P, Merrill's Wharf, 254 Commercial St, Portland ME 04101, USA
**Baldelli, Rocco D** — Baseball Player
81 Windsong Road, Cumberland RI 02864, USA
**Balderis-Sildedzis, Helmuts** — Ice Hockey Player
Hockey Federation, Raunas Lela 23, 1039 Tiga, Latvia
**Balderstone, James S** — Businessman
115 Mont Albert Road, Canterbury VIC 3126, Australia
**Baldes, Kevin** — Bassist (Lit)
Sepetys Entertainment, 5543 Edmondson Park, #8A, Nashville TN 37211, USA
**Baldeschwieler, John D** — Chemist
PO Box 50065, Pasadena CA 91115, USA
**Baldessari, John** — Conceptual Artist, Photographer
702 6th Ave, Venice CA 90291, USA

**Balding, Rebecca** — Actress
2001 Winnetka Place, Woodland Hills CA 91364, USA
**Baldinger, Brian D** — Football Player, Sportscaster
21 S Elmwood Road, Marlton NJ 08053, USA
**Baldinger, Gary T** — Football Player
114 Adam Road, Massapequa NY 11758, USA
**Baldinger, Richard L (Rich)** — Football Player
5401 Phelps Road, Kansas City MO 64136, USA
**Baldini, Ercole** — Cyclist
Viale Bologna 103, 04710 Ferli, Italy
**Baldischwiler, J Karl** — Football Player
3033 N Willow Dr, Newcastle OK 73065, USA
**Baldisseri, Lorenzo Cardinal** — Religious Leader
Synod of Bishops, Palazzo del Bramante, Via della Conciliazione 34, 00193 Rome, Italy
**Baldock, Bobby Ray** — Judge
US Court of Appeals, PO Box 2388, Roswell NM 88202, USA
**Baldoni, Justin L** — Actor
Wayfarer Entertainment, 7815 Beverly Blvd, #200, Los Angeles CA 90036, USA
**Baldschun, Jack E** — Baseball Player
311 Erie Road, Green Bay WI 54311, USA
**Balducci, Lorenzo** — Actor
Carol Levi Mgmt, Via Giuseppe Pisanelli 2, 00196 Rome, Italy
**Baldwin, Adam** — Actor
Innovative Artists, 1505 10th St, Santa Monica CA 90401 USA
**Baldwin, Alec** — Actor
N2N Entertainment, 1230 Montana Ave, #203, Santa Monica CA 90403, USA
**Baldwin, Bobby** — Poker Player
City Center Las Vegas, 3780 Las Vegas Boulevard S, Paradise NV 89109, USA
**Baldwin, Daniel** — Actor
Chaotik, 6446 Santa Monica Blvd, Los Angeles CA 90038 90038, USA
**Baldwin, David G (Dave)** — Baseball Player
PO Box 190, Yachats OR 97498, USA
**Baldwin, Hunt** — Producer, Writer
Creative Artists Agency, 2000 Ave of Stars, #100, Los Angeles CA 90067 USA
**Baldwin, Jack** — Auto Racing Driver
4748 Balmoral Way NE, Marietta GA 30068, USA
**Baldwin, Jack E** — Chemist
Oxford University, Dyson Perrins Laboratory, S Parks Road, Oxford OX1 3QY, England
**Baldwin, John A (Jack), Jr** — Navy Admiral
1371 Millersville Road, Millersville MD 21108, USA
**Baldwin, John, Jr** — Figure Skater
Lee Marshall Mgmt, 199 E Garfield Ave, Aurora OH 44202, USA
**Baldwin, Judith** — Actress
Grant Savic Kopaloff & Associates, 6399 Wilshire Blvd, #415, Los Angeles CA 90048, USA
**Baldwin, Karen D** — Beauty Queen, Actress
Miss Universe Organization, 1370 Ave of Americas, #1600, New York NY 10019 USA
**Baldwin, Keith M** — Football Player
124 Leonardville Road, Belford NJ 07718, USA
**Baldwin, Kevin** — Writer
Bloomsbury Publishing, 50 Bedford Square, London WC1B 3DP, England
**Baldwin, Margaret** — Writer
PO Box 1106, Williams Bay WI 53191, USA
**Baldwin, Randy C** — Football Player
715 Peeples St SW, #10, Atlanta GA 30310, USA
**Baldwin, Stephen** — Actor
Chaotik, 6446 Santa Monica Blvd, Los Angeles CA 90038, USA
**Baldwin, William** — Editor
Forbes, Editorial Dept, 60 5th Ave, New York NY 10011, USA
**Baldwin, William (Billy)** — Actor
Brillstein Entertainment Partners, 9150 Wilshire Blvd, #350, Beverly Hills CA 90212 USA
**Bale, Christian** — Actor
W M E Entertainment, 9601 Wilshire Blvd, #300, Beverly Hills CA 90210 USA
**Bale, John R** — Baseball Player
9017 Roberts Road, Odessa FL 33556, USA
**Bales, Michael (Mike)** — Ice Hockey Player
470 Brunswick Ave, Toronto ON M5R 2Z5, Canada
**Balestrini, Jose** — Opera Singer
I M G Artists, Hogarth Business Park, Chiswick, London W4 2TH, England
**Balfour, Earl** — Ice Hockey Player
71 Beasley Crescent, Cambridge ON N1T 1P5, Canada
**Balfour, Eric** — Actor
United Talent Agency, U T A Plaza, 9336 Civic Center Dr, Beverly Hills CA 90210 USA
**Balfour, Grant R** — Baseball Player
2678 N McMullen Booth Road, Clearwater FL 33761, USA
**Baliani, Marco** — Actor
Carol Levi Mgmt, Via Giuseppe Pisanelli 2, 00196 Rome, Italy
**Balic, Ivano** — Handball Player
Club Balonmano Atletico, Paseo del Pintor Rosales, 26 Bajos Derecha, 28008 Madrid, Spain
**Baliga, Bantval Jayant** — Electrical Engineer
2612 Bembridge Dr, Raleigh NC 27613, USA
**Baliles, Gerald L** — Governor, VA
University of Virginia, Miller Public Affairs School, Charlottesville VA 22903, USA
**Balin, Marty** — Singer, Songwriter
Joe Buchwald, 811 31st Ave, San Francisco CA 94121, USA
**Balitran, Celine** — Model
T F 6, 120 Ave Charles de Gaulle, 92522 Neuilly-sur-Seine Cedex, France
**Bality, Oded** — Photojournalist
Associated Press, Editorial Dept, 450 W 33rd St, #1500, New York NY 10001 USA
**Balk, Fairuza** — Actress
Shadow, 10 Universal City Plaza, #2000, Universal City CA 91608, USA
**Balkenhol, Klaus** — Equestrian
Narzissenweg 11A, 40723 Hilden, Germany
**Balkenhol, Stephan** — Artist
Saatchi Gallery, Duke of York's HQ, King's Road, London SW3 4RY, England
**Balkestein, Marcel** — Field Hockey Player
Oranje Zwart E M H C, Charles Roelslaan 13, 5644 Eindhoven HX, Netherlands

**Ball, Angeline** — Actress
Marfarlane Chard, 7 Adelaide St, Dun Laoghaire, Dublin, Ireland
**Ball, David** — Singer (Soft Cell), Songwriter
Susan Collier Mgmt, 6204 Jocelyn Hollow Road, Nashville TN 37205, USA
**Ball, David S (Dave)** — Football Player
208 Tarrington Court, Brentwood TN 37027, USA
**Ball, David W** — Writer
7744 Valmont Road, Boulder CO 80301, USA
**Ball, Eric C** — Football Player
10614 Margate Terrace, Cincinnati OH 45241, USA
**Ball, Jerry L** — Football Player
3311 Meadowside Dr, Sugar Land TX 77478, USA
**Ball, Larry L** — Football Player
8830 SW 57th St, Cooper City FL 33328, USA
**Ball, Marcia** — Singer, Pianist, Songwriter
Rosebud Agency, PO Box 170429, San Francisco CA 94117 USA
**Ball, Michael A** — Singer, Actor
Works Public Relations, 11 Marshalsea Road, London SE1 1EN, England
**Ball, Sam** — Actor
Robert Stein Mgmt, 1180 S Beverly Drive, #304, Los Angeles CA 90035, USA
**Ball, Taylor** — Actor
W M E Entertainment, 9601 Wilshire Blvd, #300, Beverly Hills CA 90210 USA
**Ball, Terry** — Ice Hockey Player
4502 Torrington Ave, Parma OH 44134, USA
**Ballack, Michael** — Soccer Player
International Soccer Consulting, 5 Rue des Arquebusiers, 1138 Luxembourg, Luxembourg
**Balladur, Edouard** — Prime Minister, France
5 Rue Jean Formige, 75015 Paris, France
**Ballantine, Sara** — Actress
Brady Brannon Rich, 5670 Wilshire Blvd, #820, Los Angeles CA 90036 USA
**Ballantyne, Frederick** — Governor General, St Vincent-Grenadines
Governor General's Office, Kingstown, Saint Vincent & Grenadines
**Ballard, Alimi** — Actor
Stone Manners Salners, 6100 Wilshire Blvd, #1500, Los Angeles CA 90035 USA
**Ballard, Carroll** — Director
PO Box 556, Saint Helena CA 94574, USA
**Ballard, Del, Jr** — Bowler
Ebonite International, PO Box 746, Hopkinsville KY 42241, USA
**Ballard, Donald E** — Vietnam War Navy Hero (CMH)
PO Box 34593, Kansas City MO 64116, USA
**Ballard, Frank R (Frankie), IV** — Singer, Songwriter
Reprise Records, 3300 Warner Blvd, Burbank CA 91505 USA
**Ballard, Glen** — Songwriter
Gorfaine/Schwartz, 4111 W Alameda Ave, #509, Burbank CA 91505 USA
**Ballard, Gregory (Greg)** — Basketball Player
100 Arborcrest Court, Tyrone GA 30290, USA
**Ballard, Howard L** — Football Player
PO Box 584, Ashland AL 36251, USA
**Ballard, Jeffrey S (Jeff)** — Baseball Player
4828 Rimrock Road, Billings MT 59106, USA
**Ballard, Kaye** — Actress, Comedienne
C E S D, 10635 Santa Monica Blvd, #130, Los Angeles CA 90025 USA
**Ballard, Keith** — Ice Hockey Player
2336 River Pointe Circle, Minneapolis MN 55411, USA
**Ballard, Robert D** — Oceanographer (Titanic Discoverer)
Rhode Island University, Ocean Exploration Center, 15 S Ferry Road, Narragansett RI 02882, USA
**Ballas, Mark A (Corky), Sr** — Professional Dancer
Commercial Talent, 12711 Ventura Blvd, #285, Studio City CA 91604, USA
**Ballas, Mark A, Jr** — Professional Dancer
Nocturnal Entertainment, 11735 Dorothy St, #302, Los Angeles CA 90049, USA
**Baller, Jay S** — Baseball Player
303 Spring Valley Road, Reading PA 19605, USA
**Ballerini, Edoardo** — Actor
Markham Froggatt Irwin, Julian House, 4 Windmill St, London W1P 1HF, England
**Ballestrini, Veronica** — Singer, Songwriter
11 Centre St, #6, Salem CT 06385, USA
**Ballhaus, Michael** — Cinematographer
11 Elm Place, Rye NY 10580, USA
**Ballmer, Steven A (Steve)** — Businessman
3832 Hunts Point Road, Hunts Point WA 98004, USA
**Ballou, Mark** — Actor
Total Talent Mgmt, 136 Centre St, Nutley NJ 07110, USA
**Balloun, James S** — Businessman
National Service Industry, 1420 Peachtree St NE, #200, Atlanta GA 30309, USA
**Balmaseda, Liz** — Journalist
Palm Beach Post, Editorial Dept, 2751 S Dixie Highway, West Palm Beach FL 33405, USA
**Balmer, Dan** — Jazz Guitarist
Sterling Talent, PO Box 231059, Tigard OR 97281, USA
**Balmer, Jean-Francois** — Actor
Artmedia, 20 Ave Rapp, 75007 Paris, France
**Balmond, Cecil** — Structural Engineer
University of Pennsylvania, School of Design, Philadelphia PA 19104, USA
**Balmy, Coralie** — Swimmer
Le Dauphins du Toec, 54 Rue des 7 Troubadours, 31000 Toulouse, France
**Balsam, Talia** — Actress
Gersh Agency, 9465 Wilshire Blvd, #600, Beverly Hills CA 90212 USA
**Balsley, Philip E** — Singer (Statler Brothers)
191 Abbington Road, Swoope VA 24479, USA
**Balsom, Alison** — Concert Trumpet Player
Harrison/Parrott, 5-6 Albion Court, London W6 0QT, England
**Balti, Bianca** — Model
Brave Model Mgmt, Via Imperia 22, 20142 Milan, Italy
**Baltimore, Bryon** — Ice Hockey Player
McCuaig Desrochers, 2401 10088th Ave NW, Edmonton AB T5J 2Z1, Canada
**Baltimore, Charli** — Rap Artist
The Inc Records, PO Box 40538, Glen Oaks NY 11004, USA

| | |
|---|---|
| **Baltimore, David L**<br>31460 Beach Park Road, Malibu CA 90265, USA | Nobel Medicine Laureate, Educator |
| **Baltsa, Agnes**<br>Schultz Mgmt, Rutistr 52, 8044 Zurich-Gockhausen, Switzerland | Opera Singer |
| **Baltz, Lewis**<br>23 Rue des Blancs Mantgaux, 75004 Paris, France | Photographer |
| **Balukas, Jean**<br>9818 4th Ave, Brooklyn NY 11209, USA | Billiards Player |
| **Balutin, Jacques**<br>Artmedia, 20 Ave Rapp, 75007 Paris, France | Actor |
| **Baluyut, James**<br>Ground Control Touring, 20 Jay St, #838, Brooklyn NY 11201, USA | Guitarist, Keyboardist (Versus) |
| **Baluyut, Richard**<br>Ground Control Touring, 20 Jay St, #838, Brooklyn NY 11201, USA | Singer, Guitarist (Versus) |
| **Bama, Jim**<br>27 Dunn Creek Road, Cody WY 82414, USA | Artist |
| **Bambaataa, Afrika**<br>K L B Productions, 70 Greenwich Ave, #441, New York NY 10011, USA | Rap Artist |
| **Bamber, David J**<br>Artists Partnership, 101 Finsbury Pavement, London EC2A 1RS, England | Actor |
| **Bamert, Matthias**<br>Scottish National Orchestra, 3 La Belle Place, Glasgow G3 7LH, Scotland | Conductor |
| **Bamford, Maria**<br>OmniPop Talent Group, 4605 Lankershim Blvd, #201, Toluca Lake CA 91602 USA | Actress, Comedienne |
| **Ban Ki-Moon**<br>Secretary-General's Office, 760 United Nations Plaza, New York NY 10017, USA | Government Official, South Korea |
| **Ban, Shigeru**<br>Shigeru Ban Architects, 5-2-4 Matsubara, Setagaya, Tokyo 156 0043, Japan | Architect |
| **Bana, Eric**<br>8-12 Sandilands St, #2, South Melbourne VIC 3205, Australia | Actor, Comedian |
| **Banach, Edward (Ed)**<br>2128 Country Club Blvd, Ames IA 50014, USA | Freestyle Wrestler |
| **Banach, Louis (Lou)**<br>1828 Tallgrass Circle, Waukesha WI 53188, USA | Freestyle Wrestler |
| **Banachowski, Andy**<br>University of California, Athletic Dept, Los Angeles CA 90024, USA | Volleyball Player, Coach |
| **Banas, Michaela**<br>Channel 7 Sydney, Television Center, Mobbs Lane, Epping NSW 2121, Australia | Actress |
| **Banaszak, John A**<br>420 Robinhood Lane, Canonsburg PA 15317, USA | Football Player |
| **Banaszak, Peter A (Pete)**<br>1021 Inverness Dr, Saint Augustine FL 32092, USA | Football Player |
| **Banaszek, Casimir J (Cas), II**<br>1018 Cohen Court, Petaluma CA 94952, USA | Football Player |
| **Banaszynski, Jacqui**<br>Saint Paul Pioneer Press, Editorial Dept, 345 Cedar St, Saint Paul MN 55101, USA | Journalist |
| **Bancroft, Ann**<br>Yourexpedition, 1920 Oliver Place S, Minneapolis MN 55405, USA | Explorer, Cross Country Skier |
| **Bancroft, Cameron**<br>Characters Talent Mgmt, 8 Elm St, Toronto ON M5G 1G7, Canada | Actor |
| **Bancroft, George M**<br>Western Ontario University, Chemistry Dept, London ON N6A 3K7, Canada | Chemist |
| **Band, Alexander M (Alex)**<br>Career Artist Management, 1100 Glendon Ave, #1100, Los Angeles CA 90024, USA | Singer (Calling), Songwriter |
| **Band, Jonathon**<br>Carnival P L C, 5 Gainsford St, London SE1 2NE, England | Navy Admiral, England |
| **Band, Richard H**<br>24053 Bessemer St, Woodland Hills CA 91367, USA | Composer |
| **Banderas, Antonio**<br>Media Art Mgmt, BaRbara de Braganza 11, #4 Derecha, 28004 Madrid, Spain | Actor, Singer, Director |
| **Bandholz, Willy**<br>Sonnholm 92, 24977 Westerholz, Germany | Handball Player |
| **Bando, Christopher M (Chris)**<br>638 Walsall Road, El Cajon CA 92019, USA | Baseball Player |
| **Bando, Salvatore L (Sal)**<br>W308N6225 Shore Acres Road, Hartland WI 53029, USA | Baseball Player |
| **Bandy, Moe**<br>Leroy Van Dyke Enterprises, 2900 Highway V, Smithton MO 65350, USA | Singer, Songwriter |
| **Bane, Edward N (Eddie)**<br>598 Paloma Court, Encinitas CA 92024, USA | Baseball Player |
| **Banes, Lisa**<br>Don Buchwald Talent Agency, 6500 Wilshire Blvd, #2200, Los Angeles CA 90048 USA | Actress |
| **Banfield, Ashleigh**<br>NBC-TV, News Dept, 30 Rockefeller Plaza, #270E, New York NY 10112 USA | Commentator |
| **Banfield, Bever-Leigh**<br>Gersh Agency, 9465 Wilshire Blvd, #600, Beverly Hills CA 90212 USA | Actress |
| **Banfield, J Anthony (Tony)**<br>1010 Myrtlewood Dr, Friendswood TX 77546, USA | Football Player |
| **Bang, Molly**<br>43 Drumlin Road, Falmouth MA 02540, USA | Writer, Illustrator |
| **Bangalter, Thomas**<br>Clintons, 55 Drury Lane, Covent Garden, London WC2B 5RZ, England | Musician (Daft Punk) |
| **Bangemann, Martin**<br>Telefonica, Gran Via 28, 28013 Madrid, Spain | Government Official, West Germany |
| **Bangerter, Norman H**<br>603 E South Temple, Salt Lake City UT 84102, USA | Governor, UT |
| **Banham, Frank**<br>139 W Grayling Lane, Suffield CT 06078, USA | Ice Hockey Player |
| **Bank, Melissa**<br>Rabineay Wachter Sanford, 1107 1/2 Glendon Ave, Los Angeles CA 90024, USA | Writer |
| **Banker, Ted**<br>1862 Park Ave, East Meadow NY 11554, USA | Football Player |
| **Bankhead, M Scott**<br>1236 Idlewood Dr, Asheboro NC 27205, USA | Baseball Player |
| **Banks, Anthony L (Tony)**<br>2211 Vaquero Club Dr, Westlake TX 76262, USA | Football Player |

| | |
|---|---|
| **Banks, Azealia A** | Rap Artist |
| Polydor Records, 364-366 Kensington High St, London W14 8NS, England | |
| **Banks, Barry** | Opera Singer |
| I M G Artists, Carnegie Hall Tower, 152 W 57th St, #500, New York NY 10019 USA | |
| **Banks, Carl E** | Football Player |
| 7 Glenview Dr, Warren NJ 07059, USA | |
| **Banks, Darren** | Ice Hockey Player |
| 11 Millington Road, Pleasant Ridge MI 48069, USA | |
| **Banks, Dennis** | Indian Rights Activist |
| General Delivery, Oglala SD 57764, USA | |
| **Banks, Elizabeth** | Actress, Model, Producer |
| United Talent Agency, U T A Plaza, 9336 Civic Center Dr, Beverly Hills CA 90210 USA | |
| **Banks, Ernest (Ernie)** | Baseball Player |
| 27 N Wacker Dr, #466, Chicago IL 60606, USA | |
| **Banks, Estes** | Football Player |
| 640 Gooseberry Dr, #703, Longmont CO 80503, USA | |
| **Banks, Eugene L (Gene)** | Basketball Player |
| 1210 Sloan St, Greensboro NC 27401, USA | |
| **Banks, Frederick R (Fred)** | Football Player |
| 5665 Orly Terrace, Atlanta GA 30349, USA | |
| **Banks, Gordon G** | Football Player |
| 2644 E Trinity Mills Road, Carrollton TX 75006, USA | |
| **Banks, Jillian** | Singer, Songwriter |
| Harvest Records, 415 Haywood Road, Asheville NC 28806, USA | |
| **Banks, Jonathan** | Actor |
| Lovett Mgmt, 1327 Brinkley Ave, Los Angeles CA 90049, USA | |
| **Banks, Kelcie H** | Boxer |
| Tocco's Ringside Gym, 9 W Charleston, Las Vegas NV 89102, USA | |
| **Banks, Leann** | Bassist (Von Bondies) |
| Tsunami Entertainment, 2525 Hyperion Ave, Los Angeles CA 90027, USA | |
| **Banks, Lloyd** | Rap Artist |
| Emmel Communications, 36 W 25th St, #200, New York NY 10010, USA | |
| **Banks, Lynne Reid** | Writer |
| Harper Collins Publishers, 10 E 53rd St, Cellar 1, New York NY 10022 USA | |
| **Banks, Morwenna** | Actress, Comedienne |
| I C M Partners, 10250 Constellation Blvd, #900, Los Angeles CA 90067 USA | |
| **Banks, Russell** | Writer |
| Trident Media Group, 41 Madison Ave, #3600, New York NY 10010, USA | |
| **Banks, Steven** | Actor, Comedian, Writer |
| Creative Artists Agency, 2000 Ave of Stars, #100, Los Angeles CA 90067 USA | |
| **Banks, Thomas S (Tom), Jr** | Football Player |
| 358 Wisteria St, Fairhope AL 36532, USA | |
| **Banks, Tyra** | Model, Actress |
| W M E Entertainment, 9601 Wilshire Blvd, #300, Beverly Hills CA 90210 USA | |
| **Banks, W Chip** | Football Player |
| 709 Albany Ave, Augusta GA 30901, USA | |
| **Banks, Walker B** | Basketball Player |
| 3207 Brentwood Dr, Champaign IL 61821, USA | |
| **Banks, William A (Willie), III** | Track Athlete |
| 250 Williams St NW, #6000, Atlanta GA 30303, USA | |
| **Banks, Willie A** | Baseball Player |
| 13 Michael St, Jamesburg NJ 08831, USA | |
| **Bankston, Michael** | Football Player |
| 182 N Burberry Park Circle, Spring TX 77382, USA | |
| **Bankston, Warren S** | Football Player |
| 4201 Bordeaux Dr, Kenner LA 70065, USA | |
| **Bannan, Justin L** | Football Player |
| 7625 Kreth Road, Fair Oaks CA 95628, USA | |
| **Banner, David** | Rap Artist, Actor |
| Creative Artists Agency, 2000 Ave of Stars, #100, Los Angeles CA 90067 USA | |
| **Banner, Jon** | Commentator |
| ABC-TV, News Dept, 77 W 66th St, New York NY 10023 USA | |
| **Bannerman, Isabella** | Cartoonist (Six Chix) |
| 41 South Drive, Hastings-on-Hudson NY 10706, USA | |
| **Bannerman, Murray** | Ice Hockey Player |
| 7222 Kiowa Road, Larkspur CO 80118, USA | |
| **Bannister, Alan** | Baseball Player |
| 6349 N 78th St, #129, Scottsdale AZ 85250, USA | |
| **Bannister, Brian P** | Baseball Player |
| 6701 E Caballo Dr, Paradise Valley AZ 85253, USA | |
| **Bannister, Floyd F** | Baseball Player |
| 6701 Caballo Dr, Paradise Valley AZ 85253, USA | |
| **Bannister, Kenneth (Ken)** | Basketball Player |
| 2322 Broadgreen Dr, Missouri City TX 77489, USA | |
| **Bannister, Roger G** | Track Athlete, Neurologist |
| 21 Bardwell Road, Oxford OX2 6SV, England | |
| **Bannon, Jack** | Actor |
| 6470 E Sunnyside Road, Coeur D'Alene ID 83814, USA | |
| **Bans, Jenna** | Producer |
| I C M Partners, 10250 Constellation Blvd, #900, Los Angeles CA 90067 USA | |
| **Banse, Juliane** | Opera Singer |
| Kunstler Sekretariat am Gasteig, Rosenheimer Str 52, 81669 Munich, Germany | |
| **Banta, D Bradford (Brad)** | Football Player |
| 1100 Smith Ave, Birmingham MI 48009, USA | |
| **Banta-Cain, Tully** | Football Player |
| 27 Apple Valley Dr, Sharon MA 2067, USA | |
| **Bantom, Michael A (Mike)** | Basketball Player, Executive |
| 418 Egret Lane, Secaucus NJ 07094, USA | |
| **Banton, Buju** | Singer |
| Agency Group Ltd, 142 W 57th St, #600, New York NY 10019 USA | |
| **Banville, John** | Writer |
| Gillon Aitken Assoc, 29 Fernshaw Road, London SW10 0TG, England | |
| **Bao, Joseph Y** | Microsurgeon, Orthopedist |
| 17436 Terry Lyn Lane, Cerritos CA 90703, USA | |
| **Baptiste, Marc** | Photographer |
| 420 W 14th St, #4SE, New York NY 10014, USA | |

**Baquero, Ivana** — Actress
Eduardo Gonzalez Valdivia, Isaac Peral 48, #1B, 28040 Madrid, Spain
**Baquet, Dean P** — Journalist, Editor
New York Times, Editorial Dept, 229 W 43rd St, New York NY 10036, USA
**Bar, Olaf** — Opera Singer
Opus 3 Artists, 470 Park Ave S, #900N, New York NY 10016 USA
**Baraban, Yannis** — Actor
Artmedia, 20 Ave Rapp, 75007 Paris, France
**Barac, Samir** — Water Polo Player
Ede Jardasa 1, 51000 Rijeka, Croatia
**Barajas, Rodridgo R (Rod)** — Baseball Player
8533 N 50th Place, Paradise Valley AZ 85253, USA
**Barak, Ehud** — Prime Minister, Israel; Army General
Defense Ministry, Kaplan St, Hakirya, Tel-Aviv 67659, Israel
**Baranova, Anastasia** — Actress
4 H M, 11340 Moorpark St, Studio City CA 91602, USA
**Baranski, Christine** — Actress
United Talent Agency, U T A Plaza, 9336 Civic Center Dr, Beverly Hills CA 90210 USA
**Barasso, Tom** — Ice Hockey Player
12820 Rosalie St, Raleigh NC 27614, USA
**Barats, Luke** — Actor, Comedian
Independent Artists, 9601 Wilshire Blvd, #750, Beverly Hills CA 90210, USA
**Barbacid, Mariano** — Onocologist
Spanish National Cancer Research Center, Melchor Fernandez Almagro 3, 28029 Madrid, Spain
**Barbacini, Maurizio** — Conductor
I M G Artists, Hogarth Business Park, Chiswick, London W4 2TH, England
**Barbakow, Jeffrey C** — Businessman
Tenet Healthcare Corp, 13737 Noel Road, #100, Dallas TX 75240, USA
**Barbarin, Philippe X I Cardinal** — Religious Leader
Archdiocese, 1 Place de Fourviere, 69321 Lyon Cedex 05, France
**Barbaro, Gary W** — Football Player
1000 Giuffrias Ave, Metairie LA 70001, USA
**Barbato, Randy** — Director, Producer
World of Wonder, 6650 Hollywood Blvd, #400, Los Angeles CA 90028, USA
**Barbeau, Adrienne** — Actress, Singer
B R S / Gage Talent Agency, 5757 Wilshire Blvd, #659, Los Angeles CA 90036 USA
**Barber, Aaron** — Golfer
2830 Fillmore St NE, Minneapolis MN 55418, USA
**Barber, Atiim K (Tiki)** — Football Player, Sportscaster
Greater Talent Network, 437 5th Ave, #700, New York NY 10016, USA
**Barber, Bill** — Ice Hockey Player, Coach
1112 Peppertree Court, #223, Sarasota FL 34242, USA
**Barber, Christopher E (Chris)** — Football Player
2621 Monaco Cove Circle, Orlando FL 32825, USA
**Barber, Glynis** — Actress
Waring & McKenna, Mayfair, 11-12 Dover St, London W1S 4LJ, England
**Barber, J Oronde (Ronde)** — Football Player
17119 Journeys End Dr, Odessa FL 33556, USA
**Barber, John (Skip), III** — Auto Racing Driver, Executive
497 Lime Rock Road, Lakeville CT 06039, USA
**Barber, Lance** — Actor
Paul Kohner, 9300 Wilshire Blvd, #555, Beverly Hills CA 90212 USA
**Barber, Marion, III** — Football Player
PO Box 191348, Dallas TX 75219, USA
**Barber, Marion, Jr** — Football Player
PO Box 46106, Minneapolis MN 55446, USA
**Barber, Michael D (Mike)** — Football Player
PO Box 2424, DeSoto TX 75123, USA
**Barber, Michael L (Mike)** — Football Player
43 Mill Creek Crossing, Hurricane WV 25526, USA
**Barber, Patricia** — Jazz Singer, Pianist, Composer
Blue Note Records, 304 Park Ave S, New York NY 10010, USA
**Barber, Paul** — Actor, Writer, Producer
Diamond Mgmt, 31 Percy St, London W1T 2DD, England
**Barber, Stewart C (Stew)** — Football Player
2138 Country Manor Dr, Mount Pleasant SC 29466, USA
**Barber, William** — Cinematographer
2509 White Chapel Place, Thousand Oaks CA 91362, USA
**Barberie, Bret E** — Baseball Player
11607 Bos St, Cerritos CA 90703, USA
**Barberie-Reynolds, Jillian** — Sportscaster, Actress
KTTV Fox-TV, 1999 S Bundy Dr, Los Angeles CA 90025, USA
**Barberos, Alessandro** — Businessman
Fiat Spa, Corso G Marconi 10/20, 10125 Turin, Italy
**Barbi, Shane** — Model (Barbi Twins)
A T Y, 4725 N Lois Ave, Tampa FL 33614, USA
**Barbi, Sia** — Model (Barbi Twins)
A T Y, 4725 N Lois Ave, Tampa FL 33614, USA
**Barbieri, Gato** — Jazz Saxophonist
Andi Howard Entertainment, 100 N Crescent Ave, #275, Beverly Hills CA 90210, USA
**Barbieri, Paula** — Actress, Model
Warner Books, 1271 Ave of Americas, New York NY 10020 USA
**Barbieri, Richard** — Keyboardist (Japan, Porcupine Tree)
Agency Group Ltd, 361-373 City Road, London EC1V 1PQ, England
**Barbosa, Leandro M** — Basketball Player
8046 E Vista Canyon St, Litchfield Park AZ 85340, USA
**Barbour, Haley R** — Governor, MS; Political Leader
B G R Group, Homer Building, 601 13th St NW, #1100-S, Washington DC 20005, USA
**Barbour, John** — Actor, Comedian, Writer
10309 Denman St, Las Vegas NV 89178, USA
**Barboza, David** — Journalist
New York Times, Editorial Dept, 229 W 43rd St, New York NY 10036, USA
**Barbuscia, Lisa** — Actress, Singer
Independent Talent Group, 40 Whitfield St, London W1T 2RH, England
**Barbutti, Pete** — Jazz Trumpeter
Thomas Cassidy, PO Box 1311, Tucson AZ 85702 USA

**Barch, Krystoger (Krys)** — Ice Hockey Player
Dallas Stars, 2601 Ave of Stars, #100, Frisco TX 75034 USA
**Barclay, Paris** — Director, Producer
Paradigm Agency, 360 N Crescent Dr, North Building, Beverly Hills CA 90210 USA
**Bard, Allen J** — Chemist
6202 Mountainclimb Dr, Austin TX 78731, USA
**Bard, Joshua D (Josh)** — Baseball Player
2139 Beechnut Place, Castle Rock CO 80108, USA
**Bard, Marjorie** — Social Activist
Women Organized Against Homelessness, PO Box 911, Saint Michaels MD 21663, USA
**Bardal, Anders** — Ski Jumper
Stabells Vei 7A, 7021 Trondheim, Norway
**Bardeen, William A** — Physicist
Fermi National Accelerator Laboratory, PO Box 500, Batavia IL 60510, USA
**Bardem, Javier E** — Actor
Bloom Hergott Diemer, 150 S Rodeo Dr, #300, Beverly Hills CA 90212 USA
**Barden, Brian D** — Baseball Player
10452 E Cannon Dr, Scottsdale AZ 85258, USA
**Barden, Jessica** — Actress
W M E Entertainment, 9601 Wilshire Blvd, #300, Beverly Hills CA 90210 USA
**Bardot, Brigitte** — Actress
La Madrigue, 83990 Saint Tropez, Var, France
**Bare, James** — WW II Navy Air Force Hero
3618 NW 47th St, Oklahoma City OK 73112, USA
**Bare, Richard L** — Director
700 Harbor Island Dr, Newport Beach CA 92660, USA
**Bare, Robert J (Bobby)** — Singer, Guitarist, Songwriter
Bobby Bare Enterprises, 112 The Landing, Hendersonville TN 37075, USA
**Bareikis, Arija** — Actress
Gersh Agency, 41 Madison Ave, #3301, New York NY 10010 USA
**Bareilles, Sara** — Singer, Pianist, Songwriter
Career Artist Mgmt, 1100 Glendon Ave, #1100, Los Angeles CA 90024, USA
**Barek, Djemel** — Actor
Artmedia, 20 Ave Rapp, 75007 Paris, France
**Baren, Justin** — Bassist (Redwalls)
Pinnacle Entertainment, 30 Glenn St, White Plains NY 10603, USA
**Baren, Logan** — Singer, Guitarist (Redwalls)
Pinnacle Entertainment, 30 Glenn St, White Plains NY 10603, USA
**Barenboim, Daniel** — Conductor, Concert Pianist
29 Rue de la Coulouvreeniere, 1206 Geneva, Switzerland
**Baretto, Ray** — Percussionist
Creative Music Consultants, 181 Christie St, #300, New York NY 10002, USA
**Barfield, Jesse L** — Baseball Player
5814 Spanish Moss Court, Spring TX 77379, USA
**Barfod, Hakon** — Yachtsman
Jon Ostensensv 15, 1360 Nesbru, Norway
**Barfoed, Kasper** — Director
United Talent Agency, U T A Plaza, 9336 Civic Center Dr, Beverly Hills CA 90210 USA
**Bargmann, Cornelia I (Cori)** — Neurobiologist
Rockefeller University Medical Center, Neural Circuits Dept, 1230 York Ave, New York NY 10065, USA
**Bargnani, Andrea** — Basketball Player
Toronto Raptors, Air Canada Center, 20 Bay St, Toronto ON M5J 2N8, Canada
**Barhom, Ashraf** — Actor
Zohar Ya'kobson, 136 Ben Yehuda St, Tel-Aviv 65271, Israel
**Barinholtz, Ike** — Actor, Comedian
United Talent Agency, U T A Plaza, 9336 Civic Center Dr, Beverly Hills CA 90210 USA
**Barisich, Carl J** — Football Player
16566 W Lilac St, Goodyear AZ 85338, USA
**Barjatya, Sooraj** — Director, Producer
1 Bhana, 422 Veer Sawarkar Road Prabhadevi Dadar, Mumbai MS 400024, India
**Barkauskas, Antanas S** — Chairman of Presidium, Lithuania
Akmenu Str 7A, Vilnus, Lithuania
**Barker, Bryan C** — Football Player
200 1st St, #203, Neptune Beach FL 32266, USA
**Barker, Cameron (Cam)** — Ice Hockey Player
Minnesota Wild, XCel Energy Arena, 1275 Saint Antoine W, Saint Paul MN 55104 USA
**Barker, Clive** — Writer, Director, Producer, Actor
Midnight Picture Show, PO Box 691821, West Hollywood CA 90069, USA
**Barker, Clyde F** — Surgeon
3 Coppertown Road, Haverford PA 19041, USA
**Barker, David J P** — Epidemiologist
Manor Farm, East Dean near Salisbury, Wiltshire SP5 1HB, England
**Barker, James F** — Educator
Clemson University, President's Office, Clemson SC 29634, USA
**Barker, Kevin S** — Baseball Player
PO Box 96, Mendota VA 24270, USA
**Barker, Lee** — Bass Guitar Designer
1842 SE 1st St, Redmond OR 97756, USA
**Barker, Leo** — Football Player
25 Via Lucena, San Clemente CA 92673, USA
**Barker, Leonard H (Len)** — Baseball Player
10690 Locust Grove Dr, Chardon OH 44024, USA
**Barker, Lucius** — Political Scientist
Stanford University, Political Science Dept, Stanford CA 94305, USA
**Barker, Michael** — Director
Sony Pictures Classics, 550 Madison Ave, New York NY 10022, USA
**Barker, Mike** — Producer, Writer, Actor
United Talent Agency, U T A Plaza, 9336 Civic Center Dr, Beverly Hills CA 90210 USA
**Barker, Pamela** — Boxer
1617 Mexican Poppy St, Las Vegas NV 89128, USA
**Barker, Pat** — Writer
Gillon Aitken, 29 Fernshaw Road, London SW10 0TG, England
**Barker, Robert W (Bob)** — Producer, Actor
Kazarian/Measures/Ruskin, 11969 Ventura Blvd, #300, Studio City CA 91604 USA
**Barker, Roy** — Football Player
23 Saint Marks Circle, Islandia NY 11749, USA

**Barker, Travis** — Drummer (Blink-182, +44)
7325 Seafarer Place, Carlsbad CA 92011, USA
**Barkett, Rosemary** — Judge
US Court of Appeals, 99 NE 4th St, #1223, Miami FL 33132, USA
**Barkin, Ellen** — Actress
Creative Artists Agency, 2000 Ave of Stars, #100, Los Angeles CA 90067 USA
**Barkley, Charles W** — Basketball Player, Sportscaster
7615 E Vaquero Dr, Scottsdale AZ 85258, USA
**Barkley, Douglas (Doug)** — Ice Hockey Player, Coach
523-3131 63 Ave NE, Calgary AB T3E 6N4, Canada
**Barkley, Iran** — Boxer
John Henry Reetz, 222 E 27th St, #3, New York NY 10016, USA
**Barkman Tyler, Jane (Janie)** — Swimmer
Princeton University, Athletic Dept, Princeton NJ 08544, USA
**Barkmin, Gun-Brit** — Opera Singer
Columbia Artists Mgmt Inc, 5 Columbus Circle, 1790 Broadway, #1600, New York NY 10019 USA
**Barkov, Aleksander (Sasha), Jr** — Ice Hockey Player
Florida Panthers, 1 Panthers Parkway, Sunrise FL 33323 USA
**Barks, Samantha** — Actress, Singer
United Agents, 12-26 Lexington St, London W1F 0LE, England
**Barksdale, Chuck** — Singer (Dells)
Associated Booking Corp, 501 Madison Ave, #501, New York NY 10022 USA
**Barksdale, James (Jim)** — Businessman
Barksdale Group, 2730 Sand Hill Road, Menlo Park CA 94025, USA
**Barksdale, Rhesa H** — Judge
US Court of Appeals, 245 E Capitol St, Jackson MS 39201, USA
**Barkum, Jerome P** — Football Player
2720 Palmer Dr, #15, Gulfport MS 39507, USA
**Barlett, Donald L** — Journalist
Wylie Agency, 250 W 57th St, #2114, New York NY 10107 USA
**Barletta, Joseph** — Publisher
TV Guide, Publisher's Office, 100 Matsonford Road, Wayne PA 19080, USA
**Barlow, Bob** — Ice Hockey Player
4912 Wesley Road, Victoria BC V8Y 1Y5, Canada
**Barlow, Gary** — Singer, Pianist, Songwriter
International Talent Booking, Ariel House, 74A Charlotte St, #100 London W1T 4QJ, England
**Barlow, Kevan C** — Football Player
82 Waterfront Dr, Pittsburgh PA 15222, USA
**Barlow, Lou** — Singer, Guitarist, Songwriter
Paradigm Agency, 360 N Crescent Dr, North Building, Beverly Hills CA 90210 USA
**Barlow, Michael R (Mike)** — Baseball Player
Sheftic, 4524 Francis Road, Cazenovia NY 13035, USA
**Barlow, Perry** — Cartoonist
New Yorker, Editorial Dept, 4 Times Square, Basement C1B, New York NY 10036 USA
**Barlow, Reggie D** — Football Player
8311 Timber Trace Lane, Pike Road AL 36064, USA
**Barmes, Clint H** — Baseball Player
113 Mallard Court, Mead CO 80542, USA
**Barnaby, Matthew** — Ice Hockey Player
134 King Anthony Way, Getzville NY 14068, USA
**Barnard, Aneurin** — Actor
Artists Partnership, 101 Finsbury Pavement, London EC2A 1RS, England
**Barnathan, Michael** — Producer
1492 Pictures, 4000 Warner Blvd, Building 3, Burbank CA 91522, USA
**Barndt, Thomas A (Tom)** — Football Player
11041 Romola St, Las Vegas NV 89141, USA
**Barner, Bob** — Writer
2100 Green St, #206, San Francisco CA 94123, USA
**Barnes, Aaron** — Cinematographer
Gersh Agency, 9465 Wilshire Blvd, #600, Beverly Hills CA 90212 USA
**Barnes, Benny J** — Football Player
5003 Fleming Ave, Richmond CA 94804, USA
**Barnes, Brenda C** — Businesswoman
Sara Lee Corp, 3500 Lacey Road, Downers Grove IL 60515, USA
**Barnes, Brian** — Golfer
International Golf Partners, 3300 PGA Blvd, #820, Palm Beach Gardens FL 33410, USA
**Barnes, Brian K** — Baseball Player
1006 Arrowhead Point, Anderson SC 29625, USA
**Barnes, Chris** — Bowler
Professional Bowlers Association, 719 2nd Ave, #701, Seattle WA 98104 USA
**Barnes, Christopher Daniel** — Actor
Agency S G H, 6525 Sunset Blvd, #PH9, Hollywood CA 90028, USA
**Barnes, Danny** — Singer, Musician (Bad Livers)
Red Light Mgmt, 44 Wall St, #2200, New York NY 10005, USA
**Barnes, Darian D** — Football Player
554 Clifton Ave, Toms River NJ 08753, USA
**Barnes, David M (Dave)** — Singer, Songwriter
Paradigm Agency, 360 N Crescent Dr, North Building, Beverly Hills CA 90210 USA
**Barnes, David Wilson** — Actor
Hartig-Hilepo Agency, 54 W 21st St, #610, New York NY 10010, USA
**Barnes, Demore** — Actor
S M S Talent, 8383 Wilshire Blvd, #230, Beverly Hills CA 90211 USA
**Barnes, E Randolph (Randy)** — Track Athlete
Randy Barnes Enterprises, PO Box 1373, Mechanicsburg PA 17055, USA
**Barnes, Erich T** — Football Player
712 Warburton Ave, Yonkers NY 10701, USA
**Barnes, Frank** — Baseball Player
1508 Brazil St, Greenville MS 38701, USA
**Barnes, Frank S** — Electronics Engineer
University of Colorado, Engineering Dept, Boulder CO 80309, USA
**Barnes, Gary M** — Football Player
849 Tiger Blvd, #406, Clemson SC 29631, USA
**Barnes, Harrison B** — Basketball Player
Golden State Warriors, 1011 Broadway, Oakland CA 94605 USA
**Barnes, Jeff** — Football Player
10738 Versailles Blvd, Clermont FL 34711, USA

**Barnes, Jhane E** — Fashion Designer
18 Five Ponds Dr, Waccabuc NY 10597, USA
**Barnes, Jimmy** — Singer
Harbour Agency, 135 Forbes St, Woolloomooloo NSW 2011, Australia
**Barnes, Joanna** — Actress, Writer
PO Box 1103, Gualala CA 95445, USA
**Barnes, Joey** — Drummer (Daughtry)
19 Entertainment, 8560 W Sunset Blvd, #900, Los Angeles CA 90069, USA
**Barnes, Jonathan** — Philosopher
1 Place de la Taconnerie, 1204 Geneva, Switzerland
**Barnes, Jonathan** — Writer
William Morrow Publishers, 1350 Ave of Americas, New York NY 10019 USA
**Barnes, Julian P** — Writer
Knopf Publishers, 1745 Broadway, New York NY 10019 USA
**Barnes, Khalif** — Football Player
7967 Monterey Bay Dr, Jacksonville FL 32256, USA
**Barnes, Luther** — Singer
Universal Attractions, 135 W 26th St, #1200, New York NY 10001 USA
**Barnes, Matt K** — Basketball Player
Los Angeles Clippers, Staples Center, 1111 S Figueroa St, Los Angeles CA 90015 USA
**Barnes, Michael** — Singer (Red)
Paradigm Agency, 404 W Franklin St, Monterey CA 93940 USA
**Barnes, Michael J (Mike)** — Football Player
27474 Plank Road, Guys Mills PA 16327, USA
**Barnes, Norm** — Ice Hockey Player
17 Meadow Crossing, Simsbury CT 06070, USA
**Barnes, Priscilla** — Actress, Model
Glick Agency, 347 5th Ave, #1404, New York NY 10016 USA
**Barnes, Rick** — Basketball Coach
Texas University, Athletic Dept, Austin TX 78713, USA
**Barnes, Robert H** — Psychiatrist
Texas Tech University Medical School, Psychiatry Dept, PO Box 4349, Lubbock TX 79409, USA
**Barnes, Stu** — Ice Hockey Player
5069 Royal Creek Lane, Plano TX 75093, USA
**Barnes, William H (Skeeter)** — Baseball Player
11544 Winding Wood Dr, Indianapolis IN 46235, USA
**Barnes, William R (Billy Ray)** — Football Player
518 James C Lane, Dallas NC 28034, USA
**Barnett of Heywood & Royton, Joel B** — Government Official, England
7 Hillingdon Road, Whitefield, Manchester M25 7QQ, England
**Barnett, Charlie** — Actor
Gersh Agency, 9465 Wilshire Blvd, #600, Beverly Hills CA 90212 USA
**Barnett, Douglas S (Doug), Jr** — Football Player
14105 Veracruz Dr, Bakersfield CA 93314, USA
**Barnett, Fred L** — Football Player
PO Box 604, Bala Cynwyd PA 19004, USA
**Barnett, James F (Jim)** — Basketball Player
7 Kittiwake Road, Orinda CA 94563, USA
**Barnett, Jonathan** — Architect
225 S Bonsall St, Philadelphia PA 19103, USA
**Barnett, Mandy** — Singer
Conway Entertainment Group, 1625 Broadway, #500, Nashville TN 37203, USA
**Barnett, Nathaniel (Nate)** — Basketball Player
710 N Jefferson St, Wilmington DE 19801, USA
**Barnett, Nicholas A (Nick)** — Football Player
3496 Country Winds Court, Green Bay WI 54311, USA
**Barnett, Oliver W** — Football Player
1133 Autumn Ridge Dr, Lexington KY 40509, USA
**Barnett, Pamela (Pam)** — Golfer
4908 E Rancho Tierra Dr, Cave Creek AZ 85331, USA
**Barnett, Richard (Dick)** — Basketball Player
1227 Pine Ridge, Bushkill PA 18324, USA
**Barnett, Robby** — Dance Artistic Director
Pilobolus Dance Theater, PO Box 388, Washington Depot CT 06794, USA
**Barnett, Sabrina** — Model
Next Model Mgmt, 23 Watts St, New York NY 10013 USA
**Barnett, Samuel** — Actor
I C M Partners, 10250 Constellation Blvd, #900, Los Angeles CA 90067 USA
**Barnett, Tommy** — Religious Leader
Phoenix First Assembly Church, 13613 N Cave Creek Road, Phoenix AZ 85022, USA
**Barney, Lemuel J (Lem), Jr** — Football Player
775 Kentbrook Dr, Commerce Township MI 48382, USA
**Barney, Matthew** — Performance Artist
Barbara Gladstone Gallery, 515 W 24th St, New York NY 10011, USA
**Barnhart, Nicole R** — Soccer Player
F C Kansas City, 5366 W 95th St, Prairie Village KS 66207 USA
**Barno, David W** — Army General
Center for a New American Security, 1301 Pennsylvania Ave NW, #403, Washington DC 20004, USA
**Barnow, Alex** — Producer, Writer
United Talent Agency, U T A Plaza, 9336 Civic Center Dr, Beverly Hills CA 90210 USA
**Barnum, Harvey C, Jr** — Vietnam War Marine Corps Hero (CMH)
12008 Walnut Branch Road, Reston VA 20194, USA
**Barnwell, Malcolm** — Football Player
4045 Gullah Ave, #103, North Charleston SC 29405, USA
**Barocco, Rocco** — Fashion Designer
Via Occhio Marion, 80773 Capri/Napoli, Italy
**Baron Cohen, Sacha (Borat)** — Actor, Comedian
W M E Entertainment, 9601 Wilshire Blvd, #300, Beverly Hills CA 90210 USA
**Baron Crespo, Enrique** — Government Official, Spain
European Parliament, Rue Wiertz 60, 1047 Brussels, Belgium
**Baron, Lita** — Actress
1508 S La Verne Way, Palm Springs CA 92264, USA
**Baron, Martin D** — Editor
Boston Globe, Editorial Dept, 135 William Morrissey Blvd, Dorchester MA 02125 USA
**Baron, Murray** — Ice Hockey Player
23623 N Scottsdale Road, #D3, Scottsdale AZ 85255, USA

**Baron, Natalia** — Actress
Evolution Entertainment, 901 N Highland Ave, Los Angeles CA 90038 USA

**Barone, Anita** — Actress
Paradigm Agency, 360 N Crescent Dr, North Building, Beverly Hills CA 90210 USA

**Barone, Richard A** — Singer, Guitarist, Songwriter (Bongos)
Richard Barone Music, 240 Waverly Place, #23, New York NY 10014, USA

**Baroux, Olivier** — Actor
U B B A, 6 Rue de Braque, 75003 Paris, France

**Barr, Anthony** — Football Player
Minnesota Vikings, 9520 Viking Dr, Eden Prairie MN 55344 USA

**Barr, Dave** — Ice Hockey Player
3100 Wilcrest Dr, #260, Houston TX 77042, USA

**Barr, Douglas** — Actor
Paradigm Agency, 360 N Crescent Dr, North Building, Beverly Hills CA 90210 USA

**Barr, Jean-Marc** — Actor
Zelig, 57 Rue Reaumur, 75002 Paris, France

**Barr, Julia** — Actress
Abrams Artists, 275 7th Ave, #2600, New York NY 10001 USA

**Barr, Matt** — Actor
Luber Rocklin Entertainment, 5815 Sunset Blvd, #206, Los Angeles CA 90028 USA

**Barr, Michael J (Mike)** — Basketball Player
350 38th St NW, Canton OH 44709, USA

**Barr, Nathan (Nate)** — Composer
First Artists Mgmt, 4764 Park Granada, #210, Calabasas CA 91302 USA

**Barr, Nevada** — Writer
85 Versailles Blvd, New Orleans LA 70125, USA

**Barr, Roseanne** — Actress, Comedienne
904 Silver Spur Road, #433, Rolling Hills Estates CA 90274, USA

**Barr, Tara Lynne** — Actress
Bicoastal Talent, 210 N Pass Ave, #204, Burbank CA 91505, USA

**Barr, William P** — Attorney General
Time Warner, Board of Directors, 1 Time Warner Center, New York NY 10019, USA

**Barra, Mary T** — Businesswoman
General Motors Corp, Renaissance Center, Detroit MI 48243, USA

**Barraclough, Roy** — Actor
Gavin Barker Assoc, 2D Wimpole St, London W1G 0EB, England

**Barrasso, Thomas (Tom)** — Ice Hockey Player
12820 Rosalie St, Raleigh NC 27614, USA

**Barratier, Christophe** — Director, Writer, Lyricist
Galatee Films, 19 Ave de Messine, 75008 Paris, France

**Barratt, Michael R** — Astronaut
2102 Pleasant Palm Circle, League City TX 77573, USA

**Barrault, Doug** — Ice Hockey Player
527 10th St S, Golden BC V0A 1H0, Canada

**Barraza, Adriana** — Actress, Director
Mesala Films, C/Lopez De Hoyos 384 Bis, Bajo Izq, 28043 Madrid, Spain

**Barrea, Juan J (J J)** — Basketball Player
Dallas Mavericks, Pavilion, 2909 Taylor Street, Dallas TX 75226 USA

**Barrera, Marco Antonio** — Boxer
Golden Boy Promotions, 626 Wilshire Blvd, #350, Los Angeles CA 90017, USA

**Barrere, Paul** — Singer, Guitarist, Songwriter
Skyline Music, 48 Prospect St, Whitehead NH 03598, USA

**Barrese, Sasha** — Actress
C E S D, 10635 Santa Monica Blvd, #130, Los Angeles CA 90025 USA

**Barre-Sinoussi, Francois C** — Nobel Medicine Laureate
Institut Pasteur, 25 Rue du Docteur Roux, 75724 Paris Cedex 15, France

**Barreto, Bruno** — Director
Creative Artists Agency, 2000 Ave of Stars, #100, Los Angeles CA 90067 USA

**Barrett, Christina (Tina)** — Golfer
Ladies Pro Golf Assn, 100 International Golf Dr, Daytona Beach FL 32124 USA

**Barrett, Colleen** — Businesswoman
Southwest Airlines, PO Box 36611, 2702 Love Field Dr, Dallas TX 75235, USA

**Barrett, Craig R** — Businessman
Intel Corp, 2200 Mission College Blvd, Santa Clara CA 95054, USA

**Barrett, David** — Football Player
3181 E Waterman Court, Gilbert AZ 85297, USA

**Barrett, Edward G (Ted)** — Baseball Umpire
855A Silverberry Circle SE, Albuquerque NM 87116, USA

**Barrett, Fred W** — Ice Hockey Player
3016 Leitrim Road, Gloucester ON K1T 3V9, Canada

**Barrett, George S** — Businessman
Cardinal Health, 7000 Cardinal Place, Dublin OH 43017, USA

**Barrett, Jacinda** — Actress, Model
I C M Partners, 10250 Constellation Blvd, #900, Los Angeles CA 90067 USA

**Barrett, James E** — Judge
US Court of Appeals, 2120 Capitol Ave, #2131, Cheyenne WY 82001, USA

**Barrett, Jean M, Jr** — Football Player
7494 S Sleepy Hollow Dr, Tulsa OK 74136, USA

**Barrett, Keith (K K)** — Production Designer
United Talent Agency, U T A Plaza, 9336 Civic Center Dr, Beverly Hills CA 90210 USA

**Barrett, Malcolm** — Actor
Gersh Agency, 9465 Wilshire Blvd, #600, Beverly Hills CA 90212 USA

**Barrett, Marcia** — Singer (Boney M)
International Artists, PO Box 100334, 47563 Goch, Germany

**Barrett, Martin G (Marty)** — Baseball Manager
3552 Ridge Meadow St, Las Vegas NV 89135, USA

**Barrett, Michael P** — Baseball Player
126 Circle Dr, Port Saint Joe FL 32456, USA

**Barrett, Rona** — Columnist, Commentator
Rona Barrett Foundation, PO Box 1559, Santa Ynez CA 93460, USA

**Barrett, Shirley** — Director
H L A Mgmt, PO Box 1536, Strawberry Hills NSW 2012, Australia

**Barrett, Stephen** — Psychiatrist, Social Activist
PO Box 1747, Allentown PA 18105, USA

**Barrett, Thomas J** — Coast Guard Admiral
Alyeska Pipeline Service Co, 3700 Centerpoint Dr, Anchorage AK 99503, USA

**Barrial, Henry** — Director
O'Neill Talent Group, 4150 Riverside Dr, #212, Burbank CA 91505, USA
**Barrichello, Rubens G** — Auto Racing Driver
Eng Luis Carlos Berrini 1140, 8 Andar, Sao Paulo Cep 04571 SP, Brazil
**Barrick, Matt** — Singer, Guitarist (Walkmen)
Mick Mgmt, 35 Washington St, Brooklyn NY 11201 USA
**Barrie, Amanda** — Actress
Associated International Mgmt, 7 Hatton Garden, #400, London EC1N 8AD, England
**Barrie, Barbara** — Actress
Innovative Artists, 1505 10th St, Santa Monica CA 90401 USA
**Barrie, Douglas R (Doug)** — Ice Hockey Player
12130 46th St NW, Edmonton AB T5W 2W4, Canada
**Barrie, Len** — Ice Hockey Player
Bear Mountain, 208-2800 Bryn Mawr Road, Victoria BC V9B 3T4, Canada
**Barriere, Alain** — Singer, Songwriter
Discotheque Le Stirwen, Chemin Mane Brizil, 56340 Carmac, France
**Barris, George** — Custom Car Designer
Kustom City, 10811 Riverside Dr, North Hollywood CA 91602, USA
**Barro, Robert J** — Economist
Harvard University, Economics Dept, Cambridge MA 02138, USA
**Barron, Alex B** — Football Player
630 Emerson Road, #206, Saint Louis MO 63141, USA
**Barron, Dana** — Actress
Epstein-Wyckoff, 280 S Beverly Dr, #400, Beverly Hills CA 90212 USA
**Barron, Eric J** — Educator
Pennsylvania State University, President's Office, University Park PA 16802, USA
**Barron, Kenneth (Kenny)** — Jazz Pianist, Composer
Unlimited Myles, 6 Imaginary Place, Aberdeen NJ 07747, USA
**Barron, Mark** — Football Player
Saint Louis Rams, 901 N Broadway, Saint Louis MO 63101 USA
**Barron, Steve M** — Director
United Talent Agency, U T A Plaza, 9336 Civic Center Dr, Beverly Hills CA 90210 USA
**Barros, Ana Beatriz** — Model
Elite Model Mgmt, Bridgade 23B, #400, 1260 Copenhagen, Denmark
**Barros, Dana B** — Basketball Player
10 Arborway, North Easton MA 02356, USA
**Barroso, Jose Manuel** — Prime Minister, Portugal
European Communities, Berlaymont, Rue de Loi 200, 1049 Brussels, Belgium
**Barrow, Barbara** — Golfer
11427 Mayapple Way, San Diego CA 92131, USA
**Barrow, Dean O** — Prime Minister, Belize
Prime Minister's Office, East Bloc, Belmopan, Belize
**Barrow, Geoffrey P (Geoff)** — Synthesizer Player (Portishead)
High Road Touring, 751 Bridgeway, #200, Sausalito CA 94965 USA
**Barrow, John D** — Mathematician, Templeton Prize Laureate
Cambridge University, Math Sciences Center, Cambridge CB3 0WA, England
**Barrow, Micheal C** — Football Player
1115 S Alhambra Circle, Coral Gables FL 33146, USA
**Barrowman, John** — Actor, Singer
293 Villas Road, Plumstead, London SE18 7PR, England
**Barrowman, Michael (Mike)** — Swimmer
603 S Alp St, Bay City MI 48706, USA
**Barrs, Jack L (Jay), Jr** — Archery Athlete
646 E Kings Peak Cove, Draper UT 84020, USA
**Barry, Allen (Al)** — Football Player
3760 Edgeview Dr, Pasadena CA 91107, USA
**Barry, Barbara** — Interior Designer
Barbara Barry Inc, 9526 Pico Blvd, Los Angeles CA 90035, USA
**Barry, Brandon** — Singer (Stamps Quartet)
PO Box 1471, Brentwood TN 37024, USA
**Barry, Brent R** — Basketball Player
712 The Strand, Hermosa Beach CA 90254, USA
**Barry, Daniel T (Dan)** — Astronaut
46 Ashton Lane, South Hadley MA 01075, USA
**Barry, Dave** — Journalist, Writer
6510 Granada Blvd, Coral Gables FL 33146, USA
**Barry, Ellen** — Journalist
New York Times, Editorial Dept, 229 W 43rd St, New York NY 10036 USA
**Barry, Jeff** — Composer
B M I, 8730 W Sunset Blvd, #300, Los Angeles CA 90069 USA
**Barry, Jon A** — Basketball Player
4555 Club Dr NE, Atlanta GA 30319, USA
**Barry, Jon B** — Photographer
1965 Magnolia Dr, Baton Rouge LA 70808, USA
**Barry, Kevin T** — Baseball Player
76 Amethyst Way, Franklin Park NJ 08823, USA
**Barry, Len** — Singer (Dovells)
Cape Entertainment, 8432 NW 31st Court, Sunrise FL 33351, USA
**Barry, Mark** — Cartoonist (Ernie Pook's Comeck)
PO Box 447, Footville WI 53537, USA
**Barry, Maryanne Trump** — Singer, Flutist (BBMak)
Spirit Media, PO Box 43591, Phoenix AZ 85080, USA
**Barry, Maryanne Trump** — Judge
US Court of Appeals, US Courthouse, Federal Square, #333, Newark NJ 07101, USA
**Barry, Patricia** — Actress
348 Hauser Blvd, #304, Los Angeles CA 90036, USA
**Barry, Paul F** — Football Player
409 Kingswood Dr, El Paso TX 79932, USA
**Barry, Raymond J** — Actor
Metropolitan Talent Agency, 5405 Wilshire Blvd, #218, Los Angeles CA 90036 USA
**Barry, Richard F D (Rick), III** — Basketball Player, Sportscaster
5240 Broadmoor Bluffs Dr, Colorado Springs CO 80906, USA
**Barry, Seymour (Sy)** — Cartoonist (Flash Gordon, Phantom)
225 Fairfield Dr E, Holbrook NY 11741, USA
**Barry, Thom** — Actor
Prestige Talent Agency, 9250 Wilshire Blvd, #208, Beverly Hills CA 90212, USA

**Barrymore, Drew** — Actress, Model
Creative Artists Agency, 2000 Ave of Stars, #100, Los Angeles CA 90067 USA
**Barsh, Gregory S** — Pediatrician
Stanford University Medical Center, Pediatrics Dept, Stanford CA 94305, USA
**Barshefsky, Charlene** — Government Official
Wilmer Cutler Pickering, 1875 Pennsylvania Ave NW, Washington DC 20006, USA
**Barson, Mike** — Keyboardist (Madness)
I T F, Ariel House, 74A Charlotte St, London W1T 4QJ, England
**Barstow, David** — Journalist
New York Times, Editorial Dept, 229 W 43rd St, New York NY 10036 USA
**Barstow, Josephine C** — Opera Singer
Musichall Ltd, Vicarage Way, Ringmer BN8 5LA, England
**Bart, Peter B** — Editor
Variety, 11175 Santa Monica Blvd, Los Angeles CA 90025, USA
**Bart, Roger** — Actor
Innovative Artists, 1505 10th St, Santa Monica CA 90401 USA
**Bartecko, Lubos** — Ice Hockey Player
121 Windy Acres Estates Dr, Ballwin MO 63021, USA
**Bartee, Kimera A** — Baseball Player
10808 N 57th Dr, Glendale AZ 85304, USA
**Bartee, William A** — Football Player
PO Box 730953, Ormond Beach FL 32173, USA
**Bartel, Robin** — Ice Hockey Player
210 Forsyth Court, Saskatoon SK S7N 4H2, Canada
**Barth, Francis** — Artist
7105 Jackson St, North Bergen NJ 07047, USA
**Barth, John M** — Businessman
Johnson Controls, 5757 N Green Bay Ave, PO Box 591, Milwaukee WI 53201, USA
**Barth, John S** — Writer
Wylie Agency, 250 W 57th St, #2114, New York NY 10107 USA
**Barth, T Fredrik W** — Anthropologist
Rodkleivfaret 16, 0788 Oslo, Norway
**Barth, Uta** — Conceptual Artist, Photographer
Tanya Bonakdar Gallery, 521 W 21st St, Front 1, New York NY 10011, USA
**Bartha, Justin** — Actor
Creative Artists Agency, 2000 Ave of Stars, #100, Los Angeles CA 90067 USA
**Bartholemew, Ian** — Actor
Artists Partnership, 101 Finsbury Pavement, London EC2A 1RS, England
**Bartholomew I** — Religious Leader
Eastern Orthodox Church, Rum Ortoks Patrikhanesi, 34220 Istanbul, Turkey
**Bartholomew, Dave** — Jazz Trumpeter, Singer
Paramount Entertainment, PO Box 12, Far Hills NJ 07931 USA
**Bartholomew, Logan** — Actor
J L A Talent Agency, 9151 Sunset Blvd, West Hollywood CA 90069, USA
**Bartilson, Lynsey** — Actress
C E S D, 10635 Santa Monica Blvd, #130, Los Angeles CA 90025 USA
**Bartiromo, Maria** — Commentator
Fox-TV, News Dept, 205 E 67th St, New York NY 10065 USA
**Bartkowiak, Andrzej** — Director
Paradigm Agency, 360 N Crescent Dr, North Building, Beverly Hills CA 90210 USA
**Bartkowski, Steven J (Steve)** — Football Player
10745 Bell Road, Duluth GA 30097, USA
**Bartlett, Bonnie** — Actress, Singer
12805 Hortense St, Studio City CA 91604, USA
**Bartlett, Don** — Curling Athlete
Curling Association, 1660 Vimont Court, Cumberland ON K4A 4J4, Canada
**Bartlett, Erinn** — Actress
Innovative Artists, 1505 10th St, Santa Monica CA 90401 USA
**Bartlett, Jason A** — Baseball Player
1345 Pippen Lane, Lodi CA 95242, USA
**Bartlett, Jennifer L** — Artist
134 Charles St, New York NY 10014, USA
**Bartlett, Jim** — Ice Hockey Player
8718 Chadwick Dr, Tampa FL 33635, USA
**Bartlett, Robin** — Actress
Gersh Agency, 9465 Wilshire Blvd, #600, Beverly Hills CA 90212 USA
**Bartlett, Scott** — Guitarist (Saving Abel)
Virgin Records, 338 N Foothill Road, Beverly Hills CA 90210 USA
**Bartlett, Thomas A** — Educator
1209 SW 6th St, #904, Portland OR 97204, USA
**Bartletti, Don** — Photojournalist
Los Angeles Times, Editorial Dept, 202 W 1st St, Los Angeles CA 90012 USA
**Bartley, Adam** — Actor
Gersh Agency, 9465 Wilshire Blvd, #600, Beverly Hills CA 90212 USA
**Bartley, Geoff** — Singer, Guitarist, Songwriter
Jean Schwartz Entertainment, 326 Grant St, Framingham MA 01702, USA
**Bartoe, John-David F** — Astronaut
2724 Lighthouse Dr, Houston TX 77058, USA
**Bartoletti, Louis** — Golfer
1450 Longlea Terrace, Wellington FL 33414, USA
**Bartoli, Cecilia** — Opera Singer
Mastroianni Assoc, 161 W 61st St, #32B, New York NY 10023, USA
**Bartoli, Marion** — Tennis Player
1180 Tartegnin, Switzerland
**Bartolome, Victor (Vic)** — Basketball Player
1025 Rinconada Road, #A, Santa Barbara CA 93101, USA
**Bartolomew, Kenneth (Ken)** — Speed Skater
4820 Bryant Ave S, Minneapolis MN 55419, USA
**Barton, Austin** — Sculptor
100 N Lake, Joseph OR 97846, USA
**Barton, Daric W (D B)** — Baseball Player
958 Naples Dr, Corona CA 92882, USA
**Barton, Dorie** — Actress
Abrams Artists, 9200 W Sunset Blvd, #1125, West Hollywood CA 90069 USA
**Barton, Eric** — Football Player
23 Hayes Hill Dr, Northport NY 11768, USA

**Barton, Glenys** — Artist
Angela Flowers Gallery, 199-205 Richmond Road, London E8 3NJ, England

**Barton, Gregory (Greg)** — Canoeing Athlete
6851 30th Ave NE, Seattle WA 98115, USA

**Barton, Harris S** — Football Player
334 Lincoln Ave, Palo Alto CA 94301, USA

**Barton, Jacqueline K** — Chemist
California Insitute of Techonolgy, Chemistry Dept, Pasadena CA 91125, USA

**Barton, Lou Ann** — Singer
Luther Wolf Agency, PO Box 685138, Austin TX 78718, USA

**Barton, Mischa** — Actress, Model
Domain Talent, 9229 W Sunset Blvd, #710, West Hollywood CA 90069 USA

**Barton, Peter** — Actor
2265 Westwood Blvd, #2619, Los Angeles CA 90064, USA

**Barton, Rachel** — Concert Violinist
I C M Artists, 40 W 57th St, #1800, New York NY 10019 USA

**Barton, Richard N (Rich)** — Businessman
Zillow Inc, Russell Investment Center, 1301 2nd Ave, #3100, Seattle WA 98101, USA

**Barton, Robert W (Bob)** — Baseball Player
37193 Stardust Way, Murrieta CA 92563, USA

**Bartovic, Milan** — Ice Hockey Player
141 Bennington Hills Court, West Henrietta NY 14586, USA

**Bartrum, Mike W** — Football Player
43375 Carlton Place, Pomeroy OH 45769, USA

**Bartz, Gary L** — Jazz Saxophonist, Composer
Joel Chriss Co, 300 Mercer St, #3J, New York NY 10003 USA

**Bartz, Randall (Randy)** — Speed Skater
3829 Baker Road, Hopkins MN 55305, USA

**Baruch, Jordan J** — Electrical Engineer
5630 Wisconsin Ave, #905, Chevy Chase MD 20815, USA

**Baruchel, Jay** — Actor
Thruline Entertainment, 9250 Wilshire Blvd, #100, Beverly Hills CA 90212 USA

**Barwell, Eric** — British WW II Air Force Hero
Toft, 5 Beldam's Close, Cambridge CB3 7RN, England

**Baryshnikov, Mikhail** — Ballet Dancer, Actor
Baryshnikov Arts Center, 450 W 37th St, #501, New York NY 10018, USA

**Barzelay, Eef** — Singer, Guitarist (Clem Snide)
Impact Artist Mgmt, 356 W 123rd St, New York NY 10027, USA

**Barzilauskas, Carl J** — Football Player
4444 Lower Schooner Road, Nashville IN 47448, USA

**Barzini, Benedetta** — Model
Donna Karan Co, 361 Newbury St, Boston MA 02115, USA

**Basaraba, Gary** — Actor
Stone Manners Salners, 6100 Wilshire Blvd, #1500, Los Angeles CA 90035 USA

**Basche, David Alan** — Actor
New Wave Entertainment 2660 W Olive Ave, Burbank CA 91505, USA

**Baschnagel, Brian D** — Football Player
1824 Ridgewood Lane W, Glenview IL 60025, USA

**Basco, Dante** — Actor
Dayton-Milrad-Cho, 8899 Beverly Blvd, #918, Los Angeles CA 90048, USA

**Basco, Dion** — Actor
Schiowitz Connor, 1680 N Vine St, #1016, Los Angeles CA 90028 USA

**Baselitz, Georg** — Artist
Schloss Derneberg, 31188 Holle, Germany

**Bashir, Idrees** — Football Player
5579 Mountain View Pass, Stone Mountain GA 30087, USA

**Bashir, Martin** — Commentator
ABC-TV, News Dept, 77 W 66th St, New York NY 10023 USA

**Bashmet, Yuri A** — Concert Violist, Conductor
Briyusov 7, #16, 103009 Moscow, Russia

**Bashoff, Blake** — Actor
Abrams Artists, 9200 W Sunset Blvd, #1125, West Hollywood CA 90069 USA

**Basia** — Singer
Creative Artists Agency, 2000 Ave of Stars, #100, Los Angeles CA 90067 USA

**Basilashuili, Oleg V** — Actor
Borodinskaya Str 13, #58, 196180 Saint Petersburg, Russia

**Basinger, Kim** — Actress
A P A Talent & Literary Agency, 405 S Beverly Dr, #300, Beverly Hills CA 90212 USA

**Basis, Austin** — Actor
Don Buchwald Talent Agency, 6500 Wilshire Blvd, #2200, Los Angeles CA 90048, USA

**Basler, Marianne** — Actress
Agence Artiste Adequat, 108 Rue Reaumur, 75002 Paris, France

**Basri, Gibor** — Astronomer
University of California, Astronomy Dept, Berkeley CA 94720, USA

**Bass, Gary J** — Writer
Princeton University, Bendheim Hall, Princeton NJ 08544, USA

**Bass, George F** — Underwater Archaeologist
1600 Dominik Dr, College Station TX 77840, USA

**Bass, Glenn A** — Football Player
4185 Diplomacy Circle, Tallahassee FL 32308, USA

**Bass, Hyman** — Mathematician
435 Riverside Dr, New York NY 10025, USA

**Bass, J Lance** — Singer ('N Sync)
Owen Entertainment, 1708 21st Ave S, #274, Nashville TN 37212, USA

**Bass, Kevin C** — Baseball Player
3630 Maranatha Dr, Sugar Land TX 77479, USA

**Bass, Michael T (Mike)** — Football Player
4703 NW 36th St, Gainesville FL 32605, USA

**Bass, Norman D (Norm), Jr** — Baseball, Football Player
156 E 70th St, Los Angeles CA 90003, USA

**Bass, Randy W** — Baseball Player
2709 SW Coombs Road, Lawton OK 73505, USA

**Bass, Ronald J (Ron)** — Writer
I C M Partners, 10250 Constellation Blvd, #900, Los Angeles CA 90067 USA

**Bassen, Robert P (Bob)** — Ice Hockey Player
1742 Coldstone Dr, Frisco TX 75034, USA

## B

**Bassett, Angela** — Actress
Bassett/Vance Productions, 1520 Ocean Park Blvd, #C, Santa Monica CA 90405, USA
**Bassett, Brian** — Editorial Cartoonist, Cartoonist (Adam)
Seattle Times, Editorial Dept, 1000 Denny Way, Seattle WA 98109 USA
**Bassett, E Timothy (Tim)** — Basketball Player
1143 Dorsey Place, Plainfield NJ 07062, USA
**Bassett, Leslie R** — Composer
5433 Ashmore Lane, Flowery Branch GA 30542, USA
**Bassetti, Gualtiero Cardinal** — Religious Leader
Archdiocese of Perugia-Citta della Pieve, Piazza IV Novembre 6, 06123 Perugia, Italy
**Bassett-Seguso, Carling** — Tennis Player
1008 Vista del Mar Dr, Delray Beach FL 33483, USA
**Bassey, Jennifer** — Actress
12 E 86th St, #1728, New York NY 10028, USA
**Bassey, Shirley** — Singer
La Rocca Bella, 24 Ave Princess Grace, 98000 Monte Carlo, Monaco
**Bassham, Lanny R** — Marksman
7101 Lake Mead Court, Frisco TX 75034, USA
**Basso, Dennis** — Fashion Designer
317 W 33rd St New York NY 10001, USA
**Basti, Juli** — Actress
Krecsanyi Utca 6, 1025 Budapest, Hungary
**Baston, Maceo** — Basketball Player
PO Box 4846, Troy MI 48099, USA
**Basu, Asish R** — Geochemist
University of Rochester, Geochemistry Dept, Rochester NY 14627, USA
**Batali, Dean** — Writer
A P A Talent & Literary Agency, 405 S Beverly Dr, #300, Beverly Hills CA 90212 USA
**Batali, Mario** — Restauranteur, Chef
Babbo, 110 Waverly Place, Front A, New York NY 10011, USA
**Batalli-Cosmovici, Cristiano** — Astronaut
International Astronomical Union, Via Fosso del Cavaliere 100, 00133 Rome, Italy
**Batbold, Sukhbaataryn** — Prime Minister, Mongolia
Prime Minister's Office, Great Hural, Ulan Bator 12, Mongolia
**Batch, Charles D (Charlie)** — Football Player
1844 Willow Oak Dr, Wexford PA 15090, USA
**Batchelder, Alice M** — Judge
US Court of Appeals, 143 W Liberty St, Medina OH 44256, USA
**Batchelder, Joseph L (Joe)** — Yachtsman
11004 Hard Rock Road, Austin TX 78750, USA
**Batchelor, Joy E** — Animator
Educational Film Center, 5-7 Kean St, London WC2B 4AT, England
**Bate, Jennifer L** — Concert Organist
35 Collingwood Ave, Muswell Hill, London N10 3EH, England
**Bateau, Laurent** — Actor
Voyez Mon Agent, 20 Ave Rapp, 75007 Paris, France
**Batelaan, Kelsey** — Actor
C E S D, 10635 Santa Monica Blvd, #130, Los Angeles CA 90025 USA
**Bateman, Brian** — Golfer
100 Brunswick Ave, Saint Simons Island GA 31522, USA
**Bateman, Jason** — Actor
Aggregate Films, 100 Universal City Plaza, Bungalow 414, Universal City CA 91608, USA
**Bateman, Justine** — Actress
8004 Woodrow Wilson Dr, Los Angeles CA 90046, USA
**Bateman, Marvin F (Marv)** — Football Player
1022 W Smithsonian Way, Apple Valley UT 84737, USA
**Bateman, Robert M** — Artist
PO Box 115 Fulford Harbour, Salt Spring Island BC V8K 2P2, Canada
**Bates, Billy Ray** — Basketball Player
8051 Gibbon St, Daniel Island SC 29492, USA
**Bates, Charles C** — Oceanographer
750 S La Posada Circle, #77, Green Valley AZ 85614, USA
**Bates, David M** — Artist
34 Horatio St, #4B, New York NY 10014, USA
**Bates, Doug** — Journalist
Portland Oregonian, Editorial Dept, 1320 SW Broadway, Portland OR 97201, USA
**Bates, D'Wayne L** — Football Player
1862 Sherman Ave, #1NE, Ponte Vedra Beach FL 32082, USA
**Bates, Jared L (Jerry)** — Army General
L-3 Communications Holdings, SyColeman Division, 600 3rd Ave, New York NY 10016, USA
**Bates, Kathy** — Actress
I C M Partners, 10250 Constellation Blvd, #900, Los Angeles CA 90067 USA
**Bates, Mario D** — Football Player
PO Box 5832, Scottsdale AZ 85261, USA
**Bates, Michael D** — Football Player, Track Athlete
1239 W Keuhne Court, Tucson AZ 85755, USA
**Bates, Patrick (Pat)** — Golfer
215 Ward Circle, #200, Brentwood TN 37027, USA
**Bates, Quentin** — Writer
Ampersand Agency, Ryman's Cottages, Little Tew, Oxfordshire OX7 4JJ, England
**Bates, Richard (Dick)** — Baseball Player
5858 W Cielo Grande, Glendale AZ 85310, USA
**Bates, Shawn** — Ice Hockey Player
35 Bradshaw St, Medford MA 02155, USA
**Bates, Ted D** — Football Player
4036 Paige St, Los Angeles CA 90031, USA
**Bates, Tyler** — Composer
Greenspan Kohan Management, 8760 Sunset Blvd, Los Angeles CA 90069, USA
**Bates, William F (Bill)** — Football Player
1252 Neck Road, Ponte Vedra FL 32082, USA
**Bathe, Frank** — Ice Hockey Player
2 Meadowwood Dr, Scarborough ME 04074, USA
**Bathgate, Andrew J (Andy)** — Ice Hockey Player
43 Brentwood Dr, Brampton ON L6T 1R1, Canada
**Bathory, Zoltan** — Guitarist (Five Finger Death Punch)
10th Street Entertainment, 568 Broadway, #608, New York NY 10012, USA

**Bassett - Bathory**

**Bathurst, D Benjamin** — Navy Admiral, England
British International Helicopters, Redhill Aerodrome, Redhill, Surrey RH1 5JY, England
**Bathurst, Otto** — Director
Casorotto Ramsay, Waverley House, 7-12 Noel St, London W1F 8GQ, England
**Batiashvili, Lisa** — Concert Violinist
Harrison/Parrott, 5-6 Albion Court, London W6 0QT, England
**Batinkoff, Randall** — Actor
B R S / Gage Talent Agency, 5757 Wilshire Blvd, #659, Los Angeles CA 90036 USA
**Batiste, Kimothy E (Kim)** — Baseball Player
16161 Aikens Road, Prairieville LA 70769, USA
**Batiuk, Thomas M (Tom)** — Cartoonist (Crankshaft)
Universal Press Syndicate, 4520 Main St, #700, Kansas City MO 64111 USA
**Batiz Campbell, Enrique** — Conductor
Cerrada Rancho los Colorines 11, Dele Tlalan, Mexico DF 14000, Mexico
**Batmanglij, Rostam** — Multi-Instrumentalist (Vampire Weekend)
L B I Entertainment, 2000 Ave of Stars, Los Angeles CA 90067, USA
**Batmanglij, Zal** — Director
United Talent Agency, U T A Plaza, 9336 Civic Center Dr, Beverly Hills CA 90210 USA
**Bator, Francis M** — Economist
85 Grove St, #2, Wellesley MA 02482, USA
**Batra, Pooja** — Actress, Model
403H Gokul Vihar II, Thakar Complex Kandivli (E), Mumbai MS 400068, India
**Batt, Michael P (Mike)** — Singer, Songwriter
Dramatico Entertainment, PO Box 214, Farnham, Surrey GU10 5XZ, England
**Battaglia, Jon (Bates)** — Ice Hockey Player
832 Graham St, Raleigh NC 27605, USA
**Battaglia, Marco** — Football Player
15832 79th St, Howard Beach NY 11414, USA
**Battaglia, Matt** — Actor
Matt Battaglia Productions, 8033 Sunset Blvd, #3000, Los Angeles CA 90046, USA
**Battelle, Ann** — Moguls Skier
Mogul Logic, 4279 Monroe Dr, #D, Boulder CO 80303, USA
**Batten, Kimberly (Kim)** — Track Athlete
192 Sugar Plum Dr, Tallahassee FL 32312, USA
**Battersby, Alan R** — Chemist
20 Barrow Road, Cambridge CB2 2AS, England
**Battie, D Antonio (Tony)** — Basketball Player
11264 Bridge House Road, Windermere FL 34786, USA
**Battier, Shane C** — Basketball Player
4320 Santa Maria St, Miami FL 33146, USA
**Battiste, P Francois** — Actor
Innovative Artists, 1505 10th St, Santa Monica CA 90401 USA
**Battistelli, Francesca** — Singer, Songwriter
Proper Mgmt, PO Box 150867, Nashville TN 37215, USA
**Battle, Arnaz J** — Football Player
1091 Broadmoore Lane, Prosper TX 75078, USA
**Battle, Hinton** — Dancer, Actor
McDonald Selznick Assoc, 953 Cole Ave, Los Angeles CA 90038, USA
**Battle, John S** — Basketball Player
125 Glen Beigh Run, Tyrone GA 30290, USA
**Battle, Kathleen D** — Opera Singer
Columbia Artists Mgmt Inc, 5 Columbus Circle, 1790 Broadway, #1600, New York NY 10019 USA
**Battle, Texas** — Actor
Innovative Artists, 1505 10th St, Santa Monica CA 90401 USA
**Battles, Ainsley T** — Football Player
493 Villa Dr SW, Lilburn GA 30047, USA
**Batton, Dave** — Basketball Player
6506 Bayonne Dr, Spring TX 77389, USA
**Batts, Lloyd** — Basketball Player
500 S Dante Ave, Glenwood IL 60425, USA
**Batum, Nicolas** — Basketball Player
Portland Trail Blazers, Rose Garden, 1 N Center Court St, Portland OR 97227 USA
**Baturin, Yuri M** — Cosmonaut
Cosmonaut Training Center, Star City, 141160 Zvezdny Gorodok, Moscow Oblast, Russia
**Baty, Gregory J (Greg)** — Football Player
4 King St, Redwood City CA 94062, USA
**Bauchau, Patrick** — Actor
David Shapira Assoc, 193 N Robertson Blvd, Beverly Hills CA 90211 USA
**Baudo, Serge** — Conductor
Les Hautes du Ferra, Chemin Charre, 13600 Ceyreste, France
**Baudry, Patrick** — Spatinaut, France
305 Ave Mairie, 31600 Eaunas, France
**Bauer, Chris** — Actor
Framework Entertainment, 9057 Nemo St, #C, West Hollywood CA 90069 USA
**Bauer, Erwin A** — Photographer
8880 SE 19th Avenue Road, Ocala FL 34480, USA
**Bauer, Hans-Uwe** — Actor
Fitz & Skoglund Agents, Liniestr 130, 10115 Berlin, Germany
**Bauer, Henry J (Hank)** — Football Player
11150 Alejo Place, San Diego CA 92124, USA
**Bauer, Jaime Lyn** — Actress
Gar Lester Agency, 4130 Cahuenga Blvd, #108, Universal City CA 91602, USA
**Bauer, Joy** — Writer
W M E Entertainment, 1325 Ave of Americas, New York NY 10019 USA
**Bauer, Kristin** — Actress
L I N K Entertainment, 11872 La Grange Ave, Los Angeles CA 90025 USA
**Bauer, Lukas** — Cross Country Skier
Muller Productions, Na Valech 45/32, 16000 Prague 6, Czech Republic
**Bauer, Michelle** — Actress, Model
A I Productions, 6260 Laurel Canyon Blvd, #201, North Hollywood CA 91606, USA
**Bauer, Peggy** — Photographer
8880 SE 19th Avenue Road, Ocala FL 34480, USA
**Bauer, Peter** — Bassist, Organist (Walkmen)
Mick Mgmt, 35 Washington St, Brooklyn NY 11201 USA
**Bauer, Richard E (Rick)** — Baseball Player
6805 Easthaven Way, Citrus Heights CA 95621, USA

# B

**Bauer, Steven** — Actor
Global Artists Agency, 6253 Hollywood Blvd, #508, Los Angeles CA 90028 USA
**Bauer, Viola** — Cross Country Skier
Ski Verband, Hubertusstr 1, 82152 Planegg, Germany
**Bauer, William J** — Judge
213 S Grace Ave, Elmhurst IL 60126, USA
**Baugh, Laura** — Golfer
3024 Cardinal Dr, Augusta GA 30909, USA
**Baugh, Thomas A (Tom)** — Football Player, Coach
14716 S Bynum Road, Lone Jack MO 64070, USA
**Baughan, Maxie C, Jr** — Football Player, Coach
3355 Lawndale Road, Reisterstown MD 21136, USA
**Baughman, J Ross** — Photojournalist
31101 Harbour Vista Circle, Saint Augustine FL 32080, USA
**Baughman, Ray H** — Nanotechnologist
5428 Willow Road, Dallas TX 75252, USA
**Baulcombe, David C** — Geneticist, Plant Scientist
Cambridge University, Plant Institute, Cambridge CB2 1TN, England
**Baulieu, Etienne-Emile** — Biochemist, Inventor (Abortion Pill)
Institut de France, 23 Quai de Conti, 75006 Paris, France
**Baum, Bob** — Ice Hockey Player
465 Bayle St W, Pickering ON L1W 3P6, Canada
**Baum, John (Johnny)** — Basketball Player
8216 Fenton Road, Glenside PA 19038, USA
**Baum, William W Cardinal** — Religious Leader
Apostolic Penitentiary, Palazzo della Cancelleria, 00186 Rome, Italy
**Bauman, Jon (Bowzer)** — Singer, Pianist (Sha Na Na)
David Belenzon Mgmt, PO Box 5000, PMB 67, Rancho Santa Fe CA 92067, USA
**Baumann, Alex** — Bobsled Athlete
Schnadt, 9063 Stein/AR, Switzerland
**Baumann, Dieter** — Track Athlete
Baumann Promotion, Biesingerstr 18, 72070 Tubingen, Germany
**Baumann, Frank M** — Baseball Player
7712 Sunray Lane, Saint Louis MO 63123, USA
**Baumann, Herbert K W** — Composer
Franziskaserstr 16, #1419, 81669 Munich, Germany
**Baumann, Kenny** — Actor
A K A Talent, 6310 San Vicente Blvd, #200, Los Angeles CA 90048 USA
**Baumbach, Noah** — Director, Writer
United Talent Agency, U T A Plaza, 9336 Civic Center Dr, Beverly Hills CA 90210 USA
**Baumbauer, Frank** — Director
Deutsches Schauspielhaus, Kirchenallee 39, 20099 Hamburg, Germany
**Baumgarten, Ross** — Baseball Player
399 Sunset Lane, Glencoe IL 60022, USA
**Baumgartner, Brian** — Actor
3-Bees Entertainment, 4217 Verdugo View Dr, Los Angeles CA 90065, USA
**Baumgartner, Bruce** — Freestyle Wrestler
12765 Forrest Dr, Edinboro PA 16412, USA
**Baumgartner, Felix** — Sky Diver
Red Bull Stratos Project, International Air Center, 1 Jerry Smith Circle, Roswell NM 88202, USA
**Baumgartner, Ken** — Ice Hockey Player
39 Court St, #1, Newton MA 02458, USA
**Baumgartner, Nolan** — Ice Hockey Player
Vancouver Canucks, 800 Griffiths Way, Vancouver BC V6B 6G1, Canada
**Baumgartner, Steven J (Steve)** — Football Player
144 Brookside Dr, Mandeville LA 70471, USA
**Baumhower, Robert G (Bob)** — Football Player
21201 Ayrshire Lane, Fairhope AL 36532, USA
**Baumler, Hans-Jurgen** — Figure Skater
Magt Rehling, Kirchenstr 17C, 82110 Germering, Germany
**Baumol, William J** — Economist
455 N End Ave, #1204, New York NY 10282, USA
**Baun, Robert N (Bob)** — Ice Hockey Player
35 Pittman Crescent, Ajax ON L1S 3G4, Canada
**Bauta, Eduardo G (Ed)** — Baseball Player
3786 Long Grove Lane, Port Orange FL 32129, USA
**Bautista, Daniel B (Danny)** — Baseball Player
901 E Van Buren St, #1063, Phoenix AZ 85006, USA
**Bautista, David M, Jr** — Actor, Pro Wrestler
Gersh Agency, 9465 Wilshire Blvd, #600, Beverly Hills CA 90212 USA
**Bautista, Jose A** — Baseball Player
100 Shockoe Slip, #400, Richmond VA 23219, USA
**Bautista, Jose J** — Baseball Player
15621 SW 16th Court, Pembroke Pines FL 33027, USA
**Bavaro, Mark** — Football Player
17 Long Hill, Boxford MA 01921, USA
**Bavouzet, Jean-Efflam** — Concert Pianist
Chandos Records, 1 Commerce Park, Commerce Way, Colchester, Essex CO2 8HX, England
**Bawel, Edward R (Bibbles)** — Football Player
1169 2nd Ave, Jasper IN 47546, USA
**Bawoyeu, Jean Alingue** — Prime Minister, Chad
Union for Democratic Republic, BP 1122, N'Djamena, Chad
**Bax, Adriaan (Ad)** — Biophysicist
National Institutes of Health, Biophysics Dept, 5 Memorial Dr, Building 5, Bethesda MD 20892, USA
**Bax, Kylie** — Model, Actress
Storm Model Agency, 5 Jubilee Place, Chelsea, London SW3 3TD, England
**Baxendale, Helen** — Actress
Yakety Yak, 8 Bloomsbury Square, London WC1A 2UA, England
**Baxter, Frederick D (Fred)** — Football Player
PO Box 14, Brundidge AL 36010, USA
**Baxter, Gary W** — Football Player
13749 Choctaw Dr, Tyler TX 75709, USA
**Baxter, Glen** — Artist, Cartoonist
Chris Beetle Gallery, 10 Ryder St, London SW1Y 6QB, England
**Baxter, James** — Animator
James Baxter Animation, 32 Mills Place, Pasadena CA 91105, USA

Bauer - Baxter

**Baxter, Jeff (Skunk)** — Guitarist (Doobie Brothers, Steely Dan)
Howard Rose, 9460 Wilshire Blvd, #310, Beverly Hills CA 90212, USA
**Baxter, Jennifer** — Actress
TalentWorks, 3500 W Olive Ave, #1400, Burbank CA 91505 USA
**Baxter, Kirk** — Editor
Motion Pictures Editors Guild, 7715 Sunset Blvd, #200, Los Angeles CA 90046, USA
**Baxter, Meredith** — Actress
Marshak/Zachary/Mills, 8840 Wilshire Blvd, Beverly Hills, CA 90211 USA
**Baxter, Paul** — Ice Hockey Player
1610 Saint John St, Wichita Falls TX 76302, USA
**Baxter, William E (Billy), Jr** — Poker Player
CardPlayer Media, 6940 Obannon Drive, Las Vegas NV 89117, USA
**Baxter-Johnson, Patricia** — Golfer
111 Bryn Mawr Dr, Lake Worth FL 33460, USA
**Bay, Jason R** — Baseball Player
5811 106th Ave NE, Kirkland WA 98033, USA
**Bay, Michael** — Director
W M E Entertainment, 9601 Wilshire Blvd, #300, Beverly Hills CA 90210 USA
**Bay, Susan** — Actress
Gersh Agency, 9465 Wilshire Blvd, #600, Beverly Hills CA 90212 USA
**Baye, Nathalie** — Actress
Artmedia, 20 Ave Rapp, 75007 Paris, France
**Bayh, Birch E, Jr** — Senator, IN
PO Box 3353, Easton MD 21601, USA
**Bayi, Filbert** — Track Athlete
PO Box 60240, Morogoro Road, Dar es Salaam, Tanzania
**Bayl, Benjamin** — Conductor
Harrison/Parrott, 5-6 Albion Court, London W6 0QT, England
**Bayldon, Geoffrey** — Actor
Joy Jameson, 219 Plaza, 535 Kings Road, London SW10 0SZ, England
**Bayle, Jean-Michel** — Motorcycle Racing Rider
General Delivery, 04100 Manosque, Alpes-de-Haute-Provence, France
**Bayless, Jerryd** — Basketball Player
Boston Celtics, 226 Causeway St, #4, Boston MA 02114 USA
**Bayless, Martin A** — Football Player
834 Calle Lagasca, Chula Vista CA 91910, USA
**Bayley, Clive** — Opera Singer
I M G Artists, Hogarth Business Park, Chiswick, London W4 2TH, England
**Baylor, Don E** — Baseball Player, Manager
1204 Challenger, Lakeway TX 78734, USA
**Baylor, Elgin G** — Basketball Player, Executive
2480 Briarcrest Road, Beverly Hills CA 90210, USA
**Baylor, Helen** — Singer
3037 Hartley Cove Ave, North Las Vegas NV 89081, USA
**Baylor, John M** — Football Player
211 Oak St, Hattiesburg MS 39401, USA
**Baynham, G Craig** — Football Player
1 7th St, #1102, Augusta GA 30901, USA
**Bayo, Maria** — Opera Singer
Columbia Artists Mgmt Inc, 165 W 57th St, New York NY 10019, USA
**Bayou, Bradley** — Fashion Designer
Film Fashion, 8687 Melrose Center, #G684, Los Angeles CA 90069, USA
**Bayrakdarian, Isabel** — Opera Singer
I M G Artists, Hogarth Business Park, Chiswick, London W4 2TH, England
**Bays, Carter** — Producer, Writer
United Talent Agency, U T A Plaza, 9336 Civic Center Dr, Beverly Hills CA 90210 USA
**Baz, Farouk El-** — Geologist
213 Silver Hill Road, Concord MA 01742, USA
**Baze, Russell A** — Thoroughbred Racing Jockey
22 Somerset Place, Woodside CA 94062, USA
**Bazell, Josh** — Writer
United Talent Agency, U T A Plaza, 9336 Civic Center Dr, Beverly Hills CA 90210 USA
**Bazell, Robert J** — Commentator
NBC-TV, News Dept, 4001 Nebraska Ave NW, Washington DC 20016 USA
**Bazelli, Bojan** — Cinematographer
Dattner Dispoto, 10635 Santa Monica Blvd, #165, Los Angeles CA 90025, USA
**Bazer, Fuller W** — Animal Scientist
8600 Creekview Court, College Station TX 77845, USA
**Bazzaz, Fakhri A** — Plant Biologist
Harvard University, Organismic & Evolutionary Biology Dept, Cambridge MA 02138, USA
**Beach, Adam** — Actor
A P A Talent & Literary Agency, 405 S Beverly Dr, #300, Beverly Hills CA 90212 USA
**Beach, Bill** — Bowler
3715 Lee Run Road, Hermitage PA 16148, USA
**Beach, Gary** — Actor, Singer
B R S / Gage Talent Agency, 5757 Wilshire Blvd, #659, Los Angeles CA 90036 USA
**Beach, Gary** — Actor, Singer
122 Andalusia Way, Palm Beach Gardens FL 33418, USA
**Beach, Michael** — Actor
More/Medavoy Mgmt, 10203 Santa Monica Blvd, #400, Los Angeles CA 90067 USA
**Beach, Patrick J (Pat)** — Football Player
2523 NW Beach Road, Oak Harbor WA 98277, USA
**Beach, Sanjay R** — Football Player
2989 Riviera Lane, Westlake OH 44145, USA
**Beacham, Stephanie** — Actress
United Agents, 12-26 Lexington St, London W1F 0LE, England
**Beachley, Layne** — Surfer
Aim for Stars Foundation, PO Box H67, Sydney NSW 1213, Australia
**Beadle, Michelle D** — Sportscaster
NBC-TV, Sports Dept, 30 Rockefeller Plaza, #270E, New York NY 10112 USA
**Beagle, Ronald G (Ron)** — Football Player
3830 San Ysidro Way, Sacramento CA 95864, USA
**Beah, Ishmael** — Writer
Farrar Straus Giroux, 18 W 18th St, #700, New York NY 10011 USA
**Beahan, Kate** — Actress
Management 360, 9111 Wilshire Blvd, Beverly Hills CA 90210 USA

# B

**Beal, Bradley** — Basketball Player
Washington Wizards, M C I Centre, 601 F St NW, Washington DC 20004 USA
**Beal, Jeff** — Composer
First Artists Mgmt, 4764 Park Granada, #210, Calabasas CA 91302 USA
**Beale, Simon Russell** — Actor
Richard Stone Partnership, De Walden Court, 85 New Cavendish St, London W1W 6XD, England
**Beals, Jennifer** — Actress
A P A Talent & Literary Agency, 405 S Beverly Dr, #300, Beverly Hills CA 90212 USA
**Beam, C Arlen** — Judge
US Court of Appeals, 100 Centennial Mall N, Lincoln NE 68508, USA
**Beamer, Frank** — Football Coach
Virginia Polytechnic Institute, Athletic Dept, Blacksburg VA 24061, USA
**Beamer, Lisa** — Writer
9 Cubberly Court, Cranbury NJ 08512, USA
**Beamish, Lindsay** — Actress, Dancer
Semler Entertainment, 13636 Ventura Blvd, #510, Sherman Oaks CA 91423, USA
**Beamon, Autry, Jr** — Football Player
2664 Lakeview Dr, Shakopee MN 55379, USA
**Beamon, Robert (Bob)** — Track Athlete
20533 Biscayne Blvd, #113, Miami FL 33180, USA
**Bean, Alan L** — Astronaut
9173 Briar Forest Dr, Houston TX 77024, USA
**Bean, Andy** — Golfer
2912 Grasslands Dr, Lakeland FL 33803, USA
**Bean, Dawn Pawson** — Synchronized Swimmer
11902 Red Hill Ave, Santa Ana CA 92705, USA
**Bean, Henry** — Director, Writer
Creative Artists Agency, 2000 Ave of Stars, #100, Los Angeles CA 90067 USA
**Bean, Joe** — Soccer Coach
Wheaton College, Athletic Dept, Wheaton IL 60187, USA
**Bean, Noah** — Actor
C E S D, 257 Park Ave S, #950, New York NY 10010 USA
**Bean, Orson** — Actor, Comedian
Stone Manners Salners, 6100 Wilshire Blvd, #1500, Los Angeles CA 90035 USA
**Bean, Sean** — Actor
Independent Talent Group, 40 Whitfield St, London W1T 2RH, England
**Bean, William D (Billy)** — Baseball Player, Writer
W M E Entertainment, 9601 Wilshire Blvd, #300, Beverly Hills CA 90210 USA
**Beane, William L (Billy), Jr** — Baseball Player
33 Brightwood Lane E, Danville CA 94506, USA
**Bear, Gregory D (Greg)** — Writer
506 Lakeview Road, Lynnwood WA 98087, USA
**Bearak, Barry** — Journalist
New York Times, Editorial Dept, 229 W 43rd St, New York NY 10036 USA
**Beard, Alana M** — Basketball Player
Washington Mystics, Verizon Center, 401 9th St NW, #750, Washington DC 20004 USA
**Beard, Albert (Butch)** — Basketball Player, Coach
3834 Berleigh Hill Court, Burtonsville MD 20866, USA
**Beard, Amanda** — Swimmer, Model
212 Fir Dr NW, Gig Harbor WA 98335, USA
**Beard, C David (Dave)** — Baseball Player
5325 Derby Chase Court, Alpharetta GA 30005, USA
**Beard, Edward L (Ed)** — Football Player
4110 2nd St, Chesapeake VA 23324, USA
**Beard, Frank** — Golfer
74066 De Anza Way, Palm Desert CA 92260, USA
**Beard, Frank** — Drummer (ZZ Top)
Sanctuary Mgmt, 15301 Ventura Blvd, Building B, Sherman Oaks CA 91403, USA
**Beard, Matthew** — Actor
Independent Talent Group, 40 Whitfield St, London W1T 2RH, England
**Beard, Peter H** — Photographer
Art + Commerce, 531 W 25th St, New York NY 10001, USA
**Bearse, Amanda** — Actress, Director, Producer
910 N 39th St, Seattle WA 98103, USA
**Beart, Emmanuelle** — Actress
Agence Artiste Adequat, 108 Rue Reaumur, 75002 Paris, France
**Beasley, Aaron B** — Football Player
1635 Braid Hills Dr, Pasadena MD 21122, USA
**Beasley, Allyce** — Actress
Henderson/Hogan, 850 7th Ave, #1003, New York NY 10019 USA
**Beasley, Bruce M** — Sculptor
322 Lewis St, San Francisco CA 94607, USA
**Beasley, Charles P (Charlie)** — Basketball Player
6308 Winton St, Dallas TX 75214, USA
**Beasley, Frederick J (Fred)** — Football Player
PO Box 210931, Montgomery AL 36121, USA
**Beasley, Jere L** — Attorney; Governor, AL
Beasley Allen Crow, 218 Commerce St, Montgomery AL 36104, USA
**Beasley, John** — Actor
Bauman Redanty Shaul Agency, 5757 Wilshire Blvd, #473, Los Angeles CA 90036, USA
**Beasley, John** — Composer, Musician
Donofrio Productions, 607 W Shore Road, Brigantine NJ 08203, USA
**Beasley, John** — Football Player
W3848 Turtle Patch Road, Pine River WI 54965, USA
**Beasley, John M** — Basketball Player
113 Oak Acres Dr W, Malakoff TX 75148, USA
**Beasley, Michael** — Actor
Open Range Mgmt, 2910 Fairway Drive, Baton Rouge LA 70809, USA
**Beasley, Thomas L (Tom)** — Football Player
RR 1 Box 185, Hiltons VA 24258, USA
**Beasley, Walter** — Jazz Saxophonist
Berklee College of Music, 1140 Boylston St, Boston MA 02215, USA
**Beason, Jonathan (Jon)** — Football Player
Carolina Panthers, Ericsson Stadium, 800 S Mint St, Charlotte NC 28202 USA
**Beathard, Peter F (Pete)** — Football Player
3770 Drake St, Houston TX 77005, USA

**Beaton, Frank** — Ice Hockey Player
3327 Chapel Hills Parkway, Fultondale AL 35068, USA
**Beatrix** — Queen Mother, Netherlands
Soestdijk Palace, Amsterdamsestraatweg 1, 2513 Baarn AA, Netherlands
**Beatrix, Jean-Guillaume** — Biathlete
Federation de Ski Biathlon, 50 Rue des Marquisats, 74011 Annecy, France
**Beatriz Barros, Ana** — Model
Elite Model Mgmt, 404 Park Ave S, #900, New York NY 10016 USA
**Beattie, Ann** — Writer
Janklow & Nesbit Assoc, 445 Park Ave, #1300, New York NY 10022 USA
**Beattie, Bob** — Alpine Skier
312 Aabc, #I, Aspen CO 81611, USA
**Beattie, Bruce** — Editorial Cartoonist
Daytona Beach News-Journal, Editorial Dept, 901 6th St, Daytona Beach FL 32117, USA
**Beattie, James L (Jim)** — Baseball Player
PO Box 231, Quechee VT 05059, USA
**Beattie, Joseph** — Actor
Artists Partnership, 101 Finsbury Pavement, London EC2A 1RS, England
**Beattie, Michael** — Actor
W M E Entertainment, 9601 Wilshire Blvd, #300, Beverly Hills CA 90210 USA
**Beatty, James T (Jim)** — Track Athlete
6525 Morrison Blvd, Charlotte NC 28211, USA
**Beatty, John Lee** — Stage Designer
Gersh Agency, 9465 Wilshire Blvd, #600, Beverly Hills CA 90212 USA
**Beatty, Linda** — Model
Playboy Promotions, 9346 Civic Center Dr, #200, Beverly Hills CA 90210 USA
**Beatty, Ned** — Actor
2706 N Beachwood Dr, Los Angeles CA 90068, USA
**Beatty, Warren** — Director, Producer, Actor
13671 Mulholland Dr, Beverly Hills CA 90210, USA
**Beaucham, Danny** — Model
Select Model Mgmt, 17 Ferdinand St, London NW1 8EU, England
**Beauchamp, Alfred (Al)** — Football Player
533 Pinegate Road, Peachtree City GA 30269, USA
**Beauchamp, Joseph S (Joe)** — Football Player
8896 Highwood Dr, #A, San Diego CA 92119, USA
**Beaudin, Norman J A (Norm)** — Ice Hockey Player
9595 E Thunderbird Road, #1103, Scottsdale AZ 85260, USA
**Beaudoin, Douglas L (Doug)** — Football Player
15143 Springview St, Tampa FL 33624, USA
**Beaudoin, Michelle** — Actress
Independent Artists, 9601 Wilshire Blvd, #750, Beverly Hills CA 90210 USA
**Beaufoy, Simon** — Writer
Knight Hall Agency, 7 Mallow St, London EC1Y 8RQ, England
**Beaumon, Sterling** — Actor
A P A Talent & Literary Agency, 405 S Beverly Dr, #300, Beverly Hills CA 90212 USA
**Beaumont, Jimmy** — Singer (Skyliners), Songwriter
Creative Entertainment Assoc, 1950 Old Cuthbert Road, #J, Cherry Hill NJ 08034 USA
**Beaupre, Don** — Ice Hockey Player
5020 Scriver Road, Minneapolis MN 55436, USA
**Beauregard, Robin** — Water Polo Player
467 Midvale Ave, Los Angeles CA 90024, USA
**Beauregard, Stephane** — Ice Hockey Player
175 Rue Des Plaines, Cowansville QC J2K 3T8, Canada
**Beauvais, Garcelle** — Model, Actress
S D B Partners, 315 S Beverly Dr, #411, Beverly Hills CA 90067 USA
**Beauvois, Xavier** — Actor, Writer, Director
Artmedia, 20 Ave Rapp, 75007 Paris, France
**Beavan, Jenny** — Costume Designer
United Talent Agency, U T A Plaza, 9336 Civic Center Dr, Beverly Hills CA 90210 USA
**Beaver, James N (Jim)** — Actor
House of Representatives, 1434 6th St, #1, Santa Monica CA 90401 USA
**Beaver, Joe** — Rodeo Rider
PO Box 1595, Huntsville TN 37756, USA
**Beaver, Terry L** — Actor
Paradigm Agency, 360 Park Ave S, #1600, New York NY 10010 USA
**Beban, Gary J** — Football Player
20 Timber Lane, Northbrook IL 60062, USA
**Bebington, Anna** — Rowing Athlete
Leander Club, Henly on Thames, Leander RG9 2LP, England
**Bebout, Nick** — Football Player
1606 Major Ave, Riverton WY 82501, USA
**Becaert, Sylvie** — Biathlete
F F S Biathlon, 50 Rue des Marquisats, 74011 Annecy, France
**Bechara Boutros al-Rai, Mar** — Religious Leader
Patriarchy of Maronite Catholic Church, Bkerke, Lebanon
**Bechdel, Alison** — Cartoonist, Writer
Houghton Mifflin Harcourt, 215 Park Ave S, #1200, New York NY 10003 USA
**Becherer, Hans W** — Businessman
432 Columbine St, Denver CO 80206, USA
**Becht, Anthony** — Football Player
4657 Artesian Road, Land O Lakes FL 34638, USA
**Bechtel, Riley P** — Businessman
Bechtel Group, 50 Beale St, San Francisco CA 94105, USA
**Bechtel, Stephen D, Jr** — Businessman
Bechtel Group, 50 Beale St, San Francisco CA 94105, USA
**Bechtol, T Bubba** — Actor, Comedian
The Consortium, 49 Music Square W, #210, Nashville TN 37203, USA
**Beck** — Singer, Guitarist, Songwriter
S A M, 722 Seward St, Los Angeles CA 90038, USA
**Beck, A Byron** — Basketball Player
1909 S Williams St, Kennewick WA 99338, USA
**Beck, Aaron T** — Psychiatrist
3535 Market St, #200, Philadelphia PA 19104, USA
**Beck, Barry** — Ice Hockey Player
Hong Kong Academy of Hockey, 183 Queens Road E, #64/F, Wanchai, Hong Kong, China

# B

**Beck, Charles (Charlie)** — Law Enforcement Official
Los Angeles Police Dept, 150 S Los Angeles St, Los Angeles CA 90012, USA
**Beck, Charles H (Chip)** — Golfer
11 Pembroke Dr, Lake Forest IL 60045, USA
**Beck, Christophe** — Composer
Kraft-Engel Mgmt, 15233 Ventura Blvd, #200, Sherman Oaks CA 91403 USA
**Beck, Ernest J (Ernie)** — Basketball Player
1523 Brierwood Road, Havertown PA 19083, USA
**Beck, Glenn** — Commentator
2208 Vaquero Estates Blvd, Westlake TX 76262, USA
**Beck, Jeff** — Singer, Guitarist (Yardbirds)
Coda Agency, 229 Shoreditch High St, London E1 6PJ, England
**Beck, John C** — Geriatrics Physician
1562 Casale Road, Pacific Palisades CA 90272, USA
**Beck, Maria** — Actress
Coast to Coast Talent, 3350 Barham Blvd, Los Angeles CA 90068 USA
**Beck, Martin J** — Industrial Designer
Big Red Roster, 121 Thurman Ave, Columbus OH 43206, USA
**Beck, Martina (Molly) Glagow** — Biathlete
Rehbergstr 40, 82481 Mittenwald, Germany
**Beck, Noelle** — Actress
Gersh Agency, 41 Madison Ave, #3301, New York NY 10010 USA
**Beck, Robin** — Singer
Cavaricci & White, 156 W 56th St, #1803, New York NY 10019, USA
**Beckel, Graham** — Actor, Director
Don Buchwald Talent Agency, 6500 Wilshire Blvd, #2200, Los Angeles CA 90048 USA
**Beckel, Robert D** — Air Force General
New Mexico Military Institute, Superintendent's Office, Roswell NM 88201, USA
**Beckenbauer, Franz** — Soccer Player, Coach
Posrfach 700220, 81302 Munich, Germany
**Becker, Arthur C (Art)** — Basketball Player
1879 E Bentrup Dr, Tempe AZ 85283, USA
**Becker, Boris** — Tennis Player
Ruessenstr 6, 6341 Baar, Switzerland
**Becker, Brooklyn** — Model, Actress
Gersh Agency, 9465 Wilshire Blvd, #600, Beverly Hills CA 90212 USA
**Becker, Harold** — Director
I C M Partners, 10250 Constellation Blvd, #900, Los Angeles CA 90067 USA
**Becker, Jo** — Journalist
Washington Post, Editorial Dept, 1150 15th St NW, Washington DC 20071 USA
**Becker, Karl J Cardinal** — Religious Leader
San Giuliano Martire, Via Cassia 1036, 00189 Rome Lazio, Italy
**Becker, Kuno** — Actor
A P A Talent & Literary Agency, 405 S Beverly Dr, #300, Beverly Hills CA 90212 USA
**Becker, Kurt F** — Football Player
49W412 Scott Road, Big Rock IL 60511, USA
**Becker, Quinn H** — Army General, Surgeon
2111 Peninsula Dr, San Antonio TX 78239, USA
**Becker, Richard G (Rich)** — Baseball Player
210 Mary Senica Court, LaSalle IL 61301, USA
**Becker, Richard S** — Korean War Air Force Hero
269 Woodlake Wynde, Oldsmar FL 34677, USA
**Becker, Robert J** — Allergist
2200 S Ocean Lane, #1905, Fort Lauderdale FL 33316, USA
**Becker, Walt W** — Director
Walt Becker Productions, 1680 Vine St, #1101, Los Angeles CA 90028, USA
**Becker, Walter** — Bassist, Guitarist (Steely Dan)
Front Line Mgmt, 1100 Glendon Ave, #2000, Los Angeles CA 90024 USA
**Beckert, Glenn A** — Baseball Player
1953 Arkansas Ave, Englewood FL 34224, USA
**Beckett, Bob** — Ice Hockey Player
38 Fonthill Blvd, Markham ON L3R 1V7, Canada
**Beckett, Joshua P (Josh)** — Baseball Player
1 Avery St, #20B, Boston MA 02111, USA
**Beckett, Margaret M** — Government Official, England
Foreign Ministry, 11 Downing St, London SW1A 2AA, England
**Beckett, Rogers** — Football Player
635 Gaelic Court, Apopka FL 32712, USA
**Beckett, Sister Wendy** — Art Critic
BBC TV Center, Wood Lane, London W12 7R3, England
**Beckett, William E, Jr** — Singer (Academy Is), Songwriter
Crush Music Media Mgmt, 60-62 E 11th St, #700, New York NY 10003, USA
**Beckford, Roxanne** — Actress
Abrams Artists, 9200 W Sunset Blvd, #1125, West Hollywood CA 90069 USA
**Beckford, Tyson** — Model, Actor
I C M Models, 2 Henrietta St, Covent Garden, London WC2E 8PS, England
**Beckham, Brice** — Actor, Producer, Writer
3334 Faust Ave, Long Beach CA 90808, USA
**Beckham, David R J** — Soccer Player
Creative Artists Agency, 2000 Ave of Stars, #100, Los Angeles CA 90067 USA
**Beckham, Odell, Jr** — Football Player
New York Giants, Meadowlands Stadium, 102 Route 120, East Rutherford NJ 07073 USA
**Beckinsale, Kate** — Actress
United Talent Agency, U T A Plaza, 9336 Civic Center Dr, Beverly Hills CA 90210 USA
**Becklean, William** — Rowing Athlete
30 Cambridgepark Dr, #445, Cambridge MA 02140, USA
**Beckless, Ian H** — Football Player
4915 Andros Dr, Tampa FL 33629, USA
**Beckley, Gerald L (Gerry)** — Singer, Guitarist (America), Songwriter
Morey Mgmt, 1100 Glendon Ave, #1100, Los Angeles CA 90024, USA
**Beckman, Cameron** — Golfer
23303 Wilderness Cove, San Antonio TX 78261, USA
**Beckman, Edwin J (Ed)** — Football Player
4295 18th St NE, Naples FL 34120, USA
**Beckman, Julie** — Architect
4820 Holston Heights Lane, Knoxville TN 37914, USA

**Beck - Beckman**

**Beckmann, M Patricia** — Chemist
Homestead Clinical Corp, 235 E 42nd St, Seattle WA 98102, USA
**Beckwith, T Joseph (Joe)** — Baseball Player
859 Annabrook Dr, Auburn AL 36830, USA
**Becquer, Julio V** — Baseball Player
2461 Kyle Ave N, Minneapolis MN 55422, USA
**Bedard, Emil R (Buck)** — Marine Corps General
Intellicheck Mobilisa Inc, 191 Otto St, Port Townsend WA 98368, USA
**Bedard, Eric** — Speed Skater
Speed Skating Canada, 2781 Lancaster Road, #402, Ottawa ON K1B 1A7, Canada
**Bedard, Erik J** — Baseball Player
Houston Astros, Minute Maid Park, 501 Crawford St, Houston TX 77002 USA
**Bedard, Irene** — Actress
Don Buchwald Talent Agency, 6500 Wilshire Blvd, #2200, Los Angeles CA 90048 USA
**Bedard, Myriam** — Biathlete
3329 Pinecourt, Neufchatel QC G2B 2E4, Canada
**Beddow, Cascy** — Actor
Aqua Talent Agency, 9000 Sunset Blvd, #700, Los Angeles CA 90069, USA
**Bedelia, Bonnie** — Actress
Innovative Artists, 1505 10th St, Santa Monica CA 90401 USA
**Bedell, Brad** — Football Player
545 N Altura Road, Arcadia CA 91007, USA
**Bedford, Brian** — Actor
Paradigm Agency, 360 N Crescent Dr, North Building, Beverly Hills CA 90210 USA
**Bedford, Mark (Bedders)** — Bassist (Madness)
I T F, Ariel House, 74A Charlotte St, London W1T 4QJ, England
**Bedford, Martyn** — Writer
Bloomsbury Publishing, 50 Bedford Square, London WC1B 3DP, England
**Bedford, Steuart J R** — Conductor
76 Cromwell Ave, London N6 5HQ, England
**Bedi, Bisban Singh** — Cricketer
Ispat Bhawan, Lodhi Road, New Delhi 110 003, India
**Bedi, Kabir** — Actor
9 J V P D 802, 10th NS Road, JUHU J V PD, Mumbai, Maharashtra 400049, India
**Bedia, Jose** — Artist, Sculptor
George Adams Gallery, 41 W 57th St, #700, New York NY 10019, USA
**Bedingfield, Daniel** — Singer, Songwriter
Primary Talent International, 10-11 Jockey's Fields, London WC1R 4BN, England
**Bedingfield, Natasha** — Singer, Songwriter
I/D Public Relations, 150 W 30th St, #1900, New York NY 10001, USA
**Bednarik, Charles P (Chuck)** — Football Player
6379 Winding Road, Coopersburg PA 18036, USA
**Bednarski, John** — Ice Hockey Player
22917 Forest Edge Court, Bonita Springs FL 34135, USA
**Bednob, Gerry** — Actor, Producer
Amsel Eisenstadt Frazier, 5055 Wilshire Blvd, #865, Los Angeles CA 90036 USA
**Bednorz, J Georg** — Nobel Physics Laureate
I B M Research Laboratory, Saumerstr 4, 8803 Ruschlikon, Switzerland
**Bedows, Elliott** — Oncologist
University of Nebraska Medical Center, Eppley Cancer Center, Omaha NE 68198, USA
**Bedrosian, Stephen W (Steve)** — Baseball Player
3335 Gordon Road, Senoia GA 30276, USA
**Bee, Samantha** — Actress
Parent Management, 530 Queen St, #E, Toronto, ON M5A 1V2, Canada
**Beebe, Dion** — Cinematographer
I C M Partners, 10250 Constellation Blvd, #900, Los Angeles CA 90067 USA
**Beebe, Don L** — Football Player
1246 Verona Ridge Dr, Aurora IL 60506, USA
**Beebe, Reta** — Astronomer
New Mexico State University, Astronomy Dept, Las Cruces NM 88003, USA
**Beeby, Thomas H** — Architect
Hammond Beeby Babka, 440 N Wells St, #630, Chicago IL 60654, USA
**Beede, Frank, III** — Football Player
1645 Somerset Place, Antioch CA 94509, USA
**Beedie, Ashley** — DJ Musician (X-Press 2)
International Talent Booking, Ariel House, 74A Charlotte St, #100 London W1T 4QJ, England
**Beeli, Binia** — Curling Athlete
Curling Association, PO Box 606, 3000 Bern, Switzerland
**Beem, Rich** — Golfer
104 Bella Cima Dr, Austin TX 78734, USA
**Been, Robert Levon** — Bassist (Black Rebel Motorcycle Club)
Paradigm Agency, 360 Park Ave, #1600, New York NY 10022 USA
**Beene, Frederick R (Fred)** — Baseball Player
PO Box 143, Oakhurst TX 77359, USA
**Beenie Man** — Singer
Agency Group Ltd, 142 W 57th St, #600, New York NY 10019 USA
**Beer, Donald** — Rowing Athlete
2 Governors Lane, Princeton NJ 08540, USA
**Beerbaum, Ludger** — Equestrian
Ludger Beerbaum Stables, Prozessionsweg 51B, 48477 Riesenbeck, Germany
**Beering, Steven C** — Educator
10487 Windemere, Carmel IN 46032, USA
**Beers, Betsy** — Producer
ShondaLand, 4151 Prospect Ave, #400, Los Angeles CA 90027, USA
**Beers, Bob** — Ice Hockey Player
97 Blake Road, Lexington MA 02420, USA
**Beers, Gary** — Singer, Bassist (INXS)
8 Hayes St, #1, Neutral Bay 20891 NSW, Australia
**Beers, Thom** — Producer, Actor, Writer
Fremantle Media North America, 4000 W Alameda Ave, #300, Burbank CA 91505, USA
**Beesley, Damon** — Writer
Bwark Productions, 35-47 Bethnal Green Road, London E1 6LA, England
**Beesley, Max** — Actor
Untitled Entertainment, 350 S Beverly Dr, #200, Beverly Hills CA 90212 USA
**Beeson, Terry E** — Football Player
1302 Hibbard St, Coffeyville KS 67337, USA

**B**

| | |
|---|---|
| **Beeston, Paul M** <br> Toronto Blue Jays, Skydome, 1 Blue Jay Way, Toronto ON M5V 1J1, Canada | Baseball Executive |
| **Beetem, Chris** <br> Abrams Artists, 9200 W Sunset Blvd, #1125, West Hollywood CA 90069 USA | Actor |
| **Bega, Leslie** <br> Sovereign Talent Group, 8421 Wilshire Blvd, #200, Beverly Hills CA 90211, USA | Actress |
| **Bega, Lou** <br> Ame-Media, Schloss Zweibruggen, 52531 Ubach-Palenberg, Germany | Singer |
| **Begay, Notah,III** <br> 3620 Vista del Sur St NW, Albuquerque NM 87120, USA | Golfer |
| **Beggs, Don** <br> Wichita State University, President's Office, Wichita KS 67260, USA | Educator |
| **Beggs, James M** <br> 1177 N Great Southwest Parkway, Grand Prairie TX 75050, USA | Space Engineer, Government Official |
| **Begg-Smith, Dale** <br> Ski & Snowboard, 1 Cobden St, South Melbourne VIC 3205, Australia | Freestyle Moguls Skier |
| **Beghe, Jason** <br> A P A Talent & Literary Agency, 405 S Beverly Dr, #300, Beverly Hills CA 90212 USA | Actor |
| **Beghe, Renato** <br> US Tax Court, 400 2nd St NW, Washington DC 20217, USA | Judge |
| **Begler, Michael** <br> W M E Entertainment, 9601 Wilshire Blvd, #300, Beverly Hills CA 90210 USA | Producer, Writer |
| **Begley, Ed, Jr** <br> Innovative Artists, 1505 10th St, Santa Monica CA 90401 USA | Actor |
| **Beglin, Elizabeth (Beth)** <br> 2070 Silver Maple Trail, North Liberty IA 52317, USA | Field Hockey Player |
| **Beguelin, Chad** <br> Gersh Agency, 9465 Wilshire Blvd, #600, Beverly Hills CA 90212 USA | Writer, Lyricist |
| **Behagen, Ronald M (Ron)** <br> 1101 Juniper St NE, #401, Atlanta GA 30309, USA | Basketball Player |
| **Behar, Joy** <br> Westport Entertainment Associates, 1700 Post Road, #C15, Fairfield CT 06824, USA | Actress, Comedienne |
| **Beharie, Nicole** <br> I C M Partners, 10250 Constellation Blvd, #900, Los Angeles CA 90067 USA | Actress |
| **Beharry, Johnson G** <br> Victoria Cross Assn, Old Admiralty Building, London SW1A 2BL, England | Iraq War British Army Hero (VC) |
| **Behe, Michael** <br> Lehigh University, Biochemistry Dept, Bethlehem PA 18015, USA | Biochemist, Writer |
| **Behle, Petra** <br> Sonnenhof 1, 34508 Willingen, Germany | Biathlete |
| **Behmen, Alija** <br> Prime Minister's Office, Alipasina 1, 71000 Sarajevo, Bosnia & Herzegovina | Prime Minister |
| **Behnisch, Stefan** <br> Behnisch Behnisch Partners, 6 Christophstr, 70178 Stuttgart, Germany | Architect |
| **Behnke, Elmer H** <br> 3412 Ivy Chase Circle, Birmingham AL 35226, USA | Basketball Player |
| **Behnken, Lukas** <br> Media Artists Group, 8222 Melrose Ave, #203, Los Angeles CA 90048 USA | Actor |
| **Behnken, Robert L** <br> N A S A, Johnson Space Center, 2101 NASA Road, Houston TX 77058 USA | Astronaut |
| **Behr, Jason** <br> Untitled Entertainment, 350 S Beverly Dr, #200, Beverly Hills CA 90212 USA | Actor |
| **Behrend, Marc** <br> 6805 Cross Country Road, Verona WI 53593, USA | Ice Hockey Player |
| **Behrendt, Greg** <br> Avalon Mgmt, 4A Exmoor St, London W10 6BD, England | Writer, Actor |
| **Behrendt, Jan** <br> Karl-Zink-Str 2, 96893 Ilmenau, Germany | Luge Athlete |
| **Behrendt, Wolfgang** <br> Springbornstr 204, 12487 Berlin, Germany | Boxer |
| **Behrens, Sam** <br> 530 Bryant Dr, Canoga Park CA 91304, USA | Actor |
| **Behrensmyer, Anna K** <br> Amboseli National Park, PO Box 18, Namanga, Kenya | Paleobiologist |
| **Behrman, David W (Dave)** <br> 10187 25 1/2 Mile Road, Albion MI 49224, USA | Football Player |
| **Behrman, Richard E** <br> PO Box 4446, Santa Barbara CA 93140, USA | Pediatrician |
| **Behrs, Beth** <br> Creative Artists Agency, 2000 Ave of Stars, #100, Los Angeles CA 90067 USA | Actress |
| **Beickler, Ferdinand** <br> Adam Opel AG, Bahnhofsplatz 1, 65428 Russelsheim, Germany | Businessman |
| **Beier-Sonntag, Roswitha** <br> Weneucher Str 16A, 13055 Berlin, Germany | Swimmer |
| **Beikirch, Gary B** <br> 468 Crosby Lane, Rochester NY 14612, USA | Vietnam War Army Hero (CMH) |
| **Beilein, John** <br> University of Michigan, Athletic Dept, Ann Arbor MI 48109, USA | Basketball Coach |
| **Beilina, Nina** <br> 400 W 43rd St, #7D, New York NY 10036, USA | Concert Violinist |
| **Beimel, Joseph R (Joe)** <br> 291 Fairview Road, Kersey PA 15846, USA | Baseball Player |
| **Beineix, Jean-Jacques** <br> Cargo Films, 9 Rue Ambroise Thomas, 75009 Paris, France | Director |
| **Beirne, James P (Jim)** <br> 2 Cedar Chase Place, Spring TX 77381, USA | Football Player |
| **Beisel, Monty G** <br> 5236 Cherokee Lane, McLouth KS 66054, USA | Football Player |
| **Beisler, Randall L (Randy)** <br> 899 Northgate Dr, #500, San Rafael CA 94903, USA | Football Player |
| **Beisner, Michelle** <br> Maximum Talent Agency, 1873 S Bellaire St, #915, Denver CO 80222, USA | Sportscaster |
| **Bejo, Berenice** <br> Agence Artiste Adequat, 108 Rue Reaumur, 75002 Paris, France | Actress |
| **Bekmambetov, Timur** <br> W M E Entertainment, 9601 Wilshire Blvd, #300, Beverly Hills CA 90210 USA | Director |

Beeston - Bekmambetov

**Bela, Magyari** — Cosmonaut, Hungary
Hungarian Space Office, Iskola 13, 1011 Budapest, Hungary
**Belafonte, Harry** — Singer, Actor
Belafonte Enterprises, 310 W 43rd St, #14, New York NY 10036, USA
**Belafonte, Shari** — Actress, Model
W M E Entertainment, 9601 Wilshire Blvd, #300, Beverly Hills CA 90210 USA
**Belasco, Bert** — Actor
TalentWorks, 3500 W Olive Ave, #1400, Burbank CA 91505 USA
**Belbin, Tanith J L** — Figure Skater
Detroit Skating Club, 888 Denison Court, Bloomfield Hills MI 48302, USA
**Belcher, Daniel** — Opera Singer
A D A Artist Mgmt, 4768 Broadway, #660, New York NY 10034, USA
**Belcher, Timothy W (Tim)** — Baseball Player
PO Box 153, Sparta OH 43350, USA
**Belda, Alain J P** — Businessman
Alcoa Inc, 201 Isabella St, Pittsburgh PA 15212, USA
**Belen, Ana** — Actress, Singer
Rompeolas Productions, Alabama St, #1761, San Gerardo, Rio Piedras PR 00926, USA
**Belenky, Valery** — Gymnast
Schillerstr 20, 73760 Ostfildern, Germany
**Belfi, Jordan** — Actor
Schumacher Mgmt, 10323 Santa Monica Blvd, #101, Los Angeles CA 90024, USA
**Belford, Christine** — Actress
C E S D, 10635 Santa Monica Blvd, #130, Los Angeles CA 90025 USA
**Belfour, Edward J (Ed)** — Ice Hockey Player
544 Studebaker Road, Whitewright TX 75491, USA
**Belgrave, Elliott F** — Governor General, Barbados
Governor General's Office, Bay St, Saint Michael, Bridgetown, Barbados
**Belica, Marina** — Singer, Keyboardist (October Project)
October Project, PO Box 539, Prince Street Station, New York NY 10012, USA
**Belichik, William S (Bill)** — Football Coach
116 Meadowbrook Road, Weston MA 02493, USA
**Belin, Gaspard D** — Attorney
4 Willard St, Cambridge MA 02138, USA
**Belin, Nat** — Cartoonist
Drawing Board, 820 W 7th St, #B, Winston Salem NC 27101, USA
**Belinda, Stanley P (Stan)** — Baseball Player
454 Sylvan Dr, State College PA 16803, USA
**Belinelli, Marco A** — Basketball Player
San Antonio Spurs, Alamodome, 1 AT&T Center Parkway, San Antonio TX 78219 USA
**Belisle, Matthew T (Matt)** — Baseball Player
4009 Sierra Dr, Austin TX 78731, USA
**Beliveau, Jean A** — Ice Hockey Player
155 Rue Victoria, Longuevil QC J4H 2J4, Canada
**Belk, William A (Bill)** — Football Player
12 Ricemill Ferry, Columbia SC 29229, USA
**Belknap, Anna** — Actress
S M S Talent, 8383 Wilshire Blvd, #230, Beverly Hills CA 90211 USA
**Bell, Angellica** — Entertainer
C B B C, PO Box 9989, London W12 6PA, England
**Bell, Anthony D** — Football Player
2021 Illinois St, Vallejo CA 94590, USA
**Bell, Archie** — Singer
Billy Paul Mgmt, 8215 S Winthrop St, Philadelphia PA 19136, USA
**Bell, Ashley** — Actress
Gersh Agency, 9465 Wilshire Blvd, #600, Beverly Hills CA 90212 USA
**Bell, Brad** — Golfer
6255 Oakridge Way, Sacramento CA 95831, USA
**Bell, Burwell B, III** — Army General
Mission Readiness, 1212 New York Ave NW, #300, Washington DC 20005, USA
**Bell, Byron** — Basketball Player
2546 Tech Dr, Bettendorf IA 52722, USA
**Bell, C Gordon** — Computer Scientist
Microsoft Corp, 1 Microsoft Way, Redmond WA 98052, USA
**Bell, Carl** — Guitarist (Fuel)
Media Five Entertainment, 3005 Brodhead Road, #170, Bethlehem PA 18020, USA
**Bell, Catherine** — Actress
Brillstein Entertainment Partners, 9150 Wilshire Blvd, #350, Beverly Hills CA 90212 USA
**Bell, Clyde R (Bob)** — Navy Admiral, Association Executive
1301 Harney St, Omaha NE 68102, USA
**Bell, Darrin** — Cartoonist
Washington Post Writers Group, 1150 15th St NW, Washington DC 20071 USA
**Bell, Darryl M** — Actor
Innovative Artists, 1505 10th St, Santa Monica CA 90401 USA
**Bell, David G (Buddy)** — Baseball Player, Manager
244 W Goldfinch Way, Chandler AZ 85286, USA
**Bell, David M** — Baseball Player
9710 E La Posada Circle, Scottsdale AZ 85255, USA
**Bell, Dennis R** — Basketball Player
111 Springfield Pike, Cincinnati OH 45215, USA
**Bell, Derek N** — Baseball Player
3404 Pine Top Dr, Valrico FL 33594, USA
**Bell, Drake** — Actor
Creative Artists Agency, 2000 Ave of Stars, #100, Los Angeles CA 90067 USA
**Bell, Drew Tyler** — Actor
Luber Rocklin Entertainment, 5815 Sunset Blvd, #206, Los Angeles CA 90028 USA
**Bell, Edward A (Eddie)** — Football Player
4529 Tacoma Terrace, Fort Worth TX 76123, USA
**Bell, Emma** — Actress
I C M Partners, 10250 Constellation Blvd, #900, Los Angeles CA 90067 USA
**Bell, Eric A** — Baseball Player
1140 S 124th St, Chandler AZ 85286, USA
**Bell, Gary** — Baseball Player
2107 Oak Ranch, San Antonio TX 78259, USA
**Bell, Gerald A (Jerry)** — Football Player
1347 Deerbourne Dr, Wesley Chapel FL 33543, USA

**Bell, Gregory (Greg)**
5983 E Division Road, Logansport IN 46947, USA — Track Athlete

**Bell, Gregory L (Greg)**
5849 Azalea Way, Goleta CA 93117, USA — Football Player

**Bell, Heath J**
7437 Los Brazos, San Diego CA 92127, USA — Baseball Player

**Bell, Jacob**
2175 W California St, San Diego CA 92110, USA — Football Player

**Bell, James D**
4512 San Marino Dr, Davis CA 95618, USA — Diplomat

**Bell, Jamie**
W M E Entertainment, 9601 Wilshire Blvd, #300, Beverly Hills CA 90210 USA — Actor

**Bell, Jason D**
3387 N Studebaker Road, Long Beach CA 90808, USA — Football Player

**Bell, Jay S**
PO Box 50249, Phoenix AZ 85076, USA — Baseball Player

**Bell, John**
Shore Fire Media, 32 Court St, #1600, Brooklyn NY 11201 USA — Singer (Widespread Panic)

**Bell, John Anthony**
On It Artists, 5 Heathmans Road, London SW6 4TJ, England — Director, Actor

**Bell, Jorge A M (George)**
Lamiama #14, Bell 2nd Planto, San Pedro de Macoris, Dominican Republic — Baseball Player

**Bell, Joseph (Joe)**
10522 11th Ave NE, Seattle WA 98125, USA — Ice Hockey Player

**Bell, Joshua**
Konzertdirektion Schmid, Konigstra 36, 30175 Hannover, Germany — Concert Violinist

**Bell, Kendrell A**
400 W Peachtree St NW, #1211, Atlanta GA 30308, USA — Football Player

**Bell, Kevin R**
621 Sue St, Little Chute WI 54140, USA — Baseball Player

**Bell, Kristen**
Brookside Artist Mgmt, 250 W 57th St, #2303, New York NY 10107, USA — Actress

**Bell, Lake**
United Talent Agency, U T A Plaza, 9336 Civic Center Dr, Beverly Hills CA 90210 USA — Actress

**Bell, Larry S**
PO Box 4101, Taos NM 87571, USA — Sculptor

**Bell, Lauralee**
Martin Bell Productions, 8033 Sunset Blvd, #799, West Hollywood CA 90046, USA — Actress

**Bell, Leola**
Playboy Promotions, 9346 Civic Center Dr, #200, Beverly Hills CA 90210 USA — Model

**Bell, Lynette**
149 Henry St, Merewether NSW 2200, Australia — Swimmer

**Bell, Madison Smartt**
Random House, 1745 Broadway, #1800, New York NY 10019 USA — Writer

**Bell, Mark E**
2701 Wild Rose Ave, Wichita KS 67205, USA — Football Player

**Bell, Michael P (Mike)**
4906 Encino Ave, Encino CA 91316, USA — Actor

**Bell, Michel**
Kelly Productions, 824 Munras Ave, Monterey CA 93940, USA — Actor, Singer

**Bell, Michelle**
18895 Pond Cypress Court, Jupiter FL 33458, USA — Golfer

**Bell, Mike**
American Motorcycle Assn, 13515 Yarmouth Dr, Pickerington OH 43147 USA — Motorcyle Racing Rider

**Bell, Mike J**
7405 Lakewood Circle, Wichita KS 67205, USA — Football Player

**Bell, Myron C**
3027 Crawford Ave, Gastonia NC 28052, USA — Football Player

**Bell, O'Neil**
Warrior's Boxing Promotions, 5397 Orange Dr, #202, Davie FL 33314, USA — Boxer

**Bell, Peter D**
Care, 151 Ellis St NE, Atlanta GA 30303, USA — Association Executive

**Bell, Raja**
12962 Grand Oaks Dr, Davie FL 33330, USA — Basketball Player

**Bell, Rini**
Brady Brannon & Rich Talent, 5670 Wilshire Blvd, #820, Los Angeles CA 90036, USA — Actress

**Bell, Robert A (Rob)**
28 Blossom Hill Dr, Marlboro NY 12542, USA — Baseball Player

**Bell, Robert E (Kool)**
Spirit Media, PO Box 43591, Phoenix AZ 85080 USA — Bassist (Kool & the Gang)

**Bell, Robert F (Bob)**
7415 N 12th St, Elkins Park PA 19027, USA — Football Player

**Bell, Robert H (Rob), Jr**
Mars Hill Bible Church, 3501 Fairlanes Ave, Grandville MI 49418, USA — Religious Leader

**Bell, Robert L (Bobby), Sr**
208 NW Shagbark St, Lees Summit MO 64064, USA — Football Player

**Bell, Ronald N**
Spirit Media, PO Box 43591, Phoenix AZ 85080 USA — Saxophonist (Kool & the Gang)

**Bell, Sam**
2310 E Woodstock Place, Bloomington IN 47401, USA — Track Coach

**Bell, Steve**
Guardian, Editorial Dept, 1 Scott Place, Manchester M3 3GG, England — Editorial Cartoonist

**Bell, Tatum A**
18754 E Powers Dr, Aurora CO 80015, USA — Football Player

**Bell, Thom**
B M I, 8730 W Sunset Blvd, #300, Los Angeles CA 90069 USA — Songwriter

**Bell, Tobin**
Creative Artists Mgmt, 111 Shoreditch High St, #400, London E1 6JN, England — Actor

**Bell, William**
Rodgers Redding, PO Box 4603, Macon GA 31208 USA — Singer, Pianist, Songwriter

**Bell, William Brent**
Creative Artists Agency, 2000 Ave of Stars, #100, Los Angeles CA 90067 USA — Director

**Bell, Yeremiah N**
1215 Delong Place, Lexington KY 40515, USA — Football Player

**Bell, Zoe E**
Runaway Films, 1338 Rhode Island St, San Francisco CA 94107, USA — Actress, Stuntwoman

**Bella, Brianna (Brie)** — Professional Wrestler, Model
June Entertainment, 6350 Santa Monica Blvd, Los Angeles CA 90036, USA

**Bella, Ivan** — Cosmonaut
Cosmonaut Training Center, Star City, 141160 Zvezdny Gorodok, Moscow Oblast, Russia

**Bella, Nicole (Nikki)** — Professional Wrestler, Model
June Entertainment, 6350 Santa Monica Blvd, Los Angeles CA 90036, USA

**Bellamy, Bill** — Actor, Comedian
A P A Talent & Literary Agency, 405 S Beverly Dr, #300, Beverly Hills CA 90212 USA

**Bellamy, David** — Singer (Bellamy Brothers), Songwriter
Bellamy Brothers Partners, 13917 Restless Lane, Dade City FL 33525, USA

**Bellamy, David J** — Botanist, Writer, Broadcaster
Mill House, Bedburn, Bishop Auckland, County Durham DL13 3NN, England

**Bellamy, Howard** — Singer (Bellamy Brothers), Songwriter
Bellamy Brothers Partners, 13917 Restless Lane, Dade City FL 33525, USA

**Bellamy, Matthew** — Singer, Guitarist (Muse)
Hall or Nothing P R, 35-37 Parkgate Road, London SW11 4NP, England

**Bellamy, Ned** — Actor
Global Artists Agency, 6253 Hollywood Blvd, #508, Los Angeles CA 90028 USA

**Belland, Bruce** — Singer (Four Preps)
4339 Ensenada Dr, Woodland Hills CA 91364, USA

**Belland, Neil** — Ice Hockey Player
868 Renaissance Dr, Oshawa ON L1J 8K9, Canada

**Bellar, Clara** — Actress
Julian Belfrage Assoc, 9 Argyll St, #300, London W1F 7TG, England

**Belle, Albert J** — Baseball Player
9299 E Mariposa Grande Dr, Scottsdale AZ 85255, USA

**Belle, Camilla** — Actress
United Talent Agency, U T A Plaza, 9336 Civic Center Dr, Beverly Hills CA 90210 USA

**Belle, Regina** — Singer, Songwriter
Sony Records, 2100 Colorado Ave, Santa Monica CA 90404 USA

**Bellemer, John** — Opera Singer
I M G Artists, Hogarth Business Park, Chiswick, London W4 2TH, England

**Beller, Kathleen** — Actress
PO Box 806, Half Moon Bay CA 94019, USA

**Bellhorn, Mark C** — Baseball Player
19550 N Grayhawk Dr, #1083, Scottsdale AZ 85255, USA

**Belli, Gioconda** — Writer
Carlisle Co, 121 E 17th St, New York NY 10003, USA

**Belli, Paolo** — Singer
Cicuta Produczioni, Via Barbeerini 29, 00187 Rome, Italy

**Belliard, Rafael L** — Baseball Player
10846 King Bay Dr, Boca Raton FL 33498, USA

**Belliard, Ronald (Ronnie)** — Baseball Player
2999 NW 96th St, Miami FL 33147, USA

**Bellincampi, Giordano** — Conductor
I M G Artists, Hogarth Business Park, Chiswick, London W4 2TH, England

**Bellingham, Lynda** — Actress
Artist Rights Group, 4A Exmoor St, London W10 6BD, England

**Bellingham, Norman** — Canoeing Athlete
1825 Cantwell Grove, Colorado Springs CO 80906, USA

**Bellini, Mario** — Architect
Architecture Center, 66 Portland Place, London W1, England

**Bellino, Joseph M (Joe)** — Football Player
45 Hayden Lane, Bedford MA 01730, USA

**Bellisario, Donald P** — Producer
Gelfand Rennert Feldman, 1880 Century Park E, #1600, Los Angeles CA 90067, USA

**Bellisario, Troian** — Actress
Management 360, 9111 Wilshire Blvd, Beverly Hills CA 90210 USA

**Bell-Lundy, Sandra** — Cartoonist (Between Friends)
255 Northwood Dr, Welland ON L3C 6V1, Canada

**Bellman, Gina** — Actress
Independent Talent Group, 40 Whitfield St, London W1T 2RH, England

**Bello, Frank** — Bassist (Anthrax)
Zen Media Group, 272 Grand St, #B, Brooklyn NY 11211, USA

**Bello, Maria** — Actress
Creative Artists Agency, 2000 Ave of Stars, #100, Los Angeles CA 90067 USA

**Bellocchio, Marco** — Director, Writer
Bobbio Film Festival, Piazzetta Santa Chiara, 129022 Bobbio (PC), Italy

**Bellotti, Mike** — Football Coach, Executive, Sportscaster
ESPN-TV, Sports Dept, ESPN Plaza, 935 Middle St, Bristol CT 06010 USA

**Bellovin, Steven M** — Computer Scientist
AT&T Research Laboratories, 180 Park Ave, PO Box 971, Florham Park NJ 07932, USA

**Bellows, Brian** — Ice Hockey Player
6824 Valley View Road, Minneapolis MN 55439, USA

**Bellows, Gil** — Actor
Innovative Artists, 1505 10th St, Santa Monica CA 90401 USA

**Bellucci, Monica** — Model, Actress
Creative Artists Agency, 2000 Ave of Stars, #100, Los Angeles CA 90067 USA

**Bellwood, Pamela** — Actress
1696 San Leandro Lane, Santa Barbara CA 93108, USA

**Bellynck, Lise** — Actress
Agents Associes Chen, 201 Rue Faubourg Saint-Honore, 75008 Paris, France

**Belmondo, Jean-Paul** — Actor
6 Rue Gassendi, 75014 Paris, France

**Belmondo, Olivier** — Actor
Artmedia, 20 Ave Rapp, 75007 Paris, France

**Belmont, Lara** — Actress
Markham Froggatt Irwin, Julian House, 4 Windmill St, London W1P 1HF, England

**Belo, Carlos Filipe Ximenes** — Nobel Peace Laureate, Religious Leader
Catholic Bishop, Caixa Postale 4, Dili-Leste, East Timor

**Belote Hamlin, Melissa** — Swimmer
7311 Exmore St, Springfield VA 22150, USA

**Belousova, Ludmila Y** — Figure Skater
Chalet Hubel, 3818 Grindelwald, Switzerland

**Belser, Ceaser E** — Football Player
317 Cooper Dr, Hurst TX 76053, USA

**Belser, Jason D** — Football Player
20150 Valhalla Square, Ashburn VA 20147, USA

**Beltrami, Marco** — Composer
Kraft-Engel Management, 15233 Ventura Blvd, #200, Sherman Oaks CA 91403, USA

**Beltran, Carlos I** — Baseball Player
18 Paseo Alcala, Urb Hacienda Hermanos Mena, Manati PR 00674, USA

**Beltran, Rigoberto (Rigo)** — Baseball Player
3950 Laurelwood Lane, Delray Beach FL 33445, USA

**Beltran, Robert A** — Actor
Abrams Artists, 9200 W Sunset Blvd, #1125, West Hollywood CA 90069 USA

**Beltre Perez, Adrian** — Baseball Player
Texas Rangers, Ameriquest Field, 1000 Ballpark Way, #306, Arlington TX 76011 USA

**Belushi, James** — Actor
Brillstein Entertainment Partners, 9150 Wilshire Blvd, #350, Beverly Hills CA 90212 USA

**Belvaux, Lucas** — Director
Voyez Mon Agent, 20 Ave Rapp, 75007 Paris, France

**Belzer, Richard** — Actor, Comedian
McBelz Enterprises, 1995 Broadway, #16, New York New York 10023, USA

**Beman, Deane R** — Golfer, Golf Executive
255 Deer Haven Dr, Ponte Vedra FL 32082, USA

**Bement, Linda J** — Beauty Queen
Miss Universe Organization, 1370 Ave of Americas, #1600, New York NY 10019 USA

**Bemile, Paul Cardinal** — Religious Leader
Diocese of Wa, PO Box 47, Wa, Upper West Region, Ghana

**Bemiller, Al D** — Football Player
5002 Armor-Duells Road, Orchard Park NY 14127, USA

**Ben Tre, Howard B** — Artist
Charles Cowles Gallery, 210 11th Ave, #500, New York NY 10001, USA

**Benade, Leo Edward** — Army General
417 Pine Ridge Road, #A, Carthage NC 28327, USA

**Benanti, Laura** — Actress, Singer
Brookside Artist Mgmt, 250 W 57th St, #2303, New York NY 10107, USA

**Benard, Marvin L** — Baseball Player
2806 S 38th Ave, West Richland WA 99353, USA

**Benard, Maurice** — Actor
Benard Management, 15300 Ventura Blvd, #315, Sherman Oaks CA 91403, USA

**Benassi, Benny** — DJ Musician, Producer
A M Only, 55 Washington St, #658, New York NY 10006, USA

**Benatar, Pat** — Singer, Songwriter
W M E Entertainment, 9601 Wilshire Blvd, #300, Beverly Hills CA 90210 USA

**Benavides, Fortunato P (Pete)** — Judge
US Court of Appeals, 903 San Jacinto Blvd, #400, Austin TX 78701, USA

**Benben, Brian** — Actor
Paradigm Agency, 360 N Crescent Dr, North Building, Beverly Hills CA 90210 USA

**Bench, John L (Johnny)** — Baseball Player
Johnny Bench Enterprises, 3899 Ridgedale Dr, Cincinnati OH 45247, USA

**Benchoff, Dennis L (Den)** — Army General
380 Arbor Road, Lancaster PA 17601, USA

**Bender, Gary N** — Sportscaster
TNT-TV, Sports Dept, 1050 Techwood Dr, Atlanta GA 30318 USA

**Bender, Jack** — Cartoonist (Alley Oop)
RR 1 Box 540, Terlton OK 74081, USA

**Bender, Jack** — Director
United Talent Agency, U T A Plaza, 9336 Civic Center Dr, Beverly Hills CA 90210 USA

**Bender, Jonathan R** — Basketball Player
New York Knicks, Madison Square Garden, 2 Penn Plaza, New York, NY 10121 USA

**Bender, Lawrence** — Producer, Director
W M E Entertainment, 9601 Wilshire Blvd, #300, Beverly Hills CA 90210 USA

**Bender, Lon** — Sound Editor
Soundelux, 7080 Hollywood Blvd, #1100, Los Angeles CA 90028, USA

**Bender, Thomas** — Historian
100 Sterling Place, #3F, Brooklyn NY 11217, USA

**Bendewald, Andrea** — Actress
Metropolitan Talent Agency, 5405 Wilshire Blvd, #218, Los Angeles CA 90036 USA

**Bendinger, Jessica** — Director, Writer
Creative Artists Agency, 2000 Ave of Stars, #100, Los Angeles CA 90067 USA

**Bendix, Simone** — Actress
Joy Jameson, 2/19 Plaza, 535 Kings Road, London SW10 0SZ, England

**Bendlin, Kurt** — Track Athlete
D L V, Asfelder Str 27, 64289 Leverkusen, Germany

**Ben-Dor, Gisele** — Conductor
I M G Artists, Hogarth Business Park, Chiswick, London W4 2TH, England

**Bene, B Christopher** — Architect
Chang Bene Design, 43-55 Wyndham St, Central, Hong Kong, China

**Benedek, George B** — Physicist
Massachusetts Institute of Technology, Physics Dept, Cambridge MA 02139, USA

**Benedeti, Paulo** — Actor
4201 N Ocean Blvd, #C505, Boca Raton FL 33431, USA

**Benedetti, Nicola** — Concert Violinist
I M G Artists, Hogarth Business Park, Chiswick, London W4 2TH, England

**Benedict XVI, Pope** — Religious Leader
Castel Gandolfo, 00040 Lazio, Italy

**Benedict, Bruce E** — Baseball Player
335 Quiet Water Lane, Atlanta GA 30350, USA

**Benedict, Dirk** — Actor
Arsenal Productions & Management, 8200 Wilshire Blvd, #400, Beverly Hills CA 90211, USA

**Benedict, Rob** — Actor
S M S Talent, 8383 Wilshire Blvd, #230, Beverly Hills CA 90211 USA

**Benedict-Jones, Linda** — Photographer
256 Jefferson Dr, Pittsburgh PA 15228, USA

**Benedicto, Lourdes** — Actress
23325 Collins St, Woodland Hills CA 91367, USA

**Benepe, Jim** — Golfer
602 Mountain Shadows Blvd, Sheridan WY 82801, USA

**Benero, Edward Allen** — Writer, Producer
Creative Artists Agency, 2000 Ave of Stars, #100, Los Angeles CA 90067 USA

| | |
|---|---|
| **Benes, Alan P** | Baseball Player |
| 754 Kraffel Lane, Chesterfield MO 63017, USA | |
| **Benes, Andrew C (Andy)** | Baseball Player |
| 1127 Highland Point Dr, Saint Louis MO 63131, USA | |
| **Benet, Eric** | Singer, Songwriter |
| Avnet Mgmt, 4111 W Alameda Ave, #410, Burbank CA 91505, USA | |
| **Benetton, Carlo** | Businessman |
| Benetton Group SpA, Via Minelli, 31050 Ponzano Treviso, Italy | |
| **Benetton, Gilberto** | Businessman |
| Benetton Group SpA, Via Minelli, 31050 Ponzano Treviso, Italy | |
| **Benetton, Giuliana** | Businesswoman |
| Benetton Group SpA, Via Minelli, 31050 Ponzano Treviso, Italy | |
| **Benetton, Luciano** | Businessman |
| Benetton Group SpA, Via Minelli, 31050 Ponzano Treviso, Italy | |
| **Benga** | Electronic Musician (Magnetic Man) |
| Columbia Records, 9 Derry St, London W8 5HY, England | |
| **Benglis, Lynda** | Artist, Sculptor |
| 917 Acequia Madre, Santa Fe NM 87505, USA | |
| **Bengston, Billy Al** | Artist |
| 110 Mildred Ave, Venice CA 90291, USA | |
| **Benguigui, Jean** | Actor |
| U B B A, 6 Rue de Braque, 75003 Paris, France | |
| **Benhima, Mohamed** | Prime Minister, Morocco |
| Km 5,5, Route des Zaers, Rabat, Morocco | |
| **Benichou, Maurice** | Actor |
| Voyez Mon Agent, 20 Ave Rapp, 75007 Paris, France | |
| **Benigni, Roberto** | Actor, Director |
| Melampo Cinematografica, Via Ludovisi 35, 00187 Rome, Italy | |
| **Bening, Annette** | Actress |
| 13671 Mulholland Dr, Beverly Hills CA 90210, USA | |
| **Benioff, David** | Writer, Producer |
| Creative Artists Agency, 2000 Ave of Stars, #100, Los Angeles CA 90067 USA | |
| **Beniquez Torres, Juan J** | Baseball Player |
| Villa Carolina 87-12, Calle 99A, Villa Carolina PR 00985, USA | |
| **Benirschke, Kurt** | Pathologist |
| 849 Coast Blvd, La Jolla CA 92037, USA | |
| **Benirschke, Rolf J** | Football Player |
| 4326 Vista de la Tierra, San Diego CA 92130, USA | |
| **Benish, Daniel J (Dan)** | Football Player |
| 1158 Trailblazer Way NW, Lilburn GA 30047, USA | |
| **Benitez, Armando G** | Baseball Player |
| 520 N Parkway, Golden Beach FL 33160, USA | |
| **Benitez, Elsa** | Model |
| Talent Entertainment Group, 9111 Wilshire Blvd, Beverly Hills CA 90210 USA | |
| **Benitez, Maria** | Flamenco Dancer |
| Teatro Flamenco, Institute for Spanish Arts, PO Box 8418, Santa Fe NM 87504, USA | |
| **Benitez, Wilfredo** | Boxer |
| Saint Just, 248 Calle 6, Trujilloo Alto, PR 00976, USA | |
| **Benjamin, Benoit** | Basketball Player |
| PO Box 690912, San Antonio TX 78269, USA | |
| **Benjamin, George W J** | Composer |
| Faber Music, 3 Queen Square, London WC1N 3AU, England | |
| **Benjamin, Guy E** | Football Player |
| 91-443 Ewa Beach Road, Ewa Beach HI 96706, USA | |
| **Benjamin, H Jon** | Actor, Comedian |
| Creative Artists Agency, 2000 Ave of Stars, #100, Los Angeles CA 90067 USA | |
| **Benjamin, Jill** | Actress |
| Principato-Young, 9465 Wilshire Blvd, #880, Beverly Hills CA 90212 USA | |
| **Benjamin, Julia** | Actress |
| 4054 Redwood Ave, #6, Los Angeles CA 90066, USA | |
| **Benjamin, Kelvin** | Football Player |
| Carolina Panthers, Ericsson Stadium, 800 S Mint St, Charlotte NC 28202 USA | |
| **Benjamin, Lloyd W, III** | Educator |
| Indiana State University, President's Office, Terre Haute IN 47809, USA | |
| **Benjamin, Lucy** | Actress |
| Iconic Publicity International, Wren House, #4, 334A Creek Road, London SE10 9SW, England | |
| **Benjamin, Michael P (Mike)** | Baseball Player |
| 25608 S 182nd Place, Queen Creek AZ 85142, USA | |
| **Benjamin, Regina M** | Government Official, Physician |
| Surgeon General's Office, 5600 Fishers Lane, Rockville MD 20857, USA | |
| **Benjamin, Richard** | Actor, Director |
| Gersh Agency, 9465 Wilshire Blvd, #600, Beverly Hills CA 90212 USA | |
| **Benjamin, Stephen (Steve)** | Yachtsman |
| PO Box 399, Norwalk CT 06856, USA | |
| **Benkovic, Stephen J** | Chemist |
| 771 Teaberry Lane, State College PA 16803, USA | |
| **Benmosche, Robert H** | Businessman |
| American International Group, 70 Pine St, New York NY 10270, USA | |
| **Benn, Jamie** | Ice Hockey Player |
| Randy Benn, 6290 Marie Meadows Road, Victoria BC V8Z 5Z8, Canada | |
| **Benn, Nigel** | Boxer |
| Matchroom Boxing, 10 Western Road, Romford Essex RM1 3JT, England | |
| **Bennack, Frank A, Jr** | Publisher |
| Hearst Corp, 250 W 55th St, #4200, New York NY 10019, USA | |
| **Bennet, Chloe** | Actress |
| Creative Artists Agency, 2000 Ave of Stars, #100, Los Angeles CA 90067 USA | |
| **Benneteau, Julian** | Tennis Player |
| Federation de Tenis, Stade Roland Garros, 2 Ave Gordon Bennett, 75016 Paris, France | |
| **Bennett Spector, Veronica (Ronnie)** | Singer (Ronettes) |
| Absolute Artists, 8490 W Sunset Blvd, #403, West Hollywood CA 90069, USA | |
| **Bennett, Adam** | Ice Hockey Player |
| 7 Stockman Crescent, Georgetown ON L7G 1J5, Canada | |
| **Bennett, Alan** | Writer, Actor |
| United Agents, 12-26 Lexington St, London W1F 0LE, England | |
| **Bennett, Albert F** | Physiologist |
| University of California, Biological Sciences School, Irvine CA 92697, USA | |

# B

| | |
|---|---|
| **Bennett, Andrew R (Drew)**<br>2335 Hyde St, #1, San Francisco CA 94109, USA | Football Player |
| **Bennett, Anthony**<br>Minnesota Timberwolves, Target Center, 600 1st Ave N, Minneapolis MN 55403 USA | Basketball Player |
| **Bennett, Anthony G (Tony)**<br>3408 Cesford Grange, Keswick VA 22947, USA | Basketball Player, Coach |
| **Bennett, Barry M**<br>22047 Ginseng Road, Long Prairie MN 56347, USA | Football Player |
| **Bennett, Bob**<br>Benjamin Artists Agency, PO Box 92348, Nashville TN 37209, USA | Singer, Songwriter |
| **Bennett, Brandon**<br>308 Daybrook Court, Greenville SC 29605, USA | Football Player |
| **Bennett, Brooke**<br>2585 Rowe Road, Milford MI 48380, USA | Swimmer |
| **Bennett, Charles L**<br>Johns Hopkins University, Physics/Astronomy Dept, Baltimore MD 21218, USA | Astrophysicist |
| **Bennett, Clay**<br>Christian Science Monitor, Editorial Dept, 1 Norway St, Boston MA 02136 USA | Editorial Cartoonist |
| **Bennett, Cornelius O**<br>818 S 7th Ave, Hollywood FL 33019, USA | Football Player |
| **Bennett, Curt A**<br>260 Awapuhi Place, Wailuku HI 96793, USA | Ice Hockey Player |
| **Bennett, Darren L**<br>3347 Corte del Cruce, Carlsbad CA 92009, USA | Football Player |
| **Bennett, Donnell**<br>8055 W Leitner Dr, Coral Springs FL 33067, USA | Football Player |
| **Bennett, Edgar, III**<br>1880 Horseshoe Lane, De Pere WI 54115, USA | Football Player |
| **Bennett, Eliza Hope**<br>Independent Talent Group, 40 Whitfield St, London W1T 2RH, England | Actress |
| **Bennett, Elmer J**<br>2820 Ave of the Woods, Louisville KY 40241, USA | Basketball Player |
| **Bennett, Fleur A**<br>Richard Stone Partnership, De Walden Court, 85 New Cavendish St, London W1W 6XD, England | Actress |
| **Bennett, Fran**<br>House of Representatives, 1434 6th St, #1, Santa Monica CA 90401 USA | Actress |
| **Bennett, Harvey, Jr**<br>1096 Warwick Neck Ave, Warwick RI 02889, USA | Ice Hockey Player |
| **Bennett, Hayley**<br>Schiff Co, 9465 Wilshire Blvd, #480, Beverly Hills CA 90212, USA | Actress, Singer |
| **Bennett, Hywel**<br>116 Lots Road, Chelsea Creek, London SW10, England | Actor |
| **Bennett, Jean**<br>University of Pennsylvania Medical School, 422 Curie Blvd, Philadelphia PA 19104, USA | Molecular Geneticist, Physician |
| **Bennett, Jimmy**<br>Untitled Entertainment, 350 S Beverly Dr, #200, Beverly Hills CA 90212 USA | Actor |
| **Bennett, Joan**<br>Playboy Promotions, 9346 Civic Center Dr, #200, Beverly Hills CA 90210 USA | Model |
| **Bennett, Joe C**<br>4101 Altamont Road, Birmingham AL 35213, USA | Rheumatologist, Educator |
| **Bennett, John**<br>Olympic Committee, 1 Olympic Plaza, Building 6, Colorado Springs CO 80909 USA | Track Athlete |
| **Bennett, John O, III**<br>Montclair State University, Political Science Dept, 1 Normal Ave, Upper Montclair NJ 07043, USA | Governor, NJ |
| **Bennett, Jonathan**<br>Evolution Entertainment, 901 N Highland Ave, Los Angeles CA 90038 USA | Actor |
| **Bennett, Laurence**<br>Innovative Artists, 1505 10th St, Santa Monica CA 90401 USA | Production Designer |
| **Bennett, Manu**<br>Sanders/Armstrong/Caserta Mgmt, 2120 Colorado Ave, #120, Santa Monica CA 90404 USA | Actor, Director, Producer |
| **Bennett, Matthew R**<br>Edna Talent, 318 Dundas St W, Toronto ON M5T 1G5, Canada | Actor |
| **Bennett, Michael A**<br>Minnesota Vikings, 9520 Viking Dr, Eden Prairie MN 55344 USA | Football Player |
| **Bennett, Michael V L**<br>Albert Einstein College of Medicine, Neuroscience Dept, Bronx NY 10461, USA | Neuroscientist |
| **Bennett, Michael, Jr**<br>Seattle Seahawks, 12 Seahawks Way, Renton WA 98056 USA | Football Player |
| **Bennett, Monte L**<br>2075 Ave U, Sterling KS 67579, USA | Football Player |
| **Bennett, Nigel**<br>Characters Talent, 8 Elm St, Toronto ON M5G 1G7, Canada | Actor |
| **Bennett, Patricia**<br>Lustig Talent, PO Box 770850, Orlando FL 32877 USA | Singer (Chiffons) |
| **Bennett, Robert F (Rob)**<br>Arent Fox LLP, 1050 Connecticut Ave NW, Washington DC 20036, USA | Senator, UT |
| **Bennett, Robert R**<br>Home Shopping Network, 2501 118th Ave N, Saint Petersburg FL 33716, USA | Businessman |
| **Bennett, Ronan**<br>Tavistock Wood Mgmt, 45 Conduit St, London W1S 2YN, England | Writer |
| **Bennett, Sarah**<br>Willow Personal Mgmt, 151 Main St, Yaxley, Peterborough PE7 3LD, England | Actress |
| **Bennett, Tom**<br>Susan Angel & Kevin Francis Ltd, 12 D'Arblay St, London W1F 8DU, England | Actor, Writer |
| **Bennett, Tom**<br>Bennett Gallery, 6200 Pleasant Valley Road, El Dorado CA 95623, USA | Sculptor |
| **Bennett, Tony**<br>R P M Music Productions, 48 W 10th St, #B, New York NY 10011, USA | Singer |
| **Bennett, Tony**<br>48B W 10th St, New York NY 10011, USA | Artist |
| **Bennett, Tony L**<br>7645 Ballinshire N, Indianapolis IN 46254, USA | Football Player |
| **Bennett, William J**<br>5716 3rd St NW, Washington DC 20011, USA | Secretary, Education |
| **Bennett, Winston G, III**<br>54 Barrington Circle, Paducah KY 42003, USA | Basketball Player |

**Bennett, Woodrow (Woody), Jr** — Football Player
PO Box 25022, Fort Lauderdale FL 33320, USA

**Bennetts, Leslie** — Writer
Voice/Hyperion Books, 77 W 66th St, #1100, New York NY 10023, USA

**Benning, Brian A** — Ice Hockey Player
Interstate Batteries, 11216 156th St NW, Edmonton AB T5M 1Y3, Canada

**Benning, James E (Jim)** — Ice Hockey Player
20502 SW Kruger Road, Sherwood OR 97140, USA

**Bennington, Chester** — Singer (Linkin Park)
Special Artists Agency, 9200 Sunset Blvd, #410, West Hollywood CA 90069 USA

**Benoit Samuelson, Joan** — Track Athlete
95 Lower Flying Point Road, Freeport ME 04032, USA

**Benoit, David** — Jazz Pianist, Composer
Chapman & Co Mgmt, PO Box 55246, Sherman Oaks CA 91413, USA

**Benoit, Joaquin** — Baseball Player
San Diego Padres, Petco Park, 100 Park Blvd, San Diego CA 92101 USA

**Benrubi, Abraham** — Actor
Stone Manners Salners, 6100 Wilshire Blvd, #1500, Los Angeles CA 90035 USA

**Benson, Amber N** — Actress
BenderSpink, 8447 Wilshire Blvd, #250, Beverly Hills CA 90211 USA

**Benson, Andrew A** — Marine Biologist, Plant Physiologist
6044 Folsom Dr, La Jolla CA 92037, USA

**Benson, Anna** — Model
6025 Sandy Springs Circle, #133, Atlanta GA 30328, USA

**Benson, Ashley V** — Actress
W M E Entertainment, 9601 Wilshire Blvd, #300, Beverly Hills CA 90210 USA

**Benson, Bradley W (Brad)** — Football Player
Brad Benson Mitsubishi, 3905 Route 1 S, Monmouth Junction NJ 08852, USA

**Benson, Brendan** — Singer, Guitarist, Songwriter
High Road Touring, 751 Bridgeway, #200, Sausalito CA 94965 USA

**Benson, Bruce D** — Educator
University of Colorado, President's Office, 1800 Grant St, #800, Denver CO 80203, USA

**Benson, Cedric M** — Football Player
20 Commerce Dr, #301, Cranford NJ 7016, USA

**Benson, Charles** — Football Player
1514 Hanover Lane, Van Alstyne TX 75495, USA

**Benson, Clifford A (Cliff)** — Football Player
PO Box 821957, Vancouver WA 98682, USA

**Benson, Doug** — Actor, Comedian
OmniPop Talent Group, 4605 Lankershim Blvd, #201, Toluca Lake CA 91602 USA

**Benson, Duane D** — Football Player
33053 Grit Road, Lanesboro MN 55949, USA

**Benson, Harry** — Photographer
181 E 73rd St, #18A, New York NY 10021, USA

**Benson, Herbert** — Cardiologist
Mind/Body Medical Institute, Beth Israel Hospital, Brookline MA 02146, USA

**Benson, Jodi** — Actress, Singer
319 1/2 N Church St, Grass Valley CA 95945, USA

**Benson, Jonathan (Johnny), Jr** — Auto, Truck Racing Driver
19528 Mary Ardrey Circle, Cornelius NC 28031, USA

**Benson, Kristen J (Kris)** — Baseball Player
2140 Vicki Lane, Cumming GA 30041, USA

**Benson, Linda** — Surfer
SurfHer, PO Box 1, Solana Beach CA 92075, USA

**Benson, M Kent** — Basketball Player
4315 Weymouth Lane, Bloomington IN 47408, USA

**Benson, Melissa A** — Illustrator
110 Rocky Rest Road, Shelton CT 06484, USA

**Benson, Peter** — Actor
Liebman Entertainment, 25 E 21st St, #PH, New York NY 10010 USA

**Benson, Ray** — Singer, Guitarist (Asleep at the Wheel)
Bismeaux Productions, PO Box 463, Austin TX 78767, USA

**Benson, Raymond** — Writer
Ian Fleming Foundation, PO Box 7312, Buffalo Grove IL 60089, USA

**Benson, Robby** — Actor
A K A Talent, 6310 San Vicente Blvd, #200, Los Angeles CA 90048 USA

**Benson, Stephen R (Steve)** — Editorial Cartoonist
Arizona Republic, Editorial Dept, 200 E Van Buren St, Phoenix AZ 85004, USA

**Benson, Thomas C (Tom)** — Football Player
PO Box 701341, Dallas TX 75370, USA

**Bent, Amel** — Singer
19 Music & Mgmt, 35-37 Parkgate Road, London SW11 4NP, England

**Bent, Lyriq** — Actor
Stone Manners Salners, 6100 Wilshire Blvd, #1500, Los Angeles CA 90035 USA

**Bent, Margaret H** — Musicologist
All Souls College, Oxford University, Music Dept, Oxford OX1 4AL, England

**Bent, Ridley** — Singer, Songwriter
Divine Industries, 101-1001 W Broadway, Vancouver BC V6H 4E4, Canada

**Bentas, Lily H** — Businesswoman
Cumberland Farms, 100 Crossing Blvd, Framingham MA 01702, USA

**Bentley, Albert T** — Football Player
13631 Eagle Ridge Dr, #234, Fort Myers FL 33912, USA

**Bentley, Ben** — Sportswriter
6007 N Sheridan Road, #28G, Chicago IL 60660, USA

**Bentley, Dierks** — Singer, Guitarist, Songwriter
W M E Entertainment, 1600 Division St, #300, Nashville TN 37203 USA

**Bentley, Jay D** — Bassist (Bad Religion)
Goldstar Public Relations, PO Box 130, Ross on Wye HR9 6WY, England

**Bentley, Kevin K** — Football Player
3001 Murworth Dr, #904, Houston TX 77025, USA

**Bentley, Ray** — Football Player, Sportscaster
4050 Redbush Dr SW, Granville MI 49418, USA

**Bentley, Wes** — Actor
W M E Entertainment, 9601 Wilshire Blvd, #300, Beverly Hills CA 90210 USA

**Benton, Barbi** — Model, Actress
40 N 4th St, Carbondale CO 81623, USA

# B

**Benton, Fletcher C** — Sculptor
250 Dore St, San Francisco CA 94103, USA

**Benton, Robert** — Director
Creative Artists Agency, 2000 Ave of Stars, #100, Los Angeles CA 90067 USA

**Bentsen, William** — Yachtsman
N1946 Birches Dr, Lake Geneva WI 53147, USA

**Bentyne, Cheryl** — Singer (Manhattan Transfer)
Bennett Morgan, 1022 RR 376, #3, Wappinger Falls NY 12590 USA

**Benvenuti, Giovanni (Nino)** — Boxer
V S Costanza 13, 00198 Rome, Italy

**Ben-Victor, Paul** — Actor
A P A Talent & Literary Agency, 405 S Beverly Dr, #300, Beverly Hills CA 90212 USA

**Benymon, Chico** — Actor
Don Buchwald Talent Agency, 6500 Wilshire Blvd, #2200, Los Angeles CA 90048 USA

**Benyon, Margaret** — Artist
Holography Studio, 40 Springdale, Broadstone, Dorset BH18 9EU, England

**Benz, Amy** — Golfer
2109 S Sailors Way, Gilbert AZ 85295, USA

**Benz, Edward J, Jr** — Pediatrician, Pathologist
20 Beacon St, #4, Boston MA 02108, USA

**Benz, Julie** — Actress
I C M Partners, 10250 Constellation Blvd, #900, Los Angeles CA 90067 USA

**Benz, Laura** — Ice Hockey Player
Z S C Lions Z L E Betriebs A G, Siewerdstr 105, 8050 Zurich, Switzerland

**Benz, Sara** — Ice Hockey Player
Z S C Lions Z L E Betriebs A G, Siewerdstr 105, 8050 Zurich, Switzerland

**Benza, Alfred Joseph (A J)** — Actor, Writer
Media Artists Group, 8222 Melrose Ave, #203, Los Angeles CA 90048 USA

**Benzali, Daniel** — Actor
Vanguard Management Group, 8060 Melrose Ave, #400 Los Angeles CA 90046, USA

**Benzi, Roberto** — Conductor
12 Villa Sainte Foy, 92200 Neuilly-sur-Seine, France

**Benzinger, Todd E** — Baseball Player
1047 Shore Point Court, Loveland OH 45140, USA

**Beranek, Josef** — Ice Hockey Player
Pittsburgh Penguins, Consol Energy Center, 1001 5th Ave, Pittsburgh PA 15219 USA

**Beranek, Leo** — Acoustical Engineer
10 Longwood Dr, #265, Westwood MA 2090, USA

**Berard, Bryan** — Ice Hockey Player
9 Holly Lane, Cumberland RI 02864, USA

**Berardi, Antonio** — Fashion Designer
Saint Martin's House, 59 Saint Martin's Lane, London WC2N 4JS, England

**Berben, Iris** — Actress
Moovie, Lutzowufer 12, 10785 Berlin, Germany

**Bercaw, John E** — Chemist
California Institute of Technology, Chemistry Dept, Pasadena CA 91125, USA

**Berce, Eugene D (Gene)** — Basketball Player
1119 Hawthorne Place, #6, Pewaukee WI 53072, USA

**Bercich, Peter J (Pete)** — Football Player
17448 Honeysuckle Ave, Lakeville MN 55044, USA

**Bercot, Emmanuelle** — Director, Writer
U B B A, 6 Rue de Braque, 75003 Paris, France

**Bercu, Michaela** — Model, Actress
Elite Model Mgmt, 404 Park Ave S, #900, New York NY 10016 USA

**Berdimuhammedow, Gurbanguly M** — President, Turkmenistan
President's Office, Karl Marx Str 24, 744017 Ashkabat, Turkmenistan

**Bere, Jason P** — Baseball Player
40 Berrington Place, North Andover MA 01845, USA

**Berehowsky, Drake** — Ice Hockey Player
20455 N 95th St, Scottsdale AZ 85255, USA

**Berendt, John L** — Writer
W M E Entertainment, 9601 Wilshire Blvd, #300, Beverly Hills CA 90210 USA

**Berendzen, Richard E** — Educator
1300 Crystal Dr, Arlington VA 22202, USA

**Berenger, Tom** — Actor
Brillstein Entertainment Partners, 9150 Wilshire Blvd, #350, Beverly Hills CA 90212 USA

**Berengo Gardin, Gianni** — Photographer
Via S Michele del Carso 21, 20144 Milan, Italy

**Berenguer, Juan B** — Baseball Player
8616 Alisa Court, Chanhassen MN 55317, USA

**Berenson, Gordon A (Red)** — Ice Hockey Player, Coach
3555 Daleview Dr, Ann Arbor MI 48105, USA

**Berenyi, Bruce M** — Baseball Player
10 Pine Grove Road, Exeter NH 03833, USA

**Berenzweig, Andrew** — Ice Hockey Player
4603 Brookside Road, Ottawa Hills OH 43615, USA

**Beresford, Meg** — Peace Activist
Wiston Lodge, Wiston, Biggar ML12 6HT, Scotland

**Bereta, Joe** — Actor, Comedian
Barats & Bereta Productions, 9601 Wilshire Blvd, #750, Beverly Hills CA 90210, USA

**Berezan, Perry** — Ice Hockey Player
Wellington West Capital, 1100-255 5th Ave SW, Calgary AB T2P 3G6, Canada

**Berezhnaya, Elena V** — Figure Skater
Figure Skating Federation, Luzhnetskaya Nab 8, 119871 Moscow, Russia

**Berezin, Sergei** — Ice Hockey Player
1645 SW 4th Ave, Boca Raton FL 33432, USA

**Berezovsky, Boris V** — Concert Pianist
I M G Artists, Burlington Lane, Chiswick, London W4 2TH, England

**Berfield, Justin** — Actor
Virgin Produced, 315 S Beverly D, #506, Beverly Hills CA 90212 90212, USA

**Berg, A Scott** — Writer
Creative Artists Agency, 2000 Ave of Stars, #100, Los Angeles CA 90067 USA

**Berg, Aki-Petteri** — Ice Hockey Player
Toronto Maple Leafs, AirCanada Center, 40 Bay St, Toronto ON M5J 2K2, Canada

**Berg, Alec** — Producer, Writer
United Talent Agency, U T A Plaza, 9336 Civic Center Dr, Beverly Hills CA 90210 USA

**Benton - Berg**

**Berg, Andrea** — Singer
Am Sportplatz 16, 49844 Bawinkel, Germany

**Berg, David S (Dave)** — Baseball Player
1917 Stonecastle Dr, Roanoke TX 76262, USA

**Berg, Elizabeth** — Writer
Random House, 1745 Broadway, #1800, New York NY 10019 USA

**Berg, Jeffrey S** — Businessman
Resolution, 1801 Century Park East, #2300, Los Angeles CA 90067, USA

**Berg, Laura** — Softball Player
USA Softball, 2801 NE 50th St, Oklahoma City OK 73111, USA

**Berg, Matraca** — Singer, Songwriter
Universal Publishing Group, 1904 Adelicia St, Nashville TN 37212, USA

**Berg, Paul** — Nobel Chemistry Laureate
838 Santa Fe Ave, Stanford CA 94305, USA

**Berg, Peter** — Actor, Director, Producer
W M E Entertainment, 9601 Wilshire Blvd, #300, Beverly Hills CA 90210 USA

**Berg, William D (Bill)** — Ice Hockey Player
N H L Network, 9 Channel Nine Court, Toronto ON M1S 4B5, Canada

**Berg, Yehuda** — Religious Leader
Kabbalah Centre, 1054 S Robertson Blvd, Los Angeles CA 90035, USA

**Berganio, David, Jr** — Golfer
17811 Lahey St, Granada Hills CA 91344, USA

**Berganza, Teresa** — Opera Singer
La Rossiniana, Archanda 5, 28200 San Lorenzo del Escorial, Madrid, Spain

**Berge, Francine** — Actress
Intertalent, 16 Rue Henri Barbusse, 75005 Paris, France

**Berge, Pierre V G** — Businessman
Yves Saint Laurent SA, 5 Ave Marceau, 75116 Paris, France

**Bergen, Bob** — Actor
C E S D, 10635 Santa Monica Blvd, #130, Los Angeles CA 90025 USA

**Bergen, Candice P** — Actress
51 Tradd St, Charleston SC 29401, USA

**Bergen, Gary D** — Basketball Player
1386 Graham Circle, Erie CO 80516, USA

**Berger Perdomo, Oscar J R** — President, Guatemala
President's Office, Palacio Nacional, 6 Avenida 419, Guatemala City, Guatemala

**Berger, Christian** — Cinematographer
Haus 7, 6072 Lans, Austria

**Berger, Gerhard** — Auto Racing Driver
Berger Motorsport, Postfach 1121, 9490 Vaduz, Austria

**Berger, Glenn** — Writer
W M E Entertainment, 9601 Wilshire Blvd, #300, Beverly Hills CA 90210 USA

**Berger, Helmut** — Actor
Helmut Werner Mgmt, Lugner City, Gablenzgasse 11-15, 1150 Vienna, Austria

**Berger, Howard** — Makeup Artist
K N B Effects Group, 7535 Woodman Place, Van Nuys CA 91405, USA

**Berger, John** — Writer
Quincy, Mieussy, 74440 Taninges, France

**Berger, Joseph D (Joe)** — Football Player
Minnesota Vikings, 9520 Viking Dr, Eden Prairie MN 55344 USA

**Berger, Joseph S** — Inventor (Light Can Converter)
J S B Enterprises, 12605 W North Ave, #225, Brookfield WI 53005, USA

**Berger, Lars** — Cross Country Skier
Dombas/Byaasen I L, PB 9266, Stavset, 7424 Trondheim, Norway

**Berger, Mitchell S (Mitch)** — Football Player
9108 N 118th Place, Scottsdale AZ 85259, USA

**Berger, Peter** — Opera Singer
I M G Artists, Hogarth Business Park, Chiswick, London W4 2TH, England

**Berger, Senta** — Actress, Producer
Deutsche Filmakademie, Kothener Str 44, 10963 Berlin, Germany

**Berger, Tora** — Biathlete
Teglverkstunet 6C, 7531 Meraker, Norway

**Bergere, Jenica** — Actress
Innovative Artists, 1505 10th St, Santa Monica CA 90401 USA

**Bergeron, Jean-Claude (J C)** — Ice Hockey Player
Reebok/C C M, 3400 Raymond-Lasnier St, Saint-Laurent QC H4R 3L3, Canada

**Bergeron, Michel** — Ice Hockey Player, Coach
T Q S, 612 Rue Saint-Jacques, Montreal QC H3C 5R1, Canada

**Bergeron, Patrice** — Ice Hockey Player
234 Causeway St, #1109, Boston MA 02114, USA

**Bergeron, Peter C** — Baseball Player
3495 Manatee Dr SE, Saint Petersburg FL 33705, USA

**Bergeron, Tom** — Entertainer
International Management Group, 2049 Century Park E, #2460, Los Angeles CA 90067, USA

**Bergeron, Yves** — Ice Hockey Player
1035 Clearwater Ave, Bathurst NB E2A 4H5, Canada

**Berges-Frisbey, Astrid** — Actress
Artmedia, 20 Ave Rapp, 75007 Paris, France

**Bergevin, Marc** — Ice Hockey Player
404 Canterbury Court, Hinsdale IL 60521, USA

**Bergey, John** — Inventor (Pulsar Watch)
1807 Mayflower Circle, Lancaster PA 17603, USA

**Bergey, William E (Bill)** — Football Player
2 Hickory Lane, Chadds Ford PA 19317, USA

**Berggren, Jenny** — Singer (Ace of Base)
United Stage Artists, Asogatan 142, Box 11029, 100 61 Stockholm, Sweden

**Berggren, Jonas** — Singer (Ace of Base)
United Stage Artists, Asogatan 142, Box 11029, 100 61 Stockholm, Sweden

**Berggren, Linn** — Singer (Ace of Base)
United Stage Artists, Asogatan 142, Box 11029, 100 61 Stockholm, Sweden

**Berggren, Thommy** — Actor, Director, Writer
Swedish Film Institute, PO Box 27126, 102 52, Stockholm, Sweden

**Bergh, Larry C** — Basketball Player
1849 Bent Pine Hill, Fogelsville PA 18051, USA

**Bergin, Joan** — Costume Designer
Gersh Agency, 9465 Wilshire Blvd, #600, Beverly Hills CA 90212 USA

**Bergin, Michael** — Model, Actor
Chasen Agency, 8899 Beverly Blvd, #405, Los Angeles CA 90048 USA

**Bergin, Patrick** — Actor
Sovereign Talent Group, 8421 Wilshire Blvd, #200, Beverly Hills CA 90211, USA

**Bergkamp, Dennis** — Soccer Player
Arsenal F C, Arsenal Stadium, Avenell Road, London N5 1BU, England

**Bergl, Emily** — Actress
Innovative Artists, 1505 10th St, Santa Monica CA 90401 USA

**Bergland, Robert S (Bob)** — Secretary, Agriculture
1104 7th Ave SE, Roseau MN 56751, USA

**Bergland, Tim** — Ice Hockey Player
721 Labree Ave N, Thief River Falls MN 56701, USA

**Berglund, Art** — Ice Hockey Executive
1775 Bob Johnson Dr, Colorado Springs CO 80906, USA

**Berglund, Bo** — Ice Hockey Player
Buffalo Sabres, 1 Seymour Knox Plaza, #1, Buffalo NY 14203 USA

**Berglund, Patrik** — Ice Hockey Player
Saint Louis Blues, Scottrade Center, 1401 Clark Ave, Saint Louis MO 63103 USA

**Bergman, Alan** — Lyricist
714 N Maple Dr, Beverly Hills CA 90210, USA

**Bergman, Andrew C** — Director, Writer
Creative Artists Agency, 2000 Ave of Stars, #100, Los Angeles CA 90067 USA

**Bergman, David B (Dave)** — Baseball Player
728 Canterbury Road, Grosse Pointe Woods MI 48236, USA

**Bergman, Joel D** — Architect
Bergman Walls Assoc, 2964 S Jones, Las Vegas NV 89146, USA

**Bergman, John W** — Marine Corps General
Commander, Forces Reserve, HqUSMC, 2 Navy St, Washington DC 20380 USA

**Bergman, Lowell** — Journalist
New York Times, Editorial Dept, 229 W 43rd St, New York NY 10036 USA

**Bergman, Marilyn K** — Lyricist
714 N Maple Dr, Beverly Hills CA 90210, USA

**Bergman, Martin** — Producer, Director, Writer
641 Lexington Ave, New York NY 10022, USA

**Bergman, Martin** — Actor, Producer
Martin Bregman Productions, 34-12 36th St, #2/201-2/206, New York NY 11106, USA

**Bergman, Peter** — Actor
Abrams Artists, 9200 W Sunset Blvd, #1125, West Hollywood CA 90069 USA

**Bergman, Robert G** — Chemist
501 Coventry Road, Kensington CA 94707, USA

**Bergman, Sean F** — Baseball Player
14421 Scott Road, Bryan OH 43506, USA

**Bergman, Thommie** — Ice Hockey Player
Tolvmansvagen 4, 18463 Akersberga, Sweden

**Bergmann, Barbara R** — Economist
9707 Old Georgetown Road, #2419, Bethesda MD 20814, USA

**Bergoust, Eric** — Freestyle Aerials Skier
2727 Mulberry Lane, Missoula MT 59804, USA

**Bergqvist, Kajsa M** — Track Athlete
Box 5126, 200 77 Malmo, Sweden

**Bergsma, Jorrit** — Speed Skater
K N S B, Postbus 11087, 3505 Utrecht BB, Netherlands

**Bergsten, C Fred** — Economist
4106 Sleepy Hollow Road, Annandale VA 22003, USA

**Berheim, B Douglas** — Economist
Stanford University, Economics Dept, Stanford CA 94305, USA

**Berisha, Sali** — Prime Minister, Albania
Prime Minister's Office, Keshilli i Ministrave, Tirana, Albania

**Berke, Deborah** — Architect
Deborah Berke Partners Architects, 220 5th Ave, #700, New York NY 10001, USA

**Berkeley, Michael F** — Composer
Oxford University Press, 70 Baker St, London W1U 7DN, England

**Berkley Lauren, Elizabeth** — Actress, Model
Sloane Offer Weber, 9601 Wilshire Blvd, #500, Beverly Hills CA 90210 USA

**Berkman, W Lance (Elvis)** — Baseball Player
5 Farnham Park Dr, Houston TX 77024, USA

**Berkoff, David** — Swimmer
Harvard University, Athletic Dept, Cambridge MA 02138, USA

**Berkoff, Steven** — Actor, Writer
Conway Van Gelder Grant, 8-12 Broadwick St, #300, London W1F 8HW, England

**Berkowitz, Bob** — Entertainer
CNBC-TV, 1 CNBC Plaza, Englewood Cliffs NJ 07632, USA

**Berkus, Nate** — Interior Designer
Nate Berkus Assoc, 406 N Wood St, Chicago IL 60622, USA

**Berlant, Anthony (Tony)** — Artist
Los Angeles Louver Gallery, 55 N Venice Blvd, Venice CA 90291, USA

**Berlanti, Greg** — Director, Producer, Writer
W M E Entertainment, 9601 Wilshire Blvd, #300, Beverly Hills CA 90210 USA

**Berlekamp, Elwyn R** — Mathematician
120 Hazel Lane, Piedmont CA 94611, USA

**Berlin, Eddie** — Football Player
100 Market St, #421, Des Moines IA 50309, USA

**Berlin, Jeannie** — Actress, Director
M C 2 Entertainment, 18541 Elkwood St, Reseda CA 91335, USA

**Berlin, Mike** — Bowler
12 Coventry Lane, Muscatine IA 52761, USA

**Berlin, Steve** — Singer, Saxophonist (Los Lobos)
Gold Mountain, 3940 Laurel Canyon Blvd, #444, Studio City CA 91604 USA

**Berliner, David** — Director
United Talent Agency, U T A Plaza, 9336 Civic Center Dr, Beverly Hills CA 90210 USA

**Berling, Charles** — Actor
Markham Froggat Irwin, Julian House, 4 Windmill St, London W1P 1HF, England

**Berling, Clay** — Soccer Executive, Publisher
2935 Franciscan Way, Carmel CA 93923, USA

**Berling, Peter** — Actor
12 V S Calisto, 00153 Rome, Italy

| | |
|---|---|
| **Berlinger, Warren**<br>23291 Ventura Blvd, Woodland Hills CA 91364, USA | Actor |
| **Berlinsky, Dmitri**<br>35 W 64th St, #7F, New York NY 10023, USA | Concert Violinist |
| **Berlusconi, Silvio**<br>Palazzo Grazioli, Via del Plebiscito 102, 00186 Rome, Italy | Prime Minister, Italy |
| **Berman, Andy**<br>United Talent Agency, U T A Plaza, 9336 Civic Center Dr, Beverly Hills CA 90210 USA | Actor |
| **Berman, Boris**<br>Columbia Artists Mgmt Inc, 5 Columbus Circle, 1790 Broadway, #1600, New York NY 10019 USA | Concert Pianist |
| **Berman, Christopher J (Chris)**<br>ESPN-TV, Sports Dept, ESPN Plaza, 935 Middle St, Bristol CT 06010 USA | Sportscaster |
| **Berman, David**<br>Optimism Entertainment, 303 N La Peer Dr, #205, Beverly Hills CA 90211, USA | Actor |
| **Berman, Francine**<br>San Diego Supercomputer Center, 9500 Gilman Dr, La Jolla CA 92093, USA | Computer Scientist |
| **Berman, Jennifer**<br>University of California, Women's Sexual Health Center, Los Angeles CA 90024, USA | Physician |
| **Berman, Josh**<br>Creative Artists Agency, 2000 Ave of Stars, #100, Los Angeles CA 90067 USA | Producer |
| **Berman, Julia**<br>Julia Berman Design, 947 Camino de Chelly, Santa Fe NM 87505, USA | Architect |
| **Berman, Julius**<br>Kaye Scholer Fierman, 425 Park Ave, #1200, New York NY 10022, USA | Religious Leader, Attorney |
| **Berman, Kip**<br>Slumberland Records, PO Box 19029, Oakland CA 94619, USA | Singer (Pains of Being Pure at Heart) |
| **Berman, Laura**<br>I C M Partners, 10250 Constellation Blvd, #900, Los Angeles CA 90067 USA | Psychotherapist |
| **Berman, Saul J**<br>E D A H, 1501 Broadway, #501, New York NY 10036, USA | Religious Leader, Rabbi, Writer |
| **Berman, Shari Springer**<br>Anonymous Content, 3532 Hayden Ave, Culver City CA 90232 USA | Director, Producer, Writer |
| **Berman, Shelley**<br>268 Bell Canyon Road, Bell Canyon CA 91307, USA | Actor, Comedian |
| **Berman, Zev**<br>Gersh Agency, 9465 Wilshire Blvd, #600, Beverly Hills CA 90212 USA | Writer, Producer, Director |
| **Bern, Dan**<br>Public Emily, 56 Main St, #206, Northampton MA 01060, USA | Singer, Songwriter |
| **Bernal, Gael Garcia**<br>Canana Films, Zacatecas 142A, Colonia Roma, Mexico City DF 06700, Mexico | Actor, Director |
| **Bernanke, Ben S**<br>Federal Reserve Board, 20th St & Constitution Ave NW, Washington DC 20557, USA | Government Official, Economist |
| **Bernard, Betsy**<br>American Telephone & Telegraph Corp, 32 Ave of Americas, New York NY 10013, USA | Businesswoman |
| **Bernard, Carlos**<br>Innovative Artists, 1505 10th St, Santa Monica CA 90401 USA | Actor |
| **Bernard, Crystal**<br>8436 W 3rd St, #650, Los Angeles CA 90048, USA | Actress, Singer, Songwriter |
| **Bernard, Robert (Rocky)**<br>16655 SE 69th Way, Bellevue WA 98006, USA | Football Player |
| **Bernard, Robyn**<br>3227 Cardiff Ave, Los Angeles CA 90034, USA | Actress |
| **Bernard, Rod**<br>PO Box 90665, 2410 Eraste Landry, Lafayette LA 70509, USA | Singer |
| **Bernath, Antonia**<br>Creative Artists Agency, 2000 Ave of Stars, #100, Los Angeles CA 90067 USA | Actress |
| **Bernauer, David W**<br>Walgreen Co, 200 Wilmot Road, Deerfield IL 60015, USA | Businessman |
| **Bernazard Garcia, Antonio (Tony)**<br>D25 Calle Santa Ana, Urb Santa Elvira, Caguas PR 00725, USA | Baseball Player |
| **Berne, Robert M**<br>250 Pantops Mountain Road, #5134, Charlottesville VA 22911, USA | Physiologist |
| **Bernero, Adam G**<br>11 Columbus Dr, Savannah GA 31405, USA | Baseball Player |
| **Bernero, Edward Allen**<br>Creative Artists Agency, 2000 Ave of Stars, #100, Los Angeles CA 90067 USA | Producer, Writer |
| **Berners-Lee, Timothy J**<br>20 Powder Mill Road, Concord MA 1742, USA | Computer Scientist |
| **Bernhard, Sandra**<br>6145 Shadyglade Ave, North Hollywood CA 91606, USA | Actress, Comedienne, Singer |
| **Bernhardt, Tim**<br>RR 1, Schomberg ON L0G 1T0, Canada | Ice Hockey Player |
| **Bernheimer, Martin**<br>17350 Sunset Blvd, #702C, Pacific Palisades CA 90272, USA | Music Critic |
| **Bernier, Serge J**<br>534 Rue Elisabeth, Rimouski QC G5L 3M9, Canada | Ice Hockey Player |
| **Berning, Susie Maxwell**<br>80413 Portobello Dr, Indio CA 92201, USA | Golfer |
| **Berninger, Matt**<br>Brassland Records, PO Box 76, Prince Street Station, New York NY 10012, USA | Singer (National), Songwriter |
| **Bernoldi, Enrique A L S**<br>Bartels Motor & Sport, Kobbinghausen 2, 58840 Plettenberg, Germany | Auto Racing Driver |
| **Berns, Richard R (Rick)**<br>127 Merry Trail, San Antonio TX 78232, USA | Football Player |
| **Bernsen, Corbin**<br>Home Theater Films, 12041 Maxwellton Road, Studio City CA 91604, USA | Actor |
| **Bernstein, Bonnie**<br>Monmouth County District Attorney, 71 Monmouth Park, Freehold NJ 07728, USA | Sportscaster |
| **Bernstein, Carl**<br>14 E 60th St, #705, New York NY 10022, USA | Journalist |
| **Bernstein, Charles**<br>Soundtrack Music Assoc, 1460 4th St, #308, Santa Monica CA 90401 USA | Composer |
| **Bernstein, Jake**<br>ProPublica, Editorial Dept, 1 Exchange Plaza, 55 Broadway, #2300, New York NY 10006, USA | Journalist |
| **Bernstein, Jamie**<br>Opus 3 Artists, 470 Park Ave S, #900N, New York NY 10016 USA | Concert Narrator |

**Bernstein, Jared** — Government Official, Economist
Budget & Policy Priorities Center, 820 1st St NW, #510, Washington DC 20002, USA
**Bernstein, Kenny** — Auto Racing Driver
Budweiser King Racing, 26231 Dimension Dr, Lake Forest CA 92630, USA
**Bernstine, Rod E** — Football Player
22180 E Euclid Place, Aurora CO 80016, USA
**Bernthal, Jon** — Actor
W M E Entertainment, 9601 Wilshire Blvd, #300, Beverly Hills CA 90210 USA
**Berra, Dale A** — Baseball Player
164 Eagle Rock Way, Montclair NJ 07042, USA
**Berra, Lawrence P (Yogi)** — Baseball Player, Manager
19 Highland Ave, Montclair NJ 07042, USA
**Berrian, Bernard** — Football Player
7209 Tokay Circle, Winton CA 95388, USA
**Berridge, Michael J** — Zoologist, Biologist
Babraham Institute, Babraham Hall, Cambridge CB2 4AT, England
**Berrigan, Daniel** — Clergyman, Social Activist
147 Thompson St, New York NY 10012, USA
**Berroa, Geronimo E** — Baseball Player
3681 Broadway, #23, New York NY 10031, USA
**Berry, A Kenneth (Ken)** — Baseball Player
1131 SW Camden Lane, Topeka KS 66604, USA
**Berry, Ace** — Rodeo Rider
29705 E County Road 1650, Elmore City OK 73433, USA
**Berry, Bertrand D (Bert)** — Football Player
1402 E Coral Cove Dr, Gilbert AZ 85234, USA
**Berry, Bill** — Drummer (REM)
REM/Athens Ltd, 170 College Ave, Athens GA 30601, USA
**Berry, Brad** — Ice Hockey Player
PO Box 5182, Grand Forks ND 58206, USA
**Berry, Brian J L** — Geographer, Political Economist
2404 Forest Court, McKinney TX 75070, USA
**Berry, Charles E (Chuck)** — Singer, Songwriter
Berry Park, 691 Buckner Road, Wentzville MO 63385, USA
**Berry, Cornelius J (Neil)** — Baseball Player
407 Inkster Ave, Kalamazoo MI 49001, USA
**Berry, Halle** — Actress, Model
Vincent Cirrincione Assoc, 1516 N Fairfax Ave, Los Angeles CA 90046 USA
**Berry, Jim** — Editorial Cartoonist
United Feature Syndicate, PO Box 5610, Cincinnati OH 45201 USA
**Berry, John** — Singer
Circle T Management, 44 Wiregrass Circle, Tifton GA 31794, USA
**Berry, Kenneth R (Ken)** — Actor
147 Sunny Lane, Branson West MO 65737, USA
**Berry, Marilou** — Actress
J F P M, 11 Rue Chanez, 75781 Paris Cedex 16, France
**Berry, Mark (Bez)** — Percussionist (Happy Mondays)
145 S Fairfax, #310, Los Angeles CA 90036, USA
**Berry, Michael J** — Chemist
7801 Comfort Cove, Austin TX 78731, USA
**Berry, R Stephen** — Chemist
5317 S University Ave, Chicago IL 60615, USA
**Berry, Raymond E** — Football Player, Coach
1110 SE Broad St, Murfreesboro TN 37130, USA
**Berry, Robert C (Bob)** — Football Player
1351 Wilson Circle, Gardnerville NV 89410, USA
**Berry, Robert V (Bob)** — Ice Hockey Player, Coach, Executive
640 3rd St, Hermosa Beach CA 90254, USA
**Berry, Royce E** — Football Player
PO Box 909, Comfort TX 78013, USA
**Berry, Sean R** — Baseball Player
307 Susannah Lane, Paso Robles CA 93446, USA
**Berry, Stephen J (Steve)** — Journalist
6527 Ellenview Ave, West Hills CA 91307, USA
**Berry, Walter** — Basketball Player
PO Box 81, Union City GA 30291, USA
**Berry, Wendell E** — Writer, Ecologist
PO Box 1, Port Royal KY 40058, USA
**Berryhill, Damon S** — Baseball Player
11 Springbrook Road, Laguna Niguel CA 92677, USA
**Berryman, Guy R** — Bassist (Coldplay)
Paradigm Agency, 360 N Crescent Dr, North Building, Beverly Hills CA 90210 USA
**Berryman, Michael J** — Actor
5806 Hannah Pierce Road W, #G, University Place WA 98467, USA
**Bersani, Leo** — Educator
University of California, French Dept, Berkeley CA 94720, USA
**Bersia, John** — Journalist
Orlando Sentinel, Editorial Dept, 633 N Orange Ave, Orlando FL 32801, USA
**Berson, Jerome A** — Chemist
200 Leeder Hill Dr, #205, Hamden CT 06517, USA
**Bertarelli, Ernesto** — Businessman, Yachtsman
Serono SA, Chemin des Mines 15 Bis, 1211 Geneva 20, Switzerland
**Bertello, Giuseppe Cardinal** — Religious Leader
Governatorate of Vatican City State, Urbs Salvia, 00120 Vatican City
**Bertelsen, James A (Jim)** — Football Player
2001 Days End Road, Wimberley TX 78676, USA
**Berteotti, Missie** — Golfer
300 Kane Blvd, Pittsburgh PA 15243, USA
**Berthiaume, Daniel** — Ice Hockey Player
PO Box 673, Hardy VA 24101, USA
**Berti, Marco** — Opera Singer
I M G Artists, Hogarth Business Park, Chiswick, London W4 2TH, England
**Bertil** — Crown Prince, Sweden
Hert Av Halland, Kungl Slottet, 111 30 Stockholm, Sweden
**Bertinelli, Valerie** — Actress
Innovative Artists, 1505 10th St, Santa Monica CA 90401 USA

**Bertish, Suzanne** — Actress
Jonathan Altaras Assoc, 11 Garrick St, London WC2E 9AR, England
**Berto, Andre M** — Boxer
Ray Rafoll, 1519 3rd St SE, Winterhaven FL 33880, USA
**Bertolucci, Bernardo** — Director
Via Della Lungara 3, 00165 Rome, Italy
**Bertone, Tarcisio Cardinal** — Religious Leader
Secretary of State's Office, Apostolic Palace, Palazzo Apostolico Vaticano, 00120 Vatican City
**Bertotti, Michael D (Mike)** — Baseball Player
14 Jupiter Road, Highland Mills NY 10930, USA
**Bertrup, Christina** — Curling Athlete
Masgatan 7, 856 34 Sundsvall, Sweden
**Bertsch, Jackie** — Golfer
300 Ocean Trail Way, #1304, Jupiter FL 33477, USA
**Bertsch, Shane** — Golfer
11120 Night Heron Dr, Parker CO 80134, USA
**Bertuzzi, Todd** — Ice Hockey Player
900 Deer Ridge Court, Kitchener ON N2P 2L3, Canada
**Berube, Craig** — Ice Hockey Player
1314 Durham Road, New Hope PA 18938, USA
**Berzins, Andris** — President, Latvia
President's Office, Ratslaukums 7, 1900 Riga LV, Latvia
**Berzon, Marsha S** — Judge
US Court of Appeals, Court Building, 95 7th St, San Francisco CA 94103, USA
**Beshore, Delmer (Del)** — Basketball Player
4724 N Crestmoor Ave, Clovis CA 93619, USA
**Besler, Matt** — Soccer Player
Sporting Kansas City, 210 W 19th Terrace, #200, Kansas City MO 64108 USA
**Bess, Daniel** — Actor
Coast to Coast Talent, 3350 Barham Blvd, Los Angeles CA 90068 USA
**Bess, Rufus T, Jr** — Football Player
10 Greenview Circle, Chico CA 95928, USA
**Bessmertnykh, Aleksandr A** — Government Official, Russia
International Foreign Policy Assn, Yakovo-Apostolski 10, 103604 Moscow, Russia
**Bessmertnykh, Alexander A** — Cross Country Skier
Ski Association, Luzhnetskaya Nab 8, 119270 Moscow, Russia
**Besson, Luc** — Director
Europa Corp, 137, Rue du Faubourg Saint-Honore, 75008 Paris, France
**Best, Ahmed** — Actor
PO Box 707, Renton WA 98057, USA
**Best, Ben** — Actor, Comedian, Producer
Creative Artists Agency, 2000 Ave of Stars, #100, Los Angeles CA 90067 USA
**Best, Eve** — Actress, Singer
Independent Talent Group, 40 Whitfield St, London W1T 2RH, England
**Best, Greg** — Equestrian
39 Troon Terrace, Annandale NJ 08801, USA
**Best, James** — Actor, Director, Writer
PO Box 5325, Hickory NC 28603, USA
**Best, Karl J** — Baseball Player
PO Box 1790, Snohomish WA 98291, USA
**Best, R Peter (Pete)** — Singer, Drummer (Beatles)
Splash Mgmt, 8 Hymans Green, West Derby, Liverpool L12 7JG, England
**Best, Travis E** — Basketball Player
703 Bradley Road, Springfield MA 01109, USA
**Bester, Allan** — Ice Hockey Player
12527 Crayford Ave, Orlando FL 32837, USA
**Beswicke, Martine** — Actress
4011 Primavera Road, #B, Santa Barbara CA 93110, USA
**Betancourt Perez, Yuniesky** — Baseball Player
1001 Brickell Bay Dr, #1710, Miami FL 33131, USA
**Betancourt, Rafael J** — Baseball Player
6857 Valhalla Way, Windermere FL 34786, USA
**Betancur Cuartas, Belisario** — President, Colombia
Fundacio Santilana, Calle 80, #3974, Santa Fe de Bogota, Colombia
**Bethea, Elvin L** — Football Player
16211 Leslie Lane, Missouri City TX 77489, USA
**Bethell, Tabrett** — Actress
W M E Entertainment, 9601 Wilshire Blvd, #300, Beverly Hills CA 90210 USA
**Betker, Jan** — Curling Athlete
Curling Association, 1660 Vimont Court, Cumberland ON K4A 4J4, Canada
**Betori, Giuseppe Cardinal** — Religious Leader
Archdiocese of Florence, Piazza San Giovanni 3, 50129 Florence, Italy
**Bets, Maxim** — Ice Hockey Player
5566 Candlelight Dr, La Jolla CA 92037, USA
**Bettany, Paul** — Actor
Affirmative Entertainment, 425 N Robertson Blvd, Los Angeles CA 90048 USA
**Bettencourt, Liliane** — Businesswoman
L'Oreal Group, 41 Rue Matre, 92117 Clichy, France
**Bettencourt, Nuno** — Guitarist (Extreme)
Dreamscapers International, 1701 18th Ave S, Nashville TN 37212, USA
**Bettens, Gert** — Guitarist, Keyboardist (K's Choice)
Sharpe Entertainment Services, 683 Palmera Ave, Pacific Palisades CA 90272, USA
**Bettens, Sarah** — Singer (K's Choice)
Sharpe Entertainment Services, 683 Palmera Ave, Pacific Palisades CA 90272, USA
**Betters, Doug L** — Football Player
77 Better Way, Whitefish MT 59937, USA
**Bettinger, Walter** — Financier
Charles Schwab Co, 101 Montgomery St, #200, San Francisco CA 94104, USA
**Bettini, Paolo** — Cyclist
Via Aurelia Sud 8, 77020 La California-Bibbona (LI), Italy
**Bettis, Angela** — Actress
BenderSpink, 8447 Wilshire Blvd, #250, Beverly Hills CA 90211 USA
**Bettis, Jerome A** — Football Player, Sportscaster
1651 Randall Mill Place NW, Atlanta GA 30327, USA
**Bettis, W Thomas (Tom)** — Football Player, Coach
6931 Terrace Ridge, Katy TX 77494, USA

# B

**Bettman, Gary B** — Ice Hockey Executive
National Hockey League, 1251 Ave of Americas, #4601, New York NY 10020, USA

**Betts, Daisy** — Actress
Greenlight Mgmt, 10250 Constellation Blvd, #900, Los Angeles CA 90067, USA

**Betts, F Richard (Dickie)** — Singer, Guitarist (Allman Brothers Band)
David Spero Mgmt, 1679 S Belvoir Blvd, Cleveland OH 44121, USA

**Betts, M Ladell** — Football Player
4765 W Leitner Dr, Coral Springs FL 33067, USA

**Betzig, Eric** — Nobel Chemistry Laureate
Howard Hughes Medical Institute, Janelia Farm Research Campus, 19700 Helix Drive, Ashburn VA 20147, USA

**Beuerlein, Stephen T (Steve)** — Football Player
15624 McCullers Court, Charlotte NC 28277, USA

**Beukeboom, Jeff** — Ice Hockey Player
464 Wagg Road, RR 4, Uxbridge ON L9P 1R4, Canada

**Beuron, Yann** — Opera Singer
I M G Artists, Hogarth Business Park, Chiswick, London W4 2TH, England

**Beutler, Bruce** — Nobel Medicine Laureate
Scripps Research Institute, 10550 N Torrey Pines Road, La Jolla CA 92037 USA

**Bevan, Alonzo G** — Bassist (Kula Shaker)
Little Big Man, 39A Grammercy Park N, #1C, New York NY 10010, USA

**Bevan, Tim** — Actor, Producer
Working Title Films, 26 Aybrook Str, London W1U 4AN, England

**Beverley, Nick** — Ice Hockey Player, Coach, Executive
Nashville Predators, 501 Broadway, Nashville TN 37203 USA

**Beverly, David E (Dave)** — Football Player
15 Wood Cove Dr, Spring TX 77381, USA

**Beverly, Eric R** — Football Player
PO Box 492433, Lawrenceville GA 30049, USA

**Beverly, Frankie** — Singer (Maze)
115 Cherokee Rose Lane, Fayetteville GA 30214, USA

**Beverly, Jo** — Writer
Signet Books, 375 Hudson St, New York NY 10014, USA

**Beverly, Randolph (Randy)** — Football Player
PO Box 193, Monroe Township NJ 08831, USA

**Bevill, Lisa** — Singer
Jeff Roberts, 3050 Business Park Circle, #301, Goodlettsville TN 37072, USA

**Bevington, Terry P** — Baseball Manager
2600 Halle Parkway, Collierville TN 38017, USA

**Bevis, Leslie** — Actress
Epstein-Wyckoff, 280 S Beverly Dr, #400, Beverly Hills CA 90212 USA

**Bewersdorff, Uwe** — Figure Skater
Bahnhofstr 60, 69514 Laudenbach, Germany

**Bewkes, Jeffrey L (Jeff)** — Businessman
Time Warner, 10 Columbus Circle, New York NY 10019, USA

**Bex, Shannon** — Singer (Danity Kane)
Bad Boy Entertainment, 1440 Broadway, #16, New York NY 10018 USA

**Bey, George** — Anthropologist
Millsaps College, Anthropology Dept, 1701 State St, Jackson MS 39201, USA

**Bey, Richard** — Entertainer
445 Park Ave, #1000, New York NY 10022, USA

**Beyer, Andy** — Sportswriter
4237 Lenore Lane NW, Washington DC 20008, USA

**Beyer, Brad** — Actor
Abrams Artists, 9200 W Sunset Blvd, #1125, West Hollywood CA 90069 USA

**Beyer, Frank M** — Composer
Academie der Kunste, Hanseatenweg 10, 10557 Berlin, Germany

**Beyer, Markus** — Boxer
Daniela Haak, Niederende 1, 28665 Lilienthal, Germany

**Beyer, Peter** — Biochemist
Albert-Ludwigs-Universitat, Biochemistry Dept, 79104 Freiburg, Germany

**Beyer, Tanya** — Model
Playboy Promotions, 9346 Civic Center Dr, #200, Beverly Hills CA 90210 USA

**Beyer, Troy** — Actress, Director
Independent Artists Agency, 9601 Wilshire Blvd, #750, Beverly Hills. CA 90210, USA

**Beymer, Richard** — Actor
147 N Ridgewood Place, Los Angeles CA 90004, USA

**Bezmalinovic, Mislav** — Water Polo Player
Ciovska 6A, 21000 Split, Croatia

**Bezos, Jeff** — Businessman
Amazon Inc, 1200 12th Ave S, #1200, Seattle WA 98144, USA

**Bezucha, Thomas G (Tom)** — Director, Writer
Creative Artists Agency, 2000 Ave of Stars, #100, Los Angeles CA 90067 USA

**BG** — Rap Artist (Hot Boys)
Nene Musik Productions, 1460 SW Santiago Ave, Port Saint Lucie FL 34953 USA

**Bhanupriya** — Actress
4 1st Cross St, Vijayaraghava Road, Chennai TN 600017, India

**Bhardwaj, Mohini** — Gymnast
53 Juergens Ave, Cincinnati OH 45220, USA

**Bhargava, Manjul** — Mathematician
Princeton University, Fine Hall, Princeton NJ 08544, USA

**Bhaskar, Sanjeev** — Actor
United Agents, 12-26 Lexington St, London W1F 0LE, England

**Bhattacharya, Sameer** — Guitarist (Flyleaf)
W M E Entertainment, 9601 Wilshire Blvd, #300, Beverly Hills CA 90210 USA

**Bhavsar, Natvar P** — Artist
131 Greene St, New York NY 10012, USA

**Bhraonain, Maire Ni** — Singer, Harpist (Clannad); Songwriter
Soho Agency, 55 Fulham High St, London SW6 3JJ, England

**Bhumibol Adulyadej (Rama IX)** — King, Thailand
Royal Residence, Chitralada Villa, 9 Rama VI Road, Soi 30, Bangkok 10400, Thailand

**Biafra, Jello** — Singer (Dead Kennedys), Songwriter
Agency Group Ltd, 142 W 57th St, #600, New York NY 10019 USA

**Biagiotti, Laura** — Fashion Designer
Biagiotti Group, Via Palombarese Km 17 300, 00012 Guidonia, Italy

**Biakabutuka, Tshimanga (Tim)** — Football Player
110 Sonnys Way, Fort Mill SC 29708, USA

**Biali, Laila** — Singer, Songwriter
Agency Group Ltd, 142 W 57th St, #600, New York NY 10019 USA
**Bialik, Mayim** — Actress
TalentWorks, 3500 W Olive Ave, #1400, Burbank CA 91505 USA
**Biancalana, Roland A (Buddy)** — Baseball Player
1204 Lakeview Dr, Fairfield IA 52556, USA
**Bianchi, Alfred A (Al)** — Basketball Player, Coach
Miami Heat, American Airlines Arena, 601 Biscayne Blvd, Miami FL 33132 USA
**Bianchin, Wayne** — Ice Hockey Player
2091 Wellington Road E, Nanaimo BC V9S 5V2, Canada
**Bianco, Esme** — Actress
Baker Winokur Ryder Public Relations, 9100 Wilshire Blvd, #500W, Beverly Hills CA 90212 USA
**Bianco, Lory (Bonnie)** — Singer, Actress
PO Box 218, Brinnon WA 98320, USA
**Bianco, Suzannah** — Synchronized Swimmer
Cirque du Soleil, 8400 2nd Ave, Montreal QC H1Z 4M6, Canada
**Biasucci, Dean** — Football Player
3484 Sandy Beach Dr, Canandaigua NY 14424, USA
**Bibb, Leslie** — Actress
I C M Partners, 10250 Constellation Blvd, #900, Los Angeles CA 90067 USA
**Bibby, C Henry** — Basketball Player, Coach
191 Beale St, Memphis TN 38103, USA
**Bibby, Michael (Mike)** — Basketball Player
6439 E Gelding Dr, Scottsdale AZ 85254, USA
**Bichette, A Dante, Sr** — Baseball Player
119 1st St W, Saint Petersburg FL 33715, USA
**Bichir, Demian** — Actor
Creative Artists Agency, 2000 Ave of Stars, #100, Los Angeles CA 90067 USA
**Bickerstaff, Bernard T (Bernie)** — Basketball Coach, Executive
Portland Trail Blazers, Rose Garden, 1 N Center Court St, Portland OR 97227 USA
**Bickett, Duane C** — Football Player
508 Van Dyke Ave, Del Mar CA 92014, USA
**Bickle, Richard (Rich), Jr** — Truck, Auto Racing Driver
Billy Ballew Motorsports, 802A Performance Road, Mooresville NC 28115, USA
**Bidart, Frank** — Writer
Wellesley College, English Dept, 106 Central St, Wellesley MA 02481, USA
**Bidaud, Laurence** — Curling Athlete
Curling Association, PO Box 606, 3000 Bern, Switzerland
**Biddle, Lee F (Rocky)** — Baseball Player
2031 E Rancho Culebra Dr, Covina CA 91724, USA
**Biddle, Martin** — Archaeologist
19 Hamilton Road, Oxford OX2 7OY, England
**Biden, Joseph R (Joe), Jr** — Vice President; Senator, DE
White House, 1600 Pennsylvania Ave NW, Washington DC 20502, USA
**Bidner, Todd** — Ice Hockey Player
434 Oozloffsky, Petrolia ON N0N 1R0, Canada
**Bidstrup, Jane** — Curling Athlete
Curling Association, Idraettens Hus, 2605 Brondby, Denmark
**Bidwell, Charles E** — Sociologist
5835 S Kimbark Ave, Chicago IL 60637, USA
**Bidwell, Joshua J (Josh)** — Football Player
11924 Middlebury Dr, Tampa FL 33626, USA
**Bidwell, William V** — Football Executive
Arizona Cardinals, PO Box 888, Phoenix AZ 85001 USA
**Bieber, Justin** — Singer
Creative Artists Agency, 2000 Ave of Stars, #100, Los Angeles CA 90067 USA
**Bieber, Nita** — Actress
PO Box 1889, Avalon CA 90704, USA
**Bieber, Owen F** — Labor Leader
United Auto Workers Union, 8000 E Jefferson Ave, Detroit MI 48214, USA
**Biebl-Prelevic, Heidi** — Alpine Skier
Haus Olympia, 87534 Oberstaufen, Germany
**Biedermann, Jeanette** — Singer, Actress
One Two Media, Schluter Str 51, 10629 Berlin, Germany
**Biedermann, Paul** — Swimmer
Albus Sportmanagement, Jospitalstr 7, 69115 Heidelberg, Germany
**Biedrins, Andris** — Basketball Player
Utah Jazz, Energy Solutions Arena, 301 W South Temple, Salt Lake City UT 84101 USA
**Biegel, Kevin** — Producer
I C M Partners, 10250 Constellation Blvd, #900, Los Angeles CA 90067 USA
**Biehn, Michael** — Actor
14358 Magnolia Blvd, #229, Sherman Oaks CA 91423, USA
**Bieka, Silvestre Siale** — Prime Minister, Equatorial Guinea
Prime Minister's Office, Malabo, Equatorial Guinea
**Biekert, Greg** — Football Player
2360 Fish Creek Place, Danville CA 94506, USA
**Biel, Jessica** — Actress
L B I Entertainment, 2000 Avenue of Stars, Century City CA 90067, USA
**Bielanko, Dave** — Singer, Songwriter, Guitarist (Marah)
Yep Roc Records, 449A Trollingwood Road, Haw River NC 27258, USA
**Bielanko, Serge** — Singer, Songwriter, Guitarist (Marah)
Yep Roc Records, 449A Trollingwood Road, Haw River NC 27258, USA
**Bielecki, J Krzysztof** — Prime Minister, Poland
European Reconstruction Bank, 1 Exchange Square, London EC2A 2EA, England
**Bielecki, Michael J (Mike)** — Baseball Player
1505 Habersham Place, Crownsville MD 21032, USA
**Bielema, Bret A** — Football Coach
University of Arkansas, Athletic Dept, Fayetteville AR 72701, USA
**Bieler, Christoph** — Nordic Combined Skier
Alte Arlbergstr 76, 6580 Saint Anton, Austria
**Bielke, Donald P (Don)** — Basketball Player
126 Madelia Place, San Ramon CA 94583, USA
**Biellmann, Denise** — Figure Skater
Im Brachli 25, 8053 Zurich, Switzerland
**Bielski, Richard (Dick)** — Football Player
27 Malibu Court, Towson MD 21204, USA

Biali - Bielski

**Bieniemy, Eric** — Football Player
11478 S Carbondale St, Olathe KS 66061, USA
**Bier, Susanne** — Director
Creative Artists Agency, 2000 Ave of Stars, #100, Los Angeles CA 90067 USA
**Bierhoff, Oliver** — Soccer Player
D F B, Otto-Fleck-Schneise 6, 60528 Frankkfurt/Main, Germany
**Bierko, Craig** — Actor, Singer
Impression Entertainment, 9229 W Sunset Blvd, #700 , Los Angeles CA 90069, USA
**Bierman, Bernard (Bernie)** — Songwriter
1 Penn Plaza, #4401, New York NY 10119, USA
**Bierman, Bruce** — Interior Designer
29 W 15th St, #A, New York NY 10011, USA
**Bierman, Robert** — Director
Independent Talent Group, 40 Whitfield St, London W1T 2RH, England
**Bies, Don** — Golfer
1262 NW Blakely Court, Seattle WA 98177, USA
**Biffi, Giacomo Cardinal** — Religious Leader
Archdiocese of Bologna, Via Altabella 6, 40126 Bologna, Italy
**Biffle, Gregory J (Greg)** — Auto, Truck Racing Driver
8807 Heatherstone Court, Terrell NC 28682, USA
**Big Boi** — Rap Artist (OutKast), Songwriter
4016 Elizabeth Terrace, Rex GA 30273, USA
**Big Daddy Kane** — Rap Artist, Lyricist
Betty of Troy, 100 Lincoln Ave, #12D, Mineola NY 11502, USA
**Big K R I T** — Rap Artist
Agency Group Ltd, 142 W 57th St, #600, New York NY 10019 USA
**Big Sean** — Rap Artist
Agency Group Ltd, 142 W 57th St, #600, New York NY 10019 USA
**Bigbie, Larry R** — Baseball Player
102 Brooke Lane, Centreville MD 21617, USA
**Bigelow, Kathryn A** — Director
Creative Artists Agency, 2000 Ave of Stars, #100, Los Angeles CA 90067 USA
**Biggio, Craig A** — Baseball Player
6520 Belmont St, Houston TX 77005, USA
**Biggs, Don** — Ice Hockey Player
10050 Somerset Dr, Loveland OH 45140, USA
**Biggs, Jason** — Actor
Baker Winokur Ryder Public Relations, 9100 Wilshire Blvd, #500W, Beverly Hills CA 90212 USA
**Biggs, John H** — Businessman
240 E 47th St, #47D, New York NY 10017, USA
**Biggs, Peter M** — Veterinarian
Willows, London Road, Saint Ives PE27 5ES, England
**Biggs, Tyrell (Burt)** — Boxer
Scott Schiff, 330 S High St, Columbus OH 43215, USA
**Bigham, John** — Guitarist, Keyboardist (Fishbone)
Silverback Mgmt, 9469 Jefferson Blvd, #101, Culver City CA 90232, USA
**Bigley, Thomas J** — Navy Admiral
20530 Falcons Landing Circle, #3210, Sterling VA 20165, USA
**Biittner, Lawrence D (Larry)** — Baseball Player
915 3rd Ave NW, Pocahontas IA 50574, USA
**Bikel, Theodore** — Actor, Singer
167 Langley Road, Newton Center MA 02459, USA
**Bilal** — Singer, Songwriter
Creative Artists Agency, 2000 Ave of Stars, #100, Los Angeles CA 90067 USA
**Bilardello, Dann J** — Baseball Player
4600 2nd St, Vero Beach FL 32968, USA
**Bilderback, Nicole** — Actress
Rebel Entertainment Partners, 5700 Wilshire Blvd, #456, Los Angeles CA 90036, USA
**Bildt, N D Carl** — Prime Minister, Sweden
Kreab Group, Floragatan 13, 114 75, Stockholm, Sweden
**Bileck, Pamela (Pam)** — Gymnast
2475 Redbud Court, San Jose CA 95128, USA
**Biletnikoff, Frederick (Fred)** — Football Player, Coach
1736 Avondale Dr, Roseville CA 95747, USA
**Bill, Leo** — Actor
Hamilton Hodell, 20 Golden Square, London W1F 9JL, England
**Bill, Tony** — Producer, Director, Actor
Barnstorm Films, 73 Market St, Venice CA 90291, USA
**Billick, Brian H** — Football Coach, Sportscaster
836 Stagwell Road, Queenstown MD 21658, USA
**Billing, Roy** — Actor
Sue Barnett Assoc, 1/96 Albion St, Surrey Hills, Sydney 2010, Australia
**Billingham, John E (Jack)** — Baseball Player
625 Faulkner St, New Smyrna FL 32168, USA
**Billinglsey, Ronald S (Ron)** — Football Player
PO Box 2455, Gadsden AL 35903, USA
**Billings, Earl** — Actor
Stone Manners Salners, 6100 Wilshire Blvd, #1500, Los Angeles CA 90035 USA
**Billings, Richard A (Dick)** — Baseball Player
1917 Creek Wood Dr, Arlington TX 76006, USA
**Billingslea, Beau** — Actor
Abrams Artists, 9200 W Sunset Blvd, #1125, West Hollywood CA 90069 USA
**Billingsley, Chad R** — Baseball Player
25686 N Sandstone Way, Surprise AZ 85387, USA
**Billingsley, Hobie** — Diving Coach
746 E Pepperridge Dr, Bloomington IN 47401, USA
**Billingsley, John A** — Actor
Stone Manners Salners, 6100 Wilshire Blvd, #1500, Los Angeles CA 90035 USA
**Billingsley, Peter** — Actor, Producer
Stone Meyer Genow, 9665 Wilshire Blvd, #510, Beverly Hills CA 90212 USA
**Billingsley, Ray** — Cartoonist (Curtis)
King Features Syndicate, 300 W 57th St, #1500, New York NY 10019 USA
**Billington, Craig** — Ice Hockey Player
Colorado Avalanche, Pepsi Center, 1000 Chopper Circle, Denver CO 80204 USA
**Billington, David P** — Civil Engineer
401 Webster St, #205, Palo Alto CA 94301, USA

**Billington, Kevin** — Director
Judy Daish Assoc, 2 Saint Charles Place, London W10 6EG, England

**Billups, Chauncey R** — Basketball Player
11 Sandy Lake Road, Englewood CO 80113, USA

**Bilodeau, Alexandre** — Freestyle Moguls Skier
Freestyle Ski Assn, 808 Pacific St, Vancouver BC V6Z 1C6, Canada

**Bilodeau, Jean-Luc** — Actor
Kirk Talent Agencies, 196 W 3rd Ave, #102, Vancouver BC V5Y 1E9, Canada

**Bilozertchev, Dimitri V** — Gymnast
13175 SW Yarrow Way, Portland OR 97223, USA

**Bilson, Bruce** — Director
Downwind Enterprises, 12505 Sarah St, Studio City CA 91604, USA

**Bilson, Malcolm** — Concert Pianist
132 N Sunset Dr, Ithaca NY 14850, USA

**Bilson, Rachel** — Actress
Creative Artists Agency, 2000 Ave of Stars, #100, Los Angeles CA 90067 USA

**Binder, Leonard** — Political Scientist
University of California, Political Science Dept, Los Angeles CA 90024, USA

**Binder, Mike** — Actor, Director, Writer
Verve Talent & Literary Agency, 96310 San Vicente Blvd, #100, Los Angeles CA 90048 USA

**Binder, Theodor** — Physician
Taos Canyon, Taos NM 87571, USA

**Bing, David (Dave)** — Basketball Player; Mayor, Detroit
29555 Woodhaven Lane, Southfield MI 48076, USA

**Bing, Jonathan** — Writer
Trident Media Group, 41 Madison Ave, #3600, New York NY 10010, USA

**Bingbing Fan** — Actress, Singer
W M E Entertainment, 9601 Wilshire Blvd, #300, Beverly Hills CA 90210 USA

**Binger, Brittany** — Model
Playboy Promotions, 9346 Civic Center Dr, #200, Beverly Hills CA 90210 USA

**Bingham, Craig M** — Football Player
179 Black Oak Dr, Pittsburgh PA 15220, USA

**Bingham, Gregory R (Greg)** — Football Player
3710 W Valley Dr, Missouri City TX 77459, USA

**Bingham, Guy R** — Football Player
9214 Keegan Trail, Missoula MT 59808, USA

**Bingham, Ryan** — Singer, Songwriter
Creative Artists Agency, 2000 Ave of Stars, #100, Los Angeles CA 90067 USA

**Bingham, Traci** — Actress, Model
Electra Star Mgmt, 9229 Sunset Blvd, #415, Los Angeles CA 90069, USA

**Binion, Jack B** — Poker Player
Wynn Resorts, 3131 Las Vegas Blvd S, Las Vegas NV 89109, USA

**Binkley, Gregg** — Actor
Schachter Entertainment, 1157 S Beverly Dr, #200, Los Angeles CA 90035 USA

**Binmore, Kenneth G** — Economist
Newmills, Whitebrook, Monmouth, Gwent NP5 4TY, England

**Binn, David A (Dave)** — Football Player
2005 Loring St, San Diego CA 92109, USA

**Binnie, W Brian** — Test Pilot
Scaled Composites, Mojave Airport, Hangar 78, Mojave CA 93501, USA

**Binnig, Gerd K** — Nobel Physics Laureate
I B M Research Laboratory, Saumerstr 4, 8803 Ruschlikon, Switzerland

**Binns, Malcolm** — Concert Pianist
Turner Mgmt, 223 Kingston Road, Leatherhead, Surrey KT22 7PE, England

**Binoche, Juliette** — Actress
Artmedia, 20 Ave Rapp, 75007 Paris, France

**Bintley, David** — Choreographer
Birmingham Ballet, Thorpe St, Birmingham B5 4AU, England

**Biondi, Frank J, Jr** — Businessman
Biondi Reiss Capital Mgmt, 1114 Ave of Americas, New York NY 10036, USA

**Biondi, Matthew N (Matt)** — Swimmer
Parker School, 65-1224 Lindsey Road, Mathematics Dept, Kamuela HI 96743, USA

**Birch, Diane** — Singer, Songwriter
Magus Entertainment, 158 W 23rd St, #2, New York NY 10011, USA

**Birch, L Charles** — Zoologist
5A/73 Yarranabbe Road, Darling Point NSW 2027, Australia

**Birch, Stanley F, Jr** — Judge
US Court of Appeals, 56 Forsyth St NW, Atlanta GA 30303, USA

**Birch, Thora** — Actress
Keep the Peace Productions, PO Box 691675, West Hollywood CA 90069, USA

**Birck, Michael J** — Businessman
Tellabs Inc, 1415 W Diehl Road, Naperville IL 60563, USA

**Bird, Andrew** — Singer, Guitarist, Songwriter
Ekonomisk Mgmt, 3147 W Logan Blvd, #7, Chicago IL 60647, USA

**Bird, Brad** — Animator
Pixar Animation, 1200 Park Ave, Emeryville CA 94608, USA

**Bird, Caroline** — Social Activist, Writer
60 Grammercy Park, New York NY 10010, USA

**Bird, Forrest M** — Inventor (Medical Respirators)
Percussionaire Corp, PO Box 817, Sandpoint ID 83864, USA

**Bird, J Douglas (Doug)** — Baseball Player
11821 Lady Anne Circle, Cape Coral FL 33991, USA

**Bird, Larry J** — Basketball Player, Coach, Executive
4715 Ellery Lane, Indianapolis IN 46250, USA

**Bird, R Byron** — Chemical Engineer
University of Wisconsin, Chemical Engineering Dept, Madison WI 53706, USA

**Bird, Simon** — Actor
Avalon Mgmt, 4A Exmoore St, London W10 68D, England

**Bird, Suzanne (Sue)** — Basketball Player
Seattle Storm, Key Arena, 351 Elliott Ave W, #500, Seattle WA 98119 USA

**Birden, LaJourdain J (J J)** — Football Player
27743 N 70th St, Scottsdale AZ 85266, USA

**Birdman** — Rap Artist
J L Entertainment, 18653 Ventura Blvd, #340, Los Angeles CA 91356 USA

**Birdsong, Carl** — Football Player
1807 Clubview Dr, Amarillo TX 79124, USA

# B

**Birdsong, Mary** — Actress
United Talent Agency, U T A Plaza, 9336 Civic Center Dr, Beverly Hills CA 90210 USA
**Birdsong, Otis L** — Basketball Player
PO Box 316, Little Rock AR 72203, USA
**Birdy** — Singer, Pianist, Songwriter
W M E Entertainment, 9601 Wilshire Blvd, #300, Beverly Hills CA 90210 USA
**Bires, Kelly** — Auto Racing Driver
Black Cat Racing, 200 Swiggum Road, Westby WI 54667, USA
**Birgeneau, Robert J** — Physicist, Educator
University of California, Chancellor's Office, University Hall, Berkeley CA 94720, USA
**Birgisson, Jon Thor (Jonsi)** — Singer (Sigur Ros)
Music Road Records, 5012 Brighton Road, Austin TX 78745, USA
**Birk, Matthew R (Matt)** — Football Player
5 Norfolk Court, Reisterstown MD 21136, USA
**Birk, Roger E** — Government Official, Financier
Federal National Mortgage Assn, 3900 Wisconsin Ave NW, Washington DC 20016, USA
**Birkavs, Valdis** — Prime Minister, Latvia
Justice Ministry, Brivbas Blvd 34, 1536 Riga, Latvia
**Birkbeck, Michael L (Mike)** — Baseball Player
1705 W Hill Dr, Orrville OH 44667, USA
**Birkerts, Gunnar** — Architect
Gunnar Birkerts Assoc, 65 Grove St, #241, Wellesley MA 02482, USA
**Birkett, Zoe** — Singer
Fremantle Media, 2700 Colorado Ave, #450, Santa Monica CA 90404 USA
**Birkin, Jane** — Actress
Agence Artiste Adequat, 108 Rue Reaumur, 75002 Paris, France
**Birmingham, Stephen** — Writer
Brandt & Brandt, 1501 Broadway, #2310, New York NY 10036, USA
**Birn, Laura** — Actress
Creative Artists Agency, 2000 Ave of Stars, #100, Los Angeles CA 90067 USA
**Birney, David** — Actor
Bret Adams Agency, 448 W 44th St, New York NY 10036, USA
**Birns, Jack** — Photographer
2021 Castilian Dr, Los Angeles CA 90068, USA
**Biron, Martin** — Ice Hockey Player
488 Willardshire Road, East Aurora NY 14052, USA
**Biron, Mathieu** — Ice Hockey Player
5723 NW 119th Dr, Coral Springs FL 33076, USA
**Birren, James E** — Gerontologist
University of California, Borun Gerontology Center, Los Angeles CA 90024, USA
**Birthistle, Eva** — Actress
Independent Talent Group, 40 Whitfield St, London W1T 2RH, England
**Birtsas, Timothy D (Tim)** — Baseball Player
PO Box 96, Clarkston MI 48347, USA
**Bisbal Ferre, David** — Singer
Universal Music, 420 Lincoln Road, #200, Miami Beach FL 33139, USA
**Bisby, Frank A** — Biologist
Reading University, Plant Science Laboratories, Reading Berk RG6 6AS, England
**Biscet Gonzalez, Oscar Elias** — Human Rights Activist
Lawton Foundation for Human Rights, PO Box 430905, Miami FL 33243, USA
**Bischof, Ole** — Judo Athlete
Suelburgstr 237, 50937 Cologne, Germany
**Bishe, Kerry** — Actress
Brookside Artists Mgmt, 250 W 57th St, #2303, New York NY 10107 USA
**Bishil, Summer** — Actress
Paul Kohner, 9300 Wilshire Blvd, #555, Beverly Hills CA 90212 USA
**Bishop, Blaine E** — Football Player
PO Box 3082, Brentwood TN 37024, USA
**Bishop, Elvin** — Singer, Guitarist
Blue Mountain Artists, 810 Tyvola Road, #114, Charlotte NC 28217, USA
**Bishop, Erwin W (Sonny)** — Football Player
22843 Hale Road, Land O Lakes FL 34639, USA
**Bishop, Gregory L (Greg)** — Football Player
PO Box 2263, Lodi CA 95241, USA
**Bishop, Harold L** — Football Player
2709 20th Street Ensley, Birmingham AL 35208, USA
**Bishop, J Michael** — Nobel Medicine Laureate, Educator
University of California, Chancellor's Office, San Francisco CA 94143, USA
**Bishop, Keith B** — Football Player
PO Box 131048, Spring TX 77393, USA
**Bishop, Kelly** — Actress
Abrams Artists, 9200 W Sunset Blvd, #1125, West Hollywood CA 90069 USA
**Bishop, Kevin** — Actor
Troika, 74 Clerkenwell Road, #300, London EC1M 5QA, England
**Bishop, Michael L** — Writer
PO Box 646, Pine Mountain GA 31822, USA
**Bishop, Nicholas** — Actor
United Talent Agency, U T A Plaza, 9336 Civic Center Dr, Beverly Hills CA 90210 USA
**Bishop, Richard A** — Football Player
1374 SW 142nd Terrace, Miami FL 33186, USA
**Bishop, Stephen** — Singer, Songwriter
2310 Apollo Dr, Los Angeles CA 90046, USA
**Bishops, Thom** — Actor
Brillstein Entertainment Partners, 9150 Wilshire Blvd, #350, Beverly Hills CA 90212 USA
**Biss, Jonathan** — Concert Pianist
Konzertdirektion Schmid, Konigstra 36, 30175 Hannover, Germany
**Bissell, Charles O** — Editorial Cartoonist
1006 Tower Place, Nashville TN 37204, USA
**Bissell, Charles P (Phil)** — Cartoonist
Cartoon Corner, 4 Cross Hill Circle, Forestdale MA 02644, USA
**Bissell, Jean G** — Judge
US Court of Appeals, 717 Madison Place NW, Washington DC 20439, USA
**Bissell, Mina J** — Physicist
Lawrence Berkeley Laboratory, 1 Cyclotron Road, Berkeley CA 94720, USA
**Bisset, Jacqueline** — Actress
1815 Benedict Canyon Dr, Beverly Hills CA 90210, USA

**Bisson, Thomas N** — Historian
21 Hammond St, Cambridge MA 02138, USA
**Bisson, Yannick** — Actor
Robert Stein Management, 1180 S Beverly Dr, #304, Los Angeles CA 90035, USA
**Bista, Kirti Nidhi** — Prime Minister, Nepal
Gyaneshwor, 4441009 Kathmandu, Nepal
**Bisutti, Danielle** — Actress
Prestige Talent Agency, 9250 Wilshire Blvd, #208, Beverly Hills CA 90212, USA
**Biswas, Abdul Rahmana** — President, Bangladesh
Residence Dhonmondi, Dhaka, Bangladesh
**Bitner, Rhona** — Photographer
425 Park Ave S, #12A, New York NY 10016, USA
**Bitsch, Hans-Ullrich** — Architect, Industrial Designer
Kaiser-Wilhelm-Ring 23, RiveGauche, 40545 Dusseldorf-Oberkassel, Germany
**Bittinger, Ned** — Illustrator
1323 Escalante St, Santa Fe NM 87505, USA
**Bittle, Ryan** — Actor
Bauman Redanty Shaul Agency, 5757 Wilshire Blvd, #473, Los Angeles CA 90036 USA
**Bittner, Armin** — Alpine Skier
Rauchbergstr 30, 83334 Izell, Germany
**Bitton, Joshua** — Actor
S M S Talent, 8383 Wilshire Blvd, #230, Beverly Hills CA 90211 USA
**Bitton, Raquel** — Singer
Icon Performing Arts, 1557 Westwood Blvd, #242, Los Angeles CA 90024, USA
**Bitzis, Athena Maria** — Actress
People Store, 645 Lambert Dr, Atlanta GA 30324, USA
**Biya, Paul** — President, Cameroon Republic
Palais de L'Unite, Rue de l'Exploratour, Yaounde, Cameroon
**Biyombo, Bismack** — Basketball Player
Charlotte Hornets, 333 E Trade St, #A, Charlotte NC 28202 USA
**Biz Markie** — Rap Artist, Comedian
Media Artists Group, 8222 Melrose Ave, #203, Los Angeles CA 90048 USA
**Bizarre** — Rap Artist (D-12)
Coast to Coast Talent, 3350 Barham Blvd, Los Angeles CA 90068 USA
**Bizzy Bone** — Rap Artist (Bone Thugs-N-Harmony)
Entertainment Artists, 2409 21st Ave S, #100, Nashville TN 10019 USA
**Bjedov-Gabrilo, Djurdjica** — Swimmer
Brace Santini 33, 5800 Split, Serbia
**Bjorgen, Marit** — Cross Country Skier
7295 Rognes, Norway
**Bjork** — Singer, Songwriter, Actress
Quest Mgmt, 36 Marple Way, #1D, London W3 0RG, England
**Bjorken, James D** — Physicist
Stanford Linear Accelerator Center, Stanford University, Stanford CA 94305, USA
**Bjorklund, Anders** — Neurologist
University of Lund, Neurology Dept, 221 00 Lund, Sweden
**Bjorkman, Jonas** — Tennis Player
Funke Promotions, Box 5126, 200 71 Malmo, Sweden
**Bjorkman, Olle E** — Plant Biologist
3040 Greer Road, Palo Alto CA 94303, USA
**Bjorkman, Rubin E** — Ice Hockey Player, Coach
504 Lake St NW, Warroad MN 56763, USA
**Bjorlin, Nadia** — Actress
Don Buchwald Talent Agency, 6500 Wilshire Blvd, #2200, Los Angeles CA 90048 USA
**Bjorndalen, Dag** — Biathlete
Simonstranda, Postboks 516, 3342 Amot, Norway
**Bjorndalen, Ole Einar** — Biathlete
Bergen 27, 9942 Obertilliach, Norway
**Bjornson, Eric** — Football Player
40 Orchard Road, Orinda CA 94563, USA
**Bjornson, Karen** — Model
Ford Models Inc, 111 5th Ave, #900, New York NY 10003 USA
**Bjornsso, Julius** — Actor
IceTalenta, Sua Urgata 5, Keflavak, Reykjanesbar 230, Iceland
**Bjugstad, Scott** — Ice Hockey Player
2874 Lisbon Ave N, Lake Elmo MN 55042, USA
**Blab, Uwe K** — Basketball Player
5993 Mount Gainor, Wimberley TX 78676, USA
**Blacc, Aloe** — Rap Artist
W M E Entertainment, 9601 Wilshire Blvd, #300, Beverly Hills CA 90210 USA
**Blachnik, Gabriele** — Fashion Designer
Blachnik Gabriele KG, Marstallstr 8, 80539 Munich, Germany
**Black of Crossharbour, Conrad M** — Publisher
1 Canada Square, Canary Wharf, London E14 5DT, England
**Black Thought** — Rap Artist (Roots)
Universal Attractions, 135 W 26th St, #1200, New York NY 10019, USA
**Black, Alexander (Alex)** — Actor
Hollywood Entertainment, 8306 Wilshire Blvd, #1638, Beverly Hills CA 90211, USA
**Black, B Jordan** — Football Player
4002 Tradewind Circle, Rowlett TX 75088, USA
**Black, Barbara A** — Attorney, Educator
Columbia University, Law School, 435 W 116th St, New York NY 10027, USA
**Black, Bibi** — Concert Trumpeter
Columbia Artists Mgmt Inc, 5 Columbus Circle, 1790 Broadway, #1600, New York NY 10019 USA
**Black, Cathleen P** — Publisher
Hearst Corp, Magazine Division, 250 W 55th St, New York NY 10019, USA
**Black, Cilla** — Singer, Actress
QVoice, Holborn Hall, 193-197 High Holborn, London WC1V 7BD, England
**Black, Claudia** — Actress
S M S Talent, 8383 Wilshire Blvd, #230, Beverly Hills CA 90211 USA
**Black, Clint** — Singer, Songwriter, Actor
W M E Entertainment, 1600 Division St, #300, Nashville TN 37203 USA
**Black, David** — Producer, Writer
Zero Gravity Mgmt, 1531 14th St, Santa Monica CA 90404, USA
**Black, Denise** — Actress
Cole Kitchenn Personal Mgmt, Roar House, 46 Charlotte St, London W1T 2GS, England

**Black, Dennis** — Epidemiologist
University of California Medical Center, 505 Parnassus, San Francisco CA 94122 USA

**Black, Dustin Lance** — Writer
Creative Artists Agency, 2000 Ave of Stars, #100, Los Angeles CA 90067 USA

**Black, Francis (Frank)** — Singer, Guitarist, Songwriter
X-Ray Touring, 77-79 Great Eastern St, #A, London EC2A 3HU, England

**Black, Harry R (Bud)** — Baseball Player, Manager
PO Box 2133, Rancho Santa Fe CA 92067, USA

**Black, Jack** — Actor, Singer, Comedian
W M E Entertainment, 9601 Wilshire Blvd, #300, Beverly Hills CA 90210 USA

**Black, Jake** — Singer (A3)
Conservative Mgmt, 12700 Lake Ave, #2801, Lakewood OH 44107, USA

**Black, James** — Ice Hockey Player
235 Callingwood Place NW, Edmonton AB T5T 2C6, Canada

**Black, James** — Actor
Open Entertainment, 1051 N Cole Ave, #B, Los Angeles CA 90038, USA

**Black, Jay** — Singer (Jay & the Americans)
Charles Rapp Mgmt, 10775 Santa Laguna Dr, Boca Raton FL 33428, USA

**Black, Jully** — Singer, Songwriter
Agency Group Ltd, 142 W 57th St, #600, New York NY 10019 USA

**Black, Lewis** — Actor, Comedian, Writer
A P A Talent & Literary Agency, 405 S Beverly Dr, #300, Beverly Hills CA 90212 USA

**Black, Lucas** — Actor
I C M Partners, 10250 Constellation Blvd, #900, Los Angeles CA 90067 USA

**Black, Marina** — Actress
Wright Entertainment, 3207 Winnie Dr, Los Angeles CA 90068, USA

**Black, Mary** — Singer
International Music Network, 278 Main St, #400, Gloucester MA 01930 USA

**Black, Michael Ian** — Actor, Puppeteer, Producer
United Talent Agency, U T A Plaza, 9336 Civic Center Dr, Beverly Hills CA 90210 USA

**Black, P Michael (Mike)** — Football Player
5690 Stonekirk Place NW, Acworth GA 30101, USA

**Black, Pippa** — Actress
Aran Michael Mgmt, 118 Caroline St, South Yarra VIC 3141, Australia

**Black, Robert L** — Pediatrician
976 Mesa Road, Monterey CA 93940, USA

**Black, Ron** — Religious Leader
General Baptist Ministries, 100 Stinson Dr, Poplar Bluff MO 63901, USA

**Black, Ronald J (Ronnie)** — Golfer
4355 N Rillito Creek Place, Tucson AZ 85719, USA

**Black, Roy** — Attorney
Black Strebnick Kornspan Stumpf, 201 S Biscayne Blvd, #1300, Miami FL 33131, USA

**Black, Shane** — Director, Writer
W M E Entertainment, 9601 Wilshire Blvd, #300, Beverly Hills CA 90210 USA

**Black, Susan H** — Judge
US Court of Appeals, 311 W Monroe St, Jacksonville FL 32202, USA

**Blackburn, Ade** — Singer, Guitarist (Clinic)
Windish Agency, 1658 N Milwaukee Ave, #211, Chicago IL 60647, USA

**Blackburn, Chase W** — Football Player
562 Wagonwheel Lane, Marysville OH 43040, USA

**Blackburn, Don** — Ice Hockey Player
637 S Owl Dr, Sarasota FL 34236, USA

**Blackburn, Elizabeth H** — Nobel Medicine Laureate
294 Yerba Buena Ave, San Francisco CA 94127, USA

**Blackburn, Tyler** — Actor
Gersh Agency, 9465 Wilshire Blvd, #600, Beverly Hills CA 90212 USA

**Blackburn, Woody T** — Golfer
Frank W Brown Assoc, PO Box 215, Orange Park FL 32067, USA

**Black-D'Elia, Sofia** — Actress
I C M Partners, 10250 Constellation Blvd, #900, Los Angeles CA 90067 USA

**Blackledge, Bob** — Journalist
Birmingham News, Editorial Dept, 2701 4th Ave N, Birminham AL 35203, USA

**Blackledge, Todd A** — Football Player, Sportscaster
2711 Glenmont Dr NW, Canton OH 44708, USA

**Blackley, Jamie** — Actor
United Talent Agency, U T A Plaza, 9336 Civic Center Dr, Beverly Hills CA 90210 USA

**Blackman, Cindy** — Jazz, Rock Drummer
BookArts Co, 6404 Wilshire Blvd, #1750, Los Angeles CA 90048, USA

**Blackman, Honor** — Actress
N S Mgmt, Clapham North Arts Center, Voltaire Road, London SW4 6DH, England

**Blackman, Rolando A** — Basketball Player, Sportscaster
14902 Preston Road, #404, Dallas TX 75254, USA

**Blackman, Steve** — Professional Wrestler
Steve Blackman Fighting Systems, 2200 Paxton St, Harrisburg PA 17111, USA

**Blackmar, Philip A (Phil)** — Golfer
4420 Janssen Dr, Corpus Christi TX 78411, USA

**Blackmon, Donald K (Don)** — Football Player
4340 Lansfaire Terrace, Suwanee GA 30024, USA

**Blackmon, Douglas A** — Writer
Wall Street Journal, 303 Peachtree St NE, #4200, Atlanta GA 30308, USA

**Blackmon, Larry E** — Singer (Cameo)
Mercury Records, 11150 Santa Monica Blvd, #1000, Los Angeles CA 90025 USA

**Blackmon, Robert J (Bob)** — Football Player
70 Glenwood N, Van Vleck TX 77482, USA

**Blackmore, Richard H (Ritchie)** — Singer, Guitarist (Deep Purple, Rainbow)
Performers of the World, 5657 Wilshire Blvd, #280, Los Angeles CA 90036 USA

**Blackmore, Stephanie** — Actress
Chateau-Billings, 5667 Wilshire Blvd, #340, Los Angeles CA 90036, USA

**Blackshear, Jeffrey L (Jeff)** — Football Player
9229 Christo Court, Owings Mill MD 21117, USA

**Blackthorne, Paul** — Actor
S D B Partners, 315 S Beverly Dr, #411, Beverly Hills CA 90067 USA

**Blackwelder, Myra** — Golfer
2009 Hill Gail Way, Versailles KY 40383, USA

**Blackwell, Alfonzo** — Jazz Saxophonist, Composer
Celebrity Talent Agency, 111 E 14th St, #249, New York NY 10003, USA

| | |
|---|---|
| **Blackwell, Nathaniel (Nate)** | Basketball Player |
| 1926 S 22nd St, Philadelphia PA 19145, USA | |
| **Blackwell, Simon** | Producer, Writer |
| P B J Mgmt, 5 Soho Square, London W1D 3QA, England | |
| **Blackwell, Taylor** | Actress |
| Principato-Young, 9465 Wilshire Blvd, #880, Beverly Hills CA 90212 USA | |
| **Blackwell, Timothy P (Tim)** | Baseball Player |
| 8854 Whiteport Lane, San Diego CA 92119, USA | |
| **Blackwell, William H (Will), Jr** | Football Player |
| 6168 Seneca Circle, Discovery Bay CA 94505, USA | |
| **Blackwood, Ariel** | Actress |
| Coast to Coast Talent, 3350 Barham Blvd, Los Angeles CA 90068 USA | |
| **Blackwood, Glenn A** | Football Player |
| 24 Marina Gardens Dr, Palm Beach Gardens FL 33410, USA | |
| **Blackwood, Lyle V** | Football Player |
| 4930 Stanford Ave, Dallas TX 75209, USA | |
| **Blackwood, Sarah** | Singer (Dubstar) |
| Primary Talent International, 2-12 Petonville Road, London N1 9PL, England | |
| **Blacque, Taurean** | Actor |
| 5049 Rock Springs Road, Lithonia GA 30038, USA | |
| **Bladd, Stephen Jo** | Singer, Drummer (J Geils Band) |
| Nick Ben-Meir, 652 N Doheny Dr, West Hollywood CA 90069, USA | |
| **Blade, Brian** | Jazz Drummer (Black Dub) |
| Ted Kurland, 173 Brighton Ave, Boston MA 02134 USA | |
| **Blade, Danielle** | Artist |
| Gartner & Blade, 4-1354 Kuhio Highway, Kapaa HI 96746, USA | |
| **Blades, H Benedict (Bennie)** | Football Player |
| 5124 NW 30th Lane, Fort Lauderdale FL 33309, USA | |
| **Blades, Ruben** | Singer, Songwriter, Actor |
| W M E Entertainment, 9601 Wilshire Blvd, #300, Beverly Hills CA 90210 USA | |
| **Bladon, Tom** | Ice Hockey Player |
| 2595 Wilcox Terrace, Victoria, BC V8Z 7G5, Canada | |
| **Blagden, George** | Actor |
| Paradigm Agency, 360 N Crescent Dr, North Building, Beverly Hills CA 90210 USA | |
| **Blaha, John E** | Astronaut |
| 346 Whitestone Dr, Spring Branch TX 78070, USA | |
| **Blahak, Joseph P (Joe)** | Football Player |
| 4040 N 21st St, Lincoln NE 68521, USA | |
| **Blahnik, Manolo** | Fashion Designer |
| 49-51 Old Church St, London SW3 5BS, England | |
| **Blahoski, Alana** | Ice Hockey Player |
| 60 E 9th St, #315, New York NY 10003, USA | |
| **Blaine, David** | Illusionist |
| W M E Entertainment, 9601 Wilshire Blvd, #300, Beverly Hills CA 90210 USA | |
| **Blaine, Edward H (Ed)** | Football Player |
| 4 E Clarkson Road, Columbia MO 65203, USA | |
| **Blaine, Jason** | Singer, Songwriter |
| Agency Group Ltd, 142 W 57th St, #600, New York NY 10019 USA | |
| **Blaine, Nell** | Artist |
| 210 Riverside Dr, #8A, New York NY 10025, USA | |
| **Blair, A Matthew (Matt)** | Football Player |
| 16725 43rd Ave N, Minneapolis MN 55446, USA | |
| **Blair, Anthony C L (Tony)** | Prime Minister, England |
| PO Box 60519, London W2 7JU, England | |
| **Blair, Bonnie** | Speed Skater |
| 306 White Pine Road, Delafield WI 53018, USA | |
| **Blair, Charles (Chuck)** | Ice Hockey Player |
| 869 Niagara Parkway, Fort Erie ON L2A 5M4, Canada | |
| **Blair, DeJuan L** | Basketball Player |
| Dallas Mavericks, Pavilion, 2909 Taylor Street, Dallas TX 75226 USA | |
| **Blair, Dennis** | Actor, Comedian, Writer |
| Ignite Entertainment, 201-20145 Stewart Crescent, Maple Ridge BC V2X 0T6, Canada | |
| **Blair, George** | Ice Hockey Player |
| 61 Kingsnill St, Fort Erie ON L2A 4E5, Canada | |
| **Blair, Isla** | Actress |
| Curtis Brown Group, 28-29 Haymarket St, #500, London SW1Y 4SP, England | |
| **Blair, Linda** | Actress |
| Almond Talent Agency, 8217 Beverly Blvd, #8, West Hollywood CA 90048, USA | |
| **Blair, M June** | Model, Actress |
| Playboy Promotions, 9346 Civic Center Dr, #200, Beverly Hills CA 90210 USA | |
| **Blair, Marie-Claire** | Writer |
| 4411 Rue Saint Denis, #401, Montreal QC H2J 2LN, Canada | |
| **Blair, Paul L D** | Baseball Player |
| 4177 Lotus Circle, Ellicott City MD 21043, USA | |
| **Blair, Selma** | Actress |
| Gersh Agency, 9465 Wilshire Blvd, #600, Beverly Hills CA 90212 USA | |
| **Blair, Wayne** | Director |
| Shanahan Mgmt, Berman House, 91 Campbell St, #300, Surry Hills NSW 2010, Australia | |
| **Blair, William (Bill)** | Astronomer, Space Scientist |
| Johns Hopkins University, Astronomy Dept, Baltimore MD 21218, USA | |
| **Blair, William E (Willie)** | Baseball Player |
| 62 Elder Lane, Pikeville KY 41501, USA | |
| **Blair, William M, Jr** | Attorney, Diplomat |
| 435 E 52nd St, #6B, New York NY 10022, USA | |
| **Blais, Richard** | Chef |
| Home Restaurant, 111 W Paces Ferry Road NE, Atlanta GA 30305, USA | |
| **Blaise, Kerlin** | Football Player |
| 17786 Parkshore Dr, Northville MI 48168, USA | |
| **Blake Nelson, Tim** | Actor, Director, Writer |
| Gateway Mgmt, 860 Via de la Paz, #F10, Pacific Palisades CA 90272, USA | |
| **Blake, Francis S (Frank)** | Businessman |
| Home Depot Inc, 2455 Paces Ferry Road NW, Atlanta GA 30339, USA | |
| **Blake, Geoffrey** | Actor |
| Levine Mgmt, 9028 W Sunset Blvd, #PH-1, Los Angeles CA 90069, USA | |
| **Blake, James** | Tennis Player |
| 35 Prospect Road, Westport CT 6880, USA | |

**Blake, James** — Singer, Songwriter
International Talent Booking, Ariel House, 74A Charlotte St, #100 London W1T 4QJ, England
**Blake, Jason** — Ice Hockey Player
10 Meadow Lane, Glen Head NY 11545, USA
**Blake, Jay Don** — Golfer
2859 Calle del Sol, Saint George UT 84790, USA
**Blake, Jeffrey B C (Jeff)** — Football Player
5821 Sunset Ridge, Austin TX 78735, USA
**Blake, John C** — Artist
Oz Voorburgwal 131, 1012 Amsterdam ER, Netherlands
**Blake, Johnathan** — Drummer (Donny McCaslin Trio)
Greenleaf Records, PO Box 477364, Chicago IL 60647 USA
**Blake, Megan** — Actress
Levine Communications Office, 9100 Wilshire Blvd, #540, East Tower, Beverly Hills CA 90212, USA
**Blake, Norman** — Guitarist, Mandolin Player
Scott O'Malley Assoc, PO Box 9188, Colorado Springs CO 80932, USA
**Blake, Norman** — Singer, Guitarist (Teenage Fanclub)
High Road Touring, 751 Bridgeway, #200, Sausalito CA 94965 USA
**Blake, Peter T** — Artist
Waddington Galleries, 11 Cork St, London W1X 1PD, England
**Blake, Ran** — Jazz Pianist, Composer
New England Conservatory of Music, 290 Huntington Ave, Boston MA 02115, USA
**Blake, Robert** — Actor
Thomas Mesereau, 3055 Wilshire Blvd, #600, Los Angeles CA 90010, USA
**Blake, Robert B (Rob)** — Ice Hockey Player
75 Dwyer St, Buffalo NY 14224, USA
**Blake, Stephanie** — Actress
15101 Magnolia Blvd, #E12, Sherman Oaks CA 91403, USA
**Blake, Steven H (Steve)** — Basketball Player
3479 Cascade Terrace, West Linn OR 97068, USA
**Blake, Susie** — Actress
Gavin Barker Assoc, 2D Wimpole St, London W1G 0EB, England
**Blake, W Casey** — Baseball Player
8224 150th Ave, Indianola IA 50125, USA
**Blakely, Susan** — Actress, Model
Jaffe Co, 9663 Santa Monica Blvd, #214, Beverly Hills CA 90210, USA
**Blakemore, Colin B** — Neurophysiologist, Physiologist
University Laboratory of Physiology, Parks Road, Oxford OX1 3PT, England
**Blakemore, Michael H** — Director, Actor, Writer
18 Upper Park Road, London NW3 2UP, England
**Blakeney, Larry** — Football Coach
Troy University, Athletic Dept, Troy AL 36082, USA
**Blakenham, Michael J** — Businessman
House of Lords, Westminster, London SW1A 0PW, England
**Blaker, Clay** — Singer, Songwriter
Texas Sounds Entertainment, 2317 Pecan St, Dickinson TX 77539, USA
**Blakey, G Robert** — Attorney, Educator
947 Riverside Dr, South Bend IN 46616, USA
**Blakey, Lynn** — Singer (Tres Chicas)
Conqueroo, 11271 Ventura Blvd, #522, Studio City CA 91604 USA
**Blakey, Marion** — Government Official
Aerospace Industries Assn, 1000 Wilson Blvd, #1700, Arlington VA 22209, USA
**Blakiston, Caroline** — Actress
Coolwaters Productions, 10061 Riverside Dr, Box 531, Toluca Lake CA 91602 USA
**Blakley, Ronee** — Actress, Singer
1404 Fairview Ave, Caldwell ID 83605, USA
**Blalack, Robert** — Cinematographer
12251 Huston St, Valley Village CA 91607, USA
**Blalock, Hank J** — Baseball Player
8797 Adobe Bluffs Dr, San Diego CA 92129, USA
**Blalock, Jane** — Golfer
197 8th St, #300, Charlestown MA 02129, USA
**Blalock, Jolene** — Actress
W M E Entertainment, 9601 Wilshire Blvd, #300, Beverly Hills CA 90210 USA
**Blanc, Dominique** — Actress
Les Visiteurs du Soir, 40 Rue de la Folie Regnault, 75011 Paris, France
**Blanc, Georges** — Restauranteur
Le Mere Blanc, 01540 Vonnas, Ain, France
**Blanc, Jennifer** — Actress
Blancbiehn Productions, 10990 Wilshire Blvd, #800, Los Angeles CA 90024, USA
**Blanc, Manuel** — Actor
Cineart, 28 Rue Mogador, 78009 Paris, France
**Blanc, Michael** — Actor, Director
Artmedia, 20 Ave Rapp, 75007 Paris, France
**Blanc, Raymond R A** — Restauranteur
Le Manoir, Church Road, Great Milton, Oxford OX44 7PD, England
**Blancas, Homero, Jr** — Golfer
6826 Queensclub Dr, Houston TX 77069, USA
**Blanch, Andrea** — Photographer
310 Greenwich St, New York NY 10012, USA
**Blanchard, Alana R** — Surfer, Model
Association of Surfing Professionals, 300 Pacific Coast Highway, #114, Huntington Beach CA 92648 USA
**Blanchard, James J** — Governor, MI; Diplomat
426 4th St NE, Washington DC 20002, USA
**Blanchard, Kenneth** — Writer, Business Consultant
2048 Aldergrove, #B, Escondido CA 92029, USA
**Blanchard, Olivier J** — Economist
Massachusetts Institute of Technology, Economics Dept, Cambridge MA 02139, USA
**Blanchard, R Cary** — Football Player
7528 NW 132nd St, Oklahoma City OK 73142, USA
**Blanchard, Rachel** — Actress
Luber Rocklin Entertainment, 5815 Sunset Blvd, #206, Los Angeles CA 90028 USA
**Blanchard, Tammy** — Actress, Singer
I C M Partners, 10250 Constellation Blvd, #900, Los Angeles CA 90067 USA
**Blanchard, Terence** — Jazz Trumpeter, Composer
91 English Turn Dr, New Orleans LA 70131, USA

**Blanchard, Thomas R (Tom)** — Football Player
217 Independence Dr, Grants Pass OR 97527, USA
**Blanchett, Cate** — Actress
R G M Artists, 8-12 Ann Street, Surry Hills NSW 2010, Australia
**Blanckaert, Myriam** — Actress
Agents Associes, 201 Rue du Faubourg Saint Honore, 75008 Paris, France
**Blanco, Cuauhtemoc** — Soccer Player
Chicago Fire, Toyota Park, 7000 S Harlem Ave, Bridgeview IL 60455 USA
**Blanco, Henry R** — Baseball Player
5510 N 132nd Dr, Litchfield Park AZ 85340, USA
**Blanco, Roberto** — Singer, Actor
Rotbuchenstr 25, 81547 Munich, Germany
**Blanco-Cervantes, Raul** — President, Costa Rica
Apdo 918, San Jose, Costa Rica
**Bland, Carl N** — Football Player
1985 Crossbridge Court, Saint Charles MO 63303, USA
**Bland, John** — Golfer
PO Box 451436, Westlake OH 44145, USA
**Blandford, Roger D** — Astronomer
California Institute of Technology, Astrophysics Dept, Pasadena CA 91125, USA
**Blaney, Dave** — Auto Racing Driver
211 N Emily Court, High Point NC 27265, USA
**Blanford, Lawrence J (Larry)** — Cinematographer
210 5th Ave, Venice CA 90291, USA
**Blank, Arthur M** — Businessman
1080 W Paces Ferry Road NW, Atlanta GA 30327, USA
**Blank, Boris** — Synthesizer Player (Yello)
Creative Artists Agency, 2000 Ave of Stars, #100, Los Angeles CA 90067 USA
**Blank, Rebecca M** — Secretary, Commerce
Commerce Department, 14th St & Constitution Ave NW, Washington DC 20230 USA
**Blankenbuehler, Andy** — Choreographer, Dancer
W M E Entertainment, 9601 Wilshire Blvd, #300, Beverly Hills CA 90210 USA
**Blankenship, Lance R** — Baseball Player
340 Kimberwicke Court, Alamo CA 94507, USA
**Blankfein, Lloyd C** — Financier
Goldman Sachs Co, 85 Broad St, Building 85, New York NY 10004, USA
**Blankfield, Mark** — Actor
K & K Entertainment, 1498 W Sunset Blvd, Los Angeles CA 90026 USA
**Blanks, Billie, Jr** — Actor
W M E Entertainment, 9601 Wilshire Blvd, #300, Beverly Hills CA 90210 USA
**Blanks, Billy** — Physical Fitness Expert
Tae Bo, 7095 Hollywood Blvd, #500, Los Angeles CA 90028, USA
**Blanks, Larvell** — Baseball Player
PO Box 562, Del Rio TX 78841, USA
**Blanks, Sidney (Sid)** — Football Player
4402 Warm Springs Road, Houston TX 77035, USA
**Blanton, Arell** — Actor
4191 Greenbush Ave, Sherman Oaks CA 91423, USA
**Blanton, Dain** — Volleyball Player
1615 Stoner Ave, #3, Los Angeles CA 90025, USA
**Blanton, Gerald (Jerry)** — Football Player
1942 Calumet Ave, Toledo OH 43607, USA
**Blany, David (Dave)** — Auto Racing Driver
Randy Humphrey Assoc, 18636 Starcreek Dr, Cornelius NC 28031, USA
**Blasco, Chuck** — Singer (Vogues)
Media Promotion Enterprises, 423 6th Ave, Huntington WV 25701, USA
**Blashford-Snell, John N** — Explorer
Exploration Society, Motcome, Shaftesbury, Dorset SP7 9PB, England
**Blasi, Rosa** — Actress
Untitled Entertainment, 350 S Beverly Dr, #200, Beverly Hills CA 90212 USA
**Blasingame, Wade A** — Baseball Player
5207 Riverhill Road, Marietta GA 30068, USA
**Blass, Stephen R (Steve)** — Baseball Player
1756 Quigg Dr, Pittsburgh PA 15241, USA
**Blasucci, Richard (Dick)** — Actor, Producer
A P A Talent & Literary Agency, 405 S Beverly Dr, #300, Beverly Hills CA 90212 USA
**Blatche, Andray** — Basketball Player
15053 Doral Place, Haymarket VA 20169, USA
**Blatt, David** — Basketball Coach
Cleveland Cavaliers, Gund Arena, 1 Center Court, Cleveland OH 44115 USA
**Blatt, Melanie R** — Singer
Concorde International, 101 Shepherds Bush Road, London W6 7LP, England
**Blatter, Joseph S (Sepp)** — Soccer Executive
Federation International Football Assn, Hitzigweg 11, 8030 Zurich, Switzerland
**Blatty, William Peter** — Writer
7018 Longwood Dr, Bethesda MD 20817, USA
**Blatz, Kelly** — Actor
Luber Rocklin Entertainment, 5815 Sunset Blvd, #206, Los Angeles CA 90028 USA
**Blau, Daniel** — Artist
Belgradstr 26, 80796 Munich, Germany
**Blau, Peter M** — Sociologist
7019 Old NC 86, Chapel Hill NC 27516, USA
**Blauner, Peter** — Writer
Warner Books, 1271 Ave of Americas, New York NY 10020 USA
**Blauser, Jeffrey M (Jeff)** — Baseball Player
6080 Carlisle Lane, Alpharetta GA 30022, USA
**Blaustein, Barry W** — Director
Creative Artists Agency, 2000 Ave of Stars, #100, Los Angeles CA 90067 USA
**Blaylock, Anthony D** — Football Player
88 Brighton Dr, Garner NC 27529, USA
**Blaylock, Caroline** — Golfer
232 Hennon Dr NW, Rome GA 30165, USA
**Blaylock, Daron O (Mookie)** — Basketball Player
1017 Gresham Road, Zebulon GA 30295, USA
**Blaylock, Derrick D** — Football Player
1471 Edgewater Road, Crown Point IN 46307, USA

**Blaylock, Kenneth T** — Labor Leader
American Government Employees, 80 F St NW, #700, Washington DC 20001, USA
**Blayton, Anitra** — Sculptor
Tarrant County College, Art Dept, 828 W Harwood Road, Hurst TX 76054, USA
**Blazelowski, Carol A** — Basketball Player, Executive
126 Walnut St, Nutley NJ 07110, USA
**Blechacz, Rafal** — Concert Pianist
Konzertdirektion Schmid, Konigstra 36, 30175 Hannover, Germany
**Bledel, Alexis** — Actress, Model
New Wave Entertainment, 2660 W Olive Ave, Burbank CA 91505, USA
**Bledsoe, Drew** — Football Player
845 Delrey Road, Whitefish MT 59937, USA
**Bledsoe, Tempestt** — Actress
House of Representatives, 1434 6th St, #1, Santa Monica CA 90401 USA
**Bleeth, Yasmine** — Actress
308 N Sycamore Ave, #202, Los Angeles CA 90036, USA
**Blegen, Judith** — Opera Singer
91 Central Park West, #1B, New York NY 10023, USA
**Blehm, Gary** — Cartoonist (Penmen)
PO Box 60607, Colorado Springs CO 80960, USA
**Bleibtreu, Moritz** — Actor
Agentur Players, Sophienstr 21, 10178 Berlin, Germany
**Bleier, Robert P (Rocky)** — Football Player
929 Osage Road, Pittsburgh PA 15243, USA
**Bleifeld, Stanley** — Sculptor
27 Spring Valley Road, Weston CT 06883, USA
**Bleiler, Gretchen** — Snowboard Athlete
PO Box 5774, Snowmass Village CO 81615, USA
**Blessed, Brian** — Actor
Associated International Mgmt, 7 Hatton Garden, #400, London EC1N 8AD, England
**Blessed, Rosalind** — Actress
Associated International Mgmt, 7 Hatton Garden, #400, London EC1N 8AD, England
**Blessen, Karen A** — Journalist, Illustrator
Karen Blessen Illustration, 6327 Vickery Blvd, Dallas TX 75214, USA
**Blessing, Jack** — Actor
Golan & Blumberg, 6528 W 6th St, Los Angeles CA 90048, USA
**Blethen, Frank A** — Publisher
Seattle Times, Publisher's Office, 1120 John St, Seattle WA 98109, USA
**Blethyn, Brenda A** — Actress
I C M Partners, 10250 Constellation Blvd, #900, Los Angeles CA 90067 USA
**Bleu, Corbin** — Actor, Singer
James/Levy Mgmt, 3500 W Olive Ave, #1470, Burbank CA 91505 USA
**Blevins, Ronnie Gene** — Actor
Sovereign Talent Group, 8421 Wilshire Blvd, #200, Beverly Hills CA 90211, USA
**Bley, Carla B** — Composer, Jazz Pianist
Ted Kurland, 173 Brighton Ave, Boston MA 02134 USA
**Bley, Paul** — Jazz Pianist, Composer
PO Box 4, Cherry Valley NY 13320, USA
**Blieden, Michael** — Actor, Writer
A K A Talent, 6310 San Vicente Blvd, #200, Los Angeles CA 90048 USA
**Blier, Bertrand** — Director
11 Rue Margueritte, 75017 Paris, France
**Blige, Mary J** — Rap Artist, Singer
Creative Artists Agency, 2000 Ave of Stars, #100, Los Angeles CA 90067 USA
**Blilie, Hannah** — Drummer (Gossip)
Shotclock Mgmt, 20312 NE 259th St, Battle Ground WA 98604, USA
**Blim, Richard D** — Pediatrician
304 W 172nd St, Belton MO 64012, USA
**Blinder, Alan S** — Government Official, Financier
Princeton University, Economics Dept, Fischer Hall, Princeton NJ 08544, USA
**Blinka, Stanley J (Stan)** — Football Player
3304 Carriage Dr, Export PA 15632, USA
**Blinks, Susan** — Equestrian
362 Vista del Rey Dr, Encinitas CA 92024, USA
**Bliss, Boti** — Actress
Stone Manners Salners, 6100 Wilshire Blvd, #1500, Los Angeles CA 90035 USA
**Bliss, Caroline** — Actress
Rights House, Drury House, 34-43 Russell St, London WC2B 5HA, England
**Bliss, Julian** — Concert Clarinetist
I M G Artists, Hogarth Business Park, Chiswick, London W4 2TH, England
**Bliss, Michael (Mike)** — Auto Racing Driver
156 Mariner Pointe Lane, Mooresville NC 28117, USA
**Blitt, Ricky** — Writer, Producer
Smart Entertainment, 9595 Wilshire Blvd, #900, Beverly Hills CA 90212, USA
**Blitz, Jeffrey** — Director, Writer
Creative Artists Agency, 2000 Ave of Stars, #100, Los Angeles CA 90067 USA
**Blitzer, Wolf** — Commentator
8929 Holly Leaf Lane, Bethesda MD 20817, USA
**Blix, Hans M** — Government Official
Curtis Brown Group, 28-29 Haymarket, London SW1Y 4SP, England
**Blobel, Gunter K-J** — Nobel Medicine Laureate
1100 Park Ave, #10D, New York NY 10128, USA
**Bloch, Erich** — Electrical Engineer, Computer Scientist
National Science Foundation, 1800 C St NW, Washington DC 20002, USA
**Bloch, Phillip** — Actor, Fashion Designer
Grand Central Publishing, 237 Park Ave, #1300, New York NY 10017, USA
**Block, Gene D** — Educator
University of California, Chancellor's Office, Los Angeles CA 90024, USA
**Block, Hunt** — Actor
Don Buchwald Talent Agency, 6500 Wilshire Blvd, #2200, Los Angeles CA 90048 USA
**Block, John R** — Secretary, Agriculture
National Wholesale Grocers Assn, 201 Park Washington, Falls Church VA 22046, USA
**Block, John W** — Basketball Player
1069 Santa Barbara St, San Diego CA 92107, USA
**Block, Ken** — Ice Hockey Player
15762 Bethpage Trail, Carmel IN 46033, USA

**Block, Lawrence** — Writer
299 W 12th St, #12D, New York NY 10014, USA
**Block, Ned J** — Philosopher
96 Ellery St, #2, Cambridge MA 02138, USA
**Block, Ron** — Singer, Banjo Player (Union Station)
Rounder Records, 1 Rounder Way, Burlington MA 01803 USA
**Block, Susan** — Artist
2725 Bentley Road, Highland Park IL 60035, USA
**Blocker, Dirk** — Actor
5063 La Ramada Dr, Santa Barbara CA 93111, USA
**Bloemberg, Jeff** — Ice Hockey Player
170 Diagonal Road, Wingham ON N0G 1W0, Canada
**Bloembergen, Nicolaas** — Nobel Physics Laureate
13835 E Langtree Lane, Tucson AZ 85747, USA
**Blokhuijsen, Jan** — Speed Skater
Remmersteinstraat 135, 2532 The Hague AZ, Netherlands
**Blomberg, Ronald M (Ron)** — Baseball Player
11660 Mountain Laurel Dr, Roswell GA 30075, USA
**Blomdahl, Benjamin E (Ben)** — Baseball Player
9 Emmy Lane, Ladera Ranch CA 92694, USA
**Blomkamp, Neill** — Director, Writer
W M E Entertainment, 9601 Wilshire Blvd, #300, Beverly Hills CA 90210 USA
**Blomqvist, Timo P** — Ice Hockey Player
Helsinki Ligaforeningen H I F K Road, Mantytie 23, 00270 Helsinki, Finland
**Blomstedt, Herbert T** — Conductor
Columbia Artists Mgmt Inc, 5 Columbus Circle, 1790 Broadway, #1600, New York NY 10019 USA
**Blong, Jenni** — Actress
Greene Assoc, 1901 Ave of Stars, #130, Los Angeles CA 90067 USA
**Blonsky, Nikki** — Actress, Singer
Innovative Artists, 1505 10th St, Santa Monica CA 90401 USA
**Blood, Edward J** — Skier, Skiing Official
2 Beech Hill, Durham NH 03824, USA
**Bloodgood, Moon** — Actress, Model
United Talent Agency, U T A Plaza, 9336 Civic Center Dr, Beverly Hills CA 90210 USA
**Bloom, Amy** — Writer, Psychotherapist
Gillon Aitken Assoc, 18-21 Cavaye Place, London SW10 9PT, England
**Bloom, Brian** — Actor
Osbrink Talent Agency, 4343 Lankershim Blvd, #100, North Hollywood CA 91602 USA
**Bloom, Brooke** — Actress
TalentWorks, 3500 W Olive Ave, #1400, Burbank CA 91505 USA
**Bloom, Claire** — Actress
Clive Conway, 32 Grove St, Oxford OX2 TJT, England
**Bloom, Floyd E** — Physician
628 Pacific View Dr, San Diego CA 92109, USA
**Bloom, Harold** — Educator, Writer
179 Linden St, New Haven CT 06511, USA
**Bloom, Jane Ira** — Jazz Saxophonist, Composer
Joel Chriss Co, 300 Mercer St, #3J, New York NY 10003 USA
**Bloom, Jeremy** — Alpine Skier, Football Player
PO Box 770-311, Park City UT 84060, USA
**Bloom, John** — Editor
Independent Talent Group, 40 Whitfield St, London W1T 2RH, England
**Bloom, Lindsay** — Actress
3751 Recklaw, Studio City CA 91604, USA
**Bloom, Luka** — Singer, Guitarist, Songwriter
Howlin' Wuelf Media, 527 Barclay Ave, Morrisville PA 19067, USA
**Bloom, Matthew J (Matt)** — Professional Wrestler
New Japan Dojo, PM Box 1245, 1223 Wilshire Blvd, Santa Monica CA 90403, USA
**Bloom, Mike** — Ice Hockey Player
227 School Road, Delanson NY 12053, USA
**Bloom, Orlando** — Actor
Viddywell Productions, 1041 N Formosa Ave, Formosa Building, West Hollywood CA 90046, USA
**Bloom, Scott** — Actor
11 Croydon Court, Dix Hills NY 11746, USA
**Bloom, Ursula** — Writer
Newton House, Walls Dr, Ravenglass, Cumbria CA18 1SQ, England
**Bloom, Vail** — Actress
C E S D, 10635 Santa Monica Blvd, #130, Los Angeles CA 90025 USA
**Bloom, Verna** — Actress
327 E 82nd St, New York NY 10028, USA
**Bloomberg, Michael R** — Mayor, New York City; Publisher
Bloomberg LP, 499 Park Ave, #1500, New York NY 10022, USA
**Bloomfield, Michael J (Mike)** — Astronaut
14302 Autumn Canyon Trace, Houston TX 77062, USA
**Bloomfield, Sara** — Museum Director
Holocaust Memorial Museum, 100 Wallenberg Place SW, Washington DC 20024, USA
**Bloomquist, William P (Willie)** — Baseball Player
7026 E Blue Sky Dr, Scottsdale AZ 85266, USA
**Blotzer, Robert J (Bobby)** — Drummer (Ratt)
Paradise Artists, PO Box 1821, Ojai CA 93024 USA
**Blount, Corie K** — Basketball Player
5427 Kytes Lane, Liberty Township OH 45044, USA
**Blount, Mark D** — Basketball Player
5723 High Flyer Road S, Palm Beach Gardens FL 33418, USA
**Blount, Melvin C (Mel)** — Football Player, Executive
Mel Blount Youth Home, 6 Mel Blount Dr, Claysville PA 15323, USA
**Blount, Winton M, III** — Businessman
Blount Inc, 4909 SE International Way, Portland OR 97222, USA
**Blow, Kurtis** — Rap Artist
Green Light Talent Agency, PO Box 3172, Beverly Hills CA 90212 USA
**Blowers, Michael R (Mike)** — Baseball Player
22211 42nd Ave E, Spanaway WA 98387, USA
**Blowfly** — Singer, Rap Artist
Pandisc Music, 15982 NW 48th Ave, Hialeah FL 33014, USA
**Blubaugh, Douglas M (Doug)** — Freestyle Wrestler
6640 N Utt Dr, Bloomington IN 47408, USA

# B

**Blucas, Marcus (Marc)** — Actor
Anonymous Content, 3532 Hayden Ave, Culver City CA 90232 USA
**Blue, Angel** — Opera Singer
I M G Artists, Hogarth Business Park, Chiswick, London W4 2TH, England
**Blue, Callum** — Actor
Artists Partnership, 101 Finsbury Pavement, London EC2A 1RS, England
**Blue, Vida R** — Baseball Player
PO Box 1449, Pleasanton CA 94566, USA
**Blueprint** — DJ Musician
Kork Agency, 1880 Century Park E, #711, Los Angeles CA 90067, USA
**Bluford, Guion S (Guy), Jr** — Astronaut
PO Box 549, North Olmsted OH 44070, USA
**Blum, Arlene** — Mountaineer
University of California, Biochemistry Dept, Berkeley CA 94720, USA
**Blum, Don** — Singer, Drummer (VonBondies)
Tsunami Entertainment, 2525 Hyperion Ave, Los Angeles CA 90027, USA
**Blum, Geoffrey E (Geoff)** — Baseball Player
7 Calle Angelitos, San Clemente CA 92673, USA
**Blum, H Steven** — Army General
Chief, National Guard Bureau, HqUSA, Pentagon, Washington DC 20310, USA
**Blum, John** — Ice Hockey Player
20225 Shores St, Saint Clair Shores MI 48080, USA
**Blum, Manuel** — Computer Scientist
700 Euclid Ave, Berkeley CA 94708, USA
**Blum, Stephanie** — Actress, Comedienne
Don Buchwald Talent Agency, 6500 Wilshire Blvd, #2200, Los Angeles CA 90048 USA
**Blum, Steve** — Actor
Arlene Thornton Assoc, 12711 Ventura Blvd, #490, Studio City CA 91604, USA
**Blum, Walter (Mousey)** — Thoroughbred Racing Jockey
5710 NW 65th Way, Tamarac FL 33321, USA
**Blumberg, Stuart** — Actor, Writer, Producer
Class 5 Films, 200 Park Ave S, #800, New York NY 10003, USA
**Blume, B Ray** — Basketball Player
29248 SE Powell Valley Road, Gresham OR 97080, USA
**Blume, Judy S** — Writer
W M E Entertainment, 9601 Wilshire Blvd, #300, Beverly Hills CA 90210 USA
**Blume, Martin** — Physicist
Brookhaven National Laboratory, 2 Center St, Upton NY 11973 USA
**Blumenfeld, Alan** — Actor
Stone Manners Salners, 6100 Wilshire Blvd, #1500, Los Angeles CA 90035 USA
**Blumenthal, George R** — Educator
University of California, Chancellor's Office, 1156 High St, Santa Cruz CA 95064, USA
**Blumenthal, Heston** — Chef, Restauranteur
Fat Duck Restaurant, High St, Bray on Thames West Berkshire SL6 2AQ, England
**Blumenthal, W Michael** — Secretary, Treasury; Financier
227 Ridgeview Road, Princeton NJ 08540, USA
**Blundell, Graeme** — Actor
Shanahan Mgmt, 91 Campbell St, #300, Surry Hills NSW 2010, Australia
**Blundell, Mark** — Auto Racing Driver
4001 Methanol Lane, Indianapolis IN 46268, USA
**Blundell, Pamela** — Fashion Designer
Copperwheat Blundell, 14 Cheshire St, London E2 6EH, England
**Blunstone, Colin** — Singer (Zombies)
Rhino Mgmt, 60 Babbercombe Road, Bromley, Kent BR1 3CW, England
**Blunt, Emily** — Actress
Creative Artists Agency, 2000 Ave of Stars, #100, Los Angeles CA 90067 USA
**Blunt, James** — Singer, Guitarist, Songwriter
High Road Touring, 751 Bridgeway, #200, Sausalito CA 94965 USA
**Blunt, Matthew R (Matt)** — Governor, MO
Cassidy & Assoc, 700 13th St NW, #400, Washington DC 20005, USA
**Bluteau, Lothaire** — Actor
Don Buchwald Talent Agency, 6500 Wilshire Blvd, #2200, Los Angeles CA 90048 USA
**Bluth, Ray** — Bowler
569 Beauford Dr, Saint Louis MO 63122, USA
**Bluth, Tony** — Animator
C A A T Studios, 10630 Moorpark St, #303, North Hollywood CA 91602, USA
**Bly, Donald A (Dre')** — Football Player
4312 Topsail Landing, Chesapeake VA 23321, USA
**Bly, Robert E** — Writer, Psychologist
1904 Girard Ave S, Minneapolis MN 55403, USA
**Blyleven, R Bert** — Baseball Player
14380 Riva Del Lago Dr, #2104, Fort Myers FL 33907, USA
**Blyth, Ann** — Actress, Singer
PO Box 9754, Rancho Santa Fe CA 92067, USA
**Blyth, Chay** — Yachtsman, Explorer
Inmans House, 12 London Road, Sheet, Petersfield, Hampshire GU31 4BE, England
**Blythe, Arthur M** — Jazz Saxophonist
Joel Chriss Co, 300 Mercer St, #3J, New York NY 10003 USA
**Blythe, D Randall (Randy)** — Singer (Lamb of God)
Entertainment Unlimited, 1000 Main Street Plaza, #303, Voorhees NJ 08043, USA
**Blythe, Stephanie** — Singer
Opus 3 Artists, 470 Park Ave S, #900N, New York NY 10016 USA
**Bo Bae Song** — Golfer
Ladies Pro Golf Assn, 100 International Golf Dr, Daytona Beach FL 32124 USA
**Boal, Mark** — Writer
Creative Artists Agency, 2000 Ave of Stars, #100, Los Angeles CA 90067 USA
**Board, Dwaine P** — Football Player
651 Arlington Road, Redwood City CA 94062, USA
**Boardman, Christopher M (Chris)** — Cyclist
Lindfield House, Station Approach Meols, Wirral L47 8XA, England
**Boardman, Eric** — Actor, Director
I C M Partners, 10250 Constellation Blvd, #900, Los Angeles CA 90067 USA
**Boardman, Lee** — Actor
Artists Partnership, 101 Finsbury Pavement, London EC2A 1RS, England
**Boat, William L (Billy)** — Auto Racing Driver
Boat Indy Racing, 23045 N 15th Ave, Phoenix AZ 85027, USA

Blucas - Boat

**Boatman, Michael** — Actor
1432 Sunnycrest Dr, Fullerton CA 92835, USA
**Bob, Tim** — Bassist (Rage Against the Machine)
ArtistDirect, 10900 Wilshire Blvd, #1400, Los Angeles CA 90024 USA
**Bobbie, Walter** — Director, Actor, Lyricist
B R S / Gage Talent Agency, 5757 Wilshire Blvd, #659, Los Angeles CA 90036 USA
**Bobbitt, Sean** — Cinematographer
Sandra Marsh Assoc, 9150 Wilshire Blvd, #220, Beverly Hills CA 90212 USA
**Bobby G** — Singer (Bucks Fizz)
Barry Collings Entertainment, PO 2112, Hockley, Essex SS5 4WD, England
**Bobek, Nicole** — Figure Skater
19220 Seaview Road, #100, Jupiter FL 33469, USA
**Bober, Chris** — Football Player
4406 N 195th Circle, Elkhorn NE 68022, USA
**Bobko, Karol J** — Astronaut
91 Turnberry Road, Half Moon Bay CA 94019, USA
**Bobo, Jonah** — Actor
Abrams Artists, 9200 W Sunset Blvd, #1125, West Hollywood CA 90069 USA
**Bobrova, Ekaterina A** — Figure Skater
Figure Skating Federation, Luzhnetskaya Nab 8, 119991 Moscow, Russia
**Bocachica, Hiram** — Baseball Player
2340 Carr 2, 2 Urb Rexville, Bayamon PR 00961, USA
**Bocca, Julio** — Ballet Dancer
F P S International, 150 Broadway, New York NY 10038, USA
**Boccabella, John D** — Baseball Player
1035 Lea Dr, San Rafael CA 94903, USA
**Bocchi, Nicole** — Actress
Carson Adler Agency, 250 W 57th St, #2030, New York NY 10107, USA
**Bocelli, Andrea** — Concert Singer
Konigshutter Str 9, 51065 Cologne, Germany
**Bochco, Steven** — Producer, Writer
22035 Saddle Peak Road, Topanga CA 90290, USA
**Bochenski, Brandon** — Ice Hockey Player
12962 Radisson Road NE, Minneapolis MN 55449, USA
**Bochenski, Jacek** — Writer
Ul Sonaty 6M 801, 02 744 Warsaw, Poland
**Bochner, Hart** — Actor
Integral Artists, 73 E 6th Ave, #208, Vancouver BC V5T 1M4, Canada
**Bochner, Salomon** — Mathematician
4100 Greenbriar Ave, #239, Houston TX 77098, USA
**Bochte, Bruce A** — Baseball Player
80 Century Lane, Petaluma CA 94952, USA
**Bochtler, Douglas E (Doug)** — Baseball Player
154 Narrow Gate Road, Maryville TN 37801, USA
**Bochy, Bruce D** — Baseball Player, Manager
16144 Brittany Park Lane, Poway CA 92064, USA
**Bock, Charles, Jr** — Test Pilot
PO Box 4197, Incline Village NV 89450, USA
**Bock, Dennis** — Writer
Carlisle Co, 121 E 17th St, New York NY 10003, USA
**Bock, John M** — Football Player
627 Cambridge Terrace, Weston FL 33326, USA
**Bock, Kate** — Model
Lizbell Agency, 216-309 W Cordova St, Vancouver BCV6B 1E5, Canada
**Bockhorn, Arlen (Bucky)** — Basketball Player
3540 Big Tree Road, Bellbrook OH 45305, USA
**Bockrath, Tina** — Actress, Model
755 S San Rafael Ave, Pasadena CA 91105, USA
**Bockwinkel, Nick W F** — Professional Wrestler
Cauliflower Alley Club, 383 Highway 00, Rolla MO 65401, USA
**Bocuse, Paul** — Restauranteur
Kuchenmeister, 40 Rue de la Plage, 69660 Collonges au Mont d'Or, France
**Bodden, Alonzo** — Actor, Comedian
Levity Entertainment Group, 6701 Center Drive W, #1111, Los Angeles CA 90045, USA
**Bodden, Leigh E** — Football Player
400 Foxboro Blvd, Foxborough MA 02035, USA
**Boddicker, Michael J (Mike)** — Baseball Player
11324 W 121st Terrace, Overland Park KS 66213, USA
**Boddy, Gregg** — Ice Hockey Player
2271 Sorrento Dr, Coquitlam BC V3K 6P4, Canada
**Bode, Hendrick W** — Research Engineer
Harvard University, Pierce Hall, Cambridge MA 02138, USA
**Bode, John R** — Vietnam War Air Force Hero
1100 Warm Sands Dr SE, Albuquerque NM 87123, USA
**Bode, Ken** — Commentator, Educator
Northwestern University, Journalism School, Evanston IL 60206, USA
**Boden, Lynn R** — Football Player
7103 N 146th St, Bennington NE 68007, USA
**Boden, Margaret A** — Philosopher, Psychologist
Brighton University, Cognitive Science School, Brighton BN1 9QH, England
**Bodenheimer, George** — Businessman, TV Executive
ABC-TV, Sports Dept, 77 W 66th St, New York NY 10023 USA
**Bodett, Tom** — Writer, Entertainer
PO Box 268, Putney VT 05346, USA
**Bodger, Doug** — Ice Hockey Player
Eddy's Hockey Shop, 2728 James St, Duncan BC V9L 2X9, Canada
**Bodill, Colin** — Aviator
Polar First, Onslow Gardens, #2, London SW7 3LX, England
**Bodine, Brett** — Auto Racing Driver
228 Almora Loop, Mooresville NC 28115, USA
**Bodine, Geoffrey E (Geoff)** — Auto Racing Driver
18695 Northline Dr, #C2, Cornelius NC 28031, USA
**Bodine, Todd** — Auto Racing Driver
120 Harris Farm Dr, Mooresville NC 28115, USA
**Bodmer, Walter F** — Geneticist
Oxford University, Hertford College, Oxford OX1 3BW, England

**Bodrov, Sergei V, Sr** — Director
Arlook Group, 205 S Beverly Dr, #209, Beverly Hills CA 90212, USA
**Boe, Alfie** — Singer
Agency Group Ltd, 361-373 City Road, London EC1V 1PQ, England
**Boe, Éric A** — Astronaut
N A S A, Johnson Space Center, 2101 NASA Road, Houston TX 77058 USA
**Boecher, Katherine** — Actress
Innovative Artists, 1505 10th St, Santa Monica CA 90401 USA
**Boeddeker, Steve** — Sound Designer
Skywalker Ranch, 5858 Lucas Valley Road, Nicasio CA 94946, USA
**Boeheim, James A (Jim), Jr** — Basketball Coach
701 Eagle Woods Trail, Kissimmee FL 34747, USA
**Boehm, Gottfried K** — Pritzker Architectural Laureate
Kunstgeschichtliches Seminar, Saint Alban-Graben 16, 4051 Basel, Switzerland
**Boehringer, Brian E** — Baseball Player
10 Sunset Dr, Fenton MO 63026, USA
**Boer, Margot** — Speed Skater
K N S B, Postbus 11087, 3505 Utrecht BB, Netherlands
**Boerigter, Marc R** — Football Player
210 W 2nd St, #1412, Kansas City MO 64105, USA
**Boerner, Jacqueline** — Speed Skater
Bernhard-Bastlein-Str 55, 10367 Berlin, Germany
**Boesak, Allan** — Religious Leader, Social Activist
16 Villa Bellini, Constantia St, Strand 7140, South Africa
**Boeschenstein, William W** — Businessman
10617 Cardiff Road, Perrysburg OH 43551, USA
**Boesel, Raul D** — Auto Racing Driver
150 SE 25th Road, #4E, Miami FL 33129, USA
**Boesen, Dennis L (Denny)** — Astronaut
6613 Sandra Ave NE, Albuquerque NM 87109, USA
**Boever, Joseph M (Joe)** — Baseball Player
416 Savannah Way, Franklin TN 37067, USA
**Boeving, Christian** — Actor
Diverse Talent Group, 9911 W Pico Blvd, #350W, Los Angeles CA 90035, USA
**Boff** — Guitarist (Chumbawamba)
Doug Smith Assoc, PO Box 1151, London W3 8ZJ, England
**Boff, Leonardo G D** — Theologian
Pr M Leao 12/204, Alto Vale Encantado, 20531-350 Rio de Janeiro, Brazil
**Bofill, Angela** — Singer
1385 York Ave, #6B, New York NY 10021, USA
**Bofill, Ricardo** — Architect
Taller de Arquitectura, 14 Ave de la Industria, 08960 Barcelona, Spain
**Bofinger, Helge** — Architect
Biebricher Allee 49, 65187 Wiesbaden, Germany
**Bogaliy-Titovets, Anna** — Biathlete
Biathlon Union, Luzhnetskaya Nab 8, 119992 Moscow, Russia
**Boganyi, Tibor** — Conductor
Konzertdirektion Hortnagel, Oranienburger Str 50D, 10117 Berlin, Germany
**Bogar, Timothy P (Tim)** — Baseball Player
194 Gray St, North Andover MA 01845, USA
**Bogardus, Stephen** — Actor
TalentWorks, 3500 W Olive Ave, #1400, Burbank CA 91505 USA
**Bogdanich, Walt** — Journalist
New York Times, Editorial Dept, 229 W 43rd St, New York NY 10036 USA
**Bogdanovich, Peter** — Director
A K A Talent, 6310 San Vicente Blvd, #200, Los Angeles CA 90048 USA
**Bogeberg, J B** — Bassist (A-Ha)
Bandana Mgmt, 11 Elvaston Place, #300, London SW7 5QC, England
**Boggs, Bill** — Journalist
240 Central Park S, New York NY 10019, USA
**Boggs, Danny J** — Judge
US Court of Appeals, US Courthouse, 601 W Broadway, Louisville KY 40202, USA
**Boggs, Haskell** — Cinematographer
3710 Goodland Ave, Studio City CA 91604, USA
**Boggs, Thomas W (Tommy)** — Baseball Player
1450 Long Meadow, Salado TX 76571, USA
**Boggs, Wade A** — Baseball Player
6006 Windham Place, Tampa FL 33647, USA
**Bogguss, Suzy** — Singer, Guitarist, Songwriter
Creative Artists Agency, 2000 Ave of Stars, #100, Los Angeles CA 90067 USA
**Bogle, Eric** — Singer, Songwriter
Laing Entertainment, 35 Montague St, Goulburn NSW 2580, Australia
**Bogle, John C** — Financier
320 Fishers Road, Bryn Mawr PA 19010, USA
**Boglioli, Wendy** — Swimmer
2014 210th Circle, Sammamish WA 98074, USA
**Bogner, Willy** — Producer, Fashion Designer
Firma Willy Bogner GmbH, Saint-Veit-Str 4, 81673 Munich, Germany
**Bogosian, Eric** — Performance Artist, Actor, Writer
Brookside Artists Mgmt, 250 W 57th St, #2303, New York NY 10107 USA
**Bogues, Tyrone (Muggsy)** — Basketball Player, Coach
527 E 83rd St, #2W, New York NY 10028, USA
**Boguniecki, Eric** — Ice Hockey Player
134 Buttonball Road, Orange CT 06477, USA
**Bogush, Elizabeth** — Actress
Innovative Artists, 1505 10th St, Santa Monica CA 90401 USA
**Bogut, Andrew** — Basketball Player
1660 N Prospect Ave, #2607, Milwaukee WI 53202, USA
**Bohan, Marc** — Fashion Designer
35 Rue du Bourg a Mont, 21400 Chatillon sur Seine, France
**Bohanon, Brian E** — Baseball Player
243 W Thorn Way, Houston TX 77015, USA
**Bohay, Heidi** — Actress
Brogan Agency, 1517 Park Row Dr, Venice CA 90291, USA
**Bohem, Leslie (Les)** — Writer
United Talent Agency, U T A Plaza, 9336 Civic Center Dr, Beverly Hills CA 90210 USA

**Bohigas Guardiola, Oriol** — Architect
M B M Arquitectes, Placa Reial 18, 08002 Barcelona 21, Spain

**Bohler, Stefanie** — Cross Country Skier
Miesenbacher Str 104, 83324 Ruhpolding, Germany

**Bohlin, Peter Q** — Architect
Bohlin Cywinski Jackson, 49 Geary St, #300, San Francisco CA 94108, USA

**Bohm, Daniel** — Biathlete
Am Schlagbaum 29, 38678 Clausthal-Zellerfeld, Germany

**Bohm, Uwe** — Actor
Agentur Klostermann & Thamm, Konigstr 32, 22767 Hamburg, Germany

**Bohn, Jason** — Golfer
757 Carl Sanders Dr, Acworth GA 30101, USA

**Bohn, Laura** — Interior Designer
Laura Bohn Design, 30 W 26th St, #1100, New York NY 10010, USA

**Bohn, Parker, III** — Bowler
25 Pitney Lane, Jackson NJ 08527, USA

**Bohne, Bruce** — Actor
Beacon Talent Agency, 170 Apple Ridge Road, Woodcliff Lake NJ 07677, USA

**Bohon, Justin** — Actor
Innovative Artists, 1505 10th St, Santa Monica CA 90401 USA

**Bohorquez, Claudio** — Concert Cellist
Conciertos Augusto, Calle Viento 15, 2B Majadahonda, 28220 Madrid, Spain

**Bohrer, Corinne** — Actress
Abrams Artists, 9200 W Sunset Blvd, #1125, West Hollywood CA 90069 USA

**Bohrer, Thomas** — Rowing Athlete
77 Crest St, Concord MA 01742, USA

**Bohringer, Romane** — Actress
Agence Artiste Adequat, 108 Rue Reaumur, 75002 Paris, France

**Boies, David** — Attorney
Cravath Swaine Moore, 1 Chase Manhattan Plaza, New York NY 10005, USA

**Boikov, Alexandre** — Ice Hockey Player
2138 Charleys Creek Road, Culloden WV 25510, USA

**Boileau, Linda** — Editorial Cartoonist
Frankfort State Journal, Editorial Dept, 321 W Main St, Frankfort KY 40601, USA

**Boiman, Rocky M** — Football Player
10105 County Line Road, Brookville IN 47012, USA

**Boisclair, Bruce A** — Baseball Player
5423 Spanish Oak Lane, #D, Oak Park CA 91377, USA

**Boise, Mike** — Drummer (Chesterfield Kings)
Agency Group Ltd, 142 W 57th St, #600, New York NY 10019 USA

**Boisset, Yves** — Director
61 Blvd Inkerman, 92200 Neuilly-sur-Seine, France

**Boisson, Christine** — Actress
Artmedia, 20 Ave Rapp, 75007 Paris, France

**Boisvert, Gilles** — Ice Hockey Player
10213 Greenside Dr, Cockeysville MD 21030, USA

**Boitano, Brian** — Figure Skater
1072 Inverness Way, Sunnyvale CA 94087, USA

**Boitano, Danny J** — Baseball Player
15400 Winchester Blvd, #43, Los Gatos CA 95030, USA

**Boivin, Leo J** — Ice Hockey Player
PO Box 406, Prescott ON K0E 1T0, Canada

**Bok, Chip** — Editorial Cartoonist
709 Castle Blvd, Akron OH 44313, USA

**Bok, Derek C** — Educator
Harvard University, Kennedy Government School, Cambridge MA 02138, USA

**Bok, Sissela** — Philosopher
75 Cambridge Parkway, #E610, Cambridge MA 02142, USA

**Bokamper, Kim** — Football Player
301 NW 127th Ave, Plantation FL 33325, USA

**Bokova, Irina G** — Government Official, Bulgaria
U N E S C O, Director-General's Office, 7 Place de Fontenoy, 75352 Paris 07 SP, France

**Bolam, James** — Actor
Independent Talent Group, 40 Whitfield St, London W1T 2RH, England

**Bolcom, William E** — Composer, Pianist
3080 Whitmore Lake Road, Ann Arbor MI 48105, USA

**Bolden, Charles F, Jr** — Astronaut, Marine Corps General
National Aviation & Space Administration, 300 C St SW, Washington DC 20024, USA

**Bolden, Jeanette** — Track Athlete
University of California, Athletic Dept, Los Angeles CA 90024, USA

**Bolden, Juran T** — Football Player
4618 Barkley Dr NW, Acworth GA 30101, USA

**Boldin, Anquan** — Football Player
471 E Crescent Place, Chandler AZ 85249, USA

**Boldirev, Ivan** — Ice Hockey Player
2003 Woodmere Dr E, Valparaiso IN 46383, USA

**Boldon, Ato** — Track Athlete
PO Box 3703, Santa Cruz, Trinidad, Trinidad & Tobago

**Bolduc, Danny** — Ice Hockey Player
27 Daisy Lane, Sidney ME 04330, USA

**Boles, John E, Jr** — Baseball Manager, Executive
7901 Timberlake Dr, Melbourne FL 32904, USA

**Bolger, Dermot** — Writer
A P Watt, 20 John St, London WC1N 2DR, England

**Bolger, James B (Jim)** — Prime Minister, New Zealand
New Zealand Embassy, 37 Observatory Circle NW, Washington DC 20008, USA

**Bolger, James C (Jim)** — Baseball Player
5524 Sidney Road, Cincinnati OH 45238, USA

**Bolger, Sarah L** — Actress
Hamilton Hodell, 20 Golden Square, London W1F 9JL, England

**Bolick, Frank C** — Baseball Player
381 Virginia Lane, Kulpmont PA 17834, USA

**Bolin, Bobby D** — Baseball Player
100 Medinah Dr, Easley SC 29642, USA

**Boling, David** — Writer
Bloomsbury Publishing, 50 Bedford Square, London WC1B 3DP, England

**B**

| | |
|---|---|
| **Boll, Timo**<br>B Schmittenbecher-Sportsmarketing, Erlenring 16, 61118 Bad Vilbel, Germany | Table Tennis Player |
| **Boll, Uwe**<br>Bolu Filmproduktion, Holmanstr 8-10, 97421 Schweinfurt, Germany | Director |
| **Bollen, Roger**<br>8964 Little St, Mentor OH 44060, USA | Cartoonist (Animal Crackers, Catfish) |
| **Boller, Kyle B**<br>2365 Jennifer Lane, Encinitas CA 92024, USA | Football Player |
| **Bolles, Richard N**<br>10 Stirling Dr, Danville CA 94526, USA | Writer |
| **Bollettieri, Nick**<br>Nick Bollettieri Tennis Academy, 5500 34th St W, Bradenton FL 34210, USA | Tennis Coach |
| **Bolli, Justin**<br>136 Ramsford Lane, Simpsonville SC 29681, USA | Golfer |
| **Bolling, Claude**<br>New Audiences Productions, 161 W 75th St, #9E, New York NY 10023, USA | Jazz Pianist, Composer |
| **Bolling, Dave**<br>Bloomsbury Publishing, 50 Bedford Square, London WC1B 3DP, England | Writer |
| **Bolling, Frank E**<br>171 Fenwick Road, Mobile AL 36608, USA | Baseball Player |
| **Bolling, Tiffany**<br>Tyler Kjar, 10153 1/2 Riverside Dr, #255, Toluca Lake CA 91602 USA | Actress |
| **Bollinger, Brooks**<br>3549 Birchpond Road, Saint Paul MN 55122, USA | Football Player |
| **Bollinger, Lee C**<br>Columbia University, President's Office, New York NY 10027, USA | Educator |
| **Bollinger, R Randal**<br>1120 Infinity Road, Durham NC 27712, USA | Surgeon |
| **Bolocco Fonck, Cecilia C**<br>Miss Universe Organization, 1370 Ave of Americas, #1600, New York NY 10019 USA | Beauty Queen, Actress |
| **Bologna, Joseph**<br>S M S Talent, 8383 Wilshire Blvd, #230, Beverly Hills CA 90211 USA | Actor |
| **Bolonchuk, Larry**<br>385 Woodlawn St, Winnipeg MB R3J 2J2, Canada | Ice Hockey Player |
| **Bolstorff, Douglas**<br>1553 Skyline Court, Saint Paul MN 55121, USA | Basketball Player |
| **Bolt, Mae**<br>1516 Robinhood Lane, La Grange Park IL 60526, USA | Bowler |
| **Bolt, Usain**<br>Pace Sports Mgmt, 6 Causeway, Teddington, Middlesex TW11 0HE, England | Track Athlete |
| **Boltanski, Christian**<br>146 Blvd Carmelina, 92240 Malakoff, France | Artist, Photographer |
| **Bolten, Michael C**<br>C E S D, 10635 Santa Monica Blvd, #130, Los Angeles CA 90025 USA | Actor |
| **Bolton, James R**<br>Calgon Carbon Corp, 130 Royal Crest Court, Markham ON L6G 1A8, Canada | Photochemist |
| **Bolton, Michael**<br>Works Public Relations, 11 Marshalsea Road, London SE1 1EN, England | Singer, Songwriter |
| **Bolton, Ronald C (Ron)**<br>408 Maiden Lane, Chesapeake VA 23325, USA | Football Player |
| **Bolton, Thomas E (Tom)**<br>2288 Rolling Hills Dr, Nolensville TN 37135, USA | Baseball Player |
| **Bolton-Holifield, Ruthie**<br>Sacramento Monarchs, Arco Arena, 1 Sports Parkway, Sacramento CA 95834 USA | Basketball Player |
| **Bolyard, Bob**<br>10607 Wild Flower Place, Fort Wayne IN 46845, USA | Basketball Player |
| **Bomar, Mary**<br>National Park Service, Interior Department, PO Box 37127, Washington DC 20013, USA | Government Official |
| **Bombardie, Brad**<br>8959 Baywatch Trail NW, Walker MN 56484, USA | Ice Hockey Player |
| **Bomer, Matthew (Matt)**<br>Anonymous Content, 3532 Hayden Ave, Culver City CA 90232 USA | Actor |
| **Bon Jovi, Jon**<br>Bon Jovi Mgmt, 809 Elder Circle, Austin TX 78733, USA | Singer (Bon Jovi), Songwriter, Actor |
| **Bona, Richard**<br>International Music Network, 278 Main St, Gloucester MA 01930, USA | Bassist, Singer |
| **Bonadio, Jeffrey**<br>Pacific Rim Pathology,  5325 Metro St, San Diego CA 92110, USA | Physician |
| **Bonaduce, Danny**<br>Rebel Entertainment Partners, 5700 Wilshire Blvd, #456, Los Angeles CA 90036, USA | Actor, Singer |
| **Bonaly, Surya**<br>35 Rue Felicien David, 75016 Paris, France | Figure Skater |
| **Bonamassa, Joe**<br>Premier Artists Services, 10025 Vestal Place, Coral Springs FL 33071, USA | Guitarist, Singer, Songwriter |
| **Bonanno, Louis**<br>24822 Largo Dr, Laguna Hills CA 92653, USA | Actor |
| **Bonar, Dan**<br>361 Mandeville St, Winnipeg MB R3J 2J2, Canada | Ice Hockey Player |
| **Bond, Alan**<br>89 Watkins Road, Dalkeith WA 6069, Australia | Yachtsman, Businessman |
| **Bond, Edward**<br>Casorotto Ramsay, Waverley House, 7-12 Noel St, London W1F 8GQ, England | Writer |
| **Bond, H Julian**<br>5435 41st Place NW, Washington DC 20015, USA | Civil Rights Activist |
| **Bond, Phillip (Phil)**<br>208 Northwestern Parkway, Louisville KY 40212, USA | Basketball Player |
| **Bond, Samantha**<br>Innovative Artists, 1505 10th St, Santa Monica CA 90401 USA | Actress |
| **Bond, Victoria A**<br>Roanoke Symphony, 541 Luck Ave SW, #200, Roanoke VA 24016, USA | Conductor, Composer |
| **Bond, Walter**<br>PO Box 87, Hamel MN 55340, USA | Basketball Player |
| **Bondar, Roberta L**<br>Space Agency, Rockcliffe Base, Ottawa ON K1A 1A1, Canada | Astronaut, Canada |
| **Bondarenko, Vtaly M**<br>Communal Institute, Kalitnikovskaya Str 30, 109807 Moscow, Russia | Architect |

| | |
|---|---|
| **Bonderman, Jeremy A** | Baseball Player |
| 10 Ridgeview Dr, Pasco WA 99301, USA | |
| **Bondevik, Kjell Magne** | Prime Minister, Norway |
| Oslo Peace & Human Rights Center, Box 2753 Solli, 0204 Oslo, Norway | |
| **Bondi, Viggo** | Bassist (A-Ha) |
| Bandana Mgmt, 11 Elvaston Place, London SW7 5QC, England | |
| **Bondra, Peter** | Ice Hockey Player |
| 372 Carriage Park Way, Annapolis MD 21401, USA | |
| **Bonds, Barry L** | Baseball Player |
| 3 Lagoon Dr, #400, Redwood City CA 94065, USA | |
| **Bonds, Gary U S** | Singer |
| John Regna, 8815 Conroy Windermere Road, #407, Orlando FL 32835, USA | |
| **Bondurant, Robert (Bob)** | Auto Driving Instructor |
| Firebird International Speedway, PO Box 51980, Phoenix AZ 85076, USA | |
| **Bone Crusher** | Rap Artist |
| Richard De La Font Agency, 4845 S Sheridan Road, #505, Tulsa OK 74145 USA | |
| **Bone, Ken** | Basketball Coach |
| Washington State University, Athletic Dept, Pullman WA 99164, USA | |
| **Bonebreak, Donald J (D J)** | Drummer (X) |
| A P A Talent & Literary Agency, 405 S Beverly Dr, #300, Beverly Hills CA 90212 USA | |
| **Bonehill, Richard** | Actor |
| Bosun's Nest, Carthew Way, Saint Ives, Cornwall TR26 1RJ, England | |
| **Bonell, Carlos A** | Concert Guitarist, Composer |
| Bravo Music International, PO Box 19060, London N7 0ZD, England | |
| **Bonerz, Peter** | Actor, Comedian, Director |
| Shapiro/West Assoc, 141 El Camino Dr, #205, Beverly Hills CA 90212, USA | |
| **Bones, Ricardo (Ricky)** | Baseball Player |
| 908 NW 100th Ave, Pembroke Pines FL 33024, USA | |
| **Bonet, Lisa** | Actress |
| Untitled Entertainment, 350 S Beverly Dr, #200, Beverly Hills CA 90212 USA | |
| **Bonet, Pep** | Architect |
| C/Pujades 62, 08005 Barcelona, Spain | |
| **Boneta, Diego** | Actor, Singer |
| Gersh Agency, 9465 Wilshire Blvd, #600, Beverly Hills CA 90212 USA | |
| **Bonetti, Mattia** | Designer, Interior Decorator, Artist |
| 10 Rue Rocjebrune, 75011 Paris, France | |
| **Bong Joon Ho** | Director, Writer |
| Creative Artists Agency, 2000 Ave of Stars, #100, Los Angeles CA 90067 USA | |
| **Bong Jung Keun** | Baseball Player |
| 2917 Asteria Pointe, Duluth GA 30097, USA | |
| **Bonham Carter, Helena** | Actress |
| 7 W Heath Ave, London NW11 7QS, England | |
| **Bonham, Jason** | Drummer |
| Agency Group Ltd, 142 W 57th St, #600, New York NY 10019 USA | |
| **Bonham, Ronald D (Ron)** | Basketball Player |
| 8020 S Country Road 700E, Selma IN 47383, USA | |
| **Bonham, S Shane** | Football Player |
| 321 Clover Hill Road, Maryville TN 37801, USA | |
| **Bonham, Tracy** | Singer, Musician, Songwriter |
| Big Hassle, 44 Wall St, #2200, New York NY 10005, USA | |
| **Bonhomme, Brian** | Guitarist (Roman Holliday) |
| Youngstown State University, History Dept, Youngstown OH 44555, USA | |
| **Bonhomme, Tessa** | Ice Hockey Player |
| Team Canada, 2424 University Dr NW, Calgary AB T2N 3Y9, Canada | |
| **Boni, T Yayi** | President, Benin |
| President's Office, Palais Presidentiel, BP 2028, Cotonou, Benin | |
| **Boniadi, Nazanin** | Actress |
| A K A Talent, 6310 San Vicente Blvd, #200, Los Angeles CA 90048 USA | |
| **Boniface, Bruce** | Singer, Songwriter |
| Virgin Records, 338 N Foothill Road, Beverly Hills CA 90210 USA | |
| **Bonilla, Henry** | Representative, TX |
| 2 Lake Shore Dr, Corpus Christi TX 78413, USA | |
| **Bonilla, Juan G** | Baseball Player |
| 2902 Orchidcrest Dr, Crestview FL 32539, USA | |
| **Bonilla, Michelle C** | Actress |
| Imperium 7 Artists, 5455 Wilshire Blvd, #1706, Los Angeles CA 90036 USA | |
| **Bonilla, Roberto M A (Bobby)** | Baseball Player |
| 1403 Kenilworth St, Sarasota FL 34231, USA | |
| **Bonin, Marcel** | Ice Hockey Player |
| 408 Rue Precieux-Sang, Joliette QC J6E 2M5, Canada | |
| **Bonington, Christian J S** | Mountaineer |
| Badger Hill, Hesket Newmarket, Wigton, Cumbria CA7 8LA, England | |
| **Boniol, Christopher D (Chris)** | Football Player |
| PO Box 271396, Flower Mound TX 75027, USA | |
| **Bonior, David E** | Representative, MI |
| 38875 Harper Ave, Clinton Township MI 48036, USA | |
| **Boniperti, Giampiero** | Soccer Player |
| F C Juventus, Corso Galilo Ferraris 32, 10128 Turin, Italy | |
| **Bonjour, Daniel** | Actor |
| Tinoco Mgmt, 8033 Sunset Blvd, #573, West Hollywood CA 90046, USA | |
| **Bonk, Radek** | Ice Hockey Player |
| 137 Allenhurst Circle, Franklin TN 37067, USA | |
| **Bonnaire, Sandrine** | Actress, Director, Writer |
| Artmedia, 20 Ave Rapp, 75007 Paris, France | |
| **Bonnefous, Jean-Pierre** | Ballet Dancer, Choreographer |
| Indiana University, Ballet Dept, Music School, Bloomington IN 47405, USA | |
| **Bonnefoy, Yves J** | Writer |
| College de France, Poetry Study Dept, 11 Place Marcelin Berthelot, 75005 Paris, France | |
| **Bonnell, R Barry** | Baseball Player |
| 2102 179th Court NE, Redmond WA 98052, USA | |
| **Bonner, Anthony** | Basketball Player |
| 5854 Elmbank Ave, Saint Louis MO 63120, USA | |
| **Bonner, DeWanna** | Basketball Player |
| Phoenix Mercury, American West Arena, 201 E Jefferson St, Phoenix AZ 85004 USA | |
| **Bonner, Elayna G** | Human Rights Activist |
| A D Sajharova Museum, Zemlyanoy Val 57, Building 6, 107120 Moscow, Russia | |

**Bonner, John T** — Biologist
1025 NE 33rd Ave, Portland OR 97232, USA
**Bonner, Matthew R (Matt)** — Basketball Player
San Antonio Spurs, Alamodome, 1 AT&T Center Parkway, San Antonio TX 78219 USA
**Bonner, Robert C** — Attorney, Judge
Gibson Dunn Crutcher, 333 S Grand Ave, #4400, Los Angeles CA 90071, USA
**Bonner, Steven J, Jr** — WW II Army Air Corps Hero
17043 Lakeside Dr, Carlinville IL 62626, USA
**Bonner, Tony** — Actor
Agents Associes, 201 Rue du Faubourg Saint Honore, 75008 Paris, France
**Bonness, Richard K (Rik)** — Football Player
18914 Boyle Circle, Elkhorn NE 68022, USA
**Bonneville, Hugh** — Actor
United Talent Agency, U T A Plaza, 9336 Civic Center Dr, Beverly Hills CA 90210 USA
**Bonney, Barbara** — Opera Singer
Universität Mozarteum Salzburg, Mirabellplatz 1, 5020 Salzburg, Austria
**Bono** — Singer, Songwriter (U-2)
Principle Management, 250 W 57th St, #2120, New York NY 10107, USA
**Bono, Chaz** — Entertainer
Haber Entertainment, 434 S Canon Dr, #204, Beverly Hills CA 90212, USA
**Bono, Mary** — Representative, CA
3600 S Glebe Road, #1018, Arlington VA 22202, USA
**Bono, Steven C (Steve)** — Football Player
1100 Hamilton Ave, Palo Alto CA 94301, USA
**Bonoff, Karla** — Singer, Pianist, Songwriter
2122 E Valley Road, Santa Barbara CA 93108, USA
**Bonsall, Joseph S (Joe), Jr** — Singer (Oak Ridge Boys)
88 New Shackle Island Road, Hendersonville TN 37075, USA
**Bonser, John P (Boof)** — Baseball Player
12060 Lucca St, #202, Fort Myers FL 33966, USA
**Bonsey, Don** — Photographer
3195 Tyrol Dr, Laguna Beach CA 92651, USA
**Bonsignore, Jason** — Ice Hockey Player
2152 Edgemere Dr, Rochester NY 14612, USA
**Bontemps, Ronald Y (Ron)** — Basketball Player
6358 N Allen Road, #38, Peoria IL 61614, USA
**Bonvie, Dennis** — Ice Hockey Player
670 N River St, #210, Wilkes Barre PA 18705, USA
**Bonvoisin, Berangere** — Actress
Voyez Mon Agent, 20 Ave Rapp, 75007 Paris, France
**Bonvoisin, Bernie** — Actor
U B B A, 6 Rue de Braque, 75003 Paris, France
**Bonynge, Richard A** — Conductor
Chalet Monet, Route de Sonloup, 1833 Les Avants, Switzerland
**Boo, Katherine** — Journalist
Washington Post, Editorial Dept, 1150 15th St NW, Washington DC 20071 USA
**Book, Asher M** — Actor
Paradigm Agency, 360 N Crescent Dr, North Building, Beverly Hills CA 90210 USA
**Booker, Gregory S (Greg)** — Baseball Player
1535 Charleigh Court, Elon College NC 27244, USA
**Booker, Marty M** — Football Player
15982 SW 11th St, Pembroke Pines FL 33027, USA
**Booker, Vaughn J** — Football Player
11 Page St, Hurst TX 76053, USA
**Bookwalter, J R** — Director
PO Box 6573, Akron OH 44312, USA
**Boomer, Linwood** — Actor, Producer, Writer
Greenberg Taurig, 1840 Century Park E, #1900, Los Angeles CA 90067 USA
**Boomer, Walter E** — Marine Corps General
4 Pinckney Landing Dr, Sheldon SC 29941, USA
**Boon, Dany** — Actor
W M E Entertainment, 9601 Wilshire Blvd, #300, Beverly Hills CA 90210 USA
**Boon, David C** — Cricketer
Durham Cricket Club, Chester-le-Street, County Durham DH3 3QR, England
**Boone, Aaron J** — Baseball Player
10111 E Phantom Way, Scottsdale AZ 85255, USA
**Boone, Alfonso** — Football Player
14290 W Lyle Court, Libertyville IL 60048, USA
**Boone, Brendon** — Actor
9157 W Sunset Blvd, #206, West Hollywood CA 90069, USA
**Boone, Bret R** — Baseball Player
804 Midori Court, Solana Beach CA 92075, USA
**Boone, Daneen** — Actress
Sherrida Personal Mgmt, 110 Scollard St, Toronto ON M5R 1G2, Canada
**Boone, Debby** — Singer, Actress
I C M Partners, 730 5th Ave, New York NY 10019 USA
**Boone, Megan** — Actress, Director, Writer
Gersh Agency, 9465 Wilshire Blvd, #600, Beverly Hills CA 90212 USA
**Boone, Pat** — Actor, Singer
Solters & Digney, 1680 N Vine St, #1105, Hollywood CA 90028, USA
**Boone, Robert R (Bob)** — Baseball Player, Manager
1432 Misty Sea Way, San Marcos CA 92078, USA
**Boone, Ronald B (Ron)** — Basketball Player
3877 Pheasant Ridge Road, Salt Lake City UT 84109, USA
**Boone, Steve** — Bassist, Singer (Lovin' Spoonful)
Lustig Talent, PO Box 770850, Orlando FL 32877 USA
**Boorem, Mika** — Actor
Untitled Entertainment, 350 S Beverly Dr, #200, Beverly Hills CA 90212 USA
**Boorman, John** — Director
Merlin Films, 16 Upper Pembroke St, Dublin 2, Ireland
**Booros, James** — Golfer
2615 W Pennsylvania St, Allentown PA 18104, USA
**Boosler, Elayne** — Actress, Comedienne, Writer
Levity Entertainment, 6701 Center Drive W, #1111, Los Angeles CA 90045, USA
**Bootcheck, Christopher B (Chris)** — Baseball Player
1204 Suncast Lane, #2, El Dorado Hills CA 95762, USA

**Booth, Amanda** — Model
Playboy Promotions, 9346 Civic Center Dr, #200, Beverly Hills CA 90210 USA
**Booth, Calvin L** — Basketball Player
6001 E Horseshoe Road, Paradise Valley AZ 85253, USA
**Booth, Connie** — Actress
Lip Service Casting, 60-66 Wardour St, London W1F 0TA, England
**Booth, Douglas** — Actor
United Talent Agency, U T A Plaza, 9336 Civic Center Dr, Beverly Hills CA 90210 USA
**Booth, Emma** — Actress
Robyn Gardiner Mgmt, PO Box 128, Surry Hills NSW 2010, Australia
**Booth, George** — Cartoonist
PO Box 1539, Stony Brook NY 11790, USA
**Booth, Kellee** — Golfer
4804 Goldeneyes Lane, McKinney TX 75070, USA
**Booth, Kristin** — Actress
Edna Talent, 318 Dundas St W, Toronto ON M5T 1G5, Canada
**Booth, Lindy** — Actress
Innovative Artists, 1505 10th St, Santa Monica CA 90401 USA
**Booth, Melanie L** — Soccer Player
Canadian Soccer, Place Soccer Canada, 237 Metcalfe St, Ottawa ON K2P 1R2, Canada
**Booth, Michael** — Interior Designer
Babey Mountol Jue & Booth, 510 3rd St, #110, San Francisco CA 94107, USA
**Boothe, Kevin M** — Football Player
12100 NW 18th St, Plantation FL 33313, USA
**Boothe, Powers** — Actor
Brillstein Entertainment Partners, 9150 Wilshire Blvd, #350, Beverly Hills CA 90212 USA
**Booty, John F** — Football Player
16401 Governor Bridge Road, #407, Bowie MD 20716, USA
**Booty, Joshua G (Josh)** — Football, Baseball Player
6248 N Windermere Dr, Shreveport LA 71129, USA
**Boozer, Carlos A, Jr** — Basketball Player
4550 S 700 E, Salt Lake City UT 84107, USA
**Boozer, Emerson** — Football Player
25 Windham Dr, Huntington Station NY 11746, USA
**Borbon, Pedro F, Jr** — Baseball Player
60 Enoch Crosby Road, Brewster NY 10509, USA
**Borchardt, Dirk** — Actor
Agentur Hubchen, Pariser Str 20, 10707 Berlin, Germany
**Borcherds, Richard E** — Mathematician
University of California, Mathematics Dept, Berkeley CA 94720, USA
**Borcherdt, Brian** — Singer, Songwriter
Agency Group Ltd, 142 W 57th St, #600, New York NY 10019 USA
**Bordeleau, Jean-Pierre (J P)** — Ice Hockey Player
94 Lakemist Court, Dartmouth NS B3A 4Z1, Canada
**Bordelon, Kenneth P (Ken)** — Football Player
1224 Octavia St, New Orleans LA 70115, USA
**Borden, Amanda** — Gymnast
Cincinnati Gymnastics Academy, 3536 Woodridge Blvd, Fairfield OH 45014, USA
**Borden, Robert** — Producer, Writer
United Talent Agency, U T A Plaza, 9336 Civic Center Dr, Beverly Hills CA 90210 USA
**Border, Allan R** — Cricketer
Cricket Board, 90 Jolimont St, Jolimont VIC 3002, Australia
**Borders, Patrick L (Pat)** — Baseball Player
1135 S Lakeshore Blvd, Lake Wales FL 33853, USA
**Bordi, Richard A (Rich)** — Baseball Player
1133 Hailey Court, Rohnert Park CA 94928, USA
**Bordick, Michael T (Mike)** — Baseball Player
1302 Locust Ave, Towson MD 21204, USA
**Boreanaz, David** — Actor
Creative Artists Agency, 2000 Ave of Stars, #100, Los Angeles CA 90067 USA
**Boren, David L** — Educator; Governor, Senator, OK
University of Oklahoma, President's Office, 660 Parrington, Norman OK 73019, USA
**Borg, Andy** — Singer, Entertainer
Postfach 1010, 94134 Thyrnau, Germany
**Borg, Bjorn R** — Tennis Player
Tulegatan 11, 113 53 Stockholm, Sweden
**Borg, Marcus J** — Theologian
Oregon State University, School of Religion, Corvallis OR 97331, USA
**Borges, Desmin** — Actor
Suskin Mgmt, 2 Charlton St, #5K, New York NY 10014, USA
**Borges, Jacobo** — Artist
Museo Jacobo Borges, Catia, Caracas, Venezuela
**Borghi, Frank** — Soccer Player
4123 Poepping St, Saint Louis MO 63123, USA
**Borgman, James M (Jim)** — Editorial Cartoonist
Cincinnati Enquirer, Editorial Dept, 617 Vine St, #500, Cincinnati OH 45202, USA
**Boris, Robert (Bob)** — Director, Writer
Marshak/Zachary/Mills, 8840 Wilshire Blvd, #100, Beverly Hills CA 90211 USA
**Borisenko, Andrey I** — Cosmonaut Engineer
Cosmonaut Training Center, Star City, 141160 Zvezdny Gorodok, Moscow Oblast, Russia
**Boriso-Glebsky, Nikita** — Concert Violinist
I M G Artists, The Light Box, 111 Power Road, London W4 5PY , England
**Bork, Erik** — Producer, Writer
Creative Artists Agency, 2000 Ave of Stars, #100, Los Angeles CA 90067 USA
**Borkar, Nitin** — Computer Engineer
Intel Corp, 5200 NE Elam Young Parkway, Hillsboro OR 97124, USA
**Borkh, Inge** — Opera Singer
Florentinerstr 20, #2018, D 7000 Stuttgart 75, Germany
**Borkowski, Robert V (Bob)** — Baseball Player
1031 Gerhard St, Dayton OH 45404, USA
**Borland, Chris** — Football Player
San Francisco 49ers, 4949 Centennial Blvd, Santa Clara CA 95054 USA
**Borland, Polly** — Photographer
Michael Hoppen Contemporary 3 Jubilee Place, London SW3 3TD, England
**Borland, Toby S** — Baseball Player
8642 Quitman Highway, Quitman LA 71268, USA

**Borland, Wesley L (Wes)** — Guitarist (Limp Bizkit), Songwriter
Flip/Interscope Records, 8733 Sunset Blvd, #205, West Hollywood CA 90069, USA

**Borle, Christian** — Actor
Management 360, 9111 Wilshire Blvd, Beverly Hills CA 90210 USA

**Borley, Clarence A (Spike)** — WW II Navy Air Force Hero
4337 John Luhr Road NE, Olympia WA 98516, USA

**Borman, Frank F, II** — Astronaut, Businessman
PO Box 64, Bighorn MT 59010, USA

**Born, Ruth** — Baseball Player
3307 Pines Village Circle, #183, Valparaiso IN 46383, USA

**Bornedal, Ole** — Director, Writer
Principal Entertainment, 9255 Sunset Blvd, #500, Los Angeles CA 90069 USA

**Borodina, Olga V** — Opera Singer
Mariinsky Theater, Theater Square, 1 Pl Iskusstr, 190000 Saint Petersburg, Russia

**Borofsky, Jonathan (Jon)** — Artist
11301 W Olympic Blvd, #514, Los Angeles CA 90064, USA

**Boros, Guy D** — Golfer
2900 NE 40th St, Fort Lauderdale FL 33308, USA

**Boross, Csilla** — Opera Singer
I M G Artists, Hogarth Business Park, Chiswick, London W4 2TH, England

**Boross, Peter** — Prime Minister, Hungary
Kossouth Lajos Ter 1-3, 1055 Budapest, Hungary

**Borowiak, Tony** — Singer (All-4-One)
Universal Attractions, 135 W 26th St, #1200, New York NY 10001 USA

**Borowitz, Anthony (Andy)** — Writer
Creative Artists Agency, 2000 Ave of Stars, #100, Los Angeles CA 90067 USA

**Borrego, Jesse** — Actor
550 Cascade Dr, Mill Valley CA 94941, USA

**Borrell, Jonathan E (Johnny)** — Singer, Guitarist (Razorlight)
Agency Group Ltd, 361-373 City Road, London EC1V 1PQ, England

**Borroff, Marie E** — Writer
88 Notch Hill Road, #101, North Branford CT 6471, USA

**Borsato, Luciano** — Ice Hockey Player
200-4 Tortoise Crescent, Brampton ON L6P 0A1, Canada

**Borschevsky, Nikolai** — Ice Hockey Player
3 Geranium Court, Richmond Hill ON L4C 7M7, Canada

**Borstein, Alex** — Actress, Comedienne
W M E Entertainment, 1325 Ave of Americas, New York NY 10019 USA

**Borten, Craig** — Writer, Actor
United Talent Agency, U T A Plaza, 9336 Civic Center Dr, Beverly Hills CA 90210 USA

**Bortles, Blake** — Football Player
Jacksonville Jaguars, 1 AllTel Stadium Place, Jacksonville FL 32202 USA

**Bortz, Mark S** — Football Player
PO Box 3504, Quincy IL 62305, USA

**Boruch, Robert F** — Statistician
University of Pennsylvania, Wharton Business School, Philadelphia PA 19104, USA

**Boryla, Vincent J (Vince)** — Basketball Player, Executive
5577 S Emporia Circle, Greenwood Village CO 80111, USA

**Borzov, Valeri F** — Track Athlete
National Olympic Committee, Esplanadnaya 42, 252023 Kiev, Ukraine

**Bosch, Edith** — Judo Athlete
De Korte Sport Institute, Middenbaan Zuid 402, 3191 Hoogvliet AH, Netherlands

**Boschini, Victor J, Jr** — Educator
Texas Christian University, Chancellor's Office, 2800 S University Dr, Fort Worth TX 76129, USA

**Boschman, Laurie** — Ice Hockey Player
27 Delamere Dr, Stittsville ON K2S 1G7, Canada

**Bosco, Philip** — Actor
Don Buchwald Talent Agency, 10 E 44th St, New York NY 10017 USA

**Bose, Bimal K** — Electrical Engineer
215 Ski Mountain Road, Gatlinburg TN 37738, USA

**Bose, Eleanora** — Model
I M G Models, 304 Park Ave S, #PH N, New York NY 10010 USA

**Bose, Lucia** — Actress
Anne Alvares Correa, 34 Rue Jouffroy d'Abbans, 75017 Paris, France

**Boselli, D Anthony (Tony), Jr** — Football Player
12400 W Highway 71, #350-170, Bee Cave TX 78738, USA

**Boseman, Chadwick** — Actor
Greene Assoc, 1901 Ave of Stars, #130, Los Angeles CA 90067 USA

**Bosetti, Richard A (Rick)** — Baseball Player
1471 Arroyo Manor Dr, Redding CA 96003, USA

**Bosh, Christopher W (Chris)** — Basketball Player
20 W Kinzie St, #1000, Chicago IL 60654, USA

**Bosio, Christopher L (Chris)** — Baseball Player
417 Hidden Ridges Way, Combined Locks WI 54113, USA

**Boskie, Shawn K** — Baseball Player
10220 N 55th St, Paradise Valley AZ 85253, USA

**Boskin, Michael J** — Government Official, Economist
Stanford University, Hoover Institution, Stanford CA 94305, USA

**Bosley, Thaddis (Thad), Jr** — Baseball Player
19440 Amhurst Court, Cerritos CA 90703, USA

**Bosman, Richard A (Dick)** — Baseball Player
3511 Landmark Trail, Palm Harbor FL 34684, USA

**Bosnak, Karyn** — Writer
Harper Collins Publishers, 10 E 53rd St, Cellar 1, New York NY 10022 USA

**Boso, Casper N (Cap)** — Football Player
8811 Calumet Dr, Indianapolis IN 46236, USA

**Bossard, Andre** — Law Enforcement Official
228 Rue de la Convention, 75015 Paris, France

**Bosson, Barbara** — Actress, Producer, Writer
C E S D, 10635 Santa Monica Blvd, #130, Los Angeles CA 90025 USA

**Bossy, Michael (Mike)** — Ice Hockey Player
136 Place Ducharme, Rosemere QC J7A 4H8, Canada

**Bostelle, Tom** — Artist, Sculptor
Aeolian Palace Gallery, 267 Spring Run Lane, Downingtown PA 19335, USA

**Bostic, Jeffrey L (Jeff)** — Football Player
8250 Royal Saint Georges Lane, Duluth GA 30097, USA

**Bostic, Jenn** — Singer, Songwriter
M S T B, ReverbNation, 115 N Duke St, #2A, Durham NC 27701, USA

**Bostic, Joe E, Jr** — Football Player
3507 Bromley Wood Lane, Greensboro NC 27410, USA

**Bostick, Devon** — Actor
Noble Caplan Abrams, 1260 Yonge St, #200, Toronto ON M4T 1W6, Canada

**Bostock, Roy J** — Businessman
Yahoo Inc, 701 1st Ave, Sunnyvale CA 94089, USA

**Boston, Daryl L** — Baseball Player
1016 Valley Lane, Cincinnati OH 45229, USA

**Boston, David** — Football Player
18502 Skippers Helm, Humble TX 77346, USA

**Boston, Rachel** — Actress
Core Public Relations Group, 4401 Wilshire Blvd, #400, Los Angeles CA 90010 USA

**Boston, Ralph H** — Track Athlete
3301 Woodbine Ave, Knoxville TN 37914, USA

**Bostridge, Ian** — Opera Singer
Opus 3 Artists, 470 Park Ave S, #900N, New York NY 10016 USA

**Bostwick, Barry** — Actor
Vanguard Management Group, 8060 Melrose Ave, #400, Los Angeles CA 90046, USA

**Boswell, Barbie** — Model
2046 Nellie St, Largo FL 33774, USA

**Boswell, Bobby** — Soccer Player
Houston Dynamo, 1415 Louisiana, #3400, Houston TX 77002 USA

**Boswell, Kenneth G (Ken)** — Baseball Player
1103 Live Oak Dr, Marble Falls TX 78654, USA

**Boswell, Thomas M** — Sportswriter
Washington Post, Sports Dept, 1150 15th St NW, Washington DC 20071, USA

**Boswell, Tommy G (Tom)** — Basketball Player
341 N Anton Dr, Montgomery AL 36105, USA

**Bosworth, Brian** — Football Player, Actor
4400 Arlen Court, Plano TX 75093, USA

**Bosworth, Kate** — Actress, Model
Creative Artists Agency, 2000 Ave of Stars, #100, Los Angeles CA 90067 USA

**Bosworth, Lauren O (Lo)** — Actress
Octogon Entertainment, 8687 Melrose Ave, #700, Los Angeles CA 90069, USA

**Bosworth, Libby** — Singer, Songwriter
3011 Fort Worth Trail, Austin TX 78748, USA

**Boteach, Shmuley** — Religious Leader, Rabbi, Writer
Shalom in the Home, 7700 Wisconsin Ave, Bethesda MD 20814, USA

**Botehho, Joao** — Director
Assicuacai de Realizadores, Rua de Palmeira 7, R/C, 1200 Lisbon, Portugal

**Botelho, Luciano** — Opera Singer
I M G Artists, Hogarth Business Park, Chiswick, London W4 2TH, England

**Botero, Fernando** — Artist
Nohra Haime Gallery, 41 E 57th St, #600, New York NY 10022, USA

**Both, Bjorn** — Singer, Guitarist (Santiano)
AirForce1.TV Music, Alte Schonhauser Str 44, 10119 Berlin, Germany

**Botha, Francois (Frans)** — Boxer
White Buffalo, PO Box 3982, Clearwater FL 33767, USA

**Botha, Roelof F** — Government Official, South Africa
PO Box 16176, Pretoria North 0116, South Africa

**Botham, Ian T** — Cricketer, Sportscaster
Mission Logistics, 158 Hurlington Road, Fulham, London SE6 3NGF, England

**Bothmer, Bernard V** — Museum Official, Egyptologist
Brooklyn Museum, 188 Eastern Parkway, Brooklyn NY 11238, USA

**Bothwell, Tim** — Ice Hockey Player, Coach
14 Billings Court, Burlington VT 05408, USA

**Botone, Talia** — Actress
C E S D, 10635 Santa Monica Blvd, #130, Los Angeles CA 90025 USA

**Botsford, Beth** — Swimmer
2210 River Bend Court, White Hall MD 21161, USA

**Botsford, Sara** — Actress
Kordek Agency, 8490 W Sunset Blvd, #403, West Hollywood CA 90069, USA

**Botstein, Leon** — Conductor
Columbia Artists Mgmt Inc, 5 Columbus Circle, 1790 Broadway, #1600, New York NY 10019 USA

**Botstein, Leon** — Educator
Bard College, President's Office, Annandale on Hudson NY 12504, USA

**Botta, Mario** — Architect
Via Ciani 16, 6904 Lugano, Switzerland

**Bottalico, Richard P (Ricky)** — Baseball Player
10 Rocamora Road, Rocky Hill CT 06067, USA

**Bottenfield, Kent D** — Baseball Player
12168 142nd Court N, West Palm Beach FL 33418, USA

**Botterill, Jason** — Ice Hockey Player
Pittsburgh Penguins, Consol Energy Center, 1001 5th Ave, Pittsburgh PA 15219 USA

**Botti, Chris** — Trumpeter
Colomby Group, 2110 Main St, #302, Santa Monica CA 90405, USA

**Bottin, Rob** — Director
Gersh Agency, 9465 Wilshire Blvd, #600, Beverly Hills CA 90212 USA

**Botto, Juan Diego** — Actor
Torres & Prieto, Calle Princesa 3, 28008 Madrid, Spain

**Bottom, Joe** — Swimmer
374 Spanish Garden Dr, Chico CA 95928, USA

**Bottoms, Joseph** — Actor
Bottoms Art Galleries, 1260 Channel Dr, Santa Barbara CA 93108, USA

**Bottoms, Timothy** — Actor
PO Box 15559, San Luis Obispo CA 93406, USA

**Bottum, Roddy** — Keyboardist (Faith No More)
Creative Artists Agency, 2000 Ave of Stars, #100, Los Angeles CA 90067 USA

**Bouasone Bouphavanh** — Prime Minister, Laos
Premier's Office, National Assembly, Vientiane Capital, Vientiane, Laos

**Boublil, Alain A** — Lyricist
Cameron Mackintosh Ltd, 1 Bedford Square, London WC1B 3RA, England

**Boucha, Henry C** — Ice Hockey Player
7200 Biglerville Circle, Anchorage AK 99507, USA

| | |
|---|---|
| **Bouchard, Daniel (Dan)**<br>3111 Hillsdale Court SE, Marietta GA 30067, USA | Ice Hockey Player |
| **Bouchard, Lucien**<br>Parti Quebecois, 1200 Ave Papineau, Montreal QC H2K 4R5, Canada | Government Official, Canada |
| **Bouchard, Pierre**<br>1216-1705 Ave Victoria, Saint-Lambert QC, J4R 2T7, Canada | Ice Hockey Player |
| **Bouchard, Ron**<br>300 Lunenburg St, Fitchburg MA 01420, USA | Auto Racing Driver |
| **Bouchareb, Rachid**<br>Casorotto Ramsay, Waverley House, 7-12 Noel St, London W1F 8GQ, England | Director, Writer |
| **Bouchaud, Jean**<br>Artmedia, 20 Ave Rapp, 75007 Paris, France | Actor |
| **Boucher, Brian**<br>416 Overhill Road, Haddonfield NJ 08033, USA | Ice Hockey Player |
| **Boucher, Candice**<br>Outlaws Models, 11 Wessels Road, Greenpoint 8011 Capetown, South Africa | Model |
| **Boucher, Gaetan**<br>Center Sportif, 3850 Edgar, Saint Hubert QC J4T 368, Canada | Speed Skater |
| **Boucher, Lawrence**<br>Adaptec Inc, 691 S Milpitas Blvd, Milpitas CA 95035, USA | Businessman |
| **Boucher, Philippe**<br>Dallas Stars, 2601 Ave of Stars, #100, Frisco TX 75034 USA | Ice Hockey Player |
| **Bouchez, Elodie**<br>Evolution Entertainment, 901 N Highland Ave, Los Angeles CA 90038 USA | Actress |
| **Bouchitey, Patrick**<br>Voyez Mon Agent, 20 Ave Rapp, 75007 Paris, France | Actor |
| **Boudart, Michel**<br>9636 El Venado Dr, Whittier CA 90603, USA | Chemical Engineer |
| **Boudia, David A**<br>617 Dorchester Dr, Noblesville IN 46062, USA | Diver |
| **Boudin, Michael**<br>US Court of Appeals, 1 Courthouse Way, Boston MA 02210, USA | Judge |
| **Boudreau, Bruce**<br>PO Box 27280, Anaheim CA 92809, USA | Ice Hockey Player, Coach |
| **Boudrias, Andre**<br>1008-4300 Place des Cageux, Laval QC H7W 4Z3, Canada | Ice Hockey Player |
| **Boudrias, Christine-Isabel**<br>Speed Skating Canada, 2781 Lancaster Road, #402, Ottawa ON K1B 1A7, Canada | Speed Skater |
| **Boughner, Robert (Bob)**<br>5541 La Puerta del Sol Blvd S, #414, Saint Petersburg FL 33715, USA | Ice Hockey Player |
| **Bouillon, Jean-Christophe**<br>Wildbacher 9, 8340 Hinwil, Switzerland | Auto Racing Driver |
| **Bouix, Evelyne**<br>Artmedia, 20 Ave Rapp, 75007 Paris, France | Actress |
| **Boujenah, Michel**<br>Voyez Mon Agent, 20 Ave Rapp, 75007 Paris, France | Actor |
| **Boulanger, Veronique**<br>Artmedia, 20 Ave Rapp, 75007 Paris, France | Actress |
| **Boulerice, Jesse**<br>152 McClellan Ave, West Berlin NJ 08091, USA | Ice Hockey Player |
| **Boulez, Pierre**<br>Postfach 100022, 76481 Baden-Baden, Germany | Conductor, Composer |
| **Boulmetis, Samuel A (Sam), Sr**<br>711 Academy Road, Cantonsville MD 21228, USA | Thoroughbred Racing Jockey |
| **Boulos, Frenchy**<br>20 Elvin St, Staten Island NY 10314, USA | Soccer Player |
| **Boulton, Eric**<br>41 Cove Road, Huntington NY 11743, USA | Ice Hockey Player |
| **Boulud, Daniel**<br>Daniel Restaurant, 60 E 65th St, New York NY 10065, USA | Chef |
| **Boulud, David**<br>Daniel Restaurant, 60 E 65th St, New York NY 10065, USA | Chef |
| **Boulware, Peter**<br>3791 E Millers Bridge Road, Tallahassee FL 32312, USA | Football Player |
| **Bouman, Todd**<br>2080 140th Ave, Holland MN 56139, USA | Football Player |
| **Bouquet, Carole**<br>Agence Artiste Adequat, 108 Rue Reaumur, 75002 Paris, France | Actress, Model |
| **Bourboulon, Jacques**<br>24 Rue Rennequin, 75017 Paris, France | Photographer |
| **Bource, Ludovic**<br>First Artists, 4764 Park Granada, #210, Calabasas CA 91302 USA | Composer |
| **Bourdain, Anthony**<br>Inkwell Management, 521 Fifth Ave, New York NY 10175, USA | Restauranteur, Chef, Writer |
| **Bourdais, Sebastian**<br>K V S H Racing, 4001 Methanol Lane, Indianapolis IN 46268, USA | Auto Racing Driver |
| **Bourdeaux, Brandy**<br>Coralie Junior Agency, 907 S Victory Blvd, Burbank CA 91502, USA | Actress |
| **Bourdeaux, Michael**<br>Keston College, Heathfield Road, Keston, Kent BR2 6BA, England | Templeton Religion Laureate |
| **Bourdette, Christine**<br>Elizabeth Leach Gallery, 417 NW 9th Ave, Portland OR 97209, USA | Sculptor, Artist |
| **Bourdon, Rob**<br>Artist Group International, 150 E 58th St, #1900, New York NY 10155, USA | Drummer (Linkin Park) |
| **Bourgeois, Benjamin C (Ben)**<br>Pro Surfing Mgmt, 320 High Tide Dr, #101, Saint Augustine FL 32080 USA | Surfer |
| **Bourgeois, Charles (Charlie)** | Ice Hockey Player |
| **Bourgeois, Derek D**<br>PO Box 1481, Station Main, Moncton NB E1C 8T6, Canada | Composer |
| **Bourgoin, Louise**<br>Portland House, Burton Road, Wool, Dorset BH20 6EY, England | Actress |
| **Bourn, Michael R**<br>W M E Entertainment, 9601 Wilshire Blvd, #300, Beverly Hills CA 90210 USA | Baseball Player |
| **Bourne, Bob**<br>24604 Belvon Valley Lane, Mulberry FL 33860, USA<br>Bob Bourne Realty, 1-1890 Cooper Road, Kelowna BC V1Y 8B7, Canada | Ice Hockey Player |

**Bourne, Henry R** — Pharmacologist
University of California Medical Center, Pharmacology Dept, 505 Parnassus, San Francisco CA 94122, USA
**Bourne, Shae-Lynn** — Figure Skater
Connecticut Skating Center, 300 Alumni Road, Newington CT 06111, USA
**Bournigal, Rafael A** — Baseball Player
230 Canterwood Lane, Mulberry FL 33860, USA
**Bournissen, Chantal** — Alpine Skier
1983 Evolene, Switzerland
**Bourque, Phil** — Ice Hockey Player
5117 Yale Dr, Aliquippa PA 15001, USA
**Bourque, Pierre** — Horticulturist; Mayor, Montreal
Hotel de Ville, 275 Rue Notre Dame E, Montreal QC H2Y 1C6, Canada
**Bourque, Raymond J (Ray)** — Ice Hockey Player
Tresca Restaurant, 233 Hanover St, Boston MA 02113, USA
**Bourque, Rene G W** — Ice Hockey Player
9110 93rd Ave, Lac La Biche AB T0A 2C0, Canada
**Bourret, Caprice** — Model, Actress
PO Box 509, Walton-on-Thames KT12 5XJ, England
**Boushka, Richard J (Dick)** — Basketball Player
7119 Eldorado Centre Lane, Houston TX 77069, USA
**Bousman, Darren Lynn** — Director
Verve Talent, 9696 Culver Blvd, #301, Culver City CA 90232, USA
**Bouteflika, Abdul Aziz** — President, Algeria
138 Chemin Bachir Brahimi, El Biar, Algiers, Algeria
**Boutette, Pat** — Ice Hockey Player
Doctors House Restaurant, 21 Nashville Road, Kleinburg ON L0J 1C0, Canada
**Boutilier, Paul** — Ice Hockey Player
35 Elgin Lane, Bedford NS B4A 2K2, Canada
**Bouton, Daniel** — Financier
Societe Generale, 29 Blvd Hausman, 75009 Paris, France
**Bouton, James A (Jim)** — Baseball Player, Writer
PO Box 188, North Edgemont MA 01252, USA
**Boutros-Ghali, Boutros** — Secretary-General, United Nations
2 Ave El Nil, Giza, 11221 Cairo, Egypt
**Bouvet, Didier** — Alpine Skier
Bouvet-Sports, 74360 Abondance, France
**Bouvia, Gloria** — Bowler
2072 NE Hogan Dr, Gresham OR 97030, USA
**Bouvier, Jean-Pierre** — Actor
Artmedia, 20 Ave Rapp, 75007 Paris, France
**Bouw, Carline** — Rowing Athlete
A A S R Skoll, Jan Vroegopsingel 6, 1096 Amsterdam CN, Netherlands
**Bouwmeester, Jay** — Ice Hockey Player
28 Greenoch Crescent NW, Edmonton AB T6L 1B4, Canada
**Bouwmeester, Marit** — Yachtswoman
Bouwmeester Sailing, De Greiden 14, 9003 Wartena MJ, Netherlands
**Bouza, Matthew K (Matt)** — Football Player
1042 Via Nueva, Lafayette CA 94549, USA
**Bova, Raoul** — Actor
Cristiano Cucchini Mgmt, Lungoterre dei Mellini 10, 00193 Rome, Italy
**Bovolenta, Arnaud** — Freestyle Skier
Federation de Ski, 50 Rue des Marquisats, BP 453, 74011 Annecy Cedex, France
**Bowa, Lawrence R (Larry)** — Baseball Player, Manager
129 Upper Gulph Road, Radnor PA 19087, USA
**Bowden, Craig D** — Golfer
1101 E Benson Court, Bloomington IN 47401, USA
**Bowden, James G, IV** — Baseball Executive
2333 Indian River Blvd, #501, Vero Beach FL 32960, USA
**Bowden, Katrina** — Actress
Management 360, 9111 Wilshire Blvd, Beverly Hills CA 90210 USA
**Bowden, Mark** — Writer
934 Saginaw Road, Oxford PA 19363, USA
**Bowden, Robert (Bobby)** — Football Coach
2813 Shamrock St N, Tallahassee FL 32309, USA
**Bowden, Terry** — Football Coach, Sportscaster
University of North Alabama, Athletic Dept, Florence AL 35632, USA
**Bowditch, Steven (Steve)** — Golfer
Professional Golfers Association, 100 Ave of Champions, Palm Beach Gardens FL 33418 USA
**Bowe, David** — Actor
Karg/Weissenbach, 329 N Wetherly Dr, #101, Beverly Hills CA 90211 USA
**Bowe, Dwayne L** — Football Player
4509 N Hickory Lane, Kansas City MO 64116, USA
**Bowe, Riddick L** — Boxer
714 Ahmer Dr, Fort Washington MD 20744, USA
**Bowe, Rosemarie** — Actress
321 Saint Pierre Road, Los Angeles CA 90077, USA
**Bowen, Andrea** — Actress
Domain Talent, 9229 W Sunset Blvd, #710, West Hollywood CA 90069 USA
**Bowen, Andrew** — Actor
Principato-Young, 9465 Wilshire Blvd, #880, Beverly Hills CA 90212 USA
**Bowen, Anne** — Fashion Designer
589 8th Ave, #200, New York NY 10018, USA
**Bowen, Bruce** — Basketball Player
1810 Settler Court, San Antonio TX 78258, USA
**Bowen, Cameron** — Actor
Stone Manners Salners, 6100 Wilshire Blvd, #1500, Los Angeles CA 90035 USA
**Bowen, Jason** — Ice Hockey Player
4900 W 14th Ave, Kennewick WA 99338, USA
**Bowen, Julie** — Actress, Model
Liberman/Zerman Mgmt, 252 N Larchmont Blvd, #200, Los Angeles CA 90004, USA
**Bowen, Michael** — Actor
Martin Berneman Mgmt, 5820 Wilshire Blvd, #200, Los Angeles CA 90036 USA
**Bowen, Nanci** — Golfer
201 Carolina Point Parkway, #1119, Greenville SC 29607, USA
**Bowen, Robert M (Rob)** — Baseball Player
56 Spring Dr, Ellijay GA 30536, USA

**Bowen, Ryan E** — Baseball Player
2806 Maryland Ave, Fort Worth TX 76162, USA
**Bowen, Stephen G** — Astronaut
N A S A, Johnson Space Center, 2101 NASA Road, Houston TX 77058 USA
**Bowen, Wade** — Singer
W M E Entertainment, 1600 Division St, #300, Nashville TN 37203 USA
**Bowen, William G** — Foundation Executive, Educator
Andrew Mellon Foundation, 140 E 62nd St, New York NY 10065, USA
**Bowens, David W** — Football Player
15140 SW 16th St, Weston FL 33326, USA
**Bowens, Malick** — Actor
Don Buchwald Talent Agency, 6500 Wilshire Blvd, #2200, Los Angeles CA 90048 USA
**Bowens, Timothy L (Tim)** — Football Player
PO Box 93, Okolona MS 38860, USA
**Bower, Antoinette** — Actress
1529 N Beverly Glen Blvd, Los Angeles CA 90077, USA
**Bower, Gary E** — Bowler
256 Green Lane Dr, Camp Hill PA 17011, USA
**Bower, Gordon H** — Psychologist
Stanford University, Psychology Dept, Stanford CA 94305, USA
**Bower, Jamie Campbell** — Actor
Dalzell & Beresford, 55 Charterhouse St, Paddock Suite, London EC1M 6HA, England
**Bower, Jeff** — Basketball Coach
New Orleans Pelicans, 1250 Poydras St, #101, New Orleans LA 70113 USA
**Bower, John W (Johnny)** — Ice Hockey Player
Bower Enterprises, 3937 Parkgate Dr, Mississauga ON L5N 7B4, Canada
**Bower, Robert W** — Inventor (Semiconductor Insulated Gate)
University of California, Microelectronics Dept, Davis CA 95616, USA
**Bower, Tom** — Actor
United Talent Agency, U T A Plaza, 9336 Civic Center Dr, Beverly Hills CA 90210 USA
**Bowering, Jodie** — Softball Player
Boondall, Redcliffe QLD 4020, Australia
**Bowers, Bryan** — Singer, Autoharp Player
Scott O'Malley Assoc, PO Box 9188, Colorado Springs CO 80932, USA
**Bowers, Chris** — Actor
Gersh Agency, 9465 Wilshire Blvd, #600, Beverly Hills CA 90212 USA
**Bowers, Dane** — Singer, Songwriter
79 Byrbe Blood, Mill House, Millers Way, London W6 7NH, England
**Bowers, David** — Director
Independent Talent Group, 40 Whitfield St, London W1T 2RH, England
**Bowers, Glenn** — WW II Marine Air Corps Hero
225 Mountain Road, Dillsburg PA 17019, USA
**Bowers, Mary Helen** — Ballerina
Rubenstein Public Relations, 1345 Ave of Americas, #30, New York NY 10105, USA
**Bowers-Broadbent, Christopher J** — Concert Organist, Composer
94 Colney Hatch, Muswell Hill, London N10 1EA, England
**Bowersox, Bob** — Actor
Reinhard Agency, 2021 Arch St, #400, Philadelphia PA 19103, USA
**Bowersox, Crystal L** — Singer, Songwriter
866 Lotus Dr, Erie MI 48133, USA
**Bowersox, Kenneth D** — Astronaut
16907 Soaring Forest Dr, Houston TX 77059, USA
**Bowes, Bill** — Financier
US Venture Partners, 2735 San Hill Road, Menlo Park CA 94025, USA
**Bowie, David** — Singer, Actor
Maine Road Mgmt, 195 Chrystie St, #901F, New York NY 10001, USA
**Bowie, Heather** — Golfer
3017 Elm River Dr, Fort Worth TX 76116, USA
**Bowie, Larry G** — Football Player
739 Echo Shores Court, Saint Paul MN 55115, USA
**Bowie, Micah A** — Baseball Player
2039 Small Town Dr, New Braunfels TX 78130, USA
**Bowie, Samuel P (Sam)** — Basketball Player
901 The Curtilage, Lexington KY 40502, USA
**Bowker, Judi** — Actress
Howes & Prior, 66 Berkeley House, Hay Hill, London W1X 7LH, England
**Bowlby, April** — Model, Actress
L I N K Entertainment, 11872 La Grange Ave, Los Angeles CA 90025 USA
**Bowler, Grant** — Actor
Don Buchwald Talent Agency, 6500 Wilshire Blvd, #2200, Los Angeles CA 90048 USA
**Bowles, Erskine B** — Government Official
Forstman Little Co, 767 5th Ave, #4500, New York NY 10153, USA
**Bowles, Lauren** — Actress
Main Title Entertainment, 8383 Wilshire Blvd, #408, Beverly Hills CA 90211, USA
**Bowlin, Michael R** — Businessman
Atlantic Richfield Co, 333 S Hope St, Los Angeles CA 90071, USA
**Bowling, Orbie L** — Basketball Player
10179 Frank Road, Collierville TN 38017, USA
**Bowman, Elizabeth** — Golfer
82 Davidson St, Chula Vista CA 91910, USA
**Bowman, Eric** — Artist
Brian Markel Fine Art, 2236 NE Broadway, Portland OR 97232, USA
**Bowman, Harry W** — Businessman
Outboard Marine, 1325 Remington Road, #H, Schaumburg IL 60173, USA
**Bowman, James E (Jim)** — Football Player
12 Stony Field Road, Norton MA 02766, USA
**Bowman, Joshua** — Actor
Sutton-Barth Vennari, 5900 Wilshire Blvd, #700, Los Angeles CA 90036 USA
**Bowman, Kenneth B (Ken)** — Football Player
13664 N Placita Montansas de Oro, Tucson AZ 85755, USA
**Bowman, Kirk** — Ice Hockey Player
740 Pointe Pelee Dr, RR 1, Leamington ON N8H 3V4, Canada
**Bowman, Maddie** — Freestyle Skier
US Ski & Snowboarding Assn, 1 Victory Lane, Box 100, Park City UT 84060, USA
**Bowman, Pasco M, II** — Judge
US Court of Appeals, US Courthouse, 811 Grand Ave, Kansas City MO 64106, USA

**Bowman, Rob**
W M E Entertainment, 9601 Wilshire Blvd, #300, Beverly Hills CA 90210 USA — Director, Producer
**Bowman, W Scott (Scotty)** — Ice Hockey Coach, Executive
56 Halston Parkway, East Amherst NY 14051, USA
**Bown, Jane H** — Photographer
Old Mill House, 50 Broad St, Alresford, Hants SO24 9AN, England
**Bown, R Charles (Chuck), Jr** — Auto Racing Driver
Stock Car Racing Career Development, 5082 Old NC Highway 49, Asheboro NC 27203, USA
**Bowness, Richard G (Rick)** — Ice Hockey Player, Coach
10 Shadowstone Lane, Lawrence Township NJ 08648, USA
**Bowsfield, Edward O (Ted)** — Baseball Player
980 Briar Rose Lane, Nipomo CA 93444, USA
**Bowyer, C Stuart** — Astronaut, Astronomer
34 Seascape Dr, Muir Beach CA 94965, USA
**Bowyer, Clint** — Auto, Truck Racing Driver
Clint Bowyer Enterprises, 6221 Ramada Dr, Clemmons NC 27012, USA
**Bowyer, William** — Artist
12 Cleveland Ave, Chiswick, London W4 1SN, England
**Box, C J** — Writer
Penguin Books, 375 Hudson St, Basement 1, New York NY 10014 USA
**Boxberger, Loa** — Bowler
PO Box 708, Russell KS 67665, USA
**Boxx, Gillian** — Softball Player
15111 Chelsea Dr, San Jose CA 95124, USA
**Boxx, Shannon** — Soccer Player
2321 SW Montgomery Dr, Portland OR 97201, USA
**Boyadjiev, Latchezar** — Sculptor
48 Mark Dr, San Rafael CA 94903, USA
**Boyarsky, Gerald M J (Jerry)** — Football Player
229 Boyarsky Road, Scott Township PA 18447, USA
**Boyarsky, Konstantin** — Concert Violinist, Composer
Grant Rogers Mgmt, 8 Wren Crescent, Bushey Heath, Hertfordshire WD23 1AN, England
**Boyce of Pimlico, Baron Michael C** — Navy Admiral, England
House of Lords, Westminster, London SW1A 0PW, England
**Boyce, Kim** — Singer
200 Nathan Dr, Hollister MO 65672, USA
**Boyd, Alan S** — Secretary, Transportation
116 Fairview Ave N, #735, Seattle WA 98109, USA
**Boyd, Brandon C** — Singer, Percussionist (Incubus)
Creative Artists Agency, 2000 Ave of Stars, #100, Los Angeles CA 90067 USA
**Boyd, Brent V** — Football Player
948 N Coast Highway 101, #185, Encinitas CA 92024, USA
**Boyd, Cayden** — Actor
Gersh Agency, 9465 Wilshire Blvd, #600, Beverly Hills CA 90212 USA
**Boyd, Darren** — Actor
Independent Talent Group, 40 Whitfield St, London W1T 2RH, England
**Boyd, David** — Cinematographer
Montana Artists Agency, 625 Montana Ave, Santa Monica CA 90403 USA
**Boyd, Dennis R (Oil Can)** — Baseball Player
45 Swan St, East Providence RI 02914, USA
**Boyd, Douglas** — Conductor
Ingpen & Williams, 131 Putney Bridge Road, London SW15 2PA, England
**Boyd, Fred L** — Basketball Player
10915 Open Trail Road, Bakersfield CA 93311, USA
**Boyd, Guy** — Actor
Stone Manners Salners, 6100 Wilshire Blvd, #1500, Los Angeles CA 90035 USA
**Boyd, Jenna** — Actress
Gersh Agency, 9465 Wilshire Blvd, #600, Beverly Hills CA 90212 USA
**Boyd, John** — Actor
Dontanville/Frattaroli, 315 S Beverly Dr, #201, Beverly Hills CA 90212, USA
**Boyd, Liona M C** — Concert Guitarist
B C Fiedler Mgmt, 53 Seton Park Road, Montreal ON M3C 3Z8, Canada
**Boyd, Lynda** — Actress
Greene Assoc, 1901 Ave of Stars, #130, Los Angeles CA 90067 USA
**Boyd, Malcolm** — Writer, Religious Leader
Saint Augustine by Sea Episcopal Church, 1227 4th St, Santa Monica CA 90401, USA
**Boyd, Randy** — Ice Hockey Player
1769 Blackwillow Dr, Marietta GA 30066, USA
**Boyd, Robert** — Golfer
828 Robert E Lee Dr, Wilmington NC 28412, USA
**Boyd, Robert D (Bobby)** — Football Player
2105 Lansdown Dr, Garland TX 75040, USA
**Boyd, Russell S** — Cinematographer
52 Sutherland St, Cremorne NSW 2090, Australia
**Boyd, Stephen G** — Football Player
1268 Marginal Road, Atlantic Beach NY 11509, USA
**Boyd, Tanya** — Actress
Vincent Cirrincione Assoc, 1516 N Fairfax Ave, Los Angeles CA 90046 USA
**Boyd, Willard L** — Educator, Museum Executive
3800 N Lake Shore Dr, #3A, Chicago IL 60613, USA
**Boyd, William A M** — Writer
The Agency, 24 Pottery Lane, Holland Park, London W11 4LZ, England
**Boyden, Frank D** — Artist
1914 N Three Rocks Road, Otis OR 97368, USA
**Boyega, John** — Actor
Identity Agency Group, 11-15 Betterton St, Covent Garden, London WC2H 9BP, England
**Boyens, Philippa** — Producer
I C M Partners, 10250 Constellation Blvd, #900, Los Angeles CA 90067 USA
**Boyer, Blaine T** — Baseball Player
133 Johnson Ferry Road, #108, Marietta GA 30068, USA
**Boyer, Brant T** — Football Player
1683 Old Lake Lane, Kaysville UT 84037, USA
**Boyer, Cloyd** — Baseball Player
14528 County Road 210, Jasper MO 64755, USA
**Boyer, Herbert W** — Biochemist, Inventor
PO Box 7318, Rancho Santa Fe CA 92067, USA

**Boyer, Mark** — Football Player
21942 Kaneohe Lane, Huntington Beach CA 92646, USA
**Boyer, Paul D** — Nobel Chemistry Laureate
1033 Somera Road, Los Angeles CA 90077, USA
**Boyer, Wally** — Ice Hockey Player
400 Manly St, Midland ON L4R 3E3, Canada
**Boyes, Brad** — Ice Hockey Player
11711 Fawnridge Dr, Saint Louis MO 63131, USA
**Boyette, Garland D** — Football Player
4003 E Valley Dr, Missouri City TX 77459, USA
**Boykins, Earl A** — Basketball Player
7572 Sanctuary Circle, Brecksville OH 44141, USA
**Boyko, Darren** — Ice Hockey Player
1341 Wolseley Ave, Winnipeg MB R3G 1H8, Canada
**Boylan, Eileen April** — Actress
S M S Talent, 8383 Wilshire Blvd, #230, Beverly Hills CA 90211 USA
**Boylan, Jeanne M** — Forensics Artist
W M E Entertainment, 9601 Wilshire Blvd, #300, Beverly Hills CA 90210 USA
**Boylan, Jennifer Finney** — Writer
Colby College, English Dept, 4000 Mayflower Hill, Waterville ME 04901, USA
**Boylan, John** — Actor
Noble Caplan Abrams, 1260 Younge St, #200, Toronto ON M4T 1WG, Canada
**Boylan, Orla** — Opera Singer
Harrison/Parrott, 5-6 Albion Court, London W6 0QT, England
**Boyle, Barbara D** — Businesswoman
Boyle-Taylor Productions, 5200 Lankershim Blvd, #700, North Hollywood CA 91601, USA
**Boyle, Consolata** — Costume Designer
Independent Talent Group, 40 Whitfield St, London W1T 2RH, England
**Boyle, Daniel (Dan)** — Ice Hockey Player
18232 Daves Ave, Monte Sereno CA 95030, USA
**Boyle, Danny** — Director
Independent Talent Group, 40 Whitfield St, London W1T 2RH, England
**Boyle, Jerry** — Sculptor
Jerry Boyle Studio, 926 3rd Ave, Longmont CO 80501, USA
**Boyle, Lara Flynn** — Actress
Kazarian/Measures/Ruskin, 11969 Ventura Blvd, #300, Studio City CA 91604 USA
**Boyle, Lisa D** — Model, Actress
7336 Santa Monica Blvd, #776, West Hollywood CA 90046, USA
**Boyle, Susan** — Singer
Andy Stephens Mgmt, 60A Highgate Hight St, London N6 5HX, England
**Boyle, T Coraghessan** — Writer
Creative Artists Agency, 2000 Ave of Stars, #100, Los Angeles CA 90067 USA
**Boylen, Jim** — Basketball Coach
University of Utah, Athletic Dept, Salt Lake City UT 84112, USA
**Boyne, Walter** — Museum Executive, Writer
10833 Margate Road, Silver Spring MD 20901, USA
**Boynes, Winford G** — Basketball Player
8979 Haflinger Way, Elk Grove CA 95757, USA
**Boynton, Nicholas (Nick)** — Ice Hockey Player
3326 N Valencia Lane, Phoenix AZ 85018, USA
**Boynton, Robert M** — Psychologist
6632 Grulla St, Carlsbad CA 92009, USA
**Boynton, Sandra** — Graphic Artist
Recycled Paper Products, 111 N Canal St, #700, Chicago IL 60606, USA
**Boysen, Sarah** — Psychologist
Ohio State University, Psychology Dept, Columbus OH 43210, USA
**Boyum, Steve** — Director, Producer
Creative Artists Agency, 2000 Ave of Stars, #100, Los Angeles CA 90067 USA
**Bozanic, Josip Cardinal** — Religious Leader
Archdiocese of Zagreb, Kaptol 31, PP 553, 10001 Zagreb Hrvatska, Croatia
**Bozek, Megan** — Ice Hockey Player
1936 Beverly Lane, Buffalo Grove IL 60089, USA
**Bozek, Steve** — Ice Hockey Player
8410 E Whispering Wind Dr, Scottsdale AZ 85255, USA
**Bozeman, Todd** — Basketball Coach
Morgan State University, Athletic Dept, Baltimore MD 21251, USA
**Bozzio, Dale** — Singer, Model
11935 Laurel Hills, Studio City CA 91604, USA
**Bozzo, Laura C** — Entertainer
Televisa, Blvd A Lopez Mateos 232, Colonia San Angel, Mexico City DF 01060 CP, Mexico
**Braase, Ordell** — Football Player
204 3rd St W, #201, Bradenton FL 34205, USA
**Braaten, Josh** — Actor
A P A Talent/Literary Agency, 250 W 57th St, #1701, New York NY 10107 USA
**Brabants, Tim** — Canoeing Athlete
Nottingham Canoe Club, Trentside North, Nottingham NG2 5FA, England
**Brabham, Geoff** — Auto Racing Driver
B M W Group Australia, 783 Springvale Road, Mulgrave VIC 3170, Australia
**Brabo, Manu** — Photojournalist
Associated Press, Editorial Dept, 450 W 33rd St, #1500, New York NY 10001 USA
**Bracco, Lorraine** — Actress
Innovative Artists, 1505 10th St, Santa Monica CA 90401 USA
**Bracegirdle, Nick (Chicane)** — Musician
W M E Entertainment, Centrepoint Tower, 103 New Oxford St, London WC1A 1DD, England
**Bracelin, Gregory L (Greg)** — Football Player
5465 Calumet Ave, La Jolla CA 92037, USA
**Bracey, Luke** — Actor
Creative Artists Agency, 2000 Ave of Stars, #100, Los Angeles CA 90067 USA
**Bracey, Stephen H (Steve)** — Basketball Player
560 Lincoln Ave, Brooklyn NY 11208, USA
**Bracher, Karl D** — Political Scientist, Historian
Universitat Bonn, Stationsweg 17, 53127 Bonn, Germany
**Bracht, Stephanie** — Golfer
2004 Delancey Dr, Norman OK 73071, USA
**Brack, Kenny** — Auto Racing Driver
Allen Farst Mgmt, PO Box 90383, Dayton OH 45490, USA

| | |
|---|---|
| **Brackenbury, Curt**<br>W378N5861 Valley Road, Oconomowoc WI 53066, USA | Ice Hockey Player |
| **Brackens, Tony L, Jr**<br>193 Private Road 407, Fairfield TX 75840, USA | Football Player |
| **Brackett, Gary**<br>3591 Hintocks Circle, Carmel IN 46032, USA | Football Player |
| **Bradbury, Janette Lane**<br>10817 Kling St, North Hollywood CA 91602, USA | Actress |
| **Braddy, Johanna E**<br>Innovative Artists, 1505 10th St, Santa Monica CA 90401 USA | Actress |
| **Brademas, John**<br>New York University, President's Emeritus Office, New York NY 10012, USA | Educator; Representative, NY |
| **Braden, Dallas L**<br>1459 W Walnut St, Stockton CA 95203, USA | Baseball Player |
| **bradford,**<br>Fentress Bradburn Assoc, 421 Broadway, Denver CO 80203, USA | Architect |
| **Bradford, Barbara Taylor**<br>Bradford Enterprises, 450 Park Ave, #2303, New York NY 10022, USA | Writer |
| **Bradford, Chadwick L (Chad)**<br>3867 Bill Downing Road, Raymond MS 39154, USA | Baseball Player |
| **Bradford, Charles W (Buddy)**<br>6440 Springpark Ave, Los Angeles CA 90056, USA | Baseball Player |
| **Bradford, Corey L**<br>13002 Highway 955 E, Ethel LA 70730, USA | Football Player |
| **Bradford, Richard**<br>2511 Canyon Dr, Los Angeles CA 90068, USA | Actor |
| **Bradford, Ronnie**<br>965 Allen Lake Lane, Suwanee GA 30024, USA | Football Player, Coach |
| **Bradford, Samuel J (Sam)**<br>Saint Louis Rams, 901 N Broadway, Saint Louis MO 63101 USA | Football Player |
| **Bradford, Sarah**<br>Penguin Books, 375 Hudson St, Basement 1, New York NY 10014 USA | Writer |
| **Bradley, Alonzo**<br>1713 Briaroaks Dr, Flower Mound TX 75028, USA | Basketball Player |
| **Bradley, Bob**<br>Club Deportivo Chivas, 18400 Avalon Blvd, #500, Carson CA 90746 USA | Soccer Player, Coach |
| **Bradley, Brian**<br>6417 MacLaurin Dr, Tampa FL 33647, USA | Ice Hockey Player |
| **Bradley, Bruce**<br>262 Saint Joseph Ave, Long Beach CA 90803, USA | Water Polo Player |
| **Bradley, Carlos H**<br>1316 E Cliveden St, Philadelphia PA 19119, USA | Football Player |
| **Bradley, Charles W**<br>10810 Mountshire Circle, Highlands Ranch CO 80126, USA | Basketball Player |
| **Bradley, Christopher**<br>Ford/Robert Black Agency, 4032 N Miller Road, #104, Scottsdale AZ 85251, USA | Actor |
| **Bradley, Dan**<br>W M E Entertainment, 9601 Wilshire Blvd, #300, Beverly Hills CA 90210 USA | Director |
| **Bradley, David**<br>United Agents, 12-26 Lexington St, London W1F 0LE, England | Actor |
| **Bradley, Dick**<br>10176 Corporate Square Dr, #200, Saint Louis MO 63132, USA | Sports Cartoonist |
| **Bradley, Dudley L**<br>9830 Clanford Road, Randallstown MD 21133, USA | Basketball Player |
| **Bradley, Edward W (Ed), Jr**<br>187 Fryes Creek Lane, Clemmons NC 27012, USA | Football Player |
| **Bradley, Everett**<br>Fretland Productions Mgmt, 70A Greenwich Ave, PMB 212, New York NY 10011, USA | Singer, Songwriter |
| **Bradley, James**<br>PO Box 367, Rye NY 10580, USA | Writer |
| **Bradley, James**<br>Spotlight, 7 Leicester Place, London WC2H 7RJ, England | Actor |
| **Bradley, Kathleen**<br>8412 S Denker Ave, Los Angeles CA 90047, USA | Actress |
| **Bradley, Keegan H**<br>Altus Marketing & Managing, 177 Huntington Ave, Boston MA 02115, USA | Golfer |
| **Bradley, Lonnie**<br>405 Edgecombe Ave, New York NY 10032, USA | Boxer |
| **Bradley, Michael (Mike)**<br>5501 Branch Oak Place, Lithia FL 33547, USA | Golfer |
| **Bradley, Michael T**<br>6150 Blackjack Court N, Punta Gorda FL 33982, USA | Basketball Player |
| **Bradley, Milton O, Jr**<br>5359 Oak Park Ave, Encino CA 91316, USA | Baseball Player |
| **Bradley, Patricia E (Pat)**<br>PO Box 248, West Hyannisport MA 02672, USA | Golfer |
| **Bradley, Paul C (Gus)**<br>Jacksonville Jaguars, 1 AllTel Stadium Place, Jacksonville FL 32202 USA | Football Coach |
| **Bradley, Philip P (Phil)**<br>6950 Seminole Court, Columbia MO 65203, USA | Baseball Player |
| **Bradley, Rebecca**<br>7501 Alderwood Dr, Garland TX 75044, USA | Golfer |
| **Bradley, Robert A**<br>2465 S Downing St, Denver CO 80210, USA | Physician |
| **Bradley, Ryan**<br>Colorado Springs World Arena & Ice Hall, 3185 Venetucci Blvd, Colorado Springs, CO 80906, USA | Figure Skater |
| **Bradley, Sam**<br>Agency Group Ltd, 142 W 57th St, #600, New York NY 10019 USA | Singer, Songwriter |
| **Bradley, Scott W**<br>43 Chicory Lane, Pennington NJ 08534, USA | Baseball Player |
| **Bradley, Shawn P**<br>606 Sunny Flowers Lane, Salt Lake City UT 84107, USA | Basketball Player |
| **Bradley, Thomas W (Tom)**<br>4104 Woodberry St, University Park MD 20782, USA | Baseball Player |
| **Bradley, Timothy**<br>Top Rank Inc, 3908 Howard Hughes Parkway, #580, Las Vegas NV 89169 USA | Boxer |

| | |
|---|---|
| **Bradley, William C (Bill)**<br>1505 Whispering Water, Spring Branch TX 78070, USA | Football Player |
| **Bradley, William W (Bill)**<br>7 Kips Ridge, Verona NJ 07044, USA | Senator, NJ; Basketball Player |
| **Bradshaw, Ahmad**<br>Indianapolis Colts, 7001 W 56th St, Indianapolis IN 46254 USA | Football Player |
| **Bradshaw, James A**<br>5653 Eagle Harbor Dr, Westerville OH 43081, USA | Football Player |
| **Bradshaw, John E**<br>Becsey/Wisdom/Kalajian, 849 S Wooster St, #7, Los Angeles CA 90035, USA | Writer, Theologian |
| **Bradshaw, Morris, Jr**<br>82 Steuben Bay, Alameda CA 94502, USA | Football Player |
| **Bradshaw, Sufe**<br>Affinity Artists Agency, 5724 W 3rd St, #511, Los Angeles CA 90036, USA | Actress |
| **Bradshaw, Terry P**<br>12221 Merit Dr, #750, Dallas TX 75251, USA | Football Player, Sportscaster |
| **Brady, Ed J**<br>5755 White Path Lane, Liberty Township OH 45011, USA | Football Player |
| **Brady, Jeffrey T (Jeff)**<br>1506 NW 37th Place, Cape Coral FL 33993, USA | Football Player |
| **Brady, Kyle J**<br>2221 Alicia Lane, Atlantic Beach FL 32233, USA | Football Player |
| **Brady, Nicholas F**<br>Darby Overseas Investments, 1133 Connecticut NW, #400, Washington DC 20036, USA | Secretary, Treasury; Senator, NJ |
| **Brady, Orla**<br>Independent Talent Group, 40 Whitfield St, London W1T 2RH, England | Actress |
| **Brady, Pat**<br>United Feature Syndicate, PO Box 5610, Cincinnati OH 45201 USA | Cartoonist (Rose Is Rose) |
| **Brady, Patrick H**<br>10419 Felsblock Lane, New Braunfels TX 78132, USA | Vietnam War Army Hero (CMH), General |
| **Brady, Paul J**<br>Asgard Promotions, 125 Parkway, London NW1 7PS, England | Singer, Songwriter |
| **Brady, Ray**<br>CBS-TV, News Dept, 524 W 57th St, New York NY 10019, USA | Commentator |
| **Brady, Roscoe O**<br>6026 Valerian Lane, Rockville MD 20852, USA | Neurogeneticist |
| **Brady, Sarah**<br>Handgun Control, 1225 I St NW, #1100, Washington DC 20005, USA | Social Activist |
| **Brady, Sean B Cardinal**<br>Archbishop's House, Ara Coeli, Cathedral Road, Armagh BT6 7QY, Ireland | Religious Leader |
| **Brady, Thomas (Tom)**<br>310 Beacon St, #4, Boston MA 02116, USA | Football Player |
| **Brady, Wayne**<br>Creative Artists Agency, 2000 Ave of Stars, #100, Los Angeles CA 90067 USA | Actor, Comedian, Singer |
| **Braeden, Eric**<br>Harrison Stokes, 8730 W Sunset Blvd, #270, West Hollywood CA 90069, USA | Actor |
| **Braff, Zach**<br>Creative Artists Agency, 2000 Ave of Stars, #100, Los Angeles CA 90067 USA | Actor, Director |
| **Braga, Alice**<br>Roar Mgmt, 9701 Wilshire Blvd, #800, Beverly Hills CA 90212 USA | Actress |
| **Braga, Brannon**<br>W M E Entertainment, 9601 Wilshire Blvd, #300, Beverly Hills CA 90210 USA | Writer, Producer |
| **Braga, Sonia**<br>Framework Entertainment, 9057 Nemo St, #C, West Hollywood CA 90069 USA | Actress |
| **Bragg of Wigton, Melvyn**<br>12 Hampstead Hill Gardens, London NW3 2PL, England | Writer |
| **Bragg, Billy**<br>Sincere Mgmt, 35 Bravington Road, #6, London W9 3AB, England | Singer, Guitarist, Songwriter |
| **Bragg, Darren W**<br>163 Patriot Road, Southbury CT 06488, USA | Baseball Player |
| **Bragg, Donald G (Don)**<br>965 Oak St, Clayton CA 94517, USA | Track Athlete |
| **Bragg, Michael E (Mike)**<br>PO Box 4842, Falls Church VA 22044, USA | Football Player |
| **Bragg, Todd**<br>Breen Agency, 25 Music Square W, Nashville TN 37203, USA | Drummer (Caedmon's Call) |
| **Braggs, Glenn E**<br>28369 Falcon Crest Dr, Canyon Country CA 91351, USA | Baseball Player |
| **Braggs, Stephen**<br>120 Power House Road, Lawndale NC 28090, USA | Football Player |
| **Bragnalo, Rick**<br>515 Christina St E, Thunder Bay ON P7E 4P3, Canada | Ice Hockey Player |
| **Braham, Rich**<br>19 Miramichi Trail, Morgantown WV 26508, USA | Football Player |
| **Brahaney, Thomas F (Tom)**<br>1602 W Cuthbert Ave, Midland TX 79701, USA | Football Player |
| **Brainerd, Clayton**<br>Columbia Artists Mgmt Inc, 5 Columbus Circle, 1790 Broadway, #1600, New York NY 10019 USA | Opera Singer |
| **Braly, Angela**<br>WellPoint Inc, 120 Monument Circle, #200, Indianapolis IN 46204, USA | Businesswoman |
| **Bramall of Busfield, Edwin N W**<br>House of Lords, Westminster, London SW1A 0PW, England | Army Field Marshal, England |
| **Brambilla, Marco**<br>Creative Artists Agency, 2000 Ave of Stars, #100, Los Angeles CA 90067 USA | Director |
| **Bramhill, Gina**<br>United Agents, 12-26 Lexington St, London W1F 0LE, England | Actress |
| **Bramlett, Bonnie**<br>Mutual Central Mgmt, 9 Music Square S, #316, Nashville TN 37203, USA | Singer, Actress |
| **Bramlett, David A (Dave)**<br>61-100 Iliohu Way, Haleiwa HI 96712, USA | Army General |
| **Brammell, Abby**<br>Paul Kohner, 9300 Wilshire Blvd, #555, Beverly Hills CA 90212 USA | Actress |
| **Branagh, Kenneth**<br>Troika, 74 Clerkenwell Road, #300, London EC1M 5QA, England | Director, Actor |
| **Branca, John G**<br>Ziffren Brittenham Branca, 1801 Century Park West, #700, Los Angeles CA 90067, USA | Attorney |

**Branca, Ralph T J**
Westchester Country Club, 99 Biltmore Ave, Rye NY 10580, USA — Baseball Player

**Brancato, John**
United Talent Agency, U T A Plaza, 9336 Civic Center Dr, Beverly Hills CA 90210 USA — Writer, Producer, Actor

**Branch, A Deion, Jr**
New England Patriots, 1 Patriot Place, Foxboro MA 02035 USA — Football Player

**Branch, Adrian F**
18008 Fence Post Court, Gaithersburg MD 20877, USA — Basketball Player

**Branch, Alan K**
3076 E Kesler Lane, Gilbert AZ 85295, USA — Football Player

**Branch, Anthony (Deion)**
13382 W Sherbern Dr, Carmel IN 46032, USA — Football Player

**Branch, Clifford (Cliff)**
2071 Stonefield Lane, Santa Rosa CA 95403, USA — Football Player, Coach

**Branch, John**
New York Times, Editorial Dept, 229 W 43rd St, New York NY 10036 USA — Journalist

**Branch, Michelle**
A2 Mgmt, 1316 Sherman Ave, #215, Evanston IL 60201, USA — Singer, Songwriter

**Branch, Reginald E (Reggie)**
515 San Lanta Circle, Sanford FL 32771, USA — Football Player

**Branch, Taylor**
Larjansoff & Verrill, 179 Franklin St, New York NY 10013, USA — Historian

**Branco, Joaquim Rafael**
Prime Minister's Office, CP 38, Sao Tome, Sao Tome & Principe — Prime Minister, Sao Tome & Principe

**Brand, Elton T**
1077 Sentry Lane, Gladwyne PA 19035, USA — Basketball Player

**Brand, Esther C**
PO Box 11115, 9321 Universitas, South Africa — Track Athlete

**Brand, Joshua**
United Talent Agency, U T A Plaza, 9336 Civic Center Dr, Beverly Hills CA 90210 USA — Producer, Director

**Brand, Oscar**
Douglas A Yeager Productions, 300 W 55th St, New York NY 10019, USA — Singer, Songwriter

**Brand, Ronald G (Ron)**
4421 Staten Island Dr, Plano TX 75024, USA — Baseball Player

**Brand, Russell**
W M E Entertainment, 9601 Wilshire Blvd, #300, Beverly Hills CA 90210 USA — Actor, Comedian

**Brand, Stewart**
E Gate 5 Road, Sausalito CA 94965, USA — Editor, Writer

**Brand, Vance D**
21825 Hidden Canyon Dr, Tehachapi CA 93561, USA — Astronaut

**Brandauer, Klaus Maria**
Meyer Arts Mgmt, Dolderstr 18, 8032 Zurich, Switzerland — Actor

**Brandenstein, Daniel C**
648 N Tailwind Dr, Blanco TX 78606, USA — Astronaut

**Brandes, Christine**
I M G Artists, Hogarth Business Park, Chiswick, London W4 2TH, England — Opera Singer

**Brandes, John W**
905 Ashland Court, Mansfield TX 76063, USA — Football Player

**Brandi**
Next Model Mgmt, 23 Watts St, New York NY 10013 USA — Model

**Brandmeier, Jonathon**
C E S D, 10635 Santa Monica Blvd, #130, Los Angeles CA 90025 USA — Entertainer

**Brandmuller, Walter Cardinal**
Roman Curia, 00120 Vatican City — Religious Leader

**Brandom, Robert B**
University of Pittsburgh, Philosophy Dept, Pittsburgh PA 15260, USA — Philosopher

**Brandon, Barbara**
Universal Press Syndicate, 4520 Main St, #700, Kansas City MO 64111 USA — Cartoonist (Where I'm Coming From)

**Brandon, Christopher**
Artists Partnership, 101 Finsbury Pavement, London EC2A 1RS, England — Actor

**Brandon, Clark**
9000 W Sunset Blvd, #801, West Hollywood CA 90069, USA — Actor

**Brandon, Darrell G**
590 White Cliff Dr, Plymouth MA 02360, USA — Baseball Player

**Brandon, Michael**
TalentWorks, 3500 W Olive Ave, #1400, Burbank CA 91505 USA — Actor

**Brandon, Samuel T (Sam)**
5412 Norris Dr, The Colony TX 75056, USA — Football Player

**Brandon, T Terrell**
3310 NE Shaver St, Portland OR 97212, USA — Basketball Player

**Brands, Henry W (H W)**
University of Texas, Government Dept, Austin TX 78712, USA — Writer

**Brands, Terry**
4595 Hazelwood Ave SW, Iowa City IA 52240, USA — Freestyle Wrestler

**Brands, Tom**
4494 Taft Ave SE, Iowa City IA 52240, USA — Freestyle Wrestler, Coach

**Brandt, Betsy**
TalentWorks, 3500 W Olive Ave, #1400, Burbank CA 91505 USA — Actress

**Brandt, Brandi**
Esterman Entertainment, 220 Park Road, Riva MD 21140, USA — Model, Actress

**Brandt, Carlo**
Artmedia, 20 Ave Rapp, 75007 Paris, France — Actor

**Brandt, John G (Jackie), Jr**
5 Rabbit Trail, Wildwood FL 34785, USA — Baseball Player

**Brandt, Kyle**
Sweeney Mgmt, 8755 Lookout Mountain Ave, Los Angeles CA 90046, USA — Actor

**Brandt, Lesley-Ann**
Karen Kay Mgmt, 2/25 Strate St, Aukland 1010, New Zealand — Actress

**Brandt, Matthew**
Yossi Milo Gallery, 245 10th Ave, New York NY 10001, USA — Photographer

**Brandt, Paul R**
Warner Bros Records, 3300 Warner Blvd, Burbank CA 91505 USA — Singer, Songwriter

**Brandt, Thordis**
8171 Mannix Dr, Los Angeles CA 90046, USA — Actress

**Branduardi, Angelo**
Studio Legale Costa, Via Azzo Gardino 54, 40122 Bologna, Italy — Singer, Songwriter

**Brandy** — Singer, Actress
Norwood & Norwood, 22187 Ventura Blvd, #432, Woodland Hills CA 91364, USA

**Brandywine, Marcia** — Commentator
1428 Rising Glen, Los Angeles CA 90069, USA

**Brannagh, Brigid** — Actress
Innovative Artists, 1505 10th St, Santa Monica CA 90401 USA

**Brannan, Charles F** — Secretary, Agriculture
3131 E Alameda Ave, Denver CO 80209, USA

**Branscomb, Lewis M** — Physicist, Computer Scientist
Harvard University, Kennedy School of Government, Cambridge MA 02138, USA

**Branshaw, David** — Golfer
16220 Sierra de Avila, Tampa FL 33613, USA

**Branson, Jeff** — Actor
Creative Partners Group, 1522 2nd St, Santa Monica CA 90402, USA

**Branson, Jeffrey G (Jeff)** — Baseball Player
10749 Spokane Court, Union KY 41091, USA

**Branson, Richard** — Businessman, Balloonist
Virgin, 10-14 Bartley Wood Business Park, Hook RG27 9UP, England

**Branstad, Terry E** — Governor, IA
Regency West 5, #201, 4500 Westown Parkway, West Des Moines IA 50266, USA

**Brant, Tim** — Sportscaster
12416 Ansin Circle Dr, Potomac MD 20854, USA

**Brantley, Jeffrey H (Jeff)** — Baseball Player
104 Cherry Laurel Cove, Ridgeland MS 39157, USA

**Brantley, Larry** — Actor
Home Agency, 4420 W Lovers Lane, Dallas TX 75209, USA

**Brantley, Scot E** — Football Player
326 SE 32nd Ave, Ocala FL 34471, USA

**Branton, Daniel** — Biophysicist
Harvard Medical School, Molecular & Cell Biology Dept, 25 Shattuck St, Boston MA 02115, USA

**Branyan, Russell O (Russ)** — Baseball Player
3301 Running Spring Court, Franklin TN 37064, USA

**Brasar, Per-Olov** — Ice Hockey Player
Brasar Trav A B, Heden 99, 793 29 Leksand, Sweden

**Brasco, James J (Jim)** — Basketball Player
225 W Neck Road, Huntington NY 11743, USA

**Brashares, Ann** — Writer
Delacorte Press, 1540 Broadway, New York NY 10036 USA

**Brasseur, Claude** — Actor
Artmedia, 20 Ave Rapp, 75007 Paris, France

**Braswell, Joseph** — Interior Designer
Joseph Braswell Assoc, 1148 E Jordan St, Pensacola FL 32503, USA

**Brathwaite, Edward** — Writer
University of West Indies, History Dept, Mona, Kingston 7, Jamaica

**Brathwaite, Nicholas A** — Prime Minister, Grenada
House of Representatives, Grenada Trade Center, Grand Anse, Saint George's, Grenada

**Bratkowski, Edmund R (Zeke)** — Football Player, Coach
224 Anchors Lake Dr N, Santa Rosa Beach FL 32459, USA

**Bratt, Benjamin** — Actor
Arcieri Assoc, 305 Madison Ave, #2315, New York NY 10165 USA

**Bratt, Peter** — Actor
Five Sick Films, 1438 N Gower St, Building 38, Los Angeles CA 90028, USA

**Bratton, Creed** — Actor, Guitarist (Grass Roots)
Artistry Mgmt, 340 N Camden Dr, #302, Beverly Hills CA 90210, USA

**Bratton, Joseph K** — Army General
5902 Blakeford Dr, Windermere FL 34786, USA

**Bratton, William J** — Law Enforcement Official
Altergrity Corp, 7799 Leesburg Pike, #1100 North, Falls Church VA 22043, USA

**Bratz, Michael L (Mike)** — Basketball Player
7503 Tillman Hill Road, Colleyville TX 76034, USA

**Bratzke, Chad A** — Football Player
1478 Landings Circle, Sarasota FL 34231, USA

**Brauckmann, Linda** — Figure Skating Coach
Center of Excellence, 6501 Sprott St, #2, Burnaby BC V5B 3B8, Canada

**Braude, Peter R** — Obstetrician, Gynecologist
King's College, Women's Health Dept, Strand, London WC2R 2LS, England

**Brauer, Arik** — Artist
Academy of Fine Arts, Schillerplatz 3, 1010 Vienna, Austria

**Brauer, Denny** — Fisherman
405 Agua Dulce Trail, Del Rio TX 78840, USA

**Brauer, William (Bill)** — Artist
Bill Brauer Studios, 4368 E Warren Road, Warren VT 05674, USA

**Braugher, Andre** — Actor
Principato-Young, 9465 Wilshire Blvd, #880, Beverly Hills CA 90212 USA

**Brauman, John I** — Chemist
849 Tolman Dr, Stanford CA 94305, USA

**Braun, Allen** — Neuroscientist
National Institute on Deafness, 9000 Rockville Pike, Bethesda MD 20892, USA

**Braun, Colin** — Truck Racing Driver
4502 Raceway Drive, Concord NC 28027, USA

**Braun, Nicholas** — Actor
United Talent Agency, U T A Plaza, 9336 Civic Center Dr, Beverly Hills CA 90210 USA

**Braun, Rick** — Jazz Trumpeter
Chapman Mgmt, 14011 Venture Blvd, #405, Sherman Oaks CA 91423, USA

**Braun, Russell** — Opera, Concert Singer
Columbia Artists Mgmt Inc, 5 Columbus Circle, 1790 Broadway, #1600, New York NY 10019 USA

**Braun, Ryan J** — Baseball Player
8926 38th Ave, #8W, Kenosha WI 53142, USA

**Braun, Steve** — Actor
TalentWorks, 3500 W Olive Ave, #1400, Burbank CA 91505 USA

**Braun, Tamara** — Actress
John Carrabino Mgmt, 5900 Wilshire Blvd, #406, Los Angeles CA 90036 USA

**Braun, Wendy** — Actress
C E S D, 10635 Santa Monica Blvd, #130, Los Angeles CA 90025 USA

**Braun, Zev** — Producer
Zev Braun Pictures, 1438 N Gower St, #26, Los Angeles CA 90028, USA

**Braunfels, Michael** — Composer, Concert Pianist
Dransdorferstr 40, 50968 Cologne, Germany
**Braunwald, Eugene** — Physician
Partners Healthcare, 800 Boylston St, Boston MA 02199, USA
**Braver, Rita** — Commentator
CBS-TV, News Dept, 2020 M St NW, Washington DC 20036 USA
**Braverman, Bart** — Actor
House of Representatives, 1434 6th St, #1, Santa Monica CA 90401 USA
**Braverman, Nachum** — Religious Leader, Rabbi
Aish Hatorah, 9106 W Pico Blvd, Los Angeles CA 90035, USA
**Bravman, John C** — Educator
Bucknell University, President's Office, Marts Hall, Lewisburg PA 17837, USA
**Bravo, Ciara** — Actress
Savage Agency, 6212 Banner Ave, Los Angeles CA 90038 USA
**Braxton, Anthony** — Jazz Saxophonist, Composer
Berkeley Agency, 2608 9th St, #301, Berkeley CA 94710 USA
**Braxton, David H** — Football Player
6406 Donnegal Farm Road, Charlotte NC 28270, USA
**Braxton, Kara** — Basketball Player
Phoenix Mercury, American West Arena, 201 E Jefferson St, Phoenix AZ 85004 USA
**Braxton, Toni** — Singer, Songwriter
L M A Productions, 998C Old Country Road, #409, Plainview NY 11803, USA
**Braxton, Tyrone S** — Football Player
455 Kearney St, Denver CO 80220, USA
**Bray, Robert** — Interior Designer
Bray-Schaible Design, 80 W 40th St, #800, New York NY 10018, USA
**Bray, Thomas E (Thom)** — Actor
7006 SE 29th Ave, Portland OR 97202, USA
**Brayton, Tyler** — Football Player
91 W Fremont Ave, Littleton CO 80120, USA
**BrazDeAviz, Joao Cardinal** — Religious Leader
Institutes of Consecrated Life, Palazzo della Congregazioni, Piazza Pio XII 3, 00193 Rome, Italy
**Brazelton, Dewon C** — Baseball Player
107 Scenic Dr, Tullahoma TN 37388, USA
**Brazelton, T Berry** — Pediatrician
23 Hawthorn St, Cambridge MA 02138, USA
**Braziel, Larry** — Football Player
7616 Carriage Lane, Fort Worth TX 76112, USA
**Brazile, Robert L, Jr** — Football Player
813 Felder Ave, Fort Worth TX 76112, USA
**Brazile, Trevor** — Rodeo Rider
715 County Road 3051, Decatur TX 76234, USA
**Brazoban, Yhency J** — Baseball Player
13609 N 20th St, Tampa FL 33613, USA
**B-Real** — Rap Artist (Cypress Hill)
W M E Entertainment, 9601 Wilshire Blvd, #300, Beverly Hills CA 90210 USA
**Bream, Julian A** — Concert Guitarist
Hazard Chase, 25 City Road, Cambridge CB1 1DP, England
**Bream, Sidney E (Sid)** — Baseball Player
115 Sable Run, Zelienople PA 16063, USA
**Breathed, Berkeley** — Cartoonist (Bloom County, Outland)
Washington Post Writers Group, 1150 15th St NW, Washington DC 20071, USA
**Breathnach, Paddy** — Director
I C M Partners, 10250 Constellation Blvd, #900, Los Angeles CA 90067 USA
**Breaux, Jimmey** — Accordian Player (BeauSoleil)
Rosebud Agency, PO Box 170429, San Francisco CA 94117, USA
**Breaux, John B** — Senator, LA
Lousiana State University, Mass Communications School, Baton Rouge LA 70803, USA
**Breaux, Timothy (Tim)** — Basketball Player
845 Augusta Dr, #E75, Houston TX 77057, USA
**Brebner, Morwyn** — Producer, Writer, Actress
Gary Goddard Agency, 10 Sainte Mary St, #305, Toronto ON M4Y 1P9, Canada
**Brecher, John** — Writer
I C M Partners, 10250 Constellation Blvd, #900, Los Angeles CA 90067 USA
**Brechignac, Catherine** — Physicist
Scientifique Recherche Centre, 3 Rue Michel Ange, 75794 Paris, France
**Breckenridge, Alexandra** — Actress
Gersh Agency, 9465 Wilshire Blvd, #600, Beverly Hills CA 90212 USA
**Brecker, Randy** — Jazz Trumpeter
Michael Bloom Media Relations, PO Box 41380, Los Angeles CA 90041, USA
**Bredahl, Charlotte** — Equestrian
PO Box 318, Solvang CA 93464, USA
**Bredesen, Espen** — Ski Jumper
Hellerud Gardsvei 18, 0671 Oslo, Norway
**Bredow, Reinhard** — Luge Athlete
Bert-Heller Str 12, 38855 Wernigerode, Germany
**Breech, James T (Jim)** — Football Player
5461 Union Centre Dr, West Chester OH 45069, USA
**Breeden, Harold N (Hal)** — Baseball Player
665 Middle Road S, Leesburg GA 31763, USA
**Breeden, Louis E** — Football Player
4982 Lord Alfred Court, Cincinnati OH 45241, USA
**Breeden, Richard C** — Government Official
Coopers & Lybrand, 1800 M St NW, Washington DC 20036, USA
**Breedlove, N Craig** — Auto Racing Driver
World Speedway Team, 200 N Front St, Rio Vista CA 94571, USA
**Breedlove, Rodney W (Rod)** — Football Player
264 New Valley Road, Conowingo MD 21918, USA
**Breen, Bobby** — Singer, Actor
3701 W McNab Road, #206, Pompano Beach FL 33069, USA
**Breen, Edward D, Jr** — Businessman
Tyco International, 273 Corporate Dr, #100, Portsmouth NH 03801, USA
**Breen, George** — Swimmer
425 Pepper Mill Court, Sewell NJ 08080, USA
**Breen, J Eugene (Gene)** — Football Player
1018 Henley Downs Place, Lake Mary FL 32746, USA

Braunfels - Breen

**Breen, Mike** — Sportscaster
ABC-TV, Sports Dept, 77 W 66th St, New York NY 10023 USA

**Breen, Patrick** — Actor
Gersh Agency, 9465 Wilshire Blvd, #600, Beverly Hills CA 90212 USA

**Breen, Shelley L P** — Singer (Point of Grace)
Blanton Harrell Cooke Corzine, 1014 Cross Bow Court, Hendersonville TN 37075 USA

**Breen, Stephen P (Steve)** — Editorial Cartoonist
San Diego Union-Tribune, Editorial Dept, 350 Camino Reina, San Diego CA 92108 USA

**Breer, Murle** — Golfer
7008 Sand Road, Savannah GA 31410, USA

**Brees, Drew C** — Football Player
5500 Prytania St, New Orleans LA 70115, USA

**Bregman Recht, Tracey E** — Actress
Bell-Bregman Productions, 7800 Beverly Blvd, #3371, Los Angeles CA 90036, USA

**Bregman, Anthony** — Producer, Actor
Likely Story, 150 W 22nd St, #900, New York NY 10011, USA

**Bregman, Buddy** — Director, Producer, Composer
Paul Lane Entertainment, 468 N Camden Dr, Beverly Hills CA 90210, USA

**Bregman, Martin** — Producer
Martin Bregman Productions, 100 Universal City Plaza, Universal City CA 91608, USA

**Bregvadze, Nani G** — Singer
Irakly Abashidze Str 18A, #10, 380079 Tbilisi, Georgia

**Brehaut, Jeff** — Golfer
1085 Leonello Ave, Los Altos CA 94024, USA

**Breidenbach, Warren** — Surgeon
Jewish Hospital, Surgery Dept, 217 E Chestnut, Louisville KY 40202, USA

**Breiman, Valerie** — Director, Actress
Creative Artists Agency, 2000 Ave of Stars, #100, Los Angeles CA 90067 USA

**Breining, Fred L** — Baseball Player
2120 Ticonderoga Dr, San Mateo CA 94402, USA

**Breitenbach, Ken** — Ice Hockey Player
8 Greenvale Court, SS 1, Fonthill ON L0S 1E1, Canada

**Breitenstein, Robert C (Bob)** — Football Player
4215 E 95th St, Tulsa OK 74137, USA

**Breitman, Zabou** — Actress, Director, Writer
U B B A, 6 Rue de Braque, 75003 Paris, France

**Breitner, Paul** — Soccer Player
Kuckucksweg 4, 85649 Brunnthal, Germany

**Breitschwerdt, Werner** — Businessman
Daimler-Benz AG, Mercedesstr 136, 70322 Stuttgart, Germany

**Breland, Mark** — Boxer, Trainer
20514 Heritage Highway, Denmark SC 29042, USA

**Bremers, Peter** — Artist
PO Box 27, 6120 Born AA, Netherlands

**Bremner, Ewen** — Actor
Independent Talent Group, 40 Whitfield St, London W1T 2RH, England

**Brenciu, Marius** — Opera Singer
I M G Artists, Hogarth Business Park, Chiswick, London W4 2TH, England

**Brendel, Alfred** — Concert Pianist
Ingpen & Williams, 131 Putney Bridge Road, London SW15 2PA, England

**Brendel, Wolfgang** — Opera Singer
Manuela Kursidem, Wasagasse 12/1/3, 1090 Vienna, Austria

**Brendlinger, Kai** — Model
Playboy Promotions, 9346 Civic Center Dr, #200, Beverly Hills CA 90210 USA

**Brendon, Nicholas** — Actor
Webster Talent Mgmt, 1155 Homer St, #1702, Vancouver BC V6B 2Y1, Canada

**Breneman, Curtis E** — Chemist
47 Farrell Road, Troy NY 12180, USA

**Brener, Shirly** — Actress, Model
Jackoway Tyerman Wertheimer, 1925 Century Park E, #2200, Los Angeles CA 90067 USA

**Brenes Solorzano, Leopoldo Jose Cardinal** — Religious Leader
Archdiocese of Managua, Apartado 3058, Managua, Nicaragua

**Brengarth, Didier** — Actor
Angy Co, 85 Rue Saint Honore, 75001 Paris, France

**Brenly, Robert E (Bob)** — Baseball Player, Manager
9726 E Laurel Lane, Scottsdale AZ 85260, USA

**Brennan, Bernard F** — Businessman
B V-Cornerstone Ventures, 11001 W 120th St, #300, Broomfield CO 80021, USA

**Brennan, Brian M** — Football Player
2961 Edgewood Road, Cleveland OH 44124, USA

**Brennan, Christine** — Sportswriter
Washington Post, Sports Dept, 1150 15th Ave NW, Washington DC 20071, USA

**Brennan, Dan** — Ice Hockey Player
1912 108th Ave, Dawson Creek BC V1G 2T8, Canada

**Brennan, Gabriele** — Actress
C E S D, 10635 Santa Monica Blvd, #130, Los Angeles CA 90025 USA

**Brennan, George** — Harness Racing Driver
2 Millpond Road, Millstone Township NJ 08535, USA

**Brennan, Joseph E** — Governor, ME
104 Frances St, Portland ME 04102, USA

**Brennan, Richard (Rich)** — Ice Hockey Player
14 Reflection Way, South Yarmouth MA 02664, USA

**Brennan, Shane** — Producer, Writer
Paradigm Agency, 360 N Crescent Dr, North Building, Beverly Hills CA 90210 USA

**Brennan, Terrance** — Restauranteur, Chef
Pichoine Restaurant, 35 W 64th St, New York NY 10023, USA

**Brennan, Terrance P (Terry)** — Football Player, Coach
1731 Wildberry Dr, #C, Glenview IL 60025, USA

**Brennan, Thomas M (Tom)** — Baseball Player
8204 Millbank Dr, Orland Park IL 60462, USA

**Brenneman, Amy** — Actress
Creative Artists Agency, 2000 Ave of Stars, #100, Los Angeles CA 90067 USA

**Brenneman, Gregory D** — Businessman
C C M P Capital, 245 Park Ave, New York NY 10029, USA

**Brenneman, John** — Ice Hockey Player
247 Radley Road, Mississauga ON L5G 2R6, Canada

**Brenner, Carol** — Actress
Jean-François Pignard de Mart, 11 Rue Chanez, 75781 Paris Cedex 16, France

**Brenner, Hoby F J** — Football Player
40 Calle Ameno, San Clemente CA 92672, USA

**Brenner, Sydney** — Nobel Medicine Laureate
Molecular Sciences Institute, 2168 Shattuck Ave, #200, Berkeley CA 94704, USA

**Brenner, Teddy** — Boxing Promoter
24 W 55th St, #9C, New York NY 10019, USA

**Bresee, Bobbie** — Actress
PO Box 1222, Los Angeles CA 90078, USA

**Breslik, Pavel** — Opera Singer
I M G Artists, Hogarth Business Park, Chiswick, London W4 2TH, England

**Breslin, Abigail K** — Actress
Creative Artists Agency, 2000 Ave of Stars, #100, Los Angeles CA 90067 USA

**Breslin, Jimmy** — Journalist
Newsday, Editorial Dept, 235 Pinelawn Road, Melville NY 11747, USA

**Breslin, Spencer** — Actor
Baker Winokur Ryder Public Relations, 9100 Wilshire Blvd, #500W, Beverly Hills CA 90212 USA

**Breslow, Craig A** — Baseball Player
26 Finchwood Dr, Trumbull CT 06611, USA

**Breslow, Ronald C** — Chemist
295 Three Mile Harbor Road, East Hampton NY 11937, USA

**Bresnik, Randolph J (Randy)** — Astronaut
N A S A, Johnson Space Center, 2101 NASA Road, Houston TX 77058 USA

**Bressoud, Edward F (Eddie)** — Baseball Player
515 Marble Canyon Lane, San Ramon CA 94582, USA

**Brest, Martin** — Director, Producer
I C M Partners, 10250 Constellation Blvd, #900, Los Angeles CA 90067 USA

**Bretos, Conchy** — Social Activist
M I A Consulting, 5208 Aston Road, Miami Beach Fl 33140, USA

**Brett, George H** — Baseball Player, Executive
6528 Seneca Road, Mission Hills KS 66208, USA

**Brett, Jan** — Writer
132 Pleasant St, Norwell MA 02061, USA

**Brettschneider, Carl** — Football Player
4649 Bird View Court, Las Vegas NV 89129, USA

**Bretz, Gabor** — Opera Singer
I M G Artists, Hogarth Business Park, Chiswick, London W4 2TH, England

**Breuer, Randall W (Randy)** — Basketball Player
10481 Misty Morning Lane, Eden Prairie MN 55347, USA

**Breunig, Robert P (Bob)** — Football Player
9215 Westview Circle, Dallas TX 75231, USA

**Brewer, Albert P** — Governor, AL
201 University Park Dr, Birmingham AL 35209, USA

**Brewer, Christine** — Opera Singer
I M G Artists, Hogarth Business Park, Chiswick, London W4 2TH, England

**Brewer, Craig** — Director, Writer
W M E Entertainment, 9601 Wilshire Blvd, #300, Beverly Hills CA 90210 USA

**Brewer, David L** — Navy Admiral
Commander, Military Sealift Command, Washington DC 20398 USA

**Brewer, Donald** — Drummer (Grand Funk Railroad)
Lustig Talent, PO Box 770850, Orlando FL 32877 USA

**Brewer, Eric C** — Ice Hockey Player
634 Riviera Dr, Tampa FL 33606, USA

**Brewer, James T (Jim)** — Basketball Player, Coach
1814 S 23rd Ave, Maywood IL 60153, USA

**Brewer, Madeline** — Actress, Singer
I C M Partners, 10250 Constellation Blvd, #900, Los Angeles CA 90067 USA

**Brewer, Ronnie** — Basketball Player
Chicago Bulls, United Center, 1901 W Madison St, Chicago IL 60612 USA

**Brewer, Thomas A (Tom)** — Baseball Player
409 State Road, Cheraw SC 29520, USA

**Brewer, William R (Billy)** — Baseball Player
7405 Woodway Dr, Woodway TX 76712, USA

**Brewster, Darrel B (Pete)** — Football Player
PO Box 183, Peculiar MO 64078, USA

**Brewster, Jordana** — Actress
Creative Artists Agency, 2000 Ave of Stars, #100, Los Angeles CA 90067 USA

**Brewster, Lamon T** — Boxer
Don King Productions, 501 Fairway Dr, Deerfield Beach FL 33441 USA

**Brewster, Lincoln** — Singer, Guitarist, Songwriter
G O A Inc, 1710 General George Patten Dr, #104, Brentwood TN 37027, USA

**Brewster, Paget** — Actress
Burstein Co, 15304 W Sunset Blvd, #208, Pacific Palisades CA 90272, USA

**Brewster, Patience** — Artist, Writer
World Media Communications, PO Box 689, Skaneateles NY 13152, USA

**Brewster, Tom** — Curling Athlete
Curl Aberdeen, Eday Walk off Lang Stracht, Summerhill, Aberdeen AB15 6LN, Scotland

**Brey, Mike** — Basketball Coach
Notre Dame University, Athletic Dept, Notre Dame IN 46556, USA

**Breyer, Stephen G** — Supreme Court Justice
US Supreme Court, 1 1st St NE, Washington DC 20543 USA

**Breytenbach, Breyten** — Writer, Political Activist
Houghton Mifflin Harcourt, 215 Park Ave S, #1200, New York NY 10003 USA

**Brezec, Primoz** — Basketball Player
10030 Hazelview Dr, Charlotte NC 28277, USA

**Brezina, Gregory (Greg)** — Football Player
155 Tillinghurst Trace, Newnan GA 30265, USA

**Brezina, Robert P (Bobby)** — Football Player
1204 Pine Hollow Dr, Friendswood TX 77546, USA

**Breziner, Salome** — Director, Writer
Rosen Law Group, 15 Brooks Ave, Venice CA 0291, USA

**Brezis, Haim** — Mathematician
18 Rue de la Glaciere, 75640 Paris Cedex 13, France

**Brezner, Larry** — Producer
M B S T Entertainment, 345 N Maple Dr, #200, Beverly Hills CA 90210, USA

# B

**Brian, Frank S (Frankie)** — Basketball Player
4425 40th St, Zachary LA 70791, USA
**Brice, Lee** — Singer, Songwriter
377 Mgmt, 209 10th Ave, #332, Nashville TN 37203, USA
**Brice, Pierre** — Actor
Agentur Ebisch, Schellingstr 124, 80798 Munich, Germany
**Brickel, James R** — Air Force General, Hero
4798 Hanging Moss Lane, Sarasota FL 34238, USA
**Brickell, Beth** — Director, Producer, Actress
9630 Arby Dr, Beverly Hills CA 90210, USA
**Brickell, Edie** — Singer (New Bohemians), Songwriter
Sachs Co, 427 W 14th St, #300, New York NY 10014, USA
**Bricker, Neal S** — Physician, Nephrologist
727 S Orange Grove Blvd, #6, Pasadena CA 91105, USA
**Brickley, Andy** — Ice Hockey Player
5 Mill River Lane, Hingham MA 02043, USA
**Bricklin, Daniel S** — Computer Software Designer (VisiCalc)
Trellix Corp, 300 Bahr Ave, Concord MA 01742, USA
**Brickman, Jim** — Pianist, Composer
Lucid Artists Mgmt, 54 Music Square E, #200, Nashville TN 37203, USA
**Brickman, Marshall** — Writer
I C M Partners, 10250 Constellation Blvd, #900, Los Angeles CA 90067 USA
**Brickman, Paul M** — Director, Producer, Writer
Creative Artists Agency, 2000 Ave of Stars, #100, Los Angeles CA 90067 USA
**Brickowski, Frank A** — Basketball Player
589 7th St, Lake Oswego OR 97034, USA
**Bricusse, Leslie** — Composer, Lyricist
8730 W Sunset Blvd, #300W, West Hollywood CA 90069, USA
**Bridgeman, Ulysses L (Junior)** — Basketball Player
1604 Cherokee Road, Louisville KY 40205, USA
**Bridges, Alicia** — Singer, Songwriter
Richard Walters, PO Box 2789, Toluca Lake CA 91610 USA
**Bridges, Angelica** — Actress, Model
Universal Attractions, 135 W 26th St, #1200, New York NY 10001 USA
**Bridges, Beau** — Actor
Creative Artists Agency, 2000 Ave of Stars, #100, Los Angeles CA 90067 USA
**Bridges, Chloe** — Actress
A P A Talent & Literary Agency, 405 S Beverly Dr, #300, Beverly Hills CA 90212 USA
**Bridges, Everett L (Rocky)** — Baseball Player
1128 W Shane Dr, Coeur D'Alene ID 83815, USA
**Bridges, Jeff** — Actor, Singer
Creative Artists Agency, 2000 Ave of Stars, #100, Los Angeles CA 90067 USA
**Bridges, Jeremy E** — Football Player
4502 E Ivanhoe St, Gilbert AZ 85295, USA
**Bridges, Jordan** — Actor
Mavrick Artists Agency, 6100 Wilshire Blvd, #550, Los Angeles CA 90048, USA
**Bridges, Krista** — Actress
TalentWorks, 3500 W Olive Ave, #1400, Burbank CA 91505 USA
**Bridges, Marilyn** — Photographer
PO Box 269, Warwick NY 10990, USA
**Bridges, Mark** — Costume Designer
W M E Entertainment, 9601 Wilshire Blvd, #300, Beverly Hills CA 90210 USA
**Bridges, Roy D, Jr** — Astronaut, Air Force General
113 William Barksdale, Williamsburg VA 23185, USA
**Bridges, Ruby** — Civil Rights Activist, Writer
Ruby Bridges Foundation, PO Box 870248, New Orleans LA 70187, USA
**Bridges, Todd A** — Actor
16002 Nordhoff St, North Hills CA 91343, USA
**Bridges, William C (Bill)** — Basketball Player
2322 33rd St, Santa Monica CA 90405, USA
**Bridgewater, Brad M** — Swimmer
3843 Echo Brook Lane, Dallas TX 75229, USA
**Bridgewater, Dee Dee** — Singer, Actress
Ted Kurland, 173 Brighton Ave, Boston MA 02134 USA
**Bridgewater, Theodore (Teddy)** — Football Player
Minnesota Vikings, 9520 Viking Dr, Eden Prairie MN 55344 USA
**Bridgman, Mel** — Ice Hockey Player
221 Concord St, El Segundo CA 90245, USA
**Bridwell, Norman** — Writer
PO Box 869, Edgartown MA 02539, USA
**Brie, Alison** — Actress
W M E Entertainment, 9601 Wilshire Blvd, #300, Beverly Hills CA 90210 USA
**Briem, Anita** — Actress
Baker Winokur Ryder Public Relations, 9100 Wilshire Blvd, #500W, Beverly Hills CA 90212 USA
**Brien, Douglas R Z (Doug)** — Football Player
55 Cambrian Ave, Piedmont CA 94611, USA
**Briere, Daniel** — Ice Hockey Player
17 S Hinchman Ave, Haddonfield NJ 08033, USA
**Briesewitz, Uta** — Cinematographer
W M E Entertainment, 9601 Wilshire Blvd, #300, Beverly Hills CA 90210 USA
**Briest, Anne-Sophie** — Actress
Kick Mgmt, Burgunderstr 8, 50677 Cologne, Germany
**Brigati, Eddie** — Singer, Percussionist (Rascals)
Dassinger Creative, 172 2nd Ave, Little Falls NJ 07424, USA
**Briggs of Lewes, Asa** — Historian
Caprons, Keere Saint Lewes, Sussex BN7 1TX, England
**Briggs, Daniel L (Dan)** — Baseball Player
8270 Rookery Way, Westerville OH 43082, USA
**Briggs, Edward S** — Navy Admiral
3648 Lago Sereno, Escondido CA 92029, USA
**Briggs, John E (Johnny)** — Baseball Player
238 Wall Ave, Paterson NJ 07504, USA
**Briggs, John T** — Baseball Player
216 Tom Bell Road, #133, Murphys CA 95247, USA
**Briggs, Johnny** — Actor
Associated International Mgmt, 7 Hatton Garden, #400, London EC1N 8AD, England

**Briggs, Lance M** — Football Player
225 NE Mizner Blvd, #685, Boca Raton FL 33432, USA
**Briggs, Raymond R** — Writer, Illustrator, Cartoonist
Weston, Underhill Lane, Westmeston near Hassocks, Sussex, England
**Briggs, Shannon** — Boxer
22114 N Flamingo Road, Pembroke Pines FL 33028, USA
**Briggs, William R** — Biologist
480 Hale St, Palo Alto CA 94301, USA
**Briggs, Wilma** — Baseball Player
111 Summit Ave, Wakefield RI 02879, USA
**Brigham, Kenneth (Dr Ken)** — Singer
805 Peachtree St NE, #404, Atlanta GA 30308, USA
**Bright, Leon, Jr** — Football Player
1183 Dutton Ave, Deland FL 32720, USA
**Bright, Myron H** — Judge
655 1st Ave N, #340, Fargo ND 58102, USA
**Bright, Torah J** — Snowboarding Athlete
Ski & Snowboard Australia, 1 Cobden St, South Melbourne VIC 3205, Australia
**Brightman, Sarah** — Singer
The Mill, Mill Lane, Cockham SL6 9QT, England
**Brighton, Connie** — Model, Actress
Playboy Promotions, 9346 Civic Center Dr, #200, Beverly Hills CA 90210 USA
**Brigman, D J** — Golfer
8304 Calle Soquelle NE, Albuquerque NM 87113, USA
**Briles, Arthur R (Art)** — Football Coach
Baylor University, Athletic Dept, Waco TX 76798, USA
**Briley, Gregory (Greg)** — Baseball Player
2170 Sunnybrook Road, Greenville NC 27834, USA
**Brill, Charlie** — Actor
3635 Wrightwood Dr, Studio City CA 91604, USA
**Brill, Francesca** — Actress
Kate Feast, Primrose Hill Studios, Fitzroy Road, London NW1 8TR, England
**Brill, Steven** — Editor, Publisher
American Lawyer, Editorial Dept, 600 3rd Ave, New York NY 10016, USA
**Brill, Steven (Steve)** — Director, Writer
United Talent Agency, U T A Plaza, 9336 Civic Center Dr, Beverly Hills CA 90210 USA
**Brill, Winston J** — Bacteriologist
12529 237th Way NE, Redmond WA 98053, USA
**Brillinger, Alysha** — Singer, Songwriter
Agency Group Ltd, 142 W 57th St, #600, New York NY 10019 USA
**Brilmayer, Roberta L** — Attorney, Educator
Yale University, Law School, 127 Wall St, New Haven CT 06511, USA
**Brimanis, Aris** — Ice Hockey Player
12909 Badger Lane, Anchorage AK 99516, USA
**Brimble, Nick** — Actor
Curtis Brown Group, 28-29 Haymarket St, #500, London SW1Y 4SP, England
**Brimblecombe, Richard** — Actor
Associated International Mgmt, 7 Hatton Garden, #400, London EC1N 8AD, England
**Brimhall, Cynthia** — Actress, Model
Playboy Promotions, 9346 Civic Center Dr, #200, Beverly Hills CA 90210 USA
**Brimley, Wilford** — Actor
Blake Agency, 23441 Malibu Colony Road, Malibu CA 90265, USA
**Brin, Sergey** — Businessman, Computer Engineer
Google Inc, 1600 Amphitheatre Parkway, #41, Mountain View CA 94043, USA
**Brind'Amour, Rod** — Ice Hockey Player
1153 Four Wheel Dr, Wake Forest NC 27587, USA
**Brink, Andre P** — Writer
University of Cape Town, English Dept, Rondebosch 7700, South Africa
**Brink, Bernhard** — Singer
One Two Media, Gervinusstr 12, 10629 Berlin, Germany
**Brink, Elisabeth** — Writer
Houghton Mifflin Harcourt, 215 Park Ave S, #1200, New York NY 10003 USA
**Brink, Evelien** — Balloonist
Sikelalodge, PO Box 2277, Hazyview 1242, South Africa
**Brink, Henk** — Balloonist
Sikelalodge, PO Box 2277, Hazyview 1242, South Africa
**Brink, Lawrence (Larry)** — Football Player
13310 Tierra Heights Road, Redding CA 96003, USA
**Brink, R Alexander** — Geneticist
8301 Old Sauk Road, #326, Middleton WI 53562, USA
**Brinker, Nancy Goodman** — Foundation Executive
Komen Breast Cancer Foundation, 5005 LBJ Freeway, #250, Dallas TX 75244, USA
**Brinkley, Christine (Christie)** — Model, Actress
Ford Models, 9200 Sunset Blvd, #805, West Hollywood CA 90069, USA
**Brinkley, Douglas** — Historian
Harper Collins Publishers, 10 E 53rd St, Cellar 1, New York NY 10022 USA
**Brinkman, Charles E (Chuck)** — Baseball Player
126 Country Club Road, Bryan OH 43506, USA
**Brinkman, John A** — Historian
1321 E 56th St, #4, Chicago IL 60637, USA
**Brinkman, Joseph N (Joe)** — Baseball Umpire
10351 NW 70th St, Chiefland FL 32626, USA
**Brinkman, William F** — Physicist
1177 22nd St NW, #2C, Washington DC 20037, USA
**Brinkmann, Robert S** — Cinematographer
Mirisch Agency, 1025 Colorado Ave, #B, Santa Monica CA 90211 USA
**Brinson, Gary** — Financier
Brinson Partners, 1 N Wacker Dr, #3000, Chicago IL 60606, USA
**Brion, Francoise** — Actress
11 Rue de Seine, 75006 Paris, France
**Brion, Jon** — Composer
Kraft-Engel Mgmt, 15233 Ventura Blvd, #200, Sherman Oaks CA 91403 USA
**Brisby, Vincent C** — Football Player
1926 Norfolk St, #19, Houston TX 77098, USA
**Brisco, Valerie A** — Track Athlete
USA Track & Field, 4341 Starlight Dr, Indianapolis IN 46239 USA

**B**

**Briscoe, Brent** — Actor, Writer
Moxie Agency, PO Box 791576, New Orleans LA 70179, USA
**Briscoe, Conie** — Writer
Random House, 1745 Broadway, #1800, New York NY 10019 USA
**Briscoe, John E** — Baseball Player
2705 Arbor Court, Richardson TX 75082, USA
**Briscoe, Marlin O** — Football Player
675 Coronado Ave, Long Beach CA 90814, USA
**Briscoe, Mary Beck** — Judge
US Appeals Court, 4839 Billings Parkway, Lawrence KS 66049, USA
**Briscoe, Ryan** — Auto Racing Driver
Penske Racing, Penske Plaza, 366 Riverfront, Reading PA 19602, USA
**Brisebois, Danielle** — Actress, Singer
1311 Broadway, Santa Monica CA 90404, USA
**Brisebois, Patrice** — Ice Hockey Player
4723 Castle Circle, Broomfield CO 80023, USA
**Briski, Zana** — Photographer, Cinematographer
Kids with Cameras, 341 Lafayette St, #4407, New York NY 10012, USA
**Brister, Walter A (Bubby), III** — Football Player
139 Fontainebleau Dr, Mandeville LA 70471, USA
**Bristol, J David (Dave)** — Baseball Player, Manager
1748 Fairview Road, Andrews NC 28901, USA
**Bristow, Allan M** — Basketball Player, Coach, Executive
510 Sand Hill Court, Marco Island FL 34145, USA
**Britt, Chris** — Editorial Cartoonist
State Journal-Register, Editorial Dept, 1 Copley Plaza, Springfield IL 62701, USA
**Britt, James E** — Football Player
PO Box 371202, Decatur GA 30037, USA
**Britt, May** — Actress
5059 Enfield Ave, Encino CA 91316, USA
**Britt, Michael** — Guitarist (Lonestar)
Borman Entertainment, 4322 Harding Pike, #429, Nashville TN 37205, USA
**Britt, Thomas** — Interior Designer
136 E 57th St, #700, New York NY 10022, USA
**Brittain, Paul** — Actor, Comedian
W M E Entertainment, 9601 Wilshire Blvd, #300, Beverly Hills CA 90210 USA
**Brittan of Spennithorne, Leon** — Government Official, England
1 Finsbury Ave, London EC2M 2PP, England
**Brittany, Morgan** — Actress, Model
Scott Stander Assoc, 4533 Van Nuys Blvd, #401, Sherman Oaks CA 91403 USA
**Brittenham, Harry** — Attorney
Ziffren Brittenham Branca, 1801 Century Park West, #700, Los Angeles CA 90067, USA
**Brittingham, Eric** — Singer, Bassist (Cinderella)
Union Entertainment Group, 1323 Newbury Road, #104, Thousand Oaks CA 91320, USA
**Britton, Benjamin** — Inventor (Lascaux Virtual Reality Cave)
University of Cincinnati, Fine Arts Dept, Cincinnati OH 45221, USA
**Britton, Connie** — Actress
W M E Entertainment, 9601 Wilshire Blvd, #300, Beverly Hills CA 90210 USA
**Britton, Tony** — Actor
Shepherd Mgmt, 45 Maddox St, #400, London W1S 2PE, England
**Britz, Jerilyn** — Golfer
415 E Lincoln St, #7, Luverne MN 56156, USA
**Brixius, Liz** — Producer, Writer
W M E Entertainment, 9601 Wilshire Blvd, #300, Beverly Hills CA 90210 USA
**Broad, Eli** — Businessman
SunAmerica Inc, 10900 Wilshire Blvd, #1200, Los Angeles CA 90024, USA
**Broad, Molly Corbett** — Educator
American Council on Education, 1 Dupont Circle, #800, Washington DC 20036, USA
**Broadbent, Harry** — Keyboardist (Kula Shakur)
Little Big Man, 39A Grammercy Park N, #1C, New York NY 10010, USA
**Broadbent, Jim** — Actor
Independent Talent Group, 40 Whitfield St, London W1T 2RH, England
**Broadbent, John Edward** — Government Official, Canada
1386 Nicola, #30, Vancouver BC V6G 2G2, Canada
**Broadhead, James L** — Businessman
F P L Group, 700 Universe Blvd, North Palm Beach FL 33408, USA
**Broadie, Sarah W** — Philosopher
Saint Andrews University, Philosophy Dept, Fife KY16 9AJ, Scotland
**Brobeck, John R** — Physiologist
224 Vassar Ave, Swarthmore PA 19081, USA
**Broberg, Peter S (Pete)** — Baseball Player
220 Monterey Road, Palm Beach FL 33480, USA
**Brocail, Douglas K (Doug)** — Baseball Player
8011 Meadow Vista Dr, Missouri City TX 77459, USA
**Broch, Hugo** — WW II German Luftwaffe Hero
Zedernweg 4, 51381 Leverkusen, Germany
**Broch, Nicolai Cleve** — Actor
Panorama Agency, Ryesgade 103B, 2100 Copenhagen, Denmark
**Brochere, Lizzie** — Actress
Conway Van Gelder Grant, 8-12 Broadwick St, #300, London W1F 8HW, England
**Brochet, Anne** — Actress
Artmedia, 20 Ave Rapp, 75007 Paris, France
**Brochtrup, William (Bill)** — Actor
S D B Partners, 315 S Beverly Dr, #411, Beverly Hills CA 90067 USA
**Brochu, Devin** — Actor
Greene Assoc, 1901 Ave of Stars, #130, Los Angeles CA 90067 USA
**Brochu, Doug** — Actor
A P A Talent & Literary Agency, 405 S Beverly Dr, #300, Beverly Hills CA 90212 USA
**Brochu, Jim** — Actor, Writer, Director
Dulcina Eisen Agency, 154 E 61st St, New York NY 10024, USA
**Brock, Chad** — Singer
Collingsworth Bright, 209 10th Ave S, #216, Nashville TN 37203, USA
**Brock, Gregory A (Greg)** — Baseball Player
3727 Valley Oak Dr, Loveland CO 80538, USA
**Brock, Louis C (Lou)** — Baseball Player
61 Barkley Place, Saint Charles MO 63301, USA

**Brock, Matthew L (Matt)** — Football Player
3105 SW 98th Ave, Portland OR 97225, USA

**Brock, Peter A (Pete)** — Football Player
111 Main St, Topsfield MA 01983, USA

**Brock, Raheem F** — Football Player
1017 Serpentine Lane, Wyncote PA 19095, USA

**Brock, Stanley J (Stan)** — Football Player, Coach
2555 SW 81st Ave, Portland OR 97225, USA

**Brock, T Christopher (Chris)** — Baseball Player
7684 Markham Bend Place, Sanford FL 32771, USA

**Brock, Tarrik** — Baseball Player
8111 Fairchild Ave, Winnetka CA 91306, USA

**Brock, Tricia** — Director
I C M Partners, 10250 Constellation Blvd, #900, Los Angeles CA 90067 USA

**Brock, William E (Bill), III** — Secretary of Labor; Senator, TN
16 Revell St, Annapolis MD 21401, USA

**Brockermeyer, Blake W** — Football Player
PO Box 789, Wilson WY 83014, USA

**Brockers, Michael S** — Football Player
Saint Louis Rams, 901 N Broadway, Saint Louis MO 63101 USA

**Brockert, Richard C** — Labor Leader
United Telegraph Workers, 701 E Gude Dr, Rockville MD 20850, USA

**Brockhaus, Wendy** — Artist
1210 Aldrich Court NW, Salem OR 97304, USA

**Brockington, John S** — Football Player
1835 Fort Stockton Dr, San Diego CA 92103, USA

**Brockington, Ryan** — Actor
C E S D, 10635 Santa Monica Blvd, #130, Los Angeles CA 90025 USA

**Brockovich-Ellis, Erin** — Legal Activist, Writer
Masry & Vititoe, 5707 Corsa Ave, #200, Westlake Village CA 91362, USA

**Brodbin, Kevin** — Writer
Creative Artists Agency, 2000 Ave of Stars, #100, Los Angeles CA 90067 USA

**Broder, Samuel** — Medical Administrator
I V A X Corp, 4400 Biscayne Blvd, Miami FL 33137, USA

**Broderick, Beth** — Actress
Vox Inc, 6420 Wilshire Blvd, #1080, Los Angeles CA 90048 USA

**Broderick, J M** — Artist
8825 SE 32nd Ave, Portland OR 97222, USA

**Broderick, Kenneth L (Ken)** — Ice Hockey Player
5142 Citation Road, Niagara Falls ON L2H 3H7, Canada

**Broderick, Matthew** — Actor
246 W 44th St, New York NY 10036, USA

**Brodeur, Martin (Marty)** — Ice Hockey Player
22 Baxter Lane, West Orange NJ 07052, USA

**Brodeur, Richard** — Ice Hockey Player
5007 Angus Dr, Vancouver BC V6M 3M6, Canada

**Brodhead, Richard H** — Educator
Duke University, President's Office, Durham NC 27708, USA

**Brodie, H Keith H** — Psychiatrist
63 Beverly Dr, Durham NC 27707, USA

**Brodie, John R** — Football Player, Sportscaster, Golfer
49350 Avenida Fernando, La Quinta CA 92253, USA

**Brodie, Kevin** — Actor
3925 Big Oak Dr, #5, Studio City CA 91604, USA

**Brodie-Sangster, Thomas** — Actor, Producer
Curtis Brown Group, 28-29 Haymarket St, #500, London SW1Y 4SP, England

**Brodka, Zbigniew** — Speed Skater
P S P Lowicz, Ul Seminaryjna 4, 99 400 Lowicz, Poland

**Brodowski, Richard S (Dick)** — Baseball Player
120 Pine St, Manchester MA 01944, USA

**Brody, Adam** — Actor
United Talent Agency, U T A Plaza, 9336 Civic Center Dr, Beverly Hills CA 90210 USA

**Brody, Adrien** — Actor
Paradigm Agency, 360 N Crescent Dr, North Building, Beverly Hills CA 90210 USA

**Brody, Jane E** — Journalist
4508 Cedros Ave, Sherman Oaks CA 91403, USA

**Brody, Kenneth D** — Financier
Export-Import Bank, 811 Vermont Ave NW, Washington DC 20571, USA

**Brody, Lane** — Singer, Songwriter
Center Stage Attractions, 20 Music Square W, #208, Nashville TN 37203, USA

**Brody, William R** — Educator
Biological Studies Institute, 10100 N Torrey Pines Road, La Jolla CA 92037, USA

**Broecker, Wallace S** — Geologist, Geochemist
Lamont-Doherty Earth Observatory, PO Box 1000, Palisades NY 10964, USA

**Broelsch, Christopher E** — Surgeon
University of Chicago Medical Center, Surgery Dept, Chicago IL 60690, USA

**Brogdon, Cinderella J (Cindy)** — Basketball Player
4162 Anson Trail, Suwanee GA 30024, USA

**Broglio, Ernest G (Ernie)** — Baseball Player
2838 Via Carmen, San Jose CA 95124, USA

**Brogna, Rico J** — Baseball Player
2 Gate Post Lane, Woodbury CT 06798, USA

**Brohamer, John A (Jack), Jr** — Baseball Player
39017 Narcissus Dr, Palm Desert CA 92211, USA

**Brohawn, M Troy** — Baseball Player
1619 Taylors Island Road, Woolford MD 21677, USA

**Brokaw, Thomas J (Tom)** — Commentator
941 Park Ave, #14C, New York NY 10028, USA

**Brokop, Lisa** — Singer, Songwriter
Libre Entertainment, 313-2906 W Broadway, Vancouver BC V6K 2G8, Canada

**Brolin, James** — Actor
Jeff Wald Entertainment, 176 Acari Dr, Los Angeles CA 90049, USA

**Brolin, Josh** — Actor
Creative Artists Agency, 2000 Ave of Stars, #100, Los Angeles CA 90067 USA

**Brolly, Shane** — Actor
Luber Rocklin Entertainment, 5815 Sunset Blvd, #206, Los Angeles CA 90028 USA

**Bromberg, David** — Guitarist, Songwriter
Apex Artists, 818 N Market St, Wilmington DE 19801, USA

**Bromell, Lorenzo A** — Football Player
250 Parkwood Circle, Niceville FL 32578, USA

**Bromley, Gary** — Ice Hockey Player
1130 Munro St, Victoria BC V9A 5P1, Canada

**Bromley, R Scott** — Interior Designer
Bromley Caldari Architects, 242 W 27th St, #200, New York NY 10001, USA

**Bromstad, David** — Actor, Interior Designer
W M E Entertainment, 9601 Wilshire Blvd, #300, Beverly Hills CA 90210 USA

**Bron, Eleanor** — Actress
Rebecca Blond, 69A King's Road, London SW3 4NX, England

**Bronars, Edward J** — Marine Corps General
3354 Rose Lane, Falls Church VA 22042, USA

**Bronfman, Charles R** — Businessman, Baseball Executive
Koor Industries, 14 Hamelacha St, Rosh Ha'ayin 48091, Israel

**Bronfman, Yefin** — Concert Pianist
Opus 3 Artists, 470 Park Ave S, #900N, New York NY 10016 USA

**Bronleewe, Matt** — Guitarist (Jars of Clay)
Creative Artists Agency, 2000 Ave of Stars, #100, Los Angeles CA 90067 USA

**Bronner, Till** — Jazz Singer, Trumpeter, Composer
Bam Bam Music, Alte Schonhauser Str 44, 10119 Berlin, Germany

**Bronson, Po** — Writer
Random House, 1745 Broadway, #1800, New York NY 10019 USA

**Bronson, R Zack** — Football Player
5735 Jackie Lane, Beaumont TX 77713, USA

**Bronstein, Elizabeth** — Producer
Creative Artists Agency, 2000 Ave of Stars, #100, Los Angeles CA 90067 USA

**Brook, Jayne** — Actress
Gersh Agency, 9465 Wilshire Blvd, #600, Beverly Hills CA 90212 USA

**Brook, Kelly** — Model, Actress
Curtis Brown Group, 28-29 Haymarket St, #500, London SW1Y 4SP, England

**Brook, Michael** — Composer
First Artists, 4764 Park Granada, #210, Calabasas CA 91302 USA

**Brook, Peter S P** — Director
C I C T, 37 Bis Blvd de la Chapelle, 75010 Paris, France

**Brook, Robert H** — Physician
1474 Bienvenida Ave, Pacific Palisades CA 90272, USA

**Brooke, Bob** — Ice Hockey Player
2994 Hilltop Dr, Chaska MN 55318, USA

**Brooke, Edward W, III** — Senator, MA
808 Brickell Key Dr, #3204, Miami FL 33131, USA

**Brooke, Jonatha** — Singer (Story), Songwriter
Patrick Rains Assoc, 1255 5th Ave, #7K, New York NY 10029, USA

**Brooke, Paul** — Actor
C D A, 167-169 Kensington High St, London W8 6SH, England

**Brookens, Thomas D (Tom)** — Baseball Player
488 Black Gap Road, Fayetteville PA 17222, USA

**Brooker, Gary** — Singer (Procol Harum), Songwriter
195 Sandycombe Road, Kew TW9 2EW, England

**Brooker, W Thomas (Tommy)** — Football Player
306 Woodridge Dr, Tuscaloosa AL 35406, USA

**Brookes, Harvey** — Physicist
Harvard University, Aiken Computation Laboratory, Cambridge MA 02138, USA

**Brookes, Peter** — Editorial Cartoonist
London Times, Editorial Dept, 1 Pennington St, London E98 1S5, England

**Brooke-Taylor, Tim** — Actor, Comedian
Jill Foster Ltd, 3 Lonsdale Road, London SW13 9ED, England

**Brookhart, Maurice S** — Chemist
University of North Carolina, Chemistry Dept, Chapel Hill NC 27514, USA

**Brooking, Keith H** — Football Player
15400 Emerald Coast Parkway, #1207, Destin FL 32541, USA

**Brookins, Clarence** — Basketball Player
8266 Fayette St, Philadelphia PA 19150, USA

**Brookins, Gary** — Editorial Cartoonist
Richmond Newspapers, Editorial Dept, PO Box 85333, Richmond VA 23293, USA

**Brookner, Anita** — Writer
68 Elm Park Gardens, #6, London SW10 9PB, England

**Brooks, Aaron J** — Basketball Player
Chicago Bulls, United Center, 1901 W Madison St, Chicago IL 60612 USA

**Brooks, Aaron L** — Football Player
1005 Middle Quarter Court, Henrico VA 23238, USA

**Brooks, Albert** — Director, Writer, Actor
W M E Entertainment, 9601 Wilshire Blvd, #300, Beverly Hills CA 90210 USA

**Brooks, Amanda** — Actress
United Agents, 12-26 Lexington St, London W1F 0LE, England

**Brooks, Avery** — Actor
Lynn Coles Productions, PO Box 1918, El Cerrito CA 94530, USA

**Brooks, Barrett** — Football Player
11 Berkshire Dr, #25, Voorhees NJ 08043, USA

**Brooks, Cindy** — Model
Playboy Promotions, 9346 Civic Center Dr, #200, Beverly Hills CA 90210 USA

**Brooks, Clifford (Cliff), Jr** — Football Player
12023 Briar Forest Dr, Houston TX 77077, USA

**Brooks, Conrad** — Actor
PO Box 264, Inwood WV 25428, USA

**Brooks, Danielle** — Actress
Innovative Artists, 1505 10th St, Santa Monica CA 90401 USA

**Brooks, Danny** — Singer (Dovells)
Lustig Talent, PO Box 770850, Orlando FL 32877 USA

**Brooks, Darin L** — Actor
United Talent Agency, U T A Plaza, 9336 Civic Center Dr, Beverly Hills CA 90210 USA

**Brooks, Deanna** — Model, Actress
Playboy Promotions, 9346 Civic Center Dr, #200, Beverly Hills CA 90210 USA

**Brooks, Derrick D** — Football Player
12815 Pacifica Place, Tampa FL 33625, USA

**Bromberg - Brooks**

**Brooks, Diana D** — Businesswoman
Sotheby's Holdings, 1334 York Ave, New York NY 10021, USA
**Brooks, Dolores (Lala)** — Singer (Crystals)
Superstars Unlimited, PO Box 371371, Las Vegas NV 89137, USA
**Brooks, Ed** — Golfer
6604 Augusta Road, Fort Worth TX 76132, USA
**Brooks, Elbert D** — Educator
2820 E 6th St, #128, Tucson AZ 85716, USA
**Brooks, Ethan B** — Football Player
8 Gatewood, Avon CT 06001, USA
**Brooks, Frederick P, Jr** — Mathematician, Computer Scientist
413 Granville Road, Chapel Hill NC 27514, USA
**Brooks, Garth** — Singer, Songwriter
Red Strokes Entertainment, 9465 Wilshire Blvd, #319, Beverly Hills CA 90212, USA
**Brooks, Geraldine** — Writer
PO Box 5056, Vineyard Haven MA 02568, USA
**Brooks, Golden** — Actress
Vincent Cirrincione Assoc, 1516 N Fairfax Ave, Los Angeles CA 90046 USA
**Brooks, Hubert (Hubie)** — Baseball Player
15001 Olive St, Hesperia CA 92345, USA
**Brooks, James L** — Director, Producer, Writer
W M E Entertainment, 9601 Wilshire Blvd, #300, Beverly Hills CA 90210 USA
**Brooks, James R** — Football Player
2876 Sycamore Creek Dr, Independence KY 41051, USA
**Brooks, Jason** — Actor
289 S Robertson Blvd, #424, Beverly Hills CA 90211, USA
**Brooks, Jessica** — Actress
United Agents, 12-26 Lexington St, London W1F 0LE, England
**Brooks, Kevin C** — Football Player
8201 Lighthouse Dr, Rowlett TX 75089, USA
**Brooks, Kimberly A** — Actress
Metropolitan Talent Agency, 5405 Wilshire Blvd, #218, Los Angeles CA 90036 USA
**Brooks, Kimberly D** — Actress
Sutton-Barth Vennari, 5900 Wilshire Blvd, #700, Los Angeles CA 90036 USA
**Brooks, Kix** — Singer (Brooks & Dunn), Songwriter
Team 2 Entertainment, 6345 Balboa Blvd, Building 4, #375, Encino CA 91316, USA
**Brooks, Lawrence L (Larry), Sr** — Football Player, Coach
11200 NE 53rd St, Kirkland WA 98033, USA
**Brooks, Lonnie** — Singer, Guitarist
Alligator Records & Mgmt, PO Box 60234, Chicago IL 60660, USA
**Brooks, Mark** — Golfer
1712 S Adams St, Fort Worth TX 76110, USA
**Brooks, Max** — Writer
Creative Artists Agency, 2000 Ave of Stars, #100, Los Angeles CA 90067 USA
**Brooks, Mehcad** — Actor
Mosiac Media Group, 9200 W Sunset Blvd, #1000, Los Angeles CA 90069 USA
**Brooks, Mel** — Director, Actor, Composer
Brooksfilms, 9336 W Washington Blvd, Culver City CA 90232, USA
**Brooks, Meredith** — Singer, Songwriter, Guitarist
Imago Mgmt, 11400 W Olympic Blvd, #200, Los Angeles CA 90064, USA
**Brooks, Michael (Mike)** — Football Player
716 2nd Ave, Ruston LA 71270, USA
**Brooks, Michael A** — Basketball Player
495 Bethany St, San Diego CA 92114, USA
**Brooks, Nathan** — Boxer
21274 Ellacott Parkway, #M208, Warrensville Heights OH 44128, USA
**Brooks, Randi** — Actress, Model
3205 Evergreen Point Road, Medina WA 98039, USA
**Brooks, Ray** — Actor
Artists Partnership, 101 Finsbury Pavement, London EC2A 1RS, England
**Brooks, Rich** — Football Coach
88725 Sky High Dr, Springfield OR 97478, USA
**Brooks, Richard** — Actor
Greene Assoc, 1901 Ave of Stars, #130, Los Angeles CA 90067 USA
**Brooks, Robert D** — Football Player
8611 N 17th Place, Phoenix AZ 85020, USA
**Brooks, Rodney** — Computer Scientist
Massachusetts Institute of Technology, Computer Science Dept, Cambridge MA 02139, USA
**Brooks, Ross** — Ice Hockey Player
196 Old River Road, #215, Lincoln RI 02865, USA
**Brooks, Scott W (Scottie)** — Basketball Player, Coach
Oklahoma City Thunder, 211 N Robinson Ave, #300, Oklahoma City OK 73102 USA
**Brooks, Terry** — Writer
PO Box 244, 1150 Vienna, Austria
**Brooks, Vincent K (Vince)** — Army General
Commanding General, US Army Pacific, Building T100, Fort Shafter HI 96858 USA
**Brooks, William (Bill), Jr** — Football Player
1088 Laurelwood, Carmel IN 46032, USA
**Brooks, William M (Billy)** — Football Player
313 E Garrett Run, Austin TX 78753, USA
**Broome, David M** — Equestrian
Mount Ballan Manor, Crick, Caldicot, Monmouthshire NP26 XP, Wales
**Broota, Rameshwar** — Artist, Photographer
Triveni Kala Sangam, 205 Tansen Marg, Near Mandi House, New Delhi 110001, India
**Brophy, Kevin** — Actor
15010 Hamlin St, Van Nuys CA 91411, USA
**Brorby, Wade** — Judge
US Court of Appeals, 2120 Capitol Ave, #2131, Cheyenne WY 82001, USA
**Bros, Jose** — Opera Singer
Opera et Concert, 37 Rue de la Chaussee d'Antin, 75009 Paris, France
**Broshears, Robert** — Sculptor
Robert Broshears Studio, 8020 NW Holly Road, Bremerton WA 98312, USA
**Brosius, Scott D** — Baseball Player
1780 NW Troon Court, McMinnville OR 97128, USA
**Broski, David C** — Educator
University of Illinois, President's Office, Chicago IL 60607, USA

# B

| | |
|---|---|
| **Brosnahan, Rachel**<br>Innovative Artists, 1505 10th St, Santa Monica CA 90401 USA | Actress |
| **Brosnan, Pierce**<br>31118 Broad Beach Road, Malibu CA 90265, USA | Actor |
| **Brosnan, Sean**<br>Sages Entertainment Group, 9107 Wilshire Blvd, #450, Beverly Hills CA 90210, USA | Actor |
| **Bross, Michael**<br>1243 Promenade St, Hercules CA 94547, USA | Composer |
| **Brossart, Willy**<br>9318 Susquehanna Trail, Ashland VA 23005, USA | Ice Hockey Player |
| **Brostek, Bern**<br>PO Box 44552, Kamuela HI 96743, USA | Football Player |
| **Broten, Aaron**<br>7488 Long Point Dr NW, Williams MN 56686, USA | Ice Hockey Player |
| **Broten, Neal**<br>N8216 690th St, River Falls WI 54022, USA | Ice Hockey Player |
| **Broten, Paul**<br>2971 Jordan Court, Saint Paul MN 55125, USA | Ice Hockey Player |
| **Broth, Ed**<br>Trident Media Group, 41 Madison Ave, #3600, New York NY 10010, USA | Writer |
| **Brother Ali**<br>Agency Group Ltd, 142 W 57th St, #600, New York NY 10019 USA | Rap Artist |
| **Brotman, Jeffrey**<br>Costco Wholesale Corp, 999 Lake Dr, #200, Issaquah WA 98027, USA | Businessman |
| **Broughton, Willie L**<br>1724 Lacy Lane, Mesquite TX 75181, USA | Football Player |
| **Brouhard, Mark S**<br>6289 Jackie Ave, Woodland Hills CA 91367, USA | Baseball Player |
| **Brouse, Sharon**<br>I K A R, 5870 W Olympic Blvd, Los Angeles CA 90036, USA | Religious Leader, Rabbi |
| **Broussard, Benjamin I (Ben)**<br>8917 Old Lampasas Trail, #14, Austin TX 78750, USA | Baseball Player |
| **Broussard, Israel**<br>Paradigm Agency, 360 N Crescent Dr, North Building, Beverly Hills CA 90210 USA | Actor |
| **Broussard, Marc**<br>Paradigm Agency, 404 W Franklin St, Monterey CA 93940 USA | Singer, Songwriter |
| **Broussard, Rebecca**<br>9911 W Pico Blvd, #PH A, Los Angeles CA 90035, USA | Actress |
| **Browder, Ben**<br>Gersh Agency, 9465 Wilshire Blvd, #600, Beverly Hills CA 90212 USA | Actor |
| **Browder, Felix E**<br>4 Foulet Dr, Princeton NJ 08540, USA | Mathematician |
| **Brower, James R (Jim)**<br>4947 Green Valley Road, Minnetonka MN 55345, USA | Baseball Player |
| **Brown Heritage, Doris**<br>Seattle Pacific College, Athletic Dept, Seattle WA 98119, USA | Track Athlete |
| **Brown, Aaron C**<br>3922 W Robson St, Tampa FL 33614, USA | Football Player |
| **Brown, Alec**<br>Phoenix Suns, 201 E Jefferson St, Phoenix AZ 85004 USA | Basketball Player |
| **Brown, Alex J**<br>Coyote Logistics, 2545 W Diversey Ave, Chicago IL 60647, USA | Football Player |
| **Brown, Alison**<br>Jensen Music International, PO Box 3445, Charlottetown PE C1A 8W5, Canada | Singer, Songwriter, Banjo Player |
| **Brown, Alton**<br>42 West, 220 W 42nd St, #1200, New York NY 10036 USA | Chef |
| **Brown, Amanda**<br>E P Dutton, 375 Hudson St, New York NY 10014 USA | Writer |
| **Brown, Andre L**<br>11245 S Emerald Ave, Chicago IL 60628, USA | Football Player |
| **Brown, Andy**<br>6243 S 125th W, Trafalgar IN 46181, USA | Ice Hockey Player |
| **Brown, Angela**<br>Columbia Artists Mgmt Inc, 5 Columbus Circle, 1790 Broadway, #1600, New York NY 10019 USA | Opera Singer |
| **Brown, Anthony**<br>5565 Mansions Bluffs, #4305, San Antonio TX 78245, USA | Football Player |
| **Brown, Antron**<br>Antron Brown Racing, 1681 E Northfield Drive, #A, Brownsburg IN 46112, USA | Drag Racing Driver, Motorcycle Rider |
| **Brown, Arnie**<br>General Delivery, Woodview ON K0L 3E0, Canada | Ice Hockey Player |
| **Brown, Arthur E, Jr**<br>35 Fairway Winds Place, Hilton Head Island SC 29928, USA | Army General |
| **Brown, Ashley Nicole**<br>Hervey/Grimes Talent, 10561 Missouri Ave, #2, Los Angeles CA 90025 USA | Actress |
| **Brown, Billy**<br>TalentWorks, 3500 W Olive Ave, #1400, Burbank CA 91505 USA | Actor |
| **Brown, Billy Aaron**<br>Stone Manners Salners, 6100 Wilshire Blvd, #1500, Los Angeles CA 90035 USA | Actor |
| **Brown, Billy Ray**<br>7502 Whitman Lane, Sugar Land TX 77479, USA | Golfer |
| **Brown, Blair**<br>Innovative Artists, 1505 10th St, Santa Monica CA 90401 USA | Actress |
| **Brown, Bobby**<br>M E Entertainment, 722 Varsity Road, South Orange NJ 07079, USA | Singer, Dancer, Songwriter |
| **Brown, Brant M**<br>40756 Balch Park Road, Springville CA 93265, USA | Baseball Player |
| **Brown, Brett**<br>Philadelphia 76ers, 1st Union Center, 3601 S Broad St, Philadelphia PA 19148 USA | Basketball Coach |
| **Brown, Brianna**<br>Pakula/King, 9229 W Sunset Blvd, #315, West Hollywood CA 90069 USA | Actress |
| **Brown, Bruce**<br>3858 W Carson St, Torrance CA 90503, USA | Photographer, Surfer |
| **Brown, Bryan**<br>New Town Films, 12/37 Nicholson St, East Balmain NSW 2041, Australia | Actor |
| **Brown, Bryan D (Doug)**<br>Tier 4 Consultng LLC, 13435 Carnoustie Circle, Dade City FL 33525, USA | Army General |

**Brown, Carlinhos**
Tempest Entertainment, 245 W 25th St, #BD, New York NY 10001, USA — Percussionist, Composer
**Brown, Cedric W**
PO Box 23201, Oklahoma City OK 73123, USA — Football Player
**Brown, Chadwick**
SirenSong Entertainment, PO Box 2919, New York NY 10163, USA — Actor
**Brown, Chadwick E (Chad)**
10287 Dowling Way, Littleton CO 80126, USA — Football Player
**Brown, Charles (Charlie)**
3113 Cherry Valley Circle, Fairfield CA 94534, USA — Football Player
**Brown, Charles E**
7676 Ranier Lane N, Osseo MN 55311, USA — Ice Hockey Player
**Brown, Charles E (Charlie)**
7317 S Merrill Ave, Chicago IL 60649, USA — Football Player
**Brown, Christopher M (Chris)**
Tina Davis Co, 96 Linwood Plaza, #454, Fort Lee NJ 07024, USA — Singer, Rap Artist, Actor
**Brown, Christopher R (Chris)**
251 Riverbend Dr, Franklin TN 37064, USA — Football Player
**Brown, Clancy**
I C M Partners, 10250 Constellation Blvd, #900, Los Angeles CA 90067 USA — Actor
**Brown, Clare**
A M Heath Co, 79 Saint Martin's Lane, London WC2N 4RE, England — Writer
**Brown, Clarence (Chucky)**
102 Balsamwood Court, Cary NC 27513, USA — Basketball Player
**Brown, Cleophus**
3912 Sharon Church Road, Pinson AL 35126, USA — Baseball Player
**Brown, Clifton**
Alvin Ailey American Dance Theater, 405 W 55th St, New York NY 10019, USA — Dancer
**Brown, Collier (P J)**
2142 Hampshire Dr, Slidell LA 70461, USA — Basketball Player
**Brown, Cornell D**
1600 Sangloe Place, Lynchburg VA 24502, USA — Football Player
**Brown, Corwin A**
1124 E 90th St, Chicago IL 60619, USA — Football Player
**Brown, Courtney L**
1133 Schurlknight Road, Saint Stephen SC 29479, USA — Football Player
**Brown, Curtis**
467 Carroll St, Sunnyvale CA 94086, USA — Ice Hockey Player
**Brown, Curtis J**
1600 N 2nd St, #A, Saint Charles MO 63301, USA — Football Player
**Brown, Curtis L, Jr**
204 Starrwood, Hudson WI 54016, USA — Astronaut
**Brown, Cynthia G (Cindy)**
Playboy Promotions, 9346 Civic Center Dr, #200, Beverly Hills CA 90210 USA — Model
**Brown, Dale**
Renaissance Literary & Talent, PO Box 17379, Beverly Hills CA 90209, USA — Writer
**Brown, Damone L**
83 Greenfield St, Buffalo NY 14214, USA — Basketball Player
**Brown, Dan**
Atria/Washington Square Press, 1230 Ave of Americas, New York NY 10020, USA — Writer
**Brown, Dave**
Philadelphia Flyers, 1st Union Center, 3601 S Broad St, Philadelphia PA 19148 USA — Ice Hockey Player
**Brown, David M (Dave)**
216 Watchung Fork, Westfield NJ 07090, USA — Football Player
**Brown, David T**
Owings Corning, 1 Owens Corning Parkway, Toledo OH 43659, USA — Businessman
**Brown, Denise Scott**
Venturi Scott Brown Assoc, 4236 Main St, Philadelphia PA 19127, USA — Architect
**Brown, Derek V**
13 Four Leaf Manor, Rexford NY 12148, USA — Football Player
**Brown, Dermal B (Dee)**
2626 Balmoral Court, Kissimmee FL 34744, USA — Baseball Player
**Brown, Donald David**
6511 Abbey View Way, Baltimore MD 21212, USA — Biologist
**Brown, Donald J**
Yale University, Rosencrantz Hall, 28 Hillhouse Ave, New Haven CT 06520, USA — Economist, Mathematician
**Brown, Doug**
3188 Bradway Blvd, Bloomfield Hills MI 48301, USA — Ice Hockey Player
**Brown, Dustin J**
1717 8th St, Manhattan Beach CA 90266, USA — Ice Hockey Player
**Brown, Dwier**
House of Representatives, 1434 6th St, #1, Santa Monica CA 90401 USA — Actor
**Brown, Eddie L**
628 Cedar Park Dr, Daytona Beach FL 32114, USA — Football Player
**Brown, Edward R**
3925 S Jones Blvd, #1011, Las Vegas NV 89103, USA — Cinematographer
**Brown, Emil Q**
18361 Olde Farm Road, Lansing IL 60438, USA — Baseball Player
**Brown, Eric G**
2226 Drake Falls Dr, Pearland TX 77584, USA — Football Player
**Brown, Ewart F, Jr**
Premier's Office, Cabinet Building, 105 Front St, Hamilton HM 12, Bermuda — Prime Minister, Bermuda
**Brown, Faith**
Million Dollar Music Co, 12 Praed Mews, London W2 1QY, England — Actress
**Brown, Foxy**
J L Entertainment, 18653 Ventura Blvd, #340, Los Angeles CA 91356 USA — Rap Artist
**Brown, Fred**
3696 72nd Place SE, Mercer Island WA 98040, USA — Basketball Player, Coach
**Brown, Fred R**
4128 Rigel Ave, Lompoc CA 93436, USA — Football Player
**Brown, G Hanks (Hank)**
Daniels Fund, 101 Monroe St, Denver CO 80206, USA — Senator, CO; Educator
**Brown, Gary L**
1605 Coyote Court, Keller TX 76248, USA — Football Player
**Brown, Georg Stanford**
2565 Greenvalley Road, Los Angeles CA 90046, USA — Actor

**Brown, George R** — Basketball Player
24652 Santa Barbara St, Southfield MI 48075, USA

**Brown, Glenn** — Artist
Gagosian Gallery, 6-24 Britannia St, London WC1X 9JD, England

**Brown, Greg** — Ice Hockey Player
43 Trysting Road, Scituate MA 02066, USA

**Brown, Greg** — Businessman
Motorola Inc, 1303 E Algonquin Blvd, Schaumburg IL 60196, USA

**Brown, Gregory (Greg)** — Football Player
1016 Hartley Court, Sicklerville NJ 08081, USA

**Brown, Guy, III** — Football Player
2233 Forest Hollow Park, Dallas TX 75228, USA

**Brown, H Harold (Hal)** — Baseball Player
4216 Henderson Road, Greensboro NC 27410, USA

**Brown, Harold** — Secretary, Defense
Institute for the Analysis of Global Security, 7811 Montrose Road, #505, Potomac MD 20854, USA

**Brown, Henry** — Actor
1101 E Pike St, #300, Seattle WA 98122, USA

**Brown, Henry Lee** — Baseball Player
4075 N 61st St, Milwaukee WI 53216, USA

**Brown, Henry W** — WW II Army Air Force Hero
2825 Carter Road, #117, Sumter SC 29150, USA

**Brown, Hubie** — Basketball Coach
120 Foxridge Road NW, Atlanta GA 30327, USA

**Brown, Hyman** — Civil Engineer
Colorado State University, Civil Engineering Dept, Box 428, Fort Collins CO 80523, USA

**Brown, Ian A** — Singer, Bassist (Stone Roses)
13 Artists, 11-14 Kensington St, Brighton BN1 4AJ, England

**Brown, Ivory L** — Football Player
9811 Dale Crest Dr, #126, Dallas TX 75220, USA

**Brown, J Gordon** — Prime Minister, England
Prime Minister's Office, 10 Downing St, London SW1A 0AA, England

**Brown, J Kevin** — Baseball Player
105 Browns Ridge, Macon GA 31210, USA

**Brown, James (J B)** — Sportscaster
CBS-TV, Sports Dept, 51 W 52nd St, New York NY 10019 USA

**Brown, James H (J B)** — Football Player
12520 Woodsong Lane, Bowie MD 20721, USA

**Brown, James N (Jim)** — Football Player, Actor
100 Alfred Lerner Way, Cleveland OH 44114, USA

**Brown, James R** — Air Force General
18286 Buccaneer Terrace, Leesburg VA 20176, USA

**Brown, Jamie S** — Football Player
25023 Riding Center Dr, Chantilly VA 20152, USA

**Brown, Jammal F** — Football Player
2223 NE 36th St, Lawton OK 73507, USA

**Brown, Janice Rogers** — Judge
US Court of Appeals, 333 Constitution Ave NW, #4400, Washington DC 20001, USA

**Brown, Jarvis A** — Baseball Player
4201 S Decatur Blvd, #1161, Las Vegas NV 89103, USA

**Brown, Jason** — Figure Skater
24300 Southfield Road, Southfield MI 48075, USA

**Brown, Jason W** — Football Player
8810 Gilly Way, Randallstown MD 21133, USA

**Brown, Jeff** — Ice Hockey Player
800 Tara Oaks Dr, Chesterfield MO 63005, USA

**Brown, Jim Ed** — Singer
Joe Taylor Artist Agency, 2802 Columbine Place, Nashville TN 37204 USA

**Brown, John C** — Football Player
101 Gadshill Place, Pittsburgh PA 15237, USA

**Brown, John Y** — Basketball Player
1523 Oak Forest Dr, Rolla MO 65401, USA

**Brown, John Y, Jr** — Governor, KY
1990 Fort Harrods Dr, Lexington KY 40503, USA

**Brown, Jonathan Daniel** — Actor
I C M Partners, 10250 Constellation Blvd, #900, Los Angeles CA 90067 USA

**Brown, Julie** — Actress, Comedienne, Singer
11288 Ventura Blvd, #728, Studio City CA 91604, USA

**Brown, Julie (Downtown)** — Actress, Producer
Independent Management Group, 8444 Wilshire Blvd, #500, Beverly Hills CA 90211, USA

**Brown, Julie Caitlin** — Actress, Singer
2109 S Wilbur Ave, Walla Walla WA 99362, USA

**Brown, June** — Actress
Associated International Mgmt, 7 Hatton Garden, #400, London EC1N 8AD, England

**Brown, Junior** — Singer, Guitarist
Paradigm Agency, 124 12th Ave S, #410, Nashville TN 37203, USA

**Brown, Keith** — Ice Hockey Player
8515 Woodland Brooke Trail, Cumming GA 30028, USA

**Brown, Kenneth J** — Labor Leader
Graphic Communications International Union, 1900 L St NW, #800, Washington DC 20036, USA

**Brown, Kevin L** — Baseball Player
10400 Wolfinger Road, Mount Vernon IN 47620, USA

**Brown, Kimberly J** — Actress
Gemstone Talent, 27943 Seco Canyon Road, #212, Los Angeles CA 91350, USA

**Brown, Kristopher C (Kris)** — Football Player
712 Holly St, Bellaire TX 77401, USA

**Brown, Kwame** — Basketball Player
7685 Veragua Dr, Playa del Rey CA 90293, USA

**Brown, Larry** — Football Player
1377 Glencoe Ave, Pittsburgh PA 15205, USA

**Brown, Larry L** — Baseball Player
13158 La Mirada Circle, Wellington FL 33414, USA

**Brown, Larry, Jr** — Football Player
5603 Sycamore Dr, Colleyville TX 76034, USA

**Brown, Lawrence (Larry), Jr** — Football Player
4390 Parliament Place, #A, Lanham MD 20706, USA

**Brown - Brown**

**Brown, Lawrence H (Larry)** — Basketball Player, Coach, Executive
1030 Green Valley Road, Bryn Mawr PA 19010, USA
**Brown, Lester R** — Ecologist
Worldwatch Institute, 1776 Massachusetts Ave NW, #800, Washington DC 20036, USA
**Brown, Lomas, Jr** — Football Player
5049 Elizabeth Lake Road, Waterford MI 48327, USA
**Brown, Marc** — Artist, Writer
Little Brown, 3 Center Plaza, #100, Boston MA 02108 USA
**Brown, Marcia Joan** — Writer
165 Avenida Majorca, #B, Laguna Hills CA 92637, USA
**Brown, Mark A** — Football Player
2761 SW 81st Way, Davie FL 33328, USA
**Brown, Mark N** — Astronaut
80 Earlsgate Road, Dayton OH 45440, USA
**Brown, Markel** — Basketball Player
Brooklyn Nets, 15 Metro Tech Center, #1100, Brooklyn NY 11201 USA
**Brown, Marty** — Singer, Guitarist
PO Box 190515, Nashville TN 37219, USA
**Brown, Matthew B (Matt)** — Baseball Player
11259 N Cutlass St, Hayden ID 83835, USA
**Brown, Max** — Actor
United Agents, 12-26 Lexington St, London W1F 0LE, England
**Brown, Melanie J** — Singer (Spice Girls)
Paradigm Agency, 360 N Crescent Dr, North Building, Beverly Hills CA 90210 USA
**Brown, Michael (Mike)** — Basketball Player
304 Rays Mill Road, Aberdeen NC 28315, USA
**Brown, Michael C (Mike)** — Baseball Player
2904 E Minton St, Mesa AZ 85213, USA
**Brown, Michael D** — Government Official
OnScreen Technologies, 600 NW 14th Ave, Portland OR 97209, USA
**Brown, Michael E (Mike)** — Astronomer
California Institute of Technology, Geological & Planetary Sciences Division, Pasadena CA 91125, USA
**Brown, Michael G (Mike)** — Baseball Player
710 95th Ave N, Naples FL 34108, USA
**Brown, Michael S** — Nobel Medicine Laureate
5719 Redwood Lane, Dallas TX 75209, USA
**Brown, Miguel** — Singer
International Artists, PO Box 32, Grave 5369 AA, Netherlands
**Brown, Mike** — Football Executive
Cincinnati Bengals, 1 Paul Brown Stadium, Cincinnati OH 45202 USA
**Brown, Nancy E** — Navy Admiral
Director, Communications & Computers, Joint Staff, Pentagon, Washington DC 20310 USA
**Brown, Neil, Jr** — Actor
Pantheon Talent, 1801 Century Park E, #1910, Los Angeles CA 90067, USA
**Brown, Norman** — Singer, Guitarist
A P A Talent & Literary Agency, 405 S Beverly Dr, #300, Beverly Hills CA 90212 USA
**Brown, Olivia** — Actress
Bill Rogin Mgmt, 427 N Canon Dr, #215, Beverly Hills CA 90210, USA
**Brown, Ollie L** — Baseball Player
8462 Country Club Dr, Buena Park CA 90621, USA
**Brown, Orlando** — Actor
Abrams Artists, 9200 W Sunset Blvd, #1125, West Hollywood CA 90069 USA
**Brown, Oscar L** — Baseball Player
19113 Gunlock Ave, Carson CA 90746, USA
**Brown, Patricia** — Baseball Player
821 Solar Lane, Glenview IL 60025, USA
**Brown, Patrick** — Biochemist
Stanford University Medical School, Biochemistry Dept, Stanford CA 94305, USA
**Brown, Patrick (Sleepy)** — Singer, Songwriter
J Erving Group, 555 Whitehall St SW, #N, Atlanta GA 30303, USA
**Brown, Paul** — Jazz Guitarist
Chapman & Co Mgmt, PO Box 55246, Sherman Oaks CA 91413, USA
**Brown, Peter** — Actor
Special Artists Agency, 9200 Sunset Blvd, #410, West Hollywood CA 90069 USA
**Brown, Peter R L** — Historian
Princeton University, History Dept, Princeton NJ 08544, USA
**Brown, Philip** — Actor
8721 W Sunset Blvd, #200, West Hollywood CA 90069, USA
**Brown, Pieta** — Singer, Guitarist, Songwriter
Blind Ambition Mgmt, 6 Courthouse Way, Jonesboro GA 30236, USA
**Brown, Preston M** — Football Player
6804 Jones Valley Dr SE, Huntsville AL 35802, USA
**Brown, R Anthony B (Tony), Jr** — Football Player
PO Box 7122, Branson MO 65615, USA
**Brown, R Hanbury** — Astronomer
White Cottage, Penton Mewsey, Andover, Hampshire SP11 0RQ, England
**Brown, Ralph, III** — Football Player
9395 Old Post Dr, Rancho Cucamonga CA 91730, USA
**Brown, Randy** — Basketball Player
Chicago Bulls, United Center, 1901 W Madison St, Chicago IL 60612 USA
**Brown, Raymond M** — Football Player
4936 Lake Fjord Pass, Marietta GA 30068, USA
**Brown, Reggie V** — Football Player
1325 Oxford Lane, Union NJ 07083, USA
**Brown, Rhyon Nicole** — Actress
HeyGurl, 335 E Albertoni St, Carson CA 90746, USA
**Brown, Richard S** — Football Player
5652 Alfred Ave, Westminster CA 92683, USA
**Brown, Rita Mae** — Writer, Social Activist
Wendy Weill Agency, 232 Madison Ave, New York NY 10016, USA
**Brown, Rob** — Ice Hockey Player
5204 84th St, Edmonton AB T6E 5N8, Canada
**Brown, Robert (Rob)** — Actor
W M E Entertainment, 9601 Wilshire Blvd, #300, Beverly Hills CA 90210 USA
**Brown, Robert A** — Chemical Engineer, Educator
Boston University, President's Office, 1 Sherborn St, Boston MA 02215, USA

# B

**Brown, Robert B** — Army General
Commanding General, I Corps, Joint Base Lewis-McChord WA 98433, USA

**Brown, Robert D** — Businessman
Milacron Inc, 2090 Florence Ave, Cincinnati OH 45206, USA

**Brown, Robert E (Bob)** — Football Player
PO Box 211081, Saint Louis MO 63121, USA

**Brown, Robert S (Bob)** — Football Player
1628 Fairmont Dr, San Leandro CA 94578, USA

**Brown, Robert W (Bobby)** — Baseball Player, Executive
4100 Clark Ave, Fort Worth TX 76107, USA

**Brown, Roger Aaron** — Actor
Innovative Artists, 1505 10th St, Santa Monica CA 90401 USA

**Brown, Roger L** — Football Player
9 N Point Dr, Portsmouth VA 23703, USA

**Brown, Rogers L (Bobby)** — Baseball Player
112 Avonlea Dr, Chesapeake VA 23322, USA

**Brown, Ron J** — Football Player, Track Athlete
2212 Radcourt Dr, Hacienda Heights CA 91745, USA

**Brown, Ronald K** — Choreographer, Dance Executive
Evidence, 80 Hanson Place, #605, Brooklyn NY 11217, USA

**Brown, Ronnie G, Jr** — Football Player
3445 Stratford Road NE, #3707, Atlanta GA 30326, USA

**Brown, Ruben** — Football Player
170 Fox Meadow Lane, Orchard Park NY 14127, USA

**Brown, Rupert A** — Educator
Boston University, President's Office, 1 Silber Way, Boston MA 02215, USA

**Brown, Ryan** — Actor
Side by Side Literary Productions, 15 W 26th St, #200, New York NY 10010, USA

**Brown, Sandra** — Writer
1306 W Abram St, Arlington TX 76013, USA

**Brown, Sara Suzanne** — Actress
Media Artists Group, 8222 Melrose Ave, #203, Los Angeles CA 90048 USA

**Brown, Sheldon D** — Football Player
6 Tuxedo Court, Marlton NJ 08053, USA

**Brown, Shirley** — Singer
Rodgers Redding, PO Box 4603, Macon GA 31208 USA

**Brown, Sophina** — Actress
Peter Strain, 5455 Wilshire Blvd, #1812, Los Angeles CA 90036 USA

**Brown, Sterling K** — Actor
Innovative Artists, 1505 10th St, Santa Monica CA 90401 USA

**Brown, Steve** — Football Player
2207 Osage St, Saint Louis MO 63118, USA

**Brown, Susan** — Actress
Hamilton Hodell, 20 Golden Square, London W1F 9JL, England

**Brown, T Edward (Ted)** — Football Player
7320 130th St W, Saint Paul MN 55124, USA

**Brown, T Graham** — Singer
Cody Entertainment, PO Box 456, Winchester VA 22604, USA

**Brown, Terry L** — Football Player
401 N 6th St, Marlow OK 73055, USA

**Brown, Theotis, II** — Football Player
9604 W 121st Terrace, Overland Park KS 66213, USA

**Brown, Thomas A (Timmy)** — Football Player
505 S Farrell Dr, #E28, Palm Springs CA 92264, USA

**Brown, Thomas M (Tommy)** — Baseball Player
8119 Shady Place, Brentwood TN 37027, USA

**Brown, Thomas W (Tom)** — Football, Baseball Player
27981 Nanticoke Road, Salisbury MD 21801, USA

**Brown, Timothy D (Tim)** — Football Player
1107 W Pleasant Run Road, De Soto TX 75115, USA

**Brown, Tom** — Football Player
679 Aldford Ave, Delta BC V3M 5P5, Canada

**Brown, Trisha** — Choreographer, Dancer
Trisha Brown Dance Co, 341 W 38th St, #8L, New York NY 10018, USA

**Brown, Troy F** — Football Player
PO Box 452, Foxboro MA 02035, USA

**Brown, Vincent B** — Football Player
PO Box 71268, Henrico VA 23255, USA

**Brown, W Earl** — Actor
Greene Assoc, 1901 Ave of Stars, #130, Los Angeles CA 90067 USA

**Brown, Wayne** — Ice Hockey Player
50 Montgomery Blvd, Belleville ON K8N 1H9, Canada

**Brown, William D (Bill)** — Football Player
9365 Libby Lane, Eden Prairie MN 55347, USA

**Brown, William F (Willie)** — Football Player, Coach
27138 Lillegard Court, Tracy CA 95304, USA

**Brown, Yvette Nicole** — Actress
Kazarian/Measures/Ruskin, 11969 Ventura Blvd, #300, Studio City CA 91604 USA

**Brown, Zac** — Singer, Guitarist
Roar Mgmt, 9701 Wilshire Blvd, #800, Beverly Hills CA 90212, USA

**Browne, Byron E** — Baseball Player
2831 S 83rd Dr, Tolleson AZ 85353, USA

**Browne, Chris** — Cartoonist (Hagar the Horrible)
King Features Syndicate, 300 W 57th St, #1500, New York NY 10019 USA

**Browne, Gerald** — Writer
Warner Books, 1271 6th Ave, New York NY 10020, USA

**Browne, Gordon W (Gordie)** — Football Player
1001 Lakeridge Court, Colleyville TX 76034, USA

**Browne, Herbert A, Jr** — Navy Admiral
A F C E A International, 4400 Fair Lakes Court, #104, Fairfax VA 22033, USA

**Browne, Jackson** — Singer, Songwriter
Donald Miller Mgmt, 12746 Kling St, Studio City CA 91604, USA

**Browne, Jann** — Singer
Tracy Gershon Mgmt, PO Box 158400, Nashville TN 37215, USA

**Browne, Jerome A (Jerry)** — Baseball Player
2102 Company St, #1, Christiansted VI 00820, USA

*Brown - Browne*

Browne, Leslie — Ballerina, Actress
2025 Broadway, #6F, New York NY 10023, USA
Browne, Olin — Golfer
9562 SE Sandpine Lane, Hobe Sound FL 33455, USA
Browner, Carol M — Government Official
White House, 1600 Pennsylvania Ave NW, Washington DC 20500, USA
Browner, Jimmie L (Jim) — Football Player
3369 Peachtree Corners Circle, Norcross GA 30092, USA
Browner, Joey M — Football Player
PO Box 22721, Saint Paul MN 55122, USA
Browner, Keith T — Football Player
5017 Chesley Ave, Los Angeles CA 90043, USA
Browner, Ross — Football Player
7900 Indian Springs Dr, Nashville TN 37221, USA
Brown-Findlay, Jessica — Actress
Troika, 74 Clerkenwell Road, #300, London EC1M 5QA, England
Browning Chris — Actor
Don Buchwald Talent Agency, 6500 Wilshire Blvd, #2200, Los Angeles CA 90048 USA
Browning, David (Dave) — Football Player
10117 S Lambs Lane, Mica WA 99023, USA
Browning, Edmond L — Religious Leader
5164 Imai Road, Hood River OR 97031, USA
Browning, Emily — Actress
Signpost Mgmt, 1641 Ivar Ave, Los Angeles CA 90028, USA
Browning, Kurt — Figure Skater
International Management Group, 175 Bloor St E, #400S, Toronto ON M4W 3R8, Canada
Browning, Logan — Actress, Singer
Kazarian/Measures/Ruskin, 11969 Ventura Blvd, #300, Studio City CA 91604 USA
Browning, Ricou — Actor
5221 SW 196th Lane, Southwest Ranches FL 33332, USA
Browning, Thomas L (Tom) — Baseball Player
1110 Grindstone Court, Union KY 41091, USA
Brownlee, Alistair E — Triathlete
23 Manor Road N, Esher Surrey KT10 0AA, England
Brownlee, Don — Astronomer
University of Washington, Astronomy Dept, PO Box 351580, Seattle WA 98195, USA
Brownlee, Jonathan — Triathlete
Leeds Metropolitan University, Carnegie High Performance Center, Leeds LS1 3HE, England
Brownlee, Lawrence — Opera Singer
I M G Artists, Hogarth Business Park, Chiswick, London W4 2TH, England
Brownlee, Shannon — Writer
New America Foundation, 1899 L St NW, #400, Washington DC 20036 20036, USA
Brown-Miller, Lisa — Ice Hockey Player
Olympic Committee, 1 Olympic Plaza, Building 6, Colorado Springs CO 80909 USA
Brownmiller, Susan — Social Activist
61 Jane St, New York NY 10014, USA
Brownschidle, Jack — Ice Hockey Player
35 Hidden Pines Court, East Amherst NY 14051, USA
Brownstein, Carrie — Singer, Guitarist (Sleater-Kinney)
High Road Touring, 751 Bridgeway, #200, Sausalito CA 94965 USA
Broza, David — Singer, Songwriter
Gold Village Entertainment, 72 Madison Ave, #800, New York NY 10016, USA
Brozer, Kim — Golfer
2700 N 16th St, Beaumont TX 77703, USA
Brubaker, Charles W — Architect
82 Essex Road, Winnetka IL 60093, USA
Brubaker, Ed — Cartoonist, Writer
United Talent Agency, U T A Plaza, 9336 Civic Center Dr, Beverly Hills CA 90210 USA
Brubaker, Jeff — Ice Hockey Player
1827 Oak Ridge Road, #A, Oak Ridge NC 27310, USA
Bruce Bruce — Actor, Comedian
I C M Partners, 10250 Constellation Blvd, #900, Los Angeles CA 90067 USA
Bruce, Aundray — Football Player
1730 Wentworth Dr, Montgomery AL 36106, USA
Bruce, Christopher — Choreographer
Rambert Dance Co, 94 Chiswick High Road, London W4 1SH, England
Bruce, David — Ice Hockey Player
975 Grand Blvd, Bellingham WA 98229, USA
Bruce, Dylan — Actor
Resolution, 1801 Century Park E, #2300, Los Angeles CA 90067 USA
Bruce, Ed — Singer
1022 16th Ave S, Nashville TN 37212, USA
Bruce, Isaac I — Football Player
PO Box 550141, Fort Lauderdale FL 33355, USA
Bruce, Lorraine — Actress
Curtis Brown Group, 28-29 Haymarket St, #500, London SW1Y 4SP, England
Bruce, Robert J (Bob) — Baseball Player
800 E 15th St, #207, Plano TX 75074, USA
Bruce, Thomas E (Tom) — Swimmer
122 Sea Terrace Way, Aptos CA 95003, USA
Bruckheimer, Jerry — Producer
Jerry Bruckheimer Films, 1631 10th St, Santa Monica CA 90404, USA
Bruckner, Agnes — Actress
A P A Talent & Literary Agency, 405 S Beverly Dr, #300, Beverly Hills CA 90212 USA
Bruckner, Greg — Golfer
3906 E Potter Dr, Phoenix AZ 85050, USA
Bruckner, Leslie C (Les) — Football Player
1325 Valley View Road, #307, Glendale CA 91202, USA
Brudzinski, Robert L (Bob) — Football Player
4607 Gleneagles Dr, Boynton Beach FL 33436, USA
Brue, Robert A (Bobby) — Golfer
5699 N Centerpark Way, #414, Milwaukee WI 53217, USA
Brueckner, Keith A — Physicist
7723 Ludington Place, La Jolla CA 92037, USA
Brueggemann, Walter — Theologian
701 S Columbia Dr, Decatur GA 30030, USA

**Brueggergosman - Brunner**

**Brueggergosman, Measha** — Opera Singer
I M G Artists, Hogarth Business Park, Chiswick, London W4 2TH, England
**Bruel, Patrick** — Singer, Actor
Voyez Mon Agent, 20 Ave Rapp, 75007 Paris, France
**Brueland, Lowell K** — WW II Army Air Corps Hero
420 La Z Acres Road, Westminster SC 29693, USA
**Bruen, John D** — Army General, Businessman
6104 Greenlawn Court, Springfield VA 22152, USA
**Bruener, Mark F** — Football Player
19860 NE 133rd St, Woodinville WA 98077, USA
**Bruening, Justin** — Actor
Innovative Artists, 1505 10th St, Santa Monica CA 90401 USA
**Bruer, Robert A (Bob)** — Football Player
2406 Oakridge Road, Stillwater OK 55082, USA
**Bruetti, Dana** — Producer
Creative Artists Agency, 2000 Ave of Stars, #100, Los Angeles CA 90067 USA
**Bruford, Bill** — Drummer (U K, Yes)
Ted Kurland, 173 Brighton Ave, Boston MA 02134 USA
**Brugge, Joan S** — Cell Biologist
Harvard Medical School, Cell Biology Dept, 240 Longwood Ave, Boston MA 02115, USA
**Brugge, Pieter Jan** — Director
Innovative Artists, 1505 10th St, Santa Monica CA 90401 USA
**Bruggen, Frans** — Concert Recorder Player, Flutist
Askonas Holt, Lincoln House, 300 High Holborn, London WC1V 7JH, England
**Bruggink, Eric G** — Judge
US Claims Court, 717 Madison Place NW, Washington DC 20439, USA
**Bruguera, Sergi** — Tennis Player
C'Escipion 42, 08023 Barcelona, Spain
**Bruhl, Daniel** — Actor
Players Agentur Mgmt, Sophienstr 21, 10178 Berlin, Germany
**Bruininks, Robert H** — Educator
University of Minnesota, Humphries Institute, Saint Paul MN 55104, USA
**Brukner, Caslav** — Physicist
Quantum Foundations Theory, Boltzmanngasse 5, 1090 Vienna, Austria
**Brumfield, Jacob D** — Baseball Player
208 Wrights Mill Circle NE, Atlanta GA 30324, USA
**Brumfield, Scott** — Football Player
1150 E 900 S, Spanish Fork UT 84660, USA
**Brumfield-White, Dolores (Dolly)** — Baseball Player
1604 Millcreek Dr, Arkadelphia AR 71923, USA
**Brumley, A Michael (Mike)** — Baseball Player
112 Corral Dr, Keller TX 76244, USA
**Brumm, Donald D (Don)** — Football Player
511 County Road 442, New Franklin MO 65274, USA
**Brummer, Glenn E** — Baseball Player
1830 Dalton Dr, Belleville IL 62226, USA
**Brummer, Renate L** — Astronaut, Germany
Global Systems Division, 325 Broadway, Boulder CO 80305, USA
**Brumwell, Murray** — Ice Hockey Player
3036 Lloyd Mangrum Lane, Billings MT 59106, USA
**Brunansky, Thomas A (Tom)** — Baseball Player
15444 Harrow Lane, Poway CA 92064, USA
**Brunckhorst, Natja** — Actress
Above the Line, Wielandstr 5, 10625 Berlin, Germany
**Brundage, Howard D** — Publisher
RR 2 Box 332-47, Old Lyme CT 06371, USA
**Brundage, Jackson** — Actor
Kazarian/Measures/Ruskin, 11969 Ventura Blvd, #300, Studio City CA 91604 USA
**Brundage, Jennifer** — Softball Player
4487 Augusta Court, Ann Arbor MI 48108, USA
**Brundige, William G (Bill)** — Football Player
40 Corbett St, Salem VA 24153, USA
**Brundy, Stanley D (Stan)** — Basketball Player
4644 Stephen Girard Ave, New Orleans LA 70126, USA
**Brunell, Mark A** — Football Player
3861 Ortega Blvd, Jacksonville FL 32210, USA
**Brunelli, Samuel A (Sam)** — Football Player
1080 Wisconsin Ave NW, #104W, Washington DC 20007, USA
**Bruner, Jack C (Teel)** — Football Player
518 Oak, Kamiah ID 83536, USA
**Bruner, Michael L (Mike)** — Swimmer
339 Garcia Ave, Half Moon Bay CA 94019, USA
**Brunet, Robert P (Bob)** — Football Player
149 Aspen Square, Denham Springs LA 70726, USA
**Brunet, Yasmine** — Model
One Mgmt, 42 Bond St, #200, New York NY 10012 USA
**Brunette, Andrew** — Ice Hockey Player
2392 Morgan Ave N, Stillwater MN 55082, USA
**Brunetti, Dana** — Producer
Creative Artists Agency, 2000 Ave of Stars, #100, Los Angeles CA 90067 USA
**Bruney, Brian A** — Baseball Player
1471 SW Pine Dr, Warrenton OR 97146, USA
**Bruney, Fred** — Football Player, Coach
800 Mountain Creek Trace NW, Atlanta GA 30328, USA
**Brungardt, Kurt** — Physical Fitness Trainer, Writer
Trident Media Group, 41 Madison Ave, #3600, New York NY 10010, USA
**Bruni Tedeschi, Valeria** — Actress
Carol Levi Mgmt, Via Giuseppe Pisanelli 2, 00196 Rome, Italy
**Bruni, Emily** — Actress
Markham Froggatt Irwin, Julian House, 4 Windmill St, London W1P 1HF, England
**Bruni-Sarkozy, Carla** — Model, Singer, Songwriter
Zzo Talent, 8 Rue Royale, 75008 Paris, France
**Brunkhorst, Brian J** — Basketball Player
6182 Brumder Dr, Hartland WI 53029, USA
**Brunner, Jerome S** — Psychologist
200 Mercer St, New York NY 10012, USA

| | |
|---|---|
| **Bruno, Chris**<br>S D B Partners, 315 S Beverly Dr, #411, Beverly Hills CA 90067 USA | Actor, Producer, Director |
| **Bruno, Dylan**<br>Gersh Agency, 41 Madison Ave, #3301, New York NY 10010 USA | Actor |
| **Bruno, Gioia**<br>T-Best Talent Agency, 508 Honey Lake Court, Danville CA 94506 USA | Singer (Expose), Songwriter |
| **Bruns, George W**<br>16 E Poplar St, Floral Park NY 11001, USA | Basketball Player |
| **Brunson, Larry R**<br>6104 E Peakview Place, Centennial CO 80111, USA | Football Player |
| **Bruntlett, Eric K**<br>4445 Montecito Ave, Santa Rosa CA 95404, USA | Baseball Player |
| **Brupbacher, Ross A**<br>200 Pembroke Lane, Lafayette LA 70508, USA | Football Player |
| **Bruschi, Tedy L**<br>31 Jeffrey Dr, North Attleboro MA 02760, USA | Football Player |
| **Bruske, James S (Jim)**<br>5242 N Quail Run Place, Paradise Valley AZ 85253, USA | Baseball Player |
| **Bruskin, Grisha**<br>236 W 26th St, #705, New York NY 10001, USA | Artist, Sculptor |
| **Bruson, Renato**<br>Columbia Artists Mgmt Inc, 5 Columbus Circle, 1790 Broadway, #1600, New York NY 10019 USA | Opera Singer |
| **Brusstar, Warren S**<br>3320 Redwood Road, Napa CA 94558, USA | Baseball Player |
| **Brustein, Robert S**<br>Harvard University, Loeb Drama Center, 64 Brattle St, Cambridge MA 02138, USA | Educator, Producer, Critic |
| **Bruton, John G**<br>Dail Eireann, Leinster House, Dublin 2, Ireland | Prime Minister, Ireland |
| **Bruvel, Gil**<br>PO Box 2843, Wimberley TX 78676, USA | Artist |
| **Bry, Ellen**<br>Media Artists Group, 8222 Melrose Ave, #203, Los Angeles CA 90048 USA | Actress |
| **Bryan, Alan**<br>University of Alberta, Archaeology Dept, Edmonton AB T6G 2J8, Canada | Archaeologist |
| **Bryan, David**<br>Bon Jovi Mgmt, 809 Elder Circle, Austin TX 78733, USA | Keyboardist (Bon Jovi) |
| **Bryan, Donald S**<br>108 Ridgewood Dr, Euless TX 76039, USA | WW II Army Air Corps Hero |
| **Bryan, James**<br>Chris Smith Mgmt, 21 Camden St, #500, Toronto ON M5V 1V2, Canada | Fiddler |
| **Bryan, Luke**<br>Red Light Mgmt, 124 12th Ave, #600, Nashville TN 37203, USA | Singer, Guitarist, Songwriter |
| **Bryan, Mark**<br>FishCo Mgmt, 2519 Devine Street  Columbia SC 29205, USA | Guitarist (Hootie & the Blowfish) |
| **Bryan, Michael C (Mike)**<br>PO Box 91, Bailey MI 49303, USA | Tennis Player |
| **Bryan, Richard H**<br>Lionel Sawyer Collins, Bank America Plaza, 300 S 4th St, Las Vegas NV 89101, USA | Governor, Senator, NV |
| **Bryan, Robert C (Bob)**<br>PO Box 91, Bailey MI 49303, USA | Tennis Player |
| **Bryan, Sabrina**<br>Puravida Enterprises, 2480 Corinth Ave, #3, Los Angeles CA 90064, USA | Actress, Singer (Cheetah Girls) |
| **Bryan, William K (Billy)**<br>3408 Creekwood Dr, Tuscaloosa AL 35453, USA | Football Player |
| **Bryan, William R (Billy)**<br>3001 Hickory Lane, Opelika AL 36801, USA | Baseball Player |
| **Bryan, Wright**<br>3747 Peachtree Road NE, #516, Atlanta GA 30319, USA | Journalist |
| **Bryan, Zachary Ty**<br>Vision Entertainment Group, 4404 Riverside Dr, #200, Toluca Lake CA 91505, USA | Actor |
| **Bryant Clark, Rosalyn**<br>3901 Somerset Dr, Los Angeles CA 90008, USA | Track Athlete |
| **Bryant, Anita**<br>Blackwood Mgmt, PO Box 5331, Sevierville TN 37864, USA | Social Activist, Singer |
| **Bryant, Bart H**<br>Professional Golfer's Assn, PO Box 109601, Palm Beach Gardens FL 33410, USA | Golfer |
| **Bryant, Bobby L**<br>13437 Lochrin Lane, Sylmar CA 91342, USA | Football Player |
| **Bryant, Bradley D (Brad)**<br>900 Mulberry Bush Court, Orlando FL 32828, USA | Golfer |
| **Bryant, Clara**<br>Paradigm Agency, 360 N Crescent Dr, North Building, Beverly Hills CA 90210 USA | Actress |
| **Bryant, Desmond D (Dez)**<br>Dallas Cowboys, 1 Cowboys Parkway, Irving TX 75063 USA | Football Player |
| **Bryant, Edward E (Junior), Jr**<br>2906 S 102nd St, Omaha NE 68124, USA | Football Player |
| **Bryant, Emmette (Em)**<br>PO Box 6229, Chicago IL 60680, USA | Basketball Player |
| **Bryant, Fernando A**<br>2336 Emerald Dr, Jonesboro GA 30236, USA | Football Player |
| **Bryant, Jeffrey D (Jeff)**<br>2665 Tilson Road, Decatur GA 30032, USA | Football Player |
| **Bryant, Joseph A (Red)**<br>Jacksonville Jaguars, 1 AllTel Stadium Place, Jacksonville FL 32202 USA | Football Player |
| **Bryant, Joseph W (Joe)**<br>1835 N 72nd St, Philadelphia PA 19151, USA | Basketball Player, Coach |
| **Bryant, Joy**<br>Resolution, 1801 Century Park E, #2300, Los Angeles CA 90067 USA | Actress, Model |
| **Bryant, Karyn**<br>Serendipity Entertainment, 9107 Wilshire Blvd, #400, Beverly Hills CA 90210, USA | Actress, Producer, Commentator |
| **Bryant, Kelvin L**<br>701 E Church St, Tarboro NC 27886, USA | Football Player |
| **Bryant, Kobe B**<br>Los Angeles Lakers, Staples Center, 1111 S Figueroa St, Los Angeles CA 90015 USA | Basketball Player |
| **Bryant, Mark C**<br>3300 Everett Dr, Edmond OK 73013, USA | Basketball Player |

| | |
|---|---|
| **Bryant, Robert L** <br> Duke University, Math-Science Research Institute, Box 90220, Durham NC 27708, USA | Mathematician |
| **Bryant, S Matt** <br> 5689 Legends Club Circle, Braselton GA 30517, USA | Football Player |
| **Bryant, Sharon** <br> Betty of Troy, 15 Meritoria Dr, East Williston NY 11596, USA | Singer (Atlantic Starr) |
| **Bryant, Stephen (Steve)** <br> 3602 George Washington Lane, Missouri City TX 77459, USA | Football Player |
| **Bryant, Tony** <br> 2351 Sombrero Blvd, Marathon FL 33050, USA | Football Player |
| **Bryant, Trent B** <br> 4801 S Tierney Dr, Independence MO 64055, USA | Football Player |
| **Bryars, R Gavin** <br> Schott Co, 48 Great Marlborough St, London W1V 2BN, England | Composer |
| **Bryce, Quentin A L** <br> Governor General's Office, Government House, Canberra ACT 2600, Australia | Governor General, Australia |
| **Bryce, Scott** <br> Don Buchwald Talent Agency, 6500 Wilshire Blvd, #2200, Los Angeles CA 90048 USA | Actor |
| **Brydon, Rob** <br> United Agents, 12-26 Lexington St, London W1F 0LE, England | Actor, Comedian |
| **Brye, Stephen R (Steve)** <br> 621 S Spring St, #603, Los Angeles CA 90014, USA | Baseball Player |
| **Bryers, Paul** <br> Bloomsbury Publishing, 50 Bedford Square, London WC1B 3DP, England | Writer |
| **Brylin, Sergei** <br> 32 Robert Dr, Short Hills NJ 07078, USA | Ice Hockey Player |
| **Bryson, A Shawn** <br> 418 Heatherstone Dr, Franklin NC 28734, USA | Football Player |
| **Bryson, David** <br> Geffen Records, 10900 Wilshire Blvd, #1000, Los Angeles CA 90024 USA | Singer, Guitarist (Counting Crowes) |
| **Bryson, Jim** <br> What Mgmt, 906A Logan Ave, Toronto ON M4K 3E4, Canada | Singer, Songwriter |
| **Bryson, Peabo** <br> A P A Talent & Literary Agency, 405 S Beverly Dr, #300, Beverly Hills CA 90212 USA | Singer, Songwriter |
| **Bryson, William Curtis** <br> US Appeals Court, 717 Madison Place NW, Washington DC 20439, USA | Judge |
| **Bryzgalov, Ilya N** <br> 4092 Santa Anita Lane, Yorba Linda CA 92886, USA | Ice Hockey Player |
| **Brzeska, Magdalena** <br> Vitesse Karcher GmbH, Porscestr 6, 70736 Fellbach, Germany | Rhythmic Gymnast |
| **Brzezinski, Douglas G (Doug)** <br> 329 Greenhill Way, Silver Spring MD 20904, USA | Football Player |
| **Brzezinski, Zbigniew** <br> Strategic/International Studies Center, 1800 K NW, #400, Washington DC 20006, USA | Government Official, Educator |
| **Buanne, Patrizio** <br> Agency Group Ltd, 142 W 57th St, #600, New York NY 10019 USA | Singer |
| **Buatta, Mario** <br> 120 E 80th St, New York NY 10075, USA | Interior Designer |
| **Bubas, Vic** <br> 12960 Crescent Green, #104, Midlothian VA 23114, USA | Basketball Player, Coach |
| **Bubka, Sergei N** <br> Olympic Committee, 39-41 Khoryva St, 04071 Kiiev, Ukraine | Track Athlete |
| **Bubla, Jiri** <br> 405-1050 Bowron Crescent, North Vancouver BC V7H 2X7, Canada | Ice Hockey Player |
| **Buble, Michael** <br> Creative Artists Agency, 2000 Ave of Stars, #100, Los Angeles CA 90067 USA | Singer, Songwriter |
| **Bucannon, Deone A** <br> Arizona Cardinals, PO Box 888, Phoenix AZ 85001 USA | Football Player |
| **Bucatinsky, Dan** <br> Creative Artists Agency, 2000 Ave of Stars, #100, Los Angeles CA 90067 USA | Actor |
| **Buccellato, Benedetta** <br> Carol Levi Mgmt, Via Giuseppe Pisanelli 2, 00196 Rome, Italy | Actress |
| **Bucchieri, Stephen** <br> Bucchieri Architects, 2026 Murray Hill, Cleveland,OH 44106, USA | Architect |
| **Bucha, Paul W** <br> 822 N Salem Road, Ridgefield CT 06877, USA | Vietnam War Army Hero (CMH) |
| **Buchan, William Carl** <br> 826 Evergreen Point Road, Medina WA 98039, USA | Yachtsman |
| **Buchan, William Eastman** <br> 7100 NE 42nd St, Bellevue WA 98004, USA | Yachtsman |
| **Buchanan, Brian J** <br> 136 Steeple Circle, Jupiter FL 33458, USA | Baseball Player |
| **Buchanan, Edna** <br> PO Box 403556, Miami Beach FL 33140, USA | Journalist |
| **Buchanan, Ian** <br> TalentWorks, 3500 W Olive Ave, #1400, Burbank CA 91505 USA | Actor, Model |
| **Buchanan, Isobel** <br> Marks Mgmt, 14 New Burlington St, London W1X 1FF, England | Opera Singer |
| **Buchanan, J Robert** <br> 19 Shipway Place, Charlestown MA 02129, USA | Physician |
| **Buchanan, Jeff** <br> 220 Cedar Ave, Hershey PA 17033, USA | Ice Hockey Player |
| **Buchanan, Jensen** <br> Paradigm Agency, 360 N Crescent Dr, North Building, Beverly Hills CA 90210 USA | Actress |
| **Buchanan, John M** <br> 56 Meriam St, Lexington MA 02420, USA | Biochemist |
| **Buchanan, Ken** <br> 45 Marmion Road, Greenfaulds, Cumbernaul G67 4AN, Scotland | Boxer |
| **Buchanan, Lachlan** <br> 8203 Blackburn Ave, #D, Los Angeles CA 90048, USA | Actor |
| **Buchanan, Patrick J (Pat)** <br> 8233 Old Courthouse Road, #200, Vienna VA 22182, USA | Commentator, Government Official |
| **Buchanan, Raymond L (Ray)** <br> 2423 Strand Ave, Lawrenceville GA 30043, USA | Football Player |
| **Buchanan, Ron** <br> 200 Telluride Trail, Ruidoso NM 88345, USA | Ice Hockey Player |

**Buchanan, Simone** — Actress
McMahon Mgmt, 2/24 Brereton St, South Brisbane QED 4101, Australia
**Buchanan, Thomas (Tom)** — Educator
University of Wyoming, President's Office, 1000 E University Ave, Laramie WY 82071, USA
**Buchanon, Phillip D** — Football Player
6425 Emerald Pines Circle, Fort Myers FL 33966, USA
**Buchanon, Willie J** — Football Player
2742 Mesa Dr, Oceanside CA 92054, USA
**Buchberger, Kelly** — Ice Hockey Player
Edmonton Oilers, 11230 110th St, Edmonton AB T5G 3H7, Canada
**Buchek, Gerald P (Jerry)** — Baseball Player
123 Royal Vista Dr, #502, Branson MO 65616, USA
**Buchel, Marco** — Alpine Skier
Ramschwagweg 55, 9496 Balzers, Switzerland
**Buchholz, Clay D** — Baseball Player
630 King Oaks St, Lumberton TX 77657, USA
**Buchholz, Taylor** — Baseball Player
194 Powell Road, Springfield PA 19064, USA
**Buchli, James F (Jim)** — Astronaut
14761A Innerarity Point Road, Pensacola FL 32507, USA
**Buchmann, Rainer** — Auto Racing Executive
Project Indy, 434 E Main St, Brownsburg IN 46112, USA
**Buchwald, Ephraim** — Religious Leader, Rabbi
National Jewish Outreach, 989 Ave of Americas, #1000, New York NY 10018, USA
**Buchwald, Stephen L** — Chemist
Massachusetts Institute of Technology, Chemistry Dept, Cambridge MA 02139, USA
**Buck 65** — Rap Artist
Agency Group Ltd, 142 W 57th St, #600, New York NY 10019 USA
**Buck, Chris** — Writer, Director, Animator
Newhouse/Porter/Hubbard, 333 S Hope St, #4000, Los Angeles CA 90071, USA
**Buck, Craig** — Volleyball Player
9611 Burberry Lane, Highlands Ranch CO 80129, USA
**Buck, Jason O** — Football Player
4797 Vista Dr, Highland UT 84003, USA
**Buck, Joe** — Sportscaster
18 Upper Warson Road, Saint Louis MO 63124, USA
**Buck, John E** — Sculptor
11229 Cottonwood Road, Bozeman MT 59718, USA
**Buck, Jonathan R (John)** — Baseball Player
15068 Desert Eagle Circle, Riverton UT 84065, USA
**Buck, Linda B** — Nobel Medicine Laureate
14295 Sherwood Road NW, Seattle WA 98177, USA
**Buck, Mike E** — Football Player
269 Matthews Road, Oakdale NY 11769, USA
**Buck, Peter** — Businessman
Subway Restaurants, 325 Bic Dr, Milford CT 06461, USA
**Buck, Peter L** — Guitarist (REM)
REM/Athens Ltd, 170 College Ave, Athens GA 30601, USA
**Buck, Scott** — Producer
Creative Artists Agency, 2000 Ave of Stars, #100, Los Angeles CA 90067 USA
**Buck, Tara** — Actress
C E S D, 10635 Santa Monica Blvd, #130, Los Angeles CA 90025 USA
**Buck, Travis G** — Baseball Player
1443 W Roadrunner Dr, Chandler AZ 85286, USA
**Buck, Vincent L (Vince)** — Football Player
1005 Vintage Dr, Kenner LA 70065, USA
**Buckens, Celine** — Actress
Creative Artists Agency, 2000 Ave of Stars, #100, Los Angeles CA 90067 USA
**Buckey, Jay C, Jr** — Astronaut
1 Sargent St, Hanover NH 03755, USA
**Buckfield, Clare** — Actress
Associated International Mgmt, 7 Hatton Garden, #400, London EC1N 8AD, England
**Buckhalter, Correll** — Football Player
2614 Broadway Dr, Trophy Club TX 76262, USA
**Buckhalter, Joseph (Joe)** — Basketball Player
3900 Rose Hill Ave, #201A, Hanover NH 03755, USA
**Buckingham, Amyand D** — Chemist
Crossways, 23 The Ave, Newmarket CB8 9AA, England
**Buckingham, Gregory (Greg)** — Swimmer
338 Ridge Road, San Carlos CA 94070, USA
**Buckingham, Lindsey** — Guitarist, Singer (Fleetwood Mac)
Front Line Mgmt, 1100 Glendon Ave, #2000, Los Angeles CA 90024 USA
**Buckinghams** — Pop, Rock Music Group
PO Box 220082, Great Neck NY 11022, USA
**Buckland, Jonathan M (Jonny)** — Guitarist (Coldplay)
Paradigm Agency, 360 N Crescent Dr, North Building, Beverly Hills CA 90210 USA
**Buckley, A J** — Actor
Thruline Entertainment, 9250 Wilshire Blvd, #100, Beverly Hills CA 90212 USA
**Buckley, Andy** — Actor
Coronel Group, 1100 Glendon Ave, #1700, Los Angeles CA 90046, USA
**Buckley, Betty L** — Actress, Singer, Director
Parseghian/Planco, 388 2nd Ave, #506, New York, NY 10010 USA
**Buckley, Carol** — Elephant Conservationist
Elephant Sanctuary, PO Box 393, Hohenwald TN 38462, USA
**Buckley, Curtis L** — Football Player
2208 Cantura Dr, Mesquite TX 75181, USA
**Buckley, D Terrell** — Football Player
19106 S Gardenia Ave, Weston FL 33332, USA
**Buckley, Dan** — Publisher
Marvel Comics, Publisher's Office, 417 5th Ave, New York NY 10016, USA
**Buckley, David** — Composer
Kraft-Engel Mgmt, 15233 Ventura Blvd, #200, Sherman Oaks CA 91403 USA
**Buckley, Dick** — Director
I C M Partners, 10250 Constellation Blvd, #900, Los Angeles CA 90067 USA
**Buckley, George** — Businessman
Minnesota Mining & Manufacturing, 3-M Center, Saint Paul MN 55144, USA

# B

| | |
|---|---|
| **Buckley, James L**<br>PO Box 597, Sharon CT 06069, USA | Senator, NY; Judge |
| **Buckley, Jean**<br>143 Monarch Dr, Fortuna CA 95540, USA | Baseball Player |
| **Buckley, Jerome H**<br>52 Waverley St, Belmont MA 02478, USA | Educator |
| **Buckley, Marcus W**<br>240 Yukon Court, Weatherford TX 76087, USA | Football Player |
| **Buckley, Richard E**<br>310 W 55th St, #1K, New York NY 10019, USA | Conductor |
| **Buckley, Robert E**<br>W M E Entertainment, 9601 Wilshire Blvd, #300, Beverly Hills CA 90210 USA | Actor |
| **Buckley, Roy**<br>6900 Lee Road, Westerville OH 43081, USA | Bowler |
| **Buckman, Phil**<br>S M S Talent, 8383 Wilshire Blvd, #230, Beverly Hills CA 90211 USA | Actor |
| **Buckner, Cleveland**<br>19227 S Grandee Ave, Carson CA 90746, USA | Basketball Player |
| **Buckner, Gregory D (Greg)**<br>4129 Catawba Ave, Carrollton TX 75010, USA | Basketball Player |
| **Buckner, Pam**<br>645 Utah St, Reno NV 89506, USA | Bowler |
| **Buckner, Paul E**<br>2322 Rockwood Ave, Eugene OR 97405, USA | Sculptor |
| **Buckner, Shelley**<br>Baker Winokur Ryder Public Relations, 9100 Wilshire Blvd, #500W, Beverly Hills CA 90212 USA | Actress |
| **Buckner, W Quinn**<br>857 Valencia Blvd, Irving TX 75039, USA | Basketball Player, Coach |
| **Buckner, William J (Bill)**<br>4405 E Wild Horse Lane, Boise ID 83712, USA | Baseball Player |
| **Bucknor, C B**<br>46 Midwood St, Brooklyn NY 11225, USA | Baseball Umpire |
| **Buckson, David P**<br>60 Exchange Dr, Camden Wyoming DE 19934, USA | Governor, DE |
| **Buckwheat Zydeco**<br>Ted Fox Mgmt, PO Box 561, Rhinebeck NY 12572, USA | Singer, Accordionist |
| **Bucyk, John P (Chief)**<br>17 Boren Lane, Boxford MA 01921, USA | Ice Hockey Player |
| **Budaj, Peter**<br>10140 Ridgegate Circle, Lone Tree CO 80124, USA | Ice Hockey Player |
| **Budarin, Nikolai M**<br>Cosmonaut Training Center, Star City, 141160 Zvezdny Gorodok, Moscow Oblast, Russia | Cosmonaut |
| **Budd Pieterse, Zola**<br>Coastal Carolina University, Athletic Dept, Myrtle Beach CA 29578, USA | Track Athlete |
| **Budd, David L (Dave)**<br>40 N Woodland Ave, Woodbury NJ 08096, USA | Basketball Player |
| **Budd, Harold**<br>Opal/Warner Bros Records, 6834 Camrose Dr, Los Angeles CA 90068, USA | Composer, Writer |
| **Budd, Jersey**<br>Agency Group Ltd, 361-373 City Road, London EC1V 1PQ, England | Singer, Songwriter |
| **Budd, Julie**<br>Herb Bernstein Mgmt, 180 W End Ave, #2A, New York NY 10023, USA | Actress, Singer |
| **Budde, Brad E**<br>5121 W 159th Terrace, Stilwell KS 66085, USA | Football Player |
| **Budde, Edward L (Ed)**<br>5121 W 159th Terrace, Stilwell KS 66085, USA | Football Player |
| **Budden, Joseph A (Joe), II**<br>I C M Partners, 10250 Constellation Blvd, #900, Los Angeles CA 90067 USA | Rap Artist, Songwriter |
| **Buddie, Michael J (Mike)**<br>157 Scottsdale Dr, Advance NC 27006, USA | Baseball Player |
| **Buddon, Joseph A (Joe), II**<br>I C M Partners, 10250 Constellation Blvd, #900, Los Angeles CA 90067 USA | Rap Artist |
| **Budig, Eugene A (Gene)**<br>5 Sandwedge Lane, Isle of Palms SC 29451, USA | Baseball Executive, Educator |
| **Budig, Rebecca**<br>A P A Talent & Literary Agency, 405 S Beverly Dr, #300, Beverly Hills CA 90212 USA | Actress |
| **Budimir, Zivko**<br>President's Office, Marsala Titz 7, 71000 Sarajevo, Bosnia & Herzegovina | President, Bosnia-Herzegovia |
| **Budko, Walter (Walt)**<br>7 Drumlin Dr, Morris Plains NJ 07950, USA | Basketball Player, Coach |
| **Budness, William W (Bill)**<br>401 Huckle Hill Road, Bernardston MA 01337, USA | Football Player |
| **Buechele, Steven B (Steve)**<br>1104 Arlena Dr, Arlington TX 76012, USA | Baseball Player |
| **Buechler, John Carl**<br>12031 Vose, #19-21, North Hollywood CA 91605, USA | Director |
| **Buehler, George S**<br>201 E Grant Line Road, #16, Tracy CA 95376, USA | Football Player |
| **Buehler, Judson D (Jud)**<br>1515 West Lane, Del Mar CA 92014, USA | Basketball Player |
| **Buehler, Rachel**<br>1571 Luneta Drive, Del Mar CA 92014, USA | Soccer Player |
| **Buehrle, Mark A**<br>51 Long Cove Dr, Lemont IL 60439, USA | Baseball Player |
| **Buell, Bebe**<br>International Management Group, 767 5th Ave, New York NY 10153, USA | Model, Singer, Actress |
| **Buell, Garett**<br>Breen Agency, 25 Music Square W, Nashville TN 37203, USA | Percussionist (Caedmon's Call) |
| **Bueno, Maria E**<br>TV Global, Rua Evandro Carlos de Andrade 160, Vila Cordeiro, Sao Paulo SP 04583 115, Brazil | Tennis Player |
| **Buffa, Dudley W**<br>William Morrow Publishers, 1350 Ave of Americas, New York NY 10019 USA | Writer |
| **Buffenbarger, R Thomas**<br>International Machinists Assn, 9000 Machinists Place, Upper Marlboro MD 20772, USA | Labor Leader |
| **Buffer, Michael**<br>Buffer Enterprises, 131 Fleet St, Marina del Rey CA 90292, USA | Boxing Commentator |

Buckley - Buffer

**Buffett, Jimmy** — Singer, Songwriter
Margaritaville, 424 Flemming St, #A, Key West FL 33040, USA
**Buffett, Warren E** — Businessman
Berkshire Hathaway, 1440 Kiewit Plaza, 3555 Farnam St, Omaha NE 68131, USA
**Buffkins, Archie Lee** — Performing Arts Administrator
Kennedy Center, Executive Suite, 2700 F St NW, Washington DC 20566, USA
**Buffone, Douglas J (Doug)** — Football Player
1272 W Lexington St, Chicago IL 60607, USA
**Bufman, Zev** — Producer
520 Brickell Key Dr, #612, Miami FL 33131, USA
**Buford, Damon J** — Baseball Player
5055 W Ray Road, #2, Chandler AZ 85226, USA
**Buford, Donald A (Don)** — Baseball Player
15412 Valley Vista Blvd, Sherman Oaks CA 91403, USA
**Buford, Jason (Brooks)** — Rap Artist
50 Murray St, #415, New York NY 10007, USA
**Buford, Maury A** — Football Player
2901 Sweet Briar St, Grapevine TX 76051, USA
**Bugg, Jake** — Singer, Songwriter
Kitchenware Records, 7 Stables, Saint Thomas St, Newcastle upon Tyne NE1 4LE, England
**Buggs, Daniel (Danny)** — Football Player
3186 Evans Mill Road, Lithonia GA 30038, USA
**Buggy, Regina** — Field Hockey Player
550 Limekiln Road, Oley PA 19547, USA
**Bugliosi, Vincent T** — Attorney, Writer
663 Arbor St, Pasadena CA 91105, USA
**Bugner, Joe** — Boxer
22 Buckingham St, Surrey Hills NSW 2010, Australia
**Bugnon, Alex** — Jazz Pianist, Composer
Entertainment Consultants, 1207 Penshurst Court, Abingdon MD 21009, USA
**Buhari, Muhammadu** — President, Nigeria; Army General
G R A, PO Box 2010, Daura, Katsina State, Nigeria
**Buhler, Urs** — Singer (Il Divo)
Octagon, 81-83 Fulham High St, London SW6 3JW, England
**Buhner, Jay C** — Baseball Player
3219 300th Ave SE, Fall City WA 98024, USA
**Bujnoch, Glenn** — Football Player
7598 Fairway Glen Dr, Cincinnati OH 45248, USA
**Bujold, Genevieve** — Actress
C C A Mgmt, Garden Level, 32 Charlwood St, London SW1V 2DY, England
**Bujold, Lois McMaster** — Writer
184 Peninsula Road, Minneapolis MN 55441, USA
**Buker, Heinz** — Canoeing Athlete
Hofgewann 10, 55624 Bollenbach, Germany
**Bukic, Perica** — Water Polo Player
Hercegovacka 59, 10000 Zagreb, Croatia
**Bukich, Rudolph A (Rudy)** — Football Player
7910 Ivanhoe Ave, #333, La Jolla CA 92037, USA
**Bukin, Andrei A** — Ice Dancer
Skating Federation, Lucjneskraia Nab 8, 119871 Moscow, Russia
**Buktenica, Raymond** — Actor
Special Artists Agency, 9200 Sunset Blvd, #410, West Hollywood CA 90069 USA
**Bukvich, Ryan A** — Baseball Player
200 Apple Blossom Circle, Brandon MS 39047, USA
**Bulaich, Norman B (Norm)** — Football Player
421 Lynndale Court, Hurst TX 76054, USA
**Bulatov, Erik** — Artist
Arndt Gallery, Potsdamer Str 96, 10785 Berlin, Germany
**Bulatovic, Andjela** — Handball Player
Z R L Buducnost, Ivana Milutinovica B B, 81000 Podgorica, Montenegro
**Bulatovic, Katarina** — Handball Player
C S Oltchim Ramnicu Valcea, Str Uzinel #1, 240007 Ramnicu Valcea, Romania
**Bulbrook, Anna** — Violist (Airborne Toxic Event)
Island Def Jam Records, 8920 W Sunset Blvd, #200, West Hollywood CA 90069 USA
**Bulger, Jason** — Baseball Player
1898 Harbour Oaks Dr, Snellville GA 30078, USA
**Bulger, Marc R** — Football Player
2701 S Lindbergh Blvd, Saint Louis MO 63131, USA
**Bulifant, Joyce** — Actress
301 Red Tail Court, Basalt CO 81621, USA
**Bulimar, Diana** — Gymnast
C S Dinamo Bucharest, Soseaua Stefan cel Mare 7-9, 020121 Bucharest, Romania
**Bulis, Jan** — Ice Hockey Player
Vancouver Canucks, 800 Griffiths Way, Vancouver BC V6B 6G1, Canada
**Buljubasic, Ivan** — Water Polo Player
Vaterpolski Klub Primorje Rijeka, Podkoludricu 2, 51000 Rijeka, Croatia
**Buljung, Erich** — Marksman
7570 Stampede Dr, Colorado Springs CO 80920, USA
**Bull, Ronald D (Ronnie)** — Football Player
15 Redspire Court, Bolingbrook IL 60490, USA
**Bullard, Matthew G (Matt)** — Basketball Player
10 Balmoral Place, Spring TX 77382, USA
**Bullard, Mike** — Ice Hockey Player
1170 Shillington Ave, Ottawa ON K1Z 7Z4, Canada
**Bullet, Scott D** — Baseball Player
218 Vicky Bullett St, Martinsburg WV 25404, USA
**Bullinger, James E (Jim)** — Baseball Player
2504 Elise Ave, Metairie LA 70003, USA
**Bullinger, Kirk M** — Baseball Player
3608 David Dr, Metairie LA 70003, USA
**Bullington, Bryan P** — Baseball Player
20116 Oakwood Dr, Mokena IL 60448, USA
**Bullins, Ed** — Writer
Northeastern University, English Dept, Boston MA 02115, USA
**Bullo, Nicole** — Ice Hockey Player
H C Lugano, Casekka Postale 4226, 6904 Lugano, Switzerland

| | |
|---|---|
| **Bulloch, Jeremy** | Actor |
| Fett Photos, 10 Birchwood Road, London SW17 9BQ, England | |
| **Bullock, Bruce J** | Ice Hockey Player |
| 5226 W Redbird Road, Phoenix AZ 85083, USA | |
| **Bullock, Eric J** | Baseball Player |
| 17503 Harwick Court, Carson CA 90746, USA | |
| **Bullock, Jim J** | Actor |
| Connor Ankrum & Associates, 1680 Vine St, #1016, Los Angeles CA 90028, USA | |
| **Bullock, Reggie** | Basketball Player |
| Los Angeles Clippers, Staples Center, 1111 S Figueroa St, Los Angeles CA 90015 USA | |
| **Bullock, Sandra** | Actress |
| Creative Artists Agency, 2000 Ave of Stars, #100, Los Angeles CA 90067 USA | |
| **Bullock, Susan** | Opera Singer |
| Harrison/Parrott, 5-6 Albion Court, London W6 0QT, England | |
| **Bulluck, Keith J** | Football Player |
| 874 Nialta Lane, Brentwood TN 37027, USA | |
| **Bumbeck, David A** | Artist |
| 435 Farmers Dell Lane, Deltaville VA 23043, USA | |
| **Bumbry, Alonzo B (Al)** | Baseball Player |
| 28 Tremblant Court, Lutherville MD 21093, USA | |
| **Bumbry, Grace** | Opera Singer |
| I M G Artists, Carnegie Hall Tower, 152 W 57th St, #500, New York NY 10019 USA | |
| **Bump, Dennis** | Mathematician |
| Stanford University, Mathematics Dept, Stanford CA 94305, USA | |
| **Bump, J D** | Sculptor |
| Onda Gallery, 220 A Ave, 104, Lake Oswego OR 97034, USA | |
| **Bumpass, Rodger** | Actor |
| W M E Entertainment, 9601 Wilshire Blvd, #300, Beverly Hills CA 90210 USA | |
| **Bumpers, Dale L** | Governor, Senator, AR |
| 12723 Hunters Field Road, Little Rock AR 72211, USA | |
| **Bunch, Melvin L** | Baseball Player |
| 12 Tyler Lane, Hooks TX 75561, USA | |
| **Bund, Karlheinz** | Businessman |
| Huyssenallee 82-84, 45128 Essen Ruhr, Germany | |
| **Bundchen, Gisele** | Model, Actress |
| I M G Models, 304 Park Ave S, #PH N, New York NY 10010 USA | |
| **Bundy, Brooke** | Actress |
| 1801 Ave of Stars, #1250, Los Angeles CA 90067, USA | |
| **Bundy, Laura Bell** | Actress, Singer |
| Sanctuary Mgmt, 15301 Ventura Blvd, Building B, Sherman Oaks CA 91403, USA | |
| **Bunetta, Bill** | Bowler |
| 1176 E San Bruno Ave, Fresno CA 93710, USA | |
| **Bunin, Michael** | Actor |
| Circle Talent, 433 N Camden Dr, #400, Beverly Hills CA 90210 USA | |
| **Bunker, Wallace E (Wally)** | Baseball Player |
| 622 E Coeur D'Alene Ave, Coeur D'Alene ID 83814, USA | |
| **Bunkley, Brodrick** | Football Player |
| New Orleans Saints, 5800 Airline Highway, Metairie LA 70003 USA | |
| **Bunkowsky-Scherbak, Barb** | Golfer |
| 8725 Marlamoor Lane, West Palm Beach FL 33412, USA | |
| **Bunnell, Dewey** | Singer, Guitarist (America) |
| Morey Mgmt, 1100 Glendon Ave, #1100, Los Angeles CA 90024, USA | |
| **Bunnett, Joseph F** | Chemist |
| 608 Arroyo Seca, Santa Cruz CA 95060, USA | |
| **Bunning, James P D (Jim)** | Senator, KY; Baseball Player |
| 4 Fairway Dr, Southgate KY 41071, USA | |
| **Bunting, Eve** | Writer |
| 1512 Rose Villa St, Pasadena CA 91106, USA | |
| **Bunting, John S** | Football Player, Coach |
| 134 Soundview Dr, Hampstead NC 28443, USA | |
| **Bunting, William C (Bill)** | Basketball Player |
| 11000 Pacer Court, Raleigh NC 27614, USA | |
| **Bunton, Emma L** | Singer (Spice Girls) |
| Hall of Nothing, Poplar Mews, Uxbridge Road, London W12 7JS, England | |
| **Bunz, Dan** | Football Player |
| 4230 Rocklin Road, #2, Rocklin CA 95677, USA | |
| **Bunzow, John** | Singer, Songwriter |
| T K O Artist Mgmt, 2303 21st Ave S, #300, Nashville TN 37212, USA | |
| **Buoniconti, Nicholas A (Nick)** | Football Player, Businessman |
| 445 Grand Bay Dr, #803, Key Biscayne FL 33149, USA | |
| **Buono, Cara** | Actress |
| C E S D, 257 Park Ave S, #950, New York NY 10010 USA | |
| **Burba, David A (Dave)** | Baseball Player |
| 378 N Shore Lane, Gilbert AZ 85233, USA | |
| **Burba, Edwin H, Jr** | Army General |
| 256 Montrose Dr, McDonough GA 30253, USA | |
| **Burbank, Daniel C (Dan)** | Astronaut |
| 364 Route 6A, Yarmouth Port MA 02675, USA | |
| **Burbidge, E Margaret P** | Astronomer |
| 423 Washington St, #600, San Francisco CA 94111, USA | |
| **Burbules, Peter G** | Army General |
| 8287 Chestnut Point Lane, Hayes VA 23072, USA | |
| **Burch, Paul** | Singer |
| Silverleaf Booking, 589 W 1st St, Boiling Springs PA 17007, USA | |
| **Burch, Rick** | Bassist (Jimmy Eat World) |
| S A M, 722 Seward St, Los Angeles CA 90038, USA | |
| **Burch, Tory** | Fashion Designer |
| 11 W 19th St, #400, New York, NY 10011, USA | |
| **Burcham, David W** | Educator |
| Loyola Marymount University, President's Office, Loyola Marymount University Dr, Los Angeles CA 90045, USA | |
| **Burchfiel, Burrell C** | Geologist |
| 9 Robinson Park, Winchester MA 01890, USA | |
| **Burchuladze, Paata** | Opera Singer |
| Askonas Holt, Lincoln House, 300 High Holborn, London WC1V 7JH, England | |
| **Burckhalter, Joseph H** | Inventor (Florescent Dyes) |
| 734 Green Valley Lane, Melbourne FL 32940, USA | |

**Burckle, Caroline** — Swimmer
Premier Management Group, 115 Crescent Commons, #250, Cary, NC 27518 USA
**Burd, Steven A** — Businessman
Safeway Inc, 5918 Stoneridge Mall Road, Pleasanton CA 94588, USA
**Burden, Luther D (Ticky)** — Basketball Player
4332 Grove Ave, #C, Winston Salem NC 27105, USA
**Burden, William** — Singer
Opus 3 Artists, 470 Park Ave S, #900N, New York NY 10016 USA
**Burdette, Mallory** — Tennis Player
105 Winter Chase Lane, Brunswick GA 31520, USA
**Burdick, Clinton D** — WW II Army Air Corps Hero
1134 26th St, #4, Santa Monica CA 90403, USA
**Burditt, Joyce** — Writer
Jeff Ross Entertainment, 14560 Benefit St, #206, Sherman Oaks CA 91403, USA
**Burdon, Eric** — Singer (Animals, War); Songwriter
Lustig Talent, PO Box 770850, Orlando FL 32877 USA
**Bure, Pavel V** — Ice Hockey Player
11091 Redhawk St, Plantation FL 33324, USA
**Bure, Valeri V** — Ice Hockey Player
237 Monte Grigio Dr, Pacific Palisades CA 90272, USA
**Burfeindt, Betty** — Golfer
70 San Simeon Place, Rancho Mirage CA 92270, USA
**Burford, Christopher W (Chris)** — Football Player
1215 Broken Feather Court, Reno NV 89511, USA
**Burg, Mark** — Producer
Evolution Entertainment, 901 N Highland Ave, Los Angeles CA 90038 USA
**Burgee, John H** — Architect
Perelanda Farm, Skunks Misery Road, Millerton NY 12546, USA
**Burger, Leslie** — Association Executive, Librarian
Princeton Public Library, 65 Witherspoon St, Princeton NJ 08542, USA
**Burger, Neil** — Director, Writer
Creative Artists Agency, 2000 Ave of Stars, #100, Los Angeles CA 90067 USA
**Burgess, Adrian** — Mountaineer
324 G St, Anderson SC 29625, USA
**Burgess, Albert A (Sonny)** — Singer, Guitarist, Songwriter
AristoMedia, PO Box 22765, Nashville TN 37202, USA
**Burgess, Christian** — Actor
33 Gastein Road, London W6 8LT, England
**Burgess, Derrick L** — Football Player
New England Patriots, 1 Patriot Place, Foxboro MA 02035 USA
**Burgess, Don** — Cinematographer
Gersh Agency, 9465 Wilshire Blvd, #600, Beverly Hills CA 90212 USA
**Burgess, Mitchell** — Writer, Producer
I C M Partners, 10250 Constellation Blvd, #900, Los Angeles CA 90067 USA
**Burgess, Neil** — Electrical Engineer
201 E 5th St, #2200, Cincinnati OH 45202, USA
**Burgess, Ronald L, Jr** — Army General
Director, Defense Intelligence Agency, Pentagon, Washington DC 20340 USA
**Burgess, Timothy A (Tim)** — Singer (Charlatans)
Solo Agency, 53-55 Fulham High St, #200, London SW6 3JJ, England
**Burghard, Maria** — Actress
Angentur Retzlaff, Kurfuerstenstra 34, 10785 Berlin, Germany
**Burghoff, Gary** — Actor
Scott Stander Assoc, 4533 Van Nuys Blvd, #401, Sherman Oaks CA 91403 USA
**Burgi, Richard W** — Actor
1019 Baja St, Laguna Beach CA 92651, USA
**Burgmeier, Thomas H (Tom)** — Baseball Player
13118 Walmer St, Leawood KS 66209, USA
**Burhoe, Ralph Wendell** — Templeton Religion Laureate
Montgomery Place, 5550 S South Shore Dr, #715, Chicago IL 60637, USA
**Buribayev, Alan** — Conductor
I M G Artists, Hogarth Business Park, Chiswick, London W4 2TH, England
**Buring, MyAnna** — Actress
Artists Partnership, 101 Finsbury Pavement, London EC2A 1RS, England
**Burka, Petra** — Figure Skater
Skate Canada, 865 Shefford Road, Ottawa ON K1J 1H9, Canada
**Burkart, Phil, Jr** — Drag Racing Driver
Phil Burkart Racing, 114 Oriskany Blvd, Yorkville NY 13495, USA
**Burke Charvet, Brooke** — Actress, Model
Bx2 Mgmt, 1333 2nd St, #620, Santa Monica CA 90401, USA
**Burke Hederman, Lynn** — Swimmer
26 White Oak Tree Road, Syosset NY 11791, USA
**Burke, Alfonso C (Trey), III** — Basketball Player
Utah Jazz, Energy Solutions Arena, 301 W South Temple, Salt Lake City UT 84101 USA
**Burke, Bernard F** — Physicist, Astrophysicist
10 Bloomfield St, Lexington MA 02421, USA
**Burke, Billy** — Actor
Ellen Meyer Entertainment, 8899 Beverly Blvd, #616, Los Angeles CA 90048, USA
**Burke, Cheryl B** — Dancer
Cheryl Burke Dance, 1400 N Shoreline Blvd, #A1, Mountain View CA 94043, USA
**Burke, Chris** — Actor
Abrams Artists, 9200 W Sunset Blvd, #1125, West Hollywood CA 90069 USA
**Burke, Christopher A (Chris)** — Baseball Player
15415 Crystal Springs Way, Louisville KY 40245, USA
**Burke, Clement (Clem)** — Drummer (Blondie)
Agency Group Ltd, 142 W 57th St, #600, New York NY 10019 USA
**Burke, David** — Actor
Stone Manners Salners, 6100 Wilshire Blvd, #1500, Los Angeles CA 90035 USA
**Burke, Delta** — Actress
Shelter Entertainment, 9255 Sunset Blvd, #300, Los Angeles CA 90069 USA
**Burke, Doris** — Sportscaster
ABC-TV, Sports Dept, 77 W 66th St, New York NY 10023 USA
**Burke, James** — Commentator
Henley House, Terrace Barnes, London SW13 0NP, England
**Burke, James E (Jamie)** — Baseball Player
374 W Lilburn Ave, Rosenburg OR 97470, USA

| | |
|---|---|
| **Burke, James Lee**<br>Simon & Schuster, 1230 Ave of Americas, Concourse 1, New York NY 10020, USA | Writer |
| **Burke, Jan**<br>12437 Seal Beach Blvd, #101, Seal Beach CA 90740, USA | Writer |
| **Burke, Jim**<br>Ad Hominem Enterprises, 506 Santa Monica Blvd, #400, Santa Monica CA 90401, USA | Producer, Actor |
| **Burke, John J (Jack), Jr**<br>5602 Glen Pines Dr, Houston TX 77069, USA | Golfer |
| **Burke, Kathy**<br>Hatton McEwan, 3 Chocolate Studios, 7 Shepherdess Place, London N1 7LJ, England | Actress |
| **Burke, Kelly**<br>Playboy Promotions, 9346 Civic Center Dr, #200, Beverly Hills CA 90210 USA | Model |
| **Burke, Kelly H**<br>803 Choctaw Lane, Shalimar FL 32579, USA | Air Force General |
| **Burke, Kevin**<br>Consolidated Edison, 4 Irving Place, New York NY 10003, USA | Businessman |
| **Burke, Leo P**<br>3395 Torrey Pines Circle, Riner VA 24149, USA | Baseball Player |
| **Burke, Michael Reilly**<br>Domain Talent, 9229 W Sunset Blvd, #710, West Hollywood CA 90069 USA | Actor |
| **Burke, Phil**<br>Lisa Richards Agency, 108 Upper Leeson St, Dublin 4, Ireland | Actor |
| **Burke, Raymond L Cardinal**<br>Apostolic Signatura, Palazzo della Cancelleria, Piazza della Cancelleria 1, 00185 Rome, Italy | Religious Leader |
| **Burke, Robert John**<br>Equitable Stewardship for Artists, 10317 Jefferson Blvd, Culver City CA 90232, USA | Actor |
| **Burke, Sean**<br>9016 N 60th St, Paradise Valley AZ 85253, USA | Ice Hockey Player |
| **Burke, Simon**<br>United Agents, 12-26 Lexington St, London W1F 0LE, England | Actor |
| **Burke, Tim**<br>Rocket Science Talent, 5023 N Parkway Calabasas, Calabasas CA 91302, USA | Visual Effects Designer |
| **Burke, Timothy P (Tim)**<br>12108 W Ida Lane, Littleton CO 80127, USA | Baseball Player |
| **Burke, Will**<br>United Talent Agency, U T A Plaza, 9336 Civic Center Dr, Beverly Hills CA 90210 USA | Writer, Director, Actor |
| **Burkett, Bunny**<br>Bunny Burkett Racing Team, 8314 Robert E Lee Dr, Spotsylvania VA 22551, USA | Drag Racing Driver |
| **Burkett, Chris**<br>296 Dover Lane, Madison MS 39110, USA | Football Player |
| **Burkett, John D**<br>1404 Laurel Lane, Southlake TX 76092, USA | Baseball Player |
| **Burkett, W Jackson (Jackie)**<br>957 Holbrook Circle, Fort Walton Beach FL 32547, USA | Football Player |
| **Burkhalter, Edward A, Jr**<br>4128 Fort Washington Place, Alexandria VA 22304, USA | Navy Admiral |
| **Burkhard, Gedeon**<br>Elisabeth von Molo, Nymphenburger Str 154, 80635 Munich, Germany | Actor |
| **Burkhardt, Francois**<br>3 Rue de Venise, 75004 Paris, France | Architect |
| **Burkhart, Kathe**<br>Moti Hasson Gallery, 230 Arabian Road, Palm Beach FL 33480, USA | Artist |
| **Burkholder, JoAnn**<br>North Carolina State University, Botany Dept, Raleigh NC 27695, USA | Medical Activist, Physician |
| **Burkholder, Max**<br>Principato-Young, 9465 Wilshire Blvd, #880, Beverly Hills CA 90212 USA | Actor |
| **Burks, Audra**<br>2821 Crown Point, Springfield IL 62704, USA | Golfer |
| **Burks, Ellis R**<br>115 South Lane, Chagrin Falls OH 44022, USA | Baseball Player |
| **Burleson, Nate**<br>15508 SE 79th Place, Newcastle WA 98059, USA | Football Player |
| **Burleson, Richard P (Rick)**<br>241 E Country Hills Dr, La Habra CA 90631, USA | Baseball Player |
| **Burleson, Tommy L (Tom)**<br>PO Box 596, Newland NC 28657, USA | Basketball Player |
| **Burley, Gary**<br>514 Bristol Lane, Birmingham AL 35226, USA | Football Player |
| **Burman, Alexandra**<br>Group Model Mmgt, Po de Gracia 67, Pral 1A, 08008 Barcelona, Spain | Model |
| **Burman, George R**<br>1646 James St, Syracuse NY 13203, USA | Football Player |
| **Burn, Malcolm**<br>Anthem Entertainment, 189 Carlton St, Toronto ON M5A 2K7, Canada | Singer |
| **Burnell, Jocelyn Bell**<br>Bell Open University, Physics Dept, Milton Keynes MK7 6AA, England | Astronomer |
| **Burner, David L**<br>B F Goodrich Co, 3 Coliseum Centre, 2550 W Tyvola Road, Charlotte NC 28205, USA | Businessman |
| **Burnes, Karen**<br>CBS-TV, News Dept, 51 W 52nd St, New York NY 10019 USA | Commentator |
| **Burnet, Guy**<br>Resolution, 1801 Century Park E, #2300, Los Angeles CA 90067 USA | Actor |
| **Burnett, Allan J (A J)**<br>15208 Jarrettsville Pike, Monkton MD 21111, USA | Baseball Player |
| **Burnett, Carol**<br>I C M Partners, 10250 Constellation Blvd, #900, Los Angeles CA 90067 USA | Actress, Comedienne |
| **Burnett, Kevin B**<br>2938 S Sunbeck Circle, Dallas TX 75234, USA | Football Player |
| **Burnett, Sean R**<br>14016 Aster Ave, Wellington FL 33414, USA | Baseball Player |
| **Burnett, T-Bone**<br>Creative Artists Agency, 2000 Ave of Stars, #100, Los Angeles CA 90067 USA | Singer, Songwriter, Producer |
| **Burnette, Olivia**<br>Almond Talent Agency, 8217 Beverly Blvd, #8, West Hollywood CA 90048, USA | Actress |
| **Burnette, Rocky**<br>1900 Ave of Stars, #2530, Los Angeles CA 90067, USA | Singer |

**Burning Spear** — Singer
Burning Spear Mgmt, 130-34 231st St, Springfield Gardens NY 11413, USA
**Burningham, John** — Writer
Conville & Walsh, 118-120 Wardour St, London W1V 3LA, England
**Burnitz, Jeromy N** — Baseball Player
PO Box 676032, Rancho Santa Fe CA 92067, USA
**Burnley, James H, IV** — Secretary, Transportation
Venable LLP, 575 7th St NW, #1, Washington DC 20004, USA
**Burns, Annie** — Singer (Burns Sisters), Songwriter
Burns Sisters Band, PO Box 845, Ithaca NY 14851, USA
**Burns, Bob** — Drummer (Lynyrd Skynyrd)
Vector Mgmt, PO Box 120479, Nashville TN 37212 USA
**Burns, Bob** — Golfer
12512 Fraser Ave, Granada Hills CA 91344, USA
**Burns, Brooke** — Actress
A P A Talent & Literary Agency, 405 S Beverly Dr, #300, Beverly Hills CA 90212 USA
**Burns, Charles F (Charlie)** — Ice Hockey Player, Coach
7 Fawn Dr, Wallingford CT 06492, USA
**Burns, Christian** — Singer, Guitarist (BBMak)
Spirit Media, 34 Salisbury St, London NW8 8QE, England
**Burns, David D** — Psychiatrist
Stanford University, Psychiatry/Behavioral Science Dept, Stanford CA 94305, USA
**Burns, Edward** — Director, Actor
Marlboro Road Gang Productions, 334 E 90th St, New York NY 10128, USA
**Burns, Eric A** — Entertainer
Fox News, 1211 Ave of Americas, Lower C3R, New York NY 10036, USA
**Burns, Eric D (Ric)** — Director
Steeplechase Films, 2095 Broadway, #503, New York NY 10023, USA
**Burns, George** — Golfer
403 S Sapodilla Ave, #516, West Palm Beach FL 33401, USA
**Burns, Heather** — Actress
I C M Partners, 10250 Constellation Blvd, #900, Los Angeles CA 90067 USA
**Burns, Jeannie** — Singer (Burns Sisters), Songwriter
Burns Sisters Band, PO Box 845, Ithaca NY 14851, USA
**Burns, Jere, II** — Actor
Innovative Artists, 1505 10th St, Santa Monica CA 90401 USA
**Burns, Jimmy** — Writer
Bloomsbury Publishing, 50 Bedford Square, London WC1B 3DP, England
**Burns, Joey** — Singer, Guitarist (Calexico)
Billions Corp, 3522 W Armitage Ave, Chicago IL 60647 USA
**Burns, Keith B** — Football Player
13572 Heritage Farms Dr, Gainesville VA 20155, USA
**Burns, Kenneth L (Ken)** — Director
Florentine Films, 59 Maple Grove Road, Walpole NH 03608, USA
**Burns, M Anthony** — Businessman
Ryder System Inc, 11690 NW 105th St, Medley FL 33178, USA
**Burns, Marie** — Singer (Burns Sisters), Songwriter
Burns Sisters Band, PO Box 845, Ithaca NY 14851, USA
**Burns, Marilyn** — Writer
Marilyn Burns Educational Assoc, 150 Gate 5 Road, #101, Sausalito CA 94965, USA
**Burns, Megan** — Actress
Rights House, Drury House, 34-43 Russell St, London WC2B 5HA, England
**Burns, R Britt** — Baseball Player
1550 Katy Gap Road, #903, Katy TX 77494, USA
**Burns, Regan** — Actor, Comedian
OmniPop Talent Group, 4605 Lankershim Blvd, #201, Toluca Lake CA 91602 USA
**Burns, Robin** — Ice Hockey Player
186 Sherwood Road, Beaconsfield QC H9W 2G8, Canada
**Burns, Steve** — Actor
Paradigm Agency, 360 N Crescent Dr, North Building, Beverly Hills CA 90210 USA
**Burns, Todd E** — Baseball Player
PO Box 111, Princeton AL 35766, USA
**Burns, Ursula M** — Businesswoman
Xerox Corp, 800 Long Ridge Road, Stamford CT 06092, USA
**Burns, W Brent** — Ice Hockey Player
1460 Newport Ave, San Jose CA 95125, USA
**Burnside, Iain** — Concert Pianist, Commentator
Askonas Holt, Lincoln House, 300 High Holborn, London WC1V 7JH, England
**Burnside, Peter W (Pete)** — Baseball Player
1765 Washington Ave, Wilmette IL 60091, USA
**Burr, Bill** — Actor, Comedian
A P A Talent & Literary Agency, 405 S Beverly Dr, #300, Beverly Hills CA 90212 USA
**Burr, Matthew** — Drummer (Grace Potter & the Nocturnals)
Paradigm Agency, 404 W Franklin St, Monterey CA 93940 USA
**Burrell Wiley, Kim** — Singer, Pianist, Songwriter
Universal Attractions, 135 W 26th St, #1200, New York NY 10001 USA
**Burrell, Garland L, Jr** — Judge
US District Court, 501 I St, #3200, Sacramento CA 95814, USA
**Burrell, Gary** — Businessman
Garmin International, 1200 E 151st St, Olathe KS 66062, USA
**Burrell, John B (Johnny)** — Football Player
376 Park Lake Dr, Mead OK 73449, USA
**Burrell, Kenneth E (Kenny)** — Jazz Guitarist, Composer
Joel Chriss Co, 300 Mercer St, #3J, New York NY 10003 USA
**Burrell, Leroy** — Track Athlete
University of Houston, Athletic Dept, Houston TX 77023, USA
**Burrell, Patrick B (Pat), III** — Baseball Player
PO Box 1770, Boulder Creek CA 95006, USA
**Burrell, Scott D** — Basketball Player
331 Evergreen Ave, Hamden CT 06518, USA
**Burrell, Ty** — Actor
I C M Partners, 10250 Constellation Blvd, #900, Los Angeles CA 90067 USA
**Burres, Brian** — Baseball Player
350 SE 2nd St, #1420, Fort Lauderdale FL 33301, USA
**Burress, Plaxico A** — Football Player
47 Huntington Terrace, Totowa NJ 07512, USA

# B

**Burridge, Pam** — Surfer
Mark Rabbidge, 441B Bendalong Road, Bendalong NSW 2539, Australia
**Burridge, Randy** — Ice Hockey Player
1911 Nuevo Road, Henderson NV 89014, USA
**Burris, Jeffrey L (Jeff)** — Football Player
8074 Hopkins Lane, Indianapolis IN 46250, USA
**Burrough, Kenneth O (Ken)** — Football Player
5823 Tallow Lane, Indianapolis IN 46250, USA
**Burroughs, Augusten X** — Writer
Picador/Saint Martin's Press, 175 5th Ave, New York NY 10010, USA
**Burroughs, Jeffrey A (Jeff)** — Baseball Player
6155 Laguna Court, Long Beach CA 90803, USA
**Burroughs, Sean** — Baseball Player
6155 Laguna Court, Long Beach CA 90803, USA
**Burrow, Kenneth R (Ken)** — Football Player
5371 Dunwoody Club Creek, Atlanta GA 30360, USA
**Burrows, Darren E** — Actor
Writers & Artists, 360 N Crescent Dr, Building North, Beverly Hills CA 90210, USA
**Burrows, David J (Dave)** — Ice Hockey Player
RR 1, Lake Harris ON P2A 2W7, Canada
**Burrows, Edwin G** — Writer
Oxford University Press, 198 Madison Ave, #800, New York NY 10016 USA
**Burrows, Eva E** — Religious Leader
Domain Park, 193 Domain Road, #102, South Yarra VIC 3141, Australia
**Burrows, J Stuart** — Opera Singer
29 Blackwater Grove, Alderholt, Dorset SP6 3AD, England
**Burrows, James E (Jim)** — Director
Charles Brothers, 5555 Melrose Ave, Shulberg Building, Los Angeles CA 90038, USA
**Burrows, Saffron** — Actress
United Agents, 12-26 Lexington St, London W1F 0LE, England
**Burrows, Stephen** — Fashion Designer
10 W 57th St, New York NY 10019, USA
**Burrs, Marcia Ann** — Actress
Torque Entertainment, 3118 Wilshire Blvd, #160, Santa Monica CA 90403, USA
**Burrus, William** — Labor Leader
American Postal Workers Union, 1300 L St NW, #200, Washington DC 20005, USA
**Burruss, Kandi** — Singer (Xscape)
Richard Walters, PO Box 2789, Toluca Lake CA 91610 USA
**Burry, Collin** — Interior Designer
Gensler Architecture Design & Planning, 2 Harrison St, San Francisco CA 94105, USA
**Bursch, Daniel W** — Astronaut
1305 Buena Vista Ave, Pacific Grove CA 93950, USA
**Burshnick, Anthony J (Tony)** — Air Force General
7715 Carrleigh Parkway, Springfield VA 22152, USA
**Burson, Clare** — Singer, Songwriter
Rounder Records, 1 Rounder Way, Burlington MA 01803 USA
**Burson, Harold** — Businessman
30 W 63rd St, #7H, New York NY 10023, USA
**Burson, James O (Jimmy)** — Football Player
351 Heath Road, Dawsonville GA 30534, USA
**Burstyn, Ellen** — Actress
300 Central Park W, #12E, New York NY 10024, USA
**Burt, Adam** — Ice Hockey Player
34 Smull Ave, Caldwell NJ 07006, USA
**Burt, Donald Graham** — Art Director
Skouras Agency, 1149 3rd St, #300, Santa Monica CA 90403 USA
**Burt, James P (Jim)** — Football Player
10 River Farms Lane, Saddle River NJ 07458, USA
**Burton, Brandie** — Golfer
3480 Pleasant Hill Dr, Highland CA 92346, USA
**Burton, Ellis N** — Baseball Player
15621 Beach Blvd, #SP7, Westminster CA 92683, USA
**Burton, F Shane** — Football Player
PO Box 522, Hewitt Road, Catawba NC 28609, USA
**Burton, Gary** — Jazz Vibist
Berklee College of Music, 1140 Boylston St, Boston MA 02215, USA
**Burton, Hilarie** — Actress
Principal Entertainment, 9255 Sunset Blvd, #500, Los Angeles CA 90069 USA
**Burton, Jake** — Snowboard Skier
Burton Snowboards, 80 Industrial Parkway, Burlington VT 05401, USA
**Burton, Jeffrey B (Jeff)** — Auto Racing Driver
6000 Fairview Road, #635, Charlotte NC 28210, USA
**Burton, Kate** — Actress, Singer
Gersh Agency, 9465 Wilshire Blvd, #600, Beverly Hills CA 90212 USA
**Burton, L Jared** — Baseball Player
PO Box 506, Westminster SC 29693, USA
**Burton, Lance** — Illusionist
Monte Carlo Hotel, 3770 S Las Vegas Blvd, Las Vegas NV 89109, USA
**Burton, Lawrence G (Larry), Jr** — Football Player
41 San Gabriel, Rancho Santa Margarita CA 92688, USA
**Burton, Leonard B (Len)** — Football Player
3436 Beech Grove Road, Rancho Santa Margarita CA 92688, USA
**Burton, LeVar** — Actor
Sovereign Talent Group, 8421 Wilshire Blvd, #200, Beverly Hills CA 90211 USA
**Burton, Nelson, Jr** — Bowler
9359 SW Eagles Landing, Stuart FL 34997, USA
**Burton, Richard S V** — Architect
1B Lady Margaret Road, London NW5 2NE, England
**Burton, Steve** — Actor
James/Levy Mgmt, 3500 W Olive Ave, #1470, Burbank CA 91505 USA
**Burton, Thomas M** — Journalist
Wall Street Journal, Editorial Dept, 1 World Financial Center, New York NY 10281, USA
**Burton, Timothy W (Tim)** — Director
Tim Burton Productions, 8033 W Sunset Blvd, #7500, West Hollywood CA 90046, USA
**Burton, Ward** — Auto Racing Driver
2046 Myers Road, Halifax VA 24550, USA

Burridge - Burton

|  |  |
|---|---|
| **Burton, Willie R**<br>18900 Fleming St, Detroit MI 48234, USA | Basketball Player |
| **Burtt, Ben, Jr**<br>Skywalker Sound, Skywalker Ranch, 5858 Lucas Valley Road, Nicasio CA 94946, USA | Sound Editor |
| **Burtt, Steven D (Steve)**<br>200 W 143rd St, #12D, New York NY 10030, USA | Basketball Player |
| **Burum, Stephen H**<br>Mirisch Agency, 1025 Colorado Ave, #B, Santa Monica CA 90211 USA | Cinematographer |
| **Burwell, Carter**<br>Body Studio, 105 Hudson St, New York NY 10013, USA | Composer |
| **Burwitz, Nils**<br>Calle Rosa 22, 07170 Valldemossa, Majorca, Spain | Artist, Sculptor |
| **Bury, Pol**<br>236 Blvd Raspail, 75014 Paris, France | Sculptor |
| **Busby, Cindy**<br>Play Mgmt, 807 Powell St, #220, Vancouver BC V6A 1H7, Canada | Actress |
| **Busby, Steven L (Steve)**<br>2701 Brittany Lane, Grapevine TX 76051, USA | Baseball Player |
| **Buscemi, Steve**<br>Gotham Group, 7250 Melrose Ave, Los Angeles CA 90046, USA | Actor, Director |
| **Busch, Adam**<br>Don Buchwald Talent Agency, 6500 Wilshire Blvd, #2200, Los Angeles CA 90048 USA | Actor, Director, Producer |
| **Busch, August A, III**<br>Anheuser-Busch Cos, 1 Busch Place, Saint Louis MO 63118, USA | Businessman, Baseball Executive |
| **Busch, Charles**<br>Creative Artists Agency, 2000 Ave of Stars, #100, Los Angeles CA 90067 USA | Actor, Writer |
| **Busch, Kurt T**<br>128 Landover Lane, Mooresville NC 28117, USA | Auto, Truck Racing Driver |
| **Busch, Kyle T**<br>Kyle Busch Motorsports, 559 Pitts School Road, Concord NC 28027, USA | Auto, Truck Racing Driver |
| **Buse, Donald R (Don)**<br>7300 W State Road 64, Huntingburg IN 47542, USA | Basketball Player |
| **Busemann, Frank**<br>Borkumstr 13A, 45665 Recklinghausen, Germany | Track Athlete |
| **Buser, Martin**<br>PO Box 520997, Big Lake AK 99652, USA | Dog Sled Racer |
| **Busey, Gary**<br>Global Artists Agency, 6253 Hollywood Blvd, #508, Los Angeles CA 90028 USA | Actor |
| **Busey, Jake**<br>TalentWorks, 3500 W Olive Ave, #1400, Burbank CA 91505 USA | Actor |
| **Busfield, Timothy**<br>Paradigm Agency, 360 N Crescent Dr, North Building, Beverly Hills CA 90210 USA | Actor, Producer, Director |
| **Bush, Barbara P**<br>10000 Memorial Dr, #900, Houston TX 77024, USA | Wife of US President |
| **Bush, Blair W**<br>16911 SE 32nd Place, Bellevue WA 98008, USA | Football Player |
| **Bush, David T (Dave)**<br>8 Stevens Cove Road, Bridgton ME 04009, USA | Baseball Player |
| **Bush, Devin M**<br>10278 Laurel Road, Davie FL 33328, USA | Football Player |
| **Bush, George H W**<br>10000 Memorial Dr, #900, Houston TX 77024, USA | President, USA |
| **Bush, George W**<br>Prairie Chapel Ranch, Crawford TX 76638, USA | President, USA |
| **Bush, Guy L**<br>Michigan State University, Zoology Dept, East Lansing MI 48824, USA | Zoologist |
| **Bush, Homer G**<br>1402 Exeter Court, Southlake TX 76092, USA | Baseball Player |
| **Bush, Jim**<br>5106 Bounty Lane, Culver City CA 90230, USA | Track Coach |
| **Bush, Johnny**<br>Texas Sounds Entertainment, 957 N A S A Parkway, #542, Houston TX 77058, USA | Singer, Guitarist, Songwriter |
| **Bush, Katherine (Kate)**<br>Meads, Leengate, Nottingham Nottinghamshire NG7 2GB, England | Singer, Songwriter |
| **Bush, Kristian**<br>Gail Gellman Mgmt, 23852 Pacific Coast Highway, #920, Malibu CA 90265, USA | Singer (Billy Pilgrim, Sugarland) |
| **Bush, Laura**<br>Prairie Chapel Ranch, Crawford TX 76638, USA | Wife of US President |
| **Bush, Lesley L**<br>1451 Coconut Dr, Fort Myers FL 33901, USA | Diver |
| **Bush, R Randall (Randy)**<br>37 Kings Canyon Dr, New Orleans LA 70131, USA | Baseball Player |
| **Bush, Reggie**<br>Detroit Lions, 222 Republic Dr, Allen Park MI 48101 USA | Football Player |
| **Bush, Sam**<br>Samanda Lynn Music, PO Box 50962, Nashville TN 37205, USA | Singer, Mandolinist (New Grass Revival) |
| **Bush, Sophia**<br>Joan Green Mgmt, 1836 Courtney Terrace, Los Angeles CA 90046 USA | Actress |
| **Bush, Walter L, Jr**<br>5200 Malibu Dr, Minneapolis MN 55436, USA | Ice Hockey Executive |
| **Bush, William Green**<br>TalentWorks, 3500 W Olive Ave, #1400, Burbank CA 91505 USA | Actor |
| **Bushinsky, Joseph M (Jay)**<br>Rehov Hatsafon 5, Savyon 56540, Israel | Commentator |
| **Bushland, Raymond C**<br>200 Concord Plaza Dr, San Antonio TX 78216, USA | Entomologist |
| **Bushnell, Bill**<br>2751 Pelham Place, Los Angeles CA 90068, USA | Director |
| **Bushnell, Candace**<br>Greater Talent Network, 437 5th Ave, #700, New York NY 10016, USA | Writer |
| **Bushnell, Nolan K**<br>UWink, 2100 N Main St, #A14, Los Angeles CA 90031, USA | Businessman |
| **Bushwick Bill**<br>Richard Walters, PO Box 2789, Toluca Lake CA 91610 USA | Rap Artist (Geto Boys) |
| **Bushy, Ronald (Ron)**<br>Lustig Talent, PO Box 770850, Orlando FL 32877 USA | Drummer (Iron Butterfly) |

| | |
|---|---|
| **Busick, Steve R** <br> 6246 W Long Dr, Littleton CO 80123, USA | Football Player |
| **Busino, Orlando F** <br> 12 Shadblow Hill Road, Ridgefield CT 06877, USA | Cartoonist (Mugsy) |
| **Buskas, Rod** <br> 182 Wentworth Dr, Henderson NV 89074, USA | Ice Hockey Player |
| **Buslje, Sandro** <br> Busljeno 8, 20236 Cajkovica, Croatia | Water Polo Player |
| **Busniuk, Ron** <br> 540 Laurentian Dr, Thunder Bay ON P7C 5J8, Canada | Ice Hockey Player |
| **Buss, David M** <br> University of Texas, Psychology Dept, Austin TX 78712, USA | Psychologist, Writer |
| **Busse, Keith E** <br> Steel Dynamics, 7575 W Jefferson Blvd, Fort Wayne IN 46804, USA | Businessman |
| **Bussell, Darcey A** <br> 155 New King's Road, London SW6 4SJ, England | Ballerina |
| **Bussey, Barney A** <br> 5059 Park Ridge Court, West Chester OH 45069, USA | Football Player |
| **Bussey, Dexter M** <br> American/S C I, 888 W Beaver Road, Troy MI 48084, USA | Football Player |
| **Bustamante, Carlos** <br> University of California, Howard Hughes Medical Institute, Berkeley CA 94720, USA | Molecular Scientist |
| **Bustamante, Hector Luis** <br> Diverse Talent Group, 9911 Pico Blvd, #350W, Los Angeles CA 90035 USA | Actor |
| **Bustamante, Sergio** <br> Independence 238, Col Centro, Tlaquepaque CP 45500 Jalisco, Mexico | Artist, Sculptor |
| **Butala, Tony** <br> PO Box 151, McKees Rocks PA 15136, USA | Singer (Lettermen) |
| **Butcher, Adam** <br> I C M Partners, 10250 Constellation Blvd, #900, Los Angeles CA 90067 USA | Actor |
| **Butcher, Garth** <br> 1524 Maple Lane, Bellingham WA 98229, USA | Ice Hockey Player |
| **Butcher, John D** <br> 4245 Trillium Lane E, Mound MN 55364, USA | Baseball Player |
| **Butcher, Page** <br> Next Model Mgmt, 23 Watts St, New York NY 10013 USA | Model |
| **Butcher, Paul M** <br> 32060 Pacific Coast Highway, Malibu CA 90265, USA | Football Player |
| **Butcher, Rodney** <br> 27211 Iron Gate Lane, Wesley Chapel FL 33544, USA | Golfer |
| **Butcher-Marsh, Mary** <br> 1119 Cedar St, Carson City NV 89701, USA | Baseball Player |
| **Butera, Salvatore P (Sal)** <br> 324 Tersas Court, Lake Mary FL 32746, USA | Baseball Player |
| **Buthelezi, Chief Mangosuthu G** <br> Home Affairs Ministry, Private Bag X741, Pretoria 0001, South Africa | Chief Minister, KwaZulu/Natal |
| **Butkus, Richard M (Dick)** <br> Butkus Foundation, 18920 NE 227th Ave, Brush Prairie WA 98606, USA | Football Player, Actor |
| **Butler of Brockwell, F E Robin** <br> Master's Residence, University College, Oxford OX1 4BH, England | Government Official, England |
| **Butler, Austin R** <br> Anonymous Content, 3532 Hayden Ave, Culver City CA 90232 USA | Actor |
| **Butler, Bill C** <br> 1097 Aviation Blvd, Hermosa Beach CA 90254, USA | Cinematographer |
| **Butler, Brett** <br> A P A Talent & Literary Agency, 405 S Beverly Dr, #300, Beverly Hills CA 90212 USA | Actress, Comedienne |
| **Butler, Brett M** <br> 9512 E Canyon View Road, Scottsdale AZ 85255, USA | Baseball Player |
| **Butler, Chad M** <br> Universal Attractions, 135 W 26th St, #1200, New York NY 10001 USA | Drummer, Percussionist (Switchfoot) |
| **Butler, Cher** <br> Playboy Promotions, 9346 Civic Center Dr, #200, Beverly Hills CA 90210 USA | Model |
| **Butler, Chris** <br> C E S D, 10635 Santa Monica Blvd, #130, Los Angeles CA 90025 USA | Guitarist (Waitresses), Songwriter |
| **Butler, Clay** <br> PO Box 245, Capitola CA 95010, USA | Cartoonist |
| **Butler, Dan** <br> Innovative Artists, 1505 10th St, Santa Monica CA 90401 USA | Actor |
| **Butler, Dean** <br> Peak Moore Enterprises, 3233 Donald Douglas Loop S, #B, Santa Monica CA 90405, USA | Actor, Producer, Writer |
| **Butler, Edwin F (Win), III** <br> Billions Corp, 3522 W Armitage Ave, Chicago IL 60647 USA | Singer (Arcade Fire), Songwriter |
| **Butler, Gayle Goodson** <br> Better Homes & Gardens, Editor's Office, 1716 Locust St, Des Moines IA 50309, USA | Editor |
| **Butler, George L (Lee)** <br> Peter Kiewit & Sons, 11122 William Plaza, Omaha NE 68144, USA | Air Force General |
| **Butler, Gerard** <br> Creative Artists Agency, 2000 Ave of Stars, #100, Los Angeles CA 90067 USA | Actor, Singer, Producer |
| **Butler, J Caron** <br> 3802 Millard Way, Fairfax VA 22033, USA | Basketball Player |
| **Butler, J Keith** <br> 805 Cavan Dr, Cranberry Township PA 16066, USA | Football Player |
| **Butler, James (Cannonball)** <br> 1261 Cahaba Dr SW, Atlanta GA 30311, USA | Football Player |
| **Butler, James W** <br> Valley Farm Studios, Radway, Warwick CV35 0UJ, England | Sculptor |
| **Butler, Jerome P (Jerry)** <br> 3595 Eldridge Ave, Winnipeg MB R3R 0L5, Canada | Ice Hockey Player |
| **Butler, Jerry (Iceman), Jr** <br> Entertainment Consultants, 1207 Penhurst Court, Abingdon MD 21009, USA | Singer, Songwriter |
| **Butler, Jerry O** <br> 17117 Shaker Blvd, Cleveland OH 44120, USA | Football Player |
| **Butler, Jonathan** <br> Creative Artists Agency, 2000 Ave of Stars, #100, Los Angeles CA 90067 USA | Guitarist, Singer, Songwriter |
| **Butler, Joseph C (Joe)** <br> Lustig Talent, PO Box 770850, Orlando FL 32877 USA | Drummer, Singer (Lovin'Spoonful) |

|  |  |
|---|---|
| **Butler, Kevin G**<br>3256 Bagley Passage, Duluth GA 30097, USA | Football Player |
| **Butler, LeRoy**<br>2812 Eagle Preserve Blvd, Jacksonville FL 32226, USA | Football Player |
| **Butler, Martin**<br>University of Sussex, Music Dept, Brighton BN1 9RH, England | Composer |
| **Butler, Michael A**<br>3107 Magdalene Forest Court, Tampa FL 33618, USA | Football Player |
| **Butler, Mitchell L**<br>3526 Ocean View Ave, Los Angeles CA 90066, USA | Basketball Player |
| **Butler, Raymond L (Ray)**<br>1300 Woodcrest Dr, Houston TX 77018, USA | Football Player |
| **Butler, Robert**<br>650 Club View Dr, Los Angeles CA 90024, USA | Director |
| **Butler, Robert C (Bobby)**<br>5567 Naylor Court, Norcross GA 30092, USA | Football Player |
| **Butler, Robert Olen**<br>3909 Reserve Dr, #1611, Tallahassee FL 32311, USA | Writer |
| **Butler, Samuel C**<br>Cravath Swain Moore, 825 8th Ave, New York NY 10019, USA | Attorney |
| **Butler, Terence M J (Geezer)**<br>Sharon Osborne Mgmt, 8899 Beverly Blvd, #905, West Hollywood CA 90048, USA | Bassist (Black Sabbath), Songwriter |
| **Butler, William F (Bill)**<br>141 Buckskin Lane, Berkeley Springs WV 25411, USA | Baseball Player |
| **Butler, William F (Skip)**<br>1311 Spyglass Dr, Mansfield TX 76063, USA | Football Player |
| **Butler, William R (Bill)**<br>200 E Liberty St, Berlin WI 54923, USA | Football Player |
| **Butler, Yancy**<br>Mavrick Artists Agency, 6100 Wilshire Blvd, #550, Los Angeles CA 90048, USA | Actress |
| **Butor, Michel**<br>A l'Ecart, 216 Place de L'Eglise, 74380 Lucinges, France | Writer |
| **Butt, Yondani**<br>Gurtman & Murtha, 450 Fashion Ave, #603, New York NY 10123, USA | Conductor |
| **Butterfield, Alexander P**<br>9237 Regents Road, #323, La Jolla CA 92037, USA | Government Official |
| **Butterfield, Benjamin**<br>I M G Artists, Hogarth Business Park, Chiswick, London W4 2TH, England | Opera Singer |
| **Butterfield, Deborah K**<br>11229 Cottonwood Road, Bozeman MT 59718, USA | Sculptor |
| **Buttle, Gregory E (Greg)**<br>5 Hollacher Dr, Northport NY 11768, USA | Football Player |
| **Buttle, Jeffrey**<br>International Management Group, 304 Park Ave, #PH N, New York NY 10010, USA | Figure Skater |
| **Button, Jenson A L**<br>Jenson Racing, 67 Valkenburgerweg, 6419 Heerlen AP, Netherlands | Auto Racing Driver |
| **Button, Richard T (Dick)**<br>Candio Productions, 765 Park Ave, #6B, New York NY 10021, USA | Figure Skater, Producer |
| **Butts, James**<br>16950 Belforest Dr, Carson CA 90746, USA | Track Athlete |
| **Butz, David E (Dave)**<br>746 E Adams St, Belleville IL 62220, USA | Football Player |
| **Butz, Norbert Leo**<br>Creative Artists Agency, 2000 Ave of Stars, #100, Los Angeles CA 90067 USA | Actor, Singer |
| **Buxbaum, Richard M**<br>University of California, Law School, Boalt Hall, Berkeley CA 94720, USA | Attorney, Educator |
| **Buxton, Sarah**<br>Origin Talent Mgmt, 4705 Laurel Canyon BLvd, #306, Valley Village CA 91607, USA | Actress, Singer |
| **Buy, Margherita**<br>Carol Levi Mgmt, Via Giuseppe Pisanelli 2, 00196 Rome, Italy | Actress |
| **Buyers, William**<br>Atomic Energy of Canada, 2251 Speakman Dr, Mississauga ON L5K 1B2, Canada | Physicist |
| **Buynak, Gordie**<br>11512 Douglas Lake Road, Pellston MI 49769, USA | Ice Hockey Player |
| **Buzzi, Ruth**<br>31159 N State Highway 108, Mingus TX 76463, USA | Actress, Comedienne |
| **Byambasuren, Dashiin**<br>C D S S R, Sergen Mandakh Gudamj 13, #4 Gin Hurd, Uuriin Javar, Mongolia | Prime Minister, Mongolia |
| **Byars, Betsy C**<br>401 Rudder Ridge, Seneca SC 29678, USA | Writer |
| **Byars, Keith**<br>23307 Boca Trace Dr, Boca Raton FL 33433, USA | Football Player |
| **Byas, Richard R (Rick), Jr**<br>19925 Greenwald Dr, Southfield MI 48075, USA | Football Player |
| **Byatt, Antonia Susan (A S)**<br>37 Rusholme Road, London SW15 3LF, England | Writer |
| **Bybee, Catherine**<br>Dystel & Goderich Literary Mgmt, 1 Union Square W, #904, New York NY 10003, USA | Writer |
| **Bybee, Jay**<br>US Court of Appeals, Courthouse, 333 Las Vegas Blvd S, Las Vegas NV 89101, USA | Judge |
| **Bychkov, Semyon**<br>Buffalo Symphony Orchestra, 499 Franklin St, Buffalo NY 14202, USA | Conductor |
| **Bye, Kermit E**<br>US Court of Appeals, 657 2nd Ave N, Fargo ND 58102, USA | Judge |
| **Bye-Dietz, Karyn**<br>322 Gandy Dancer Circle, Hudson WI 54016, USA | Ice Hockey Player |
| **Byer, Renee C**<br>Sacramento Bee, Editorial Dept, 2100 Q St, Sacramento CA 95816 USA | Photojournalist |
| **Byers, Michael A (Mike)**<br>28 Presidio Dr, Novato CA 94949, USA | Ice Hockey Player |
| **Byers, Nina**<br>University of California, Physics Dept, Los Angeles CA 90024, USA | Physicist |
| **Byers, Steve**<br>TalentWorks, 3500 W Olive Ave, #1400, Burbank CA 91505 USA | Actor |
| **Byers, Walter**<br>25707 Aiken Switch Road, Emmett KS 66422, USA | Athletic Association Executive |

**Bykovsky, Valeri F** — Cosmonaut
Cosmonaut Training Center, Star City, 141160 Zvezdny Gorodok, Moscow Oblast, Russia

**Bylsma, Dan** — Ice Hockey Player
12637 Broadmoor Place, Grand Haven MI 49417, USA

**Byman, Robert T (Bob)** — Golfer
9325 Eagle Ridge Dr, Las Vegas NV 89134, USA

**Byner, Earnest A** — Football Player
1016 Sattui Court, Franklin TN 37064, USA

**Byner, John** — Actor, Comedian, Impressionist
American Mgmt, 19948 Mayall St, Chatsworth CA 91311, USA

**Bynes, Amanda** — Actress, Comedienne
Baker Winokur Ryder Public Relations, 9100 Wilshire Blvd, #500W, Beverly Hills CA 90212 USA

**Bynum, Andrew L** — Basketball Player
7412 Denrock Ave, Los Angeles CA 90045, USA

**Bynum, Caroline W** — Historian
Institute for Advanced Study, Einstein Dr, Princeton NJ 08540 USA

**Byrd, Chris** — Boxer
1181 Heatherwood Court, Flint MI 48532, USA

**Byrd, Dan** — Actor
Creative Artists Agency, 2000 Ave of Stars, #100, Los Angeles CA 90067 USA

**Byrd, Donald** — Choreographer
Spectrum Dance Theater, 800 Lake Washington Blvd, Seattle WA 98122, USA

**Byrd, Eugene** — Actor
Sanders/Armstrong/Caserta Mgmt, 2120 Colorado Ave, #120, Santa Monica CA 90404 USA

**Byrd, George E (Butch)** — Football Player
23 Wayside Road, Westborough MA 01581, USA

**Byrd, Gill A** — Football Player
5347 Notting Hill Road, Gurnee IL 60031, USA

**Byrd, Isaac, III** — Football Player
5712 Astra Ave, Saint Louis MO 63147, USA

**Byrd, Jonathan C** — Golfer
110 Meadow Brook, Saint Simons Island GA 31522, USA

**Byrd, Marlon J** — Baseball Player
3105 N Ashland Ave, Chicago IL 60657, USA

**Byrd, Paul G** — Baseball Player
910 Foxhollow Run, Alpharetta GA 30004, USA

**Byrd, Richard** — Football Player
2230 Haley Road, Terry MS 39170, USA

**Byrd, Tracy** — Singer
Star Keeper Public Relations, 4695 Monticello St, Beaumont TX 77706, USA

**Byrdak, Timothy C (Tim)** — Baseball Player
16721 W Seneca Dr, Lockport IL 60441, USA

**Byrne, Alexandra** — Costume Designer
Independent Talent Group, 40 Whitfield St, London W1T 2RH, England

**Byrne, Brendan T** — Governor, NJ
6 Becker Farm Road, Roseland NJ 07068, USA

**Byrne, David** — Singer (Talking Heads), Songwriter
Luaka Bop, 195 Christie St, #901, New York NY 10002, USA

**Byrne, Gabriel** — Actor
Paradigm Agency, 360 N Crescent Dr, North Building, Beverly Hills CA 90210 USA

**Byrne, Gerry** — Publisher
Penske Media Corporation, 9800 S La Cienega Blvd, #1400, Los Angeles CA 90301, USA

**Byrne, Josh** — Actor
Hervey/Grimes Talent, 10561 Missouri Ave, #2, Los Angeles CA 90025 USA

**Byrne, Martha** — Actress
Innovative Artists, 1505 10th St, Santa Monica CA 90401 USA

**Byrne, Megan** — Actress
Douglas Gorman Rothacker Wilhelm, 1501 Broadway, #703, New York NY 10036 USA

**Byrne, Michael** — Actor
Conway Van Gelder Grant, 8-12 Broadwick St, #300, London W1F 8HW, England

**Byrne, Nicholas B J A (Nicky), Jr** — Actor, Singer, Songwriter, Dancer
Solo Agency, 53-55 Fulham High St, #200, London SW6 3JJ, England

**Byrne, Rose** — Actress
Creative Artists Agency, 2000 Ave of Stars, #100, Los Angeles CA 90067 USA

**Byrnes, Edd** — Actor
PO Box 1623, Beverly Hills CA 90213, USA

**Byrnes, Eric J** — Baseball Player
16030 Ventura Blvd, Encino CA 91436, USA

**Byrnes, James T (Jim)** — Actor, Singer
Characters Talent Agency, 8 Elm St, Toronto ON M5G 1G7, Canada

**Byrnes, Martin W (Marty)** — Basketball Player
8739 3rd Ave, Pleasant Prairie WI 53158, USA

**Byrom, Monty** — Singer (Big House), Songwriter
Gurley & Co, 1204 Cedar Lane, #B, Nashville TN 37212 USA

**Byron, Don** — Jazz Clarinetist
Hans Wendl Productions, 2220 California St, Berkeley CA 94703, USA

**Byron, Jeffrey** — Actor
Visionary Artists, 7162 Beverly Blvd, #324, Los Angeles CA 90036, USA

**Byrum, Curt A** — Golfer
12441 N 86th St, Scottsdale AZ 85260, USA

**Byrum, John W** — Director
Creative Artists Agency, 2000 Ave of Stars, #100, Los Angeles CA 90067 USA

**Byrum, Thomas E (Tom)** — Golfer
734 Sentry Hill, San Antonio TX 78260, USA

**Bystrom, Martin E (Marty)** — Baseball Player
PO Box 89, Geigertown PA 19523, USA

**Byun Chun-Sa** — Speed Skater
Skating Union, 88 Bangyee-Dong, Songpaku, Seoul 138 749, South Korea

**Byzantine, Julian S** — Concert Guitarist
42 Ennismore Gardens, #1, London SW7 1AQ, England

**Bzdelik, Jeff** — Basketball Coach
Wake Forest University, Athletic Dept, Winston-Salem NC 27109, USA

**Caan, James** — Actor
Rogers & Cowan, 8687 Melrose Ave, #G700, West Hollywood CA 90069 USA
**Caan, Scott** — Actor
Paradigm Agency, 360 N Crescent Dr, North Building, Beverly Hills CA 90210 USA
**Caballe, Montserrat** — Opera Singer
Avenida Madronos 27, Madrid 28043, Spain
**Caballero, Katia** — Actress
Agence Elisabeth Simpson, 62 Boul du Montparnasse, 75015 Paris, France
**Caballero, Ralph J (Putsy)** — Baseball Player
6773 Milne Blvd, New Orleans LA 70124, USA
**Caballero, Tara** — Model
2134 Carol View Dr, Cardiff CA 92007, USA
**Cabana, Robert D** — Astronaut
Kennedy Space Center, Director's Office, Kennedy Space Center FL 32899, USA
**Cabannes, Henri** — Mathematician
University of Marie & Pierre Curie, Mathematics Dept, 4 Place Jussieu 75005 Paris, France
**Cabarga, Leslie** — Cartoonist
451 S Padre Juan Ave, Ojai CA 93023, USA
**Cabas** — Singer, Musician
J E P Entertainment, 16027 Ventura Blvd, #510, Encino CA 91436, USA
**Cabell, Enos M** — Baseball Player
4103 Frost Lake Court, Missouri City TX 77459, USA
**Cabell, Nicole** — Opera Singer
Columbia Artists Mgmt Inc, 5 Columbus Circle, 1790 Broadway, #1600, New York NY 10019 USA
**Cabellut, Lita** — Artist
Bill Lowe Gallery, 1555 Peachtree NE, #100, Atlanta GA 30309, USA
**Cable, Byrum W (Barney)** — Basketball Player
1134 S Main St, #69, Hampstead MD 21074, USA
**Cable, Tawnni** — Actress, Model
Playboy Promotions, 9346 Civic Center Dr, #200, Beverly Hills CA 90210 USA
**Cable, Thomas L (Tom), Jr** — Football Player, Coach
Oakland Raiders, 1220 Harbor Bay Parkway, Alameda CA 94502 USA
**Cabral, Angelique** — Actress
Pakula/King, 9229 W Sunset Blvd, #315, West Hollywood CA 90069 USA
**Cabral, Travis** — Moguls Skier
Police Department, 1352 Johnson Blvd, South Lake Tahoe NV 96150, USA
**Cabranes, Jose A** — Judge
US Court of Appeals, 141 Church St, New Haven CT 06510, USA
**Cabrera, Angel L** — Golfer
Professional Golfers Association, 100 Ave of Champions, Palm Beach Gardens FL 33418 USA
**Cabrera, Daniel A** — Baseball Player
Washington Nationals, 1500 S Capitol St SE, Washington DC 20003 USA
**Cabrera, J Miguel T** — Baseball Player
3339 Virginia St, #PH2, Miami FL 33133, USA
**Cabrera, Orlando L** — Baseball Player
9248 Scarlette Oak Ave, Fort Myers FL 33967, USA
**Cabrera, Ryan** — Singer, Guitarist
Luber Rocklin Entertainment, 5815 Sunset Blvd, #206, Los Angeles CA 90028 USA
**Cabrera, Santiago** — Actor
Conway Van Gelder Grant, 8-12 Broadwick St, #300, London W1F 8HW, England
**Cabrinha, Pete** — Kiteboarding Athlete
245A Kane Road, Haiku HI 96708, USA
**Cabtaline, Anita** — Bowler
32455 Pinto Dr, Warren MI 48093, USA
**Cacciavillan, Agostino Cardinal** — Religious Leader
Patrimony of Holy See, Palazzo Apostolico, 00120 Vatican City
**Caceres, Kurt** — Actor
Rebel Entertainment Partners, 5700 Wilshire Blvd, #456, Los Angeles CA 90036, USA
**Cackowski, Liz** — Actress, Comedienne
United Talent Agency, U T A Plaza, 9336 Civic Center Dr, Beverly Hills CA 90210 USA
**Cadaret, Gregory J (Greg)** — Baseball Player
22636 Bridlewood Lane, Palo Cedro CA 96073, USA
**Caddell, Patrick H** — Statistician
Cambridge Research Inc, 1625 I St NW, Washington DC 20006, USA
**Cadell, Ava** — Actress, Model
Levin, 8484 Wilshire Blvd, #745, Beverly Hills CA 90211, USA
**Cadiff, Andy** — Director
United Talent Agency, U T A Plaza, 9336 Civic Center Dr, Beverly Hills CA 90210 USA
**Cadigan, Dave** — Football Player
14416 Katie Road, Phoenix MD 21131, USA
**Cadile, James D (Jim)** — Football Player
1738 Spring St, Medford OR 97504, USA
**Cadman, Sam** — Director, Producer, Actor
United Talent Agency, U T A Plaza, 9336 Civic Center Dr, Beverly Hills CA 90210 USA
**Cadogan, William J** — Businessman
A D C Telecommunications, PO Box 1101, Minneapolis MN 55440, USA
**Cadrez, Glenn E** — Football Player
PO Box 130818, Carlsbad CA 92013, USA
**Caesar, Shirley** — Singer
Shu-Bel Music, PO Box 3336, Durham NC 27702, USA
**Cafagna, Ashley** — Actress
Tesoro Entertainment, 205 N Stephanie St, #D115, Henderson NV 89074, USA
**Caffarelli, Luis A** — Mathematician
University of Texas, Mathematics Dept, 1 University Station, Austin TX 78712, USA
**Caffari, Denise (Dee)** — Yachtswoman
Caroline Rose Mgmt, Peter House, Oxford St, Manchester M1 5AN, England
**Caffarra, Carlo Cardinal** — Religious Leader
Archdiocese of Bologna, Via Altabella 6, 40126 Bologna, Italy
**Cafferata, Hector A, Jr** — Korean War Marine Corps Hero (CMH)
1807 Plum Lane, Venice FL 34293, USA
**Caffey, Charlotte** — Guitarist (Go-Go's)
Direct Management Group, 947 N La Cienega Blvd, #G, West Hollywood CA 90069, USA
**Caffey, Jason A** — Basketball Player
PO Box 131, Roswell GA 30077, USA
**Caffie, Joseph C (Joe)** — Baseball Player
PO Box 1932, Warren OH 44482, USA

# C

**Cafu** — Soccer Player
F C Milan, Via Filippo Turati 3, 20121 Milan, Italy

**Cagatay, Mustafa** — Prime Minister, Cyprus Federated State
60 Cumhuriyet Caddesi, 900 Kyrenia, Cyprus

**Cage** — Rap Artist
Agency Group Ltd, 142 W 57th St, #600, New York NY 10019 USA

**Cage, Byron** — Singer
Mahgonany Entertainment, 12201 Pleasant Prospect Road, Mitchellville MD 20721, USA

**Cage, Michael J** — Basketball Player
21163 Newport Coast Dr, Newport Coast CA 92657, USA

**Cage, Nicolas** — Actor
Creative Artists Agency, 2000 Ave of Stars, #100, Los Angeles CA 90067 USA

**Cagle, Chris** — Singer, Songwriter
McGhee Entertainment, 8730 Sunset Blvd, #200, West Hollywood CA 90069, USA

**Cagle, Myrtle K** — Astronaut Candidate
RR 3, Lake Tobesofkee, Lizella GA 31052, USA

**Cagle, Yvonne D** — Astronaut
N A S A, Johnson Space Center, 2101 NASA Road, Houston TX 77058 USA

**Cahill, Eddie** — Actor
Management 360, 9111 Wilshire Blvd, Beverly Hills CA 90210 USA

**Cahill, Laura** — Writer
I C M Partners, 10250 Constellation Blvd, #900, Los Angeles CA 90067 USA

**Cahill, Michael (Mike)** — Director
W M E Entertainment, 9601 Wilshire Blvd, #300, Beverly Hills CA 90210 USA

**Cahill, Sarah** — Pianist
KPFA-FM, 1929 Martin Luther King Way, Berkeley CA 94704, USA

**Cahill, Teresa M** — Opera, Concert Singer
65 Leyland Road, London SE12 8DW, England

**Cahill, Thomas** — Writer
Doubleday Press, 1540 Broadway, New York NY 10036, USA

**Cahill, Timothy F (Tim)** — Soccer Player
Red Bulls New York, 600 Cape May St, Harrison, NJ 07029 USA

**Cahill, Trevor J** — Baseball Player
Arizona Diamondbacks, Chase Field, 401 E Jefferson, Phoenix AZ 85003 USA

**Cahn, John W** — Metallurgist
2032 43rd Ave E, #18, Seattle WA 98112, USA

**Cahouet, Frank V** — Financier
Mellon Bank Corp, 1 Mellon Bank Center, 500 Grant St, #1, Pittsburgh PA 15219, USA

**Cahow, Caitlin** — Ice Hockey Player
USA Hockey, 1775 Bob Johnson Dr, Colorado Springs CO 80906 USA

**Caillat, Colbie M** — Singer, Songwriter
Fitzgerald Hartley, 34 N Palm St, #100, Ventura CA 93001, USA

**Caillon, Anne** — Actress
U B B A, 6 Rue de Braque, 75003 Paris, France

**Cain, Carl** — Basketball Player
3045 Sun Valley Dr, Pickerington OH 43147, USA

**Cain, Chelsea** — Writer
Saint Martin's Press, 175 5th Ave, #400, New York NY 10010 USA

**Cain, Dean** — Actor
W M E Entertainment, 9601 Wilshire Blvd, #300, Beverly Hills CA 90210 USA

**Cain, Matthew T (Matt)** — Baseball Player
1331 N 104th Place, Mesa AZ 85207, USA

**Caine, Michael** — Actor
42 Mgmt, 8 Flitcroft St, London WC2H 8DL, England

**Cainero, Chiara** — Markswoman
Comitato Olimpico Nazionale, Largo Lauro de Bocsis 15, 00194 Rome, Italy

**Caio, Francesco** — Businessman
Netscalibur, 9 Selsdon Way, Cityharbour, London E14 9GL, England

**Caird, John** — Director, Lyricist
Gersh Agency, 9465 Wilshire Blvd, #600, Beverly Hills CA 90212 USA

**Cairns, Eric** — Ice Hockey Player
1291 Treeland St, Burlington ON L7R 3T5, Canada

**Cairns, Ian** — Surfer
868 Wilson St, Laguna Beach CA 92651, USA

**Cairo, Miguel J** — Baseball Player
209 Highland Woods Dr, Safety Harbor FL 34695, USA

**Caivano, Ernesto** — Artist
Guild & Greyshkul, 131 Prince St, #4F, New York NY 10012, USA

**Cajanek, Petr** — Ice Hockey Player
Saint Louis Blues, Scottrade Center, 1401 Clark Ave, Saint Louis MO 63103 USA

**Cake, Jonathan** — Actor
Independent Talent Group, 40 Whitfield St, London W1T 2RH, England

**Calabrese, Gerald A (Gerry)** — Basketball Player
351 Esplanade Place, Cliffside Park NJ 07010, USA

**Calabresi, Guido** — Judge
US Court of Appeals, 157 Church St, #1800, New Haven CT 06510, USA

**Calabro, Thomas** — Actor
A K A Talent, 6310 San Vicente Blvd, #200, Los Angeles CA 90048 USA

**Calame, Ingrid** — Artist
Cohen Gallery, 533 W 26th St, New York NY 10001, USA

**Calamos, John P, Sr** — Financier
Calamos Asset Management, 1111 E Warrenville Road, Naperville IL 60563, USA

**Calarco, Vincent A** — Businessman
Crompton Corp, 199 Benson Road, Waterbury CT 06749, USA

**Calatrava, Santiago** — Architect, Engineer
Santiago Calatrava SA, Hoschgasse 5, 8008 Zurich, Switzerland

**Calcagno, Domenico Cardinal** — Religious Leader
Administration of Patrimony, Palazzo Apostolico, 00120 Vatican City

**Calcevecchi, Mark** — Golfer
2741 E Bighorn Ave, Phoenix AZ 85048, USA

**Calder, Kyle** — Ice Hockey Player
19 Trumpet Vine St, Ladera Ranch CA 92694, USA

**Calderon Borrallo, Jose M** — Basketball Player
New York Knicks, Madison Square Garden, 2 Penn Plaza, New York, NY 10121 USA

**Calderon Fournier, Rafael A** — President, Costa Rica
Partido Unidad Social Cristiana, San Jose, Costa Rica

**Calderon, Mark**
J-Bird Entertainment, 4905 S Atlantic Ave, Ponce Inlet FL 32127 USA — Singer (Color Me Badd)

**Calderon, Paul**
TalentWorks, 220 E 23rd St, #303, New York NY 10010, USA — Actor

**Caldicott, Helen**
Physicians for Responsibility, 639 Massachusetts Ave, Cambridge MA 02139, USA — Social Activist, Pediatrician

**Caldwell Dyson, Tracy E**
N A S A, Johnson Space Center, 2101 NASA Road, Houston TX 77058 USA — Astronaut

**Caldwell, Adrian B**
10990 West Road, #311, Houston TX 77064, USA — Basketball Player

**Caldwell, Andrew**
Management 101, 11271 Ventura Blvd, #102, Studio City CA 91604 USA — Actor

**Caldwell, Bobby**
Universal Attractions, 135 W 26th St, #1200, New York NY 10001 USA — Singer, Musician, Songwriter

**Caldwell, Gail**
Boston Globe, Editorial Dept, 135 William Morrissey Blvd, Dorchester MA 02125 USA — Journalist

**Caldwell, Isaiah (Mike), Jr**
646 Robertsville Road, Oak Ridge TN 37830, USA — Football Player

**Caldwell, James (Jim)**
Detroit Lions, 222 Republic Dr, Allen Park MI 48101 USA — Football Coach

**Caldwell, James W (Jim)**
705 Freedom Lane, Roswell GA 30075, USA — Basketball Player

**Caldwell, Joe L**
15 E Pebble Beach Dr, Tempe AZ 85282, USA — Basketball Player

**Caldwell, John**
King Features Syndicate, 300 W 57th St, #1500, New York NY 10019 USA — Cartoonist

**Caldwell, Kimberly**
PO Box 8158, The Woodland TX 77387, USA — Singer, Actress

**Caldwell, L Scott**
Innovative Artists, 1505 10th St, Santa Monica CA 90401 USA — Actor

**Caldwell, Nicholas**
Pyramid Entertainment Group, 377 Rector Place, #21A, New York NY 10280 USA — Singer (Whispers)

**Caldwell, R Michael (Mike)**
1645 Brook Run Dr, Raleigh NC 27614, USA — Baseball Player

**Caldwell, Ravin C, Jr**
4415 Johnson St, Fort Smith AR 72904, USA — Football Player

**Caldwell, Rex**
260 El Dorado Blvd, #3006, Webster TX 77598, USA — Golfer

**Caldwell, Stephen (Steve)**
Lustig Talent, PO Box 770850, Orlando FL 32877 USA — Singer (Orlons)

**Caldwell, Toy**
Ron Rainey Mgmt, 315 S Beverly Dr, #407, Beverly Hills CA 90212, USA — Guitarist (Marshall Tucker Band)

**Caldwell, Zoe**
Whitehead-Stevens, 1501 Broadway, New York NY 10036, USA — Actress

**Caldwell-Pope, Kentavious**
Detroit Pistons, Palace, 4 Championship Dr, Auburn Hills MI 48326 USA — Basketball Player

**Cale, Paula**
Gersh Agency, 9465 Wilshire Blvd, #600, Beverly Hills CA 90212 USA — Actress

**Calegari, Maria**
404 Richardsville Road, Carmel NY 10512, USA — Ballerina

**Caleo, Michael**
I C M Partners, 10250 Constellation Blvd, #900, Los Angeles CA 90067 USA — Director, Writer

**Calero, Enrique N (Kiko)**
1465 65th St, Emeryville CA 94608, USA — Baseball Player

**Caley, Don**
7127 E Aloe Vera Dr, Scottsdale AZ 85266, USA — Ice Hockey Player

**Calfa, Marian**
Calfa, Pravni Kancela Premyslovska 28, 130 00 Prague 3, Czech Republic — President, Czechoslovakia

**Calfan, Nicole**
Agents Associes, 201 Rue du Faubourg Saint Honore, 75008 Paris, France — Actress

**Calhoon, Jesse M**
Marine Engineers Union, 17 Battery Place, New York NY 10004, USA — Labor Leader

**Calhoun, David L (Corky)**
17912 Lafayette Dr, Olney MD 20832, USA — Basketball Player

**Calhoun, Donald C (Don)**
PO Box 49104, Wichita KS 67201, USA — Football Player

**Calhoun, James A (Jim)**
PO Box 379, Pomfret Center CT 06259, USA — Basketball Coach

**Calhoun, Jeffrey W (Jeff)**
10002 Springwood Forest Dr, Houston TX 77080, USA — Baseball Player

**Calhoun, Monica**
Abrams Artists, 9200 W Sunset Blvd, #1125, West Hollywood CA 90069 USA — Actress

**Calhoun, Troy**
US Air Force Academy, Athletic Dept, Colorado Springs CO 80840, USA — Football Coach

**Calhoun, Will**
Entertainment Artists, 2409 21st Ave S, #100, Nashville TN 10019 USA — Drummer (Living Colour)

**Calhoun, William C (Bill)**
3740 El Cerro View Circle, Reno NV 89509, USA — Basketball Player

**Cali, Joseph**
25630 Edenwild Road, Calabasas CA 91302, USA — Actor

**Caliendo, Frank**
Gersh Agency, 9465 Wilshire Blvd, #600, Beverly Hills CA 90212 USA — Actor, Comedian, Writer

**Califano, Joseph A, Jr**
Casa at Columbia, 633 3rd Ave, #1900, New York NY 10017, USA — Secretary, Health Education & Welfare

**Calipari, John**
University of Kentucky, Athletic Dept, Lexington KY 40506, USA — Basketball Coach

**Calis, Natasha**
Creative Artists Agency, 2000 Ave of Stars, #100, Los Angeles CA 90067 USA — Actress

**Call, Kevin B**
839 Carey Road, Carmel IN 46033, USA — Football Player

**Callahan, Daniel J**
Hastings Center, 255 Elm Road, Briarcliff Manor NY 10510, USA — Educator

**Callahan, John**
Levin Representatives, 2402 4th St, #6, Santa Monica CA 90405, USA — Actor

**Callahan, Ryan**
Tampa Bay Lightning, 401 Channelside Dr, Tampa FL 33602 USA — Ice Hockey Player

V.I.P. Address Book

**Calderon - Callahan**

**Callahan, William E (Bill)** — Football Coach
623 Lake Point Dr, Irving TX 75039, USA

**Callan, K** — Actress
A M T International, 15260 Ventura Blvd, #1200, Sherman Oaks CA 91403, USA

**Callan, Michael** — Actor, Director, Producer
4440 Talofa Ave, #102, Toluca Lake CA 91602, USA

**Calland, Albert M, III** — Navy Admiral
Central Intelligence Agency, Deputy Director's Office, Washington DC 20505, USA

**Calland, Lee** — Football Player
6624 Windwood Circle, Douglasville GA 30135, USA

**Callard, Rebecca** — Actress
Curtis Brown Group, 28-29 Haymarket St, #500, London SW1Y 4SP, England

**Callas, John L** — Space Scientist, Physicist
Jet Propulsion Laboratory, 4800 Oak Grove Dr, Pasadena CA 91109 USA

**Callaway, Ann Hampton** — Jazz Singer, Pianist, Composer
Miller Wright Assoc, 1650 Broadway, #1210, New York NY 10019, USA

**Callaway, Michael C (Mickey)** — Baseball Player
8061 Stonewyck Road, Germantown TN 38138, USA

**Callaway, Thomas V** — Actor
House of Representatives, 1434 6th St, #1, Santa Monica CA 90401 USA

**Callen Jones, Gloria** — Swimmer
1508 Chafton Road, Charleston WV 25314, USA

**Callen, Bryan C** — Actor, Comedian
Innovative Artists, 1505 10th St, Santa Monica CA 90401 USA

**Callender, William D (Jock)** — Ice Hockey Player
388 Lear Road, Avon Lake OH 44012, USA

**Callery, Sean** — Composer
Gorfaine/Schwartz, 4111 W Alameda Ave, #509, Burbank CA 91505 USA

**Callicutt, Ken B** — Football Player
919 Suchava Dr, White Lake MI 48386, USA

**Callie, Dayton** — Actor
Abrams Artists, 9200 W Sunset Blvd, #1125, West Hollywood CA 90069 USA

**Callies, Sarah Wayne** — Actress
I C M Partners, 10250 Constellation Blvd, #900, Los Angeles CA 90067 USA

**Callighen, Brett** — Ice Hockey Player
PO Box 249, Bala ON P0C 1A0, Canada

**Callis, James** — Actor
Alan Siegel Entertainment, 345 N Maple Dr, #375, Beverly Hills CA 90210, USA

**Callow, Simon** — Actor
Paradigm Agency, 360 N Crescent Dr, North Building, Beverly Hills CA 90210 USA

**Calloway, Christopher F (Chris)** — Football Player
1213 Dawnview Dr, Locust Grove GA 30248, USA

**Calloway, Jordan** — Actor
Gold Levin, 8424A Santa Monica Blvd, #706, Los Angeles CA 90069, USA

**Calloway, Vanessa Bell** — Actress
Luber Rocklin Entertainment, 5815 Sunset Blvd, #206, Los Angeles CA 90028 USA

**Calman, Robert F** — Businessman
241 S 6th St, #2302, Philadelphia PA 19106, USA

**Calmus, Rocky A** — Football Player
4131 Trinity Road, Franklin TN 37067, USA

**Calne, Roy Y** — Surgeon
Douglas House Annexe, 18 Trumpington Road, Cambridge CB2 2AS, England

**Caltabiano, Tom** — Actor, Comedian, Producer, Writer
United Talent Agency, U T A Plaza, 9336 Civic Center Dr, Beverly Hills CA 90210 USA

**Calvaer, Andre J** — Electrical Engineer
Blvd Louis Mettewie 270, 1080 Molenbeek-Saint-Jean, Belgium

**Calvert, Mark** — Baseball Player
908 W Waco St, Broken Arrow OK 74011, USA

**Calvet, Jacques** — Businessman, Financier
Bazar de L'Hotel de Ville, 14 Rue du Temple, 75189 Paris, France

**Calvin, Brian** — Artist
David Kordansky Gallery, 3143 S La Cienega Blvd, #A, Los Angeles CA 90016, USA

**Calvin, John** — Actor
445 Sudden Valley, Bellingham WA 98229, USA

**Calvin, William H** — Neurobiologist, Writer
University of Washington, Neurobiology Dept, Seattle WA 98195, USA

**Calzaghe, Joseph W (Joe)** — Boxer
Newbridge Boxing Gym, Bridge St, Newbridge, Caerphily South Wales NP11 5FR, Wales

**Camacho, Carlos A** — Actor
Telemundo Network Group, 2470 W 8th Ave, Hialeah FL 33010 USA

**Camacho, Ernest C (Ernie)** — Baseball Player
746 Saint Regis Way, Salinas CA 93905, USA

**Camacho, Felix** — Boxer
Lisa Terlizzi, 14 Fulton St, Weehawken NJ 07086, USA

**Camacho, Jesse** — Actor
Amanda Rosenthal Agency, 543 Richmond St W, #123, Toronto, ON M5V 1Y6, Canada

**Camacho, Jessie** — Actress, Comedienne
Laura Lichen Mgmt, PO Box 33051, Granada Hills CA 91394, USA

**Camarda, Charles J** — Astronaut
2301 Beach Haven Dr, #102, Virginia Beach VA 23451, USA

**Camargo, Christian** — Actor
Innovative Artists, 1505 10th St, Santa Monica CA 90401 USA

**Camarillo, Richard J (Rich)** — Football Player
1941 E Clubhouse Dr, Phoenix AZ 85048, USA

**Camastra, Danielle** — Actress
Don Buchwald Talent Agency, 6500 Wilshire Blvd, #2200, Los Angeles CA 90048 USA

**Cambage, Elizabeth (Liz)** — Basketball Player
Zhejiang Golden Bulls, 153 Administrative Building 6, Tiyu Chang Rd, Hangzhou Zhejiang, China

**Camberling, Sylvain** — Conductor
S W R Orchestra, 76550 Baden-Baden, Germany

**Cambor, Kathleen** — Writer
Farrar Straus Giroux, 18 W 18th St, #700, New York NY 10011 USA

**Cambor, Peter** — Actor
Brillstein Entertainment Partners, 9150 Wilshire Blvd, #350, Beverly Hills CA 90212 USA

**Cambre, Ronald C** — Businessman
Newmont Mining, 1700 Lincoln St, Denver CO 80203, USA

**Cambreling, Sylvain** — Conductor
Van Walsum Mgmt, Tower Building, 11 York Road, London SE1 7NX, England

**Cambria, John** — Cinematogapher
9939 Topanga Canyon Blvd, #11, Chatsworth CA 91311, USA

**Camby, Marcus D** — Basketball Player
6725 Fite Road, Pearland TX 77584, USA

**Camdessus, Michel J** — Financier
27 Rue de Valois, 75001 Paris, France

**Cameron Bure, Candance** — Actress
Abrams Artists, 9200 W Sunset Blvd, #1125, West Hollywood CA 90069 USA

**Cameron, Al** — Ice Hockey Player
1225 Ormsby Lane NW, Edmonton AB T5T 6R2, Canada

**Cameron, Ann** — Writer
Foster Books/Farrar Straus Giroux, 18 W 18th St, New York NY 10011, USA

**Cameron, Cam** — Football Coach
Miami Dolphins, 7500 SW 30th St, Davie FL 33314, USA

**Cameron, Caressa** — Beauty Queen
Miss America Organization, 1370 Ave of Americas, #1600, New York NY 10019 USA

**Cameron, David** — Prime Minister, England
Prime Minister's Office, 10 Downing St, London SW1A 0AA, England

**Cameron, David** — Fashion Designer
Schauspielschule Krauss, Weihburggasse 19, 1010 Vienna, Austria

**Cameron, Dean** — Actor
Maverick Artists, 6100 Wilshire Blvd, #550, Los Angeles CA 90048, USA

**Cameron, Don R** — Educator, Labor Leader
National Education Association, 1201 16th St NW, Washington DC 20036, USA

**Cameron, Glenn S** — Football Player
250 S Australian Ave, West Palm Beach FL 33401, USA

**Cameron, James** — Director, Producer
Cameron/Pace Group, 2020 N Lincoln St, Burbank CA 91504, USA

**Cameron, Joanna** — Actress
PO Box 198900-9MB 808, Hawi HI 96719, USA

**Cameron, John** — Composer, Conductor
David Wilkinson Assoc, 115 Hazlebury Road, London SW6 2LX, England

**Cameron, Julia** — Writer
Tarcher/Penguin Books, 375 Hudson St, Basement 1, New York NY 10014, USA

**Cameron, Kenneth D** — Astronaut
11333 Gulf Beach Highway, Pensacola FL 32507, USA

**Cameron, Kirk** — Actor
Mark Craig Productions, 1383 Callens, Ventura CA 93003, USA

**Cameron, Michael T (Mike)** — Baseball Player
615 Champions Dr, McDonough GA 30253, USA

**Cameron, Michelle** — Synchronized Swimmer
Box 2 Site 1SS3, Calgary AB T3C 3N9, Canada

**Cameron, Nancy** — Model
Playboy Promotions, 9346 Civic Center Dr, #200, Beverly Hills CA 90210 USA

**Cameron, Stephanie** — Actress
Innovative Artists, 1505 10th St, Santa Monica CA 90401 USA

**Cameron, Tassie** — Producer
Creative Artists Agency, 2000 Ave of Stars, #100, Los Angeles CA 90067 USA

**Camerota, Brett** — Nordic Combined Athlete
Park City Nordic Ski Club, PO Box 682722, Park City UT 84081, USA

**Camil, Jaime** — Singer, Actor
Roar Mgmt, 9701 Wilshire Blvd, #800, Beverly Hills CA 90212 USA

**Camilleri, Andrea** — Writer
Viking Press, 375 Hudson St, New York NY 10014, USA

**Camilleri, Louis C** — Businessman
Kraft Foods Inc, 3 Lake Dr, Northfield IL 60093, USA

**Camilli, Douglas J (Doug)** — Baseball Player
4245 61st Ave, Vero Beach FL 32967, USA

**Camilo, Michel** — Jazz Pianist
Redondo Music & Mgmt, PO Box 216, Katonah NY 10536, USA

**Caminito, Jerry** — Auto Racing Driver
Blue Thunder Racing, 480 Hyson Road, Jackson NJ 08527, USA

**Cammalleri, Michael (Mike)** — Ice Hockey Player
43 Stockdale Crescent, Richmond Hill ON L4C 3T1, Canada

**Cammarata, Bernard** — Businessman
T J X Companies, 770 Cochituate Road, Framingham MA 01701, USA

**Cammuso, Frank** — Cartoonist
1725 James St, #1, Syracuse NY 13206, USA

**Camp, Anna** — Actress
United Talent Agency, U T A Plaza, 9336 Civic Center Dr, Beverly Hills CA 90210 USA

**Camp, Bill** — Actor
Innovative Artists, 1505 10th St, Santa Monica CA 90401 USA

**Camp, Colleen** — Actress
Colleen Camp Productions, 6464 Sunset Blvd, #800, Los Angeles CA 90028, USA

**Camp, Greg** — Guitarist (Smash Mouth)
Creative Artists Agency, 2000 Ave of Stars, #100, Los Angeles CA 90067 USA

**Camp, Jeffrey B** — Artist
Browse & Darby, 19 Cork St, London W1X 2LP, England

**Camp, Jeremy T** — Singer, Actor
Third Coast Artists Agency, 2021 21st Ave S, #220, Nashville TN 37212, USA

**Camp, Shawn** — Singer, Guitarist, Songwriter
Tamara Saviano Media, 1603 Horton Ave, Nashville TN 37212, USA

**Camp, Shawn** — Baseball Player
9416 Deep Creek Lane, Fredericksburg VA 22407, USA

**Camp, Steve** — Singer
Third Coast Artists Agency, 2021 21st Ave S, #220, Nashville TN 37212, USA

**Campanella, Joseph** — Actor
4196 Colfax Ave, Studio City CA 91604, USA

**Campaneris, B Dagoberto (Bert)** — Baseball Player
9797 N 105th Place, Scottsdale AZ 85258, USA

**Campanis, James A (Jim)** — Baseball Player
17082 Cascades Ave, Yorba Linda CA 92886, USA

**Campau, Thomas E** — Cinematographer
2000 S Hammond Lake Dr, West Bloomfield MI 48324, USA

**Campbell - Campbell**

|  |  |
|---|---|
| **Campbell, A P D Kim** | Prime Minister, Canada |
| Club de Madrid, C/Goya 5-7, Pasaje 2, 28001 Madrid, Spain | |
| **Campbell, Alan** | Actor |
| Douglas Gorman Rothacker Wilhelm, 1501 Broadway, #703, New York NY 10036 USA | |
| **Campbell, Allan McCulloch** | Biologist |
| 947 Mears Court, Stanford CA 94305, USA | |
| **Campbell, Andy** | Actor, Comedian |
| OmniPop Talent Group, 4605 Lankershim Blvd, #201, Toluca Lake CA 91602 USA | |
| **Campbell, Brian W** | Ice Hockey Player |
| Florida Panthers, 1 Panthers Parkway, Sunrise FL 33323 USA | |
| **Campbell, Bruce** | Actor |
| A P A Talent & Literary Agency, 405 S Beverly Dr, #300, Beverly Hills CA 90212 USA | |
| **Campbell, Bruce A** | Geophysicist |
| National Air/Space Museum, Smithsonian Institution, Earth/Planetary Studies, Washington DC 20560, USA | |
| **Campbell, Bryan A** | Ice Hockey Player |
| 10895 Tamoron Lane, Boca Raton FL 33498, USA | |
| **Campbell, Calais** | Football Player |
| Arizona Cardinals, PO Box 888, Phoenix AZ 85001 USA | |
| **Campbell, Cassie** | Ice Hockey Player |
| Team Canada, 2424 University Dr NW, Calgary AB T2N 3Y9, Canada | |
| **Campbell, Cheryl** | Actress |
| Amanda Howard, 74 Clerkenwell Road, London EC1M 5QA, England | |
| **Campbell, Christa** | Actress, Model |
| Sovereign Talent Group, 8421 Wilshire Blvd, #200, Beverly Hills CA 90211, USA | |
| **Campbell, Christian** | Actor |
| Don Buchwald Talent Agency, 6500 Wilshire Blvd, #2200, Los Angeles CA 90048 USA | |
| **Campbell, Clifton** | Producer |
| I C M Partners, 10250 Constellation Blvd, #900, Los Angeles CA 90067 USA | |
| **Campbell, Colin** | Ice Hockey Player |
| National Hockey League, 50 Bay St, #1100, Toronto ON M5J 2X8, Canada | |
| **Campbell, Colin G** | Foundation Executive |
| Colonial Williamsburg Foundation, PO Box 1776, Williamsburg VA 23187, USA | |
| **Campbell, Conchita** | Actress |
| Red Management, Box 3, 415 W Esplanade, North Vancouver BC V7M, Canada | |
| **Campbell, D Chad** | Golfer |
| 200 Glade Road, Colleyville TX 76034, USA | |
| **Campbell, Daniel A (Dan)** | Football Player |
| PO Box 977, County Road 2111, Meridian TX 76665, USA | |
| **Campbell, David** | Actor, Singer |
| Caplice Mgmt, PO Box 381, Darlinghurst NSW 1300, Australia | |
| **Campbell, David W** | Baseball Player |
| 726 N Dundee Dr, Post Falls ID 83854, USA | |
| **Campbell, Derrick** | Speed Skater |
| Skate Canada, 865 Shefford Road, Ottawa ON K1J 1H9, Canada | |
| **Campbell, Earl C** | Football Player |
| 4305 Verano Dr, Austin TX 78735, USA | |
| **Campbell, Elden J** | Basketball Player |
| 17252 Hawthorne Blvd, #493, Torrance CA 90504, USA | |
| **Campbell, Eugene E (Gene)** | Ice Hockey Player |
| 6149 Sugar Mill Lane, Mound MN 55364, USA | |
| **Campbell, Gary K** | Football Player |
| PO Box 775353, Steamboat Springs CO 80477, USA | |
| **Campbell, Glen** | Singer, Guitarist |
| Gursey Schneider, 1888 Century Park E, #900, Los Angeles CA 90067, USA | |
| **Campbell, Gregory** | Ice Hockey Player |
| PO Box 342, Tilsonburg ON N4G 4H8, Canada | |
| **Campbell, Ian** | Singer |
| Act 1 Entertainment, PO Box 1079, New Haven CT 06504, USA | |
| **Campbell, Isobel** | Singer, Cellist (Belle & Sebastian) |
| Red Ryder Entertainment, 1532 N Milwaukee Ave, #207, Chicago IL 60622, USA | |
| **Campbell, Jason** | Football Player |
| Cincinnati Bengals, 1 Paul Brown Stadium, Cincinnati OH 45202 USA | |
| **Campbell, Jeff** | Football Player |
| 10205 Birdlip Circle, Austin TX 78733, USA | |
| **Campbell, Jennifer L** | Actress, Model |
| 9200 W Sunset Blvd, #1130, West Hollywood CA 90069, USA | |
| **Campbell, Jim** | Ice Hockey Player |
| 32 Lemp Road, Saint Louis MO 63122, USA | |
| **Campbell, John** | Bassist (Lamb of God) |
| Entertainment Services, 1000 Main Street Plaza, #303, Voorhees NJ 08043, USA | |
| **Campbell, John** | Harness Racing Driver |
| John D Campbell Stable, 823 Allison Dr, River Vale NJ 07675, USA | |
| **Campbell, John F** | Army General |
| I S A Force/US Forces Afghanistan, N A T O Headquarters, Blvd Leopold III, 1110 Brussels, Belgium | |
| **Campbell, John W** | Football Player |
| 12908 Welcome Lane, Burnsville MN 55337, USA | |
| **Campbell, Jonny** | Director |
| Independent Talent Group, 40 Whitfield St, London W1T 2RH, England | |
| **Campbell, Julia** | Actress |
| Innovative Artists, 1505 10th St, Santa Monica CA 90401 USA | |
| **Campbell, Kate** | Singer, Songwriter |
| Large River Music, PO Box 121743, Nashville TN 37212, USA | |
| **Campbell, Kevin W** | Baseball Player |
| 207 Ridout Dr, Des Arc AR 72040, USA | |
| **Campbell, L Arthur** | Molecular Geneticist |
| Rockefeller University Medical Center, 1230 York Ave, New York NY 10065 USA | |
| **Campbell, LaMar** | Football Player |
| 2511 W 7th St, Chester PA 19013, USA | |
| **Campbell, Larry Joe** | Actor |
| A P A Talent & Literary Agency, 405 S Beverly Dr, #300, Beverly Hills CA 90212 USA | |
| **Campbell, Levin H** | Judge |
| US Court of Appeals, 1 Courthouse Way, #9400, Boston MA 02210, USA | |
| **Campbell, Lewis B** | Businessman |
| Textron Inc, 40 Westminster St, #500, Providence RI 02903, USA | |
| **Campbell, Luther (Skywalker)** | Rap Artist (2 Live Crew) |
| 8000 Governors Square Blvd, #304, Hialeah FL 33016, USA | |

**Campbell, Marion**
351 Marsh Point Circle, Saint Augustine FL 32080, USA — Football Player, Coach

**Campbell, Martin**
Independent Talent Group, 40 Whitfield St, London W1T 2RH, England — Director

**Campbell, Mary Schmidt**
New York University, Tisch Art School, 721 Broadway, New York NY 10003, USA — Art Historian

**Campbell, Menzies**
House of Commons, Westminster, London SW1A 0AA, England — Government Official, England

**Campbell, Michael**
Master's International, Hurst Grove, Sandford Lane, Hurst, Berkshire R10 0SQ, England — Golfer

**Campbell, Naomi**
I M G Models, 304 Park Ave S, #PH N, New York NY 10010 USA — Model, Singer, Actress

**Campbell, Natalie**
Playboy Promotions, 9346 Civic Center Dr, #200, Beverly Hills CA 90210 USA — Model

**Campbell, Nathaniel (Nate)**
Don King Productions, 501 Fairway Dr, Deerfield Beach FL 33441 USA — Boxer

**Campbell, Neve**
United Talent Agency, U T A Plaza, 9336 Civic Center Dr, Beverly Hills CA 90210 USA — Actress

**Campbell, Nicholas**
Noble Caplan Abrams, 1260 Yonge St, #200, Toronto ON M4T 1W6, Canada — Actor

**Campbell, Paul**
Pacific Artists Mgmt, 112 E 3rd Ave, #210, Vancouver BC V5T 1C8, Canada — Actor

**Campbell, Richard**
National Hockey League, 50 Bay St, #1100, Toronto ON M5J 2X8, Canada — Ice Hockey Player, Coach

**Campbell, Robert**
54 Antrim St, Cambridge MA 02139, USA — Architectural Critic

**Campbell, Tevin**
Universal Attractions, 135 W 26th St, #1200, New York NY 10001 USA — Singer

**Campbell, Tisha**
Paul Kohner, 9300 Wilshire Blvd, #555, Beverly Hills CA 90212 USA — Actress, Singer

**Campbell, Tracyanne**
Ground Control Touring, 20 Jay St, #826, Brooklyn NY 11201 USA — Singer, Guitarist (Camera Obscura)

**Campbell, Vivian**
Front Line Mgmt, 1100 Glendon Ave, #2000, Los Angeles CA 90024 USA — Guitarist (Def Leppard, Whitesnake)

**Campbell, William**
Intuit Inc, PO Box 7850, Mountain View CA 94039, USA — Businessman

**Campbell, William J**
3267 Alex Findlay Place, Sarasota FL 34240, USA — Air Force General

**Campbell, William O (Billy)**
L I N K Entertainment, 11872 La Grange Ave, Los Angeles CA 90025 USA — Actor

**Campbell, William R (Bill)**
133 S Hale St, Palatine IL 60067, USA — Baseball Player

**Campbell, Woodrow L (Woody)**
9122 Weymouth Dr, Houston TX 77031, USA — Football Player

**Campbell-Bower, Jamie**
Dalzell & Beresford, 55 Charterhouse St, Paddock Suite, London EC1M 6HA, England — Actor

**Campbell-Hughes, Antonia**
Independent Talent Group, 40 Whitfield St, London W1T 2RH, England — Actress

**Campbell-Martin, Tisha**
Paul Kohner, 9300 Wilshire Blvd, #555, Beverly Hills CA 90212 USA — Actress, Singer

**Campedelli, Dominic**
732 Jerusalem Road, Cohasset MA 02025, USA — Ice Hockey Player

**Campen, James F**
2789 Ichabod Lane, Green Bay WI 54313, USA — Football Player

**Campese, David I**
D C Management Group, 870 Pacific Highway, #4, Gordon NSW 2072, Australia — Rugby Player

**Campfield, William (Billy)**
930 Glenmore Way, #K, Westerville OH 43082, USA — Football Player

**Campi, Ray**
2872 1/2 W Ave 35, Los Angeles CA 90065, USA — Singer, Guitarist

**Campion, Cris**
Artmedia, 20 Ave Rapp, 75007 Paris, France — Actor

**Campion, Jane**
H L A Mgmt, PO Box 1536, Strawberry Hills, Sydney NSW 2012, Australia — Director

**Campion, Robert T**
4170 Kraft Ave, Studio City CA 91604, USA — Businessman

**Campisi, Amber**
Playboy Promotions, 9346 Civic Center Dr, #200, Beverly Hills CA 90210 USA — Model

**Campo, David C (Dave)**
Dallas Cowboys, 1 Cowboys Parkway, Irving TX 75063 USA — Football Coach

**Campos, Alana**
10925 Bluffside Dr, #203, Studio City CA 91604, USA — Model

**Campos, Antonio**
United Talent Agency, U T A Plaza, 9336 Civic Center Dr, Beverly Hills CA 90210 USA — Director, Producer

**Campos, Jorge**
Federacion de Futbol Association, Colima 373, Col Roma N, Del Cuauhtemoc DF 06700 CP, Mexico — Soccer Player

**Campos, Tony**
Warner Bros Records, 3300 Warner Blvd, Burbank CA 91505 USA — Bassist (Static-X, Soulfly, Asesino)

**Campuzano Lopez, Felipe**
Urbanizacion Cumbres de Marbella 47, 29601 Los Naguelos, Marbella, Spain — Composer

**Cam'ron**
I C M Partners, 10250 Constellation Blvd, #900, Los Angeles CA 90067 USA — Rap Artist, Actor

**Camus, Philippe**
Alcatel-Lucent, 54 Rue Le Boetie, 75006 Paris, France — Businessman

**Canada, Geoffrey**
Harlem Children's Zone Project, 35 E 125th St, New York NY 10035, USA — Educator, Social Activist

**Canada, Ron**
C E S D, 10635 Santa Monica Blvd, #130, Los Angeles CA 90025 USA — Actor

**Canadas, Esther**
Wilhelmina Models, 300 Park Ave S, #200, New York NY 10010 USA — Model, Actress

**Canady, Alexa I**
6064 Forest Green Road, Pensacola FL 32505, USA — Pediatric Neurosurgeon

**Canals-Barrera, Maria**
A P A Talent & Literary Agency, 405 S Beverly Dr, #300, Beverly Hills CA 90212 USA — Actress

**Canary, David**
698 W End Ave, #1B, New York NY 10025, USA — Actor

# C

**Canby, William C, Jr** — Judge
US Court of Appeals, US Courthouse, 401 W Washington St, #1, Phoenix AZ 85003, USA

**Cancellara, Fabian** — Cyclist
Team C S C, Riis Cycling, Firskovvej 36, 2800 Lyngby, Denmark

**Candaele, Casey T** — Baseball Player
251 Broad St, San Luis Obispo CA 93405, USA

**Candelaria, John R** — Baseball Player
3122 Elroy Ave, Pittsburgh PA 15227, USA

**Candelaria, Richard G** — WW II Army Air Corps Hero
3812 Conough Lane, Las Vegas NV 89129, USA

**Candelo, Juan Carlos (J C)** — Boxer
T's K O Fight Club, 3730 Wheeling St, #10, Denver CO 80239, USA

**Candiotti, Thomas C (Tom)** — Baseball Player
6061 E Jenan Dr, Scottsdale AZ 85254, USA

**Candyman** — Rap Artist
Groove Entertainment, 1005 N Alfred St, #2, West Hollywood CA 90069, USA

**Cane, Louis P J** — Artist
37 Rue D'Enghien, 75010 Paris, France

**Cane, Mark A** — Oceanographer, Climatologist
Lamont Doherty Earth Observatory, Route 9W, Palisades NY 10964, USA

**Canella, Guido** — Architect
Via Revere 7, 20123 Milan, Italy

**Canepa, John C** — Financier
Crowe Chizek, 400 Riverfront Plaza, Grand Rapids MI 49503, USA

**Canestri, Giovanni Cardinal** — Religious Leader
Archdiocese of Genoa-Bobbio, Piazza Matteotti 4, 16123 Genoa, Italy

**Canet, Guillaume** — Actor, Director
U B B A, 6 Rue de Braque, 75003 Paris, France

**Canete, Ariel** — Golfer
Advantage International, 1751 Pinnacle Dr, #1500, McLean VA 22102 USA

**Canfield, Jack** — Writer
PO Box 30880, Santa Barbara CA 93130, USA

**Canfield, Paul** — Physicist
Iowa State University, Physics Dept, Ames IA 50011, USA

**Canfield, William N (Bill)** — Editorial Cartoonist
Star Ledger, Editorial Dept, 1 Star Ledger Plaza, Newark NJ 07102, USA

**Cangelosi, John A** — Baseball Player
10914 Caribou Lane, Orland Park IL 60467, USA

**Cangemi, Joseph P** — Psychologist
1409 Mount Ayr Circle, Bowling Green KY 42103, USA

**Canibus** — Rap Artist
J L Entertainment, 18653 Ventura Blvd, #340, Los Angeles CA 91356 USA

**Canin, Ethan** — Writer
Rogers Coleridge White, 20 Powis Mews, London W11 1JN, England

**Canin, Serena** — Concert Violinist
David Rowe Artists, 24 Bessom St, #2, Marblehead MA 01945, USA

**Canizales, Jose (Gaby)** — Boxer
4215 Santa Marie Ave, Laredo TX 78041, USA

**Canizales, Orlando** — Boxer
17542 College Port Dr, Laredo TX 78045, USA

**Canizares Llovera, Antonio Cardinal** — Religious Leader
Divine Worship Congregation, Palazzo delle Congregazioni, Piazza Pio XII 10, 00193 Rome, Italy

**Cannavale, Bobby** — Actor
I C M Partners, 730 5th Ave, New York NY 10019 USA

**Cannavaro, Fabio** — Soccer Player
F C Real Madrid, Avda Concha Espana 1, 28036 Madrid, Spain

**Cannida, James T, II** — Football Player
4504 Harmony Place, Rohnert Park CA 94928, USA

**Cannizzaro, Christopher J (Chris)** — Baseball Player
13597 Grain Lane, San Diego CA 92129, USA

**Cannom, Greg** — Makeup Artist
223 Alameda Ave, #1, Burbank CA 91502, USA

**Cannon, Danny** — Director
Steve Kenis Co, 95 Barkston Gardens, London SW5 0EU, England

**Cannon, Dyan** — Actress
1100 Alta Loma Road, #808, West Hollywood CA 90069, USA

**Cannon, Freddy (Boom Boom)** — Singer, Songwriter
5119 Surfrider Way, Oxnard CA 93035, USA

**Cannon, Joe** — Soccer Player
Vancouver Whitecaps, 375 Water St, #550, Vancouver V6B 5C6, Canada

**Cannon, John (Ace)** — Saxophonist
J L Entertainment, 18653 Ventura Blvd, #340, Los Angeles CA 91356 USA

**Cannon, John R** — Football Player
2911 W Bay Vista Ave, Tampa FL 33611, USA

**Cannon, Katherine** — Actress
1310 S Westholme Ave, Los Angeles CA 90024, USA

**Cannon, Mark M** — Football Player
2604 Riveroaks Dr, Arlington TX 76006, USA

**Cannon, Nick** — Actor, Comedian, Writer
I C M Partners, 10250 Constellation Blvd, #900, Los Angeles CA 90067 USA

**Cannon, Robert H, Jr** — Aerospace Engineer
Stanford University, Aeronautics/Astronautics Dept, Stanford CA 94305, USA

**Cannon, William A (Billy)** — Football Player
8851 Sage Hill Dr, Saint Francisville LA 70775, USA

**Cano Mercedes, Robinson J** — Baseball Player
Seattle Mariners, Safeco Field, PO Box 4100, Seattle WA 98194 USA

**Cano, Pablo D** — Sculptor
501 SW 24th Ave, Miami FL 33135, USA

**Cano, Roberto** — Actor
C F Representaciones, Carrera 13A, #97-82,Oficina 306, Bogota, Cundinamarca 00000, Colombia

**Canogar, Rafael** — Artist
Calle de la Bolsa 14, 28012 Madrid, Spain

**Canonero, Milena** — Costume Designer
I C M Partners, 10250 Constellation Blvd, #900, Los Angeles CA 90067 USA

**Canova, Diana** — Actress
TalentWorks, 3500 W Olive Ave, #1400, Burbank CA 91505 USA

**Canby - Canova**

**Canseco, Jose, Jr** — Baseball Player
Canseco Inc, 112 Panlock Court, Irmo SC 29063, USA
**Cantaline, Anita** — Bowler
31455 Pinto Dr, Warren MI 48093, USA
**Canterbury, Chandler** — Actor
United Talent Agency, U T A Plaza, 9336 Civic Center Dr, Beverly Hills CA 90210 USA
**Cantey, Charlsie** — Sportscaster
ABC-TV, Sports Dept, 77 W 66th St, New York NY 10023 USA
**Cantley, Lewis C** — Cell Biologist, Biochemist
Cornell University, Weill Cornell Medical College, 1300 York Ave, New York NY 10065, USA
**Canto, Adan** — Actor
United Talent Agency, U T A Plaza, 9336 Civic Center Dr, Beverly Hills CA 90210 USA
**Canton, Joanna** — Actress
7790 Via Belfiore, #1, San Diego CA 92129, USA
**Canton, Mark** — Businessman, Producer
Atmosphere Entertainment, 4751 Wilshire Blvd, #300, Los Angeles CA 90010, USA
**Cantona, Eric** — Soccer Player
Mikado, 105 Ave Raymond Poincare, 75016 Paris, France
**Cantone, Mario** — Actor, Comedian
Gersh Agency, 9465 Wilshire Blvd, #600, Beverly Hills CA 90212 USA
**Cantor, Charles R** — Molecular Biologist
Sequenom Inc, 3595 John Hopkins Court, San Diego CA 92121, USA
**Cantor, Geoffrey** — Actor
Stone Manners Salners, 6100 Wilshire Blvd, #1500, Los Angeles CA 90035 USA
**Cantor, Nancy E** — Educator
Syracuse University, Chancellor's Office, Syracuse NY 13244, USA
**Cantor, Tim** — Artist
527 4th Ave, San Diego CA 92101, USA
**Cantrell, Blu** — Singer
Universal Attractions, 135 W 26th St, #1200, New York NY 10001 USA
**Cantrell, Cady** — Model
Playboy Promotions, 9346 Civic Center Dr, #200, Beverly Hills CA 90210 USA
**Cantrell, Jerry F, Jr** — Singer, Guitarist (Alice in Chains)
Core Entertainment Organization, 14724 Ventura Blvd, #PH, Sherman Oaks CA 91403, USA
**Cantrell, Lana** — Singer
300 E 71st St, #91A, New York NY 10021, USA
**Cantu Guzman, Jorge L** — Baseball Player
5015 24th Ave S, Tampa Bay FL 33619, USA
**Canty, Christopher L (Chris)** — Football Player
Baltimore Ravens, Ravens Stadium, 1 Winning Dr, Baltimore MD 21230 USA
**Canup, Robin** — Astronomer
Southwest Research Institute, 1050 Walnut St, #300, Boulder CO 80302, USA
**Capaldi, Peter** — Actor, Writer, Director
United Agents, 12-26 Lexington St, London W1F 0LE, England
**Caparulo, John** — Actor, Comedian, Writer
Parallel Entertainment, 9420 Wilshire Blvd, #250, Beverly Hills CA 90212, USA
**Capasso, Federico** — Physicist
Lucent Technologies, Bell Laboratories, 600 Mountain Ave, New Providence NJ 07974, USA
**Capecchi, Mario R** — Nobel Medicine Laureate
778 E 13800 S, Draper UT 84020, USA
**Capellas, Michael** — Businessman
M C I, 500 Clinton Center Dr, #2200, Clinton MS 39056, USA
**Capellino, Ally** — Fashion Designer
N1R, Metropolitan Wharf, Wapping Wall, London E1 9SS, England
**Capellmann, Nadine** — Equestrian
Haller Str 46, 52325 Wurselen, Germany
**Capello, Fabio** — Soccer Player, Manager
F C Real Madrid, Avda Concha Espana 1, 28036 Madrid, Spain
**Capers, Dom** — Football Coach
814 Hilltop Dr, Walpole MA 02081, USA
**Caperton, W Gaston, III** — Governor, WV; Foundation Executive
College Board, President's Office, 45 Columbus Ave, New York NY 10023, USA
**Capilouto, Eli** — Educator
University of Kentucky, President's Office, Lexington KY 40506, USA
**Caplan, Lizzy** — Actress
Mosiac Media Group, 9200 W Sunset Blvd, #1000, Los Angeles CA 90069 USA
**Capleton** — Singer
Agency Group Ltd, 142 W 57th St, #600, New York NY 10019 USA
**Caplin, Mortimer M** — Government Official
5610 Wisconsin Ave NW, #18E, Chevy Chase MD 20815, USA
**Capobianco, Tito** — Opera Director
Pittsburgh Opera Co, 711 Penn Ave, #800, Pittsburgh PA 15222, USA
**Caponera, John** — Actor, Comedian
Messina Baker Entertainment, 955 Carillo Dr, #100, Los Angeles CA 90048, USA
**Caponi-Byrnes, Donna** — Golfer
2731 Silver River Trail, Orlando FL 32828, USA
**Caponigro, Paul** — Photographer
73 Cross Road, Cushing ME 04563, USA
**Capovilla, Loris Francesco Cardinal** — Religious Leader
Prelate of Loreto, Piazza della Madonna 1, 60025 Loteto [Ancona], Italy
**Cappelletti, Gino R M** — Football Player
19 Louis Dr, Wellesley MA 02481, USA
**Cappelletti, John R** — Football Player
23791 Brant Lane, Laguna Niguel CA 92677, USA
**Capps, Matthew D (Matt)** — Baseball Player
6348 S Summers Circle, Douglasville GA 30135, USA
**Capps, Ron** — Drag Racing Driver
Copenhagen Racing, 1232 Distribution Way, Vista CA 92081, USA
**Capps, Steve** — Computer Software Designer
Microsoft Corp, 1 Microsoft Way, Redmond WA 98052, USA
**Capra, Francis** — Actor
Curtis Talent Mgmt, 9607 Arby Dr, Beverly Hills CA 90210, USA
**Capra, Fritjof** — Physicist, Systems Theorist
PO Box 9066, Berkeley CA 94709, USA
**Capra, Lee W (Buzz)** — Baseball Player
15039 W Keswick Place, Lockport IL 60441, USA

# C

**Capriati, Jennifer**
PO Box 7078, Wesley Chapel FL 33545, USA — *Tennis Player*

**Caprice**
Select Model Mgmt, 43 King St, London WC2E, England — *Model, Singer, Songwriter*

**Caprioli, Anita**
Carol Levi Mgmt, Via Giuseppe Pisanelli 2, 00196 Rome, Italy — *Actress*

**Capron, Robert**
Generation TV, 20 W 20th St, #1008, New York NY 10011, USA — *Actor*

**Capshaw, Jessica**
Creative Artists Agency, 2000 Ave of Stars, #100, Los Angeles CA 90067 USA — *Actress*

**Capshaw, Kate**
PO Box 491356, Los Angeles CA 90049, USA — *Actress*

**Capuano, Christopher F (Chris)**
10953 E Tusayan Trail, Scottsdale AZ 85255, USA — *Baseball Player*

**Capuano, Dave, Jr**
145 Capuano Ave, Cranston RI 02920, USA — *Ice Hockey Player*

**Capuano, Jack**
New York Islanders, 1255 Hempstead Turnpike, Uniondale NY 11553 USA — *Ice Hockey Player, Coach*

**Capucon, Gautier**
Columbia Artists Mgmt Inc, 5 Columbus Circle, 1790 Broadway, #1600, New York NY 10019 USA — *Concert Cellist*

**Capucon, Renaud**
Columbia Artists Mgmt Inc, 5 Columbus Circle, 1790 Broadway, #1600, New York NY 10019 USA — *Concert Violinist*

**Capurro, Scott**
Coolwaters Productions, 10061 Riverside Dr, Box 531, Toluca Lake CA 91602 USA — *Actor*

**Cara, Irene**
Caramel Productions, 2143 SR 54, #116, New Port Richey FL 34653, USA — *Singer, Actress, Songwriter*

**Carafotes, Paul**
C E S D, 10635 Santa Monica Blvd, #130, Los Angeles CA 90025 USA — *Actor*

**Caramanlis, Costas**
Prime Minister's Office, Maximos Mansion, 19 Irodou Attikou St, 10674 Athens, Greece — *Prime Minister, Greece*

**Carano, Gina J**
Syndicate, 8265 Sunset Blvd, #205, Los Angeles CA 90046, USA — *Actress, Mixed Martial Artist*

**Carano, Glenn T**
2551 Lakeridge Shores E, Reno NV 89519, USA — *Football Player*

**Carapella, Alfred R (Al)**
10 Woodlot Road, Eastchester NY 10709, USA — *Football Player*

**Carasco, Joe (King)**
Texas Sounds, 2317 Pecan St, Dickinson TX 77539, USA — *Singer*

**Carax, Leos**
Artmedia, 20 Ave Rapp, 75007 Paris, France — *Director*

**Caray, Harry C (Chip), III**
1302 Azalea Lane, Maitland FL 32751, USA — *Sportscaster*

**Carbajal, Michael**
PO Box 510, Phoenix AZ 85001, USA — *Boxer*

**Carberry, Deirdre**
American Ballet Theater, 890 Broadway, #300, New York NY 10003, USA — *Ballerina*

**Carbo, Bernardo (Bernie)**
6352 Woodside Dr S, Theodore AL 36582, USA — *Baseball Player*

**Carbonara, David**
Creative Artists Agency, 2000 Ave of Stars, #100, Los Angeles CA 90067 USA — *Composer*

**Carbonell, Nestor**
Paradigm Agency, 360 N Crescent Dr, North Building, Beverly Hills CA 90210 USA — *Actor*

**Carcaterra, Lorenzo**
Pitt Group, 9465 Wilshire Blvd, #420, Beverly Hills CA 90212, USA — *Writer*

**Card, Andrew H, Jr**
1207 Buchana St, McLean VA 22101, USA — *Secretary, Transportation*

**Card, Michael**
Michael Card Music, PO Box 586, Franklin TN 37065, USA — *Singer, Musician, Songwriter*

**Card, Orson Scott**
401 Willoughby Blvd, Greensboro NC 27408, USA — *Writer*

**Cardamone, Richard J**
US Court of Appeals, 10 Broad St, #322, Utica NY 13501, USA — *Judge*

**Cardellini, Linda**
I/D Public Relations, 7060 Hollywood Blvd, #800, Los Angeles CA 90028 USA — *Actress*

**Carden, Joan M**
Avere Artists Mgmt, 26 Oxley Dr, Bowral NSW 2576, Australia — *Opera Singer*

**Carden, Michael (Mike)**
Crush Music Media Mgmt, 60-62 E 11th St, #700, New York NY 10003, USA — *Guitarist (Academy Is), Songwriter*

**Cardenal, Jose D**
118 Bridgewater Court, Bradenton FL 34212, USA — *Baseball Player*

**Cardenas, Leonardo L (Chico)**
5412 Ravenna St, Cincinnati OH 45227, USA — *Baseball Player*

**Cardenas, Robert L**
6143 Madra Ave, San Diego CA 92129, USA — *Test Pilot, Air Force General*

**Cardin, Claude**
13 Rue Boucher, Sorel QC J3P 1E7, Canada — *Ice Hockey Player*

**Cardin, Pierre**
59 Rue du Faubourg-Saint-Honore, 75008 Paris, France — *Fashion Designer*

**Cardinal, Brian L**
15615 Shining Spring Dr, Westfield IN 46074, USA — *Basketball Player*

**Cardinal, Douglas J**
7011A Manchester Blvd, #315, Alexandria VA 22310, USA — *Architect*

**Cardinale, Claudia**
Agence A2, 139 Boul Magenta, 75010 Paris, France — *Actress*

**Cardona, Manolo**
D2 Management, 9255 Sunset Blvd, #600, West Hollywood CA 90069, USA — *Actor*

**Cardona, Manuel**
Max-Planck-Institut, Heisenbergstr 1, 70569 Stuttgart, Germany — *Physicist*

**Cardona, Prudencio**
4845 NW 7th St, #402, Miami FL 33126, USA — *Boxer*

**Cardone, Vivian**
C E S D, 10635 Santa Monica Blvd, #130, Los Angeles CA 90025 USA — *Actress*

**Cardow, Cameron (Cam)**
Ottawa Sentinental, 11 Baxter Road, Box 5020, Ottawa ON K2C 3M4, Canada — *Editorial Cartoonist*

**Cardoza, Dennis A**
Manatt Phelps Phillips, 700 12th St NW, #1100, Washington DC 20005, USA — *Representative, CA*

**Capriati - Cardoza**

**C**

|  |  |
|---|---|
| **Care, Peter**<br>Bob Industries, 1313 5th St, Santa Monica CA 90401, USA | Director, Producer, Writer |
| **Carell, Steve**<br>W M E Entertainment, 9601 Wilshire Blvd, #300, Beverly Hills CA 90210 USA | Actor, Writer |
| **Carelli, Rick**<br>PO Box 1000, Arvada CO 80001, USA | Truck Racing Driver |
| **Caretto-Brown, Patty**<br>16079 Mesquite Circle, Fountain Valley CA 92708, USA | Swimmer |
| **Carew, Rodney C (Rod)**<br>1171 Via Santiago, Corona CA 92882, USA | Baseball Player |
| **Carey, Clare**<br>Baker Winokur Ryder Public Relations, 9100 Wilshire Blvd, #500W, Beverly Hills CA 90212 USA | Actress |
| **Carey, Danny**<br>Volcano Records, 3375 Cahuenga Blvd, #590, Los Angeles CA 90068, USA | Drummer (Tool) |
| **Carey, Drew**<br>Gersh Agency, 9465 Wilshire Blvd, #600, Beverly Hills CA 90212 USA | Actor, Comedian |
| **Carey, Duane G**<br>5938 Instone Circle, Colorado Springs CO 80922, USA | Astronaut |
| **Carey, Ezekiel**<br>509 E Ridge Crest Blvd, #A, Ridge Crest CA 93555, USA | Singer (Flamingos) |
| **Carey, George L**<br>Gloucestershire University, Chancellory, Cheltenham GL50 2RH, England | Religious Leader |
| **Carey, Gerard**<br>Gavin Barker Assoc, 2D Wimpole St, London W1G 0EB, England | Actor |
| **Carey, Jim**<br>5351 Hunt Club Way, Sarasota FL 34238, USA | Ice Hockey Player |
| **Carey, Maggie**<br>United Talent Agency, U T A Plaza, 9336 Civic Center Dr, Beverly Hills CA 90210 USA | Director, Producer, Writer |
| **Carey, Mariah**<br>Creative Artists Agency, 2000 Ave of Stars, #100, Los Angeles CA 90067 USA | Singer, Songwriter |
| **Carey, Matthew**<br>J K A Talent, 12725 Ventura Blvd, #H, Studio City CA 91604, USA | Actor |
| **Carey, Peter**<br>I C M Partners, 730 5th Ave, New York NY 10019 USA | Writer |
| **Carey, Vernon A**<br>5321 Thoroughbred Lane, Southwest Ranches FL 33330, USA | Football Player |
| **Caria, Marco**<br>I M G Artists, Hogarth Business Park, Chiswick, London W4 2TH, England | Opera Singer |
| **Carides, Gia**<br>Innovative Artists, 1505 10th St, Santa Monica CA 90401 USA | Actress |
| **Caridis, Miltiades**<br>Himmelhofgasse 10, 1130 Vienna, Austria | Conductor |
| **Carillo, Mary**<br>822 Boylston St, #203, Chestnut Hill PA 02467, USA | Sportscaster, Tennis Player |
| **Carillo, Tony**<br>United Feature Syndicate, PO Box 5610, Cincinnati OH 45201 USA | Cartoonist (F Minus) |
| **Carimi, Gabe**<br>Atlanta Falcons, 4400 Falcon Parkway, Flowery Branch GA 30542 USA | Football Player |
| **Carion, Christian**<br>Film Talents, 34 Rue du Louvre, 75001 Paris, France | Director, Writer |
| **Carioti, Ricky**<br>Washington Post, Editorial Dept, 1150 15th St NW, Washington DC 20071 USA | Photographer |
| **Cariou, Len**<br>7004 Blvd E, #17D, West New York NJ 07093, USA | Actor |
| **Carithers, William C, Jr**<br>817 The Alameda, Berkeley CA 94707, USA | Physicist |
| **Carkner, Terry**<br>4 Remington Lane, Malvern PA 19355, USA | Ice Hockey Player |
| **Carl XVI Gustaf**<br>Kungliga Slottet, Slottsbacken, 111 30 Stockholm, Sweden | King, Sweden |
| **Carle, Eric**<br>PO Box 485, Northampton MA 01061, USA | Artist |
| **Carlei, Carlo**<br>Bloom Hergott Diemer, 150 S Rodeo Dr, #300, Beverly Hills CA 90212 USA | Director |
| **Carles Gordo, Ricardo M Cardinal**<br>Archdiocese of Barcelona, Carrer del Bisbe 5, 08002 Barcelona, Spain | Religious Leader |
| **Carlesimo, Pete J (P J)**<br>1429 Willard Ave W, Seattle WA 98119, USA | Basketball Coach, Sportscaster |
| **Carleson, Lennart A E**<br>Royal Institute, Kungl Tekniska Hogskloan SE 100 44, Stockholm, Sweden | Abel Mathematics Laureate |
| **Carlestrom, John E**<br>University of Chicago, Astronomy Dept, 5640 S Ellis Ave, Chicago IL 60637, USA | Astronomer |
| **Carleton, K Wayne**<br>9846 Highway 26 E, RR 2 LCD Collingwood, Collingwood ON L9Y 3Z1, Canada | Ice Hockey Player |
| **Carley, Christopher**<br>Untitled Entertainment, 350 S Beverly Dr, #200, Beverly Hills CA 90212 USA | Actor |
| **Carlile, Brandi**<br>A2 Mgmt, 1316 Sherman Ave, #215, Evanston IL 60201, USA | Singer, Guitarist, Songwriter |
| **Carlile, Forbes**<br>16 Cross St, Ryde NSW 2112, Australia | Swimming Coach |
| **Carlin, Amanda**<br>Greene Assoc, 1901 Ave of Stars, #130, Los Angeles CA 90067 USA | Actress |
| **Carlin, Brian**<br>103 Mount Norquay Park SE, Calgary AB T2Z 2R3, Canada | Ice Hockey Player |
| **Carlin, John W**<br>1208 Wyndham Heights Dr, Manhattan KS 66503, USA | Governor, KS |
| **Carling, William D C**<br>Mike Burton Mgmt, Brunswick Road, Gloucester GL1 1JJ, England | Rugby Player, Sportscaster |
| **Carlisle, Belinda**<br>Tony Denton Promotions, Charter House, 157/159 High St, London N14 7DY, England | Singer, Songwriter, Model |
| **Carlisle, Bob**<br>Ray Ware Artist Mgmt, 3108 Saint Stephens Way, Franklin TN 37064, USA | Singer, Songwriter |
| **Carlisle, Cooper M**<br>1693 SW 188th St, Newberry FL 32669, USA | Football Player |
| **Carlisle, Herbert J (Hawk)**<br>Commander, Air Combat Command, Langley Air Force Base VA 23665 USA | Air Force General |

*V.I.P. Address Book*

**Care - Carlisle**

155

# C

**Carlisle, Jodi** — Actress, Comedienne
I C M Partners, 10250 Constellation Blvd, #900, Los Angeles CA 90067 USA

**Carlisle, Mary** — Actress
517 N Rodeo Dr, Beverly Hills CA 90210, USA

**Carlisle, Richard P (Rick)** — Basketball Player, Coach
3925 Greenbrier Dr, Dallas TX 75225, USA

**Carll, Hayes** — Singer, Guitarist, Songwriter
Crowley Artists Mgmt, 602 Wayside Dr, Wimberley TX 78676, USA

**Carlos Moco, Marcolino Jose** — Prime Minister, Angola
Movimento Popular de Libertacao de Angola, Luanda, Angola

**Carlos, Bun E** — Drummer (Cheap Trick)
Oakie Dokie Mgmt, 6090 Central Ave, Saint Petersburg FL 33707, USA

**Carlos, John** — Track Athlete
160 Palisade Point Dr, Ellenwood GA 30294, USA

**Carlos, Wendy** — Composer
B M I, 8730 W Sunset Blvd, #300, Los Angeles CA 90069 USA

**Carlson, Amy** — Actress
Principal Entertainment, 9255 Sunset Blvd, #500, Los Angeles CA 90069 USA

**Carlson, Arne H** — Governor, MN
145 Holly Lane N, Minneapolis MN 55447, USA

**Carlson, Dudley L** — Navy Admiral
Navy League, 2300 Wilson Blvd, #210, Arlington VA 22201, USA

**Carlson, Jack** — Ice Hockey Player
8335 Cedarview Circle, Savage MN 55378, USA

**Carlson, Jesse C** — Baseball Player
654 High Road, Berlin CT 06037, USA

**Carlson, John A** — Businessman
Cray Research, 655 Lone Oak Dr, #A, Saint Paul MN 55121, USA

**Carlson, K C** — Cartoonist (Legion of Super Heroes)
D C Comics, 1700 Broadway, #400, New York NY 10019 USA

**Carlson, Karen** — Actress, Producer, Director
Lisa Lax Agency, 304 Park Ave S, #1100, New York NY 10013, USA

**Carlson, Kelly** — Actress
Gersh Agency, 9465 Wilshire Blvd, #600, Beverly Hills CA 90212 USA

**Carlson, Kent** — Ice Hockey Player
58 Branch Turnpike, #74, Concord NH 03301, USA

**Carlson, Lane** — Model
Warning Models, 1590 S Lewis St, Anaheim CA 92805, USA

**Carlson, M Cody** — Football Player
3417 Foothill Terrace, Austin TX 78731, USA

**Carlson, Mark C** — Baseball Umpire
354 Tall Oak Trail, Tarpon Springs FL 34688, USA

**Carlson, Michael** — Chef
Schwa Restaurant, 1466 N Ashland Ave, Chicago IL 60622, USA

**Carlson, Monica** — Model, Actress
Sports Unlimited, 1732 NW Quimby St, Portland OR 97209, USA

**Carlson, Paulette** — Singer
Fat City Artists, 1906 Chet Atkins Place, #502, Nashville TN 37212 USA

**Carlson, Richard A** — Interior Designer
Swanke Hayden Connell Architects, 295 Lafayette St, New York NY 10012, USA

**Carlson, Shane** — Model
Warning Models, 1590 S Lewis St, Anaheim CA 92805, USA

**Carlson, Steve** — Auto Racing Driver
539 Brickel Road, West Salem WI 54669, USA

**Carlson, Steve E** — Ice Hockey Player
PO Box 3476, Rancho Cordova CA 95741, USA

**Carlson, Tucker** — Commentator
Fox-TV, News Dept, 205 E 67th St, New York NY 10065 USA

**Carlson, Veronica** — Actress
7844 Kavanagh Court, Sarasota FL 34240, USA

**Carlsson, Arvid** — Nobel Medicine Laureate
Gothenborg University, Sahlgrenska Academy, Box 100, 405 30 Gothenborg Sweden

**Carlsson, Ingvar G** — Prime Minister, Sweden
Riksdagen, 100 12 Stockholm, Sweden

**Carlton, Carl** — Singer
Universal Attractions, 135 W 26th St, #1200, New York NY 10001 USA

**Carlton, Hope Marie** — Actress, Model
Playboy Promotions, 9346 Civic Center Dr, #200, Beverly Hills CA 90210 USA

**Carlton, L Wray** — Football Player
29 Pine Terrace, Orchard Park NY 14127, USA

**Carlton, Larry** — Jazz Guitarist, Composer
W B A Entertainment, PO Box 291802, Nashville TN 37229, USA

**Carlton, Paul K, Jr** — Air Force General, Surgeon
ImmuneRegen BioSciences, 8777 Via de Ventura, #280, Scottsdale AZ 85258, USA

**Carlton, Steven N (Steve)** — Baseball Player
G W Sports, 555 S Camino del Rio, #B2, Durango CO 81303, USA

**Carlton, Vanessa** — Singer, Songwriter
Creative Artists Agency, 2000 Ave of Stars, #100, Los Angeles CA 90067 USA

**Carlucci, Dave** — Singer (Danny & the Juniors)
Joe Terry Mgmt, PO Box 279, Williamstown NJ 08094, USA

**Carlucci, Frank C, III** — Secretary, Defense; Businessman
Carlyle Group, 1001 Pennsylvania Ave NW, #220S, Washington DC 20004, USA

**Carlyle, Earl L (Buddy)** — Baseball Player
205 Ashmere Court, Tyrone GA 30290, USA

**Carlyle, Joan H** — Opera Singer
Laundry Cottage, Hammer, North Wales SY13 4QX, England

**Carlyle, Liz** — Writer
1939 High House Road, #185, Cary NC 27519, USA

**Carlyle, Randy** — Ice Hockey Player, Coach
180 S Lakeview Ave, Anaheim CA 92807, USA

**Carlyle, Robert** — Actor
Hamilton Hodell, 20 Golden Square, London W1F 9JL, England

**Carmack, Chris** — Actor
Luber Rocklin Entertainment, 5815 Sunset Blvd, #206, Los Angeles CA 90028 USA

**Carman** — Singer
Carman World Outreach, PO Box 470470, Tulsa OK 74147, USA

**Carman, Brian**
Bill Hollingshead Productions, 1010 Anderson Road, Davis CA 95616 USA — Singer, Guitarist (Chantays)

**Carman, Donald W (Don)**
555 Murex Dr, Naples FL 34102, USA — Baseball Player

**Carman, Gregory W**
US Court of International Trade, 1 Federal Plaza, New York NY 10278, USA — Judge; Representative, NY

**Carmel, Leon J (Duke)**
116 Spring Lake Blvd, Waretown NJ 08758, USA — Baseball Player

**Carmen, Eric**
David Spero Mgmt, 1679 S Belvoir Blvd, Cleveland OH 44121, USA — Singer, Songwriter

**Carmen, Julie**
Greene Assoc, 1901 Ave of Stars, #130, Los Angeles CA 90067 USA — Actress

**Carmichael, Albert R (Hoagy)**
78641 Hampshire Ave, Palm Desert CA 92211, USA — Football Player

**Carmichael, Clint**
Kazarian/Measures/Ruskin, 11969 Ventura Blvd, #300, Studio City CA 91604 USA — Actor

**Carmichael, Daniel A (Dan), Jr**
2764 Elm Ave, Columbus OH 43209, USA — WW II Navy Air Force Hero

**Carmichael, Jesse**
J Records, 745 5th Ave, #600, New York NY 10151 USA — Keyboardist (Maroon 5)

**Carmichael, Katy**
Shining Mgmt, 12 D'Arblay St, London W1F 8DU, England — Actress

**Carmichael, L Harold**
38 Birch Lane, Glassboro NJ 08028, USA — Football Player

**Carmichael, Laura**
Curtis Brown Group, 28-29 Haymarket St, #500, London SW1Y 4SP, England — Actress

**Carmichael, Ricky**
1219 Shady Rest Road, Havana FL 32333, USA — Motorcycle Racing Rider

**Carmine, Michael**
3615 West Dr, Little Neck NY 11363, USA — Cinematographer

**Carmody, Matt**
Metropolitan Talent Agency, 5405 Wilshire Blvd, #218, Los Angeles CA 90036 USA — Actor

**Carmona, Richard H**
Canyon Ranch Wellness Center, 8600 E Rockcliff Road, Tucson AZ 85750, USA — Physician, Government Official

**Carmona, Wayne**
W M E Entertainment, 9601 Wilshire Blvd, #300, Beverly Hills CA 90210 USA — Producer

**Carnahan, Joe**
Creative Artists Agency, 2000 Ave of Stars, #100, Los Angeles CA 90067 USA — Director, Producer, Writer

**Carnahan, Matthew Michael**
W M E Entertainment, 9601 Wilshire Blvd, #300, Beverly Hills CA 90210 USA — Writer

**Carne, Jean**
Walt Reeder Productions, 93 Old York Road, #1-604, Jenkintown PA 19046, USA — Singer

**Carneiro, Joana**
I M G Artists, Hogarth Business Park, Chiswick, London W4 2TH, England — Conductor

**Carner, Charles Robert**
4172 Sandy Hollow Court, Moorpark CA 93021, USA — Director, Producer, Writer

**Carner, JoAnne Gunderson**
3030 S Ocean Blvd, Palm Beach FL 33480, USA — Golfer

**Carnes, Kim**
1829 Tyne Blvd, Nashville TN 37215, USA — Singer, Songwriter

**Carnes, Ryan**
Vincent Cirrincione Assoc, 1516 N Fairfax Ave, Los Angeles CA 90046 USA — Actor

**Carnesale, Albert**
University of California, Chancellor's Office, Los Angeles CA 90024, USA — Educator

**Carnesecca, Luigi (Lou)**
18247 Midland Parkway, Jamaica NY 11432, USA — Basketball Coach

**Carnevale, Mark**
24 Loggerhead Lane, Ponte Vedra Beach FL 32082, USA — Golfer

**Carney, Jay**
White House, 1600 Pennsylvania Ave NW, Washington DC 20500 USA — Government Official, Journalist

**Carney, John**
Casorotto Ramsay, Waverley House, 7-12 Noel St, London W1F 8GQ, England — Director, Writer, Actor

**Carney, John M**
2950 Wishbone Way, Encinitas CA 92024, USA — Football Player

**Carney, Keith E**
8701 N 55th Place, Paradise Valley AZ 85253, USA — Ice Hockey Player

**Carney, Lester N (Les)**
978 Seward Ave, Akron OH 44320, USA — Track Athlete

**Carney, Patrick J**
Q-Prime South, 131 S 11th St, Nashville TN 37206 USA — Drummer (Black Keys)

**Carney, Quinn**
University of Maryland, Athletic Dept, College Park MD 20742, USA — Lacrosse Player

**Carney, Reeve**
Paradigm Agency, 360 N Crescent Dr, North Building, Beverly Hills CA 90210 USA — Actor

**Carney, Thomas P**
3928 Forest Glen Blvd, #102, Naples FL 34114, USA — Army General

**Carnoy, Martin**
Stanford University, Economic Studies Center, Stanford CA 94305, USA — Economist

**Carns, Michael P C (Mike)**
966 Coral Dr, Pebble Beach CA 93953, USA — Air Force General

**Caro, Niki**
I C M Partners, 10250 Constellation Blvd, #900, Los Angeles CA 90067 USA — Director, Writer

**Caro, Robert A**
Robert A Caro Assoc, 250 W 57th St, #2215, New York NY 10107, USA — Writer

**Caroit, Phillipe**
Voyez Mon Agent, 20 Ave Rapp, 75007 Paris, France — Actor

**Carol, Linda**
William Kerwin Agency, 1605 N Cahuenga Blvd, #202, Los Angeles CA 90028, USA — Actress

**Carolin, Heather M**
Playboy Promotions, 9346 Civic Center Dr, #200, Beverly Hills CA 90210 USA — Model

**Caroline**
Villa Le Clos Saint Pierre, Ave San-Martin, 98000 Monte Carlo, Monaco — Heir Presumptive, Monaco

**Caroline, James C (J C)**
2501 Stanford Dr, Champaign IL 61820, USA — Football Player

**Carolla, Adam**
Dixon Talent, 375 Greenwich St, #500, New York NY 10013, USA — Actor, Comedian

# C

**Carollo, Joseph P (Joe)** — Football Player
4634 Meyer Way, Carmichael CA 95608, USA

**Caron, Glenn Gordon** — Producer, Writer
Picturemaker Productions, 1600 Rosecrans Ave, Building 2A, Manhattan Beach CA 90266, USA

**Caron, Jacques** — Ice Hockey Player
11105 Bullrush Terrace, Lakewood Ranch FL 34202, USA

**Caron, Jean-Claude** — Actor
Artmedia, 20 Ave Rapp, 75007 Paris, France

**Caron, Leslie** — Actress, Dancer
6 Rue De Bellechaisse, 75007 Paris, France

**Carothers, Veronica** — Actress
535 N Heatherstone Dr, Orange CA 92869, USA

**Carp, Daniel A (Dan)** — Businessman
Delta Air Lines, Hartsfield International Airport, Atlanta GA 30320, USA

**Carpani, Rachael** — Actress
Lisa Mann Agency, 99 Spring St, #100, Bondi Junction NSW 2022, Australia

**Carpendale, Howard** — Singer
Helmat 2050 Verlags, Postfach 113407, 20434 Hamburg, Germany

**Carpendale, Wayne** — Actor
Actors Connection Agentur, Kuckucksberg 9, 22952 Lutjensee bei Hamburg, Germany

**Carpenter, Alexandra** — Ice Hockey Player
Bob Carpenter, 71 Chestnut St, North Reading MA 01864, USA

**Carpenter, Andrew (Drew)** — Baseball Player
1894 SW Mistybrook Dr, Grants Pass OR 97527, USA

**Carpenter, Bobby** — Ice Hockey Player
71 Chestnut St, North Reading MA 01864, USA

**Carpenter, Carleton** — Actor
RR 2, Chardavoyne Road, Warwick NY 10990, USA

**Carpenter, Chad** — Cartoonist
Tundra Comics, PO Box 871354, Wasilla AK 99687, USA

**Carpenter, Charisma** — Actress, Model
John Carrabino Mgmt, 5900 Wilshire Blvd, #406, Los Angeles CA 90036 USA

**Carpenter, Christopher J (Chris)** — Baseball Player
809 S Warson Road, Saint Louis MO 63124, USA

**Carpenter, Cris H** — Baseball Player
1484 Heritage Place, Gainesville GA 30501, USA

**Carpenter, Ed** — Auto Racing Driver
Vision Racing, 4760 Kingsway Dr, #B, Indianapolis IN 46205, USA

**Carpenter, Jack** — Actor
I C M Partners, 10250 Constellation Blvd, #900, Los Angeles CA 90067 USA

**Carpenter, Jennifer** — Actress
W M E Entertainment, 9601 Wilshire Blvd, #300, Beverly Hills CA 90210 USA

**Carpenter, John H** — Director, Writer
Echo Lake Mgmt, 421 S Beverly Dr, #800, Beverly Hills CA 90212, USA

**Carpenter, Keion E** — Football Player
2009 Shin Court, Buford GA 30519, USA

**Carpenter, Kip** — Speed Skater
W375S10897 Prairie Lane, Eagle WI 53119, USA

**Carpenter, Mary Chapin** — Singer, Guitarist, Songwriter
Paradigm Agency, 360 N Crescent Dr, North Building, Beverly Hills CA 90210 USA

**Carpenter, Richard L** — Pianist, Singer, Songwriter
960 Country Valley Road, Westlake Village CA 91362, USA

**Carpenter, Robert J (Bobby), III** — Football Player
103 Graeser Acres, Saint Louis MO 63146, USA

**Carpenter, Robert J (Rob), Jr** — Football Player
1601 Wheeling Road NE, Lancaster OH 43130, USA

**Carpenter, Russell P** — Cinematographer
Worldwide Production Agency, 144 N Robertson Blvd, #200, West Hollywood CA 90048, USA

**Carpenter, Stephen** — Guitarist (Deftones)
Velvet Hammer Music, 9014 Melrose Ave, West Hollywood CA 90069, USA

**Carpenter, W Kyle** — Afghanistan War Marine Hero (CMH)
University of South Carolina, Psychology Dept, Columbia SC 29208, USA

**Carpenter, William S (Bill), Jr** — Army General, Hero, Football Player
PO Box 4067, Whitefish MT 59937, USA

**Carpenter-Phinney, Connie** — Cyclist
470 Juniper Ave, Boulder CO 80304, USA

**Carpentier, Alain** — Heart Surgeon
Hospital Broussais, 96 Rue Didot, 75674 Bris Cedex 14, France

**Carpentier, Patrick** — Auto Racing Driver
S A M A X Motorsports, 203 NW 16th St, Pompano Beach FL 33060, USA

**Carpinello, James** — Actor, Singer
A P A Talent & Literary Agency, 405 S Beverly Dr, #300, Beverly Hills CA 90212 USA

**Carr, Antoine L** — Basketball Player
5724 Croyden Circle, Wichita KS 67220, USA

**Carr, Austin G** — Basketball Player
4547 Saint Germain Blvd, Cleveland OH 44128, USA

**Carr, Brandon C** — Football Player
Dallas Cowboys, 1 Cowboys Parkway, Irving TX 75063 USA

**Carr, Caleb** — Writer
Grand Central Publishing, 237 Park Ave, #1300L, New York NY 10017, USA

**Carr, Catherine (Cathy)** — Swimmer
409 10th St, Davis CA 95616, USA

**Carr, Charles L G (Chuck), Jr** — Baseball Player
5419 E Greenway St, Mesa AZ 85205, USA

**Carr, David** — Football Player
4771 Sweetwater Blvd, #226, Sugar Land TX 77479, USA

**Carr, Fred A** — Football Player
6274 S 17th Place, Phoenix AZ 85042, USA

**Carr, Gary** — Actor
Markham Froggatt Irwin, Julian House, 4 Windmill St, London W1P 1HF, England

**Carr, Gene** — Ice Hockey Player
13529 Leadwell St, #1, Van Nuys CA 91405, USA

**Carr, Gerald P (Jerry)** — Astronaut
Camus Inc, 49 Maple St, #123, Manchester Center VT 05255, USA

**Carr, Henry** — Track Athlete, Football Player
1612 Pinebrook Dr, Griffin GA 30224, USA

**Carr, Jane** — Actress
Sovereign Talent Group, 8421 Wilshire Blvd, #200, Beverly Hills CA 90211 USA

**Carr, Jimmy** — Actor
P F D, Drury House, 34-43 Russell St, London WC2B 5HA, England

**Carr, Katie** — Actress
S M S Talent, 8383 Wilshire Blvd, #230, Beverly Hills CA 90211 USA

**Carr, Kenneth A (Kenny)** — Basketball Player
24421 SW Valley View Dr, West Linn OR 97068, USA

**Carr, Kenneth M** — Navy Admiral
16600 Warren Court, #302, Chagrin Falls OH 44023, USA

**Carr, Michael Leon (M L)** — Basketball Player, Coach, Executive
168 Beaver Road, Weston MA 02493, USA

**Carr, Robyn** — Writer
Nancy Berland Public Relations, 2816 NW 57th St, #101, Oklahoma City OK 73112, USA

**Carr, Roger D** — Football Player
222 Broken Arrow Trail, Petal MS 39465, USA

**Carr, Steve** — Director, Producer
Rumpus Entertainment, 9000 W Sunset Blvd, #650, Los Angeles CA 90048, USA

**Carr, Vikki** — Singer
Vi-Carr Entertainment, 3102 Iron Stone Lane, San Antonio TX 78230, USA

**Carrabba, Christopher A (Chris)** — Singer (Dashboard Confessional)
Hard 8 Mgmt, 2118 Wilshire Blvd, #361, Santa Monica CA 90403, USA

**Carrack, Paul** — Singer, Songwriter
Alan Wood Agency, 346 Gleadless Road, Sheffield, South York S2 3AJ, England

**Carradine, Ever** — Actress
Management 360, 9111 Wilshire Blvd, Beverly Hills CA 90210 USA

**Carradine, Keith** — Actor, Singer, Songwriter
355 S Grand Ave, #1710, Los Angeles CA 90071, USA

**Carradine, Robert** — Actor
Triple Tap Productions, 5850 Canoga Ave, #200, Woodland Hills CA 91367, USA

**Carrasco, Daniel J (D J)** — Baseball Player
508 Lonesome Trail, Haslet TX 76052, USA

**Carre, Isabelle** — Actress
Agence Artiste Adequat, 108 Rue Reaumur, 75002 Paris, France

**Carreker, Alphonso** — Football Player
5599 Asheforde Lane, Marietta GA 30068, USA

**Carreon, Mark S** — Baseball Player
413 Ashland Creek, Victoria TX 77901, USA

**Carrera, Barbara** — Actress, Model
Alan David Mgmt, 8840 Wilshire Blvd, #200, Beverly Hills CA 90211, USA

**Carrera, Carlos** — Director
Creative Artists Agency, 2000 Ave of Stars, #100, Los Angeles CA 90067 USA

**Carrera, Christy** — Actress
Michael Scott, PO Box 683, Lewis Center OH 43035, USA

**Carreras, Jose** — Opera Singer
Fundacion Jose Carreras, Calle Muntaner 383, 08021 Barcelona, Spain

**Carrere, Emmanuel** — Writer
Bloomsbury Publishing, 50 Bedford Square, London WC1B 3DP, England

**Carrere, Tia** — Actress, Model
Arlook Group, 205 S Beverly Dr, #209, Beverly Hills CA 90212, USA

**Carretto, Joseph A, Jr** — Astronaut
Space Missile Systems Center, 483 N Aviation Blvd, El Segundo CA 90245, USA

**Carrey, Jim** — Actor, Comedian
J C 23 Entertainment, 1925 Century Park E, #200, Los Angeles CA 90067, USA

**Carrick, Charlie** — Actor
United Talent Agency, U T A Plaza, 9336 Civic Center Dr, Beverly Hills CA 90210 USA

**Carrick, Ted** — Clinical Neurologist
Carrick Graduate Studies Institute, 203-8941 Lake Dr, Cape Canaveral FL 32920, USA

**Carrier, J Darel** — Basketball Player
4224 Glasgow Road, Oakland KY 42159, USA

**Carrier, J Mark** — Football Player
4115 Highland Park Circle, Lutz FL 33558, USA

**Carrier, Mark A** — Football Player
8501 Wilton Ave, Cincinnati OH 45236, USA

**Carriere, Jean P J** — Writer
Le Devois, Super Camprieu, 30750 Treves, France

**Carriere, Larry** — Ice Hockey Player
94 Dawnbrook Lane, Buffalo NY 14221, USA

**Carriere, Mathieu** — Actor
Agence Elizabeth Simpson, 32 Blvd du Montparnasse, 75015 Paris, France

**Carril, Pete** — Basketball Coach
372 Carter Road, Princeton NJ 08540, USA

**Carrillo, Elpidia** — Actress
Bresler Kelly Assoc, 11500 W Olympic Blvd, #400, Los Angeles CA 90064 USA

**Carrington, Alan** — Chemist
46 Lakewood Road, Chandler's Ford, Hampshire SO53 1EX, England

**Carrington, Darren R** — Football Player
14097 Montfort Court, San Diego CA 92128, USA

**Carrington, Debbie Lee** — Actress
PO Box 9897, Marina del Rey CA 90295, USA

**Carrington, Kelly** — Model
Playboy Promotions, 9346 Civic Center Dr, #200, Beverly Hills CA 90210 USA

**Carrington, Paul D** — Attorney, Educator
Duke University, Law School, Durham NC 27708, USA

**Carrington, Peter A R** — Government Official, England
32A Ovinton Square, London SW3 1LR, England

**Carrington, Robert F (Bob)** — Basketball Player
PO Box 13191, Carlsbad CA 92013, USA

**Carrington, Rodney** — Actor, Comedian
P M G Entertainment Group, 1505 S Atlantic St, Melbourne Beach FL 32951, USA

**Carrington, Terri Lyne** — Jazz Drummer
Stax/Concord Records, 270 N Canon Dr, #1212, Beverly Hills CA 90210 USA

**Carroll, Aaron E** — Pediatrician
Indiana University, Health Policy Center, 410 W 10th St, Indianapolis IN 46202, USA

**Carroll, Brett M** — Baseball Player
1916 Hidden Meadow Dr, Knoxville TN 37922, USA

**C**

**Carroll, Charles C (Corky)** — Surfer
624 20th St, Huntington Beach CA 92648, USA
**Carroll, Clay P** — Baseball Player
3052 22nd St, Sarasota FL 34234, USA
**Carroll, Diahann** — Singer, Actress
C E S D, 10635 Santa Monica Blvd, #130, Los Angeles CA 90025 USA
**Carroll, James S (Jim)** — Football Player
3101 N State Road 7, Hollywood FL 33021, USA
**Carroll, Jamey B** — Baseball Player
2789 Wyndham Way, Melbourne FL 32940, USA
**Carroll, Jason Michael** — Singer, Songwriter
Paradigm Agency, 360 Park Ave, #1600, New York NY 10022 USA
**Carroll, John** — Attorney
Rogers & Wells, 31 W 52nd St, #300, New York NY 10019, USA
**Carroll, John B** — Psychologist
2158 Penrose Lane, Fairbanks AK 99709, USA
**Carroll, John S** — Editor
Harvard University, John F Kennedy Government School, Cambridge MA 02138, USA
**Carroll, Joseph B (Joe Barry)** — Basketball Player
5220 Cascade Road SW, Atlanta GA 30331, USA
**Carroll, Julian M** — Governor, KY
Carroll Assoc, PO Box 1491, Frankfort KY 40602, USA
**Carroll, Kent J** — Navy Admiral
Country Club of North Carolina, 1600 Morganton Road, #30X, Pinehurst NC 28374, USA
**Carroll, Lester (Les)** — Cartoonist (Our Boarding House)
1715 Ivyhill Loop N, Columbus OH 43229, USA
**Carroll, Liz** — Fiddler
Mike Green Assoc, 339 E Liberty St, #220, Ann Arbor MI 48104, USA
**Carroll, Peter C (Pete)** — Football Coach
Seattle Seahawks, 12 Seahawks Way, Renton WA 98056 USA
**Carroll, Philip J** — Businessman
10314 Crimston Canyon Dr, Houston TX 77098, USA
**Carroll, Roscoe (Rocky)** — Actor
L I N K Entertainment, 11872 La Grange Ave, Los Angeles CA 90025 USA
**Carroll, Thomas (Tom)** — Surfer
Quiksilver, 363 George St, Sydney NSW 2000, Australia
**Carroll, Willard** — Director
Hyperion Pictures, 7510 Sunset Blvd, #228, Los Angeles CA 90046, USA
**Carrot Top** — Actor, Comedian
420 Sylvan Dr, Winter Park FL 32789, USA
**Carrozzini, Francesco** — Photographer, Director
92 W Houston St, #PH #3, New York NY 10012, USA
**Carruthers, Alastair** — Dermatologist
943 W Broadway, #820, Vancouver BC V5Z 4E1, Canada
**Carruthers, Caitlin (Kitty)** — Figure Skater
2106 White Eagle Lane, Katy TX 77450, USA
**Carruthers, Dwight** — Ice Hockey Player
9513 W Nelson Dr, Nine Mile Falls WA 99026, USA
**Carruthers, Garrey E** — Governor, NM
4405 Echo Canyon Road, Las Cruces NM 88011, USA
**Carruthers, Jean** — Opthamalogist
943 W Broadway, #820, Vancouver BC V5Z 4E1, Canada
**Carruthers, Peter** — Figure Skater
239 Via Monterey, Newbury Park CA 91320, USA
**Carsey, Marcia L P** — Producer
Carsey-Warner Productions, 4024 Radford Ave, Building 3, Studio City CA 91604, USA
**Carson, Adam** — Drummer, Singer (AFI)
S A M, 722 Seward St, Los Angeles CA 90038, USA
**Carson, Benjamin S** — Neurosurgeon
Johns Hopkins University Medical Center, Pediatry Surgery Dept, Baltimore MD 21218, USA
**Carson, Carlos A** — Football Player
4747 W 150th Terrace, Overland Park KS 66224, USA
**Carson, David** — Director
Creative Artists Agency, 2000 Ave of Stars, #100, Los Angeles CA 90067 USA
**Carson, Essence** — Basketball Player
New York Liberty, Madison Square Garden, 2 Penn Plaza, New York NY 10121 USA
**Carson, Harold D (Harry)** — Football Player
PO Box 852, Westwood NJ 07675, USA
**Carson, James (Jimmy)** — Ice Hockey Player
1154 Ridgeway Dr, Rochester MI 48307, USA
**Carson, Jeff** — Singer
Buddy Lee Attractions, 38 Music Square E, #300, Nashville TN 37203 USA
**Carson, Kendel** — Singer, Songwriter
Train Wrecks Records, 218 Tallwood Dr, Hartsdale NY 10530, USA
**Carson, Leonardo T** — Football Player
800 Ross Ave, #3125, Dallas TX 75202, USA
**Carson, Lisa Nicole** — Actress
Beth Rosner Management, 4 Stuyvesant Oval, #10H, New York NY 10009, USA
**Carson, William H (Willie)** — Thoroughbred Racing Jockey
Minster House, Barnsley, Cirencester, Gloucestershire GL7 5DZ, England
**Carswell, Dwyane** — Football Player
PO Box 2488, Immokalee FL 34143, USA
**Cartagena, Victoria** — Actress
Gersh Agency, 9465 Wilshire Blvd, #600, Beverly Hills CA 90212 USA
**Cartellone, Michael** — Drummer (Lynyrd Skynyrd, Damn Yankees)
Vector Mgmt, PO Box 120479, Nashville TN 37212, USA
**Carter, Aaron C** — Singer, Actor
Roger Paul, 1650 Broadway, #304, New York NY 10019, USA
**Carter, Adrienne** — Actress
Characters Talent Mgmt, 8 Elm St, Toronto ON M5G 1G7, Canada
**Carter, Alex** — Actor
Emmerdale Production Center, 27 Burley Lane, Leeds LS3 1JT, England
**Carter, Anson** — Ice Hockey Player
820 Haven Oaks Court NE, Atlanta GA 30342, USA
**Carter, Anthony** — Football Player
4314 Danielson Dr, Lake Worth FL 33467, USA

**Carroll - Carter**

*V.I.P. Address Book*

**Carter, Anthony B**
15250 E Caley Ave, Centennial CO 80016, USA — Basketball Player
**Carter, Antonio M (Tony)**
7839 Maple Grove Dr, Lewis Center OH 43035, USA — Football Player
**Carter, Carlene**
Roots Agency, 177 Woodland Ave, Westwood NJ 07675, USA — Singer, Songwriter
**Carter, Cheryl**
C E S D, 10635 Santa Monica Blvd, #130, Los Angeles CA 90025 USA — Actress
**Carter, Christopher C (Chris)**
Creative Artists Agency, 2000 Ave of Stars, #100, Los Angeles CA 90067 USA — Producer, Writer
**Carter, Christopher G (Chris)**
1500 Mill Creek Dr, De Soto TX 75115, USA — Football Player
**Carter, Clarence**
Rodgers Redding, PO Box 4603, Macon GA 31208 USA — Singer
**Carter, Clarence E (Butch)**
900 Legacy Park Dr, Lawrenceville GA 30043, USA — Basketball Player, Coach
**Carter, Cristopher D (Cris)**
2943 NW 46th St, Boca Raton FL 33431, USA — Football Player, Sportscaster
**Carter, Cy**
Archetype, 1608 Argyle Ave, Los Angeles CA 90028, USA — Actor
**Carter, Dale L**
10416 Magnolia Heights Circle, Covington GA 30014, USA — Football Player
**Carter, Darren**
A K A Talent, 6310 San Vicente Blvd, #200, Los Angeles CA 90048 USA — Actor, Comedian
**Carter, David**
2401 Long Reach Dr, Sugar Land TX 77478, USA — Football Player
**Carter, Deana**
Peters Mgmt, PO Box 1710, Topanga CA 90290, USA — Singer, Songwriter
**Carter, Dexter A**
7130 Nesters Dr, Tallahassee FL 32312, USA — Football Player
**Carter, Dixie**
T N A Wrestling, 209 10th Ave S, #302, Nashville TN 37203, USA — Professional Wrestler
**Carter, Duane (Pancho), Jr**
32 Forest Dr, Brownsburg IN 46112, USA — Auto Racing Driver
**Carter, E Graydon**
Vanity Fair, Editorial Dept, 4 Times Square, Basement C1B, New York NY 10036, USA — Editor
**Carter, Elan**
Playboy Promotions, 9346 Civic Center Dr, #200, Beverly Hills CA 90210 USA — Model, Actress
**Carter, Finn**
Front Line Entertainment, 867 S Muirfield Road, Los Angeles CA 90005, USA — Actress
**Carter, Frederick J (Fred)**
2979 W School House Lane, #703K, Philadelphia PA 19144, USA — Basketball Player, Coach
**Carter, Gerald L**
3917 Cheshire Court, Bryan TX 77802, USA — Football Player
**Carter, Howard O**
7572 Hanks Dr, Baton Rouge LA 70812, USA — Basketball Player
**Carter, Jack**
1023 Chevy Chase Dr, Beverly Hills CA 90210, USA — Actor, Comedian
**Carter, James (Larry)**
American International Artists, 356 Pine Valley Road, Hoosick Falls NY 12090, USA — Jazz Saxophonist, Composer
**Carter, James E (Jimmy), Jr**
Carter Center, 453 Freedom Parkway NE, Atlanta GA 30307, USA — President, USA; Nobel Peace Laureate
**Carter, Jay**
PO Box 5357, Spring Hill FL 34611, USA — Singer (Crests)
**Carter, Jeff**
Los Angeles Kings, Staples Center, 1111 S Figueroa St, Los Angeles CA 90015 USA — Ice Hockey Player
**Carter, Jeffrey A (Jeff)**
4625 River Overlook Dr, Valrico FL 33596, USA — Baseball Player
**Carter, Jim**
12575 N 130th Way, Scottsdale AZ 85259, USA — Golfer
**Carter, Jim**
C D A, 167-169 Kensington High St, London W8 6SH, England — Actor
**Carter, Joelle**
Innovative Artists, 1505 10th St, Santa Monica CA 90401 USA — Actress
**Carter, John**
27 Country Lane, Sharon MA 02067, USA — Ice Hockey Player
**Carter, John**
Harden-Curtis Associates, 850 7th Ave, #903, New York NY 10019 — Actor
**Carter, John D (Jake)**
5102 80th St, #132, Lubbock TX 79424, USA — Basketball Player
**Carter, Joseph C (Joe)**
3000 W 117th St, Leawood KS 66211, USA — Baseball Player
**Carter, Joseph T (Jodie)**
5921 Timberview Road, Little Rock AR 72204, USA — Football Player
**Carter, Ki-Jana**
1236 NW 121st Ave, Plantation Fl 33323, USA — Football Player
**Carter, Lance D**
306 74th Street Court NW, Bradenton FL 34209, USA — Baseball Player
**Carter, Lynda**
Potomac Productions, PO Box 59110, Potomac MD 20859, USA — Actress, Singer
**Carter, Mel**
Cape Entertainment, 4799 Coconut Creek Parkway, #258, Coconut Creek FL 33063, USA — Actor, Singer
**Carter, Michael D**
901 Red Oak Creek Dr, Red Oak TX 75154, USA — Football Player, Track Athlete
**Carter, Nicholas G (Nick)**
E M C Bowery, 8145 Santa Monica Blvd, #200, West Hollywood CA 90046, USA — Singer (Backstreet Boys), Songwriter
**Carter, Powell F, Jr**
699 Fillmore St, Harpers Ferry WV 25425, USA — Navy Admiral
**Carter, Regina**
Depth of Field Mgmt, 1501 Broadway, #1304, New York NY 10036, USA — Jazz, Concert Violinist
**Carter, Ronald L (Ron)**
Bridge Agency, 35 Clark St, #A5, Brooklyn NY 11201, USA — Jazz Bassist, Composer
**Carter, Rosalynn S**
Carter Center, 453 Freedom Parkway NE, Atlanta GA 30307, USA — Wife of US President
**Carter, Rubin**
1793 Vineyard Way, Tallahassee FL 32317, USA — Football Player, Coach

**Carter, Sarah** — Actress
A P A Talent & Literary Agency, 405 S Beverly Dr, #300, Beverly Hills CA 90212 USA

**Carter, Shawn C (Jay-Z)** — Rap Artist, Songwriter, Record Producer
Roc Nation, 1411 Broadway, #3800, New York NY 10018, USA

**Carter, Stephen L** — Attorney, Educator, Writer
Yale University, Law School, 127 Wall St, New Haven CT 06511, USA

**Carter, Terry** — Actor, Producer
244 Madison Ave, #332, New York NY 10016, USA

**Carter, Thomas** — Director
Kazarian/Measures/Ruskin, 11969 Ventura Blvd, #300, Studio City CA 91604 USA

**Carter, Thomas (Tom), III** — Football Player
4548 Bristol Lane, Cincinnati OH 45229, USA

**Carter, Timothy M (Tim)** — Football Player
4860 26th Court S, Saint Petersburg FL 33712, USA

**Carter, Tom** — Golfer
3787 County Lane Road, Quakertown PA 18951, USA

**Carter, Ty** — Afghanistan War Army Hero (CMH)
US Army 7th Infantry Division, Joint Base Lewis-McChord WA 98433, USA

**Carter, Vincent L (Vince)** — Basketball Player
1978 Country Club Dr, Port Orange FL 32128, USA

**Carter, Virgil R (Virg)** — Football Player
2010 Whitebluff Dr, San Dimas CA 91773, USA

**Carter, W Hodding, III** — Government Official
214 N Columbus St, Alexandria VA 22314, USA

**Carter, W Patrick (Pat)** — Football Player
11321 Cambray Creek Loop, Riverview FL 33579, USA

**Carteri, Rosana** — Opera Singer
Angel Records, 150 5th Ave, New York NY 10011 USA

**Carteris, Gabrielle** — Actress
4019 Longridge Ave, Sherman Oaks CA 91423, USA

**Carter-Williams, Michael** — Basketball Player
Philadelphia 76ers, 1st Union Center, 3601 S Broad St, Philadelphia PA 19148 USA

**Cartes Jara, Horacio M** — President, Paraguay
Palacio de Gobinerno, Ave Mariscal Lopez, 1807 Asuncion, Paraguay

**Carthon, Maurice** — Football Player
2040 E Indigo Dr, Chandler AZ 85286, USA

**Carthy, Eliza** — Singer, Fiddler, Songwriter
Glass Ceiling, 50 Stroud Green Road, London N4 3ES, England

**Carthy, Martin** — Singer, Guitarist, Songwriter
Moneypenny Agency, Westwood House, North Dalton, Driffield East Yorkshire YO25 9XA, England

**Carthy-Deu, Deborah F** — Beauty Queen, Actress
Deborah Carthy-Deu Studio, 353 F Calder St, Urb Roosevelt, San Juan, PR 00918, USA

**Cartwright, Angela** — Actress
Rubber Boots, 11333 Moorpark St, #433, North Hollywood CA 91602, USA

**Cartwright, Catherine** — Golfer
4505 SE County Road 760, Arcadia FL 34266, USA

**Cartwright, J William (Bill)** — Basketball Player, Coach
1839 Wedgewood Court, Lake Forest IL 60045, USA

**Cartwright, Justin** — Writer
P F D, Drury House, 34-43 Russell St, London WC2B 5HA, England

**Cartwright, Nancy** — Actress
Innovative Artists, 1505 10th St, Santa Monica CA 90401 USA

**Cartwright, Nancy D** — Philosopher
London School of Economics, Houghton St, London WC2A 2AE, England

**Cartwright, Roderick R (Rock)** — Football Player
231 Interstate 45 N, #21115, Conroe TX 77304, USA

**Cartwright, Veronica** — Actress
Mitch Clem Mgmt, 2600 W Olive Ave #500, Burbank CA 91505, USA

**Carty, Donald J** — Businessman
Dell Inc, 1 Dell Way, Round Rock TX 78682, USA

**Carty, Jay J** — Basketball Player
5425 Lower Honopaiilani Road, Lahaina HI 96761, USA

**Carty, Ricardo A J (Rico)** — Baseball Player
5 Ens Enriquillo, San Pedro de Macoris, Dominican Republic

**Carty, Todd** — Actor
Associated International Mgmt, 7 Hatton Garden, #400, London EC1N 8AD, England

**Caruana, Patrick P (Pat)** — Air Force General
1922 Havemeyer Lane, Redondo Beach CA 90278, USA

**Caruana, Peter R** — Chief Minister, Gibraltar
Chief Minister's Office, 10/3 Irish Town, Gibraltar

**Carucci, Elinor** — Photographer
School of Visual Arts, 209 E 23rd St, New York NY 10010, USA

**Caruncho, Fernando** — Landscape Architect
Paseo del Narcea 17, San Sebastian de los Reyes, 28707 Madrid, Spain

**Caruso, D J** — Director
Creative Artists Agency, 2000 Ave of Stars, #100, Los Angeles CA 90067 USA

**Caruso, David** — Actor
Untitled Entertainment, 350 S Beverly Dr, #200, Beverly Hills CA 90212 USA

**Carver, Brent** — Actor, Singer
Live Entertainment, 1500 Broadway, #902, New York NY 10036, USA

**Carver, Johnny** — Singer
Ace Productions, PO Box 428, Portland TN 37148, USA

**Carver, Melvin (Mel)** — Football Player
10840 Breaking Rocks Dr, Tampa FL 33647, USA

**Carver, Randall** — Actor
Kazarian/Measures/Ruskin, 11969 Ventura Blvd, #300, Studio City CA 91604 USA

**Carveth-Dunn, Betty** — Baseball Player
11531 77th Ave, Edmonton AB T6G 0M2, Canada

**Carvey, Dana** — Actor, Comedian
Baker Winokur Ryder Public Relations, 9100 Wilshire Blvd, #500W, Beverly Hills CA 90212 USA

**Carville, C James, Jr** — Political Consultant
424 S Washington St, Alexandria VA 22314, USA

**Cary, Caitlin** — Singer, Fiddler
Conqueroo, 11271 Ventura Blvd, #522, Studio City CA 91604 USA

**Cary, Charles D (Chuck)** — Baseball Player
1016 Stephen Dr, Niceville FL 32578, USA

**Cary, W Sterling** — Religious Leader
2344 Vardon Lane, Flossmoor IL 60422, USA
**Cary-Williams, Robert** — Fashion Designer
1A Wellington Row, London E2 7BB, England
**Casablancas, Julian** — Singer (Strokes), Songwriter
Wiz Kid Management, 123 E 7th St, New York NY 10009, USA
**Casadesus, Jean-Claude** — Conductor
23 Blvd de la Liberte, 59800 Lille, France
**Casady, Jack** — Bassist (Jefferson Airplane, Hot Tuna)
Mission Control, 15030 Ventura Blvd, #541, Sherman Oaks CA 91403, USA
**Casale, Jerry J** — Baseball Player
600 County Ave, #408, Secaucus NJ 07094, USA
**Casali, Kim** — Cartoonist (Love Is)
Times-Mirror Syndicate, Times-Mirror Square, Los Angeles CA 90053 USA
**Casals, Rosemary (Rosie)** — Tennis Player
Women's Tennis Assn, 1 Progress Plaza, #1500, Saint Petersburg FL 33701 USA
**Casamayor Johnson, Joel** — Boxer
Luis de Cubas, 19220 E Saint Andrews, Miami FL 33015, USA
**Casanova, O Paulino (Paul)** — Baseball Player
5370 NW 183rd St, Miami Gardens FL 33055, USA
**Casanova, Raul** — Baseball Player
1441 Ortiz Ave, Fort Myers FL 33905, USA
**Casanova, Thomas H (Tommy)** — Football Player
345 Casanova Road, Crowley LA 70526, USA
**Casar, Amira** — Actress
Conway Van Gelder Grant, 8-12 Broadwick St, #300, London W1F 8HW, England
**Casbarian, John** — Architect
Taft Architects, 2370 Rice Blvd, #112, Houston TX 77005, USA
**Cascadden, Chad** — Football Player
2611 Windsor Dr, Eau Claire WI 54703, USA
**Casdin-Silver, Hariet** — Artist
99 Pond Ave, #D403, Brookline MA 02445, USA
**Case** — Singer
Celebrity Talent Agency, 111 E 14th St, #249, New York NY 10003 USA
**Case, Christopher** — Producer, Writer
Evolution Entertainment, 901 N Highland Ave, Los Angeles CA 90038 USA
**Case, J Scott** — Football Player
4930 Price Dr, Suwanee GA 30024, USA
**Case, John** — Writer
Random House, 1745 Broadway, #1800, New York NY 10019 USA
**Case, Neko** — Singer (New Pornographers), Songwriter
Beekeeper Corp, 1005 Reagan Terrace, Austin TX 78704, USA
**Case, Peter** — Singer, Guitarist
Eastern Star Productions, 2625 Alcatraz Ave, #302, Berkeley CA 94705, USA
**Case, Sharon** — Actress
Innovative Artists, 1505 10th St, Santa Monica CA 90401 USA
**Case, Stephen M (Steve)** — Businessman
8619 Westwood Center Dr, Vienna VA 22182, USA
**Case, Stoney J** — Football Player
4824 Travis Oaks Dr, Marble Falls TX 78654, USA
**Case, Walter H, Jr** — Harness Racing Driver
8795 Crow Dr, Macedonia OH 44056, USA
**Casell, John W** — Actor
3746 Willowcrest Ave, Studio City CA 91604, USA
**Caselli, Chiara** — Actress
Artmedia, 20 Ave Rapp, 75007 Paris, France
**Casey, Bernie** — Football Player, Actor
6145 Flight Ave, Los Angeles CA 90056, USA
**Casey, Brandon** — Singer (Jagged Edge)
Entertainment Artists, 2409 21st Ave S, #100, Nashville TN 10019 USA
**Casey, Brian** — Singer (Jagged Edge)
Entertainment Artists, 2409 21st Ave S, #100, Nashville TN 10019 USA
**Casey, Conor** — Soccer Player
Colorado Rapids, 1000 Chopper Circle, Denver CO 80204 USA
**Casey, Daniel** — Actor
Curtis Brown Group, 28-29 Haymarket St, #500, London SW1Y 4SP, England
**Casey, Dillon** — Actor
A P A Talent & Literary Agency, 405 S Beverly Dr, #300, Beverly Hills CA 90212 USA
**Casey, Dwane** — Basketball Player, Coach
Toronto Raptors, Air Canada Center, 20 Bay St, Toronto ON M5J 2N8, Canada
**Casey, George W, Jr** — Army General
90 Morse Ave, Attleboro MA 02703, USA
**Casey, Harry W (K C)** — Singer (K C & the Sunshine Band)
7530 Loch Ness Dr, Hialeah FL 33014, USA
**Casey, James B** — Football Player
Philadelphia Eagles, 1 Novacare Way, Philadelphia PA 19145 USA
**Casey, John D** — Writer
University of Virginia, English Dept, Bryan Hall, Charlottesville VA 22903, USA
**Casey, Jon** — Ice Hockey Player
651 Bluffs View Court, Eureka MO 63025, USA
**Casey, Patrick (Paddy)** — Singer, Songwriter
Principal Mgmt, 30-32 John Robertson's Quay, Dublin 2, Ireland
**Casey, Paul A** — Golfer
Paul Casey Foundation, 72 Salcott Road, London SW11 6DF, England
**Casey, Peter** — Director
Creative Artists Agency, 2000 Ave of Stars, #100, Los Angeles CA 90067 USA
**Casey, Sean T** — Baseball Player
271 Trotwood Dr, Pittsburgh PA 15241, USA
**Cash, Aya** — Actress
United Talent Agency, U T A Plaza, 9336 Civic Center Dr, Beverly Hills CA 90210 USA
**Cash, David (Dave), Jr** — Baseball Player
16308 Birkdale Dr, Odessa FL 33556, USA
**Cash, Keith L** — Football Player
9839 Heritage Farm Road, San Antonio TX 78245, USA
**Cash, Kerry L** — Football Player
9839 Heritage Farm Road, San Antonio TX 78245, USA

# C

**Cash, Kevin F**
32256 Woodfield Dr, Avon Lake OH 44012, USA — Baseball Player

**Cash, Pat**
Patrick Cash Assoc, PO Box 2238, Footscray 3011, Australia — Tennis Player

**Cash, Richard F (Rick)**
203 E Benton St, Savannah MO 64485, USA — Football Player

**Cash, Rosanne**
Cross Road Mgmt, 45 W 11th St, #7B, New York NY 10011, USA — Singer, Songwriter

**Cash, Swintayla M (Swin)**
Atlanta Dream, 83 Walton St NW, #400, Atlanta, GA 30303 USA — Basketball Player

**Cashell, Sophie**
I M G Artists, Hogarth Business Park, Chiswick, London W4 2TH, England — Concert Pianist

**Cashin, Patrick (Pat)**
Kelly-Miller Circus, 2581 E 2070 Road, Hugo OK 74743, USA — Clown

**Cashman, John**
Boeing Commerical Airplane Group, PO Box 3707, Seattle WA 98124, USA — Test Pilot

**Cashman, Terry**
Metrostar Records, PO Box 5807, Englewood NJ 07631, USA — Singer (Buchanan Brothers)

**Cashman, Wayne J**
5150 NW 80th Avenue Road, Ocala FL 34482, USA — Ice Hockey Player

**Casian, Lawrence P (Larry)**
1939 Popcorn St NW, Salem OR 97304, USA — Baseball Player

**Casida, John E**
1570 La Vereda Road, Berkeley CA 94708, USA — Entomologist

**Casile, Genevieve**
Agents Associes, 201 Rue du Faubourg Saint Honore, 75008 Paris, France — Actress

**Casillas, Tony S**
6201 Bay Valley Court, Flower Mound TX 75022, USA — Football Player

**Caslavska, Vera**
Olympic Committee, Benesovska 6, 101 00 Prague 10, Czech Republic — Gymnast

**Casnoff, Philip**
Don Buchwald Talent Agency, 6500 Wilshire Blvd, #2200, Los Angeles CA 90048 USA — Actor

**Cason, Aveion M**
5936 N 64th St, Milwaukee WI 53218, USA — Football Player

**Casorati, Francesco**
Corso So Kossuth 19, 10131 Turin, Italy — Artist

**Caspar, Donald L D**
911 Gardenia Dr, Tallahassee FL 32312, USA — Biophysicist

**Caspe, David**
W M E Entertainment, 9601 Wilshire Blvd, #300, Beverly Hills CA 90210 USA — Producer, Writer

**Casper, David J (Dave)**
1525 Alamo Way, Alamo CA 94507, USA — Football Player

**Casper, John H**
4414 Village Corner Dr, Houston TX 77059, USA — Astronaut

**Casper, William E (Billy)**
2561 Stonebury Loop Road, Springville UT 84663, USA — Golfer

**Cass, Christopher**
Halpern Assoc, PO Box 5597, Santa Monica CA 90409 USA — Actor

**Cassady, Howard (Hopalong)**
Tails Sports Mgmt, PO Box 7828, Columbus OH 43207, USA — Football Player

**Cassavetes, Nick**
L B I Entertainment, 2000 Avenue of Stars, Century City CA 90067, USA — Actor, Director

**Cassel, Matthew B (Matt)**
150 Street of Dreams, Village Loch Loyd MO 64012, USA — Football Player

**Cassel, Seymour**
Abrams Artists, 9200 W Sunset Blvd, #1125, West Hollywood CA 90069 USA — Actor

**Cassel, Vincent**
Agence Artiste Adequat, 108 Rue Reaumur, 75002 Paris, France — Actor

**Cassell, Samuel J (Sam)**
5205 N Charles St, Baltimore MD 21210, USA — Basketball Player

**Cassels, Andrew W**
6697 Duffy Road, Delaware OH 43015, USA — Ice Hockey Player

**Casserino, Frank J**
Office of Under Secretary of Air Force, HqUSAF, Pentagon, Washington DC 20330, USA — Astronaut, Air Force General

**Casserly, Charley**
N F L Network, 10950 Washington Blvd, #100, Culver City CA 90232 USA — Football Executive, Sportscaster

**Casseus, Gabriel**
Don Buchwald Talent Agency, 6500 Wilshire Blvd, #2200, Los Angeles CA 90048 USA — Actor

**Cassidy, Bruce**
174 Irving Ave, Providence RI 02906, USA — Ice Hockey Player

**Cassidy, Candice**
Playboy Promotions, 9346 Civic Center Dr, #200, Beverly Hills CA 90210 USA — Model

**Cassidy, Christopher J (Chris)**
N A S A, Johnson Space Center, 2101 NASA Road, Houston TX 77058 USA — Astronaut

**Cassidy, David**
J A G Entertainment, 4265 Hazeltine Ave, Sherman Oaks CA 91423, USA — Actor, Singer

**Cassidy, Edward I Cardinal**
Promoting Christian Unity Council, Via della Conciliazione 5, 00193 Rome, Italy — Religious Leader

**Cassidy, Elaine**
Rights House, Drury House, 34-43 Russell St, London WC2B 5HA, England — Actress

**Cassidy, Joanna**
Stone Manners Salners, 6100 Wilshire Blvd, #1500, Los Angeles CA 90035 USA — Actress

**Cassidy, Katherine E (Katie)**
Anonymous Content, 3532 Hayden Ave, Culver City CA 90232 USA — Actress, Model, Singer

**Cassidy, Michael**
Principal Entertainment, 9255 Sunset Blvd, #500, Los Angeles CA 90069 USA — Actor

**Cassidy, Patrick**
979 E 42nd St, Brooklyn NY 11210, USA — Actor

**Cassidy, Ronald G (Ron)**
2214 W 171st St, Torrance CA 90504, USA — Football Player

**Cassidy, Shaun**
Shaun Cassidy Productions, 8530 Wilshire Blvd, #200, Beverly Hills CA 90211, USA — Actor, Singer

**Cassie**
42 West, 220 W 42nd St, #1200, New York NY 10036 USA — Rap Artist, Model, Singer

**Cassignard, Pierre**
Artmedia, 20 Ave Rapp, 75007 Paris, France — Actor

Cash - Cassignard

| | |
|---|---|
| **Cassolato, Tony** | Ice Hockey Player |
| 576 Camino El Dorado, Encinitas CA 92024, USA | |
| **Casspi, Omri** | Basketball Player |
| Cleveland Cavaliers, Gund Arena, 1 Center Court, Cleveland OH 44115 USA | |
| **Cast, Edward** | Actor |
| 4 Bankside Dr, Thames Ditton, Surrey KT7 0AQ, England | |
| **Cast, Tricia** | Actress |
| 20 Georgette Road, Rolling Hills Estates CA 90274, USA | |
| **Casta, Laetitia** | Model, Actress |
| D Management Group, 13 Via Forcella, 20144 Milan, Italy | |
| **Castaneda, Cameron** | Actor |
| Lewis & Beal Talent Agency, 15303 Ventura Blvd, #900, Sherman Oaks CA 91403, USA | |
| **Castaneda, Jorge A** | Government Official, Mexico |
| Anillo Periferico Sur 3180, #1120, Jardines del Pedregal, 01900 Mexico | |
| **Castellaneta, Dan** | Actor |
| Foster Entertainment, 12533 Woodgreen St, Building B, Los Angeles CA 90066, USA | |
| **Castellanos, Jonathan** | Actor |
| Jaime Ferrar Agency, 4741 Laural Canyon Blvd, #110, Valley Village CA 91607, USA | |
| **Castellaw, John G** | Marine Corps General |
| Deputy Commandant, Aviation, HqUSMC, 2 Navy St, Washington DC 20380 USA | |
| **Castelli, Marissa** | Figure Skater |
| 159 Marlow St, Cranston RI 02920, USA | |
| **Castelluccio, Federico** | Actor |
| Barry Haft Brown Artists Agency, 165 W 46th St, #908, New York NY 10036, USA | |
| **Caster, Richard C (Rich)** | Football Player |
| 41 Lincoln Court, Rockville Centre NY 11570, USA | |
| **Castiglioni, Consuelo** | Fashion Designer |
| Marni International, Palazzo Torre Delta, La Sguancia 23, 6902 Lugano, Switzerland | |
| **Castilla Soria, Vinicio S (Vinny)** | Baseball Player |
| 7680 Polo Ridge Dr, Littleton CO 80128, USA | |
| **Castile, Jeremiah** | Football Player |
| 2904 Kirkcaldy Lane, Birmingham AL 35242, USA | |
| **Castillo, Alberto T** | Baseball Player |
| 400 SW Lakota Ave, Port Saint Lucie FL 34953, USA | |
| **Castillo, Jose Luis** | Boxer |
| Top Rank Inc, 3908 Howard Hughes Parkway, #580, Las Vegas NV 89169 USA | |
| **Castillo, M Carmelo (Carmen)** | Baseball Player |
| 344 Prospect Ave, #6A, Hackensack NJ 07601, USA | |
| **Castillo, Robert E (Bobby), Jr** | Baseball Player |
| 316 Calle Amraillo SW, Albuquerque NM 87121, USA | |
| **Castino, John A** | Baseball Player |
| 3465 Crystal Place, Wayzata MN 55391, USA | |
| **Castle, John** | Actor |
| Larry Dalzell, 91 Regent St, London W1R 7TA, England | |
| **Castle, Michael N** | Governor, Representative, DE |
| Castle Campaign Fund, PO Box 133, Wilmington DE 19899, USA | |
| **Castle, Nick C, Jr** | Director |
| Jackoway Tyerman Wertheimer, 1925 Century Park E, #2200, Los Angeles CA 90067 USA | |
| **Castle-Hughes, Keisha** | Actress |
| Gail Cowan Mgmt, 21 Village Fields Road, Waiau Pa, RD4, Pukekohe 2679, New Zealand | |
| **Castleman, Foster E** | Baseball Player |
| 8250 Graves Road, Cincinnati OH 45243, USA | |
| **Castrale, Nicole** | Golfer |
| Ladies Pro Golf Assn, 100 International Golf Dr, Daytona Beach FL 32124 USA | |
| **Castrillon Hoyos, Dario Cardinal** | Religious Leader |
| Ecclesia Dei Pontifical Commission, Piazza del S Uffizio 11, 00193 Rome, Italy | |
| **Castro Ruz, Fidel A** | President, Cuba |
| Palacio de Gobierno, Cibsejo de la Revolucion, Havana, Cuba | |
| **Castro Ruz, Raul** | President, Prime Minister, Cuba |
| Palacio de Gobierno, Cibsejo de la Revolucion, Havana, Cuba | |
| **Castro, Cristian** | Singer |
| Generamusica Mgmt, C Arcniegae 29A, Col Mixcoac, Naucalpan 03910, Mexico | |
| **Castro, Joseph I** | Educator |
| California State University, President's Office, 5241 N Maple Ave, Fresno CA 93740, USA | |
| **Castro, Ramon A** | Baseball Player |
| 1230 Windway Circle, Kissimmee FL 34744, USA | |
| **Castro, Raquel** | Actress |
| Abrams Artists, 275 7th Ave, #2600, New York NY 10001 USA | |
| **Castro, Raul H** | Governor, AZ; Diplomat |
| 429 W Crawford St, Nogales AZ 85621, USA | |
| **Castro, Ruy** | Writer |
| Bloomsbury Publishing, 50 Bedford Square, London WC1B 3DP, England | |
| **Castro, Tommy** | Singer, Guitarist, Band Leader |
| Rosebud Agency, PO Box 170429, San Francisco CA 94117 USA | |
| **Castro, Williams R (Bill)** | Baseball Player |
| 5217 W Harvard Dr, Franklin WI 53132, USA | |
| **Castroneves, Helio** | Auto Racing Driver |
| 386 Isla Dorada Blvd, Coral Gables FL 33143, USA | |
| **Caswell, Ben** | Actor |
| Progressive Artists Agency, 1041 N Formosa Ave, West Hollywood CA 90046, USA | |
| **Caswell, Dean** | WW II Marine Corps Air Force Hero |
| 2309 Village Way Dr, Austin TX 78745, USA | |
| **Cat Power** | Singer, Songwriter, Actress |
| Management Production Entertainment, 9229 Sunset Blvd, #301, West Hollywood CA 90069, USA | |
| **Catalanotto, Frank J** | Baseball Player |
| 4 Muffins Meadows, Saint James NY 11780, USA | |
| **Catalifo, Patrick** | Actor |
| Artmedia, 20 Ave Rapp, 75007 Paris, France | |
| **Catalino, Ken** | Editorial Cartoonist |
| Creators Syndicate, 737 3rd St, Hermosa Beach CA 90254 USA | |
| **Catano, Mark** | Football Player |
| 9036 Walton St, Indianapolis IN 46231, USA | |
| **Catanzaro, Tony** | Dancer |
| 8915 SW 207th St, Cutler Bay FL 33189, USA | |
| **Catchings, Harvey L** | Basketball Player |
| 17406 Edenwalk, Spring TX 77379, USA | |

**Catchings, Tamika D** — Basketball Player
3429 Windham Lake Place, Indianapolis IN 46214, USA
**Cate, Earl** — Singer, Songwriter (Cate Brothers)
1606 Cartwright Circle, Springdale AR 72762, USA
**Cate, Ernie** — Singer, Pianist (Cate Brothers)
17464 Highway 90 W, Ravenden Springs AR 72460, USA
**Cate, Field** — Actor
J L A Talent Agency, 9151 Sunset Blvd, West Hollywood CA 90069, USA
**Cater, Danny A** — Baseball Player
3268 Candlewood Trail, Plano TX 75023, USA
**Cater, Gregory W (Greg)** — Football Player
19 Warwick Way SE, Rome GA 30161, USA
**Cates, Darlene** — Actress
13340 FM 740, Forney TX 75126, USA
**Cates, Phoebe** — Actress
Hofflund/Polone, 9465 Wilshire Blvd, #420, Beverly Hills CA 90212 USA
**Cathcart, Patti** — Singer (Tuck & Patti)
T & P Productions, PO Box 1363, Menlo Park CA 94026, USA
**Catherine** — Singer
Artery Foundation, 1412 S St, Sacramento CA 95811, USA
**Cathey, Reg E** — Actor
Paradigm Agency, 360 N Crescent Dr, North Building, Beverly Hills CA 90210 USA
**Catillon, Brigitte** — Actress
Artmedia, 20 Ave Rapp, 75007 Paris, France
**Catlett, Mary Jo** — Actress
Robert Yacko, 4375 Farmdale Ave, Studio City CA 91604, USA
**Catlett, Sidney L (Sid)** — Basketball Player
3110 Scottish Ave, Suitland MD 20746, USA
**Catley, Glenn** — Boxer
Bristol Gym, Trinity Road, Saint Phillips, Bristol BS2 0NW, England
**Cato, Kelvin T** — Basketball Player
13607 Winter Creek Court, Houston TX 77077, USA
**Caton-Jones, Michael** — Director
Gersh Agency, 9465 Wilshire Blvd, #600, Beverly Hills CA 90212 USA
**Catrow, David** — Editorial Cartoonist
Springfield News-Sun, Editorial Dept, 202 N Limestone St, Springfield OH 45503, USA
**Cattage, Robert L (Bobby)** — Basketball Player
4838 US Highway 29 S, Auburn AL 36830, USA
**Cattaneo, Peter** — Director
Independent Talent Group, 40 Whitfield St, London W1T 2RH, England
**Catta-Preta, Jade** — Actress
Levity Entertainment Group, 6701 Center Dr W, #1100, Los Angeles CA 90045, USA
**Cattelan, Maurizio** — Artist
Galleria Massimo De Carlo, Via Privata Giovanni Ventura, 5, 20134 Milan, Italy
**Cattell, Christine** — Actress
Epstein-Wyckoff, 280 S Beverly Dr, #400, Beverly Hills CA 90212 USA
**Cattrall, Kim** — Actress, Model
I C M Partners, 10250 Constellation Blvd, #900, Los Angeles CA 90067 USA
**Catz, Caroline** — Actress
Independent Talent Group, 40 Whitfield St, London W1T 2RH, England
**Caudill, William H (Bill)** — Baseball Player
11605 NE 41st St, Kirkland WA 98033, USA
**Cauffiel, Jessica** — Actress
Greene Assoc, 1901 Ave of Stars, #130, Los Angeles CA 90067 USA
**Caufield, Jay** — Ice Hockey Player
106 Quail Hollow Lane, Wexford PA 15090, USA
**Caughthran, Matt** — Singer (Bronx)
Crush Music Mgmt, 60-62 E 11th St, #700, New York NY 10003, USA
**Caulfield, Emma** — Actress
Crazy 8 Entertainment, 8581 Santa Monica Blvd, West Hollywood CA 90069, USA
**Caulfield, Maxwell** — Actor
Connor Ankrum & Associates, 1680 Vine St, #1016, Los Angeles CA 90028, USA
**Causey, J Wayne** — Baseball Player
2905 Paynter Dr, Ruston LA 71270, USA
**Causwell, Duane** — Basketball Player
3 Pierce Dr, Stony Point NY 10980, USA
**Caute, J David** — Writer
41 Westcroft Square, London W6 0TA, England
**Cauthen, Stephen M (Steve)** — Thoroughbred Racing Jockey
15541 Porter Road, Verona KY 41092, USA
**Cauthen, Terrance** — Boxer
953 Beatty St, Trenton NJ 08611, USA
**Cauty, James F (Jimmy)** — Musician (KLF)
Nene Musik Productions, 1460 SW Santiago Ave, Port Saint Lucie FL 34953 USA
**Cavalera, Max** — Singer, Guitrist
Oasis Mgmt, 3010 E Bloomfield Road, Phoenix AZ 85032, USA
**Cavaliere, Felix** — Singer, Keyboardist, Composer (Rascals)
Brothers Management Assoc, 141 Dunbar Ave, Fords NJ 08863 USA
**Cavaliero, Rosie** — Actress
Another Tongue, 10-11 D'Arblay St, London W1F 8DS, England
**Cavallari, Kristin** — Actress
W M E Entertainment, 9601 Wilshire Blvd, #300, Beverly Hills CA 90210 USA
**Cavalli, Roberto** — Fashion Designer
Via Senato 8, 20121 Milan, Italy
**Cavallini, Gino** — Ice Hockey Player
6614 Clayton Road, #315, Saint Louis MO 63117, USA
**Cavalli-Sforza, Luigi L** — Geneticist
Stanford University, Human Population Genetics Laboratory, Stanford CA 94305, USA
**Cavallo, Domingo F** — Government Official, Argentina
Hipolito Yrigoyen 250, 1310 Buenos Aires, Argentina
**Cavanagh, Thomas (Tom)** — Actor
United Talent Agency, U T A Plaza, 9336 Civic Center Dr, Beverly Hills CA 90210 USA
**Cavanaugh, Kasie** — Body Builder
PO Box 21882, El Cajon CA 92021, USA
**Cavanaugh, Matthew A (Matt)** — Football Player
8 Barstad Court, Lutherville Timon MD 21093, USA

| | |
|---|---|
| **Cavaney, Red** | Association Executive |
| ConocoPhillips, 600 N Dairy Ashford Road, Houston TX 77079, USA | |
| **Cavazos, Lauro F** | Secretary, Education |
| 173 Annursnac Hill Road, Concord MA 01742, USA | |
| **Cavazos, Lumi** | Actress |
| Talent on Road Mgmt, Av Revolucion 1716 Y\O Sagredo #155, Mexico City DF 03900, Mexico | |
| **Cavazos, Richard E** | Army General |
| Texas Tech University, Board of Regents, Lubbock TX 79409, USA | |
| **Cave, Nick** | Singer, Songwriter |
| Creative Artists Agency, 2000 Ave of Stars, #100, Los Angeles CA 90067 USA | |
| **Caveness, Ronald G (Ronnie)** | Football Player |
| 684 N Cliffside Dr, Fayetteville AR 72701, USA | |
| **Caves, Richard E** | Economist |
| Harvard University, Economics Dept, Cambridge MA 02138, USA | |
| **Cavett, Richard A (Dick)** | Entertainer |
| 1044 Northern Blvd, #304, Roslyn NY 11576, USA | |
| **Cavezza, Carmen J** | Army General |
| Columbus State University, Leadership Development Center, Columbus GA 31907, USA | |
| **Caviezel, James** | Actor |
| Tencer Assoc, 9777 Wilshire Blvd, #1005, Beverly Hills CA 90212, USA | |
| **Cavill, Henry** | Actor |
| United Agents, 12-26 Lexington St, London W1F 0LE, England | |
| **Cawley, Tucker** | Writer, Producer |
| Creative Artists Agency, 2000 Ave of Stars, #100, Los Angeles CA 90067 USA | |
| **Cawley, Warren (Rex)** | Track Athlete |
| 17741 Miller Dr, Tustin CA 92780, USA | |
| **Caws, Matthew** | Singer, Guitarist (Nada Surf) |
| M-Squared Mgmt, 201 W 72nd St, #12G, New York NY 10023, USA | |
| **Cayne, James E (Jimmy)** | Financier |
| Bear Stearns Co, 383 Madison Ave, New York NY 10179, USA | |
| **Cazalot, Clarence P, Jr** | Businessman |
| Marathon Oil, 5555 San Felipe Road, Basement B114, Houston TX 77056, USA | |
| **Ceballos, Cedric Z** | Basketball Player |
| 2068 FM 1252 W, Kilgore TX 75662, USA | |
| **Ceberano, Kate** | Singer, Songwriter |
| Ralph Carr Mgmt, Lennox House, 229 Lennox St, Richmond VIC 3121, Australia | |
| **Ceccarelli, Arthur E (Art)** | Baseball Player |
| 63 Hall Dr, Orange CT 06477, USA | |
| **Ceccato, Aldo** | Conductor |
| Chaunt da Crusch, 7524 Zuoz, Switzerland | |
| **Cecchi, Carlo** | Actor |
| Carol Levi Mgmt, Via Giuseppe Pisanelli 2, 00196 Rome, Italy | |
| **Cech, Thomas R** | Nobel Chemistry Laureate |
| Howard Hughes Medical Institute, 4000 Tones Bridge Road, Chevy Chase MD 20815, USA | |
| **Cechmanek, Roman** | Ice Hockey Player |
| Los Angeles Kings, Staples Center, 1111 S Figueroa St, Los Angeles CA 90015 USA | |
| **Cechvala, Dean** | Actor |
| Geddes Agency, 8430 Santa Monica Blvd, #201, West Hollywood CA 90069 USA | |
| **Cecil, Charles D (Chuck)** | Football Player |
| 2008 Waterstone Dr, Franklin TN 37069, USA | |
| **Cecil, Derek** | Actor |
| One Entertainment, 347 5th Ave, #1404, New York NY 10016 USA | |
| **Cecil, Francesca** | Actress |
| Cinematic Mgmt, 249 1/2 E 13th St, New York NY 10003, USA | |
| **Cedar, Joseph** | Director |
| Kneller Artists Agency, Hayarkon 169, #420, Tel Aviv 63453, Israel | |
| **Cedarstrom, Gary L** | Baseball Umpire |
| 1610 18th St SE, Minot ND 58701, USA | |
| **Cedeno, Cesar E** | Baseball Player |
| 2112 Marisol Loop, Kissimmee FL 34743, USA | |
| **Cedeno, Matt** | Actor, Model |
| Luber Rocklin Entertainment, 5815 Sunset Blvd, #206, Los Angeles CA 90028 USA | |
| **Cedeno, Roger L** | Baseball Player |
| 9325 Byron Ave, Surfside FL 33154, USA | |
| **Cederqvist, Jane** | Swimmer |
| National Museum of Antiquities, PO Box 5428, 114 84 Stockholm, Sweden | |
| **Cedillo, Julio Cesar** | Actor |
| Judy Fox Mgmt, 1525 1/2 S Beverly Dr, Los Angeles CA 90035, USA | |
| **Cedolins, Fiorenza** | Opera Singer |
| Columbia Artists Mgmt Inc, 5 Columbus Circle, 1790 Broadway, #1600, New York NY 10019 USA | |
| **Cedric the Entertainer** | Actor, Comedian |
| Creative Artists Agency, 2000 Ave of Stars, #100, Los Angeles CA 90067 USA | |
| **Cee-Lo** | Singer, Rap Artist, Songwriter |
| Primary Wave Music Publishing, 116 E 16th St, #900, New York NY 10003, USA | |
| **Cefalo, James C (Jimmy)** | Football Player |
| 6675 Roxbury Lane, Miami Beach FL 33141, USA | |
| **Ceglarski, Leonard (Len)** | Ice Hockey Player, Coach |
| 61 Lantern Lane, Duxbury MA 02332, USA | |
| **Cejka, Alexander** | Golfer |
| 9484 S Eastern Ave, Las Vegas NV 89123, USA | |
| **Cejudo, Henry** | Freestyle Wrestler |
| USA Wrestling, 6155 Lehman Dr, Colorado Springs CO 80918, USA | |
| **Celestin, Oliver, Jr** | Football Player |
| 635 Hendee St, New Orleans LA 70114, USA | |
| **Cellier, Caroline** | Actress |
| Artmedia, 20 Ave Rapp, 75007 Paris, France | |
| **Celmins, Vija** | Artist |
| 49 Crosby St, New York NY 10012, USA | |
| **Celski, John R (J R)** | Speed Skater |
| Legacy Mgmt, 1500 Broadway, #2500, New York NY 10036, USA | |
| **Cena, John** | Actor, Professional Wrestler |
| I C M Partners, 10250 Constellation Blvd, #900, Los Angeles CA 90067 USA | |
| **Cenac, Wyatt** | Actor, Comedian, Writer |
| United Talent Agency, U T A Plaza, 9336 Civic Center Dr, Beverly Hills CA 90210 USA | |
| **Cencig, Julia** | Actress |
| Agentur Kelterborn, Schwedter Str 77, 10437 Berlin, Germany | |

**C**

| | |
|---|---|
| **Cenker, Robert J**<br>G O R C A Inc, 155 Hickory Corner Road, East Windsor NJ 08520, USA | Astronaut |
| **Centers, Larry E**<br>5023 Stagecoach Way, Grand Prairie TX 75052, USA | Football Player |
| **Cenziper, Debbie**<br>Miami Herald, Editorial Dept, 1 Herald Plaza, Miami FL 33132 USA | Journalist |
| **Cepeda, Angie**<br>Kuranda Mgmt, Santo Angel 84, 28043 Madrid, Spain | Actress |
| **Cepeda, Orlando M**<br>2305 Palmer Court, Fairfield CA 94534, USA | Baseball Player |
| **Cepero, Jaime**<br>Hartig-Hilepo Agency, 54 W 21st St, #610, New York NY 10010 USA | Actor |
| **Cepicky, Matthew W (Matt)**<br>7 Upper Bluffs View Court, Eureka MO 63025, USA | Baseball Player |
| **Cera, Michael**<br>Thruline Entertainment, 9250 Wilshire Blvd, #100, Beverly Hills CA 90212 USA | Actor |
| **Cerami, Anthony**<br>Ram Island Dr, Shelter Island NY 11964, USA | Biochemist |
| **Ceresino, Ray**<br>13282 Ocean Vista Road, San Diego CA 92130, USA | Ice Hockey Player |
| **Cerezo Arevalo, M Vinicio**<br>Party of Christian Democracy, Avda Elena 20-66, Zone 3, Guatemala City, Guatemala | President, Guatemala |
| **Cerf, Vinton G**<br>3614 Camelot Dr, Annandale VA 22003, USA | Inventor (Internet) |
| **Cerha, Friedrich**<br>Kupelwiesergasse 14, 1010 Vienna, Austria | Composer, Conductor |
| **Cerne, Joseph (Joe)**<br>408 Prospect Ave, Minneapolis MN 55419, USA | Football Player |
| **Cerone, Laura**<br>Don Buchwald Talent Agency, 6500 Wilshire Blvd, #2200, Los Angeles CA 90048 USA | Actress |
| **Cerone, Richard A (Rick)**<br>34 Winding Way, West Paterson NJ 07424, USA | Baseball Player |
| **Cerra, Erica**<br>Trisko Talent Mgmt, 1140 Homer St, #270,Vancouver BC V6B 2X6, Canada | Actress |
| **Cerrone, Christopher**<br>Project Schott, 254 W 31st St, #1500, New York NY 10001, USA | Composer |
| **Cerrudo, Ronald J (Ron)**<br>7 Fox Briar Court, Hilton Head Island SC 29926, USA | Golfer |
| **Cerruti, Nino**<br>Via A Saffi 25, 20121 Milan, Italy | Fashion Designer |
| **Cerry, Amanda**<br>Playboy Promotions, 9346 Civic Center Dr, #200, Beverly Hills CA 90210 USA | Model |
| **Certo, Tish**<br>151 Buffalo Ave, #211, Niagara Falls NY 14303, USA | Golfer |
| **Cerv, Robert H (Bob)**<br>805 N 22nd St, #1A, Blair NE 68008, USA | Baseball Player |
| **Cervantes, Hector**<br>Proper Mgmt, PO Box 150867, Nashville TN 37215, USA | Guitarist (Casting Crowns) |
| **Cervenka, Exene**<br>A P A Talent & Literary Agency, 405 S Beverly Dr, #300, Beverly Hills CA 90212 USA | Singer (X) |
| **Cerveris, Michael**<br>Innovative Artists, 1505 10th St, Santa Monica CA 90401 USA | Actor, Singer |
| **Cervi, Valentina**<br>T N A, Via Parioli 41, 00197 Rome, Italy | Actress |
| **Cesaire, Jacques E**<br>13388 Greenstone Court, San Diego CA 92131, USA | Football Player |
| **Cesarani, Sal**<br>S J C Concepts, 40 E 80th St, New York NY 10075, USA | Fashion Designer |
| **Cesare, William J (Billy)**<br>1655 Hendry Isles Blvd, Clewiston FL 33440, USA | Football Player |
| **Cesario, Jeff**<br>A P A Talent & Literary Agency, 405 S Beverly Dr, #300, Beverly Hills CA 90212 USA | Actor, Comedian |
| **Cetera, Peter**<br>M P I Talent, 9255 Sunset Blvd, #407, West Hollywood CA 90069, USA | Singer, Bassist, Songwriter |
| **Cetlinski, Matthew (Matt)**<br>13121 SE 93rd Terrace Road, Summerfield FL 34491, USA | Swimmer |
| **CeU**<br>Six Degrees Records/A-Train Entertainment, PO Box 29242, Oakland CA 94604, USA | Singer, Songwriter |
| **Cey, Ronald C (Ron)**<br>22714 Creole Road, Woodland Hills CA 91364, USA | Baseball Player |
| **Ceylan, Nuri Bilge**<br>N B C Film, Baskurt Sok 19/4, Urgup Palas Apt, 34433 Cihangir, Istanbul, Turkey | Actor, Director |
| **Chabat, Alain**<br>Chez Wham, 18 Blvd Montmartre, 75009 Paris, France | Actor |
| **Chaber, Madelyn J**<br>101 California St, San Francisco CA 94111, USA | Attorney |
| **Chabert, Lacey**<br>Innovative Artists, 1505 10th St, Santa Monica CA 90401 USA | Actress |
| **Chabon, Michael**<br>United Talent Agency, U T A Plaza, 9336 Civic Center Dr, Beverly Hills CA 90210 USA | Writer |
| **Chabraja, Nicholas D**<br>General Dynamics, 2941 Fairview Park Dr, #100, Falls Church VA 22042, USA | Businessman |
| **Chacon, Alex Pineda**<br>Los Angeles Galaxy, Home Depot Center, 18400 Avalon Blvd, Carson CA 90746 USA | Soccer Player |
| **Chacon, Bobby**<br>3010 Wilshire Blvd, #491, Los Angeles CA 90010, USA | Boxer |
| **Chacon, Shawn A**<br>162 50th Avenue Place, Greeley CO 80634, USA | Baseball Player |
| **Chacurian, Efrain (Chico)**<br>96 Stratford Road, Stratford CT 06615, USA | Soccer Player |
| **Chad**<br>Icon Performing Arts, 1557 Westwood Blvd, #242, Los Angeles CA 90024, USA | Singer, Guitarist (Chad & Jeremy) |
| **Chadbon, Tom**<br>C D A, 167-169 Kensington High St, London W8 6SH, England | Actor |
| **Chadha, Gurinder**<br>I C M Partners, 10250 Constellation Blvd, #900, Los Angeles CA 90067 USA | Director |

**Cenker - Chadha**

**Chadli, Bendjedid**
Palace Emir Abedelkader, Algiers, Algeria — President, Algeria; Army Officer

**Chadwick, Ed**
12 Bowen Road, Fort Erie ON L2A 2Y4, Canada — Ice Hockey Player

**Chadwick, J Leslie (Les)**
Barry Collins, 21A Cliftown Road, Southend on Sea, Essex SS1 1AB, England — Bassist (Gerry & the Pacemakers)

**Chadwick, Jeffrey A (Jeff)**
23062 Village Dr, #A, Lake Forest CA 92630, USA — Football Player

**Chadwick, June**
Independent Artists, 9601 Wilshire Blvd, #750, Beverly Hills CA 90210, USA — Actress

**Chadwick, Justin**
Independent Talent Group, 40 Whitfield St, London W1T 2RH, England — Director, Actor

**Chadwick, Paul**
Dark Horse Publishing, 10956 SE Main St, Portland OR 97222 USA — Cartoonist (Concrete)

**Chae Ji Hoon**
Skating Union, 88 Bangyee-Dong, Songpaku, Seoul 138 749, South Korea — Speed Skater

**Chafee, Lincoln D**
Brown University, International Studies Institute, Providence RI 02912, USA — Senator, RI

**Chafer, Derek**
Ugly Enterprises, Tigis House, 256 Edgware Road, London W2 1DS, England — Actor

**Chafetz, Sidney**
Ohio State University, Art Dept, Columbus OH 43210, USA — Artist

**Chaffee, Don**
7020 La Presa Dr, Los Angeles CA 90068, USA — Director

**Chaffee, Susan (Suzy)**
55 Roadrunner Road, Sedona AZ 86336, USA — Alpine Skier

**Chagaev, Ruslan**
Universum Box-Promotion, Am Stadtrand 27, 22047 Hamburg, Germany — Boxer

**Chagoya, Enrique**
59 Arroyo Way, San Francisco CA 94127, USA — Artist

**Chaiken, Ilene**
W M E Entertainment, 9601 Wilshire Blvd, #300, Beverly Hills CA 90210 USA — Producer, Writer

**Chaikin, Carly**
Paradigm Agency, 360 N Crescent Dr, North Building, Beverly Hills CA 90210 USA — Actress

**Chailly, Riccardo**
Royal Concertgebrew, Jacob Obrechtstraat 51, 1071 KJ Amsterdam 41, Holland — Conductor

**Chakiris, George**
7266 Clinton St, Los Angeles CA 90036, USA — Actor, Singer, Dancer

**Chakvetadze, Anna D**
Best, 303 E Main St, #200, Louisville KY 40202 USA — Tennis Player

**Chalayan, Hussein**
71 Endell Road, London WC2 9AJ, England — Fashion Designer

**Chalenski, Michael (Mike)**
225 S Michigan Ave, Kenilworth NJ 07033, USA — Football Player

**Chalfant, Kathleen**
Douglas Gorman Rothacker Wilhelm, 1501 Broadway, #703, New York NY 10036 USA — Actress

**Chalfie, Martin**
15 Claremont Ave, New York NY 10027, USA — Nobel Chemistry Laureate

**Chalfont, A G (Arthur)**
House of Lords, Westminster, London SW1A 0PW, England — Government Official, England

**Chali 2na**
Vision Entertainment Group, 1100 Glendon Ave, #1100, Los Angeles CA 90024, USA — Rap Artist

**Chalk, David L (Dave)**
137 Cross Timbers Trail, Coppell TX 75019, USA — Baseball Player

**Chalke, Sarah**
John Carrabino Mgmt, 5900 Wilshire Blvd, #406, Los Angeles CA 90036 USA — Actress

**Challenger, James**
Challenger Gray Christmas, 1200 Smith St, #1600, Houston TX 77002, USA — Businessman

**Chalmers, Iain G**
James Lind Initiative, Summertown Pavilion, Oxford OX2 7LG, England — Medical Research Executive

**Chaloner, William G**
20 Parke Road, London SW13 9NG, England — Botanist

**Chalsty, John S**
68 Church St, Charleston SC 29401, USA — Financier

**Chalupny, Lori C**
Octagon Worldwide, 1751 Pinnacle Dr, #1500, McLean VA 22102 USA — Soccer Player

**Chamarande, Brigitte**
Artmedia, 20 Ave Rapp, 75007 Paris, France — Actress

**Chamberlain, Byron**
PO Box 326, Montclair CA 91763, USA — Football Player

**Chamberlain, Cliff**
Brillstein Entertainment Partners, 9150 Wilshire Blvd, #350, Beverly Hills CA 90212 USA — Actor

**Chamberlain, Dean**
1795 Washington Way, Venice CA 90291, USA — Photographer, Artist

**Chamberlain, Gary E**
Harvard University, Littauer Center, Cambridge MA 02138, USA — Economist

**Chamberlain, Jeffrey S**
University of Michigan Medical Center, 301 E Liberty St, Ann Arbor MI 48104, USA — Geneticist

**Chamberlain, Justin L (Joba)**
1504 Kara Lane, Lincoln NE 68522, USA — Baseball Player

**Chamberlain, Richard**
Framework Entertainment, 9057 Nemo St, #C, West Hollywood CA 90069 USA — Actor

**Chamberlain, Spencer**
Red Light Mgmt, 44 Wall St, #2200, New York NY 10005, USA — Singer (Underoath)

**Chamberlain, Wesley P (Wes)**
PO Box 1358, Homewood IL 60430, USA — Baseball Player

**Chamberlin, Beth**
Paradigm Agency, 360 N Crescent Dr, North Building, Beverly Hills CA 90210 USA — Actress

**Chamberlin, James J (Jimmy)**
535 W Basil Road, Lake Bluff IL 60044, USA — Drummer (Smashing Pumpkins)

**Chambers, Anne Cox**
Cox Enterprises, 1400 Lake Hearn Dr NE, Atlanta GA 30319, USA — Businesswoman, Diplomat

**Chambers, Christina**
Don Buchwald Talent Agency, 6500 Wilshire Blvd, #2200, Los Angeles CA 90048 USA — Actress

**Chambers, Jerome P (Jerry)**
4135 Don Diablo Dr, Los Angeles CA 90008, USA — Basketball Player

# C

**Chambers, John T** — Businessman
Cisco Systems, 170 W Tasman Dr, San Jose CA 95134, USA

**Chambers, Justin** — Actor, Model
Gersh Agency, 41 Madison Ave, #3301, New York NY 10010 USA

**Chambers, Kasey** — Singer
Premier Artists, 9 Dundas Lane, Albert Park VIC 3206, Australia

**Chambers, Kirk** — Football Player
1294 Lakeview Dr, Provo UT 84604, USA

**Chambers, Lester** — Singer (Chambers Brothers)
Lustig Talent, PO Box 770850, Orlando FL 32877 USA

**Chambers, Martin** — Drummer (Pretenders)
Gailforce Mgmt, 91 Peterborough Road, London SW6 3BU, England

**Chambers, Nancy** — Actress
United Talent Agency, U T A Plaza, 9336 Civic Center Dr, Beverly Hills CA 90210 USA

**Chambers, Raymond G** — Businessman, Social Activist
Malaria No More, 432 Park Ave S, #400, New York NY 10016, USA

**Chambers, Shawn R** — Ice Hockey Player
9999 Wood Ridge, Pequot Lakes MN 56472, USA

**Chambers, Thomas D (Tom)** — Basketball Player
7437 E Via Dona Road, Scottsdale AZ 85266, USA

**Chambers, Wallace H (Wally)** — Football Player
1838 Joslin St, Saginaw MI 48602, USA

**Chambers, Willie** — Singer, Guitarist (Chambers Brothers)
Lustig Talent, PO Box 770850, Orlando FL 32877 USA

**Chamblee, Brandel E** — Golfer
Golf Channel, 7580 Golf Channel Drive, Orlando FL 32819, USA

**Chambliss, C Christopher (Chris)** — Baseball Player
9100 Otter Creek Dr, #L, Charlotte NC 28277, USA

**Chambliss, Scott** — Art Director
Innovative Artists, 1505 10th St, Santa Monica CA 90401 USA

**Chambon, Pierre H** — Biochemist
Institute of Genetics Molecular & Cellular Biology, 1 Rue Laurent Fries, 67404 Illkirch, France

**Chamillionaire** — Rap Artist
Universal Records, 70 Universal City Plaza, Universal City CA 91608 USA

**Chamitoff, Gregory E** — Astronaut
N A S A, Johnson Space Center, 2101 NASA Road, Houston TX 77058 USA

**Chammah, Walid A** — Financier
Morgan Stanley Co Inc, 1585 Broadway, New York NY 10036, USA

**Champine, Robert** — Test Pilot
205 Tipton Road, Newport News VA 23606, USA

**Champion, B Billy** — Baseball Player
240 Triple H Farm Road, Inman SC 29349, USA

**Champion, Marge** — Dancer, Actress
484 W 43rd St, New York NY 10036, USA

**Champion, William (Will)** — Drummer (Coldplay)
Paradigm Agency, 360 N Crescent Dr, North Building, Beverly Hills CA 90210 USA

**Champlin, James L** — Vietnam War Air Force Hero
Distinguished Flying Cross Society, PO Box 530250, San Diego CA 92153, USA

**Champoux, Robert (Bob)** — Ice Hockey Player
8861 Centuras Way, San Diego CA 92126, USA

**Chan, Ernie** — Cartoonist (Conan the Barbarian)
4131 Vale Ave, Oakland CA 94619, USA

**Chan, Jackie** — Actor
Jackie Chan Cinema, 70 Pak To Ave, Clearwater Bay Road, Kowloon, Hong Kong 852, China

**Chan, Julius** — Prime Minister, Papua New Guinea
PO Box 6030, Boroto, Papua New Guinea

**Chan, Margaret F C** — Government Official, China
World Health Organization, Ave Appia 20, 1211 Geneva 27, Switzerland

**Chan, Michael Paul** — Actor
Tyler Kjar, 10153 1/2 Riverside Dr, #255, Toluca Lake CA 91602 USA

**Chan, Patrick L W-K** — Figure Skater
Detroit Skating Club, 888 Denison Court, Bloomfield Hills MI 48302, USA

**Chance, Greyson** — Singer
W M E Entertainment, 9601 Wilshire Blvd, #300, Beverly Hills CA 90210 USA

**Chance, Larry** — Singer (Earls)
Brothers Management Assoc, 141 Dunbar Ave, Fords NJ 08863 USA

**Chance, Robert (Bob)** — Baseball Player
2258 Oakridge Dr, Charleston WV 25311, USA

**Chance, W Dean** — Baseball Player
9505 W Smithville Western Road, Wooster OH 44691, USA

**Chancellor, Van** — Basketball Coach
Lousiana State University, Athletic Dept, Baton Rouge LA 70803, USA

**Chancey, Robert D** — Football Player
PO Box 212, Coosada AL 36020, USA

**Chanchez, Hosea** — Actor
A P A Talent & Literary Agency, 405 S Beverly Dr, #300, Beverly Hills CA 90212 USA

**Chandler, Carrol H (Howie)** — Air Force General
Vice Chief of Staff, HqUSAF, Pentagon, Washington DC 20330 USA

**Chandler, Christopher M (Chris)** — Football Player
1625 Lugano Lane, Del Mar CA 92014, USA

**Chandler, Dianne** — Model
110 River Oaks Dr, Woodstock GA 30188, USA

**Chandler, Gene** — Singer
8829 S Bishop St, Chicago IL 60620, USA

**Chandler, Jeff** — Boxer
6242 Horner St, Philadelphia PA 19144, USA

**Chandler, Karl V** — Football Player
5 Plymouth Road, Newtown Square PA 19073, USA

**Chandler, Kyle** — Actor
Gersh Agency, 9465 Wilshire Blvd, #600, Beverly Hills CA 90212 USA

**Chandler, Tyson C** — Basketball Player
21731 Ventura Blvd, #300, Woodland Hills CA 91364, USA

**Chandler, Wesley S (Wes)** — Football Player
207 Howard St, New Smyrna Beach FL 32168, USA

**Chandler, Wilson** — Basketball Player
Denver Nuggets, Pepsi Center, 1000 Chopper Circle, Denver CO 80204 USA

**Chandola, Walter** — Photographer
50 Spring Hill Road, Annandale NJ 08801, USA
**Chandor, J C** — Director, Writer
W M E Entertainment, 9601 Wilshire Blvd, #300, Beverly Hills CA 90210 USA
**Chandrasekar** — Actor
34 Senthil Nagar Main Road, Chinna Porur, Chennai TN 600116, India
**Chaney, Darrel L** — Baseball Player
10 Fawn Circle, Sautee Nacoochee GA 30571, USA
**Chaney, Donald R (Don)** — Basketball Player, Coach
20711 Park Pine Dr, Katy TX 77450, USA
**Chaney, John** — Basketball Coach
7840 Gilbert St, Philadelphia PA 19150, USA
**Chaney, Rebekah** — Actress
Polimedia Communications, 1010 Wilshire Blvd, Los Angeles CA 90017, USA
**Chang, Christina** — Actress, Producer
Silver Lining Entertainment, 421 S Beverly Drive, #700, Beverly Hills CA 90212 USA
**Chang, David** — Chef, Restauranteur
Momofuku Sam Bar, 207 2nd Ave, Front 1, New York NY 10003, USA
**Chang, Han-Na** — Conductor, Concert Cellist
Harrison/Parrott, 5-6 Albion Court, London W6 0QT, England
**Chang, Jeannette** — Publisher
Harper's Bazaar, Publisher's Office, 1700 Broadway, New York NY 10019, USA
**Chang, Katie** — Actress
I C M Partners, 10250 Constellation Blvd, #900, Los Angeles CA 90067 USA
**Chang, Michael** — Tennis Player
Chang Foundation, 28562 Oso Parkway, #D343, Rancho Santa Margarita CA 92688, USA
**Chang, Sarah** — Concert Violinist
Opus 3 Artists, 470 Park Ave S, #900N, New York NY 10016 USA
**Chang, Shirley** — Architect
Chang Bene Design, 43-55 Wyndham St, Central, Hong Kong, China
**Chang-Diaz, Franklin R** — Astronaut
Ad Astra Rocket Co, 141 W Bay Area Blvd, Webster TX 77598, USA
**Changeux, Jean-Pierre G** — Molecular Biologist
47 Rue du Four, 75006 Paris, France
**Chanik, Evan M** — Navy Admiral
Commander, 2nd Fleet, FPO AE 09506 USA
**Channing, Carol** — Actress, Singer
Dramatic Artists Agency, 103 W Alameda, #139, Burbank CA 91502, USA
**Channing, Stockard** — Actress
Paradigm Agency, 360 N Crescent Dr, North Building, Beverly Hills CA 90210 USA
**Chante, Keshia** — Singer, Songwriter
Agency Group Ltd, 142 W 57th St, #600, New York NY 10019 USA
**Chan-Wook, Park** — Director
W M E Entertainment, 9601 Wilshire Blvd, #300, Beverly Hills CA 90210 USA
**Chao, Charles** — Businessman
Sina, 37F Jinmao Tower, 88 Century Blvd, Pudong, Shanghai 200121, China
**Chao, Manu** — Singer, Guitarist
Cookman Mgmt, 10627 Burbank Blvd, North Hollywood CA 91601, USA
**Chao, Rosalind** — Actress
Don Buchwald Talent Agency, 6500 Wilshire Blvd, #2200, Los Angeles CA 90048 USA
**Chaovarat Chanweerakul** — Prime Minister, Thailand
Prime Minister's Office, Thanon Nakhon Patnom, Bangkok 10300, Thailand
**Chapdelaine, Rene** — Ice Hockey Player
662 S Division Road, Petoskey MI 49770, USA
**Chapin, Jen** — Singer, Songwriter
Admire Entertainment, PO Box 152, Palisades NY 10964, USA
**Chapin, Lauren** — Actress
726 63rd Ave, Vero Beach FL 32968, USA
**Chapin, Tom** — Singer, Songwriter
Charles Rothschild, 330 E 48th St, #2D, New York NY 10017 USA
**Chaplin, Ben** — Actor
Independent Talent Group, 40 Whitfield St, London W1T 2RH, England
**Chaplin, Carmen** — Actress
Kwanon Films, 20-21 Wolsey Mews, London NW5 2DX, England
**Chaplin, Geraldine** — Actress
Agence Artcine, 15 Rue Romain Rolland, 94250 Gentilly, France
**Chaplin, Kiera** — Actress, Model
Limelight Films, 8913 1/2 W Sunset Blvd, West Hollywood CA 90069, USA
**Chaplin, Oona** — Actress
Troika, 74 Clerkenwell Road, #300, London EC1M 5QA, England
**Chapman, Beth Nielsen** — Singer, Songwriter
PO Box 121551, Nashville TN 37212, USA
**Chapman, Blair** — Ice Hockey Player
2086 Redcoach Road, Allison Park PA 15101, USA
**Chapman, Candace M M** — Soccer Player
Canadian Soccer, Place Soccer Canada, 237 Metcalfe St, Ottawa ON K2P 1R2, Canada
**Chapman, Clarence W** — Football Player
14820 Parkside St, Detroit MI 48238, USA
**Chapman, Dinos** — Artist
Chapman Fine Arts, 49 Fashion St, London E1 6PX, England
**Chapman, Gary W** — Singer, Songwriter, Entertainer
PO Box 25330, Nashville TN 37202, USA
**Chapman, Georgina** — Fashion Designer (Marchesa), Actress
Marchesa, 60 W 26th St, #1425, New York NY 10001, USA
**Chapman, Jake** — Artist
Chapman Fine Arts, 49 Fashion St, London E1 6PX, England
**Chapman, John** — Actor
Elliott Agency, 94 Roundhill Crescent, Brighton BN2 3FR, England
**Chapman, Judith** — Actress
McCabe Group, 3211 Cahuenga Blvd W, #104, Los Angeles CA 90068, USA
**Chapman, Kevin** — Actor
TalentWorks, 3500 W Olive Ave, #1400, Burbank CA 91505 USA
**Chapman, Lanei** — Actress
Mitchell K Stubbs Assoc, 8695 W Washington Blvd, #204, Culver City CA 90232 USA
**Chapman, Marshall** — Singer, Guitarist, Songwriter
1906 South St, #704, Nashville TN 37212, USA

**Chapman, Max C, Jr** — Financier
Nomura Securities, 1 World Financial Center, #200, New York NY 10281, USA

**Chapman, Michael G (Mike)** — Football Player
8731 Avator Circle, Boerne TX 78015, USA

**Chapman, Michael J** — Director, Cinematographer
United Talent Agency, U T A Plaza, 9336 Civic Center Dr, Beverly Hills CA 90210 USA

**Chapman, Nicki** — Actress, Entertainer
19 Music & Mgmt, 35-37 Parkgate Road, London SW11 4NP, England

**Chapman, Orville L** — Chemist
1213 Roscomare Road, Los Angeles CA 90077, USA

**Chapman, Philip K** — Astronaut
11460 E Helm Dr, Scottsdale AZ 85255, USA

**Chapman, Rex E** — Basketball Player
16600 N Thompson Peak Parkway, #2043, Scottsdale AZ 85260, USA

**Chapman, Robert F** — Judge
707 N Summit Crest Court, Spartanburg SC 29307, USA

**Chapman, Steven Curtis** — Singer, Guitarist, Songwriter
Creative Trust, 5141 Virginia Way, #320, Brentwood TN 37027, USA

**Chapman, Tracy** — Singer, Songwriter
Macklam/Feldman Mgmt, 1505 W 2nd Ave, #200, Vancouver BC V6H 3Y4, Canada

**Chapman, Wayne G** — Basketball Player
3593 Salisbury Dr, Lexington KY 40510, USA

**Chapman, Wes** — Ballet Dancer
American Ballet Theater, 890 Broadway, #300, New York NY 10003, USA

**Chapot, Francis D (Frank)** — Equestrian
1075 Opie Road, Branchburg NJ 08853, USA

**Chappell, Crystal** — Actress
Stone Manners Salners, 6100 Wilshire Blvd, #1500, Los Angeles CA 90035 USA

**Chappell, Fred D** — Writer
305 Kensington Road, Greensboro NC 27403, USA

**Chappell, Gregory S (Greg)** — Cricketer
Greg Chappell Cricket Centre, 30 Crosby Road, Albion QLD 4010, Australia

**Chappell, Lenonard R (Len)** — Basketball Player
7624 Chestnut Lane, Waterford WI 53185, USA

**Chappelle, David** — Actor, Comedian
Gersh Agency, 9465 Wilshire Blvd, #600, Beverly Hills CA 90212 USA

**Chapuisat, Stephane** — Soccer Player
Borussia Dortmund S C, Strobelallee, 44139 Dortmund, Germany

**Chaput, Charles J** — Religious Leader
Archdiocese, 222 N 17th St, Philadelphia PA 19103, USA

**Chaquico, Craig** — Guitarist (Jefferson Starship)
Maximus Entertainment, PO Box 27517, Austin TX 78755, USA

**Chara, Zdeno** — Ice Hockey Player
343 Commercial St, #211-213, Boston MA 02109, USA

**Charbonneau, Patricia** — Actress
Mary Harden-Curtis Assoc, 850 7th Ave, #903, New York NY 10019, USA

**Charbonneau, Stephane** — Ice Hockey Player
1 Wilderness Dr, Voorhees NJ 08043, USA

**Chardin, Germain** — Rowing Athlete
10 Ave Meurthe, 54320 Maxeville, France

**Charest, Benoit** — Composer
I C M Partners, 10250 Constellation Blvd, #900, Los Angeles CA 90067 USA

**Charest, Isabelle** — Speed Skater
Speed Skating Canada, 2781 Lancaster Road, #402, Ottawa ON K1B 1A7, Canada

**Chargin, Don** — Boxing Promoter
Don Chargin Productions, 1241 Knollwood Dr, #134, Cambria CA 93428, USA

**Charhi, Liraz** — Actress
Paradigm Agency, 360 N Crescent Dr, North Building, Beverly Hills CA 90210 USA

**Charice** — Actress, Singer
W M E Entertainment, 9601 Wilshire Blvd, #300, Beverly Hills CA 90210 USA

**Charlap, William M (Bill)** — Jazz Pianist
Ted Kurland, 173 Brighton Ave, Boston MA 02134 USA

**Charlene** — Princess Consort, Monaco
Palais de Monaco, BP 518, 98015 Monaco Cedex, Monaco

**Charles** — Prince of Wales, England
Saint James's Palace, London SW1A 1BS, England

**Charles, Caroline** — Fashion Designer
56/57 Beauchamp Place, London SW3, England

**Charles, Craig** — Actor
P F D, Drury House, 34-43 Russell St, London WC2B 5HA, England

**Charles, Edwin D (Ed)** — Baseball Player
57 Park Terrace E, #B58, New York NY 10034, USA

**Charles, Fran** — Sportscaster
N F L Network, 10950 Washington Blvd, #100, Culver City CA 90232 USA

**Charles, Gaius** — Actor
Gersh Agency, 9465 Wilshire Blvd, #600, Beverly Hills CA 90212 USA

**Charles, John C (J C)** — Football Player
5644 Westheimer Road, #164, Houston TX 77056, USA

**Charles, Josh A** — Actor
Arcieri Assoc, 305 Madison Ave, #2315, New York NY 10165 USA

**Charles, Kenneth M (Ken)** — Basketball Player
621 Putnam Ave, Brooklyn NY 11221, USA

**Charles, Larry** — Director
W M E Entertainment, 9601 Wilshire Blvd, #300, Beverly Hills CA 90210 USA

**Charles, Robert J (Bob)** — Golfer
5329 Sea Biscuit Road, Palm Beach Gardens FL 33418, USA

**Charles, Tanika** — Singer, Songwriter
Agency Group Ltd, 142 W 57th St, #600, New York NY 10019 USA

**Charles, Tina** — Basketball Player
Connecticut Sun, 1 Mohegan Sun Blvd, Uncasville CT 06382 USA

**Charles, Tina** — Pop, Disco Singer
International Artists, PO Box 32, 5360 Grave AA, Netherlands

**Charles-Furlow, Daedra** — Basketball Player
19414 Spencer St, Detroit MI 48234, USA

**Charleson, Leslie** — Actress
4851 Cromwell Ave, Los Angeles CA 90027, USA

**Charles-Roux, Edmonde** — Writer
Editions Grasset, 61 Rue des Saints-Peres, 75006 Paris, France
**Charlesworth, Brian** — Evolutionary Biologist
Edinburgh University, Biology Institute, Edinburgh EH1 1HT, Scotland
**Charlesworth, Todd** — Ice Hockey Player
2240 Pleasant Hill Dr, Muskegon MI 49441, USA
**Charli XCX** — Singer, Songwriter
Iamsound Records, 830 Traction Ave, Los Angeles CA 90013, USA
**Charlone, Cesar** — Cinematographer
I C M Partners, 10250 Constellation Blvd, #900, Los Angeles CA 90067 USA
**Charlton, Norman W (Norm)** — Baseball Player
312 Estes Dr, Rockport TX 78382, USA
**Charlton, Robert (Bobby)** — Soccer Player
Garthollerton, Cleford Road, Ollerton, Cheshire WA16 8RY, England
**Charnin, Martin** — Producer, Director, Lyricist
Richard Ticktin, 1345 Ave of Americas, New York NY 10105, USA
**Charno, Stuart** — Actor, Comedian
4147 Sunnyside Ave, Los Angeles CA 90066, USA
**Charo** — Singer, Guitarist
Charo Entertainment, 1801 Lexington Road, Beverly Hills CA 90210, USA
**Charron, Paul R** — Businessman
44 Contentment Island Road, Darien CT 06820, USA
**Chartier, Dave** — Ice Hockey Player
SW 13-19-28 W, Binscarth MB R0J 0G0, Canada
**Chartoff, Melanie** — Actress
Artists Agency, 9430 Olympic Blvd, Beverly Hills CA 90212 USA
**Chartraw, Rick** — Ice Hockey Player
600 Chaparral Road, Sierra Madre CA 91024, USA
**Charvet, David** — Actor
Chasen Agency, 8899 Beverly Blvd, #405, Los Angeles CA 90048 USA
**Charyk, Joseph V** — Businessman
790 Andrews Ave, #A302, Delray Beach FL 33483, USA
**Charyn, Jerome** — Writer
Bloomsbury Publishing, 50 Bedford Square, London WC1B 3DP, England
**Chase, Alison** — Dance Artistic Director
Apogee Arts, PO Box 224, Brooksville ME 04617, USA
**Chase, Alston** — Writer
Bohrman Agency, 3141 Ellington Dr, Los Angeles CA 90068, USA
**Chase, Bailey** — Actor
Gersh Agency, 9465 Wilshire Blvd, #600, Beverly Hills CA 90212 USA
**Chase, Barrie** — Actress, Dancer
446 Carrol Canal, Venice CA 90291, USA
**Chase, Brian** — Drummer (Yeah Yeah Yeahs)
C E S D, 10635 Santa Monica Blvd, #130, Los Angeles CA 90025 USA
**Chase, Chevy** — Actor, Comedian
A P A Talent & Literary Agency, 405 S Beverly Dr, #300, Beverly Hills CA 90212 USA
**Chase, Daveigh** — Actress
Brillstein Entertainment Partners, 9150 Wilshire Blvd, #350, Beverly Hills CA 90212 USA
**Chase, David** — Producer, Writer
United Talent Agency, U T A Plaza, 9336 Civic Center Dr, Beverly Hills CA 90210 USA
**Chase, Debra Martin** — Producer
Martin Chase Productions, 500 S Buena Vista St, Burbank CA 91521, USA
**Chase, Jonathan** — Actor
Main Title Mgmt, 8383 Wilshire Blvd, #408, Beverly Hills CA 90211 USA
**Chase, Kelly W** — Ice Hockey Player
16476 Horseshoe Ridge Road, Chesterfield MO 63005, USA
**Chase, Lori** — Actress, Comedienne
OmniPop Talent Group, 4605 Lankershim Blvd, #201, Toluca Lake CA 91602 USA
**Chase, Lorraine** — Actress
Burnett Granger Assoc, 3 Clifford St, London W1S 2LF, England
**Chase, Qiana** — Model
Playboy Promotions, 9346 Civic Center Dr, #200, Beverly Hills CA 90210 USA
**Chase, Steve** — Interior Designer
Chase Design Assoc, 70005 Mirage Cove Dr, Rancho Mirage CA 92270, USA
**Chasez, Joshua Scott (J C)** — Singer ('N Sync)
Podwall Entertainment, 710 N Orlando Ave, #203, West Hollywood CA 90069, USA
**Chass, Murray** — Sportswriter
New York Times, Editorial Dept, 229 W 43rd St, New York NY 10036 USA
**Chassagne, Regine** — Musician (Arcade Fire), Actress
Billions Corp, 3522 W Armitage Ave, Chicago IL 60647 USA
**Chast, Roz** — Cartoonist
New Yorker, Editorial Dept, 4 Times Square, Basement C1B, New York NY 10036 USA
**Chastain, Brandi** — Soccer Player, Sportscaster
1661 University Way, San Jose CA 95126, USA
**Chastain, Jessica** — Actress
Mosiac Media Group, 9200 W Sunset Blvd, #1000, Los Angeles CA 90069 USA
**Chastel, Andre** — Writer
30 Rue de Lubeck, 75116 Paris, France
**Chater, Eos** — Violinist (Bond)
Mel Bush, Ranglewood, Arrowsmith Road, Wimborne, Dorset BH21 3B5, England
**Chatham, Matthew (Matt)** — Football Player
2502 Old Bridge Lane, Bellingham MA 02019, USA
**Chatham, Russell** — Artist
Clark City Press, PO Box 1358, Livingston MT 59047, USA
**Chatham, Wes** — Actor
Gersh Agency, 9465 Wilshire Blvd, #600, Beverly Hills CA 90212 USA
**Chatroit, Francois** — Auto Racing Driver
Artmedia, 20 Ave Rapp, 75007 Paris, France
**Chattaway, Jay** — Composer
May Artist Mgmt, 8491 W Sunset Blvd, #228, West Hollywood CA 90069, USA
**Chatwin, Justin** — Actor
Alchemy Entertainment, 7024 Melrose Ave, #420, Los Angeles CA 90038 USA
**Chaudhry, Iftikhar Mohammed** — Judge
Supreme Court, Constitution Ave, Islamabad, Pakistan
**Chaudhry, Mahendra P** — Prime Minister, Fiji
Fiji Labor Party, PO Box 2162, Suva, Fiji

**Chaumette, Monique** — Actress
Voyez Mon Agent, 20 Ave Rapp, 75007 Paris, France

**Chauvin, Yves** — Nobel Chemistry Laureate
10 Place Francois Sicard, 37000 Tours, France

**Chauvire, Yvette** — Ballerina
21 Place du Commerce, 75015 Paris, France

**Chaves, Richard** — Actor
Media Artists Group, 8222 Melrose Ave, #203, Los Angeles CA 90048 USA

**Chavez Ramirez, Darvin F** — Soccer Player
C F Monterrey, Ave Revolucion 846B, C Jardin Espanol, 63820 Monterrey Nuevo Leon, Mexico

**Chavez, Endy D** — Baseball Player
1406 Bonnie Lane, Bayside NY 11360, USA

**Chavez, Jorge F** — Thoroughbred Racing Jockey
106 John St, Garden City NY 11530, USA

**Chavez, Julio Cesar, Jr** — Boxer
Team Chavez, 12620 Washington Blvd, Los Angeles CA 90066, USA

**Chavira, Ricardo Antonio** — Actor
Innovative Artists, 1505 10th St, Santa Monica CA 90401 USA

**Chavous, Barney L** — Football Player, Coach
601 Chavous Road, Aiken SC 29803, USA

**Chavous, Corey L** — Football Player
1218 S Main St, Saint Charles MO 63301, USA

**Chawla, Juhi** — Actress
153 Oxford Tower, Yamuna Nagar, Oshiwara Andheri (W), Mumbai 40058, India

**Chayanne** — Singer, Actress
Chaf Enterprises, 1717 N Bayshore Dr, #2146, Miami FL 33132, USA

**Chbosky, Stephen** — Writer, Producer
W M E Entertainment, 9601 Wilshire Blvd, #300, Beverly Hills CA 90210 USA

**Cheadle, Don** — Actor
United Talent Agency, U T A Plaza, 9336 Civic Center Dr, Beverly Hills CA 90210 USA

**Cheaney, Calbert N** — Basketball Player
2103 Finchley Road, Carmel IN 46032, USA

**Cheatham, Maree** — Actress
Sutton-Barth Vennari, 5900 Wilshire Blvd, #700, Los Angeles CA 90036 USA

**Checker, Chubby** — Singer, Songwriter
Twisted Entertainment, 320 Fayette St, #200, Conshohocken PA 19428, USA

**Checkley, Laura** — Actress
Gavin Barker Assoc, 2D Wimpole St, London W1G 0EB, England

**Cheechoo, Jonathan** — Ice Hockey Player
707 Iris Gardens Court, San Jose CA 95125, USA

**Cheek, Jimmy G** — Educator
University of Tennessee, Chancellor's Office, Andy Holt Tower, Knoxville TN 37996, USA

**Cheek, Joey** — Speed Skater
Q Sports Marketing, 534 W Evergreen St, Wheaton IL 60187 USA

**Cheek, Louis R, Jr** — Football Player
545 Woelke Road, Seguin TX 78155, USA

**Cheek, Molly** — Actress
Kazarian/Measures/Ruskin, 11969 Ventura Blvd, #300, Studio City CA 91604 USA

**Cheeks, Maurice E (Mo)** — Basketball Player, Coach
709 Broad Acres Road, Penn Valley PA 19072, USA

**Cheena, Parvesh** — Actor
Global Artists Agency, 6253 Hollywood Blvd, #508, Los Angeles CA 90028 USA

**Cheeseborough, Chandra** — Track Athlete
104 W Harbor, Hendersonville TN 37075, USA

**Cheesman, Barry** — Golfer
2901 Theresa Lane, Sarasota FL 34239, USA

**Cheetham, Jay (Jay Kay)** — Singer
Merlin Elite, Hammersmith Studios, 55 Yelman Road, London W6 8JF, England

**Cheever, Eddie** — Auto Racing Driver
8227 N West Blvd, #300, Indianapolis IN 46278, USA

**Cheever, Susan** — Writer
Simon & Schuster, 1230 Ave of Americas, Concourse 1, New York NY 10020 USA

**Cheevers, Gerald M (Gerry)** — Ice Hockey Player, Coach
106 Appleton St, North Andover MA 01845, USA

**Chee-Yun** — Concert Violinist
Opus 3 Artists, 470 Park Ave S, #900N, New York NY 10016 USA

**Chef, Genia** — Artist
Leibnizstr 61, 10629 Berlin, Germany

**Chekamauskas, Vitautas** — Architect
State Arts Academy, Maironio 6, 2600 Vilnius, Lithuania

**Chelberg, Robert D** — Army General
Cubic Applications, Patch Community, Unit 30400, Box R65, APO AE 09131, USA

**Cheli, Maurizio** — Astronaut, Italy
Alenia Aeronautica, Via Campania 45, 00187 Rome RM, Italy

**Cheli-Merchez, Marianne** — Astronaut, Belgium
38 Via Ciro Sant'agata, 40019 Modena, Italy

**Chelios, Christos K (Chris)** — Ice Hockey Player
790 Falmouth Dr, Bloomfield Hills MI 48304, USA

**Chellas, Semi** — Producer
United Talent Agency, U T A Plaza, 9336 Civic Center Dr, Beverly Hills CA 90210 USA

**Chellgren, Paul W** — Businessman
Ashland Inc, PO Box 15391, Covington KY 41015, USA

**Chelsom, Peter** — Director
Principato-Young, 9465 Wilshire Blvd, #880, Beverly Hills CA 90212 USA

**Chemetov, Paul** — Architect
Chemetov-Huidobro, 4 Square Massena, 75013 Paris, France

**Chen Kaige** — Director
I C M Partners, 10250 Constellation Blvd, #900, Los Angeles CA 90067 USA

**Chen Lu** — Figure Skater
World Ice Arena, 1881th Bao'an Road, Luohu District, Shenzhen 518000 , China

**Chen Wenbo** — Artist
P K M Gallery, 7-32 Samcheongro, Jongnogu, Seoul 110 230 South Korea

**Chen Xieyang** — Conductor
Shanghai Symphony Orchestra, 105 Hunan Road, Shanghai 200031, China

**Chen Yi** — Composer
University of Missouri, Music Conservatory, Kansas City MO 64110, USA

**Chen Yibing**
Beijing Normal University, 19 Xin Jie Kou Wai St, Hai Dian District, Beijing 100875 PR, China — Gymnast

**Chen Zuohuang**
Wichita Symphony Orchestra, Concert Hall, 225 W Douglas St, Wichita KS 67202, USA — Conductor

**Chen, Bruce K**
18372 W Ivy Lane, Surprise AZ 85388, USA — Baseball Player

**Chen, Daniel (Dan)**
PO Box 41513, Eugene OR 97404, USA — Sculptor, Artist

**Chen, Edison**
Fulong Production, 8/F Baskerville House, 13 Duddell St, Central, Hong Kong, China — Actor

**Chen, Irvin S Y**
University of California Medical Center, Hematology Dept, Los Angeles CA 90024, USA — Geneticist

**Chen, Joan**
2601 Filbert St, San Francisco CA 94123, USA — Actress, Director

**Chen, Joie**
CNN-TV, News Dept, 190 Marietta Ave SW, Atlanta GA 30303 USA — Commentator

**Chen, Julie**
CBS-TV, News Dept, 51 W 52nd St, New York NY 10019 USA — Commentator

**Chen, Lincoln C**
302 Dean Road, Brookline MA 02445, USA — Nutritionist

**Chen, Steve**
YouTube, 1000 Cherry Ave, #200, San Bruno CA 94066, USA — Businessman

**Chen, Steve S**
Chen Systems Corp, 1414 W Hamilton Ave, Eau Claire WI 54701, USA — Computer Engineer

**Chen, Steven**
Island Def Jam Records, 8920 W Sunset Blvd, #200, West Hollywood CA 90069 USA — Keyboardist (Airline Toxic Event)

**Chenchikova, Olga**
Kirov Ballet Theater, 1 Pl Iskusstr, 190000 Saint Petersburg, Russia — Ballerina

**Chenery, Penny**
20 Roberts Lane, Saratoga Springs NY 12866, USA — Thoroughbred Racing Owner

**Cheney, Dorothy B (Dodo)**
442 Woodland Hills Dr, Escondido CA 92029, USA — Tennis Player

**Cheney, Lauren**
Boston Breakers, 400 Blue Hill Dr, #302, Westwood, MA 02090 USA — Soccer Player

**Cheney, Lynne V**
American Enterprise Institute, 1150 17th St NW, Washington DC 20036, USA — Government Official

**Cheney, Richard B**
6613 Madison Dr, McLean VA 22101, USA — Vice President; Secretary, Defense

**Cheng, Andy**
Paradigm Agency, 360 N Crescent Dr, North Building, Beverly Hills CA 90210 USA — Director

**Chenier, Philip (Phil)**
7807 Arbor Grove Dr, #407, Hanover MD 21076, USA — Basketball Player

**Chennault, Anna Chan**
T A C International, Chennault Building, 1049 30th St NW, Washington DC 20007, USA — Businesswoman, Writer

**Chenoweth, Kristin**
Creative Artists Agency, 2000 Ave of Stars, #100, Los Angeles CA 90067 USA — Actress, Singer

**Cheong Jin-Suk, Nicholas Cardinal**
Archdiocese of Seoul, Chunggu Myongdong 2-1, Seoul 100 809, South Korea — Religious Leader

**Chepik, Sergei**
Galerie Guiter, 23 Rue Guenegaud, 75006 Paris, France — Artist

**Cher**
Schiff Co, 9220 Sunset Blvd, #106, West Hollywood CA 90069 USA — Actress, Singer

**Cherestal, Jean Marie**
Villa d'Accueil, Delmas 60, Mousseau, Port-au-Prince 6110, Haiti — Prime Minister, Haiti

**Cherlin, Andrew J**
Johns Hopkins University, Sociology Dept, Baltimore MD 21218, USA — Sociologist

**Chermayeff, Peter**
Chermayeff Sollogub Poolle, 51 Melcher St, #902, Boston MA 02210, USA — Architect

**Chernicky, Laura**
PO Box 39723, Los Angeles CA 90039, USA — Actress

**Chernin, Peter**
Chernin Entertainment, 1733 Ocean Ave, Santa Monica CA 90401, USA — Businessman

**Chernoff, Herman**
44 Allandale St, #311, Jamaica Plain MA 02130, USA — Applied Mathematician/Statistician

**Chernousov, Ilia G**
Reto Burgermeister, Lengmattastr 3, 7276 Davos Frauenkirch, Switzerland — Cross Country Skier

**Chernow, Ron**
105 State St, Brooklyn NY 11201, USA — Writer

**Chernus, Michael**
United Talent Agency, U T A Plaza, 9336 Civic Center Dr, Beverly Hills CA 90210 USA — Actor

**Cherrelle**
Green Light Talent Agency, PO Box 3172, Beverly Hills CA 90212 USA — Singer

**Cherry, Byron**
Talent Bin, 5270 Railview Court, #238, Shelby Township MI 48316, USA — Actor, Producer

**Cherry, Deron L**
13800 S Pebblebrook Lane, Greenwood MO 64034, USA — Football Player

**Cherry, Dick**
Box 346 RR 1, Bath ON K0H 1G0, Canada — Ice Hockey Player

**Cherry, Don**
928 Pinehurst Dr, Las Vegas NV 89109, USA — Singer, Golfer

**Cherry, Don S**
CBC-TV, PO Box 500, Station A, Toronto ON M5W 1E6, Canada — Ice Hockey Player, Coach, Sportscaster

**Cherry, Eagle-Eye L**
Umbrella Group, 1 West St, #3506, New York NY 10004, USA — Singer

**Cherry, Fred V**
720 Dale Dr, Silver Spring MD 20910, USA — Vietnam War Air Force Hero

**Cherry, Jake**
United Talent Agency, U T A Plaza, 9336 Civic Center Dr, Beverly Hills CA 90210 USA — Actor

**Cherry, Je'rod L**
993 Mimosa Dr, Macedonia OH 44056, USA — Football Player

**Cherry, Jonathan**
Roar, 2400 Broadway, #330, Santa Monica CA 90404, USA — Actor

**Cherry, Marc**
Paradigm Agency, 360 N Crescent Dr, North Building, Beverly Hills CA 90210 USA — Producer

**Cherry, Neneh**
Paradigm Agency, 360 Park Ave, #1600, New York NY 10022 USA — Singer

# C

**Chertoff, Michael** — Secretary, Homeland Security; Judge
Covington & Burling, 1201 Pennsylvania Ave NW, Washington DC 20004, USA

**Cherundolo, Charles J (Chuck), Jr** — Football Player
4230 Simms Road, Lakeland FL 33810, USA

**Cherundolo, Steve** — Soccer Player
Hanover 96, Arthur-Menge Ufer 5, 30169 Hannover, Germany

**Chervin, Stan** — Writer
I C M Partners, 10250 Constellation Blvd, #900, Los Angeles CA 90067 USA

**Chesnais, Patrick** — Actor
Artmedia, 20 Ave Rapp, 75007 Paris, France

**Chesnes, Shelby** — Model
Playboy Promotions, 9346 Civic Center Dr, #200, Beverly Hills CA 90210 USA

**Chesney, Kenny** — Singer
Morris Management Group, 818 19th Ave S, Nashville TN 37203, USA

**Chesnutt, Mark N** — Singer, Songwriter
Music City News Media, 38 Music Square E, #200, Nashville TN 37203, USA

**Chester, Colby** — Actor
Brady Brannon Rich, 5670 Wilshire Blvd, #820, Los Angeles CA 90036 USA

**Chester, Larry T** — Football Player
14121 SW 33rd Court, Davie FL 33330, USA

**Chester, Raymond T** — Football Player
4722 Grass Valley Road, Oakland CA 94605, USA

**Chestnut, Mary Boykin** — Educator
Sweet Briar College, President's Office, Sweet Briar VA 24595, USA

**Chestnut, Morris** — Actor
Gersh Agency, 9465 Wilshire Blvd, #600, Beverly Hills CA 90212 USA

**Chet, Ilan** — Microbiologist
Weizmann Science Institute, President's Office, Rehovot 76100, Israel

**Chetry, Kiran** — Commentator
CNN-TV, News Dept, 190 Marietta Ave SW, Atlanta GA 30303 USA

**Chetwynd, Lionel** — Writer, Producer, Director
Creative Artists Agency, 2000 Ave of Stars, #100, Los Angeles CA 90067 USA

**Cheung, Maggie** — Actress
Schachter Entertainment, 1157 S Beverly Dr, Los Angeles CA 90035, USA

**Chevrier, Alain** — Ice Hockey Player
5138 Greenwich Preserve Court, Boynton Beach FL 33436, USA

**Chew, Geoffrey F** — Physicist
10 Maybeck Twin Dr, Berkeley CA 94708, USA

**Cheyunski, James M (Jim)** — Football Player
821 W Locust St, Seaford DE 19973, USA

**Chi Haotian** — Army General, China
National Defense Ministry, Jingshanqia Jie, Beijing 100009, China

**Chi, Chen** — Artist
23 Washington Square N, New York NY 10011, USA

**Chi, Tony** — Interior Designer
Tony Chi & Assoc, 121 Varick St, #500, New York NY 10013, USA

**Chia, Sandro** — Artist
601 W 26th St, #12, New York NY 10001, USA

**Chiacchia, Darren** — Equestrian
PO Box 278, East Aurora NY 14052, USA

**Chianese, Dominic** — Actor
S M S Talent, 8383 Wilshire Blvd, #230, Beverly Hills CA 90211 USA

**Chiao, Leroy** — Astronaut
2108 Butler Dr, Friendswood TX 77546, USA

**Chiara, Maria** — Opera Singer
Narodni Divado, Ostrovni 1, 11230 Prague 1, Czech Republic

**Chiarelli, Peter W** — Army General
One Mind for Research, 120 Lakeside Ave, #200, Seattle WA 98122, USA

**Chichkan, Ilya** — Artist, Sculptor
Victor Pinchuk Foundation, 2 Mechnikova St, 01601 Kiev, Ukraine

**Chick, Austin** — Director
Bloom Hergott Diemer, 150 S Rodeo Dr, #300, Beverly Hills CA 90212 USA

**Chihara, Charles S** — Philosopher
567 Cragmont Ave, Berkeley CA 94708, USA

**Chihuly, Dale P** — Artist, Sculptor
Chihuly Inc, 1111 NW 50th St, Seattle WA 98107, USA

**Chikezie, Caroline** — Actress
Paradigm Agency, 360 N Crescent Dr, North Building, Beverly Hills CA 90210 USA

**Chiklis, Michael** — Actor
W M E Entertainment, 9601 Wilshire Blvd, #300, Beverly Hills CA 90210 USA

**Child, Desmond** — Singer, Songwriter
D S W Entertainment, 116 E 16th St, #900, New York NY 10003, USA

**Child, Jane** — Singer, Keyboardist, Songwriter
7095 Hollywood Blvd, #747, Los Angeles CA 90028, USA

**Child, Lee** — Writer
Delacorte Press, 1540 Broadway, New York NY 10036 USA

**Childers, Ambyr** — Actress
W M E Entertainment, 9601 Wilshire Blvd, #300, Beverly Hills CA 90210 USA

**Childress, Joshua M (Josh)** — Basketball Player
1433 Cherokee Trail, Lawrenceville GA 30043, USA

**Childress, Kallie Flynn** — Actress
Amsel Eisenstadt Frazier, 5055 Wilshire Blvd, #865, Los Angeles CA 90036 USA

**Childress, Raymond C (Ray), Jr** — Football Player
639 Shady Hill St, Houston TX 77056, USA

**Childress, Richard (R C)** — Auto Racing Executive
Childress Racing, 236 Industrial Dr, Welcome NC 27374, USA

**Childs, Billy** — Jazz Pianist
Unlimited Myles, 6 Imaginery Place, Aberdeen NJ 07747, USA

**Childs, Chris** — Basketball Player
10830 Willow Meadow Circle, Alpharetta GA 30022, USA

**Childs, David M** — Architect
Skidmore Owings Merrill, 14 Wall St, #2500, New York NY 10005, USA

**Childs, Henry** — Football Player
8304 Allman Road, Lenexa KS 66219, USA

**Childs, Martin** — Art Director
Independent Talent Group, 40 Whitfield St, London W1T 2RH, England

**Childs, Toni** — Singer, Songwriter
Studio C Communications, 324 Sunset Ave, Venice CA 90291, USA

**Chiles, Henry G (Hank), Jr** — Navy Admiral
6436 Pima St, Alexandria VA 22312, USA

**Chiles, Linden** — Actor
2521 Topanga Skyline Dr, Topanga CA 90290, USA

**Chiles, Lois** — Actress, Model
Abrams Artists, 9200 W Sunset Blvd, #1125, West Hollywood CA 90069 USA

**Chiles, Richard F (Rich)** — Baseball Player
18147 Mallard St, Woodland CA 95695, USA

**Chillar, Brandon O** — Football Player
1030 Iris Court, Carlsbad CA 92011, USA

**Chillemi, Connie** — Golfer
2701 NE 10th St, #705, Ocala FL 34470, USA

**Chilstom, Ken** — Test Pilot
20 Selby Lane, Palm Beach Gardens FL 33418, USA

**Chilton, Gene A** — Football Player
45828 US Highway 69 N, Jacksonville TX 75766, USA

**Chilton, Karen** — Actress
Innovative Artists, 1505 10th St, Santa Monica CA 90401 USA

**Chilton, Kevin P** — Astronaut, Air Force General
2555 Talleson Court, Colorado Springs CO 80919, USA

**Chilton, W Alexander (Alex)** — Singer, Guitarist (Box Tops, Big Star)
High Road Touring, 751 Bridgeway, #200, Sausalito CA 94965 USA

**Chiminazzo, Jeisa** — Model
I M G Models, 304 Park Ave S, #PH N, New York NY 10010 USA

**Chiminello, Bianca** — Actress
Vox Inc, 6420 Wilshire Blvd, #1080, Los Angeles CA 90048 USA

**Chin, Lonny** — Actress, Model
Playboy Promotions, 9346 Civic Center Dr, #200, Beverly Hills CA 90210 USA

**Chinchilla Miranda, Laura** — President, Costa Rica
Casa Presidencial, Apdo 520-2010, San Jose 1000, Costa Rica

**Ching, Brian** — Soccer Player
Houston Dynamo, 1415 Louisiana, #3400, Houston TX 77002 USA

**Chingy** — Rap Artist
Central Entertainment Group Talent, 251 W 39th St, New York NY 10018, USA

**Chinlund, Nick** — Actor
Innovative Artists, 1505 10th St, Santa Monica CA 90401 USA

**Chinn, Simon** — Producer, Writer
Red Box Films, Kirkman House, 12-14 Whitfield St, #300, London W1T 2RF, England

**Chipchura, Kyle D G** — Ice Hockey Player
Arizona Coyotes, 6751 N Sunset Blvd, #200, Glendale AZ 85305 USA

**Chipperfield, David** — Architect
Chipperfield Architects, Cobham Mews, Agar Grove, London NW1 9SB, England

**Chipperfield, Ron** — Ice Hockey Player
Optima World Sports, Box 248, Wilcox SK S0G 5E0, Canada

**Chirac, Jacques R** — President, France
110 Rue du Bac, 75007 Paris, France

**Chirico, Emanuel** — Businessman
Phillips-Van Heusen Corp, 200 Madison Ave, Basement 1, New York NY 10016, USA

**Chisholm, Melanie J** — Singer (Spice Girls)
45 Mgmt, 13 Tottenham Mews, London W1T 4AG, England

**Chisholm, Sallie W (Penny)** — Biological Oceanographer
Massachusetts Institute of Technology, Engineering Dept, Cambridge MA 02139, USA

**Chislett, Michael Guy** — Guitarist (Academy Is)
Decaydance Records, 9229 Sunset Blvd, #900, West Hollywood CA 90069, USA

**Chissano, Joaquim A** — President, Mozambique
Rua Pereira do Lago 10, Bairro de Sommerschield, Maputo, Mozambique

**Chitalada, Sot** — Boxer
Home Express Co, 242/19 Moo 10, Sukhumvit Road, Cholburi 20210, Thailand

**Chittenden, Khan** — Actor
Lisa Mann Creaqtive Mgmt, 99 Spring St, Bondi Junction NSW 2022, Australia

**Chittister, Joan D** — Social Psychologist
Saint Scholastica Priory, 335 E 9th St, Erie PA 16503, USA

**Chitty, Dennis** — Animal Ecologist
1602-5775 Hampton Place, Vancouver BC V6T 2G6, Canada

**Chitwood, Joey, Jr** — Stunt Car Driver
5324 Golden Isles Dr, Apollo Beach FL 33572, USA

**Chiu, Raymond J** — Heart Surgeon
9075 Rue Omega, Brossard QC J4Y 3A9, Canada

**Chivian, Eric** — Psychiatrist, Social Activist
Harvard University, Health & Global Environment Center, Cambridge MA 02138, USA

**Chizevsky, Kim** — Body Builder
PO Box 9101, Springfield MO 65801, USA

**Chladek, Dana** — Canoeing Athlete
5302 Flanders Ave, Kensington MD 20895, USA

**Chlumsky, Anna** — Actress
Innovative Artists, 235 Park Ave S, #1000, New York NY 10003 USA

**Chmerkovskiy, Maksim** — Dancer, Choreographer
Rising Stars Dance Academy, 479 N Midland Ave, #H, Saddlebrook NJ 07663, USA

**Chmerkovskiy, Val** — Dancer
Lizzie Grubman Mgmt, 424 W 33 St, #110, New York NY 10001, USA

**Chmura, Mark W** — Football Player
S18W28948 Price Court, Waukesha WI 53188, USA

**Cho Ha-Ri** — Speed Skater
Skating Union, 88 Bangyee-Dong, Songpaku, Seoul 138 749, South Korea

**Cho Na-Yeon** — Golfer
Ladies Pro Golf Assn, 100 International Golf Dr, Daytona Beach FL 32124 USA

**Cho, Alfred Y** — Electrical Engineer
A T & T Bell Lucent Laboratory, 600 Mountain Ave, New Providence NJ 07974 USA

**Cho, Frank** — Cartoonist (Liberty Meadows)
Creators Syndicate, 737 3rd St, Hermosa Beach CA 90254 USA

**Cho, Fujio** — Businessman
Toyota Motor Corp, 1 Toyotacho, Toyota City, Aichi Pref 471 8701, Japan

**Cho, John** — Actor
United Talent Agency, U T A Plaza, 9336 Civic Center Dr, Beverly Hills CA 90210 USA

**Cho, Margaret**
W M E Entertainment, 9601 Wilshire Blvd, #300, Beverly Hills CA 90210 USA
Actress, Comedienne

**Cho, Paul Y**
Full Gospel Central Church, 12 Yoido-dong, #1100, Youngdungpoku, Seoul 150 869, Korea
Evangelist

**Cho, Simon**
U S Speedskating, 5662 S Cougar Lane, Salt Lake City UT 84118 USA
Speed Skater

**Cho, Smith**
Gersh Agency, 9465 Wilshire Blvd, #600, Beverly Hills CA 90212 USA
Actress

**Choate, Jerry D**
Allstate Insurance, Allstate Plaza, 2775 Sanders Road, Northbrook IL 60062, USA
Businessman

**Choate, Randol D (Randy)**
6610 Cobia Circle, Boynton Beach FL 33437, USA
Baseball Player

**Chodron, Pemo**
Gampo Abbey, Pleasant Bay, Cape Breton NS B0E 2P0, Canada
Religious Leader

**Choi Eun-Kyung**
Skating Union, 88 Bangyee-Dong, Songpaku, Seoul 138 749, South Korea
Speed Skater

**Choi Min-Kyung**
Skating Union, 88 Bangyee-Dong, Songpaku, Seoul 138 749, South Korea
Speed Skater

**Choi, Kenneth**
TalentWorks, 3500 W Olive Ave, #1400, Burbank CA 91505 USA
Actor

**Choi, Kyung-Ju (K J)**
2205 Vaquero Estates Blvd, Westlake TX 76262, USA
Golfer

**Chojnacka, Elisabeth**
17 Rue Emile Dubois, 75014 Paris, France
Concert Harpsichordist

**Chojnowska-Liskiewicz, Krystyna**
Ul Norblina 29 m 50, 80 304 Gdansk-Oliwa, Poland
Yachtswoman

**Chokachi, David**
Abrams Artists, 9200 W Sunset Blvd, #1125, West Hollywood CA 90069 USA
Actor

**Chomet, Sylvain**
I C M Partners, 10250 Constellation Blvd, #900, Los Angeles CA 90067 USA
Animator, Lyricist

**Chomski, Alejandro**
Gersh Agency, 9465 Wilshire Blvd, #600, Beverly Hills CA 90212 USA
Director, Producer, Writer

**Chomsky, A Noam**
15 Suzanne Road, Lexington MA 02420, USA
Linguist

**Chomsky, Marvin J**
15200 W Sunset Blvd, #209, Pacific Palisades CA 90272, USA
Director

**Chon, Justin**
A P A Talent & Literary Agency, 405 S Beverly Dr, #300, Beverly Hills CA 90212 USA
Actor

**Chonacas, Katie**
K Star Productions, 8491 Sunset Blvd, #549, Los Angeles CA 90069, USA
Actress, Model

**Chones, James B (Jim)**
26400 George Zeiger Dr, #405, Beachwood OH 44122, USA
Basketball Player

**Chong, Rae Dawn**
Metropolitan Talent Agency, 5405 Wilshire Blvd, #218, Los Angeles CA 90036 USA
Actress

**Chong, Thomas (Tommy)**
1625 Casale Road, Pacific Palisades CA 90272, USA
Actor, Comedian (Cheech & Chong)

**Chontosh, Brian R**
1009 Harbour Dr, Stafford VA 22554, USA
Marine Corps Iraq War Hero

**Choper, Jesse H**
University of California, Law School, Boalt Hall, Berkeley CA 94720, USA
Attorney, Educator

**Chopp, Rebecca S**
University of Denver, Chancellor's Office, 2199 S University Blvd, Denver CO 80208, USA
Educator

**Chopra, Daniel**
9838 Laurel Valley Dr, Windermere FL 34786, USA
Golfer

**Chopra, Deepak**
Trident Media Group, 41 Madison Ave, #3600, New York NY 10010, USA
Writer

**Chopra, Prem**
144A Nibbana Pali Hill, Bandra, Mumbai MS 400050, India
Actor

**Chopra, Priyanka**
Creative Artists Agency, 2000 Ave of Stars, #100, Los Angeles CA 90067 USA
Beauty Queen, Actress

**Chopra, Sherlyn**
People Tree Wellness, 124 E 40th St, #704, New York NY 10016, USA
Actress

**Chopra, Vidhu Vinod**
Bhagtani Krishang, RH1, Plot 16C, Dattatray Road, Santacruz (West), Mumbai 400054, India
Director, Producer

**Chorley of Kendal, Roger R E**
50 Kensington Place, London W8 7PW, England
Businessman

**Chorske, Tom**
23 Cooper Circle, Minneapolis MN 55436, USA
Ice Hockey Player

**Chorvat, Scarlett**
Innovative Artists, 1505 10th St, Santa Monica CA 90401 USA
Actress

**Chorzempa, Daniel W**
Kunstleragentur Raab & Bohm, Plankengasse 7, 1010 Vienna, Austria
Concert Organist, Composer

**Choudhury, Sarita**
Don Buchwald Talent Agency, 6500 Wilshire Blvd, #2200, Los Angeles CA 90048 USA
Actress

**Chouinard, Guy**
P E I Rocket, 46 Kensington Road, Charlottetown PE C1A 5H7, Canada
Ice Hockey Player

**Chouinard, Marie**
Compagnie Chouinard, 3981 Boul Saint-Laurent, Montreal QC H2W 1Y5, Canada
Dancer, Choreographer

**Chouinard, Robert W (Bobby)**
6024 S Paris Place, Englewood CO 80111, USA
Baseball Player

**Choummali Sayasone**
Presidential House, Vientiane Capital, Vientiane, Laos
President, Laos; Army General

**Chow Yun-Fat**
2/F 192 Prince Edward Road W, Kowloon, Hong Kong, China
Actor

**Chow, Amy Y Y**
Lucille Packard Children's Hospital, Pediatrics Dept, Palo Alto CA 94304, USA
Gymnast

**Chow, China**
Creative Artists Agency, 2000 Ave of Stars, #100, Los Angeles CA 90067 USA
Actress, Model

**Chow, Jeffrey**
Jeffrey Chow Inc, 525 E 82nd St, New York NY 10028, USA
Fashion Designer

**Chow, Kelsey**
Coast to Coast Talent, 3350 Barham Blvd, Los Angeles CA 90068 USA
Actress

**Chow, Raymond**
Golden Harvest, 16/F Peninsula Office Tower, Tsim Sha Tsui, Kowloon, Hong Kong, China
Producer

**Chow, Stephen**
Creative Artists Agency, 2000 Ave of Stars, #100, Los Angeles CA 90067 USA
Actor, Director

| | |
|---|---|
| **Chowdhury, A Q M Badruddoza** | President, Bangladesh |
| Residence Bari Dhara near Gulshan, Dhaka 1212, Bangladesh | |
| **Chrebet, Wayne** | Football Player |
| 147 Heulitt Road, Colts Neck NJ 07722, USA | |
| **Chretien, Jean J J** | Prime Minister, Canada |
| 541 Acacia Ave, Ottawa ON K1A 0A6, Canada | |
| **Chretien, Jean-Loup** | Spatinaut, France; Air Force General |
| Tietronix Software, 1331 Gemini Ave, #300, Houston TX 77058, USA | |
| **Chriqui, Emmanuelle** | Actress |
| Agence Artiste Adequat, 108 Rue Reaumur, 75002 Paris, France | |
| **Chrisman, Paul W (Woody Paul)** | Singer, Fiddler (Riders in the Sky) |
| New Frontier Mgmt, 1921 Broadway, Nashville TN 37203, USA | |
| **Christ, Dorothy** | Baseball Player |
| 1700 I St, #18, La Porte IN 46350, USA | |
| **Christakis, Nicholas A** | Internist, Sociologist |
| Harvard University, Sociology Dept, Cambridge MA 02115, USA | |
| **Christensen, Calvin L (Cal)** | Basketball Player |
| 395 Canal Road, #419, Waterville OH 43566, USA | |
| **Christensen, Erika** | Actress |
| Brillstein Entertainment Partners, 9150 Wilshire Blvd, #350, Beverly Hills CA 90212 USA | |
| **Christensen, Hayden** | Actor |
| Forest Park Pictures, 11210 Briarcliff Lane, Studio City CA 91604, USA | |
| **Christensen, Helena** | Model, Photographer |
| Panorama Agency, Ryesgade 103B, 2100 Copenhagen, Denmark | |
| **Christensen, Jesper** | Actor |
| Conway Van Gelder Grant, 8-12 Broadwick St, #300, London W1F 8HW, England | |
| **Christensen, Joss** | Slopestyle Skier |
| Park City Freestyle Team, PO Box 982857, Park City UT 84098, USA | |
| **Christensen, Kai** | Architect |
| 100 Vester Voldgade, 1552 Copenhagen V, Denmark | |
| **Christensen, Shawn** | Singer, Guitarist (Stellarstarr*) |
| +1 Management/Public Relations, 242 Wythe Ave, #6, Brooklyn NY 11211, USA | |
| **Christensen, Tonja M** | Model |
| Playboy Promotions, 9346 Civic Center Dr, #200, Beverly Hills CA 90210 USA | |
| **Christenson, Ryan A** | Baseball Player |
| 7513 Terry John Ave, Bakersfield CA 93308, USA | |
| **Christian, Ash** | Actor, Director, Producer |
| Ironclad Pictures, 25 Broadway, #1200, New York NY 10004, USA | |
| **Christian, Claudia** | Actress |
| Abrams Artists, 9200 W Sunset Blvd, #1125, West Hollywood CA 90069 USA | |
| **Christian, David W (Dave)** | Ice Hockey Player |
| 513 Queens Court, Moorhead MN 56560, USA | |
| **Christian, Gordon** | Ice Hockey Player |
| 604 Lake St NW, Warroad MN 56763, USA | |
| **Christian, Robert D (Bob)** | Football Player |
| 9450 Lincolnwood Dr, Evanston IL 60203, USA | |
| **Christian, Stephen T E** | Singer (Anberlin) |
| Arson Media Group, 23 N Summerlin Ave, #200, Orlando FL 32801, USA | |
| **Christian, William (Bill)** | Ice Hockey Player |
| 502 Carrol St NW, Warroad MN 56763, USA | |
| **Christians, F Wilhelm** | Financier |
| Konigsallee 51, 40212 Dusseldorf, Germany | |
| **Christiansen, Jason S** | Baseball Player |
| 3428 E Jasmine Circle, Mesa AZ 85213, USA | |
| **Christiansen, Keith R (Huffer)** | Ice Hockey Player |
| 1023 Timberline Lane, Duluth MN 55811, USA | |
| **Christianson, Claude V (Chris)** | Army General |
| Director, National Defense University, Fort Lesley J McNair, Washington DC 20319, USA | |
| **Christie, Douglas D (Doug)** | Basketball Player |
| 13812 NE 40th St, Bellevue WA 98005, USA | |
| **Christie, G Stephen (Steve)** | Football Player |
| PO Box 646, Buffalo NY 14231, USA | |
| **Christie, Gwendoline** | Actress |
| Artists Partnership, 101 Finsbury Pavement, London EC2A 1RS, England | |
| **Christie, Julie** | Actress, Model |
| Curtis Brown Group, 28-29 Haymarket St, #500, London SW1Y 4SP, England | |
| **Christie, Linford** | Track Athlete |
| Nuff Respect, 107 Sherland Road, Twickenham, Middlesex TW9 4HB, England | |
| **Christie, Lou** | Singer |
| Fox Entertainment, 1650 Broadway, #303, New York NY 10019, USA | |
| **Christie, Mike** | Ice Hockey Player |
| 6093 S Krameria St, Centennial CO 80111, USA | |
| **Christie, Perry G** | Prime Minister, Bahamas |
| Prime Minister's Office, Rawson Square, PO Box N8301, Nassau NP, Bahamas | |
| **Christie, Tony** | Singer |
| Amarillo Music, 31 Kensington Oval, Lichfield, Staffs WS13 6ND, England | |
| **Christie, Warren** | Actor |
| I F A Talent Agency, 8730 W Sunset Blvd, #490, West Hollywood CA 90069 USA | |
| **Christie, William** | Concert Harpsichordist |
| 81 Ave Victor Hugo, 75116 Paris, France | |
| **Christin, Judith** | Opera Singer |
| Columbia Artists Mgmt Inc, 5 Columbus Circle, 1790 Broadway, #1600, New York NY 10019 USA | |
| **Christine, Andrew (Andy)** | Cartoonist (Man Called Horse) |
| King Features Syndicate, 300 W 57th St, #1500, New York NY 10019 USA | |
| **Christl, Lisy** | Costume Designer |
| Claire Best Assoc, 736 Seward St, Los Angeles CA 90038, USA | |
| **Christlieb, Peter (Pete)** | Jazz Saxophonist |
| J V C Music, 3800 Barham Blvd, #409, Los Angeles CA 90068, USA | |
| **Christman, Daniel W (Dan)** | Army General, Educator |
| US Chamber of Commerce, 1615 H St NW, Washington DC 20062, USA | |
| **Christman, Kevin** | Artist, Sculptor |
| 714 S Pacific Highway, Talent OR 97540, USA | |
| **Christmas, G Ronald (Ron)** | Marine Corps General |
| 3809 Spicewood Springs Road, Stafford VA 22554, USA | |
| **Christo** | Sculptor |
| 48 Howard St, New York NY 10013, USA | |

**Christoff, Steven (Steve)** — Ice Hockey Player
542 Fairview Ave S, Saint Paul MN 55116, USA

**Christon, Shameka D** — Basketball Player
Chicago Sky, 20 W Kinzie St, #1010, Chicago IL 60654 USA

**Christopher** — Cartoonist (Ghouly Boys)
Colden McKuin Frankel, 141 El Camino Dr, #100, Beverly Hills CA 90212, USA

**Christopher, Ann** — Sculptor
Stable Block, Hay St, Marshfield near Chippenham SN14 8PF, England

**Christopher, Dennis** — Actor
B R & S, 5757 Wilshire Blvd, #473, Los Angeles CA 90036, USA

**Christopher, Gretchen** — Singer (Fleetwoods)
509 E Ridgecrest Blvd, #A, Ridgecrest CA 93555, USA

**Christopher, Joseph O (Joe)** — Baseball Player
PO Box 65240, Baltimore MD 21209, USA

**Christopher, Tyler** — Actor
Paradigm Agency, 360 N Crescent Dr, North Building, Beverly Hills CA 90210 USA

**Christopherson, James (Jim)** — Football Player, Coach
526 Queens Court, Moorhead MN 56560, USA

**Christy, James W** — Astronomer
Hollinghead, 7285 Golden Eagle Dr, Flagstaff AZ 86004, USA

**Christy, Jeffrey A (Jeff)** — Football Player
138 Horseshoe Dr, Freeport PA 16229, USA

**Chromy, Bronislaw** — Sculptor
Ul Halki 5, 30 228 Cracow, Poland

**Chu, Julie** — Ice Hockey Player
145 Primrose Lane, Fairfield CT 06825, USA

**Chu, Paul Ching-Wu** — Physicist
University of Houston, Center for Superconductivity, Houston TX 77204, USA

**Chu, Steven** — Nobel Laureate; Secretary, Energy
42 Bishop Lane, Menlo Park CA 94025, USA

**Chua, Amy L** — Writer
Yale University, Law School, New Haven CT 06520, USA

**Chua, Leon O** — Electrical Engineer
University of California, Electrical Engineering Dept, Berkeley CA 94720, USA

**Chuan Leekpai** — Prime Minister, Thailand
Prachatipat, 67 Thanon Setsiri, Samsen Nai, Bangkok 10300, Thailand

**Chubais, Anatoly B** — Government Official, Russia
United Power Grids, Kitaigorodsky Proyezd 7, 103074 Moscow, Russia

**Chuck D** — Rap Artist (Public Enemy)
Richard Walters, PO Box 2789, Toluca Lake CA 91610 USA

**Chuck, Wendy** — Costume Designer
A P A Talent & Literary Agency, 405 S Beverly Dr, #300, Beverly Hills CA 90212 USA

**Chudacoff, Katy** — Interior Designer
Dovetail Design Works, 1005 Buckworth Ave, Franklin TN 37064, USA

**Chukwurah, Patrick C** — Football Player
6757 Camino Real, Irving TX 75039, USA

**Chulack, Christopher** — Producer, Director, Writer
Ken Gross Mgmt, 12135 Stanwood Drive, Los Angeles CA 90066, USA

**Chulk, C Vincent (Vinnie)** — Baseball Player
4607 Ballstonefield Lane, Katy TX 77494, USA

**Chun Lee-Kyung** — Speed Skater
Skating Union, 88 Bangyee-Dong, Songpaku, Seoul 138 749, South Korea

**Chun, Tze** — Writer
Gramercy Park Entertainment, 9701 Wilshire Blvd, #1000, Beverly Hills CA 90212, USA

**Chung, Constance Y (Connie)** — Commentator
Creative Artists Agency, 2000 Ave of Stars, #100, Los Angeles CA 90067 USA

**Chung, Kyung-Wha** — Concert Violinist
Harrison/Parrott, 5-6 Albion Court, London W6 0QT, England

**Chung, Myung-Whun** — Concert Pianist, Conductor
Askonas Holt, Lincoln House, 300 High Holborn, London WC1V 7JH, England

**Chupack, Cindy** — Writer, Producer
W M E Entertainment, 9601 Wilshire Blvd, #300, Beverly Hills CA 90210 USA

**Church, Charlotte** — Singer, Actress
Creative Artists Agency, 2000 Ave of Stars, #100, Los Angeles CA 90067 USA

**Church, Eric** — Singer, Songwriter
Q Prime South, 131 A 11th St, Nashville TN 37206, USA

**Church, George** — Molecular Geneticist
Harvard Medical School, Genetics Dept, 77 Ave Louis Pasteur, Boston MA 02115, USA

**Church, Ryan M** — Baseball Player
3500 Thurloe Dr, Rockledge FL 32955, USA

**Church, Thomas Haden** — Actor
Creative Artists Agency, 2000 Ave of Stars, #100, Los Angeles CA 90067 USA

**Churchill, Caryl** — Writer
Casarotto Ramsay, Waverley House, 7-12 Noel St, London W1F 8GQ, England

**Churchill, Kim** — Singer, Songwriter
Agency Group Ltd, 142 W 57th St, #600, New York NY 10019 USA

**Churla, Shane** — Ice Hockey Player
31826 Scotch Pine Lane, Bigfork MT 59911, USA

**Chute, Robert M** — Biologist, Writer
68 Schellinger Road, Poland ME 04274, USA

**Chuy, Donald J (Don)** — Football Player
11690 Oxnard St, North Hollywood CA 91606, USA

**Chwast, Seymour** — Artist, Illustrator
Push Pin Group, 38 W 26th St, #5A, New York NY 10010, USA

**Chychrun, Jeff** — Ice Hockey Player
6423 NW 32nd Way, Boca Raton FL 33496, USA

**Chynoweth, Dean** — Ice Hockey Player
131 Shawnee Rise SW, Calgary AB T2Y 2S3, Canada

**Chyzowski, David B (Dave)** — Ice Hockey Player
Kamloops Blazers, 300 Lorne St, Kamloops BC V2C 1W3, Canada

**Cialini, Julie Lynn** — Model, Actress
PO Box 55536, Valencia CA 91385, USA

**Cianfrance, Derek** — Director
Creative Artists Agency, 2000 Ave of Stars, #100, Los Angeles CA 90067 USA

**Cianfrocco, Angelo D (Archi)** — Baseball Player
12424 Addax Court, San Diego CA 92129, USA

**Christoff - Cianfrocco**

**Ciani, Suzanne** — Composer
Musica International, 20 Sunnyside Ave, #A197, Mill Valley CA 94941, USA

**Ciara** — Singer, Songwriter
W M E Entertainment, 9601 Wilshire Blvd, #300, Beverly Hills CA 90210 USA

**Ciaramello, Benjamin (Benny)** — Actor
A P A Talent & Literary Agency, 405 S Beverly Dr, #300, Beverly Hills CA 90212 USA

**Ciavaglia, Peter** — Ice Hockey Player
1137 Carrie Court, Rochester Hills MI 48309, USA

**Cibani, Tia** — Fashion Designer
601 W 26th St, #875, New York NY 10001, USA

**Cibrian, Eddie** — Actor
I C M Partners, 10250 Constellation Blvd, #900, Los Angeles CA 90067 USA

**Ciccarelli, Dino** — Ice Hockey Player
37934 Lakeshore Dr, Harrison Township MI 48045, USA

**Ciccolella, Jude** — Actor
McKeon-Myrones Mgmt, 3500 Olive Ave, #770, Burbank CA 91505 USA

**Ciccolini, Aldo** — Concert Pianist
Gerhild Baron Mgmt, Dornbacher Str 41/III/3, 1170 Vienna, Austria

**Ciccone, Enrico** — Ice Hockey Player
Sports Prospects, 77 Rue de Bleury, Rosemere QC J7A 4L9, Canada

**Cicero, Roger** — Singer, Songwriter
Heinrich & de Wall, Ulmenstr 8, 22299 Hamburg, Germany

**Cicerone, Ralph J** — Environmental Scientist
University of California, Earth Science Dept, Rowland Hall, Irvine CA 92717, USA

**Cichocki, Chris J** — Ice Hockey Player
3955 Pine Lake Circle, Stockton CA 95219, USA

**Cichy, Joseph J (Joe)** — Football Player
1220 N Mandan St, Bismarck ND 58501, USA

**Ciechanover, Aaron** — Nobel Chemistry Laureate
Technion-Israel Institute, Box 9649, Bat Galim, Haifa 31096, Israel

**Cienfuegos, Mauricio** — Soccer Player
Los Angeles Galaxy, Home Depot Center, 18400 Avalon Blvd, Carson CA 90746 USA

**Cierpinski, Waldemar** — Track Athlete
Sport GmbH, Grosse Ulrichstr 60, 06108 Halle/Saale, Germany

**Cigliuti, Natalia** — Actress
Sager Mgmt, 260 S Beverly Dr, #205, Beverly Hills CA 90212, USA

**Cimino, Michael** — Director, Writer
9015 Alto Cedro, Beverly Hills CA 90210, USA

**Cincotta, Anthony H** — Biotechnologist
VeroScience, 1334 Main Road, Tiverton RI 02878, USA

**Cincotti, Peter** — Singer, Pianist, Songwriter
Morey Management Group, 1100 Glendon Ave, #1100, Los Angeles CA 90024, USA

**Cink, Stewart** — Golfer
2195 Lockett Court, Duluth GA 30097, USA

**Cintron, Alexander (Alex)** — Baseball Player
HC 2 Box 8575, Yabuccoa PR 00767, USA

**Cintron, Kermit (Killer)** — Boxer
DiBella Entertainment, 350 7th Ave, #800, New York NY 10001, USA

**Cioffi, Charles** — Actor
Paradigm Agency, 360 N Crescent Dr, North Building, Beverly Hills CA 90210 USA

**Ciokey, Janna** — Actress
J Michael Bloom, 9255 W Sunset Blvd, #710, West Hollywood CA 90069 USA

**Ciorbea, Victor** — Prime Minister, Romania
C D N P P, Bd Carol I34, 73231 Bucharest, Romania

**Cipriani Thorne, Juan Luis Cardinal** — Religious Leader
Archdiocese of Lima, Plaza de Armas S/N, Apartado 1512, Lima 100, Peru

**Cirella, Joe** — Ice Hockey Player
Teranet 600-1 Adelaide St E, Toronto ON M5C 2V9, Canada

**Ciriani, Henri** — Architect
61 Rue Pascal, 75013 Paris, France

**Cirici, Cristian** — Architect
Cirici Arquitecte, Carrer de Pujades 63 2-N, 08005 Barcelona, Spain

**Cirillo, Jeffrey H (Jeff)** — Baseball Player
604 Elmwood Lane, Celina OH 45822, USA

**Cirio, Chuck** — Composer, Director, Producer
B M I, 8730 W Sunset Blvd, #300, Los Angeles CA 90069 USA

**Ciry, Michel** — Artist
La Bergerie, 76119 Varengeville sur Mer, Seine-Maritime, France

**Cisco, Galen B** — Baseball Player
604 Elmwood Lane, Celina OH 45822, USA

**Cisneros, Evelyn** — Ballerina
San Francisco Ballet, 455 Franklin St, San Francisco CA 94102, USA

**Cisneros, Henry G** — Secretary, Housing & Urban Development
2002 W Houston St, San Antonio TX 78207, USA

**Citerne, Philippe** — Financier
Societe Generale, 29 Blvd Haussman, 75009 Paris, France

**Citizen Cope** — Singer, Songwriter
Agency Group Ltd, 142 W 57th St, #600, New York NY 10019 USA

**Citro, Ralph** — Boxing Historian
32 N Black Horse Pike, Blackwood NJ 08012, USA

**Citron, Martin** — Neurobiologist
Amgen Co, 152A 226 Amgen Center, Thousand Oaks CA 91320, USA

**Citterio, Antonio** — Architect, Interior Designer
Antonio Citterio Partners, Via Cerva 4, 20122 Milan, Italy

**Citti, Christine** — Actress
Artmedia, 20 Ave Rapp, 75007 Paris, France

**Ciuha, Joze** — Artist
Presernov 12, 61000 Ljubljana, Slovenia

**Civiletti, Benjamin R** — Attorney General
5900 Old Ocean Blvd, #B3, Boynton Beach FL 33435, USA

**Cizik, Robert** — Businessman
Cizik Interests, Chase Tower, 600 Travis St, #3628, Houston TX 77002, USA

**Claassen, Yann** — Actor
Artmedia, 20 Ave Rapp, 75007 Paris, France

**Clackson, Kim** — Ice Hockey Player
342 Thomas Road, Canonsburg PA 15317, USA

**Claes, Willy** — Government Official, Belgium
Berkenlaan 23, 3500 Hasselt, Belgium

**Claflin, Bruce L** — Businessman
Advanced Micro Devices, 1 A M D Plaza, Sunnyvale CA 94088, USA

**Claflin, Sam** — Actor
Creative Artists Agency, 2000 Ave of Stars, #100, Los Angeles CA 90067 USA

**Claiborne, Chris** — Football Player
Premier Sports Mgmt, 1000 N Green Valley Parkway, #440, Henderson NV 89074, USA

**Claiborne, Morris L** — Football Player
Dallas Cowboys, 1 Cowboys Parkway, Irving TX 75063 USA

**Claire, Julie** — Actress
I C M Partners, 10250 Constellation Blvd, #900, Los Angeles CA 90067 USA

**Clamp, Shirley** — Singer
Lionheart, PO Box 11108, Nytogstan 40A, 100 61 Stockholm, Sweden

**Clampett, Robert D (Bobby), Jr** — Golfer, Sportscaster
10600 Golf Link Dr, Raleigh NC 27617, USA

**Clancy, Abigail R** — Model
Money Mgmt, 42A Berwick St, London W1F 8RZ, England

**Clancy, Aoife** — Singer
Producers Inc, 11806 N 56th St, Tampa FL 33617 USA

**Clancy, James (Jim)** — Baseball Player
177 Lance Dr, Twin Lakes WI 53181, USA

**Clancy, Sam** — Football Player
1308 Crest Lane, Oakdale PA 15071, USA

**Clancy, Terry** — Ice Hockey Player
65 Golfdale Road, Toronto ON M4N 2B5, Canada

**Clancy, William (Liam)** — Singer (Clancy Brothers)
Charles Rothschild, 330 E 48th St, #2D, New York NY 10017 USA

**Clanton, Jimmy** — Singer
Neal Hollander Agency, 9966 Majorca Place, Boca Raton FL 33434 USA

**Clapp, Gordon** — Actor
Cynthia Snyder Public Relations, 5739 Colfax Ave, North Hollywood CA 91601, USA

**Clapp, Joss** — Singer, Guitaist (Tarras)
Rounder Records, 1 Rounder Way, Burlington MA 01803 USA

**Clapp, Nicholas R** — Explorer (Ubar), Producer
PO Box 1019, Borrego Springs CA 92004, USA

**Clapper, James R (Jim), Jr** — Government Official, Air Force General
National Intelligence Department, 725 17th St NW, Washington DC 20523 USA

**Clapton, Eric** — Singer, Guitarist
Michael Eaton, 22 Blades Court, Deodar Road, London SW15 2NU, England

**Clardy, Jon C** — Chemist
Cornell University, Chemistry Dept, Ithaca NY 14853, USA

**Clare, Jillian** — Actress
Greene Assoc, 1901 Ave of Stars, #130, Los Angeles CA 90067 USA

**Clarizio, Louis** — Baseball Player
133 Lela Lane, Schaumburg IL 60193, USA

**Clark, A Keon** — Basketball Player
Phoenix Suns, 201 E Jefferson St, Phoenix AZ 85004 USA

**Clark, Alan** — Pianist (Dire Straits)
Damage Mgmt, 16 Lambton Place, London W11 2SH, England

**Clark, Alan M (Allie)** — Baseball Umpire
1185 SW 5th Ave, Boca Raton FL 33432, USA

**Clark, Anthony** — Actor, Comedian
Innovative Artists, 1505 10th St, Santa Monica CA 90401 USA

**Clark, Anthony C (Tony)** — Baseball Player
14125 N 65th Ave, Glendale AZ 85306, USA

**Clark, Archie L** — Basketball Player
4268 10th St, Ecorse MI 48229, USA

**Clark, Bob** — Commentator
ABC-TV, News Dept, 5010 Creston St, Hyattsville MD 20781 USA

**Clark, Brady W** — Baseball Player
19275 Green Lakes Loop, Bend OR 97702, USA

**Clark, Brett** — Ice Hockey Player
8745 Aberdeen Circle, Littleton CO 80130, USA

**Clark, Brian M** — Football Player
811 Wonderland Forest Dr, Waxhaw NC 28173, USA

**Clark, Bryan D** — Baseball Player
508 E Clark St, Madera CA 93638, USA

**Clark, C Joseph (Joe)** — Prime Minister, Canada
Joe Clark Assoc, 237 4th Ave SW, #3000, Calgary AB T2P 4X7, Canada

**Clark, Candace J (Candy)** — Actress
PO Box 3421, Memorial Station, Montclair NJ 07043, USA

**Clark, Carol Higgins** — Writer
524 E 72nd St, #28DE, New York NY 10021, USA

**Clark, Chris** — Ice Hockey Player
71 Grand View Dr, Dedham ME 04429, USA

**Clark, Colin W** — Mathematician
9531 Finn Road, Richmond BC V7A 2L3, Canada

**Clark, Dallas D** — Football Player
2995 Belle Maison Dr, Zionsville IN 46077, USA

**Clark, Daniel** — Actor
Brightline Education, 3200 Port Royale Dr N, #906, Fort Lauderdale FL 33308, USA

**Clark, Danny, IV** — Football Player
213 Seneca Trail, Bloomington IL 60108, USA

**Clark, David E (Dave)** — Baseball Player, Manager
4842 Mayfield Road W, Collierville TN 38017, USA

**Clark, Doran** — Actress
Paul Kohner, 9300 Wilshire Blvd, #555, Beverly Hills CA 90212 USA

**Clark, Dwight E** — Football Player, Executive
2511 Sedley Road, Charlotte NC 28211, USA

**Clark, Elbernita (Twinkie)** — Gospel Singer (Clark Sisters)
Universal Attractions, 135 W 26th St, #1200, New York NY 10001 USA

**Clark, Gary C** — Football Player
PO Box 202, Dublin VA 24084, USA

**Clark, Guy** — Singer, Songwriter
Keith Case Assoc, 1025 17th Ave S, #200, Nashville TN 37212 USA

**Clark, Hamish**
Artists Partnership, 101 Finsbury Pavement, London EC2A 1RS, England — Actor

**Clark, Helen E**
Labour Party, 160-62 Willis St, Wellington 6011, New Zealand — Prime Minister, New Zealand

**Clark, Herbert H**
Stanford University, Psychology Dept, Jordan Hall, Stanford CA 94305, USA — Pscycholinguist

**Clark, Howard R (Howie)**
14202 439th Ave SE, North Bend WA 98045, USA — Baseball Player

**Clark, Jack A**
6541 Scottsdale Way, Frisco TX 75034, USA — Baseball Player

**Clark, James (Jim)**
Neoteris, 940 Stewart Dr, Sunnyvale CA 94085, USA — Businessman

**Clark, Jerald D**
12325 Crisscross Lane, San Diego CA 92129, USA — Baseball Player

**Clark, Jessie L**
411 E Indian School Road, #2089, Phoenix AZ 85012, USA — Football Player

**Clark, Jim**
International Union of Electronic Workers, 401 3rd St NW, Washington DC 20001, USA — Labor Leader

**Clark, Joe**
1856 Clarence Dr, Hellertown PA 18055, USA — Educator

**Clark, Kelly**
Kelly Clark Foundation, PO Box 725, West Dover VT 05356, USA — Snowboarding Athlete

**Clark, Kelvin**
3812 Evesham Dr, Plano TX 75025, USA — Football Player

**Clark, L Hill**
Crane Co, 100 Stamford Place, #300, Stamford CT 06902, USA — Businessman

**Clark, Larry**
Killer/Moxie Mgmt, 5890 W Jefferson Blvd, Los Angeles CA 90016, USA — Director

**Clark, Louis S**
6149 Kissengen Springs Court, Jacksonville FL 32258, USA — Football Player

**Clark, Marcia R**
A P A Talent & Literary Agency, 405 S Beverly Dr, #300, Beverly Hills CA 90212 USA — Attorney

**Clark, Mario S**
48100 Sandia Creek Dr, Temecula CA 92590, USA — Football Player

**Clark, Martin**
Knopf Publishers, 1745 Broadway, New York NY 10019 USA — Writer, Judge

**Clark, Mary Ellen**
90 Irving St, Waltham MA 02451, USA — Diver

**Clark, Mary Higgins**
15 Werimus Brook Road, Saddle River NJ 07458, USA — Writer

**Clark, Mary Jane**
Saint Martin's Press, 175 5th Ave, #400, New York NY 10010 USA — Writer

**Clark, Matt**
1199 Park Ave, #15D, New York NY 10128, USA — Actor, Director

**Clark, Michael, II**
4007 Pintail Circle, Rocky Face GA 30740, USA — Golfer

**Clark, Mystro**
I C M Partners, 10250 Constellation Blvd, #900, Los Angeles CA 90067 USA — Actor

**Clark, Oliver**
House of Representatives, 1434 6th St, #1, Santa Monica CA 90401 USA — Actor

**Clark, Perry**
Miami University, Athletic Dept, Coral Gables FL 33124, USA — Basketball Coach

**Clark, Peter B**
7675 La Jolla Blvd, #203, La Jolla CA 92037, USA — Publisher

**Clark, Petula**
15 Chemin Rieu Coligny, 1208 Geneva, Switzerland — Singer, Actress

**Clark, Philip E (Phil)**
208 George St, Barrington IL 60010, USA — Football Player

**Clark, Phillip B (Phil)**
PO Box 620612, Orlando FL 32862, USA — Baseball Player

**Clark, Ricardo**
Eintracht Frankfurt S C, Morfelder Landstr 362, 60528 Frankfurt, Germany — Soccer Player

**Clark, Richard C (Dick)**
4424 Edmunds St NW, #1070, Washington DC 20007, USA — Senator, IA

**Clark, Rickey C**
8953 Emerald Waters Court, Las Vegas NV 89147, USA — Baseball Player

**Clark, Robert A**
Munstead Wood, Godalming, Surrey GU7 1UN, England — Businessman

**Clark, Robert C**
34 Monterey Court, Manhattan Beach CA 90266, USA — Artist

**Clark, Robert C (Bobby)**
1030 Perrisito St, Perris CA 92570, USA — Baseball Player

**Clark, Ronald B (Ron)**
700 Starkey Road, #511, Largo FL 33771, USA — Baseball Player

**Clark, Roy**
Ro-Bar, 3225 S Norwood Ave, #101, Tulsa OK 74135, USA — Singer, Guitarist

**Clark, Ryan T**
1236 Camarta Dr, Pittsburgh PA 15227, USA — Football Player

**Clark, Sharon**
Playboy Promotions, 9346 Civic Center Dr, #200, Beverly Hills CA 90210 USA — Model, Actress

**Clark, Spencer Trent**
Untitled Entertainment, 350 S Beverly Dr, #200, Beverly Hills CA 90212 USA — Actor

**Clark, Stephen E (Steve)**
29 Martling Road, San Anselmo CA 94960, USA — Swimmer

**Clark, Susan**
13400 Riverside Dr, #308, Sherman Oaks CA 91423, USA — Actress

**Clark, Terri**
Spalding Entertainment, 54 Music Square E, #200, Nashville TN 37203, USA — Singer, Songwriter

**Clark, Terry L**
1607 E Tam O'Shanter St, Ontario CA 91761, USA — Baseball Player

**Clark, Timothy H (Tim)**
Professional Golfers Association, 100 Ave of Champions, Palm Beach Gardens FL 33418 USA — Golfer

**Clark, Vernon E (Vern)**
Raytheon Co, 870 Winter St, Waltham MA 02451, USA — Navy Admiral

**Clark, Victoria**
Untitled Entertainment, 350 S Beverly Dr, #200, Beverly Hills CA 90212 USA — Actress, Singer

# C

**Clark, W G** — Architect
Clark & Menefee Architects, 4048 E Main St, Charlottesville VA 22902, USA

**Clark, W Ramsey** — Attorney General
37 W 12th St, #2B, New York NY 10011, USA

**Clark, Wayne M** — Football Player
14241 Lambeth Way, Tustin CA 92780, USA

**Clark, Wendel L** — Ice Hockey Player
Toronto Maple Leafs, AirCanada Center, 40 Bay St, Toronto ON M5J 2K2, Canada

**Clark, Wesley Curley (W C)** — Guitarist
Crossfire Productions, 304 Braeswood Road, Austin TX 78704, USA

**Clark, Wesley K (Wes)** — Army General
1 Crestmont Dr, Little Rock AR 72227, USA

**Clark, William N (Will), Jr** — Baseball Player
36170 Pleasant Hill Court, Prairieville LA 70769, USA

**Clark-Chisholm, Jacky** — Singer (Clark Sisters)
Universal Attractions, 135 W 26th St, #1200, New York NY 10001 USA

**Clark-Cole, Dorinda** — Singer (Clark Sisters)
Universal Attractions, 135 W 26th St, #1200, New York NY 10001 USA

**Clarke, Allan** — Singer, Musician (Hollies)
Hill Farm, Hackleton, Northamptonshire NN7 2DH, England

**Clarke, Brian** — Artist
Tony Shafrazi Gallery, 544 W 26th St, #2, New York NY 10001, USA

**Clarke, Brian Patrick** — Actor
2102 Clubside Dr, Longwood FL 32779, USA

**Clarke, Cam** — Actor
Sutton-Barth Vennari, 5900 Wilshire Blvd, #700, Los Angeles CA 90036 USA

**Clarke, Darren C** — Golfer
Darren Clarke Golf School, The Lodge, Greenmount Campus, Antrim BT41 4PU, England

**Clarke, Emilia** — Actress
Creative Artists Agency, 2000 Ave of Stars, #100, Los Angeles CA 90067 USA

**Clarke, Emmy** — Actress
Global Creative, 1051 N Cole Ave, #B, Los Angeles CA 90038, USA

**Clarke, Frank D** — Football Player
3121 NE 34th Ave, Portland OR 97212, USA

**Clarke, Gary** — Actor, Writer
1113 Heep Run, Buda TX 78610, USA

**Clarke, Geoffrey** — Artist, Sculptor
Stowe Hill, Hartest, Bury Saint Edmunds, Suffolk IP29 4EQ, England

**Clarke, Gilby** — Singer, Guitarist (Guns N' Roses)
Central Entertainment Group, 165 5th Ave, #400, New York NY 10010, USA

**Clarke, Hagood, III** — Football Player
2500 NE 37th Dr, Fort Lauderdale FL 33308, USA

**Clarke, Horace M** — Baseball Player
PO Box 891, Frederiksted VI 00841, USA

**Clarke, Jacqueline (Jackie)** — Actress
Paradigm Agency, 360 N Crescent Dr, North Building, Beverly Hills CA 90210 USA

**Clarke, Jason** — Actor, Producer
Creative Artists Agency, 2000 Ave of Stars, #100, Los Angeles CA 90067 USA

**Clarke, John** — Actor
8350 Santa Monica Blvd, #206A, West Hollywood CA 90069, USA

**Clarke, Judy** — Attorney
Clarke & Rice, 1010 2nd Ave, #1800, San Diego CA 92101, USA

**Clarke, Justine** — Actress
Shanahan Mgmt, Berman House, 91 Campbell St, #300, Surry Hills NSW 2010, Australia

**Clarke, Kathy Kiera** — Actress
Emptage Hallett, 14 Rathbone Place, London W1T 1HT, England

**Clarke, Keith R** — Writer
Resolution, 1801 Century Park E, #2300, Los Angeles CA 90067 USA

**Clarke, Kenneth H** — Government Official, England
House of Commons, Westminster, London SW1A 0AA, England

**Clarke, Kenneth M (Ken)** — Football Player
7610 Willoughby Court, Alpharetta GA 30005, USA

**Clarke, Lenny** — Actor
Paradigm Agency, 360 N Crescent Dr, North Building, Beverly Hills CA 90210 USA

**Clarke, Martha** — Dancer, Choreographer
Columbia Artists Mgmt Inc, 5 Columbus Circle, 1790 Broadway, #1600, New York NY 10019 USA

**Clarke, Melinda** — Actress
Innovative Artists, 1505 10th St, Santa Monica CA 90401 USA

**Clarke, Noel A** — Actor
Independent Talent Group, 40 Whitfield St, London W1T 2RH, England

**Clarke, Paul Charles** — Singer
Welsh National Opera, Millennium Centre, Bute Place, Cardiff Bay, Cardiff CF10 5AL, Wales

**Clarke, Richard A** — Government Official
Simon & Schuster, 1230 Ave of Americas, Concourse 1, New York NY 10020 USA

**Clarke, Robert E (Bobby)** — Ice Hockey Player, Executive
420 Beechwood Ave, Haddonfield NJ 08033, USA

**Clarke, Robert L** — Government Official
Bracewell & Patterson, 711 Louisiana St, #2900, Houston TX 77002, USA

**Clarke, Ronald (Ron)** — Track Athlete
1 Bay St, Brighton VIC 3186, Australia

**Clarke, Sarah** — Actress
Levine Mgmt, 9028 W Sunset Blvd, #PH1, Los Angeles CA 90069, USA

**Clarke, Stanley M** — Jazz Bassist, Composer
4786 Topanga Canyon Blvd, Woodland Hills CA 91364, USA

**Clarke, Stanley M (Stan)** — Baseball Player
5533 Sanders Dr, Toledo OH 43615, USA

**Clarke, Susanna** — Writer
Curtis Brown Group, 28-29 Haymarket St, #500, London SW1Y 4SP, England

**Clarke, Thomas E** — Businessman
Nike Inc, 1 SW Bowerman Dr, Beaverton OR 97005, USA

**Clark-Sheard, Karen** — Singer (Clark Sisters)
Universal Attractions, 135 W 26th St, #1200, New York NY 10001 USA

**Clarkson, Jordan** — Basketball Player
Los Angeles Lakers, Staples Center, 1111 S Figueroa St, Los Angeles CA 90015 USA

**Clarkson, Kelly** — Singer
Starstruck Entertainment, 40 Music Square W, Nashville TN 37203, USA

**Clarkson, Patricia** — Actress
Anonymous Content, 3532 Hayden Ave, Culver City CA 90232 USA

**Claro, Manuel Alberto** — Cinematographer
Sheldon Prosnit Agency, 800 S Robertson Blvd, #6, Los Angeles CA 90035, USA

**Clary, Robert** — Actor
10001 Sundial Lane, Beverly Hills CA 90210, USA

**Clary, Tyler** — Swimmer
Premier Management Group, 115 Crescent Commons, #250, Cary, NC 27518 USA

**Clasby, Robert J (Bob)** — Football Player
8180 E Shea Blvd, #1090, Scottsdale AZ 85260, USA

**Clash, Kevin** — Puppeteer
W M E Entertainment, 9601 Wilshire Blvd, #300, Beverly Hills CA 90210 USA

**Clatterbuck, Tamara** — Actress
House of Representatives, 1434 6th St, #1, Santa Monica CA 90401 USA

**Clatworthy, Robert** — Sculptor
Moelfre, Cynghordy, Landovery, Carmarthenshire SA20 OUW, Wales

**Claure, Marcelo** — Businessman
Sprint Corp, 6391 Sprint Parkway, Overland Park KS 66251, USA

**Clauser, Francis H** — Aeronautical Engineer, Educator
842 E Villa St, #161, Pasadena CA 91101, USA

**Clauss, Jared** — Football Player
215 S 82nd St, West Des Moines IA 50266, USA

**Claver Arocas, Victor** — Basketball Player
Portland Trail Blazers, Rose Garden, 1 N Center Court St, Portland OR 97227 USA

**Clavier, Christian** — Actor
Ouille, 7 Rue des Dames Agustines, 92200 Neuilly, France

**Clawson, John R** — Basketball Player
30 Eagle Lake Place, #31, San Ramon CA 94582, USA

**Claxton, Craig (Speedy)** — Basketball Player
11215 Fairhaven Dr, Riverside CA 92505, USA

**Claxton, Paul** — Golfer
PO Box 485, Claxton GA 30417, USA

**Clay, Andrew Dice** — Actor, Comedian
Vox Inc, 6420 Wilshire Blvd, #1080, Los Angeles CA 90048 USA

**Clay, Bryan E T** — Track Athlete
Doyle Mgmt, 952 Chippendale Trail, Marietta GA 30064, USA

**Clay, Eric L** — Judge
US Court of Appeals, 231 W Lafayette Blvd, #564, Detroit MI 48226, USA

**Clay, Kenneth E (Ken)** — Baseball Player
4523 60th Street Court W, Bradenton FL 34210, USA

**Clay, Otis** — Singer
Universal Attractions, 135 W 26th St, #1200, New York NY 10001 USA

**Clayborn, Raymond D (Ray)** — Football Player
20610 Aspen Canyon Dr, Katy TX 77450, USA

**Claycomb, Laura** — Opera Singer
I M G Artists, Hogarth Business Park, Chiswick, London W4 2TH, England

**Clayderman, Richard** — Pianist
World Entertainment, 8815 Conroy Windermeer Road, #407, Orlando FL 32835, USA

**Claye, Will** — Track Athlete
44754 W Desert Garden Road, Maricopa AZ 85139, USA

**Clayman, Ralph V** — Surgeon
Barnes Hospital, Surgery Dept, 416 S Kingshighway Blvd, Saint Louis MO 63110, USA

**Claypool, James (Jim)** — Ice Hockey Executive
302 Paine Farm Road, Duluth MN 55804, USA

**Claypool, Leslie E (Les)** — Singer, Bassist (Primus, Oysterhead)
Red Light Mgmt, PO Box 1467, Charlottesville VA 22902, USA

**Claypool, Philip** — Singer, Songwriter
B L T Mgmt, 2953 Sidco Dr, Nashville TN 37204, USA

**Clayson, Jane** — Commentator
CBS-TV, News Dept, 51 W 52nd St, New York NY 10019 USA

**Clayton, Adam** — Bassist (U-2)
Principle Mgmt, 30-32 Sir John Rogerson's Quay, Dublin 2, Ireland

**Clayton, Beth** — Opera Singer
I M G Artists, Hogarth Business Park, Chiswick, London W4 2TH, England

**Clayton, Donald D** — Astrophysicist
Clemson University, Physics/Astrophysics Dept, Clemson SC 29634, USA

**Clayton, Harvey J** — Football Player
15303 SW 143rd St, Miami FL 33196, USA

**Clayton, Mark G** — Football Player
16426 Canyon Chase Dr, Houston TX 77095, USA

**Clayton, Mark J** — Football Player
9407 Manor Forge Way, Owings Mill MD 21117, USA

**Clayton, Michael R** — Football Player
10406 Oak Canopy Junction, Thonotosassa FL 33592, USA

**Clayton, Robert N** — Geochemist
5201 S Cornell Ave, Chicago IL 60615, USA

**Clayton, Royce S** — Baseball Player
5924 Paseo Canyon Dr, Malibu CA 90265, USA

**Clayton, Willie** — Singer, Songwriter
Universal Attractions, 135 W 26th St, #1200, New York NY 10001 USA

**Clayton-Thomas, David** — Singer (Blood Sweat & Tears)
Live Tour Artists, 1451 White Oaks Blvd, Oakville ON L6H 4R9, Canada

**Claywell, Brett** — Actor
Stone Meyer Genow, 9665 Wilshire Blvd, #510, Beverly Hills CA 90212 USA

**Cleamons, James M (Jim)** — Basketball Player, Coach
29 Sausalito Circle W, Manhattan Beach CA 90266, USA

**Clear, Jacob** — Canoeing Athlete
Gold Coast Kayak & Canoe, 18 Kiers Road, Miami QLD 4220, Australia

**Clear, Mark A** — Baseball Player
15654 S Rene St, Olathe KS 66062, USA

**Clearwater, Keith A** — Golfer
967 N 900 W, Orem UT 84057, USA

**Cleary, Beverly A** — Writer
Harper Collins Publishers, 10 E 53rd St, Cellar 1, New York NY 10022 USA

**Cleary, Jon** — Pianist, Composer
Rosebud Agency, PO Box 170429, San Francisco CA 94117, USA

**C**

**Clarkson - Cleary**

**Cleary, Robert B (Bob)** — Ice Hockey Player
680 South Ave, #8, Weston MA 02493, USA
**Cleary, Robert J** — Attorney
Proskauer Rose, 1585 Broadway, #2700, New York NY 10036, USA
**Cleary, William J (Bill), Jr** — Ice Hockey Player, Coach
27 Kingswood Road, Auburndale MA 02466, USA
**Cleave, Mary L** — Astronaut
1901 E Belair Dr, Mount Vernon WA 98273, USA
**Cleaver, Alan R** — Fashion Designer
Byblos, Via Maggini 126, 60127 Ancona, Italy
**Cleaves, Slaid** — Singer, Songwriter
Keith Case Assoc, 1025 17th Ave S, #200, Nashville TN 37212 USA
**Cleeland, Cameron S (Cam)** — Football Player
23160 Lanyard Lane, Mount Vernon WA 98274, USA
**Cleese, John** — Actor, Comedian, Writer
Anonymous Content, 3532 Hayden Ave, Culver City CA 90232 USA
**Clegg, Johnny** — Singer
Monterey International, 200 W Superior St, #202, Chicago IL 60654 USA
**Cleghorne, Ellen** — Actress, Comedienne
Management 101, 468 N Camden Dr, #200, Beverly Hills CA 90210, USA
**Cleland, J Maxwell (Max)** — Senator, GA
2460 Peachtree Road NW, #1406, Atlanta GA 30305, USA
**Clemens, Clarence (Big Man)** — Saxophonist (E Street Band)
Vineberg Communications, 1695 Beach St, #303, San Francisco CA 94123, USA
**Clemens, Donella** — Religious Leader
Mennonite Church, 722 N Main St, Newton KS 67114, USA
**Clemens, Douglas H (Doug)** — Baseball Player
4799 Lower Mountain Road, New Hope PA 18938, USA
**Clemens, J Barry** — Basketball Player
3111 Clinton Ave, Cleveland OH 44113, USA
**Clemens, W Roger** — Baseball Player
8572 Katy Freeway, #106, Houston TX 77024, USA
**Clemenson, Christian** — Actor
Stone Manners Salners, 6100 Wilshire Blvd, #1500, Los Angeles CA 90035 USA
**Clement, Anthony** — Football Player
141 Navajo Lane, Opelousas LA 70570, USA
**Clement, Aurore** — Actress
Artmedia, 20 Ave Rapp, 75007 Paris, France
**Clement, Bill** — Ice Hockey Player
8 Elfreths Court, Newtown PA 18940, USA
**Clement, Edith Brown** — Judge
US Court of Appeals, 600 Camp St, New Orleans LA 70130, USA
**Clement, Jemaine** — Singer (Flight of the Conchords), Actor
Creative Artists Agency, 2000 Ave of Stars, #100, Los Angeles CA 90067 USA
**Clement, John** — Businessman
Tuddenham Hall, Tuddenham, Ipswich, Suffolk IP6 9DD, England
**Clement, Kerron** — Track Athlete
University of Florida, Athletic Dept, Gainesville FL 32611, USA
**Clement, Matthew P (Matt)** — Baseball Player
143 Milt Miller Road, Renfrew PA 16053, USA
**Clement, Paul D** — Government Official, Attorney
Georgetown University, Law Center, Washington DC 20057, USA
**Clemente, Carmine D** — Anatomist
11737 Bellagio Road, Los Angeles CA 90049, USA
**Clemente, Francesco** — Artist
684 Broadway, New York NY 10012, USA
**Clements, Ashley** — Actress
Resolution, 1801 Century Park E, #2300, Los Angeles CA 90067, USA
**Clements, John A** — Physiologist
University of California, Cardiovascular Institute, San Francisco CA 94143, USA
**Clements, Kim** — Writer
Creative Artists Agency, 2000 Ave of Stars, #100, Los Angeles CA 90067 USA
**Clements, Lennie** — Golfer
PO Box 182197, Coronado CA 92178, USA
**Clements, Nathan D (Nate)** — Football Player
Cincinnati Bengals, 1 Paul Brown Stadium, Cincinnati OH 45202 USA
**Clements, Patrick B (Pat)** — Baseball Player
166 Lazy S Lane, Chico CA 95928, USA
**Clements, Ronald F (Ron)** — Animator, Director
Creative Artists Agency, 2000 Ave of Stars, #100, Los Angeles CA 90067 USA
**Clements, Suzanne** — Fashion Designer
Clements Ribeiro Ltd, 48 S Molton St, London W1X 1HE, England
**Clemmensen, Scott L** — Ice Hockey Player
7 Woodbridge Court, Saratoga Springs NY 12886, USA
**Clemons, Charlie F** — Football Player
569 Inman Road, Fayetteville GA 30215, USA
**Clemons, Craig L** — Football Player
1517 D Ave NE, Cedar Rapids IA 52402, USA
**Clemons, Duane** — Football Player
7512 Dr Phillips Blvd, #50-908, Orlando FL 32819, USA
**Clendenin, Robert T (Bob)** — Actor
Stone Manners Salners, 6100 Wilshire Blvd, #1500, Los Angeles CA 90035 USA
**Clennon, David** — Actor
Greene Assoc, 1901 Ave of Stars, #130, Los Angeles CA 90067 USA
**Cleobury, Nicholas R** — Conductor
Ben Rayfield, Southbank House, Black Prince Road, London SE1 7SJ, England
**Cleobury, Stephen J** — Conductor, Organist
King's College, Music Dept, Cambridge CB2 1ST, England
**Clermont, Herve** — Actor
Arch Talent Group, 117 N Robertson Blvd, Los Angeles CA 90048, USA
**Clervoy, Jean-Francois** — Spatinaut, France
European Space Center, Linder Hohe, Box 906096, 51127 Cologne, Germany
**Clery, Corinne** — Actress
C D A Studio di Nardo, 12 Cavour 171, 00184 Rome, Italy
**Cleve, George W** — Conductor
Columbia Artists Mgmt Inc, 5 Columbus Circle, 1790 Broadway, #1600, New York NY 10019 USA

**Cleveland, Ashley** — Singer, Songwriter
Street Level Artists Agency, 107 E Center St, Warsaw IN 46580, USA

**Cleveland, Charles G (Chick)** — Air Force General, Hero
3603 Thomas Ave, Montgomery AL 36111, USA

**Cleveland, Davis** — Actor
Coast to Coast Talent, 3350 Barham Blvd, Los Angeles CA 90068 USA

**Cleveland, Pat** — Model
Ford Models Inc, 111 5th Ave, #900, New York NY 10003 USA

**Cleveland, Patience** — Actress
PO Box 490, Richland MO 65556, USA

**Cleveland, Reginald L (Reggie)** — Baseball Player
202 Creekview Dr, Anna TX 75409, USA

**Cleven, Harry** — Actor
U B B A, 6 Rue de Braque, 75003 Paris, France

**Clevenger, Raymond C, III** — Judge
US Court of Appeals, 717 Madison Place NW, Washington DC 20439, USA

**Clevenger, Truman E (Tex)** — Baseball Player
31727 Country Club Dr, Porterville CA 93257, USA

**Clevers, Johannes C (Hans)** — Molecular Geneticist
Hubrecht Institute, Uppsalalaan 8, 3584 Utrecht CT, Netherlands

**Clexton, Edward W, Jr** — Navy Admiral
1000 Bobolink Dr, Virginia Beach VA 23451, USA

**Cliff, Jimmy** — Singer, Songwriter
51 Lady Musgrave Road, Kingston 10, Jamaica

**Clifford, Keith** — Actor
Jonathan Altaras Assoc, 11 Garrick St, London WC2E 9AR, England

**Clifford, Linda** — Singer
T-Best Talent Agency, 508 Honey Lake Court, Danville CA 94506 USA

**Clifford, M Richard (Rich)** — Astronaut
N A S A, Johnson Space Center, 2101 NASA Road, Houston TX 77058 USA

**Clifford, Michael** — Singer, Guitarist (5 Seconds of Summer)
Wonder Mgmt, Philips House, 17/617 Elizabeth St, Redfern NSW 2016, Australia

**Clift, William B, III** — Photographer
PO Box 6035, Santa Fe NM 87502, USA

**Clifton, J Chad** — Football Player
1641 Whispering Hills Dr, Franklin TN 37069, USA

**Clifton, James** — Actor
500 W 43rd St, #26J, New York NY 10036, USA

**Clifton, Kyle** — Football Player
777 South Point Court, Aledo TX 76008, USA

**Clifton, Scott** — Actor
Innovative Artists, 1505 10th St, Santa Monica CA 90401 USA

**Clifton, Shaw** — Religious Leader
Salvation Army International, 101 Queen Victoria St, London EC4 4EP, England

**Clijsters, Kim A L** — Tennis Player
Omselweg 37, 3960 Bree, Belgium

**Cline, Richard** — Cartoonist
New Yorker, Editorial Dept, 4 Times Square, Basement C1B, New York NY 10036 USA

**Cline, Tyrone A (Ty)** — Baseball Player
37 Wappoo Creek Place, Charleston SC 29412, USA

**Clines, Eugene A (Gene)** — Baseball Player
5303 9th Ave Dr W, Bradenton FL 34209, USA

**Clingan, Bruce W** — Navy Admiral
US Naval Forces Europe/African Command, PSC 809 Box 70, FPO AE 09626, USA

**Clinger, Debra** — Actress
1206 Chickasaw Dr, Brentwood TN 37027, USA

**Clinkscale, F Dextor** — Football Player
206 Michaux Dr, Greenville SC 29605, USA

**Clinton, George** — Singer, Synthesizer Player, Songwriter
Agency Group, 1100 Century Park E, #711, Los Angeles CA 90067 USA

**Clinton, George S** — Composer
First Artists Mgmt, 4764 Park Granada, #210, Calabasas CA 91302 USA

**Clinton, Hillary Rodham** — Secretary, State; Senator, NY
15 Old House Lane, Chappaqua NY 10514, USA

**Clinton, Kate** — Actress, Comedienne, Writer
Beachfront Productions, PO Box 13218, Portland OR 97213, USA

**Clinton, William J (Bill)** — President, USA
15 Old House Lane, Chappaqua NY 10514, USA

**Clinton-Dix, Ha'Sean (Ha Ha)** — Football Player
Green Bay Packers, 1265 Lombardi Ave, Green Bay WI 54304 USA

**Clippard, Tyler L** — Baseball Player
13575 58th St N, #199, Clearwater FL 33760, USA

**Clivilles, Robert M** — Music Producer (C & C Music Factory)
Brothers Management Assoc, 141 Dunbar Ave, Fords NJ 08863 USA

**Clodagh** — Interior Designer
Clodagh Design International, 670 Broadway, #300, New York NY 10012, USA

**Cloepfil, Brad** — Architect
4505 SW Bernard Dr, Portland OR 97239, USA

**Clohessy, Robert** — Actor
Don Buchwald Talent Agency, 6500 Wilshire Blvd, #2200, Los Angeles CA 90048 USA

**Cloke, Kristen** — Actress
Mitchell K Stubbs Assoc, 8695 W Washington Blvd, #204, Culver City CA 90232 USA

**Cloninger, Tony L** — Baseball Player
PO Box 1500, Denver NC 28037, USA

**Clontz, J Bradley (Brad)** — Baseball Player
General Delivery, Alpharetta GA 30009, USA

**Clooney, George** — Actor, Director, Writer
Stan Rosenfield Assoc, 2029 Century Park E, #1190, Los Angeles CA 90067 USA

**Close, Charles T (Chuck)** — Artist
20 Bond St, New York NY 10012, USA

**Close, Eric** — Actor
Untitled Entertainment, 350 S Beverly Dr, #200, Beverly Hills CA 90212 USA

**Close, Glenn** — Actress
Trillium Productions, PO Box 1560, #200, New Canaan CT 06840, USA

**Close, Joshua** — Actor
Untitled Entertainment, 350 S Beverly Dr, #200, Beverly Hills CA 90212 USA

# C

**Closs, William T (Bill)** — Basketball Player
555 Byron St, #409, Palo Alto CA 94301, USA

**Closton, Cory** — Ice Hockey Coach
Ottawa Senators, Scotia Bank Place, Kanata ON K2V 1A5, Canada

**Clotet, Lluis** — Architect
Studio P E R, Caspe 151, 08013 Barcelona, Spain

**Clottey, Joshua** — Boxer
Top Rank Inc, 3908 Howard Hughes Parkway, #580, Las Vegas NV 89169 USA

**Clotworthy, Robert** — Actor
Amsel Eisenstadt Frazier, 5055 Wilshire Blvd, #865, Los Angeles CA 90036 USA

**Clotworthy, Robert L (Bob)** — Diver, Coach
2301 Moss Rose Lane, Fort Collins CO 80526, USA

**Cloud, Michael A (Mike)** — Football Player
5126 Miller Ave, Dallas TX 75206, USA

**Clough, G Wayne** — Educator, Administrator
Smithsonian Institution, 100 Jefferson Dr SW, Washington DC 20560, USA

**Clough, Ray W, Jr** — Structural Engineer
19800 SW Touchmark Way, #280, Bend OR 97702, USA

**Cloutier, Jacques** — Ice Hockey Player
12172 Triple Crown Dr, Parker CO 80134, USA

**Clowes, Daniel** — Cartoonist (Ghost World), Writer
United Talent Agency, U T A Plaza, 9336 Civic Center Dr, Beverly Hills CA 90210 USA

**Clowney, Jadeveon** — Football Player
Houston Texans, 2 Reliant Park, Houston TX 77054 USA

**Clunes, Martin** — Actor
Independent Talent Group, 40 Whitfield St, London W1T 2RH, England

**Clunie, Michelle** — Actress
Abrams Artists, 9200 W Sunset Blvd, #1125, West Hollywood CA 90069 USA

**Cluzet, Francois** — Actor
Voyez Mon Agent, 20 Ave Rapp, 75007 Paris, France

**Clyde, David E (Dave)** — Baseball Player
7806 Pinehurst Shadows Dr, Humble TX 77346, USA

**Clymer, Ben** — Ice Hockey Player
2713 Plaza Verde, Lake Havasu City AZ 86406, USA

**Clyne, Patricia** — Fashion Designer
353 W 39th St, New York NY 10018, USA

**Coakley, W Dexter** — Football Player
1304 Sunset Ridge Circle, Cedar Hill TX 75104, USA

**Coan, E Bert, III** — Football Player
14517 N US Highway 59, Nacogdoches TX 75965, USA

**Coan, Gilbert F (Gil)** — Baseball Player
70 Beach Lane, Brevard NC 28712, USA

**Coates, Anne V** — Film Editor, Producer
United Talent Agency, U T A Plaza, 9336 Civic Center Dr, Beverly Hills CA 90210 USA

**Coates, Ben T** — Football Player, Coach
461 Havenbrook Way NW, Concord NC 28027, USA

**Coates, James A (Jim)** — Baseball Player
1098 Oak Hill Road, Lancaster VA 22503, USA

**Coates, Kim** — Actor
Oscars Abrams Zimel, 438 Queen St E, Toronto ON M5A 1T4, Canada

**Coates, Phyllis** — Actress
PO Box 1969, Boyes Hot Springs CA 95416, USA

**Coates, Steve J** — Ice Hockey Player, Sportscaster
102 Stoney Creek Dr, Egg Harbor Township NJ 08234, USA

**Coats, Kristi** — Golfer
185 Wildwood Place, Petal MS 39465, USA

**Coats, Michael L** — Astronaut
3203 Acorn Wood Way, Houston TX 77059, USA

**Cobb, Garry W** — Football Player
112 Society Hill Blvd, Cherry Hill NJ 08003, USA

**Cobb, Geraldyn M (Jerrie)** — Astronaut Candidate
1006 Beach Blvd, Sun City Center FL 33573, USA

**Cobb, Henry N** — Architect
Pei Cobb Freed Partners, 88 Pine St, Lobby 1, New York NY 10005, USA

**Cobb, Jewel Plummer** — Biologist, Cell Physiologist, Educator
California State University, Biology Dept, PO Box 3480, Fullerton CA 92834, USA

**Cobb, John B, Jr** — Social Activist
Claremont Graduate School, Center for Process Studies, Claremont CA 91711, USA

**Cobb, Julie** — Actress
C E S D, 10635 Santa Monica Blvd, #130, Los Angeles CA 90025 USA

**Cobb, Keith Hamilton** — Actor
B R S / Gage Talent Agency, 1650 Broadway, #1410, New York NY 10019 USA

**Cobb, Marvin L** — Football Player
655 S Flower St, #290, Los Angeles CA 90017, USA

**Cobb, Reginald J (Reggie)** — Football Player
PO Box 17416, Sugar Land TX 77496, USA

**Cobbin, W Jim (James)** — Baseball Player
121 E Rayen Ave, Youngstown OH 44503, USA

**Cobbs, Bill** — Actor
Stone Manners Salners, 6100 Wilshire Blvd, #1500, Los Angeles CA 90035 USA

**Coben, Harlan** — Writer
E P Dutton, 375 Hudson St, New York NY 10014 USA

**Cobert, Bob** — Composer
B M I, 8730 W Sunset Blvd, #300, Los Angeles CA 90069 USA

**Cobham, William C (Billy)** — Jazz Drummer, Composer
Joel Chriss Co, 300 Mercer St, #3J, New York NY 10003 USA

**Coble, G Drew** — Baseball Umpire
205 80th Ave N, Myrtle Beach SC 29572, USA

**Coblenz, Walter** — Director, Producer
4310 Cahuenga Blvd, #401, Toluca Lake CA 91602, USA

**Cobos, Alberto** — Paleontologist
Teruel-Dinopolis Museum, Poligono de los Planos, 44002 Teruel, Spain

**Cobos, Jesus Lopez** — Conductor
Cincinnati Symphony, 1241 Elm St, Cincinnati OH 45202, USA

**Coburn, Braydon** — Ice Hockey Player
523 Chews Landing Road, Haddonfield NJ 8033, USA

**Coburn, Doris**
130 Dalton Dr, Buffalo NY 14223, USA — Bowler

**Coburn, John G**
7717 Island Creek Court, Alexandria VA 22315, USA — Army General

**Coccopalmerio, Francesco Cardinal**
Legislative Texts Council, Palazzo delle Congregazioni, Piazza Pio XII 10, 00193 Rome, Italy — Religious Leader

**Cochinescu, Ioan Mihai**
CP 1-151, 2000 Ploiesti 1, Prahova, Romania — Photographer, Writer

**Cochran, Antonio D**
PO Box 9644, Columbus GA 31908, USA — Football Player

**Cochran, Barbara Ann**
Cochran's Ski Area, PO Box 789, Richmond VT 05477, USA — Skier

**Cochran, John**
ABC-TV, News Dept, 5010 Creston St, Hyattsville MD 20781 USA — Commentator

**Cochran, Robert**
A P A Talent & Literary Agency, 405 S Beverly Dr, #300, Beverly Hills CA 90212 USA — Writer, Producer

**Cochran, Russ**
23 Bayview Road, Jupiter FL 33469, USA — Golfer

**Cochran, Shannon**
Mitchell K Stubbs Assoc, 8695 W Washington Blvd, #204, Culver City CA 90232 USA — Actress

**Cochran, Stacy**
I C M Partners, 10250 Constellation Blvd, #900, Los Angeles CA 90067 USA — Director

**Cochran, Tammy**
Consortium, 49 Music Square W, #210, Nashville TN 37203, USA — Singer, Songwriter

**Cochrane, David C (Dave)**
126 Silver Eagle Lane, Mooresville NC 28117, USA — Baseball Player

**Cochrane, Glen M**
405 Collett Road, Kelowna BC V1W 1K6, Canada — Ice Hockey Player

**Cochrane, Rory**
Untitled Entertainment, 350 S Beverly Dr, #200, Beverly Hills CA 90212 USA — Actor

**Cockburn, Bruce**
Finkelstein Mgmt, 137 Berkeley St, Toronto ON M5V 2X1, Canada — Singer, Songwriter, Guitarist

**Cocker, Jarvis**
X-Ray Touring, Nena House, 77-79 Great Eastern St, London EC2A 3HU, England — Singer (Pulp), Songwriter

**Cocker, Joe**
Mad Dog Ranch, 43401 Cottonwood Creek Road, Crawford CO 81415, USA — Singer

**Cockerill, Franklin**
Mayo Clinic, Microbiology Dept, 200 1st St SW, Rochester MN 55905, USA — Microbiologist

**Cockerill, Kay**
131 Beulah St, San Francisco CA 94117, USA — Golfer

**Cockey, Tim**
Hyperion Books, 114 5th Ave, New York NY 10011 USA — Writer

**Cockrell, Kenneth D**
2300 Richmond Ave, #350, Houston TX 77098, USA — Astronaut

**Cockroft, Donald L (Don)**
2418 Dunkeith Dr NW, Canton OH 44708, USA — Football Player

**Coco, Lea**
Gersh Agency, 9465 Wilshire Blvd, #600, Beverly Hills CA 90212 USA — Actor, Writer

**Cocroft, Sherman**
2504 Christopher Lane, Costa Mesa CA 92626, USA — Football Player

**Codiroli, Christopher A (Chris)**
2700 Hillcrest Dr, Cameron Park CA 95682, USA — Baseball Player

**Codrescu, Andrei**
Louisiana State University, English Dept, Baton Rouge LA 70803, USA — Writer

**Coduri, Camille**
Independent Talent Group, 40 Whitfield St, London W1T 2RH, England — Actress

**Cody, Diablo**
W M E Entertainment, 9601 Wilshire Blvd, #300, Beverly Hills CA 90210 USA — Producer, Writer

**Cody, Richard A**
L-3 Communications Holdings, 1215 S Clark St, #1205, Arlington VA 22202, USA — Army General

**Cody, William E (Bill)**
209 Orleans Dr, Fairhope AL 36532, USA — Football Player

**Coe of Ranmore, Sebastian N**
Starswood, High Barn Road, Effingham, Surrey KT24 5PW, England — Track Athlete

**Coe, David Allan**
Conqueroo, 11271 Ventura Blvd, #522, Studio City CA 91604, USA — Singer, Guitarist, Songwriter

**Coe, George**
A M T Artists, 15260 Ventura Blvd, #1200, Sherman Oaks CA 91403, USA — Actor

**Coe, Sue**
Galerie Saint Etienne, 24 W 57th St, New York NY 10019, USA — Artist

**Coe-Jones, Dawn**
2945 SW 39th Ave, Gainesville FL 32608, USA — Golfer

**Coelho, Paulo**
Caixa Postal 43003, Rio de Janiero 22052-970, Brazil — Writer

**Coelho, Susie**
3565 Meadowview Dr, Riverside CA 92503, USA — Actress

**Coen, Ethan**
United Talent Agency, U T A Plaza, 9336 Civic Center Dr, Beverly Hills CA 90210 USA — Director, Writer

**Coen, Joel**
United Talent Agency, U T A Plaza, 9336 Civic Center Dr, Beverly Hills CA 90210 USA — Director, Writer

**Coetzee, Gergardus C (Gerrie)**
22 Sydney Road, Ravenswood, Boksburg 1460, South Africa — Boxer

**Coetzee, John M**
PO Box 92, Rondebosch, Cape Province 7700, South Africa — Nobel Literature Laureate

**Coetzer, Amanda**
PO Box 686, Florida Hills 1716, South Africa — Tennis Player

**Coeur De Pirate**
Agency Group Ltd, 142 W 57th St, #600, New York NY 10019 USA — Singer, Songwriter

**Cofer, J Michael (Mike)**
Racing West, 1772 Los Arboles, #J186, Thousand Oaks CA 91362, USA — Football Player, Truck Racing Driver

**Cofer, Michael L (Mike)**
110 Bridgestone Cove, Fayetteville GA 30215, USA — Football Player

**Coffee, Claire**
Domain Talent, 9229 W Sunset Blvd, #710, West Hollywood CA 90069 USA — Actress

**Coffey, J Todd**
320 Widd Lawing Lane, Union Mills NC 28167, USA — Baseball Player

# C

**Coffey, Jeffrey (King)** — Drummer (Butthole Surfers)
Kork Agency, 1880 Century Park E, #711, Los Angeles CA 90067, USA
**Coffey, John L** — Judge
US Court of Appeals, US Courthouse, 517 E Wisconsin Ave, Milwaukee WI 53202, USA
**Coffey, Junior L** — Football Player
17228 32nd Ave S, #E12, Seatac WA 98188, USA
**Coffey, Kellie** — Singer, Songwriter
W M E Entertainment, 1600 Division St, #300, Nashville TN 37203 USA
**Coffey, Paul D** — Ice Hockey Player
Bolton Toyota, 12050 Albion Vaughan Road, Bolton ON L7E 1S7, Canada
**Coffin, Edmund (Tad)** — Equestrian
1151 Dairy Road, Ruckersville VA 22968, USA
**Coffin, Peter** — Artist, Sculptor
Venus Over Manhattan Gallery, 980 Madison Ave, #300, New York NY 10075, USA
**Coffman, Paul R** — Football Player
14103 E 195th St, Peculiar MO 64078, USA
**Cogan, Kevin** — Auto Racing Driver
205 Rocky Point Road, Palos Verdes Estates CA 90274, USA
**Cogdill, Gail R** — Football Player
12922 E 36th Ave, Spokane Valley WA 99206, USA
**Coggins, Richard A (Rich)** — Baseball Player
4095 Fruit St, #219, La Verne CA 91750, USA
**Coghill, Jonathan R (Jon)** — Drummer (Powderfinger)
Secret Service, PO Box 401, Fortitude Valley QLD 4006, Australia
**Coghlan, Eamon** — Track Athlete
International Mangement Group, 1 Erieview Plaza, 1360 E 9th St, #100, Cleveland OH 44114 USA
**Cogollo, Heriberto** — Artist
54 Rue Faubourg du Courreau, 34000 Montpelier (Herault), France
**Cohan, Lauren** — Actress
Creative Artists Agency, 2000 Ave of Stars, #100, Los Angeles CA 90067 USA
**Cohan, Robert P** — Choreographer
The Place, 17 Dukes Road, London WC1H 9AB, England
**Coheleach, Guy J** — Artist
Pandion Art, PO Box 96, Bernardsville NJ 07924, USA
**Cohen, Adam** — Singer, Guitarist, Songwriter
Paquin Entertainment Agency, 219 Dufferin St, #206B, Toronto ON M6K 3J1, Canada
**Cohen, Alexandra P (Sasha)** — Figure Skater
International Mangement Group, 1 Erieview Plaza, 1360 E 9th St, #100, Cleveland OH 44114 USA
**Cohen, Arnaldo** — Concert Pianist
Arts Management Group, 1133 Broadway, #1025, New York NY 10010, USA
**Cohen, Avishai** — Jazz Bassist
Janet Williamson Music Agency, PO Box 27114, Los Angeles CA 90027, USA
**Cohen, Bernard W** — Artist
80 Camberwell Grove, London SE5 8RF, England
**Cohen, Bruce** — Producer
Bruce Cohen Productions, 8292 Hollywood Blvd, Los Angeles CA 90069, USA
**Cohen, David** — Keyboardist (Country Joe & the Fish)
I C M Partners, 10250 Constellation Blvd, #900, Los Angeles CA 90067 USA
**Cohen, David X** — Producer, Writer
Creative Artists Agency, 2000 Ave of Stars, #100, Los Angeles CA 90067 USA
**Cohen, Emory** — Actor
Harvest Talent Management, 124 W 80th St, #1, New York NY 10024, USA
**Cohen, Etan** — Producer, Writer
Creative Artists Agency, 2000 Ave of Stars, #100, Los Angeles CA 90067 USA
**Cohen, Jerome A** — Attorney, Educator
New York University, Law School, 40 Washington Square, New York NY 10012, USA
**Cohen, Joshua** — Philosopher
Stanford University, Philosophy Dept, Stanford CA 94305, USA
**Cohen, Larry** — Labor Leader
Communications Workers of America, 501 3rd St NW, #C1, Washington DC 20001, USA
**Cohen, Larry** — Director, Writer
Larco Productions, 2111 Coldwater Canyon, Beverly Hills CA 90210, USA
**Cohen, Leonard N** — Writer, Singer, Songwriter
S L Feldman Mgmt, 1505 W 2nd Ave, #200, Vancouver BC V6H 3Y4, Canada
**Cohen, Lynn** — Actress
Paradigm Agency, 360 Park Ave S, #1600, New York NY 10010 USA
**Cohen, Marshall H** — Astronomer
California Institute of Technology, Astronomy Dept, Pasadena CA 91125, USA
**Cohen, Marvin** — Pharmacologist
Triumph Pharmaceuticals, 10403 Baur Blvd, #A, Saint Louis MO 63132, USA
**Cohen, Marvin L** — Physicist
10 Forest Lane, Berkeley CA 94708, USA
**Cohen, Matt** — Actor
Stone Manners Salners, 6100 Wilshire Blvd, #1500, Los Angeles CA 90035 USA
**Cohen, Peter M** — Director, Producer, Writer
United Talent Agency, U T A Plaza, 9336 Civic Center Dr, Beverly Hills CA 90210 USA
**Cohen, Rachel Leah** — Actress
Avalon Artists Group, 143 W 29th St, #1103, New York NY 10001, USA
**Cohen, Rob** — Director
Nowita Pictures, 2900 Olympic Blvd, #345, Santa Monica CA 90404, USA
**Cohen, Robert** — Concert Cellist
15 Birchwood Ave, London N10 3BE, England
**Cohen, Sacha Baron** — Actor, Comedian
W M E Entertainment, 9601 Wilshire Blvd, #300, Beverly Hills CA 90210 USA
**Cohen, Sarah** — Journalist
Washington Post, Editorial Dept, 1150 15th St NW, Washington DC 20071 USA
**Cohen, Scott** — Actor
One Entertainment, 347 5th Ave, #1404, New York NY 10016 USA
**Cohen, Sheldon S** — Government Official
5518 Trent St, Chevy Chase MD 20815, USA
**Cohen, Stanley** — Nobel Medicine Laureate
106 Mint Spring Circle, Brentwood TN 37027, USA
**Cohen, Stanley N** — Geneticist, Inventor
Stanford University Medical Center, Genetics Dept, Stanford CA 94305, USA
**Cohen, William S** — Secretary, Defense; Senator, ME
Cohen Group, 600 13th St NW, #640, Washington DC 20005, USA

| | |
|---|---|
| **Cohen-Tannoudji, Claude K** | Nobel Physics Laureate |
| 38 Rue des Cordelieres, 75013 Paris, France | |
| **Cohn, Alfred (Al)** | Bowler |
| 85 Odyssey Dr, Tinley Park IL 60477, USA | |
| **Cohn, Gary** | Financier |
| Goldman Sachs Co, 85 Broad St, Building 85, New York NY 10004, USA | |
| **Cohn, Gary** | Journalist |
| Baltimore Sun, Editorial Dept, 501 N Calvert St, Baltimore MD 21278, USA | |
| **Cohn, Marc** | Singer, Songwriter |
| Michael Hausman Mgmt, 511 Ave of Americas, #197, New York NY 10011, USA | |
| **Cohn, Mindy** | Actress |
| Allegory Creative Mgmt, 13261 Moorpark St, #103, Sherman Oaks CA 91423, USA | |
| **Coia, Arthur A** | Labor Leader |
| Laborers' International Union, 905 16th St NW, #600, Washington DC 20006, USA | |
| **Coifman, Ronald R** | Computer Scientist |
| 11 Hickory Road, North Haven CT 06473, USA | |
| **Cojocaru, Steven** | Entertainer |
| Selverne Co, 650 Rose Ave, #2, Venice CA 90291, USA | |
| **Coker, Larry E** | Football Coach, Sportscaster |
| University of Texas, Athletic Dept, San Antonio TX 78249, USA | |
| **Cokes, Curtis** | Boxer |
| 3540 Durango Dr, Dallas TX 75220, USA | |
| **Colander-Richardson, LaTasha** | Track Athlete |
| 26 E Myrtle Dr, Angier NC 27501, USA | |
| **Colangelo, Jerry J** | Basketball, Baseball Executive |
| 70 E Country Club Dr, Phoenix AZ 85014, USA | |
| **Colantoni, Enrico** | Actor |
| Innovative Artists, 1505 10th St, Santa Monica CA 90401 USA | |
| **Colao, Vittorio** | Businessman |
| Vodaphone Group, Connection, Newbury, Berkshire RG14 2FN, England | |
| **Colbert, Jim** | Golfer |
| 118 Wanish Place, Palm Desert CA 92260, USA | |
| **Colbert, Nathan (Nate)** | Baseball Player |
| 2756 N Green Valley Parkway, Henderson NV 89014, USA | |
| **Colbert, Stephen** | Actor, Comedian, Writer |
| Dixon Talent Agency, 375 Greenwich St, #500, New York NY 10013, USA | |
| **Colborn, James W (Jim)** | Baseball Player |
| 2932 Solimar Beach Dr, Ventura CA 93001, USA | |
| **Colbrunn, Gregory J (Greg)** | Baseball Player |
| 1544 Wellesley Circle, Mount Pleasant SC 29466, USA | |
| **Colburn, Richard** | Drummer (Belle & Sebastian) |
| Ground Control Touring, 20 Jay St, #826, Brooklyn NY 11201 USA | |
| **Colclough, Henry** | Singer |
| 3040 Fontain St, Philadelphia PA 19121, USA | |
| **Cold 187um** | Rap Artist (Above the Law) |
| Green Light Talent Agency, PO Box 3172, Beverly Hills CA 90212 USA | |
| **Cole, Alexander (Alex)** | Baseball Player |
| 6545 N Stevens Hollow Dr, Chesterfield VA 23832, USA | |
| **Cole, Anne** | Fashion Designer |
| Cole of California, 6040 Bandini Blvd, Los Angeles CA 90040, USA | |
| **Cole, Artemas** | Cartoonist |
| 15 Regency Manor, #15-8, Rutland VT 05701, USA | |
| **Cole, Ashley** | Soccer Player |
| Arsenal London, Avenell Road, Highbury, London N5 1BU, England | |
| **Cole, Bobby** | Golfer |
| 204 W 2nd Ave, Windermere FL 34786, USA | |
| **Cole, Bradley** | Actor |
| Leading Artists, 145 W 45th St, #1000, New York NY 10036 10036, USA | |
| **Cole, Carolyn** | Photojournalist |
| Los Angeles Times, Editorial Dept, 202 W 1st St, Los Angeles CA 90012 USA | |
| **Cole, Cheryl A (Tweedy)** | Singer (Girls Aloud) |
| Concorde International, 101 Shepherds Bush Road, London W6 7LP, England | |
| **Cole, Christina** | Actress |
| Conway Van Gelder Grant, 8-12 Broadwick St, #300, London W1F 8HW, England | |
| **Cole, Danton** | Ice Hockey Player |
| 7180 Wapiti Way, Saline MI 48176, USA | |
| **Cole, David D** | Attorney |
| Georgetown University, Law School, Washington DC 20057, USA | |
| **Cole, Erik** | Ice Hockey Player |
| 1112 Stonekirk, Raleigh NC 27614, USA | |
| **Cole, Freddy** | Singer |
| Producers Inc, 11806 N 56th St, Tampa FL 33617 USA | |
| **Cole, Gary** | Actor |
| Danis Panaro Nist Talent, 9201 W Olympic Blvd, Beverly Hills CA 90212 USA | |
| **Cole, George E** | Actor |
| Joy Jameson, PO Box 68182, London N1P 2BN, England | |
| **Cole, Holly** | Singer |
| Alert Music, 51 Hillsview Ave, Toronto ON M6P 1J4, Canada | |
| **Cole, Jasper** | Actor |
| Newman-Thomas Mgmt, 8306 Wilshire Blvd, #996 Beverly Hills CA 90211, USA | |
| **Cole, Joanna** | Writer |
| Scholastic Press, 555 Broadway, New York NY 10012, USA | |
| **Cole, John** | Editorial Cartoonist |
| Scranton Times-Tribune, Editorial Dept, 149 Penn Ave, Scranton PA 18503, USA | |
| **Cole, Johnnetta B** | Museum Executive, Educator |
| National African Art Museum, 950 Independence Ave SW, Washington DC 20560, USA | |
| **Cole, Julie Dawn** | Actress |
| Joy Jameson, PO Box 68182, London N1P 2BN, England | |
| **Cole, Kenneth** | Fashion Designer |
| Kenneth Cole Productions, 601 W 50th St, New York NY 10019, USA | |
| **Cole, Keyshia** | Singer, Actress |
| Creative Artists Agency, 2000 Ave of Stars, #100, Los Angeles CA 90067 USA | |
| **Cole, Larry R** | Football Player |
| 400 Country Place, Colleyville TX 76034, USA | |
| **Cole, Lily** | Model, Actress |
| I M G Models, 304 Park Ave S, #PH N, New York NY 10010 USA | |

**Cole, Marilyn** — Model
Playboy Promotions, 9346 Civic Center Dr, #200, Beverly Hills CA 90210 USA

**Cole, Michael** — Psychologist
University of California, Communications Dept, La Jolla CA 92093, USA

**Cole, Michael** — Actor
J K A Talent Agency, 12725 Ventura Blvd, #H, Studio City CA 91604, USA

**Cole, Nadine E L** — Singer (Girls Aloud)
Concorde International, 101 Shepherds Bush Road, London W6 7LP, England

**Cole, Natalie** — Singer, Actress
Moir/Borman Entertainment, 1250 6th St, #401, Santa Monica CA 90401, USA

**Cole, Nigel** — Director, Writer
Independent Talent Group, 40 Whitfield St, London W1T 2RH, England

**Cole, Olivia** — Actress
Century Artists, PO Box 59747, Santa Barbara CA 93150 USA

**Cole, Paula** — Singer, Songwriter
Skyline Music, 48 Prospect St, Whitefield NH 03598, USA

**Cole, Ralph, Jr** — Actor
Prestige Talent Agency, 9250 Wilshire Blvd, #208, Beverly Hills CA 90212, USA

**Cole, Richard (Richie)** — Jazz Saxophonist
Abby Hoffer Enterprises, 223 1/2 E 48th St, New York NY 10017 USA

**Cole, Richard E** — WW II Army Air Corps Hero
48 Blaschke Road, Comfort TX 78013, USA

**Cole, Richard R (Dick)** — Baseball Player
3149 Madeira Ave, Costa Mesa CA 92626, USA

**Cole, Robert C (Bob)** — Sportscaster
CBC-TV, PO Box 500 Station A, Toronto ON M5W 1E6, Canada

**Cole, Robin** — Football Player
9 Brook Lane, Eighty Four PA 15330, USA

**Cole, Steve** — Jazz Saxophonist
Great Scott Productions, 4750 Lincoln Blvd, #229, Marina del Rey CA 90292, USA

**Cole, Steven** — Opera Singer
Columbia Artists Mgmt Inc, 5 Columbus Circle, 1790 Broadway, #1600, New York NY 10019 USA

**Cole, Susan A** — Educator
Montclair State University, President's Office, Montclair NJ 07043, USA

**Cole, Taylor** — Actress
TalentWorks, 3500 W Olive Ave, #1400, Burbank CA 91505 USA

**Cole, Tina** — Actress, Singer
4603 Edison Ave, Sacramento CA 95821, USA

**Cole, Trent** — Football Player
Philadelphia Eagles, 1 Novacare Way, Philadelphia PA 19145 USA

**Colella, Richard (Rick)** — Swimmer
217 19th Place, Kirkland WA 98033, USA

**Coleman, Andre C** — Football Player
1616 Mulligan Place, Manhattan KS 66502, USA

**Coleman, Benjamin (Ben)** — Basketball Player
14211 Fisher Ave NE, Prior Lake MN 55372, USA

**Coleman, Bill** — Dance Company Executive, Choreographer
Coleman Lemieux Compagnie, 304 Paliament St, Toronto M5A 3A4, Canada

**Coleman, Bobby** — Actor
Coast to Coast Talent, 3350 Barham Blvd, Los Angeles CA 90068 USA

**Coleman, Brian** — Artist
900 Old Evans Road, Watsonville CA 95076, USA

**Coleman, Catherine G (Cady)** — Astronaut
30 Frank Williams Road, Shelburne Falls MA 01370, USA

**Coleman, Chad** — Actor
TalentWorks, 3500 W Olive Ave, #1400, Burbank CA 91505 USA

**Coleman, Cosey C** — Football Player
11901 Northumberland Dr, Tampa FL 33626, USA

**Coleman, Dabney** — Actor
Michael Black Mgmt, 9701 Wilshire Blvd, 1000, Beverly Hills CA 90212, USA

**Coleman, David L (Dave)** — Baseball Player
4303 Delhi Dr, Dayton OH 45432, USA

**Coleman, Deborah** — Singer, Guitarist
Piedmont Talent, PO Box 680006, Charlotte NC 28216, USA

**Coleman, Don E** — Football Player
424 McPherson Ave, Lansing MI 48915, USA

**Coleman, E C, Jr** — Basketball Player
370 E Harmon Ave, Las Vegas NV 89169, USA

**Coleman, George E** — Jazz Saxophonist
Maurice Montoya Music Agency, 1133 Broadway, #1608, New York NY 10010, USA

**Coleman, Greg J** — Football Player
2313 River Pointe Circle, Minneapolis MN 55411, USA

**Coleman, Jack** — Actor
Domain Talent, 9229 W Sunset Blvd, #710, West Hollywood CA 90069 USA

**Coleman, Jenna** — Actress
Troika, 74 Clerkenwell Road, #300, London EC1M 5QA, England

**Coleman, Jeremy (Jaz)** — Singer (Killing Joke), Songwriter
Agency Group, 1100 Century Park E, #711, Los Angeles CA 90067 USA

**Coleman, Joseph H (Joe)** — Baseball Player
17851 Eagle View Lane, Cape Coral FL 33909, USA

**Coleman, Kari** — Actress
C E S D, 10635 Santa Monica Blvd, #130, Los Angeles CA 90025 USA

**Coleman, Kelly** — Basketball Player
PO Box 183, Higgins Lake MI 48627, USA

**Coleman, Kenyon O** — Football Player
35723 Stock St, Murrieta CA 92562, USA

**Coleman, Leonard D** — Football Player
125 NE 13th Ave, Boynton Beach FL 33435, USA

**Coleman, Marco D** — Football Player
105 Monarch Court, Saint Augustine FL 32095, USA

**Coleman, Marcus** — Football Player
1736 Mapleleaf Dr, Wylie TX 75098, USA

**Coleman, Marissa** — Basketball Player
Los Angeles Sparks, 888 S Figueroa St, #2010, Los Angeles CA 90017 USA

**Coleman, Mary Sue** — Educator
University of Michigan, President's Office, Ann Arbor MI 48109, USA

**Coleman, Monique**
Magnolia Entertainment, 9595 Wilshire Blvd, #601, Beverly Hills CA 90212, USA — Actress

**Coleman, Norman B, Jr**
American Action Forum, 1455 Pennsylvania Ave NW, #350, Washington DC 20004, USA — Senator, MN

**Coleman, Ornette**
Ted Kurland, 173 Brighton Ave, Boston MA 02134 USA — Jazz Saxophonist, Composer

**Coleman, Phyllis**
Playboy Promotions, 9346 Civic Center Dr, #200, Beverly Hills CA 90210 USA — Model

**Coleman, Roderick D (Rod)**
6735 Great Water Dr, Flowery Branch GA 30542, USA — Football Player

**Coleman, Ronnie L**
16039 Williwaw Dr, Houston TX 77083, USA — Football Player

**Coleman, Rowan**
Pocket Books, 1230 Ave of Americas, New York NY 10020 USA — Writer

**Coleman, Sidney**
15083 Highway 39 N, DeKalb MS 39328, USA — Football Player

**Coleman, Signy**
Abrams Artists, 9200 W Sunset Blvd, #1125, West Hollywood CA 90069 USA — Actress

**Coleman, Vincent M (Vince)**
7271 Primrose Lane, San Diego CA 92129, USA — Baseball Player

**Coleman, William T, Jr**
O'Melveny & Myers, 1625 I St NW, Washington DC 20006, USA — Secretary, Transportation

**Coleman, Zendaya**
Monster Talent Mgmt, 6333 W 3rd St, #912, Los Angeles CA 90036, USA — Actress

**Coles, Darnell**
10021 Brompton Dr, Tampa FL 33626, USA — Baseball Player

**Coles, Janet**
6083 Alumni Gym, Hanover NH 3755, USA — Golfer

**Coles, Julie**
6780 N Casa Real Place, Boise ID 83714, USA — Actress

**Coles, Kim**
Abrams Artists, 9200 W Sunset Blvd, #1125, West Hollywood CA 90069 USA — Actress, Comedienne

**Coles, Laveranues L**
1 Sagamore Dr, Plainview NY 11803, USA — Football Player

**Coles, Robert M**
81 Carr Road, Concord MA 01742, USA — Psychiatrist

**Coles, Vernell E (Bimbo)**
203 E Washington St, Lewisburg WV 24901, USA — Basketball Player

**Colescott, Warrington W**
8788 County Road A, Hollandale WI 53544, USA — Artist

**Coley, Daryl**
Daryl Coley Ministries, 417 E Regent St, Inglewood CA 90301, USA — Clarinetist, Pianist

**Coley, John Ford**
Utopia Artists, PO Box 1821, Ojai CA 93024, USA — Singer, Songwriter

**Colfer, Chris**
Coast to Coast Talent, 3350 Barham Blvd, Los Angeles CA 90068 USA — Actor

**Colicchio, Thomas P (Tom)**
Colicchio & Sons, 85 10th Ave, New York NY 10011, USA — Chef, Restauranteur

**Colin, Charlie**
Jon Landau, 80 Main St, Greenwich CT 06830, USA — Bassist (Train)

**Colin, Margaret**
Innovative Artists, 1505 10th St, Santa Monica CA 90401 USA — Actress

**Colinet, Stalin**
3 Mohawk Dr, Framingham MA 01701, USA — Football Player

**Coll, Ashley**
1419 Chetwynd Ave, Plainfield NJ 07060, USA — Artist

**Coll, Ivonne**
Don Buchwald Talent Agency, 6500 Wilshire Blvd, #2200, Los Angeles CA 90048 USA — Actress

**Coll, Stephen W**
New America Foundation, 1899 L St, NW, #400, Washington DC 20036, USA — Journalist

**Collard, Jean-Philippe**
Caroline Martin Musique, 126 Rue Vielle du Temple, 75003 Paris, France — Concert Pianist

**Collet-Serra, Jaume**
Ombra Films, 12444 Ventura Blvd, #103, Studio City CA 91604, USA — Director

**Collett, C Elmer**
PO Box 522, 10 Avenida Farralone, Stinson Beach CA 94970, USA — Football Player

**Collett, Jason**
Agency Group Ltd, 142 W 57th St, #600, New York NY 10019 USA — Singer, Songwriter

**Collette, Toni**
Viking Entertainment, 445 W 23rd St, #1A, New York NY 10011, USA — Actress

**Colletti, Stephen**
Core Public Relations Group, 4401 Wilshire Blvd, #400, Los Angeles CA 90010 USA — Actor

**Colley, Dana**
48 Laight St, New York NY 10013, USA — Saxophonist (Morphine)

**Colley, Ed**
11 Blaisdell Terrace, Ipswich MA 01938, USA — Cartoonist (Suburban Cowgirls)

**Colley, Kenneth**
Artists Partnership, 101 Finsbury Pavement, London EC2A 1RS, England — Actor

**Colley, Michael C**
12022 Forest St, Thornton CO 80241, USA — Navy Admiral

**Colley, Tom**
71 Dillon Dr, Collingwood ON L9Y 4S4, Canada — Ice Hockey Player

**Collie, Bruce S**
9595 Ranch Road 12, #13, Wimberley TX 78676, USA — Football Player

**Collie, Mark**
Dreamcatcher Artist Mgmt, 2908 Poston Ave, Nashville TN 37203, USA — Singer, Songwriter, Actor

**Collier, Charles (Charlie)**
A M C Networks, 11 Penn Plaza, New York NY 10001, USA — Businessman

**Collier, Don**
9024 E 21st St, Tucson AZ 85710, USA — Actor

**Collier, James Lincoln**
71 Barrow St, New York NY 10014, USA — Writer

**Collier, Lesley F**
Royal Ballet, Covent Garden, Bow St, London WC2E 9DD, England — Ballerina

**Collier, Louis K (Lou)**
6409 S Kenwood Ave, Chicago IL 60637, USA — Baseball Player

**Collier, Timothy (Tim)** — Football Player
3116 50th St, Dallas TX 75216, USA

**Colligan, Edward T** — Businessman
Equity Partners, 70 E 55th St, New York NY 10022, USA

**Colligan, John (Bud)** — Businessman
Macromedia Inc, 600 Townsend St, San Francisco CA 94103, USA

**Collin, Aurelien** — Soccer Player
Sporting Kansas City, 210 W 19th Terrace, #200, Kansas City MO 64108 USA

**Collingwood, Chris** — Singer (Fountains of Wayne), Songwriter
Big Hassle, 157 Chambers St, #1200, New York NY 10007, USA

**Collins, Anthony (Tony)** — Football Player
2712 Gulfstream Dr, Miramar FL 33023, USA

**Collins, Arthur W (Bud), Jr** — Sportscaster
822 Boylston St, #203, Chestnut Hill MA 02467, USA

**Collins, Bernard** — Singer (Abyssinians)
Fast Lane International, 4856 Haygood Road, #200, Virginia Beach VA 23455, USA

**Collins, Candace L** — Model
Playboy Promotions, 9346 Civic Center Dr, #200, Beverly Hills CA 90210 USA

**Collins, Carla** — Comedienne, Actress
Agency Group Ltd, 142 W 57th St, #600, New York NY 10019 USA

**Collins, Clifton G, Jr** — Actor
Industry Entertainment, 955 Carillo Dr, #300, Los Angeles CA 90048 USA

**Collins, David J** — Inventor (Bar Code)
A2B Tracking Solutions, 207 Highpoint Ave, Portsmouth RI 02871, USA

**Collins, David S (Dave)** — Baseball Player
206 N East St, #15, Mason OH 45040, USA

**Collins, Dean** — Actor
A P A Talent & Literary Agency, 405 S Beverly Dr, #300, Beverly Hills CA 90212 USA

**Collins, Eileen M** — Astronaut
2024 Pebble Beach Dr, League City TX 77573, USA

**Collins, Francis S** — Geneticist
National Institutes of Health, 9000 Rockville Pike, Bethesda MD 20892, USA

**Collins, Gary** — Ice Hockey Player
1908-1320 Islington Ave, Etobicoke M9A 5C6, Canada

**Collins, Gary J** — Football Player
221 Lamp Post Lane, Hershey PA 17033, USA

**Collins, George F, III** — Football Player
2043 Northside Road, Perry GA 31069, USA

**Collins, Heidi** — Commentator
CNN-TV, News Dept, 820 1st St NE, #1000, Washington DC 20002 USA

**Collins, J Maxwell S (Max), III** — Singer, Bassist (Eve 6)
Agency Group Ltd, 1880 Century Park E, #711, Los Angeles CA 90067 USA

**Collins, Jackie** — Writer
10624 Wellworth Ave, Los Angeles CA 90024, USA

**Collins, James B (Jim)** — Football Player
2140 E Oceanfront, Newport Beach CA 92661, USA

**Collins, Jarron T** — Basketball Player
11173 Cashmere St, Los Angeles CA 90049, USA

**Collins, Jason P** — Basketball Player
13120 Constable Ave, Granada Hills CA 91344, USA

**Collins, Jeff** — Rodeo Rider
1429 Limestone Road, Redfield KS 66769, USA

**Collins, Jerry** — Actor, Writer, Producer
United Talent Agency, U T A Plaza, 9336 Civic Center Dr, Beverly Hills CA 90210 USA

**Collins, Jessica** — Actress
Innovative Artists, 1505 10th St, Santa Monica CA 90401 USA

**Collins, Jim** — Writer, Management Consultant
Harper Business Books, 10 E 53rd St, Cellar 1, New York NY 10022, USA

**Collins, Jo** — Model, Actress
Playboy Promotions, 9346 Civic Center Dr, #200, Beverly Hills CA 90210 USA

**Collins, Joan** — Actress
Peter Charlesworth, 67 Holland Park Mews, London W11 3SS, England

**Collins, Joely** — Actress
Kirk Talent Agencies, 196 W 3rd Ave, #102, Vancouver BC V5Y 1E9, Canada

**Collins, John** — Bassist (Powderfinger)
Secret Service, PO Box 401, Fortitude Valley QLD 4006, Australia

**Collins, John W** — Businessman
Clorox Co, 1221 Broadway, Oakland CA 94612, USA

**Collins, Judy** — Singer, Songwriter
American Program Bureau, 313 Washington St, #225, Newton MA 02458, USA

**Collins, K C** — Actor
A Mgmt, 12001 Ventura Place, #340, Studio City CA 91604 USA

**Collins, Kate** — Actress
1410 York Ave, #4D, New York NY 10021, USA

**Collins, Kayla** — Model
Playboy Promotions, 9346 Civic Center Dr, #200, Beverly Hills CA 90210 USA

**Collins, Kerry M** — Football Player
1090 Stockett Dr, Nashville TN 37221, USA

**Collins, Kevin M** — Baseball Player
9121 Point Charity Dr, Pigeon MI 48755, USA

**Collins, Lauren** — Actress
A M I Artist Management, 464 King St E, Toronto ON M5A 1L7, Canada

**Collins, Lily J** — Actress, Model
Creative Artists Agency, 2000 Ave of Stars, #100, Los Angeles CA 90067 USA

**Collins, Mark A** — Football Player
2568 Baseline St, #155, Highland CA 92346, USA

**Collins, Martha Layne** — Governor, KY; Educator
921 Taborlake Court, Lexington KY 40502, USA

**Collins, Marva** — Educator
1507 E 53rd St, Chicago IL 60615, USA

**Collins, Michael** — Writer
Viking Penguin Books, 375 Hudson St, Basement 1, New York NY 10014 USA

**Collins, Michael** — Conductor, Concert Clarinetist
Hazard Chase, 72 Charlotte St, London W1T 4QQ, England

**Collins, Michael** — Astronaut, Air Force General
272 Polynesia Court, Marco Island FL 34145, USA

**Collins, Misha** — Actor
Framework Entertainment, 9057 Nemo St, #C, West Hollywood CA 90069 USA

**Collins, Mo** — Actress, Comedienne
C E S D, 10635 Santa Monica Blvd, #130, Los Angeles CA 90025 USA

**Collins, Nancy A** — Writer
Harper Collins Publishers, 10 E 53rd St, Cellar 1, New York NY 10022 USA

**Collins, P Douglas (Doug)** — Basketball Player, Coach, Sportscaster
10040 E Happy Valley Road, #617, Scottsdale AZ 85255, USA

**Collins, Patrick** — Actor
Tisherman Agency, 6767 Forest Lawn Dr, #101, Los Angeles CA 90068 USA

**Collins, Pauline** — Actress
Independent Talent Group, 40 Whitfield St, London W1T 2RH, England

**Collins, Phil** — Singer, Songwriter, Drummer
Alfred House, 23-24 Cromwell Place, #300, London SW7 2LD, England

**Collins, Randall** — Sociologist
University of Pennsylvania, Sociology Dept, Philadelphia PA 19104, USA

**Collins, Shanna** — Actress
A K A Talent, 6310 San Vicente Blvd, #200, Los Angeles CA 90048 USA

**Collins, Shawn** — Football Player
PO Box 711933, San Diego CA 92171, USA

**Collins, Sherron M** — Basketball Player
Charlotte Hornets, 333 E Trade St, #A, Charlotte NC 28202 USA

**Collins, Steve** — Boxer
Rock Solid Productions, PO Box 70642, Houston TX 77270, USA

**Collins, Terry L** — Baseball Manager
40992 Hollydale, Novi MI 48375, USA

**Collins, Thomas C Cardinal** — Religious Leader
Archdiocese of Toronto, Chancery Office, 1155 Yonge St, Toronto ON M4T 1W2, Canada

**Collins, Thomas H** — Coast Guard Admiral
E I D Passport, 5800 NW Pinefarm Place, Hillsboro OR 97124, USA

**Collins, Todd S** — Football Player
26 Cambridge Circle, Victor NY 14564, USA

**Collins, William (Billy)** — Writer
RR 202, Somers NY 10589, USA

**Collins, William E (Bill)** — Ice Hockey Player
5000 Town Center, #505, Southfield MI 48075, USA

**Collins, William E (Bootsy)** — Singer, Bassist
Agency Group Ltd, 1880 Century Park E, #711, Los Angeles CA 90067 USA

**Collinson, Madeleine** — Model, Actress
Playboy Promotions, 9346 Civic Center Dr, #200, Beverly Hills CA 90210 USA

**Collinson, Mary** — Model, Actress
Playboy Promotions, 9346 Civic Center Dr, #200, Beverly Hills CA 90210 USA

**Collinsworth, A Cris** — Football Player, Sportscaster
31 Crow Hill Road, Fort Thomas KY 41075, USA

**Collison, Darren M** — Basketball Player
Sacramento Kings, Arco Arena, 1 Sports Parkway, Sacramento CA 95834 USA

**Collison, Frank** — Actor
Amsel Eisenstadt Frazier, 5055 Wilshire Blvd, #865, Los Angeles CA 90036 USA

**Collison, Nicholas J (Nick)** — Basketball Player
16 Comstock St, Seattle WA 98109, USA

**Collister, Christine** — Singer
Running Media, 14 Victoria Road, Douglas, Isle of Man IM2 4ER, England

**Collman, James P** — Chemist
794 Tolman Dr, Stanford CA 94305, USA

**Collomb, Bertrand P** — Businessman
4 Rue de Lota, 75116 Paris, France

**Collyer, Laurie** — Director, Writer, Actress
Gersh Agency, 9465 Wilshire Blvd, #600, Beverly Hills CA 90212 USA

**Colman, Booth** — Actor
2160 Century Park E, #603, Los Angeles CA 90067, USA

**Colman, Oliva** — Actress
United Agents, 12-26 Lexington St, London W1F 0LE, England

**Colman, Paul** — Singer, Guitarist, Pianist, Composer
W M E Entertainment, 9601 Wilshire Blvd, #300, Beverly Hills CA 90210 USA

**Colman, Philip E, Jr** — WW II, Korean War Air Force Hero
630 Cambridge Road, Augusta GA 30909, USA

**Colman, Wayne C** — Football Player
604 N Somerset Ave, Ventnor NJ 08406, USA

**Colmes, Alan** — Commentator
Fox-TV, News Dept, 1211 Ave of Americas, New York NY 10036, USA

**Colo, Donald R (Don)** — Football Player
7355 E Claremont St, Scottsdale AZ 85250, USA

**Cologna, Dario** — Cross Country Skier
Tabla Nov, 7532 Tschierv, Switzerland

**Coloma, Marcus** — Actor
Don Buchwald Talent Agency, 6500 Wilshire Blvd, #2200, Los Angeles CA 90048 USA

**Colombo, Marc E** — Football Player
7219 Marigold Dr, Irving TX 75063, USA

**Colomby, Scott** — Actor
Grant Savic Kopaloff & Associates, 6399 Wilshire Blvd, #415, Los Angeles CA 90048 90048, USA

**Colon, Bartolo** — Baseball Player
14 Federal St, #1, Passaic NJ 07055, USA

**Colon, Willie A** — Singer, Trombonist, Composer
Universal Attractions, 135 W 26th St, #1200, New York NY 10001 USA

**Colosimo, Vince** — Actor
Robyn Gardiner Mgmt, 397 Riley St, Surry Hills NSW 2010, Australia

**Colquitt, Dustin F** — Football Player
1905 Pitts Field Lane, Knoxville TN 37922, USA

**Colquitt, J Craig** — Football Player
1905 Pitts Field Lane, Knoxville TN 37922, USA

**Colson, Elizabeth F** — Anthropologist
University of California, Anthropology Dept, Berkeley CA 94720, USA

**Colston, Marques** — Football Player
New Orleans Saints, 5800 Airline Highway, Metairie LA 70003 USA

**Colter, Jessie** — Singer
Bobby Roberts, PO Box 1547, Goodlettsville TN 37070, USA

**Colter, Steve** — Basketball Player
802 E Mountain Sage Dr, Phoenix AZ 85048, USA
**Colton, Graham** — Singer, Songwriter
Back Bay Mgmt, 397 Little Neck Road, Virginia Beach VA 23452, USA
**Coltrane, Chi** — Singer, Pianist, Songwriter
5955 Tuxedo Terrace, Los Angeles CA 90068, USA
**Coltrane, Ravi** — Jazz Saxophonist
Ted Kurland, 173 Brighton Ave, Boston MA 02134 USA
**Coltrane, Robbie** — Actor, Comedian
C D A, 167-169 Kensington High St, London W8 6SH, England
**Coluccio, Robert P (Bob)** — Baseball Player
369 Flower St, Costa Mesa CA 92627, USA
**Columbo, Marc E** — Football Player
Miami Dolphins, 7500 SW 30th St, Davie FL 33314 USA
**Columbu, Franco** — Body Builder
2265 Westwood Blvd, #A, Los Angeles CA 90064, USA
**Columbus, Christopher J (Chris)** — Director, Writer
1492 Pictures, 4000 Warner Blvd, Building 3, Burbank CA 91522, USA
**Colvin, James R (Jim)** — Football Player
1310 Rancho Vista Dr, McKinney TX 75070, USA
**Colvin, John O** — Judge
US Tax Court, 400 2nd St NW, Washington DC 20217, USA
**Colvin, Roosevelt, III** — Football Player
9340 Sargent Road, Indianapolis IN 46256, USA
**Colvin, Shawn** — Singer, Songwriter
Vector Mgmt, PO Box 120479, Nashville TN 37212 USA
**Colvin, Shelly** — Singer, Songwriter
Parallel Entertainment, 209 10th Ave S, #506, Nashville TN 37203, USA
**Colwell, John A** — Association Executive, Physician
American Diabetes Assn, 1701 N Beauregard St, #100, Alexandria VA 22311, USA
**Colwell, Rita R** — Microbiologist, Foundation Executive
5010 River Hill Road, Bethesda MD 20816, USA
**Colwill, Les** — Ice Hockey Player
714 20th St, North Lethbridge AB T1H 3N6, Canada
**Comaneci, Nadia** — Gymnast
4421 Hidden Hill Road, Norman OK 73072, USA
**Comart, Jean-Paul** — Actor
Artmedia, 20 Ave Rapp, 75007 Paris, France
**Comastri, Angelo Cardinal** — Religious Leader
Fabric of Saint Peter, Basilica di San Pietro, 00120 Vatican City
**Combas, Robert** — Artist
Galleries D'Arte Elysees, 26 Ave des Champs-Elysees, 75008 Paris, France
**Combeau, Muriel** — Actress
Voyez Mon Agent, 20 Ave Rapp, 75007 Paris, France
**Combes, Willard W** — Editorial Cartoonist
1266 Oakridge Dr, Cleveland OH 44121, USA
**Combs, David** — Actor
Special Artists Agency, 9200 Sunset Blvd, #410, West Hollywood CA 90069 USA
**Combs, Glenn** — Basketball Player
3627 Dogwood Lane SW, Roanoke VA 24015, USA
**Combs, Holly Marie** — Actress
Gersh Agency, 9465 Wilshire Blvd, #600, Beverly Hills CA 90212 USA
**Combs, Jeffrey** — Actor
Bleu, 5225 Wilshire Blvd, #401, Los Angeles CA 90036, USA
**Combs, Rodney** — Auto Racing Driver
American Diecast, 16173 Edgemont Dr, Fort Myers FL 33908, USA
**Combs, Sean, (Puff Daddy, P Diddy)** — Rap Artist, Actor
Creative Artists Agency, 2000 Ave of Stars, #100, Los Angeles CA 90067 USA
**Comeau, Andy** — Actor
TalentWorks, 3500 W Olive Ave, #1400, Burbank CA 91505 USA
**Comeau, Ray** — Ice Hockey Player
4 Rue de Cernay, Lorraine QC J6Z 2Z1, Canada
**Comeaux, Darren** — Football Player
6313 Kristie Lane, Brusly LA 70719, USA
**Comegys, Dallas A** — Basketball Player
4330 Wayne Ave, Philadelphia PA 19140, USA
**Comella, Greg** — Football Player
90 Fairbanks Ave, Wellesley Hills MA 02481, USA
**Comer, H Wayne** — Baseball Player
145 Marcus St, Shenandoah VA 22849, USA
**Comer, Steven M (Steve)** — Baseball Player
525 Lake Dr, #377, Chanhassen MN 55317, USA
**Comess, Aaron** — Musician (Spin Doctors)
D A S Communications, 83 Riverside Dr, New York NY 10024 USA
**Comi, Paul** — Actor
2395 Ridgeway Road, San Marino CA 91108, USA
**Commander Cody** — Musician
Jacobson & Colfin, 60 Madison Ave, #1026, New York NY 10010, USA
**Commissiong, Janelle** — Beauty Queen
Bowen Marine, Western Main Road, Chaguaramas, Trinidad
**Commodore, Michael (Mike)** — Ice Hockey Player
12017 Fern Dr, Detroit Lakes MN 56501, USA
**Common** — Rap Artist, Actor
42 West, 220 W 42nd St, #1200, New York NY 10036 USA
**Compagnon, Antoine M T** — Educator, Writer
875 W End Ave, #15D, New York NY 10025, USA
**Compagnoni, Deborah** — Alpine Skier
Benetton Group SpA, Via Minelli, 31050 Ponzano Treviso, Italy
**Compte, Maurice** — Actor
Don Buchwald Talent Agency, 6500 Wilshire Blvd, #2200, Los Angeles CA 90048 USA
**Compton, Ann Woodruff** — Commentator
ABC-TV, News Dept, 3361 75th Ave, #X, Hyattsville MD 20785, USA
**Compton, Richard** — Actor
A P A Talent & Literary Agency, 405 S Beverly Dr, #300, Beverly Hills CA 90212 USA
**Compton, Richard L (Dick)** — Football Player
3408 S Briarcliff Court, Irving TX 75062, USA

**Comrie, Michael W (Mike)**
10800 Wilshire Blvd, #1703, Los Angeles CA 90024, USA — Ice Hockey Player

**Comstock, Harold**
2809 Aberdeen Lane, El Dorado Hills CA 95762, USA — Air Force Hero

**Comstock, Keith M**
9615 E Desert Trail, Scottsdale AZ 85260, USA — Baseball Player

**Comte, Claudia**
BolteLang, Limmatstr 214, 8005 Zurich, Switzerland — Artist, Sculptor

**Comte, Michel**
Guy Hepner Gallery, 300 N Robertson Blvd, West Hollywood CA 90048, USA — Photographer

**Cona, Louis**
New Yorker, Publisher's Office, 4 Times Square, New York NY 10036, USA — Publisher

**Conacher, Brian**
202-500 Avenue Road, Toronto ON M4V 2J6, Canada — Ice Hockey Player

**Conacher, Jim**
422-980 Lynn Valley Road, West Vancouver BC V7J 3V7, Canada — Ice Hockey Player

**Conacher, Pat**
18371 W Sweet Acacia Dr, Goodyear AZ 85338, USA — Ice Hockey Player

**Conacher, Pete**
3 Conifer Dr, Etobicoke ON M9C 1X3, Canada — Ice Hockey Player

**Conant, Kenneth J**
3 Carlton Village, #T105, Bedford MA 01730, USA — Archaeologist

**Conatsor, Clinton A (Connie)**
26701 Quail Creek, #191, Laguna Hills CA 92656, USA — Baseball Player

**Conaty, William B (Billy), Jr**
203 Country Club Dr, Moorestown NJ 08057, USA — Football Player

**Conaway, Cristi**
1759 Old Ranch Road, Los Angeles CA 90049, USA — Actress

**Conaway, John B**
Spectrum Group, 11 Canal Center Plaza, #103, Alexandria VA 22314, USA — Air Force General

**Conaway, Ronald C**
Stowers Medical Research Institute, 1000 E 50th St, Kansas City MO 64110, USA — Geneticist

**Concepcion Benitez, David I (Davey)**
Urb el Castano Botalon 5D, Maracay 5, Venezuela — Baseball Player

**Concepcion Cardona, Onix C**
1486 Steeplechase Lane, Deltona FL 32725, USA — Baseball Player

**Conde, Alpha**
President's Office, Palais Presidentiel, Cite des Nations, Conakry, Guinea — President, Guinea

**Conde, Ninel H**
Apodaca Promotions, 717 E Tidwell Road, Houston TX 77022, USA — Actress, Singer

**Condit, Gary A**
2509 Acorn Lane, Ceres CA 95307, USA — Representative, CA

**Condo, George**
108 E 78th St, New York NY 10075, USA — Artist

**Condon of Langton Green, Paul L**
I C C, Clock Tower, Lord's Cricket Ground, London NW8 8QN, England — Law Enforcement Official

**Condon, Kerry**
I C M Partners, 10250 Constellation Blvd, #900, Los Angeles CA 90067 USA — Actress

**Condon, Thomas J (Tom)**
99 Oakleigh Lane, Saint Louis MO 63124, USA — Football Player

**Condon, William (Bill)**
Anonymous Content, 3532 Hayden Ave, Culver City CA 90232 USA — Director, Writer

**Condon, Zach**
Ba Da Bing Records, 181 Clermont Ave, #403, Brooklyn NY 11205, USA — Singer (Beirut), Songwriter

**Condren, Glen P**
8557 N 175th East Ave, Owasso OK 74055, USA — Football Player

**Condrey, Clayton L (Clay)**
412 N 8th St, Navasota TX 77868, USA — Baseball Player

**Cone Vanderbush, Carin**
47 Rose Dr, Highland Falls NY 10928, USA — Swimmer

**Cone, David B**
219 Dolphin Cove Quay, Stamford CT 6902, USA — Baseball Player

**Cone, Fred**
111 Elizabeth Lane, Pickens SC 29671, USA — Football Player

**Confino, Edmond**
676 N Saint Clair St, #1845, Chicago IL 60611, USA — Obstetrician, Gynecologist

**Conforti, Gino**
Orange Grove Group, 12178 Ventura Blvd, #205, Studio City CA 91604 USA — Actor

**Congdon, Jeffrey D (Jeff)**
505 Highway View Court, Mesquite NV 89027, USA — Basketball Player

**Conigliaro, William M (Billy)**
501 Cabot St, #2, Beverly MA 01915, USA — Baseball Player

**Conine, Jeffrey G (Jeff)**
3166 Iverness, Weston FL 33332, USA — Baseball Player

**Conkey, Margaret**
University of California, Archaeological Research Facility, Berkeley CA 94720, USA — Archaeologist

**Conklin, Harold C**
200 Leeder Hill Dr, #607, Hamden CT 06517, USA — Anthropologist

**Conklin, Ty**
PO Box 472, New Castle NH 03854, USA — Ice Hockey Player

**Conlan, Shane P**
521 East Dr, Sewickley PA 15143, USA — Football Player

**Conlee, Jenny**
Big Hassle, 44 Wall St, #2200, New York NY 10005, USA — Organist, Accordianist (Decemberists)

**Conlee, John**
John Conlee Enterprises, 38 Music Square E, #117, Nashville TN 37203, USA — Singer

**Conley, Clare D**
Hemlock Farms, Hawley PA 18428, USA — Editor

**Conley, D Eugene (Gene)**
400 Foxboro Blvd, #3102, Foxboro MA 02035, USA — Baseball, Basketball Player

**Conley, Earl Thomas**
657 Baker Road, Smyrna TN 37167, USA — Singer, Songwriter

**Conley, Mike, Jr**
3496 Windgarden Cove, Memphis TN 38125, USA — Basketball Player

**Conley, Wayne**
Paradigm Agency, 360 Park Ave S, #1600, New York NY 10010 USA — Writer

# C

**Conlin, Edward J (Ed)**  Basketball Player
153 N Mountain Ave, Montclair NJ 07042, USA
**Conlin, Michaela**  Actress
Evolution Entertainment, 901 N Highland Ave, Los Angeles CA 90038 USA
**Conlon, Edward W**  Writer
Random House, 1745 Broadway, #1800, New York NY 10019 USA
**Conlon, James J**  Conductor
Shuman Assoc, 120 W 58th St, #8D, New York NY 10019, USA
**Conlon, Martin M (Marty)**  Basketball Player
204 Head of Pond Road, Water Mill NY 11976, USA
**Conn, Didi**  Actress, Singer
C E S D, 10635 Santa Monica Blvd, #130, Los Angeles CA 90025 USA
**Conn, Richard R (Dick)**  Football Player
144 Sugarmill Lane, Moore SC 29369, USA
**Conn, Shelley**  Actress
United Agents, 12-26 Lexington St, London W1F 0LE, England
**Conneff, Kevin**  Singer, Percussionist (Chieftains)
Macklam/Feldman Mgmt, 1505 W 2nd Ave, #200, Vancouver BC V6H 3Y4, Canada
**Connell, Albert G A**  Football Player
3522 Ruth St, Houston TX 77004, USA
**Connell, Desmond Cardinal**  Religious Leader
Archbishop's House, Drumcondra, Dublin 9, Ireland
**Connelly, Jennifer**  Actress
Creative Artists Agency, 2000 Ave of Stars, #100, Los Angeles CA 90067 USA
**Connelly, Michael**  Writer
Little Brown, 3 Center Plaza, #100, Boston MA 02108 USA
**Connelly, Wayne F**  Ice Hockey Player
RR 2 Site 2, Box 61, Swastika ON P0K 1T0, Canada
**Conner, Bart**  Gymnast
4421 Hidden Hill Road, Norman OK 73072, USA
**Conner, Chris**  Actor
A K A Talent, 6310 San Vicente Blvd, #200, Los Angeles CA 90048 USA
**Conner, Clyde R**  Football Player
510 Valencia Dr, Los Altos Hills CA 94022, USA
**Conner, Darion**  Football Player
9553 Prairie Point Road, Macon MS 39341, USA
**Conner, Dennis W**  Yachtsman
881 Golden Park Ave, San Diego CA 92106, USA
**Conner, Lester A**  Basketball Player
10392 Erin Place, Lone Tree CO 80124, USA
**Conner, Lois**  Photographer
36 Gramercy Park E, #4E, New York NY 10003, USA
**Conners, Daniel J (Dan)**  Football Player
1032 Chorro St, San Luis Obispo CA 93401, USA
**Conners, Sheralee**  Model
Playboy Promotions, 9346 Civic Center Dr, #200, Beverly Hills CA 90210 USA
**Connery, Jason**  Actor
C A M, 111 Shoreditch High St, #400, London E1 6JN, England
**Connery, Sean**  Actor
Lyford Cay, PO Box N7776, Nassau, Bahamas
**Connery, Vincent L**  Labor Leader
National Treasury Employees Union, 1730 K St NW, Washington DC 20006, USA
**Connes, Alain**  Mathematician
Leon Motchane l'H E S, 35 Route Chartres, 91440 Bures-sur-Yvette, France
**Connick, Harry, Jr**  Pianist, Singer, Actor
Creative Artists Agency, 2000 Ave of Stars, #100, Los Angeles CA 90067 USA
**Conniff, Cal**  Skier
157 Pleasantview Ave, Longmeadow MA 01106, USA
**Connolly, Billy**  Actor
Julian Belfrage Assoc, 9 Argyll St, #300, London W1F 7TG, England
**Connolly, John**  Writer
Simon & Schuster, 1230 Ave of Americas, Concourse 1, New York NY 10020 USA
**Connolly, Kevin**  Actor
Creative Artists Agency, 2000 Ave of Stars, #100, Los Angeles CA 90067 USA
**Connolly, Kristen**  Actress
Untitled Entertainment, 350 S Beverly Dr, #200, Beverly Hills CA 90212 USA
**Connolly, Nathan**  Singer, Guitarist (Snow Patrol)
Big Life Mgmt, 67-69 Charlton St, London NW1 1HY, England
**Connolly, Olga Fikotova**  Track Athlete
931 W 19th St, #35, Costa Mesa CA 92627, USA
**Connolly, Theodore W (Ted)**  Football Player
1805 N Carson St, #86, Carson City NV 89701, USA
**Connolly, Timothy L (Tim)**  Ice Hockey Player
1266 Greenfield Lane, Skaneateles NY 13152, USA
**Connolly, Tom**  Actor
Innovative Artists, 1505 10th St, Santa Monica CA 90401 USA
**Connor, Cam**  Ice Hockey Player
1331 Leeward Way, Qualicum Beach BC V9K 2M1, Canada
**Connor, Daniel M (Dan)**  Football Player
1032 Chorro St, San Luis Obispo CA 93401, USA
**Connor, Kate**  Actress
Jay Schwartz Assoc, 3151 Cahuenga Blvd, W, #220, Los Angeles CA 90068, USA
**Connor, Linda S**  Photographer
San Francisco Art Institute, Photography Dept, 800 Chestnut St, San Francisco CA 94133, USA
**Connor, Paolo**  Actor
Abrams Artists, 275 7th Ave, #2600, New York NY 10001 USA
**Connor, Sarah**  Singer, Songwriter
Live Legend Entertainment, Kurfurstendamm 186, 10707 Berlin, Germany
**Connors, Carol**  Songwriter
1709 Ferrari Dr, Beverly Hills CA 90210, USA
**Connors, James S (Jimmy)**  Tennis Player
1962 E Valley Road, Santa Barbara CA 93108, USA
**Connors, Mike**  Actor
4810 Louise Ave, Encino CA 91316, USA
**Connors, Norman**  Jazz Drummer
Universal Attractions, 135 W 26th St, #1200, New York NY 10001 USA

Conlin - Connors

**Connors, William A (Bill)**
Michael Bloom Media Relations, PO Box 41380, Los Angeles CA 90041, USA — Jazz Guitarist

**Conover, K Scott**
28 Windsor Terrace, #B, Freehold NJ 07728, USA — Football Player

**Conover, Lloyd H**
1095 Pinellas Point Dr S, #404, Saint Petersburg FL 33705, USA — Inventor (Tetracycline)

**Conquest, G Robert A**
52 Peter Coutts Circle, Stanford CA 94305, USA — Historian

**Conrad, Brooks L**
3672 E Robin Lane, Gilbert AZ 85296, USA — Baseball Player

**Conrad, David**
Gersh Agency, 9465 Wilshire Blvd, #600, Beverly Hills CA 90212 USA — Actor

**Conrad, Fred**
New York Times, Editorial Dept, 229 W 43rd St, New York NY 10036, USA — Photographer

**Conrad, James A**
Source One Mortgage, 100 Galleria Officentre, #300, Southfield MI 48034, USA — Financier

**Conrad, Jimmy**
Sporting Kansas City, 210 W 19th Terrace, #200, Kansas City MO 64108 USA — Soccer Player

**Conrad, Lauren K**
United Talent Agency, U T A Plaza, 9336 Civic Center Dr, Beverly Hills CA 90210 USA — Actress, Model

**Conrad, Robert**
6320 Via Cataldo St, Malibu CA 90265, USA — Actor

**Conrad, Robert J (Bobby Joe)**
148 County Road 3270, Clifton TX 76634, USA — Football Player

**Conrad, Shane**
Sutton-Barth Vennari, 5900 Wilshire Blvd, #700, Los Angeles CA 90036 USA — Actor

**Conrad, Steve**
2640 N Wayne Ave, Chicago IL 60614, USA — Director, Writer

**Conradt, Jody**
9614 Leaning Rock Circle, Austin TX 78730, USA — Basketball Coach

**Conran, Jasper A T**
1-7 Rostrevor Mews, Fulham, London SW6 5AZ, England — Fashion Designer

**Conran, Kerry**
Paradigm Agency, 360 N Crescent Dr, North Building, Beverly Hills CA 90210 USA — Director, Writer

**Conran, Philip J**
4706 Calle Reina, Santa Barbara CA 93110, USA — Vietnam War Air Force Hero

**Conran, Terence O**
22 Shad Thames, London SE1 2YU, England — Interior Designer

**Conroy, Craig**
PO Box 549, Henderson Harbor NY 13651, USA — Ice Hockey Player

**Conroy, D Patrick (Pat)**
247 Brighton Road NE, Atlanta GA 30309, USA — Writer

**Conroy, Frances**
Paradigm Agency, 360 N Crescent Dr, North Building, Beverly Hills CA 90210 USA — Actress

**Conroy, Kevin**
Imperium 7 Talent, 5455 Wilshire Blvd, #1706, Los Angeles CA 90036, USA — Actor

**Conroy, Patricia**
Live Tour Artists, 1451 White Oaks Blvd, Oakville ON L6H 4R9, Canada — Singer, Songwriter

**Conroy, Timothy J (Tim)**
109 Moonlight Dr, Monroeville PA 15146, USA — Baseball Player

**Considine, Paddy**
Creative Artists Agency, 2000 Ave of Stars, #100, Los Angeles CA 90067 USA — Actor, Director

**Considine, Tim**
3708 Mountain View Ave, Los Angeles CA 90066, USA — Actor, Writer, Director

**Constantine II**
4 Linnell Dr, Hampstead Way, London NW11 7LN, England — King, Greece

**Constantine, Kevin L**
5928 Jenny Lind Court, San Jose CA 95120, USA — Ice Hockey Coach

**Constantine, Michael**
6861 Colbath Ave, Van Nuys CA 91405, USA — Actor

**Constantine, Susannah**
Paradigm Agency, 360 N Crescent Dr, North Building, Beverly Hills CA 90210 USA — Actress

**Constantinescu, Roxana**
Harrison/Parrott, 5-6 Albion Court, London W6 0QT, England — Opera Singer

**Consuelos, Mark**
Milojo Productions, 270 Lafayette St, #702, New York NY 10012, USA — Actor, Model

**Contador Velasco, Alberto**
Team Saxo Bank, Firskowej 38, 2800 KGS Lynby, Denmark — Cyclist

**Conte, Paolo**
Partisan Arts, PO Box 5085, Larkspur CA 94977, USA — Singer, Pianist, Composer

**Conteh, John**
8 Cedar Dr, Hatch End, Pinner, Middlesex HA5 4DE, England — Boxer

**Conti, Bill**
117 Fremont Place W, Los Angeles CA 90005, USA — Composer

**Conti, Jason**
740 N April Dr, Chandler AZ 85226, USA — Baseball Player

**Conti, Tom**
Gersh Agency, 9465 Wilshire Blvd, #600, Beverly Hills CA 90212 USA — Actor

**Contino, Dick**
3355 Nahatan Way, Las Vegas NV 89169, USA — Singer, Accordianist

**Contner, James A**
3020 Kensington Ave, Richmond VA 23221, USA — Cinematographer

**Contreras Camejo, Jose A**
1001 Brickell Bay Dr, #1710, Miami FL 33131, USA — Baseball Player

**Contreras, Narciso**
Associated Press, Editorial Dept, 450 W 33rd St, #1500, New York NY 10001 USA — Photojournalist

**Contz, William (Bill)**
106 Grace Dr, Cranberry Township PA 16066, USA — Football Player

**Converse, Frank**
I C M Partners, 10250 Constellation Blvd, #900, Los Angeles CA 90067 USA — Actor

**Converse, James D (Jim)**
11865 Cobble Brook Dr, Rancho Cordova CA 95742, USA — Baseball Player

**Converse-Roberts, William**
Don Buchwald Talent Agency, 6500 Wilshire Blvd, #2200, Los Angeles CA 90048 USA — Actor

**Convertino, John**
Billons Corp, 3522 W Armitage Ave, Chicago IL 60647 USA — Drummer, Percussionist (Calexico)

Connors - Convertino

# C

**Convertino, Michael** — Composer
Soundtrack Music Assoc, 1460 4th St, #308, Santa Monica CA 90401 USA

**Conway Mitchell, Susan** — Actress
70 Highbourne Road, Toronto ON M5R 3H8, Canada

**Conway, Billy** — Drummer (Morphine)
Spivak Entertainment, 11845 W Olympic Blvd, Los Angeles CA 90064, USA

**Conway, Brett A** — Football Player
630 Virginia Ave NE, Atlanta GA 30306, USA

**Conway, Craig** — Actor
Artists Partnership, 101 Finsbury Pavement, London EC2A 1RS, England

**Conway, Curtis L** — Football Player
446 E Phelps St, Gilbert AZ 85295, USA

**Conway, Gary** — Actor
11240 Chimney Rock Road, Paso Robles CA 93446, USA

**Conway, James L** — Director
Kaplan-Stahler Agency, 8383 Wilshire Blvd, #923, Beverly Hills CA 90211 USA

**Conway, James T** — Marine Corps General
8164 Ambach Way, Hypoluxo FL 33462, USA

**Conway, Jill K** — Educator, Historian
65 Commonwealth Ave, #8B, Boston MA 02116, USA

**Conway, Joe** — Writer
Gersh Agency, 9465 Wilshire Blvd, #600, Beverly Hills CA 90212 USA

**Conway, John Horton** — Mathematician
120 Prospect Ave, #1A, Princeton NJ 08540, USA

**Conway, Karla (Sachi)** — Model, Artist
PO Box 249, Honaunau HI 96726, USA

**Conway, Kevin** — Actor
Innovative Artists, 1505 10th St, Santa Monica CA 90401 USA

**Conway, Robert T, Jr** — Navy Admiral
Commander, Installations Command, 2713 Mitscher Road SW, Anacostia Annex DC 20373, USA

**Conway, Tim** — Actor, Comedian
Innovative Artists, 1505 10th St, Santa Monica CA 90401 USA

**Conwell, Angell** — Actress
Media Artists Group, 8222 Melrose Ave, #203, Los Angeles CA 90048 USA

**Conwell, Ernest H (Ernie)** — Football Player
5301 McGavock Road, Brentwood TN 37027, USA

**Conwell, Tommy** — Guitarist
Brothers Management Assoc, 141 Dunbar Ave, Fords NJ 08863 USA

**Coo Coo Cal** — Rap Artist
Celebrity Talent Agency, 111 E 14th St, #249, New York NY 10003, USA

**Cooder, Ry** — Singer, Guitarist, Composer
326 Entrada Dr, Santa Monica CA 90402, USA

**Coody, B Charles** — Golfer
1555 Oldham Lane, Abilene TX 79602, USA

**Coogan, Keith** — Actor
Elev8, 489 S Robertson Blvd, #206, Beverly Hills CA 90211, USA

**Coogan, Steve** — Actor, Comedian, Writer
Independent Talent Group, 40 Whitfield St, London W1T 2RH, England

**Coogler, Ryan** — Director
W M E Entertainment, 9601 Wilshire Blvd, #300, Beverly Hills CA 90210 USA

**Cook, Aaron L** — Baseball Player
6113 Liberty Fairfield Road, Liberty Township OH 45011, USA

**Cook, Andrea Joy (A J)** — Actress
Paradigm Agency, 360 N Crescent Dr, North Building, Beverly Hills CA 90210 USA

**Cook, Anthony A** — Football Player
PO Box 961404, Riverdale GA 30296, USA

**Cook, Barbara** — Singer, Actress
Jeff Berger Mgmt, 301 W 53rd St, #10J, New York NY 10019, USA

**Cook, Brian J** — Basketball Player
24 Malaga Place E, Manhattan Beach CA 90266, USA

**Cook, Carole** — Actress, Comedienne
8829 Ashcroft Ave, West Hollywood CA 90048, USA

**Cook, Chris** — Singer, Guitarist, Songwriter
214 Ferstl Ave, #1, Belmont NC 28012, USA

**Cook, Claire** — Writer
Voice/Hyperion Books, 77 W 66th St, #1100, New York NY 10023, USA

**Cook, Daequan** — Basketball Player
Houston Rockets, 1730 Jefferson St, Houston TX 77003 USA

**Cook, Dane J** — Actor, Comedian
United Talent Agency, U T A Plaza, 9336 Civic Center Dr, Beverly Hills CA 90210 USA

**Cook, Darwin L** — Basketball Player
1840 W Avenue J12, #103, Lancaster CA 93534, USA

**Cook, David R** — Singer, Guitarist, Songwriter
19 Entertainment, 8560 W Sunset Blvd, #900, Los Angeles CA 90069 USA

**Cook, Dennis B** — Baseball Player
3413 Serene Hills Court, Austin TX 78738, USA

**Cook, Doris** — Baseball Player
1059 Airport Road, Muskegon MI 49441, USA

**Cook, Elizabeth** — Singer
Thirty Tigers Mgmt, 1604 8th Ave S, #200, Nashville TN 37203, USA

**Cook, Frederick H (Fred), III** — Football Player
4402 Market St, Pascagoula MS 39567, USA

**Cook, Gareth** — Journalist
Boston Globe, Editorial Dept, 135 William Morrissey Blvd, Dorchester MA 02125 USA

**Cook, Jamie R** — Guitarist (Arctic Monkeys)
Wildlife Entertainment, 21 Heathmans Road, London SW6 4TJ, England

**Cook, Jeffrey A (Jeff)** — Singer, Guitarist (Alabama)
Cook Sound Studio, PO Box 680067, Fort Payne AL 35968, USA

**Cook, Jeffrey J (Jeff)** — Basketball Player
4908 E Doubletree Ranch Road, Paradise Valley AZ 85253, USA

**Cook, Jesse** — Jazz, Latin Guitarist
Paul Mercs Concerts, 3355 W Broadway, #200, Vancouver BC V6R 2B1, Canada

**Cook, John N** — Golfer
8815 Conroy Windermere Road, #40, Orlando FL 32835, USA

**Cook, Kristy Lee** — Singer
Arista/RCA Records, 1400 18th Ave S, Nashville TN 37212, USA

Convertino - Cook

**Cook, Marvin E (Marv)** — Football Player
425 Butternut Lane, Iowa City IA 52246, USA
**Cook, Paul** — Drummer (Sex Pistols)
Solo Agency, 53-55 Fulham High St, #200, London SW6 3JJ, England
**Cook, Paul M** — Businessman
S R I International, 333 Ravenswood Ave, Menlo Park CA 94025, USA
**Cook, Peter F C** — Architect
54 Compayne Gardens, London NW6 3RY, England
**Cook, R Clifford (Cliff)** — Baseball Player
6009 Fantail Dr, Fort Worth TX 76179, USA
**Cook, Rachel Leigh** — Actress
James/Levy Mgmt, 3500 W Olive Ave, #1470, Burbank CA 91505 USA
**Cook, Rebecca** — Director, Actress
G Williams Agency, 525 S 4th St, #365, Philadelphia PA 19147, USA
**Cook, Robert** — Opera Singer
Quavers, 53 Friars Ave, Fiern Barnet, London N2O OXG, England
**Cook, Robin** — Writer
10 Louisburg Square, Boston MA 02108, USA
**Cook, Stanton R** — Publisher
224 Raleigh Road, Kenilworth IL 60043, USA
**Cook, Stephen A** — Computer Scientist, Mathematician
6 Indian Valley Crescent, Toronto M6R 1Y6, Canada
**Cook, Steve** — Bowler
1209 Devonshire Court, Roseville CA 95661, USA
**Cook, Terry** — Auto, Truck Racing Driver
PO Box 86, Mount Mourne NC 28123, USA
**Cook, Thomas A** — Writer
Bantam Books, 1745 Broadway, New York NY 10019 USA
**Cook, Timothy D (Tim)** — Businessman
Apple Computer, 1 Infinite Loop, Cupertino CA 95014, USA
**Cook, Toi F** — Football Player
8430 Winnetka Ave, #20, Winnetka CA 91306, USA
**Cook, Victor Trent** — Singer, Actor
C D Enterprises Mgmt, 7531 Leesburg Pike, #200, Falls Church VA 22043, USA
**Cooke, Amelia** — Actress
John Pierce Agency, 800 S Robertson Blvd, #5, Los Angeles CA 90035, USA
**Cooke, Christian L** — Actor
United Agents, 12-26 Lexington St, London W1F 0LE, England
**Cooke, Christopher (Chris)** — Editor
2157 Ridgeview Ave, Los Angeles CA 90041, USA
**Cooke, David D** — Basketball Player
PO Box 270591, San Diego CA 92198, USA
**Cooke, Edward G (Ed)** — Football Player
2093 Wake Forest St, Virginia Beach VA 23451, USA
**Cooke, Janis** — Journalist
Washington Post, Editorial Dept, 1150 15th St NW, Washington DC 20071, USA
**Cooke, John P** — Rower
290 Old Branchville Road, Ridgefield CT 06877, USA
**Cooke, Josh** — Actor
Gersh Agency, 9465 Wilshire Blvd, #600, Beverly Hills CA 90212 USA
**Cooke, Michael (Mick)** — Trumpet Player (Belle & Sebastian)
Ground Control Touring, 20 Jay St, #826, Brooklyn NY 11201 USA
**Cooke, Nicole D** — Cyclist
PO Box 38, Cowbridge CF71 7XU, England
**Cooke, Pamela D (Pam)** — Animator
1809 San Jacinto St, Los Angeles CA 90026, USA
**Cooke, Sasha** — Opera Singer
I M G Artists, Hogarth Business Park, Chiswick, London W4 2TH, England
**Cooke, Steven M (Steve)** — Baseball Player
20709 SW Trails End Dr, Sherwood OR 97140, USA
**Cooke, Victoria** — Model, Actress
Playboy Promotions, 9346 Civic Center Dr, #200, Beverly Hills CA 90210 USA
**Cooke, William M (Bill)** — Football Player
1851 Hillside Road, Fairfield CT 06824, USA
**Cooks, Brandin** — Football Player
New Orleans Saints, 5800 Airline Highway, Metairie LA 70003 USA
**Cooks, Johnie E** — Football Player
1305 Meadow Creek Dr, #111, Irving TX 75038, USA
**Cool, Tre** — Drummer (Green Day)
P M C, 5900 Wilshire Blvd, #1720, Los Angeles CA 90036, USA
**Cooley, Chelsea** — Beauty Queen
Miss Universe Organization, 1370 Ave of Americas, #1600, New York NY 10019 USA
**Cooley, Cheryl** — Guitarist (Klymaxx)
R D M J Entertainment Mgmt, 3619 Rose Ave, Long Beach CA 90807 USA
**Cooley, Denton A** — Surgeon
3014 Del Monte Dr, Houston TX 77019, USA
**Coolidge, Charles H** — WW II Army Hero (CMH)
1054 Balmoral Dr, Signal Mountain TN 37377, USA
**Coolidge, Harold J** — Conservationist
38 Standley St, Beverly MA 01915, USA
**Coolidge, Jennifer** — Actress, Comedienne
Mannic Productions, 1170 26th St, #600, New York NY 10001, USA
**Coolidge, Martha** — Director
A P A Talent & Literary Agency, 405 S Beverly Dr, #300, Beverly Hills CA 90212 USA
**Coolidge, Rita** — Singer, Actress
Axis Artist Mgmt, 9715 Belmar Ave, Northridge CA 91324, USA
**Coolio** — Rap Artist, Actor
Haber Entertainment, 434 S Canon Ave, #204, Beverly Hills CA 90212, USA
**Coombs, Daniel B (Danny)** — Baseball Player
14130 Cleobrook Dr, Houston TX 77070, USA
**Coombs, Stephen** — Concert Pianist
Wordplay, 35 Lisbon St, Blackheath, London SE3 8SS, England
**Coombs, Torrance** — Actor
D2 Mgmt, 9255 Sunset Blvd, #600, West Hollywood CA 90069, USA
**Coombs-Mueller, Carol** — Actress
772 Tyrol Court, Crestline CA 92325, USA

# C

| | |
|---|---|
| **Coomer, Ronald B (Ron)**<br>7021 Howard Lane, Eden Prairie MN 55346, USA | Baseball Player |
| **Coon, Charles (Chuck), Sr**<br>9433 E Shady Grove Court, White Lake MI 48386, USA | Harness Racing Executive |
| **Cooney, Gerry**<br>PO Box 525, Fanwood NJ 07023, USA | Boxer |
| **Cooney, Joan Ganz**<br>Children's TV Workshop, 1 Lincoln Plaza, New York NY 10023, USA | Educator, Businesswoman |
| **Cooney, Thomas M**<br>854 Country Club Dr, Cincinnati OH 45245, USA | Businessman |
| **Coonts, Stephen**<br>109 Marland Road S, Colorado Springs CO 80906, USA | Writer |
| **Cooper, A Louis**<br>200 Gregg Ave, Marion SC 29571, USA | Football Player |
| **Cooper, A Wayne**<br>5013 Millstone Way, Granite Bay CA 95746, USA | Basketball Player |
| **Cooper, Abraham**<br>Simon Wiesental Center, 1399 S Roxbury, #100, Los Angeles CA 90035, USA | Religious Leader, Rabbi |
| **Cooper, Adam**<br>Diamond Mgmt, 31 Percy St, London W1T 2DD, England | Actor, Singer |
| **Cooper, Adrian**<br>3120 Saint Paul St, Denver CO 80205, USA | Football Player |
| **Cooper, Alice**<br>Bx2 Management, PO Box 989, Woodland Hills CA 91365, USA | Singer, Songwriter |
| **Cooper, Amy Levin**<br>60 Sutton Place S, #16C, New York NY 10022, USA | Editor |
| **Cooper, Anderson**<br>CNN-TV, News Dept, 190 Marietta Ave SW, Atlanta GA 30303 USA | Commentator |
| **Cooper, Bernadette**<br>R D M J Entertainment Mgmt, 3619 Rose Ave, Long Beach CA 90807 USA | Musician (Klymaxx) |
| **Cooper, Bradley**<br>22 & Indiana Pictures, 10640 Rochester Ave, Los Angeles CA 90024, USA | Actor |
| **Cooper, Brian J**<br>346 W Ada Ave, Glendora CA 91741, USA | Baseball Player |
| **Cooper, Camille**<br>New York Liberty, Madison Square Garden, 2 Penn Plaza, New York NY 10121 USA | Basketball Player |
| **Cooper, Cecil C**<br>24802 Boulder Lakes Court, Katy TX 77494, USA | Baseball Player, Manager |
| **Cooper, Charles G**<br>3410 Barger Dr, Falls Church VA 22044, USA | Marine Corps General |
| **Cooper, Chris**<br>Untitled Entertainment, 350 S Beverly Dr, #200, Beverly Hills CA 90212 USA | Actor |
| **Cooper, Christin**<br>1001 E Hyman Ave, Aspen CO 81611, USA | Alpine Skier |
| **Cooper, Daniel L**<br>400 Willow Valley Square, #GA110, Lancaster PA 17602, USA | Navy Admiral |
| **Cooper, Dominic**<br>Markham Froggatt Irwin, Julian House, 4 Windmill St, London W1P 1HF, England | Actor |
| **Cooper, Eric R**<br>4330 NW 169th Court, Clive IA 50325, USA | Baseball Umpire |
| **Cooper, Helene**<br>New York Times, Editorial Dept, 229 W 43rd St, New York NY 10036 USA | Writer, Journalist |
| **Cooper, Imogen**<br>Askonas Holt, Lincoln House, 300 High Holborn, London WC1V 7JH, England | Concert Pianist |
| **Cooper, James A (Jim)**<br>12910 Low Meadow Court, Charlotte NC 28277, USA | Football Player |
| **Cooper, Jilly**<br>Curtis Brown Group, 28-29 Haymarket St, #500, London SW1Y 4SP, England | Writer |
| **Cooper, John**<br>ESPN-TV, Sports Dept, ESPN Plaza, 935 Middle St, Bristol CT 06010 USA | Football Coach |
| **Cooper, John M**<br>182 Western Way, Princeton NJ 08540, USA | Philosopher |
| **Cooper, Leon N**<br>49 Intervale Road, Providence RI 02906, USA | Nobel Physics Laureate |
| **Cooper, Lester I**<br>45 Morningside Dr S, Westport CT 06880, USA | Producer |
| **Cooper, Lynn A**<br>Columbia University, Psychology Dept, 1190 Amsterdam Ave, New York NY 10027, USA | Psychologist |
| **Cooper, M Earl**<br>2224 E Highway 21, Lincoln TX 78948, USA | Football Player |
| **Cooper, Martha**<br>City Lore, 56 E 1st St, New York NY 10003, USA | Photojournalist |
| **Cooper, Martin**<br>ArrayComm, 2480 N 1st St, #200, San Jose CA 95131, USA | Inventor (Cell Phone) |
| **Cooper, Matthew T**<br>9326 Fairfax St, Alexandria VA 22309, USA | Marine Corps General |
| **Cooper, Pat**<br>243 W 70th St, #8D, New York NY 10023, USA | Actor, Comedian |
| **Cooper, Richard N**<br>33 Washington Ave, Cambridge MA 02140, USA | Economist |
| **Cooper, Roxanne**<br>Freemantle Media, 2700 Colorado Ave, #450, Santa Monica CA 90404, USA | Singer |
| **Cooper, Stuart**<br>Creative Artists Agency, 2000 Ave of Stars, #100, Los Angeles CA 90067 USA | Director, Actor |
| **Cooper, Susan M**<br>Simon & Schuster, 1230 Ave of Americas, Concourse 1, New York NY 10020 USA | Writer |
| **Cooper, Wayne**<br>PO Box 106, Depew OK 74028, USA | Artist, Sculptor |
| **Cooper, William A (Bill)**<br>16056 Greenwood Road, Monte Sereno CA 95030, USA | Football Player |
| **Cooper-Dyke, Cynthia**<br>University of North Carolina, Athletic Dept, Wilmington NC 28403, USA | Basketball Player, Coach |
| **Coor, Lattie F**<br>Arizona State University, Public Affairs School, Tempe AZ 85287, USA | Educator |
| **Coors, William K**<br>Adolph Coors Co, 311 10th St, Golden CO 80401, USA | Businessman |

**Coote, Alice**
I M G Artists, Hogarth Business Park, Chiswick, London W4 2TH, England — Opera Singer

**Coover, Robert**
Brown University, Linden Press, 49 George St, Providence RI 02912, USA — Writer

**Cope, Derrike**
103 Turnerlair Court, Mooresville NC 28117, USA — Auto Racing Driver

**Cope, Jonathan**
Royal Ballet, Covent Garden, Bow St, London WC2E 9DD, England — Ballet Dancer

**Copeland, Horace C**
4195 Blakemore Place, Spring Hill FL 34609, USA — Football Player

**Copeland, Kenneth**
Kenneth Copeland Ministries, PO Box 2908, Fort Worth TX 76113, USA — Evangelist

**Copeland, Shemekia**
Alligator Records, PO Box 60234, Chicago IL 60660, USA — Singer

**Copeland, Stewart**
2420 Arbutus Dr, Los Angeles CA 90049, USA — Drummer (Police, Oysterhead), Composer

**Copeland, William Edward (Ed)**
9998 E Purdue Ave, Scottsdale AZ 85258, USA — WW II Navy Air Force Hero

**Coples, Quinton**
New York Jets, 1 Jets Dr, Florham Park NJ 07932 USA — Football Player

**Copley, Teri**
13351 Riverside Dr, #D513, Sherman Oaks CA 91423, USA — Actress, Model

**Copley, William**
1 Frisbie Road, Roxbury CT 06783, USA — Artist

**Copon, Michael S**
Don Buchwald Talent Agency, 6500 Wilshire Blvd, #2200, Los Angeles CA 90048 USA — Actor, Model, Singer

**Copp, D Harold**
4755 Belmont Ave, Vancouver BC V6T 1A8, Canada — Physiologist

**Coppa, Giovanni Cardinal**
Apostolic Nuncio, Vorsilska Ul 12, 11000 Prague 1, Czech Republic — Religious Leader

**Coppens, Yves**
4 Rue du Pont-aux-Choux, 75003 Paris, France — Anthropologist

**Copperfield, David**
Magic Arts Entertainment, 10145 Philipp Parkway, #A, Streetsboro OH 44241, USA — Illusionist

**Copperwheat, Lee**
Copperwheat Blundell, 14 Cheshire St, London E2 6EH, England — Fashion Designer

**Coppinger, John T (Rocky)**
7280 Alto Rey Ave, El Paso TX 79912, USA — Baseball Player

**Coppo, Paul**
3458 Solitude Road, De Pere WI 54115, USA — Ice Hockey Player

**Coppola, Alicia**
A P A Talent & Literary Agency, 405 S Beverly Dr, #300, Beverly Hills CA 90212 USA — Actress

**Coppola, Francis Ford**
Niebaum-Coppola Estate, 1991 Saint Helena Highway, Rutherford CA 94573, USA — Director

**Coppola, Imani**
International Talent Booking, Ariel House, 74A Charlotte St, #100 London W1T 4QJ, England — Singer, Songwriter

**Coppola, Sofia**
I C M Partners, 10250 Constellation Blvd, #900, Los Angeles CA 90067 USA — Actress, Director, Writer

**Copps Michael J**
Federal Communications Commission, 1919 M St NW, Washington DC 20036, USA — Government Official

**Cora, Catherine (Cat)**
I/D Public Relations, 7060 Hollywood Blvd, #800, Los Angeles CA 90028 USA — Chef

**Cora, J Alexander (Alex)**
150 Brookline Ave, Boston MA 02215, USA — Baseball Player

**Cora, Jose M (Joey)**
17734 SW 47th St, Miramar FL 33029, USA — Baseball Player

**Corabi, John**
Union Entertainment Group, 1323 Newbury Road, #104, Newbury Park CA 91320, USA — Singer, Guitarist (Motley Crue)

**Coraci, Frank**
I C M Partners, 10250 Constellation Blvd, #900, Los Angeles CA 90067 USA — Director

**Corbat, Michael L (Mike)**
Citigroup Inc, 55 E 52nd St, New York NY 10055, USA — Financier

**Corbato, Fernando J**
88 Temple St, West Newton MA 02465, USA — Computer Scientist

**Corbet, Brady**
W M E Entertainment, 9601 Wilshire Blvd, #300, Beverly Hills CA 90210 USA — Actor, Director

**Corbett, Douglas M (Doug)**
75083 Edwards Road, Yulee FL 32097, USA — Baseball Player

**Corbett, Gretchen**
S D B Partners, 315 S Beverly Dr, #411, Beverly Hills CA 90067 USA — Actress

**Corbett, John**
Gersh Agency, 9465 Wilshire Blvd, #600, Beverly Hills CA 90212 USA — Actor

**Corbett, Michael**
Innovative Artists, 1505 10th St, Santa Monica CA 90401 USA — Actor

**Corbett, Mike**
41828 Road 600, Ahwahnee CA 93601, USA — Rock Climber

**Corbett, Ronnie**
International Artistes, 235 Regent St, London W1R 8AX, England — Actor, Comedian

**Corbijn, Anton**
Independent Talent Group, 40 Whitfield St, London W1T 2RH, England — Photographer, Cinematographer

**Corbin, A Ray**
65 Moore St, Franklin NC 28734, USA — Baseball Player

**Corbin, Barry**
Linda McAlister Talent, 530 S Lake Ave, #435, Pasadena CA 91101, USA — Actor

**Corbin, Tom**
201 Wyandotte St, #102, Kansas City MO 64105, USA — Sculptor

**Corbin, Tyrone K**
301 Oakbrook Dr, Columbia SC 29223, USA — Basketball Player, Coach

**Corbitt, Jerry**
First Rainbow, 1650 Barnes Mill Road, #1214, Marietta GA 30062, USA — Singer, Guitarist (Youngbloods)

**Corchiani, Christopher (Chris)**
1106 Harvey St, Raleigh NC 27608, USA — Basketball Player

**Corcoran, Barbara**
W M E Entertainment, 9601 Wilshire Blvd, #300, Beverly Hills CA 90210 USA — Writer

**Corcoran, Kevin**
8617 Balcom Ave, Northridge CA 91325, USA — Actor

V.I.P. Address Book

**Corcoran, Norm** — Ice Hockey Player
20 Nickerson Ave, Saint Catherines ON L2N 3L4, Canada

**Corcoran, Roy E** — Baseball Player
PO Box 173, Slaughter LA 70777, USA

**Corcoran, Timothy M (Tim)** — Baseball Player
4349 Friar Circle, La Verne CA 91750, USA

**Cord, Alex** — Actor
Cord Equestrian, 7639 FM 2071, Gainesville TX 76240, USA

**Cordalis, Costa** — Singer
Concorda Kunstler Mgmt, Rippoldsauer Str 32, 72250 Freudenstadt, Germany

**Corday, Barbara** — Businesswoman, Writer, Producer
317 N Van Ness Ave, Los Angeles CA 90004, USA

**Corday, Ken** — Producer
Corday Productions, 3400 W Olive Ave, #170, Burbank CA 91505, USA

**Corday, Mara** — Actress, Model
29532 Mendoze Dr, Valencia CA 91355, USA

**Corddry, Nathan (Nate)** — Actor
Baker Winokur Ryder Public Relations, 9100 Wilshire Blvd, #500W, Beverly Hills CA 90212 USA

**Corddry, Rob** — Actor, Comedian
Principato-Young, 9465 Wilshire Blvd, #880, Beverly Hills CA 90212 USA

**Corden, James G** — Actor, Writer, Producer
United Agents, 12-26 Lexington St, London W1F 0LE, England

**Cordero Lanza di Montezemolo, Andrea** — Religious Leader
Saint Paul Outside-the-Walls Basilica, 00120 Vatican City

**Cordero, Angel T, Jr** — Thoroughbred Racing Jockey
4 Osborne Lane, Greenvale NY 11548, USA

**Cordero, Chad P** — Baseball Player
13305 Noble Place, Chino CA 91710, USA

**Cordero, Francisco J** — Baseball Player
5811 Falling Brook Dr, Mason OH 45040, USA

**Cordero, Sebastian** — Director, Writer
Creative Artists Agency, 2000 Ave of Stars, #100, Los Angeles CA 90067 USA

**Cordero, Wilfredo N (Wil)** — Baseball Player
25844 Kensington Dr, Westlake OH 44145, USA

**Cordes, Paul J Cardinal** — Religious Leader
Pontifical Council Cor Unum, Palazzo San Pio X, Via della Conciliazione 5, 00193 Rome, Italy

**Cordes-Elliott, Gloria** — Baseball Player
86 Malone Ave, Staten Island NY 10306, USA

**Cordingly, Beth** — Actress
Hatton McEwan, 3 Chocolate Studios, 7 Shepherdess Place, London N1 7LJ, England

**Cordova, France A** — Educator
Purdue University, President's Office, West Lafayette IN 47907, USA

**Cordova, Martin K (Marty)** — Baseball Player
47 Club Vista Dr, Henderson NV 89052, USA

**Corduner, Allan** — Actor
Conway Van Gelder Grant, 8-12 Broadwick St, #300, London W1F 8HW, England

**Core, Ericson** — Director, Cinematographer
Gersh Agency, 9465 Wilshire Blvd, #600, Beverly Hills CA 90212 USA

**Corea, Armando A (Chick)** — Jazz Pianist, Composer
D L Media, 124 N Highland Ave, Bala Cynwyd PA 19004, USA

**Corey, Bryan S** — Baseball Player
7829 E Riverdale Circle, Mesa AZ 85207, USA

**Corey, Clint** — Rodeo Rider
30635 W Mission Road, Powell Butte OR 97753, USA

**Corey, Elias J** — Nobel Chemistry Laureate
20 Avon Hill St, Cambridge MA 02140, USA

**Corey, Irwin (Professor)** — Actor, Comedian
Worlds Foremost Mgmt, 165 W 21st St, New York NY 10011, USA

**Corey, Jill** — Singer
64 Division Ave, Levittown NY 11756, USA

**Corey, Walter M (Walt)** — Football Player
26007 Timber Meadow Dr, Lees Summit MO 64086, USA

**Corfield, Kenneth G** — Businessman
10 Chapel Place, Rivington St, London EC2A 3DQ, England

**Corgan, William P (Billy), Jr** — Singer (Smashing Pumpkins), Songwriter
Evolution Music Partners, 1680 N Vine St, #500, Los Angeles CA 90028, USA

**Corigliano, John P** — Composer
365 W End Ave, New York NY 10024, USA

**Corinealdi, Emayatzy** — Actress
I C M Partners, 10250 Constellation Blvd, #900, Los Angeles CA 90067 USA

**Corkins, Michael P (Mike)** — Baseball Player
3760 Chemehuevi Blvd, Lake Havasu City AZ 86406, USA

**Corley, Al** — Actor
1177 Embury St, Pacific Palisades CA 90272, USA

**Corley, W Gene** — Structural Engineer
2491 Indigo Lane, Glenview IL 60026, USA

**Cormack, Danielle** — Actress
Johnson & Laird Mgmt, PO Box 78340, Grey Lynn, Auckland 1002, New Zealand

**Corman, Roger W** — Director, Producer
Concorde New Horizons, 11600 San Vicente Blvd, Los Angeles CA 90049, USA

**Cormier, Lance R** — Baseball Player
3630 Windy Ridge, Tuscaloosa AL 35406, USA

**Cormier, Rheal P** — Baseball Player
2640 Cody Circle, Park City UT 84098, USA

**Corn, Alfred** — Writer
350 W 14th St, #6A, New York NY 10014, USA

**Cornelison, Jerry G** — Football Player
12713 Cedar St, Leawood KS 66209, USA

**Cornelius** — Singer, Guitarist
Magnum Public Relations, 32 E 31st St, #900, New York NY 10016, USA

**Cornelius, Helen** — Singer, Songwriter
PO Box 12089, Nashville TN 37212, USA

**Cornelius, James M** — Businessman
Bristol-Myers Squibb, 345 Park Ave, New York NY 10154, USA

**Cornelius, Kathy** — Golfer
5744 W Dek Rio St, Chandler AZ 85226, USA

**Cornelius, Peter** — Singer, Songwriter, Guitarist
Master Fader Records, 3002 Purkersdorf, Austria
**Cornell, Brian** — Businessman
Target Corp, 1000 Nicollet Mall, Minneapolis MN 55403, USA
**Cornell, Chris** — Singer, Drummer (Soundgarden)
W M E Entertainment, 9601 Wilshire Blvd, #300, Beverly Hills CA 90210 USA
**Cornell, Eric A** — Nobel Physics Laureate
University of Colorado, Physics Dept, PO Box 440, Boulder CO 80328, USA
**Cornell, Harry M, Jr** — Businessman
Leggett & Platt Inc, 1 Leggett Road, Carthage MO 64836, USA
**Cornell, Lydia** — Actress
J K A Talent, 12725 Ventura Blvd, #H, Studio City CA 91604, USA
**Cornell, Robert P (Bo)** — Football Player
2605 239th Ave SE, Sammamish WA 98075, USA
**Cornet, Alize** — Tennis Player
11 Ave Jean Medecin, 06000 Nice, France
**Cornette, Jim** — Wrestler
PO Box 436963, Louisville KY 40253, USA
**Cornforth, Mark** — Ice Hockey Player
11 Indian Spring Road, Milton MA 02186, USA
**Cornish, Abbie** — Actress
W M E Entertainment, 9601 Wilshire Blvd, #300, Beverly Hills CA 90210 USA
**Cornish, Frank E, III** — Football Player
1024 Inca Dr, #A, Harvey LA 70058, USA
**Cornish, Nick** — Actor
James Levy Jacobson Mgmt, 3500 W Olive Ave, #900, Burbank CA 91505, USA
**Cornwell, Bernard** — Writer
Harper Collins Publishers, 10 E 53rd St, Cellar 1, New York NY 10022 USA
**Cornwell, Frederick K (Fred)** — Football Player
2107 Windward Lane, Newport Beach CA 92660, USA
**Cornwell, Hugh** — Singer, Guitarist (Stranglers)
Red Entertainment, 16 Penn Plaza, #824, New York NY 10001, USA
**Cornwell, Patricia D** — Writer
G P Putnam's Sons, 375 Hudson St, New York NY 10014 USA
**Cornwell, Peter** — Director, Producer, Writer
I C M Partners, 10250 Constellation Blvd, #900, Los Angeles CA 90067 USA
**Corona, Jose de Jesus** — Soccer Player
C D Cruz Azul, San Pablo 100, C La Nora Xochimilco, 16030 DF Mexico City, Mexico
**Corr, Andrea** — Singer, Tin Whistle Player (Corrs)
John Hughes, 6 Martello Terrace, Sandycove, Dunlaoughaire, Dublin, Ireland
**Corr, Caroline** — Singer, Percussionist, Pianist (Corrs)
John Hughes, 6 Martello Terrace, Sandycove, Dunlaoughaire, Dublin, Ireland
**Corr, Jim** — Singer, Keyboardist, Guitarist (Corrs)
John Hughes, 6 Martello Terrace, Sandycove, Dunlaoughaire, Dublin, Ireland
**Corr, Karen** — Billiards Player
PO Box 285, Feasterville Trevose PA 19053, USA
**Corr, Sharon** — Singer, Violinist (Corrs)
John Hughes, 6 Martello Terrace, Sandycove, Dunlaoughaire, Dublin, Ireland
**Corraface, Georges** — Actor
Agents Associes, 201 Rue du Faubourg Saint Honore, 75008 Paris, France
**Corrales, Patrick (Pat)** — Baseball Player, Manager
2 W Wesley Road NW, #18, Atlanta GA 30305, USA
**Correa Delgado, Rafael V** — President, Ecuador
Palacio de Gobierno, Garcia Moreno 1043, Quito, Ecuador
**Correa, Charles M** — Architect
Sonmarg, Napean Sea Road, Mumbai 400006, India
**Correia, Amy** — Singer, Guitarist, Songwriter
Season of Mist Records, 111 Rt de la Valentinell, 13011 Marseille, France
**Correia, Kevin J** — Baseball Player
2081 Gatun St, Del Mar CA 92014, USA
**Correll, Victor C (Vic)** — Baseball Player
119 Kentucky Downs, Perry GA 31069, USA
**Corretja, Alex** — Tennis Player
Association of Tennis Professionals, 201 A T P Blvd, Ponte Vedra Beach FL 32082 USA
**Corri, Adrienne** — Actress
Rolf & Rachel Kruger, 205 Chudleigh Road, London SE4 1EG, England
**Corrie, Emily** — Actress
United Agents, 12-26 Lexington St, London W1F 0LE, England
**Corrigan, E Gerald** — Government Official, Financier
Goldman Sachs Co, 85 Broad St, Building 85, New York NY 10004, USA
**Corrigan, Kevin** — Actor
Innovative Artists, 1505 10th St, Santa Monica CA 90401 USA
**Corrigan, Michale D (Mike)** — Ice Hockey Player
21 Birchwood Road, Enfield CT 06082, USA
**Corrigan, Patrick** — Editorial Cartoonist
Toronto Star, Editorial Dept, 1 Yonge St, Toronto ON M5E 1E5, Canada
**Corrigan-Maguire, Mairead** — Nobel Peace Laureate
Peace People, 224 Lisburn Road, Belfast BT9 6GE, Northern Ireland
**Corriveau, Yvon** — Ice Hockey Player
396 Willard Ave, #A2, Newington CT 06111, USA
**Corsaro, Frank A** — Director
33 Riverside Dr, New York NY 10023, USA
**Corsi, James B (Jim)** — Baseball Player
6 Edwards Circle, Bellingham MA 02019, USA
**Corso, John A** — Cinematographer
241 W 13th St, #21, New York NY 10011, USA
**Corso, Leland (Lee)** — Sportscaster
ESPN-TV, Sports Dept, ESPN Plaza, 935 Middle St, Bristol CT 06010 USA
**Corson, Shayne** — Ice Hockey Player
Tappo Restaurant, 3-55 Mill St, Toronto ON M5A 3C4, Canada
**Cort, Bud** — Actor
2609 Lake View Ave, Los Angeles CA 90039, USA
**Cortazar, Esteban** — Fashion Designer
111 NE 1st St, #900, Miami FL 33132, USA
**Cortes Granados, Javier** — Soccer Player
Tigres U A N L, Estadio Universitario, 66451 San Nicolas de los Garza, Mexico

Cornelius - Cortes Granados

**Cortes, Joaquin** — Flamenco Dancer, Choreographer
W M E Entertainment, 9601 Wilshire Blvd, #300, Beverly Hills CA 90210 USA

**Cortes, Ron** — Journalist
Philadelphia Inquirer, Editorial Dept, 400 N Broad St, Philadelphia PA 19130, USA

**Cortese, Dan** — Actor
Glick Agency, 347 5th Ave, #1404, New York NY 10016 USA

**Cortese, Federico** — Conductor
Boston Youth Symphony, 855 Commonwealth Ave, Boston MA 02215, USA

**Cortese, Genevieve** — Actress
Innovative Artists, 1505 10th St, Santa Monica CA 90401 USA

**Cortese, Joe** — Actor
100 S Hayworth Ave, #201, Los Angeles CA 90048, USA

**Cortese, Valentina** — Actress
Pretta S Erasmo 6, 20121 Milan, Italy

**Cortez, Alfonso** — Actor, Producer
C E S D, 10635 Santa Monica Blvd, #130, Los Angeles CA 90025 USA

**Cortright, Edgar M, Jr** — Aerospace Engineer
9701 Calvin St, Northridge CA 91324, USA

**Corvo, Joseph (Joe)** — Ice Hockey Player
2012 N 77th Court, Elmwood Park IL 60707, USA

**Corwin, Jeff** — Actor
Jeff Corwin Experience, PO Box 2904, Toluca Lake CA 91610, USA

**Corwin, Morena** — Model
Playboy Promotions, 9346 Civic Center Dr, #200, Beverly Hills CA 90210 USA

**Coryatt, Quentin J** — Football Player
611 Cannon Lane, Sugar Land TX 77479, USA

**Coryell, Larry** — Guitarist
Jazz-Map, Hans Bredow Str 32A, 65189 Weisbaden, Germany

**Corzine, David J (Dave)** — Basketball Player
1161 W Hunting Dr, Palatine IL 60067, USA

**Cosbie, Douglas D (Doug)** — Football Player
1503 Fordham Court, Mountain View CA 94040, USA

**Cosby, Bill** — Actor, Comedian
PO Box 808, Bardwell Ferry Road, Greenfield MA 01302, USA

**Coscina, Dennis** — Golfer
211 Main St, East Windsor CT 06088, USA

**Cosgrave, Liam** — Prime Minister, Ireland
Beech Park, Templeogue County, Dublin 6W, Ireland

**Cosgriff, Kevin J** — Navy Admiral
Deputy Commander, Fleet Forces Command, Norfolk VA 23551, USA

**Cosgrove, Daniel** — Actor
James/Levy Mgmt, 3500 W Olive Ave, #1470, Burbank CA 91505 USA

**Cosgrove, Miranda** — Actress, Singer
W M E Entertainment, 9601 Wilshire Blvd, #300, Beverly Hills CA 90210 USA

**Coslet, Bruce N** — Football Player, Coach
1778 Ivy Pointe Court, Naples FL 34109, USA

**Cosmo, James** — Actor
United Agents, 12-26 Lexington St, London W1F 0LE, England

**Cosmos, Jean** — Writer
57 Rue de Versailles, 92410 Ville d'Avray, France

**Cosmovici, Cristiano B** — Astronaut, Italy
Instituto Fisica Spazio Interplanetario, CP 27, 00044 Frascati, Italy

**Cosper, Kina** — Singer (Brownstone), Songwriter
Richard Walters, PO Box 2789, Toluca Lake CA 91610 USA

**Cossack, Roger** — Attorney, Commentator
ESPN-TV, Sports Dept, ESPN Plaza, 935 Middle St, Bristol CT 06010 USA

**Cosso, Pierre** — Actor
Agents Associes, 201 Rue du Faubourg Saint Honore, 75008 Paris, France

**Cossotto, Fiorenza** — Opera Singer
Via Ezio Biondi 1, 21 Milan, Italy

**Costa, Manuel Rui** — Soccer Player
F C Milan, Via Filippo Turati 3, 20121 Milan, Italy

**Costa, Mary** — Opera Singer
California Artists Mgmt, 41 Sutter St, #420, San Francisco CA 94104, USA

**Costa, Nikka** — Singer, Songwriter
Front Line Mgmt, 1100 Glendon Ave, #2000, Los Angeles CA 90024 USA

**Costa, S Paul** — Football Player
8017 Kristina Lane, North Richland Hills TX 76182, USA

**Costabile, David** — Actor
Innovative Artists, 1505 10th St, Santa Monica CA 90401 USA

**Costa-Gavras, Konstaninos** — Director
Artmedia, 20 Ave Rapp, 75007 Paris, France

**Costanzo, Paulo** — Actor
Principato-Young, 9465 Wilshire Blvd, #880, Beverly Hills CA 90212 USA

**Costanzo, Robert** — Actor, Producer, Director
TalentWorks, 3500 W Olive Ave, #1400, Burbank CA 91505 USA

**Costas, Robert Q (Bob)** — Sportscaster
W M E Entertainment, 9601 Wilshire Blvd, #300, Beverly Hills CA 90210 USA

**Costello, Barry M** — Navy Admiral
A D S Ventures, 500 New Jersey Ave NW, #400, Washington DC 20001 20001, USA

**Costello, Elvis** — Singer, Guitarist, Songwriter
I C M Partners, 10250 Constellation Blvd, #900, Los Angeles CA 90067 USA

**Costello, Murray** — Ice Hockey Player, Executive
105 Kenilworth St, Ottawa ON K1Y 3Y8, Canada

**Costello, Vince** — Football Player
9914 W 125th Terrace, Overland Park KS 66213, USA

**Costelloe, Paul** — Fashion Designer
30 Westminster Palace Gardens, Artillery Row, London SW1P 1RR, England

**Coster, Nicolas** — Actor
Momentum Talent, 9401 Wilshire Blvd, 501, Beverly Hills CA 90212, USA

**Coster, Ritchie** — Actor
Gersh Agency, 9465 Wilshire Blvd, #600, Beverly Hills CA 90212 USA

**Coster-Waldau, Nikolaj** — Actor
Lindberg Mgmt, Lavendelstr 5-7, Baghuset, 4 Sal, 1462 Copenhagen K, Denmark

**Costigan, C C** — Actress
I C M Partners, 10250 Constellation Blvd, #900, Los Angeles CA 90067 USA

**Costle, Douglas M**
Harvard University, Public Health School, Cambridge MA 02138, USA — Government Official, Educator

**Costner, Kevin**
Treehouse Films, 4450 Lakeside Dr, #225, Burbank CA 91505, USA — Actor, Director

**Cota, Chad G**
216 Island Pointe Dr, Medford OR 97504, USA — Football Player

**Cotchery, Jerricho**
79 Carriage Lane, Plainview NY 11803, USA — Football Player

**Cote, Alain**
1352 Rue Gabrielle Roy, Quebec QC G1Y 3K3, Canada — Ice Hockey Player

**Cote, David M**
Honeywell International, 61 Columbia Road, Morristown NJ 07960, USA — Businessman

**Cote, Laurence**
Agents Associes, 201 Rue du Faubourg Saint Honore, 75008 Paris, France — Actress

**Cote, Sylvain**
1432 Wild Cranberry Court, Crownsville MD 21032, USA — Ice Hockey Player

**Cothran, Sherry**
Turner Management Group, 9200 W Sunset Blvd, #600, West Hollywood CA 90069, USA — Singer (EvinRudes)

**Cotillard, Marion**
Agence Artiste Adequat, 108 Rue Reaumur, 75002 Paris, France — Actress

**Cotroneo, Vince**
4455 E Palmdale Lane, Gilbert AZ 85298, USA — Sportscaster

**Cotrubas, Ileana**
Royal Opera House, Covent Garden, Bow St, London WC2, England — Opera Singer

**Cotte, Pascal**
Lumiere Technology, 215 Bis Blvd Saint Germain, 75007 Paris, France — Engineer

**Cottee, Kay**
Showboat Productions, 113 Willoughby Road, Crows Nest NSW 2065, Australia — Yachtswoman

**Cottencon, Fanny**
Agence Artiste Adequat, 108 Rue Reaumur, 75002 Paris, France — Actress, Producer

**Cotterill, Tim (Frogman)**
518 Victoria Ave, Venice CA 90291, USA — Sculptor

**Cotti, Flavio**
Christian Democratic Party, Klaraweg 6, 3001 Bern, Switzerland — President, Switzerland

**Cottier, Charles K (Chuck)**
7129 Lake Ballinger Way, Edmonds WA 98026, USA — Baseball Player, Manager

**Cottier, Georges-Marie-Martin Cardinal**
Convento Santa Sabina, Piazza Pierro d'Illiria, 00193 Rome, Italy — Religious Leader

**Cottingham, Robert**
PO Box 604, Blackman Road, Newtown CT 06470, USA — Artist

**Cottle, Tameka**
Richard Walters, PO Box 2789, Toluca Lake CA 91610 USA — Singer (Xscape)

**Cotto, Miguel**
Top Rank Inc, 3908 Howard Hughes Parkway, #580, Las Vegas NV 89169 USA — Boxer

**Cotton, Blaine**
Jack Scagnetti Talent, 5118 Vineland Ave, #102, North Hollywood CA 91601, USA — Actor

**Cotton, James**
Jacklyn Hairston Mgmt, PO Box 150402, Austin TX 78715, USA — Singer, Harmonica Player

**Cotton, John G**
Commander, Naval Reserve Force, HqUSN, Pentagon, Washington DC 20350 USA — Navy Admiral

**Cotton, John J (Jack)**
11426 Country Road 4 S, Alamosa CO 81101, USA — Basketball Player

**Cotton, Joseph F**
20 Linda Vista Ave, Atherton CA 94027, USA — Test Pilot

**Cotton, Maxwell Perry**
Greene Assoc, 1901 Ave of Stars, #130, Los Angeles CA 90067 USA — Actor

**Cotton, Shamika**
Don Buchwald Talent Agency, 6500 Wilshire Blvd, #2200, Los Angeles CA 90048 USA — Actress

**Cottrell, Erin**
TalentWorks, 3500 W Olive Ave, #1400, Burbank CA 91505 USA — Actress

**Cottrell, William H (Bill)**
39675 Patterson Lane, Solon OH 44139, USA — Football Player

**Couch, Chris**
307 Johns Creek Parkway, Saint Augustine FL 32092, USA — Golfer

**Couch, Timothy S (Tim)**
3041 Brookmonte Lane, Lexington KY 40515, USA — Football Player

**Couchepin, Pascal**
Federal Chancellery, Bundeshaus-W, Bundesgasse, 3033 Berne, Switzerland — President, Switzerland

**Couelle, Savin**
Localita Abbiadori CP 4, 07020 Porto Cervo, Italy — Architect

**Couffer, Jack**
Original Artists, 9465 Wilshire Blvd, #324, Beverly Hills CA 90212, USA — Cinematographer

**Coughlan, Marisa**
Mosaic Media Group, 9200 W Sunset Blvd, #1000, Los Angles CA 90069, USA — Actress

**Coughlin, Jeg (Jeggy), Jr**
Jeg's High Performance Racing, 751 E 11th Ave, Columbus OH 43211, USA — Auto Racing Driver

**Coughlin, Natalie**
4139 Coralee Lane, Lafayette CA 94549, USA — Swimmer

**Coughlin, Shaun R**
University of California Medical Center, Box 1753, San Francisco CA 94143, USA — Cardiovascular Biologist

**Coughlin, Tom**
New York Giants, Meadowlands Stadium, 102 Route 120, East Rutherford NJ 07073 USA — Football Coach

**Coughran, John W**
5476 Morningside Dr, San Jose CA 95138, USA — Basketball Player

**Coulby, Angel**
Curtis Brown Group, 28-29 Haymarket St, #500, London SW1Y 4SP, England — Actress

**Coulier, David**
Brillstein Entertainment Partners, 9150 Wilshire Blvd, #350, Beverly Hills CA 90212 USA — Actor

**Coulson, Catherine E**
1115 Terra Ave, Ashland OR 97520, USA — Actress

**Coulter, Ann H**
Crown Publishing Group, 1745 Broadway, #1300, New York NY 10019 USA — Commentator, Writer

**Coulter, Catherine**
PO Box 17, Mill Valley CA 94942, USA — Writer

**Coulter, Michael**
35 Carlton Mansions, Randolph Ave, London W9 1NP, England — Cinematographer

Costle - Coulter

**Coulthard, David M**
Red Bull, Am Brunnen 1, 5330 Puschi am See, Austria — Auto Racing Driver

**Coulthard, Raymond**
United Agents, 12-26 Lexington St, London W1F 0LE, England — Actor

**Counsell, Craig J**
992 E Circle Dr, Milwaukee WI 53217, USA — Baseball Player

**Countryman, Michael**
Paradigm Agency, 360 N Crescent Dr, North Building, Beverly Hills CA 90210 USA — Actor

**Counts, Mel G**
1581 Matheny Road, Gervais OR 97026, USA — Basketball Player

**Coupe, Eliza**
Kirsten Ames Mgmt, 8111 Beverly Blvd, #201, Los Angeles CA 90048, USA — Actress

**Coupland, Douglas**
United Talent Agency, U T A Plaza, 9336 Civic Center Dr, Beverly Hills CA 90210 USA — Writer, Producer, Actor

**Couples, Fredrederick S (Fred)**
Players Group, 1851 Alexander Bell Dr, #410, Reston VA 20191, USA — Golfer

**Courant, Ernest D**
40 W 72nd St, #4I, New York NY 10023, USA — Physicist

**Couric, Katherine (Katie)**
1155 Park Ave, #2SW, New York NY 10128, USA — Commentator

**Courier, James S (Jim), Jr**
9533 Blandford Road, Orlando FL 32827, USA — Tennis Player

**Cournoyer, Charle**
Ice Complex, Winter Park, 88 Canada Olympic Road SW, Calgary AB T3B 5R5, Canada — Speed Skater

**Cournoyer, Yvan S**
104 Boul Des Chateaux, Blainville QC J7B 1K6, Canada — Ice Hockey Player

**Courreges, Andre**
27 Rue Delabordere, 92 Neuilly-sur-Seine, France — Fashion Designer

**Court, Charles**
21 Lewanna Way, City Beach, Perth WA 9060, Australia — Government Official, Australia

**Courtenay, Tom**
Jonathan Altaras Assoc, 11 Garrick St, London WC2E 9AR, England — Actor

**Courtnall, Geoffrey L (Geoff)**
2730 Queenswood Dr, Victoria BC V8N 1X5, Canada — Ice Hockey Player

**Courtnall, Russ**
398 W Stafford Road, Thousand Oaks CA 91361, USA — Ice Hockey Player

**Courtney, Jai**
United Talent Agency, U T A Plaza, 9336 Civic Center Dr, Beverly Hills CA 90210 USA — Actor

**Courtney, Joel**
676 W Pullman Road, #301, Moscow ID 83841, USA — Actor

**Courtney, Stephanie**
Greene Assoc, 1901 Ave of Stars, #130, Los Angeles CA 90067 USA — Actress

**Courtney, Thomas W (Tom)**
336 Edgemere Way E, Naples FL 34105, USA — Track Athlete

**Coury, Fred**
Union Entertainment Group, 1323 Newbury Road, #104, Thousand Oaks CA 91320, USA — Singer, Drummer (Cinderella)

**Cousin, Philip R**
African Methodist Episcopal Church, 2625 Orange Picker Road, Jacksonville FL 32223, USA — Religious Leader

**Cousin, Terry S**
9213 Everwood Court, Tampa FL 33647, USA — Football Player

**Cousineau, Tom**
645 Ridgecrest Road, Akron OH 44303, USA — Football Player

**Cousino, Tishara**
T L C, 1602 Alton Road, Miami Beach FL 33139, USA — Model, Actress

**Cousins, Christopher**
DiSante Frank, 10061 Riverside Dr, #377, Toluca Lake CA 91602, USA — Actor

**Cousins, Derryl**
78136 Desert Mountain Circle, Bermuda Dunes CA 92203, USA — Baseball Umpire

**Cousins, Robin**
Billy Marsh, 174-8 N Gower St, London NW1 2NB, England — Figure Skater

**Cousins, Rose**
Old Farm Pony Records, PO Box 36054, RPO Spring Garden Road, Halifax NS B3J 3S9, Canada — Singer, Songwriter, Guitarist

**Cousins, Tina**
Tony Denton Promotions, Charter House, 157-159 High St, London N14 6BP, England — Singer, Model

**Cousteau, Jean-Michel**
Ocean Futures Society, 325 Chapala St, Santa Barbara CA 93101, USA — Oceanographer

**Cousy, Robert J (Bob)**
427 Salisbury St, Worcester MA 01609, USA — Basketball Player

**Coutterand, Leslie**
Agence Elisabeth Simpson, 62 Boulevard Du Montparnasse, 75015 Paris, France — Actress

**Couture, Barbara**
Association of Public & Land Grant Universities, 1307 New York Ave NW, #400, Washington DC 20005, USA — Educator

**Couture, Randy D (Natural)**
Xtreme Couture, 4055 W Sunset Road, Las Vegas NV 89118, USA — Martial Arts Fighter, Wrestler, Actor

**Covay, Don**
Rawstock, PO Box 110002, Cambria Heights NY 11411, USA — Singer, Songwriter

**Coventry, Kirsty**
Octagon Worldwide, 1751 Pinnacle Dr, #1500, McLean VA 22102 USA — Swimmer

**Coveny, John**
Creative Artists Agency, 2000 Ave of Stars, #100, Los Angeles CA 90067 USA — Producer, Writer

**Coverdale, David**
Agency Group Ltd, 142 W 57th St, #600, New York NY 10019 USA — Singer (Whitesnake, Deep Purple)

**Coverly, David C (Dave)**
221 8th St, Ann Arbor MI 48103, USA — Editorial Cartoonist, Cartoonist

**Covert, Allen**
Baker Winokur Ryder Public Relations, 9100 Wilshire Blvd, #500W, Beverly Hills CA 90212 USA — Actor

**Covert, James P (Jimbo)**
2647 Nelson Court, Weston FL 33332, USA — Football Player

**Covey, Richard O**
United Space Alliance, 1102 John Glenn Blvd, Titusville FL 32780, USA — Astronaut

**Covic, Nebojsa**
Prime Minister's Office, Nemanjina 11, 11000 Belgrade, Serbia — Prime Minister, Serbia & Montenegro

**Coville, Bruce**
Oddly Enough, PO Box 6110, Syracuse NY 13217, USA — Writer

**Covington, Bucky**
30141 Deercroft Dr, Wagram NC 28396, USA — Singer

| | |
|---|---|
| **Covington, Warren**<br>1627 Open Field Loop, Brandon FL 33510, USA | Orchestra Leader |
| **Covino, William A**<br>California State University, President's Office, 5151 State University Dr, Los Angeles CA 90032, USA | Educator |
| **Cowan, Billy R**<br>PO Box 1087, Palos Verdes Estates CA 90274, USA | Baseball Player |
| **Cowan, John**<br>Squire Mgmt, 3960 Radio Road, #206, Naples FL 34104, USA | Singer, Bassist (John Cowan Band) |
| **Cowan, Ralph Wolfe**<br>243 29th St, West Palm Beach FL 33407, USA | Artist |
| **Cowart, Sam, III**<br>11110 Fallgate Point Court, Jacksonville FL 32256, USA | Football Player |
| **Cowell, Simon P**<br>J G M, 15 Lexham Mews, London W8 6JW, England | Actor |
| **Cowen, Robert E**<br>US Court of Appeals, Judicial Complex, 402 E State St, Trenton NJ 08608, USA | Judge |
| **Cowen, Scott S**<br>Tulane University, President's Office, New Orleans LA 70118, USA | Educator |
| **Cowens, David W (Dave)**<br>132 Deep Cove, Raymond ME 04071, USA | Basketball Player, Coach |
| **Cowher, William L (Bill)**<br>1225 Briar Patch Lane, Raleigh NC 27615, USA | Football Player, Coach; Sportscaster |
| **Cowhill, William J**<br>9428 Vernon Dr, Great Falls VA 22066, USA | Navy Admiral |
| **Cowie, Lennox L**<br>University of Hawaii, Astronomy Dept, 2600 Campus Road, Honolulu HI 96822, USA | Astronomer |
| **Cowin, Dana**<br>Food & Wine, Editor's Office, 1120 Ave of Americas, New York NY 10036, USA | Editor |
| **Cowley, Anthony (Tony)**<br>Innovative Artists, 1505 10th St, Santa Monica CA 90401 USA | Art Director |
| **Cowley, John M**<br>Arizona State University, Physics & Astronomy Dept, Tempe AZ 85287, USA | Physicist |
| **Cowley, Joseph A (Joe)**<br>904 Andover Garden, Lexington KY 40509, USA | Baseball Player |
| **Cowlings, Allen G (A C)**<br>PO Box 1064, Pacific Palisades CA 90272, USA | Football Player |
| **Cowper, Nicola**<br>Brunskill Mgmt, 169 Queens Gate, #A8, London SW7 5EH, England | Actress |
| **Cowper, Stephen C (Steve)**<br>PO Box A, Juneau AK 99811, USA | Governor, AK |
| **Cox, Archibald, Jr**<br>998 5th Ave, #6W, New York NY 10028, USA | Financier |
| **Cox, Brian**<br>Conway Van Gelder Grant, 8-12 Broadwick St, #300, London W1F 8HW, England | Actor |
| **Cox, Brian E**<br>Sue Rider Mgmt, PO Box 49175, London SW19 3WY, England | Physicist |
| **Cox, Bryan K**<br>2845 Eudora Trail, Duluth GA 30097, USA | Football Player |
| **Cox, C Christopher**<br>4000 MacArthur Blvd, #430, Newport Beach CA 92660, USA | Government Official |
| **Cox, Charlie**<br>United Agents, 12-26 Lexington St, London W1F 0LE, England | Actor |
| **Cox, Chris**<br>T-Best Talent Agency, 508 Honey Lake Court, Danville CA 94506 USA | DJ Musician, Music Producer |
| **Cox, Christina**<br>Global Artists Agency, 6253 Hollywood Blvd, #508, Los Angeles CA 90028 USA | Actress |
| **Cox, Courteney**<br>W M E Entertainment, 9601 Wilshire Blvd, #300, Beverly Hills CA 90210 USA | Actress |
| **Cox, Craig**<br>Kaplan/Perrone Entertainment, 9744 Wilshire Blvd, #300, Beverly Hills CA 90212, USA | Writer, Producer |
| **Cox, Danny B**<br>306 Feagin Mill Road, Warner Robins GA 31088, USA | Baseball Player, Manager |
| **Cox, David R**<br>Nuffield College, Statistics Dept, Oxford OX1 1NF, England | Statistician |
| **Cox, David R**<br>Stanford University, Human Genome Center, Stanford CA 94305, USA | Geneticist |
| **Cox, DeAnna**<br>McFadden Artists, 818 18th Ave S, Nashville TN 37203, USA | Singer |
| **Cox, Deborah**<br>Abrams Artists, 275 7th Ave, #2600, New York NY 10001 USA | Singer, Songwriter |
| **Cox, Don**<br>Stellar Entertainment, 1019 17th Ave S, Nashville TN 37212, USA | Singer |
| **Cox, Emmett R**<br>US Court of Appeals, 113 Saint Joseph St, #433, Mobile AL 36602, USA | Judge |
| **Cox, Frederick W (Fred)**<br>401 E River St, Monticello MN 55362, USA | Football Player |
| **Cox, Gary W**<br>University of California, Political Science Dept, La Jolla CA 92093, USA | Political Scientist |
| **Cox, Gerald**<br>McMasters University Medical School, Respirology Division, Hamilton ON L85 4L8, Canada | Respirologist |
| **Cox, Harvey G, Jr**<br>Harvard University, Divinity School, Cambridge MA 02140, USA | Educator, Theologian |
| **Cox, J Casey**<br>2840 La Concha Dr, Clearwater FL 33762, USA | Baseball Player |
| **Cox, Jennifer Elise**<br>Don Buchwald Talent Agency, 6500 Wilshire Blvd, #2200, Los Angeles CA 90048 USA | Actress |
| **Cox, Joel**<br>Gersh Agency, 9465 Wilshire Blvd, #600, Beverly Hills CA 90212 USA | Editor |
| **Cox, Johnny W**<br>849 N Main St, Hazard KY 41701, USA | Basketball Player, Coach |
| **Cox, Kris**<br>2009 Lunenburg Dr, Allen TX 75013, USA | Golfer |
| **Cox, Laverne**<br>Hartig-Hilepo Agency, 54 W 21st St, #610, New York NY 10010 USA | Actress |
| **Cox, Lynne**<br>Martha Kaplan Agency, 115 W 29th St, #3, New York NY 10001, USA | Swimmer |

Covington - Cox

**C**

| | |
|---|---|
| **Cox, Paul**<br>Illumination Films, 1 Victoria Ave, Albert Park VIC 3208, Australia | Director, Producer, Writer |
| **Cox, Philip S**<br>Cox Richardson Architects, 204 Clarence St, Sydney NSW 2000, Australia | Architect |
| **Cox, Ralph**<br>8R Rolfes Lane, Newbury MA 01951, USA | Ice Hockey Player |
| **Cox, Robert J (Bobby)**<br>2190 Heathermoor Hill Dr, Marietta GA 30062, USA | Baseball Manager, Executive |
| **Cox, Ronny**<br>A P A Talent & Literary Agency, 405 S Beverly Dr, #300, Beverly Hills CA 90212 USA | Actor |
| **Cox, Stephanie R**<br>Atlanta Beat, 1955 Vaughn Road, #209, Kennesaw GA 30144, USA | Soccer Player |
| **Cox, Stephen J**<br>154 Barnsbury Road, Islington, London N1 0ER, England | Artist |
| **Cox, Steve**<br>1001 E Lakeshore Dr, Jonesboro AR 72401, USA | Football Player |
| **Cox, Tony**<br>New Wave Entertainment, 2660 W Olive Ave, Burbank CA 91505, USA | Actor |
| **Cox, Torrie T**<br>42 NW 92nd St, Miami Shores FL 33150, USA | Football Player |
| **Cox, W Ted**<br>109 W Pratt Dr, Oklahoma City OK 73110, USA | Baseball Player |
| **Cox, Warren J**<br>3111 N St NW, Washington DC 20007, USA | Architect |
| **Coxe, Craig**<br>Teddy Griffin Arena, 3450M 119th, Harbor Springs MI 49740, USA | Ice Hockey Player |
| **Coxon, Graham L**<br>X-Ray Touring, 77-79 Great Eastern St, #A, London EC2A 3HU, England | Singer, Guitarist (Blur), Actor |
| **Coyle, Brendan**<br>Rights House, Drury House, 34-43 Russell St, London WC2B 5HA, England | Actor |
| **Coyle, Richard**<br>Troika, 74 Clerkenwell Road, #300, London EC1M 5QA, England | Actor |
| **Coyne, Colleen**<br>3 Baldwin Lane, North Reading MA 01864, USA | Ice Hockey Player |
| **Coyne, Jonny**<br>Belfield & Ward, 80-81 Saint Martin Lane, Top Level, London WC2N 4AA, England | Actor |
| **Coyne, Kendall**<br>John Coyne, 10629 S Keeler Ave, Oak Lawn IL 60453, USA | Ice Hockey Player |
| **Coyne, Wayne M**<br>World's Fair Mgmt, 1208 Chowning Ave, Edmond OK 73034, USA | Singer, Guitarist (Flaming Lips) |
| **Coyote, Peter**<br>Untitled Entertainment, 350 S Beverly Dr, #200, Beverly Hills CA 90212 USA | Actor |
| **Coz, Steve**<br>National Enquirer, 1000 American Media Way, Boca Raton FL 33464, USA | Editor |
| **Cozier, Jimmy**<br>Padell Nadell Fine Wineberger, 59 Maiden Lane, #2700, New York NY 10038 USA | Singer, Songwriter |
| **Crabbe, Claude C**<br>49581 Wayne St, Indio CA 92201, USA | Football Player |
| **Crable, Robert E (Bob)**<br>564 Miami Trace Court, Loveland OH 45140, USA | Football Player |
| **Crabtree, Colleen**<br>A P A Talent & Literary Agency, 405 S Beverly Dr, #300, Beverly Hills CA 90212 USA | Actress |
| **Crabtree, Eric L**<br>3101 Walnut St, Denver CO 80205, USA | Football Player |
| **Crabtree, Michael**<br>San Francisco 49ers, 4949 Centennial Blvd, Santa Clara CA 95054 USA | Football Player |
| **Crabtree, Timothy L (Tim)**<br>1503 Kingswood Lane, Colleyville TX 76034, USA | Baseball Player |
| **Cracknell, James**<br>Headway, 190 Bagnall Road, Old Basford, Nottingham, Nottinghamshire NG6 8SF, England | Rowing Athlete |
| **Craddock, Bantz J**<br>Military Professional Resources, 1320 Braddock Place, Alexandria VA 22314, USA | Army General |
| **Craddock, Billy (Crash)**<br>3007 Old Martinsville Road, Greensboro NC 27455, USA | Singer, Songwriter |
| **Craft, Christine**<br>KRBK-TV, News Dept, 500 Media Place, Sacramento CA 95815, USA | Commentator |
| **Craft, Jason D A**<br>11688 Armistad Court, Jacksonville FL 32256, USA | Football Player |
| **Crafter, Jane**<br>317 W Almeria Road, Phoenix AZ 85003, USA | Golfer |
| **Cragg, Anthony D (Tony)**<br>Lise-Meitner-Str 33, 42119 Wuppertal, Germany | Sculptor |
| **Cragg, Stephen**<br>Thrive Entertainment, 1093 Broxton Ave, Ste 228, Los Angeles CA 90024, USA | Director |
| **Craggs, George**<br>6223 6th Ave NW, Seattle WA 98107, USA | Soccer Player |
| **Craig of Radley, David B**<br>House of Lords, Westminster, London SW1A 0PW, England | Air Force Marshal, England |
| **Craig, Adam Jamal**<br>Keyword Entertainment, 1015 Gayley Ave, #601, Los Angeles CA 90024, USA | Actor |
| **Craig, Carly**<br>A P A Talent & Literary Agency, 405 S Beverly Dr, #300, Beverly Hills CA 90212 USA | Actress, Comedienne |
| **Craig, Cornelius (Neal), Jr**<br>2231 Crane Ave, Cincinnati OH 45207, USA | Football Player |
| **Craig, Daniel**<br>Independent Talent Group, 40 Whitfield St, London W1T 2RH, England | Actor |
| **Craig, Eli**<br>Creative Artists Agency, 2000 Ave of Stars, #100, Los Angeles CA 90067 USA | Director, Producer |
| **Craig, Elijah**<br>Gilbertson Entertainment, 1334 3rd Street Promenade, #201, Santa Monica CA 90401 USA | Actor |
| **Craig, James D (Jim)**<br>PO Box 1199, Mattapoisett MA 02739, USA | Ice Hockey Player |
| **Craig, Jenny**<br>5770 Fleet St, Carlsbad CA 92008, USA | Nutritionist |
| **Craig, Jonny**<br>Artery Foundation, 142 S St, Sacramento CA 95811, USA | Singer |

**Cox - Craig**

**Craig, Judy**
Lustig Talent, PO Box 770850, Orlando FL 32877 USA — Singer (Chiffons)

**Craig, Keren**
Marquesa, 60 W 26th St, #1425, New York NY 10001, USA — Fashion Designer (Marchesa), Model

**Craig, Larry E**
PO Box 2271, Eagle ID 83616, USA — Senator, ID

**Craig, Michael**
Chatto & Linnit, 123A King's Road, London SW3 4PL, England — Actor

**Craig, Mike**
29907 County Road 3, Merrifield MN 56465, USA — Ice Hockey Player

**Craig, Richard**
Pacific Northwest National Laboratory, 902 Battelle Blvd, Richland WA 99354, USA — Inventor (Land-Mine Detector)

**Craig, Roger L**
2925 County Road 30, Craig CO 81625, USA — Baseball Player, Manager

**Craig, Roger T**
271 Vista Verde Way, Portola Valley CA 94028, USA — Football Player

**Craig, Ryan**
United Agents, 12-26 Lexington St, London W1F 0LE, England — Director, Writer

**Craig, Stuart**
Skouras Agency, 1149 3rd St, #300, Santa Monica CA 90403 USA — Production Designer

**Craig, William (Bill)**
PO Box 629, Newport Beach CA 92661, USA — Swimmer

**Craig, Yvonne**
Y C/M C Ltd, PO Box 827, Pacific Palisades CA 90272, USA — Actress

**Craighead, John J**
5125 Orchard Ave, Missoula MT 59803, USA — Ecologist

**Crain, Jesse A**
20702 Hartford Way, Lakeville MN 55044, USA — Baseball Player

**Crain, William**
Contemporary Artists, 610 Santa Monica Blvd, #202, Santa Monica CA 90401 USA — Director

**Crais, Robert**
12829 Landale St, Studio City CA 91604, USA — Writer

**Cramer, Darrell**
708 E 150 N, Springville UT 84663, USA — Hero

**Cramer, Grant**
9911 W Pico Blvd, #1060, Los Angeles CA 90035, USA — Actor

**Cramer, James J (Jim)**
W M E Entertainment, 9601 Wilshire Blvd, #300, Beverly Hills CA 90210 USA — Actor

**Cramer, Tom**
Mark Wooley Gallery, 120 NW 9th, Portland OR 97209, USA — Artist

**Crampton, Barbara**
Amsel Eisenstadt Frazier, 5055 Wilshire Blvd, #865, Los Angeles CA 90036 USA — Actress

**Crampton, Bruce**
225 Winter Crest Lane, Severna Park MD 21146, USA — Golfer

**Cramton, Roger C**
475 Savage Farm Dr, Ithaca NY 14850, USA — Attorney, Educator

**Crandall, Bruce P**
PO Box 736, Manchester WA 98353, USA — Vietnam War Air Force Hero (CMH)

**Crandall, Delmar W (Del)**
807 Azalea Lane, Vero Beach FL 32963, USA — Baseball Player

**Crandall, Stephen H**
PO Box 898, Westwood MA 02090, USA — Mechanical Engineer

**Crane, Benjamin M (Ben)**
2223 Cedar Elm Terrace, Westlake TX 76262, USA — Golfer

**Crane, Brian**
PO Box 51771, Sparks NV 89435, USA — Cartoonist (Pickles)

**Crane, David**
W M E Entertainment, 9601 Wilshire Blvd, #300, Beverly Hills CA 90210 USA — Writer, Director, Producer

**Crane, Paul E**
12 N Monterey St, Mobile AL 36604, USA — Football Player

**Crane, Tony**
Abrams Artists, 9200 W Sunset Blvd, #1125, West Hollywood CA 90069 USA — Actor

**Cranham, Kenneth**
Markham Froggatt Irwin, Julian House, 4 Windmill St, London W1P 1HF, England — Actor

**Cranston, Bryan**
United Talent Agency, U T A Plaza, 9336 Civic Center Dr, Beverly Hills CA 90210 USA — Actor

**Cranston, Toller**
International Management Group, 1 Saint Clair Ave E, Toronto ON M4T 2V7, Canada — Figure Skater

**Crary, Dan**
Rob Hall Acoustic Music, PO Box 2105, Ringwood North VIC 3134, Australia — Singer, Guitarist

**Crashley, Bart**
90 Goacher Road, Campbellford ON K0L 1L0, Canada — Ice Hockey Player

**Craven, Matt**
Paradigm Agency, 360 N Crescent Dr, North Building, Beverly Hills CA 90210 USA — Actor

**Craven, Murray**
2814 Rest Haven Dr, Whitefish MT 59937, USA — Ice Hockey Player

**Craven, Richard A (Ricky)**
3585 Boy Scout Camp Road, Kannapolis NC 28081, USA — Auto Racing Driver

**Craven, Wesley E (Wes)**
2419 Solar Dr, Los Angeles CA 90046, USA — Director

**Craver, Aaron L**
821 W Maple St, Compton CA 90220, USA — Football Player

**Crawford Stanley, Marianne**
Washington Mystics, Verizon Center, 401 9th St NW, #750, Washington DC 20004 USA — Basketball Coach

**Crawford, A Jamal**
Los Angeles Clippers, Staples Center, 1111 S Figueroa St, Los Angeles CA 90015 USA — Basketball Player

**Crawford, Billy J**
Concorde International, 101 Shepherds Bush Road, London W6 7LP, England — Singer

**Crawford, Bob**
6 Progress Dr, Cromwell CT 06416, USA — Ice Hockey Player

**Crawford, Brad**
RR 2, Winamac IN 46996, USA — Football Player

**Crawford, Carl D**
15618 Bristol Lake Dr, Houston TX 77070, USA — Baseball Player

**Crawford, Chace**
Podwall Entertainment, 710 N Orbach Ave, #203, West Hollywood CA 90069, USA — Actor

**Crawford, Christina**
Seven Springs Farm, Sanders Road, Tensed ID 83870, USA — Writer
**Crawford, Chuck**
Country Thunder Records, 1016 17th Ave S, Nashville TN 37212, USA — Fiddler, Singer (Heartland)
**Crawford, Cindy**
Creative Artists Agency, 2000 Ave of Stars, #100, Los Angeles CA 90067 USA — Model, Actress
**Crawford, Clayne**
A P A Talent & Literary Agency, 405 S Beverly Dr, #300, Beverly Hills CA 90212 USA — Actor
**Crawford, Eve**
Nobel Caplan Abrams, 1260 Younge St, #200, Toronto ON M4T 1W6, Canada — Actress
**Crawford, Frederick R (Fred)**
24 W Lawn Dr, Teaneck NJ 07666, USA — Basketball Player
**Crawford, Gerald J (Gerry)**
111 9th St E, Saint Petersburg FL 33715, USA — Baseball Umpire
**Crawford, Joan**
4748 S Harvard Ave, #80, Tulsa OK 74135, USA — Basketball Player
**Crawford, John E (Johnny)**
PO Box 1851, Los Angeles CA 90078, USA — Actor, Singer
**Crawford, Keith L**
119 A N County Road 2203, Palestine TX 75803, USA — Football Player
**Crawford, Kirsty**
All Terrain Music Rights, 53 Chandos Place, London WC2N 4HS, England — Singer, Songwriter
**Crawford, Lavell**
Anonymous Content, 3532 Hayden Ave, Culver City CA 90232 USA — Actor, Comedian
**Crawford, Mac**
C V S/Caremark Corp, 1 C V S/Caremark Dr, Woonsocket RI 02895, USA — Businessman
**Crawford, Michael**
W M E Entertainment, 9601 Wilshire Blvd, #300, Beverly Hills CA 90210 USA — Actor, Singer
**Crawford, Nancy**
Playboy Promotions, 9346 Civic Center Dr, #200, Beverly Hills CA 90210 USA — Model, Actress
**Crawford, Rachel**
Edna Talent Mgmt, 318 Dundas St W, Toronto ON M5T 1G5, Canada — Actress
**Crawford, Randy**
Performers of the World, 5657 Wilshire Blvd, #280, Los Angeles CA 90036 USA — Singer
**Crawford, Steve**
4011 Hillman Way, #100, Youngstown OH 44512, USA — Singer (Annointed), Songwriter
**Crawford, Steven R (Steve)**
6122 E 480, Salina OK 74365, USA — Baseball Player
**Crawley, Sylvia**
Ohio University, Athletic Dept, Athens OH 45701, USA — Basketball Player, Coach
**Cray, Robert**
Conquero Public Relations, 11271 Ventura Blvd, #522, Studio City CA 91604, USA — Singer, Guitarist
**Crayton, Patrick J**
2831 Merlins Rock Lane, Lewisville TX 75056, USA — Football Player
**Crazy Mohan**
5 Hokkalingam St, Mandavelli, Chennai TN 600028, India — Actor, Comedian
**Creadon, Patrick**
Paradigm Agency, 360 N Crescent Dr, North Building, Beverly Hills CA 90210 USA — Director
**Creager, Melora**
Ken-Ran Entertainment, 418 S Barton St, Grapevine TX 76051, USA — Singer, Cellist, Songwriter
**Creamer, Paula**
4705 Joanna Garden Court, Windermere FL 34786, USA — Golfer
**Creamer, Roger W**
180 E Hartsdale Ave, #2E, Hartsdale NY 10530, USA — Sportswriter
**Creamer, Timothy J**
5103 Carefree Dr, League City TX 77573, USA — Astronaut
**Crear, Mark**
27023 McBean Parkway, Valencia CA 91355, USA — Track Athlete
**Crebassa, Marianne**
I M G Artists, Hogarth Business Park, Chiswick, London W4 2TH, England — Opera Singer
**Crede, Joseph (Joe)**
42 Dry Creek Trail, Linn MO 65051, USA — Baseball Player
**Creech, Morri**
Waywiser Press, PO Box 6205, Baltimore MD 21206, USA — Writer
**Creech, Sharon**
Harper Collins Publishers, 10 E 53rd St, Cellar 1, New York NY 10022 USA — Writer
**Creeggan, Jim**
Nettwerk Mgmt, 6525 W Sunset Blvd, #800, Los Angeles CA 90028 USA — Bassist (Barenaked Ladies)
**Creek, P Douglas (Doug)**
17500 White Water Court, Punta Gorda FL 33982, USA — Baseball Player
**Creekmore, Nathaniel R (Nate)**
Universal Press Syndicate, 4520 Main St, #700, Kansas City MO 64111 USA — Cartoonist (Maintaining)
**Creel, Gavin**
Bill Silva Mgmt, 8225 Santa Monica Blvd, West Hollywood CA 90046, USA — Actor, Singer
**Creel, Monica**
Amsel Eisenstadt Frazier, 5055 Wilshire Blvd, #865, Los Angeles CA 90036 USA — Actress
**Cregeen, Peter**
Associated International Mgmt, 7 Hatton Garden, #400, London EC1N 8AD, England — Director, Producer
**Cregger, Zach**
Baker Winokur Ryder Public Relations, 9100 Wilshire Blvd, #500W, Beverly Hills CA 90212 USA — Actor, Producer, Director, Writer
**Creighton, Adam**
5202 Spectacular Bid Dr, Wesley Chapel FL 33544, USA — Ice Hockey Player
**Creighton, David T (Dave), Sr**
5202 Spectacular Bid Dr, Wesley Chapel FL 33544, USA — Ice Hockey Player, Coach
**Creighton, Jim**
5297 S Geneva St, Englewood CO 80111, USA — Basketball Player
**Creighton, Joanne V**
Mount Holyoke College, President's Office, South Hadley MA 01075, USA — Educator
**Creighton, John O**
2111 SW 174th St, Burien WA 98166, USA — Astronaut
**Crennel, Romeo**
200 E 89th St, #41A, New York NY 10128, USA — Football Coach
**Crensha, George**
22 Morning State Way, Sequim WA 98382, USA — Cartoonist (Belvedere)
**Crenshaw, Ben D**
2610 Kenmore Court, Austin TX 78703, USA — Golfer

**Crenshaw, Lewis W, Jr** — Navy Admiral
D C N O, Resource/Warfare Requirements, HqUSN, Pentagon, Washington DC 20350, USA

**Crenshaw, Marshall** — Singer, Songwriter
Rascoff/Zysblat Organization, 250 W 57th St, New York NY 10107 USA

**Crenshaw, Willis C** — Football Player
21 Carly Dr, Woodstock NY 12498, USA

**Creskoff, Rebecca** — Actress
Innovative Artists, 1505 10th St, Santa Monica CA 90401 USA

**Crespo Claudio, Felipe J** — Baseball Player
PO Box 592363, Orlando FL 32859, USA

**Crespo, Elvis** — Singer
A-P R Media, 8334 Lefferts Blvd, #3C, Kew Gardens NY 11415, USA

**Crespo, Hernan** — Soccer Player
Chelsea F C, Stamford Bridge, Fulham Road, London SW6 1HS, England

**Cressend, Jack** — Baseball Player
723 Libby Lane, Mandeville LA 70471, USA

**Cressida, Kathryn** — Actress
W M E Entertainment, 9601 Wilshire Blvd, #300, Beverly Hills CA 90210 USA

**Cresson, Edith** — Prime Minister, France
Mairie, 86018 Chatellerault Cedex, France

**Cretier, Jean-Luc** — Alpine Skier
153 Ave du Marechal Leclerc, BP 20, 73700 Bourq Saint Maurice, France

**Cretton, Destin Daniel** — Director
W M E Entertainment, 9601 Wilshire Blvd, #300, Beverly Hills CA 90210 USA

**Creveling, Christopher** — Speed Skater
U S Speedskating, 5662 S Cougar Lane, Salt Lake City UT 84118 USA

**Crew, Amanda** — Actress
United Talent Agency, U T A Plaza, 9336 Civic Center Dr, Beverly Hills CA 90210 USA

**Crewdson, Gregory** — Photographer
247 16th St, Brooklyn NY 11215, USA

**Crewe, Candida** — Writer
Bloomsbury Publishing, 50 Bedford Square, London WC1B 3DP, England

**Crews, David P** — Psychobiologist
University of Texas, Biological Science Division, Zoology Dept, Austin TX 78712, USA

**Crews, Frederick C** — Educator, Writer
636 Vicente Ave, Berkeley CA 94707, USA

**Crews, Phillip** — Chemist
University of California, Chemistry Dept, 1156 High St, Santa Cruz CA 99064, USA

**Crews, Terry A, Jr** — Actor, Football Player
3 Arts Entertainment, 9460 Wilshire Blvd, #700, Beverly Hills CA 90212 USA

**Crewson, Wendy** — Actress
Oscars Abrams Zimel, 438 Queen St E, Toronto ON M5A 1T4, Canada

**Crha, Jiri** — Ice Hockey Player
16390 Braeburn Ridge Trail, Delray Beach FL 33446, USA

**Cribbins, Bernard** — Actor
Gavin Barker Assoc, 2D Wimpole St, London W1G 0EB, England

**Cribbs, Joe S** — Football Player
5333 Creekside Loop, Birmingham AL 35244, USA

**Cribbs, Joshua** — Football Player
9333 W Hampton Dr, North Royalton OH 44133, USA

**Crichlow, Lenora** — Actress
B W H Agency, 117 Shaftesbury Ave, London WC2H 8AD, England

**Crickhowell of Pont Esgob, Nicholas E** — Government Leader, England
4 Henning St, London SW11 3DR, England

**Crider, Melissa (Missy)** — Actress
Mavrick Artists Agency, 6100 Wilshire Blvd, #550, Los Angeles CA 90048, USA

**Crier, Catherine** — Commentator
Crier Communications, PO Box 627, Katonah NY 10536, USA

**Crile, Susan** — Artist
168 W 86th St, New York NY 10024, USA

**Crilley, Mark** — Writer
PO Box 103, Walled Lake MI 48390, USA

**Crim, Charles R (Chuck)** — Baseball Player
50039 Golden Horse Dr, Oakhurst CA 93644, USA

**Crippen, Robert L** — Astronaut
781 Harbour Isle Place, West Palm Beach FL 33410, USA

**Crisostomo, Manny** — Photojournalist
Pacific Daily News, PO Box DN, Hagatna GU 96932, USA

**Crisp, Covelli L (Coco)** — Baseball Player
15 Evening Star Dr, Rancho Mirage CA 92270, USA

**Crisp, Terry A** — Ice Hockey Player, Coach
805 Cherry Laurel Court, Nashville TN 37215, USA

**Criss, Charles W (Charlie)** — Basketball Player
4310 Melanie Lane, Atlanta GA 30349, USA

**Criss, Darren** — Actor
C E S D, 10635 Santa Monica Blvd, #130, Los Angeles CA 90025 USA

**Criss, Peter** — Singer, Drummer (Kiss)
2111 Friar Court, Wall Township NJ 07719, USA

**Crist, Charles T (Chuck)** — Football Player
PO Box 369, Greenhurst NY 14742, USA

**Crist, George B** — Marine Corps General
406 East St, Beaufort SC 29902, USA

**Crist, Myndy** — Actress
Abrams Artists, 9200 W Sunset Blvd, #1125, West Hollywood CA 90069 USA

**Crista, Heloise** — Sculptor
Taliesin West, PO Box 4430, Scottsdale AZ 85261, USA

**Cristal, Linda** — Actress
9129 Hazen Dr, Beverly Hills CA 90210, USA

**Cristofer, Michael** — Writer, Director, Actor
Gersh Agency, 9465 Wilshire Blvd, #600, Beverly Hills CA 90212 USA

**Cristol, Stanley J** — Chemist
1638 W 3rd Ave, Durango CO 81301, USA

**Criswell, Jeffrey L (Jeff)** — Football Player
811 Walnut St, Kansas City MO 64106, USA

**Critelli, Michael** — Businessman
Pitney Bowes Inc, 1 Elmcroft Road, Stamford CT 06926, USA

**C**

**Crenshaw - Critelli**

**Criter, Kenneth W (Ken)** — Football Player
PO Box 441343, Aurora CO 80044, USA

**Crittenton, Javaris C** — Basketball Player
Washington Wizards, M C I Centre, 601 F St NW, Washington DC 20004 USA

**Croasdell, Adam** — Actor
Artists Partnership, 101 Finsbury Pavement, London EC2A 1RS, England

**Croce, Adrian J (A J)** — Singer
Railway Tour Consultants, 800 W 3rd St, #2308, Austin TX 78701, USA

**Croce, Joseph** — Singer (Chimes)
Wolfman Jack Entertainment, 105 Rivershore Dr, Hertford NC 27944 USA

**Crocicchia, Olivia** — Actress
United Talent Agency, U T A Plaza, 9336 Civic Center Dr, Beverly Hills CA 90210 USA

**Crocker, Ian** — Swimmer
8901 Ovalia Ave, Austin TX 78749, USA

**Crocker, J Dillard** — Basketball Player
5601 Holiday Park Blvd, North Port FL 34287, USA

**Crocker, Mary Lou** — Golfer
1403 Sutton Dr, Carrollton TX 75006, USA

**Crocker, Ryan C** — Diplomat
State Department, 2201 C St NW, Washington DC 20520 USA

**Crockett, Affion** — Actor
Lejan Entertainment, 11271 Ventura Blvd, #186, Studio City CA 91604, USA

**Crockett, Billy** — Singer, Songwriter
McGuckin Entertainment Public Relations, 500 Riverside Dr, #160, Austin TX 78704, USA

**Crockett, Zack** — Football Player
3301 NE 183rd St, #604, Aventura FL 33160, USA

**Croel, Mike** — Football Player
8305 Lookout Mountain Ave, Los Angeles CA 90046, USA

**Croft, Dwayne** — Opera Singer
I M G Artists, Carnegie Hall Tower, 152 W 57th St, #500, New York NY 10019 USA

**Croft, Laura** — Model
Playboy Promotions, 9346 Civic Center Dr, #200, Beverly Hills CA 90210 USA

**Croft, Richard** — Opera Singer
I M G Artists, Hogarth Business Park, Chiswick, London W4 2TH, England

**Crofts, Dash** — Singer, Songwriter (Seals & Crofts)
4Star Entertainment, 1675 York Ave, #32C, New York NY 10128, USA

**Croker, Stephen B (Steve)** — Air Force General
2 Byford Court, Chestertown MD 21620, USA

**Cromartie, Antonio** — Football Player
Arizona Cardinals, PO Box 888, Phoenix AZ 85001 USA

**Crombeen, Mike** — Ice Hockey Player
817 Foxcroft Blvd, Newmarket ON L3X 1MB, Canada

**Crombey, Bernard** — Actor
Artmedia, 20 Ave Rapp, 75007 Paris, France

**Crombie, Jonathan** — Actor
B R S / Gage Talent Agency, 5757 Wilshire Blvd, #659, Los Angeles CA 90036 USA

**Cromer, Roy B (Tripp), III** — Baseball Player
32 W Tombee Lane, Columbia SC 29209, USA

**Cromme, Gerhard** — Businessman
Siemens AG, Wittelsbacherplatz 2, 80333 Munich, Germany

**Crompton, Alfred W** — Archaeologist, Ethnologist, Biologist
Harvard University, Museum of Comparative Zoology, Cambridge MA 02138, USA

**Crompton, Steven S** — Cartoonist (Demi the Demoness)
PO Box 2018, Scottsdale AZ 85252, USA

**Cromwell, James** — Actor
Koshari Films, 13251 Ventura Blvd, #1, Studio City CA 91604, USA

**Cromwell, Nolan** — Football Player, Coach
2624 140th Ave NE, Bellevue WA 98005, USA

**Cronan, Peter J (Pete)** — Football Player
13 Saddle Hill Road, Hopkinton MA 01748, USA

**Cronbach, Lee J** — Psychologist
2614 Oregon St, Union City CA 94587, USA

**Crone, Raymond H (Ray)** — Baseball Player
508 Panarama, Waxahachie TX 75165, USA

**Cronenberg, David** — Director
Sentient Entertainment, 8840 Wilshire Blvd, #200, Beverly Hills CA 90211, USA

**Cronenweth, Jeffrey S (Jeff)** — Cinematographer
2241 Corinth Ave, Los Angeles CA 90064, USA

**Cronin, Anthony** — Writer
30 Oakley Road, Dublin 6, Ireland

**Cronin, Eugene E (Gene)** — Football Player
2445 37th Ave, Sacramento CA 95822, USA

**Cronin, James W** — Nobel Physics Laureate
175 N Harbor Dr, #4902, Chicago IL 60601, USA

**Cronin, Shawn** — Ice Hockey Player
4163 SE Oakland St, Stuart FL 34997, USA

**Cronk, William F (Rick), III** — Businessman, Non-Profit Executive
Boy Scouts of America, National Council, PO Box 152079, Irving TX 75015, USA

**Crook, Mackenzie** — Actor, Comedian
Karushi Mgmt, 7 Wenlock Road, #10, London N1 7SL, England

**Croom, Sylvester** — Football Player, Coach
3909 12th St NE, Tuscaloosa AL 35404, USA

**Crosbie, Annette** — Actress
Independent Talent Group, 40 Whitfield St, London W1T 2RH, England

**Crosbie, John C** — Political Leader, Canada
Scotia Center, 235 Water St, Saint John's NF A1C 5L3, Canada

**Crosby, Alfred W** — Historian
2506 Bowman Ave, Austin TX 78703, USA

**Crosby, Caitlin** — Actress
Paradigm Agency, 360 N Crescent Dr, North Building, Beverly Hills CA 90210 USA

**Crosby, Cathy Lee** — Actress
Epstein Wyckoff Corsa Ross, 11350 Ventura Blvd, #100, Studio City CA 91604, USA

**Crosby, David** — Singer (Byrds, Crosby Stills Nash)
Lookout Mgmt, 1460 4th St, #300, Santa Monica CA 90401 USA

**Crosby, Denise** — Actress, Model
Rebel Entertainment Partners, 5700 Wilshire Blvd, #456, Los Angeles CA 90036, USA

| | |
|---|---|
| **Crosby, Edward C (Ed)** | Baseball Player |
| 6952 Brightwood Lane, #9, Garden Grove CA 92845, USA | |
| **Crosby, Elaine** | Golfer |
| 2580 Meadowbrook Lane, Jackson MI 49201, USA | |
| **Crosby, Kathryn Grant** | Actress |
| 508 W 3rd St, Carson City NV 89703, USA | |
| **Crosby, Mary** | Actress |
| 2875 S Barrymore Dr, Malibu CA 90265, USA | |
| **Crosby, Robert E (Bobby)** | Baseball Player |
| 11463 Anticost Way, Cypress CA 90630, USA | |
| **Crosby, Sidney P** | Ice Hockey Player |
| Pittsburgh Penguins, Consol Energy Center, 1001 5th Ave, Pittsburgh PA 15219 USA | |
| **Croshere, Austin** | Basketball Player |
| 21766 Azurelee Dr, Malibu CA 90265, USA | |
| **Cross, Ben** | Actor |
| Shepherd & Ford, 13 Radnor Walk, London SW3 4BP, England | |
| **Cross, Christopher** | Singer, Guitarist, Songwriter |
| Front Line Mgmt, 1100 Glendon Ave, #2000, Los Angeles CA 90024 USA | |
| **Cross, Cory** | Ice Hockey Player |
| 2963 Bayshore Pointe Dr, Tampa FL 33611, USA | |
| **Cross, David** | Actor, Comedian |
| Brillstein Entertainment Partners, 9150 Wilshire Blvd, #350, Beverly Hills CA 90212 USA | |
| **Cross, Donna Woolfolk** | Writer |
| Onondaga Community College, English Dept, Syracuse NY 13202, USA | |
| **Cross, Helen** | Writer |
| Rogers Coleridge White, 20 Powis Mews, London W11 1JN, England | |
| **Cross, Irv A** | Football Player, Sportscaster |
| 2196 Marion Road, Roseville MN 55113, USA | |
| **Cross, Jeffrey A (Jeff)** | Football Player |
| 8045 SW 100th St, Miami FL 33156, USA | |
| **Cross, Joseph** | Actor |
| United Talent Agency, U T A Plaza, 9336 Civic Center Dr, Beverly Hills CA 90210 USA | |
| **Cross, Justin A** | Football Player |
| PO Box 1967, New London NH 03257, USA | |
| **Cross, Marcia** | Actress |
| Gersh Agency, 9465 Wilshire Blvd, #600, Beverly Hills CA 90212 USA | |
| **Cross, Mike** | Guitarist, Fiddler |
| Blade Agency, PO Box 1556, Gainesville FL 32602, USA | |
| **Cross, Randall L (Randy)** | Football Player, Sportscaster |
| 155 Travertine Trail, Alpharetta GA 30022, USA | |
| **Cross, Shauna** | Writer |
| Wolf Kasteler Public Relations, 9350 Wilshire Blvd, #450, Beverly Hills CA 90212 USA | |
| **Crossan, David H (Dave)** | Football Player |
| 3314 Emory Dr, Winston Salem NC 27103, USA | |
| **Crosse, Clay** | Singer |
| Breen Agency, 110 30th Ave N, #3, Nashville TN 37203, USA | |
| **Crosse, Liris** | Model, Actress |
| Britto Agency, 234 W 56th St, #PH, New York NY 10019, USA | |
| **Crossett, Howard W** | Bobsled Athlete |
| Bobsled & Skeleton Federation, 1631 Mesa Ave, #A, Colorado Springs CO 80906 USA | |
| **Crossley, Paul C R** | Concert Pianist |
| Connaught Artists, 2 Molasses Row, London SW11 3UX, England | |
| **Crossley-Mercer, Edwin** | Opera Singer |
| I M G Artists, Hogarth Business Park, Chiswick, London W4 2TH, England | |
| **Crossman, Doug** | Ice Hockey Player |
| 107 Franklin Road, Glassboro NJ 08028, USA | |
| **Crosta, Roger** | Artist, Sculptor |
| PO Box 204, Manzanita OR 97130, USA | |
| **Croteau, Gary P** | Ice Hockey Player |
| 8380 E Hinsdale Ave, Centennial CO 80112, USA | |
| **Crothers, Donald M** | Chemist |
| Yale University, Biophysical Chemistry Dept, New Haven CT 06520, USA | |
| **Crothers, Will** | Rowing Athlete |
| Kingston Rowing Club, 1 Cataraqui, Kingston ON K7K 1Z7, Canada | |
| **Crotty, John K** | Basketball Player |
| 370 NE Edgewater Dr, #404, Stuart FL 34996, USA | |
| **Crouch, Andrae** | Singer, Pianist, Songwriter |
| Universal Attractions, 135 W 26th St, #1200, New York NY 10001 USA | |
| **Crouch, Eric E** | Football Player |
| 19453 Walnut Circle, Omaha NE 68130, USA | |
| **Crouch, Roger K** | Astronaut |
| 120 6th St NE, Washington DC 20002, USA | |
| **Crouch, Sandra** | Drummer, Songwriter |
| Sparrow Communications Group, 101 Winners Circle, Brentwood TN 37027, USA | |
| **Crouch, Stanley** | Writer, Columnist |
| Georges Borchardt Agency, 136 E 57th St, #1400, New York NY 10022, USA | |
| **Crouch, William W (Bill)** | Army General |
| Isilon Systems, 3101 Western Ave, Seattle WA 98121, USA | |
| **Croucier, Juan C** | Bassist (Dokken, Ratt) |
| 45 Cayuse Lane, Rancho Palos Verdes CA 90275, USA | |
| **Crouse, Lindsay** | Actress |
| 28 Leonard St, Gloucester MA 01930, USA | |
| **Crouther, Lance** | Actor |
| Circle of Confusion, 8548 Washington Blvd, Culver City CA 90232, USA | |
| **Crow, Ashley** | Actress |
| Don Buchwald Talent Agency, 6500 Wilshire Blvd, #2200, Los Angeles CA 90048 USA | |
| **Crow, Harlan R** | Businessman |
| Trammell Crow Co, Trammell Crow Center, 2001 Ross Ave, #325, Dallas TX 75201, USA | |
| **Crow, John David** | Football Player, Coach |
| 5004 Augusta Circle, College Station TX 77845, USA | |
| **Crow, Kim** | Rowing Athlete |
| Melbourne University Boat Club, Boathouse Dr, Melbourne VIC 3004, Australia | |
| **Crow, Lindon** | Football Player |
| 6800 S Strand Ave, #481, Yuma AZ 85364, USA | |
| **Crow, Mark H** | Basketball Player |
| 501 W Bay St, Jacksonville FL 32202, USA | |

**C**

**Crosby - Crow**

**Crow, Michael M** — Educator
Arizona State University, President's Office, Tempe AZ 85287, USA

**Crow, Sheryl** — Singer, Songwriter, Actress
W Mgmt, 75 E 4th St, Front 1, New York NY 10003, USA

**Crow, Thomas E** — Art Historian
New York University, Art History Institute, New York NY 10012, USA

**Crow, William R (Bill)** — Basketball Player
21300 River Road, #15, Perris CA 92570, USA

**Crowder, Bruce** — Ice Hockey Player
7 Kyle Dr, Nashua NH 03062, USA

**Crowder, David** — Singer, Guitarist, Pianist
Media Collective, PO Box 273, Franklin TN 37065, USA

**Crowder, J Corey** — Basketball Player
725 Ballard Bridge Road, Carrollton GA 30117, USA

**Crowder, Keith** — Ice Hockey Player
PO Box 95 Station Main, Essex ON N8M 2Y1, Canada

**Crowder, R Channing, Jr** — Football Player
8921 Southern Orchard Road, Davie FL 33328, USA

**Crowder, Randolph C (Randy)** — Football Player
803 Strawberry Lane, Brandon FL 33511, USA

**Crowder, Troy** — Ice Hockey Player
103 Panache North Shore Road, Whitefish ON P0M 3E0, Canada

**Crowder, William D** — Navy Admiral
Deputy CNO, Operations Plans & Strategy, HqUSN, Pentagon, Washington DC 20350 USA

**Crowe, Cameron** — Director, Writer
1016 Amalfi Dr, Pacific Palisades CA 90272, USA

**Crowe, Martin D** — Cricketer
PO Box 109302, Newmarket, Auckland 1149, New Zealand

**Crowe, Mia** — Actress
C E S D, 10635 Santa Monica Blvd, #130, Los Angeles CA 90025 USA

**Crowe, Phil** — Ice Hockey Player
204 Duffield St, Willow Grove PA 19090, USA

**Crowe, Russell** — Actor
W M E Entertainment, 9601 Wilshire Blvd, #300, Beverly Hills CA 90210 USA

**Crowe, Tonya** — Actress, Writer
13030 Mindanao Way, #4, Marina del Rey CA 90292, USA

**Crowell, Angelo D** — Football Player
PO Box 38203, Tallahassee FL 32315, USA

**Crowell, Germane L** — Football Player
195 Everidge Road, Winston Salem NC 27103, USA

**Crowell, John C** — Geologist
300 Hot Springs Road, Santa Barbara CA 93108, USA

**Crowell, Rodney J** — Singer, Songwriter
Maine Road Mgmt, 195 Chrystie St, #901F, New York NY 10002, USA

**Crowley, Ben** — Actor
Glick Agency, 347 5th Ave, #1404, New York NY 10016 USA

**Crowley, Dermot** — Actor
United Agents, 12-26 Lexington St, London W1F 0LE, England

**Crowley, Mart** — Writer
I C M Partners, 10250 Constellation Blvd, #900, Los Angeles CA 90067 USA

**Crowley, Michael** — Columnist, Writer
Three Rivers Press, 1745 Broadway, New York NY 10019, USA

**Crowley, Patricia** — Actress
T M C E, 270 N Canon Dr, #1064, Beverly Hills CA 90210, USA

**Crowley, Terrence M (Terry)** — Baseball Player
18405 Ensor Farm Court, Parkton MD 21120, USA

**Crown, David A** — Criminologist
100 Macoma Court, Fort Myers FL 33908, USA

**Crowson, Richard** — Editorial Cartoonist
Wichita Eagle-Beacon, Editorial Dept, 825 E Douglas Ave, Wichita KS 67202, USA

**Crowton, Gary** — Football Coach
Brigham Young University, Athletic Dept, Provo UT 84602, USA

**Croyle, J Brodie** — Football Player
105 Apple Blossom Dr, Brandon MS 39047, USA

**Croze, Marie-Josee** — Actress
U B B A, 6 Rue de Braque, 75003 Paris, France

**Crozier, Joseph R (Joe)** — Ice Hockey Player, Coach
299 Randwood Dr, Buffalo NY 14221, USA

**Crudup, Billy** — Actor
Creative Artists Agency, 2000 Ave of Stars, #100, Los Angeles CA 90067 USA

**Cruickshank, John A** — WW II Air Force Hero (VC)
Victoria Cross Assn, Old Admiralty Building, London SW1A 2BL, England

**Cruikshank, Thomas H** — Businessman
5949 Sherry Lane, #1035, Dallas TX 75225, USA

**Cruise, Tom** — Actor
42 West, 220 W 42nd St, #1200, New York NY 10036 USA

**Crum, E Denzel (Denny)** — Basketball Coach
6901 Routt Road, Louisville KY 40299, USA

**Crumb, George H** — Composer
240 Kirk Lane, Media PA 19063, USA

**Crumb, Robert (R)** — Cartoonist (Keep on Truckin')
20 Rue du Pont Vieux, 30610 Sauve, France

**Crump, Benjamin L** — Attorney
Parks & Crump, 240 N Magnolia Drive, Tallahassee FL 32301, USA

**Crump, Simon** — Writer
A M Heath Co, 79 Saint Martin's Lane, London WC2N 4RE, England

**Crumpler, Algernon D (Alge)** — Football Player
2155 Enclave Mill Dr, Dacula GA 30019, USA

**Crumpler, Carlester, Jr** — Football Player
4355 River Gate Lane, #B, Little River SC 29566, USA

**Crusan, Douglas G (Doug), Jr** — Football Player
6263 Hanover Court, Fishers IN 46038, USA

**Crutcher, Chris** — Writer
3405 E Marion Court, Spokane WA 99223, USA

**Crutzen, Paul J** — Nobel Chemistry Laureate
Am Fort Gonsenheim 36, 55122 Mainz, Germany

**Cruyff, Johan** — Soccer Player, Coach
Koninklijke Nederk Voetbalbod, Postbus 515, 3700 Zeist AM, Netherlands

**Cruz Dilan, Jose L, Sr** — Baseball Player
2309 Delta Bridge Dr, Pearland TX 77584, USA

**Cruz Garcia, Deivi** — Baseball Player
611 Woodward Ave, Detroit MI 48226, USA

**Cruz Martinez, Nelson R** — Baseball Player
Baltimore Orioles, Oriole Park, 333 W Camden St, Baltimore MD 21201 USA

**Cruz Smith, Martin** — Writer
Simon & Schuster, 1230 Ave of Americas, Concourse 1, New York NY 10020 USA

**Cruz, Alexis** — Actor
Defining Artists, 4370 Tujunga Ave, #120, Studio City CA 91604, USA

**Cruz, Anthony** — Singer
Latin Artist Group, 11271 Ventura Blvd, #151, Studio City CA 91604, USA

**Cruz, Brandon** — Actor, Musician
Taang Records & Retail, 706 Pismo Court, San Diego CA 92109, USA

**Cruz, Hector L** — Baseball Player
1646 N Monticello Ave, Chicago IL 60647, USA

**Cruz, Jacob** — Baseball Player
1582 W Commerce Ave, Gilbert AZ 85233, USA

**Cruz, Jose L, Jr** — Baseball Player
8475 SW 53rd Ave, Miami FL 33143, USA

**Cruz, Julio L** — Baseball Player
12212 164th Court NE, Redmond WA 98052, USA

**Cruz, Nilo** — Writer
Paradigm Agency, 360 N Crescent Dr, North Building, Beverly Hills CA 90210 USA

**Cruz, Penelope** — Actress, Model
Kuranda Mgmt, Santo Angel 84, 28043 Madrid, Spain

**Cruz, Raymond** — Actor
Media Artists Group, 8222 Melrose Ave, #203, Los Angeles CA 90048 USA

**Cruz, Taio** — Singer, Songwriter
Helter Skelter, 347-353 Chiswick High Road, London W4 4HS, England

**Cruz, Valerie** — Actress
Innovative Artists, 1505 10th St, Santa Monica CA 90401 USA

**Cruz, Victor M** — Football Player
New York Giants, Meadowlands Stadium, 102 Route 120, East Rutherford NJ 07073 USA

**Cruzado, Waded** — Educator
Montana State University, President's Office, Bozeman MT 59717, USA

**Cruz-Diez, Carlos** — Artist
23 Rue Pierre Semard, 75009 Paris, France

**Crvenkovski, Branko** — President, Macedonia
Bihacka 8, 1000 Skopje, Macedonia

**Cryder, Robert J (Bob)** — Football Player
17411 NE 129th St, Redmond WA 98052, USA

**Cryer, Gretchen** — Writer, Lyricist, Actress
885 W End Ave, New York NY 10025, USA

**Cryer, Jon** — Actor
United Talent Agency, U T A Plaza, 9336 Civic Center Dr, Beverly Hills CA 90210 USA

**Cryer, Suzanne** — Actress
Essential Talent Mgmt, 3151 Cahuenga Blvd W, #220, Los Angeles CA 90068, USA

**Crystal, Billy** — Actor, Comedian
P M K-B N C, 622 3rd Ave, #800, New York NY 10017 USA

**Crystal, Ronald G** — Molecular Biologist
435 E 70th St, #34B, New York NY 10021, USA

**Csikszentmihalyi, Mihaly** — Psychologist
700 Alamosa Dr, Claremont CA 91711, USA

**Csokas, Marton** — Actor
Sue Barnett Assoc, 1/96 Albion St, Surry Hills NSW 2010, Australia

**Csonka, Lawrence R (Larry)** — Football Player
6940 Stella Place, Anchorage AK 99507, USA

**Csupo, Gabor** — Director
Grand Allure Entertainment, 12835 Mulholland Drive, Beverly Hills CA 90210, USA

**Ctvrtlik, Robert (Bob)** — Volleyball Player
22 Leon Way, Rancho Mirage CA 92270, USA

**Cua, Rick** — Singer, Pianist
Greg Menza, 1086 Rip Steele Road, Columbia TN 38401, USA

**Cuaron Orozoco, Carlos J** — Director, Producer, Writer
Esperanto Filmoj, 37 W 20th St, New York NY 10011, USA

**Cuaron, Alfonso** — Director, Producer
United Talent Agency, U T A Plaza, 9336 Civic Center Dr, Beverly Hills CA 90210 USA

**Cuba, Alex** — Singer, Songwriter
Agency Group Ltd, 1880 Century Park E, #711, Los Angeles CA 90067 USA

**Cuban, Mark** — Basketball Executive, Businessman
Dallas Mavericks, Pavilion, 2909 Taylor Street, Dallas TX 75226 USA

**Cubbage, Michael L (Mike)** — Baseball Player, Manager
3349 Carroll Creek Road, Keswick VA 22947, USA

**Cubitt, David** — Actor
Resolution, 1801 Century Park E, #2300, Los Angeles CA 90067 USA

**Cuccarini, Lorella** — Actress
Assoziazione Italia, CP 6323, 00100 Rome-Prati, Italy

**Cucchi, Enzo** — Artist
Galerie Bruno Bischofberger, Weissenrainstr 1, 8708 Mannedorf, Switzerland

**Cuccurullo, Warren** — Guitarist (Duran Duran)
D D Productions, 93A Westbourne Park Villas, London W2 5ED, England

**Cuche, Didier** — Alpine Skier
Bonne Auberge, 2058 Les Bugnenets, Switzerland

**Cucinotta, Maria Grazia** — Actress, Model
Class Mgmt, Pizza Cavour 66, 02100 Rieti, Italy

**Cudahy, Richard D** — Judge
US Court of Appeals, 219 S Dearborn St, #2302B, Chicago IL 60604, USA

**Cuddy, Jim** — Singer, Guitarist (Blue Rodeo)
Starfish Entertainment, 906A Logan Ave, Toronto ON M4K 3E4, Canada

**Cuddyer, Michael B** — Baseball Player
10240 Washington Palm Way, Malverne NY 11565, USA

**Cudlitz, Michael** — Actor
Gold Coast, 1023 1/2 Abbot Kinney Blvd, Venice CA 90291, USA

**Cudmore, Daniel** — Actor
Characters Talent Agency, 1505 W 2nd Ave, #200, Vancouver, BC V6H 3Y4, Canada
**Cuesta, Michael** — Director
W M E Entertainment, 9601 Wilshire Blvd, #300, Beverly Hills CA 90210 USA
**Cuevas, Beto** — Singer, Actor, Composer
Espada-Zimmatore, PO Box 6577, Burbank CA 91510, USA
**Cuevas, Jose Luis** — Artist
Galeana 109, San Angel Inn, Mexico City 20 DF, Mexico
**Culbertson, Brian** — Jazz Musician
Stiletto Entertainment, 8295 S La Cienega Blvd, Inglewood CA 90301, USA
**Culbertson, Frank L, Jr** — Astronaut
15500 Meherrin Dr, Centreville VA 20120, USA
**Culbreath, Joshua (Josh)** — Track Athlete
Central State University, Athletic Dept, Wilberforce OH 45384, USA
**Culbreth, Fieldin H, III** — Baseball Umpire
224 Claiborne Court, Spartanburg SC 29301, USA
**Culea, Melinda** — Actress
Blueline Productions, 212 26th St, #295, Santa Monica CA 90402, USA
**Culhane, Jim** — Ice Hockey Player
8547 Hathaway Road, Kalamazoo MI 49009, USA
**Culkin, Courtney Rachel** — Model
Playboy Promotions, 9346 Civic Center Dr, #200, Beverly Hills CA 90210 USA
**Culkin, Kieran** — Actor
Brookside Artists Mgmt, 250 W 57th St, #2303, New York NY 10107, USA
**Culkin, Macaulay** — Actor
Brookside Artists Mgmt, 250 W 57th St, #2303, New York NY 10107 USA
**Culkin, Rory** — Actor
Brookside Artists Mgmt, 450 N Roxbury Dr, #400, Beverly Hills CA 90210, USA
**Cullen, Barry** — Ice Hockey Player
Cullen Motors, 905 Woodlawn Road W, Guelph ON N1K 1B7, Canada
**Cullen, Brett** — Actor
Lovett Mgmt, 1327 Brinkley Ave, Los Angeles CA 90049, USA
**Cullen, Brian** — Ice Hockey Player
Brian Cullen Motors, 386 Ontario St, Saint Catherines ON L2R 6S8, Canada
**Cullen, Crista K (Chay)** — Field Hockey Player
5 Holford Way, Queen Mary's Place, Roehampton, London SW15 5GB, England
**Cullen, John** — Ice Hockey Player
1002 Legacy Hills Dr, McDonough GA 30253, USA
**Cullen, Matthew (Matt)** — Ice Hockey Player
6008 Over Hadden Court, Raleigh NC 27614, USA
**Cullen, Ray** — Ice Hockey Player
20 Sydenham Dr, RR 2, Iderton ON N0M 2A0, Canada
**Cullen, Sean M** — Actor
Henderson Hogan Agency, 850 7th Ave, #1003, New York NY 10019, USA
**Cullen, Timothy L (Tim)** — Baseball Player
159 W G St, Benicia CA 94510, USA
**Cullen, Tom** — Actor
United Agents, 12-26 Lexington St, London W1F 0LE, England
**Culler, Glen** — Computer Scientist
Culler Scientific Systems Corp, 100 Burns Place, Goleta CA 93117, USA
**Culligan, Joe** — Private Investigator, Writer
Research Investigative Services, 650 NE 126th St, North Miami FL 33161, USA
**Cullimore, Jassen A** — Ice Hockey Player
8610 Dolce Vita Lane, Odessa FL 33556, USA
**Cullinan, Edward H** — Architect
Wharf, 1 Baldwin Terrace, London N1 7RU, England
**Cullum, Jamie** — Jazz Pianist, Singer, Songwriter
Direct Management Group, 947 La Cienega Blvd, #G, West Hollywood CA 90069, USA
**Cullum, John** — Actor, Singer
Stone Manners Salners, 6100 Wilshire Blvd, #1500, Los Angeles CA 90035 USA
**Cullum, Mark E** — Editorial Cartoonist
5401 Forest Acres Dr, Nashville TN 37220, USA
**Culp, Joseph** — Actor, Director, Producer
A M T Artists, 15260 Ventura Blvd, #1200, Sherman Oaks CA 91403, USA
**Culp, Ray L** — Baseball Player
7400 Waterline Road, Austin TX 78731, USA
**Culp, Steven** — Actor
Miriam Milgrom Entertainment, 3614 Lankershim Blvd, Los Angeles CA 90068, USA
**Culpepper, Daunte** — Football Player
3429 NW 82nd Terrace, Pembroke Pines FL 33024, USA
**Culpepper, J Broward (Brad)** — Football Player
60 Bahama Circle, Tampa FL 33606, USA
**Culpepper, James** — Drummer (Flyleaf)
W M E Entertainment, 9601 Wilshire Blvd, #300, Beverly Hills CA 90210 USA
**Culpepper, R Edward (Ed)** — Football Player
811 Bluewater Dr, Sun City Center FL 33573, USA
**Culpo, Olivia** — Beauty Queen
Miss Universe Organization, 1370 Ave of Americas, #1600, New York NY 10019 USA
**Culver, George R** — Baseball Player
5409 Rustic Canyon St, Bakersfield CA 93306, USA
**Culver, John C** — Senator, IA
5409 Spangler Ave, Bethesda MD 20816, USA
**Culver, Michael** — Actor
Waring & McKenna, 22 Grafton St, London W1S 4EX, England
**Culver, Molly** — Actress
Jonas Public Relations, 240 26th St, #3, Santa Monica CA 90402, USA
**Cumberbatch, Benedict** — Actor
United Talent Agency, U T A Plaza, 9336 Civic Center Dr, Beverly Hills CA 90210 USA
**Cumberland, John S** — Baseball Player
19417 Golden Slipper Place, Lutz FL 33558, USA
**Cumby, George E** — Football Player
12090 Cross Fence Trail, Tyler TX 75706, USA
**Cuming, Ry** — Singer, Songwriter
Agency Group Ltd, 142 W 57th St, #600, New York NY 10019 USA
**Cumming, Alan** — Actor, Singer, Director
Troika, 74 Clerkenwell Road, #300, London EC1M 5QA, England

**Cumming, Charles** — Writer
Jankow & Nesbit, 33 Drayson Mews, London W8 4LY, England
**Cumming, Ian M** — Businessman
Leucadia National Corp, 315 Park Ave S, New York NY 10010, USA
**Cummings, Burton** — Singer (Guess Who), Songwriter
S L Feldman Mgmt, 1505 W 2nd Ave, #200, Vancouver BC V6H 3Y4, Canada
**Cummings, Erin** — Actress
Paradigm Agency, 360 N Crescent Dr, North Building, Beverly Hills CA 90210 USA
**Cummings, James J (Jim)** — Actor
Atlas Talent Agency, 15 E 32nd St, #600, New York NY 10016, USA
**Cummings, John R** — Baseball Player
21 Park Paseo, Laguna Beach CA 92677, USA
**Cummings, Midre A** — Baseball Player
17741 Jamestown Way, Lutz FL 33558, USA
**Cummings, Quinn** — Actress, Writer
HipHugger Inc, PO Box 93963, Pasadena CA 91109, USA
**Cummings, Stephen P (Steve)** — Cyclist
Barloworld, 1800 Katherine St, Sandton 2146, Scotland
**Cummings, T Terrell (Terry)** — Basketball Player
12820 W Golden Lane, San Antonio TX 78249, USA
**Cummings, Whitney** — Actress, Comedienne
Creative Artists Agency, 2000 Ave of Stars, #100, Los Angeles CA 90067 USA
**Cummins, Barry** — Ice Hockey Player
155 Marsden St, Kimberley BC V1A 1G8, Canada
**Cummins, Corryn** — Actress
Mitchell K Stubbs Assoc, 8695 W Washington Blvd, #204, Culver City CA 90232 USA
**Cummins, Gregory Scott** — Actor
Schiowitz Connor, 1680 N Vine St, #1016, Los Angeles CA 90028 USA
**Cummins, Jim** — Ice Hockey Player
15 W Quincy St, #B, Westmont IL 60559, USA
**Cummins, Peggy** — Actress
17 Brockley Road, Bexhill on Sea, Sussex TN39 4TT, England
**Cumpsty, Michael** — Actor
Innovative Artists, 1505 10th St, Santa Monica CA 90401 USA
**Cundey, Dean R** — Cinematographer
250 S De Lacey Ave, #207, Pasadena CA 91105, USA
**Cundieff, Rusty** — Actor, Director
Code Entertainment, 9229 Sunset Blvd, #615, Los Angeles CA 90069, USA
**Cundiff, William A (Billy)** — Football Player
Cleveland Browns, 76 Lou Groza Blvd, Berea OH 44017 USA
**Cunnane, William J (Will)** — Baseball Player
123 Sleepy Hollow Lane, Congers NY 10920, USA
**Cunneyworth, Randy W** — Ice Hockey Player, Coach
141 Caversham Woods, Pittsford NY 14534, USA
**Cunningham, Bennie L** — Football Player
Quincy Road, Seneca SC 29672, USA
**Cunningham, Bill** — Singer, Bassist, Pianist (Box Tops)
Horizon Mgmt, PO Box 8770, Endwell NY 13762, USA
**Cunningham, Carl M** — Football Player
4471 Saddleworth Circle, Orlando FL 32826, USA
**Cunningham, Danny** — Actor
United Agents, 12-26 Lexington St, London W1F 0LE, England
**Cunningham, David L** — Director
United Talent Agency, U T A Plaza, 9336 Civic Center Dr, Beverly Hills CA 90210 USA
**Cunningham, J Douglas (Doug)** — Football Player
5060 Harling Place, Jackson MS 39211, USA
**Cunningham, Jared** — Basketball Player
Dallas Mavericks, Pavilion, 2909 Taylor Street, Dallas TX 75226 USA
**Cunningham, John** — Actor
B R S / Gage Talent Agency, 1650 Broadway, #1410, New York NY 10019 USA
**Cunningham, Joseph R (Joe)** — Baseball Player
RR 1 Box 80A, Koshkonong MO 65692, USA
**Cunningham, Liam** — Actor
Management 360, 9111 Wilshire Blvd, Beverly Hills CA 90210 USA
**Cunningham, Michael** — Writer
Columbia University, Creative Writing Center, Lewisohn Hall, New York NY 10014, USA
**Cunningham, R Walter (Walt)** — Astronaut
5110 San Felipe, #162W, Houston TX 77056, USA
**Cunningham, Randall** — Football Player
380 E Robindale Road, Las Vegas NV 89123, USA
**Cunningham, Richard A (Richie)** — Football Player
610 Cheyenne Dr, Houma LA 70360, USA
**Cunningham, Richard K (Dick)** — Football Player
100 Rosewood Court, Peachtree City GA 30269, USA
**Cunningham, Samuel L (Sam), Jr** — Football Player
9316 S 4th Ave, Inglewood CA 90305, USA
**Cunningham, Sean S** — Director, Producer
Crystal Lake Entertainment, 4420 Hayvenhurst Ave, Encino CA 91436, USA
**Cunningham, Wallace E** — Architect
PO Box 371493, San Diego CA 92137, USA
**Cunningham, William J (Billy)** — Basketball Player, Coach, Executive
Court Restaurant, 31 Front St, #33, Conshohocken PA 19428, USA
**Cuoco, Kaley** — Actress, Comedienne
S D B Partners, 315 S Beverly Dr, #411, Beverly Hills CA 90067 USA
**Cuomo, Andrew M** — Governor, NY; Secretary, HUD
Governor's Office, State Capitol, Albany NY 12224 USA
**Cuomo, Christopher** — Commentator
ABC-TV, News Dept, 147 Columbus Ave, New York NY 10023, USA
**Cuomo, Jerome J** — Inventor (Read-Write Optical Storage)
I B M Watson Research Center, PO Box 218, Yorktown Heights NY 10598 USA
**Cuomo, Mario M** — Governor, NY
50 Sutton Place S, #11G, New York NY 10022, USA
**Cuomo, Rivers** — Singer, Guitarist (Weezer), Songwriter
W M E Entertainment, 1600 Division St, #300, Nashville TN 37203 USA
**Cuozzo, Gary S** — Football Player
4 Swimming River Road, #4, Lincroft NJ 07738, USA

**Cupich, Blase J** — Religious Leader
Archdiocese of Chicago, 835 Rush St, Chicago IL 60611, USA
**Cura, Jose** — Opera Singer
Columbia Artists Mgmt Inc, 5 Columbus Circle, 1790 Broadway, #1600, New York NY 10019 USA
**Curatola, Vincent** — Actor
Stone Manners Salners, 6100 Wilshire Blvd, #1500, Los Angeles CA 90035 USA
**Curb, Michael (Mike)** — Composer, Businessman
3907 W Alameda Ave, #2, Burbank CA 91505, USA
**Curbeam, Robert L, Jr** — Astronaut
15806 Virginia Fern Way, Houston TX 77059, USA
**Curci, Francis (Fran)** — Football Player, Coach
14707 Croydon Place, Tampa FL 33618, USA
**Cureton, Earl** — Basketball Player
31190 Country Way, Farmington Hills MI 48331, USA
**Curfman, Shannon** — Singer, Guitarist
A R M Entertainment, 1257 Arcade St, Saint Paul MN 55106, USA
**Curl, Carolyn** — Speed Skier, Mountain Cyclist
Robert U Curl, 405 N Westridge Dr, Idaho Falls ID 83402, USA
**Curl, Robert F, Jr** — Nobel Chemistry Laureate
1824 Bolsover St, Houston TX 77005, USA
**Curlander, Paul J** — Businessman
Lexmark International, 740 W New Circle Road, Lexington KY 40550, USA
**Curless, Ann** — Singer (Expose), Songwriter
Richard Walters, PO Box 2789, Toluca Lake CA 91610 USA
**Curley, Cindy** — Ice Hockey Player
166 Barton Road, Stow MA 01775, USA
**Curley, Edwin M** — Philosopher
2645 Pin Oak Dr, Ann Arbor MI 48103, USA
**Curley, John** — Bassist (Afghan Whigs)
Rascoff/Zysblat Organization, 250 W 57th St, New York NY 10107 USA
**Curley, John J** — Publisher
Gannett Co, 1100 Wilson Blvd, Arlington VA 22209, USA
**Curley, William M (Bill)** — Basketball Player
377 Autumn Ave, Duxbury MA 02332, USA
**Curnen, Monique Gabriela** — Actress
Don Buchwald Talent Agency, 6500 Wilshire Blvd, #2200, Los Angeles CA 90048 USA
**Curnin, Thomas F** — Attorney
Cahill Gordon Reindel, 80 Pine St, #1700, New York NY 10005, USA
**Curran, Brian** — Ice Hockey Player
Kalamazoo Wings, 3600 Vanrick Dr, Kalamazoo MI 49001, USA
**Curran, Brittany** — Actress
More/Medavoy Mgmt, 10203 Santa Monica Blvd, #400, Los Angeles CA 90067 USA
**Curran, Charles E** — Theologian
Southern Methodist University, Theology Dept, Dallas Hall, Dallas TX 75275, USA
**Curran, John** — Director
H L A Mgmt, PO Box 1536, Strawberry Hills NSW 2012, Australia
**Curran, Kelly** — Actress
J K A Talent, 12725 Ventura Blvd, #H, Studio City CA 91604 91604, USA
**Curran, Michael V (Mike)** — Ice Hockey Player
7615 Lanewood Lane N, Osseo MN 55311, USA
**Curran, Patrick M (Pat)** — Football Player
3195 Avenida Magoria, Escondido CA 92029, USA
**Curran, Paul** — Director
National Opera, Millenium Centre, Bute Place, Cardiff CF10 5AL, Wales
**Curran, Sean** — Dancer
Sean Curran Co, 21 1st Ave, #18, New York NY 10003, USA
**Curran, Tony** — Actor
Paradigm Agency, 360 N Crescent Dr, North Building, Beverly Hills CA 90210 USA
**Curren, Thomas R (Tom)** — Surfer
Troubadour Entertainment, 3732 Gregory Way, #4, Santa Barbara CA 93105, USA
**Currentzis, Teodor** — Conductor
I M G Artists, Hogarth Business Park, Chiswick, London W4 2TH, England
**Curreri, Lee** — Composer
Gorfaine/Schwartz, 4111 W Alameda Ave, #509, Burbank CA 91505 USA
**Currey, Francis S** — WW II Army Hero (CMH)
PO Box 515, Selkirk NY 12158, USA
**Currie, Cherie** — Singer, Actress
Times Productions, 520 Washington Blvd, #199, Marina del Rey CA 90292, USA
**Currie, Daniel G (Dan)** — Football Player
6650 W Flamingo Road, #152, Las Vegas NV 89103, USA
**Currie, Gordon** — Actor
Characters Talent Agency, 8 Elm St, Toronto ON M5G 1G7, Canada
**Currie, Louise** — Actress
1317 Delresto Dr, Beverly Hills CA 90210, USA
**Currie, Monique** — Basketball Player
Washington Mystics, Verizon Center, 401 9th St NW, #750, Washington DC 20004 USA
**Currie, Nancy J** — Astronaut
1023 Knoll Bridge Lane, Friendswood TX 77546, USA
**Currie, Sondra** — Actress
Geddes Agency, 8430 Santa Monica Blvd, #201, West Hollywood CA 90069 USA
**Currier, William F (Bill)** — Football Player
8661 Monticello Road, Columbia SC 29203, USA
**Currington, William M (Billy)** — Singer, Songwriter
Parallel Entertainment, 209 10th Ave S, #506, Nashville TN 37203, USA
**Curry, Aaron** — Football Player
Seattle Seahawks, 12 Seahawks Way, Renton WA 98056 USA
**Curry, Adrianne** — Model, Actress
Wilhelmina Models, 300 Park Ave S, #200, New York NY 10010 USA
**Curry, Alana** — Actress
Sovereign Talent Group, 8421 Wilshire Blvd, #200, Beverly Hills CA 90211 USA
**Curry, Ann** — Commentator
NBC-TV, News Dept, 30 Rockefeller Plaza, #270E, New York NY 10112 USA
**Curry, Anne E** — Actress
Edna Talent Mgmt, 318 Dundas St West, Toronto ON M5T 1G5, Canada
**Curry, Christopher** — Actor
Darlene Kaplan, 4450 Balboa Ave, Encino CA 91316, USA

**Curry, Clifford** — Singer
Fat City Artists, 1906 Chet Atkins Place, #502, Nashville TN 37212 USA

**Curry, Denise** — Basketball Player, Coach
21 Maple Dr, Aliso Viejo CA 92656, USA

**Curry, Don (DC)** — Actor, Comedian
Rush Hour Productions, 6464 Sunset Blvd, #750, Los Angeles CA 90028, USA

**Curry, Donald (Don)** — Boxer
41 Woodland Ave, West Orange NJ 07052, USA

**Curry, Eddy, Jr** — Basketball Player
17 Magnolia Dr, Purchase NY 10577, USA

**Curry, Eric F** — Football Player
PO Box 17321, Jacksonville FL 32245, USA

**Curry, George J (Buddy)** — Football Player
4407 Trestle Way, Buford GA 30518, USA

**Curry, John A H** — Tennis Executive
All England Lawn Tennis Club, Church Road, Wimbledon, London SW19 5AE, England

**Curry, Mark** — Actor
Nine Yards Entertainment, 8530 Wilshire Blvd, #500, Beverly Hills CA 90211 USA

**Curry, Michael E (Mike)** — Basketball Player, Coach
2880 Wells Dr, Augusta GA 30906, USA

**Curry, Stephen** — Actor, Comedian
R G M Assoc, 64076 Kippax St, #202, Surry Hills NSW 2010, Australia

**Curry, Tim** — Singer, Actor
Innovative Artists, 1505 10th St, Santa Monica CA 90401 USA

**Curry, Valorie** — Actress
I C M Partners, 10250 Constellation Blvd, #900, Los Angeles CA 90067 USA

**Curry, Wardell S (Dell)** — Basketball Player
1615 Rutledge Ave, Charlotte NC 28211, USA

**Curry, William A (Bill)** — Football Player, Coach
2660 Peachtree Road NW, #27H, Atlanta GA 30305, USA

**Curtin, David S** — Journalist
Colorado Springs Gazette Telegraph, 30 S Prospect, Colorado Springs CO 80903, USA

**Curtin, Jane T** — Actress
I C M Partners, 10250 Constellation Blvd, #900, Los Angeles CA 90067 USA

**Curtin, John J, Jr** — Attorney
Bingham Dana Gould, 100 High St, #1500, Boston MA 02110, USA

**Curtin, Phyllis** — Opera Singer
Boston University, Fine Arts College, 855 Commonwealth Ave, Boston MA 02215, USA

**Curtin, Valerie** — Actress
15622 Meadowgate Road, Encino CA 91436, USA

**Curtis, A Scott** — Football Player
31661 Prairie Dunes Court, Evergreen CO 80439, USA

**Curtis, Ben** — Golfer
8959 Bevington Lane, Orlando FL 32827, USA

**Curtis, Benjamin B (Ben)** — Actor
Hatton McEwan, PO Box 37385, London N1 7XF, England

**Curtis, Catie** — Singer, Guitarist, Songwriter
Deep Blue Arts, 4440 Morse Ave, Studio City CA 91604, USA

**Curtis, Chad D** — Baseball Player
1400 Buttrick Ave SE, Ada MI 49301, USA

**Curtis, Christopher Paul** — Writer
Random House, 1745 Broadway, #1800, New York NY 10019 USA

**Curtis, Cliff** — Actor
Abrams Artists, 9200 W Sunset Blvd, #1125, West Hollywood CA 90069 USA

**Curtis, Isaac F** — Football Player
711 Clinton Springs Ave, Cincinnati OH 45229, USA

**Curtis, J Michael (Mike)** — Football Player
5101 River Road, #1803, Bethesda MD 20816, USA

**Curtis, Jamie Lee** — Actress
Creative Artists Agency, 2000 Ave of Stars, #100, Los Angeles CA 90067 USA

**Curtis, John D, II** — Baseball Player
1800 Roundhill Road, #1207, Charleston WV 25314, USA

**Curtis, Kenneth M** — Governor, ME; Diplomat
1211 Southport Dr, Sarasota FL 34242, USA

**Curtis, Kevin D** — Football Player
Tennessee Titans, 460 Great Circle Road, Nashville TN 37228 USA

**Curtis, Paul E** — Ice Hockey Player
PO Box 6325, Abilene TX 79608, USA

**Curtis, Richard** — Director, Writer
United Agents, 12-26 Lexington St, London W1F 0LE, England

**Curtis, Simon** — Director
United Talent Agency, U T A Plaza, 9336 Civic Center Dr, Beverly Hills CA 90210 USA

**Curtis, Thomas N (Tom)** — Football Player
5433 NW 94th Doral Place, Doral FL 33178, USA

**Curtis-Hall, Vondie** — Actor, Director
Film Independent, 9911 W Pico Blvd, #1100, Los Angeles CA 90035, USA

**Curtiss, Shelley Smith** — Sculptor
PO Box 497, Joseph OR 97846, USA

**Cusack, Ann** — Actress
Innovative Artists, 1505 10th St, Santa Monica CA 90401 USA

**Cusack, Joan** — Actress, Comedienne
W M E Entertainment, 9601 Wilshire Blvd, #300, Beverly Hills CA 90210 USA

**Cusack, John** — Actor
New Crime Productions, 1041 N Formosa Ave, Formosa Building, West Hollywood CA 90046, USA

**Cusack, Sinead M** — Actress
Dalzell & Beresford, 55 Charterhouse St, Paddock Suite, London EC1M 6HA, England

**Cuse, Carlton** — Writer, Producer
W M E Entertainment, 9601 Wilshire Blvd, #300, Beverly Hills CA 90210 USA

**Cushenan, Ian** — Ice Hockey Player
4014 Dryden Dr, North Olmsted OH 44070, USA

**Cushing, Matthew J (Matt)** — Football Player
5752 Lyman Ave, Downers Grove IL 60516, USA

**Cushman, Karen** — Writer
17804 Thorsen Road SW, Vashon WA 98070, USA

**Cusick, Henry Ian** — Actor
Artists Partnership, 101 Finsbury Pavement, London EC2A 1RS, England

## C

**Cussler, Clive E**
13835 N Tatum Blvd, #9-421, Phoenix AZ 85032, USA — Writer

**Cust, John J (Jack), III**
9 Club House Dr, Whitehouse Station NJ 08889, USA — Baseball Player

**Custom**
ArtistDirect, 10900 Wilshire Blvd, #1400, Los Angeles CA 90024 USA — Singer

**Cut Chemist**
Vision Entertainment Group, 1100 Glendon Ave, #1100, Los Angeles 90024, USA — DJ, Rap Musician

**Cutcliffe, David**
Duke University, Athletic Dept, Durham NC 27708, USA — Football Coach

**Cutell, Lou**
Conan Carroll Assoc, 11350 Ventura Blvd, #200, Studio City CA 91604, USA — Actor

**Cuthbert, Elisha**
John Carrabino Mgmt, 5900 Wilshire Blvd, #406, Los Angeles CA 90036 USA — Actress

**Cuthbeth, Elizabeth (Betty)**
4/7 Karara Close, Hall's Head, Mandurah WA 6210, Australia — Track Athlete

**Cutler, Eric**
I M G Artists, Hogarth Business Park, Chiswick, London W4 2TH, England — Opera Singer

**Cutler, James**
Cutler Anderson Architects, 135 Parfitt Way, Bainbridge Island WA 98110, USA — Architect

**Cutler, Jay C**
39 Bancroft Place, Nashville TN 37215, USA — Football Player

**Cutler, Laurel**
Foote Cone Belding, 767 5th Ave, New York NY 10153, USA — Businesswoman

**Cutler, R J**
Creative Artists Agency, 2000 Ave of Stars, #100, Los Angeles CA 90067 USA — Director, Producer, Actor

**Cutler, Walter L**
Meridian International Center, 1630 Crescent Place NW, Washington DC 20009, USA — Diplomat

**Cutrone, Angela**
Speed Skating Canada, 2781 Lancaster Road, #402, Ottawa ON K1B 1A7, Canada — Speed Skater

**Cutrufello, Mary**
Mercury Records, 11150 Santa Monica Blvd, #1000, Los Angeles CA 90025 USA — Singer, Songwriter

**Cutsinger, Gary L**
600 Mountain Dew Road, Horseshoe Bay TX 78657, USA — Football Player

**Cutter, Lise**
PO Box 2665, Sag Harbor NY 11963, USA — Actress

**Cuyler, Milton (Milt), Jr**
962 Lamar Road, Macon GA 31210, USA — Baseball Player

**Cuzin, Francois**
Instit Pasteur, 25 Rue du Docteur Roux, 75724 Paris Cedex 15, France — Cell Biologist

**Cuzzi, Philip (Phil)**
32 Maples Ave, Nutley NJ 07110, USA — Baseball Umpire

**Cvijanovic, Adam**
Bellwether Gallery, 134 10th St, Front A, New York NY 10011, USA — Artist

**Cwiklinski, Stanley**
728 W Washington St, San Diego CA 92103, USA — Rowing Athlete

**Cymphonique**
I C M Partners, 10250 Constellation Blvd, #900, Los Angeles CA 90067 USA — Singer, Songwriter, Actress

**Cypher, Jon**
PO Box 25040, Ventura CA 93002, USA — Actor

**Cyphers, Charles**
C R Mgmt, 23852 Pacific Coast Highway, #627, Malibu CA 90265, USA — Actor

**Cyr, Denis**
9816 N Townsend Dr, Peoria IL 61615, USA — Ice Hockey Player

**Cyr, Myriam**
John DeHority Mgmt, 125 Christopher St, #6C, New York NY 10014, USA — Actress

**Cyrus, Billy Ray**
C E S D, 10635 Santa Monica Blvd, #130, Los Angeles CA 90025 USA — Singer, Guitarist, Songwriter

**Cyrus, Miley**
Creative Artists Agency, 2000 Ave of Stars, #100, Los Angeles CA 90067 USA — Actress, Singer

**Czapsky, Stefan**
RR 3 Box 278, Unadilla NY 13849, USA — Cinematographer

**Czerny, Henry**
Oscars Abrams Zimel, 438 Queen St E, Toronto ON M5A 1T4, Canada — Actor

**Czerwinska, Anna**
Anamax-Import-Export, Ul Lomianska 10 m 4, 01 685 Warsaw, Poland — Mountaineer

**Czerwonka, Natalia**
Piotr Wyszynski, Ul Matarewicza 4D, 05 230 Kobylka, Ossow, Poland — Speed Skater

**Czisny, Alissa**
Detroit Skating Club, 888 Denison Court, Bloomfield Hills MI 48302, USA — Figure Skater

**Czuchry, Matt**
Gersh Agency, 9465 Wilshire Blvd, #600, Beverly Hills CA 90212 USA — Actor

**Cussler - Czuchry**

| | |
|---|---|
| **Da Brat** | Rap Artist |
| Mauldin Brand Agency, 1280 W Peachtree St NW, #300, Atlanta GA 30309, USA | |
| **Daal, Omar J** | Baseball Player |
| 3859 E Bellerive Dr, Queen Creek AZ 85142, USA | |
| **Daane, James D** | Financier, Government Official |
| 102 Westhampton Place, Nashville TN 37205, USA | |
| **D'Abaldo, Chris** | Guitarist (Saliva) |
| Helter Skelter, 347-353 Chiswick High Road, London W4 4HS, England | |
| **Dabich, Mike** | Basketball Player |
| PO Box 236, Hudson WY 82515, USA | |
| **D'Abo, Maryam** | Actress |
| Diamond Mgmt, 31 Percy St, London W1T 2DD, England | |
| **D'Abo, Olivia** | Actress |
| Great Vision Artists Talent Agency, 8981 Sunset Blvd, #101, Los Angeles CA 90069, USA | |
| **Dabul, Brian** | Tennis Player |
| Octagon Worldwide, 1751 Pinnacle Dr, #1500, McLean VA 22102 USA | |
| **D'Accone, Frank A** | Music Educator |
| 725 Fontana Way, Laguna Beach CA 92651, USA | |
| **Dacic, Ivica** | Prime Minister, Serbia |
| Prime Minister's Office, Nemanjina 11, 11000 Belgrade, Serbia | |
| **DaCorte, Alex** | Artist |
| Joe Sheftel Gallery, 24A Orchid St, New York NY 10002, USA | |
| **DaCosta, Rebecca** | Actress |
| Resolution, 1801 Century Park E, #2300, Los Angeles CA 90067 USA | |
| **DaCosta, Yaya** | Actress, Model |
| Gersh Agency, 41 Madison Ave, #3301, New York NY 10010 USA | |
| **D'Acquisto, John F** | Baseball Player |
| 32010 N 20th Lane, Phoenix AZ 85085, USA | |
| **Daddario, Alexandra** | Actress |
| United Talent Agency, U T A Plaza, 9336 Civic Center Dr, Beverly Hills CA 90210 USA | |
| **Daddo, Cameron** | Actor |
| Innovative Artists, 1505 10th St, Santa Monica CA 90401 USA | |
| **Daddy Yankee** | Reggaeton Singer |
| Nevarez Communications, 6020 NW 99th Ave, #307, Doral FL 33178, USA | |
| **Dade, L Paul** | Baseball Player |
| 5212 66th Street Court W, University Place WA 98467, USA | |
| **Daehlie, Bjorn** | Cross Country Skier |
| Cathinka Guldbergs Veg 64, 2034 Holter, Norway | |
| **Dafoe, Bryon** | Ice Hockey Player |
| 6620 Lakeshore Road, Kelowna BC V1W 4J5, Canada | |
| **Dafoe, Willem** | Actor |
| I C M Partners, 10250 Constellation Blvd, #900, Los Angeles CA 90067 USA | |
| **Daggett, Timothy (Tim)** | Gymnast |
| 134 Country Club Dr, East Longmeadow MA 01028, USA | |
| **Daghe, Noelle** | Golfer |
| 1300 Tamarac St, Denver CO 80220, USA | |
| **D'Agostino, James S, Jr** | Businessman |
| Encore Bank, 1220 Augusta Dr, Houston TX 77057, USA | |
| **D'Agosto, Nicholas (Nick)** | Actor |
| Emerald Talent Group, 15260 Ventura Blvd, #1200, Sherman Oaks CA 91403, USA | |
| **D'Aguanno, Emanuele** | Opera Singer |
| I M G Artists, Hogarth Business Park, Chiswick, London W4 2TH, England | |
| **Dagworthy Prew, Wendy A** | Fashion Designer |
| Royal College of Art, Kensington Gore, London SW7 3EU, England | |
| **Dahal, Pushpa Kamal (Prachanda)** | Prime Minister, Nepal |
| Premier's Office, Central Secretariat, Singha Durbar, Kathmandu, Nepal | |
| **Dahl, Arlene** | Actress |
| Dahlmark Productions, PO Box 116, Rockland Road, Sparkill NY 10976, USA | |
| **Dahl, John** | Director, Writer |
| United Talent Agency, U T A Plaza, 9336 Civic Center Dr, Beverly Hills CA 90210 USA | |
| **Dahl, Kevin C** | Ice Hockey Player |
| 4000 Astoria Way, Avon OH 44011, USA | |
| **Dahl, Lawrence F** | Chemist |
| 4817 Woodburn Dr, Madison WI 53711, USA | |
| **Dahl, Sophie** | Model, Actress |
| Ed Victor, 6 Bayley St, London WC18 3HE, England | |
| **Dahlberg Olsson, Anna** | Cross Country Skiing |
| Skiforbundet, Riksskistadion, 79119 Falun, Sweden | |
| **Dahlberg, James E** | Biomolecular Chemist |
| University of Wisconsin, Biochemical Sciences Building, Madison WI 53706, USA | |
| **Daigle, Alain** | Ice Hockey Player |
| 3510 Rue Bordeaux, Trois-Rivieres-Ouest QC G8Y 3P7, Canada | |
| **Daigle, Alexandre** | Ice Hockey Player |
| 3510 Rue Bordeaux, Trois-Rivieres-Ouest QC G8Y 3P7, Canada | |
| **Daigle, Sylvie** | Speed Skater |
| Speed Skating Canada, 2781 Lancaster Road, #402, Ottawa ON K1B 1A7, Canada | |
| **Daigneault, Jean-Jacques (J J)** | Ice Hockey Player |
| Hartford Wolf Pack, 196 Trumbull St, #300, Hartford CT 06103, USA | |
| **Dailey, Benjamin P** | Chemist |
| 440 Riverside Dr, New York NY 10027, USA | |
| **Dailey, John R** | Marine Corps General |
| National Air & Space Museum, Director's Office, Independence Ave, Washington DC 20472, USA | |
| **Dailor, Brann** | Drummer, Singer (Mastodon) |
| Pinnacle Entertainment, 30 Glenn St, White Plains NY 10603, USA | |
| **Daily, Bill** | Actor |
| 1331 Park Ave SW, #802, Albuquerque NM 87102, USA | |
| **Daily, Bob** | Producer |
| Gersh Agency, 9465 Wilshire Blvd, #600, Beverly Hills CA 90212 USA | |
| **Daily, E G** | Singer, Songwriter, Actress |
| 369 Universal Artists, 468 N Camden Dr, #200, Beverly Hills CA 90210, USA | |
| **Daish, Charles** | Actor |
| Gavin Barker Assoc, 2D Wimpole St, London W1G 0EB, England | |
| **Dajani, Nadia** | Actress |
| Innovative Artists, 1505 10th St, Santa Monica CA 90401 USA | |
| **Dalai Lama** | Religious Leader; Nobel Peace Laureate |
| Thekchen Choeling, McLeod Ganj 176219, Dharamsal, Himachal Pradesh, India | |

# D

**Dalberto, Michel** — Concert Pianist
13 Blvd Henri Plumhof, 1800 Vevey, Switzerland

**Daldry, Stephen** — Director
Creative Artists Agency, 2000 Ave of Stars, #100, Los Angeles CA 90067 USA

**Dale, Alan** — Actor
Management 360, 9111 Wilshire Blvd, Beverly Hills CA 90210 USA

**Dale, Bruce** — Photographer
National Geographic, Editorial Dept, 1145 17th St NW, Washington DC 20036 USA

**Dale, Carroll W** — Football Player
Clinch Valley College, Athletic Dept, 1 College Ave, Wise VA 24293, USA

**Dale, Dick** — Singer, Guitarist, Songwriter
Dick Dale Mgmt, PO Box 1713, Twentynine Palms CA 92277, USA

**Dale, Ian Anthony** — Actor
Paul Kohner, 9300 Wilshire Blvd, #555, Beverly Hills CA 90212 USA

**Dale, James Badge** — Actor
M J Mgmt, 130 W 57th St, New York NY 10019, USA

**Dale, Jim** — Actor, Comedian
C E S D, 10635 Santa Monica Blvd, #130, Los Angeles CA 90025 USA

**Dalembert, Samuel D (Sam)** — Basketball Player
899 NE Orchid Bay Dr, Boca Raton FL 33487, USA

**D'Alemberte, Talbot (Sandy)** — Educator
Florida State University, Law College, 425 W Jefferson, Tallahassee FL 32301, USA

**D'Aleo, Angelo** — Singer (Dion & the Belmonts)
Paramount Entertainment, PO Box 12, Far Hills NJ 07931 USA

**Dalesandro, Mark A** — Baseball Player
1908 Arbor Fields Dr, Plainfield IL 60586, USA

**Daley, Joe** — Golfer
10015 E Mountain View Road, #2126, Scottsdale AZ 85258, USA

**Daley, Joe** — Ice Hockey Player
Joe Daley's Cards, 666 Saint James St, Winnipeg MB R3G 3J6, Canada

**Daley, John Francis** — Actor
United Talent Agency, U T A Plaza, 9336 Civic Center Dr, Beverly Hills CA 90210 USA

**Daley, Leavitt L (Buddy)** — Baseball Player
922 Moose Dr, Riverton WY 82501, USA

**Daley, Patrick** — Ice Hockey Player
118 Mount Olive Dr, Toronto ON M9V 2E2, Canada

**Daley, Peter H (Pete)** — Baseball Player
4019 Calle Mira Monte, Newbury Park CA 91320, USA

**Daley, Richard M** — Mayor, Chicago
University of Chicago, Harris Public Policy School, Chicago IL 60637, USA

**Daley, Rosie** — Chef, Writer
Harpo Productions, 110 N Carpenter St, Chicago IL 60607, USA

**DalFabbro, Corrado** — Bobsled Athlete
Olympic Committee, Foro Italico, Largo Lauro de Bosis 15, 00135 Rome, Italy

**Dalgarno, Alexander** — Astronomer
27 Robinson St, Cambridge MA 02138, USA

**Dalgarno, Brad** — Ice Hockey Player
1146 Fairfield Place, Oakville ON L6M 2L9, Canada

**Dalglish, Kenneth M (Kenny)** — Soccer Player, Manager
Celtic F C, Celtic Park, Glasgow G4O 3RE, Scotland

**Dalhausser, Philip** — Volleyball Player
593 Citation Way, Newbury Park CA 91320, USA

**Dalheimer, Patrick** — Musician (Live)
Freedman & Smith, 350 W End Ave, #1, New York NY 10024, USA

**Dali, Tracy** — Actress, Model
PO Box 69541, West Hollywood CA 90069, USA

**Dalis, Irene** — Opera Singer, Executive
San Jose Opera, 2149 Paragon Dr, San Jose CA 95131, USA

**Dalkas, Nicole** — Golfer
288 Green Mountain Dr, Palm Desert CA 92211, USA

**Dall, Bobby** — Bassist (Poison)
Front Line Mgmt, 1100 Glendon Ave, #2000, Los Angeles CA 90024 USA

**Dallafior, Kenneth R (Ken)** — Football Player
188 Four Seasons Dr, Lake Orion MI 48360, USA

**Dallara, Charles H** — Government Official, Financier
International Finance Institute, 2000 Pennsylvania Ave NW, Washington DC 20006, USA

**Dalle, Beatrice** — Actress
Artmedia, 20 Ave Rapp, 75007 Paris, France

**Dallek, Robert** — Historian
2138 Cathedral Ave NW, Washington DC 20008, USA

**Dallenbach, Wally** — Auto Racing Executive
5315 Stowe Lane, Harrisburg NC 28075, USA

**Dallman, Marty** — Ice Hockey Player
3843 Main St, Niagara Falls ON L2G 6B4, Canada

**Dalrymple, Clayton E (Clay)** — Baseball Player
28248 Mateer Road, Gold Beach OR 97444, USA

**Dalrymple, Gary B** — Geologist
1847 NW Hillcrest Dr, Corvallis OR 97330, USA

**Dalton, Audrey** — Actress
2241 Labrusca, Mission Viejo CA 92692, USA

**Dalton, James E** — Air Force General
61 Misty Acres Road, Rolling Hills Estates CA 90274, USA

**Dalton, John H** — Government Official
3710 University Ave NW, Washington DC 20016, USA

**Dalton, Kristen** — Actress
Daniel Hoff Agency, 5455 Wilshire Blvd, #1100, Los Angeles CA 90036, USA

**Dalton, Lacy J** — Singer
Bobby Roberts, 3050 Business Park Circle, #303, Goodlettsville TN 37221 USA

**Dalton, Lional D** — Football Player
9858 Clint Moore Road, #128, Boca Raton FL 33496, USA

**Dalton, Nic** — Bassist (Lemonheads)
Agency Group Ltd, 142 W 57th St, #600, New York NY 10019 USA

**Dalton, Nicole** — Actress
Domain Talent, 9229 W Sunset Blvd, #710, West Hollywood CA 90069 USA

**Dalton, Suzy** — Singer
Gold Dust Talent, Route 78, Exit 19, Straußstown PA 19559, USA

**Dalton, Timothy**
Independent Talent Group, 40 Whitfield St, London W1T 2RH, England — Actor

**Daltrey, Roger**
TalentWorks, 3500 W Olive Ave, #1400, Burbank CA 91505 USA — Singer (Who), Actor

**Daluiso, Bradley W (Brad)**
13258 Glencliff Way, San Diego CA 92130, USA — Football Player

**Daly, Andrew (Andy)**
Creative Artists Agency, 2000 Ave of Stars, #100, Los Angeles CA 90067 USA — Actor, Comedian, Writer

**Daly, Carson**
Dixon Talent, 375 Greenwich St, #500, New York NY 10013, USA — Actor, Entertainer

**Daly, Herman**
6934 Pineway, University Park MD 20782, USA — Social Activist

**Daly, Jim**
Focus on the Family, 8605 Explorer Drive, Colorado Springs CO 80920, USA — Religious Leader

**Daly, John P**
1009 Par St, Dardanelle AR 72834, USA — Golfer

**Daly, Lance**
FastNet Films, 75-76 Camden St, Lower, Dublin 2, Ireland — Director, Writer

**Daly, Timothy (Tim)**
Gateway Mgmt, 860 Via de la Paz, #F10, Pacific Palisades CA 90272, USA — Actor

**Daly, Tyne**
405 E 54th St, #12D, New York NY 10022, USA — Actress

**Daly-Donofrio, Heather**
414 Long Cove Court, Ormond Beach FL 32174, USA — Golfer

**Dalziel, Ryan**
S A M A X Motorsports, 203 NW 16th St, Pompano Beach FL 33060, USA — Auto Racing Driver

**Dam, Kenneth W**
University of Chicago, Law School, 1111 E 60th St, #1, Chicago IL 60637, USA — Government Official

**Damadian, Raymond V**
F O N A R Corp, 110 Marcus Dr, Melville NY 11747, USA — Inventor (Cancer Tissue Detector-M R I)

**Damas, Bertila**
Craig Wyckoff Assoc, 11350 Ventura Blvd, #100, Studio City CA 91604, USA — Actress

**D'Amato, Alfonse M**
Park Strategies, 101 Park Ave, #2506, New York NY 10178, USA — Senator, NY

**DaMatta, Cristiano M**
Newman-Haas Racing, 50 Tower Parkway, Lincolnshire IL 60069, USA — Auto Racing Driver

**D'Amboise, Charlotte**
Don Buchwald Talent Agency, 10 E 44th St, New York NY 10017 USA — Actress, Dancer

**D'Amboise, Jacques J**
National Dance Institute, 594 Broadway, #805, New York NY 10012, USA — Dancer, Choreographer

**Dame Edna**
P B J Mgmt, 22 Rathbone St, London W1T 1LA, England — Actor, Comedian

**Dameshek, David**
Creative Artists Agency, 2000 Ave of Stars, #100, Los Angeles CA 90067 USA — Actor, Writer

**Damian, Michael**
United Talent Agency, U T A Plaza, 9336 Civic Center Dr, Beverly Hills CA 90210 USA — Actor, Singer

**Damiano, Edward R**
Boston University, Biomedical Engineering Dept, 44 Cummington St, Boston MA 02215, USA — Biomedical Engineer

**Damiano, Jennifer**
Innovative Artists, 1505 10th St, Santa Monica CA 90401 USA — Actress

**Damiao, Leandro**
Confederacion de Futebol, Rua Victor Civita 66, #1, Rio de Janeiro 22775 044, Brazil — Soccer Player

**D'Amico, Jeffrey C (Jeff)**
2223 Muirfield Way, Oldsmar FL 34677, USA — Baseball Player

**D'Amico, Marcus**
26 Astwood Mews, London SW7 4DE, England — Actor

**D'Amico, Mike**
Paradise Artists, PO Box 1821, Ojai CA 93024 USA — Percussionist (Wondermints)

**Dam-Jensen, Inger**
Hollaendervej 4A, 1855 Frederiksberg C, Denmark — Opera Singer

**Damon, Grey**
Paradigm Agency, 360 N Crescent Dr, North Building, Beverly Hills CA 90210 USA — Actor

**Damon, Johnny D**
904 Main St, Windermere FL 34786, USA — Baseball Player

**Damon, Mark**
2781 Benedict Canyon Dr, Beverly Hills CA 90210, USA — Actor, Producer

**Damon, Matt**
Pearl Street Productions, 517 N Robertson, #200, West Hollywood CA 90048, USA — Actor, Producer

**Damon, Una**
DeWalt & Muzik Mgmt, 623 N Parish Place, Burbank CA 91506, USA — Actress, Director, Writer

**Damone, Vic**
International Ventures, 25864 Tournament Road, #L, Valencia CA 91355, USA — Singer, Actor

**D'Amore, Caroline**
Stiefel Entertainment, 21731 Ventura Blvd, #300, Woodland Hills CA 91364, USA — Actress

**Damphousse, Vincent**
Le Scandinave Spa, 4280 Montee Ryan, Mont-Tremblant QC J8E 1S4, Canada — Ice Hockey Player

**Dampier, Erick T**
18724 Wainsborough Lane, Dallas TX 75287, USA — Basketball Player

**Dampier, Louie (Lou)**
Dampier Distributing, 2808 New Moody Lane, La Grange KY 40031, USA — Basketball Player

**Damrosch, Leo**
Harvard Extension School, 51 Brattle St, Cambridge MA 02138, USA — Writer

**Damson, Barrie M**
1720 Post Road E, #215, Westport CT 06880, USA — Businessman

**Damus, Mike**
Untitled Entertainment, 350 S Beverly Dr, #200, Beverly Hills CA 90212 USA — Actor

**Dana, Bill**
Amsel Eisenstadt Frazier, 5055 Wilshire Blvd, #865, Los Angeles CA 90036 USA — Actor, Comedian

**Danby, Gordon T**
PO Box 12, Wading River NY 11792, USA — Inventor (Magnetic Levitation Train)

**Dance, Charles**
Tavistock Wood Mgmt, 45 Conduit St, London W1S 2YN, England — Actor

**Dancy, Hugh**
United Agents, 12-26 Lexington St, London W1F 0LE, England — Actor, Model

**Dancy, John**
Harvard University, Kennedy Government School, Cambridge MA 02138, USA — Commentator

| | |
|---|---|
| **Dando, Carolyn** | Actress |
| Red11 Mgmt, 441 Queen St, Auckland 1010, New Zealand | |
| **Dando, Evan** | Singer (Lemonheads), Songwriter |
| Agency Group Ltd, 142 W 57th St, #600, New York NY 10019 USA | |
| **Dandridge, Robert L (Bob)** | Basketball Player |
| 1708 Saint Denis Ave, Norfolk VA 23509, USA | |
| **Dandry, Evelyne** | Actress |
| Artmedia, 20 Ave Rapp, 75007 Paris, France | |
| **Dane, Eric** | Actor |
| Management 360, 9111 Wilshire Blvd, Beverly Hills CA 90210 USA | |
| **Dane, Paul** | Test Pilot |
| 17105 Ambassador Dr, #515, Colorado Springs CO 80921, USA | |
| **Dane, Shelton** | Actor |
| Innovative Artists, 235 Park Ave S, #1000, New York NY 10003 USA | |
| **Danelli, Dino** | Drummer (Rascals) |
| Thomas Cassidy, PO Box 1311, Tucson AZ 85702 USA | |
| **Danelo, Joseph P (Joe)** | Football Player |
| 3601 Roxbury St, San Pedro CA 90731, USA | |
| **Danes, Claire** | Actress |
| W M E Entertainment, 9601 Wilshire Blvd, #300, Beverly Hills CA 90210 USA | |
| **Daneyko, Ken** | Ice Hockey Player |
| 11 Combs Hollow Road, Mendham NJ 07945, USA | |
| **Danforth, Douglas D** | Businessman, Baseball Executive |
| 8787 Bay Colony Dr, #1002, Naples FL 34108, USA | |
| **Danforth, Fred** | Artist |
| PO Box 828, Middlebury VT 05753, USA | |
| **Danforth, John C (Jack)** | Senator, MO |
| Bryan Cave LLP, 211 N Broadway, #3600, Saint Louis MO 63102, USA | |
| **D'Angelo** | Singer, Songwriter |
| W M E Entertainment, 9601 Wilshire Blvd, #300, Beverly Hills CA 90210 USA | |
| **D'Angelo, Beverly** | Actress |
| I C M Partners, 10250 Constellation Blvd, #900, Los Angeles CA 90067 USA | |
| **Danger Mouse** | Rap Artist (Gnarls Barkley) |
| Hall or Nothing, Poplar Mews, Uxbridge Road, London W12 7JS, England | |
| **D'Angio, Giulio J** | Radiation Therapist |
| 201 S 18th St, #1818, Philadelphia PA 19103, USA | |
| **Daniel** | Prince, Sweden |
| Royal Palace, Kundg Slottet, Stottsbacken, 111 30 Stockholm, Sweden | |
| **Daniel, Brittany** | Actress, Model |
| A P A Talent & Literary Agency, 405 S Beverly Dr, #300, Beverly Hills CA 90212 USA | |
| **Daniel, Elizabeth A (Beth)** | Golfer |
| 219 Palm Trail, Delray Beach FL 33483, USA | |
| **Daniel, Eugene, Jr** | Football Player |
| PO Box 80345, Baton Rouge LA 70898, USA | |
| **Daniel, J Britt** | Singer, Guitarist (Spoon) |
| Legends of 21st Century, 7 Trinity Row, Florence MA 01062, USA | |
| **Daniel, Jeffrey** | Singer (Shalamar) |
| Green Light Talent Agency, PO Box 3172, Beverly Hills CA 90212 USA | |
| **Daniel, Paul W** | Conductor |
| Ingpen & Williams, 131 Putney Bridge Road, London SW15 2PA, England | |
| **Daniel, William P (Willie)** | Football Player |
| 1711 Oktoc Road, Starkville MS 39759, USA | |
| **Daniele, Graciela** | Director, Choreographer |
| Abrams Artists, 9200 W Sunset Blvd, #1125, West Hollywood CA 90069 USA | |
| **Danielpour, Richard** | Composer |
| Sony Classics Records, 2100 Colorado Ave, Santa Monica CA 90404, USA | |
| **Daniels, Anthony** | Actor |
| Artists First International, 45 Monmouth St, London WC2H 9DG, England | |
| **Daniels, Antonio** | Basketball Player |
| Philadelphia 76ers, 1st Union Center, 3601 S Broad St, Philadelphia PA 19148 USA | |
| **Daniels, Ben** | Actor |
| Hamilton Hodell, 20 Golden Square, London W1F 9JL, England | |
| **Daniels, Bennie, Jr** | Baseball Player |
| 938 W 156th St, Compton CA 90220, USA | |
| **Daniels, Charlie** | Singer, Songwriter |
| C D B Inc, 17060 Central Pike, Lebanon TN 37090, USA | |
| **Daniels, Cheryl** | Bowler |
| 6574 Crest Top Dr, West Bloomfield MI 48322, USA | |
| **Daniels, Clemon (Bo)** | Football Player |
| 8683 Mountain Road, Oakland CA 94605, USA | |
| **Daniels, David** | Opera Singer |
| Askonas Holt, Lincoln House, 300 High Holborn, London WC1V 7JH, England | |
| **Daniels, DeAndre M** | Basketball Player |
| Toronto Raptors, Air Canada Center, 20 Bay St, Toronto ON M5J 2N8, Canada | |
| **Daniels, Erin** | Actress, Director, Writer |
| Framework Entertainment, 9057 Nemo St, #C, West Hollywood CA 90069, USA | |
| **Daniels, Faith** | Commentator |
| CBS-TV, News Dept, 51 W 52nd St, New York NY 10019 USA | |
| **Daniels, Greg** | Actor, Director, Producer, Writer |
| W M E Entertainment, 9601 Wilshire Blvd, #300, Beverly Hills CA 90210 USA | |
| **Daniels, Jeff** | Actor |
| I C M Partners, 10250 Constellation Blvd, #900, Los Angeles CA 90067 USA | |
| **Daniels, Jeff** | Ice Hockey Player |
| 108 Delaplane Court, Morrisville NC 27560, USA | |
| **Daniels, Kalvoski (Kal)** | Baseball Player |
| PO Box 9632, Warner Robins GA 31095, USA | |
| **Daniels, Kevin** | Actor |
| TalentWorks, 3500 W Olive Ave, #1400, Burbank CA 91505 USA | |
| **Daniels, Lee** | Director, Producer |
| Lee Daniels Entertainment, 315 W 36th St, #1002 , New York NY 10037, USA | |
| **Daniels, Marquis A** | Basketball Player |
| 2501 Sutton Place Dr S, Carmel IN 46032, USA | |
| **Daniels, Melvin J (Mel)** | Basketball Player |
| 19789 Centennial Road, Sheridan IN 46069, USA | |
| **Daniels, Mitchell E (Mitch), Jr** | Governor, IN |
| Purdue University, West Lafayette IN 47907 USA | |

**Daniels, Owen** — Football Player
5425 Inwood Dr, Houston TX 77056, USA

**Daniels, Quincey** — Boxer
112 Sunny Meadows Dr, Blackshear GA 31516, USA

**Daniels, Scott** — Ice Hockey Player
36 Deer Run, Southwick MA 01077, USA

**Daniels, Travis A** — Football Player
4665SW 75th Way, #104, Davie FL 33314, USA

**Daniels, William** — Actor
S L J Mgmt, 833 N Edinburgh Ave, #203, Los Angeles CA 90046 90046, USA

**Daniels, William B** — Physicist
1100 Lovering Ave, #1208, Wilmington DE 19806, USA

**Danielsen, Egil** — Track Athlete
Roreks Gate 9, 2300 Hamar, Norway

**Danielson, Gary D** — Football Player
10112 Magnolia Bend, Bonita Springs FL 34135, USA

**Danielsson, Bengt F** — Anthropologist
PO Box 558, Papette, Tahiti

**Danilo Luiz da Silva (Danilo)** — Soccer Player
F C Porto, Estadio do Dragao, Via F C Porto, Entrada Nascente, 4350 415 Porto, Portugal

**Daniloff, Nicholas** — Journalist
PO Box 892, Chester VT 05143, USA

**Danko, William D** — Writer
PO Box 9125, Niskayuna NY 12309, USA

**Danks, John W** — Baseball Player
702 Oaklands Dr, Round Rock TX 78681, USA

**Danley, Kerwin J** — Baseball Umpire
2455 E Desert Broom Place, Chandler AZ 85286, USA

**Danmeier, Richard C (Rick)** — Football Player
4917 Ridge Road, Minneapolis MN 55436, USA

**Danneels, Godfried Cardinal** — Religious Leader
Archdiocese of Malines-Brussels, Wollemarkt 15, 2800 Mechelen, Belgium

**Dannelly, Brian** — Director, Writer
Creative Artists Agency, 2000 Ave of Stars, #100, Los Angeles CA 90067 USA

**Dannemann, Don** — Singer, Guitarist
8 Brant Court, Middletown DE 19709, USA

**Danner, Blythe** — Actress
Anonymous Content, 3532 Hayden Ave, Culver City CA 90232 USA

**Danning, Sybil** — Actress, Model
Adventuress Production, 8491 Sunset Blvd, #361, West Hollywood CA 90069, USA

**Dano, Linda** — Actress
70 Riverside Lane, Riverside CT 06878, USA

**Dano, Paul F** — Actor
Anonymous Content, 3532 Hayden Ave, Culver City CA 90232 USA

**Dansby, Karlos M** — Football Player
2844 E Honeysuckle Place, Chandler AZ 85286, USA

**Danson, Ted** — Actor
W M E Entertainment, 9601 Wilshire Blvd, #300, Beverly Hills CA 90210 USA

**Dante, Joe** — Director
Renfield Productions, 1041 N Formosa Ave, Writers Building, West Hollywood CA 90046, USA

**Dantley, Adrian D** — Basketball Player, Coach
9 Barn Ridge Court, Silver Spring MD 20906, USA

**D'Antoni, Mike** — Basketball Player, Coach
116 25th St, Manhattan Beach CA 90266, USA

**D'Antoni, Philip** — Producer, Director
Saint Andrews, 10 Old Jackson Ave, Hastings on Hudson NY 10706, USA

**Dantonio, Mark** — Football Coach
Michigan State University, Athletic Dept, East Lansing MI 48824, USA

**Dantzscher, Jamie A** — Gymnast
Arizona State University, Athletic Dept, Tempe AZ 85287, USA

**Danvers, Tasha** — Track Athlete
Shaftesbury Barnet, Greenlands Lane, Herndon, London NW 1RL, England

**Danz, Ingeborg** — Opera Singer
Kunstler Sekretariat am Gasteig, Rosenheimer Str 52, 81669 Munich, Germany

**Danz, Shirley** — Baseball Player
330 Greystone Dr, Hendersonville NC 28792, USA

**Danza, Tony** — Actor
Farah Films & Mgmt, 11640 Mayfield Ave, #208, Brentwood CA 90049, USA

**Danzenie, Billy** — Rap Artist (M O P)
Pyramid Entertainment Group, 377 Rector Place, #21A, New York NY 10280 USA

**Danziger, Jeff** — Editorial Cartoonist
RFD, Plainfield VT 05667, USA

**Danziger, Sheldon H** — Economist
University of Michigan, Public Policy School, Ann Arbor MI 48109, USA

**Daoust, Dan A** — Ice Hockey Player
55 John Silver Crescent, Markham ON L3R 9B, Canada

**Daoust, Melodie** — Ice Hockey Player
McGill Martlets, Martlet House, 1430 Rue Peel, Montreal QC H3A 3T3, Canada

**Dapper, Marco** — Actor, Model
Himber Entertainment, PO Box 950, South Orange NJ 07079 USA

**D'Aquino, Carl** — Interior Designer
D'Aquino Monaco Inc, 214 W 29th St, #1202, New York NY 10001, USA

**Darabont, Frank** — Director, Writer
Darkwoods Productions, 301 E Colorado Blvd, #705, Pasadena CA 91101, USA

**D'Arbanville-Quinn, Patti** — Actress
Hartig-Hilepo Agency, 54 W 21st St, #610, New York NY 10010 USA

**Darbinyan, Armen R** — Prime Minister, Armenia
19 Str Sayat Nova, 375001 Yerevan, Armenia

**Darby, Chartric T** — Football Player
14335 Simonds Road NE, Bothell WA 98011, USA

**Darby, Craig** — Ice Hockey Player
40 Vista Dr, Saratoga Springs NY 12866, USA

**Darby, Kim** — Actress
Au Courant, 6705 Sunset Blvd, #200, Hollywood CA 90028, USA

**Darby, Matthew L (Matt)** — Football Player
501 Sagecreek Court, Winter Springs FL 32708, USA

**Darby, Rhys**
Creative Artists Agency, 2000 Ave of Stars, #100, Los Angeles CA 90067 USA — Actor

**D'Arby, Terence Trent**
Agency Group Ltd, 142 W 57th St, #600, New York NY 10019 USA — Singer

**Darc, Mireille**
Agents Associes, 201 Faubourg Saint Honore, 75008 Paris, France — Actress

**D'Arcangelo, Ildebrando**
I M G Artists, Hogarth Business Park, Chiswick, London W4 2TH, England — Opera Singer

**D'Arcevia, Bruno**
Via Luigi Angeloni 29, 00149 Rome, Italy — Artist, Sculptor

**Darche, Jean-Philippe**
9507 W 160th Terrace, Stilwell KS 66085, USA — Football Player

**Darchinyan, Vic**
Billy Hussein, 49 The Avenue, Yagoona NSW 2199, Australia — Boxer

**Darcy, Dame**
22 W Bryan St, #185, Savannah GA 31401, USA — Cartoonist, Artist

**D'Arcy, James**
Creative Artists Agency, 2000 Ave of Stars, #100, Los Angeles CA 90067 USA — Actor

**Darden, Christopher**
9551 Baden Ave, Chatsworth CA 91311, USA — Attorney, Actor

**Darden, Thomas V (Thom)**
637 20th Ave SW, Cedar Rapids IA 52404, USA — Football Player

**Darensbourg, Victor A (Vic)**
4151 Abernethy Forest Place, Las Vegas NV 89141, USA — Baseball Player

**Darin, Ricardo**
Media Art Mgmt, BaRbara de Braganza 11, #4 Derecha, 28004 Madrid, Spain — Actor

**Darius, Donovin (Don)**
12051 Scarsdale Dr, Jacksonville FL 32246, USA — Football Player

**Darlan, Eva**
Agents Associes, 201 Rue du Faubourg Saint Honore, 75008 Paris, France — Actress

**Darling, Alistair M**
Chancellory of Exchequer, 1 Horse Guards Road, London SW1A 2HQ, England — Government Official, England

**Darling, Charles (Chuck)**
8066 S Kramerie Way, Centennial CO 80112, USA — Basketball Player

**Darling, David**
John Wiley & Sons, 111 River St, Hoboken NJ 07030 USA — Astronomer, Writer

**Darling, Devard L**
4234 NE Park Springs Dr, Lees Summit MO 64064, USA — Football Player

**Darling, Gary R**
16609 S 32nd Lane, Phoenix AZ 85045, USA — Baseball Umpire

**Darling, Jennifer**
C E S D, 10635 Santa Monica Blvd, #130, Los Angeles CA 90025 USA — Actress

**Darling, Katrina**
Playboy Promotions, 9346 Civic Center Dr, #200, Beverly Hills CA 90210 USA — Dancer, Model

**Darling, Ronald M (Ron)**
10 Barclay St, #34C, New York NY 10007, USA — Baseball Player

**Darlington, Jonathan**
I M G Artists, Hogarth Business Park, Chiswick, London W4 2TH, England — Conductor

**Darmaatmadja, Julius Riyadi Cardinal**
Archdiocese of Jakarta, Keuskupan Agung, J I Katedral 7, Jakarta 10710, Indonesia — Religious Leader

**Darnell, August**
Ron Rainey Mgmt, 315 S Beverly Dr, #407, Beverly Hills CA 90212, USA — Singer (Kid Creole & the Coconuts)

**Darnell, Bruce**
Fashion4Art, Ingendorfer Str 34, 50529 Pulheim, Germany — Model

**Darnell, Daniel J**
Deputy Commander, Pacific Command, Camp H M Smith HI 96861, USA — Air Force General

**Darnell, Erik**
Darmer Motorsports, 3627 Washington St, Park City IL 60085, USA — Truck Racing Driver

**Darnell, James E, Jr**
Rockefeller University Medical Center, 1230 York Ave, New York NY 10065 USA — Molecular Biologist

**Darnton, John**
New York Times, Editorial Dept, 229 W 43rd St, New York NY 10036 USA — Journalist, Writer

**Darnton, Robert C**
985 Memorial Dr, #403, Cambridge MA 02138, USA — Historian

**Darr, Lisa**
Stone Manners Salners, 6100 Wilshire Blvd, #1500, Los Angeles CA 90035 USA — Actress

**Darrell, Katrina**
Avo Talent, 8500 Melrose Ave, #212, West Hollywood CA 90069, USA — Singer, Actress

**Darren, James**
PO Box 1088, Beverly Hills CA 90213, USA — Singer, Actor

**Darrow, Henry**
Hervey/Grimes Talent, 10561 Missouri Ave, #2, Los Angeles CA 90025 USA — Actor

**Darvill, Arthur**
Independent Talent Group, 40 Whitfield St, London W1T 2RH, England — Actor

**Darvish, Yu**
Texas Rangers, Ameriquest Field, 1000 Ballpark Way, #306, Arlington TX 76011 USA — Baseball Player

**Darwin, Daniel W (Danny)**
6489 Stags Leap Road, Sanger TX 76266, USA — Baseball Player

**Darwin, Matthew W (Matt)**
414 Love Bird Lane, Murphy TX 75094, USA — Football Player

**Darwitz, Natalie**
4655 Pine Cone Circle, Saint Paul MN 55123, USA — Ice Hockey Player

**Dascascos, Mark**
Three-X Vision, 18850 Vista del Canon, #A, Newhall CA 91321, USA — Actor

**D'Ascoli, Bernard**
C L B Mgmt, 28 Earlswood Road, London NW10 5QB, England — Concert Pianist

**Dash, Damon**
Dash Films, 825 8th Ave, #2900, New York NY 10019, USA — Actor, Director, Producer

**Dash, Leon D, Jr**
Washington Post, Editorial Dept, 1150 15th Ave NW, Washington DC 20071, USA — Journalist

**Dash, Stacey**
Prestige Talent Agency, 9250 Wilshire Blvd, #208, Beverly Hills CA 90212, USA — Actress, Model

**DaSilva, Danilo L**
Confederacion de Futebol, Rua Victor Civita 66, #1, Rio de Janeiro 22775 044, Brazil — Soccer Player

**DaSilva, Rafael Pereira**
Manchester United, Busby Way, Old Trafford, Manchester M16 0RA, England — Soccer Player

| | |
|---|---|
| **Dassler, Uwe** <br> Stolze-Schrey-Str 6, 15745 Wilday, Germany | Swimmer |
| **Dastmalchian, David** <br> C E S D, 10635 Santa Monica Blvd, #130, Los Angeles CA 90025 USA | Actor |
| **Dater, Judy L** <br> 2430 5th St, #J, Berkeley CA 94710, USA | Photographer |
| **Datsyuk, Pavel V** <br> 3166 Rosedale St, Ann Arbor MI 48108, USA | Ice Hockey Player |
| **Daub, Matthew** <br> A C A Galleries, 529 W 20th St, #500, New York NY 10011, USA | Artist |
| **Daubach, Brian M** <br> 2709 Timberline Dr, Belleville IL 62226, USA | Baseball Player |
| **Daubechies, Ingrid C** <br> Princeton University, Mathematics Dept, Princeton NJ 08544, USA | Computer Mathematician, Physicist |
| **Dauer, Richard F (Rich)** <br> 2510 Brook Haven Lane, Hinckley OH 44233, USA | Baseball Player |
| **Daughaday, William H** <br> 1840 N Prospect Ave, #322, Milwaukee WI 53202, USA | Endocrinologist |
| **Daugherty, Bradley L (Brad)** <br> 10 Inspiration Way, Swananoa NC 28778, USA | Basketball Player, Sportscaster |
| **Daugherty, George** <br> I M G Artists, Hogarth Business Park, Chiswick, London W4 2TH, England | Conductor |
| **Daugherty, John M (Jack)** <br> 20360 N 95th Place, Scottsdale AZ 85255, USA | Baseball Player |
| **Daugherty, Michael** <br> Argo London Records, 810 7th Ave, New York NY 10019, USA | Composer |
| **Daughtrey, Martha Craig** <br> US Court of Appeals, 701 Broadway, #207, Nashville TN 37203, USA | Judge |
| **Daughtry, Christopher (Chris)** <br> 19 Music & Mgmt, 35-37 Parkgate Road, London SW11 4NP, England | Singer, Guitarist, Songwriter |
| **Daugman, John** <br> Cambridge University, Computer Laboratory, Cambridge CB3 0FD, England | Inventor (Scan Security System) |
| **Dauline, Marie** <br> Todo Mundo, PO Box 319, New York NY 10012, USA | Singer (Zap Mama) |
| **Dault, Julia** <br> Marianne Boelsky Gallery, 509 W 24th St, New York NY 10011, USA | Artist |
| **Daulton, Darren A** <br> 643 Woodbridge Dr, Melbourne FL 32940, USA | Baseball Player |
| **Dauterive, Jim** <br> United Talent Agency, U T A Plaza, 9336 Civic Center Dr, Beverly Hills CA 90210 USA | Producer, Writer |
| **Davalillo Romero, Victor J (Vic)** <br> Calle Trujillo 7, Mariperez QV, Caracas, Venezuela | Baseball Player |
| **Davalos, Alexa** <br> United Talent Agency, U T A Plaza, 9336 Civic Center Dr, Beverly Hills CA 90210 USA | Actress |
| **Davalos, Richard** <br> 23388 Mulholland Dr, #28, Woodland Hills CA 91364, USA | Actor |
| **Davanger, Flemming** <br> Curling Assn, Sognsveien 75, Serviceboks 1, 0840 Oslo, Norway | Curling Athlete |
| **Davanon, F Jeffrey (Jerry)** <br> 350 Greypine W, Montgomery TX 77356, USA | Baseball Player |
| **Davanon, Jeffrey G (Jeff)** <br> 731 E Buena Vista Dr, Chandler AZ 85249, USA | Baseball Player |
| **Davenport, Ian** <br> Paul Kasmin Gallery, 293 10th Ave, New York NY 10001, USA | Artist |
| **Davenport, Jack** <br> Hamilton Hodell, 20 Golden Square, London W1F 9JL, England | Actor |
| **Davenport, James H (Jim)** <br> 1016 Hewitt Dr, San Carlos CA 94070, USA | Baseball Player, Manager |
| **Davenport, Jeremy** <br> Columbia Artists Mgmt Inc, 5 Columbus Circle, 1790 Broadway, #1600, New York NY 10019 USA | Trumpeter, Singer |
| **Davenport, Jessica** <br> Indiana Fever, Conseco Fieldhouse, 125 S Pennsylvania, Indianapolis IN 46204 USA | Basketball Player |
| **Davenport, Lindsay** <br> PO Box 10179, Newport Beach CA 92658, USA | Tennis Player |
| **Davenport, Madison** <br> C E S D, 10635 Santa Monica Blvd, #130, Los Angeles CA 90025 USA | Actress |
| **Davenport, Najeh T M** <br> 12622 SW 28th St, Miramar FL 33027, USA | Football Player |
| **Davenport, N'Dea** <br> Sangfroid Music Group, 24 Caradoc St, Greenwich, London SE10 9AG, England | Singer, Dancer |
| **Davenport, N'Dea** <br> David Levin Business Mgmt, 200 W 57th St, #1101, New York NY 10019, USA | Singer (Brand New Heavies), Songwriter |
| **Davenport, Wilbur B, Jr** <br> 1120 Skyline Dr, Medford OR 97504, USA | Electrical Engineer |
| **Daves, Michael** <br> Paradigm Agency, 360 N Crescent Dr, North Building, Beverly Hills CA 90210 USA | Singer |
| **Davey, Donald V (Don)** <br> 1525 Beach Ave, Atlantic Beach FL 32233, USA | Football Player |
| **Davi, Robert** <br> Binder & Assoc, 1465 Lindacrest Dr, Beverly Hills CA 90210 USA | Actor |
| **Daviau, Allen** <br> 2249 Bronson Hill Dr, Los Angeles CA 90068, USA | Cinematographer |
| **Davich, Marty** <br> 530 S Greenwood Lane, Pasadena CA 91107, USA | Composer |
| **David Mohato** <br> Royal Palace, PO Box 524, Maseru, Lesotho | Crown Prince, Lesotho |
| **David, Anna** <br> 8424 Santa Monica Blvd, #A754, West Hollywood CA 90069, USA | Columnist, Writer |
| **David, Craig A** <br> Creative Artists Agency, 2000 Ave of Stars, #100, Los Angeles CA 90067 USA | Singer, Songwriter |
| **David, Edward E, Jr** <br> E E D Inc, PO Box 435, Bedminster NJ 07921, USA | Underwater Sound, Electrical Engineer |
| **David, George A L** <br> United Technologies Corp, United Technologies Building, 1 Financial Plaza, Hartford CT 06103, USA | Businessman |
| **David, John R** <br> Harvard Public Health School, Tropical Health Dept, 665 Huntington Ave, Boston MA 02115, USA | Internist |

|  |  |
|---|---|
| **David, Keith**<br>Stone Manners Salners, 6100 Wilshire Blvd, #1500, Los Angeles CA 90035 USA | Actor, Producer |
| **David, Larry**<br>L D Productions, 3000 Olympic Blvd, Santa Monica CA 90404, USA | Writer, Actor, Producer |
| **David, Michael Stahl**<br>Management 360, 9111 Wilshire Blvd, Beverly Hills CA 90210 USA | Actor |
| **Davidoff, Dov**<br>United Talent Agency, U T A Plaza, 9336 Civic Center Dr, Beverly Hills CA 90210 USA | Actor, Comedian |
| **Davidovich, Bella**<br>Agnes Bruneau Assoc, 155 W 68th St, #1010, New York NY 10023, USA | Concert Pianist |
| **Davidovich, Lolita**<br>Mavrick Artists Agency, 6100 Wilshire Blvd, #550, Los Angeles CA 90048, USA | Actress |
| **Davidovici, Brigette**<br>W M E Entertainment, 9601 Wilshire Blvd, #300, Beverly Hills CA 90210 USA | Actress |
| **Davidovsky, Mario**<br>490 W End Ave, New York NY 10024, USA | Composer |
| **Davids, Edgar**<br>F C Juventus, Corso Galilo Ferraris 32, 10128 Turin, Italy | Soccer Player |
| **Davidson, Adam**<br>Creative Artists Agency, 2000 Ave of Stars, #100, Los Angeles CA 90067 USA | Director |
| **Davidson, Amy**<br>Stone Manners Salners, 6100 Wilshire Blvd, #1500, Los Angeles CA 90035 USA | Actress |
| **Davidson, Andrew**<br>Doubleday Press, 1745 Broadway, New York NY 10019 USA | Writer |
| **Davidson, Barbara**<br>Los Angeles Times, Editorial Dept, 202 W 1st St, Los Angeles CA 90012 USA | Photographer |
| **Davidson, Bruce O**<br>RR 842, Unionville PA 19375, USA | Equestrian |
| **Davidson, Diane Mott**<br>William Morrow Publishers, 1350 Ave of Americas, New York NY 10019 USA | Writer |
| **Davidson, Eileen**<br>Media Artists Group, 8222 Melrose Ave, #203, Los Angeles CA 90048 USA | Actress |
| **Davidson, Ernest R**<br>5051 50th Ave NE, #22, Seattle WA 98105, USA | Chemist |
| **Davidson, Francis M (Cotton)**<br>435 Old Osage Road, Gatesville TX 76528, USA | Football Player |
| **Davidson, Gordon**<br>165 Mabery Rd, Santa Monica CA 90402, USA | Producer, Director |
| **Davidson, J Mark**<br>996 Old Mountain Road, Statesville NC 28677, USA | Baseball Player |
| **Davidson, Jeff**<br>Breathing Space Institute, 3202 Ruffin St, Raleigh NC 27607, USA | Motivational Speaker |
| **Davidson, Jeremy**<br>Innovative Artists, 1505 10th St, Santa Monica CA 90401 USA | Actor |
| **Davidson, John**<br>6 Briarbrook Trail, Saint Louis MO 63131, USA | Ice Hockey Player, Executive |
| **Davidson, John**<br>8605 Santa Monica Blvd, West Hollywood CA 90069, USA | Singer, Actor |
| **Davidson, Justin**<br>New York Newsday, Editorial Dept, 235 Pinelawn Road, Melville NY 11747 USA | Journalist |
| **Davidson, Kenneth D (Kenny)**<br>1922 Thompson Crossing Dr, Richmond TX 77406, USA | Football Player |
| **Davidson, Owen**<br>39 N Lakemist Harbour Place, Spring TX 77381, USA | Tennis Player |
| **Davidson, Philip**<br>Commander, Naval Forces Mid East Force & 6th Fleet, FPO AE 09501 USA | Navy Admiral |
| **Davidson, Richard**<br>University of Wisconsin, Keck Brain Imaging & Behavior Laboratory, Madison WI 53706, USA | Neuroplastic Surgeon |
| **Davidson, Tommy**<br>Integrated Public Relations, 9025 Wilshire Blvd, Beverly Hills CA 90211, USA | Actor, Comedian |
| **David-Weill, Michel**<br>Lazard, 121 Blvd Haussmann, 75008 Paris, France | Financier |
| **Davie, J Alan**<br>Gamels Studio, Rush Green, Hertfordshire SG13 7SB, England | Artist |
| **Davie, Karin**<br>James Harris Gallery, 309 3rd Ave S, #A, Seattle WA 98104, USA | Artist, Sculptor |
| **Davie, Robert (Bob)**<br>University of New Mexico, Athletic Dept, Albuquerque NM, USA | Football Coach, Sportscaster |
| **Davies, Alan**<br>Rights House, Drury House, 34-43 Russell St, London WC2B 5HA, England | Actor |
| **Davies, Caryn**<br>Columbia University, Law School, New York NY 10027, USA | Rowing Athlete |
| **Davies, Dave**<br>Talent Consultants International, 105 Shad Row, #B, Piermont NY 10968 USA | Singer, Guitarist (Kinks) |
| **Davies, David R**<br>4224 Franklin St, Kensington MD 20895, USA | Biophysicist |
| **Davies, Dennis Russell**<br>Columbia Artists Mgmt Inc, 5 Columbus Circle, 1790 Broadway, #1600, New York NY 10019 USA | Conductor, Concert Pianist |
| **Davies, Gail**<br>246 Cherokee Road, Nashville TN 37205, USA | Singer, Guitarist, Songwriter |
| **Davies, Geraint Wyn**<br>Oscars Abrams Zimel, 438 Queen St W, Toronto ON M5A 1T4, Canada | Actor |
| **Davies, H Kyle**<br>1495 E Lake Road, McDonough GA 30252, USA | Baseball Player |
| **Davies, Jeremy**<br>Paradigm Agency, 360 N Crescent Dr, North Building, Beverly Hills CA 90210 USA | Actor |
| **Davies, John G**<br>520 Madeline Dr, Pasadena CA 91105, USA | Judge, Swimmer |
| **Davies, Karle**<br>Curtis Brown Group, 28-29 Haymarket St, #500, London SW1Y 4SP, England | Actor |
| **Davies, Laura**<br>Tytherington Club, Tytherington Macclesfield SK10 2JP, England | Golfer |
| **Davies, Linda**<br>Calle Once 286, La Molona, Lima, Peru | Writer |
| **Davies, Matt**<br>Journal News, Editorial Dept, 1 Gannett Dr, West Harrison NY 10604, USA | Editorial Cartoonist |

**Davies, Mike**
Rogers Partnership, Thames Wharf, Rainville Road, London N6 94A, England — Architect

**Davies, Paul C W**
PO Box 389, Burnside SA 5066, Australia — Mathematical Physicist

**Davies, Peter Maxwell**
Judy Arnold, 50 Hogarth Road, London SW5 OPU, England — Composer

**Davies, Raymond D (Ray)**
Agency Group Ltd, 1880 Century Park E, #711, Los Angeles CA 90067 USA — Singer, Guitarist (Kinks)

**Davies, Ryland**
71 Fairmile Lane, Cobham, Surrey KT11 2DG, England — Opera Singer

**Davies, S Howard**
Royal National Theater, South Bank, London SE 19PX, England — Director

**Davies, William**
United Talent Agency, U T A Plaza, 9336 Civic Center Dr, Beverly Hills CA 90210 USA — Writer

**Davila, Robert**
Gallaudet University, President's Office, 800 Florida NW, Washington DC 20002, USA — Educator

**Davis, Alia**
Universal Attractions, 135 W 26th St, #1200, New York NY 10001 USA — Singer (Allure)

**Davis, Alvin G**
7983 Armagosa Dr, Riverside CA 92508, USA — Baseball Player

**Davis, Andre' N**
11407 Jutland Road, Houston TX 77048, USA — Football Player

**Davis, Andrew**
Chicago Pacific Entertainment, 1475 Hillcrest Road, Santa Barbara CA 93103, USA — Director

**Davis, Andrew F**
Columbia Artists Mgmt Inc, 5 Columbus Circle, 1790 Broadway, #1600, New York NY 10019 USA — Conductor

**Davis, Angela Y**
Speakout, PO Box 22748, Oakland CA 94609, USA — Political Activist, Educator

**Davis, Anthony**
8011 Carter Ave, #2606, Overland Park KS 66204, USA — Football Player

**Davis, Anthony**
Andriolo Communications, 115 E 9th St, New York NY 10003, USA — Jazz Pianist, Composer

**Davis, Anthony, Jr**
New Orleans Pelicans, 1250 Poydras St, #101, New Orleans LA 70113 USA — Basketball Player

**Davis, Antone**
2252 Red Bud Road, Sevierville TN 37876, USA — Football Player

**Davis, Antonio L**
1883 Cedar Glenn Way, Atlanta GA 30339, USA — Basketball Player

**Davis, Baron W L**
PO Box 12109, Marina del Rey CA 90295, USA — Basketball Player

**Davis, Barry**
417 N High Point Road, Madison WI 53717, USA — Freestyle Wrestler

**Davis, Benjamin (Ben)**
Encompass Arts, 119 W 72nd St, 371, New York NY 10023, USA — Opera Singer

**Davis, Benjamin F (Ben)**
1144 Brandon Road, Cleveland OH 44112, USA — Football Player

**Davis, Benjamin Jay**
Untitled Entertainment, 350 S Beverly Dr, #200, Beverly Hills CA 90212 USA — Actor

**Davis, Bennie L**
101 Golden Road, Georgetown TX 78633, USA — Air Force General

**Davis, Bill**
Bill Davis Racing, 810 Newport Road, Batesville AR 72501, USA — Auto Racing Executive

**Davis, Billy, Jr**
Brokaw Co, 9255 W Sunset Blvd, #804, West Hollywood CA 90069 USA — Singer (Fifth Dimension)

**Davis, Bradley E (Brad)**
2703 Ridge Top Lane, Arlington TX 76006, USA — Basketball Player

**Davis, Bradley J (Brad)**
Houston Dynamo, 1415 Louisiana, #3400, Houston TX 77002 USA — Soccer Player

**Davis, Brian W**
3847 E Hiddenview Dr, Phoenix AZ 85048, USA — Football Player

**Davis, Brianne**
Sager Mgmt, 260 S Beverly Dr, #205, Beverly Hills CA 90212, USA — Actress

**Davis, Bryshear B (Brock)**
23759 Heliotrope Way, Moreno Valley CA 92557, USA — Baseball Player

**Davis, Charles A**
201 E 19th St, #9E, New York NY 10003, USA — Jazz Saxophonist

**Davis, Charles E (Charlie)**
615 Main St, Nashville TN 37206, USA — Basketball Player

**Davis, Charles F**
N F L Network, 10950 Washington Blvd, #100, Culver City CA 90232 USA — Sportscaster

**Davis, Charles M (Charlie)**
2400 Bowler Road, Waller TX 77484, USA — Football Player

**Davis, Charles T (Chili)**
4625 Lake Washington Blvd SE, Bellevue WA 98006, USA — Baseball Player

**Davis, Clarence E**
171 Longleaf St, Pickerington OH 43147, USA — Football Player

**Davis, Clifton**
C E S D, 10635 Santa Monica Blvd, #130, Los Angeles CA 90025 USA — Actor

**Davis, Clive J**
R C A Records, 8750 Wilshire Blvd, Beverly Hills CA 90211 USA — Businessman

**Davis, Dana**
Marshak/Zachary/Mills, 8840 Wilshire Blvd, #100, Beverly Hills CA 90211 USA — Actress

**Davis, Daniel**
Innovative Artists, 1505 10th St, Santa Monica CA 90401 USA — Actor

**Davis, Daniel M**
Imperial College, Biological Sciences Dept, London SW7 2AZ, England — Immunologist

**Davis, David (Dave)**
DeStasio, 710 Shore Road, Spring Lake Heights NJ 07762, USA — Bowler

**Davis, David Brion**
783 Lambert Road, Orange CT 06477, USA — Writer, Historian

**Davis, Debbie**
Playboy Promotions, 9346 Civic Center Dr, #200, Beverly Hills CA 90210 USA — Model

**Davis, DeRay**
Principato-Young, 9465 Wilshire Blvd, #880, Beverly Hills CA 90212 USA — Actor

**Davis, Destiny**
10624 S Eastern Ave, #A157, Henderson NV 89052, USA — Model

**Davis, Dexter W**
7580 Hunters Woods Dr, Atlanta GA 30350, USA — Football Player

**Davis, Diane**
Paradigm Agency, 360 N Crescent Dr, North Building, Beverly Hills CA 90210 USA — Actress

**Davis, Don**
15910 FM 529, #219, Houston TX 77095, USA — Golfer

**Davis, Douglas N (Doug)**
26125 N 116th St, Scottsdale AZ 85255, USA — Baseball Player

**Davis, E Lydell (Dale)**
2000 Westwood Circle SE, Smyrna GA 30080, USA — Basketball Player

**Davis, Edgar**
Jet Propulsion Laboratory, 4800 Oak Grove Dr, Pasadena CA 91109 USA — Space Scientist

**Davis, Elliot M**
1328 Arch St, Berkeley CA 94708, USA — Cinematographer

**Davis, Eric K**
6203 Variel Ave, #118, Woodland Hills CA 91367, USA — Baseball Player

**Davis, Eric W**
236 S Oakhurst Dr, Beverly Hills CA 90212, USA — Football Player

**Davis, Essie**
R G M Artists, 8-12 Ann Street, Surry Hills NSW 2010, Australia — Actress

**Davis, Gary C**
10750 San Marcus Road, Atascadero CA 93422, USA — Football Player

**Davis, Geena**
Creative Artists Agency, 2000 Ave of Stars, #100, Los Angeles CA 90067 USA — Actress

**Davis, George E (Storm)**
7931 Dawsons Creek Dr, Jacksonville FL 32222, USA — Baseball Player

**Davis, Gerald S (Gerry)**
Gerry Davis Sports, 2420 W Nordale Drive, Appleton WI 54914 54914, USA — Baseball Umpire

**Davis, Glenn E**
27 Cascade Road, Columbus GA 31904, USA — Baseball Player

**Davis, Gregory B (Greg)**
793 Vernon Road NE, Rome GA 30165, USA — Football Player

**Davis, H Thomas (Tommy)**
9767 Whirlaway St, Rancho Cucamonga CA 91737, USA — Baseball Player

**Davis, Harry A**
1966 E 75th St, Cleveland OH 44103, USA — Basketball Player

**Davis, Harry R, Jr**
Schering-Plough Research, 2000 Galloping Hill Road, Kenilworth NJ 07033, USA — Chemist

**Davis, Hope**
United Talent Agency, U T A Plaza, 9336 Civic Center Dr, Beverly Hills CA 90210 USA — Actress

**Davis, Hubert I**
4320 Trenton Road, Chapel Hill NC 27517, USA — Basketball Player

**Davis, J Graham (Gray), Jr**
Loeb & Loeb, 10100 Santa Monica Blvd, #2200, Los Angeles CA 90067, USA — Governor, CA

**Davis, James B**
3600 Wimber Blvd, Palm Harbor FL 34685, USA — Air Force General

**Davis, James O**
612 Maplewood Dr, Columbia MO 65203, USA — Physician

**Davis, James R (Jim)**
Paws Inc, 5440 E Country Road 450 N, Albany IN 47320, USA — Cartoonist (Garfield)

**Davis, James S**
5701 S Saint Andrews Place, Los Angeles CA 90062, USA — Football Player

**Davis, Jamie**
Curtis Brown Group, 28-29 Haymarket St, #500, London SW1Y 4SP, England — Actress

**Davis, Jason T**
474 Leatha Lane NW, Cleveland TN 37312, USA — Baseball Player

**Davis, Jay**
2152 S State St, Springfield IL 62704, USA — Golfer

**Davis, Jeff**
Magnet Mgmt, 11704 Wilshire Blvd, #210, Los Angeles CA 90025, USA — Producer, Writer

**Davis, Jeff (Stick)**
Gen-X Entertainment, PO Box 128164, Nashville TN 37212, USA — Bassist (Amazing Rhythm Aces)

**Davis, Jeff Bryan**
Domain Talent, 9229 W Sunset Blvd, #710, West Hollywood CA 90069 USA — Actor, Comedian, Director

**Davis, Jeffrey E (Jeff)**
106 Sycamore Dr, Clemson SC 29631, USA — Football Player

**Davis, Jesse**
Concord Records, 100 N Crescent Dr, #275, Beverly Hills CA 90210 USA — Jazz Saxophonist

**Davis, Jill A**
Random House, 1745 Broadway, #1800, New York NY 10019 USA — Writer

**Davis, Jody R**
PO Box 93157, Phoenix AZ 85070, USA — Baseball Player

**Davis, John A**
W M E Entertainment, 9601 Wilshire Blvd, #300, Beverly Hills CA 90210 USA — Actor, Director, Producer, Writer

**Davis, John H**
901 Forest Pond Dr, Marietta GA 30068, USA — Football Player

**Davis, John K**
303 Calle Empalome, San Clemente CA 92672, USA — Marine Corps General

**Davis, Johnny L**
100 Winston Dr, #7CN, Cliffside Park NJ 07010, USA — Football Player

**Davis, Johnny R**
135 W Market St, #2D, Indianapolis IN 46204, USA — Basketball Player, Coach

**Davis, Jonathan H**
Kraft-Engel Mgmt, 15233 Ventura Blvd, #200, Sherman Oaks CA 91403, USA — Singer (Korn), Bagpipe Player

**Davis, Josh**
USA Swim Clinics, 3332 Dornoch Dr, Edmond OK 73034, USA — Swimmer

**Davis, Josie**
Brady Brannon Rich, 5670 Wilshire Blvd, #820, Los Angeles CA 90036 USA — Actress, Producer

**Davis, Judy**
Shanahan Mgmt, PO Box 1509, Darlinghurst NSW 1300, Australia — Actress

**Davis, Julie**
Felker Toczak Gellman, 10880 Wilshire Blvd, #2070, Los Angeles CA 90024 USA — Director, Writer

**Davis, Kane**
1558 Noble Ridge, Reedy WV 25270, USA — Baseball Player

**Davis, Keith B**
1343 Marvin Gardens, Lancaster TX 75134, USA — Football Player

**Davis, Keno**
Providence College, Athletic Dept, Providence RI 02918, USA — Basketball Coach

**Davis, Kim**
14 Shorecrest Dr, Winnipeg MB R3P 1N2, Canada — Ice Hockey Player

**Davis, Kristin**
Mosiac Media Group, 9200 W Sunset Blvd, #1000, Los Angeles CA 90069 USA — Actress, Model

**Davis, Kyle**
Global Artists Agency, 6253 Hollywood Blvd, #508, Los Angeles CA 90028, USA — Actor

**Davis, Lance**
5845 Old Berkley Road, Auburdale FL 33823, USA — Baseball Player

**Davis, Lance E**
9717 Thistle Court, Fort Smith AR 72908, USA — Economist

**Davis, Lauren**
2302 NE 5th Ave, Boca Raton FL 33431, USA — Tennis Player

**Davis, Lee C**
5024 Fieldgreen Crossing, #82, Stone Mountain GA 30088, USA — Basketball Player

**Davis, Linda K**
Alkahest Artists, 1709 Verona Dr, Chattanooga TN 37421, USA — Singer

**Davis, Louis (Chip), Jr**
Sound Trak, 9120 Mormon Bridge Road, Omaha NE 68152, USA — Musician

**Davis, Lowell**
1070 3rd St, #E, Carthage MO 64836, USA — Artist, Sculptor

**Davis, Lucy**
Melanie Greene Mgmt, 425 N Robertson Blvd, West Hollywood CA 90048 USA — Actress

**Davis, Lynn**
Galerie Karsten Greve, 5 Rue DeBelleyme, 75003 Paris, France — Photographer

**Davis, Mac**
Abrams Artists, 9200 W Sunset Blvd, #1125, West Hollywood CA 90069 USA — Singer, Songwriter, Actor

**Davis, Mackenzie**
United Talent Agency, U T A Plaza, 9336 Civic Center Dr, Beverly Hills CA 90210 USA — Actress

**Davis, Mark A**
108 Government Circle, #A, Thibodaux LA 70301, USA — Basketball Player

**Davis, Mark C (Ben)**
416 Homestead Dr, West Chester PA 19382, USA — Baseball Player

**Davis, Mark M**
Stanford University Medical Center, Microbiology Dept, Stanford CA 94305, USA — Microbiologist

**Davis, Mark W**
8867 E Sierra Pinta Dr, Scottsdale AZ 85255, USA — Baseball Player

**Davis, Martha**
Paradise Artists, PO Box 1821, Ojai CA 93024 USA — Singer (Motels)

**Davis, Matthew (Matt)**
Brillstein Entertainment Partners, 9150 Wilshire Blvd, #350, Beverly Hills CA 90212 USA — Actor

**Davis, Melvyn J (Mel)**
PO Box 29, Suffern NY 10901, USA — Basketball Player

**Davis, Meryl**
Artic Edge Ice Skating Club, 46615 Michigan Ave, Canton MI 48188, USA — Ice Dancer

**Davis, Michael**
I C M Partners, 10250 Constellation Blvd, #900, Los Angeles CA 90067 USA — Director, Producer, Writer

**Davis, Michael D (Mike)**
2491 San Ramon Valley Blvd, #1407, San Ramon CA 94583, USA — Baseball Player

**Davis, Michael L (Mike)**
37039 N 109th St, Scottsdale AZ 85262, USA — Football Player

**Davis, N Jan**
4105 Cumberland Pass, #814, Fort Worth TX 76116, USA — Astronaut

**Davis, Oliver J**
245 Pinehaven St, Seale AL 36875, USA — Football Player

**Davis, Philip (Phil)**
Yakety Yak, 7A Bloomsbury Square, London WC1A 2LP, England — Actor, Director, Producer

**Davis, Phyllis**
29330 SE Hillyard Dr, #D14, Boring OR 97009, USA — Actress

**Davis, Preston**
Vincent Cirrincione Assoc, 1516 N Fairfax Ave, Los Angeles CA 90046 USA — Actor

**Davis, R Glen (Big Baby)**
Performance Sports Mgmt, PO Box 270715, Houston TX 77277, USA — Basketball Player

**Davis, Rajal L**
31 Pond Edge Dr, Waterford CT 06385, USA — Baseball Player

**Davis, Reuben C**
4424 Lystra Road, Chapel Hill NC 27517, USA — Football Player

**Davis, Richard**
S R O Artists, 6629 University Ave, #206, Middleton WI 53562, USA — Jazz Bassist

**Davis, Richard D (Rick)**
12501 Isis Ave, Hawthorne CA 90250, USA — Soccer Player

**Davis, Richard E (Dick)**
11091 Sultan St, Moreno Valley CA 92557, USA — Baseball Player

**Davis, Richard K (Ted)**
5401 Riverbend Dr, Knoxville TN 37919, USA — Football Player

**Davis, Robert E (Bob), Jr**
500 W 111th St, #4F, New York NY 10025, USA — Football Player

**Davis, Robert J E (Bob)**
PO Box 198, Locust Grove OK 74352, USA — Baseball Player

**Davis, Roger W**
17522 Harvard Ave, Cleveland OH 44128, USA — Football Player

**Davis, Ronald (Ron)**
PO Box 293, Arroyo Hondo NM 87513, USA — Artist

**Davis, Ronald G (Ron)**
11748 N 90th Place, Scottsdale AZ 85260, USA — Baseball Player

**Davis, Ronald H**
5668 W Evergreen Road, Glendale AZ 85302, USA — Basketball Player

**Davis, Russell M**
605 Jones Ferry Road, Carrboro NC 27510, USA — Football Player

**Davis, Russell S (Russ)**
3351 Crescent Dr, Bessemer AL 35023, USA — Baseball Player

**Davis, Sammy J, Jr**
4020 Murphy Canyon Road, San Diego CA 92123, USA — Football Player

**Davis, Sammy L**
3376 N 100th St, Flat Rock IL 62427, USA — Vietnam War Army Hero (CMH)

**D**

**Davis, Sampson**
Three Doctors Foundation, 65 Hazelwood Ave, Newark NJ 07106, USA — Physician
**Davis, Samuel R (Sam)**
423 Edgemont St, Mount Washington PA 15211, USA — Football Player
**Davis, Scott**
5308 Worthington Dr, Bethesda MD 20816, USA — Figure Skater, Coach
**Davis, Shani**
7639 N Eastlake Terrace, #1A, Chicago IL 60626, USA — Speed Skater
**Davis, Sharen**
Sandra Marsh & Associates, 9150 Wilshire Blvd, #220, Beverly Hills CA 90212, USA — Costume Designer
**Davis, Spencer**
Alan Cottam Agency, 19 Charles St, Lancashire, Wigan WN1 2BP, England — Singer, Guitarist
**Davis, Stephen H**
2735 Simpson St, Evanston IL 60201, USA — Mathematician, Engineer
**Davis, Stephen L**
PO Box 31847, Saint Louis MO 63131, USA — Football Player
**Davis, Steve**
Matchroom Snooker, 10 Western Road, Romford, Essex RM1 3JT, England — Snooker Player
**Davis, Tamra**
Paradigm Agency, 360 N Crescent Dr, North Building, Beverly Hills CA 90210 USA — Director, Cinematographer
**Davis, Tania**
Mel Bush, Tanglewood, Arrowsmith Road, Wimborne, Dorset BH21 3BG, England — Violist (Bond)
**Davis, Terrell L**
19750 E Geddes Place, Centennial CO 80016, USA — Football Player, Sportscaster
**Davis, Terry R**
2933 Kenmore Road, Richmond VA 23225, USA — Basketball Player
**Davis, Vernon**
San Francisco 49ers, 4949 Centennial Blvd, Santa Clara CA 95054 USA — Football Player
**Davis, Viola**
Wolf Kasteler Public Relations, 9350 Wilshire Blvd, #450, Beverly Hills CA 90212 USA — Actress
**Davis, W Eugene**
US Court of Appeals, 800 Lafayette St, #2100, Lafayette LA 70501, USA — Judge
**Davis, Wallace M (Butch)**
1108 Brucemont Dr, Garner NC 27529, USA — Baseball Player
**Davis, Walter F (Buddy)**
5200 E Donald Ave, #A, Denver CO 80222, USA — Track Athlete, Basketball Player
**Davis, Walter P**
5200 E Donald Ave, #A, Denver CO 80222, USA — Basketball Player
**Davis, Warwick A**
Independent Talent Group, 40 Whitfield St, London W1T 2RH, England — Actor
**Davis, Wendy**
Pakula/King, 9229 W Sunset Blvd, #315, West Hollywood CA 90069 USA — Actress
**Davis, William A (Billy), III**
5813 Tautoga Dr, El Paso TX 79924, USA — Football Player
**Davis, William D (Willie)**
100 Corporate Pointe, #310, Culver City CA 90230, USA — Football Player
**Davison, Bruce**
Innovative Artists, 1505 10th St, Santa Monica CA 90401 USA — Actor
**Davison, Fred C**
National Science Foundation, 1 7th St, #502, Augusta GA 30901, USA — Foundation Executive, Educator
**Davison, Peter**
Conway Van Gelder Grant, 8-12 Broadwick St, #300, London W1F 8HW, England — Actor
**Davison, Ronald K**
11/217 Kupe St Orakei, Auckland 1071, New Zealand — Governor General, New Zealand; Judge
**Davison, Rosana D**
Storm Model Agency, 5 Jubilee Place, Chelsea, London SW3 3TD, England — Beauty Queen, Model
**Davis-Wrightsil, Clarissa**
Phoenix Mercury, American West Arena, 201 E Jefferson St, Phoenix AZ 85004 USA — Basketball Player
**Davitian, Ken**
Luber Rocklin Entertainment, 5815 Sunset Blvd, #206, Los Angeles CA 90028 USA — Actor
**Davuluri, Nina**
Miss America Organization, 1370 Ave of Americas, #1600, New York NY 10019 USA — Beauty Queen
**Davutoglu, Ahmet**
Prime Minister's Office, Eski Basbakanlik Binasi, Bakanliklar, 06573 Ankara, Turkey — Prime Minister, Turkey
**Davydova, Yelena V**
Gemini Gymnastics Association, 1000 Stevenson Road N, Oshawa ON L1J 5P5, Canada — Gymnast
**Dawber, Pam**
TalentWorks, 3500 W Olive Ave, #1400, Burbank CA 91505 USA — Actress
**Dawe, Jason**
9077 Drayton Lane, Fort Mill SC 29707, USA — Ice Hockey Player
**Dawes, Dominque M**
5484 Randolph Road, Rockville MD 20852, USA — Gymnast
**Dawes, Scott**
Dawes Construction Co, 1122 W 156th St, #100, Glenpool OK 74033, USA — Construction Engineer
**Dawid, Igor B**
Tufts Regenerative & Developmental Biology Center, 200 Boston Ave, #4600, Medford , MA 02155, USA — Molecular Geneticist
**Dawkins, Brian P**
9874 Red Sumac Place, Parker CO 80138, USA — Football Player
**Dawkins, C Richard**
Oxford University, Museum, Parks Road, Oxford OX1 3PW, England — Biologist, Ethologist, Writer
**Dawkins, Darryl**
1708 Glacier Court, Allentown PA 18104, USA — Basketball Player
**Dawkins, Johnny E**
40 Sunkist Lane, Los Altos CA 94022, USA — Basketball Player, Coach
**Dawkins, Peter M (Pete)**
80 W River Road, Rumson NJ 07760, USA — Football Player, Businessman
**Dawkins, Sean R**
826 Weichert Dr, Morgan Hill CA 95037, USA — Football Player
**Dawkins, Travis S (Gookie)**
106 Hunter Ridge Court, Boiling Springs SC 29316, USA — Baseball Player
**Dawley, Joseph W (Joe)**
13 Holly St, Cranford NJ 07016, USA — Artist
**Dawley, William C (Bill)**
8127 Landau Park Lane, Spring TX 77379, USA — Baseball Player
**Dawsey, Lawrence**
4341 Cheval Blvd, Lutz FL 33558, USA — Football Player

V.I.P. Address Book

| | |
|---|---|
| **Dawson, Andre N**<br>10601 SW 74th Ave, Miami FL 33156, USA | Baseball Player |
| **Dawson, Carol**<br>Simon & Schuster, 1230 Ave of Americas, Concourse 1, New York NY 10020 USA | Writer |
| **Dawson, Chad**<br>Gary Shaw Productions, 555 Preakness Ave, #9, Totowa NJ 07502, USA | Boxer |
| **Dawson, Dermontti F**<br>PO Box 712481, San Diego CA 92171, USA | Football Player |
| **Dawson, Douglas A (Doug)**<br>Dawson Financial Services, 1 Riverway, #900, Houston TX 77056, USA | Football Player |
| **Dawson, J Cutler, Jr**<br>Navy Federal Credit Union, PO Box 3000, Merrifield VA 22119, USA | Navy Admiral |
| **Dawson, James C (Jim)**<br>61 Glendale Road, Rye NY 10580, USA | Basketball Player |
| **Dawson, Leonard R (Lenny)**<br>1030 W 59th Terrace, Kansas City MO 64113, USA | Football Player, Sportscaster |
| **Dawson, Lynne**<br>I M G Artists, Hogarth Business Park, Chiswick, London W4 2TH, England | Opera Singer |
| **Dawson, Marco**<br>4360 Stillwater Dr, Merritt Island FL 32952, USA | Golfer |
| **Dawson, Philip D (Phil)**<br>4000 Dunning Lane, Austin TX 78746, USA | Football Player |
| **Dawson, Rosario**<br>Creative Artists Agency, 2000 Ave of Stars, #100, Los Angeles CA 90067 USA | Actress, Singer |
| **Dawson, Roxann**<br>Andrea Simon Entertainment, 4230 Woodman Ave, Sherman Oaks CA 91423, USA | Actress, Director |
| **Dawson, Thomas C, II**<br>1183 Dolores St, San Francisco CA 94110, USA | Economist |
| **Dawson, Trent**<br>Innovative Artists, 1505 10th St, Santa Monica CA 90401 USA | Actor |
| **Day George, Lynda**<br>10310 Riverside Dr, #104, Toluca Lake CA 91602, USA | Actress |
| **Day, Bill**<br>Cagle Cartoons, PO Box 22342, Santa Barbara CA 93121 USA | Editorial Cartoonist |
| **Day, Charles F (Boots)**<br>1154 Vespasian Way, Chesterfield MO 63017, USA | Baseball Player |
| **Day, Doris**<br>C W P Public Relations, 901 Hancock Ave, #312, West Hollywood CA 90069, USA | Singer, Actress |
| **Day, Felicia**<br>W M E Entertainment, 9601 Wilshire Blvd, #300, Beverly Hills CA 90210 USA | Actress |
| **Day, Glen**<br>6 Hickory Hills Circle, Little Rock AR 72212, USA | Golfer |
| **Day, Jason**<br>Professional Golfers Association, 100 Ave of Champions, Palm Beach Gardens FL 33418 USA | Golfer |
| **Day, Joe**<br>805 Shoreline Road, Lake Barrington IL 60010, USA | Ice Hockey Player |
| **Day, Julian**<br>Kmart, 3000 W 14 Mile Road, Royal Oak MI 48073, USA | Businessman |
| **Day, Laura**<br>Harper Collins Publishers, 10 E 53rd St, Cellar 1, New York NY 10022 USA | Writer |
| **Day, Matt**<br>United Agents, 12-26 Lexington St, London W1F 0LE, England | Actor |
| **Day, Patrick (Pat)**<br>14703 Isleworth Court, Louisville KY 40245, USA | Thoroughbred Racing Jockey |
| **Day, Peter R**<br>8200 Tarsier Ave, New Port Richey FL 34653, USA | Agricultural Scientist |
| **Day, Robert**<br>8832 Ferncliff Ave NE, Bainbridge Island WA 98110, USA | Director |
| **Day, S Zachary (Zach)**<br>9663 Lupine Dr, Cincinnati OH 45241, USA | Baseball Player |
| **Day, Skyler**<br>I C M Partners, 10250 Constellation Blvd, #900, Los Angeles CA 90067 USA | Actress |
| **Dayal, Manish**<br>United Talent Agency, U T A Plaza, 9336 Civic Center Dr, Beverly Hills CA 90210 USA | Actor |
| **Daye, Darren K**<br>21 Elderberry, Irvine CA 92603, USA | Basektball Player |
| **Dayett, Brian K**<br>276 Phillips Dr, Winchester TN 37398, USA | Baseball Player |
| **Daykin, Anthony A (Tony)**<br>5204 Cross Ridge Circle, Woodstock GA 30188, USA | Football Player |
| **Day-Lewis, Daniel**<br>Julian Belfrage Assoc, 9 Argyll St, #300, London W1F 7TG, England | Actor |
| **Dayley, Kenneth G (Ken)**<br>1300 Wingate Way Court, Chesterfield MO 63005, USA | Baseball Player |
| **Dayne, Ron**<br>2135 Regent St, Madison WI 53726, USA | Football Player |
| **Dayne, Taylor**<br>Almond Talent Agency, 8217 Beverly Blvd, #8, West Hollywood CA 90048, USA | Singer, Songwriter, Actress |
| **Days, Drews S, III**<br>Yale University, Law School, New Haven CT 06520, USA | Government Official |
| **Dayton, Jonathan**<br>United Talent Agency, U T A Plaza, 9336 Civic Center Dr, Beverly Hills CA 90210 USA | Director |
| **Dea, Billy**<br>2636 W Bartlett Way, Queen Creek AZ 85142, USA | Ice Hockey Player |
| **Deacon, Max**<br>Julian Belfrage Assoc, 9 Argyll St, #300, London W1F 7TG, England | Actor |
| **Deacon, Richard**<br>Lisson Gallery, 67 Lisson St, London NW1 5DA, England | Sculptor |
| **Deadmarsh, Adam**<br>PO Box 3346, Coeur D'Alene ID 83816, USA | Ice Hockey Player |
| **Deadmarsh, Ernest C (Butch)**<br>282 Diamond Dr SE, Calgary AB T2J 7E2, Canada | Ice Hockey Player |
| **Deadmau5**<br>W M E Entertainment, 9601 Wilshire Blvd, #300, Beverly Hills CA 90210 USA | Electronic Musician |
| **DeAgostini-Rossetti, Doris**<br>Strada de Valle, 6780 Airolo, Switzerland | Alpine Skier |

Dawson - DeAgostini-Rossetti

**Deakin, Julia** — Actress
Curtis Brown Group, 28-29 Haymarket St, #500, London SW1Y 4SP, England
**Deakin, Paul** — Drummer (Mavericks)
AristoMedia, 1620 16th Ave S, Nashville TN 37212, USA
**Deakins, Roger A** — Cinematographer
I C M Partners, 10250 Constellation Blvd, #900, Los Angeles CA 90067 USA
**Deal, Kimberly A (Kim)** — Singer, Bassist (Pixies, Breeders)
X-Ray Touring, 77-79 Great Eastern St, London EC2A 3HU, England
**Deal, Lance** — Track Athlete
845 Park Ave, Eugene OR 97404, USA
**DeAlmeida, Joaquim** — Actor
A P A Talent & Literary Agency, 405 S Beverly Dr, #300, Beverly Hills CA 90212 USA
**Dean, Barry** — Ice Hockey Player
315 Marsh St, Maple Creek SK S0N 1N0, Canada
**Dean, Billy** — Singer, Songwriter
Graham Brothers Entertainment, 6999 E Highway 80, Odessa TX 79762, USA
**Dean, Christopher** — Ice Dancer
4575 Governors Point, Colorado Springs CO 80906, USA
**Dean, David** — Football Coach
Valdosta State University, Athletic Dept, Valdosta GA 31698, USA
**Dean, Frederick G (Fred)** — Football Player, Coach
3911 Whitchurch Dr, Houston TX 77066, USA
**Dean, Fredrick R (Fred)** — Football Player
2411 Highway 3061, Ruston LA 71270, USA
**Dean, Graham** — Artist
Lacey Gallery, 1 Crawford Passage, Bay Street, London EC1R 3DP, England
**Dean, Hazell** — Singer, Songwriter
7 Kentish Town Road, London NW1 8N4, England
**Dean, Ira** — Singer (Trick Pony)
Warner Bros Records, 20 Music Square East, Nashville TN 37203 USA
**Dean, John G** — Diplomat
Chalet Crettaz, BP 1318, 1936 Verbier Valais, Switzerland
**Dean, John W, III** — Watergate Figure
9496 Rembert Lane, Beverly Hills CA 90210, USA
**Dean, Kevin** — Ice Hockey Player
1905 Wayzata Blvd, Wayzata MN 55391, USA
**Dean, Kiley** — Singer
Music World Entertainment, 1505 Hadley St, Houston TX 77002, USA
**Dean, Laura** — Choreographer, Composer
Dean Dance & Music Foundation, 552 Broadway, #400, New York NY 10012, USA
**Dean, Mark E** — Inventor (Electronic Tablet)
2184 N Ridge Dr, Jefferson City TN 37760, USA
**Dean, Stafford R** — Opera Singer
I M G Artists, Burlington Lane, Chiswick, London W4 2TH, England
**Dean, Theodore C (Ted)** — Football Player
16474 W Lava Dr, Surprise AZ 85374, USA
**Dean, Vernon D** — Football Player
2345 Hemlock St, Beaumont TX 77701, USA
**DeAnda, Paula** — Singer
I C M Partners, 10250 Constellation Blvd, #900, Los Angeles CA 90067 USA
**DeAndrea, John** — Artist
2220 Suncrest Dr, Loveland CO 80537, USA
**Deane, William Patrick** — Governor General, Australia
PO Box 4168, Manu Ka 2603 ACT, Australia
**DeAngelis, Beverly** — Psychiatrist
505 S Beverly Dr, #1017, Beverly Hills CA 90212, USA
**DeAngelis, William R (Billy)** — Basketball Player
14 Pickering Dr, Trenton NJ 08691, USA
**DeAngelo, Nino** — Singer
Ina Zimmermann, Neues Land 152, 29227 Celler, Germany
**DeAragon, Maria** — Actress
1159 10th Ave, San Diego CA 92101, USA
**DeAraujo, Serafim Fernandes Cardinal** — Religious Leader
Archdiocese of Belo Horizonte, Av Brasil 2079, 30140-002 Belo Horizonte MG, Brazil
**Dearborn, Matthew (Matt)** — Producer, Writer
Original Artists, 9465 Wilshire Blvd, #324, Beverly Hills CA 90212
**Deardurff-Schmidt, Deena** — Swimmer
742 Murray Dr, El Cajon CA 92020, USA
**Dearman, John** — Guitarist (LAGQ)
California State University, Music Dept, 18111 Nordhoff St, Northridge CA 91330, USA
**DeArmond, Frank M** — Astronaut
3086 Ravencrest Circle, Prescott AZ 86303, USA
**Deas, Justin** — Actor
I C M Partners, 10250 Constellation Blvd, #900, Los Angeles CA 90067 USA
**D'Eath, Tom** — Boat Racing Driver
435 Bay Road, Mount Dora FL 32757, USA
**Deaton, Brady J** — Educator
University of Missouri, Chancellor's Office, Jesse Hall, Columbia MO 65211, USA
**Deaver, Jeffrey** — Writer
Simon & Schuster, 1230 Ave of Americas, Concourse 1, New York NY 10020 USA
**DeBankole, Isaach** — Actor
Magrit Polak Mgmt, 1411 Carroll Ave, Los Angeles CA 90026, USA
**DeBarge, Chico** — Singer, Songwriter
Entertainment Artists, 2409 21st Ave S, #100, Nashville TN 10019 USA
**DeBarge, Eldra P (El)** — Singer, Pianist, Songwriter
Universal Attractions, 135 W 26th St, #1200, New York NY 10001 USA
**DeBarge, Kristina** — Singer, Songwriter
Soda Pop/Def Soul Records, 825 8th Ave, #2700, New York NY 10019, USA
**Debarr, Dennis L (Denny)** — Baseball Player
33843 Juliet Circle, Fremont CA 94555, USA
**Debbie Deb** — Singer
Harmony Artists, 6399 Wilshire Blvd, #914, Los Angeles CA 90048, USA
**Debbouze, Jamel** — Actor
Artmedia, 20 Ave Rapp, 75007 Paris, France
**DeBeaufort, India** — Actress, Singer
Safron Co, 2000 Ave of Stars, #600N, Los Angeles CA 90067, USA

| | |
|---|---|
| **DeBellevue, Charles B** <br> 916 Huntsman Road, Edmond OK 73003, USA | Vietnam War Air Force Hero |
| **Debello, James** <br> Full Circle Mgmt, 4932 Lankershim Blvd, #202, North Hollywood CA 91601, USA | Actor |
| **Debenedet, Nelson** <br> 38142 N Vista Dr, Livonia MI 48152, USA | Ice Hockey Player |
| **DeBenning, Burr** <br> 4235 Kingfisher Road, Calabasas CA 91302, USA | Actor |
| **DeBerg, Steve** <br> 17920 Simms Road, Odessa FL 33556, USA | Football Player, Coach |
| **Debie, Benoit** <br> I C M Partners, 10250 Constellation Blvd, #900, Los Angeles CA 90067 USA | Cinematographer |
| **Debison, Aselin (Azi)** <br> S L Feldman Mgmt, 1505 W 2nd Ave, #200, Vancouver BC V6H 3Y4, Canada | Singer |
| **DeBlaeij, Merel** <br> Larensche Mixed Hockey Club, Postbus 105, 1250 Laren AC, Netherlands | Field Hockey Player |
| **DeBlasio, Bill** <br> Mayor's Office, Gracie Mansion, New York NY | Mayor, New York City |
| **DeBlois, Dean** <br> W M E Entertainment, 9601 Wilshire Blvd, #300, Beverly Hills CA 90210 USA | Director, Writer |
| **Deblois, Lucien** <br> 407-350 Boul Graham, Mont Royal QC H3P 2C8, Canada | Ice Hockey Player |
| **Debney, John** <br> First Artists Mgmt, 4764 Park Granada, #210, Calabasas CA 91302 USA | Composer |
| **DeBoer, Nicole** <br> Characters Talent Agency, 8 Elm St, Toronto ON M5G 1G7, Canada | Actress |
| **DeBoer, Peter** <br> New Jersey Devils, Arena, 50 State Route 120, East Rutherford NJ 07073 USA | Ice Hockey Coach |
| **DeBont, Jan** <br> Blue Tulip Productions, 2202 Main St, Santa Monica CA 90405, USA | Cinematographer, Director |
| **DeBoor, Carl-Wilhelm R** <br> University of Wisconsin, Mathematics Dept, Madison WI 53706, USA | Mathematician |
| **Debre, Michel** <br> 20 Rue Jacob, 75006 Paris, France | Prime Minister, France |
| **DeBruijn, Inge** <br> Alsemhof 6, 2991 Barendrecht HA, Netherlands | Swimmer |
| **DeBrunhoff, Laurent** <br> Mary Ryan Gallery, 527 W 26th St, New York NY 10001, USA | Writer, Illustrator (Babar) |
| **Debrusk, Louie** <br> 27502 N 84th Dr, Peoria AZ 85383, USA | Ice Hockey Player |
| **DeBurgh, Chris** <br> Kenny Thomson Mgmt, 754 Fulham Road, London SW6 5SH, England | Singer, Songwriter |
| **Deby Itno, Idriss** <br> President's Office, Presidential Palace, BP 74, N'Djamena, Chad | President, Chad; Army General |
| **DeCaestecker, Iain** <br> W M E Entertainment, 9601 Wilshire Blvd, #300, Beverly Hills CA 90210 USA | Actor |
| **DeCamilli, Pietro V** <br> Yale University Medical School, Cell Biology Dept, New Haven CT 06512, USA | Biologist |
| **DeCarlo, Arthur A (Art), Jr** <br> 9030 Manordale Lane, Ellicott City MD 21042, USA | Football Player |
| **DeCarlo, Mark** <br> 3292 Carse Dr, Los Angeles CA 90068, USA | Actor |
| **Decarnin, Christophe** <br> Balmain, 44 Rue Francois, 75008 Paris, France | Fashion Designer |
| **DeCaro, Frank** <br> Sirius, 1221 Ave of Americas, #1900, New York NY 10020, USA | Actor, Comedian |
| **DeCasabianca, Camille** <br> Artmedia, 20 Ave Rapp, 75007 Paris, France | Actress |
| **DeCastella, F Robert** <br> Smart Start, PO Box 3808, Weston ACT 2611, Australia | Track Athlete |
| **DeCastro, David** <br> Pittsburgh Steelers, 3400 S Water St, Pittsburgh PA 15203 USA | Football Player |
| **DeCercio, Tom** <br> Farah Films Mgmt, 11640 Mayfield, #208, Brentwood CA 90049, USA | Director |
| **DeCinces, Douglas V (Doug)** <br> 124 Riviera Way, Laguna Beach CA 92651, USA | Baseball Player |
| **Decker, Brianna** <br> John Decker, S46W38746 County Road Z, Dousman WI 53118, USA | Ice Hockey Player |
| **Decker, Brooklyn** <br> Place Model Mgmt, Am Felde 29, 22765 Hamburg, Germany | Model, Actress |
| **Decker, Steven M (Steve)** <br> 1024 Laurelridge St NE, Keizer OR 97303, USA | Baseball Player |
| **Declan** <br> PO Box 161, Market Rasen LN8 6EX, England | Singer, Guitarist, Pianist |
| **Decoder** <br> Moskaha Mgmt, PO Box 102, London E15 2HH, England | Drum, Bass Producer (Kosheen) |
| **DeConcini, Dennis** <br> 6014 Chesterbrook Road, McLean VA 22101, USA | Senator, AZ |
| **DeCosta, Sara** <br> 200 Cowesett Green Dr, Warwick RI 02886, USA | Ice Hockey Player |
| **DeCoster, Roger** <br> M C Sports, 1919 Torrance Blvd, Torrance CA 90501, USA | Motorcycle Racing Rider |
| **DeCrane, Alfred C, Jr** <br> 30 Wax Myrtle Way, Vero Beach FL 32963, USA | Businessman |
| **Decrem, Bart** <br> Tapulous, 854 High St, Palo Alto CA 94301, USA | Educator, Social Activist |
| **Decter, Midge** <br> 120 E 81st St, New York NY 10028, USA | Writer, Journalist |
| **Dedes, Spero** <br> N F L Network, 10950 Washington Blvd, #100, Culver City CA 90232 USA | Sportscaster |
| **Dedkov, Anatoli I** <br> Cosmonaut Training Center, Star City, 141160 Zvezdny Gorodok, Moscow Oblast, Russia | Cosmonaut |
| **Dedmon, Jeffrey L (Jeff)** <br> 21102 Broadwell Ave, Torrance CA 90502, USA | Baseball Player |
| **Dee, Donald M (Don)** <br> 7924 N Pennsylvania Ave, Kansas City MO 64118, USA | Basketball Player |

**Dee, Joey**
Universal Attractions, 135 W 26th St, #1200, New York NY 10001 USA — Singer

**Dee, Kiki**
Alan Cottam Agency, 19 Charles St, Lancashire Wigam WN1 2BP, England — Singer, Songwriter

**Dee, Sally**
3508 W Barcelona St, Tampa FL 33629, USA — Golfer

**Dee, Wanda**
Universal Attractions, 135 W 26th St, #1200, New York NY 10001 USA — Singer, Songwriter

**Deeb, Gary**
Chicago Sun-Times, Editorial Dept, 401 N Wabash Ave, Chicago IL 60611 USA — Television Critic

**Deeley, Catherine E (Cat)**
Maydew & Golenberg, 8383 Wilshire Blvd, #1050, Beverly Hills CA 90211, USA — Actress, DJ Musician, Model

**Deeley, Justin**
Arlook Group, 205 S Beverly Dr, #209, Beverly Hills CA 90212, USA — Actor

**Deemer, Audrey**
4401 Country Club Dr, #30, Steubenville OH 43953, USA — Baseball Player

**Deen, Paula H**
102 W Congress St, Savannah GA 31401, USA — Chef, Restaurateur, Writer

**Deep Roy**
C E S D, 10635 Santa Monica Blvd, #130, Los Angeles CA 90025 USA — Actor

**Deer, Ada E**
2537 Mutchler Road, Fitchburg WI 53711, USA — Government Official

**Deer, Robert G (Rob)**
22217 N 78th St, Scottsdale AZ 85255, USA — Baseball Player

**Deering, John**
6701 Westover Dr, Little Rock AR 72207, USA — Editorial Cartoonist

**Deery, Tom**
49 Yale Square, Morton PA 19070, USA — Football Player

**Dees, Archie W**
4405 N Hillview Dr, Bloomington IN 47408, USA — Basketball Player

**Dees, Charles H (Charlie)**
1064 Allison Woods Court, Lawrenceville GA 30043, USA — Baseball Player

**Dees, Morris S, Jr**
Southern Poverty Law Center, PO Box 548, Montgomery AL 36101, USA — Attorney, Civil Rights Activist

**Dees, Rick**
Dees Entertainment, 3601 W Olive St, #675, Burbank CA 91505, USA — Entertainer, Singer

**Deese, Derrick**
PO Box 3356, Cerritos CA 90703, USA — Football Player

**Deezen, Eddie**
Coolwaters Productions, 10061 Riverside Dr, Box 531, Toluca Lake CA 91602 USA — Actor

**Deezer D**
Acme Talent Agency, 4727 Wilshire Blvd, #333, Los Angeles CA 90010, USA — Actor, Rap Artist

**Def Jef**
Turner Accountancy, 13245 Riverside Dr, #330, Sherman Oaks CA 91423, USA — Rap Artist

**DeFanti, Sylvia**
Fox & Gould Mgmt, Via Arenula 29, 00186 Rome, Italy — Actress

**DeFanti, Thomas A (Tom)**
University of Illinois, Electronic Visualization Laboratory, 842 W Taylor St, Chicago IL 60607, USA — Inventor (Cave Electronic Visualization)

**DeFelitta, Raymond**
Paradigm Agency, 360 N Crescent Dr, North Building, Beverly Hills CA 90210 USA — Director, Writer

**DeFer, Kaylee**
Innovative Artists, 1505 10th St, Santa Monica CA 90401 USA — Actress

**DeFerran, Gil**
524 Royal Plaza Dr, Fort Lauderdale FL 33301, USA — Auto Racing Driver

**DeFilippo, Jacy**
C E S D, 10635 Santa Monica Blvd, #130, Los Angeles CA 90025 USA — Actress

**Deford, Frank**
23 W 73rd St, #4, New York NY 10023, USA — Sportswriter

**DeFrance, Cecile**
Margrit Polak Mgmt, 1920 Hillhurst, #405, Los Angeles CA 90027, USA — Actress

**DeFranceschi, Alexandre**
I C M Partners, 10250 Constellation Blvd, #900, Los Angeles CA 90067 USA — Editor

**DeFrancisco, Joseph E (Joe)**
1201 N Nash St, #203, Arlington VA 22209, USA — Army General

**DeFranco, Buddy**
978 Colorado Ave, #A, Whitefish MT 59937, USA — Jazz Clarinetist

**DeFrank, Joe**
PO Box 655, Lake Pleasant NY 12108, USA — Harness Racing Official

**DeFreitas, Eric**
175 W 12th St, New York NY 10011, USA — Bowler

**DeGale, James**
Amateur Boxing Assn, National Sports Centre, London SE19 2B8, England — Boxer

**DeGarmo, Diana K**
Mauldin Brand Agency, 1280 W Peachtree St, #300, Atlanta GA 30309, USA — Singer, Actress, Songwriter

**DeGarmo, Todd**
Studios Architecture, 1625 M St NW, Washington DC 20036, USA — Architect, Interior Designer

**DeGeneres, Ellen**
I C M Partners, 10250 Constellation Blvd, #900, Los Angeles CA 90067 USA — Actress, Comedienne

**Degerick, Michael A (Mike)**
2702 Lake Osborne Dr, Lake Worth FL 33461, USA — Baseball Player

**DeGiorgi, Salvatore Cardinal**
Archdiocese of Palermo, Corso Vittorio Emanuele 461, 90134 Palermo, Italy — Religious Leader

**DeGivenchy, Hubert T**
3 Ave George V, 75008 Paris, France — Fashion Designer

**Degler, Carl N**
907 Mears Court, Stanford CA 94305, USA — Historian

**Degout, Stephane**
I M G Artists, Hogarth Business Park, Chiswick, London W4 2TH, England — Opera Singer

**DeGouw, Jessica**
R G M Artists, 8-12 Ann Street, Surry Hills NSW 2010, Australia — Actress

**DeGraw, Gavin**
C E S D, 257 Park Ave S, #950, New York NY 10010 USA — Singer, Songwriter

**Degray, Dale**
Owen Sound Attack, Box 1420 Station Main, Owen Sound ON N4K 6T5, Canada — Ice Hockey Player

**DeHaan, Dane**
Creative Artists Agency, 2000 Ave of Stars, #100, Los Angeles CA 90067 USA — Actor

**Dehart, Richard A (Rick)** — Baseball Player
811 NE Wabash Ave, Topeka KS 66616, USA

**DeHaven, Gloria** — Actress
2223 W San Miguel Ave, North Las Vegas NV 89032, USA

**DeHavilland, Olivia** — Actress
BP 156-16, 75764 Paris Cedex 16, France

**Dehmelt, Hans G** — Nobel Physics Laureate
1600 43rd Ave E, #211, Seattle WA 98112, USA

**Dehner, Dorothy** — Artist
33 5th Ave, New York NY 10003, USA

**DeHomem Christo, Guy-Manuel** — Musician (Daft Punk)
Clintons, 55 Drury Lane, Covent Garden, London WC2B 5RZ, England

**Deibert, Charles (Larry)** — Vietnam War Army Hero
201 NE Saizman Road, Corbett OR 97019, USA

**Deibold, Alex** — Snowboard Athlete
PO Box 1544, Manchester Center VT 05255, USA

**Deidel, James L (Jim)** — Baseball Player
14312 Wright Way, Broomfield CO 80023, USA

**Deighton, Leonard C (Len)** — Writer
Fairymount, Blackrock, Dundalk, County Louth, Ireland

**Deininger, Svenja** — Artist
Marianne Boesky Gallery, 118 E 64th St, New York NY 10065, USA

**Deisenhofer, Johann** — Nobel Chemistry Laureate
3860 Echo Brook Lane, Dallas TX 75229, USA

**Deitch, Donna** — Director
Paradigm Agency, 360 N Crescent Dr, North Building, Beverly Hills CA 90210 USA

**Deja, Andreas** — Animator
Disney Animation, PO Box 10200, Orlando FL 32830, USA

**DeJager, Cornelis** — Astronomer
Zonnenburg 1, 352 Utrecht NL Netherlands

**DeJesus, Ivan** — Baseball Player
14608 Velleux Dr, Orlando FL 32837, USA

**DeJesus, Wanda** — Actress
McGowan Mgmt, 8733 W Sunset Blvd, #103, West Hollywood CA 90069, USA

**DeJohnette, Jack** — Jazz Drummer, Composer
Silver Hollow Road, Willow NY 12495, USA

**DeJong, Bob J C** — Speed Skater
Drechtlaan 131, 2451 Leimuiden CL, Netherlands

**DeJong, Pierre** — Geneticist
Lawrence Livermore Laboratory, 7000 East St, Livermore CA 94550, USA

**DeJonge, Peter** — Writer
Little Brown, 3 Center Plaza, #100, Boston MA 02108 USA

**DeJongh, John P, Jr** — Governor, Virgin Islands
Governor's Office, 21-2 Kongens Gade, Charlotte Amalie, Saint Thomas VI 00802 USA

**DeJordy, Denis E** — Ice Hockey Player
472 Chemin Des-Patriotes, Saint Charles QC J0L 2G0, Canada

**DeJurnett, Charles R** — Football Player
1355 Heritage Court, Escondido CA 92027, USA

**Dekker, Thomas** — Actor
Schiff Co, 9220 Sunset Blvd, #106, West Hollywood CA 90069 USA

**DeKlerk, Albert** — Concert Organist, Composer
Crayenesterlaan 22, 2012 Haarlem DK, Netherlands

**DeKlerk, Frederik W** — Nobel Laureate; President, South Africa
DeKlerk Foundation, PO Box 15785, Panorama, Cape Town 7506, South Africa

**Deklin, Mark** — Actor
Michael Black Mgmt, 9701 Wilshire Blvd, #1000, Beverly Hills CA 90212, USA

**DeKnight, Steven S** — Producer, Writer
Creative Artists Agency, 2000 Ave of Stars, #100, Los Angeles CA 90067 USA

**DeLaBilliere, Peter** — Army General, England
Naval & Military Club, 4 Saint James's Square, London SW1Y 4JU, England

**Delacote, Jacques** — Conductor
Dr Hilbert Maximilianstr 22, 80539 Munich, Germany

**DeLaCruz, Rosie** — Model
Wilhelmina Models, 300 Park Ave S, #200, New York NY 10010 USA

**DeLaFuente, Cristian** — Actor
Abrams Artists, 9200 W Sunset Blvd, #1125, West Hollywood CA 90069 USA

**DeLaFuente, Marian** — Commentator
Latin World Entertainment, 2601 S Bayshore Dr, #235, Miami FL 33133, USA

**DelaGarza, Alana** — Actress
Brillstein Entertainment Partners, 9150 Wilshire Blvd, #350, Beverly Hills CA 90212 USA

**Delahoussay, Edward (Eddie)** — Thoroughbred Racing Jockey
1024 S 4th Ave, Arcadia CA 91006, USA

**Delahoussaye, Ryan** — Violinist (Blue October)
Rainmaker Artists, PO Box 551665, Dallas TX 75355, USA

**DeLaHoya, Oscar** — Boxer
Golden Boy Promotions, 626 Wilshire Blvd, #350, Los Angeles CA 90017, USA

**DeLaHoz, Miguel A (Mike)** — Baseball Player
PO Box 441233, Miami FL 33144, USA

**DeLaHuerta, Paz** — Actress
T C A/Jed Root, 9220 Sunset Blvd, #315, Los Angeles CA 90069, USA

**Delahunt, William D (Bill)** — Representative, MA
Prime Policy Group LLP, 1110 Vermont Ave NW, #1000, Washington DC 20005, USA

**Delainey, Gary** — Cartoonist (Bub Slug, Betty)
United Feature Syndicate, PO Box 5610, Cincinnati OH 45201 USA

**Delaire, Suzy** — Actress, Singer
46 Rue de Varenne, 75007 Paris, France

**DeLaMaza, Roland** — Baseball Player
28533 Silverking Trial, Santa Clarita CA 91390, USA

**DeLamielleure, Joseph M (Joe)** — Football Player
7818 Ridgeloch Place, Charlotte NC 28226, USA

**DeLancey, William J, III** — Businessman
200 Public Square, #1950, Cleveland OH 44114, USA

**DeLancie, John** — Actor
S D B Partners, 315 S Beverly Dr, #411, Beverly Hills CA 90067 USA

**Delaney, Frank** — Writer
Random House, 1745 Broadway, #1800, New York NY 10019 USA

**Delaney, Jeffrey J (Jeff)** — Football Player
215 Village Green Dr, Canonsburg PA 15317, USA

**Delaney, Kim** — Actress, Model
Gersh Agency, 9465 Wilshire Blvd, #600, Beverly Hills CA 90212 USA

**Delaney, Simon** — Actor, Writer
Lorraine Brennan Mgmt, Greenmount Industrial Estate, #22, Harold's Cross, Dublin 6, Ireland

**DeLange, Titia** — Cell Biologist, Geneticist
Rockefeller University Medical Center, Anderson Cancer Research Center, 1230 York Ave, New York NY 10065, USA

**Delano, Diane** — Actress
Abrams Artists, 9200 W Sunset Blvd, #1125, West Hollywood CA 90069 USA

**Delano, Robert B** — Association Executive
American Farm Bureau, 1501 E Woodfield Road, #300W, Schaumburg IL 60173, USA

**Delany, Dana** — Actress
United Talent Agency, U T A Plaza, 9336 Civic Center Dr, Beverly Hills CA 90210 USA

**Delany, Samuel R** — Writer
Vintage Books, 1745 Broadway, New York NY 10019 USA

**DeLap, Tony** — Artist, Sculptor
225 Jasmine St, Corona del Mar CA 92625, USA

**DeLaParra, Alondra** — Conductor
I M G Artists, Hogarth Business Park, Chiswick, London W4 2TH, England

**DeLaPena, Gemmenne** — Actress
Corsa Agency, 11704 Wilshire Blvd, #204, Los Angeles CA 90025 90025, USA

**DelArco, Jonathan** — Actor
S D B Partners, 315 S Beverly Dr, #411, Beverly Hills CA 90067 USA

**DeLaria, Lea** — Actress, Writer
Katz Co, 1674 Broadway, #700, New York NY 10019, USA

**Delarme, Julie** — Actress
Artmedia, 20 Ave Rapp, 75007 Paris, France

**DeLaRocha, Zack** — Singer (Rage Against the Machine)
Creative Artists Agency, 2000 Ave of Stars, #100, Los Angeles CA 90067 USA

**DeLaRosa, Evelyn** — Opera Singer
Dorothy Cone Artists, 150 W 55th St, New York NY 10019, USA

**DeLaRosa, Pedro M** — Auto Racing Driver
P D L R, Pedro de la Creu, 08017 Barcelona, Spain

**DeLaSalle, Lise** — Concert Pianist
Frank Salomon, 121 W 27th St, #703, New York NY 10001 USA

**Delasin, Dorothy** — Golfer
20 Longview Dr, Daly City CA 94015, USA

**DeLaTour, Frances** — Actress
Independent Talent Group, 40 Whitfield St, London W1T 2RH, England

**Delaughter, Tim** — Singer, Musician (Polyphonic Spree)
Gorfaine/Schwartz, 4111 W Alameda Ave, #509, Burbank CA 91505 USA

**DeLaurentiis, Giada** — Chef, Writer
W M E Entertainment, 9601 Wilshire Blvd, #300, Beverly Hills CA 90210 USA

**DeLautour, David** — Actor, Writer, Producer
Karen Kay Mgmt, 2/25 Sale St, Freemans Bay, Auckland 1010, New Zealand

**Delavan, Mark** — Opera Singer
Columbia Artists Mgmt Inc, 5 Columbus Circle, 1790 Broadway, #1600, New York NY 10019 USA

**Delbanco, Nicholas** — Writer
Warner Books, 1271 Ave of Americas, New York NY 10020 USA

**Delbonnel, Bruno** — Cinematographer
Cosmic, 7 Rue Jean Ferrandi, 75006 Paris, France

**DelBuono, Brett** — Actor
C E S D, 10635 Santa Monica Blvd, #130, Los Angeles CA 90025 USA

**DelCarlo, John** — Singer
Opus 3 Artists, 470 Park Ave S, #900N, New York NY 10016 USA

**Delcarmen, Manny** — Baseball Player
68 Surrey Lane, East Bridgewater MA 02333, USA

**DelCastillo Galvez, Jorge A A** — Prime Minister, Peru
Premier's Office, Urb Corpac, Calle 1 Oeste, San Isidro, Lima 27, Peru

**DelCastillo, Kate** — Actress
Creative Artists Agency, 2000 Ave of Stars, #100, Los Angeles CA 90067 USA

**DeLeeuw, Ton** — Composer
Costeruslaan 4, 1217 Hilversum JT, Netherlands

**DeLeeuw-Chapman, Dianne M** — Figure Skater
3857 Birch St, #141, New Beach CA 92660, USA

**Delehanty, Hugh** — Editor
A A R P Publications, Editorial Dept, 601 E St NW, Washington DC 20049, USA

**DeLeo, Dean** — Guitarist (Stone Temple Pilots)
Q Prime, 729 7th Ave, #1600, New York NY 10019 USA

**DeLeo, Robert** — Bassist (Stone Temple Pilots), Composer
Q Prime, 729 7th Ave, #1600, New York NY 10019 USA

**Deleon, Luis A** — Baseball Player
120 Calle San Antonio, Bda Clausells, Ponce PR 00730, USA

**DeLeone, Thomas D (Tom)** — Football Player
PO Box 681472, Park City UT 84068, USA

**Delerm, Graziella** — Actress
Artmedia, 20 Ave Rapp, 75007 Paris, France

**Delfino, Carlos F** — Basketball Player
Milwaukee Bucks, Bradley Center, 1001 N 4th St, #2, Milwaukee WI 53203 USA

**Delgado, Alvaro** — Artist
Biarritz 5, Parque de las Avenidas, 28028 Madrid, Spain

**Delgado, Carlos J** — Baseball Player
9 Repto Ramos Bo Borinquen, Aguadilla PR 00603, USA

**Delgado, Emilio** — Actor
About Artists Agency, 1650 Broadway, #1406, New York NY 10019, USA

**Delgado, Isaac** — Singer, Orchestra Leader
Second Octave Talent, 720 South Point Blvd, #A200, Petaluma CA 94954, USA

**DelGreco, Albert L (Al), Jr** — Football Player
1012 Little Turtle Circle, Birmingham AL 35242, USA

**DelGreco, Robert G (Bobby)** — Baseball Player
625 Southview Dr, Pittsburgh PA 15226, USA

**Delhomme, Jake C** — Football Player
1459 Mills Highway, Breaux Bridge LA 70517, USA

**D'Elia, Bill** — Director, Producer, Writer
W M E Entertainment, 9601 Wilshire Blvd, #300, Beverly Hills CA 90210 USA

**D'Elia, Chris** — Actor, Writer
United Talent Agency, U T A Plaza, 9336 Civic Center Dr, Beverly Hills CA 90210 USA
**Deligne, Pierre R** — Mathematician
Institute for Advanced Study, Math School, Einstein Dr, Princeton NJ 08540, USA
**DeLillo, Don** — Writer
57 Rossmore Ave, Bronxville NY 10708, USA
**DeLint, Derek** — Actor
Features Creative Mgmt, Entrepotdok 76A, 101 Amsterdam AD, Netherlands
**DeLisle, Paul** — Bassist (Smash Mouth), Actor
Interscope Records, 2220 Colorado Ave, Santa Monica CA 90404 USA
**Delk, Denny** — Actor
Innovative Artists, 235 Park Ave S, #700, New York NY 10003, USA
**Delk, Joan** — Golfer
830 Forest Path Lane, Alpharetta GA 30022, USA
**Delk, Tony L** — Basketball Player
1843 Glenhill Dr, Lexington KY 40502, USA
**Dell, Charlie** — Actor
Scott Stander Assoc, 4533 Van Nuys Blvd, #401, Sherman Oaks CA 91403 USA
**Dell, Donald L** — Tennis Player, Attorney
Blue Entertainment, 333 E Main St, #200, Louisville KY 40202 USA
**Dell, Michael S** — Businessman
Dell Inc, 1 Dell Way, Round Rock TX 78682, USA
**Dellacqua, Casey** — Tennis Player
107 Alana Road, Gibson WA 6448, Australia
**Dellanos, Myrka** — Actress
United Talent Agency, U T A Plaza, 9336 Civic Center Dr, Beverly Hills CA 90210 USA
**DelleDonne, Elena** — Basketball Player
Chicago Sky, 20 W Kinzie St, #1010, Chicago IL 60654 USA
**Dellenbach, Jeffrey A (Jeff)** — Football Player
1002 Pine Branch Dr, Weston FL 33326, USA
**Dellinger, Walter** — Educator, Attorney
Duke University, Law School, Durham NC 27706, USA
**Dellinger, William (Bill)** — Track Athlete, Coach
1993 Fircrest Dr, Eugene OR 97403, USA
**Dellorco, Chris** — Artist
Rebecca Molayem Gallery, 306 Robertson Blvd, West Hollywood CA 90048, USA
**Dell'Orefice, Carmen** — Model
Ford Models Inc, 111 5th Ave, #900, New York NY 10003 USA
**Dellucci, David M** — Baseball Player
5512 Summer Lake Dr, Baton Rouge LA 70817, USA
**Dellums, Ronald V (Ron)** — Representative, CA
658 Santa Ray Ave, Oakland,CA 94610, USA
**DelNegro, Vincent J (Vinny)** — Basketball Player, Coach
58 Bagnell Dr, Pembroke MA 02359, USA
**DeLoach, Nikki** — Singer (Innosense), Actress
R C A Records, 8750 Wilshire Blvd, Beverly Hills CA 90211 USA
**Delock, Ivan M (Ike)** — Baseball Player
433 Cypress Way E, Naples FL 34110, USA
**Delon, Alain** — Actor
Alain Delon International, 7 Rue des Battoirs, 1205 Geneva, Switzerland
**Delong, Gregory A (Greg)** — Football Player
4960 Shady Maple Lane, Winston-Salem NC 27106, USA
**DeLong, Keith A** — Football Player
1850 Greywell Road, Knoxville TN 37922, USA
**DeLong, Michael P** — Marine Corps General
Deputy Commander, US Central Command, MacDill Air Force Base, Tampa FL 33621, USA
**Delong, Nathan J (Nate)** — Basketball Player
PO Box 485, Hayward WI 54843, USA
**DeLonge, Tom** — Singer, Guitarist, Songwriter
1665 Neptune Ave, Encinitas CA 92024, USA
**DeLorenzo, Michael** — Actor
Opus Entertainment, 5225 Wilshire Blvd, #905, Los Angeles CA 90036, USA
**Delorme, Daniele** — Actress
Gueville Productions, 16 Rue de Marignan, 75008 Paris, France
**Delorme, Ronald (Ron)** — Ice Hockey Player
94 Ravine Dr, Port Moody BC V3H 4T8, Canada
**Delors, Jacques L J** — Government Official, France
Notre Europe Assn, 41 Blvd des Capucines, 75002 Paris, France
**DeLosReyes, Kamar** — Actor
TalentWorks, 3500 W Olive Ave, #1400, Burbank CA 91505 USA
**DeLosSantos, Becky** — Model
Playboy Promotions, 9346 Civic Center Dr, #200, Beverly Hills CA 90210 USA
**DeLosSantos, Marisa** — Writer
Hudson Street Press, 375 Hudson St, Basement 3, New York NY 10014, USA
**DeLosSantos, Valerio L** — Baseball Player
9838 N 119th Place, Scottsdale AZ 85259, USA
**Delpeyrat, Scali** — Actor
U B B A, 6 Rue de Braque, 75003 Paris, France
**DelPiero, Alessandro** — Soccer Player
F C Juventus, Corso Galilo Ferraris 32, 10128 Turin, Italy
**Delpino, Robert L** — Football Player
9569 Calle Del Casa, Riverside CA 92503, USA
**DelPonte, Carla** — Attorney
War Crimes Tribunal, Churchilluplein 1, 2517 The Hague JW, Netherlands
**DelPorto, Juan Martin** — Tennis Player
Association of Tennis Professionals, Palliser Road, London W14 9EB, England
**Delpy, Julie** — Actress, Director, Writer
Markham Froggatt Irwin, Julian House, 4 Windmill St, London W1P 1HF, England
**DelRey, Lana** — Singer, Songwriter, Model
Next Model Mgmt, 23 Watts St, New York NY 10013 USA
**DelRio, David** — Actor
Paradigm Agency, 360 N Crescent Dr, North Building, Beverly Hills CA 90210 USA
**DelRio, Jack** — Football Player, Coach
285 Twisted Pine Trail, Santa Rosa Beach FL 32459, USA
**Delsing, Jay** — Golfer
14020 Woods Mill Cove Dr, Chesterfield MO 63017, USA

# D

## D'Elia - Delsing

**Delson, Brad** — Guitarist (Linkin Park)
Artist Group International, 150 E 58th St, #1900, New York NY 10155, USA

**Delson, Rudolph** — Writer
Houghton Mifflin Harcourt, 215 Park Ave S, #1200, New York NY 10003 USA

**DelToro, Benicio** — Actor
Creative Artists Agency, 2000 Ave of Stars, #100, Los Angeles CA 90067 USA

**DelToro, Guillermo** — Director, Writer
W M E Entertainment, 9601 Wilshire Blvd, #300, Beverly Hills CA 90210 USA

**DelTredici, David** — Composer
463 West St, #G121, New York NY 10014, USA

**DeLuca, Fred** — Businessman
3550 Galt Ocean Dr, #301, Fort Lauderdale FL 33308, USA

**DeLuca, Rocco** — Singer, Dobro Player
Primary Talent International, 10-11 Jockey's Fields, London WC1R 4BN, England

**DeLucas, Lawrence J** — Astronaut
909 19th St S, Birmingham AL 35205, USA

**DeLucca, Gerald D (Jerry)** — Football Player
27 Pulaski St, Peabody MA 01960, USA

**DeLucchi, Michele** — Architect
Via Cenisio 40, 20154 Milan, Italy

**Delugg, Milton** — Accordionist, Band Leader, Composer
2740 Claray Dr, Los Angeles CA 90077, USA

**DeLuise, David** — Actor, Director, Producer
Stone Manners Salners, 6100 Wilshire Blvd, #1500, Los Angeles CA 90035 USA

**DeLuise, Michael** — Actor, Director, Producer
Stone Manners Salners, 6100 Wilshire Blvd, #1500, Los Angeles CA 90035 USA

**DeLuise, Peter** — Actor, Director, Producer
A P A Talent & Literary Agency, 405 S Beverly Dr, #300, Beverly Hills CA 90212 USA

**DelVecchi, Mauro** — Army General, Italy
Senato Della Repubblica, Piazza Madama, 00196 Rome, Italy

**Delvecchio, Alexander P (Alex)** — Ice Hockey Player
Pen Pro, 2602 Stoodleigh Dr, Rochester Hills MI 48309, USA

**Demaestri, Joseph P (Joe)** — Baseball Player
50 Fairway Dr, Novato CA 94949, USA

**DeMaistre, Xavier** — Concert Harpist
Konzertdirektion Schmid, Konigstra 36, 30175 Hannover, Germany

**DeMaiziere, K E Thomas** — Government Official, Germany
Salgasse 2, 01558 Grossenhain, Germany

**DeMaiziere, Lothar** — Prime Minister, East Germany
Buro Berlin Mitte, Chausseestr 128A, 10115 Berlin, Germany

**Demarchelier, Patrick** — Photographer
162 W 21st St, New York NY 10011, USA

**DeMarco, Albert (Ab), Jr** — Ice Hockey Player
211 Regal Road, North Bay ON P1B 8G4, Canada

**DeMarco, Jean** — Sculptor
Cervaro 03044, Prov-Frosinore, Italy

**DeMarco, Robert A (Bob)** — Football Player
13055 Midfield Terrace, Saint Louis MO 63146, USA

**DeMarco, Tony** — Boxer
150 Staniford St, #709, Boston MA 02114, USA

**DeMarcus, Jay** — Singer, Bassist (Rascal Flatts)
Turner & Nichols, 49 Music Square W, #500, Nashville TN 37203, USA

**Demarest, Arthur A** — Archaeologist
Vanderbilt University, Anthropology Dept, Nashville TN 37235, USA

**Demarie, John E** — Football Player
736 Magazine St, Lake Charles LA 70607, USA

**Demars, Bruce** — Navy Admiral
41 Manters Point Road, Plymouth MA 02360, USA

**Demars, William L (Billy)** — Baseball Player
770 Island Way, #305, Clearwater Beach FL 33767, USA

**DeMartini, Warren J (Torch)** — Guitarist (Ratt)
2666 Carmar Dr, Los Angeles CA 90046, USA

**DeMartino, Jules** — Drummer (Ting Tings)
Paradigm Agency, 404 W Franklin St, Monterey CA 93940 USA

**DeMatteo, Drea** — Actress
Gersh Agency, 9465 Wilshire Blvd, #600, Beverly Hills CA 90212 USA

**Dembo, Fennis M** — Basketball Player
430 N Pine St, San Antonio TX 78202, USA

**Demchenko, Albert M** — Luge Athlete
All-Russian Luge Federation, Luzhnetskaja Nab 8, 119992 Moscow, Russia

**DeMedeiros, Maria** — Actress
Alsira Garcia-Maroto Talent Agency, Calle de Los Invencibles 8, Bajo, Madrid 28019, Spain

**DeMenezes, Fradique B M** — President, Sao Tome & Principe
President's Office, Pargo do Povo, Sao Tome, Sao Tome & Principe

**DeMent, Iris** — Singer, Songwriter
Nick Ben-Meir, 652 N Doheny Dr, West Hollywood CA 90069, USA

**DeMent, Jack** — Chemist
Oregon Health Care Center, 11325 NE Weidler St, #44, Portland OR 97220, USA

**Dementieva, Elena V** — Tennis Player
Myasnitskaya Str, #6/7, 10100 Moscow, Russia

**DeMerit, Jay** — Soccer Player
Watford F C, Vicarage Stadium, Vicarage Road, Watford, Hertfordshire WD18 0ER, England

**Demery, Lawrence C (Larry)** — Baseball Player
10407 Pinnacle Ridge Ave, Bakersfield CA 93311, USA

**Demet-Barry, Dede** — Cyclist
2607 Thornbird Place, Boulder CO 80304, USA

**Demeter, Donald L (Don)** — Baseball Player
6240 S Country Club Dr, Oklahoma City OK 73159, USA

**Demetral, Christopher (Chris)** — Actor
J M G Mgmt, 18000 Coastline Dr, #8, Malibu CA 90265, USA

**Demetrios** — Religious Leader
Greek Orthodox Church, 89 E 79th St, #19, New York NY 10075, USA

**Demetrius, Duppy** — Writer
Creative Artists Agency, 2000 Ave of Stars, #100, Los Angeles CA 90067 USA

**Demetz, Peter** — Educator
Rutgers State University, German Dept, 172 College Ave, New Brunswick NJ 08901, USA

**Demeulmeester, Ann** — Fashion Designer
6 Rue Milne Edwards, 75017 Paris, France
**DeMeuron, Pierre** — Pritzker Architectural Laureate
Herzog & DeMeuron Architekten, Rheinschanze 6, 4056 Basel, Switzerland
**Demic, Lawrence C (Larry)** — Basketball Player
680 S Lassen Court, Anaheim CA 92804, USA
**DeMicco, Kirk** — Director, Writer
Gersh Agency, 9465 Wilshire Blvd, #600, Beverly Hills CA 90212 USA
**DeMille, Nelson** — Writer
61 Hilton Ave, #23, Garden City NY 11530, USA
**Demin, Lev S** — Cosmonaut
Cosmonaut Training Center, Star City, 141160 Zvezdny Gorodok, Moscow Oblast, Russia
**Deming, Peter** — Cinematographer
Sandra Marsh Assoc, 9150 Wilshire Blvd, #220, Beverly Hills CA 90212 USA
**DeMita, L Ciriaco** — Prime Minister, Italy
Partito Democrazia Cristiana, Piazza de Gesu 46, 00186 Rome, Italy
**Demme, Jonathan** — Director
Clinica Estetico, 319 Lafayette St, #144, New York NY 10012, USA
**DeMol, Johannes H H (John)** — Producer, Director
Talpa, Zevenend 45-IV, PO Box 154, Laren, Noord Holland 1250 AD, Netherlands
**Demola, Donald J (Don)** — Baseball Player
352 Village Dr, Hauppauge NY 11788, USA
**DeMonaco, James** — Writer, Producer, Director
United Talent Agency, U T A Plaza, 9336 Civic Center Dr, Beverly Hills CA 90210 USA
**Demong, Bill** — Nordic Combined Skier
N Y S E F, Route 86, PO Box 300, Wilmington NY 12997, USA
**Demongeot, Mylene** — Actress
Artmedia, 20 Ave Rapp, 75007 Paris, France
**DeMont, Rick** — Swimmer
84-596 Upena St, Waianae HI 96792, USA
**DeMontebello, Philippe L** — Museum Executive
40 E 94th St, #11G, New York NY 10128, USA
**DeMoraes, Ronaldo (Ron)** — Producer
W M E Entertainment, 9601 Wilshire Blvd, #300, Beverly Hills CA 90210 USA
**DeMornay, Rebecca** — Actress
Binder & Assoc, 1465 Lindacrest Dr, Beverly Hills CA 90210, USA
**DeMoss, Harold R, Jr** — Judge
US Court of Appeals, 515 Rusk Ave, #12015, Houston TX 77002, USA
**Demoustier, Anais** — Actress
I M G Models, 8 Rue Danielle Casanova, 75001 Paris, France
**Demps, Jeffery (Jeff)** — Track Athlete, Football Player
Tampa Bay Buccaneers, 1 W Buccaneer Place, Tampa FL 33607 USA
**Dempsey, Clint** — Soccer Player
Fulham F C, Craven Cottage, Stevenage Road, London SW6 6HH, England
**Dempsey, George P** — Basketball Player
6945 Cedar Ave, Pennsauken NJ 08109, USA
**Dempsey, J Rikard (Rick)** — Baseball Player
3081 Township Ave, Simi Valley CA 93063, USA
**Dempsey, M Clinton (Clint)** — Soccer Player
New England Revolution, 1 Patriot Place, Foxboro MA 02035 USA
**Dempsey, Martin E** — Army General
Chairman, Joint Chiefs of Staff, Pentagon, Washington DC 20318 USA
**Dempsey, Michael** — Bassist (Cure)
Primary Talent International, 10-11 Jockey's Fields, London WC1R 4BN, England
**Dempsey, Patrick** — Actor
Burstein Co, 15304 Sunset Blvd, #208, Pacific Palisades CA 90272, USA
**Dempsey, Thomas (Tom)** — Football Player
541 Julius Ave, New Orleans LA 70121, USA
**Dempsie, Joseph** — Actor
Troika, 74 Clerkenwell Road, #300, London EC1M 5QA, England
**Dempster, Ryan S** — Baseball Player
3537 N Greenview Ave, Chicago IL 60657, USA
**Demsetz, Harold** — Economist
University of California, Economics Dept, Los Angeles CA 90024, USA
**Demsey, Todd** — Golfer
Gaylord Sports Mgmt, 13845 N Northsight Blvd, #200, Scottsdale AZ 85260 USA
**DeMulder, Frank** — Photographer
TeNeues Publishing Group, 7 W 18th St, New York NY 10011, USA
**DeMulder, Kim** — Cartoonist, Illustrator
76 Lafayette Ave, Coxsackie NY 12051, USA
**DeMunn, Jeffrey (Jeff)** — Actor
Davis Spylios Agency, 244 W 54th St, #707, New York NY 10019, USA
**Demuro, Francesco** — Opera Singer
I M G Artists, Hogarth Business Park, Chiswick, London W4 2TH, England
**Demus, Chaka** — Singer (Chaka Demus & Pliers)
Mission Control, City Business Center, Lower Road, London SE16 2XB, England
**Demus, Jorg** — Concert Pianist
Lyra Artists Mgmt, Doblinger Hauptstr 77A/10, 1190 Vienna, Austria
**Demuth, Richard H** — Attorney, Financier
7 Eliot Road, Lexington MA 02421, USA
**Denault, Jim** — Cinematographer
Gersh Agency, 9465 Wilshire Blvd, #600, Beverly Hills CA 90212 USA
**Denberg, Susan** — Model
Playboy Promotions, 9346 Civic Center Dr, #200, Beverly Hills CA 90210 USA
**Dench, Judi** — Actress
Julian Belfrage, 9 Argyll St, London W1F 7TG, England
**Dencik, David** — Actor
A P A Talent & Literary Agency, 405 S Beverly Dr, #300, Beverly Hills CA 90212 USA
**Deneriaz, Antoine** — Alpine Skier
775 Ave de la Republique, 74300 Cluses, France
**Denes, Agnes C** — Artist
595 Broadway, New York NY 10012, USA
**Deneuve, Catherine** — Actress
Artmedia, 20 Ave Rapp, 75007 Paris, France
**Denevan, William M** — Geographer, Ecologist
University of Wisconsin, Geography Dept, Madison, WI 53706, USA

# D

**Deneve, Stephane** — Conductor
I C M Artists, 40 W 57th St, #1800, New York NY 10019 USA

**Deng Yaping** — Table Tennis Player
International Olympic Committee, Chateau de Vidy, 1007 Lausanne, Switzerland

**Deng, Luol** — Basketball Player
3280 Sunset Trail, Northbrook IL 60062, USA

**Dengler, Carlos** — Bassist (Interpol)
Flowerbooking, 1532 N Milwaukee Ave, #201, Chicago IL 60622, USA

**Denham, Alice** — Model
Playboy Promotions, 9346 Civic Center Dr, #200, Beverly Hills CA 90210 USA

**Denhardt, David T** — Biologist
Rutgers University, Nelson Biological Laboratories, Piscataway NJ 08855, USA

**DenHerder, Vern W** — Football Player
2342 Riviera Road, Sioux Center IA 51250, USA

**Denicourt, Marianne** — Actress
Artmedia, 20 Ave Rapp, 75007 Paris, France

**DeNiese, Danielle** — Opera Singer
I M G Artists, Hogarth Business Park, Chiswick, London W4 2TH, England

**DeNiro, Robert** — Actor
Stan Rosenfield Assoc, 2029 Century Park E, #1190, Los Angeles CA 90067, USA

**Denis, Catalina** — Actress
A C T 1, 83 Rue Saint Honore, 75001 Paris, France

**Denisof, Alexis** — Actor
A P A Talent & Literary Agency, 405 S Beverly Dr, #300, Beverly Hills CA 90212 USA

**Denisov, Edison V** — Composer
Studentcheskaia 44/28, #35, 121165 Moscow, Russia

**Denisse, Francois-Jean** — Astronomer
48 Rue Monsieur Le Prince, 75006 Paris, France

**Denisyev, Alexander** — Luge Athlete
All-Russian Luge Federation, Luzhnetskaja Nab 8, 119992 Moscow, Russia

**Denisyuk, Yuri N** — Optical Engineer
Vavilov Optical Institute, 12 Burzhevaya, 199034 Saint Petersburg, Russia

**Denk, Jeremy** — Concert Pianist
Opus 3 Artists, 470 Park Ave S, #900N, New York NY 10016 USA

**Denman, David** — Actor
Hofflund/Polone, 9465 Wilshire Blvd, #420, Beverly Hills CA 90212 USA

**Dennard, Mark W** — Football Player
4990 Afton Oaks Dr, College Station TX 77845, USA

**Dennard, Preston** — Football Player
4545 Greene Ave NW, Albuquerque NM 87114, USA

**Dennard, Robert H** — Inventor (Random Access Memory Cell)
2054 Quaker Ridge Road, Croton-on-Hudson NY 10520, USA

**Dennehy, Brian** — Actor
C E S D, 10635 Santa Monica Blvd, #130, Los Angeles CA 90025 USA

**Dennehy, Elizabeth** — Actress
Kazarian/Measures/Ruskin, 11969 Ventura Blvd, #300, Studio City CA 91604 USA

**Dennen, Brett** — Singer
Mick Mgmt, 35 Washington St, Brooklyn NY 11201, USA

**Dennerlein, Barbara** — Jazz Organist
Tsingtauer Str 66, 81827 Munich, Germany

**Dennett, Daniel C** — Philosopher
20 Ironwood Road, North Andover MA 01845, USA

**Denney, Kyle** — Baseball Player
PO Box 300, Prague OK 74864, USA

**Denney, Ryan C** — Football Player
351 Silver Circle, Alpine UT 84004, USA

**Denning, Blaine** — Basketball Player
1283 NW Bentley Circle, #A, Port Saint Lucie FL 34986, USA

**Dennings, Kat** — Actress
Management 360, 9111 Wilshire Blvd, Beverly Hills CA 90210 USA

**Dennis, Cathy** — Singer
19 Mgmt, Ransomes Dock, 35-37 Parkgate Road, London SW11 4NP, England

**Dennis, Clark** — Golfer
4117 Sarita Dr, Fort Worth TX 76109, USA

**Dennis, Donna F** — Sculptor, Artist
131 Duane St, New York NY 10013, USA

**Dennis, Gabrielle** — Actress
Pantheon Talent Group, 1900 Ave of the Stars, #2840, Los Angeles CA 90064, USA

**Dennis, Guy D** — Football Player
PO Box 2500, Hawthorne FL 32640, USA

**Dennis, James L** — Judge
US Court of Appeals, 600 Camp St, New Orleans LA 70130, USA

**Dennis, Jim** — Harness Racing Driver, Trainer
1810 Little Masters Corner Road, Harrington DE 19952, USA

**Dennis, Mark F** — Football Player
7533 Bittersweet Dr, Gurnee IL 60031, USA

**Dennis, Mike** — Singer (Dovells)
American Promotions, 2011 Ferry Ave, #U19, Camden NJ 08104, USA

**Dennis, Norm** — Ice Hockey Player
1531 Highway 3B, Fruitvale BC V0G 1L0, Canada

**Dennis, Pamela** — Fashion Designer
10 McGuirk Lane, West Orange NJ 7052, USA

**Dennis, Rowly** — Actor
Henderson Represents, 100 Universal City Plaza, #7152, Universal City CA 91608, USA

**Dennis, Wesley** — Singer, Guitarist
Mercury Records, 401 Commerce St, #1100, Nashville TN 37219 USA

**Dennison, George M** — Educator
International Heart Institute Foundation, 500 W Broadway, #350, Missoula MT 59802, USA

**Dennison, W Douglas (Doug)** — Football Player
2309 Daybreak Trail, Plano TX 75093, USA

**Denny, Floyd W, Jr** — Pediatrician
1 Carolina Meadows, #308, Chapel Hill NC 27517, USA

**Denny, John A** — Baseball Player
13750 W Colonial Dr, #350, Winter Garden FL 34787, USA

**Denny, Robyn** — Artist
20/30 Wilds Rents, #4B, London SE1 4QG, England

|  |  |
|---|---|
| **DeNooijer, Teun**<br>H C Bloemendaal, Aelbertsbergweg 3, 2061 Bloemendaal AA, Netherlands | Field Hockey Player |
| **Denorfia, Christopher A (Chris)**<br>3468 Longmeadow, Sarasota FL 34235, USA | Baseball Player |
| **Densham, Gary**<br>28397 Jenny Lane, Menifee CA 92584, USA | Auto Racing |
| **Densmore, John**<br>Doors Music, 8899 Beverly Blvd, #812, Los Angeles CA 90048, USA | Drummer (Doors) |
| **Denson, Alfred F (Al)**<br>10838 Naples Court S, Jacksonville FL 32218, USA | Football Player |
| **Denson, Karl**<br>Madison House, 2060 Broadway, #225, Boulder CO 80302, USA | Musician, Singer |
| **Dent, Burnell J**<br>2904 Essex Ave, La Place LA 70068, USA | Football Player |
| **Dent, Catherine**<br>S D B Partners, 315 S Beverly Dr, #411, Beverly Hills CA 90067 USA | Actress |
| **Dent, Frederick B**<br>221 Montgomery St, Spartanburg SC 29302, USA | Secretary, Commerce |
| **Dent, James L (Jim)**<br>12449 Kelso Road, Thonotosassa FL 33592, USA | Golfer |
| **Dent, Kevin**<br>221 Brannan Ave, Byram MS 39272, USA | Football Player |
| **Dent, Richard L**<br>R L D Resources, 333 N Michigan Ave, #2800, Chicago IL 60601, USA | Football Player, Coach |
| **Dent, Russell E (Bucky)**<br>8895 Indian River Run, Boynton Beach FL 33472, USA | Baseball Player, Manager |
| **Denton, Derek A**<br>816 Irring Road, Toorak VIC 3142, Australia | Physiologist |
| **Denton, James**<br>Paradigm Agency, 360 N Crescent Dr, North Building, Beverly Hills CA 90210 USA | Actor |
| **Denton, Randall D (Randy)**<br>515 Sunnybrook Road, Raleigh NC 27610, USA | Basketball Player |
| **Denton, Robert (Bob)**<br>6669 Embarcadero Dr, #7, Stockton CA 95219, USA | Football Player |
| **Denton, Sandi (Pepa)**<br>Richard Walters, PO Box 2789, Toluca Lake CA 91610 USA | Rap Artist (Salt'N'Pepa) |
| **Denton, Will**<br>Gersh Agency, 9465 Wilshire Blvd, #600, Beverly Hills CA 90212 USA | Actor |
| **Deodato, Eumir**<br>Carlini Group, 445 Park Ave, #900, New York NY 10022, USA | Keyboardist, Composer, Producer |
| **Deol, Sunny**<br>Plot 22 11th Road, J V P D Scheme Juhu, Mumbai MS 400049, India | Actor, Director |
| **DeOliveira, Manoel**<br>Rua H Lopes Mendoca, 4010 Porto, Portugal | Director, Writer |
| **DeOre, Bill**<br>Dallas News, Editorial Dept, Communications Center, Dallas TX 75265, USA | Editorial Cartoonist |
| **DeOssie, Steven L (Steve)**<br>835 Chestnut St, North Andover MA 01845, USA | Football Player |
| **DePaiva, James**<br>PO Box 11152, Greenwich CT 06831, USA | Actor |
| **DePaiva, Kassie**<br>CornerStone Talent Agency, 37 W 20th St, #1108, New York NY 10011, USA | Actress, Singer |
| **DePalma, Brian R**<br>I C M Partners, 10250 Constellation Blvd, #900, Los Angeles CA 90067 USA | Director |
| **DePaolis, Luciano**<br>Olympic Committee, Foro Italico, Largo Lauro de Bosis 15, 00135 Rome, Italy | Bobsled Athlete |
| **DePaolis, Velasio Cardinal**<br>Economic Affairs Prefecture, Palazzo Congregazioni, Largo Colonnato 3, 00193 Rome, Italy | Religious Leader |
| **Depardieu, Elisabeth**<br>Artmedia, 20 Ave Rapp, 75007 Paris, France | Actress, Writer |
| **Depardieu, Gerard X M**<br>Artmedia, 20 Ave Rapp, 75007 Paris, France | Actor |
| **Depardieu, Julie**<br>Cineart, 28 Rue Mogador, 78009 Paris, France | Actress |
| **Depardon, Raymond**<br>18 Bis Rue Henri Barbusse, 75005 Paris, France | Photographer |
| **Depenbusch, Anna**<br>105 Music GmbH, Hopfensack 20, 20457 Hamburg, Germany | Singer |
| **DePencier, Miranda**<br>United Talent Agency, U T A Plaza, 9336 Civic Center Dr, Beverly Hills CA 90210 USA | Producer |
| **DePeyer, Gervase**<br>42 Tower Bridge Wharf, Saint Katherine's Way, London E1 9UR, England | Concert Clarinetist, Conductor |
| **DePortzamparc, Christian**<br>Architecte D P L G, 1 Rue de l'Aude, 75014 Paris, France | Pritzker Architectural Laureate |
| **Depp, John C (Johnny)**<br>United Talent Agency, U T A Plaza, 9336 Civic Center Dr, Beverly Hills CA 90210 USA | Actor, Director |
| **Depre, Joe**<br>59 Oneida St, Rochester NY 14621, USA | Basketball Player |
| **Depres, Cyril**<br>Red Bull GmbH, Am Brunnen 1, 5330 Fuschl am See Austria | Motorcycle Racing Rider |
| **DePriest, Tommy Lee**<br>Schiowitz Artists Management, 14 Bond St, #228, Great Neck NY 11021 11021, USA | Actor |
| **Deptula, David A**<br>Deputy CofS, Intelligence & Survelliance, HqUSAF, Pentagon, Washington DC 20310, USA | Air Force General |
| **Dequenne, Emilie**<br>Cineart, 28 Rue Mogador, 78009 Paris, France | Actress |
| **Der, Lambert**<br>Houston Post, Editorial Dept, 4888 Loop Central Dr, #390, Houston TX 77081, USA | Editorial Cartoonist |
| **DeRakoff, Alex**<br>W M E Entertainment, 9601 Wilshire Blvd, #300, Beverly Hills CA 90210 USA | Director, Writer |
| **DeRavin, Emilie**<br>Gersh Agency, 41 Madison Ave, #3301, New York NY 10010 USA | Actress |
| **Derby, C Dean**<br>1682 Corkrum Road, Walla Walla WA 99362, USA | Football Player |
| **Derbyshire, Andrew G**<br>4 Sunnyfield, Hatfield, Hertsforshire AL9 5DX, England | Architect |

|  |  |
|---|---|
| **Dercho, Natalia**<br>I M G Artists, Hogarth Business Park, Chiswick, London W4 2TH, England | Opera Singer |
| **Derek, Bo**<br>Guttman Assoc, 118 S Beverly Dr, #201, Beverly Hills CA 90212 USA | Actress, Model |
| **DeRist, Joseph**<br>University of California Medical Center, 505 Parnassus, San Francisco CA 94122 USA | Molecular Biologist |
| **Dern, Bruce**<br>Pure Arts, 9925 Jefferson Blvd, Culver City CA 90232, USA | Actor |
| **Dern, Laura**<br>Creative Artists Agency, 2000 Ave of Stars, #100, Los Angeles CA 90067 USA | Actress |
| **Dernesch, Helga**<br>Salztogasse 8/11, 1013 Vienna, Austria | Opera Singer |
| **Dernier, Robert E (Bob)**<br>1242 SW Arbormill Terrace, Lees Summit MO 64082, USA | Baseball Player |
| **Deromedi, Herbert**<br>885 Hiawatha Dr, Mount Pleasant MI 48858, USA | Football Coach |
| **DeRoo, David C (Dave)**<br>Novi Entertainment, PO Box 17077, Beverly Hills CA 90209, USA | Bassist (Adema) |
| **Deroo, Romain**<br>Artmedia, 20 Ave Rapp, 75007 Paris, France | Actor |
| **DeRosa, Mark T**<br>58 Avalon Way, Waretown NJ 08758, USA | Baseball Player |
| **DeRosier, David**<br>27 Chesterfield Road, West Newton MA 02465, USA | Biophysicist |
| **Derosier, Michael**<br>Borman Entertainment, 1250 6th St, #401, Santa Monica CA 90401, USA | Drummer (Heart) |
| **DeRossi, Massimo**<br>Carol Levi Mgmt, Via Giuseppe Pisanelli 2, 00196 Rome, Italy | Actor |
| **DeRossi, Portia**<br>I/D Public Relations, 7060 Hollywood Blvd, #800, Los Angeles CA 90028 USA | Actress, Model |
| **Derow, Peter A**<br>PO Box 534, Bedford NY 10506, USA | Publisher |
| **Deroyer, Jean**<br>I M G Artists, Hogarth Business Park, Chiswick, London W4 2TH, England | Conductor |
| **DeRozan, DeMar D**<br>Toronto Raptors, Air Canada Center, 20 Bay St, Toronto ON M5J 2N8, Canada | Basketball Player |
| **Derr, Kenneth T**<br>Chevron Corp, 6001 Bollinger Canyon Road, San Ramon CA 94583, USA | Businessman |
| **Derricks, Cleavant**<br>Kazarian/Measures/Ruskin, 11969 Ventura Blvd, #300, Studio City CA 91604 USA | Actor |
| **Derrickson, Scott**<br>W M E Entertainment, 9601 Wilshire Blvd, #300, Beverly Hills CA 90210 USA | Director, Writer |
| **D'Errico, Donna**<br>Michael Forman Agency, 409 N Camden Drive, #205, Beverly Hills CA 90210, USA | Model, Actress |
| **Derringer, Rick**<br>Lustig Talent, PO Box 770850, Orlando FL 32877 USA | Singer, Guitarist |
| **Derrington, C James (Jim)**<br>107 Oliver St, West Columbia SC 29169, USA | Baseball Player |
| **Derry, Kathy**<br>Co-Ed Trainers Club, PO Box 785, New York NY 10101, USA | Physical Fitness Instructor |
| **Dersch, Hans**<br>7217 E 55th Place, Tulsa OK 74145, USA | Swimmer |
| **Dershowitz, Alan M**<br>1563 Massachusetts Ave, Cambridge MA 02138, USA | Attorney, Educator |
| **Derulo, Jason**<br>Creative Artists Agency, 2000 Ave of Stars, #100, Los Angeles CA 90067 USA | Singer, Songwriter, Actor |
| **Dervan, Peter B**<br>California Institute of Technology, Chemistry Dept, Pasadena CA 91125, USA | Chemist |
| **Derwin, Mark**<br>Innovative Artists, 1505 10th St, Santa Monica CA 90401 USA | Actor |
| **Dery, Vincent**<br>Warner Bros Records, 3300 Warner Blvd, Burbank CA 91505 USA | Rap Artist, Singer (Nico & Vinz) |
| **Desai, Anita**<br>Deborah Rogers Ltd, 20 Powis Mews, London W11 1JN, England | Writer |
| **Desailly, Marcel**<br>Chelsea F C, Stamford Bridge, Fulham Road, London SW6 1HS, England | Soccer Player |
| **DeSalvo, Anne**<br>Don Buchwald Talent Agency, 6500 Wilshire Blvd, #2200, Los Angeles CA 90048 USA | Actress, Director |
| **DeSalvo, Matthew T (Matt)**<br>10 Village Gate Blvd, Delaware OH 43015, USA | Baseball Player |
| **DeSanctis, Roman W**<br>5 Thoreau Circle, Winchester MA 01890, USA | Cardiologist |
| **DeSando, Anthony**<br>D2 Mgmt, 9255 Sunset Blvd, #600, West Hollywood CA 90069, USA | Actor |
| **Desante, Michael**<br>Talent House, 3000 Olympic Blvd, #2226, Santa Monica CA 90404, USA | Actor, Producer |
| **DeSantis, Jaclyn**<br>Hess Entertainment, 195 S Beverly Dr, #401, Beverly Hills CA 90212, USA | Actress |
| **DeSanto, Greg**<br>Big Apple Circus, 505 8th Ave, #1900, New York NY 10018 USA | Clown |
| **DeSanto, Karen**<br>Big Apple Circus, 505 8th Ave, #1900, New York NY 10018 USA | Clown |
| **Desarthe, Gerard**<br>National Conservatory of Dramatic Art, 2 Bis Rue du Conservatoire, 75009 Paris, France | Actor |
| **Deschamps, Didier C**<br>Monaco Association Sportive, 7 Ave des Castelans, 98000 Monaco | Soccer Player |
| **Deschanel, Caleb**<br>Optimism Entertainment, 303 N La Peer Dr, #205, Beverly Hills CA 90211, USA | Cinematographer |
| **Deschanel, Emily**<br>Management 360, 9111 Wilshire Blvd, Beverly Hills CA 90210 USA | Actress |
| **Deschanel, Zooey**<br>Creative Artists Agency, 2000 Ave of Stars, #100, Los Angeles CA 90067 USA | Actress, Model, Singer |
| **Deser, Stanley**<br>Brandeis University, Physics Dept, Waltham MA 02254, USA | Physicist |
| **Desfor, Max**<br>15115 Interlachen Dr, #1018, Silver Spring MD 20906, USA | Photojournalist |

**Desfosses, Erik** — Actor
Artmedia, 20 Ave Rapp, 75007 Paris, France

**Deshaies, James J (Jim)** — Baseball Player
151 N Taylor Point Dr, Spring TX 77382, USA

**DeShields, Delino L** — Baseball Player
1051 Heathchase Dr, Suwanee GA 30024, USA

**DeShon, Michelle** — Actress
L B Talent Agency, 15303 Ventura Blvd, #900, Sherman Oaks CA 91403, USA

**Deshorties, Alexandra** — Singer
Opus 3 Artists, 470 Park Ave S, #900N, New York NY 10016 USA

**Desiderio, Robert** — Actor
2934 N Beverly Glen Circle, Los Angeles CA 90077, USA

**DeSilva, John R** — Baseball Player
32750 Airport Road, Fort Bragg CA 95437, USA

**DeSilvestro, Simona** — Auto Racing Driver
K V Racing Technology, 4001 Methanol Lane, Indianapolis IN 46268, USA

**Desjardins, Eric** — Ice Hockey Player
9 Woodglen Lane, Voorhees NJ 08043, USA

**Desjardins, Gerry** — Ice Hockey Player
252 Suffolk Place, London ON N6G 3S4, Canada

**Desjardins, Willie** — Ice Hockey Coach
Vancouver Canucks, 800 Griffiths Way, Vancouver BC V6B 6G1, Canada

**DesLauriers, Kit** — Free Skier
Teton Village, Jackson Hole WY 83001, USA

**Deslongchamps, Pierre** — Chemist
RR 1, 11 Church McFarland, North Hatley QC J0B 2C0, Canada

**Desormeaux, Kent** — Thoroughbred Racing Jockey
292 W Carter Ave, Sierra Madre CA 91024, USA

**DeSousa, Mauricio** — Cartoonist (Monica)
Mauricio de Sousa Producoes, Rua do Curtume 745, Sao Paulo SP, Brazil

**DeSousa, Melissa** — Actress
Stone Manners Salners, 6100 Wilshire Blvd, #1500, Los Angeles CA 90035 USA

**Desplat, Alexandre** — Composer
B M I, 8730 W Sunset Blvd, #300, Los Angeles CA 90069 USA

**Des'ree** — Singer
Creative Artists Agency, 2000 Ave of Stars, #100, Los Angeles CA 90067 USA

**Desrosiers, David P** — Bassist (Simple Plan)
Depot Sainte-Dorothee, PO Box 223, Lavel QC H7X 2T4, Canada

**Dess, Darrell C** — Football Player
224 Summer Ave, New Castle PA 16105, USA

**Desselle, Natalie** — Actress
Innovative Artists, 1505 10th St, Santa Monica CA 90401 USA

**Dessens Jusaino, Elmer** — Baseball Player
5427 E Sheena Dr, Scottsdale AZ 85254, USA

**Dessner, Bryce** — Guitarist (National)
Brassland Records, PO Box 76, Prince Street Station, New York NY 10012, USA

**Destrade, Orestes** — Baseball Player
10653 Garda Dr, Trinity FL 34655, USA

**Destri, James (Jimmy)** — Keyboardist (Blondie)
Agency Group Ltd, 142 W 57th St, #600, New York NY 10019 USA

**Desurvive, Emmanuel** — Optical Fiber Engineer
Alcatel Submarine Networks, Villarceaux Centre, 91625 Nozay, France

**DeTar, Dean E** — Vietnam War Air Force Hero
7785 Portwood Road, Azle TX 76020, USA

**DeThe, Guy Blaudin** — Oncologist, Biologist
14 Rue Le Regrattier, 75004 Paris, France

**Detmer, Amanda** — Actress
John Carrabino Mgmt, 5900 Wilshire Blvd, #406, Los Angeles CA 90036 USA

**Detmer, Koy D** — Football Player
2906 Spring Bend St, San Antonio TX 78209, USA

**Detmer, Ty H** — Football Player
18449 Flagler Dr, Austin TX 78738, USA

**Detmers, Maruschka** — Actress
Agence Metropolitan Paris, 23 Blvd des Capucines, 75002 Paris, France

**Detorie, Rick** — Cartoonist (One Big Happy)
Creators Syndicate, 737 3rd St, Hermosa Beach CA 90254 USA

**Detroit, Marcella** — Singer, Songwriter, Guitarist
Dawson Breed Music, Spenser House, London SE24 0NR, England

**Dettlaff, Bill** — Golfer
133 Clearlake Dr, Ponte Vedra Beach FL 32082, USA

**DeTurck, Dennis** — Mathematician
University of Pennsylvania, Arts & Sciences College, Philadelphia PA 19104, USA

**Detwiler, Ross** — Baseball Player
359 Brown Swiss Circle, Duncansville PA 16635, USA

**Deukmejian, C George** — Governor, CA
Sidley & Austin, 555 W 5th St, #3900, Los Angeles CA 90013, USA

**Deutch, Howard** — Director, Producer, Writer
I C M Partners, 10250 Constellation Blvd, #900, Los Angeles CA 90067 USA

**Deutch, John M** — Government Official
51 Clifton St, Belmont MA 02478, USA

**Deutch, Zoey** — Actress
Gilbertson Entertainment, 1334 3rd Street Promenade, #201, Santa Monica CA 90401 USA

**Deutekom, Cristina** — Opera Singer
Lancasterdreef 41, Dronten 8251 TG, Holland

**Deutsch, David (Dave)** — Basketball Player
315 Fairmount Road, Long Valley NJ 07853, USA

**Dev** — Singer, Rap Artist, Songwriter
Paradigm Agency, 360 N Crescent Dr, North Building, Beverly Hills CA 90210 USA

**Dev, Mukul** — Actor
Karan Apts, #500, Yari Road Versova, Mumbai MS 400061, India

**Deva, Prabhu** — Actor, Dancer, Director
68 T T K Road, Alwarpet, Chennai TN 600018, India

**DeValeria, Dennis** — Sportswriter
213 Hillendale Road, Pittsburgh PA 15237, USA

**Devane, William** — Actor
Shelter Entertainment, 9255 Sunset Blvd, #300, Los Angeles CA 90069 USA

# D

**Devarez, Cesar S** — Baseball Player
35 Arden St, #B, New York NY 10040, USA
**DeVarona, Donna** — Swimmer, Sportscaster
3 Avon Lane, Greenwich CT 06830, USA
**DeVasquez, Devin** — Model, Actress
9903 Santa Monica Blvd, #169, Beverly Hills CA 90212, USA
**Devault, Calvin** — Actor
Amsel Eisenstadt Frazier, 5055 Wilshire Blvd, #865, Los Angeles CA 90036 USA
**Devayani** — Actress
51 Indira Gandhi St, Saligramam, Chennai TN 600093, India
**Devendorf, Bryan** — Drummer (National)
Brassland Records, PO Box 76, Prince Street Station, New York NY 10012, USA
**Devendorf, Scott** — Guitarist (National)
Brassland Records, PO Box 76, Prince Street Station, New York NY 10012, USA
**DeVenzio, Dick** — Basketball Player
1116 Home Place, Matthews NC 28105, USA
**Dever, Barbara** — Opera Singer
Wolf Artists Mgmt, 13 E 69th St, #3R, New York NY 10021, USA
**Dever, Kaitlyn** — Actress
United Talent Agency, U T A Plaza, 9336 Civic Center Dr, Beverly Hills CA 90210 USA
**Dever, Seamus** — Actor
A P A Talent & Literary Agency, 405 S Beverly Dr, #300, Beverly Hills CA 90212 USA
**Deveraux, Jude** — Writer
Atria/Simon & Schuster, 1230 Ave of Americas, Concourse 1, New York NY 10020, USA
**Devereaux, Michael (Mike)** — Baseball Player
2236 W Doublegrove St, West Covina CA 91790, USA
**Devers, Gail** — Track Athlete
G B M Mgmt, 4207 Corrales Dr, #100, Florissant MO 63034, USA
**DeVevo, Juan** — Guitarist (Casting Crowns)
Proper Mgmt, PO Box 150867, Nashville TN 37215, USA
**DeVevo, Melodee** — Violinist (Casting Crowns)
Proper Mgmt, PO Box 150867, Nashville TN 37215, USA
**Devgan, Ajay** — Actor, Director, Producer
5/6 Sheetak Apts, Opp Chandand Cinema, Juhu, Mumbai MS 400049, India
**DeVicenzo, Roberto** — Golfer
Noni Lann, 5025 Veloz Ave, Tarzana CA 91356, USA
**DeVilla, Alfredo** — Director
Underground Films & Mgmt, 447 S Highland Ave, Los Angeles CA 90036, USA
**DeVille, Cecil (C C)** — Guitarist (Poison)
Esterman.Com, PO Box 514, Riva MD 21140, USA
**Deville, Michel** — Director
36 Rue Reinhardt, 92100 Boulogne, France
**Devin, Anna** — Opera Singer
I M G Artists, Hogarth Business Park, Chiswick, London W4 2TH, England
**DeVine, Adam** — Actor, Writer
W M E Entertainment, 9601 Wilshire Blvd, #300, Beverly Hills CA 90210 USA
**Devine, Aidan** — Actor
S M S Talent, 8383 Wilshire Blvd, #230, Beverly Hills CA 90211 USA
**Devine, Elizabeth** — Writer, Producer
Creative Artists Agency, 2000 Ave of Stars, #100, Los Angeles CA 90067 USA
**Devine, Joseph N (Joey)** — Baseball Player
2616 Long Pointe, Roswell GA 30076, USA
**Devine, Loretta** — Actress
Essential Talent Mgmt, 3151 Cahuenga Blvd W, #220, Los Angeles CA 90068, USA
**Devine, P Adrian** — Baseball Player
271 Timber Laurel Lane, Lawrenceville GA 30043, USA
**DeVita, Vincent T, Jr** — Oncologist
Yale Comprehensive Cancer Center, 333 Cedar St, New Haven CT 06510, USA
**DeVito, Danny** — Actor, Comedian, Director
1028 Ridgedale Dr, Beverly Hills CA 90210, USA
**DeVito, Joe** — Actor, Comedian
OmniPop Talent Group, 4605 Lankershim Blvd, #201, Toluca Lake CA 91602 USA
**Devitt, John** — Swimmer
46 Beacon Ave, Beacon Hill NSW 2100, Australia
**Devlin, Bruce** — Golfer
3601 Foot Hills Dr, Weatherford TX 76087, USA
**Devlin, Christopher J (Chris)** — Football Player
100 Meadowlark Lane, Boalsburg PA 16827, USA
**Devlin, Dean** — Director, Producer, Actor
Electric Entertainment, 940 N Highland Ave, #A, Los Angeles CA 90038, USA
**Devlin, Joseph (Joe)** — Football Player
3815 Schintzius Road, Eden NY 14057, USA
**Devlin, Peter J** — Sound Mixer
Doug Apatow Agency, 12049 Jefferson Blvd, #200, Culver City CA 90230, USA
**Devlin, Ryan** — Actor
Michelle Grant Mgmt, 1158 26th St, #414, Santa Monica CA 90403, USA
**DeVoe, Ronald (Ronnie)** — Singer (New Edition, Bell Biv DeVoe)
Pyramid Entertainment Group, 377 Rector Place, #21A, New York NY 10280 USA
**Devoll, Hal** — Basketball Player
8928 Fox Ave, Allen Park MI 48101, USA
**DeVoogd, Bob** — Field Hockey Player
Oanje-Zwart M H C, Charles Roelslaan 13, 5644 Eindhoven NX, Netherlands
**Devor, Robinson** — Director, Writer
United Talent Agency, U T A Plaza, 9336 Civic Center Dr, Beverly Hills CA 90210 USA
**Devore, Doug** — Baseball Player
5247 Willow Grove Place S, Dublin OH 43017, USA
**DeVorzon, Barry** — Songwriter
MasterWriter, 70 State St, Santa Barbara CA 93101, USA
**Devos, Emmanuelle** — Actress
Zelig, 57 Rue Reaumur, 75002 Paris, France
**DeVos, Richard M** — Businessman, Philanthropist
6565 Otis Lane, Harbor Springs MI 49740, USA
**DeVries, Greg** — Ice Hockey Player
25 Colonel Winstead Dr, Brentwood TN 37027, USA
**Devries, Jared** — Football Player
15342 Lambert Dr, Clear Lake IA 50428, USA

**DeVries, Jill** — Model
Playboy Promotions, 9346 Civic Center Dr, #200, Beverly Hills CA 90210 USA

**DeVries, Marius** — Composer
Gorfaine/Schwartz, 4111 W Alameda Ave, #509, Burbank CA 91505 USA

**DeVries, William C** — Surgeon
Hardin Memorial Hospital, 913 N Dixie Ave, Elizabethtown KY 42701, USA

**DeWaal, Frans** — Primatologist
Emory University, Primate Behavior Dept, Atlanta GA 30322, USA

**DeWaart, Edo** — Conductor
Milwaukee Symphony, 700 N Water St, #700, Milwaukee, WI 53202, USA

**DeWaele, Ellen** — Producer, Production Manager
Serendipity Films, Huigeveldstraat 37, 9550 Saint-Antelinks, Belgium

**Dewan-Tatum, Jenna** — Actress, Producer
Sanders/Armstrong/Caserta Mgmt, 2120 Colorado Ave, #120, Santa Monica CA 90404 USA

**Dewar, Susan** — Cartoonist (Us & Them)
Universal Press Syndicate, 4520 Main St, #700, Kansas City MO 64111 USA

**DeWarren, Patrick** — Photographer
153 Roebling St, #100, Brooklyn NY 11211, USA

**Dewdney, Christopher** — Writer
Bloomsbury Publishing, 50 Bedford Square, London WC1B 3DP, England

**DeWet, Shaun** — Model
Elite Model Mgmt, 404 Park Ave S, #900, New York NY 10016 USA

**Dewey, Duane E** — Korean War Marine Corps Hero (CMH)
10550 N Forman Road, Irons MI 49644, USA

**Dewey, Mark A** — Baseball Player
28150 Rivermont Dr, Meadowview VA 24361, USA

**DeWijn, Sander** — Field Hockey Player
S V Kampong Hockey, Postbus 85219, 3508 Utrecht AE, Netherlands

**DeWilde, Edy** — Museum Executive
Stedelijk Museum, Oosterdokskade 5, 1011 Amsterdam AD, Netherlands

**DeWillis, Jeffrey A (Jeff)** — Baseball Player
8918 Wind Side Dr, Richmond Hill ON L4C 1T4, Canada

**DeWinne, Frank** — Cosmonaut, Belgium
349th Squadron, Vliegbasis 10W T A C Kleine Brogel, 3990 Peer, Belgium

**DeWit, Peter** — Cartoonist
Galerie Lambiek, Kerkstaat 78, 1017 GP Amsterdam, Netherlands

**DeWit, William T (Willie)** — Boxer
Wolch Hursh DeWit, 1500-633 6th Ave SW, Calgary AB T2P 2Y5, Canada

**DeWitt, Doug** — Boxer
176 Garth Road, #TM, Scarsdale NY 10583, USA

**DeWitt, Joyce** — Actress, Model
PO Box 7309, Santa Monica CA 90406, USA

**DeWitt, Rosemarie** — Actress
I C M Partners, 10250 Constellation Blvd, #900, Los Angeles CA 90067 USA

**Dewitt, Willie** — Boxer
605 N Water St, Burnet TX 78611, USA

**DeWitt-Morette, Cecile** — Physicist
2411 Vista Lane, Austin TX 78703, USA

**Dews, Peter B** — Psychiatrist
99 Norumbega Road, #231, Weston MA 02493, USA

**DeWulf, Noureen** — Actress
Evolution Entertainment, 901 N Highland Ave, Los Angeles CA 90038 USA

**DeWyze, Lee** — Singer, Songwriter
Sony Records, 2100 Colorado Ave, Santa Monica CA 90404 USA

**Dexter, Mary** — Director
Hank Tani, 14542 Delaware Dr, Moorpark CA 93021, USA

**Dexter, N Colin** — Writer
456 Banbury Road, Oxford 0X2 7RG, England

**Dexter, Peter W** — Writer, Columnist
Sacramento Bee, Editorial Dept, 21st & Q Sts, Sacramento CA 95852, USA

**Dey, Charles** — Association Executive
Start on Success, 910 16th Ave NW, Washington DC 20006, USA

**Dey, Susan** — Actress
I C M Partners, 10250 Constellation Blvd, #900, Los Angeles CA 90067 USA

**Dey, Tom** — Director
W M E Entertainment, 9601 Wilshire Blvd, #300, Beverly Hills CA 90210 USA

**DeYoung, Cliff** — Actor
Geddes Agency, 8430 Santa Monica Blvd, #201, West Hollywood CA 90069 USA

**DeYoung, Michelle** — Singer
Opus 3 Artists, 470 Park Ave S, #900N, New York NY 10016 USA

**DeZarn, Tim** — Actor
C E S D, 10635 Santa Monica Blvd, #130, Los Angeles CA 90025 USA

**Dezhurov, Vladimir N** — Cosmonaut
Cosmonaut Training Center, Star City, 141160 Zvezdny Gorodok, Moscow Oblast, Russia

**Dhabhara, Firdaus S** — Neuroscientist
Rockefeller University, Neurology Dept, 1230 York Ave, New York NY 10065, USA

**Dhalia, Heitor** — Director
W M E Entertainment, 9601 Wilshire Blvd, #300, Beverly Hills CA 90210 USA

**Dhaliwal, Daljit** — Commentator
Knight Ayton Mgmt, 114 Saint Martin's Lane, London WC2N 4BE, England

**Dhanapala, Jayantha C P** — Government Official, Sri Lanka
United Nations, Sri Lanka Delegation, United Nations Plaza, New York NY 10007, USA

**Dharker, Ayesha** — Actress
Independent Talent Group, 40 Whitfield St, London W1T 2RH, England

**Dharma Master Cheng Yen** — Religious Leader
Tzu Chi Foundation, 701 Zhongyang Road, Hualien 97004, Taiwan

**Dhawan, Sacha** — Actress
Troika, 74 Clerkenwell Road, #300, London EC1M 5QA, England

**Dhoinine, Ikililou** — President, Comores
President's Office, Palais de Beit Salam, BP 421, Moroni, Grand Comoro, Comoros

**Dhoni, Mahendra Singh** — Cricket Player
Chennai Super Kings, Gummidipundi, Tamil Nadu 132400 India

**Diadkova, Larissa** — Opera Singer
I M G Artists, Hogarth Business Park, Chiswick, London W4 2TH, England

**Diamantopoulos, Chris** — Actor
Untitled Entertainment, 350 S Beverly Dr, #200, Beverly Hills CA 90212 USA

DeVries - Diamantopoulos

**Diamond, Abel J** — Architect
Diamond Schmitt Co, 2 Berkeley St, #600, Toronto ON M5A 2W3, Canada
**Diamond, Jared M** — Biologist
University of California Medical School, Physiology Dept, Los Angeles CA 90024, USA
**Diamond, Marian C** — Neuroanatomist
100 Bay Place, #804, Oakland CA 94610, USA
**Diamond, Michael (Mike D)** — Rap Artist (Beastie Boys)
Nasty Little Man, 110 Greene St, #605, New York NY 10012, USA
**Diamond, Neil L** — Singer, Songwriter
Richard De La Font Agency, 4845 S Sheridan Road, #505, Tulsa OK 74145 USA
**Diamond, Peter A** — Nobel Economics Laureate
Massachusetts Institute of Technology, Economics Dept, Cambridge MA 02139, USA
**Diamond, Reed** — Actor
Paradigm Agency, 360 N Crescent Dr, North Building, Beverly Hills CA 90210 USA
**Diamond, Seymour** — Physician
Diamond Headache Clinic, 467 W Deming Place, #500, Chicago IL 60614, USA
**Diamond, William** — Financier
28 Preakness Court, Owings Mills MD 21117, USA
**Diamont, Anita** — Writer
Charles Scribner's Sons, 866 3rd Ave, New York NY 10022 USA
**Diamont, Don** — Actor, Model
Craig Mgmt, 2240 Miramonte Circle E, #C, Palm Springs CA 92264 USA
**Dias, Ivan Cardinal** — Religious Leader
Evangelization of Peoples Congregation, Piazza di Spagna 48, 00187 Rome, Italy
**DiasDosSantos, Fernando da Piedade** — Prime Minister, Angola
Prime Minister's Office, Avda 4 de Fevereiro, Luanda CP 2723, Angola
**Diaw, Boris** — Basketball Player
10430 N 108th Place, Scottsdale AZ 85259, USA
**Diaz, Alex** — Photojournalist
Associated Press, Editorial Dept, 450 W 33rd St, #1500, New York NY 10001 USA
**Diaz, Cameron** — Actress, Model
Creative Artists Agency, 2000 Ave of Stars, #100, Los Angeles CA 90067 USA
**Diaz, Carlos A** — Baseball Player
45-236 Ka Hanahou Circle, Kaneohe HI 96744, USA
**Diaz, David** — Boxer
1524 N Avers Ave, Chicago IL 60651, USA
**Diaz, Einar A** — Baseball Player
4315 70th Ave E, Ellenton FL 34222, USA
**Diaz, Gloria M A** — Beauty Queen, Actress
Miss Universe Organization, 1370 Ave of Americas, #1600, New York NY 10019 USA
**Diaz, Guillermo** — Actor
Innovative Artists, 1505 10th St, Santa Monica CA 90401 USA
**Diaz, Jorge A** — Football Player
10801 Starkey Road, Seminole FL 33777, USA
**Diaz, Juan** — Boxer
13616 Monarch Road, Houston TX 77047, USA
**Diaz, Julio** — Boxer
40795 Adriatico Ct, Indio CA 92203, USA
**Diaz, Junot** — Writer
Riverhead/Penguin Books, 375 Hudson St, Basement 1, New York NY 10014, USA
**Diaz, Laura** — Golfer
Ladies Pro Golf Assn, 100 International Golf Dr, Daytona Beach FL 32124 USA
**Diaz, Maggie** — Photographer
Gwendolen De Lacy, Dream Cave, PO Box 124, The Patch VIC 3792, Australia
**Diaz, Manuel A (Manny)** — Mayor, Miami
Mayor's Office, 3500 Pan American Dr, Miami FL 33133, USA
**Diaz, Matthew E (Matt)** — Baseball Player
1124 Afton St, Lakeland FL 33803, USA
**Diaz, Melonie** — Actress
Gersh Agency, 9465 Wilshire Blvd, #600, Beverly Hills CA 90212 USA
**Diaz, Michael A (Mike)** — Baseball Player
1113 Everglades Dr, Pacifica CA 94044, USA
**Diaz-Balart, Jose** — Commentator
Telmundo, 2470 W 8th Ave, Hialeah FL 33010, USA
**Diaz-Infante, G David M** — Football Player
24723 E Park Crescent Dr, Aurora CO 80016, USA
**Diaz-Rahi, Yamila** — Model
Next Model Mgmt, 9 Boul de la Madeleine, 75001 Paris, France
**Dibaba, Tirunesh** — Track Athlete
Global Athletics & Marketing, 437 Boylston St, #400, Boston MA 02116, USA
**Dibb, Sam** — Director
Casorotto Ramsay, Waverley House, 7-12 Noel St, London W1F 8GQ, England
**Dibble, Dorne A** — Football Player
18601 Jamestown Circle, Northville MI 48168, USA
**Dibble, Robert K (Rob)** — Baseball Player
30020 Trail Creek Dr, Agoura Hills CA 91301, USA
**DiBeligiojoso, Lodovico B** — Architect
8 Via Perugia, 20121 Milan, Italy
**DiBenedetto, Kaitlyn** — Instrumentalist (Just Kait)
Transfer Media Group, 5200 Lankershim Blvd, #400, North Hollywood CA 91601, USA
**DiBlasio, Raul** — Singer
World Entertainment Assoc, 8815 Conroy Windermere Road, #407, Orlando FL 32835, USA
**DiBona, Craig** — Cinematographer
333 E 66th St, #7-O, New York NY 10065, USA
**DiBonaventura, Lorenzo** — Producer
Rogers & Cowan, 8687 Melrose Ave, #G700, West Hollywood CA 90069 USA
**Dibos, Alicia** — Golfer
1465 E Putnam Ave, #112E, Old Greenwich, T 06870, USA
**Dibowski, Andreas** — Equestrian
Waldwinkel 2, 21272 Egestorf, Germany
**Dibra, Bash** — Dog Trainer
3476 Bailey Ave, Bronx NY 10463, USA
**DiCamillo, Gary T** — Businessman
1001 Saint Georges Road, Baltimore MD 21210, USA
**DiCamillo, Katrice E (Kate)** — Writer
Candlewick Press, 99 Dover St, Somerville MA 02144, USA

**DiCaprio, Leonardo** — Actor
L B I Entertainment, 2000 Avenue of Stars, Century City CA 90067, USA

**DiCenta, Giorgio** — Cross Country Skier
33020 Treppo Carnico (UD), Italy

**Dichter, Misha** — Concert Pianist
Columbia Artists Mgmt Inc, 5 Columbus Circle, 1790 Broadway, #1600, New York NY 10019 USA

**Dick, Andrew R (Andy)** — Actor, Comedian
A P A Talent & Literary Agency, 405 S Beverly Dr, #300, Beverly Hills CA 90212 USA

**Dick, Bryan** — Actor
Markham Froggatt Irwin, Julian House, 4 Windmill St, London W1P 1HF, England

**Dick, Douglas** — Actor, Writer
604 S Gretna Green Way, Los Angeles CA 90049, USA

**Dickau, Daniel D (Dan)** — Basketball Player
190 Marietta St SW, Atlanta GA 30303, USA

**Dickel, Daniel L (Dan)** — Football Player
970 Maplewood Dr, Coralville IA 52241, USA

**Dicken, Paul** — Baseball Player
4421 NW Blitchton Road, Ocala FL 34482, USA

**Dickens, Kim** — Actress
Gersh Agency, 41 Madison Ave, #3301, New York NY 10010 USA

**Dickens, Little Jimmy** — Singer
5010 W Concord Road, Brentwood TN 37027, USA

**Dickenson, Gary** — Bowler
501 Wade Martin Dr, Edmond OK 73034, USA

**Dickenson, Herb** — Ice Hockey Player
240 Jerseyville Road, RR 8 Station Main, Brantford ON N3T 5M1, Canada

**Dickerson, Christopher C (Chris)** — Baseball Player
Milwaukee Brewers, Miller Park, 1 Brewers Way, Milwaukee WI 53214 USA

**Dickerson, Eric D** — Football Player, Sportscaster
516 Dickerson St, Sealy TX 77474, USA

**Dickerson, Ernest R** — Director
Untitled Entertainment, 350 S Beverly Dr, #200, Beverly Hills CA 90212 USA

**Dickerson, Marty** — Golfer
4225 Luzon Way, Sarasota FL 34241, USA

**Dickerson, Sandra** — Actress
Howes & Prior, Berkeley House, Hay Hill, London W1X 7LH, England

**Dickey, Boh A** — Businessman
Safeco Corp, Safeco Plaza, 1001 4th Ave, #800, Seattle WA 98154, USA

**Dickey, C Lynn** — Football Player
9220 Pawnee Lane, Leawood KS 66206, USA

**Dickey, Curtis R** — Football Player
1817 Sheehan Court, Arlington TX 76012, USA

**Dickey, Doug** — Football Coach
11677 Thornapple Dr, Jacksonville FL 32223, USA

**Dickey, Eric Jerome** — Writer
E P Dutton, 375 Hudson St, New York NY 10014 USA

**Dickey, Robert A (R A)** — Baseball Player
1015 Lynnwood Blvd, Nashville TN 37215, USA

**Dickinson, Amy** — Columnist
Tribune Media Services, 435 N Michigan Ave, #1500, Chicago IL 60611 USA

**Dickinson, Angie** — Actress
1715 Carla Ridge, Beverly Hills CA 90210, USA

**Dickinson, Bruce** — Singer (Iron Maiden)
Chipster, 100 Village Square Crossing, Palm Beach Gardens FL 33410 USA

**Dickinson, Gary** — Bowler
501 Wade Martin Road, Edmond OK 73034, USA

**Dickinson, Janice** — Model, Actress, Photographer
Total Talent Mgmt, 11005 Morrison St, #105, North Hollywood CA 91601, USA

**Dickinson, Judy** — Golfer
18277 SE Heritage Dr, Jupiter FL 33469, USA

**Dickinson, Peter** — Writer
Mysterious Press, Warner Books, 1271 Ave of Americas, New York NY 10020 USA

**Dickinson, Richard L (Bo)** — Football Player
PO Box 166, New Augusta MS 39462, USA

**Dickinson, Rob** — Singer, Guitarist (Catherine Wheel)
Paradigm Agency, 360 Park Ave, #1600, New York NY 10022 USA

**Dickinson, Sandra** — Actress
Associated International Mgmt, 7 Hatton Garden, #400, London EC1N 8AD, England

**Dickinson, Steve** — Cartoonist (Tar Pit)
King Features Syndicate, 300 W 57th St, #1500, New York NY 10019 USA

**Dickman, James B (Jay)** — Photographer
3176 S Vine St, Englewood CO 80113, USA

**Dickson, Barbara R** — Actress, Singer
Kennedy Street Enterprises, 31 Stamford St, Altrincham, Cheshire WA14 1ES, Scotland

**Dickson, Billy** — Director, Cinematographer
Global Artists Agency, 6253 Hollywood Blvd, #508, Los Angeles CA 90028 USA

**Dickson, Chris** — Yachtsman
International Mangement Group, 1 Erieview Plaza, 1360 E 9th St, #100, Cleveland OH 44114 USA

**Dickson, Jason R** — Baseball Player
15 Edison St, Sainte Margarets NB E1N 5B4, Canada

**Dickson, Jennifer** — Artist, Photographer
20 Osborne St, Ottawa ON K1S 4Z9, Canada

**Dickson, Neil** — Actor
Clear Talent Group, 10950 Ventura Blvd, Studio City CA 91604, USA

**Dickson, Ngila** — Costume Designer
Weta Workshop, PO Box 15208, Miramar, Wellington, New Zealand

**DiCorcia, Philip-Lorca** — Photographer
55 Hudson St, #8D, New York NY 10013, USA

**Dicus, Charles W (Chuck)** — Football Player
852 N Mansfield Ave, Los Angeles CA 90038, USA

**Dicus, John C** — Financier
Capitol Federal Savings & Loan, 700 S Kansas Ave, #100, Topeka KS 66603, USA

**Diczfalusy, Egon R** — Endocrinologist
Ronninger 21, 144 61 Ronninge, Sweden

**Didier, Clint** — Football Player
8770 N Glade Road, Pasco WA 99301, USA

**D**

# D

**Didier, Robert D (Bob)** — Baseball Player
1819 N Lynch, Mesa AZ 85207, USA
**Didion, Joan** — Writer
Creative Artists Agency, 2000 Ave of Stars, #100, Los Angeles CA 90067 USA
**Dido** — Singer, Songwriter
Paradigm Agency, 360 N Crescent Dr, North Building, Beverly Hills CA 90210 USA
**Diduck, Gerald** — Ice Hockey Player
4555 Elsby Ave, Dallas TX 75209, USA
**Diebel, John C** — Businessman
Meade Instruments Corp, 27 Hubble, #100, Irvine CA 92618, USA
**Diebel, Nelson** — Swimmer
401 Webb Road, Newark DE 19711, USA
**Diegel, Adam** — Opera Singer
I M G Artists, Hogarth Business Park, Chiswick, London W4 2TH, England
**Diehl, David M** — Football Player
116 Liberty Ridge Trail, Totowa NJ 07512, USA
**Diehl, Digby R** — Journalist
788 S Lake Ave, Pasadena CA 91106, USA
**Diehl, John** — Actor
Don Buchwald Talent Agency, 6500 Wilshire Blvd, #2200, Los Angeles CA 90048 USA
**Dieken, Doug H** — Football Player
29876 Lake Road, Bay Village OH 44140, USA
**Diemberger, Kurt** — Mountaineer
Via Amola 23/1, 40050 Calderino (BO), Italy
**Diemecke, Enrique Arturo** — Conductor
Barrett Vantage Artists, 508 8th Ave, #12A00, New York NY 10018 USA
**Diemer, Brian** — Track Athlete
Calvin College, Athletic Dept, Grand Rapids MI 49506, USA
**Diener, Theodor O** — Plant Virologist
PO Box 272, 11711 Battersea Dr, Beltsville MD 20704, USA
**Dieng, Gorgui** — Basketball Player
Utah Jazz, Energy Solutions Arena, 301 W South Temple, Salt Lake City UT 84101 USA
**Dier, Brett** — Actor
Gersh Agency, 9465 Wilshire Blvd, #600, Beverly Hills CA 90212 USA
**Dierdorf, Daniel L (Dan)** — Football Player, Sportscaster
13302 Buckland Hall Road, Saint Louis MO 63131, USA
**Dierker, Lawrence E (Larry)** — Baseball Player, Manager
8318 N Tahoe Dr, Houston TX 77040, USA
**Dierking, Scott E** — Football Player
1862 Wingate Lane, Wheaton IL 60189, USA
**Dierkop, Charles R** — Actor
10 Town Plaza, #428, Durango CO 81301, USA
**Diesel, Vin** — Director, Actor
One Race Productions, 9100 Wilshire Blvd, 535 East Tower, Beverly Hills CA 90212, USA
**Dieterich, Christian J (Chris)** — Football Player
804 Edisto River Road, Myrtle Beach SC 29588, USA
**Diethart, Thomas** — Ski Jumper
Wienerstr 36, 3451 Michelhausen, Austria
**Dietrich, Don** — Ice Hockey Player
310 Finlay Avenue E, Deloraine MB R0M 0M0, Canada
**Dietrich, William A (Bill)** — Journalist
Seattle Times, Editorial Dept, 1000 Denny Way, Seattle WA 98109 USA
**Dietrick, Coby J** — Basketball Player
644 Patterson Ave, San Antonio TX 78209, USA
**Dietz, Michael** — Actor
Michael Bruno Group, 13576 Cheltenham Dr, Sherman Oaks CA 91423, USA
**Difelice, Michael W (Mike)** — Baseball Player
3980 Mimosa Place, Palm Harbor FL 34685, USA
**Diffie, Joe** — Singer, Songwriter
Bobby Roberts, 3050 Business Park Circle, #303, Goodlettsville TN 37221 USA
**Diffie, Whitfield** — Inventor (Public Key Cryptology)
Sun Microsystems, 4150 Network Circle, Santa Clara CA 95054, USA
**DiFiore, Vince** — Trumpeter, Keyboardist (Bush)
Umbrella Group, 1 West St, #3506, New York NY 10004, USA
**DiFranco, Ani** — Singer, Songwriter, Musician
Scot Fisher PO Box 95, Ellicott Station, Buffalo NY 14205, USA
**Digby, Marie** — Singer, Guitarist
Hollywood Records, 1851 Ivar, #500, Los Angeles CA 90028, USA
**DiGenova, Joseph E** — Attorney
DiGenova & Toensing, 1776 K St NW, #700, Washington DC 20006, USA
**Diggins, Skylar K** — Basketball Player, Model
Tulsa Shock, B O K Center, 200 S Denver, Tulsa OK 74103 USA
**Diggle, Steve** — Guitarist, Bassist (Buzzcocks)
Free Trade Agency, Chapel Place, Rivington St, London EC2A 3DQ, England
**Diggs, Na'il R** — Football Player
2006 Connonade Dr, Waxhaw NC 28173, USA
**Diggs, Taye** — Actor, Singer
O'Taye Productions, 12001 Ventura Place, #340, Studio City CA 91604, USA
**DiGiallonardo, Rick** — Keyboardist (Quarterflash)
Pacific Talent Agency, PO Box 19145, Portland OR 97280, USA
**DiGiovanni, Janine** — Journalist, Writer
David Godwin Assoc, 55 Monmouth St, London WC2H 9DG, England
**DiGregorio, Ernest (Ernie)** — Basketball Player
60 Chestnut Ave, Narragansett RI 02882, USA
**Dijkstra, Rineke** — Photographer
Marian Goodman Gallery, 24 W 57th St, New York NY 10019, USA
**Dilba** — Singer, Musician, Songwriter
United Stage Production, PO Box 11029, 100 61 Stockholm, Sweden
**Dildarian, Steve** — Producer, Writer, Actor
W M E Entertainment, 9601 Wilshire Blvd, #300, Beverly Hills CA 90210 USA
**Dileita, Dileita Mohamed** — Prime Minister, Djibouti
Prime Minister's Office, BP 2086, Djibouti City, Djibouti
**Dilfer, Trent F** — Football Player, Sportscaster
15288 Quito Road, Saratoga CA 95070, USA
**Dilger, Kennth R (Ken)** — Football Player
10403 Windemere, Carmel IN 46032, USA

**Dill, Craig H** — Basketball Player
10200 Thomas Woods Road, Saginaw MI 48609, USA

**Dill, Guy** — Artist, Sculptor
13215 Innes Place, Venice CA 90291, USA

**Dill, Laddie John** — Artist
1625 Electric Ave, Venice CA 90291, USA

**Dillane, Stephen** — Actor
W M E Entertainment, 9601 Wilshire Blvd, #300, Beverly Hills CA 90210 USA

**Dillard, Alex** — Businessman
Dillard's Inc, 1600 Cantrell Road, Little Rock AR 72201, USA

**Dillard, Annie** — Writer
Russell Volkering, 50 W 29th St, New York NY 10001, USA

**Dillard, D Donald (Don)** — Baseball Player
160 Orchard Park Dr, Greenwood SC 29649, USA

**Dillard, Stephen B (Steve)** — Baseball Player
154 Drive 841, Saltillo MS 38866, USA

**Dillard, Victoria** — Actress
Alliance Talent, 2734 E Oakland Park Blvd, #101, Fort Lauderdale FL 33306 USA

**Dillard, W Harrison** — Track Athlete
3449 Glencairn Road, Shaker Heights OH 44122, USA

**Dillard, William T, Jr** — Businessman
Dillard's Inc, 1600 Cantrell Road, Little Rock AR 72201, USA

**Dillehay, Thomas (Tom)** — Anthropologist
University of Kentucky, Anthropology Dept, Lexington KY 40506, USA

**Diller, Barry** — Businessman
I A C/InterActive Corp, 152 W 57th St, #4200, New York NY 10019, USA

**Diller, Elizabeth** — Architect, Designer
Diller Scofidio & Renfro, 601 W 26th St, #1815, New York NY 10001, USA

**Dillman, Bradford** — Actor
770 Hot Springs Road, Santa Barbara CA 93108, USA

**Dillon, Bobby D** — Football Player
1289 Morgan Dr, Temple TX 76502, USA

**Dillon, Corey** — Football Player
31 Marlboro Road, Woburn MA 01801, USA

**Dillon, Joseph W (Joe)** — Baseball Player
2360 Water Way, Rockwall TX 75087, USA

**Dillon, Kevin** — Actor
I C M Partners, 10250 Constellation Blvd, #900, Los Angeles CA 90067 USA

**Dillon, Matt** — Actor, Director
Untitled Entertainment, 350 S Beverly Dr, #200, Beverly Hills CA 90212 USA

**Dillon, Melinda** — Actress
Innovative Artists, 1505 10th St, Santa Monica CA 90401 USA

**Dillon, Shawn** — Model
Playboy Promotions, 9346 Civic Center Dr, #200, Beverly Hills CA 90210 USA

**Dillon, Wayne** — Ice Hockey Player
Hockey Development, 301-1185 Eglinton E, North York ON M3C 3C6, Canada

**Dilly, Erin** — Actress, Singer
Paradigm Agency, 360 N Crescent Dr, North Building, Beverly Hills CA 90210 USA

**Dilone, Miguel A** — Baseball Player
Calle El Sol, #190, Santiago, Dominican Republic

**DiLoreto, Dante** — Producer
Creative Artists Agency, 2000 Ave of Stars, #100, Los Angeles CA 90067 USA

**Dils, Stephen W (Steve)** — Football Player
10285 Midway Ave, Alpharetta GA 30022, USA

**DiMaggio, John** — Actor
Gersh Agency, 9465 Wilshire Blvd, #600, Beverly Hills CA 90212 USA

**Dimaio, Robert (Rob)** — Ice Hockey Player
Saint Louis Blues, Scottrade Center, 1401 Clark Ave, Saint Louis MO 63103 USA

**DiMarco, Chris** — Golfer
3545 Rice Lake Loop, Longwood FL 32779, USA

**Dimas, Trent** — Gymnast
Gold Cup Gymnastics School, 6009 Carmel Ave NE, Albuquerque NM 87113, USA

**Dimbleby, David** — Journalist, Commentator
14 King St, Richmond, Surrey TW9 1NF, England

**DiMeco, Allie** — Singer (Naked Brothers Band)
Untitled Entertainment, 350 S Beverly Dr, #200, Beverly Hills CA 90212 USA

**DiMeola, Al** — Jazz Guitarist
Georg Leitner Productions, Huetteldorfer Str 259, 1140 Vienna, Austria

**Dimitrakos, Niko** — Ice Hockey Player
71 Pennsylvania Ave, Somerville MA 02145, USA

**Dimmel, Michael W (Mike)** — Baseball Player
526 Country Lane, Coppell TX 75019, USA

**Dimmock, Jessica** — Photojournalist
Foley Gallery, 547 W 27th St, #500, New York NY 10011, USA

**Dimon, James (Jamie)** — Businessman
J P Morgan Chase, 270 Park Ave, #1200, New York NY 10017, USA

**Dimry, Charles L, III** — Football Player
PO Box 461266, Escondido CA 92046, USA

**DiNardo, Daniel N Cardinal** — Religious Leader
Archdiocese of Galvelston-Houston, 1700 San Jacinto St, Houston TX 77002, USA

**Dinardo, Lenny** — Baseball Player
10000 SW 52nd Ave, #164, Gainesville FL 32608, USA

**Dindal, Mark** — Animator, Director
I C M Partners, 10250 Constellation Blvd, #900, Los Angeles CA 90067 USA

**Dine, James (Jim)** — Artist, Sculptor, Photographer
Pace Wildenstein Gallery, 32 E 57th St, #400, New York NY 10022, USA

**Dineen, Gord** — Ice Hockey Player
51 Fitzgerald Road, Queensbury NY 12804, USA

**Dineen, Kevin** — Ice Hockey Player, Coach
149 Birdsall Road, Queensbury NY 12804, USA

**Dineen, William P (Bill)** — Ice Hockey Player, Executive
18 Fairwood Dr, Queensbury NY 12804, USA

**Dinello, Paul** — Director, Actor, Writer
United Talent Agency, U T A Plaza, 9336 Civic Center Dr, Beverly Hills CA 90210 USA

**Dinerstein, James** — Sculptor
Salander-O'Reilly Gallery, 22 E 71st St, New York NY 10021, USA

**Dingle, Adrian K** — Football Player
3228 W Canyon Ave, San Diego CA 92123, USA

**Dingman, Christographer R (Chris)** — Ice Hockey Player
9220 Pine Island Court, Tampa FL 33647, USA

**Dingman, Craig** — Baseball Player
3573 W Del Sienno St, Wichita KS 67203, USA

**Dinicol, Joe** — Actor
I C M Partners, 10250 Constellation Blvd, #900, Los Angeles CA 90067 USA

**Dinkel, Thomas (Tom)** — Football Player
877 Squire Lake Court, Villa Hills KY 41017, USA

**Dinkeloo, John** — Architect
Roche & Dinkeloo, 20 Davis St, Hamden CT 06517, USA

**Dinkins, Byron** — Basketball Player
10326 Tallent Lane, Huntersville NC 28078, USA

**Dinkins, Darnell J** — Football Player
9006 Pembroke Court, Pittsburgh PA 15237, USA

**Dinklage, Peter** — Actor
Arcieri Assoc, 305 Madison Ave, #2315, New York NY 10165 USA

**Dinnel, Harry** — Basketball Player
1427 El Nido Dr, Fallbrook CA 92028, USA

**Dinner, Michael** — Director
Creative Artists Agency, 2000 Ave of Stars, #100, Los Angeles CA 90067 USA

**Dinnerstein, Simone** — Concert Pianist
I M G Artists, Hogarth Business Park, Chiswick, London W4 2TH, England

**Dinnigan, Collette** — Fashion Designer
22-24 Hutchinson St, Surry Hills, Sydney NSW 2010, Australia

**Diogu, Ikechukwa S (Ike)** — Basketball Player
2052 W Lagoon Road, Pleasanton CA 94566, USA

**DioGuardi, Kara** — Songwriter, Producer, Entertainer
Arthouse Entertainment, PO Box 3900, Los Angeles CA 90078, USA

**Dion** — Singer
Lustig Talent, PO Box 770850, Orlando FL 32877 USA

**Dion, Celine** — Singer
Feeling Productions, 2540 Blvd Daniel-Johnson, #755, Lavel QC H7T 2S3, Canada

**Dion, Michel** — Ice Hockey Player
33 Mulrain Way, Bluffton SC 29910, USA

**Dionisi, Stefano** — Actor
Media Art Mgmt, BaRbara de Braganza 11, #4 Derecha, 28004 Madrid, Spain

**Dionne, Marcel E** — Ice Hockey Player
4424 Montrose Road, Niagara Falls ON L2H 1K2, Canada

**Diop, Bineta** — Human Rights Activist
Femmes Africa Solidarite, 8 Rue du Vieux-Billard, Box 5037, 1211 Geneva 11, Switzerland

**Diop, DeSagana N** — Basketball Player
4300 Haddonfield Road, #309, Pennsauken NJ 8109, USA

**DiOrio, Nicholas (Nick)** — Soccer Player
273 Clark St, Lemoyne PA 17043, USA

**Dipino, Frank M** — Baseball Player
5479 Pebble Beach Dr, Camillus NY 13031, USA

**Dipoto, Gerald P (Jerry)** — Baseball Player
15130 E Camelview Dr, Fountain Hills AZ 85268, USA

**DiPrete, Edward D** — Governor, RI
555 Wilbur Ave, Cranston RI 02921, USA

**Dirda, Michael** — Journalist
Washington Post, Editorial Dept, 1150 15th St NW, Washington DC 20071 USA

**Dirie, Waris** — Model, Human Rights Activist, Actress
Media Pros Handels, Ungargasse 24/6, 1030 Vienna, Austria

**Dirk, Robert** — Ice Hockey Player
4441 Lee Ave, Groves TX 77619, USA

**Dirnt, Mike** — Bassist (Green Day)
P M C, 5900 Wilshire Blvd, #1720, Los Angeles CA 90036, USA

**Disarcina, Gary T** — Baseball Player
141 Martingale Lane, Plymouth MA 2360, USA

**Dischinger, Terry G** — Basketball Player
1739 Oak Ave, Northbrook IL 60062, USA

**Dishman, Cris E** — Football Player
5019 Mariposa Circle, Fresno TX 77545, USA

**Dishman, Gleneig E (Glenn)** — Baseball Player
5400 Fairway Dr, San Jose CA 95127, USA

**Diskin, Ben** — Actor
C E S D, 10635 Santa Monica Blvd, #130, Los Angeles CA 90025 USA

**Disl, Ursula (Uschi)** — Biathlete, Cross Country Skier
Powerplay Mgmt, Seepromenade 53, 14467 Gross Glienicke, Germany

**Disney, Anthea** — Editor
News America Corp, 1211 Ave of Americas, #700, New York NY 10036, USA

**Disney, William** — Speed Skater
1610 Kirk Dr, Lake Havasu City AZ 86404, USA

**DiSpirito, Rocco** — Chef, Restauranteur
Linda Lisco Mgmt, 360 E Randolph St, #3203, Chicago IL 60601, USA

**DiStefano, Andrea** — Actor
W M E Entertainment, 9601 Wilshire Blvd, #300, Beverly Hills CA 90210 USA

**DiStefano, Philip P** — Educator
University of Colorado, Chancellor's Office, 914 Broadway St, Boulder CO 80309, USA

**Disterheft, Brandi** — Bassist, Composer
Agency Group Ltd, 1880 Century Park E, #711, Los Angeles CA 90067 USA

**Distler, Natalie** — Actress
A P A Talent & Literary Agency, 405 S Beverly Dr, #300, Beverly Hills CA 90212 USA

**DiSuvero, Mark** — Sculptor
PO Box 2218, Astoria NY 11102, USA

**Ditka, Michael K (Mike)** — Football Player, Coach, Sportscaster
161 E Chicago Ave, #39F, Chicago IL 60611, USA

**Ditmar, Arthur J (Art)** — Baseball Player
6687 Wisteria Dr, Myrtle Beach SC 29588, USA

**Dittl, Ursula** — Sculptor
216 Munsel Creek Road, Florence OR 97439, USA

**Dittmer, Andreas** — Canoeing Athlete
Fischerbank 5, 17033 Neubrandenburg, Germany

**Dittmer, Edward C**
702 Old Mescalero Road, Tularosa NM 88352, USA — Space Scientist

**Dittmer, John D (Jack)**
200 S Main St, Elkader IA 52043, USA — Baseball Player

**Ditz, Nancy**
524 Moore Road, Woodside CA 94062, USA — Track Athlete

**Divac, Vlade**
811 Haverford Ave, Pacific Palisades CA 90272, USA — Basketball Player

**Divakaruni, Chitra Banerjee**
Doubleday Press, 1745 Broadway, New York NY 10019 USA — Writer

**Divoff, Andrew**
Marshak/Zachary/Mills, 8840 Wilshire Blvd, #100, Beverly Hills CA 90211 USA — Actor

**Dix, Drew D**
HC 68, Box 70, Mimbres NM 88049, USA — Vietnam War Army Hero (CMH)

**Dixit, Avinash K**
36 Gordon Way, Princeton NJ 08540, USA — Economist

**Dixit, Madhuri**
Vijaydeep, #300, Iris Park, Juhu, Mumbai MS 400049, India — Actress

**Dixon, Alesha**
Independent Talent Group, 40 Whitfield St, London W1T 2RH, England — Singer (Mis-Teeq)

**Dixon, Becky**
ABC-TV, Sports Dept, 77 W 66th St, New York NY 10023 USA — Sportscaster

**Dixon, Blake**
Virgin Records, 338 N Foothill Road, Beverly Hills CA 90210 USA — Drummer (Saving Abel)

**Dixon, Calvert R (Cal)**
179 Las Palmas, Merritt Island FL 32953, USA — Football Player

**Dixon, Craig**
10630 Wellworth Ave, Los Angeles CA 90024, USA — Track Athlete

**Dixon, D Jeremy**
44 Gloucester Ave, #6C, London NW1 8JD, England — Architect

**Dixon, David T**
4795 W 131 1/2 St, Savage MN 55378, USA — Football Player

**Dixon, Donna**
Applied Action Research, 859 N Hollywood Way, #497, Burbank CA 91505, USA — Actress

**Dixon, Hanford**
2034 Acadia Trace, Westlake OH 44145, USA — Football Player

**Dixon, Jack E**
Howard Hughes Medical Institute, 4000 Jones Bridge Road, Chevy Chase MD 20815, USA — Biochemist

**Dixon, Jamie**
University of Pittsburgh, Athletic Dept, Pittsburgh PA 15260, USA — Basketball Coach

**Dixon, Kenneth J (Ken)**
4317 Highview Ave, Baltimore MD 21229, USA — Baseball Player

**Dixon, Larry**
Willow Oak Court, Avon IN 46123, USA — Drag Racing Driver

**Dixon, Leslie**
Creative Artists Agency, 2000 Ave of Stars, #100, Los Angeles CA 90067 USA — Writer, Producer, Director

**Dixon, Mark K**
4016 Ivy Lane, Kitty Hawk NC 27949, USA — Football Player

**Dixon, Michael**
Markham Froggatt Irwin, Julian House, 4 Windmill St, London W1P 1HF, England — Actor

**Dixon, Randolph C (Randy)**
9910 Summerlakes Dr, Carmel IN 46032, USA — Football Player

**Dixon, Rodney P (Rod)**
22 Entrican Ave, Remuera, Auckland 1050, New Zealand — Track Athlete

**Dixon, Ronnie C**
1440 W Kemper Road, #510, Cincinnati OH 45240, USA — Football Player

**Dixon, Scott R**
7161 Zionville Road, Indianapolis IN 45250, USA — Auto Racing Driver

**Dixon, Thomas F**
1761 Cuba Island Lane, Hayes VA 23072, USA — Aerospace Engineer

**Dixon, Zachary**
19365 Hottinger Circle, Germantown MD 20874, USA — Football Player

**Dizon, Jesse**
PO Box 572105, Tarzana CA 91357, USA — Actor

**DJ Babu**
W M E Entertainment, 9601 Wilshire Blvd, #300, Beverly Hills CA 90210 USA — Rap Artist (Dilated Peoples)

**DJ Champion**
Agency Group Ltd, 142 W 57th St, #600, New York NY 10019 USA — DJ Musician

**DJ Clue**
Roc-A-Fella Records, 825 8th Ave, #2900, New York NY 10019, USA — DJ Musician

**DJ Diesel**
International Talent Booking, Ariel House, 74A Charlotte St, #100 London W1T 4QJ, England — DJ Musician (X-Press 2)

**DJ Enuff**
J L Entertainment, 18653 Ventura Blvd, #340, Los Angeles CA 91356 USA — DJ Musician

**DJ Green Lantern**
Central Entertainment Group, 166 5th Ave, #400, New York NY 10010, USA — DJ Musician

**DJ Jazzy Jeff**
Coast to Coast Entertainment, 8671 Wilshire Blvd, Beverly Hills, CA 90211, USA — Rap Artist

**DJ Kool**
2 Bala Plaza, #300, Bala Cynwyd PA 19004, USA — DJ Musician, Rap Artist

**DJ Kool Herc**
Kool Herc Productions, PO Box 20472, Huntington Station NY 11746, USA — Rap Artist

**DJ Magic Mike**
Entertainment Artists, 2409 21st Ave S, #100, Nashville TN 10019 USA — DJ Musician

**DJ Muggs**
Regime Mgmt, 150 W Alameda, #230, Burbank CA 91502, USA — Rap Artist (Cypress Hill)

**DJ Pam**
Windish Agency, 1658 N Milwaukee Ave, #211, Chicago IL 60647, USA — DJ Musician (Coup)

**DJ Quik**
A P A Talent & Literary Agency, 405 S Beverly Dr, #300, Beverly Hills CA 90212 USA — Rap Artist, Record Producer

**DJ Rocky**
International Talent Booking, Ariel House, 74A Charlotte St, #100 London W1T 4QJ, England — DJ Musician (X-Press 2)

**DJ Shadow**
Universal/Island Records, 1755 Broadway, #600, New York NY 10019, USA — Rap Artist

**DJ Spooky**
Music & Art Mgmt, 9 W Walnut St, #2D, Asheville NC 28801, USA — Electronica Musician

**DJ Total K-Oss** — Rap Artist (Above the Law)
Green Light Talent Agency, PO Box 3172, Beverly Hills CA 90212 USA

**DJ Virman** — Singer (Far East Movement)
Stampede Mgmt, 12530 Beatrice St, Los Angeles CA 90066, USA

**Djalili, Omid** — Actor
Independent Talent Group, 40 Whitfield St, London W1T 2RH, England

**Djawadi, Ramin** — Composer
Gorfaine/Schwartz, 4111 W Alameda Ave, #509, Burbank CA 91505 USA

**Djebar, Assia** — Writer
13 University Place, #621, New York, New York NY 1003, USA

**Djerassi, Carl** — Inventor (Oral Contraceptive)
2325 Bear Gulch Road, Redwood City CA 94062, USA

**Djerassi, Isaac** — Physician
2034 Delancey Place, Philadelphia PA 19103, USA

**Djokovic, Novak** — Tennis Player
Novak Tennis Academy, 63A Tadeusa Koscucka, 11000 Belgrade, Serbia

**Djou, Charles K** — Representative, HI
Majority Group LLP, 1701 Pennsylvania Ave NW, #300, Washington DC 20006, USA

**Dlamini, A Themba** — Prime Minister, Swaziland
Prime Minister's Office, PO Box 395, Mbabane, Swaziland

**D'Lyn, Shae** — Actress
Talent House,3000 Olympic Blvd, #2226, Santa Monica CA 90404, USA

**Dmitriev, Artur** — Figure Skater
Skating Federation, Luchneksaia Nab 8, 119871 Moscow, Russia

**DMX** — Rap Artist (Ruff Ryders), Actor
Media Artists Group, 8222 Melrose Ave, #203, Los Angeles CA 90048 USA

**Do Amaral, Diogo F** — Government Official, Portugal
Ave Fontes Pereira de Melo 35, #13A, 1050 Lisbon, Portugal

**Do Carma Silveira, Maria** — Prime Minister, Sao Tome & Principe
Prime Minister's Office, CP 38, Sao Tome, Sao Tome & Principe

**Do Muoi** — Secretary General, Vietnam
Communist Party, 1 Hoang Van Thu, Hanoi, Vietnam

**Do Nascimento, Alexandre Cardinal** — Religious Leader
Archdiocese of Luanda, Largo do Palacio 9, CP 87, 1230C Luanda, Angola

**Doak, Gary W** — Ice Hockey Player
47 Highland Ave, Lynnfield MA 1940, USA

**Doane, Melanie** — Singer, Songwriter
Live Tour Artists, 1451 White Oak Blvd, Oakville ON L6H 4R9, Canada

**Dobbek, Daniel J (Dan)** — Baseball Player
4042 SE Yamhill St, Portland OR 97214, USA

**Dobbin, Brian** — Ice Hockey Player
5075 Shiloh Line, Petrolia ON N0N 1R0, Canada

**Dobbs, Greg S** — Baseball Player
2255 Richey Dr, La Canada Flintridge CA 91011, USA

**Dobbs, Louis C (Lou)** — Commentator
Fox-TV, News Dept, 205 E 67th St, New York NY 10065 USA

**Dobbs, Mattiwilda** — Opera Singer
1101 S Arlington Ridge Road, #301, Arlington VA 22202, USA

**Dobek, Michelle** — Golfer
292 Chicopee St, Chicopee MA 01013, USA

**Dobey, James K** — Financier
26611 Carmel Center Place, Carmel CA 93923, USA

**Dobie, Alan** — Actor
Pontus Molash, Kent CT4 8HW, England

**Dobkins, Carl, Jr** — Singer
5618 Harbourside Dr, Mason OH 45040, USA

**Dobler, Conrad F** — Football Player
6227 W 126th Terrace, Leawood KS 66209, USA

**Dobo, Kata** — Actress
Paradigm Agency, 360 N Crescent Dr, North Building, Beverly Hills CA 90210 USA

**Dobrev, Nina** — Actress
Noble Caplan Abrams, 1260 Yonge St, #200, Toronto ON M4T 1W6, Canada

**Dobrin, Tory** — Choreographer, Dance Executive
Les Ballets Trockadero de Monte Carlo, Box 46 Cathedral Station, New York City, NY 10025, USA

**Dobroshi, Arta** — Actress
U B B A, 6 Rue de Braque, 75003 Paris, France

**Dobslow, Bill** — Singer (Rivieras)
945 Handlebar Road, Mishawaka IN 46544, USA

**Dobson, Anita** — Actress
I T G, 1 Stedham Place, London W1CA 1HU, England

**Dobson, Charles T (Chuck)** — Baseball Player
4208 Locust St, Kansas City MO 64110, USA

**Dobson, Dominic** — Auto Racing Executive
PacWest Racing Group, PO Box 1717, Bellevue WA 98009, USA

**Dobson, FeFe** — Singer, Songwriter
Chris Smith Mgmt, 21 Camden St, #500, Toronto ON M5V 1V2, Canada

**Dobson, Helen** — Golfer
7638 Eagle Creek Dr, Sarasota FL 34243, USA

**Dobson, James C** — Religious Leader
Focus on the Family, 8605 Explorer Dr, Colorado Springs CO 80920, USA

**Dobson, Kevin** — Actor
Rothman/Andres Entertainment, 4400 Coldwater Canyon Ave, #125, Studio City CA 91604, USA

**Dobson, Peter** — Actor, Writer, Producer
Sovereign Talent Group, 8421 Wilshire Blvd, #200, Beverly Hills CA 90211, USA

**Dobtcheff, Vernon** — Actor
Actors International, Via Fosso Del Poggio, 141 00189 Rome, Italy

**Dobud, Niksa** — Water Polo Player
Iva Dulcica 35, 20000 Dubrovnik, Croatia

**Dockery, John P** — Football Player
360 Furman St, #1208, Brooklyn NY 11201, USA

**Dockery, Michelle** — Actress
Hamilton Hodell, 20 Golden Square, London W1F 9JL, England

**Dockett, Darnell** — Football Player
2197 E Teakwood Place, Chandler AZ 85249, USA

**Dockser, Amy** — Journalist
Wall Street Journal, Editorial Dept, 1 World Financial Center, New York NY 10281, USA

**Dockstader, Frederick J** — Museum Executive
165 W 66th St, New York NY 10023, USA
**Doctorow, Edgar Lawrence (E L)** — Writer
333 E 57th St, #118, New York NY 10022, USA
**Doda, Carol** — Exotic Dancer, Actress
PO Box 387, Fremont CA 94537, USA
**Dodd, Christina** — Writer
Pocket Books, 1230 Ave of Americas, New York NY 10020 USA
**Dodd, Deryl** — Singer, Songwriter
Ken-Ran Entertainment, 418 S Barton St, Grapevine TX 76051, USA
**Dodd, Kenneth A** — Actor, Comedian
Michael O'Mara Books, 9 Lion Yard, Tremadoc Road, London SW4 7NQ, England
**Dodd, Lois** — Artist
30 E 2nd St, New York NY 10003, USA
**Dodd, Michael T (Mike)** — Volleyball Player
1017 Manhattan Ave, Manhattan Beach CA 90266, USA
**Dodd, Patty Orozco** — Volleyball Player
1017 Manhattan Ave, Manhattan Beach CA 90266, USA
**Dodds, Megan** — Actress
Independent Talent Group, 40 Whitfield St, London W1T 2RH, England
**Dodds, Trevor** — Golfer
13103 Beaver Dam Road, Saint Louis MO 63131, USA
**Dodge, Brooks** — Skier
PO Box C, Jackson NH 03846, USA
**Dodge, Charles M** — Composer
Brooklyn College, Center for Computer Music, Brooklyn NY 11210, USA
**Dodge, Dedrick A** — Football Player
1109 Bowlin Dr, Locust Grove GA 30248, USA
**Dodge, Geoffrey A** — Publisher
Business Week, Publisher's Office, 1221 Ave of Americas, New York NY 10020, USA
**Dodge, Marcia Milgrom** — Director, Choreographer
Abrams Artists, 275 7th Ave, #2600, New York NY 10001, USA
**Dodik, Milorad** — Prime Minister, Serb Republic
Prime Minister's Office, Nemanjina 11, 11000 Belgrade, Serbia
**Dodrill, Dale F** — Football Player
2579 S Independence St, Lakewood CO 80227, USA
**Dods, Walter A, Jr** — Financier
Banc West Corp, PO Box 3200, Honolulu HI 96847, USA
**Dodson, Patrick N (Pat)** — Baseball Player
4104 Holly Hill Road, Mebane NC 27302, USA
**Doe, John** — Actor
TalentWorks, 3500 W Olive Ave, #1400, Burbank CA 91505 USA
**Doering, Christopher P (Chris)** — Football Player
3723 SW 20th St, Gainesville FL 32608, USA
**Doering-Powell, Mark** — Cinematographer
Paradigm Agency, 360 N Crescent Dr, North Building, Beverly Hills CA 90210 USA
**Doerr, Robert P (Bobby)** — Baseball Player
94449 Territorial Highway, Junction City OR 97448, USA
**Doherty, John H** — Baseball Player
202 Alpine Place, Tuckahoe NY 10707, USA
**Doherty, Matt** — Basketball Player, Coach
Southern Methodist University, Athletic Dept, Dallas TX 75275, USA
**Doherty, Pete** — Singer (Libertines, Babyshambles)
Primary Talent International, 10-11 Jockey's Fields, London WC1R 4BN, England
**Doherty, Peter C** — Nobel Medicine Laureate
262 Danny Thomas Place, Memphis TN 38105, USA
**Doherty, Shannen** — Actress, Model
Rebel Entertainment Partners, 5700 Wilshire Blvd, #456, Los Angeles CA 90036, USA
**Dohle, Markus** — Businessman, Publisher
Random House, 1745 Broadway, #1800, New York NY 10019 USA
**Dohmann, Scott** — Baseball Player
3222 W Paxton Ave, Tampa FL 33611, USA
**Dohring, Jason** — Actor
Innovative Artists, 1505 10th St, Santa Monica CA 90401 USA
**Dohrmann, Angela** — Actress
Innovative Artists, 235 Park Ave S, #1000, New York NY 10003 USA
**Dohrmann, George** — Journalist
Saint Paul Pioneer Press, Editorial Dept, 345 Cedar St, Saint Paul MN 55101, USA
**Doi, Takao** — Astronaut, Japan
Japanese Aerospace Exploration Agency, 2-1-1 Sengen, Tsukuba, Ibaraki 305 8505, Japan
**Doig, Ivan** — Writer
University of Washington, English Dept, Seattle WA 98195, USA
**Doig, Jason** — Ice Hockey Player
2153 Broderick Ave, Duarte CA 91010, USA
**Doig, Lexa** — Actress
TalentWorks, 3500 W Olive Ave, #1400, Burbank CA 91505 USA
**Doig, Stephen G (Steve)** — Football Player
PO Box 206, North Reading MA 01864, USA
**Doillon, Lou** — Actress, Model
Gersh Agency, 41 Madison Ave, #3301, New York NY 10010 USA
**Dokey, Merritt (Butch)** — Harness Racing Owner
14109 B Dr, Plymouth MI 48170, USA
**Dokic, Jelena** — Tennis Player
Octagon Worldwide, 800 Connecticut Ave, #200, Norwalk CT 06854 USA
**Dokish, Wanita** — Baseball Player
2480 S Grande Blvd, Greensburg PA 15601, USA
**Dokiwari, Duncan** — Boxer
Thell Torrence Enterprises, 5449 S Eastern Ave, #3, Las Vegas NV 89119, USA
**Dokovic, Novak (Nole)** — Tennis Player
Studio Magnet, Milan Marijanac, Sime Solaje 55A, 21410 Futog, Serbia
**Doky, Niels Lan** — Jazz Pianist, Composer
P D H Dansk Musikformidling, Dag Hammerskjolds Alle 42G, 2100 Copenhagen, Denmark
**Dolan, Charles F** — Businessman
Cablevision Systems Corp, 1111 Stewart Ave, Bethpage NY 11714, USA
**Dolan, James** — Businessman
Cablevision Systems Corp, 1111 Stewart Ave, Bethpage NY 11714, USA

**Dolan, Julie** — Actress
Laura Lichen Mgmt, PO Box 33051, Granada Hills CA 91394, USA

**Dolan, Louise A** — Physicist
University of North Carolina, Physics Dept, Chapel Hill NC 27599, USA

**Dolan, Mary Anne** — Editor
M A D Inc, 1033 Gayley Ave, #205, Los Angeles CA 90024, USA

**Dolan, Michael P** — Government Official
Internal Revenue Service, 1111 Constitution Ave NW, Washington DC 20224, USA

**Dolan, Timothy M Cardinal** — Religious Leader
Archdiocese of New York, 1011 First St, New York NY 10022, USA

**Dolan, Tom** — Swimmer
610 Poplar Dr, Falls Church VA 22046, USA

**Dolan, Xavier** — Actor
W M E Entertainment, 9601 Wilshire Blvd, #300, Beverly Hills CA 90210 USA

**Dolbin, John T (Jack)** — Football Player
1775 Howard Ave, Pottsville PA 17901, USA

**Dolby, Thomas** — Singer, Songwriter
International Talent Group, 729 7th Ave, #1600, New York NY 10019 USA

**Dolce, Domenico** — Fashion Designer
Dolce & Gabbana, Via Santa Cecilia 7, 20122 Milan, Italy

**Dold, R Bruce** — Journalist
501 N Park Road, #HSE, La Grange Park IL 60526, USA

**Dole, Elizabeth H** — Secretary, Transportation & Labor
Wings of Hope, 18370 Wings of Hope Blvd, Saint Louis MO 63005, USA

**Dole, Kathryn** — Landscape Architect
512 Brinkerhoff Ave, Santa Barbara CA 93101, USA

**Dole, Robert J** — Senator, KS
Verner Liipfert Berhard, 1200 19th St NW, Washington DC 20036, USA

**Doleac, Michael S** — Basketball Player
1155 Old Rail Lane, Park City UT 84098, USA

**Doleman, Christopher J (Chris)** — Football Player
1025 Leadenhall St, Alpharetta GA 30022, USA

**Dolenz, Ami** — Actress
K C Talent, 2408 W 8th Ave, Vancouver BC V6K 2B1, Canada

**Dolenz, Micky** — Actor, Singer, Drummer (Monkees)
Amsel Eisenstadt Frazier, 5055 Wilshire Blvd, #865, Los Angeles CA 90036 USA

**Dolgen, Jonathan L** — Businessman
Viacom Inc, 1515 Broadway, New York NY 10036, USA

**D'Oliveira, Damon** — Actor, Film Producer
LeFeaver Talent Agency, 2 College St, #202, Toronto ON M5G 1K5, Canada

**Doll, W Richard S** — Epidemiologist
12 Rawlinson Road, Oxford OX2 6UE, England

**Dollar, Jawole Willa Jo** — Dancer, Dance Executive
Urban Bush Women, 138 S Oxford St, #4B, Brooklyn, NY 11217, USA

**Dollar, Linda** — Volleyball Coach
Southwest Missouri State University, Athletic Dept, Springfield MO 65804, USA

**Dolley, Jason S** — Actor
Gersh Agency, 9465 Wilshire Blvd, #600, Beverly Hills CA 90212 USA

**Dolman, Bob** — Director, Writer, Actor
United Talent Agency, U T A Plaza, 9336 Civic Center Dr, Beverly Hills CA 90210 USA

**Dolmayan, John** — Drummer (System of a Down)
Velvet Hammer Music, 9014 Melrose Ave, West Hollywood CA 90069, USA

**Dombasle, Arielle** — Actress
Agence Intertalent, 5 Rue Clement Marot, 75008 Paris, France

**Dombroski, Paul M** — Football Player
19122 Beckett Dr, Odessa FL 33556, USA

**Dombrowski, James M (Jim)** — Football Player
220 Evangeline Dr, Mandeville LA 70471, USA

**Domenichelli, Hnat A** — Ice Hockey Player
H C Lugano, Casella Postale 4226, 6904 Lugano, Switzerland

**Dominczyk, Dagmara** — Actress
Paradigm Agency, 360 N Crescent Dr, North Building, Beverly Hills CA 90210 USA

**Dominczyk, Marika** — Actress
I C M Partners, 10250 Constellation Blvd, #900, Los Angeles CA 90067 USA

**Domingo, Colman** — Actor
Wolf Talent Group, 165 West 46, #1104, New York NY 10036, USA

**Domingo, Placido** — Opera Singer
2728 Thomson Ave, #712, Long Island City NY 11101, USA

**Dominguez, Adolfo** — Fashion Designer
Polingono Industrial Calle 4, 32901 San Ciprian de Vinas, Ourense, Spain

**Dominguez, Mario** — Auto Racing Driver
Herdez Competition, 57 Gasoline Alley, #A, Indianapolis IN 46222, USA

**Dominik, Andrew** — Director
Creative Artists Agency, 2000 Ave of Stars, #100, Los Angeles CA 90067 USA

**Domino, Antoine (Fats)** — Singer, Pianist
9 Wedgwood Court, Harvey LA 70058, USA

**Dominy, Charles E (Chuck)** — Army General
300 Fox Mill Road, Oakton VA 22124, USA

**Domracheva, Darya** — Biathlete
Biathlon Federation, Raubitchi Sport Complex, Ul Karl Marx 1016, 223068 Minsk, Belarus

**Domres, Martin F (Marty)** — Football Player
Deutsche Bank, 1 South St, #2400, Baltimore MD 21202, USA

**Donahoe, John** — Businessman
eBay, 2125 Hamilton Ave, San Jose CA 95125, USA

**Donahue, Ann M** — Producer, Writer
W M E Entertainment, 9601 Wilshire Blvd, #300, Beverly Hills CA 90210 USA

**Donahue, Claire** — Swimmer
408 Olympia Dr, Maryville TN 37804, USA

**Donahue, Kenneth** — Museum Executive
245 S Westgate Ave, Los Angeles CA 90049, USA

**Donahue, Phil** — Entertainer
244 Madison Ave, #707, New York NY 10016, USA

**Donahue, Terry** — Football Coach, Sportscaster
707 N Bayfront, Newport Beach CA 92662, USA

**Donahue, Thomas R** — Labor Leader
2425 L St NW, #326, Washington DC 20037, USA

**Dolan - Donahue**

**Donaire, Nonito**
Golden Boy Promotions, 626 Wilshire Blvd, #350, Los Angeles CA 90017 USA — Boxer

**Donald, Aaron C**
Saint Louis Rams, 901 N Broadway, Saint Louis MO 63101 USA — Football Player

**Donald, Jason T**
Cleveland Indians, Jacobs Field, 2401 Ontario St, Cleveland OH 44115 USA — Baseball Player

**Donald, Luke**
8 Bristol Road, Northfield IL 60093, USA — Golfer

**Donald, Michael W (Mike)**
2400 NW 65th Way, Hollywood FL 33024, USA — Golfer

**Donaldson, James L, III**
2843 34th Ave W, Seattle WA 98199, USA — Basketball Player

**Donaldson, Jeffery M (Jeff)**
PO Box 270634, Fort Collins CO 80527, USA — Football Player

**Donaldson, Lily**
I M G Models, 304 Park Ave S, #PH N, New York NY 10010 USA — Model

**Donaldson, Mark G S**
Victoria Cross Assn, Old Admiralty Building, London SW1A 2BL, England — Afghanistan War R A F Hero (VC)

**Donaldson, Roger**
Cameron Creswell, 61 Marlborough St, #700, Surry Hills NSW 2010, Australia — Director

**Donaldson, Samuel A (Sam)**
1125 Crest Lane, McLean VA 22101, USA — Commentator

**Donaldson, Simon K**
Imperial College, 180 Queen's Gate, London SW7 2BZ, England — Mathematician

**Donan, Holland R (Hollie)**
213 Southwinds, Tinton Falls NJ 7753, USA — Football Player

**Donat, Peter**
Gersh Agency, 9465 Wilshire Blvd, #600, Beverly Hills CA 90212 USA — Actor

**Donatelli, Clark**
1101 Curtis Corner Road, Wakefield RI 02879, USA — Ice Hockey Player

**Donath, Helen**
Hannagret Bueker Agentur, Fuhsestr 2, 30419 Hannover, Germany — Opera Singer

**Donato, Marc**
C E S D, 10635 Santa Monica Blvd, #130, Los Angeles CA 90025 USA — Actor

**Donato, Ted**
34 Whitcomb Road, Scituate MA 02066, USA — Ice Hockey Player

**Done, Kenneth S (Ken)**
17 Thurlow St, Redfern NSW 2016, Australia — Graphic Artist

**Donegan, Dan**
Agency Group Ltd, 142 W 57th St, #600, New York NY 10019 USA — Guitarist (Disturbed)

**Donella, Chad E**
TalentWorks, 3500 W Olive Ave, #1400, Burbank CA 91505 USA — Actor

**Donelly, Tanya**
Helter Skelter, 347-353 Chiswick High Road, London W4 4HS, England — Singer, Songwriter

**Donen, Stanley**
30 W 63rd St, #25, New York NY 10023, USA — Director

**Doniger, Wendy**
1319 E 55th St, Chicago IL 60615, USA — Theologian, Historian

**Donlan, Yolande**
11 Mellina Place, Belgravia, London NW8 9SA, England — Actress

**Donleavy, James Patrick (J P)**
Levington Park, Mullingar, County Westmeath, Ireland — Writer

**Donlon, Christine**
Nu Talent, 117 N Robertson Blvd, Los Angeles CA 90048, USA — Actress

**Donlon, Roger H C**
2101 Wilson Ave, Leavenworth KS 66048, USA — Vietnam War Army Hero (CMH)

**Donnalley, W Frederick (Rick)**
485 Gramercy Dr NE, Marietta GA 30068, USA — Football Player

**Donnell, Colin**
Gersh Agency, 9465 Wilshire Blvd, #600, Beverly Hills CA 90212 USA — Actor

**Donnellan, Declan**
Cheek by Jowl Theatre Co, Aveline St, London SW11 5DQ, England — Director

**Donnelly, Brendan K**
2815 E Arrowhead Trail, Gilbert AZ 85297, USA — Baseball Player

**Donnelly, Declan**
Baker Winokur Ryder Public Relations, 9100 Wilshire Blvd, #500W, Beverly Hills CA 90212 USA — Actor

**Donnelly, Gord**
110 Ave Claude, Dorval QC H9S 3A7, Canada — Ice Hockey Player

**Donnelly, John J**
Commander, Submarine Command Atlantic, 7958 Blandy Road, Norfolk VA 23511 USA — Navy Admiral

**Donnelly, Rick**
1796 Danforth Dr, Marietta GA 30062, USA — Football Player

**Donnelly, Russell J**
2175 Olive St, Eugene OR 97405, USA — Physicist

**Donnelly, Tanya**
High Road Touring, 751 Bridgeway, #200, Sausalito CA 94965 USA — Singer, Guitarist

**Donnels, Chris B**
5 Stone Pine, Aliso Viejo CA 92656, USA — Baseball Player

**Donner, Jorn J**
Pohjoisranta 12, 00170 Helsinki 17, Finland — Director

**Donner, Richard D**
Donners' Co, 9465 Wilshire Blvd, #420, Beverly Hills CA 90212, USA — Director

**D'Onofrio, Vincent**
United Talent Agency, U T A Plaza, 9336 Civic Center Dr, Beverly Hills CA 90210 USA — Actor

**Donoghue, Denis**
Gaybrook, North Ave, Mount Merrion, County Dublin, Ireland — Writer

**Donoghue, Mary Agnes**
Gersh Agency, 9465 Wilshire Blvd, #600, Beverly Hills CA 90212 USA — Writer

**Donoghue, Paul**
Sony Music, 9 Derry St, London W8 5HY, England — Singer, Bassist (Glasvegas)

**Donohoe, Amanda**
Artist Rights Group, 4A Exmoor St, London W10 6BD, England — Actress

**Donohoe, Michael P (Mike)**
1110 E Acacia Circle, Litchfield Park AZ 85340, USA — Football Player

**Donohoe, Peter H**
82 Hampton Lane, Solihull, West Midlands B91 2RS, England — Concert Pianist

V.I.P. Address Book

# D

**Donohue, James T (Jim)**
16 Huntleigh Downs, Saint Louis MO 63131, USA — Baseball Player

**Donohue, Leon**
1904 Bechelli Lane, Redding CA 96002, USA — Football Player

**Donohue, Peter M**
Villanova University, President's Office, 800 Lancaster Ave, Villanova PA 19085, USA — Educator

**Donohue, Thomas J (Tom)**
249 Liberty Ave, Westbury NY 11590, USA — Baseball Player

**Donohue, Timothy**
Nextel Communications, 2001 Edmund Halley Dr, Reston VA 20191, USA — Businessman

**Donose, Ruxandra**
Columbia Artists Mgmt Inc, 5 Columbus Circle, 1790 Broadway, #1600, New York NY 10019 USA — Opera Singer

**Donovan**
PO Box 1119, London SW9 9JW, England — Singer, Songwriter, Actor

**Donovan, Anne**
123 Ledgewood Road, #310, Groton CT 06340, USA — Basketball Player, Coach

**Donovan, Brian**
Newsday, Editorial Dept, 235 Pinelawn Road, Melville NY 11747, USA — Journalist

**Donovan, Daisy**
Independent Talent Group, 40 Whitfield St, London W1T 2RH, England — Actress

**Donovan, Elisa**
DiSante Frank Co, 10061 Riverside Dr, #377, Toluca Lake, CA 91602 91602, USA — Actress, Producer

**Donovan, Francis R (Frank)**
9216 Dellwood Dr, Vienna VA 22180, USA — Navy Admiral

**Donovan, H Harry**
8303 Bayonet Point Court, #C, Gainesville FL 32608, USA — Basketball Player

**Donovan, Jason S**
United Agents, 12-26 Lexington St, London W1F 0LE, England — Singer, Actor

**Donovan, Jeffrey**
Paradigm Agency, 360 Park Ave S, #1600, New York NY 10010 USA — Actor

**Donovan, Landon**
Los Angeles Galaxy, Home Depot Center, 18400 Avalon Blvd, Carson CA 90746 USA — Soccer Player

**Donovan, Martin**
Parseghian/Planco, 388 2nd Ave, #506, New York, NY 10010 USA — Actor

**Donovan, Patrick E (Pat)**
113 S Prairiesmoke Circle, Whitefish MT 59937, USA — Football Player

**Donovan, Raymond J**
1600 Paterson Park Road, Secaucus NJ 07094, USA — Secretary, Labor

**Donovan, Shaun L S**
Housing & Urban Development Department, 451 7th SW, Washington DC 20410 USA — Secretary, Housing & Urban Development

**Donovan, Tate**
Gersh Agency, 9465 Wilshire Blvd, #600, Beverly Hills CA 90212 USA — Actor

**Donovan, William J (Billy)**
8515 SW 31st Ave, Gainesville FL 32608, USA — Basketball Player, Coach

**Donowho, Ryan**
Schiff Co, 9220 Sunset Blvd, #106, West Hollywood CA 90069 USA — Actor, Producer

**Donzelli, Valerie**
U B B A, 6 Rue de Braque, 75003 Paris, France — Director

**Donziger, Stephen R**
Donziger & Assoc, 245 W 104th St, #7D New York NY 10025, USA — Attorney

**Doo Ri Chung**
Doo Ri Fashions, 831 Madison Ave, New York NY 10021, USA — Fashion Designer

**Doody, Alison**
Commercial Agency, 16 Harcourt Terrace, London SW1W 9JR, England — Actress

**Doolan, Wendy**
3353 Turnberry Dr, Lakeland FL 33803, USA — Golfer

**Dooley, David M**
University of Rhode Island, President's Office, 6 Rhodney Ram Way, Kingston RI 02881, USA — Educator

**Dooley, James M (Jim)**
Gorfaine/Schwartz, 4111 W Alameda Ave, #509, Burbank CA 91505 USA — Composer

**Dooley, Paul**
Innovative Artists, 1505 10th St, Santa Monica CA 90401 USA — Actor

**Dooley, Taylor M**
Evolution Entertainment, 901 N Highland Ave, Los Angeles CA 90038 USA — Actress

**Dooley, Thomas**
242 Montana Dr, Rancho Santa Margarita CA 92688, USA — Soccer Player

**Dooley, Vincent J (Vince)**
University of Georgia, Athletic Dept, PO Box 1472, Athens GA 30603, USA — Football Player, Coach, Administrator

**Dooling, Keyon L**
2016 NW 3rd Court, Fort Lauderdale FL 33311, USA — Basketball Player

**Doolittle, Eliza**
Insanity Artists, 5 Little Portland St, London W1W 7JD, England — Singer, Songwriter

**Doolittle, Melinda**
1524 Braden Circle, Franklin TN 37067, USA — Singer

**Doorman, Dana**
David Binkley, 201 W Big Beaver Road, #500, Troy MI 48084, USA — Golfer

**Doornink, Daniel E (Dan)**
401 S 12th Ave, Yakima WA 98902, USA — Football Player

**Dopson, John R**
3337 Old Gambler Road, Finksburg MD 21048, USA — Baseball Player

**Dor, Karin**
Nordliche Munchner Str 43, 82031 Grunwald, Germany — Actress

**Doran, William P (Bill)**
5720 Grand Legacy Dr, Maineville OH 45039, USA — Baseball Player

**Doran-Webb, James**
Matthew Upham Antiques, 584 King's Road, London SW6 2DX, England — Artist

**Dore, Andre**
73 Betsys Lane, Kingston ON K7M 7B6, Canada — Ice Hockey Player

**Dore, Jon**
Gersh Agency, 9465 Wilshire Blvd, #600, Beverly Hills CA 90212 USA — Actor, Comedian

**Dore, Ronald Philip**
157 Surrenden Road, Brighton, East Sussex BN1 6ZA, England — Sociologist

**Dorensky, Sergey L**
Bryusov Per 8/10, #75, 103009 Moscow, Russia — Concert Pianist

**Dorey, Jim**
105 Aaron Place, Amherstview ON K7N 2A1, Canada — Ice Hockey Player

**Dorff, Stephen**
I C M Partners, 10250 Constellation Blvd, #900, Los Angeles CA 90067 USA — Actor
**Dorfman, Ariel**
Duke University, International Studies Center, 2122 Campus Dr, Durham NC 27708, USA — Writer
**Dorfman, David**
Abrams Artists, 9200 W Sunset Blvd, #1125, West Hollywood CA 90069 USA — Actor
**Dorfmeister, Michaela**
Quellenstr 12, 2763 Neusiedl, Austria — Alpine Skier
**Dorgan, Byron L**
Arent Fox LLP, 1050 Connecticut Ave NW, Washington DC 20036, USA — Senator, ND
**Dorian, Antonia**
3940 Laurel Canyon Blvd, PO Box 342, Studio City CA 91604, USA — Actress
**Dorin, Marie**
Le Ruisseay, 38190 Laval, France — Biathlete
**Dorin-Ballard, Carolyn**
Del Ballard, Ebonite International, PO Box 746, Hopkinsville KY 42241, USA — Bowler
**Dorion, Dan**
3910 28th St, Long Island City NY 11101, USA — Ice Hockey Player
**Dority, Douglas H**
United Food/Commercial Workers Union, 1775 K St NW, Washington DC 20006, USA — Labor Leader
**Dorman, Dave**
Rolling Thunder, 405 Windham Trail, Carpentersville IL 60110, USA — Illustrator
**Dormann, Dana**
4887 Arlene Place, Pleasanton CA 94566, USA — Golfer
**Dormer, Natalie**
United Agents, 12-26 Lexington St, London W1F 0LE, England — Actress
**Dorn, Michael**
Innovative Artists, 1505 10th St, Santa Monica CA 90401 USA — Actor
**Dornan, Jamie**
United Agents, 12-26 Lexington St, London W1F 0LE, England — Actor, Model
**Dorney, Keith R**
2450 Blucher Valley Road, Sebastopol CA 95472, USA — Football Player
**Dornhelm, Robert**
Paradigm Agency, 360 N Crescent Dr, North Building, Beverly Hills CA 90210 USA — Actor
**Dornhoefer, Gary**
267 Chestnut Neck Road, Port Republic NJ 08241, USA — Ice Hockey Player
**Doronina, Tatyana V**
Gorky Arts Theater, 22 Tverskoi Blvd, 119146 Moscow, Russia — Actress
**Dorough, Howie**
World Concerts, Hamburger Str 273a, 38114 Braunschweig, Germany — Singer (Backstreet Boys)
**Dorris, Andrew M (Andy)**
12391 Ike White Road, Conroe TX 77303, USA — Football Player
**Dorroh, Jefferson D**
10032 136th Ave NE, Kirkland WA 98033, USA — WW II Marine Corps Air Force Hero
**Dorrough, Holley Ann**
D G I Mgmt, 609 Greenwich St, #600, New York NY 10014, USA — Model
**D'Orsay, Brooke**
M B S T Entertainment, 345 N Maple Dr, #200, Beverly Hills CA 90210, USA — Actress
**Dorsaz, Damien**
Artmedia, 20 Ave Rapp, 75007 Paris, France — Actor
**Dorsen, Norman**
146 Central Park W, New York NY 10023, USA — Attorney
**Dorsett, Anthony D (Tony)**
Tony Dorsett Foods, 321 High St, Burlington NJ 08016, USA — Football Player
**Dorsett, Anthony, Jr**
3817 Bowser Ave, #C, Dallas TX 75219, USA — Football Player
**Dorsey, Eric H**
5 London Court, Teaneck NJ 07666, USA — Football Player
**Dorsey, Glenn J**
4616 Triangle Ave, #4202, Austin TX 78751, USA — Football Player
**Dorsey, Jack**
Twitter Inc, 795 Folsom St, #600, San Francisco CA 94107, USA — Businessman
**Dorsey, Jacky**
1231 S Teal Estates Circle, Fresno TX 77545, USA — Basketball Player
**Dorsey, James E (Jim)**
335 Elm St, Seekonk MA 02771, USA — Baseball Player
**Dorsey, John M**
3100 W 68th St, Mission Hills KS 66208, USA — Football Player
**Dorsey, Kenneth S (Ken)**
7108 Presidio Glen, Lakewood Ranch FL 34202, USA — Football Player
**Dorsey, Kerris Lilla**
W M E Entertainment, 9601 Wilshire Blvd, #300, Beverly Hills CA 90210 USA — Actress
**Dorsey, Richard E (Joey)**
Houston Rockets, 1730 Jefferson St, Houston TX 77003 USA — Basketball Player
**Dorsey, Ryan**
Defining Artists, 4370 Tujunga Ave, #120, Studio City CA 91604 91604, USA — Actor
**Dorta, Melvin**
1351 Cambridge Court, Palmyra PA 17078, USA — Baseball Player
**Doshi, Balkrishna V**
14 Shree Sadma Society, Navrangpura, Ahmedabad 380009, India — Architect
**Dosoretz, Daniel E**
1120 Lee Blvd, Lehigh Acres FL 33936, USA — Physician, Businessman
**Doss, Terri Lynn**
PO Box 18185, Irvine CA 92623, USA — Actress, Model
**DosSantos Ramirez, Giovani**
Federacion de Futbol, Colima 373 Colonia Roma, Delegacion Cuauhtemoc, Mexico City DF 06700, Mexico — Soccer Player
**DosSantos, Alexandre J M Cardinal**
Archdiocese of Maputo, Avenida Eduardo Mondlane 1448, CP 258 Maputo, Mozambique — Religious Leader
**DosSantos, Jose Eduardo**
President's Office, Palacio do Povo, Luanda, Angola — President, Angola
**Dost, Andrew P**
Fueled by Ramen, 1290 Ave of Americas, #2800, New York NY 10104, USA — Musician (Fun), Songwriter
**Dostal, Josef**
A S O Dukla Prague, Cisarska Iouka 1, 15500 Prague, Czech Republic — Canoeing Athlete
**Dotel, Octavio E**
382 Oakland Road, Lawrenceville GA 30044, USA — Baseball Player

D

**Dorff - Dotel**

# D

**Dotrice, Roy** — Actor
Lord, 6 Meadow Lane, Leasingham, Sleaford, Lincolnshire NG34 8LL, England
**Dotson, Earl C** — Football Player
1112 Azalea Dr, Longview TX 75601, USA
**Dotson, Richard E (Rich)** — Baseball Player
7 Colonel Watson Dr, New Richmond OH 45157, USA
**Dotson, Santana N** — Football Player
PO Box 79134, Houston TX 77279, USA
**Dotter, Bobby** — Auto, Truck Racing Driver
3630 N Pacific Ave, Chicago IL 60634, USA
**Dotter, Gary R** — Baseball Player
7413 Ravenswood Road, Granbury TX 76049, USA
**Dottley, Jason** — Actor
Baker Winokur Ryder Public Relations, 9100 Wilshire Blvd, #500W, Beverly Hills CA 90212 USA
**Doty, Mark** — Writer
Rutgers State University, English Dept, New Brunswick NJ 08903, USA
**Douaihy, Saliba** — Artist
Vining Road, Windham NY 12496, USA
**Doucet, David** — Singer, Guitarist (BeauSoleil)
Rosebud Agency, PO Box 170429, San Francisco CA 94117 USA
**Doucet, Michael** — Singer, Fiddler (BeauSoleil)
Rosebud Agency, PO Box 170429, San Francisco CA 94117 USA
**Doucett, Linda** — Actress, Model
Michael Slessinger, 8730 W Sunset Blvd, #220W, West Hollywood CA 90069 USA
**Doucette, Jeff** — Actor
C E S D, 10635 Santa Monica Blvd, #130, Los Angeles CA 90025 USA
**Doufexis, Stella** — Opera Singer
Kunstler Sekretariat am Gasteig, Rosenheimer Str 52, 81669 Munich, Germany
**Doug, Doug E** — Actor, Comedian
Brillstein Entertainment, 375 Greenwich St, New York NY 10013, USA
**Dougherty, Dennis A** — Chemist
1817 Bushnell Ave, South Pasadena CA 91030, USA
**Dougherty, Ed** — Golfer
448 SW Fairway Vista, Port Saint Lucie FL 34986, USA
**Dougherty, James E (Jim)** — Baseball Player
102 Pinnacle Court, Kitty Hawk NC 27949, USA
**Dougherty, Joseph (Joe)** — Producer, Director, Writer
Katz Golden Sullivan Rosenman, 2001 Wilshire Blvd, #400, Santa Monica CA 90403, USA
**Dougherty, Mike** — Guitarist, Songwriter
High Road Touring, 751 Bridgeway, #200, Sausalito CA 94965 USA
**Dougherty, Tom** — Clown
Ringling Bros Barnum & Bailey, 8607 Westwood Circle Dr, Vienna VA 22182 USA
**Dougherty, William A, Jr** — Navy Admiral
1505 Colonial Court, Arlington VA 22209, USA
**Doughty, Andrew P (Drew)** — Ice Hockey Player
1322 Basswood Road, London ON N5V 4C3, Canada
**Doughty, Glenn** — Football Player
8808 Saint Charles Rock Road, Saint Louis MO 63114, USA
**Doughty, Kenny** — Actor
United Agents, 12-26 Lexington St, London W1F 0LE, England
**Doughty, Neal** — Keyboardist (REO Speedwagon)
Front Line Mgmt, 1100 Glendon Ave, #2000, Los Angeles CA 90024 USA
**Doughty, Reed** — Football Player
Washington Redskins, 21300 Redskin Park Dr, Ashburn VA 20147 USA
**Douglas, Andrew** — Director
W M E Entertainment, 9601 Wilshire Blvd, #300, Beverly Hills CA 90210 USA
**Douglas, Anslem** — Composer, Entertainer
J W Records, 2833 Church Ave, Brooklyn NY 11226, USA
**Douglas, Barry** — Concert Pianist
I M G Artists, Hogarth Business Park, Chiswick, London W4 2TH, England
**Douglas, Bobby** — Wrestler, Coach
Bobby Douglas Wrestling Camps, 5520 Hickory Hills Dr, Ames IA 50014, USA
**Douglas, Brandon** — Actor
1546 Caitlyn Circle, Westlake Village CA 91361, USA
**Douglas, Cameron** — Actor
Creative Management Group, 8522 National Blvd, #108, Culver City CA 90232 USA
**Douglas, Charles W (Whammy)** — Baseball Player
1711 Caterine Lake Road, Jacksonville NC 28540, USA
**Douglas, Cullen** — Actor
Greene Assoc, 1901 Ave of Stars, #130, Los Angeles CA 90067 USA
**Douglas, David A (Dave)** — Drummer (Relient K, Attack Cat)
Janlyn Public Relations, 106 Cabrini Blvd, #4-I, New York NY 10033, USA
**Douglas, David G** — Football Player
605 Snowshill Way, Maryville TN 37803, USA
**Douglas, Denzil L** — Prime Minister, Saint Kitts & Nevis
Prime Minister's Office, Government Building, Waterfront, Basseterre, Saint Kitts & Nevis
**Douglas, Donna** — Actress
B G A Music, PO Box 1038, Lincolnton NC 28093, USA
**Douglas, Gabriel C V (Gabby)** — Gymnast
Buckeye Gymnastics, 7159 Northgate Way, Westerville OH 43082, USA
**Douglas, Illeana** — Actress
Eleven Minutes Entertainment, 11812 San Vicente Blvd, Los Angeles CA 90049, USA
**Douglas, James (Buster)** — Boxer
545 Towne Court N, Gahanna OH 43230, USA
**Douglas, Jerry** — Actor
Stone Manners Salners, 6100 Wilshire Blvd, #1500, Los Angeles CA 90035 USA
**Douglas, Jordy** — Ice Hockey Player
Courts Financial Group, 5-2727 Portage Ave, Winnipeg MB R3J 0R2, Canada
**Douglas, Kirk** — Actor
805 N Rexford Dr, Beverly Hills CA 90210, USA
**Douglas, Leon** — Basketball Player
6265 Sun Blvd, #402G, Saint Petersburg FL 33715, USA
**Douglas, Merrill G** — Football Player
2185 E 3970 S, Salt Lake City UT 84124, USA
**Douglas, Michael K** — Actor, Director, Producer
Further Films, 100 Universal City Plaza, Building 5174, Universal City CA 91608, USA

| | |
|---|---|
| **Douglas, Sarah**<br>R D F Mgmt, 3-6 Kenrick Place, London W1U 6HD, England | Actress |
| **Douglas, Sherman**<br>10401 Stapleford Hall Dr, Potomac MD 20854, USA | Basketball Player |
| **Douglas, Toney B**<br>Miami Heat, American Airlines Arena, 601 Biscayne Blvd, Miami FL 33132 USA | Basketball Player |
| **Douglass, Dale**<br>6601 E San Miguel Ave, Paradise Valley AZ 85253, USA | Golfer |
| **Douglass, Maurice G**<br>1021 Sunset Dr, Englewood OH 45322, USA | Football Player |
| **Douglass, Robert G (Bobby)**<br>151 E Laurel Ave, #203, Lake Forest IL 60045, USA | Football Player |
| **Doumbia, Mariam**<br>Partisan Arts, PO Box 5085, Larkspur CA 94977, USA | Singer (Amadou & Mariam) |
| **Doumit, Ryan M**<br>5232 Ridgeview Dr Loop NE, Moses Lake WA 98837, USA | Baseball Player |
| **Doumit, Sam**<br>Baker Winokur Ryder Public Relations, 9100 Wilshire Blvd, #500W, Beverly Hills CA 90212 USA | Actress |
| **Dourdan, Gary**<br>TalentWorks, 3500 W Olive Ave, #1400, Burbank CA 91505 USA | Actor |
| **Dourif, Bradford C (Brad)**<br>Innovative Artists, 1505 10th St, Santa Monica CA 90401 USA | Actor |
| **Dourif, Fiona**<br>Innovative Artists, 1505 10th St, Santa Monica CA 90401 USA | Actress, Producer |
| **Douris, Peter W**<br>PO Box 113, Cape Neddick ME 03902, USA | Ice Hockey Player |
| **Dove, Dennis**<br>144 Kirk Lane, Ocilla GA 31774, USA | Baseball Player |
| **Dove, Edward E (Eddie)**<br>1750 Poppy Ave, Menlo Park CA 94025, USA | Football Player |
| **Dove, Rita F**<br>1757 Lambs Road, Charlottesville VA 22901, USA | Writer |
| **Dove, Ronnie**<br>Ken Keene Artists, PO Box 1875, Gretna LA 70054, USA | Singer |
| **Dovolani, Driton (Tony)**<br>Abrams Artists, 9200 W Sunset Blvd, #1125, West Hollywood CA 90069 USA | Dancer |
| **Dow, Ellen Albertini**<br>Greene Assoc, 1901 Ave of Stars, #130, Los Angeles CA 90067 USA | Actress |
| **Dow, Peggy**<br>2121 S Yorktown Ave, Tulsa OK 74114, USA | Actress |
| **Dow, Tony**<br>Imperium 7 Artists, 5455 Wilshire Blvd, #1706, Los Angeles CA 90036 USA | Actor |
| **Dowd, Ann**<br>Innovative Artists, 1505 10th St, Santa Monica CA 90401 USA | Actress |
| **Dowd, James T (Jim)**<br>708 New Jersey Ave, Point Pleasant Beach NJ 08742, USA | Ice Hockey Player |
| **Dowd, Maureen**<br>New York Times, Editorial Dept, 229 W 43rd St, New York NY 10036 USA | Columnist |
| **Dowding, Leilani**<br>A C Talent Agency, 9595 Wilshire Blvd, #900, Beverly Hills CA 90212, USA | Model, Actress |
| **Dowdle, Walter R**<br>8555 Morven Road, Hahira GA 31632, USA | Microbiologist |
| **Dowell, Anthony J**<br>Royal Ballet, Covent Garden, Bow St, London WC2E 9DD, England | Ballet Dancer |
| **Dowell, Kenneth A (Ken)**<br>5221 Helen Way, Sacramento CA 95822, USA | Baseball Player |
| **Dower, John W**<br>Massachusetts Institute of Technology, History Dept, Cambridge MA 02139, USA | Writer |
| **Dowle, David**<br>International Talent Booking, Ariel House, 74A Charlotte St, #100 London W1T 4QJ, England | Drummer (Whitesnake) |
| **Dowler, Boyd H**<br>5309 Creek Heights Dr, Midlothian VA 23112, USA | Football Player |
| **Dowling, David B (Dave)**<br>173 Whelan Way, Manteca CA 95336, USA | Baseball Player |
| **Dowling, John E**<br>135 Charles St, Boston MA 02114, USA | Biologist, Neurobiologist |
| **Dowling, Timothy (Tim)**<br>Mosiac Media Group, 9200 W Sunset Blvd, #1000, Los Angeles CA 90069 USA | Actor, Writer |
| **Down, Lesley-Anne**<br>6252 Paseo Canyon Dr, Malibu CA 90265, USA | Actress |
| **Down, Sarah**<br>Playboy, Reader Services, 680 N Lake Shore Dr, Chicago IL 60611, USA | Cartoonist (Betsey's Buddies) |
| **Downes, Lorraine E**<br>Miss Universe NZ, PO Box 39624, Howick, Auckland 2145, New Zealand | Beauty Queen |
| **Downes, Terry**<br>Oaklea, 29 Meadowsbank, Watford WD19 4NP, England | Boxer |
| **Downey, Chris**<br>Creative Artists Agency, 2000 Ave of Stars, #100, Los Angeles CA 90067 USA | Producer, Writer |
| **Downey, Raymond**<br>Boxing Canada, 888 Belfast Road, Ottawa ON K1G 0Z6, Canada | Boxer |
| **Downey, Robert J**<br>I C M Partners, 10250 Constellation Blvd, #900, Los Angeles CA 90067 USA | Director |
| **Downey, Robert, Jr**<br>McDaniel Entertainment, 1311 Broadway, Santa Monica CA 90404, USA | Actor, Singer, Songwriter |
| **Downey, Roma**<br>Abrams Artists, 9200 W Sunset Blvd, #1125, West Hollywood CA 90069 USA | Actress |
| **Downey, William K (Bill)**<br>1035 S Moorings Dr, Arlington Heights IL 60005, USA | Basketball Player |
| **Downie, Gordon**<br>Bobby Breen Mgmt, 13 Blackburn St, #300, Toronto ON M4M 2B3, Canada | Singer, Guitarist (Tragically Hip) |
| **Downing, Alphonso E (Al)**<br>25343 Silver Aspen Way, #735, Valencia CA 91381, USA | Baseball Player |
| **Downing, Brian J**<br>8095 County Road 135, Celina TX 75009, USA | Baseball Player |
| **Downing, George**<br>Get Wet!, 3021 Waialae Ave, Honolulu HI 96816, USA | Surfer, Surfing Executive |

**Downing, James (Jim)** — Auto Racing Driver
5096 Peachtree Road, Atlanta GA 30341, USA

**Downing, Kenneth K (K K), Jr** — Guitarist (Judas Priest)
Trinifold Mgmt, 12 Oval Road, #300, Camden, London NW1 7D4, England

**Downing, Sara** — Actress
Amsel Eisenstadt Frazier, 5055 Wilshire Blvd, #865, Los Angeles CA 90036 USA

**Downing, Vern** — Bowler
523 Napa St, Rodeo CA 94572, USA

**Downing, Walter T (Walt)** — Football Player
1141 Durham Circle NW, Massillon OH 44646, USA

**Downs, Anthony** — Political Scientist
Brookings Institute, 1775 Massachusetts Ave NW, Washington DC 20036 USA

**Downs, David R (Dave)** — Baseball Player
925 E 1050 N, Bountiful UT 84010, USA

**Downs, Gary M** — Football Player
3953 Balleycastle Dr, Duluth GA 30097, USA

**Downs, Hugh M** — Commentator
7993 N Ridgeview Dr, Paradise Valley AZ 85253, USA

**Downs, Kelly R** — Baseball Player
6459 Willow Creek Road, Morgan UT 84050, USA

**Downs, Michael (Mike)** — Football Player
1405 Knob Hill Dr, DeSoto TX 75115, USA

**Downs, Scott** — Baseball Player
6814 Barbrook Road, Louisville KY 40258, USA

**Dowse, Michael** — Director
United Talent Agency, U T A Plaza, 9336 Civic Center Dr, Beverly Hills CA 90210 USA

**Dowson, Philip M** — Architect
Royal Academy of Arts, Piccadilly, London W1V 0DS, England

**Doyle, Allan** — Singer (Great Big Sea)
Fleming Assoc, 167 Little Lake Dr, Ann Arbor MI 48103, USA

**Doyle, Allen** — Golfer
512 Riverside Dr, LaGrange GA 30240, USA

**Doyle, Brian R** — Baseball Player
1310 Meadown Circle NE, Winter Haven FL 33881, USA

**Doyle, Christopher** — Cinematographer
I C M Partners, Marlborough House, 10 Earlham St, #300, London WC2H 9LNP, England

**Doyle, J Patrick** — Businessman
Domino's Pizza, PO Box 997, Ann Arbor MI 48106, USA

**Doyle, James H, Jr** — Navy Admiral
6200 Oregon Ave NW, #420, Washington DC 20015, USA

**Doyle, Jeffrey D (Jeff)** — Baseball Player
830 SE Bayshore Circle, Corvallis OR 97333, USA

**Doyle, Patrick** — Composer
Air Edel, 9100 Wilshire Blvd, #350E, Beverly Hills CA 90212 USA

**Doyle, R Dennis (Denny)** — Baseball Player
PO Box 9156, Winter Haven FL 33883, USA

**Doyle, Roddy** — Writer
Random House, 1745 Broadway, #1800, New York NY 10019 USA

**Doyle, Shawn** — Actor
Paul Kohner, 9300 Wilshire Blvd, #555, Beverly Hills CA 90212 USA

**Doyle-Murray, Brian** — Actor, Comedian
Abrams Artists, 9200 Sunset Blvd, #625, Los Angeles CA 90069, USA

**Doyne, Cory** — Baseball Player
20229 County Line Road, Lutz FL 33558, USA

**Dozier, James L** — Army General
1387 Wales Dr, Fort Myers FL 33901, USA

**Dozier, Lamont** — Singer, Songwriter
320 E Charleston Blvd, #205-130, Las Vegas NV 89104, USA

**Dozier, Terry** — Basketball Player
1037 Congress Road, Arlington Heights IL 60005, USA

**Dozier, Thomas D (Tom)** — Baseball Player
1231 Willow Ave, #D7, Hercules CA 94547, USA

**Dozier, William H (D J)** — Football, Baseball Player
PO Box 2722, Norfolk VA 23501, USA

**Dozy** — Bassist (Dave Dee Dozy Beaky Mick Tich)
Gerd Kehren Mgmt, Postfach 1408, 41804 Erkelenz, Germany

**Dr Demento** — Entertainer
Skyline Music, 48 Prospect St, Whitefield NH 03598, USA

**Dr Dre** — Rap Artist, Record Producer, Actor
Aftermath Entertainment, 2220 Colorado Ave, Santa Monica CA 90404, USA

**Dr John** — Jazz Pianist, Singer, Songwriter
Impact Artists Mgmt, 356 W 123rd St, New York NY 10027, USA

**Drabble, Margaret** — Writer
Penguin Books, 375 Hudson St, Basement 1, New York NY 10014 USA

**Drabek, Douglas D (Doug)** — Baseball Player
2 Peony Springs Court, Spring TX 77382, USA

**Drabinsky, Garth H** — Producer
Livent Inc, 165 Avenue Road, #600, Toronto ON M5R 3S4, Canada

**Draffen, Willis** — Singer (Bloodstone)
16103 Vista Del Mar Dr, Houston TX 77083, USA

**Draft, Christopher M (Chris)** — Football Player
970 E Oak St, Anaheim CA 92805, USA

**Draganja, Duje** — Swimmer
Plivacki Klub Dubrava, Stefanovecka Cesta 67/1, 10000 Zagreb Dubrava, Croatia

**Dragic, Goran** — Basketball Player
Phoenix Suns, 201 E Jefferson St, Phoenix AZ 85004 USA

**Draglia, Stacy** — Track Athlete
PO Box 30931, Phoenix AZ 85046, USA

**Drago, Billy** — Actor
Deborah Miller, 9454 Wilshire Blvd, #715, Beverly Hills CA 90212, USA

**Drago, Richard A (Dick)** — Baseball Player
4703 Belle Chase Circle, Tampa FL 33634, USA

**Dragon, Daryl** — Musician (Captain & Tennille)
Greenlaw, 1251 S Cimarron Road, #22, Las Vegas NV 89117, USA

**Dragoti, Stan** — Director
1800 Ave of Stars, #430, Los Angeles CA 90067, USA

**Drahman, Brian S** — Baseball Player
46 Mariner Green Dr, Corte Madera CA 94925, USA
**Drahos, Nicholas (Nick)** — Football Player
3158 State Route 90, Aurora NY 13026, USA
**Draiman, Dave** — Singer (Disturbed)
Agency Group Ltd, 142 W 57th St, #600, New York NY 10019 USA
**Drake** — Singer, Rap Artist, Actor
Bryant Mgmt, 800 Brickell Ave, #550, Miami FL 33131, USA
**Drake, Bebe** — Actress
Ashby/Rojo Entertainment, 1485 S Beverly Dr, Los Angeles CA 90035, USA
**Drake, Dallas** — Ice Hockey Player
11472 E Cedar Bay Trail, Traverse City MI 49684, USA
**Drake, Frank D** — Astronomer
Search for ExtraTerrestrial Intelligence Institute, 515 N Whisman Road, Mountain View CA 94043, USA
**Drake, Jamie** — Interior Designer
Drake Design Assoc, 315 E 62nd St, #500, New York NY 10065, USA
**Drake, Jeremy** — Astronomer
Harvard University, Smithsonian Center for Astrophysics, Cambridge MA 02138, USA
**Drake, Judith** — Actress
Schiowitz Connor, 1680 N Vine St, #1016, Los Angeles CA 90028 USA
**Drake, Julius** — Concert Pianist
I M G Artists, Hogarth Business Park, Chiswick, London W4 2TH, England
**Drake, Kenneth** — Artist, Sculptor
Carrer D'es Port 2, #6, 07720 Es Castell, Minorca, Balearic Islands, Spain
**Drake, Larry** — Actor
Amsel Eisenstadt Frazier, 5055 Wilshire Blvd, #865, Los Angeles CA 90036 USA
**Drake, Michael V** — Educator
University of California, Chancellor's Office, Irvine CA 92697, USA
**Drake, Solomon L (Solly)** — Baseball Player
1732 S Corning St, Los Angeles CA 90035, USA
**Drake, Thomas** — Basketball Coach
Drake University, Athletic Dept, Des Moines IA 50311, USA
**Drane, Dwight** — Football Player
200 NW 107th Ave, Plantation FL 33324, USA
**Draper, Courtnee** — Actress
C E S D, 10635 Santa Monica Blvd, #130, Los Angeles CA 90025 USA
**Draper, Dave** — Body Builder
837 California St, Santa Cruz CA 95060, USA
**Draper, Kris** — Ice Hockey Player
3418 Westchester Road, Bloomfield Hills MI 48304, USA
**Draper, Michael H (Mike)** — Baseball Player
18317 Manor Church Road, Boonsboro MD 21713, USA
**Draper, Polly** — Actress
Innovative Artists, 1505 10th St, Santa Monica CA 90401 USA
**Draper, Timothy C** — Financier
Draper Fisher Jurvetson, 2802 Sand Hill Road, Menlo Park CA 94025, USA
**Draper, Tom** — Ice Hockey Player
76 Blackstone Ave, Binghamton NY 13903, USA
**Draper, William H, III** — Financier
91 Tallwood Court, Atherton CA 94027, USA
**Dratch, Rachel** — Actress, Comedienne
Paradigm Agency, 360 N Crescent Dr, North Building, Beverly Hills CA 90210 USA
**Dravecky, David F (Dave)** — Baseball Player
475 W 12th Ave, #8F, Denver CO 80204, USA
**Draxl, Tim** — Actor
Management 360, 9111 Wilshire Blvd, Beverly Hills CA 90210 USA
**Dray, Albert** — Actor
Artmedia, 20 Ave Rapp, 75007 Paris, France
**Drayton, Kia** — Model
Playboy Promotions, 9346 Civic Center Dr, #200, Beverly Hills CA 90210 USA
**Drayton, T Anthony (Troy)** — Football Player
31 Oak St, #1, Patchogue NY 11772, USA
**Drechsler, Heike** — Track Athlete
Neblund Sportsnetwork, Lichstr 43G, 50825 Cologne, Germany
**Drecker, Anneli M** — Singer (Bel Canto)
Kjell Kalleklev Mgmt, Georgernes Verft 12N, 5011 Bergen, Norway
**Drees, Thomas K (Tom)** — Baseball Player
18638 Bearpath Trail, Eden Prairie MN 55347, USA
**Dreesen, Tom** — Actor, Comedian
14538 Benefit St, #301, Sherman Oaks CA 91403, USA
**Dreier, David T** — Representative, CA
Brookings Institute, 1775 Massachusetts Ave NW, Washington DC 20036 USA
**Dreier, R Chad** — Businessman
Ryland Group, 6300 Canoga Ave, Woodland Hills CA 91367, USA
**Dreifort, Darren J** — Baseball Player
463 Wynola St, Pacific Palisades CA 90272, USA
**Dreiling, Gregory A (Greg)** — Basketball Player
5952 Willowross Way, Plano TX 75093, USA
**Dreiskens, Daumants** — Bobsled Athlete
Bobsled Federation, Roberta Feldmana 11, 1014 Riga, Latvia
**Drell, Persis** — Physicist
Stanford University, Linear Accelerator Center, Stanford CA 94305, USA
**Drell, Sidney D** — Physicist
620 Sand Hill Road, #420D, Palo Alto CA 94304, USA
**Drescher, Fran** — Actress
Manatt Phelps Phillips, 11355 W Olympic Blvd, #20, Los Angeles CA 90064 USA
**Drese, Ryan T** — Baseball Player
2201 Bear Lake Dr, Euless TX 76039, USA
**Dressel, Chris** — Football Player
410 Whiskey Hill Road, Woodside CA 94062, USA
**Dresselhaus, Mildred S** — Physicist, Electrical Engineer
Energy Department, 1000 Independence Ave SW, Washington DC 20585, USA
**Dressendorfer, Kirk R** — Baseball Player
1004 Oaklands Dr, Round Rock TX 78681, USA
**Dressler, Alan M** — Astronomer
Carnegie Observatories, 813 Santa Barbara St, Pasadena CA 91101, USA

**D**

| | |
|---|---|
| **Dressler, Douglas J (Doug)**<br>118 Frostwood Dr, Westwood CA 96137, USA | Football Player |
| **Dressler, Robert A (Rob)**<br>2037 17th Ave, Forest Grove OR 97116, USA | Baseball Player |
| **Drew, B Alvin, Jr**<br>2814 Lighthouse Dr, Houston TX 77058, USA | Astronaut |
| **Drew, David J (J D)**<br>5006 Old US Highway 41 N, Hahira GA 31632, USA | Baseball Player |
| **Drew, Griffin**<br>9066 Cambridge Circle, Vallejo CA 94591, USA | Actress, Model |
| **Drew, Heather**<br>76160 Desert Mountain Circle, Indio CA 92203, USA | Golfer |
| **Drew, John E**<br>2303 W Tidwell Road, #3404, Houston TX 77091, USA | Basketball Player |
| **Drew, Larry D**<br>4942 Densmore Ave, Encino CA 91436, USA | Basketball Player, Coach |
| **Drew, Sarah**<br>Innovative Artists, 1505 10th St, Santa Monica CA 90401 USA | Actress |
| **Drew, Tim**<br>5006 Old US Highway 41N, Hahira GA 31632, USA | Baseball Player |
| **Drewrey, Willie J**<br>2714 Cheryl Court, Missouri City TX 77459, USA | Football Player |
| **Drexler Prada, Jorge A**<br>Morgan Britos Mgmt, Calle Princesa 3, Depdo Ofic 1331, 28008 Madrid, Spain | Singer, Songwriter |
| **Drexler, Clyde A**<br>4045 Piping Rock Lane, Houston TX 77027, USA | Basketball Player, Coach |
| **Drexler, Millard S (Mickey)**<br>J Crew, 770 Broadway, #1200, New York NY 10003, USA | Businessman |
| **Dreyer, Steven W (Steve)**<br>6018 Greywood Circle, Johnston IA 50131, USA | Baseball Player |
| **Dreyfus, George**<br>3 Grace St, Camberwell VIC 3124, Australia | Composer |
| **Dreyfus, Hubert L**<br>University of California, Industrial Engineering Dept, Berkeley CA 94720, USA | Philosopher |
| **Dreyfuss, Richard S**<br>A P A Talent & Literary Agency, 405 S Beverly Dr, #300, Beverly Hills CA 90212 USA | Actor |
| **Drickamer, Harry G**<br>7008 Knotty Pine Dr, Chapel Hill NC 27517, USA | Chemical Engineer |
| **Driessen, Daniel (Dan)**<br>208 Mitchellville Road, Hilton Head Island SC 29926, USA | Baseball Player |
| **Drinfeld, Vladimir**<br>Steklov Mathematics Institute, 42 Vavilova, 117966 ESP-1 Moscow, Russia | Mathematician |
| **Drinkwater, Carol**<br>Artists Partnership, 101 Finsbury Pavement, London EC2A 1RS, England | Actress |
| **Driscoll, Edward C (Terry)**<br>101 Taylor Circle, Williamsburg VA 23185, USA | Basketball Player |
| **Driscoll, James B (Jim)**<br>18 Coyne Road, Waban MA 02468, USA | Baseball Player |
| **Driscoll, Jean**<br>Pat Fettig, 8142 Traverse Court, Cincinnati OH 45242, USA | Track Athlete |
| **Driskill, Travis**<br>800 Blue Spring Circle, Round Rock TX 78681, USA | Baseball Player |
| **Driver, Adam**<br>Gersh Agency, 9465 Wilshire Blvd, #600, Beverly Hills CA 90212 USA | Actor |
| **Driver, Bruce**<br>21A Crest Terrace, Montville NJ 07045, USA | Ice Hockey Player |
| **Driver, Donald J**<br>1501 Noble Way, Flower Mound TX 75022, USA | Football Player |
| **Driver, Minnie**<br>Untitled Entertainment, 350 S Beverly Dr, #200, Beverly Hills CA 90212 USA | Actress, Singer |
| **D'Rivera, Paquito**<br>Charismic Productions, 2604 Mozart Place NW, Washington DC 20009, USA | Jazz, Concert Saxophonist |
| **Drmanac, Radoje (Rade)**<br>Complete Genomics, 2071 Stierlin Court, Mountain View CA 94043, USA | Research Scientist |
| **Droge, Pete**<br>1423 34th Ave, Seattle WA 98122, USA | Singer, Songwriter |
| **Drolet, Francois L**<br>Speed Skating Canada, 2781 Lancaster Road, #402, Ottawa ON K1B 1A7, Canada | Speed Skater |
| **Drolet, Marie-Eve**<br>1870 Blvd PieXi N, Quebec QC G3J 1N9, Canada | Speed Skater |
| **Drollinger, Ralph K**<br>22831 Market St, Newhall CA 91321, USA | Basketball Player |
| **Drosdick, John G**<br>Sunoco Inc, 10 Penn Center, 1801 Market St, Philadelphia PA 19103, USA | Businessman |
| **Drougas, Thomas C (Tom)**<br>PO Box 1596, Sun Valley ID 83353, USA | Football Player |
| **Droughns, Reuben**<br>5955 S Elkhart Court, Centennial CO 80016, USA | Football Player |
| **Drouin, Derek**<br>321 Brentwood Crescent, Corunna ON N0N 1G0, Canada | Track Athlete |
| **Drouin, Jude**<br>44479 Maltese Falcon Square, Ashburn VA 20147, USA | Ice Hockey Player |
| **Drozd, Steven D**<br>World's Fair Mgmt, 1208 Chowning Ave, Edmond OK 73034, USA | Drummer, Guitarist (Flaming Lips) |
| **Drozdova, Inga**<br>Playboy Promotions, 9346 Civic Center Dr, #200, Beverly Hills CA 90210 USA | Model |
| **Drozdova, Margarita S**<br>Stanislavsky Musical Theater, Pushkinskaya Str 17, 143900 Moscow, Russia | Ballerina |
| **Druce, John**<br>Freedom 55 Financial, 405-360 George St N, Peterborough ON K9H 7E7, Canada | Ice Hockey Player |
| **Drucker, Eugene**<br>I M G Artists, Burlington Lane, Chiswick, London W4 2TH, England | Violinist (Emerson String Quartet) |
| **Drukarova, Dinara**<br>Voyez Mon Agent, 20 Ave Rapp, 75007 Paris, France | Actress |
| **Druken, Harold**<br>16 Shaw Dr, Wayland MA 01778, USA | Ice Hockey Player |

**Dressler - Druken**

**Druker, Brian J** — Oncologist, Hematologist
Oregon Health Science University, Cancer Research Center, Portland OR 97201, USA

**Drummond, Alice** — Actress
351 E 50th St, New York NY 10022, USA

**Drummond, Greg** — Curling Athlete
Curl Aberdeen, Eday Walk off Lang Stracht, Summerhill, Aberdeen AB15 6LN, Scotland

**Drummond, Jonathan (Jon)** — Track Athlete
PO Box 982, Arlington TX 76004, USA

**Drummond, Lauren** — Actress
Independent Talent Group, 40 Whitfield St, London W1T 2RH, England

**Drummond, Ryan** — Actor
Artists Management Agency, 835 5th Ave, #411, San Diego CA 92101, USA

**Drummond, Timothy D (Tim)** — Baseball Player
102 Haldane Court, La Plata MD 20646, USA

**Drummond, Tom** — Singer, Bassist (Better Than Ezra)
Uppercut Mgmt, 805 N Milwaukee Ave, #401, Chicago IL 60642, USA

**Drummond, William E (Bill)** — Guitarist (KLF), Record Producer
Nene Musik Productions, 1460 SW Santiago Ave, Port Saint Lucie FL 34953 USA

**Drury, Chris** — Ice Hockey Player
145 Parsonage Road, Greenwich CT 06830, USA

**Drury, James** — Actor
100 Spring Lake Dr, Montgomery TX 77356, USA

**Drury, Theodore E (Ted)** — Ice Hockey Player
305 Hibbard Road, Wilmette IL 60091, USA

**Drut, Guy J** — Track Athlete
Mairie, 77120 Coulommiers, France

**Dryburgh, Stuart** — Cinematographer
Gersh Agency, 9465 Wilshire Blvd, #600, Beverly Hills CA 90212 USA

**Dryden, Kenneth W (Ken)** — Ice Hockey Player
58 Poplar Plains Road, Toronto ON M4V 2M8, Canada

**Dryer, J Frederick (Fred)** — Football Player, Actor
Greater Vision Artists Talent Agency, 8981 Sunset Blvd, #101, Los Angeles CA 90069, USA

**Dryke, Matthew (Matt)** — Marksman
292 Dryke Road, Sequim WA 98382, USA

**Drysdale, Cliff** — Tennis Player, Sportscaster
A T Y, 4725 N Lois Ave, Tampa FL 33614, USA

**Duany, Andres** — Architect
Duany & Plater-Zyberk Architects, 1023 SW 25th Ave, Miami FL 33135, USA

**Duarte, Chris** — Musician
Intrepid Artists, Midtown Plaza, 1300 Baxter St, #405, Charlotte NC 28204, USA

**Duato, Nacho** — Ballet Dancer, Choreographer
Compania Nacional de Danza, Paseo de la Chopera 4, 28045 Madrid, Spain

**Dubberley, Emily** — Writer, Journalist
Fox & Howard Literary Agency, 39 Eland Road, London SW11 5JX, England

**Dube, Desmond** — Actor
Mahogany, PO Box 3085, Saxonwold, Johannesburg 2132, South Africa

**Dubenion, Elbert (Duby)** — Football Player
610 E Walnut St, Westerville OH 43081, USA

**Duberman, Justin** — Ice Hockey Player
4004 Avalon Pointe Dr, Boca Raton FL 33496, USA

**Dubia, John A** — Army General
10095 Cover Place, Fairfax VA 22030, USA

**Dubik, James M** — Army General
Institute for Study of War, 1400 16th St NW, #515 Washington DC 20036, USA

**Dubinbaum, Gail** — Opera Singer
Metropolitan Opera Assn, Lincoln Center Plaza, New York NY 10023 USA

**Dubinsky, Steve** — Ice Hockey Player
939 Central Ave, Highland Park IL 60035, USA

**Dublinski, Thomas E (Tom), Jr** — Football Player
15918 El Lago Blvd, Fountain Hills AZ 85268, USA

**Dubner, Stephen J** — Economist, Writer
William Morrow Publishers, 1350 Ave of Americas, New York NY 10019 USA

**Dubnyk, Devan** — Ice Hockey Player
Montreal Canadiens, 1275 Saint Antoine St W, Montreal QC H3C 5L2, Canada

**Dubois, Brian A** — Baseball Player
3 Spartan Place, Springfield IL 62703, USA

**DuBois, G Macy** — Architect
175 Carlton St, Toronto ON M5A 2K3, Canada

**DuBois, Ja'Net** — Actress
C E S D, 10635 Santa Monica Blvd, #130, Los Angeles CA 90025 USA

**Dubois, Jason** — Baseball Player
2204 Lord Seaton Circle, Virginia Beach VA 23454, USA

**Dubois, Marie** — Actress
Artmedia, 20 Ave Rapp, 75007 Paris, France

**DuBois, Marta** — Actress
Orange Grove Group, 12178 Ventura Blvd, #205, Studio City CA 91604, USA

**Dubose, Eric** — Baseball Player
326 County Road 8, Gilbertown AL 36908, USA

**Dubreuil, Maroussia** — Actress
Agence Artistique Sophie Lemaitre, 9 Rue de Mubeuge, 75009 Paris, France

**Dubus, Andre, III** — Writer
Penguin Group, 375 Hudson St, Basement 1, New York NY 10014, USA

**Ducasse, Alain** — Chef
Groupe Alain Ducasse, 25 Ave Montaigne, 75008 Paris, France

**Duce, Sharon** — Actress
Castaway Voice Overs, 15 Broad Court, #3, London WC2B 5QN, England

**Ducey, Caroline** — Actress
Vefour Mgmt, 12 Rue Pelouze, 75008 Paris, France

**Ducey, Robert T (Rob)** — Baseball Player
699 Richmond Close, Tarpon Springs FL 34688, USA

**Duchene, Matthew (Matt)** — Ice Hockey Player
Vince Duchene, 191 Highland St, Box 330, Ha;onurton ON K0M 1S0, Canada

**Duchesnay, Isabelle** — Ice Dancer
Im Steinach 30, 87561 Oberstdorf, Germany

**Duchesnay, Paul** — Ice Dancer
Bundesleistungszentrum, Rossbichstr 2-6, 87561 Oberstdorf, Germany

Druker - Duchesnay

# D

| | |
|---|---|
| **Duchesne, Steve** | Ice Hockey Player |
| 2104 Cedar Elm Terrace, Westlake TX 76262, USA | |
| **Duchin, Peter** | Jazz Pianist, Orchestra Leader |
| Peter Duchin Music, 244 Madison Ave, #333, New York NY 10016, USA | |
| **Duchovny, David** | Actor, Director |
| Affirmative Entertainment, 425 N Robertson Blvd, Los Angeles CA 90048 USA | |
| **Duchscherer, Justin C** | Baseball Player |
| 975 E Runaway Bay Place, Chandler AZ 85249, USA | |
| **DuCille, Michel** | Photojournalist |
| 9571 Pine Meadow Lane, Burke VA 22015, USA | |
| **Duckett, Todd J (T J)** | Football Player |
| Seattle Seahawks, 12 Seahawks Way, Renton WA 98056 USA | |
| **Duckworth, Brandon J** | Baseball Player |
| 106 Carrie Lynne Court, Mullica Hill NJ 08062, USA | |
| **Duckworth, Charles** | Actor |
| Landis-Simon Productions, 3625 E Thousand Oaks Blvd, #279, Thousand Oaks CA 91362, USA | |
| **Duckworth, Marilyn** | Writer |
| 41 Queen St, Mount Victoria, Wellington 6001, New Zealand | |
| **Ducornet, Rikki** | Writer |
| University of Louisiana, English Dept, 104 E University Circle, Lafayette LA 70503, USA | |
| **Ducsmal Jaroszewska, Agnieszka** | Conductor |
| Polish Radio Orchestra, Al Marchinkowskiego 3, 61745 Pozna, Poland | |
| **Dudek, Anne** | Actress |
| Innovative Artists, 1505 10th St, Santa Monica CA 90401 USA | |
| **Dudek, Joseph A (Joe)** | Football Player |
| 31 Ryan Road, Auburn NH 03032, USA | |
| **Duden, H Richard (Dick), Jr** | Football Player |
| 11 Old Station Road, Severna Park MD 21146, USA | |
| **Duderstadt, James J** | Educator, Government Official |
| National Science Foundation, 1800 G St NW, Washington DC 20006, USA | |
| **Dudikoff, Michael** | Actor |
| 4341 Birch St, #201, Newport Beach CA 92660, USA | |
| **Dudley, Anne** | Keyboardist (Art of Noise), Composer |
| Cool Music, 1-A Fishers Lane, Chiswick London W4 1RX, England | |
| **Dudley, Charles** | Basketball Player |
| 4032 42nd Ave S, Seattle WA 98118, USA | |
| **Dudley, Christen G (Chris)** | Basketball Player |
| PO Box 703, Rancho Santa Fe CA 92067, USA | |
| **Dudley, Jaquelin** | Microbiologist |
| University of Texas, Microbiology Dept, Austin TX 78712, USA | |
| **Dudley, Jared A** | Basketball Player |
| Los Angeles Clippers, Staples Center, 1111 S Figueroa St, Los Angeles CA 90015 USA | |
| **Dudley, Rick** | Ice Hockey Player, Coach |
| 5150 Oakhill Dr, Lewiston NY 14092, USA | |
| **Dudley, Rickey D** | Football Player |
| 4529 Mahogany Lane, Lewisville TX 75077, USA | |
| **Dudman, Nick** | Makeup Artist |
| Pigs Might Fly, Gawithfield Barn, Arrad Foot, Ulverston, Cumbria LA12 7SL, England | |
| **Duenkel Fuldner, Virginia (Ginny)** | Swimmer |
| 2132 NE 17th Terrace, #500, Wilton Manors FL 33305, USA | |
| **Duensing, Brian** | Baseball Player |
| 524 S 198th St, Elkhorn NE 68022, USA | |
| **Duerod, Terry** | Basketball Player |
| 6542 Chirrewa St, Westland MI 48185, USA | |
| **Duesenberry, James S** | Economist |
| 514 Harvard St, #3B, Brookline MA 02446, USA | |
| **Dufay, Rick** | Guitarist (Aerosmith) |
| H K Mgmt, 9200 W Sunset Blvd, #530, West Hollywood CA 90069 USA | |
| **Dufek, Donald P (don)** | Football Player |
| 570 S Maple Road, Ann Arbor MI 48103, USA | |
| **Duff, Anne-Marie** | Actress |
| Gordon & French, 12-13 Poland St, London W1F 8QB, England | |
| **Duff, Haylie** | Actress, Singer, Songwriter |
| Curtis Talent Mgmt, 9607 Arby Dr, Beverly Hills CA 90210, USA | |
| **Duff, Hilary** | Actress, Singer, Model |
| Creative Artists Agency, 2000 Ave of Stars, #100, Los Angeles CA 90067 USA | |
| **Duff, John E** | Sculptor |
| 5 Doyers St, New York NY 10013, USA | |
| **Duff, T Richard (Dick)** | Ice Hockey Player |
| 4-7 Elmwood Ave S, Mississauga ON L5G 3J6, Canada | |
| **Duffalo, James F (Jim)** | Baseball Player |
| 1505 Savannah St, Mesquite TX 75149, USA | |
| **Duffey, Joseph D** | Educator |
| 2891 New Mexico Ave NW, #311, Washington DC 20007, USA | |
| **Duffie, John B** | Baseball Player |
| 177 Lakeside Circle, Douglas GA 31535, USA | |
| **Duffield, Burkely** | Actor |
| United Talent Agency, U T A Plaza, 9336 Civic Center Dr, Beverly Hills CA 90210 USA | |
| **Duffner, Christof** | Ski Jumper |
| Am Sagebauer 1, 78141 Schonwald, Germany | |
| **Duffner, Mark** | Football Coach |
| University of Maryland, Athletic Dept, College Park MD 20740, USA | |
| **Duffus, Parris** | Ice Hockey Player |
| 8609 Timbermill Place, Fort Wayne IN 46804, USA | |
| **Duffy** | Singer, Songwriter |
| 13 Artists, 11-14 Kensington St, Brighton BN1 4AJ, England | |
| **Duffy, Brian** | Editorial Cartoonist |
| Des Moines Register, Editorial Dept, PO Box 957, Des Moines IA 50306, USA | |
| **Duffy, Brian** | Astronaut |
| 16410 Heather Bend Court, Houston TX 77059, USA | |
| **Duffy, Carol Ann** | Writer |
| Manchester Metropolitan University, English Dept, All Saints, Manchester M15 6BH, England | |
| **Duffy, Francis (Frank)** | Architect |
| Three Ways, Street, Walberswick near Southwold, Suffolk IP18 6UE, England | |
| **Duffy, Frank T** | Baseball Player |
| 1740 E Silver St, Tucson AZ 85719, USA | |

**Duchesne - Duffy**

**Duffy, J C**
Universal Press Syndicate, 4520 Main St, #700, Kansas City MO 64111 USA — Cartoonist (Fusco Brothers)

**Duffy, John**
Meet the Composer, 2112 Broadway, New York NY 10023, USA — Composer

**Duffy, Julia**
C E S D, 10635 Santa Monica Blvd, #130, Los Angeles CA 90025 USA — Actress

**Duffy, Keith**
Carol/War Mgmt, Bushy Park Road, 57 Meadowgate, Dublin 6, Ireland — Singer (Boyzone)

**Duffy, Maureen P**
18 Fabian Road, London SW6 7TZ, England — Writer

**Duffy, Patrick**
Bx2 Mgmt, 15304 Sunset Blvd, #202, Pacific Palisades VA 90272, USA — Actor

**Duffy, Roger T**
6509 Lutz Ave NW, Massillon OH 44646, USA — Football Player

**Duffy, Troy**
Original Artists, 9465 Wilshire Blvd, #324, Beverly Hills CA 90212, USA — Actor, Director, Writer

**Duffy, William H (Billy)**
Tom Vitorino Mgmt, 11606 Viny Road, Granada Hills CA 91344, USA — Guitarist (Cult)

**Duflo, Esther**
Massachusetts Institute of Technology, Economics Dept, Cambridge MA 02139, USA — Economist

**Dufner, Jason**
2002 Saint Patrick Court, Auburn AL 36830, USA — Golfer

**Dufour, Marc**
1065 Rue Des Saules, Trois-Reivieres QC G8Y 2K6, Canada — Ice Hockey Player

**Dufour-Lapointe, Chloe**
Freestyle Ski Assn, 808 Pacific St, Vancouver BC V6Z 1C5, Canada — Freestyle Skier

**Dufour-Lapointe, Justine**
Freestyle Ski Assn, 808 Pacific St, Vancouver BC V6Z 1C5, Canada — Freestyle Skier

**Dufresne, Donald**
Hamilton Bulldogs, 101 York Blvd, Hamilton ON L8R 3L4, Canada — Ice Hockey Player

**Dufresne, John**
W W Norton, 500 5th Ave, #600, New York NY 10110 USA — Writer

**Dufresne, Mark**
Bobby Roberts, 3050 Business Park Circle, #303, Goodlettsville TN 37221 USA — Drummer (Confederate Railroad)

**Dugan, Dennis**
United Talent Agency, U T A Plaza, 9336 Civic Center Dr, Beverly Hills CA 90210 USA — Actor, Director

**Dugan, J Fred**
1827 Tamiami Trail N, Nokomia FL 34275, USA — Football Player

**Dugan, Jeffrey S (Jeff)**
13701 Ashcroft Road, Savage MN 55378, USA — Football Player

**Dugan, Michael J**
36 James Court, Dillon CO 80435, USA — Air Force General, Association Executive

**Dugdale, John**
Holden Luntz Gallery, 332 Worth Ave, Palm Beach FL 33480, USA — Photographer

**Duggan, James S (Hacksaw Jim)**
1328 Hornsby Circle, Lugoff SC 29078, USA — Professional Wrestler, Football Player

**Duggan, Meghan**
115 Burley St, Danvers MA 01923, USA — Ice Hockey Player

**Dugger, John Scott**
410 Evelyn Ave, #201, Albany CA 94706, USA — Artist

**Dugoni, Robert**
Warner Books, 1271 Ave of Americas, New York NY 10020 USA — Writer

**Duguay, Christian**
Gersh Agency, 9465 Wilshire Blvd, #600, Beverly Hills CA 90212 USA — Director

**Duguay, Ron**
14 Sea Winds Lane N, Ponte Vedra Beach FL 32082, USA — Ice Hockey Player

**Duhamel, Josh**
John Carrabino Mgmt, 5900 Wilshire Blvd, #406, Los Angeles CA 90036 USA — Actor

**Duhamel, Meagan**
Club De Patinage Artisique, 4365 Cartier, Montreal QC H2H 1W6, Canada — Figure Skater

**Duhe, Adam J (A J), Jr**
379 Coconut Circle, Weston FL 33326, USA — Football Player

**Duhe, John M, Jr**
US Court of Appeals, 556 Jefferson St, Lafayette LA 70501, USA — Judge

**Duho, Veselin**
V K Jug Dubrovnik, Dr Ante Starcevica 22, 20000 Dubrovnik, Croatia — Water Polo Player

**Duigan, John**
54A Tite St, London SW3 4JA, England — Director

**Dujardin, Jean**
W M E Entertainment, 9601 Wilshire Blvd, #300, Beverly Hills CA 90210 USA — Actor, Comedian

**Dujmovits, Julia**
Sulz 84, 7542 Gerersdorf-Sulz, Austria — Snowboard Athlete

**Duk Kim, Randall**
Charles Bright, 135 Houpe Road, Great Meadows NJ 07838, USA — Actor

**Duka, Dominik J Cardinal**
Archdiocese, Hradcanske Nam 16, 11902 Prague 1, Czech Republic — Religious Leader

**Dukakis, Michael S**
85 Perry St, Brookline MA 02446, USA — Governor, MA

**Dukakis, Olympia**
Innovative Artists, 235 Park Ave S, #1000, New York NY 10003 USA — Actress

**Duke, Annie**
Federated Sports & Gaming, Palms Casino & Resort, 4301 W Flamingo Road, Las Vegas NV 89103, USA — Poker Player

**Duke, Bill**
Duke Media, 7510 Sunset Blvd, #523, Los Angeles CA 90046, USA — Director

**Duke, Charles M, Jr**
Duke Ministry for Christ, PO Box 310345, New Braunfels TX 78131, USA — Astronaut, Air Force General

**Duke, Clark**
W M E Entertainment, 9601 Wilshire Blvd, #300, Beverly Hills CA 90210 USA — Actor, Director, Writer

**Duke, Elizabeth**
Federal Reserve System, 20th St & Constitution Ave NW, Washington DC 20551, USA — Government Official, Financier

**Duke, Kenneth W (Ken)**
3612 SW Rivers End Way, Palm City FL 34990, USA — Golfer

**Duke, Norm**
719 2nd Ave, #701, Seattle WA 98104, USA — Bowler

**Duke, Patty**
Mitchell K Stubbs Assoc, 8695 W Washington Blvd, #204, Culver City CA 90232 USA — Actress

**Duke, Robin Chandler** — Association Executive, Diplomat
435 E 52nd St, New York NY 10022, USA

**Duke, Zachary T (Zach)** — Baseball Player
2517 County Road 4240, Clifton TX 76634, USA

**Dukes, Jamie D** — Football Player, Sportscaster
2553 Northern Oak Dr, Braselton GA 30517, USA

**Dukes, Thomas E (Tom)** — Baseball Player
325 Monte Vista Road, Arcadia CA 91007, USA

**Dukuchitz, Jonathan** — Actor, Singer
Innovative Artists, 235 Park Ave S, #1000, New York NY 10003 USA

**Dukurs, Martins** — Skeleton Athlete
Skeleton Federation, Annas Sakses 19, 1014 Riga, Latvia

**Dulany, Caitlin** — Actress
TalentWorks, 3500 W Olive Ave, #1400, Burbank CA 91505 USA

**Dulery, Antoine** — Actor
Artmedia, 20 Ave Rapp, 75007 Paris, France

**Dulfer, Candy** — Musician, Actress
Sun Music, PO Box 130, 3235 Erlach, Switzerland

**Duliba, Robert J (Bob)** — Baseball Player
327 Philadelphia Ave, West Pittston PA 18643, USA

**Dullea, Keir** — Actor
Bret Adams Agency, 448 W 44th St, New York NY 10036, USA

**Dulli, Gregory (Greg)** — Singer, Guitarist (Twilight Singers)
Rascoff/Zysblat Organization, 250 W 57th St, New York NY 10107 USA

**Dumars, Joe, III** — Basketball Player
3499 Franklin Road, Bloomfield Hills MI 48302, USA

**Dumaux, Christophe** — Opera Singer
I M G Artists, Hogarth Business Park, Chiswick, London W4 2TH, England

**Dumerc, Celine** — Basketball Player
Atlanta Dream, 83 Walton St NW, #400, Atlanta, GA 30303 USA

**Dumervil, Elvis K** — Football Player
6115 Trailhead Road, Littleton CO 80130, USA

**Dumont, J P** — Ice Hockey Player
1512 Kimberleigh Court, Franklin TN 37069, USA

**DuMont, James** — Actor
House of Representatives, 1434 6th St, #1, Santa Monica CA 90401 USA

**Dumoulin, Daniel L (Dan)** — Baseball Player
202 Nancy Dr, Kokomo IN 46901, USA

**Dunaev, Andrej** — Opera Singer
I M G Artists, Hogarth Business Park, Chiswick, London W4 2TH, England

**Dunagin, Ralph** — Cartoonist (Dunagin's People)
North American Syndicate, 235 E 45th St, New York NY 10017 USA

**Dunaway, Faye** — Actress
Mavrick Artists Agency, 6100 Wilshire Blvd, #550, Los Angeles CA 90048, USA

**Dunaway, James E (Jim)** — Football Player
170 Mount Carmel Church Road, Sandy Hook MS 39478, USA

**Dunbar, Bonnie J** — Astronaut
2200 Todville Road, Seabrook TX 77586, USA

**Dunbar, Dale** — Ice Hockey Player
41 Nahant Ave, Winthrop MA 02152, USA

**Dunbar, Gavin** — Bassist (Camera Obscura)
Ground Control Touring, 20 Jay St, #826, Brooklyn NY 11201 USA

**Dunbar, Jo-Lonn D** — Football Player
Saint Louis Rams, 901 N Broadway, Saint Louis MO 63101 USA

**Dunbar, Matt** — Baseball Player
6328 County Donegal Court, Charlotte NC 28277, USA

**Dunbar, Rockmond** — Actor
Untitled Entertainment, 350 S Beverly Dr, #200, Beverly Hills CA 90212 USA

**Duncan Nalasco, Mariano** — Baseball Player
Ingenio Angelina #137, San Pedro de Macoris, Dominican Republic

**Duncan, Arne** — Secretary, Education
Education Department, 400 Maryland Ave SW, Washington DC 20202 USA

**Duncan, Charles W, Jr** — Secretary, Energy
9 Briarwood Court, Houston TX 77019, USA

**Duncan, Christopher E (Chris)** — Baseball Player
6421 N Foothills Dr, Tucson AZ 85718, USA

**Duncan, Curtis E** — Football Player
4915 Glen Hollow St, Sugar Land TX 77479, USA

**Duncan, David Douglas** — Photojournalist
Castellaras Mouans-Sartoux 06370, France

**Duncan, David E (Dave)** — Baseball Player
6547 N Trunberry Dr, Tucson AZ 85718, USA

**Duncan, Giles** — Fashion Designer
Giles, Arnold Circus, London E2 7ES, England

**Duncan, Glen** — Writer
Knopf Publishers, 1745 Broadway, New York NY 10019 USA

**Duncan, Ian** — Actor
Artists Partnership, 101 Finsbury Pavement, London EC2A 1RS, England

**Duncan, Jamie R** — Football Player
217 Remi Dr, New Castle DE 19720, USA

**Duncan, Jeff** — Baseball Player
825 Lincoln Lane, Frankfort IL 60423, USA

**Duncan, Leslie H (Speedy)** — Football Player
1607 Porter Way, Stockton CA 95207, USA

**Duncan, Lindsay V** — Actress
Dalzell & Beresford, 55 Charterhouse St, Paddock Suite, London EC1M 6HA, England

**Duncan, Melvin L (Buck)** — Baseball Player
470 Bedford St, PO Box 980407, Ypsilanti MI 48198, USA

**Duncan, Peter** — Director
Cameron Creswell, 61 Marlborough St, #700, Surry Hills NSW 2010, Australia

**Duncan, Robert** — Actor
Artists Partnership, 101 Finsbury Pavement, London EC2A 1RS, England

**Duncan, Robert C** — Astrophysicist
University of Texas, Astronomy Dept, Austin TX 78712, USA

**Duncan, Robert W** — WW II Navy Air Force Hero
1511 Ryder Cup Blvd, Marion IL 62959, USA

| | |
|---|---|
| **Duncan, Sandy**<br>Douglas Gorman Rothacker Wilhelm, 1501 Broadway, #703, New York NY 10036, USA | Actress, Comedienne |
| **Duncan, Scott D**<br>Enterprise Products Partners, 1100 Louisiana St, Houston TX 77002, USA | Businessman |
| **Duncan, Shelley**<br>6421 N Foothills Dr, Tucson AZ 85718, USA | Baseball Player |
| **Duncan, Timothy T (Tim)**<br>13215 Vista del Mundo, San Antonio TX 78216, USA | Basketball Player |
| **Duncan, Whitney**<br>W B R Nashville, 20 Music Square E, Nashville TN 37203, USA | Singer, Songwriter |
| **Duncanson, Craig**<br>Laurentian University, Athletic Dept, Sudbury ON P3E 2C6, Canada | Ice Hockey Player |
| **Dundas, Jennifer**<br>Paradigm Agency, 360 N Crescent Dr, North Building, Beverly Hills CA 90210 USA | Actress |
| **Dundas, Peter H**<br>Palazzo Pucci, 6 Via de Pucci, 50122 Florence, Italy | Fashion Designer |
| **Dundas, Rocky**<br>14 Nantucket Dr, Richmond Hill ON L4E 3V1, Canada | Ice Hockey Player |
| **Dunegan, James W (Jim)**<br>20246 180th St, New London IA 52645, USA | Baseball Player |
| **Dunford, Joseph F, Jr**<br>Commandant, HqUSMC, 2 Navy Annex, Washington DC 20380 USA | Marine Corps General |
| **Dungan, Fred L (Buck)**<br>205 1/2 Avenida San Pablo, #1, San Clemente CA 92672, USA | WW II Navy Air Force Hero |
| **Dungey, Lon**<br>Auckland Actors, PO Box 56460, Auckland 1030, New Zealand | Actor |
| **Dungey, Merrin**<br>Gersh Agency, 9465 Wilshire Blvd, #600, Beverly Hills CA 90212 USA | Actress |
| **Dungy, Tony**<br>16604 Villalenda de Avila, Tampa FL 33613, USA | Football Coach |
| **Dunham, Archie W**<br>ConocoPhillips Inc, 600 N Dairy Ashford, Houston TX 77079, USA | Businessman |
| **Dunham, Chip**<br>Universal Press Syndicate, 4520 Main St, #700, Kansas City MO 64111 USA | Cartoonist (Overboard) |
| **Dunham, Lena**<br>United Talent Agency, U T A Plaza, 9336 Civic Center Dr, Beverly Hills CA 90210 USA | Writer, Film Director, Actress |
| **Dunham, Michael (Mike)**<br>39 Garfield Road, Concord MA 01742, USA | Ice Hockey Player |
| **Dunigan, Tim**<br>Hervey/Grimes Talent, 10561 Missouri Ave, #2, Los Angeles CA 90025 USA | Actor |
| **Dunitz, Jack D**<br>Obere Heslibachstr 77, 8700 Kusnacht, Switzerland | Chemist |
| **Dunkle, Nancy**<br>1350 Lorawood St, La Habra CA 90631, USA | Basketball Player |
| **Dunlap, Alexander W**<br>N A S A, Johnson Space Center, 2101 NASA Road, Houston TX 77058 USA | Astronaut |
| **Dunleavy, Mary**<br>Fletcher Artist Mgmt, 809 W 181st St, #274, New York NY 10033, USA | Opera Singer |
| **Dunleavy, Michael J (Mike), Jr**<br>Chicago Bulls, United Center, 1901 W Madison St, Chicago IL 60612 USA | Basketball Player |
| **Dunleavy, Michael J (Mike), Sr**<br>127 S Carmelina Ave, Los Angeles CA 90049, USA | Basketball Player, Coach |
| **Dunlop, Andy**<br>Wildlife Entertainment, 21 Heathmans Road, London SW6 4TJ, England | Guitarist (Travis) |
| **Dunlop, Blake**<br>8112 Maryland Ave, Saint Louis MO 63105, USA | Ice Hockey Player |
| **Dunmore, Laurence**<br>Independent Talent Group, 40 Whitfield St, London W1T 2RH, England | Director |
| **Dunn, Adam T**<br>533 Tusculum Ave, Cincinnati OH 45226, USA | Baseball Player |
| **Dunn, Andrew W**<br>525 Broadway, #250, Santa Monica CA 90401, USA | Cinematographer |
| **Dunn, Colton**<br>Paradigm Agency, 360 N Crescent Dr, North Building, Beverly Hills CA 90210 USA | Actor |
| **Dunn, Dave**<br>1433 Hamilton St, Regina SK S4H 7V4, Canada | Ice Hockey Player |
| **Dunn, Gary E**<br>243 Navajo St, Tavernier FL 33070, USA | Football Player |
| **Dunn, Holly**<br>8624 Poplar Creek Road, Nashville TN 37221, USA | Singer, Songwriter |
| **Dunn, John M**<br>Western Michigan University, President's Office, Kalamazoo MI 49008, USA | Educator |
| **Dunn, Jourdan**<br>Storm Model Agency, 5 Jubilee Place, Chelsea, London SW3 3TD, England | Model |
| **Dunn, Keldrick D (K D)**<br>1640 Township Terrace, McDonough GA 30252, USA | Football Player |
| **Dunn, Kevin**<br>Gersh Agency, 9465 Wilshire Blvd, #600, Beverly Hills CA 90212 USA | Actor |
| **Dunn, Larry**<br>Spirit Media, PO Box 43591, Phoenix AZ 85080, USA | Pianist (Earth Wind & Fire), Songwriter |
| **Dunn, Lin**<br>Indiana Fever, Conseco Fieldhouse, 125 S Pennsylvania, Indianapolis IN 46204 USA | Basketball Coach |
| **Dunn, Mignon**<br>Bloch Artists Mgmt, 360 W 28th St, #6B, New York NY 10001, USA | Opera Singer |
| **Dunn, Mike**<br>PO Box 128, Wrightsville PA 17368, USA | Drag Racing Driver |
| **Dunn, Moira**<br>15803 Bridgewater Lane, Tampa FL 33624, USA | Golfer |
| **Dunn, Nora**<br>Lighthouse Entertainment, 9220 W Sunset Blvd, #200, West Hollywood CA 90069 USA | Actress, Comedienne |
| **Dunn, Perry L**<br>64 Glenway Place, Brandon MS 39042, USA | Football Player |
| **Dunn, Richard (Richie)**<br>12229 Clarence Center Road, Akron NY 14001, USA | Ice Hockey Player |
| **Dunn, Robert F**<br>Lexington Institute, 1600 Wilson Blvd, #900, Arlington VA 22209 USA | Navy Admiral |

**D**

|  | |  |
|---|---|---|
| **Dunn, Ronald R (Ron)** | 1161 Husted Ave, San Jose CA 95125, USA | Baseball Player |
| **Dunn, Ronnie** | Spalding Entertainment, 54 Music Square E, #200, Nashville TN 37203, USA | Singer (Brooks & Dunn), Songwriter |
| **Dunn, Scott** | 1331 Arizona Ash St, San Antonio TX 78232, USA | Baseball Player |
| **Dunn, Stephen** | Stockton State College, Humanities & Fine Arts Dept, Pomona NJ 08240, USA | Writer |
| **Dunn, Steven R (Steve)** | 484 Broadmoor Dr, Maryville TN 37803, USA | Baseball Player |
| **Dunn, Susan** | Duke University, Music Dept, Durham NC 27708, USA | Opera Singer |
| **Dunn, Teala** | Abrams Artists, 275 7th Ave, #2600, New York NY 10001 USA | Actress, Singer |
| **Dunn, Theodore R (T R)** | 1014 19th St SW, Birmingham AL 35211, USA | Basketball Player |
| **Dunn, Todd K** | 12030 London Lake Dr W, Jacksonville FL 32258, USA | Baseball Player |
| **Dunn, Warrick D** | 6016 Beacon Shores St, Tampa FL 33616, USA | Football Player |
| **Dunne, Colin** | I M G Artists, Hogarth Business Park, Chiswick, London W4 2TH, England | Dancer |
| **Dunne, Griffin** | Arcieri Assoc, 305 Madison Ave, #2315, New York NY 10165 USA | Actor, Director |
| **Dunne, Michael D (Mike)** | 5115 W Ancient Oak Dr, Peoria IL 61615, USA | Baseball Player |
| **Dunne, Robin** | Empera Southpaw Productions, #317 1275 W 6th Ave, Vancouver BC V6H 1A6, Canada | Actor, Writer, Producer |
| **Dunning, Jeanne** | 2438 N Bernard St, Chicago IL 60647, USA | Artist, Photographer |
| **Dunning, John** | Pocket Books, 1230 Ave of Americas, New York NY 10020 USA | Writer |
| **Dunning, Steven J (Steve)** | 35 Prairie, Irvine CA 92618, USA | Baseball Player |
| **Dunn-Luoma, Tricia** | 4 Huson Ave, Derry NH 03038, USA | Ice Hockey Player |
| **Duno, Milka** | S A M A X Motorsports, 203 NW 16th St, Pompano Beach FL 33060, USA | Auto Racing Driver |
| **Dunphy, Marv** | 33370 Decker School Road, Malibu CA 90265, USA | Volleyball Coach |
| **Dunsky, Evan** | Creative Artists Agency, 2000 Ave of Stars, #100, Los Angeles CA 90067 USA | Director |
| **Dunsmore, Barrie** | ABC-TV, News Dept, 5010 Creston St, Hyattsville MD 20781 USA | Commentator |
| **Dunst, Kirsten** | United Talent Agency, U T A Plaza, 9336 Civic Center Dr, Beverly Hills CA 90210 USA | Actress |
| **Dunstan, A H Bernard** | 10 High Park Road, Kew, Richmond, Surrey TW9 4BH, England | Artist |
| **Dunstan, William E (Bill)** | PO Box 514, Rancho Mirage CA 92270, USA | Football Player |
| **Dunston, Shawon D** | 957 Corte del Sol, Fremont CA 94539, USA | Baseball Player |
| **Dunwoody, Ann E** | 2802 Shore Breeze Dr. Tampa FL 33611, USA | Army General |
| **Dunwoody, T Richard** | Sports Marketing, Litten, Newtown Road, Newbury, Berkshire RG14 7BB, England | Thoroughbred Racing Jockey |
| **Dunwoody, Todd F** | 1704 King Eider Dr, West Lafayette IN 47906, USA | Baseball Player |
| **DuPage, Julie** | Artmedia, 20 Ave Rapp, 75007 Paris, France | Actress |
| **Dupard, J Reginald (Reggie)** | 1316 Green Hills Court, Duncanville TX 75137, USA | Football Player |
| **Duper, Mark K** | 1905 Banks Road, Margate FL 33063, USA | Football Player |
| **Dupere, Denis** | 26 Lorraine Ave, Kitchener ON N2B 2M8, Canada | Ice Hockey Player |
| **Duperey, Anny** | Agents Associes, 201 Rue du Faubourg Saint Honore, 75008 Paris, France | Actress |
| **Duplaix, Daphnee Lynn** | Greene Assoc, 1901 Ave of Stars, #130, Los Angeles CA 90067 USA | Actress, Model |
| **Duplass, Jay** | I C M Partners, 10250 Constellation Blvd, #900, Los Angeles CA 90067 USA | Writer, Director, Actor |
| **Duplass, Mark D** | Brigade Marketing, 548 W 28th St, #670, New York NY 10001, USA | Writer, Director, Actor |
| **Dupont, Jerry** | 216 Rosemar Gardens, Richmond Hill ON L4C 3Z9, Canada | Ice Hockey Player |
| **DuPont, Pierre S, IV** | Richards Layton Finger, 1 Rodney Square, PO Box 551, Wilmington DE 19899, USA | Governor, DE |
| **Dupont, Tiffany** | Paradigm Agency, 360 N Crescent Dr, North Building, Beverly Hills CA 90210 USA | Actress |
| **Dupre, John** | University of Exeter, Genomics Center, Exeter, Devon EX4 4QJ, England | Philosopher |
| **DuPree, Billy Joe** | 3621 Llano River Trail, McKinney TX 75070, USA | Football Player |
| **Dupree, Candice** | Phoenix Mercury, American West Arena, 201 E Jefferson St, Phoenix AZ 85004 USA | Basketball Player |
| **Dupree, Mike** | 2358 E Richmond Ave, Fresno CA 93720, USA | Baseball Player |
| **DuPrez, John** | Air Edel, 18 Rodmarton St, London W1U 8BJ, England | Composer |
| **Dupri, Jermaine** | Three Rings Projects, 111 Westwood Place, #101, Brentwood TN 37027, USA | Rap Artist, Singer |
| **Dupuis, Bob** | 446 Algonquin Ave, North Bay ON P1B 4W5, Canada | Ice Hockey Player |
| **Dupuis, Roy** | Agence Premier Role, 3451 Hotel de Ville, Montreal QC H2X 3B5, Canada | Actor |

**Dunn - Dupuis**

**Duque, Pedro** — Astronaut, Spain
European Space Center, Linder Hohe, Box 906096, 51127 Cologne, Germany
**Durack, David T** — Physician, Microbiologist, Internist
3306 Pinafore Dr, Durham NC 27705, USA
**Duran, Daniel J (Dan)** — Baseball Player
493 Maxine Court, Sunnyvale CA 94086, USA
**Duran, Elise** — Producer, Director, Writer
Creative Artists Agency, 2000 Ave of Stars, #100, Los Angeles CA 90067 USA
**Duran, Roberto** — Boxer
Calle F El Cangrejo, Casa 33, Panama City, Panama
**Durance, Erica** — Actress
Gersh Agency, 9465 Wilshire Blvd, #600, Beverly Hills CA 90212 USA
**Durand, Kevin** — Actor
Alchemy Entertainment, 7024 Melrose Ave, #420, Los Angeles CA 90038 USA
**Durang, Christopher** — Writer
I C M Partners, 730 5th Ave, New York NY 10019 USA
**Durant, Graham J** — Inventor (Antiulcer Compound)
Cambridge NeuroScience, 333 Boston Providence Turnpike, Norwood MA 02062, USA
**Durant, Joseph S (Joe)** — Golfer
PO Box 910, Gulf Breeze FL 32562, USA
**Durant, Kevin** — Basketball Player
Oklahoma City Thunder, 211 N Robinson Ave, #300, Oklahoma City OK 73102 USA
**Durant, Michael J (Mike)** — Baseball Player
7520 Marston Lane, Dublin OH 43016, USA
**Durante, Viviana P** — Ballerina
20 Bristol Gardens, Little Venice, London W9, England
**Durazo Cardenas, Erubiel** — Baseball Player
3800 S Cantabria Circle, #1079, Chandler AZ 85248, USA
**Durban, Manfred** — Singer (Die Flippers)
Die Flippers, August Lammle Str 14, 75438 Knittlingen, Germany
**Durbin, Chad G** — Baseball Player
17918 Jefferson Ridge Dr, Baton Rouge LA 70817, USA
**Durbin, Michael W (Mike)** — Bowler
1042 Wilshire Dr, Roanoke TX 76262, USA
**Duren, Clarence E** — Football Player
201 W 54th St, Los Angeles CA 90037, USA
**Duren, John T** — Basketball Player
1107 1st St NW, Washington DC 20001, USA
**Durham, Joseph V (Joe)** — Baseball Player
9715 Mendoza Road, Randallstown MD 21133, USA
**Duris, Romain** — Actor
Agents Associes, 201 Rue du Faubourg Saint Honore, 75008 Paris, France
**Duritz, Adam** — Singer (Counting Crowes), Lyricist
Interscope/Geffen Records, 2220 Colorado Ave, #300, Santa Monica CA 90404, USA
**Durjan'narc, Ogan** — Conductor, Composer
Moscow Symphony Orchestra, Gorky Park, 9 Krymsky Val, 119049 Moscow, Russia
**Durkin, Clare** — Model
Models 1, 12 Macklin St, Covent Garden, London WC2B 5SZ, England
**Durr Browning, Francoise** — Tennis Player
195 Rue de Lourmel, 75015 Paris, France
**Durr, Jason** — Actor
S D B Partners, 315 S Beverly Dr, #411, Beverly Hills CA 90067 USA
**Durrance, Samuel T** — Astronaut, Astronomer
770 Kerry Downs Circle, Melbourne FL 32940, USA
**Durrant, Jennifer A** — Artist
9-10 Holly Grove, London SE15 5DF, England
**Durrett, Richard T** — Mathematician
Duke University, Mathematics Dept, Durham NC 27708, USA
**Durrington, Trent J** — Baseball Player
499 N Canon Dr, #400, Beverly Hills CA 90210, USA
**Durst, W Frederick (Fred)** — Musician (Limp Bizkit), Director
KillerMoxie Mgmt, 5890 W Jefferson Blvd, #J, Los Angeles CA 90016, USA
**Durst, Will** — Actor, Comedian
Entertainment Alliance, PO Box 1544, Mendocino CA 95460, USA
**Dusard, Jay** — Photogapher
5261 N Stewart Ranch Road, Douglas AZ 85607, USA
**Dusay, Marj** — Actress
1964 Westwood Blvd, #6F, New York NY 10025, USA
**Dusek, J Bradley (Brad)** — Football Player
4th Quarter Ranch, 8311 FM 2086, Temple TX 76501, USA
**Dusenberg, Walter** — Sculptor
Stone Mill Hall, 109 Cemetery Road, Fly Creek NY 13337, USA
**Dusenberry, Ann** — Actress
1615 San Leandro Lane, Santa Barbara CA 93108, USA
**Duser, Carl R** — Baseball Player
3021 Cornwall Road, Bethlehem PA 18017, USA
**Dushku, Eliza** — Actress, Producer, Director
United Talent Agency, U T A Plaza, 9336 Civic Center Dr, Beverly Hills CA 90210 USA
**Dussault, Jean H** — Endocrinologist
Laval Medical Center, 2705 Blvd Laurier, Sainte Foy QC G1V 4G2, Canada
**Dussault, Nancy** — Actress, Singer
4406 Moorpark Way, Toluca Lake CA 91602, USA
**Dussollier, Andre** — Actor
Artmedia, 20 Ave Rapp, 75007 Paris, France
**Dustal, Robert A (Bob)** — Baseball Player
625 Marian Lane, Lakeland FL 33813, USA
**Dutch, Deborah** — Actress
Jack Scagnetti Talent Agency, 5118 Vineland Ave, North Hollywood CA 91601, USA
**Dutoit, Charles E** — Conductor
Montreal Symphony, 260 Blvd Maisonneuve W, Montreal QC H2X 1Y9, Canada
**DuToit, Elize** — Actress
Special Artists Agency, 9200 Sunset Blvd, #410, West Hollywood CA 90069 USA
**Dutronc, Jacques** — Actor
Voyez Mon Agent, 20 Ave Rapp, 75007 Paris, France
**Dutrow, Richard E (Rick), Jr** — Thoroughbred Racing Trainer
2 The Howl W, East Norwich NY 11732, USA

**Dutt, Hank** — Concert Violist (Kronos Quartet)
Kronos Quartet, 1235 9th Ave, San Francisco CA 94122, USA

**Dutt, Sanjay** — Actor
58 Smt Nargis Dutt Road, Pali Hill Bandra (W), Mumbai MS 400050, India

**Dutta Bhupathi, Lara** — Beauty Queen, Actress, Model
401 Merry Ville, 25 Saint Andrews Road, Bandra (W), Mumbai 400050, India

**Dutton, Charles S** — Actor, Director
Greene Assoc, 1901 Ave of Stars, #130, Los Angeles CA 90067 USA

**Dutton, James P (Jim), Jr** — Astronaut
1604 Mossy Stone Dr, Friendswood TX 77546, USA

**Dutton, John O** — Football Player
5706 Moss Creek Trail, Dallas TX 75252, USA

**Dutton, Lawrence** — Violist (Emerson String Quartet)
I M G Artists, Burlington Lane, Chiswick, London W4 2TH, England

**Dutton, Simon** — Actor
Marmont Mgmt, Langham House, 302/8 Regent St, London W1R 5AL, England

**Duty, Kenton** — Actor
Osbrink Talent Agency, 4343 Lankershim Blvd, #100, North Hollywood CA 91602 USA

**Duva, Louis (Lou)** — Boxing Promoter, Trainer, Manager
Main Events, 811 Totowa Road, #100, Totowa NJ 07512, USA

**Duval, David R** — Golfer
11 Parkway Dr, Englewood CO 80113, USA

**Duval, Dennis** — Basketball Player
8105 Verbeck Dr, Manlius NY 13104, USA

**Duval, Helen** — Bowler
PO Box 2071, Oakland CA 94604, USA

**Duval, James** — Actor
Artistry Mgmt, 340 N Camden Dr, #302, Beverly Hills CA 90210, USA

**Duval, Michael A (Mike)** — Baseball Player
2743 Nature Pointe Loop, Fort Myers FL 33905, USA

**DuVall, Clea** — Actress
Framework Entertainment, 9057 Nemo St, #C, West Hollywood CA 90069 USA

**Duvall, Jed** — Commentator
ABC-TV, News Dept, 5010 Creston St, Hyattsville MD 20781 USA

**Duvall, Robert** — Actor
I C M Partners, 10250 Constellation Blvd, #900, Los Angeles CA 90067 USA

**Duvall, Sammy** — Water Skier
PO Box 871, Windermere FL 34786, USA

**Duvall, Vincent** — Actor, Producer, Director
Cenzo Media, 8721 Santa Monica Blvd, #332, Los Angeles CA 90069, USA

**Duvauchelle, Nicolas** — Actor
U B B A, 6 Rue de Braque, 75003 Paris, France

**DuVernay, Ava** — Director
DuVernay Agency, 4515 Van Nuys Blvd, #402, Sherman Oaks CA 91403, USA

**Duvert, Michael** — Actor
Liebman Entertainment, 25 E 21st St, #PH, New York NY 10010, USA

**Duvillard, Henri** — Alpine Skier
Le Mont d'Arbois, 74120 Megere, France

**Duwelius, Rich** — Volleyball Player
266 Stoddards Wharf Road, Gales Ferry CT 06335, USA

**Dvorak, Radek** — Ice Hockey Player
10342 Lexington Estates Blvd, Boca Raton FL 33428, USA

**Dvorak, Tomas** — Track Athlete
Stadium Juliska, 16000 Prague 6, Czech Republic

**Dvorak, Wayne C** — Actor
2204 Stanley Hills Dr, Los Angeles CA 90046, USA

**Dvorsky, Peter** — Opera Singer
J Hronca 1A, 84102 Bratislava, Slovakia

**Dweck, Michael** — Photographer
Staley-Wise Gallery, 560 Broadway, New York NY 10012, USA

**Dwight, Edward, Jr** — Astronaut
4022 Montview Blvd, Denver CO 80207, USA

**Dwight, Timothy J (Tim), Jr** — Football Player
26164 Indigo Dr, Park Rapids MN 56470, USA

**Dworaczyk, Hope** — Model
Playboy Promotions, 9346 Civic Center Dr, #200, Beverly Hills CA 90210 USA

**Dwork, Melvin** — Interior Designer
Melvin Dwork Inc, 50 Murray St, #1710, New York NY 10007, USA

**Dworkin, Martin** — Microbiologist
2123 Hoyt Ave W, Saint Paul MN 55108, USA

**Dworkins, Lenny** — Cartoonist (Buck Rogers)
2906 Wilmette Ave, Wilmette IL 60091, USA

**Dworsky, Daniel L (Dan)** — Football Player, Architect
9225 Nightingale Dr, Los Angeles CA 90069, USA

**Dwurnik, Edward** — Artist
Ul Podgorska 5, 02 921 Warsaw, Poland

**Dwyer, James E (Jim)** — Baseball Player
826 Hancock Bridge Parkway, Cape Coral FL 33990, USA

**Dwyer, Jim** — Journalist
New York Times, Editorial Dept, 229 W 43rd St, New York NY 10036 USA

**Dwyer, Karyn** — Actress
Oscars Abrams Zimel, 438 Queen St E, Toronto ON M5A 1T4, Canada

**Dyas, Guy Hendrix** — Production Designer
United Talent Agency, U T A Plaza, 9336 Civic Center Dr, Beverly Hills CA 90210 USA

**Dybzinski, Jerome M (Jerry)** — Baseball Player
1626 Haywood Place, Fort Collins CO 80526, USA

**Dychtwald, Ken** — Psychologist
Age Wave Inc, 1900 Powell St, Emeryville CA 94608, USA

**Dye, Ernest T** — Football Player
580 Bienville Court, Alpharetta GA 30004, USA

**Dye, Ian** — Composer
Gorfaine/Schwartz, 4111 W Alameda Ave, #509, Burbank CA 91505, USA

**Dye, Jermaine T** — Baseball Player
18776 Heritage Dr, Poway CA 92064, USA

**Dye, Lee** — Golf Course Architect
Dye Designs, 5500 E Yale Ave, #300, Denver CO 80222, USA

**Dye, Melissa Dori** — Singer, Songwriter
Dye Productions, 5403 Everhart Road, #140, Corpus Christi TX 78411, USA

**Dye, Paul B (Pete)** — Golf Course Architect
3247 Polo Dr, Delray Beach FL 33483, USA

**Dyer, Danny** — Actor
Independent Talent Group, 40 Whitfield St, London W1T 2RH, England

**Dyer, Donald R (Duffy)** — Baseball Player
742 W Las Palmaritas Dr, Phoenix AZ 85021, USA

**Dyk, Timothy B** — Judge
US Court of Appeals, 717 Madison Place NW, Washington DC 20439, USA

**Dyka, Oksana** — Opera Singer
I M G Artists, Hogarth Business Park, Chiswick, London W4 2TH, England

**Dyke, Charles W** — Army General, Association Executive
International Technical/Trade Assoc, 1330 Connecticut NW, Washington DC 20036, USA

**Dykema, Craig** — Basketball Player
10525 Destino St, Bellflower CA 90706, USA

**Dykers, Craig** — Architect
Snohetta, Skur 39, Vippetangen, 0150 Oslo, Norway

**Dykes Bower, John** — Concert Organist
42 Artillery Mansions, Westminster, London SW1P 1RR, England

**Dykinga, Jack** — Photojournalist
1519 E Tascal Loop, Tucson AZ 85737, USA

**Dykstra, John** — Artist, Animator, Cinematographer
15060 Encanto Dr, Sherman Oaks CA 91403, USA

**Dykstra, Leonard K (Lenny)** — Baseball Player
10550 Wilshire Blvd, #1203, Los Angeles CA 90024, USA

**Dylan, Bob** — Singer, Songwriter
Creative Artists Agency, 2000 Ave of Stars, #100, Los Angeles CA 90067 USA

**Dylan, Jakob** — Singer, Guitarist (Wallflowers)
Paradigm Agency, 360 N Crescent Dr, North Building, Beverly Hills CA 90210 USA

**Dylan, Jesse** — Director
Creative Artists Agency, 2000 Ave of Stars, #100, Los Angeles CA 90067 USA

**Dymott, Adiam** — Singer
Agency Group Ltd, 361-373 City Road, London EC1V 1PQ, England

**Dynarski, Eugene (Gene)** — Actor
Victor Kruglov Talent Mgmt, 6565 Sunset Blvd, #280, Los Angeles CA 90028, USA

**Dyrason, Orri Pall** — Drummer, Keyboardist (Sigur Ros)
Music Road Records, 5012 Brighton Road, Austin TX 78745, USA

**Dyrdek, Robert D (Rob)** — Skateboarder, Actor
I C M Partners, Marlborough House, 10 Earlham St, #300, London WC2H 9LNP, England

**Dyroen-Lancer, Rebekah (Becky)** — Sychronized Swimmer
31101 Via Madera, San Juan Capistrano CA 92675, USA

**Dysart, Richard** — Actor
654 Copeland Court, Santa Monica CA 90405, USA

**Dyson, Andre** — Football Player
3367 N Shoreline Circle, Layton UT 84040, USA

**Dyson, Esther** — Businesswoman, Writer
Edventure Holdings, 104 5th Ave, #2000, New York NY 10011, USA

**Dyson, Freeman J** — Physicist, Templeton Religion Laureate
105 Battle Road Circle, Princeton NJ 08540, USA

**Dyson, James** — Industrial Designer
Dyson Appliances, Tetbury Hill, Malmesbury Wiltshire SN16 0RP, England

**Dyson, Kevin T** — Football Player
3109 Chase Point Dr, Franklin TN 37067, USA

**Dyson, Michael Eric** — Writer
DePaul University, English Dept, Chicago IL 60604, USA

**Dzau, Victor J** — Molecular Biologist
Duke University Health System, Chancellor's Office, Durham NC 27708, USA

**Dzhanibekov, Vladimir A** — Cosmonaut, Air Force General
Cosmonaut Training Center, Star City, 141160 Zvezdny Gorodok, Moscow Oblast, Russia

**Dzhyma, Juliya** — Biathlete
Biathlon Federation, Vul Dimitrova 6, 03680 Kiev, Ukraine

**Dziedzic, Joe** — Ice Hockey Player
2195 Marion Road, Saint Paul MN 55113, USA

**Dziedzic, Stanley** — Freestyle Wrestler
835 Hedgegate Court, Roswell GA 30075, USA

**Dziena, Alexis** — Actress
Paradigm Agency, 360 N Crescent Dr, North Building, Beverly Hills CA 90210 USA

**Dziewonski, Adam M** — Seismologist, Geophysicist
Harvard University, Seismology Dept, Cambridge MA 02138, USA

**Dziubinska, Anulka** — Model, Actress
Playboy Promotions, 9346 Civic Center Dr, #200, Beverly Hills CA 90210 USA

**Dziwisz, Stanislaw Cardinal** — Religious Leader
Archdiocese of Cracow, Ul Franciszkanska 3, 31004 Cracow, Poland

**Dzomba, Mirza** — Handball Player
Antuna Branko Simica 27, 51000 Rijeka, Croatia

**Dzundza, George** — Actor
PO Box 133, Netarts OR 97143, USA

**Dzyaloshinskii, Igor E** — Physicist
University of California, Physics Dept, Irvine CA 92697, USA

# E

| | |
|---|---|
| **Eackles, Ledell** | Basketball Player |
| 9134 Elmgrove Garden Dr, Baton Rouge LA 70807, USA | |
| **Eade, George J** | Air Force General |
| 1131 Sunnyside Dr, Healdsburg CA 95448, USA | |
| **Eads, George** | Actor |
| Innovative Artists, 1505 10th St, Santa Monica CA 90401 USA | |
| **Eagle, Ian** | Sportscaster |
| CBS-TV, Sports Dept, 51 W 52nd St, New York NY 10019 USA | |
| **Eagles, Mike** | Ice Hockey Player |
| 59 Abbott Court, Fredericton NB E3B 5V8, Canada | |
| **Eagling, Wayne J** | Ballet Dancer, Choreographer |
| Postbus 16486, 1001 Amsterdam RN, Netherlands | |
| **Eakes, Bobbie** | Actress, Singer |
| Bauman Redanty Shaul Agency, 5757 Wilshire Blvd, #473, Los Angeles CA 90036 USA | |
| **Eakin, Thomas C** | Businessman |
| 245 Sandover Dr, Aurora OH 44202, USA | |
| **Eakins, Dallas F** | Ice Hockey Player, Coach |
| 19705 N 84th Way, Scottsdale AZ 85255, USA | |
| **Eakins, James S (Jim)** | Basketball Player |
| 2575 Little Cottonwood Road, Sandy UT 84092, USA | |
| **Ealy, Michael** | Actor |
| Epidemic Pictures, 1635 N Cahuenga Blvd, #500, Los Angeles CA 90028, USA | |
| **Eanes, Antonio dos Santos Ramalho** | President, Portugal; Army General |
| Partido Renovador Democratico, Travessa do Falo 9, 1200 Lisbon, Portugal | |
| **Earl, Anthony S** | Governor, WI |
| Quarles & Brady, 1st Wisconsin Plaza, 1 S Pinckney St, Madison WI 53703, USA | |
| **Earl, Robin D** | Football Player |
| 395 Oak Creek Dr, #415, Wheeling IL 60090, USA | |
| **Earl, Roger** | Drummer (Foghat) |
| Lustig Talent, PO Box 770850, Orlando FL 32877 USA | |
| **Earle Mead, Sylvia A** | Oceanographer |
| 12812 Skyline Blvd, Oakland CA 94619, USA | |
| **Earle, Acie B** | Basketball Player |
| 2301 14th Ave, Moline IL 61265, USA | |
| **Earle, Steve** | Singer, Guitarist, Songwriter |
| Gold Village Entertainment, 72 Madison Ave, #800, New York NY 10016, USA | |
| **Earles, Jason** | Actor |
| C E S D, 10635 Santa Monica Blvd, #130, Los Angeles CA 90025 USA | |
| **Earley, Liz** | Golfer |
| 24 Morton Dr, Buffalo NY 14226, USA | |
| **Early, Gerald L** | Writer, Educator |
| Washington University, English Dept, McMillan Hall, Saint Louis MO 63130, USA | |
| **Early, Quinn R** | Football Player |
| PO Box 675752, Rancho Santa Fe CA 92067, USA | |
| **Earnhardt, R Dale, Jr** | Auto Racing Driver |
| 955 Shinnville Road, Mooresville NC 28115, USA | |
| **Earp, Mildred** | Baseball Player |
| 217 Dolly, West Fork AR 72774, USA | |
| **Easler, Michael A (Mike)** | Baseball Player |
| 2824 White Peaks Ave, North Las Vegas NV 89081, USA | |
| **Easley, Bill** | Jazz Saxophonist, Clarinetist, Flutist |
| Hot Jazz Mgmt, 116 E 27th St, New York NY 10016, USA | |
| **Easley, J Damion** | Baseball Player |
| 6420 W Line Dr, Glendale AZ 85310, USA | |
| **Easley, Kenny M (Ken)** | Football Player |
| 3906 Kegagie Dr, Norfolk VA 23518, USA | |
| **Eason, Bo** | Football Player, Actor, Writer |
| Creative Artists Agency, 2000 Ave of Stars, #100, Los Angeles CA 90067 USA | |
| **Eason, Charles C (Tony), IV** | Football Player |
| PO Box 340, Walnut Grove CA 95690, USA | |
| **East, Clyde B** | WW II Army Air Corps Hero |
| 21301 Erwin St, #221, Woodland Hills CA 91367, USA | |
| **East, Jeff** | Actor |
| 99 Spinfdrift Dr, Rancho Palos Verdes CA 90275, USA | |
| **East, Ronald A (Ron)** | Football Player |
| PO Box 3442, Redmond WA 98073, USA | |
| **Easter, Robert A** | Educator |
| University of Illinois, President's Office, 506 S Wright St, Urbana IL 61801, USA | |
| **Easterbrook, Frank H** | Judge |
| US Court of Appeals, 219 S Dearborn St, #2302B, Chicago IL 60604, USA | |
| **Easterbrook, Leslie** | Actress, Singer |
| Tufield Entertainment, 19521 Rosita St, Tarzana CA 91356, USA | |
| **Easterlin, Richard A** | Economist |
| 329 Patrician Way, Pasadena CA 91105, USA | |
| **Easterly, James M (Jamie)** | Baseball Player |
| 1306 Plantation Dr, Crockett TX 75835, USA | |
| **Eastin, Jeff** | Producer, Writer |
| Creative Artists Agency, 2000 Ave of Stars, #100, Los Angeles CA 90067 USA | |
| **Eastman, Dean E** | Physicist |
| 336 Coonley Road, Riverside IL 60546, USA | |
| **Eastman, John** | Attorney |
| Eastman & Eastman, 39 W 54th St, #200, New York NY 10019, USA | |
| **Eastman, Kevin** | Cartoonist (Ninja Turtles) |
| 1527 N Wickiup Road, Apache Junction AZ 85119, USA | |
| **Eastman, Marilyn** | Actress |
| Greater Talent Network, 437 5th Ave, #700, New York NY 10016, USA | |
| **Easton, David Anthony** | Interior Designer |
| 72 Spring St, #700, New York NY 10012, USA | |
| **Easton, Michael** | Actor |
| 2810 Baseline Trail, Los Angeles CA 90068, USA | |
| **Easton, Sheena** | Singer, Actress |
| Vox Inc, 6420 Wilshire Blvd, #1080, Los Angeles CA 90048 USA | |
| **Eastwick, Rawlins J (Rawly)** | Baseball Player |
| 10 River Meadow Dr, West Newbury MA 01985, USA | |
| **Eastwood, Clint** | Director, Actor |
| Hogs Breath Inn, Carlos St, PO Box 4366, Carmel by the Sea CA 93921, USA | |

**Eastwood, Jayne** — Actress
Premier Artists Mgmt, 273 Eglinton Ave E, Toronto ON M4P 1L3, Canada

**Eastwood, Kyle** — Jazz Guitarist
Chapman Co, 14011 Ventura Blvd, #405, Sherman Oaks CA 91403, USA

**Eastwood, Michael B (Mike)** — Ice Hockey Player
Sports Radio 1200 the Team, 87 George St, Ottawa ON K1N 9H7, Canada

**Eastwood, Robert F (Bob)** — Golfer
PO Box 14769, Haltom City TX 76117, USA

**Easum, Donald B** — Diplomat
1940 Inverness Dr, Scotch Plains NJ 07076, USA

**Eathorne, A J** — Golfer
23023 N 25th Place, Phoenix AZ 85024, USA

**Eaton, Adam T** — Baseball Player
17404 NE 126th Place, Redmond WA 98052, USA

**Eaton, Ashton E** — Decathlete
Oregon Track Club, PO Box 11364, Eugene OR 97440, USA

**Eaton, John C** — Composer
4585 N Hartstrait Road, Bloomington IN 47404, USA

**Eaton, Mark A** — Ice Hockey Player
3 Fieldstone Circle, Greenville RI 02828, USA

**Eaton, Mark E** — Basketball Player
2104 Dayton Ave NE, Renton WA 98056, USA

**Eaton, Meredith** — Actress
Amsel Eisenstadt Frazier, 5055 Wilshire Blvd, #865, Los Angeles CA 90036 USA

**Eaton, Rebecca** — Producer
Masterpiece Theater, WGBH-TV, 1 Guest St, Brighton MA 02135, USA

**Eaton, Shirley** — Actress
Diamond Mgmt, 31 Percy St, London W1T 2DD, England

**Eaton, T Scott** — Football Player
3950 W Lake Sammamish Parkway SE, Bellevue WA 98008, USA

**Eaton, Tracey B** — Football Player
PO Box 881, Preston WA 98050, USA

**Eatough, Jeff** — Ice Hockey Player
2050 Insley Road, Mississauga ON L4Y 1P9, Canada

**Eaves, Jerry L** — Basketball Player
10 Perch Place, Greensboro NC 27455, USA

**Eaves, Michael G (Mike)** — Ice Hockey Player, Coach
3615 Culver Trail, Faribault MN 55021, USA

**Eaves, Patrick C** — Ice Hockey Player
18125 Laurel Springs Court, Northville MI 48168, USA

**Ebadi, Shirin** — Nobel Peace Laureate
University of Tehran, Enghelab Ave & 16 Azar St, 14174 Tehran, Iran

**Ebanks, Selita** — Model
Women Model Mgmt, 199 Lafayette St, #700, New York NY 10012 USA

**Ebashi, Setsuro** — Biophysicist, Pharmacologist
17-503 Nagaizumi Myodaiji, Okazaki 444 0864, Japan

**Ebbesen, Thomas W** — Physical Chemist
Louis Pasteur University, 4 rue Blaise Pascal, 67081 Strasbourg Cedex 2010, France

**Ebel, David M** — Judge
US Court of Appeals, US Courthouse, 1929 Stout St, Denver CO 80294, USA

**Eberhart, Ralph E (Ed)** — Air Force General
Armed Forces Benefit Assn, 909 N Washington St, #767, Alexandria VA 22314, USA

**Eberharter, Stephan (Steff)** — Alpine Skier
Dorfstr 21, 6272 Stumm, Austria

**Eberle, Markus** — Alpine Skier
Unterwestweg 27, 87567 Riezlern, Germany

**Ebersol, Dick** — Businessman
174 West St, #54, Litchfield CT 06759, USA

**Ebersole, Christine** — Actress, Singer
A P A Talent & Literary Agency, 405 S Beverly Dr, #300, Beverly Hills CA 90212 USA

**Ebersole, John J** — Football Player
1470 Village Square, Mount Pleasant SC 29464, USA

**Ebert, Alex** — Singer (Edward Sharpe & Magnetic Zeroes)
KillerMoxie Management, 5890 W Jefferson Blvd, #J, Los Angeles CA 90016, USA

**Ebert, Peter** — Opera Director
Col di Mura, 06010 Lippiano, Italy

**Ebnoether, Luzia** — Curling Athlete
Curling Association, PO Box 606, 3000 Bern, Switzerland

**Ebsen, Bonnie** — Actress
PO Box 356, Agoura CA 91376, USA

**Ebstein, Katja** — Singer
Katja Ebstein Stiftung, Competence Center, Gotlandstr 5, 10439 Berlin, Germany

**Eby, Betsy** — Artist
Winston Wachter Fine Art, 39 E 78th St, New York NY 10075, USA

**Eccles, Spencer F** — Financier
Wells Fargo Bank, 299 S Main St, #400, Salt Lake City UT 84111, USA

**Eccleston, Christopher** — Actor
Independent Talent Group, 40 Whitfield St, London W1T 2RH, England

**Ecclestone, Bernie** — Auto Racing Executive
Formula One Ltd, 6 Prince's Gate, London SW7 1QJ, England

**Ecclestone, Tamara** — Actress, Model
Lucy Hibbard, 6 Princes Gate, London SW7 1QJ, England

**Ecclestone, Timothy J (Tim)** — Ice Hockey Player
10095 Fairway Village Dr, Roswell GA 30076, USA

**Echevarria, Angel S** — Baseball Player
23830 231st Place SE, Maple Valley WA 98038, USA

**Echeverria Alvarez, Luis** — President, Mexico
Magnolia 131, San Jeronimo Lidice, Magdalena Contreras CP 10200, Mexico

**Echikunwoke, Megalyn** — Actress
United Talent Agency, U T A Plaza, 9336 Civic Center Dr, Beverly Hills CA 90210 USA

**Eckbauer, Edith** — Rowing Athlete
Dreisbuschstr 15, 82327 Tutzing, Germany

**Ecker, Haylie** — Violinist
Mel Bush, Tanglewood, Arrowsmith Road, Wimborne, Dorset BH21 2BS, England

**Eckersley, Dennis L** — Baseball Player
6 Macy Lane, Ipswich MA 01938, USA

# E

|  |  |
|---|---|
| **Eckert, Shari**<br>PO Box 5761, Sherman Oaks CA 91413, USA | Actress, Model |
| **Eckhart, Aaron**<br>Creative Artists Agency, 2000 Ave of Stars, #100, Los Angeles CA 90067 USA | Actor |
| **Eckhoff, Tiril K**<br>Underhaugsvegen 12, 7023 Trondheim, Norway | Biathlete |
| **Eckholdt, Steven**<br>Brady Brannon Rich, 5670 Wilshire Blvd, #820, Los Angeles CA 90036 USA | Actor, Producer |
| **Eckstein, David M**<br>6969 Sylvan Woods Dr, Sanford FL 32771, USA | Baseball Player |
| **Eco, Umberto**<br>Piazza Castello 13, 20121 Milan, Italy | Writer, Educator |
| **Edberg, Stefan**<br>Storgatan 8, 352 31 Vaxjo, Sweden | Tennis Player |
| **Eddery, Patrick J**<br>Musk Hill Farm, Nether Winchendon, Aylesbury, Bucks HP18 0DT, England | Thoroughbred Racing Jockey |
| **Eddings, Douglas L (Doug)**<br>8072 Constitution Road, Las Cruces NM 88007, USA | Baseball Umpire |
| **Eddington, Roderick I (Rod)**<br>British Airways, Waterside, PO Box 365, Harmondsworth UB7 0GB, England | Businessman |
| **Eddy, Duane**<br>1906 Chet Atkins Blvd, #502, Nashville TN 37212, USA | Singer, Songwriter, Guitarist |
| **Edel, Uli**<br>Gersh Agency, 9465 Wilshire Blvd, #600, Beverly Hills CA 90212 USA | Director |
| **Edell, Marc Z**<br>Budd Larner Gross, 150 John F Kennedy Parkway, #301, Short Hills NJ 07078, USA | Attorney |
| **Edelman, Brad M**<br>828 Royal St, #410, New Orleans LA 70116, USA | Football Player |
| **Edelman, Elazer R**<br>Harvard-MIT Biomedical Center, 77 Massachusetts Ave, Cambridge MA 02139, USA | Cardiologist |
| **Edelman, Ian**<br>United Talent Agency, U T A Plaza, 9336 Civic Center Dr, Beverly Hills CA 90210 USA | Producer, Writer |
| **Edelman, Marian Wright**<br>Children's Defense Fund, 25 E St NW, Washington DC 20001, USA | Association Executive |
| **Edelman, Pawel**<br>I C M Partners, 10250 Constellation Blvd, #900, Los Angeles CA 90067 USA | Cinematographer |
| **Edelman, Randy**<br>Gorfaine/Schwartz, 4111 W Alameda Ave, #509, Burbank CA 91505 USA | Composer |
| **Edelstein, Jean**<br>48 Brooks Ave, Venice CA 90291, USA | Artist |
| **Edelstein, Lisa**<br>Water Street Anthem Entertainment, 5225 Wilshire Blvd, #615, Los Angeles CA 90036 USA | Actress |
| **Edelstein, Victor A**<br>3 Stanhope Mews West, London SW7 5RB, England | Fashion Designer, Artist |
| **Eden, Barbara**<br>9816 Denbigh Dr, Beverly Hills CA 90210, USA | Actress |
| **Eden, Richard**<br>Abrams Artists, 9200 W Sunset Blvd, #1125, West Hollywood CA 90069 USA | Actor |
| **Edens, Thomas P (Tom)**<br>2033 Quailridge Court, Clarkston WA 99403, USA | Baseball Player |
| **Eder, Simon**<br>Obsmarkstr 14/4, 5760 Saalfeldem, Austria | Biathlete |
| **Edestrand, Darryl**<br>391 Beechwood Ave, London ON N6J 3J9, Canada | Ice Hockey Player |
| **Edgar, David**<br>Alan Brodie Representation, 211 Piccadilly, London W1V 9LD, England | Writer |
| **Edgar, David (Dave)**<br>2633 Middle River Dr, #3, Fort Lauderdale FL 33306, USA | Swimmer |
| **Edgar, James (Jim)**<br>University of Illinois, Public Affairs Institute, Urbana IL 61801, USA | Governor, IL |
| **Edgar, Ross**<br>Ashwood Laboratories, Brockhall Village, Blackburn, Lancashire BB6 8BB, England | Cyclist |
| **Edge**<br>Regine Moylet, 9 Ivebury Court, 325 Latimer Road, London W10 6RA, England | Guitarist (U-2), Singer |
| **Edge, Graeme**<br>Insight Mgmt, 1222 16th Ave S, #300, Nashville TN 37212, USA | Drummer (Moody Blues) |
| **Edge, Mitzi**<br>118 Kings Chapel Road, Augusta GA 30907, USA | Golfer |
| **Edgerson, Booker T**<br>68 Union Common, Buffalo NY 14221, USA | Football Player |
| **Edgerton, Joel**<br>Blue-Tongue Films, PO Box 873, Darlinghurst, Sydney NSW 1300, Australia | Actor |
| **Edgley, Gigi**<br>Soverign Talent Group, 8421 Wilshire Blvd, #200, Beverly Hills CA 90211, USA | Actress, Singer |
| **Edin, Niklas**<br>Brogatan 5, 654 55 Karlstad, Sweden | Curling Athlete |
| **Edinger, Paul E, IV**<br>2313 York Place, Lakeland FL 33810, USA | Football Player |
| **Edler, Alexander**<br>Taptogrand 8, 831 38 Ostersund, Sweden | Ice Hockey Player |
| **Edlund, Ben**<br>United Talent Agency, U T A Plaza, 9336 Civic Center Dr, Beverly Hills CA 90210 USA | Comic Book Artist, Animator |
| **Edlund, Richard P**<br>2710 Wilshire Blvd, Santa Monica CA 90403, USA | Cinematographer |
| **Edmonds, Albert J (Al)**<br>Military Officers Assn, 201 N Washington St, Alexandria VA 22314, USA | Air Force General |
| **Edmonds, Jacque**<br>Collective, 8383 Wilshire Blvd, #1050, Beverly Hills CA 90211 USA | Producer, Writer |
| **Edmonds, James P (Jim)**<br>25 Boulder View, Irvine CA 92603, USA | Baseball Player |
| **Edmonds, Kenneth (Babyface)**<br>Creative Artists Agency, 2000 Ave of Stars, #100, Los Angeles CA 90067 USA | Singer, Keyboardist, Songwriter |
| **Edmonds, Tracey E**<br>Our Stories Films, 1635 N Cahuenga Blvd, Los Angeles CA 90028, USA | Actress, Producer |
| **Edmondson, Adrian**<br>Jonathan Altaras Assoc, 11 Garrick St, London WC2E 9AR, England | Actor, Writer, Director |

**Edmondson, Jaime Faith** — Model
Playboy Promotions, 9346 Civic Center Dr, #200, Beverly Hills CA 90210 USA
**Edmondson, James L (J L)** — Judge
US Court of Appeals, 56 Forsyth St NW, Atlanta GA 30303, USA
**Edmondson, Sarah** — Actress
Characters Talent Mgmt, 8 Elm St, Toronto ON M5G 1G7, Canada
**Edmunds, Dave** — Singer, Guitarist, Songwriter
A B S Agency, PO Box 932A, Sirbiton KT1 9QR, England
**Edmunds, Ferrell, Jr** — Football Player
PO Box 414, Blairs VA 24527, USA
**Edmundson, Gary** — Ice Hockey Player
Silvercrest Western Homes, 299 N Smith Ave, Corona CA 92880, USA
**Edner, Ashley** — Actress
10061 Riverside Dr, #341, North Hollywood CA 91602, USA
**Edney, Leon A (Bud)** — Navy Admiral
1037 Encino Row, Coronado CA 92118, USA
**Edney, Tyus D** — Basketball Player
1800 S Floyd Court, La Habra CA 90631, USA
**Edsall, Randy D** — Football Coach
University of Maryland, Athletic Dept, College Park MD 20742, USA
**Eduardo dos Santos, Jose** — President, Angola
President's Office, Palacio do Povo, Luanda, Angola
**Edur, Tom** — Ice Hockey Player
Puhanzu 77, 10316 Talinn, Estonia
**Edward** — Prince, England
Bagshot, Bagshot Park, Surrey GU19 5PN, England
**Edward, John** — Psychic
Berkley Publishing Group, 375 Hudson St, Basement 1, New York NY 10014 USA
**Edwards, Anthony** — Actor
Gersh Agency, 9465 Wilshire Blvd, #600, Beverly Hills CA 90212 USA
**Edwards, Antuan M** — Football Player
8108 Connestee Dr, McKinney TX 75070, USA
**Edwards, Barbara** — Model, Actress
Hansen, 7767 Hollywood Blvd, #202, Los Angeles CA 90046, USA
**Edwards, Braylon J** — Football Player
32388 Legacy Pointe Parkway, Avon Lake OH 44012, USA
**Edwards, Carl M** — Auto, Truck Racing Driver
3910 Trinity Church Road, Concord NC 28027, USA
**Edwards, Chris** — Bassist (Kasabian)
Independent Talent Group, 40 Whitfield St, London W1T 2RH, England
**Edwards, Cleophus (Cid)** — Football Player
5343 Adobe Fall Road, San Diego CA 92120, USA
**Edwards, David** — Golfer
5 Champion Place, Stillwater OK 74074, USA
**Edwards, David L (Dave)** — Baseball Player
5059 Quail Run Road, #75, Riverside CA 92507, USA
**Edwards, Dennis** — Singer (Temptations)
Paradise Artists, PO Box 1821, Ojai CA 93024 USA
**Edwards, Don** — Singer
Scott O'Malley Assoc, PO Box 9188, Colorado Springs CO 80932, USA
**Edwards, Don** — Ice Hockey Player
530 Saint Andrews Road, #4, Saginaw MI 48638, USA
**Edwards, Earl** — Football Player
1534 W Saint Thomas Dr, Gilbert AZ 85233, USA
**Edwards, Eddie** — Football Player
2701 NW 1st St, #2, Pompano Beach FL 33069, USA
**Edwards, Eric** — Cinematographer
3404 SW Water Ave, Portland OR 97239, USA
**Edwards, Gareth** — Director, Writer
W M E Entertainment, 9601 Wilshire Blvd, #300, Beverly Hills CA 90210 USA
**Edwards, Gareth O** — Rugby Player
Hamdden Ltd, Plas y Ffynnon, Cambrian Way, Brecon Powys LD3 7HP, Wales
**Edwards, Gary** — Ice Hockey Player
6818 Pecan Ave, Moorpark CA 93021, USA
**Edwards, Glen** — Football Player
4115 31st St S, Saint Petersbug FL 33712, USA
**Edwards, Harry** — Educator, Social Activist
University of California, Sociology Dept, Berkeley CA 94720, USA
**Edwards, Harry T** — Judge
US Court of Appeals, 333 Constitution Ave NW, #4400, Washington DC 20001, USA
**Edwards, Herman L (Herm)** — Football Player, Coach, Sportscaster
433 Ward Parkway, #1, Kansas City MO 64112, USA
**Edwards, Howard R (Doc)** — Baseball Player, Manager
3706 Driftwood Dr, San Angelo TX 76904, USA
**Edwards, James B** — Secretary, Energy; Governor, SC
100 Venning St, Mount Pleasant SC 29464, USA
**Edwards, Jay C** — Basketball Player
121 N Washington St, #506, Marion IN 46952, USA
**Edwards, Jennifer** — Actress
I C M Partners, 10250 Constellation Blvd, #900, Los Angeles CA 90067 USA
**Edwards, Joe F, Jr** — Astronaut
National Sciences Center, 1 7th St, #502, Augusta GA 30901, USA
**Edwards, Joel** — Golfer
5809 Shoreside Bend, Irving TX 75039, USA
**Edwards, John** — Singer (Spinners)
Buddy Allen Mgmt, 3750 Hudson Manor Terrace, #3AE, Bronx NY 10463, USA
**Edwards, John A (Johnny)** — Baseball Player
2511 E Blue Lake Dr, Magnolia TX 77354, USA
**Edwards, John R** — Senator, NC
North Carolina University, Work Poverty Center, Chapel Hill NC 27599, USA
**Edwards, Jonathan** — Track Athlete
Jonathan Marks, 20 York St, London W1U 6PU, England
**Edwards, Jonathan** — Singer, Songwriter
Northern Lights, 437 Live Oak Loop NE, Albuquerque NM 87122, USA
**Edwards, Kalimba** — Football Player
6140 Sibling Pine Dr, Durham NC 27705, USA

**Edwards, Kathleen** — Singer, Songwriter
Potty Mouth, 13 Blackburn St, #300, Toronto ON M4M 2B3, Canada
**Edwards, Kevin** — Basketball Player
821 Reilly Lane, Lake Forest IL 60045, USA
**Edwards, Kim** — Writer
Penguin Books, 375 Hudson St, Basement 1, New York NY 10014 USA
**Edwards, Luke** — Actor, Producer, Writer
Abrams Artists, 9200 W Sunset Blvd, #1125, West Hollywood CA 90069 USA
**Edwards, Mario L** — Football Player
PO Box 216, Prosper TX 75078, USA
**Edwards, Mark J** — Navy Admiral
Deputy CNO, Communications Networks, HqUSN, Pentagon, Washington DC 20350, USA
**Edwards, R LaVell** — Football Player, Coach
Brigham Young University, Athletic Dept, Provo UT 84602, USA
**Edwards, Robert** — Director, Producer, Writer
Creative Artists Agency, 2000 Ave of Stars, #100, Los Angeles CA 90067 USA
**Edwards, Robert A (Bob)** — Commentator
Sirius XM Satellite Radio, 1500 Eckington Place NE, Washington DC 20002, USA
**Edwards, Sandra** — Model, Actress
Playboy Promotions, 9346 Civic Center Dr, #200, Beverly Hills CA 90210 USA
**Edwards, Sian** — Conductor
70 Twisden Road, London NW5 1DN, England
**Edwards, Stacy** — Actress
TalentWorks, 3500 W Olive Ave, #1400, Burbank CA 91505 USA
**Edwards, Stephen (Steve)** — Composer
3980 Royal Oak Place, Encino CA 91436, USA
**Edwards, Teresa** — Basketball Player, Coach
600 1st Ave N, #Sky, Minneapolis MN 55403, USA
**Edwards, Theodore (Blue)** — Basketball Player
1103 Hart Circle, Snow Hill NC 28580, USA
**Edwards, Tommy Lee** — Illustrator
D C Comics, 1700 Broadway, #400, New York NY 10019 USA
**Edwards, Wayne** — Guitarist
PO Box 153, 2441Q Old Fort Parkway, Murfreesboro TN 37133, USA
**Edwin, Colin** — Bassist (Porcupine Tree)
Agency Group Ltd, 361-373 City Road, London EC1V 1PQ, England
**Efremova, Svetlana** — Actress
Greene Assoc, 1901 Ave of Stars, #130, Los Angeles CA 90067 USA
**Efron, Zac** — Actor
Ninjas Runnin' Wild Productions, 7024 Melrose Ave, #420, Los Angeles CA 90038, USA
**Egan, Christopher (Chris)** — Actor
Troika, 74 Clerkenwell Road, #300, London EC1M 5QA, England
**Egan, Edward M Cardinal** — Religious Leader
Archdiocese of New York, 1011 1st St, New York NY 10022, USA
**Egan, Jennifer** — Writer
Knopf Publishers, 1745 Broadway, New York NY 10019 USA
**Egan, John F (Johnny)** — Basketball Player, Coach
2124 Nantucket Dr, #B, Houston TX 77057, USA
**Egan, John L** — Businessman
Inchape PLC, 33 Cavendish Square, London W1M 9HF, England
**Egan, Melissa Claire** — Actress
Don Buchwald Talent Agency, 6500 Wilshire Blvd, #2200, Los Angeles CA 90048 USA
**Egan, Richard W (Dick)** — Baseball Player
709 Carnoustie Court, Garland TX 75044, USA
**Egan, Susan** — Actress, Singer, Dancer
13801 Ventura Blvd, Sherman Oaks CA 91423, USA
**Egan, Thomas P (Tom)** — Baseball Player
184 E Myrna Lane, Tempe AZ 85284, USA
**Egdahl, Richard H** — Surgeon
640 Bridgeway Lane, Naples FL 34108, USA
**Eger, David B** — Golfer
4300 Sharon Road, #302, Charlotte NC 28211, USA
**Egers, Jack** — Ice Hockey Player
24 Zinkann Crescent Gardens, Wellesley ON 0B 2T0, Canada
**Egerszegi, Krisztina** — Swimmer
Budapest Spartacus, Koer Utca 1/A, 1103 Budapest, Hungary
**Egerton, Tamsin** — Actress
Independent Talent Group, 40 Whitfield St, London W1T 2RH, England
**Eggar, Samantha** — Actress
5005 Varna Ave, Sherman Oaks CA 91423, USA
**Eggby, David** — Cinematographer
4344 Promenade Way, #209, Marina del Rey CA 90292, USA
**Eggeling, Dale** — Golfer
8918 Magnolia Chase Circle, Tampa FL 33647, USA
**Eggers, Dave** — Writer, Publisher, Social Activist
Voice of Witness, 848 Valencia St, San Francisco CA 94110, USA
**Eggers, Douglas B (Doug)** — Football Player
12803 Cedarbrook Lane, Laurel MD 20708, USA
**Eggert, Nicole** — Actress
Sloane Offer Weber, 9601 Wilshire Blvd, #500, Beverly Hills CA 90210 USA
**Eggert, Robert J** — Economist
Eggert Economic Enterprises, 1195 S Bates Road, Cottonwood AZ 86326, USA
**Eggimann, Romy** — Ice Hockey Player
E H C Bulach, Postfach 661, 8180 Bulach, Switzerland
**Eggler, Markus** — Curling Athlete
Bruckfeldstr 2, 4142 Munchenstein BL, Switzerland
**Egglesfield, Colin** — Actor
United Talent Agency, U T A Plaza, 9336 Civic Center Dr, Beverly Hills CA 90210 USA
**Eggleston, William** — Photographer, Artist
Robert Miller Gallery, 526 W 26th St, #10A, New York NY 10001, USA
**Eggleton, Arthur C** — Government Official, Canada
National Defense Ministry, 101 Colonel By Dr, Ottawa ON K1A 0K2, Canada
**Eggold, Ryan J** — Actor
Gersh Agency, 9465 Wilshire Blvd, #600, Beverly Hills CA 90212 USA
**Egielski, Richard** — Illustrator
525 B St, #1900, San Diego CA 92101, USA

| | |
|---|---|
| **Egington, Richard P**<br>Leander Club, Henley-on-Thames, Oxfordshire, Leander RG9 2LP, England | Rowing Athlete |
| **Egli, Beatrice**<br>Postlagernd, 8808 Pfaffikon SZ, Switzerland | Singer |
| **Egloff, Bruce E**<br>3136 S Emporia Court, Denver CO 80231, USA | Baseball Player |
| **Egon, Nicholas**<br>Villa Aetos, Katakali, Corinthia 20100, Greece | Artist |
| **Ehart, Phil**<br>Lustig Talent, PO Box 770850, Orlando FL 32877 USA | Drummer (Kansas) |
| **Eheart, Brenda Krause**<br>Hope Meadows, 1530 Fairway Dr, Rantoul IL 61666, USA | Social Activist |
| **Ehle, Jennifer**<br>I C M Partners, 10250 Constellation Blvd, #900, Los Angeles CA 90067 USA | Actress |
| **Ehlert, Lois**<br>Scholastic Press, 555 Broadway, New York NY 10012 USA | Writer |
| **Ehlo, J Craig**<br>3323 E 77th Ave, Spokane WA 99223, USA | Basketball Player |
| **Ehrenfeld, Rachel**<br>American Center for Democracy, 330 W 56th St, #24E, New York NY 10019, USA | Writer |
| **Ehrenkrantz, Dan**<br>Reconstructionist Rabbinical College, 1299 Church Road, Wyncote PA 19095, USA | Religious Leader, Rabbi, Educator |
| **Ehrenreich, Alden**<br>Creative Artists Agency, 2000 Ave of Stars, #100, Los Angeles CA 90067 USA | Actor |
| **Ehrenreich, Barbara**<br>I C M Partners, 10250 Constellation Blvd, #900, Los Angeles CA 90067 USA | Women's Activist, Writer |
| **Ehret, Gloria**<br>3335 Royal Lane, Dallas TX 75229, USA | Golfer |
| **Ehrhoff, Christian**<br>4517 Carlyle Court, Santa Clara CA 95054, USA | Ice Hockey Player |
| **Ehrlich, Paul R**<br>Stanford University, Biological Sciences Dept, Stanford CA 94305, USA | Population Biologist |
| **Ehrlich, Thomas**<br>Carnegie Teaching Foundation, 51 Vista Lane, Stanford CA 94305, USA | Educator |
| **Ehrmann, Joseph C (Joe)**<br>5 Elmhurst Road, Baltimore MD 21210, USA | Football Player |
| **Eichelberger, Charles B**<br>California Microwave, 124 Sweetwater Oaks, Peachtree City GA 30269, USA | Army General |
| **Eichelberger, David**<br>1947 Judd Hillside Road, Honolulu HI 96822, USA | Golfer |
| **Eichelberger, Juan T**<br>14674 Silverset St, Poway CA 92064, USA | Baseball Player |
| **Eichhorn, Lisa**<br>Conway Van Gelder Grant, 8-12 Broadwick St, #300, London W1F 8HW, England | Actress |
| **Eichhorn, Mark A**<br>147 Norma Court, Aptos CA 95003, USA | Baseball Player |
| **Eichhorst, Richard A (Dick)**<br>2701 Sheridan Road, Saint Louis MO 63125, USA | Basketball Player |
| **Eigen, Manfred**<br>Georg-Dehio-Weg 4, 37075 Gottingen, Germany | Nobel Chemistry Laureate |
| **Eigenberg, David**<br>Paul Kohner, 9300 Wilshire Blvd, #555, Beverly Hills CA 90212 USA | Actor |
| **Eijk, Willem J (Wim) Cardinal**<br>Archdiocese of Utrecht, Maliebaan 38-40, 3581 Utrecht CR, Netherlands | Religious Leader |
| **Eikenberry, Jill**<br>PO Box 843, Santa Ynez CA 93460, USA | Actress |
| **Eikenberry, Karl W**<br>State Department, 2201 C St NW, Washington DC 20520 USA | Army General |
| **Eiland, David W (Dave)**<br>2824 Blue Springs Place, Wesley Chapel FL 33544, USA | Baseball Player |
| **Eilbacher, Lisa**<br>Metropolitan Talent Agency, 5405 Wilshire Blvd, #218, Los Angeles CA 90036 USA | Actress |
| **Eilber, Janet**<br>Irv Schechter, 9460 Wilshire Blvd, #300, Beverly Hills CA 90212 USA | Actress |
| **Eilers, David L (Dave)**<br>602 Perkins Lane, Brenham TX 77833, USA | Baseball Player |
| **Eilers, Patrick C (Pat)**<br>177 De Windt Road, Winnetka IL 60093, USA | Football Player |
| **Eine, Simon**<br>Anne Alvares Correa, 34 Rue Jouffroy d'Abbans, 75017 Paris, France | Actor |
| **Einhorn, Lawrence**<br>Indiana University Medical School, Oncology Dept, Bloomington IN 47405, USA | Oncologist |
| **Einhorn, Richard**<br>320 Riverside Dr, #15C, New York NY 10025, USA | Composer |
| **Einstein, Bob (Super Dave Osbourne)**<br>9842 Cardigan Place, Beverly Hills CA 90210, USA | Actor, Comedian |
| **Einziger, Mike**<br>Variety Artists, 1924 Spring St, Paso Robles CA 93446 USA | Guitarist (Incubus), Songwriter |
| **Eischeid, Michael D (Mike)**<br>306 Auburn St, West Union IA 52175, USA | Football Player |
| **Eischen, Joseph R (Joey)**<br>3678 E Thornton Ave, Gilbert AZ 85297, USA | Baseball Player |
| **Eisen, Herman N**<br>75 Cambridge Parkway, #E806, Cambridge MA 02142, USA | Immunologist |
| **Eisen, Rich**<br>N F L Network, 10950 Washington Blvd, #100, Culver City CA 90232 USA | Sportscaster |
| **Eisen, Tripp**<br>United Talent Agency, U T A Plaza, 9336 Civic Center Dr, Beverly Hills CA 90210 USA | Guitarist (Static-X) |
| **Eisenach, Kathleen**<br>University of Arkansas Medical Sciences, 4301 W Markham, Little Rock AR 72205, USA | Pathologist |
| **Eisenberg, David S**<br>University of California, Chemisty & Biochemistry Dept, Los Angeles CA 90024, USA | Chemist |
| **Eisenberg, Hallie Kate**<br>Abrams Artists, 9200 W Sunset Blvd, #1125, West Hollywood CA 90069 USA | Actress |
| **Eisenberg, Jesse A**<br>Creative Artists Agency, 2000 Ave of Stars, #100, Los Angeles CA 90067 USA | Actor |

**Eisenberg, Lee**
W M E Entertainment, 9601 Wilshire Blvd, #300, Beverly Hills CA 90210 USA — Actor, Comedian, Writer

**Eisenberg, Melvin A**
1197 Keeler Ave, Berkeley CA 94708, USA — Attorney, Educator

**Eisenhauer, Lawrence C (Larry)**
19 Hobart Lane, Cohasset MA 02025, USA — Football Player

**Eisenhauer, Stephen S (Steve)**
105 Abbey Road, Winchester VA 22602, USA — Football Player

**Eisenman, Peter D**
Eisenman Architects, 40 W 25th St, New York NY 10010, USA — Architect

**Eisenreich, James M (Jim)**
11 Emerald Shore Dr, Blue Springs MO 64015, USA — Baseball Player

**Eisenstein, Michael**
Little Big Man, 155 Ave of Americas, #700, New York NY 10013, USA — Guitarist (Letters to Cleo)

**Eisert, Sandra**
13315 NE 77th St, Redmond WA 98052, USA — Photographer

**Eisinger, Jesse**
ProPublica, Editorial Dept, 1 Exchange Plaza, 55 Broadway, #2300, New York NY 10006, USA — Journalist

**Eisler, Barry**
Penguin Group, 375 Hudson St, Basement 1, New York NY 10014, USA — Writer

**Eisler, Lloyd E**
Los Angeles Kings Valley Ice Center, 8750 Van Nuys Blvd, Panorama City CA 91402, USA — Figure Skater

**Eisley, Howard J**
20250 Rodeo Court, Southfield MI 48075, USA — Basketball Player

**Eisley, India**
I C M Partners, 10250 Constellation Blvd, #900, Los Angeles CA 90067 USA — Actress

**Eisman, Hy**
99 Boulevard, Glen Rock NJ 07452, USA — Cartoonist (Katzenjammer Kids)

**Eisner, Breck**
Creative Artists Agency, 2000 Ave of Stars, #100, Los Angeles CA 90067 USA — Director

**Eisner, Michael D**
233 S Beverly Dr, #B, Beverly Hills CA 90212, USA — Businessman

**Eitner, Lorenz E A**
684 Mirada Ave, Stanford CA 94305, USA — Art Historian

**Eitzel, Mark**
Gearbox Agency, Halmtonvet 29, Bygning 12A, 1799 Copenhagen, Denmark — Singer, Songwriter

**Eizenstat, Stuart E**
5610 Wisconsin Ave, #603, Chevy Chase MD 20815, USA — Government Official, Diplomat

**Ejiofor, Chiwetel**
Markham Froggatt Irwin, Julian House, 4 Windmill St, London W1P 1HF, England — Actor

**Ejogo, Carmen**
I C M Partners, 10250 Constellation Blvd, #900, Los Angeles CA 90067 USA — Actress

**Ek, Klara**
Harrison/Parrott, 5-6 Albion Court, London W6 0QT, England — Opera Singer

**Ekberg, Anita**
Via Aspro N 1, 00045 Genzano di Rome, Italy — Actress, Model

**Ekberg, Niclas**
T H W Kiel Handball, Herzog-Friedrich-Str 52, 24103 Kiel, Germany — Handball Player

**Ekberg, Ulf**
United Stage Artists, Asogatan 142, Box 11029, 100 61 Stockholm, Sweden — Singer (Ace of Base)

**Ekimov, Viatcheslav V**
TeamRadio Shack, Capital Sports & Mgmt, 98 San Jacinto Blvd, #430, Austin, TX 78701, USA — Cyclist

**Eklund, Greg**
Pinnacle Entertainment, 30 Glenn St, White Plains NY 10603, USA — Drummer (Everclear)

**Eklund, Per-Erik (Pelle)**
Sunnanangyttervagen 67, 793 90 Leksand, Sweden — Ice Hockey Player

**Ekman, Paul**
University of California Medical Center, 505 Parnassus, San Francisco CA 94122 USA — Psychologist

**Ekman-Larsson, Oliver**
Stigamovagen 1, 363 21 Tingsryd, Sweden — Ice Hockey Player

**Ekstrom, Michael**
1616 SE 282nd Ave, Gresham OR 97080, USA — Baseball Player

**Ekuban, Ebenezer, Jr**
5391 Moonlight Way, Parker CO 80134, USA — Football Player

**El DeBarge**
205 Hill St, Santa Monica CA 90405, USA — Singer

**El Fadil, Siddig**
Paramount, 5555 Melose Ave, Los Angeles CA 90038, USA — Actor

**El Fassi, Abbas**
Prime Minister's Office, Palais Royal, Le Mechouar, Rabat, Morocco — Prime Minister, Morocco

**Elam, Jason**
PO Box 1425, Soldotna AK 99669, USA — Football Player

**Elam, Katrina**
PO Box 209, Marlow OK 73055, USA — Singer

**Elarton, V Scott**
12835 Daisy Place, Bradenton FL 34212, USA — Baseball Player

**Elba, Idris**
W M E Entertainment, 9601 Wilshire Blvd, #300, Beverly Hills CA 90210 USA — Actor

**ElBaradei, Mohamed M**
Constitution Party, Abdin, Qasr El-Nile St, Cairo 002, Egypt — Nobel Peace Laureate

**Eldard, Ron**
United Talent Agency, U T A Plaza, 9336 Civic Center Dr, Beverly Hills CA 90210 USA — Actor

**Elder, Lee E**
PO Box 667200, Pompano Beach FL 33066, USA — Golfer

**Elder, Mark P**
Ingpen & Williams, 131 Putney Bridge Road, London SW15 2PA, England — Conductor

**Elders, M Jocelyn**
810 Marcia Cove, Little Rock AR 72206, USA — Pediatrician, Government Official

**Eldon, Kevin**
R D F Mgmt, 3-6 Kendrick Place, London W1U 6HD, England — Actor

**Eldred, Calvin J (Cal)**
1893 Horn Road, Mount Vernon IA 52314, USA — Baseball Player

**Eldredge, Todd**
2463 N Lake Angelus Road W, Auburn Hills MI 48326, USA — Figure Skater

**Electra, Carmen**
E M C Bowery, 5971 W 3rd St, Los Angeles CA 90036, USA — Actress, Singer, Model

**Eleniak, Erika**
Kirk Talent Agencies, 196 W 3rd Ave, #102, Vancouver BC V5Y 1E9, Canada — Model, Actress

**Elephant Man**
Bad Boy Entertainment, 1440 Broadway, #16, New York NY 10018 USA — Singer

**Elfman, Bodhi**
Lewis & Beal Talent Agency, 15303 Ventura Blvd, #900, Sherman Oaks CA 91403, USA — Actor

**Elfman, Danny**
Musica de la Muerte, 1901 Ave of Stars, #1450, Los Angeles CA 90067, USA — Singer, Composer

**Elfman, Jenna**
Brillstein Entertainment Partners, 9150 Wilshire Blvd, #350, Beverly Hills CA 90212 USA — Actress, Model

**Elg, Taina**
789 W End Ave, New York NY 10025, USA — Actress

**Elgart, Larry J**
2065 Gulf of Mexico Dr, Longboat Key FL 34228, USA — Orchestra Leader

**Elgort, Ansel**
42 West, 11400 W Olympic Blvd, #1100, Los Angeles CA 90064 USA — Actor

**Eli, Mike**
Triple 8 Mgmt, 1611 6th St, Austin TX 78703, USA — Singer, Guitarist (Eli Youn Band)

**Elia, Lee C**
11613 Innfields Dr, Odessa FL 33556, USA — Baseball Player, Manager

**Elia, Nicolas**
Red Management, Box 3, 415 W Esplanade, North Vancouver BC V7M, Canada — Actor

**Eliane, Elias**
RR 376 Box 1282, Wappingers FL 12590, USA — Singer, Pianist, Composer

**Elias, Antonio L**
Orbital Sciences Corp, 21839 Atlantic Blvd, Dulles VA 20166, USA — Space Scientist

**Elias, Eliane**
Axis Artists Mgmt, 9715 Belmar Ave, Northridge CA 91324, USA — Jazz Pianist, Singer, Composer

**Elias, Hector**
C E S D, 10635 Santa Monica Blvd, #130, Los Angeles CA 90025 USA — Actor

**Elias, Jonathan**
Elias Arts, 2219 Main St, Santa Monica CA 90405, USA — Composer

**Elias, Keith H**
4507 Norma Place, Toms River NJ 08755, USA — Football Player

**Elias, Patrik**
1005 Smith Manor Blvd, #98, West Orange NJ 07052, USA — Ice Hockey Player

**Elias, Rosalind**
Robert Lombardo Assoc, Harkness Plaza, 61 W 62nd St, #6F, New York NY 10023 USA — Opera Singer

**Eliasson, Olafur**
Studio Olafur Eliasson, Christinenstr 18/19, #2, 10119 Berlin, Germany — Sculptor

**Elice, Rick**
I C M Partners, 10250 Constellation Blvd, #900, Los Angeles CA 90067 USA — Writer

**Elicker, Paul H**
10213 Montgomery Ave, Kensington MD 20895, USA — Businessman

**Elie, Mario A**
1 Mott Lane, Houston TX 77024, USA — Basketball Player

**Elinson, Jack**
655 Pomander Walk, #210, Teaneck NJ 07666, USA — Sociomedical Scientist

**Eliot, Darren J**
1100 Grayton St, Grosse Pointe Park MI 48230, USA — Ice Hockey Player

**Eliot, Jan**
PO Box 50032, Eugene OR 97405, USA — Cartoonist (Stone Soup)

**Eliot, Peter**
University of Adelaide, Mineralogy Dept, Adelaide SA 5000, Australia — Mineralogist

**Elise, Christine**
Sovereign Talent Group, 8421 Wilshire Blvd, #200, Beverly Hills CA 90211 USA — Actress

**Elise, Kimberly**
Untitled Entertainment, 350 S Beverly Dr, #200, Beverly Hills CA 90212 USA — Actress

**Elistratov, Semion**
All-Russian Skating Union, Luzhnetskaia Nab 8, 119992 Moscow, Russia — Speed Skater

**Eliuk, Dallas**
Portland LumberJax, Rose Garden Arena, 1 N Center Court, Portland OR 97227, USA — Lacrosse Player

**Elizabeth II**
Buckingham Palace, London SW1A 1AA, England — Queen, England

**Elizabeth, Sarah**
Playboy Promotions, 9346 Civic Center Dr, #200, Beverly Hills CA 90210 USA — Model

**Elizabeth, Shannon**
Ganesh Productions, 7119 W Sunset Blvd, #369, Los Angeles CA 90046, USA — Actress, Model, Producer

**Elizondo, Hector**
Gersh Agency, 9465 Wilshire Blvd, #600, Beverly Hills CA 90212 USA — Actor

**Elkaim, Jeremie**
Artmedia, 20 Ave Rapp, 75007 Paris, France — Actor

**Elkes, Joel**
University of Louisville, Psychiatry & Behavioral Science Dept, Louisville KY 40292, USA — Psychiatrist

**Elkind, Mortimer M**
10234 Rue Chamonix, San Diego CA 92131, USA — Biophysicist

**Elkington, Steve**
7010 Kelsey Rae Court, Houston TX 77069, USA — Golfer

**Elkins, Lawrence C (Larry)**
1 Keats Ave, Norden, Rochdale, Lancashire OL12 7PZ, England — Football Player

**Ellard, Henry A**
5800 Airline Dr, Metairie LA 70003, USA — Football Player

**Ellena, Jack D**
73164 Monterra Circle N, Palm Desert CA 92260, USA — Football Player

**Ellenshaw, Harrison**
2060 Avenida de los Arboles, #D317, Thousand Oaks CA 91362, USA — Special Effects Artist

**Ellenson, David**
Hebrew Union College, Jewish Religious Institute, 1 W 4th St, New York NY 10012, USA — Religious Leader, Rabbi, Educator

**Eller, Carl**
1035 Washburn Ave N, Minneapolis MN 55411, USA — Football Player, Executive

**Eller, Claudia**
Variety, 11175 Santa Monica Blvd, Los Angeles CA 90025, USA — Editor

**Eller, Walter (Glenn), III**
US Army Marksmanship Unit, Fort Benning GA 31905, USA — Marksman

**Ellerbee, Linda**
Lucky Duck Productions, 96 Morton St, #400, New York NY 10014, USA — Commentator

**E**

|  |  |
|---|---|
| **Ellerson, Rich**<br>US Military Academy, Athletic Dept, West Point NY 10996, USA | Football Coach |
| **Ellett, David D G (Dave)**<br>36611 N 51st St, Cave Creek AZ 85331, USA | Ice Hockey Player |
| **Ellickson, Robert C**<br>Yale University, Law School, 127 Wall St, New Haven CT 06511, USA | Attorney, Educator |
| **Elliman, Yvonne**<br>Diva Central, 7510 W Sunset Blvd, #1445, Los Angeles CA 90046, USA | Singer |
| **Ellin, Doug**<br>Leverage Mgmt, 3030 Pennsylvania Ave, Santa Monica CA 90404, USA | Director, Producer |
| **Elling, Kurt**<br>Jazz Tree, 648 Broadway, #303, New York NY 10012, USA | Singer |
| **Ellingson, Evan**<br>Innovative Artists, 1505 10th St, Santa Monica CA 90401 USA | Actor |
| **Ellingson, Lindsay**<br>D N A Model Mgmt, 555 W 25th St, #600, New York NY 10001, USA | Model |
| **Elliot, Adam**<br>I C M Partners, 10250 Constellation Blvd, #900, Los Angeles CA 90067 USA | Director, Writer |
| **Elliot, Janet**<br>Kirkwood Stables, 21 Mount Eden Road, Kirkwood PA 17536, USA | Steeplechase Racing Trainer |
| **Elliot, Lawrence L (Larry)**<br>13010 Caminito Bracho, San Diego CA 92128, USA | Baseball Player |
| **Elliott, Alecia**<br>Creative Artists Agency, 2000 Ave of Stars, #100, Los Angeles CA 90067 USA | Singer, Actress |
| **Elliott, Alison**<br>Innovative Artists, 1505 10th St, Santa Monica CA 90401 USA | Actress |
| **Elliott, Andrea**<br>New York Times, Editorial Dept, 229 W 43rd St, New York NY 10036 USA | Journalist |
| **Elliott, Brennan**<br>Red Management, Box 3, 415 W Esplanade, North Vancouver, BC V7M, Canada | Actor |
| **Elliott, Brooke**<br>Innovative Artists, 1505 10th St, Santa Monica CA 90401 USA | Actress, Singer |
| **Elliott, Chalmers (Bump)**<br>1 Oaknoll Court, Iowa City IA 52246, USA | Football Player, Coach |
| **Elliott, Chris**<br>Mosiac Media Group, 9200 W Sunset Blvd, #1000, Los Angeles CA 90069 USA | Actor, Comedian |
| **Elliott, David James**<br>Paradigm Agency, 360 N Crescent Dr, North Building, Beverly Hills CA 90210 USA | Actor |
| **Elliott, Dennis**<br>Hard to Handle Mgmt, 16501 Ventura Blvd, #602, Encino CA 91436, USA | Drummer (Foreigner) |
| **Elliott, Donald G (Donnie)**<br>1206 Bayou Vista Dr, Deer Park TX 77536, USA | Baseball Player |
| **Elliott, E Matthew (Matt)**<br>7453 Coventry Woods Dr, Dublin OH 43017, USA | Football Player |
| **Elliott, Gordon**<br>Food Network, 1180 Ave of Americas, #1200, New York NY 10036 USA | Chef |
| **Elliott, Harry L**<br>9608 Los Coches Road, Lakeside CA 92040, USA | Baseball Player |
| **Elliott, Herbert (Herb)**<br>Fortescue Metals Group, 87 Adelaide Terrace, East Perth WA 6004, Australia | Track Athlete |
| **Elliott, Ira S**<br>M-Squared Mgmt, 201 W 72nd St, #12G, New York NY 10023, USA | Drummer (Fuzztones, Nada Surf) |
| **Elliott, Joe**<br>Front Line Mgmt, 1100 Glendon Ave, #2000, Los Angeles CA 90024 USA | Singer, Musician (Def Leppard) |
| **Elliott, John H**<br>122 Church Way, Iffley, Oxford OX4 4EG, England | Historian |
| **Elliott, John S (Jumbo)**<br>17 Fieldstone Lane, Oyster Bay NY 11771, USA | Football Player |
| **Elliott, Mekissa A (Missy)**<br>Monami Entertainment, 649 W 27th St, New York NY 10001, USA | Singer, Songwriter, Actress |
| **Elliott, Paul H**<br>Sandra Marsh Assoc, 9150 Wilshire Blvd, #220, Beverly Hills CA 90212 USA | Cinematographer |
| **Elliott, Ralph E**<br>5150 Damascus Road S, Jacksonville FL 32207, USA | WW II Navy Air Force Hero |
| **Elliott, Ramblin' Jack**<br>Keith Case Assoc, 1025 17th Ave S, #200, Nashville TN 37212 USA | Singer, Songwriter, Guitarist |
| **Elliott, Rand**<br>Elliott Assoc, 35 Harrison Ave, Oklahoma City OK 73104, USA | Architect |
| **Elliott, Randy L**<br>1002 Steuben St, Wausau WI 54403, USA | Baseball Player |
| **Elliott, Robert A (Bob)**<br>6760 E Fieldstone Lane, Tucson AZ 85750, USA | Basketball Player |
| **Elliott, Ronald C (Ron)**<br>1532 Dale Ave, San Mateo CA 94401, USA | Singer, Guitarist (Beau Brummels) |
| **Elliott, Sam**<br>33050 Pacific Coast Highway, Malibu CA 90265, USA | Actor |
| **Elliott, Sean M**<br>1726 Greystone Ridge, San Antonio TX 78258, USA | Basketball Player |
| **Elliott, Steve**<br>36 Brookwood Road, Mount Laurel NJ 8054, USA | Harness Racing Driver, Trainer |
| **Elliott, Ted A**<br>Creative Artists Agency, 2000 Ave of Stars, #100, Los Angeles CA 90067 USA | Writer, Producer |
| **Elliott, William C (Bill)**<br>Bill Elliott Racing, 200 Woodhaven Lane, Ball Ground GA 30107, USA | Auto Racing Driver |
| **Ellis Bextor, Sophie**<br>Primary Talent International, 10-11 Jockey's Fields, London WC1R 4BN, England | Singer |
| **Ellis, Anita**<br>130 E End Ave, New York NY 10028, USA | Jazz Singer |
| **Ellis, Aunjanue**<br>I C M Partners, 10250 Constellation Blvd, #900, Los Angeles CA 90067 USA | Actress |
| **Ellis, Bob**<br>2401 Village Lane, #A7, Ardmore OK 73401, USA | Professional Wrestler |
| **Ellis, Bret Easton**<br>Vintage Books, 1745 Broadway, New York NY 10019 USA | Writer |
| **Ellis, Caroline**<br>8060 Saint Clair Ave, North Hollywood CA 91605, USA | Actress |

**Ellis, Chris**
Bauman Redanty Shaul Agency, 5757 Wilshire Blvd, #473, Los Angeles CA 90036 USA — Actor
**Ellis, Cliff**
Auburn University, Athletic Dept, Auburn AL 36831, USA — Basketball Coach
**Ellis, Dale**
3564 W Hampton Dr NW, Marietta GA 30064, USA — Basketball Player
**Ellis, Danny**
1543 Cherry Lake Way, Lake Mary FL 32746, USA — Golfer
**Ellis, Don**
34 Crestwood Circle, Sugar Land TX 77478, USA — Bowler
**Ellis, Elmer**
3300 New Haven Ave, #223, Columbia MO 65201, USA — Historian, Educator
**Ellis, F (Cot)**
9505 N Silver Lake Dr, Oklahoma City OK 73162, USA — Baseball Player
**Ellis, George F R**
3 Marlowe Road, Capetown 7700, South Africa — Mathematician, Templeton Laureate
**Ellis, Gerry L**
250 Cavil Way, De Pere WI 54115, USA — Football Player
**Ellis, Greg**
Gersh Agency, 9465 Wilshire Blvd, #600, Beverly Hills CA 90212 USA — Actor
**Ellis, Gregory L (Greg)**
PO Box 96075, Southlake TX 76092, USA — Football Player
**Ellis, Harold**
9420 Parkwood Ave, Douglasville GA 30135, USA — Basketball Player
**Ellis, Hunter**
Ideal Mgmt, 5780 W Centennial Ave, #313, Los Angeles CA 90045, USA — Actor
**Ellis, James O, Jr**
Institute of Nuclear Power Operations, 700 Galleria Parkway SE, #100, Atlanta GA 30339, USA — Navy Admiral
**Ellis, James R**
4213 Swann Ave, Tampa FL 33609, USA — Army General
**Ellis, James R (Jim)**
13608 Ave 24, Tulare CA 93274, USA — Baseball Player
**Ellis, Janet**
Arlington Entertainments, 1/3 Charlotte St, London W1P 1HD, England — Actress
**Ellis, John C**
14 Marina Point Dr, Old Saybrook CT 06475, USA — Baseball Player
**Ellis, Joseph J**
Mount Holyoke College, History Dept, South Hadley MA 01075, USA — Writer
**Ellis, K Ray**
4666 E Olney Ave, Gilbert AZ 85234, USA — Football Player
**Ellis, Kenneth A (Ken)**
2700 Gulf Freeway, #2111, Texas City TX 77591, USA — Football Player
**Ellis, LaPhonso**
51215 Shannon Brook Court, Granger IN 46530, USA — Basketball Player
**Ellis, Larry R**
3425 SW 2nd Ave, Gainesville FL 32607, USA — Army General
**Ellis, Mary Elizabeth**
Danis Panaro Nist Talent, 9201 W Olympic Blvd, Beverly Hills CA 90212 USA — Actress
**Ellis, MeShaunda P (Shaun)**
26 Green St, Newbury MA 01951, USA — Football Player
**Ellis, Monta**
Dallas Mavericks, Pavilion, 2909 Taylor Street, Dallas TX 75226 USA — Basketball Player
**Ellis, Nelsan**
I C M Partners, 10250 Constellation Blvd, #900, Los Angeles CA 90067 USA — Actor
**Ellis, Osian G**
90 Chandos Ave, London N20 9DZ, England — Concert Harpist
**Ellis, Richard S**
California Institute of Technology, Astronomy Dept, Pasadena CA 91125, USA — Astronomer
**Ellis, Robert**
Vector Mgmt, PO Box 120479, Nashville TN 37212 USA — Singer
**Ellis, Robin**
Artists Partnership, 101 Finsbury Pavement, London EC2A 1RS, England — Actor
**Ellis, Romallis**
2062 San Marco Dr, Ellenwood GA 30294, USA — Boxer
**Ellis, Ronald J E (Ron)**
Hockey Hall of Fame, Brookfield Place, 30 Yonge St, Toronto ON M5E 1X8, Canada — Ice Hockey Player
**Ellis, Rosemary**
Good Housekeeping, Editor's Office, 300 W 57th St, New York NY 10019, USA — Editor
**Ellis, Samuel J (Sam)**
12511 Forest Highlands Dr, Dade City FL 33525, USA — Baseball Player
**Ellis, Scott**
301 W 118th St, #10-I, New York NY 10026, USA — Director
**Ellis, Sean**
I C M Partners, 10250 Constellation Blvd, #900, Los Angeles CA 90067 USA — Director, Producer, Writer
**Ellis, Terry**
Green Light Talent Agency, PO Box 3172, Beverly Hills CA 90212 USA — Singer (En Vogue)
**Ellis, Tom**
Hamilton Hodell, 20 Golden Square, London W1F 9JL, England — Actor
**Ellison, Brady**
PO Box 277, Claypool AZ 85532, USA — Archer
**Ellison, Brooke**
Hyperion Books, 114 5th Ave, New York NY 10011 USA — Writer
**Ellison, Harlan J**
Kilimanjaro Group, PO Box 55548, Sherman Oaks CA 91413, USA — Writer
**Ellison, Jason J**
3745 248th Ave SE, Issaquah WA 98029, USA — Baseball Player
**Ellison, Jennifer**
C A M, 55-59 Shaftsbury Ave, London W1D 6LD, England — Actress
**Ellison, Keith**
Buffalo Bills, 1 Bills Dr, Orchard Park NY 14127 USA — Football Player
**Ellison, Lawrence J**
Oracle Systems, 500 Oracle Parkway, Redwood Shores CA 94065, USA — Businessman, Yachtsman
**Ellison, Megan**
I/D Public Relations, 7060 Hollywood Blvd, #800, Los Angeles CA 90028 USA — Producer
**Ellison, Pervis**
4602 Kettering Dr NE, Roswell GA 30075, USA — Basketball Player

**Ellison, William H (Willie)** — Football Player
3503 Mosley Court, Houston TX 77004, USA

**Elliss, Luther J** — Football Player
118 E 3200 N, Kamas UT 84036, USA

**Ellmann, Lucy** — Writer
David Godwin Assoc, 55 Monmouth St, London WC2H 9DG, England

**Ellroy, James** — Writer
Sobel Weber Assoc, 146 E 19th St, New York NY 10003, USA

**Ellsberg, Daniel** — Political Activist
90 Norwood Ave, Kensington CA 94707, USA

**Ellsbury, Jacoby M** — Baseball Player
1204 Suncast Lane, #2, El Dorado Hills CA 95762, USA

**Ellsworth, Frank L** — Educator
11205 Ettrick St, Oakland CA 94605, USA

**Ellsworth, Kiko** — Actor
Stone Manners Salners, 6100 Wilshire Blvd, #1500, Los Angeles CA 90035 USA

**Ellsworth, Percy D** — Football Player
11261 Fortsville Road, Capron VA 23829, USA

**Ellsworth, Richard C (Dick)** — Baseball Player
1099 W Morris Ave, Fresno CA 93711, USA

**Ellwood, Paul M, Jr** — Physician
68 Dell Creek Road, Bondurant WY 82922, USA

**Ellyson, Erica** — Model
9850 S Maryland Parkway, #A5-446, Las Vegas NV 89183, USA

**Elmaleh, Gad** — Actor, Comedian
Thruline Entertainment, 9250 Wilshire Blvd, #100, Beverly Hills CA 90212 USA

**Elmendorf, David C (Dave)** — Football Player
17990 FM 1452 W, Normangee TX 77871, USA

**Elmes, Fredrick** — Cinematographer
Mirisch Agency, 1025 Colorado Ave, #B, Santa Monica CA 90211 USA

**Elmore, Leonard J (Len)** — Basketball Player, Sportscaster
PO Box 22, Highland MD 20777, USA

**Elrod, Jack** — Cartoonist (Mark Trail)
7240 Hunter's Branch Dr NE, Atlanta GA 30328, USA

**Elrod, Scott** — Actor
Independent Group, 8444 Wilshire Blvd, #500, Beverly Hills CA 90211, USA

**Els, T Ernest (Ernie)** — Golfer
Ernie Els Design, PO Box 73, Virginia Water GU25 4ZS, England

**Elsasser, Kurt** — Singer
Karat Promotion, Schloss Johannesberg, Braubacher Str 58, 56130 Bad Ems/Lahn, Germany

**Elshire, Neil J** — Football Player
2441 NW Torsway St, Bend OR 97701, USA

**Elsley, Bryan** — Producer
The Agency, 24 Pottery Lane, London W11 4LZ, England , USA

**Elsna, Hebe** — Writer
Curtis Brown Group, 28-29 Haymarket St, #500, London SW1Y 4SP, England

**Elsner, Christian** — Opera Singer
Kunstler Sekretariat am Gasteig, Rosenheimer Str 52, 81669 Munich, Germany

**Elson, Francisco** — Basketball Player
92 Foxton Dr, San Antonio TX 78258, USA

**Elson, Karen** — Model
Elite Model Mgmt, 404 Park Ave S, #900, New York NY 10016 USA

**Elster, Jennifer** — Director
P M K-B N C, 622 3rd Ave, #800, New York NY 10017 USA

**Elstner, Frank** — Actor
Elstnertainment, Postfach 100568, 76486 Baden-Baden, Germany

**Elswit, Richard (Rik)** — Singer, Guitarist (Dr Hook)
Artists International Mgmt, 9850 Sandalwood Blvd, #458, Boca Raton FL 33428, USA

**Elswit, Robert** — Cinematographer
United Talent Agency, U T A Plaza, 9336 Civic Center Dr, Beverly Hills CA 90210 USA

**Elton, Ben** — Actor, Comedian
Phil McIntyre Mgmt, 35 Soho Square, London W1D 3QX, England

**Elts, Olari** — Conductor
Van Walsum Mgmt, Tower Building, 11 York Road, London SE1 7NX, England

**Elvin, Violetta** — Ballerina
Marina di Equa, 80066 Seiano, Bay of Naples, Italy

**Elvin-Lewis, Memory** — Ethnobotanist
7915 Park Dr, Saint Louis MO 63117, USA

**Elvira, (Cassandra Peterson)** — Actress
Queen B Productions, PO Box 38246, Los Angeles CA 90038, USA

**Elway, John A** — Football Player
13644 E Dole Valley, Englewood CO 80112, USA

**Elwes, Cary** — Actor
L I N K Entertainment, 11872 La Grange Ave, Los Angeles CA 90025 USA

**Elwood, Hugh M** — WW II Marine Corps Air Force Hero
1 Fleet Landing Blvd, Atlantic Beach FL 32233, USA

**Ely, Alexandre (Alex)** — Soccer Player
5526 N 2nd St, Philadelphia PA 19120, USA

**Ely, Jack** — Singer, Guitarist
Rolling Highway Mgmt, PO Box 1176, Marfa TX 79843, USA

**Ely, Joe** — Singer, Guitarist, Songwriter
L C Media, PO Box 965, Antioch TN 37011, USA

**Ely, Ron** — Actor
4161 Mariposa Dr, Santa Barbara CA 93110, USA

**Ely, Shyra** — Basketball Player
Indiana Fever, Conseco Fieldhouse, 125 S Pennsylvania, Indianapolis IN 46204 USA

**Elynuik, Patrick G (Pat)** — Ice Hockey Player
143 Aspen Green, Calgary AB T3Z 3B9, Canada

**Emanuel, Alphonsia** — Actress
Marina Martin, 12/13 Poland St, London W1V 3DE, England

**Emanuel, Bert T** — Football Player
15 Bees Creek Court, Missouri City TX 77459, USA

**Emanuel, David** — Fashion Designer
David Emanuel Couture, Lanesborough Hotel, London SW1X 7TA, England

**Emanuel, Elizabeth F** — Fashion Designer
Sew Forth Productions, 26 Chiltern St, London W1M 1PF, England

**Emanuel, Kerry A**
Massachusetts Institute of Technology, Atmospheric Science Center, Cambridge MA 02139, USA — Meteorologist

**Emanuel, Rahm**
Mayor's Office, 121 N La Salle St, #507, Chicago IL 60602, USA — Mayor, Chicago; Government Official

**Emanuel, T Frank**
10211 Deercliff Dr, Tampa FL 33647, USA — Football Player

**Embach, Carsten**
B S R Rennsteig e V, Grafenrodaer Str 2, 98559 Oberhof, Germany — Bobsled Athlete

**Emberg, Kelly**
PO Box 675401, Rancho Santa Fe CA 92067, USA — Actress, Model

**Embery, Joan**
American Zoo Keepers Assn, 3601 SW 29th St, #133, Topeka KS 66614, USA — Animal Activist

**Embiid, Joel H**
Philadelphia 76ers, 1st Union Center, 3601 S Broad St, Philadelphia PA 19148 USA — Basketball Player

**Embree, Ainslie T**
PO Box 433, Centerville MA 02632, USA — Historian

**Embree, Alan D**
238 NW Outlook Vista Dr, Bend OR 97701, USA — Baseball Player

**Embree, Jon W**
9450 Owl Lane, Boulder CO 80301, USA — Football Player, Coach

**Embry, Ethan**
A P A Talent & Literary Agency, 405 S Beverly Dr, #300, Beverly Hills CA 90212 USA — Actor

**Embry, Wayne R**
1101-211 Queens Quay W, Toronto ON M5J 2M6, Canada — Basketball Player, Executive

**Emburey, John E**
Middlesex Cricket Club, Lord's Cricket Ground, London NW8 8QN, England — Cricketer

**Emerick, Kate**
Matt Sherman Mgmt, 9107 Wilshire Blvd, #225, Beverly Hills CA 90210, USA — Actress

**Emerick, Scotty**
Paradise Artists, PO Box 1821, Ojai CA 93024 USA — Singer, Songwriter

**Emerson, Claudia**
Mary Washington University, English Dept, 1301 College, Fredericksburg VA 22401, USA — Writer

**Emerson, David F**
211 E 18th St, #5O, New York NY 10003, USA — Navy Admiral

**Emerson, Keith**
Asia, 9 Hillgate St, London W8 7SP, England — Keyboardist (Emerson Lake & Palmer)

**Emerson, Michael**
Innovative Artists, 1505 10th St, Santa Monica CA 90401 USA — Actor

**Emerson, Nelson**
717 33rd St, Manhattan Beach CA 90266, USA — Ice Hockey Player

**Emerson, Roy**
2221 Alta Vista Dr, Newport Beach CA 92660, USA — Tennis Player

**Emery, Gideon**
Greene Assoc, 1901 Ave of Stars, #130, Los Angeles CA 90067 USA — Actor

**Emery, John**
Bobsled Canada, 140 Canada Olympic Road SW, Calgary AB T3B 5R5, Canada — Bobsled Athlete

**Emery, Julie Ann**
Principal Entertainment, 9255 Sunset Blvd, #500, Los Angeles CA 90069 USA — Actress

**Emery, Lin**
7520 Dominican St, New Orleans LA 70118, USA — Artist, Sculptor

**Emery, R Lee**
Bill Rogin Mgmt, 427 N Canon Dr, #215, Beverly Hills CA 90210, USA — Actor

**Emery, Ralph**
RFD-TV, Rural Media Group, 1 Valmont Plaza, #400, Omaha NE 68154, USA — Entertainer

**Emery, Ray**
1723 Haldimand Road 20, Cayuga ON N0A 1E0, Canada — Ice Hockey Player

**Emery, Victor (Vic)**
Bobsled Canada, 140 Canada Olympic Road SW, Calgary AB T3B 5R5, Canada — Bobsled Athlete

**Emick, Jarrod**
Douglas Gorman Rothacker Wilhelm, 1501 Broadway, #703, New York NY 10036 USA — Actor

**Emilio**
Refugee Mgmt, 209 10th Ave S, #347 Cummins Station, Nashville TN 37203, USA — Singer

**Eminem**
I C M Partners, 10250 Constellation Blvd, #900, Los Angeles CA 90067 USA — Rap Artist, Actor

**Emma, David**
193 Eugenia Dr, Naples FL 34108, USA — Ice Hockey Player

**Emmanuel**
Sendyk Leonard, 532 Colorado Ave, Santa Monica CA 90401, USA — Singer

**Emmanuel, Tommy**
Gina Mendello, C P R Entertainment, PO Box 121983, Nashville TN 37212, USA — Guitarist

**Emme**
EmmeNation, PO Box 546, Closter NJ 07624, USA — Model

**Emmerich, Noah J**
Gersh Agency, 9465 Wilshire Blvd, #600, Beverly Hills CA 90212 USA — Actor

**Emmerich, Roland**
Creative Artists Agency, 2000 Ave of Stars, #100, Los Angeles CA 90067 USA — Director, Producer

**Emmerich, Toby**
New Line Cinema, 888 7th Ave, #1900, New York NY 10106, USA — Producer, Writer

**Emmert, Mark A**
National Collegiate Athletic Assn, President's Office, 700 W Washington St, Indianapolis IN 46204, USA — Association Executive, Educator

**Emmett, John C**
Oak House, Hatfield Broad Oak, Bishop's Stortford, Hertfordshire CM22 7HG, England — Inventor (Antiulcer Compound)

**Emmett, Rik**
Agency Group Ltd, 142 W 57th St, #600, New York NY 10019 USA — Singer, Guitar Player

**Emond, Linda**
Innovative Artists, 1505 10th St, Santa Monica CA 90401 USA — Actress

**Emory, Sonny**
Great Scott Productions, 4750 Lincoln Blvd, #229, Marina del Rey CA 90292, USA — Drummer (Earth Wind & Fire)

**Emrich, W Thomas (Tom)**
725 S Santa Ana Dr, Tucson AZ 85710, USA — WW II Marine Air Corps Hero

**Emtman, Steven C (Steve)**
19601 S Cheney Spangle Road, Cheney WA 99004, USA — Football Player

**Enberg, Dick**
1275 Virginia Way, La Jolla CA 92037, USA — Sportscaster

**Encarnacion, Juan D**
Toronto Blue Jays, Skydome, 1 Blue Jay Way, Toronto ON M5V 1J1, Canada — Baseball Player

Emanuel - Encarnacion

**Endelman, Stephen** — Composer
First Artists Mgmt, 4764 Park Granada, #210, Calabasas CA 91302 USA

**Ender Grummt, Kornelia** — Swimmer
D S V, Postfach 420140, 34070 Kassel, Germany

**Enders, Anthony T** — Financier
Brown Brothers Harriman, 59 Wall St, New York NY 10005, USA

**Enders, Thomas** — Businessman
Airbus Industrie, Ronde Point Maurice Bellont 1, 31707 Blagnac, France

**Endicott, Lori** — Volleyball Player
351 Dogwood Ridge, Rogersville MO 65742, USA

**Endicott, Sam** — Singer, Guitarist (Bravery)
+1 Mgmt, 242 Wythe Ave, #6, Brooklyn NY 11211, USA

**Endicott, William F (Bill)** — Baseball Player
14219 Oak Knoll Road, Sonora CA 95370, USA

**Endre, Lena** — Actress
Actors in Scandinavia, Jaakarinkatu 10, 00150 Helsinki, Finland

**Enevoldsen, Einar** — Test Pilot
103 City Limits Circle, Emeryville CA 94608, USA

**Enfeldt, Monique Gabrecht** — Speedskater
Rosenthaler Str 40-41, Hackesche Hofe, 10178 Berlin, Germany

**Enfield, Andrew W (Andy)** — Basketball Coach
University of Southern California, Heritage Hall, Los Angeles CA 90089, USA

**Enfield, Jill** — Photographer
Tilt Gallery, 919 W Fillmore St, Phoenix AZ 85007, USA

**Engberg, Lotta** — Singer
Gallviksvagen 20, 44163 Alingsas, Sweden

**Engblom, Brian** — Ice Hockey Player
601 W Burgundy St, #B, Highlands Ranch CO 80129, USA

**Engel, Albert J, Jr** — Judge
5497 Forest Bend Dr SE, Ada MI 49301, USA

**Engel, Georgia** — Actress
C E S D, 10635 Santa Monica Blvd, #130, Los Angeles CA 90025 USA

**Engelberger, John A** — Football Player
8176 Cliffview Ave, Springfield VA 22153, USA

**Engelberger, Joseph F** — Robotics Engineer
HelpMate Robotics, Shelter Rock Lane, Danbury CT 06810, USA

**Engelhardt, Thomas A (Tom)** — Editorial Cartoonist
Saint Louis Post-Dispatch, Editorial Dept, 900 N Tucker, Saint Louis MO 63101, USA

**Engels, Sarah** — Singer
Xtrasystem, Durener Str 221, 50931 Cologne, Germany

**Engen, D Travis** — Businessman
I T T Industries, 4 W Red Oak Lane, #200, West Harrison NY 10604, USA

**Enger, Leif** — Writer
Grove/Atlantic Monthly Press, 841 Broadway, New York NY 10003, USA

**Engerman, Stanley L** — Economist, Historian
181 Warrington Dr, Rochester NY 14618, USA

**Engh, Michael E** — Educator
Santa Clara University, President's Office, 500 El Camino Real, Santa Clara CA 95053, USA

**Engibous, Thomas J** — Businessman
Texas Instruments, 8505 Forest Lane, PO Box 660199, Dallas TX 75266, USA

**England, Anthony W** — Astronaut, Geophysicist
7949 Ridgeway Court, Dexter MI 48130, USA

**England, Richard** — Architect
The Gardens, 8 Oleander St, Saint Julians SJ 12, Malta

**England, Tyler (Ty)** — Singer, Guitarist, Songwriter
Harmony Artists, 6399 Wilshire Blvd, #914, Los Angeles CA 90048, USA

**England, Yan** — Actor, Director, Writer
Arlook Group, 205 S Beverly Dr, #209, Beverly Hills CA 90212, USA

**Englander, Harold R** — Public Health Dentist
625 Baldwin Ave, Charlotte NC 28204, USA

**Engle, Eleanor** — Baseball Player
725 Heiden Dr, Hummelstown PA 17036, USA

**Engle, Joe H** — Astronaut, Air Force General
PO Box 58386, Houston TX 77258, USA

**Engle, Robert F** — Nobel Economics Laureate
New York University, Stern Business School, 44 W 4th St, New York NY 10012, USA

**Englehart, Robert W (Bob), Jr** — Editorial Cartoonist
Hartford Courant, Editorial Dept, 280 Broad St, Hartford CT 06105, USA

**Englehorn, Shirley** — Golfer
849 Shrine View, Colorado Springs CO 80906, USA

**Engler, Erich** — Space Scientist
80 Valley Way Circle SE, Huntsville AL 35802, USA

**Engler, Michael** — Director
United Talent Agency, U T A Plaza, 9336 Civic Center Dr, Beverly Hills CA 90210 USA

**Englert, Alice** — Actress
Creative Artists Agency, 2000 Ave of Stars, #100, Los Angeles CA 90067 USA

**Englert, Francois** — Nobel Physics Laureate
Physique Theorique Service, CP225, Blvd du Triomphe, 1050 Bruxelles, Belgium

**English, Alexander (Alex)** — Basketball Player
596 Rimer Pond Road, Blythewood SC 29016, USA

**English, Bill** — Actor
Innovative Artists, 1505 10th St, Santa Monica CA 90401 USA

**English, CariDee** — Model
Elite Model Mgmt, 404 Park Ave S, #900, New York NY 10016 USA

**English, Diane** — Writer
Shukovsky-English Entertainment, 4024 Radford Ave, Studio City CA 91604, USA

**English, Harris** — Golfer
Professional Golfers Association, 100 Ave of Champions, Palm Beach Gardens FL 33418 USA

**English, James F, Jr** — Educator
31 Potter St, Groton CT 06340, USA

**English, Joseph T** — Psychiatrist
Saint Vincent's Hospital, 203 W 12th St, New York NY 10011, USA

**English, Kim** — Singer
Universal Attractions, 135 W 26th St, #1200, New York NY 10001 USA

**English, L Douglas (Doug)** — Football Player
Lone Star Paralysis, 1215 Red River St, Austin TX 78701, USA

**English, Michael** — Singer
Trifecta Entertainment, 209 10th Ave S, #302, Nashville TN 37203, USA
**English, Mitch** — Actor, Writer, Producer
Abrams Artists, 9200 W Sunset Blvd, #1125, West Hollywood CA 90069 USA
**Englund, Robert** — Actor
1278 Glenneyre, #73, Laguna Beach CA 92651, USA
**Engram, Simon J (Bobby), III** — Football Player
2009 High Pointe Court, Murrysville PA 15668, USA
**Engstrom, Erik** — Businessman
General Atlantic Partners, 3 Pickwick Plaza, #8, Greenwich CT 06830, USA
**Engstrom, Molly** — Ice Hockey Player
7582 Southshore Dr, Siren WI 54872, USA
**Engstrom, Royce C** — Educator
University of Montana, President's Office, 32 Campus Dr, Missoula MT 59812, USA
**Engvall, Bill** — Actor, Comedian
Paradigm Agency, 360 N Crescent Dr, North Building, Beverly Hills CA 90210 USA
**Enkhsaikhan, Mendsaikhany** — Prime Minister, Mongolia
Pease Ave 11A, Ulan Bator 210648, Mongolia
**Ennis, Garth** — Cartoonist, Writer
Avatar Press, 515 N Century Blvd, Rantoul IL 61866, USA
**Ennis, Jessica** — Track Athlete
J C C M Ltd, Matrix Studios, 91 Peterborough Road, London SW6 3BU, England
**Ennis, John** — Baseball Player
14255 Dearborn St, Panorama City CA 91402, USA
**Ennis, Ralph** — Singer, Guitarist
2 Kirklake Bank, Formby, Liverpool L37 2Y5, England
**Ennis, Raymond V (Ray)** — Singer, Guitarist
2 Kirklake Bank, Formby, Liverpool L37 2Y5, England
**Ennis,Victor Ray** — Sound Editor
Soundelux, 7080 Hollywood Blvd, #1100, Los Angeles CA 90028, USA
**Eno, Brian** — Composer, Keyboardist
Creative Artists Agency, 2000 Ave of Stars, #100, Los Angeles CA 90067 USA
**Enoch, Ed** — Singer (Stamps Quartet)
PO Box 1471, Brentwood TN 37024, USA
**Enos, Clay** — Photographer
96 5th Ave, #2, New York NY 10011, USA
**Enos, John, III** — Actor
I C M Partners, 10250 Constellation Blvd, #900, Los Angeles CA 90067 USA
**Enos, Mark** — Interior Designer
Enos Co, 8659 Holloway Plaza Drive, West Hollywood CA 90069, USA
**Enos, Mireille** — Actress
Gartner/Green Entertainment, 5225 Wilshire Blvd, #1200, Los Angeles CA 90036, USA
**Enos, Randall** — Cartoonist, Illustrator
402 N Park Ave, Easton CT 06612, USA
**Enrico, Roger A** — Businessman
PepsiCo Inc, 700 Anderson Hill Road, Purchase NY 10577, USA
**Enright, Agnes Leahy** — Singer, Keyboardist (Leahy)
PO Box 716, Lakefield ON K0L 2H0, Canada
**Enright, Anne** — Writer
Jonathan Cape Ltd, 20 Vauxhall Bridge Road, London SW1V 2SA, England
**Enright, Barbara** — Poker Player
All American Speakers, 437 5th Ave, New York NY 10016, USA
**Enright, George A** — Baseball Player
3075 Strawflower Way, Lake Worth FL 33467, USA
**Enriquez Garcia, Jorge** — Soccer Player
Club Deportivo Guadalajara, Av Aviacion 3800, #20, Col De Ocot, Zapopan Jalisco 45018, Mexico
**Enriquez, Jocelyn** — Singer
Nene Musik Productions, 1460 SW Santiago Ave, Port Saint Lucie FL 34953 USA
**Enriquez, Joy** — Singer
W M E Entertainment, 9601 Wilshire Blvd, #300, Beverly Hills CA 90210 USA
**Enroth, Jhonas** — Ice Hockey Player
Lovtaktsvagen 37, 141 42 Huddinge, Sweden
**Enroth-Cugell, Christina A E** — Neurophysiologist
Northwestern University, Engineering School, 2145 Sheridan, Evanston IL 60208, USA
**Ensberg, Morgan P** — Baseball Player
5535 Memorial Dr, #F114, Houston TX 77007, USA
**Ensher, Jason R** — Physicist
University of Colorado, Physics Dept, Boulder CO 80309, USA
**Ensign, Michael** — Actor
Abrams Artists, 9200 W Sunset Blvd, #1125, West Hollywood CA 90069 USA
**Ensler, Eve** — Actress, Comedienne, Writer
Grand Central Publishing, 237 Park Ave, New York NY 10017, USA
**Ensler, Jason** — Director
Pitt Group, 9465 Wilshire Blvd, #420, Beverly Hills CA 90212, USA
**Enthoven, Alain C** — Economist
1 McCormick Lane, Atherton CA 94027, USA
**Entner, Warren** — Singer, Guitarist (Grass Roots)
Thomas Cassidy, PO Box 1311, Tucson AZ 85702 USA
**Entremont, Philippe** — Conductor, Concert Pianist
Columbia Artists Mgmt Inc, 5 Columbus Circle, 1790 Broadway, #1600, New York NY 10019 USA
**Enya** — Singer, Composer
Manderley, Victoria Road, Killiney, County Dublin, Ireland
**Enyart, William (Bill)** — Football Player
61070 Parrell Road, Bend OR 97702, USA
**Enzensberger, Hans M** — Writer
Lindenstr 29, 60325 Frankfurt am Maim, Germany
**Eotvos, Peter** — Composer, Conductor
Naardeweg 56, 1261 Blaircum BV, Netherlands
**Ephron, Hallie** — Writer
William Morrow Publishers, 1350 Ave of Americas, New York NY 10019 USA
**Epic** — Rap Artist (Crazy Town)
Wyze Mgmt, 34 Maple St, London W1 5GD, England
**Epley, John M** — Otologist, Inventor
Portland Otologic Clinic, 52657 NE 2nd St, Scappoose OR 97056, USA
**Eppard, James G (Jim)** — Baseball Player
23115 153rd Ave, Rapid City SD 57703, USA

# E

**Epperson-Doumani, Brenda** — Actress
Kazarian/Measures/Ruskin, 11969 Ventura Blvd, #300, Studio City CA 91604 USA

**Eppinger, Dale L** — Vietnam War Air Force Hero
4100 Colina Cove, Round Rock TX 78681, USA

**Epple, Maria** — Alpine Skier
Gunzesried 3, 87544 Blaicach, Germany

**Epps, Mike** — Actor, Comedian
Creative Artists Agency, 2000 Ave of Stars, #100, Los Angeles CA 90067 USA

**Epps, Omar** — Actor
Anonymous Content, 3532 Hayden Ave, Culver City CA 90232 USA

**Epps, Phillip E (Phil)** — Football Player
212 Boulder Creek Dr, DeSoto TX 75115, USA

**Epps, Raymond E (Ray)** — Basketball Player
4030 Old Warwick Road, Richmond VA 23234, USA

**Epps, Shareeka** — Actress
Innovative Artists, 1505 10th St, Santa Monica CA 90401 USA

**Epstein, Daniel M** — Writer
843 W University Parkway, Baltimore MD 21210, USA

**Epstein, Emmanuel** — Plant Nutritionist, Microbiologist
University of California, Land Air Water Resources Dept, Davis CA 95616, USA

**Epstein, Jason** — Editor
PO Box 1143, Sag Harbor NY 11963, USA

**Epstein, Joseph** — Writer, Educator
522 Church St, #6B, Evanston IL 60201, USA

**Epstein, Michael P (Mike)** — Baseball Player
6384 S Blackhawk Way, Aurora CO 80016, USA

**Erat, Martin** — Ice Hockey Player
4 Crooked Stick Lane, Brentwood TN 37027, USA

**Erautt, Edward L S (Eddie)** — Baseball Player
7252 Waite Dr, La Mesa CA 91941, USA

**Erb, Fred** — Lyricist
I C M Partners, 10250 Constellation Blvd, #900, Los Angeles CA 90067 USA

**Erb, Richard D** — Government Official
University of Montana, Business School, Missoula MT 59807, USA

**Erbe, Kathryn** — Actress
Innovative Artists, 1505 10th St, Santa Monica CA 90401 USA

**Ercegan, Milan** — Wrestling Executive
F I L A, Rue du Chateau 6, 1804 Corsier-sur-Vevey, Switzerland

**Erdman, Dennis** — Actor, Director, Producer
Creative Artists Agency, 2000 Ave of Stars, #100, Los Angeles CA 90067 USA

**Erdman, Richard** — Sculptor
3188 S Brownell Road, Williston VT 05495, USA

**Erdman, Richard** — Actor
5655 Greenbush Ave, Van Nuys CA 91401, USA

**Erdmann, Susi-Lisa** — Bobsled Athlete
Karwendelstr 8A, 81369 Munich, Germany

**Erdo, Peter Cardinal** — Religious Leader
Archdiocese of Esztergom-Budapest, Uri Utca 62, Pf 1, 1024 Budapest, Hungary

**Erdogan, Recep Tayyip** — President, Prime Minister, Turkey
President's Office, Cumhurbaskanlgl Kosku, Cankaya, 06689 Ankara, Turkey

**Erdos, Todd M** — Baseball Player
118 Windsor Court, Cranberry Township PA 16066, USA

**Erdrich, K Louise** — Writer
Andrew Wylie Agency, 250 W 57th St, #2114, New York NY 10107, USA

**Erevia, Santiago J** — Vietnam War Army Hero (CMH)
311 Felps Blvd, San Antonio TX 78221, USA

**Ergen, Charles W** — Businessman
EchoStar Corporation, 100 Inverness Terrace E, Englewood CO 80112, USA

**Eric B** — Rap Artist (Eric B & Rakim)
Richard Walters, PO Box 2789, Toluca Lake CA 91610 USA

**Ericks, John E** — Baseball Player
17000 Oketo Ave, Tinley Park IL 60477, USA

**Erickson, Bryan L** — Ice Hockey Player
114 3rd St NW, #A, Roseau MN 56751, USA

**Erickson, Craig N** — Football Player
420 N Country Club Dr, Lake Worth FL 33462, USA

**Erickson, Dennis** — Football Coach
911 W Kidd Island Road, Coeur D'Alene ID 83814, USA

**Erickson, Ethan** — Actor
Greater Visions Artists Talent Agency, 8981 W Sunset Blvd, #101, West Hollywood CA 90069 USA

**Erickson, Grant** — Ice Hockey Player
222 Parks St, Whitewood SK S0G 5C0, Canada

**Erickson, Keith R** — Basketball, Volleyball Player
333 23rd St, Santa Monica CA 90402, USA

**Erickson, Roger F** — Baseball Player
PO Box 235, Sautee Nacoochee GA 30571, USA

**Erickson, Roger K (Roky)** — Singer, Guitarist, Songwriter
Ten Pin Mgmt, 176 Park Ave, Warwick RI 02889, USA

**Erickson, Scott** — Actor
I C M Partners, 10250 Constellation Blvd, #900, Los Angeles CA 90067 USA

**Erickson, Scott G** — Baseball Player
1183 Corral Ave, Sunnyvale CA 94086, USA

**Ericson, John** — Actor
7 Avenida Vista Grande, #310, Santa Fe NM 87508, USA

**Ericsson, Jimmie** — Ice Hockey Player
Skelleftea A I K Hockey, Skelleftea Kraft Arena, Mossgatan 27E, 931 22, Skelleftea, Sweden

**Ericsson, Jonathan** — Ice Hockey Player
Detroit Red Wings, Joe Louis Arena, 600 Civic Center Dr, Detroit MI 48226 USA

**Erika Jo** — Singer
Universal South Artists, 2303 21st Ave S, #400, Nashville TN 37212, USA

**Eriksen, Stein** — Skier
7700 Stein Way, Park City UT 84060, USA

**Erikson, Duke** — Bassist, Keyboardist (Garbage)
Borman Entertainment, 1250 6th St, #401, Santa Monica CA 90401, USA

**Erikson, Raymond L** — Medical Researcher
Harvard University Medical School, Biology Dept, 25 Shattuck St, Boston MA 02115, USA

**Eriksson, Aleksandra** — Model
Elite Model Mgmt, 404 Park Ave S, #900, New York NY 10016 USA
**Eriksson, Anders** — Ice Hockey Player
2259 Arlington Ave, Columbus OH 43221, USA
**Eriksson, Oskar** — Curling Athlete
Farjestadsvagen 19, 654 65 Karlstad, Sweden , USA
**Eriksson, Per-Olaf** — Businessman
Hedasvagen 57, 811 61 Sandviken, Sweden
**Eriksson, Peter K** — Ice Hockey Player
Vastra Storgatan 10, 553 15 Jonokoping, Sweden
**Erixon, Jan** — Ice Hockey Player
Stenbackav 58, Skelleftea 931 42, Sweden
**Erland, Jonathan** — Visual Effects Artist
Composite Components Co, 134 N Ave 61, #102-103, Los Angeles CA 90042, USA
**Erlandson, Eric** — Guitarist (Hole), Songwriter
Artist Group International, 9560 Wilshire Blvd, #400, Beverly Hills CA 90212 USA
**Erlandson, Thomas D (Tom), Sr** — Football Player
1045 E Possee Road, Castle Rock CO 80108, USA
**Erman, John** — Director
Creative Artists Agency, 2000 Ave of Stars, #100, Los Angeles CA 90067 USA
**Ermey, R Lee** — Actor
Bill Rogin Mgmt, 427 N Canon Dr, #215, Beverly Hills CA 90210, USA
**Erna, Salvatore P (Sully)** — Singer, Guitarist (Godsmack); Songwriter
Front Line Mgmt, 1100 Glendon Ave, #2000, Los Angeles CA 90024 USA
**Ernaga, Frank J** — Baseball Player
50 N Roop St, Susanville CA 96130, USA
**Ernst, Bret** — Actor, Comedian
United Talent Agency, U T A Plaza, 9336 Civic Center Dr, Beverly Hills CA 90210 USA
**Ernst, Richard R** — Nobel Chemistry Laureate
Kurlistr 24, 8404 Winterthur, Switzerland
**Ernst, Wallace Gary** — Geologist
Stanford University, Earth & Environment Sciences Dept, Stanford CA 94305, USA
**Eroglu, Dervis** — President, Turkish Northern Cyprus
President's Office, Via Mersin 10, Lefkosa, Turkish Northern Cyprus, Turkey
**Errazuriz Ossa, Francisco J Cardinal** — Religious Leader
Archdiocese of Santiago, Erasmo Escala 1872, Santiago, Chile
**Errey, Bob** — Ice Hockey Player
213 Fuji Dr, Canonsburg PA 15317, USA
**Errico, Melissa** — Actress, Singer
Right Side Mgmt, PO Box 250806, New York NY 10025, USA
**Erskine, Carl D** — Baseball Player
4031 Fallbrook Lane, Anderson IN 46011, USA
**Erskine, Peter** — Jazz Drummer, Composer
1727 Hill St, Santa Monica CA 90405, USA
**Erstad, Darin C** — Baseball Player
6230 Doe Creek Circle, Lincoln NE 68516, USA
**Ertegun, Mica** — Interior Designer
M A C II, 125 E 81st St, New York NY 10028, USA
**Ertl, Gerhard L** — Nobel Chemistry Laureate
Garystr 18, 14195 Berlin, Germany
**Ertl, Martina** — Alpine Skier
Ertlrenz, Brienner Str 13, 80333 Munich, Germany
**Ertl, Sue** — Golfer
4707 Sabal Key Dr, Bradenton FL 34203, USA
**Eruzione, Michael (Mike)** — Ice Hockey Player
40 Floyd St, Winthrop MA 02152, USA
**Erving, Julius W (Dr J)** — Basketball Player
108 Windrush Road, Winston-Salem NC 27106, USA
**Ervins, Ricky** — Football Player
20984 Nightshade Place, Ashburn VA 20147, USA
**Erwin, Mike** — Actor
Leverage Mgmt, 3030 Pennsylvania Ave, Santa Monica CA 90404 USA
**Erwitt, Elliott R** — Photographer
88 Central Park West, #1S, New York NY 10023, USA
**Erxleban, Russell A** — Football Player
2031 Beth Lane, Shreveport LA 71118, USA
**Esaki, Reona (Leo)** — Nobel Physics Laureate
12-6 Sanbancho, Chiyodaku, Tokyo 102 0075, Japan
**Esasky, Nicholas A (Nick)** — Baseball Player
1779 Starlight Dr, Marietta GA 30062, USA
**Escalera, Alfredo, Jr** — Boxer
Star Boxing, 991 Morris Park Ave, Bronx NY 10462, USA
**Escamilla, Michael Ray** — Actor, Director
Bauman Redanty Shaul Agency, 5757 Wilshire Blvd, #473, Los Angeles CA 90036 USA
**Escarpeta, Arlen** — Actor
Karen Forman Mgmt, 17547 Ventura Blvd, #102, Encino CA 91316, USA
**Esche, Robert** — Ice Hockey Player
6750 W Carter Road, Rome NY 13440, USA
**Eschenbach, Christoph** — Conductor, Concert Pianist
National Symphony Orchestra, Kennedy Performing Arts Center, 2700 F St NW, Washington, DC 20566, USA
**Eschenmoser, Albert J** — Chemist
Bergstra 9, 8700 Kusnacht ZH, Switzerland
**Eschert, Jurgen** — Canoeing Athlete
Tornowstr 8, 14473 Potsdam, Germany
**Escobar, Yunel** — Baseball Player
15763 SW 43rd St, Miami FL 33185, USA
**Escovedo, Alejandro** — Singer, Songwriter
MongrelMusic, 746 Center Blvd, Fairfax CA 94930, USA
**Escovedo, Peter (Pete)** — Percussionist
Universal Attractions, 135 W 26th St, #1200, New York NY 10001 USA
**Eselin, Caroline** — Costume Designer
United Talent Agency, U T A Plaza, 9336 Civic Center Dr, Beverly Hills CA 90210 USA
**Esfahani, Mahan** — Concert Harpsichordist
Borletti-Buitoni Trust, 20 Leythe Road, London W3 8AW, England
**Eshelman, Vaughn M** — Baseball Player
30106 Falher Dr, Spring TX 77386, USA

# E

**Esiason, Norman J (Boomer)** — Football Player, Sportscaster
25 Heights Road, Manhasset NY 11030, USA
**Esipovich, Alla** — Photographer
Maya Polsky Gallery, 215 W Superior St, Chicago IL 60654, USA
**Eskew, Michael L** — Businessman
United Parcel Service, 55 Glenlake Parkway NE, Atlanta GA 30328, USA
**Eskridge, William N, Jr** — Attorney, Educator
Yale University, Law School, 127 Wall St, New Haven CT 06511, USA
**Esler-Smith, Frank** — Keyboardist (Air Supply)
PO Box 3367, Beverly Hills CA 90212, USA
**Esparza, Raul** — Actor, Singer
Elin Flack Mgmt, 435 W 57th St, #3M, New York NY 10019, USA
**Esper, Michael** — Actor
Gersh Agency, 9465 Wilshire Blvd, #600, Beverly Hills CA 90212 USA
**Esperian, Kallen R** — Opera Singer
514 Lindseywood Cove, Memphis TN 38117, USA
**Espineli, Geno** — Baseball Player
1222 Park Lane, Katy TX 77450, USA
**Espinosa, Daniel** — Director
United Talent Agency, U T A Plaza, 9336 Civic Center Dr, Beverly Hills CA 90210 USA
**Espinosa, Eden** — Actress, Singer
Gersh Agency, 41 Madison Ave, #3301, New York NY 10010 USA
**Espinoza, Alvaro A** — Baseball Player
2374 SW Freeman St, Port Saint Lucie FL 34953, USA
**Esposito, Anthony J (Tony)** — Ice Hockey Player
418 55th Ave, Saint Pete Beach FL 33706, USA
**Esposito, Frank** — Bowling Executive
200 N State Route 17, Paramus NJ 07652, USA
**Esposito, Jennifer** — Actress
Washington Square Arts, 1041 N Formosa Ave, Formosa Building, West Hollywood CA 90046, USA
**Esposito, Philip A (Phil)** — Ice Hockey Player, Coach
4003 W Tacon St, Tampa FL 33629, USA
**Esposito, Samuel (Sammy)** — Baseball Player
PO Box 1826, Banner Elk NC 28604, USA
**Espy, A Michael (Mike)** — Secretary, Agriculture
Commodity Credit Corp, PO Box 2415, Washington DC 20013, USA
**Espy, Cecil E** — Baseball Player
5480 Encina Dr, San Diego CA 92114, USA
**Esquivel, Manuel** — Prime Minister, Belize
United Democratic Party, 19 King St, PO Box 1143, Belize City, Belize
**Essandoh, Ato** — Actor
S M S Talent, 8383 Wilshire Blvd, #230, Beverly Hills CA 90211 USA
**Essegian, Charles A (Chuck)** — Baseball Player
15639 Bronco Dr, Canyon Country CA 91387, USA
**Essensa, Bob** — Ice Hockey Player
1130 Iroquois Trail, Oxford MI 48371, USA
**Esser, Mark G** — Baseball Player
717 S US Highway 1, #708, Jupiter FL 33477, USA
**Essex, David** — Singer, Actor, Composer
Stratford Saye, 20 Wellington Road, Bournemouth, Dorset BG8 8JN, England
**Essex, Myron E** — Microbiologist
Harvard School of Public Health, 665 Huntington Ave, Boston MA 02115, USA
**Essian, James S (Jim)** — Baseball Player, Manager
134 Eckford Dr, Troy MI 48085, USA
**Essick, Todd** — Photographer
PO Box 2376, West Palm Beach FL 33402, USA
**Essink, Ronald A** — Football Player
PO Box 265, Hamilton MI 49419, USA
**Esslinger, Hartmut** — Industrial Designer
FrogDesign, 3460 Hillview Ave, Palo Alto CA 94304, USA
**Essman, Susan (Susie)** — Actress, Comedienne
Paradigm Agency, 360 N Crescent Dr, North Building, Beverly Hills CA 90210 USA
**Esswood, Paul L V** — Opera Singer
Jasmine Cottage, 42 Ferring Lane, Ferring, West Sussex BN12 6QT, England
**Estabrook, Christine** — Actress
Don Buchwald Talent Agency, 6500 Wilshire Blvd, #2200, Los Angeles CA 90048 USA
**Estabrook, Michael J (Mike)** — Baseball Umpire
110 Grove Way, Delray Beach FL 33444, USA
**Estalella, Robert M (Bobby)** — Baseball Player
3612 Churchill Downs Dr, Davie FL 33328, USA
**Esteban, Manuel A** — Educator
California State University, O'Connell Hall, Chico CA 95929, USA
**Estefan, Emilio, Jr** — Musician, Producer
Estefan Enterprises, 420 Jefferson Ave, Miami Beach FL 33139, USA
**Estefan, Gloria** — Singer, Songwriter
39 Star Island Dr, Miami Beach FL 33139, USA
**Estefan, Lili** — Actress
T G A Voice, 100 Lincoln Road, #928, Miami Beach FL 33178, USA
**Estelle** — Singer
I C M Partners, 10250 Constellation Blvd, #900, Los Angeles CA 90067 USA
**Esten, Charles (Chip)** — Actor, Comedian
Stone Manners Salners, 6100 Wilshire Blvd, #1500, Los Angeles CA 90035 USA
**Estepa Llaurens, Jose M Cardinal** — Religious Leader
Military Ordinariate of Spain Military, Calle Nuncio 13, 28005 Madrid, Spain
**Estern, Neil** — Sculptor
432 Cream Hill Road, West Cornwall CT 06796, USA
**Estes, A Shawn** — Baseball Player
9694 E Legacy Lane, Scottsdale AZ 85255, USA
**Estes, Bob** — Golfer
4408 Long Champ Dr, #21, Austin TX 78746, USA
**Estes, Clarissa Pinkola** — Psychologist, Writer
Knopf Publishers, 201 E 50th St, New York NY 10022, USA
**Estes, Jacob Aaron** — Director, Writer
Management 360, 9111 Wilshire Blvd, Beverly Hills CA 90210 USA
**Estes, James** — Cartoonist
1103 Callahan St, Amarillo TX 79106, USA

|  |  |
|---|---|
| **Estes, Lawrence G (Larry)**<br>115 Alida St, Hammond LA 70403, USA | Football Player |
| **Estes, Richard**<br>PO Box 685, Northeast Harbour ME 04662, USA | Artist |
| **Estes, Robert (Rob)**<br>Thruline Entertainment, 9250 Wilshire Blvd, #100, Beverly Hills CA 90212 USA | Actor |
| **Estes, Simon L**<br>Hochstr 43, 8706 Feldmeilen, Switzerland | Opera Singer |
| **Estes, Will**<br>Paradigm Agency, 360 N Crescent Dr, North Building, Beverly Hills CA 90210 USA | Actor |
| **Estes, William K**<br>65 Gaston Road, Morristown NJ 07960, USA | Psychologist |
| **Esteve-Coll, Elizabeth**<br>27 Ursula St, London SW11 3DW, England | Museum Executive |
| **Estevez, Emilio**<br>Alchemy Entertainment, 7024 Melrose Ave, #420, Los Angeles CA 90038 USA | Actor, Director |
| **Estevez, Luis**<br>122 E 7th St, Los Angeles CA 90014, USA | Fashion Designer |
| **Estevez, Ramon L**<br>Special Artists Agency, 9200 Sunset Blvd, #410, West Hollywood CA 90069 USA | Actor |
| **Estevez, Renee**<br>House of Representatives, 1434 6th St, #1, Santa Monica CA 90401 USA | Actress |
| **Esthero**<br>ArtistDirect, 10900 Wilshire Blvd, #1400, Los Angeles CA 90024 USA | Singer |
| **Estil, Frode**<br>7530 Meraker, Norway | Cross Country Skier |
| **Estill, Michelle**<br>613 N 6th St Circle, Princeton IA 52768, USA | Golfer |
| **Estleman, Loren Daniel**<br>5552 Walsh Road, Whitmore Lake MI 48189, USA | Writer |
| **Estrada, Charles L (Chuck)**<br>1289 Manzanita Way, San Luis Obispo CA 93401, USA | Baseball Player |
| **Estrada, Erik**<br>Creative Talent Group, 1900 Ave of Stars, #2475, Los Angeles CA 90067, USA | Actor, Producer |
| **Estrada, Erik-Michael**<br>Trans Continental Records, 127 W Church St, #350, Orlando FL 32801, USA | Singer (O-Town) |
| **Estrada, Johnny P**<br>20 Winged Foot Ridge, Newnan GA 30265, USA | Baseball Player |
| **Estrich, Susan R**<br>947 Berkeley St, Santa Monica CA 90403, USA | Attorney |
| **Estrin, Zack**<br>W M E Entertainment, 9601 Wilshire Blvd, #300, Beverly Hills CA 90210 USA | Producer, Writer |
| **Eswaran, Vijay**<br>Q I Group, Bank of China Tower, #5500, Hong Kong Central, China | Businessman |
| **E-Swift**<br>Likwit Entertainment, PO Box 360713, Los Angeles CA 90036, USA | Rap Artist |
| **Eszterhas, Joseph A**<br>Baumgarten Mgmt, 406 Wilshire Blvd, Santa Monica CA 90401, USA | Writer |
| **Etaix, Pierre**<br>Editions du Seuil, 27 Rue Jacob, 75261 Paris Cedex 06, France | Director, Actor |
| **Etchebarren, Andrew A (Andy)**<br>1488 Vermeer Dr, Nokomis FL 34275, USA | Baseball Player |
| **Etchegaray, Roger Cardinal**<br>Council for Justice & Peace, Piazza San Calisto 16, 00153 Rome, Italy | Religious Leader |
| **Etcheverry, Marco**<br>D C United, R F K Stadium, 2400 E Capitol St SE, Washington DC 20003 USA | Soccer Player |
| **Etcoff, Nancy**<br>Harvard Medical School, Mind Brain Behavior Initiative, 25 Shattuck St, Boston MA 02115, USA | Psychologist |
| **Etel, Alex**<br>Independent Talent Group, 40 Whitfield St, London W1T 2RH, England | Actor |
| **Etheridge, Melissa L**<br>Creative Artists Agency, 2000 Ave of Stars, #100, Los Angeles CA 90067 USA | Singer, Songwriter, Guitarist |
| **Ethier, Andre E**<br>21423 S 147th St, Gilbert AZ 85298, USA | Baseball Player |
| **Ethier, Linda**<br>2846 NE Glissan St, Portland OR 97232, USA | Artist |
| **Ethridge, Mark F, III**<br>5516 Gorham Dr, Charlotte NC 28226, USA | Editor |
| **Etienne, Jean-Louis**<br>Musee Oceanographique de Monaco, Ave Saint-Martin, 98000 Monaco | Explorer |
| **Etienne, Pauline**<br>A C T I, 83 Rue Saint Honore, 75001 Paris, France | Actress |
| **Etsel, Edward (Ed)**<br>University of Virginia, Athletic Dept, Charlottesville VA 22906, USA | Marksman |
| **Ettinger, Cynthia**<br>Thruline Entertainment, 9250 Wilshire Blvd, #100, Beverly Hills CA 90212 USA | Actress |
| **Ettinger, Dan**<br>Mannheim Opera House, Mozartstr 9, 68161 Mannheim, Germany | Conductor |
| **Ettles, Mark**<br>3-10 Rose Ave, Perth WA 6151, Australia | Baseball Player |
| **Ettlin, Lukas**<br>Mirisch Agency, 1025 Colorado Ave, #B, Santa Monica CA 90211 USA | Cinematographer |
| **Etura, Marta**<br>Kuranda Mgmt, Santo Angel 84, 28043 Madrid, Spain | Actress |
| **Etzel, Gregory A M**<br>7822 Wonder St, Citrus Heights CA 95610, USA | Vietnam War Air Force Hero |
| **Etzioni, Amitai W**<br>George Washington University, Sociology Dept, Washington DC 20052, USA | Sociologist |
| **Eubank, Chris**<br>3 Vallensdean Cottages, Hangleton Lane, Portslade, Sussex BN41 2FQ, England | Boxer |
| **Eubanks, Kevin**<br>Blue Note Records, 6920 W Sunset Blvd, Los Angeles CA 90028 USA | Jazz Guitarist |
| **Eubanks, Robert L (Bob)**<br>Cheryl Kagan Public Relations, 4422 E 103rd St, Tulsa OK 74137, USA | Actor, Producer |
| **Eubesio, R Antonio (Tony)**<br>2078 Shannon Lakes Blvd, Kissimmee FL 34743, USA | Baseball Player |

**Euge Groove** — Jazz Saxophonist
Variety Artists, 1924 Spring St, Paso Robles CA 93446 USA

**Eugenides, Jeffrey** — Writer
Janklow & Nesbit Assoc, 445 Park Ave, #1300, New York NY 10022 USA

**Eustis, Joshua** — Musician (Telefon Tel Aviv)
Aero Booking, 8008 Greenwood Ave N, #3, Seattle WA 98103, USA

**Evancho, Jackie** — Singer
W M E Entertainment, 9601 Wilshire Blvd, #300, Beverly Hills CA 90210 USA

**Evangelista, Christine** — Actress
M J Management, 130 W 57th St, #11A, New York NY 10019, USA

**Evangelista, Linda** — Model
D N A Model Mgmt, 520 Broadway, #1100, New York NY 10012, USA

**Evanovich, Janet** — Writer
PO Box 2889, Naples FL 34106, USA

**Evans, Aja** — Bobsled Athlete
11 Saint Joseph's Terrace, Albany NY 12210, USA

**Evans, Alice** — Actress
Domain Talent, 9229 W Sunset Blvd, #710, West Hollywood CA 90069 USA

**Evans, B Heath** — Football Player
16633 Bienveneda Place, Pacific Palisades CA 90272, USA

**Evans, Barry S** — Baseball Player
128 Russell Dr, McDonough GA 30252, USA

**Evans, Bill** — Jazz Saxophonist, Keyboardist, Composer
Sony Records, 2100 Colorado Ave, Santa Monica CA 90404 USA

**Evans, Byron N** — Football Player
1763 E Carter Road, Phoenix AZ 85042, USA

**Evans, Cadell** — Cyclist
B M C Racing Team, Sportstr 49, 2540 Grenchen, Switzerland

**Evans, Christine** — Singer, Songwriter
Jane Harbury Publicity, 1290 Dundas St E, Toronto ON M4M 1S6, Canada

**Evans, Daniel** — Actor, Singer
Hamilton Hodell, 20 Golden Square, London W1F 9JL, England

**Evans, Daniel A** — Organic Chemist
Harvard University, Evans Group, 12 Oxford St, Cambridge MA 02138, USA

**Evans, Daniel E** — Businessman
Bob Evans Farms, 3776 S High St, Columbus OH 43207, USA

**Evans, Daniel J** — Governor, Senator, WA; Educator
Daniel J Evans Assoc, 1111 3rd Ave, #3400, Seattle WA 98101, USA

**Evans, Danielle** — Model
Click Model Mgmt, 881 7th Ave, New York NY 10019 USA

**Evans, Darrell W** — Baseball Player
1400 E Tahquitz Canyon Way, Palm Springs CA 92262, USA

**Evans, Daryl** — Ice Hockey Player
22403 Marjorie Ave, Torrance CA 90505, USA

**Evans, David A** — Chemist
Harvard University, Chemistry & Chemical Biology Dept, Cambridge MA 02138, USA

**Evans, Demetric U** — Football Player
PO Box 2256, Allen TX 75013, USA

**Evans, Dick** — Bowling Columnist
121 Morning Dove Court, Daytona Beach FL 32119, USA

**Evans, Donald L** — Football Player
12407 Beauvoir St, Raleigh NC 27614, USA

**Evans, Donald L** — Secretary, Commerce
Financial Services Forum, 601 13th Street NW, #750 South, Washington DC 20005, USA

**Evans, Douglas E (Doug)** — Football Player
8099 Highway 534, Haynesville LA 71038, USA

**Evans, Dwight M** — Baseball Player
123 Johnson Woods Dr, Reading MA 01867, USA

**Evans, Evans** — Actress
3114 Abington Dr, Beverly Hills CA 90210, USA

**Evans, Faith** — Singer, Songwriter
Padell Nadell Fine, 59 Maiden Lane, #2700, New York NY 10038, USA

**Evans, Frederick H (Fred)** — Football Player
Minnesota Vikings, 9520 Viking Dr, Eden Prairie MN 55344 USA

**Evans, Gareth** — Director
Management 360, 9111 Wilshire Blvd, Beverly Hills CA 90210 USA

**Evans, George** — Cartoonist (Anna & Corrigan)
King Features Syndicate, 300 W 57th St, #1500, New York NY 10019 USA

**Evans, Glen** — Molecular Biologist
Salk Institute, 10100 N Torrey Pines Road, La Jolla CA 92037 USA

**Evans, Greg** — Cartoonist (Luann)
216 Country Garden Lane, San Marcos CA 92069, USA

**Evans, Harold J** — Plant Physiologist
17360 Holy Names Dr, #2037, Lake Oswego OR 97034, USA

**Evans, J Thomas** — Freestyle Wrestler
607 S Fir Court, Broken Arrow OK 74012, USA

**Evans, Jahri** — Football Player
New Orleans Saints, 5800 Airline Highway, Metairie LA 70003 USA

**Evans, James B (Jim)** — Baseball Umpire
1801 Rogge Lane, Austin TX 78723, USA

**Evans, Janet** — Swimmer
8 Barneburg, Trabuco Canyon CA 92679, USA

**Evans, John R** — Foundation Executive
Rockefeller Foundation, 1133 Ave of Americas, New York NY 10036, USA

**Evans, Jonathan** — Law Enforcement Official
Security Service (MI-5), Thames House, 11 Millbank, London SW1P AQJ, England

**Evans, Lee** — Actor
Off the Kerb Productions, Hammer House, 113-117 Wardour St, #300, London W1F 0UN, England

**Evans, Lee E** — Track Athlete
250 S Sage Ave, Mobile AL 36606, USA

**Evans, Linda** — Actress
PO Box 29, Rainier WA 98576, USA

**Evans, Lindsey Gayle** — Model
Playboy Promotions, 9346 Civic Center Dr, #200, Beverly Hills CA 90210 USA

**Evans, Luke** — Actor
United Agents, 12-26 Lexington St, London W1F 0LE, England

**Evans, Lynn** — Singer (Chordettes)
Richard Paul Assoc, 16207 Mott Dr, Macomb Township MI 48044, USA
**Evans, M Terry** — Baseball Player
1049 Dunedin Trail, Woodstock GA 30188, USA
**Evans, Marc** — Director
Tessa Sayle Agency, 11 Jubilee Place, London SW3 3TE, England
**Evans, Martin J** — Nobel Medicine Laureate
Cardiff University Museum, PO Box 911, Cardiff CF10 3US, Wales
**Evans, Martina** — Writer
Sayle Literary Agency, 25-27 Bickerton Road, London N19 5JT, England
**Evans, Mary Beth** — Actress
Michael Bruno Group, 13576 Cheltenham Dr, Sherman Oaks CA 91423, USA
**Evans, Michael L (Mike)** — Football Player
Tampa Bay Buccaneers, 1 W Buccaneer Place, Tampa FL 33607 USA
**Evans, Mijoshki A (Josh)** — Football Player
PO Box 273309, Boca Raton FL 33427, USA
**Evans, Nathan** — Keyboardist (Neon Trees)
Creative Artists Agency, 2000 Ave of Stars, #100, Los Angeles CA 90067 USA
**Evans, Nicholas (Nick)** — Writer
Signet Books, 375 Hudson St, New York NY 10014 USA
**Evans, Nicky** — Actor
Associated International Mgmt, 7 Hatton Garden, #400, London EC1N 8AD, England
**Evans, Norm E** — Football Player
360 NW Boulder Place, Issaquah WA 98027, USA
**Evans, Richard** — Sports Executive
Madison Square Garden, 4 Pennsylvania Plaza, New York NY 10001, USA
**Evans, Richard Paul** — Writer
PO Box 712137, Salt Lake City UT 84171, USA
**Evans, Robert J (Bob)** — Producer
Robert Evans Productions, Paramount Pictures, 5555 Melrose, Los Angeles, CA 90038, USA
**Evans, Robert S** — Businessman
Crane Co, 100 Stamford Plaza, Stamford CT 06902, USA
**Evans, Ronald M** — Geneticist
Salk Institute, 10100 N Torrey Pines Road, La Jolla CA 92037 USA
**Evans, Roy** — WW II Army Air Corps Hero
15221 Lime St, Hesperia CA 92345, USA
**Evans, Rupert** — Actor
Curtis Brown Group, 28-29 Haymarket St, #500, London SW1Y 4SP, England
**Evans, Sara E** — Singer, Songwriter
Gersh Agency, 9465 Wilshire Blvd, #600, Beverly Hills CA 90212 USA
**Evans, Shaun** — Actor
Hamilton Hodell, 20 Golden Square, London W1F 9JL, England
**Evans, Sian** — Singer, Songwriter (Kosheen)
Moksha Mgmt, PO Box 102, London E15 2HH, England
**Evans, Terence T** — Judge
US Court of Appeals, 517 E Wisconsin Ave, Milwaukee WI 53202, USA
**Evans, Tiffany** — Singer, Actress
W M E Entertainment, 9601 Wilshire Blvd, #300, Beverly Hills CA 90210 USA
**Evans, Troy** — Actor
Stone Manners Salners, 6100 Wilshire Blvd, #1500, Los Angeles CA 90035 USA
**Evans, Tyreke** — Basketball Player
New Orleans Pelicans, 1250 Poydras St, #101, New Orleans LA 70113 USA
**Evans, Vincent T (Vince)** — Football Player
14084 Bronte Dr, Whittier CA 90602, USA
**Evans, Walker** — Truck, Off-Road Racing Driver
Walker Evans Racing, PO Box 2469, Riverside CA 92516, USA
**Evans, William (Billy)** — Basketball Player
24369 Sandpiper Isle Way, #105, Bonita Springs FL 34134, USA
**Evason, Dean C** — Ice Hockey Player
Washington Capitals, 627 N Glebe Road, #850, Arlington VA 22203 USA
**Evatt, Christopher** — Motivational Speaker
P O Box 294, 06101 Porvoo, Finland
**Eve** — Rap Artist (Ruff Ryders), Actress
1438 N Gower St, #115, Los Angeles CA 90028, USA
**Eve, Alice** — Actress
Independent Talent Group, 40 Whitfield St, London W1T 2RH, England
**Eve, Trevor J** — Actor
Insight Entertainment, 1134 S Cloverdale Ave, Los Angeles CA 90019, USA
**Eveland, Dana J** — Baseball Player
17530 Ventura Blvd, #201, Encino CA 91316, USA
**Evensen, Johan Remen** — Ski Jumper
Molde og Omega I F, PB 2326, 6402 Molde, Norway
**Everett, Carl E** — Baseball Player
19108 Harborbridge Lane, Lutz FL 33558, USA
**Everett, Danny** — Track Athlete
Santa Monica Track Club, 1801 Ocean Park Ave, #112, Santa Monica CA 90405, USA
**Everett, J Adam** — Baseball Player
4374 Oglethorpe Loop NW, Acworth GA 30101, USA
**Everett, James S (Jim)** — Football Player
555 N El Camino Real, #A445, San Clemente CA 92672, USA
**Everett, Major D** — Football Player
PO Box 1441, Pine Lake GA 30072, USA
**Everett, Mark Oliver (E, Eels)** — Singer, Guitarist, Songwriter
International Talent Booking, Ariel House, 74A Charlotte St, #100 London W1T 4QJ, England
**Everett, Rupert** — Actor
Tavistock Wood Mgmt, 45 Conduit St, London W1S 2YN, England
**Everett, Thomas G** — Football Player
PO Box 795337, Dallas TX 75379, USA
**Everhard, Nancy** — Actress
Talent Management Group, 339 E 3900 S, #200, Salt Lake City UT 84107, USA
**Everhart, Angie** — Model, Actress
2961 Dona Emilia Dr, Studio City CA 91604, USA
**Everhart, Thomas E** — Educator
705 Poinsettia Way, Santa Barbara CA 93111, USA
**Everitt, Steven M (Steve)** — Football Player
17252 Snapper Lane, Summerland Key FL 33042, USA

**Everlast**
A A Music Mgmt, 1100 Glendon Ave, #2000, Los Angeles CA 90024, USA — Rap Artist, Actor, Songwriter

**Everly, Donald (Don)**
401 W 9th St, Columbia TN 38401, USA — Singer (Everly Brothers)

**Evers, Charles**
1018 Pecan Park Dr, Jackson MS 39209, USA — Civil Rights Activist

**Eversgerd, Bryan D**
9212 Huey Road, Centralia IL 62801, USA — Baseball Player

**Eversley, Frederick J**
1110 W Abbot Kinney Blvd, Venice CA 90291, USA — Sculptor

**Eversman, Nick**
More/Medavoy Mgmt, 10203 Santa Monica Blvd, #400, Los Angeles CA 90067 USA — Actor

**Everson, Corinna (Cory)**
23705 Van Owen St, West Hills CA 91307, USA — Body Builder

**Evers-Williams, Myrlie**
15 SW Colorado Ave, #310, Bend OR 97702, USA — Association Executive

**Evert, Ray F**
810 Woodward Dr, Madison WI 53704, USA — Botanist

**Evert-Mill, Christine M (Chris)**
8563 Horseshoe Lane, Boca Raton FL 33496, USA — Tennis Player

**Evidence**
W M E Entertainment, 9601 Wilshire Blvd, #300, Beverly Hills CA 90210 USA — Rap Artist (Dilated Peoples)

**Evigan, Briana**
A P A Talent & Literary Agency, 405 S Beverly Dr, #300, Beverly Hills CA 90212 USA — Actress

**Evigan, Greg**
Stone Manners Salners, 6100 Wilshire Blvd, #1500, Los Angeles CA 90035 USA — Actor, Singer

**Evren, Kenan**
Beyaz Ev Sokak 21, Armutalan, 48700 Marmaris, Turkey — President, Turkey; Army General

**Ewald, Elwyn**
Free Lutheran Congregations, 12015 Manchester Road, Saint Louis MO 63131, USA — Religious Leader

**Ewald, Reinhold**
D L R Astronauterburo WT/AN, Linder Hohe, 51140 Cologne, Germany — Cosmonaut, Germany

**Ewell, Kayla**
Innovative Artists, 1505 10th St, Santa Monica CA 90401 USA — Actress

**Ewen, Harold I**
60 Hillcrest Dr, South Deerfield MA 01373, USA — Astronomer, Physicist

**Ewen, Paterson**
1015 Wellington St, London ON N6A 3T5, Canada — Artist

**Ewen, Todd**
420 Thunderhead Canyon Dr, Ballwin MO 63011, USA — Ice Hockey Player

**Ewing, Barbara**
1 Candover St, #4, London W1W 7DG, England — Actress

**Ewing, Donald Ralph (Skip)**
Sussman Assoc, 1222 16th Ave S, #300, Nashville TN 37212, USA — Singer, Songwriter

**Ewing, Maria L**
Mitchell-Godfrey Mgmt, 48 Gary's Inn Road, London WC1X 8LT, England — Opera Singer

**Ewing, Patrick A**
Orlando Magic, 8701 Maitland Summit Blvd, Orlando FL 32810 USA — Basketball Player

**Ewing, Reid**
United Talent Agency, U T A Plaza, 9336 Civic Center Dr, Beverly Hills CA 90210 USA — Actor

**Exarchopoulos, Adele**
Creative Artists Agency, 2000 Ave of Stars, #100, Los Angeles CA 90067 USA — Actress

**Exelby, Garnet**
1182 Saint Louis Place NE, Atlanta GA 30306, USA — Ice Hockey Player

**Exum, Dante**
Utah Jazz, Energy Solutions Arena, 301 W South Temple, Salt Lake City UT 84101 USA — Basketball Player

**Eyharts, Leopold**
49 Rue Desnouttes, 75015 Paris, France — Spatinaut, France

**Eyoghe Ndong, Jean**
Prime Minister's Office, BP 91, Immeuble du 2 Decembre, Libreville, Gabon — Prime Minister, Gabon

**Eyre, Chris**
Critical Mass Mgmt, 1158 26th St, #414, Santa Monica CA 90403, USA — Actor, Director, Producer

**Eyre, Ivan**
1098 Des Trappistes St, Winnipeg MB R3V 1B8, Canada — Artist

**Eyre, Richard**
Judy Daish Assoc, 2 Saint Charles Place, London W10 6EG, England — Director, Writer

**Eyre, Scott A**
7010 190th St E, Bradenton FL 34211, USA — Baseball Player

**Eyring, Henry B**
Church of Latter Day Saints, 50 E North Temple, Salt Lake City UT 84150, USA — Religious Leader

**Eyskens, Mark M F**
Graaf de Grunnelaan 17, 3001 Heverlee-Leuven, Belgium — Prime Minister, Belgium

**Eytchison, Ronald M**
11 Prentice Lane, Signal Mountain TN 37377, USA — Navy Admiral

**Ezeli, I Festus**
Golden State Warriors, 1011 Broadway, Oakland CA 94605 USA — Basketball Player

**Ezersky, John J (Johnny)**
2564 Walnut Blvd, #103, Walnut Creek CA 94596, USA — Basketball Player

**Ezra, Derek**
2 Salisbury Road, Wimbledon, London SW19 4EZ, England — Government Official, Businessman

**Ezzati Andrello, Ricardo Cardinal**
Archdiocese of Santiago del Cile, Erasmo Escala 1872, Santiago, Chile — Religious Leader

**Fabares, Shelley** — Actress, Singer
Innovative Artists, 1505 10th St, Santa Monica CA 90401 USA
**Fabbricini, Tiziana** — Opera Singer
Gianni Testa, Via Wrenteggio 31/6, 20146 Milan, Italy
**Faber, Michel** — Writer
Canongate Books, 14 High St, Edinburgh EH1 1TE, Scotland
**Faber, Sandra M** — Astronomer
16321 Ridgecrest Ave, Monte Sereno CA 95030, USA
**Faber, Steve** — Writer, Producer
McKuin Frankel Whitehead, 141 El Camino Drive, #100, Beverly Hills CA 90212 USA
**Fabian** — Singer
Universal Attractions, 135 W 26th St, #1200, New York NY 10001 USA
**Fabian DeLa Mora, Marco J** — Soccer Player
Club Deportivo Guadalajara, Av Aviacion 3800, Col De Ocot, Zapopan Jalisco 45019, Mexico
**Fabian, Ava** — Actress, Model
Playboy Enterprises, 680 N Lake Shore Dr, Chicago IL 60611 USA
**Fabian, John M** — Astronaut
100 Shine Road, Port Ludlow WA 98365, USA
**Fabian, Lara** — Singer, Songwriter
Productions Clandestines, 1 Place du Commerce, #400, Ile des Soeurs QC H3E 1A2, Canada
**Fabian, Patrick** — Actor
Essential Talent Mgmt, 7958 Beverly Blvd, Los Angeles CA 90048, USA
**Fabini, Jason** — Football Player
8701 Wheelock Road, Fort Wayne IN 46835, USA
**Fabio** — Model, Actor
Premier Talent Group, 4370 Tujunga Ave, #110, Studio City CA 91604, USA
**Fabiola Mora y Aragon, Dona** — Queen Mother, Belgium
Royal Palace of Laeken, Avenue du Parc, 1020 Laeken-Brussels, Belgium
**Fabius, Laurent** — Premier, France
National Assembly, Casier de la Poste, Paris Bourbon, 75355 Paris, France
**Fabjan, Vesna** — Cross Country Skier
Pod Gozdom 29, 4201 Spodnja Besnica, Slovenia
**Fabolous** — Rap Artist, Actor
Artist Representation Group, 9701 Wilshire Blvd, #1000, Beverly Hills CA 90212, USA
**Fabray, Nanette** — Singer, Actress
13834 Magnolia Blvd, Sherman Oaks CA 91423, USA
**Fabre, Jan** — Artist
Pastorihstaat 23, 2060 Antwerp, Belgium
**Fabregas, Jorge** — Baseball Player
10249 SW 77th Court, Miami FL 33156, USA
**Face, Elroy L (Roy)** — Baseball Player
608 Della Dr, #5F, North Versailles PA 15137, USA
**Fachinetti, Alessandra** — Fashion Designer
Gucci Group, 1 Amstelplein, 10966 Amsterdam HA, Netherlands
**Facinelli, Peter** — Actor
A P A Talent & Literary Agency, 405 S Beverly Dr, #300, Beverly Hills CA 90212 USA
**Fadden, Jimmie** — Musician (Nitty Gritty Dirt Band)
W M E Entertainment, 9601 Wilshire Blvd, #300, Beverly Hills CA 90210 USA
**Faddeyev, Ludwig D** — Mathematician, Physicist
Steklov Mathematics Institute, Gubkina Str 8, 119991 Moscow, Russia
**Faddis, Jonathan (Jon)** — Jazz Trumpeter, Flugelhorn Player
Carolyn McClair, PO Box 55, Radio Station, New York NY 10101, USA
**Fadek, Timothy** — Photographer
Polaris Images, 259 W 30th St, #1300, New York NY 10001, USA
**Fadem, Josh** — Actor
United Talent Agency, U T A Plaza, 9336 Civic Center Dr, Beverly Hills CA 90210 USA
**Fadeyechev, Alexei** — Ballet Dancer
Karenty Ryad Str 5/10, #20, 103006 Moscow Russia
**Fadeyechev, Nicolai B** — Ballet Dancer
Bolshoi Theater, Teatralnaya Pl 1, 103009 Moscow, Russia
**Fadiman, Anne** — Editor, Writer
Farrar Straus Giroux, 18 W 18th St, #700, New York NY 10011 USA
**Faedo, Leonardo L (Lenny)** — Baseball Player
2920 W Collins St, Tampa FL 33607, USA
**Faerch, Daeg** — Actor
Stone Manners Salners, 6100 Wilshire Blvd, #1500, Los Angeles CA 90035 USA
**Fagan, Garth** — Choreographer
Garth Fagan Dance, 50 Chestnut Plaza, #1, Rochester NY 14604, USA
**Fagan, Giles** — Actor
Artists Partnership, 101 Finsbury Pavement, London EC2A 1RS, England
**Fagan, Kevin** — Cartoonist (Drabble)
26771 Ashford, Mission Viejo CA 92692, USA
**Fagan, Kevin S** — Football Player
21555 SW 106th Lane Road, Dunnellon FL 34431, USA
**Fagen, Donald** — Singer (Steely Dan); Songwriter
Creative Artists Agency, 2000 Ave of Stars, #100, Los Angeles CA 90067 USA
**Fagenson, Anthony E (Tony)** — Drummer (Eve 6)
Agency Group Ltd, 1880 Century Park E, #711, Los Angeles CA 90067 USA
**Fagerbakke, Bill** — Actor
Main Title Mgmt, 8383 Wilshire Blvd, #408, Beverly Hills CA 90211 USA
**Fagg, George G** — Judge
US Court of Appeals, US Courthouse, 110 E Court Ave, Des Moines IA 50309, USA
**Faggin, Federico** — Co-Inventor (Microprocessor)
27910 Roble Blanco Dr, Los Altos Hills CA 94022, USA
**Faggins, DeMarcus** — Football Player
3002 Southworth Lane, Manvel TX 77578, USA
**Fagin, Claire M** — Educator
200 Central Park S, #12E, New York NY 10019, USA
**Fagin, Dan** — Writer
New York University, Carter Journalism Institute, New York NY 10012, USA
**Fahey, Damien** — Actor
Creative Artists Agency, 2000 Ave of Stars, #100, Los Angeles CA 90067 USA
**Fahey, Jeff** — Actor
Jeff Goldberg Mgmt, 817 Monte Leon Dr, Beverly Hills CA 90210, USA
**Fahey, John M, Jr** — Association Executive
National Geographic, President's Office, 1145 17th St NW, Washington DC 20036, USA

**F**

**Fabares - Fahey**

**Fahey, William R (Bill)**
5740 Mona Lane, Dallas TX 75236, USA — Baseball Player

**Fahl, Mary**
Invasion Group, 133 W 25th St, #500, New York NY 10001, USA — Singer

**Fahn, Stanley**
155 Edgars Lane, Hastings on Hudson NY 10706, USA — Neurologist

**Fahnhorst, James J (Jim)**
2365 Brockton Lane N, Minneapolis MN 55447, USA — Football Player

**Fahnhorst, Keith V**
12216 Chadwick Lane, Eden Prairie MN 55344, USA — Football Player

**Faibisovich, Semyon**
Regina Gallery, 1, 4 Syromyatnichesky Pereulok, 105120 Moscow, Russia — Artist, Photographer

**Fainaru, Steve**
Washington Post, Editorial Dept, 1150 15th St NW, Washington DC 20071 USA — Journalist

**Fair, Lorrie**
300 3rd St, #1515, San Francisco CA 94107, USA — Soccer Player

**Fair, Terrtance D (Terry)**
12910 W Monte Vista Road, Avondale AZ 85392, USA — Football Player

**Fairbairn, Bruce**
975 N Vendome St, #214, Los Angeles CA 90026, USA — Actor

**Fairbairn, William J (Bill)**
Box 55, Site 30, RR 3 Station Main, Brandon MB R7A 5Y6, Canada — Ice Hockey Player

**Fairbank, Richard D**
Capital One Financial, 1680 Capital One Dr, #1, McLean VA 22102, USA — Financier

**Fairbrass, Craig**
Screen 360, 145-157 Saint John St, London EC1V 4PW, England — Actor

**Fairchild, Barbara**
Artist Direction Agency, PO Box 40, Bremen GA 30110, USA — Singer, Songwriter

**Fairchild, John B**
Chalet Bianchina, Talstr GR, 7250 Klosters, Switzerland — Publisher

**Fairchild, Morgan**
Greene Assoc, 1901 Ave of Stars, #130, Los Angeles CA 90067 USA — Actress

**Fairchild, Paul J**
PO Box 25442, Overland Park KS 66225, USA — Football Player

**Fairchild, Shelly**
Creative Artists Agency, 2000 Ave of Stars, #100, Los Angeles CA 90067 USA — Singer

**Faircloth, D McLauchlin (Lauch)**
PO Box 496, Clinton NC 28329, USA — Senator, NC

**Fairley, Michelle**
Paradigm Agency, 360 N Crescent Dr, North Building, Beverly Hills CA 90210 USA — Actress

**Fairley, Nick**
Detroit Lions, 222 Republic Dr, Allen Park MI 48101 USA — Football Player

**Fairly, Ronald R (Ron)**
75369 Spyglass Dr, Indian Wells CA 92210, USA — Baseball Player, Sportscaster

**Fairs, Eric J**
32707 Wales Circle, Fulshear TX 77441, USA — Football Player

**Fairstein, Linda**
I C M Partners, 10250 Constellation Blvd, #900, Los Angeles CA 90067 USA — Writer, Attorney

**Faison, Donald**
A P A Talent & Literary Agency, 405 S Beverly Dr, #300, Beverly Hills CA 90212 USA — Actor

**Faison, W Earl**
2279 N Sequoia Dr, Prescott AZ 86301, USA — Football Player

**Faithfull, Marianne**
Republic Media, Westbourne Studios, 242 Acklam Road, #202, London W10 5JJ, England — Singer, Songwriter, Actress

**Fakhri, Nargis**
Ford Models Inc, 111 5th Ave, #900, New York NY 10003 USA — Actress

**Fakir, Abdul (Duke)**
I C M Partners, 730 5th Ave, New York NY 10019 USA — Singer (Four Tops)

**Falana, Lola**
Capital Entertainment, 217 Seaton Place NE, Washington DC 20002, USA — Singer, Dancer

**Falardeau, Philippe**
United Talent Agency, U T A Plaza, 9336 Civic Center Dr, Beverly Hills CA 90210 USA — Director

**Falcao, Jose Freire Cardinal**
Archdiocese of Brasilia, Esplanada dos Ministerios, Emi Lote 12, Brasilia DF 70050 000, Brazil — Religious Leader

**Falchi, Anna**
A Movie Productions, Via Filippo Corridoni 15, 00195 Rome, Lazio, Italy — Model, Actress, Producer

**Falchuk, Brad**
W M E Entertainment, 9601 Wilshire Blvd, #300, Beverly Hills CA 90210 USA — Producer, Director, Writer

**Falco, Ed**
Virginia Polytechnic Institute, English Dept, Blacksburg VA 24060, USA — Writer

**Falco, Edie**
I C M Partners, 10250 Constellation Blvd, #900, Los Angeles CA 90067 USA — Actress

**Falcon, Rose**
Show Dog/Universal Records, 70 Universal City Plaza, Universal City CA 91608, USA — Singer, Songwriter

**Falcone, Ben**
Creative Artists Agency, 2000 Ave of Stars, #100, Los Angeles CA 90067 USA — Actor

**Falcone, Meghan M**
Aligned Entertainment, 201 Wilshire Blvd, Santa Monica CA 90401, USA — Actress

**Falcone, Peter F (Pete)**
2232 Thornton Court, Alexandria LA 71301, USA — Baseball Player

**Falconer, Eric**
United Talent Agency, U T A Plaza, 9336 Civic Center Dr, Beverly Hills CA 90210 USA — Producer, Writer, Actor

**Falconer, Ian W**
Simon & Schuster, 1230 Ave of Americas, Concourse 1, New York NY 10020 USA — Writer, Illustrator

**Faldo, Nicholas A (Nick)**
Elizabeth House, 18-20 Sheet St, Windsor Berkshire SL4 1BG, England — Golfer, Sportscaster

**Falk, Adam F**
Williams College, President's Office, 880 Main St, Williamstown MA 01267, USA — Educator

**Falk, David B**
Falk Assoc, 5335 Wisconsin Ave NW, #850, Washington DC 20015, USA — Sports Attorney

**Falk, Dean**
Florida State University, Anthropology Dept, Tallahassee FL 32306, USA — Anthropologist

**Falk, Ingrid**
FA+, Drottninggatan 71A, 111 36 Stockholm, Sweden — Photographer, Artist

**Falk, Lisanne**
9255 W Sunset Blvd, #515, West Hollywood CA 90069, USA — Actress

**Falk, Paul** — Figure Skater
Sybelstr 21, 40239 Dusseldorf, Germany
**Falk, Thomas J** — Businessman
Kimberly-Clark Corp, 351 Phelps Dr, Irving TX 75038, USA
**Falkenborg, Brian T** — Baseball Player
30223 N 125th Dr, Peoria AZ 85383, USA
**Falkenburg, Robert (Bob)** — Tennis Player
PO Box 1837, Santa Ynez CA 93460, USA
**Falkow, Stanley** — Microbiologist
Stanford University Medical School, Microbiology Dept, Stanford CA 94305, USA
**Fall, Timothy** — Actor
Greenberg Glusker, 1900 Ave of Stars, #2100, Los Angeles CA 90067 USA
**Falla, Maiken Caspersen** — Cross Country Skier
Gjerdrum I L, Postbus 93, 2024 Gjerdrum, Norway
**Falldin, N O Thorbjorn** — Prime Minister, Sweden
As, 870 16 Ramvik, Sweden
**Fallon, Brian** — Singer, Guitarist (Gaslight Anthem)
Esther Creative Group, 27 W 24th St, #404, New York NY 10010, USA
**Fallon, James T (Jimmy), Jr** — Actor, Comedian
Creative Artists Agency, 2000 Ave of Stars, #100, Los Angeles CA 90067 USA
**Fallon, Robert J (Bob)** — Baseball Player
801 Somerset Circle, Hanover Park IL 60133, USA
**Fallon, Tiffany** — Model, Actress
Enter Talking Client Relations, 645 W 9th St, #110, Los Angeles CA 90010, USA
**Fallon, William J** — Navy Admiral
Business Executives for National Security, 1030 15th St NW, #200 East, Washington DC 20005, USA
**Falloon, Pat** — Ice Hockey Player
112-155 10th St, Birtle MB R0M 0C0, Canada
**Falls, Kevin** — Producer, Writer
W M E Entertainment, 9601 Wilshire Blvd, #300, Beverly Hills CA 90210 USA
**Falls, Robert A** — Director
Creative Artists Agency, 2000 Ave of Stars, #100, Los Angeles CA 90067 USA
**Falls, Sam** — Artist, Sculptor
American Contemporary Gallery, 4 E 2nd St, New York NY 10003, USA
**Faloona, Christopher J** — Cinematographer
Paradigm Agency, 360 N Crescent Dr, North Building, Beverly Hills CA 90210 USA
**Falsani, Cathleen** — Columnist
Chicago Sun-Times, Editorial Dept, 401 N Wabash Ave, Chicago IL 60611 USA
**Faltings, Gerd** — Mathematician
Princeton University, Mathematics Dept, Princeton NJ 08544, USA
**Faltskog, Agnetha (Anna)** — Singer (ABBA)
Sodra Brobanken 41A, 111 49 Stockholm, Sweden
**Faludi, Susan C** — Writer, Journalist
Sandra Dijkstra Literary Agency, 1155 Camino del Mar, #515, Del Mar CA 92014, USA
**Fama, Eugene F (Gene)** — Nobel Economics Laureate
University of Chicago, Booth Business School, 5807 S Woodlawn Ave, Chicago IL 60637, USA
**Fambrough, Henry** — Singer (Spinners)
Whitepine Entertainment, 398 Whitepine Creek Road, Trout Creek MT 59874, USA
**Famechon, Johnny** — Boxer
9 Wandana Court, Frankston VIC 3199, Australia
**Famie, Keith** — Chef, Director, Producer
W M E Entertainment, 9601 Wilshire Blvd, #300, Beverly Hills CA 90210 USA
**Famiglietti, Mark** — Actor
Hofflund/Polone, 9465 Wilshire Blvd, #420, Beverly Hills CA 90212 USA
**Fanaro, Barry** — Writer, Producer
I C M Partners, 10250 Constellation Blvd, #900, Los Angeles CA 90067 USA
**Fancher, Hampton** — Director, Writer, Actor
Earthbourne Films, 1810 14th St, #214, Santa Monica CA 90404, USA
**Fancy, Richard** — Actor
Bauman Redanty Shaul Agency, 5757 Wilshire Blvd, #473, Los Angeles CA 90036 USA
**Faneca, Alan J, Jr** — Football Player
3800 S Clubhouse Dr, #6, Chandler AZ 85248, USA
**Fang Lijun** — Artist
Max Protetch Gallery, 511 W 22nd St, New York NY 10011, USA
**Fankhauser, Merrell** — Guitarist, Composer
Franklyn Agency, 1010 Hammond St, #312, West Hollywood CA 90069, USA
**Fankhouser, Scott** — Ice Hockey Player
2043 Crippled Oak Trail, Jasper GA 30143, USA
**Fann, Al** — Actor
6051 Hollywood Blvd, #207, Los Angeles CA 90028, USA
**Fanning, Bernard** — Singer (Powderfinger)
Secret Service, PO Box 401, Fortitude Valley QLD 4006, Australia
**Fanning, Dakota** — Actress
W M E Entertainment, 9601 Wilshire Blvd, #300, Beverly Hills CA 90210 USA
**Fanning, Elle** — Actress
W M E Entertainment, 9601 Wilshire Blvd, #300, Beverly Hills CA 90210 USA
**Fanning, Michael L (Mike)** — Football Player
28808 S 4190 Road, Inola OK 74036, USA
**Fanning, W James (Jim)** — Baseball Player, Manager
154 Tiner Ave, Dorchester ON N0L 1G2, Canada
**Fano, Robert M** — Computer Scientist, Electrical Engineer
80 Deaconess Road, #227, Concord MA 01742, USA
**Fantetti, Ken M** — Football Player
4652 Sunvalley Dr, Loveland CO 80538, USA
**Fantoni, Sergio** — Actor
Via del Cappellari 35, 00186 Rome, Italy
**Fanzone, Carmen R** — Baseball Player
5114 Ranchito Ave, Sherman Oaks CA 91423, USA
**Faraci, John V, Jr** — Businessman
International Paper Corp, 2 Manhattanville Road, Purchase NY 10577, USA
**Faracy, Stephanie** — Actress
S D B Partners, 315 S Beverly Dr, #411, Beverly Hills CA 90067 USA
**Faragalli, Lindy** — Bowler
113 N 5th Ave, Manville NJ 08835, USA
**Farah** — Queen, Iran
Hellen Medien Projekte, Kornweg 1G, 44805 Bochum, Germany

**Farah, Mohammed (Mo)** — Track Athlete
Pace Sports Mgmt, 6 Causeway, Teddington, Middlesex TW11 0HE, England
**Farar, Hassan Abshir** — Prime Minister, Somalia
Prime Minister's Office, People's Palace, Mogadishu, Somalia
**Farenthold, Frances T** — Women's Activist, Educator
2929 Buffalo Speedway, #18B, Houston TX 77098, USA
**Farentino, Debrah** — Actress
Innovative Artists, 1505 10th St, Santa Monica CA 90401 USA
**Fares, Muhammad Ahmed Al** — Cosmonaut, Syria
PO Box 1272, Aleppo, Syria
**Fargis, Joseph H (Joe), IV** — Equestrian
25 Hampton Road, Southampton NY 11968, USA
**Fargo, Donna** — Singer, Guitarist
Prima Donna Entertainment, PO Box 150527, Nashville TN 37215, USA
**Fargo, Thomas B** — Navy Admiral
Trex Enterprises, 10455 Pacific Center Court, San Diego CA 92121, USA
**Farha, Ihsam (Sam)** — Poker Player
14027 Memorial Dr, #234, Houston TX 77079, USA
**Farhadi, Asghar** — Director, Producer, Writer
United Talent Agency, U T A Plaza, 9336 Civic Center Dr, Beverly Hills CA 90210 USA
**Farham, John P** — Singer
Gotham/B M G Records, 69-79 Fulham High St, London SW6 3JW, England
**Farhi, Nicole** — Fashion Designer
16 Foubert's Place, London W1F 7PJ, England
**Farina, Johnny** — Guitarist (Santo & Johnny)
Bellrose Music, 308 E 6th St, #13, New York NY 10003, USA
**Farina, Raffaele Cardinal** — Religious Leader
Vatican Library, Cortile del Belvedere, 00120 Vatican City
**Farino, Julian** — Director
Independent Talent Group, 40 Whitfield St, London W1T 2RH, England
**Faris, Al** — Actor
Chaotik, 6446 Santa Monica Blvd, Los Angeles CA 90038, USA
**Faris, Anna** — Actress
Anonymous Content, 3532 Hayden Ave, Culver City CA 90232 USA
**Faris, Sean H** — Actor
Gersh Agency, 9465 Wilshire Blvd, #600, Beverly Hills CA 90212 USA
**Faris, Valerie** — Director
United Talent Agency, U T A Plaza, 9336 Civic Center Dr, Beverly Hills CA 90210 USA
**Farish, William S** — Diplomat
W S Farish Co, 1100 Louisiana St, #2200, Houston TX 77002, USA
**Fariss, Monty T** — Baseball Player
PO Box 249, Leedey OK 73654, USA
**Farkas, Bertalan** — Cosmonaut, Hungary
A Magyar Koztarsasag, Kutato Urhajosa, Pf 25, 1885 Budapest, Hungary
**Farkas, Ferenc** — Composer
Nagyatai Utca 12, 1026 Budapest, Hungary
**Farkas, Jeff** — Ice Hockey Player
284 Patrice Terrace, Buffalo NY 14221, USA
**Farley, Carole** — Opera, Concert Singer
270 Riverside Dr, New York NY 10025, USA
**Farley, Kevin P** — Actor
Glick Agency, 347 5th Ave, #1404, New York NY 10016 USA
**Farley, Terrence M** — Financier
Brown Brothers Harriman, 59 Wall St, New York NY 10005, USA
**Farmar, Jordan R** — Basketball Player
2625 Zinfandel Dr, Rancho Cordova CA 95670, USA
**Farmer, Charles (Red)** — Auto Racing Driver
Talladega Walk of Fame, PO Drawer 1179, Talladega AL 35161, USA
**Farmer, D Michael (Mike)** — Basketball Player, Coach
2520 Lakeview Dr, Santa Rosa CA 95405, USA
**Farmer, Edward J (Ed)** — Baseball Player
4581 Camino del Sol, Calabasas CA 91302, USA
**Farmer, Gary** — Actor
Gonzo Drive Records, PO Box 31096, Santa Fe NM 87594, USA
**Farmer, George T** — Football Player
332 Lorraine Blvd, Los Angeles CA 90020, USA
**Farmer, George, III** — Football Player
12422 S Denker Ave, Los Angeles CA 90047, USA
**Farmer, James H (Jim)** — Basketball Player
214 Ashborough Circle, Dothan AL 36301, USA
**Farmer, John, Jr** — Governor, NJ
Attorney General's Office, Hughes Justice Complex, Trenton NJ 08625, USA
**Farmer, Paul** — Physician, Anthropologist
Partners in Health, 641 Huntington Ave, #100, Boston MA 02115, USA
**Farmiga, Talissa** — Actress
I C M Partners, 10250 Constellation Blvd, #900, Los Angeles CA 90067 USA
**Farmiga, Vera A** — Actress, Director
Creative Artists Agency, 2000 Ave of Stars, #100, Los Angeles CA 90067 USA
**Farner, Mark** — Singer, Guitarist
Bobby Roberts, 3050 Business Park Circle, #303, Goodlettsville TN 37221 USA
**Farnham, John P** — Singer, Actor
Talentworks, PO Box 246, South Yarra VIC 3141, Australia
**Farnon, Shannon** — Actress
12743 Milbank St, Studio City CA 91604, USA
**Farnsworth, Kyle L** — Baseball Player
1163 Wilde Dr, Kissimmee FL 34747, USA
**Farquhar, John W** — Physician
Stanford University Medical School, Disease Prevention Center, Stanford CA 94305, USA
**Farquhar, Kurt** — Composer
First Artists Mgmt, 4764 Park Granada, #210, Calabasas CA 91302 USA
**Farquhar, Marilyn G** — Cell Biologist, Pathologist
12894 Via Latina, Del Mar CA 92014, USA
**Farr, David N** — Businessman
Emerson Electric, 800 S Florissant Ave, Saint Louis MO 63135, USA
**Farr, Felicia** — Actress
1143 Tower Road, Beverly Hills CA 90210, USA

**Farr, James A (Jimmy)**
3 Tyndal Court, Williamsburg VA 23188, USA — Baseball Player

**Farr, Jamie**
51 Ranchero Road, Bell Canyon CA 91307, USA — Actor

**Farr, Melvin (Mel), Sr**
5000 Town Center, #2803, Southfield MI 48075, USA — Football Player

**Farr, Norman (Rocky)**
3850 Overton Park Dr W, Fort Worth TX 76109, USA — Ice Hockey Player

**Farr, Shonda**
Creative Artists Agency, 2000 Ave of Stars, #100, Los Angeles CA 90067 USA — Actress

**Farr, Steven M (Steve)**
126 Chicahauk Trail, Kitty Hawk NC 27949, USA — Baseball Player

**Farr, Tyler**
Columbia Records, 34 Music Square E, Nashville TN 37203 USA — Singer, Guitarist, Songwriter

**Farrakhan, Louis**
Nation of Islam, 734 W 79th St, Chicago IL 60620, USA — Religious Leader

**Farrar, Frank L**
PO Box 1029, Britton SD 57430, USA — Governor, SD

**Farrar, Jay**
Steel Toe Artist Mgmt, PO Box 3165, Jersey City NJ 07303, USA — Singer (Uncle Tupelo, Son Volt)

**Farrell, Colin**
Creative Artists Agency, 2000 Ave of Stars, #100, Los Angeles CA 90067 USA — Actor

**Farrell, Gemma Lee**
Playboy Promotions, 9346 Civic Center Dr, #200, Beverly Hills CA 90210 USA — Model

**Farrell, John E**
PO Box 3519, Clearwater Beach FL 33767, USA — Baseball Player, Manager

**Farrell, Mike**
Innovative Artists, 1505 10th St, Santa Monica CA 90401 USA — Actor

**Farrell, Perry**
Paradigm Agency, 360 N Crescent Dr, North Building, Beverly Hills CA 90210 USA — Singer (Jane's Addiction)

**Farrell, Sean W**
PO Box 21426, Tampa FL 33622, USA — Football Player

**Farrell, Sharon**
Wallis Agency, 210 Pass Ave, Burbank CA 91505, USA — Actress

**Farrell, Suzanne**
Kennedy Center for Performing Arts, 2700 F St NW, Washington DC 20566, USA — Ballet Dancer

**Farrell, Terence (Terry)**
Terry Farrell Partners, 7 Hatton St, London NW8 8PL, England — Architect

**Farrell, Terry**
Don Buchwald Talent Agency, 6500 Wilshire Blvd, #2200, Los Angeles CA 90048 USA — Actress

**Farrelly, Bernard (Midget)**
Parkes Australia, PO Box 505, Byron Bay NSW 2481, Australia — Surfer

**Farrelly, Bobby**
Conundrum Entertainment, 130 E Main St, Rochester NY 14604, USA — Director

**Farrelly, Peter J**
Conundrum Entertainment, 325 Wilshire Blvd, #201, Santa Monica CA 90401, USA — Director

**Farrimond, Richard A**
Metra Marconi Center, Gunnels Wood Road, Stevenage, Hertsfordshire SG1 2AS, England — Astronaut, England

**Farrington, Kaitlyn**
Ski & Snowboard Association, 1 Victory Lane, Box 100, Park City UT 84060, USA — Snowboarding Athlete

**Farrington, Robert G (Bob)**
105 Country Place, Sanford FL 32771, USA — Harness Racing Driver

**Farrior, James A**
5925 Almeda Road, #11115, Houston TX 77004, USA — Football Player

**Farris, Dionne**
Creative Artists Agency, 2000 Ave of Stars, #100, Los Angeles CA 90067 USA — Singer (Arrested Development)

**Farris, Isaac Newton, Jr**
Southern Christian Leadership Conference, 320 Auburn Ave NE, Atlanta GA 30303, USA — Religious Leader

**Farris, J Jerome**
US Court of Appeals, US Courthouse, 1010 5th Ave, Seattle WA 98104, USA — Judge

**Farris, Joseph**
Long Meadow Lane, Bethel CT 06801, USA — Cartoonist

**Farris, Rachel**
5708 Burnet Ave, Van Nuys CA 91411, USA — Singer, Pianist

**Farris, Roy Wayne**
H T M Enterprises, 4655 E Harwell St, Gilbert AZ 85234, USA — Professional Wrestler

**Farriss, Andrew**
8 Hayes St, #1, Neutral Bay 20891 NSW, Australia — Keyboardist (INXS)

**Farriss, Jon**
8 Hayes St, #1, Neutral Bay 20891 NSW, Australia — Drummer, Singer (INXS)

**Farrow, Mallory**
Hervey/Grimes Talent, 10561 Missouri Ave, #2, Los Angeles CA 90025 USA — Actress

**Farrow, Mia V**
Berwick & Kovacik, 6300 Wilshire Blvd, #1410, Los Angeles CA 90048, USA — Actress, Social Activist

**Faryniarz, Brett A**
1021 S Patrick Way, Anaheim CA 92808, USA — Football Player

**Fasano, Salvatore F (Sal)**
905 Catherine Glenn, Minooka IL 60447, USA — Baseball Player

**Fasman, Gerald D**
180 Wells Ave, #106, Newton Center MA 02459, USA — Biochemist

**Fassbaender, Brigitte**
Sekretariat, Haiming 2, 83119 Obing, Germany — Opera Singer

**Fassbender, Michael**
Troika, 74 Clerkenwell Road, #300, London EC1M 5QA, England — Actor

**Fassell, James E (Jim)**
56 Jacquelin Ave, Ho Ho Kus NJ 07423, USA — Football Player, Coach

**Fassero, Jeffrey J (Jeff)**
9841 N 56th St, Paradise Valley AZ 85253, USA — Baseball Player

**Fassio, Anne**
U B B A, 6 Rue de Braque, 75003 Paris, France — Actress

**Fast, Alexia**
Sanders/Armstrong/Caserta Mgmt, 2120 Colorado Ave, #120, Santa Monica CA 90404 USA — Actress

**Fat Joe**
Universal Media Artists, 8222 Melrose Ave, #203, Los Angeles CA 90048, USA — Rap Artist (Terror Squad), Actor

**Fatkulina, Olga A**
All-Russian Skating Federation, Luzhnetskaja Nab 8, 119992 Moscow, Russia — Speed Skater

V.I.P. Address Book

**Fatmi, Mourir** — Artist
Galerie Hussenot, 5 bis Rue des Haudriettes, 75003 Paris, France

**Fatone, Joseph (Joey), Jr** — Singer ('N Sync)
P M K-B N C, 8687 Melrose Ave, #800, Los Angeles CA 90069 USA

**Fauci, Anthony S** — Immunologist
3012 43rd St NW, Washington DC 20016, USA

**Faucon, Bernard** — Photographer
6 Rue Barbanegre, 75019 Paris, France

**Faulk, Kevin T** — Football Player
249 Magellan Road, Carencro LA 70520, USA

**Faulk, Marshall** — Football Player, Sportscaster
6340 Clayton Road, #305, Saint Louis MO 63117, USA

**Faulkner, Frank** — Artist
Arden Gallery, 129 Newbury St, Mezzanine 2, Boston MA 02116, USA

**Faulkner, Newton** — Singer, Guitarist, Songwriter
Sony-BMG Records, 69-79 Fulham High St, London SW8 3JW, England

**Faulkner, Shannon** — Educational Activist
Woodmont High School, 2831 W Georgia Road, Piedmont SC 29673, USA

**Faure, Margot** — Actress
Artmedia, 20 Ave Rapp, 75007 Paris, France

**Fauria, Christian** — Football Player
51 Jeffrey Dr, North Attleboro MA 02760, USA

**Fauser, Mark** — Actor
United Talent Agency, U T A Plaza, 9336 Civic Center Dr, Beverly Hills CA 90210 USA

**Faussart, Helene** — Singer
Evolution Talent Agency, 1501 Broadway, #1301, New York NY 10036, USA

**Faust, Chad** — Actor
Untitled Entertainment, 350 S Beverly Dr, #200, Beverly Hills CA 90212 USA

**Faust, Chris** — Photographer
308 Prince St, Saint Paul MN 55101, USA

**Faust, Drew Gilpin** — Educator
Harvard University, President's Office, 33 Elmwood Ave, Cambridge MA 02138, USA

**Faustino, David** — Actor
Abrams Artists, 9200 W Sunset Blvd, #1125, West Hollywood CA 90069 USA

**Fauza, Dario O** — Surgeon
Harvard Medical School, Surgery Dept, 25 Shattuck St, Boston MA 02115, USA

**Favier, Jean-Jacques** — Spatinaut, France
Technologies Avances, 17 Ave des Martys, 38054 Grenoble Cedex, France

**Favor, Mike** — Football Player
Robinsdale Cooper High School, 8230 47th Ave N, New Hope MN 55428, USA

**Favors, Derrick B** — Basketball Player
Utah Jazz, Energy Solutions Arena, 301 W South Temple, Salt Lake City UT 84101 USA

**Favors, Gregory B (Greg)** — Football Player
1990 Sandgate Circle, Atlanta GA 30349, USA

**Favre, Brett L** — Football Player
7698 US Highway 98W, Sumrall MS 39482, USA

**Favreau, Jon** — Actor, Writer, Director
Creative Artists Agency, 2000 Ave of Stars, #100, Los Angeles CA 90067 USA

**Fawcett, Don W** — Anatomist
3710 American Way, #325, Missoula MT 59808, USA

**Fawcett, Joy** — Soccer Player
11 Calle Marta, Rancho Santa Margarita CA 92688, USA

**Fawcett, Sherwood L** — Physicist
1800 Riverside Dr, #2314, Columbus OH 43212, USA

**Faxon, Brad** — Golfer
85 Nayatt Road, Barrington RI 02806, USA

**Faxon, Nat** — Actor, Writer
Innovative Artists, 1505 10th St, Santa Monica CA 90401 USA

**Fay, James A** — Mechanical Engineer
100 Newbury Court, #406, Concord MA 01742, USA

**Fay, Johnny** — Drummer (Tragically Hip)
Bobby Breen Mgmt, 13 Blackburn St, #300, Toronto ON M4M 2B3, Canada

**Fay, Meagen** — Actress
Main Title Mgmt, 8383 Wilshire Blvd, #408, Beverly Hills CA 90211 USA

**Fay, Peter T** — Judge
US Court of Appeals, 36 NE 1st St, #300, Miami FL 33132, USA

**Faydoedeelay** — Rap Artist, Bassist (Crazy Town)
Q Prime, 729 7th Ave, #1600, New York NY 10019, USA

**Fayed, Mohamed al-** — Businessman
Craven Cottage, Stevenage Road, Fulham, London SW6 6HH, England

**Fazio, Ernest J (Ernie)** — Baseball Player
2310 Royal Oaks Dr, Alamo CA 94507, USA

**Fazio, Tom** — Golf Course Architect
Fazio Golf Course Designers, 401 N Main St, #400, Hendersonville NV 28792, USA

**Fazzini, Enrico** — Neurologist
New York University Medical Center, Neurology Dept, 353 Lexington Ave, #101, New York NY 10016, USA

**Fazzino, Charles** — Artist
32 Relyea Place, #2, New Rochelle NY 10801, USA

**Feachem, Richard** — Foundation Executive
Global Fund, Chemin de Blandonnet 8, 1214 Vernier, Switzerland

**Feagles, Jeffrey A (Jeff)** — Football Player
326 W End Ave, Ridgewood NJ 07450, USA

**Fearnley, James** — Accordianist (Pogues)
Agency Group Ltd, 361-373 City Road, London EC1V 1PQ, England

**Fearnley-Whittingstall, Hugh** — Writer, Chef
Bloomsbury Publishing, 50 Bedford Square, London WC1B 3DP, England

**Featherman, David L** — Sociologist
46515 Arboretum Circle, Plymouth MI 48170, USA

**Featherstone, Glen** — Ice Hockey Player
8 Larrabee Ave, Danvers MA 01923, USA

**Feck, Luke M** — Editor
6366 Grassmere Dr, Westerville OH 43082, USA

**Fedak, Chris** — Producer, Writer
W M E Entertainment, 9601 Wilshire Blvd, #300, Beverly Hills CA 90210 USA

**Federer, Michelle** — Actress, Singer
Gotham Talent Agency, 570 7th Ave, New York NY 10018, USA

|  |  |
|------|-----------|
| **Federer, Roger** Postfach, 4103 Bottmingen, Switzerland | Tennis Player |
| **Federighi, Christine M** 1315 Obispo Ave, Coral Gables FL 33134, USA | Sculptor |
| **Federko, Bernie** 2219 Devonsbrook Dr, Chesterfield MO 63005, USA | Ice Hockey Player |
| **Federspiel, Joseph M (Joe)** 2016 Lakeside Dr, Lexington KY 40502, USA | Football Player |
| **Fedewa, Tim** 1737 Onondaga Road, Holt MI 48842, USA | Auto Racing Driver |
| **Fedorov, Sergei V** Metallurg Magnitogorsk, Pr Lenin 105, 455000, Magnitogorsk, Chelysbinsk Oblast, Russia | Ice Hockey Player |
| **Fedoseyev, Vladimir I** Recording/Broadcasting House, Malaya Nikitskaya 24, 121069 Moscow, Russia | Conductor |
| **Fedotenko, Ruslan V** 130 S 18th St, #1402, Philadelphia PA 19103, USA | Ice Hockey Player |
| **Fedotov, Maxim V** Tolbukhin Str 8, Korp 1, #6, 121596 Moscow, Russia | Concert Violinist |
| **Feehan, Christine** PO Box 181, Mendocino CA 95460, USA | Writer |
| **Feehery, Gerald (Gerry)** 5 Sharpless Lane, Media PA 19063, USA | Football Player |
| **Feehily, Mark** Solo Agency, 53-55 Fulham High St, #200, London SW6 3JJ, England | Singer (Westlife) |
| **Feeley, Adam J (A J)** 19062 Park Ridge St, Weston FL 33332, USA | Football Player |
| **Feely, T James (Jay)** 15923 Noting Hill Dr, Lutz FL 33548, USA | Football Player |
| **Feeney, Mark** Boston Globe, Editorial Dept, 135 William Morrissey Blvd, Dorchester MA 02125 USA | Journalist |
| **Fegan, Roshon B** W M E Entertainment, 9601 Wilshire Blvd, #300, Beverly Hills CA 90210 USA | Actor |
| **Feher, George** University of California, Physics Dept, 9500 Gilman Dr, La Jolla CA 92093, USA | Physicist |
| **Feher, Raymond** 62 Cool Springs Road, Signal Mountain TN 37377, USA | Basketball Player |
| **Feherty, David** 6422 Prestonshire Lane, Dallas TX 75225, USA | Golfer |
| **Fehr, Brendan** Roar Mgmt, 9701 Wilshire Blvd, #800, Beverly Hills CA 90212 USA | Actor |
| **Fehr, Oded** I F A Talent Agency, 8730 W Sunset Blvd, #490, West Hollywood CA 90069 USA | Actor |
| **Fehr, Richard E (Rick)** 2869 W Haley Dr, Anthem AZ 85086, USA | Golfer |
| **Fehr, Steve** 1329 Castlebridge Court, Cincinnati OH 45233, USA | Bowler |
| **Fei Junlong** Japanese Aerospace Exploration Agency, 2-1-1 Sengen, Tsukuba, Ibaraki 305 8505, Japan | Taikonaut |
| **Feiffer, Halley** Gersh Agency, 9465 Wilshire Blvd, #600, Beverly Hills CA 90212 USA | Actress |
| **Feiffer, Jules** 35 Cosdrew Lane, East Hampton NY 11937, USA | Cartoonist |
| **Feig, Paul S** Creative Artists Agency, 2000 Ave of Stars, #100, Los Angeles CA 90067 USA | Actor, Director, Writer |
| **Feigenbaum, Armand V** General Systems, 2 South St, #235, Pittsfield MA 01201, USA | Businessman, Systems Engineer |
| **Feigenbaum, Edward A** 1017 Cathcart Way, Stanford CA 94305, USA | Computer Scientist |
| **Feign, Larry** Heineman Educational Books, GPO Box 6086, Tsim Sha Tsui Post Office, Kowloon, Hong Kong, China | Cartoonist (World of Lily Wong) |
| **Feigum, Christopher** I M G Artists, Hogarth Business Park, Chiswick, London W4 2TH, England | Opera Singer |
| **Feild, J J** Artists Partnership, 101 Finsbury Pavement, London EC2A 1RS, England | Actor |
| **Feilden, Richard J R** Bradley Architects, Bath Brewery, Toll Bridge Road, Bath BA1 7DE, England | Architect |
| **Feinberg, Alan** C M Artists, 127 W 96th St, #13B, New York NY 10025 USA | Concert Pianist |
| **Feiner, Edward F** General Services Administration, 1800 F St NW, #3341, Washington DC 20405, USA | Architect |
| **Feinstein, A Richard** 1760 2nd Ave, #32C, New York NY 10128, USA | Epidemiologist |
| **Feinstein, Alan** Connor Ankrum & Associates, 1680 Vine St, #1016, Los Angeles CA 90028, USA | Actor |
| **Feinstein, John** Little Brown, 1271 Ave of Americas, New York NY 10020, USA | Sportswriter, Commentator |
| **Feinstein, Michael** Paradigm Agency, 360 N Crescent Dr, North Building, Beverly Hills CA 90210 USA | Singer, Pianist |
| **Feist, Leslie** Interscope Records, 2220 Colorado Ave, Santa Monica CA 90404 USA | Singer, Songwriter |
| **Feitl, Dave S** 12255 Highway 62 E, Harrison AR 72601, USA | Basketball Player |
| **Felber, Dean** FishCo Mgmt, 2519 Devine Street Columbia SC 29205, USA | Bassist (Hootie & the Blowfish) |
| **Felch, William C** 8545 Carmel Valley Road, Carmel CA 93923, USA | Physician |
| **Feld, Eliot** Feld Ballet, 890 Broadway, #800, New York NY 10003, USA | Dancer, Choreographer |
| **Feld, Steven** New Mexico University, Anthropology Dept, Albuquerque NM 87131, USA | Ethnomusicologist, Anthropologist |
| **Felder, Donald W (Don)** Renaissance Literary & Talent, PO Box 17379, Beverly Hills CA 90209, USA | Singer, Guitarist (Eagles) |
| **Felder, Michael O (Mike)** 322 S 17th St, Richmond CA 94804, USA | Baseball Player |
| **Felder, Raoul Lionel** 437 Madison Ave, #3000, New York NY 10022, USA | Attorney |

**F**

**Feldman - Feng Ying**

| | |
|---|---|
| **Feldman, Bella**<br>12 Summit Lane, Berkeley CA 94708, USA | Artist |
| **Feldman, Corey**<br>Scott Carlson Entertainment, 5739 Bucknell Ave, Valley Village CA 91607, USA | Actor |
| **Feldman, Donna**<br>Across the Board Talent, 22543 Ventura Blvd, #225, Woodland Hills CA 91364, USA | Actress, Model |
| **Feldman, Ed**<br>Gersh Agency, 9465 Wilshire Blvd, #600, Beverly Hills CA 90212 USA | Actor |
| **Feldman, Jerome M**<br>2744 Sevier St, Durham NC 27705, USA | Physician |
| **Feldman, Jon H**<br>Gersh Agency, 9465 Wilshire Blvd, #600, Beverly Hills CA 90212 USA | Producer, Writer |
| **Feldman, Kurt**<br>Slumberland Records, PO Box 19029, Oakland CA 94619, USA | Drummer (Pains of Being Pure at Heart) |
| **Feldman, Marcus W**<br>Stanford University, Biological Sciences Dept, Stanford CA 94305, USA | Biological Scientist |
| **Feldman, Michael**<br>Inphenate, 9701 Wilshire Blvd, #1000, Beverly Hills CA 90212 USA | Producer, Writer |
| **Feldman, Michelle**<br>Gary Feldman, PO Box 713, Skaneateles NY 13152, USA | Bowler |
| **Feldman, Scott W**<br>1021 Balboa Ave, Burlingame CA 94010, USA | Baseball Player |
| **Feldman, Tamara**<br>Leverage Mgmt, 3030 Pennsylvania Ave, Santa Monica CA 90404 USA | Actress |
| **Feldmann, Marc**<br>Charing Cross Hospital, Saint Dunstan's Road, London W6 8RP, England | Rheumatologist |
| **Feldmann, Sabine**<br>Shape, Publisher's Office, 1 Park Ave, New York NY 10016, USA | Publisher |
| **Feldon, Barbara**<br>Creative Artists Agency, 2000 Ave of Stars, #100, Los Angeles CA 90067 USA | Actress, Model |
| **Feldshuh, Tovah S**<br>B R S / Gage Talent Agency, 5757 Wilshire Blvd, #659, Los Angeles CA 90036 USA | Actress |
| **Feldstein, Martin S**<br>147 Clifton St, Belmont MA 02478, USA | Government Official, Economist |
| **Feliciano, Jose**<br>Feliciano Enterprises, 606 Boston Post Road E, #880, Westport CT 06880, USA | Singer, Guitarist |
| **Felipe VI**<br>Palacio de la Zarzuela, Carretera del Pardo S/N, 28071 Madrid, Spain | King, Spain |
| **Felix Sanchez, Junior F**<br>7545 Treadway Road, Gresham SC 29546, USA | Baseball Player |
| **Felix, Kelvin Edward Cardinal**<br>Archdiocese of Castries, Nelson Mandela Drive, PO Box 267, Castries, Saint Lucia | Religious Leader |
| **Felke, Petra**<br>S C Motor Jena, Wollnitzevstr 42, 07749 Jena, Germany | Track Athlete |
| **Fellag, Mohamed**<br>Agence Artiste Adequat, 108 Rue Reaumur, 75002 Paris, France | Actor |
| **Feller, Anke**<br>Heinrich-Claes Str 11, 51373 Leverkusen, Germany | Track Athlete, Model |
| **Fellmeth, Catherine**<br>Professional Bowlers Association, 719 2nd Ave, #701, Seattle WA 98104 USA | Bowler |
| **Fellner, Eric**<br>Working Title Films, 26 Aybrook St, London W1U 4AN, England | Producer |
| **Fellner, Till**<br>Ingpen & Williams, 131 Putney Bridge Road, London SW15 2PA, England | Concert Pianist |
| **Fellowes, Julian**<br>Independent Talent Group, 40 Whitfield St, London W1T 2RH, England | Director, Writer |
| **Fellows, Ron**<br>PO Box 564, RPO Turtle Creek, Mississauga ON L5J 4S6, Canada | Auto Racing Driver |
| **Fellows, Ronald L (Ron)**<br>202 Creekview Dr, Wylie TX 75098, USA | Football Player |
| **Fellows, Simon**<br>United Agents, 12-26 Lexington St, London W1F 0LE, England | Director |
| **Felmy, Hansjorg**<br>Berghofen, 84174 Eching, Germany | Actor |
| **Felsenfeld, Gary**<br>National Institutes of Health, Physical Chemistry Section, 5 Memorial Dr, Bethesda MD 20892, USA | Molecular Biologist |
| **Felsenstein, Lee**<br>1479 Regent St, Redwood City CA 94061, USA | Inventor (Portable Computer) |
| **Felske, John F**<br>3804 Ridge Road, Spring Grove IL 60081, USA | Baseball Player, Manager |
| **Felton, Dennis**<br>University of Georgia, Athletic Dept, Athens GA 30602, USA | Basketball Coach |
| **Felton, John**<br>G M S, PO Box 1031, Montrose CA 91021, USA | Singer (Diamonds) |
| **Felton, Lindsay**<br>Geddes Agency, 8430 Santa Monica Blvd, #201, West Hollywood CA 90069 USA | Actress |
| **Felton, Raymond B**<br>15814 Sullivan Ridge Road, Charlotte NC 28277, USA | Basketball Player |
| **Felton, Tom**<br>Troika, 74 Clerkenwell Road, #300, London EC1M 5QA, England | Actor |
| **Felts, Narvel**<br>Joe Taylor Artist Agency, 2802 Columbine Place, Nashville TN 37204 USA | Singer, Songwriter |
| **Feltus, Alan E**<br>Porziano 68, 06081 Assisi, Italy | Artist |
| **Fencik, J Gary**<br>1134 W Schubert Ave, Chicago IL 60614, USA | Football Player |
| **Fendrich, Rainhard J**<br>Management Agnes Rehling, Kirchenstras 17C, 82110 Germering, Germany | Singer, Actor, Composer |
| **Fenech Adami, Edward (Eddie)**<br>176 Main St, Birkikara, Malta | President, Malta |
| **Fenech, Edwige**<br>Carol Levi Mgmt, Via G Pisanelli 2, 00196 Rome, Italy | Actress, Producer |
| **Fenech, Jeff**<br>Team Fenech, PO Box 66, Millers Point NSW 2000, Australia | Boxer, Trainer |
| **Feng Ying**<br>Central Ballet of China, 3 Taiping St, Beijing 100050, China | Ballerina |

**Feng Zhengjie**, Artist
Primo Marella Gallery, Viale Stelvio 66, 20159 Milan, Italy

**Feng-Hsiung Hsu**, Computer Engineer
I B M Watson Research Center, PO Box 218, Yorktown Heights NY 10598 USA

**Fenical, William**, Organic Chemist
Scripps Institution of Oceanography, Organic Chemistry Dept, La Jolla CA 92093, USA

**Fenn, Sherilyn**, Actress
Water Street Anthem Entertainment, 5225 Wilshire Blvd, #615, Los Angeles CA 90036 USA

**Fenner, Derrick S**, Football Player
7533 33rd Ave NW, Seattle WA 98117, USA

**Fenninger, Anna**, Alpine Skier
Waidach 197, 5421 Adnet, Austria

**Fenson, Pete**, Curling Athlete
3760 Crest Court NE, Bemidji MN 56601, USA

**Fenton, George**, Composer
Gorfaine/Schwartz, 4111 W Alameda Ave, #509, Burbank CA 91505 USA

**Fenton, James**, Writer
Farrar Straus Giroux, 18 W 18th St, #700, New York NY 10011 USA

**Fenton, Paul**, Ice Hockey Player
16 Bridle Path Road, Brewster MA 02631, USA

**Fentress, Curtis W**, Architect
Fentress Bradburn Assoc, 421 Broadway, Denver CO 80203, USA

**Fenty, Adrian**, Mayor, Washington DC
Mayor's Office, 1 Judiciary Square, 414 4th St NW, Washington DC 20001, USA

**Fenwick, Robert R (Bobby)**, Baseball Player
51201 Hutchinson Road, Three Rivers MI 49093, USA

**Fenyves, Dave**, Ice Hockey Player
940 Parish Place, Hummelstown PA 17036, USA

**Feore, Colm**, Actor
Coronel Group, 1100 Glendon Ave, #1700, Los Angeles CA 90046, USA

**Feranec, Peter**, Conductor
Bolshoi Theater, Teatralnaya Pl 1, 103009 Moscow, Russia

**Feraud, Gianfranco**, Fashion Designer
25 Rue Saint Honore, 75001 Paris, France

**Ferdinand, Ron**, Inventor (Portable Computer)
PO Box 1997, Monterey CA 93942, USA

**Ference, Andrew**, Ice Hockey Player
220 Commercial St, Boston MA 02109, USA

**Ferentz, Kirk J**, Football Coach
University of Iowa, Athletic Dept, Iowa City IA 52242, USA

**Fergie**, Rap Artist
13701 Ventura Blvd, #800, Sherman Oaks CA 91423, USA

**Fergon, Vicki**, Golfer
44 Partridge Lane, Aliso Viejo CA 92656, USA

**Fergus, Keith C**, Golfer
11903 Royal Rose Dr, Houston TX 77082, USA

**Fergus, Tom**, Ice Hockey Player
Blue Leaf Ltd, 2134 Speers Road, Oakville ON L6L 2X8, Canada

**Ferguson Cullum, Cathy**, Swimmer
515 Amanda Dr, Bear DE 19701, USA

**Ferguson, Alexander C (Alex)**, Soccer Player, Manager
Manchester United, Busby Way, Old Trafford, Manchester M16 0RA, England

**Ferguson, Charles A**, Editor
123 Walnut St, #801, New Orleans LA 70118, USA

**Ferguson, Charles E (Charley)**, Football Player
81 Stonecroft Lane, Buffalo NY 14226, USA

**Ferguson, Charles H**, Director
Representational Pictures, 75 E 4th St, #83, New York NY 10003, USA

**Ferguson, Christopher J**, Astronaut
2405 Airline Dr, Friendswood TX 77546, USA

**Ferguson, Colin**, Actor, Comedian
United Talent Agency, U T A Plaza, 9336 Civic Center Dr, Beverly Hills CA 90210 USA

**Ferguson, Craig**, Actor, Comedian
Green Mountain Werst, 7800 Beverly Blvd, Los Angeles CA 90036, USA

**Ferguson, D'Brickashaw M**, Football Player
New York Jets, 1 Jets Dr, Florham Park NJ 07932 USA

**Ferguson, Frederick E**, Vietnam War Army Hero (CMH)
5420 E Lincoln Dr, Paradise Valley AZ 85253, USA

**Ferguson, James (Jim)**, Water Polo Player
2404 Stonybrook Road, Opelika AL 36804, USA

**Ferguson, James L**, Businessman
General Foods Corp, 800 Westchester Ave, Rye Brook NY 10573, USA

**Ferguson, Jay R**, Actor
I F A Talent Agency, 8730 W Sunset Blvd, #490, West Hollywood CA 90069 USA

**Ferguson, Jesse Tyler**, Actor
I C M Partners, 10250 Constellation Blvd, #900, Los Angeles CA 90067 USA

**Ferguson, Joe C, Jr**, Football Player, Coach
12 Mason Lane, Bella Vista AR 72715, USA

**Ferguson, Joseph V (Joe)**, Baseball Player
11322 River Run Lane, Berlin MO 21811, USA

**Ferguson, Keith T**, Football Player
PO Box 19006, Sugar Land TX 77496, USA

**Ferguson, Kent**, Diver, Model
199 Tiffany Ave, #407, San Francisco CA 94110, USA

**Ferguson, Lynnda**, Actress
606 N Larchmont Blvd, #309, Los Angeles CA 90004, USA

**Ferguson, M Paul**, Drummer (Killing Joke)
Agency Group, 1100 Century Park E, #711, Los Angeles CA 90067 USA

**Ferguson, Mark E, III**, Navy Admiral
Vice Chief of Naval Operations, HqUSN, Pentagon, Washington DC 20350 USA

**Ferguson, Megan**, Actress
Don Buchwald Talent Agency, 6500 Wilshire Blvd, #2200, Los Angeles CA 90048 USA

**Ferguson, Nick**, Football Player
114 Arlington Ave SW, Atlanta GA 30310, USA

**Ferguson, Rebecca C**, Singer, Songwriter
RCA Label Group, 9 Derry St, London W8 5HY, England

| | |
|---|---|
| **Ferguson, Rebecca L** Tavistock Wood Mgmt, 45 Conduit St, London W1S 2YN, England | Actress |
| **Ferguson, Robert A** Columbia University, Jerome Green Hall, New York NY 10027, USA | Educator, Attorney |
| **Ferguson, Robert C** 15102 Oldtown Bridge Court, Sugar Land TX 77498, USA | Football Player |
| **Ferguson, Sarah** Birchhall, Windlesham, Surrey GU20 6BN, England | Duchess of York, England |
| **Ferguson, Stacy** Paradigm Agency, 360 N Crescent Dr, North Building, Beverly Hills CA 90210 USA | Actress |
| **Ferguson, Thomas A, Jr** Newell Rubbermaid Inc, Newell Center, 29 E Stephenson St, Freeport IL 61032, USA | Businessman |
| **Ferguson, Tom** General Delivery, Miami OK 74354, USA | Rodeo Rider |
| **Fergus-Thompson, Gordon** 12 Audley Road, Hendon, London NW4 3EY, England | Concert Pianist |
| **Ferilli, Sabrina** Camelia Srl, Via Giorgio Vasari 4, 00196 Rome, Italy | Actress |
| **Feringa, Ben L** University of Groningen, Chemistry Dept, Nijenborgh 4, 9747 Groningen AG, Netherlands | Chemist |
| **Ferland, E James** Public Service Enterprise, 80 Park Plaza, PO Box 1171, Newark NJ 07101, USA | Businessman |
| **Ferland, Guy V** W M E Entertainment, 9601 Wilshire Blvd, #300, Beverly Hills CA 90210 USA | Director |
| **Ferland, Jodelle** Play Mgmt, 807 Powell St, #220, Vancouver BC V6A 1H7, Canada | Actress |
| **Ferlinghetti, Lawrence** City Lights Booksellers, 261 Columbus Ave, San Francisco CA 94133, USA | Writer, Publisher |
| **Ferlito, Vanessa** Alchemy Entertainment, 7024 Melrose Ave, #420, Los Angeles CA 90038 USA | Actress |
| **Fermin, Felix J** Akron Aeros, 300 S Main St, Akron OH 44308, USA | Baseball Player |
| **Fernandez de Kirchner, Cristina E** Casa de Gobierno, Balcarce 50, Buenos Aires 1064, Argentina | President, Argentina |
| **Fernandez Krupij, Stefania** Miss Universe Organization, 1370 Ave of Americas, #1600, New York NY 10019 USA | Beauty Queen |
| **Fernandez Molinos, Begona** R K Zajecar, Dositejeva 11, 19000 Zajecar, Serbia | Handball Player |
| **Fernandez, Adrian** Fernandez Racing, PO Box 68828, Indianapolis IN 46268, USA | Auto Racing Driver |
| **Fernandez, Alejandro** Creative Artists Agency, 2000 Ave of Stars, #100, Los Angeles CA 90067 USA | Singer, Actor |
| **Fernandez, Alexander (Alex)** 12323 SW 55th St, #1007, Cooper City FL 33330, USA | Baseball Player |
| **Fernandez, C Sidney (Sid)** 25 Aulike St, #218, Kailua HI 96734, USA | Baseball Player |
| **Fernandez, Emmanuel (Manny)** Boston Bruins, 100 Legends Way, #250, Boston MA 02114 USA | Ice Hockey Player |
| **Fernandez, Ferdinand F** US Court of Appeals, 125 S Grand Ave, Pasadena CA 91105, USA | Judge |
| **Fernandez, Frank** 37 Couglan Ave, Staten Island NY 10310, USA | Baseball Player |
| **Fernandez, Gigi** US Lawn Tennis Assn, 1212 Ave of Americas, New York NY 10036, USA | Tennis Player |
| **Fernandez, Humberto P (Chico)** 8401 NW 40th Court, Sunrise FL 33351, USA | Baseball Player |
| **Fernandez, James W** University of Chicago, Anthropology Dept, 1126 E 59th St, Chicago IL 60637, USA | Anthropologist |
| **Fernandez, Jared W** 4298 S 4625 West, Salt Lake City UT 84120, USA | Baseball Player |
| **Fernandez, Karina** United Agents, 12-26 Lexington St, London W1F 0LE, England | Actress |
| **Fernandez, Lisa** 1460 Homewood Road, #95B, Seal Beach CA 90740, USA | Softball Player |
| **Fernandez, Lujan** Fashion Model Mgmt, 40 Ang Via Monte Rosa, 20149 Milan, Italy | Model, Actress |
| **Fernandez, Manuel J (Manny)** 5805 SW 120th St, Cooper City FL 33330, USA | Football Player |
| **Fernandez, Mariestela** Sandra Marsh Assoc, 9150 Wilshire Blvd, #220, Beverly Hills CA 90212 USA | Costume Designer |
| **Fernandez, Mary Joe** 1121 Crandon Blvd, #D606, Key Biscayne FL 33149, USA | Tennis Player |
| **Fernandez, Mervyn** 1454 Hicks Ave, San Jose CA 95125, USA | Football Player |
| **Fernandez, O Antonio (Tony)** Tony Fernandez Foundation, 19232 N Gardenia Ave, Weston FL 33332, USA | Baseball Player |
| **Fernandez, Pedro** S D L Productions, PO Box 65948, Los Angeles CA 90065, USA | Singer, Songwriter |
| **Fernandez, Raul** F C Dallas, 9200 World Cup Way, #202, Frisco TX 75034 USA | Soccer Player |
| **Fernandez, Shiloh** W M E Entertainment, 9601 Wilshire Blvd, #300, Beverly Hills CA 90210 USA | Actor |
| **Fernandez, Vicente** Hauser Entertainment, 3703 San Gabriel River Parkway, Pico Rivera CA 90660, USA | Singer |
| **Ferneyhough, Brian J P** 848 Allardice Way, Stanford CA 94305, USA | Composer |
| **Ferns, Alex** Artists Partnership, 101 Finsbury Pavement, London EC2A 1RS, England | Actor |
| **Fernsten, Eric R** 5634 Linden St, Dublin CA 94568, USA | Basketball Player |
| **Ferragamo, Vince A** Touchdown Real Estate, 6200 E Canyon Rim Road, #204, Anaheim CA 92807, USA | Football Player |
| **Ferrara, Abel** I C M Partners, 10250 Constellation Blvd, #900, Los Angeles CA 90067, USA | Director |
| **Ferrara, Adam** Gersh Agency, 9465 Wilshire Blvd, #600, Beverly Hills CA 90212 USA | Actor, Comedian |

**Ferrara, Alfred J (Al)**
4901 Whitsett Ave, #207, Valley Village CA 91607, USA — Baseball Player

**Ferrara, Jerry**
W M E Entertainment, 9601 Wilshire Blvd, #300, Beverly Hills CA 90210 USA — Actor

**Ferrara, Stephane**
Artmedia, 20 Ave Rapp, 75007 Paris, France — Actress

**Ferrare, Cristina**
10727 Wilshire Blvd, #1602, Los Angeles CA 90024, USA — Model, Entertainer

**Ferrarese, Donald H (Don)**
15290 Myalon Road, Apple Valley CA 92307, USA — Baseball Player

**Ferrari, Albert R (Al)**
5911 Bristlecone Court, Saint Louis MO 63129, USA — Basketball Player

**Ferrari, Gillian**
Team Canada, 2424 University Dr NW, Calgary AB T2N 3Y9, Canada — Ice Hockey Player

**Ferrari, Michael R, Jr**
570 Greenway Dr, Lake Forest IL 60045, USA — Educator

**Ferrari, Tina**
2901 S Las Vegas Blvd, Las Vegas NV 89109, USA — Dancer, Wrestler

**Ferraro, Dave**
672 E Chester St, Kingston NY 12401, USA — Bowler

**Ferraro, Michael D (Mike)**
5201 Rim View Lane, Las Vegas NV 89130, USA — Baseball Player, Manager

**Ferraro, Raymond (Ray)**
Team 1040 Sports Radio, 30-380 W 2nd Ave, Vancouver BC V5Y 1C8, Canada — Ice Hockey Player, Sportscaster

**Ferrarone, Jessica**
Evolution Entertainment, 901 N Highland Ave, Los Angeles CA 90038 USA — Actress

**Ferratti, Rebecca M**
10061 Riverside Dr, #721, Toluca Lake CA 91602, USA — Model, Actress

**Ferrazzi, Pierpaolo**
EuroGrafica, Via del Progresso, 36035 Marano Vicenza, Italy — Canoeing Athlete

**Ferree, Jim**
12 Kings Tree Road, Hilton Head Island SC 29928, USA — Golfer

**Ferreira, Gabriel Vasconcellos**
Confederacion de Futebol, Rua Victor Civita 66, #1, Rio de Janeiro 22775 044, Brazil — Soccer Player

**Ferreira, Wayne**
International Mangement Group, 1 Erieview Plaza, 1360 E 9th St, #100, Cleveland OH 44114 USA — Tennis Player

**Ferrell Edmonson, Barbara A**
University of Nevada, Athletic Dept, Las Vegas NV 89154, USA — Track Athlete

**Ferrell, Conchata**
B R S / Gage Talent Agency, 1650 Broadway, #1410, New York NY 10019 USA — Actress

**Ferrell, Earl T**
107 E Forest Trail, South Boston VA 24592, USA — Football Player

**Ferrell, Perry**
DeMann Entertainment, 1017 N La Cienega Blvd, #103, West Hollywood CA 90069, USA — Singer (Porno for Pyros)

**Ferrell, Rachelle**
Wenig-LaMonica Associates, 580 White Plains Road, #130, Tarrytown NY 10591 USA — Singer

**Ferrell, Robert S (Bobby)**
1090 N Shooting Star Dr, Beaumont CA 92223, USA — Football Player

**Ferrell, Tyra**
Gersh Agency, 9465 Wilshire Blvd, #600, Beverly Hills CA 90212 USA — Actress

**Ferrell, Will**
Mosiac Media Group, 9200 W Sunset Blvd, #1000, Los Angeles CA 90069 USA — Actor, Comedian

**Ferreol, Andrea**
Artmedia, 20 Ave Rapp, 75007 Paris, France — Actress

**Ferrer Ern, David**
Association of Tennis Professionals, 201 A T P Blvd, Ponte Vedra Beach FL 32082 USA — Tennis Player

**Ferrer, Danay**
R C A Records, 8750 Wilshire Blvd, Beverly Hills CA 90211 USA — Singer (Innosense)

**Ferrer, Miguel**
Danis Panaro Nist, 9201 W Olympic Blvd, Beverly Hills CA 90212, USA — Actor

**Ferrera, America**
I C M Partners, 10250 Constellation Blvd, #900, Los Angeles CA 90067 USA — Actress

**Ferreras, Francisco (Pipin)**
7548 W Treasure Dr, North Bay Village FL 33141, USA — Free Diver

**Ferrero, Juan Carlos**
Echegaray 2, 468 70 Ontynent, Spain — Tennis Player

**Ferres, Veronica**
Resolution, 1801 Century Park East, #2300, Los Angeles CA 90067, USA — Actress

**Ferretti, Alberta**
Via delle Querce 51, 47842 San Giovanni in Marignano, Italy — Fashion Designer

**Ferretti, Dante**
Cinecitta Studios, Via Tuscolana, 1055, 00173 Rome Italy — Art Director

**Ferrick, Melissa**
Agency Group Ltd, 142 W 57th St, #600, New York NY 10019 USA — Singer, Songwriter

**Ferrigno, Lou**
Lou Ferrigno Enterprises, PO Box 1671, Santa Monica CA 90406, USA — Actor, Body Builder

**Ferrigno, Robert**
Charles Scribner's Sons, 866 3rd Ave, New York NY 10022 USA — Writer

**Ferrin, Arnold (Arnie)**
2104 S Barona Road, Palm Springs CA 92264, USA — Basketball Player

**Ferrin, Jennifer**
Gersh Agency, 9465 Wilshire Blvd, #600, Beverly Hills CA 90212 USA — Actress

**Ferris, Charles D**
Mintz Levin Ferris Assoc, 701 Pennsylvania Ave NW, Washington DC 20004, USA — Government Official

**Ferris, John**
1961 Klamath River Dr, Rancho Cordova CA 95670, USA — Swimmer

**Ferris, Keltie**
Mitchell-Innes & Nash Gallery, 1018 Madison Ave, New York NY 10075, USA — Artist

**Ferris, Michael (Mike)**
United Talent Agency, U T A Plaza, 9336 Civic Center Dr, Beverly Hills CA 90210 USA — Writer, Producer, Actor

**Ferriss, David M (Boo)**
510 Robinson Dr, Cleveland MS 38732, USA — Baseball Player

**Ferro, Cindy**
1901 Brookside Dr, Scotch Plains NJ 07076, USA — Golfer

**Ferro, Tiziano**
EMI Italiana, Via Bergamo 315, 21402 Coronno Pertusella, Italy — Singer, Songwriter

**Ferron** — Singer, Synthesizer Player, Songwriter
Silverleaf Booking, 589 W 1st St, Bolling Springs PA 17007, USA

**Ferry, April** — Costume Designer
United Talent Agency, U T A Plaza, 9336 Civic Center Dr, Beverly Hills CA 90210 USA

**Ferry, Bjorn** — Biathlete
Hojdvagen 24G, 923 31 Storuman, Sweden

**Ferry, Bryan** — Singer, Songwriter
Agency Group Ltd, 142 W 57th St, #600, New York NY 10019 USA

**Ferry, Daniel J W (Danny)** — Basketball Player, Executive
145 Blackland Road NW, Atlanta GA 30342, USA

**Ferry, David R** — Writer
Wellesley College, English Dept, Wellesley MA 02181, USA

**Ferry, Robert D (Bob)** — Basketball Player
2129 Beach Haven Road, Annapolis MD 21409, USA

**Fersht, Alan R** — Organic Chemist
2 Barrow Close, Cambridge CB2 2AT, England

**Fert, Albert** — Nobel Physics Laureate
C N R S/Thales, Domaine de Corbeville, 91404 Orsay Cedex, France

**Fery, John B** — Businessman
PO Box 15407, Boise ID 83715, USA

**Ferzetti, Gabriele** — Actor
NCE Italiana, Viale Bruno Buozzi 53, 00197 Rome, Italy

**Fessel, Craig** — Cartoonist (Sandman)
40 Camino Alto, #2306, Mill Valley CA 94941, USA

**Fessel, Nicole** — Cross Country Skier
Erlenweg 10, 87544 Blaichach, Germany

**Fessenden, Larry** — Director, Writer
Glass Eye Pix, 18 Bridge St, #2G, Brooklyn NY 11201, USA

**Fest, Howard A** — Football Player
133 Forest Circle, Bandera TX 78003, USA

**Feste, Shana** — Writer, Director
Creative Artists Agency, 2000 Ave of Stars, #100, Los Angeles CA 90067 USA

**Festinger, Leon** — Psychologist
37 W 12th St, New York NY 10011, USA

**Fetisov, Vyacheslav A (Slava)** — Ice Hockey Player
196 Rensselaer Road, Essex Falls NJ 07021, USA

**Fetter, Laurie** — Model
Playboy Promotions, 9346 Civic Center Dr, #200, Beverly Hills CA 90210 USA

**Fetterman, John H (Jack), Jr** — Navy Admiral
Naval Aviation Museum Foundation, 1750 Radford Blvd, Pensacola FL 32508, USA

**Fetters, Michael L (Mike)** — Baseball Player
2411 E Cedar Place, Chandler AZ 85249, USA

**Fettig, Jeff M** — Businessman
Whirlpool Corp, 2000 N State St, RR 63, Benton Harbor MI 49022, USA

**Fetting, Katie** — Actress, Writer
United Talent Agency, U T A Plaza, 9336 Civic Center Dr, Beverly Hills CA 90210 USA

**Fetting, Rainer** — Artist, Sculptor
Andino Fine Arts, 2450 Virginia Ave NW, Washington DC 20037, USA

**Fettman, Martin J** — Astronaut, Veterinarian
1572 N Saguaro Cliffs Court, Tucson AZ 85745, USA

**Feuer, Debra** — Actress
United Talent Agency, U T A Plaza, 9336 Civic Center Dr, Beverly Hills CA 90210 USA

**Feuerman, Carole A** — Sculptor
200 Mercer St, #1F, New York NY 10012, USA

**Feuerstein, Mark** — Actor
United Talent Agency, U T A Plaza, 9336 Civic Center Dr, Beverly Hills CA 90210 USA

**Feuerwerker, Albert** — Historian
827 Asa Gray Dr, #356, Ann Arbor MI 48105, USA

**Feuerzeig, Jeff** — Director, Writer
W M E Entertainment, 9601 Wilshire Blvd, #300, Beverly Hills CA 90210 USA

**Feustel, Andrew J (Drew)** — Astronaut
4003 Elm Crest Trail, Houston TX 77059, USA

**Feuti, Norm** — Cartoonist (Gil)
King Features Syndicate, 300 W 57th St, #1500, New York NY 10019 USA

**Fewx, Gene** — Sculptor
666 15th St NE, Salem OR 97301, USA

**Fexler, Forrest O** — Golfer
6270 Old Water Oak Road, Tallahassee FL 32312, USA

**Fey** — Singer
R A C, Paseo Palmas 1005, Chapultapec Lomas, Mexico City DF 11000, Mexico

**Fey, Michael** — Cartoonist (Committed)
United Feature Syndicate, PO Box 5610, Cincinnati OH 45201 USA

**Fey, Tina** — Actress, Comedienne, Producer
3 Arts Entertainment, 9460 Wilshire Blvd, #700, Beverly Hills CA 90212 USA

**Fezler, Forrest O** — Golfer
1523 Pine St, Tallahassee FL 32303, USA

**Fforde, Jasper** — Writer
Viking Press, 375 Hudson St, New York NY 10014, USA

**Fiala, John C** — Football Player
12113 268th Dr NE, Duvall WA 98019, USA

**Fialkowska, Janina** — Concert Pianist
Ingpen & Williams, 131 Putney Bridge Road, London SW15 2PA, England

**Fiasco, Lupe** — Rap Artist, Songwriter
1st & 15th Records, 437 Brookwood Dr, Olympia Fields IL 60461, USA

**Ficarra, Glenn** — Writer, Director
W M E Entertainment, 9601 Wilshire Blvd, #300, Beverly Hills CA 90210 USA

**Ficatier, Carol** — Model, Actress
Playboy Promotions, 9346 Civic Center Dr, #200, Beverly Hills CA 90210 USA

**Ficca, Billy** — Drummer (Television, Waitresses)
Primary Talent International, 10-11 Jockey's Fields, London WC1R 4BN, England

**Ficca, Daniel R (Dan)** — Football Player
151 Kansas Lane, Kulpmont PA 17834, USA

**Fichaud, Eric** — Ice Hockey Player
191 Rue Charron, Lemoyne QC J4R 2K6, Canada

**Fichtel-Mauritz, Anja** — Fencer
Stauferring 104, 97941 Taunerbischofsheim, Germany

**Fichter, Michael (Mike)** — Baseball Umpire
2942 192nd Place, Lansing IL 60438, USA

**Fichter, Rick T** — Cinematographer
318 1st Ave S, #406, Seattle WA 98104, USA

**Fichtner, Ross W** — Football Player
46833 Danbridge St, Plymouth MI 48170, USA

**Fichtner, William (Bill)** — Actor
Paradigm Agency, 360 N Crescent Dr, North Building, Beverly Hills CA 90210 USA

**Fick, Robert C** — Baseball Player
832 Dolores Dr, Santa Barbara CA 93109, USA

**Fickman, Andy** — Director
W M E Entertainment, 9601 Wilshire Blvd, #300, Beverly Hills CA 90210 USA

**Fico, Robert** — Prime Minister, Slovakia
Prime Minister's Office, Nam Slobody, 81370 Bratislava 1, Slovakia

**Fiddler, Vernon (Vern)** — Ice Hockey Player
3659 Hickory Grove Lane, Frisco TX 75033, USA

**Fiedler, Jay B** — Football Player
25 Russell Road, Garden City NY 11530, USA

**Fieger, Geoffrey** — Attorney
Fieger Fieger Schwartz, 19390 W Ten Mile Road, Southfield MI 48075, USA

**Field, Arabella** — Actress
S M S Talent, 8383 Wilshire Blvd, #230, Beverly Hills CA 90211 USA

**Field, Ayda** — Actress, Comedienne
Paradigm Agency, 360 N Crescent Dr, North Building, Beverly Hills CA 90210 USA

**Field, Chelsea** — Actress
Allegory Creative Mgmt, 13261 Moorpark St, #103, Sherman Oaks CA 91423, USA

**Field, David** — Actor
Sue Barnett & Associates, 1/96 Albion St, Surry Hills NSW 2010, Australia

**Field, George B** — Theoretical Astrophysicist
Harvard University Observatory, 60 Garden St, Cambridge MA 02138, USA

**Field, Helen** — Opera Singer
Athole Still, Foresters Hall, 25-27 Weston St, London SE19 3RV, England

**Field, John J (J J)** — Actor
Artists Partnership, 101 Finsbury Pavement, London EC2A 1RS, England

**Field, Nathan P (Nate)** — Baseball Player
1040 W Ridge Road, Littleton CO 80120, USA

**Field, Sally** — Actress
Hofflund/Polone, 9465 Wilshire Blvd, #420, Beverly Hills CA 90212 USA

**Field, Shirley Ann** — Actress
Roger Carey Assoc, Old House, Shepperton Film Studios, Shepperton, Middlesex TW17 0QD, England

**Field, Todd** — Actor, Director, Writer
Smuggler, 38 W 21st St, #1200, New York NY 10010, USA

**Fielder, Cecil G** — Baseball Player
6907 Smokey Brook Lane, Katy TX 77494, USA

**Fielder, Harry** — Actor
Guild House, Upper Saint Martins, London WC2H 9EG, England

**Fielder, Prince S** — Baseball Player
Texas Rangers, Ameriquest Field, 1000 Ballpark Way, #306, Arlington TX 76011 USA

**Fielding, Fred F** — Attorney, Government Official
Wiley Rein Fielding, 1776 K St NW, #300, Washington DC 20006, USA

**Fielding, Helen** — Writer
Creative Artists Agency, 2000 Ave of Stars, #100, Los Angeles CA 90067 USA

**Fielding, Joy** — Writer
Atria Books, 1230 Ave of Americas, New York NY 10020, USA

**Fields, Alexis** — Actress
Rookery, 8200 Wilshire Blvd, #100, Beverly Hills CA 90212, USA

**Fields, Bertram (Bert)** — Attorney
Greenberg Glusker, 1900 Ave of Stars, #2100, Los Angeles CA 90067 USA

**Fields, Edgar E** — Football Player
435 Musket Entry, Roswell GA 30076, USA

**Fields, Harold T, Jr** — Army General
126 Deer Run Strut, Enterprise AL 36330, USA

**Fields, Johnny** — Singer (Blind Boys of Alabama)
Blind Ambition Mgmt, 6 Courthouse Way, Jonesboro GA 30236, USA

**Fields, Joseph C (Joe), Jr** — Football Player
Widener University, Alumni Association, 1 University Place, Chester PA 19013, USA

**Fields, Joshua D (Josh)** — Baseball Player
4819 61st Ave Dr W, Bradenton FL 34210, USA

**Fields, Kenny** — Basketball Player
1050 E Ramon Road, #81, Palm Springs CA 92264, USA

**Fields, Kim** — Actress
Rookery, 8200 Wilshire Blvd, #100, Beverly Hills CA 90212, USA

**Fields, Mark** — Businessman
Ford Motor Co, Dearborn Road, Dearborn MI 48121, USA

**Fields, Mark L** — Football Player
887 W Palo Brea Dr, Litchfield Park AZ 85340, USA

**Fields, Stanley** — Microbiologist
University of Washington Medical School, Microbiology Dept, Seattle WA 98195, USA

**Fiennes, Joseph** — Actor
Artists Partnership, 101 Finsbury Pavement, London EC2A 1RS, England

**Fiennes, Ralph N** — Actor
Dalzell & Beresford, 55 Charterhouse St, Paddock Suite, London EC1M 6HA, England

**Fiennes, Ranulph T-W** — Transglobal Explorer
Greenlands, Exford, Minehead, West Sussex TA24 7NU, England

**Fierek, Wolfgang** — Singer, Actor
Scenario Agentur, Rambergstr 5, 80799 Munich, Germany

**Fierstein, Harvey F** — Actor, Singer, Writer
10106 Empyrean Way, #101, Los Angeles CA 90067, USA

**Fieser, Louis** — Inventor (Napalm)
58 Medford St, Arlington MA 02474, USA

**Fifty Cent** — Rap Artist, Actor
Shady Records, 151 Lafayette St, #6, New York NY 10013, USA

**Figaro, Cedric N** — Football Player
205 Staten St, Lafayette LA 70501, USA

**Figga, Mike** — Baseball Player
16434 Turnbury Oak Dr, Odessa FL 33556, USA

**Figg-Currier, Cindy**
109 Blue Jay Dr, Lakeway TX 78734, USA — Golfer

**Figgins, D DeChone (Chone)**
16 San Sovino, Newport Coast CA 92657, USA — Baseball Player

**Figgis, Michael (Mike)**
Red Mullet, Waterside, 44-48 Wharf Road, #22, London N1 7UX, England — Director

**Figo, Luis**
F C Real Madrid, Avda Concha Espana 1, 28036 Madrid, Spain — Soccer Player

**Figueroa, Eduardo (Ed)**
Calle 41, #AN15, Santa Juanita PR 00619, USA — Baseball Player

**Figueroa, Nelson, Jr**
1950 E Woodsman Place, Chandler AZ 85286, USA — Baseball Player

**Fike, Dan C, Jr**
23479 Wingedfoot Dr, Westlake OH 44145, USA — Football Player

**Fikrig, Erol**
Yale University Medical Center, Infectious Disease Dept, New Haven CT 06510, USA — Immunologist

**Filali, Yasmina**
Agency GmbH, Under Krahnenbaeumer 9, 50688 Cologne, Germany — Actress

**Filat, Vladimir (Vlad)**
Prime Minister's Office, Piata Marii Adunari Nacional, 227033 Chishinev, Moldova — Prime Minister, Moldova

**Filatova-Kourbatova Maria**
Kour Gymnastics, 121 Lincoln Ave, Rochester NY 14611, USA — Gymnast

**Filer, Thomas C (Tom)**
425 Fox Hollow Dr, Feasterville Terrace PA 19053, USA — Baseball Player

**Filicia, Thom**
Artist & Brand Management, 9320 Wilshire Blvd, #212, Beverly Hills CA 90212, USA — Actor, Interior Designer

**Filigno, Jonelle**
Canadian Soccer, Place Soccer Canada, 237 Metcalfe St, Ottawa ON K2P 1R2, Canada — Soccer Player

**Filion, Herve**
18 Evans Ave, Albertson NY 11507, USA — Harness Racing Driver

**Filipacchi, Daniel**
Hachette Filipacchi, 149-51 Rue Anatole-France, 92534 Levallois, France — Publisher

**Filipchenko, Anatoli N**
Cosmonaut Training Center, Star City, 141160 Zvezdny Gorodok, Moscow Oblast, Russia — Cosmonaut; Air Force General

**Fillion, Nathan**
I C M Partners, 10250 Constellation Blvd, #900, Los Angeles CA 90067 USA — Actor

**Fillmore, Charles J**
University of California, Linguistics Dept, Berkeley CA 94720, USA — Linguist

**Fillon, Francois-Charles A**
Prime Minister's Office, Hotel Matignon, 57 Rue de Varenne, 75700 Paris, France — Prime Minister, France

**Filo, David**
Yahoo, 701 1st Ave, Sunnyvale CA 94089, USA — Businessman, Computer Scientist

**Filoni, Fernando Cardinal**
Evangelization of Peoples, Piazza di Spagna 48, 00187 Rome, Italy — Religious Leader

**Filson, W Peter (Pete)**
1034 10th Ave, Folsom PA 19033, USA — Baseball Player

**Fimbres, Andrea**
Bad Boy Entertainment, 1440 Broadway, #16, New York NY 10018 USA — Singer (Danity Kane)

**Fimmel, Travis**
Paradigm Agency, 360 N Crescent Dr, North Building, Beverly Hills CA 90210 USA — Model, Actor

**Fina, John J**
5180 E Fort Lowell Road, Tucson AZ 85712, USA — Football Player

**Finch, David**
D C Comics, 1700 Broadway, #400, New York NY 10019 USA — Cartoonist (Wonder Woman)

**Finch, Jennie**
3265 W Bird Haven Place, Tucson AZ 85745, USA — Softball Player, Model

**Finch, Joel D**
68571 Oak Spring Road, Edwardsburg MI 49112, USA — Baseball Player

**Finch, Jon N**
London Mgmt, 2-4 Noel St, London W1V 3RB, England — Actor

**Finch, Linda**
World Flight, 211 Switch Oak, Shavano Park TX 78230, USA — Aviatrix

**Finch, Meredith**
D C Comics, 1700 Broadway, #400, New York NY 10019 USA — Writer (Wonder Woman)

**Finchem, Timothy W**
Professional Golfer's Assn, Sawgrass, Ponte Vedra Beach FL 32082, USA — Golf Executive

**Finck, George C**
143 Beaver Lane, Benton LA 71006, USA — Vietnam War Air Force Hero

**Fincke, E Michael (Mike)**
15819 El Dorado Oaks Dr, Houston TX 77059, USA — Astronaut

**Finckel, David**
I M G Artists, Burlington Lane, Chiswick, London W4 2TH, England — Cellist (Emerson String Quartet)

**Finder, Joseph**
United Talent Agency, U T A Plaza, 9336 Civic Center Dr, Beverly Hills CA 90210 USA — Writer

**Findlay, Conn F**
1920 Oak Knoll, Belmont CA 94002, USA — Rowing Athlete, Yachtsman

**Findlay, Jessica Brown**
Troika, 74 Clerkenwell Road, #300, London EC1M 5QA, England — Actress

**Findley, Vern M (Rusty), II**
Vice Commander, Air Mobility Command, Scott Air Force Base IL 62225 USA — Air Force General

**Fine, Jud**
1366 Appleton Way, Venice CA 90291, USA — Sculptor

**Fine, Russell Lee**
Creative Artists Agency, 2000 Ave of Stars, #100, Los Angeles CA 90067 USA — Cinematographer

**Finer, Jeremy (Jem)**
Agency Group Ltd, 361-373 City Road, London EC1V 1PQ, England — Banjoist (Pogues)

**Finer, Lawrence**
Guttmacher Institute, 120 Wall St, #2100, New York NY 10005, USA — Sociologist

**Fingaz, Sticky**
Major Independents, 22425 Ventura Blvd, #106, Woodland Hills CA 91364, USA — Rap Artist, Actor

**Fingers, Roland G (Rollie)**
PO Box 230729, Las Vegas NV 89105, USA — Baseball Player

**Fink, Kenneth**
United Talent Agency, U T A Plaza, 9336 Civic Center Dr, Beverly Hills CA 90210 USA — Director, Producer, Writer

**Fink, Michael**
B U F, 7720 W Sunset Blvd, Los Angeles CA 90046, USA — Visual Effects Editor

**Fink, Natascha** — Golfer
Golfclub Murhof, Adriach 54, 8130 Irohnleiten, Austria

**Finkel, David** — Journalist
Washington Post, Editorial Dept, 1150 15th St NW, Washington DC 20071 USA

**Finkel, Fyvush** — Actor
C E S D, 10635 Santa Monica Blvd, #130, Los Angeles CA 90025 USA

**Finkel, Henry J (Hank)** — Basketball Player
2 Pocahontas Way, Lynnfield MA 01940, USA

**Finkel, Sheldon (Shelly)** — Boxing Promoter, Manager
Shelly Finkel Mgmt, 110 Greene St, #403, New York NY 10012, USA

**Finkelstein, Joel S** — Endocrinologist
Masssachusetts General Hospital, Endocrinology Dept, 55 Fruit St, Boston MA 02114, USA

**Finlay, Frank** — Actor
Artists Partnership, 101 Finsbury Pavement, London EC2A 1RS, England

**Finley, Charles E (Chuck)** — Baseball Player
500 McCormick Road, West Monroe LA 71291, USA

**Finley, David** — Astronaut, Astronomer
1642 Milvia St, #3S, Berkeley CA 94709, USA

**Finley, Gerard H** — Opera Singer
I M G Artists, Hogarth Business Park, Chiswick, London W4 2TH, England

**Finley, Greg** — Actor
Paul Kohner, 9300 Wilshire Blvd, #555, Beverly Hills CA 90212 USA

**Finley, Karen** — Conceptual Artist
Creative Time, 59 E 4th St, #6E, New York NY 10003, USA

**Finley, Michael H** — Basketball Player
6600 Sudbury Road, Plano TX 75024, USA

**Finley, Steven A (Steve)** — Baseball Player
PO Box 2101, Rancho Santa Fe CA 92067, USA

**Finn, Charlie** — Actor
Brillstein Entertainment Partners, 9150 Wilshire Blvd, #350, Beverly Hills CA 90212 USA

**Finn, Craig** — Singer, Guitarist (Hold Steady)
Paradigm Agency, 360 N Crescent Dr, North Building, Beverly Hills CA 90210 USA

**Finn, James (Jim)** — Football Player
12-14 Western Dr, Fair Lawn NJ 07410, USA

**Finn, John** — Actor, Director, Writer
Domain Talent, 9229 W Sunset Blvd, #710, West Hollywood CA 90069 USA

**Finn, Neil** — Singer (Split Enz, Crowded House)
Ignition Mgmt, 54 Linhope St, London NW1 7JQ, England

**Finn, Patrick** — Actor
Brillstein Entertainment Partners, 9150 Wilshire Blvd, #350, Beverly Hills CA 90212 USA

**Finn, Tim** — Singer (Split Enz, Crowded House)
Harbour Agency, 135 Forbes St, Woolloomoloo NSW 2011, Australia

**Finn, Veronica** — Singer (Innosense)
R C A Records, 8750 Wilshire Blvd, Beverly Hills CA 90211 USA

**Finn, William** — Composer, Lyricist
New York University, Music Dept, New York NY 10012, USA

**Finn-Burrell, Michelle** — Track Athlete
1801 Ocean Park Blvd, #112, Santa Monica CA 90405, USA

**Finnegan, Cortland T** — Football Player
9280 Exton Lane, Brentwood TN 37027, USA

**Finneran, Katie** — Actress
Innovative Artists, 1505 10th St, Santa Monica CA 90401 USA

**Finneran, Siobhan** — Actress
Shane Collins Assoc, 11-15 Betterton St, Covent Garden, London WC2H 9BP, England

**Finnerty, Dan** — Actor, Comedian, Musician
Gersh Agency, 9465 Wilshire Blvd, #600, Beverly Hills CA 90212 USA

**Finney, Albert** — Actor
Simpkins Partnership, 45/51 Whitfield St, London W1P 4HB, England

**Finney, Allison** — Golfer
78160 Desert Mountain Circle, Bermuda Dunes CA 92203, USA

**Finnie, Linda A** — Concert Singer
16 Golf Course, Girvan, Ayrshire KA26 9HW, England

**Finnie, Roger L** — Football Player
937 NW 58th St, Miami FL 33127, USA

**Finnigan, Jennifer** — Actress
I C M Partners, 10250 Constellation Blvd, #900, Los Angeles CA 90067 USA

**Finsterwald, Dow** — Golfer
2772 Fawn Grove Court, Colorado Springs CO 80906, USA

**Fiona, Melanie** — Singer
Creative Artists Agency, 2000 Ave of Stars, #100, Los Angeles CA 90067 USA

**Fionda, Andrew** — Fashion Designer
Pearce Fionda, Loft, 27 Horsell Road, Highbury, London N5 1XL, England

**Fiordaliso, Marina** — Singer
Mithos Agency, Via Koristka 8, 20154 Milan, Italy

**Fiore, David A (Dave)** — Football Player
868 Southampton Dr, Palo Alto CA 94303, USA

**Fiore, Kathryn** — Actress
TalentWorks, 3500 W Olive Ave, #1400, Burbank CA 91505 USA

**Fiore, Mark** — Editorial Cartoonist
265 Frisco St, San Francisco CA 94133, USA

**Fiore, Michael G J (Mike)** — Baseball Player
17 Silver St, Malverne NY 11565, USA

**Fiore, William J (Bill)** — Actor
Access Talent Mgmt, 171 Madison Ave, #910, New York NY 10016, USA

**Fiori, Edward R (Ed)** — Golfer
4411 Winding River Dr, Richmond TX 77406, USA

**Fiorillo, Elisbetta** — Opera Singer
I U M A Mgmt, Via E Filiberto 125, 00185 Rome, Italy

**Fire, Andrew Z** — Nobel Medicine Laureate
Stanford University Medical School, Pathology Dept, 3000 Pasteur Dr, Stanford CA 94305, USA

**Firek, Marc** — Producer, Writer
United Talent Agency, U T A Plaza, 9336 Civic Center Dr, Beverly Hills CA 90210 USA

**Fireman, Paul B** — Businessman
Reebok International, 1895 J W Foster Blvd, Canton MA 02021, USA

**Fireovid, Stephen J (Steve)** — Baseball Player
1408 Woodstream Dr, Bryan OH 43506, USA

# F

| | |
|---|---|
| **Fires, Earlie S** 2603 Arlingdale Dr, Palatine IL 60067, USA | Thoroughbred Racing Jockey |
| **Firestone, Andrew** Paradigm Agency, 360 N Crescent Dr, North Building, Beverly Hills CA 90210 USA | Actor |
| **Firestone, Roy** Fat City Sports, 1906 Chet Atkins Place, #502, Nashville TN 37212, USA | Sportscaster, Actor |
| **Firth, Colin** Independent Talent Group, 40 Whitfield St, London W1T 2RH, England | Actor |
| **Firth, Peter** Markham Froggatt Irwin, Julian House, 4 Windmill St, London W1P 1HF, England | Actor |
| **Fisch, Asher** Opus 3 Artists, 470 Park Ave S, #900N, New York NY 10016 USA | Conductor |
| **Fisch, Jonas** Joel Stevens Entertainment, 750 Fairmont Ave, #100, Glendale CA 91203, USA | Actor, Comedian |
| **Fischbacher, Andrea** 5531 Eben im Pongau, Salzburg, Austria | Alpine Skier |
| **Fischer Schmidt, Birgit** Kuckuckswald 11, 14532 Kleinmachnow, Germany | Canoeing Athlete |
| **Fischer, Adam** Askonas Holt, Lincoln House, 300 High Holborn, London WC1V 7JH, England | Conductor |
| **Fischer, Alain** Hospitalier Necker-Enfants-Malades, 149 Rue Sevres, 75015 Paris, France | Pediatric Immunologist |
| **Fischer, Edmond H** 5540 N Windermere Road, Seattle WA 98105, USA | Nobel Medicine Laureate |
| **Fischer, Fanny** Kanu Club Potsdam, Am Luftschiffhafen 2, 14471 Potsdam, Germany | Canoeing Athlete |
| **Fischer, Gotthilf** Buro Gotthilf Fischer, Postfach 45, 71715 Berlin, Germany | Composer |
| **Fischer, Heinz** Prasidentschaftskanzlei, Hofburg, Alderstiege, 1010 Vienna, Austria | President, Austria |
| **Fischer, Helene** Kunstlermanagement Uwe Kanthak, Postfach 113124, 20431 Hamburg, Germany | Singer |
| **Fischer, Henry W (Hank)** 10367 Big Canoe, Big Canoe GA 30143, USA | Baseball Player |
| **Fischer, Ivan** 1 Andrassy Utca 27, 1061 Budapest, Hungary | Conductor |
| **Fischer, Jenna** Odenkirk Provissiero Entertainment, 1936 N Bronson Ave, Los Angeles CA 90069 USA | Actress |
| **Fischer, Joschka** Princeton University, Liechtenstein Institute, Princeton NJ 08544, USA | Government Official, Germany |
| **Fischer, Julia** Kunstler Sekretariat am Gasteig, Rosenheimer Str 52, 81669 Munich, Germany | Concert Violinist |
| **Fischer, Lisa** Alive Enterprises, 3264 S Kihei Road, Kihei HI 96753, USA | Singer |
| **Fischer, Patrick (Pat)** 45800 Jona Dr, #314, Sterling VA 20165, USA | Football Player |
| **Fischer, Stanley** Bank of Israel, PO Box 780, 91007 Jerusalem, Israel | Economist |
| **Fischer, Sven (Fritz)** Schillerhoehe 7, 98574 Schmalkalden, Germany | Biathlete |
| **Fischer, Todd** 7347 Linwood Court, Pleasanton CA 94588, USA | Golfer |
| **Fischer, Urs** Gavin Brown Gallery, 620 Greenwich St, New York NY 10014, USA | Sculptor |
| **Fischer, Veronika** B 2 K Media, Brandenburgische Str 38, 10707 Berlin, Germany | Singer |
| **Fischer, William A (Moose)** 23191 Shady Oak Lane, Estero FL 33928, USA | Football Player |
| **Fischer, William C (Bill)** 139 Upland Dr, Council Bluffs IA 51503, USA | Baseball Player |
| **Fischer-Nielsen, Joachim** Heslegardsvej 8-2, 2900 Hellerup, Denmark | Badminton Player |
| **Fischetti, Brad** Evolution Talent Agency, 1501 Broadway, #1301, New York NY 10036 USA | Singer, Rap Artist |
| **Fischetti, Vincent A** Rockefeller University Medical Center, 1230 York Ave, New York NY 10065 USA | Microbiologist |
| **Fischl, Eric** Mary Boone Gallery, 745 5th Ave, #405, New York NY 10151, USA | Artist |
| **Fischlin, Michael T (Mike)** 1010 Curtright Place, Greensboro GA 30642, USA | Baseball Player |
| **Fish, Ginger** Interscope Records, 2220 Colorado Ave, Santa Monica CA 90404 USA | Drummer (Marilyn Manson) |
| **Fish, Howard M** 15797 Dockside Court, Tyler TX 75703, USA | Air Force General |
| **Fish, Mardy** S F X Sports, 846 Lincoln Road, #500, Miami Beach Fl 33139 USA | Tennis Player |
| **Fishburne, Laurence** Paradigm Agency, 360 N Crescent Dr, North Building, Beverly Hills CA 90210 USA | Actor |
| **Fishburne, Rodes** Delacorte Press, 1540 Broadway, New York NY 10036 USA | Writer |
| **Fishel, Danielle** Levity Entertainment Group, 6701 Center Dr W, #1111, Los Angeles CA 90045, USA | Actress |
| **Fisher Hartman, Sarah** Sarah Fisher Racing, 1255 Main St, Indianapolis IN 46224, USA | Auto Racing Driver |
| **Fisher, Allison** Bailey's Sports Bar, 8500 Pineville-Mathew Road, Charlotte NC 28226, USA | Billiards Player |
| **Fisher, Anna L** 1912 Elmen St, Houston TX 77019, USA | Astronaut |
| **Fisher, Bernard** 5636 Aylesboro Ave, Pittsburgh PA 15217, USA | Surgeon |
| **Fisher, Brian K** 3660 S Uravan St, Aurora CO 80013, USA | Baseball Player |
| **Fisher, Carrie** 1700 Coldwater Canyon Road, Beverly Hills CA 90210, USA | Actress, Writer |
| **Fisher, Debra Mae** 2150 NW Hill St, #2, Bend OR 97701, USA | Artist |

| | |
|---|---|
| **Fisher, Derek L** | Basketball Player, Coach |
| New York Knicks, Madison Square Garden, 2 Penn Plaza, New York, NY 10121 USA | |
| **Fisher, Eddie G** | Baseball Player |
| 408 Cardinal Circle S, Altus OK 73521, USA | |
| **Fisher, Edwin L (Ed)** | Football Player |
| 4734 E Redfield Road, Phoenix AZ 85032, USA | |
| **Fisher, Elder A (Bud)** | Bowling Executive |
| 7551 Brackenwood Circle N, Indianapolis IN 46260, USA | |
| **Fisher, Evan** | Singer (Diamonds) |
| G E M S, PO Box 1031, Montrose CA 91021, USA | |
| **Fisher, Frances** | Actress |
| Greene Assoc, 1901 Ave of Stars, #130, Los Angeles CA 90067 USA | |
| **Fisher, Frederick** | Interior Designer, Architect |
| Frederick Fisher Partners, 12248 Santa Monica Blvd, Los Angeles CA 90025, USA | |
| **Fisher, Isla** | Actress |
| Creative Artists Agency, 2000 Ave of Stars, #100, Los Angeles CA 90067 USA | |
| **Fisher, Jeffrey M (Jeff)** | Football Player, Coach |
| Saint Louis Rams, 901 N Broadway, Saint Louis MO 63101 USA | |
| **Fisher, Jeremy** | Singer, Songwriter |
| Agency Group Ltd, 142 W 57th St, #600, New York NY 10019 USA | |
| **Fisher, Joel** | Sculptor |
| PO Box 65, Palisades NY 10964, USA | |
| **Fisher, Joely** | Actress |
| John Carrabino Mgmt, 5900 Wilshire Blvd, #406, Los Angeles CA 90036 USA | |
| **Fisher, John H (Jack)** | Baseball Player |
| 4407 Nicholas St, Easton PA 18045, USA | |
| **Fisher, John Norwood** | Bassist (Fishbone) |
| Silverback Mgmt, 9469 Jefferson Blvd, #101, Culver City CA 90232, USA | |
| **Fisher, Kimberly** | Model, Actress |
| PO Box 69330, #436, West Hollywood CA 90069, USA | |
| **Fisher, Mary** | AIDS Activist |
| Charles Scribner's Sons, 866 3rd Ave, New York NY 10022 USA | |
| **Fisher, Matthew** | Organist (Procol Harum), Songwriter |
| 39 Croham Road, South Croydon CR2 7HD, England | |
| **Fisher, Noel** | Actor |
| United Talent Agency, U T A Plaza, 9336 Civic Center Dr, Beverly Hills CA 90210 USA | |
| **Fisher, Raymond C** | Judge |
| US Court of Appeals, 125 S Grand Ave, Pasadena CA 91105, USA | |
| **Fisher, Red** | Sportswriter |
| Montreal Gazette, 250 Saint Antoine W, Montreal QC H2Y 3R7, Canada | |
| **Fisher, Richard W** | Financier, Government Official |
| Dallas Federal Reserve Bank, 2200 N Pearl St, Dallas TX 75201, USA | |
| **Fisher, Rob** | Conductor |
| I M G Artists, Carnegie Hall Tower, 152 W 57th St, #500, New York NY 10019 USA | |
| **Fisher, Robert J** | Businessman |
| Gap Inc, 2 Folsom St, San Francisco CA 94105, USA | |
| **Fisher, Roger** | Guitarist (Heart) |
| PO Box 1162, Woodinville WA 98072, USA | |
| **Fisher, Scott** | Astronomer |
| Gemini Observatory, Mauna Kea, Hilo HI 96720, USA | |
| **Fisher, Steve** | Basketball Coach |
| San Diego State University, Athletic Dept, San Diego CA 92182, USA | |
| **Fisher, Todd** | Producer |
| Paradigm Agency, 360 N Crescent Dr, North Building, Beverly Hills CA 90210 USA | |
| **Fisher, William F** | Astronaut |
| 1119 Woodbank Dr, Seabrook TX 77586, USA | |
| **Fishman, Alan F** | Financier |
| Columbia Financial Partners, 195 Montague St, Brooklyn NY 11201, USA | |
| **Fishman, Bill** | Director |
| Fallout Entertainment, 3100 Airport Ave, Santa Monica CA 90405, USA | |
| **Fishman, James H (Jim)** | Publisher |
| A A R P Magazine, Publisher's Office, 601 E St NW, Washington DC 20049, USA | |
| **Fishman, Jay S** | Businessman |
| Saint Paul Travelers, 388 Greenwich St, #3900, New York NY 10013, USA | |
| **Fishman, Jon** | Drummer (Phish) |
| Dionysian Productions, 431 Pine St, Burlington VT 05401, USA | |
| **Fishman, Mark C** | Cardiologist |
| Novartis BioMedical Research Institute, 250 Massachusetts Ave, Cambridge MA 02139, USA | |
| **Fishman, Michael** | Actor |
| 4141 Ball Road, Cypress CA 90630, USA | |
| **Fisichella, Giancarlo** | Auto Racing Driver |
| Movie & Sport Mgmt, Finsgate, 5-7 Cranwood St, London EC1V 9EE, England | |
| **Fisk, Carlton E** | Baseball Player |
| 18705 63rd Ave E, Bradenton FL 34211, USA | |
| **Fisk, Jason** | Football Player |
| 2619 Regatta Lane, Davis CA 95618, USA | |
| **Fisk, Sari K** | Ice Hockey Player |
| Ice Hockey Association, Veturitie 13H, 00240 Helsinki, Finland | |
| **Fisk, Schuyler** | Actress, Singer |
| Innovative Artists, 1505 10th St, Santa Monica CA 90401 USA | |
| **Fiske, James (Jim)** | Electrical Engineer |
| Launchpoint Technologies, 5735 Hollister Ave, #B, Goleta CA 93117, USA | |
| **Fiske, Robert B, Jr** | Attorney |
| 19 Juniper Road, Darien CT 06820, USA | |
| **Fister, Bruce L** | Air Force General |
| 400 Regatta Dr, Niceville FL 32578, USA | |
| **Fister, Douglas W (Doug)** | Baseball Player |
| Washington Nationals, 1500 S Capitol St SE, Washington DC 20003 USA | |
| **Fistric, Mark** | Ice Hockey Player |
| Anaheim Ducks, 2695 E Katella Ave, Anaheim CA 92806 USA | |
| **Fitch, Janet** | Writer |
| Little Brown, 3 Center Plaza, #100, Boston MA 02108 USA | |
| **Fitch, Val L** | Nobel Physics Laureate |
| 292 Hartley Ave, Princeton NJ 08540, USA | |
| **Fitch, William C (Bill)** | Basketball Coach |
| 627 Nerita St, #A, Sanibel FL 33957, USA | |

**F**

## F

|  |  |
|---|---|
| **Fites, Donald V** | Businessman |
| 9943 Brassie Bend, Naples FL 34108, USA | |
| **Fittipaldi, Christian** | Auto Racing Driver |
| 282 Alphaville Barueri, Sao Paulo 0640 500, Brazil | |
| **Fittipaldi, Emerson** | Auto Racing Driver |
| Ave Reboucas 3551, Jardim Paulistano, Sao Paulo 05401 400, Brazil | |
| **Fittipaldi, Lisa** | Artist |
| Mind's Eye Foundation, 215 Beauregard, San Antonio TX 78204, USA | |
| **Fitts, Rick** | Actor |
| A M T Artists, 15260 Ventura Blvd, #1200, Sherman Oaks CA 91403, USA | |
| **Fitzgerald, Annie** | Actress |
| Stone Manners Salners, 6100 Wilshire Blvd, #1500, Los Angeles CA 90035 USA | |
| **Fitzgerald, Caitlin** | Actress, Model |
| I C M Partners, 730 5th Ave, New York NY 10019 USA | |
| **Fitzgerald, Christopher** | Actor |
| United Talent Agency, U T A Plaza, 9336 Civic Center Dr, Beverly Hills CA 90210 USA | |
| **FitzGerald, Edward R (Ed)** | Baseball Player |
| 431 Christopher St, Folsom CA 95630, USA | |
| **Fitzgerald, Fern** | Actress |
| 7409 Leescott Ave, Van Nuys CA 91406, USA | |
| **FitzGerald, Frances** | Writer |
| Simon & Schuster, 1230 Ave of Americas, Concourse 1, New York NY 10020, USA | |
| **Fitzgerald, Frankie** | Actor |
| Creative Artists Agency, 2000 Ave of Stars, #100, Los Angeles CA 90067 USA | |
| **FitzGerald, Helen** | Actress |
| Paul Kohner, 9300 Wilshire Blvd, #555, Beverly Hills CA 90212 USA | |
| **Fitzgerald, Jack** | Actor |
| William Kerwin Agency, 1605 N Cahuenga, #202, Los Angeles CA 90028, USA | |
| **Fitzgerald, John R** | Football Player |
| 408 Arborcrest Dr, Richardson TX 75080, USA | |
| **Fitzgerald, Larry D, Jr** | Football Player |
| 15832 S 22nd St, Phoenix AZ 85048, USA | |
| **Fitzgerald, Michael R (Mike)** | Baseball Player |
| 502 Flint Ave, Long Beach CA 90814, USA | |
| **Fitzgerald, Pat** | Football Player, Coach |
| Northwestern University, Athletic Dept, Evanston IN 60208, USA | |
| **Fitzgerald, Patrick J** | Attorney, Government Official |
| Justice Dept, Dirksen Building, 219 S Dearborn St, #500, Chicago IL 60604, USA | |
| **Fitzgerald, Tara** | Actress |
| United Agents, 12-26 Lexington St, London W1F 0LE, England | |
| **FitzGerald, Thomas** | Environmentalist |
| Kentucky Resources Council, 213 Saint Clair St, Frankfort KY 40601, USA | |
| **Fitzgerald, Tom** | Ice Hockey Player |
| 3 Samuel Phelps Way, North Reading MA 01864, USA | |
| **Fitzgerald, Willa** | Actress |
| Paradigm Agency, 360 N Crescent Dr, North Building, Beverly Hills CA 90210 USA | |
| **Fitzgerald, William H G** | Diplomat |
| 25 Carrington Dr, Greenwich CT 06831, USA | |
| **Fitzgerald-Brown, Benita** | Track Athlete |
| Women in Cable/Telecommunications, 14555 Avion Parkway, Chantilly VA 20151, USA | |
| **Fitzmaurice, David J** | Labor Leader |
| Electrical Radio & Machinists Union, 11256 156th St NW, Washington DC 20005, USA | |
| **Fitzmaurice, Deanne** | Photojournalist |
| San Francisco Chronicle, Editorial Dept, 925 Mission, San Francisco CA 94103 USA | |
| **Fitzmaurice, Michael J** | Vietnam War Army Hero (CMH) |
| PO Box 178, Hartford SD 57033, USA | |
| **Fitzmorris, Alan J (Al)** | Baseball Player |
| 17512 W 159th Terrace, Olathe KS 66062, USA | |
| **Fitzpatrick, Leo** | Actor |
| Don Buchwald Talent Agency, 6500 Wilshire Blvd, #2200, Los Angeles CA 90048 USA | |
| **Fitzpatrick, Stephen** | Guitarist (Veruca Salt, Ashtar Command) |
| S T C Entertainment, 5627 Sepulveda Blvd, #230, Van Nuys CA 91411, USA | |
| **FitzRandolph, Casey** | Speed Skater |
| Janey Miller Mgmt, 1435 Cherryvale Dr, Boulder CO 80303, USA | |
| **Fitzsimmons, Greg** | Actor, Comedian |
| United Talent Agency, U T A Plaza, 9336 Civic Center Dr, Beverly Hills CA 90210 USA | |
| **Fitzsimonds, Roger L** | Financier |
| Firstar Corp, 777 E Wisconsin Ave, Milwaukee WI 53202, USA | |
| **FitzSimons, Dennis J** | Publisher |
| Tribune Co, 435 N Michigan Ave, Chicago IL 60611, USA | |
| **Fitzwater, Marlin** | Government Official |
| 851 Cedar Dr, Deale MD 20751, USA | |
| **Fitzwilliam, Wendy M** | Beauty Queen |
| Evolving TecKnologies, Don Miguel Road Extension, El Socorro, Trinidad | |
| **Fix, Oliver** | Canoeing Athlete |
| Ringstr 6, 86391 Stadtbergen, Germany | |
| **Fixman, Marshall** | Chemist |
| Colorado State University, Chemistry Dept, Fort Collins CO 80523, USA | |
| **Fjuioka, Sachio** | Conductor |
| I M G Artists, Hogarth Business Park, Chiswick, London W4 2TH, England | |
| **Flacco, Joe V** | Football Player |
| Baltimore Ravens, Ravens Stadium, 1 Winning Dr, Baltimore MD 21230 USA | |
| **Flach, Ken** | Tennis Player, Coach |
| Vanderbilt University, Athletic Dept, Nashville TN 37240, USA | |
| **Flach, Thomas** | Yachtsman |
| Johanna-Resch-Str 13, 12439 Berlin, Germany | |
| **Flack, Enya** | Actress |
| Marv Dauer Mgmt, 11661 San Vicente Blvd, #104, Los Angeles CA 90049, USA | |
| **Flack, Roberta** | Singer, Songwriter |
| Red Entertainment Agency, 505 8th Ave, #1004, New York NY 10018, USA | |
| **Flade, H Klaus-Dietrich** | Cosmonaut, Germany |
| Airbus Industries, 1 Rond Point M Bellonte, 31707 Blagnac Cedex, France | |
| **Flagg, Fannie** | Actress, Comedienne |
| Creative Artists Agency, 2000 Ave of Stars, #100, Los Angeles CA 90067 USA | |
| **Flaherty, Joe** | Actor, Comedian |
| S M S Talent, 8383 Wilshire Blvd, #230, Beverly Hills CA 90211 USA | |

**Fites - Flaherty**

**Flaherty, John T**
17 Joseph Bow Court, Pearl River NY 10965, USA — Baseball Player
**Flaherty, Stephen**
W M E Entertainment, 9601 Wilshire Blvd, #300, Beverly Hills CA 90210 USA — Composer
**Flaim, Eric J**
52 East St, Rutland VA 05701, USA — Speed Skater
**Flair, Ric**
5701 Providence Country Club Dr, Charlotte NC 28277, USA — Professional Wrestler
**Flamand, Didier**
U B B A, 6 Rue de Braque, 75003 Paris, France — Actor
**Flanagan, Crista**
Liberman-Zerman Mgmt, 252 N Larchmont Blvd, #200, Los Angeles CA 90004 USA — Actress
**Flanagan, Edward J (Ed)**
10981 Clayton St, Northglenn CO 80233, USA — Football Player
**Flanagan, Edward M, Jr**
Parade Rest, 12 Oyster Catcher Road, Beaufort SC 29907, USA — Army General
**Flanagan, Fionnula**
Lisa Richards Agency, 108 Upper Leeson St, Dublin 4, Ireland — Actress
**Flanagan, Michael C (Mike)**
5 Moss Springs Court, Henderson NV 89052, USA — Football Player
**Flanagan, Richard M**
Penguin/Random House, 100 Pacific Highway, #300, North Sydney NSW 2060, Australia — Writer
**Flanagan, Shalane**
410 NW 18th Ave, Portland OR 97209, USA — Track Athlete
**Flanagan, Tommy**
Untitled Entertainment, 350 S Beverly Dr, #200, Beverly Hills CA 90212 USA — Actor
**Flanery, Bridget**
Sovereign Talent Group, 8421 Wilshire Blvd, #200, Los Angeles CA 90211, USA — Actress
**Flanery, Sean Patrick**
A P A Talent & Literary Agency, 405 S Beverly Dr, #300, Beverly Hills CA 90212 USA — Actor
**Flanigan, James M (Jim)**
3820 Sand Point Road, Sturgeon Bay WI 54235, USA — Football Player
**Flanigan, James M (Jim), Jr**
4511 Wyandot Trail, Green Bay WI 54313, USA — Football Player
**Flanigan, Joe**
C E S D, 10635 Santa Monica Blvd, #130, Los Angeles CA 90025 USA — Actor, Writer
**Flanigan, Lauren**
Robert Lombardo Assoc, Harkness Plaza, 61 W 62nd St, #6F, New York NY 10023 USA — Opera Singer
**Flannery, John M**
9002 Scottish Pastures Dr, Austin TX 78750, USA — Baseball Player
**Flannery, Kate**
Marleah Leslie & Associates, 1645 N Vine St, #712, Los Angeles CA 90028, USA — Actress
**Flannery, Susan**
Bell-Phillip Television Productions, 7800 Beverly Blvd, #3371, Los Angeles CA 90036, USA — Actress
**Flannery, Thomas**
911 Dartmouth Glen Way, Baltimore MD 21212, USA — Editorial Cartoonist
**Flannery, Timothy E (Tim)**
715 Hymettus Ave, Encinitas CA 92024, USA — Baseball Player
**Flannigan, Maureen**
Don Buchwald Talent Agency, 10 E 44th St, New York NY 10017 USA — Actress
**Flansburgh, John C**
Hornblow Group, PO Box 176, Palisades NY 10964, USA — Singer, Guitarist (They Might Be Giants)
**Flathman, Richard E**
112 Rafael Dr, San Rafael CA 94901, USA — Political Scientist
**Flatland, Ann Kristin Aafeldt**
Jaerbubratet 6, 4330 Algard, Norway — Biathlete
**Flatley, Michael**
Unicorn Entertainments, 19 Portland Place, London W1B 1PX, England — Dancer
**Flatley, Paul R**
795 Woods Road, Richmond IN 47374, USA — Football Player
**Flaum, Joel M**
US District Court, 219 S Dearborn St,, #2302B, Chicago IL 60604, USA — Judge
**Flavell, Richard A**
Yale University Medical Center, Immunology Dept, New Haven CT 06520, USA — Immunologist
**Flavin, Jennifer**
30 Beverly Park, Beverly Hills CA 90210, USA — Model
**Flavor Flav**
Media Artists Group, 8222 Melrose Ave, #203, Los Angeles CA 90048 USA — Rap Artist, Actor, Comedian
**Flaxey, Caleb**
Team Brad Jacobs, 38 Barber Blvd, Sault Sainte Marie ON P6A 5T8, Canda — Curling Athlete
**Flay, Bobby**
Bold Food, PO Box 1102, New York NY 10159, USA — Restauranteur, Chef
**Flea**
Innovative Artists, 1505 10th St, Santa Monica CA 90401 USA — Bassist (Red Hot Chili Peppers)
**Fleck, Bela**
Shore Fire Media, 32 Court St, #1600, Brooklyn NY 11201 USA — Guitarist, Banjoist, Composer
**Fleck, John**
Greater Vision Artists Talent, 8981 Sunset Blvd, #101, Los Angeles CA 90069, USA — Performance Artist, Actor
**Fleck, Ryan**
Management 360, 9111 Wilshire Blvd, Beverly Hills CA 90210 USA — Director, Writer
**Fleder, Gary R**
Mojo Films, Animation Building, 500 S Buena Vista St, Burbank CA 91521, USA — Director
**Fleeshman, Richard**
Independent Talent Group, 40 Whitfield St, London W1T 2RH, England — Actor
**Fleetwood, Mick J K**
Sabre Entertainment, 5737 Kanan Road, #237, Agoura Hills CA 91301, USA — Drummer (Fleetwood Mac)
**Fleischer, Ari**
Harper Collins Publishers, 10 E 53rd St, Cellar 1, New York NY 10022 USA — Government Official, Journalist
**Fleischer, Ruben**
United Talent Agency, U T A Plaza, 9336 Civic Center Dr, Beverly Hills CA 90210 USA — Director, Writer
**Fleischman, Paul**
PO Box 646, Aromas CA 95004, USA — Writer
**Fleischmann, Peter**
Filmzentrum Babelsberg, August-Bebel-Str 26-53, 14482 Potsdam, Germany — Director, Producer
**Fleisher, Bruce L**
127 Via Isabela, Jupiter FL 33458, USA — Golfer

| | |
|---|---|
| **Fleisher, Leon** 20 Merrymount Road, Baltimore MD 21210, USA | Concert Pianist, Conductor |
| **Fleiss, Michael** Creative Artists Agency, 2000 Ave of Stars, #100, Los Angeles CA 90067 USA | Producer, Writer |
| **Fleming Jenkins, Peggy** 16387 Aztec Ridge Dr, Los Gatos CA 95030, USA | Figure Skater |
| **Fleming, Andrew M (Andy)** I/D Public Relations, 7060 Hollywood Blvd, #800, Los Angeles CA 90028 USA | Director |
| **Fleming, Anne Taylor** Janklow & Nesbit Assoc, 445 Park Ave, #1300, New York NY 10022 USA | Journalist, Writer |
| **Fleming, David A** PO Box 692, Lincolndale NY 10540, USA | Baseball Player |
| **Fleming, Eric** A P A Talent & Literary Agency, 405 S Beverly Dr, #300, Beverly Hills CA 90212 USA | Actor |
| **Fleming, Jacky** Bloomsbury Publishing, 50 Bedford Square, London WC1B 3DP, England | Writer |
| **Fleming, James P** PO Box 487, Manvel TX 77578, USA | Vietnam War Air Force Hero (CMH) |
| **Fleming, Joy** Bernd Liebenow Kunstlervermittl, Cherry Str 28, 74889 Hilsbach, Germany | Singer |
| **Fleming, Marvin (Marv)** 909 Howard St, Marina del Rey CA 90292, USA | Football Player |
| **Fleming, Renee** Gorfaine/Schwartz, 4111 W Alameda Ave, #509, Burbank CA 91505 USA | Opera Singer |
| **Fleming, Rhonda** 10281 Century Woods Dr, Los Angeles CA 90067, USA | Actress |
| **Fleming, Scott** 2425 Elendil Lane, Davis CA 95616, USA | Government Official |
| **Fleming, Valerie** Q Sports Marketing, 534 W Evergreen St, Wheaton IL 60187 USA | Bobsled Athlete |
| **Fleming, Vern** 10713 Brixton Lane, Fishers IN 46037, USA | Basketball Player |
| **Flemings, Merton C** 975 Memorial Dr, #608, Cambridge MA 02138, USA | Materials Engineer |
| **Flemming, John** 1409 Cambronne St, New Orleans LA 70118, USA | Artist |
| **Flemyng, Jason** Conway Van Gelder Grant, 8-12 Broadwick St, #300, London W1F 8HW, England | Actor |
| **Flender, Rodman** Apostle Mgmt, 9696 Culver Blvd, #110, Culver City CA 90232, USA | Director, Producer, Actor |
| **Flesch, Steve** PO Box 440, Union KY 41091, USA | Golfer |
| **Fletcher, Andrew J (Andy)** Reach Media, 295 Greenwich St. #109, New York NY 10007, USA | Synthesizer Musician (Depeche Mode) |
| **Fletcher, Anne** United Talent Agency, U T A Plaza, 9336 Civic Center Dr, Beverly Hills CA 90210 USA | Director, Choreographer |
| **Fletcher, Christopher C (Chris)** 4818 La Cruz Dr, La Mesa CA 91941, USA | Football Player |
| **Fletcher, Cliff** 19980 N 94th Way, Scottsdale AZ 85255, USA | Ice Hockey Executive |
| **Fletcher, Darrin G** 9146 E 2100 North Road, Oakwood IL 61858, USA | Baseball Player |
| **Fletcher, Dexter** Independent Talent Group, 40 Whitfield St, London W1T 2RH, England | Actor |
| **Fletcher, Diane** Gavin Barker Assoc, 2D Wimpole St, London W1G 0EB, England | Actress |
| **Fletcher, E Paul** 548 Mockingbird Way, Warrington PA 18976, USA | Baseball Player |
| **Fletcher, Guy** Air Edel, 9100 Wilshire Blvd, #350E, Beverly Hills CA 90212 USA | Keyboardist (Dire Straits) |
| **Fletcher, Jamar M** 11063 Worchester Dr, Saint Louis MO 63136, USA | Football Player |
| **Fletcher, London L** 300 Oakmont Lane, Waxhaw NC 28173, USA | Football Player |
| **Fletcher, Louise** 1520 Camden Ave, #105, Los Angeles CA 90025, USA | Actress |
| **Fletcher, Martin** NBC-TV, News Dept, 4001 Nebraska Ave NW, Washington DC 20016 USA | Commentator |
| **Fletcher, Scott B** 300 Birkdale Dr, Fayetteville GA 30215, USA | Baseball Player |
| **Fletcher, Terrell A** 13889 Etude Road, San Diego CA 92128, USA | Football Player |
| **Fletcher, Thomas M (Tom)** Helter Skelter, 347-353 Chiswick High Road, London W4 4HS, England | Singer, Guitarist (McFly); Songwriter |
| **Fletcher, Thomas W (Tom)** 9287 E 2085 North Road, Oakwood IL 61858, USA | Baseball Player |
| **Fletcher, William A** US Court of Appeals, Court Building, 95 7th St, San Francisco CA 94103, USA | Judge |
| **Fleury, Marc-Andre** 1123 Castletown Court, Sewickley PA 15143, USA | Ice Hockey Player |
| **Fleury, Sylvie** Spruth Magers Gallery, Oranienburger Str 18, 10178 Berlin, Germany | Sculptor |
| **Fleury, Theoren W (Theo)** Concrete Coatings, 4519 Manhattan Road SE, Calgary AB T2G 4B3, Canada | Ice Hockey Player |
| **Flick, Bob** Bob Flick Productions, 300 Vine St, #14, Seattle WA 98121, USA | Singer, Fiddle Player (Brothers Four) |
| **Flicker, John** National Audubon Society, 225 Varick St, #700, New York NY 10014, USA | Association Executive |
| **Flindt, George H** PO Box 2486, Prescott AZ 86302, USA | Football Player |
| **Flint, Jill** Innovative Artists, 1505 10th St, Santa Monica CA 90401 USA | Actress |
| **Flint, Keith** Maverick Records, 3300 Warner Blvd, Burbank CA 91505, USA | Dancer, Singer (Prodigy) |
| **Flipkens, Kirsten** Autohandel Marino Flipkens, Saint Janstraat 22, 2400 Moi, Belgium | Tennis Player |

**Flippin, Lucy Lee**  
713 Eagle Road, Fleetwood PA 19522, USA — *Actress*

**Fliter, Ingrid**  
C M Artists, 127 W 96th St, #13B, New York NY 10025 USA — *Concert Pianist*

**Flitter, Josh**  
Abrams Artists, 9200 W Sunset Blvd, #1125, West Hollywood CA 90069 USA — *Actor*

**Float, Jeffrey (Jeff)**  
1906 University Park Dr, Sacramento CA 95825, USA — *Swimmer*

**Flockhart, Calista**  
Industry Entertainment, 955 Carillo Dr, #300, Los Angeles CA 90048 USA — *Actress*

**Flood, Debbie**  
Leander Club, Henley on Thames, Leander RG9 2LP, England — *Rowing Athlete*

**Flor, Claus Peter**  
I M G Artists, Hogarth Business Park, Chiswick, London W4 2TH, England — *Conductor*

**Florance, Sheila**  
Melbourne Artists, 643 Saint Kikla Road, Melbourne VIC 3004, Australia — *Actress*

**Florek, Dann**  
Access Talent Mgmt, 171 Madison Ave, #910, New York NY 10016, USA — *Actor*

**Florence, David**  
Frasser Florence, 160 Wilford Grove, Nottingham, Nottinghamshire NG2 2DW, England — *Canoeing Athlete*

**Flores, Gene**  
Portland Community College, Art Dept, 1200 SW 49th Ave, Portland OR 97219, USA — *Artist*

**Flores, Randy A**  
23 Keepsake, Irvine CA 92618, USA — *Baseball Player*

**Flores, Rosie**  
Rounder Records, 1 Rounder Way, Burlington MA 01803 USA — *Singer, Guitarist*

**Flores, Thomas R (Tom)**  
77741 Cove Point Circle, Indian Wells CA 92210, USA — *Football Player, Coach, Executive*

**Florie, Bryce B**  
1118 Lands End Dr, Hanahan SC 29410, USA — *Baseball Player*

**Florijn, Ronald**  
H J Z Sport, Sporthallen Zuid, Burgerweehuispad 54, 1076 Amsterdam EP, Netherlands — *Rowing Athlete*

**Florio, James J (Jim)**  
Mudge Rose Guthrie, Corporate Center 2, 1673 E 16th St, #16, Brooklyn NY 11229, USA — *Governor, NJ*

**Florio, Thomas A**  
New Yorker, Publisher's Office, 4 Times Square, New York NY 10036, USA — *Publisher*

**Florschuetz, Thomas**  
Gary Tatintsian Gallery, 526 W 26th St, New York NY 10001, USA — *Photographer*

**Flowers, Brandon**  
W M E Entertainment, 9601 Wilshire Blvd, #300, Beverly Hills CA 90210 USA — *Singer, Pianist (Killers)*

**Flowers, Brandon L**  
San Diego Chargers, 4020 Murphy Canyon Road, San Diego CA 92123 USA — *Football Player*

**Flowers, Bruce**  
276 W Grantley Ave, Elmhurst IL 60126, USA — *Basketball Player*

**Flowers, Charles (Charlie)**  
6170 Mountain Brook Way NW, Atlanta GA 30328, USA — *Football Player*

**Flowers, Frank E**  
Brillstein Entertainment Partners, 9150 Wilshire Blvd, #350, Beverly Hills CA 90212 USA — *Director, Writer*

**Flowers, Richmond M, Jr**  
3434 Indian Lake Dr, Pelham AL 35124, USA — *Football Player*

**Floyd, C Clifford (Cliff), Jr**  
3283 Birch Terrace, Davie FL 33330, USA — *Baseball Player*

**Floyd, Carlisle**  
3552 Trillium Court, Tallahassee FL 32312, USA — *Composer*

**Floyd, Eddie**  
J W Entertainment, PO Box 78904, Atlanta GA 30357 USA — *Singer, Songwriter*

**Floyd, Elson S**  
Washington State University, President's Office, Pullman WA 99164, USA — *Educator*

**Floyd, Eric A (Sleepy)**  
3191 Ivy Creek Road, Gastonia NC 28056, USA — *Basketball Player*

**Floyd, Eric C**  
18047 Sailfish Dr, Lutz FL 33558, USA — *Football Player*

**Floyd, Gavin C**  
9809 Milano Dr, Trinity FL 34655, USA — *Baseball Player*

**Floyd, George, Jr**  
8621 Heritage Dr, Florence KY 41042, USA — *Football Player*

**Floyd, Heather**  
W M E Entertainment, 1600 Division St, #300, Nashville TN 37203 USA — *Singer (Point of Grace)*

**Floyd, Marlene**  
Marlene Floyd Golf School, 5370 Club House Lane, Hope Mills NC 28348, USA — *Golfer*

**Floyd, Michael**  
Arizona Cardinals, PO Box 888, Phoenix AZ 85001 USA — *Football Player*

**Floyd, Raymond (Ray)**  
505 S Flagler Dr, #910, West Palm Beach FL 33401, USA — *Golfer*

**Floyd, Robert**  
C E S D, 10635 Santa Monica Blvd, #130, Los Angeles CA 90025 USA — *Actor*

**Floyd, Robert N (Bobby)**  
1757 SE Dominic Ave, Port Saint Lucie FL 34952, USA — *Baseball Player*

**Floyd, Susan**  
Untitled Entertainment, 350 S Beverly Dr, #200, Beverly Hills CA 90212 USA — *Actress*

**Floyd, Tim**  
University of Texas, Athletic Dept, El Paso TX 79968, USA — *Basketball Coach*

**Floyd, William A**  
PO Box 784767, Winter Garden FL 34778, USA — *Football Player*

**Fluckey, Tim**  
Novi Entertainment, PO Box 17077, Beverly Hills CA 90209, USA — *Guitarist, Pianist (Adema)*

**Fluegel, Darlanne**  
Shelter Entertainment, 9255 Sunset Blvd, #300, Los Angeles CA 90069 USA — *Actress*

**Flueger, Patrick John**  
United Talent Agency, U T A Plaza, 9336 Civic Center Dr, Beverly Hills CA 90210 USA — *Actor*

**Flutie, Douglas R (Doug)**  
22 Chieftain Lane, Natick MA 01760, USA — *Football Player, Sportscaster*

**Flynn, Barbara**  
Rights House, Drury House, 34-43 Russell St, London WC2B 5HA, England — *Actress*

**Flynn, George W**  
382 Summit Ave, Leonia NJ 07605, USA — *Chemist*

**Flynn, Jackie** — Actress, Comedienne
Don Buchwald Talent Agency, 6500 Wilshire Blvd, #2200, Los Angeles CA 90048 USA

**Flynn, Johnny** — Singer, Musician, Actor
Agency Group Ltd, 1880 Century Park E, #711, Los Angeles CA 90067 USA

**Flynn, Matt** — Drummer (Maroon 5)
J Records, 745 5th Ave, #600, New York NY 10151 USA

**Flynn, Matthew C (Matt)** — Football Player
Green Bay Packers, 1265 Lombardi Ave, Green Bay WI 54304 USA

**Flynn, Michael D (Mike)** — Basketball Player
3934 E Battala Ave, Gilbert AZ 85297, USA

**Flynn, Michael P (Mike)** — Football Player
1922 Clifden Road, Catonsville MD 21228, USA

**Flynn, Neil** — Actor
A P A Talent & Literary Agency, 405 S Beverly Dr, #300, Beverly Hills CA 90212 USA

**Flynn, R Douglas (Doug), Jr** — Baseball Player
2465 Vale Dr, Lexington KY 40514, USA

**Flynn, Raymond L** — Mayor, Boston; Diplomat
Catholic Alliance, Via Catholic City, PO Box 1872, Chesapeake VA 23327, USA

**Flynn, Sean** — Actor
Innovative Artists, 1505 10th St, Santa Monica CA 90401 USA

**Flynn, Thomas J (Tom)** — Football Player
4008 Holiday Park Dr, Murrysville PA 15668, USA

**Flynt, Larry** — Publisher
Larry Flynt Publications Inc, 8484 Wilshire Blvd, #900, Beverly Hills CA 90211, USA

**Fo, Dario** — Nobel Literature Laureate
C T F R, Corso di Porta Romana 132, 20122 Milan, Italy

**Foa, Barrett** — Actor
Jackoway Tyerman Wertheimer, 1925 Century Park E, #2200, Los Angeles CA 90067 USA

**Foad, James** — Rowing Athlete
Molesey Boat Club, Barge Walk, East Molesey KT8 9AJ, England

**Foale, C Michael (Mike)** — Astronaut
2101 Todville Road, #11, Seabrook TX 77586, USA

**Foale, Marion A** — Fashion Designer
Foale Ltd, 133A Long St, Atherstone, Warwicks CV9 1AD, England

**Fobbs, Brandon** — Actor
Stone Manners Salners, 6100 Wilshire Blvd, #1500, Los Angeles CA 90035 USA

**Foege, William H** — Public Health Executive
PO Box 450989, Atlanta GA 31145, USA

**Foer, Jonathan Safran** — Writer
Little Brown, 237 Park Ave, #1300, New York NY 10017, USA

**Foerster, Paul** — Yachtsman
126 Dunford Dr, Rockwall TX 75032, USA

**Fofana, Mohamed Said** — Prime Minister, Guinea
Prime Minister's Office, PO Box 5141, Cite des Nations, Conakry, Guinea

**Fogarty, Thomas J** — Inventor (Embolectomy Catheter)
205 South Dr, #B, Mountain View CA 94040, USA

**Fogel, Daniel M** — Educator
University of Vermont, President's Office, Burlington VT 05405, USA

**Fogerty, John** — Singer, Guitarist, Songwriter
Paradigm Agency, 360 N Crescent Dr, North Building, Beverly Hills CA 90210 USA

**Fogg, Joshua S (Josh)** — Baseball Player
4910 S Quincy St, Tampa FL 33611, USA

**Fogle, Larry** — Basketball Player
72 Beechwood St, Rochester NY 14609, USA

**Fogleman, Ronald R (Ron)** — Air Force General
406 Snowshoe Lane, Durango CO 81301, USA

**Fogler, Dan** — Actor
W M E Entertainment, 9601 Wilshire Blvd, #300, Beverly Hills CA 90210 USA

**Fogler, Eddie** — Basketball Coach
University of South Carolina, Athletic Dept, Columbia SC 53233, USA

**Foglesong, Robert H (Doc)** — Air Force General, Educator
Council on Foreign Relations, 58 E 68th St, New York NY 10065, USA

**Fohrer, Alan J** — Businessman
Edison International, 2244 Walnut Grove Ave, Rosemead CA 91770, USA

**Foiles, Henry L (Hank), Jr** — Baseball Player
4333 Silverleaf Court, Virginia Beach VA 23462, USA

**Fois, Marina** — Actress
U B B A, 6 Rue de Braque, 75003 Paris, France

**Fok, Clarence** — Director
Becsey Wisdom Kalajian, 849 S Wooster St, #7, Los Angeles CA 90035, USA

**Fokin, Vitold P** — Prime Minister, Ukraine
Vezkhovna Rada, M Hrushevskoho Rul 5, 252019 Kiev, Ukraine

**Folau, Spencer S** — Football Player
14003 Woodens Lane, Reisterstown MD 21136, USA

**Folds, Ben** — Singer, Pianist, Songwriter
Primary Talent International, 10-11 Jockey's Fields, London WC1R 4BN, England

**Foley, Alina** — Actress
Seven Summits Mgmt, 8906 W Olympic Blvd, Beverly Hills CA 90211 USA

**Foley, Dave** — Football Player
4500 Redmond Road, Springfield OH 45505, USA

**Foley, David S (Dave)** — Actor, Comedian
A P A Talent & Literary Agency, 405 S Beverly Dr, #300, Beverly Hills CA 90212 USA

**Foley, Gerry** — Ice Hockey Player
352 Skead Road, Garson ON P3L 1N4, Canada

**Foley, James** — Director
W M E Entertainment, 9601 Wilshire Blvd, #300, Beverly Hills CA 90210 USA

**Foley, Kathleen** — Neurologist
Memorial Sloan Kettering Cancer Center, 1275 York Ave, New York NY 10065 USA

**Foley, Mark A** — Representative, FL; Commentator
WSVU-FM, News Dept, 8895 N Military Trail, West Palm Beach FL 33410, USA

**Foley, Marvis E (Marv)** — Baseball Player
10166 Glenmore Ave, Bradenton FL 34202, USA

**Foley, Maurice B** — Judge
US Tax Court, 400 2nd St NW, Washington DC 20217, USA

**Foley, Robert F** — Vietnam War Army Hero (CMH), General
2121 Jamieson Ave, #606, Alexandria VA 22314, USA

**Foley, Scott** — Actor
I C M Partners, 10250 Constellation Blvd, #900, Los Angeles CA 90067 USA
**Foley, Stephen J (Steve)** — Football Player
6321 S Newport Circle, Centennial CO 80111, USA
**Foley, Sue** — Singer, Guitarist, Songwriter
Agency Group, 2 Berkeley St, #202, Toronto ON M5A 4J5, Canada
**Foley, Sylvester R, Jr** — Navy Admiral
50 Apple Hill Dr, Tewksbury MA 01876, USA
**Foley, Thomas D (Tim)** — Football Player
3029 Isola Bella Blvd, Mount Dora FL 32757, USA
**Foley, Thomas M (Tom)** — Baseball Player
5237 Karlsburg Place, Palm Harbor FL 34685, USA
**Folger, Franklin** — Cartoonist
King Features Syndicate, 300 W 57th St, #1500, New York NY 10019 USA
**Folguera, Ruy** — Composer
Gorfaine/Schwartz, 4111 W Alameda Ave, #509, Burbank CA 91505 USA
**Foli, Timothy J (Tim)** — Baseball Player
525 Timberline Dr, Lenoir City TN 37772, USA
**Folk, Nicholas A (Nick)** — Football Player
New York Jets, 1 Jets Dr, Florham Park NJ 07932 USA
**Folk, Robert** — Composer
A S C A P, 7920 Sunset Blvd, #300, Los Angeles CA 90046, USA
**Folkenberg, Robert S** — Religious Leader
Seventh-Day Adventists, 12501 Old Columbia Pike, Silver Spring MD 20904, USA
**Folkers, Richard N (Rich)** — Baseball Player
7100 3rd Ave N, Saint Petersburg FL 33710, USA
**Folkerts, Ulrike** — Actress
Agentur Carola Studlar, Agnesstr 47, 80798 Munich, Germany
**Folkins, L Leroy (Lee)** — Football Player
8749 The Esplanade, #13, Orlando FL 32836, USA
**Folkson, Sheree** — Director
Casorotto Ramsay, Waverley House, 7-12 Noel St, London W1F 8GQ, England
**Follesdal, Dagfinn K** — Philosopher
Staverhagen 7, 1312 Slepemdem, Norway
**Follett, Ken** — Writer
Follett House, Primett Road, Stevenage, Hertfordshire Sg1 3EE, England
**Followill, Caleb** — Singer (Kings of Leon)
Vector Mgmt, 1100 Glendon Ave, #2000, Los Angeles CA 90024, USA
**Followill, Jared** — Bassist (Kings of Leon)
Vector Mgmt, 1100 Glendon Ave, #2000, Los Angeles CA 90024, USA
**Followill, Matthew** — Guitarist (Kings of Leon)
Vector Mgmt, 1100 Glendon Ave, #2000, Los Angeles CA 90024, USA
**Followill, Nathan** — Drummer (Kings of Leon)
Vector Mgmt, 1100 Glendon Ave, #2000, Los Angeles CA 90024, USA
**Follows, Megan** — Actress
Greene Assoc, 1901 Ave of Stars, #130, Los Angeles CA 90067 USA
**Folman, Ari** — Director, Writer
Creative Artists Agency, 2000 Ave of Stars, #100, Los Angeles CA 90067 USA
**Folsom, James E (Jim), Jr** — Governor, AL
1482 Orchard Dr NE, Cullman AL 35055, USA
**Folsome, Claire** — Microbiologist
University of Hawaii, Microbiology Dept, 2600 Campus Road, Honolulu HI 96822, USA
**Folta, Danelle M** — Model
537 S Highland Ave, Winter Garden FL 34787, USA
**Fonda, Bridget** — Actress
I F A Talent Agency, 8730 W Sunset Blvd, #490, West Hollywood CA 90069 USA
**Fonda, Jane** — Actress
Fonda Foundation, PO Box 5840, Atlanta GA 31107, USA
**Fonda, Peter** — Actor
Indian Hills Ranch, RR 38G, Box 2024, Livingston MT 59047, USA
**Fondren, Debra Jo** — Model, Actress
Playboy Promotions, 9346 Civic Center Dr, #200, Beverly Hills CA 90210 USA
**Foner, Eric** — Historian
606 W 116th St, New York NY 10027, USA
**Fonoimoana, Eric** — Volleyball Player
Manhattan Beach Properties, 2501 N Sepulveda Blvd, #200, Manhattan Beach CA 90266, USA
**Fonseca, Adriana** — Actress
Aquos Entertainment Group, 20533 Biscayne Blvd, #153, Aventura FL 33180, USA
**Fonseca, Caio** — Artist
Paul Kasmin Gallery, 293 10th Ave, New York NY 10001, USA
**Fonseca, Lyndsy** — Actress
I C M Partners, 10250 Constellation Blvd, #900, Los Angeles CA 90067 USA
**Fonsi, Luis** — Singer, Songwriter
Tony Mojena Entertainment, 463 Sergio Cuevas Bustamante, San Juan PR 00198, USA
**Fontaine, Levi** — Basketball Player
25 11th Ave, San Mateo CA 94401, USA
**Fontaine, Lucien** — Thoroughbred Racing Jockey
1680 Riverwood Lane, Coral Springs FL 33071, USA
**Fontaine, Maurice A** — Physiologist
25 Rue Pierre Nicole, 75005 Paris, France
**Fontana, Arianna** — Speed Skater
23010 Berbenno di Valtellina (SO), Italy
**Fontana, Isabeli** — Model
Women Model Mgmt, 199 Lafayette St, #700, New York NY 10012 USA
**Fontana, Wayne** — Singer
Brian Gannon Mgmt, PO Box 106, Rochdale OL16 4HW, England
**Fontas, Jon** — Ice Hockey Player
38a Worthen Road, #1, Lexington MA 02421, USA
**Fontenot, Albert P (Al)** — Football Player
4919 Gammage St, Houston TX 77021, USA
**Fontenot, Jerry P** — Football Player
938 Bristol Dr, Deerfield IL 60015, USA
**Fontenot, S Ray** — Baseball Player
1674 N Crestview Dr, Lake Charles LA 70605, USA
**Fontes, Wayne H** — Football Player, Coach
2043 Harbour Watch Circle, Tarpon Springs FL 34689, USA

**Fonteyne, Valere R (Val)** — Ice Hockey Player
5403 52nd Ave, Wetaskiwin AB T9A 0X8, Canada
**Fonville, Chad E** — Baseball Player
2338 Piney Green Road, Midway Park NC 28544, USA
**Fonville, Charles** — Track Athlete
1845 Wintergreen Court, Ann Arbor MI 48103, USA
**Foo, Sharin** — Singer, Guitarist, Bassist (Raveonettes)
Orchard, 100 Park Ave, #200, New York NY 10017, USA
**Foor, James E (Jim)** — Baseball Player
2018 Bolsover St, Houston TX 77005, USA
**Foote, Adam D V** — Ice Hockey Player
4656 S Ogden St, Englewood CO 80113, USA
**Foote, Barry C** — Baseball Player
92 Lassiter Pond Road, Smithfield NC 27577, USA
**Foote, Chris D** — Football Player
1431 Springpointe Way, Knoxville TN 37931, USA
**Foote, Dan** — Editorial Cartoonist
Dallas Times Herald, Editorial Dept, Herald Square, Dallas TX 75202, USA
**Foote, Lawrence E (Larry), Jr** — Football Player
24605 Franklin Farms Dr, Franklin MI 48025, USA
**Foppert, Jesse** — Baseball Player
PO Box 150682, San Rafael CA 94915, USA
**Foray, June** — Actress
22745 Erwin St, Woodland Hills CA 91367, USA
**Forbert, Steve** — Singer, Guitarist, Songwriter
W N S Group, 6 Rolyn Hills Dr, Orangeburg NY 10962, USA
**Forbes, James A, Jr** — Religious Leader
Riverside Church, Senior Minister Office, 490 Riverside Dr, New York NY 10027, USA
**Forbes, Malcolm S (Steve), Jr** — Editor
Forbes, President's Office, 60 5th Ave, New York NY 10011, USA
**Forbes, Maya** — Producer, Writer
I C M Partners, 10250 Constellation Blvd, #900, Los Angeles CA 90067 USA
**Forbes, Michelle R** — Actress
Hofflund/Polone, 9465 Wilshire Blvd, #420, Beverly Hills CA 90212 USA
**Forbes, West** — Singer (Five Satins)
Paramount Entertainment, PO Box 12, Far Hills NJ 07931 USA
**Forbes-Robinson, Elliott** — Auto Racing Driver
7118 Vinewood Road, Sherrills Ford NC 28673, USA
**Forbis, Clifton** — Opera Singer
Columbia Artists Mgmt Inc, 5 Columbus Circle, 1790 Broadway, #1600, New York NY 10019 USA
**Force, John** — Drag Racing Driver
John Force Racing, 22722 Old Canal Road, Yorba Linda CA 92887, USA
**Forciniti, Rosalba** — Judo Athlete
Federazione Judo Lotta Karate, Via dei Sandolini 79, 00122 Rome, Italy
**Ford, Alissa** — Actress
Innovative Artists, 1505 10th St, Santa Monica CA 90401 USA
**Ford, Atina** — Curling Athlete
Curling Association, 1660 Vimont Court, Cumberland ON K4A 4J4, Canada
**Ford, Benjamin C (Ben)** — Baseball Player
1717 Applewood Place NE, Cedar Rapids IA 52402, USA
**Ford, Bette** — Actress
Innovative Artists, 1505 10th St, Santa Monica CA 90401 USA
**Ford, Bruce** — Opera Singer
Athole Still, Foresters Hall, 25-27 Wistrow St, London SE19 3BY, England
**Ford, Candy** — Actress
C E S D, 10635 Santa Monica Blvd, #130, Los Angeles CA 90025 USA
**Ford, Charles G (Charlie)** — Football Player
2995 South St, Beaumont TX 77702, USA
**Ford, Cheryl** — Basketball Player
New York Liberty, Madison Square Garden, 2 Penn Plaza, New York NY 10121 USA
**Ford, Christopher J (Chris)** — Basketball Player, Coach
424 N Vendome Ave, Margate City NJ 08402, USA
**Ford, Colin** — Actor
Management 360, 9111 Wilshire Blvd, Beverly Hills CA 90210 USA
**Ford, Courtney** — Actress
Main Title Mgmt, 8383 Wilshire Blvd, #408, Beverly Hills CA 90211 USA
**Ford, Curtis G (Curt)** — Baseball Player
6306 Sprig Oak Court, #B, Saint Louis MO 63128, USA
**Ford, Darnell G (Dan)** — Baseball Player
1271 Linton Road, Benton LA 71006, USA
**Ford, Dee** — Football Player
Kansas City Chiefs, 1 Arrowhead Dr, Kansas City KS 64129 USA
**Ford, Donald (Don)** — Basketball Player
519 W Quinto St, #B, Santa Barbara CA 93105, USA
**Ford, Douglas (Doug)** — Golfer
3737 Gulfstream Road, Delray Beach FL 33483, USA
**Ford, Edward C (Whitey)** — Baseball Player
PO Box 160, Sea Cliff NY 11579, USA
**Ford, Faith** — Actress
Hofflund/Polone, 9465 Wilshire Blvd, #420, Beverly Hills CA 90212 USA
**Ford, Frankie** — Singer, Songwriter
Sea Cruise Productions, PO Box 1875, Gretna LA 70054, USA
**Ford, Gilbert (Gib)** — Basketball Player, Coach
264 Edgemere Way E, Naples FL 34105, USA
**Ford, Harrison** — Actor
3555 N Moose Wilson Road, Jackson Hole WY 83001, USA
**Ford, Henry** — Football Player
7222 Shannon Road, Verona PA 15147, USA
**Ford, J Lewis (Lew)** — Baseball Player
2201 Lady Cornwall Dr, Lewisville TX 75056, USA
**Ford, Jack** — Commentator
CBS-TV, News Dept, 51 W 52nd St, New York NY 10019 USA
**Ford, Katie** — Businesswoman
Ford Models Inc, 111 5th Ave, #900, New York NY 10003 USA
**Ford, Kevin A** — Astronaut
3526 E 200 N, Hartford City IN 47348, USA

**Ford, Lita** — Singer, Guitarist (Runaways)
Monterey International, 200 W Superior St, #202, Chicago IL 60654 USA

**Ford, Luke** — Actor
Wolf Kasteler Public Relations, 9350 Wilshire Blvd, #450, Beverly Hills CA 90212 USA

**Ford, Maria** — Actress
Momentum Talent, 9401 Wilshire Blvd, #501, Beverly Hills CA 90212, USA

**Ford, Mark** — Publisher
Time Inc Sports Group, Publisher's Office, Time-Life Building, New York NY 10020, USA

**Ford, Melyssa** — Model, Actress
Don Buchwald Talent Agency, 6500 Wilshire Blvd, #2200, Los Angeles CA 90048 USA

**Ford, Phil J, Jr** — Basketball Player
2928 Cone Manor Lane, Raleigh NC 27613, USA

**Ford, Ray** — Actor
Rectangle Entertainment, 357 S Fairfax Ave, #414, Los Angeles CA 90036, USA

**Ford, Richard** — Writer
Ecco/Harper Collins Publishers, 10 E 53rd St, Cellar 1, New York NY 10022, USA

**Ford, Robben** — Jazz Guitarist (Yellowjackets)
Maria Matias Music, 316 Mid Valley Center, #203, Carmel CA 93922, USA

**Ford, Robert A (Bob)** — Basketball Player
202 Pathway Lane, West Lafayette IN 47906, USA

**Ford, Scott** — Businessman
Alltel Corp, PO Box 94255, Palatine IL 60094, USA

**Ford, Susan** — Photojournalist
Susan Ford Photography, 1825 La Costa Dr, Rockwall TX 75032, USA

**Ford, Thomas Mikal** — Actor
TalentWorks, 3500 W Olive Ave, #1400, Burbank CA 91505 USA

**Ford, Tom** — Fashion Designer, Director
Creative Artists Agency, 2000 Ave of Stars, #100, Los Angeles CA 90067 USA

**Ford, Trent** — Actor
TalentWorks, 3500 W Olive Ave, #1400, Burbank CA 91505 USA

**Ford, Wendell H** — Governor, Senator, KY
423 Frederica St, #314, Owensboro KY 42301, USA

**Ford, Willa** — Singer, Model, Actress
A P A Talent & Literary Agency, 405 S Beverly Dr, #300, Beverly Hills CA 90212 USA

**Ford, William Clay, Jr** — Businessman
Ford Motor Co, American Road, Dearborn MI 48121, USA

**Fordham, Julia** — Singer, Songwriter
Lori Levee Mgmt, 1366 Miller Dr, West Hollywood CA 90069, USA

**Fordyce, Brook A** — Baseball Player
5 River Crest, Stuart FL 34996, USA

**Foreman, Amanda** — Actress
Abrams Artists, 9200 W Sunset Blvd, #1125, West Hollywood CA 90069 USA

**Foreman, Carol L T** — Government Official
5600 Wisconsin Ave, #502, Chevy Chase MD 20815, USA

**Foreman, Chris (Chrissie Boy)** — Guitarist (Madness)
I T F, Ariel House, 74A Charlotte St, London W1T 4QJ, England

**Foreman, George** — Boxer
PO Box 1405, Huffman TX 77336, USA

**Foreman, Michael J** — Astronaut
N A S A, Johnson Space Center, 2101 NASA Road, Houston TX 77058 USA

**Foreman, Walter E (Chuck)** — Football Player
9716 Mill Creek Dr, Eden Prairie MN 55347, USA

**Foremsky, Fred (Skee)** — Bowler
914 Manchester Dr, Conroe TX 77304, USA

**Forest, Michael** — Actor
1327 N Vista, #203, Los Angeles CA 90046, USA

**Forester, Nicole** — Actress
Thruline Entertainment, 9250 Wilshire Blvd, #100, Beverly Hills CA 90212 USA

**Foret, Mickey P** — Businessman
7829 Brookhollow Blvd, Frisco TX 75034, USA

**Foret, Sarah** — Actress
Baker Winokur Ryder Public Relations, 9100 Wilshire Blvd, #500W, Beverly Hills CA 90212 USA

**Forgeard, Noel** — Businessman
85 Ave de Wagram, 75017 Paris, France

**Forget, Guy** — Tennis Player
Rue des Pacs 2, 2000 Neuchatel, Switzerland

**Forke, Farrah** — Actress
Pop Art Mgmt, 9615 Brighton Way, #426, Beverly Hills CA 90210, USA

**Forlani, Arnaldo** — Prime Minister, Italy
Piazzale Schumann 15, 00187 Rome, Italy

**Forlani, Claire** — Actress
Independent Talent Group, 40 Whitfield St, London W1T 2RH, England

**Forman, Donald J (Donnie)** — Basketball Player
1532 Gormican Lane, Naples FL 34110, USA

**Forman, Milos** — Director
Aspland Mgmt, 245 W 55th St, #1102, New York NY 10019, USA

**Forman, Stanley** — Photojournalist
17 Cherry Road, Beverly MA 01915, USA

**Forman, Tom** — Cartoonist (Motley's Crew)
10544 James Road, Celina TX 75009, USA

**Formia, Osvaldo** — Harness Racing Trainer
6501 Winfield Blvd, #A10, Margate FL 33063, USA

**Forney, G David, Jr** — Computer Scientist
6 Coolidge Hill Road, Cambridge MA 02138, USA

**Forney, Kynan L** — Football Player
2046 Skybrooke Lane, Hoschton GA 30548, USA

**Fornos, Werner H** — Association Executive
Population Institute, 107 2nd St NE, Washington DC 20002, USA

**Foronjy, Richard** — Actor
House of Representatives, 1434 6th St, #1, Santa Monica CA 90401 USA

**Forrest, Bayard** — Basketball Player
300A Squaw Valley Place, Pagosa Springs CO 81147, USA

**Forrest, Emma** — Writer
Lutyens & Rubinstein, 231 Westbourne Park Road, London W11 1EB, England

**Forrest, Frederic** — Actor
11300 W Olympic Blvd, #610, Los Angeles CA 90064, USA

V.I.P. Address Book

# F

**Forrest, Sally** — Actress
1125 Angelo Dr, Beverly Hills CA 90210, USA

**Forrest, Steve** — Drummer (Placebo)
Riverman Records, George House, Brecon Road, London W6 8PY, England

**Forrestal, Robert P** — Government Official, Financier
1200 Brookhaven Park Place NE, Atlanta GA 30319, USA

**Forrester, Jay W** — Inventor (Digital Storage Device)
Massachusetts Institute of Technology, Management School, Cambridge MA 02139, USA

**Forrester, Patrick G** — Astronaut
3923 Park Circle Way, Houston TX 77059, USA

**Forsberg, Fred C** — Football Player
1727 223rd Ave SE, Sammamish WA 98075, USA

**Forsberg, Peter M** — Ice Hockey Player
1155 Sherman St, Denver CO 80203, USA

**Forsch, Kenneth R (Ken)** — Baseball Player
881 S Country Glen Way, Anaheim CA 92808, USA

**Forsee, Gary D** — Businessman, Educator
University of Missouri System, President's Office, University Hall, Columbia MO 65211, USA

**Forslund, Constance** — Actress
165 W 46th St, #1109, New York NY 10036, USA

**Forsman, Dan** — Golfer
88 W 4500 N, Provo UT 84604, USA

**Forst, Bill** — Cartoonist
2320 Byer Road, Santa Cruz CA 95062, USA

**Forstemann, Robert** — Cyclist
SSV Gera 1990 E V, Vollersdorfer Str 32, 07548 Gera, Germany

**Forster, Marc** — Director, Producer
Management 360, 9111 Wilshire Blvd, Beverly Hills CA 90210 USA

**Forster, Robert** — Actor
Don Buchwald Talent Agency, 6500 Wilshire Blvd, #2200, Los Angeles CA 90048 USA

**Forster, Sarah** — Ice Hockey Player
H C Ajoie, Case Postale 1329, 2900 Porrentruy, Switzerland

**Forster, Terry J** — Baseball Player
PO Box 711658, Santee CA 92072, USA

**Forster, William H** — Army General
10245 Fairfax Dr, Fort Belvoir VA 22060, USA

**Forsyth, Bill** — Director
20 Winton Dr, Glasgow G12 0QA, Scotland

**Forsyth, Bruce** — Actor, Comedian
Straidarran, Wentworth Dr, Virginia Water, Surrey GU25 4NY, England

**Forsyth, David** — Actor
C E S D, 10635 Santa Monica Blvd, #130, Los Angeles CA 90025 USA

**Forsyth, Frederick** — Writer
Trans World Publishers, 61-63 Oxbridge Road, Ealing, London W5 5SA, England

**Forsyth, Rosemary** — Actress
1591 Benedict Canyon, Beverly Hills CA 90210, USA

**Forsythe, Gerald (Gary)** — Auto Racing Executive
Forsythe Racing, 7231 Georgetown Road, Indianapolis IN 46268, USA

**Forsythe, William** — Choreographer
Frankfurt Ballet, Untermainanlage 11, 60311 Frankfurt, Germany

**Forsythe, William** — Actor
Innovative Artists, 1505 10th St, Santa Monica CA 90401 USA

**Fort-Brescia, Bernardo** — Architect
Arquitectonica International, 801 Brickell Ave, #1100, Miami FL 33131, USA

**Forte, Allen** — Musicologist
Columbia University, Music Dept, New York NY 10027, USA

**Forte, Donald R (Ike)** — Football Player
5811 Winchester Dr, Texarkana TX 75503, USA

**Forte, Marlene** — Actress, Producer, Director
Greater Visions Artists Talent Agency, 8981 W Sunset Blvd, #101, West Hollywood CA 90069 USA

**Forte, Matthew G (Matt)** — Football Player
2067 N Laurel Valley Dr, Vernon Hills IL 60061, USA

**Forte, Will** — Actor, Comedian
Mosiac Media Group, 9200 W Sunset Blvd, #1000, Los Angeles CA 90069 USA

**Fortier, David E (Dave)** — Ice Hockey Player
150 Kingsmount Blvd, Sudbury ON P3E 1K9, Canada

**Fortier, Laurie** — Actress
Vincent Cirrincione Assoc, 1516 N Fairfax Ave, Los Angeles CA 90046 USA

**Fortin, Roman B** — Football Player
10741 Bell Road, Duluth GA 30097, USA

**Fortino, Laura** — Ice Hockey Player
Cornell University, Athletic Dept, Teagle Hall, Ithaca NY 14853, USA

**Fortner, Nell** — Basketball Coach
Auburn University, Athletic Dept, Auburn AL 36849, USA

**Fortson, Daniel A (Danny)** — Basketball Player
3447 W Blaine St, Seattle WA 98199, USA

**Fortunato, Joseph F (Joe)** — Football Player
PO Box 934, Natchez MS 39121, USA

**Fortunato, Ron** — Cinematographer
1 Columbus Place, #N5G, New York NY 10019, USA

**Fortune, Jimmy** — Singer (Statler Brothers)
American Major Talent, 8747 Highway 304, Hernando MS 38632, USA

**Fortuno Burset, Luis G** — Governor, Representative, PR
Governor's Office, La Fortaleza, PO Box 9020082, San Juan PR 00902 USA

**Fosbury, Richard D (Dick)** — Track Athlete
708 Canyon Run Blvd, Ketchum ID 83340, USA

**Foss, Anita** — Baseball Player
452 S Highland Ave, Los Angeles CA 90036, USA

**Foss, Eric** — Businessman
Pepsi Bottling Group, 1 Pepsi Way, #1, Somers NY 10589, USA

**Foss, John W, II** — Army General
16 Hampton Key, Williamsburg VA 23185, USA

**Fosse, Raymond E (Ray)** — Baseball Player
PO Box 567, Diablo CA 94528, USA

**Fossey, Brigitte** — Actress
Anne Alvares Correa, 34 Rue Jouffroy d'Abbans, 75017 Paris, France

| | |
|---|---|
| **Fossum, Casey P** | Baseball Player |
| 1087 White Bluff Dr, Whitney TX 76692, USA | |
| **Fossum, Michael E** | Astronaut |
| 822 Rolling Run Court, Houston TX 77062, USA | |
| **Foster of Thames Bank, Norman R** | Architect |
| Foster Assoc, Riverside 3, 22 Hester Road, London SW11 4AN, England | |
| **Foster, Alan B** | Baseball Player |
| 10330 Grandview Dr, La Mesa CA 91941, USA | |
| **Foster, Alan Dean** | Writer |
| Thranx Inc, PO Box 12757, Prescott AZ 86304, USA | |
| **Foster, Barry** | Football Player |
| PO Box 750, Colleyville TX 76034, USA | |
| **Foster, Ben** | Actor |
| United Talent Agency, U T A Plaza, 9336 Civic Center Dr, Beverly Hills CA 90210 USA | |
| **Foster, Catherine** | Artist |
| 19689 7th Ave NE, #351, Poulsbo WA 98370, USA | |
| **Foster, Corey J** | Ice Hockey Player |
| 71 Pine Ridge Dr, Arnprior ON K7S 3G8, Canada | |
| **Foster, Coy** | Balloonist |
| 5486 Glen Lakes Dr, Dallas TX 75231, USA | |
| **Foster, David** | Producer |
| Paradigm Agency, 360 N Crescent Dr, North Building, Beverly Hills CA 90210 USA | |
| **Foster, David** | Songwriter, Musician |
| 3903 Carbon Canyon Road, Malibu CA 90265, USA | |
| **Foster, DeShaun X** | Football Player |
| 2391 Apple Tree Dr, Tustin CA 92780, USA | |
| **Foster, George** | Football Player |
| 4057 Meadowbrook Dr, Macon GA 31204, USA | |
| **Foster, George A** | Baseball Player |
| 15 E Putnam Ave, #320, Greenwich CT 06830, USA | |
| **Foster, Hunter** | Actor, Singer |
| Gersh Agency, 41 Madison Ave, #3301, New York NY 10010 USA | |
| **Foster, Jeffrey D (Jeff)** | Basketball Player |
| 333 Pickwick Court, Noblesville IN 46062, USA | |
| **Foster, Jodie** | Actress, Director |
| I C M Partners, 10250 Constellation Blvd, #900, Los Angeles CA 90067 USA | |
| **Foster, Jon** | Actor |
| Gersh Agency, 9465 Wilshire Blvd, #600, Beverly Hills CA 90212 USA | |
| **Foster, Karen** | Model, Actress |
| Playboy Promotions, 9346 Civic Center Dr, #200, Beverly Hills CA 90210 USA | |
| **Foster, Lawrence T** | Conductor |
| Opus 3 Artists, 470 Park Ave S, #900N, New York NY 10016 USA | |
| **Foster, Leonard N (Leo)** | Baseball Player |
| 699 Glensprings Dr, Cincinnati OH 45246, USA | |
| **Foster, Meg** | Actress |
| C R Mgmt, 22631 Pacific Coast Hwy, #627, Malibu CA 90265, USA | |
| **Foster, Radney (Randy)** | Singer, Songwriter |
| 326 Lauderdale Road, Nashville TN 37205, USA | |
| **Foster, Robert W (Bob)** | Boxer |
| 913 Valencia Dr NE, Albuquerque NM 87108, USA | |
| **Foster, Roderick A (Rod)** | Basketball Player |
| 1246 Armacost Ave, #105, Los Angeles CA 90025, USA | |
| **Foster, Roy A** | Football Player |
| 12110 Salem Dr, Granada Hills CA 91344, USA | |
| **Foster, Ruthie** | Singer, Songwriter |
| Blind Ambition Mgmt, 6 Courthouse Way, Jonesboro GA 30236, USA | |
| **Foster, Sara** | Actress |
| Innovative Artists, 1505 10th St, Santa Monica CA 90401 USA | |
| **Foster, Scott Michael** | Actor |
| United Talent Agency, U T A Plaza, 9336 Civic Center Dr, Beverly Hills CA 90210 USA | |
| **Foster, Stan** | Actor, Writer, Producer, Director |
| I C M Partners, 10250 Constellation Blvd, #900, Los Angeles CA 90067 USA | |
| **Foster, Sutton** | Actress, Singer |
| Creative Artists Agency, 2000 Ave of Stars, #100, Los Angeles CA 90067 USA | |
| **Foster, Todd (Kid)** | Boxer |
| 303 13th St NW, Great Falls MT 59404, USA | |
| **Foster, William E (Bill)** | Basketball Coach |
| 152 Hollywood Dr, Coppell TX 75019, USA | |
| **Fosterling, Karsten** | Rowing Athlete |
| 13 Elder Corners, Nowra NSW 2541, Australia | |
| **Fotiu, Nicholas E (Nick)** | Ice Hockey Player |
| 16 Backus River Road, East Falmouth MA 02536, USA | |
| **Foucault, Steven R (Steve)** | Baseball Player |
| 24353 Rolling View Court, Lutz FL 33559, USA | |
| **Foudy Sawyers, Judy (Julie)** | Soccer Player, Model, Sportscaster |
| 6208 Colina Pacifica, San Clemente CA 92673, USA | |
| **Fought, John, III** | Golfer |
| 5010 E Shea Blvd, #A217, Scottsdale AZ 85254, USA | |
| **Foules, Elbert** | Football Player |
| 633 E Ohea St, Greenville MS 38701, USA | |
| **Foulke, Keith C** | Baseball Player |
| 4844 W Electra Lane, Glendale AZ 85310, USA | |
| **Foulkes, Arthur A** | Governor General, Bahamas |
| Governor General's Office, Government House, PO Box N8301, Nassau NP, Bahamas | |
| **Foulkes, Cathy** | Model, Actress |
| C E S D, 10635 Santa Monica Blvd, #130, Los Angeles CA 90025 USA | |
| **Foulkes, Llyn** | Artist |
| 6010 Eucalyptus Lane, Los Angeles CA 90042, USA | |
| **Fountain, Clarence** | Singer (Blind Boys of Alabama) |
| Blind Ambition Mgmt, 6 Courthouse Way, Jonesboro GA 30236, USA | |
| **Fountain, Peter D (Pete), Jr** | Jazz Clarinetist |
| Kuoni Destination Mgmt, 650 Poydras St, #2050, New Orleans LA 70130, USA | |
| **Fourcade, Martin** | Biathlete |
| Allee des Marquisats, 74000 Annecy, France | |
| **Fournier, Evan** | Basketball Player |
| Denver Nuggets, Pepsi Center, 1000 Chopper Circle, Denver CO 80204 USA | |

**Foust, Nina** — Golfer
901 East Dr, Morehead City NC 28557, USA

**Fouts, Daniel F (Dan)** — Football Player, Sportscaster
16820 Varco Road, Bend OR 97701, USA

**Fowke, Philip F** — Concert Pianist
Patrick Garvey, 59 Lansdowne Place, Hove, East Sussex BN3 1FL, England

**Fowler, Beth** — Actress, Singer
B R S / Gage Talent Agency, 1650 Broadway, #1410, New York NY 10019 USA

**Fowler, Calvin B (Cal)** — Basketball Player
10121 Godspeed Dr, Ocean City MD 21842, USA

**Fowler, Damon** — Guitarist, Singer
Blind Pig Records, 1233 17th St, San Francisco CA 94107, USA

**Fowler, E Michael C** — Architect
Branches, Giffords Road, RD 3, Blenheim, New Zealand

**Fowler, Mark S** — Government Official
Latham & Watkins, 555 11th St NW, #1000, Washington DC 20004, USA

**Fowler, Rick Y (Rickie)** — Golfer
Professional Golfers Association, 100 Ave of Champions, Palm Beach Gardens FL 33418 USA

**Fowler, Ryan O** — Football Player
1713 Montclair Blvd, Brentwood TN 37027, USA

**Fowler, W Wyche, Jr** — Senator, GA; Diplomat
701 A St NE, Washington DC 20002, USA

**Fowles, Sylvia** — Basketball Player
2116 NW 96th Terrace, Miami FL 33147, USA

**Fowlkes, Curtis** — Trombonist (Jazz Passengers)
Cross Road Mgmt, 45 W 11th St, #7B, New York NY 10011, USA

**Fox Quesada, Vicente** — President, Mexico
San Francisco del Rincon, San Cristobal, Guanajuato 36440 CP, Mexico

**Fox, Andy** — Baseball Player
9087 Tarmac Court, Fair Oaks CA 95628, USA

**Fox, Bernard** — Actor
6601 Burnet Ave, Van Nuys CA 91405, USA

**Fox, Chad D** — Baseball Player
15 Tannery Hill Road, Tomball TX 77375, USA

**Fox, Charles I** — Composer, Conductor
American International Artists, 356 Pine Valley Road, Hoosick Falls NY 12090, USA

**Fox, Edward** — Actor
25 Maida Ave, London W2 1ST, England

**Fox, Emilia** — Actress
Tavistock Wood Management, 45 Conduit St, London W1S 2YN, England

**Fox, George** — Singer, Songwriter
Agency Group, 2 Berkeley St, #202, Toronto On M5A 4J5, Canada

**Fox, Greg** — Ice Hockey Player
323 Resource Parkway # 6A, Winder GA 30680, USA

**Fox, Harold** — Basketball Player
6511 Wilburn D, Capitol Heights MD 20743, USA

**Fox, J Carter** — Businessman
1439 Floyd Ave, Richmond VA 23220, USA

**Fox, Jack** — Actor
I C M Partners, 10250 Constellation Blvd, #900, Los Angeles CA 90067 USA

**Fox, James** — Actor
Dalzell & Beresford, 55 Charterhouse St, Paddock Suite, London EC1M 6HA, England

**Fox, James L (Jim)** — Basketball Player
4136 N 52nd St, Phoenix AZ 85018, USA

**Fox, Jessica** — Canoeing Athlete
Penrith Valley Canoeing, PO Box 92, Penrith NSW 2751, Australia

**Fox, Jessica** — Actress
Associated International Mgmt, 7 Hatton Garden, #400, London EC1N 8AD, England

**Fox, John** — Football Coach
7512 Baltusrol Lane, Charlotte NC 28210, USA

**Fox, Jorja** — Actress
Framework Entertainment, 9057 Nemo St, #C, West Hollywood CA 90069 USA

**Fox, Kerry** — Actress
R G M Artists, 8-12 Ann Street, Surry Hills NSW 2010, Australia

**Fox, Marye Anne P** — Educator, Organic Chemist
5926 Sagebrush Road, La Jolla CA 92037, USA

**Fox, Matthew** — Actor
Management 360, 9111 Wilshire Blvd, Beverly Hills CA 90210 USA

**Fox, Maurice S** — Molecular Biologist, Geneticist
1573 Cambridge St, #405, Cambridge MA 02138, USA

**Fox, Megan** — Actress
I C M Partners, 10250 Constellation Blvd, #900, Los Angeles CA 90067 USA

**Fox, Michael J** — Actor
Baker Winokur Ryder Public Relations, 9100 Wilshire Blvd, #500W, Beverly Hills CA 90212 USA

**Fox, Neil** — Actor, Entertainer
Magic 105.4, Mappin House, 4 Winsley St, London W1W 8HF, England

**Fox, Paula** — Writer
Robert Lescher, 47 E 19th St, New York NY 10003, USA

**Fox, Rachel G** — Actress
Paradigm Agency, 360 N Crescent Dr, North Building, Beverly Hills CA 90210 USA

**Fox, Samantha K** — Singer, Model
Global Entertainments, PO Box 6945, Beeston, Nottingham NG9 4WA, England

**Fox, Terrence E (Terry)** — Baseball Player
2312 Sugar Mill Road, New Iberia LA 70563, USA

**Fox, Timothy R (Tim)** — Football Player
11 Glover Ave, Hull MA 02045, USA

**Fox, Tom** — Opera Singer
Columbia Artists Mgmt Inc, 5 Columbus Circle, 1790 Broadway, #1600, New York NY 10019 USA

**Fox, Ulrich A (Rick)** — Basketball Player, Actor
17530 Ventura Blvd, #201, Encino CA 91316, USA

**Fox, Vernon L, III** — Football Player
6704 Willow Run Court, Las Vegas NV 89108, USA

**Fox, Vivica A** — Actress
Foxy Brown Productions, PO Box 6305, Woodland Hills CA 91365, USA

**Fox, Wesley L** — Vietnam War Marine Corps Hero (CMH)
855 Deercraft Dr, Blacksburg VA 24060, USA

**Fox-Pitt, William S**
Barled Farmhouse, Hinton-Sainte-Mary/Sturminster Newton, Dorset DT10 1NA, England — Equestrian

**Foxworth, Dominique**
7568 Morris St, Fulton MD 20759, USA — Football Player

**Foxworth, Robert**
C E S D, 10635 Santa Monica Blvd, #130, Los Angeles CA 90025 USA — Actor

**Foxworthy, Jeff**
Parallel Entertainment, 9420 Wilshire Blvd, #250, Beverly Hills CA 90212 USA — Actor, Comedian

**Foxx, Anthony R**
Transportation Department, 400 7th St SW, Washington DC 20590 USA — Secretary, Transportation

**Foxx, Jamie**
4477 Sherman Oaks Circle, Sherman Oaks CA 91403, USA — Actor, Comedian, Singer

**Foye, Randy**
Denver Nuggets, Pepsi Center, 1000 Chopper Circle, Denver CO 80204 USA — Basketball Player

**Foyle, Adonal D**
174 Crestview Dr, Orinda CA 94563, USA — Basketball Player

**Foyt, Anthony J (A J), Jr**
Foyt Racing, 19480 Stokes Road, Waller TX 77484, USA — Auto Racing Driver

**Foytack, Paul E**
1910 Portview Dr, Spring Hill TX 37174, USA — Baseball Player

**Frabotta, Don**
PO Box 962, Douglas MA 01516, USA — Actor

**Fraccaro, Walter**
Opera et Concert, 37 Rue de la Chaussee d'Antin, 75009 Paris, France — Opera Singer

**Fradon, Dana**
2 Brushy Hill Road, Newtown CT 06470, USA — Cartoonist

**Fradon, Ramona**
Tribune Media Services, 435 N Michigan Ave, #1500, Chicago IL 60611 USA — Cartoonist (Brenda Starr)

**Frafjord, Marit Malm**
Viborg H K, Tingvej 7, 8800 Viborg, Denmark — Handball Player

**Frahm, Donald R**
82 Jericho Road, Weston MA 02493, USA — Businessman

**Frailing, Kenneth D (Ken)**
2150 Shadow Oaks Road, Sarasota FL 34240, USA — Baseball Player

**Frain, James**
A P A Talent & Literary Agency, 405 S Beverly Dr, #300, Beverly Hills CA 90212 USA — Actor

**Fraisse, Robert**
Paradigm Agency, 360 N Crescent Dr, North Building, Beverly Hills CA 90210 USA — Cinematographer

**Fraiture, Nikolai**
M V O Ltd, 370 7th Ave, #807, New York NY 10001, USA — Bassist (Strokes)

**Frakes, Jonathan**
Paradigm Agency, 360 N Crescent Dr, North Building, Beverly Hills CA 90210 USA — Actor, Director

**Fraley, Mark**
Northern Iowa University, Athletic Dept, Cedar Falls IA 50614, USA — Football Coach

**Fralic, William (Bill)**
280 Galsworthy Court, Roswell GA 30075, USA — Football Player

**Frampton, Peter**
W M E Entertainment, 1325 Ave of Americas, New York NY 10019 USA — Singer, Guitarist, Songwriter

**France, Brian**
1151 N Halifax Ave, Daytona Beach FL 32118, USA — Auto Racing Executive

**France, David**
W M E Entertainment, 9601 Wilshire Blvd, #300, Beverly Hills CA 90210 USA — Producer, Director, Writer

**France, F Douglas (Doug), Jr**
6056 Great Falls Ave, Las Vegas NV 89110, USA — Football Player

**Francella, Meaghan**
16 Maywood Ave, Port Chester NY 10573, USA — Golfer

**Franchitti, G Dario M**
G P Sports Mgmt, 299 Milwaukee St, #329, Denver CO 80020, USA — Auto Racing Driver

**Francia, Susan**
1022 Kipling Road, Jenkintown PA 19046, USA — Rowing Athlete

**Francis**
Apostolic Palace, Vatican Square, 00120 Vatican City — Pope of Catholic Church

**Francis, Clarence (Bevo)**
18340 Steubenville Pike Road, Salineville OH 43945, USA — Basketball Player

**Francis, Connie**
6413 NW 102nd, Pompano Beach FL 33076, USA — Singer, Actress

**Francis, Emile P**
7220 Crystal Lake Dr, West Palm Beach FL 33411, USA — Ice Hockey Player, Coach

**Francis, Genie**
A M T Artists, 15260 Ventura Blvd, #1200, Sherman Oaks CA 91403 USA — Actress

**Francis, Hubert**
I M G Artists, Hogarth Business Park, Chiswick, London W4 2TH, England — Opera Singer

**Francis, James**
2727 Crossview Dr, Houston TX 77063, USA — Football Player

**Francis, Jeffrey W (Jeff)**
3191 Quitman St, Denver CO 80212, USA — Baseball Player

**Francis, Mark**
Maureen Paley Gallery, 21 Herald St, London E2 6JT, England — Artist

**Francis, Norman C**
Xavier University, President's Office, New Orleans LA 70125, USA — Educator

**Francis, Robert**
Aeronaut Records, PO Box 361432, Los Angeles CA 90036, USA — Singer

**Francis, Robert E (Bob)**
23725 N 75th Place, Scottsdale AZ 85255, USA — Ice Hockey Player, Coach

**Francis, Ron**
12312 Birchfalls Dr, Raleigh NC 27614, USA — Ice Hockey Player

**Francis, Russell R (Russ)**
800 Putney Road, Brattleboro VT 05301, USA — Football Player

**Francis, Steve D**
632 Pifer Road, Houston TX 77024, USA — Basketball Player

**Francis, Wallace D (Wally)**
2452 Wilshire Way, Douglasville GA 30135, USA — Football Player

**Francis, William (Bill)**
Artists International, 9850 Sandalwood Blvd, #458, Boca Raton FL 33428, USA — Keyboardist, Singer

**Francisco, Aaron**
5064 W Geronimo St, Chandler AZ 85226, USA — Football Player

**F**

| | |
|---|---|
| **Francisco, Don**<br>Univision, 605 3rd Ave, #1200, New York NY 10158, USA | Entertainer |
| **Francisco, Franklin (Frank)**<br>Texas Rangers, Ameriquest Field, 1000 Ballpark Way, #306, Arlington TX 76011 USA | Baseball Player |
| **Francks, Rainbow Sun**<br>Characters Talent Mgmt, 8 Elm St, Toronto ON M5G 1G7, Canada | Actor |
| **Franco, Carlos**<br>10561 NW 51st St, Doral FL 33178, USA | Golfer |
| **Franco, Dave**<br>Paradigm Agency, 360 N Crescent Dr, North Building, Beverly Hills CA 90210 USA | Actor |
| **Franco, David**<br>Global Artists Agency, 6253 Hollywood Blvd, #508, Los Angeles CA 90028 USA | Cinematographer |
| **Franco, James**<br>Creative Artists Agency, 2000 Ave of Stars, #100, Los Angeles CA 90067 USA | Actor, Director |
| **Franco, John A**<br>111 Helena Road, Staten Island NY 10309, USA | Baseball Player |
| **Franco, Julio C**<br>651 NE 23rd Court, Pompano Beach FL 33064, USA | Baseball Player |
| **Franco, Matthew N (Matt)**<br>1008 Clear Sky Place, Simi Valley CA 93065, USA | Baseball Player |
| **Franco, Ramon**<br>Greene Assoc, 1901 Ave of Stars, #130, Los Angeles CA 90067 USA | Actor |
| **Francoeur, Jeffrey B (Jeff)**<br>3111 Willowstone Dr, Duluth GA 30096, USA | Baseball Player |
| **Francois, Jacques**<br>Artmedia, 20 Ave Rapp, 75007 Paris, France | Actor |
| **Francois, Mike**<br>PO Box 3184, Westerville OH 43086, USA | Body Builder |
| **Francona, John P (Tito)**<br>1109 Penn Ave, New Brighton PA 15066, USA | Baseball Player |
| **Francona, Terry J (Tito)**<br>750 Newton St, Chestnut Hill MA 02467, USA | Baseball Player, Manager |
| **Frandsen, Kevin V**<br>2521 Coffee Ave, San Jose CA 95125, USA | Baseball Player |
| **Frangilli, Michele**<br>Frangilli Vittorio, Via Filzi F45, 21013 Gallarate (VA), Italy | Archery Athlete |
| **Frank Chang ting Hsieh**<br>Premier's Office, 1 Chunghsiao East Road, Section 1, Taipei, Taiwan | Prime Minister, Taiwan |
| **Frank, Anthony A**<br>Colorado State University, President's Office, Fort Collins CO 80523, USA | Educator |
| **Frank, Anthony M**<br>Independent Bancorp, 3800 N Central, Phoenix AZ 85012, USA | Government Official, Financier |
| **Frank, Charles**<br>S D B Partners, 315 S Beverly Dr, #411, Beverly Hills CA 90067 USA | Actor |
| **Frank, Claude**<br>Columbia Artists Mgmt Inc, 5 Columbus Circle, 1790 Broadway, #1600, New York NY 10019 USA | Concert Pianist |
| **Frank, David Michael**<br>Soundtrack Music, 229 Cloverfield Blvd, Santa Monica CA 90405, USA | Composer |
| **Frank, Diana**<br>The Agency, 3711 Ocean Front Walk, #1, Marina del Rey CA 90292 USA | Actress |
| **Frank, Donald L**<br>2039 Weston Green Loop, Cary NC 27513, USA | Football Player |
| **Frank, Gary**<br>861 S Bundy Dr, Los Angeles CA 90049, USA | Actor |
| **Frank, Joanna**<br>1274 Capri Dr, Pacific Palisades CA 90272, USA | Actress |
| **Frank, Joe**<br>I C M Partners, 10250 Constellation Blvd, #900, Los Angeles CA 90067 USA | Actor |
| **Frank, John E**<br>Medical Hair Restoration, 150 Central Park S, #299, New York NY 10019, USA | Football Player |
| **Frank, Louis A**<br>University of Iowa, Astronomy Dept, Iowa City IA 52242, USA | Astronomer |
| **Frank, Pamela**<br>Opus 3 Artists, 470 Park Ave S, #900N, New York NY 10016 USA | Concert Violinist |
| **Frank, Scott**<br>Creative Artists Agency, 2000 Ave of Stars, #100, Los Angeles CA 90067 USA | Director, Writer |
| **Frank, Tellis S**<br>4936 Van Noord Ave, Sherman Oaks CA 91423, USA | Basketball Player |
| **Franke, William A (Bill)**<br>Spirit Airlines, 2800 Executive Way, Miramar FL 33025, USA | Businessman |
| **Frankee**<br>Levine Communication Office, 10333 Ashton Ave, Los Angeles CA 90024, USA | Singer |
| **Frankel, Bethenny**<br>Creative Artists Agency, 2000 Ave of Stars, #100, Los Angeles CA 90067 USA | Chef, Entertainer, Writer |
| **Frankel, Max**<br>New York Times, Editorial Dept, 229 W 43rd St, New York NY 10036, USA | Editor |
| **Frankel, Neil**<br>Frankel & Coleman, 727 S Dearborn St, #412, Chicago IL 60605, USA | Interior Designer |
| **Franken, Al**<br>US Senate, Hart Office Building, Washington DC 20510 USA | Senator, Actor, Comedian, Writer |
| **Frankfort, Lew**<br>Coach Inc, 516 W 34th St, Basement 5, New York NY 10001, USA | Businessman |
| **Frankie J**<br>Esterman Entertainment, PO Box 514, Riva MD 21140, USA | Singer, Songwriter |
| **Franklin, Anthony R (Tony)**<br>117 Shady Trail St, San Antonio TX 78232, USA | Football Player |
| **Franklin, Aretha**<br>8450 Linwood St, Detroit MI 48206, USA | Singer |
| **Franklin, Aubrayo R**<br>1 Castleton Court, Johnson City TN 37615, USA | Football Player |
| **Franklin, Barbara Hackman**<br>1875 Perkins St, Bristol CT 06010, USA | Secretary, Commerce |
| **Franklin, Bobby R**<br>384 Country Club Dr, Senatobia MS 38668, USA | Football Player |
| **Franklin, Byron P**<br>1917 Eagle Circle Road, Demopolis AL 36732, USA | Football Player |

V.I.P. Address Book

**Franklin, Carl M** — Director, Writer
I C M Partners, 10250 Constellation Blvd, #900, Los Angeles CA 90067 USA
**Franklin, Diane** — Actress
Third Hill Entertainment, 195 S Beverly Dr, #400, Beverly Hills CA 90212, USA
**Franklin, Don** — Actor
Bauman Redanty Shaul Agency, 5757 Wilshire Blvd, #473, Los Angeles CA 90036 USA
**Franklin, G Wayne** — Baseball Player
925 McManness Ave, Findlay OH 45840, USA
**Franklin, Howard** — Director, Writer
W M E Entertainment, 9601 Wilshire Blvd, #300, Beverly Hills CA 90210 USA
**Franklin, James** — Football Coach
Pennsylvania State University, Athletic Dept, University Park PA 16802, USA
**Franklin, John** — Actor
Gilla Roos, 9744 Wilshire Blvd, #203, Beverly Hills CA 90212 USA
**Franklin, Jon D** — Journalist
9650 Strickland Road, Raleigh NC 27615, USA
**Franklin, Kirk** — Singer, Songwriter
Paradigm Agency, 360 N Crescent Dr, North Building, Beverly Hills CA 90210 USA
**Franklin, Marcus Carl** — Actor, Singer
Don Buchwald Talent Agency, 10 E 44th St, New York NY 10017 USA
**Franklin, Melissa** — Physicist
Harvard University, Physics Dept, Cambridge MA 02138, USA
**Franklin, Melissa J (Missy)** — Swimmer
Colorado Stars Swim Club, 6400 S Lewiston Way, Aurora CO 80016, USA
**Franklin, Micah I** — Baseball Player
3948 E Lafayette Ave, Gilbert AZ 85298, USA
**Franklin, Nelson** — Actor
W M E Entertainment, 9601 Wilshire Blvd, #300, Beverly Hills CA 90210 USA
**Franklin, Robert M, Jr** — Educator
Morehouse College, President's Office, 830 Westview Dr SW, Atlanta GA 30314, USA
**Franklin, Ronnie** — Thoroughbred Racing Jockey
Max Bauer's Cabinet Shop, 12811 Folly Quarter Road, Ellicott City MD 21042, USA
**Franklin, Roshawn** — Actor
Baker Winokur Ryder Public Relations, 9100 Wilshire Blvd, #500W, Beverly Hills CA 90212 USA
**Franklin, Ryan R** — Baseball Player
PO Box 723, Shawnee OK 74802, USA
**Franklin, Scott** — Producer
Protozoa Films, 104 N 7th St, Brooklyn NY 11211, USA
**Franklin, Shirley** — Mayor, Atlanta
Mayor's Office, City Hall, 55 Trinity Ave S, Atlanta GA 30303, USA
**Franklin, William** — Bowling Executive
920 La Sombra Dr, San Marcos CA 92078, USA
**Franklyn, Sabina** — Actress
C C A Mgmt, 4 Court Lodge, 48 Sloane Square, London SW1W 8AT, England
**Franks, Daniel L (Bubba)** — Football Player
108 Solomon Lane, Midland TX 79705, USA
**Franks, Elvis** — Football Player
2147 Rusk St, Beaumont TX 77701, USA
**Franks, Frederick M, Jr** — Army General
5016 Kensington High St, Naples FL 34105, USA
**Franks, Lucinda L** — Journalist
64 E 86th St, New York NY 10028, USA
**Franks, Michael** — Singer, Songwriter, Guitarist
A P A Talent & Literary Agency, 405 S Beverly Dr, #300, Beverly Hills CA 90212 USA
**Franks, Tommy R (Tom)** — Army General
Franks Assoc, 15273 N 2280 Road, Roosevelt OK 73564, USA
**Frankston, Robert M (Bob)** — Computer Software Designer (VisiCalc)
Software Arts Inc, 675 Massachusetts Ave, Boston MA 02118, USA
**Franquin, Andre** — Cartoonist
21 Ave Belelaere, 1170 Brussels, Belgium
**Franti, Michael** — Singer (Spearhead)
Guerilla Mangement Collective, 2180 Bryant St, #206, San Francisco CA 94110, USA
**Frantz, Adrienne** — Actress
Innovative Artists, 1505 10th St, Santa Monica CA 90401 USA
**Frantz, Chris** — Drummer (Talking Heads, Tom Tom Club)
Premier Talent, 3 E 54th St, #1100, New York NY 10022 USA
**Frantz, Justus** — Concert Pianist
Osterbekstr 90B, 22083 Hamburg, Germany
**Franz, Dennis** — Actor
PO Box 5370, Santa Barbara CA 93150, USA
**Franz, Judy R** — Physicist
American Physical Society, 1 Physics Eclipse, College Park MD 20740, USA
**Franz, Ron** — Basketball Player
8590 Beaverwood Dr, Germantown TN 38138, USA
**Franz, S Todd** — Football Player
5629 N Classen Blvd, Oklahoma City OK 73118, USA
**Franzen, Johan** — Ice Hockey Player
1043 Fairfax St, Birmingham MI 48009, USA
**Franzen, Jonathan** — Writer
Farrar Straus Giroux, 18 W 18th St, #700, New York NY 10011 USA
**Franzese, Daniel** — Actor, Producer, Director
Advanced Mgmt, 8033 Sunset Blvd, #935, Los Angeles CA 90046, USA
**Frasca, Robert J** — Architect
Zimmer Gunsul Frasca, 1223 SW Washington St, #200, Portland OR 97205, USA
**Frascatore, John V** — Baseball Player
PO Box 1411, Brooksville FL 34605, USA
**Frase, Paul M** — Football Player
124 Crossroad Lakes Dr, Ponte Vedra FL 32082, USA
**Fraser, Antonia** — Writer
Orion Publishing Group, Orion House, 5 Upper Saint Martin's Lane, London WC2H 9EA, England
**Fraser, Brad** — Writer
Great North Artists Mgmt, 350 Dupont Ave, Toronto ON M5R 1V9, Canada
**Fraser, Brendan** — Actor
Brillstein Entertainment Partners, 9150 Wilshire Blvd, #350, Beverly Hills CA 90212 USA
**Fraser, Curt M** — Ice Hockey Player, Coach
2205 Whitney Pointe Dr, Chesterfield MO 63005, USA

**Fraser, Dawn**
87 Birchgrove Road, Balmain NSW 2041, Australia — Swimmer

**Fraser, Elisabeth**
International Talent Booking, Ariel House, 74A Charlotte St, #100 London W1T 4QJ, England — Singer (Cocteau Twins)

**Fraser, Honor**
Select Model Mgmt, Archer House, 43 King St, London WC2E 8RJ, England — Model

**Fraser, Hugh**
3 Gate Apartments, 2 Chepstow Road, London W2 5BH, England — Actor

**Fraser, J Malcolm**
101 Collins St, Level 2, Melbourne VIC 3000, Australia — Prime Minister, Australia

**Fraser, Laura**
Grotto Writers Workshop, 490 2nd St, #200, San Francisco CA 94107, USA — Writer

**Fraser, Laura**
Emptage Hallett, 14 Rathbone Place, London W1T 1HT, England — Actress

**Fraser, Neale A**
21 Bolton Ave, Hampton VIC 3188, Australia — Tennis Player

**Fraser, Toa**
I C M Partners, 10250 Constellation Blvd, #900, Los Angeles CA 90067 USA — Director

**Fraser, William M, III**
Commander, Air Combat Command, Langley Air Force Base VA 23665 USA — Air Force General

**Frasor, Jason A**
15043 Landings Lane, Oak Forest IL 60452, USA — Baseball Player

**Frassinelli, Adriano**
Olympic Committee, Foro Italico, Largo Lauro de Bosis 15, 00135 Rome, Italy — Bobsled Athlete

**Fratello, Michael R (Mike)**
7642 Fisher Island Dr, Miami Beach FL 33109, USA — Basketball Coach, Sportscaster

**Fratianne Maricich, Linda S**
3352 Whispering Glen Court, Simi Valley CA 93065, USA — Figure Skater

**Frautschi, Angela**
Z S C Lions Z LA Betriebs, Siewerdtstr 105, 8050 Zurich, Switzerland — Ice Hockey Player

**Frayn, Michael**
Greene & Heaton, 37A Goldhawk Road, London W12 8QQ, England — Writer

**Frazar, Harrison**
3208 Villanova St, Dallas TX 75225, USA — Golfer

**Frazier, A Louis (Lou)**
557 N Mondel Dr, Gilbert AZ 85233, USA — Baseball Player

**Frazier, Amy**
Octagon Worldwide, 1751 Pinnacle Dr, #1500, McLean VA 22102 USA — Tennis Player

**Frazier, Andre**
4295 Cross Creek Court, Liberty Township OH 45011, USA — Football Player

**Frazier, Charles**
I C M Partners, 10250 Constellation Blvd, #900, Los Angeles CA 90067 USA — Writer

**Frazier, Charles D (Charlie0**
4018 Brookston St, Houston TX 77045, USA — Football Player

**Frazier, Dallas**
RR 5 Box 133, Longhollow Pike, Gallatin TN 37066, USA — Singer, Songwriter

**Frazier, George A**
6886 S Evanston Ave, Tulsa OK 74136, USA — Baseball Player

**Frazier, Guy S**
3944 Dickson Ave, Cincinnati OH 45229, USA — Football Player

**Frazier, Herman**
1024 E Frye Road, #1011, Phoenix AZ 85048, USA — Track Athlete

**Frazier, Ian**
Farrar Straus Giroux, 18 W 18th St, #700, New York NY 10011 USA — Writer

**Frazier, Kevin**
250 President St, #201, Baltimore MD 21202, USA — Actor

**Frazier, Leslie A**
867 Normandy Trace Road, Tampa FL 33602, USA — Football Player, Coach

**Frazier, Owsley B**
Brown-Forman Corp, 850 Dixie Highway, Louisville KY 40210, USA — Businessman

**Frazier, Sheila**
J K A Talent Agency, 12725 Ventura Blvd, #H, Studio City CA 91604, USA — Actress

**Frazier, Stan**
Lava/Atlantic Records, 9229 W Sunset Blvd, #900, West Hollywood CA 90069, USA — Drummer (Sugar Ray)

**Frazier, Walter (Clyde), II**
200 E 82nd St, New York NY 10028, USA — Basketball Player

**Frazier, Willie**
6203 Bankside Dr, Houston TX 77096, USA — Football Player

**Frears, Stephen A**
Casorotto Ramsay, Waverley House, 7-12 Noel St, London W1F 8GQ, England — Director

**Freberg, Stanley V (Stan)**
Radio Spirits, PO Box 3107, Wallingford CT 06494, USA — Actor, Comedian

**Frechette, Sylvie**
Cirque du Soleil, 8400 2nd Ave, Montreal QC H1Z 4M6, Canada — Synchronized Swimmer

**Frecheville, James**
United Talent Agency, U T A Plaza, 9336 Civic Center Dr, Beverly Hills CA 90210 USA — Actor

**Frederick, Andrew B (Andy)**
7247 Alexander Dr, Dallas TX 75214, USA — Football Player

**Frederick, Kevin**
5701 Foxlake Dr, #A, North Fort Myers FL 33917, USA — Baseball Player

**Frederick-Blanchette, Marcia**
105 High St, Assonet MA 02702, USA — Gymnast

**Fredericks, Frank (Frankie)**
4497 Wimbledon Dr, Provo UT 84604, USA — Track Athlete

**Fredericks, Fred**
PO Box 475, Eastham MA 02642, USA — Cartoonist (Mandrake the Magician)

**Frederickson, Ivan C (Tucker)**
12414 Indian Road, North Palm Beach FL 33408, USA — Football Player

**Frederickson, Scott E**
20703 Turning Leaf Lake Court, Cypress TX 77433, USA — Baseball Player

**Frederik**
Amalienborg Palace, 1257 Copenhagen K, Denmark — Prince, Denmark

**Fredette, James T (Jimmer)**
New Orleans Pelicans, 1250 Poydras St, #101, New Orleans LA 70113 USA — Basketball Player

**Fredrickson, Robert J (Rob)**
8312 N 50th St, Paradise Valley AZ 85253, USA — Football Player

| | |
|---|---|
| **Fredriksson, Marie**<br>D & D Mgmt, Drottninggatan 55, 111 21 Stockholm, Sweden | Singer, Songwriter (Roxette) |
| **Free, Helen M**<br>3752 E Jackson Blvd, Elkhart IN 46516, USA | Chemist, Inventor (Glucose Detector) |
| **Free, Lloyd B (World)**<br>1131 E County Lane Road, Lakewood NJ 08701, USA | Basketball Player, Coach, Executive |
| **Freed, Jack H**<br>108 Homestead Circle, Ithaca NY 14850, USA | Chemist |
| **Freedman, Alix M**<br>Wall Street Journal, Editorial Dept, 1 World Financial Center, New York NY 10281 USA | Journalist |
| **Freedman, Eric**<br>Detroit News, Editorial Dept, 615 W Lafayette Blvd, Detroit MI 48226, USA | Journalist |
| **Freedman, Ronald**<br>1200 Earhart Road, #228, Ann Arbor MI 48105, USA | Sociologist |
| **Freeh, Louis J**<br>Saint Martin's Press, 175 5th Ave, #400, New York NY 10010 USA | Law Enforcement Official |
| **Freehan, William A (Bill)**<br>6999 Indian Garden Road, Petoskey MI 49770, USA | Baseball Player |
| **Freelon, Nnenna**<br>Ed Keene Assoc, 573 Pleasant St, Winthrop MA 02152, USA | Singer |
| **Freeman, Antonio M**<br>PO Box 450718, Fort Lauderdale FL 33345, USA | Football Player |
| **Freeman, Arturo C**<br>PO Box 551612, Fort Lauderdale FL 33355, USA | Football Player |
| **Freeman, Bobby**<br>First Class Entertainment, 483 Ridgewood Road, Maplewood NJ 07040, USA | Singer |
| **Freeman, Cassidy**<br>Paul Kohner, 9300 Wilshire Blvd, #555, Beverly Hills CA 90212 USA | Actress |
| **Freeman, Catherine A (Cathy)**<br>Jane Cowmeadow, Bron Madigan, PO Box 5138, Ringwood VIC 3134, Australia | Track Athlete |
| **Freeman, Charles W, Jr**<br>Project International, 1800 K St NW, #1010, Washington DC 20006, USA | Diplomat |
| **Freeman, Gary C**<br>PO Box 1399, Albany OR 97321, USA | Basketball Player |
| **Freeman, Gregory A**<br>PO Box 680922, Marietta GA 30068, USA | Writer |
| **Freeman, Harold P**<br>Lauren Cancer Prevention Center, 1919 Madison Ave, New York NY 10035, USA | Oncologist |
| **Freeman, Isaac**<br>Keith Case Assoc, 1025 17th Ave S, #200, Nashville TN 37212 USA | Singer |
| **Freeman, Jennifer**<br>Pakula/King, 9229 W Sunset Blvd, #315, West Hollywood CA 90069 USA | Actress, Model |
| **Freeman, Jimmy L**<br>4716 E 106th St, Tulsa OK 74137, USA | Baseball Player |
| **Freeman, Jonathan**<br>Bauman Redanty Shaul Agency, 5757 Wilshire Blvd, #473, Los Angeles CA 90036 USA | Actor |
| **Freeman, Joshua T (Josh)**<br>New York Giants, Meadowlands Stadium, 102 Route 120, East Rutherford NJ 07073 USA | Football Player |
| **Freeman, LaVel M**<br>8941 Laguna Place Way, Elk Grove CA 95758, USA | Baseball Player |
| **Freeman, Martin**<br>United Talent Agency, U T A Plaza, 9336 Civic Center Dr, Beverly Hills CA 90210 USA | Actor |
| **Freeman, Marvin**<br>20135 Mohawk Trail, Olympia Fields IL 60461, USA | Baseball Player |
| **Freeman, Morgan**<br>Creative Artists Agency, 2000 Ave of Stars, #100, Los Angeles CA 90067 USA | Actor |
| **Freeman, R Matthew (Matt)**<br>Leave Home Booking, 10 W Broadway, #608, Salt Lake City UT 84101, USA | Singer, Bassist (Rancid) |
| **Freeman, Rich**<br>Paramount Entertainment, PO Box 12, Far Hills NJ 07931 USA | Singer (Five Satins) |
| **Freeman, Richard**<br>Economic Research Bureau, 1050 Massachusetts Ave, Cambridge MA 02138, USA | Economist |
| **Freeman, Rodney L (Rod)**<br>6308 Murray Lane, Brentwood TN 37027, USA | Basketball Player |
| **Freeman, Yvette**<br>Stone Manners Salners, 6100 Wilshire Blvd, #1500, Los Angeles CA 90035 USA | Actress, Singer |
| **Freemantle, Glenn**<br>Sound 24, Pinewood Road, Iver, Buckinghamshire SL0 0NH, England | Sound Editor |
| **Freeney, Dwight J**<br>11021 Hintocks Circle, Carmel IN 46032, USA | Football Player |
| **Freese, David R**<br>Los Angeles Angels, Angel Stadium, 2000 E Gene Autry Way, Anaheim CA 92806 USA | Baseball Player |
| **Freeway**<br>Agency Group Ltd, 142 W 57th St, #600, New York NY 10019 USA | Rap Artist |
| **Freeze, Hugh**<br>University of Mississippi, Athletic Dept, University MS 38677, USA | Football Coach |
| **Frehley, Paul D (Ace)**<br>Creative Artists Agency, 2000 Ave of Stars, #100, Los Angeles CA 90067 USA | Singer, Guitarist (Kiss) |
| **Frei Ruiz-Tagle, Eduardo**<br>Christian Democratic Party, O'Higgins 1460, #20, Santiago, Chile | President, Chile |
| **Frei, Tanya**<br>Curling Association, PO Box 606, 3000 Bern, Switzerland | Curling Athlete |
| **Freiberger, Marcus**<br>985 US Highway 64 W, Mocksville NC 27028, USA | Basketball Player |
| **Freidheim, Cyrus**<br>Chiquita Brands International, 250 E 5th St, #2600, Cincinnati OH 45202, USA | Businessman |
| **Freilicher, Jane**<br>51 5th Ave, New York NY 10003, USA | Artist |
| **Freire, Nelson**<br>Columbia Artists Mgmt Inc, 5 Columbus Circle, 1790 Broadway, #1600, New York NY 10019 USA | Concert Pianist |
| **Freireich, Emil J**<br>M D Anderson Medical Center, 1515 Holcombe Blvd, #207, Houston TX 77030 USA | Physician |
| **Freisleben, David J (Dave)**<br>1326 Diamante Dr, Pasadena TX 77504, USA | Baseball Player |
| **Freitas, Acelino (Popo)**<br>Banner Promotions, 1231 Bainbridge St, Philadelphia PA 19147, USA | Boxer |

**Freitas, Rockne C (Rocky)** — Football Player
2667 E Manoa Road, Honolulu HI 96822, USA

**Fremaux, Louis J F** — Conductor
25 Edencroft, Wheeley's Road, Birmingham B15 2LW, England

**French, Dawn** — Actress, Comedienne
United Agents, 12-26 Lexington St, London W1F 0LE, England

**French, Heather R** — Beauty Queen
567 Circle Dr, Maysville KY 41056, USA

**French, Jay Jay** — Singer, Guitarist (Twisted Sister)
Rebellion Entertainment, 2440 Broadway, #111, New York NY 10024, USA

**French, Kate** — Actress
Caliber Media, 9229 W Sunset Blvd, #705, West Hollywood CA 90069, USA

**French, Nicola S (Niki)** — Singer
Energise Records, 347 Caspian Way, Purfleet, Essex RM19 1LB, England

**French, Paige** — Actress
Collier Talent Agency, 2313 Lake Austin Blvd, #103, Austin TX 78703, USA

**French, R James (Jim)** — Baseball Player
PO Box 6452, Chicago IL 60680, USA

**French, Tara** — Writer
Viking Press, 375 Hudson St, New York NY 10014 USA

**Frenette, Matt** — Drummer (Loverboy)
Loverboy Touring Offices, 425 Carrall St, Vancouver BC V6A 6E3, Canada

**Freni, Mirella** — Opera Singer
I M G Artists, Hogarth Business Park, Chiswick, London W4 2TH, England

**Frenkel, Jacob A** — Economist
J P MorganChase Co, 270 Park Ave, New York NY 10017, USA

**Frenkiel, Richard H** — Systems Engineer, Inventor
Rutgers University, WinLab, PO Box 909, Piscataway NJ 08855, USA

**Frentzen, Heinz-Harald** — Auto Racing Driver
Jordan Grand Prix, Silverstone Circuit, Towcester Northhamptonshire NN12 8TN, England

**Frenzel, Eric** — Nordic Combined Skier
Wiesenstr 11, 09468 Geyer, Germany

**Frerotte, Gustave J (Gus)** — Football Player
10040 Litzsinger Road, Saint Louis MO 63124, USA

**Fresco, Michael** — Director
I C M Partners, 10250 Constellation Blvd, #900, Los Angeles CA 90067 USA

**Fresco, Paolo** — Businessman
Fiat SpA, Corso Marconi 10/20, 10125 Turin, Italy

**Fresh, Doug E** — Rap Artist
Pyramid Entertainment Group, 377 Rector Place, #21A, New York NY 10280 USA

**Fresnadillo, Juan Carlos** — Director
United Talent Agency, U T A Plaza, 9336 Civic Center Dr, Beverly Hills CA 90210 USA

**Fretton, Anthony (Tony)** — Architect
49-59 Old St, London EC1V 9XH, England

**Freud, Bella L** — Fashion Designer
21 Saint Charles Square, London W10 6EF, England

**Freudenberg, Ute** — Singer
Postfach 2660, 99407 Weimar, Germany

**Freudenberger, Nell** — Writer
Harper Collins Publishers, 10 E 53rd St, Cellar 1, New York NY 10022 USA

**Freund, Lambert B** — Mechanical Engineer
3 Palisade Lane, Barrington RI 02806, USA

**Freund, Severin** — Ski Jumper
Leopoldstr 173D, 80804 Munich, Germany

**Freundlich, Bart** — Director
Creative Artists Agency, 2000 Ave of Stars, #100, Los Angeles CA 90067 USA

**Frewer, Matt** — Actor
Gilbertson Entertainment, 1334 3rd Street Promenade, #201, Santa Monica CA 90401 USA

**Frey, Glenn** — Singer (Eagles), Songwriter, Actor
I C M Partners, 10250 Constellation Blvd, #900, Los Angeles CA 90067 USA

**Frey, James G (Jim)** — Baseball Manager
12101 Tullamore Court, #406, Lutherville Timonium MD 21093, USA

**Frey, Sami** — Actor
Les Visiteurs du Soir, 40 Rue de la Folie Regnault, 75011 Paris, France

**Frey, Steven F (Steve)** — Baseball Player
1414 2nd Street Pike, Southampton PA 18966, USA

**Freytag, Arny** — Photographer
22735 MacFarlane Dr, Woodland Hills CA 91364, USA

**Frias, Arturo** — Boxer
12418 Penn St, Whittier CA 90602, USA

**Frick, Stephen N** — Astronaut
27998 Mercurio Road, Carmel CA 93923, USA

**Fricke, Janie** — Singer, Guitarist
Janie Fricke Concerts, PO Box 798, Lancaster TX 75146, USA

**Fricker, Brenda** — Actress
Aegis Entertainment Group, 7510 Sunset Blvd, #275, Los Angeles CA 90046, USA

**Frickman, Andrew J (Andy)** — Director, Producer
W M E Entertainment, 9601 Wilshire Blvd, #300, Beverly Hills CA 90210 USA

**Friday, Gavin** — Singer, Composer, Artist
Bloomsbury Publishing, 50 Bedford Square, London WC1B 3DP, England

**Friday, Nancy** — Writer
Harper Collins Publishers, 10 E 53rd St, Cellar 1, New York NY 10022 USA

**Fridell, Squire** — Actor
Stars Agency, 23 Grant Ave, #400, San Francisco CA 94108, USA

**Fridovich, David P** — Army General
Special Operations Center, 7701 Tampa Point Blvd, McDill Air Force Base FL 33621, USA

**Fried, Charles** — Government Official, Judge, Educator
Harvard University, Law School, Cambridge MA 02138, USA

**Fried, Miriam** — Concert Violinist
Opus 3 Artists, 470 Park Ave S, #900N, New York NY 10016 USA

**Friedberg, Rick** — Director
A P A Talent & Literary Agency, 405 S Beverly Dr, #300, Beverly Hills CA 90212 USA

**Friedberger, Eleanor** — Singer (Fiery Furnaces)
High Road Touring, 751 Bridgeway, #200, Sausalito CA 94965 USA

**Friedberger, Matthew** — Singer, Drummer (Fiery Furnaces)
High Road Touring, 751 Bridgeway, #200, Sausalito CA 94965 USA

**Frieden, Tanja** — Snowboard Athlete
Kari Frieden, Freisestr 29A, 3604 Thun, Switzerland
**Frieden, Thomas R** — Government Official, Physician
Centers for Disease Control, 1600 Clifton Road NE, Atlanta GA 30329 USA
**Friedericy, Bonita** — Actress
Amsel Eisenstadt Frazier, 5055 Wilshire Blvd, #865, Los Angeles CA 90036 USA
**Friedkin, William** — Director
10741 Levico Way, Los Angeles CA 90077, USA
**Friedlaender, Jonathan** — Biological Anthropologist
3401 N Broad St, Philadelphia PA 19140, USA
**Friedlander, Judah** — Actor, Comedian
Cohen & Gardner, 345 N Maple Drive, #181, Beverly Hills CA 90210, USA
**Friedlander, Lee** — Artist, Photographer
Janet Borden, 560 Broadway, #601, New York NY 10012, USA
**Friedlander, Liz** — Director
Gersh Agency, 9465 Wilshire Blvd, #600, Beverly Hills CA 90212 USA
**Friedlander, Saul** — Writer
University of California, History Dept, Los Angeles CA 90024, USA
**Friedle, Will** — Actor
Innovative Artists, 1505 10th St, Santa Monica CA 90401 USA
**Friedman, Bruce Jay** — Writer
Biblioasis, PO Box 92, Emeryville ON N0R 1C0, Canada
**Friedman, Emanuel A** — Obstetrician
Beth-Israel Hospital, 330 Brookline Ave, Boston MA 02215, USA
**Friedman, Jeffrey M** — Molecular Geneticist
Rockefeller University Hughes Medical Institute, Molecular Genetics Laboratory, New York NY 10021, USA
**Friedman, Jeremiah** — Writer
United Talent Agency, U T A Plaza, 9336 Civic Center Dr, Beverly Hills CA 90210 USA
**Friedman, Jerome I** — Nobel Physics Laureate
44 Allandale St, #408, Jamaica Plain MA 02130, USA
**Friedman, Kinky** — Singer, Songwriter, Writer
1101 Crown Ridge Path, Austin TX 78753, USA
**Friedman, Leonard L (Lennie)** — Football Player
1000 Cross Clay Court, Raleigh NC 27614, USA
**Friedman, Maggie** — Producer
Ensemble Entertainment, 280 S Beverly Dr, #402, Beverly Hills CA 90212, USA
**Friedman, Mal** — Actor
J E Talent, 323 Geary St, #302, San Francisco CA 94102, USA
**Friedman, Mark** — Writer, Producer
United Talent Agency, U T A Plaza, 9336 Civic Center Dr, Beverly Hills CA 90210 USA
**Friedman, Michael** — Composer, Lyricist
I C M Partners, 10250 Constellation Blvd, #900, Los Angeles CA 90067 USA
**Friedman, Peter** — Actor, Singer
J Michael Bloom, 233 Park Ave S, #1000, New York NY 10003 USA
**Friedman, Philip** — Writer
Ivy Books/Random House, 1745 Broadway, #B1, New York NY 10019, USA
**Friedman, Sonya** — Psychologist, Entertainer
111 S Old Woodward Ave, #212B, Birmingham MI 48009, USA
**Friedman, Thomas L** — Journalist
New York Times, Editorial Dept, 229 W 43rd St, New York NY 10036 USA
**Friedman, Tom** — Sculptor
Luhring Augustine Gallery, 531 W 24th St, New York NY 10011, USA
**Friedrich, Hans-Peter** — Government Official, Germany
Bundestag, Platz der Republik 1, 10557 Berlin, Germany
**Friel, Anna** — Actress
Artists Partnership, 101 Finsbury Pavement, London EC2A 1RS, England
**Friel, Brian** — Writer
Drumaweir House, Greencastle, County Donegal, Ireland
**Frielinghaus, Paul** — Actor
Agentur Gotha, Elisabethstr 19, 80796 Munich, Germany
**Friels, Colin** — Actor
129 Brooke St, Woollomooloo, Sydney NSW 2011, Australia
**Friend, Robert B (Bob)** — Baseball Player
4 Salem Circle, Pittsburgh PA 15238, USA
**Friend, Rupert** — Actor
Creative Artists Agency, 2000 Ave of Stars, #100, Los Angeles CA 90067 USA
**Friesen, Jeff D** — Ice Hockey Player
96 Dornoch Way, Trabuco Canyon CA 92679, USA
**Friesinger-Postma, Anna (Anni)** — Speed Skater
Am Bichl 4, 83334 Inzell, Germany
**Friesz, John M** — Football Player
1454 E W Pebblestone Court, Hayden ID 83835, USA
**Frigo, Francesco** — Model, Actress
Playboy Promotions, 9346 Civic Center Dr, #200, Beverly Hills CA 90210 USA
**Frimout, Dirk D** — Astronaut, Belgium
Flanders Language Foundation, Merghelynckstraat 4, 8900 Iper, Belgium
**Fripp, Robert** — Guitarist (King Crimson), Songwriter
Agency Group Ltd, 361-373 City Road, London EC1V 1PQ, England
**Frischmann, Justine** — Singer (Elastica)
C M O Mgmt, Studio 2.6, Shepherds East, Richmond Way, London W14 0DQ, England
**Frisell, Sonja** — Director
Columbia Artists Mgmt Inc, 5 Columbus Circle, 1790 Broadway, #1600, New York NY 10019 USA
**Frisell, William R (Bill)** — Jazz Guitarist
Rosebud Agency, PO Box 170429, San Francisco CA 94117 USA
**Frishberg, David L** — Jazz Singer, Pianist, Composer
Irvin Arthur Assoc, 550 Okeechobee Blvd, #1711, West Palm Beach FL 33401 USA
**Frist, William H (Bill), Sr** — Senator, TN
V O L P A C, PO Box 15852, Nashville TN 37215, USA
**Fristsche, Jim** — Basketball Player
470 Emerson Ave W, Saint Paul MN 55118, USA
**Fritsch, Theodore E (Ted), Jr** — Football Player
5014 Odins Way, Marietta GA 30068, USA
**Fritsche, Dan** — Ice Hockey Player
116 Olentangy Point, Columbus OH 43202, USA
**Fritts, Debra** — Artist
Chase Gallery, 129 Newbury St, Mezzanine, Boston MA 02116, USA

**Fritz, Harold A** — Vietnam War Army Hero (CMH)
1017 W Scottwood Dr, Peoria IL 61615, USA
**Fritz, Laurence J (Larry)** — Baseball Player
2632 Schrage Ave, Whiting IN 46394, USA
**Fritz, Nikki** — Actress
1158 28th St, #683, Santa Monica CA 90403, USA
**Frizza, Riccardo** — Conductor
I M G Artists, Hogarth Business Park, Chiswick, London W4 2TH, England
**Frizzell, David** — Singer
Symons Adams Myers Promotions, PO Box 30, Fostoria OH 44830, USA
**Frizzell, John** — Composer
First Artists Mgmt, 4764 Park Granada, #210, Calabasas CA 91302 USA
**Frizzelle, William J** — Football Player
8001 Tylerton Dr, Raleigh NC 27613, USA
**Frobel, Douglas S (Doug)** — Baseball Player
169 Springwater Dr, Kanata ON K2K 1Z8, Canada
**Froboess, Cornelia** — Singer, Actress
Rinkhof Kleinholzhausen, 83064 Raubling, Germany
**Froch, Carl** — Boxer
Gedling Road, Carlton, Nottingham NG4 3FG, England
**Froemming, Bruce N** — Baseball Umpire
702 W Haddonstone Place, Thiensville WI 53092, USA
**Froese, Bob** — Ice Hockey Player
11701 Clarence Center Road, Akron NY 14001, USA
**Froggatt, Joanne** — Actress
Conway Van Gelder Grant, 8-12 Broadwick St, #300, London W1F 8HW, England
**Frohnmayer, John E** — Government Official
38511 Kelly Road, Jefferson OR 97352, USA
**Frohwirth, Todd G** — Baseball Player
S66W24360 Skyline Ave, Waukesha WI 53189, USA
**Froines, John R** — Social Activist, Educator
University of California Public Health School, Environmental Health Science Dept, Los Angeles CA 90024, USA
**Frolov, Alexander** — Ice Hockey Player
1467 3rd St, Manhattan Beach CA 90266, USA
**Fromm, Fritz** — Handball Player
An der Bismarckschule 64, 30173 Hannover, Germany
**Frongillo, John R** — Football Player
10230 Elmhurst Dr NW, Albuquerque NM 87114, USA
**Fronius, Hans** — Artist
Guggenberggasse 18, 2380 Perchtoldadorf bei Vienna, Austria
**Froome, Chris** — Cyclist
Team Sky, National Cycling Centre, Stuart St, Great Manchester M11 4DQ, England
**Frosch, Robert A** — Government Official, Space Scientist
18 Heritage Hills Dr, Somers NY 10589, USA
**Frost, Alex** — Actor
Industry Entertainment, 955 Carillo Dr, #300, Los Angeles CA 90048 USA
**Frost, C David (Dave)** — Baseball Player
2206 Ocana Ave, Long Beach CA 90815, USA
**Frost, David L** — Golfer
5836 Royal Lane, Dallas TX 75230, USA
**Frost, Lindsay** — Actress
Glick Agency, 347 5th Ave, #1404, New York NY 10016 USA
**Frost, Mark** — Writer
Mark Frost Productions, PO Box 1723, Studio City CA 91614, USA
**Frost, Martin** — Concert Clarinetist
Kunstlermanagement Till Doench, Roegergasse 24-26/G2, 1090 Vienna, Austria
**Frost, Nick** — Actor, Comedian, Writer
Hamilton Hodell, 20 Golden Square, London W1F 9JL, England
**Frost, Sadie** — Actress
Money Mgmt, 22 Noel St, London W1F 8GS, England
**Frost, Scott A** — Football Player
99 Thomas Lake, Ashland NE 68003, USA
**Fruhwirth, Amy** — Golfer
26431 N 44th Way, Phoenix AZ 85050, USA
**Frusciante, John A** — Guitarist (Red Hot Chili Peppers)
Q Prime, 729 7th Ave, #1600, New York NY 10019 USA
**Fry Irvin, Shirley** — Tennis Player
540 Village Place, #112, Longwood FL 32779, USA
**Fry, Jerry R** — Baseball Player
3300 Stanton St, Springfield IL 62703, USA
**Fry, John A** — Educator
Drexel University, President's Office, 3141 Chestnut St, #103, Philadelphia PA 19104, USA
**Fry, Lyndsey** — Ice Hockey Player
Douglas W Fry, 4880 W Geronimo St, Chandler AZ 85226, USA
**Fry, Michael** — Cartoonist (Committed, Over the Hedge)
United Feature Syndicate, PO Box 5610, Cincinnati OH 45201 USA
**Fry, Robert N (Bob)** — Football Player
1604 Bexley Dr, Wilmington NC 28412, USA
**Fry, Ryan B** — Curling Athlete
Team Brad Jacobs, 38 Barber Blvd, Sault Sainte Marie ON P6A 5T5, Canada
**Fry, Stephen J** — Actor, Comedian, Director
Hamilton Hodell, 20 Golden Square, London W1F 9JL, England
**Fryar, Chris** — Drummer (Zac Brown Band)
Roar, 9701 Wilshire Blvd, #800, Beverly Hills CA 90212, USA
**Fryar, Irving D** — Football Player, Sportscaster
51 Applegate Road, Jobstown NJ 08041, USA
**Frye, Channing T** — Basketball Player
Phoenix Suns, 201 E Jefferson St, Phoenix AZ 85004 USA
**Frye, Jarem** — Inventor (Prosthetic Knee)
K12 Prosthetics, 212 E SR-73, #141, Saratoga Springs UT 84043, USA
**Frye, Jeffrey A (Jeff)** — Baseball Player
6833 Lahontan Dr, Fort Worth TX 76132, USA
**Frye, Soliel Moon** — Actress
42 West, 220 W 42nd St, #1200, New York NY 10036 USA
**Fryling, Victor J** — Businessman
C M S Energy, Fairlane Plaza South, 330 Town Center Dr, Dearborn MI 48126, USA

| | |
|---|---|
| **Fryman, D Travis**<br>2600 Highway 196, Molino FL 32577, USA | Baseball Player |
| **Ftorek, Robert B (Robbie)**<br>79 Sunset Point Road, Wolfeboro NH 03894, USA | Ice Hockey Player, Coach |
| **Fu Mingxia**<br>General Physical Culture Bureau, 9 Tiyuguan Road, Dongcheng District, Beijing 100061, China | Diver |
| **Fu, Haijing**<br>I M G Artists, Hogarth Business Park, Chiswick, London W4 2TH, England | Opera Singer |
| **Fucarino, Frank A**<br>21 Heathcote Court, Shirley NY 11967, USA | Basketball Player |
| **Fuchs, Florian**<br>U H C Hamburg, Wesselblek 8, 22339 Hamburg, Germany | Field Hockey Player |
| **Fuchs, Victor R**<br>796 Cedro Way, Stanford CA 94305, USA | Economist |
| **Fudenberg, Drew**<br>Harvard University, Economics Dept, Littauer Center, Cambridge MA 02138, USA | Economist |
| **Fuente, David I**<br>Office Depot Inc, 6600 N Military Trail, Boca Raton FL 33496, USA | Businessman |
| **Fuentes Fache, Andrea**<br>Club Natcio Sincronizada Kallipolis, Calle dels Esports S/N, 08017 Barcelona, Spain | Synchronized Swimmer |
| **Fuentes, Brian C**<br>1342 El Portal Dr, Merced CA 95340, USA | Baseball Player |
| **Fuentes, Daisy**<br>Shelter Entertainment, 9255 Sunset Blvd, #300, Los Angeles CA 90069 USA | Actress, Model |
| **Fuentes, Julio M**<br>US Court of Appeals, US Courthouse, 50 Walnut St, #5032, Newark NJ 07102, USA | Judge |
| **Fuentes, Rigoberto B (Tito)**<br>61 S Maddux Dr, Reno NV 89512, USA | Baseball Player |
| **Fuentes, Val**<br>Tabletop Productions, PO Box 698, Carson City NV 89702, USA | Drummer (It's a Beautiful Day) |
| **Fugard, Athol H**<br>PO Box 5090, Walmer, Port Elizabeth 6065, South Africa | Writer |
| **Fugate, Katherine**<br>Stakevich-Gothman, 9777 Wilshire Blvd, #550, Beverly Hills CA 90212, USA | Producer, Writer |
| **Fugelsang, John**<br>Brillstein Entertainment Partners, 9150 Wilshire Blvd, #350, Beverly Hills CA 90212 USA | Actor, Comedian |
| **Fugett, Jean S, Jr**<br>4801 Westparkway, Baltimore MD 21229, USA | Football Player |
| **Fugit, Patrick**<br>Levin/Brown Mgmt, M M Productions, 1351 4th St, #201, Santa Monica CA 90401, USA | Actor |
| **Fuglesang, A Christer**<br>PO Box 555, Bellaire TX 77402, USA | Astronaut, Sweden |
| **Fuhrman, Isabelle**<br>Trilogy Talent, 13425 Ventura Blvd, #200, Sherman Oaks CA 91423, USA | Actress |
| **Fujita, Hiroyuki**<br>Fujita Laboratory, 4-6-1 Komaba, Meguroku, Tokyo 153 8505, Japan | Microbiotics Engineer |
| **Fukada, Kyoko**<br>Horipro, 2-5-1 Shimo-Meguro, Meguroku, Meguro, Tokyo 153 8660, Japan | Actress, Singer |
| **Fuksas, Massimiliano**<br>Piazzi del Monte di Pieta 30, 00186 Rome, Italy | Architect |
| **Fukuda, Yasuo**<br>4-20-7 Nazawa, Setagayaku, Tokyo 154 0003, Japan | Prime Minister, Japan |
| **Fukui, Takeo**<br>Honda Motor Co, 2-1-1 Minami-Aoyama, Minatoku, Tokyo 107 8556, Japan | Businessman |
| **Fukumoto, Miho**<br>Football Association, 3-10-15 Hongo, Bunkyoku, Tokyo 113 0033 Japan | Soccer Player |
| **Fukunaga, Cary J**<br>Anonymous Content, 3532 Hayden Ave, Culver City CA 90232 USA | Director |
| **Fukuyama, Francis**<br>George Mason University, Public Policy Dept, Fairfax VA 22030, USA | Social Scientist |
| **Fulcher, David D**<br>All Pro Sports, PO Box 378, Mason OH 45040, USA | Football Player |
| **Fulcher, Rich**<br>United Talent Agency, U T A Plaza, 9336 Civic Center Dr, Beverly Hills CA 90210 USA | Actor |
| **Fuld, Samuel B (Sam)**<br>8 Meadow Road, Durham NH 03824, USA | Baseball Player |
| **Fulghum, Robert**<br>Random House, 1745 Broadway, #1800, New York NY 10019 USA | Writer, Religious Leader |
| **Fulgoni, Sara**<br>I M G Artists, Hogarth Business Park, Chiswick, London W4 2TH, England | Opera Singer |
| **Fulhage, Scott A**<br>2430 N Road, Beloit KS 67420, USA | Football Player |
| **Fulks, Robbie**<br>Mongrel Music, 743 Center Blvd, Fairfax CA 94930, USA | Singer, Songwriter |
| **Fulle, Siegfried**<br>Gerolstr 30A, 80339 Munich, Germany | Gymnast |
| **Fuller, Charles**<br>Creative Artists Agency, 2000 Ave of Stars, #100, Los Angeles CA 90067 USA | Writer |
| **Fuller, Cindy**<br>Playboy Promotions, 9346 Civic Center Dr, #200, Beverly Hills CA 90210 USA | Model |
| **Fuller, Corey**<br>626 Raspberry Way, Tallahassee FL 32312, USA | Football Player |
| **Fuller, Delores**<br>3628 Ottawa Circle, Las Vegas NV 89169, USA | Actress, Songwriter |
| **Fuller, Drew**<br>Gersh Agency, 9465 Wilshire Blvd, #600, Beverly Hills CA 90212 USA | Actor |
| **Fuller, James H (Jim)**<br>5107 Bur Oak Dr, Pasadena TX 77505, USA | Baseball Player |
| **Fuller, John C (Johnny)**<br>1925 Highland Dr, Salado TX 76571, USA | Football Player |
| **Fuller, John E**<br>31912 Paseo Terraza, San Juan Capistrano CA 92675, USA | Baseball Player |
| **Fuller, Kathryn S**<br>World Wildlife Fund, 1250 24th St NW, #600, Washington DC 20037, USA | Association Executive |
| **Fuller, Kyle B**<br>Chicago Bears, 1000 Football Dr, Lake Forest IL 60045 USA | Football Player |

|  |  |
|---|---|
| **Fuller, Linda**<br>Habitat for Humanity, 121 Habitat St, Americus GA 31709, USA | Association Executive, Social Activist |
| **Fuller, Mark**<br>Wet Design, 90 Universal City Plaza, Universal City CA 91608, USA | Sculptor |
| **Fuller, Marvin D**<br>6799 Patton Dr, Fort Hood TX 76544, USA | Army General |
| **Fuller, Michael D (Mike)**<br>4241 Abingdon Trail, Birmingham AL 35243, USA | Football Player |
| **Fuller, Penny**<br>Paradigm Agency, 360 N Crescent Dr, North Building, Beverly Hills CA 90210 USA | Actress |
| **Fuller, Randy L**<br>2257 Patsy Lane, Columbus GA 31903, USA | Football Player |
| **Fuller, Robert (Bob)**<br>5012 Auckland Ave, North Hollywood CA 91601, USA | Actor |
| **Fuller, Rod**<br>David Powers Motorsports, 10205 Westheimer Road, Houston TX 77042, USA | Drag Racing Driver |
| **Fuller, Simon**<br>Creative Artists Agency, 2000 Ave of Stars, #100, Los Angeles CA 90067 USA | Producer, Writer |
| **Fuller, Stephen R (Steve)**<br>81 Oak Tree Lane, Bluffton SC 29910, USA | Football Player |
| **Fuller, Todd D**<br>Miami Heat, American Airlines Arena, 601 Biscayne Blvd, Miami FL 33132 USA | Basketball Player |
| **Fuller, Vernon G (Vern)**<br>155 Ironwood Circle, Aurora OH 44202, USA | Baseball Player |
| **Fuller, Victoria**<br>PO Box 6010-513, Sherman Oaks CA 91453, USA | Model, Actress |
| **Fuller, William H, Jr**<br>4025 Church Point Road, Virginia Beach VA 23455, USA | Football Player |
| **Fullerton, Larry**<br>Time Domain, 6700 Odyssey Dr NW, Huntsville AL 35806, USA | Inventor (Low Power Pulses for Messages) |
| **Fullington, Darrell**<br>1023 W Patrick Circle, Daytona Beach FL 32117, USA | Football Player |
| **Fullmer, Bradley R (Brad)**<br>400 S Barrington Ave, #202, Los Angeles CA 90049, USA | Baseball Player |
| **Fullmer, Gene**<br>9217 S Covered Wagon Circle, #B, West Jordan UT 84088, USA | Boxer |
| **Fulmer, Phillip**<br>CBS-TV, Sports Dept, 51 W 52nd St, New York NY 10019 USA | Football Coach, Sportscaster |
| **Fulton, Christina**<br>Innovative Artists, 1505 10th St, Santa Monica CA 90401 USA | Actress |
| **Fulton, Eileen**<br>60 E 42nd St, #305, New York NY 10165, USA | Actress, Singer |
| **Fulton, Fitzhugh L, Jr**<br>1023 E Ave J, #5, Lancaster CA 93535, USA | Test Pilot |
| **Fulton, Hamish**<br>John Weber Gallery, 529 W 20th St, New York NY 10011, USA | Artist |
| **Fulton, Keith**<br>Sloss Law Office, 555 W 25th St, #400, New York NY 10001, USA | Director |
| **Fulton, Robert D**<br>PO Box 2634, Waterloo IA 50704, USA | Governor, IA |
| **Fulton, Soren**<br>Paradigm Agency, 360 N Crescent Dr, North Building, Beverly Hills CA 90210 USA | Actor |
| **Fulton, William D (Bill)**<br>3001 Lexington Dr, Export PA 15632, USA | Baseball Player |
| **Fultz, Jeff**<br>J C R 3 Racing, PO Box 561001, Charlotte NC 28256, USA | Auto Racing Driver |
| **Fultz, Michael D (Mike)**<br>1900 W Foothills Road, Lincoln NE 68523, USA | Football Player |
| **Fultz, R Aaron**<br>151 Grannys Path, Millington TN 38053, USA | Baseball Player |
| **Fumusa, Dominic**<br>Gersh Agency, 9465 Wilshire Blvd, #600, Beverly Hills CA 90212 USA | Actor |
| **Funaro, Frank**<br>Back Bay Mgmt, 397 Little Neck Road, #305, Virginia Beach VA 23452 USA | Drummer (Cracker) |
| **Funchess, Thomas (Tom)**<br>1015 Funchess St, Crystal Springs MS 39059, USA | Football Player |
| **Funderburk, Leonard J**<br>2311 Lathan Road, Monroe NC 28112, USA | Vietnam War Air Force Hero |
| **Funderburke, Lawrence**<br>1688 Meadoway Court, Blacklick OH 43004, USA | Basketball Player |
| **Funk, Eric**<br>PO Box 1073, Helena MT 59624, USA | Composer |
| **Funk, Fred**<br>24729 Harbour View Dr, Ponte Vedra FL 32082, USA | Golfer |
| **Funk, Mary Wallace (Wally)**<br>243 Oak Hill Dr, Roanoke TX 76262, USA | Astronaut Candidate |
| **Funk, Thomas J (Tom)**<br>6952 N Olive St, Kansas City MO 64118, USA | Baseball Player |
| **Funke, Alex**<br>1176 Fiske St, Pacific Palisades CA 90272, USA | Cinematographer |
| **Fuqua, Antoine**<br>Creative Artists Agency, 2000 Ave of Stars, #100, Los Angeles CA 90067 USA | Director |
| **Fuqua, Johnny W Frenchy)**<br>13983 Glastonbury Ave, Detroit MI 48223, USA | Football Player |
| **Furay, Richie**<br>Agency Group, 9348 Civic Center Dr, #200, Beverly Hills CA 90210, USA | Singer (Buffalo Springfield, Poco) |
| **Furcal, Rafael A**<br>2489 Provence Circle, Weston FL 33327, USA | Baseball Player |
| **Furie, Sidney J**<br>I C M Partners, 10250 Constellation Blvd, #900, Los Angeles CA 90067 USA | Director |
| **Furlan, Mira**<br>Imperium 7 Artists, 5455 Wilshire Blvd, #1706, Los Angeles CA 90036 USA | Actress |
| **Furler, Sia**<br>Paradigm Agency, 360 N Crescent Dr, North Building, Beverly Hills CA 90210 USA | Singer, Songwriter |
| **Furlong, Edward**<br>Titus Production & Mgmt, 8335 Winnetka Ave, #277, Winnetka CA 91306, USA | Actor |

|  |  |
|------|-----------|
| **Furlong, Shirley**<br>6251 S Kimberlee Way, Chandler AZ 85249, USA | Golfer |
| **Furman, Brad**<br>Atlas Entertainment, 9200 W Sunset Blvd, Los Angeles CA 90069, USA | Director, Producer, Writer |
| **Furmaniak, Jason J (J J)**<br>184 Nottingham Dr, Bolingbrook IL 60440, USA | Baseball Player |
| **Furmann, Benno**<br>Tavistock Wood Management, 45 Conduit St, London W1S 2YN, England | Actor |
| **Furmanovsky, Jill**<br>National Portrait Gallery, Saint Martin's Place, London WC2H 0HE, England | Photographer |
| **Furnas, Barnaby**<br>Marianne Boesky Gallery, 509 W 24th St, New York NY 10011, USA | Artist |
| **Furness, Deborra-Lee**<br>Lou Coulson Assoc, 37 Berwick St, London W1V 8RS, England | Actress |
| **Furniss, Bruce M**<br>1 Segada, Rancho Santa Margarita CA 92688, USA | Swimmer |
| **Furniss, Steve**<br>6478 Frampton Circle, Huntington Beach CA 92648, USA | Swimmer |
| **Furno, Carlo Cardinal**<br>Equestrian Order of the Holy Sepulchre of Jerusalem, 00120 Vatican City | Religious Leader |
| **Furrey, Michael T (Mike)**<br>12397 Steeplechase Lane, Strongsville OH 44149, USA | Football Player |
| **Furshpan, Edwin J**<br>27 Stonewall Lane, Falmouth MA 02540, USA | Neurobiologist |
| **Furst, Alan**<br>Random House, 1745 Broadway, #1800, New York NY 10019 USA | Writer |
| **Furst, Stephen**<br>Marshak/Zachary/Mills, 8840 Wilshire Blvd, #100, Beverly Hills CA 90211 USA | Actor, Comedian |
| **Furste, Moritz**<br>U H C Hamburg, Wesselblek 8, 22339 Hamburg, Germany | Field Hockey Player |
| **Furstenberg, Frank F, Jr**<br>University of Pennsylvania, Population Studies Center, Phildelphia PA 19104, USA | Sociologist |
| **Furstenfeld, Jeremy**<br>Rainmaker Artists, PO Box 551665, Dallas TX 75355, USA | Drummer (Blue October) |
| **Furstenfeld, Justin**<br>Rainmaker Artists, PO Box 551665, Dallas TX 75355, USA | Singer, Guitarist (Blue October) |
| **Furtado, Nelly**<br>Chris Smith Mgmt, 21 Camden St, #500, Toronto ON M5V 1V2, Canada | Singer, Songwriter |
| **Furtsch Ojeda, Evelyn**<br>841 Clemenson Ave, Santa Ana CA 92705, USA | Track Athlete |
| **Furuholmen, Magne**<br>Agency Group Ltd, 361-373 City Road, London EC1V 1PQ, England | Singer, Keyboardist (A-Ha) |
| **Furukawa, Satoshi**<br>Japanese Aerospace Exploration Agency, 2-1-1 Sengen, Tsukuba, Ibaraki 305 8505, Japan | Astronaut |
| **Furuseth, Ole Christian**<br>John Colletts Alle 74, 0854 Oslo, Norway | Alpine Skier |
| **Furyk, James M (Jim)**<br>240 Deer Haven Dr, Ponte Vedra FL 32082, USA | Golfer |
| **Fusco, Mark E**<br>155 Grove St, Westwood MA 02090, USA | Ice Hockey Player |
| **Fusco, Scott M**<br>25083 Pioneer Way NW, Poulsbo WA 98370, USA | Ice Hockey Player |
| **Fusco, Simona**<br>Scott Stander Assoc, 4533 Van Nuys Blvd, #401, Sherman Oaks CA 91403 USA | Actress, Model |
| **Fusina, Charles A (Chuck)**<br>1548 King James St, Pittsburgh PA 15237, USA | Football Player |
| **Fuss, Adam**<br>151 Ave B, New York NY 10009, USA | Photographer |
| **Futey, Bohdan A**<br>US Claims Court, 717 Madison Place NW, Washington DC 20439, USA | Judge |
| **Futia, Leo R**<br>18 Interlaken Road, Greenwich CT 06830, USA | Businessman |
| **Futral, Elizabeth**<br>Neil Funkhouser Mgmt, 105 Arden St, #5G, New York NY 10040, USA | Opera Singer |
| **Futterman, Daniel (Dan)**<br>Principal Entertainment, 9255 Sunset Blvd, #500, Los Angeles CA 90069 USA | Actor, Writer |
| **Future**<br>Freebandz/Epic Records, 9830 Wilshire Blvd, Beverly Hills CA | Rap Artist, Singer |
| **Fyfe, William S**<br>1 Joanna Dr, Sainte Catherines ON L2N 1V1, Canada | Geochemist, Geologist |
| **Fyhie, Michael E (Mike)**<br>4 Wellesley Court, Trabuco Canyon CA 92679, USA | Baseball Player |
| **Fylstra, Daniel**<br>Frontline Systems, PO Box 4288, Incline Village CA 89450, USA | Computer Software Designer |
| **Fywell, Tim**<br>I C M Partners, 10250 Constellation Blvd, #900, Los Angeles CA 90067 USA | Director |

Gabaldon, Diana — Writer
PO Box 584, Scottsdale AZ 85252, USA
Gabalier, Andrea — Singer
Adlmann Musik Promotion, Deutschfeistriltz 468, 8121 Deutschfeistriltz, Austria
Gabarra, Carin L — Soccer Player, Coach
305 Rosslare Dr, Arnold MD 21012, USA
Gabbana, Stefano — Fashion Designer
Dolce & Gabbana, Via Santa Cecilia 7, 20122 Milan, Italy
Gabel, Seth — Actor
Management 360, 9111 Wilshire Blvd, Beverly Hills CA 90210 USA
Gabelli, Mario J — Financier
Gabelli Asset Mgmt, 1 Corporate Center, Rye NY 10580, USA
Gabellini, Michael — Interior Designer
Gabellini-Sheppard Assoc, 665 Broadway, #706, New York NY 10012, USA
Gabetta, Sol — Concert Cellist
Harrison/Parrott, Lucile-Grahn-Str 37, 81675 Munich, Germany
Gable, Daniel M (Danny) — Freestyle Wrestler, Coach
4343 Treefarm Lane NE, Iowa City IA 52240, USA
Gabor, William A (Billy) — Basketball Player
101 Ocean Bluffs Blvd, #501, Jupiter FL 33477, USA
Gabor, Zsa Zsa — Actress
1001 Bel Air Road, Los Angeles CA 90077, USA
Gabriel, Ana B — Singer, Composer, Actress
A G Musicales, Peten 117 Col Narvarte, Mexico City DF 03020, Mexico
Gabriel, Jani — Model
Premier Model Mgmt, 40-42 Parker St, London WC2B 5PQ, England
Gabriel, John — Actor
Access Talent Voice Overs, 171 Madison Ave, #910, New York NY 10016, USA
Gabriel, Juan — Singer, Songwriter
J E P Entertainment Group, 16027 Ventura Blvd, #510, Encino CA 91436, USA
Gabriel, Mike — Director, Animator
I C M Partners, 10250 Constellation Blvd, #900, Los Angeles CA 90067 USA
Gabriel, Peter — Singer, Keyboardist, Songwriter
Box Mill, Mill Lane, Corsham SN13 8PL, England
Gabriel, Roman I, Jr — Football Player
PO Box 4173, Calabash NC 28467, USA
Gabriela — Circus Trapeze Artist
Ringling Bros Barnum & Bailey, 8607 Westwood Circle Dr, Vienna VA 22182 USA
Gabrielle, Monique — Model, Actress
Purrfect Productions, 1231 NE 28th Ave, Pompano Beach FL 33062 USA
Gabrielson, Leonard G (Len) — Baseball Player
24230 Hillview Road, Los Altos Hills CA 94024, USA
Gaddis, John L — Historian
Ohio University, Contemporary History Institute, Brown House, Athens OH 45701, USA
Gadhia, Sameer — Singer (Young the Giant)
Foundations Artists Mgmt, 628 Broadway, #503, New York NY 10012, USA
Gadot, Gal — Actress, Model
I C M Partners, 10250 Constellation Blvd, #900, Los Angeles CA 90067 USA
Gadsby, William A (Bill) — Ice Hockey Player
28765 E Kalong Circle, Southfield MI 48034, USA
Gadzuric, Dan — Basketball Player
1312 Villa Barolo Ave, Henderson NV 89052, USA
Gaebel, Tom — Singer
Public Entertainment, Liebigstr 29, 49074 Osnabruck, Germany
Gaechter, Michael T (Mike) — Football Player
13 Horizon Point, Frisco TX 75034, USA
Gaeta, Alexander L — Optical Engineer
Cornell University, Applied & Engineering Physics Dept, Clark Hall, Ithaca NY 14853, USA
Gaeta, John — Special Effects Designer
Creative Artists Agency, 2000 Ave of Stars, #100, Los Angeles CA 90067 USA
Gaetti, Gary J — Baseball Player
7819 Silent Forest Dr, Sugar Land TX 77479, USA
Gaffigan, James — Conductor
C M Artists, 127 W 96th St, #13B, New York NY 10025 USA
Gaffigan, Jim — Actor, Comedian
Creative Artists Agency, 2000 Ave of Stars, #100, Los Angeles CA 90067 USA
Gaffney, D Jabar — Football Player
11750 Cherry Bark Dr E, Jacksonville FL 32218, USA
Gaffney, Derrick T — Football Player
11750 Cherry Bark Dr E, Jacksonville FL 32218, USA
Gaffney, F Andrew (Drew) — Astronaut
2311 Pierce Ave, Nashville TN 37232, USA
Gaffney, Mo — Actor
Stone Manners Salners, 6100 Wilshire Blvd, #1500, Los Angeles CA 90035 USA
Gage, Fred H — Neurobiologist
Salk Biological Study Institute, 10110 N Torrey Pines Road, La Jolla CA 92037, USA
Gage, John — Labor Leader
American Government Employees Federation, 80 F St NW, #700, Washington DC 20001, USA
Gage, Nathaniel L — Educator
6033 45th Ave NE, Seattle WA 98115, USA
Gage, Nicholas — Columnist, Writer
37 Nelson St, North Grafton MA 01536, USA
Gage, Paul — Computer Scientist
Crag Research, Highway 178 N, Chippewa Falls WI 55402, USA
Gaghan, Stephen — Director, Writer
Unsupervised, 10201 W Pico Blvd, #75, Los Angeles CA 90035, USA
Gagliano, Philip J (Phil) — Baseball Player
1095 Crescent Dr, Hollister MO 65672, USA
Gagliano, Robert F (Bob) — Football Player
1064 Dover Lane, Ventura CA 93001, USA
Gagne, Greg C — Baseball Player
746 Whetstone Hill Road, Somerset MA 02726, USA
Gagne, Simon — Ice Hockey Player
601 Laurel Oak Road, Voorhees NJ 08043, USA
Gagner, Larry J — Football Player
205 W Curtis St, Tampa FL 33603, USA

**Gagnon, Marc**
Speed Skating Canada, 2781 Lancaster Road, #402, Ottawa ON K1B 1A7, Canada — Speed Skater

**Gahan, David**
Mute Records, 429 Harrow Road, London W10 4RE, England — Singer (Depeche Mode)

**Gail, Max**
28198 Rey de Copas Lane, Malibu CA 90265, USA — Actor

**Gailes, Jason**
17 Mark Vincent Dr, Westford MA 01886, USA — Rowing Athlete

**Gailey, T Chandler (Chan)**
176 Rocky Branch Road, Clarkesville GA 30523, USA — Football Player, Coach

**Gaillard, Bob**
Lewis & Clark University, Athletic Dept, Pamplin Sports Center, Portland OR 97219, USA — Basketball Coach

**Gain, Robert (Bob)**
11 Nokomis Dr, Eastlake OH 44095, USA — Football Player

**Gainer, Derrick**
420 Elcino Dr, Pensacola FL 32526, USA — Boxer

**Gaines Miller, Chryste**
5408 E Saddleridge Lane, Lithonia GA 30038, USA — Track Athlete

**Gaines, Ambrose (Rowdy), IV**
6800 Hawaii Kai Dr, Honolulu HI 96825, USA — Swimmer

**Gaines, Boyd P**
9220 Sunset Blvd, #625, West Hollywood CA 90069, USA — Actor, Singer

**Gaines, C Reece**
Milwaukee Bucks, Bradley Center, 1001 N 4th St, #2, Milwaukee WI 53203 USA — Basketball Player

**Gaines, Clark**
21364 Scara Place, Broadlands VA 20148, USA — Football Player

**Gaines, Corey Y**
3968 Windansea St, Las Vegas NV 89147, USA — Basketball Player, Coach

**Gaines, Davis**
Bobby Roberts, 3050 Business Park Circle, #303, Goodlettsville TN 37221 USA — Actor, Singer

**Gaines, Ernest J**
PO Box 81, Oscar LA 70762, USA — Writer

**Gaines, William C**
Chicago Tribune, Editorial Dept, 435 N Michigan Ave, #1, Chicago IL 60611, USA — Journalist

**Gainey, Kathleen**
Director, Defense Logistics Agency, Joint Staff, Pentagon, Washington DC 20318 USA — Army General

**Gainey, Robert M (Bob)**
PO Box 829, Coppell TX 75019, USA — Ice Hockey Player, Coach

**Gainsbourg, Charlotte**
U B B A, 6 Rue de Braque, 75003 Paris, France — Actress, Singer

**Gait, Gary**
Colorado Mammouth, Pepsi Center, 1000 Chopper Circle, Denver CO 80204, USA — Lacrosse Player, Coach

**Gaiter, Dorothy J**
I C M Partners, 10250 Constellation Blvd, #900, Los Angeles CA 90067 USA — Writer

**Gaither, Gloria S**
Gaither Music Co, PO Box 737, Alexandria IN 46001, USA — Singer, Songwriter

**Gaither, Israel L**
Salvation Army USA, 615 Slaters Lane, Alexandria VA 22314, USA — Religious Leader

**Gaither, William J (Bill)**
Gaither Concerts, PO Box 178, Alexandria IN 46001, USA — Singer, Songwriter

**Gaitskill, Mary**
Pantheon/Random House, 1745 Broadway, New York NY 10019, USA — Writer

**Gajarsa, Arthur J**
US Court of Appeals, 717 Madison Place NW, Washington DC 20439, USA — Judge

**Gal, Edward**
Maatschap Dressuurstall Werner/Gal, Laarweg 15, 6732 Harskamp DG, Netherlands — Equestrian

**Galan, Nely**
Galan Entertainment, 523 Victoria Ave, Venice CA 90291, USA — Actress, Writer

**Galanos, James**
1316 Sunset Plaza Dr, Los Angeles CA 90069, USA — Fashion Designer

**Galanos, Mike**
CNN-TV, News Dept, 190 Marietta Ave SW, Atlanta GA 30303 USA — Commentator

**Galanter, Marc S**
University of Wisconsin, Law School, Madison WI 53706, USA — Attorney, Educator

**Galarraga, Andres J P**
1639 Enclave Circle, West Palm Beach FL 33411, USA — Baseball Player

**Galbraith, A Scott**
149 Arleta Ave, San Francisco CA 94134, USA — Football Player

**Galbraith, Clint**
PO Box 902, Edwardsville IL 62025, USA — Harness Racing Driver

**Galbreath, Anthony D (Tony)**
411 W 9th St, Fulton MO 65251, USA — Football Player

**Galdikas, Birute M F**
Orangutan Foundation International, 822 Wellesley Ave, Los Angeles CA 90049, USA — Anthropologist

**Gale, Michael E (Mike)**
18003 4th Ave S, Burien WA 98148, USA — Basketball Player

**Gale, Richard B (Rich)**
869 Center Park St, Daniel Island SC 29492, USA — Baseball Player

**Gale, Tristan**
Ego Sports Mgmt, PO Box 680051, Park City UT 84068, USA — Skeleton Athlete

**Galella, Ronald E (Ron)**
Ron Galella Ltd, 12 Nelson Lane, Montville NJ 07045, USA — Photographer

**Galiazzo, Marco**
Via Sorio 80/B, 35141 Padua (PD), Italy — Archery Athlete

**Galifianakis, Zachary K (Zach)**
Brillstein Entertainment Partners, 9150 Wilshire Blvd, #350, Beverly Hills CA 90212 USA — Actor, Comedian, Pianist

**Galina, Stacy**
11400 Cashmere St, Los Angeles CA 90049, USA — Actress

**Galindo, Rudy**
1115 E Haley St, Santa Barbara CA 93103, USA — Figure Skater

**Gall, Hugues R**
Opera National de Paris, 120 Rue de Lyon, 75012 Paris, France — Opera Executive

**Gall, Joseph G**
5702 Ainsley Garth, Baltimore MD 21212, USA — Biologist

**Gallacher, Kevin**
Blackburn Rovers, Ewood Park, Blackburn, Lancashire BB2 4JF, England — Soccer Player

**Gallagher**
14984 Roan Court, Wellington FL 33414, USA — Actor, Writer, Producer

**Gallagher, Brian**
United Way of America, 701 N Fairfax Ave, Lobby, Alexandria VA 22314, USA — Association Executive

**Gallagher, Bronagh**
Hamilton Hodell, 20 Golden Square, London W1F 9JL, England — Actor

**Gallagher, Chad A**
482 Wynstone Way, Rockton IL 61072, USA — Basketball Player

**Gallagher, David T (Dave)**
29 Carrs Tavern Road, Millstone Township NJ 08510, USA — Baseball Player

**Gallagher, Frank J**
6572 Enclave Dr, Clarkston MI 48348, USA — Football Player

**Gallagher, Gus**
Artists Partnership, 101 Finsbury Pavement, London EC2A 1RS, England — Actor

**Gallagher, Helen**
260 W End Ave, New York NY 10023, USA — Singer, Actress

**Gallagher, Jim, Jr**
PO Box 507, Greenwood MS 38935, USA — Golfer

**Gallagher, John, Jr**
Gersh Agency, 9465 Wilshire Blvd, #600, Beverly Hills CA 90212 USA — Actor, Singer

**Gallagher, Kathleen**
Milwaukee Journal Sentinel, Editorial Dept, PO Box 371, Milwaukee WI 53201 USA — Journalist

**Gallagher, Liam**
Beady Eye Records, PO Box 14877, London NW1 62X, England — Singer (Oasis)

**Gallagher, Megan**
Shelter Entertainment, 9454 Wilshire Blvd, #715, Beverly Hills CA 90212, USA — Actress

**Gallagher, Noel T D**
Ignition Mgmt, 54 Linhope St, London NW1 6HL, England — Singer, Guitarist (Oasis), Songwriter

**Gallagher, Peter**
Gersh Agency, 9465 Wilshire Blvd, #600, Beverly Hills CA 90212 USA — Actor, Singer

**Gallagher-Smith, Jackie**
193 Paradise Circle, Jupiter FL 33458, USA — Golfer

**Gallant, Gerard**
Montreal Canadiens, 1275 Saint Antoine St W, Montreal QC H3C 5L2, Canada — Ice Hockey Player, Coach

**Gallardo, Yovani**
Milwaukee Brewers, Miller Park, 1 Brewers Way, Milwaukee WI 53214 USA — Baseball Player

**Gallatin, Harry J**
2010 Madison Ave, Edwardsville IL 62025, USA — Basketball Player, Coach

**Gallego, Gina**
Ellis Talent Group, 4705 Laurel Canyon Blvd, #300, Valley Village CA 91607, USA — Actress

**Gallego, Michael A (Mike)**
20205 Chandler Dr, Yorba Linda CA 92887, USA — Baseball Player

**Gallegos, Reynaldo**
Greater Vision Talent Agency, 8981 Sunset Blvd, #101, Los Angeles CA 90069, USA — Actor

**Gallena, Anna**
Artmedia, 20 Ave Rapp, 75007 Paris, France — Actress

**Gallery, Robert J**
3163 210th St, Masonville IA 50654, USA — Football Player

**Galles, Rick**
Galles Racing, PO Box 2507, Albuquerque NM 87165, USA — Auto Racing Executive

**Galley, Garry M**
CBC-TV, PO Box 500, Station A, Toronto ON M5W 1E6, Canada — Ice Hockey Player

**Galli, Joseph, Jr**
Newell Rubbermaid Co, Newell Center, 29 E Stephenson St, Freeport IL 61032, USA — Businessman

**Gallico, Gregory, III**
Massachusetts General Hospital, 275 Cambridge St, Boston MA 02114, USA — Surgeon, Inventor (Synthetic Skin)

**Galligan, Zach**
Innovative Artists, 1505 10th St, Santa Monica CA 90401 USA — Actor

**Gallinari, Danilo**
Denver Nuggets, Pepsi Center, 1000 Chopper Circle, Denver CO 80204 USA — Basketball Player

**Gallion, Billy Ray**
Sovereign Talent Group, 8421 Wilshire Blvd, #200, Beverly Hills CA 90211 USA — Actor

**Gallison, Joseph**
PO Box 10187, Wilmington NC 28404, USA — Actor

**Gallo, Frank**
T R A Art Group, 1700 Stutz Dr, #15, Troy MI 48084, USA — Sculptor

**Gallo, Richard L**
University of California Medical Center, Dermatology Dept, 200 W Arbor Dr, San Diego CA 92103, USA — Dermatologist

**Gallo, Robert C**
University of Maryland, Study of Viruses Institute, Baltimore MD 21228, USA — Research Scientist

**Gallo, Valentino**
Circolo Nautico Posillipo, Via Posillipo 5, 80123 Naples, Italy — Water Polo Player

**Gallo, Vincent**
Gray Daisy Films, 8033 W Sunset Blvd, #833, Los Angeles CA 90046, USA — Actor, Director, Producer

**Gallois, Louis**
Airbus E A D S, Ronde Point Maurice Bellont 1, 31207 Blagnac, France — Businessman

**Gallop, Tom**
A P A Talent & Literary Agency, 405 S Beverly Dr, #300, Beverly Hills CA 90212 USA — Actor

**Galloway, David L**
19331 NW 19th Ave, Miami Gardens FL 33056, USA — Football Player

**Galloway, George**
Talk Sport Radio, 18 Hatfields, London SE1 8DJ, England — Government Official, England

**Galloway, Joseph S (Joey)**
ESPN-TV, Sports Dept, ESPN Plaza, 935 Middle St, Bristol CT 06010 USA — Football Player

**Gallucci, Robert L**
MacArthur Foundation, 140 S Dearborn St, Chicago IL 60603, USA — Foundation Executive

**Galvez, Balvino**
3986 SW 190th St, Miramar FL 33029, USA — Baseball Player

**Galvin, James**
University of Iowa, Writers' Workshop, Iowa City IA 52242, USA — Writer

**Galvin, John R**
2714 Lake Jodeco Dr, Jonesboro GA 30236, USA — Army General

**Galway, James**
Benseholzstr 11, 6045 Meggan, Switzerland — Concert Flutist, Conductor

**Galyon, Scott**
758 Deep Woods Lane, Seymour TN 37865, USA — Football Player

**Gam, Rita** — Actress
180 W 58th St, #8B, New York NY 10019, USA

**Gamache, Joey** — Boxer
60 Pettingill St, #2, Lewiston ME 4240, USA

**Gamba, Rumon** — Conductor
NorrlandsOperan, Operaplan 5, 901 08 Umea, Sweden

**Gamba, Veronica** — Actress, Model
32230 Alvarado Blvd, #128, Union City CA 94587, USA

**Gambee, David P (Dave)** — Basketball Player
6175 SW Arrow Wood Lane, Portland OR 97223, USA

**Gambino, Richard J** — Inventor (Read-Write Optical Storage)
State University of New York, Materials Science Dept, Stony Brook NY 11794, USA

**Gamble, Chris L** — Football Player
111 Harbor Shore Court, Mooresville NC 28117, USA

**Gamble, Ed** — Editorial Cartoonist
Florida Times-Union, Editorial Dept, 1 Riverside Ave, Jacksonville FL 32202, USA

**Gamble, John R** — Baseball Player
369 Caliente St, Reno NV 89509, USA

**Gamble, Kenneth (Kenny)** — Songwriter
W M E Entertainment, 9601 Wilshire Blvd, #300, Beverly Hills CA 90210 USA

**Gamble, Kenneth P (Kenny)** — Football Player
4 Algonquin Dr, Wilbraham MA 01095, USA

**Gamble, Kevin D** — Basketball Player
2366 Sandstone Dr, Mount Pleasant MI 48858, USA

**Gamble, Mason** — Actor
Bresler Kelly Assoc, 11500 W Olympic Blvd, #400, Los Angeles CA 90064 USA

**Gamble, Nathan** — Actor
Paradigm Agency, 360 N Crescent Dr, North Building, Beverly Hills CA 90210 USA

**Gamble, Oscar C** — Baseball Player
9705 Bent Brook Dr, Montgomery AL 36117, USA

**Gamble, Patrick K** — Air Force General, Educator
PO Box 107500, Anchorage AK 99510, USA

**Gamble, Richard F (Dick)** — Ice Hockey Player
1 Vantage Dr, Pittsford NY 14534, USA

**Gamblin, Jacques** — Actor
Agence Artiste Adequat, 108 Rue Reaumur, 75002 Paris, France

**Gamblin, Kip** — Actor
Lisa Mann Creative Mgmt, 99 Spring St, Bondi Junction NSW 2022, Australia

**Gambon, Michael J** — Actor
Independent Talent Group, 40 Whitfield St, London W1T 2RH, England

**Gambrell, David H** — Senator, GA
3205 Arden Road NW, Atlanta GA 30305, USA

**Gambrell, William E (Billy)** — Football Player
341 Osceola Ave, Bogart GA 30622, USA

**Gambril, Don** — Swimming Coach
4409 Spring Row, Northport AL 35473, USA

**Gambucci, Andre P (Andy)** — Ice Hockey Player, Coach
9241 Yukon Ave S, Minneapolis MN 55438, USA

**Gambucci, Gary A** — Ice Hockey Player
9241 Yukon Ave S, Minneapolis MN 55438, USA

**Game** — Rap Artist
I C M Partners, 10250 Constellation Blvd, #900, Los Angeles CA 90067 USA

**Gamez, Robert** — Golfer
Team Gamez Foundation, PO Box 690362, Orlando FL 32869, USA

**Gammon, Kendall R** — Football Player
14429 Maple St, Overland Park KS 66223, USA

**Gammons, Peter** — Sportswriter
Boston Globe, Editorial Dept, 135 William Morrissey Blvd, Dorchester MA 02125 USA

**Ganassi, Floyd (Chip)** — Auto Racing Driver, Executive
Chip Ganassi Racing, 8500 Westmoreland Dr, Concord NC 28027, USA

**Ganassi, Sonia** — Opera Singer
Columbia Artists Mgmt Inc, 5 Columbus Circle, 1790 Broadway, #1600, New York NY 10019 USA

**Ganatra, Nitin C** — Actor
United Agents, 12-26 Lexington St, London W1F 0LE, England

**Ganchar, Perry** — Ice Hockey Player
8043 Summerhouse Dr W, Dublin OH 43016, USA

**Gand, Gayle** — Chef
674 N Saint Clair St, Chicago IL 60611, USA

**Gandee, Sherman H (Sonny)** — Football Player
1525 Hinton St, Port Charlotte FL 33952, USA

**Gandhi, Sonia** — Government Official, India
All India Congress Party, 24 Akbar Road, New Delhi 110011, India

**Gandy, Mike J** — Football Player
8508 E Sweetwater Ave, Scottsdale AZ 85260, USA

**Gandy, Wayne L** — Football Player
6 Pinecrest Road NE, Atlanta GA 30342, USA

**Ganellin, C Robin** — Inventor (Antiulcer Compound)
University College, Chemistry Dept, 20 Gordon, London WC1H 0AJ, England

**Ganem, Edy** — Actress
McKeon-Myrones Mgmt, 3500 Olive Ave, #770, Burbank CA 91505 USA

**Gangel, Geraldine (Gig)** — Model, Actress
Playboy Promotions, 9346 Civic Center Dr, #200, Beverly Hills CA 90210 USA

**Gangloff, Mark** — Swimmer
5318 Camden Dr, Stow OH 44224, USA

**Gann, Jason W** — Actor, Writer
W M E Entertainment, 9601 Wilshire Blvd, #300, Beverly Hills CA 90210 USA

**Gann, Mike A** — Football Player
1479 Ashford Place NE, Atlanta GA 30319, USA

**Gann, Pamela B** — Educator
Claremont McKenna College, President's Office, 500 E 9th, Claremont CA 91711, USA

**Gannascoli, Joseph R** — Actor, Writer
Acme Talent Agency, 4727 Wilshire Blvd, #333, Los Angeles CA 90010 USA

**Gannaway, Preston** — Photojournalist
Concord Monitor, Editorial Dept, 1 Monitor Dr, Concord NH 03301, USA

**Gannon, Richard J (Rich)** — Football Player, Sportscaster
6472 Smithtown Road, Atlanta GA 30319, USA

**Ganso, Paulo Henrique** — Soccer Player
Confederacion de Futebol, Rua Victor Civita 66, #1, Rio de Janeiro 22775 044, Brazil
**Gant, Harry P** — Auto Racing Driver
7531 Millersville Road, Taylorsville NC 28681, USA
**Gant, Kenneth D (Kenny)** — Football Player
1820 W 10th St, Lakeland FL 33805, USA
**Gant, Reuben C** — Football Player
PO Box 3051, Tulsa OK 74101, USA
**Gant, Richard** — Actor
Pakula/King, 9229 W Sunset Blvd, #315, West Hollywood CA 90069 USA
**Gant, Robert** — Actor
Mythgarden, 960 N Ridgewood Place, Los Angeles CA 90038, USA
**Gant, Ronald E (Ron)** — Baseball Player
1027 Wellesley Crest Dr, Woodstock GA 30189, USA
**Gantz, Robert J** — Cinematographer
20 Kettle Creek Road, Weston CT 06883, USA
**Ganz, Bruno** — Actor
Braumbauer Actors, Hanfelderstr 32, 82319 Starnberg, Germany
**Ganzel, Teresa** — Actress
I C M Partners, 10250 Constellation Blvd, #900, Los Angeles CA 90067 USA
**Gao Min** — Diver
Olympic Committee, 9 Tiyuguan Road, Chongwen District, Beijing 100763, China
**Gao Xingjian** — Nobel Literature Laureate
Editions l'Aube, Le Moulin de Chateau, 84240 Le Tour d'Aigues, France
**Gao, Xiang** — Concert Violinist
Columbia Artists Mgmt Inc, 5 Columbus Circle, 1790 Broadway, #1600, New York NY 10019 USA
**Gaona, Tito** — Circus Trapeze Artist
432 Spadora Dr, Venice FL 34285, USA
**Gara, Jeremy** — Musician (Arcade Fire)
Billions Corp, 3522 W Armitage Ave, Chicago IL 60647 USA
**Garagiola, Joseph H (Joe)** — Sportscaster, Baseball Player
4555 E Mayo Blvd, #3331, Phoenix AZ 85050, USA
**Garagozzo, Keith J** — Baseball Player
16 Foxcroft Way, Mount Laurel NJ 08054, USA
**Garai, Romola** — Actress
Artist Rights Group, 4A Exmoor St, London W10 6BD, England
**Garan, Ronald J, Jr** — Astronaut
2002 Sea Cove Court, Houston TX 77058, USA
**Garant, Robert Ben** — Actor
Creative Artists Agency, 2000 Ave of Stars, #100, Los Angeles CA 90067 USA
**Garant, Sylvie** — Model, Actress
Playboy Promotions, 9346 Civic Center Dr, #200, Beverly Hills CA 90210 USA
**Garas, Kaz** — Actor
400 W 43rd St, #42L, New York NY 10036, USA
**Garavito, R Michael** — Biochemist
Michigan State University, Biochemistry Dept, East Lansing MI 48824, USA
**Garbacz, Lori** — Golfer
777 Albany Post Road, Briarcliff Manor NY 10510, USA
**Garber, H Eugene (Gene)** — Baseball Player
771 Stonemill Dr, Elizabethtown PA 17022, USA
**Garber, Helen K** — Photographer
Helen K Garber Studio, 801 Ocean Front Walk, #9, Venice Beach CA 90291, USA
**Garber, Terri** — Actress
38 E 1st St, #2B, New York NY 10003, USA
**Garber, Victor** — Actor
United Talent Agency, U T A Plaza, 9336 Civic Center Dr, Beverly Hills CA 90210 USA
**Garces, Paula** — Actress
Baker Winokur Ryder Public Relations, 9100 Wilshire Blvd, #500W, Beverly Hills CA 90212 USA
**Garces, Richard A (Rich)** — Baseball Player
605 Swigert St, Kerrville TX 78028, USA
**Garci, Jose Luis** — Director, Producer, Writer
Direccion General del Libro, Paseo de la Castellana 109, 20846 Madrid, Spain
**Garcia Bernal, Gael** — Actor, Director, Producer
Canana Films, San Luis Potosi, #211 Piso 8, Colonia Roma, Mexico City  DF 06700, Mexico
**Garcia Swisher, Joanna** — Actress
John Carrabino Mgmt, 5900 Wilshire Blvd, #406, Los Angeles CA 90036 USA
**Garcia, Adam G** — Actor
I C M Partners, 10250 Constellation Blvd, #900, Los Angeles CA 90067 USA
**Garcia, Aimee** — Actress
Paradigm Agency, 360 N Crescent Dr, North Building, Beverly Hills CA 90210 USA
**Garcia, Alfonso R (Kiko)** — Baseball Player
526 Trailview Circle, Martinez CA 94553, USA
**Garcia, Andy** — Actor
CineSon Entertainment, 4519 Varna Ave, Sherman Oaks CA 91423, USA
**Garcia, Carlos J** — Baseball Player
5208 William St, Lancaster NY 14086, USA
**Garcia, Danna** — Actress, Singer, Model
Innovative Artists, 1505 10th St, Santa Monica CA 90401 USA
**Garcia, Danny (Swift)** — Boxer
Golden Boy Promotions, 626 Wilshire Blvd, #350, Los Angeles CA 90017 USA
**Garcia, David (Dave)** — Baseball Manager
17842 Avenida Cordillera, #28, San Diego CA 92128, USA
**Garcia, Eric** — Writer
W M E Entertainment, 9601 Wilshire Blvd, #300, Beverly Hills CA 90210 USA
**Garcia, Freddy A** — Baseball Player
Quisquella Gta Etapa M22, #52, La Ramana, Dominican Republic
**Garcia, G Karim** — Baseball Player
38 Agnew Farm Road, Armonk NY 10504, USA
**Garcia, Gina** — Artist
Garcia Art Glass, 123 Losoya St, #5, San Antonio TX 78205, USA
**Garcia, Gregory Thomas** — Producer, Writer
Creative Artists Agency, 2000 Ave of Stars, #100, Los Angeles CA 90067 USA
**Garcia, Guillermo A** — Baseball Player
3806 Shoma Dr, West Palm Beach FL 33414, USA
**Garcia, Jeffrey J (Jeff)** — Football Player
PO Box 8977, Rancho Santa Fe CA 92067, USA

**Garcia, Jesse** — Actor
Evolution Entertainment, 901 N Highland Ave, Los Angeles CA 90038 USA

**Garcia, Jesus** — Singer
Columbia Artists Mgmt Inc, 5 Columbus Circle, 1790 Broadway, #1600, New York NY 10019 USA

**Garcia, Jorge** — Actor
L I N K Entertainment, 11872 La Grange Ave, Los Angeles CA 90025 USA

**Garcia, Juan Carlos** — Actor
Gabriel Blanco, Rio Balsas 35-32, Colonia Cuauhtemoc DF 6500, Mexico

**Garcia, Lucrezia** — Opera Singer
I M G Artists, Hogarth Business Park, Chiswick, London W4 2TH, England

**Garcia, Mayte** — Actress
C E S D, 10635 Santa Monica Blvd, #130, Los Angeles CA 90025 USA

**Garcia, Miguel A (Mike)** — Baseball Player
28428 Eagle St, Moreno Valley CA 92555, USA

**Garcia, Nicole** — Actress
Voyez Mon Agent, 20 Ave Rapp, 75007 Paris, France

**Garcia, Pedro M** — Baseball Player
Parque del Condado L4, Urb Bairoa Park, Caguas PR 00725, USA

**Garcia, Richard R (Rich)** — Baseball Umpire
769 Harbor Isle, Clearwater FL 33767, USA

**Garcia, Rodrigo** — Director, Producer
W I G S C O, 3815 Hughes Ave, Culver City CA 90232, USA

**Garcia, Rupert** — Artist
Aurobora Press, 370 Brannan St, #100, San Francisco CA 94107, USA

**Garcia, Sergio** — Golfer
International Mangement Group, 1 Erieview Plaza, 1360 E 9th St, #100, Cleveland OH 44114 USA

**Garcia-Bellido, Antonio** — Biologist
Spanish National Research Council, Serrano 117, 28006 Madrid, Spain

**Garcia-Lorido, Dominik** — Actress
McKeon-Myrones Mgmt, 3500 Olive Ave, #770, Burbank CA 91505 USA

**Garciaparra, A Nomar** — Baseball Player
613 15th St, Manhattan Beach CA 90266, USA

**Garcon, Pierre** — Football Player
Washington Redskins, 21300 Redskin Park Dr, Ashburn VA 20147 USA

**Gard, Robert G, Jr** — Army General
Center for Arms Control, 322 4th St NE, Washington DC 20002, USA

**Gard, Toby** — Video Games Designer (Lara Croft)
SCi Entertainment Group, 1 Hartfield Road, London SW19 3RU, England

**Gardell, Billy** — Actor, Comedian
Creative Artists Agency, 2000 Ave of Stars, #100, Los Angeles CA 90067 USA

**Gardener, Daryl R** — Football Player
8925 Legacy Court, #106, Kissimmee FL 34747, USA

**Gardener, Jason** — Track Athlete
Athletics World Mgmt, 7097 Alvern St, #308, Los Angeles CA 90045 USA

**Gardenhire, Ronald C (Ron)** — Baseball Player, Manager
585 County Road B2 E, Saint Paul MN 55117, USA

**Gardiner, Greg** — Cinematographer
Paradigm Agency, 360 N Crescent Dr, North Building, Beverly Hills CA 90210 USA

**Gardiner, John Eliot** — Conductor
Monteverdi Choir & Orchestra, 25 Cabot Square, Canary Wharf, London E14 4QA, England

**Gardiner, Margaret** — Beauty Queen
Andre Nel, 200 UCLA Medical Plaza, Los Angeles CA 90095, USA

**Gardiner, Michael J (Mike)** — Baseball Player
26 Read Dr, Hanover MA 02339, USA

**Gardner, Ashley** — Actress
S M S Talent, 8383 Wilshire Blvd, #230, Beverly Hills CA 90211 USA

**Gardner, Barry A** — Football Player
24964 S Willow Brook Trail, Crete IL 60417, USA

**Gardner, Brett M** — Baseball Player
117 Drake St, Charleston SC 29403, USA

**Gardner, Carwell E** — Football Player
9603 Galene Dr, Louisville KY 40299, USA

**Gardner, David P** — Educator, Foundation Executive
2989 American Saddler Dr, Park City UT 84060, USA

**Gardner, Dede** — Producer
Plan B Entertainment, 9150 Wilshire Blvd, #350, Beverly Hills CA 90212, USA

**Gardner, Emerson N, Jr** — Marine Corps General
Deputy CofS, Programs & Resources, HqUSMC, 2 Navy St, Washington DC 20380 USA

**Gardner, Guy S** — Astronaut
N A S A, Johnson Space Center, 2101 NASA Road, Houston TX 77058 USA

**Gardner, Howard E** — Psychologist, Neurobiologist
Harvard University, Graduate Education School, Cambridge MA 02138, USA

**Gardner, James** — Director
Shapiro-Lichtman, 8827 Beverly Blvd, Los Angeles CA 90048 USA

**Gardner, Jeffrey S (Jeff)** — Baseball Player
1906 Port Weybridge Place, Newport Beach CA 92660, USA

**Gardner, John** — Ballet Dancer
American Ballet Theatre, 890 Broadway, #300, New York NY 10003 USA

**Gardner, Lisa** — Writer
Jane Rotrosen Agency, 318 E 51st St, New York NY 10022, USA

**Gardner, Mark A** — Baseball Player
15216 Mesa View Ave, Friant CA 93626, USA

**Gardner, Randy** — Figure Skater
4640 Glencoe Ave, #6, Marina del Rey CA 90292, USA

**Gardner, Robert G** — Educator
Harvard University, Visual & Environmental Studies Dept, Cambridge MA 02138, USA

**Gardner, Roderick F (Rod)** — Football Player
1883 Executive Dr, Duluth GA 30096, USA

**Gardner, Rulon** — Greco-Roman Wrestler
Elite Training Center, 981 S Main St, #130, Logan UT 84321, USA

**Gardner, Tom** — Editor
124 N Pitt St, Alexandria VA 22314, USA

**Gardner, Wesley B (Wes)** — Baseball Player
305 Ruth, Benton AR 72019, USA

**Gardner, Wilford R** — Physicist
University of California, Natural Resources College, Berkeley CA 94720, USA

**Gardner, William F (Billy)** — Baseball Player, Manager
35 Dayton Road, Waterford CT 06385, USA

**Gardocki, Christopher A (Chris)** — Football Player
63 Yorkshire Dr, Hilton Head Island SC 29928, USA

**Gardot, Melody** — Singer, Pianist, Guitarist
W M E Entertainment, 9601 Wilshire Blvd, #300, Beverly Hills CA 90210 USA

**Gare, Danny** — Ice Hockey Player
950 Hopkins Road, #F, Buffalo NY 14221, USA

**Garelick, Jeremy** — Producer, Writer
United Talent Agency, U T A Plaza, 9336 Civic Center Dr, Beverly Hills CA 90210 USA

**Garfat, Jance** — Bassist, Singer (Dr Hook)
Artists Int'l Mgmt, 9850 Sandalwood Road, #458, Boca Raton FL 33428, USA

**Garfield, Allen** — Actor
8271 Melrose Ave, #203, Los Angeles CA 90046, USA

**Garfield, Andrew** — Actor
Gordon & French, 12-13 Poland St, London W1F 8QB, England

**Garfunkel, Art** — Singer, Actor
Metropolitan Talent Agency, 5405 Wilshire Blvd, #218, Los Angeles CA 90036 USA

**Garity, Troy** — Actor
Untitled Entertainment, 350 S Beverly Dr, #200, Beverly Hills CA 90212 USA

**Garko, Ryan F** — Baseball Player
1120 Saxon Way, Menlo Park CA 94025, USA

**Garland, Alex** — Writer
Creative Artists Agency, 2000 Ave of Stars, #100, Los Angeles CA 90067 USA

**Garland, George D** — Geophysicist
5 Mawhiney Court, Huntsville ON P0A 1K0, Canada

**Garland, Jon S** — Baseball Player
2924 Summerwood Dr, Springfield IL 62712, USA

**Garland, Nicholas** — Editorial Cartoonist
Daily Telegraph, 111 Buckingham Palace Road, London SW1W 0DT, England

**Garland, R Wayne** — Baseball Player
7556 Mossback St, Las Vegas NV 89123, USA

**Garland, Winston K** — Basketball Player
1512 Southoak Dr, Nashville TN 37211, USA

**Garlin, Jeff** — Actor, Producer
I C M Partners, 10250 Constellation Blvd, #900, Los Angeles CA 90067 USA

**Garlits, Donald G (Big Daddy)** — Drag Racing Driver
Garlits Racing Museum, 13700 SW 16th Ave, Ocala FL 34473, USA

**Garmaker, Richard E (Dick)** — Basketball Player
5824 E 111th St, Tulsa OK 74137, USA

**Garman, Michael D (Mike)** — Baseball Player
15144 Kings Row Road, Caldwell ID 83607, USA

**Garn, E Jacob (Jake)** — Senator, UT; Astronaut
1267 Chalder Circle, Salt Lake City UT 84103, USA

**Garn, Stanley M** — Anthropologist
1200 Earhart Road, #223, Ann Arbor MI 48105, USA

**Garneau, Marc** — Astronaut, Canada
Space Agency, 6767 Route de Aeroport, Sainte-Hubert QC J3Y 8Y9, Canada

**Garner, Charlie, III** — Football Player
16220 Nottingham Park Way, Tampa FL 33647, USA

**Garner, Jennifer** — Actress
Vandalia Films, 9100 Wilshire Blvd, #1000W, Beverly Hills CA 90212, USA

**Garner, Kelli** — Actress
John Carrabino Mgmt, 5900 Wilshire Blvd, #406, Los Angeles CA 90036 USA

**Garner, Philip M (Phil)** — Baseball Player, Manager
2 Sapling Place, Spring TX 77382, USA

**Garner, Wendell R** — Psychologist
105 Northcreek Circle, Walnut Creek CA 94598, USA

**Garner, William S** — Editorial Cartoonist
Memphis Commercial Appeal, Editorial Dept, 495 Union Ave, Memphis TN 38103, USA

**Garnes, Sam A** — Football Player
7322 S Valdai Circle, Aurora CO 80016, USA

**Garnett, Kevin M** — Basketball Player
101 1st St, #44, Cambridge MA 02141, USA

**Garofalo, Janeane** — Actress, Comedienne
I C M Partners, 10250 Constellation Blvd, #900, Los Angeles CA 90067 USA

**Garouste, Gerard** — Artist
La Mesangere, 27810 Marcilly-sur-Eure, France

**Garr, Ralph A** — Baseball Player
22314 Auburn Canyon Lane, Richmond TX 77469, USA

**Garr, Teri** — Actress
Paradigm Agency, 360 N Crescent Dr, North Building, Beverly Hills CA 90210 USA

**Garrard, David D** — Football Player
4372 Hunterston Lane, Jacksonville FL 32224, USA

**Garrard, Rose** — Artist, Sculptor
105 Carpenters Road, #21, London E18, England

**Garre, Gregory G** — Government Official, Attorney
George Washington University, Law Center, Washington DC 20052, USA

**Garrel, Louis** — Actor
Agence Artiste Adequat, 108 Rue Reaumur, 75002 Paris, France

**Garrelts, Scott W** — Baseball Player
11070 Ashland Way, Shreveport LA 71106, USA

**Garrett, Brad** — Actor, Comedian
United Talent Agency, U T A Plaza, 9336 Civic Center Dr, Beverly Hills CA 90210 USA

**Garrett, Carl L** — Football Player
203 S Crawford St, Denton TX 76205, USA

**Garrett, David** — Concert Violinist
Music & Media Partnership, 126-129 Power Road, London W4 5PY, England

**Garrett, Eldo (Dick)** — Basketball Player
7100 N Park Manor Dr, Milwaukee WI 53224, USA

**Garrett, H Adrian (Ade)** — Baseball Player
PO Box 201, Manchaca TX 78652, USA

**Garrett, H Lawrence, III** — Government Official
RR 1 Box 136-18, Boyce VA 22620, USA

**Garrett, Jason C** — Football Player, Coach
3656 Maplewood Ave, Dallas TX 75205, USA

**Garrett, Jeremy** — Actor
W M E Entertainment, 9601 Wilshire Blvd, #300, Beverly Hills CA 90210 USA

**Garrett, John M** — Ice Hockey Player
Rogers Sportsnet, 181 Keefer Place, #221, Vancouver BC V6B 6C1, Canada

**Garrett, Kathleen** — Actress
Don Buchwald Talent Agency, 10 E 44th St, New York NY 10017 USA

**Garrett, Kenneth** — Photographer
National Geographic, Editorial Dept, 1145 17th St NW, Washington DC 20036 USA

**Garrett, Kenny** — Jazz Saxophonist, Flutist
Management Ark, 116 Village Blvd, #200, Princeton NJ 08540, USA

**Garrett, LaMonica** — Actor
Elevate Entertainment, 1925 Century Park E, #2320 Los Angeles CA 90067, USA

**Garrett, Leif** — Actor, Singer
Barbara Papageorge, 790 Amsterdam Ave, #4E, New York NY 10025, USA

**Garrett, Leonard N (Len)** — Football Player
9413 W Tampa Dr, Baton Rouge LA 70815, USA

**Garrett, Lesley** — Opera Singer
Music Partnership, 41 Aldebert Terrace, London SW8 1BH, England

**Garrett, Maureen** — Actress
Paradigm Agency, 360 N Crescent Dr, North Building, Beverly Hills CA 90210 USA

**Garrett, Megan** — Keyboardist (Casting Crowns)
Proper Mgmt, PO Box 150867, Nashville TN 37215, USA

**Garrett, Pat** — Singer, Guitarist, Songwriter
Gold Dust Talent/Records, RR 78, Exit 19, Strausstown PA 19559, USA

**Garrett, Peter R** — Singer, Government Official
806-812 Anzac Parade, #600, PO Box 249, Maroubra NSW 2035, Australia

**Garrett, R Wayne** — Baseball Player
4331 Linwood St, Sarasota FL 34232, USA

**Garrett, Siedah** — Singer (Brand New Heavies), Songwriter
McClure & Associates Public Relations, 5225 Wilshire Blvd, #909, Los Angeles CA 90036, USA

**Garrett, Spencer** — Actor
Stone Manners Salners, 6100 Wilshire Blvd, #1500, Los Angeles CA 90035 USA

**Garrett, Wilbur E (Bill)** — Editor
209 Seneca Road, Great Falls VA 22066, USA

**Garrick, Barbara** — Actress
CornerStone Talent, 37 W 20th St, #1108, New York NY 10011, USA

**Garrick, Thomas S (Tom)** — Basketball Player
235 Providence St, West Warwick RI 02893, USA

**Garrido Davidds, Norberto, Jr** — Football Player
15633 Briarbank St, La Puente CA 91744, USA

**Garrido, Gil G** — Baseball Player
11311 SW 200th St, #110D, Miami FL 33157, USA

**Garrigus, Thomas** — Marksman
PO Box 681, Plains MT 59859, USA

**Garriott, Owen K** — Astronaut
111 Lost Tree Dr SW, Huntsville AL 35824, USA

**Garriott, Richard A** — Tourist Cosmonaut
NCsoft, 6801 N Capital of Texas Highway, #1-102, Austin TX 78731, USA

**Garris, Mick** — Director
Paradigm Agency, 360 N Crescent Dr, North Building, Beverly Hills CA 90210 USA

**Garrison, David** — Actor
S M S Talent, 8383 Wilshire Blvd, #230, Beverly Hills CA 90211 USA

**Garrison, Gary L** — Football Player
7757 Caminito Encanto Lane, #102, Carlsbad CA 92009, USA

**Garrison, Lane** — Actor, Writer
Untitled Entertainment, 350 S Beverly Dr, #200, Beverly Hills CA 90212 USA

**Garrison, Walter B (Walt)** — Football Player
3475 E Hickory Hill Road, Argyle TX 76226, USA

**Garrison, Webster L** — Baseball Player
2038 Rue Racine, Marrero LA 70072, USA

**Garrison, Zina** — Tennis Player
All Court Tennis Foundation, 12335 Kingsride, #106, Houston TX 77024, USA

**Garrity, Gregg D** — Football Player
86 Seldom Seen Road, Bradfordwoods PA 15015, USA

**Garrity, John (Jack)** — Ice Hockey Player
1530 Beacon St, #1201, Brookline MA 02446, USA

**Garrity, Patrick J (Pat)** — Basketball Player
6126 Ches Court, Orlando FL 32819, USA

**Garrix, Martin** — DJ Musician
Ace Agency, Tuinstraat 237, 1015 Amsterdam PD, Netherlands

**Garro, Julia** — Actress
Innovative Artists, 1505 10th St, Santa Monica CA 90401 USA

**Garron, Lawrence (Larry), Jr** — Football Player
3 Debra Lane, Framingham MA 01701, USA

**Garrone, Matteo** — Director
Archimede, Via Tiburtina 521, 00159 Rome, Italy

**Garson, Willie** — Actor
John Carrabino Mgmt, 5900 Wilshire Blvd, #406, Los Angeles CA 90036 USA

**Garten, Ina** — Food Expert
46 Newton Ave, #3, East Hampton NY 11937, USA

**Garth, Jennie** — Actress
Paradigm Agency, 360 N Crescent Dr, North Building, Beverly Hills CA 90210 USA

**Garth, Leonard I** — Judge
US Court of Appeals, US Courthouse, 50 Walnut St, #5040, Newark NJ 07102, USA

**Gartner, Claus-Theo** — Actor
Postfach 230313, 45071 Essen, Germany

**Gartner, James** — Director
I C M Partners, 10250 Constellation Blvd, #900, Los Angeles CA 90067 USA

**Gartner, Michael A (Mike)** — Ice Hockey Player
N H L Players Assn, 1700-20 Bay St, Toronto ON M5J 2N8, Canada

**Gartner, Michael G** — Publisher, Editor, Businessman
100 Market St, #515, Des Moines IA 50309, USA

**Gartner, Stephen** — Artist
Gartner & Blade, 4-1354 Kuhio Highway, Kapaa HI 96746, USA

**Garver, Kathy** — Actress
PO Box 117345, Burlingame CA 94011, USA

**Garver, Ned F** — Baseball Player
1121 Town Line Road, #164, Bryan OH 43506, USA
**Garvey, Rea** — Singer, Guitarist, Songwriter
Jewelmusic, Dresdener Str 109, 10179 Berlin, Germany
**Garvey, Steven P (Steve)** — Baseball Player
Athlete Promotions, 2247 Rickover Place, Winter Garden FL 34787, USA
**Garwin, Richard L** — Physicist
1 Christie Place, #402W, Scarsdale NY 10583, USA
**Gary, Keith J** — Football Player
1401 N Taft St, #821, Arlington VA 22201, USA
**Gary, Lorraine** — Actress
1158 Tower Dr, Beverly Hills CA 90210, USA
**Garza, David** — Singer
Partisan Arts, PO Box 5085, Larkspur CA 94977, USA
**Garza, Emilio M** — Judge
US Court of Appeals, US Courthouse, 8200 I-10 W, San Antonio TX 78230, USA
**Garza, Henry** — Guitarist (Los Lonely Boys)
Loophole Entertainment, PO Box 162045, Austin TX 78716, USA
**Garza, JoJo** — Bassist (Los Lonely Boys)
Loophole Entertainment, PO Box 162045, Austin TX 78716, USA
**Garza, Loreto** — Boxer
6 Napa Place, Woodland CA 95695, USA
**Garza, Matthew S (Matt)** — Baseball Player
Milwaukee Brewers, Miller Park, 1 Brewers Way, Milwaukee WI 53214 USA
**Garza, Nicole** — Actress, Model
N T A Talent Agency, 1445 N Stanley Ave, #200, Los Angeles CA 90046, USA
**Garza, Ringo** — Drummer (Los Lonely Boys)
Loophole Entertainment, PO Box 162045, Austin TX 78716, USA
**Garzon, Baltasar** — Judge
Audiencia Nacional, Garcia Gutierrez 1, 28004 Madrid, Spain
**Gascoigne, Paul J** — Soccer Player
Robertson Craig Co, Clairmont Gardens, Glasgow G3 7LW, Scotland
**Gascoine, Jill** — Actress
Marina Martin, 12/13 Poland St, London W1V 3DE, England
**Gash, Samuel L (Sam)** — Football Player
18549 Steep Hollow Court, Northville MI 48168, USA
**Gaskell, Anna** — Photographer
Albright-Kerr Gallery, 1285 Elmwood Ave, Buffalo NY 14222, USA
**Gaskin, F Neal, Jr** — Architect
Gaskin Architectural, 2900 S Rancho Drive, #101, Las Vegas NV 89102, USA
**Gaskins, Reggie** — Actor, Director, Writer
I C M Partners, 10250 Constellation Blvd, #900, Los Angeles CA 90067 USA
**Gasol I Saez, Pau** — Basketball Player
Chicago Bulls, United Center, 1901 W Madison St, Chicago IL 60612 USA
**Gasol I Sasez, Marc** — Basketball Player
Memphis Grizzlies, 191 Beale St, Memphis TN 38103 USA
**Gaspar, Rodney E (Rod)** — Baseball Player
28771 Peach Blossom, Mission Viejo CA 92692, USA
**Gasparovic, Ivan** — President, Slovakia
President's Office, Hodzova Namestie 2978/1, 81006 Bratislava, Slovakia
**Gasquet, Richard** — Tennis Player
49 Rue Gaite, 92140 Clamart, France
**Gass, Kyle R** — Actor, Singer, Guitarist
Greene Assoc, 1901 Ave of Stars, #130, Los Angeles CA 90067 USA
**Gass, William H** — Philosopher, Writer
6304 Westminster Place, Saint Louis MO 63130, USA
**Gass-Donnelly, Ed** — Director
I C M Partners, 10250 Constellation Blvd, #900, Los Angeles CA 90067 USA
**Gassiyev, Nikolai T** — Opera Singer
Mariinsky Theater, Teatralnaya Square 1, 190000 Saint Petersburg, Russia
**Gassner, Dave** — Baseball Player
N1376 Woodland Dr, Greenville WI 54942, USA
**Gast, Alice P** — Educator
Lehigh University, President's Office, 27 Memorial Dr W, Bethlehem PA 18015, USA
**Gasteyer, Ana K** — Actress, Comedienne
Gersh Agency, 9465 Wilshire Blvd, #600, Beverly Hills CA 90212 USA
**Gastineau, Marcus D (Mark)** — Football Player
22202 N 48th St, Phoenix AZ 85054, USA
**Gaston, Clarence E (Cito)** — Baseball Player, Manager
1454 Woodstream Dr, Oldsmar FL 34677, USA
**Gaston, Marilyn H** — Physician, Administrator
Gaston-Porter Health Improvement Center, 8612 Timber Hill, Potomac MD 20854, USA
**Gaston, Michael** — Actor
A P A Talent & Literary Agency, 405 S Beverly Dr, #300, Beverly Hills CA 90212 USA
**Gate, Aaron** — Cyclist
6 Kipling Ave, Epsom Auckland 1023, New Zealand
**Gates, Antonio M** — Football Player
PO Box 11369, Charlotte NC 28220, USA
**Gates, Brent R** — Baseball Player
4229 Haralson Court SE, Grand Rapids MI 49546, USA
**Gates, David** — Singer, Keyboardist (Bread), Songwriter
Icon Performing Arts, 1557 Westwood Blvd, #242, Los Angeles CA 90024, USA
**Gates, Gareth P** — Singer
Insanity Artists, 5 Little Portland St, London W1W 7JD, England
**Gates, Henry Lewis, Jr** — Educator
Harvard University, Afro-American Studies Dept, Cambridge MA 02138, USA
**Gates, Marshall D, Jr** — Chemist
41 W Brook Road, Pittsford PA 14534, USA
**Gates, Tucker** — Director, Producer
United Talent Agency, U T A Plaza, 9336 Civic Center Dr, Beverly Hills CA 90210 USA
**Gates, William H (Bill), III** — Computer Software Designer, Businessman
Bill & Melinda Gates Foundation, 500 5th Ave N, Seattle WA 98102, USA
**Gatewood, Mark** — Artist
Gatewood Studio, 211 SE Morrison St, Portland OR 97214, USA
**Gathegi, Edi** — Actor
Framework Entertainment, 9057 Nemo St, #C, West Hollywood CA 90069 USA

**Gathright, Joey R**
9100 Dr Martin Luther King Jr St N, #902, Saint Petersburg FL 33702, USA
Baseball Player

**Gatien, Elise**
Carrie Wheeler Mgmt, 101-1001 W Broadway, #338, Vancouver BC V6H 4E4, Canada
Actress

**Gatins, John**
United Talent Agency, U T A Plaza, 9336 Civic Center Dr, Beverly Hills CA 90210 USA
Actor, Writer

**Gatlin, Justin**
6979 Raburn Road, Pensacola FL 32526, USA
Track Athlete

**Gatlin, Larry W**
Press Office, 1009 16th Ave S, Nashville TN 37212, USA
Singer, Songwriter (Gatlin Brothers)

**Gatling, Chris R**
175 Canon Dr, Orinda CA 94563, USA
Basketball Player

**Gatos, Harry C**
20 Indian Hill Road, Weston MA 02493, USA
Electrical Engineer

**Gatti, Daniele**
Via Scaglia Est 134, 41100 Modena, Italy
Conductor

**Gatti, Jennifer**
S D B Partners, 315 S Beverly Dr, #411, Beverly Hills CA 90067 USA
Actress

**Gatting, Michael W**
Middlesex Cricket Club, Saint John's Wood Road, London NW8 8QN, England
Cricketer

**Gattison, Kenneth A (Kenny)**
1115 I St NE, Washington DC 20002, USA
Basketball Player

**Gaubatz, Dennis E**
1250 County Road 943, West Columbia TX 77486, USA
Football Player

**Gauci, Miriam**
Kunstleragentur Raab & Bohm, Plankengasse 7, 1010 Vienna, Austria
Opera Singer

**Gauck, Joachim**
Bundespraesidialamt, Spreeweg 1, 10557 Berlin, Germany
President, Germany; Political Activist

**Gaudin, Chad E**
511 Vecino St, Benicia CA 94510, USA
Baseball Player

**Gaudio, Robert J (Bob)**
I C M Partners, 10250 Constellation Blvd, #900, Los Angeles CA 90067 USA
Singer, Organist (Four Seasons)

**Gaughan, Brendan**
Germain Racing, 218 Raceway Drive, Mooresville NC 28117, USA
Truck Racing Driver

**Gault, Scott**
Roger A Gault, 615 Park Way, Piedmont CA 94611, USA
Rowing Athlete

**Gault, William Campbell**
481 Mountain Dr, Santa Barbara CA 93103, USA
Writer

**Gault, Willie J**
15460 La Maida St, Sherman Oaks CA 91403, USA
Football Player

**Gaultier, Jean-Paul**
30 Rue Saint Martin, 75003 Paris, France
Fashion Designer

**Gauthier, Dan**
Michael Einfeld Mgmt, 10630 Moorpark Ave, #101, Toluca Lake CA 91602, USA
Actor

**Gauthier, Daniel**
Cirque du Soleil, 8400 2nd Ave, Montreal QC H1Z 4M6, Canada
Circus Executive

**Gauthier, Jean P**
415 Vinet Ave, Dorval QC H9S 2M7, Canada
Ice Hockey Player

**Gauthier, Mary**
Mark Spector Co, 100 5th Ave, #1100, New York NY 10011
Singer, Songwriter

**Gautier, Dick**
11333 Moorpark St, #59, North Hollywood CA 91602, USA
Actor

**Gava, Cassandra**
1745 Camino Palmero St, #210, Los Angeles CA 90046, USA
Actress

**Gavanelli, Paolo**
I M G Artists, Hogarth Business Park, Chiswick, London W4 2TH, England
Opera Singer

**Gavankar, Janina**
TalentWorks, 3500 W Olive Ave, #1400, Burbank CA 91505 USA
Actress

**Gavaris, Jason**
Gary Goddard Agency, 149 Church St, #200, Toronto ON M5B 1Y4, Canada
Actor

**Gavaskar, Sunil M**
Nirlon Synthetics, Annie Besant Road, #254B, Worli, Mumbai 400025, India
Cricketer

**Gavey, Aaron**
84 Park Place Dr, Sault Sainte Marie ON P6B 6L3, Canada
Ice Hockey Player

**Gavin, John**
606 N Larchmont Blvd, #210, Los Angeles CA 90004, USA
Actor, Diplomat

**Gaviria Trujillo, Cesar**
Club de Madrid, C/Goya 5-7, Pasaje 2, 28001 Madrid, Spain
President, Colombia

**Gavrilov, Andrei V**
Konzertdirektion Schlote, Danreitergasse 4, 5020 Salzburg, Austria
Concert Pianist

**Gavron, Rafi**
Affirmative Entertainment, 425 N Robertson Blvd, Los Angeles CA 90048 USA
Actor

**Gay, Don**
1818 Rodeo Dr, Mesquite TX 75149, USA
Rodeo Rider

**Gay, Gerald H (Jerry)**
2121 Madison St, #C, Everett WA 98203, USA
Photojournalist

**Gay, J Brian**
Professional Golfers Association, 100 Ave of Champions, Palm Beach Gardens FL 33418 USA
Golfer

**Gay, Peter J**
270 Riverside Dr, #8C, New York NY 10025, USA
Historian

**Gay, Randall J, Jr**
6706 Joyce Dr, #3C, Addis LA 70710, USA
Football Player

**Gay, Rudy C, Jr**
91 W Galloway Dr, Memphis TN 38111, USA
Basketball Player

**Gay, Tyson**
Global Athletics & Marketing, 437 Boylston St, #400, Boston MA 02116, USA
Track Athlete

**Gay, William H (Bill)**
8200 E Jefferson Ave, #804, Detroit MI 48214, USA
Football Player

**Gaydukov, Sergei N**
Cosmonaut Training Center, Star City, 141160 Zvezdny Gorodok, Moscow Oblast, Russia
Cosmonaut

**Gayheart, Rebecca**
Gersh Agency, 9465 Wilshire Blvd, #600, Beverly Hills CA 90212 USA
Actress, Model

**Gayl, Franz**
5823 Crowfoot Dr, Burke VA 22015, USA
Military Activist

**Gayle, Crystal**
Gayle Enterprises, 51 Music Square E, Nashville TN 37203, USA
Singer

**Gayle, Michelle P** — Singer, Actress
Mission Control, City Business Center, Lower Road, London SE16 2XB, England
**Gayle, Robyn K** — Soccer Player
Canadian Soccer, Place Soccer Canada, 237 Metcalfe St, Ottawa ON K2P 1R2, Canada
**Gayle, Shaun L** — Football Player
1530 N Elk Grove Ave, #1, Chicago IL 60622, USA
**Gaylor, Christopher J (Chris)** — Drummer (All-American Rejects)
Creative Artists Agency, 2000 Ave of Stars, #100, Los Angeles CA 90067 USA
**Gaylord, Frank** — Sculptor
2844 Vermont Route 14, Williamstown VT 05679, USA
**Gaylord, Mitchell J (Mitch)** — Gymnast, Actor
9601 Bowman Dr, Fort Worth TX 76244, USA
**Gaynes, George** — Actor
Innovative Artists, 1505 10th St, Santa Monica CA 90401 USA
**Gaynor, Gloria** — Singer
Red Entertainment Agency, 505 8th Ave, #1004, New York NY 10018, USA
**Gaynor, Mitzi** — Actress, Dancer, Singer
517 N Bedford Dr, Beverly Hills CA 90210, USA
**Gayoom, Maumoon Abdul** — President, Maldives
Ma Ki'nbigasdhoshuge, Male 20229, Maldives
**Gayson, Eunice** — Actress
Spotlight, 7 Leicester Place, London WC2H 7BP, England
**Gayton, Joe** — Producer, Writer
United Talent Agency, U T A Plaza, 9336 Civic Center Dr, Beverly Hills CA 90210 USA
**Gayton, Tony** — Producer, Writer
United Talent Agency, U T A Plaza, 9336 Civic Center Dr, Beverly Hills CA 90210 USA
**Gazarek, Sara** — Singer, Guitarist
Stiletto Entertainment, 5200 W 83rd St, #G, Los Angeles CA 90045, USA
**Gaze, Andrew** — Basketball Player
Basketball Resources, PO Box 2222, Ivanhoe East VIC 3029, Australia
**Gazit, Doron** — Artist
Air Dimensional Inc, 14141 Covello St, Building 1, Van Nuys CA 91405, USA
**Gazzaniga, Michael S** — Psychologist
University of California, Study of Mind Center, Santa Barbara CA 93106, USA
**Gbaja-Biamila, Akbar O** — Football Player
1050 Armitage St, Alameda CA 94502, USA
**Gbowee, Leymah R** — Nobel Peace Activist
Women's Peace & Security Network, 68 Onyankle St, Abelempke, Accra, Ghana
**Geale, Daniel** — Boxer
Team Fenech, PO Box 66, Millers Point NSW 2000, Australia
**Gearhart, G David** — Educator
University of Arkansas, Chancellor's Office, Administration Building, Fayetteville AR 72701, USA
**Gearhart, John P** — Neurologist, Biologist
Johns Hopkins University Medical Center, Urology Dept, 600 N Wolfe St, Baltimore MD 21218, USA
**Gearing, Ashley** — Singer
W M E Entertainment, 1600 Division St, #300, Nashville TN 37203 USA
**Geary, Anthony (Tony)** — Actor
7010 Pacific View Dr, Los Angeles CA 90068, USA
**Geary, Cynthia** — Actress
Baumgarten/Prophet, 1041 N Formosa Ave, #200, West Hollywood CA 90046, USA
**Geary, Geoffrey M (Geoff)** — Baseball Player
175 Maple Ave, #2, Carlsbad CA 92008, USA
**Geary, Nancy** — Writer
Nicholas Ellison, 55 5th Ave, #1500, New York NY 10003, USA
**Geathers, Robert L, Jr** — Football Player
1 Dab Dr, Georgetown SC 29440, USA
**Gebhard, Robert H (Bob)** — Baseball Player, Executive
5242 E Otero Place, Littleton CO 80122, USA
**Gebo, Daniel** — Paleontologist
Northern Illinois University, Paleontology Dept, DeKalb IL 60115, USA
**Gebrselassie, Haile** — Track Athlete
Waterdelweg 14, 5427 LS Boehel 98007, Monaco
**Gedda, Nicolai** — Opera Singer
Valhavagen 128, 114 41 Stockholm, Sweden
**Geddes, Anne** — Photographer
K Geddes Mgmt, 2 York St, Parnell 1001, Auckland, New Zealand
**Geddes, James L (Jim)** — Baseball Player
6738 Harrisburg London Road, Orient OH 43146, USA
**Geddes, Jane** — Golfer
72 Shady Knoll Lane, New Canaan CT 06840, USA
**Geddes, Kenneth L (Ken)** — Football Player
7702 147th Ave NE, Redmond WA 98052, USA
**Geddis, Peter** — Actor
Brown & Simcocks, 109 Blackfriars Road, London SE1 8HW, England
**Gedeck, Martina** — Actress
Postfach 370521, 14135 Berlin, Germany
**Gedman, Richard L (Rich)** — Baseball Player
10 Parmenter Road, Framingham MA 01701, USA
**Gedney, Christopher J (Chris)** — Football Player
4881 Excalibur Dr, Syracuse NY 13215, USA
**Gedrick, Jason** — Actor
I F A Talent Agency, 8730 W Sunset Blvd, #490, West Hollywood CA 90069 USA
**Gee, E Gordon** — Educator
West Virginia University, President's Office, Morgantown WV 26506, USA
**Gee, Prunella** — Actress
Michael Ladkin Mgmt, 1 Duchess St, #1, London W1N 3DE, England
**Geer, Charlotte** — Rowing Athlete
PO Box 324, Hinesburg VT 05461, USA
**Geer, Ellen** — Actress
Kyle Fritz Mgmt, 6325 Heather Dr, Los Angeles CA 90068 USA
**Geer, Josh** — Baseball Player
10836 Peach Circle, Forney. TX 75126, USA
**Geesaman, Lynn** — Photographer
Thomas Barry Fine Arts, 530 N 3rd St, #B10, Minneapolis MN 55401, USA
**Geesen, Masha** — Writer
Bloomsbury Publishing, 50 Bedford Square, London WC1B 3DP, England

**Geeson, Judy** — Actress
Bauman Redanty Shaul Agency, 5757 Wilshire Blvd, #473, Los Angeles CA 90036 USA
**Geffen, David** — Producer, Businessman
22108 Pacific Coast Highway, Malibu CA 90265, USA
**Gehring, Frederick W** — Mathematician
1200 Earhart Road, Ann Arbor MI 48105, USA
**Gehring, Lana** — Speed Skater
U S Speedskating, 5662 S Cougar Lane, Salt Lake City UT 84118 USA
**Gehring, Walter J** — Geneticist
Hochfeldstr 32, 4106 Therwil, Switzerland
**Gehry, Frank O** — Pritzker Architectural Laureate
Gehry Partners, 12541 Beatrice St, Los Angeles CA 90066, USA
**Geiberger, Al** — Golfer
80555 Tangelo Court, Indio CA 92201, USA
**Geiduschek, E Peter** — Biologist
University of California, Biology Dept, 9500 Gilman Dr, La Jolla CA 92093, USA
**Geier, Philip H, Jr** — Businessman
Geier Group, Heron Tower, 70 E 55th St, #1500, New York NY 10022, USA
**Geiger, Ken** — Photojournalist
National Geographic Magazine, Editorial Dept, PO Box 98199, Washington DC 20090, USA
**Geiger, Matthew A (Matt)** — Basketball Player
3385 Old Keystone Road, Tarpon Springs FL 34688, USA
**Geiger, Teddy** — Singer, Songwriter, Actor
I C M Partners, 10250 Constellation Blvd, #900, Los Angeles CA 90067 USA
**Geisel, J David (Dave)** — Baseball Player
4 Blacksmith Lane, Media PA 19063, USA
**Geisenberger, Natalie** — Luge Athlete
On the Green 35, 83714 Miesbach, Germany
**Geismar, Thomas H** — Architect
Chermayeff & Geismar, 15 E 26th St, #1200, New York NY 10010, USA
**Geiss, Johannes** — Physicist
International Space Science Institute, Hallestr 6, 3012 Berne, Switzerland
**Geist, William (Willie)** — Commentator
NBC-TV, News Dept, 30 Rockefeller Plaza, #270E, New York NY 10112 USA
**Geithner, Timothy F** — Financier; Secretary, Treasury
Warburg Pincus LLC, 450 Lexington Ave, New York, NY 10017, USA
**Gelana, E Tiki** — Track Athlete
Global Sports Communication, Snelliustraat 10, 6533 Nijmegen NV, Netherlands
**Gelb, Leslie H** — Educator
Council on Foreign Relations, 58 E 68th St, New York NY 10065, USA
**Gelb, Peter** — Opera Executive
Metropolitan Opera Assn, Lincoln Center Plaza, New York NY 10023 USA
**Gelbaugh, Stanley M (Stan)** — Football Player
10819 Hob Nail Court, Potomac MD 20854, USA
**Geldof, Bob** — Singer, Songwriter
Finch Partners, 4 Rue de la Paix, 75002 Paris, France
**Gellar, Sarah Michelle** — Actress
I C M Partners, 10250 Constellation Blvd, #900, Los Angeles CA 90067 USA
**Geller, Margaret J** — Astronomer
Harvard University, Astronomy Dept, 60 Garden St, Cambridge MA 02138, USA
**Geller, Uri** — Psychic, Illusionist
Celeb Agents, 77 Oxford St, London W1D 2ES, England
**Gellman, Marc** — Religious Leader, Rabbi, Commentator
Temple Beth Torah, 35 Bagatelle Road, Melville NY 11747, USA
**Gell-Mann, Murray** — Nobel Physics Laureate
Santa Fe Institute, 1399 Hyde Park Road, Santa Fe NM 87501, USA
**Gelman, Barton** — Journalist
Washington Post, Editorial Dept, 1150 15th St NW, Washington DC 20071 USA
**Gelman, Larry** — Actor
5121 Greenbush Ave, Sherman Oaks CA 91423, USA
**Gelman, Michael S** — Producer
7 W 63rd St, #500, New York NY 10023, USA
**Gelnar, John R** — Baseball Player
300 N Hitchcock St, Hobart OK 73651, USA
**Gemar, Charles D** — Astronaut
7660 N 159th St Court E, Benton KS 67017, USA
**Gemignani, Alexander** — Actor, Singer
Innovative Artists, 1505 10th St, Santa Monica CA 90401 USA
**Gemma** — Model
I M G Models, 304 Park Ave S, #PH N, New York NY 10010 USA
**Gemmell, Ruth** — Actress
Hamilton Hodell, 20 Golden Square, London W1F 9JL, England
**Genaux, Vivica** — Opera Singer
K K N Enterprises, 277 W End Ave, #11A, New York NY 10023, USA
**Gendron, George M** — Editor, Educator
Clark University, Graduate Management School, 950 Main St, Worcester MA 01610, USA
**Genest, Veronique** — Actress
Artmedia, 20 Ave Rapp, 75007 Paris, France
**Genova, Lisa** — Writer
Pocket Books, 1230 Ave of Americas, New York NY 10020 USA
**Genovese, George M** — Baseball Player
11474 Erwin St, North Hollywood CA 91606, USA
**Genscher, Hans-Dietrich** — Government Official, Germany
Am Kottenforst 16, 53343 Wachtberg-Pech, Germany
**Genser, Eli Morgan** — Actor
Innovative Artists, 1505 10th St, Santa Monica CA 90401 USA
**Genshaft, Judy L** — Educator
University of South Florida, President's Office, Tampa FL 33620, USA
**Gensler, M Arthur, Jr** — Architect
Gensler & Assoc Architects, 550 Kearny St, San Francisco CA 94108, USA
**Genthe, Eva Z** — Photographer
C A 1 Photography, Scholdstr 1, 76227 Karlsruhe-Durlach, Germany
**Gentile, James E (Jim)** — Baseball Player
1016 W Neptune Road, Edmond OK 73003, USA
**Gentry, Alvin** — Basketball Coach, Executive
Los Angeles Clippers, Staples Center, 1111 S Figueroa St, Los Angeles CA 90015 USA

**G**

**Geeson - Gentry**

**Gentry, Dennis L** — Football Player
916 Queen Elizabeth Dr, McGregor TX 76657, USA

**Gentry, Gary E** — Baseball Player
301 W Lawrence Lane, Phoenix AZ 85021, USA

**Gentry, Teddy W** — Singer, Guitarist (Alabama)
Alabama Band Promotions, PO Box 680529, Fort Payne AL 35968, USA

**Gentry, Troy** — Singer (Montgomery Gentry)
Parallel Entertainment, 209 10th Ave S, #506, Nashville TN 37203, USA

**Genzel, Carrie** — Actress
Pakula/King, 9229 W Sunset Blvd, #315, West Hollywood CA 90069 USA

**Genzel, Reinhard** — Astrophysicist
Extraterrestrial Institute, Schwarzschild Str 1, 85741 Garching, Germany

**Geoffroy, Gregory** — Educator
Iowa State University, President's Office, Ames IA 50011, USA

**George, Anton H (Tony)** — Auto Racing Executive
Vision Racing, 6803 Coffman Road, Indianapolis IN 46268, USA

**George, Christopher S (Chris)** — Baseball Player
7703 Goldengrove Dr, Spring TX 77379, USA

**George, Devean J** — Basketball Player
14001 53rd Ave N, Minneapolis MN 55446, USA

**George, Edward N (Eddie)** — Football Player, Actor
9538 Sanctuary Place, Brentwood TN 37027, USA

**George, Elizabeth** — Writer
Byron's Mgmt, 76 Saint James Lane, London N10 3DF, England

**George, Eric** — Actor
Ziffren Brittenham Branca, 1801 Century Park W, #700, Los Angeles CA 90067 USA

**George, Francis E Cardinal** — Religious Leader
Archdiocese of Chicago, 835 Rush St, Chicago IL 60611, USA

**George, Helen** — Actress
D A A Management, Welbeck House, 66-67 Wells St, London WIT 3PY, England

**George, Inara** — Singer, Guitarist (Bird & the Bee)
Blue Note Records, 6920 W Sunset Blvd, Los Angeles CA 90028 USA

**George, James (Jim)** — Weightlifter
4319 Regal Dr, Akron OH 44321, USA

**George, Jason Winston** — Actor
Management 360, 9111 Wilshire Blvd, Beverly Hills CA 90210 USA

**George, Jeffrey S (Jeff)** — Football Player
3577 Hintocks Circle, Carmel IN 46032, USA

**George, Madeleine** — Writer
Gersh Agency, 41 Madison Ave, #3301, New York NY 10010 USA

**George, Maximillian A (Max)** — Singer (Wanted)
Industry Music Group, 128 Regent Road, Hanley Stoke, Trent ST1 3AY, England

**George, Melissa** — Actress
I C M Partners, 10250 Constellation Blvd, #900, Los Angeles CA 90067 USA

**George, Oorlagh** — Producer
Northwood Productions, 2901 Ocean Park Blvd, #217, Santa Monica CA 90405, USA

**George, Phyllis** — Entertainer, Beauty Queen
C E S D, 10635 Santa Monica Blvd, #130, Los Angeles CA 90025 USA

**George, Rocky** — Guitarist (Fishbone)
Silverback Mgmt, 9469 Jefferson Blvd, #101, Culver City CA 90232, USA

**George, Ronald L (Ron)** — Football Player
13720 Piedmont Vista Dr, Haymarket VA 20169, USA

**George, Susan** — Actress
McKorkindale & Holton, 1-2 Langham Place, London W1A 3DD, England

**George, Tate** — Basketball Player
55 Georgetown Road, Bristol CT 06010, USA

**George, Terry** — Director, Writer
Independent Talent Group, 40 Whitfield St, London W1T 2RH, England

**George, William W** — Businessman, Educator
Harvard University, Business School, Cambridge MA 02138, USA

**Georgel, Pierre** — Museum Official
41 Blvd Saint-Germain, 75005 Paris, France

**Georgi, Howard** — Physicist
Harvard University, Physics Dept, Lyman Laboratory, Cambridge MA 02138, USA

**Georgian, Theodore J** — Religious Leader
Orthodox Presbyterian Church, PO Box P, Willow Grove PA 19090, USA

**Georgije, Bishop** — Religious Leader
Serbian Orthodox Church, Sava Monastery, PO Box 519, Libertyville IL 60048, USA

**Georgis, William T** — Architect
233 E 72nd St, New York NY 10021, USA

**Geraci, Sonny** — Singer (Outsiders, Climax)
Precious Time Productions, 30799 Pine Tree Road, #135, Pepper Pike OH 44124, USA

**Geraghty, Brian T** — Actor
United Talent Agency, U T A Plaza, 9336 Civic Center Dr, Beverly Hills CA 90210 USA

**Geragos, Mark J** — Attorney
Geragos & Geragos, 2 California Plaza, 350 S Grand Ave, Los Angeles CA 90071, USA

**Gerard, Cindy** — Writer
Pocket/Star Books, 1230 Ave of Americas, New York NY 10020, USA

**Gerard, Daniel J (Gus)** — Basketball Player
614 Cypresswood Dr, Spring TX 77388, USA

**Gerard, Gil** — Actor, Producer, Director
Michael Einfeld Mgmt, 10630 Moorpark Ave, #101, Toluca Lake CA 91602, USA

**Gerard, Leo W** — Labor Leader
United Steel Workers of America, 5 Gateway Center, Pittsburgh PA 15222, USA

**Gerardo** — Rap Artist
Nene Musik Productions, 1460 SW Santiago Ave, Port Saint Lucie FL 34953 USA

**Gerber, Craig S** — Baseball Player
4297 N Pershing Ave, San Bernardino CA 92407, USA

**Gerber, H Joseph** — Businessman
Gerber Scientific Inc, 83 Gerber Road W, South Windsor CT 06074, USA

**Gerber, Joel** — Judge
US Tax Court, 400 2nd St NW, Washington DC 20217, USA

**Gerberding, Julie L** — Government Official, Physician
Emory University Medical School, Infectious Disease Dept, Atlanta GA 30322, USA

**Gere, Richard** — Actor
Hirsch Wallerstein Hayum, 10100 Santa Monica Blvd, #1700, Los Angeles CA 90067 USA

| | |
|---|---|
| **Gerela, Roy** | Football Player |
| 3933 Ramrod Forge, Las Cruces NM 88012, USA | |
| **Geren, Robert P (Bob)** | Baseball Player, Manager |
| 2710 Bay Canyon Court, San Diego CA 92117, USA | |
| **Gerety, Tom, Jr** | Educator |
| Amherst College, President's Office, Amherst MA 01002, USA | |
| **Gerg, Hilde** | Alpine Skier |
| Richard-Voss-Str 63, 83471 Schonau am Konigssee, Germany | |
| **Gergen, David R** | Editor |
| 31 Ash St, Cambridge MA 02138, USA | |
| **Gergiev, Valery A** | Conductor |
| Kirov Ballet Theater, 1 Pl Iskusstr, 190000 Saint Petersburg, Russia | |
| **Gergov, Rossen** | Conductor |
| Harrison/Parrott, 5-6 Albion Court, London W6 0QT, England | |
| **Gerhaher, Christian** | Opera Singer |
| Kunstler Sekretariat am Gasteig, Rosenheimer Str 52, 81669 Munich, Germany | |
| **Gerideau-Squires, Wilda** | Photographer |
| PO Box 1515, Andover MA 01810, USA | |
| **Gering, Jenna** | Actress |
| Paradigm Agency, 360 N Crescent Dr, North Building, Beverly Hills CA 90210 USA | |
| **Germann, Greg** | Actor |
| Innovative Artists, 1505 10th St, Santa Monica CA 90401 USA | |
| **Germano, Lisa** | Singer, Violinist, Songwriter |
| Artists & Audience Entertainment, PO Box 35, Pawling NY 12564 USA | |
| **Germany, Willie** | Football Player |
| 4401 Pratt St, Omaha NE 68111, USA | |
| **Germeshausen, Bernhard** | Bobsled Athlete |
| Hinter Dem Salon 39, 99195 Schwansee, Germany | |
| **Gernert, Richard E (Dick)** | Baseball Player |
| 1801 Cambridge Ave, #C12, Reading PA 19610, USA | |
| **Gernhardt, Michael L** | Astronaut |
| 2705 Lighthouse Dr, Houston TX 77058, USA | |
| **Gero, Gary D** | Cinematographer |
| 2 McLaren, #A, Irvine CA 92618, USA | |
| **Gerring, Cathy** | Golfer |
| 3328 Tarrant Springs Trail, Fort Wayne IN 46804, USA | |
| **Gerrish, Brian A** | Theologian |
| 9142 Sycamore Hill Place, Mechanicsville VA 23116, USA | |
| **Gerritsen, Tess** | Writer |
| 11 Pleasant Ridge Dr, Camden ME 04843, USA | |
| **Gersbach, Carl R** | Football Player |
| PO Box 433, Devon PA 19333, USA | |
| **Gershon, Gina** | Actress |
| Apostle Management, 9696 Culver Blvd, #108, Culver City CA 90232, USA | |
| **Gerson, Mark** | Photographer |
| 3 Regal Lane, Regent's Park, London NW1 7TH, England | |
| **Gerst, Alexander** | Astronaut, Germany |
| European Space Center, Linder Hohe, Box 906096, 51127 Cologne, Germany | |
| **Gerstein, Kirill** | Concert Pianist |
| I M G Artists, Hogarth Business Park, Chiswick, London W4 2TH, England | |
| **Gerstell, A Frederick** | Businessman |
| CalMat Co, 3200 San Fernando Road, Los Angeles CA 90065, USA | |
| **Gerth, Jeff** | Journalist |
| New York Times, Editorial Dept, 229 W 43rd St, New York NY 10036 USA | |
| **Gertz, Jami** | Actress |
| Innovative Artists, 1505 10th St, Santa Monica CA 90401 USA | |
| **Gerut, Joseph D (Jody)** | Baseball Player |
| 623 Rochdale Circle, Lombard IL 60148, USA | |
| **Gervais, Ricky** | Actor, Comedian, Producer, Director |
| United Agents, 12-26 Lexington St, London W1F 0LE, England | |
| **Gervin, George** | Basketball Player, Coach |
| 44 Gervin Pass, Spring Branch TX 78070, USA | |
| **Gerwick, Ben C, Jr** | Construction Engineer |
| 5727 Country Club Dr, Oakland CA 94618, USA | |
| **Gerwig, Greta** | Actress, Writer |
| United Talent Agency, U T A Plaza, 9336 Civic Center Dr, Beverly Hills CA 90210 USA | |
| **Gerzmava, Hibla** | Opera Singer |
| Elena Kharakidzyan Art-Brand Artists, 6/66 Klimentovsky Per, 115184 Moscow, Russia | |
| **Geschke, Charles** | Businessman |
| Adobe Systems, 375 Park Ave, San Jose CA 95110, USA | |
| **Gesek, John C, Jr** | Football Player |
| 105 Sand Point Court, Coppell TX 75019, USA | |
| **Gesinger, Michael** | Photographer |
| 1136 Umatilla Ave, Port Townsend WA 98368, USA | |
| **Gesner, Zen** | Actor |
| Jenny Delaney Mgmt, 3238 Fond Dr, Encino CA 91436, USA | |
| **Gessendorf, Mechthild** | Opera Singer |
| Columbia Artists Mgmt Inc, 5 Columbus Circle, 1790 Broadway, #1600, New York NY 10019 USA | |
| **Gessle, Per** | Singer, Guitarist (Roxette) |
| D & D Mgmt, Drottninggatan 55, 111 21 Stockholm, Sweden | |
| **Gethard, Chris** | Actor |
| Creative Artists Agency, 2000 Ave of Stars, #100, Los Angeles CA 90067 USA | |
| **Gets, Malcolm** | Actor, Singer |
| Viking Entertainment, 445 W 23rd St, #1A, New York NY 10011, USA | |
| **Gettelfinger, Ron** | Labor Leader |
| United Auto Workers Union, 800 E Jefferson Ave, Detroit MI 48214, USA | |
| **Gettis, Byron** | Baseball Player |
| 6313 Whalen Ave, East Saint Louis IL 62207, USA | |
| **Getty, Balthazar** | Actor |
| Patricola Public Relations, 9171 Wilshire Blvd, #441, Beverly Hills CA 90210 USA | |
| **Getty, Charles M (Charlie)** | Football Player |
| 3736 W Morningside St, Springfield MO 65807, USA | |
| **Getz, John** | Actor |
| Beddingfield Co, 13600 Ventura Blvd, #B, Sherman Oaks CA 91423, USA | |
| **Getzenberg, Robert** | Urologist |
| Johns Hopkins University Medical Center, Urological Institute, Baltimore MD 21218, USA | |

**Geyer, Hugh** — Singer (Vogues)
2218 Ridge Road, McKeesport PA 15135, USA

**Ghaffari, Matt** — Greco-Roman Wrestler
32834 Fox Chappel Lane, Avon Lake OH 44012, USA

**Ghai, Subhash** — Director, Producer
Mount Saint Mary Church Road, #12, Bandra (W), Mumbai MS 400050, India

**Ghauri, Yasmeen** — Model
Next Model Mgmt, 23 Watts St, New York NY 10013 USA

**Ghedi, Ali Muhammad** — Prime Minister, Somalia
Prime Minister's Office, People's Palace, Mogadishu, Somalia

**Ghelfi, Anthony P (Tony)** — Baseball Player
3414 Geneva Lane, La Crosse WI 54601, USA

**Gheorghiu, Angela** — Opera Singer
Askonas Holt, Lincoln House, 300 High Holborn, London WC1V 7JH, England

**Gheorghiu, Ion A** — Artist
6 Aviator Petre Cretu St, 012151 Bucharest, Romania

**Gheorghiu, Teo** — Concert Pianist
Harrison/Parrott, 5-6 Albion Court, London W6 0QT, England

**Ghesquiere, Nicolas** — Fashion Designer
Angie Rubioni, 40 Rue du Cherche-Midi, 75006 Paris, France

**Ghez, Andrea M** — Physicist, Astronomer
University of California, Physics & Astronomy Dept, Los Angeles CA 90024, USA

**Ghiardi, John F L** — Government Official, Economist
12 Park Overlook Court, Bethesda MD 20817, USA

**Ghomeshi, Jian** — Broadcaster, Writer, Musician
Agency Group Lts, 2 Berkeley St, #202, Toronto ON M5A 4J5, Canada

**Ghormley, Antony** — Sculptor
European Graduate School, Alter Kehr 20, 3953 Leuk-Stadt, Switzerland

**Ghosh, Amitrav** — Writer
Farrar Straus Giroux, 18 W 18th St, #700, New York NY 10011 USA

**Ghosh, Gautam** — Director
28/1A Gariahat Road, Block 5, #50, Mumbai WB 700029, India

**Ghosn, Carlos** — Businessman
Nissan Motor Co, 1-1-1 Takashima, Nishi-ku, Yokohamashi, Kanagawa 220 8686, Japan

**Ghostface Killa** — Rap Artist (Wu-Tang Clan)
Agency Group Ltd, 142 W 57th St, #600, New York NY 10019 USA

**Ghribi, Habiba** — Track Athlete
Demadonnathletics, Via Zanella 4, 38100 Trento, Italy

**Ghuman, J B, Jr** — Actor, Director
W M E Entertainment, 9601 Wilshire Blvd, #300, Beverly Hills CA 90210 USA

**Giacchino, Michael** — Composer
Gorfaine/Schwartz, 4111 W Alameda Ave, #509, Burbank CA 91505 USA

**Giacconi, Riccardo** — Nobel Physics Laureate
7157 Fay Ave, La Jolla CA 92037, USA

**Giacomin, Edward (Ed)** — Ice Hockey Player
6575 Red Maple Lane, Bloomfield MI 48301, USA

**Giacoppo, Massimo** — Water Polo Player
A S D Pro Recco, Via Biagio Assereto 10/A, 16036 Recco (GE), Italy

**Giaever, Ivar** — Nobel Physics Laureate
2080 Van Antwerp Road, Schenectady NY 12309, USA

**Giamatti, Paul** — Actor
United Talent Agency, U T A Plaza, 9336 Civic Center Dr, Beverly Hills CA 90210 USA

**Giambastiani, Edmund P, Jr** — Navy Admiral
Business Executives for National Security, 1030 15th St NW, #200 East, Washington DC 20005, USA

**Giambi, Jason G** — Baseball Player
34 Iselworth Dr, Henderson NV 89052, USA

**Giambi, Jeremy D** — Baseball Player
23360 S Power Road, Gilbert AZ 85298, USA

**Giambra, Joey** — Boxer
4673 Ashington St, Las Vegas NV 89147, USA

**Giammarese, Carl** — Guitarist (Buckinghams)
Thomas Cassidy, PO Box 1311, Tucson AZ 85702 USA

**Gianelli, John A** — Basketball Player
28241 Pine Ave, Pinecrest CA 95364, USA

**Giangrande, Meredith** — Actress
Allen Edelman Mgmt, 6230 Wilshire Blvd, #175, Los Angeles CA 90048, USA

**Giannelli, Raymond J (Ray)** — Baseball Player
56 E Saltaire Road, Lindenhurst NY 11757, USA

**Giannini, Adriano** — Actor
Media Art Mgmt, BaRbara de Braganza 11, #4 Derecha, 28004 Madrid, Spain

**Giannini, Alfreda** — Fashion Designer
Gucci Group, 1 Amstelplein, 1096 Amsterdam HA, Netherlands

**Giannini, Giancarlo** — Actor
Via Salaria 292, 00199 Rome, Italy

**Giannoni, Giovani** — Co-Regent, San Marino
Co-Regent's Office, Government Palace, 47031 San Marino

**Giannulli, Mossimo** — Fashion Designer
Mossimo Supply, 2450 White Road, #200, Irvine CA 92614, USA

**Gianopulos, Mimi** — Actress
I C M Partners, 10250 Constellation Blvd, #900, Los Angeles CA 90067 USA

**Gianotti, Fabiola** — Physicist
C E R N, Large Hadron Collider, 1211 Geneva 23, Switzerland

**Gibara, Samir** — Businessman
Goodyear Tire & Rubber, 1144 E Market St, Akron OH 44316, USA

**Gibb, Barry** — Singer (Bee Gees), Songwriter
Rhino Entertainment, 3400 Olive Ave, #400, Burbank CA 91505, USA

**Gibb, Cynthia** — Actress
Scott Hart Mgmt, 14622 Ventura Blvd, #746, Sherman Oaks CA 91403, USA

**Gibb, Donald** — Actor
Ashby/Rojo Entertainment, 1485 S Beverly Dr, Los Angeles CA 90035, USA

**Gibbard, Allan F** — Philosopher
University of Michigan, Philosophy Dept, Ann Arbor MI 48109, USA

**Gibbard, Benjamin (Ben)** — Singer (Death Cab for Cutie)
Zeitgeist Artist Mgmt, 660 York St, #216, San Francisco CA 94110, USA

**Gibbon, Joseph C (Joe)** — Baseball Player
26 County Road 24142, Newton MS 39345, USA

**Gibbons, Beth** — Singer (Portishead), Songwriter
High Road Touring, 751 Bridgeway, #200, Sausalito CA 94965 USA
**Gibbons, Billy** — Singer, Guitarist (ZZ Top)
Sanctuary Mgmt, 15301 Ventura Blvd, Building B, Sherman Oaks CA 91403, USA
**Gibbons, Gail** — Writer, Illustrator
1 Goose Green St, Corinth VT 05039, USA
**Gibbons, Gemma J** — Judo Athlete
Metro Judo Club, Mycenae House, 90 Mycenae Road, London SE3 7SE, England
**Gibbons, James E (Jim)** — Football Player
9 Sagewood Court, Basalt CO 81621, USA
**Gibbons, James F** — Electrical Engineer
15 Red Berry Ridge, Portola Valley CA 94028, USA
**Gibbons, Jason** — Drummer (Neon Trees)
Creative Artists Agency, 2000 Ave of Stars, #100, Los Angeles CA 90067 USA
**Gibbons, Jay J** — Baseball Player
758 Donnington Court, Simi Valley CA 93065, USA
**Gibbons, John D** — Prime Minister, Bermuda
Leeward, 5 Leeside Dr, Pembroke HM 05, Bermuda
**Gibbons, John M (Gibby)** — Baseball Player, Manager
3602 Hunters Quail, San Antonio TX 78230, USA
**Gibbons, Julia Smith** — Judge
US Court of Appeals, 167 N Main St, #970, Memphis TN 38103, USA
**Gibbons, Kaye** — Writer
Houghton Mifflin Harcourt, 215 Park Ave S, #1200, New York NY 10003 USA
**Gibbons, Leeza** — Actress, Producer
9025 Ashcroft Ave, West Hollywood CA 90048, USA
**Gibbs, Freddie** — Rap Artist
Agency Group Ltd, 1880 Century Park E, #711, Los Angeles CA 90067 USA
**Gibbs, Jerry D (Jake)** — Football, Baseball Player
223 Saint Andres Circle, Oxford MS 38655, USA
**Gibbs, Joe J** — Football Coach, Auto Racing Executive
19133 Penisula Point Dr, Cornelius NC 28031, USA
**Gibbs, Marla** — Actress, Singer
Momentum Talent, 9401 Wilshire Blvd, #501, Beverly Hills CA 90212, USA
**Gibbs, Martin** — Biologist
5 Arbor Court, Burlington MA 01803, USA
**Gibbs, Terri** — Singer, Songwriter
P O Box 2100, Thomson GA 30824, USA
**Gibbs, Terry** — Jazz Vibist, Drummer
Thomas Cassidy, PO Box 1311, Tucson AZ 85702 USA
**Gibbs, Timothy B** — Actor
Jefferson Rilke Cooper, 50 Lexington Ave, #23D, New York NY 10010, USA
**Gibgot, Jennifer** — Producer
Offspring Entertainment, 8755 Colgate Ave, Los Angeles CA 90048, USA
**Giblett, Eloise R** — Hematologist
2518 3rd Ave W, Seattle WA 98119, USA
**Giblin, Vincent J** — Labor Leader
International Union of Operating Engineers, 1125 17th St NW, Washington DC 20036, USA
**Gibney, Alex** — Director
I C M Partners, 10250 Constellation Blvd, #900, Los Angeles CA 90067 USA
**Gibney, Susan** — Actress
Insight Mgmt, 11245 Cloverdale Ave, Los Angeles CA 90019, USA
**Gibran, Kahlil G** — Sculptor
160 W Canton St, Boston MA 02118, USA
**Gibson, Antonio M** — Football Player
2320 Jaguar Dr, #502, Bryan TX 77807, USA
**Gibson, Beau** — Opera Singer
I M G Artists, Hogarth Business Park, Chiswick, London W4 2TH, England
**Gibson, Brandon L** — Football Player
Miami Dolphins, 7500 SW 30th St, Davie FL 33314 USA
**Gibson, Charles D** — Commentator
ABC-TV, News Dept, 47 W 66th St, New York NY 10023, USA
**Gibson, Claude** — Football Player
47 Gladstone Road, Asheville NC 28805, USA
**Gibson, Deborah** — Singer, Actress, Model
David Shapira Assoc, 193 N Robertson Blvd, Beverly Hills CA 90211 USA
**Gibson, Dennis M** — Football Player
6900 NE 11th Court, Ankeny IA 50023, USA
**Gibson, Derrick A** — Baseball Player
303 Ave O NW, Winter Haven FL 33881, USA
**Gibson, Ernest G** — Football Player
6518 Paradise Point Road, Flowery Branch GA 30542, USA
**Gibson, Fred** — Golfer
2006 Avenel St, Orlando FL 32828, USA
**Gibson, Gregory A (Greg)** — Baseball Umpire
5222 Dog Fork Laurel Road, Catlettsburg KY 41129, USA
**Gibson, John R** — Judge
US Court of Appeals, US Courthouse, 811 Grand Ave, Kansas City MO 64106, USA
**Gibson, Kelly** — Golfer
13 Wisteria Lane, Covington LA 70433, USA
**Gibson, Kirk H** — Baseball, Football Player
15135 Charlevoix St, Grosse Pointe Park MI 48230, USA
**Gibson, Leah D** — Actress
Play Mgmt, 07 Powell St, #220, Vancouver BC V6A 1H7, Canada
**Gibson, Mel** — Actor, Director
Icon Productions, 808 Wilshire Blvd, #400, Santa Monica CA 90401, USA
**Gibson, Oliver D** — Football Player
1448 E 52nd St, #406, Chicago IL 60615, USA
**Gibson, Paul M** — Baseball Player
23421 Water Circle, Boca Raton FL 33486, USA
**Gibson, Quentin H** — Biochemist
5 Carrot Hill Road, Woods Hole MA 02543, USA
**Gibson, Ralph H** — Photographer
331 W Broadway, #400, New York NY 10013, USA
**Gibson, Raquel** — Model
Playboy Promotions, 9346 Civic Center Dr, #200, Beverly Hills CA 90210 USA

**Gibson, Reginald W** — Judge
US Claims Court, 717 Madison Place NW, Washington DC 20439, USA
**Gibson, Robert (Bob)** — Baseball Player
215 Bellevue Blvd S, Bellevue NE 68005, USA
**Gibson, Robert L (Bob)** — Baseball Player
751 W Rolling Road, Springfield PA 19064, USA
**Gibson, Robert L (Hoot)** — Astronaut
1709 Shagbark Trail, Murfreesboro TN 37130, USA
**Gibson, Thomas** — Actor
Paradigm Agency, 360 N Crescent Dr, North Building, Beverly Hills CA 90210 USA
**Gibson, Thomas A (Tom)** — Football Player
5940 E Sandra Terrace, Scottsdale AZ 85254, USA
**Gibson, Tyrese D** — Singer, Songwriter, Actor, Producer
H Q Pictures, 15260 Ventura Blvd, #2100, Sherman Oaks CA 91403, USA
**Gibson, William Ford** — Writer, Photographer
G P Putnam's Sons, 375 Hudson St, New York NY 10014 USA
**Giddins, Gary** — Writer, Columnist
Oxford University Press, 198 Madison Ave, #800, New York NY 10016 USA
**Giddish, Kelli** — Actress
Paradigm Agency, 360 N Crescent Dr, North Building, Beverly Hills CA 90210 USA
**Gideon, Raynold** — Actor, Writer
3524 Multiview Dr, Los Angeles CA 90068, USA
**Gidley, Pamela** — Actress
32 Cliff Ave, Hampton NH 03842, USA
**Gidzenko, Yuri P** — Cosmonaut
Cosmonaut Training Center, Star City, 141160 Zvezdny Gorodok, Moscow Oblast, Russia
**Gielen, Michael A** — Conductor, Composer
Ingpen & Williams, 131 Putney Bridge Road, London SW15 2PA, England
**Giella, Joseph** — Cartoonist (Mary Worth)
191 Morris Dr, East Meadow NY 11554, USA
**Gien, Pamela** — Actress
I C M Partners, 10250 Constellation Blvd, #900, Los Angeles CA 90067 USA
**Gienger, Eberhard** — Gymnast
Pkeidelsheimer Str 11, 74321 Bietigheim-Bissingen, Germany
**Gierasch, Adam** — Director, Writer
Gersh Agency, 9465 Wilshire Blvd, #600, Beverly Hills CA 90212 USA
**Gierer, Vincent A, Jr** — Businessman
U S T Inc, 100 W Putnam Ave, Greenwich CT 06830, USA
**Gierowski, Stefan** — Artist
Ul Gagarina 15 m 97, 00 753 Warsaw, Poland
**Giesler, Jon W** — Football Player
141 Via Isabela, Jupiter FL 33458, USA
**Gietz, Gordon** — Opera Singer
I M G Artists, Hogarth Business Park, Chiswick, London W4 2TH, England
**Giff, Patricia Reilly** — Writer
Bantam Books, 1745 Broadway, New York NY 10019 USA
**Gifford, Barry** — Writer
Creative Artists Agency, 2000 Ave of Stars, #100, Los Angeles CA 90067 USA
**Gifford, Frank N** — Football Player, Sportscaster
I C M Partners, 10250 Constellation Blvd, #900, Los Angeles CA 90067 USA
**Gifford, Gloria** — Actress
Gloria Gifford Theater, 6468 Santa Monica Blvd, Los Angeles CA 90038, USA
**Gifford, Kathie Lee** — Entertainer
Artist Brand Alliance, 11 E 86th St, #900, New York NY 10028, USA
**Gift, Roland** — Singer (Fine Young Cannibals), Actor
Primary Talent International, 10-11 Jockey's Fields, London WC1R 4BN, England
**Gigandet, Cam** — Actor
United Talent Agency, U T A Plaza, 9336 Civic Center Dr, Beverly Hills CA 90210 USA
**Giggie, Robert T (Bob)** — Baseball Player
89 McAndrew Road, Braintree MA 02184, USA
**Gigli, Romeo** — Fashion Designer
37 W 57th St, #900, New York NY 10019, USA
**Gigliotti, Donna** — Producer
Bloom Hergott Diemer, 150 S Rodeo Dr, #300, Beverly Hills CA 90212 USA
**Gigon, Norman P (Norm)** — Baseball Player
2503 Rio Vista Dr, Mahwah NJ 07430, USA
**Gigot, Paul A** — Journalist
Wall Street Journal, Editorial Dept, 1 World Financial Center, New York NY 10281, USA
**Giguere, Jean-Sebastien** — Ice Hockey Player
Colorado Avalanche, Pepsi Center, 1000 Chopper Circle, Denver CO 80204 USA
**Giguere, Russ** — Singer, Guitarist (Association)
Variety Artists, 1924 Spring St, Paso Robles CA 93446 USA
**Gil, Gilberto** — Singer, Songwriter, Guitarist
M G Ltd, 520 8th Ave, #2205, New York NY 10010, USA
**Gil, Maria Luisa** — Model
Playboy Promotions, 9346 Civic Center Dr, #200, Beverly Hills CA 90210 USA
**Gil, R Benjamin (Benji)** — Baseball Player
1654 Paseo Aurora, San Diego CA 92154, USA
**Gilbert, Bradley (Brad)** — Tennis Player
ProServe, 1101 Woodrow Wilson Blvd, #1800, Arlington VA 22209 USA
**Gilbert, Chris** — Football Player
Greenbriar Mgmt, 4422 FM 1960 Road W, Houston TX 77068, USA
**Gilbert, David** — Cartoonist (Buckles)
King Features Syndicate, 300 W 57th St, #1500, New York NY 10019 USA
**Gilbert, Drew E (Buddy)** — Baseball Player
1913 Belcaro Dr, Knoxville TN 37918, USA
**Gilbert, Elizabeth** — Writer
Penguin Books, 375 Hudson St, Basement 1, New York NY 10014 USA
**Gilbert, Greg** — Ice Hockey Player, Coach
Toronto Marlies, 100 Princess Blvd, Toronto ON M6K 3C3, Canada
**Gilbert, J Freeman** — Geophysicist
780 Kalamath Dr, Del Mar CA 92014, USA
**Gilbert, Joe D** — Baseball Player
512 W Martin Luther King Blvd, Jasper TX 75951, USA
**Gilbert, Jonathan** — Actor
PO Box 15583, Newport Beach CA 92659, USA

**Gilbert, Justin R** — Football Player
Cleveland Browns, 76 Lou Groza Blvd, Berea OH 44017 USA
**Gilbert, Kenneth A** — Concert Harpsichordist
11 Rue Ernest-Psichari, 75007 Paris, France
**Gilbert, Lawrence I** — Biologist
857 Fearrington Post, Pittsboro NC 27312, USA
**Gilbert, Lewis** — Director, Producer
19 Blvd de Suisse, 98000 Monte Carlo, Monaco
**Gilbert, Martin J** — Historian
Merton College, History Dept, Oxford OX1 4JD, England
**Gilbert, Melissa** — Actress, Labor Leader
Innovative Artists, 1505 10th St, Santa Monica CA 90401 USA
**Gilbert, Rodrique G (Rod)** — Ice Hockey Player
52 E End Ave, #33A, New York NY 10028, USA
**Gilbert, Ronnie** — Singer
Donna Korones Mgmt, 1031 Merced St, Berkeley CA 94707, USA
**Gilbert, S J, Sr** — Religious Leader
Baptist Convention of America, 6717 Centennial Blvd, Nashville TN 37209, USA
**Gilbert, Sara** — Actress
Framework Entertainment, 9057 Nemo St, #C, West Hollywood CA 90069 USA
**Gilbert, Sean** — Football Player
7912 N Baltusrol Lane, Charlotte NC 28210, USA
**Gilbert, Simon** — Drummer (Suede)
Interceptor Enterprises, 98 White Lion St, London N1 9PF, England
**Gilbert, Walter** — Nobel Chemistry Laureate
15 Gray Gardens W, Cambridge MA 02138, USA
**Gilberto, Astrud** — Singer
Absolute Artists, 530 Howard Ave, #200, San Francisco CA 94105, USA
**Gilberto, Bebel** — Singer
Umbrella Group, 20 West St, #30E, New York NY 10002, USA
**Gilbertson, Bob** — Drag Racing Driver, Owner
Terminator Motorsports, 2250 Toomey Ave, Charlotte NC 28203, USA
**Gilbreath, Rodney J (Rod)** — Baseball Player
1438 Ridgeland Way SW, Lilburn GA 30047, USA
**Gilbride, Kevin** — Football Player, Coach
New York Giants, Meadowlands Stadium, 102 Route 120, East Rutherford NJ 07073 USA
**Gilburg, Thomas D (Tom)** — Football Player
29 Valley Road, Warminster PA 18974, USA
**Gilchrist, Brent** — Ice Hockey Player
Bank of Montreal, 200-3200 30th Ave, Vernon BC V1T 2C5, Canada
**Gilchrist, Guy** — Cartoonist (Nancy, Mudpie)
20 Bristol Dr, Canton CT 06019, USA
**Gilchrist, Keir** — Actor
I C M Partners, 10250 Constellation Blvd, #900, Los Angeles CA 90067 USA
**Gilchrist, Lara** — Actress
Lauren Levitt Assoc, 1525 W 8th Ave, #300, Vancouver BC V6J 1T5, Canada
**Gilchrist, Paul R** — Religious Leader
Presbyterian Church in America, 1862 Century Place, Atlanta GA 30345, USA
**Gilder, Bob** — Golfer
1977 NW Bonney Dr, Corvallis OR 97330, USA
**Gilder, George F** — Economist
Gilder Publishing, 291A Main St, Great Barrington MA 01230, USA
**Gildon, Jason L** — Football Player
1562 Barrington Dr, Wexford PA 15090, USA
**Giles, Brian J** — Baseball Player
136 Coronation Ave, Las Vegas NV 89123, USA
**Giles, Brian S** — Baseball Player
4130 Rancho Las Brisas Trail, San Diego CA 92130, USA
**Giles, Curtis J (Curt)** — Ice Hockey Player
5225 Grandview Square, #402, Minneapolis MN 55436, USA
**Giles, Jimmie, Jr** — Football Player
10429 Greenmont Dr, Tampa FL 33626, USA
**Giles, Marcus W** — Baseball Player
26132 Old Highway 80, Descanso CA 91916, USA
**Giles, Nancy** — Actress
12047 178th St, Jamaica NY 11434, USA
**Giles, William Y (Bill)** — Baseball Executive
1400 Waverly Road, #B317, Gladwyne PA 19035, USA
**Giletti, Alain** — Figure Skater
103 Place de L'Eglise, 74400 Chamonix, France
**Gilfillan, Jason** — Baseball Player
153 Gilfillan Road, Blacksburg SC 29702, USA
**Gilford, Zach** — Actor
W M E Entertainment, 9601 Wilshire Blvd, #300, Beverly Hills CA 90210 USA
**Gilfry, Rodney** — Opera Singer
Askonas Holt, Lincoln House, 300 High Holborn, London WC1V 7JH, England
**Gilham, David R** — Writer
Berkley/Penguin Group, 375 Hudson St, New York NY 10014, USA
**Gilhousen, Klein** — Inventor
Qualcomm, 5775 Morehouse Dr, San Diego CA 92121, USA
**Gilkey, O Bernard** — Baseball Player
11463 Patty Ann Dr, Saint Louis MO 63146, USA
**Gill, Harold P (Hal)** — Ice Hockey Player
1 Fairfield Place, #4, Boston MA 02109, USA
**Gill, Janis** — Singer (Sweethearts of the Rodeo)
2803 Bransford Ave, Nashville TN 37204, USA
**Gill, Johnny** — Singer, Songwriter
Universal Attractions, 135 W 26th St, #1200, New York NY 10001 USA
**Gill, Kendall C** — Basketball Player
3133 S Calumet Ave, Chicago IL 60616, USA
**Gill, Tim** — Computer Software Designer (Quark)
Gill Foundation, 2215 Market St, Denver CO 80205, USA
**Gill, Tonya** — Golfer
3655 Habersham Road NE, #B229, Atlanta GA 30305, USA
**Gill, Turner H** — Football Player, Coach
University of Kansas, Athletic Dept, Lawrence KS 66045, USA

# G

**Gill, Vince** — Singer, Songwriter, Guitarist
Fitzgerald Hartley Co, 1908 Wedgewood Ave, Nashville TN 37212, USA

**Gill, William A, Jr** — Labor Leader, Government Official
15975 Cove Lane, Dumfries VA 22025, USA

**Gillan, Ian** — Singer, Musician (Deep Purple)
Coda Agency, 229 Shoreditch High St, London E1 6PJ, England

**Gillan, Karen S** — Actress
United Talent Agency, U T A Plaza, 9336 Civic Center Dr, Beverly Hills CA 90210 USA

**Gillanders, J David** — Swimmer
1617 Briarwood Dr, Jonesboro AR 72401, USA

**Gille, Bertrand** — Handball Player
Chambery Savoie H B, 688 Ave des Follaz, 73000 Chambery, France

**Gille, Guillaume A** — Handball Player
Chambery Savoie H B, 688 Ave des Follaz, 73000 Chambery, France

**Gillen, Aidan** — Actor
Independent Talent Group, 40 Whitfield St, London W1T 2RH, England

**Gilles, Frederic** — Actor
Martinez Creative Mgmt, 6856 Saint-Laurent Blvd, #205, Montreal QC H2S 3C7, Canada

**Gilles, Thomas B (Tom)** — Baseball Player
14615 W Southern St, Princeville IL 61559, USA

**Gillespie, Aaron R** — Singer, Drummer (Underoath)
Force Media Mgmt, 135 Voorhis Ave, Rockville Centre NY 11570, USA

**Gillespie, Jack A** — Basketball Player
1104 37th Ave NE, Great Falls MT 59404, USA

**Gillespie, Jim** — Director
Creative Artists Agency, 2000 Ave of Stars, #100, Los Angeles CA 90067 USA

**Gillespie, Rhondda M** — Concert Pianist
2 Princess Road, Saint Leonards on Sea, East Sussex TN37 6EL, England

**Gillespie, Robert W** — Financier
KeyCorp, 127 Public Square, Cleveland OH 44114, USA

**Gillespie, Ronald J** — Chemist
150 Wilson St W, Ancaster ON L9G 4E7, Canada

**Gillette, Anita** — Actress
Harden-Curtis Assoc, 214 W 29th St, #1203, New York NY 10001, USA

**Gillette, James (Jim)** — Singer (Tuff, Nitro)
Nene Musik Productions, 1460 SW Santiago Ave, Port Saint Lucie FL 34953 USA

**Gillette, Walker A** — Football Player
401 N College Dr, Franklin VA 23851, USA

**Gilley, J Wade** — Educator
University of Tennessee, President's Office, Knoxville TN 37996, USA

**Gilley, Mickey L** — Singer, Pianist, Songwriter
Mickey Gilley Interests, PO Box 1242, Pasadena TX 77501, USA

**Gilliam, Elijah** — Baseball Player
1617 5th Ave N, Birmingham AL 35203, USA

**Gilliam, Jon R** — Football Player
802 Wandering Court, Granbury TX 76049, USA

**Gilliam, Sam** — Artist
Lou Stovall Workshop, 3145 Newark St NW, Washington DC 20008, USA

**Gilliam, Seth** — Actor
Gersh Agency, 9465 Wilshire Blvd, #600, Beverly Hills CA 90212 USA

**Gilliam, Terry V** — Actor, Animator, Writer (Monty Python)
Old Hall, South Grove, Highgate, London N6 6BP, England

**Gilliard, Lawrence (Larry), Jr** — Actor
Innovative Artists, 1505 10th St, Santa Monica CA 90401 USA

**Gillick, L Patrick D (Pat)** — Baseball Executive
Philadelphia Phillies, 1 Citizens Bank Way, Philadelphia PA 19148 USA

**Gillies, Ben** — Drummer (Silverchair)
John Watson Mgmt, PO Box 281, Sunny Hills NSW 2010, Australia

**Gillies, Clark (Jethro)** — Ice Hockey Player
17 Pinta Court, Greenlawn NY 11740, USA

**Gillies, Daniel** — Actor
A P A Talent & Literary Agency, 405 S Beverly Dr, #300, Beverly Hills CA 90212 USA

**Gillies, Isabel** — Actress, Writer
Charles Scribner's Sons, 866 3rd Ave, New York NY 10022 USA

**Gilliford, Paul G** — Baseball Player
7 Woodland Dr, Malvern PA 19355, USA

**Gilligan, Carol** — Educator
Harvard University, Gender Studies Dept, Cambridge MA 02138, USA

**Gilligan, Paul** — Cartoonist
160 Baldwin St, #607, Toronto ON M5T 1L8, Canada

**Gilligan, Vince** — Producer
I C M Partners, 10250 Constellation Blvd, #900, Los Angeles CA 90067 USA

**Gillilan, William J, III** — Businessman
Centex Corp, PO Box 199000, Dallas TX 75219, USA

**Gilliland, David** — Auto Racing Driver
8556 Dog Leg Road, Sherrills Ford NC 28673, USA

**Gilliland, Richard** — Actor
9145 W Sunset Blvd, #228, West Hollywood CA 90069, USA

**Gilliland, Robert J (Bob)** — Test Pilot
PO Box 84, Palm Desert CA 92261, USA

**Gillingham, Charles T (Charlie)** — Musician (Counting Crowes)
Geffen Records, 10900 Wilshire Blvd, #1000, Los Angeles CA 90024 USA

**Gillispie, Billy C** — Basketball Coach
Texas Tech University, Athletic Dept, Lubbock TX 79409, USA

**Gillom, Jennifer** — Basketball Player
Washington Mystics, Verizon Center, 401 9th St NW, #750, Washington DC 20004 USA

**Gilman, Alfred G** — Nobel Medicine Laureate
10996 Crooked Creek Dr, Dallas TX 75229, USA

**Gilman, Jared** — Actor
D-mand Talent Agency, 85 S Broadway, #4, Nyack NY 10960, USA

**Gilman, Richard C** — Educator
131 Annandale Road, Pasadena CA 91105, USA

**Gilman, Richard H** — Publisher
Boston Globe, Publisher's Office, 135 Morrissey Blvd, Dorchester MA 02125, USA

**Gilman, Ronald Lee** — Judge
US Court of Appeals, 167 N Main St, #1176, Memphis TN 38103, USA

**Gilman, Sid** — Neurologist
3441 Geddes Road, Ann Arbor MI 48105, USA

**Gilmartin, Paul** — Actor, Comedian, Producer, Writer
Gersh Agency, 9465 Wilshire Blvd, #600, Beverly Hills CA 90212 USA

**Gilmer, Harry V** — Football Player
7467 Highway N, O'Fallon MO 63368, USA

**Gilmore, Alexie** — Actress
Paradigm Agency, 360 N Crescent Dr, North Building, Beverly Hills CA 90210 USA

**Gilmore, Artis** — Basketball Player
11043 Turnbridge Dr, Jacksonville FL 32256, USA

**Gilmore, Bryan** — Football Player
PO Box 815, Prosper TX 75078, USA

**Gilmore, Jimmie Dale** — Singer, Songwriter
Maine Road Mgmt, 195 Chrystie St, #901F, New York NY 10002, USA

**Gilmore, John** — Computer Software Designer, Activist
Electronic Frontier Foundation, 815 Eddy St, San Francisco CA 94109, USA

**Gilmore, John H, Jr** — Football Player
Gilmore/Henne Community Fund, Berks County Community Foundation, 237 Court St, Reading PA 19601, USA

**Gilmore, Stephanie** — Surfer
International Surfing Association, 5580 La Jolla Blvd, #145, La Jolla CA 92037 USA

**Gilmore, Stephone** — Football Player
Buffalo Bills, 1 Bills Dr, Orchard Park NY 14127 USA

**Gilmore, Thea** — Singer, Songwriter
Mongrel Music, 743 Center Blvd, Fairfax CA 94930, USA

**Gilmore, Walt** — Basketball Player
257 Benjamin Blvd, Bear DE 19701, USA

**Gilmour, Buddy** — Harness Racing Driver
50 Merrick Ave, #410, East Meadow NY 11554, USA

**Gilmour, David** — Singer, Guitarist (Pink Floyd)
One Fifteen, 1 Globe House, Middle Lane Mews, London 8N 8PN, England

**Gilmour, Doug** — Ice Hockey Player
Octagon Worldwide, 1751 Pinnacle Dr, #1500, McLean VA 22102 USA

**Gilmur, Charles E (Chuck)** — Basketball Player
230 Farallone Ave, Fircrest WA 98466, USA

**Gilot, Fabien** — Swimmer
C N Marseille, Extremite Blvd Charles Livon, 13007 Marseille, France

**Gilpin, Peri** — Actress
Burstein Co, 15304 W Sunset Blvd, #208, Pacific Palisades CA 90272 USA

**Gilpin, Robert G, Jr** — Political Scientist
133 Covington Lane, Shelburne VT 05482, USA

**Gilroy, Frank D** — Writer
8 Mangin Road, Monroe NY 10950, USA

**Gilroy, Tom** — Actor, Director, Producer, Writer
Sweet 180, 141 W 28th St, #300, New York NY 10001, USA

**Gilroy, Tony** — Writer, Director, Producer
Creative Artists Agency, 2000 Ave of Stars, #100, Los Angeles CA 90067 USA

**Gilsean, Matthew** — Singer (Celtic Tenors)
PO Box 32, Kells, County Meath, Ireland

**Gilsig, Jessalyn** — Actress
Paradigm Agency, 360 N Crescent Dr, North Building, Beverly Hills CA 90210 USA

**Gilyard, Clarence, Jr** — Actor, Director, Producer
Dick Delson Assoc, 4520 Bakman Ave, Studio City CA 91602, USA

**Gimble, Johnny** — Fiddle Player
Nancy Fly Agency, 6618 Wolfcreek Pall, Austin TX 78749, USA

**Gimbrone, Michael A, Jr** — Pathologist
Brigham & Women's Hospital, Vascular Pathology Dept, Boston MA 02115, USA

**Gimeno, Andres** — Tennis Player
Paseo de la Bonanova 38, Barcelona 6, Spain

**Gimpel, Erica** — Actress
Innovative Artists, 1505 10th St, Santa Monica CA 90401 USA

**Gina G** — Singer
What Mgmt, PO Box 1463, Culver City CA 90232, USA

**Ginepri, Robby** — Tennis Player
Olde Towne Athletic Club, 4950 Olde Towne Parkway, Marietta GA 30068, USA

**Ging, Jack** — Actor
48701 San Pedro St, La Quinta CA 92253, USA

**Ginger Fish** — Drummer (Marilyn Manson)
Coast II Coast Entertainment, 8671 Wilshire Blvd, Beverly Hills, CA 90211, USA

**Gingrich, Newton L (Newt)** — Representative, GA; Speaker
7410 Windy Hill Court, McLean VA 22102, USA

**Ginibre, Jean-Louis** — Editor
Hachette Filipacchi, Editorial Dept, 1633 Broadway, #4001, New York NY 10019, USA

**Ginn, Chad** — Golfer
Signature Sports Group, 4150 Olson Memorial Highway, #110, Minneapolis, MN 55422, USA

**Ginn, Drew C** — Rowing Athlete
Mercantile Rowing Club, 5 Boathouse Dr, Melbourne VIC 3000, Australia

**Ginn, Hubert (Hubie)** — Football Player
16 Egrets Nest Dr, Savannah GA 31406, USA

**Ginn, Theodore (Ted), Jr** — Football Player
18289 SW 54th St, Savannah GA 31406, USA

**Ginobili, Emmanuel (Manny)** — Basketball Player
10 Queens Hill, San Antonio TX 78257, USA

**Ginsburg, Ruth Bader** — Supreme Court Justice
US Supreme Court, 1 1st St NE, Washington DC 20543 USA

**Ginter, Keith** — Baseball Player
2907 Maple Ave, Fullerton CA 92835, USA

**Ginter, Matthew S (Matt)** — Baseball Player
3320 Boonesboro Road, Winchester KY 40391, USA

**Ginuwine** — Singer
Universal Attractions, 135 W 26th St, #1200, New York NY 10001 USA

**Giocante, Vahina** — Actress
Artmedia, 20 Ave Rapp, 75007 Paris, France

**Giola, Dana** — Government Official, Writer
National Endowment for Arts, 1100 Pennsylvania Ave NW, Washington DC 20004, USA

**Gionta, Brian** — Ice Hockey Player
PO Box 16499, Rochester NY 14616, USA

G

Gilman - Gionta

# G

**Giorgetti, Alex** — Water Polo Player
A S D Pro Recco, Via Biagio Assereto 10/A, 16036 Recco, Italy

**Giovanelli, Gordon** — Rowing Athlete
332 Ouci de la Loma, Escondido CA 92029, USA

**Giovanni, Joseph** — Architect
Giovanni Assoc, 140 E 40th St, New York NY 10016, USA

**Giovanni, Nikki E** — Writer
Virginia Polytechnic Institute, English Dept, Blacksburg VA 24061, USA

**Giovanola, Edward T (Ed)** — Baseball Player
1741 Nomark Court, San Jose CA 95125, USA

**Giovi, Andrea** — Volleyball Player
Sir Safety Perugio, Viale Giontella 1, 06083 Bastia Umbra, Italy

**Giovinazzo, Carmine** — Actor
Paradigm Agency, 360 N Crescent Dr, North Building, Beverly Hills CA 90210 USA

**Gipson, Charles W** — Baseball Player
632 S Earlham St, Orange CA 92869, USA

**Gipson, Dre** — Singer, Keyboardist (Fishbone)
Silverback Mgmt, 9469 Jefferson Blvd, #101, Culver City CA 90232, USA

**Giradelli, Marc** — Alpine Skier
Marc Giradelli Sport AG, Wiesentalstr 6, 9445 Reibstein, Switzerland

**Giraldo, Neil** — Producer, Composer
Bel Chiasso Entertainment, 7956 Glade Ave, Canoga Park CA 91304, USA

**Girard, Christine** — Weightlifter
British Columbia Weightlifting Assn, 1449 Hornby St, Vancouver BC V6Z 1W8, Canada

**Girard, Ken** — Ice Hockey Player
6-519 Riverside Dr, London ON N6H 5J3, Canada

**Girardi, Joseph E (Joe)** — Baseball Player, Manager
7320 Wisteria Ave, Parkland FL 33076, USA

**Girardin, Ray** — Actor
Academy of Performing Arts, PO Box 1843, Orleans MA 02653, USA

**Girardot, Hippolyte** — Actor
Artmedia, 20 Ave Rapp, 75007 Paris, France

**Giraud, Joyce** — Actress
C E S D, 10635 Santa Monica Blvd, #130, Los Angeles CA 90025 USA

**Giri, Tulsi** — Prime Minister, Nepal
Jawakpurdham, District Dhanuka, Nepal

**Girone, Remo** — Actor
Cristiano Cucchino Mgmt, Lungotevere dei Mellini 10, 00193 Rome, Italy

**Giscard d'Estaing, Valery M R** — President, France
11 Rue Benouville, 75116 Paris, France

**Gisele** — Model
I M G Models, 304 Park Ave S, #PH N, New York NY 10010 USA

**Gish, Annabeth** — Actress
Innovative Artists, 1505 10th St, Santa Monica CA 90401 USA

**Gisin, Dominique** — Alpine Skier
Schwandstr 4A, 6390 Engelberg, Switzerland

**Gisler, Michael (Mike)** — Football Player
407 Tampa Dr, Victoria TX 77904, USA

**Gisondo, Skyler** — Actor
Paradigm Agency, 360 N Crescent Dr, North Building, Beverly Hills CA 90210 USA

**Gitlin, Todd** — Historian
New York University, Culture & Communications Dept, New York NY 10012, USA

**Gittins, Jeremy** — Actor
Associated International Mgmt, 7 Hatton Garden, #400, London EC1N 8AD, England

**Gitto, Niccolo** — Water Polo Player
A S D Pro Recco, Via Biagio Assereto 10/A, 16036 Recco (GE), Italy

**Giuliani, Rudolph W** — Mayor, New York City
Giuliani Partners, 5 Times Square, Converse Level 1, New York NY 10036, USA

**Giuliano, Louis J** — Businessman
I T T Industries, 4 W Red Oak Lane, #200, West Harrison NY 10604, USA

**Giuliano, Tom** — Singer (Happenings)
6929 N Hayden Road, Scottsdale AZ 85250, USA

**Giuntoli, David** — Actor
C E S D, 10635 Santa Monica Blvd, #130, Los Angeles CA 90025 USA

**Giuranna, Bruno** — Concert Violist
Via Bembo 96, 31011 Asolo TV, Italy

**Giurescu, Dino** — Historian
3033 32nd St, Astoria NY 11102, USA

**Giusti, David J (Dave)** — Baseball Player
524 Clair Dr, Pittsburgh PA 15241, USA

**Giusti, Katy** — Foundation Executive
Multiple Myeloma Research Consortium, 383 Main Ave, #500, Norwalk CT 06851, USA

**Givens, Adele** — Actress, Comedienne
Artistry Mgmt, 340 N Camden Dr, #302, Beverly Hills CA 90210, USA

**Givens, David L** — Football Player
1117 Lochland Dr, Gallatin TN 37066, USA

**Givens, Robin** — Actress, Model
Marshak/Zachary/Mills, 8840 Wilshire Blvd, #100, Beverly Hills CA 90211 USA

**Givhan, Robin** — Journalist
Washington Post, Editorial Dept, 1150 15th St NW, Washington DC 20071 USA

**Givins, Brian A** — Baseball Player
719 Stonemont Court, Castle Rock CO 80108, USA

**Givins, Ernest P, Jr** — Football Player
3115 48th Ave S, Saint Petersburg FL 33712, USA

**Gizenga, Antoine** — Premier, Congo Democratic Republic
Palais de la Primature, BP 1354, Brazzaville, Congo Republic

**Gizyn, Louie** — Artist
1161 NW Taylor Ave, Corvallis OR 97330, USA

**Gjertsen, Douglas (Doug)** — Swimmer
7130 Havenridge Way, McDonough GA 30253, USA

**Gjokaj, Enver** — Actor
Suskin Mgmt, 2 Charlton St, #5K, New York NY 10014, USA

**Gladden, C Daniel (Dan)** — Baseball Player
6543 Pinnacle Dr, Eden Prairie MN 55346, USA

**Gladding, Fred E** — Baseball Player
436 Marsh Pointe Dr, Columbia SC 29229, USA

| | |
|---|---|
| **Gladis, Michael** | Actor |
| Stone Manners Salners, 6100 Wilshire Blvd, #1500, Los Angeles CA 90035 USA | |
| **Gladwell, Malcolm** | Writer |
| Black Bay/Little Brown, 3 Center Plaza, Boston MA 02108, USA | |
| **Glaesser, Jasmin** | Cyclist |
| National Cycling Assn, 2197 Riverside Dr, #203, Ottawa ON K1H 7X3, Canada | |
| **Glaister, Lesley** | Writer |
| A M Heath Co, 79 Saint Martin's Lane, London WC2N 4RE, England | |
| **Glance, Harvey** | Track Athlete |
| 2408 Old Creek Road, Montgomery AL 36117, USA | |
| **Glanfield, Joe** | Yachtsman |
| W N W Design, 24A Upper Church St, Exmouth, Devon EX8 2TA, England | |
| **Glanville, Brian L** | Writer |
| 160 Holland Park Ave, London W11 4UH, England | |
| **Glanville, Douglas M (Doug)** | Baseball Player |
| 2043 W McLean Ave, Chicago IL 60647, USA | |
| **Glanville, Jerry** | Football Coach, Auto Racing Driver |
| Jerry Glanville Motorsports, 550 Twinflower Court, Roswell GA 30075, USA | |
| **Glasbergen, Randy** | Cartoonist (Better Half) |
| King Features Syndicate, 300 W 57th St, #1500, New York NY 10019 USA | |
| **Glaser, Daniel** | Sociologist |
| 63 Walk Hill St, Jamaica Plain MA 02130, USA | |
| **Glaser, Jim** | Singer |
| Joe Taylor Artist Agency, 2802 Columbine Place, Nashville TN 37204 USA | |
| **Glaser, Jon** | Actor, Writer |
| Creative Artists Agency, 2000 Ave of Stars, #100, Los Angeles CA 90067 USA | |
| **Glaser, Milton** | Graphic Artist |
| Milton Glaser Assoc, 207 E 32nd St, New York NY 10016, USA | |
| **Glaser, Paul Michael** | Actor, Director |
| 11939 Weddington St, #106, Valley Village CA 91607, USA | |
| **Glaser, Rob** | Businessman, Inventor |
| Real Networks, 2601 Elliott Ave, Seattle WA 98121, USA | |
| **Glaser, Robert J** | Foundation Executive |
| 868 Boyce Ave, Palo Alto CA 94301, USA | |
| **Glaser, Rose Mary** | Baseball Player |
| 8929 Long Lane, Cincinnati OH 45231, USA | |
| **Glasgow, Nesby L** | Football Player |
| 8402 165th Ave NE, #106, Redmond WA 98052, USA | |
| **Glasgow, Walter** | Yachtsman |
| 781 Silver Spur Dr, Weatherford TX 76087, USA | |
| **Glashow, Jonathan L** | Sports Medicine Surgeon |
| 737 Park Ave, New York NY 10021, USA | |
| **Glashow, Sheldon Lee** | Nobel Physics Laureate |
| 30 Prescott St, Brookline MA 02446, USA | |
| **Glasper, Robert** | Jazz Pianist |
| Second Son Productions, 5500 Prytania St, #142, New Orleans LA 70115, USA | |
| **Glaspie, April** | Diplomat |
| State Department, 2201 C St NW, Washington DC 20520 USA | |
| **Glass, Charles (Chip)** | Football Player |
| 23704 Lake Dr E, Bothell WA 98021, USA | |
| **Glass, David D** | Businessman |
| Wal-Mart Stores, 702 SW 8th St, Bentonville AK 72712, USA | |
| **Glass, Gerald** | Basketball Player |
| 1123 Tillman Road, Port Gibson MS 39150, USA | |
| **Glass, Glenn M** | Football Player |
| 301 Portsmouth Road, Knoxville TN 37909, USA | |
| **Glass, Leland S** | Football Player |
| 9 Bayou Court, Sacramento CA 95831, USA | |
| **Glass, Mona** | Actress |
| Agentur Eberstein, Mullenhoffstr 2, 10967 Berlin, Germany | |
| **Glass, Philip** | Composer |
| 48 E 3rd St, #2, New York NY 10003, USA | |
| **Glass, Ron** | Actor |
| Mitchell K Stubbs Assoc, 8695 W Washington Blvd, #204, Culver City CA 90232 USA | |
| **Glass, William S (Bill)** | Football Player |
| Bill Glass Ministries, PO Box 761101, Dallas TX 75376, USA | |
| **Glasser, Ira S** | Attorney |
| American Civil Liberties Union, 132 W 43rd St, New York NY 10036, USA | |
| **Glassic, Thomas J (Tom)** | Football Player |
| 1030 S Pine Dr, Bailey CO 80421, USA | |
| **Glassner, Barry** | Educator, Sociologist |
| Lewis & Clark College, President's Office, 0615 SW Palatine Hill Road, Portland OR 97219, USA | |
| **Glasson, Bill** | Golfer |
| 5819 W Villas Court, Stillwater OK 74074, USA | |
| **Glasson, Stephanie** | Model |
| Playboy Promotions, 9346 Civic Center Dr, #200, Beverly Hills CA 90210 USA | |
| **Glätter, Lesli Linka** | Director, Producer |
| Anonymous Content, 3532 Hayden Ave, Culver City CA 90232 USA | |
| **Glau, Summer L** | Actress |
| Schiff Co, 9220 Sunset Blvd, #106, West Hollywood CA 90069 USA | |
| **Glauber, Robert R** | Businessman |
| National Association of Securities Dealers, 33 Whitehall St, New York NY 10004, USA | |
| **Glauber, Roy J** | Nobel Physics Laureate |
| 221 Pleasant St, Arlington MA 02476, USA | |
| **Glaudini, Lola** | Actress |
| Paul Kohner, 9300 Wilshire Blvd, #555, Beverly Hills CA 90212 USA | |
| **Glaus, Troy E** | Baseball Player |
| 4300 Bibleway Court, Holly Springs NC 27540, USA | |
| **Glave, Matthew** | Actor |
| Sanders/Armstrong/Caserta Mgmt, 2120 Colorado Ave, #120, Santa Monica CA 90404 USA | |
| **Glaviano, Marco** | Photographer |
| 150 W 56th St, New York NY 10019, USA | |
| **Glavine, Thomas M (Tom)** | Baseball Player |
| 920 Hurleston Lane, Alpharetta GA 30022, USA | |
| **Glazer, Eugene Robert** | Actor |
| 20058 Ventura Blvd, #61, Woodland Hills CA 91364, USA | |

**G**

**Gladis - Glazer**

**Glazer, Jay** — Sportscaster
Fox-TV, Sports Dept, 205 W 67th St, New York NY 10065 USA

**Glazer, Jonathan** — Director
Independent Talent Group, 40 Whitfield St, London W1T 2RH, England

**Glazer, Nathan** — Sociologist
12 Scott St, Cambridge MA 02138, USA

**Glazunov, Ilya S** — Artist
Academy of Painting, Myasnitskaya Str 21, 101000 Moscow, Russia

**Gleason, Joanna** — Actress
Innovative Artists, 1505 10th St, Santa Monica CA 90401 USA

**Gleason, Timothy (Tim)** — Ice Hockey Player
2908 Spaldwick Court, Raleigh NC 27613, USA

**Gleason, Vanessa** — Model, Actress
4821 Lankershim Blvd, #F, North Hollywood CA 91601, USA

**Gleaton, Jerry Don** — Baseball Player
3008 Ave K, Brownwood TX 76801, USA

**Glebova, Natalie** — Beauty Queen
Miss Universe Organization, 1370 Ave of Americas, #1600, New York NY 10019 USA

**Gleeson, Brendan** — Actor, Director, Writer
The Agency, 9 Upper Fitzwilliam St, Dublin 2, Ireland

**Gleeson, Domhnall** — Actor, Writer, Director
The Agency, 9 Upper Fitzwilliam St, Dublin 2, Ireland

**Glen, Iain** — Actor
Independent Talent Group, 40 Whitfield St, London W1T 2RH, England

**Glen, John** — Director
Skouras Agency, 1149 3rd St, #300, Santa Monica CA 90403 USA

**Glen, Marla** — Singer
Mom Productions, 20 Rue de la Providence, 75013 Paris, France

**Glendon, Mary Ann** — Attorney, Educator
Harvard University, Law School, Cambridge MA 02138, USA

**Glenesk, Dean** — Modern Pentathlete
1705 Ben Crenshaw Way, Austin TX 78746, USA

**Glenister, Philip** — Actor
Artists Partnership, 101 Finsbury Pavement, London EC2A 1RS, England

**Glenn, Aaron D** — Football Player
30 Commanders Cove, Missouri City TX 77459, USA

**Glenn, Devon** — Drummer (Buckcherry)
10th Street Mgmt, 700 N San Vicente Blvd, #G410, West Hollywood CA 90069, USA

**Glenn, Jason** — Football Player
15530 Ella Blvd, #501, Houston TX 77090, USA

**Glenn, John** — Baseball Player
32 Edgewater Ave, Beverly NJ 08010, USA

**Glenn, John** — Director, Writer
Brian Lutz Mgmt, 6565 Sunset Blvd, #416, Los Angeles CA 90028, USA

**Glenn, John H, Jr** — Senator, OH; Astronaut
Ohio State University, Stillman Hall, 1810 S College Road, Columbus OH 43210, USA

**Glenn, Mike T** — Basketball Player
3571 Kilpatrick Lane, Snellville GA 30039, USA

**Glenn, Scott** — Actor
Innovative Artists, 1505 10th St, Santa Monica CA 90401 USA

**Glenn, Tarik** — Football Player
2224 Ward St, Berkeley CA 94705, USA

**Glenn, Terrance T (Terry)** — Football Player
Dallas Cowboys, 1 Cowboys Parkway, Irving TX 75063 USA

**Glenn, Tyler** — Keyboardist, Singer (Neon Trees)
Creative Artists Agency, 2000 Ave of Stars, #100, Los Angeles CA 90067 USA

**Glenn, Wendy** — Actress
Paradigm Agency, 360 N Crescent Dr, North Building, Beverly Hills CA 90210 USA

**Glennie, Brian A** — Ice Hockey Player
4 Curling Road, Bracebridge ON P1L 1M6, Canada

**Glennie, Evelyn E A** — Concert Percussionist
PO Box 6, Sawtry, Huntingdon, Cambridgeshire PE17 5WE, England

**Glennie-Smith, Nick** — Composer
First Artists Mgmt, 4764 Park Granada, #210, Calabasas CA 91302 USA

**Gless, Sharon** — Actress
Domain Talent, 9229 W Sunset Blvd, #710, West Hollywood CA 90069 USA

**Glick, Frederick C (Freddy)** — Football Player
4226 Antlers Court, Fort Collins CO 80526, USA

**Glick, Gary G** — Football Player
2801 Middlesborough Court, Fort Collins CO 80525, USA

**Glicker, Daniel (Danny)** — Costume Designer
I C M Partners, 10250 Constellation Blvd, #900, Los Angeles CA 90067 USA

**Glickman, Andrew Z** — Photographer
4903 Newport Ave, Bethesda MD 20816, USA

**Glickman, Daniel R** — Secretary, Agriculture
Motion Picture Association, 4635 Ashby St NW, Washington DC 20007, USA

**Glidden, Bob** — Auto Racing Driver
Route 1, Box 236, Whiteland IN 46184, USA

**Glidewell, Iain** — Judge
Rough Heys Farm, Macclesfield, Cheshire SK11 9PF, England

**Glier, Seth** — Singer, Songwriter
Mpress Records, 200 E 10th St, #106, New York NY 10003, USA

**Glimcher, Arnold O (Arne)** — Director, Producer, Composer
Paradigm Agency, 360 N Crescent Dr, North Building, Beverly Hills CA 90210 USA

**Glimcher, Laurie H** — Rheumatologist
Weill Cornell Medical College, Dean's Office, 1300 York Ave, New York NY 10065, USA

**Glimm, James G** — Mathematician
State University of New York, Applied Mathematics Dept, Stony Brook NY 11794, USA

**Glinatsis, George** — Baseball Player
13742 W 59th Ave, Arvada CO 80004, USA

**Glisson, Henry T (Tom)** — Army General
V T Services, 40 E 52nd St, #1400, New York NY 10022, USA

**Glitter, Gary** — Singer, Songwriter
Jef Hanlon Mgmt, 1 York St, London W1H 1PZ, England

**Glitter, Lesli Linka** — Director
Anonymous Content, 3532 Hayden Ave, Culver City CA 90232 USA

| | |
|---|---|
| **Gload, Ross P** <br> 23 Harrison Ave, East Hampton NY 11937, USA | Baseball Player |
| **Globus, Yoram** <br> Pathe International, 8670 Wilshire Blvd, Beverly Hills CA 90211, USA | Producer |
| **Glocer, Tom** <br> Reuters Group PLC, Canary Wharf, South Colonnade, London E14 5EP, England | Businessman |
| **Glockner, Michael** <br> Kaiserslautener Str 54, 66123 Saarbrucken, Germany | Cyclist |
| **Gloor, Olga** <br> Professional Bowlers Association, 719 2nd Ave, #701, Seattle WA 98104 USA | Bowler |
| **Glouberman, Michael** <br> Creative Artists Agency, 2000 Ave of Stars, #100, Los Angeles CA 90067 USA | Producer, Writer |
| **Glover, Andrew L** <br> 33226 Magnolia Circle, Magnolia TX 77354, USA | Football Player |
| **Glover, Bloc** <br> American Motorcycle Assn, 13515 Yarmouth Dr, Pickerington OH 43147 USA | Motorcycle Racing Rider |
| **Glover, Bruce** <br> 11449 Woodbine St, Los Angeles CA 90066, USA | Actor |
| **Glover, Clarence** <br> 811 Lake Forest Parkway, Louisville KY 40245, USA | Basketball Player |
| **Glover, Corey** <br> Entertainment Artists, 2409 21st Ave S, #100, Nashville TN 10019 USA | Singer (Living Colour), Actor |
| **Glover, Crispin** <br> A P A Talent & Literary Agency, 405 S Beverly Dr, #300, Beverly Hills CA 90212 USA | Actor |
| **Glover, Danny** <br> Carrie Productions, 3200 College Ave, Berkeley CA 94705, USA | Actor |
| **Glover, Dion** <br> 3691 Seton Hall Way, Decatur GA 30034, USA | Basketball Player |
| **Glover, Donald** <br> Creative Artists Agency, 2000 Ave of Stars, #100, Los Angeles CA 90067 USA | Actor |
| **Glover, Helen** <br> Minerva Bath Rowing Club, 11 Bathwick St, #5, Bath BA2 6NX, England | Rowing Athlete |
| **Glover, Jane A** <br> Askonas Holt, Lincoln House, 300 High Holborn, London WC1V 7JH, England | Conductor |
| **Glover, John** <br> Innovative Artists, 1505 10th St, Santa Monica CA 90401 USA | Actor |
| **Glover, Julian** <br> Conway Van Gelder Grant, 8-12 Broadwick St, #300, London W1F 8HW, England | Actor |
| **Glover, Kevin B** <br> 11553 Manorstone Lane, Columbia MD 21044, USA | Football Player |
| **Glover, La'Roi D** <br> PO Box 410589, Saint Louis MO 63141, USA | Football Player |
| **Glover, Lucas** <br> 105 Annas Place, Simpsonville SC 29681, USA | Golfer |
| **Glover, M Dionae (Dion)** <br> 2052 Channing Dr, Conyers GA 30094, USA | Basketball Player |
| **Glover, Martin (Youth)** <br> Agency Group, 1100 Century Park E, #711, Los Angeles CA 90067 USA | Bassist (Killing Joke) |
| **Glover, Richard E (Rich)** <br> 215 Claremont Ave, Jersey City NJ 07305, USA | Football Player |
| **Glover, Roger D** <br> Thames Talent, 1720 Post Road E, #101, Westport CT 06880, USA | Bassist (Deep Purple) |
| **Glover, Savion** <br> Savion Glover Productions, 131 Brunswick St, Newark NJ 07114, USA | Dancer, Choreographer, Actor |
| **Glover, Stephen (Steve-O)** <br> I C M Partners, 10250 Constellation Blvd, #900, Los Angeles CA 90067 USA | Actor, Writer |
| **Glowacki, Janusz** <br> 845 W End Ave, #4B, New York NY 10025, USA | Writer |
| **Glowinski, Jacques** <br> Unite INSERM College de France, 111 Pl M Berthelot, 75005 Paris, France | Neuropharmacologist |
| **Gluck, Carol** <br> 440 Riverside Dr, New York NY 10027, USA | Historian |
| **Gluck, Louise E** <br> 14 Ellsworth Park, Cambridge MA 02139, USA | Writer |
| **Gluck, Will** <br> Olive Bridge Entertainment, 10202 W Washington Blvd, Hepburn West Bldg, Culver City CA 90232, USA | Director |
| **Gluckman, Richard** <br> Gluckman Mayer Architects, 250 Hudson Ave, New York NY 10013, USA | Architect |
| **Glueck, Lawrence D (Larry)** <br> 10 Cooper Road, East Falmouth MA 02536, USA | Football Player |
| **Glushchenko, Fedor I** <br> 1st Pryadilnaya Str 11, #5, 105037 Moscow, Russia | Conductor |
| **Glushenko, Yevgenia K** <br> 1905 Goda Str 3, #91, 123100 Moscow, Russia | Actress |
| **Glynn, Brian** <br> Prince Albert Police Dept, 1084 Central, Prince Albert SK S6V 7P3, Canada | Ice Hockey Player |
| **Glynn, Carlin** <br> 1165 5th Ave, New York NY 10029, USA | Actress |
| **Glynn, Edward P (Ed)** <br> 157 San Carlos St, Toms River NJ 08757, USA | Baseball Player |
| **Glynn, Ian M** <br> Daylesford, Conduit Head Road, Cambridge CB3 0EY, England | Physiologist |
| **Glynn, Ryan D** <br> 1226 Melaleuca Lane, Fort Myers FL 33901, USA | Baseball Player |
| **Gminski, Michael T (Mike)** <br> 1309 Canterbury Hill Circle, Charlotte NC 28211, USA | Basketball Player, Sportscaster |
| **Gnedovsky, Yuri P** <br> Union of Architects, Granatny Per 22, 103001 Moscow, Russia | Architect |
| **Goad, Jim** <br> Simon & Schuster, 1230 Ave of Americas, Concourse 1, New York NY 10020 USA | Journalist, Writer |
| **Goad, Timothy R (Tim)** <br> 138 Birchwood Dr, Pittsboro NC 27312, USA | Football Player |
| **Goalby, Bob** <br> 904 Briar Hill Road, Belleville IL 62223, USA | Golfer |
| **Goapele** <br> I C M Partners, 10250 Constellation Blvd, #900, Los Angeles CA 90067 USA | Singer |

**Gobble, B James (Jimmy)** — Baseball Player
150 Lake View Estates Dr, Bristol TN 37620, USA

**Gober, Robert** — Sculptor
Matthew Marks Gallery, 523 W 24 St, New York NY 10011, USA

**Goberville, Celine** — Markswoman
Federation de Tir, 38 Rue Brunel, 75017 Paris, France

**Goc, Marcel** — Ice Hockey Player
36 Reichert Circle, Westport CT 06880, USA

**Gocong, Christopher A (Chris)** — Football Player
PO Box 93, Berea OH 44017, USA

**Godal, Tore** — Physician
World Health Organization, 20 Ave Appia, 1211 Geneva 27, Switzerland

**Godard, Jean-Luc** — Director
26 Ave Pierre 1er de Serbie, 75116 Paris, France

**Godber, John** — Writer
Alan Brodie, Fairgate House, 78 New Oxford St, London WC1A 1HB, England

**Godby, Danny R** — Baseball Player
RR 2 Box 17A, Chapmanville WV 25508, USA

**Godchaux, Stephen** — Producer
Paradigm Agency, 360 N Crescent Dr, North Building, Beverly Hills CA 90210 USA

**Goddard, Joseph H (Joe)** — Baseball Player
304 Ridgepark Dr, Beckley WV 25801, USA

**Goddet, Michelle** — Actress
Artmedia, 20 Ave Rapp, 75007 Paris, France

**Goderie, Maartje** — Field Hockey Player
H C Den Bosch, Oosterplasweg 35, 5215 'S-Hertgebosch HT, Netherlands

**Godfread, Dan** — Basketball Player
622 Michigan St, Eagle River WI 54521, USA

**Godfrey** — Actor, Comedian
Paradigm Agency, 360 N Crescent Dr, North Building, Beverly Hills CA 90210 USA

**Godfrey, Christopher J (Chris)** — Football Player
52383 Swanson Dr, South Bend IN 46635, USA

**Godfrey, Paul V** — Businessman
Postmedia Network, 1450 Don Mills Road, Don Mills ON M3B 3R5, Canada

**Godfrey, Randall E** — Football Player
4102 Mount Zion Church Road, South Bend IN 46635, USA

**Godin, Elodie** — Basketball Player
Familia Basket Schio, Viale Dell'Industria, 36025 Schio, France

**Godley, Georgina** — Fashion Designer
42 Bassett Road, London W10 6UL, England

**Godmanis, Ivars** — Prime Minister, Latvia
Palasta St 1, 1954 Riga, Latvia

**Godovsky, Yan** — Ballet Dancer, Executive
Bolshoi Theater, Teatralnaya Pl 1, 103009 Moscow, Russia

**Godwin, Gail K** — Writer
PO Box 946, Woodstock NY 12498, USA

**Godwin, Linda M** — Astronaut, Physicist
3801 Eagle View Court, Columbia MO 65203, USA

**Godynyuk, Alexander** — Ice Hockey Player
217 Follen Road, Lexington MA 02421, USA

**Goeas, Leo D** — Football Player
95-104 Hiilei Place, Mililani HI 96789, USA

**Goebel, Timothy** — Figure Skater
Lee Marshall Mgmt, 199 E Garfield Road, Aurora OH 44202, USA

**Goeddeke, George A** — Football Player
1227 Pinecrest Dr, White Lake MI 48386, USA

**Goeddel, David V N** — Biochemist
Tularik Inc, 270 Grand Ave, San Francisco CA 94108, USA

**Goedgedrag, Frits M D L S** — Governor, Netherlands Antilles
Governor's Office, Fort Amsterdam 2, Willemstad, Netherlands Antilles

**Goehr, P Alexander** — Composer
University of Cambridge, Music Faculty, 11 West Road, Cambridge CB3 9DP, England

**Goellner, Marc-Kevin** — Tennis Athlete
Blau-Weiss Neuss, Tennishall Jahnstra, 41464 Neuss, Germany

**Goelz, Dave (Gonzo)** — Puppeteer
Jim Henson Productions, 117 E 69th St, New York NY 10021, USA

**Goen, Robert K (Bob)** — Entertainer
Rebel Entertainment Partners, 5700 Wilshire Blvd, #456, Los Angeles CA 90036, USA

**Goerke, Christine** — Opera Singer
I M G Artists, Hogarth Business Park, Chiswick, London W4 2TH, England

**Goerke, Glenn A** — Educator
University of Houston, President's Office, Houston TX 77204, USA

**Goerne, Matthias** — Opera Singer
I M G Artists, Hogarth Business Park, Chiswick, London W4 2TH, England

**Goertz, LeRoy** — Sculptor, Jewelry Designer, Composer
Refiner's Fire, PO Box 66612, Portland OR 97290, USA

**Goestschi, Renate** — Alpine Skier
Schwarzenbach 3, 8742 Obdach, Austria

**Goetz, Dick** — Golfer
4301 Fillbrook Lane, Tyler TX 75707, USA

**Goetz, Eric** — Yacht Builder
Eric Goetz Marine & Technology, 15 Broad Common Road, Bristol RI 02809, USA

**Goetz-Ackerman, Vicki** — Golfer
3621 Sally Parrish Trail, Valrico FL 33596, USA

**Goetzman, Gary M** — Producer
Playtone Productions, PO Box 7340, Santa Monica CA 90406, USA

**Goff, Michael J (Mike)** — Football Player
2225 5th St, Peru IL 61354, USA

**Goffin, Louise L** — Singer, Songwriter
Evolution Music, 1680 N Vine St, #500, Los Angeles CA 90028, USA

**Gogan, Kevin P** — Football Player
4643 286th Ave E, Fall City MA 98024, USA

**Goganious, Keith L** — Football Player
4173 Cheswick Lane, Virginia Beach VA 23455, USA

**Gogel, Matt** — Golfer
3509 W 68th St, Mission Hills KS 66208, USA

**Goggin, Charles F (Chuck)** — Baseball Player
1224 Roundhouse Lane, Alexandria VA 22314, USA

**Goggins, Walton** — Actor
I C M Partners, 10250 Constellation Blvd, #900, Los Angeles CA 90067 USA

**Gogo, David** — Guitarist
Cordova Bay Entertainment, 2750 Quadra St, #209, Victoria BC V8T 4EB, Canada

**Gogolak, Charles P (Charlie)** — Football Player
PO Box 361, Northeast Harbor ME 04662, USA

**Gogolak, Peter (Pete)** — Football Player
24 Arrowhead Way, Darien CT 06820, USA

**Gogolewski, William J (Bill)** — Baseball Player
1522 Graham Ave, Oshkosh WI 54902, USA

**Gogue, Jay** — Educator
Auburn University, President's Office, Auburn AL 36849, USA

**Goh Chok Tong** — Prime Minister, Singapore
Senior Minister's Office, Istana Annexe, 238823 Singapore, Singapore

**Goh, Rex** — Guitarist (Air Supply)
PO Box 3367, Beverly Hills CA 90212, USA

**Gohl, Matthias** — Composer
I C M Artists, 40 W 57th St, #1800, New York NY 10019 USA

**Gohlke, Frank** — Photographer
Howard Greenberg Gallery, 41 E 57th St, #1406, New York NY 10022, USA

**Gohr, Gregory J (Greg)** — Baseball Player
77 Scotland Road, Reading MA 01867, USA

**Goich, Daniel J (Dan)** — Football Player
PO Box 19068, Las Vegas NV 89132, USA

**Goicolea, Anthony** — Photographer
149-151 Grand St, #1, Brooklyn NY 11211, USA

**Goin, Suzanne** — Restauranteur
Lucques, 8484 Melrose Ave, West Hollywood CA 90069, USA

**Goines, Siena** — Actress
Don Buchwald Talent Agency, 6500 Wilshire Blvd, #2200, Los Angeles CA 90048 USA

**Going, Joanna** — Actress
Vanguard Management Group, 8060 Melrose Ave, #400, Los Angeles CA 90046, USA

**Goings, E V** — Businessman
Tupperware Corp, PO Box 2353, Orlando FL 32802, USA

**Goings, Nick A** — Football Player
660 Caicos Court, Wilmington NC 28405, USA

**Goitschel-Beranger, Marielle** — Alpine Skier
Val Thorens, 73440 Saint-Martin de Belleville, France

**Gojun, Jakov** — Handball Player
Club Balonmano Athletico, Paseo del Pintor Rosales 26, 28008 Madrid, Spain

**Golay, Jeanne** — Cyclist
1125 Red Mountain Dr, Glenwood Springs CO 81601, USA

**Gold, Christina A** — Businesswoman
Western Union, 12500 Belford Ave, Englewood CO 80112, USA

**Gold, Elon** — Actor, Comedian
Gersh Agency, 9465 Wilshire Blvd, #600, Beverly Hills CA 90212 USA

**Gold, Gracie** — Figure Skater
International Management Group, 50 Main St, #1625, White Plains NY 10606, USA

**Gold, Herbert** — Writer
1051 Broadway, #A, San Francisco CA 94133, USA

**Gold, Ian M** — Football Player
10275 Tradition Place, Lone Tree CO 80124, USA

**Gold, Jack** — Director
The Agency, 24 Pottery Lane, Holland Park,London W11 4LZ, England

**Gold, Jonathan** — Journalist
L A Weekly, Editorial Dept, 6715 Sunset Blvd, Los Angeles CA 90028, USA

**Gold, Tracey** — Actress
TalentWorks, 3500 W Olive Ave, #1400, Burbank CA 91505 USA

**Goldberg, Adam C** — Actor
Luber Rocklin Entertainment, 5815 Sunset Blvd, #206, Los Angeles CA 90028 USA

**Goldberg, Bernard R** — Commentator
CBS-TV, News Dept, 51 W 52nd St, New York NY 10019 USA

**Goldberg, Daryl** — Director, Producer
Pipeline Entertainment, 305 2nd Ave, #302, New York NY 10003, USA

**Goldberg, Eric** — Animator
Walt Disney Studios, Animation Dept, 500 S Buena Vista St, Burbank CA 91521, USA

**Goldberg, Evan** — Producer, Director
United Talent Agency, U T A Plaza, 9336 Civic Center Dr, Beverly Hills CA 90210 USA

**Goldberg, Fred T, Jr** — Government Official
Skadden Arps Slate, 1440 New York Ave NW, #600, Washington DC 20005, USA

**Goldberg, Harris** — Director, Writer
Key Creatives, 1800 N Highland Ave, Los Angeles CA 90028, USA

**Goldberg, Iddo** — Actor
Gordon & French, 12-13 Poland St, London W1F 8QB, England

**Goldberg, Jim** — Photographer
California College of Arts, Fine Arts Dept, San Francisco CA 94107, USA

**Goldberg, Leonard** — Producer
Spectradyne Inc, 1198 Commerce Dr, Richardson TX 75081, USA

**Goldberg, Lucianne S** — Publisher
4 Oak St, Weehawken NJ 7086, USA

**Goldberg, Luella G** — Educator
7019 Tupa Dr, Minneapolis MN 55439, USA

**Goldberg, Myla** — Writer
Doubleday Press, 1745 Broadway, New York NY 10019, USA

**Goldberg, Richard W** — Judge
US International Trade Court, 1 Federal Plaza, New York NY 10278, USA

**Goldberg, Stan** — Cartoonist (Archie)
8 White Birch Lane, Scarsdale NY 10583, USA

**Goldberg, Whoopi** — Actress, Comedienne, Writer, Producer
Whoop/One Ho Productions, 333 W 52nd St, #602, New York NY 10019, USA

**Goldberg, William S (Bill)** — Professional Wrestler, Football Player
L I N K Entertainment, 11872 La Grange Ave, Los Angeles CA 90025 USA

**Goldberg, Andreas** — Ski Jumper
Bleckenwegen 4, 4924 Waldzell, Austria

# G

**Goldberger, Marvin L** — Physicist, Educator
5205 Pacifica Dr, San Diego CA 92109, USA

**Goldberger, Paul J** — Journalist, Architectural Critic
New York Times, Editorial Dept, 229 W 43rd St, New York NY 10036, USA

**Goldblatt, David** — Photographer
South Picture Portal, Box 91776, Auckland Park, 2006 Gauteng, South Africa

**Goldblatt, Stephen L** — Cinematographer
Skouras Agency, 1149 3rd St, #300, Santa Monica CA 90403 USA

**Goldblum, Jeff** — Actor
I C M Partners, 10250 Constellation Blvd, #900, Los Angeles CA 90067 USA

**Golden, Alfred J (Al)** — Football Player, Coach
University of Miami, Athletic Dept, Coral Gables FL 33124, USA

**Golden, Arthur** — Writer
Vintage Books, 1745 Broadway, New York NY 10019 USA

**Golden, Daniel** — Journalist
Wall Street Journal, Editorial Dept, 1 World Financial Center, New York NY 10281, USA

**Golden, Harry** — Bowling Executive
Professional Bowlers Association, 719 2nd Ave, #701, Seattle WA 98104 USA

**Golden, James E (Jim)** — Baseball Player
8630 SW 10th Ave, Topeka KS 66615, USA

**Golden, Kate** — Golfer
969 Hunterwood Dr, Jasper TX 75951, USA

**Golden, William Lee** — Singer (Oak Ridge Boys); Songwriter
329 Rockland Road, Hendersonville TN 37075, USA

**Goldenhersh, Heather** — Actress
Gersh Agency, 9465 Wilshire Blvd, #600, Beverly Hills CA 90212 USA

**Goldenthal, Elliot** — Composer
Gorfaine/Schwartz, 4111 W Alameda Ave, #509, Burbank CA 91505 USA

**Goldfaden, Benjamin P (Ben)** — Basketball Player
5819 Bounty Circle, Tavares FL 32778, USA

**Goldfinger, June** — Interior Designer
June Goldfinger Designs, 109 Katonah Ave, Katonah NY 10536, USA

**Goldfinger, Myron** — Architect
PO Box 53, Waccabuc NY 10597, USA

**Goldfinger, Sarah** — Actress, Producer
Creative Artists Agency, 2000 Ave of Stars, #100, Los Angeles CA 90067 USA

**Goldhor, David** — Director
Eagle Eye, 4013 Topanga Ave, Studio City CA 91604, USA

**Goldin, Claudia D** — Economist
Harvard University, Economics Dept, Cambridge MA 02138, USA

**Goldin, Judah** — Educator
3300 Darby Road, Haverford PA 19041, USA

**Goldin, Nan** — Photographer
334 Bowery, New York NY 10012, USA

**Goldin, Ricky Paull** — Actor
Stone Manners Salners, 6100 Wilshire Blvd, #1500, Los Angeles CA 90035 USA

**Golding, Anders** — Marksman
Skytte Union, Idraettens Hus, Broendby Stadion 20, 2605 Brondby, Denmark

**Golding, Meta** — Actress
I F A Talent Agency, 8730 W Sunset Blvd, #490, West Hollywood CA 90069 USA

**Golding, O Bruce** — Prime Minister, Jamaica
Prime Minister's Office, 1 Devon Road, PO Box 272, Kingston 6, Jamaica

**Goldman, Bo** — Writer
Creative Artists Agency, 2000 Ave of Stars, #100, Los Angeles CA 90067 USA

**Goldman, Dan** — Writer
I C M Partners, 10250 Constellation Blvd, #900, Los Angeles CA 90067 USA

**Goldman, Jean-Jacques** — Singer, Guitarist, Songwriter
J S M Music, 73 Ave de la Republique, 92120 Montrouge, France

**Goldman, Julie** — Actress, Comedienne
427 Union St, #3, Brooklyn NY 11231, USA

**Goldman, Matt** — Entertainer (Blue Man Group)
Blue Man Group Productions, 411 Lafayette St, #300, New York NY 10003, USA

**Goldman, William** — Writer
Janklow & Nesbit Assoc, 445 Park Ave, #1300, New York NY 10022 USA

**Goldreich, Peter M** — Astronomer
471 S Catalina Ave, Pasadena CA 91106, USA

**Goldsboro, Bobby** — Singer, Songwriter
Jim Stephany Mgmt, 1021 Preston Dr, Nashville TN 37206, USA

**Goldschmidt, Neil E** — Secretary, Transportation; Governor, OR
1150 SW King Ave, Portland OR 97205, USA

**Goldsman, Akiva** — Director, Writer
Weed Road Pictures, 4000 Warner Blvd, Building 81, Burbank CA 91522, USA

**Goldsmith, Barbara** — Writer
Janklow Nesbit Assocs, 445 Park Ave, #1300, New York NY 10022, USA

**Goldsmith, Clio** — Actress
Elephant Family, 81 Gower St, London WC1E 6HJ, England

**Goldsmith, Judy** — Social Activist
National Organization for Women, 425 13th St NW, Washington DC 20002, USA

**Goldsmith, Myron** — Architect
Skidmore Owings Merrill, 224 S Michigan Ave, #1000, Chicago IL 60604, USA

**Goldsmith, Paul** — Auto Racing Driver, Motorcycle Rider
1705 E Main St, Griffith IN 46319, USA

**Goldsmith, Timothy H** — Biologist
Yale University, Biology Dept, New Haven CT 06520, USA

**Goldson, Dashon H** — Football Player
Tampa Bay Buccaneers, 1 W Buccaneer Place, Tampa FL 33607 USA

**Goldstein, Allan A** — Director
7017 Murietta Ave, Van Nuys CA 91405, USA

**Goldstein, Allan L** — Biochemist, Immunologist
PO Box 296, Reedville VA 22539, USA

**Goldstein, Alon** — Concert Pianist
Frank Salomon, 121 W 27th St, #703, New York NY 10001 USA

**Goldstein, Avram** — Pharmacologist
355 S Grand Ave, #2600, Los Angeles CA 90071, USA

**Goldstein, Joseph L** — Nobel Medicine Laureate
3831 Turtle Creek Blvd, #22B, Dallas TX 75219, USA

**Goldstein, Lisa** — Actress
Harrison Stokes, 8730 W Sunset Blvd, #270, West Hollywood CA 90069, USA
**Goldstein, Murray** — Physician, Association Executive
United Cerebral Palsy Foundation, 1660 L St NW, #700, Washington DC 20036, USA
**Goldstein, Rebecca** — Writer, Philosopher
2 Payamel Lane, Truro MA 02666, USA
**Goldstone, Jeffrey** — Physicist
77 Massachusetts Ave, #6-313, Cambridge MA 02139, USA
**Goldstone, Richard J** — Judge
Constitutional Court, Private Bag X32, Braamfontein 2017, South Africa
**Goldsworthy, Andrew C (Andy)** — Artist, Photographer
Hue-Williams Fine Art, 21 Cork St, London W1X 1HB, England
**Goldthwait, Bob (Bobcat)** — Actor, Comedian, Director
Gersh Agency, 9465 Wilshire Blvd, #600, Beverly Hills CA 90212 USA
**Goldwyn, Samuel J, Jr** — Producer
Samuel Goldwyn Co, 9570 W Pico Blvd, #400, Los Angeles CA 90035, USA
**Goldwyn, Tony** — Actor, Director
Creative Artists Agency, 2000 Ave of Stars, #100, Los Angeles CA 90067 USA
**Golic, Mike** — Football Player
108 Westland Road, Avon CT 06001, USA
**Golic, Robert P (Bob)** — Football Player, Sportscaster
6130 Loch Lomond Court, Solon OH 44139, USA
**Golijov, Osvaldo** — Composer
116 Thorndike St, Brookline MA 02446, USA
**Golimowski, David A** — Astronomer
515 Holden Road, Towson MD 21286, USA
**Golino, Valeria** — Actress
Cineart, 28 Rue Mogador, 78009 Paris, France
**Golisano, B Thomas** — Businessman
Paychex Inc, 911 Panorama Trail S, Rochester NY 14625, USA
**Golonka, Arlene** — Actress
H David Moss, 733 Seward St, #PH, Los Angeles CA 90038 USA
**Golota, Andrzej** — Boxer
26852 W Apple Tree Lane, Barrington IL 60010, USA
**Golovkin, Gennady G** — Boxer
Spotlight Boxing, Am Stadtrand 27, 22047 Hamburg, Germany
**Golson, Benny** — Jazz Saxophonist, Composer
Bridge Agency, 35 Clark St, #A5, Brooklyn Heights NY 11201, USA
**Golsteyn, Jerry M** — Football Player
2620 Lockwood Road, #202, Fayetteville NC 28303, USA
**Goltz, David A (Dave)** — Baseball Player
1009 Stonybrook Manor, Fergus Falls MN 56537, USA
**Golub, Jeff** — Jazz Guitarist
Chapman & Co Mgmt, 14011 Ventura Blvd, #405, Sherman Oaks CA 91423, USA
**Golubeva, Yekatarina** — Actress
Artmedia, 20 Ave Rapp, 75007 Paris, France
**Goluboff, Bryan** — Writer, Director
Paradigm Agency, 360 N Crescent Dr, North Building, Beverly Hills CA 90210 USA
**Golzari, Sam** — Actor
Innovative Artists, 1505 10th St, Santa Monica CA 90401 USA
**Gomes Junior, Carlos D** — Prime Minister, Guinea-Bissau
Premier's Office, Ave Unidad Africana, CP 137, Bissau, Guinea-Bissau
**Gomes, Jessica** — Model
Vivien's Model Mgmt, 43 Bay St, Double Bay, Sydney NSW 2028, Australia
**Gomes, Jonathan J (Jonny)** — Baseball Player
7901 Garden Dr N, Saint Petersburg FL 33710, USA
**Gomes, Wayne M** — Baseball Player
5104 W Creek Court, Suffolk VA 23435, USA
**Gomez Noya, Francisco Javier** — Triathlete
Mourente 9, 36164 Mourente, Spain
**Gomez, Andres** — Tennis Player
ProServe, 1101 Woodrow Wilson Blvd, #1800, Arlington VA 22209 USA
**Gomez, Carlos** — Actor
Stone Manners Salners, 6100 Wilshire Blvd, #1500, Los Angeles CA 90035 USA
**Gomez, Chris C** — Baseball Player
8 Vernal Spring, Irvine CA 92603, USA
**Gomez, Christian** — Soccer Player
D C United, R F K Stadium, 2400 E Capitol St SE, Washington DC 20003 USA
**Gomez, Ian** — Actor
A P A Talent & Literary Agency, 405 S Beverly Dr, #300, Beverly Hills CA 90212 USA
**Gomez, Jaime P** — Actor
Susan Nathe Assoc, 8281 Melrose Ave, #200, Los Angeles CA 90046, USA
**Gomez, Jeff** — Cartoonist
Starlight Runner Entertainment, 5 Union Square, #400, New York NY 10003, USA
**Gomez, Jill** — Opera Singer
16 Milton Park, London N6 5QA, England
**Gomez, Joshua E** — Actor
Progressive Artists Agency, 9696 Culver Blvd, #110, Culver City CA 90232 USA
**Gomez, Leonardo (Leo)** — Baseball Player
273 Portofino Dr, North Venice FL 34275, USA
**Gomez, Luis J** — Baseball Player
676 Chesterfield Dr, Lawrenceville GA 30044, USA
**Gomez, Mariette Himes** — Interior Designer
504 E 74th St, #300, New York NY 10021, USA
**Gomez, Randall S (Rocky)** — Baseball Player
50 Oak St, San Martin CA 95046, USA
**Gomez, Rick** — Actor, Writer, Producer
A P A Talent & Literary Agency, 405 S Beverly Dr, #300, Beverly Hills CA 90212 USA
**Gomez, Scott** — Ice Hockey Player
14121 Thunder Road, Anchorage AK 99516, USA
**Gomez, Selena M** — Actress, Singer
July Moon Productions, 10100 Santa Monica Blvd, #1300, Los Angeles CA 90067, USA
**Gomez, Wilfredo** — Boxer
U E C A, Edificio 54 Apt 01, Trujillo Alto PR 00976, USA
**Gomez-Preston, Reagan** — Actress
Innovative Artists, 1505 10th St, Santa Monica CA 90401 USA

**Gomis, Emilie** — Basketball Player
Federation de Basketball, Rue du Chateau des Rentiers 117, 75013 Paris, France

**Gomory, Ralph E** — Foundation Executive, Mathematician
Alfred P Sloan Foundation, President's Office, 630 5th Ave, New York NY 10111, USA

**Gompf, Thomas (Tom)** — Diver
2716 Barret Ave, Plant City FL 33566, USA

**Gomyo, Karen** — Concert Violinist
Seldy Cramer Artists, 3439 Springhill Road, Lafayette CA 94549, USA

**Gonchar, Sergei V** — Ice Hockey Player
7 Kevin Dr, Sewickley PA 15143, USA

**Gonchor, Jess** — Art Director
Murtha Agency, 4240 Promenade Way, #232, Marina del Rey CA 90292, USA

**Gondoline, Michel** — Actor
Alais Agence Artisqaue, 13 Rue Chevreul, 75011 Paris, France

**Gondrezick, Grant** — Basketball Player
5906 Etiwanda Ave, #19, Tarzana CA 91356, USA

**Gondry, Michel** — Director
Creative Artists Agency, 2000 Ave of Stars, #100, Los Angeles CA 90067 USA

**Gonet, Stella** — Actress
Markham Froggatt Irwin, Julian House, 4 Windmill St, London W1P 1HF, England

**Gong Li** — Actress, Model
I C M Partners, 10250 Constellation Blvd, #900, Los Angeles CA 90067 USA

**Gongora, Omar** — Drummer (Kinky)
Marcella C Public Relations, 646 S Barrington Ave, #206, Brentwood CA 90049, USA

**Gonick, Larry** — Cartoonist (Prehistoric Animals)
247 Missouri St, San Francisco CA 94107, USA

**Gonnenwein, Wolfgang** — Conductor
Buro Beate Gienger, Im Boblinger 2, 71636 Ludwigsburg, Germany

**Gonsalves, Ralph E** — Premier, Saint Vincent & Grenadines
Prime Minister's Office, Administration Centre, Kingstown, Saint Vincent & Grenadines

**Gonshaw, Francesca** — Actress
Greg Mellard, 12 D'Arblay St, #200, London W1V 3FP, England

**Gonzales, Carlos** — Cinematographer
3850 Tracy St, Los Angeles CA 90027, USA

**Gonzales, Chilly** — Singer, Songwriter
Agency Group Ltd, 1880 Century Park E, #711, Los Angeles CA 90067 USA

**Gonzales, Rene A** — Baseball Player
755 E Orangewood Dr, Covina CA 91723, USA

**Gonzalez Echevarria, Roberto** — Educator
Yale University, Hispanic/Comparative Literature Dept, New Haven CT 06520, USA

**Gonzalez Inarritu, Alejandro** — Director
Creative Artists Agency, 2000 Ave of Stars, #100, Los Angeles CA 90067 USA

**Gonzalez Marquez, Felipe** — Prime Minister, Spain
Fundacion Socialismo XXI, Gobelas 31, 28023 Madrid, Spain

**Gonzalez Zumarraga, Antonio J Cardinal** — Religious Leader
Arzobispado, Apartado 17-01-00106, Called Chile 1140, Quito, Ecuador

**Gonzalez, A Antonio (Tony)** — Baseball Player
8011 SW 196th Terrace, Cutler Bay FL 33189, USA

**Gonzalez, Adrian** — Baseball Player
Los Angeles Dodgers, Stadium, 1000 Elysian Park Ave, Los Angeles CA 90090 USA

**Gonzalez, Alex** — Actor
Kuranda Mgmt, Santo Angel 84, 28043 Madrid, Spain

**Gonzalez, Alexander S (Alex)** — Baseball Player
192 Acorn Trail, Fleetwood NC 28626, USA

**Gonzalez, Anthony D (Tony)** — Football Player
18935 Evening Breeze Circle, Huntington Beach CA 92648, USA

**Gonzalez, Arthur** — Judge
US Bankruptcy Court, 1 Bowling Green, #534, New York NY 10004, USA

**Gonzalez, Ashie** — Bowler
Professional Bowlers Association, 719 2nd Ave, #701, Seattle WA 98104 USA

**Gonzalez, Carlos A** — Baseball Player
Colorado Rockies, Coors Field, 2001 Blake St, #A, Denver CO 80205 USA

**Gonzalez, Fredi J** — Baseball Manager
2768 Pete Shaw Road, Marietta GA 30066, USA

**Gonzalez, Giovanny A (Gio)** — Baseball Player
Oakland Athletics, McAfee Coliseum, 7000 Coliseum Way, #3, Oakland CA 94621 USA

**Gonzalez, Hector** — Religious Leader
Baptist Churches USA, PO Box 851, Valley Forge PA 19482, USA

**Gonzalez, Jaslene** — Model
Elite Model Mgmt, 404 Park Ave S, #900, New York NY 10016 USA

**Gonzalez, Juan A** — Baseball Player
Ext Catoni A9, Vega Baja PR 00693, USA

**Gonzalez, Lissette** — Commentator, Model
CBS4-TV, 8900 NW 18th Terrace, Doral FL 33172, USA

**Gonzalez, Michael V (Mike)** — Baseball Player
2414 Pine Brook Court, Deer Park TX 77536, USA

**Gonzalez, Nicholas** — Actor
Pakula/King, 9229 W Sunset Blvd, #315, West Hollywood CA 90069 USA

**Gonzalez, Omar** — Soccer Player
Los Angeles Galaxy, Home Depot Center, 18400 Avalon Blvd, Carson CA 90746 USA

**Gonzalez, Pedro O** — Baseball Player
104 Gen Cabral, San Pedro de Macoris, Dominican Republic

**Gonzalez, Raul** — Soccer Player
F C Real Madrid, Avda Concha Espana 1, 28036 Madrid, Spain

**Gonzalez, Rick** — Actor
Framework Entertainment, 9057 Nemo St, #C, West Hollywood CA 90069 USA

**Gonzalo, Julie** — Actress
United Talent Agency, U T A Plaza, 9336 Civic Center Dr, Beverly Hills CA 90210 USA

**Gonzi, Lawrence** — Prime Minister, Malta
Prime Minister's Office, Auberge de Castille, 13 Saint Paul's St, Valletta VLT 1210, Malta

**Gooch, Jeffrey L (Jeff)** — Football Player
12709 Seronera Valley Court, Spring Hill FL 34610, USA

**Gooch, Rich** — Bassist (Quarterflash)
Pacific Talent Agency, PO Box 19145, Portland OR 97280, USA

**Good, Andrew R** — Baseball Player
1433 S Belcher Road, #G4, Clearwater FL 33764, USA

**Good, Hugh W**
Primitive Advent Christian Church, 6403 Frame Road, Elkview WV 25071, USA — Religious Leader

**Good, Meagan**
Untitled Entertainment, 350 S Beverly Dr, #200, Beverly Hills CA 90212 USA — Actress

**Good, Michael T**
2617 Broussard Court, Seabrook TX 77586, USA — Astronaut

**Goodacre Connick, Jill**
Harry Connick, Wilkins Mgmt, 323 Broadway, Cambridge MA 02139, USA — Model

**Goodacre, Glenna**
1202 Ojo Verde, Santa Fe NM 87501, USA — Sculptor

**Goodall, Caroline**
United Agents, 12-26 Lexington St, London W1F 0LE, England — Actress

**Goodall, V Jane**
Jane Goodall Institute, 4245 N Fairfax Dr, #600, Arlington VA 22203, USA — Ethologist, Primatologist

**Goodburn, Kelly J**
3710 W 52nd Place, Mission KS 66205, USA — Football Player

**Goode, Chris K**
1428 Egret Lane, Birmingham AL 35214, USA — Football Player

**Goode, David R**
Norfolk Southern Corp, 3 Commercial Place, #100, Norfolk VA 23510, USA — Businessman

**Goode, Donald R (Don)**
30177 Tattersall Way, Menifee CA 92584, USA — Football Player

**Goode, Irvin L (Irv)**
1030 Schnucks Woodsmill Plaza, Chesterfield MO 63017, USA — Football Player

**Goode, Joe**
PO Box 10372, Playa del Rey CA 90291, USA — Artist

**Goode, Matthew**
Dalzell & Beresford, 55 Charterhouse St, Paddock Suite, London EC1M 6HA, England — Actor

**Goode, Richard S**
Frank Salomon, 121 W 27th St, #703, New York NY 10001 USA — Concert Pianist

**Goode, W Wilson**
Amachi, 2000 Market St, #600, Philadelphia PA 19103, USA — Mayor, Philadelphia; Social Activist

**Goodell, Brian S**
27040 S Ridge Dr, Mission Viejo CA 92692, USA — Swimmer

**Goodell, Roger**
National Football League, 280 Park Ave, #12W, New York NY 10017, USA — Football Executive

**Gooden, Dwight E**
20114 Nob Oak Ave, Tampa FL 33647, USA — Baseball Player

**Goodenough, Ward H**
3300 Darby Road, #5306, Haverford PA 19041, USA — Anthropologist

**Goodfellow, Peter N**
Cancer Research Fund, Lincoln Inn Fields, London WC2A 3PX, England — Geneticist

**Goodfriend, Lynda**
338 S Beachwood Dr, Burbank CA 91506, USA — Actress

**Gooding, Cuba, Jr**
14320 W Sunset Blvd, Pacific Palisades CA 90272, USA — Actor

**Gooding, Cuba, Sr**
Universal Attractions, 135 W 26th St, #1200, New York NY 10001 USA — Singer (Main Ingredient)

**Gooding, Omar**
Innovative Artists, 1505 10th St, Santa Monica CA 90401 USA — Actor

**Goodison, Paul**
Utley Sailing Club, Pleasley Road, Aughton, Sheffield S26 3XL, England — Yachtsman

**Goodkind, Terry**
G P Putnam's Sons, 375 Hudson St, New York NY 10014 USA — Writer

**Goodman, Alfred**
Bodenstedtstr 31, 81241 Munich, Germany — Composer

**Goodman, Allegra**
Dial Press, 375 Hudson St, New York NY 10014, USA — Writer

**Goodman, Brian**
Nine Yards Entertainment, 8530 Wilshire Blvd, #500, Beverly Hills CA 90211 USA — Actor

**Goodman, Corey S**
Howard Hughes Medical Institute, Molecular/Cell Biology Dept, Berkeley CA 94720, USA — Neurobiologist

**Goodman, Eli**
Maverick Artists Agency, 1680 N Vine St, #802, Los Angeles CA 90028, USA — Actor

**Goodman, Ellen H**
Boston Globe, Editorial Dept, 135 William Morrissey Blvd, Dorchester MA 02125 USA — Columnist

**Goodman, Gregory (Greg)**
I C M Partners, 10250 Constellation Blvd, #900, Los Angeles CA 90067 USA — Producer

**Goodman, Hazelle**
C E S D, 10635 Santa Monica Blvd, #130, Los Angeles CA 90025 USA — Actress

**Goodman, John**
Gersh Agency, 9465 Wilshire Blvd, #600, Beverly Hills CA 90212 USA — Actor

**Goodman, John F**
Commander, Marine Forces Pacific, Camp H M Smith HI 96861 USA — Marine Corps General

**Goodman, John R**
800 E 9th St, Edmond OK 73034, USA — Football Player

**Goodman, Joseph W**
570 University Terrace, Los Altos CA 94022, USA — Electrical Engineer

**Goodman, Katy (La Sera)**
Agency Group Ltd, 1880 Century Park E, #711, Los Angeles CA 90067 USA — Singer, Songwriter

**Goodman, Len**
Strictly Come Dancing, BBC Television, Wood Lane, London W12 7RJ, England — Dance Judge

**Goodman, Oscar**
520 S 4th St, Las Vegas NV 89101, USA — Attorney

**Goodrem, Delta**
Harbour Agency, 135 Forbes St, Woolloomooloo NSW 2011, Australia — Singer, Pianist

**Goodrich, Gail C, Jr**
PO Box 4969, Greenwich CT 06831, USA — Basketball Player

**Goodridge, Robin J**
Front Line Mgmt, 1100 Glendon Ave, #2000, Los Angeles CA 90024 USA — Drummer (Bush)

**Goodrum, Charles L (Charlie)**
117 Pico Road, East Palatka FL 32131, USA — Football Player

**Goodson, J Edward (Ed)**
PO Box 1655, Palatka FL 32178, USA — Baseball Player

**Goodwin, Carly**
3624 Westbrook Ave, Nashville TN 37205, USA — Singer

**Goodwin, Danny K** — Baseball Player
1555 Linksview Close, Stone Mountain GA 30088, USA

**Goodwin, Doris Kearns** — Historian, Commentator
1649 Monument Lane, Concord MA 01742, USA

**Goodwin, Frederick Tutu** — Queen's Representative, Cook Islands
Queen's Representative's Office, Avarua, Rarotonga, Cook Islands

**Goodwin, Ginnifer** — Actress
John Carrabino Mgmt, 5900 Wilshire Blvd, #406, Los Angeles CA 90036 USA

**Goodwin, Gordon** — Jazz Orchestra Leader
Randex Communications, 906 Jonathan Lane, Marlton NJ 08053, USA

**Goodwin, Malcolm J** — Actor
I F A Talent Agency, 8730 W Sunset Blvd, #490, West Hollywood CA 90069 USA

**Goodwin, Michael** — Labor Leader
Office & Professional Employees, 1660 L St NW, #801, Washington DC 20036, USA

**Goodwin, Michael** — Actor
Rosella Olson Mgmt, 319 W 105th St, #1F, New York NY 10025, USA

**Goodwin, R Hunter** — Football Player
1011 Lyceum Court, College Station TX 77840, USA

**Goodwin, Raven** — Actress
C E S D, 10635 Santa Monica Blvd, #130, Los Angeles CA 90025 USA

**Goodwin, Ronald R (Ronnie)** — Football Player
3702 Sul Ross St, San Angelo TX 76904, USA

**Goodwin, Thomas J (Tom)** — Baseball Player
8 Maple St, Massapequa NY 11758, USA

**Goodwin, Trudie** — Actress
Bosun House, 1 Deer Park Road, Merton, London SW19 3TL, England

**Goodwyn, Myles** — Singer, Guitarist (April Wine)
S L Feldman Mgmt, 1505 W 2nd Ave, #200, Vancouver BC V6H 3Y4, Canada

**Goody, Joan E** — Architect
Goody Clancy Assoc, 334 Boylston St, Boston MA 02116, USA

**Goodyear, Scott** — Auto Racing Driver
Scott Goodyear Racing, PO Box 589, Carmel IN 46082, USA

**Goodyear, Stewart** — Concert Pianist
Columbia Artists Mgmt Inc, 5 Columbus Circle, 1790 Broadway, #1600, New York NY 10019 USA

**Goolagong Cawley, Yvonne F** — Tennis Player
PO Box 1347, Noosa Heads QLD 4567, Australia

**Goolrick, Robert** — Writer
Algonquin Books, PO Box 27515, Chapel Hill NC 27515 USA

**Goolsby, Austan D** — Government Official, Economist
White House, 1600 Pennsylvania Ave NW, Washington DC 20500 USA

**Goorjian, Michael** — Actor
Lyceum Entertainment, 4221 Hollis St, Emeryville CA 94608, USA

**Goose, Claire** — Actress
C A M, 55-59 Shaftesbury Ave, London W1D 6LD, England

**Goosen, Retief** — Golfer
9228 Sloane St, Orlando FL 32827, USA

**Goossen, Jeananne** — Actress
Characters Talent Agency, 8 Elm St, Toronto, ON M5G 1G7, Canada

**Gopnik, Adam** — Writer
New Yorker, Editorial Dept, 4 Times Square, Basement C1B, New York NY 10036 USA

**Gora, Jo Ann M** — Educator
Ball State University, President's Office, A D Building, Muncie IN 47306, USA

**Goranson, Alicia** — Actress
Paradigm Agency, 360 Park Ave S, #1600, New York NY 10010 USA

**Gorbachev, Mikhail S** — Nobel Peace Laureate; Gen Sec, USSR
Leningradsky Prospekt 39, 125167 Moscow, Russia

**Gorbachev, Yuri** — Artist
Adrienne Editions, 377 Geary St, San Francisco CA 94102, USA

**Gorbatko, Viktor V** — Cosmonaut; Air Force General
Cosmonaut Training Center, Star City, 141160 Zvezdny Gorodok, Moscow Oblast, Russia

**Gorchakova, Galina** — Opera Singer
Kirov Opera, Mariinsky Theater, Teatralnaya Pl 1, 190000 Saint Petersburg, Russia

**Gordeeva, Ekaterina** — Figure Skater, Model
Anaheim Ice, 300 W Lincoln Ave, Anaheim CA 92805, USA

**Gordeyev, Vyacheslav M** — Ballet Dancer, Choreographer
Tverskaya Str 9, #78, 103009 Moscow, Russia

**Gordley, James R** — Attorney, Educator
University of California, Law School, Boalt Hall, Berkeley CA 94720, USA

**Gordon, Aaron A** — Basketball Player
Orlando Magic, 8701 Maitland Summit Blvd, Orlando FL 32810 USA

**Gordon, Barry** — Actor, Singer
1912 Kaweah Dr, Pasadena CA 91105, USA

**Gordon, Benjamin (Ben)** — Basketball Player
4300 Sharon Road, #418, Charlotte NC 28211, USA

**Gordon, Bert I** — Director
9640 Arby Dr, Beverly Hills CA 90210, USA

**Gordon, Bridgette** — Basketball Player
Pattonville High School, 2497 Creve Coeur Mill Road, Maryland Heights MO 63043, USA

**Gordon, Bryan** — Director, Producer, Writer
Creative Artists Agency, 2000 Ave of Stars, #100, Los Angeles CA 90067 USA

**Gordon, Christopher** — Composer
I C M Partners, 10250 Constellation Blvd, #900, Los Angeles CA 90067 USA

**Gordon, Cornell K** — Football Player
4029 Spring Meadow Crescent, Chesapeake VA 23321, USA

**Gordon, Dan** — Director, Producer, Writer
I C M Partners, 10250 Constellation Blvd, #900, Los Angeles CA 90067 USA

**Gordon, Danso** — Actor
Evolution Entertainment, 901 N Highland Ave, Los Angeles CA 90038 USA

**Gordon, Darrien X J** — Football Player
1500 Pecos Dr, Southlake TX 76092, USA

**Gordon, David** — Choreographer
47 Great Jones St, #2, New York NY 10012, USA

**Gordon, Dennie** — Director, Producer, Actress
Creative Artists Agency, 2000 Ave of Stars, #100, Los Angeles CA 90067 USA

**Gordon, Don** — Actor
10576 Rocca Way, Los Angeles CA 90077, USA

**Gordon, Donald T (Don)** — Baseball Player
711 Sunset Mountain Dr, Chattanooga TN 37421, USA
**Gordon, Douglas** — Artist
Gagosian Gallery, 6-24 Britannia St, London WC1X 9JD, England
**Gordon, Ed** — Commentator
NBC-TV, News Dept, 30 Rockefeller Plaza, #270E, New York NY 10112 USA
**Gordon, Eric, Jr** — Basketball Player
Los Angeles Clippers, Staples Center, 1111 S Figueroa St, Los Angeles CA 90015 USA
**Gordon, Eve** — Actress
TalentWorks, 3500 W Olive Ave, #1400, Burbank CA 91505 USA
**Gordon, Hannah Taylor** — Actress
Olivia Bell Mgmt, 193 Wardour St, London W1F 8ZF, England
**Gordon, Harold P** — Businessman
Hasbro Inc, 1027 Newport Ave, Pawtucket RI 02861, USA
**Gordon, Howard** — Writer, Producer
W M E Entertainment, 9601 Wilshire Blvd, #300, Beverly Hills CA 90210 USA
**Gordon, Josh** — Director, Producer, Writer
Creative Artists Agency, 2000 Ave of Stars, #100, Los Angeles CA 90067 USA
**Gordon, Keith** — Director
Arlook Group, 205 S Beverly Dr, #209, Beverly Hills CA 90212, USA
**Gordon, Keith B** — Baseball Player
4601 Thornhurst St, Olney MD 20832, USA
**Gordon, Kim** — Singer, Bassist (Sonic Youth)
Silva Artist Mgmt, 722 Seward St, Los Angeles CA 90038, USA
**Gordon, Kiowa** — Actor
A P A Talent & Literary Agency, 405 S Beverly Dr, #300, Beverly Hills CA 90212 USA
**Gordon, Lalonde** — Track Athlete
National Athletics, PO Box 605, Port-of-Spain, Trinidad & Tobago
**Gordon, Lamar D** — Football Player
5428 N 19th St, Milwaukee WI 53209, USA
**Gordon, Lancaster** — Basketball Player
550 Robinhood Road, Jackson MS 39206, USA
**Gordon, Lawrence** — Businessman
Largo Entertainment, 20th Century Fox, 10201 W Pico Blvd, Los Angeles CA 90064, USA
**Gordon, Mark** — Producer
Mark Gordon Productions, 12200 W Olympic Blvd, #250, Los Angeles CA 90064, USA
**Gordon, Mary C** — Writer
Viking Penguin Press, 375 Hudson St, New York NY 10014, USA
**Gordon, Matt** — Actor
Edna Talent Mgmt, 318 Dundas St W, Toronto, ON M5T 1G5, Canada
**Gordon, Michael E (Mike)** — Bassist (Phish)
PO Box 4400, Burlington VT 05404, USA
**Gordon, Milton A** — Educator
California State University, President's Office, Fullerton CA 99264, USA
**Gordon, Nina** — Singer, Guitarist, Songwriter
Paradigm Agency, 360 Park Ave S, #1600, New York NY 10010 USA
**Gordon, Pamela F** — Prime Minister, Bermuda
United Bermuda Party, Chancery Lane, Box HM715, Hamilton HM CX, Bermuda
**Gordon, Phil** — Actor
Alexandria Alvarez, 3145 Geary Blvd, #744, San Francisco CA 94118, USA
**Gordon, Richard** — Writer, Anesthetist
1 Craven Hill, London W2 3EN, England
**Gordon, Richard F (Dick)** — Football Player
7119 Sandy Springs Road, Maumee OH 43537, USA
**Gordon, Richard F, Jr** — Astronaut
65 Woodside Dr, Prescott AZ 86305, USA
**Gordon, Robert W (Robby)** — Auto Racing Driver
19525 Mary Ardrey Circle, Cornelius NC 28031, USA
**Gordon, Stuart** — Director
Red Hen Productions, 3607 W Magnolia, #L, Burbank CA 91505, USA
**Gordon, Thomas (Tom)** — Baseball Player
2006 Lake Lotela Dr, Avon Park FL 33825, USA
**Gordon, Zachary** — Actor
Industry Entertainment, 955 Carillo Dr, #300, Los Angeles CA 90048 USA
**Gordon-Levitt, Joseph** — Actor
W M E Entertainment, 9601 Wilshire Blvd, #300, Beverly Hills CA 90210 USA
**Gordon-Reed, Annette** — Writer, Educator
New York University, Law School, 57 Worth St, New York NY 10013, USA
**Gordy, Berry, Jr** — Businessman, Composer
878 Stradella Road, Los Angeles CA 90077, USA
**Gordy, Walter** — Physicist
2521 Perkins Road, Durham NC 27705, USA
**Gore, Albert A, Jr** — Nobel Peace Laureate, Vice President
Wylie Agency, 250 W 57th St, #2114, New York NY 10107, USA
**Gore, Frank** — Football Player
6641 SW 159th Place, Miami FL 33193, USA
**Gore, Lesley** — Singer, Songwriter, Actress
228 W 71st St, #1E, New York NY 10023, USA
**Gore, Michael** — Composer
Soundtrack Music Assoc, 1460 4th St, #308, Santa Monica CA 90401 USA
**Gore, Robert W** — Inventor (Gore-Tex)
W L Gore Assoc, 555 Paper Mill Road, Newark DE 19711, USA
**Gorence, Tom** — Ice Hockey Player
56205 Village Dr, La Quinta CA 92253, USA
**Gorenstein, Mark B** — Conductor
Rublevskoye Shosse 28, #25, 121609 Moscow, Russia
**Gorfinkel, Jordan (Gorf)** — Cartoonist
2427 White Road, Cleveland OH 44118, USA
**Gorgal, Kenneth R (Ken)** — Football Player
4 The Court of Harborside, Northbrook IL 60062, USA
**Gorgl, Elisabeth** — Alpine Skier
Helmut Zangerl, Innrain 15/4/32, 6020 Innsbruck, Austria
**Gorham, Christopher** — Actor
Creative Artists Agency, 2000 Ave of Stars, #100, Los Angeles CA 90067 USA
**Gorie, Dominic L** — Astronaut
13656 Hidden Valley Lane, Salida CO 81201, USA

**Gorilla Zoe**
Multi Entertainment Group, 4044 W Lake Mary Blvd, #104-324, Lake Mary FL 32746, USA — Rap Artist

**Gorin, Brandon M**
5277 N College Ave, Indianapolis IN 46220, USA — Football Player

**Goring, Robert T (Butch)**
245 W 5th Ave, #108, Anchorage AK 99501, USA — Ice Hockey Player, Coach

**Gorinski, Robert J (Bob)**
PO Box 133, Calumet PA 15621, USA — Baseball Player

**Goris, Eva**
I C M Partners, 10250 Constellation Blvd, #900, Los Angeles CA 90067 USA — Actress

**Gorka, John**
Roots Agency, 177 Woodland Ave, Westwood NJ 07675, USA — Singer, Songwriter

**Gorlatch, Alexej**
Freitag Artists, Sophienstr 95, 60487 Frankfurt am Main, Germany — Concert Pianist

**Gorlin, Alexander**
Alexander Gorlin Architect, 137 Varick St, #500, New York NY 10013, USA — Architect

**Gorman, Bryan**
Auld Course, 525 Hunte Parkway, Chula Vista CA 91914, USA — Golfer

**Gorman, E J**
PO Box 669, Cedar Rapids IA 52406, USA — Writer

**Gorman, John G**
Mediware Information Systems, 11711 W 79th St, Lenexa KS 66214, USA — Pathologist

**Gorman, Joseph T**
T R W Inc, 1900 Richmond Road, Cleveland OH 44124, USA — Businessman

**Gorman, Leigh**
M O B Agency, 6404 Wilshire Blvd, #505, Los Angeles CA 90048 USA — Bassist (Bow Wow Wow)

**Gorman, Patrick**
Circle Talent Assoc, 520 Broadway, #350, Santa Monica CA 90401, USA — Actor

**Gorman, Paul F, Jr**
9175 Batesville Road, Afton VA 22920, USA — Army General

**Gorman, Steve**
Angeles Entertainment, 16000 Ventura Blvd, #600, Encino CA 91436, USA — Drummer (Black Crowes)

**Gorman, Suzy**
Suzy Gorman Studios, 2508 N Broadway, Saint Louis MO 63102, USA — Photographer

**Gorman, Thomas P (Tom)**
1615 SW 5th Ave, Portland OR 97201, USA — Baseball Player

**Gorman, Tom**
ProServe, 1101 Woodrow Wilson Blvd, #1800, Arlington VA 22209 USA — Tennis Player

**Gormley, Antony**
13 South Villas, London NW1 9BS, England — Sculptor

**Gorneault, Nick**
94 Seymour Ave, Springfield MA 01109, USA — Baseball Player

**Gorney, Karen Lynn**
Karen Company, PO Box 231060, New York NY 10023, USA — Actress, Model

**Gorouuch, Edward Lee**
University of Alaska, President's Office, Anchorage AK 99508, USA — Educator

**Gorrell, Bob**
Creators Syndicate, 737 3rd St, Hermosa Beach CA 90254 USA — Editorial Cartoonist

**Gorrell, Fred**
501 E Port au Prince Lane, Phoenix AZ 85022, USA — Balloonist

**Gorris, Marleen**
Gersh Agency, 9465 Wilshire Blvd, #600, Beverly Hills CA 90212 USA — Director

**Gorshkov, Aleksandr G**
Skating Federation, Luchnesksaia Nab 8, 119871 Moscow, Russia — Ice Dancer

**Gorsky, Alex**
Johnson & Johnson, 1 Johnson & Johnson Plaza, New Bruswick NJ 08993, USA — Businessman

**Gortat, Marcin**
Washington Wizards, M C I Centre, 601 F St NW, Washington DC 20004 USA — Basketball Player

**Gortney, William E**
Commander, US Northern Command, Peterson Air Force Base CO 80914 USA — Navy Admiral

**Goryl, John A**
528 Dry Run Road, Monongahela PA 15063, USA — Baseball Player, Manager

**Gosger, James C (Jim)**
1823 7th St, Port Huron MI 48060, USA — Baseball Player

**Gosling, James**
Sun Microsystems, 2550 Garcia Ave, Mountain View CA 94043, USA — Computer Software Designer (Java)

**Gosling, Ryan T**
Anonymous Content, 3532 Hayden Ave, Culver City CA 90232 USA — Actor

**Gosnell, Raja**
Creative Artists Agency, 2000 Ave of Stars, #100, Los Angeles CA 90067 USA — Director

**Goss, Fred**
A P A Talent & Literary Agency, 405 S Beverly Dr, #300, Beverly Hills CA 90212 USA — Actor, Director

**Goss, Luke**
Luber Rocklin Entertainment, 5815 Sunset Blvd, #206, Los Angeles CA 90028 USA — Actor

**Gossage, John**
Light Work, 316 Waverly Ave, Syracuse NY 13210, USA — Photographer

**Gossage, Richard M (Goose)**
35 Marland St, Colorado Springs CO 80906, USA — Baseball Player

**Gossard, Stone**
Curtis Mgmt, 1900 S Corgiat Dr, Seattle WA 98108, USA — Guitarist (Green River, Pearl Jam)

**Gosselaar, Mark-Paul**
Paradigm Agency, 360 N Crescent Dr, North Building, Beverly Hills CA 90210 USA — Actor

**Gosselin, Katie I (Kate)**
The Alexander, 201 W 72nd St, New York NY 10023, USA — Actress

**Gosselin, Mario**
Energie Ecole, 70 Rue Favvettes, Saint Basile Grand QC J3N 1P4, Canada — Ice Hockey Player

**Gossett, D Bruce**
6109 Puerto Dr, Rancho Murieta CA 95683, USA — Football Player

**Gossett, David S**
3405 Normandy Ridge Lane, Austin TX 78738, USA — Golfer

**Gossett, Jeffery A (Jeff)**
6 Lake Forest Court, Roanoke TX 76262, USA — Football Player

**Gossett, Louis, Jr**
Logo Entertainment, 22337 Pacific Coast Highway, #202, Malibu CA 90265, USA — Actor

**Gossett, Robert**
Stone Manners Salners, 6100 Wilshire Blvd, #1500, Los Angeles CA 90035 USA — Actor

**Gossick Crockatt, Sue** — Diver
11738 Villageview Court, Moorpark CA 93021, USA

**Gossner, Miriam** — Cross Country Skier
Rheinstalstr 3, 82467 Garmisch-Partenkirchen, Germany

**Gostowski, Stephen C (Steve)** — Football Player
18 Rhodes Dr, Wrentham MA 02093, USA

**Gotschlich, Emil C** — Internist
1435 Lexington Ave, New York NY 10128, USA

**Gotshalk, Leonard W (Len)** — Football Player
1200 Butler Creek Road, Ashland OR 97520, USA

**Gott, James W (Jim)** — Baseball Player
860 La Vina Lane, Altadena CA 91001, USA

**Gott, Karel** — Singer
Auf der Kante 85, 42349 Wuppertal, Germany

**Gottfried, Brian** — Tennis Player
PO Box 417, Ponte Vedra Beach FL 32004, USA

**Gottfried, Gilbert** — Actor, Comedian
W M E Entertainment, 1325 Ave of Americas, New York NY 10019 USA

**Gotti, Yo** — Rap Artist
J Records, 745 5th Ave, #600, New York NY 10151 USA

**Gottlieb, Lisa** — Director
Stone Manners Salners, 6100 Wilshire Blvd, #1500, Los Angeles CA 90035 USA

**Gottschalk, Thomas J** — Actor, Writer, Director
Agenehme Unterhaultungs, Von-Simolin-Str 1, 82402 Seeshaupt, Germany

**Gottwald, Felix** — Nordic Combined Skier
Rosengasse 12, 5700 Zell am See, Austria

**Gotye** — Singer, Musician, Songwriter
Agency Group Ltd, 361-373 City Road, London EC1V 1PQ, England

**Gotz, George** — Actor
Terrassenstr 32, 14129 Berlin, Germany

**Gough, Alfred, III** — Producer, Writer
Millar Gough Ink, 500 S Buena Vista St, Animations 1E17, Burbank CA 91521, USA

**Gough, Darren** — Cricketer
Octagon, 81-83 Fulham High St, London SW6 3JW, England

**Goulart, Izabel** — Model
Women Model Mgmt, 199 Lafayette St, #700, New York NY 10012 USA

**Goulart, Ron** — Writer, Cartoonist (Star Hawks)
232 Georgetown Road, Weston CT 06883, USA

**Gould, Alexander** — Actor
Coast to Coast Talent, 3350 Barham Blvd, Los Angeles CA 90068 USA

**Gould, Dana** — Actor, Writer, Producer
United Talent Agency, U T A Plaza, 9336 Civic Center Dr, Beverly Hills CA 90210 USA

**Gould, Elliott** — Actor
A P A Talent & Literary Agency, 405 S Beverly Dr, #300, Beverly Hills CA 90212 USA

**Gould, Georgia** — Cyclist
540 N Hollywood St, Fort Collins CO 80521, USA

**Gould, Nolan** — Actor
Stone Manners Salners, 6100 Wilshire Blvd, #1500, Los Angeles CA 90035 USA

**Gould, Peter** — Writer
Larchmont Literary Agency, 444 N Larchmont Blvd, #200, Los Angeles CA 90004, USA

**Gould, Robert P (Robbie)** — Football Player
544 Cliffwood Lane, Gurnee IL 60031, USA

**Gould, Ronald M** — Judge
US Court of Appeals, US Courthouse, 1010 5th Ave, Seattle WA 98104, USA

**Gould, Tony** — Writer
Rogers Coleridge White, 20 Powis Court, London W11 1JN, England

**Goulding, Ellie** — Singer, Songwriter
W M E Entertainment, Centrepoint Tower, 103 New Oxford St, London WC1A 1DD, England

**Goulet, Michel** — Ice Hockey Player
PO Box 656, Sedalia CO 80135, USA

**Goulet-Nadon, Amelie** — Speed Skater
Speed Skating Canada, 2781 Lancaster Road, #402, Ottawa ON K1B 1A7, Canada

**Goulian, Mehran K** — Physician, Biochemist
8433 Prestwick Dr, La Jolla CA 92037, USA

**Goulston, Mark** — Psychiatrist, Commentator
1150 Yale St, #3, Santa Monica CA 90403, USA

**Gourley, Roark** — Artist
Roark Gourley Art Gallery, 33151 Paso Dr, South Laguna Beach CA 92677, USA

**Gourmet, Olivier** — Actor
Artmedia, 20 Ave Rapp, 75007 Paris, France

**Gouveia, Kurt K** — Football Player
138 Seagrove Lane, Mooresville NC 28117, USA

**Govan, Gerald** — Basketball Player
30 Newport Parkway, #2112, Jersey City NJ 07310, USA

**Govan, Michael** — Museum Director
Los Angeles County Museum of Art, 5905 Wilshire Blvd, Los Angeles CA 90036, USA

**Govich, Milena** — Actress
A P A Talent & Literary Agency, 405 S Beverly Dr, #300, Beverly Hills CA 90212 USA

**Govinda** — Actor
105 Jal Darshan, A Wing Ruia Park, Juhu, Mumbai MS 400049, India

**Gowan, Caroline** — Golfer
209 Crescent Ave, Greenville SC 29605, USA

**Gowan, James** — Architect
2 Linden Gardens, London W2 4ES, England

**Gowariker, Ashutosh** — Director
I C M Partners, 10250 Constellation Blvd, #900, Los Angeles CA 90067 USA

**Gowda, H D Deve** — Prime Minister, India
5 Safdarjung Lane, New Delhi 110011, India

**Gower, David I** — Cricketer
David Gower Promotions, 6 George St, Nottingham NG1 3BE, England

**Gowers, W Timothy** — Mathematician
Math Services Centre, Wilberforce Road, Cambridge CB3 0WB, England

**Gowin, Toby** — Football Player
847 Fort Worth St, Jacksonville TX 75766, USA

**Gowon, Yakub** — President, Nigeria; Army General
National Oil & Chemical Marketing Co, 38-39 Marina, 2052 Lagos, Nigeria

# G

| | |
|---|---|
| **Gowrie, Earl of**<br>Government Securities, Stag Place, London SW1E 5DS, England | Government Official, England |
| **Goycoechea, Sergio J**<br>Football Assn, Via Monte 1366-76, Buenos Aires 1053, Argentina | Soccer Player |
| **Goydos, Paul**<br>1864 Stearnlee Ave, Long Beach CA 90815, USA | Golfer |
| **Goyer, David S**<br>Holmes Defender of the Faith, 1559 7th St, Santa Monica CA 90401, USA | Director, Writer |
| **Goyette, Danielle**<br>Team Canada, 2424 University Dr NW, Calgary AB T2N 3Y9, Canada | Ice Hockey Player |
| **Goyette, Philippe J G (Phil)**<br>815 38 E Ave, Lachine QC H8T 2C4, Canada | Ice Hockey Player |
| **Goyo, Dakota**<br>W M E Entertainment, 9601 Wilshire Blvd, #300, Beverly Hills CA 90210 USA | Actor |
| **Gozlan, Yann**<br>Gersh Agency, 9465 Wilshire Blvd, #600, Beverly Hills CA 90212 USA | Writer, Director |
| **Gozney, Richard H T**<br>Governor General's Office, 11 Langton Hill, Pembroke HM 13, Bermuda | Governor General, Bermuda |
| **Gozzo, Mauro P**<br>156 Newton St, Berlin CT 06037, USA | Baseball Player |
| **Grabarkewitz, Billy C**<br>2162 Estes Park Road, Southlake TX 76092, USA | Baseball Player |
| **Grabarz, Robert K**<br>Newham & Essex Beeagles, 1000 Dockside Road, London  E16 2QU, England | Track Athlete |
| **Grabe, Ronald J**<br>3380 S Price Road, Chandler AZ 85248, USA | Astronaut |
| **Grabeel, Lucas**<br>Paradigm Agency, 360 N Crescent Dr, North Building, Beverly Hills CA 90210 USA | Actor, Singer |
| **Graber, Rodney B (Rod)**<br>4674 Mount Armet Dr, San Diego CA 92117, USA | Baseball Player |
| **Graber, Susan P**<br>US Court of Appeals, Pioneer Courthouse, 555 SW Yamhill St, Portland OR 97204, USA | Judge |
| **Grabois, Neil R**<br>Colgate University, President's Office, Hamilton NY 13346, USA | Educator |
| **Grabow, John W**<br>6810 S Amethyst Dr, Chandler AZ 85249, USA | Baseball Player |
| **Grabow, Volker**<br>Institute for Sport & Sport Science, Otto-Hahn-Str 3, 44227 Dortmund, Germany | Rowing Athlete |
| **Grabowski, James S (Jim)**<br>1523 Withorn Lane, Inverness IL 60067, USA | Football Player |
| **Grace, Alana**<br>Creative Artists Agency, 2000 Ave of Stars, #100, Los Angeles CA 90067 USA | Actress, Singer, Songwriter |
| **Grace, April**<br>Innovative Artists, 1505 10th St, Santa Monica CA 90401 USA | Actress |
| **Grace, Bud**<br>King Features Syndicate, 300 W 57th St, #1500, New York NY 10019 USA | Cartoonist (Ernie, Piranha Club) |
| **Grace, Dick**<br>Grace Vineyards, 1210 Rockland Dr, Saint Helena CA 94574, USA | Businessman, Social Activist |
| **Grace, Emily**<br>Bad Girl Productions, 14 Parkside Court, Brooklyn NY 11225, USA | Actress |
| **Grace, Helen**<br>Gavin Barker Assoc, 2D Wimpole St, London W1G 0EB, England | Actress |
| **Grace, Jillian**<br>Playboy Promotions, 9346 Civic Center Dr, #200, Beverly Hills CA 90210 USA | Model, Actress |
| **Grace, Maggie**<br>United Talent Agency, U T A Plaza, 9336 Civic Center Dr, Beverly Hills CA 90210 USA | Actress |
| **Grace, Mark E**<br>5624 E Via Buena Vista, Paradise Valley AZ 85253, USA | Baseball Player |
| **Grace, Michael J (Mike)**<br>1156 Buell Ave, Joliet IL 60435, USA | Baseball Player |
| **Grace, Nancy**<br>Breaking News Public Relations, 9601 Wilshire Blvd, #1106, Beverly Hills CA 90210, USA | Commentator |
| **Grace, Topher**<br>I C M Partners, 10250 Constellation Blvd, #900, Los Angeles CA 90067 USA | Actor |
| **Gracen, Elizabeth**<br>James Levy Mgmt, 3500 W Olive Ave, #920, Burbank CA 91505, USA | Actress, Beauty Queen, Model |
| **Gracey, James S**<br>1 Westin Center, 2445 M St NW, #260, Washington DC 20037, USA | Coast Guard Admiral, Businessman |
| **Grach, Eduard D**<br>1st Smolensky Per 9, #98, 121099 Moscow, Russia | Concert Violinist |
| **Gracheva, Nadezhda A**<br>1st Truzhennikov Per 17, #49, 119121 Moscow, Russia | Ballerina |
| **Gracias, Oswald Cardinal**<br>Archdiocese of Bombay, 1 Nathalal Parekh Marg, Mumbai 40001, India | Religious Leader |
| **Gracie, Charlie**<br>Joe Taylor Artist Agency, 2802 Columbine Place, Nashville TN 37204 USA | Singer, Guitarist |
| **Gracin, Joshua M (Josh)**<br>Buddy Lee Attractions, 38 Music Square E, #300, Nashville TN 37203 USA | Singer |
| **Grad, Harold**<br>248 Overlook Road, New Rochelle NY 10804, USA | Mathematician |
| **Graddy, Sam**<br>4792 Brasac Dr, Stone Mountain GA 30083, USA | Football Player, Track Athlete |
| **Gradishar, Randy C**<br>7628 Pineridge Terrace, Castle Rock CO 80108, USA | Football Player |
| **Grady, Michael**<br>I C M Partners, 10250 Constellation Blvd, #900, Los Angeles CA 90067 USA | Actor |
| **Grady, Michael P**<br>1808 Pine Ave, Manhattan Beach CA 90266, USA | Cinematographer |
| **Grady, Wayne**<br>PO Box 78, Coolum Beach QLD 4573, Australia | Golfer |
| **Graebner, Clark**<br>411 Harbor Road, Fairfield CT 06431, USA | Tennis Player |
| **Graebner, Norman A**<br>University of Virginia, History Dept, Charlottesville VA 22903, USA | Historian |
| **Graef, Jed**<br>PO Box 880, Shelburne VT 05482, USA | Swimmer |

**Gowrie - Graef**

**Graells, Francisco (Pancho)** — Editorial Cartoonist
Le Monde, Editorial Dept, 21 Bis Rue Claude Bernard, 75005 Paris, France
**Graf, David F (Dave)** — Football Player
1825 Bel Air Ave, Pompano Beach FL 33062, USA
**Graf, Hans** — Conductor
Konzertdirektion Schmid, Konigstra 36, 30175 Hannover, Germany
**Graf, Jim** — Space Scientist
Jet Propulsion Laboratory, 4800 Oak Grove Dr, Pasadena CA 91109 USA
**Graf, Richard G (Rick)** — Football Player
6609 Biscayne Blvd, Minneapolis MN 55436, USA
**Graf, Stefanie M (Steffi)** — Tennis Player
9804 Camden Hills Ave, Las Vegas NV 89145, USA
**Graff, Ilene** — Actress
Sovereign Talent Group, 8421 Wilshire Blvd, #200, Beverly Hills CA 90211, USA
**Graff, Randy** — Actress
Lava Entertainment, 1560 Broadway, #1001, New York NY 10036, USA
**Graff, Todd** — Director, Writer, Actor
United Talent Agency, U T A Plaza, 9336 Civic Center Dr, Beverly Hills CA 90210 USA
**Graffanino, Anthony J (Tony)** — Baseball Player
16 Amberfield Lane, Hockessin DE 19707, USA
**Graffe, Anne-Caroline** — Taekwondo Athlete
Aix Universite Club Taekwondo, 33 Chemin des Infirmeries, 13100 Aix-en-Provence, France
**Graffeo, Karen C** — Photographer
University of Montevallo, Fine Arts Dept, Montevallo, AL 35115, USA
**Graffin, Gregory W (Greg)** — Singer (Bad Religion), Songwriter
Goldstar Public Relations, PO Box 130, Ross on Wye HR9 6WY, England
**Graffin, Guillaume** — Ballet Dancer
American Ballet Theatre, 890 Broadway, #300, New York NY 10003, USA
**Graffman, Gary** — Concert Pianist
Curtis Institute of Music, 1726 Locust St, Philadelphia PA 19103, USA
**Grafstein, Bernice** — Neurologist, Physiologist
Weill Medical College, Physiology Dept, 1300 York Ave, New York NY 10065, USA
**Grafton, Anthony T** — Historian
Princeton University, History Dept, Dickinson Hall, Princeton NJ 08544, USA
**Grafton, Sue** — Writer
PO Box 41446, Santa Barbara CA 93140, USA
**Gragg, Scott** — Football Player
583 Cash Nichols Road, Stevensville MT 59870, USA
**Graham, Alex** — Cartoonist (Fred Basset)
Tribune Media Services, 435 N Michigan Ave, #1500, Chicago IL 60611 USA
**Graham, Arthur W (Art), III** — Football Player
PO Box 785, South Orleans MA 02662, USA
**Graham, Charles P** — Army General
134 Warbler Way, Georgetown TX 78633, USA
**Graham, Currie** — Actor
Paradigm Agency, 360 N Crescent Dr, North Building, Beverly Hills CA 90210 USA
**Graham, David** — Golfer
4201 Lomo Alto Dr, #305, Dallas TX 75219, USA
**Graham, Detrice A (Derrick)** — Football Player
203 Pine Hill Road, West End NC 27376, USA
**Graham, Dirk M** — Ice Hockey Player
17001 S Blackfoot Dr, Lockport IL 60441, USA
**Graham, Donald E** — Publisher
Washington Post Co, 1150 15th St NW, Washington DC 20071, USA
**Graham, Franklin** — Religious Leader
Samaritan's Purse, PO Box 3000, Boone NC 28607, USA
**Graham, Gary** — Actor
Amsel Eisenstadt Frazier, 5055 Wilshire Blvd, #865, Los Angeles CA 90036 USA
**Graham, Gerrit** — Actor
S M S Talent, 8383 Wilshire Blvd, #230, Beverly Hills CA 90211 USA
**Graham, Glen** — Drummer (Blind Melon)
Shapiro Co, 9229 W Sunset Blvd, #607, West Hollywood CA 90069 USA
**Graham, Heather** — Actress
Gersh Agency, 9465 Wilshire Blvd, #600, Beverly Hills CA 90212 USA
**Graham, Jack** — Religious Leader
Prestonwood Baptist Church, 6801 W Park Blvd, Plano TX 75093, USA
**Graham, Jeffrey T (Jeff)** — Football Player
1849 Infirmary Road, Dayton OH 45417, USA
**Graham, Jimmy** — Football Player
New Orleans Saints, 5800 Airline Highway, Metairie LA 70003 USA
**Graham, Joey J** — Basketball Player
Cleveland Cavaliers, Gund Arena, 1 Center Court, Cleveland OH 44115 USA
**Graham, Jorie** — Writer
12 Quincy St, Cambridge MA 02138, USA
**Graham, Julie** — Actress
Troika, 74 Clerkenwell Road, #300, London EC1M 5QA, England
**Graham, Kate** — Actress
Gavin Barker Assoc, 2D Wimpole St, London W1G 0EB, England
**Graham, Katerina (Kat)** — Actress
W M E Entertainment, 9601 Wilshire Blvd, #300, Beverly Hills CA 90210 USA
**Graham, Kenneth J (Kenny)** — Football Player
PO Box 7402, Santa Monica CA 90406, USA
**Graham, Kent D** — Football Player
1001 N Washington St, Wheaton IL 60187, USA
**Graham, Larry** — Guitarist (Sly & Family Stone), Singer
Groove Entertainment, 1005 N Alfred St, #2, West Hollywood CA 90069, USA
**Graham, Lauren** — Actress
John Carrabino Mgmt, 5900 Wilshire Blvd, #406, Los Angeles CA 90036 USA
**Graham, Lee W** — Baseball Player
481 Richmond Road, Cleveland OH 44143, USA
**Graham, Linda** — Bowler
4147 E Seneca Ave, Des Moines IA 50317, USA
**Graham, Loren R** — Historian
7 Francis Ave, Cambridge MA 02138, USA
**Graham, Louis K (Lou)** — Golfer
85 Concord Park W, Nashville TN 37205, USA

G

Graells - Graham

# G

**Graham, Marcus** — Actor
Shanahan Mgmt, Berman House, 91 Campbell St, #300, Surry Hills NSW 2010, Australia

**Graham, Mary Lou** — Bowler
Professional Bowlers Association, 719 2nd Ave, #701, Seattle WA 98104 USA

**Graham, Michael J** — Educator
Xavier University, President's Office, 3800 Victory Parkway, Cincinnati OH 45207, USA

**Graham, Mikey** — Singer (Boyzone)
J C Music, 84A Strand-on-the-Green, London W43 PU, England

**Graham, Nancy Perry** — Editor
A A R P Magazine, Editorial Dept, 601 E St NW, Washington DC 20049, USA

**Graham, Norma V** — Psychologist
Columbia University, Psychology Dept, New York NY 10027, USA

**Graham, Patricia A** — Educator
Harvard University, Graduate School of Education, Cambridge MA 02138, USA

**Graham, Patrick** — Artist, Writer
Jack Rutberg Fine Arts, 357 N La Brea Ave, Los Angeles CA 90036, USA

**Graham, Rodney** — Artist
Hauser & Wirth Limmatstr 270, 8005 Zurich, Switzerland

**Graham, Ronald L** — Mathematician
University of California, Computer & Information Science Dept, La Jolla CA 92093, USA

**Graham, Stephen** — Actor
Independent Talent Group, 40 Whitfield St, London W1T 2RH, England

**Graham, Susan** — Opera Singer
I M G Artists, Hogarth Business Park, Chiswick, London W4 2TH, England

**Graham, Susan L** — Computer Scientist
University of California, Computer Science Dept, Soda Hall, Berkeley CA 94720, USA

**Graham, Thomas L (Tom)** — Football Player
4084 S Wisteria Way, Denver CO 80237, USA

**Graham, Wayne L** — Baseball Player
2017 Dryden Road, Houston TX 77030, USA

**Graham, William F (Billy)** — Evangelist
Billy Graham Evangelistic Assn, 1 Billy Graham Parkway, Charlotte NC 28201, USA

**Graham, William R (Bill)** — Football Player
11013 Sierra Verde Trail, Austin TX 78759, USA

**Grahame, Ron** — Ice Hockey Player
9000 E Jewell Circle, Denver CO 80231, USA

**Grahe, Joseph M (Joe)** — Baseball Player
2317 N Wallen Dr, West Palm Beach FL 33410, USA

**Grahn, Nancy Lee** — Actress
Innovative Artists, 1505 10th St, Santa Monica CA 90401 USA

**Grainger, Holliday** — Actress
Troika, 74 Clerkenwell Road, #300, London EC1M 5QA, England

**Grainger, Katherine** — Rowing Athlete
Saint Andrews Boat Club, Meggetland, 60F Colinton Road, Edinburgh EH14 1AS, Scotland

**Grainger, Sebastien A** — Singer, Drummer (Death from Above 1979)
Biz 3 Publicity, 1321 N Milwaukee Ave, #452, Chicago IL 60622, USA

**Grais, Michael** — Writer
Metropolitan Talent Agency, 5405 Wilshire Blvd, #218, Los Angeles CA 90036 USA

**Gralish, Tom** — Photojournalist
203 E Cottage Ave, Haddonfield NJ 08033, USA

**Graman, Alex** — Baseball Player
450 E Sunset Dr, Huntingburg IN 47542, USA

**Gramatica, Martin** — Football Player
3912 Northampton Way, Tampa FL 33618, USA

**Gramly, B Thomas (Tommy)** — Baseball Player
16485 Red Wood Circle W, McKinney TX 75071, USA

**Gramm, Lou** — Singer (Foreigner)
Elite Talent Agency, 1208 17th Ave S, Nashville TN 37212, USA

**Gramm, W Philip (Phil)** — Senator, TX
U B S Securities, 299 Park Ave, New York NY 10171, USA

**Gramm, Wendy L** — Government Official, Economist
George Mason University, 3301 N Fairfax Dr, #450, Arlington VA 22201, USA

**Grammas, Alexander P (Alex)** — Baseball Player, Manager
4030 Vestview Dr, Vestavia AL 35242, USA

**Grammelknodel, Sascha** — Ventriloquist, Puppeteer, Comedian
Josie, Therese-Pohler-Weg 1, 33100 Paderborn, Germany

**Grammer, Kathy** — Actress
Artists Agency, 9430 Olympic Blvd, Beverly Hills CA 90212 USA

**Grammer, Kelsey** — Actor
Grammnet Productions, 2461 Santa Monica Blvd, #521, Santa Monica CA 90404, USA

**Grammer, Spencer** — Actress
United Talent Agency, U T A Plaza, 9336 Civic Center Dr, Beverly Hills CA 90210 USA

**Grammer, Tracy** — Singer, Violinist
PO Box 831, Greenfield MA 01302, USA

**Granada, Julieta** — Golfer
Ladies Pro Golf Assn, 100 International Golf Dr, Daytona Beach FL 32124 USA

**Granato, Anthony L (Tony)** — Ice Hockey Player, Coach
1481 Hollow Tree Dr, Pittsburgh PA 15241, USA

**Granby, John E, Jr** — Football Player
8905 Melwood Oak Dr, Arlington TN 38002, USA

**Grandage, Michael** — Director
Donmar Warehouse, 41 Earlham St, Seven Dials, London WC2H 9LX, England

**Grande, Ariana** — Actress, Singer
Creative Artists Agency, 2000 Ave of Stars, #100, Los Angeles CA 90067 USA

**Granderson, Curtis** — Baseball Player
1450 S Emerald St, Chicago IL 60607, USA

**Grandholm, Jim** — Basketball Player
211 Spring Park Ave, Sawyer MI 49125, USA

**Grandin, Temple** — Animal Scientist
2918 Silver Plume Dr, #C3, Fort Collins CO 80526, USA

**Grandison, Ronnie** — Basketball Player
6151 Chappellfield Dr, West Chester OH 45069, USA

**Grandmaster Flash** — Rap Artist
K L B Production, 302A W 12th St, #296, New York NY 10014, USA

**Grandmaster Mele-Mel** — Rap Artist
Groove Entertainment, 1005 N Alfred St, #2, West Hollywood CA 90069 USA

**Graham - Grandmaster Mele-Mel**

| | |
|---|---|
| **Grandmaster Roc Raida**<br>Agency Group Ltd, 142 W 57th St, #600, New York NY 10019 USA | Rap Artist (X-Ecutioners) |
| **Grandmont, Jean-Michel**<br>55 Blvd de Charonne, Les Doukas 23, 75011 Paris, France | Economist |
| **Grandpa Pike**<br>PO Box 3008, Hillsborough NB E4H 4W5, Canada | Singer |
| **GrandPre, Mary**<br>Scholastic Press, 555 Broadway, New York NY 10012 USA | Illustrator |
| **Grandy, Fred**<br>10806 Waring Place, Charlotte NC 28277, USA | Actor; Representative, IA |
| **Granger, Danny**<br>141 S Meridian St, #602, Indianapolis IN 46225, USA | Basketball Player |
| **Granger, Hoyle J**<br>13427 Paradise Valley Dr, Houston TX 77069, USA | Football Player |
| **Granger, Jeffrey A (Jeff)**<br>2905 Glasgow Dr, Arlington TX 76015, USA | Baseball Player |
| **Granger, Stewart F**<br>552 E 53rd St, Brooklyn NY 11203, USA | Basketball Player |
| **Granger, Wayne A**<br>133 Redtail Place, Winter Springs FL 32708, USA | Baseball Player |
| **Granholm, Jennifer M**<br>University of California, Law & Public Policy Dept, Berkeley CA 94720, USA | Governor, MI |
| **Granier-Deferre, Celia**<br>Artmedia, 20 Ave Rapp, 75007 Paris, France | Actress |
| **Granik, Debra**<br>Gersh Agency, 9465 Wilshire Blvd, #600, Beverly Hills CA 90212 USA | Director, Writer, Cinematographer |
| **Granlund, Mikael A**<br>Minnesota Wild, XCel Energy Arena, 1275 Saint Antoine W, Saint Paul MN 55104 USA | Ice Hockey Player |
| **Grannan, Katy**<br>Fraenkel Gallery, 49 Geary St, 400, San Francisco CA 94108, USA | Photographer |
| **Grannis, Kina**<br>Agency Group Ltd, 142 W 57th St, #600, New York NY 10019 USA | Singer, Songwriter |
| **Grannis, Paul D**<br>Fermi National Accelerator Laboratory, C D F Collaboration, PO Box 500, Batavia IL 60510, USA | Physicist |
| **Grant Walsh, Margo**<br>Gensler & Associates/Architects, 1 Rockefeller Plaza, #500, New York NY 10020, USA | Interior Designer |
| **Grant, Alan**<br>148 Cisco Road, Asheville NC 28805, USA | Football Player |
| **Grant, Allie**<br>Sweeney Entertainment, 6253 Hollywood Blvd, #201, Los Angeles CA 90028, USA | Actress |
| **Grant, Amy L**<br>Creative Artists Agency, 3310 W End Ave, #500, Nashville TN 37203 USA | Singer, Songwriter |
| **Grant, B Rosemary**<br>Princeton University, Ecology & Evolution Biology Dept, Princeton NJ 08544, USA | Evolutionary Biologist |
| **Grant, Beth**<br>Don Buchwald Talent Agency, 6500 Wilshire Blvd, #2200, Los Angeles CA 90048 USA | Actress |
| **Grant, Boyd**<br>Colorado State University, Athletic Dept, Fort Collins CO 80523, USA | Basketball Coach |
| **Grant, Brea**<br>Baker Winokur Ryder Public Relations, 9100 Wilshire Blvd, #500W, Beverly Hills CA 90212 USA | Actress |
| **Grant, Brian W, III**<br>24152 SW Petes Mountain Road, West Linn OR 97068, USA | Basketball Player |
| **Grant, Charles**<br>Spotlight, 7 Leicester Place, London WC2H 7RJ, England | Actor |
| **Grant, Daniel F (Danny)**<br>1163 Route 101 Highway, Nasonworth NB E3C 2C3, Canada | Ice Hockey Player |
| **Grant, Darryl**<br>6931 Compton Lane, Centreville VA 20121, USA | Football Player |
| **Grant, David Marshall**<br>Creative Artists Agency, 2000 Ave of Stars, #100, Los Angeles CA 90067 USA | Actor, Writer |
| **Grant, Deon D**<br>4465 Cape Cod Dr, Evans GA 30809, USA | Football Player |
| **Grant, Edmond (Eddy)**<br>B1 Represents, 8 Hornton Place, Kensington, London W8 4LZ, England | Singer, Songwriter |
| **Grant, Faye**<br>S M S Talent, 8383 Wilshire Blvd, #230, Beverly Hills CA 90211 USA | Actress |
| **Grant, Frank**<br>PO Box 14536, Myrtle Beach SC 29587, USA | Football Player |
| **Grant, Gil**<br>Paradigm Agency, 360 N Crescent Dr, North Building, Beverly Hills CA 90210 USA | Producer, Writer |
| **Grant, Gogi**<br>10323 Alamo Ave, #202, Los Angeles CA 90064, USA | Singer |
| **Grant, Harold P (Bud)**<br>8134 Oakmere Road, Minneapolis MN 55438, USA | Football, Basketball Player, Coach |
| **Grant, Harvey**<br>15604 Marathon Circle, #401, Gaithersburg MD 20878, USA | Basketball Player |
| **Grant, Horace J**<br>195 Michael Lane, Arroyo Grande CA 93420, USA | Basketball Player |
| **Grant, Hugh**<br>42 West, 220 W 42nd St, #1200, New York NY 10036 USA | Actor |
| **Grant, Hugh, Jr**<br>35 E 84th St, #8B, New York NY 10028, USA | Harness Racing Executive |
| **Grant, James T (Mudcat)**<br>1020 S Dunsmuir Ave, Los Angeles CA 90019, USA | Baseball Player |
| **Grant, Jennifer**<br>Teitelbaum Artists, 8840 Wilshire Blvd, Beverly Hills CA 90212, USA | Actress |
| **Grant, Jerami**<br>Philadelphia 76ers, 1st Union Center, 3601 S Broad St, Philadelphia PA 19148 USA | Basketball Player |
| **Grant, John D**<br>6365 S Harrison Court, Centennial CO 80121, USA | Football Player |
| **Grant, Joshua D (Josh)**<br>3191 S Davis Blvd, Bountiful UT 84010, USA | Basketball Player |
| **Grant, Kate Jennings**<br>Melanie Greene Mgmt, 425 N Robertson Blvd, West Hollywood CA 90048 USA | Actress |
| **Grant, Lee**<br>Fleury/Grant Entertainment, 610 W End Ave, #7B, New York NY 10024, USA | Actress, Director |

V.I.P. Address Book

# G

## Grant - Gray

**Grant, Mark A**
2837 Via Dieguenos, Alpine CA 91901, USA — Baseball Player

**Grant, Mickie**
250 W 94th St, #6G, New York NY 10025, USA — Actress

**Grant, Natalie**
Maximum Artist Mgmt, 1305 Clinton St, #200A, Nashville TN 37203, USA — Singer, Songwriter

**Grant, Peter R**
Princeton University, Ecology & Evolutionary Biology Dept, Princeton NJ 08544, USA — Evolutionary Biologist

**Grant, Quiana**
Traffic Models, Pasaje Sert, 2, 08010 Barcelona, Spain — Model

**Grant, Richard E**
Artist Rights Group, 4A Exmoor St, London W10 6BD, England — Actor, Director

**Grant, Rodney A**
Omar, 526 N Larchmont Blvd, Los Angeles CA 90004, USA — Actor

**Grant, Stephen M (Steve)**
20134 SW 123rd Dr, Miami FL 33177, USA — Football Player

**Grant, Susannah**
Creative Artists Agency, 2000 Ave of Stars, #100, Los Angeles CA 90067 USA — Writer, Director

**Grant, Teach**
K C Talent, #109-119 W Pender St, Vancouver BC V6B 1S5, Canada — Actor

**Grant, Tom**
Brad Simon Organization, 445 E 80th St, #4C, New York NY 10075 USA — Jazz Musician

**Grant, Toni**
610 S Ardmore Ave, Los Angeles CA 90005, USA — Radio Psychologist

**Grant, Travis**
3314 Pointe Bleue Court, Decatur GA 30034, USA — Basketball Player

**Grantham, George**
Rick Alter Mgmt, 1018 17th Ave S, #12, Nashville TN 37212, USA — Singer, Drummer (Poco)

**Grantham, J Larry**
312 Wicklow Cove, Brandon MS 39047, USA — Football Player

**Grantham, Victoria**
VGrantham, Via Morimondo 2/3, 20143 Milan, Italy — Fashion Designer

**Grapenthin, Richard R (Dick)**
5040 170th Ave, Linn Grove IA 51033, USA — Baseball Player

**Grapey, Marc**
TalentWorks, 3500 W Olive Ave, #1400, Burbank CA 91505 USA — Actor

**Grasmanis, Paul R**
1073 Watkins Creek Dr, Franklin TN 37067, USA — Football Player

**Grasmick, Louis J (Lou)**
6715 Quad Ave, Rosedale MD 21237, USA — Baseball Player

**Grass, Frank J**
Chief, National Guard Bureau, HqUSA, Pentagon, Washington DC 20310, USA — Army General

**Grass, Gunter**
G Kiepenheuer Buhnenvertrieb, Schweinfurthstr 60, 14195 Berlin, Germany — Nobel Literature Laureate

**Grassle, Karen**
J E Talent, 323 Geary St, #302, San Francisco CA 94102, USA — Actress, Writer

**Grata, Enrique**
Univision, 605 3rd Ave, #1200, New York NY 10158, USA — Actor

**Grate, Donald (Don)**
1245 NW 203rd St, Miami FL 33169, USA — Baseball, Basketball Player

**Grater, Mark A**
1136 Indiana Ave, Monaca PA 15061, USA — Baseball Player

**Grattard, Adeline**
Yam'Tacha Restaurant, 4 Rue Sauval, 75001 Paris, France — Chef

**Grau, Shirley Ann**
12 Nassau Dr, Metairie LA 70005, USA — Writer

**Grauer, Ona**
Performers Mgmt, 258 E 3rd St, #B, Vancouver BC V7W 1E7, Canada — Actress

**Grausman, Phillip**
21 Barnes Road, Washington CT 06793, USA — Sculptor

**Gravel, Maurice R (Mike)**
1600 N Oak St, #1412, Arlington VA 22209, USA — Senator, AK

**Graveline, Duane E**
PO Box 92, Underhill Center VT 05490, USA — Astronaut

**Gravelle, Gordon C**
186 Kuss Road, Danville CA 94526, USA — Football Player

**Graves, Adam**
574 Lis Crescent, Windsor ON N9G 2M5, Canada — Ice Hockey Player

**Graves, Alex**
Creative Artists Agency, 2000 Ave of Stars, #100, Los Angeles CA 90067 USA — Director, Producer, Writer

**Graves, Daniel P (Danny)**
5041 Rishley Run Way, Mount Dora FL 32757, USA — Baseball Player

**Graves, Denyce A**
I M G Artists, Carnegie Hall Tower, 152 W 57th St, #500, New York NY 10019 USA — Opera Singer

**Graves, Earl G (Butch), Jr**
123 Random Farms Dr, Chappaqua NY 10514, USA — Basketball Player

**Graves, Ernest, Jr**
2328 S Nash St, Arlington VA 22202, USA — Army General

**Graves, Harold N, Jr**
PO Box 8390, Gaithersburg MD 20898, USA — Journalist, Government Official

**Graves, Liza**
The Kirby Organization, 9200 Sunset Blvd, #600, Los Angeles CA 90069, USA — Singer (Civet)

**Graves, Michael**
Michael Graves Assoc, 341 Nassau St, Princeton NJ 08540, USA — Architect

**Graves, Ray**
420 Bay Ave, #821, Clearwater FL 33756, USA — Football Coach

**Graves, Richard G**
6101 Bannocks Dr, San Antonio TX 78239, USA — Army General

**Graves, Rupert**
A P A Talent & Literary Agency, 405 S Beverly Dr, #300, Beverly Hills CA 90212 USA — Actor

**Graves, Thomas E (Tom)**
1902 Montclair Ave, Norfolk VA 23523, USA — Football Player

**Gravett, Michael G**
University of Washington Medical Center, Obstetrics Dept, PO Box 356460, Seattle WA 98195, USA — Obstetrician

**Gray, Aaron M**
Sacramento Kings, Arco Arena, 1 Sports Parkway, Sacramento CA 95834 USA — Basketball Player

**Gray, Alasdair J** — Writer
Rogers Coleridge White, 20 Powis Mews, London W11 1JN, England

**Gray, Alfred M, Jr** — Marine Corps General
6317 Chaucer View Circle, Alexandria VA 22304, USA

**Gray, Billy** — Actor
19612 Grandview Dr, Topanga Canyon CA 90290, USA

**Gray, C Boyden** — Government Official
Wilmer Cutler Pickering, 1875 Pennsylvania Ave NW, Washington DC 20006, USA

**Gray, Carleton P** — Football Player
11981 Kenn Road, Cincinnati OH 45240, USA

**Gray, Chad (Kud)** — Singer (Mudvayne)
Agency Group Ltd, 142 W 57th St, #600, New York NY 10019 USA

**Gray, Cleve** — Artist, Sculptor
102 Melius Road, Warren CT 06754, USA

**Gray, Coleen** — Actress
2841 Roscomare Road, Los Angeles CA 90077, USA

**Gray, David** — Singer, Songwriter
Mondo Mgmt, Clatham Nove Art Centre, 26-32 Voltaire Road, London SW4 6DH, England

**Gray, Del** — Drummer (Little Texas)
Splash Public Relations, 1520 16th Ave S, #2, Nashville TN 37212, USA

**Gray, Doug** — Singer (Marshall Tucker Band)
Ron Rainey Mgmt, 315 S Beverly Dr, #407, Beverly Hills CA 90212, USA

**Gray, D'Wayne** — Marine Corps General
3423 Barger Dr, Falls Church VA 22044, USA

**Gray, Earnest** — Football Player
6746 Kirby Oaks Lane, Memphis TN 38119, USA

**Gray, Edward (Ed)** — Basketball Player
Houston Rockets, 1730 Jefferson St, Houston TX 77003 USA

**Gray, Erin** — Actress, Model
10921 Alta View Dr, Studio City CA 91604, USA

**Gray, F Gary** — Director
United Talent Agency, U T A Plaza, 9336 Civic Center Dr, Beverly Hills CA 90210 USA

**Gray, Fred, Sr** — Attorney
1005 Lakeshore Dr, Tuskegee AL 36083, USA

**Gray, Gary G** — Baseball Player
PO Box 98, La Place LA 70069, USA

**Gray, George W** — Organic Chemist
Juniper House, Furzehill, Wimborne, Dorset BH21 4HD, England

**Gray, Harry B** — Chemist
1415 E California Blvd, Pasadena CA 91106, USA

**Gray, James** — Director, Writer
Creative Artists Agency, 2000 Ave of Stars, #100, Los Angeles CA 90067 USA

**Gray, Jamie Lynn B** — Markswoman
3522 Bridgewater Road, Columbus GA 31909, USA

**Gray, Jerry** — Football Player
27 Birdsong Parkway, Orchard Park NY 14127, USA

**Gray, John** — Director, Writer
John Gray's Mars Venus, 20 Sunnyside Ave, #A130, Mill Valley CA 94941, USA

**Gray, John E** — WW II, Korean & Vietnam Army Hero
4115 Bloomdale Dr, #16, Charlotte NC 28211, USA

**Gray, John L (Johnny)** — Baseball Player
10645 Greenbriar Court, Boca Raton FL 33498, USA

**Gray, Johnnie L** — Football Player
535 Brule Road, #13, De Pere WI 54115, USA

**Gray, Kenneth D (Ken)** — Football Player
356 Campa Pajama Lane, Kingsland TX 78639, USA

**Gray, Lauren** — Curling Athlete
Curling Association, 14 Donnelly Dr, Bedford, Bedfordshire MK4 9TU, England

**Gray, Linda** — Actress
PO Box 5064, Sherman Oaks CA 91413, USA

**Gray, Lorenzo** — Baseball Player
2680 E 19th St, #1, Signal Hill CA 90755, USA

**Gray, Macy** — Singer, Songwriter, Actress
Vox Inc, 6420 Wilshire Blvd, #1080, Los Angeles CA 90048 USA

**Gray, Melvin D (Mel)** — Football Player
4507 Skyline Dr, Rockford IL 61107, USA

**Gray, Melvin J (Mel)** — Football Player
137 Winterset Pass, Williamsburg VA 23188, USA

**Gray, Shan R** — Sculptor
The American, 3600 E 32nd St, Edmond OK 73013, USA

**Gray, Stuart A** — Basketball Player
909 Andover Green, Lexington KY 40509, USA

**Gray, Tamyra M** — Singer, Actress
19 Music & Mgmt, 35-37 Parkgate Road, London SW11 4NP, England

**Gray, Timothy (Tim)** — Football Player
6109 Crane St, Houston TX 77026, USA

**Gray, Tom** — Guitarist, Keyboardist (Gomez)
Red Light Mgmt, 44 Wall St, #2200, New York NY 10005, USA

**Graybiel, Ann M** — Anatomist
Massachusetts Institute of Technology, Cognitive Science Dept, Cambridge MA 02139, USA

**Gray-Cabey, Noah** — Actor
L I N K Entertainment, 11872 La Grange Ave, Los Angeles CA 90025 USA

**Grayden, Sprague** — Actress
Untitled Entertainment, 350 S Beverly Dr, #200, Beverly Hills CA 90212 USA

**Graydon, Michael J** — Air Force Marshal, England
Lloyds Bank, Cox & King's Branch, 7 Pall Mall, London SW1Y 5NA, England

**Grayer, Jeffrey (Jeff)** — Basketball Player
1617 Barbara Dr, Flint MI 48504, USA

**Gray-Garcia, Lisa (Tiny)** — Social Activist
City Lights Books, 261 Columbus Ave, San Francisco CA 94133, USA

**Grayling, A C** — Philosopher, Writer
Bloomsbury Publishing, 50 Bedford Square, London WC1B 3DP, England

**Graynor, Ari** — Actress
United Talent Agency, U T A Plaza, 9336 Civic Center Dr, Beverly Hills CA 90210 USA

**Graysmith, Robert** — Editorial Cartoonist, Writer
Berkley Publishing Group, 375 Hudson St, Basement 1, New York NY 10014 USA

Gray - Graysmith

**Grayson, C Jackson, Jr** — Government Official, Educator
123 N Post Oak Lane, Houston TX 77024, USA

**Grayson, David L (Dave), Jr** — Football Player
5962 Rancho Mission Road, #218, San Diego CA 92108, USA

**Grayson, David L (Dave), Sr** — Football Player
PO Box 601292, San Diego CA 92160, USA

**Gray-Stanford, Jason** — Actor
Headline Talent Agency, 138 W 25th St, #1000, New York NY 10001, USA

**Grazer, Brian** — Producer
Imagine Entertainment, 9465 Wilshire Blvd, #700, Beverly Hills CA 90212, USA

**Graziadei, Michael** — Actor
Main Title Mgmt, 8383 Wilshire Blvd, #408, Beverly Hills CA 90211 USA

**Grazzola, Kenneth E** — Publisher
Aviation Week, Publisher's Office, 1221 Ave of Americas, New York NY 10020, USA

**Grba, Eli** — Baseball Player
106 Fox Run, Florence AL 35633, USA

**Grbac, Elvis** — Football Player
17361 Coldwater Trail, Chagrin Falls OH 44023, USA

**Greason, William H (Bill)** — Baseball Player
4536 Hillman Dr NW, Birmingham AL 35221, USA

**Grebeck, Craig A** — Baseball Player
27856 Homestead Road, Laguna Nigel CA 92677, USA

**Grebenshchikov, Boris** — Singer, Guitarist (Akvarium)
2 Marata St, #3, 191025 Saint Petersburg, Russia

**Greceanii, Zinaida** — Prime Minister, Moldova
Prime Minister's Office, Piata Marii Adunari Nacional, 227033 Chishinev, Moldova

**Grech, Prosper (Stanley) Cardinal** — Religious Leader
Order of Saint Augustine, Via Paolo VI, #25, 00193 Rome, Italy

**Grechko, Georgi M** — Cosmonaut
Cosmonaut Training Center, Star City, 141160 Zvezdny Gorodok, Moscow Oblast, Russia

**Greco, Buddy** — Singer, Pianist
Fast Forward Communications, PO Box 1655, Troy NY 12181, USA

**Greco, Emilio** — Sculptor
Viale Cortina d'Ampezzo 132, 00135 Rome, Italy

**Greco, Joel S (Joey)** — Actor, Producer, Writer
Linda McAlister Talent, 30 N Raymond, #409, Pasadena CA 91103, USA

**Greco, Juliette** — Actress, Singer
Productions Gerald Meys, 110 Rue Saint Florentin, 75001 Paris, France

**Greco, Marco** — Auto Racing Driver
11717 W Rockville Road, Indianapolis IN 46232, USA

**Greco, Michael** — Actor
Greg Millard Mgmt, 38 Barton House, Sable St, London N1 2AF, England

**Greczyn, Alice** — Actress
A P A Talent & Literary Agency, 405 S Beverly Dr, #300, Beverly Hills CA 90212 USA

**Greed-Miles, Charlie** — Actor, Writer, Director
C A M, 111 Shoreditch High St, #400, London E1 6JN, England

**Greehey, William E** — Businessman
Valero Energy Corp, 530 McCullough Ave, San Antonio TX 78215, USA

**Green, A C** — Basketball Player
904 Silver Spur Road, Rolling Hills Estates CA 90274, USA

**Green, Adam** — Director, Writer
ArieScope Pictures, 10750 Cumpston St, North Hollywood CA 91601, USA

**Green, Ahman R** — Football Player
1750 Limestone Trail, De Pere WI 54115, USA

**Green, Al** — Singer, Songwriter
Al Green Music, PO Box 456, Millington TN 38083, USA

**Green, Andy D** — Land Speed Racing Driver
London Speaker Bureau, Elsinore House, 77 Fulham Palace Road, London W6 8JA, England

**Green, Anthony W (Bubba)** — Football Player
9611 Wesland Circle, Randallstown MD 21133, USA

**Green, Art** — Religious Leader, Rabbi, Educator
Hebrew College, Rabbinical School, 160 Herrick Road, Newton Centre MA 02459, USA

**Green, B Eric** — Football Player
13131 Luntz Point Lane, Windermere FL 34786, USA

**Green, Barrett** — Football Player
2650 Lake Shore Dr, #705, Riviera Beach FL 33404, USA

**Green, Barry** — Auto Racing Executive
Team Green, 7615 Zionsville Road, Indianapolis IN 46268, USA

**Green, Belina R** — Beauty Queen
Wildlife Information Rescue & Education Service, PO Box 260, Forestville NSW 2087, Australia

**Green, Benny** — Jazz Pianist
Thomas Cassidy, PO Box 1311, Tucson AZ 85702 USA

**Green, Beth** — Photojournalist
Beth Green Studios, 60 Riverside Dr, New York NY 10024, USA

**Green, Boyce K** — Football Player
18812 Parting Oaks Lane, Davidson NC 28036, USA

**Green, Brian Austin** — Actor, Producer, Director
I C M Partners, 10250 Constellation Blvd, #900, Los Angeles CA 90067 USA

**Green, Brunson** — Producer
Slate Public Relations, 9000 Sunset Blvd, #915, West Hollywood CA 90069 USA

**Green, Charles H (Charlie)** — Football Player
255 S Kyrene Road, #214, Chandler AZ 85226, USA

**Green, Cornell D** — Football Player
2106 Trinidad Dr, Dallas TX 75232, USA

**Green, D Jacquez** — Football Player
5102 Madison Lakes Circle W, Davie FL 33328, USA

**Green, Dallas** — Singer, Songwriter
Agency Group Ltd, 142 W 57th St, #600, New York NY 10019 USA

**Green, Darrell R** — Football Player
20998 Rostormel Court, Ashburn VA 20147, USA

**Green, David** — Director
September Films, Glen House, 22 Glenthorne Road, London W6 0NG, England

**Green, David A** — Auto Racing Driver
118 Reel Brook Lane, Mooresville NC 28117, USA

**Green, David A** — Baseball Player
Colinia Managua Grupo H407, Managua, Nicaragua

| | |
|---|---|
| **Green, David E**<br>8311 Pat Blvd, Tampa FL 33615, USA | Football Player |
| **Green, David E**<br>5339 Brody Dr, Madison WI 53705, USA | Chemist |
| **Green, David Gordon**<br>Rough House, 1722 Whitley Ave, Los Angeles CA 90028, USA | Director, Writer |
| **Green, David T**<br>401 Black Rock Turnpike, Easton CT 06612, USA | Inventor (Surgical Instruments) |
| **Green, Debbie**<br>239 5th St, Seal Beach CA 90740, USA | Volleyball Player |
| **Green, Dennis**<br>3930 Torrey Hill Lane, San Diego CA 92130, USA | Football Coach |
| **Green, Donnie G**<br>PO Box 685, Hagerstown MD 21741, USA | Football Player |
| **Green, Douglas B (Ranger Doug)**<br>New Frontier Mgmt, 1921 Broadway, Nashville TN 37203, USA | Singer (Riders in the Sky), Songwriter |
| **Green, Eric**<br>National Institutes of Health, 50 South Dr, Bethesda MD 20892, USA | Medical Administrator |
| **Green, Ernest (Ernie)**<br>424 Rue Marseille, Dayton OH 45429, USA | Football Player |
| **Green, Eva**<br>8 Bis Blvd de Courcelles, 75017 Paris, France | Actress |
| **Green, G Dallas**<br>846 Conowingo Road, Conowingo MD 21918, USA | Baseball Player, Manager, Executive |
| **Green, Gary A**<br>939 Kennebec St, Pittsburgh PA 15217, USA | Baseball Player |
| **Green, Gary F**<br>16330 Walnut Creek Dr, San Antonio TX 78247, USA | Football Player |
| **Green, Gaston A, III**<br>13524 Stanford Ave, Los Angeles CA 90059, USA | Football Player |
| **Green, Gerald, Jr**<br>Phoenix Suns, 201 E Jefferson St, Phoenix AZ 85004 USA | Basketball Player |
| **Green, Hamilton**<br>Plot D Lodge, Georgetown, Guyana | Prime Minister, Guyana |
| **Green, Harold, Jr**<br>145 Folk Road, Blythewood SC 29016, USA | Football Player |
| **Green, Howard**<br>Harvard Medical School, Physiology & Biophysics Dept, Boston MA 02115, USA | Cellular Physiologist |
| **Green, Hubert (Hubie)**<br>Assured Management Co, 1901 W 47th Place, #200, Mission KS 66205, USA | Golfer |
| **Green, Hugh D**<br>4758 Highway 61, Fayette MS 39069, USA | Football Player |
| **Green, Jacob C**<br>4921 Whistling Straits Loop, College Station TX 77845, USA | Football Player |
| **Green, Janine**<br>Don Buchwald Talent Agency, 6500 Wilshire Blvd, #2200, Los Angeles CA 90048 USA | Actress |
| **Green, Jarvis P**<br>3804 Ole Miss Dr, Kenner LA 70065, USA | Football Player |
| **Green, Jeffrey (Jeff)**<br>Haas C N C Racing, 6001 Haas Way, Kanapolis NC 28081, USA | Auto Racing Driver |
| **Green, Jeffrey L (Jeff)**<br>Boston Celtics, 226 Causeway St, #4, Boston MA 02114 USA | Basketball Player |
| **Green, Jimmy**<br>30808 Pine Court, Spanish Fort AL 36527, USA | Golfer |
| **Green, John M**<br>Dutton Books for Young Readers, 345 Hudson St, New York NY 10014, USA | Writer |
| **Green, John M (Johnny)**<br>9 Susan Lane, Dix Hills NY 11746, USA | Basketball Player |
| **Green, John N (Jack), Jr**<br>516 Esplanade, #E, Redondo Beach CA 90277, USA | Cinematographer |
| **Green, Lamar**<br>PO Box 490208, Chicago IL 60649, USA | Basketball Player |
| **Green, Leonard C (Lenny)**<br>18693 Sunset St, Detroit MI 48234, USA | Baseball Player |
| **Green, Leonard I**<br>Rite Aid Corp, 30 Hunter Lane, Camp Hill PA 17011, USA | Businessman |
| **Green, Litterial**<br>1500 N Opdyke Road, Auburn Hills MI 48326, USA | Basketball Player |
| **Green, Mark J**<br>Democracy Project, 43 E 19th St, #300, New York NY 10003, USA | Activist, Attorney, Writer |
| **Green, Michael**<br>11 Stevenson Lane, Upper Saddle River NJ 07458, USA | Cinematographer |
| **Green, Pat**<br>Spaulding Entertainment, 54 Music Square E, #200, Nashville TN 37203, USA | Singer, Songwriter |
| **Green, Richard D (Rick)**<br>RR 1, Peterborough ON K9J 6X2, Canada | Ice Hockey Player |
| **Green, Richard L (Dick)**<br>3924 Ridemoor Dr, Rapid City SD 57702, USA | Baseball Player |
| **Green, Rickey**<br>20584 Tyler Dr, Lynwood IL 60411, USA | Basketball Player |
| **Green, Robson**<br>Creative Artists Agency, 2000 Ave of Stars, #100, Los Angeles CA 90067 USA | Actor |
| **Green, Seth**<br>United Talent Agency, U T A Plaza, 9336 Civic Center Dr, Beverly Hills CA 90210 USA | Actor, Comedian |
| **Green, Shawn D**<br>1430 Village Way, Santa Ana CA 92705, USA | Baseball Player |
| **Green, Tammie**<br>4990 Township Road 147 NE, Somerset OH 43783, USA | Golfer |
| **Green, Timothy J (Tim)**<br>1194 Greenfield Lane, Skaneateles NY 13152, USA | Football Player, Sportscaster, Writer |
| **Green, Tom**<br>I C M Partners, 10250 Constellation Blvd, #900, Los Angeles CA 90067 USA | Actor, Comedian |
| **Green, Travis**<br>2 Riverside, Irvine CA 92602, USA | Ice Hockey Player |
| **Green, Trent J**<br>12109 Alhambra St, Leawood KS 66209, USA | Football Player |

G

Green - Green

V.I.P. Address Book

**G**

G

Green, Victor B
10 Dover Cliff Way, Alpharetta GA 30022, USA — Football Player

Green, Vivian
I C M Partners, 10250 Constellation Blvd, #900, Los Angeles CA 90067 USA — Singer, Songwriter, Actress

Green, William D
Accenture, 50 W San Fernando St, #1200, San Jose CA 95113, USA — Businessman

Green, Willie A
152 Farmington Road, Shelby NC 28150, USA — Football Player

Green, Willie J
Los Angeles Clippers, Staples Center, 1111 S Figueroa St, Los Angeles CA 90015 USA — Basketball Player

Greenawalt, Kent
Columbia University, Law School, 435 W 116th St, New York NY 10027, USA — Attorney, Educator

Greenaway, Peter
V U E, Gabriel Metsu Straat 34, #100, 1071 Amsterdam EC, Netherlands — Director

Greenbaum, Michael
Jewish Theological Seminary, 3080 Broadway, New York NY 10027, USA — Religious Leader, Rabbi, Educator

Greenbaum, Norman
Greenbaum Music, 2513 Saddleback Court, Santa Rosa CA 95401, USA — Singer, Songwriter

Greenberg, Adam
Gersh Agency, 9465 Wilshire Blvd, #600, Beverly Hills CA 90212 USA — Cinematographer

Greenberg, Adam D
79 Fernwood Dr, Guilford CT 06437, USA — Baseball Player

Greenberg, Bernard
1463 E 55th Place, Chicago IL 60637, USA — Biological Scientist, Entomologist

Greenberg, Bryan
Gersh Agency, 9465 Wilshire Blvd, #600, Beverly Hills CA 90212 USA — Actor

Greenberg, Carl
6001 Canterbury Dr, Culver City CA 90230, USA — Journalist

Greenberg, Evan
American International Group, 70 Pine St, New York NY 10270, USA — Businessman

Greenberg, Jack
118 Riverside Dr, New York NY 10024, USA — Attorney, Educator

Greenberg, Jay
I M G Artists, Carnegie Hall Tower, 152 W 57th St, #500, New York NY 10019 USA — Composer

Greenberg, Kathy
Kaplan/Perrone Entertainment, 9744 Wilshire Blvd, #300, Beverly Hills CA 90212, USA — Writer, Producer

Greenberg, Morton I
US Court of Appeals, Judicial Complex, 402 E State St, Trenton NJ 08608, USA — Judge

Greenberg, Peter S
CBS-TV, News Dept, 51 W 52nd St, New York NY 10019 USA — Travel Commentator, Producer, Actor

Greenberg, Robbie S
11 Reef St, Marina del Rey CA 90292, USA — Cinematographer

Greenblatt, Stephen J
Harvard University, English Dept, Cambridge MA 02138, USA — Writer

Greenburg, Dan
323 E 50th St, New York NY 10022, USA — Writer

Greenburg, Jill
Apostrophe, 217 Centre St, #700, New York NY 10013, USA — Photographer, Artist

Greenburg, Paul
5900 Scenic Dr, Little Rock AR 72207, USA — Journalist

Greenbush, Rachel Lindsay
Inmotion Management, 5200 Kanan Road, Agoura Hills CA 91377, USA — Actress

Greenbush, Sidney Robin
Inmotion Management, 5200 Kanan Road, Agoura Hills CA 91377, USA — Actress

Greene, Anthony (Tony)
1890 Briarcliff Circle NE, #D, Atlanta GA 30329, USA — Football Player

Greene, Ashley
McKeon-Myrones Mgmt, 3500 Olive Ave, #770, Burbank CA 91505 USA — Actress

Greene, Bob
Simon & Schuster Books, 1230 Ave of Americas, Concourse 1, New York NY 10020, USA — Exercise Physiologist, Writer

Greene, Brian
Columbia University, Physics Dept, New York NY 10027, USA — Physicist, Mathematician

Greene, Charles E (Charlie)
PO Box 6938, Lincoln NE 68506, USA — Track Athlete

Greene, Charles P (Charlie)
1449 Oldfield Dr, Tallahassee FL 32308, USA — Baseball Player

Greene, Daniel
Michael Slessinger, 8730 W Sunset Blvd, #220W, West Hollywood CA 90069 USA — Actor

Greene, Ellen
Innovative Artists, 1505 10th St, Santa Monica CA 90401 USA — Actress, Singer

Greene, Graham
Greene Assoc, 1901 Ave of Stars, #130, Los Angeles CA 90067 USA — Actor

Greene, Herb
PO Box 1141, Vineyard Haven MA 02568, USA — Photographer

Greene, I Thomas (Tommy)
PO Box 10, Warrington PA 18976, USA — Baseball Player

Greene, Jack P
1974 Division Road, East Greenwich RI 02818, USA — Historian

Greene, James
TalentWorks, 3500 W Olive Ave, #1400, Burbank CA 91505 USA — Actor

Greene, Joseph E (Mean Joe)
PO Box 270953, Flower Mound TX 75027, USA — Football Player, Coach

Greene, Kenneth E (Ken)
5569 Nevil Point, Brentwood TN 37027, USA — Football Player

Greene, Kevin D
928 Bambi Dr, Destin FL 32541, USA — Football Player

Greene, Khalil T
10 Green Hill Dr, Simpsonville SC 29681, USA — Baseball Player

Greene, Kim Morgan
Kazarian/Measures/Ruskin, 11969 Ventura Blvd, #300, Studio City CA 91604 USA — Actress

Greene, Maurice
H S I Sports Mgmt, 9871 Irvine Center Dr, Irvine CA 92618, USA — Track Athlete

Greene, Michele
PO Box 382, Skyforest CA 92385, USA — Actress, Singer, Writer

Greene, Robert B (Bob), Jr
Chicago Tribune, Editorial Dept, 435 N Michigan Ave, #1, Chicago IL 60611, USA — Columnist

Green - Greene

378

V.I.P. Address Book

**Greene, Shecky** — Actor, Comedian
Charles Rapp Enterprises, 55 Broad St, #2600, New York NY 10004, USA

**Greene, Todd A** — Baseball Player
725 Pine Leaf Court, Alpharetta GA 30022, USA

**Greene, William L (Willie)** — Baseball Player
1044 Georgia Highway 22 E, Haddock GA 31033, USA

**Green-Ellis, BenJarvus** — Football Player
Cincinnati Bengals, 1 Paul Brown Stadium, Cincinnati OH 45202 USA

**Greenert, Jonathan W** — Navy Admiral
Chief of Naval Operations, HqUSN, Pentagon, Washington DC 20350 USA

**Greenfield, James L** — Journalist
470 Park Ave, #9A, New York NY 10022, USA

**Greenfield, Jeff** — Commentator
CNN-TV, News Dept, 820 1st St NE, #1000, Washington DC 20002 USA

**Greenfield, Lauren** — Photographer, Filmmaker, Director
Gersh Agency, 9465 Wilshire Blvd, #600, Beverly Hills CA 90212 USA

**Greenfield, Luke** — Director
Creative Artists Agency, 2000 Ave of Stars, #100, Los Angeles CA 90067 USA

**Greenfield, Max** — Actor
W M E Entertainment, 9601 Wilshire Blvd, #300, Beverly Hills CA 90210 USA

**Greengard, Paul** — Nobel Medicine Laureate
450 E 63rd St, #11J, New York NY 10065, USA

**Greengrass, James R (Jim)** — Baseball Player
232 Rock Creek Road, Chatsworth CA 30705, USA

**Greengrass, Paul** — Director
Creative Artists Agency, 2000 Ave of Stars, #100, Los Angeles CA 90067 USA

**Greenhouse, Linda** — Journalist
New York Times, Editorial Dept, 229 W 43rd St, New York NY 10036, USA

**Greenland, Seth** — Writer
R W S H Agency, 1107 1/2 Glendon Ave, Los Angeles CA 90024, USA

**Greenough, George** — Filmmaker, Surfer
PO Box 611, Byron Bay NSW 2481, Australia

**Greenquist, Brad** — Actor
A M T Artists, 15260 Ventura Blvd, #1200, Sherman Oaks CA 91403, USA

**Greenspan, Alan** — Producer
International Arts Entertainment, 8899 Beverly Blvd, #800, Los Angeles CA 90048, USA

**Greenspan, Alan** — Government Official, Financier
Greenspan Assoc, 1133 Connecticut Ave NW, Washington DC 20036, USA

**Greenspan, Gerald (Jerry)** — Basketball Player
291 County Line Road, Riegelsville PA 18077, USA

**Greenspoon, Jimmy** — Organist (Three Dog Night)
McKenzie Accountancy, 5171 Caliente St, #134, Las Vegas NV 89119, USA

**Greenstein, Barry** — Poker Player, Writer
3303 Palos Verdes Dr, Rancho Palos Verdes CA 90272, USA

**Greenstein, Fred I** — Political Scientist
1 Conifer Court, Princeton NJ 08540, USA

**Greenstein, Jeff** — Producer
I C M Partners, 10250 Constellation Blvd, #900, Los Angeles CA 90067 USA

**Greenville, Georgina** — Model
Next Model Mgmt, 188 Rue de Rivoli, 75001 Paris, France

**Greenwald, Alex** — Actor, Model, Singer (Phantom Planet)
C A M, 10635 Santa Monica Blvd W, #340, Los Angeles CA 90025, USA

**Greenwald, Milton** — Paleontologist
University of California, Museum of Paleontology, Berkeley CA 94720, USA

**Greenwald, Robert** — Director
Brave New Films, 10510 Culver Blvd, Culver City CA 90232, USA

**Greenwald, Todd J** — Producer, Writer
Creative Artists Agency, 2000 Ave of Stars, #100, Los Angeles CA 90067 USA

**Greenway, Chad** — Football Player
39448 250th St, Mount Vernon SD 57363, USA

**Greenwell, Michael L (Mike)** — Baseball Player, Auto Racing Driver
20150 S River Road, Alva FL 33920, USA

**Greenwood, Bruce** — Actor
Binder & Assoc, 1465 Lindacrest Dr, Beverly Hills CA 90210 USA

**Greenwood, Colin C** — Bassist (Radiohead)
Courtyard, 21 Nursery, Sutton Courtenay, Abingdon, Oxfordshire OX14 4UA, England

**Greenwood, David K** — Basketball Player
4991 Glenview St, Chino Hills CA 91709, USA

**Greenwood, James C (Jim)** — Representative, PA
Biotechnology Industry, 1201 Maryland Ave SW, Washington DC 20024, USA

**Greenwood, Jonathan R G (Jonny)** — Guitarist (Radiohead)
Courtyard, 21 Nursery, Sutton Courtenay, Abingdon, Oxfordshire OX14 4UA, England

**Greenwood, Kerry** — Writer
Allen & Unwin, 83 Alexander St, Crows Nest NSW 2065, Australia

**Greenwood, Lee** — Singer, Songwriter
Umberger Agency, 1562 Steele Drive NW, Atlanta GA 30309, USA

**Greenwood, Morlon O** — Football Player
1131 Wigwam Parkway, #19209, Henderson NV 89074, USA

**Greenwood, Norman** — Chemist
University of Leeds, Chemistry Dept, Leeds LS2 9JT, England

**Greer, David S** — Internist
447 Albany St, Fall River MA 02720, USA

**Greer, Donovan O** — Football Player
3423 Shadowside Court, Houston TX 77082, USA

**Greer, Germaine** — Social Activist, Writer
University of Warwick, English Literature Dept, Coventry CV4 7AL, England

**Greer, Harold E (Hal)** — Basketball Player
7900 E Princess Dr, #1021, Scottsdale AZ 85255, USA

**Greer, Howard E (Howie)** — Navy Admiral
2845 Granada Blvd Apt 2C, Coral Gables FL 33134, USA

**Greer, Judy** — Actress
Creative Artists Agency, 2000 Ave of Stars, #100, Los Angeles CA 90067 USA

**Greer, Kenneth W (Kenny)** — Baseball Player
17 Hill St, Cohasset MA 02025, USA

**Greer, Thurman C (Rusty), III** — Baseball Player
4793 Patterson Lane, Colleyville TX 76034, USA

**Gregg, A Forrest** — Football Player, Coach, Administrator
926 Summer Spring View, Colorado Springs CO 80906, USA
**Gregg, Clark** — Actor
United Talent Agency, U T A Plaza, 9336 Civic Center Dr, Beverly Hills CA 90210 USA
**Gregg, John** — Actor
International Casting Service, 2/218 Crown St, Darlinghurst NSW 2010, Australia
**Gregg, Kelly M** — Football Player
13800 Hollow Glen Road, Edmond OK 73013, USA
**Gregg, Kevin M** — Baseball Player
1907 SW Brooklane Dr, Corvallis OR 97333, USA
**Gregg, Ricky Lynn** — Singer
E R Rimes Mgmt, 1103 Bell Grimes Lane, Nashville TN 37207, USA
**Gregg, Stephen** — Writer
Creative Artists Agency, 2000 Ave of Stars, #100, Los Angeles CA 90067 USA
**Gregg, W Thomas (Tommy)** — Baseball Player
531 Timbercreek Estates Dr, Sharpsburg GA 30277, USA
**Gregga, Bruce** — Interior Designer
Gregga Jordan Smieszny, 1255 N State Parkway, Chicago IL 60610, USA
**Gregor, Gary W** — Basketball Player
444 Dove Ridge Road, Columbia SC 29223, USA
**Gregorian, Vartan** — Educator
Carnegie Corp, President's Office, 437 Madison Ave, New York NY 10022, USA
**Gregorio, Rose** — Actress
Bauman Redanty Shaul Agency, 5757 Wilshire Blvd, #473, Los Angeles CA 90036 USA
**Gregorio, Tom** — Baseball Player
66 McArthur Ave, Staten Island NY 10312, USA
**Gregorios, Metropolitan Paulos M** — Religious Leader
Orthodox Seminary, PO Box 98, Kottayam, Kerala 686001, India
**Gregory, Alex** — Rowing Athlete
Leander Rowing Club, Henley-on-Thames Oxfordshire RG9 2LP, England
**Gregory, Bettina L** — Commentator
ABC-TV, News Dept, 3361 75th Ave, #X, Hyattsville MD 20785, USA
**Gregory, Claude** — Basketball Player
14621 Blackburn Road, Burtonsville MD 20866, USA
**Gregory, Cynthia** — Ballet Dancer
American Ballet Theatre, 890 Broadway, #300, New York NY 10003 USA
**Gregory, David** — Commentator
NBC-TV, News Dept, 4001 Nebraska Ave NW, Washington DC 20016 USA
**Gregory, Dick** — Actor, Comedian, Social Activist
Dick Gregory Health Enterprises, PO Box 3270, Plymouth MA 02361, USA
**Gregory, E Jackson (Jack), Jr** — Football Player
108 Robertson St, Okolona MS 38860, USA
**Gregory, Frederick D** — Astronaut
506 Tulip Road, Annapolis MD 21403, USA
**Gregory, G Leroy (Lee)** — Baseball Player
6456 N Teilman Ave, Fresno CA 93711, USA
**Gregory, James M (Jim)** — Ice Hockey Executive
National Hockey League, 75 International Blvd, Rexdale ON M9W 6L9, Canada
**Gregory, Kathy** — Cartoonist
Playboy, Reader Services, 680 N Lake Shore Dr, Chicago IL 60611, USA
**Gregory, Leo** — Actor
Artists Partnership, 101 Finsbury Pavement, London EC2A 1RS, England
**Gregory, Philippa** — Writer, Historian
Simon & Schuster, 222 Gray's Inn Road, London WC1X 8HE, England
**Gregory, Richard** — Religious Leader
Independent Fundamental Churches, 2684 Meadow Ridge, Byron Center MI 49315, USA
**Gregory, Sebastian** — Actor
Active Artists Mgmt, 43/38 Manchester Lane, Melbourne VIC 3000, Australia
**Gregory, William G** — Astronaut
2027 E Freeport Lane, Gilbert AZ 85234, USA
**Gregory, William P (Bill), Jr** — Football Player
4317 Cityview Dr, Plano TX 75093, USA
**Gregory, Wilton D** — Religious Leader
Illinois Diocese, Chancery Office, 222 S 3rd St, Belleville IL 62220, USA
**Gregson Wagner, Natasha** — Actress
1014 N Doheny Dr, #8, West Hollywood CA 90069, USA
**Gregson, Wallace C** — Marine Corps General
Commander, Marine Forces Pacific, Camp H M Smith HI 96861 USA
**Gregson-Williams, Harry** — Composer
Gorfaine/Schwartz, 4111 W Alameda Ave, #509, Burbank CA 91505 USA
**Grehl, Michael** — Editor
Memphis Commercial Appeal, Editorial Dept, 495 Union Ave, Memphis TN 38103, USA
**Greider, Carolyn W (Carol)** — Nobel Medicine Laureate
Johns Hopkins University Medical Center, Greider Laboratory, 725 N Wolfe Ave, Baltimore MD 21205, USA
**Greif, Matthew** — Guitarist (LAGQ)
Jana Jae Enterprises, PO Box 35726, Tulsa OK 74153, USA
**Greif, Michael** — Director
I C M Partners, 730 5th Ave, New York NY 10019 USA
**Greif, William B (Bill)** — Baseball Player
807 E 31st St, Austin TX 78705, USA
**Greifeld, Robert A** — Financier
NASDAQ OMX Group, 1 Liberty Plaza, 165 Broadway, New York NY 10006, USA
**Greig, John W** — Basketball Player
2031 218th Place NE, Sammamish WA 98074, USA
**Greilsammer, David** — Conductor, Concert Pianist
I M G Artists, The Light Box, 111 Power Road, London W4 5PY, England
**Greiner, William R** — Educator
80 Aspenwood Dr, East Amherst NY 14051, USA
**Greinke, D Zackary (Zack)** — Baseball Player
8629 Vista Pine Court, Orlando FL 32836, USA
**Greis, Michael** — Biathlete
Postfach 1120, 83318 Ruhpolding, Germany
**Greisen, Nick A** — Football Player
525 Kedzie St, #403, Evanston IL 60202, USA
**Greisinger, Seth A** — Baseball Player
6460 Overbrook St, Falls Church VA 22043, USA

**Greist, Kim** — Actress
Jeffrey Leavitt Agency, 11500 W Olympic Blvd, #400, Los Angeles CA 90064, USA
**Grenier, Adrian** — Actor
Leverage Mgmt, 3030 Pennsylvania Ave, Santa Monica CA 90404 USA
**Grenier, Sylvain** — Professional Wrestler
World Wrestling Entertainment, Titan Towers, 1241 E Main St, Stamford CT 06902 USA
**Grenier, Zach** — Actor
Stone Meyer Genow, 9665 Wilshire Blvd, #510, Beverly Hills CA 90212 USA
**Grentz, Theresa Shank** — Basketball Coach
University of Illinois, Athletic Dept, Champaign IL 61820, USA
**Greschner, Ron** — Ice Hockey Player
PO Box 4513, Greenwich CT 6831, USA
**Gresham, Robert C (Bob)** — Football Player
2428 Portstewart Lane, Charlotte NC 28270, USA
**Gretsch, Joel J** — Actor
A P A Talent & Literary Agency, 405 S Beverly Dr, #300, Beverly Hills CA 90212 USA
**Gretzky, Wayne D** — Ice Hockey Player, Coach
6436 E Gainsborough Road, Scottsdale AZ 85251, USA
**Greutert, Kevin** — Director, Editor
United Talent Agency, U T A Plaza, 9336 Civic Center Dr, Beverly Hills CA 90210 USA
**Grevelius, Anna** — Opera Singer
I M G Artists, Hogarth Business Park, Chiswick, London W4 2TH, England
**Grevers, Matthew (Matt)** — Swimmer
821 N Waukegan Road, Lake Forest IL 60045, USA
**Grevey, Kevin M** — Basketball Player
528 River Bend Road, Great Falls VA 22066, USA
**Grevill, Laurent** — Actor
Artmedia, 20 Ave Rapp, 75007 Paris, France
**Grewal, Alexi** — Cyclist
US Cycling Federation, 1750 E Boulder, Colorado Springs CO 80909, USA
**Grey, Beryl E** — Ballerina
Fernhill, Priory Road, Forest Row, East Sussex RH18 5JE, England
**Grey, Brad** — Businessman, Producer, Agent
Paramount Pictures, 5555 Melrose Ave, Los Angeles CA 90038, USA
**Grey, Jennifer** — Actress
United Talent Agency, U T A Plaza, 9336 Civic Center Dr, Beverly Hills CA 90210 USA
**Grey, Joel** — Actor
Innovative Artists, 1505 10th St, Santa Monica CA 90401 USA
**Grey, Sasha** — Actress, Model
A P A Talent & Literary Agency, 405 S Beverly Dr, #300, Beverly Hills CA 90212 USA
**Grey, Skylar** — Singer, Songwriter
Rogers & Cowan, 8687 Melrose Ave, #G700, West Hollywood CA 90069 USA
**Greyeyes, Michael** — Actor
TalentWorks, 3500 W Olive Ave, #1400, Burbank CA 91505 USA
**Gribble, David** — Cinematographer
Sheldon Prosnit Agency, 800 S Robertson Blvd, Los Angeles CA 90035, USA
**Grich, Robert A (Bobby)** — Baseball Player
31 Madison Lane, Trabuco Canyon CA 92679, USA
**Grichting, Damian** — Curling Athlete
Curling Association, PO Box 606, 3000 Bern, Switzerland
**Grider, Robbin** — Keyboardist (Klymaxx)
R D M J Entertainment Mgmt, 3619 Rose Ave, Long Beach CA 90807 USA
**Grieco, Richard** — Actor
Independent Artists, 9601 Wilshire Blvd, #750, Beverly Hills CA 90210 USA
**Grieder, William** — Journalist
Simon & Schuster, 1230 Ave of Americas, Concourse 1, New York NY 10020, USA
**Grier, David Alan** — Actor, Comedian
Innovative Artists, 1505 10th St, Santa Monica CA 90401 USA
**Grier, J A D** — Businessman
Cincinnati Milacron Inc, 4701 Marbury Ave, Cincinnati OH 45209, USA
**Grier, Mike** — Ice Hockey Player
72 Stonecrest Dr, Needham MA 2492, USA
**Grier, Pam** — Actress
TalentWorks, 3500 W Olive Ave, #1400, Burbank CA 91505 USA
**Grier, Roosevelt (Rosey)** — Football Player, Actor
1250 4th St, #600, Santa Monica CA 90401, USA
**Griese, Brian D** — Football Player
17 Polo Club Dr, Denver CO 80209, USA
**Griese, Robert A (Bob)** — Football Player, Sportscaster
3195 Ponce de Leon Blvd, #412, Coral Gables FL 33134, USA
**Griesemer, John N** — Government Official
RR 2 Box 204B, Springfield MO 65802, USA
**Grieve, Benjamin (Ben)** — Baseball Player
6906 Fairway Road, La Jolla CA 92037, USA
**Grieve, Pierson M** — Businessman
Ecolab Inc, Ecolab Center, 370 Wabasha St N, Saint Paul MN 55102, USA
**Griffen, Everson** — Football Player
Minnesota Vikings, 9520 Viking Dr, Eden Prairie MN 55344 USA
**Griffey, G Kenneth (Ken)** — Baseball Player
1102 Portmoor Way, Winter Garden FL 34787, USA
**Griffey, G Kenneth (Ken), Jr** — Baseball Player
8815 Conroy Windermere Road, Orlando FL 32835, USA
**Griffin, Adrian D** — Basketball Player
2909 Taylor St, Dallas TX 75226, USA
**Griffin, Alfredo C** — Baseball Player
9731 NW 41st St, Doral FL 33178, USA
**Griffin, Archie M** — Football Player
6845 Temperance Point Place, Westerville OH 43082, USA
**Griffin, Benjamin S** — Army General
Institute for Strategic & Innovative Technologies, 2600 McHale Court, Austin TX 78758, USA
**Griffin, Blake A** — Basketball Player
Los Angeles Clippers, Staples Center, 1111 S Figueroa St, Los Angeles CA 90015 USA
**Griffin, Cedric L** — Football Player
3015 Garwood St, Austin TX 78702, USA
**Griffin, Cornelius** — Football Player
224 Countryside Dr, Troy AL 36079, USA

| | |
|---|---|
| **Griffin, Douglas L (Doug)**<br>15811 El Soneto Dr, Whittier CA 90603, USA | Baseball Player |
| **Griffin, Eddie**<br>Front Of The Bus, 7400 Hollywood Blvd, #626, Los Angeles CA 90046, USA | Actor, Comedian |
| **Griffin, Greg**<br>12051 Bayport St, #1-208, Garden Grove CA 92840, USA | Basketball Player |
| **Griffin, John**<br>David Shapira Assoc, 193 N Robertson Blvd, Beverly Hills CA 90211 USA | Actor, Writer, Producer |
| **Griffin, John-Ford**<br>PO Box 1359, Sarasota FL 34230, USA | Baseball Player |
| **Griffin, Kathleeen (Kathy)**<br>W M E Entertainment, 9601 Wilshire Blvd, #300, Beverly Hills CA 90210 USA | Actress, Comedienne |
| **Griffin, Keith**<br>4330 Canada Hills Court, Waldorf MD 20602, USA | Football Player |
| **Griffin, Kevin**<br>Uppercut Mgmt, 805 N Milwaukee Ave, #401, Chicago IL 60642, USA | Singer, Guitarist (Better Than Ezra) |
| **Griffin, Khamani**<br>Commercial Talent, 12711 Ventura Blvd, #285, Studio City CA 91604, USA | Actor |
| **Griffin, Larry A**<br>5617 Silchester Lane, Charlotte NC 28215, USA | Football Player |
| **Griffin, Leonard J, Jr**<br>PO Box 480, Calhoun LA 71225, USA | Football Player |
| **Griffin, Michael D (Mike)**<br>University of Alabama, Mechanical & Aerospace Engineering Dept, Huntsville AL 35805, USA | Government Official |
| **Griffin, Michael L (Mike)**<br>1620 Grove Ave, Woodland CA 95695, USA | Baseball Player |
| **Griffin, Nikki**<br>Corsa Agency, 11704 Wilshire Blvd, #204, Los Angeles CA 90025, USA | Actress |
| **Griffin, Patty**<br>High Road Touring, 751 Bridgeway, #200, Sausalito CA 94965 USA | Singer, Songwriter, Guitarist |
| **Griffin, Paul A**<br>903 Great Tree Dr, San Antonio TX 78260, USA | Basketball Player |
| **Griffin, Raymond (Ray)**<br>2304 Somersworth Dr, Columbus OH 43219, USA | Football Player |
| **Griffin, Robert L, III**<br>Washington Redskins, 21300 Redskin Park Dr, Ashburn VA 20147 USA | Football Player |
| **Griffin, Robert P**<br>Michigan Supreme Court, PO Box 30052, Lansing MI 48909, USA | Senator, MI; Judge |
| **Griffin, Thomas J (Tom)**<br>13147 Avenida La Valencia, Poway CA 92064, USA | Baseball Player |
| **Griffin, Thomas N, Jr**<br>9749 S Park Circle, Fairfax Station VA 22039, USA | Army General |
| **Griffin, Tim**<br>Untitled Entertainment, 350 S Beverly Dr, #200, Beverly Hills CA 90212 USA | Actor |
| **Griffin, W E B**<br>Penguin Books, 375 Hudson St, Basement 1, New York NY 10014 USA | Writer |
| **Griffin, Wade H, Jr**<br>2937 Highway 72, Holly Springs MS 38635, USA | Football Player |
| **Griffith, Anastasia**<br>Paradigm Agency, 360 Park Ave S, #1600, New York NY 10010 USA | Actress |
| **Griffith, Anthony**<br>Spivak Sobol Entertainment, 11845 W Olympic Blvd, #1125, Los Angeles CA 90064, USA | Actor |
| **Griffith, Bill**<br>Pinhead Productions, PO Box 88, Hadlyme CT 06439, USA | Cartoonist (Zippy the Pinhead) |
| **Griffith, Darrell S**<br>PO Box 24841, Louisville KY 40224, USA | Basketball Player |
| **Griffith, Howard T**<br>9152 S Clyde Ave, Chicago IL 60617, USA | Football Player |
| **Griffith, James**<br>eBay, 2145 Hamilton Ave, San Jose CA 95125, USA | Businessman |
| **Griffith, James**<br>Timken Co, 1835 Dueber Ave SW, Canton OH 44706, USA | Businessman |
| **Griffith, Melanie**<br>Green Moon Productions, Paseo Maritimo, Ciudad de Melilla 23, 29016 Malaga, Spain | Actress, Model |
| **Griffith, Nanci**<br>Gold Mountain, 11 Music Square E, #103, Nashville TN 37203, USA | Singer, Songwriter |
| **Griffith, R Derrell**<br>201 E Central Blvd, Anadarko OK 73005, USA | Baseball Player |
| **Griffith, Richard P (Rich)**<br>9368 Stoneglen Dr, Colorado Springs CO 80920, USA | Football Player |
| **Griffith, Robert O**<br>3525 Del Mar Heights Road, #331, San Diego CA 92130, USA | Football Player |
| **Griffith, Ronald H (Ron)**<br>Military Professional Resources, 1320 Braddock Place, Alexandria VA 22314, USA | Army General |
| **Griffith, Thomas B**<br>US Court of Appeals, 333 Constitution Ave NW, #4400, Washington DC 20001, USA | Judge |
| **Griffith, Thomas Ian**<br>Pitt Group, 9465 Wilshire Blvd, #420, Beverly Hills CA 90212, USA | Actor |
| **Griffith, Tom W**<br>Rural Letter Carriers Assn, 1448 Duke St, #100, Alexandria VA 22314, USA | Labor Leader |
| **Griffith, Tracy**<br>Rodriguez Mgmt, 223 S Beverly Dr, #207, Beverly Hills CA 90212, USA | Actress |
| **Griffiths, Jeremy**<br>120 Beachdale Dr, Avon Lake OH 44012, USA | Baseball Player |
| **Griffiths, Phillip A**<br>Advanced Study Institute, Director's Office, Olden Lane, Princeton NJ 08540, USA | Mathematician, Educator |
| **Griffiths, Rachel**<br>W M E Entertainment, 9601 Wilshire Blvd, #300, Beverly Hills CA 90210 USA | Actress |
| **Griggs, Andrew T (Andy)**<br>Splash Public Relations, 1520 16th Ave S, #2, Nashville TN 37212, USA | Singer |
| **Griggs, William E (Bill), III**<br>18 Summerhill Lane, Medford NJ 08055, USA | Football Player |
| **Grigorev, Vladimir**<br>All-Russian Skating Union, Luzhnetskaia Nab 8, 119992 Moscow, Russia | Speed Skater |
| **Grijalva, Lucy**<br>PO Box 1634, Benicia CA 94510, USA | Writer |

| | |
|---|---|
| **Grijalva, Victor E**<br>Schlumberger Ltd, 277 Park Ave, New York NY 10172, USA | Businessman |
| **Grilli, Jason**<br>9037 Point Cypress Dr, Orlando FL 32836, USA | Baseball Player |
| **Grillo, Frank**<br>Creative Artists Agency, 2000 Ave of Stars, #100, Los Angeles CA 90067 USA | Actor |
| **Grim, Robert L (Bob)**<br>18 NW Saginaw Ave, Bend OR 97701, USA | Football Player |
| **Grimaldi, Dan**<br>Kingsborough Community College, Mathematics Dept, Brooklyn NY 11235, USA | Actor |
| **Grimaldi, James V**<br>Washington Post, Editorial Dept, 1150 15th St NW, Washington DC 20071 USA | Journalist |
| **Grimaldi, Martina**<br>Swimming Federation, Stadio Olimpico, Curve Nord, 00194 Rome, Italy | Swimmer |
| **Grimaud, Helene**<br>Harm's Way Mgmt, Fritschestr 27/28, Fabrik 2, Aufgang C, 10585 Berlin, Germany | Concert Pianist |
| **Grimes, Brent O**<br>Miami Dolphins, 7500 SW 30th St, Davie FL 33314 USA | Football Player |
| **Grimes, Kareem**<br>Coast to Coast Talent, 3350 Barham Blvd, Los Angeles CA 90068 USA | Actor |
| **Grimes, Karolyn**<br>PO Box 432, Manchester WA 98353, USA | Actress |
| **Grimes, Luke**<br>Global Creative, 1051 N Cole Ave, #B, Los Angeles CA 90038, USA | Actor |
| **Grimes, Martha**<br>115 D St SE, #G6, Washington DC 20003, USA | Writer |
| **Grimes, Randall C (Randy)**<br>13214 Halifax St, Houston TX 77015, USA | Football Player |
| **Grimes, Scott**<br>Abrams Artists, 9200 W Sunset Blvd, #1125, West Hollywood CA 90069 USA | Actor |
| **Grimes, Shenae**<br>Gersh Agency, 9465 Wilshire Blvd, #600, Beverly Hills CA 90212 USA | Actress |
| **Grimes, Tammy**<br>Artist Group, 1650 Broadway, #1105, New York NY 10019, USA | Actress, Singer |
| **Grimes, Tinsely**<br>Innovative Artists, 1505 10th St, Santa Monica CA 90401 USA | Actress |
| **Grimm, Alexander**<br>Wallgauer Weg 7A, 86163 Augsburg, Germany | Canoeing Athlete |
| **Grimm, Daniel J (Dan)**<br>2514 Smith Harbour Dr, Denver NC 28037, USA | Football Player |
| **Grimm, Oliver**<br>Kronberger Str 15, 94086 Bad-Griesbach, Germany | Actor |
| **Grimm, Russ**<br>2654 E Mead Place, Chandler AZ 85249, USA | Football Player, Coach |
| **Grimm, Tim**<br>Abrams Artists, 9200 W Sunset Blvd, #1125, West Hollywood CA 90069 USA | Actor, Singer |
| **Grimmette, Mark**<br>21 Snowberry Lane, Lake Placid NY 12946, USA | Luge Athlete |
| **Grimsbo, Kari Aalvik**<br>Klaebuveien 157, 7037 Trondheim, Norway | Handball Player |
| **Grimshaw, Nicholas T**<br>Fitzroy Square, 1 Conway St, London W1P 5HA, England | Architect |
| **Grimsley, Jason A**<br>13315 Timberwild Court, Tomball TX 77375, USA | Baseball Player |
| **Grimsley, Ross A**<br>92 Conewago Court, Owings Mill MD 21117, USA | Baseball Player |
| **Grimsmo, Anthon**<br>Curling Assn, Sognsveien 75, Serviceboks 1, 0840 Oslo, Norway | Curling Athlete |
| **Grimson, A Stuart (Stu)**<br>999 Jones Parkway, Brentwood TN 37027, USA | Ice Hockey Player |
| **Grimsson, Olafur Ragnar**<br>President's Office, Stadastadur, Soleyjargata 1, 150 Reykjavik, Iceland | President, Iceland |
| **Grinberg, Anouk**<br>Voyez Mon Agent, 20 Ave Rapp, 75007 Paris, France | Actress |
| **Grindenko, Tatyana T**<br>Moscow State Philharmonic, Tverskaya Str 31, 103050 Moscow, Russia | Concert Violinist |
| **Griner, Brittney**<br>Phoenix Mercury, American West Arena, 201 E Jefferson St, Phoenix AZ 85004 USA | Basketball Player |
| **Griner, Paul**<br>Random House, 1745 Broadway, #1800, New York NY 10019 USA | Writer |
| **Grinham Rawley, Judy**<br>103 Green Lane, Northwood, Middlesex HA6 1AP, England | Swimmer |
| **Grinnage, Jack**<br>Discover Mgmt, 11624 Moorpark St, Studio City CA 91602, USA | Actor |
| **Grinnell, Alan D**<br>University of California Medical School, Lewis Center, Los Angeles CA 90024, USA | Physiologist |
| **Grinnell, Todd A**<br>Gersh Agency, 9465 Wilshire Blvd, #600, Beverly Hills CA 90212 USA | Actor |
| **Grinney, Jay**<br>Healthsouth Corp, 3660 Grandview Parkway, #200, Birmingham AL 35243, USA | Businessman |
| **Grinstead, Irish**<br>Richard Walters, PO Box 2789, Toluca Lake CA 91610, USA | Singer (702) |
| **Grinstead, LeMisha**<br>Richard Walters, PO Box 2789, Toluca Lake CA 91610, USA | Singer (702) |
| **Grint, Rupert**<br>Gersh Agency, 9465 Wilshire Blvd, #600, Beverly Hills CA 90212 USA | Actor |
| **Grinville, Patrick**<br>Academie Goncourt, 38 Rue du Faubourg Saint Jacques, 75014 Paris, France | Writer |
| **Grione, Remo**<br>Cristiano Cucchino Mgmt, Lungotevere dei Mellini 10, 00193 Rome, Italy | Actor |
| **Grippe, Peter**<br>1190 Boylston St, Newton Upper Falls MA 02464, USA | Artist, Sculptor |
| **Grisanti, Eugene P**<br>International Flavors, 521 W 57th St, New York NY 10019, USA | Businessman |
| **Grisdale, John R**<br>A-455 Bromley St, Coquitlam BC V3K 6N7, Canada | Ice Hockey Player |

# G

**Grisez, Germain** — Theologian
Mount Saint Mary's College, Christian Ethics Dept, Emmitsburg MD 21727, USA

**Grisham, John** — Writer
Gernert Co, 136 E 57th St, New York NY 10022, USA

**Grishin, Aleksei** — Freestyle Aerials Skier
Olympic Committee, Ul Ya Kolas 2, 220005 Minsk, Belarus

**Grishuk, Oksana (Pasha)** — Ice Dancer, Actress
PO Box 420, Beverly Hills CA 90213, USA

**Grisman, David** — Singer, Mandolin Player, Composer
C M Mgmt, 5749 Larryan Dr, Woodland Hills CA 91367, USA

**Grissom, Marquis D** — Baseball Player
694 Highway 279, Fayetteville GA 30214, USA

**Grissom, Steve** — Auto Racing Driver
5901 Orr Road, Charlotte NC 28211, USA

**Groat, Richard M (Dick)** — Baseball, Basketball Player
320 Beech St, Pittsburgh PA 15218, USA

**Grob, Mike** — Golfer
3611 Quimet Circle, Billings MT 59106, USA

**Groban, Joshua W (Josh)** — Singer, Actor, Songwriter
W M E Entertainment, 9601 Wilshire Blvd, #300, Beverly Hills CA 90210 USA

**Grobe, Jim** — Football Coach
Wake Forest University, Athletic Dept, Winston-Salem NC 27109, USA

**Grobert, Xavier Perez** — Cinematographer
Dattner Dispoto, 10635 Santa Monica Blvd, #165, Los Angeles CA 90025, USA

**Groce, Clifton A (Clif)** — Football Player
1632 Park Place, College Station TX 77840, USA

**Grocholewski, Zenon Cardinal** — Religious Leader
Catholic Education Congregation, Palazzo della Congregazioni, Piazzo Pio XII, 00193 Rome, Italy

**Grodin, Charles** — Actor
187 Chestnut Hill Road, Wilton CT 06897, USA

**Grodnikaite, Liora** — Opera Singer
I M G Artists, Hogarth Business Park, Chiswick, London W4 2TH, England

**Groening, Matthew (Matt)** — Cartoonist (Life in Hell, Simpsons)
1650 21st St, Santa Monica CA 90404, USA

**Groetzinger, Jon, Jr** — Businessman
American Greetings Corp, 1 American Road, Cleveland OH 44144, USA

**Groff, Jonathan** — Actor, Singer
W M E Entertainment, 9601 Wilshire Blvd, #300, Beverly Hills CA 90210 USA

**Grogan, Clare** — Actress
United Agents, 12-26 Lexington St, London W1F 0LE, England

**Grogan, John** — Writer
Harper Collins Publishers, 10 E 53rd St, Cellar 1, New York NY 10022 USA

**Grogan, Steven J (Steve)** — Football Player
PO Box 530, Foxboro MA 02035, USA

**Groh, Gary** — Golfer
331 Signe Court, Lake Bluff IL 60044, USA

**Grohl, David E (Dave)** — Singer, Songwriter, Drummer
S A M, 722 Seward St, Los Angeles CA 90038, USA

**Grohmann, Tim** — Rowing Athlete
Dresden Rowing Club, Hamburger Str 74, 01157 Dresden, Germany

**Grol, Hindrik H A (Henk)** — Judo Athlete
Junoplantsoen 15, 2024 Haarlem RL, Netherlands

**Gromada, John** — Sound Designer, Composer
I C M Partners, 10250 Constellation Blvd, #900, Los Angeles CA 90067 USA

**Groman, William F (Bill)** — Football Player
7906 Scherzo Lane, Houston TX 77040, USA

**Gromov, Mikhael L** — Abel Mathematics Laureate
91 Rue de la Sante, 75013 Paris, France

**Grondin, Marc-Andre** — Actor
United Talent Agency, U T A Plaza, 9336 Civic Center Dr, Beverly Hills CA 90210 USA

**Gronemeyer, Herbert** — Actor, Composer
Postfach 100969, 44709 Bochum, Germany

**Gronk** — Artist
Daniel Saxon Gallery, 7000 Romaine St, #211, West Hollywood CA 90038, USA

**Gronkowski, Rob** — Football Player
New England Patriots, 1 Patriot Place, Foxboro MA 02035 USA

**Gronman, Tuomas O** — Ice Hockey Player
Pittsburgh Penguins, Consol Energy Center, 1001 5th Ave, Pittsburgh PA 15219 USA

**Gronvole, Audun** — Freestyle Cross Skier
Ski Federation, Ulleval Stadion, 0840 Oslo, Norway

**Groom, Sam** — Actor
8730 W Sunset Blvd, #440, West Hollywood CA 90069, USA

**Groom, Wedsel G (Buddy)** — Baseball Player
1991 Saint Andrews Dr, Red Oak TX 75154, USA

**Grooms, Charles R (Red)** — Artist
85 Walker St, New York NY 10013, USA

**Groop, Monica** — Opera Singer
I M G Artists, Hogarth Business Park, Chiswick, London W4 2TH, England

**Groopman, Jerome** — Hematologist
Beth Israel Deaconess Medical Center, 330 Brookline Ave, Boston MA 02215, USA

**Gropper, Steven L (Steve)** — Guitarist (Mar-Keys), Songwriter
Insomnia Studios, 119 17th Ave S, Nashville TN 37203, USA

**Gros, Earl R** — Football Player
17424 Airline Highway, #12, Prairieville LA 70769, USA

**Grosek, Michal** — Ice Hockey Player
5 Samba Circle, Sandwich MA 02563, USA

**Gross, Alfred E (Al), Jr** — Football Player
8227 Grandstaff Dr, Sacramento CA 95823, USA

**Gross, Arye** — Actor
S D B Partners, 315 S Beverly Dr, #411, Beverly Hills CA 90067 USA

**Gross, Brian** — Actor
Amsel Eisenstadt Frazier, 5055 Wilshire Blvd, #865, Los Angeles CA 90036 USA

**Gross, Charles G** — Psychologist
18 E Shore Dr, Princeton NJ 08540, USA

**Gross, Clayton K** — WW II Army Air Corps Hero
2306 SE Spyglass Dr, Vancouver WA 98683, USA

**Grisez - Gross**

| | |
|---|---|
| **Gross, David**<br>Creative Artists Agency, 2000 Ave of Stars, #100, Los Angeles CA 90067 USA | Actor, Comedian, Writer |
| **Gross, David J**<br>30 Pueblo Vista Road, Santa Barbara CA 93103, USA | Nobel Physics Laureate |
| **Gross, Gabriel J (Gabe)**<br>1756 Raymer Place, Auburn AL 36830, USA | Baseball Player |
| **Gross, Gregory E (Greg)**<br>802 Hallowell Dr, West Chester PA 19382, USA | Baseball Player |
| **Gross, Henry**<br>Zelda Mgmt, PO Box 150163, Nashville TN 37215, USA | Singer, Guitarist (Sha Na Na) |
| **Gross, Jordan A**<br>12725 Ninebark Trail, Charlotte NC 28278, USA | Football Player |
| **Gross, Kevin F**<br>117 Principia Court, Claremont CA 91711, USA | Baseball Player |
| **Gross, Kip L**<br>2015 Ridgeview Court, Redlands CA 92373, USA | Baseball Player |
| **Gross, Lance**<br>Schiff Co, 9220 Sunset Blvd, #106, West Hollywood CA 90069 USA | Actor |
| **Gross, Mary**<br>Pakula/King, 9229 W Sunset Blvd, #315, West Hollywood CA 90069 USA | Actress, Comedienne |
| **Gross, Michael**<br>Stone Manners Salners, 6100 Wilshire Blvd, #1500, Los Angeles CA 90035 USA | Actor |
| **Gross, Michael**<br>Altkonigstr 50, 61462 Konigstein, Germany | Swimmer |
| **Gross, Paul**<br>Bresler Kelly Assoc, 11500 W Olympic Blvd, #400, Los Angeles CA 90064 USA | Actor |
| **Gross, Ricco**<br>Sports2Business, Erlenring 16, 61118 Bad Vilbel, Germany | Biathlete |
| **Gross, Robert A**<br>14 Sunnyside Way, New Rochelle NY 10804, USA | Physicist |
| **Gross, Robert E (Bob)**<br>13466 SE Red Rose Lane, Happy Valley OR 97086, USA | Basketball Player |
| **Gross, Sam**<br>New Yorker, Editorial Dept, 4 Times Square, Basement C1B, New York NY 10036 USA | Cartoonist |
| **Gross, Terry R**<br>WHYY-Radio, News Dept, Independence Mall W, Philadelphia PA 19104, USA | Commentator |
| **Gross, Wayne D**<br>45 Leonard Court, Danville CA 94526, USA | Baseball Player |
| **Grossfeld, Stanley**<br>Boston Globe, Editorial Dept, 135 William Morrissey Blvd, Dorchester MA 02125 USA | Photojournalist |
| **Grossheusch, Leroy (Lee)**<br>1239 Kupau St, Kailua HI 96734, USA | WW II Army Air Corps Hero |
| **Grossman, Austin**<br>Pantheon/Random House, 1745 Broadway, New York NY 10019, USA | Writer |
| **Grossman, Ben**<br>Syndicate, 100 Universal City Plaza, #6148, Universal City CA 91608, USA | Visual Effects Designer |
| **Grossman, Burt**<br>2595 Oak Springs Dr, Chula Vista CA 91915, USA | Football Player |
| **Grossman, C Randy**<br>204 Ridge Road, Pittsburgh PA 15238, USA | Football Player |
| **Grossman, David**<br>United Talent Agency, U T A Plaza, 9336 Civic Center Dr, Beverly Hills CA 90210 USA | Director, Producer |
| **Grossman, David**<br>Bloomsbury Publishing, 50 Bedford Square, London WC1B 3DP, England | Writer |
| **Grossman, Eric**<br>Sharpe Entertainment Services, 683 Palmera Ave, Pacific Palisades CA 90272, USA | Bassist (K's Choice) |
| **Grossman, Gene M**<br>Princeton University, Economics Dept, Princeton NJ 08544, USA | Economist |
| **Grossman, Judith**<br>Warren Wilson College, English Dept, Swannanoa NC 28778, USA | Writer |
| **Grossman, Leslie**<br>Marsh Entertainment, 12444 Ventura Blvd, #203, Sherman Oaks CA 91604, USA | Actress |
| **Grossman, Rex D**<br>17230 Crawley Road, Odessa FL 33556, USA | Football Player |
| **Grossman, Robert**<br>19 Crosby St, New York NY 10013, USA | Illustrator |
| **Grosvenor, Benjamin**<br>Hazard Chase, 25 City Road, Cambridge CB1 1DP, England | Concert Pianist |
| **Grosvenor, Gilbert M**<br>National Geographic, Editorial Dept, 1145 17th St NW, Washington DC 20036 USA | Foundation Executive, Publisher |
| **Grote, Gerald W (Jerry)**<br>2608 N Main St, #B, Belton TX 76513, USA | Baseball Player |
| **Grotenfelt, Georg E J**<br>Kapteeninkatu 20D, 00140 Helsinki, Finland | Architect |
| **Groth, Jacob**<br>Air Edel, 18 Rodmarton St, London W1U 8BJ, England | Composer |
| **Groth, Jeffrey E (Jeff)**<br>13824 Driftwood Dr, Carmel IN 46033, USA | Football Player |
| **Groth, John T (Johnny)**<br>170 N Ocean Blvd, #307, Palm Beach FL 33480, USA | Baseball Player |
| **Grotjahn, Mark**<br>Blum & Poe Gallery, 2727 S La Cienega Blvd, Los Angeles CA 90034, USA | Artist |
| **Grott, Matthew A (Matt)**<br>19431 N Concho Circle, Sun City AZ 85373, USA | Baseball Player |
| **Grouch, Roger K**<br>Life/Microgravity Sciences Office, NASA Headquarters, Washington DC 20546, USA | Astronaut |
| **Grove, Andrew S**<br>Intel Corp, 2200 Mission College Blvd, Santa Clara CA 95054, USA | Businessman |
| **Grove, Jill**<br>I M G Artists, Hogarth Business Park, Chiswick, London W4 2TH, England | Opera Singer |
| **Groves, Kristina**<br>Agenda Sport Marketing, 119-9A St NE, Calgary AB T2E 9C5, Canada | Speed Skater |
| **Groves, Ray J**<br>Marsh Inc, 1166 Ave of Americas, Converse Level 1, New York NY 10036, USA | Businessman |
| **Groves, Richard H**<br>9110 Belvoir Woods Parkway, #216, Fort Belvoir VA 22060, USA | Army General |

**Groves, Robert M** — Government Official, Statistician
Georgetown University, Provost's Office, Washington DC 20057, USA

**Groves, S Russell** — Architect
210 11th Ave, New York NY 10001, USA

**Growney, Robert L** — Businessman
Motorola Inc, 1303 E Algonquin Road, Schaumburg IL 60196, USA

**Grubb, John M** — Baseball Player
6618 Bel Lac Dr, Chester VA 23831, USA

**Grubbs, Benjamin R (Ben)** — Football Player
New Orleans Saints, 5800 Airline Highway, Metairie LA 70003 USA

**Grubbs, Gary** — Actor
TalentWorks, 3500 W Olive Ave, #1400, Burbank CA 91505 USA

**Grubbs, Robert H** — Nobel Chemistry Laureate
1700 Spruce St, South Pasadena CA 91030, USA

**Gruber, Bernhard** — Nordic Combined Skier
Dr Lechnerweg 25, 5310 Mondsee, Austria

**Gruber, J Mackye** — Director
New Wave Entertainment, 2660 W Olive Ave, Burbank CA 91505, USA

**Gruber, Kelly W** — Baseball Player
17718 Linkview Dr, Dripping Springs TX 78620, USA

**Gruber, Michael** — Writer
William Morrow Publishers, 1350 Ave of Americas, New York NY 10019 USA

**Gruber, Paul B** — Football Player
PO Box 4239, Edwards CO 81632, USA

**Gruberova, Edita** — Opera Singer
Theateragentur Hilbert, Maximilianstr 22, 80539 Munich, Germany

**Grubinger, Martin** — Concert Percussionist
Harrison/Parrott, 5-6 Albion Court, London W6 0QT, England

**Grubman, Allen J** — Attorney
Grubman Indursky Schindler Goldstein, 152 W 57th St, New York NY 10019, USA

**Grubnic, Dave** — Drag Racing Driver
Kalitta Motorsports, 1010 James L Hart Parkway, Ypsilanti MI 48197, USA

**Gruda, Sandrine** — Basketball Player
Los Angeles Sparks, 888 S Figueroa St, #2010, Los Angeles CA 90017 USA

**Gruden, Jay** — Football Coach
Washington Redskins, 21300 Redskin Park Dr, Ashburn VA 20147 USA

**Gruden, Jon** — Football Coach, Sportscaster
709 Guisando de Avila, Tampa FL 33613, USA

**Grudt, Mona** — Beauty Queen
Ditt Bryllup, Editor's Office, PO Box 24, 1485 Hakadal, Norway

**Grudzielanek, Mark J** — Baseball Player
833 Aspen Peak Loop, #1113, Henderson NV 89011, USA

**Gruenberg, Erich** — Concert Violinist
80 Northway, Hampstead Garden Suburb, London NW11 6PA, England

**Gruenberg, Peter** — Nobel Physics Laureate
Solid State Research Institute, Wilhelm-Johnen-Str, 52425 Juelich, Germany

**Gruevski, Nikola** — Prime Minister, Macedonia
Prime Minister's Office, Ilindenska BB, 1000 Skopje, Macedonia

**Gruffudd, Ioan** — Actor
Framework Entertainment, 9057 Nemo St, #C, West Hollywood CA 90069 USA

**Grum, Clifford J** — Businessman
Temple-Inland Inc, 303 S Temple Dr, Diboll TX 75941, USA

**Grumman, Cornelia** — Journalist
Chicago Tribune, Editorial Dept, 350 N Orleans St, Chicago IL 60654 USA

**Grummer, Elisabeth** — Opera Singer
Am Schlachtensee 104, 14163 Berlin, Germany

**Grunberg-Manago, Marianne** — Biochemist
80 Boulevard Pasteur, 75015 Paris, France

**Grundfest, Joseph A** — Government Official
Stanford University, Law School, Stanford CA 94305, USA

**Grundhofer, Jerry A** — Financier
US Bancorp, 601 2nd Ave S, Minneapolis MN 55402, USA

**Grundhofer, John F** — Financier
Donaldson Co, 1400 W 94th St, Minneapolis MN 55431, USA

**Grundman, Bernie** — Music Executive
Bernie Grundman Mastering, 1640 N Gower St, Los Angeles CA 90028, USA

**Grundt, Kenneth A (Ken)** — Baseball Player
4814 W Parker Ave, Chicago IL 60639, USA

**Grundy, Hugh** — Drummer (Zombies)
Lustig Talent, PO Box 770850, Orlando FL 32877 USA

**Grune, George V** — Publisher, Foundation Executive
PO Box 2348, Ponte Vedra Beach FL 32004, USA

**Gruneisen, Samuel K (Sam)** — Football Player
569 Finsbay Court, Ocoee FL 34761, USA

**Grunfeld, Ernest (Ernie)** — Basketball Player, Executive
10121 Counselman Road, Potomac MD 20854, USA

**Grunhard, Timothy G (Tim)** — Football Player
2005 Arno Road, Mission Hills KS 66208, USA

**Grunsfeld, John M** — Astronaut
PO Box 279, Highland MD 20777, USA

**Grunstein, Michael** — Biological Chemist
University of California, Biological Chemistry Dept, Los Angeles CA 90024, USA

**Grunwald, Ernie** — Actor
Stone Manners Salners, 6100 Wilshire Blvd, #1500, Los Angeles CA 90035 USA

**Grupp, Robert W (Bob)** — Football Player
305 Hill Ave, Langhorne PA 19047, USA

**Grush, Stephen Louis** — Actor
W M E Entertainment, 9601 Wilshire Blvd, #300, Beverly Hills CA 90210 USA

**Grushecky, Joe** — Singer (Iron City Houserockers)
Brothers Management Assoc, 141 Dunbar Ave, Fords NJ 08863 USA

**Grusin, Dave** — Composer, Pianist
Kraft-Engel Mgmt, 15233 Ventura Blvd, #200, Sherman Oaks CA 91403 USA

**Grutman, N Roy** — Attorney
Grutman Miller Greenspoon Hendler, 505 Park Ave, New York NY 10022, USA

**Gruttadauria, Michael J (Mike)** — Football Player
4250 Swift Road, Sarasota FL 34231, USA

| | |
|---|---|
| **Grybauskaite, Dalia** | President, Lithuania |
| President's Office, Gediminas 53, 232026 Vilnius, Lithuania | |
| **Gryboski, Kevin** | Baseball Player |
| 127 Castlebrooke Dr, Venetia PA 15367, USA | |
| **Grylls, Edward M (Bear)** | Entertainer, Writer, Mountaineer |
| Second Assn, Gilwell Park, Chingford, London E4 7QW, England | |
| **Grzanich, Michael E (Mike)** | Baseball Player |
| 176 Holliday Trace, Raymond MS 39154, USA | |
| **Guang Yang** | Opera Singer |
| Columbia Artists Mgmt Inc, 5 Columbus Circle, 1790 Broadway, #1600, New York NY 10019 USA | |
| **Guanlao, Christopher** | Drummer (Silversun Pickups) |
| Ink Tank Public Relations, 1824 W Sunset Blvd, #102, Los Angeles CA 90026, USA | |
| **Guard, Christopher** | Actor |
| 76 Oxford St, London W1N 0AX, England | |
| **Guardado, Edward A (Eddie)** | Baseball Player |
| 11268 Overlook Point, Tustin CA 92782, USA | |
| **Guare, John** | Writer |
| R Andrew Boose, 1 Dag Hammarskjold Plaza, New York NY 10017, USA | |
| **Guarini, Justin** | Singer |
| Axis Artist Management, 9715 Belmar Ave, Northridge CA 91324, USA | |
| **Guaty, Camille** | Actress |
| A P A Talent & Literary Agency, 405 S Beverly Dr, #300, Beverly Hills CA 90212 USA | |
| **Guay, Paul F** | Ice Hockey Player |
| 34 Kirkbrae Dr, Lincoln RI 02865, USA | |
| **Gubaidulina, Sofia A** | Composer |
| 2D Pugachevskaya 8, Korp 5, #130, 107061 Moscow, Russia | |
| **Gubanich, Creighton W** | Baseball Player |
| 10 Galicia Dr, Phoenixville PA 19460, USA | |
| **Gubanova, Ekaterina** | Opera Singer |
| Mariinsky Theater, Theater Square, 1 Pl Iskusstr, 190000 Saint Petersburg, Russia | |
| **Gubarev, Aleksei A** | Cosmonaut; Air Force General |
| Cosmonaut Training Center, Star City, 141160 Zvezdny Gorodok, Moscow Oblast, Russia | |
| **Guber, Peter** | Producer |
| Mandalay Entertainment, 10202 W Washington Blvd, #1070, Culver City CA 90232, USA | |
| **Gubicza, Mark S** | Baseball Player |
| 11808 Macoda Lane, Chatsworth CA 91311, USA | |
| **Gubler, Matthew Gray** | Actor |
| Creative Artists Agency, 2000 Ave of Stars, #100, Los Angeles CA 90067 USA | |
| **Guccione, Christopher (Chris)** | Baseball Umpire |
| 15362 W Iliff Dr, Denver CO 80228, USA | |
| **Guckel, Henry** | Microbiotics Engineer |
| University of Wisconsin, Engineering Dept, Madison WI 53706, USA | |
| **Gudereit, Marcia** | Curling Athlete |
| Curling Association, 1660 Vimont Court, Cumberland ON K4A 4J4, Canada | |
| **Gudgeon, Simon** | Sculptor |
| Halcyon Gallery, 144-146 New Bond St, London W1S 2PF, England | |
| **Gudmundsson, Petur** | Basketball Player |
| 2423 Vibrant Oak, San Antonio TX 78232, USA | |
| **Guebuza, Armando** | President, Mozambique |
| President's Office, Avenida Julius Nyerere 1780, Maputo, Mozambique | |
| **Guelleh, Ismail Omar** | President, Djibouti |
| President's Office, 8-10 Ahmed Nessin St, BP 109, Djibouti City, Djibouti | |
| **Guennel, Joe** | Soccer |
| 835 Front Range Road, Littleton CO 80120, USA | |
| **Gueno, James A (Jim)** | Football Player |
| 6939 General Haig St, New Orleans LA 70124, USA | |
| **Guenot, Steeve** | Greco-Roman Wrestler |
| Federation de Lutte, 2 Rue Louis Pergaud, 94706 Maisons Alfort Cedex, France | |
| **Guenther, Johnny** | Bowler |
| 23826 115th Place W, Woodway WA 98020, USA | |
| **Guerard, Michel E** | Chef |
| Les Pres d'Eugenie, 40320 Eugenie les Bains, France | |
| **Guerdat, Steve** | Equestrian |
| Rutihof 1560, 8704 Herrliberg, Switzerland | |
| **Guerin, Richard V (Richie)** | Basketball Player |
| 1355 Bear Island Dr, West Palm Beach FL 33409, USA | |
| **Guerin, Wiliam R (Bill)** | Ice Hockey Player |
| 12 North Road, Oyster Bay NY 11771, USA | |
| **Guerra, Andrea** | Composer |
| First Artists, 4764 Park Granada, #210, Calabasas CA 91302 USA | |
| **Guerra, Eddie** | Actor |
| Creative Artists Agency, 2000 Ave of Stars, #100, Los Angeles CA 90067 USA | |
| **Guerra, Juan Luis** | Singer, Songwriter |
| Joyce Agency Entertainment, 370 Harrison Ave, Harrison NY 10528, USA | |
| **Guerra, Vida** | Actress, Model, Singer |
| It Girl Public Relations, 225 1/2 Howland Canal, Venice CA 90291, USA | |
| **Guerrero Coles, Lisa** | Sportscaster, Actress, Model |
| Lorraine Berglund Mgmt, 11537 Hesby St, North Hollywood CA 91601, USA | |
| **Guerrero, Giancarlo** | Conductor |
| Opus 3 Artists, 470 Park Ave S, #900N, New York NY 10016 USA | |
| **Guerrero, Julen** | Soccer Player |
| A C Bilbao, Alameda Mazarredo 23, 48009 Bilbao, Spain | |
| **Guerrero, Mario M** | Baseball Player |
| Calle Duarte 450, 10211 Santo Domingo, Dominican Republic | |
| **Guerrero, Pedro** | Baseball Player |
| 10720 NW 66th St, #408, Doral FL 33178, USA | |
| **Guerrero, Robert J (Ghost)** | Boxer |
| 14810 Delano St, Van Nuys CA 91411, USA | |
| **Guerrero, Roberto J** | Auto Racing Driver |
| 31642 Via Cervantes, San Juan Capistrano CA 92675, USA | |
| **Guerrero, Vladimir A** | Baseball Player |
| 5160 E Copa de Oro Dr, Anaheim CA 92807, USA | |
| **Guerrier, Matthew O (Matt)** | Baseball Player |
| 200 Highland View Dr, Birmingham AL 35242, USA | |
| **Guers, Paul** | Actor |
| 40 Rue de Buci, 75006 Paris, France | |

G

Grybauskaite - Guers

# G

**Guesmi, Samir** — Actor
Artmedia, 20 Ave Rapp, 75007 Paris, France

**Guest, Christopher H** — Director, Actor, Comedian
United Talent Agency, U T A Plaza, 9336 Civic Center Dr, Beverly Hills CA 90210 USA

**Guest, Cornelia** — Actress, Model, Socialite
Brillstein Entertainment Partners, 9150 Wilshire Blvd, #350, Beverly Hills CA 90212 USA

**Guest, Lance** — Actor
2269 La Granada Dr, Los Angeles CA 90068, USA

**Guetary, Francois** — Actor
Paola Bonelli Consuelenza Cinematografica, 50, Viale Parioli, 00197 Rome, Italy

**Guetta, David** — DJ Musician, Songwriter
Creative Artists Agency, 2000 Ave of Stars, #100, Los Angeles CA 90067 USA

**Guettel, Adam** — Composer, Lyricist
Gersh Agency, 9465 Wilshire Blvd, #600, Beverly Hills CA 90212 USA

**Guetterman, A Lee** — Baseball Player
108 1/2 E Broadway St, Lenoir City TN 37771, USA

**Guffey, John W, Jr** — Businessman
Coltec Industries, 2550 W Tyvola Road, Charlotte NC 28217, USA

**Gugelmin, Mauricio** — Auto Racing Driver
Ave 7 de Septembre 4476-60-62, Cuiriba PR 80250210, Brazil

**Guggenheim, Alan** — Inventor (Hydrogen Energy Processor)
Northwest Power Systems, PO Box 5339, Bend OR 97708, USA

**Guggenheim, Davis** — Director
Electric Kinney Films, 1661 Lincoln Blvd, #101, Santa Monica CA 90404, USA

**Gugino, Carla** — Actress
Untitled Entertainment, 350 S Beverly Dr, #200, Beverly Hills CA 90212 USA

**Guglielmi, Ralph V** — Football Player
159 Red Berry Dr, Wallace NC 28466, USA

**Gugliotta, Thomas J (Tom)** — Basketball Player
1267 Francis St NW, Atlanta GA 30318, USA

**Guice, Jackson** — Cartoonist (Resurrection Man)
D C Comics, 1700 Broadway, #400, New York NY 10019 USA

**Guida, Gloria** — Actress
C D A Studio di Nardo, Via Cavour 171, 00184 Rome, Italy

**Guida, Louis P (Lou)** — Harness Racing Driver, Trainer
173 San Remo Dr, Jupiter FL 33458, USA

**Guidarini, Marco** — Conductor
I M G Artists, Hogarth Business Park, Chiswick, London W4 2TH, England

**Guidinger, Jay P** — Basketball Player
N39W22702 Grandview Dr, Pewaukee WI 53072, USA

**Guidolin, Aldo** — Ice Hockey Player
34 Blair Dr, Guelph ON N1L 1N7, Canada

**Guidoni, Umberto** — Astronaut, Italy
European Space Center, Linder Hohe, Box 906096, 51127 Cologne, Germany

**Guidry, Mark** — Thoroughbred Racing Jockey
102 S William Dr, Lafayette LA 70506, USA

**Guidry, N T** — Aeronautical Engineer
23971 Coral Springs Lane, Tehachapi CA 93561, USA

**Guidry, Paul M** — Football Player
880 Noel Dr, Mount Juliet TN 37122, USA

**Guidry, Ronald A (Ron)** — Baseball Player
PO Box 278, Scott LA 70583, USA

**Guiel, Aaron** — Baseball Player
18944 69th Ave, Surrey BC V4N 5K1, Canada

**Guigou, Michael** — Handball Player
Montpellier Agglomeration H B, 1000 Ave du Val de Montferrand, 34090 Montpellier, France

**Guilbert, Ann** — Actress
550 Erskine Dr, Pacific Palisades CA 90272, USA

**Guilfoyle, Paul** — Actor
S M S Talent, 8383 Wilshire Blvd, #230, Beverly Hills CA 90211 USA

**Guill, Julianna** — Actress
Luber Rocklin Entertainment, 5815 Sunset Blvd, #206, Los Angeles CA 90028 USA

**Guillaume** — Hereditary Grand Duke, Luxembourg
Palais Grand-Ducal, 17 Rue du Marche-aux-Herbes, 1728 Luxembourg-Ville, Luxembourg

**Guillaume, Robert** — Actor
Alan David Mgmt, 8840 Wilshire Blvd, #200, Beverly Hills CA 90211, USA

**Guillem, Sylvie** — Ballerina
Royal Ballet, Covent Garden, Bow St, London WC2E 9DD, England

**Guillemin, Roger C L** — Nobel Medicine Laureate
7316 Encelia Ave, La Jolla CA 92037, USA

**Guillen, Oswaldo J (Ozzie)** — Baseball Player, Manager
19462 38th Court, Golden Beach FL 33160, USA

**Guillerman, John** — Director
309 S Rockingham Ave, Los Angeles CA 90049, USA

**Guillo, Dominque** — Actor
Agence Artiste Adequat, 108 Rue Reaumur, 75002 Paris, France

**Guillory, Sienna** — Actress
United Talent Agency, U T A Plaza, 9336 Civic Center Dr, Beverly Hills CA 90210 USA

**Guilmette, Jonathan** — Speed Skater
Speed Skating Canada, 2781 Lancaster Road, #402, Ottawa ON K1B 1A7, Canada

**Guindon, Richard G** — Cartoonist (Guindon)
321 W Lafayette Blvd, Detroit MI 48226, USA

**Guindon, Robert J (Bob)** — Baseball Player
437 Marsh Creek Road, Venice FL 34292, USA

**Guinee, Tim** — Actor
Innovative Artists, 1505 10th St, Santa Monica CA 90401 USA

**Guinier, Lani** — Attorney, Educator
University of Pennsylvania, Law School, 3400 Chestnut, Philadelphia PA 19104, USA

**Guinn, Drannon E (Skip)** — Baseball Player
PO Box 911, Stilwell OK 74960, USA

**Guirgis, Stephen Adly** — Actor, Comedian
Anonymous Content, 3532 Hayden Ave, Culver City CA 90232 USA

**Guiry, Tom** — Actor
Gersh Agency, 9465 Wilshire Blvd, #600, Beverly Hills CA 90212 USA

**Guisewite, Cathy L** — Cartoonist (Cathy)
4039 Camilla Ave, Studio City CA 91604, USA

| | |
|---|---|
| **Guiter, Sophie** | Actress |
| Artmedia, 20 Ave Rapp, 75007 Paris, France | |
| **Gulan, Michael W (Mike)** | Baseball Player |
| 4409 Fairway Dr, Steubenville OH 43953, USA | |
| **Gulbinowicz, Henryk Roman Cardinal** | Religious Leader |
| Archdiocese of Wroclaw, Ul Katedraina 11, 50328 Wroclaw, Poland | |
| **Gulbis, Natalie** | Golfer, Model |
| 7733 Glenn Ave, Citrus Heights CA 95610, USA | |
| **Gulden, Bradford L (Brad)** | Baseball Player |
| 15820 Lundstead Road, Carver MN 55315, USA | |
| **Guleghina, Maria** | Opera Singer |
| I M G Artists, Carnegie Hall Tower, 152 W 57th St, #500, New York NY 10019 USA | |
| **Gulledge, Dustyn** | Actor |
| Judy Boals, 307 W 38th St, #812, New York NY 10018 | |
| **Gullett, Donald E (Don)** | Baseball Player |
| 194 Kingsway Dr, South Shore KY 41175, USA | |
| **Gullickson, William L (Bill)** | Baseball Player |
| 3 Banchory Court, Palm Beach Gardens FL 33418, USA | |
| **Gulliver, Harold** | Editor |
| Atlanta Constitution, 223 Perimeter Center Parkway NE, Atlanta GA 30346, USA | |
| **Gullotta, Leo** | Actor |
| Carol Levi Mgmt, Via Giuseppe Pisanelli 2, 00196 Rome, Italy | |
| **Guloien, Krista** | Rowing Athlete |
| Rowing Canada Aviron, 100-4636 Elk Lake Dr, Victoria V8Z 5M1, Canada | |
| **Gulyas, Denes** | Opera Singer |
| Hungarian State Opera, Andrassy Utca 22, 1061 Budapest, Hungary | |
| **Gulzar** | Director, Songwriter |
| Boskiyana Pali Hill, Bandra (W), Mumbai MS 400050, India | |
| **Guman, Michael D (Mike)** | Football Player |
| 3913 Pleasant Ave, Allentown PA 18103, USA | |
| **Gumbel, Bryant C** | Commentator |
| Home Box Office, 1100 Ave of Americas, Front 300, New York NY 10036 USA | |
| **Gumbel, Greg** | Sportscaster |
| 10372 N Lake Vista Circle, Davie FL 33328, USA | |
| **Gummer, Grace** | Actress |
| Creative Artists Agency, 2000 Ave of Stars, #100, Los Angeles CA 90067 USA | |
| **Gummer, Mamie** | Actress |
| Creative Artists Agency, 2000 Ave of Stars, #100, Los Angeles CA 90067 USA | |
| **Gummersall, Devon** | Actor |
| Don Buchwald Talent Agency, 6500 Wilshire Blvd, #2200, Los Angeles CA 90048 USA | |
| **Gump, Scott** | Golfer |
| 14346 Deer Court, Mishawaka IN 46545, USA | |
| **Gumpert, David L (Dave)** | Baseball Player |
| 68371 Fleetwood Dr, South Haven MI 49090, USA | |
| **Gund, Graham** | Architect |
| 47 Thorndike St, #1, Cambridge MA 02141, USA | |
| **Gunderson, Eric A** | Baseball Player |
| 19809 SE 10th St, Camas WA 98607, USA | |
| **Gundi** | Artist |
| RR 1, Roseneath ON K0K 2X0, Canada | |
| **Gunesekera, Romesh** | Writer |
| A M Heath Co, 79 Saint Martin's Lane, London WC2N 4RE, England | |
| **Gunn, Anna** | Actress |
| United Talent Agency, U T A Plaza, 9336 Civic Center Dr, Beverly Hills CA 90210 USA | |
| **Gunn, Chanda L** | Ice Hockey Player |
| 74 Rockcroft Road, Weymouth MA 02188, USA | |
| **Gunn, James E** | Astrophysicist |
| Princeton University, Astrophysics Dept, Princeton NJ 08544, USA | |
| **Gunn, Janet** | Actress |
| David Shapira Assoc, 193 N Robertson Blvd, Beverly Hills CA 90211 USA | |
| **Gunn, Lee F** | Navy Admiral |
| Public Research Institute, CNA Corp, 4825 Mark Center Dr, Alexandria VA 22311, USA | |
| **Gunn, Nathan** | Concert, Opera Singer |
| Opus 3 Artists, 470 Park Ave S, #900N, New York NY 10016 USA | |
| **Gunn, Richard** | Actor |
| Pantheon Talent, 1801 Century Park E, #1910, Los Angeles CA 90067, USA | |
| **Gunn, Sean** | Actor, Writer, Producer |
| 1111 Magnolia St, South Pasadena CA 91030, USA | |
| **Gunnarsson, Martin** | Marksman |
| 3536 Saint Marys Road, #D24, Columbus GA 31906, USA | |
| **Gunnell, Owen** | Concert Percussionist (O Duo) |
| Sony/BMI Records, 550 Madison Ave, #600, New York NY 10022, USA | |
| **Gunnell, Sally** | Track Athlete |
| Old School Cottage, School Lane, Pycombe, West Sussex BN45 7FQ, England | |
| **Gunnels, J Riley** | Football Player |
| 606 Wesley Ave, Ocean City NJ 08226, USA | |
| **Gunnestad, Stig-Arne** | Curling Athlete |
| Curling Assn, Sognsveien 75, Serviceboks 1, 0840 Oslo, Norway | |
| **Gunnlaugsson, Sigmundur David** | Prime Minister, Iceland |
| Prime Minister's Office, Stornarroshusino v/Laekjartou, 150 Reykjavik, Iceland | |
| **Gunther, Dan** | Actor |
| Century Artists, PO Box 59747, Santa Barbara CA 93150 USA | |
| **Gunther, David C (Dave)** | Basketball Player |
| 4510 Cherry St, Grand Forks ND 58201, USA | |
| **Gunton, Bob** | Actor |
| Abrams Artists, 275 7th Ave, #2600, New York NY 10001 USA | |
| **Guokas, Matthew G (Matt), Jr** | Basketball Player, Coach, Executive |
| 2410 S 19th St, Philadelphia PA 19145, USA | |
| **Guolla, Steve** | Ice Hockey Player |
| 733 Spartan Dr, Rochester Hills MI 48309, USA | |
| **Gupta, Amit** | Director |
| United Agents, 12-26 Lexington St, London W1F 0LE, England | |
| **Gupta, Modugu V** | Aquaculturist |
| Jalan Batu Maung, Batu Maung 11960 Bayan Lepas, Penang, Malaysia | |
| **Gupta, Raj** | Businessman |
| Rohm & Haas Co, 100 S Independence Mall W, #1A, Philadelphia PA 19106, USA | |

# G

**Gupta, Subodh** — Artist
Hauser & Wirth Art Gallery, 32 E 69th St, New York NY 10021, USA

**Gupta, Sudhir** — Immunologist
University of California, Medicine Dept, Irvine CA 92717, USA

**Gupton, Damon** — Actor
Harden-Curtis Associates, 850 7th Ave, #903, New York NY 10019, USA

**Gur, Mordechai** — Army General, Israel
25 Mishmeret St, Afeka, Tel-Aviv 69694, Israel

**Gura, Larry C** — Baseball Player
PO Box 94, Litchfield Park AZ 85340, USA

**Gurdon, John B** — Nobel Medicine Laureate
Whittlesford Grove, Whittlesford, Cambridge CB2 4W2, England

**Guren, Peter** — Cartoonist (Ask Shagg, Committed)
Creators Syndicate, 737 3rd St, Hermosa Beach CA 90254 USA

**Gurewitz, Brett W** — Guitarist (Bad Religion)
Goldstar Public Relations, PO Box 130, Ross on Wye HR9 6WY, England

**Gurian, Michael** — Psychotherapist, Social Philosopher
417 W 32nd Ave, Spokane WA 99203, USA

**Gurira, Danai Jekesai** — Actress
United Talent Agency, U T A Plaza, 9336 Civic Center Dr, Beverly Hills CA 90210 USA

**Gurnah, Abdulrazak** — Writer
Roger Coleridge White, 20 Powis Mews, London W11 1KN, England

**Gurnett, Jane** — Actress
Hamilton Hodell, 20 Golden Square, London W1F 9JL, England

**Gurney, Albert R (A R), Jr** — Writer
Gersh Agency, 9465 Wilshire Blvd, #600, Beverly Hills CA 90212 USA

**Gurney, Daniel S (Dan)** — Auto Racing Driver, Executive
All-American Racers Inc, 2334 S Broadway, Santa Ana CA 92707, USA

**Gurney, Hilda** — Equestrian
8430 Waters Road, Moorpark CA 93021, USA

**Gurney, James** — Writer, Illustrator
PO Box 693, Rhinebeck NY 12572, USA

**Gurraggchaa, Jugderdemidijn** — Cosmonaut, Mongolia; Air Force General
Lyotchik Kosmonavt, MNR, Central Post Office Box 378, Ulan Bator, Mongolia

**Gursky, Andreas** — Photographer
Matthew Marks Gallery, 523 W 24th St, New York NY 10011, USA

**Gurung, Prabal** — Fashion Designer
247 W 37th St, #1501, New York NY 10018, USA

**Gurwitch, Annabelle** — Actress
Global Artists Agency, 6253 Hollywood Blvd, #508, Los Angeles CA 90028 USA

**Guryakova, Olga** — Opera Singer
I M G Artists, Hogarth Business Park, Chiswick, London W4 2TH, England

**Gusarov, Alexei** — Ice Hockey Player
1168 Yankee Creek Road, Evergreen CO 80439, USA

**Gusella, James** — Biologist
Harvard Medical School, 25 Shattuck St, Boston MA 02115, USA

**Gusenbauer, Alfred** — Chancellor, Austria
Chancellor's Office, Ballhausplatz 2, 1014, Vienna, Austria

**Gushue, Brad** — Curling Athlete
Curling Association, 1660 Vimont Court, Cumberland ON K4A 4J4, Canada

**Gusmao, Jose Alexandre (Xanana)** — Prime Minister, Timor-Leste
Prime Minister's Office, Government Palace, President Nicolau Lobato Ave, Dili, Timor-Leste

**Gustafson, Elisabet** — Curling Athlete
Curling Association, Idrottshuser, Marbackagatan 19, 123 43 Farsta, Sweden

**Gustafson, Kathryn** — Landscape Architect
Gustafson Guthrie Nichol, Pier 55, #31101, Alaskan Way, Seattle WA 98101, USA

**Gustafson, Steven** — Bassist (10000 Maniacs)
Geffen Records, 10900 Wilshire Blvd, #1000, Los Angeles CA 90024 USA

**Gustafsson, Jan-Ake** — Biologist
University of Houston, Biosciences Dept, 4800 Calhoun Road, Houston TX 77004, USA

**Gustafsson, Mattias** — Handball Player
TuS Nettelstedt-Lubbecke, Gerichtsstr 1A, 31312 Lubbecke, Germany

**Gustafsson, Per** — Ice Hockey Player
5605 NE 3rd Ave, Fort Lauderdale FL 33334, USA

**Gustin, Grant** — Actor
C E S D, 10635 Santa Monica Blvd, #130, Los Angeles CA 90025 USA

**Gut, Laura** — Alpine Skier
Grafenauweg 2, 6304 Zug, Switzerland

**Guterres, Antonio Manuel de Oliveira** — Prime Minister, Portugal
United Nations High Commission for Refugees, CP 2500, 1211 Geneva 2, Switzerland

**Guterson, David** — Writer
Georges Borchardt, 136 E 57th St, #1400, New York NY 10022, USA

**Guth, Alan H** — Astrophysicist
Massachusetts Institute of Technology, Physics Dept, Cambridge MA 02139, USA

**Guthe, Manfred** — Cinematographer
122 Collier St, Toronto ON M4W 1M3, Canada

**Guthe, Nick** — Writer, Director, Producer
Artist International Mgmt, 9107 Wilshire Blvd, #600, Beverly Hills CA 90210, USA

**Guthrie of Cragiebank, Charles R L** — Army Field Marshal, England
International Strategic Studies Institute, 13 Arundel St, Temple Place, London WC2R 3DX, England

**Guthrie, Arlo** — Singer, Guitarist, Songwriter
Rising Son Records, 218 Beach Road, Washington MA 01223, USA

**Guthrie, Janet** — Auto Racing Driver
PO Box 505, Aspen CO 81612, USA

**Guthrie, Jeremy S** — Baseball Player
1004 Clay St, Ashland OR 97520, USA

**Guthrie, Mark A** — Baseball Player
3129 Donald Rosse Road E, Sarasota FL 34240, USA

**Guthrie, Savannah C** — Commentator
NBC-TV, News Dept, 30 Rockefeller Plaza, #270E, New York NY 10112 USA

**Guthy, Jackson** — Singer
Creative Artists Agency, 2000 Ave of Stars, #100, Los Angeles CA 90067 USA

**Gutierrez, Brock** — Football Player
1040 Pueblo Pass, Weidman MI 48893, USA

**Gutierrez, Carlos M** — Businessman
Woodrow Wilson Center, 1300 Pennsylvania Ave NW, #300, Washington DC 20004, USA

**Gupta - Gutierrez**

**Gutierrez, Diego**
Creative Artists Agency, 2000 Ave of Stars, #100, Los Angeles CA 90067 USA
Producer, Writer

**Gutierrez, F Javier**
Paradigm Agency, 360 N Crescent Dr, North Building, Beverly Hills CA 90210 USA
Director

**Gutierrez, Franklin R**
5130 Preferred Place, Hilliard OH 43026, USA
Baseball Player

**Gutierrez, Gustavo**
Instituto Bartolome Las Casas-Rimac, Apartado 3090, Lima 100, Peru
Theologian

**Gutierrez, Horacio**
C M Artists, 127 W 96th St, #13B, New York NY 10025 USA
Concert Pianist

**Gutierrez, Joaquin F (Jackie)**
10631 SW 126th Ave, Miami FL 33186, USA
Baseball Player

**Gutierrez, Ricardo (Ricky)**
7100 NW 173rd Dr, #1304, Hialeah FL 33015, USA
Baseball Player

**Gutierrez, Sidney M**
324 Sarah Lane NW, Albuquerque NM 87114, USA
Astronaut

**Gutman, Natalia G**
Augstein & Hahn, Tal 28, 80331 Munich, Germany
Concert Cellist

**Gutman, Roy W**
1349 Windy Hill Road, McLean VA 22102, USA
Journalist

**Gutmann, Amy**
University of Pennsylvania, President's Office, 3451 Walnut St, Philadelphia PA 19104, USA
Educator

**Gutsche, Torsten**
Hans-Marchwitza-Ring 51, 14473 Potsdam, Germany
Canoeing Athlete

**Gutsu, Tatiana K**
30979 Country Bluff, Farmington Hills MI 48331, USA
Gymnast

**Gutt, Fred E**
116 Fairview Ave N, #624, Seattle WA 98109, USA
WW II Marine Corps Air Force Hero

**Guttenberg, Steve**
Binder & Assoc, 1465 Lindacrest Dr, Beverly Hills CA 90210 USA
Actor

**Guttentag, Bill**
W M E Entertainment, 9601 Wilshire Blvd, #300, Beverly Hills CA 90210 USA
Director, Writer

**Guttman, Ronald**
Don Buchwald Talent Agency, 6500 Wilshire Blvd, #2200, Los Angeles CA 90048 USA
Actor

**Guy, Buddy**
Buddy Guy's Legends, 754 S Wabash Ave, Chicago IL 60605, USA
Singer, Guitarist

**Guy, Francois-Frederic**
Van Walsum Mgmt, Tower Building, 11 York Road, London SE1 7NX, England
Concert Pianist

**Guy, Jasmine**
Kass Management, 501 Santa Monica Blvd, #604, Los Angeles CA 90401, USA
Actress

**Guy, Ralph B, Jr**
US Court of Appeals, PO Box 7910, Ann Arbor MI 48107, USA
Judge

**Guy, W Ray**
936 Central Road SW, Thomson GA 30824, USA
Football Player

**Guyer, Cindy**
2 Lincoln Square, New York NY 10023, USA
Model, Producer

**Guyer, David B**
Save the Children Foundation, 514 2nd St, Owyhee NV 89832, USA
Foundation Executive

**Guyot, Paul**
Gersh Agency, 9465 Wilshire Blvd, #600, Beverly Hills CA 90212 USA
Actor, Writer

**Guyton, Myron M**
PO Box 3481, Thomasville GA 31799, USA
Football Player

**Guzman Pinal, Alejandra G**
O C E S A Seitrack Mgmt, Av Industria Militar S/N Col, Mexico City 11200, Mexico
Singer, Actress

**Guzman, Andrea**
Fox TeleColombia, Cra 50, #17-77, 4174200 Bogota, Colombia
Actress

**Guzman, Jose A**
4401 Shadycreek Lane, Colleyville TX 76034, USA
Baseball Player

**Guzman, Juan A**
176 Dockside Circle, Weston FL 33327, USA
Baseball Player

**Guzman, Luis**
PO Box 21, Peacham VT 05862, USA
Actor

**Guzman, Santiago D**
1712 N Douty St, Hanford CA 93230, USA
Baseball Player

**Guzy, Carol**
2412 Fort Scott Dr, Arlington VA 22202, USA
Photojournalist

**Gwinn, Mary Ann**
Seattle Times, Editorial Dept, 1000 Denny Way, Seattle WA 98109 USA
Journalist

**Gwynn, Christopher K (Chris)**
10975 Hillside Road, Rancho Cucamonga CA 91737, USA
Baseball Player

**Gwynn, Darrell**
Darrell Gwynn Ventures, 4850 SW 52nd St, Davie FL 33314, USA
Drag Racing Driver

**Gyanendra**
Royal Palace, Narayanhiti, Durbag Marg, Kathmandu, Nepal
King, Nepal

**Gyll, J Soren**
Volvo AB, Torslanda, 405 08 Gothenborg, Sweden
Businessman

**Gyllenhaal, Jake**
W M E Entertainment, 9601 Wilshire Blvd, #300, Beverly Hills CA 90210 USA
Actor

**Gyllenhaal, Maggie**
Schiff Co, 9220 Sunset Blvd, #106, West Hollywood CA 90069 USA
Actress

**Gyllenhaal, Stephen**
Gersh Agency, 9465 Wilshire Blvd, #600, Beverly Hills CA 90212 USA
Director, Writer, Actor

**Gyllenhammar, Pehr G**
C G U, Saint Helen's, 1 Undershaft, London EC3P 3DQ, England
Businessman

**Gysi, Gregor**
Fraktion Die Linke, Platz der Repubik 1, 11011 Berlin, Germany
General Secretary, East Germany

**Gyurcsany, Ferenc**
Prime Minister's Office, Kossuth Lajos Ter 1-3, 1055 Budapest, Hungary
Prime Minister, Hungary

**Gyurta, Daniel**
Jovo SC Veolia, Hangyalepcso Utca 6, 1121 Budapest, Hungary
Swimmer

**Gutierrez - Gyurta**

## H

**Ha Jin** — Writer
Emory University, English Dept, Atlanta GA 30332, USA

**Haack, Susan** — Philosopher
University of Miami, Philosophy Dept, Coral Gables FL 33124, USA

**Haacke, Hans C** — Artist
Paula Cooper Gallery, 534 W 21st St, New York NY 10011, USA

**Haag, Anna M** — Cross Country Skier
Ski Federation, Riksskidstadion, 791 19 Falun, Sweden

**Haag, Rudolf** — Theoretical Physicist
Waldschmidt Str 4B, 83727 Schliersee-Neuhaus, Germany

**Haakon** — Crown Prince, Norway
Royal Palace, Det Kongelige Slott, Drammensveien 1, 0010 Oslo, Norway

**Haarhuis, Paul** — Tennis Player
Octagon Worldwide, 1751 Pinnacle Dr, #1500, McLean VA 22102 USA

**Haas, Bryan E (Moose)** — Baseball Player
4351 E Lariat Lane, Phoenix AZ 85050, USA

**Haas, Carl** — Auto Racing Executive
Newman-Haas Racing, 500 Tower Parkway, Lincolnshire IL 60069, USA

**Haas, Ed** — Photographer
180 W End Ave, #11C, New York NY 10023, USA

**Haas, G Edwin (Eddie)** — Baseball Player, Manager
8314 Alpena Way, Louisville KY 40242, USA

**Haas, Hunter J** — Golfer
6424 Barkwood Lane, Dallas TX 75248, USA

**Haas, Jay D** — Golfer
4 Tuscany Court, Greer SC 29650, USA

**Haas, Lukas** — Actor
Innovative Artists, 1505 10th St, Santa Monica CA 90401 USA

**Haas, R David (Dave)** — Baseball Player
160 E 6th Place, Mesa AZ 85201, USA

**Haas, Richard J** — Artist
361 W 36th St, #5A, New York NY 10018, USA

**Haas, Robert D** — Businessman
Levi Strauss Assoc, 1155 Battery St, San Francisco CA 94111, USA

**Haas, Thomas M (Tommy)** — Tennis Player
4715 67th Ave Terrace W, Bradenton FL 34210, USA

**Haas, William H** — Golfer
Professional Golfers Association, 100 Ave of Champions, Palm Beach Gardens FL 33418 USA

**Haataja, Samuli (J J)** — Singer, Bassist (Crash)
Welldone Agency, Hameentie 15, 00500 Helsinki, Finland

**Haavisto, Nina** — Body Builder
Aleksanterinkatu 29 B 29, 15040 Lahti, Finland

**Habek, Janine** — Model
Playboy Promotions, 9346 Civic Center Dr, #200, Beverly Hills CA 90210 USA

**Habel, Karl** — Medical Researcher
Reading Institute of Rehabilitation, RR 1 Box 252, Reading PA 19607, USA

**Habel, Sarah** — Actress
A P A Talent & Literary Agency, 405 S Beverly Dr, #300, Beverly Hills CA 90212 USA

**Habeler, Peter** — Mountaineer
Apinschule Mount Everest, Haupstra 458, 6290 Mayrhofen Zillertal, Austria

**Haber, Karen** — Writer
2270 N Beachwood Terrace, Los Angeles CA 90068, USA

**Haber, Norman** — Inventor (Electromolecular Propulsion)
Haber Inc, 470 Main Road, Towaco NJ 07082, USA

**Haberlandt, Fritzi** — Actress
Die Agenten, Ackerstr 11B, 10115 Berlin, Germany

**Habib, Brian R** — Football Player
17235 Sangallo Lane, San Diego CA 92127, USA

**Habib, Hasan** — Poker Player
World Poker Tour Enterprises, 5700 Wilshire Blvd, #350, Los Angeles CA 90036 USA

**Habib, Munir** — Cosmonaut, Syria
Cosmonaut Training Center, Star City, 141160 Zvezdny Gorodok, Moscow Oblast, Russia

**Habibie, Baharuddin Jusuf** — President, Indonesia
Bina Craha, Istana Negana, Jarkata 10110, Indonesia

**Habiger, Eugene E (Gene)** — Air Force General
University of Georgia, International Trade & Security Center, Athens GA 30602, USA

**Habumuremyi, Pierre Damien** — Prime Minister, Rwanda
Prime Minister's Office, Kigali, Rwanda

**Habyan, John G** — Baseball Player
4 Dorfer Lane, Nesconset NY 11767, USA

**Hachette, Jean-Louis** — Publisher
Hachette Livre, 83 Ave Marceau, 75116 Paris, France

**Hack, Shelley** — Actress, Model
Deborah Miller, 9454 Wilshire Blvd, #715, Beverly Hills CA 90212, USA

**Hackbart, Dale L** — Football Player
2541 Cowley Dr, Lafayette CO 80026, USA

**Hacke, Axel** — Writer
Bloomsbury Publishing, 50 Bedford Square, London WC1B 3DP, England

**Hacker, Alan** — Concert Clarinetist, Composer
Royal Academy of Music, Marylebone Road, London NW1 5HT, England

**Hacker, Joseph** — Actor
University of Southern California, Theater School, Los Angeles CA 90089, USA

**Hackett, B Dean (Dino)** — Football Player
1152 Kearns Hackett Road, Pleasant Garden NC 27313, USA

**Hackett, Grant** — Swimmer
Swimming Australia, PO Box 3286, Belconnen ACT 2617, Australia

**Hackett, James T** — Businessman
Anadarko Petroleum, 1201 Lake Robbins Dr, Spring TX 77380, USA

**Hackett, Jeff** — Ice Hockey Player
Colorado Avalanche, Pepsi Center, 1000 Chopper Circle, Denver CO 80204 USA

**Hackett, Steve** — Guitarist (Genesis)
Publicity Connection, Haversham Lodge, Melrose Ave, London NW2 4JS, England

**Hackford, Taylor** — Director, Producer
2003 La Brea Terrace, Los Angeles CA 90046, USA

**Hackl, Georg** — Luge Athlete
Caftehaus Soamatl, Ramsauerstr 100, 83470 Berchtesgaden-Engedey, Germany

**Hackman, Gene**
Guttman Assoc, 118 S Beverly Dr, #201, Beverly Hills CA 90212 USA — Actor

**Hackman, Luther G**
1406 12th Ave N, #16G, Columbus MS 39701, USA — Baseball Player

**Hackney, F Sheldon**
University of Pennsylvania, History Dept, Philadelphia PA 19104, USA — Educator

**Hadas, Rachel C**
838 W End Ave, #3A, New York NY 10025, USA — Writer, Educator

**Haddix, Michael M**
465 Tanners Bridge Road NW, Monroe GA 30656, USA — Football Player

**Haddock, Laura**
Independent Talent Group, 40 Whitfield St, London W1T 2RH, England — Actress

**Haddock, Marcus**
Columbia Artists Mgmt Inc, 5 Columbus Circle, 1790 Broadway, #1600, New York NY 10019 USA — Opera Singer

**Haddon, Dayle**
Hyperion Books, 114 5th Ave, New York NY 10011 USA — Actress, Model

**Hadek, Krystof**
Markham Froggatt Irwin, Julian House, 4 Windmill St, London W1P 1HF, England — Actor

**Haden, Patrick C (Pat)**
1525 Wilson Ave, San Marino CA 91108, USA — Football Player, Sportscaster

**Hader, Bill**
Odenkirk Provissiero Entertainment, 1936 N Bronson Ave, Los Angeles CA 90069 USA — Actor, Comedian

**Hadfield, Chris A**
N A S A, Johnson Space Center, 2101 NASA Road, Houston TX 77058 USA — Astronaut, Canada

**Hadid, Zaha**
Studio 9, 10 Bowling Green Lane, London WC1R 0BD, England — Pritzker Architectural Laureate

**Hadjii**
Paradigm Agency, 360 N Crescent Dr, North Building, Beverly Hills CA 90210 USA — Director, Writer

**Hadl, John W**
3700 Quail Creek Court, Lawrence KS 66047, USA — Football Player

**Hadlee, Richard J**
PO Box 29186, Fendalton, Christchurch 8540, New Zealand — Cricketer

**Hadley, Chesson T**
North Ridge Country Club, 6612 Falls of Neuse Road, Raleigh NC 27615, USA — Golfer

**Hadley, Stephen**
White House, 1600 Pennsylvania Ave NW, Washington DC 20500, USA — Government Official

**Hadley, Tony**
Tony Denton Promotions, Charter House, 157-159 High St, London N14 6BP, England — Singer (Spandau Ballet)

**Hadnot, J Rex, Jr**
2677 Center Court Dr, Weston FL 33332, USA — Football Player

**Haebler, Ingrid**
5412 Saint Jakob am Thurn, Post Puch Bei Hallein, 5020 Land Salzburg, Austria — Concert Pianist

**Haefliger, Andrea**
Opus 3 Artists, 470 Park Ave S, #900N, New York NY 10016 USA — Concert Pianist

**Haenchen, Hartmut**
Van Walsum Mgmt, Tower Building, 11 York Road, London SE1 7NX, England — Conductor

**Haenning, Gitte**
Agentur Charis Eike Koch, Kleine Brunnenstr 16B, 22765 Hamburg, Germany — Singer, Actress

**Haensch, Theodor W**
Ludwig-Maximilian University, Geschwister-Scholl, 80539 Munich, Germany — Nobel Physics Laureate

**Hafer, Fred D**
G P U Inc, 300 Madison Ave, Morristown NJ 07960, USA — Businessman

**Haffner, Scott R**
5062 Sweetwater Dr, Noblesville IN 46062, USA — Basketball Player

**Hafner, Dudley H**
140 Estrada Maya, Santa Fe NM 87506, USA — Foundation Executive

**Hafner, Travis L**
32696 Lake Road, Avon Lake OH 44012, USA — Baseball Player

**Hagan, Clifford O (Cliff)**
8839 Lakeside Circle, Vero Beach FL 32963, USA — Basketball Player, Coach

**Hagan, Derek S, Jr**
14611 SW 7th St, Pembroke Pines FL 33027, USA — Football Player

**Hagan, Glenn**
34 Roth St, Rochester NY 14621, USA — Basketball Player

**Hagan, Molly**
Paul Kohner, 9300 Wilshire Blvd, #555, Beverly Hills CA 90212 USA — Actress

**Hagan, Victoria**
Victoria Hagan Interiors, 654 Madison Ave, #2201, New York NY 10065, USA — Interior Designer

**Hagar, Sammy**
Front Line Mgmt, 1100 Glendon Ave, #2000, Los Angeles CA 90024 USA — Singer, Songwriter, Guitarist

**Hagee, Michael W**
Rackable Systems, 46600 Landing Parkway, Fremont CA 94538, USA — Marine Corps General

**Hagegard, Hakan**
Gunnarsbyn, 670 30 Edane, Sweden — Opera Singer

**Hageman, Fred J**
4608 Merion Court, Lawrence KS 66047, USA — Football Player

**Hagemeister, Charles C**
1908 Canterbury Court, Leavenworth KS 66048, USA — Vietnam War Army Hero (CMH)

**Hagen, Carl R**
University of Rochester, Physics Dept, Bausch & Lomb Hall, Rochester NY 14627, USA — Physicist

**Hagen, Halvor R**
PO Box 911711, Saint George UT 84791, USA — Football Player

**Hagen, Nina**
Hanns Wolters International, 501 5th Ave, #2112A, New York NY 10017, USA — Singer

**Hagen, Reinhard**
I M G Artists, Hogarth Business Park, Chiswick, London W4 2TH, England — Opera Singer

**Hagenbeck, Franklin L**
Superintendent's Office, US Military Academy, West Point NY 10996 USA — Army General, Educator

**Hager, Britt H**
6200 Indian Canyon Dr, Austin TX 78746, USA — Football Player

**Hager, Kristen**
Paul Kohner, 9300 Wilshire Blvd, #555, Beverly Hills CA 90212 USA — Actress

**Hagerman, Jamie**
USA Hockey, 1775 Bob Johnson Dr, Colorado Springs CO 80906 USA — Ice Hockey Player

**Hagerty, Julie**
Framework Entertainment, 9057 Nemo St, #C, West Hollywood CA 90069 USA — Actress

**Hagerty, Michael (Mike)** — Actor
Mark Holder Mgmt, 5225 Wilshire Blvd, #600, Los Angeles CA 90036, USA

**Haggard, Merle** — Singer, Songwriter
Department 56, 22410 Collins St, Woodland Hills CA 91367, USA

**Haggard, Piers** — Director
Casorotto Ramsay, Waverley House, 7-12 Noel St, London W1F 8GQ, England

**Hagge, Marlene Bauer** — Golfer
PO Box 570, La Quinta CA 92247, USA

**Haggerty, Dan** — Actor
Blind Squirrel Entertainment, 155 Bent Oak, Palm Beach FL 33411, USA

**Haggerty, Dylan** — Actor, Writer, Director
KillerMoxie Mgmt, 5890 W Jefferson Blvd, #J, Los Angeles CA 90016, USA

**Haggerty, Tim** — Cartoonist (Ground Zero)
PO Box 4203, New York NY 10163, USA

**Haggis, Paul E** — Director, Writer
Hwy61, 1660 Euclid, Santa Monica CA 90404, USA

**Hagins, Isaac B (Ike)** — Football Player
9008 Tudor Dr, #105, Tampa FL 33615, USA

**Hagler, Marvin** — Boxer
Valerie Sweet, 1 Design Center Place, #600, Boston MA 02210, USA

**Haglund, Kirsten** — Beauty Queen
Miss America Organization, 1370 Ave of Americas, #1600, New York NY 10019 USA

**Hagman, Niklas O** — Ice Hockey Player
48 Crimson Rose, Irvine CA 92603, USA

**Hagn, Johanna** — Judo Athlete
A S G Elsdorf, Behrgasse 6, 50198 Elsdorf, Germany

**Hagner, Meredith** — Actress
Abrams Artists, 9200 W Sunset Blvd, #1125, West Hollywood CA 90069 USA

**Hagner, Viviane** — Concert Violinist
Kirshbaum Demler, 711 W End Ave, #5KN, New York NY 10025, USA

**Hagon, Garrick** — Actor
Castaway Voice Overs, 15 Broad Court, #3, London WC2B 5QN, England

**Hague, William J** — Government Official, England
House of Commons, Westminster, London SW1A 0AA, England

**Hahn, Beatrice H** — Microbiologist
University of Alabama Medical School, Microbiology Dept, Birmingham AL 35294, USA

**Hahn, Donald A (Don)** — Baseball Player
1046 Boise Dr, Campbell CA 95008, USA

**Hahn, Erwin L** — Physicist
69 Stevenson Ave, Berkeley CA 94708, USA

**Hahn, Frank H** — Economist
16 Adams Road, Cambridge CB3 9AD, England

**Hahn, Hilary** — Concert Violinist
Lovell House, 616 Chiswick High Road, London W4 5RX, England

**Hahn, Jessica** — Model, Actress
6345 Balboa Blvd, #375, Encino CA 91316, USA

**Hahn, Joseph** — DJ Musician (Linkin Park)
United Talent Agency, U T A Plaza, 9336 Civic Center Dr, Beverly Hills CA 90210 USA

**Hahn, Kathryn** — Actress
Gersh Agency, 41 Madison Ave, #3301, New York NY 10010 USA

**Haid, Charles** — Actor, Director
4376 Forman Ave, Toluca Lake CA 91602, USA

**Haiduk, Stacy** — Actress
Stone Manners Salners, 6100 Wilshire Blvd, #1500, Los Angeles CA 90035 USA

**Haig, Matt** — Writer
A P Watt, 20 John St, London WC1N 2DR, England

**Haig, Sid** — Actor
Don Buchwald Talent Agency, 6500 Wilshire Blvd, #2200, Los Angeles CA 90048 USA

**Haigh, Juliette** — Rowing Athlete
West End Rowing Club, 26 Saunders Place, Avondale, Auckland 1026, New Zealand

**Haight, Michael (Mike)** — Football Player
2401 Biltmore Lane, Coralville IA 52241, USA

**Haignere, Jean-Pierre** — Spatinaut, France
C N E S, 2 Place Maurice Quentin, 75039 Paris Cedeux, France

**Hailemaria-Mariam Desalegn** — Prime Minister, Ethiopia
Prime Minister's Office, PO Box 1031, Addis Ababa, Ethiopia

**Hailey, Cedric (K-Ci)** — Singer (Jodeci, Ki-C & JoJo)
Red Entertainment Agency, 505 8th Ave, #1004, New York NY 10018, USA

**Hailey, Joel L (JoJo)** — Singer (Jodeci, K-Ci & JoJo)
Creative Artists Agency, 2000 Ave of Stars, #100, Los Angeles CA 90067 USA

**Hailey, Leisha** — Singer (Murmurs), Songwriter, Actress
L W 1, 9378 Wilshire Blvd, #310, Beverly Hills CA 90212, USA

**Hailston, Earl B** — Marine Corps General
Commanding General, Marine Force Central Asia, HqUSMC, Washington DC 20380, USA

**Haines, Randa** — Director
1429 Avon Park Terrace, Los Angeles CA 90026, USA

**Hairer, Martin** — Mathematician
University of Warwick, Mathematics Department, Coventry CV4 7AL, England

**Hairston, Carl B** — Football Player, Coach
6448 Chartwell Dr, Virginia Beach VA 23464, USA

**Hairston, Jerry W, Jr** — Baseball Player
6 Austringer Court, Pikesville MD 21208, USA

**Hairston, Jerry W, Sr** — Baseball Player
7831 W Peace Pipe Road, Tucson AZ 85743, USA

**Hairston, Samuel P (P J), Jr** — Basketball Player
Charlotte Hornets, 333 E Trade St, #A, Charlotte NC 28202 USA

**Hairston, Scott A** — Baseball Player
4658 S Banning Dr, Gilbert AZ 85297, USA

**Haise, Fred W, Jr** — Astronaut, Test Pilot
PO Box 5765, Pasadena TX 77508, USA

**Haislett, Nicole** — Swimmer
275 N Poplar St, Massapequa NY 11758, USA

**Haislip, Marcus L** — Basketball Player
Milwaukee Bucks, Bradley Center, 1001 N 4th St, #2, Milwaukee WI 53203 USA

**Haith, Frank** — Basketball Coach
University of Missouri, Athletic Dept, Columbia MO 65211, USA

**Haitink, Bernard J H** — Conductor
Askonas Holt, Lincoln House, 300 High Holborn, London WC1V 7JH, England

**Haje, Khrystyne** — Actress
C E S D, 10635 Santa Monica Blvd, #130, Los Angeles CA 90025 USA

**Hajek, Andreas** — Rowing Athlete
Weissbundenweg 18, 06128 Halle/Saale, Germany

**Haji-Sheikh, Ali** — Football Player
550 S Spinningwheel Lane, Bloomfield Township MI 48304, USA

**Hakkinen, Henri** — Marksman
Joensuun Ampujat Ry, Sepankatu 18A B15, 80110 Joensuu, Finland

**Hakkinen, Mika P** — Auto Racing Driver
Le Scguylkill, Blvd de Suisse 8, 98000 Monte Carlo, Monaco

**Halama, John T** — Baseball Player
7615 Fort Hamilton Parkway, Brooklyn NY 11228, USA

**Halas, John** — Animator
Educational Film Center, 5-7 Kean St, London WC2B 4AT, England

**Halbert, Charles P (Chuck)** — Basketball Player
100 E Whidbey Ave, #35, Oak Harbor WA 98277, USA

**Haldeman, Charles (Ed), Jr** — Financier, Government Official
McGraw-Hill, 1221 Avenue of Americas, #4700, New York NY 10020, USA

**Haldorson, Burdette (Burdie)** — Basketball Player
2868 Stonewall Heights, Colorado Springs CO 80909, USA

**Hale, Alan** — Astronomer
Southwest Space Research Institute, 15 E Spur Road, Cloudcraft NM 88317, USA

**Hale, Amanda** — Actress
Gordon & French, 12-13 Poland St, London W1F 8QB, England

**Hale, Barbara** — Actress
PO Box 6061-261, Sherman Oaks CA 91413, USA

**Hale, David** — Ice Hockey Player
3470 Cortina Dr, Colorado Springs CO 80918, USA

**Hale, David R (Dave)** — Football Player
1204 S Maple St, #B, Ottawa KS 66067, USA

**Hale, Georgina** — Actress
74A Saint John's Wood, High St, London NW8, England

**Hale, John S** — Baseball Player
2200 Pine St, Bakersfield CA 93301, USA

**Hale, Lucy K** — Actress
W M E Entertainment, 9601 Wilshire Blvd, #300, Beverly Hills CA 90210 USA

**Hale, Robert H (Bob)** — Baseball Player
616 Overhill Ave, Park Ridge IL 60068, USA

**Hale, Tony** — Actor
United Talent Agency, U T A Plaza, 9336 Civic Center Dr, Beverly Hills CA 90210 USA

**Hale, Walter W (Chip)** — Baseball Player, Manager
190 Driftwood Court, Aptos CA 95003, USA

**Halep, Simona** — Tennis Player
Virginia Ruzici, 9 Boul Chateau, 92200 Neuilly sur Seine, France

**Haley, Charles L** — Football Player
3787 Royal Cove Dr, Dallas TX 75229, USA

**Haley, Jackie Earle** — Actor
Leslie Allan-Rice Mgmt, 1007 Maybrooke Dr, Beverly Hills CA 90210, USA

**Haley, Jermaine** — Football Player
16806 Heather Knolls Place, Hamilton VA 20158, USA

**Haley, Shay** — Singer, Rap Artist (NERD)
Virgin Records, 338 N Foothill Road, Beverly Hills CA 90210 USA

**Haley, Todd** — Football Coach
Pittsburgh Steelers, 3400 S Water St, Pittsburgh PA 15203 USA

**Halford, Robert J A (Rob)** — Singer (Judas Priest)
Trinifold Mgmt, 12 Oval Road, Camden, London NW1 7DH, England

**Halfpenny, Jill** — Actress
Artists Partnership, 101 Finsbury Pavement, London EC2A 1RS, England

**Halfvarson, Eric F** — Opera Singer
1264 Harwood Road, #100, Bedford, TX 76021, USA

**Hali, Tamba B** — Football Player
13227 Outlook Dr, Leawood KS 66209, USA

**Halicki, Edward L (Ed)** — Baseball Player
19605 Paddlewheel Lane, Reno NV 89521, USA

**Halimon, Shaler** — Basketball Player
9535 SW Millen Dr, Portland OR 97224, USA

**Hall Greff, Kaye** — Swimmer
906 3rd St, Mukilteo WA 98275, USA

**Hall, Ahmard R** — Football Player
8402 Cruit Isle, Missouri City TX 77459, USA

**Hall, Albert** — Actor
Stone Manners Salners, 6100 Wilshire Blvd, #1500, Los Angeles CA 90035 USA

**Hall, Albert** — Baseball Player
1628 Spaulding Ishkooda Road, Birmingham AL 35211, USA

**Hall, Andrew C (Drew)** — Baseball Player
4107 Spreading Oaks Court, Waxhaw NC 28173, USA

**Hall, Anthony Michael** — Actor, Comedian
I C M Partners, 10250 Constellation Blvd, #900, Los Angeles CA 90067 USA

**Hall, Arsenio** — Actor, Producer, Writer
Harper Public Relations, 3940 Laurel Canyon Blvd, #1010, Studio City CA 91604, USA

**Hall, Brad, II** — Actor, Comedian
W M E Entertainment, 9601 Wilshire Blvd, #300, Beverly Hills CA 90210 USA

**Hall, Bridget** — Model
I M G Models, 304 Park Ave S, #PH N, New York NY 10010 USA

**Hall, Bruce** — Guitarist (REO Speedwagon)
Front Line Mgmt, 1100 Glendon Ave, #2000, Los Angeles CA 90024 USA

**Hall, Charles** — Inventor (Waterbed)
Basic Designs, 5815 Bennett Valley Road, Santa Rosa CA 95404, USA

**Hall, Charles L (Charlie)** — Football Player
602 Lavaca St, Yaokum TX 77995, USA

**Hall, Daryl F** — Singer (Hall & Oates), Songwriter
Doyle-Kos Entertainment, 1 Penn Plaza, 2107, New York, NY 10119, USA

**Hall, DeAngelo E** — Football Player
5553 Legends Dr, Braselton GA 30517, USA

**Hall, Deidre** — Actress
PO Box 715, 11041 Santa Monica Blvd, Los Angeles CA 90078, USA
**Hall, Delton D** — Football Player
9 Mystic Court, Greensboro NC 27406, USA
**Hall, Donald** — Writer
Eagle Point Farm, Wilmot NH 03287, USA
**Hall, Donald J** — Businessman
Hallmark Cards, 2501 McGee St, Kansas City MO 64108, USA
**Hall, Donald R (Dino)** — Football Player
355 Chestnut Neck Road, Port Republic NJ 08241, USA
**Hall, Esther** — Actress
United Agents, 12-26 Lexington St, London W1F 0LE, England
**Hall, Galen** — Football Player, Coach
Pennsylvania State University, Athletic Dept, Greenberg Complex, University Park PA 16802, USA
**Hall, Gary** — Swimmer
151 Kahiki Dr, Tavernier FL 33070, USA
**Hall, Gary, Jr** — Swimmer
2409 E Luke Ave, Phoenix AZ 85016, USA
**Hall, Glenn H** — Ice Hockey Player
PO Box 2483, Main Station, Stony Plain AB T7Z 1X, Canada
**Hall, Hanna** — Actress
Baron Entertainment, 13848 Ventura Blvd, #A, Sherman Oaks CA 91423, USA
**Hall, James E (Jim)** — Auto Racing Driver, Executive
Jim Hall Kart Racing School, 1555 Morse Ave, #G, Ventura CA 93003, USA
**Hall, Jerry** — Model, Actress
Ford Models, 9200 Sunset Blvd, #805, West Hollywood CA 90069, USA
**Hall, Jimmie R** — Baseball Player
8622 Carter Grove Dr, Elm City NC 27822, USA
**Hall, Joe B** — Basketball Coach
Central Bank & Trust Co, 300 W Vine St, #3, Lexington KY 40507, USA
**Hall, John L** — Nobel Physics Laureate
3748 Davidson Place, Boulder CO 80305, USA
**Hall, Joseph G (Joe)** — Baseball Player
961 Preachers Mill Road, Clarksville TN 37042, USA
**Hall, Kevan** — Fashion Designer
Kevan Hall Studio, 756 S Spring St, #11E, Los Angeles CA 90014, USA
**Hall, Kristen** — Singer, Guitarist (Sugarland)
Gail Gelman Mgmt, 23852 Pacific Coast Highway, #920, Malibu CA 90265, USA
**Hall, Lani** — Singer
31930 Pacific Coast Highway, Malibu CA 90265, USA
**Hall, Lawrence** — Physicist
University of California, Physics Dept, Berkeley CA 94720, USA
**Hall, Lemanski S** — Football Player
238 Wardington Pass, Franklin TN 37069, USA
**Hall, Leon L L** — Football Player
2343 Clydes Crossing, Cincinnati OH 45244, USA
**Hall, Lloyd M, Jr** — Religious Leader
Congregation Christian Church Assn, PO Box 1620, Oak Creek MI 53154, USA
**Hall, M Darren** — Baseball Player
5008 Townsend Dr, Flower Mound TX 75028, USA
**Hall, Mark** — Singer (Casting Crowns)
Proper Mgmt, PO Box 150867, Nashville TN 37215, USA
**Hall, Michael C** — Actor
Hamilton Hodell, 20 Golden Square, London W1F 9JL, England
**Hall, Nigel J** — Artist
11 Kensington Park Gardens, London W11 3HD, England
**Hall, Peter R F** — Director
68 Lamont Road, London SW10 0HX, England
**Hall, Philip Baker** — Actor
Paradigm Agency, 360 N Crescent Dr, North Building, Beverly Hills CA 90210 USA
**Hall, Rebecca M** — Actress
Julian Belfrage Assoc, 9 Argyll St, #300, London W1F 7TG, England
**Hall, Regina** — Actress
I C M Partners, 10250 Constellation Blvd, #900, Los Angeles CA 90067 USA
**Hall, Richard W (Dick)** — Baseball Player
403 Plumbridge Court, #202, Lutherville Timonium MD 21093, USA
**Hall, Robert David** — Actor
C E S D, 10635 Santa Monica Blvd, #130, Los Angeles CA 90025 USA
**Hall, Robert E (Bob)** — Economist
Stanford University, Hoover Institution, Stanford CA 94305, USA
**Hall, Robert N** — Inventor (Semiconductor Injection Laser)
325 Kings Road, #8, Schenectady NY 12304, USA
**Hall, Ronald G (Ronnie)** — Football Player
14008 NE 162nd St, Kearney MO 64060, USA
**Hall, Samuel (Sam)** — Diver
5759 Wilcke Way, Dayton OH 45459, USA
**Hall, Sonny** — Labor Leader
AFL-CIO, 815 16th St, NW, Washington DC 20006, USA
**Hall, Thomas E (Tom)** — Baseball Player
3592 Lillian St, Riverside CA 92504, USA
**Hall, Thomas F (Tom)** — Football Player
PO Box 60441, Longmeadow MA 01116, USA
**Hall, Toby J** — Baseball Player
3814 Evergreen Oaks Dr, Lutz FL 33558, USA
**Hall, Tom T** — Singer, Guitarist, Songwriter
John D Lentz, PO Box 198888, Nashville TN 37219, USA
**Hall, Trevor** — Singer, Guitarist, Songwriter
Monterey International, 200 W Superior St, #202, Chicago IL 60654 USA
**Hall, Willie C** — Football Player
717 S Hacienda St, Anaheim CA 92804, USA
**Halla, Brian L** — Businessman
National Semiconductor, 2900 Semiconductor Dr, Santa Clara CA 95051, USA
**Halladay, H Leroy (Roy), III** — Baseball Player
18509 Council Crest Dr, Odessa FL 33556, USA
**Halldorson, Daniel A (Dan)** — Golfer
209 South Road, Cambridge IL 61238, USA

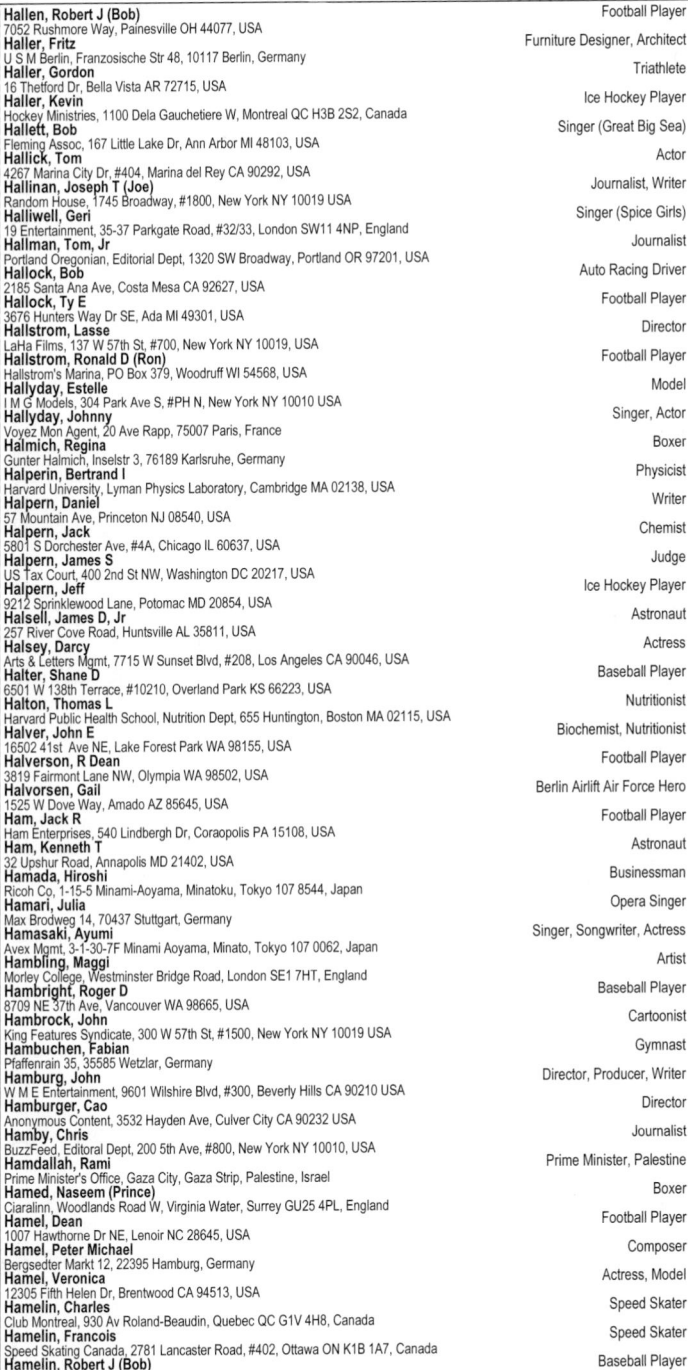

**Hallen, Robert J (Bob)** — Football Player
7052 Rushmore Way, Painesville OH 44077, USA

**Haller, Fritz** — Furniture Designer, Architect
U S M Berlin, Franzosische Str 48, 10117 Berlin, Germany

**Haller, Gordon** — Triathlete
16 Thetford Dr, Bella Vista AR 72715, USA

**Haller, Kevin** — Ice Hockey Player
Hockey Ministries, 1100 Dela Gauchetiere W, Montreal QC H3B 2S2, Canada

**Hallett, Bob** — Singer (Great Big Sea)
Fleming Assoc, 167 Little Lake Dr, Ann Arbor MI 48103, USA

**Hallick, Tom** — Actor
4267 Marina City Dr, #404, Marina del Rey CA 90292, USA

**Hallinan, Joseph T (Joe)** — Journalist, Writer
Random House, 1745 Broadway, #1800, New York NY 10019 USA

**Halliwell, Geri** — Singer (Spice Girls)
19 Entertainment, 35-37 Parkgate Road, #32/33, London SW11 4NP, England

**Hallman, Tom, Jr** — Journalist
Portland Oregonian, Editorial Dept, 1320 SW Broadway, Portland OR 97201, USA

**Hallock, Bob** — Auto Racing Driver
2185 Santa Ana Ave, Costa Mesa CA 92627, USA

**Hallock, Ty E** — Football Player
3676 Hunters Way Dr SE, Ada MI 49301, USA

**Hallstrom, Lasse** — Director
LaHa Films, 137 W 57th St, #700, New York NY 10019, USA

**Hallstrom, Ronald D (Ron)** — Football Player
Hallstrom's Marina, PO Box 379, Woodruff WI 54568, USA

**Hallyday, Estelle** — Model
I M G Models, 304 Park Ave S, #PH N, New York NY 10010 USA

**Hallyday, Johnny** — Singer, Actor
Voyez Mon Agent, 20 Ave Rapp, 75007 Paris, France

**Halmich, Regina** — Boxer
Gunter Halmich, Inselstr 3, 76189 Karlsruhe, Germany

**Halperin, Bertrand I** — Physicist
Harvard University, Lyman Physics Laboratory, Cambridge MA 02138, USA

**Halpern, Daniel** — Writer
57 Mountain Ave, Princeton NJ 08540, USA

**Halpern, Jack** — Chemist
5801 S Dorchester Ave, #4A, Chicago IL 60637, USA

**Halpern, James S** — Judge
US Tax Court, 400 2nd St NW, Washington DC 20217, USA

**Halpern, Jeff** — Ice Hockey Player
9212 Sprinklewood Lane, Potomac MD 20854, USA

**Halsell, James D, Jr** — Astronaut
257 River Cove Road, Huntsville AL 35811, USA

**Halsey, Darcy** — Actress
Arts & Letters Mgmt, 7715 W Sunset Blvd, #208, Los Angeles CA 90046, USA

**Halter, Shane D** — Baseball Player
6501 W 138th Terrace, #10210, Overland Park KS 66223, USA

**Halton, Thomas L** — Nutritionist
Harvard Public Health School, Nutrition Dept, 655 Huntington, Boston MA 02115, USA

**Halver, John E** — Biochemist, Nutritionist
16502 41st Ave NE, Lake Forest Park WA 98155, USA

**Halverson, R Dean** — Football Player
3819 Fairmont Lane NW, Olympia WA 98502, USA

**Halvorsen, Gail** — Berlin Airlift Air Force Hero
1525 W Dove Way, Amado AZ 85645, USA

**Ham, Jack R** — Football Player
Ham Enterprises, 540 Lindbergh Dr, Coraopolis PA 15108, USA

**Ham, Kenneth T** — Astronaut
32 Upshur Road, Annapolis MD 21402, USA

**Hamada, Hiroshi** — Businessman
Ricoh Co, 1-15-5 Minami-Aoyama, Minatoku, Tokyo 107 8544, Japan

**Hamari, Julia** — Opera Singer
Max Brodweg 14, 70437 Stuttgart, Germany

**Hamasaki, Ayumi** — Singer, Songwriter, Actress
Avex Mgmt, 3-1-30-7F Minami Aoyama, Minato, Tokyo 107 0062, Japan

**Hambling, Maggi** — Artist
Morley College, Westminster Bridge Road, London SE1 7HT, England

**Hambright, Roger D** — Baseball Player
8709 NE 37th Ave, Vancouver WA 98665, USA

**Hambrock, John** — Cartoonist
King Features Syndicate, 300 W 57th St, #1500, New York NY 10019 USA

**Hambuchen, Fabian** — Gymnast
Pfaffenrain 35, 35585 Wetzlar, Germany

**Hamburg, John** — Director, Producer, Writer
W M E Entertainment, 9601 Wilshire Blvd, #300, Beverly Hills CA 90210 USA

**Hamburger, Cao** — Director
Anonymous Content, 3532 Hayden Ave, Culver City CA 90232 USA

**Hamby, Chris** — Journalist
BuzzFeed, Editoral Dept, 200 5th Ave, #800, New York NY 10010, USA

**Hamdallah, Rami** — Prime Minister, Palestine
Prime Minister's Office, Gaza City, Gaza Strip, Palestine, Israel

**Hamed, Naseem (Prince)** — Boxer
Ciaralinn, Woodlands Road W, Virginia Water, Surrey GU25 4PL, England

**Hamel, Dean** — Football Player
1007 Hawthorne Dr NE, Lenoir NC 28645, USA

**Hamel, Peter Michael** — Composer
Bergsedter Markt 12, 22395 Hamburg, Germany

**Hamel, Veronica** — Actress, Model
12305 Fifth Helen Dr, Brentwood CA 94513, USA

**Hamelin, Charles** — Speed Skater
Club Montreal, 930 Av Roland-Beaudin, Quebec QC G1V 4H8, Canada

**Hamelin, Francois** — Speed Skater
Speed Skating Canada, 2781 Lancaster Road, #402, Ottawa ON K1B 1A7, Canada

**Hamelin, Robert J (Bob)** — Baseball Player
51 Patton Court SE, Concord NC 28025, USA

**Hamhuis, Dan** — Ice Hockey Player
9553 Hampton Reserve Dr, Brentwood TN 37027, USA

**Hamill, Dorothy S** — Figure Skater
10045 Red Run Blvd, #250, Owings Mills MD 21117, USA

**Hamill, Mark** — Actor
Danis Panaro Nist Talent, 9201 W Olympic Blvd, Beverly Hills CA 90212, USA

**Hamill, W Pete** — Writer, Editor
8 Whiskey Hill Road, Wallkill NY 12589, USA

**Hamilton** — Guitarist (British Sea Power)
Agency Group Ltd, 361-373 City Road, London EC1V 1PQ, England

**Hamilton, Allan G (Al)** — Ice Hockey Player
2452 115th St, Edmonton AB T6J 3S1, Canada

**Hamilton, Ann** — Sculptor
64 Smith Place, Columbus OH 43201, USA

**Hamilton, Anthony** — Singer, Rap Artist
Special Assignment Operations, 269 S Beverly Drive, #1173, Beverly Hills CA 90212, USA

**Hamilton, Arthur Lee** — Baseball Player
4374 Woodley Creek Road, Jacksonville FL 32218, USA

**Hamilton, Ashley G** — Actor
Mavrick Artists Agency, 6100 Wilshire Blvd, #550, Los Angeles CA 90048, USA

**Hamilton, Benjamin T (Ben)** — Football Player
5240 Golden Ridge Court, Parker CO 80134, USA

**Hamilton, C Robert (Bobby), Jr** — Auto Racing Driver
Motorsports Decisions, 1435 W Morehead St, #190, Charlotte NC 28208, USA

**Hamilton, Claire** — Curling Athlete
Curling Association, 14 Donnelly Dr, Bedford, Bedfordshire MK4 9TU, England

**Hamilton, Clyde H** — Judge
US Appeals Court, Federal Courthouse, 1100 Laurel St, Columbia SC 29201, USA

**Hamilton, Conrad** — Football Player
19619 N 35th Place, Phoenix AZ 85050, USA

**Hamilton, Darryl Q** — Baseball Player
4721 Southwind Dr, Baton Rouge LA 70816, USA

**Hamilton, David** — Photographer, Writer, Producer
41 Blvd du Montparnasse, 75006 Paris, France

**Hamilton, David E (Dave)** — Baseball Player
9464 Cherry Hills Lane, San Ramon CA 94583, USA

**Hamilton, De'Marr** — Drummer (Plain White T's), Songwriter
One Moment Mgmt, PO Box 55156, Sherman Oaks CA 91413 USA

**Hamilton, George** — Actor
C E S D, 10635 Santa Monica Blvd, #130, Los Angeles CA 90025 USA

**Hamilton, Guy** — Director
Palma de Mallorca, Apartado III, 01753 Andratz, Baleric Islands, Spain

**Hamilton, Harry E** — Football Player
PO Box 986, Lemont PA 16851, USA

**Hamilton, Hugo** — Writer
Harper Collins Publishers, 10 E 53rd St, Cellar 1, New York NY 10022 USA

**Hamilton, J Joseph (Joey)** — Baseball Player
4035 Wellington Mist Point, Duluth GA 30097, USA

**Hamilton, Jane** — Writer
Doubleday Press, 1540 Broadway, New York NY 10036, USA

**Hamilton, Jeffrey R (Jeff)** — Baseball Player
2485 Golfview Circle, Fenton MI 48430, USA

**Hamilton, Jim** — Ice Hockey Player
2906 Glasgow St, Pittsburgh PA 15204, USA

**Hamilton, Josh** — Actor
Paradigm Agency, 360 N Crescent Dr, North Building, Beverly Hills CA 90210 USA

**Hamilton, Joshua H (Josh)** — Baseball Player
4317 Willowdale Court, Apex NC 27539, USA

**Hamilton, Keith L** — Football Player
6 Bonnieview Lane, Towaco NJ 07082, USA

**Hamilton, Laird J** — Surfer
Ziffren Brittenham Branca, 1801 Century Park W, #700, Los Angeles CA 90067 USA

**Hamilton, Laurell K** — Writer
PO Box 190306, Saint Louis MO 63119, USA

**Hamilton, Leonard** — Basketball Coach
Florida State University, Athletic Dept, Tallahassee FL 32306, USA

**Hamilton, Lewis C D** — Auto Racing Driver
Mercedes A M G Petronas, Operation Centre, Brackley Northantshire NN13 7BD, England

**Hamilton, Linda** — Actress
Innovative Artists, 1505 10th St, Santa Monica CA 90401 USA

**Hamilton, Lisa Gay** — Actress
Paradigm Agency, 360 N Crescent Dr, North Building, Beverly Hills CA 90210 USA

**Hamilton, Marcus** — Cartoonist (Dennis the Menance)
12225 Ranburne Road, Charlotte NC 28227, USA

**Hamilton, Melinda Page** — Actress
Don Buchwald Talent Agency, 6500 Wilshire Blvd, #2200, Los Angeles CA 90048 USA

**Hamilton, Michael** — Artist
2012 N 19th St, Boise ID 83702, USA

**Hamilton, Milo** — Sportscaster
2001 Holcombe Blvd, #901, Houston TX 77030, USA

**Hamilton, Page** — Guitarist (Band of Susans, Helmet)
Maine Road Mgmt, 195 Chrystie St, #901F, New York NY 10002, USA

**Hamilton, Richard C** — Basketball Player
2301 W Big Beaver Road, #535, Troy MI 48084, USA

**Hamilton, Roy Lee** — Basketball Player
1644 Del Mar Road, Oceanside CA 92057, USA

**Hamilton, Ruffin, III** — Football Player
236 Sumac Trail, Woodstock GA 30188, USA

**Hamilton, Scott S** — Figure Skater
2451 Hidden River Lane, Franklin TN 37069, USA

**Hamilton, Suzanna** — Actress
Julian Belfrage Assoc, 9 Argyll St, #300, London W1F 7TG, England

**Hamilton, Thomas W (Tom)** — Bassist (Aerosmith)
Front Line Mgmt, 1100 Glendon Ave, #2000, Los Angeles CA 90024 USA

**Hamilton, Todd** — Golfer
2004 Rock Dove Court, Westlake TX 76262, USA

| | |
|---|---|
| **Hamilton, Tom**<br>31704 Sailors Cove, Avon Lake OH 44012, USA | Sportscaster |
| **Hamilton, Tyler**<br>32 Russell St, Marblehead MA 01945, USA | Cyclist |
| **Hamilton, Victoria**<br>Paradigm Agency, 360 Park Ave S, #1600, New York NY 10010 USA | Actress |
| **Hamilton, Wendy**<br>Playboy Promotions, 9346 Civic Center Dr, #200, Beverly Hills CA 90210 USA | Model, Actress |
| **Hamilton, William**<br>17 E 95th St, #3F, New York NY 10128, USA | Cartoonist, Writer |
| **Hamlett, Denis**<br>Chicago Fire, Toyota Park, 7000 S Harlem Ave, Bridgeview IL 60455 USA | Soccer Coach |
| **Hamlin, Brooke**<br>Piper Kaniecki Mgmt, 13273 Ventura Blvd, #104, Studio City CA 91604, USA | Actress |
| **Hamlin, Catherine**<br>Addis Adaba Fistula Hospital, PO Box 5066 Turramurra NSW 2074, Australia | Obstetrician, Gynecologist |
| **Hamlin, Erin**<br>171 W 57th St, #8A, New York NY 10019, USA | Luge Athlete |
| **Hamlin, Harry**<br>Paradigm Agency, 360 N Crescent Dr, North Building, Beverly Hills CA 90210 USA | Actor |
| **Hamlin, J Dennis A (Denny)**<br>19135 Pennsylvanis Point Dr, Cornelius NC 29031, USA | Auto Racing Driver |
| **Hamlin, Kenneth L (Ken)**<br>5242 County Road 413, McMillan MI 49853, USA | Baseball Player |
| **Hamlin, Shelley**<br>4311 W Ardmore Road, Laveen AZ 85339, USA | Golfer |
| **Hamm, Jon**<br>Creative Artists Agency, 2000 Ave of Stars, #100, Los Angeles CA 90067 USA | Actor |
| **Hamm, Mia**<br>613 15th St, Manhattan Beach CA 90266, USA | Soccer Player, Model |
| **Hamm, Morgan**<br>171 W 57th St, #8A, New York NY 10019, USA | Gymnast |
| **Hamm, Nick**<br>I C M Partners, 10250 Constellation Blvd, #900, Los Angeles CA 90067 USA | Director |
| **Hamm, Paul**<br>171 W 57th St, #8A, New York NY 10019, USA | Gymnast |
| **Hammaker, C Atlee**<br>12740 Manning Lane, Knoxville TN 37932, USA | Baseball Player |
| **Hammel, Eugene A**<br>2332 Piedmont Ave, Berkeley CA 94720, USA | Anthropologist |
| **Hammell, Penny**<br>4786 Orchard Lane, Delray Beach FL 33445, USA | Golfer |
| **Hammer**<br>Media Artists Group, 8222 Melrose Ave, #203, Los Angeles CA 90048 USA | Rap Artist |
| **Hammer, A J**<br>CNN-TV, News Dept, 190 Marietta Ave SW, Atlanta GA 30303 USA | Commentator |
| **Hammer, Armie**<br>W M E Entertainment, 9601 Wilshire Blvd, #300, Beverly Hills CA 90210 USA | Actor |
| **Hammer, Jan, Jr**<br>2 W 45th St, #1102, New York NY 10036, USA | Jazz Keyboardist, Composer |
| **Hammer, Sarah K**<br>1960 Knoxville Ave, Long Beach CA 90815, USA | Cyclist |
| **Hammer, Victor S**<br>Gersh Agency, 9465 Wilshire Blvd, #600, Beverly Hills CA 90212 USA | Cinematographer |
| **Hammergren, John H**<br>McKesson Inc, 1 Post St, #1800, San Francisco CA 94104, USA | Businessman |
| **Hammes, Gordon G**<br>11 Staley Place, Durham NC 27705, USA | Chemist |
| **Hammett, Kirk**<br>2505 Divisadero St, San Francisco CA 94115, USA | Guitarist (Metallica) |
| **Hammock, Robert W (Robby)**<br>8644 S 21st Place, Phoenix AZ 85042, USA | Baseball Player |
| **Hammond, Albert, Jr**<br>Albert Hammond Music, 10100 Santa Moncia Blvd, #1050, Los Angeles CA 90067, USA | Guitarist (Strokes) |
| **Hammond, Christopher A (Chris)**<br>116144 Palomino Valley Road, San Diego CA 92127, USA | Baseball Player |
| **Hammond, Darrell**<br>W M E Entertainment, 1325 Ave of Americas, New York NY 10019 USA | Actor, Comedian |
| **Hammond, Donald W (Donnie)**<br>8518 Cypress Hollow Court, Sanford FL 32771, USA | Golfer |
| **Hammond, Fred**<br>Face to Face Ministries, 21421 Hilltop St, #20, Southfield MI 48033, USA | Singer, Bassist (Radical for Christ) |
| **Hammond, Gary A**<br>5321 Seascape Lane, Plano TX 75093, USA | Football Player |
| **Hammond, George S**<br>27 Timber Lane, Painted Post NY 14870, USA | Chemist |
| **Hammond, Joan H**<br>Private Bag 101, Geelong Mail Center VIC 3221, Australia | Opera Singer |
| **Hammond, John P**<br>Rosebud Agency, PO Box 170429, San Francisco CA 94117 USA | Singer, Guitarist |
| **Hammond, Josh**<br>Hines & Hurt Entertainment, 1213 W Magnolia Blvd, Burbank CA 91506, USA | Actor, Producer |
| **Hammond, Julian H (Julie)**<br>2943 S Ulster St, Denver CO 80231, USA | Basketball Player |
| **Hammond, L Blaine, Jr**<br>Gulfstream Aircraft, 4150 E Donald Douglas Dr, #926, Long Beach CA 90808, USA | Astronaut |
| **Hammond, Philip**<br>Foreign Minister's Office, 11 Downing St, London SW1A 0AA, England | Government Official, England |
| **Hammond, Richard**<br>Independent Talent Group, 40 Whitfield St, London W1T 2RH, England | Actor, Producer |
| **Hammond, Robert D**<br>219 Del Mesa Carmel, Carmel CA 93923, USA | Army General |
| **Hammond, Robert L (Bobby)**<br>2535 Butler St, East Elmhurst NY 11369, USA | Football Player |
| **Hammond, Steven B (Steve)**<br>11104 Lake Butler Road, Windermere FL 34786, USA | Baseball Player |

H

Hamilton - Hammond

**Hammond, Tom** — Sportscaster
NBC-TV, Sports Dept, 30 Rockefeller Plaza, #270E, New York NY 10112 USA
**Hammonds, Bruce** — Businessman
M B N A Corp, 1100 N King St, Wilmington DE 19884, USA
**Hammonds, Jeffrey B (Jeff)** — Baseball Player
2950 Meadow Lane, Weston FL 33331, USA
**Hammonds, Tom E** — Basketball Player
122 Windsor Dr, Crestview FL 32539, USA
**Hammons, David** — Sculptor
Studio Museum in Harlem, 144 W 125th St, #200, New York NY 10027, USA
**Hamner, Earl, Jr** — Producer, Writer
11575 Amanda Dr, Studio City CA 91604, USA
**Hamnett, Katharine** — Fashion Designer
Aberdeen Studios, 22-24 Highbury Grove, #3D, London N5 2EA, England
**Hamon, Lucienne** — Actress
Agents Associes, 201 Rue du Faubourg Saint Honore, 75008 Paris, France
**Hamp, Eric P** — Language Educator
1190 Railroad Trail, Beulah MI 49617, USA
**Hampe, Michael** — Director
Tiergartenstr 36, 01219 Dresden, Germany
**Hampshire, Susan** — Actress
Rob Groves Personal Management, 33 Glasshouse St, Soho London W1B 5DG, England
**Hampson, Edward G (Ted)** — Ice Hockey Player
4436 Claremore Dr, Minneapolis MN 55435, USA
**Hampson, Justin M** — Baseball Player
7018 Richmond Dr, Glen Carbon IL 62034, USA
**Hampson, Thomas** — Opera Singer
Starkfriedgasse 53, 1180 Vienna, Austria
**Hampton, Brenda** — Producer
Paradigm Agency, 360 N Crescent Dr, North Building, Beverly Hills CA 90210 USA
**Hampton, Casey, Jr** — Football Player
105 Conover Road, Pittsburgh PA 15208, USA
**Hampton, Christopher J** — Writer
Casorotto Ramsay, Waverley House, 7-12 Noel St, London W1F 8GQ, England
**Hampton, Daniel O (Dan)** — Football Player
9191 Falling Waters Dr E, Burr Ridge IL 60527, USA
**Hampton, Isaac B (Ike)** — Baseball Player
4415 E Ridge Gate Road, Anaheim CA 92807, USA
**Hampton, J J** — Rodeo Rider
Barbara Hampton Assoc, 1702 W South Loop, Stephenville TX 76401, USA
**Hampton, James** — Actor
102 Forest Hill Dr, Roanoke TX 76262, USA
**Hampton, Locksley W (Slide)** — Jazz Trombonist
Thomas Cassidy, PO Box 1311, Tucson AZ 85702 USA
**Hampton, Lorenzo T** — Football Player
16231 NW 77th Place, Hialeah FL 33016, USA
**Hampton, Mark G** — Architect
Mark Hampton Architect, 3900 Loquat Ave, Miami FL 33133, USA
**Hampton, Michael W (Mike)** — Baseball Player
8601 N 59th Place, Paradise Valley AZ 85253, USA
**Hampton, Millard** — Track Athlete
201 W Mission St, San Jose CA 95110, USA
**Hampton, Ralph C, Jr** — Religious Leader
Free Will Baptist Bible College, 3606 W End Ave, Nashville TN 37205, USA
**Hampton, Rodney C** — Football Player
5603 Grand Floral Blvd, Houston TX 77041, USA
**Hamra, Khalil** — Photojournalist
Associated Press, Editorial Dept, 450 W 33rd St, #1500, New York NY 10001 USA
**Hamri, Sanaa** — Director
Creative Artists Agency, 2000 Ave of Stars, #100, Los Angeles CA 90067 USA
**Hamrlik, Roman** — Ice Hockey Player
56 Alhambra Dr, Oceanside NY 11572, USA
**Hamulack, Tim** — Baseball Player
530 Campbell Road, York PA 17402, USA
**Han Seung-Soo** — Prime Minister, South Korea
Prime Minister's Office, 77 Sejong-no, Chongnogu, Seoul 110 760, South Korea
**Han, Jefferson Y (Jeff)** — Computer Scientist
New York University, Courant Math Sciences Institute, New York NY 10012, USA
**Hanafusa, Hidesaburo** — Microbiologist
500 E 63rd St, New York NY 10065, USA
**Hanauer, Lee E (Chip)** — Boat Racing Driver
Hanauer Enterprises, 2702 NE 88th St, Seattle WA 98115, USA
**Hanburger, Christian (Chris), Jr** — Football Player
125 Wyandot St, Darlington SC 29532, USA
**Hancock, Anthony D** — Football Player
8233 Corteland Dr, Knoxville TN 37909, USA
**Hancock, Herbert J (Herbie)** — Jazz Pianist, Composer
Red Light Mgmt, PO Box 1467, Charlottesville VA 22902, USA
**Hancock, John** — Opera Singer
Columbia Artists Mgmt Inc, 5 Columbus Circle, 1790 Broadway, #1600, New York NY 10019 USA
**Hancock, John D** — Director, Producer, Writer
7355 N Fail Road, La Porte IN 46350, USA
**Hancock, John Lee** — Director
Creative Artists Agency, 2000 Ave of Stars, #100, Los Angeles CA 90067 USA
**Hancock, Lee** — Baseball Player
8338 Brentwood Blvd, Brentwood CA 94513, USA
**Hancock, Phillip** — Golfer
3339 Handy Road, #728, Tampa FL 33618, USA
**Hancock, R Garry** — Baseball Player
2217 Greenhills Dr, Valrico FL 33596, USA
**Hancock, Sheila** — Actress, Writer
Independent Talent Group, 40 Whitfield St, London W1T 2RH, England
**Hancock, Vincent** — Marksman
8889 Cook Ranch Road, Benbrook TX 76126, USA
**Hand, Elizabeth** — Writer
Editions Denoel, 9 Rue du Cherche-Midi, 75278 Paris Cedex 06, France

**Hand, Joey** — Auto Racing Driver
Joey Hand Racing, 5877 Power Inn Road, Sacramento CA 95824, USA
**Hand, Jon T** — Football Player
PO Box 40296, Indianapolis IN 46240, USA
**Hand, Richard A (Rich)** — Baseball Player
3824 Bay Court, Fort Worth TX 76179, USA
**Handelsman, Walt** — Editorial Cartoonist
Newsday, Editorial Dept, 235 Pinelawn Road, Melville NY 11747, USA
**Handford, Martin** — Cartoonist (Where's Waldo)
Walker Books, 87 Vauxhall Walk, London SE11 5HU, England
**Handke, Peter** — Writer
Farrar Straus Giroux, 18 W 18th St, #700, New York NY 10011 USA
**Handler, Chelsea** — Actress, Comedienne
Borderline Amazing Productions, 12312 W Olympic Blvd, Los Angeles CA 90064, USA
**Handler, Daniel** — Writer
Harper Collins Publishers, 10 E 53rd St, Cellar 1, New York NY 10022 USA
**Handler, Evan** — Actor
Gersh Agency, 9465 Wilshire Blvd, #600, Beverly Hills CA 90212 USA
**Handley, Robert R (Ray)** — Football Coach
PO Box 275, Glenbrook NV 89413, USA
**Handley, Taylor** — Actor
Paradigm Agency, 360 N Crescent Dr, North Building, Beverly Hills CA 90210 USA
**Hands, Guy** — Businessman
Terra Firma Capital, 2 More London Riverside, London SE1 2AP, England
**Hands, Terence D** — Director
Clwyd Theater Cymru, Mold, Flintshire CH7 1YA, North Wales
**Hands, William A (Bill)** — Baseball Player
PO Box 334, Orient NY 11957, USA
**Handy, James** — Actor
C E S D, 10635 Santa Monica Blvd, #130, Los Angeles CA 90025 USA
**Handy, John** — Jazz Saxophonist
Integrity Talent, 1 Westcroft Court, Cockeysville MD 21030 USA
**Haneef-Park, Tayyiba M** — Volleyball Player
USA Volleyball, 4065 Sinton Road, #200, Colorado Springs CO 80907, USA
**Haneke, Michael** — Director, Writer
Filmakademie Vienna, Metternichgasse 12, 1030 Vienna, Austria
**Haner, Josh** — Photojournalist
New York Times, Editorial Dept, 229 W 43rd St, New York NY 10036 USA
**Haner, Martin** — Field Hockey Player
Berlin Hockey Club, Wilskistr 70, 14163 Berlin, Germany
**Hanevold, Halvard** — Biathlete
Barlindbakken 23, 1388 Borgen, Norway
**Haney, Cecil E D** — Navy Admiral
U S Strategic Command, 901 S A C Blvd, Offutt Air Force Base NE 68113 USA
**Haney, Christopher D (Chris)** — Baseball Player
PO Box 135, Barboursville VA 22923, USA
**Haney, Lee** — Body Builder
Lee Haney Enterprises, 105 Trail Point Circle, Fayetteville GA 30214, USA
**Haney, Todd M** — Baseball Player
5404 Pointwood Circle, Waco TX 76710, USA
**Hanft, Ruth S** — Medical Researcher
606 Rainier Road, Charlottesville VA 22903, USA
**Hangartner, Geoffrey T (Geoff)** — Football Player
805 Park Slope Dr, Charlotte NC 28209, USA
**Hanggi, Kristin** — Director
Wonderfalls Entertainment, 1041 N Formosa Ave, Formosa Building, Los Angeles CA 90067, USA
**Hanifan, James M (Jim)** — Football Coach
1217 Grey Fox Run, Weldon Spring MO 63304, USA
**Hanigan, Ryan M** — Baseball Player
55 Bailey Road, Andover MA 01810, USA
**Hanin, Roger** — Actor, Writer, Director
Artmedia, 20 Ave Rapp, 75007 Paris, France
**Hanisch, Cornelia** — Fencer
Rosemarie Hanisch, Via San Rocco 25, 18017 Lingueglietta/Imperia, Italy
**Hankin, Larry** — Actor, Writer, Producer
Amsel Eisenstadt Frazier, 5055 Wilshire Blvd, #865, Los Angeles CA 90036 USA
**Hankinson, Tim** — Soccer Coach
Columbus Crew, 1 Black & Gold Blvd, Columbus OH 43211 USA
**Hankowsky, William** — Financier
Liberty Property Trust, 7201 Wayne Ave, Philadelphia PA 19119, USA
**Hanks, Colin** — Actor
United Talent Agency, U T A Plaza, 9336 Civic Center Dr, Beverly Hills CA 90210 USA
**Hanks, Merton E** — Football Player
62 Oakland Ave, Bloomfield NJ 07003, USA
**Hanks, Tom** — Actor, Director, Producer
Playtone Productions, PO Box 7340, Santa Monica CA 90406, USA
**Hankton, Karl C** — Football Player
7024 Indian Ridge Lane, Charlotte NC 28214, USA
**Hanley, Charles** — Journalist
Associated Press, Editorial Dept, 450 W 33rd St, #1500, New York NY 10001 USA
**Hanley, Frank** — Labor Leader
International Union of Operating Engineers, 1125 17th St NW, Washington DC 20036, USA
**Hanley, Jenny** — Actress
M G A, Southbank House, Black Prince Road, London SE1 7SJ, England
**Hanley, Kay** — Singer (Letters to Cleo)
Creamer Mgmt, 32 Oak Square Ave, Brighton MA 02135, USA
**Hanley, Richard D (Dick)** — Swimmer
2343 Old Glenview Road, Wilmette IL 60091, USA
**Hanlon, Glenn A** — Ice Hockey Player, Coach
8781 Piney Orchard Parkway, Odenton MD 21113, USA
**Hanna, Preston L** — Baseball Player
5555 Mayfair Dr, Pensacola FL 32506, USA
**Hannah, Bob** — Baseball Coach
University of Delaware, Athletic Dept, Newark DE 19716, USA
**Hannah, Charles A (Charley)** — Football Player
PO Box 2671, Lutz FL 33548, USA

# H

**Hannah, Daryl** — Actress, Model
Binder & Assoc, 1465 Lindacrest Dr, Beverly Hills CA 90210 USA
**Hannah, John** — Actor
Artist Rights Group, 4A Exmoor St, London W10 6BD, England
**Hannah, John A** — Football Player
2407 Hideaway Place SE, Decatur AL 35603, USA
**Hannah, Kristin** — Writer
Saint Martin's Press, 175 5th Ave, #400, New York NY 10010 USA
**Hannah, Robert (Bob)** — Motorcycle Racing Rider
Bob Hannah Aviation, 22499 Channel Road, Caldwell ID 83607, USA
**Hannahan, John J (Jack), IV** — Baseball Player
1995 Bayard Ave, Saint Paul MN 55116, USA
**Hannan, David P (Dave)** — Ice Hockey Player
408 Timberlake Dr, Venetia PA 15367, USA
**Hannan, James J (Jim)** — Baseball Player
3907 Cherry Hill Way, Annandale VA 22003, USA
**Hannan, K Scott** — Ice Hockey Player
19145 Graystone Lane, San Jose CA 95120, USA
**Hannan, Mary Claire** — Costume Designer
Dattner Dispoto, 10635 Santa Monica Blvd, #165, Los Angeles CA 90025, USA
**Hannawald, Sven** — Ski Jumper
W H Sport International GmbH, Im Sabel 4, 54294 Trier, Germany
**Hanneman, Craig L** — Football Player
4350 Gibson Road NW, Salem OR 97304, USA
**Hanni, Luca** — Singer
3661 Uetendorf, Switzerland
**Hannibal, Lars** — Concert Guitarist
Nordskraenten 3, 2980 Kokkedal, Denmark
**Hannigan, Alyson** — Actress
A P A Talent & Literary Agency, 405 S Beverly Dr, #300, Beverly Hills CA 90212 USA
**Hannigan, Barbara** — Opera Singer, Conductor
Harrison/Parrott, 5-6 Albion Court, London W6 0QT, England
**Hanning, Rob** — Producer, Writer
Ziffren Brittenham Branca, 1801 Century Park W, #700, Los Angeles CA 90067 USA
**Hannity, Sean** — Commentator
Hannity & Colmes, Fox-TV, News Dept, 1211 Ave of Americas, New York NY 10036, USA
**Hannon, Thomas E (Tom)** — Football Player
17398 Roxbury Ave, Southfield MI 48075, USA
**Hannula, Dick** — Swimming Coach
1021 Westley Dr, Tacoma WA 98465, USA
**Hannum, Taimie** — Actress, Model
7095 Hollywood Blvd, #762, Los Angeles CA 90028, USA
**Hano, Gregg R** — Publisher
Popular Science, Publisher's Office, 2 Park Ave, #900, New York NY 10016, USA
**Hanold, Marilyn** — Model, Actress
Playboy Promotions, 9346 Civic Center Dr, #200, Beverly Hills CA 90210 USA
**Hanover, Donna** — Commentator
Helen Brezinsky, 1301 Ave of Americas, New York NY 10019, USA
**Hanrahan, Joel R** — Baseball Player
2488 Captain Hook Dr, Fernandina Beach FL 32034, USA
**Hanratty, Samantha (Sammi)** — Actress
Paradigm Agency, 360 N Crescent Dr, North Building, Beverly Hills CA 90210 USA
**Hanratty, Terrance R (Terry)** — Football Player
31 Gower Road, New Canaan CT 06840, USA
**Hans-Adam II** — Prince, Liechtenstein
Prince's Residence, Schloss Vaduz, 9490 Vaduz, Liechtenstein
**Hansard, Glen** — Actor, Singer, Songwriter
Frames, PO Box 67 Gorey, County Wexford, Ireland
**Hansbrough, A Tyler** — Basketball Player
Indiana Pacers, Conseco Fieldhouse, 125 S Pennsylvania, Indianapolis IN 46204 USA
**Hansch, Theodor W** — Nobel Physics Laureate
Max Plack Institut, Hans-Kopermann-Str 1, 85748 Garching, Germany
**Hansen, Alfred G** — Air Force General, Businessman
Lockheed Aero Systems, 86 S Cobb Dr, Marietta GA 30063, USA
**Hansen, Barbara C** — Neuroscientist
University of Maryland, Obesity/Diabetes Research Center, Baltimore MD 21201, USA
**Hansen, Brendan J** — Swimmer
8704 Framdale Cove, Austin TX 78749, USA
**Hansen, Brian** — Speed Skater
U S Speedskating, 5662 S Cougar Lane, Salt Lake City UT 84118 USA
**Hansen, Brian D** — Football Player
101 W Hazletine Lane, Sioux Falls SD 57108, USA
**Hansen, Chris** — Commentator
NBC-TV, News Dept, 30 Rockefeller Plaza, #270E, New York NY 10112 USA
**Hansen, David A (Dave)** — Baseball Player
9852 Orchard Lane, Villa Park CA 92861, USA
**Hansen, Donald R (Don)** — Football Player
3390 Spain Road, Snellville GA 30039, USA
**Hansen, Frederick M (Fred)** — Track Athlete
201 Vanderpool Lane, #12, Houston TX 77024, USA
**Hansen, Gale** — Actress
Relativity Media, 9242 Beverly Blvd, #300, Beverly Hills CA 90210, USA
**Hansen, Gunnar** — Actor
Amsel Eisenstadt Frazier, 5055 Wilshire Blvd, #865, Los Angeles CA 90036 USA
**Hansen, J Stanley (Stan)** — Professional Wrestler
233 Fannin Dr, Hewitt TX 76643, USA
**Hansen, James Lee** — Sculptor
28219 NE 63rd Ave, Battle Ground WA 98604, USA
**Hansen, Joseph T** — Labor Leader
United Food/Commercial Workers Union, 1775 K St NW, Washington DC 20006, USA
**Hansen, Lars Peter** — Nobel Economics Laureate
University of Chicago, Economics Dept, 1126 E 59th St, Chicago IL 60637, USA
**Hansen, Lasse Norman** — Cyclist
Team Concordia-Himmerland, Vestergade 20, 9620 Aalestrup, Denmark
**Hansen, Mark Victor** — Motivational Speaker, Writer
PO Box 7665, Newport Beach CA 92658, USA

**Hansen, Monica**
Playboy Promotions, 9346 Civic Center Dr, #200, Beverly Hills CA 90210 USA — Model

**Hansen, Patti**
Redlands, West Wittering, Chichester, Sussex PO20 8QE, England — Model, Actress

**Hansen, Peter**
Stone Manners Salners, 6100 Wilshire Blvd, #1500, Los Angeles CA 90035 USA — Actor

**Hansen, Phillip A (Phil)**
24921 N Melissa Dr, Detroit Lakes MN 56501, USA — Football Player

**Hansen, Robert L (Bob)**
710 36th St, West Des Moines IA 50265, USA — Basketball Player

**Hansen, Ronald L (Ron)**
13602 Alliston Dr, Baldwin MD 21013, USA — Baseball Player

**Hansen, Ryan**
Gersh Agency, 9465 Wilshire Blvd, #600, Beverly Hills CA 90212 USA — Actor

**Hanshaw, Anthony L**
Gary Shaw Productions, 555 Preakness Ave, #9, Totowa NJ 07502, USA — Boxer

**Hanson, Carl T**
3377 E Arroyo Chico, Tucson AZ 85716, USA — Navy Admiral

**Hanson, Curtis**
United Talent Agency, U T A Plaza, 9336 Civic Center Dr, Beverly Hills CA 90210 USA — Director, Writer

**Hanson, Dian**
Taschen GmbH, Hohenzollernring 53, 50672 Cologne, Germany — Writer

**Hanson, Erik B**
20333 N 83rd Place, Scottsdale AZ 85255, USA — Baseball Player

**Hanson, Hart**
W M E Entertainment, 9601 Wilshire Blvd, #300, Beverly Hills CA 90210 USA — Producer, Writer

**Hanson, Isaac**
10th Street Entertainment, 700 San Vicente Blvd, #G410, West Hollywood CA 90069, USA — Singer, Guitarist (Hanson); Songwriter

**Hanson, J Taylor**
10th Street Entertainment, 700 San Vicente Blvd, #G410, West Hollywood CA 90069, USA — Singer, Keyboardist (Hanson); Songwriter

**Hanson, Janine**
Winnipeg Rowing Club, 20 Lyndale Dr, Saint Boniface MB R2H 3H2, Canada — Rowing Athlete

**Hanson, Jason D**
27272 Ovid Court, Franklin MI 48025, USA — Football Player

**Hanson, Jennifer K**
Mission Mgmt, 24 Middleton St, Nashville TN 37210, USA — Singer

**Hanson, Joselio B**
2531 Hudspeth St, Inglewood CA 90303, USA — Football Player

**Hanson, Marcy**
8721 W Sunset Blvd, #101, West Hollywood CA 90069, USA — Model, Actress

**Hanson, Robert A**
PO Box 990, Moline IL 61266, USA — Businessman

**Hanson, Ronald**
Delft Technology University, Kavil Nanoscience Institute, Postbus 5, 2600 Delft AA, Netherlands — Nanoscientist, Physicist

**Hanson, Scott**
N F L Network, 10950 Washington Blvd, #100, Culver City CA 90232 USA — Sportscaster

**Hanson, Zachary**
10th Street Entertainment, 700 San Vicente Blvd, #G410, West Hollywood CA 90069, USA — Singer, Drummer (Hanson); Songwriter

**Hanson-Sfingi, Beverly**
79915 Horseshoe Road, La Quinta CA 92253, USA — Golfer

**Hanus, Tomas**
I M G Artists, Hogarth Business Park, Chiswick, London W4 2TH, England — Conductor

**Hanway, H Edward**
C I G N A Corp, 1 Liberty Place, 1650 Market St, Philadelphia PA 19103, USA — Businessman

**Hanzlik, William H (Bill)**
5701 Green Oaks Dr, Greenwood Village CO 80121, USA — Basketball Player, Coach

**Hape, Patrick S**
105 Sutton Circle, Birmingham AL 35242, USA — Football Player

**Happ, James A (J A)**
902 14th St, Peru IL 61354, USA — Baseball Player

**Harad, George J**
Boise Cascade Corp, 1111 W Jefferson St, Boise ID 83728, USA — Businessman

**Harada, Ann**
Davis Spylios Management, 244 W 54th St, #707, New York NY 10019, USA — Actress

**Harada, Masahiko (Fighting)**
Boxing Commission, Tokyo Dome, 1-3-61, Koraku, Bunkyoku, Tokyo 112 8562 , Japan — Boxer

**Harald V**
Royal Palace, Henrik Ibsens Gate 1, 0010 Oslo, Norway — King, Norway

**Haraldsen, Katrine Lunde**
Gyori Audi E T O, Kiskutliget Magvassy Mihaly Sportcsarnok, 9027 Gyor, Hungary — Handball Player

**Harang, Aaron M**
7828 Sendero Angelica, San Diego CA 92127, USA — Baseball Player

**Harangody, Luke C**
Cleveland Cavaliers, Gund Arena, 1 Center Court, Cleveland OH 44115 USA — Basketball Player

**Harareet, Haya**
Herons Flight, Marlow, Buckinghamshire SL7 2LE, England — Actress

**Harbaugh, Gregory J**
1936 Thornwood Ave, Wilmette IL 60091, USA — Astronaut

**Harbaugh, James J (Jim)**
San Francisco 49ers, 4949 Centennial Blvd, Santa Clara CA 95054 USA — Football Player, Coach

**Harbaugh, John**
Baltimore Ravens, Ravens Stadium, 1 Winning Dr, Baltimore MD 21230 USA — Football Coach

**Harbison, John H**
479 Franklin St, Cambridge MA 02139, USA — Composer

**Harbour, David**
Lou Coulson Assoc, 37 Berwick St, London W1V 8RS, England — Actor

**Harcourt, Ed**
Nice Mgmt, 2109 Cooley Place, Pasadena CA 91104, USA — Singer, Songwriter

**Hard, Darlene R**
22924 Erwin St, Woodland Hills CA 91367, USA — Tennis Player

**Hardaway, Anfernee D (Penny)**
3217 Point Hill Cove, Memphis TN 38125, USA — Basketball Player

**Hardaway, Timothy D (Tim)**
10050 SW 62nd Ave, Miami FL 33156, USA — Basketball Player

**Hardaway, Timothy D (Tim), Jr**
New York Knicks, Madison Square Garden, 2 Penn Plaza, New York, NY 10121 USA — Basketball Player

**Hardee, James E (Trey), III** — Decathlete
2409 E 9th St, Austin TX 78702, USA

**Hardeman, Donald R (Don)** — Football Player
901 S Valley Mills Dr, #207B, Waco TX 76711, USA

**Harden, J Richard (Rich)** — Baseball Player
Texas Rangers, Ameriquest Field, 1000 Ballpark Way, #306, Arlington TX 76011 USA

**Harden, James** — Basketball Player
Houston Rockets, 1730 Jefferson St, Houston TX 77003 USA

**Harden, Marcia Gay** — Actress
Framework Entertainment, 9057 Nemo St, #C, West Hollywood CA 90069 USA

**Harden, Michael (Mike)** — Football Player
21512 E Portland Place, Aurora CO 80016, USA

**Hardesty, Brandon A** — Actor
Strong Mgmt, 9350 Wilshire Blvd, #224, Beverly Hills CA 90212, USA

**Hardin, Meghan** — Golfer, Model
Lake Arrowhead Country Club, 250 Golf Course Road, Lake Arrowhead CA 92352, USA

**Hardin, Melora** — Actress, Singer, Director
Paul Kohner, 9300 Wilshire Blvd, #555, Beverly Hills CA 90212 USA

**Harding, C B** — Director, Producer, Writer
Passenger Films, 1901 Ave of Stars, #1050, Los Angeles CA 90067, USA

**Harding, Daniel** — Conductor
Columbia Artists Mgmt Inc, 5 Columbus Circle, 1790 Broadway, #1600, New York NY 10019 USA

**Harding, Ian** — Actor
Gersh Agency, 9465 Wilshire Blvd, #600, Beverly Hills CA 90212 USA

**Harding, John Wesley** — Singer, Guitarist, Songwriter, Writer
Concerted Efforts, PO Box 440326, Somerville MA 02144, USA

**Harding, Joshua J (Josh)** — Ice Hockey Player
1415 Brown St, Regina SK S4N 5C9, Canada

**Harding, Lindsey M** — Basketball Player
Minnesota Lynx, Target Center, 600 1st Ave N, Minneapolis MN 55403 USA

**Harding, Peter R** — Air Force Marshal, England
Avalon House, Marnhull, Dorset DT10 1PT, England

**Harding, Sarah N** — Actress, Singer (Girls Aloud)
Concorde International, 101 Shepherds Bush Road, London W6 7LP, England

**Harding, Tonya M** — Figure Skater, Actress
11805 Bastrop St, Manor TX 78653, USA

**Hardis, Stephen R** — Businessman
Eaton Corp, Eaton Center, 1111 Superior Ave, #1900, Cleveland OH 44114, USA

**Hardison, Bethann** — Producer
Bethann Entertainment, 388 2nd Ave, #223, New York NY 10010, USA

**Hardison, Kadeem** — Actor
Peter Strain, 5455 Wilshire Blvd, #1812, Los Angeles CA 90036 USA

**Hardison, W David (Dee)** — Football Player
756 Belvin Maynard Road, Harrells NC 28444, USA

**Hardman, Cedrick W** — Football Player
364 Myrtle St, Laguna Beach CA 92651, USA

**Hardnett, Charles (Charlie)** — Basketball Player, Coach
1906 Swainsboro Dr, Louisville KY 40218, USA

**Hardrict, Cory** — Actor
Luber Rocklin Entertainment, 5815 Sunset Blvd, #206, Los Angeles CA 90028 USA

**Hardt, Michael** — Educator
Duke University, English Dept, Durham NC 27708, USA

**Hardwick, Catherine** — Director
Creative Artists Agency, 2000 Ave of Stars, #100, Los Angeles CA 90067 USA

**Hardwick, Chris** — Actor, Comedian (Hard n Phirm)
Brillstein Entertainment Partners, 9150 Wilshire Blvd, #350, Beverly Hills CA 90212 USA

**Hardwick, Gary C** — Director, Writer
Gersh Agency, 9465 Wilshire Blvd, #600, Beverly Hills CA 90212 USA

**Hardwick, Johnny** — Writer
Creative Artists Agency, 2000 Ave of Stars, #100, Los Angeles CA 90067 USA

**Hardwick, Nicholas A (Nick)** — Football Player
San Diego Chargers, 4020 Murphy Canyon Road, San Diego CA 92123 USA

**Hardwicke, Catherine** — Director, Writer
Creative Artists Agency, 2000 Ave of Stars, #100, Los Angeles CA 90067 USA

**Hardy, Bruce A** — Football Player
252 W 325 N, Ivins UT 84738, USA

**Hardy, Carroll W** — Football, Baseball Player
1514 Whitehall Dr, Longmont CO 80504, USA

**Hardy, Francoise** — Singer, Songwriter
Voyez Mon Agent, 20 Ave Rapp, 75007 Paris, France

**Hardy, Gregory M (Greg)** — Football Player
Carolina Panthers, Ericsson Stadium, 800 S Mint St, Charlotte NC 28202 USA

**Hardy, Hagood** — Vibrist, Composer
S O C A N, 41 Valleybrook Dr, Don Mills ON M3B 2S6, Canada

**Hardy, Hugh** — Architect
Hardy Holzman Pfeiffer, 902 Broadway, #1900, New York NY 10010, USA

**Hardy, James F (Jim)** — Football Player
48490 San Vicente St, La Quinta CA 92253, USA

**Hardy, James J (J J)** — Baseball Player
5070 S Roosevelt St, Tempe AZ 85282, USA

**Hardy, Jessica A** — Swimmer
218 Rivo Alto Canal, Long Beach CA 90803, USA

**Hardy, Kevin L** — Football Player
1228 Windsor Harbor Dr, Jacksonville FL 32225, USA

**Hardy, Kevin T** — Football Player
298 Paraiso Dr, Danville CA 94526, USA

**Hardy, Robert** — Actor
Chatto & Linnit, 123A King's Road, London SW3 4PL, England

**Hardy, Robert B (Bob)** — Bassist (Franz Ferdinand)
M A M A Group, 57-65 Worship Ave, London EC2A 2DU, England

**Hardy, Thomas A (Tom)** — Sculptor
1530 SW Harrison, #203, Portland OR 97201, USA

**Hardy, Tom** — Actor
United Agents, 12-26 Lexington St, London W1F 0LE, England

**Hardy, Willis (Bill)** — WW II Navy Air Force Hero
26523 Called Lorenzo, San Juan Capistrano CA 92675, USA

**Hare, David** — Writer, Director
Casorotto Ramsay, Waverley House, 7-12 Noel St, London W1F 8GQ, England
**Haren, Daniel J (Dan)** — Baseball Player
7724 E Santa Catalina Dr, Scottsdale AZ 85255, USA
**Harewood, David** — Actor
A P A Talent & Literary Agency, 405 S Beverly Dr, #300, Beverly Hills CA 90212 USA
**Harewood, Dorian** — Actor
S M S Talent, 8383 Wilshire Blvd, #230, Beverly Hills CA 90211 USA
**Hargan, Steven L (Steve)** — Baseball Player
2502 E Morongo Trail, Palm Springs CA 92264, USA
**Harge, Ira L** — Basketball Player
328 Yucca Dr NW, Albuquerque NM 87105, USA
**Hargett, Edward E (Edd)** — Football Player
379 County Road 222, Nacogdoches TX 75965, USA
**Hargis, V Burns** — Educator
Oklahoma State University, President's Office, Stillwater OK 74078, USA
**Hargitay, Mariska** — Actress
Creative Artists Agency, 2000 Ave of Stars, #100, Los Angeles CA 90067 USA
**Hargreaves, Brad** — Drummer (Third Eye Blind)
Eric Godtland Mgmt, 1040 Mariposa St, #200, San Francisco CA 94107, USA
**Hargrove, Brian** — Director
Broder Webb Chervin Silbermann, 9242 Beverly Blvd, Beverly Hills CA 90210 USA
**Hargrove, D Michael (Mike)** — Baseball Player, Manager
3925 Ramblewood Dr, Richfield OH 44286, USA
**Harikkala, Timothy A (Tim)** — Baseball Player
W6132 Everglade Road, Greenville WI 54942, USA
**Haring, Robert W** — Editor
Tulsa World, Editorial Dept, 315 S Boulder Ave, Tulsa OK 74103, USA
**Harington, Kit** — Actor
Creative Artists Agency, 2000 Ave of Stars, #100, Los Angeles CA 90067 USA
**Hariri, Ayman R** — Businessman
Saudi Oger, PO Box 1449, Riyadh 11431, Saudi Arabia
**Hariri, Gisue** — Architect
Hariri & Hariri, 39 W 29th St, #1200, New York NY 10001, USA
**Hariri, Mojgan** — Architect
Hariri & Hariri, 39 W 29th St, #1200, New York NY 10001, USA
**Harker, Patrick T** — Educator
University of Delaware, President's Office, Newark DE 19716, USA
**Harker, Susannah** — Actress
55 Ashburnham Grove, Greenwich, London SW10 8UL, England
**Harket, Morten** — Singer (A-Ha)
Agency Group Ltd, 361-373 City Road, London EC1V 1PQ, England
**Harkey, Michael A (Mike)** — Baseball Player
2344 Eaglewood Dr, Chino Hills CA 91709, USA
**Harkleroad, Ashley** — Tennis Player, Model
Women's Tennis Assn, 1 Progress Plaza, #1500, Saint Petersburg FL 33701 USA
**Harkness, Jerald B (Jerry)** — Basketball Player
8340 Misty Dr, Indianapolis IN 46236, USA
**Harlan, Jack R** — Plant Geneticist
University of Illinois, Agronomy Dept, Urbana IL 61801, USA
**Harlan, Kevin** — Sportscaster
CBS-TV, Sports Dept, 51 W 52nd St, New York NY 10019 USA
**Harley, Carol** — Singer, Guitarist (Misty River)
1111B NW 131st Way, Vancouver WA 98685, USA
**Harley, Steve** — Singer (Steve Harley & Cockney Rebel)
Work Hard, 19D Pinfold Road, London SW16 2SL, England
**Harlin, Renny** — Director, Producer
Midnight Sun Pictures, 10960 Wilshire Blvd, #700, Los Angeles CA 90024, USA
**Harlock, David A** — Ice Hockey Player
3234 Chamberlain Circle, Ann Arbor MI 48103, USA
**Harlow, Bill** — Writer
Charles Scribner's Sons, 866 3rd Ave, New York NY 10022 USA
**Harlow, Larry D** — Baseball Player
26348 W Burnett Road, Buckeye AZ 85396, USA
**Harlow, Patrick C (Pat)** — Football Player
230 W Avenida San Antonio, San Clemente CA 92672, USA
**Harlow, Shalom** — Model, Actress
United Talent Agency, U T A Plaza, 9336 Civic Center Dr, Beverly Hills CA 90210 USA
**Harman, Brian** — Golfer
Professional Golfers Association, 100 Ave of Champions, Palm Beach Gardens FL 33418 USA
**Harman, Denham** — Biochemist
6804 Creekside Lane, Plano TX 75023, USA
**Harman, Jennifer** — Poker Player
Prince Marketing Group, 18 Carillon Circle, Livingston NJ 07039 USA
**Harman, Katie** — Beauty Queen, Singer
3631 NW 1st Court, Gresham OR 97030, USA
**Harmel, Pierre C J M** — Prime Minister, Belgium
8 Ave de l'Horizon, 1150 Brussels, Belgium
**Harmer, Nicholas (Nick)** — Bassist (Death Cab for Cutie)
Zeitgeist Artist Mgmt, 660 York St, #216, San Francisco CA 94110, USA
**Harmer, Sarah** — Singer, Songwriter
Agency Group Ltd, 2 Berkeley St, #202, Toronto ON M5A 4J5, Canada
**Harmon, Amy** — Journalist
New York Times, Editorial Dept, 229 W 43rd St, New York NY 10036 USA
**Harmon, Andrew P (Andy)** — Football Player
1258 Waters Edge Dr, Dayton OH 45458, USA
**Harmon, Angie** — Actress, Model
John Carrabino Mgmt, 5900 Wilshire Blvd, #406, Los Angeles CA 90036 USA
**Harmon, Charles B (Chuck)** — Baseball Player
6035 Ridgeacres Dr, #A, Cincinnati OH 45237, USA
**Harmon, Clarence, Jr** — Football Player
PO Box 571, Verona MS 38879, USA
**Harmon, Curtis** — Drummer (Pieces of a Dream)
23309 Commerce Park Road, Cleveland OH 44122, USA
**Harmon, Dan** — Producer, Writer, Actor
United Talent Agency, U T A Plaza, 9336 Civic Center Dr, Beverly Hills CA 90210 USA

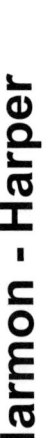

**Harmon - Harper**

| | |
|---|---|
| **Harmon, Joy** | Actress |
| 9901 Poole Ave, Sunland CA 91040, USA | |
| **Harmon, Mark** | Actor |
| Wings Inc, 2236 Encinitas Blvd, #A, Encinitas CA 92024, USA | |
| **Harmon, Noah** | Bassist (Airborne Toxic Event) |
| Island Def Jam Records, 8920 W Sunset Blvd, #200, West Hollywood CA 90069 USA | |
| **Harmon, Robert** | Director |
| Paradigm Agency, 360 N Crescent Dr, North Building, Beverly Hills CA 90210 USA | |
| **Harmon, Ronnie K** | Football Player |
| 13022 218th St, Springfield Gardens NY 11413, USA | |
| **Harmotta, Christa D** | Volleyball Player |
| Universal Volley Modena, Viale dello Sport 25, 41122 Modena, Italy | |
| **Harms, Alfred G, Jr** | Navy Admiral |
| Commander, Education & Training Command, Naval Air Station, Pensacola FL 32508 USA | |
| **Harms, Joni** | Singer, Songwriter |
| PO Box 272, Canby OR 97013, USA | |
| **Harner, Jason Butler** | Actor |
| I C M Partners, 10250 Constellation Blvd, #900, Los Angeles CA 90067 USA | |
| **Harner, Levi** | Harness Racing Driver |
| RR 1, Millville PA 17846, USA | |
| **Harney, Corinna** | Model, Actress |
| Playboy Promotions, 9346 Civic Center Dr, #200, Beverly Hills CA 90210 USA | |
| **Harnick, Sheldon M** | Writer, Lyricist |
| Deutsch Deutsch & Blasband, 800 3rd Ave, New York NY 10022, USA | |
| **Harnisch, Peter T (Pete)** | Baseball Player |
| 35 Brentwood Dr S, Colts Neck NJ 07722, USA | |
| **Harnois, Elisabeth R** | Actress |
| Schachter Entertainment, 1157 S Beverly Dr, #200, Los Angeles CA 90035 USA | |
| **Harnois, Marlene** | Taekwondo Athlete |
| INSEP, 11 Ave du Tremblay, 75012 Paris, France | |
| **Harnoncourt, Nikolaus** | Conductor |
| 38 Piaristangasse, 1080 Vienna, Austria | |
| **Harnoy, Ofra** | Concert Cellist |
| 437 Spadina Road, PO Box 23046, Toronto ON M5P 2W0, Canada | |
| **Haro, Melissa** | Model, Actress |
| Elite Model Mgmt, 119 Washington Ave, #501, Miami Beach FL 33139, USA | |
| **Harold, Erika N L** | Beauty Queen |
| 115 E Holmes St, Urbana IL 61801, USA | |
| **Harold, Gale** | Actor |
| Gersh Agency, 9465 Wilshire Blvd, #600, Beverly Hills CA 90212 USA | |
| **Harouche, Serge** | Nobel Physics Laureate |
| College de France, 11 Place Marcelin Berthelot, 75231 Paris Cedex 05, France | |
| **Harout, Magda** | Actress |
| 13452 Vose St, Van Nuys CA 91405, USA | |
| **Harp, Everette** | Jazz Saxophonist |
| Universal Attractions, 135 W 26th St, #1200, New York NY 10001 USA | |
| **Harper, Alvin C** | Football Player |
| 501 Harry S Truman Dr, #109, Upper Marlboro MD 20774, USA | |
| **Harper, Ben** | Singer, Guitarist, Songwriter |
| Red Light Mgmt, 44 Wall St, #2200, New York NY 10005, USA | |
| **Harper, Billy** | Jazz Saxophonist |
| Joel Chriss Co, 300 Mercer St, #3J, New York NY 10003 USA | |
| **Harper, Bob** | Physical Fitness Instructor, Actor |
| Entertainment Fusion Group, 8899 Beverly Blvd, #412, West Hollywood CA 90046, USA | |
| **Harper, Brian D** | Baseball Player |
| 8319 E Shetland Trail, Scottsdale AZ 85258, USA | |
| **Harper, Bruce S** | Football Player |
| 311 Lindbergh Ave, Closter NJ 07624, USA | |
| **Harper, Bryce A M** | Baseball Player |
| Washington Nationals, 1500 S Capitol St SE, Washington DC 20003 USA | |
| **Harper, Charles L (Charlie)** | Football Player |
| 2115 Augusta, McKinney TX 75070, USA | |
| **Harper, Charles M** | Businessman |
| 6625 State St, Omaha NE 68152, USA | |
| **Harper, Dawn** | Track Athlete |
| USA Track & Field, RCA Dome, PO Box 140, Indianapolis IN 46225 USA | |
| **Harper, Derek R** | Basketball Player |
| 5665 Arapaho Road, #1223, Dallas TX 75248, USA | |
| **Harper, Deveron A** | Football Player |
| 2749 Huntsville St, Kenner LA 70062, USA | |
| **Harper, Donald D W (Don)** | Diver |
| 1765 Lynnhaven Dr, Columbus OH 43221, USA | |
| **Harper, Dwayne A** | Football Player |
| 104 Cue St, Orangeburg SC 29115, USA | |
| **Harper, Heather M** | Opera Singer |
| Royal Academy of Music/Drama, 100 Renfrew St, Glasgow G2 3DB, England | |
| **Harper, Helen** | Actress |
| Gavin Barker Assoc, 2D Wimpole St, London W1G 0EB, England | |
| **Harper, Hill** | Actor |
| Innovative Artists, 1505 10th St, Santa Monica CA 90401 USA | |
| **Harper, Jessica** | Actress, Singer |
| 2337 Roscomare Road, #2-244, Los Angeles CA 90077, USA | |
| **Harper, Judson M** | Chemical Engineer |
| 1818 Westview Road, Fort Collins CO 80524, USA | |
| **Harper, Mark** | Football Player |
| 2162 Albany Ave, Memphis TN 38108, USA | |
| **Harper, Michael S** | Writer |
| Brown University, English Dept, Providence RI 02912, USA | |
| **Harper, Roland** | Football Player |
| 207 Grandview Court, Algonquin IL 60102, USA | |
| **Harper, Ron** | Actor |
| 13317 Ventura Blvd, #1, Sherman Oaks CA 91423, USA | |
| **Harper, Ronald (Ron)** | Basketball Player |
| 8934 Brecksville Road, #417, Brecksville OH 44141, USA | |
| **Harper, Stephen J** | Prime Minister, Canada |
| Prime Minister's Office, Langevin Block, Ottawa ON K1A 0A1, Canada | |

**Harper, Terry J** — Baseball Player
4225 Jailette Road, Atlanta GA 30349, USA

**Harper, Tess** — Actress
Bauman Redanty Shaul Agency, 5757 Wilshire Blvd, #473, Los Angeles CA 90036 USA

**Harper, Thomas (Tommy)** — Baseball Player
5 Cow Hill Road, Sharon MA 02067, USA

**Harper, Tom** — Actor
Artists Partnership, 101 Finsbury Pavement, London EC2A 1RS, England

**Harper, Travis B** — Baseball Player
3222 Whitings Neck Road, Martinsburg WV 25404, USA

**Harper, Valerie** — Actress
David Shapira Assoc, 193 N Robertson Blvd, Beverly Hills CA 90211 USA

**Harpring, Matthew H (Matt)** — Basketball Player
4550 Stella Dr NW, Atlanta GA 30327, USA

**Harrah, Colbert D (Toby)** — Baseball Player, Manager
316 Leewood Circle, Azle TX 76020, USA

**Harrah, Dennis W** — Football Player
925 Rockin One Way, Paso Robles CA 93446, USA

**Harrell, Lynn M** — Concert Cellist, Conductor
Opus 3 Artists, 470 Park Ave S, #900N, New York NY 10016 USA

**Harrell, Maestro** — Actor
C E S D, 10635 Santa Monica Blvd, #130, Los Angeles CA 90025 USA

**Harrell, Willard R** — Football Player
8 Scarlet Oak Court, Lake Saint Louis MO 63367, USA

**Harrelson, Derrell M (Bud)** — Baseball Player, Manager
357 Ridgefield Road, Hauppauge NY 11788, USA

**Harrelson, Kenneth S (Ken)** — Baseball Player
90006 Shawn Park Place, Orlando FL 32819, USA

**Harrelson, Woody** — Actor
Creative Artists Agency, 2000 Ave of Stars, #100, Los Angeles CA 90067 USA

**Harries, Kathryn** — Opera Singer
Ingpen & Williams, 131 Putney Bridge Road, London SW15 2PA, England

**Harrigan, Lori** — Softball Player
828 Rainbow Rock St, Las Vegas NV 89123, USA

**Harring, Laura E** — Actress, Beauty Queen
Brillstein Entertainment Partners, 9150 Wilshire Blvd, #350, Beverly Hills CA 90212 USA

**Harring, Laura E** — Actress, Beauty Queen
Amsel Eisenstadt Frazier, 5055 Wilshire Blvd, #865, Los Angeles CA 90036 USA

**Harrington, Albert F (Al)** — Basketball Player
16124 Chancellors Ridge Way, Noblesville IN 46062, USA

**Harrington, Dan** — Poker Player, Writer
Poker Gives, Nevada Community Foundation, 1635 Village Center Circle, #160, Las Vegas NV 89134, USA

**Harrington, Desmond** — Actor
Untitled Entertainment, 350 S Beverly Dr, #200, Beverly Hills CA 90212 USA

**Harrington, Donald J** — Educator
Saint John's University, President's Office, 8000 Utopia Parkway, Queens NY 11439, USA

**Harrington, Jay** — Actor
A Mgmt, 12001 Ventura Place, #340, Studio City CA 91604 USA

**Harrington, John** — Ice Hockey Player, Coach
8138 Golden Valley Road, Minneapolis MN 55427, USA

**Harrington, Laura** — Actress
Creative Artists Agency, 2000 Ave of Stars, #100, Los Angeles CA 90067 USA

**Harrington, Othella F** — Basketball Player
1602 Rika Point, Houston TX 77077, USA

**Harrington, Padraig** — Golfer
International Mgmt Group, Pier House, Strand on the Green, London W4 3NN, England

**Harrington, Pat** — Actor
730 Marzella Ave, Los Angeles CA 90049, USA

**Harrington, Pat, Jr** — Actor
C E S D, 10635 Santa Monica Blvd, #130, Los Angeles CA 90025 USA

**Harrington, Perry D** — Football Player
1302 Roxbury Court, Jackson MS 39211, USA

**Harris, Alfred C (Al)** — Football Player
12 Stone Ridge Dr, South Barrington IL 60010, USA

**Harris, Barbara C** — Religious Leader, Social Activist
Episcopal Diocese of Massachusetts, 138 Tremont St, Boston MA 02111, USA

**Harris, Barry** — Jazz Pianist
Thomas Cassidy, PO Box 1311, Tucson AZ 85702 USA

**Harris, Bernard A, Jr** — Astronaut
1330 Post Oak Blvd, #2550, Houston TX 77056, USA

**Harris, Brendon M** — Baseball Player
30 Fox Hollow Lane, Queensbury NY 12804, USA

**Harris, Callard** — Actor
United Talent Agency, U T A Plaza, 9336 Civic Center Dr, Beverly Hills CA 90210 USA

**Harris, Carter** — Producer, Director, Writer
W M E Entertainment, 9601 Wilshire Blvd, #300, Beverly Hills CA 90210 USA

**Harris, Charlaine** — Writer
PO Box 354, Magnolia AR 71754, USA

**Harris, Clifford A (Cliff)** — Football Player
722 Kentwood Dr, Rockwall TX 75032, USA

**Harris, Corey** — Guitarist
Blue Mountain Artists, 810 Tyvola Road, #114, Charlotte NC 28217, USA

**Harris, Corey L** — Football Player
933 N Tremont St, Indianapolis IN 46222, USA

**Harris, Cynthia** — Actress
Paradigm Agency, 360 N Crescent Dr, North Building, Beverly Hills CA 90210 USA

**Harris, Damian** — Director
I C M Partners, 10250 Constellation Blvd, #900, Los Angeles CA 90067 USA

**Harris, Daniel P (Dan)** — Director, Writer
Chasen Agency, 8899 Beverly Blvd, #405, Los Angeles CA 90048 USA

**Harris, Danielle** — Actress
Advanced Mgmt, 7805 Sunset Blvd, #201, Los Angeles CA 90046, USA

**Harris, Delmar (Del)** — Basketball Coach
1229 Ducks Landing, Frisco TX 75034, USA

**Harris, Devin** — Basketball Player
4875 Gramercy Oaks Dr, #253, Dallas TX 75287, USA

**Harris, Duriel L, Jr** — Football Player
3875 San Pablo Road S, #1212, Jacksonville FL 32224, USA

**Harris, Ed** — Actor
Special Artists Agency, 9200 Sunset Blvd, #410, West Hollywood CA 90069 USA

**Harris, Emmylou** — Singer, Songwriter
Vector Mgmt, PO Box 120479, Nashville TN 37212 USA

**Harris, Estelle** — Actress
Danis Panaro Nist, 9201 W Olympic Blvd, Beverly Hills CA 90212, USA

**Harris, Franco** — Football Player
200 Chaucer Court S, Sewickley PA 15143, USA

**Harris, Gail** — Actress
Don Gerler, 3349 Cahuenga Blvd W, #1, Los Angeles CA 90068 USA

**Harris, Greg A** — Baseball Player
10262 Mardel Dr, Cypress CA 90630, USA

**Harris, Gregory W (Greg)** — Baseball Player
6708 Green Hollow Court, Wake Forest NC 27587, USA

**Harris, Harry B, Jr** — Navy Admiral
Commander, U S Pacific Fleet, 250 Makalapa Drive, Pearl Harbor HI 96860, USA

**Harris, Henry** — Cell Biologist
William Dunn Pathology School, South Parks Road, Oxford OX1 3RE, England

**Harris, Hollis L** — Businessman
608 Wingspread, Peachtree City GA 30269, USA

**Harris, Hugh** — Ice Hockey Player
150 Sycamore Dr, Carmel IN 46033, USA

**Harris, Jackie B** — Football Player
7905 Haydenberry Court, Nashville TN 37221, USA

**Harris, James L** — Football Player
9838 Old Baymeadows Road, Jacksonville FL 32256, USA

**Harris, Jamie** — Actor
Innovative Artists, 1505 10th St, Santa Monica CA 90401 USA

**Harris, Jared** — Actor
Paradigm Agency, 360 N Crescent Dr, North Building, Beverly Hills CA 90210 USA

**Harris, Jay** — Cartoonist (Better Half)
King Features Syndicate, 300 W 57th St, #1500, New York NY 10019 USA

**Harris, Joanne** — Writer
Knopf Publishers, 1745 Broadway, New York NY 10019 USA

**Harris, Joe Frank** — Governor, GA
712 West Ave, Cartersville GA 30120, USA

**Harris, Joe M** — Basketball Player
Cleveland Cavaliers, Gund Arena, 1 Center Court, Cleveland OH 44115 USA

**Harris, John E** — Football Player
270 NW 120th St, Miami FL 33168, USA

**Harris, John R** — Golfer
4316 Fremont Ave S, Minneapolis MN 55409, USA

**Harris, John R** — Architect
24 Devonshire Place, London W1N 2BX, England

**Harris, Joseph A (Joe)** — Football Player
4747 River Road, Ellenwood GA 30294, USA

**Harris, Joshua** — Actor
TalentWorks, 3500 W Olive Ave, #1400, Burbank CA 91505 USA

**Harris, Lara** — Actress
Arlook Group, 205 S Beverly Dr, #209, Beverly Hills CA 90212, USA

**Harris, Lee** — Dance Executive
Pilobolus Dance Theater, PO Box 388, Washington Depot CT 06794, USA

**Harris, Leon** — Commentator
CNN-TV, News Dept, 190 Marietta Ave SW, Atlanta GA 30303 USA

**Harris, Leonard A (Lenny)** — Baseball Player
7435 N Augusta Dr, Hialeah FL 33015, USA

**Harris, Leroy** — Football Player
1919 Live Oak St, Savannah GA 31404, USA

**Harris, Leroy, Jr** — Football Player
890 Arlington Heights Dr, Brentwood TN 37027, USA

**Harris, Louis** — Statistician
200 E 66th St, #2004, New York NY 10065, USA

**Harris, Lucious H** — Basketball Player
1149 W 62nd St, Los Angeles CA 90044, USA

**Harris, Mark Jonathan** — Director
Principato-Young, 9465 Wilshire Blvd, #880, Beverly Hills CA 90212 USA

**Harris, Mark Yale** — Sculptor
Artwork, 170 Lena St, #A, Santa Fe NM 87505, USA

**Harris, Mel** — Actress
Abrams Artists, 9200 W Sunset Blvd, #1125, West Hollywood CA 90069 USA

**Harris, Michael L (M L)** — Football Player
M L Harris Outreach, 15589 Apple Valley Road, Apple Valley CA 92307, USA

**Harris, Mike** — Curling Athlete
Curling Association, 1660 Vimont Court, Cumberland ON K4A 4J4, Canada

**Harris, Naomie M** — Actress
United Talent Agency, U T A Plaza, 9336 Civic Center Dr, Beverly Hills CA 90210 USA

**Harris, Napoleon B** — Football Player
Napoleon Harris Foundation, 15774 S LaGrange Road, #214, Orland Park IL 60462, USA

**Harris, Neil** — Historian
5555 S Everett Ave, Chicago IL 60637, USA

**Harris, Neil Patrick** — Actor
Creative Artists Agency, 2000 Ave of Stars, #100, Los Angeles CA 90067 USA

**Harris, Nicholas J (Nick)** — Football Player
2035 Kingsway Dr, Troy MI 48098, USA

**Harris, Paul** — Sculptor
200 Ocean Parkway, Bolinas CA 94924, USA

**Harris, Quentin H** — Football Player
3013 W Glass Lane, Phoenix AZ 85041, USA

**Harris, Rachael E** — Actress, Comedienne
A K A Talent, 6310 San Vicente Blvd, #200, Los Angeles CA 90048 USA

**Harris, Raymont L** — Football Player
1144 Aroya Court, New Albany OH 43054, USA

**Harris, Reginald A (Reggie)** — Baseball Player
133 Paige St, Waynesboro VA 22980, USA

| | |
|---|---|
| **Harris, Richard**<br>Paramount Entertainment, PO Box 12, Far Hills NJ 07931 USA | Singer (Jive Five) |
| **Harris, Rickie C**<br>613 Q St NW, Washington DC 20001, USA | Football Player |
| **Harris, Robert D**<br>Inkwell Mgmt, 521 5th Ave, New York NY 10175, USA | Writer |
| **Harris, Robert L**<br>2711 13th St SW, Lehigh Acres FL 33976, USA | Football Player |
| **Harris, Rolf**<br>Billy Marsh, 76A Grove End Road, Saint John's Wood, London NW8 9ND, England | Actor |
| **Harris, Rosemary**<br>Independent Talent Group, 40 Whitfield St, London W1T 2RH, England | Actress |
| **Harris, Sam**<br>Bauman Redanty Shaul Agency, 5757 Wilshire Blvd, #473, Los Angeles CA 90036 USA | Singer, Actor |
| **Harris, Samantha**<br>E! Network, 5750 Wilshire Blvd, Los Angeles CA 90036, USA | Actress, Model |
| **Harris, Sean**<br>Troika, 74 Clerkenwell Road, #300, London EC1M 5QA, England | Actor |
| **Harris, Sidney**<br>302 W 86th St, #9A, New York NY 10024, USA | Cartoonist |
| **Harris, Stefon**<br>Unlimited Myles, 6 Imaginary Place, Aberdeen NJ 07747, USA | Jazz Vibraphone Player |
| **Harris, Stephen E**<br>Stanford University, Ginzton Laboratory, 450 Via Palou, Stanford CA 94305, USA | Electrical Engineer, Physicist |
| **Harris, Steve**<br>Sanctuary Music Mgmt, 82 Bishop's Bridge Road, London W2 6BB, England | Bassist (Iron Maiden) |
| **Harris, Steve**<br>Brillstein Entertainment Partners, 9150 Wilshire Blvd, #350, Beverly Hills CA 90212 USA | Actor |
| **Harris, Steven D (Steve)**<br>3005 W Fort Worth St, Broken Arrow OK 74012, USA | Basketball Player |
| **Harris, T Eugene (Gene)**<br>1267 NE 16th Ave, Okeechobee FL 34972, USA | Baseball Player |
| **Harris, Ted**<br>1 Stonegate Court, Blackwood NJ 08012, USA | Ice Hockey Player |
| **Harris, Thomas**<br>Creative Artists Agency, 2000 Ave of Stars, #100, Los Angeles CA 90067 USA | Writer |
| **Harris, Timothy D (Tim)**<br>843 N N St, Livermore CA 94551, USA | Football Player |
| **Harris, Tommie, Jr**<br>San Diego Chargers, 4020 Murphy Canyon Road, San Diego CA 92123 USA | Football Player |
| **Harris, Victor L (Vic)**<br>5420 S Garth Ave, Los Angeles CA 90056, USA | Baseball Player |
| **Harris, Walt**<br>Akron University, Athletic Dept, Akron OH 44325, USA | Football Coach |
| **Harris, Walter F (Buddy)**<br>2305 Carol Lane, Norristown PA 19401, USA | Baseball Player |
| **Harris, Walter L (Walt)**<br>4103 Shinault Lane, Olive Branch MS 38654, USA | Football Player |
| **Harris, William C (Willie)**<br>1176 Willie C Harris Dr, Cairo GA 39828, USA | Baseball Player |
| **Harris, William E (Billy)**<br>Muskoka Candle Co, PO Box 233, Rosseau ON P0C 1J0, Canada | Ice Hockey Player |
| **Harris, Wood**<br>Gersh Agency, 9465 Wilshire Blvd, #600, Beverly Hills CA 90212 USA | Actor |
| **Harrison Breetzke, Joan**<br>16 Clevedon Road, East London 5201, South Africa | Swimmer |
| **Harrison, Alvin**<br>Octagon Worldwide, 800 Connecticut Ave, #200, Norwalk CT 06854 USA | Track Athlete |
| **Harrison, Audley**<br>Thell Torrence, 5449 S Eastern Ave, #3, Las Vegas NV 89119, USA | Boxer |
| **Harrison, Bret**<br>United Talent Agency, U T A Plaza, 9336 Civic Center Dr, Beverly Hills CA 90210 USA | Actor |
| **Harrison, C Richard**<br>Parametric Technology, 140 Kendrick St, #C120, Needham Heights MA 02494, USA | Businessman |
| **Harrison, Charles (Tex)**<br>Harlem Globetrotters, 400 E Van Buren St, #300, Phoenix AZ 85004, USA | Basketball Player, Coach |
| **Harrison, Charles W (Chuck)**<br>222 Buckskin Road, Abilene TX 79602, USA | Baseball Player |
| **Harrison, Christopher (Chris)**<br>Allure Model & Talent, 5556 S Centinela Ave, Los Angeles CA 90066, USA | Actor |
| **Harrison, Claudia**<br>Markham Froggatt Irwin, Julian House, 4 Windmill St, London W1P 1HF, England | Actress |
| **Harrison, Colin**<br>Farrar Straus Giroux, 18 W 18th St, #700, New York NY 10011 USA | Writer |
| **Harrison, Dennis**<br>1048 Hickory Hollow Road, Nashville TN 37221, USA | Football Player |
| **Harrison, Donald (Duck)**<br>Carolyn McClair, PO Box 55, Radio City Station, New York NY 10101, USA | Jazz Saxophonist |
| **Harrison, Dwight W**<br>5550 Harvest Hill Road, #W118, Dallas TX 75230, USA | Football Player |
| **Harrison, Fiona**<br>California Institute of Technology, Physics Dept, Pasadena CA 91125, USA | Physicist |
| **Harrison, Gregory**<br>Himber Entertainment, PO Box 950, South Orange NJ 07079 USA | Actor |
| **Harrison, James D (Jim)**<br>102-645 Barrera Road, Kelowna BC V1W 3C9, Canada | Ice Hockey Player |
| **Harrison, James, Jr**<br>2525 Matterhorn Dr, Wexford PA 15090, USA | Football Player |
| **Harrison, Jenilee**<br>J Lee Corp, 19528 Ventura Blvd, #365, Tarzana CA 91356, USA | Actress |
| **Harrison, Jim**<br>Grove Press, 841 Broadway, New York NY 10003 USA | Writer |
| **Harrison, Kathryn**<br>Random House, 1745 Broadway, #1800, New York NY 10019 USA | Writer |
| **Harrison, Kayla**<br>9 Summer St, Wakefield MA 01880, USA | Judo Athlete |

**Harrison, Linda** — Actress
10370 Ashton Ave, Los Angeles CA 90024, USA

**Harrison, Marvin D** — Football Player
928 Morgan Road, Jenkintown PA 19046, USA

**Harrison, Matthew** — Director
Trisko Talent Management, 209 Carrall St, #240, Vancouver, BC V6B 2J2, Canada

**Harrison, Michael Allen** — Pianist, Composer
M A H Records, 828 NE Prescott St, Portland OR 97211, USA

**Harrison, Nolan** — Football Player
19964 Interlachen Circle, Ashburn VA 20147, USA

**Harrison, Paul D** — Ice Hockey Player
5-215 Royale St, Timmins ON P4N 8S7, Canada

**Harrison, Randy** — Actor
Paradigm Agency, 360 N Crescent Dr, North Building, Beverly Hills CA 90210 USA

**Harrison, Robert L (Bob)** — Baseball Player
1104 N Meridian St, Lebanon IN 46052, USA

**Harrison, Robert L (Bob), Jr** — Football Player
3 Westwind Circle, Stamford TX 79553, USA

**Harrison, Robert W (Bob)** — Basketball Player
Harbour Ridge, 13405 NW Wax Myrtle Trail, Palm City FL 34990, USA

**Harrison, Rodney** — Football Player, Sportscaster
24 Country Club Dr, Olympia Fields IL 60461, USA

**Harrison, Roric E** — Baseball Player
2932 Channing Way, Los Alamitos CA 90720, USA

**Harrison, Sabrina Ward** — Writer
Chronicle Books, 680 2nd St, San Francisco CA 94107 USA

**Harrison, Teri Marie** — Model, Actress
2973 Harbor Blvd, #350, Costa Mesa CA 92626, USA

**Harrison, Thomas J (Tom)** — Baseball Player
2932 Channing Way, Los Alamitos CA 90720, USA

**Harrison, Tony** — Writer
Gordon Dickinson, 2 Crescent Grove, London SW4 7AH, England

**Harrison, William B, Jr** — Financier
J P Morgan Chase Corp, 270 Park Ave, #1200, New York NY 10017, USA

**Harrison, William H** — Army General
7302 Amber Lane SW, Lakewood WA 98498, USA

**Harris-Stewart, Lusia M (Lucy)** — Basketball Player
1002 Cherry St, Greenwood MS 38930, USA

**Harrold, Kathryn** — Actress
9255 W Sunset Blvd, #901, West Hollywood CA 90069, USA

**Harron, Mary** — Director
Circle of Confusion, 315 S Beverly Dr, #201, Beverly Hills CA 90212, USA

**Harrower, Kristi** — Basketball Player
Bendigo Spirit, PO Box 282, Eaglehawk VIC 3556, Australia

**Harrowyn, Danni** — Drummer (Civet)
The Kirby Organization, 9200 Sunset Blvd, #600, Los Angeles CA 90069, USA

**Harry** — Prince, England
Clarence House, Stable Yard Gate, London SW1A 1BA, England

**Harry, Deborah A (Debbie)** — Singer, Songwriter, Actress
Tavistock Wood Mgmt, 45 Conduit St, London W1S 2YN, England

**Harry, Emile M** — Football Player
34 Villa Vista Dr, Brownsville TX 78520, USA

**Harsch, Eddie** — Keyboardist (Black Crowes)
Mitch Schneider Organization, 14724 Ventura Blvd, #500, Sherman Oaks CA 91403 USA

**Harshman, John E (Jack)** — Baseball Player
1010 Baywood Circle, #E, Chula Vista CA 91915, USA

**Harshman, Margo** — Actress
A P A Talent & Literary Agency, 405 S Beverly Dr, #300, Beverly Hills CA 90212 USA

**Hart, Ann Weaver** — Educator
Temple University, President's Office, 1801 N Broad St, Philadelphia PA 19122, USA

**Hart, Beth** — Singer, Songwriter
W M E Entertainment, 1600 Division St, #300, Nashville TN 37203 USA

**Hart, Bob** — Bowler
5740 Laurel Oak Dr, Suwanee GA 30024, USA

**Hart, Bobby** — Singer, Composer
1422 LaMar Ave, #613, Memphis TN 38104, USA

**Hart, Bodhi J (Bo)** — Baseball Player
1815 Portola Dr, #A, Santa Cruz CA 95062, USA

**Hart, Bret (Hitman)** — Professional Wrestler
435 Patina Place SW, Calgary AB T3H 2P5, Canada

**Hart, Carolyn G** — Writer
1705 Drakestone Ave, Nichols Hills OK 73120, USA

**Hart, Charles** — Lyricist
London Mgmt, 2-4 Noel St, London W1V 3RB, England

**Hart, Christopher** — Actor
203 Las Gallinas Ave, San Rafael CA 94903, USA

**Hart, Clinton G** — Football Player
2894 County Road 730, Webster FL 33597, USA

**Hart, Corey M** — Singer, Songwriter
PO Box 1100, Station A, Montreal QC H3C 2X6, Canada

**Hart, Dolores (Mother Dolores)** — Actress
Regina Laudis Abbey, 275 Flanders Road, Bethlehem CT 06751, USA

**Hart, Doris** — Tennis Player
600 Biltmore Way, #306, Coral Gables FL 33134, USA

**Hart, Douglas W (Doug)** — Football Player
2192 Medina Road, Long Lake MN 55356, USA

**Hart, Dru** — Model
Playboy Promotions, 9346 Civic Center Dr, #200, Beverly Hills CA 90210 USA

**Hart, Dudley** — Golfer
5130 Rockledge Dr, Clarence NY 14031, USA

**Hart, Emerson** — Singer, Guitarist (Tonic), Songwriter
Sanctuary Artist Mgmt, 54 Music Square E, #300, Nashville TN 37203, USA

**Hart, Freddie** — Singer, Songwriter, Guitarist
317 N Kenwood St, Burbank CA 91505, USA

**Hart, Gary W** — Senator, CO
730 17th St, #300, Denver CO 80202, USA

**Hart, Harold J** — Football Player
2004 E Caracas St, Tampa FL 33610, USA
**Hart, Ian** — Actor
A P A Talent & Literary Agency, 405 S Beverly Dr, #300, Beverly Hills CA 90212 USA
**Hart, J Corey** — Baseball Player
808 Oakwood Dr, Waukesha WI 53186, USA
**Hart, James V** — Writer, Director, Producer
Creative Artists Agency, 2000 Ave of Stars, #100, Los Angeles CA 90067 USA
**Hart, James W (Jim)** — Football Player, Sports Administrator
3141 Dominica Way, Naples FL 34119, USA
**Hart, Jason W** — Baseball Player
3202 S Westwood Ave, Springfield MO 65807, USA
**Hart, Jeff** — Golfer
105 Guanajuato Court, Solana Beach CA 92075, USA
**Hart, Jeffery A (Jeff)** — Football Player
1307 SE 14th Ave, Canby OR 97013, USA
**Hart, Jessica** — Model
Chadwick Models, 351 Elizabeth St, #400, Melbourne VIC 3000, Australia
**Hart, John R** — Commentator
I C M Partners, 730 5th Ave, New York NY 10019 USA
**Hart, Kevin** — Actor, Comedian, Producer
3 Arts Entertainment, 9460 Wilshire Blvd, #700, Beverly Hills CA 90212 USA
**Hart, Kevin** — Baseball Player
5605 Plantation Circle, Plano TX 75093, USA
**Hart, Mary** — Entertainer
Brokaw Co, 9255 W Sunset Blvd, #804, West Hollywood CA 90069 USA
**Hart, Melissa Joan** — Actress
Hartbreak Productions, 14622 Ventura Blvd, #102, Sherman Oaks CA 91403, USA
**Hart, Mickey** — Drummer (Grateful Dead)
Pinnacle Entertainment, 30 Glenn St, White Plains NY 10603, USA
**Hart, Parker T** — Diplomat
8904 Longstreet Dr, Manassas VA 20110, USA
**Hart, Roxanne** — Actress
Abrams Artists, 9200 W Sunset Blvd, #1125, West Hollywood CA 90069 USA
**Hart, Stanley R** — Geologist
PO Box 625, Green Valley AZ 85622, USA
**Hart, Terry J** — Astronaut
PO Box V, Hellertown PA 18055, USA
**Hart, Tommy L** — Football Player
3503 Highland Ave, Redwood City CA 94062, USA
**Harte, Houston H** — Publisher
Harte-Hanks Communications, 200 Concord Plaza Dr, San Antonio TX 78216, USA
**Hartenstein, Charles O (Chuck)** — Baseball Player
10735 Cassia Dr, Austin TX 78759, USA
**Hartenstine, Michael A (Mike)** — Football Player
322 Winchester Court, Lake Bluff IL 60044, USA
**Harting, Robert** — Track Athlete
S C Charlottenburg Berlin, Waldschulallee 34, 14055 Berlin, Germany
**Hartings, Jeffrey A (Jeff)** — Football Player
171 Manchester Circle, Pittsburgh PA 15237, USA
**Hartley, Bridgitte** — Canoeing Athlete
PO Box 102982, Meerensee, Richards Bay 3901, South Africa
**Hartley, Hal** — Director
True Fiction Pictures, 39 W 14th St, #406, New York NY 10011, USA
**Hartley, Harry J** — Educator
University of Connecticut, President's Office, Storrs CT 06269, USA
**Hartley, Justin S** — Actor, Director, Writer
Innovative Artists, 1505 10th St, Santa Monica CA 90401 USA
**Hartley, Mariette** — Actress
J Michael Bloom, 9255 W Sunset Blvd, #710, West Hollywood CA 90069 USA
**Hartley, Michael E (Mike)** — Baseball Player
9845 Quail Canyon Road, El Cajon CA 92021, USA
**Hartley, Robert (Bob)** — Ice Hockey Coach
2713 Bonar Hall Path, Duluth GA 30097, USA
**Hartline, Brian** — Football Player
Miami Dolphins, 7500 SW 30th St, Davie FL 33314 USA
**Hartman Black, Lisa** — Actress
Innovative Artists, 1505 10th St, Santa Monica CA 90401 USA
**Hartman, Arthur A** — Diplomat
A P C O Consulting Group, 1615 L St NW, Washington DC 20036, USA
**Hartman, David** — Actor, Commentator
3215 Stoneybrook Dr, Durham NC 27705, USA
**Hartman, Elmer E (Butch), IV** — Animator, Composer, Director
Gotham Group, 9255 Sunset Blvd, #515, Los Angeles CA 90069, USA
**Hartman, Geoffrey H** — Language Educator
200 Leeder Hill Dr, #2401, Hamden CT 6517, USA
**Hartman, George E** — Architect
1657 31st St, Washington DC 20007, USA
**Hartman, J C** — Baseball Player
3425 Rosedale St, Houston TX 77004, USA
**Hartman, Kevin** — Soccer Player
Sporting Kansas City, 210 W 19th Terrace, #200, Kansas City MO 64108 USA
**Hartman, William K (Bill)** — Astrophysicist
Planetary Science Institute, 1700 E Fort Lowell Road, #106, Tucson AZ 85719, USA
**Hartmanis, Juris** — Computer Scientist
43 Janivar Dr, Ithaca NY 14850, USA
**Hartman-Smith, Rhonda** — Auto Racing Driver
Hart Enterprises, 5611 Highway 81 N, Williamston SC 29697, USA
**Hartnell, Scott** — Ice Hockey Player
111 Church St, Philadelphia PA 19106, USA
**Hartner, Rona** — Actress
Artmedia, 20 Ave Rapp, 75007 Paris, France
**Hartnett, Josh** — Actor
Management 360, 9111 Wilshire Blvd, Beverly Hills CA 90210 USA
**Harts, Gregory R (Greg)** — Baseball Player
829 Humphries St SW, Atlanta GA 30310, USA

**Hartsburg, Craig W** — Ice Hockey Player, Coach
Columbus Blue Jackets, Arena, 200 W Nationwide Blvd, #1, Columbus OH 43215 USA

**Hartsock, Jeffrey R (Jeff)** — Baseball Player
1720 Swannanoa Dr, Greensboro NC 27410, USA

**Hartung, James** — Gymnast
6426 Tanglewood Lane, Lincoln NE 68516, USA

**Hartwell, Edgerton (Ed), II** — Football Player
3830 Galendo Dr, N Las Vegas NV 89032, USA

**Hartwell, Leland H (Lee)** — Nobel Medicine Laureate
Hutchinson Cancer Research Center, PO Box 19024, Seattle WA 98109, USA

**Hartwig, Justin J** — Football Player
2250 Mary St, #117, Pittsburgh PA 15203, USA

**Hartzell, Paul F** — Baseball Player
1 Hays Mews, London W1J 5PU, England

**Hartzog, William W (Bill)** — Army General
Burdeshaw Assoc, 9781 Blue Larkspur Lane, Monterey CA 93940, USA

**Haruf, Kent** — Writer
Southern Illinois University, English Dept, Carbondale IL 62901, USA

**Harutyunyan, Arayik** — Prime Minister, Nagorno-Karabakh
Premier's Office, Nagorno-Karabakh, Stepanarket, Nagornyi, Azerbaijan

**Harvey, Adam Paul** — Actor
Associated International Mgmt, 7 Hatton Garden, #400, London EC1N 8AD, England

**Harvey, Anthony** — Director
Arthur Greene, 101 Park Ave, #2607, New York NY 10178, USA

**Harvey, Antonio** — Basketball Player
5906 Yaupon Ave, Moss Point MS 39563, USA

**Harvey, Brian** — Photographer, Explorer
National Geographic, Editorial Dept, 1145 17th St NW, Washington DC 20036 USA

**Harvey, Bryan S** — Baseball Player
152 Windemere Isle Road, Statesville NC 28677, USA

**Harvey, Cynthia T** — Ballerina
American Ballet Theater, 890 Broadway, #300, New York NY 10003, USA

**Harvey, H Douglas (Doug)** — Baseball Umpire
32398 River Island Dr, Springville CA 93265, USA

**Harvey, Harry** — Harness Racing Driver, Trainer
34 Deep Hollow Lane N, Columbus NJ 08022, USA

**Harvey, James B (Jim), Jr** — Football Player
3685 Clarice Cove, Memphis TN 38133, USA

**Harvey, James Michael** — Religious Leader
Saint Paul Outside-the-Walls Basilica, 00120 Vatican City

**Harvey, John C, Jr** — Navy Admiral
Veterans Affairs & Homeland Security, 1111 East Broad St, #300, Richmond VA 23219, USA

**Harvey, Kenneth E (Ken)** — Baseball Player
5012 Grand Ave, #C, Kansas City MO 64112, USA

**Harvey, Kenneth R (Ken)** — Football Player
11600 Great Falls Way, Great Falls VA 22066, USA

**Harvey, Nancy** — Golfer
7006 E Jensen St, #62, Mesa AZ 85207, USA

**Harvey, Polly Jean (P J)** — Singer, Guitarist, Songwriter
Creative Artists Agency, 2000 Ave of Stars, #100, Los Angeles CA 90067 USA

**Harvey, Richard C** — Football Player
3414 Baltimore Ave, Pascagoula MS 39581, USA

**Harvey, Stephen P** — Archaeologist
University of Chicago, Oriental Institute, 1155 E 58th St, Chicago IL 60637, USA

**Harvey, Steve** — Actor, Comedian
W M E Entertainment, 9601 Wilshire Blvd, #300, Beverly Hills CA 90210 USA

**Harvick, Kerry** — Singer
L G B Media, 861 High Point Ridge Road, Franklin TN 37069, USA

**Harvick, Kevin M** — Auto Racing Driver
PO Box 938, Oak Ridge NC 27310, USA

**Harville, Chad A** — Baseball Player
261 Farmington Road, Savannah TN 38372, USA

**Harvin, W Percy, III** — Football Player
New York Jets, 1 Jets Dr, Florham Park NJ 07932 USA

**Harwell, Steve** — Singer (Smash Mouth)
Creative Artists Agency, 2000 Ave of Stars, #100, Los Angeles CA 90067 USA

**Harwood, Ronald** — Writer
Judy Daish Assoc, 2 Saint Charles Place, London W10 6EG, England

**Harzbecker, Astrid** — Singer, Songwriter
Postfach 1209, 83602 Holzkirchen, Germany

**Hase, Dagmar** — Swimmer
Niederndodeleber Str 14, 29110 Magdeburg, Germany

**Hasegawa, Shigetoshi** — Baseball Player
110 Newport Center Dr, #200, Newport Beach CA 92660, USA

**Haselkorn, Robert** — Virologist
5834 S Stony Island Ave, Chicago IL 60637, USA

**Haselman, William J (Bill)** — Baseball Player
14501 SE 85th St, Newcastle WA 98059, USA

**Haselrig, Carlton L** — Football Player, Wrestler
386 William Penn Ave, Johnstown PA 15901, USA

**Haseltine, Daniel P (Dan)** — Singer (Jars of Clay)
Nettwerk Mgmt, 1650 W 2nd Ave, Vancouver BC V6J 4R3, Canada

**Haseltine, William A** — Molecular Biologist
Human Genome Sciences, 14200 Shady Grove Road, Rockville MD 20850, USA

**Hasen, Irvin H** — Cartoonist (Goldbergs, Dondi)
68 E 79th St, #E, New York NY 10075, USA

**Hasenmayer, Donald I (Don)** — Baseball Player
721 Golf Dr, Warrington PA 18976, USA

**Hasina Wajed, Sheikh** — Prime Minister, Bangladesh
Sere-e Bangla Nagar, Gono, Bhaban, Sher-e-Banglanagar, Dhakar 1207, Bangladesh

**Haskins, Clem S** — Basketball Player, Coach
2632 Roberts Road, Campbellsville KY 42718, USA

**Haskins, Dennis** — Actor
Maverick Artists Agency, 1680 N Vine St, #802, Los Angeles CA 90028, USA

**Haslem, Udonis J** — Basketball Player
3489 Gulfstream Way, Davie FL 33328, USA

|  |  |
|---|---|
| **Haslett, James D (Jim)**<br>118 Crandon Dr, Saint Louis MO 63105, USA | Football Player, Coach |
| **Hass, Robert**<br>University of California, English Dept, Berkeley CA 94720, USA | Writer |
| **Hassan Ibn Talal**<br>Deputy King's Office, Royal Palace, Amman, Jordan | Crown Prince, Jordan |
| **Hassan, Fred**<br>Schering-Plough Corp, 2000 Galloping Hill Road, Kenilworth NJ 07033, USA | Businessman |
| **Hassan, Kamal**<br>63 Lutz Church Road, Chennai TN 600004, India | Actor, Director |
| **Hassan, Mohammed Waheed**<br>Presidential Palace, Orchid Magu, Male 20208, Maldives | President, Maldives |
| **Hassanal Bolkiah**<br>Istana Darul Hana, Bandar Seri Begawan, BA 1000 Brunei | Sultan, Brunei |
| **Hassel, Gerald L**<br>Bank of New York, 1 Wall St, #200, New York NY 10286, USA | Financier |
| **Hasselbeck, Donald W (Don)**<br>38 Noon Hill Ave, Norfolk VA 02056, USA | Football Player |
| **Hasselbeck, Mattthew M (Matt)**<br>9027 NE 1st St, Bellevue WA 98004, USA | Football Player |
| **Hasselbeck, Timothy T (Tim)**<br>38 Noon Hill Ave, Norfolk VA 02056, USA | Football Player, Sportscaster |
| **Hasselhoff, David**<br>Panacea Entertainment, 13587 Andalusia Dr E, Santa Rosa Valley CA 93012, USA | Actor, Singer, Producer |
| **Hasselmo, Nils**<br>Association of American Universities, 1200 New York Ave, #550, Washington DC 20005, USA | Educator |
| **Hassenfeld, Alan G**<br>Hasbro Inc, 1027 Newport Ave, Pawtucket RI 02861, USA | Businessman |
| **Hassett, Joseph P (Joey)**<br>28 Marigold Circle, Providence RI 02904, USA | Basketball Player |
| **Hassett, Marilyn**<br>8905 Rosewood Ave, West Hollywood CA 90048, USA | Actress |
| **Hassler, Andrew E (Andy)**<br>PO Box 15932, Phoenix AZ 85060, USA | Baseball Player |
| **Hassler, Thomas**<br>M T M Music & Publishing, Pariser Str 1, 81669 Munich, Germany | Soccer Player |
| **Hasson, Maddie**<br>Coast to Coast Talent, 3350 Barham Blvd, Los Angeles CA 90068 USA | Actress |
| **Hasson, Maurice**<br>18 West Heath Court, North End Road, London NW11, England | Concert Violinist |
| **Hastings, Andre O**<br>700 N Dobson Road, #17, Chandler AZ 85224, USA | Football Player |
| **Hastings, Barry G**<br>Northern Trust Corp, 50 S La Salle St, #1, Chicago IL 60603, USA | Financier |
| **Hastings, Don**<br>524 W 57th St, #5330, New York NY 10019, USA | Actor |
| **Hastings, Natasha M**<br>540 Vickers Lane, Locust Grove GA 30248, USA | Track Athlete |
| **Hastings, Reed**<br>Netflix Inc, 100 Winchester Circle, Los Gatos CA 95032, USA | Businessman |
| **Hastings, Scott A**<br>10210 Ridgegate Circle, Lone Tree CO 80124, USA | Basketball Player |
| **Hasty, James E**<br>8212 127th Ave SE, Newcastle WA 98056, USA | Football Player |
| **Hatch, Annia P**<br>1800 Sans Souci Blvd, #239, North Miami FL 33181, USA | Gymnast |
| **Hatch, Harold A**<br>8655 White Beach Way, Vienna VA 22182, USA | Marine Corps General |
| **Hatch, Henry J**<br>2715 Silkwood Court, Oakton VA 22124, USA | Army General |
| **Hatch, Monroe W, Jr**<br>8210 Thomas Ashleigh Lane, Clifton VA 20124, USA | Air Force General |
| **Hatch, Richard**<br>Omniquest Media, 1416 N La Brea Ave, Hollywood CA 90028, USA | Actor |
| **Hatchell, Sylvia**<br>University of North Carolina, Athletic Dept, Chapel Hill NC 27515, USA | Basketball Coach |
| **Hatcher, Derian**<br>567 Chews Landing Road, Haddonfield NJ 08033, USA | Ice Hockey Player |
| **Hatcher, Jason D**<br>Washington Redskins, 21300 Redskin Park Dr, Ashburn VA 20147 USA | Football Player |
| **Hatcher, Kevin J**<br>1225 S Water St, Marine City MI 48039, USA | Ice Hockey Player |
| **Hatcher, Michael V (Mickey)**<br>1179 N Williams Dr, Queen Valley AZ 85118, USA | Baseball Player |
| **Hatcher, R Dale**<br>906 White Plains Road, Gaffney SC 29340, USA | Football Player |
| **Hatcher, Teri**<br>United Talent Agency, U T A Plaza, 9336 Civic Center Dr, Beverly Hills CA 90210 USA | Actress |
| **Hatcher, William A (Billy)**<br>7079 Shawnee Run Road, Cincinnati OH 45243, USA | Baseball Player |
| **Hatchett, Joseph W**<br>9119 Shoal Creek Dr, Tallahassee FL 32312, USA | Judge |
| **Hatchette, Matthew (Matt)**<br>3222 Winding Pine Trail, Longwood FL 32779, USA | Football Player, Actor |
| **Hatfield, Juliana**<br>Ye Olde Records, PO Box 398110, Cambridge MA 02139, USA | Singer, Songwriter |
| **Hathaway, Amy**<br>Peter Strain, 5455 Wilshire Blvd, #1812, Los Angeles CA 90036 USA | Actress |
| **Hathaway, Anne**<br>Management 360, 9111 Wilshire Blvd, Beverly Hills CA 90210 USA | Actress |
| **Hathaway, Lalah**<br>Agency Group Ltd, 1880 Century Park E, #711, Los Angeles CA 90067 USA | Singer |
| **Hatori, Miho**<br>Billions Corp, 3522 W Armitage Ave, Chicago IL 60647, USA | Singer (Cibo Matto) |
| **Hatosy, Shawn**<br>Vox Inc, 6420 Wilshire Blvd, #1080, Los Angeles CA 90048 USA | Actor |

**Hatoum, Milton** — Writer
Rogers Coleridge White, 20 Powis Mews, London W11 1JN, England

**Hatsopoulos, George N** — Businessman, Mechanical Engineer
Thermo Electron Corp, 81 Wyman St, PO Box 9046, Waltham MA 02454, USA

**Hatteberg, Scott A** — Baseball Player
802 Berg Court NW, Gig Harbor WA 98335, USA

**Hatten, Tom** — Actor
1759 Sunset Plaza Dr, Los Angeles CA 90069, USA

**Hattersley, Roy S G** — Government Official, England
House of Lords, Westminster, London SW1A 0PW, England

**Hattestad, Ola Vigen** — Cross Country Skier
Ski Federation, Ulleval Stadion, 0840 Oslo, Norway

**Hattestad, Stine Lise** — Moguls Skier
Sundlia 1B, 1315 Nesoya, Norway

**Hatton, Ricky** — Boxer
Heart Break Hotel, 47 Rock St, Hyde, Cheshire SK14 5JH, England

**Hatton, W Vernon (Vern)** — Basketball Player
PO Box 8405, Lexington KY 40533, USA

**Hatzigiannis, Mihalis** — Singer
Universal Records, 70 Universal City Plaza, Universal City CA 91608 USA

**Hau, Lene Vestergaard** — Physicist
Harvard University, Applied Physics Dept, Cambridge MA 02138, USA

**Hauck, Frederick H (Rick)** — Astronaut
2 Redwood Lane, Falmouth ME 04105, USA

**Hauck, Timothy C (Tim)** — Football Player
2410 42nd St, Missoula MT 59803, USA

**Hauer, Brett** — Ice Hockey Player
2921 Branch St, Duluth MN 55812, USA

**Hauer, Rutger** — Actor
Glick Agency, 347 5th Ave, #1404, New York NY 10016 USA

**Hauerwas, Stanley** — Theologian
Duke University, Divinity School, Durham NC 27706, USA

**Haug, Ian** — Guitarist (Powderfinger)
Secret Service, PO Box 401, Fortitude Valley QLD 4006, Australia

**Haug, Norbert F** — Auto Racing Executive
Mercedes-Benz Motorsport, Brackley, Northantshire UNN 13 7BD, England

**Haugedal, Majken** — Model
Playboy Promotions, 9346 Civic Center Dr, #200, Beverly Hills CA 90210 USA

**Haugen, Greg** — Boxer
PO Box 155, 1802 A St SE, Auburn WA 98002, USA

**Hauke, Tobias C** — Field Hockey Player
Harvestehuder T H C, Barmbeker Str 106, 22303 Hamburg, Germany

**Haukohl, Guenter** — Space Scientist
714 Watts Dr SE, Huntsville AL 35801, USA

**Haun, Lindsey** — Actress
TalentWorks, 3500 W Olive Ave, #1400, Burbank CA 91505 USA

**Hauptman, Micah A** — Actor
Chaiotek, 6446 Santa Monica Blvd, Los Angeles CA 90038, USA

**Haus, Hermann A** — Electrical Engineer, Computer Scientist
38 Jeffrey Terrace, Lexington MA 02420, USA

**Hauser, Arthur A (Art)** — Football Player
2816 Walsh Road, Cincinnati OH 45208, USA

**Hauser, Cole** — Actor
A P A Talent & Literary Agency, 405 S Beverly Dr, #300, Beverly Hills CA 90212 USA

**Hauser, Erich** — Sculptor
Saline 36, 78628 Rottweil, Germany

**Hauser, Marc D** — Ethnologist, Neurologist
Harvard University, Cognitive Evolution Laboratory, 33 Kirkland, Cambridge MA 02138, USA

**Hauser, Wings** — Actor
David Shapira Assoc, 193 N Robertson Blvd, Beverly Hills CA 90211 USA

**Hausman, Jerry A** — Economist
Massachusetts Institute of Technology, Economics Dept, Cambridge MA 02139, USA

**Hausman, Thomas M (Tom)** — Baseball Player
3165 Westfield Circle, Las Vegas NV 89121, USA

**Hauss, Lenard M (Len)** — Football Player
110 Portmere Dr, Jesup GA 31546, USA

**Hauswald, Simone H** — Biathlete
Robert-Schumannstr 15, 78141 Schoenwald, Germany

**Hauver, Charles D** — Hero
6250 S Commerce Court, #1118, Tucson AZ 85746, USA

**Havel, Daniel** — Canoeing Athlete
A S O Dukla Prague, Cisarska Louka 1, 15500 Prague, Czech Republic

**Havelid, A Niclas** — Ice Hockey Player
PO Box 129, Point Roberts WA 98281, USA

**Havens, Bradley D (Brad)** — Baseball Player
3227 Eden Trail, Brighton MI 48114, USA

**Havens, Frank B** — Canoeing Athlete
PO Box 55, Harborton VA 23389, USA

**Havergal, Giles** — Actor, Director
Gavin Barker Assoc, 2D Wimpole St, London W1G 0EB, England

**Havig, Dennis E** — Football Player
5964 Old Stilesboro Road NW, Acworth GA 30101, USA

**Havlicek, John J** — Basketball Player
Naismith Basketball Hall of Fame, 1150 W Columbus Ave, Springfield MA 01105 USA

**Havlish, Jean** — Bowler, Baseball Player
PO Box 122, Rockville MN 56369, USA

**Havnevik, Kate** — Singer, Songwriter
Continentica Records, 1/710 Fulham Road, London SW6 5SB, England

**Havok, Davey** — Singer (AFI)
S A M, 722 Seward St, Los Angeles CA 90038, USA

**Havrilak, Samuel C (Sam)** — Football Player
1 Trojan Horse Dr, Phoenix MD 21131, USA

**Hawerchuk, Dale** — Ice Hockey Player
Grande Farms, RR 5 LCD Main, Orangeville ON L9W 2Z2, Canada

**Hawes, Keeley** — Actress
Troika, 74 Clerkenwell Road, #300, London EC1M 5QA, England

| | |
|---|---|
| **Hawes, Roy L** | Baseball Player |
| PO Box 854, Ringgold GA 30736, USA | |
| **Hawes, Spencer** | Basketball Player |
| Los Angeles Clippers, Staples Center, 1111 S Figueroa St, Los Angeles CA 90015 USA | |
| **Hawes, Steven S (Steve)** | Basketball Player |
| 400 W Highland Dr, Seattle WA 98119, USA | |
| **Hawk, Aaron James (A J)** | Football Player |
| 460 B Olden Glen, De Pere WI 54115, USA | |
| **Hawk, Kali** | Actress |
| Intellectual Artists Management, 10585 Santa Monica Blvd, #135, Los Angeles CA 90025 | |
| **Hawk, Tony** | Skateboarder, Actor |
| 900 Films, 1203 Activity Dr, Vista CA 92081, USA | |
| **Hawke, Ethan** | Actor, Writer |
| I/D Public Relations, 7060 Hollywood Blvd, #800, Los Angeles CA 90028 USA | |
| **Hawke, Robert J L (Bob)** | Prime Minister, Australia |
| Westfield Towers, 100 William St, Level 13, Sydney NSW 2001, Australia | |
| **Hawkes, John** | Actor |
| Innovative Artists, 1505 10th St, Santa Monica CA 90401 USA | |
| **Hawkes, Rechelle M** | Field Hockey Player |
| I C M I, PO Box 2311, Praham VIC 3181, Australia | |
| **Hawking, Stephen W** | Theoretical Physicist |
| University of Cambridge, Applied Math Dept, Cambridge CB3 9EW, England | |
| **Hawkins, Artrell** | Football Player |
| 12166 Peak Dr, Cincinnati OH 45246, USA | |
| **Hawkins, Barbara** | Singer (Dixie Cups) |
| Superstars Unlimited, PO Box 371371, Las Vegas NV 89137, USA | |
| **Hawkins, Benjamin C (Ben)** | Football Player |
| 104 Deforest St, Roslindale MA 02131, USA | |
| **Hawkins, C Alexander (Alex)** | Football Player |
| 215 Bonanza Road, Denmark SC 29042, USA | |
| **Hawkins, Cornelius L (Connie)** | Basketball Player, Executive |
| 33 W Missouri Ave, #27, Phoenix AZ 85013, USA | |
| **Hawkins, Courtney T, Jr** | Football Player |
| 8305 Gale Road, Goodrich MI 48438, USA | |
| **Hawkins, Dan** | Guitarist (Darkness) |
| Whitehouse Mgmt, PO Box 43829, London NW6 3PJ, England | |
| **Hawkins, Edwin** | Gospel Musician |
| Sierra Mgmt, 1035 Bates Court, Hendersonville TN 37075, USA | |
| **Hawkins, Frank** | Football Player |
| 2300 Alta Dr, Las Vegas NV 89107, USA | |
| **Hawkins, Hersey R, Jr** | Basketball Player |
| 2687 Beacon Hill Dr, West Linn OR 97068, USA | |
| **Hawkins, Jennifer** | Beauty Queen, Model, Actress |
| 22 Mgmt, 34 Darling St, #B, Balmain NSW 2041, Australia | |
| **Hawkins, Justin** | Singer (Darkness) |
| Whitehouse Mgmt, PO Box 43829, London NW6 3PJ, England | |
| **Hawkins, LaTroy (Roy)** | Baseball Player |
| 3521 Amberwood Lane, Prosper TX 75078, USA | |
| **Hawkins, M Andrew (Andy)** | Baseball Player |
| PO Box 1595, Bruceville TX 76630, USA | |
| **Hawkins, Michael Daly** | Judge |
| US Court of Appeals, 230 N 1st St, Phoenix AZ 85004, USA | |
| **Hawkins, Ronnie** | Singer |
| Live Tour Artists, 1454 White Oaks Blvd, Oakville ON L6H 4R9, Canada | |
| **Hawkins, Rosa** | Singer (Dixie Cups) |
| Superstars Unlimited, PO Box 371371, Las Vegas NV 89137, USA | |
| **Hawkins, Ross C (Rip)** | Football Player |
| 910 Prairie Ave, Cheyenne WY 82009, USA | |
| **Hawkins, Sally** | Actress |
| Conway Van Gelder Grant, 8-12 Broadwick St, #300, London W1F 8HW, England | |
| **Hawkins, Sophie B** | Singer, Songwriter |
| Trumpet Swan Productions, 520 Washington Blvd, #337, Marina del Rey CA 90292, USA | |
| **Hawkins, Taylor** | Drummer (Foo Fighters), Actor |
| Silva Artist Mgmt, 722 Seward St, Los Angeles CA 90038, USA | |
| **Hawkins, Thomas J (Tommy)** | Basketball Player, Sportscaster |
| 1745 Manzanita Park Ave, Malibu CA 90265, USA | |
| **Hawkins, Wayne A** | Football Player |
| 1 Dogwood Court, San Ramon CA 94583, USA | |
| **Hawkins, Wynn F** | Baseball Player |
| 5326 Cottage Dr, Cortland OH 44410, USA | |
| **Hawkinson, Tim** | Artist |
| Ace Gallery, 5514 Wilshire Blvd, #200, Los Angeles CA 90036, USA | |
| **Hawlata, Franz** | Opera Singer |
| Columbia Artists Mgmt Inc, 5 Columbus Circle, 1790 Broadway, #1600, New York NY 10019 USA | |
| **Hawley, D Sanford (Sandy)** | Thoroughbred Racing Jockey |
| 9625 Merrill Road, Silverwood MI 48760, USA | |
| **Hawley, Frank** | Auto Racing Driver |
| Frank Hawley Racing School, 3300 Hamilton Mill Road, #102, Buford, GA 30519, USA | |
| **Hawley, Noah** | Producer, Writer |
| 26 Keys Productions, 500 S Buena Vista St, Old Animation Building, Burbank CA 91521, USA | |
| **Hawley, Steven A** | Astronaut |
| 3303 Calvin Dr, Lawrence KS 66049, USA | |
| **Hawn, Goldie** | Actress |
| Renaissance Literary & Talent, PO Box 17379, Beverly Hills CA 90209, USA | |
| **Haworth, Alan** | Ice Hockey Player |
| 845 112E Ave, Drummondville QC J2B 4K5, Canada | |
| **Hawpe, David V** | Editor |
| 507 Penwood Road, Louisville KY 40206, USA | |
| **Hawthorne, Chris** | Artist |
| Hawthorne Gallery, 517 Jefferson St, Port Orford OR 97465, USA | |
| **Hawthorne, Gregory D (Greg)** | Football Player |
| 1428 E Jefferson Ave, Fort Worth TX 76104, USA | |
| **Hawthorne, Julie** | Artist |
| Hawthorne Gallery, 517 Jefferson St, Port Orford OR 97465, USA | |
| **Hawthorne, Mayer** | Singer, Songwriter |
| Creative Artists Agency, 2000 Ave of Stars, #100, Los Angeles CA 90067 USA | |

**H**

**H**

**Hax - Hayes**

| | |
|---|---|
| **Hax, Carolyn** <br> Washington Post, Editorial Dept, 1150 15th St NW, Washington DC 20071 USA | Columnist |
| **Hay, Colin** <br> Fleming Artists, 543 N Main St, Ann Arbor MI 48104, USA | Singer (Men at Work) |
| **Hay, Louise L** <br> Hay House, PO Box 5100, Carlsbad CA 92018, USA | Writer |
| **Haya Rashed Al Khalifa, Sheikha** <br> General Assemby, United Nations, United Nations Plaza, New York NY 10017, USA | Government Official, Bahrain |
| **Hayaishi, Osamu** <br> 1-29 Izumigawacho, Shimogamo Sakyoku, Kyoto 606 0807, Japan | Biochemist |
| **Hayashi, Izuo** <br> OptoElectrics Research Laboratory, 5-5 Tohkodai, Tsukuba, Ibaraki 300 26, Japan | Engineer |
| **Hayashida, Erika** <br> 1470 NW 107th St, Doral FL 33172, USA | Golfer |
| **Haydee, Marcia** <br> Stuttgart Ballet, Oberer Schlossgarten 6, 70173 Stuttgart, Germany | Ballerina |
| **Haydel, J Harold (Hal)** <br> 304 Lynwood Dr, Houma LA 70360, USA | Baseball Player |
| **Hayden** <br> Fat Possum Records, PO Box 1923, Oxford MS 38655, USA | Singer |
| **Hayden, Brent M** <br> 2770 Sophia St, #605, Vancouver BC V5T 0A4, Canada | Swimmer |
| **Hayden, Dennis** <br> Susan J Talent Agency, 13273 Ventura Blvd, #104, Sherman Oaks CA 91604, USA | Actor, Producer |
| **Hayden, J Michael (Mike)** <br> 5809 Sagamore Court, Lawrence KS 66047, USA | Governor, KS |
| **Hayden, Jim** <br> Philadelphia Inquirer, 400 N Broad St, Philadelphia PA 19130, USA | Publisher |
| **Hayden, Linda** <br> Michael Ladkin Mgmt, 1 Duchess St, #1, London W1N 3DE, England | Actress |
| **Hayden, Michael** <br> H W A Talent, 3500 W Olive Ave, #1400, Burbank CA 91505 USA | Actor |
| **Hayden, Neil Steven** <br> 1755 York Ave, #19A, New York NY 10128, USA | Publisher |
| **Hayden, Pamela** <br> W M E Entertainment, 9601 Wilshire Blvd, #300, Beverly Hills CA 90210 USA | Actress |
| **Hayden, Tom** <br> 152 Wadsworth Ave, Santa Monica CA 90405, USA | Political Activist |
| **Hayden, William George** <br> GPO Box 7829, Waterfront Place, Brisbane QLD 4001, Australia | Governor General, Australia |
| **Haydon Jones, Ann** <br> 85 Westerfield Road, Edge Aston, Birmingham, West Midlands B15 3JF, England | Tennis Player |
| **Haye, David D** <br> Golden Boy Promotions, 626 Wilshire Blvd, #350, Los Angeles CA 90017 USA | Boxer |
| **Hayek, Salma** <br> Management 360, 9111 Wilshire Blvd, Beverly Hills CA 90210 USA | Actress, Model |
| **Hayers, Sidney A** <br> John Redway, 5 Denmark St, London WC2H 8LP, England | Director |
| **Hayes, Amy** <br> PO Box 717, Burgin KY 40310, USA | Model, Sportscaster |
| **Hayes, Amy Beth** <br> Hamilton Hodell, 20 Golden Square, London W1F 9JL, England | Actress |
| **Hayes, Anthony** <br> Lou Coulson Assoc, 37 Berwick St, London W1V 8RS, England | Actor |
| **Hayes, Ben J** <br> 3501 10th St NE, Saint Petersburg FL 33704, USA | Baseball Player |
| **Hayes, Bill** <br> 4528 Beck Ave, North Hollywood CA 91602, USA | Singer, Actor |
| **Hayes, Cathy Lind** <br> Talent Agency, 6310 San Vicente Blvd, #200, Los Angeles CA 90048, USA | Actress |
| **Hayes, Charles D (Charlie)** <br> 22503 Holy Creek Trail, Tomball TX 77377, USA | Baseball Player |
| **Hayes, Darren** <br> Harbour Agency, 135 Forbes St, Woolloomooloo NSW 2011, Australia | Singer (Savage Garden) |
| **Hayes, Denis A** <br> Bullitt Foundation, 1212 Minor Ave, Seattle WA 98101, USA | Environmentalist |
| **Hayes, Dennis C** <br> Hayes Microcomputer Products, 945 E Paces Ferry Road NE, Atlanta GA 30326, USA | Engineer, Co-Inventor (Modem) |
| **Hayes, Elvin E** <br> 14 Canaveral Creek Lane, Sugar Land TX 77479, USA | Basketball Player |
| **Hayes, Erinn** <br> United Talent Agency, U T A Plaza, 9336 Civic Center Dr, Beverly Hills CA 90210 USA | Actress |
| **Hayes, Gemma** <br> Paradigm Agency, 360 N Crescent Dr, North Building, Beverly Hills CA 90210 USA | Singer, Songwriter |
| **Hayes, Gerald B** <br> 3841 E Windsong Dr, Phoenix AZ 85048, USA | Football Player |
| **Hayes, Jarvis J** <br> 4495 Greycliff Pointe, Douglasville GA 30135, USA | Basketball Player |
| **Hayes, Joanna D** <br> Brentwood School, 100 S Barrington Place, Los Angeles CA 90049, USA | Track Athlete |
| **Hayes, John** <br> Oceanographic Institution, 266 Woods Hole Road, Woods Hole MA 02543, USA | Geologist, Geophysicist |
| **Hayes, John P (J P)** <br> 740 Camino Real Ave, El Paso TX 79922, USA | Golfer |
| **Hayes, Jonathan M** <br> 9632 W 116th Place, Overland Park KS 66210, USA | Football Player |
| **Hayes, Julia** <br> Carolina Moon Enterprises, PO Box 2571, Columbia SC 29202, USA | Actress, Model |
| **Hayes, Laura** <br> Performance Artists Agency, 137 Goswell Road, London EC1V 7ET, England | Actress |
| **Hayes, Louis S** <br> Abby Hoffer Enterprises, 223 1/2 E 48th St, New York NY 10017 USA | Jazz Drummer |
| **Hayes, Mark S** <br> 1014 Saint Andrews Dr, Edmond OK 73025, USA | Golfer |
| **Hayes, Patty** <br> 3436 Sipsey St, Villages FL 32162, USA | Golfer |

**Hayes, Peter**
Paradigm Agency, 360 Park Ave, #1600, New York NY 10022 USA — Guitarist (Black Rebel Motorcycle Club)

**Hayes, Reginald C (Reggie)**
Ellis Talent Group, 4705 Laurel Canyon Blvd, #300, Valley Village CA 91607, USA — Actor

**Hayes, Robert M**
National Coalition for the Homeless, 105 E 22nd St, New York NY 10010, USA — Social Activist

**Hayes, Sean P**
Hazy Mills Productions, 4024 Radford Ave, Studio City CA 91604, USA — Actor

**Hayes, Steven L (Steve)**
1630 Mercoal Dr, Spring TX 77386, USA — Basketball Player

**Hayes, Terry**
Danny Greene Talent, 9601 Wilshire Blvd, #300, Beverly Hills CA 90210, USA — Writer, Producer

**Hayes, Von F**
314 Circle Dr, Lake Bluff IL 60044, USA — Baseball Player

**Hayes, Wade**
Morris Management Group, 818 19th Ave S, Nashville TN 37203, USA — Singer

**Hayes, Wendell**
1935 E 30th St, #23, Oakland CA 94606, USA — Football Player

**Hayhoe, William (Bill), II**
5146 Santa Anita Dr, Sparks NV 89436, USA — Football Player

**Hayhurst, Dirk V**
570 Harvey St, Kent OH 44240, USA — Baseball Player

**Hayhurst, John O**
14741 SE Wanda Dr, Portland OR 97267, USA — Inventor (Bone Tissue Reattachment)

**Hayman, Conway**
6811 Stiller Dr, Missouri City TX 77489, USA — Football Player

**Hayman, David T**
Markham Froggatt Irwin, Julian House, 4 Windmill St, London W1P 1HF, England — Actor, Director

**Hayman, Fred**
6946 Wildlife Road, Malibu CA 90265, USA — Fashion Designer

**Hayman, Gordon I**
54 Lakes Lane, Beaconsfield, Buckinghamshire HP9 2LB, England — Cinematographer

**Hayman, James**
Paradigm Agency, 360 N Crescent Dr, North Building, Beverly Hills CA 90210 USA — Producer, Director

**Haymond, Alvin H (Juggie)**
2857 Mantis Dr, San Jose CA 95148, USA — Football Player

**Haynes, Abner**
1950 FM 489, Oakwood TX 75855, USA — Football Player

**Haynes, Al**
4410 S 182nd St, Seatac WA 98188, USA — Airline Pilot Hero

**Haynes, Betsy**
2355 Lebanon Road, #2108, Frisco TX 75034, USA — Writer

**Haynes, Colton**
I C M Partners, 10250 Constellation Blvd, #900, Los Angeles CA 90067 USA — Actor

**Haynes, Cotton**
Podwall Entertainment, 710 N Orlando Ave, #203, West Hollywood CA 90069, USA — Actor

**Haynes, Gibson J (Gibby)**
Agency Group Ltd, 142 W 57th St, #600, New York NY 10019 USA — Singer, Guitarist (Butthole Surfers)

**Haynes, Jimmy W**
2601 N John B Dennis Highway, #1108, Kingsport TN 37660, USA — Baseball Player

**Haynes, Mark**
220 S Oneida St, Denver CO 80230, USA — Football Player

**Haynes, Marques O**
954 Taylor Dr, Winnsboro TX 75494, USA — Basketball Player, Coach

**Haynes, Michael D**
2375 Saddlesprings Dr, Alpharetta GA 30004, USA — Football Player

**Haynes, Michael J (Mike)**
7931 Entrada Lazanja, San Diego CA 92127, USA — Football Player

**Haynes, Richard**
2701 Fannin St, Houston TX 77002, USA — Attorney

**Haynes, Roy O**
Ted Kurland, 173 Brighton Ave, Boston MA 02134 USA — Jazz Drummer

**Haynes, Todd**
Creative Artists Agency, 2000 Ave of Stars, #100, Los Angeles CA 90067 USA — Director

**Haynes, Verron U**
2500 Northwinds Parkway, #275, Alpharetta GA 30009, USA — Football Player

**Haynes, Warren**
Hard Head Productions, PO Box 651, New York NY 10014, USA — Singer, Guitarist, Songwriter

**Haynesworth, Albert (Al), III**
5060 Abington Ridge Lane, Franklin TN 37067, USA — Football Player

**Haynie, Jim**
2721 Reynier Ave, Los Angeles CA 90034, USA — Actor

**Haynie, Kristin**
Sacramento Monarchs, Arco Arena, 1 Sports Parkway, Sacramento CA 95834 USA — Basketball Player

**Haynie, Sandra J**
301 Stockade Lane, Denton TX 76205, USA — Golfer

**Hays, Kathryn**
Look Talent Agency, 166 Geary St, San Francisco CA 94108, USA — Actress

**Hays, L Harold**
10410 Ravenswood Road, Granbury TX 76049, USA — Football Player

**Hays, Robert**
Fran Saperstein Organization, 919 Victoria Ave, Venice CA 90291, USA — Actor

**Hays, Ronald J**
869 Kamoi Place, Honolulu HI 96825, USA — Navy Admiral

**Hays, Todd**
Bobsled & Skeleton Federation, 1631 Mesa Ave, #A, Colorado Springs CO 80906 USA — Bobsled Athlete

**Haysbert, Dennis**
G S Mgmt, 861 S Windsor Blvd, #105, Los Angeles CA 90005, USA — Actor

**Hayter, David**
United Talent Agency, U T A Plaza, 9336 Civic Center Dr, Beverly Hills CA 90210 USA — Director, Writer, Actor

**Haythe, Justin**
Creative Artists Agency, 2000 Ave of Stars, #100, Los Angeles CA 90067 USA — Writer

**Hayward, Jimmy**
United Talent Agency, U T A Plaza, 9336 Civic Center Dr, Beverly Hills CA 90210 USA — Animator, Director, Actor

**Hayward, Justin**
Threshold Records, 54 High St, Cobham, Surrey KT11 3DP, England — Singer, Guitarist (Moody Blues)

**Hayward, Kara** — Actress
I C M Partners, 10250 Constellation Blvd, #900, Los Angeles CA 90067 USA
**Hayward, Matt** — Drummer (Band of Skulls)
Pias Entertainment Group, Trading Centre, 101 Farm Lane, #24, London SW6 1QJ, England
**Hayward, Reginald J (Reggie), Jr** — Football Player
4651 Swilcan Bridge Lane S, Jacksonville FL 32224, USA
**Hayward, Thomas B** — Navy Admiral
2200 Ross Ave, #3800, Dallas TX 75201, USA
**Haywood, Brendan T** — Basketball Player
4514 Lawndale Dr, #E, Greensboro NC 27455, USA
**Haywood, Dave** — Singer, Musician (Lady Antebellum)
Capitol Records, 3322 West End Ave, #1100, Nashville TN 37203 USA
**Haywood, Hurley** — Auto Racing Driver
1445 Ponte Vedra Blvd, Ponte Vedra Beach FL 32082, USA
**Haywood, Spencer** — Basketball Player
49447 Plymouth Way, Plymouth MI 48170, USA
**Hayworth, Tracy K** — Football Player
528 Knights Church Road, Decherd TN 37324, USA
**Hazanavicius, Michel** — Director, Editor, Writer
Creative Artists Agency, 2000 Ave of Stars, #100, Los Angeles CA 90067 USA
**Hazard, Geoffrey C, Jr** — Attorney, Educator
200 W Willow Grove Ave, Philadelphia PA 19118, USA
**Haze, Angel** — Rap Artist, Lyricist
Republic Records, 755 Broadway, #700, New York NY 10019, USA
**Hazell, Keeley R** — Model, Singer
98 De Beauvoir Road, London N1 4EN, England
**Hazelwood, Rebecca** — Actress
Don Buchwald Talent Agency, 6500 Wilshire Blvd, #2200, Los Angeles CA 90048 USA
**Hazen, Maya** — Actress, Model
K Dash, 2-7-10-5F, Higashi, Shibuya Tokyo 150 0011, Japan
**Haziza, Shlomi** — Artist
H Studio, 8421 Lankershim Blvd, Sun Valley CA 91352, USA
**Hazzard, Shirley** — Writer
200 E 66th St, New York NY 10065, USA
**Head, Anthony Stewart** — Actor
Gordon & French, 12-13 Poland St, London W1F 8QB, England
**Head, Dena** — Basketball Player
Central Connecticut State University, Athletic Dept, New Britain CT 06050, USA
**Head, Donald C (Don)** — Ice Hockey Player
15240 NE Knott St, Portland OR 97230, USA
**Head, Emily** — Actress
United Talent Agency, U T A Plaza, 9336 Civic Center Dr, Beverly Hills CA 90210 USA
**Head, Glenn O** — Financier
First Investors Corp, 95 Wall St, #2200, New York NY 10005, USA
**Head, Luther D** — Basketball Player
2714 Defoe Dr, Katy TX 77449, USA
**Head, Roy** — Singer
Texas Sounds Entertainment, 2317 Pecan, Dickinson TX 77539, USA
**Head, Tim D** — Artist
271 Eversholt St, London NW1 1BA, England
**Headden, Susan M** — Journalist
US News & World Report, 2400 N St NW, Washington DC 20037, USA
**Headen, Andrew R (Andy)** — Football Player
PO Box 821, Liberty NC 27298, USA
**Headey, Lena** — Actress
Troika, 74 Clerkenwell Road, #300, London EC1M 5QA, England
**Headley, Chase J** — Baseball Player
3221 Baker Lane, Franklin TN 37064, USA
**Headley, Heather** — Singer, Actress
Creative Artists Agency, 2000 Ave of Stars, #100, Los Angeles CA 90067 USA
**Headly, Glenne** — Actress
I C M Partners, 10250 Constellation Blvd, #900, Los Angeles CA 90067 USA
**Headon, Nicky (Topper)** — Drummer (Clash)
Clash, 268 Camden Road, London NW1 9AB, England
**Heald, Anthony** — Actor
Abrams Artists, 9200 W Sunset Blvd, #1125, West Hollywood CA 90069 USA
**Healey, Denis W** — Government Official, England
Pingles Place, Alfriston, East Sussex BN26 5TT, England
**Healey, Derek E** — Composer
29 Stafford Road, Ruislip Gardens, Middlesex H4A 6PB, England
**Healey, John G** — Association Executive
Amnesty International USA, 322 8th Ave, New York NY 10001, USA
**Healy, Cornelius T** — Labor Leader
Plate Die Engravers Union, 228 S Swarthmore Ave, Ridley Park PA 19078, USA
**Healy, Fran** — Singer (Travis)
Wildlife Entertainment, 21 Heathmans Road, London SW6 4TJ, England
**Healy, Francis X (Fran)** — Baseball Player, Sportscaster
1 Primrose Lane, Holyoke MA 01040, USA
**Healy, Jane E** — Journalist
Orlando Sentinel, Editorial Dept, 633 N Orange Ave, Lobby, Orlando FL 32801, USA
**Healy, M Donald (Don)** — Football Player
3427 Boca Ciega Dr, Naples FL 34112, USA
**Healy, Patricia** — Actress
McCabe Group, 3211 Cahuenga Blvd W, #104, Los Angeles CA 90068, USA
**Healy, Timothy M (Tim)** — Actor
Artists Partnership, 101 Finsbury Pavement, London EC2A 1RS, England
**Heap, Imogen** — Singer (Frou Frou)
Primary Talent International, 10-11 Jockey's Fields, London WC1R 4BN, England
**Heap, Mark** — Actor, Comedian
Curtis Brown Group, 28-29 Haymarket St, #500, London SW1Y 4SP, England
**Heap, Todd B** — Football Player
7634 E Summit Trail St, Mesa AZ 85207, USA
**Heard, Amber** — Actress
W M E Entertainment, 9601 Wilshire Blvd, #300, Beverly Hills CA 90210 USA
**Heard, Garfield (Gar)** — Basketball Player, Coach
1735 Peachtree St NE, #133, Atlanta GA 30309, USA

Heard, Herman W, Jr — Football Player
PO Box 938, Broomfield CO 80038, USA
Heard, Jerry — Golfer
PO Box 429, Central Lake MI 49622, USA
Heard, John — Actor
Forster Entertainment, 12533 Woodgreen St, Building B, Los Angeles CA 90066, USA
Hearn, Edward J (Ed) — Baseball Player
5737 Theden St, Shawnee KS 66218, USA
Hearn, George — Actor, Singer
Paradigm Agency, 360 Park Ave S, #1600, New York NY 10010 USA
Hearn, J Woodrow — Religious Leader
62 Campeche Circle, Galveston TX 77554, USA
Hearn, Kevin — Musician (Barenaked Ladies)
Shore Fire Media, 32 Court St, #1600, Brooklyn NY 11201 USA
Hearne, Bill — Singer, Guitarist
Class Act Entertainment, PO Box 160236, Nashville TN 37216, USA
Hearney, Richard D — Marine Corps General
Armed Forces Y M C A, PO Box 555028, Building 16144, Camp Pendleton CA 92055, USA
Hearns, Thomas (Tommy) — Boxer
20551 S Norwood St, Southfield MI 48075, USA
Hearron, Jeffrey V (Jeff) — Baseball Player
5820 Hill Road, Powder Springs GA 30127, USA
Hearst Shaw, Patricia C (Patty) — Writer
110 5th St, San Francisco CA 94103, USA
Hearst, G Garrison — Football Player
3753 Augusta Highway, Lincolnton GA 30817, USA
Hearst, Richard C (Rick) — Actor
Debbie O'Connor, PO Box 16212, Irvine CA 92623, USA
Heat, Reverend Horton — Singer, Guitarist, Songwriter
Atomic Music Group, 9836 Gloucester Dr, Beverly Hills CA 90210, USA
Heath, Albert (Tootie) — Jazz Drummer (Modern Jazz Quarter)
Ted Kurland, 173 Brighton Ave, Boston MA 02134 USA
Heath, Brandon — Singer, Guitarist, Songwriter
Creative Trust, 5141 Virginia Way, #320, Brentwood TN 37027, USA
Heath, James E (Jimmy) — Jazz Saxophonist, Composer
Ted Kurland, 173 Brighton Ave, Boston MA 02134 USA
Heath, Liam — Canoeing Athlete
6 Dunsdon Ave, Guildford GU2 7NX, England
Heath, Michael T (Mike) — Baseball Player
2107 Timothy Terrace, Valrico FL 33594, USA
Heath, Stanley (Stan), III — Basketball Player, Coach
University of South Florida, Athletic Dept, Tampa FL 33620, USA
Heath, Tobin P — Soccer Player
USA Soccer Federation, 1801 S Prairie Ave, Chicago IL 60616 USA
Heath, William C (Bill) — Baseball Player
1626 Lake Charlotte Lane, Richmond TX 77406, USA
Heathcock, Clayton H — Chemist
5235 Alhambra Valley Road, Martinez CA 94553, USA
Heathcock, R Jeffrey (Jeff) — Baseball Player
24962 Calle Vecindad, Lake Forest CA 92630, USA
Heathcote, Alastair — Rowing Athlete
Amateur Rowing Assn, 6 Lower Mall, London W6 9DJ, England
Heathcote, Jud — Basketball Coach
5418 S Quail Ridge Circle, Spokane WA 99223, USA
Heatherly, Eric — Singer
A P A Talent & Literary Agency, 405 S Beverly Dr, #300, Beverly Hills CA 90212 USA
Heatley, Daniel J (Dany) — Ice Hockey Player
686 Leguime Road, #306, Kelowna BC V1W 1A4, Canada
Heaton, Neal — Baseball Player
3 Nursery Court, East Patchogue NY 11772, USA
Heaton, Patricia — Actress
Creative Artists Agency, 2000 Ave of Stars, #100, Los Angeles CA 90067 USA
Heaverlo, David W (Dave) — Baseball Player
3720 W Lakeshore Dr, Moses Lake WA 98837, USA
Hebert, Bobby J, Jr — Football Player
855 Walker St, New Orleans LA 70124, USA
Hebert, Doug — Auto Racing Driver
1443 E Gastib St, Lincolnton NC 28092, USA
Hebert, Guy — Ice Hockey Player
8 Gleneagles Dr, Newport Beach CA 92660, USA
Hebert, Johnny — Auto Racing Driver
Team Lotus, Kettering Hamm Hall, Wymondham, Norfolk NR18 7HW, England
Hebner, Richard J (Richie) — Baseball Player
6 Tetreault Dr, Walpole MA 02081, USA
Hebron, Vaughn H — Football Player
800 Summit Trace Road, Langhorne PA 19047, USA
Hebson, Bryan — Baseball Player
1151 Fairmont Lane, Auburn AL 36830, USA
Heche, Anne — Actress
United Talent Agency, U T A Plaza, 9336 Civic Center Dr, Beverly Hills CA 90210 USA
Hecht, Duvall — Rower
2910 W Garry Ave, Santa Ana CA 92704, USA
Hecht, Gina — Actress
House of Representatives, 1434 6th St, #1, Santa Monica CA 90401 USA
Hecht, Jessica — Actress
Innovative Artists, 1505 10th St, Santa Monica CA 90401 USA
Hecht, William F — Businessman
P P & L Resources, 2 N 9th St, Allentown PA 18101, USA
Heck, Andrew R (Andy) — Football Player
1 Bullrush Court, Stafford VA 22554, USA
Heck, Ralph A — Football Player
1906 Wicks Ridge Lane, Marietta GA 30062, USA
Hecke, Christina — Actress
Agentur Scenario, Rambergstr 5, 80799 Munich, Germany
Hecker, Zvi — Architect
19 Elzar St, Tel Aviv 65157, Israel

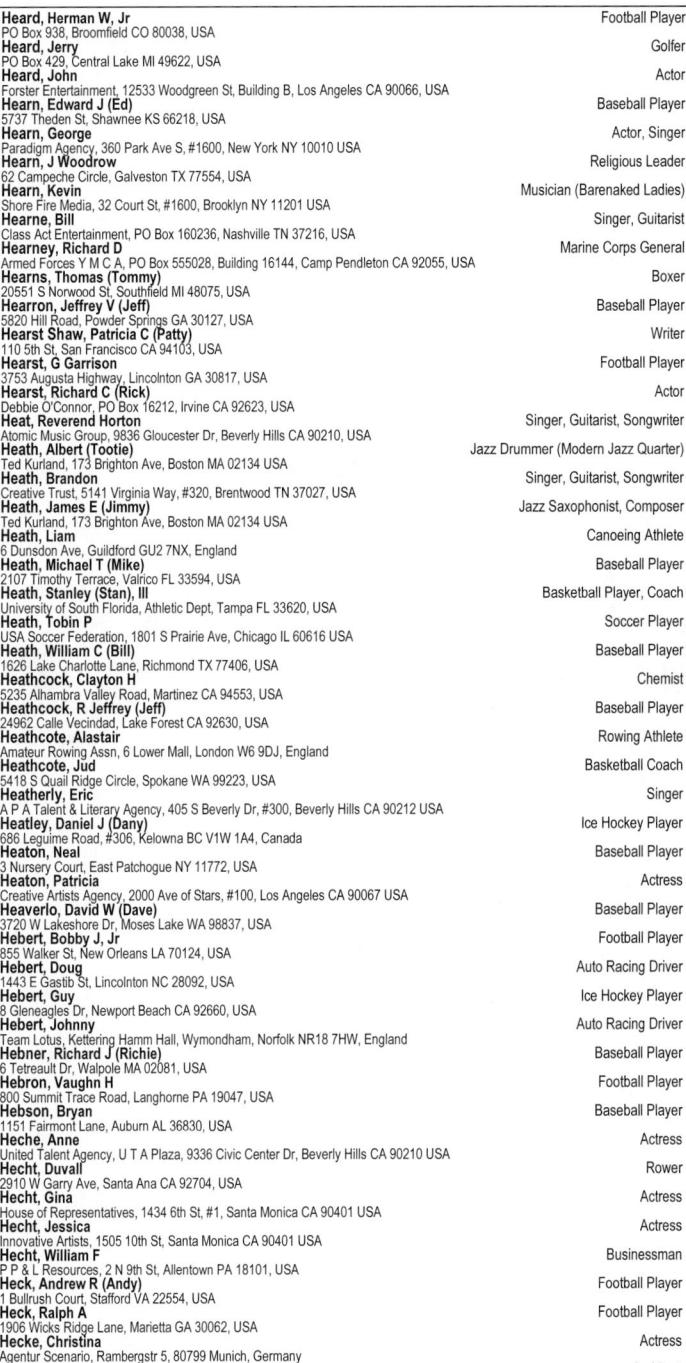

H

Heard - Hecker

**Heckerling, Amy** — Director, Producer
1330 Schuyler Road, Beverly Hills CA 90210, USA
**Heckler, Margaret M** — Secretary, Health & Human Services
1401 N Oak St, Arlington VA 22209, USA
**Heckman, James J** — Nobel Economics Laureate
4807 S Greenwood Ave, Chicago IL 60615, USA
**Heckscher, August** — Writer
333 E 68th St, New York NY 10065, USA
**Hector, Jamie** — Actor
T C A/Jed Root, 9220 Sunset Blvd, #315, Los Angeles CA 90069, USA
**Hector, Johnny L** — Football Player
525 Caroline St, New Iberia LA 70560, USA
**Hedaya, Dan** — Actor
Gersh Agency, 9465 Wilshire Blvd, #600, Beverly Hills CA 90212 USA
**Hedberg, Johan** — Ice Hockey Player
20 Indian Lane, Florham Park NJ 07932, USA
**Hedeman, Richard (Tuff)** — Rodeo Bull Rider
PO Box 224, Morgan Mill TX 76465, USA
**Heder, Jon** — Actor
Baker Winokur Ryder Public Relations, 9100 Wilshire Blvd, #500W, Beverly Hills CA 90212 USA
**Hedford, Eric** — Singer, Drummer (Dandy Warhols)
Monqui Mgmt, PO Box 5908, Portland OR 97228, USA
**Hedgepeth, Whitney** — Swimmer
9801 Westward Dr, Austin TX 78733, USA
**Hedges, Peter** — Director, Writer
Creative Artists Agency, 2000 Ave of Stars, #100, Los Angeles CA 90067 USA
**Hedican, Bret** — Ice Hockey Player
290 Las Quebradas Lane, Alamo CA 94507, USA
**Hedison, David** — Actor
Ambrosio/Mortimer, 165 W 46th St, New York NY 10036 USA
**Hedlund, Garrett** — Actor, Singer
Brillstein Entertainment Partners, 9150 Wilshire Blvd, #350, Beverly Hills CA 90212 USA
**Hedlund, Michael D (Mike)** — Baseball Player
2412 Klinger Road, Arlington TX 76016, USA
**Hedren, Tippi** — Actress
PO Box 189, Acton CA 93510, USA
**Hedrick, Chad** — Speed Skater
5504 Fellowship Lane, Spring TX 77379, USA
**Hedrick, Jerry L** — Biochemist
5831 Constitution Ave, Fairfield CA 94533, USA
**Hedrick, Joan D** — Writer
Trinity College, Women's Studies Program, 300 Summit St, Hartford CT 06106, USA
**Heeger, Alan J** — Nobel Chemistry Laureate
1042 Las Alturas Road, Santa Barbara CA 93103, USA
**Heelan, Briga** — Actress
Gersh Agency, 9465 Wilshire Blvd, #600, Beverly Hills CA 90212 USA
**Heemskerk, Frederike J M (Femke)** — Swimmer
K N Z B, Postbus 7217, 3430 Nieuwegein JE, Netherlands
**Heep, Daniel W (Dan)** — Baseball Player
18610 Crosstimber, San Antonio TX 78258, USA
**Heery, Gary** — Photographer
Kitchen, 43 Bridge Road, Stanmore NSW 2048, Australia
**Heeschen, David S** — Radio Astronomer
702 Copa de Oro, Marathon FL 33050, USA
**Heesters, Nicole** — Actress
Dirk Fehrecke Agentur, Ludwigkirchplatz 2, 10719 Berlin, Germany
**Heeter, Carrie** — Inventor (Sign-Language Software)
Michigan State University, Communication Technology Laboratory, East Lansing MI 48824, USA
**Heffernan, Bertram A (Bert)** — Baseball Player
130 Eagle Court, Locust Grove VA 22508, USA
**Heffernan, John** — Actor
Artists Partnership, 101 Finsbury Pavement, London EC2A 1RS, England
**Heffernan, Kevin** — Actor, Comedian
Broken Lizard Industries, PO Box 642809, Los Angeles CA 90064, USA
**Heffner, Robert F (Bob)** — Baseball Player
910 N 12th St, Allentown PA 18102, USA
**Hefford, Jayna** — Ice Hockey Player
Team Canada, 2424 University Dr NW, Calgary AB T2N 3Y9, Canada
**Heffron, John** — Actor, Comedian
Conversation Co, 1044 Northern Blvd, #304, Roslyn NY 11576, USA
**Heflin, Vincent G (Vince)** — Football Player
5603 Regency Park Court, #3, Suitland MD 20746, USA
**Hefner, Hugh M** — Publisher, Editor
10236 Charing Cross Road, Los Angeles CA 90024, USA
**Hegamin, George R** — Football Player
1409 S Lamar St, #512, Dallas TX 75215, USA
**Hegarty, John F** — Labor Leader
National Postal Mail Handlers Union, 1101 Connecticut Ave NW, #500, Washington DC 20036, USA
**Hegman, Michael W (Mike)** — Football Player
2958 Suesand Dr, Memphis TN 38128, USA
**Hegman, Robert H (Bob)** — Baseball Player
3529 NW Winding Woods Dr, Lees Summit MO 64064, USA
**Hegre, Petter** — Photographer
Ocinum, Rua das Hortas 55, 9050-024 Funchal Madeira, Portugal
**Heidemann, Britta** — Fencer
Schinkelstr 10, 50933 Cologne, Germany
**Heidemann, Jack S** — Baseball Player
1816 S Salida del Sol Circle, Mesa AZ 85202, USA
**Heiden, Elizabeth L (Beth)** — Speed Skater
915 Swarthmore Court, Madison WI 53705, USA
**Heiden, Eric A** — Speed Skater, Cyclist
1219 Cottonwood Lane, Park City UT 84098, USA
**Heiden, Steve A** — Football Player
12047 Tivoli Park Row, #3, San Diego CA 92128, USA
**Heidler, Betty** — Track Athlete
Eintracht Frankfurt, Gustav-Behringer-Str, 60386 Frankfurt, Germany

| | |
|---|---|
| **Heigl, Katherine**<br>Jason Heigl Foundation, 3450 Cahuenga Blvd W, #905, Los Angeles CA 90068, USA | Actress, Model |
| **Heil, Jennifer**<br>Newport Sports Mgmt, 201 City Centre Dr, #400, Missisauga ON L5B 2T4, Canada | Freestyle Moguls Skier |
| **Heil, Reinhold**<br>First Artists, 4764 Park Granada, #210, Calabasas CA 91302 USA | Composer |
| **Heilman, Aaron M**<br>9314 Aboite Center Road, Fort Wayne IN 46804, USA | Baseball Player |
| **Heimbold, Charles A, Jr**<br>Bristol-Myers Squibb, 345 Park Ave, Basement LC3, New York NY 10154, USA | Businessman |
| **Heimlich, Henry J**<br>3939 Erie Ave, #4060, Cincinnati OH 45208, USA | Physician |
| **Heimueller, Gorman J**<br>2148 Glen Ave, Riverton UT 84065, USA | Baseball Player |
| **Hein, Jeppe**<br>Karriere Bar, Bacon Square 57-67, 1711 Copenhagen V, Denmark | Artist |
| **Heine, Jutta**<br>Blaue Muhle, 57614 Burglahr, Germany | Track Athlete |
| **Heineman, Kenneth R (Ken)**<br>300 Innis Free Circle, #C4, Rogers AR 72758, USA | Football Player |
| **Heinen, Mike**<br>4518 E Meadow Lane, Lake Charles LA 70605, USA | Golfer |
| **Heinkel, Donald E (Don)**<br>508 Covington Ave, Birmingham AL 35206, USA | Baseball Player |
| **Heinle, Amelia**<br>Don Buchwald Talent Agency, 6500 Wilshire Blvd, #2200, Los Angeles CA 90048 USA | Actress |
| **Heino**<br>Postfach 1270, 53896 Bad Muenstereifel, Germany | Singer |
| **Heinrich, Stephanie**<br>294 S Beverly Dr, Beverly Hills CA 90212, USA | Model |
| **Heinrichs, Albert M**<br>Harvard University, Classics Dept, Cambridge MA 02138, USA | Philologist |
| **Heinrichs, Rick**<br>Sandra Marsh & Associates, 9150 Wilshire Blvd, #220, Beverly Hills CA 90212, USA | Art Director, Production Designer |
| **Heins, Thorsten**<br>BlackBerry, Research in Motion, 295 Phillip St, Waterloo ON N2L 3W8, Canada | Businessman |
| **Heins, Trevor**<br>Abrams Artists, 275 7th Ave, #2600, New York NY 10001 USA | Actor |
| **Heinsohn, Thomas W (Tom)**<br>15 Hunters Way, Needham Heights MA 02494, USA | Basketball Player, Coach |
| **Heintz, Christopher J (Chris)**<br>6002 Laketree Lane, #N, Tampa FL 33617, USA | Baseball Player |
| **Heinz, Andras**<br>Luber Rocklin Entertainment, 5815 Sunset Blvd, #206, Los Angeles CA 90028 USA | Writer |
| **Heinz, Robert K (Bob)**<br>516 Mansion Court, #502, Santa Clara CA 95054, USA | Football Player |
| **Heinzmann, Stefanie**<br>Universal Music Group, 401 Commerce St, #1100, Nashville TN 37219 USA | Singer |
| **Heise, Robert L (Bob)**<br>537 Live Oak Dr, Angels Camp CA 95222, USA | Baseball Player |
| **Heiser, Rolland V**<br>4721 Ocean Blvd, #W7, Sarasota FL 34242, USA | Army General |
| **Heisler, Eileen**<br>United Talent Agency, U T A Plaza, 9336 Civic Center Dr, Beverly Hills CA 90210 USA | Producer |
| **Heisler, Gregory**<br>Hallmark Institute of Photography, 241 Millers Falls Road, Turners Falls MA 01376, USA | Photographer |
| **Heisler, Todd**<br>Rocky Mountain News, Editorial Dept, 101 W Colfax Ave, Denver CO 80202, USA | Photojournalist |
| **Heiss Jenkins, Carol**<br>3183 Regency Place, Westlake OH 44145, USA | Figure Skater |
| **Heist, Ari**<br>Agency Group Ltd, 142 W 57th St, #600, New York NY 10019 USA | Singer, Songwriter |
| **Heist, Hans-Joachim**<br>H B Mgmt, Marsiliusstr 36, 50937 Cologne, Germany | Actor |
| **Heitman, Dana C**<br>Paradise Artists, PO Box 1821, Ojai CA 93024 USA | Trumpeter (Cherry Poppin' Daddies) |
| **Heitmann, Eric**<br>8510 Madrone Meadow Court, Katy TX 77494, USA | Football Player |
| **Hejda, Jan**<br>9929 Sara Gulch Circle, Parker CO 80138, USA | Ice Hockey Player |
| **Hejduk, Milan**<br>7895 Forest Keep Circle, Parker CO 80134, USA | Ice Hockey Player |
| **Hejlik, Dennis J**<br>Commander, Marine Forces Command, 1468 Ingram St, Norfolk VA 23511 USA | Marine Corps General |
| **Hejnova, Zuzana**<br>Zeyerova 296, 46001 Liberec 1, Czech Republic | Track Athlete |
| **Hekman, Peter M, Jr**<br>5021 Via Papel, San Diego CA 92122, USA | Navy Admiral |
| **Helberg, Simon**<br>Brillstein Entertainment Partners, 9150 Wilshire Blvd, #350, Beverly Hills CA 90212 USA | Actor, Comedian |
| **Held, Alan**<br>Opus3 Artists, 470 Park Ave S, #900, New York NY 10016, USA | Opera Singer |
| **Held, Archie**<br>A New Leaf Garden, 1286 Gilman St, Albany CA 94706, USA | Sculptor |
| **Held, Carl**<br>1551 E Chevy Chase Dr, #313, Glendale CA 91206, USA | Actor |
| **Held, Franklin (Bud)**<br>13367 Caminito Mar Villa, Del Mar CA 92014, USA | Track Athlete |
| **Held, Ingrid**<br>Agents Associes, 201 Rue du Faubourg Saint Honore, 75008 Paris, France | Actress |
| **Held, Mara**<br>Garth Greenan Gallery, 529 W 20th St, #1000, New York NY 10011, USA | Artist |
| **Held, Richard M**<br>Massachusetts Institute of Technology, Psychology Dept, Cambridge MA 02139, USA | Psychologist |
| **Helders, Matthew (Matt)**<br>Wildlife Entertainment, 21 Heathmans Road, London SW6 4TJ, England | Drummer (Arctic Monkeys) |

**Helfand, Eric J** — Baseball Player
7314 Jackson Dr, San Diego CA 92119, USA

**Helfer, Ricki Tigert** — Government Official, Financier
Federal Deposit Insurance, 550 17th St NW, Washington DC 20429, USA

**Helfer, Tricia** — Model, Actress
Gilbertson Entertainment, 1334 3rd Street Promenade, #201, Santa Monica CA 90401 USA

**Helfgott, David** — Concert Pianist
PO Box 264, Vellengen NSW 2454, Australia

**Helford, Bruce** — Producer, Writer
United Talent Agency, U T A Plaza, 9336 Civic Center Dr, Beverly Hills CA 90210 USA

**Helgeland, Brian** — Director, Writer
Brillstein Entertainment Partners, 9150 Wilshire Blvd, #350, Beverly Hills CA 90212 USA

**Helgen, Kristofer M** — Vertebrate Zoologist
Smithsonian Institution, PO Box 37012, MRC 108, Washington DC 20013, USA

**Helgenberger, Marg** — Actress
Sanders/Armstrong/Caserta Mgmt, 2120 Colorado Ave, #120, Santa Monica CA 90404 USA

**helilaj, Nik** — Actor
Cinematography National Center, Blvd Aleksander Mojsiu 77, 1012 Tirana, Albania

**Heline, DeAnn** — Producer, Writer
United Talent Agency, U T A Plaza, 9336 Civic Center Dr, Beverly Hills CA 90210 USA

**Hell, Stefan W** — Nobel Chemistry Laureate, Physicist
Max Planck Biophysical Chemistry Institute, NanoBiophotonics Dept, 37077 Gottingen, Germany

**Helland, J Roy** — Make-Up Artist
Crew Co, 3941 E Chandler Blvd, #106-259, Phoenix AZ 85048, USA

**Hellawell, Keith** — Law Enforcment Official
Government Offices, Great George St, London SW1A 2AL, England

**Hellberg, Nisse** — Singer, Guitarist (Wilmer X)
United Stage Artists, Asogatan 142, Box 11029, 100 61 Stockholm, Sweden

**Hellekant, Charlotte** — Opera Singer
Harrison/Parrott, 5-6 Albion Court, London W6 0QT, England

**Heller, Andre** — Actor, Entertainer, Writer
Singerstr 8, 1010 Vienna, Austria

**Heller, Jane** — Writer
1014 Ladera Lane, Santa Barbara CA 93108, USA

**Heller, Jeffrey M** — Businessman
Electronic Data Systems, 5400 Legacy Dr, Plano TX 75024, USA

**Heller, Joe** — Editorial Cartoonist
Green Bay Press-Gazette, Editorial Dept, 435 E Walnut St, Green Bay WI 54301, USA

**Heller, John H** — Physician, Research Scientist
74 Horseshoe Road, Wilton CT 06897, USA

**Heller, Ronald J (Ron)** — Football Player
3894 Nathan Road, Santa Barbara CA 93110, USA

**Heller, Ronald R (Ron)** — Football Player
538 Stillwater River Road, Absarokee MT 59001, USA

**Hellerman, Fred** — Singer (Weavers), Songwriter
83 Good Hill Road, Weston CT 06883, USA

**Hellestrae, Dale R** — Football Player
4960 E Fellars Dr, Scottsdale AZ 85254, USA

**Hellickson, Russell (Russ)** — Freestyle Wrestler
6893 Lauren Place, Columbus OH 43235, USA

**Helliker, Kevin** — Journalist
Wall Street Journal, Editorial Dept, 1 World Financial Center, New York NY 10281, USA

**Helling, Ricky A (Rick)** — Baseball Player
3672 Landings Dr, Excelsior MN 55331, USA

**Hellman, Bonnie** — Actress
C E S D, 257 Park Ave S, #950, New York NY 10010 USA

**Hellman, Martin E** — Inventor (Public Key Cryptology)
855 Serra St, Stanford CA 94305, USA

**Hellman, Monte** — Director
8588 Appian Way, Los Angeles CA 90046, USA

**Hellmuth, Phil** — Poker Player
World Poker Tour, 1041 N Formosa, Building 99, West Hollywood CA 90046, USA

**Hellner, Marcus** — Cross Country Skier
Haglofs, Henry Bergstens Vag 3, #Hus B, 176 69 Jarfalla, Sweden

**Hellstrand, Kristoffer** — Microbiologist
Goteborg University, Vice Dean's Office, 405 03 Goteborg, Sweden

**Helluin, F Jerome (Jerry)** — Football Player
3930 Southdown Mandalay Road, Houma LA 70360, USA

**Hellwig, Margot** — Singer
Torsten Nitsche, Gabelsberger Str 33, 64521 Gross-Gerau, Germany

**Hellyer, Paul T** — Government Official, Canada
65 Harbour Square, #506, Toronto ON M5J 2L4, Canada

**Helm, Amy** — Singer (Ollabelle)
Columbia Records, 9830 Wilshire Blvd, Beverly Hills CA 90212 USA

**Helm, Zach** — Director, Writer
Gang of Two Productions, 8750 Wilshire Blvd, Beverly Hills CA 90211, USA

**Helmberger, Don V** — Seismologist
California Institute of Technology, Seismology Dept, Pasadena CA 91125, USA

**Helmer, Thomas** — Soccer Player
Rosenthaler Str 40-41, Hackesche Hofe, 10178 Berlin, Germany

**Helmerich, Hans C** — Businessman
Helmerich & Payne Inc, 1437 S Boulder Ave, #1400, Tulsa OK 74119, USA

**Helmerich, Walter H, III** — Businessman
Helmerich & Payne Inc, 1437 S Boulder Ave, #1400, Tulsa OK 74119, USA

**Helmick, Frank** — Army General
Multi-National Security Transition Command, Bagdad Iraq, APO AE 09348, USA

**Helminen, Raimo I** — Ice Hockey Player
269 N Regent St, Port Chester NY 10573, USA

**Helmond, Katherine** — Actress
14170 Montecito Place, Victorville CA 92395, USA

**Helmreich, Ernst J M** — Chemist
University of Wurzburg Biozentrum, Am Hubland, 97074 Wurzburg, Germany

**Helms, Cory** — Writer
Writers Guild of America, 700 W 3rd St, Los Angeles CA 90071, USA

**Helms, Edward P (Ed)** — Actor, Comedian
Creative Artists Agency, 2000 Ave of Stars, #100, Los Angeles CA 90067 USA

| | |
|---|---|
| **Helms, Susan J**<br>Commander, 14th Air Force, Vandenberg Air Force Base CA 93437 USA | Astronaut, Air Force General |
| **Helms, Tommy V**<br>5427 Blue Sky Dr, Cincinnati OH 45247, USA | Baseball Player, Manager |
| **Helms, Wesley R (Wes)**<br>9314 Bear Creek Road, Sterrett AL 35147, USA | Baseball Player |
| **Helnwein, Gottfried**<br>Auf der Burg 2, 56659 Burgbrohl, Germany | Artist |
| **Heloise, (Cruse Evans)**<br>PO Box 795000, San Antonio TX 78279, USA | Columnist, Writer |
| **Helpern, Joan G**<br>Joan & David Helpern Inc, 46 W 55th St, #200, New York NY 10019, USA | Fashion Designer |
| **Helseth, Tine Ting**<br>I M G Artists, Hogarth Business Park, Chiswick, London W4 2TH, England | Concert Trumpeter |
| **Helton, Michael (Mike)**<br>National Association of Stock Car Racing, 1801 Speedway Blvd, Daytona Beach FL 32114 USA | Auto Racing Executive |
| **Helton, Todd L**<br>8720 E 127th Court, Brighton CO 80602, USA | Baseball Player |
| **Helvin, Marie**<br>I M G Models, 131-151 Great Titchfield St, London W1W 5BB, England | Model |
| **Helwig, David G**<br>General Delivery, Belfast PE C0A 1A0, Canada | Writer |
| **Hely, Steve**<br>W M E Entertainment, 9601 Wilshire Blvd, #300, Beverly Hills CA 90210 USA | Actor |
| **Heman, Russell F (Russ)**<br>5555 Canyon Crest Dr, #30, Riverside CA 92507, USA | Baseball Player |
| **Hemingway, Gerardine**<br>Red or Dead Ltd, Courtney Road, Building 201, Wembley, Middlesex HA9 7PP, England | Fashion Designer |
| **Hemingway, Mariel**<br>21300 Victory Blvd, Woodland Hills CA 91367, USA | Model, Actress |
| **Hemingway, Toby**<br>United Talent Agency, U T A Plaza, 9336 Civic Center Dr, Beverly Hills CA 90210 USA | Actor |
| **Hemingway, Wayne**<br>15 Wembley Park Dr, Wembley, Middlesex HA9 8HD, England | Fashion Designer |
| **Hemme, Christy (Sunni)**<br>Strachota Insurance Agency, 43500 Ridge Park Dr, #203, Temecula CA 92590, USA . | Wrestler, Model, Actress |
| **Hemmens, Heather**<br>Untitled Entertainment, 350 S Beverly Dr, #200, Beverly Hills CA 90212 USA | Actress |
| **Hemmer, Bill**<br>Fox-TV, News Dept, 205 E 67th St, New York NY 10065 USA | Commentator |
| **Hemmi, Heini**<br>Chalet Bel-Lia, 7077 Valbella, Switzerland | Alpine Skier |
| **Hemming, Lindy**<br>Independent Talent Group, 40 Whitfield St, London W1T 2RH, England | Costume Designer |
| **Hemmings, Fred, Jr**<br>45-075 Auloa Road, Kaneohe HI 96744, USA | Surfer, Surfing Executive |
| **Hemmings, Luke**<br>Wonder Mgmt, Philips House, 17/617 Elizabeth St, Redfern NSW 2016, Australia | Singer, Guitarist (5 Seconds of Summer) |
| **Hemmis, Paige**<br>Tuff Chix, 22817 Ventura Blvd, #317, Woodland Hills CA 91364, USA | Actress |
| **Hemond, Scott M**<br>263 Florida Ave, Dunedin FL 34698, USA | Baseball Player |
| **Hempel, Amy**<br>Charles Scribner's Sons, 866 3rd Ave, New York NY 10022 USA | Writer |
| **Hemphill, Joel**<br>PO Box 656, Joelton TN 37080, USA | Singer, Songwriter |
| **Hemphill, Labreeska**<br>PO Box 656, Joelton TN 37080, USA | Singer |
| **Hemric, N Dixon (Dick)**<br>1220 7th St NE, North Canton OH 44720, USA | Basketball Player |
| **Hemse, Rebecka**<br>A I S Agency, Bergmansgatan 20, 00150 Helsinfors, Finland | Actress |
| **Hemsky, Ales**<br>16390 Braeburn Ridge Tail, Delray Beach FL 33446, USA | Ice Hockey Player |
| **Hemsley, Stephen J**<br>United HealthCare Corp, Opus Center, 9900 Bren Road E, Hopkins MN 55343, USA | Businessman |
| **Hemsworth, Chris**<br>Roar Mgmt, 9701 Wilshire Blvd, #800, Beverly Hills CA 90212 USA | Actor |
| **Hemsworth, Liam**<br>Roar Mgmt, 9701 Wilshire Blvd, #800, Beverly Hills CA 90212 USA | Actor |
| **Hemsworth, Martin C**<br>11200 Springfield Pike, Cincinnati OH 45246, USA | Mechanical Engineer |
| **Hemus, Solomon J (Solly)**<br>5100 San Felipe St, #194E, Houston TX 77056, USA | Baseball Player, Manager |
| **Henao, Zulay**<br>Creative Artists Agency, 2000 Ave of Stars, #100, Los Angeles CA 90067 USA | Actress |
| **Henchy, Chris**<br>Mosiac Media Group, 9200 W Sunset Blvd, #1000, Los Angeles CA 90069 USA | Actor, Producer, Writer |
| **Hencken, John F**<br>PO Box 2540, Weaverville NC 28787, USA | Swimmer |
| **Henderson, Alan L**<br>8080 N Pennsylvania St, Indianapolis IN 46260, USA | Basketball Player |
| **Henderson, Bruce**<br>Fitch Thomas Mgmt, 75 E End Ave, #4C, New York NY 10028, USA | Singer, Songwriter |
| **Henderson, Cathy**<br>W Mgmt, 266 Elizabeth St, #1A, New York NY 10012, USA | Guitarist (Antigone Rising) |
| **Henderson, Cedric**<br>PO Box 148, Smyrna GA 30081, USA | Basketball Player |
| **Henderson, Craig**<br>Lee Morgan Management, 4 Bloomsbury Square, London WC1A 2RP, England | Actor |
| **Henderson, David L (Dave)**<br>6004 142nd Court SE, Bellevue WA 98006, USA | Baseball Player |
| **Henderson, David M (Dave)**<br>805 Sweet Hollow Court, Middletown DE 19709, USA | Basketball Player |
| **Henderson, Devery V, Jr**<br>835 E Bellevue St, Opelousas LA 70570, USA | Football Player |

**Henderson, Donald A (D A)** — Epidemologist, Educator
1055 W Joppa Road, #710, Towson MD 21204, USA

**Henderson, Felicia D** — Producer, Director, Writer
Paradigm Agency, 360 N Crescent Dr, North Building, Beverly Hills CA 90210 USA

**Henderson, Fergus** — Chef, Writer
Lutyens & Rubinstein, 231 Westbourne Park Road, London W11 1EB, England

**Henderson, Florence** — Actress, Singer
F H B Productions, PO Box 11295, Marina del Rey CA 90295, USA

**Henderson, Gordon** — Fashion Designer
World Hong Kong, 80 W 40th St, New York NY 10018, USA

**Henderson, James A** — Businessman
Cummins Engine Co, PO Box 3005, 500 Jackson St, Columbus IN 47201, USA

**Henderson, Jerome M (Gerald)** — Basketball Player
185 Birkdale Dr, Blue Bell PA 19422, USA

**Henderson, Jerome M (Gerald), Jr** — Basketball Player
Charlotte Hornets, 333 E Trade St, #A, Charlotte NC 28202 USA

**Henderson, John W** — Football Player
11667 Blackstone River Dr, Jacksonville FL 32256, USA

**Henderson, Joseph L (Jose)** — Baseball Player
525 Agua Clara St, El Paso TX 79928, USA

**Henderson, Josh** — Actor
Impression Entertainment, 9229 W Sunset Blvd, #700, Los Angeles CA 90069, USA

**Henderson, Kara** — Sportscaster
N F L Network, 10950 Washington Blvd, #100, Culver City CA 90232 USA

**Henderson, Karen LeCraft** — Judge
US Court of Appeals, 333 Constitution Ave NW, #4400, Washington DC 20001, USA

**Henderson, Kenneth J (Ken)** — Baseball Player
182 La Montagne Court, Los Gatos CA 95032, USA

**Henderson, Kristen** — Guitarist (Antigone Rising)
W Mgmt, 266 Elizabeth St, #1A, New York. NY 10012, USA

**Henderson, Martin** — Actor
Management 360, 9111 Wilshire Blvd, Beverly Hills CA 90210 USA

**Henderson, Melissa** — Soccer Player
Sky Blue F C, 80 Cottontail Lane, #400, Somerset NJ 08873 USA

**Henderson, Michael (Mike)** — Singer, Guitarist, Songwriter
Press Network, PO Box 176, Pleasant Shade TN 37145, USA

**Henderson, Paul, III** — Journalist
Seattle Times, Editorial Dept, 1000 Denny Way, Seattle WA 98109 USA

**Henderson, Pete** — Comedian (Skiles & Henderson)
Jack Grenier Productions, 32630 Concord Dr, Madison Heights MI 48071 USA

**Henderson, Rickey H** — Baseball Player
10561 Englewood Dr, Oakland CA 94605, USA

**Henderson, Shirley** — Actress
Hamilton Hodell, 20 Golden Square, London W1F 9JL, England

**Henderson, Stephen** — Journalist
Detroit Free Press, Editorial Dept, 600 W Fort St, Detroit MI 48226 USA

**Henderson, Stephen C (Steve)** — Baseball Player
10509 Gretna Green Dr, Tampa FL 33626, USA

**Henderson, Tareva** — Singer
PO Box 17678, Nashville TN 37217, USA

**Henderson, Thomas E (Hollywood)** — Football Player
3106 E 13th St, Austin TX 78702, USA

**Henderson, Thomas E (Tom)** — Basketball Player
6822 Baron Gate Court, Spring TX 77379, USA

**Henderson, Wymon** — Football Player
634 Braidwood Dr NW, Acworth GA 30101, USA

**Hendrick, George A, Jr** — Baseball Player
72 Wildwing Court, Las Vegas NV 89135, USA

**Hendricks, Barbara** — Opera Singer
Ingpen & Williams, 131 Putney Bridge Road, London SW15 2PA, England

**Hendricks, Barkley L** — Artist
Connecticut College, Art Dept, 270 Mohegan Ave, New London CT 06320, USA

**Hendricks, Christina** — Actress
42 West, 11400 W Olympic Blvd, #1100, Los Angeles CA 90064 USA

**Hendricks, Jon** — Singer
7437 Savanna Dr, Temperance MI 48182, USA

**Hendricks, Theodore P (Ted)** — Football Player
PO Box 7470, Buffalo Grove IL 60089, USA

**Hendrickson, Darby J** — Ice Hockey Player
3939 Huntingdon Dr, Hopkins MN 55305, USA

**Hendrickson, Elizabeth** — Actress
TalentWorks, 3500 W Olive Ave, #1400, Burbank CA 91505 USA

**Hendrickson, Mark A** — Baseball, Basketball Player
1585 Wyndham Dr, York PA 17403, USA

**Hendrickson, Steven D (Steve)** — Football Player
2558 Miller Ave, Escondido CA 92029, USA

**Hendrie, Phil** — Actor
I C M Partners, 10250 Constellation Blvd, #900, Los Angeles CA 90067 USA

**Hendrix, Elaine** — Actress
Innovative Artists, 1505 10th St, Santa Monica CA 90401 USA

**Hendrix, John W** — Army General
Military Officers Assn, 201 N Washington St, Alexandria VA 22314, USA

**Hendry, Gloria** — Actress
H David Moss, 733 Seward St, #PH, Los Angeles CA 90038 USA

**Hendryx, Nona** — Singer, Songwriter
Take Out Productions, 630 9th Ave, #603, New York NY 10036, USA

**Henenlotter, Frank** — Director
81 Bedford St, #6E, New York NY 10014, USA

**Hengel, David L (Dave)** — Baseball Player
2642 Kingfisher Lane, Lincoln CA 95648, USA

**Hengst, Bernd** — Singer (Die Flippers)
Die Flippers, August Lammle Str 14, 75438 Knittlingen, Germany

**Henin, Justine** — Tennis Player
Blue Entertainment, 333 E Main St, #200, Louisville KY 40202 USA

**Henke, Brad William** — Actor
I F A Talent Agency, 8730 W Sunset Blvd, #490, West Hollywood CA 90069 USA

Henke, Edgar E (Ed) — Football Player
769 Lisa Lane, Ashland OR 97520, USA
Henke, Nolan — Golfer
1323 Florida Ave, Fort Myers FL 33901, USA
Henke, Thomas A (Tom) — Baseball Player
6200 Saint Francis Dr, Jefferson City MO 65101, USA
Henkel, Andrea — Biathlete
Tri: ceps GmbH, Homberger Str 105D, 47441 Moers, Germany
Henkel, Heike — Track Athlete
Tannenbergstr 57, 51373 Leverkusen, Germany
Henkel, Herbert L — Businessman
Ingersoll-Rand Co, PO Box 6820, Piscataway NJ 08855, USA
Henle, Gertrude — Virologist
533 Ott Road, Bala Cynwyd PA 19004, USA
Henley, Don — Singer (Eagles), Songwriter
Front Line Mgmt, 1100 Glendon Ave, #2000, Los Angeles CA 90024 USA
Henley, Drewe — Actor
1 Granary Cottages, Combpyne, Axminster, Devon EX13 8SX, England
Henley, Elizabeth B (Beth) — Writer
W M E Entertainment, 9601 Wilshire Blvd, #300, Beverly Hills CA 90210 USA
Henley, Gail C — Baseball Player
7338 Alta Vista, La Verne CA 91750, USA
Henley, Georgie — Actress
Hamilton Hodell, 20 Golden Square, London W1F 9JL, England
Henley, Jeff — Businessman
Oracle Systems, 500 Oriole Parkway, Redwood Shores CA 94065, USA
Henley, Larry — Composer
Creative Directions, PO Box 335, Brentwood TN 37024, USA
Henley, Patricia — Writer
4229 Florida Ave, Cincinnati OH 45223, USA
Henley, Robert C (Bob) — Baseball Player
11050 Moreland Dr E, Grand Bay AL 36541, USA
Henley, Virginia — Writer
Penguin Putnam Press, 375 Hudson St, New York NY 10014, USA
Henn, Mark — Animator (Little Mermaid)
Walt Disney Animation, PO Box 10200, Orlando FL 32830, USA
Henn, Sean M — Baseball Player
4747 Kelly Road, Aledo TX 76008, USA
Hennagan, Monique — Track Athlete
505 Winter View Way, Stockbridge GA 30281, USA
Henne, Chad S — Football Player
Jacksonville Jaguars, 1 AllTel Stadium Place, Jacksonville FL 32202 USA
Henneman, Brian — Singer, Guitarist (Bottle Rockets)
Undertow, 2307 Milan Court, Champaign IL 61822, USA
Henneman, Michael A (Mike) — Baseball Player
806 Lake Creek Dr, McKinney TX 75070, USA
Hennen, Thomas J — Astronaut
16315 Cascade Caverns Lane, Houston TX 77044, USA
Henner, Marilu — Actress
Gutmann Assoc, 188 S Bevery Dr, Beverly Hills CA 90212, USA
Hennessey, Brad — Baseball Player
6657 Brentridge Lane, Lambertville MI 48144, USA
Hennessey, Debbie — Singer, Songwriter
Rustic Music, 10736 Jefferson Blvd, #777, Culver City CA 90230, USA
Hennessey, Walter (Wally) — Harness Racing Driver
4141 NW 9th Court, Coconut Creek FL 33066, USA
Hennessy, Angelique — Actress, Model
2107 Spring St, Eureka CA 95501, USA
Hennessy, Jill — Actress, Model
Paradigm Agency, 360 N Crescent Dr, North Building, Beverly Hills CA 90210 USA
Hennessy, John L — Educator
Stanford University, President's Office, Stanford CA 94305, USA
Henney, Daniel — Actor
Creative Artists Agency, 2000 Ave of Stars, #100, Los Angeles CA 90067 USA
Hennig, Larry — Wrestler
7426 43rd Ave SE, Saint Cloud MN 56304, USA
Hennigan, Charles T (Charley) — Football Player
3875 Line Ave, #108, Shreveport LA 71106, USA
Hennigan, Phillip W (Phil) — Baseball Player
PO Box 1212, Cookeville TN 38503, USA
Hennigan, T Michael (Mike) — Football Player, Coach
456 Loweland Road, Cookeville TN 38501, USA
Henning, Cameron — Swimmer
Swimming Canada, 2197 Riverside Dr, #700, Ottawa ON K1H 7X3, Canada
Henning, Dan — Football Player, Coach
116 Meeting Way, Ponte Vedra Beach FL 32082, USA
Henning, Linda — Actress
Trinkets & Treasures, 4342 Tujunga Ave, Studio City CA 91604, USA
Henning, Lorne E — Ice Hockey Player, Coach
18 Coldbrook, Irvine CA 92604, USA
Henning, Megan — Actress
Greene Assoc, 1901 Ave of Stars, #130, Los Angeles CA 90067 USA
Henninger, Brian — Golfer
25481 SW Newland Road, Wilsonville OR 97070, USA
Henninger, Egon — Swimmer
Imbiss Uhle, Heuweg 3, 18181 Graal-Muritz, Germany
Hennings, Chad W — Football Player
6101 Bay Valley Court, Flower Mound TX 75022, USA
Hennings, Sam — Actor
S M S Talent, 8383 Wilshire Blvd, #230, Beverly Hills CA 90211 USA
Henning-Walker, Anne — Speed Skater
12359 E LaSalle Place, Aurora CO 80014, USA
Hennis, Randall P (Randy) — Baseball Player
1747 Sienna Dr, Melbourne FL 32934, USA
Henri — Grand Duke, Luxembourg
Palais Grand-Ducal, 17 Rue du Marche-aux-Herbes, 1728 Luxembourg-Ville, Luxembourg

# H

**Henrich, Robert E (Bobby)**
1531 Via Los Coyotes, La Habra CA 90631, USA — Baseball Player

**Henrichs, April**
Olympic Committee, 1 Olympic Plaza, Building 6, Colorado Springs CO 80909 USA — Soccer Player, Coach

**Henricks, Jon N**
254 Laurel Ave, Des Plaines IL 60016, USA — Swimmer

**Henricks, Terence T (Tom)**
Aviation Week, President's Office, 1200 G St NW, #922, Washington DC 20005, USA — Astronaut

**Henrie, David**
Untitled Entertainment, 350 S Beverly Dr, #200, Beverly Hills CA 90212 USA — Actor

**Henrik**
Amalienborg Palace, 1257 Copenhagen K, Denmark — Prince Consort, Denmark

**Henriksen, Donald A (Don)**
18160 Cottonwood Road, Bend OR 97707, USA — Basketball Player

**Henriksen, Lance**
Henriksen Talent Management, 13024 Hesby St, Sherman Oaks CA 91423, USA — Actor

**Henriquez, Ron**
PO Box 38027, Los Angeles CA 90038, USA — Actor

**Henry, Albert J (Al)**
2410 N 52nd St, Philadelphia PA 19131, USA — Basketball Player

**Henry, Alex**
Montreal Canadiens, 1275 Saint Antoine St W, Montreal QC H3C 5L2, Canada — Ice Hockey Player

**Henry, Anthony D**
1619 N La Brea Ave, #511, Los Angeles CA 90028, USA — Football Player

**Henry, Boris**
Semperstr 18, 66123 Saarbrucken, Germany — Track Athlete

**Henry, Buck**
117 E 57th St, New York NY 10022, USA — Actor, Writer

**Henry, Clarence (Frogman)**
3309 Lawrence St, New Orleans LA 70114, USA — Singer, Pianist, Songwriter

**Henry, Dale (Hank)**
8611 Datapoint Dr, #43, San Antonio TX 78229, USA — Ice Hockey Player

**Henry, David**
Rights House, Drury House, 34-43 Russell St, London WC2B 5HA, England — Actor

**Henry, Dwayne A**
407 E Hampstead Court, Middletown DE 19709, USA — Baseball Player

**Henry, F Buford (Butch), III**
12072 Paseo de Amor Lane, El Paso TX 79936, USA — Baseball Player

**Henry, Gloria**
849 N Harper Ave, Los Angeles CA 90046, USA — Actress

**Henry, Gregg**
Domain Talent, 9229 W Sunset Blvd, #710, West Hollywood CA 90069 USA — Actor

**Henry, J J**
6901 Sanctuary Lane, Fort Worth TX 76132, USA — Golfer

**Henry, Joe**
Maine Road Mgmt, 195 Chrystie St, #901F, New York NY 10002, USA — Singer, Guitarist, Songwriter

**Henry, Joseph L**
60 Marinita Ave, San Rafael CA 94901, USA — Dentist

**Henry, Justin**
Metropolitan Talent Agency, 5405 Wilshire Blvd, #218, Los Angeles CA 90036 USA — Actor

**Henry, Kevin L**
1428 Mill Pointe Court, Lawrenceville GA 30043, USA — Football Player

**Henry, Lenny**
P B J Management Ltd, 5 Soho St, London W1D 3QA, England — Actor, Comedian

**Henry, Michael (Mike)**
United Talent Agency, U T A Plaza, 9336 Civic Center Dr, Beverly Hills CA 90210 USA — Producer, Writer, Actor

**Henry, Michael D (Mike)**
10803 Blix St, #3, North Hollywood CA 91602, USA — Football Player, Actor

**Henry, Nicole**
NikiSings, PO Box 192011, Miami Beach FL 33119, USA — Singer

**Henry, R Douglas (Doug)**
1804 Burries Road, Hartland WI 53029, USA — Baseball Player

**Henry, Robert H**
US Court of Appeals, PO Box 1767, Oklahoma City OK 73101, USA — Judge

**Henry, Steve A**
1907 Darlene Way, Emporia KS 66801, USA — Football Player

**Henry, Thierry D (Titi)**
Red Bulls New York, 600 Cape May St, Harrison, NJ 07029 USA — Soccer Player

**Henry, Wallace (Wally)**
3444 Bernadette Court, #A, West Covina CA 91792, USA — Football Player

**Hensby, Mark A**
20802 N Grayhawk Dr, #1024, Scottsdale AZ 85255, USA — Golfer

**Henshall, Douglas**
Artists Partnership, 101 Finsbury Pavement, London EC2A 1RS, England — Actor

**Henshall, Ruthie**
Roar Global Entertainment, 34-35 Eastcastle St, Oxford Circle, London W1W 8DW, England — Singer, Dancer, Actress

**Hensilwood, Christopher**
Iziko Museum, 25 Queen Victoria St, Cape Town, South Africa — Anthropologist

**Henske, Judy**
Fair Star Music, PO Box 326, Plaza Station, Pasadena CA 91102, USA — Singer

**Hensley, Charles F (Chuck)**
259 Bonanza Dr, Erie CO 80516, USA — Baseball Player

**Hensley, Clayton A (Clay)**
3601 Dogwood Blossom Court, Pearland TX 77581, USA — Baseball Player

**Hensley, Jimmy**
2570 Horsepasture Price Road, Ridgeway VA 24148, USA — Auto, Truck Racing Driver

**Hensley, John C**
A P A Talent & Literary Agency, 405 S Beverly Dr, #300, Beverly Hills CA 90212 USA — Actor

**Hensley, Pamela**
Overlook Press, 141 Wooster St, #4B, New York NY 10012, USA — Actress

**Hensley, Shuler**
Paradigm Agency, 360 N Crescent Dr, North Building, Beverly Hills CA 90210 USA — Actor, Singer

**Henson, Darrin Dewitt**
T C A/Jed Root, 9220 Sunset Blvd, #315, Los Angeles CA 90069 90069, USA — Actor, Choreographer

**Henson, Robby**
New Wave Entertainment, 2660 W Olive Ave, Burbank CA 91505, USA — Director, Writer

**Henson, Samuel (Sammy)**
U S Military Academy, Athletic Dept, West Point NY 10996, USA — Freestyle Wrestler
**Henson, Taraji P**
Vincent Cirrincione Assoc, 1516 N Fairfax Ave, Los Angeles CA 90046 USA — Actress, Singer
**Henstridge, Elizabeth**
Evolution Entertainment, 901 N Highland Ave, Los Angeles CA 90038 USA — Actress
**Henstridge, Natasha**
Mosiac Media Group, 9200 W Sunset Blvd, #1000, Los Angeles CA 90069 USA — Actress, Model
**Hentgen, Patrick G (Pat)**
14451 Knightsbridge Dr, Shelby Township MI 48315, USA — Baseball Player
**Hentoff, Nathan I (Nat)**
Village Voice, Editorial Dept, 36 Cooper Square, Front 1, New York NY 10003, USA — Jazz Critic
**Hentrich, Craig A**
9130 Old Smyrna Road, Brentwood TN 37027, USA — Football Player
**Hepburn, Michael**
Cycling Australia, PO Box 6310, Alexandria NSW 2015, Australia — Cyclist
**Hephner, Jeff**
W M E Entertainment, 9601 Wilshire Blvd, #300, Beverly Hills CA 90210 USA — Actor
**Hepler, William L (Bill)**
12518 Fort King Road, Dade City FL 33525, USA — Baseball Player
**Heppel, Leon A**
Cornell University, Biochemistry Dept, Ithaca NY 14850, USA — Biochemist
**Heppner, Ben**
Columbia Artists Mgmt Inc, 5 Columbus Circle, 1790 Broadway, #1600, New York NY 10019 USA — Opera Singer
**Heras-Casado, Pablo**
21C Media Group, 162 W 56th Street, #506, New York NY 10019, USA — Conductor
**Herbers, Ian**
1135 Ridgeway Road, Brookfield WI 53045, USA — Ice Hockey Player
**Herbert of Hemingford, D Nicholas**
Old Rectory, Hemingford Abbots, Huntington Cambridgeshire PE18 9AN, England — Publisher
**Herbert, Bob**
New York Times, Editorial Dept, 229 W 43rd St, New York NY 10036 USA — Columnist
**Herbert, Doug**
Herbert Performance Parts, 4030 Concord Parkway S, Concord NC 28027, USA — Drag Racing Driver
**Herbert, Johnny**
P P Sayber AG, Wildbachstr 9, 8340 Hinwil, Switzerland — Auto Racing Driver
**Herbert, Michael K**
990 Grove St, Evanston IL 60201, USA — Editor
**Herbert, Raymond E (Ray)**
9360 Taylors Turn, Gadsden AL 35901, USA — Baseball Player
**Herbig, Gunther**
Toronto Symphony, 60 Simcoe St, #C116, Toronto ON MJ5 2H5, Canada — Conductor
**Herbig, Michael (Bully)**
HerbX Medienproduktions, Bavariafilmplatz 7, 82031 Geiselgasteig, Germany — Actor, Comedian, Director
**Herbst, Jeffrey**
Colgate University, President's Office, 13 Oak Dr, Hamilton NY 13346, USA — Educator
**Herbst, Susan**
University of Connecticut, President's Office, Storrs CT 06269, USA — Educator
**Herbst, William**
Wesleyan University, Astronomy Dept, Middletown CT 06459, USA — Astronomer
**Herbstreit, Kirk**
ESPN-TV, ESPN Plaza, 935 Middle St, Bristol CT 06010, USA — Sportscaster
**Herczegh, Gezar G**
International Justice Court, Carnegieplein 2, 2517 Hague KJ, Netherlands — Judge
**Herd, Richard**
PO Box 56297, Sherman Oaks CA 91413, USA — Actor
**Herda, Frank A**
PO Box 30967, Cleveland OH 44130, USA — Vietnam War Army Hero (CMH)
**Heredia, Felix P**
PO Box 4842, Hialeah FL 33014, USA — Baseball Player
**Heredia, Gilbert (Gil)**
4233 E Pontatoc Dr, Tucson AZ 85718, USA — Baseball Player
**Heredia, Wilson Jermaine**
Shadow, 10 Universal City Plaza, #2000, Universal City CA 91608, USA — Actor, Singer
**Herek, Stephen R**
Howard Entertainment, 16530 Ventura Blvd, #305, Encino CA 91436 USA — Director
**Herforth, Ralph**
Agentur Velvet, Dieffenbachstr 33, Hof Aufgang C, 10967 Berlin, Germany — Actor
**Herges, Matthew T (Matt)**
21029 N 79th Place, Scottsdale AZ 85255, USA — Baseball Player
**Herheim, Stefan**
Berlin Opera, Behrenstra 55-57, 10117 Berlin, Germany — Opera Director
**Herincx, Raimund**
Monks' Vineyard, Larkbarrow, Shepton Mallet, Somerset BA4 4NR, England — Opera Singer
**Herkenhoff, Matthew B (Matt)**
16000 Baywood Lane, Eden Prairie MN 55346, USA — Football Player
**Herlihy, Tim**
W M E Entertainment, 9601 Wilshire Blvd, #300, Beverly Hills CA 90210 USA — Writer, Actor
**Herman, Bill**
200 Laurel Lake Dr, #305, Hudson OH 44236, USA — Basketball Player
**Herman, David**
Gersh Agency, 9465 Wilshire Blvd, #600, Beverly Hills CA 90212 USA — Actor
**Herman, David J (Dave)**
19 Stephens Lane, Valhalla NY 10595, USA — Football Player
**Herman, Jerry**
5801 Collins Ave, #1400, Miami Beach FL 33140, USA — Composer, Lyricist
**Herman, Mark**
United Agents, 12-26 Lexington St, London W1F 0LE, England — Director
**Herman, Pee Wee, (Paul Reubens)**
PO Box 29373, Los Angeles CA 90029, USA — Actor, Comedian
**Herman, Susan**
American Civil Liberties Union, 125 Broad St, #1800, New York NY 10004, USA — Social Activist
**Hermann, Allen M**
2704 Lookout View Dr, Golden CO 80401, USA — Physicist
**Hermann, Peter**
Gersh Agency, 41 Madison Ave, #3301, New York NY 10010 USA — Actor

H

Henson - Hermann

**Hermansen - Herring**

**Hermansen, Chad B** — Baseball Player
2104 Rhonda Terrace, Henderson NV 89074, USA

**Hermanson, Dustin M** — Baseball Player
9002 E Rimrock Dr, Scottsdale AZ 85255, USA

**Herman-Wurmfeld, Charles** — Director
A P A Talent & Literary Agency, 405 S Beverly Dr, #300, Beverly Hills CA 90212 USA

**Hermaszewski, Miroslav** — Cosmonaut, Poland; Air Force General
Ul Zwirki Wigury 105A, 00912 Warsaw, Poland

**Hermeling, Terry A** — Football Player
PO Box 7321, Bend OR 97708, USA

**Hermesh, Michael** — Sculptor
104-800 Macleod Trail SE, Calgary AB T2G 5E6, Canada

**Hermida, Jeremy R** — Baseball Player
3728 Paces Park Circle SE, Smyrna GA 30080, USA

**Herms, George** — Artist, Sculptor
Tobey Moss Gallery, 7321 Beverly Blvd, Los Angeles CA 90036, USA

**Hernandez Colon, Rafael** — Governor, PR
Puerta de Tierra, PO Box 5788, San Juan PR 00906, USA

**Hernandez Navarro, Agustin** — Architect, Sculptor
Bosque de Acacias 61, Bosques de las Lomas, Mexico City DF 11700, Mexico

**Hernandez, Carlos** — Boxer
2038 Milan, San Antonio TX 78258, USA

**Hernandez, David** — Singer
Jeff Ballard Public Relations, 4814 N Lemona Ave, Sherman Oaks CA 91403, USA

**Hernandez, E Livan** — Baseball Player
560 Gate Lane, Miami FL 33137, USA

**Hernandez, Gerard** — Actor
Artmedia, 20 Ave Rapp, 75007 Paris, France

**Hernandez, Guillermo (Willie)** — Baseball Player
Calle C Buzon, PO Box 125, Bo Espina, Aguada PR 00602, USA

**Hernandez, Jay** — Actor
Alchemy Entertainment, 7024 Melrose Ave, #420, Los Angeles CA 90038 USA

**Hernandez, Jose A** — Baseball Player
22 Calle Sur, Vega Alta PR 00692, USA

**Hernandez, Jose M** — Astronaut
N A S A, Johnson Space Center, 2101 NASA Road, Houston TX 77058 USA

**Hernandez, Keith** — Baseball Player
14 Woodland Court, Southampton NY 11968, USA

**Hernandez, Lazaro** — Fashion Designer
Proenza Schouler, 120 Walker St, #1600, New York NY 10013, USA

**Hernandez, Orlando (El Duque)** — Baseball Player
1001 Brickell Bay Dr, #1710, Miami FL 33131, USA

**Hernandez, Robert J** — Businessman
U S X Corp, 600 Grant St, #450, Pittsburgh PA 15219, USA

**Hernandez, Roberto M** — Baseball Player
5969 Bayview Circle S, Saint Petersburg FL 33707, USA

**Herndon, Junior** — Baseball Player
1477 Sequoia Ave, Craig CO 81625, USA

**Herndon, Kelly E** — Football Player
8932 Merryvale Dr, Twinsburg OH 44087, USA

**Herndon, Larry D** — Baseball Player
6149 Brunswick Road, Arlington TN 38002, USA

**Herndon, Mark J** — Singer, Drummer (Alabama)
Alabama Band Promotions, PO Box 680529, Fort Payne AL 35968, USA

**Herndon, Ty** — Singer
Cody Entertainment Group, PO Box 456, Winchester VA 22604, USA

**Herold, Catherine** — Actress
Agence Peggy Fischer, 11 Rue Du Bouloi, 75001 Paris, France

**Herr, Matt** — Ice Hockey Player
1951 Holly Creek Place, Concord CA 94521, USA

**Herr, Michael** — Writer
I C M Partners, 730 5th Ave, New York NY 10019 USA

**Herr, Thomas M (Tommy)** — Baseball Player
1077 Olde Forge Crossing, Lancaster PA 17601, USA

**Herranz Casado, Julian Cardinal** — Religious Leader
Legislative Texts Curia, Palazzo delle Congregazioni, Piazza Pio XII, #10, 00193 Rome, Italy

**Herre, Maximilian (Max)** — Singer, Songwriter
Nesola GmbH, Stralauer Allee 1, 10245 Berlin, Germany

**Herrem, Camilla** — Handball Player
Byasen Handball Elite, Idrettens Hus, 7495 Trondheim, Norway

**Herremans, Todd** — Football Player
Philadelphia Eagles, 1 Novacare Way, Philadelphia PA 19145 USA

**Herrera Lopez, Hector M** — Soccer Player
F C Porto, Estadio do Drago, Entreda Poente Piso 3, 4350 451 Porto, Portugal

**Herrera, Carl V** — Basketball Player
1201 Dulles Ave, #6305, Stafford TX 77477, USA

**Herrera, Carolina** — Fashion Designer
Carolina Herrera Ltd, 501 Fashion Ave, #1700, New York NY 10018, USA

**Herrera, Efren** — Football Player
861 Atlanta Court, Claremont CA 91711, USA

**Herrera, Kristin** — Actress
Innovative Artists, 1505 10th St, Santa Monica CA 90401 USA

**Herrera, Michael A (Mike)** — Singer, Guitarist (MxPx)
W M E Entertainment, 9601 Wilshire Blvd, #300, Beverly Hills CA 90210 USA

**Herrera, Paloma** — Ballerina
American Ballet Theatre, 890 Broadway, #300, New York NY 10003 USA

**Herriage, W Troy** — Baseball Player
238 California Ave, Oakdale CA 95361, USA

**Herriman, Damon** — Actor
Lisa Mann Creative Mgmt, 99 Spring St, Bondi Junction, NSW 2022, Australia

**Herring, Hayim** — Religious Leader, Rabbi
S T A R, 1660 S Highway 100, #344, Saint Louis Park MO 55416, USA

**Herring, Kimani M (Kim)** — Football Player
6503 Cartmel Lane, Windermere FL 34786, USA

**Herring, Lynn** — Actress
Cynthia Snyder Public Relations, 5739 Colfax Ave, North Hollywood CA 91601, USA

**Herrington, John B** — Astronaut
University of Colorado, Space Studies Center, Colorado Springs CO 80918, USA
**Herrington, John S** — Secretary, Energy; Businessman
Vic Stewart's Steakhouse, 850 S Broadway, Walnut Creek CA 94596, USA
**Herrmann, Donald B (Don)** — Football Player
PO Box 318, Brookside NJ 07926, USA
**Herrmann, Edward** — Actor
Paul Kohner, 9300 Wilshire Blvd, #555, Beverly Hills CA 90212 USA
**Herrmann, Edward M (Ed)** — Baseball Player
13153 Tobiasson Road, Poway CA 92064, USA
**Herrmann, Mark D** — Football Player
8525 Tidewater Dr W, Indianapolis IN 46236, USA
**Herron, Bruce W** — Football Player
8504 S Calumet Ave, Chicago IL 60619, USA
**Herron, Denis** — Ice Hockey Player
12841 Marsh Pointe Way, West Palm Beach FL 33418, USA
**Herron, Keith O** — Basketball Player
5374 Chew Ave, #G2, Philadelphia PA 19138, USA
**Herron, Robert J** — Architect
Herron Assoc, 28-30 Rivington St, London EC2A 3DU, England
**Herron, Tim (Lumpy)** — Golfer
20440 Linden Road, Excelsior MN 55331, USA
**Herron-Braggs, Cindy** — Singer (En Vogue)
28396 Falcon Crest Dr, Canyon Country CA 91351, USA
**Herrscher, Richard F (Rick)** — Baseball Player
7714 Marquette St, Dallas TX 75225, USA
**Hersch, Fred** — Jazz Pianist
Bennett Morgan, 1022 RR 376, #3, Wappinger Falls NY 12590 USA
**Hersch, Michael** — Composer
21C Music Publishing, 30 W 63rd St, #15S, New York NY 10023, USA
**Herschbach, Dudley R** — Nobel Chemistry Laureate
116 Conanat Road, Lincoln MA 01773, USA
**Herschberger, Gary** — Actor
Goodloe Law, 2029 Century Park E, #1400, Los Angeles CA 90067, USA
**Herscher, Uri D** — Religious Leader, Rabbi
Skirball Cultural Center, 2701 N Sepulveda Blvd, Los Angeles CA 90049, USA
**Herschler, E David** — Artist
New Horizon Gallery, PO Box 5859, Santa Barbara CA 93150, USA
**Herschman, Adam** — Actor
Kazarian/Measures/Ruskin, 11969 Ventura Blvd, #300, Studio City CA 91604 USA
**Hersh, Kristin** — Singer, Guitarist (Throwing Muses)
Throwing Mgmt, PO Box 248, Batesville VA 22924, USA
**Hersh, Seymour M** — Writer, Journalist
1211 Connecticut Ave NW, #320, Washington DC 20036, USA
**Hershey, Barbara** — Actress
Independent Artists, 9601 Wilshire Blvd, #750, Beverly Hills CA 90210 USA
**Hershiser, Orel L Q** — Baseball Player, Sportscaster
2167 Orchard Mist St, Las Vegas NV 89135, USA
**Hershko, Avram** — Nobel Chemistry Laureate
Rappaport Family Institute, Institute of Technology, Haifa 32000, Israel
**Herskovitz, Marshall** — Director
Bedford Falls Co, 409 Santa Monica Blvd, #PH, Santa Monica CA 90401, USA
**Herta, Bryan J** — Auto Racing Driver
24803 Los Altos Dr, Santa Clarita CA 91355, USA
**Herthum, Louis** — Actor
Ransack Films, 10000 Celtic Drive, #504, Baton Rouge LA 70809, USA
**Hertling, Mark P** — Army General
Deputy Commanding General, Initial Military Training, TraDoc, Fort Monroe VA 23651, USA
**Hertweck, Neal C** — Baseball Player
111 Leesburg Lane, Troutman NC 28166, USA
**Hertz, C Hellmuth** — Physicist
Lund Institute of Technology, Physics School, 221 00 Lund, Sweden
**Hertz, Stephen A (Steve)** — Baseball Player
10211 SW 96th Terrace, Miami FL 33176, USA
**Hertz, Tom** — Producer, Writer
W M E Entertainment, 9601 Wilshire Blvd, #300, Beverly Hills CA 90210 USA
**Hertzberg, Daniel** — Journalist
Wall Street Journal, Editorial Dept, 1 World Financial Center, #900, New York NY 10281, USA
**Hervey, Jason** — Actor
Hervey/Grimes Talent, 10561 Missouri Ave, #2, Los Angeles CA 90025 USA
**Herzfeld, John M** — Director
New Redemption Pictures, 3000 W Olympic Blvd, Building 3, Santa Monica CA
**Herzigova, Eva** — Model
Czechoslovak Models, Palac Adria, Narodni 40, 11000 Prague 1, Czech Republic
**Herzog, Dorrel N E (Whitey)** — Baseball Player, Manager, Executive
9426 Sappington Estates Dr, Saint Louis MO 63127, USA
**Herzog, Jacques** — Pritzker Architectural Laureate
Herzog & De Meuron Architekten, Rheinschanze 6, 4056 Basel, Switzerland
**Herzog, Roman** — President, Germany
Roman Herzog Institut, Max-Joseph Str 5, 80333 Munich, Germany
**Herzog, Werner** — Director
Werner Herzog Film, Spiegelgasse 9, 1010 Vienna, Austria
**Hesburgh, Theodore M** — Educator
University of Notre Dame, President Emeritus Office, 1301 Hesburgh Library, Notre Dame IN 46556, USA
**Heseltine, Michael R D** — Government Official, England
Thenford House, Banbury, Oxfordshire OX17 2BX, England
**Hesketh, Joseph T (Joe)** — Baseball Player
202 Glenridge Road, East Aurora NY 14052, USA
**Heskett, Myles** — Drummer (Wolfmother)
John Watson Mgmt, PO Box 281, Surry Hills NSW 2010, Australia
**Heskin, Kam** — Actress
Thruline Entertainment, 9250 Wilshire Blvd, #100, Beverly Hills CA 90212 USA
**Heslov, Grant A** — Actor, Producer, Writer
Gold Coast Mgmt, 438 S Venice Blvd #5, Venice CA 90291, USA
**Hesme, Clotilde** — Actress
Artmedia, 20 Ave Rapp, 75007 Paris, France

**Hess, Erika** — Alpine Skier
Aeschi, 6388 Gratenort, Switzerland

**Hess, Jared** — Director, Writer, Actor
United Talent Agency, U T A Plaza, 9336 Civic Center Dr, Beverly Hills CA 90210 USA

**Hess, John B** — Businessman
Amerada Hess Corp, 1185 Ave of Americas, #3900, New York NY 10036, USA

**Hess, Robert** — Sculptor
2661 Dorfs Ave NE, Salem OR 97301, USA

**Hess, Robert G (Bob)** — Ice Hockey Player
PO Box 598, Chesterfield MO 63006, USA

**Hess, Sandra** — Actress
2336 W Irwin Way, Eugene OR 97402, USA

**Hesse, Jonathan A (Jon)** — Football Player
3401 S 30th St, Lincoln NE 68502, USA

**Hesseman, Howard** — Actor
Kass Management, 501 Santa Monica Blvd, #604, Los Angeles CA 90401, USA

**Hessler, Gordon** — Director
8910 Holly Place, Los Angeles CA 90046, USA

**Hessler, Robert R** — Oceanographer
Scripps Institute of Oceanography, Biodiversity Dept, La Jolla CA 92037, USA

**Hester, Carl** — Equestrian
Oaklebrook Mill, Hooks Lane, Malswick, Newent Gloucestershire GL18 1HD, England

**Hester, Dan** — Basketball Player
13846 N Sunset Dr, Fountain Hills AZ 85268, USA

**Hester, Devin** — Football Player
11103 Bridge House Road, Windermere FL 34786, USA

**Hester, Jessie L** — Football Player
12813 Pineacre Court, Wellington FL 33414, USA

**Hester, Phil** — Businessman
Advanced Micro Devices, 1 A M D Place, PO Box 3453, Sunnyvale CA 94088, USA

**Hetfield, James** — Singer, Guitarist (Metallica)
Q Prime Inc, 729 7th Ave, #1400, New York NY 10019, USA

**Hetki, John E (Johnny)** — Baseball Player
4004 Stary Dr, Cleveland OH 44134, USA

**Hetland, Tor Arne** — Cross Country Skier
Leirbruveien 24, 7026 Trondheim, Norway

**Hetrick, Jennifer** — Actress
Liberman/Zerman Mgmt, 252 N Larchmont Blvd, #200, Los Angeles CA 90004, USA

**Hetson, Greg** — Guitarist (Red Kross, Circle Jerks)
Goldstar Public Relations, PO Box 130, Ross on Wye HR9 6WY, England

**Hettich, Georg** — Nordic Combined Skier
Albert-Schweitzer-Str 1, 78136 Schonach, Germany

**Hetzel, Eric P** — Baseball Player
2271 Hetzel Road, Crowley LA 70526, USA

**Hetzel, Fred** — Basketball Player
40290 Iron Liege Court, Leesburg VA 20176, USA

**Heuer, Rolf** — Physicist
C E R N, Large Hadron Collider, 1211 Geneva 23, Switzerland

**Heughan, Sam** — Actor
United Talent Agency, U T A Plaza, 9336 Civic Center Dr, Beverly Hills CA 90210 USA

**Heuring, Lori** — Actress
Baker Winokur Ryder Public Relations, 9100 Wilshire Blvd, #500W, Beverly Hills CA 90212 USA

**Heusinger, Patrick** — Actor
Group Entertainment, 115 W 29th St, #1102, New York NY 10001, USA

**Heward, Jamie** — Ice Hockey Player
159 Bentley Dr, Regina SK S4N 4S7, Canada

**Hewer, Mitch** — Actor
United Agents, 12-26 Lexington St, London W1F 0LE, England

**Hewett, Howard** — Singer (Shalamar)
Wenig-LaMonica Associates, 580 White Plains Road, #130, Tarrytown NY 10591 USA

**Hewish, Anthony** — Nobel Physics Laureate
Pryor's Cottage, Kingston, Cambridge CB3 7NQ, England

**Hewitt, Angela** — Concert Pianist
Opus 3 Artists, 470 Park Ave S, #900N, New York NY 10016 USA

**Hewitt, Jennifer Love** — Actress, Singer
11601 Wilshire Blvd, #1840, Los Angeles CA 90025, USA

**Hewitt, Lleyton** — Tennis Player
PO Box 1235, North Sydney NSW 2059, Australia

**Hewitt, Martin** — Actor
1147 Horn Ave, #3, West Hollywood CA 90069, USA

**Hewitt, Paul** — Basketball Coach
Georgia Institute of Technology, Athletic Dept, Atlanta GA 30332, USA

**Hewitt, Peter** — Director
Casorotto Ramsay, Waverley House, 7-12 Noel St, London W1F 8GQ, England

**Hewlett, David** — Actor
Northern Exposure Talent, 2888 Birch St, Vancouver BC V6H 2T6, Canada

**Hewlett, Jamie C** — Cartoonist (Tank Girl)
Nasty Little Man, 110 Greene St, #605, New York NY 10012 USA

**Hewson, John** — Government Official, Australia
A B N Amro Australia, 10 Spring St, #14, Sydney NSW 2000, Australia

**Hewson, John G (Jack)** — Basketball Player
114 Tahlequah Lane, Loudon TN 37774, USA

**Hextall, Dennis H** — Ice Hockey Player
2631 Harvest Hill Dr, Brighton MI 48114, USA

**Hextall, Ronald (Ron)** — Ice Hockey Player, Executive
118 Calico Court, Paupack PA 18451, USA

**Hexum, Nicholas L (Nick)** — Singer, Songwriter (311)
311 Hive, 8904 Florence Dr, Omaha NE 68147, USA

**Hey, Virginia** — Actress
Anthony Williams Mgmt, 50 Oxford St, Paddington NSW 2021, Australia

**Heydeman, Gregory G (Greg)** — Baseball Player
702 Ramona Ave, Monterey CA 93940, USA

**Heyer, Ingeburg** — Astronomer
PO Box 143, Burtonsville MD 20866, USA

**Heyland, Rob** — Actor
United Agents, 12-26 Lexington St, London W1F 0LE, England

|  |  |
|---|---|
| **Heylen, Ilse**<br>Judo Centrum Leuven, Waversebaan 46, 3001 Leuven, Belgium | Judo Athlete |
| **Heyman, David**<br>Bloom Hergott Diemer, 150 S Rodeo Dr, #300, Beverly Hills CA 90212 USA | Producer |
| **Heyman, Mark**<br>Protozoa Pictures, 104 N 7th St, Brooklyn NY 11211, USA | Writer |
| **Heyman, Richard**<br>Ligand Pharmaceuticals, 9393 Town Center Dr, #100, San Diego CA 92121, USA | Geneticist |
| **Heymans, Emilie**<br>1926 Victoria, Greenfield Park QC J4B 1M6, Canada | Diver |
| **Heynckes, Josef (Jupp)**<br>Fischeln 16, 41366 Schwalmtal, Germany | Soccer Player, Manager |
| **Heynert, Josef**<br>Agentur Gottschalk & Behrens, Sillemstr 60A, 20257 Hamburg, Germany | Actor |
| **Heywood, Anne**<br>9966 Liebe Dr, Beverly Hills CA 90210, USA | Actress |
| **Hiassen, Carl**<br>Knopf Publishers, 1745 Broadway, New York NY 10019 USA | Writer |
| **Hiatt, Andrew**<br>Scripps Research Foundation, 10666 N Torrey Pines Road, La Jolla CA 92037, USA | Molecular Biologist |
| **Hiatt, Fred**<br>Washington Post, Editorial Dept, 1150 15th St NW, Washington DC 20071 USA | Journalist |
| **Hiatt, Jack E**<br>1408 Fisher Road, Roseburg OR 97471, USA | Baseball Player |
| **Hiatt, John**<br>United Talent Agency, U T A Plaza, 9336 Civic Center Dr, Beverly Hills CA 90210 USA | Singer, Guitarist, Songwriter |
| **Hiatt, Philip A (Phil)**<br>30 Littleton St, Cantonment FL 32533, USA | Baseball Player |
| **Hiatt, Shana**<br>Shandrew Public Relations, 1050 S Stanley Ave, Los Angeles CA 90019 USA | Model |
| **Hibbard, J Gregory (Greg)**<br>5287 Conifer View Lane, Lakeland TN 38002, USA | Baseball Player |
| **Hibbert, Edward**<br>Sovereign Talent Group, 8421 Wilshire Blvd, #200, Beverly Hills CA 90211 USA | Actor |
| **Hibbert, Frederick N (Toots)**<br>Keep on Kicking Music, 330 84th St, #9, Miami Beach FL 33141, USA | Singer, Orchestra Leader |
| **Hibbert, Roy D**<br>Indiana Pacers, Conseco Fieldhouse, 125 S Pennsylvania, Indianapolis IN 46204 USA | Basketball Player |
| **Hibbs, James K (Jim)**<br>4659 Foothill Road, Ventura CA 93003, USA | Baseball Player |
| **Hibel, Edna**<br>1530 53rd St, West Palm Beach FL 33407, USA | Artist |
| **Hick, Graeme A**<br>Worcestershire County Cricket Club, New Road, Worcester WR2 4QQ, England | Cricketer |
| **Hickam, Homer H, Jr**<br>9532 Hemlock Dr SE, Huntsville AL 35803, USA | Writer |
| **Hicke, Ernie**<br>5287 S Sugarberry Court, Gilbert AZ 85298, USA | Ice Hockey Player |
| **Hickerson, Bryan D**<br>275 S Hunters Ridge, Warsaw IN 46582, USA | Baseball Player |
| **Hickey, David L**<br>Security Police Fire Professional Union, 25510 Kelly Road, Roseville MI 48066, USA | Labor Leader |
| **Hickey, John Benjamin**<br>Paradigm Agency, 360 N Crescent Dr, North Building, Beverly Hills CA 90210 USA | Actor |
| **Hickey, Thomas H (Bo)**<br>94 Field Crest Road, New Canaan CT 06840, USA | Football Player |
| **Hickey, Thomas J**<br>2127 Bobbyber Dr, Vienna VA 22182, USA | Air Force General |
| **Hickey, William V**<br>Sealed Air Corp, Park 80 E, Saddle Brook NJ 07663, USA | Businessman |
| **Hickland, Catherine**<br>255 W 84th St, #2A, New York NY 10024, USA | Actress |
| **Hickman, Ana**<br>I D Model Mgmt, 137 Varick St, New York NY 10013, USA | Model |
| **Hickman, Dallas M**<br>6521 E Dreyfus Dr, Scottsdale AZ 85254, USA | Football Player |
| **Hickman, Darryl**<br>171 Hermosillo Road, Santa Barbara CA 93108, USA | Actor |
| **Hickman, Dwayne**<br>PO Box 17226, Encino CA 91416, USA | Actor |
| **Hickman, Fred**<br>Atlanta Braves, Turner Field, 755 Hank Aaron Dr, Atlanta GA 30315 USA | Sportscaster |
| **Hickman, James L (Jim)**<br>PO Box 455, Henning TN 38041, USA | Baseball Player |
| **Hickman, Johnny**<br>Back Bay Mgmt, 397 Little Neck Road, #305, Virginia Beach VA 23452 USA | Singer, Guitarist (Cracker) |
| **Hickman, Sara**<br>Roots Agency, 177 Woodland Ave, Westwood NJ 07675, USA | Singer, Songwriter |
| **Hickox, Anthony**<br>United Agents, 12-26 Lexington St, London W1F 0LE, England | Director |
| **Hickox, Marc**<br>Creative Drive Artists, 166 King St E, #400, Toronto ON M5A 1J3, Canada | Actor |
| **Hicks, Artis**<br>1804 Woods Edge Dr NE, Leesburg VA 20176, USA | Football Player |
| **Hicks, Bill**<br>Keith Case Assoc, 1025 17th Ave S, #200, Nashville TN 37212 USA | Fiddler (Red Clay Ramblers) |
| **Hicks, Catherine**<br>S M S Talent, 8383 Wilshire Blvd, #230, Beverly Hills CA 90211 USA | Actress |
| **Hicks, Clifford W (Cliff), Jr**<br>8967 Windham Court, Spring Valley CA 91977, USA | Football Player |
| **Hicks, Dan**<br>NBC-TV, Sports Dept, 30 Rockefeller Plaza, #270E, New York NY 10112 USA | Sportscaster |
| **Hicks, Daniel I (Dan)**<br>Dave Kaplan Mgmt, 1126 S Coast Highway, #101, Encinitas CA 92024, USA | Singer |
| **Hicks, Dwight**<br>PO Box 342, Sierra Madre CA 91025, USA | Football Player |

H

**Hicks - Higgins**

**Hicks, Elizabeth (Betty)** — Golfer
669 Canyon View Dr, Laguna Beach CA 92651, USA

**Hicks, Eric D** — Football Player
6714 W 148th Terrace, Overland Park KS 66223, USA

**Hicks, India A C** — Model, Interior Designer
Storm Model Agency, 5 Jubilee Place, Chelsea, London SW3 3TD, England

**Hicks, J Stephen** — Photographer
2445 Kanan Road, Agoura Hills CA 91301, USA

**Hicks, James E (Jim)** — Baseball Player
9331 Portal Dr, Houston TX 77031, USA

**Hicks, John C, Jr** — Football Player
3287 Green Cook Road, Johnstown OH 43031, USA

**Hicks, Michelle** — Actress, Model
Domain Talent, 9229 W Sunset Blvd, #710, West Hollywood CA 90069 USA

**Hicks, Robert** — Writer
Warner Books, 1271 Ave of Americas, New York NY 10020 USA

**Hicks, Scott** — Director, Writer
PO Box 824, Kent Town 5071, South Africa

**Hicks, Sylvester** — Football Player
1891 W Fletcher Run Circle, #103, Cordova TN 38016, USA

**Hicks, Taylor** — Singer
19 Entertainment, 8560 W Sunset Blvd, #900, West Hollywood CA 90069, USA

**Hicks, Thomas L (Tom)** — Football Player
207 Rivershire Lane, #106, Lincolnshire IL 60069, USA

**Hicks, Tyler** — Photojournalist
New York Times, Editorial Dept, 229 W 43rd St, New York NY 10036 USA

**Hicks, W Joseph (Joe)** — Baseball Player
2707 Brookmere Road, Charlottesville VA 22901, USA

**Hicks, Wayne W** — Ice Hockey Player
7726 E Buteo Dr, Scottsdale AZ 85255, USA

**Hicks, Wilmer Kenzie (W K)** — Football Player
10149 Kemp Forest Dr, Houston TX 77080, USA

**Hickson, James E (J J), Jr** — Basketball Player
Denver Nuggets, Pepsi Center, 1000 Chopper Circle, Denver CO 80204 USA

**Hidalgo, David** — Singer (Los Lobos), Songwriter
Gold Mountain, 3940 Laurel Canyon Blvd, #444, Studio City CA 91604 USA

**Hidalgo, John** — Government Official
Mays Valentine Davenport Moore, 1899 L St NW, Washington DC 20036, USA

**Hiddleston, Thomas W (Tom)** — Actor
W M E Entertainment, 9601 Wilshire Blvd, #300, Beverly Hills CA 90210 USA

**Hide, Herbie** — Boxer
Lionheart Boxing, 415 Argyle Road, #5M, Brooklyn NY 11218, USA

**Hide, Raymond** — Geophysicist
17 Clinton Ave, East Molesey, Surrey KT8 0HS, England

**Hieb, Richard J** — Astronaut
N A S A, Johnson Space Center, 2101 NASA Road, Houston TX 77058 USA

**Hiebert, Erwin N** — Historian
40 Payson Road, Belmont MA 02478, USA

**Hiegel, Catherine** — Actress
Artmedia, 20 Ave Rapp, 75007 Paris, France

**Hier, Marvin** — Religious Leader, Rabbi, Social Activist
Simon Wiesenthal Holocaust Center, 9766 W Pico Blvd, Los Angeles CA 90035, USA

**Hieronymus, Clara W** — Journalist
50 Spring St, Savannah TN 38372, USA

**Hietanen, Juuso** — Ice Hockey Player
H V 71, Kinnarps Arena, 554 54 Jonkoping, Sweden

**Hietpas, Joseph C (Joe)** — Baseball Player
611 E Timberline Dr, Appleton WI 54913, USA

**Higareda, Martha** — Actress
I C M Partners, 10250 Constellation Blvd, #900, Los Angeles CA 90067 USA

**Higdon, Bruce** — Cartoonist
210 Canvasback Court, Murfreesboro TN 37130, USA

**Higgenson, Tom** — Singer, Songwriter (Plain White T's)
One Moment Mgmt, PO Box 55156, Sherman Oaks CA 91413 USA

**Higginbotham, Joan E** — Astronaut
1409 Mija Lane, Seabrook TX 77586, USA

**Higginbotham, Patrick E** — Judge
US Court of Appeals, US Courthouse, 1100 Commerce St, Dallas TX 75242, USA

**Higgins, Alan J** — Producer
Creative Artists Agency, 2000 Ave of Stars, #100, Los Angeles CA 90067 USA

**Higgins, Anthony** — Actor
I C M Partners, 10250 Constellation Blvd, #900, Los Angeles CA 90067 USA

**Higgins, Bertie** — Singer, Songwriter
J-Bird Entertainment, 248 W Park Ave, #180, Long Beach NY 11561 USA

**Higgins, Chester, Jr** — Photographer
New York Times, Editorial Dept, 229 W 43rd St, New York NY 10036, USA

**Higgins, David Anthony** — Actor, Writer, Producer
Stone Manners Salners, 6100 Wilshire Blvd, #1500, Los Angeles CA 90035 USA

**Higgins, Dennis D** — Baseball Player
1123 Boonville Road, Jefferson Cty MO 65109, USA

**Higgins, J Kenneth** — Test Pilot
Boeing Commercial Airplane Group, PO Box 3707, Seattle WA 98124, USA

**Higgins, Jack** — Editorial Cartoonist
59 Waverly Ave, Clarendon Hills IL 60514, USA

**Higgins, Jack** — Writer
September Tide, Mont de la Roque, Jersey, Channel Islands JE3 8BQ, England

**Higgins, Joel** — Actor, Singer
Gage Group, 450 7th Ave, #1809, New York NY 10123 USA

**Higgins, Joel** — Actor, Singer
B R S / Gage Talent Agency, 1650 Broadway, #1410, New York NY 10019 USA

**Higgins, John** — Swimmer, Swimming Coach
40 Williams Dr, Annapolis MD 21401, USA

**Higgins, John Michael** — Actor
Magnolia Entertainment, 9595 Wilshire Blvd, #601, Beverly Hills CA 90212, USA

**Higgins, Melissa (Missy)** — Singer, Songwriter
John Watson Mgmt, PO Box 281 Surry Hills NSW 2010, Australia

432                                                                 V.I.P. Address Book

| | |
|---|---|
| **Higgins, Michael D** | President, Ireland |
| President's Office, 'Áras an Uachtaráin, Phoenix Park, Dublin 8, Ireland | |
| **Higgins, Michael S (Mike)** | Basketball Player |
| 137 48th Ave, Greeley CO 80634, USA | |
| **Higgins, Robert** | Businessman |
| Fleet Boston Corp, PO Box 55850, Boston MA 02205, USA | |
| **Higgins, Roderick D (Rod)** | Basketball Player |
| 743 Mendenhall Court, Fort Mill SC 29715, USA | |
| **Higgins, Rosalyn** | Judge |
| International Court of Justice, Peace Palace, 2517 The Hague KJ, Netherlands | |
| **Higgins, Steve** | Actor |
| Creative Artists Agency, 2000 Ave of Stars, #100, Los Angeles CA 90067 USA | |
| **Higginson, John** | Pathologist |
| 16 Sundew Road, Savannah GA 31411, USA | |
| **Higginson, Torri** | Actress |
| Don Buchwald Talent Agency, 6500 Wilshire Blvd, #2200, Los Angeles CA 90048 USA | |
| **Higgs, Kenny** | Basketball Player |
| 746 Sargent Dr, Owensboro KY 42301, USA | |
| **Higgs, Mark D** | Football Player |
| 10829 NW 5th St, Plantation FL 33324, USA | |
| **Higgs, Peter W** | Nobel Physics Laureate |
| University of Edinburgh, Physics & Astronomy School, Edinburgh EH9 3JZ, Scotland | |
| **Higham, Scott** | Journalist |
| Washington Post, Editorial Dept, 1150 15th St NW, Washington DC 20071 USA | |
| **Highmore, Freddie** | Actor |
| Artist Rights Group, 4A Exmoor St, London W10 6BD, England | |
| **Highsmith, Alonzo W** | Football Player |
| 28 Warwick Lane, Missouri City TX 77459, USA | |
| **Hightower, Chelsie K** | Dancer |
| Abrams Artists, 9200 W Sunset Blvd, #1125, West Hollywood CA 90069 USA | |
| **Hightower, Rosetta** | Singer (Orlons) |
| Lustig Talent, PO Box 770850, Orlando FL 32877 USA | |
| **Higuera, Joel** | Singer (Los Tucanes de Tijuana) |
| Tucanes Inc, 6055 E Washington Blvd, #455, Commerce CA 90040, USA | |
| **Higuera, Teodoro V** | Baseball Player |
| 1567 S Sycamore Place, Chandler AZ 85286, USA | |
| **Hilario, Maybyner R (Nene)** | Basketball Player |
| 300 W 11th Ave, #18C, Denver CO 80204, USA | |
| **Hilbert, Andy** | Ice Hockey Player |
| 419 N Michigan Ave, Howell MI 48843, USA | |
| **Hildebrand, Roger H** | Astronomer, Astrophysicist |
| University of Chicago, Fermi Institute, 5640 S Ellis Ave, Chicago IL 60637, USA | |
| **Hildebrandt, Greg** | Cartoonist (Terry & the Pirates) |
| Spiderweb Art, 5 Waterloo Road, Hopatcong NJ 07843, USA | |
| **Hildreth, Eugene A (Pat)** | Physician |
| 2000 Cambridge Ave, #103, Reading PA 19610, USA | |
| **Hildreth, Mark** | Actor |
| Characters Talent Agency, 8 Elm St, Toronto ON M5G 1G7, Canada | |
| **Hilfiger, Tommy** | Fashion Designer |
| Tommy Hilfiger USA, 601 W 26th St, #500, New York NY 10001, USA | |
| **Hilgenberg, Jay W** | Football Player |
| 1296 Kimmer Court, Lake Forest IL 60045, USA | |
| **Hilgenberg, Joel** | Football Player |
| 2027 Ridgeway Dr, Iowa City IA 52245, USA | |
| **Hilgenbrinck, Tad** | Actor |
| Innovative Artists, 1505 10th St, Santa Monica CA 90401 USA | |
| **Hilgendorf, Thomas E (Tom)** | Baseball Player |
| PO Box 124, Camanche IA 52730, USA | |
| **Hilger, Russell T (Rusty)** | Football Player |
| 2625 SW 67th St, Oklahoma City OK 73159, USA | |
| **Hiljus, Eric K** | Baseball Player |
| 2253 Demaray Dr, Grants Pass OR 97527, USA | |
| **Hill Smith, Marilyn** | Opera Singer |
| Music International, 13 Ardilaun Road, Highbury, London N5 2QR, England | |
| **Hill, Aaron W** | Baseball Player |
| 4741 W Addisyn Court, Visalia CA 93291, USA | |
| **Hill, Achim** | Rowing Athlete |
| Dahmestr 94, 12526 Berlin, Germany | |
| **Hill, Al D** | Ice Hockey Player |
| 4807 Margaret Lane, Harrisburg PA 17110, USA | |
| **Hill, Amy** | Actress |
| J G M, 15 Lexham Mews, London W8 6JW, England | |
| **Hill, Anita** | Educator |
| Brandeis University, Heller Law School, Waltham MA 02254, USA | |
| **Hill, Armond G** | Basketball Player |
| 1626 Laurens Way SW, Atlanta GA 30311, USA | |
| **Hill, Bernard** | Actor |
| Optimism Entertainment, 3383 Robertson Place, #2, Los Angeles CA 90034, USA | |
| **Hill, Bob** | Basketball Coach |
| 205 Rio Cordillera, Boerne TX 78006, USA | |
| **Hill, Brendan C C** | Drummer (Blues Traveler) |
| C3 Presents, 98 San Jacinto Blvd, #400, Austin TX 78701, USA | |
| **Hill, Brian** | Basketball Coach |
| Detroit Pistons, Palace, 4 Championship Dr, Auburn Hills MI 48326 USA | |
| **Hill, Bruce E** | Football Player |
| 1919 E Citation Lane, Tempe AZ 85284, USA | |
| **Hill, Calvin** | Football Player, Executive |
| 10300 Walker Lake Dr, Great Falls VA 22066, USA | |
| **Hill, Carolyn** | Golfer |
| 5906 Summer Point Blvd S, Gulfport FL 33707, USA | |
| **Hill, Damon G D** | Auto Racing Driver |
| B R D C, Silverstone, Towcester, Northamptonshire NN12 8TN, England | |
| **Hill, Dan** | Singer, Songwriter |
| Paquin Entertainment, 1067 Sherwin Road, Winnipeg MB R3H 1C1, Canada | |
| **Hill, Dave** | Actor, Comedian |
| C E S D, 10635 Santa Monica Blvd, #130, Los Angeles CA 90025 USA | |

**H**

**Higgins - Hill**

**H**

| | |
|---|---|
| **Hill, David**<br>13844 Buckhart St, Corona CA 92880, USA | Football Player |
| **Hill, David H (Dave)**<br>402 Le Grand Dr, Panama City Beach FL 32413, USA | Football Player |
| **Hill, Donald E (Donnie)**<br>6 Knob Hill, Laguna Niguel CA 92677, USA | Baseball Player |
| **Hill, Draper**<br>1818 Northbrook Dr, Lancaster PA 17601, USA | Editorial Cartoonist |
| **Hill, Dule**<br>I C M Partners, 10250 Constellation Blvd, #900, Los Angeles CA 90067 USA | Actor |
| **Hill, Dusty**<br>Sanctuary Mgmt, 15301 Ventura Blvd, Building B, Sherman Oaks CA 91403, USA | Singer, Bassist (ZZ Top) |
| **Hill, Eddie**<br>Eddie Hill's Fun Cycles, 401 N Scott Ave, Wichita Falls TX 76306, USA | Drag Racing Driver |
| **Hill, Edwin D**<br>International Brotherhood of Electrical Workers, 1125 15th St NW, Washington DC 20005, USA | Labor Leader |
| **Hill, Eric D**<br>PO Box 870637, New Orleans LA 70187, USA | Football Player |
| **Hill, Erica R**<br>CNN-TV, News Dept, 190 Marietta Ave SW, Atlanta GA 30303 USA | Commentator |
| **Hill, Faith**<br>Creative Artists Agency, 2000 Ave of Stars, #100, Los Angeles CA 90067 USA | Singer, Actress |
| **Hill, Frederick G (Fred)**<br>31441 Paseo Riobo, San Juan Capistrano CA 92675, USA | Football Player |
| **Hill, Garry A**<br>9602 Willowglen Trail, Charlotte NC 28215, USA | Baseball Player |
| **Hill, Gary**<br>Donald Young Gallery, 224 S Michigan Ave, #266, Chicago IL 60604, USA | Artist |
| **Hill, Geoffrey W**<br>Boston University, University Professors, 745 Commonwealth St, Boston MA 02215, USA | Writer |
| **Hill, George J, Jr**<br>Indiana Pacers, Conseco Fieldhouse, 125 S Pennsylvania, Indianapolis IN 46204 USA | Basketball Player |
| **Hill, Gerald A (Jerry)**<br>300 Hudson St, #202, Denver CO 80220, USA | Football Player |
| **Hill, Glenallen**<br>2913 Cortez Court, College Station TX 77845, USA | Baseball Player |
| **Hill, Grant H**<br>9600 McCormick Place, Windermere FL 34786, USA | Basketball Player |
| **Hill, Gregory M (Greg)**<br>8014 Downington Court, Spring TX 77379, USA | Football Player |
| **Hill, Harry**<br>4225 Shore Dr, #147, Virginia Beach VA 23455, USA | Hero |
| **Hill, Ian**<br>Trinifold Mgmt, 12 Oval Road, #300, Camden, London NW1 7DH, England | Bassist (Judas Priest) |
| **Hill, J D**<br>2375 W Comstock Dr, Chandler AZ 85224, USA | Football Player |
| **Hill, Jack**<br>5310 Clear Run Dr, Wilmington NC 28403, USA | Director, Producer, Writer |
| **Hill, James C**<br>US Court of Appeals, PO Box 52598, Jacksonville FL 32201, USA | Judge |
| **Hill, James J**<br>1518 Crain St, Evanston IL 60202, USA | WW II Marine Corps Hero |
| **Hill, Jane H**<br>University of Arizona, Language Dept, Tucson AZ 85721, USA | Language Educator |
| **Hill, Jeremy D**<br>10050 Gooding Dr, Dallas TX 75229, USA | Baseball Player |
| **Hill, Jim**<br>4120 Parva Ave, Los Angeles CA 90027, USA | Football Player, Sportscaster |
| **Hill, Jody**<br>Rough House, 1722 Whitley Ave, Los Angeles CA 90028, USA | Actor, Producer, Director |
| **Hill, John S**<br>2005 Boyce Bridge Road, Creedmoor NC 27522, USA | Football Player |
| **Hill, Jon Michael**<br>CornerStone Talent Agency, 37 West 20th St, #1108, New York NY 10011, USA | Actor |
| **Hill, Jonah**<br>W M E Entertainment, 9601 Wilshire Blvd, #300, Beverly Hills CA 90210 USA | Actor |
| **Hill, Jordan**<br>Los Angeles Lakers, Staples Center, 1111 S Figueroa St, Los Angeles CA 90015 USA | Basketball Player |
| **Hill, Jordan**<br>143/Atlantic Records, 9229 W Sunset Blvd, #900, West Hollywood CA 90069, USA | Singer, Songwriter |
| **Hill, Judith**<br>W M E Entertainment, 9601 Wilshire Blvd, #300, Beverly Hills CA 90210 USA | Singer, Songwriter |
| **Hill, Julia Butterfly**<br>Circle of Life Foundation, PO Box 6747, Albany CA 94706, USA | Environmentalist |
| **Hill, Kenneth W (Ken)**<br>1360 Shady Oaks Dr, Southlake TX 76092, USA | Baseball Player |
| **Hill, Kenneth W (Kenny)**<br>121 Hawkins Place, Boonton NJ 07005, USA | Football Player |
| **Hill, Kent A**<br>630 Hawthorne Place, Fayetteville GA 30214, USA | Football Player |
| **Hill, Kim**<br>Breen Agency, 110 30th Ave, #3, Nashville TN 37203, USA | Singer, Guitarist |
| **Hill, Koyie D**<br>1704 NW 146th St, Edmond OK 73013, USA | Baseball Player |
| **Hill, Lauren Michelle**<br>Playboy Promotions, 9346 Civic Center Dr, #200, Beverly Hills CA 90210 USA | Model, Actress |
| **Hill, Lauryn**<br>Press Here, 138 W 25th St, #700, New York NY 10001, USA | Rap Artist (Fugees), Actress |
| **Hill, Marc K**<br>203 Maple St, Elsberry MO 63343, USA | Baseball Player |
| **Hill, Michael J (Mike)**<br>6750 Jefferson Road, Brooklyn MI 49230, USA | Golfer |
| **Hill, Pat**<br>California State University, Athletic Dept, Fresno CA 93740, USA | Football Coach |
| **Hill, Phelan**<br>Leander Rowing Club, Henley-on-Thames, Oxfordshire RG9 2LP, England | Rowing Athlete |

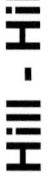

**Hill, Randal T**
18101 SW 112th Ave, Miami FL 33157, USA — Football Player

**Hill, Richard J (Rich)**
17 Spafford Road, Milton MA 02186, USA — Baseball Player

**Hill, Ron**
PO Box 11, Hyde, Cheshire SK14 1RD, England — Track Athlete

**Hill, Sean**
2735 E Carob Dr, Chandler AZ 85286, USA — Ice Hockey Player

**Hill, Shaun**
4956 Shorewood Dr, Osage Beach MO 65065, USA — Football Player

**Hill, Solomon**
Indiana Pacers, Conseco Fieldhouse, 125 S Pennsylvania, Indianapolis IN 46204 USA — Basketball Player

**Hill, Steven**
18 Jill Lane, Monsey NY 10952, USA — Actor

**Hill, Susan E**
Longmoor Farmhouse, Ebrington, Chipping Campden, Gloucestershire GL55 6NW, England — Writer

**Hill, Talmaldga L (Ike)**
412 Randolph St, Oak Park IL 60302, USA — Football Player

**Hill, Terence**
Iniziative Promozioni Cinematografiche, Via Francesco Siacci 38, 00197 Rome, Italy — Actor

**Hill, Terrell L**
5320 Fox Hollow Road, Eugene OR 97405, USA — Biophysicist, Chemist

**Hill, Thomas (Tom)**
428 Elmcrest Dr, Norman OK 73071, USA — Track Athlete

**Hill, Tim**
Gersh Agency, 9465 Wilshire Blvd, #600, Beverly Hills CA 90212 USA — Director, Producer, Writer

**Hill, Tyrone**
Atlanta Hawks, Centennial Tower, 101 Marietta St NW, #1900, Atlanta GA 30303 USA — Basketball Player

**Hill, Virgil**
Timothy Downey, PO Box 442, Oceanville NJ 08231, USA — Boxer

**Hill, Virgil L, Jr**
1000 Glendevon Court, Ambler PA 19002, USA — Navy Admiral, Educator

**Hill, W Robert (Bobby)**
1874 Dry Creek Road, San Jose CA 95124, USA — Baseball Player

**Hill, Walter**
836 Greenway Dr, Beverly Hills CA 90210, USA — Director

**Hill, Warren**
Air Tight Mgmt, PO Box 113, Winchester Center MA 01748, USA — Jazz Saxophonist

**Hill, Winston C**
1900 E Girard Place, #605, Englewood CO 80113, USA — Football Player

**Hillaby, John**
Constable Co, Lanchesters, 102 Fulham Palace Road, London W6 9ER, England — Writer

**Hillary, Barbara**
Playboy Promotions, 9346 Civic Center Dr, #200, Beverly Hills CA 90210 USA — Model

**Hillcoat, John**
Creative Artists Agency, 2000 Ave of Stars, #100, Los Angeles CA 90067 USA — Director

**Hille, Bertil**
10630 Lakeside Ave NE, Seattle WA 98125, USA — Physiologist

**Hille, Einar**
8862 La Jolla Scenic Dr N, La Jolla CA 92037, USA — Mathematician

**Hillebrand, Gerald J (Jerry)**
23 Madison Circle, Davenport IA 52806, USA — Football Player

**Hillegas, Shawn P**
870 Rockville Road, South Fork PA 15956, USA — Baseball Player

**Hillel, Shlomo**
14 Gelber St, Jerusalem 96755, Israel — Government Official, Israel

**Hillen, Bobby, Jr**
Donleavy Racing, 5011 Midlothian Turnpike, Richmond VA 23225, USA — Auto Racing Driver

**Hillenbrand, Daniel A**
Hillenbrand Industries, 700 State RR 46 E, Batesville IN 47006, USA — Businessman

**Hillenbrand, Laura**
Jankow & Nesbitt, 445 Park Ave, New York NY 10022, USA — Writer

**Hillenbrand, Shea M**
PO Box 9526, Chandler Heights AZ 85127, USA — Baseball Player

**Hiller, Arthur**
1218 Benedict Canyon, Beverly Hills CA 90210, USA — Director

**Hiller, David D**
Chicago Tribune, Publisher's Office, 435 N Michigan Ave, Chicago IL 60611, USA — Publisher

**Hiller, John F**
W8085 Becker Dr, Iron Mountain MI 49801, USA — Baseball Player

**Hillerman, John**
Prager & Hillerman, 12424 Wilshire Blvd, #1000, Los Angeles CA 90025, USA — Actor

**Hilliard, Dalton**
23 Hermitage Dr, Destrehan LA 70047, USA — Football Player

**Hilliard, Isaac J (Ike)**
17020 SW 74th Ave, Palmetto Bay FL 33157, USA — Football Player

**Hillier, Bevis**
Maggie Noach Literary Agency, 21 Redan St, London W14 0AB, England — Writer

**Hillier, Paul D**
Hazard Chase, 25 City Road, Cambridge CB1 1DP, England — Concert Singer, Music Director

**Hillier, Steve**
Primary Talent, 2-12 Petonville Road, London N1 9PL, England — Keyboardist (Dubstar)

**Hillis, Ali**
Luber Rocklin Entertainment, 5815 Sunset Blvd, #206, Los Angeles CA 90028 USA — Actress

**Hillis, David M**
University of Texas, Computational Biology Center, Austin TX 78712, USA — Integrative Biologist

**Hillis, Peyton**
New York Giants, Meadowlands Stadium, 102 Route 120, East Rutherford NJ 07073 USA — Football Player

**Hillis, W Daniel (Danny)**
Applied Minds, 1209 Grand Central Ave, Glendale CA 91201, USA — Computer Scientist

**Hillman, Chris**
New Frontier Touring, 1503 17th Ave S, Nashville TN 37212, USA — Singer, Bassist (Byrds)

**Hillman, Darius D (Dave)**
849 Mimosa Dr, Kingsport TN 37660, USA — Baseball Player

**Hillman, Darnell**
6011 Medora Dr, Indianapolis IN 46228, USA — Basketball Player

**Hillman, Larry M** — Ice Hockey Player
57 Westland St, Sainte Catharine's ON L2S 3W8, Canada

**Hills, Anthony T (Tony)** — Football Player
Buffalo Bills, 1 Bills Dr, Orchard Park NY 14127 USA

**Hills, Carla A** — Secretary, Housing & Urban Development
3125 Chain Bridge Road NW, Washington DC 20016, USA

**Hills, Douglas** — Architect
Douglas Hills Assoc, 920 S Waukegan Road, #300, Lake Forest IL 60045, USA

**Hills, Hollis H** — WW II Navy Air Force Hero
570 Marnie Circle, Melbourne FL 32904, USA

**Hilmers, David C** — Astronaut
2846 Bellefontaine St, Houston TX 77025, USA

**Hilmes, Jerome B** — Army General
4900 Windsor Park, Sarasota FL 34235, USA

**Hilson, Keri** — Singer, Songwriter
I C M Partners, 10250 Constellation Blvd, #900, Los Angeles CA 90067 USA

**Hilton, Barron** — Businessman
Hilton Hotels Corp, 7930 Jones Branch Dr, #100, McLean VA 22102, USA

**Hilton, J David (Dave)** — Baseball Player
4910 E Sunnyside Dr, Scottsdale AZ 85254, USA

**Hilton, John J** — Football Player
3911 S Fairway Dr, Powhatan VA 23139, USA

**Hilton, Paris** — Model, Actress
Paris Hilton Entertainment, 250 N Canon Dr, #100, Beverly Hills CA 90210, USA

**Hilton, Roy L** — Football Player
8332 Merrymount Dr, Windsor Mill MD 21244, USA

**Hilton, Tyler** — Actor, Singer
Emblem Mgmt, 22315 Mulholland Highway, Calabasas CA 91302, USA

**Hilty, Megan** — Actress, Singer
Gersh Agency, 9465 Wilshire Blvd, #600, Beverly Hills CA 90212 USA

**Hiltz, Nichole** — Actress
Sanders/Armstrong/Caserta Mgmt, 2120 Colorado Ave, #120, Santa Monica CA 90404 USA

**Hiltzik, Michael A** — Journalist
Los Angeles Times, Editorial Dept, 202 W 1st St, Los Angeles CA 90012 USA

**Himelstein, Aaron** — Actor
Innovative Artists, 1505 10th St, Santa Monica CA 90401 USA

**Himes Gomez, Margaret** — Interior Designer
Gomez Assoc, 504 E 74th St, #300, New York NY 10021, USA

**Himes, Richard D (Dick)** — Football Player
431 Prairie Lane, Luxemburg WI 54217, USA

**Hinault, Bernard** — Cyclist
Quest Levure, 7 Rue de la Sauvaie, 21 Sud-Est, 35000 Rennes, France

**Hinch, Andrew Jay (A J)** — Baseball Player
7010 Fairway Road, La Jolla CA 92037, USA

**Hinchcliffe, James** — Auto Racing Driver
Andretti Audiosport, 7615 Zionsville Road, Indianapolis IN 46268, USA

**Hinchliffe, Dickon** — Composer
First Artists Mgmt, 4764 Park Granada, #210, Calabasas CA 91302 USA

**Hindes, Philip** — Cyclist
Cycling Federation, National Cycling Centre, Stuart St, Manchester M11 4DQ, England

**Hindle, Art** — Actor
Independent Artists, 9601 Wilshire Blvd, #750, Beverly Hills CA 90210 USA

**Hindman, Stanley C (Stan)** — Football Player
824 Creed Road, Oakland CA 94610, USA

**Hindmarch, Anya** — Fashion Designer
Plough Brewery, 516 Wandsworth Road, London SW8 3JX, England

**Hinds, Aisha** — Actress
Greene Assoc, 1901 Ave of Stars, #130, Los Angeles CA 90067 USA

**Hinds, Brent** — Guitarist, Singer (Mastodon)
Pinnacle Entertainment, 30 Glenn St, White Plains NY 10603, USA

**Hinds, Ciaran** — Actor
Dalzell & Beresford, 55 Charterhouse St, Paddock Suite, London EC1M 6HA, England

**Hinds, David** — Singer, Guitarist (Steel Pulse)
Steel Pulse Ltd, 33 Kersley Road, London N16 0NT, England

**Hinds, Samuel A A** — Prime Minister, Guyana
Prime Minister's Office, Wights Lane, Georgetown, Guyana

**Hinds, Samuel R (Sam)** — Baseball Player
320 S 56th Terrace, Hollywood FL 33023, USA

**Hinds, William E (Bill)** — Cartoonist (Tank McNamara)
1301 Spring Oaks Circle, Houston TX 77055, USA

**Hine, Maynard K** — Dentist
1121 W Michigan St, Indianapolis IN 46202, USA

**Hine, Patrick** — Air Force Marshal, England
Lloyd's Bank, Cox's & Kings, 7 Pall Mall, London SW1 5NA, England

**Hiner, Glen H, Jr** — Businessman
Owens-Corning, 1 Owens Corning Parkway, Toledo OH 43659, USA

**Hines, Brendan** — Actor
TalentWorks, 3500 W Olive Ave, #1400, Burbank CA 91505 USA

**Hines, Cheryl** — Actress, Comedienne
W M E Entertainment, 9601 Wilshire Blvd, #300, Beverly Hills CA 90210 USA

**Hines, Deni** — Singer
Entertainment Consulting, 15 Alice St, Padstow NSW 2211, Australia

**Hines, Garrett** — Bobsled Athlete
Bobsled & Skeleton Federation, 1631 Mesa Ave, #A, Colorado Springs CO 80906 USA

**Hines, Glen R** — Football Player
861 N Queen Annes Lace Dr, Fayetteville AR 72704, USA

**Hines, Mimi** — Actress, Comedienne
Scott Stander Assoc, 4533 Van Nuys Blvd, #401, Sherman Oaks CA 91403 USA

**Hingis, Martina** — Tennis Player
Inselweg 28, 8640 Hurden, Switzerland

**Hingorani, Narain G** — Electrical Engineer
835 W Big Sand Place, Oro Valley AZ 85755, USA

**Hingsen, Jurgen** — Track Athlete
655 Circle Dr, Santa Barbara CA 93108, USA

**Hinkle, Bryan E** — Football Player
1402 Missouri Ave, Bridgeville PA 15017, USA

**Hinkle, George A**
4998 Willowford Road, Robertsville MO 63072, USA — Football Player

**Hinkle, Lon**
PO Box 1347, Bigfork MT 59911, USA — Golfer

**Hinkle, Marin**
Innovative Artists, 1505 10th St, Santa Monica CA 90401 USA — Actress

**Hinnant, Michael W (Mike)**
43 Ashford Way, Schwenksville PA 19473, USA — Football Player

**Hino, Kazuyoshi**
Hino & Malee Inc, 3701 N Ravenswood Ave, Chicago IL 60613, USA — Fashion Designer

**Hinojosa, Ricardo H**
US District Court, PO Box 5007, McAllen TX 78502, USA — Judge

**Hinojosa, Tish**
PO Box 3304, Austin TX 78764, USA — Singer, Songwriter

**Hinote, Daniel C (Dan)**
4323 Forest Park Ave, Saint Louis MO 63108, USA — Ice Hockey Player

**Hinrich, Kirk J**
1886 Hilltop Lane, Bannockburn IL 60015, USA — Basketball Player

**Hinrichs, Fabian**
Heppeler Agency, Steinstr 54, 81667 Munich, Germany — Actor

**Hinse, Andre**
PO Box 237, Fort Cobb OK 73038, USA — Ice Hockey Player

**Hinske, Eric S**
10222 E Southwind Lane, #1041, Scottsdale AZ 85262, USA — Baseball Player

**Hinson, Jordan D**
Inphenate, 9701 Wilshire Blvd, #1000, Beverly Hills CA 90212 USA — Actress

**Hinson, Larry**
3179 Highway 32 E, Douglas GA 31533, USA — Golfer

**Hinson, Roy M**
8167 Quail Meadow Way, West Palm Beach FL 33412, USA — Basketball Player

**Hinterseer, Ernst**
Hahnenkammstr, 6370 Kitzbuhel, Austria — Alpine Skier

**Hinton, Christopher J (Chris)**
374 Citadella Court, Alpharetta GA 30022, USA — Football Player

**Hinton, Eddie**
34 Auburn Ridge, Spring Branch TX 78070, USA — Football Player

**Hinton, Jerrika**
Greene Assoc, 1901 Ave of Stars, #130, Los Angeles CA 90067 USA — Actress

**Hinton, Jessa**
Playboy Promotions, 9346 Civic Center Dr, #200, Beverly Hills CA 90210 USA — Model

**Hinton, Richard M (Rich)**
7447 Hawkins Road, Sarasota FL 34241, USA — Baseball Player

**Hinton, Susan Eloise (S E)**
Delacorte Press, 1540 Broadway, New York NY 10036, USA — Writer

**Hintz, Donald C**
Entergy Corp, 10055 Grogans Mill Road, #150, Spring TX 77380, USA — Businessman

**Hinze, Kristy**
Ford Models Inc, 111 5th Ave, #900, New York NY 10003 USA — Model, Actress

**Hinzo, Thomas L (Tommy)**
635 Imperial Beach Blvd, Imperial Beach CA 91932, USA — Baseball Player

**Hiort, Esbjorn**
Bel Colles Farm, Parkvej 6, 2960 Rungsted Kyst, Denmark — Architect

**Hipp, Paul**
Stone Manners Salners, 6100 Wilshire Blvd, #1500, Los Angeles CA 90035 USA — Actor

**Hipple, Eric E**
7155 Driftwood Dr, Fenton MI 48430, USA — Football Player

**Hirai, Kazuo (Kaz)**
Sony Corporation, 1-7-1 Konan Minatoku, Tokyo 108 0075, Japan — Businessman

**Hire, Kathryn P (Kay)**
PO Box 580146, Houston TX 77258, USA — Astronaut

**Hirsch, Corey**
Saint Louis Blues, Scottrade Center, 1401 Clark Ave, Saint Louis MO 63103 USA — Ice Hockey Player

**Hirsch, E D, Jr**
University of Virginia, Education Dept, Charlottesville VA 22906, USA — Educator

**Hirsch, Emile**
Silver Lining Entertainment, 421 S Beverly Drive, #700, Beverly Hills CA 90212 USA — Actor

**Hirsch, Hallee**
Baker Winokur Ryder Public Relations, 9100 Wilshire Blvd, #500W, Beverly Hills CA 90212 USA — Actress

**Hirsch, Howard**
Hirsch/Bedner Assoc, 3216 Nebraska Ave, Santa Monica CA 90404, USA — Interior Designer

**Hirsch, Janis**
Creative Artists Agency, 2000 Ave of Stars, #100, Los Angeles CA 90067 USA — Writer, Producer

**Hirsch, Judd**
Joan Sittenfield Talent Mgmt, 1064 S Ogden Dr, Los Angeles CA 90019, USA — Actor

**Hirsch, Laurence E**
Centex Corp, 2728 N Harwood, #200, Dallas TX 75201, USA — Businessman

**Hirsch, Leon C**
150 Glover Ave, Norwalk CT 06850, USA — Inventor (Surgical Stapler)

**Hirsch, Paul**
Innovative Artists, 1505 10th St, Santa Monica CA 90401 USA — Editor

**Hirsch, Robert P**
1 Place du Palais Bourbon, 75007 Paris, France — Actor

**Hirsch, Sherre**
Canyon Ranch, 8600 E Rockcliffe Road, Tucson AZ 85750, USA — Writer, Religious Leader, Rabbi

**Hirschbeck, Mark**
12 Isinglass Terrace, Trumbull CT 06611, USA — Baseball Umpire

**Hirschbiegel, Oliver**
United Talent Agency, U T A Plaza, 9336 Civic Center Dr, Beverly Hills CA 90210 USA — Director, Actor

**Hirscher, Marcel**
Altausseer Stra 182/3, 8990 Bad Aussee, Austria — Alpine Skier

**Hirschfeld, Gerald J**
826 Pavilion Place, Ashland OR 97520, USA — Cinematographer

**Hirschfeld, Alan J**
PO Box 7443, Jackson WY 83002, USA — Businessman

**Hirschfeld, Bradley**
Center for Learning & Leadership, 440 Park Ave S, #400, New York NY 10016, USA — Religious Leader, Rabbi

**Hirst, Damien** — Sculptor
White Cube Gallery, Saint James's, 44 Duke St, London SW1Y 6DD, England

**Hirtz, Dagmar** — Director
Jollystr 45, 81545 Munich, Germany

**Hiscock, Norm** — Producer
Vanguarde Artists Mgmt, 119 Spadina Ave, #501, Toronto ON M5V 2L1, Canada

**Hiser, Gene T** — Baseball Player
1450 Caldwell Lane, Hoffman Estates IL 60169, USA

**Hiskey, Bryant (Babe)** — Golfer
4046 Pirates Beach, Galveston TX 77554, USA

**Hisle, Larry E** — Baseball Player
10603 N Hidden Reserve Circle, Mequon WI 53092, USA

**Hitchcock, Ken** — Ice Hockey Coach
11118 Valleydale Dr, #C, Dallas TX 75230, USA

**Hitchcock, Robyn** — Singer (Soft Boys), Songwriter
High Road Touring, 751 Bridgeway, #200, Sausalito CA 94965 USA

**Hitchcock, Russell C** — Singer (Air Supply)
PO Box 3367, Beverly Hills CA 90212, USA

**Hitchcock, Sterling A** — Baseball Player
5129 River Lakes Parkway, Whitefish MT 59937, USA

**Hitchcock, Sylvia L** — Beauty Queen
Miss Universe Organization, 1370 Ave of Americas, #1600, New York NY 10019 USA

**Hite, Robert L** — WW II Army Air Corps Hero
112 Elaine Ave, Camden AR 71701, USA

**Hite, Shere D** — Writer
75 Haywood St, #312, Asheville NC 28801, USA

**Hite, William P** — Labor Leader
United Plumbing/Pipefitters Association, 3 Park Place, Annapolis MD 21401, USA

**Hitsujia, Shirotama** — Director
Yubiwa Hotel, 4-41-15-701, Yoyogi Shibuyaku, Tokyo 151 0053, Japan

**Hitt, John C** — Educator
University of Central Florida, President's Office, Orlando FL 32816, USA

**Hix, Charles** — Fashion Expert, Writer
Simon & Schuster, 1230 Ave of Americas, Concourse 1, New York NY 10020, USA

**Hjalmarsson, Niklas** — Ice Hockey Player
Chicago Blackhawks, United Center, 1901 W Madison St, Chicago IL 60612 USA

**Hjejle, Iben** — Actress
Tavistock Wood, 45 Conduit St, London W1S 2YN, England

**Hjelt, Caroline** — Singer (Icona Pop)
United Stage, Box 11029, 100 61 Stockholm, Sweden

**Hjorth, Maria A (Mimmi)** — Golfer
608 Henley Circle, Davenport FL 33896, USA

**Hlavackova, Andrea** — Tennis Player
Na Zahonech 1303/45, 14100 Prague, Czech Republic

**Hlinka, Nichol** — Ballerina
New York City Ballet, Lincoln Center Plaza, New York NY 10023 USA

**Hnatiuk, Glen** — Golfer
8746 Mississippi Run, Weeki Wachee FL 34613, USA

**Hnidy, Shane** — Ice Hockey Player
1704 Silvermere Court, Duluth GA 30097, USA

**Ho, David** — Medical Researcher
Aaron Diamond AIDS Research Center, 455 1st Ave, New York NY 10016, USA

**Ho, Derek K** — Surfer
Association of Surfing Professionals, PO Box 309, Huntington Beach CA 92648, USA

**Ho, Josie** — Actress
I C M Partners, 10250 Constellation Blvd, #900, Los Angeles CA 90067 USA

**Ho, Tao** — Architect
499 King's Road, #8/B, North Point, Hong Kong Special Region, China

**Hoag, Judith W** — Actress
Bauman Redanty Shaul Agency, 5757 Wilshire Blvd, #473, Los Angeles CA 90036 USA

**Hoag, Peter C** — Test Pilot
3655 Little Rock Dr, Provo UT 84604, USA

**Hoag, Tami** — Writer
Bantam/Dell Books, 1745 Broadway, New York NY 10019, USA

**Hoage, Terrell L (Terry)** — Football Player
870 Arbor Road, Paso Robles CA 93446, USA

**Hoagland, Edward** — Writer
PO Box 51, Barton VT 05822, USA

**Hoagland, Jimmie L (Jim)** — Journalist
Washington Post, Editorial Dept, 1150 15th St NW, Washington DC 20071, USA

**Hoaglin, G Frederick (Fred)** — Football Player, Coach
7 Governors Road, Hilton Head SC 29928, USA

**Hoak, Richard j (Dick)** — Football Player
162 Crest View Dr, Greensburg PA 15601, USA

**Hoar, Joseph P** — Marine Corps General
386 13th St, Del Mar CA 92014, USA

**Hoard, Leroy** — Football Player
13141 NW 8th Court, Sunrise FL 33325, USA

**Hoare, C Antony R** — Computer Engineer
Oxford University, Computing Laboratory, Parks Road, Oxford OX1 3QD, England

**Hobaugh, Charles O** — Astronaut
N A S A, Johnson Space Center, 2101 NASA Road, Houston TX 77058 USA

**Hobault, John** — Space Scientist
15 Piper Road, #K319, Scarborough ME 04074, USA

**Hobbie, Glen F** — Baseball Player
RR 2 Box 234A, Ramsey IL 62080, USA

**Hobbs, Becky** — Singer, Pianist
Entertainment Artists, 2409 21st Ave S, #100, Nashville TN 10019 USA

**Hobbs, Chelsea** — Actress
Paradigm Agency, 360 N Crescent Dr, North Building, Beverly Hills CA 90210 USA

**Hobbs, David** — Auto Racing Driver, Sportscaster
David Hobbs Honda, 6100 N Green Bay Ave, Glendale WI 53209, USA

**Hobbs, Ellis, III** — Football Player
8885 Old Southwick Pass, Alpharetta GA 30022, USA

**Hobbs, Jeff** — Writer
Simon & Schuster, 1230 Ave of Americas, Concourse 1, New York NY 10020 USA

**Hobbs, John D (Jack)** — Baseball Player
3 Wade Dr, Cherry Hill NJ 08034, USA

**Hoberman, David** — Producer
Mandeville Films, 500 S Buena Vista St, Animation Building 2G, Burbank CA 91521, USA

**Hobert, Billy J** — Football Player
255 Portofino Way, Redondo Beach CA 90277, USA

**Hoblit, Gregory (Greg)** — Director
W M E Entertainment, 9601 Wilshire Blvd, #300, Beverly Hills CA 90210 USA

**Hobolt, John C** — Space Scientist
15 Piper Road, #K319, Scarborough ME 04074, USA

**Hobson, Clell L (Butch)** — Baseball Player, Manager
6302 Catarata St, Bakersfield CA 93311, USA

**Hobson, Helen** — Actress
Gavin Barker Assoc, 2D Wimpole St, London W1G 0EB, England

**Hobson, Jeff** — Illusionist
Jack Grenier Productions, 32630 Concord Dr, Madison Heights MI 48071 USA

**Hobson, Victor B** — Football Player
505 Gracelyn Court SW, Atlanta GA 30331, USA

**Hobson, Will** — Journalist
Tampa Bay Times, Editorial Dept, 401 Channelside Dr, Tampa FL 33602 USA

**Hoch, Carin** — Golfer
International Mangement Group, 1 Erieview Plaza, 1360 E 9th St, #100, Cleveland OH 44114 USA

**Hoch, Danny** — Performance Artist, Actor
Gersh Agency, 9465 Wilshire Blvd, #600, Beverly Hills CA 90212 USA

**Hoch, Scott** — Golfer
9239 Cypress Cove Dr, Orlando FL 32819, USA

**Hochevar, Luke A** — Baseball Player
2452 Glen Meadow Road, Knoxville TN 37909, USA

**Hochhuth, Rolf** — Writer
PO Box 661, 4002 Basel, Switzerland

**Hochschorner, Pavol** — Canoeing Athlete
Mlynarovicova 17, 851 03 Bratislava, Slovakia

**Hochstein, Russ** — Football Player
43 Massand Road, North Attleboro MA 02760, USA

**Hock, Dee Ward** — Businessman
Visa International, 900 Metro Center Blvd, Foster City CA 94404, USA

**Hocke, Stefan** — Ski Jumper
Sportgymnasium, Am Harzwald 3, 98558 Oberhof, Germany

**Hockenbery, Charles M (Chuck)** — Baseball Player
1546 Birka Lane, Onalaska WI 54650, USA

**Hockfield, Susan** — Educator
Massachusetts Institute of Technology, President's Office, Cambridge MA 02139, USA

**Hocking, Amanda** — Writer
Saint Martin's Press, 175 5th Ave, #400, New York NY 10010 USA

**Hocking, Dennis L (Denny)** — Baseball Player
7384 E Villanueva Dr, Orange CA 92867, USA

**Hockney, David** — Artist, Photographer
Tradhart Ltd, 19B Buckingham Ave, Slough SL1 4QB, England

**Hodder, Kane W** — Actor, Stuntman
Amsel Eisenstadt Frazier, 5055 Wilshire Blvd, #865, Los Angeles CA 90036 USA

**Hoddle, Glenn** — Soccer Player, Manager
Football Assn, 16 Lancaster Gate, London W2 3LW, England

**Hodel, Donald P** — Secretary, Energy; Labor
1801 Sara Dr, #L, Chesapeake VA 23320, USA

**Hodel, Nathan W** — Football Player
2411 Goldenrod Way, Wauconda IL 60084, USA

**Hodge, Aldis** — Actor
Paradigm Agency, 360 N Crescent Dr, North Building, Beverly Hills CA 90210 USA

**Hodge, Chad** — Writer, Producer
W M E Entertainment, 9601 Wilshire Blvd, #300, Beverly Hills CA 90210 USA

**Hodge, Charles E (Charlie)** — Ice Hockey Player
27111 25A Ave, Aldergrove BC V4W 3N4, Canada

**Hodge, Daniel A (Dan)** — Freestyle Wrestler
914 Jackson St, Perry OK 73077, USA

**Hodge, Douglas** — Actor
United Agents, 12-26 Lexington St, London W1F 0LE, England

**Hodge, Ed O** — Baseball Player
127 Jedwell St, Johnson City TN 37601, USA

**Hodge, Edwin** — Actor
Luber Rocklin Entertainment, 5815 Sunset Blvd, #206, Los Angeles CA 90028 USA

**Hodge, John** — Producer
United Agents, 12-26 Lexington St, London W1F 0LE, England

**Hodge, Kenneth R (Ken), Sr** — Ice Hockey Player
13 Longfellow Dr, Newburyport MA 01950, USA

**Hodge, Megan** — Volleyball Player
USA Volleyball, 4065 Sinton Road, #200, Colorado Springs CO 80907, USA

**Hodge, Patricia** — Actress
I C M Partners, Marlborough House, 10 Earlham St, #300, London WC2H 9LNP, England

**Hodge, Sedrick J** — Football Player
120 Victoria Place, Fayetteville GA 30214, USA

**Hodges, Bill** — Basketball Coach
Georgia College, Athletic Dept, Milledgeville GA 31061, USA

**Hodges, Craig A** — Basketball Player
67 Elm St, Park Forest IL 60466, USA

**Hodges, J T** — Singer, Songwriter
Show Dog/Universal Music, 2303 21st Ave S, #400, Nashville TN 37212 USA

**Hodges, Mike** — Director
Wesley Farm, Durweston, Blanford Forum, Dorset DT11 0QG, England

**Hodges, Robert H, Jr** — Judge
US Claims Court, 717 Madison Place NW, Washington DC 20439, USA

**Hodges, Ronald W (Ron)** — Baseball Player
110 Hajo Lane, Rocky Mount VA 24151, USA

**Hodges, Roneeka** — Basketball Player
Indiana Fever, Conseco Fieldhouse, 125 S Pennsylvania, Indianapolis IN 46204 USA

**Hodges, Trey** — Baseball Player
19506 Kuykendahl Road, Spring TX 77379, USA

**Hodgins, William**
232 Clarendon St, Boston MA 02116, USA — Interior Designer

**Hodgman, John**
United Talent Agency, U T A Plaza, 9336 Civic Center Dr, Beverly Hills CA 90210 USA — Actor, Writer

**Hodgson, Nicholas J D (Nick)**
Red Light Mgmt, 8439 Sunset Blvd, West Hollywood CA 90069, USA — Singer, Drummer (Kaiser Chiefs)

**Hodgson, Roger**
Agency Group Ltd, 142 W 57th St, #600, New York NY 10019 USA — Guitarist (Supertramp)

**Hoechlin, Tyler**
United Talent Agency, U T A Plaza, 9336 Civic Center Dr, Beverly Hills CA 90210 USA — Actor

**Hoeg, Peter**
Farrar Straus Giroux, 18 W 18th St, #700, New York NY 10011 USA — Writer

**Hoeks, Sylvia**
Copper En Co, Wamondstraat 73-1, 1058 Amsterdam KR, Netherlands — Actress

**Hoelsher, Vanessa**
Playboy Promotions, 9346 Civic Center Dr, #200, Beverly Hills CA 90210 USA — Model

**Hoelzer, Margaret**
535 N Coast Highway, Laguna Beach CA 92651, USA — Swimmer

**Hoenig, Heinz**
Society Relations, Mundsburger Damm 2, 22087 Hamburg, Germany — Actor

**Hoenig, Thomas M**
444 W 60th Terrace, Kansas City MO 64113, USA — Government Official, Financier

**Hoest, Bunny**
William Hoest Enterprises, 27 Watch Way, Lloyd Neck, Huntington NY 11743, USA — Cartoonist (Lockhorns)

**Hoewing, Gerald L**
Navy Mutual Aid Assn, 29 Carpenter Road, Arlington VA 22214, USA — Navy Admiral

**Hoey, George W**
4171 Westcliffe Court, Boulder CO 80301, USA — Football Player

**Hofer, Paul D**
981 June Road, Memphis TN 38119, USA — Football Player

**Hoff, Kathryn (Katie)**
106 Kenilworth Park, #4D, Towson MD 21204, USA — Swimmer

**Hoff, Lawrence C**
8720 Cypress Club Dr, Raleigh NC 27615, USA — Businessman

**Hoff, Marcian E (Ted), Jr**
26541 Taafe Road, Los Altos Hills CA 94022, USA — Inventor (Microprocessor)

**Hoff, Max**
Siegburger Str 112, 50679 Cologne, Germany — Canoeing Athlete

**Hoff, Michael**
University of Nebraska, Art & Art History Dept, 120 Richards Hall, Lincoln NE 68588, USA — Art Historian

**Hoff, Philip H**
Hoff Wilson Powell Lang, PO Box 123, Essex Junction VT 05453, USA — Governor, VT

**Hoffa, James P**
2593 Hounds Chase Dr, Troy MI 48098, USA — Labor Leader

**Hoffa, Reese**
425 Oak Grove Road, Athens GA 30607, USA — Track Athlete

**Hoffman, Alan J**
I B M Research Center, PO Box 218, Yorktown Heights NY 10598, USA — Mathematician

**Hoffman, Alice**
32 Lowell Road, Concord MA 01742, USA — Writer

**Hoffman, Basil**
26 Aller Court, Glendale CA 91206, USA — Actor

**Hoffman, Charley L**
Professional Golfers Association, 100 Ave of Champions, Palm Beach Gardens FL 33418 USA — Golfer

**Hoffman, Darleane C**
Lawrence Berkeley Laboratory, 1 Cyclotron Road, Berkeley CA 94720, USA — Nuclear Physicist

**Hoffman, David**
Mavrick Artists Agency, 6100 Wilshire Blvd, #550, Los Angeles CA 90048, USA — Actor

**Hoffman, Dustin L**
Punch Productions, 11661 San Vicente Blvd, #222, Los Angeles CA 90049, USA — Actor

**Hoffman, Gaby**
Innovative Artists, 235 Park Ave S, #1000, New York NY 10003 USA — Actress

**Hoffman, Glenn E**
201 S Old Bridge Road, Anaheim CA 92808, USA — Baseball Player, Manager

**Hoffman, Guy A**
313 Fairway Dr, #S, Bloomington IL 61701, USA — Baseball Player

**Hoffman, Jackie**
Don Buchwald Talent Agency, 6500 Wilshire Blvd, #2200, Los Angeles CA 90048 USA — Actress

**Hoffman, Jake**
W M E Entertainment, 9601 Wilshire Blvd, #300, Beverly Hills CA 90210 USA — Actor

**Hoffman, Jeffrey A**
US Embassy, 2 Ave Gabriel, PSC 116/NASA, 75382 Paris Cedex, France — Astronaut

**Hoffman, John Robert**
Creative Artists Agency, 2000 Ave of Stars, #100, Los Angeles CA 90067 USA — Director, Writer

**Hoffman, Matt**
D D K Talent, 16255 Ventura Blvd, #525, Encino CA 91436, USA — Actor

**Hoffman, Michael**
United Talent Agency, U T A Plaza, 9336 Civic Center Dr, Beverly Hills CA 90210 USA — Director, Writer

**Hoffman, Reid G**
LinkedIn, 2029 Stierlin Court, #200, Mountain Valley CA 94043, USA — Businessman

**Hoffman, Rick**
Framework Entertainment, 9057 Nemo St, #C, West Hollywood CA 90069 USA — Actor

**Hoffman, Robert James, III**
Impression Entertainment, 9229 W Sunset Blvd, #700, Los Angeles CA 90069, USA — Actor

**Hoffman, Ted, Jr**
1568 Partarian Way, San Jose CA 95129, USA — Bowling Executive

**Hoffman, Thom**
Anne Alvares Correa, 34 Rue Jouffroy d'Abbans, 75017 Paris, France — Actor

**Hoffman, William M**
190 Prince St, New York NY 10012, USA — Lyricist, Writer

**Hoffmann, Ambrosi**
Talstrasse 63, 7250 Davos Dorf, Switzerland — Alpine Skier

**Hoffmann, Christian**
Frunwald 7, 4160 Aigen, Austria — Cross Country Skier

**Hoffmann, Gaby**
I C M Partners, 10250 Constellation Blvd, #900, Los Angeles CA 90067 USA — Actress

| | |
|---|---|
| **Hoffmann, Jan**<br>Ice Skating Union, Menzinger Str 68, 80992 Munich, Germany | Figure Skater |
| **Hoffmann, Jules A**<br>Biologie Moléculaire & Cellulaire Institut, 15 Rue Descartes, 67084 Strasbourg Cedex, France | Nobel Medicine Laureate |
| **Hoffmann, Roald**<br>4 Sugarbush Lane, Ithaca NY 14850, USA | Nobel Chemistry Laureate |
| **Hoffmann, Robert**<br>Agentur Rehling, Mommsenstr 47, 10629 Berlin, Germany | Actor |
| **Hoffmann, Stanley H**<br>Harvard University, Government Dept, Cambridge MA 02138, USA | Political Scientist |
| **Hoffpauir, Jarrett L**<br>2043 Viking St, Vidalia LA 71373, USA | Baseball Player |
| **Hoffs, Susanna**<br>Creative Artists Agency, 2000 Ave of Stars, #100, Los Angeles CA 90067 USA | Singer, Guitarist (Bangles) |
| **Hofheimer, Charlie**<br>Innovative Artists, 1505 10th St, Santa Monica CA 90401 USA | Actor |
| **Hoflehner, Rudolf**<br>Ottensteinstr 62, 2344 Maria Enzersdorf, Austria | Artist |
| **Hofman, Rogier**<br>H C Bloemendaal, Aelbertsbergweg 3, 2061 Bloemendaal AA, Netherlands | Field Hockey Player |
| **Hofmann, Detlef**<br>Saarlandstr 164, 76187 Karlsruhe, Germany | Canoeing Athlete |
| **Hofmann, Douglas W**<br>15 W Mount Vernon Place, Baltimore MD 21201, USA | Artist |
| **Hofmann, Isabella**<br>Daniel Hoff Agency, 5455 Wilshire Blvd, #1100, Los Angeles CA 90036, USA | Actress |
| **Hofmeister, John**<br>Shell Oil Co, PO Box 2463, Houston TX 77252, USA | Businessman |
| **Hofschneider, Marco**<br>Agent U Nicolai, Schorlemerallee 16, 14195 Berlin, Germany | Actor |
| **Hogan, Brooke**<br>Sovereign Talent Group, 8421 Wilshire Blvd, #200, Beverly Hills CA 90211, USA | Singer, Actress |
| **Hogan, Chris**<br>Creative Artists Agency, 2000 Ave of Stars, #100, Los Angeles CA 90067 USA | Actor |
| **Hogan, Darrell**<br>14988 Scenic Loop Road, Helotes TX 78023, USA | Football Player |
| **Hogan, Erin Marie**<br>Michael Zanuck Agency, 28035 Dorothy Dr, #120, Agoura Hills CA 91301, USA | Actress |
| **Hogan, Gabriel**<br>Characters Talent Mgmt, 8 Elm St, Toronto ON M5G 1G7, Canada | Actor |
| **Hogan, Hulk**<br>756 Eldorado Ave, Clearwater Beach FL 33767, USA | Professional Wrestler, Actor |
| **Hogan, Jack**<br>22 Altura Road, Santa Fe NM 87508, USA | Actor |
| **Hogan, Linda**<br>University of Colorado, English Dept, Boulder CO 80309, USA | Writer |
| **Hogan, Nick**<br>Sovereign Talent Group, 8421 Wilshire Blvd, #200, Beverly Hills CA 90211, USA | Actor |
| **Hogan, Paul**<br>18 Marshall Crescent, Beacon Hill NSW 2060, Australia | Actor |
| **Hogan, Paul J (P J)**<br>Creative Artists Agency, 2000 Ave of Stars, #100, Los Angeles CA 90067 USA | Director, Writer |
| **Hogan, Robert J (Bob)**<br>Hartig-Hilepo Agency, 54 W 21st St, #610, New York NY 10010 USA | Actor |
| **Hoge, Merril D**<br>155 W Maple Ave, Fort Mitchell KY 41011, USA | Football Player, Sportscaster |
| **Hogeboom, Gary K**<br>13635 Hofma Court, Grand Haven MI 49417, USA | Football Player |
| **Hogestyn, Drake**<br>28913 W Beach Lane, Malibu CA 90265, USA | Actor |
| **Hogg, Christopher A**<br>Financial Reporting Council, 71-91 Aldwych, London WC2B 4HN, England | Businessman |
| **Hogg, James R**<br>Prescott Farm, 2556 W Main Road, Portsmouth RI 02871, USA | Navy Admiral |
| **Hoggard, Jay**<br>Wesleyan University, Music Dept, Middletown CT 06459, USA | Jazz Vibraphonist |
| **Hogh-Christensen, Jonas**<br>Dag Hammarskjolds Allee 3, #4, 2100 Copenhagen, Denmark | Yachtsman |
| **Hogland, M Douglas (Doug)**<br>1514 4th St, Tillamook OR 97141, USA | Football Player |
| **Hogue, Benoit**<br>488 Village Oaks Lane, Babylon NY 11702, USA | Ice Hockey Player |
| **Hohlmayer, Alice (Lefty)**<br>5155 Cedarwood Road #47, Bonita CA 91902, USA | Baseball Player |
| **Hoiberg, Frederick K (Fred)**<br>2129 Quail Ridge Road, Ames IA 50010, USA | Basketball Player, Coach |
| **Hoiles, Christopher A (Chris)**<br>8688 Jersey City Road, Wayne OH 43466, USA | Baseball Player |
| **Hoke, Christopher L (Chris)**<br>121 Cardinal Circle, Pittsburgh PA 15237, USA | Football Player |
| **Holbert, Jerry**<br>Boston Herald, Editorial Dept, 1 Herald St, Boston MA 02118, USA | Editorial Cartoonist |
| **Holbert, Ray A, III**<br>13981 W Desert Cove Road, Surprise AZ 85379, USA | Baseball Player |
| **Holbrook, Bill**<br>King Features Syndicate, 300 W 57th St, #1500, New York NY 10019 USA | Cartoonist (Safe Havens) |
| **Holbrook, Boyd**<br>Creative Artists Agency, 2000 Ave of Stars, #100, Los Angeles CA 90067 USA | Actor |
| **Holbrook, Hal**<br>Abrams Artists, 9200 W Sunset Blvd, #1125, West Hollywood CA 90069 USA | Actor |
| **Holbrook, Karen A**<br>University of South Florida, Research & Innovation Dept, 42-2 E Fowler Ave, Tampa FL 33620, USA | Educator |
| **Holcomb, B Kelly**<br>114 Spence Creek Lane, Murfreesboro TN 37128, USA | Football Player |
| **Holcomb, Steven**<br>Team Holcomb, PO Box 118, Oakley UT 84055, USA | Bobsled Athlete |

## H

**Holcombe, Robert W** — Football Player
2611 Hardy St, Houston TX 77009, USA

**Holden, Alexandra** — Actress
Abrams Artists, 9200 W Sunset Blvd, #1125, West Hollywood CA 90069 USA

**Holden, Amanda** — Actress
Artist Rights Group, 4A Exmoor St, London W10 6BD, England

**Holden, Laurie** — Actress
A P A Talent & Literary Agency, 405 S Beverly Dr, #300, Beverly Hills CA 90212 USA

**Holden, Mari K** — Cyclist
11160 Vista Sorrento Parkway, #302, San Diego CA 92130, USA

**Holden, Marjean** — Actress
Defining Artists Agency, 4370 Tujunga Ave, #120, Studio City CA 91604 USA

**Holden, Rebecca** — Actress, Singer, Model
Box Office, 5207 Rustic Way, Old Hickory TN 37138, USA

**Holden, Robert L (Bob)** — Governor, MO
Webster University, Political Science Dept, 470 E Lockwood Ave, Saint Louis MO 63119, USA

**Holden, Steven A (Steve)** — Football Player
1202 N Nevada Way, Mesa AZ 85203, USA

**Holden, Warrick D** — Football Player
17202 Stratford Green Dr, Sugar Land TX 77498, USA

**Holden-Reid, Kris** — Actress
Oscars Abrams Zimel, 438 Queen St E, Toronto ON M5A 1T4, Canada

**Holdsclaw, Chamique** — Basketball Player
San Antonio Silver Stars, 1 AT&T Center, San Antonio TX 78219 USA

**Holdsworth, Frederick W (Fred)** — Baseball Player
578 Upland Hills Dr, Chelsea MI 48118, USA

**Holecek, John F** — Football Player
1828 Prairie St, Glenview IL 60025, USA

**Holiday, Phillip** — Boxer
Pacific Boxing Club, 14 Channel St, Cleveland QLD, Australia

**Holl, Steven M** — Architect
Steven Holl Architects, 435 Hudson St, #400, New York NY 10014, USA

**Holladay, Wilhelmina Cole** — Museum Executive
National Museum of Women in Arts, 1250 New York NW, Washington DC 20005, USA

**Holland, Agnieszka** — Director, Writer
Field Entertainment, 1240 N Wetherly Dr, Los Angeles CA 90069, USA

**Holland, Alfred W (Al)** — Baseball Player
443 Lewiston St NW, Roanoke VA 24017, USA

**Holland, Brian** — Songwriter
9912 Cozy Glen Circle, Las Vegas NV 89117, USA

**Holland, Darius J** — Football Player
13972 Meadowbrook Dr, Broomfield CO 80020, USA

**Holland, Dexter** — Singer (Offspring)
Rebel Waltz, 31652 2nd Ave, Laguna Beach CA 92651, USA

**Holland, Edward (Eddie), Jr** — Songwriter
555 S Burlingame Ave, Los Angeles CA 90049, USA

**Holland, James F** — Oncologist
Mount Sinai Medical Center, Oncology Dept, 1190 5th Ave, New York NY 10029, USA

**Holland, Jamie L** — Football Player
4025 Jonesville Road, Wake Forest NC 27587, USA

**Holland, Johnny R** — Football Player, Coach
6210 Woodvale Terrace, Dublin CA 94568, USA

**Holland, Jolie** — Singer (Be Good Tanyas), Songwriter
525 Worldwide Music Co, PO Box 957, Salem MA 01945, USA

**Holland, Julian M (Jools)** — Pianist (Squeeze, The The)
One Fifteen, Globe House, Middle Lane Mews, London N8 8PN, England

**Holland, Ken** — Ice Hockey Player, Executive
19022 Oak Leaf Lane, Northville MI 48168, USA

**Holland, Kimberly** — Model
Playboy Promotions, 9346 Civic Center Dr, #200, Beverly Hills CA 90210 USA

**Holland, Montrae R** — Football Player
1096 Sendero Dr, Keller TX 76248, USA

**Holland, Richard J** — Art Director
Screen Talent Agency, Rich Mix Building, 35-47 Bethnal Green Road, London E1 6LA, England

**Holland, Tara Dawn** — Beauty Queen
9050 Carothers Parkway, #104, Franklin TN 37067, USA

**Holland, Terry** — Basketball Player, Coach, Administrator
East Carolina University, Athletic Dept, Greenville NC 27858, USA

**Holland, Todd** — Director, Producer
W M E Entertainment, 9601 Wilshire Blvd, #300, Beverly Hills CA 90210 USA

**Holland, Tom** — Director
Dead Rabbit Films, 215 Zelley Ave, Moorestown NJ 08057, USA

**Holland, Wilbur** — Basketball Player
538 Georgia Dr, Columbus GA 31907, USA

**Holland, Willa** — Actress, Model
United Talent Agency, U T A Plaza, 9336 Civic Center Dr, Beverly Hills CA 90210 USA

**Holland, Willard R, Jr** — Businessman
FirstEnergy Corp, 76 S Main St, Akron OH 44308, USA

**Hollande, Francois G G** — President, France
Palais de l'Elysee, 55 Rue Faubourg Saint Honore, 75008 Paris, France

**Hollander, Edmund D** — Landscape Architect
Hollander Landscape Design, 200 Park Ave S, New York NY 10003, USA

**Hollander, Lorin** — Concert Pianist
I C M Artists, 40 W 57th St, #1800, New York NY 10019 USA

**Hollander, Nicole** — Cartoonist (Sylvia)
Sylvia Syndicate, 1440 N Dayton St, Chicago IL 60642, USA

**Hollander, Tom** — Actor, Producer, Writer
United Talent Agency, U T A Plaza, 9336 Civic Center Dr, Beverly Hills CA 90210 USA

**Hollandsworth, Todd M** — Baseball Player
1310 MacAlpin Court, Inverness IL 60010, USA

**Hollas, Donald W** — Football Player
1811 Mayweather Lane, Richmond TX 77406, USA

**Holldobler, Berthold K** — Writer, Biologist, Zoologist
University of Wurzburg, Zoology Dept, Am Nubland, 97074 Wurzburg, Germany

**Holler, J Edward (Ed)** — Football Player
4500 Ivy Hall Dr, Columbia SC 29206, USA

**Holleran, Leslie** — Producer
United Talent Agency, U T A Plaza, 9336 Civic Center Dr, Beverly Hills CA 90210 USA

**Hollerer, Walter F** — Writer
Heerstr 99, 14055 Berlin, Germany

**Holliday, Cheryl** — Writer, Producer
W M E Entertainment, 9601 Wilshire Blvd, #300, Beverly Hills CA 90210 USA

**Holliday, D Giovonni (Vonnie)** — Football Player
1060 Canter Road NE, Atlanta GA 30324, USA

**Holliday, Jennifer Y** — Singer, Actress
Holliday 6 Entertainment, 3330 Cumberland Blvd, #500, Atlanta GA 30339, USA

**Holliday, Matthew T (Matt)** — Baseball Player
4 Ravenswood Road, Englewood CO 80113, USA

**Holliday, Polly D** — Actress, Singer
Blake Agency, 23441 Malibu Colony Road, Malibu CA 90265 USA

**Hollier, Dwight L** — Football Player
5012 Woodview Lane, Matthews NC 28104, USA

**Holliger, Heinz** — Concert Oboist, Composer
Konzertgellschaft, Hochstr 51, 4002 Basel, Switzerland

**Holliman, Earl** — Actor
PO Box 1969, Studio City CA 91614, USA

**Hollimon, Mike** — Baseball Player
9922 Glenn Canyon Dr, Dallas TX 75243, USA

**Hollings, Michael R** — Religious Leader
Saint Mary of Angels, Moorhouse Road, Bayswater, London W2 5DJ, England

**Hollingsworth, David S** — Space Scientist
Orbital Sciences Corp, 21839 Atlantic Blvd, Dulles VA 20166, USA

**Hollinquest, Lamont** — Football Player
13709 S San Pedro St, Los Angeles CA 90061, USA

**Hollins, David M (Dave)** — Baseball Player
3221 Southwestern Blvd, Orchard Park NY 14127, USA

**Hollins, Lionel E** — Basketball Player, Coach
7594 Tagg Dr, Germantown TN 38138, USA

**Hollis, Michael S (Mike)** — Football Player
124 Sawbill Palm Dr, Ponte Vedra Beach FL 32082, USA

**Hollister, Dave** — Singer, Actor
I C M Partners, 10250 Constellation Blvd, #900, Los Angeles CA 90067 USA

**Holloman, Gus M** — Football Player
2489 County Road 139, Cameron TX 76520, USA

**Holloman, Laurel** — Actress
Sanders/Armstrong/Caserta Mgmt, 2120 Colorado Ave, #120, Santa Monica CA 90404 USA

**Holloway, Brenda** — Singer
Universal Attractions, 135 W 26th St, #1200, New York NY 10001 USA

**Holloway, Brian D** — Football Player
4110 Heritage Lake Court, Lutz FL 33558, USA

**Holloway, Glen L** — Football Player
2737 N Columbus Blvd, #6, Tucson AZ 85712, USA

**Holloway, James L, III** — Navy Admiral
4800 Fillmore Ave, #1058, Alexandria VA 22311, USA

**Holloway, Jennifer** — Opera Singer
I M G Artists, Carnegie Hall Tower, 152 W 57th St, #500, New York NY 10019 USA

**Holloway, Joshua L (Josh)** — Actor, Model
W M E Entertainment, 9601 Wilshire Blvd, #300, Beverly Hills CA 90210 USA

**Holloway, Ken** — Singer, Songwriter
Terajay Music, PO Box 1283, White House TN 37188, USA

**Holloway, Matt** — Writer
Creative Artists Agency, 2000 Ave of Stars, #100, Los Angeles CA 90067 USA

**Holloway, Robin G** — Composer
Boosey & Hawkes Music Publishers, 71-91 Aldwych, London WC2B 4HN, England

**Hollstein, Martin** — Canoeing Athlete
S C Neubrandenburg, Werderstr 5, 17033 Neubrandenburg, Germany

**Hollweg, Ryan** — Ice Hockey Player
190 John Olds Dr, #212, Manchester CT 06042, USA

**Holly, Lauren** — Actress
Gilbertson Entertainment, 1334 3rd St Promenade, #207, Santa Monica CA 90401, USA

**Hollyday, Christopher** — Jazz Saxophonist
Ted Kurland, 173 Brighton Ave, Boston MA 02134 USA

**Holm, Anders** — Actor, Writer
United Talent Agency, U T A Plaza, 9336 Civic Center Dr, Beverly Hills CA 90210 USA

**Holm, Dorthe Elisabeth** — Curling Athlete
Curling Association, Idraettens Hus, 2605 Brondby, Denmark

**Holm, Georg** — Bassist (Sigur Ros)
Music Road Records, 5012 Brighton Road, Austin TX 78745, USA

**Holm, Ian** — Actor
Markham Froggatt Irwin, Julian House, 4 Windmill St, London W1P 1HF, England

**Holm, Joan** — Bowler
3639 S 61st Court, Cicero IL 60804, USA

**Holm, Peter** — Singer
1 Rue de Fer Achevel Port Grimaud, 83310 Cogolin, France

**Holman, Brian S** — Baseball Player
23595 W 223rd St, Spring Hill KS 66083, USA

**Holman, C Ray** — Businessman
Mallinckrodt Inc, 675 McDonnell Blvd, Saint Louis MO 63134, USA

**Holman, Clare** — Actress
United Agents, 12-26 Lexington St, London W1F 0LE, England

**Holman, Marshall** — Bowler
3753 Windgate St, Medford OR 97504, USA

**Holman, Ralph T** — Biochemist
3900 Bethel Dr, Saint Paul MN 55112, USA

**Holman, Rodney A** — Football Player
41460 Herwig Bluff Road, Slidell LA 70461, USA

**Holman, Shawn L** — Baseball Player
105 Edgewood Road, Sewickley PA 15143, USA

**Holmberg, Jonas** — Drummer (Komeda)
M O B Agency, 6404 Wilshire Blvd, #505, Los Angeles CA 90048 USA

**Holmberg, Marcus** — Bassist (Komeda)
M O B Agency, 6404 Wilshire Blvd, #505, Los Angeles CA 90048 USA

**Holmberg, Robert A (Rob)** — Football Player
611 Richfield Court, Greensburg PA 15601, USA
**Holmes, Amy M (A M)** — Writer
Princeton University, Creative Writing Program, Princeton NJ 08544, USA
**Holmes, Andre (PaDre)** — Musician (Fishbone)
Silverback Mgmt, 9469 Jefferson Blvd, #101, Culver City CA 90232, USA
**Holmes, Ashton** — Actor
Baker Winokur Ryder Public Relations, 9100 Wilshire Blvd, #500W, Beverly Hills CA 90212 USA
**Holmes, Clint** — Singer
Park Avenue Talent, 1560 Broadway, #1211, New York NY 10036, USA
**Holmes, Darren L** — Baseball Player
1 Emerald Court, Arden NC 28704, USA
**Holmes, David** — Music Producer, Composer
First Artists Mgmt, 4764 Park Granada, #210, Calabasas CA 91302 USA
**Holmes, Earl L** — Football Player
2978 Stonybrook Court, Tallahassee FL 32309, USA
**Holmes, J Patrick (Pat)** — Football Player
221 Mack Hollimon Dr, Kerrville TX 78028, USA
**Holmes, Jennifer** — Actress
PO Box 6303, Carmel CA 93921, USA
**Holmes, Jerry** — Football Player
107 Chatham Terrace, Hampton VA 23666, USA
**Holmes, John B (J B)** — Golfer
5175 Latrobe Dr, Windermere FL 34786, USA
**Holmes, Katie** — Actress
I C M Partners, 10250 Constellation Blvd, #900, Los Angeles CA 90067 USA
**Holmes, Kelly** — Track Athlete
Talk Mgmt, 26/28 Hammersmith Grove, London W6 7BA, England
**Holmes, Kenneth (Kenny)** — Football Player
6103 Aqua Ave, #PH, Miami Beach FL 33141, USA
**Holmes, Larry** — Boxer
228 W Canal St, Easton PA 18042, USA
**Holmes, Lester** — Football Player
3760 Motor Ave, Los Angeles CA 90034, USA
**Holmes, Pete** — Actor
W M E Entertainment, 9601 Wilshire Blvd, #300, Beverly Hills CA 90210 USA
**Holmes, Priest A** — Football Player
9937 Spring Beauty, San Antonio TX 78254, USA
**Holmes, Robert** — Sculptor
PO Box 244, Sheep Ranch CA 95246, USA
**Holmes, Rupert** — Singer, Songwriter, Writer
Creative Artists Agency, 2000 Ave of Stars, #100, Los Angeles CA 90067 USA
**Holmes, Santonio, Jr** — Football Player
PO Box 1959, Burleson TX 76097, USA
**Holmes, Tina** — Actress
Abrams Artists, 9200 W Sunset Blvd, #1125, West Hollywood CA 90069 USA
**Holmgren, Michael G (Mike)** — Football Coach, Executive
905 Lake St S, #101, Kirkland WA 98033, USA
**Holmgren, Paul H** — Ice Hockey Player, Coach, Executive
724 Southwick Circle, Somerdale NJ 08083, USA
**Holmlund, Anna** — Freestyle Skier
Sundsvall Salomklubb, Mogatan 60, 85460 Sundsvall, Sweden
**Holmquest, Donald L** — Astronaut
205 Princeton Road, Menlo Park CA 94025, USA
**Holmstrom, B Tomas** — Ice Hockey Player
43479 McLean Court, Novi MI 48375, USA
**Holmstrom, Bengt R** — Economist
Massachusetts Institute of Technology, Economics Dept, Cambridge MA 02139, USA
**Holofcener, Nicole** — Director
United Talent Agency, U T A Plaza, 9336 Civic Center Dr, Beverly Hills CA 90210 USA
**Holohan, Peter J (Pete)** — Football Player
2945 Curie St, San Diego CA 92122, USA
**Holonyak, Nick, Jr** — Inventor (Light Emitting Diode)
101 W Windsor Road, Urbana IL 61802, USA
**Holroyd, Michael D** — Writer
85 Saint Marks Road, London W10 6JS England
**Holroyd, Scott** — Actor
Stone Manners Salners, 6100 Wilshire Blvd, #1500, Los Angeles CA 90035 USA
**Holscher, Mark** — Attorney
O'Melveny & Meyers, 400 S Hope St, Los Angeles CA 90071, USA
**Holsinger, James W, Jr** — Physician
University of Kentucky Medical School, Public Health College, Lexington KY 40506, USA
**Holst, Per** — Producer
Per Holst Film A/S, Rentemestervej 69A, 2400 Copenhagen NV, Denmark
**Holt, Christopher M (Chris)** — Baseball Player
152 Hollywood Dr, Coppell TX 75019, USA
**Holt, David Lee** — Guitarist (Mavericks)
AristoMedia, 1620 16th Ave S, Nashville TN 37212, USA
**Holt, Issiac, III** — Football Player
4028 Fairmont Place, Birmingham AL 35207, USA
**Holt, James W (Jim)** — Baseball Player
150 Judge Sharpe Road, Graham NC 27253, USA
**Holt, Lester** — Commentator
NBC-TV, News Dept, 30 Rockefeller Plaza, #270E, New York NY 10112 USA
**Holt, Pierce** — Football Player
3840 County Road 339, Christoval TX 76935, USA
**Holt, Sandrine** — Actress
A P A Talent & Literary Agency, 405 S Beverly Dr, #300, Beverly Hills CA 90212 USA
**Holt, Terrence** — Football Player
9924 Thoughtful Spot Way, Raleigh NC 27614, USA
**Holt, Torrance J (Torry)** — Football Player
2604 Prosser Court, Raleigh NC 27614, USA
**Holten, Kasper** — Director
Royal Danish Theatre, Postbox 2185, 1017 Copenhagen K, Denmark
**Holtermann, E Louis, Jr** — Publisher
Glamour, Publisher's Office, 350 Madison Ave, New York NY 10017, USA

| | |
|---|---|
| **Holton, A Linwood, Jr** | Governor, VA |
| 3883 Black Stump Road, Weems VA 22576, USA | |
| **Holton, Brian J** | Baseball Player |
| 213 Overcup Loop, Summerville SC 29483, USA | |
| **Holton, Gerald** | Physicist |
| 64 Francis Ave, Cambridge MA 02138, USA | |
| **Holton, Michael D** | Basketball Player, Coach |
| 5822 NW Redfox Dr, Portland OR 97229, USA | |
| **Holtz, Louis L (Lou)** | Football Coach, Sportscaster |
| 9201 Cromwell Park Place, Orlando FL 32827, USA | |
| **Holtz, Michael J (Mike)** | Baseball Player |
| 243 Goodridge Road, Northern Cambria PA 15714, USA | |
| **Holtzman, David** | Neurologist |
| Washington University Medical Center, 660 S Euclid Ave, Saint Louis MO 63110, USA | |
| **Holtzman, Kenneth D (Ken)** | Baseball Player |
| 256 Waterside Dr, Grover MO 63040, USA | |
| **Holub, Emil Joe (E J)** | Football Player |
| 2311 S County Road 1120, Midland TX 79706, USA | |
| **Holub, Robert C** | Educator |
| University of Massachusetts, Chancellor's Office, Whitmore Building, Amherst MA 01003, USA | |
| **Holum, Dianne** | Speed Skater |
| 2835 W 32nd Ave, #89, Denver CO 80211, USA | |
| **Holum, Kristin** | Speed Skater |
| 2835 W 32nd Ave, #89, Denver CO 80211, USA | |
| **Holway, Jerome F** | Cinematographer |
| 448 Spruce Dr, Exton PA 19341, USA | |
| **Holyfield, Evander** | Boxer |
| PO Box 143420, Fayetteville GA 30214, USA | |
| **Holz, Gordon F (Gordy)** | Football Player |
| 730 S Plaza Dr, #222, Saint Paul MN 55120, USA | |
| **Holzdeppe, Raphael M** | Track Athlete |
| Marc Osenberg Athletics, Altenbach 14, 42799 Leichlingen, Germany | |
| **Holzemer, Mark H** | Baseball Player |
| 10044 S MacAlister Trail, Littleton CO 80129, USA | |
| **Holzer, Helmut** | Space Scientist |
| 2403 Little Cove Road, Owens Crossroads AL 35763, USA | |
| **Holzer, Jenny** | Artist |
| 80 Hewitt Road, Hoosick Falls NY 12090, USA | |
| **Holzinger, Brian A** | Ice Hockey Player |
| 1005 Ledgemont Dr, Broadview Heights OH 44147, USA | |
| **Holzl, Kathrin (Katy)** | Alpine Skier |
| Urbanweg 25A, 83483 Bischofswiesen, Germany | |
| **Holzmair, Wolfgang** | Opera Singer |
| Augstein & Hahn, Tal 28, 80331 Munich, Germany | |
| **Holzman, Malcolm** | Architect |
| Hardy Holzman Pfeiffer, 902 Broadway, #1900, New York NY 10010, USA | |
| **Homan, Dennis** | Football Player |
| 1950 Charlotte Court, Florence AL 35630, USA | |
| **Homewrecker, Suzi** | Singer, Guitarist (Civet) |
| The Kirby Organization, 9200 Sunset Blvd, #600, Los Angeles CA 90069, USA | |
| **Homfeld, Conrad** | Equestrian |
| Sandron, 11744 Marblestone Court, Wellington FL 33414, USA | |
| **Honda, Yuka** | Singer (Cibo Matto) |
| Billions Corp, 3522 W Armitage Ave, Chicago IL 60647, USA | |
| **Honeck, Manfred** | Conductor |
| Pittsburgh Symphony, Heinz Hall, 600 Penn Ave, Pittsburgh PA 15222, USA | |
| **Honeycutt, Frederick W (Rick)** | Baseball Player |
| 207 Forrest Road, Fort Oglethorpe GA 30742, USA | |
| **Honeycutt, Van B** | Businessman |
| Computer Sciences Corp, 2100 E Grand Ave, El Segundo CA 90245, USA | |
| **Honeyghan, Lloyd** | Boxer |
| 50 Barnfield Wood Road, Park Langley, Beckenham, Kent BR3 6SZ, England | |
| **Hong Chih-Kuo** | Baseball Player |
| Seattle Mariners, Safeco Field, PO Box 4100, Seattle WA 98194 USA | |
| **Hong, James** | Actor, Producer, Director |
| Stage 9 Talent 1249 N Lodi Place, Hollywood CA 90038, USA | |
| **Hongsakula, Apasra (Pook)** | Beauty Queen |
| Slimming Spa, 95 Ladprao Soi 23, Chatuchak, Bangkok 10900, Thailand | |
| **Honore, Russel L** | Army General |
| Keppler Speakers, 4350 N Fairfax Dr, #700, Arlington VA 22203, USA | |
| **Honrubia, Samuel** | Handball Player |
| Paris Saint Germain Handball, 82 Ave Georges Lafont, 75016 Paris, France | |
| **Honti, Zolton** | Cinematographer |
| Gersh Agency, 9465 Wilshire Blvd, #600, Beverly Hills CA 90212 USA | |
| **Hood, Calum** | Singer, Bassist (5 Seconds of Summer) |
| Wonder Mgmt, Philips House, 17/617 Elizabeth St, Redfern NSW 2016, Australia | |
| **Hood, Donald H (Don)** | Baseball Player |
| 20753 Charing Cross Circle, Estero FL 33928, USA | |
| **Hood, Estus, III** | Football Player |
| 2105 W Grace St, Kankakee IL 60901, USA | |
| **Hood, Gavin** | Director |
| Anonymous Content, 3532 Hayden Ave, Culver City CA 90232 USA | |
| **Hood, Kenneth** | Religious Leader |
| 5799 Bloomfield Ave, Verona NJ 07044, USA | |
| **Hood, Leroy E** | Inventor (DNA Sequencer), Geneticist |
| Institutions for Systems Biology, 1441 N 34th St, Seattle WA 98103, USA | |
| **Hood, Robin** | Golfer |
| 6705 Shoal Creek Dr, Arlington TX 76001, USA | |
| **Hood, Rodney** | Basketball Player |
| Utah Jazz, Energy Solutions Arena, 301 W South Temple, Salt Lake City UT 84101 USA | |
| **Hood, Walter** | Landscape Designer |
| Hood Studio, 3016 Filbert St, Oakland CA 94608, USA | |
| **Hood, Winford D** | Football Player |
| 79 Anderson Ave NW, Atlanta GA 30314, USA | |
| **Hoog, Ellen** | Field Hockey Player |
| Amsterdam Hockey & Bandy Club, Postbus 7843, 1008 Amsterdam AA, Netherlands | |

# H

**Hook, James W (Jay)** — Baseball Player
PO Box 90, Maple City MI 49664, USA
**Hooker, Charles R** — Artist
28 Whippingham Road, Brighton, Sussex BN2 3PG, England
**Hooker, Destinee D** — Volleyball Player
USA Volleyball, 4065 Sinton Road, #200, Colorado Springs CO 80907, USA
**Hooker, Fair, Jr** — Football Player
3728 Rutherford Court, Inglewood CA 90305, USA
**Hooker, Jake** — Journalist
New York Times, Editorial Dept, 229 W 43rd St, New York NY 10036 USA
**Hooks, Bell** — Writer
291 W 12th St, New York NY 10014, USA
**Hooks, Brian** — Actor
Don Buchwald Talent Agency, 6500 Wilshire Blvd, #2200, Los Angeles CA 90048 USA
**Hooks, Kevin** — Director, Producer
Gyre Entertainment, 4119 W Burbank Blvd, Burbank CA 91505, USA
**Hooks, Robert** — Actor
145 N Valley St, Burbank CA 91505, USA
**Hooks, Roland** — Football Player
3724 Calgary Dr, Reno NV 89511, USA
**Hooper, Bobby Joe** — Basketball Player
825 Ivywood St, #4, Dayton OH 45420, USA
**Hooper, Brandon** — Actor, Writer, Producer
United Talent Agency, U T A Plaza, 9336 Civic Center Dr, Beverly Hills CA 90210 USA
**Hooper, C Darrow** — Track Athlete
6 Braemore Place, Dallas TX 75230, USA
**Hooper, Ella** — Singer (Killing Heidi)
Harbour Agency, 135 Forbes St, Woolloomooloo NSW 2011, Australia
**Hooper, Kay** — Writer
Bantam/Dell Books, 1745 Broadway, New York NY 10019, USA
**Hooper, Thomas G (Tom)** — Director
I C M Partners, 10250 Constellation Blvd, #900, Los Angeles CA 90067 USA
**Hooper, Tobe** — Director
Gersh Agency, 9465 Wilshire Blvd, #600, Beverly Hills CA 90212 USA
**Hoopes, Chad** — Concert Violinist
I M G Artists, Carnegie Hall Tower, 152 W 57th St, #500, New York NY 10019 USA
**Hooser, Carroll L** — Basketball Player
925 Edgefield Trail, Flower Mound TX 75028, USA
**Hooton, Burt C** — Baseball Player
3619 Granby Court, San Antonio TX 78217, USA
**Hoover, Alice** — Baseball Player
340 Roosevelt Ave, Reading PA 19605, USA
**Hoover, Bradley R (Brad)** — Football Player
2130 Climbing Rose Lane, Matthews NC 28104, USA
**Hoover, Houston R** — Football Player
1216 Mareed Ave, Yazoo City MS 39194, USA
**Hoover, Paul C** — Baseball Player
2320 Anderson Road, Cuyahoga Falls OH 44221, USA
**Hoover, Richard** — Scenic Designer
I C M Partners, 10250 Constellation Blvd, #900, Los Angeles CA 90067 USA
**Hoover, Robert A (Bob)** — Test Pilot
Bob Hoover Airshows, 1100 E Imperial Ave, El Segundo CA 90245, USA
**Hoover, Thomas L (Tom)** — Basketball Player
9 Apple Manor Lane, East Brunswick NJ 08816, USA
**Hopcroft, John E** — Computer Scientist
Cornell University, Engineering College, Carpenter Hall, Ithaca NY 14853, USA
**Hope, Amanda** — Model
Playboy Promotions, 9346 Civic Center Dr, #200, Beverly Hills CA 90210 USA
**Hope, David (Dave)** — Bassist (Kansas)
Immanuel Angelican Church, 250 Indian Bayou Trail, Destin FL 32541, USA
**Hope, Jim** — Producer, Writer
A P A Talent & Literary Agency, 405 S Beverly Dr, #300, Beverly Hills CA 90212 USA
**Hope, Leslie** — Actress
Oscars Abrams Zimel, 438 Queen St E, Toronto ON M5A 1T4, Canada
**Hope, William (Bill)** — Actor
Artists Partnership, 101 Finsbury Pavement, London EC2A 1RS, England
**Hopkins Dent, Jennifer** — Tennis Player
4312 W 110 St, Leawood KS 66211, USA
**Hopkins, Anthony** — Actor
United Talent Agency, U T A Plaza, 9336 Civic Center Dr, Beverly Hills CA 90210 USA
**Hopkins, Antony** — Composer, Writer
Woodyard Cottage, Ashridge Park, Little Gaddesden, Berkhamsted HP4 1PS, England
**Hopkins, Bo** — Actor
6628 Ethel Ave, North Hollywood CA 91606, USA
**Hopkins, Bradley D (Brad)** — Football Player
95 Timberline Dr, Nashville TN 37221, USA
**Hopkins, Donald (Don)** — Baseball Player
PO Box 8817, Benton Harbor MI 49023, USA
**Hopkins, Gail E** — Baseball Player
120 Canterbury Dr, Parkersburg WV 26104, USA
**Hopkins, Godfrey T** — Photographer
Wilmington Cottage, Wilmington Road, Seaford, East Sussex BN25 2EH, England
**Hopkins, James** — Artist, Sculptor
Saatchi Gallery, Duke Of York's HQ, King's Road, London SW3 4RY, England
**Hopkins, Jan** — Commentator
CNN-TV, News Dept, 190 Marietta Ave SW, Atlanta GA 30303 USA
**Hopkins, Jerry W** — Football Player
1025 Burberry, Woodway TX 76712, USA
**Hopkins, John** — Bassist (Zac Brown Band)
Shore Fire Media, 32 Court St, #1600, Brooklyn NY 11201 USA
**Hopkins, Jonathan J (Jon)** — Musician, Producer
Domino Recording, PO Box 47029, London SW18 1EG, England
**Hopkins, Josh** — Actor
Gersh Agency, 9465 Wilshire Blvd, #600, Beverly Hills CA 90212 USA
**Hopkins, Joshua** — Opera Singer
I M G Artists, Hogarth Business Park, Chiswick, London W4 2TH, England

**Hopkins, Kaitlin** — Actress
B R S / Gage Talent Agency, 1650 Broadway, #1410, New York NY 10019 USA

**Hopkins, Linda** — Singer, Actress
Scott Stander Assoc, 4533 Van Nuys Blvd, #401, Sherman Oaks CA 91403 USA

**Hopkins, Michael J** — Architect
27 Broadley Terrace, London NW1 6LG, England

**Hopkins, Michael J** — Mathematician
Harvard University, Mathematics Dept, Cambridge MA 02138, USA

**Hopkins, Michael N** — Astronaut
N A S A, Johnson Space Center, 2101 NASA Road, Houston TX 77058 USA

**Hopkins, Nancy** — Geneticist, Biologist
Massachusetts Institute of Technology, Biology Dept, Cambridge MA 02139, USA

**Hopkins, Paul** — Actor
Edna Talent Mgmt, 318 Dundas St W, Toronto ON M5T 1G5, Canada

**Hopkins, Robert M (Bob)** — Basketball Player
8421 SE 71st St, Mercer Island WA 98040, USA

**Hopkins, Stephen J** — Director
Creative Artists Agency, 2000 Ave of Stars, #100, Los Angeles CA 90067 USA

**Hopkins, Sy** — Singer (Five Satins)
Paramount Entertainment, PO Box 12, Far Hills NJ 07931 USA

**Hopkins, Telma** — Actress, Singer
Innovative Artists, 1505 10th St, Santa Monica CA 90401 USA

**Hopkins, Tom** — Writer
7531 E 2nd St, Scottsdale AZ 85251, USA

**Hopkins, Wesley (Wes)** — Football Player
7412 White Oak Road, Fairfield AL 35064, USA

**Hoppe, Fred** — Sculptor
PO Box 42, Milford NE 68405, USA

**Hoppe, Wolfgang** — Bobsled Athlete
Dieterstedter Str 11, 99510 Apolda, Germany

**Hoppen, David D (Dave)** — Basketbal Player
16341 Webster St, Omaha NE 68118, USA

**Hopper, Heather** — Actress
Baron Entertainment, 13848 Ventura Blvd, #A, Sherman Oaks CA 91423, USA

**Hopper, Norris S** — Baseball Player
902 Hampton St, Shelby NC 28152, USA

**Hopperdeitz, Anna** — Actress
Agentur Fuhrmann, Lindenstr 8A, 84424 Isen-Pemmering, Germany

**Hoppus, Mark** — Bassist (Blink-182, +44)
14015 Chestnut Hill Lane, San Diego CA 92128, USA

**Hopson, Dennis** — Basketball Player
7229 Donnybrook Dr, Dublin OH 43017, USA

**Hora, Jeremy** — Guitarist (Default)
Union Entertainment, 1323 Newbury Road, #104, Newbury Park CA 91320, USA

**Horan, Dennis, Jr** — Bowler
32458 Galatina St, Temecula CA 92592, USA

**Horan, James** — Actor
Angel City Talent, 8318 Kirkwood Dr, Los Angeles CA 90046, USA

**Horan, Michael W (Mike)** — Football Player
7235 E La Cumbre Dr, Orange CA 92869, USA

**Horan, Monica** — Actress
Creative Artists Agency, 2000 Ave of Stars, #100, Los Angeles CA 90067 USA

**Horbiger, Christiane** — Actress
Agentur Alexander, Lamontstr 9, 81679 Munich, Germany

**Horford Reynoso, Alfred J (Al)** — Basketball Player
Atlanta Hawks, Centennial Tower, 101 Marietta St NW, #1900, Atlanta GA 30303 USA

**Horgan, Joe** — Baseball Player
2039 Kellogg Way, Rancho Cordova CA 95670, USA

**Horgan, Patrick** — Actor
I C M Partners, 10250 Constellation Blvd, #900, Los Angeles CA 90067 USA

**Horgan, Sharon** — Actress, Comedienne
United Agents, 12-26 Lexington St, London W1F 0LE, England

**Horinek, Ramon A** — Vietnam War Air Force Hero
184 National Blvd, Universal City TX 78148, USA

**Horlen, Joel E (Joe)** — Baseball Player
3718 Chartwell Dr, San Antonio TX 78230, USA

**Horlock, John H** — Mechanical Engineer, Educator
2 The Avenue, Ampthill, Bedford MK45 2NR, England

**Horn, Donald G (Don)** — Football Player
2229 Wynterbrook Dr, Littleton CO 80126, USA

**Horn, Joseph (Joe)** — Football Player
3919 Nemours Trail NW, Kennesaw GA 30152, USA

**Horn, Marian Blank** — Judge
US Claims Court, 717 Madison Place NW, Washington DC 20439, USA

**Horn, Samuel L (Sam)** — Baseball Player
1305 Narragansett Blvd, Cranston RI 02905, USA

**Hornacek, Jeffrey J (Jeff)** — Basketball Player, Coach
5821 N 37th St, Paradise Valley AZ 85253, USA

**Hornaday, Jeffrey** — Choreographer
I C M Partners, 10250 Constellation Blvd, #900, Los Angeles CA 90067 USA

**Hornaday, Ronald (Ron), Jr** — Truck, Auto Racing Driver
116 Courtney Lane, Mooresville NC 28117, USA

**Hornbacher, Scott** — Producer
United Talent Agency, U T A Plaza, 9336 Civic Center Dr, Beverly Hills CA 90210 USA

**Hornbuckle, Linda** — Singer
Pacific Talent, PO Box 19145, Portland OR 97280, USA

**Hornby, Nick** — Writer
Penguin Books, 80 Stand, London WC2R 0RL, England

**Horne, Jimmy Bo** — Singer, Dancer
Talent Consultants International, 105 Shad Row, #B, Piermont NY 10968 USA

**Horne, John R** — Businessman
Navistar International, PO Box 1488, Warrenville IL 60555, USA

**Horne, Marilyn** — Opera Singer
Marilyn Horne Foundation, 315 W 86th St, #2D, New York NY 10024, USA

**Horne, Steve** — Auto Racing Executive
Tasman Motor Sports Group, 4192 Weaver Court, Hilliard OH 43026, USA

|  |  |
|------|-----------|
| **Horneber, Petra**<br>Ringstr 77, 85402 Kranzberg, Germany | Markswoman |
| **Horneff, Will**<br>Abrams Artists, 9200 W Sunset Blvd, #1125, West Hollywood CA 90069 USA | Actor |
| **Horner, Alex Kapp**<br>Innovative Artists, 1505 10th St, Santa Monica CA 90401 USA | Actress |
| **Horner, Charles A (Chuck)**<br>2824 Jack Nicklaus Way, Shalimar FL 32579, USA | Air Force General |
| **Horner, Craig**<br>Marquee Mgmt, 188 Oxford St, Paddington NSW 2021, Australia | Actor |
| **Horner, J Robert (Bob)**<br>209 Steeplechase Dr, Irving TX 75062, USA | Baseball Player |
| **Horner, James**<br>Gorfaine/Schwartz, 4111 W Alameda Ave, #509, Burbank CA 91505 USA | Composer |
| **Horner, John R (Jack)**<br>70 Cougar Dr, Bozeman MT 59718, USA | Paleontologist |
| **Horner, Martina S**<br>T I A A-C R E F, 730 3rd Ave, New York NY 10017, USA | Educator, Businesswoman |
| **Hornish, Samuel J (Sam), Jr**<br>Joe Gibbs Racing, 13415 Reese Blvd W, Huntersville NC 28078, USA | Auto Racing Driver |
| **Hornlein, Horst**<br>Tambascherstr 13, 98559 Oberhoff, Germany | Luge Athlete |
| **Hornsby, Bruce**<br>Red Light Mgmt, PO Box 1467, Charlottesville VA 22902, USA | Singer, Pianist, Actor |
| **Hornsby, David**<br>Schachter Entertainment, 1157 S Beverly Dr, #200, Los Angeles CA 90035 USA | Actor |
| **Hornsby, Russell**<br>I C M Partners, 10250 Constellation Blvd, #900, Los Angeles CA 90067 USA | Actor |
| **Hornsey, Kate**<br>Mercantile Rowing Club, Boathouse Drive, Melbourne VIC 3004, Australia | Rowing Athlete |
| **Hornung, Paul V**<br>3115 Arden Road, Louisville KY 40222, USA | Football Player |
| **Horovitz, Adam (King Ad-Rock)**<br>Capitol Records, 810 7th Ave, New York NY 10019 USA | Rap Artist (Beastie Boys) |
| **Horovitz, Israel A**<br>Washington Square Arts, 310 Bowery, #200, New York NY 10012, USA | Writer |
| **Horovitz, Joseph**<br>Royal College of Music, Prince Consort Road, London SW7 2BS, England | Composer |
| **Horovitz, Rachael**<br>Creative Artists Agency, 2000 Ave of Stars, #100, Los Angeles CA 90067 USA | Producer, Actress |
| **Horowitz, Ben**<br>Esther Creative Group, 27 W 24th St, #404, New York NY 10010, USA | Drummer (Gaslight Anthem) |
| **Horowitz, David C**<br>Fight Back Productions, 139 S Beverly Dr, #233, Beverly Hills CA 90210, USA | Commentator |
| **Horowitz, Jerome P**<br>Wayne State University Medical School, 540 E Canfield Ave, Detroit MI 48201, USA | Internist |
| **Horowitz, Paul**<br>111 Chilton St, Cambridge MA 02138, USA | Physicist, Electrical Engineer |
| **Horowitz, Sari**<br>Washington Post, Editorial Dept, 1150 15th St NW, Washington DC 20071 USA | Journalist |
| **Horowitz, Scott J**<br>5491 Freestyle Way, Park City UT 84098, USA | Astronaut |
| **Horrigan, Sam**<br>Prestige Talent Agency, 9250 Wilshire Blvd, #208, Beverly Hills CA 90212, USA | Actor, Producer |
| **Horrocks, Jane**<br>United Agents, 12-26 Lexington St, London W1F 0LE, England | Actress, Singer |
| **Horry, Robert K**<br>2126 Countryshire Lane, Richmond TX 77406, USA | Basketball Player |
| **Horschel, William J (Billy)**<br>Professional Golfers Association, 100 Ave of Champions, Palm Beach Gardens FL 33418 USA | Golfer |
| **Horsey, David**<br>Los Angeles Times, Editorial Dept, 202 W 1st St, Los Angeles CA 90012 USA | Editorial Cartoonist |
| **Horsford, Anna Maria**<br>Innovative Artists, 1505 10th St, Santa Monica CA 90401 USA | Actress |
| **Horsley, Jack**<br>608 N Sampson St, Ellensburg WA 98926, USA | Swimmer |
| **Horsley, Lee A**<br>Central Artists, 3310 W Burbank Blvd, Burbank CA 91505, USA | Actor |
| **Horsman, Vincent S J (Vince)**<br>1941 Pinehurst Dr, Clearwater FL 33763, USA | Baseball Player |
| **Horton, Anthony D (Tony)**<br>17001 Livorno Dr, Pacific Palisades CA 90272, USA | Baseball Player |
| **Horton, Ethan S**<br>4602 Fairvista Dr, Charlotte NC 28269, USA | Football Player |
| **Horton, Frank E**<br>288 River Ranch Circle, Bayfield CO 81122, USA | Educator |
| **Horton, Gregory K (Greg)**<br>1053 Lytle St, Redlands CA 92374, USA | Football Player |
| **Horton, Peter**<br>W M E Entertainment, 9601 Wilshire Blvd, #300, Beverly Hills CA 90210 USA | Actor |
| **Horton, Raymond A (Ray)**<br>3400 S Water St, Pittsburgh PA 15203, USA | Football Player |
| **Horton, Ricky N**<br>16026 Aston Court, Chesterfield MO 63005, USA | Baseball Player |
| **Horton, Robert**<br>5317 Andasol Ave, Encino CA 91316, USA | Actor |
| **Horton, William W (Willie)**<br>5655 Woodland Pass, Bloomfield Hills MI 48301, USA | Baseball Player |
| **Horvat, Zlatko**<br>R K Zagreb, Verprinacka 16, 10000 Zagreb, Croatia | Handball Player |
| **Horvath, Bronco J**<br>27 Oliver St, South Yarmouth MA 02664, USA | Ice Hockey Player |
| **Horvitz, H Robert**<br>34 Pilgrim Road, Wellesley Hills MA 02481, USA | Nobel Medicine Laureate |
| **Horvitz, Louis J**<br>Gersh Agency, 9465 Wilshire Blvd, #600, Beverly Hills CA 90212 USA | Director |

**Horwitz, Dominique** — Actress, Singer
Agentur Patricia Horwitz, Erdmannstra 10, 22765 Hamburg, Germany

**Horwitz, Morton J** — Attorney, Educator
Harvard University, Law School, Cambridge MA 02138, USA

**Horwitz, Tony** — Journalist, Writer
PO Box 5056, Vineyard Haven MA 02568, USA

**Hosey, Dwayne S** — Baseball Player
164 N Plum Ave, Ontario CA 91764, USA

**Hoshide, Akihiko (Aki)** — Astronaut, Japan
J A X A, Tsukuba Space Center, 2-1-1 Sengen, Tsukubashi, Ibaraki 305 8505, Japan

**Hosket, Wilmer F (Bill)** — Basketball Player
4721 Bayford Court, Columbus OH 43220, USA

**Hosking, Sophie** — Rowing Athlete
British Rowing, 6 Lower Mall, London W6 9DJ, England

**Hoskins, Derrick** — Football Player
10491 Road 842, Philadelphia MS 39350, USA

**Hosley, Timothy K (Tim)** — Baseball Player
112 Elena Dr, Moore SC 29369, USA

**Hosmer, Bradley C (Brad)** — Air Force General
PO Box 1128, Cedar Crest NM 87008, USA

**Hosp, Nicole** — Alpine Skier
Kirchhif 36, 6621 Bichlbach, Austria

**Hospodar, Edward D (Ed)** — Ice Hockey Player
217 Orchard Way, Wayne PA 19087, USA

**Hossa, Marian** — Ice Hockey Player
270 E Pearson St, #1402, Chicago IL 60611, USA

**Hossack, Allison** — Actress
Characters Talent Mgmt, 8 Elm St, Toronto ON M5G 1G7, Canada

**Hossein, Robert** — Actor, Director
Ghislaine de Wing, 10 Rue du Docteur Roux, 75015 Paris, France

**Hosseini, Khaled** — Writer
Riverhead/Penguin Group, 375 Hudson St, Basement 1, New York NY 10014, USA

**Hostak, Martin** — Ice Hockey Player
Ceska Televize, Kavci Hory, 14070 Prague 4, Czech Republic

**Hostetler, David A (Dave)** — Baseball Player
3404 Steeplechase Trail, Arlington TX 76016, USA

**Hostetler, David L** — Sculptor
PO Box 989, Athens OH 45701, USA

**Hostetler, Jeff W** — Football Player
2032 Magnolia Dr, Morgantown WV 26508, USA

**Hostetter, G Richard** — Religious Leader
Presbyterian Church in America, 1852 Century Place NE, #201, Atlanta GA 30345, USA

**Hotani, Hirokazu** — Microbiotics Engineer
Teikyo University, Biosciences Dept, Toyosatodai, Utsunomiya 320 0003, Japan

**Hotchkiss, Rob** — Guitarist (Train)
Jon Landau, 150 Rowayton Ave, Norwalk CT 06853, USA

**Hotez, Peter** — Microbiologist, Immunologist
Sabin Vaccine Institute, 2000 Pennsylvania Ave NW, #7100, Washington DC 20006, USA

**Hottelet, Richard C** — Commentator
120 Chestnut Hill Road, Wilton CT 06897, USA

**Hotten, Terry** — Chemist
Eli Lilly Wood Laboratory, Windlesham, Surrey GO20 6PH, England

**Hottman, Kenneth (Ken)** — Baseball Player
9537 2nd Ave, Elk Grove CA 95624, USA

**Hoty, Dee** — Actress, Singer
B R S / Gage Talent Agency, 1650 Broadway, #1410, New York NY 10019 USA

**Hotz, Kenneth J (Kenny)** — Actor, Director, Writer
Paradigm Agency, 360 N Crescent Dr, North Building, Beverly Hills CA 90210 USA

**Hou, Ya-Ming** — Biologist
Massachusetts Institute of Technology, Biology Dept, Cambridge MA 02139, USA

**Houcke, Sara** — Circus Animal Trainer
Ringling Bros Barnum & Bailey, 8607 Westwood Circle Dr, Vienna VA 22182 USA

**Houellebecq, Michel** — Writer, Director
Green Ufos, Parque Pisa, C/Exposicion, 1 Izq, 41927 Mairena del Aljarafe, Spain

**Hough, Charles O (Charlie)** — Baseball Player
2266 Shade Tree Circle, Brea CA 92821, USA

**Hough, Derek** — Dancer, Choreographer
Brillstein Entertainment Partners, 9150 Wilshire Blvd, #350, Beverly Hills CA 90212 USA

**Hough, James H (Jim)** — Football Player
2440 Christian Dr, Chaska MN 55318, USA

**Hough, Joseph C, Jr** — Educator
Union Theological Seminary, President's Office, New York NY 10027, USA

**Hough, Julianne M** — Dancer, Singer, Actress
Creative Artists Agency, 2000 Ave of Stars, #100, Los Angeles CA 90067 USA

**Hough, Stephen A G** — Concert Pianist
C M Artists, 127 W 96th St, #13B, New York NY 10025 USA

**Houghton, Frances** — Rowing Athlete
Tyrian Club, 6 Lower Mall, Hammersmith W6 9DJ, England

**Houghton, Israel** — Singer, Songwriter, Guitarist
Integrity Music, 1000 Cody Road, Mobile AL 36695, USA

**Houghton, J Nicholas R (Nick)** — Army General, England
Chief of Defense Staff, Whitehall, London SW1A 2HB, England

**Houghton, James R** — Businessman
36 Spencer Hill Road, Corning NY 14830, USA

**Houghton, John T** — Physicist, Climatologist
Hadley Center, London Broad, Bracknell, Berkshire RG12 2SZ, England

**Houghton, Katharine** — Actress
Ambrosio/Mortimer, 165 W 46th St, New York NY 10036 USA

**Houghton, Michael** — Geneticist
Chiron Corp, 4560 Horton St, Emeryville CA 94608, USA

**Hougland, William M (Bill)** — Basketball Player
PO Box 2629, Edwards CO 81632, USA

**Houle, Rejean** — Ice Hockey Player
7941 Boul Lasalle, Lasalle QC H8P 3R1, Canada

**Hoult, Nicholas** — Actor
United Talent Agency, U T A Plaza, 9336 Civic Center Dr, Beverly Hills CA 90210 USA

| | |
|---|---|
| **Houlton, D J**<br>2357 N Campus Ave, Upland CA 91784, USA | Baseball Player |
| **Houngbo, Gilbert**<br>Prime Minister's Office, BP 5618, Lome, Togo | Prime Minister, Togo |
| **Hounslow, Richard**<br>Canoe Union, Adbolton Lane/West Bridgford, Nottingham NG2 5AS, England | Canoeing Athlete |
| **Hounsou, Djimon**<br>Creative Artists Agency, 2000 Ave of Stars, #100, Los Angeles CA 90067 USA | Actor, Model |
| **House, David (Dave)**<br>Nortel Networks Corp, 8200 Dixie Road, Brampton ON L6T 5P6, Canada | Businessman |
| **House, Edward L (Eddie)**<br>Miami Heat, American Airlines Arena, 601 Biscayne Blvd, Miami FL 33132 USA | Basketball Player |
| **House, James R (J R)**<br>34 River Ridge Trail, Ormond Beach FL 32174, USA | Baseball Player |
| **House, James S**<br>University of Michigan, Social Research Institute, Ann Arbor MI 48106, USA | Psychologist |
| **House, Karen Eliot**<br>58 Cleveland Lane, Princeton NJ 08540, USA | Journalist |
| **House, Thomas R (Tom)**<br>12794 Via Felino, Del Mar CA 92014, USA | Baseball Player |
| **House, Yoanna**<br>I M G Models, 304 Park Ave S, #PH N, New York NY 10010 USA | Model |
| **Householder, Paul W**<br>521 N Swinton Ave, Delray Beach FL 33444, USA | Baseball Player |
| **Housekat, D Jane**<br>Alex Sinner Artist Mmgt, Postfach 1247, 64319 Pfungstadt, Germany | Singer, DJ Musician |
| **Houser, Jerry**<br>4050 Woodman Canyon, Sherman Oaks CA 91423, USA | Actor |
| **Houser, John W, Jr**<br>2197 Creekside Dr, Solvang CA 93463, USA | Football Player |
| **Houser, Kevin J**<br>941 Montclair Circle, Westlake OH 44145, USA | Football Player |
| **Houser, Randy**<br>Fitzgerald Hartley, 1964 Wedgewood Ave, Nashville TN 37212 USA | Singer, Songwriter |
| **Houshmandzadeh, Touraj (T J), Jr**<br>16703 Greenbrook Circle, Cerritos CA 90703, USA | Football Player |
| **Housley, Phil**<br>2877 Itasca Ave S, Lakeland MN 55043, USA | Ice Hockey Player |
| **Houston, Allan W**<br>Allan Houston Foundation, 350 5th Ave, #5900, New York NY 10118, USA | Basketball Player |
| **Houston, Bobby**<br>4640 Vendue Range Dr, Raleigh NC 27604, USA | Football Player |
| **Houston, Cissy**<br>Nippy Inc, 60 Park Place, #1800, Newark NJ 07102, USA | Singer |
| **Houston, James E (Jim)**<br>925 Trimble Place, Northfield OH 44067, USA | Football Player |
| **Houston, Kenneth R (Ken)**<br>3603 Forest Village Dr, Kingwood TX 77339, USA | Football Player |
| **Houston, Marques B**<br>Pyramid Entertainment Group, 377 Rector Place, #21A, New York NY 10280 USA | Singer, Actor |
| **Houston, Penelope**<br>Absolute Artists, 8490 W Sunset Blvd, #403, West Hollywood CA 90069, USA | Singer |
| **Houston, Russell**<br>General Delivery, Eagar AZ 85925, USA | Artist |
| **Houston, Stephen D**<br>Brown University, Anthropology Dept, Providence RI 02912, USA | Anthropologist, Social Scientist |
| **Houston, Thelma**<br>Diva Central, 7510 W Sunset Blvd, #1445, Los Angeles CA 90046, USA | Singer |
| **Houston, Tyler S**<br>325 Pleasant Summit Dr, Henderson NV 89012, USA | Baseball Player |
| **Houston, Wade**<br>University of Tennessee, Athletic Dept, Knoxville TN 37901, USA | Basketball Coach |
| **Hout, Michael**<br>University of California, Demography Center, 2538 Channing, Berkeley CA 94720, USA | Demographer |
| **Houtzager, Marc**<br>Royal Dutch Equestrian, De Beek 125, PO Box 3040, 3852 Ermelo PL, Netherlands | Equestrian |
| **Hovan, Christopher J (Chris)**<br>17301 Ladera Estates Blvd, Lutz FL 33548, USA | Football Player |
| **Hove, Andrew C (Skip), Jr**<br>Promontory Financial Group, 1201 Pennsylvania NW, #617, Washington DC 20004, USA | Government Official, Financier |
| **Hovind, David J**<br>Paccar Inc, 777 106th Ave NE, Bellevue WA 98004, USA | Businessman |
| **Hovland, Tim**<br>Association of Volleyball Professionals, 2183 Fairview Road, #222, Costa Mesa CA 92627 USA | Volleyball Player |
| **Hovsepian, Vatche**<br>Armenian Church of America West, 1201 N Vine St, Los Angeles CA 90038, USA | Religious Leader |
| **Howard, Adina**<br>A&M Entertainment, 13280 NW Freeway, #F328, Houston TX 77040, USA | Singer |
| **Howard, Alan M**<br>Julian Belfrage Assoc, 9 Argyll St, #300, London W1F 7TG, England | Actor |
| **Howard, Andrew**<br>Julian Belfrage Assoc, 9 Argyll St, #300, London W1F 7TG, England | Actor |
| **Howard, Ann**<br>Stafford Law Assoc, 6 Barham Close, Weybridge, Surrey KT13 9PR, England | Opera Singer |
| **Howard, Arliss**<br>Innovative Artists, 235 Park Ave S, #1000, New York NY 10003 USA | Actor, Director |
| **Howard, Barbara**<br>PO Box 459, Chelsea MI 48118, USA | Actress |
| **Howard, Bruce E**<br>8705 Misty Creek Dr, Sarasota FL 34241, USA | Baseball Player |
| **Howard, Bryce Dallas**<br>Management 360, 9111 Wilshire Blvd, Beverly Hills CA 90210 USA | Actress |
| **Howard, Christian (Chris)**<br>11 Hawser Lane, Swampscott MA 01907, USA | Baseball Player |
| **Howard, Christopher H (Chris)**<br>8655 Jones Road, #301, Houston TX 77065, USA | Baseball Player |

| | |
|---|---|
| **Howard, Clark**<br>WSB-AM, 1601 West Peachtree St, Atlanta GA 30309, USA | Entertainer |
| **Howard, Clint**<br>4286 Clybourn Ave, Burbank CA 91505, USA | Actor |
| **Howard, David**<br>5516 E Rosedale St, Fort Worth TX 76112, USA | Football Player |
| **Howard, David W**<br>22846 Chesterview Loop, #111, Land O Lakes FL 34639, USA | Baseball Player |
| **Howard, Desmond K**<br>Prince Promotions, 9663 Santa Monica Blvd, #324, Beverly Hills CA 90210, USA | Football Player |
| **Howard, Douglas L (Doug)**<br>8038 Deer Creek Road, Salt Lake City UT 84121, USA | Baseball Player |
| **Howard, Dwight D**<br>3565 Rice Lake Loop, Longwood FL 32779, USA | Basketball Player |
| **Howard, Eugene (Gene)**<br>11051 Lavender Ave, Fountain Valley CA 92708, USA | Football Player |
| **Howard, Frank O**<br>24178 Lenah Woods Place, Aldie VA 20105, USA | Baseball Player |
| **Howard, George**<br>David Rubinson, PO Box 411197, San Francisco CA 94141, USA | Jazz Saxophonist |
| **Howard, George**<br>8415 Brookwood Dr, Portage MI 49024, USA | Bowler |
| **Howard, Greg**<br>4517 W 16th Place, #2, Los Angeles CA 90019, USA | Basketball Player |
| **Howard, Greg**<br>1900 N Atlantic Ave, #604, Daytona Beach FL 32118, USA | Cartoonist (Sally Forth) |
| **Howard, Harry N**<br>6508 Greentree Road, Bradley Hills Grove, Bethesda MD 20817, USA | Historian |
| **Howard, Hobie**<br>O-Seven Artist Mgmt, PO Box 210586, Nashville TN 37221, USA | Singer (Sawyer Brown) |
| **Howard, James J, III**<br>Northern States Power, 414 Nicollett Mall, Minneapolis MN 55401, USA | Businessman |
| **Howard, James Newton**<br>Gorfaine/Schwartz, 4111 W Alameda Ave, #509, Burbank CA 91505 USA | Composer |
| **Howard, Jan**<br>Tessier-Marsh Talent, 2825 Blue Brick Dr, Nashville TN 37214, USA | Singer, Songwriter |
| **Howard, Jason**<br>I M G Artists, Hogarth Business Park, Chiswick, London W4 2TH, England | Opera Singer |
| **Howard, Jeffrey R**<br>US Court of Appeals, US Courthouse, 55 Pleasant St, Concord NH 03301, USA | Judge |
| **Howard, Jeremy**<br>Stone Manners Salners, 6100 Wilshire Blvd, #1500, Los Angeles CA 90035 USA | Actor |
| **Howard, John W**<br>GPO Box 59, Sydney NSW 2001, Australia | Prime Minister, Australia |
| **Howard, Joshua J (Josh)**<br>6306 Linden Lane, Dallas TX 75230, USA | Basketball Player |
| **Howard, Juwan A**<br>11714 Bistro Lane, Houston TX 77082, USA | Basketball Player |
| **Howard, Ken**<br>Screen Actors Guild, 5757 Wilshire Blvd, Los Angeles CA 90036, USA | Actor, Labor Leader |
| **Howard, Kyle**<br>United Talent Agency, U T A Plaza, 9336 Civic Center Dr, Beverly Hills CA 90210 USA | Actor, Writer, Director |
| **Howard, Linda**<br>Ballatine Books, 1745 Broadway, New York NY 10019 USA | Writer |
| **Howard, Michael**<br>House of Lords, Westminster, London SW1A 0PW, England | Government Official, England |
| **Howard, Michelle J**<br>Deputy Commander, Fleet Forces Command, 1562 Mitscher Ave, Norfolk VA 23551 USA | Navy Admiral |
| **Howard, Michelle J**<br>Vice Chief of Naval Operations, HqUSN, Pentagon, Washington DC 20350 USA | Navy Admiral |
| **Howard, Miki**<br>Majestic Entertainment Group, 3645 Marketplace Blvd, #130-40, East Point GA 30344, USA | Singer, Actress |
| **Howard, Otis**<br>231 Manhattan Ave, Oak Ridge TN 37830, USA | Basketball Player |
| **Howard, Paul G**<br>10859 W 85th Place, Arvada CO 80005, USA | Football Player |
| **Howard, Rance**<br>4286 Clybourn Ave, Burbank CA 91505, USA | Actor |
| **Howard, Rebecca Lynn**<br>W M E Entertainment, 1600 Division St, #300, Nashville TN 37203 USA | Singer |
| **Howard, Reginald C (Reggie)**<br>PO Box 382666, Germantown TN 38183, USA | Football Player |
| **Howard, Richard**<br>23 Waverly Place, #5X, New York NY 10003, USA | Writer |
| **Howard, Robert E**<br>Dark House Publishing, 10956 SE Main St, Portland OR 97222, USA | Cartoonist (Conan) |
| **Howard, Ronald F (Ron)**<br>14701 NE 61st Court, Redmond WA 98052, USA | Football Player |
| **Howard, Ronald W (Ron)**<br>Imagine Entertainment, 9465 Wilshire Blvd, #700, Beverly Hills CA 90212, USA | Actor, Director |
| **Howard, Russ**<br>Curling Association, 1660 Vimont Court, Cumberland ON K4A 4J4, Canada | Curling Athlete |
| **Howard, Ryan J**<br>1630 Bentshire Court, Ballwin MO 63011, USA | Baseball Player |
| **Howard, Sherri**<br>14059 Bridle Ridge Road, Sylmar CA 91342, USA | Track Athlete |
| **Howard, Sophie**<br>International Model Mgmt, Elysium Gate, 126-128 New Kings Road, London SW6 4LZ, England | Model |
| **Howard, Steven B (Steve)**<br>4712 Shetland Ave, Oakland CA 94605, USA | Baseball Player |
| **Howard, Susan**<br>PO Box 1456, Boerne TX 78006, USA | Actress |
| **Howard, Terrence D**<br>Creative Artists Agency, 2000 Ave of Stars, #100, Los Angeles CA 90067 USA | Actor |
| **Howard, Thomas S**<br>822 8th Ave, Middletown OH 45044, USA | Baseball Player |

**H**

**Howard - Howard**

**H**

**Howard, Tish** — Model
Playboy Promotions, 9346 Civic Center Dr, #200, Beverly Hills CA 90210 USA

**Howard, Traylor** — Actress
John Carrabino Mgmt, 5900 Wilshire Blvd, #406, Los Angeles CA 90036 USA

**Howard, Walker** — Actor
Stone Manners Salners, 6100 Wilshire Blvd, #1500, Los Angeles CA 90035 USA

**Howard, Walter I (Todd)** — Football Player
1300 Bienville Ave, Ruston LA 71270, USA

**Howard, Wilbur L** — Baseball Player
643 Walston Lane, Houston TX 77060, USA

**Howard, William W, Jr** — Association Executive
National Wildlife Federation, 11100 Wildlife Center Dr, Reston VA 20190, USA

**Howarth, Elgar** — Composer
27 Cromwell Ave, London N6 5HN, England

**Howarth, James E (Jim)** — Baseball Player
PO Box 401, 1 Hancock Plaza, Gulfport MS 39502, USA

**Howarth, Roger** — Actor
McGowan Mgmt, 8733 W Sunset Blvd, #103, West Hollywood CA 90069, USA

**Howarth, Thomas** — Architect
131 Bloor St W, #1001, Toronto ON M5S 1R1, Canada

**Howatch, Susan** — Writer
Aitken & Stone, 29 Fernshaw Road, London SW10 0TG, England

**Howatt, Glenn** — Journalist
Minneapolis Star Tribune, Editorial Dept, 425 Portland Ave S, Minneapolis MN 55488 USA

**Howe of Aberavon, R E Geoffrey** — Government Official, England
Barclays Bank, Cavendish Square Branch, 4 Vere St, London W1, England

**Howe, Arthur** — Journalist
Philadelphia Inquirer, Editorial Dept, 400 N Broad St, Philadelphia PA 19130, USA

**Howe, Arthur H (Art), Jr** — Baseball Player, Manager
17214 Calico Peak Way, Cypress TX 77433, USA

**Howe, Brian** — Singer (Bad Company)
Artists International Mgmt, 9850 Sandalfoot Blvd, #458, Boca Raton FL 33428 USA

**Howe, Daniel Walker** — Writer
Oxford University Press, 198 Madison Ave, #800, New York NY 10016 USA

**Howe, Gordon (Gordie)** — Ice Hockey Player
Power Play International, 1119 Rochester Road, Troy MI 48083, USA

**Howe, Jonathan T** — Navy Admiral
Arthur Vining Davis Foundation, 225 Water St, #1510, Jacksonville FL 32202, USA

**Howe, Mark S** — Ice Hockey Player
106 Barrington Road, Bloomfield Hills MI 48302, USA

**Howe, Oscar** — Artist
5900 S Prairie View Court, Sioux Falls SD 57108, USA

**Howe, Tina** — Writer
333 W End Ave, New York NY 10023, USA

**Howell, Alex** — Cartoonist (Butch & Dougie)
King Features Syndicate, 300 W 57th St, #1500, New York NY 10019 USA

**Howell, Anthony** — Actor
Artists Partnership, 101 Finsbury Pavement, London EC2A 1RS, England

**Howell, Bailey E** — Basketball Player
1989 S Montgomery St, Starkville MS 39759, USA

**Howell, C Thomas** — Actor
Innovative Artists, 1505 10th St, Santa Monica CA 90401 USA

**Howell, Charles, III** — Golfer
5187 Vardon Dr, Windermere FL 34786, USA

**Howell, Delles R** — Football Player
910 Stubbs Vinson Road, Monroe LA 71203, USA

**Howell, Henry V (Harry)** — Ice Hockey Player
401-49 Robinson St, Hamilton ON L8P 1Y7, Canada

**Howell, Jack R** — Baseball Player
822 S Lehigh Dr, Tucson AZ 85710, USA

**Howell, James P (J P)** — Baseball Player
808 46th St, Sacramento CA 95819, USA

**Howell, Jay C** — Baseball Player
4560 Colony Point, Suwanee GA 30024, USA

**Howell, Jefferson D, Jr** — Marine Corps General
2207 Villa Rose Dr, Houston TX 77062, USA

**Howell, John T** — Football Player
8276 San Dollar Dr, Windsor CO 80528, USA

**Howell, Kathleen** — Aeronautical Engineer
Purdue University, Aeronautical Engineering Dept, West Lafayette IN 47907, USA

**Howell, Kenneth (Ken), Jr** — Baseball Player
29512 Bradmoor Court, Farmington Hills MI 48334, USA

**Howell, Margaret** — Actress
Chateau/Billings Agency, 8489 W 3rd St, #1032, Los Angeles CA 90048, USA

**Howell, Margaret** — Fashion Designer
5 Garden House, 8 Battersea Park Road, London SW8 4BG, England

**Howell, Michael L (Mike)** — Football Player
200 Charlotte St, Monroe LA 71202, USA

**Howell, Pat G** — Football Player
7692 N Kincaid Ave, Fresno CA 93711, USA

**Howell, Porter** — Guitarist (Little Texas)
Splash Public Relations, 1520 16th Ave S, #2, Nashville TN 37212, USA

**Howell, Roy L** — Baseball Player
413 N Daisy St, Lompoc CA 93436, USA

**Howell, William R** — Businessman
J C Penney Co, PO Box 10001, Dallas TX 75301, USA

**Howells, Anne E** — Opera Singer
Milestone, Broom Close, Esher, Surrey KT10 9NP, England

**Howerton, Glenn** — Producer, Writer, Actor
W M E Entertainment, 9601 Wilshire Blvd, #300, Beverly Hills CA 90210 USA

**Howes, Sally Ann** — Actress, Singer
Palm Beach Theater Guild, PO Box 667, Palm Beach FL 33480, USA

**Howey, Steve** — Actor
United Talent Agency, U T A Plaza, 9336 Civic Center Dr, Beverly Hills CA 90210 USA

**Howfield, Robert (Bobby)** — Football Player
5529 S Lowell Blvd, Littleton CO 80123, USA

**Howard - Howfield**

|  |  |
|------|-----------|
| **Howison, Ryan**<br>245 Barbados Dr, Jupiter FL 33458, USA | Golfer |
| **Howitt, Dann P J**<br>PO Box 565, Douglas MI 49406, USA | Baseball Player |
| **Howitt, Peter**<br>Industry Entertainment, 955 Carillo Dr, #300, Los Angeles CA 90048 USA | Director |
| **Howland, Beth**<br>Access Talent Voice Overs, 171 Madison Ave, #910, New York NY 10016, USA | Actress, Singer |
| **Howland, Rick**<br>Oscars Abrams Zimel, 438 Queen St E, Toronto ON M5A 1T4, Canada | Actor |
| **Howle, Paul**<br>United Feature Syndicate, PO Box 5610, Cincinnati OH 45201 USA | Cartoonist (In Their Own Words) |
| **Howlett, Liam P**<br>Midi Mgmt, Jenkins Lane, Great Hallinsbury, Essex CM22 7QL, England | Musician (Prodigy), Composer |
| **Howley, Charles L (Chuck)**<br>Happy Hollow Ranch, 26875 FM 47, Wills Point TX 75169, USA | Football Player |
| **Howley, Peter M**<br>Harvard Medical School, 200 Longwood Ave, Boston MA 02115, USA | Pathologist |
| **Howry, Bobby D (Bob)**<br>24108 N 73rd Lane, Peoria AZ 85383, USA | Baseball Player |
| **Howson, Peter**<br>Flowers East, 82 Kingsland Road, London E2 8DP, England | Artist |
| **Howton, William H (Bill)**<br>1796 County Road 10, Plainview TX 79072, USA | Football Player |
| **Howze, Leonard Earl**<br>L I N K Entertainment, 11872 La Grange Ave, Los Angeles CA 90025 USA | Actor |
| **Hoxby, Caroline M**<br>Stanford University, Institute for Economic Policy Research, Stanford CA 94305, USA | Educational Economist |
| **Hoy, Christopher A (Chris)**<br>27A Alva St, Edinburgh EH2 4PS, Scotland | Cyclist |
| **Hoy, Peter A**<br>26 Woods Dr, Canton NY 13617, USA | Baseball Player |
| **Hoying, Robert C (Bobby)**<br>Crawford Hoying Real Estate, 555 Metro Place N, #600, Dublin OH 43017, USA | Football Player |
| **Hoyle, Dan**<br>Gersh Agency, 41 Madison Ave, #3301, New York NY 10010 USA | Actor, Comedian |
| **Hoyt, D'LaMarr**<br>500 Harbison Blvd, #1002, Columbia SC 29212, USA | Baseball Player |
| **Hozumi, Masako**<br>Skating Federation, 1-1-1 Jinnan, #414, Shibuyaku, Tokyo 150 8050, Japan | Speed Skater |
| **Hrabosky, Alan T (Al)**<br>9 Frontenac Estates Dr, Saint Louis MO 63131, USA | Baseball Player, Sportscaster |
| **Hrabowski, Freeman A, III**<br>University of Maryland Baltimore County, President's Office, 1000 Hilltop Circle, Baltimore MD 21250, USA | Educator |
| **Hradecka, Lucie**<br>C T L K Prague, Stvanice 38, 17000 Prague 7, Czech Republic | Tennis Player |
| **Hradilek, Vavrinec**<br>U S K Prague, Na Folimance 2, 12000 Prague 2, Czech Republic | Canoeing Athlete |
| **Hrbaty, Dominik**<br>Octagon Worldwide, 800 Connecticut Ave, #200, Norwalk CT 06854 USA | Tennis Player |
| **Hrbek, Kent A**<br>Hrbek Outdoors, 5500 Lincoln Dr, #150, Edina MN 55436, USA | Baseball Player |
| **Hrdy, Sarah Blaffer**<br>University of California, Anthropology Dept, Davis CA 95616, USA | Anthropologist |
| **Hriniak, Walter J (Walt)**<br>18 Stacy Dr, North Andover MA 01845, USA | Baseball Player |
| **Hristov, Momchil**<br>Hristo Vakavelski Str Bl 5, #3, 1700 Sofia, Bulgaria | Photographer |
| **Hrkac, Anthony J (Tony)**<br>6818 Kasota Court, Mequon WI 53092, USA | Ice Hockey Player |
| **Hrudey, Kelly**<br>CBC-TV, PO Box 500, Station A, Toronto ON M5W 1E6, Canada | Ice Hockey Player |
| **Hrusa, Jakub**<br>I M G Artists, Hogarth Business Park, Chiswick, London W4 2TH, England | Conductor |
| **Hruska, Carrie B**<br>Mayo Clinic, Biomedical Engineering Dept, 200 1st St SW, Rochester MN 55905, USA | Biomedical Engineer |
| **Hsiang, Wu-chung**<br>Princeton University, Mathematics Dept, Princeton NJ 08544, USA | Mathematician |
| **Hsiao, Rita**<br>W M E Entertainment, 9601 Wilshire Blvd, #300, Beverly Hills CA 90210 USA | Writer |
| **Hsuan Yu Chen**<br>Taiwan University Medical Center, Roosevelt Road, Taipei 10517, Taiwan | Oncologist |
| **Hu Jintao**<br>Chairman's Office, Zhongnanhai, Beijing 100017, China | President, China |
| **Hu Qili**<br>Consultative Conference, 23 Taipingqiao St, Beijing 100283, China | Government Official, China |
| **Hu Shuli**<br>Caijing Media, Winterless Center, 1 Xidawanglu, Chaoyang District, Beijing 100026 PR, China | Editor |
| **Hu, Ann**<br>C E S D, 10635 Santa Monica Blvd, #130, Los Angeles CA 90025 USA | Director, Writer |
| **Hu, Kelly**<br>Don Buchwald Talent Agency, 6500 Wilshire Blvd, #2200, Los Angeles CA 90048 USA | Actress |
| **Huan, Zhang**<br>Pace Gallery, 32 E 57th St, New York NY 10022 USA | Artist, Sculptor |
| **Huang Qun**<br>Global Athletics & Marketing, 611 Tremont St, #400, Boston MA 02118, USA | Gymnast |
| **Huang, Helen**<br>I C M Artists, 40 W 57th St, #1800, New York NY 10019 USA | Concert Pianist |
| **Huang, Henry**<br>Washington University, McDonnell Pediatrics Dept, Saint Louis MO 63110, USA | Inventor (DNA Sequencer), Biologist |
| **Huang, James**<br>Kazarian/Measures/Ruskin, 11969 Ventura Blvd, #300, Studio City CA 91604 USA | Actor, Producer |
| **Huang, Kerson**<br>Massachusetts Institute of Technology, Physics Dept, 77 Massachusetts, #6309, Cambridge MA 02139, USA | Physicist |
| **Huang, Ying**<br>Columbia Artists Mgmt Inc, 5 Columbus Circle, 1790 Broadway, #1600, New York NY 10019 USA | Opera Singer |

**Huard, Damon P** — Football Player
9508 NE 18th St, Clyde Hill WA 98004, USA

**Huarte, John G** — Football Player
14959 La Cumbre Dr, Pacific Palisades CA 90272, USA

**Hub** — Bassist (Roots)
W M E Entertainment, 1325 Ave of Americas, New York NY 10019 USA

**Hubbard, Elizabeth (Liz)** — Actress
Liebman Entertainment, 25 E 21st St, #PH, New York NY 10010, USA

**Hubbard, Erica** — Actress
Pantheon Talent, 1801 Century Park E, #1910, Los Angeles CA 90067, USA

**Hubbard, Glenn D** — Baseball Player
1515 Kings Crossing, Stone Mountain GA 30087, USA

**Hubbard, Gregg (Hobie)** — Singer, Keyboardist (Sawyer Brown)
O-Seven Artist Mgmt, PO Box 210586, Nashville TN 37221, USA

**Hubbard, John** — Artist
Chilcombe House, Chilcombe near Bridport, Dorset DT6 4PN, England

**Hubbard, Marvin R (Marv)** — Football Player
5804 Dawn View Court, Castro Valley CA 94552, USA

**Hubbard, Michael W (Mike)** — Baseball Player
2552 Brookstone Lane, Richmond VA 23233, USA

**Hubbard, Phillip G (Phil)** — Basketball Player, Coach
5130 Pleasant Forest Dr, Centreville VA 20120, USA

**Hubbard, R Glenn** — Government Official, Economist
Columbia University, Graduate Management School, New York NY 10027, USA

**Hubbard, Robert** — Basketball Player
353 Piper Road, West Springfield MA 01089, USA

**Hubbard, Trenidad A (Trent)** — Baseball Player
4206 Clearwater Court, Missouri City TX 77459, USA

**Hubbard, William N, Jr** — Businessman
3634 Woodcliff Dr, Kalamazoo MI 49008, USA

**Hubby, Sandra** — Model
Playboy Promotions, 9346 Civic Center Dr, #200, Beverly Hills CA 90210 USA

**Huber, Anja** — Skeleton Athlete
Loslerstr 48, 83471 Schonau am Konigssee, Germany

**Huber, Anke** — Tennis Player
Dieselstr 10, 76689 Karlsdorf-Neuthard, Germany

**Huber, Gunther** — Bobsled Athlete
Olympic Committee, Foro Italico, Largo Lauro de Bosis 15, 00135 Rome, Italy

**Huber, Hans** — Boxer
Lindenallee 5, 93173 Wenzenbach, Germany

**Huber, Jon** — Baseball Player
4409 S Angeline St, Seattle WA 98118, USA

**Huber, Liezel** — Tennis Player
14423 Middle Bluff Trail, Cypress TX 77429, USA

**Huber, Robert** — Nobel Chemistry Laureate
Planck Biochemie Institut, Am Klopferspitz, 82152 Martinsried, Germany

**Hubert, Janet L** — Actress
Michael Slessinger, 8730 W Sunset Blvd, #220W, West Hollywood CA 90069 USA

**Hubley, Season** — Actress
47 Pleasant St, Essex Junction VT 05452, USA

**Hubley, Whip** — Actor
Geddes Agency, 8430 Santa Monica Blvd, #201, West Hollywood CA 90069 USA

**Huck, A Francis (Fran)** — Ice Hockey Player
313-2505 11th Ave, Regina SK S4P 0K6, Canada

**Huck, John Lloyd** — Businessman
233 Lion's Hill Road, State College PA 16803, USA

**Huckabee, Cooper** — Actor
Kazarian/Measures/Ruskin, 11969 Ventura Blvd, #300, Studio City CA 91604 USA

**Huckabee, Michael (Mike)** — Governor, AR
Fox-TV, News Dept, 5151 Wisconsin Ave NW, #100, Washington DC 20016 USA

**Huckaby, Ken** — Baseball Player
4490 S Rio Dr, Chandler AZ 85249, USA

**Hucknall, Michael J (Mick)** — Singer (Simply Red)
Sideways Mgmt, Junction Mews, Paddington, London WC1E 7EA, England

**Huckstep, Ronald L** — Orthopedic Surgeon
108 Sugarloaf Crescent, Castlecrag, Syndey NSW 2068, Australia

**Hucles, Angela** — Soccer Player
8 Worcester Square, #1, Boston MA 02118, USA

**Hucul, Fred** — Ice Hockey Player
4550 N Flowing Wells Road, #279, Tucson AZ 85705, USA

**Hudd, Roy** — Actor
Associated International Mgmt, 7 Hatton Garden, #400, London EC1N 8AD, England

**Huddleston, David** — Actor
3101 Old Pecos Trail, #677, Santa Fe NM 87505, USA

**Huddleston, Mark W** — Educator
University of New Hampshire, President's Office, Durham NH 03824, USA

**Huddy, Charlie** — Ice Hockey Player
9114 100 A Ave, Edmonton AB T5H 4N7, Canada

**Hudec, Jan, Jr** — Alpine Skier
Alpine Skiing, 151 Canada Olympic Road SW, #302, Calgary AB T3B 5R5, Canada

**Hudecek, Vaclav** — Concert Violinist
Londynska 25, 12000 Prague 2, Czech Republic

**Hudek, John R** — Baseball Player
7603 Shady Way Dr, Sugar Land TX 77479, USA

**Hudepohl, Joe** — Swimmer
10437 Greendale Dr, Tampa FL 33626, USA

**Hudgens, Vanessa A** — Singer, Actress, Model
Untitled Entertainment, 350 S Beverly Dr, #200, Beverly Hills CA 90212 USA

**Hudler, Jiri** — Ice Hockey Player
555 S Old Woodward Ave, Birmingham MI 48009, USA

**Hudler, Rex A** — Baseball Player
9430 W 157th Court, Overland Park KS 66221, USA

**Hudner, Thomas J, Jr** — Korean War Navy Hero (CMH)
31 Allen Farm Lane, Concord MA 01742, USA

**Hudson, C B, Jr** — Businessman
Torchmark Corp, 2001 3rd Ave S, Birmingham AL 35233, USA

**Hudson, Cary** — Singer, Songwriter
Michelle Roche Media Relations, 360 University Circle, Athens GA 30605, USA
**Hudson, Charles (Charlie)** — Baseball Player
32 W Hooker Ave, Coalgate OK 74538, USA
**Hudson, Charles L** — Baseball Player
PO Box 368, Oakwood TX 75855, USA
**Hudson, Clifford G** — Financier
Securities Investor Protection, 805 15th St NW, #800, Washington DC 20005, USA
**Hudson, Ernie** — Actor
TalentWorks, 3500 W Olive Ave, #1400, Burbank CA 91505 USA
**Hudson, Garth** — Organist (Band)
Skyline Music, 32 Clayton St, Portland ME 04103, USA
**Hudson, Gordon L** — Football Player
5350 Edgewood Circle, Salt Lake City UT 84117, USA
**Hudson, Hugh** — Director
Jenks & Partners, 37 W 28th St, #7, New York NY 10001, USA
**Hudson, James** — Psychiatrist
Harvard Medical School, Psychiatry Dept, 25 Shattuck St, Boston MA 02115, USA
**Hudson, Jennifer** — Actress, Singer
Creative Artists Agency, 2000 Ave of Stars, #100, Los Angeles CA 90067 USA
**Hudson, Jessie J (Jesse)** — Baseball Player
341 Albert Lewis Way, Mansfield LA 71052, USA
**Hudson, John L** — Football Player
3320 Highway 77, Paris TN 38242, USA
**Hudson, Joseph P (Joe)** — Baseball Player
109 Pine Valley Dr, Medford NJ 08055, USA
**Hudson, Kate** — Actress
Creative Artists Agency, 2000 Ave of Stars, #100, Los Angeles CA 90067 USA
**Hudson, Luke** — Baseball Player
9912 Aster Circle, Fountain Valley CA 92708, USA
**Hudson, Oliver** — Actor
Management 360, 9111 Wilshire Blvd, Beverly Hills CA 90210 USA
**Hudson, Orlando T** — Baseball Player
PO Box 1888, Darlington SC 29540, USA
**Hudson, Ray** — Soccer Player, Coach
D C United, R F K Stadium, 2400 E Capitol St SE, Washington DC 20003 USA
**Hudson, Richard S (Dick)** — Football Player
3320 Highway 77, Paris TN 38242, USA
**Hudson, Robert W (Bob)** — Football Player
3408 Dalrock Road, Rowlett TX 75088, USA
**Hudson, Sally** — Skier
PO Box 2343, Olympic Valley CA 96146, USA
**Hudson, Timothy A (Tim)** — Baseball Player
600 Graystone Court, Peachtree City GA 30269, USA
**Hudson, Troy** — Basketball Player
6040 Earle Brown Dr, #450, Minneapolis MN 55430, USA
**Hudspeth, Mark** — Football Coach
University of Louisiana, Athletic Dept, 104 University Circle, Lafayette LA 70504, USA
**Huebel, Rob** — Actor
Creative Artists Agency, 2000 Ave of Stars, #100, Los Angeles CA 90067 USA
**Huefner, Tatjana** — Luge Athlete
Welfenstr 32, 38889 Blankenburg/Harz, Germany
**Huerta, Dolores** — Labor Activist
United Farm Workers, 29700 Woodford Tehachapi Road, Keene CA 93531, USA
**Huertas, Jon** — Actor
Innovative Artists, 1505 10th St, Santa Monica CA 90401 USA
**Huett, Zane** — Actor
Coast to Coast Talent, 3350 Barham Blvd, Los Angeles CA 90068 USA
**Huey** — Rap Artist
Multi Entertainment Group, 4044 W Lake Mary Blvd, #104-324, Lake Mary FL 32746, USA
**Huff, Aubrey L, III** — Baseball Player
471 H C R 3121, Hillsboro TX 76645, USA
**Huff, Brent** — Actor
Vox Inc, 6420 Wilshire Blvd, #1080, Los Angeles CA 90048 USA
**Huff, Gary E** — Football Player
3175 Hawks Landing Dr, Tallahassee FL 32309, USA
**Huff, Kenneth W (Ken)** — Football Player
74003 Harvey, Chapel Hill NC 27517, USA
**Huff, Leon A** — Songwriter, Pianist, Businessman
W M E Entertainment, 9601 Wilshire Blvd, #300, Beverly Hills CA 90210 USA
**Huff, Michael K (Mike)** — Baseball Player
PO Box 6176, Woodridge IL 60517, USA
**Huff, Robert L (Sam)** — Football Player
8 N Jay St, Middleburg VA 20117, USA
**Huffington, Arianna S** — Writer
3299 K St NW, #402, Washington DC 20007, USA
**Huffins, Chris** — Track Athlete
1319 Wildcliff Parkway NE, Atlanta GA 30329, USA
**Huffman, Cady** — Actress, Singer
Don Buchwald Talent Agency, 6500 Wilshire Blvd, #2200, Los Angeles CA 90048 USA
**Huffman, Chris** — Bassist (Casting Crowns)
Proper Mgmt, PO Box 150867, Nashville TN 37215, USA
**Huffman, Felicity K** — Actress
Creative Artists Agency, 2000 Ave of Stars, #100, Los Angeles CA 90067 USA
**Huffman, Kerry** — Ice Hockey Player
5557 Sea Forest Dr, #215, New Port Richey FL 34652, USA
**Huffman, Logan** — Actor
Gersh Agency, 9465 Wilshire Blvd, #600, Beverly Hills CA 90212 USA
**Huffman, Phillip L (Phil)** — Baseball Player
194 Paxton Road, Rochester NY 14617, USA
**Huffman, Timothy P (Tim)** — Football Player
3365 Jubilee Trail, Dallas TX 75229, USA
**Hufner, Tatjana** — Luge Athlete
Welfenstr 32, 38889 Blankenburg/Harz, Germany
**Hufsey, Billy** — Actor, Singer
11725 Greystone Pt, Strongsville OH 44149, USA

**H**

**Hufstedler - Huisgen**

**Hufstedler, Shirley M** — Secretary, Education; Judge
720 Iverness Dr, La Canada Flintridge CA 91011, USA
**Hug, Procter R, Jr** — Judge
US Court of Appeals, Courthouse, 400 S Virginia St, Reno NV 89501, USA
**Huggins, Bob** — Basketball Coach
West Virginia University, Athletic Dept, Morgantown WV 26506, USA
**Hughes, Albert** — Director, Producer, Writer
W M E Entertainment, 9601 Wilshire Blvd, #300, Beverly Hills CA 90210 USA
**Hughes, Alfredrick (Alfred)** — Basketball Player
5024 S Kildare Ave, Chicago IL 60632, USA
**Hughes, Allen** — Director, Producer, Writer
W M E Entertainment, 9601 Wilshire Blvd, #300, Beverly Hills CA 90210 USA
**Hughes, Bradley** — Golfer
204 Easton Court, Simpsonville SC 29680, USA
**Hughes, Bronwen** — Director
Gersh Agency, 9465 Wilshire Blvd, #600, Beverly Hills CA 90212 USA
**Hughes, Chris** — Businessman, Publisher, Editor
New Republic, 1400 K St NW, #1200, Washington DC 20005, USA
**Hughes, Clara** — Speed Skater, Cyclist
Speed Skating Canada, 2781 Lancaster Road, #402, Ottawa ON K1B 1A7, Canada
**Hughes, Dan** — Basketball Coach, Executive
San Antonio Silver Stars, 1 AT&T Center, San Antonio TX 78219 USA
**Hughes, David A** — Football Player
5307 240th Ave NE, Redmond WA 98053, USA
**Hughes, Eddie** — Basketball Player
4253 Deerfield Hills Road, Colorado Springs CO 80916, USA
**Hughes, Ernest L (Ernie)** — Football Player
2116 Camino Brazos, Pleasanton CA 94566, USA
**Hughes, Finola** — Actress
Harrison Stokes, 8730 W Sunset Blvd, #270, West Hollywood CA 90069, USA
**Hughes, Frank John** — Actor
A P A Talent & Literary Agency, 405 S Beverly Dr, #300, Beverly Hills CA 90212 USA
**Hughes, H Richard** — Architect
47 Chiswick Quay, London W4 3UR, England
**Hughes, Harold R (Harry)** — Governor, MD
Patton Boggs Blow, 2550 M St NW, #500, Washington DC 20037, USA
**Hughes, J Randell (Randy)** — Football Player
17608 Cedar Creek Canyon Dr, Dallas TX 75252, USA
**Hughes, James M (Jim)** — Baseball Player
7526 El Manor Ave, Los Angeles CA 90045, USA
**Hughes, John** — Ice Hockey Player
317 Laudholm Farm Road, Wells ME 04090, USA
**Hughes, Karen** — Government Official
Harper Collins Publishers, 10 E 53rd St, Cellar 1, New York NY 10022 USA
**Hughes, Kathleen** — Actress
8818 Rising Glen Place, Los Angeles CA 90069, USA
**Hughes, Kim G** — Basketball Player, Coach
2232 NE 8th Ave, Portland OR 97212, USA
**Hughes, Larry D** — Basketball Player
3 Hanna Court, Cleveland OH 44108, USA
**Hughes, Mervyn G** — Cricketer
Australian Cricket Board, 90 Jollimant St, Melbourne VIC 3002, Australia
**Hughes, Miko** — Actor
Jamieson Assoc, 53 Sunrise Road, Superior MT 59872, USA
**Hughes, Nicola** — Actress
Gavin Barker Assoc, 2D Wimpole St, London W1G 0EB, England
**Hughes, Pat** — Ice Hockey Player
8388 Webster Hills Road, Dexter MI 48130, USA
**Hughes, Philip J (Phil)** — Baseball Player
275 Bayshore Blvd, #501, Tampa FL 33606, USA
**Hughes, Richard D** — Drummer (Keane)
Agency Group Ltd, 361-373 City Road, London EC1V 1PQ, England
**Hughes, Richard H (Dick)** — Baseball Player
PO Box 598, Stephens AR 71764, USA
**Hughes, Sally** — Actress
Associated International Mgmt, 7 Hatton Garden, #400, London EC1N 8AD, England
**Hughes, Sarah E** — Figure Skater
John Hughes, 12 Channel Dr, Great Neck NY 11024, USA
**Hughes, Terry** — Director
Creative Artists Agency, 2000 Ave of Stars, #100, Los Angeles CA 90067 USA
**Hughes, Terry W** — Baseball Player
532 Pierpoint Avenue Extension, Spartanburg SC 29303, USA
**Hughes, Thomas E (Tom)** — Baseball Player
610 Kimswick Court, Deer Park TX 77536, USA
**Hughes, Thomas J, Jr** — Navy Admiral
400 Mar Vista Dr, #4, Monterey CA 93940, USA
**Hughes, Tom** — Actor
Gordon & French, 12-13 Poland St, London W1F 8QB, England
**Hughes, Tyrone C** — Football Player
6581 Rue Louis Phillipe, Marrero LA 70072, USA
**Hughes, W Patrick (Pat)** — Football Player
4 Woodside Dr, Stratham NH 03885, USA
**Hughes-Fulford, Millie** — Astronaut
Veterans Affairs Dept, Medical Center, 4150 Clement St, San Francisco CA 94121, USA
**Hughey, Gary H** — Marine Corps General
Deputy CinC, US Transportation Command, Scott Air Force Base IL 62225 USA
**Hughley, D L** — Actor, Comedian
Five Timz Productions, 22817 Ventura Blvd, #872, Woodland Hills CA 91364, USA
**Hugo, Chad** — Singer, Rap Artist (NERD)
Virgin Records, 338 N Foothill Road, Beverly Hills CA 90210 USA
**Huguenin, G Richard** — Inventor (Portable Gun Detector Camera)
Millitech Corp, 5 North St, South Deerfield MA 01373, USA
**Huh, John** — Golfer
Professional Golfers Association, 100 Ave of Champions, Palm Beach Gardens FL 33418 USA
**Huisgen, Rolf** — Chemist
Kaulbachstr 10, 80539 Munich, Germany

| | |
|---|---|
| **Huish, Justin**<br>3475 Indian Mesa Dr, Thousand Oaks CA 91360, USA | Archer |
| **Huisman, Justin R**<br>8713 Forest Glen Court, Saint John IN 46373, USA | Baseball Player |
| **Huisman, Michiel**<br>Conway Van Gelder Grant, 8-12 Broadwick St, #300, London W1F 8HW, England | Actor |
| **Huisman, Richard A (Rick)**<br>17W25 Oak Lane, Bensenville IL 60106, USA | Baseball Player |
| **Huismann, Mark L**<br>5751 NW Plantation Lane, Lees Summit MO 64064, USA | Baseball Player |
| **Huizenga, H Wayne**<br>1575 Ponce del Leon Dr, Fort Lauderdale FL 33316, USA | Businessman |
| **Hulbert, Mike**<br>7770 Apple Tree Circle, Orlando FL 32819, USA | Golfer |
| **Hulbig, Joe**<br>11 Bragg Road, Foxboro MA 02035, USA | Ice Hockey Player |
| **Hulce, Tom**<br>Anonymous Content, 3532 Hayden Ave, Culver City CA 90232 USA | Actor |
| **Hulk**<br>Zenit Saint Petersburg, Galermaya 5, 190000 Saint Petersburg, Russia | Soccer Player |
| **Hull, Brett A**<br>8025 Maryland Ave, #7D, Saint Louis MO 63105, USA | Ice Hockey Player |
| **Hull, Dennis W**<br>11642 County Road 29, Roseneath ON K0K 2X0, Canada | Ice Hockey Player |
| **Hull, Eric**<br>803 N 4th St, Selah WA 98942, USA | Baseball Player |
| **Hull, Frank M**<br>US Court of Appeals, 56 Forsyth St NW, Atlanta GA 30303, USA | Judge |
| **Hull, Gina**<br>479 Arricola Ave, Saint Augustine FL 32080, USA | Golfer |
| **Hull, Lisa**<br>Maitland Mgmt, PO Box 364, Esher KT10 9XZ, England | Actress, Singer |
| **Hull, Mike**<br>3809 Vista Azul, San Clemente CA 92672, USA | Football Player |
| **Hull, Robert M (Bobby)**<br>6916 Lennox Place, University Park FL 34201, USA | Ice Hockey Player |
| **Hull, Roger H**<br>Union College, Chancellor's Office, Schenectady NY 12308, USA | Educator |
| **Hullar, Theodore L**<br>3 Lowell Place, Ithaca NY 14850, USA | Educator |
| **Hulme, Keri**<br>PO Box 1, Whataroa, South Westland, Aotearoa 7587, New Zealand | Writer |
| **Hulse, Cale**<br>9290 E Thompson Peak Parkway, #107, Scottsdale AZ 85255, USA | Ice Hockey Player |
| **Hulse, David L**<br>1301 Kenwood Dr, San Angelo TX 76903, USA | Baseball Player |
| **Hulse, Russell A**<br>PO Box 451, Princeton NJ 08542, USA | Nobel Physics Laureate |
| **Hulsey, Corey S**<br>178 Pine Needle Trail, Villa Rica GA 30180, USA | Football Player |
| **Hulten, Jens**<br>T C G Artists Mgmt, 14A Goodwin's Court, Covent Garden, London WC2N 4LL, England | Actor |
| **Hultqvist, Bengt K G**<br>Gronstensv 2, 981 40 Kiruna, Sweden | Space Physicist |
| **Hultz, W Donald (Don)**<br>5078 Pleasant Ridge Road, Millington TN 38053, USA | Football Player |
| **Huly, Jan C**<br>M B O Partners, 13454 Sunrise Valley Dr, #550, Herndon VA 20171, USA | Marine Corps General |
| **Humala, Ollanta**<br>Palacio de Gobierno S/N, Plaza de Armas S/N, Lima 1, Peru | President, Peru |
| **Humann, L Phillip**<br>SunTrust Banks, 303 Peachtree St NE, Atlanta GA 30308, USA | Financier |
| **Humayan, Mark S**<br>University of Southern California, Doheny Eye Institute, Los Angeles CA 90033, USA | Ophthalmologist |
| **Humber, Philip**<br>PO Box 130788, Tyler TX 75713, USA | Baseball Player |
| **Humbert, John O**<br>Christian Church Disciples of Christ, 130 E Washington, Indianapolis IN 46204, USA | Religious Leader |
| **Hume, A Britton (Brit)**<br>1401 N Oak St, #608, Arlington VA 22209, USA | Commentator |
| **Hume, Gary**<br>Kentmere Photographic Ltd, Staveley, Kendal LA8 9PB, England | Artist |
| **Hume, John**<br>Constituency, 5 Bayview Terrace, Derry BT48 7EE, Northern Ireland | Nobel Peace Laureate |
| **Hume, Kirsty**<br>Elite Model Mgmt, 404 Park Ave S, #900, New York NY 10016 USA | Model |
| **Hume, Thomas H (Tom)**<br>3810 Redfish Court, Palmetto FL 34221, USA | Baseball Player |
| **Humenik, Ed**<br>4746 SW Hammock Creek Dr, Palm City FL 34990, USA | Golfer |
| **Humes, Edward**<br>Simon & Schuster, 1230 Ave of Americas, Concourse 1, New York NY 10020, USA | Journalist |
| **Humes, H David**<br>University of Michigan Medical Center, 1500 E Medical Center Dr, Ann Arbor MI 48109, USA | Surgeon, Nephrologist |
| **Humes, Mary-Margaret**<br>Stone Manners Salners, 6100 Wilshire Blvd, #1500, Los Angeles CA 90035 USA | Actress, Model |
| **Humes, Steven**<br>Opera et Concert, 37 Rue de la Chaussee d'Antin, 75009 Paris, France | Opera Singer |
| **Humm, David H**<br>4301 Via Olivero Ave, Las Vegas NV 89102, USA | Football Player |
| **Hummer, John R**<br>2640 Baker St, San Francisco CA 94123, USA | Basketball Player |
| **Hummes, Claudio Cardinal**<br>Congregation for Clergy, Palazzo delle Congregazioni, Piazza Pio XII 3, 00193 Rome, Italy | Religious Leader |
| **Humperdinck, Engelbert**<br>Jones Entertainment Group, 550 Wellington St, London ON N6A 3P9, Canada | Singer |

| | |
|---|---|
| **Humphrey, Claude B**<br>3399 Lord Dunmore Cove, Memphis TN 38134, USA | Football Player |
| **Humphrey, Gordon J**<br>78 Garvin Hill Road, Chichester NH 03258, USA | Senator, NH |
| **Humphrey, Jackie**<br>616 Powder Horn Road, Richmond KY 40475, USA | Track Athlete |
| **Humphrey, Neil D**<br>963 Ridgeview Dr, Reno NV 89511, USA | Educator |
| **Humphrey, Terryal G (Terry)**<br>7 Oakmont, Trabuco Canyon CA 92679, USA | Baseball Player |
| **Humphreys, Matthew**<br>Don Buchwald Talent Agency, 6500 Wilshire Blvd, #2200, Los Angeles CA 90048 USA | Actor |
| **Humphreys, Michael B (Mike)**<br>1402 Lost Creek Dr, De Soto TX 75115, USA | Baseball Player |
| **Humphreys, Robert W (Bob)**<br>1803 Oakwood St, Bedford VA 24523, USA | Baseball Player |
| **Humphries, J Jay**<br>22107 N 37th Terrace, Phoenix AZ 85050, USA | Basketball Player |
| **Humphries, Kaillie**<br>Alberta Bobsled, Niven Center, 140 Canada Olympic Road, Calgary AB T3B 5RS, Canada | Bobsled Athlete |
| **Humphries, Stefan G**<br>8708 E Redwood Lane, Spokane WA 99217, USA | Football Player |
| **Humphries, W Stanley (Stan)**<br>4100 Chauvin Lane, Monroe LA 71201, USA | Football Player |
| **Humphry, Derek**<br>Euthanasia Research & Guidance Organization, 24828 Norris Lane, Junction City OR 97448, USA | Social Activist |
| **Hun Sen, Samdech**<br>Prime Minister's Office, Supreme National Council, Phnom Penh, Cambodia | Prime Minister, Cambodia |
| **Hundley, C Randolph (Randy)**<br>122 E Forest Lane, Palatine IL 60067, USA | Baseball Player |
| **Hundley, Rodney C (Hot Rod)**<br>29769 N 130th Dr, Peoria AZ 85383, USA | Basketball Player, Sportscaster |
| **Hundley, Todd R**<br>21691 W Swan Court, Kildeer IL 60047, USA | Baseball Player |
| **Hundt, Reed E**<br>6416 Brookside Dr, Chevy Chase MD 20815, USA | Government Official |
| **Hung, Sammo**<br>Blue Stone Entertainment, 9000 Sunset Blvd, #515, Los Angeles CA 90069, USA | Actor |
| **Hunger, Daniela**<br>S V Preussen, Hansastr 190, 13088 Berlin, Germany | Swimmer |
| **Hunger, Sophie**<br>Agency Group Ltd, 142 W 57th St, #600, New York NY 10019 USA | Singer |
| **Huniford, James (Ford)**<br>Huniford Design Studio, 210 11th Ave, #601, New York NY 10001, USA | Interior Designer, Architect |
| **Hunkapiller, Michael**<br>Applied Biosystems, 850 Lincoln Centre Dr, Foster City CA 94404, USA | Inventor (DNA Sequencer), Biochemist |
| **Hunley, Leann**<br>Mitchell K Stubbs Assoc, 8695 W Washington Blvd, #204, Culver City CA 90232 USA | Actress |
| **Hunley, Rickard C (Ricky)**<br>4435 Circle View Blvd, Los Angeles CA 90043, USA | Football Player |
| **Hunnam, Charlie**<br>Creative Artists Agency, 2000 Ave of Stars, #100, Los Angeles CA 90067 USA | Actor |
| **Hunnicutt, Gayle**<br>174 Regents Park Road, London NW1 8XP, England | Actress |
| **Hunold, Joachim**<br>Air Berlin PLC, Saatwinkler Damm 42-43, 13627 Berlin, Germany | Businessman |
| **Hunt, Bonnie**<br>W M E Entertainment, 9601 Wilshire Blvd, #300, Beverly Hills CA 90210 USA | Actress, Director |
| **Hunt, Bruce**<br>I C M Partners, 10250 Constellation Blvd, #900, Los Angeles CA 90067 USA | Director |
| **Hunt, Bryan**<br>9 White St, New York NY 10013, USA | Artist, Sculptor |
| **Hunt, Byron R**<br>PO Box 281, Rutherford NJ 07070, USA | Football Player |
| **Hunt, Caroline R**<br>100 Crescent Court, #1700, Dallas TX 75201, USA | Businesswoman |
| **Hunt, Cletidus M**<br>58 S Walnut Bend Road, Cordova TN 38018, USA | Football Player |
| **Hunt, Courtney**<br>W M E Entertainment, 9601 Wilshire Blvd, #300, Beverly Hills CA 90210 USA | Writer |
| **Hunt, Crystal**<br>Amatruda Benson Assoc, 433 N Camden Drive, #400, Beverly Hills CA 90210, USA | Actress, Producer |
| **Hunt, Darlene**<br>United Talent Agency, U T A Plaza, 9336 Civic Center Dr, Beverly Hills CA 90210 USA | Producer, Writer, Actress |
| **Hunt, David**<br>Artists Partnership, 101 Finsbury Pavement, London EC2A 1RS, England | Actor, Director |
| **Hunt, Helen**<br>Creative Artists Agency, 2000 Ave of Stars, #100, Los Angeles CA 90067 USA | Actress |
| **Hunt, J Randall (Randy)**<br>324 Holly Ridge Dr, Montgomery AL 36109, USA | Baseball Player |
| **Hunt, James B, Jr**<br>Womble Carlyle Sandridge Rice, 150 Fayetteville St Mall, Raleigh NC 27601, USA | Governor, NC |
| **Hunt, Johnny M**<br>First Baptist Church, 11905 Highway 92, Woodstock GA 30188, USA | Religious Leader |
| **Hunt, Joseph (Joe)**<br>Iron Workers Union, 1750 New York Ave NW, #400, Washington DC 20006, USA | Labor Leader |
| **Hunt, Linda**<br>W M E Entertainment, 9601 Wilshire Blvd, #300, Beverly Hills CA 90210 USA | Actress |
| **Hunt, R Kevin**<br>11 Royal Lane, Londonderry NH 03053, USA | Football Player |
| **Hunt, R Timothy**<br>Rose Cottage, Ridge, Hertfordshire EN6 3LH, England | Nobel Medicine Laureate |
| **Hunt, Rameck**<br>Three Doctors Foundation, 65 Hazelwood Ave, Newark NJ 07106, USA | Physician |
| **Hunt, Richard H**<br>1017 W Lill Ave, Chicago IL 60614, USA | Sculptor |

**Humphrey - Hunt**

**Hunt, Robert K (Bobby)** — Football Player
5928 Bentway Dr, Charlotte NC 28226, USA
**Hunt, Ronald K (Ron)** — Baseball Player
2806 Jackson Road, Wentzville MO 63385, USA
**Hunt, Samuel K (Sam)** — Football Player
1708 Eliza St, Nacogdoches TX 75961, USA
**Hunt, Stephanie** — Actress
Innovative Artists, 1505 10th St, Santa Monica CA 90401 USA
**Hunten, Donald M** — Astronomer
1828 E Barn Swallow Lane, Green Valley AZ 85614, USA
**Hunter, Anthony R (Tony)** — Molecular Biologist
4578 Vista de la Patria, Del Mar CA 92014, USA
**Hunter, Brian L** — Baseball Player
8349 S Aberdeen St, Chicago IL 60620, USA
**Hunter, Brian R** — Baseball Player
12141 Centralia St, #219, Lakewood CA 90715, USA
**Hunter, Charlie** — Jazz Guitarist (Charlie Hunter Quartet)
Mongrel Music, 743 Center Blvd, Fairfax CA 94930, USA
**Hunter, Daniel L** — Football Player
210 N Lakeview Dr, Farmerville LA 71241, USA
**Hunter, Dave** — Ice Hockey Player
53350 Range Road 220, Androssan AB T8E 2B5, Canada
**Hunter, G William (Billy)** — Baseball Player, Manager
104 E Seminary Ave, Lutherville MD 21093, USA
**Hunter, Harold J (Buddy)** — Baseball Player
14616 Fir Circle, Plattsmouth, NE 68048, USA
**Hunter, Holly** — Actress
Special Artists Agency, 9200 Sunset Blvd, #410, West Hollywood CA 90069 USA
**Hunter, Ian** — Singer, Songwriter (Mott the People)
High Road Touring, 751 Bridgeway, #200, Sausalito CA 94965 USA
**Hunter, J Scott** — Football Player
6386 Dolive Court, Daphne AL 36526, USA
**Hunter, James** — Singer, Guitarist
Large Public Relations, 1 Brickfield Cottages High Road, Thornwood, London CM 16TH, England
**Hunter, James M (Jim)** — Baseball Player
12939 Penshurst Lane, Windermere FL 34786, USA
**Hunter, Jeffrey O (Jeff)** — Football Player
2004 Barton Court, Augusta GA 30906, USA
**Hunter, Jesse** — Singer, Guitarist
Friedman & LaRosa, 1334 Lexington Ave, New York NY 10128, USA
**Hunter, Jim** — Skier
Jungle Jim Hunter Mgmt, 864 Woodpark Way SW, Calgary AB T2W 2V8, Canada
**Hunter, John** — Rocket Engineer
Lawrence Livermore Laboratory, 7000 East St, Livermore CA 94550, USA
**Hunter, Leslie (Les)** — Basketball Player
8712 W 92nd St, Overland Park KS 66212, USA
**Hunter, Lindsey B** — Basketball Player, Coach
4355 Hickory Ridge Court, Plymouth MI 48170, USA
**Hunter, Mark J** — Rowing Athlete
Leander Rowing Club, Henley-on-Thames, Oxfordshire RG9 2LP, England
**Hunter, Patrick E** — Football Player
8901 S 10th Dr, Phoenix AZ 85041, USA
**Hunter, Rachel** — Model, Actress
23 Beverly Park Terrace, Beverly Hills CA 90210, USA
**Hunter, Robert** — Songwriter (Grateful Dead)
Agency Group Ltd, 1880 Century Park E, #711, Los Angeles CA 90067 USA
**Hunter, Simon** — Director
United Talent Agency, U T A Plaza, 9336 Civic Center Dr, Beverly Hills CA 90210 USA
**Hunter, Stephen** — Writer
Washington Post, Editorial Dept, 1150 15th St NW, Washington DC 20071 USA
**Hunter, Tab** — Actor, Singer
PO Box 50308, Santa Barbara CA 93150, USA
**Hunter, Tim** — Ice Hockey Player
Toronto Maple Leafs, AirCanada Center, 40 Bay St, Toronto ON M5J 2K2, Canada
**Hunter, Tim** — Director
A P A Talent/Literary Agency, 250 W 57th St, #1701, New York NY 10107 USA
**Hunter, Torii K** — Baseball Player
7164 Richmond Dr, Frisco TX 75035, USA
**Hunter, Willard M** — Baseball Player
2562 Poppleton Ave, Omaha NE 68105, USA
**Hunter-Gault, Charlayne** — Commentator, Writer
News Hour Show, 2700 S Quincy St, #250, Arlington VA 22206, USA
**Hunthausen, Raymond G** — Religious Leader
Catholic Archdiocese of Seattle, 710 9th Ave, Seattle WA 98104, USA
**Huntington, Sam** — Actor
United Talent Agency, U T A Plaza, 9336 Civic Center Dr, Beverly Hills CA 90210 USA
**Huntington-Whiteley, Rosie** — Model, Actress
Women Model Mgmt, 199 Lafayette St, #700, New York NY 10012 USA
**Huntley, Joni** — Track Athlete
7148 SW 4th Ave, Portland OR 97219, USA
**Huntley, Richard E** — Football Player
7123 Rumple Road, Charlotte NC 28262, USA
**Huntsman, Jon M, Jr** — Diplomat; Governor, UT
Brookings Institute, 1775 Massachusetts Ave NW, Washington DC 20036 USA
**Huntsman, Stanley H** — Track Coach
5532 Timbercrest Trail, Knoxville TN 37909, USA
**Huntz, Stephen M (Steve)** — Baseball Player
3303 Linden Road, #405, Rocky River OH 44116, USA
**Hunyadfi, Steven** — Swimming Coach
838 Ridgewood Dr, #12, Fort Wayne IN 46805, USA
**Hunyady, Emese** — Speed Skater
Beim Spitzriegel 1/2/9, 2500 Baden, Austria
**Hunziker, Terry** — Interior Designer
208 3rd Ave S, Seattle WA 98104, USA
**Hupp, Jana Marie** — Actress
A P A Talent & Literary Agency, 405 S Beverly Dr, #300, Beverly Hills CA 90212 USA

**H**

**Huppert - Husmann**

**Huppert, David B (Dave)** — Baseball Player
6732 Stephens Path, Zephyrhills FL 33542, USA
**Huppert, Isabelle** — Actress
Voyez Mon Agent, 20 Ave Rapp, 75007 Paris, France
**Hurd of Westwell, Douglas R** — Government Official, England
Hawkpoint, Crosby Court, 4 Great Saint Helens, London EC3A 6HA, England
**Hurd, Gale Anne** — Producer
Valhalla Motion Pictures, 3201 Cahuenga Blvd W, Los Angeles CA 90068, USA
**Hurd, Michelle** — Actress
T M T Entertainment, 648 Broadway, #1002, New York NY 10012, USA
**Hurdle, Clinton M (Clint)** — Baseball Player, Manager
9068 Sturbridge Place, Littleton CO 80129, USA
**Hurd-Wood, Rachel C** — Actress
Troika, 74 Clerkenwell Road, #300, London EC1M 5QA, England
**Hurford, Peter J** — Concert Organist
Broom House, Saint Bernard's Road, Saint Albans, Hertfordshire AL3 5RA, England
**Hurlbert, Jacquline (Jackie)** — Artist
Studio Ten XIII, 16396 SW Kimball Ave, Lake Oswego OR 97035, USA
**Hurlbut, Laura** — Golfer
6609 Jamieson Ave, Reseda CA 91335, USA
**Hurley, Alfred F** — Educator, Historian
3505 Turtle Creek Blvd, #6A, Dallas TX 75219, USA
**Hurley, Andrew (Andy)** — Drummer (Fall Out Boy)
PO Box 219, 1187 Wilmette Ave, Wilmette IL 60091, USA
**Hurley, Bob** — Surfing Executive
Hurley International, 1945 Placentia Ave, Costa Mesa CA 92627, USA
**Hurley, Bob** — Basketball Coach
Saint Anthony High School, Athletic Dept, 175 8th St, Jersey City NJ 07302, USA
**Hurley, Chad** — Businessman
YouTube, 1000 Cherry Ave, #200, San Bruno CA 94066, USA
**Hurley, Courtney** — Fencer
2607 Menard, San Antonio TX 78251, USA
**Hurley, Craig** — Actor
Avo Talent, 8500 Melrose Ave, #212, West Hollywood CA 90069, USA
**Hurley, Douglas G** — Astronaut
1848 Lake Landing Dr, League City TX 77573, USA
**Hurley, Elizabeth** — Model, Actress
United Talent Agency, U T A Plaza, 9336 Civic Center Dr, Beverly Hills CA 90210 USA
**Hurley, Kelley** — Fencer
2607 Menard, San Antonio TX 78251, USA
**Hurley, Robert M (Bobby)** — Basketball Player, Coach
State University of New York, Athletic Dept, Buffalo NY 14260, USA
**Hurn, David** — Photographer
Prospect Cottage, Tintern, Chepstow, Gwent NP16 6SG, Wales
**Hurran, Nick** — Director
Independent Talent Group, 40 Whitfield St, London W1T 2RH, England
**Hurst, Bruce V** — Baseball Player
1080 N Riata St, Gilbert AZ 85234, USA
**Hurst, Geoff** — Soccer Player
Dragonwyck, Saint George's Hill, Weybridge, Surrey KT13 0PY, England
**Hurst, Maurice R** — Football Player
3520 Leonidas St, New Orleans LA 70118, USA
**Hurst, Michael** — Actor, Director, Producer
Johnson & Laird Mgmt, PO Box 78340, Grey Lynn, Auckland 1245, New Zealand
**Hurst, Pat** — Golfer
730 Camino Amigo, Danville CA 94526, USA
**Hurst, Rick** — Actor
1230 N Horn Road, West Hollywood CA 90069, USA
**Hurst, Ryan D** — Actor
Piper Kaniecki Mgmt, 13273 Ventura Blvd, #104, Studio City CA 91604, USA
**Hurst, William H (Bill)** — Baseball Player
9331 SW 192nd Dr, Cutler Bay FL 33157, USA
**Hurston, Charles F (Chuck)** — Football Player
9360 Prestwick Club Dr, Duluth GA 30097, USA
**Hurt, John** — Actor
Independent Talent Group, 40 Whitfield St, London W1T 2RH, England
**Hurt, Mary Beth** — Actress
I C M Partners, 10250 Constellation Blvd, #900, Los Angeles CA 90067 USA
**Hurt, Weston** — Opera Singer
Opus 3 Artists, 470 Park Ave S, #900N, New York NY 10016 USA
**Hurt, William** — Actor
I C M Partners, 10250 Constellation Blvd, #900, Los Angeles CA 90067 USA
**Hurtado Larrea, Oswaldo** — President, Ecuador
Suecia 277 y Av Los Shyris, Quito, Ecuador
**Hurtado, Edwin A** — Baseball Player
1202 15th Ave N, Lake Worth FL 33460, USA
**Hurvich, Leo M** — Psychologist
276 5th Ave, #306, New York NY 10001, USA
**Hurwitz, Charles E** — Businessman
Maxxam Inc, 1330 Post Oak Blvd, #2000, Houston TX 77056, USA
**Hurwitz, Jerard** — Molecular Biologist
Memorial Sloan Kettering Cancer Center, 1275 York Ave, New York NY 10065, USA
**Hurwitz, Mitchell (Mitch)** — Producer, Writer
Creative Artists Agency, 2000 Ave of Stars, #100, Los Angeles CA 90067 USA
**Husa, Karel J** — Composer, Conductor
3417 Foy Glen Court, Apex NC 27539, USA
**Husar, Lubomyr Cardinal** — Religious Leader
Archdiocese of Kiev, Vul Riznytcka 11-B/28-29, 01011 Kiev, Ukraine
**Huscroft, Jamie** — Ice Hockey Player
3024 38th St SE, Puyallup WA 98374, USA
**Huselius, Kristian** — Ice Hockey Player
Columbus Blue Jackets, Arena, 200 W Nationwide Blvd, #1, Columbus OH 43215 USA
**Husen, Torsten** — Educator
Armfeltsgatan 10, 115 34 Stockholm, Sweden
**Husmann, Edward E (Ed)** — Football Player
27266 Orth Lane, Conroe TX 77385, USA

| | |
|---|---|
| **Huson, Jeffrey K (Jeff)** | Baseball Player |
| 10349 Rowlock Way, Parker CO 80134, USA | |
| **Huss, Toby** | Actor |
| Abrams Artists, 9200 W Sunset Blvd, #1125, West Hollywood CA 90069 USA | |
| **Hussain, Mamnoon** | President, Pakistan |
| President's Office, Aiwan-e-Sadr, Mall & Mayo Roads, Islamabad, Pakistan | |
| **Hussey, Olivia** | Actress |
| Frozen Flame Entertainment, 8033 Sunset Blvd, #247, Los Angeles CA 90046, USA | |
| **Husted, Wayne D** | Artist |
| Keep Homestead Museum, Ely Road, Monson MA 01057, USA | |
| **Huster, Marc** | Weightlifter |
| Grundstr 111, 0132 Dresden, Germany | |
| **Huston, Anjelica** | Actress, Director |
| 57 Windward Ave, Venice CA 90291, USA | |
| **Huston, Daniel (Danny)** | Director, Actor |
| Julian Belfrage Assoc, 9 Argyll St, #300, London W1F 7TG, England | |
| **Huston, Geoff A** | Basketball Player |
| 1960 Ellis Ave, Bronx NY 10472, USA | |
| **Huston, Jack** | Actor |
| United Talent Agency, U T A Plaza, 9336 Civic Center Dr, Beverly Hills CA 90210 USA | |
| **Huston, John** | Golfer |
| 1134 Skye Lane, Palm Harbor FL 34683, USA | |
| **Hutcherson, Josh** | Actor |
| JetLag Productions, 11812 San Vicente Blvd, Los Angeles CA | |
| **Hutcherson, Robert (Bobby)** | Jazz Vibraphonist |
| Blue Note Records, 6920 W Sunset Blvd, Los Angeles CA 90028 USA | |
| **Hutchins, Melvin R (Mel)** | Basketball Player |
| 160 Sherri Lane, Oceanside CA 92054, USA | |
| **Hutchins, Will** | Actor |
| PO Box 371, Glen Head NY 11545, USA | |
| **Hutchinson, Andrew** | Ice Hockey Player |
| 1350 Dennison Road, East Lansing MI 48823, USA | |
| **Hutchinson, Barbara** | Labor Leader |
| American Federation of Labor, 815 15th St NW, Washington DC 20005, USA | |
| **Hutchinson, Chad M** | Football, Baseball Player |
| 1388 Elder Ave, Menlo Park CA 94025, USA | |
| **Hutchinson, Eric** | Singer, Pianist, Songwriter |
| W F Leopold Mgmt, 4425 Riverside Dr, #102, Burbank CA 91505, USA | |
| **Hutchinson, Frederick E** | Educator |
| University of Maine, President's Office, Orono ME 04469, USA | |
| **Hutchinson, J Maxwell** | Architect |
| 58 Hatton Garden, London EC1N 8LX, England | |
| **Hutchinson, Michelle** | Actress |
| Wehmann Models & Talent, 1128 Harmon Place, #202, Minneapolis MN 55403, USA | |
| **Hutchinson, Scott R** | Football Player |
| 1223 Northern Way, Winter Springs FL 32708, USA | |
| **Hutchinson, Steven J (Steve)** | Football Player |
| 16119 Crosby Cove Road, Wayzata MN 55391, USA | |
| **Hutchison, Dave** | Ice Hockey Player |
| Re/Max Realty, 3922 Hamilton Road, Dorchester ON N0L 1G2, Canada | |
| **Hutchison, Fiona** | Actress |
| Don Buchwald Talent Agency, 6500 Wilshire Blvd, #2200, Los Angeles CA 90048 USA | |
| **Huth, Edward J** | Editor, Physician |
| 1124 Morris Ave, Bryn Mawr PA 19010, USA | |
| **Huther, Bruce A** | Football Player |
| 1156 N Bonnie Brae St, Denton TX 76201, USA | |
| **Hutman, Jon** | Production Designer |
| Gersh Agency, 9465 Wilshire Blvd, #600, Beverly Hills CA 90212 USA | |
| **Hutsell, Melanie** | Actress, Comedienne |
| Greene Assoc, 1901 Ave of Stars, #130, Los Angeles CA 90067 USA | |
| **Hutshing, Joe** | Editor |
| Gersh Agency, 9465 Wilshire Blvd, #600, Beverly Hills CA 90212 USA | |
| **Hutson, G Herbert (Herb)** | Baseball Player |
| 7203 W Sugar Tree Court, Savannah GA 31410, USA | |
| **Hutson, Martin** | Actor |
| Artists Partnership, 101 Finsbury Pavement, London EC2A 1RS, England | |
| **Hutt, Peter B** | Attorney |
| 124 S Fairfax St, Alexandria VA 22314, USA | |
| **Hutter, Mark** | Actor |
| Judy Fox Mgmt, 1525 1/2 S Beverly Dr, Los Angeles, CA 90035, USA | |
| **Hutter, Sidney** | Artist |
| Sidney Hutter Glass & Light, 225 Riverside Ave, Auburndale MA 02466, USA | |
| **Hutto, James N (Jim)** | Baseball Player |
| 1317 John Carroll Dr, Pensacola FL 32504, USA | |
| **Hutton, Danny** | Singer (Three Dog Night) |
| 2437 Horseshoe Canyon Road, Los Angeles CA 90046, USA | |
| **Hutton, Lauren** | Model, Actress |
| Untitled Entertainment, 350 S Beverly Dr, #200, Beverly Hills CA 90212 USA | |
| **Hutton, Mark S** | Baseball Player |
| 6 Corfu Court, Westlakes, Adelaide SA 5021, Australia | |
| **Hutton, Thomas G (Tommy)** | Baseball Player, Sportscaster |
| 18 Huntly Dr, Palm Beach Gardens FL 33418, USA | |
| **Hutton, Timothy** | Actor |
| W M E Entertainment, 9601 Wilshire Blvd, #300, Beverly Hills CA 90210 USA | |
| **Hutton, W Thomas (Tom)** | Football Player |
| 400 S Shady Grove Road, Memphis TN 38120, USA | |
| **Huxhold, Kenneth W (Ken)** | Football Player |
| 5007 Prairie Rose Court, Middleton WI 53562, USA | |
| **Huxley, Hugh E** | Biologist |
| 349 Nashawtuc Road, Concord MA 01742, USA | |
| **Huynh, Carol** | Freestyle Wrestler |
| Amateur Wrestling Assoc, 5370 Canotek Road, #7, Gloucester ON K1J 9E6, Canada | |
| **Hvorostovsky, Dmitri** | Opera Singer |
| Askonas Holt, Lincoln House, 300 High Holborn, London WC1V 7JH, England | |
| **Hwang Seok-Ho** | Soccer Player |
| Football Association, 1-131 Sinmunno, 2-Ga Jongno-Gu, Seoul 110 062, South Korea | |

**H**

**Huson - Hwang Seok-Ho**

# H

**Hwang, David Henry** — Writer
Bobbi Thompson Mgmt, 870 Galloway St, Pacific Palisades CA 90272, USA

**Hyams, Peter** — Director
627 San Lorenzo St, Santa Monica CA 90402, USA

**Hyatt, Fred P (Freddie)** — Football Player
19350 SE 52nd Place, Morriston FL 32668, USA

**Hyatt, Joel Z** — Attorney, Businessman
Hyatt Legal Services, 1215 Superior Ave E, Cleveland OH 44114, USA

**Hybl, William J** — Foundation, Sports Executive
El Pomar Foundation, 10 Lake Circle, Colorado Springs CO 80906, USA

**Hyde, Christopher** — Writer
Onyx Penguin Putnam, 375 Hudson St, New York NY 10014, USA

**Hyde, Glenn T** — Football Player
955 Eudora St, #201, Denver CO 80220, USA

**Hyde, James** — Actor
Innovative Artists, 1505 10th St, Santa Monica CA 90401 USA

**Hyde, Jonathan** — Actor
Artist Rights Group, 4A Exmoor St, London W10 6BD, England

**Hyde, Richard E (Dick)** — Baseball Player
1506 Cambridge Dr, Champaign IL 61821, USA

**Hyder, Greg** — Basketball Player
16228 Wato Road, #A, Apple Valley CA 92307, USA

**Hyde-White, Alex** — Actor
Amsel Eisenstadt Frazier, 5055 Wilshire Blvd, #865, Los Angeles CA 90036 USA

**Hyers, Timothy J (Tim)** — Baseball Player
241 Ridge Road, Covington GA 30016, USA

**Hyland, Brian** — Singer
Stone Buffalo, PO Box 101, Silver Lakes CA 92342, USA

**Hyland, Robert J (Bob)** — Football Player
30 Colonial Road, White Plains NY 10605, USA

**Hyland, Sarah** — Actress
R K M, 400 N Mansfield Ave, Los Angeles CA 90036, USA

**Hylton, James** — Auto Racing Driver
15 Avalon Road, Martin GA 30557, USA

**Hylton, Thomas J** — Journalist
Pottstown Mercury, Editorial Dept, Hanover & King Sts, Pottstown PA 19464, USA

**Hyman, B D** — Evangelist, Writer
PO Box 7107, Charlottesville VA 22906, USA

**Hyman, Earle** — Actor
PO Box 650188, Sterling VA 20165, USA

**Hyman, Misty** — Swimmer
3826 E Lupine Ave, Phoenix AZ 85028, USA

**Hyman, Richard R (Dick)** — Jazz Pianist, Composer
Abby Hoffer Enterprises, 223 1/2 E 48th St, New York NY 10017 USA

**Hyman, Timothy** — Artist
62 Muddelton Square, London EC1, England

**Hymes, Dell H** — Anthropologist
20 Mountvue Dr, Charlottesville VA 22901, USA

**Hynd, Noel** — Writer
I C M Partners, 10250 Constellation Blvd, #900, Los Angeles CA 90067 USA

**Hynd, Ronald** — Ballet Dancer, Choreographer
Fern Cottage, U Somerton, Bury Saint Edmonds, Suffolk IP29 4ND, England

**Hynde, Christine E (Chrissie)** — Singer, Guitarist, Songwriter
Gailforce Mgmt, 91 Peterborough Road, London SW6 3BU, England

**Hynes, Garry** — Director
Druid Theater Co, Druid Lane & Flood St, North County Galway, Ireland

**Hynes, Jessica** — Actress, Comedienne, Writer
Independent Talent Group, 40 Whitfield St, London W1T 2RH, England

**Hynes, Richard O** — Biologist
Massachusetts Institute of Technology, Cancer Research Center, Cambridge MA 02139, USA

**Hynes, Samuel** — Writer
130 Moore St, Princeton NJ 08540, USA

**Hynes, Tyler** — Actor
Butler Ruston Bell, 10 Sainte Mary St, #310, Toronto ON M4Y 1P9, Canada

**Hynoski, Henry, Jr** — Football Player
New York Giants, Meadowlands Stadium, 102 Route 120, East Rutherford NJ 07073 USA

**Hysong, Nick** — Track Athlete
10424 N 38th St, Phoenix AZ 85028, USA

**Hytner, Nicholas R** — Director
United Agents, 12-26 Lexington St, London W1F 0LE, England

**Hyzdu, Adam** — Baseball Player
7823 E Red Hawk Circle, Mesa AZ 85207, USA

## Hwang - Hyzdu

**Iacobellis, Sam F** — Businessman, Aeronautical Engineer
Rockwell International, PO Box 5090, Costa Mesa CA 92628, USA

**Iacocca, Lido A (Lee)** — Businessman
75252 Pepperwood Dr, Indian Wells CA 92210, USA

**Iaconio, Frank** — Auto Racing Driver
250 US Highway 206, Flanders NJ 07836, USA

**Iafrate, Al A** — Ice Hockey Player
6990 Spring Meadow Lane, Plymouth MI 48170, USA

**Ian, Janis** — Singer, Songwriter
S R O Artists, 6629 University Ave, #206, Middleton WI 53562, USA

**Iannetta, Christopher D (Chris)** — Baseball Player
7422 E 7th Ave, #14, Denver CO 80230, USA

**Iassonga, Daniel (Dan)** — Baseball Umpire
1501 Bailey Farm Court SW, Marietta GA 30064, USA

**Iavarone, Michael** — Thoroughbred Racing Executive
I E A H Stables, 595 Stewart Ave, #450, Garden City NY 11530, USA

**Iavaroni, Marcus J (Marc)** — Basketball Player, Coach
8129 N Via de Lago, Scottsdale AZ 85258, USA

**Ibaka Ngobila, Serge J** — Basketball Player
Oklahoma City Thunder, 211 N Robinson Ave, #300, Oklahoma City OK 73102 USA

**Ibanez, Raul J** — Baseball Player
26004 SE 23rd Place, Sammamish WA 98075, USA

**Ibbetson, Bruce** — Rowing Athlete
424 San Bernardino Ave, Newport Beach CA 92663, USA

**Ibragimov, Sultan** — Boxer
Warrior's Boxing Promotions, 5397 Orange Dr, #202, Davie FL 33314, USA

**Ibrahim, Abdullah, (Dollar Brand)** — Jazz Pianist, Composer
Brad Simon Organization, 445 E 80th St, #4C, New York NY 10075 USA

**Ibrahim, Nizar** — Paleontologist, Explorer
University of Chicago, Paleontology Dept, 5801 S Ellis Ave, Chicago IL 60637, USA

**Icahn, Carl C** — Businessman
Icahn Co, 445 Hamilton Ave, #1210, White Plains NY 10601, USA

**Ice Cube** — Rap Artist, Actor, Director
Cube Vision, 9000 W Sunset Blvd, West Hollywood CA 90069, USA

**Ice T** — Rap Artist, Actor
Jorge Hinojosa Mgmt, 6606 Maryland Dr, Los Angeles CA 90048, USA

**Ickx, Jacques B (Jacky)** — Auto Racing Driver
171 Chaussee de la Hulpe, 1170 Brussels, Belgium

**Idle, Eric** — Actor, Comedian (Monty Python)
Mayday Mgmt, 68A Delancey St, Camden Town, London NW1 7RY, England

**Idol, Billy** — Singer, Songwriter
East End Mgmt, 13721 Ventura Blvd, #200, Sherman Oaks CA 91423, USA

**Idowu, Phillips** — Track Athlete
Belgrave Harriers, Denmark Road, London SW19 4PG, England

**Ielemia, Apisai** — Prime Minister, Tuvalu
Prime Minister's Office, Vaiaku, Funafuti, Tuvalu

**Ieronymous II** — Religious Leader
Archdiocese of Athens, Hatzichristou 8, 53212 Athens, Greece

**Ifans, Rhys** — Actor
Brillstein Entertainment Partners, 9150 Wilshire Blvd, #350, Beverly Hills CA 90212 USA

**Ifill, Gwen** — Commentator
Public Broadcasting System, 1320 Braddock Place, Alexandria VA 22314 USA

**Iger, Robert A** — Businessman
Walt Disney Co, 500 S Buena Vista St, Burbank CA 91521, USA

**Iginla, Jarome A A** — Ice Hockey Player
Colorado Avalanche, Pepsi Center, 1000 Chopper Circle, Denver CO 80204 USA

**Iglesias, Enrique** — Singer
4535 Sabal Palm Road, Miami FL 33137, USA

**Iglesias, Gabriel** — Comedian, Actor
Creative Artists Agency, 2000 Ave of Stars, #100, Los Angeles CA 90067 USA

**Iglesias, Julio** — Singer
Doyle-Kos Entertainment, Penn Plaza, #2107, New York NY 10119, USA

**Iglesias, Julio, Jr** — Singer, Songwriter
A R Entertainment, 3400 Coral Way, #404, Miami FL 33145, USA

**Ignarro, Louis J** — Nobel Medicine Laureate
C H A, 10833 La Conte Ave, Los Angeles CA 90095, USA

**Ignasiak, Michael J (Mike)** — Baseball Player
8473 Dixie Highway, Ira MI 48023, USA

**Ignatius Zakka I Iwas, Patriarch** — Religious Leader
Syrian Orthodox Patriarchate, Bab Touma, BP 914, Damascus, Syria

**Ignatius, David** — Writer, Columnist
W W Norton, 500 5th Ave, #600, New York NY 10110 USA

**Ignatius, Paul R** — Government Official
2700 Calvert St NW, #416, Washington DC 20008, USA

**Ignizo, Mildred** — Bowler
241 Shore Acres Dr, Rochester NY 14612, USA

**Iguodala, Andre T** — Basketball Player
1111 Riverview Lane, West Conshohocken PA 19428, USA

**Igwebuike, Donald A** — Football Player
1118 Tumlin Court, Lawrenceville GA 30045, USA

**Iha, James Y** — Guitarist (Smashing Pumpkins)
Spivak Sobol Entertainment, 11845 W Olympic Blvd, #1125, Los Angeles CA 90064, USA

**Ihle, Andreas** — Canoeing Athlete
Wiesenweg 5, 39114 Magedburg, Germany

**Ikeda, Daisaku** — Religious Leader, Philosopher
Soka Gakkai, 32 Shinanomachi, Shinjuku, Tokyo 160 8583, Japan

**Ikeda, Kazuyosi** — Physicist, Writer
Osaka University, 2-1 Yamadaoka Suita-Si, Osaka 565 0871, Japan

**Ikenberry, Stanley O** — Educator
University of Illinois, Education Dept, 1310 S 6th St, Champaign IL 61820, USA

**Ikola, Willard** — Ice Hockey Player, Coach
5697 Green Circle Drive, #316, Hopkins MN 55343, USA

**Iler, Robert** — Actor
Baker Winokur Ryder Public Relations, 9100 Wilshire Blvd, #500W, Beverly Hills CA 90212 USA

**Iles, Greg** — Writer
Creative Artists Agency, 2000 Ave of Stars, #100, Los Angeles CA 90067 USA

**Ilg, Raymond P**
591 Camino de la Reina, #300, San Diego CA 92108, USA — Navy Admiral

**Ilgauskas, Zydrunas**
32654 Lake Road, Avon Lake OH 44012, USA — Basketball Player

**Iliff, W Peter**
Hard Noir Films, 660 Iliff St, Pacific Palisades CA 90272, USA — Director, Writer

**Ilinykh, Elena R**
Figure Skating Federation, Luzhnetskaya Nab 8, 119991 Moscow, Russia — Ice Dancer

**Ilitch, Michael (Mike)**
23670 Woodlyne Dr, Bingham Farms MI 48025, USA — Ice Hockey, Baseball Executive

**Ilken, Tunch A**
1000 Grandview Ave, #1103, Pittsburgh PA 15211, USA — Football Player

**Ilonzeh, Annie**
Vincent Cirrincione Assoc, 1516 N Fairfax Ave, Los Angeles CA 90046 USA — Actress

**Ilunga-Mbenga, Didier (D J)**
Los Angeles Lakers, Staples Center, 1111 S Figueroa St, Los Angeles CA 90015 USA — Basketball Player

**Ilves, Toomas Hendrik**
President's Office, 39 Av Weizenbergi, 15050 Tallinn, Estonia — President, Estonia

**Imada, Ryuji**
16204 Sierra de Avila, Tampa FL 33613, USA — Golfer

**Imai, Nobuko**
Conservatorium van Amsterdam, Oosterdokskade 151, Postbus 78022, 1070 Amsterdam LP, Netherlands — Concert Violist

**Iman**
Essex House, 160 Central Park S, New York NY 10019, USA — Model, Actress

**Imbruglia, Natalie**
Untitled Entertainment, 350 S Beverly Dr, #200, Beverly Hills CA 90212 USA — Singer, Songwriter, Actress

**Imhoff, Darrall T**
3637 Sterling Woods Dr, Eugene OR 97408, USA — Basketball Player

**Imhoff, Gary**
Samantha Group, 300 S Raymond Ave, Pasadena CA 91105, USA — Actor

**Immelman, Trevor J**
5174 Vardon Dr, Windermere FL 34786, USA — Golfer

**Immelt, Jeffrey (Jeff)**
General Electric Co, 3135 Easton Turnpike, Fairfield CT 06828, USA — Businessman

**Immonen, Jarkko**
Ak Bars H K, Tatneft Arena, Ul Chistopolskaja 42, 420126 Kazan, Tatarstan, Russia — Ice Hockey Player

**Imperioli, Michael**
T M T Entertainment Group, 648 Broadway, #1002, New York NY 10012, USA — Actor

**Imus, Don**
I C M Partners, 10250 Constellation Blvd, #900, Los Angeles CA 90067 USA — Actor

**In Kyung Kim**
Ladies Pro Golf Assn, 100 International Golf Dr, Daytona Beach FL 32124 USA — Golfer

**Inaba, Carrie Ann**
EnterMediArts, 800 S Main St, #200, Burbank CA 91506, USA — Dancer, Choreographer, Singer

**Inamori, Kazuo**
R D D I Corp, 3-22 Nishi-Shinjuku, Shinjuku, Tokyo 163 8003, Japan — Businessman

**Inarritu, Alejandro Gonzalez**
Gang Tyrer Ramer, 132 S Rodeo Dr, #306, Beverly Hills CA 90212 USA — Director

**Inbal, Eliahu**
Askonas Holt, Lincoln House, 300 High Holborn, London WC1V 7JH, England — Conductor

**Incandela, Joseph (Joe)**
University of California, Physics Dept, Broida Hall, Santa Barbara CA 93106, USA — Particle Physicist

**Incaviglia, Peter J (Pete)**
PO Box 1047, Argyle TX 76226, USA — Baseball Player

**Incognito, Richard D (Richie)**
3231 NW 125th Ave, Sunrise FL 33323, USA — Football Player

**India**
Granada Entertainment, 480 NE 30th St, #101, Miami FL 33137, USA — Singer

**India.Arie**
Creative Artists Agency, 2000 Ave of Stars, #100, Los Angeles CA 90067 USA — Singer, Guitarist, Songwriter

**Indiana, Robert**
Star of Hop, Press Box 464, Vinalhaven ME 04863, USA — Artist

**Indovina, Lorenza**
Carol Levi Mgmt, Via Giuseppe Pisanelli 2, 00196 Rome, Italy — Actress

**Indurain, Miguel**
Avenida Villava, 31013 Pamplona, Navarra, Spain — Cyclist

**Infante, Lindy**
6780 A1A S, Saint Augustine FL 32080, USA — Football Coach

**Infante, Omar R**
Kansas City Royals, Kauffman Stadium, 1 Royal Way, Kansas City MO 64129 USA — Baseball Player

**Ingarfield, Earl, Sr**
1715 Lakehill Crescent S, Lethbridge AB T1K 3R2, Canada — Ice Hockey Player

**Inge of Richmond, Peter A**
Aegis Defence Services, 84 Eccleston Square, London SW1V 1PX, England — Army Field Marshal, England

**Inge, C Brandon**
5003 Windsong Trail, Salem SC 29676, USA — Baseball Player

**Ingels, Marty**
4531 Noeline Way, Encino CA 91436, USA — Actor, Comedian

**Ingelsby, Tom**
1507 Canterbury Lane, Berwyn PA 19312, USA — Basketball Player

**Ingersoll, Andrew P**
California Institute of Technology, Geological/Planetary Sciences Division, Pasadena CA 91125, USA — Meteorologist, Climatologist

**Inghram, Mark G**
PO Box 771721, Eagle River AK 99577, USA — Physicist

**Ingle, Doug**
Entertainment Services International, 6400 Pleasant Park Dr, Chanhassen MN 55317 USA — Singer, Keyboardist (Iron Butterfly)

**Ingman, Einar H, Jr**
W4053 N Silver Lake Road, Irma WI 54442, USA — Korean War Army Hero (CMH)

**Ingraham, Laura**
Sirius XM Radio, 1221 Ave of Americas, New York NY 10020, USA — Commentator

**Ingram, Alfred**
983 Oakland Dr, Atlanta GA 30315, USA — Baseball Player

**Ingram, Jack**
699 Brevard Road, Asheville NC 28806, USA — Auto Racing Driver

**Ingram, James**
867 S Muirfield Road, Los Angeles CA 90005, USA — Singer, Songwriter

**Ingram, Marv**
4339 Ensenada Dr, Woodland Hills CA 91364, USA — Singer (Four Preps)

**Ingram, Melvin**
San Diego Chargers, 4020 Murphy Canyon Road, San Diego CA 92123 USA — Football Player

**Ingram, Preston**
174 Douglas St SE, Atlanta GA 30317, USA — Baseball Player

**Ingrassia, Paul J**
111 Division Ave, New Providence NJ 07974, USA — Journalist

**Inkeles, Alex**
32 Plaza Dr, Berkeley CA 94705, USA — Sociologist

**Inkster, Juli Simpson**
23140 Mora Glen Dr, Los Altos Hills CA 94024, USA — Golfer

**Inman, Bobby Ray**
Arboretum Plaza, 9442 N Capital of Texas Highway, #685, Austin TX 78759, USA — Navy Admiral, Government Official

**Inman, Jerry F**
PO Box 1113, Battle Ground WA 98604, USA — Football Player

**Inman, John S**
2210 Chase St, Durham NC 27707, USA — Golfer

**Inman, Joseph C (Joe), Jr**
3599 Tuckers Farm SE, Marietta GA 30067, USA — Golfer

**Innauer, Anton (Toni)**
Steinbruckstr 8/II, 6024 Innsbruck, Austria — Ski Jumper, Coach

**Innaurato, Albert F**
325 W 22nd St, New York NY 10011, USA — Writer

**Innerhofer, Christoff**
Via Gisse 37, 39030 Gais (BZ), Italy — Alpine Skier

**Innes, Laura**
Creative Artists Agency, 2000 Ave of Stars, #100, Los Angeles CA 90067 USA — Actress

**Innis, Jeffrey D (Jeff)**
4920 Woodlong Lane, Cumming GA 30040, USA — Baseball Player

**Innis, Roy E A**
817 Broadway, New York NY 10003, USA — Civil Rights Activist

**Inogradov, Pavel**
Cosmonaut Training Center, Star City, 141160 Zvezdny Gorodok, Moscow Oblast, Russia — Cosmonaut

**Inoni, Ephraim**
Palais de L'Unite, Rue de l'Exploratour, Yaounde, Cameroon — Prime Minister, Cameroon Republic

**Inoue, Hirochika**
University of Tokyo, Mechano-Informatics Dept, 7-3-1 Hongo, 113 8654 Tokyo, Japan — Robotics Engineer

**Inoue, Rena**
Lee Marshall Mgmt, 199 E Garfield Road, Aurora OH 44202, USA — Figure Skater

**Inoue, Shinya**
Marine Biological Laboratory, 167 Water St, Woods Hole MA 02543, USA — Biologist, Photographer

**Insalaco, Kim**
USA Hockey, 1775 Bob Johnson Dr, Colorado Springs CO 80906 USA — Ice Hockey Player

**Insko, Delmer M (Del)**
2360 Fischer Road, South Beloit IL 61080, USA — Harness Racing Driver

**Insley, Will**
231 Bowery, New York NY 10002, USA — Artist

**Inspectah Deck**
A&E Entertainment, 13280 NE Freeway, #F328, Houston TX 77040, USA — Rap Artist (Wu-Tang Clan)

**Insulza, Jose Miguel**
Organization of American States, 17th St & Constitution Ave, Washington DC 20006, USA — Government Official, Chile

**Intriligator, Michael D**
140 Foxtail Dr, Santa Monica CA 90402, USA — Economist

**Inui, Kumiko**
Showa Women's University, 1-7 Taishide, Satagayaku, Tokyo 154 8533, Japan — Architect

**Inzaghi, Filippo (Pippo)**
F C Milan, Via Filippo Turati 3, 20121 Milan, Italy — Soccer Player

**Inzko, Valentin**
Emerika Bluma 1, 71000 Sarajevo, Bosnia-Herzegovia — High Representative, Bosnia-Herzegovina

**Iohannis, Klaus W**
President's Office, Calea Victoriei 59-53, 76258 Bucharest, Romania — President, Romania

**Iommi, F Anthony (Tony)**
Sharon Osborne Mgmt, 8899 Beverly Blvd, #905, West Hollywood CA 90048, USA — Guitarist (Black Sabbath), Songwriter

**Iooss, Walter**
152 DeForest Road, Montauk NY 11954, USA — Photographer

**Iordache, Larisa**
C S Dinamo Bucherest, Soseaua Stefan cel Mare 7-9, 20121 Bucharest, Romania — Gymnast

**Iorg, Dane C**
5358 W Evergreen Circle, American Fork UT 84003, USA — Baseball Player

**Iorg, Garth R**
10635 Alameda Dr, Knoxville TN 37932, USA — Baseball Player

**Iovine, Vicki**
Trident Media Group, 41 Madison Ave, #3600, New York NY 10010, USA — Writer, Columnist, Model

**Ipcar, Dahlov**
Thomas Crotty Frost Gully Gallery, 1159 US Route 1, Freeport ME 04032, USA — Illustrator, Artist, Writer

**Ipsen, Kristian**
Kent Ipsen, 6061 Clayton View Lane, Clayton CA 94517, USA — Diver

**Iraheta, Allison**
Jive Records, 137-39 W 25th St, #1100, New York NY 10001 USA — Singer

**Irani, Ray R**
Occidental Petroleum, 10889 Wilshire Blvd, #1000, Los Angeles CA 90024, USA — Businessman

**Iraschko-Stolz, Daniela**
W S V Eisenerz, Spitalgrund 1, 8790 Eisenerz, Austria — Ski Jumper

**Irbe, Arturs**
10733 Trego Trail, Raleigh NC 27614, USA — Ice Hockey Player

**Iredale, Randle W**
1151 W 8th Ave, Vancouver BC V6H 1C5, Canada — Architect

**Ireland, Dan**
Gersh Agency, 9465 Wilshire Blvd, #600, Beverly Hills CA 90212 USA — Director, Producer, Writer

**Ireland, Julius W (Buck)**
4389 Malaai St, #324, Honolulu HI 96818, USA — WW II Marine Corps Hero

**Ireland, Kathy**
Guttman Assoc, 118 S Beverly Dr, #201, Beverly Hills CA 90212 USA — Model, Actress

**Ireland, Marin**
I C M Partners, 10250 Constellation Blvd, #900, Los Angeles CA 90067 USA — Actress

Ingram - Ireland

| | | |
|---|---|---|
| **Ireland, Patricia**<br>Katz Kutter Haigler Assoc, 801 Pennsylvania Ave NW, #750, Washington DC 20004, USA | Association Executive | |
| **Irglova, Marketa**<br>Billions Corp, 3522 W Armitage Ave, Chicago IL 60647 USA | Actress, Pianist, Songwriter | |
| **Irie, Saaya**<br>Ace Crew, Minatoku, 6-12-11 Akasaka Koyo Building, #7F, 107-0052 Tokyo Akasaka, Japan | Actress, Singer | |
| **Irigoyen, Adam**<br>Amatruda Benson, 433 N Camden Drive, #400, Beverly Hills CA 90210, USA | Actor | |
| **Irimia, Gabriela**<br>Concorde International, 101 Shepherds Bush Road, London W6 7LP, England | Singer (Cheeky Girls) | |
| **Irimia, Monica**<br>Concorde International, 101 Shepherds Bush Road, London W6 7LP, England | Singer (Cheeky Girls) | |
| **Irina**<br>Marilyn Model Agency, 32 Union Square E, #PH, New York NY 10003 USA | Model | |
| **Iris, Donnie**<br>807 Darlington Road, Beaver Falls PA 15010, USA | Singer, Songwriter | |
| **Irons, Eddie**<br>5720 Guilford Forest Dr SW, Atlanta GA 30331, USA | Singer, Drummer, Keyboardist (Brick) | |
| **Irons, Gerald D**<br>30010 E Legends Trail Court, Spring TX 77386, USA | Football Player | |
| **Irons, Grant M**<br>30010 E Legends Trail Court, Spring TX 77386, USA | Football Player | |
| **Irons, Jeremy**<br>Artists Partnership, 101 Finsbury Pavement, London EC2A 1RS, England | Actor | |
| **Irons, Max**<br>United Talent Agency, U T A Plaza, 9336 Civic Center Dr, Beverly Hills CA 90210 USA | Actor, Model | |
| **Ironside, Michael**<br>Abrams Artists, 9200 W Sunset Blvd, #1125, West Hollywood CA 90069 USA | Actor | |
| **Irrera, Domenick J (Dom)**<br>Metropolitan Talent Agency, 5405 Wilshire Blvd, #218, Los Angeles CA 90036 USA | Actor, Comedian, Writer, Producer | |
| **Irvan, V Earnest (Ernie)**<br>9939 Troutman Road, Midland NC 28107, USA | Auto Racing Driver | |
| **Irvin, Cal**<br>1311 Julian St, Greensboro NC 27406, USA | Baseball Player, Basketball Coach | |
| **Irvin, John**<br>6 Lower Common South, London SW15 1BP, England | Director | |
| **Irvin, Kenneth P (Ken)**<br>8151 Nesbit Ferry Road, Atlanta GA 30350, USA | Football Player | |
| **Irvin, LeRoy, Jr**<br>2905 Ruby Dr, #C, Fullerton CA 92831, USA | Football Player | |
| **Irvin, Michael J**<br>2339 Aberdeen Bend, Carrolton TX 75007, USA | Football Player, Sportscaster | |
| **Irvin, Monford M (Monte)**<br>1815 Enclave Parkway, #6203, Houston TX 77077, USA | Baseball Player | |
| **Irvin, Sandora**<br>San Antonio Silver Stars, 1 AT&T Center, San Antonio TX 78219 USA | Basketball Player | |
| **Irvine, Edmund (Eddie), Jr**<br>Jaguar Racing, Browns Lane, Allesley Coventry CV5 9DR, England | Auto Racing Driver | |
| **Irvine, Edward A (Ted)**<br>5-2727 Portage Ave, Winnipeg MB R3J 0R2, Canada | Ice Hockey Player | |
| **Irvine, Jeremy**<br>Hatton McEwan, 3 Chocolate Studios, 7 Shepherdess Place, London N1 7LJ, England | Actor | |
| **Irving, Amy**<br>TalentWorks, 3500 W Olive Ave, #1400, Burbank CA 91505 USA | Actress, Producer | |
| **Irving, John W**<br>Turnbull Agency, PO Box 757, Dorset VT 05251, USA | Writer | |
| **Irving, K Stuart (Stu)**<br>93 Hart St, Beverly MA 01915, USA | Ice Hockey Player | |
| **Irving, Kyrie A**<br>Cleveland Cavaliers, Gund Arena, 1 Center Court, Cleveland OH 44115 USA | Basketball Player | |
| **Irving, Paul H**<br>Manatt Phelps Phillips, 11355 W Olympic Blvd, #20, Los Angeles CA 90064, USA | Attorney | |
| **Irwin, Ashton**<br>Wonder Mgmt, Philips House, 17/617 Elizabeth St, Redfern NSW 2016, Australia | Singer, Drummer (5 Seconds of Summer) | |
| **Irwin, Elaine**<br>Innovative Artists, 1505 10th St, Santa Monica CA 90401 USA | Model | |
| **Irwin, Hale S**<br>5720 N Saguaro Road, Paradise Valley AZ 85253, USA | Golfer | |
| **Irwin, Haley**<br>Hockey Canada, 151 Canada Olympic Road SW, #201, Calgary AB T3B 6B7, Canada | Ice Hockey Player | |
| **Irwin, Heath S**<br>5530 N 115th St, Longmont CO 80504, USA | Football Player | |
| **Irwin, Jennifer**<br>Gersh Agency, 9465 Wilshire Blvd, #600, Beverly Hills CA 90212 USA | Actress | |
| **Irwin, Mark**<br>1260 Coast Village Circle, Santa Barbara CA 93108, USA | Cinematographer | |
| **Irwin, Paul G**<br>Humane Society of the United States, PO Box 9100, League City TX 77574, USA | Association Executive | |
| **Irwin, Robert W**<br>501 S Beverly Dr, Beverly Hills CA 90212, USA | Artist | |
| **Irwin, Terence H**<br>University of California, Philosophy Dept, Irvine CA 92697, USA | Philosopher | |
| **Irwin, Timothy E (Tim)**<br>5512 River Point Cove Road, Knoxville TN 37919, USA | Football Player | |
| **Irwin, Tom, II**<br>Framework Entertainment, 9057 Nemo St, #C, West Hollywood CA 90069 USA | Actor | |
| **Irwin, William M (Bill)**<br>Innovative Artists, 1505 10th St, Santa Monica CA 90401 USA | Clown, Actor | |
| **Isaac, Oscar**<br>United Talent Agency, U T A Plaza, 9336 Civic Center Dr, Beverly Hills CA 90210 USA | Actor | |
| **Isaacs, Jason**<br>Gersh Agency, 9465 Wilshire Blvd, #600, Beverly Hills CA 90212 USA | Actor | |
| **Isaacs, Jeremy I**<br>Royal Opera House, Covent Garden, Bow St, London WC2E 9DD, England | Director | |
| **Isaacs, Levie**<br>Innovative Artists, 1505 10th St, Santa Monica CA 90401 USA | Cinematographer | |

| | |
|---|---|
| **Isaacs, Susan**<br>Harper Collins Publishers, 10 E 53rd St, Cellar 2, New York NY 10022, USA | Writer |
| **Isaacson, Walter S**<br>I C M Partners, 10250 Constellation Blvd, #900, Los Angeles CA 90067 USA | Journalist |
| **Isaak, Chris**<br>W M E Entertainment, 9601 Wilshire Blvd, #300, Beverly Hills CA 90210 USA | Singer, Songwriter, Actor |
| **Isacco, Jennifer**<br>Olympic Committee, Foro Italico, Largo Lauro de Bosis 15, 00135 Rome, Italy | Bobsled Athlete |
| **Isacksen, Peter**<br>Sutton-Barth Vennari, 5900 Wilshire Blvd, #700, Los Angeles CA 90036 USA | Actor |
| **Isaksson, Irma Sara**<br>United Stage Artists, PO Box 11029, 100 61, Stockholm, Sweden | Singer, Songwriter |
| **Isbell, Jason**<br>Ground Control Touring, 20 Jay St, #826, Brooklyn NY 11201 USA | Singer, Guitarist, Songwriter |
| **Isbell, Stewart**<br>Retna, 24 W 25th St, #1200, New York NY 10010, USA | Photographer |
| **Isbin, Sharon**<br>Columbia Artists Mgmt Inc, 5 Columbus Circle, 1790 Broadway, #1600, New York NY 10019 USA | Concert Guitarist |
| **Isbister, Brad**<br>1818 Lakeview Dr, Fort Wayne IN 46808, USA | Ice Hockey Player |
| **Iscove, Robert (Rob)**<br>Course Mgmt, 15159 Greenleaf St, Sherman Oaks CA 91403, USA | Director |
| **Isham, Mark**<br>23679 Calabasas Road, #522, Calabasas CA 91302, USA | Composer |
| **Ishibashi, Brittany**<br>Abrams Artists, 9200 W Sunset Blvd, #1125, West Hollywood CA 90069 USA | Actress |
| **Ishida, Jim**<br>871 N Vail Ave, Montebello CA 90640, USA | Actor |
| **Ishida, Nobuhiro**<br>Golden Boy Promotions, 626 Wilshire Blvd, #350, Los Angeles CA 90017 USA | Boxer |
| **Ishiguro, Kazuo**<br>Rogers Coleridge White, 20 Powis Mews, London W11 1JN, England | Writer |
| **Ishihara, Satomi**<br>Horipro, 2-5-1 Shimo-Meguro, Meguroku, Meguro, Tokyo 153 8660, Japan | Actress |
| **Ishii, Ken**<br>3-5-12 Yakumo, Meguroku, Tokyo 152 0023, Japan | Composer |
| **Ishikawa, Shigeru**<br>19-8-4 Chome Kugayama, Suginamiku, Tokyo 168 0082, Japan | Economist |
| **Ishikawa, Travis T**<br>324 Violetta Court, San Ramon CA 94582, USA | Baseball Player |
| **Ishimaru, Akira**<br>2913 165th Place NE, Bellevue WA 98008, USA | Electrical Engineer |
| **Ishizaka, Kimishige**<br>Allergy/Immunology Institute, 11149 N Torrey Pines Road, La Jolla CA 92037, USA | Allergist |
| **Ishizaka, Teruko**<br>Good Samaritan Hospital, 5601 Loch Raven Blvd, Baltimore MD 21239, USA | Allergist |
| **Isikoff, Michael**<br>6209 Meadowbrook Lane, Chevy Chase MD 20815, USA | Writer, Journalist |
| **Isinbayeva, Yelena G**<br>Podium Management Group, 3 Ave de Grande Bretagne, 98000 Monte Carlo, Monaco | Track Athlete |
| **Iskander, Fazil A**<br>Leningradski Prosp Korp 2, #67, 125040 Moscow, Russia | Writer |
| **Isler, Gabriela**<br>Miss Universe Organization, 1370 Ave of Americas, #1600, New York NY 10019 USA | Beauty Queen |
| **Isler, Jennifer (J J)**<br>6828 Country Club Dr, La Jolla CA 92037, USA | Yachtswoman |
| **Isley, Ronald (Ron)**<br>Walt Reeder Productions, 93 Old York Road, #I-604, Jenkintown PA 19046, USA | Singer (Isley Brothers) |
| **Ismail, Qadry R**<br>1506 Sunningdale Way, Bel Air MD 21015, USA | Football Player |
| **Ismail, Raghib R (Rocket)**<br>7423 Marigold Dr, Irving TX 75063, USA | Football Player |
| **Isner, John R**<br>5700 Saddlebrook Way, Wesley Chapel FL 33543, USA | Tennis Player |
| **Ison, Christopher J**<br>Minneapolis-Saint Paul Star Tribune, 425 Portland Ave, Minneapolis MN 55488, USA | Journalist |
| **Isozaki, Arata**<br>5-12-9 Akasaka, Minatoku, Tokyo 107 0052, Japan | Architect |
| **Israel, Alex**<br>Reena Spaulings Fine Art, 185 E Broadway, New York NY 10002, USA | Video Artist |
| **Israel, Werner**<br>2323 Hamiota St, #401, Victoria BC V8R 2N1, Canada | Physicist |
| **Isringhausen, Jason D**<br>550 E Lake Dr, Tarpon Springs FL 34688, USA | Baseball Player |
| **Issel, Daniel P (Dan)**<br>325 E Palace Ave, Santa Fe NM 87501, USA | Basketball Player, Coach, Executive |
| **Isserlis, Steven**<br>I M G Artists, Hogarth Business Park, Chiswick, London W4 2TH, England | Concert Cellist |
| **Italeli, Iakoba T**<br>Governor General's Office, Government House, Vaiaku, Funafuti, Tuvalu | Governor General, Tuvalu |
| **Itin, Ilya**<br>Jonathan Wentworth Assoc, 10 Fiske Place, #530, Mount Vernon NY 10550 USA | Concert Pianist |
| **Ito, Lance**<br>Los Angeles Superior Court, 210 W Temple St, #M6, Los Angeles CA 90012, USA | Judge |
| **Ito, Masao**<br>Riken Brain Science Institute, 2-1 Hirosawa Wako City, Saitama 351 0198, Japan | Physiologist |
| **Ito, Midori**<br>Prince Hotel Skate Club, 3-4 Shin Yokohama, Kanagawa 222 8533, Japan | Figure Skater |
| **Ito, Misaki**<br>Ken-On, 7-10-9 Akasaka, Minatoku, Tokyo 107 8415, Japan | Actress, Model |
| **Ito, Robert**<br>843 N Sycamore Ave, Los Angeles CA 90038, USA | Actor |
| **Ito, Takenobu**<br>Honda Motor Co, 2-1-1 Minami-Aoyama, Minatoku, Tokyo 107 8556, Japan | Businessman |
| **Iu, Carolyn**<br>Iu & Bibliowicz, 57 E 11th St, #700, New York NY 10003, USA | Interior Designer |

**I**

**Isaacs - Iu**

| | | |
|---|---|---|
| **I** | **Ivanchenkov, Aleksandr S**<br>Cosmonaut Training Center, Star City, 141160 Zvezdny Gorodok, Moscow Oblast, Russia | Cosmonaut |
| | **Ivanek, Zeljko**<br>Leading Artists, 145 W 45th St, #1000, New York NY 10036, USA | Actor |
| | **Ivanisevic, Goran**<br>Alijnoviceva 28, 58000 Split, Serbia | Tennis Player |
| | **Ivanishvili, Bidzina**<br>Prime Minister's Office, Government House, Ingorokva 7, 380034 Tbilsi, Georgia | President, Georgia |
| | **Ivanov, Georgi I**<br>Air Sofia Ltd, Sofia Airport, 1 Brussels Blvd, 1540 Sofia, Bulgaria | Cosmonaut, Bulgaria |
| | **Ivanov, Gjorge**<br>President's Office, Villa Vodno, Aco Karamanov BB, 1000 Skopje, Macedonia | President, Macedonia |
| | **Ivanov, Igor S**<br>Moscow State Institute, Vernadskogo Prospekt 76, 119454 Moscow, Russia | Government Official, Russia |
| | **Ivanovic, Ana**<br>D H Mgmt, Holeestra 86, 4054 Basel, Switzerland | Tennis Player |
| | **Ivar, Stan**<br>Rogers Orion Talent Agency, 13731 Ventura Blvd, #D, Sherman Oaks CA 91423, USA | Actor |
| | **Ivens, Terri**<br>Paul Kohner, 9300 Wilshire Blvd, #555, Beverly Hills CA 90212 USA | Actress |
| | **Iveri, Tamar**<br>I M G Artists, Hogarth Business Park, Chiswick, London W4 2TH, England | Opera Singer |
| | **Ivers, Eileen**<br>Roots Agency, 177 Woodland Ave, Westwood NJ 07675, USA | Fiddler |
| | **Iversen, Leslie M**<br>Oxford University, Pharmacology Dept, Oxford OX1 3QT, England | Pharmacologist |
| | **Iverson, Allen**<br>308 Harper Dr, #210, Moorestown NJ 8057, USA | Basketball Player |
| | **Iverson, Becky**<br>4723 Poplar Creek Dr, Madison WI 53718, USA | Golfer |
| | **Ivery, Eddie Lee**<br>1080 Wrightsboro Road, Thomson GA 30824, USA | Football Player |
| | **Ivey, Dana**<br>Paradigm Agency, 360 N Crescent Dr, North Building, Beverly Hills CA 90210 USA | Actress |
| | **Ivey, James B (Jim)**<br>5840 Dahlia Dr, #7, Orlando FL 32807, USA | Editorial Cartoonist |
| | **Ivey, Judith**<br>Abrams Artists, 9200 W Sunset Blvd, #1125, West Hollywood CA 90069 USA | Actress |
| | **Ivey, Royal T**<br>6080 Indian Wood Circle SE, Mableton GA 30126, USA | Basketball Player |
| | **Ivey, Susan**<br>Reynolds American, PO Box 2990, Winston-Salem NC 27102, USA | Businesswoman |
| | **Ivie, Michael W (Mike)**<br>PO Box 1565, Loganville GA 30052, USA | Baseball Player |
| | **Ivins, Marsha S**<br>2811 Timber Briar Circle, Houston TX 77059, USA | Astronaut |
| | **Ivins, Michael L**<br>World's Fair Mgmt, 1208 Chowning Ave, Edmond OK 73034, USA | Bassist, Keyboardist (Flaming Lips) |
| | **Ivory, Horace O**<br>5321 Diaz Ave, Fort Worth TX 76107, USA | Football Player |
| | **Ivory, James (Sap)**<br>3026 Wenonah Park Road SW, Birmingham AL 35211, USA | Baseball Player |
| | **Ivory, James F**<br>18 Patroon St, Claverack NY 12513, USA | Director, Producer |
| | **Ivy Queen**<br>I C M Partners, 10250 Constellation Blvd, #900, Los Angeles CA 90067 USA | Reggaeton, Rap Artist, Songwriter |
| | **Iwan, Dafydd**<br>Carrog, Rhos-Bach, Caeathro, Caernarfon, Gwynedd LL55 2TF, Wales | Singer, Songwriter |
| | **Iwaniec, Henryk**<br>Rutgers State University, Mathematics Dept, New Brunswick NJ 08903, USA | Mathematician |
| | **Iwasa, Mayuko**<br>Platinum Production, 3-26-16-6F, Shibuya, Tokyo 150 0002, Japan | Actress, Model |
| | **Iwata, Satoru**<br>Nintendo, 11-1 Kamitoba Hokotatecho, Minamiku, Kyoto 601 8501, Japan | Businessman |
| | **Iwatani, Toru**<br>Tokyo Polytechnic University, 1583 Iiyama, Atsugi Kanagawa 243 0297, Japan | Computer Game Inventor |
| | **Iwerks, Donald W**<br>Iwerks Entertainment, 4520 W Valerio St, Burbank CA 91505, USA | Businessman |
| | **Izambard, Sebastien**<br>Octagon, 81-83 Fulham High St, London SW6 3JW, England | Singer (Il Divo) |
| | **Izbasa, Sandra**<br>C S S 3 Steaua, Sectia de Gimnastica, B Dul Ghencea, #35, 61692 Bucherest, Romania | Gymnast |
| | **Izo, George W**<br>PO Box 325, Alexandria VA 22313, USA | Football Player |
| | **Izon, David**<br>Stanley Levin, 226 Palafox Place, Pensacola FL 32502, USA | Boxer |
| | **Izzard, Eddie**<br>A P A Talent & Literary Agency, 405 S Beverly Dr, #300, Beverly Hills CA 90212 USA | Actor, Comedian |
| | **Izzo, Lawrence A (Larry)**<br>1 Snowbird Place, Spring TX 77381, USA | Football Player |
| | **Izzo, Tom**<br>Michigan State University, Athletic Dept, Breslin Center, East Lansing MI 48824, USA | Basketball Coach |

**J Splif** — Singer (Far East Movement)
Stampede Mgmt, 12530 Beatrice St, Los Angeles CA 90066, USA

**Ja Rule** — Pop, Rap Artist; Actor
Universal Media Artists, 8222 Melrose Ave, #203, Los Angeles CA 90048, USA

**Jaafari, Ibrahim al-** — Prime Minister, Iraq
Parliament, Karradat Mariam, Baghdad, Iraq

**Jaar, Alfredo** — Photographer, Sculptor, Filmmaker
252 Lafayette St, #3G, New York NY 10012, USA

**Jablonski, Joseph** — Concert Pianist
Carlscrona Chamber Music Festival, Verstorp Skarfva, 371 91 Karlskrona, Sweden

**Jablonski, Patrick D (Pat)** — Ice Hockey Player
18814 Wimbledon Circle, Lutz FL 33558, USA

**Jabs, Matthias** — Guitarist
M J Guitars, Pariser Str 32, 81667 Munich, Germany

**Jace, Michael** — Actor
Blueprint Mgmt, 5670 Wilshire Blvd, #2525, Los Angeles CA 90036, USA

**Jack, Jarrett M** — Basketball Player
Brooklyn Nets, 15 Metro Tech Center, #1100, Brooklyn NY 11201 USA

**Jacke, Christopher L (Chris)** — Football Player
1158 S Taylor St, #C, Green Bay WI 54304, USA

**Jackee** — Actress
Metropolitan Talent Agency, 5405 Wilshire Blvd, #218, Los Angeles CA 90036 USA

**Jackendoff, Ray S** — Language Educator
Brandies University, Linguistics & Cognitive Dept, Waltham MA 02254, USA

**Jackiw, Roman W** — Physicist
Massachusetts Institute of Technology, Physics Dept, Cambridge MA 02139, USA

**Jackiw, Stefan** — Concert Violinist
Opus 3 Artists, 470 Park Ave S, #900N, New York NY 10016 USA

**Jacklin, Bill** — Artist
62 Bank St, New York NY 10014, USA

**Jacklin, Tony** — Golfer, Sportscaster
1175 51st St W, Bradenton FL 34209, USA

**Jackman, Hugh** — Actor, Singer, Dancer
W M E Entertainment, 9601 Wilshire Blvd, #300, Beverly Hills CA 90210 USA

**Jackson Hoye, Rose** — Actress
Haldeman Business Mgmt, 1137 2nd St, #119, Santa Monica CA 90403, USA

**Jackson Nelson, Marjorie** — Track Athlete
Athletics Australia, 431 Saint Kilda Road, Melbourne VIC 3004, Australia

**Jackson, Ed, Jr** — Architect
ArchD Consulting, PO Box 1345, Fairfax VA 22038

**Jackson, Alan** — Singer, Guitarist, Songwriter
Co-Op, 1510 16th Ave S, Nashville TN 37212, USA

**Jackson, Alfred** — Football Player
1811 Kirby Dr, Houston TX 77019, USA

**Jackson, Alvin N (Al)** — Baseball Player
3221 SE Morningside Blvd, Port Saint Lucie FL 34952, USA

**Jackson, Andrea** — Actress
Scott Schwimer Assoc, 183 Pecos Way, Las Vegas NV 89121, USA

**Jackson, Anne** — Actress
TalentWorks, 3500 W Olive Ave, #1400, Burbank CA 91505 USA

**Jackson, Arthur J** — WW II Marine Corps Hero (CMH)
1290 E Spring Court, Boise ID 83712, USA

**Jackson, Betty** — Fashion Designer
Betty Jackson Ltd, 1 Netherwood Place, London W14 0BW, England

**Jackson, Bobby** — Basketball Player
Houston Rockets, 1730 Jefferson St, Houston TX 77003 USA

**Jackson, Brandon T** — Actor
Class Clown Entertainment, 14622 Ventura Blvd, #1002, Sherman Oaks CA 91403, USA

**Jackson, Calvin B** — Football Player
250 SW 28th Terrace, Fort Lauderdale FL 33312, USA

**Jackson, Charles M** — Football Player
PO Box 888285, Atlanta GA 30356, USA

**Jackson, Cheyenne** — Actor
Schiff Co, 9220 Sunset Blvd, #106, West Hollywood CA 90069 USA

**Jackson, Chuck** — Singer
Universal Attractions, 135 W 26th St, #1200, New York NY 10001 USA

**Jackson, Colin R** — Track Athlete
4 Jackson Close, Rhoose, Vale of Glamorgan CF62 3DQ, England

**Jackson, Danny L** — Baseball Player
16332 Larsen St, Overland Park KS 66062, USA

**Jackson, Darrell L** — Football Player
Darrell Jackson Family Foundation, 720 E Fletcher Ave, #202, Tampa FL 33612, USA

**Jackson, Darrell P** — Baseball Player
PO Box 4424, Downey CA 90241, USA

**Jackson, Darrin J** — Baseball Player
432 E Mead Dr, Chandler AZ 85249, USA

**Jackson, DeSean** — Football Player
Washington Redskins, 21300 Redskin Park Dr, Ashburn VA 20147 USA

**Jackson, Earnest (Ernie)** — Football Player
938 Pisgah N, Eads TN 38028, USA

**Jackson, Eddie** — Bowler
3961 Glenmore Ave, Cincinnati OH 45211, USA

**Jackson, Edwin** — Baseball Player
6955 Setter Dr, Columbus GA 31909, USA

**Jackson, Elly** — Singer, Keyboardist (La Roux)
Beatnik Public Relations, 5 Little Portland St, London W1W 7JD, England

**Jackson, Eric (E J)** — Canoeing Athlete
Jackson Kayak, 325 Iris Dr, Sparta TN 38583, USA

**Jackson, Francis A** — Concert Organist, Composer
Nether Garth, East Acklam, Malton, North Yorkshire YO17 9RG, England

**Jackson, Frank H** — Football Player
2812 Boll St, Dallas TX 7504, USA

**Jackson, Freddie** — Singer, Songwriter
Orpheus, 630 9th Ave, #1101, New York NY 10036, USA

**Jackson, Gildart** — Actor
Ellis Talent Agency, 4705 Laurel Canyon Blvd, #300, Valley Village CA 91607, USA

**Jackson, Glenda**
Agents Associes, 201 Rue du Faubourg Saint Honore, 75008 Paris, France — Actress

**Jackson, Glenda**
Lionel Larner Ltd, 119 W 57th St, New York NY 10019, USA — Actress

**Jackson, Grady O**
PO Box 841, Braselton GA 30517, USA — Football Player

**Jackson, Grant D**
212 Mesa Circle, Pittsburgh PA 15241, USA — Baseball Player

**Jackson, Harold**
57 Fox Hollow Lane, Sewell NJ 08080, USA — Journalist

**Jackson, Harold L**
Jackson State University, Athletic Dept, Jackson MS 39217, USA — Football Player, Coach

**Jackson, James A (Jim)**
17827 Windflower Way, Dallas TX 75252, USA — Basketball Player

**Jackson, Janet**
Guttman Assoc, 118 S Beverly Dr, #201, Beverly Hills CA 90212 USA — Singer, Actress, Dancer

**Jackson, Jaren**
7728 Solana Dr, Indianapolis IN 46240, USA — Basketball Player

**Jackson, Javon**
Palmetto Records, 67 Hill Road, Redding CT 06896, USA — Jazz Saxophonist

**Jackson, Jeff**
Furman University, Athletic Dept, Greenville SC 29613, USA — Basketball Coach

**Jackson, Jeff**
1119 Parkview Dr, Griffin GA 30224, USA — Ice Hockey Player

**Jackson, Jeremy**
International Talent Agency, 9701 Wilshire Blvd, Beverly Hills CA 90212, USA — Actor

**Jackson, Jermaine**
Entertainment Artists, 2409 21st Ave S, #100, Nashville TN 10019 USA — Singer, Guitarist, Songwriter

**Jackson, Jesse L**
Operation Push, 930 E 50th St, Chicago IL 60615, USA — Civil Rights Activist, Evangelist

**Jackson, Joanne**
Nova Centurion S C, Beechdale Road, Bilborough, Nottingham NG8 3LL, England — Swimmer

**Jackson, Joe**
Big Hassle, 44 Wall St, #2200, New York NY 10005, USA — Singer, Pianist, Songwriter

**Jackson, Joe M**
25320 38th Ave S, Kent WA 98032, USA — Vietnam War Air Force Hero (CMH)

**Jackson, John**
PO Box 898, Hodge LA 71247, USA — Baseball Player

**Jackson, John**
8183 Alpine Aster Court, Liberty Township OH 45044, USA — Football Player

**Jackson, John David**
1022 S State St, Tacoma WA 98405, USA — Boxer

**Jackson, Jonathan**
Echo Lake Management, 421 S Beverly Dr, #800, Beverly Hills CA 90212, USA — Actor

**Jackson, Joshua**
Anonymous Content, 3532 Hayden Ave, Culver City CA 90232 USA — Actor

**Jackson, Julian**
Sugar Estate Branc, PO Box 10246, Charlotte Amalie VI 00801, USA — Boxer

**Jackson, Kate**
Greater Talent Network, 437 5th Ave, #700, New York NY 10016, USA — Actress

**Jackson, Keith J**
PO Box 241695, Little Rock AR 72223, USA — Football Player

**Jackson, Keith M**
ABC-TV, Sports Dept, 77 W 66th St, New York NY 10023 USA — Sportscaster

**Jackson, Kenneth B (Ken)**
PO Box 613, Waskom TX 75692, USA — Baseball Player

**Jackson, Kevin**
7215 Montarbor Dr, Colorado Springs CO 80918, USA — Freestyle Wrestler

**Jackson, Kirby**
3575 Candytuft Run, Auburn GA 30011, USA — Football Player

**Jackson, Larron D**
20000 Mitchell Place, #56, Denver CO 80249, USA — Football Player

**Jackson, Larry R**
Grain Millers Federation, 14115 Lincoln St NE, #200, Andover MN 55304, USA — Labor Leader

**Jackson, LaToya**
Chuck Jones Public Relations, 150 W 51st, #802, New York NY 10019, USA — Singer, Model

**Jackson, Lauren**
Seattle Storm, Key Arena, 351 Elliott Ave W, #500, Seattle WA 98119 USA — Basketball Player

**Jackson, Lillian**
1050 W Camino Velesquez, Green Valley AZ 85622, USA — Baseball Player

**Jackson, Lisa**
Signet Books, 375 Hudson St, New York NY 10014 USA — Writer

**Jackson, Lucious B (Luke)**
4580 Cartwright St, Beaumont TX 77707, USA — Basketball Player

**Jackson, Luke R**
7711 County Road 511, Rosharon TX 77583, USA — Basketball Player

**Jackson, Mannie**
Harlem Globetrotters, 400 E Van Buren, #300, Phoenix AZ 85004, USA — Basketball Player, Executive

**Jackson, Mark A**
25548 Kingston Court, Calabassas CA 91302, USA — Basketball Player, Coach

**Jackson, Mark A**
2585 E Flamingo Road, Las Vegas NV 89101, USA — Football Player

**Jackson, Mary Ann**
30108 Village 30, #30, Camarillo CA 93012, USA — Actress

**Jackson, Matthew Day**
Hauser & Wirth, 32 E 69th St, New York NY 10021, USA — Artist

**Jackson, Mel**
101 E 119th St, #2D, New York NY 10035, USA — Actor

**Jackson, Melvin (Mel), Jr**
4345 Enoro Dr, Los Angeles CA 90008, USA — Football Player

**Jackson, Mervin P (Merv)**
16638 Kildare Court, Tinley Park IL 60477, USA — Basketball Player

**Jackson, Michael A**
PO Box 473, Tangiaphoa LA 70465, USA — Football Player

**Jackson, Michael D (Mike)**
P A Consulting Group, 123 Buckingham Palace Road, London SW1W 9SR, England — Army General, England

**Jackson, Michael R (Mike)** — Baseball Player
17214 Oak Dale Dr, Spring TX 77379, USA
**Jackson, Mick** — Director
1349 Berea Place, Pacific Palisades CA 90272, USA
**Jackson, Millie** — Singer, Songwriter, Actress
Associated Booking Corp, 501 Madison Ave, #501, New York NY 10022 USA
**Jackson, Monte C** — Football Player
7646 Westbrook Ave, San Diego CA 92139, USA
**Jackson, Noah D** — Football Player
1640 Milburne Road, Lake Forest IL 60045, USA
**Jackson, Peter** — Director, Producer
Park Road Post, 141 Park Road, PO Box 15132, Miramar, Wellington 6022, New Zealand
**Jackson, Philip** — Actor
Markham Froggatt Irwin, Julian House, 4 Windmill St, London W1P 1HF, England
**Jackson, Philip D (Phil)** — Basketball Player, Coach
18942 Medicine Rock Lane, Lakeside MT 59922, USA
**Jackson, Quinton (Rampage)** — Ultimate Fighter, Actor
Roar Mgmt, 9701 Wilshire Blvd, #800, Beverly Hills CA 90212 USA
**Jackson, R Graham** — Architect
Calhoun Tungate Jackson Dill Architects, 6200 Savoy Dr, Houston TX 77036, USA
**Jackson, Ralph A** — Basketball Player
3235 W 11th Place, Inglewood CA 90303, USA
**Jackson, Randall B (Randy)** — Football Player
747 Musago Run, Lake Mary FL 32746, USA
**Jackson, Randall D (Randy)** — Bassist, Entertainer
Dream Merchant 21 Entertainment, 1416 N La Brea Ave, Hollywood CA 90028, USA
**Jackson, Ransom J (Randy)** — Baseball Player
250 Hunnicutt Dr, Athens GA 30606, USA
**Jackson, Rebbie** — Singer, Songwriter
Groove Entertainment, 1005 N Alfred St, #2, West Hollywood CA 90069, USA
**Jackson, Reginald M (Reggie)** — Baseball Player
305 Amador Ave, Seaside CA 93955, USA
**Jackson, Richard Lee** — Actor
1815 Butler Ave, #120, Los Angeles CA 90025, USA
**Jackson, Rickey A** — Football Player
3701 Lake Catherine Dr, Harvey LA 70058, USA
**Jackson, Robert C (Bobby)** — Football Player
47 Tippin Dr, Huntington Station NY 11746, USA
**Jackson, Roland T (Sonny)** — Baseball Player
117 Palm Bay Dr, #B, Palm Beach Gardens FL 33418, USA
**Jackson, Roy Lee** — Baseball Player
8269 Lee Road 54, Auburn AL 36830, USA
**Jackson, S Randall (Randy)** — Singer
Big J Productions, 854 Florida Blvd, New Orleans LA 70124 USA
**Jackson, Samuel L** — Actor
Anonymous Content, 3532 Hayden Ave, Culver City CA 90232 USA
**Jackson, Sharisse (Shar)** — Actress, Singer
Sovereign Talent Group, 8421 Wilshire Blvd, #200, Beverly Hills CA 90211, USA
**Jackson, Sherry** — Actress
13082 Mindanao Way, #54, Marina Del Rey CA 90292, USA
**Jackson, Shirley Ann** — Educator, Theoretical Physicist
Rensselaer Polytechnic Institute, President's Office, Troy NY 12180, USA
**Jackson, Stephen J** — Basketball Player
10541 Titan Run, Carmel IN 46032, USA
**Jackson, Steven W (Steve)** — Football Player
43752 Lees Mill Square, Leesburg VA 20176, USA
**Jackson, Stonewall** — Singer, Guitarist, Songwriter
6007 Cloverland Dr, Brentwood TN 37027, USA
**Jackson, Stoney** — Actor
1602 N Fuller Ave, #102, Los Angeles CA 90046, USA
**Jackson, Stu** — Basketball Coach, Executive
National Basketball Assn, 645 5th Ave, #1900, New York NY 10022, USA
**Jackson, Tarvaris F** — Football Player
11171 Sun Center Dr, #290, Rancho Cordova CA 95670, USA
**Jackson, Terence L (Terry)** — Football Player
2269 Glenmore Terrace, Rockville MD 20850, USA
**Jackson, Thomas (Tom)** — Football Player, Sportscaster
7475 Brill Road, Cincinnati OH 45243, USA
**Jackson, Tiffany** — Basketball Player
Tulsa Shock, B O K Center, 200 S Denver, Tulsa OK 74103 USA
**Jackson, Tito** — Singer (Jackson Five)
2467 Taylor Ave, Corona CA 92882, USA
**Jackson, Tony** — Basketball Player
1009 Trevey Point, Lexington KY 40515, USA
**Jackson, Tracey** — Writer
Arlook Group, 205 S Beverly Drive, #209, Beverly Hills CA 90212, USA
**Jackson, Trina** — Swimmer
9271 Saltwater Way, Jacksonville FL 32256, USA
**Jackson, Tyoka** — Football Player
16312 Birkdale Dr, Odessa FL 33556, USA
**Jackson, Vestee, II** — Football Player
2800 S Eastern Ave, #410, Las Vegas NV 89169, USA
**Jackson, Victoria** — Actress, Comedienne
Breen Agency, 25 Music Square W, Nashville TN 37203, USA
**Jackson, Vincent** — Football Player
Tampa Bay Buccaneers, 1 W Buccaneer Place, Tampa FL 33607 USA
**Jackson, Vincent E (Bo)** — Football, Baseball Player
100 Oak Ridge Dr, Burr Ridge IL 60527, USA
**Jackson, Wanda** — Singer
Wanda Jackson Enterprises, 11700 S Western Ave, Oklahoma City OK 73170, USA
**Jackson, Wardell** — Basketball Player
PO Box 164142, Columbus OH 43216, USA
**Jackson, Wilbur** — Football Player
PO Box 1571, Ozark AL 36361, USA
**Jackson, Willie B, Jr** — Football Player
PO Box 12643, Gainesville FL 32604, USA

Jackson - Jackson

**Jackson, Zachary T (Zach)** — Baseball Player
7630 Menler Dr, Austin TX 78735, USA
**Jaco, Charles** — Commentator, Writer
PO Box 220182, Saint Louis MO 63122, USA
**Jacob, Irene** — Actress
Paradigm Agency, 360 N Crescent Dr, North Building, Beverly Hills CA 90210 USA
**Jacob, Jacob-Farj-Rafael (J F R)** — Army General, India
Roli Press, M-75 Greater Kailash 2 Market, New Delhi 110048, India
**Jacob, John E** — Civil Rights Activist
Anheuser-Busch, 1 Busch Place, Saint Louis MO 63118, USA
**Jacob, Stanley W** — Surgeon
1055 SW Westwood Court, Portland OR 97239, USA
**Jacobellis, Lindsey** — Snowboard Athlete
30648 E Ski Bowl Way, Government Camp OR 97028, USA
**Jacobi, Derek G** — Actor
Independent Talent Group, 40 Whitfield St, London W1T 2RH, England
**Jacobi, Doreen** — Actress
Agentur Breilmann, Toppenstedter Kirchweg 11, 21376 Salzhausen, Germany
**Jacobi, Walter** — Space Scientist
2004 Max Luther Dr NW, #419, Huntsville AL 35810, USA
**Jacobs, Allen W** — Football Player
3050 Tolcate Lane, Salt Lake City UT 84121, USA
**Jacobs, Arnold S (A J), Jr** — Writer
Simon & Schuster, 1230 Ave of Americas, Concourse 1, New York NY 10020 USA
**Jacobs, Brad** — Curling Athlete
Curling Association, 1660 Vimont Court, Cumberland ON K4A 4J4, Canada
**Jacobs, Brandon** — Football Player
New York Giants, Meadowlands Stadium, 102 Route 120, East Rutherford NJ 07073 USA
**Jacobs, David J (Dave)** — Football Player
8388 Glen Eagle Dr, Manlius NY 13104, USA
**Jacobs, Debbie** — Singer
T-Best Talent Agency, 508 Honey Lake Court, Danville CA 94506 USA
**Jacobs, Dennis G** — Judge
US Appeals Court, Moynihan Courthouse, 500 Pearl St, New York NY 10007, USA
**Jacobs, Gillian** — Actress
United Talent Agency, U T A Plaza, 9336 Civic Center Dr, Beverly Hills CA 90210 USA
**Jacobs, Glenn** — Professional Wrestler
World Wrestling Entertainment, Titan Towers, 1241 E Main St, Stamford CT 06902 USA
**Jacobs, H Ray** — Football Player
2402 W 5th Ave, Corsicana TX 75110, USA
**Jacobs, Harry E** — Football Player
108 Lenora Dr, Hamburg NY 14075, USA
**Jacobs, Howard L** — Attorney
Forgie Jacobs Leonard, 4165 E Thousand Oaks Blvd, Westlake Village CA 91362, USA
**Jacobs, Irwin M** — Businessman
Qualcomm Inc, 5775 Morehouse Dr, San Diego CA 92121, USA
**Jacobs, Jack H** — Vietnam War Army Hero (CMH)
Bankers Trust Co, 1 Appold St, London EC2A 2HE, England
**Jacobs, Jeremy M** — Businessman, Hockey Executive
1300 N Davis Road, East Aurora NY 14052, USA
**Jacobs, Jim** — Writer, Composer, Actor
Ronald Taft, 18 W 55th St, New York NY 10019, USA
**Jacobs, Julien I** — Judge
US Tax Court, 400 2nd St NW, Washington DC 20217, USA
**Jacobs, Kate** — Singer, Guitarist, Songwriter
East Central One, All Saints Road, Suffolk 1P6 8PR, England
**Jacobs, Katie** — Writer, Producer
Heel & Toe Films, 2058 Broadway, Santa Monica CA 90404, USA
**Jacobs, Lawrence-Hilton** — Actor
PO Box 67905, Los Angeles CA 90067, USA
**Jacobs, Lloyd A** — Educator
University of Toledo, President's Office, 2801 W Bancroft, Toledo OH 43606, USA
**Jacobs, Marc** — Fashion Designer
72 Spring St, New York NY 10012, USA
**Jacobs, Michael J (Mike)** — Baseball Player
1583 Hikers Trail Dr, Chula Vista CA 91915, USA
**Jacobs, Paul E** — Businessman
Qualcomm, 5775 Morehouse Dr, San Diego CA 92121, USA
**Jacobs, Proverb G** — Football Player
4369 Detroit Ave, Oakland CA 94619, USA
**Jacobs, Robert Nathan** — Writer
Gersh Agency, 9465 Wilshire Blvd, #600, Beverly Hills CA 90212 USA
**Jacobs, Taylor H** — Football Player
8083 Longmeadow Dr, Tallahassee FL 32312, USA
**Jacobs, Timothy J (Tim)** — Football Player
7306 Finns Lane, Lanham MD 20706, USA
**Jacobsen, Anders** — Ski Jumper
Ringkollen Skilubb, Owrensgt 28, 3510 Honefoss, Norway
**Jacobsen, Casey G** — Basketball Player
24622 Cresta Court, Laguna Hills CA 92653, USA
**Jacobsen, Hugh Newell** — Architect
Hugh Newell Jacobsen Architect, 2529 P St NW, Washington DC 20007, USA
**Jacobsen, Peter** — Golfer
27771 Marina Pointe Dr, Bonita Springs FL 34134, USA
**Jacobsen, Stephanie** — Actress
1 Mgmt, 9000 W Sunset Blvd, #1550, Los Angeles CA 90069 USA
**Jacobs-Lorena, Marcelo** — Molecular Microbiologist
Johns Hopkins University, Malaria Research Institute, Baltimore MD 21218, USA
**Jacobson, D D** — Bowler
8261 Rees St, Playa del Rey CA 90293, USA
**Jacobson, Danny** — Writer
Brillstein Entertainment Partners, 9150 Wilshire Blvd, #350, Beverly Hills CA 90212 USA
**Jacobson, Herbert L** — Diplomat, Journalist
Apartado 160, Escazu, Costa Rica
**Jacobson, Nina** — Producer
Color Force, 1524 Cloverfield Blvd, #C, Santa Monica CA 90404, USA

**Jacobson, Peter** — Actor
Innovative Artists, 235 Park Ave S, #1000, New York NY 10003 USA
**Jacoby, Brook W** — Baseball Player
21825 N Dobson Road, Scottsdale AZ 85255, USA
**Jacoby, Charles H, Jr** — Army General
Commander, US Northern Command, Peterson Air Force Base CO 80914 USA
**Jacoby, Joe** — Football Player
Jacoby Jeep/Eagle/Chrysler, 7308 Cedar Run Dr, Warrenton VA 20187, USA
**Jacoby, Mark** — Actor, Singer
TalentWorks, 3500 W Olive Ave, #1400, Burbank CA 91505 USA
**Jacoby, Scott** — Actor, Director, Writer
PO Box 5569, Sherman Oaks CA 91413, USA
**Jacome, Jason J** — Baseball Player
5115 N Camino Esplendora, Tucson AZ 85718, USA
**Jacot, Christopher** — Actor
Characters Talent Mgmt, 8 Elm St, Toronto ON M5G 1G7, Canada
**Jacot, Michele** — Alpine Skier
Residence du Brevent, 74 Chamonix, France
**Jacott, Carlos** — Actor
Thruline Entertainment, 9250 Wilshire Blvd, #100, Beverly Hills CA 90212 USA
**Jacox, Kendyl L** — Football Player
50 Schubach Dr, Sugar Land, TX 77479, USA
**Jacquemard, Simonne** — Writer
Le Verdier, 24520 Sireuil, France
**Jacques, Russell K** — Sculptor
38 Drake St, Newport Beach CA 92663, USA
**Jacquot, Benoit** — Director
Voyez Mon Agent, 20 Ave Rapp, 75007 Paris, France
**Jaczko, Gregory B** — Government Official
US Nuclear Regulatory Commission, Mail Stop 0-16G4, Washington DC 20555, USA
**Jadakiss** — Rap Artist (Ruff Ryders)
J Erving Group, 154 Krog St, #130, Atlanta GA 30307, USA
**Jaeckin, Just** — Director, Writer
Galerie Anne et Just Jaeckin, 19 Rue Guenegaud, 75006 Paris, France
**Jaeger, Aaron** — Actor
Allegory Creative Management, 13261 Moorpark St, #103, Sherman Oaks CA 91423, USA
**Jaeger, Andrea** — Tennis Player
Kids Stuff Foundation, Silver Lining Ranch, 1490 S Ute Ave, Aspen CO 81611, USA
**Jaeger, Jeff T** — Football Player
3026 Sahalee Dr W, Sammamish WA 98074, USA
**Jaeger, Sam** — Actor
Greene Assoc, 1901 Ave of Stars, #130, Los Angeles CA 90067 USA
**Jaeggi, Andreas** — Opera Singer
I M G Artists, Hogarth Business Park, Chiswick, London W4 2TH, England
**Jaenicke, Hannes** — Actor
Rough Diamond Mgmt, 1424 N Kings Road, Los Angeles CA 90069, USA
**Jaenisch, Rudolf** — Biologist
Massachusetts Institute of Technology, Biology Dept, 9 Cambridge Center, Cambridge MA 02142, USA
**Jaffe, Arthur M** — Mathematical Physicist
27 Lancaster St, Cambridge MA 02140, USA
**Jaffe, Harold W** — Epidemiologist
Centers for Disease Control, 1600 Clifton Road NE, Atlanta GA 30329 USA
**Jaffe, Robert L** — Theoretical Physicist
Massachusetts Institute of Technology, Physics Dept, Cambridge MA 02139, USA
**Jaffe, Stanley R** — Producer, Director
152 W 57th St, #5200F, New York NY 10019, USA
**Jaffe, Susan** — Ballerina
American Ballet Theatre, 890 Broadway, #300, New York NY 10003 USA
**Jaffrey, Raza** — Actor
United Agents, 12-26 Lexington St, London W1F 0LE, England
**Jaffrey, Saeed** — Actor, Comedian
503 Sejal New Link Road, Andheri, Mumbai MS 400058, India
**Jagendorf, Andre T** — Plant Physiologist
455 Savage Farm Dr, Ithaca NY 14850, USA
**Jager, Thomas (Tom)** — Swimmer
1416 Chinook St, Moscow ID 83843, USA
**Jagge, Finn Christian** — Alpine Skier
Michelets Vei 108, 1320 Stabekk, Norway
**Jagger, Bianca** — Actress, Model
Bianca Jagger Human Rights Foundation, 272 Kensington High St, #246, London, W8 6ND, England
**Jagger, Elizabeth (Lizzy)** — Model
Tess Mgmt, 9-10 Market Place, #400, London W1W 8AQ, England
**Jagger, Michael (Mick)** — Singer (Rolling Stones)
Jagged Films, 1041 N Formosa Ave, West Hollywood CA 90046, USA
**Jagland, Thorbjoern** — Prime Minister, Norway
Stortinget, Karl Johans Gate 22, 0026 Oslo, Norway
**Jaglom, Henry** — Director
9165 W Sunset Blvd, #300, West Hollywood CA 90069, USA
**Jagr, Jaromir** — Ice Hockey Player
New Jersey Devils, Arena, 50 State Route 120, East Rutherford NJ 07073 USA
**Jaha, John E** — Baseball Player
9494 SE Chatfield Court, Happy Valley OR 97086, USA
**Jahan, Marine** — Actress, Dancer
Media Artists Group, 8222 Melrose Ave, #203, Los Angeles CA 90048 USA
**Jaheim** — Singer
Universal Attractions, 135 W 26th St, #1200, New York NY 10001 USA
**Jahn, Helmut** — Architect
Murphy/Jahn, 33 E Wacker Dr, #300, Chicago IL 60601, USA
**Jahn, Robert G** — Aeronautical Engineer
Princeton University, Aerospace Sciences Dept, Princeton NJ 08544, USA
**Jahn, Sigmund** — Cosmonaut, East Germany; General
Fontanestr 35, 15344 Strausberg, Germany
**Jaidah, Ali Mohammed** — Government Official, Qatar
Qatar Petroleum Corp, PO Box 3212, Doha, Qatar
**Jakel, Bernd** — Yachtsman
Salvador-Allende-Str 48, 12559 Berlin, Germany

**Jakes - James**

| | |
|---|---|
| **Jakes, John**<br>445 Meadow Lark Dr, Sarasota FL 34236, USA | Writer |
| **Jakes, T D**<br>T D Jakes Ministries, PO Box 763518, Dallas TX 75376, USA | Religious Leader |
| **Jakes, Van K**<br>305 Worthing Lane, McDonough GA 30253, USA | Football Player |
| **Jakobs, Marco**<br>Oststr 1B, 59427 Unna, Germany | Bobsled Athlete |
| **Jakobsson, Johan M**<br>Aalborg Handbold, Willy Brandts Vej 31, 9220 Aalborg Ost, Denmark | Handball Player |
| **Jakopin, John**<br>57 Samana Dr, Miami FL 33133, USA | Ice Hockey Player |
| **Jakosits, Michael**<br>Karlsbergstr 140, 66424 Homburg/Saar, Germany | Marksman |
| **Jakub, Lisa**<br>Lafeaver Talent, 785 Carlaw Ave, #101, Toronto ON M4K 3L1, Canada | Actress |
| **Jakubowicz, Jonathan**<br>Creative Artists Agency, 2000 Ave of Stars, #100, Los Angeles CA 90067 USA | Director, Producer, Writer |
| **Jalal, Farida**<br>3B Nandini Unik Housing Society, Andheri, Mumbai MS 400058, India | Actress |
| **Jalali, Bahram**<br>University of California, Electrical Engineering Dept, Los Angeles CA 90024, USA | Electrical Engineer |
| **Jamail, Joseph D, Jr**<br>Jamail & Kolius, 500 Dallas St, #3434, Houston TX 77002, USA | Attorney |
| **Jamal, Ahmad**<br>Ellora Mgmt, PO Box 755, 11 Brook St, Lakeville CT 06039, USA | Jazz Pianist |
| **Jamelia**<br>Roar Global Entertainment, 34-35 Eastcastle St, Oxford Circus, London W1W 8DW, England | Singer, Songwriter |
| **James, Aaron (A J)**<br>3057 Orrin Ave, Youngstown OH 44505, USA | Basketball Player |
| **James, Anthony**<br>C N A Assoc, 1875 Century Park East, #2250, Los Angeles CA 90067 USA | Actor |
| **James, Arthur (Art)**<br>6935 Brown Dr S, Fairburn GA 30213, USA | Baseball Player |
| **James, Boney**<br>Direct Management Group, 947 N La Cienega Blvd, #G, West Hollywood CA 90069, USA | Saxophonist, Songwriter |
| **James, Bradie D**<br>2509 Silver Table Dr, Lewisville TX 75056, USA | Football Player |
| **James, Brett**<br>Starstruck Entertainment, 40 Music Square W, Nashville TN 37203, USA | Singer, Guitarist, Songwriter |
| **James, Brian D'Arcy**<br>Thruline Entertainment, 9250 Wilshire Blvd, #100, Beverly Hills CA 90212 USA | Actor |
| **James, Charity**<br>C E S D, 10635 Santa Monica Blvd, #130, Los Angeles CA 90025 USA | Actress |
| **James, Charmayne**<br>Gold Buckle Ranch, 2100 N Highway 360, #1207, Grand Prairie TX 75050, USA | Rodeo Rider |
| **James, Cheryl (Salt)**<br>Entertainment Artists, 2409 21st Ave S, #100, Nashville TN 10019 USA | Rap Artist (Salt'N'Pepa) |
| **James, Clifton**<br>500 W 43rd St, #26J, New York NY 10036, USA | Actor |
| **James, Colton**<br>James/Levy Mgmt, 3500 W Olive Ave, #1470, Burbank CA 91505 USA | Actor |
| **James, D Christopher (Chris)**<br>1040 County Road 2707, Alto TX 75925, USA | Baseball Player |
| **James, D Clayton**<br>106 Wagon Wheel Trail, Moneta VA 24121, USA | Historian |
| **James, Daniel J, III**<br>Director, Air National Guard, HqUSAF, Pentagon, Washington DC 20330, USA | Air Force General |
| **James, Dion**<br>5 Shelter Point Court, Sacramento CA 95831, USA | Baseball Player |
| **James, Donald M**<br>Vulcan Materials Co, 1200 Urban Center Dr, Birmingham AL 35242, USA | Businessman |
| **James, E L**<br>Vintage Books, 1745 Broadway, New York NY 10019 USA | Writer |
| **James, Edgerrin T**<br>709 Hendry St, Immokalee FL 34142, USA | Football Player |
| **James, Elgin**<br>W M E Entertainment, 9601 Wilshire Blvd, #300, Beverly Hills CA 90210 USA | Director, Writer, Actor |
| **James, Eloisa**<br>Mary Bly, Fordham University, English Dept, Lincoln Center Campus, New York NY 10023, USA | Writer |
| **James, Forrest H (Fob), Jr**<br>39 Alabama Road, Lehigh Acres FL 33936, USA | Governor, AL |
| **James, Frances C**<br>Florida State University, Biological Sciences Dept, Tallahassee FL 32306, USA | Biologist |
| **James, G William (Bill)**<br>625 Ohio St, Lawrence KS 66044, USA | Baseball Writer, Statistician |
| **James, Geraldine**<br>Denville Hall, 62 Ducks Hill Road, Northwood, Middlesex HA6 2SB, England | Actress |
| **James, Godfrey**<br>Shack, Western Road, Pevensey Bay, East Sussex BN23 6HG, England | Actor |
| **James, Henry C**<br>527 E Leith St, Fort Wayne IN 46806, USA | Basketball Player |
| **James, J Craig**<br>12714 W FM 455, Celina TX 75009, USA | Football Player, Sportscaster |
| **James, James (Boney)**<br>Direct Mgmt Group, 947 N La Cienega Blvd, #G, West Hollywood CA 90069, USA | Jazz Saxophonist |
| **James, Jenorris (Jeno)**<br>1620 NW 117th Ave, Plantation FL 33323, USA | Football Player |
| **James, Jesse**<br>Dino May Mgmt, 6362 Hollywood Blvd, #PH 422, Los Angeles CA 90028, USA | Actor |
| **James, Jesse G**<br>West Coast Choppers, 718 W Anaheim St, Long Beach CA 90813, USA | Producer |
| **James, Jessica R (Jessie)**<br>Show Dog/Universal Music, 2303 21st Ave S, #400, Nashville TN 37212, USA | Singer, Songwriter |
| **James, Jim**<br>A T O Records, 44 Wall St, #2300, New York NY 10005, USA | Singer, Guitarist (My Morning Jacket) |

**James, Jimmy** — Singer (Jimmy James & the Vagabonds)
Barry Collings Entertainments, PO Box 1151, Saint Albans, Herthshire AL1 9WB, England
**James, John** — Actor
PO Box 9, Cambridge NY 12816, USA
**James, John P (Johnny)** — Baseball Player
6037 E Larkspur Dr, Scottsdale AZ 85254, USA
**James, John W, Jr** — Football Player
23108 NE 69th Ave, Melrose FL 32666, USA
**James, Joni** — Singer
Silent Angels Productions, 439 E 74th St, #5FW, New York NY 10021, USA
**James, Kate** — Model
Men/Women Model Inc, 199 Lafayette St, New York NY 10012, USA
**James, Kevin, III** — Illusionist, Actor
Jeff Sussman Mgmt, 603 W 115th St, #282, New York NY 10025, USA
**James, LeBron R** — Basketball Player
Cleveland Cavaliers, Gund Arena, 1 Center Court, Cleveland OH 44115 USA
**James, Leela** — Singer, Songwriter
R K D Music Mgmt, PO Box 11611, Beverly Hills CA 90213, USA
**James, Lennie** — Actor
Principal Entertainment, 130 W 42nd St, #614, New York NY 10036, USA
**James, Liam** — Actor
Gersh Agency, 9465 Wilshire Blvd, #600, Beverly Hills CA 90212 USA
**James, Lionel** — Football Player
199 Woodbury Dr, Sterret AL 35147, USA
**James, M William (Billy)** — Basketball Player
12 S Sunset Dr, Lexington IN 47138, USA
**James, Marco** — Actor
Don Buchwald Talent Agency, 6500 Wilshire Blvd, #2200, Los Angeles CA 90048 USA
**James, Marianne** — Jazz Guitarist, Composer
89 Ave Charles de Gaulle, 92575 Neuilly-sur-Seine Cedex, France
**James, Michael E (Mike)** — Baseball Player
115 Austin Court, Mary Esther FL 32569, USA
**James, Oliver** — Actor
Independent Talent Group, 40 Whitfield St, London W1T 2RH, England
**James, Oliver** — Psychologist, Writer
Gillon Aitken Assoc, 18-21 Cavaye Place, London SW10 9PT, England
**James, P D** — Writer
Greene & Heaton Ltd, 37A Goldhawk Road, London W12 8QQ, England
**James, Pell** — Actress
Creative Artists Agency, 2000 Ave of Stars, #100, Los Angeles CA 90067 USA
**James, Robert (Bob)** — Jazz Keyboardist (Bob James Trio)
Monterey International, 200 W Superior St, #202, Chicago IL 60654 USA
**James, Robert D** — Football Player
1511 N Highland Ave, Murfreesboro TN 37130, USA
**James, Robert H (Bob)** — Baseball Player
15844 Cindy Court, Canyon Country CA 91387, USA
**James, Roland O** — Football Player
19 Spring Lane, Sharon MA 02067, USA
**James, Shannon** — Model
Playboy Promotions, 9346 Civic Center Dr, #200, Beverly Hills CA 90210 USA
**James, Sheryl** — Journalist
Saint Petersburg Times, Editorial Dept, 490 1st Ave, Saint Petersburg FL 33701, USA
**James, Sonny** — Singer, Guitarist, Songwriter
W M E Entertainment, 1600 Division St, #300, Nashville TN 37203 USA
**James, Thomas (Tom)** — Rowing Athlete
Molesey Boat Club, Barge Walk, East Molesey, Surrey KT8 9AJ, England
**James, Tommy** — Singer (Shondells)
Paradise Artists, PO Box 1821, Ojai CA 93024 USA
**James, Tory S** — Football Player
70 N Gary Glen Circle, Spring TX 77382, USA
**James-Collier, Rob** — Actor
Rights House, Drury House, 34-43 Russell St, London WC2B 5HA, England
**James-Kuehl, Sheila** — Actress
3201 Pearl St, Santa Monica CA 90405, USA
**Jameson, Keith** — Opera Singer
Columbia Artists Mgmt Inc, 5 Columbus Circle, 1790 Broadway, #1600, New York NY 10019 USA
**Jameson, Nick** — Actor
Danis Panaro Nist, 9201 W Olympic Blvd, Beverly Hills CA 90212, USA
**James-Rodman, Charmayne** — Rodeo Rider
General Delivery, Clayton NM 88415, USA
**Jamieson, Janet** — Baseball Player
6324 212th St SW, #3, Lynnwood WA 98036, USA
**Jamieson, John K** — Businessman
10313 Stanley Circle, Minneapolis MN 55437, USA
**Jamieson, Michael** — Swimmer
University of Bath, Sports Development Dept, Claverton Down, Bath BA2 7AY, England
**Jamison, Antawn C** — Basketball Player
6041 Providence Country Club Dr, Charlotte NC 28277, USA
**Jamison, George R, Jr** — Football Player
3430 Vineyard Hill Dr, Rochester MI 48306, USA
**Jamison, Judith** — Dancer, Choreographer
Alvin Ailey American Dance Foundation, 405 W 55th St, New York NY 10019, USA
**Jammeh, Yahya A J J** — Head of State, Gambia; Army Officer
President's Office, Private Mail Bag, State House, Banjul, Gambia
**Jammer, Quentin T** — Football Player
7815 Sendero Angelica, San Diego CA 92127, USA
**Jampolsky, Gerald** — Writer
Celestial Arts, 6001 Shellmound St, #400, Emeryville CA 94608, USA
**Janas, Elizabeth** — Actress
Don Buchwald Talent Agency, 6500 Wilshire Blvd, #2200, Los Angeles CA 90048 USA
**Janaszak, Steve** — Ice Hockey Player
42 Montrose Ave, Babylon NY 11702, USA
**Jance, J A** — Writer
William Morrow, 1350 Ave of Americas, New York NY 10019, USA
**Janda, Krystyna** — Actress
Teatr Powszechny, Ul Zamoyskiego 20, 03801 Warsaw, Poland

**J**

**James - Janda**

# J

**Jane, Thomas** — Actor
Paradigm Agency, 360 N Crescent Dr, North Building, Beverly Hills CA 90210 USA

**Janes, Dominic** — Actor
Rising Talent Mgmt, 137 S Spalding Drive, #406, Beverly Hills CA 90212, USA

**Janetti, Gary** — Producer, Writer
W M E Entertainment, 9601 Wilshire Blvd, #300, Beverly Hills CA 90210 USA

**Janeway, Richard** — Physician
PO Box 188, Blowing Rock NC 28605, USA

**Jang, Jeong (J J)** — Golfer
8749 The Esplanade, #33, Orlando FL 32836, USA

**Janic, Adrienne** — Actress
Bleu Entertainment, 5225 Wilshire Blvd, #401, Los Angeles CA 90036, USA

**Janics, Natasa Dusev-** — Canoeing Athlete
E D F Demas Szeged, PF 199, 6701 Szeged, Hungary

**Janikowski, Damian** — Greco-Roman Wrestler
Turn-Und Sportverein Adelhausen, Fahrestr 22, 79618 Rheinfelden, Germany

**Janikowski, Sebastian** — Football Player
11958 Brady Road, Jacksonville FL 32223, USA

**Janis, Byron** — Concert Pianist
Phillips Records, 810 7th Ave, New York NY 10019 USA

**Janis, Conrad** — Actor, Jazz Trombonist
Feminine Touch, 300 N Swall Dr, #251, Beverly Hills CA 90211, USA

**Janish, Paul R** — Baseball Player
11926 Deep Woods Dr, Cypress TX 77429, USA

**Janitz, John A** — Businessman
Textron Inc, 40 Westminster St, #500, Providence RI 02903, USA

**Janka, Carlo** — Alpine Skier
Miraniga, 7134 Obersaxen, Switzerland

**Jankovic, Jelena** — Tennis Player
Octagon Worldwide, 1751 Pinnacle Dr, #1500, McLean VA 22102 USA

**Jankovic, Joseph** — Neurologist
Baylor College of Medicine, Neurology Dept, Baylor Plaza, Houston TX 77030, USA

**Jankowska-Cieslak, Jadwiga** — Actress
Film Polski, Ul Mazewiecka 6/8, 00950 Warsaw, Poland

**Jankowski, Gene F** — Businessman
American Film Institute, 901 15th St NW, #700, Washington DC 20005, USA

**Jankowski, Peter** — Producer
United Talent Agency, U T A Plaza, 9336 Civic Center Dr, Beverly Hills CA 90210 USA

**Jann, Michael Patrick** — Director, Producer, Actor
Creative Artists Agency, 2000 Ave of Stars, #100, Los Angeles CA 90067 USA

**Jannazzo, Izzy** — Boxer
6924 62nd Ave, Middle Village NY 11379, USA

**Janney, Allison** — Actress
Gersh Agency, 9465 Wilshire Blvd, #600, Beverly Hills CA 90212 USA

**Janney, Craig H** — Ice Hockey Player
6424 E Exeter Blvd, Scottsdale AZ 85251, USA

**Jannot, Mark** — Editor
Popular Science, Editorial Dept, 2 Park Ave, #900, New York NY 10016, USA

**Janotta, Howard (Howie)** — Basketball Player
18118 Brookwood Forest, San Antonio TX 78258, USA

**Janov, Arthur** — Psychologist, Psychotherapist
1205 Abbot Kinney Blvd, Venice CA 90291, USA

**Janovitz, Bill** — Singer, Guitarist (Buffalo Tom)
Agency Group Ltd, 142 W 57th St, #600, New York NY 10019 USA

**Janowicz, Josh** — Actor
1 Mgmt, 9000 W Sunset Blvd, #1550, Los Angeles CA 90069 USA

**Janowitz, Gundula** — Opera Singer
3072 Kasten 75, Austria

**Janowitz, Tama** — Writer
Random House, 1745 Broadway, #1800, New York NY 10019 USA

**Janowski, Marek** — Conductor
Columbia Artists Mgmt Inc, 5 Columbus Circle, 1790 Broadway, #1600, New York NY 10019 USA

**Jansa, Janez** — Prime Minister, Slovenia
Prime Minister's Office, Gregorcicova St 20, 61000 Ljubljana, Slovenia

**Jansch, Heather** — Artist
Knowle, Rundlerohy, Newton Abbot, Devon TQ12 2PJ, England

**Jansen, Daniel E (Dan)** — Speed Skater
PO Box 3354, Mooresville NC 28117, USA

**Jansen, Janine** — Concert Violinist
Harrison/Parrott, 5-6 Albion Court, London W6 0QT, England

**Janson, Karin Stahre** — Cruise Ship Captain
Royal Carribean International, 1111 S Arroyo Parkway, #450, Pasadena CA 91105, USA

**Jansons, Mariss** — Conductor
Opus 3 Artists, 470 Park Ave S, #900N, New York NY 10016 USA

**Jansrud, Kjetil** — Alpine Skier
Vinstra, 2640 Gudbrandsdalen, Norway

**Janssen, Daniel** — Businessman
La Ronciere, 108 Ave Ernest Solvay, 1310 La Hulpe, Belgium

**Janssen, Famke** — Actress, Model
Brookside Artists Mgmt, 250 W 57th St, #2303, New York NY 10107 USA

**Janssen, Marlene** — Model, Actress
Playboy Promotions, 9346 Civic Center Dr, #200, Beverly Hills CA 90210 USA

**Janssen, Tom** — Editorial Cartoonist
Prinsengract 304, 1016 Amsterdam HW, Netherlands

**Janssens, Mark** — Ice Hockey Player
115 Central Park W, #17A, New York NY 10023, USA

**Jantz, Richard** — Anthropologist
University of Tennessee, Anthropology Dept, Knoxville TN 37996, USA

**January, Briann J** — Basketball Player
Indiana Fever, Conseco Fieldhouse, 125 S Pennsylvania, Indianapolis IN 46204 USA

**January, Donald R (Don)** — Golfer
5006 Village Place, Dallas TX 75248, USA

**Jany, Alexandre (Alex)** — Swimmer
104 Blvd Livon, 13007 Marseille, France

**Janzen, Daniel H** — Biologist
Parque Nacional Santa Rosa, #169, Liberia, Guanacaste Province, Costa Rica

**Janzen, Edmund** — Religious Leader
General Conference of Mennonite Brethren, 8000 W 21st St, Wichita KS 67205, USA
**Janzen, Lee M** — Golfer
9088 Point Cypress Dr, Orlando FL 32836, USA
**Janzen, Rhoda** — Writer
Hope College, English Dept, Holland MI 49422, USA
**Japarov, Dmitry S** — Cross Country Skier
Ski Association, Luzhnetskaya Nab 8, 119270 Moscow, Russia
**Jaquess, Lindel G (Pete)** — Football Player
631 Cunningham Lane, El Cajon CA 92019, USA
**Jaquiss, Nigel** — Journalist
Willamette Week, Editorial Dept, 822 SW 10th Ave, Portland OR 97205, USA
**Jaramillo. Jason C** — Baseball Player
6111 Madeline Lane, Caledonia WI 53108, USA
**Jardine, Alan C (Al)** — Singer, Guitarist (Beach Boys)
Edge Mgmt, 10850 Wilshire Blve, #380, Los Angeles CA 90024, USA
**Jardine, Ray** — Mountaineer, Hiker, Cyclist, Rower
Ray-Way Products, PO Box 2153, Arizona City AZ 85123, USA
**Jarecki, Andrew** — Director
Creative Artists Agency, 2000 Ave of Stars, #100, Los Angeles CA 90067 USA
**Jarecki, Nicholas** — Director, Writer
W M E Entertainment, 9601 Wilshire Blvd, #300, Beverly Hills CA 90210 USA
**Jarman, Claude, Jr** — Actor
16 Tamal Vista Lane, Axminster, Kentfield CA 94904, USA
**Jarmusch, Jim** — Director
Cinetic Mgmt, 555 W 25th St, #400, New York NY 10001, USA
**Jarosz, Sarah** — Singer, Songwriter, Musician
D S Artists Mgmt, PO Box 121499, Nashville TN 37212, USA
**Jarre, Jean M A** — Composer
Creme-Creative Mgmt, 8 Rue de Levis, 75017 Paris, France
**Jarreau, Alwyn L (Al)** — Singer
Joe Gordon Mgmt, 1954 1st St, #270, Highland Park IL 60035, USA
**Jarrell, Jessica** — Singer
Island Def Jam Records, 8920 W Sunset Blvd, #200, West Hollywood CA 90069 USA
**Jarrett, Dale A** — Auto Racing Driver
1510 46th Ave NE, Hickory NC 28601, USA
**Jarrett, Douglas W (Doug)** — Ice Hockey Player
3486 Maisonneuve Ave, Windsor ON N9E 1Y8, Canada
**Jarrett, Gabriel** — Actor
Hervey/Grimes Talent, 10561 Missouri Ave, #2, Los Angeles CA 90025 USA
**Jarrett, Gary W** — Ice Hockey Player
9662 E Peak View Road, Scottsdale AZ 85262, USA
**Jarrett, Keith** — Jazz Pianist, Composer
Stephen Cloud Presentation, PO Box 578, Santa Ynez CA 93460, USA
**Jarrett, Ned M** — Auto Racing Driver
3182 Ninth Tee Dr, Newton NC 28658, USA
**Jarriel, Thomas E (Tom)** — Commentator
ABC-TV, News Dept, 77 W 66th St, New York NY 10023 USA
**Jarrin, Jaime** — Sportscaster
Los Angeles Dodgers, Stadium, 1000 Elysian Park Ave, Los Angeles CA 90090 USA
**Jarrold, Julian** — Director, Producer, Actor
W M E Entertainment, 9601 Wilshire Blvd, #300, Beverly Hills CA 90210 USA
**Jarryd, Anders** — Tennis Player
Maaneskoldsgatan 37, 531 00 Lidkoping, Sweden
**Jarvi, Kristjan** — Conductor
I M G Artists, Hogarth Business Park, Chiswick, London W4 2TH, England
**Jarvi, Neeme** — Conductor
Harrison/Parrott, 5-6 Albion Court, London W6 0QT, England
**Jarvi, Paavo** — Conductor
Orchestre de Paris, Salle Pleyel, 252 Rue du Faubourg Saint-Honore, 75008 Paris, France
**Jarvik, Robert K** — Surgeon, Inventor (Artificial Heart)
Jarvick Heart Inc, 333 W 52nd St, New York NY 10019, USA
**Jarvis, Doug** — Ice Hockey Player
Montreal Canadiens, 1275 Saint Antoine St W, Montreal QC H3C 5L2, Canada
**Jarvis, James C (Jim)** — Basketball Player
PO Box 154, Asotin WA 99402, USA
**Jarvis, Katie** — Actress
Artist Rights Group, 4A Exmoor St, London W10 6BD, England
**Jarvis, Kevin T** — Baseball Player
1613 Whispering Hills Dr, Franklin TN 37069, USA
**Jarvis, L Raeminton (Ray)** — Football Player
19155 Hi View Dr, Brookfield WI 53045, USA
**Jarvis, R Patrick (Pat)** — Baseball Player
4201 Providence Lane, Tucker GA 30084, USA
**Jarvis, Wes** — Ice Hockey Player
National Training Rinks, 1115 Stellar Dr, Newmarket ON L3Y 7B8, Canada
**Jason, David** — Actor, Comedian
Richard Stone Partnership, De Walden Court, 85 New Cavendish St, London W1W 6XD, England
**Jason, Peter** — Actor
Greene Assoc, 1901 Ave of Stars, #130, Los Angeles CA 90067 USA
**Jasontek, Rebecca** — Synchronized Swimmer
1201 Retswood Dr, Loveland OH 45140, USA
**Jasper, Edward V (Ed)** — Football Player
113 N Price St, Troup TX 75789, USA
**Jaster, Larry E** — Baseball Player
1105 Mill Creek Dr, Saint Johns FL 32259, USA
**Jastremski, Chester A (Chet)** — Swimmer
5064 W September Dr, Bloomington IN 47404, USA
**Jastrow, Kenneth M, II** — Businessman
Temple-Inland Inc, 303 S Temple Dr, Diboll TX 75941, USA
**Jastrow, Terry L** — Director
13201 Old Oak Lane, Los Angeles CA 90049, USA
**Jata, Paul** — Baseball Player
117 Hidden Ridge Court, Highland Heights KY 41076, USA
**Jaugstetter, Robert** — Rowing Athlete
619 Mandeville St, #3, New Orleans LA 70117, USA

**Jaumotte - Jefferson**

**Jaumotte, Andre** — Mechanical Engineer
33 Ave Jeanne, Bte 17, 1050 Brussels, Belgium
**Jauron, Dick M** — Football Player, Coach
Cleveland Browns, 76 Lou Groza Blvd, Berea OH 44017 USA
**Javan, Ali** — Physicist, Inventor
12 Hawthorne St, Cambridge MA 02138, USA
**Javed Miandad Khan** — Cricketer
Cricket Control Board, Gaddafi Stadium, Lahore, Pakistan
**Javier Liranzo, M Julian** — Baseball Player
PO Box 71, San Francisco de Marcoris, Dominican Republic
**Javier, Stanley J A (Stan)** — Baseball Player
5798 Hammock Isles Dr, Naples FL 34119, USA
**Jawara, Dawda K** — President, Gambia
15 Birchen Lane, Haywards Heath, West Sussex RH16 1RY, England
**Jawo, Aino** — Singer (Icona Pop)
United Stage, Box 11029, 100 61 Stockholm, Sweden
**Jaworski, Marian Cardinal** — Religious Leader
Archdiocese of Kiev, Ploscha Katedralny 1, 79008 Kiev, Ukraina
**Jaworski, Ronald V (Ron)** — Football Player, Sportscaster
18 Brookwood Dr, Medford NJ 08055, USA
**Jax, J Garth** — Football Player
12014 E Lake Circle, Greenwood Village CO 80111, USA
**Jay, Anjali** — Actress
Independent Talent Group, 40 Whitfield St, London W1T 2RH, England
**Jay, Joseph R (Joey)** — Baseball Player
7209 Battenwood Court, Tampa FL 33615, USA
**Jay, Ken** — Drummer (Static-X)
Warner Bros Records, 3300 Warner Blvd, Burbank CA 91505 USA
**Jay, Martin E** — Historian
University of California, History Dept, Berkeley CA 94720, USA
**Jay, Peter** — Government Official, England
Hensington Farmhouse, Woodstock, Oxfordshire OX20 1LH, England
**Jay, Ricky** — Illusionist, Actor
W M E Entertainment, 9601 Wilshire Blvd, #300, Beverly Hills CA 90210 USA
**Jay, Vincent** — Biathlete
Ski Federation, 50 Rue des Marquisats, BP 2451, 74011 Annecy Cedex, France
**Jayner, Travis** — Speed Skater
US Speed Skating, PO Box 18370, Kearns UT 84118, USA
**Jayston, Michael** — Actor
Michael Whitehall, 125 Gloucester Road, London SW7 4TE, England
**Jean, B C** — Singer, Songwriter
Intellectual Artists Mgmt, 10585 Santa Monica Blvd, #135, Los Angeles CA 90025, USA
**Jean, Christiane** — Actress
C D A Studio Di Nardo, Via Cavour 171, 00184 Rome, Italy
**Jean, Kenneth** — Conductor
Columbia Artists Mgmt Inc, 5 Columbus Circle, 1790 Broadway, #1600, New York NY 10019 USA
**Jean, Michaelle** — Governor General, Canada
Governor General's Office, 1 Sussex Dr, Ottawa ON K1A 0A2, Canada
**Jean, Nikki** — Singer, Songwriter
Creative Artists Agency, 2000 Ave of Stars, #100, Los Angeles CA 90067 USA
**Jean, Olivier** — Speed Skater
Speed Skating Canada, 2781 Lancaster Road, #402, Ottawa ON K1B 1A7, Canada
**Jean, Vadim** — Director
United Agents, 12-26 Lexington St, London W1F 0LE, England
**Jean, Wyclef** — Rap Artist, Actor
W M E Entertainment, 1325 Ave of Americas, New York NY 10019, USA
**Jean-Baptiste, Marianne R** — Actress
A P A Talent & Literary Agency, 405 S Beverly Dr, #300, Beverly Hills CA 90212 USA
**Jean-Charles, Livio** — Basketball Player
San Antonio Spurs, Alamodome, 1 AT&T Center Parkway, San Antonio TX 78219 USA
**Jeangerard, Robert E (Bob)** — Basketball Player
1930 Belmont Ave, San Carlos CA 94070, USA
**Jean-Gilles, Max** — Football Player
Philadelphia Eagles, 1 Novacare Way, Philadelphia PA 19145 USA
**Jean-Louis, Jimmy** — Actor
Artists Partnership, 101 Finsbury Pavement, London EC2A 1RS, England
**Jeanmaire, Zizi** — Ballerina, Actress
Ballets Roland Petit, 20 Blvd Gabes, 13008 Marseille, France
**Jeanrenaud, Joan** — Concert Cellist (Kronos Quartet)
Kronos Quartet, 1235 9th Ave, San Francisco CA 94122, USA
**Jeantot, Philippe** — Yachtsman, Explorer
Jeantot Organization, BP 01, 85100 Les Sables D'Olonne, France
**Jee, Elizabeth** — Actress
Actors Creative Team, Panther House, 38 Mount Pleasant, London WC1X 0AN, England
**Jee, M James** — Astronomer
Johns Hopkins University, Astronomy Dept, Baltimore MD 21218, USA
**Jeelani, Abdul Q** — Basketball Player
W515 State Road 59, Palmyra WI 53156, USA
**Jeetendra** — Actor
26 Gulmohar Cross Road 5, JVPD Scheme, Mumbai MS 400049, India
**Jeezy** — Rap Artist
Def Jam Records, 828 8th Ave, New York NY 10019 USA
**Jeffcoat, Donald L (Donnie)** — Actor
Antrim Street Entertainment, 5225 Wilshire Blvd, #424, Los Angeles CA 90036, USA
**Jeffcoat, J Michael (Mike)** — Baseball Player
4224 Oak Springs Dr, Arlington TX 76016, USA
**Jeffcoat, James W (Jim)** — Football Player
5135 Summit Hill Dr, Dallas TX 75287, USA
**Jefferies, Gregory S (Greg)** — Baseball Player
7806 Bernal Ave, Pleasanton CA 94588, USA
**Jeffers, Eve** — Actress
I C M Partners, 10250 Constellation Blvd, #900, Los Angeles CA 90067 USA
**Jeffers, Patrick C** — Football Player
5810 Buckpasser Cove, Austin TX 78746, USA
**Jefferson, Al** — Basketball Player
Charlotte Hornets, 333 E Trade St, #A, Charlotte NC 28202 USA

**Jefferson, Herb, Jr** — Actor
California Paralyzed Veterans, 5901 E 7th St, Building 150, Long Beach CA 90822, USA

**Jefferson, James A, III** — Football Player
11220 NE 53rd St, Kirkland WA 98033, USA

**Jefferson, John L** — Football Player
43590 Merchant Mill Terrace, Leesburg VA 20176, USA

**Jefferson, Margo** — Journalist
New York Times, Editorial Dept, 229 W 43rd St, New York NY 10036, USA

**Jefferson, Reginal J (Reggie)** — Baseball Player
1881 Raymond Tucker Road, Tallahassee FL 32311, USA

**Jefferson, Richard A** — Basketball Player
Utah Jazz, Energy Solutions Arena, 301 W South Temple, Salt Lake City UT 84101 USA

**Jefferson, Roy L** — Football Player
8813 Queen Elizabeth Blvd, Annandale VA 22003, USA

**Jefferson, Stanley (Stan)** — Baseball Player
2420 Hunter Ave, #3E, Bronx NY 10475, USA

**Jefferts Schori, Katharine** — Religious Leader
Espicopal Church Center, 815 2nd Ave, New York NY 10017, USA

**Jeffires, Haywood F** — Football Player
2601 Courtyard Lane, Pearland TX 77584, USA

**Jeffre, Justin P** — Singer (98 Degrees)
D A S Communications, 83 Riverside Dr, New York NY 10024, USA

**Jeffrey, Arthur F** — WW II Army Air Corps Hero
7305 Englewood Hill Place, Yakima WA 98908, USA

**Jeffrey, P Michael** — Governor General, Australia
Governor General's Office, Government House, Canberra ACT 2600, Australia

**Jeffrey, Richard C** — Philosopher
55 Patton Ave, Princeton NJ 08540, USA

**Jeffreys, Alec J** — Inventor (Genetic Fingerprinting)
Leicester University, Biochemistry Dept, University Road, Leicester LE1 7RH, England

**Jeffreys, Anne** — Actress
Don Gibble Assoc, 8945 Canby Ave, Northridge CA 91325, USA

**Jeffries, Edward (Dean)** — Custom Car Painter, Stuntman
Jeffries Studio of Style, 3077 Cahuenga Blvd, Los Angeles CA 90028, USA

**Jeffries, Fran** — Singer, Actress, Model
Terry M Hill, 41910 Boardwalk, #A2, Palm Desert CA 92211 USA

**Jeffries, John T** — Astronomer
1652 E Camino Cielo, Tucson AZ 85718, USA

**Jeffries, Sabrina** — Writer
Pocket Star Books, 1230 Ave of Americas, New York NY 10020, USA

**Jeffries, Tony** — Boxer
Amateur Boxing Assn, National Sports Centre, London SE19 2B8, England

**Jeffs, Christine** — Director, Writer
United Talent Agency, U T A Plaza, 9336 Civic Center Dr, Beverly Hills CA 90210 USA

**Jeinsen, Elke E W** — Model
Playboy Promotions, 9346 Civic Center Dr, #200, Beverly Hills CA 90210 USA

**Jelen, Ben** — Singer, Musician, Songwriter, Actor
555 W 53rd St, #1252, New York NY 10019, USA

**Jelic, Christopher J (Chris)** — Baseball Player
33 Allegheny Ave, #5, Cuddy PA 15031, USA

**Jelinek, Elfriede** — Nobel Literature Laureate
Jupiterweg 40, 1140 Vienna, Austria

**Jellis, Paul** — Actor
Artists Partnership, 101 Finsbury Pavement, London EC2A 1RS, England

**Jeltz, L Steven (Steve)** — Baseball Player
608 W 28th Place, Lawrence KS 66046, USA

**Jemison, Eddie** — Actor
Don Buchwald Talent Agency, 6500 Wilshire Blvd, #2200, Los Angeles CA 90048 USA

**Jemison, Mae C** — Astronaut
Dartmouth College, Environmental Studies Dept, Hanover NH 03755, USA

**Jencks, William P** — Biochemist
11 Revere St, Lexington MA 02420, USA

**Jendresen, Erik** — Writer
W M E Entertainment, 9601 Wilshire Blvd, #300, Beverly Hills CA 90210 USA

**Jenes, Theodore G, Jr** — Army General
809 169th Place SW, Lynnwood WA 98037, USA

**Jenkin of Roding, Patrick F** — Government Official, England
703 Howard House, Dolphin Square, London SW1V 3PQ, England

**Jenkin, Warren** — Bassist (Killing Heidi)
Harbour Agency, 135 Forbes St, Woolloomooloo NSW 2011, Australia

**Jenkins, Alfred D** — Football Player
4267 Janice Dr, Atlanta GA 30337, USA

**Jenkins, Billy L** — Football Player
4761 S Atchison Court, Aurora CO 80015, USA

**Jenkins, Carter** — Actor
InMomentum Mgmt, 14622 Ventura Blvd, #778, Sherman Oaks CA 91403, USA

**Jenkins, Charles H, Jr** — Businessman
Publix Super Markets, PO Box 407, Lakeland FL 33802, USA

**Jenkins, Charles L (Charlie)** — Track Athlete, Coach
12826 Forest Creek Court, Sykesville MD 21784, USA

**Jenkins, Cullen D** — Football Player
49124 Peninsular Dr, Belleville MI 48111, USA

**Jenkins, Daniel** — Actor
S M S Talent, 8383 Wilshire Blvd, #230, Beverly Hills CA 90211 USA

**Jenkins, David W** — Figure Skater
5947 S Atlanta Ave, Tulsa OK 74105, USA

**Jenkins, Don J** — Vietnam War Army Hero (CMH)
3783 Bowling Green Road, Morgantown KY 42261, USA

**Jenkins, Eddie J (Ed)** — Football Player
PO Box 190278, Boston MA 02119, USA

**Jenkins, Ferguson A (Fergie), Jr** — Baseball Player
3655 W Anthem Way, #A109, Anthem AZ 85086, USA

**Jenkins, Geoffrey S (Geoff)** — Baseball Player
6683 E Judson Road, Paradise Valley AZ 85253, USA

**Jenkins, George** — Physician
Three Doctors Foundation, 65 Hazelwood Ave, Newark NJ 07106, USA

**Jenkins, Hayes Alan** — Figure Skater
3183 Regency Place, Westlake OH 44145, USA

**Jenkins, Izel, Jr** — Football Player
5106 Masters Lane N, Wilson NC 27896, USA

**Jenkins, Jerry B** — Writer
Tyndale House Publishers, 351 Executive Dr, PO Box 80, Wheaton IL 60187, USA

**Jenkins, Jo Ann C** — Association Executive
American Association of Retired Persons, 601 E St NW, Washington DC 20049, USA

**Jenkins, John L** — Basketball Player
Atlanta Hawks, Centennial Tower, 101 Marietta St NW, #1900, Atlanta GA 30303 USA

**Jenkins, Katherine** — Singer
247 Worldwide Mgmt, 500 Chiswick High Road, #25, London W4 5RG, England

**Jenkins, Ken** — Actor
Paradigm Agency, 360 N Crescent Dr, North Building, Beverly Hills CA 90210 USA

**Jenkins, Kerry C** — Football Player
120 Three Sons Dr, Hoover AL 35226, USA

**Jenkins, Kristopher R-C (Kris)** — Football Player
9525 Sweetleaf Place, Charlotte NC 28278, USA

**Jenkins, Larry Flash** — Actor
Baker Winokur Ryder Public Relations, 9100 Wilshire Blvd, #500W, Beverly Hills CA 90212 USA

**Jenkins, Loren** — Journalist
Washington Post, Editorial Dept, 1150 15th St NW, Washington DC 20071, USA

**Jenkins, Michael G** — Football Player
4817 Basingstoke Dr, Suwanee GA 30024, USA

**Jenkins, Mike P** — Football Player
Tampa Bay Buccaneers, 1 W Buccaneer Place, Tampa FL 33607 USA

**Jenkins, Noam** — Actor
Characters Talent Agency, 1505 W 2nd Ave, #200, Vancouver BC V6H 3Y4, Canada

**Jenkins, Patricia L (Patty)** — Director, Writer
Creative Artists Agency, 2000 Ave of Stars, #100, Los Angeles CA 90067 USA

**Jenkins, Richard** — Actor
Gersh Agency, 9465 Wilshire Blvd, #600, Beverly Hills CA 90212 USA

**Jenkins, Robert L** — Football Player
2878 Fieldview Terrace, San Ramon CA 94583, USA

**Jenkins, Sandra** — Curling Athlete
Curling Association, 1660 Vimont Court, Cumberland ON K4A 4J4, Canada

**Jenkins, Stephan D** — Singer, Guitarist (Third Eye Blind)
Eric Godtland Mgmt, 1040 Mariposa St, #200, San Francisco CA 94107, USA

**Jenkins, Tamara** — Director
Cinetic Mgmt, 555 W 25th St, #400, New York NY 10001 USA

**Jenkins, Thomas (Tomi)** — Singer (Cameo)
Reprise Records, 3300 Warner Blvd, Burbank CA 91505 USA

**Jenks, Downing B** — Businessman
1 McKnight Place, #115, Saint Louis MO 63124, USA

**Jenks, Robert S (Bobby)** — Baseball Player
8383 Wilshire Blvd, #500, Beverly Hills CA 90211, USA

**Jenneke, Michelle** — Track Athlete, Model
Six Sides Management Group, 147 Pirie St, #808, Adelaide SA 5000, Australia

**Jenner, Brianne** — Ice Hockey Player
Hockey Canada, 151 Canada Olympic Road SW, #201, Calgary AB T3B 6B7, Canada

**Jenner, Brody** — Entertainer, Model
I C M Partners, 10250 Constellation Blvd, #900, Los Angeles CA 90067 USA

**Jenner, Bruce** — Track Athlete, Actor
Commercial Talent, 12711 Ventura Blvd, #285, Studio City CA 91604, USA

**Jenness, James** — Businessman
Kellogg Co, 1 Kellogg Square, PO Box 3599, Battle Creek MI 49016, USA

**Jenney, Neil** — Artist
Barbara Mathes Gallery, 22 E 80th St, New York NY 10075, USA

**Jennings, Alex** — Actor
Royal National Theater, South Park, London SE1 9PX, England

**Jennings, Brandon** — Basketball Player
Detroit Pistons, Palace, 4 Championship Dr, Auburn Hills MI 48326 USA

**Jennings, Brian L** — Football Player
San Francisco 49ers, 4949 Centennial Blvd, Santa Clara CA 95054 USA

**Jennings, Byron** — Actor
Bauman Redanty Shaul Agency, 5757 Wilshire Blvd, #473, Los Angeles CA 90036 USA

**Jennings, Garth** — Director
Hammer & Tongs, Holborn Studios, 49-50 Eagle Wharf Road, London N1 7ED, England

**Jennings, Grant C** — Ice Hockey Player
307 Yoakum Parkway, #510, Alexandria VA 22304, USA

**Jennings, Gregory (Greg), Jr** — Football Player
4115 Oakharbor St, Kalamazoo MI 49009, USA

**Jennings, J Douglas (Doug)** — Baseball Player
PO Box 812692, Boca Raton FL 33481, USA

**Jennings, Jason R** — Baseball Player
7978 Stone River Dr, Frisco TX 75034, USA

**Jennings, Jim** — Architect
Jim Jennings Architect, 49 Rodgers Alley, San Francisco CA 94103, USA

**Jennings, Jonas D** — Football Player
123 Davis Road, Fayetteville GA 30215, USA

**Jennings, Keith O** — Football Player
119 Axtell Dr, Summerville SC 29485, USA

**Jennings, Keith R** — Basketball Player
808 Lakeland Court, Culpeper VA 22701, USA

**Jennings, Paul** — Writer
PO Box 1459, Warrnambool VIC 3280, Australia

**Jennings, Paul C** — Civil Engineer
640 S Grand Ave, Pasadena CA 91105, USA

**Jennings, Robert B** — Pathologist
Duke University Medical Center, Pathology Dept, Durham NC 27710, USA

**Jennings, Robin C** — Baseball Player
380 Parkview Dr, Park City UT 84098, USA

**Jennings, Stanford J** — Football Player
215 Jasmine Way, Alpharetta GA 30004, USA

**Jennings, Waylon A (Shooter)** — Singer, Songwriter
208 Bibb St, Campbellsville KY 42718, USA

**Jennings, Wilbur (Will)** — Composer, Songwriter
B M I, 8730 W Sunset Blvd, #300, Los Angeles CA 90069 USA
**Jenniskens, Tim** — Field Hockey Player
H C Bloemendaal, Aelbertsbergweg 3, 2061 Bloemendaal AA, Netherlands
**Jenrette, Richard H** — Businessman
67 E 93rd St, New York NY 10128, USA
**Jens, Salome** — Actress
Stagecoach Entertainment, 1526 14th St, #109, Santa Monica CA 90404, USA
**Jensen, Ashley** — Actress, Comedienne
Hamilton Hodell, 20 Golden Square, London W1F 9JL, England
**Jensen, Chris B** — Ice Hockey Player
20310 Enright Way, Farmington MI 55024, USA
**Jensen, David** — Entertainer
Capital Gold, 30 Leicester Square, London WC2H 7LA, England
**Jensen, Debra** — Model
31441 Santa Margarita Parkway, #322, Rancho Santa Margarita CA 92688, USA
**Jensen, Derrick** — Football Player
147 Downing St, Panama City FL 32413, USA
**Jensen, Eivind Gullberg** — Conductor
Ophelias Public Relations for Culture, Lucile-Grahn-Str 37, 81675 Munich, Germany
**Jensen, Iain** — Yachtsman
Middle Harbour Yacht Club, Spit, Mosman NSW 2088, Australia
**Jensen, Jacob** — Industrial Designer
Bang Olufsen, Peter Bangs Vej 15, PO Box 40, DK 7600 Struer, Denmark
**Jensen, James** — Geologist
Brigham Young University, Geology Dept, Provo UT 84602, USA
**Jensen, James C (Jim)** — Football Player
9811 N Oak Knoll Circle, Davie FL 33324, USA
**Jensen, James D (Jim)** — Football Player
1972 Cayman Dr, Windsor CO 80550, USA
**Jensen, James W, Jr** — Cinematographer
28853 Garnet Hill Court, Agoura Hills CA 91301, USA
**Jensen, Jonathan W (Jon)** — Football Player
36771 Allder School Road, Purcellville VA 20132, USA
**Jensen, Liz** — Writer
Gillon Aitken Assoc, 18-21 Cavaye Place, London SW10 9PT, England
**Jensen, Marcus C** — Baseball Player
19550 N Grayhawk Dr, #1134, Scottsdale AZ 85255, USA
**Jenson, Victoria (Vicky)** — Director, Animator
Creative Artists Agency, 2000 Ave of Stars, #100, Los Angeles CA 90067 USA
**Jenssen, Amanda** — Singer
Sony Music Sweden, Box 3187, 103 63 Stockholm, Sweden
**Jentsch, Julia** — Actress
Agentur Vogel, Katzbachstr 8, 10965 Berlin, Germany
**Jeon Da-Hye** — Speed Skater
Skating Union, 88 Bangyee-Dong, Songpaku, Seoul 138 749, South Korea
**Jeong, Ken** — Actor, Comedian
United Talent Agency, U T A Plaza, 9336 Civic Center Dr, Beverly Hills CA 90210 USA
**Jepsen, Carly Rae** — Singer, Songwriter
W M E Entertainment, 9601 Wilshire Blvd, #300, Beverly Hills CA 90210 USA
**Jepsen, Kevin M** — Baseball Player
425 Cannon Green Dr, #H, Goleta CA 93117, USA
**Jepsen, Les** — Basketball Player
8075 9th Street Way N, Saint Paul MN 55128, USA
**Jepsen, Roger W** — Senator, IA
3799 Cadbury Circle, #400, Venice FL 34293, USA
**Jepson, Mary Lou** — Computer Scientist, Social Activist
Massachusetts Institute of Technology, Media Laboratory, Cambridge MA 02139, USA
**Jepson, Mikael** — Guitarist (The Ark)
Live Nation, Linnegatan 89, Box 21451, 104 51 Stockholm, Sweden
**Jeremih** — Singer, Rap Artist, Songwriter
Def Jam Records, 828 8th Ave, New York NY 10019 USA
**Jeremy** — Singer, Guitarist (Chad & Jeremy)
Icon Performing Arts, 1557 Westwood Blvd, #242, Los Angeles CA 90024, USA
**Jerins, Ruby** — Actress
Management 360, 9111 Wilshire Blvd, Beverly Hills CA 90210 USA
**Jerkens, H Allen** — Thoroughbred Racing Trainer
9509 242nd St, Floral Park NY 11001, USA
**Jerkins, Rodney (Darkchild)** — Music Producer
Paradigm Agency, 360 N Crescent Dr, North Building, Beverly Hills CA 90210 USA
**Jernemyr, Magnus** — Handball Player
F C Barcelona Balonmano, Avda Aristides Maillol, 08028 Barcelona, Spain
**Jernigan, Tamara E (Tammy)** — Astronaut
4268 Brindisi Place, Pleasanton CA 94566, USA
**Jeru the Damaja** — Rap Artist
W M E Entertainment, 1325 Ave of Americas, New York NY 10019 USA
**Jerusalem, Siegfried** — Opera Singer
Sudring 9, 90542 Eckental, Germany
**Jervey, Travis R** — Football Player
22 Sand Dollar Dr, Isle of Palms SC 29451, USA
**Jerzak, Stephen** — Singer, Songwriter
Agency Group Ltd, 142 W 57th St, #600, New York NY 10019 USA
**Jerzembeck, Michael J (Mike)** — Baseball Player
10625 S Hall Dr, Charlotte NC 28270, USA
**Jeselnik, Anthony** — Actor, Comedian
Mosiac Media Group, 9200 W Sunset Blvd, #1000, Los Angeles CA 90069 USA
**Jessee, Michael A** — Government Official, Financier
Federal Home Loan Bank, 1 Financial Center, #2000, Boston MA 02111, USA
**Jessen, Gene Nora** — Astronaut Candidate
630 S Tiburon Ave, Meridian ID 83642, USA
**Jessie J** — Singer, Songwriter
Crown Music, Matrix Complex, 91 Peterborough Road, London SW6 3BU, England
**Jessup, Bill (Billy0** — Football Player
13341 Saint Andrews Dr, #137D, Seal Beach CA 90740, USA
**Jesus, Juan** — Soccer Player
Internazionale Milan, Corso Vittorio Emanuele II 9, 20122 Milan, Italy

# J

**Jet Li** — Actor
Current Entertainment, 9378 Wilshire Blvd, #210, Beverly Hills CA 90212, USA
**Jeter, Carmelita** — Track Athlete
408 W Ellis Ave, Inglewood CA 90302, USA
**Jeter, Derek S** — Baseball Player
845 United Nations Plaza, #888, New York NY 10017, USA
**Jeter, Gary M** — Football Player
3612 Quail Ridge Dr, Plainsboro NJ 8536, USA
**Jeter, John (Johnny)** — Baseball Player
1012 N 5th St, Monroe LA 71201, USA
**Jeter, Thomas M (Tommy)** — Football Player
2108 Estes Park Road, Southlake TX 76092, USA
**Jetsun Pema** — Queen, Bhutan
Royal Palace, Tashichhodzong, Thimphu, Bhutan
**Jett, Brent W, Jr** — Astronaut
2529 Goldsmith St, Houston TX 77030, USA
**Jett, James** — Football Player, Track Athlete
PO Box 430, Kearneysville WV 25430, USA
**Jett, Joan** — Singer, Guitarist, Songwriter
Blackheart Records, 636 Broadway, #1210, New York NY 10012, USA
**Jett, John** — Football Player
177 Crowder Point Dr, Reedville VA 22539, USA
**Jeunet, Jean-Pierre** — Director
I C M Partners, 10250 Constellation Blvd, #900, Los Angeles CA 90067 USA
**Jevanord, Oystein** — Drummer (A-Ha)
Bandana Mgmt, 11 Elvaston Place, #300, London SW7 5QC, England
**Jewel** — Singer, Songwriter, Actress
Front Line Mgmt, 1100 Glendon Ave, #2000, Los Angeles CA 90024 USA
**Jewell, Buddy, Jr** — Singer, Songwriter
Third Coast Talent, PO Box 334, Kingston Springs TN 37082, USA
**Jewison, Norman F** — Director, Producer
Yorktown Productions, 300 W Olympic Blvd, #1314, Santa Monica CA 90401, USA
**Ji Dong-Won** — Soccer Player
A F C Sunderland, Light Stadium, Sunderland SR5 1SU, England
**Ji Yai-Shin** — Golfer
Ladies Pro Golf Assn, 100 International Golf Dr, Daytona Beach FL 32124 USA
**Ji Young Oh** — Golfer
Ladies Pro Golf Assn, 100 International Golf Dr, Daytona Beach FL 32124 USA
**Jia, Li** — Hematologist
Duke University Medical Center, Hematology Dept, Durham NC 27708, USA
**Jia, Ran** — Concert Pianist
I M G Artists, Hogarth Business Park, Chiswick, London W4 2TH, England
**Jiang Tiefeng** — Artist
Jiang Publishing, 1329 San Carlos Road, Arcadia CA 91006, USA
**Jiear, Alison** — Singer, Actress
United Agents, 12-26 Lexington St, London W1F 0LE, England
**Jiggets, Daniel M (Dan)** — Football Player
4751 RFD, Long Grove IL 60047, USA
**Jiles, Dwayne** — Football Player
3712 Churchill Court, Plano TX 75075, USA
**Jillian, Ann** — Actress
PO Box 57739, Sherman Oaks CA 91413, USA
**Jim Yong Kim** — Physician
Partners in Health, 641 Huntington Ave, #100, Boston MA 02115, USA
**Jimenez Nanez, Israel S** — Soccer Player
Tigres U A N L, Estadio Universitario, 66451 San Nicolas de los Garza NL, Mexico
**Jimenez Rodriguez, Raul A** — Soccer Player
Club America, C del Toro 100, Ex Hacienda Coapa, Mexico City 14390, Mexico
**Jimenez, Carlos** — Architect
Jimenez Architectural Design Studio, 1116 Willard St, Houston TX 77006, USA
**Jimenez, Flaco** — Singer/Accordionist (Texas Tornados)
Management Plus, PO Box 132, Sequin TX 78155, USA
**Jimenez, Gladys** — Actress
Stone Manners Salners, 6100 Wilshire Blvd, #1500, Los Angeles CA 90035 USA
**Jimenez, Jessica** — Actress
A P A Talent & Literary Agency, 405 S Beverly Dr, #300, Beverly Hills CA 90212 USA
**Jimenez, Miguel Angel** — Golfer
Advantage International, 1025 Thomas Jefferson NW, #450, Washington DC 20007 USA
**Jimenez, Nicario** — Artist
3841 29th Ave SW, Naples FL 34117, USA
**Jimenez, Penelope** — Model
Playboy Promotions, 9346 Civic Center Dr, #200, Beverly Hills CA 90210 USA
**Jimenez, Santiago, Jr** — Singer, Accordian Player
Folklore Productions, PO Box 7003, Santa Monica CA 90406, USA
**Jimerson, Charlton** — Baseball Player
22048 Betlen Way, Castro Valley CA 94546, USA
**Jiminez, Joe** — Golfer
29243 Enchanted Glen, Boerne TX 78015, USA
**Jiminez, Miguel A** — Baseball Player
16 Shelley Court, Middletown NY 10941, USA
**Jimmy Jam** — Businessman, Producer, Composer
Universal Attractions, 135 W 26th St, #1200, New York NY 10001 USA
**Jimoh, Ade** — Football Player
41782 Bristow Manor Dr, Ashburn VA 20148, USA
**Jin** — Rap Artist, Actor
Great Co, 1234 Wilshire Blvd, #422, Los Angeles CA 90017, USA
**Jin Sun-Yu** — Speed Skater
Skating Union, 88 Bangyee-Dong, Songpaku, Seoul 138 749, South Korea
**Jing Haipeng** — Taikonaut
Satellite Launch Center, Jiuquan, Guangzhou Province, China
**Jinks, Dan** — Producer
Dan Jinks Co, 4024 Radford Ave, Bungalow 9, Studio City CA 91604, USA
**Jiricna, Eva M** — Architect
Jiricna Architects, 38 Warren St, #300, London W1T 6AE, England
**Jiro Ono** — Chef, Restauranteur
Sukiyabashi Jiro, Tsukamoto Sogyo Building, 2-15-4 Ginza, Chuoku, Tokyo 104 0061, Japan

*Jet Li - Jiro Ono*

**Jirov, Vassili** — Boxer
Thell Torrence, 5449 S Eastern Ave, #3, Las Vegas NV 89119, USA

**Jirtle, Randy L** — Geneticist
Duke University Medical Center, Radiation Oncology Dept, Durham NC 27708, USA

**J-Kwon** — Rap Artist
Universal Attractions, 135 W 26th St, #1200, New York NY 10001 USA

**Jo, Sumi** — Opera Singer
Askonas Holt, Lincoln House, 300 High Holborn, London WC1V 7JH, England

**Jo, Timothy W (Tim)** — Actor
Innovative Artists, 1505 10th St, Santa Monica CA 90401 USA

**Joannou, Chris** — Bassist (Silverchair)
John Watson Mgmt, PO Box 281, Sunny Hills NSW 2010, Australia

**Joanou, Phil** — Director
Todd Smith Assoc, 11835 W Olympic Blvd, #640, Los Angeles CA 90064, USA

**Job, Brian G** — Swimmer
PO Box 213, Palo Alto CA 94302, USA

**Jobe, Emmett** — Auto Racing Executive
Phoenix International Raceway, 125 S Avondale Blvd, #200, Avondale AZ 85323, USA

**Jobert, Marlene** — Actress
8-10 Blvd de Courcelles, 75008 Paris, France

**Jobrani, Maz** — Actor
Levity Entertainment, 6701 Center Drive W, #1111, Los Angeles CA 90045 USA

**Jobson, Richard** — Director, Producer, Writer
Curtis Brown Group, 28-29 Haymarket St, #500, London SW1Y 4SP, England

**Jodat, James S (Jim)** — Football Player
25032 Mammoth Circle, Lake Forest CA 92630, USA

**Jodie, Brett** — Baseball Player
1359 Corley Mill Road, Lexington SC 29072, USA

**Jodorowsky, Alejandro** — Director, Producer, Composer
Agence Josiane Stroh, 3 Allee Marie Laurent, 75020 Paris, France

**Jodzio, Rick** — Ice Hockey Player
23731 Perth Bay, Dana Point CA 92629, USA

**Joe** — Singer, Songwriter, Producer
Kedar Entertainment, 21 W 39th St, #600, New York NY 10018, USA

**Joe, Leon M** — Football Player
7917 Woodyard Road, Clinton MD 20735, USA

**Joe, William (Billy)** — Football Player, Coach
3964 Butler Springs Way, Birmingham AL 35226, USA

**Joel, Billy** — Singer, Songwriter
Maritime Inc, 34 Audrey Ave, #4, Oyster Bay NY 11771, USA

**Joel, Richard M** — Educator
Yeshiva University, President's Office, 500 W 185th St, New York NY 10033, USA

**Joerger, David (Dave)** — Basketball Coach
Memphis Grizzlies, 191 Beale St, Memphis TN 38103 USA

**Joerres, Jeffrey** — Businessman
Manpower Inc, 600 A B Data Dr, Milwaukee WI 53217, USA

**Joey Z** — Guitarist (Life of Agony, Stereomud)
Agency Group Ltd, 142 W 57th St, #600, New York NY 10019 USA

**Joffe, Roland V** — Director, Producer
Baumgartan Mgmt, 406 Wilshire Blvd, Santa Monica CA 90401, USA

**Joffin, Jon** — Cinematographer
Dattner Disposto, 10635 Santa Monica Blvd, #165, Los Angeles CA 90025, USA

**Jofre, Eder** — Boxer
Alamo de Ministero Rocha, Azevedo 373, C Cesar 21-15, Sao Paulo, Brazil

**Jogia, Avan** — Actor
Characters Talent Mgmt, 8 Elm St, Toronto ON M5G 1G7, Canada

**Johannesen, Eric** — Rowing Athlete
Ruder-Club Bergedorf, Schleusendamm 20, 21037 Hamburg, Germany

**Johannesen, Lena** — Body Builder, Model
PO Box 325, Culver City CA 90232, USA

**Johannsen, Jake** — Actor
Paradigm Agency, 360 N Crescent Dr, North Building, Beverly Hills CA 90210 USA

**Jóhannsson, Jóhann** — Composer
Agency Group Ltd, 142 W 57th St, #600, New York NY 10019 USA

**Johannsson, Kristjan** — Opera Singer
Vesturbru 1, 210 Garoabae, Iceland

**Johansen, Iris** — Writer
Jane Rotrosen Agency, 318 E 51st St, New York NY 10022, USA

**Johansen, Kari Mette** — Handball Player
Bobakken 15F, 3242 Sandefjord, Norway

**Johansen, Roy** — Writer
Saint Martin's Press, 175 5th Ave, #400, New York NY 10010 USA

**Johanson, Chris** — Artist
Jack Hanley Gallery, 327 Broome St, New York NY 10002, USA

**Johanson, Donald C** — Anthropologist
Arizona State University, Human Origins Institute, Tempe AZ 85287, USA

**Johanson, Jai Johnny (Jaimoe)** — Drummer (Allman Brothers Band)
Allman Brothers Band Inc, 18 Tamworth Road, Waban MA 02468, USA

**Johanson, Sue** — Educator, Writer, Commentator
Sunday Night Sex Show, 42 Pardee Ave, Toronto ON M6K 3H5, Canada

**Johansson, Calle** — Ice Hockey Player
1708 Mayfair Place, Crofton MD 21114, USA

**Johansson, Kathy** — Model, Body Builder
PO Box 43351, Tucson AZ 85733, USA

**Johansson, Lars-Olof** — Guitarist, Keyboardist (Cardigans)
Talent Trust, Kungsgatan 9C, 411 19 Gothenburg, Sweden

**Johansson, Marcus** — Ice Hockey Player
Washington Capitals, 627 N Glebe Road, #850, Arlington VA 22203 USA

**Johansson, Paul** — Actor
Innovative Artists, 1505 10th St, Santa Monica CA 90401 USA

**Johansson, Per-Ulik** — Golfer
18710 SE Pineneedle Lane, Jupiter FL 33469, USA

**Johansson, Scarlett** — Actress, Model, Singer
Creative Artists Agency, 2000 Ave of Stars, #100, Los Angeles CA 90067 USA

**Johansson, Stefan** — Auto Racing Driver
3546 Crownridge Dr, Sherman Oaks CA 91403, USA

| | |
|---|---|
| **Johaug, Therese**<br>Nansen I L Ski, Toini Berg Brynhildsvoll, Dalsbygda, 2550 Os I Osterdalen, Norway | Cross Country Skier |
| **Johjima, Kenji**<br>2412 109th Ave SE, Bellevue WA 98004, USA | Baseball Player |
| **John, Chris**<br>Harry's Gym, 14 Cressall Road, Balcatta, Perth WA 6021, Australia | Boxer |
| **John, David D**<br>7 Cyncoed Ave, Cardiff CF2 6ST, Wales | Museum Executive, Explorer |
| **John, Elton**<br>Rocket Music Management, 1 Blythe Road, London W14 0HG, England | Singer, Songwriter |
| **John, Thomas E (Tommy)**<br>6202 Seton House Lane, Charlotte NC 28277, USA | Baseball Player |
| **John, Tylyn**<br>813 Harbor Blvd, #133, West Sacramento CA 95691, USA | Model, Actress |
| **Johnagin, Tommy**<br>Avalon Mgmt, 4a Exmoor St, London W10 6BD, England | Actor, Comedian |
| **Johncock, Gordon**<br>649 S Fall River Dr, Coldwater MI 49036, USA | Auto Racing Driver |
| **John-Jules, Danny**<br>Jonathan Altaras Assoc, 11 Garrick St, London WC2E 9AR, England | Actor |
| **Johnny A**<br>Ralph Jaccodine Mgmt, PO Box 381982, Cambridge MA 02238, USA | Guitarist, Songwriter |
| **Johnny O**<br>Universal Attractions, 135 W 26th St, #1200, New York NY 10001 USA | Singer |
| **Johnova, Andriena**<br>Nad Kralovskou Oborou 278/15, 17000 Prague 7, Czech Republic | Artist |
| **Johns, Daniel**<br>John Watson Mgmt, PO Box 281, Sunny Hills NSW 2010, Australia | Singer, Guitarist (Silverchair) |
| **Johns, Douglas A (Doug)**<br>1131 SW 72nd Ave, Plantation FL 33317, USA | Baseball Player |
| **Johns, Glynis**<br>2051 N Highland Ave, Los Angeles CA 90068, USA | Actress |
| **Johns, Jasper**<br>97 Low Road, #642, Sharon CT 06069, USA | Artist |
| **Johns, Lori**<br>PO Box 3667, Corpus Christi TX 78463, USA | Drag Racing Driver |
| **Johns, R Keith**<br>1525 Suzanne Ridge Court, Glencoe MO 63038, USA | Baseball Player |
| **Johns, Raymond E, Jr**<br>Commander, Air Mobility Command, Scott Air Force Base IL 62225 USA | Air Force General |
| **Johns, Simon**<br>Duophonic Records, PO Box 3787, London SE22 9DZ, England | Bassist (Stereolab) |
| **Johnson Jerald, Penny**<br>Mitchell K Stubbs Assoc, 8695 W Washington Blvd, #204, Culver City CA 90232 USA | Actress |
| **Johnson Pucci, Gail**<br>2132 Ward Dr, Walnut Creek CA 94596, USA | Synchronized Swimmer |
| **Johnson, Aaron**<br>3810 Gabrielle Dr, Dublin OH 43016, USA | Ice Hockey Player |
| **Johnson, Aaron**<br>Hamilton Hodell, 20 Golden Square, London W1F 9JL, England | Actor |
| **Johnson, Adam**<br>Stanford University, English Dept, Stanford CA 94305, USA | Writer |
| **Johnson, Addison**<br>King Features Syndicate, 300 W 57th St, #1500, New York NY 10019 USA | Cartoonist (Bringing Up Father) |
| **Johnson, Alexander (Alex)**<br>18425 Bretton Dr, Detroit MI 48223, USA | Baseball Player |
| **Johnson, Alexzander S (Alexz)**<br>W M E Entertainment, 9601 Wilshire Blvd, #300, Beverly Hills CA 90210 USA | Actress |
| **Johnson, Allen**<br>Octagon Worldwide, 800 Connecticut Ave, #200, Norwalk CT 06854 USA | Track Athlete |
| **Johnson, Amy Jo**<br>Burstein Co, 15304 Sunset Blvd, #208, Pacific Palisades CA 90272, USA | Actress, Singer, Songwriter |
| **Johnson, Anderson J (Andy)**<br>PO Box 6828, Athens GA 30604, USA | Football Player |
| **Johnson, Andre L**<br>Houston Texans, 2 Reliant Park, Houston TX 77054 USA | Football Player |
| **Johnson, Andreas**<br>International Talent Booking, Ariel House, 74A Charlotte St, #100 London W1T 4QJ, England | Singer, Songwriter |
| **Johnson, Anne-Marie**<br>Diverse Talent Group, 9911 Pico Blvd, #350W, Los Angeles CA 90035 USA | Actress |
| **Johnson, Anthony C (Tony)**<br>4446 Janssen Dr, Memphis TN 38128, USA | Baseball Player |
| **Johnson, Anthony M**<br>5162 Inwood Place, Mableton GA 30126, USA | Basketball Player |
| **Johnson, Anthony S**<br>534 Magnolia Ave, Saint Johns FL 32259, USA | Football Player |
| **Johnson, Arte**<br>2725 Bottlebrush Dr, Los Angeles CA 90077, USA | Actor, Comedian |
| **Johnson, Ashley**<br>Anonymous Content, 3532 Hayden Ave, Culver City CA 90232 USA | Actress |
| **Johnson, Avery**<br>5101 Meadowside Lane, Plano TX 75093, USA | Basketball Player, Coach |
| **Johnson, Bart**<br>Baker Winokur Ryder Public Relations, 9100 Wilshire Blvd, #500W, Beverly Hills CA 90212 USA | Actor |
| **Johnson, Ben**<br>4 Saint Peter's Wharf, Hammersmith Terrace, London W6 9UD, England | Artist |
| **Johnson, Benjamin F (Ben)**<br>112 Locksley Dr, Greenwood SC 29649, USA | Baseball Player |
| **Johnson, Benjamin S (Ben), Jr**<br>Ed Futerman, 2 Saint Clair Ave E, #1500, Toronto ON M4T 2R1, Canada | Track Athlete |
| **Johnson, Bernie**<br>15 Carriage Way, Scarborough ME 04074, USA | Ice Hockey Player |
| **Johnson, Bethel**<br>1000 Crystal Oak Lane, Arlington TX 76005, USA | Football Player |
| **Johnson, Betsey L**<br>Betsey Johnson Co, 498 Fashion Ave, #2103, New York NY 10018, USA | Fashion Designer |

| | |
|---|---|
| **Johnson, Beverly** | Model, Actress |
| PO Box 1474, Rancho Mirage CA 92270, USA | |
| **Johnson, Bjorn** | Actor, Director |
| TalentWorks, 3500 W Olive Ave, #1400, Burbank CA 91505 USA | |
| **Johnson, Bob** | Monster Truck Executive |
| Bigfoot 4X4, 6311 N Lindbergh Blvd, Hazelwood MO 63042, USA | |
| **Johnson, Brad** | Model, Actor |
| Metropolitan Talent Agency, 5405 Wilshire Blvd, #218, Los Angeles CA 90036 USA | |
| **Johnson, Brandon H** | Football Player |
| 1541 W Coquina Dr, Gilbert AZ 85233, USA | |
| **Johnson, Brent** | Ice Hockey Player |
| 808 N Florida St, Arlington VA 22205, USA | |
| **Johnson, Brian** | Singer (AC/DC) |
| Alberts Music, 9 Rangers Road, Neutral Bay, Sydney NSW 2089, Australia | |
| **Johnson, Brian D** | Baseball Player |
| 17477 Plaza del Curtidor, #198, San Diego CA 92128, USA | |
| **Johnson, Bryant A** | Football Player |
| 2963 Springbluff Lane, Buford GA 30519, USA | |
| **Johnson, Bryce** | Actor |
| Untitled Entertainment, 350 S Beverly Dr, #200, Beverly Hills CA 90212 USA | |
| **Johnson, Buck** | Basketball Player |
| 701 Pine Grove Road, Harvest AL 35749, USA | |
| **Johnson, C Barth (Bart)** | Baseball Player |
| 1929 N Newland Ave, Chicago IL 60707, USA | |
| **Johnson, C Stephen (Steve)** | Basketball Player |
| 9715 SW Quail Post Road, Portland OR 97219, USA | |
| **Johnson, Calvin, Jr** | Football Player |
| 185 Roscommon Court, Tyrone GA 30290, USA | |
| **Johnson, Carolyn Dawn** | Singer, Songwriter |
| Paquin Entertainment, 468 Stradbrook Ave, Winnipeg MB R3L 0J9, Canada | |
| **Johnson, Chad J J** | Football Player |
| 1051 NW 44th St, Miami FL 33127, USA | |
| **Johnson, Charles E** | Football Player |
| 6549 Wakefalls Dr, Wake Forest NC 27587, USA | |
| **Johnson, Charles E** | Baseball Player |
| 12301 NW 7th St, Plantation FL 33325, USA | |
| **Johnson, Charles E (Charlie)** | Football Player |
| Minnesota Vikings, 9520 Viking Dr, Eden Prairie MN 55344 USA | |
| **Johnson, Charles L (Charley)** | Football Player |
| New Mexico State University, Chemical Engineering Dept, Las Cruces NM 88003, USA | |
| **Johnson, Charles R** | Writer |
| University of Washington, English Dept, Seattle WA 98105, USA | |
| **Johnson, Cheryl L** | Labor Leader |
| United American Nurses, 8515 Georgia Ave, Silver Spring MD 20910, USA | |
| **Johnson, Chris J** | Actor |
| A P A Talent & Literary Agency, 405 S Beverly Dr, #300, Beverly Hills CA 90212 USA | |
| **Johnson, Christa** | Golfer |
| 6210 W Sunset Road, Tucson AZ 85743, USA | |
| **Johnson, Clark** | Actor, Director |
| United Talent Agency, U T A Plaza, 9336 Civic Center Dr, Beverly Hills CA 90210 USA | |
| **Johnson, Clemon** | Basketball Player |
| 835 N Waukeenah St, Monticello FL 32344, USA | |
| **Johnson, Clifford (Cliff)** | Baseball Player |
| 9618 Mediator Pass, Converse TX 78109, USA | |
| **Johnson, Corey** | Actor |
| Another Tongue, 10-11 D'Arblay St, London W1F 8DS, England | |
| **Johnson, Cornelius O** | Football Player |
| 603 Dale St, Highland Springs VA 23075, USA | |
| **Johnson, Courtney** | Water Polo Player |
| 408 Tharp Dr, Moraga CA 94556, USA | |
| **Johnson, Craig** | Ice Hockey Player |
| 812 Island Dr, #A, Alameda CA 94502, USA | |
| **Johnson, Craig A** | Writer |
| Penguin Books, 375 Hudson St, Basement 1, New York NY 10014 USA | |
| **Johnson, Curtis W** | Football Player |
| PO Box 70608, Toledo OH 43607, USA | |
| **Johnson, Curtis, Jr** | Football Coach |
| Tulane University, Athletic Dept, New Orleans LA 70118, USA | |
| **Johnson, Daniel R (Dan)** | Baseball Player |
| 3355 134th Ave NE, Andover MN 55304, USA | |
| **Johnson, Darren** | Chemist |
| University of Oregon, Chemistry Dept, Eugene OR 97403, USA | |
| **Johnson, Darrius D** | Football Player |
| 402 Thomas St, Terrell TX 75160, USA | |
| **Johnson, Dave** | Labor Leader |
| United Garment Workers, 4207 Lebanon Road, Hermitage TN 37076, USA | |
| **Johnson, David A (Davey)** | Baseball Player, Manager |
| 1064 Howell Branch Road, Winter Park FL 32789, USA | |
| **Johnson, David Allen (D J)** | Football Player |
| 500 Tripoli St, Pittsburgh PA 15212, USA | |
| **Johnson, David Cay** | Journalist |
| New York Times, Editorial Dept, 229 W 43rd St, New York NY 10036 USA | |
| **Johnson, David G** | Economist |
| 5500 S Shore Dr, #1406, Chicago IL 60637, USA | |
| **Johnson, David W** | Businessman |
| Campbell Soup Co, 1 Campbell Place, Camden NJ 08103, USA | |
| **Johnson, David W (Dave)** | Baseball Player |
| 7101 Mount Vista Road, Kingsville MD 21087, USA | |
| **Johnson, Demetrios** | Football Player |
| 840 Garonne Dr, Ballwin MO 63021, USA | |
| **Johnson, DerMarr M** | Basketball Player |
| 14610 Man O War Dr, Bowie MD 20721, USA | |
| **Johnson, Derrick O** | Football Player |
| 524 Private Road 4450, Uvalde TX 78801, USA | |
| **Johnson, Diane** | Writer |
| Creative Artists Agency, 2000 Ave of Stars, #100, Los Angeles CA 90067 USA | |

**J**

Johnson - Johnson

**Johnson, Don**
Actor
Don Johnson Productions, 9663 Santa Monica Blvd, #278, Beverly Hills CA 90210, USA

**Johnson, Donald (Groundhog)**
Baseball Player
3935 King Place, Cincinnati OH 45223, USA

**Johnson, Donald R (Don)**
Baseball Player
1529 NE 21st Ave, #205, Portland OR 97232, USA

**Johnson, Dwayne D (The Rock)**
Actor, Professional Wrestler
White Buffalo Entertainment, One State Street Plaza, #2400, New York NY 10004, USA

**Johnson, Dwight O**
Football Player
1812 King Cole Dr, Waco TX 76705, USA

**Johnson, Earvin (Magic), Jr**
Basketball Player, Coach
Magic Johnson Foundation, 9100 Wilshire Blvd, #700E, Beverly Hills CA 90212, USA

**Johnson, Echo L**
Model
2402 Jarratt Ave, #B, Austin TX 78703, USA

**Johnson, Edward (Eddie)**
Soccer Player
Seattle Sounders, 12 Seahawks Way, Renton WA 98056 USA

**Johnson, Edward A (Eddie)**
Basketball Player
6133 N 61st Place, Paradise Valley AZ 85253, USA

**Johnson, Edward L (Eddie), Jr**
Basketball Player
PO Box 542, Weirsdale FL 32195, USA

**Johnson, Edward S (Tre), III**
Football Player
680 Harrison Ave, Peekskill NY 10566, USA

**Johnson, Emma**
Concert Clarinetist
Columbia Artists Mgmt Inc, 5 Columbus Circle, 1790 Broadway, #1600, New York NY 10019 USA

**Johnson, Eric**
Golfer
893 Chateau Meadows Dr, Eugene OR 97401, USA

**Johnson, Eric**
Writer
Verve Talent & Literary Agency, 96310 San Vicente Blvd, #100, Los Angeles CA 90048 USA

**Johnson, Eric**
Guitarist
Joe Priesnitz Artist Mgmt, PO Box 5249, Austin TX 78763, USA

**Johnson, Eric**
Actor
Brillstein Entertainment Partners, 9150 Wilshire Blvd, #350, Beverly Hills CA 90212 USA

**Johnson, Erik**
Ice Hockey Player
Colorado Avalanche, Pepsi Center, 1000 Chopper Circle, Denver CO 80204 USA

**Johnson, Ernest T (Ernie), Jr**
Sportscaster
TNT-TV, Sports Dept, 1050 Techwood Dr, Atlanta GA 30318 USA

**Johnson, Ervin**
Basketball Player
Minnesota Timberwolves, Target Center, 600 1st Ave N, Minneapolis MN 55403 USA

**Johnson, Essex L**
Football Player
1633 E Dimondale Dr, Carson CA 90746, USA

**Johnson, Ezra R**
Football Player
330 Millhaven Landing, Fayetteville GA 30215, USA

**Johnson, Frank**
Cartoonist (Bringing Up Father)
King Features Syndicate, 300 W 57th St, #1500, New York NY 10019 USA

**Johnson, Frank A**
Baseball Player
1151 Cypress Hill Lane, Stockton CA 95206, USA

**Johnson, Franklin L (Frank)**
Basketball Player, Coach
4320 N 40th St, Phoenix AZ 85018, USA

**Johnson, Fred**
Singer (Marcels)
5501 Camelia St, Pittsburgh PA 15201, USA

**Johnson, Gary**
Baseball Player
50 Tallwood Court, Atherton CA 94027, USA

**Johnson, Gene**
Guitarist, Mandolin Player (Diamond Rio)
Modern Mgmt, 1625 Broadway, #600, Nashville TN 37203, USA

**Johnson, Georgann**
Actress
218 Glenroy Place, Los Angeles CA 90049, USA

**Johnson, George**
Singer, Guitarist (Brothers Johnson)
Green Light Talent Agency, PO Box 3172, Beverly Hills CA 90212 USA

**Johnson, George T**
Basketball Player
630 Highland Overlook, Atlanta GA 30349, USA

**Johnson, George W**
Educator
George Mason University, President's Office, Fairfax VA 22030, USA

**Johnson, Glen**
Boxer
DiBella Entertainment, 350 7th Ave, #800, New York NY 10001, USA

**Johnson, Gregory C**
Astronaut
N A S A, Johnson Space Center, 2101 NASA Road, Houston TX 77058 USA

**Johnson, Gregory C (Greg)**
Ice Hockey Player
1058 Runyon Road, Rochester Hills MI 48306, USA

**Johnson, Gregory G**
Navy Admiral
Snow Ridge Assoc, 69 Shore Road, Harpswell ME 04079, USA

**Johnson, Gregory H**
Astronaut
N A S A, Johnson Space Center, 2101 NASA Road, Houston TX 77058 USA

**Johnson, Hansford T**
Air Force General
U S A A Capital Corp, 9800 Fredericksburg Road, San Antonio TX 78240, USA

**Johnson, Harold**
Boxer
2964 N Bambrey St, Philadelphia PA 19132, USA

**Johnson, Holly**
Singer (Frankie Goes to Hollywood)
Wolfgang Kuhle Artist Mgmt, PO Box 425, London SW6 3TX, England

**Johnson, Howard M (Hojo)**
Baseball Player
8597 SE Coconut St, Hobe Sound FL 33455, USA

**Johnson, Hugh T**
Director, Cinematographer
Mirisch Agency, 1025 Colorado Ave, #B, Santa Monica CA 90211 USA

**Johnson, Ian**
Journalist
Wall Street Journal, Editorial Dept, 1 World Financial Center, New York NY 10281, USA

**Johnson, J Bradley (Brad)**
Football Player
1911 Nellie Gray Court, Athens GA 30606, USA

**Johnson, J Curley**
Football Player
5512 Wedgefield Road, Granbury TX 76049, USA

**Johnson, J Seward, II**
Sculptor
Grounds for Sculpture, 18 Fairgrounds Road, Hamilton NJ 08619, USA

**Johnson, Jack**
Singer, Guitarist, Songwriter
Universal Republic Records, 1755 Broadway, #800, New York NY 10019 USA

**Johnson, James A**
Government Official, Financier
Perseus LLC, 1325 Ave of Americas, #2500, New York NY 10019, USA

**Johnson, James E (Jimmy)**
Football Player
656 Amaranth Blvd, Mill Valley CA 94941, USA

**Johnson, James W (Jimmy)** — Football Coach, Sportscaster
Fox-TV, Sports Dept, 205 W 67th St, New York NY 10065 USA
**Johnson, Jamey** — Singer, Songwriter
Vector Mgmt, PO Box 120479, Nashville TN 37212 USA
**Johnson, Jarret W** — Football Player
437 Evans Road, Niceville FL 32578, USA
**Johnson, Jason M** — Baseball Player
18122 Emerald Bay St, Tampa FL 33647, USA
**Johnson, Jay** — Actor, Comedian, Ventriloquist
Comedians USA, 1308 Sumac Drive, Knoxville TN 37919, USA
**Johnson, Jay Kenneth** — Actor
A P A Talent & Literary Agency, 405 S Beverly Dr, #300, Beverly Hills CA 90212 USA
**Johnson, Jay L** — Navy Admiral, Businessman
General Dynamics, 2941 Fairview Park Dr, #100, Falls Church VA 22042, USA
**Johnson, Jenna** — Swimmer, Coach
University of Tennessee, Athletic Dept, PO Box 15016, Knoxville TN 37901, USA
**Johnson, Jennifer** — Producer, Writer
W M E Entertainment, 9601 Wilshire Blvd, #300, Beverly Hills CA 90210 USA
**Johnson, Jerome L** — Navy Admiral
Navy-Marine Corps Relief Society, 801 N Randolph St, Arlington VA 22203, USA
**Johnson, Jerry M** — Baseball Player
16670 Espola Road, Poway CA 92064, USA
**Johnson, Jesse** — Football Player
102 Rosegill Road, Richmond VA 23236, USA
**Johnson, Jimmie K** — Auto Racing Driver
PO Box 4283, Mooresville NC 28117, USA
**Johnson, Jimmy** — Cartoonist (Arlo & Janis)
United Media Syndicate, PO Box 5610, Cincinnati OH 45201 USA
**Johnson, Joe M** — Basketball Player
2704 Wolf Lake Dr SW, Atlanta GA 30349, USA
**Johnson, Johari** — Actress
H W A Talent, 3500 W Olive Ave, #1400, Burbank CA 91505 USA
**Johnson, John H** — Basketball Player
4751 N 18th St, Milwaukee WI 53209, USA
**Johnson, John Henry** — Baseball Player
3345 Delna, Sparks NV 89431, USA
**Johnson, John J (Jack), III** — Ice Hockey Player
Los Angeles Kings, Staples Center, 1111 S Figueroa St, Los Angeles CA 90015 USA
**Johnson, Johnnie, Jr** — Football Player
3540 W Sahara Ave, #780, Las Vegas NV 89102, USA
**Johnson, Johnny** — Football Player
PO Box 13301, Tempe AZ 85284, USA
**Johnson, Jonathan K** — Baseball Player
101 Broad Bluff Point, Irmo SC 29063, USA
**Johnson, Joseph E, III** — Physician
187 Sea Hammock Way, Ponte Vedra Beach FL 32082, USA
**Johnson, Joshua M (Josh)** — Baseball Player
10855 S 94th East Place, Tulsa OK 74133, USA
**Johnson, K Lance** — Baseball Player
5712 Foxfire Road, Mobile AL 36618, USA
**Johnson, Kate Lang** — Actress
Innovative Artists, 1505 10th St, Santa Monica CA 90401 USA
**Johnson, Kathy** — Gymnast
2102 Clubside D, Longwood FL 32779, USA
**Johnson, Keith** — Labor Leader
Woodworkers of America Union, 1622 N Lombard St, Portland OR 97217, USA
**Johnson, Kenneth A (Kenny)** — Actor
L I N K Entertainment, 11872 La Grange Ave, Los Angeles CA 90025 USA
**Johnson, Kenneth H (Ken)** — Basketball Player
1401 N Wheeler Ave, Portland OR 97227, USA
**Johnson, Kenneth T (Ken)** — Baseball Player
121 Myrtlewood Dr, Pineville LA 71360, USA
**Johnson, Kevin M** — Basketball Player, Sportscaster, Mayor
Mayor's Office, City Hall, 915 I St, #500, Sacramento CA 95814, USA
**Johnson, Keyshawn** — Football Player, Sportscaster
19232 Northfleet Way, Tarzana CA 91356, USA
**Johnson, Kylie** — Model
Playboy Promotions, 9346 Civic Center Dr, #200, Beverly Hills CA 90210 USA
**Johnson, Kym** — Dancer, Model
Rothman Patino Andres Entertainment, 4370 Tujunga Ave, #120, Studio City CA 91604, USA
**Johnson, Lamar** — Baseball Player
4105 Sangre Trail, Arlington TX 76016, USA
**Johnson, Landon T** — Football Player
7556 Fox Chase Dr, West Chester OH 45069, USA
**Johnson, Larry A, Jr** — Football Player
340 Glengarry Lane, State College PA 16801, USA
**Johnson, Larry D** — Baseball Player
5111 Hector Ave, #405, Cleveland OH 44127, USA
**Johnson, Larry D** — Basketball Player
Larry Johnson's R W A C, 15303 Dallas Parkway, #970, Addison TX 75001, USA
**Johnson, Laura** — Actress
Geddes Agency, 8430 Santa Monica Blvd, #201, West Hollywood CA 90069 USA
**Johnson, Laurie** — Composer
Priority House, Camp Hill, Stanmore, Middlesex HA7 3JQ, England
**Johnson, LeShon E** — Football Player
15102 Beverly St, Overland Park KS 66223, USA
**Johnson, Levi** — Football Player
1202 Craig Dr, Westland MI 48186, USA
**Johnson, Linda** — Poker Player
Poker Gives, PO Box 434, Conyers NY 10920, USA
**Johnson, Lonnie D** — Football Player
8500 Amber Ridge Court, Sanford FL 32771, USA
**Johnson, Louis** — Singer, Bassist (Brothers Johnson)
Green Light Talent Agency, PO Box 3172, Beverly Hills CA 90212 USA
**Johnson, Louis B (Lou)** — Baseball Player
4532 Valley Ridge Ave, Los Angeles CA 90008, USA

| | |
|---|---|
| **Johnson, Lynn-Holly** | Actress |
| 2109 S Wilbur Ave, Walla Walla WA 99362, USA | |
| **Johnson, Manuel H, Jr** | Government Official, Economist |
| Johnson Smick Int'l, 2099 Pennsylvania Ave NW, #950, Washington DC 20006, USA | |
| **Johnson, Marc** | Jazz Bassist, Composer |
| Word of Mouth Music, 235 E 22nd St, #9F, New York NY 10010, USA | |
| **Johnson, Marcia Thornton** | Writer |
| Scholastic Press, 555 Broadway, New York NY 10012 USA | |
| **Johnson, Mark** | Boxer |
| 1204 Howison Place SW, Washington DC 20081, USA | |
| **Johnson, Mark** | Journalist |
| Milwaukee Journal Sentinel, Editorial Dept, PO Box 371, Milwaukee WI 53201 USA | |
| **Johnson, Mark** | Producer |
| Gran Via Productions, 1888 Century Park E, #1400, Los Angeles CA 90067, USA | |
| **Johnson, Mark E** | Ice Hockey Player |
| 1609 Hidden Hill Dr, Verona WI 53593, USA | |
| **Johnson, Mark P** | Baseball Player |
| 40 Helen Ave, Rye NY 10580, USA | |
| **Johnson, Mark Steven** | Director, Writer |
| Creative Artists Agency, 2000 Ave of Stars, #100, Los Angeles CA 90067 USA | |
| **Johnson, Marques K** | Basketball Player |
| 5133 Dawn View Place, Los Angeles CA 90043, USA | |
| **Johnson, Marvin** | Boxer |
| 5452 Turfway Circle, Indianapolis IN 46228, USA | |
| **Johnson, Marvin M** | Chemical Engineer |
| 3055 SE Bison Road, Bartlesville OK 74006, USA | |
| **Johnson, Matt** | Singer, Guitarist (The The); Songwriter |
| Free Trade Agency, Chapel Place, Rivington St, London EC2A 3DQ, England | |
| **Johnson, Michael** | Singer, Guitarist, Songwriter |
| A R T R A-Artists Mgmt, 130 S Canal St, #211, Chicago IL 60606, USA | |
| **Johnson, Michael D** | Track Athlete |
| Baylor University, Athletic Dept, 150 Bear Run, Waco TX 76711, USA | |
| **Johnson, Michael K (Mike)** | Baseball Player |
| 446 23rd Place, Manhattan Beach CA 90266, USA | |
| **Johnson, Michael M (Butch)** | Football Player |
| 9719 S Red Oakes Dr, Littleton CO 80126, USA | |
| **Johnson, Michelle** | Actress, Model |
| Angel City Talent, 4741 Laurel Canyon Blvd, Valley Village CA 91607, USA | |
| **Johnson, Mike** | Animator, Director |
| Paradigm Agency, 360 N Crescent Dr, North Building, Beverly Hills CA 90210 USA | |
| **Johnson, Monte C** | Football Player |
| 2349 Hurst Dr NE, Atlanta GA 30305, USA | |
| **Johnson, N James (Jim)** | Ice Hockey Player |
| Interactive Coaching, 34522 N Scottsdale Road, #D8, Scottsdale AZ 85266, USA | |
| **Johnson, Nancy L** | Representative, CT |
| Baker Donelson Bearman Caldwell Berkowitz, 901 K St NW, #900,Washington DC 20001, USA | |
| **Johnson, Neil A** | Basketball Player |
| 821 Plymouth Lane, Virginia Beach VA 23451, USA | |
| **Johnson, Nicholas R (Nick)** | Baseball Player |
| 8008 Sacramento St, Fair Oaks CA 95628, USA | |
| **Johnson, Nick** | Basketball Player |
| Houston Rockets, 1730 Jefferson St, Houston TX 77003 USA | |
| **Johnson, Nicole Randall** | Actress |
| Greene Assoc, 1901 Ave of Stars, #130, Los Angeles CA 90067 USA | |
| **Johnson, Norman D (Norm)** | Football Player |
| 8523 NW Anderson Hill Road, Silverdale WA 98383, USA | |
| **Johnson, Ollie** | Basketball Player |
| 1700 Spring Garden St, Philadelphia PA 19130, USA | |
| **Johnson, Ora J** | Religious Leader |
| General Baptists Ministries, 100 Stinson Dr, Poplar Bluff MO 63901, USA | |
| **Johnson, Paatricia M (Trish)** | Golfer |
| Encompass, 121 Hook Road, Epsom, Surrey KT19 8TU, England | |
| **Johnson, Patricia (Tish)** | Bowler |
| Professional Bowlers Association, 719 2nd Ave, #701, Seattle WA 98104 USA | |
| **Johnson, Patrick** | Actor |
| A P A Talent & Literary Agency, 405 S Beverly Dr, #300, Beverly Hills CA 90212 USA | |
| **Johnson, Paul** | Football Coach |
| Georgia Institute of Technology, Athletic Dept, Atlanta GA 30332, USA | |
| **Johnson, Paul B** | Historian |
| 29 Newton Road, London W2 5JR, England | |
| **Johnson, Paul H** | Ice Hockey Player |
| 1719 Yale Ave, Burley ID 83318, USA | |
| **Johnson, Penny** | Actress |
| Mitchell K Stubbs Assoc, 8695 W Washington Blvd, #204, Culver City CA 90232 USA | |
| **Johnson, Pete** | Football Player |
| 6304 Misty Cove Lane, Columbus OH 43231, USA | |
| **Johnson, R E** | Labor Leader |
| Train Dispatchers Assn, 4239 W 150th St, #1, Cleveland OH 44135, USA | |
| **Johnson, R Keith** | Baseball Player |
| PO Box 4122, Park City UT 84060, USA | |
| **Johnson, Rafer L** | Track Athlete, Actor |
| 4217 Woodcliff Road, Sherman Oaks CA 91403, USA | |
| **Johnson, Randall D (Randy)** | Baseball Player |
| 8404 N El Maro Circle, Paradise Valley AZ 85253, USA | |
| **Johnson, Raylee T** | Football Player |
| 2010 Black Fox Dr NE, Atlanta GA 30345, USA | |
| **Johnson, Rebecca** | Actress |
| United Agents, 12-26 Lexington St, London W1F 0LE, England | |
| **Johnson, Reed C** | Baseball Player |
| 10008 Mirada Dr, Las Vegas NV 89144, USA | |
| **Johnson, Reggie D (Sweet)** | Boxer |
| Puglistic Drama, 1029 Highway 6 N, #650-150, Houston TX 77079, USA | |
| **Johnson, Reginald R (Reggie)** | Football Player |
| 17907 Souter Lane, Land O'Lakes FL 34638, USA | |
| **Johnson, Richard** | Archer |
| 234 Route 197, Woodstock CT 06281, USA | |

**Johnson, Richard A (Dick)** — Baseball Player
5001 E Main St, #762, Mesa AZ 85205, USA
**Johnson, Richard J** — Football Player
926 Peachwood Bend Dr, Houston TX 77077, USA
**Johnson, Richard K** — Actor
Conway Van Gelder Grant, 8-12 Broadwick St, #300, London W1F 8HW, England
**Johnson, Richard S** — Golfer
Professional Golfers Association, 100 Ave of Champions, Palm Beach Gardens FL 33418 USA
**Johnson, Rob C** — Football Player
26635 Aracena Dr, Mission Viejo CA 92691, USA
**Johnson, Robert D (Bob)** — Baseball Player
650 Caves Highway, Cave Junction OR 97523, USA
**Johnson, Robert D (Bob)** — Football Player
165 Magnolia Ave, Cincinnati OH 45246, USA
**Johnson, Robert G (Junior), Jr** — Auto Racing Driver, Executive
3200 Seven Eagles Road, Charlotte NC 28210, USA
**Johnson, Robert L** — Businessman, Basketball Executive
Black Entertainment TV, 1900 W Place NE, Washington DC 20018, USA
**Johnson, Robert Sherlaw** — Composer, Concert Pianist
Omnibus Press, 14/15 Berners St, London W1T 3LJ, England
**Johnson, Robert W (Bob)** — Baseball Player
1474 Barclay St, Saint Paul MN 55106, USA
**Johnson, Romina** — Singer
Mission Control, City Business Center, Lower Road, London SE16 2XB, England
**Johnson, Ron, Sr** — Football Player
1080 Stafford Place, Detroit MI 48207, USA
**Johnson, Ronald A (Ron)** — Football Player
226 Summit Ave, Summit NJ 07901, USA
**Johnson, Roy** — Labor Leader
Roofers & Waterproofers Union, 1125 17th St NW, Washington DC 20036, USA
**Johnson, Rudi A** — Football Player
5177 Rollman Estates Dr, Cincinnati OH 45236, USA
**Johnson, Rupert** — Financier
Franklin Resources, 277 Mariners Island Blvd, San Mateo CA 94404, USA
**Johnson, Samuel L (Sammy)** — Football Player
142 Old Mill Road, #B, High Point NC 27265, USA
**Johnson, Sandy** — Model, Actress
Playboy Promotions, 9346 Civic Center Dr, #200, Beverly Hills CA 90210 USA
**Johnson, Sankey Anton (S A)** — Businessman
PO Box 976, Trabuco Canyon CA 92678, USA
**Johnson, Scott** — Guitarist (Gin Blossoms/Low Watts)
W M E Entertainment, 1600 Division St, #300, Nashville TN 37203 USA
**Johnson, Scott** — Composer
Tzadik Records, 200 E 10th St, Box 126, New York, NY 10003, USA
**Johnson, Scott** — Gymnast
PO Box 195222, Winter Springs FL 32719, USA
**Johnson, Seleena** — Singer, Songwriter
Shanachie Records, 37 E Clinton St, #1, Newton NJ 07860 USA
**Johnson, Shawn** — Gymnast
171 W 57th St, #8A, New York NY 10019, USA
**Johnson, Sonia** — Women's, Religious Activist
3318 2nd St S, Arlington VA 22204, USA
**Johnson, Spencer** — Writer
G P Putnam's Sons, 375 Hudson St, New York NY 10014 USA
**Johnson, Stanley L (Stan)** — Baseball Player
56 Moringside Dr, Daly City CA 94015, USA
**Johnson, Steffond** — Basketball Player
10525 Marsh Lane, Dallas TX 75229, USA
**Johnson, Syl** — Singer, Songwriter, Producer
Blue Sky Artists, 761 Washington Ave N, Minneapolis MN 55401, USA
**Johnson, Syleena** — Singer, Songwriter
Rodgers Redding, PO Box 4603, Macon GA 31208 USA
**Johnson, Ted C** — Football Player
44 Lincoln Road, Wayland MA 01778, USA
**Johnson, Temeko** — Basketball Player
Phoenix Mercury, American West Arena, 201 E Jefferson St, Phoenix AZ 85004 USA
**Johnson, Terry** — Ice Hockey Player
Endev Energy, 200-207 9th Ave SW, Calgary AB T2P 1K3, Canada
**Johnson, Terry (Buzzy)** — Singer (Flamingos)
Resort Attractions, 2375 E Tropicana Ave, #304, Las Vegas NV 89119, USA
**Johnson, Thomas (Pepper)** — Football Player
New England Patriots, 1 Patriot Place, Foxboro MA 02035 USA
**Johnson, Thomas F** — Baseball Player
1611 Constitution Blvd, Rock Hill SC 29732, USA
**Johnson, Thomas R (Tom)** — Baseball Player
2700 Knox Ave N, Minneapolis MN 55411, USA
**Johnson, Timothy (Tim)** — Football Player
2839 Dorell Ave, Orlando FL 32814, USA
**Johnson, Timothy E (Tim)** — Baseball Player, Manager
2550 E River Road, #3205, Tucson AZ 85718, USA
**Johnson, Tom** — Sound Editor
Ardmore Sound, Ardmore Studios, Herbert Road, Bray, County Wicklow, Ireland
**Johnson, Tommy** — Musician (Brothers Johnson)
Green Light Talent Agency, PO Box 3172, Beverly Hills CA 90212 USA
**Johnson, Torrence V** — Astronomer, Space Scientist
Jet Propulsion Laboratory, 4800 Oak Grove Dr, Pasadena CA 91109 USA
**Johnson, Trent** — Basketball Coach
Stanford University, Athletic Dept, Stanford CA 94305, USA
**Johnson, Vance E** — Football Player
PO Box 606, Parachute CO 81635, USA
**Johnson, Vaughan M** — Football Player
4915 Arendell St, #253, Morehead City NC 28557, USA
**Johnson, Victoria** — Physical Fitness Instructor
V J International, PO Box 1744, Lake Oswego OR 97035, USA
**Johnson, Vincent (Vinnie)** — Basketball Player
5236 Elmsgate Dr, Orchard Lake MI 48324, USA

Johnson - Johnson

**J**

| | |
|---|---|
| **Johnson, Virginia** <br> Dance Theatre of Harlem, 466 W 152nd St, New York NY 10031, USA | Ballerina |
| **Johnson, W Bruce** <br> Sears Holdings, 3333 Beverly Road, Hoffman Estates IL 60179, USA | Businessman |
| **Johnson, W Leon** <br> 813 Vine Arden Road, Morganton NC 28655, USA | Football Player |
| **Johnson, W Russell (Russ)** <br> 3542 Russell Road, Green Cove Springs FL 32043, USA | Baseball Player |
| **Johnson, Wallace D** <br> 5210 S Campbell Ave, Chicago IL 60632, USA | Baseball Player |
| **Johnson, Wallace E (Mickey)** <br> 3642 W Grenshaw St, Chicago IL 60624, USA | Basketball Player |
| **Johnson, Warren** <br> Warren Johnson Enterprises, 700 N Price Road, Sugar Hill GA 30518, USA | Auto Racing Driver |
| **Johnson, Warren C** <br> 946 Bellclair Road SE, Grand Rapids MI 49506, USA | Chemist |
| **Johnson, Wendy** <br> 126 Red Brook Lane, Mooresville NC 28117, USA | Auto Racing Driver |
| **Johnson, Wilko** <br> A B S Agency, PO Box 932A, Surbiton KT1 9QR, England | Guitarist (Dr Feelgood) |
| **Johnson, William A (Billy White Shoes)** <br> 3701 Whitney Place, Duluth GA 30096, USA | Football Player |
| **Johnson, William B** <br> Ritz-Carlton Hotels, 4445 Willard Ave, #800, Chevy Chase MD 20815, USA | Businessman |
| **Johnson, William E (Bill)** <br> 3399 Hartwood Road, Cleveland Heights OH 44112, USA | Football Player |
| **Johnson, William Merritt** <br> Creative Artists Agency, 2000 Ave of Stars, #100, Los Angeles CA 90067 USA | Writer |
| **Johnson, William R** <br> H J Heinz Co, PO Box 57, Pittsburgh PA 15230, USA | Businessman |
| **Johnson, Zach** <br> 267 Saint Andrews, Saint Simons Island GA 31522, USA | Golfer |
| **Johnson-Scharpf, Brandy** <br> Brandy Johnson's Global Gymnastics, 1945 Don Wickham Dr, Clermont FL 34711, USA | Gymnast |
| **Johnsson, Kim** <br> 5308 Oaklawn Ave, Minneapolis MN 55424, USA | Ice Hockey Player |
| **Johnstad, Kurt** <br> W M E Entertainment, 9601 Wilshire Blvd, #300, Beverly Hills CA 90210 USA | Writer |
| **Johnston McKay, Mary H** <br> University of Tennessee, Space Institute, Tullahoma TN 37388, USA | Astronaut |
| **Johnston, Abigail L (Abby)** <br> Duke Aquatics, 3020 Pickett Road, #424, Durham NC 27705, USA | Diver |
| **Johnston, Allen H** <br> Bishop's House, 3 Wymer Terrace, PO Box 21, Chartwell, Hamilton 3210, New Zealand | Religious Leader |
| **Johnston, Bruce** <br> I C M Partners, 10250 Constellation Blvd, #900, Los Angeles CA 90067 USA | Singer (Beach Boys) |
| **Johnston, Daniel D** <br> Dog Day Press, Finsbury Centre, 40 Bowling Green Lane, London EC1R 0NE, England | Singer, Songwriter |
| **Johnston, Daryl P (Moose)** <br> 4414 Woodfin Dr, Dallas TX 75220, USA | Football Player |
| **Johnston, Freedy** <br> High Road Touring, 751 Bridgeway, #200, Sausalito CA 94965 USA | Singer, Songwriter |
| **Johnston, Gerald A** <br> McDonnell Douglas Corp, PO Box 516, Saint Louis MO 63166, USA | Businessman |
| **Johnston, Gerald E** <br> Clorox Co, 1221 Broadway, Oakland CA 94612, USA | Businessman |
| **Johnston, Harold S** <br> 285 Franklin St, Harrisonburg VA 22801, USA | Chemist |
| **Johnston, J Bennett, Jr** <br> Johnston Assoc, 900 19th St NW, #800, Washington DC 20006, USA | Senator, LA |
| **Johnston, Jimmy** <br> Pro's Inc, 9 S 12th St, #300, Richmond VA 23219, USA | Golfer |
| **Johnston, Joanna** <br> Independent Talent Group, 40 Whitfield St, London W1T 2RH, England | Costume Designer |
| **Johnston, Joel R** <br> 1318 Meadowview Dr, #M, Pottstown PA 19464, USA | Baseball Player |
| **Johnston, John Dennis** <br> S D B Partners, 315 S Beverly Dr, #411, Beverly Hills CA 90067 USA | Actor |
| **Johnston, Joseph E (Joe)** <br> Resolution, 1801 Century Park E, #2300, Los Angeles CA 90067 USA | Director |
| **Johnston, Kristen** <br> Paradigm Agency, 360 N Crescent Dr, North Building, Beverly Hills CA 90210 USA | Actress |
| **Johnston, L Marshall** <br> 3933 Waville Road NE, Bemidji MN 56601, USA | Ice Hockey Player |
| **Johnston, Lynn** <br> Universal Press Syndicate, 4520 Main St, #700, Kansas City MO 64111 USA | Cartoonist (For Better or For Worse) |
| **Johnston, Mark R** <br> 609 Carolyn Ave, Austin TX 78705, USA | Football Player |
| **Johnston, Nate** <br> 8870 Fontainbleau Blvd, #301, Miami FL 33172, USA | Basketball Player |
| **Johnston, Rebecca** <br> Team Canada, 2424 University Dr NW, Calgary AB T2N 3Y9, Canada | Ice Hockey Player |
| **Johnston, Rex D** <br> 15117 Illinois Ave, Paramount CA 90723, USA | Football, Baseball Player |
| **Johnston, S K, Jr** <br> Coca-Cola Enterprises, 2500 Windy Ridge Parkway, #700, Atlanta GA 30339, USA | Businessman |
| **Johnston, Steven E (Stevie)** <br> Silverhawk Boxing, 10120 S Eastern Ave, #200, Henderson NV 89052, USA | Boxer |
| **Johnstone, John W** <br> 9330 Clubside Circle, #3305, Sarasota FL 34238, USA | Baseball Player |
| **Johnstone, John W (Jay), Jr** <br> 853 Chapea Road, Pasadena CA 91107, USA | Baseball Player |
| **Johnstone, John W, Jr** <br> 467 Carter St, New Canaan CT 06840, USA | Businessman |
| **Johnstone, Parker, III** <br> Parker Johnstone Honda, 30600 SW Parkway Ave, Wilsonville OR 97070, USA | Auto Racing Driver |

**Johnston-Forbes, Cathy** — Golfer
5104 Lunar Dr, Kitty Hawk NC 27949, USA
**Johnston-Ulrich, Kim** — Actress
S D B Partners, 315 S Beverly Dr, #411, Beverly Hills CA 90067 USA
**Joiner, Charles (Charlie), Jr** — Football Player, Coach
16935 W Bernardo Dr, #107, San Diego CA 92127, USA
**Joiner, J Russell (Rusty)** — Actor, Model
TalentWorks, 3500 W Olive Ave, #1400, Burbank CA 91505 USA
**JoJo** — Singer, Songwriter, Actress
Universal Records, 70 Universal City Plaza, Universal City CA 91608 USA
**Jokinen, Jussi** — Ice Hockey Player
Pittsburgh Penguins, Consol Energy Center, 1001 5th Ave, Pittsburgh PA 15219 USA
**Jokinen, Olli** — Ice Hockey Player
6501 N Federal Highway, #2, Boca Raton FL 33487, USA
**Jokovic, Maro** — Water Polo Player
V K Jug Dubrovnik, Dr Ante Starcevica 22, 20000 Dubrovnik, Croatia
**Jokowi (Joko Widodo)** — President, Indonesia
President's Office, 15 Jalam Merdeka Utara, Jarkata, Indonesia
**Jokubonis, Gediminas** — Sculptor
V Kudirkos 4-3, 2009 Vilnius, Lithuania
**Jolas, Betsy M** — Composer
Nat Superieur Musique Conservatoire, 209 Ave Jaures, 75019 Paris, France
**Joli, France** — Singer
Brothers Management Assoc, 141 Dunbar Ave, Fords NJ 08863 USA
**Joli, Guillaume** — Handball Player
Dunkirk H B Grand Littoral, Ave de Rosendael, BP 4197, 59378 Dunkirk, France
**Joli, Wouter** — Field Hockey Player
H C Bloemendaal, Aelbertsbergweg 3, 2061 Bloemendaal AA, Netherlands
**Jolicoeur, David** — Rap Artist (DeLaSoul)
Entertainment Artists, 2409 21st Ave S, #100, Nashville TN 10019 USA
**Jolie, Angelina** — Actress, Model, Director
Media Talent Group, 9200 W Sunset Blvd, #550, West Hollywood CA 90069 USA
**Joliff, Howard (Howie)** — Basketball Player
2346 Fallen Oak Circle NE, Massillon OH 44646, USA
**Joliot, Pierre A** — Biologist
16 Rue de la Glaciere, 75013 Paris, France
**Jollett, Mikel** — Singer, Guitarist (Airborne Toxic Event)
Island Def Jam Records, 8920 W Sunset Blvd, #200, West Hollywood CA 90069 USA
**Jolley, Gordon H** — Football Player
1459 Navajo Dr, Saint George UT 84790, USA
**Jolly, Allison** — Yachtswoman
27122 Benidorm, Mission Viejo CA 92692, USA
**Jolly, E Grady** — Judge
US Court of Appeals, Eastland Courthouse, 245 E Capitol St, Jackson MS 39201, USA
**Jolovitz, Jenna** — Actress, Writer
Creative Artists Agency, 2000 Ave of Stars, #100, Los Angeles CA 90067 USA
**Joltz, Joachim** — Electrical Engineer
A M Forsthof 16, 42119 Wuppertal, Germany
**Jomaa, Mehdi** — Prime Minister, Tunisia
Prime Minister's Office, Place du Gouvernement, La Kasbah, 1008 Tunis, Tunisia
**Jon B** — Singer, Songwriter
Entertainment Artists, 2409 21st Ave S, #100, Nashville TN 10019 USA
**Jonas, Joseph A (Joe)** — Singer, Guitarist (Jonas Brothers)
Philymack Inc, 11661 San Vicente Blvd, #609, Los Angeles CA 90049, USA
**Jonas, Nicholas J (Nick)** — Singer, Guitarist (Jonas Brothers)
Jonas Group, 6725 W Sunset Blvd, #350, Los Angeles CA 90028, USA
**Jonas, P Kevin** — Singer, Guitarist (Jonas Brothers)
Philymack Inc, 11661 San Vicente Blvd, #609, Los Angeles CA 90049, USA
**Jonathan, Wesley** — Actor
Marsh Entertainment, 12444 Ventura Blvd, #203, Studio City CA 91604, USA
**Jones Gillian** — Actress
Shanahan Mgmt, Berman House, 91 Campbell St, #300, Surry Hills NSW 2010, Australia
**Jones, Aaron D, II** — Football Player
7677 Torino Court, Orlando FL 32835, USA
**Jones, Adam B (Pacman)** — Football Player
4282 N Chapel Road, Franklin TN 37067, USA
**Jones, Adam L** — Baseball Player
Baltimore Orioles, Oriole Park, 333 W Camden St, Baltimore MD 21201 USA
**Jones, Adam T** — Guitarist (Tool)
Volcano Records, 3575 Cahuenga Blvd W, #590, Los Angeles CA 90068, USA
**Jones, Aled** — Singer
Agency Group Ltd, 361-373 City Road, London EC1V 1PQ, England
**Jones, Alex S** — Journalist
1 Waterhouse St, #61, Cambridge MA 02138, USA
**Jones, Alfred** — Boxer
19610 Northbrook Dr, Southfield MI 48076, USA
**Jones, Allen C** — Artist
41 Charterhouse Square, London EC1M 6EA, England
**Jones, Andruw R** — Baseball Player
2931 Grey Moss Pass, Duluth GA 30097, USA
**Jones, Angus T** — Actor
Paradigm Agency, 360 N Crescent Dr, North Building, Beverly Hills CA 90210 USA
**Jones, Anthony H** — Basketball Player
44 Hempstead Dr, Newark DE 19702, USA
**Jones, Antonia** — Actress
Baron Entertainment, 13848 Ventura Blvd, #A, Sherman Oaks CA 91423, USA
**Jones, Asjha T** — Basketball Player
Connecticut Sun, 1 Mohegan Sun Blvd, Uncasville CT 06382 USA
**Jones, Barry L** — Baseball Player
411 S Morton Ave, Centerville IN 47330, USA
**Jones, Ben** — Representative, GA; Actor
Cooter's Place, 157 Parkway, Gatlinburg TN 37738, USA
**Jones, Bertram H (Bert)** — Football Player
133 Pinecrest Dr, Ruston LA 71270, USA
**Jones, Bill T** — Choreographer
219 W 19th St, New York NY 10011, USA

| | |
|---|---|
| **Jones, Booker T** | Singer, Guitarist (Booker T & the MG's) |
| Wenig-LaMonica Associates, 580 White Plains Road, #130, Tarrytown NY 10591 USA | |
| **Jones, Brad** | Bassist (Jazz Passengers) |
| Cross Road Mgmt, 45 W 11th St, #7B, New York NY 10011, USA | |
| **Jones, Brad** | Ice Hockey Player |
| International Hockey League, PO Box 175, Bedford MI 49020, USA | |
| **Jones, Brandon V** | Football Player |
| 1070 Randall Road, Texarkana TX 75501, USA | |
| **Jones, Brent M** | Football Player, Sportscaster |
| 756 El Pintado Road, Danville CA 94526, USA | |
| **Jones, Caleb Landry** | Actor |
| Paradigm Agency, 360 N Crescent Dr, North Building, Beverly Hills CA 90210 USA | |
| **Jones, Calvin (Fuzz)** | Singer, Musician (Legendary Blues Band) |
| J W Entertainment, PO Box 78904, Atlanta GA 30357 USA | |
| **Jones, Carnetta** | Actress |
| C E S D, 10635 Santa Monica Blvd, #130, Los Angeles CA 90025 USA | |
| **Jones, Cedric D** | Football Player |
| 804 Hawkesbury Park, Norman OK 73072, USA | |
| **Jones, Charles A** | Basketball Player |
| 304 Chestnut St, Elizabethtown KY 42701, USA | |
| **Jones, Cherry** | Actress |
| W M E Entertainment, 9601 Wilshire Blvd, #300, Beverly Hills CA 90210 USA | |
| **Jones, Christine** | Scenic Designer |
| Abrams Artists, 275 7th Ave, #2600, New York NY 10001 USA | |
| **Jones, Cleon J** | Baseball Player |
| 751 Edwards St, Mobile AL 36610, USA | |
| **Jones, Cleve** | Social Activist |
| Names Project Foundation, 637 Hope St, Atlanta GA 30310, USA | |
| **Jones, Clinton (Clint)** | Football Player |
| 16555 Sherman Way, #C, Lake Balboa CA 91406, USA | |
| **Jones, Cobi** | Soccer Player, Coach |
| 501 N Edinburgh Ave, Los Angeles CA 90048, USA | |
| **Jones, Courtney J L** | Figure Skating Executive |
| National Skating Assn, 15-27 Gee St, London EC1V 3RE, England | |
| **Jones, Cullen A** | Swimmer |
| Premier Management Group, 115 Crescent Commons, #250, Cary, NC 27518 USA | |
| **Jones, Dahntay L** | Basketball Player |
| PO Box 9984, Trenton NJ 8650, USA | |
| **Jones, Damon** | Basketball Player |
| 10703 Karter Court, Houston TX 77064, USA | |
| **Jones, Damon** | Football Player |
| 12690 Copper Springs Road, Jacksonville FL 32246, USA | |
| **Jones, Daniel A D (Danny)** | Singer, Guitarist (McFly), Songwriter |
| Helter Skelter, 347-353 Chiswick High Road, London W4 4HS, England | |
| **Jones, Daniel W** | Educator |
| University of Mississippi, Chancellor's Office, 1848 University Circle, Oxford MS 38677, USA | |
| **Jones, Dante D** | Football Player |
| 328 Partridge Run Dr, Duncanville TX 75137, USA | |
| **Jones, Darryl** | Bassist (Rolling Stones) |
| Rascoff/Zysblat Organization, 250 W 57th St, New York NY 10107 USA | |
| **Jones, Darryl L** | Baseball Player |
| 15628 King Dr, Meadville PA 16335, USA | |
| **Jones, David** | Conductor |
| Owen White Mgmt, 22 Brunswick Terrace, Hove, East Sussex BN3 1HJ, England | |
| **Jones, David A** | Businessman |
| Humana Corp, 500 W Main St, Louisville KY 40202, USA | |
| **Jones, Davy** | Auto Racing Driver |
| T R W Racing, 2000 Jaguar Dr, Valparaiso IN 46383, USA | |
| **Jones, Dean** | Actor, Singer |
| Dean Jones Productions, PO Box 570276, Tarzana CA 91357, USA | |
| **Jones, Denise R M** | Singer (Point of Grace) |
| Blanton Harrell Cooke Corzine, 1014 Cross Bow Court, Hendersonville TN 37075 USA | |
| **Jones, Dhani M** | Football Player |
| 20550 Falcons Landing Circle, #5403, Sterling VA 20165, USA | |
| **Jones, Donell** | Singer, Songwriter |
| Universal Attractions, 135 W 26th St, #1200, New York NY 10001 USA | |
| **Jones, Dot-Marie** | Actress |
| Levin Agency, 8484 Wilshire Blvd, #750, Beverly Hills CA 90211, USA | |
| **Jones, Doug** | Actor |
| Coolwaters Productions, 10061 Riverside Dr, Box 531, Toluca Lake CA 91602 USA | |
| **Jones, Douglas R (Doug)** | Baseball Player |
| 129 E Navilla Place, Covina CA 91723, USA | |
| **Jones, Dwight E** | Basketball Player |
| 28926 Enchanted Dr, Shenandoah TX 77381, USA | |
| **Jones, Eddie** | Actor |
| A M T Artists, 15260 Ventura Blvd, #1200, Sherman Oaks CA 91403, USA | |
| **Jones, Eddie** | Architect |
| Jones Studio, 4450 N 12th St, Phoenix AZ 85014, USA | |
| **Jones, Eddie C** | Basketball Player |
| 3400 Paddock Road, Weston FL 33331, USA | |
| **Jones, Edith H** | Judge |
| US Court of Appeals, US Courthouse, 515 Rusk Ave, #12015, Houston TX 77002, USA | |
| **Jones, Edward L (Too Tall)** | Football Player |
| 1 Lost Valley Dr, Dallas TX 75234, USA | |
| **Jones, Edward M** | Architect |
| Jones Studios, 4450 N 12th St, Phoenix AZ 85014, USA | |
| **Jones, Edward P** | Writer |
| Amistad/Harper Collins Publishers, 10 E 53rd St, New York NY 10022, USA | |
| **Jones, Ellis B** | Financier |
| Wasserstein & Co, 1999 Ave of Stars, #2840, Los Angeles CA 90067, USA | |
| **Jones, Ernest L (Ernie)** | Football Player |
| 17410 SW 109th Ave, Miami FL 33157, USA | |
| **Jones, Evan** | Actor |
| A P A Talent & Literary Agency, 405 S Beverly Dr, #300, Beverly Hills CA 90212 USA | |
| **Jones, Fay** | Artist |
| Grover Thurston Gallery, 309 Occidental Ave S, Seattle WA 98104, USA | |

Jones, Felicity — Actress
Independent Talent Group, 40 Whitfield St, London W1T 2RH, England
Jones, Finn — Actor
A P A Talent & Literary Agency, 405 S Beverly Dr, #300, Beverly Hills CA 90212 USA
Jones, Freddie — Actor
Diamond Mgmt, 31 Percy St, London W1T 2DD, England
Jones, Freddie R, Jr — Football Player
151 S 111th Place, Mesa AZ 85208, USA
Jones, Garrett T — Baseball Player
670 W Wayman St, #1306, Chicago IL 60661, USA
Jones, Gary D — Football Player
3510 Rosedale St, Houston TX 77004, USA
Jones, Gemma — Actress
Conway Van Gelder Grant, 8-12 Broadwick St, #300, London W1F 8HW, England
Jones, Glenn — Singer
Andi Howard Entertainment, 30765 Pacific Coast Highway, #134, Malibu CA 90265, USA
Jones, Gordon — Football Player
18919 Fishermans Bend Dr, Lutz FL 33558, USA
Jones, Grace — Model, Actress, Singer
Raphael Santin Celebrity Services, 35 Rue Oberkampf, 75011 Paris, France
Jones, Greg — Skier
PO Box 500, Tahoe City CA 96145, USA
Jones, Greg P — Football Player
2331 S Fenton Dr, Lakewood CO 80227, USA
Jones, Grover W (Deacon) — Baseball Player
1015 Goldfinch Ave, Sugar Land TX 77478, USA
Jones, Gwyneth — Opera Singer
Opera et Concert, 37 Rue de la Chaussee d'Antin, 75009 Paris, France
Jones, Hassan A — Football Player
1010 Eldridge St, Clearwater FL 33755, USA
Jones, Hayes W — Track Athlete
408 Stonewood Dr, Peachtree City GA 30269, USA
Jones, Homer C — Football Player
408 S Texas St, Pittsburg TX 75686, USA
Jones, Horace A — Football Player
7925 Hobart Ave, Pensacola FL 32534, USA
Jones, Howard — Singer, Songwriter
F M L, 33 Alexander Road, Aylesbury, Buckinghamshire HP20 2NR, England
Jones, J Dalton — Baseball Player
4688 S Dixon Lane, Liberty MS 39645, USA
Jones, Jack — Singer
6 Exeter Court, Rancho Mirage CA 92270, USA
Jones, Jacque D — Baseball Player
347 Saint Rita Court, San Diego CA 92113, USA
Jones, Jacqueline — Historian
University of Texas, History Dept, Austin TX 78712, USA
Jones, Jade — Taekwondo Athlete
British Taekwondo, 4 Tinshill Lane, Leeds LS16 7AP, England
Jones, James (Jimmy) — Basketball Player
319 Salinas Dr, Henderson NV 89014, USA
Jones, James A (J J) — Football Player
PO Box 16, Bettendorf IA 52722, USA
Jones, James C (Jimmy) — Baseball Player
3054 Newcastle Dr, Dallas TX 75220, USA
Jones, James C (Jimmy) — Football Player
2 Odyssey Dr, Tinley Park IL 60477, USA
Jones, James D — Football Player
Oakland Raiders, 1220 Harbor Bay Parkway, Alameda CA 94502 USA
Jones, James Earl — Actor
Paradigm Agency, 360 N Crescent Dr, North Building, Beverly Hills CA 90210 USA
Jones, James R — Football Player
18130 Palm Breeze Dr, Tampa FL 33647, USA
Jones, Jamie — Singer (All-4-One), Songwriter
Big Machine Media, 575 Lexington Ave, #400, New York NY 10022, USA
Jones, Janet — Actress, Producer
9100 Wilshire Blvd, #1000W, Beverly Hills CA 90212, USA
Jones, January — Actress
Mosiac Media Group, 9200 W Sunset Blvd, #1000, Los Angeles CA 90069, USA
Jones, Jason — Actor, Writer
United Talent Agency, U T A Plaza, 9336 Civic Center Dr, Beverly Hills CA 90210 USA
Jones, Jason D — Football Player
Detroit Lions, 222 Republic Dr, Allen Park MI 48101 USA
Jones, Jeffrey A (Jeff) — Basketball Coach
Old Dominion University, Athletic Dept, Norfolk VA 23529, USA
Jones, Jeffrey A (Jeff) — Baseball Player
2200 Ready Road, Carleton MI 48117, USA
Jones, Jeffrey D — Actor
Leading Artists, 145 W 45th St, #1000, New York NY 10036, USA
Jones, Jennifer — Curling Athlete
Team Jennifer Jones, 246 Jacques Ave, Winnipeg MB R3W 1S9, Canada
Jones, Jenny — Entertainer, Comedienne
600 Plum Tree Road, Barrington IL 60010, USA
Jones, Jenny — Slopestyle Skier
Olympic Committee, 60 Charlotte St, London W1T 2NU, England
Jones, Jerrauld C (Jerry) — Football Executive
4400 Preston Road, Dallas TX 75205, USA
Jones, Jill Marie — Actress
Global Artists Agency, 6253 Hollywood Blvd, #508, Los Angeles CA 90028 USA
Jones, Jim — Rap Artist
A&M Entertainment, 13280 NW Freeway, #F328, Houston TX 77040, USA
Jones, Jimmie — Football Player
2658 Unicorn Court, Herndon VA 20171, USA
Jones, Jimmie S — Football Player
204 Moss Dr, Cedar Hill TX 75104, USA
Jones, John E, III — Judge
US District Court, Federal Building, 240 W 3rd St, Williamsport PA 17701, USA

**Jones, John Paul** — Bassist, Keyboardist (Led Zeppelin)
Opium Arts, 49 Portland Road, London W11 4LJ, England
**Jones, Johnny (Lam)** — Football Player, Track Athlete
1903 Pachea Trail, Round Rock TX 78665, USA
**Jones, Julia** — Actress
Mavrick Artists Agency, 6100 Wilshire Blvd, #550, Los Angeles CA 90048, USA
**Jones, Julius A M** — Football Player
517 Northwood Trail, Southlake TX 76092, USA
**Jones, June S, III** — Football Player, Coach
June Jones Foundation, PO Box 753139, Dallas TX 75275, USA
**Jones, Junior** — Boxer
Golden Boy Promotions, 626 Wilshire Blvd, #350, Los Angeles CA 90017, USA
**Jones, Kelly** — Singer, Guitarist (Stereophonics)
Marsupial Mgmt, Home Farm, Welfor, Newbury, Berkshire RG20 8HR, England
**Jones, Ken** — Football Player
4455 Porter Road, Niagara Falls NY 14305, USA
**Jones, Kim R** — Football Player
1396 Madison Ave, #150, Loveland CO 80537, USA
**Jones, Kimberly** — Sportscaster
YES Network, 405 Lexington Ave, #3600, New York NY 10174, USA
**Jones, Kirk** — Director, Writer
Creative Artists Agency, 2000 Ave of Stars, #100, Los Angeles CA 90067 USA
**Jones, L Q** — Actor
Sovereign Talent Group, 8421 Wilshire Blvd, #200, Beverly Hills CA 90211, USA
**Jones, Larry** — Basketball Player
1442 Cottingham Court, Columbus OH 43209, USA
**Jones, Larry W (Chipper)** — Baseball Player
5015 Heatherwood Court, Roswell GA 30075, USA
**Jones, Leisel M** — Swimmer
Swimming Australia, 12/7 Beissel St, Belconnen ACT 2617, Australia
**Jones, LeRoy** — Football Player
347 Kantor Blvd, Casselberry FL 32707, USA
**Jones, Leslie** — Actress
I C M Partners, 10250 Constellation Blvd, #900, Los Angeles CA 90067 USA
**Jones, Levi J** — Football Player
1448 W Bahia Court, Gilbert AZ 85233, USA
**Jones, Lori (Lolo)** — Track, Bobsled Athlete; Model
Lolo Jones Foundation, Hurdles of Hope, PO Box 82221, Baton Rouge LA 70884, USA
**Jones, Lupita** — Beauty Queen
Miss Universe Organization, 1370 Ave of Americas, #1600, New York NY 10019 USA
**Jones, Lynn M** — Baseball Player
9959 Dicksonburg Road, Conneautville PA 16406, USA
**Jones, M Donta'** — Football Player
4495 Jimmy Greens Place, La Plata MD 20646, USA
**Jones, Major J B** — Basketball Player
2475 Brandy Mill Road, Houston TX 77067, USA
**Jones, Marcus E** — Football Player
18701 Pepper Pike, Lutz FL 33558, USA
**Jones, Marilyn** — Actress
Kaplan-Stahler Agency, 8383 Wilshire Blvd, #923, Beverly Hills CA 90211, USA
**Jones, Marion L** — Track Athlete, Basketball Player
PO Box 3065, Cary NC 27519, USA
**Jones, Marvin M** — Football Player
8891 Brighton Lane, #114, Bonita Springs FL 34135, USA
**Jones, Matt** — Actor
Paradigm Agency, 360 N Crescent Dr, North Building, Beverly Hills CA 90210 USA
**Jones, Matthew (Matt)** — Golfer
Professional Golfers Association, 100 Ave of Champions, Palm Beach Gardens FL 33418 USA
**Jones, Maxine** — Singer (En Vogue)
East West Records, 75 Rockefeller Plaza, #1200, New York NY 10019, USA
**Jones, Michael D (Mike)** — Football Player
Lincoln University, Athletic Dept, Jefferson MO 65101, USA
**Jones, Michael G (Mick)** — Singer, Guitarist (Clash, Foreigner)
Function, 8330 W 3rd St, Los Angeles CA 90048, USA
**Jones, Mickey** — Actor, Musician
Hervey/Grimes Talent, 10561 Missouri Ave, #2, Los Angeles CA 90025 USA
**Jones, Nate** — Boxer
7801 South Shore Dr, Chicago IL 60649, USA
**Jones, Nathaniel R** — Judge
201 E 5th St, #1700, Cincinnati OH 45202, USA
**Jones, Newton B** — Labor Leader
International Brotherhood of Boilermakers, 753 State Ave, #570, Kansas City KS 66101, USA
**Jones, Norah** — Singer, Pianist; Songwriter
Creative Artists Agency, 2000 Ave of Stars, #100, Los Angeles CA 90067 USA
**Jones, Odell** — Baseball Player
5831 Opal Ave, Palmdale CA 93552, USA
**Jones, Orlando** — Actor
Paradigm Agency, 360 N Crescent Dr, North Building, Beverly Hills CA 90210 USA
**Jones, P J** — Auto Racing Driver
Gurney Racing, 2334 S Broadway, #2186, Santa Ana CA 92707, USA
**Jones, Parnelli** — Auto Racing Driver, Executive
20550 Earl St, Torrance CA 90503, USA
**Jones, Paul** — Guitarist (Elastica)
Chatto & Linnit, 123A King's Road, London SW3 4PL, England
**Jones, Perry J, III** — Basketball Player
Oklahoma City Thunder, 211 N Robinson Ave, #300, Oklahoma City OK 73102 USA
**Jones, Pete** — Director, Writer
Creative Artists Agency, 2000 Ave of Stars, #100, Los Angeles CA 90067 USA
**Jones, Quincy D, Jr** — Composer, Conductor
Quincy Jones Productions, 6671 W Sunset Blvd, #1574A, Los Angeles CA 90028, USA
**Jones, Quintorris L (Julio)** — Football Player
Atlanta Falcons, 4400 Falcon Parkway, Flowery Branch GA 30542 USA
**Jones, Randall L (Randy)** — Baseball Player
2638 Cranston Dr, Escondido CA 92025, USA
**Jones, Randy** — Bobsled Athlete
Bobsled & Skeleton Federation, 1631 Mesa Ave, #A, Colorado Springs CO 80906 USA

**Jones, Rashida** — Actress, Writer
United Talent Agency, U T A Plaza, 9336 Civic Center Dr, Beverly Hills CA 90210 USA
**Jones, Renee** — Actress
256 S Robertson Blvd, #700, Beverly Hills CA 90211, USA
**Jones, Richard T** — Actor
Mavrick Artists Agency, 6100 Wilshire Blvd, #550, Los Angeles CA 90048, USA
**Jones, Richard W (Rich)** — Basketball Player
101 Luna Way, #232, Las Vegas NV 89145, USA
**Jones, Rickie Lee** — Singer, Songwriter
Esther Creative Group, 27 W 24th St, #404, New York NY 10010, USA
**Jones, Robbie** — Actor
Untitled Entertainment, 350 S Beverly Dr, #200, Beverly Hills CA 90212 USA
**Jones, Robert (K C)** — Basketball Player, Coach
13405 NW Spirit Court W, Silverdale WA 98383, USA
**Jones, Robert C (Bobby)** — Basketball Player
7413 Valleybrook Road, Charlotte NC 28270, USA
**Jones, Robert E (Bobby)** — Football Player
6824 Stewart Sharon Road, Brookfield OH 44403, USA
**Jones, Robert J (Bobby)** — Baseball Player
10222 N Whitney Ave, Fresno CA 93730, USA
**Jones, Robert L** — Football Player
405 Aria Dr, Austin TX 78738, USA
**Jones, Robert M (Bobby)** — Baseball Player
32 Elm St, Rutherford NJ 07070, USA
**Jones, Robert O (Bobby)** — Baseball Player
7809 S Oxford Ave, Tulsa OK 74136, USA
**Jones, Rod** — Guitarist (Idlewild)
Agency Group Ltd, 361-373 City Road, London EC1V 1PQ, England
**Jones, Roderick W (Rod)** — Football Player
517 Tealridge Lane, De Soto TX 75115, USA
**Jones, Roger C** — Football Player
712 Trebor Dr, Goodlettsville TN 37072, USA
**Jones, Ronald J (Popeye)** — Basketball Player
29 Bass Pond Dr, Frisco TX 75034, USA
**Jones, Rondell T** — Football Player
423 Competition Road, Raleigh NC 27603, USA
**Jones, Rosie** — Golfer
4895 High Point Road, Atlanta GA 30342, USA
**Jones, Rosie** — Model
Samantha Bond Mgmt, Elysium Gate, 126-128 New Kings Road, London SW6 4LZ, England
**Jones, Ross A** — Baseball Player
4135 Eastridge Circle, Pompano Beach FL 33064, USA
**Jones, Roy, Jr** — Boxer
4590 Isbella Ingram Dr, Pensacola FL 32504, USA
**Jones, Rulon K** — Football Player
4003 N 3775 E, Eden UT 84310, USA
**Jones, Rupert Penry** — Actor
Artist Rights Group, 4A Exmoor St, London W10 6BD, England
**Jones, Ruppert S** — Baseball Player
17925 Valle de Lobo Dr, Poway CA 92064, USA
**Jones, Sam J** — Actor
A K A Talent, 6310 San Vicente Blvd, #200, Los Angeles CA 90048 USA
**Jones, Sam, III** — Actor
Pantheon Talent, 1801 Century Park E, #1910, Los Angeles CA 90067, USA
**Jones, Samuel (Sam)** — Basketball Player
338 S Hampton Club Way, Saint Augustine FL 32092, USA
**Jones, Sarah** — Actress
Management 360, 9111 Wilshire Blvd, Beverly Hills CA 90210 USA
**Jones, Scott A** — Inventor (LED Video Animation)
Dittoe Public Relations, 2815 E 62nd St, #300, Indianapolis IN 46220, USA
**Jones, Sean** — Football Player
4602 McKeever Lane, Missouri City TX 77459, USA
**Jones, Serene** — Educator
Union Theological Seminary, President's Office, 3041 Broadway, New York NY 10027, USA
**Jones, Sharon** — Singer
Motormouth Media, 2525 Hyperion Ave, #1, Los Angeles CA 90027, USA
**Jones, Shirley** — Actress, Singer
Suchin Co, 16501 Ventura Blvd, #504, Encino CA 91436, USA
**Jones, Simon** — Actor
Innovative Artists, 1505 10th St, Santa Monica CA 90401 USA
**Jones, Stacy** — Singer, Guitarist, Songwriter
Crush Music, 584 Broadway, #1102, New York NY 10012, USA
**Jones, Stephen** — Attorney
Jones & Wyatt, PO Box 472, Enid OK 73702, USA
**Jones, Stephen H (Steve)** — Basketball Player
26 Kingwood Greens Dr, Kingwood TX 77339, USA
**Jones, Stephen J M** — Fashion Designer
Steve Jones Millinery, 36 Great Queen St, London WC1E 6BT, England
**Jones, Steve** — Guitarist (Sex Pistols)
Solo Agency, 53-55 Fulham High St, #200, London SW6 3JJ, England
**Jones, Steve** — Golfer
Whirlwind Golf Club, 5200 Grand Del Mar Way, San Diego CA 92130, USA
**Jones, Steve H** — Football Player
12774 Fee Fee Road, Saint Louis MO 63146, USA
**Jones, Steven** — Physicist
Brigham Young University, Physics Dept, Provo UT 84602, USA
**Jones, Steven H (Steve)** — Baseball Player
8116 Kingsdale Dr, Knoxville TN 37919, USA
**Jones, Stewart** — Architect
Meyer/Gifford/Jones, 270 Lafayette St, New York NY 10012, USA
**Jones, Suranne** — Actress
Shepherd Mgmt, Joel House, 17-21 Garrick St, London WC2E 9BL, England
**Jones, T Frederick (Rick)** — Baseball Player
6319 Nancy Dr, Jacksonville FL 32244, USA
**Jones, Tamala** — Actress
A P A Talent & Literary Agency, 405 S Beverly Dr, #300, Beverly Hills CA 90212 USA

| | |
|---|---|
| **Jones, Taylor**<br>Cagle Cartoons, PO Box 22342, Santa Barbara CA 93121 USA | Editorial Cartoonist |
| **Jones, Tebucky S**<br>55 Brentwood Dr, Avon CT 06001, USA | Football Player |
| **Jones, Terrence**<br>Houston Rockets, 1730 Jefferson St, Houston TX 77003 USA | Basketball Player |
| **Jones, Terry**<br>Python Pictures, 34 Thistlewaite Road, London E5 QQQ, England | Animator, Director (Monty Python) |
| **Jones, Thomas D**<br>N A S A, Johnson Space Center, 2101 NASA Road, Houston TX 77058 USA | Astronaut |
| **Jones, Thomas Q**<br>2742 Clinch Haven Road, Big Stone Gap VA 24219, USA | Football Player |
| **Jones, Timothy B (Tim)**<br>6049 Roloff Way, Orangevale CA 95662, USA | Baseball Player |
| **Jones, Toby**<br>United Talent Agency, U T A Plaza, 9336 Civic Center Dr, Beverly Hills CA 90210 USA | Actor |
| **Jones, Todd B G**<br>421 Eagle Point Dr, Pell City AL 35128, USA | Baseball Player |
| **Jones, Tom**<br>W M E Entertainment, 9601 Wilshire Blvd, #300, Beverly Hills CA 90210 USA | Singer |
| **Jones, Tommy Lee**<br>Creative Artists Agency, 2000 Ave of Stars, #100, Los Angeles CA 90067 USA | Actor, Director |
| **Jones, Tracy D**<br>101 Harbor Green Dr, #602, Bellevue KY 41073, USA | Baseball Player |
| **Jones, Trevor**<br>46 Ave Road, Highgate, London N6 5DR, England | Composer |
| **Jones, Tyler Patrick**<br>House of Representatives, 1434 6th St, #1, Santa Monica CA 90401 USA | Actor |
| **Jones, Vaughan F R**<br>University of California, Mathematics Dept, Berkeley CA 94720, USA | Mathematician |
| **Jones, Victor P**<br>9710 Sunset Grove Dr, Huntersville NC 28078, USA | Football Player |
| **Jones, Victor T**<br>PO Box 132241, Dallas TX 75313, USA | Football Player |
| **Jones, Vinnie**<br>Cole Kitchenn Personal Mgmt, 212 Strand, London WC2R 1AP, England | Actor |
| **Jones, W Timothy (Tim)**<br>30 Chicot Dr, Maumelle AR 72113, USA | Baseball Player |
| **Jones, Walter (Wali)**<br>3160 SW 132nd Ave, Miramar FL 33027, USA | Basketball Player |
| **Jones, Walter J**<br>520 Raymond Place NW, Renton WA 98057, USA | Football Player |
| **Jones, Wesley**<br>Holt Hinshaw Jones, 320 Florida St, San Francisco CA 94110, USA | Architect |
| **Jones, Wilbert (Wil)**<br>3360 Idlecreek Way, Decatur GA 30034, USA | Basketball Player |
| **Jones, William A (Dub)**<br>904 Glendale Dr, Ruston LA 71270, USA | Football Player |
| **Jones, Zoe Lister**<br>W M E Entertainment, 9601 Wilshire Blvd, #300, Beverly Hills CA 90210 USA | Actress, Writer |
| **Jones-Doxey, Marilyn C**<br>320 15th Street Court W, Bradenton FL 34205, USA | Baseball Player |
| **Jones-Drew, Maurice C**<br>Jacksonville Jaguars, 1 AllTel Stadium Place, Jacksonville FL 32202 USA | Football Player |
| **Jong, Erica M**<br>PO Box 1434, New York NY 10021, USA | Writer |
| **Jonker, Kelly**<br>Amsterdamsche Hockey & Bandy Club, Postbus 7843, 1008 Amsterdam AA, Netherlands | Field Hockey Player |
| **Jonrowe, Dee Dee**<br>PO Box 272, Willow AK 99688, USA | Dog Sled Racer |
| **Jonsen, Albert R**<br>1383 Jones St, #502, San Francisco CA 94109, USA | Physician |
| **Jonsson, U P Jorgen**<br>Anaheim Ducks, 2695 E Katella Ave, Anaheim CA 92806 USA | Ice Hockey Player |
| **Jonze, Spike**<br>Creative Artists Agency, 2000 Ave of Stars, #100, Los Angeles CA 90067 USA | Director, Actor, Writer |
| **Joo Hyong-Jun**<br>Skating Union, 88 Bangyee-Dong, Songpaku, Seoul 138 749, South Korea | Speed Skater |
| **Joo Min-Jin**<br>Skating Union, 88 Bangyee-Dong, Songpaku, Seoul 138 749, South Korea | Speed Skater |
| **Joop, Jette**<br>Jette Design Group, Parkallee 53, 20144 Hamburg, Germany | Fashion Designer |
| **Joop, Wolfgang**<br>Seestr 35-37, 14467 Potsdam, Germany | Fashion Designer |
| **Jopling of Alnderby Quernhow, T Michael**<br>Ainderby Hall, Thirsk, North Yorkshire YO7 4HZ, England | Government Official, England |
| **Joppich, Peter**<br>Untermarkstr 3, 56073 Koblenz, Germany | Fencer |
| **Joppy, William T**<br>5107 Cansing Dr, Camp Springs MD 20748, USA | Boxer |
| **Jorda, Claude J C**<br>International Criminal Tribunal, PO Box 13888, 2501 The Hague EW, Netherlands | Judge |
| **Jordan, Alex**<br>Gregga Jordan Smieszny, 1225 N State Parkway, Chicago IL 60610, USA | Interior Designer |
| **Jordan, Alexis**<br>Roc Nation, 1411 Broadway, #3800, New York NY 10018, USA | Singer |
| **Jordan, Brian O**<br>2631 Trailing Ivy Way, Buford GA 30519, USA | Football, Baseball Player |
| **Jordan, Claudia**<br>C E S D, 10635 Santa Monica Blvd, #130, Los Angeles CA 90025 USA | Model, Entertainer |
| **Jordan, Curtis W**<br>629 Surfside Ave, Virginia Beach VA 23451, USA | Football Player |
| **Jordan, Darin G**<br>44 Connell Dr, Stoughton MA 02072, USA | Football Player |
| **Jordan, Dion**<br>Miami Dolphins, 7500 SW 30th St, Davie FL 33314 USA | Football Player |

| | |
|---|---|
| **Jordan, Don D** | Businessman |
| Reliant Energy, 1111 Louisiana Ave, Houston TX 77002, USA | |
| **Jordan, Edward M (Eddie)** | Basketball Player, Coach |
| 158 Monroe Ave, Belle Mead NJ 08502, USA | |
| **Jordan, Glenn** | Director |
| 9401 Wilshire Blvd, #700, Beverly Hills CA 90212, USA | |
| **Jordan, Gregor** | Director |
| H L A Mgmt, PO Box 1536, Strawberry Hills, Sydney NSW 2012, Australia | |
| **Jordan, H DeAndre, Jr** | Basketball Player |
| Los Angeles Clippers, Staples Center, 1111 S Figueroa St, Los Angeles CA 90015 USA | |
| **Jordan, Jeremy** | Actor, Singer |
| Schachter Entertainment, 1157 S Beverly Dr, #200, Los Angeles CA 90035 USA | |
| **Jordan, Kathy** | Tennis Player |
| 114 Walter Hays Dr, Palo Alto CA 94303, USA | |
| **Jordan, Kevin W** | Baseball Player |
| 127 Ney St, San Francisco CA 94112, USA | |
| **Jordan, LaMont D** | Football Player |
| 1407 Alberta Dr, District Heights MD 20747, USA | |
| **Jordan, Lee Roy** | Football Player |
| 7710 Caruth Blvd, Dallas TX 75225, USA | |
| **Jordan, Leslie** | Actor |
| Michael Slessinger, 8730 W Sunset Blvd, #220W, West Hollywood CA 90069 USA | |
| **Jordan, Marc** | Singer, Songwriter |
| Live Tour Artists, 1451 White Oaks Blvd, Oakville ON L6H 4R9, Canada | |
| **Jordan, Mary** | Journalist |
| Washington Post, Editorial Dept, 1150 15th St NW, Washington DC 20071 USA | |
| **Jordan, Michael B** | Actor |
| W M E Entertainment, 9601 Wilshire Blvd, #300, Beverly Hills CA 90210 USA | |
| **Jordan, Michael J** | Basketball Player |
| David Falk Mgmt, 5335 Wisconsin Ave, #850, Washington DC 20015, USA | |
| **Jordan, Montell** | Singer, Songwriter |
| Red Entertainment Agency, 505 8th Ave, #1004, New York NY 10018, USA | |
| **Jordan, Neil P** | Director |
| 2 Martello Terrace, Strand Road, Bray, County Wicklow, Ireland | |
| **Jordan, P Buford** | Football Player |
| 11 Acadia St, Kenner LA 70065, USA | |
| **Jordan, Paul S (Ricky)** | Baseball Player |
| 5691 Power Inn Road, #A, Sacramento CA 95824, USA | |
| **Jordan, Philippe** | Conductor |
| I M G Artists, Hogarth Business Park, Chiswick, London W4 2TH, England | |
| **Jordan, Randy L** | Football Player |
| 514 Mountain Laurel, Chapel Hill NC 27517, USA | |
| **Jordan, Ronny** | Jazz Guitarist |
| Universal Attractions, 135 W 26th St, #1200, New York NY 10001 USA | |
| **Jordan, Sass** | Singer, Songwriter |
| Management Trust, 411 Queen St W, #300, Toronto ON M5V 2A5, Canada | |
| **Jordan, Sheila J** | Singer, Songwriter |
| F A M, 4102 Rue Saint Urbain, Montreal QC H2W 1V3, Canada | |
| **Jordan, Shelby L** | Football Player |
| 29208 Posey Way, Rancho Palos Verdes CA 90275, USA | |
| **Jordan, Steven R (Steve)** | Football Player |
| 581 W San Marcos Dr, Chandler AZ 85225, USA | |
| **Jordan, Thomas J (Tom)** | Baseball Player |
| 2909 S Wyoming Ave, Roswell NM 88203, USA | |
| **Jordan, Tina Marie** | Model |
| Playboy Promotions, 9346 Civic Center Dr, #200, Beverly Hills CA 90210 USA | |
| **Jordan, Vernon E, Jr** | Civil Rights Activist |
| 2940 Benton Place NW, Washington DC 20008, USA | |
| **Jordanova, Vera** | Actress, Model |
| Special Artists Agency, 9200 Sunset Blvd, #410, West Hollywood CA 90069 USA | |
| **Jordi, Francine** | Singer |
| Management Kaminski, Unterer Ahlenbergweg 47A, 58313 Herdecke, Germany | |
| **Jordyn, Shanice** | Model |
| Playboy Promotions, 9346 Civic Center Dr, #200, Beverly Hills CA 90210 USA | |
| **Jorge, Seu** | Singer, Songwriter, Actor |
| Windish Agency, 1658 N Milwaukee Ave, #211, Chicago IL 60647, USA | |
| **Jorgensen, Anker** | Prime Minister, Denmark |
| Borgbjergvej 1, 2450 SV Copenhagen, Denmark | |
| **Jorgensen, Michael (Mike)** | Baseball Player, Manager |
| 1820 Harbor Mill Dr, Fenton MO 63026, USA | |
| **Jorgensen, Morten** | Rowing Athlete |
| Forening for Rosport, Skovalleen 38A, Postboks 74, 2880 Bagsvaerd, Denmark | |
| **Jorgensen, Roger K** | Basketball Player |
| 642 Woodcrest Dr, Pittsburgh PA 15205, USA | |
| **Jorgenson, Dale W** | Economist |
| Harvard University, Economics Dept, 1010 Memorial Dr, #14C, Cambridge MA 02138, USA | |
| **Jorgenson, John** | Guitarist (Desert Rose Band) |
| T G Squared Artist Representation, 201 Rainbow Dr, Carrboro NC 27510, USA | |
| **Jorginho de Amorim Campos** | Soccer Player |
| Rua Levi Carneiro 420, Barra dd Tijuca 22630 150, Brazil | |
| **Jorndt, L Daniel** | Businessman |
| Walgreen Co, 200 Wilmot Road, Deerfield IL 60015, USA | |
| **Jose, D Felix A** | Baseball Player |
| 9825 Equus Circle, Boynton Beach FL 33472, USA | |
| **Jose, Jose** | Singer |
| Joyce Agency Entertainment Services, 370 Harrison Ave, Harrison NY 10528, USA | |
| **Josefowicz, Leila** | Concert Violinist |
| C M Artists, 127 W 96th St, #13B, New York NY 10025 USA | |
| **Joseph Wenzel** | Prince, Liechtenstein |
| Prince's Residence, Schloss Vaduz, 9490 Vaduz, Liechtenstein | |
| **Joseph, Amin** | Actor |
| Jay Schachter Entertainment, 28994 Sam Place, Canyon Country CA 91387, USA | |
| **Joseph, Curtis S** | Ice Hockey Player |
| Newport Sports Mgmt, 601-201 City Centre, Mississauga ON L5B 2T4, Canada | |
| **Joseph, Daryl J** | Astronaut |
| 615 Peachtree Court, Campbell CA 95008, USA | |

V.I.P. Address Book

Jordan - Joseph

**Joseph, James** — Football Player
8942 Stoneridge Place, Montgomery AL 36117, USA

**Joseph, Johnathan** — Football Player
Houston Texans, 2 Reliant Park, Houston TX 77054 USA

**Joseph, Joseph E, III** — Physician
University of Michigan, Taubman Center, Ann Arbor MI 48109, USA

**Joseph, Kimberly** — Actress, Director, Writer
Creative Representation, 1/44 Derby St, Collingwood VIC 3065, Australia

**Joseph, R Christopher (Chris)** — Ice Hockey Player
17 L'Hirondelle Court, Saint Albert AB T8N 5X9, Canada

**Joseph, Shalrie** — Soccer Player
New England Revolution, 1 Patriot Place, Foxboro MA 02035 USA

**Joseph, Stephen** — Physician
New York City Health Department, 125 Worth St, New York NY 10013, USA

**Joseph, William** — Football Player
1071 NE 107th St, Miami FL 33161, USA

**Josephson, Brian D** — Nobel Physics Laureate
Cavendish Laboratory, Madingley Road, Cambridge CB3 0HE, England

**Josephson, Karen** — Synchronized Swimmer
1923 Junction Dr, Concord CA 94518, USA

**Josephson, Lester J (Josey)** — Football Player
5388 N Genematas Dr, Tucson AZ 85704, USA

**Josephson, Sarah** — Synchronized Swimmer
1923 Junction Dr, Concord CA 94518, USA

**Joshi, Indira** — Singer
B B C Artist Mail, PO Box 116, Belfast BT2 7AJ, Northern Ireland

**Joshi, Pallavi** — Actress, Entertainer
23 Veer Savarkar Road, Mahim, Mumbai MS 400016, India

**Joshua, Anthony O O** — Boxer
Finchley & District Amateur Boxing, Bulwer Road, New Barnet, London EN5 5EX, England

**Joshua, Von E** — Baseball Player
20922 E Glen Haven Circle, Northville MI 48167, USA

**Josipovic, Ivo** — President, Croatia
Presidential Palace, Banski Dvori, Zagreb 10000, Croatia

**Jospin, Lionel R** — Prime Minister, France
Parti Socialiste, 10 Rue de Solfarino, 75333 Paris Cedex 07, France

**Josserand, Marion** — Freestyle Cross Skier
Ski Federation, 50 Rue des Marquisats, BP 2451 , 74011 Annecy Cedex, France

**Joubert, Beverly** — Photographer
National Geographic, Editorial Dept, 1145 17th St NW, Washington DC 20036 USA

**Joubert, Dereck** — Photographer
National Geographic, Editorial Dept, 1145 17th St NW, Washington DC 20036 USA

**Joulwan, George A** — Army General
1348 S 19th St, Arlington VA 22202, USA

**Jourdain, Michel, Jr** — Auto Racing Driver
Team Rahal, 4601 Lyman Dr, Hilliard OH 43026, USA

**Jourdan, Louis** — Actor
1139 Maybrook Dr, Beverly Hills CA 90210, USA

**Jourgensen, Al** — Singer, Guitarist (Ministry)
First Row Talent, 6220 Lemona Ave, #8, Van Nuys CA 91411, USA

**Journell, Jimmy** — Baseball Player
1511 Eastgate Road, Springfield OH 45503, USA

**Jousset, Anne** — Actress
Artmedia, 20 Ave Rapp, 75007 Paris, France

**Jovanotti** — Singer, Rap Artist, Songwriter, Actor
Trident Mgmt, Corso Europa 13, 20122 Milan, Italy

**Jovanovich, Brandon** — Opera Singer
I M G Artists, Hogarth Business Park, Chiswick, London W4 2TH, England

**Jovanovich, Peter W** — Publisher
Pearson Education, 1 Lake St, Upper Saddle River NJ 07458, USA

**Jovanovski, Edward (Ed)** — Ice Hockey Player
5224 NW 27th Court, Margate FL 33063, USA

**Jovich, John B** — Historian
1342 Rosepointe Dr, York PA 17404, USA

**Jovovich, Milla** — Actress, Model, Singer
Untitled Entertainment, 350 S Beverly Dr, #200, Beverly Hills CA 90212 USA

**Joy, Mike** — Sportscaster
111 Mystic Lake Loop, Mooresville NC 28117, USA

**Joyal, Edward A (Eddie)** — Ice Hockey Player
6469 Wandermere Dr, San Diego CA 92120, USA

**Joyce, Andrea** — Sportscaster, Commentator
Arts & Entertainment, 235 E 45th St, #200, New York NY 10017, USA

**Joyce, James A** — Baseball Umpire
9785 SW 167th Place, Beaverton OR 97007, USA

**Joyce, Joan** — Softball Player, Golfer
9504 Amberleigh Lane, #L, Perry Hall MD 21128, USA

**Joyce, John T (Jack)** — Labor Leader
Bricklayers & Allied Craftsmen, 815 15th St NW, Washington DC 20005, USA

**Joyce, Kara Lynn** — Swimmer
5973 Cedar Ridge Dr, Ann Arbor MI 48103, USA

**Joyce, Kevin F** — Basketball Player
420 W Olive St, #9, Long Beach NY 11561, USA

**Joyce, Matt** — Football Player
6330 E Wilshire Dr, Scottsdale AZ 85257, USA

**Joyce, Matthew R (Matt)** — Baseball Player
Tampa Bay Rays, 1 Tropicana Dr, Saint Petersburg FL 33705 USA

**Joyce, Tom** — Sculptor
21 Likely Road, Santa Fe NM 87508, USA

**Joyce, William** — Artist, Writer
2911 Centenary Blvd, PO Box 4188, Shreveport LA 71104, USA

**Joyce, William H** — Businessman
Union Carbide, 39 Old Ridgebury Road, #1, Danbury CT 06810, USA

**Joyeux, Odette** — Actress
Agents Associes, 201 Rue du Faubourg Saint Honore, 75008 Paris, France

**Joyner, Alrederick (Al)** — Track Athlete
10500 Crosspoint Blvd, Indianapolis IN 46256, USA

|  |  |
|---|---|
| **Joyner, Michelle**<br>A M T Artists, 15260 Ventura Blvd, #1200, Sherman Oaks CA 91403, USA | Actress |
| **Joyner, Seth**<br>502 E Bishop Dr, Tempe AZ 85282, USA | Football Player, Sportscaster |
| **Joyner, Wallace K (Wally)**<br>516 E 2800 S, Mapleton UT 84664, USA | Baseball Player |
| **Joyner-Kersee, Jacqueline (Jackie)**<br>1049 Bristol Manor Dr, Ballwin MO 63011, USA | Track Athlete |
| **Jozwiak, Brian J**<br>668 Alvarado, North Port FL 34287, USA | Football Player, Coach |
| **J-Ro**<br>Likwit Entertainment, PO Box 360713, Los Angeles CA 90036, USA | Rap Artist |
| **Ju Ming**<br>208 No 2 She-shi-hu, Chin-shan, Taipei, Taiwan | Sculptor |
| **Juan Carlos I**<br>Palacio de la Zarzuela, 28671 Madrid, Spain | King, Spain |
| **Juanes**<br>Fernan Martinez Mgmt, 4141 NE 2nd Ave, #106C, Miami FL 33137, USA | Singer, Guitarist |
| **Juantorena Danger, Alberto**<br>National Institute for Sports, Sports City, Havana, Cuba | Track Athlete |
| **Juarez, Ricardo (Rocky)**<br>3916 Weems St, Houston TX 77009, USA | Boxer |
| **Juby, Marcus L**<br>Reformed Church of Latter-Day Saints, 801 E 23rd St, Independence MO 64055, USA | Religious Leader |
| **Juchhelm, Alwin M, Jr**<br>939 Ave of Pines, Grenada MS 38901, USA | WW II Army Air Corps Hero |
| **Judah, Zab**<br>Prize Fight Boxing, 7160 Tchulahoma Road, #A1, Southhaven MS 38671, USA | Boxer |
| **Judd, Ashley**<br>PO Box 1569, Franklin TN 37065, USA | Actress, Model |
| **Judd, Bob**<br>Harper Collins Publishers, 10 E 53rd St, Cellar 1, New York NY 10022 USA | Writer |
| **Judd, Harry M C**<br>Helter Skelter, 347-353 Chiswick High Road, London W4 4HS, England | Drummer (McFly) |
| **Judd, Jackie**<br>ABC-TV, News Dept, 77 W 66th St, New York NY 10023 USA | Commentator |
| **Judd, Michael G (Mike)**<br>9805 Shadow Road, La Mesa CA 91941, USA | Baseball Player |
| **Judd, Naomi**<br>Gary Good Entertainment, 2614 NW 62nd St, Oklahoma City OK 73112, USA | Singer (Judds), Songwriter |
| **Judd, Wynonna**<br>Big Enterprises, PO Box 682708, Franklin TN 37068, USA | Singer, Guitarist |
| **Juden, Jeffrey D (Jeff)**<br>85 Proctor St, Salem MA 01970, USA | Baseball Player |
| **Judge, George**<br>University of California, Economics Dept, Berkeley CA 94720, USA | Economist |
| **Judge, Mike**<br>3 Arts Entertainment, 9460 Wilshire Blvd, #700, Beverly Hills CA 90212 USA | Animator (Beavis & Butt-Head), Actor |
| **Judkins, Jeffrey R (Jeff)**<br>3471 S 3570 E, Salt Lake City UT 84109, USA | Basketball Player, Coach |
| **Judson, Howard K (Howie)**<br>239 Fairway Circle NE, Winter Haven FL 33881, USA | Baseball Player |
| **Judson, William T**<br>652 Sinclair Way, Jonesboro GA 30238, USA | Football Player |
| **Jue, Blawoh P**<br>4514 Billingham St, Fairfax VA 22030, USA | Football Player |
| **Jugnauth, Anerood**<br>President's Office, Government Centre, Port Louis, Mauritius | President, Mauritius |
| **Jugnot, Gerard**<br>J G P M, 11 Rue Chavez, 75016 Paris, France | Director, Actor |
| **Ju-Ju**<br>Agency Group Ltd, 142 W 57th St, #600, New York NY 10019 USA | Rap Artist (Beatnuts) |
| **Julavits, Heidi**<br>G P Putnam's Sons, 375 Hudson St, New York NY 10014 USA | Writer |
| **Julfalakyam, Arsen**<br>K S V Aalen 05, Friedrichstr 52, 73430 Aalen, Germany | Greco-Roman Wrestler |
| **Julian, Alexander, II**<br>323 Florida Hill Road, Ridgefield CT 6877, USA | Fashion Designer |
| **Julian, Jose**<br>Paradigm Agency, 360 N Crescent Dr, North Building, Beverly Hills CA 90210 USA | Actor |
| **Julien, Claire**<br>Creative Artists Agency, 2000 Ave of Stars, #100, Los Angeles CA 90067 USA | Actress |
| **Julien, Claude**<br>3 Myrna Road, Lexington MA 02420, USA | Ice Hockey Player, Coach |
| **Julius, DeAnne**<br>Bank of England, Threadneedle St, London EC2R 8AH, England | Economist |
| **July, Miranda**<br>United Talent Agency, U T A Plaza, 9336 Civic Center Dr, Beverly Hills CA 90210 USA | Actor, Director, Writer |
| **Jumaliyev, Kubanychbek M**<br>Transport Ministry, Isanova Str 42, 720017 Bishkek, Kyrgyzstan | Prime Minister, Kyrgyzstan |
| **Junck, Mary E**<br>Lee Enterprises, 201 N Harrison St, #600, Davenport IA 52801, USA | Businesswoman |
| **Juncker, Jean-Claude**<br>Prime Minister's Office, 33 Boul Roosevelt, 1728 Luxembourg-Ville, Luxembourg | Prime Minister, Luxembourg |
| **June, Carl H**<br>University of Pennsylvania Medical School, 421 Curie Blvd, Philadelphia PA 19104, USA | Pathologist |
| **June, Cato N**<br>13500 Van Brady Road, Upper Marlboro MD 20772, USA | Football Player |
| **June, Valerie**<br>Billions Corp, 3522 W Armitage Ave, Chicago IL 60647 USA | Singer, Songwriter |
| **Juneau, Joseph (Joe)**<br>Harlem Technologies, 100-2 Rue du Jardin, Pont Rouge QC G3H 3R7, Canada | Ice Hockey Player |
| **Jung Sung-Ryong**<br>Football Association, 1-131 Sinmunno, 2-Ga Jongno-Gu, Seoul 110 062, South Korea | Soccer Player |
| **Jung Woo-Young**<br>Football Association, 1-131 Sinmunno, 2-Ga Jongno-Gu, Seoul 110 062, South Korea | Soccer Player |

**J**

**Joyner - Jung Woo-Young**

**Jung, Andrea** — Businesswoman
Avon Products, 1345 Ave of Americas Basement Concourse 9, New York NY 10105, USA
**Jung, Ernst** — Writer
88515 Lagenensligen/Wiltlingen, Germany
**Jung, Michael** — Equestrian
Joachim Jung, Sportplatzweg, 72160 Horb-Altheim, Germany
**Jung, Richard** — Neurologist
Waldhofstr 42, 71691 Freiburg, Germany
**Junge, Daniel** — Director
Milkhaus/Jungefilm, 3059 Vine St, Denver CO 80205, USA
**Junger Witt, Paul** — Producer, Director
Creative Artists Agency, 2000 Ave of Stars, #100, Los Angeles CA 90067 USA
**Junger, Gil** — Director, Producer
Intellectual Artists Mgmt, 10585 Santa Monica Blvd, #135, Los Angeles CA 90025, USA
**Junger, Sebastian** — Writer, Director
United Talent Agency, U T A Plaza, 9336 Civic Center Dr, Beverly Hills CA 90210 USA
**Junior, Ester J (E J)** — Football Player
911 W Summit St, Bolivar MO 65613, USA
**Junker, Steve N** — Football Player
5660 Julmar Dr, Cincinnati OH 45238, USA
**Junkie XL** — Keyboardist, Guitarist, Drummer
Primary Talent International, 10-11 Jockey's Fields, London WC1R 4BN, England
**Junkin, Abner K (Trey)** — Football Player
5 Lakeside Lane, Newport AR 72112, USA
**Junkin, Michael W (Mike)** — Football Player
1002 Whitehall Dr, Doylestown PA 18901, USA
**Junqueira, Bruno** — Auto Racing Driver
3669 Royal Palm Ave, Miami FL 33133, USA
**Juntunen, Helena** — Opera Singer
Harrison/Parrott, 5-6 Albion Court, London W6 0QT, England
**Juppe, Alain M** — Prime Minister, France
Mairie, Place Pey-Berland, 33077 Bordeaux Cedex, France
**Jur, Jeffrey** — Cinematographer
4438 Wortser Ave, Studio City CA 91604, USA
**Jurado, Jeanette L** — Singer (Expose), Songwriter
Richard Walters, PO Box 2789, Toluca Lake CA 91610 USA
**Jurak, Edward J (Ed)** — Baseball Player
3650 S Walker Ave, San Pedro CA 90731, USA
**Jurasik, Peter** — Actor
2109 S Wilbur Ave, Walla Walla WA 99362, USA
**Jurevicius, Joseph M (Joe)** — Football Player
3310 Brainard Road, Pepper Pike OH 44142, USA
**Jurgens, Udo** — Singer, Pianist, Songwriter
Freddy Burger Mgmt, Carmentstr 12, 8032 Zurich, Switzerland
**Jurgensen, Christian A (Sonny), III** — Football Player
6963 Greentree Dr, Naples FL 34108, USA
**Jurgensmeier-Carroll, Margaret** — Baseball Player
5245 Rowena Dr, Roscoe IL 61073, USA
**Juri, Carla** — Actress
Curtis Brown Group, 28-29 Haymarket St, #500, London SW1Y 4SP, England
**Jurin, Michael** — Guitarist (Stellarstar)
+1 Management/Public Relations, 242 Wythe Ave, #6, Brooklyn NY 11211, USA
**Jurkovic, John I** — Football Player
2212 June Dr, Schereville IN 46375, USA
**Jurowski, Michail** — Conductor
Amalienhof 20, 13581 Berlin, Germany
**Jurowski, Vladimir** — Conductor
I M G Artists, Hogarth Business Park, Chiswick, London W4 2TH, England
**Jurrjens, Jair F** — Baseball Player
Atlanta Braves, Turner Field, 755 Hank Aaron Dr, Atlanta GA 30315 USA
**Just, Ward S** — Writer
Janklow & Nesbit Assoc, 445 Park Ave, #1300, New York NY 10022 USA
**Juster, Norton** — Writer, Architect
55 Kellogg Ave, Amherst MA 01002, USA
**Justice, David C** — Baseball Player
18570 Old Coach Way, Poway CA 92064, USA
**Justice, Victoria** — Actress, Singer
United Talent Agency, U T A Plaza, 9336 Civic Center Dr, Beverly Hills CA 90210 USA
**Justin, Kerry J** — Football Player
13331 W Marlette Court, Litchfield Park AZ 85340, USA
**Justman, Seth** — Singer, Keyboardist (J Geils Band)
Nick Ben-Meir, 652 N Doheny Dr, West Hollywood CA 90069, USA
**Jutze, Alfred H (Skip)** — Baseball Player
3395 Zephry Court, Wheat Ridge CO 80033, USA
**Juvenile** — Rap Artist
Pretty Special, 200 W 72nd St, #64, New York NY 10023, USA

**K**

**Kaake, Jeff** — Actor
2533 N Carson St, #3105, Carson City NV 89706, USA

**Kaas, Carmen** — Model
Men/Women Model Inc, 199 Lafayette St, #700, New York NY 10012 USA

**Kaas, Patricia** — Singer
Attitude, 71 Rue Robespierre, 93100 Montreuil, France

**Kaat, James L (Jim)** — Baseball Player
PO Box 1130, Port Salerno FL 34992, USA

**Kabakov, Ilya** — Artist
Gladstone Gallery, 515 W 52nd St, New York NY 10019, USA

**Kaberle, Frantisek** — Ice Hockey Player
3105 Briar Stream Run, Raleigh NC 27612, USA

**Kaberle, Tomas** — Ice Hockey Player
Montreal Canadiens, 1275 Saint Antoine St W, Montreal QC H3C 5L2, Canada

**Kabila, Joseph** — President, Congo; Army General
President's Office, Mont Ngaliema, Kinshasa, Congo Democratic Republic

**Kabui, Frank** — Governor General, Soloman Islands
Governor General's House, Box 252, Honiara, Guadacanal, Solomon Islands

**Kac, Eduardo** — Artist
Chicago Art Institute, 112 S Michigan Ave, #400, Chicago IL 60603, USA

**Kaci** — Singer, Songwriter, Dancer
Spectrum Talent Agency, 1650 Broadway, #1105, New York NY 10019, USA

**Kacyvenski, Isaiah J** — Football Player
1081 Beacon St, #8, Brookline MA 02446, USA

**Kaczmarek, Jane** — Actress
Greenlight Mgmt, 13848 Valleyheart Drive, Sherman Oaks CA 91423, USA

**Kaczur, Nick** — Football Player
17K Marie Dr, Attleboro MA 02703, USA

**Kad** — Actor, Writer, Director
1 Mgmt, 9000 W Sunset Blvd, #1550, Los Angeles CA 90069 USA

**Kadanoff, Leo P** — Physicist
5421 S Cornell Ave, Chicago IL 60615, USA

**Kadare, Ismail** — Writer
40 Rue Violet, 75015 Paris, France

**Kadena, Reon** — Model, Actress
Oscar Promotion, 3-6-7-5F Kita Aoyama, Minato, Tokyo 107 0061, Japan

**Kadenyuk, Leonid K** — Cosmonaut
Cosmonaut Training Center, Star City, 141160 Zvezdny Gorodok, Moscow Oblast, Russia

**Kadish, Michael S (Mike)** — Football Player
7941 Sudbury Lane SE, Ada MI 49301, USA

**Kadison, Joshua** — Singer, Songwriter, Pianist
Nick Bode, 1265 Electric Ave, Venice CA 90291, USA

**Kaeding, Nathaniel J (Nate)** — Football Player
1528 1st Ave, #A, Coralville IA 52241, USA

**Kaestle, Carl F** — Historian
35 Charlesfield St, Providence RI 02906, USA

**Kaesviharn, Kevin R** — Football Player
6334 Merrimac Lane N, Osseo MN 55311, USA

**Kafatos, Fotis C** — Biologist
Imperial College, Cell/Molecular Biology Dept, London SW7 2AZ, England

**Kafelnikov, Yevgeny A** — Tennis Player
International Mgmt Group, 26 Riverside Dr, Rumson NJ 07760, USA

**Kaftan, George A** — Basketball Player
2591 Lantern Light Way, Manasquan NJ 08736, USA

**Kagan, Daryn** — Commentator
CNN-TV, News Dept, 190 Marietta Ave SW, Atlanta GA 30303 USA

**Kagan, Elaine** — Actress, Writer
Greene Assoc, 1901 Ave of Stars, #130, Los Angeles CA 90067 USA

**Kagan, Elena** — Supreme Court Justice
US Supreme Court, 1 1st St NE, Washington DC 20543 USA

**Kagan, Henri Boris** — Chemist
Universite Paris-Sud, Institut de Chimie Moleculaire, 91405 Orsay, France

**Kagan, Jeremy Paul** — Director
2024 N Curson Ave, Los Angeles CA 90046, USA

**Kagan, Robert A** — Attorney, Educator
University of California, Law School, Boalt Hall, Berkeley CA 94720, USA

**Kagasoff, Daren** — Actor
Anderson Group Public Relations, 8060 Melrose Ave, #400, Los Angeles CA 90046, USA

**Kagge, Erling** — Polar Skier
Munkedamsveien 86, 0270 Oslo, Norway

**Kahane, Gabriel** — Composer
I M G Artists, Hogarth Business Park, Chiswick, London W4 2TH, England

**Kahane, Jeffrey** — Concert Pianist, Conductor
C M Artists, 127 W 96th St, #13B, New York NY 10025 USA

**Kahin, Brian** — Educator
Harvard University, Information Infrastructure Project, Cambridge MA 02138, USA

**Kahin, Dahir Riyale** — President, Somaliland Republic
President's Office, Hargiesa, Somaliland Republic

**Kahler, Eric** — Educator
University of Minnesota, President's Office, 176 N Mississippi River Blvd, Saint Paul MN 55104, USA

**Kahn, David R** — Publisher
New Yorker, Publisher's Office, 4 Times Square, New York NY 10036, USA

**Kahn, Harold** — Businessman
Wet Seal Inc, 26972 Burbank, Foothill Ranch CA 92610, USA

**Kahn, Joseph** — Journalist
New York Times, Editorial Dept, 229 W 43rd St, New York NY 10036 USA

**Kahn, Joseph** — Director
I C M Partners, 10250 Constellation Blvd, #900, Los Angeles CA 90067 USA

**Kahn, Nikki** — Photographer
Washington Post, Editorial Dept, 1150 15th St NW, Washington DC 20071 USA

**Kahn, Oliver** — Soccer Player
Titaneon Media, Oskar-Schlemmer-Str 11,80807 Munich, Germany

**Kahn, Robert E** — Inventor (Internet Protocol)
909 Lynton Place, McLean VA 22102, USA

**Kahn, Roger** — Writer
PO Box 556, Stone Ridge NY 12484, USA

**Kaake - Kahn**

**Kahn, Si** — Singer, Musician, Songwriter
Real People's Music, 520 S Clinton Ave, Oak Park IL 60304, USA

**Kahn, Wyatt** — Artist, Sculptor
T293 Gallery, Via G M Crescimbeni 11, 00184 Rome, Italy

**Kahne, Kasey K** — Auto Racing Driver
265 Cayuga Dr, Mooresville NC 28117, USA

**Kahneman, Daniel** — Nobel Economics Laureate
70 E 10th St, #HD, New York NY 10003, USA

**Kaifu, Toshiki** — Prime Minister, Japan
House of Representatives, Diet, Tokyo 100 0014, Japan

**Kaihori, Ayumi** — Soccer Player
Football Association, 3-10-15 Hongo, Bunkyoku, Tokyo 113 0033 Japan

**Kailath, Thomas** — Electrical Engineer
346 Greenoaks Dr, Atherton CA 94027, USA

**Kain, Karin A** — Ballet Dancer
National Ballet of Canada, 470 Queens Quay, Toronto ON M5V 3K4, Canada

**Kain, Khalil** — Actor
Envision Entertainment, 8840 Wilshire Blvd, Beverly Hills CA 90211 USA

**Kaine, Whitney** — Model
Playboy Promotions, 9346 Civic Center Dr, #200, Beverly Hills CA 90210 USA

**Kaiser, A Dale** — Biochemist
832 Santa Fe Ave, Stanford CA 94305, USA

**Kaiser, George B** — Financier
Bank of Oklahoma, Bank of Oklahoma Tower, PO Box 2300, Tulsa OK 74102, USA

**Kaiser, Jeffrey P (Jeff)** — Baseball Player
26227 James Dr, Grosse Isle MI 48138, USA

**Kaiser, Joseph** — Opera Singer, Actor
I M G Artists, Carnegie Hall Tower, 152 W 57th St, #500, New York NY 10019 USA

**Kaiser, Michael M** — Concert Executive
Kennedy Center for Performing Arts, 2700 F St NW, Washington DC 20566, USA

**Kaiser, R Thomas (Tom)** — Baseball Player
8 Independence Way, Southampton NJ 08088, USA

**Kaiser, Raf** — Physical Chemist
University of Hawaii, Physical Chemistry Dept, Honolulu HI 96822, USA

**Kaiser, Roland** — Singer, Songwriter
Semmel Concerts, Lutzplatz 15, 10785 Berlin, Germany

**Kaiser, Suki** — Actress
Greene Assoc, 1901 Ave of Stars, #130, Los Angeles CA 90067 USA

**Kaiser, Tim** — Producer
Vision Art Mgmt, 530 N Larchmont Blvd, #2, Los Angeles CA 90004, USA

**Kaiser-Brown, Natasha** — Track Athlete
2601 Hickman Road, Des Moines IA 50310, USA

**Kaiserman, William** — Fashion Designer
29 W 56th St, New York NY 10019, USA

**Kaji, Gautam S** — Government Official, Financier
World Bank Group, 1818 H St NW, Washington DC 20433, USA

**Kajlich, Bianca** — Model, Actress
United Talent Agency, U T A Plaza, 9336 Civic Center Dr, Beverly Hills CA 90210 USA

**Kajol** — Actress
Craving Dreams, 304 Oberoi Chambers II, B Wing off New Link Road, Andheri W, Mumbai 400053, India

**Kaka, Ricardo** — Soccer Player
Orlando City Lions, 618 E South St, #510, Orlando FL 32801 USA

**Kakhidze, Djansug I** — Conductor
Leselidze St 18, 380005 Tbilisi, Georgia

**Kaku, Michio** — Theoretical Physicist
City University of New York, Physics Dept, New York NY 10031, USA

**Kakutani, Michiko** — Journalist
New York Times, Editorial Dept, 229 W 43rd St, New York NY 10036, USA

**Kalainov, Samuel C** — Businessman
American Mutual Life, 611 5th Ave, Des Moines IA 50309, USA

**Kalb, Marvin L** — Commentator, Educator
1717 Massachusetts Ave NW, #610, Washington DC 20036, USA

**Kaldor, Connie** — Singer, Songwriter
Fleming Artists, 543 N Main St, Ann Arbor MI 48104, USA

**Kalem, Toni** — Actress
Creative Artists Agency, 2000 Ave of Stars, #100, Los Angeles CA 90067 USA

**Kalember, Patricia** — Actress
Innovative Artists, 1505 10th St, Santa Monica CA 90401 USA

**Kalen, Herbert D** — Vietnam War Air Force Hero
General Delivery, Angel Fire NM 87710, USA

**Kaler, Jamie** — Actor, Comedian
Paradigm Agency, 360 N Crescent Dr, North Building, Beverly Hills CA 90210 USA

**Kaleri, Aleksandr Y (Sasha)** — Cosmonaut
141 160 Svyosdny Gorodok, Moskovskoi Oblasti, Potchta Kosmonavtor, Russia

**Kalesniko, Michael** — Director, Writer
Creative Artists Agency, 2000 Ave of Stars, #100, Los Angeles CA 90067 USA

**Kalichstein, Joseph** — Concert Pianist
Opus 3 Artists, 470 Park Ave S, #900N, New York NY 10016 USA

**Kalikow, Peter S** — Publisher
H J Kalikow Co, 101 Park Ave, #2500, New York NY 10178, USA

**Kalina, Mike** — Chef
Travelin' Gourmet Show, PBS-TV, 1320 Braddock Place, Alexandria VA 22314, USA

**Kalina, Richard** — Artist
44 King St, New York NY 10014, USA

**Kaline, Albert W (Al)** — Baseball Player
3613 York Court, Bloomfield Hills MI 48301, USA

**Kaling, Mindy** — Actress, Comedienne, Writer
3 Arts Entertainment, 9460 Wilshire Blvd, #700, Beverly Hills CA 90212 USA

**Kalinin, Dmitri** — Ice Hockey Player
555 Pleasantville Road, #210N, Briarcliff NY 10510, USA

**Kalis, Todd A** — Football Player
127 Majestic Dr, Mars PA 16046, USA

**Kalish, Martin** — Labor Leader
School Administrators Federation, 853 Broadway, New York NY 10003, USA

**Kalish, Robert P** — Government Official, Financier
Government National Mortgage Assn, 451 7th St SW, Washington DC 20410, USA

**Kalitta, Connie** — Auto Racing Driver
Kalitta Motorsports, 1010 James L Hart Parkway, Ypsilanti MI 48197, USA
**Kalitta, Doug** — Drag Racing Driver
Kalitta Motorsports, 1010 James L Hart Prkway, Ypsilanta MI 49197, USA
**Kaljuste, Tonu** — Conductor
Konzertdirektion Hortnagel, Oranienburgen Str 50D, 10117 Berlin, Germany
**Kalla, Charlotte** — Cross Country Skier
Core Talent, Vibyvagen 14, 155 91 Nykvarn, Sweden
**Kallaugher, Kevin (Kall)** — Editorial Cartoonist
Baltimore Sun, Editorial Dept, 501 N Calvert St, Baltimore MD 21278, USA
**Kallen, Jackie** — Boxing Manager
Trident Media, 41 Madison Ave, #3600, New York NY 10010, USA
**Kallen, Kitty** — Singer, Actress
35 Winthrop Place, Englewood NJ 07631, USA
**Kallin, Catherine** — Physicist
224 Hillcrest Ave, Hamilton ON L8P 2X5, Canada
**Kallisch, Cornelia** — Opera Singer
Kunstler Sekretariat am Gasteig, Rosenheimer Str 52, 81669 Munich, Germany
**Kallita, Doug** — Auto Racing Driver
Kalitta Motorsports, 1010 James L Hart Parkway, Ypsilanti MI 48197, USA
**Kallman, Jonas** — Handball Player
Kunsvagen 54, 541 32 Slovde, Sweden
**Kallosh, Renata** — Physicist
Stanford University, Physics Dept, Stanford CA 94305, USA
**Kallur, Anders** — Ice Hockey Player
Utsiktsvagen 14, 791 31 Falun, Sweden
**Kalman, Rudolf E** — Mathematician
E T H Zentrum, 8092 Zurich, Switzerland
**Kalmoe, Megan** — Rowing Athlete
152 Old Beekman Road, Monmouth Junction NJ 08852, USA
**Kalonji, Sizzla** — Singer
Agency Group Ltd, 142 W 57th St, #600, New York NY 10019 USA
**Kalpokas, Donald M** — Prime Minister, Vanuatu
Vanuaaku Pati, PO Box 472, Port Vila, Vanuatu
**Kaltenegger, Lisa** — Astrobiologist, Astrophysicist
Max Planck Astrophysics Institute, Koenigstuhl 17, 69117 Heidelberg, Germany
**Kalu, Ndukwe D (N D)** — Football Player
3719 Popular Springs Dr, Missouri City TX 77459, USA
**Kalule, Ayub** — Boxer
Palie, Skjulet, Bagsvaert 12, Copenhagen 2880, Denmark
**Kalyan, Adhir** — Actor
United Talent Agency, U T A Plaza, 9336 Civic Center Dr, Beverly Hills CA 90210 USA
**Kamal, Gray** — Keyboardist (Roots)
Helter Skelter, 347-353 Chiswick High Road, London W4 4HS, England
**Kamali, Norma** — Fashion Designer
O M O Norma Kamali, 11 W 56th St, New York NY 10019, USA
**Kaman, Christopher Z (Chris)** — Basketball Player
300 N Dianthus St, Manhattan Beach CA 90266, USA
**Kamano, Stacy** — Actress, Model
Vision Mgmt, 8500 Steller Dr, Building 8, Culver City CA 90232, USA
**Kamarck, Andrew M** — Financier, Diplomat
PO Box 1267, Brewster MA 02631, USA
**Kamarck, Martin A** — Government Official, Financier
Export-Import Bank, 811 Vermont Ave NW, Washington DC 20571, USA
**Kamb, Alexander** — Geneticist
300 Alberta Way, Hillsborough CA 94010, USA
**Kamen, Dean** — Inventor (Portable Dialysis Machine)
D E K A Research & Development, 340 Commercial St, Manchester NH 03101, USA
**Kamen, Robert Mark** — Writer
Paradigm Agency, 360 N Crescent Dr, North Building, Beverly Hills CA 90210 USA
**Kamensky, Valeri** — Ice Hockey Player
4 Stonehedge Dr S, Greenwich CT 06831, USA
**Kamieniecki, Scott A** — Baseball Player
7800 Somerhill Lane, Clarkston MI 48348, USA
**Kamin, Aaron K** — Guitarist (Calling), Songwriter
Prince Promotions, 9663 Santa Monica Blvd, #324, Beverly Hills CA 90210, USA
**Kamin, Blair** — Architectural Critic
Chicago Tribune, Editorial Dept, 350 N Orleans St, Chicago IL 60654 USA
**Kaminir, Lisa** — Actress
Ellis Talent Group, 4705 Laurel Canyon Blvd, #300, Valley Village CA 91607, USA
**Kaminski, Jake** — Archer
US Olympic Training Center, 2800 Olympic Parkway, Chula Vista CA 91915, USA
**Kaminski, Janusz Z** — Cinematographer
23801 Calabasas Road, #2004, Calabasas CA 91302, USA
**Kaminski, Larry M** — Football Player
31423 State Highway 3 NE, Poulsbo WA 98370, USA
**Kaminski, Marek** — Explorer
Ul Dickmana 14/15, 80339 Gdansk, Poland
**Kaminsky, James** — Editor
Maxim, Dennis Publishing, 1040 Ave of Americas, #1500, New York NY 10018, USA
**Kaminsky, Kevin S** — Ice Hockey Player
162 Dryad Woods Road, Raymond ME 04071, USA
**Kaminsky, Walter** — Chemist
Hamburg University, Chemistry Dept, Martin-Luther-King Platz 6, 20146 Hamburg, Germany
**Kamisar, Yale** — Attorney, Educator
2910 Daleview Dr, Ann Arbor MI 48105, USA
**Kamm, Henry** — Journalist
New York Times, Editorial Dept, 229 W 43rd St, New York NY 10036, USA
**Kammer, Jerry** — Journalist
San Diego Union-Tribune, Editorial Dept, 350 Camino Reina, San Diego CA 92108 USA
**Kammerer, Carlton C (Carl)** — Football Player
6941 Brooks Road, Highland MD 20777, USA
**Kammerer, Zoltan** — Canoeing Athlete
Cserfa Utca 11, 2131 God, Hungary
**Kammerlander, Hansjorg (Hans)** — Mountaineer
Hotel Kammerlander, #69A, 6274 Aschau im Zillertal (T), Austria

**K**

**Kamp, Alexandra** — Actress, Model
Agentur Aziel, Pfarrstr 94, 10317 Berlin, Germany
**Kampman, Aaron A** — Football Player
PO Box 246, Solon IA 52333, USA
**Kampmeier, Deborah** — Director, Writer
I C M Partners, 10250 Constellation Blvd, #900, Los Angeles CA 90067 USA
**Kamu, Okko T** — Conductor
Calle Mozart 7, Rancho Domingo, 29639 Benalmedina Pueblo, Spain
**Kan, Yuet Wai** — Geneticist
20 Yerba Buena Ave, San Francisco CA 94127, USA
**Kanakaredes, Melina** — Actress
W M E Entertainment, 9601 Wilshire Blvd, #300, Beverly Hills CA 90210 USA
**Kanal, Tony** — Bassist, Songwriter (No Doubt)
Rebel Waltz, 31652 2nd Ave, Laguna Beach CA 92651, USA
**Kanaly, Steve** — Actor
C E S D, 10635 Santa Monica Blvd, #130, Los Angeles CA 90025 USA
**Kanamori, Hiroo** — Geophysicist
California Institute of Technology, Geophysics Dept, Pasadena CA 91125, USA
**Kanan, Sean** — Actor
Stone Manners Salners, 6100 Wilshire Blvd, #1500, Los Angeles CA 90035 USA
**Kananin, Roman G** — Architect
Joint-Stock Mosprojekt, 13/14 1 Brestkaya Str, 125190 Moscow, Russia
**Kancheli, Giya A (Georgy)** — Composer
Tovstonogov Str 6, 380064 Tbilisi, Georgia
**Kandel, Eric R** — Nobel Medicine Laureate
9 Sigma Place, Bronx NY 10471, USA
**Kander, John H** — Composer
146 Central Park W, #14D, New York NY 10023, USA
**Kandil, Hesham** — Prime Minister, Egypt
Prime Minister's Office, PO Box 191, 1 Majlis El-Shaab St, Cairo CA104, Egypt
**Kane Elson, Marion** — Synchronized Swimmer
4669 Badger Road, Santa Rosa CA 95409, USA
**Kane, Adelaide** — Actress
Frog Mgmt, 120 Lake St, #11, Northbridge WA 6865, Australia
**Kane, Carol** — Actress
Diamond Mgmt, 31 Percy St, London W1T 2DD, England
**Kane, Chelsea** — Actress, Singer
United Talent Agency, U T A Plaza, 9336 Civic Center Dr, Beverly Hills CA 90210 USA
**Kane, Christian** — Actor, Singer, Songwriter
Sutton-Barth Vennari, 5900 Wilshire Blvd, #700, Los Angeles CA 90036 USA
**Kane, Howie** — Singer (Jay & the Americans)
T C I, 105 Shad Row, #D, Piermont NY 10968, USA
**Kane, John C** — Businessman
Cardinal Health, 7000 Cardinal Place, Dublin OH 43017, USA
**Kane, Kelly** — Actress
D H Talent, 1800 N Highland Ave, #300, Los Angeles CA 90028 USA
**Kane, Lorie** — Golfer
101-5397 Eglinton Ave W, Etobicoke ON M9C 5K6, Canada
**Kane, Matt** — Actor
United Talent Agency, U T A Plaza, 9336 Civic Center Dr, Beverly Hills CA 90210 USA
**Kane, Nick** — Singer (Mavericks)
AstroMedia, 1620 16th Ave S, Nashville TN 37212, USA
**Kane, Patrick T, II** — Ice Hockey Player
213 McKinley Parkway, Buffalo NY 14220, USA
**Kane, Robert H** — Philosopher
University of Texas, Philosophy Dept, Austin TX 78712, USA
**Kanell, Daniel P (Danny)** — Football Player
4631 NE 25th Ave, Fort Lauderdale FL 33308, USA
**Kanellis, Maria** — Professional Wrestler, Model
World Wrestling Entertainment, Titan Towers, 1241 E Main St, Stamford CT 06902 USA
**Kanengiser, William** — Guitarist (LAGQ)
Besen Arts, 77 Park Ave, #128, Hoboken NJ 07030, USA
**Kanerva, Silja** — Yachtswoman
Pajalahdentie 4A16, 00200 Helsinki, Finland
**Kaneswaren, Siva** — Singer (Wanted), Model
Industry Music Group, 128 Regent Road, Hanley Stoke, Trent ST1 3AY, England
**Kang, Dong-Suk** — Concert Violinist
Clarion/Seven Muses, 47 Whitehall Park, London N19 3TW, England
**Kang, Jimin** — Golfer
8539 E Cactus Wren Circle, Scottsdale AZ 85266, USA
**Kang, Kourtney** — Producer
United Talent Agency, U T A Plaza, 9336 Civic Center Dr, Beverly Hills CA 90210 USA
**Kang, Tim** — Actor
Vincent Cirrincione Assoc, 1516 N Fairfax Ave, Los Angeles CA 90046 USA
**Kanicki, James H (Jim)** — Football Player
Tackle Hill Farm, 4590 Schramling Road, Pierpont OH 44082, USA
**Kanievska, Marek** — Director
I C M Partners, 10250 Constellation Blvd, #900, Los Angeles CA 90067 USA
**Kann Valar, Paula** — Alpine Skier
34 Hubertus Ring, Franconia NH 03580, USA
**Kann, Peter R** — Businessman, Publisher, Journalist
Dow Jones Co, 1 World Financial Center, #900, New York NY 10281, USA
**Kanne, Michael S** — Judge
US Court of Appeals, PO Box 1340, Lafayette IN 47902, USA
**Kannenberg, Bernd** — Track Athlete
Sportschule, 87527 Sonthofen/Allgau, Germany
**Kanouse, Lyle** — Actor
Avalon Artists Group, 5455 Wilshire Blvd, #900, Los Angeles CA 90036, USA
**Kanter, Gerd** — Track Athlete
Parnu Spordiklubi Altius, Kooli 5-9, 80019 Parnu, Estonia
**Kantner, Paul L** — Guitarist (Jefferson Airplane, Starship)
Mission Control, 15030 Ventura Blvd, #300, Sherman Oaks CA 91403, USA
**Kantor, Michael (Mickey)** — Secretary, Commerce
2709 Olive Ave NW, Washington DC 20007, USA
**Kao, Archie** — Actor
C E S D, 10635 Santa Monica Blvd, #130, Los Angeles CA 90025 USA

**Kao, Charles K**
Yee Foundation, 1 Harbour Road, #1708, Wan Chai, Hong Kong, China — Nobel Physics Laureate

**Kao, Min H**
Garmin International, 1200 E 151st St, Olathe KS 66062, USA — Businessman

**Kapadia, Asif**
Independent Talent Group, 40 Whitfield St, London W1T 2RH, England — Actor, Writer, Director

**Kapadia, Dimple**
201A Vastu Building, Military Road Juhu, Mumbai MS 400049, India — Actress

**Kapanen, Niko K P**
Ak Bars Kazan, Tatneff Arena, Kazan, Tatarstan, Russia — Ice Hockey Player

**Kapanen, Sami H K**
Kalpa Hockey, Sairaalakatu 15, 70110 Kuopio, Finland — Ice Hockey Player

**Kapches, Ko**
Agency Group Ltd, 142 W 57th St, #600, New York NY 10019 USA — Singer, Songwriter

**Kapelos, John**
Axiom Mgmt, 10701 Wilshire Blvd, #1202, Los Angeles CA 90024, USA — Actor

**Kapilow, Robert (Rob)**
I M G Artists, Hogarth Business Park, Chiswick, London W4 2TH, England — Conductor, Composer

**Kapinos, Tom**
Creative Artists Agency, 2000 Ave of Stars, #100, Los Angeles CA 90067 USA — Producer, Writer

**Kapioitas, John**
I T T Sheraton Corp, 1111 Westchester Ave, West Harrison NY 10604, USA — Businessman

**Kaplan, Fred M**
Simon & Schuster, 1230 Ave of Americas, Concourse 1, New York NY 10020 USA — Writer

**Kaplan, Gabe**
9551 Hidden Valley Road, Beverly Hills CA 90210, USA — Actor, Comedian

**Kaplan, Jonathan S**
4323 Ben Ave, Studio City CA 91604, USA — Director

**Kaplan, Kyle**
Michael Adams Group, 2934 Beverly Glen Circle, #453, Bel Air CA 90077, USA — Actor

**Kaplan, Marvin**
D D O Artists, 4605 Lankershim Blvd, #340, North Hollywood CA 91602, USA — Actor, Writer, Producer

**Kaplan, Nathan O**
8587 La Jolla Scenic Dr, La Jolla CA 92037, USA — Biochemist

**Kaplan, Paul**
Old Coat Music, 203 Heatherstone Road, Amherst MA 01002, USA — Singer, Songwriter

**Kaplansky, Lucy**
Fleming Artists, 543 N Main St, Ann Arbor MI 48104, USA — Singer, Guitarist, Songwriter

**Kapler, Gabriel S (Gabe)**
18316 Palomar Place, Tarzana CA 91356, USA — Baseball Player

**Kapnek, Emily**
Gotham Group, 9255 Sunset Blvd, #515, Los Angeles CA 90069, USA — Producer, Wrtiter

**Kapoor, Anil**
I C M Partners, 10250 Constellation Blvd, #900, Los Angeles CA 90067 USA — Actor

**Kapoor, Anish**
33 Coleherne Road, London SW10, England — Sculptor

**Kapoor, Kareena**
2B/110/1201 Excellency 4th Cross Road, Mumbai MS 400058, India — Actress

**Kapoor, Rishi**
27 Krishna Raj, Pali Hill Bandra, Mumbai MS 400058, India — Actor

**Kapoor, Shashi**
112 Atlas Apartments, Mumbai 400006, India — Actor

**Kapor, Mitchell D**
Open Source Application Foundation, 177 Post St, #900, San Francisco CA 94108, USA — Computer Programmer

**Kapp, Joseph (Joe)**
PO Box 1973, Los Gatos CA 95031, USA — Football Player, Coach

**Kappe, Ron**
715 Brooktree Road, Pacific Palisades CA 90272, USA — Architect

**Kapranos, Alexander P (Alex)**
M A M A Group, 59-65 Worship St, London EC2A 2DU, England — Singer, Guitarist (Franz Ferdinand)

**Kaprisky, Valerie**
Artmedia, 20 Ave Rapp, 75007 Paris, France — Actress

**Kapture, Mitzi**
Lovett Mgmt, 1327 Brinkley Ave, Los Angeles CA 90049 USA — Actress

**Kapur, Shekhar**
Sentient Entertainment, 8840 Wilshire Blvd, #200, Beverly Hills CA 90211, USA — Director

**Karabatic, Nikola**
F C Barcelona Balonmano, Aristides Maillol S/N, 08028 Barcelona, Spain — Handball Player

**Karabits, Kirill**
Bournemouth Symphony Orchestra, 2 Seldown Lane, Poole, Dorset BH15 1UF, England — Conductor

**Karaboue, Daouda**
580 Route Prades, 34730 Saint Vincent de Barbeyrargues, France — Handball Player

**Karadaglic, Milos**
I M G Artists, Hogarth Business Park, Chiswick, London W4 2TH, England — Concert Guitarist

**Karaev, Anatol**
I M G Artists, Hogarth Business Park, Chiswick, London W4 2TH, England — Concert Violinist

**Karageorghis, Vassos**
Foundation Anastasios Leventis, 28 Sofoulis St, Nicosia, Cyprus — Archaeologist

**Karagias, Evan**
2009 Tomshire Dr, Gastonia NC 28056, USA — Professional Wrestler

**Karamanov, Alemdar S**
Voykova Str 2, #4, Simferopol, Crimea, Ukraine — Composer

**Karamesines, Chris**
7444 S Claremont Ave, Chicago IL 60636, USA — Drag Racing Driver

**Karan, Amara**
Curtis Brown Group, 28-29 Haymarket St, #500, London SW1Y 4SP, England — Actress

**Karan, Donna**
Donna Karan Co, 361 Newbury St, Boston MA 02115, USA — Fashion Designer

**Karasev, Sergey V**
Brooklyn Nets, 15 Metro Tech Center, #1100, Brooklyn NY 11201 USA — Basketball Player

**Karath, Kym**
Dykema Gossett, 333 S Grand Ave, #2100, Los Angeles CA 90071, USA — Actress

**Karathanasis, Sotirios K**
AstraZeneca, Bioscience Dept, Pepparedsleden 1, 431 83 Molndal, Sweden — Physiologist

**Karbacher, Bernd**
Hufnagelstra 13, 80686 Munich, Germany — Tennis Player

# K

**Karchner, Matthew D (Matt)** — Baseball Player
401 E 2nd St, Berwick PA 18603, USA
**Kardashian, Khloe A** — Actress, Producer
W M E Entertainment, 9601 Wilshire Blvd, #300, Beverly Hills CA 90210 USA
**Kardashian, Kimberly (Kim)** — Actress, Model
W M E Entertainment, 9601 Wilshire Blvd, #300, Beverly Hills CA 90210 USA
**Kardashian, Kourtney** — Actress
W M E Entertainment, 9601 Wilshire Blvd, #300, Beverly Hills CA 90210 USA
**Kardashian, Robert A (Rob), Jr** — Actor
A P A Talent & Literary Agency, 405 S Beverly Dr, #300, Beverly Hills CA 90212 USA
**Karelin, Alesander A** — Greco-Roman Wrestler
State Duma, Yedinstvo Faction, Okhotny Ryad 1, 103265 Moscow, Russia
**Karelskaya, Rimma K** — Ballerina
Bolshoi Theater, Teatralnaya Pl 1, 103009 Moscow, Russia
**Karen, James** — Actor
Amsel Eisenstadt Frazier, 5055 Wilshire Blvd, #865, Los Angeles CA 90036 USA
**Karieva, Bernara** — Ballerina
National Ballet Theater, 28 MK Otaturk St, 700029 Tashkent, Uzbekistan
**Karim, Jawed** — Businessman
YouTube, 1000 Cherry Ave, #200, San Bruno CA 94066, USA
**Karim-Lamrani, Mohammed** — Prime Minister, Morocco
Rue du Mont Saint Michel, Anfa Superieur, Casablanca 21300, Morocco
**Karimov, Islom M** — President, Uzbekistan
President's Office, Uzbekistansky Prosp 45, 700163 Tashkent, Uzbekistan
**Karina, Anna** — Actress
Artmedia, 20 Ave Rapp, 75007 Paris, France
**Kariya, Paul T** — Ice Hockey Player
2493 Aquasanta, Tustin CA 92782, USA
**Karkovice, Ronald J (Ron)** — Baseball Player
3201 Oakstand Lane, Orlando FL 32812, USA
**Karl, Benjamin M** — Snowboarding Skier
Snowboard Federation, Olympic St 10, 6010 Innsbruck, Austria
**Karl, George M** — Basketball Coach, Executive
145 Kearney St, Denver CO 80220, USA
**Karl, R Scott** — Baseball Player
11765 Costa Blanca Ave, Las Vegas NV 89138, USA
**Karle, Isabella** — Chemist
6304 Lakeview Dr, Falls Church VA 22041, USA
**Karlen, John** — Actor
2940 N Verdugo Road, #202, Glendale CA 91208, USA
**Karlic, Estanislao E Cardinal** — Religious Leader
Archdiocese of Parana, Monte Caseris 77, 3100 Parana (Entre Rios), Argentina
**Karlin, Ben** — Writer, Producer
United Talent Agency, U T A Plaza, 9336 Civic Center Dr, Beverly Hills CA 90210 USA
**Karlis, Richard J (Rich)** — Football Player
9947 Arthur Lane, Highlands Ranch CO 80130, USA
**Karlsson, Erik** — Ice Hockey Player
Ottawa Senators, Scotia Bank Place, Kanata ON K2V 1A5, Canada
**Karlsson, Lena** — Singer (Komeda)
M O B Agency, 6404 Wilshire Blvd, #505, Los Angeles CA 90048 USA
**Karlstad, Geir** — Speed Skater
Hamarveien 5A, 1472 Fjellhamar, Norway
**Karlzen, Mary** — Singer, Songwriter
Little Big Man, 155 Ave of Americas, #700, New York NY 10013, USA
**Karman, Tawakul** — Nobel Peace Laureate
Al-Islah Party, Parliament Building, Sana's, Yemen
**Karmann, Sam** — Actor
Les Films A4, 41 Rue Vivienne 75002 Paris, France
**Karmanos, Peter, Jr** — Businessman, Hockey Executive
Compuware Corp, 1 Campus Martius, Detroit MI 48226, USA
**Karmazin, Mel** — Businessman
Sirius Satelite Radio, 1221 Avenue of Americas, #3600, New York NY 10020, USA
**Karmi-Melamede, Ada** — Architect
Karmi Architects, 17 Kaplan St, Tel Aviv 64734, Israel
**Karn, Richard** — Actor
Stone Manners Salners, 6100 Wilshire Blvd, #1500, Los Angeles CA 90035 USA
**Karnes, David K** — Senator, NE
9639 Oak Circle, Omaha NE 68124, USA
**Karnes, Jay** — Actor
Innovative Artists, 1505 10th St, Santa Monica CA 90401 USA
**Karneus, Katarina** — Opera Singer
Ingpen & Williams, 131 Putney Bridge Road, London SW15 2PA, England
**Karolyi, Bela** — Gymnastics Coach
171 W 57th St, #8A, New York NY 10019, USA
**Karolyi, Marta** — Gymnastics Coach
World Gymnastics Academy, 1937 W Parker Road, Plano TX 75023, USA
**Karon, Jan** — Writer
7060 Esmont Farm, Esmont VA 22937, USA
**Karp, Peter** — Singer, Songwriter
Road Dawg Touring, PO Box 2835, Evergreen CO 80437, USA
**Karp, Richard M** — Computer Scientist, Engineer
University of Washington, Computer Science Dept, Seattle WA 98195, USA
**Karpa, Dave** — Ice Hockey Player
23668 N Lookout Pointe Road, Port Barrington IL 60010, USA
**Karpati, Gyorgy** — Water Polo Player
Il Liva Utca 1, 1025 Budapest, Hungary
**Karpatkin, Rhoda H** — Publisher, Consumers Activist
280 Riverside Drive, New York NY 10025, USA
**Karpluk, Erin** — Actress
Play Mgmt, 807 Powell St, #220, Vancouver BC V6A 1H7, Canada
**Karplus, Martin** — Nobel Chemistry Laureate
Harvard University, Chemistry & Chemical Biology Dept, 12 Oxford St, Cambridge MA 02138, USA
**Karponosov, Gennadiy** — Ice Dancer, Coach
146 Dallam Road, Newark DE 19711, USA
**Karpovsky, Alex** — Actor, Director
Mosiac Media Group, 9200 W Sunset Blvd, #1000, Los Angeles CA 90069 USA

**Karchner - Karpovsky**

**Karr, Mary** — Writer
Syracuse University, English Dept, Syracuse NY 13244, USA

**Karrass, Chester L** — Writer
1633 Stanford St, Santa Monica CA 90404, USA

**Karros, Eric P** — Baseball Player
1170 Longfellow Dr, Manhattan Beach CA 90266, USA

**Karrys, George** — Curling Athlete
Curling Association, 1660 Vimont Court, Cumberland ON K4A 4J4, Canada

**Karsay, Stefan A (Steve)** — Baseball Player
20244 N 102nd Place, Scottsdale AZ 85255, USA

**Karsenty, Gerard** — Geneticist
Columbia University Medical Center, 701 W 168th St, #1602A, New York NY 10032, USA

**Karsh, Jonathan** — Producer, Director
Relativity Real, 1040 N Las Palmas Ave, Los Angeles CA 90038, USA

**Karst, Kenneth L** — Attorney, Educator
University of California, Law School, PO Box 951476, Los Angeles CA 90095, USA

**Karstens, Jeffrey W (Jeff)** — Baseball Player
212 S Moody Ave, #3, Tampa FL 33609, USA

**Kartheiser, Vincent P** — Actor
Paradigm Agency, 360 N Crescent Dr, North Building, Beverly Hills CA 90210 USA

**Kartz, Keith L** — Football Player
19232 E Hinsdale Lane, Centennial CO 80016, USA

**Karume, Amani Abeid** — President, Zanzibar
President's Office, State House, PO Box 776, Zanzibar, Tanzania

**Karusseit, Ursula** — Actress
FilmArtists Katja Ohneck, Hauptstr 7, 21514 Hornbek, Germany

**Karvan, Claudia** — Actress, Writer, Producer
Robyn Gardiner Mgmt, 64-76 Kippax St, Surry Hills NSW 2010, Australia

**Karyo, Tcheky** — Actor
Artmedia, 20 Ave Rapp, 75007 Paris, France

**Kasaks, Sally Frame** — Businesswoman
AnnTaylor Stores, 7 Times Square, #4, New York NY 10036, USA

**Kasarova, Vesselina** — Opera Singer
Opera et Concert, 37 Rue de la Chaussee d'Antin, 75009 Paris, France

**Kasatkina, Natalya K** — Ballerina, Choreographer
Karietny Riad, H 5/10, #37, 103006 Moscow, Russia

**Kasatonov, Alexei V** — Ice Hockey Player
153 Eagle Rock Way, Montclair NJ 07042, USA

**Kasay, John D** — Football Player
8711 Lake Challis Lane, Charlotte NC 28226, USA

**Kasch, Cody** — Actor
TalentWorks, 3500 W Olive Ave, #1400, Burbank CA 91505 USA

**Kasch, Max** — Actor
Abrams Artists, 9200 W Sunset Blvd, #1125, West Hollywood CA 90069 USA

**Kasdan, Jacob (Jake)** — Director, Actor
W M E Entertainment, 9601 Wilshire Blvd, #300, Beverly Hills CA 90210 USA

**Kasdan, Lawrence E** — Director, Writer
Kasdan Pictures, PO Box 17578, Beverly Hills CA 90209, USA

**Kaselawski, Bradley R (Brad)** — Auto Racing Driver
K Auto Motorsports, 2790 Auburn Road, Auburn Hills MI 48326, USA

**Kasem, Jean** — Actress
138 N Mapleton Dr, Los Angeles CA 90077, USA

**Kaseman, Keith** — Architect
4820 Holston Heights Lane, Knoxville TN 37914, USA

**Kaser, Helmut A** — Soccer Executive
Hitzigweg 11, 8032 Zurich, Switzerland

**Kasha, Al** — Composer, Lyricist
458 N Oakhurst Dr, #102, Beverly Hills CA 90210, USA

**Kasher, Tim** — Singer, Guitarist (Cursive)
Ground Control Touring, 20 Jay St, #826, Brooklyn NY 11201 USA

**Kashiwara, Masaki** — Mathematician
Mathematical Science Institute, Kyoto University, Kyoto 606 8502, Japan

**Kashkari, Neel** — Financier, Government Official
Treasury Department, 1500 Pennsylvania Ave NW, Washington DC 20220 USA

**Kashkashian, Kim** — Concert Violist
Musicians Corporate Mgmt, PO Box 825, Highland NY 12528, USA

**Kaskey, Raymond J** — Sculptor, Architect
2221 Hiatt Place NW, Washington DC 20007, USA

**Kasko, Edward M (Eddie)** — Baseball Player, Manager
32 Major Ginter Court, Richmond VA 23227, USA

**Kasling, Dagmar Luhenschloss** — Track Athlete
Hollehocjstr 27E, 39110 Magdeburg, Germany

**Kasman, Yakov** — Concert Pianist
Jonathan Wentworth Assoc, 10 Fiske Place, #530, Mount Vernon NY 10550 USA

**Kasparov, Garry K** — Chess Player
Kasparov Agency, 3114 45th St, #8, West Palm Beach FL 33407, USA

**Kasper, Kevin J** — Football Player
3119 Landore Dr, Naperville IL 60564, USA

**Kasper, Steve** — Ice Hockey Player, Coach
6 Swan Lane, Andover MA 01810, USA

**Kasper, Walter Cardinal** — Religious Leader
Promoting Christian Unity Council, Via della Conciliazione 5, 00193 Rome, Italy

**Kaspszyk, Jacek** — Conductor
Teatr Wielki, Pl Teatralny 1, 00077 Warsaw, Poland

**Kasrashvili, Makvala** — Opera Singer
Bolshoi Theater, Teatralnaya Pl 1, 103009 Moscow, Russia

**Kass, Carmen** — Model, Actress
Women Model Mgmt, 199 Lafayette St, #700, New York NY 10012 USA

**Kass, Daniel (Danny)** — Snowboard Skier
4315 NE Laurelhurst Place, Portland OR 97213, USA

**Kass, Leon R** — Bioethicist
1150 17th St NW, #AE1, Washington DC 20036, USA

**Kass, Nikolaj Lie** — Actor, Director, Writer
Lindberg Mgmt, Lavendelstaede 5-7, Baghuset 4 Sal, 1462 Copenhagen K, Denmark

**Kass, Patricia** — Singer, Actress
Talent Sorcier, 56 Rue Notre Dame de Nazareth, 75003 Paris, France

# K

**Kassay, Jacob** — Artist
Eleven Rivington, 11 Rivington St & 195 Chrystie St, New York NY 10002, USA

**Kassebaum, Nancy Landon** — Senator, KS
Robert Wood Johnson Foundation, College Road E, Princeton NJ 08543, USA

**Kassell, Brad** — Football Player
20117 Rancho Cielo Court, Lago Vista TX 78645, USA

**Kassell, Carl** — Commentator
National Public Radio, 635 Massachusetts Ave NW, #1, Washington DC 20001, USA

**Kassell, Nicole** — Director, Writer
Washington Square Arts, 1041 N Formosa Ave, Formosa Building, West Hollywood CA 90046, USA

**Kassen, Mark** — Actor, Producer, Director
Kassen Brothers Production, 348 Hauser Blvd, Los Angeles CA 90036, USA

**Kassir, John** — Actor, Producer
Vincent Cirrincione Assoc, 1516 N Fairfax Ave, Los Angeles CA 90046 USA

**Kassoma, A Paulo** — Prime Minister, Angola
National Assemby, Rua do 1 Confresso do M P L A, CP 1204 Luanda, Angola

**Kassorla, Irene C** — Psychologist
908 N Roxbury Dr, Beverly Hills CA 90210, USA

**Kasten, Robert W, Jr** — Senator, WI
Kasten Co, 888 16th St NW, #700, Washington DC 20006, USA

**Kastor, Deena** — Track Athlete
1208 Majestic Pines Dr, Mammoth Lakes CA 93546, USA

**Kasulke, Benjamin** — Cinematographer
United Talent Agency, U T A Plaza, 9336 Civic Center Dr, Beverly Hills CA 90210 USA

**Kasyanov, Mikhail M** — Prime Minister, Russia
House of Government, Krasnopresneskaya Nab 2, 103274 Moscow, Russia

**Kata, Matthew J (Matt)** — Baseball Player
7050 Tunbridge Dr, Mentor OH 44060, USA

**Katagas, Anthony G** — Producer
Keep Your Head Productions, 349 Broadway, New York NY 10013, USA

**Katainen, Jyrki T** — Prime Minister, Finland
Prime Minister's Office, Snellmaninkatu 1A, 00170, Helsinki, Finland

**Katchor, Ben** — Cartoonist (Julius Knipl)
Wylie Agency, 250 W 57th St, #2114, New York NY 10107 USA

**Kate** — Duchess of Cambridge
Clarence House, Stable Yard Gate, London SW1A 1BA, England

**Katehi, Linda P B** — Educator
University of California, Chancellor's Office, 1 Shields Ave, Davis CA 95616, USA

**Kates, Kimberley** — Actress
David Talent, 116 S Gardner St, Los Angeles CA 90036, USA

**Kates, Robert W** — Geographer
1081 Bar Harbor Road, Trenton ME 04605, USA

**Kathpalia, Rajeev** — Architect
Vastu Shilpa Consultants, Sangath, Thaltej Road, Ahmedabad 380054, India

**Katic, Stana J** — Actress
Sine Timore, 195 S Beverly Dr, #400, Beverly Hills CA 90212 90212, USA

**Katims, Jason** — Producer
Creative Artists Agency, 2000 Ave of Stars, #100, Los Angeles CA 90067 USA

**Katin, Peter R** — Concert Pianist
4 Clarence Road, Croydon, Surrrey CR0 2EN, England

**Katleman, Michael** — Director
United Talent Agency, U T A Plaza, 9336 Civic Center Dr, Beverly Hills CA 90210 USA

**Kato, Masaya** — Actor
Burning Productions, 7-6-11-1F, Akasaka, Minatoku, Tokyo 107 0052 , Japan

**Katon, Rosanne** — Actress, Model
407 Ocean Front Walk, #5, Venice CA 90291, USA

**Katona, Kerry J E** — Entertainer, Singer
Flood Bumstead McCready McCarthy, 1700 Hayes St, #304, Nashville TN 37203 USA

**Katritzky, Alan R** — Chemist
1221 SW 21st Ave, Gainesville FL 32601, USA

**Katsalapov, Nikita G** — Ice Dancer
Figure Skating Federation, Luzhnetskaya Nab 8, 119991 Moscow, Russia

**Katsoudas, Stella** — Singer (Sister Soleil), Songwriter
Ashley Talent, 2002 Hogback Road, #20, Ann Arbor MI 48105 USA

**Katt, Nicholas L (Nicky)** — Actor, Producer
Paradigm Agency, 360 N Crescent Dr, North Building, Beverly Hills CA 90210 USA

**Katt, William** — Actor, Writer, Director
Horne Agency, 4420 W Lovers Lane, Dallas TX 75209, USA

**Kattan, Chris** — Actor, Comedian
A P A Talent & Literary Agency, 405 S Beverly Dr, #300, Beverly Hills CA 90212 USA

**Kattan, Mohammed Imad** — Architect
PO Box 950846, Amman 11195, Jordan

**Katula, Matthew C (Matt)** — Football Player
14 Victoria Court, #21, Reisterstown MD 21136, USA

**Katz, Aaron** — Director, Writer
Creative Artists Agency, 2000 Ave of Stars, #100, Los Angeles CA 90067 USA

**Katz, Abraham** — Diplomat
US Council for International Business, 1212 Ave of Americas, New York NY 10036, USA

**Katz, Alex** — Artist
435 W Broadway, New York NY 10012, USA

**Katz, Bernard** — Sculptor
PO Box 41064, Philadelphia PA 19127, USA

**Katz, Cindy** — Actress
Harden-Curtis Assoc, 214 W 29th St, #1203, New York NY 10001, USA

**Katz, Donald L** — Petroleum Engineer
2011 Washtenaw Ave, Ann Arbor MI 48104, USA

**Katz, Douglas J (Doug)** — Navy Admiral
1530 Gordon Cove Dr, Annapolis MD 21403, USA

**Katz, Harold** — Basketball Executive
Philadelphia 76ers, 1st Union Center, 3601 S Broad St, Philadelphia PA 19148 USA

**Katz, Hilda** — Artist
915 W End Ave, #5D, New York NY 10025, USA

**Katz, Jonathan** — Actor, Comedian, Animator
Creative Artists Agency, 2000 Ave of Stars, #100, Los Angeles CA 90067 USA

**Katz, Michael** — Pediatrician
200 E 57th St, #11K, New York NY 10022, USA

**Kassay - Katz**

**Katz, Omri** — Actor
J H Productions, 23679 Calabasas Road, #333, Calabasas CA 91302, USA
**Katz, Ross** — Producer, Director, Writer
Ross Katz Films, 200 Park Ave S, #800, New York NY 10003, USA
**Katz, Samuel L** — Pediatrician
1917 Wildcat Creek Road, Chapel Hill NC 27516, USA
**Katz, Stanley N** — Attorney, Educator
American Council on Learned Societies, 228 E 45th St, New York NY 10017, USA
**Katz, Stephen M** — Cinematographer
C E S D, 10635 Santa Monica Blvd, #130, Los Angeles CA 90025 USA
**Katzenberg, David** — Producer, Writer
Katz/Smith Productions, 8447 Wilshire Blvd, #210, Beverly Hills CA 90211, USA
**Katzenberg, Jeffrey** — Businessman, Philanthropist
DreamWorks SKG, 100 Flower St, Glendale CA 91201, USA
**Katzenmoyer, Andrew W (Andy)** — Football Player
5764 Salem Dr, Westerville OH 43082, USA
**Katzmann, Robert A** — Judge
US Court of Appeals, Moynihan Courthouse, 500 Pearl St, New York NY 10007, USA
**Katzur, Klaus** — Swimmer
Robert-Siewart-Str 76, 09120 Chemnitz, Germany
**Kauffman, Marta** — Writer, Producer
W M E Entertainment, 9601 Wilshire Blvd, #300, Beverly Hills CA 90210 USA
**Kauffman, Stuart A A** — Biologist
Biocomplexity Institute, 2500 University NW, Calgary AB T2N 1N4, Canada
**Kaufman, Adam** — Actor
S D B Partners, 315 S Beverly Dr, #411, Beverly Hills CA 90067 USA
**Kaufman, Charles S (Charlie)** — Director, Producer, Writer
W M E Entertainment, 9601 Wilshire Blvd, #300, Beverly Hills CA 90210 USA
**Kaufman, Dan S** — Hematologist
University of Wisconsin Medical School, Hematology Dept, Madison WI 53706, USA
**Kaufman, Donald** — Writer
United Talent Agency, U T A Plaza, 9336 Civic Center Dr, Beverly Hills CA 90210 USA
**Kaufman, Henry** — Financier
Henry Kaufman Co, 65 E 55th St, New York NY 10022, USA
**Kaufman, Moises** — Director, Writer
Gersh Agency, 41 Madison Ave, #3301, New York NY 10010 USA
**Kaufman, Napoleon** — Football Player
1913 Via Di Salerno, Pleasanton CA 94566, USA
**Kaufman, Philip** — Director, Writer
I C M Partners, 10250 Constellation Blvd, #900, Los Angeles CA 90067 USA
**Kaufman, Thomas C (Thom)** — Biologist
Indiana University, Biology Dept, Bloomington IN 47405, USA
**Kaufmann, Christine** — Actress
Agentur Alexander, Lamontstr 9, 81679 Munich, Germany
**Kaufmann, Robert (Bob)** — Basketball Player
1677 Rivermist Dr SW, Lilburn GA 30047, USA
**Kaukonen, Jorma L, Jr** — Guitarist (Jefferson Airplane, Hot Tuna)
Moneypenny Agency, Westwood House, Main St, Driffield, East Yorkshire YO25 9XA, England
**Kaunda, Kenneth D** — President, Zambia
21A Serval Road, Private Bag E501, Lusaka, Zambia
**Kaurismaki, Aki** — Director, Producer, Writer
Sputnik, Museokato 13A, 00100 Helsinki, Finland
**Kausalya** — Actress
15A-2 Akshar, Palace Road, Bangalore JA 52, India
**Kaushal, Kamini** — Actress, Dancer
B2 Anita Mount Pleasant Road, Malabar Hill, Mumbai MS 400006, India
**Kauth, Kathleen** — Ice Hockey Player
13 Hillcrest Lane, Saratoga Springs NY 12866, USA
**Kava, Caroline** — Actress
TalentWorks, 3500 W Olive Ave, #1400, Burbank CA 91505 USA
**Kavanaugh, Brett M** — Judge
US Appellate Court, 333 Constitution Ave NW, #4400, Washington DC 20001, USA
**Kavanaugh, John** — Actor
The Agency, 9 Upper Fitzwilliam St, Dublin 2, Ireland
**Kavandi, Janet L** — Astronaut
3907 Park Circle Way, Houston TX 77059, USA
**Kavner, Julie** — Actress
Martino Mgmt, 149 W 72nd St, #1D, New York NY 10023, USA
**Kavovit, Andrew** — Actor, Producer
Thruline Entertainment, 9250 Wilshire Blvd, #100, Beverly Hills CA 90212 USA
**Kavrakos, Dimitri** — Opera Singer
Columbia Artists Mgmt Inc, 5 Columbus Circle, 1790 Broadway, #1600, New York NY 10019 USA
**Kawakubo, Rei** — Fashion Designer
Comme des Garcons, 16 Place Vendome, 75001 Paris, France
**Kawasumi, Nahomi** — Soccer Player
Football Association, 3-10-15 Hongo, Bunkyoku, Tokyo 113 0033 Japan
**Kay, Alan C** — Computer Scientist
Viewpoints Research Institute, 1209 Grand Capital Ave, Glendale CA 91201, USA
**Kay, Clarence H** — Football Player
1648 Lansing St, Aurora CO 80010, USA
**Kay, Dianne** — Actress
1565 Calle Del Estribo, Pacific Palisades CA 90272, USA
**Kay, Dominic Scott** — Actor
Paradigm Agency, 360 N Crescent Dr, North Building, Beverly Hills CA 90210 USA
**Kay, Herma H** — Attorney, Educator
University of California, Law School, Boalt Hall, Berkeley CA 94720, USA
**Kay, Jason (Jay)** — Singer (Jamiroquai)
Nettwerk Mgmt, 6525 W Sunset Blvd, #800, Los Angeles CA 90028 USA
**Kay, John** — Singer, Guitarist (Steppenwolf)
Paradise Artists, PO Box 1821, Ojai CA 93024 USA
**Kay, Lesli** — Actress
Innovative Artists, 1505 10th St, Santa Monica CA 90401 USA
**Kay, Stephen T** — Actor
I C M Partners, 10250 Constellation Blvd, #900, Los Angeles CA 90067 USA
**Kaye, Carol** — Guitarist, Bassist
25852 McBean Parkway, #200, Valencia CA 91355, USA

K

Katz - Kaye

**Kaye, Jonathan** — Golfer
328 W El Camino, Phoenix AZ 85021, USA
**Kaye, Paul** — Actor, Writer, Composer
Richard Stone Partnership, De Walden Court, 85 New Cavendish St, London W1W 6XD, England
**Kaye, Thorsten** — Actor
I C M Partners, 10250 Constellation Blvd, #900, Los Angeles CA 90067 USA
**Kaymer, Martin** — Golfer
Weimar Str 65, 40822 Mettmann, Germany
**Kayne** — Singer, Songwriter
Agency Group Ltd, 142 W 57th St, #600, New York NY 10019 USA
**Kays, Roland W** — Zoologist
Nature Research Center, 121 W Jones St, Raleigh NC 27603, USA
**Kayser, Manfred** — Molecular Biologist
Erasmus University Medical Center, 3013 Rotterdam GE, Netherlands
**Kazakevic, Aleksandr** — Greco-Roman Wrestler
Olympic Committee, 15 Rue Olimpieciu, 09200 Vilnius, Lithuania
**Kazan, Lainie** — Singer, Actress
Greene Assoc, 1901 Ave of Stars, #130, Los Angeles CA 90067 USA
**Kazan, Zoe** — Actress
United Talent Agency, U T A Plaza, 9336 Civic Center Dr, Beverly Hills CA 90210 USA
**Kazankina, Tatyana** — Track Athlete
Hoshimina St, 111211 Saint Petersburg, Russia
**Kazanski, Theodore S (Ted)** — Baseball Player
1544 Dormie Dr, Gladwin MI 48624, USA
**Kazantsov, Kira** — Beauty Queen
Miss America Organization, 1370 Ave of Americas, #1600, New York NY 10019 USA
**Kazee, Steve** — Actor
Innovative Artists, 1505 10th St, Santa Monica CA 90401 USA
**Kazer, Beau** — Actor
139A N San Fernando Blvd, Burbank CA 91502, USA
**Kazinsky, Robert (Rob)** — Actor
C A M, 111 Shoreditch High St, #400, London E1 6JN, England
**Kazmir, Scott E** — Baseball Player
9206 Point Park Dr, Houston TX 77095, USA
**Kazurinsky, Tim** — Actor, Comedian
Geddes Agency, 1633 N Halsted St, #300, Chicago IL 60614, USA
**Ke$ha** — Singer, Songwriter
Creative Artists Agency, 2000 Ave of Stars, #100, Los Angeles CA 90067 USA
**Keach, James** — Actor
Catfish Productions, 22631 Pacific Coast Highway, #313, Malibu CA 90265, USA
**Keach, Stacy** — Actor
Lionel Larner Ltd, 119 W 57th St, New York NY 10019, USA
**Keady, L Eugene (Gene)** — Basketball Coach
Saint John's University, Athletic Dept, 8000 Utopia Parkway, Queens NY 11439, USA
**Keaggy, Phil** — Guitarist
Ray Ware Artist Mgmt, 3108 Saint Stephens Way, Franklin TN 37064, USA
**Kealey, Steven W (Steve)** — Baseball Player
1080 1700 Ave, Abilene KS 67410, USA
**Kean, Laurel** — Golfer
11831 Forest Mere Dr, Bonita Springs FL 34135, USA
**Kean, Thomas H** — Governor, NJ; Educator
PO Box 332, Far Hills NJ 07931, USA
**Keanan, Staci** — Actress
Vox Inc, 6420 Wilshire Blvd, #1080, Los Angeles CA 90048 USA
**Keane, Dolores** — Singer, Musician
Kieren Cavanaugh Promotions, PO Box 5639, Dublin 4, Ireland
**Keane, Glen** — Animator
Walt Disney Studios, Animation Dept, 500 S Buena Vista St, Burbank CA 91521, USA
**Keane, John** — Writer
Bloomsbury Publishing, 50 Bedford Square, London WC1B 3DP, England
**Keane, John M** — Film Composer
United Talent Agency, U T A Plaza, 9336 Civic Center Dr, Beverly Hills CA 90210 USA
**Keane, John M (Jack)** — Army General
Institute for Study of War, 1400 16th St NW, #515 Washington DC 20036, USA
**Keane, Kerrie** — Actress
S D B Partners, 315 S Beverly Dr, #411, Beverly Hills CA 90067 USA
**Keane, Louis M (Dillie)** — Actress, Singer, Comedienne
Gavin Barker Assoc, 2D Wimpole St, London W1G 0EB, England
**Keane, Roy M** — Soccer Player
Manchester United, Busby Way, Old Trafford, Manchester M16 0RA, England
**Keane, Sean** — Fiddler (Chieftains)
Macklam/Feldman Mgmt, 1505 W 2nd Ave, #200, Vancouver BC V6H 3Y4, Canada
**Keane, William** — Actor
C E S D, 10635 Santa Monica Blvd, #130, Los Angeles CA 90025 USA
**Kear, David** — Geologist
34 W End, Ohope 3121, New Zealand
**Kearney, Hannah** — Moguls Skier
Waterville Valley B B T S, Box 277, Waterville Valley NH 03215, USA
**Kearney, James L (Jim)** — Football Player
1817 E 59th St, Kansas City MO 64130, USA
**Kearney, Mat** — Singer, Songwriter
A2 Mgmt, 1316 Sherman Ave, #215, Evanston IL 60201, USA
**Kearney, Robert H (Bob)** — Baseball Player
4155 Elizabeth Dr, Stevensville MI 49127, USA
**Kearney, Timothy E (Tim)** — Football Player
2144 Dartmouth Gate Court, Ballwin MO 63011, USA
**Kearns, Austin R** — Baseball Player
719 Haverhill Dr, Lexington KY 40503, USA
**Kearns, Dennis M** — Ice Hockey Player
1292 Esquimalt Ave, West Vancouver BC V7T 1K3, Canada
**Kearse, Amalya L** — Judge
US Court of Appeals, Moynihan Courthouse, 500 Pearl St, New York NY 10007, USA
**Kearse, Jevon** — Football Player
61 Whitworth Blvd, Nashville TN 37205, USA
**Kearse, NaShawn** — Actor
Leverage Mgmt, 3030 Pennsylvania Ave, Santa Monica CA 90404 USA

**Keaser, Lloyd (Butch)** — Freestyle Wrestler
43960 Tavern Dr, Ashburn VA 20147, USA
**Keating, Christopher P (Chris)** — Football Player
741 Canton Ave, Milton MA 02186, USA
**Keating, Dominic** — Actor
TalentWorks, 3500 W Olive Ave, #1400, Burbank CA 91505 USA
**Keating, Francis A (Frank), II** — Governor, OK
American Life Insurers, 101 Constitution Ave NW, #700W, Washington DC 20001, USA
**Keating, Paul J** — Prime Minister, Australia
GPO Box 1265, Potts Point NSW 1335, Australia
**Keating, Ronan** — Singer (Boyzone)
Outside Organization, 177-178 Tottenham Court Road, London W1T 7NY, England
**Keating, Thomas A (Tom)** — Football Player
3725 W St NW, Washington DC 20007, USA
**Keating, Timothy J** — Navy Admiral
7443 Collins Meade Way, Alexandria VA 22315, USA
**Keaton, Danielle** — Actress
Imperium 7 Artists, 5455 Wilshire Blvd, #1706, Los Angeles CA 90036 USA
**Keaton, Diane** — Actress, Director
15260 Ventura Blvd, #1040, Sherman Oaks CA 91403, USA
**Keaton, Michael** — Actor
I C M Partners, 10250 Constellation Blvd, #900, Los Angeles CA 90067 USA
**Keats, Donald H** — Composer
University of Denver, Music School, Denver CO 80208, USA
**Keb' Mo'** — Singer, Songwriter
J B Mgmt, PO Box 25703, Chicago IL 60625, USA
**K'eba, Miftah Muhammed** — General Secretary, Libya
General Secretary's Office, Bab el Asiziya Barracks, Tripoli, Libya
**Kebbel, Arielle** — Actress
Paradigm Agency, 360 N Crescent Dr, North Building, Beverly Hills CA 90210 USA
**Kebbell, Toby** — Actor
Independent Talent Group, 40 Whitfield St, London W1T 2RH, England
**Kebede, Liya** — Model, Actress
I M G Models, 304 Park Ave S, #PH N, New York NY 10010 USA
**Kebich, Vyacheslav F** — Prime Minister, Belarus
National Assembly, K Marksa Str 38, Dom Urada, 220016 Minsk, Belarus
**Kechiche, Abdellatif** — Director
Quato'sous Films, 64 Rue Rebeval, 75019 Paris, France
**Keck, Donald B** — Inventor (Silica Optical Waveguide)
2877 Chequers Circle, Big Flats NY 14814, USA
**Keck, Howard B** — Philanthropist
600 Wilshire Blvd, #17, Los Angeles CA 90017, USA
**Keczmer, Daniel L (Dan)** — Ice Hockey Player
9533 Sanctuary Place, Brentwood TN 37027, USA
**Kedah** — Sultan, Kedah
Istana Anak Bukit, Alor Setar, Kedah, Darul Aman, Malaysia
**Kee, John P** — Singer
A&M Entertainment, 13280 NW Freeway, #328, Houston,TX 77040, USA
**Keefe, Adam T** — Basketball Player
15933 Alcima Ave, Pacific Palisades CA 90272, USA
**Keefe, Mike** — Editorial Cartoonist
Denver Post, Editorial Dept, PO Box 1709, Denver CO 80201, USA
**Keeffe, Bernard** — Conductor
153 Honor Oak Road, London SE23 3RN, England
**Keegan, Andrew** — Actor
C E S D, 10635 Santa Monica Blvd, #130, Los Angeles CA 90025 USA
**Keegan, Kevin J** — Soccer Player, Executive
Manchester City F C, Maine Road, Moss Side, Manchester M14 7WN, England
**Keegan, Robert J** — Businessman
Goodyear Tire & Rubber, 1144 E Market St, Akron OH 44316, USA
**Keegan, Scarlett** — Model
C E S D, 10635 Santa Monica Blvd, #130, Los Angeles CA 90025 USA
**Keehne, Virginya** — Actress
Craig Mgmt, 2240 Miramonte Circle E, #C, Palm Springs CA 92264 USA
**Keel, Alton G, Jr** — Diplomat, Businessman
Atlantic Partners, 2891 S River Road, Stanardsville VA 22973, USA
**Keelaghan, James** — Singer, Songwriter
Jensen Music International, PO Box 3445, Charlottetown PE C1A 8W5, Canada
**Keeler, Jesse F** — Electronic Musician (Mstrkrft)
Biz 3 Publicity, 1321 N Milwaukee Ave, #452, Chicago IL 60622, USA
**Keeler, William H Cardinal** — Religious Leader
Archdiocese of Baltimore, Catholic Center, 320 Cathedral St, Baltimore MD 21201, USA
**Keeley, Edmund L (Mike)** — Writer
2423 Windrow Dr, Princeton NJ 08540, USA
**Keeley, Robert V** — Diplomat
3814 Livingston St NW, Washington DC 20015, USA
**Keeley, Sam** — Actor
Paradigm Agency, 360 N Crescent Dr, North Building, Beverly Hills CA 90210 USA
**Keelor, Greg** — Singer, Guitarist (Blue Rodeo)
Starfish Entertainment, 906A Logan Ave, Toronto ON M4K 3E4, Canada
**Keen, Robert Earl** — Singer, Songwriter
C3 Presents, 98 San Jacinto Blvd, #400, Austin TX 78701, USA
**Keen, Sam** — Writer, Philosopher
16331 Norrbom Road, Sonoma CA 95476, USA
**Keena, Monica** — Actress
Greater Vision Agency, 8981 Sunset Blvd, #101, Los Angeles CA 90069, USA
**Keenan, Edward L** — Historian
Harvard University, History Dept, Robinson Hall, Cambridge MA 02138, USA
**Keenan, Joseph D** — Labor Leader
2727 29th St NW, Washington DC 20008, USA
**Keenan, Larry** — Ice Hockey Player
132 Gordon Dr, North Bay ON P1B 8B2, Canada
**Keenan, Maynard James** — Singer (Tool, Perfect Circle)
Spivak Sobol Entertainment, 11845 W Olympic Blvd, #1125, Los Angeles CA 90064, USA
**Keenan, Michael E (Mike)** — Ice Hockey Coach
PO Box 175, 1975 Duval St, Key West FL 33041, USA

K

Keaser - Keenan

**Keene Cherot, Kyera** — Producer, Writer
C C A, 7 Saint Georges Square, London SW1V 2HX, England
**Keene, Donald L** — Language Educator
Columbia University, Language Dept, Kent Hall, New York NY 10027, USA
**Keene, Phillip P** — Actor
A K A Talent, 6310 San Vicente Blvd, #200, Los Angeles CA 90048 USA
**Keene, Tommy** — Singer, Guitarist, Songwriter
Black Park Mgmt, PO Box 107, Sunbury NC 27979, USA
**Keener, Catherine** — Actress
Gersh Agency, 9465 Wilshire Blvd, #600, Beverly Hills CA 90212 USA
**Keenlyside, Simon** — Opera Singer
Askonas Holt, Lincoln House, 300 High Holborn, London WC1V 7JH, England
**Keenum, Mark E** — Educator
Mississippi State University, President's Office, Allen Hall, Mississippi State MS 39762, USA
**Keeny, Spurgeon M, Jr** — Association Executive
3600 Albemarle St NW, Washington DC 20008, USA
**Keeslar, Matt** — Actor
Martin Berneman Mgmt, 5820 Wilshire Blvd, #200, Los Angeles CA 90036 USA
**Keezer, Geoff** — Jazz Pianist
D L Media, 124 N Highland Ave, Bala Cynwyd PA 19004, USA
**Keflezighi, Mebrahtom (Meb)** — Track Athlete
Competitor Group, Running Dept, 9477 Waples St, San Diego CA 92121, USA
**Kegel, Oliver** — Canoeing Athlete
Am Bogen 23, 13589 Berlin, Germany
**Kegeles, Gerson** — Chemist
RR 1 Box 156, Groveton NH 03582, USA
**Keggi, Caroline** — Golfer
807 Westlake Dr, Ormond Beach FL 32174, USA
**Kehler, C Robert (Bob)** — Air Force General
Commander, US Strategic Command, Offutt Air Force Base NE 68113 USA
**Kehoe, Rick** — Ice Hockey Player, Coach
1027 Highland Dr, Cincinnati OH 45211, USA
**Kehoe, Robert (Bob)** — Soccer Player, Coach
4848 Towne South Road, Saint Louis MO 63128, USA
**Keibler, Stacy** — Actress, Model, Wrestler
W M E Entertainment, 9601 Wilshire Blvd, #300, Beverly Hills CA 90210 USA
**Keifer, C Tom** — Singer, Guitarist (Cinderella)
Union Entertainment Group, 1323 Newbury Road, #104, Thousand Oaks CA 91320, USA
**Keifer, Elizabeth** — Actress
Stone Manners Salners, 6100 Wilshire Blvd, #1500, Los Angeles CA 90035 USA
**Keightley, David N** — Historian
University of California, History Dept, Berkeley CA 94720, USA
**Keil, Val** — Model
Playboy Promotions, 9346 Civic Center Dr, #200, Beverly Hills CA 90210 USA
**Keillor, Garrison E** — Actor, Writer, Producer
Prairie Home Productions, 480 Cedar St, Saint Paul MN 55101, USA
**Keineg, Katell** — Singer
Headline Agency, 39 Churchfields, Milltown, Dublin 14, Ireland
**Keisel, Brett** — Football Player
2015 W Grove Dr, Gibsonia PA 15044, USA
**Keisler, Randy** — Baseball Player
6842 Durango Creek Dr, Magnolia TX 77354, USA
**Keita, Ibrahim Boubacar** — Prime Minister, Mali
Alliance pour la Demoractie au Mali, BP 1791, Bamako-Coura, Mali
**Keita, Salif** — Singer, Composer
Mad Minute Music, 5-7 Rue Paul Bert, 93400 Saint Ouen, France
**Keitel, Harvey** — Actor
I C M Partners, 10250 Constellation Blvd, #900, Los Angeles CA 90067 USA
**Keith, Damon J** — Judge
US Court of Appeals, US Courthouse, 231 W Lafayette Blvd, Detroit MI 48226, USA
**Keith, David** — Actor
L I N K Entertainment, 11872 La Grange Ave, Los Angeles CA 90025 USA
**Keith, Louis** — Physician
333 E Superior St, #476, Chicago IL 60611, USA
**Keith, Penelope** — Actress
Burnett Granger Assoc, 3 Clifford St, London W1S 2LF, England
**Keith, Toby** — Singer, Actor
T K O Artist Mgmt, 2303 21st Ave S, #300, Nashville TN 37212, USA
**Kekalainen, Jarmo** — Ice Hockey Player, Executive
Jokerit H C, Areenankuja 1, 00240 Helsinki, Finland
**Keker, John** — Attorney
710 Sansome St, San Francisco CA 94111, USA
**Kekich, Michael D (Mike)** — Baseball Player
4942 Kolopelli Dr, Rio Rancho NM 87144, USA
**Kekilli, Sibel** — Actress
Wasted Mgmt, Diffenbachstr 33, 10967 Berlin, Germany
**Kelcher, J Louie** — Football Player
10204 Carlotta Cove, Austin TX 78733, USA
**Kele** — Singer, Musician
Agency Group Ltd, 142 W 57th St, #600, New York NY 10019 USA
**Kelela** — Singer, Songwriter
Windish Agency, 1658 N Milwaukee Ave, #211, Chicago IL 60647 USA
**Keleti, Agnes** — Gymnast
Wingate Institute for Physical Education & Sport, Netanya 42902, Israel
**Kelif, Atmen** — Actor
Artmedia, 20 Ave Rapp, 75007 Paris, France
**Kelis** — Singer
Creative Artists Agency, 2000 Ave of Stars, #100, Los Angeles CA 90067 USA
**Kell, Ayla** — Actress
Savage Agency, 6212 Banner Ave, Los Angeles CA 90038 USA
**Kell, Everett L (Skeeter)** — Baseball Player
PO Box 10113, Conway AR 72034, USA
**Kellar-Duke, Rebecca D (Becky)** — Ice Hockey Player
Team Canada, 2424 University Dr NW, Calgary AB T2N 3Y9, Canada
**Kellaway, Roger** — Composer, Jazz Pianist
Joel Chriss Co, 300 Mercer St, #3J, New York NY 10003 USA

| | |
|---|---|
| **Kelleher, Herbert D** | Businessman |
| 144 Thelma Dr, San Antonio TX 78212, USA | |
| **Kelleher, Michael D (Mick)** | Baseball Player |
| 1451 Alamo Pintado Road, Solvang CA 93463, USA | |
| **Kelleher, Tim** | Actor |
| Paradigm Agency, 360 N Crescent Dr, North Building, Beverly Hills CA 90210 USA | |
| **Keller, Bill** | Journalist |
| Marshall Project, 250 W 57th St, #2514, New York NY | |
| **Keller, Erhard** | Speed Skater |
| Sudliche Munchneustr 6A, 82031 Grunwald, Germany | |
| **Keller, Jason** | Auto Racing Driver |
| Progressive Motorsports, 177 Knob Hill Road, Mooresville NC 28117, USA | |
| **Keller, Joseph B** | Mathematician |
| 820 Sonoma Terrace, Stanford CA 94305, USA | |
| **Keller, Julia** | Journalist |
| Chicago Tribune, Editorial Dept, 350 N Orleans St, Chicago IL 60654 USA | |
| **Keller, Kasey** | Soccer Player |
| Seattle Sounders, 12 Seahawks Way, Renton WA 98056 USA | |
| **Keller, Klete** | Swimmer |
| 3015 N Hozoni Road, Prescott AZ 86305, USA | |
| **Keller, Marthe** | Actress |
| Lemonstr 9, 81679 Munich, Germany | |
| **Keller, Mary Page** | Actress |
| S M S Talent, 8383 Wilshire Blvd, #230, Beverly Hills CA 90211 USA | |
| **Keller, Nino** | Drummer (Caesars) |
| Paradigm Agency, 360 Park Ave, #1600, New York NY 10022 USA | |
| **Keller, Robert P** | Marine Corps General |
| 6367 Kirby Oaks Dr, Memphis TN 38119, USA | |
| **Keller, Shawn** | Animator |
| C A A T Studios, 36 King Eider Lane, Aliso Viejo CA 92656, USA | |
| **Keller, Thomas** | Chef, Restauranteur |
| French Laundry, 6640 Washington St, Yountville CA 94599, USA | |
| **Kellerman, Ernie J** | Football Player |
| 522 Spice Bush Lane, Chagrin Falls OH 44023, USA | |
| **Kellerman, Faye** | Writer |
| Karpfinger Agency, 357 W 20th St, #A, New York NY 10011, USA | |
| **Kellerman, Jonathan S** | Writer |
| Karpfinger Agency, 357 W 20th St, #A, New York NY 10011, USA | |
| **Kellerman, Martin** | Cartoonist (Rocky) |
| Krukmakargatan 29, 118 51 Stockhom, Sweden | |
| **Kellerman, Max** | Sportscaster, Commentator |
| Fox-TV, Sports Dept, PO Box 900, Beverly Hills CA 90213 USA | |
| **Kellerman, Sally** | Actress |
| Polimedia Communications, 1010 Wilshire Blvd, Los Angeles CA 90017, USA | |
| **Kellermann, Susan** | Actress |
| C E S D, 10635 Santa Monica Blvd, #130, Los Angeles CA 90025 USA | |
| **Kelley, Brian L** | Football Player |
| 98 Constitution Way, Basking Ridge NJ 07920, USA | |
| **Kelley, David E** | Producer, Writer |
| David E Kelley Productions, 1600 Rosecrans Ave, Building 4B, Manhattan Beach CA 90266, USA | |
| **Kelley, Dean** | Basketball Player |
| 5900 Longleaf Dr, Lawrence KS 66049, USA | |
| **Kelley, Donald R** | Historian |
| 45 Jefferson Ave, New Brunswick NJ 08901, USA | |
| **Kelley, E Allen (Al)** | Basketball Player |
| 5900 Longleaf Dr, Lawrence KS 66049, USA | |
| **Kelley, Elijah** | Actor, Singer |
| Schiff Co, 9220 Sunset Blvd, #106, West Hollywood CA 90069 USA | |
| **Kelley, Gaynor N** | Businessman |
| Perkin-Elmer Corp, 710 Bridgeport Ave, Shelton CT 06484, USA | |
| **Kelley, Harold H** | Psychologist |
| 21634 Rambla Vista St, Malibu CA 90265, USA | |
| **Kelley, Josh** | Singer, Songwriter |
| Wilspro Mgmt, 1335 Martin Ave, Point Pleasant NJ 08742, USA | |
| **Kelley, Kitty** | Writer |
| 1228 Eton Court NW, Washington DC 20007, USA | |
| **Kelley, Malcolm David** | Actor |
| Amsel Eisenstadt Frazier, 5055 Wilshire Blvd, #865, Los Angeles CA 90036 USA | |
| **Kelley, Nathalie** | Actress |
| Innovative Artists, 1505 10th St, Santa Monica CA 90401 USA | |
| **Kelley, Paul X** | Marine Corps General |
| 1600 N Oak St, #1619, Arlington VA 22209, USA | |
| **Kelley, Richard R (Rich)** | Basketball Player |
| 314 Raymundo Dr, Woodside CA 94062, USA | |
| **Kelley, Robert O** | Educator |
| University of North Dakota, President's Office, Grand Forks ND 58202, USA | |
| **Kelley, Ryan J** | Actor |
| A P A Talent & Literary Agency, 405 S Beverly Dr, #300, Beverly Hills CA 90212 USA | |
| **Kelley, S R** | Sculptor |
| PO Box 682, Mendocino CA 95460, USA | |
| **Kelley, Sheila** | Actress |
| I F A Talent Agency, 8730 W Sunset Blvd, #490, West Hollywood CA 90069 USA | |
| **Kelley, Steve** | Editorial Cartoonist |
| Creators Syndicate, 737 3rd St, Hermosa Beach CA 90254 USA | |
| **Kelley, Thomas G** | Vietnam War Navy Hero (CMH) |
| 600 Washington St, #1100, Boston MA 02111, USA | |
| **Kelley, Thomas H (Tom)** | Baseball Player |
| 710 11th Ave S, North Myrtle Beach SC 29582, USA | |
| **Kelley, William G** | Businessman |
| Consolidated Stores, 1105 N Market St, Wilmington DE 19801, USA | |
| **Kelley, William N** | Biochemist, Biophysicist |
| 150 Anchor Dr, Vero Beach FL 32963, USA | |
| **Kelliher, Bill** | Guitarist, Singer (Mastodon) |
| Pinnacle Entertainment, 30 Glenn St, White Plains NY 10603, USA | |
| **Kellis, Manolis** | Electrical Engineer |
| Massachusetts Institute of Technology, Engineering Dept, Cambridge MA 02139, USA | |

Kelleher - Kellis

**Kellman, Barnet** — Director
Paradigm Agency, 360 N Crescent Dr, North Building, Beverly Hills CA 90210 USA
**Kellmeyer, Fern L (Peachy)** — Tennis Executive
Women's Tennis Assn, 1 Progress Plaza, #1500, Saint Petersburg FL 33701 USA
**Kellner, Lawrence (Larry)** — Businessman
Continental Airlines, PO Box 4607, Houston TX 77210, USA
**Kellogg, Allan J, Jr** — Vietnam War Marine Air Hero (CMH)
250 Ilihau St, Kailua HI 96734, USA
**Kellogg, Clark C** — Basketball Player, Sportscaster
5423 Medallion Dr E, Westerville OH 43082, USA
**Kellogg, David** — Director
I C M Partners, 10250 Constellation Blvd, #900, Los Angeles CA 90067 USA
**Kellogg, William S** — Businessman
Kohl's Corp, N56W17000 Ridgewood Dr, Menomonee Falls WI 53051, USA
**Kellum, Marvin L (Marv)** — Football Player
235 Jamaica Ave, Pittsburgh PA 15229, USA
**Kelly, Annese** — Bowler
3812 Bach Way, North Las Vegas NV 89032, USA
**Kelly, Arvesta** — Basketball Player
1040 Oxford St N, Saint Paul MN 55103, USA
**Kelly, Brendan** — Actor
Allman/Rea Mgmt, 141 Barrington Walk, #E, Los Angeles CA 90049, USA
**Kelly, Brian** — Football Player
325 Dark Forest Dr, Chapel Hill NC 27516, USA
**Kelly, Brian K** — Football Coach
University of Notre Dame, Athletic Dept, Notre Dame IN 46556, USA
**Kelly, Charles (Chip)** — Football Coach
Philadelphia Eagles, 1 Novacare Way, Philadelphia PA 19145 USA
**Kelly, Daniel Hugh** — Actor
Innovative Artists, 1505 10th St, Santa Monica CA 90401 USA
**Kelly, David Patrick** — Actor
Paradigm Agency, 360 N Crescent Dr, North Building, Beverly Hills CA 90210 USA
**Kelly, Eamon M** — Educator
123 Walnut St, #804, New Orleans LA 70118, USA
**Kelly, Ellsworth** — Artist
PO Box 151, Spencertown NY 12165, USA
**Kelly, Gary C** — Businessman
Southwest Airlines, PO Box 36647, Dallas TX 75235, USA
**Kelly, J Thomas (Tom)** — Baseball Player, Manager
1643 Currie St N, Saint Paul MN 55119, USA
**Kelly, James E (Jim)** — Football Player
6 Woodcrest Dr, Orchard Park NY 14127, USA
**Kelly, James M (Jim)** — Astronaut
403 S Northfield St, Mediapolis IA 52637, USA
**Kelly, Jean Louisa** — Actress
Levine/Okwu/Erickson, 6363 Wilshire Blvd, #300, Los Angeles CA 90048, USA
**Kelly, Jerry** — Golfer
531 Farwell Dr, Madison WI 53704, USA
**Kelly, Joanne** — Actress
Domain Talent, 9229 W Sunset Blvd, #710, West Hollywood CA 90069 USA
**Kelly, Joey** — Singer (Kelly Family)
Kelly Family, Wendelinusstr 5, 53809 Ruppichteroth, Germany
**Kelly, John** — Singer (Kelly Family)
E M I America Records, 6920 W Sunset Blvd, Los Angeles CA 90028 USA
**Kelly, John H** — Diplomat
John Kelly Consulting, 1808 Over Lake Dr SE, #D, Conyers GA 30013, USA
**Kelly, Joseph W (Joe)** — Football Player
PO Box 6335, Cincinnati OH 45206, USA
**Kelly, Krista** — Model
Playboy Promotions, 9346 Civic Center Dr, #200, Beverly Hills CA 90210 USA
**Kelly, Laura Michelle** — Actress
Dalzell & Beresford, 55 Charterhouse St, Paddock Suite, London EC1M 6HA, England
**Kelly, Leonard P (Red)** — Ice Hockey Player, Coach
30 Dunvegan, Toronto ON M4V 2P6, Canada
**Kelly, Leroy** — Football Player
91 Club House Dr, Willingboro NJ 8046, USA
**Kelly, Lisa** — Singer (Celtic Woman)
W M E Entertainment, 9601 Wilshire Blvd, #300, Beverly Hills CA 90210 USA
**Kelly, Mark E** — Astronaut
528 W Fork, Webster TX 77598, USA
**Kelly, Megyn M** — Commentator
Fox-TV, News Dept, 205 E 67th St, New York NY 10065 USA
**Kelly, Michael J** — Actor
Liebman Entertainment, 35 E 21st St, #PH, New York NY 10010, USA
**Kelly, Michael R (Mike)** — Baseball Player
5072 S Serpentine Road, Flagstaff AZ 86001, USA
**Kelly, Minka** — Actress
Creative Artists Agency, 2000 Ave of Stars, #100, Los Angeles CA 90067 USA
**Kelly, Moira** — Actress
Gersh Agency, 9465 Wilshire Blvd, #600, Beverly Hills CA 90212 USA
**Kelly, Patrick F (Pat)** — Baseball Player
3519 Capri Court, Philadelphia PA 19145, USA
**Kelly, Paul** — Singer, Guitarist, Songwriter
One Louder Entertainment, PO Box 989, Darlinghurst NSW 1300, Australia
**Kelly, Paul J, Jr** — Judge
US Appeals Court, 120 S Federal Plaza, Santa Fe NM 87501, USA
**Kelly, R** — Rap Artist, Singer, Songwriter
Creative Artists Agency, 2000 Ave of Stars, #100, Los Angeles CA 90067 USA
**Kelly, Raymond** — Law Enforcement Official
Police Commissioner's Office, 1 Police Plaza, New York NY 10038, USA
**Kelly, Richard** — Director, Writer
Darko Entertainment, 1041 N Formosa Ave, West Hollywood CA 90046, USA
**Kelly, Robert** — Financier
Bank of New York Mellon Corp, 1 Wall St, New York NY 10005, USA
**Kelly, Robert J (Bob)** — Ice Hockey Player
10 Peyton Court, Marlton NJ 08053, USA

Kelly, Roberto C (Bobby) — Baseball Player
510 Franklin Dr, Arlington TX 76011, USA
Kelly, Roz — Actress
5664 Fair Ave, #26, North Hollywood CA 91601, USA
Kelly, Sarah — Singer
Creative Artists Agency, 2000 Ave of Stars, #100, Los Angeles CA 90067 USA
Kelly, Scott J — Astronaut
528 W Fork, Webster TX 77598, USA
Kelly, Shane J — Cyclist
Fairsy Consultancy, 25 Kerran Crescent, Lanceston TAS 7249, Australia
Kelly, T Ross — Chemist
Boston College, Chemistry Dept, 140 Commonwealth Ave, Chestnut Hill MA 02467, USA
Kelly, Thomas J (Tom), III — Photojournalist
PO Box 2208, Sanatoga Branch, Pottstown PA 19464, USA
Kelly, Thomas J, Jr — Molecular Biologist
Memorial Sloan Kettering Cancer Center, 1275 York Ave, New York NY 10065, USA
Kelly, Thomas P — Sculptor
1518 Thurber Road, Corning NY 14830, USA
Kelly, Van H — Baseball Player
11 Beauregard Dr, Spencer NC 28159, USA
Kelm, Larry D — Football Player
67 Driftoak Circle, Spring TX 77381, USA
Kelman, Arthur — Plant Pathologist
1406 Springmoor Circle, Raleigh NC 27615, USA
Kelman, James — Writer
Weidenfeld-Nicolson, Upper Saint Martin's Lane, London WC2H 9EA, England
Kelsch, Kenneth A (Ken) — Cinematographer
PO Box 255, Budd Lake NJ 07828, USA
Kelser, Gregory (Greg) — Basketball Player
30400 Forest Dr, Franklin MI 48025, USA
Kelsey, David — Actor
Ellis Talent Group, 4705 Laurel Canyon Blvd, #300, Valley Village CA 91607, USA
Kelsey, Linda — Actress
500 S Sepulveda Blvd, #500, Los Angeles CA 90049, USA
Kelsey, Quinn — Opera Singer
Columbia Artists Mgmt Inc, 5 Columbus Circle, 1790 Broadway, #1600, New York NY 10019 USA
Kelso, Ben — Basketball Player
1877 Midchester Dr, West Bloomfield MI 48324, USA
Kelso, Mark A — Football Player
897 Luther Road, East Aurora NY 14052, USA
Kelso, Megan — Cartoonist, Writer
4416 S Othello St, Seattle WA 98118, USA
Kem — Singer, Keyboardist, Songwriter
Project Producers, 16500 N Park Dr, #101, Southfield MI 48075, USA
Kemal, Yashar — Writer
P K 14 Basinkoy, 34360 Istanbul, Turkey
Kemme, Thomas — Labor Leader
Stove Furnace & Appliance Union, 2929 S Jefferson Ave, Saint Louis MO 63118, USA
Kemmer, Heike — Equestrian
Am Amselhof 4, 47495 Rheinberg, Germany
Kemmerer, Russell P (Russ) — Baseball Player
6335 Colebrook Dr, Indianapolis IN 46220, USA
Kemner, Caren — Volleyball Player
2045 Elm St, Quincy IL 62301, USA
Kemoeatu, Ma'ake T — Football Player
8 Pellinore Court, Pikesville MD 21208, USA
Kemp, Charlotte — Model
Playboy Promotions, 9346 Civic Center Dr, #200, Beverly Hills CA 90210 USA
Kemp, Gary — Guitarist (Spandau Ballet)
International Talent Group, 729 7th Ave, #1600, New York NY 10019 USA
Kemp, Jeffrey A (Jeff) — Football Player
22101 NE 66th Place, Redmond WA 98053, USA
Kemp, Jeremy — Actor
Marina Martin, 12/13 Poland St, London W1V 3DE, England
Kemp, Perry C — Football Player
PO Box 78, Westland PA 15378, USA
Kemp, Ross — Actor, Producer
Brillstein Entertainment Partners, 9150 Wilshire Blvd, #350, Beverly Hills CA 90212 USA
Kemp, Shawn T — Basketball Player
Oskar's Kitchen, 621 1/2 Queen Anne Ave, Seattle WA 98109, USA
Kemp, Steven (Steve) F — Baseball Player
1428 Colony Plaza, Newport Beach CA 92660, USA
Kemp, Will — Actor, Dancer, Model
United Agents, 12-26 Lexington St, London W1F 0LE, England
Kemper, David W, II — Financier
Commerce Bancshares, 1000 Walnut St, Kansas City MO 64106, USA
Kemper, Ellie — Actress
Mosiac Media Group, 9200 W Sunset Blvd, #1000, Los Angeles CA 90069 USA
Kemper, Hunter C — Triathlete
1700 Piedmont Place, Lake Mary FL 32746, USA
Kemper, J Mariner, Jr — Financier
U M B Financial Corp, 1010 Grand Ave, Kansas City MO 64106, USA
Kemper, Randolph E (Randy) — Fashion Designer
Randy Kemper Corp, 530 Fashion Ave, #1400, New York NY 10018, USA
Kemper, Victor J — Cinematographer
Mirisch Agency, 1025 Colorado Ave, #B, Santa Monica CA 90211 USA
Kempermann, Robbert — Field Hockey Player
S V Kampong Hockey, Postbus 85219, 3508 Utrecht AE, Netherlands
Kempf, Cecil J — Navy Admiral
831 Olive Ave, Coronado CA 92118, USA
Kempf, Freddy — Concert Pianist
I M G Artists, Hogarth Business Park, Chiswick, London W4 2TH, England
Kempner, Patty — Swimmer
1605 Harris Dr, Fort Collins CO 80524, USA
Kempner, Walter — Nutritionist
1505 Virginia Ave, Durham NC 27705, USA

# K

**Kempthorne, Dirk A** — Secretary, Interior; Governor, Senator
2081 S White Pine Lane, Boise ID 83706, USA
**Kempton, Timothy J (Tim)** — Basketball Player
4131 N 43rd St, Phoenix AZ 85018, USA
**Kenan, Gil** — Director, Animator
W M E Entertainment, 9601 Wilshire Blvd, #300, Beverly Hills CA 90210 USA
**Kendal, Felicity** — Actress
Chatto & Linnit, 123A King's Road, London SW3 4PL, England
**Kendall, A Bruce** — Yachtsman
6 Pedersen Place, Bucklands Beach, Auckland 2012, New Zealand
**Kendall, Barbara** — Yachtswoman
Kendall Distributing, 26 Great South Road, Otahuhu 1062, New Zealand
**Kendall, David** — Producer
Rothman Brecher Agency, 9465 Wilshire Blvd, #840, Beverly Hills CA 90212 USA
**Kendall, Donald M** — Businessman
PepsiCo Inc, Anderson Hill Road, Purchase NY 10577, USA
**Kendall, Fred L** — Baseball Player
57575 Johnston Road, Anza CA 92539, USA
**Kendall, Jason D** — Baseball Player
11730 Stonehenge Lane, Los Angeles CA 90077, USA
**Kendall, Jeannie** — Singer (Kendalls)
Joe Taylor Artist Agency, 2802 Columbine Place, Nashville TN 37204 USA
**Kendall, Kerri** — Model
4128 Catalina Place, San Diego CA 92107, USA
**Kendall, Skip** — Golfer
8406 Kemper Lane, Windermere FL 34786, USA
**Kendall, Tom** — Auto Racing Driver
International Motor Sports Assn, 1394 Broadway Ave, Braselton GA 30517, USA
**Kendler, Bob** — Handball, Raquetball Player
Handball Association, 4101 Dempster St, Skokie IL 60076, USA
**Kendrick, Alex** — Religious Leader, Filmmaker, Writer
Sherwood Baptist Church, 2201 Whispering Pines Road, Albany GA 31707, USA
**Kendrick, Anna** — Actress, Singer
Creative Artists Agency, 2000 Ave of Stars, #100, Los Angeles CA 90067 USA
**Kendrick, Howard J (Howie)** — Baseball Player
4030 E Anderson Dr, Phoenix AZ 85032, USA
**Kendrick, Rodney** — Singer, Jazz Pianist, Composer
Carolyn McClair, 410 W 53rd St, #128C, New York NY 10019, USA
**Kendrick, Stephen** — Religious Leader, Writer
Sherwood Baptist Church, 2201 Whispering Pines Road, Albany GA 31707, USA
**Keneally, Thomas M** — Writer
24 Serpentine, Bilgola Beach NSW 2107, Australia
**Kenilorea, Peter** — Prime Minister, Solomon Islands
Kalala House, PO Box 535, Honiara, Guadacanal, Solomon Islands
**Kenn, Michael L (Mike)** — Football Player
360 Bardolier, Alpharetta GA 30022, USA
**Kenna, E Douglas (Doug)** — Businessman, Football Player
Carlisle Companies, 250 S Clinton Square, Syracuse NY 13202, USA
**Kennard, Derek C** — Football Player
15849 S 35th Way, Phoenix AZ 85048, USA
**Kennard, William E (Bill)** — Government Official
Carlyle Group, 1001 Pennsylvania Ave NW, #220S, Washington DC 20004, USA
**Kennaugh, Peter** — Cyclist
10 Eskdale Road, Onchan IM3 2AL, England
**Kennedy, Adam T** — Baseball Player
5025 Windhill Dr, Riverside CA 92507, USA
**Kennedy, Adrienne** — Writer
I C M Partners, 10250 Constellation Blvd, #900, Los Angeles CA 90067 USA
**Kennedy, Alan D** — Businessman
Tupperware Corp, PO Box 2353, Orlando FL 32802, USA
**Kennedy, Anthony M** — Supreme Court Justice
US Supreme Court, 1 1st St NE, Washington DC 20543 USA
**Kennedy, Cam** — Cartoonist
Dark Horse Publishing, 10956 SE Main St, Portland OR 97222 USA
**Kennedy, Caroline B** — Diplomat, Writer, Attorney
State Department, 2201 C St NW, Washington DC 20520 USA
**Kennedy, Cortez** — Football Player
121 Gary Lynn Dr, Osceola AR 72370, USA
**Kennedy, Courtney** — Ice Hockey Player
13 Whispering Hill Road, Woburn MA 01801, USA
**Kennedy, David** — Actor
Artists Partnership, 101 Finsbury Pavement, London EC2A 1RS, England
**Kennedy, David M** — Historian
Stanford University, History Dept, Stanford CA 94305, USA
**Kennedy, Dean** — Ice Hockey Player
General Delivery, Pincher Creek AB T0K 1W0, Canada
**Kennedy, Delicious** — Singer (All-4-One)
Universal Attractions, 135 W 26th St, #1200, New York NY 10001 USA
**Kennedy, Diana S** — Chef, Writer
Clarkson Potter/Crown Publishing Group, 1745 Broadway, New York NY 10019, USA
**Kennedy, Donald** — Educator
Stanford University, International Studies Institute, Stanford CA 94305, USA
**Kennedy, Ethel** — Wife of Robert Kennedy
PO Box 328, Hyannis Port MA 02647, USA
**Kennedy, Eugene (Gene)** — Basketball Player
8218 Westrock Dr, Dallas TX 75243, USA
**Kennedy, Forbes T** — Ice Hockey Player
20 Oakland Dr, Charlottetown PE C1C 1P4, Canada
**Kennedy, George** — Actor
719 N Cactus Creek Ave, Eagle ID 83616, USA
**Kennedy, Ian P** — Baseball Player
1204 Suncast Lane, #2, El Dorado Hills CA 95762, USA
**Kennedy, James C** — Businessman
1601 W Peachtree St NE, Atlanta GA 30309, USA
**Kennedy, James E (Jim)** — Baseball Player
13940 SW Lisa Lane, Beaverton OR 97005, USA

| | |
|---|---|
| **Kennedy, Jason** | Actor |
| United Talent Agency, U T A Plaza, 9336 Civic Center Dr, Beverly Hills CA 90210 USA | |
| **Kennedy, Jimmy W** | Football Player |
| New York Giants, Meadowlands Stadium, 102 Route 120, East Rutherford NJ 07073 USA | |
| **Kennedy, Joey D (Joe), Jr** | Journalist |
| 1635 11th Place S, Birmingham AL 35205, USA | |
| **Kennedy, John E** | Baseball Player |
| 2 Rodney Road, Peabody MA 01960, USA | |
| **Kennedy, John Milton** | Actor |
| 5711 Reseda Blvd, #204, Tarzana CA 91356, USA | |
| **Kennedy, Junior R** | Baseball Player |
| 6001 Eucalyptus Dr, #215, Bakersfield CA 93306, USA | |
| **Kennedy, Kathleen** | Producer |
| Lucasfilm, 5858 Lucas Valley Road, Nicasio CA 94946, USA | |
| **Kennedy, Kevin** | Producer, Writer |
| R W S H Agency, 1107 1/2 Glendon Ave, Los Angeles CA 90024, USA | |
| **Kennedy, Kevin C** | Baseball Player, Manager |
| Fox-TV, Sports Dept, 205 W 67th St, New York NY 10065 USA | |
| **Kennedy, Lee** | Businessman |
| Equifax Inc, 1550 Peachtree St NE, Atlanta GA 30309, USA | |
| **Kennedy, Leon Isaac** | Actor |
| 859 N Hollywood Way, #384, Burbank CA 91505, USA | |
| **Kennedy, M Peter** | Figure Skater |
| 7650 SE 41st, Mercer Island WA 98040, USA | |
| **Kennedy, Maria Doyle** | Actress, Singer |
| United Agents, 12-26 Lexington St, London W1F 0LE, England | |
| **Kennedy, Maura** | Singer (Kennedys) |
| PO Box 1298, New York NY 10276, USA | |
| **Kennedy, Mimi** | Actress |
| Justice & Ponder, PO Box 480033, Los Angeles CA 90048, USA | |
| **Kennedy, Myles R** | Singer, Guitarist |
| Wind-Up Records, 72 Madison Ave, #800, New York NY 10016 USA | |
| **Kennedy, Nigel** | Concert Violinist |
| George Leitner Productions, Huetteldurfer St 259, 1140 Vienna, Austria | |
| **Kennedy, Patrick** | Actor |
| Curtis Brown Group, 28-29 Haymarket St, #500, London SW1Y 4SP, England | |
| **Kennedy, Paul M** | Historian |
| 409 Humphrey St, New Haven CT 06511, USA | |
| **Kennedy, Pete** | Singer (Kennedys) |
| PO Box 1298, New York NY 10276, USA | |
| **Kennedy, Randall L** | Attorney, Educator |
| Harvard University, Law School, Cambridge MA 02138, USA | |
| **Kennedy, Ray F** | Businessman |
| Masco Corp, 21001 Van Born Road, Taylor MI 48180, USA | |
| **Kennedy, Robert A** | Educator |
| University of Maine, President's Office, 5703 Alumni Hall, Orono ME 04469, USA | |
| **Kennedy, Rory** | Director, Producer |
| Moxie Firecracker Films, 232 3rd St, #B403, Brooklyn NY 11215, USA | |
| **Kennedy, T Lincoln, Jr** | Football Player |
| 3555 E Jasmine Circle, Mesa AZ 85213, USA | |
| **Kennedy, Terrence E (Terry)** | Baseball Player |
| 333 N Pennington Dr, #23, Chandler AZ 85224, USA | |
| **Kennedy, William J** | Writer |
| New York State Writers Institute, 1400 Washington Ave, Albany NY 12222, USA | |
| **Kennedy, William R (Pickles)** | Basketball Player |
| 9927 Galleon Dr, West Palm Beach FL 33411, USA | |
| **Kennedy, X Joseph (X J)** | Writer |
| 22 Revere St, Lexington MA 02420, USA | |
| **Kennedy-Powell, Kathleen** | Judge |
| Los Angeles Municipal Court, 110 N Grand Ave, Los Angeles CA 90012, USA | |
| **Kennerly, David Hume** | Photojournalist |
| 1015 18th St, Santa Monica CA 90403, USA | |
| **Kennerty, Michael B (Mike)** | Singer, Guitarist (All-American Rejects) |
| Interscope Records, 2220 Colorado Ave, Santa Monica CA 90404 USA | |
| **Kenney, Emma** | Actress |
| Innovative Artists, 1505 10th St, Santa Monica CA 90401 USA | |
| **Kenney, Gerald T (Jerry)** | Baseball Player |
| 1980 Harrison Ave, Beloit WI 53511, USA | |
| **Kenney, Kerri** | Actress, Comedienne |
| Principato-Young, 9465 Wilshire Blvd, #880, Beverly Hills CA 90212 USA | |
| **Kenney, Stephen F (Steve)** | Football Player |
| 1105 Silver Oaks Court, Raleigh NC 27614, USA | |
| **Kenney, William P (Bill)** | Football Player |
| 2808 SW Arthur Dr, Lees Summit MO 64082, USA | |
| **Kennicott, Philip** | Architectural Critic, Journalist |
| Washington Post, Editorial Dept, 1150 15th St NW, Washington DC 20071 USA | |
| **Kenniebrew, Dolores (Dee Dee)** | Singer (Crystals) |
| Superstars Unlimited, PO Box 371371, Las Vegas NV 89137, USA | |
| **Kennison, Eddie J, III** | Football Player |
| 14813 Sherwood Road, Overland Park KS 66224, USA | |
| **Kenny G** | Saxophonist |
| Front Line Mgmt, 1100 Glendon Ave, #2000, Los Angeles CA 90024 USA | |
| **Kenny, Andrew** | Singer (American Analog Set), Songwriter |
| Flower Booking, 1532 N Milwaukee Ave, #201, Chicago IL 60622, USA | |
| **Kenny, Enda** | Prime Minister, Ireland |
| Taoiseach's Office, Government Buildings, Upper Merrion St, Dublin 2, Ireland | |
| **Kenny, Jason** | Cyclist |
| Ashwood Laboratories, Brockhall Village, Blackburn, Lancashire BB6 8BB, England | |
| **Kenny, Shirley Strum** | Educator |
| State University of New York, President's Office, Stony Brook NY 11794, USA | |
| **Kenny, Tom** | Actor, Comedian |
| Innovative Artists, 1505 10th St, Santa Monica CA 90401 USA | |
| **Kenny, Yvonne** | Opera Singer |
| I M G Artists, Burlington Lane, Chiswick, London W4 2TH, England | |
| **Kenon, Larry J** | Basketball Player |
| 25057 Toutant Beauregard Road, San Antonio TX 78255, USA | |

# K

**Kenrich, John L** — Businessman
3009 Arborcreek Lane, Montgomery OH 45242, USA

**Kenseth, Matthew R (Matt)** — Auto Racing Driver
111 Stonewall Beach Lane, Mooresville NC 28117, USA

**Kensing, Logan F** — Baseball Player
450 Rodalyn Dr, Boerne TX 78006, USA

**Kensit, Patsy** — Actress, Singer
A P A Talent & Literary Agency, 405 S Beverly Dr, #300, Beverly Hills CA 90212 USA

**Kent** — Duke, England
York House, Saint James's Palace, London SW1A 1BQ, England

**Kent, Allegra** — Ballerina
New York City Ballet, Lincoln Center Plaza, New York NY 10023 USA

**Kent, Arthur** — Commentator
2184 Torringford St, Torrington CT 06790, USA

**Kent, Hannah** — Writer
Curtis Brown, PO Box 19, Paddington NSW 2021, Australia

**Kent, Jeffrey A (Jeff)** — Baseball Player
550 Chaparral Court, Altadena CA 91001, USA

**Kent, Jonathan** — Director
International Talent Booking, Ariel House, 74A Charlotte St, #100 London W1T 4QJ, England

**Kent, Julie** — Ballerina
American Ballet Theatre, 890 Broadway, #300, New York NY 10003 USA

**Kent, Muhtar** — Businessman
Coca-Cola Co, 1 Coca-Cola Plaza, 310 North Ave NW, Atlanta GA 30313, USA

**Kent, Stacey** — Singer
John Boddy Agency, 10 Southfield Gardens, Twickenham TW1 4SZ, England

**Kentridge, William** — Artist
David Krut Projects, Box 892, Houghton, 2041 Johannesburg, South Africa

**Kenty, Hilmer** — Boxer
Escot Boxing, 19260 Bretton Dr, Detroit MI 48223, USA

**Kenville, William M (Bill)** — Basketball Player
59 Crary Ave, Binghamton NY 13905, USA

**Keny-Guyer, Neal L** — Association Executive
Mercy Corps, 45 SW Ankeny St, Portland OR 97204, USA

**Kenyon, Melvin E (Mel)** — Auto Racing Driver
2645 S 25th West, Lebanon IN 46052, USA

**Kenyon, Sherrilyn** — Writer
Pocket Books, 1230 Ave of Americas, New York NY 10020 USA

**Kenzo** — Fashion Designer
54 Rue Etienne Marcel, 75002 Paris, France

**Keogh, Lainey** — Fashion Designer
42 Dawson St, Dublin 2, Ireland

**Keoghan, Phil** — Entertainer
I C M Partners, 10250 Constellation Blvd, #900, Los Angeles CA 90067 USA

**Keon, David M (Dave)** — Ice Hockey Player
115 Brackenwood Road, Palm Beach Gardens FL 33418, USA

**Keough, Donald R (Don)** — Financier
200 Galleria Parkway, #970, Atlanta GA 30339, USA

**Keough, Matthew L (Matt)** — Baseball Player
12 Shire, Trabuco Canyon CA 92679, USA

**Keough, R Martin (Marty)** — Baseball Player
6874 E Nightingale Star Circle, Scottsdale AZ 85266, USA

**Keough, Riley** — Model, Actress
W M E Entertainment, 9601 Wilshire Blvd, #300, Beverly Hills CA 90210 USA

**Keppinger, Jeffrey S (Jeff)** — Baseball Player
1578 Cordillo Court, Dacula GA 30019, USA

**Kepros, Nicholas** — Actor
Cobalt Sky Entertainment, 48 W 21st St, #709, New York NY 10010, USA

**Kerber, Angelique** — Tennis Player
Postfach 2846, 24027 Kiel, Germany

**Kercheval, Ken** — Actor
PO Box 3371, Granada Hills CA 91634, USA

**Kerdyk, Tracy L** — Golfer
935 S Alhambra Circle, Coral Gables FL 33146, USA

**Keresztes, K Sandor** — Architect
Fo Utca 44/50, 1011 Budapest, Hungary

**Kerfeld, Charles P (Charlie)** — Baseball Player
PO Box 1666, Gig Harbor WA 98335, USA

**Kerger, Paula** — Government Official
Public Broadcasting System, 1320 Braddock Dr, Alexandria VA 22314, USA

**Kerim, Srgjan** — Government Official, Macedonia
United Nations, General Assembly, New York NY 10017, USA

**Kerkeling, Hape** — Actor
Postfach 200257, 13512 Berlin, Germany

**Kerkorian, Kirk** — Businessman
M G M/U A Communications, 2500 Broadway St, Santa Monica CA 90404, USA

**Kerkovich, Rob** — Actor
I C M Partners, 10250 Constellation Blvd, #900, Los Angeles CA 90067 USA

**Kerlikowske, R Gil** — Government, Law Enforcement Official
National Drug Control Policy Office, White House, Washington DC 20500, USA

**Kern, Geof** — Photographer
1355 Conant St, Dallas TX 75207, USA

**Kern, James L (Jim)** — Baseball Player
6009 Amberwood Court, Arlington TX 76016, USA

**Kern, Joey** — Actor
Abrams Artists, 9200 W Sunset Blvd, #1125, West Hollywood CA 90069 USA

**Kern, Olga** — Concert Pianist
Agence de Concerts Caecilia, 29 Rue de la Coulouvreniere, 1204 Geneva, Switzerland

**Kern, Otto** — Fashion Designer
Augustastr 1, 67655 Kaiserslautern, Germany

**Kern, Paul J** — Army General
A M Industries, 105 N Niles Ave, South Bend IN 46617, USA

**Kern, Rex W** — Football Player
2816 Avenida de Autlan, Camarillo CA 93010, USA

**Kernan, William F (Buck)** — Army General
30 Pinewild Dr, Pinehurst NC 28374, USA

| | |
|---|---|
| **Kernek, George B** | Baseball Player |
| 16423 Cotton Gin Ave, Wayne OK 73095, USA | |
| **Kernen, Joe** | Commentator |
| CNBC-TV, 2200 Fletcher Ave, #600, Fort Lee NJ 07024, USA | |
| **Kernis, Aaron Jay** | Composer |
| Yale University, Music Dept, New Haven CT 06520, USA | |
| **Kernochan, Sarah** | Writer, Director, Producer |
| Mange-Ment, 1103 1/2 Glendon Ave, Los Angeles CA 90024, USA | |
| **Kerns, David V, Jr** | Microbiotics Engineer |
| Vanderbilt University, Electrical Engineering Dept, Nashville TN 37235, USA | |
| **Kerns, Joanna** | Actress |
| Paradigm Agency, 360 N Crescent Dr, North Building, Beverly Hills CA 90210 USA | |
| **Keropian, Michael** | Sculptor |
| Keropian Sculpture LLC, 392 Gipsy Trail Road, Carmel NY 10512, USA | |
| **Kerr, Allen** | Plant Pathologist |
| 419 Carrington St, Adelaide SA 5000, Australia | |
| **Kerr, Anita** | Singer |
| 235 W 36th St, #321M, New York NY 10018, USA | |
| **Kerr, Brook** | Actress |
| Precision Entertainment, 6338 Wilshire Blvd, Los Angeles CA 90048, USA | |
| **Kerr, Cristie** | Golfer |
| 10810 E Addy Way, Scottsdale AZ 85262, USA | |
| **Kerr, Donald M, Jr** | Physicist |
| Science Applications International, 1241 Cave St, La Jolla CA 92037, USA | |
| **Kerr, Edward** | Actor |
| A K A Talent, 6310 San Vicente Blvd, #200, Los Angeles CA 90048 USA | |
| **Kerr, Graham** | Food Expert, Writer |
| Kerr Corp, 1020 N Sunset Dr, Camano Island WA 98282, USA | |
| **Kerr, Judy** | Actress |
| 350 Paseo de Playa, #208, Ventura CA 93001, USA | |
| **Kerr, Miranda** | Model |
| I M G Models, 179-191 New South Head Road, Edgecliff NSW 2027, Australia | |
| **Kerr, Pat** | Fashion Designer |
| Pat Kerr Inc, 200 Wagner Place, Memphis TN 38103, USA | |
| **Kerr, Philip** | Writer |
| Independent Talent Group, 40 Whitfield St, London W1T 2RH, England | |
| **Kerr, Stephen D (Steve)** | Basketball Player, Executive, Coach |
| PO Box 1964, Rancho Santa Fe CA 92067, USA | |
| **Kerr, Tim** | Ice Hockey Player |
| 335 Tom Brown Road, Moorestown NJ 08057, USA | |
| **Kerr, William T** | Businessman |
| Meredith Corp, 1716 Locust St, Des Moines IA 50309, USA | |
| **Kerrey, J Robert (Bob)** | Governor, Senator; Vietnam Hero (CMH) |
| 278 W 4th St, New York NY 10014, USA | |
| **Kerrigan, Joseph T (Joe)** | Baseball Player, Manager |
| 450 Forest Lane, North Wales PA 19454, USA | |
| **Kerrigan, Nancy A** | Figure Skater |
| 40 Salem St, #101, Lynnfield MA 01940, USA | |
| **Kerrigan, Pamela** | Golfer |
| 3205 Truckers Lane, Hingham MA 02043, USA | |
| **Kerry, Alexandra** | Actress, Producer, Director |
| Tar Art Media, 304 Hudson St, #600, New York NY 10013, USA | |
| **Kerry, James** | Astronaut |
| N A S A, Johnson Space Center, 2101 NASA Road, Houston TX 77058 USA | |
| **Kersee, Bob** | Track Coach |
| University of California, Athletic Dept, Los Angeles CA 90024, USA | |
| **Kersey, Jerome** | Basketball Player |
| 24140 SW Peters Mountain Road, West Linn OR 97068, USA | |
| **Kersey, Paul** | Actor |
| TalentWorks, 3500 W Olive Ave, #1400, Burbank CA 91505 USA | |
| **Kersh, David** | Singer |
| Mark Hybner Entertainment, 50 Music Square W, #802, Nashville TN 37203, USA | |
| **Kershaw, Clayton E** | Baseball Player |
| Los Angeles Dodgers, Stadium, 1000 Elysian Park Ave, Los Angeles CA 90090 USA | |
| **Kershaw, Douglas J (Doug)** | Singer, Fiddler, Songwriter |
| Cooking Vinyl, 10 Allied Way, London W3 0RQ, England | |
| **Kershaw, Noreen** | Director |
| Artists Partnership, 101 Finsbury Pavement, London EC2A 1RS, England | |
| **Kershaw, Sammy** | Singer |
| Sammy Kershaw Mgmt, 38 Music Square E, #111, Nashville TN 37203, USA | |
| **Kertesz, Imre** | Nobel Literature Laureate |
| Rowohit Verlage, Hamburger Str 17, 21465 Reinbeck, Germany | |
| **Kerwin, Brian** | Actor |
| Paradigm Agency, 360 Park Ave S, #1600, New York NY 10010 USA | |
| **Kerwin, Cornelius** | Educator |
| American University, President's Office, Washington DC 20006, USA | |
| **Kerwin, Joseph P** | Astronaut |
| 10411 River Road, College Station TX 77845, USA | |
| **Kerwin, Lance** | Actor |
| 26331 Osborne Lane, Homeland CA 92548, USA | |
| **Kerwin, Larkin** | Physicist |
| 2166 Bourboniere Park, Sillery QC G1T 1B4, Canada | |
| **Kerwin, Thomas V (Tom)** | Basktball Player |
| 283 Salter Path Road, #114, Atlantic Beach NC 28512, USA | |
| **Keselowski, Bradley R (Brad)** | Auto Racing Driver |
| Penske Racing, 200 Penske Way, Mooresville, NC 28115 28115, USA | |
| **Keshen, Christine** | Curling Athlete |
| Curling Association, 1660 Vimont Court, Cumberland ON K4A 4J4, Canada | |
| **Keshishian, Alek** | Director |
| Creative Artists Agency, 2000 Ave of Stars, #100, Los Angeles CA 90067 USA | |
| **Kesler, Ryan** | Ice Hockey Player |
| Vancouver Canucks, 800 Griffiths Way, Vancouver BC V6B 6G1, Canada | |
| **Kessel, Philip J (Phil), Jr** | Ice Hockey Player |
| 500 Atlantic Ave, #198, Boston MA 02210, USA | |
| **Kessinger, Donald E (Don)** | Baseball Player, Manager |
| 1306 Pelican Loop, Oxford MS 38655, USA | |

# K

**Kessler, David A** — Physician, Government Official
University of California Medical School, Dean's Office, San Francisco CA 94143, USA

**Kessler, Glenn D** — Producer, Writer
Creative Artists Agency, 2000 Ave of Stars, #100, Los Angeles CA 90067 USA

**Kessler, Jeffrey L** — Attorney
Dewey Ballantine, 1301 Ave of Americas, Basement 3, New York NY 10019, USA

**Kessler, Mikkel** — Boxer
Bettina Palle, Frederiksberg Alle 76, 1820 Frederiksberg C, Denmark

**Kessler, Ron** — Writer
Newsman.com, PO Box 20989, West Palm Beach FL 33416, USA

**Kessler, Stephen** — Director
Nikki Weiss Co, 754 N La Jolla Ave, Los Angeles CA 90046, USA

**Kessler, Todd A** — Producer, Writer
Creative Artists Agency, 2000 Ave of Stars, #100, Los Angeles CA 90067 USA

**Kessy, Jennifer A (Jen)** — Volleyball Player
32951 Avenida Descanso, San Juan Capistrano CA 92675, USA

**Kester, Richard L (Rick)** — Baseball Player
PO Box 623, Gardnerville NV 89410, USA

**Kestner, Boyd** — Actor
Mirisch Agency, 1025 Colorado Ave, #B, Santa Monica CA 90211 USA

**Ketchum, Hal** — Singer, Songwriter
602 Wayside Dr, Wimberley TX 78676, USA

**Ketchum, Howard** — Color Engineer
3800 Washington Road, West Palm Beach FL 33405, USA

**Ketchum, Robert Glenn** — Photographer
Art Source, 11901 Santa Monica Blvd, Los Angeles CA 90025, USA

**Ketilsson, Jon** — Opera Singer
I M G Artists, Hogarth Business Park, Chiswick, London W4 2TH, England

**Ketterle, Wolfgang** — Nobel Physics Laureate
25 Bellingham Dr, Brookline MA 02446, USA

**Kettle, Roger** — Cartoonist (Man Called Horse)
King Features Syndicate, 300 W 57th St, #1500, New York NY 10019 USA

**Kettner, Carla** — Producer, Writer
W M E Entertainment, 9601 Wilshire Blvd, #300, Beverly Hills CA 90210 USA

**Kev Nish** — Singer (Far East Movement)
Stampede Mgmt, 12530 Beatrice St, Los Angeles CA 90066, USA

**Keves, Gyorgy** — Architect
Keves es Epitesztarsai Rt, Melinda Utca 21, 1121 Budapest, Hungary

**Key, A Wade** — Football Player
PO Box 857, Hondo TX 78861, USA

**Key, James E (Jimmy)** — Baseball Player
128 Talavera Place, Palm Beach Gardens FL 33418, USA

**Key, John** — Prime Minister, New Zealand
Prime Minister's Office, Parliament Buildings, Wellington 6160, New Zealand

**Key, Keegan-Michael** — Actor
United Talent Agency, U T A Plaza, 9336 Civic Center Dr, Beverly Hills CA 90210 USA

**Keyes, Leroy** — Football Player
3935 Glen Eagles Place, West Lafayette IN 47906, USA

**Keyes, Nathan** — Actor
Creative Artists Agency, 2000 Ave of Stars, #100, Los Angeles CA 90067 USA

**Keyes, Robert W** — Physicist, Engineer
I B M Research Division, PO Box 218, Yorktown Heights NY 10598, USA

**Keyfitz, Nathan** — Statistician
1580 Massachusetts Ave, #7C, Cambridge MA 02138, USA

**Keynes, Skander** — Actor
Hamilton Hodell, 20 Golden Square, London W1F 9JL, England

**Keys, Alicia** — Singer, Songwriter, Pianist
Big Pita Little Pita Productions, Walt Disney Co, 500 S Buena Vista St, Burbank CA 91521, USA

**Keys, Brady, Jr** — Football Player
2931 Banchory Road, Winter Park FL 32792, USA

**Keys, Donald** — Educator
Planetary Citizens, 777 United Nations Plaza, New York NY 10017, USA

**Keys, Randolph** — Basketball Player
4308 Ludi Mae Court, Charlotte NC 28227, USA

**Keys, Tyrone P** — Football Player
5708 Clouds Peak Dr, Lutz FL 33558, USA

**Keys, William M (Bull)** — General, Marine Corps
5105 Stillhouse Road, Hume VA 22639, USA

**Keyser, F Ray, Jr** — Governor, VT
64 Warner Ave, Proctor VT 05765, USA

**Keyser, Richard L** — Businessman
W W Grainger Inc, 14441 W Illinois Route 60, Lake Forest IL 60045, USA

**Keyworth, Jonathan K (Jon)** — Football Player
1722 E Ridgefield Road, Spanish Fork UT 84660, USA

**Khabibulin, Nikolai I** — Ice Hockey Player
6451 E El Maro Circle, Paradise Valley AZ 85253, USA

**Khajag Barsamian** — Religious Leader
Armenian Church of America, Eastern Diocese, 630 2nd Ave, New York NY 10016, USA

**Khaled** — Singer
George Leitner Productions, Huetteldorfer Str 259, 1140 Vienna, Austria

**Khalfoun, Franck** — Actor, Director
United Talent Agency, U T A Plaza, 9336 Civic Center Dr, Beverly Hills CA 90210 USA

**Khali, Simbi** — Actress
I C M Partners, 10250 Constellation Blvd, #900, Los Angeles CA 90067 USA

**Khalifa, Sheikh Hamad bin Isa al-** — Emir, Bahrain
Rifa's Palace, PO Box 555, Manama, Bahrain

**Khalifa, Sheikh Khalifa bin Sulman, al-** — Prime Minister, Bahrain
Prime Minister's Office, Government House, PO Box 1000, Manama, Bahrain

**Khalifa, Sheikh Salman bin Hamad al-** — Crown Prince, Bahrain
Defense Ministry, PO Box 245, West Rif'a, Bahrain

**Khalifa, Wiz** — Rap Artist
Atlantic Records, 9229 W Sunset Blvd, #900, West Hollywood CA 90069 USA

**Khama, K Ian** — President, Botswana; Army General
President's Office, State House, Private Bag 001, Gaborone, Botswana

**Khamenei, Hojatolislam Sayyed Ali** — President, Iran
President's Office, Pastor Ave, Teheran, Iran

| | |
|---|---|
| **Khan, Aamir**<br>Aamir Khan Productions, Kuber Niwas, #2, Meera Baug Road, Santacruz (W), Mumbai 400054, India | Actor |
| **Khan, Amir I**<br>Golden Boy Promotions, 626 Wilshire Blvd, #350, Los Angeles CA 90017 USA | Boxer |
| **Khan, Amjad Ali**<br>Eye for Talent, 1139 San Carlos Abe, #310, San Carlos CA 94070, USA | Sarod Player, Composer |
| **Khan, Chaka**<br>Management for Advancement of Artists, 9100 Wilshire Blvd, #450E, Beverly Hills CA 90212, USA | Singer, Actress |
| **Khan, Irrfan**<br>Paradigm Agency, 360 N Crescent Dr, North Building, Beverly Hills CA 90210 USA | Actor |
| **Khan, Nareem**<br>Deborah Hughes, 311 W 43rd St, #1102, New York NY 10036, USA | Fashion Designer |
| **Khan, Niazi Imran**<br>Pakistan Tehreek-e-Insaf, Street #84, Ho 2, Sector G-6/4, Islamabad, Pakistan | Cricketer |
| **Khan, Salman**<br>3 Galaxy Apartments, B J Road, Band Stand Bandra, Mumbai MS 400050, India | Actor |
| **Khan, Salman A (Sal)**<br>Khan Academy Discovery Laboratory, 151 Laura Lane, Palo Alto CA 94303, USA | Educator |
| **Khan, Shahrukh**<br>Amrit Apartments, #700, 15th Carter Road Bandra, Mumbai MS 400050, India | Actor |
| **Khan, Ustad Sultan**<br>Agency Group Ltd, 1880 Century Park E, #711, Los Angeles CA 90067, USA | Sarangi Musician |
| **Khanh, Emmanuelle**<br>Emmanuelle Khanh International, 39 Ave Victor Hugo, 75116 Paris, France | Fashion Designer |
| **Khanna, Akshay**<br>13/C Elplaza, Little Gibs Road, Malabar Hill, Mumbai MS 400026, India | Actor |
| **Khanna, Rinke**<br>201A Vastu Building, Military Road Juhu, Mumbai MS 400049, India | Actress |
| **Khanzadian, Vahan**<br>PO Box 137, Jewett NY 12444, USA | Opera Singer |
| **Kharbanda, Kulbhushan**<br>501 Silver Cascade, Mount Mary Road, Bandra, Mumbai MS 400050, India | Actor |
| **Khashoggi, Adnan M**<br>La Baraka, 29604 Marbella, Spain | Businessman |
| **Khavin, Vladimir Y**<br>Glavmosarchitectura, Triumfalnaya Square 1, 103001 Moscow, Russia | Architect |
| **Khayat, Edward (Eddie)**<br>7813 Haydenberry Cove, Nashville TN 37221, USA | Football Player, Coach |
| **Khayat, Robert C (Bob)**<br>PO Box 677, Oxford MS 38655, USA | Educator, Football Player |
| **Kher, Anupam**<br>402 Marina, Juhu Tara Road Juhu Beach, Mumbai MS 400049, India | Actor |
| **Khmylev, Yuri A**<br>8236 Oakway Lane, Buffalo NY 14221, USA | Ice Hockey Player |
| **Khokhlov, Boris**<br>Myaskovsky St 11-13, #102, 121019 Moscow, Russia | Ballet Dancer |
| **Khondji, Darius**<br>Independent Talent Group, 40 Whitfield St, London W1T 2RH, England | Cinematographer |
| **Khorkina, Svetlana**<br>Gymnastics Federation, Lujnetskaya Nabererynaya 8, 119270 Moscow, Russia | Gymnast |
| **Khosla, Vinod**<br>Khosla Ventures, 3000 Sand Hill Road, Building 3, Menlo Park CA 94025, USA | Businessman |
| **Khouri, Callie**<br>Creative Artists Agency, 2000 Ave of Stars, #100, Los Angeles CA 90067 USA | Director, Writer |
| **Khoury, Raymond**<br>Penguin Books, 375 Hudson St, Basement 1, New York NY 10014 USA | Writer |
| **Khristenko, Viktor**<br>Prime Minister's Office, Krasnopresneskaya Nab 2, 103274 Moscow, Russia | Prime Minister, Russia |
| **Khristich, Dmitri**<br>5002 N Convent Lane, #E, Philadelphia PA 19114, USA | Ice Hockey Player |
| **Khrushchev, Sergei**<br>3 Laurelhurst Road, Cranston RI 02920, USA | Writer |
| **Khush, Gurdev S**<br>International Rice Institute, Box 3127, Makati City 1271, Philippines | Agricultural Researcher |
| **Ki Sung-Yueng**<br>A F C Sunderland, Stadium of Light, Sunderland 1SU 2FA, England | Soccer Player |
| **Kiarostami, Abbas**<br>Zeitgeist Films, 247 Center St, #203, New York NY 10013, USA | Director |
| **Kibaki, Mwai**<br>President's Office, Harambee House, Harambee Ave, Nairobi, Kenya | President, Kenya |
| **Kibble, Thomas W B (Tom)**<br>Imperial College, Blackett Laboratory, South Kensington, London SW7 2AZ, England | Physicist |
| **Kiberd, James**<br>Phoenix Artists, 330 W 38th St, #607, New York NY 10018, USA | Actor |
| **Kiberlain, Sandrine**<br>Voyez Mon Agent, 20 Ave Rapp, 75007 Paris, France | Actress, Singer |
| **Kibrick, Anne**<br>381 Seminary Ave, #221, Auburndale MA 02466, USA | Medical Educator |
| **Kid Capri**<br>Asti Artist Mgmt, 66 Irving Place, New York NY 10003, USA | DJ Musician, Actor |
| **Kid Rock**<br>Creative Artists Agency, 2000 Ave of Stars, #100, Los Angeles CA 90067 USA | Rap Artist |
| **Kidd, Jason F**<br>367 Cottonwood Way, Mahwah NJ 07430, USA | Basketball Player, Coach |
| **Kidd, Jodie**<br>I M G Models, 131-151 Great Titchfield St, London W1W 5BB, England | Model |
| **Kidd, M John**<br>4204 Moorland Dr, Midland MI 48640, USA | Football Player |
| **Kidd, Warren L**<br>313 River Road, Harpersville AL 35078, USA | Basketball Player |
| **Kidd, William W (Billy)**<br>Billy Kidd Racing, 2305 Mount Werner Circle, Steamboat Springs CO 80487, USA | Alpine Skier |
| **Kidder Lee, Barbara**<br>1308 W Highland, Phoenix AZ 85013, USA | Alpine Skier |
| **Kidder, Margot**<br>Muse Mgmt, 1541 Ocean Ave, #200, Santa Monica CA 90401, USA | Actress |

**Kidder, Tracy** — Writer
Random House, 1745 Broadway, #1800, New York NY 10019 USA

**Kidd-Gilchrist, Michael** — Basketball Player
Charlotte Hornets, 333 E Trade St, #A, Charlotte NC 28202 USA

**Kidjo, Angelique** — Singer, Songwriter
Vector Mgmt, PO Box 120479, Nashville TN 37212 USA

**Kidron, Beeban** — Director, Producer, Writer
Independent Talent Group, 40 Whitfield St, London W1T 2RH, England

**Kiechel, Walter, III** — Editor
929 Washington St, Hoboken NJ 07030, USA

**Kiecker, Dana E** — Baseball Player
4104 Prairie Ridge Road, Saint Paul MN 55123, USA

**Kiedis, Anthony** — Singer (Red Hot Chili Peppers)
Untitled Entertainment, 350 S Beverly Dr, #200, Beverly Hills CA 90212 USA

**Kiefel, Ronald A (Ron)** — Cyclist
3875 Field Dr, Wheat Ridge CO 80033, USA

**Kiefer, Adolph G** — Swimmer, Coach
42125 N Hunt Club Road, Wadsworth IL 60083, USA

**Kiefer, Anselm** — Artist
Gagosian Gallery, 980 Madison Ave, New York NY 10075 USA

**Kiefer, Mark A** — Baseball Player
11832 Old Fashion Way, Garden Grove CA 92840, USA

**Kiefer, Nicolas** — Tennis Player
Sports 2 Business. Erlenring 16, 61118 Bad Vibel, Germany

**Kiefer, Steven G (Steve)** — Baseball Player
12389 Cloudburst Trail, Moreno Valley CA 92555, USA

**Kieffer, James M** — Businessman
422 Stoutenburgh Lane, Pittsford NY 14534, USA

**Kiehl, Heinz** — Greco-Roman Wrestler
Am Weidenschlag 44, 67071 Ludwigshafen, Germany

**Kiehl, Marina** — Alpine Skier
Hermie-Bland Str 11, 81545 Munich, Germany

**Kiehl, Stuart** — Cinematographer
4193 Concord Ave, Santa Rosa CA 95407, USA

**Kielty, Robert M (Bobby)** — Baseball Player
21504 Appaloosa Court, Canyon Lake CA 92587, USA

**Kier, Udo** — Actor
Richard Schwartz Mgmt, 2934 N Beverly Glen Circle, #107, Los Angeles CA 90077 USA

**Kiermayer, Susanne** — Markswoman
Amthofplatz 5, 94259 Kirchberg, Germany

**Kieschnick, M Brooks** — Baseball Player
210 Joliet Ave, #A, San Antonio TX 78209, USA

**Kiesel, Theresia** — Track Athlete
Stifterstr 24, 4050 Truan, Austria

**Kiffin, Irv** — Basketball Player
1441 Trellis Lane, Pembroke Pines FL 33026, USA

**Kigeli V Ndagindurwa** — King, Rwanda
Kigeli Foundation, Fairfax Towers, 9941 Oak Creek Place, Oakton VA 22124, USA

**Kightlinger, Laura** — Actress, Comedienne
Avalon Mgmt, 8332 Melrose Ave, #200, Los Angeles CA 90069, USA

**Kihlstedt, Rya** — Actress
Brookside Mgmt, 250 W 57th St, #2303, New York NY 10107, USA

**Kihn, Greg** — Singer, Guitarist (Greg Kihn Band)
Riot Mgmt, PO Box 8553, Berkeley CA 94707, USA

**Kihune, Robert K U** — Navy Admiral
1428 Aunauna St, Kailua HI 96734, USA

**Kiick, James F (Jim)** — Football Player
2900 S University Dr, #9112, Davie FL 33328, USA

**Kiir Mayardit, Salva** — President, South Sudan
President Office, Juba, Southern Sudan

**Kiiskinen, Kalle** — Curling Athlete
Curling Association, Kalatorppa 2A62, 02230 Espoo, Finland

**Kikuchi, Rinko** — Actress
Anore, 6-17-15-9F Jingumae, Shibuya, Tokyo 150 0001, Japan

**Kikuchi, Rioko** — Astronaut, Japan; Photographer
Japanese Aerospace Exploration Agency, 2-1-1 Sengen, Tsukuba, Ibaraki 305 8505, Japan

**Kikwete, Jakaya Mrisho** — President, Tanzania
President's Office, State House, PO Box 9120, Dar es Salaam, Tanzania

**Kilar, Jason** — Businessman
Hulu, 12312 W Olympic Blvd, Los Angeles CA 90064, USA

**Kilbane, Pat** — Actor
Amsel Eisenstadt Frazier, 5055 Wilshire Blvd, #865, Los Angeles CA 90036 USA

**Kilbey, Elektra** — Singer (Say Lou Lou)
Windish Agency, 1658 N Milwaukee Ave, #211, Chicago IL 60647 USA

**Kilbey, Steven J** — Singer, Guitarist (Church); Songwriter
M O B Agency, 6404 Wilshire Blvd, #505, Los Angeles CA 90048 USA

**Kilborn, Craig** — Actor, Comedian, Writer, Producer
Apostle Management, 9696 Culver Blvd, #108, Culver City CA 90232, USA

**Kilbourne, Wendy** — Actress
9200 W Sunset Blvd, #612, West Hollywood CA 90069, USA

**Kilburn, Terry** — Actor
Oakland University, Meadowbrook Theatre, Walton & Squirrel, Rochester MI 48063, USA

**Kilby, Miranda** — Singer (Say Lou Lou)
Windish Agency, 1658 N Milwaukee Ave, #211, Chicago IL 60647 USA

**Kilcher, Q'Orianka** — Actress
I Q Films, 1705 Pico Blvd, #24, Santa Monica CA 90405, USA

**Kilcline, Thomas J (Tom), Jr** — Navy Admiral
Commander, Naval Air Force Pacific, NAS North Island, San Diego CA 92135 USA

**Kilcullen, Robert B (Bob)** — Football Player
400 E Division St, Pilot Point TX 76258, USA

**Kildea, Bobby** — Guitarist, Bassist (Belle & Sebastian)
Ground Control Touring, 20 Jay St, #826, Brooklyn NY 11201 USA

**Kiley, Ariel** — Actress
Untitled Entertainment, 350 S Beverly Dr, #200, Beverly Hills CA 90212 USA

**Kilgallon, Robert D** — Environmental Researcher
662 Park Ave, Meadville PA 16335, USA

**Kilgore, Jerry**
T B A Artist Mgmt, 300 10th Ave S, Nashville TN 37203, USA — Singer, Songwriter
**Kilgore, Jon**
2422 Glen Oaks Court NE, Atlanta GA 30345, USA — Football Player
**Kilgus, Paul N**
968 Threewood Circle, Bowling Green KY 42103, USA — Baseball Player
**Kilius, Marika**
Postfach 201151, 63271 Dreieich, Germany — Figure Skater
**Kilkenny, Michael D (Mike)**
274 Holland St W, Bradford ON L3Z 1J1, Canada — Baseball Player
**Kill, Jerry**
Legacy Agency, 230 Park Ave, #851, New York NY 10169 USA — Football Coach
**Killam, Taran**
Principato-Young, 9465 Wilshire Blvd, #880, Beverly Hills CA 90212 USA — Actor
**Killar, Wojciech**
Ul Ksciuszki 165, 40 524 Katowice, Poland — Composer
**Killeen, Denise**
803 Golden Wood Trace, Canton GA 30114, USA — Golfer
**Killen, Kyle**
W M E Entertainment, 9601 Wilshire Blvd, #300, Beverly Hills CA 90210 USA — Producer, Writer
**Killens, Terry D**
5665 Water Spring Way, Mason OH 45040, USA — Football Player
**Killer Mike**
J L Entertainment, 18653 Ventura Blvd, #340, Los Angeles CA 91356 USA — Rap Artist
**Killing, Laure**
Agence Christine Parat, 9 Rue de Maubeuge, 75009 Paris, France — Actress
**Killip, Christopher D**
Harvard University, Visual Studies Dept, 24 Quincy St, Cambridge MA 02138, USA — Photographer
**Killy, Jean-Claude**
Villa Les Oiseaux 13 Chemin Bellefontaine, 1223 Cologny GE, Switzerland — Alpine Skier
**Kilman, Sato**
Prime Minister's Office, PO Box 053, Port Vila, Vanuatu — Prime Minister, Vanuatu
**Kilmer, Val**
PO Box 364, Rowe NM 87562, USA — Actor
**Kilmer, William O (Billy)**
1853 Monte Carlo Way, #36, Coral Springs FL 33071, USA — Football Player
**Kilmore, Chris**
Variety Artists, 1924 Spring St, Paso Robles CA 93446 USA — DJ Musician, Keyboardist (Incubus)
**Kilner, Clare**
Gersh Agency, 9465 Wilshire Blvd, #600, Beverly Hills CA 90212 USA — Director, Writer
**Kilner, Kevin**
Innovative Artists, 1505 10th St, Santa Monica CA 90401 USA — Actor
**Kilpatrick, Carl**
10517 23rd Street Court E, Edgewood WA 98372, USA — Basketball Player
**Kilrain, Susan L**
2168 Lords Landing, Virginia Beach VA 23454, USA — Astronaut
**Kilrea, Brian**
2192 Saunderson Dr, Ottawa ON K1G 2G4, Canada — Ice Hockey Player, Coach
**Kilts, James M**
Centerview Partners, 31 W 52nd St, #2200, New York NY 10019, USA — Businessman
**Kilzer, Louis C (Lon)**
Minneapolis-Saint Paul Star-Tribune, Editorial Dept, 425 Portland Ave, Minneapolis MN 55488, USA — Journalist
**Kim Bo-Kyung**
Football Association, 1-131 Sinmunno, 2-Ga Jongno-Gu, Seoul 110 062, South Korea — Soccer Player
**Kim Chang-Soo**
Football Association, 1-131 Sinmunno, 2-Ga Jongno-Gu, Seoul 110 062, South Korea — Soccer Player
**Kim Cheol-Min**
Skating Union, 88 Bangyee-Dong, Songpaku, Seoul 138 749, South Korea — Speed Skater
**Kim Dong-Sung**
Skating Union, 88 Bangyee-Dong, Songpaku, Seoul 138 749, South Korea — Speed Skater
**Kim Hyun-Sung**
Football Association, 1-131 Sinmunno, 2-Ga Jongno-Gu, Seoul 110 062, South Korea — Soccer Player
**Kim Jong-Pil**
340-38, Sindang 4-Dongku, Seoul, South Korea — Prime Minister, South Korea; General
**Kim Jong-Un**
President's Office, Pyongyang, North Korea — President Designate, North Korea
**Kim Kee-Hee**
Football Association, 1-131 Sinmunno, 2-Ga Jongno-Gu, Seoul 110 062, South Korea — Soccer Player
**Kim Ki-Hoon**
Skating Union, 88 Bangyee-Dong, Songpaku, Seoul 138 749, South Korea — Speed Skater
**Kim Seoung-Il**
Skating Union, 88 Bangyee-Dong, Songpaku, Seoul 138 749, South Korea — Speed Skater
**Kim So-Hui**
Skating Union, 88 Bangyee-Dong, Songpaku, Seoul 138 749, South Korea — Speed Skater
**Kim Young-Gwon**
Football Association, 1-131 Sinmunno, 2-Ga Jongno-Gu, Seoul 110 062, South Korea — Soccer Player
**Kim Young-Sam**
7-6-1 Sangdo, Dongjakku, Seoul 156 743, South Korea — President, South Korea
**Kim Yu-Na**
Toronto C S C C, 141 Wilson Ave, Toronto ON M5M 3A3, Canada — Figure Skater
**Kim Yun-Mi**
Skating Union, 88 Bangyee-Dong, Songpaku, Seoul 138 749, South Korea — Speed Skater
**Kim, Anthony**
Professional Golfers Association, 100 Ave of Champions, Palm Beach Gardens FL 33418 USA — Golfer
**Kim, Byung-Hyun**
4601 E Skyline Dr, #1302, Tucson AZ 85718, USA — Baseball Player
**Kim, Christina**
Ladies Pro Golf Assn, 100 International Golf Dr, Daytona Beach FL 32124 USA — Golfer
**Kim, Daniel Dae**
A P A Talent & Literary Agency, 405 S Beverly Dr, #300, Beverly Hills CA 90212 USA — Actor
**Kim, Grace**
Playboy Promotions, 9346 Civic Center Dr, #200, Beverly Hills CA 90210 USA — Model
**Kim, Jacqueline**
Innovative Artists, 1505 10th St, Santa Monica CA 90401 USA — Actress
**Kim, Jaegwon**
Brown University, Philosophy Dept, Providence RI 02912, USA — Philosopher

| | |
|---|---|
| **Kim, Jim Yong** | Financier, Educator |
| World Bank Group, 1818 H St NW, Washington DC 20433, USA | |
| **Kim, John J** | Journalist |
| Chicago Sun-Times, Editorial Dept, 401 N Wabash Ave, Chicago IL 60611 USA | |
| **Kim, Kathleen** | Opera Singer |
| Harrison/Parrott, 5-6 Albion Court, London W6 0QT, England | |
| **Kim, Kwang Soo** | Neuroscientist, Psychiatrist |
| McLean Hospital, Molecular Neurobiology Laboratory, 115 Mill St, Belmont MA 02478, USA | |
| **Kim, Nelli V** | Gymnast |
| 2480 Cobblehill, #A, Alcove, Woodbury MN 55125, USA | |
| **Kim, Peter S** | Biochemist, Geneticist |
| Whitehead Institute, 9 Cambridge Center, Cambridge MA 02142, USA | |
| **Kim, Yunjin** | Actress |
| Ace Mgmt, 210 5th Ave, Venice CA 90291, USA | |
| **Kimball, Bobby** | Singer (Toto) |
| World Entertainment Assoc, 8815 Conroy Windermere Road, #407, Orlando FL 32835, USA | |
| **Kimball, Charlie** | Auto Racing Driver |
| Chip Ganassi Racing, 8500 Westmoreland Dr, Concord NC 28027, USA | |
| **Kimball, Cheyenne** | Singer, Songwriter, Actress |
| Creative Artists Agency, 2000 Ave of Stars, #100, Los Angeles CA 90067 USA | |
| **Kimball, Christopher** | Chef |
| Public Broadcasting System, 1320 Braddock Place, Alexandria VA 22314 USA | |
| **Kimball, Dick** | Diver, Diving Coach |
| 1540 Waltham Dr, Ann Arbor MI 48103, USA | |
| **Kimball, Jeffrey** | Cinematographer |
| Paradigm Agency, 360 N Crescent Dr, North Building, Beverly Hills CA 90210 USA | |
| **Kimball, Lynnda** | Model |
| Playboy Promotions, 9346 Civic Center Dr, #200, Beverly Hills CA 90210 USA | |
| **Kimball, Thomas (Toby)** | Basketball Player |
| 6859 Avenida Andorra, La Jolla CA 92037, USA | |
| **Kimball, Warren F** | Historian |
| 2540 Otter Lane, Johns Island SC 29455, USA | |
| **Kimble, Avis** | Model |
| Playboy Promotions, 9346 Civic Center Dr, #200, Beverly Hills CA 90210 USA | |
| **Kimble, Darin** | Ice Hockey Player |
| 2660 Cleveland Blvd, Granite City IL 62040, USA | |
| **Kimble, Gregory K (Bo)** | Basketball Player |
| 100 Poe Court, North Wales PA 19454, USA | |
| **Kimble, Warren** | Artist |
| RR 3 Box 1038, Brandon VT 05733, USA | |
| **Kimbrough, Charles** | Actor, Singer |
| 255 Amalfi Dr, Santa Monica CA 90402, USA | |
| **Kimbrough, Elbert L** | Football Player |
| 886 W 2nd St, Galesburg IL 61401, USA | |
| **Kimbrough, R Shane** | Astronaut |
| N A S A, Johnson Space Center, 2101 NASA Road, Houston TX 77058 USA | |
| **Kimbrough, Stan** | Basketball Player |
| 3922 Elm Ave, Cincinnati OH 45236, USA | |
| **Kimery, James L** | Association Executive |
| Veterans of Foreign Wars, 405 W 34th St, Kansas City MO 64111, USA | |
| **Kimm, Bruce E** | Baseball Player, Manager |
| 3168 121st St, Amana IA 52203, USA | |
| **Kimmel, Jimmy** | Actor, Comedian |
| Jackhole Industries, 6834 Hollywood Blvd, Los Angeles CA 90028, USA | |
| **Kimmelman, Michael** | Art Critic |
| New York Times, Editorial Dept, 229 W 43rd St, New York NY 10036 USA | |
| **Kimmet, Brian** | Actor |
| Sutton-Barth Vennari, 5900 Wilshire Blvd, #700, Los Angeles CA 90036 USA | |
| **Kimura, Doreen** | Psychologist |
| 211 Madison Ave, Toronto ON M5R 2S6, Canada | |
| **Kimura, Kazuo** | Industrial Designer |
| Japan Design Foundation, 2-2 Cenba Chuo, Higashiku, Osaka 541 0046, Japan | |
| **Kinard, A Terance (Terry)** | Football Player |
| 18 Safe Harbor Ave, Pawleys Island SC 29585, USA | |
| **Kinard, William R (Billy)** | Football Player |
| PO Box 680944, Fort Payne AL 35968, USA | |
| **Kincaid, Jamaica** | Writer |
| College Road, North Bennington VT 05257, USA | |
| **Kinchen, Arif S** | Actor |
| Xpose Talent Agency, 1055 E Colorado Blvd, #5, Pasadena CA 91106, USA | |
| **Kinchen, Brian D** | Football Player |
| 19502 E Pinnacle Circle, Baton Rouge LA 70810, USA | |
| **Kinchen, Todd W** | Football Player |
| 247 Guava Dr, Baton Rouge LA 70808, USA | |
| **Kinchla, Chandler (Chan)** | Guitarist (Blues Traveler) |
| C3 Presents, 98 San Jacinto Blvd, #400, Austin TX 78701, USA | |
| **Kinchla, Thaddeus A (Tad)** | Bassist (Blues Traveler) |
| C3 Presents, 98 San Jacinto Blvd, #400, Austin TX 78701, USA | |
| **Kincses, Veronika** | Opera Singer |
| Hungarian State Opera, Andrassy Utca 22, 1061 Budapest, Hungary | |
| **Kind, Richard** | Actor |
| Foster Entertainment, 12533 Woodgreen St, Building B, Los Angeles CA 90066, USA | |
| **Kind, Roslyn** | Actress, Singer |
| Randy Johnson Co, PO Box 69A18, West Hollywood CA 90069, USA | |
| **Kindall, Gerald D (Jerry)** | Baseball Player |
| 7220 E Grey Fox Lane, Tucson AZ 85750, USA | |
| **Kinder, Donald R** | Political Scientist |
| University of Michigan, Political Science Dept, Ann Arbor MI 48109, USA | |
| **Kinder, Melvyn** | Psychologist, Writer |
| 1951 San Ysidro Dr, Beverly Hills CA 90210, USA | |
| **Kinder, Richard D** | Businessman |
| Kinder-Morgan Inc, 500 Dallas St, #1000, Houston TX 77002, USA | |
| **Kindig, Howard W, Jr** | Football Player |
| 8740 Bayside Ave, Baton Rouge LA 70806, USA | |
| **Kindler, Damian** | Producer, Writer |
| H2F Entertainment, 644 N Cherokee Ave, Los Angeles CA 90004, USA | |

**Kindler, Jeffrey B** — Businessman
Pfizer Inc, 235 E 42nd St, New York NY 10017, USA
**Kindrachuk, Orest** — Ice Hockey Player
106 Meeshaway Trail, Medford Lakes NJ 08055, USA
**Kindred, David A** — Sportswriter
Atlanta Constitution, 223 Perimeter Center Parkway NE, Atlanta GA 30346, USA
**Kiner, Kevin** — Composer
First Artists Mgmt, 4764 Park Granada, #210, Calabasas CA 91302 USA
**Kiner, Steven A (Steve)** — Football Player
112 N Ole Hickory Trail, Carrollton GA 30117, USA
**King Hogue, Maxine (Micki)** — Diver
3509 Colt Neck Lane, Lexington KY 40502, USA
**King Tee** — Rap Artist
Likwit Entertainment, PO Box 360713, Los Angeles CA 90036, USA
**King, Albert** — Basketball Player
88 Sturbridge Circle, Wayne NJ 07470, USA
**King, Angelo T** — Football Player
2922 W Royal Lane, #2090, Irving TX 75063, USA
**King, Anthony S** — Political Scientist
Mill House, Middle Green, Wakes Colne, Colchester, Essex CP6 2BP, England
**King, B B** — Singer, Guitarist
W M E Entertainment, 9601 Wilshire Blvd, #300, Beverly Hills CA 90210 USA
**King, Ben E** — Singer
Randy Irwin, PO Box 11862, Naples FL 34101, USA
**King, Bernard** — Basketball Player
307 Jupiter Hills Dr, Duluth GA 30097, USA
**King, Billie Jean** — Tennis Player
World Team Tennis, 1776 Broadway, #600, New York NY 10019, USA
**King, Brent** — Actor
Malaky International, 205 S Beverly Dr, #211, Beverly Hills CA 90212, USA
**King, Carole** — Composer, Singer, Pianist
Carole King Productions, 11684 Ventura Blvd, #273, Studio City CA 91604, USA
**King, Carolyn Dineen** — Judge
US Court of Appeals, US Courthouse, 515 Rusk Ave, #12015, Houston TX 77002, USA
**King, Charles G (Chick)** — Baseball Player
4036 Highway 54, Paris TN 38242, USA
**King, Colbert** — Journalist
Washington Post, Editorial Dept, 1150 15th St NW, Washington DC 20071 USA
**King, Curtis E** — Baseball Player
2538 Beechwood Dr, Vineland NJ 08361, USA
**King, Dana** — Commentator
CBS-TV, News Dept, 524 W 57th St, New York NY 10019, USA
**King, Danielle (Dani)** — Cyclist
Trevor King, 11 College Close Hamble, Southampton Hampshire SO31 4QU, England
**King, David A** — Chemist
20 Glisson Road, Cambridge CB1 2EW, England
**King, Dennis** — Artist
108 Andrew Court, Mount Shasta CA 96067, USA
**King, Derek** — Ice Hockey Player
8184 E Wingspan Way, Scottsdale AZ 85255, USA
**King, Dexter Scott** — Association Executive
Martin Luther King Nonviolent Social Change Center, 449 Auburn Ave NE, Atlanta GA 30312, USA
**King, Diana** — Singer, Songwriter
Wenig-LaMonica Associates, 580 White Plains Road, #130, Tarrytown NY 10591 USA
**King, Don** — Boxing Promoter
Don King Productions, 501 Fairway Dr, Deerfield Beach FL 33441, USA
**King, Edward E (Ed)** — Football Player
9903 North Blvd, Cleveland OH 44108, USA
**King, Elizabeth (Betsy)** — Golfer
7418 E Alta Sierra Dr, Scottsdale AZ 85266, USA
**King, Emanuel** — Football Player
Hollywood Christian High School, 1708 N 60th Ave, Hollywood FL 33021, USA
**King, Eric S** — Baseball Player
1063 Stanford Dr, Simi Valley CA 93065, USA
**King, Erik** — Actor
Burstein Co, 15304 W Sunset Blvd, #208, Pacific Palisades CA 90272 USA
**King, Evelyn (Champagne)** — Singer
T-Best Talent Agency, 508 Honey Lake Court, Danville CA 94506 USA
**King, Fallon** — Singer (Cherish)
Capitol Records, 810 7th Ave, New York NY 10019 USA
**King, Farrah** — Singer (Cherish)
Capitol Records, 810 7th Ave, New York NY 10019 USA
**King, Felisha** — Singer (Cherish)
Capitol Records, 810 7th Ave, New York NY 10019 USA
**King, G Stephen (Steve)** — Football Player
45 Chipping Stone Road, North Atteboro MA 02760, USA
**King, Gary** — Political Scientist
Harvard University, Quantitative Social Science Institute, Cambridge MA 02138, USA
**King, Georgia** — Actress
Paradigm Agency, 360 N Crescent Dr, North Building, Beverly Hills CA 90210 USA
**King, Gilbert** — Writer
Chase Literary Agency, 220 E 23rd St, #1100 New York NY 10011, USA
**King, Gordon D** — Football Player
2641 Highwood Dr, Roseville CA 95661, USA
**King, Graham** — Writer, Producer
1221 2nd St, #200, Santa Monica CA 90401, USA
**King, Harold (Hal)** — Baseball Player
828 Geneva Dr, Oviedo FL 32765, USA
**King, Horace E** — Football Player
884 Fairburn Road NW, Atlanta GA 30331, USA
**King, Jaime** — Actress, Model
Gersh Agency, 9465 Wilshire Blvd, #600, Beverly Hills CA 90212 USA
**King, James** — Singer
Rounder Records, 1 Rounder Way, Burlington MA 01803 USA
**King, James H (Jim)** — Baseball Player
720 Stokenbury Road, Elkins AR 72727, USA

# K

**King, Jeff**
PO Box 48, Denali National Park AK 99755, USA — Dog Sled Racer

**King, Jeffrey F (Jeff)**
Creative Artists Agency, 2000 Ave of Stars, #100, Los Angeles CA 90067 USA — Producer, Director, Writer

**King, Jeffrey W (Jeff)**
50401 Highway 278, Wisdom MT 59761, USA — Baseball Player

**King, Joanne**
T N Enterprises, 14 Beach Grove, Blackrock County, Dublin, Ireland — Actress

**King, Joe**
A2 Mgmt, 624 Davis St, #200, Evanston IL 60201, USA — Singer, Guitarist (Fray)

**King, Joey**
Coast to Coast Talent, 3350 Barham Blvd, Los Angeles CA 90068 USA — Actress

**King, Jon**
Story Worldwide, Primrose Hill, 15B Saint George's Mews, London NW1 8XC, England — Singer (Gang of Four)

**King, Kaki**
Big Hassle, 44 Wall St, #2200, New York NY 10005, USA — Singer, Guitarist

**King, Kathryn (Katie)**
3 Birchwood Road, Salem NH 3079, USA — Ice Hockey Player

**King, Kerry R**
Work Hard Public Relations, 190 Pinfold Road, London SW16 2SL, England — Guitarist (Slayer)

**King, Kris**
National Hockey League, 50 Bay St, #1100, Toronto ON M5J 2X8, Canada — Ice Hockey Player

**King, Kristin**
USA Hockey, 1775 Bob Johnson Dr, Colorado Springs CO 80906 USA — Ice Hockey Player

**King, Lamar**
5082 Springhouse Circle, Rosedale MD 21237, USA — Football Player

**King, Larry**
Media Talent Group, 9200 Sunset Blvd, #550, West Hollywood CA 90069, USA — Commentator, Columnist

**King, Linden K**
1130 S Flower St, #418, Los Angeles CA 90015, USA — Football Player

**King, Loyd**
118 Wilde Brook Dr, Asheville NC 28806, USA — Basketball Player

**King, Mark**
Level 42, PO Box 23, Sandown PO36 0QL, Canada — Singer, Bassist (Level 42)

**King, Mark**
King Griffin Inc, 8665 Miralani Dr, #100, San Diego CA 92126, USA — Artist

**King, Mary E**
Thorn Farm Buildings, Salcombe Regis, Sidmouth, Devon EX10 0JH, England — Equestrian

**King, Mary-Claire**
University of Washington Medical School, Genetics Dept, Seattle WA 98195, USA — Geneticist

**King, Michael Patrick**
Creative Artists Agency, 2000 Ave of Stars, #100, Los Angeles CA 90067 USA — Director, Writer

**King, Michelle**
Paradigm Agency, 360 N Crescent Dr, North Building, Beverly Hills CA 90210 USA — Producer, Writer

**King, Morgana**
13327 Cheltenham Dr, Sherman Oaks CA 91423, USA — Singer, Actress

**King, Neosha**
Capitol Records, 810 7th Ave, New York NY 10019 USA — Singer (Cherish)

**King, Perry**
3647 Wrightwood Dr, Studio City CA 91604, USA — Actor

**King, Peter**
NBC-TV, Sports Dept, 30 Rockefeller Plaza, #270E, New York NY 10112 USA — Sportscaster, Sportswriter

**King, Phillip**
Royal College of Arts, Kensington Gore, London SW7 2EU, England — Sculptor

**King, Raymond K (Ray)**
4220 N 161st Ave, Goodyear AZ 85395, USA — Baseball Player

**King, Regina**
I C M Partners, 10250 Constellation Blvd, #900, Los Angeles CA 90067 USA — Actress

**King, Reginald B (Reggie)**
4716 Chouteau St, Shawnee KS 66226, USA — Basketball Player

**King, Richard L**
Albertson's Inc, 250 E Parkcenter Blvd, Boise ID 83706, USA — Businessman

**King, Robert**
Paradigm Agency, 360 N Crescent Dr, North Building, Beverly Hills CA 90210 USA — Producer, Writer

**King, Robert B**
US Court of Appeals, 300 Virginia St E, #2630, Charleston WV 25301, USA — Judge

**King, Ronette**
Gensler Assoc, 600 California St, #1000, San Francisco CA 94108, USA — Interior Designer

**King, Shaun E**
10116 Caraway Spice Ave, Riverview FL 33578, USA — Football Player, Sportscaster

**King, Stephen E**
1380 Hammond St, Bangor ME 04401, USA — Writer

**King, Stephenson T**
Prime Minister's Office, Greaham Louisy Building, #500, Waterfront, Castries, Saint Lucia — Prime Minister, Saint Lucia

**King, Theodore W (Ted)**
Brady Brannon Rich, 5670 Wilshire Blvd, #820, Los Angeles CA 90036, USA — Actor

**King, Thomas J (Tom)**
House of Commons, Westminster, London SW1A 0AA, England — Government Official, England

**King, Thomas V (Tom)**
4930 Sea Witch Dr, Fernandina Beach FL 32034, USA — Basketball Player

**King, Vania**
380 Forsyth St, Boca Raton FL 33487, USA — Tennis Player

**King, W David (Dave)**
Arizona Coyotes, 6751 N Sunset Blvd, #200, Glendale AZ 85305 USA — Ice Hockey Coach

**King, William (Bill)**
Management Assoc, 1920 Benson Ave, Saint Paul MN 55116, USA — Trumpeter (Commodores)

**King, Woodie, Jr**
417 Convent Ave, New York NY 10031, USA — Producer

**Kinga, Yukari**
Football Association, 3-10-15 Hongo, Bunkyoku, Tokyo 113 0033 Japan — Soccer Player

**Kingdom, Roger**
146 S Fairmont St, #1, Pittsburgh PA 15206, USA — Track Athlete

**Kingery, Michael S (Mike)**
51923 298th St, Grove City MN 56243, USA — Baseball Player

**King-Hele, Desmond G**
7 Hilltops Court, 65 North Lane, Buriton, Hampshire GU31 5RS, England — Writer

| | |
|---|---|
| **Kingma, Nienke**<br>A S R Nereus, Amsteldijk 130A, 1078 Amsterdam RT, Netherlands | Rowing Athlete |
| **Kingman, David A (Dave)**<br>PO Box 209, Glenbrook NV 89413, USA | Baseball Player |
| **Kingrea, Richard O (Rick)**<br>102 N Bayview St, Fairhope AL 36532, USA | Football Player |
| **Kingsale, Eugene H (Gene)**<br>105 Angelfish Lane, Jupiter FL 33477, USA | Baseball Player |
| **Kingsbury, Gina**<br>Team Canada, 2424 University Dr NW, Calgary AB T2N 3Y9, Canada | Ice Hockey Player |
| **Kingsbury, Tim**<br>Billions Corp, 3522 W Armitage Ave, Chicago IL 60647 USA | Musician (Arcade Fire) |
| **Kingsley, Ben**<br>New Penworth House, Stratford upon Avon, Warwickshire 0V3 7QX, England | Actor |
| **Kingsolver, Barbara E**<br>PO Box 160, Meadowview VA 24361, USA | Writer |
| **Kingston, Alex**<br>Principal Entertainment, 9255 Sunset Blvd, #500, Los Angeles CA 90069 USA | Actress |
| **Kingston, George**<br>235 W Camino Descanso, Palm Springs CA 92264, USA | Ice Hockey Coach |
| **Kingston, Maxine Hong**<br>University of California, English Dept, Berkeley CA 94720, USA | Writer |
| **Kingston, Sean**<br>I C M Partners, 10250 Constellation Blvd, #900, Los Angeles CA 90067 USA | Rap Artist, Songwriter, Actor |
| **Kinkade, Mike**<br>3005 SE Spyglass Dr, Vancouver WA 98683, USA | Baseball Player |
| **Kinkel, Klaus**<br>Auswartigen Amt, Adenauerallee 101, 53113 Bonn, Germany | Government Official, Germany |
| **Kinley, Heather**<br>PO Box 128501, Nashville TN 37212, USA | Singer (Kinleys) |
| **Kinley, Jennifer**<br>Sony Records, 2100 Colorado Ave, Santa Monica CA 90404 USA | Singer (Kinleys) |
| **Kinmont, Kathleen**<br>9929 Sunset Blvd, #310, Los Angeles CA 90069, USA | Actress |
| **Kinnally, Jon**<br>W M E Entertainment, 9601 Wilshire Blvd, #300, Beverly Hills CA 90210 USA | Writer, Producer |
| **Kinnaman, Joel**<br>W M E Entertainment, 9601 Wilshire Blvd, #300, Beverly Hills CA 90210 USA | Actor |
| **Kinnear, Dominic**<br>San Jose Earthquakes, 451 El Camino Real, #220, Santa Clara CA 95050 USA | Soccer Player, Coach |
| **Kinnear, Greg**<br>Creative Artists Agency, 2000 Ave of Stars, #100, Los Angeles CA 90067 USA | Actor, Comedian |
| **Kinnear, James W, III**<br>149 Taconic Road, Greenwich CT 06831, USA | Businessman |
| **Kinnear, Rory**<br>Markham Froggatt Irwin, Julian House, 4 Windmill St, London W1P 1HF, England | Actor |
| **Kinnebrew, Larry D**<br>216 Kingston Ave NE, Rome GA 30161, USA | Football Player |
| **Kinney, Dallas**<br>13010 Silver Sands Dr, Fort Myers FL 33913, USA | Photojournalist |
| **Kinney, Dennis P**<br>1981 Arundel Road, Myrtle Beach SC 29577, USA | Baseball Player |
| **Kinney, Emily**<br>Abrams Artists, 9200 W Sunset Blvd, #1125, West Hollywood CA 90069 USA | Actress |
| **Kinney, Erron Q**<br>1103 State Blvd, Franklin TN 37064, USA | Football Player |
| **Kinney, Jeff**<br>Harry N Abrams/Amulet Publishers, 115 W 18th St, New York NY 10011, USA | Writer, Cartoonist |
| **Kinney, Jeffrey B (Jeff)**<br>2720 W 161st Terrace, Stilwell KS 66085, USA | Football Player |
| **Kinney, Kathy**<br>Truhett/Garcia Mgmt, 12031 Ventura Blvd, #4, Studio City CA 91604, USA | Actress |
| **Kinney, Matt**<br>12 Owens Way, Hermon ME 04401, USA | Baseball Player |
| **Kinney, Sean H**<br>Atmosphere Artists Mgmt, 6523 California Ave SW, #348, Seattle WA 98136, USA | Drummer (Alice in Chains) |
| **Kinney, Taylor**<br>Gersh Agency, 9465 Wilshire Blvd, #600, Beverly Hills CA 90212 USA | Actor |
| **Kinney, Terry**<br>Brookside Artists Mgmt, 250 W 57th St, #2303, New York NY 10107 USA | Actor |
| **Kinnock, Neil G**<br>European Communities Commission, 200 Rue de loi, 1049 Brussels, Belgium | Government Official, England |
| **Kinsella, John P**<br>PO Box 3067, Sumas WA 98295, USA | Swimmer |
| **Kinsella, Thomas**<br>639 Addison St, Philadelphia PA 19147, USA | Writer |
| **Kinsella, William Patrick (W P)**<br>9442 Nowell, Chilliwack BC V2P 4X7, Canada | Writer |
| **Kinser, Steve**<br>Kinser Racing, 280 E Smithville Road, Bloomington IN 47401, USA | Auto Racing Driver |
| **Kinsey, Angela**<br>United Talent Agency, U T A Plaza, 9336 Civic Center Dr, Beverly Hills CA 90210 USA | Actress |
| **Kinsey, Donald**<br>Jay Reil Assoc, 3490 Bayberry Dr, Northbrook IL 60062, USA | Singer, Guitarist (Kinsey Report) |
| **Kinsey, James L**<br>Rice University, Natural Sciences School, Houston TX 77005, USA | Chemist |
| **Kinsey, Kenneth**<br>Jay Reil Assoc, 3490 Bayberry Dr, Northbrook IL 60062, USA | Bassist (Kinsey Report) |
| **Kinsey, Ralph (Woody)**<br>Jay Reil Assoc, 3490 Bayberry Dr, Northbrook IL 60062, USA | Drummer (Kinsey Report) |
| **Kinshofer-Guthlein, Christa**<br>Munchnerstr 44, 83026 Rosenheim, Germany | Alpine Skier |
| **Kinski, Nastassja**<br>Resolution, 1801 Century Park E, #2300, Los Angeles CA 90067 USA | Actress, Model |
| **Kinsler, Ian M**<br>4029 Westmont Court, Bedford TX 76021, USA | Baseball Player |

Kingma - Kinsler

|  |  |
|---|---|
| **Kinsley, Michael E**<br>14150 NE 20th St, #527, Bellevue WA 98007, USA | Editor, Commentator |
| **Kinsman, Brent**<br>Coast to Coast Talent, 3350 Barham Blvd, Los Angeles CA 90068 USA | Actor |
| **Kinsman, Shane**<br>Coast to Coast Talent, 3350 Barham Blvd, Los Angeles CA 90068 USA | Actor |
| **Kinsman, T James (Jim)**<br>111 Howe Road E, Toledo WA 98591, USA | Vietnam War Army Hero (CMH) |
| **Kiper, Mel, Jr**<br>ESPN-TV, Sports Dept, ESPN Plaza, 935 Middle St, Bristol CT 06010 USA | Sportscaster |
| **Kipketer, Wilson**<br>Atletik Forbund, Idraettens Hus, Brondby Stadion 20, 2605 Brondby, Denmark | Track Athlete |
| **Kiplinger, Austin H**<br>Montevideo, 1680 River Road, Poolesville MD 20837, USA | Publisher |
| **Kipniss, Robert**<br>Hudson House, PO Box 112, Ardsley on Hudson NY 10503, USA | Artist |
| **Kipper, Robert W (Bob)**<br>117 Tuscany Way, Greer SC 29650, USA | Baseball Player |
| **Kiprusoff, Miikka S**<br>Calgary Flames, PO Box 1540, Station M, Calgary AB T2P 3B9, Canada | Ice Hockey Player |
| **Kipyego, Sally J**<br>Oregon Track Club, PO Box 11364, Eugene OR 97440, USA | Track Athlete |
| **Kiraly, Charles F (Karch)**<br>307 Boca del Canon, San Clemente CA 92672, USA | Volleyball Player, Coach |
| **Kiraly, John**<br>Lynn Roberts, 2410 Avenue A, Bradenton Beach FL 34217, USA | Artist |
| **Kirby, Luke**<br>Parseghian/Planco, 388 2nd Ave, #506, New York, NY 10010 USA | Actor |
| **Kirby, Peter**<br>Bobsled Canada, 140 Canada Olympic Road SW, Calgary AB T3B 5R5, Canada | Bobsled Athlete |
| **Kirby, Ronald H**<br>PO Box 337, Melville, 2109 Johannesburg, South Africa | Architect |
| **Kirby, Terry G**<br>744 Michelle Dr, Newport News VA 23601, USA | Football Player |
| **Kirby, Wayne L**<br>320 Kenya Road, Las Vegas NV 89123, USA | Baseball Player |
| **Kirch, Patrick V**<br>University of California, Anthropology Dept, Kroeber Hall, Berkeley CA 94720, USA | Archaeologist |
| **Kirchbach, Gunar**<br>Georgi-Dobrowolski-Str 10, 15517 Furstenwalde, Germany | Canoeing Athlete |
| **Kirchberger, Sonja**<br>Calle C'An Sanc 14, 07001 Palma de Mallorca, Baleares, Spain | Actress |
| **Kircheisen, Bjorn**<br>Georg-Baumgarten-Str 4, 08349 Johanngeorgenstadt, Germany | Nordic Combined Skier |
| **Kirchen, Bill**<br>328 Shrike Dr, Buda TX 78610, USA | Guitarist (Twangbangers) |
| **Kirchhoff, Ulrich**<br>Hoven 258, 48720 Rosendahl, Germany | Equestrian |
| **Kirchner, Cristina F**<br>Casa de Gobierno, Balcarce 50, Buenos Aires 1064, Argentina | President, Agentina |
| **Kirchner, Jamie Lee**<br>Gersh Agency, 41 Madison Ave, #3301, New York NY 10010 USA | Actress |
| **Kirchner, Mark**<br>Hauptstr 74A, 98749 Scheibe-Alsbach, Germany | Biathlete |
| **Kirchschlager, Angelika**<br>Mastroianni Assoc, 161 W 61st St, #32B, New York NY 10023, USA | Opera Singer |
| **Kiriasis, Sandra Prokoff**<br>Bonifatiusweg 6, 59955 Winterberg, Germany | Bobsled Athlete |
| **Kirilenko, Andrei G**<br>8 Spruce St, #75M, New York NY 10038, USA | Basketball Player |
| **Kirilenko, Maria Y**<br>Women's Tennis Assn, 1 Progress Plaza, #1500, Saint Petersburg FL 33701 USA | Tennis Player, Model |
| **Kirk, Justin**<br>Management 360, 9111 Wilshire Blvd, Beverly Hills CA 90210 USA | Actor |
| **Kirk, Rahsaan Roland**<br>Atlantic Records, 9229 W Sunset Blvd, #900, West Hollywood CA 90069 USA | Jazz Musician |
| **Kirk, Tammy Joe**<br>732 Peek Road, Dalton GA 30721, USA | Motorcyle Racing Rider, Auto Driver |
| **Kirk, Thomas B**<br>Brookhaven National Laboratory, Physics Dept, 2 Center St, Upton NY 11973, USA | Physicist |
| **Kirk, Tommy**<br>833 Beacon Ave, Los Angeles CA 90017, USA | Actor |
| **Kirkby, Emma**<br>Consort of Music, 54A Leamington Road Villas, London W11 1HT, England | Opera, Concert Singer |
| **Kirkcaldy, Robert**<br>Centers for Disease Control, S T D Prevention Center, 1600 Clifton Road NE, Atlanta GA 30329, USA | Epidemiologist |
| **Kirke, Jemima**<br>Creative Artists Agency, 2000 Ave of Stars, #100, Los Angeles CA 90067 USA | Actress |
| **Kirke, Simon**<br>Tabletop Productions, PO Box 698, Carson City NV 89702, USA | Drummer (Free, Bad Company) |
| **Kirkeby, Per**<br>Margarete Roeder Gallery, 545 Broadway, New York NY 10012, USA | Artist |
| **Kirkland, Douglas**<br>9060 Wonderland Park Ave, Los Angeles CA 90046, USA | Photographer |
| **Kirkland, Gelsey**<br>Dube Zakin Mgmt, 67 Riverside Dr, #3B, New York NY 10024, USA | Ballerina |
| **Kirkland, L Levon**<br>3255 Whitman Way, Tallahassee FL 32311, USA | Football Player |
| **Kirkland, Mike**<br>Bob Flick Productions, 300 Vine St, #14, Seattle WA 98121, USA | Singer, Banjo Player (Brothers Four) |
| **Kirkland, Ric**<br>Fortune Magazine, Time-Life Building, Rockefeller Center, New York NY 10020, USA | Editor |
| **Kirkland, Sally**<br>Greene Assoc, 1901 Ave of Stars, #130, Los Angeles CA 90067 USA | Actress |
| **Kirkland, Willie C**<br>19374 Northrup St, Detroit MI 48219, USA | Baseball Player |

**Kirkman, Rick** — Cartoonist (Baby Blues)
King Features Syndicate, 300 W 57th St, #1500, New York NY 10019 USA

**Kirkpatrick, Chris** — Singer ('N Sync)
Wright Entertainment, PO Box 590009, Orlando FL 32859 USA

**Kirkpatrick, D/Andre L (Dre)** — Football Player
Cincinnati Bengals, 1 Paul Brown Stadium, Cincinnati OH 45202 USA

**Kirkpatrick, Kevin** — Actor
Stone Manners Salners, 6100 Wilshire Blvd, #1500, Los Angeles CA 90035 USA

**Kirkpatrick, Maggie** — Actress
Karen Kay Mgmt, PO Box 446, Auckland 1140, New Zealand

**Kirkwood, Curt** — Singer (Meat Puppets)
High Road Touring, 751 Bridgeway, #200, Sausalito CA 94965 USA

**Kirkwood, Donald P (Don)** — Baseball Player
455 W Elmwood Ave, Clawson MI 48017, USA

**Kirla, John A** — WW II Army Air Corps Hero
447 Main St, PO Box 396, Deep River CT 06417, USA

**Kirn, Walter** — Writer
Creative Artists Agency, 2000 Ave of Stars, #100, Los Angeles CA 90067 USA

**Kirner, Gary B** — Football Player
3507 Senasac Ave, Long Beach CA 90808, USA

**Kirrane, John J (Jack), Jr** — Ice Hockey Player
3 Country Road, Chestnut MA 02467, USA

**Kirrene, Joseph J (Joe)** — Baseball Player
2557 Kilpatrick Court, San Ramon CA 94583, USA

**Kirsch, Russell** — Inventor (Square Pixels)
4610 SW Greenhills Way, Portland OR 97221, USA

**Kirsch, Stan** — Actor
Stan Kirsch Studios, 6671 Sunset Blvd, #1584-A, Los Angeles CA 90028, USA

**Kirschke, Travis** — Football Player
10196 Crooked Stick Trail, Lone Tree CO 80124, USA

**Kirschner, Carl** — Educator
Rutgers State University College, President's Office, New Brunswick NJ 08093, USA

**Kirschner, David M** — Animator, Producer
David Kirschner Productions, 400 S June St, Los Angeles CA 90020, USA

**Kirschner, Marc W** — Cell Biologist
Harvard Medical School, Cell Biology Dept, 25 Shattuck St, Boston MA 02115, USA

**Kirschstein, Ruth L** — Physician
6 West Dr, Bethesda MD 20814, USA

**Kirshbaum, Ralph** — Concert Cellist
Ingpen & Williams, 131 Putney Bridge Road, London SW15 2PA, England

**Kirshner, Mia** — Actress
Gersh Agency, 9465 Wilshire Blvd, #600, Beverly Hills CA 90212 USA

**Kirst, Michael W** — Educator
Stanford University, Education School, Stanford CA 94305, USA

**Kirstein, Peter T** — Computer Scientist
University College, Computer Science Dept, London WC1E 6BT, England

**Kirszenstein Szewinska, Irena** — Track Athlete
Ul Bagno 5 m 80, 00112 Warsaw, Poland

**Kirtadze, Nino** — Actress
GoDigital Media Group, 233 Wilshire Blvd, #100, Santa Monica CA 90401, USA

**Kirton, Mark R** — Ice Hockey Player
251 N Service Road W, Oakville ON L6M 3E7, Canada

**Kirvesniemi, Harri** — Cross Country Skier
Karhu Ski, Henrikinkatu 2, 21100 Naantali, Finland

**Kirwan, Larry** — Singer, Guitarist (Black 47)
Skyline Music, 28 Union St, Whitefield NH 03598, USA

**Kirwan, William E, II** — Educator
3112 Old Court Road, Pikesville MD 21208, USA

**Kisabaka, Lisa** — Track Athlete
Franz-Hitze-Str 22, 51372 Leverkusen, Germany

**Kiser, Garland R** — Baseball Player
267 Carr Dr, Blountville TN 37617, USA

**Kiser, Terry** — Actor
Innovative Artists, 1505 10th St, Santa Monica CA 90401 USA

**Kishida, Shuzo** — Chef, Restauranteur
Restaurant Quintessence, 6-7-29 Garden City Shinagawa Gotenyama, Tokyo 141 0001, Japan

**Kishlansky, Mark A** — Historian
Harvard University, History Dept, Cambridge MA 02138, USA

**Kisio, Kelly W** — Ice Hockey Player
Calgary Hitmen, PO Box 1420 Station Main, Calgary AB T2P 3B9, Canada

**Kisner, Jacob** — Writer
245 Park Ave S, #PH F, New York NY 10003, USA

**Kison, Bruce E** — Baseball Player
1403 Riverview Circle, Bradenton FL 34209, USA

**Kissane, James J (Jim)** — Basketball Player
6 Mellen Lane, Wayland MA 01778, USA

**Kissin, Evgeni I** — Concert Pianist
I M G Artists, Carnegie Hall Tower, 152 W 57th St, #500, New York NY 10019 USA

**Kissinger, Henry A** — Secretary, State; Nobel Peace Laureate
PO Box 38, South Kent CT 06785, USA

**Kissling, Conny** — Freestyle Skier
Hubel, 3254 Messen, Switzerland

**Kistler, Darci** — Ballerina
New York City Ballet, Lincoln Center Plaza, New York NY 10023 USA

**Kita, Toshiyuki** — Industrial Designer
TS Bild 2F, 3-1-2 Tenma, Kitauku, Osaka 530 0043, Japan

**Kitaen, Tawny** — Actress
Brady Brannon Rich, 5670 Wilshire Blvd, #820, Los Angeles CA 90036 USA

**Kitamura, Ryuhei** — Director
Capitol Motion Pictures, 610 Brazos, #300D, Austin TX 78701, USA

**Kitano, Takeshi** — Actor, Director, Writer
Office Kitano, 5-4-14 Akasaka Minataku, 107 0052 Tokyo, Japan

**Kitaro** — Musician, Composer
Hands On Public Relations, 9800-D Topanga Canyon Blvd, #117, Chatsworth CA 91311, USA

**Kitayawa, Keiko** — Actress, Model
Stardust Promotion, 2-3-3-2F Ebisu Nishi, Shibuya, Tokyo 150 0021, Japan

Kirkman - Kitayawa

| | |
|---|---|
| **Kitayenko, Dmitri G** | Conductor |
| Chalet Kalimor, 1652 Botterens, Switzerland | |
| **Kitbunchu, M Michai Cardinal** | Religious Leader |
| Archdiocese of Bangkok, Charoenkrung Road 40, Bangrak, Bangkok 10500, Thailand | |
| **Kitchell, Sonya** | Singer, Songwriter |
| Monterey International, 200 W Superior St, #202, Chicago IL 60654 USA | |
| **Kitchen, Curtis** | Basketball Player |
| 343 19th Ave, Seattle WA 98122, USA | |
| **Kitchen, Michael** | Actor |
| Rights House, Drury House, 34-43 Russell St, London WC2B 5HA, England | |
| **Kitchen, Mike** | Ice Hockey Player, Coach |
| 5570 NE Trieste Way, Boca Raton FL 33487, USA | |
| **Kite, Gregory F (Greg)** | Basketball Player |
| 3060 Seigneury Dr, Windermere FL 34786, USA | |
| **Kite, Thomas O (Tom), Jr** | Golfer |
| 907 Terrace Mountain Dr, West Lake Hills TX 78746, USA | |
| **Kitsch, Taylor** | Actor |
| Rogers & Cowan, 8687 Melrose Ave, #G700, West Hollywood CA 90069 USA | |
| **Kitson, Linda F** | Artist |
| 1 Argyll Mansions, Kings Road, London SW3 5ER, England | |
| **Kitsopoulos, Constantine** | Conductor |
| I M G Artists, Hogarth Business Park, Chiswick, London W4 2TH, England | |
| **Kitt, A J** | Alpine Skier |
| Colt Realty Group, 509 Cascade Ave, #A, Hood River OR 97031, USA | |
| **Kittel, Charles** | Physicist |
| University of California, Physics Dept, Berkeley CA 94720, USA | |
| **Kittinger, Joseph W (Joe), Jr** | Parachutist, Balloonist |
| 608 Mariner Way, Altamonte Springs FL 32701, USA | |
| **Kittle, Ronald D (Ron)** | Baseball Player |
| 1840 Tour Trace, Chesterton IN 46304, USA | |
| **Kittles, Tory** | Actor |
| A P A Talent & Literary Agency, 405 S Beverly Dr, #300, Beverly Hills CA 90212 USA | |
| **Kittredge, William A** | Writer |
| 42 Brookside Way, Missoula MT 59802, USA | |
| **Kitum, Timothy** | Track Athlete |
| PO Box 49, Kapsowar, Marakwet District, Kenya | |
| **Kivelson, Margaret Galland** | Physicist |
| University of California, Earth & Space Sciences Dept, Los Angeles CA 90024, USA | |
| **Kiwanuka, Mathias K** | Football Player |
| 456 9th St, #13, Hoboken NJ 07030, USA | |
| **Kiyosaki, Robert T** | Writer |
| Cashflow Technologies, 4330 N Civic Center Plaza, #100, Scottsdale AZ 85251, USA | |
| **Kjall, Viktor E** | Curling Athlete |
| Curling Association, Idrottshuser, Marbackagatan 19, 123 43 Farsta, Sweden | |
| **Kjus, Lasse** | Alpine Skier |
| Rugdeveien 2C, 1404 Siggerud, Norway | |
| **Klabunde, Charles S** | Artist |
| 68 W 3rd St, New York NY 10012, USA | |
| **Klaes, Ulrich** | Field Hockey Player |
| Herbert-Albert-Str 1B, 68259 Mannheim, Germany | |
| **Klammer, Franz** | Alpine Skier |
| Mooswald 22, 9712 Friesach, Austria | |
| **Klaplisch, Cedric** | Director, Writer |
| Ce Qui Me Meut Motion Pictures, 23 Passage de la Main d'Or, 75011 Paris, France | |
| **Klapman, Lia** | Sculptor |
| 2581 Mission St, Santa Cruz CA 95060, USA | |
| **Klarik, Jeffrey** | Producer, Writer |
| W M E Entertainment, 9601 Wilshire Blvd, #300, Beverly Hills CA 90210 USA | |
| **Klas, Eri** | Conductor |
| C M Artists, 127 W 96th St, #13B, New York NY 10025 USA | |
| **Klassen, Daniel V (Danny)** | Baseball Player |
| 28925 N 111th Place, Scottsdale AZ 85262, USA | |
| **Klatt, Trent T** | Ice Hockey Player |
| 267 SW 12th Ave, Grand Rapids MN 55744, USA | |
| **Klattenhoff, Diego** | Actor |
| Amanda Rosenthal, 543 Richmond St W, #123, PO Box 205, Toronto ON M5V 1Y6, Canada | |
| **Klausing, Chuck** | Football Coach |
| 2115 Lazor St, Indiana PA 15701, USA | |
| **Klausner, Julie** | Actress, Writer |
| Avalon Mgmt, 8332 Melrose Ave, #200, Los Angeles CA 90069, USA | |
| **Klausner, Richard D** | Cell Biologist |
| Column Group, 1700 Owens Street, #500, San Francisco CA 94158, USA | |
| **Klavan, Andrew** | Writer |
| Gersh Agency, 9465 Wilshire Blvd, #600, Beverly Hills CA 90212 USA | |
| **Klaveno, Mariana** | Actress |
| A P A Talent & Literary Agency, 405 S Beverly Dr, #300, Beverly Hills CA 90212 USA | |
| **Klawe, Maria** | Educator |
| Harvey Mudd College, President's Office, Claremont CA 91711, USA | |
| **Klawitter, Thomas C (Tom)** | Baseball Player |
| 605 Foxglove Lane, Whitewater WI 53190, USA | |
| **Klaws, Alexander** | Singer, Actor |
| Cruiser Entertainment, Neuer Pferdemarkt 1, 20359 Hamburg, Germany | |
| **Klecko, Joseph E (Joe)** | Football Player |
| 6 Victorian Way, Colts Neck NJ 07722, USA | |
| **Klee, Ken** | Ice Hockey Player |
| 78 W Ranch Trail, Morrison CO 80465, USA | |
| **Klees, Christian** | Marksman |
| Eutiner Sportschutzen, Schutzenweg 26, 23701 Eutin, Germany | |
| **Kleibeuker, Carien** | Speed Skater |
| K N S B, Postbus 1120, 3800 Arnesfoort BC, Netherlands | |
| **Kleibrink, Benjamin** | Fencer |
| F C Tauberbischofsheim, Pestalozziallee 12, 97941 Tauberbischofsheim, Germany | |
| **Kleibrink, Shannon** | Curling Athlete |
| Curling Association, 1660 Vimont Court, Cumberland ON K4A 4J4, Canada | |
| **Klein, Abigail** | Actress |
| Brillstein Entertainment Partners, 9150 Wilshire Blvd, #350, Beverly Hills CA 90212 USA | |

**Klein, Calvin R** — Fashion Designer
650 Meadow Lane, Southampton NY 11968, USA

**Klein, Chris** — Actor
I C M Partners, 10250 Constellation Blvd, #900, Los Angeles CA 90067 USA

**Klein, Dale E** — Government Official
US Nuclear Regulatory Commission, 11555 Rockville Pike, Rockville MD 20852, USA

**Klein, Danny** — Bassist (J Geils Band)
Nick Ben-Meir, 652 N Doheny Dr, West Hollywood CA 90069, USA

**Klein, David** — Geneticist
National Child Health Institute, 49 Convent Dr, Bethesda MD 20892, USA

**Klein, Edward** — Writer
Random House, 1745 Broadway, #1800, New York NY 10019 USA

**Klein, Emilee** — Golfer
5350 E Deer Valley Dr, #1431, Phoenix AZ 85054, USA

**Klein, George** — Tumor Biologist
Kottlavagen 10, 181 61 Lidingo, Sweden

**Klein, Hans-Joachim** — Swimmer
Schuchardstr 7, 64283 Darmstadt, Germany

**Klein, Jess** — Singer, Guitarist, Songwriter
Invasion Group, 133 W 25th St, #500, New York NY 10001, USA

**Klein, Joe** — Journalist, Writer
Time, Editorial Dept, Time-Life Building, 1271 Ave of Americas, New York NY 10020, USA

**Klein, Joel** — Attorney, Government Official, Educator
New York City Schools, Chancellor's Office, 110 Livingston, Brooklyn NY 11201, USA

**Klein, Lester A** — Urologist
Scripps Clinic, Urology Dept, 10666 N Torrey Pines Road, La Jolla CA 92037, USA

**Klein, Marci** — Producer
Slate Public Relations, 9000 Sunset Blvd, #915, West Hollywood CA 90069 USA

**Klein, Richard G** — Paleoanthropologist
Stanford University, Anthropology Services Dept, Stanford CA 94305, USA

**Klein, Robert** — Actor, Comedian
Park Avenue Talent, 1560 Broadway, #1211, New York NY 10036, USA

**Klein, Robert O (Bob)** — Football Player
15263 Friends St, Pacific Palisades CA 90272, USA

**Kleine, Joseph W (Joe)** — Basketball Player
53 Hickory Hills Circle, Little Rock AR 72212, USA

**Kleiner, Jeremy** — Producer
Plan B Entertainment, 9150 Wilshire Blvd, #350, Beverly Hills CA 90212, USA

**Kleinert, Harold E** — Microsurgeon
225 Abraham Flexner Way, #700, Louisville KY 40202, USA

**Kleinfeld, Andrew J** — Judge
US Court of Appeals, Courthouse Square, 250 Cushman St, Fairbanks AK 99701, USA

**Kleinfeld, Klaus C** — Businessman
Alcoa Global Center, 390 Park Ave, New York NY 10022, USA

**Kleinman, Arthur M** — Anthropologist, Psychiatrist
Harvard University, Anthropology Dept, Cambridge MA 02138, USA

**Kleinrock, Leonard** — Computer Scientist, Engineer
601 N Elm Dr, Beverly Hills CA 90210, USA

**Kleinsasser, Jimmy C (Jim)** — Football Player
6835 Cardinal Cove Dr, Mound MN 55364, USA

**Kleinsmith, Bruce** — Cartoonist
PO Box 1083, San Juan Bautista CA 95045, USA

**Kleintank, Luke** — Actor
Robert Stein Management, 345 N Maple Dr, #317, Beverly Hills CA 90210, USA

**Kleiser, Randal** — Director
3050 Runyan Canyon Road, Los Angeles CA 90046, USA

**Kleiza, Linas** — Basketball Player
Toronto Raptors, Air Canada Center, 20 Bay St, Toronto ON M5J 2N8, Canada

**Klembaum, Sharon** — Religious Leader, Rabbi
Congregation Beth Simchat Torah, 57 Bethune St, New York NY 10014, USA

**Klemm, Adrian W** — Football Player
900 W Olympic Blvd, #43D, Los Angeles CA 90015, USA

**Klemm, Jon** — Ice Hockey Player
400 61st St, Willowbrook IL 60527, USA

**Klemmer, John** — Jazz Saxophonist
Boardman, 10548 Clearwood Court, Los Angeles CA 90077, USA

**Klemperer, William** — Chemist
53 Shattuck Road, Watertown MA 02472, USA

**Klemt, Becky** — Attorney
Pence & MacMillan, PO Box 1285, Laramie WY 82073, USA

**Klesko, Ryan A** — Baseball Player
735 Henderson Mill Road, Covington GA 30014, USA

**Klesla, Rotislav** — Ice Hockey Player
6751 N Sunset Blvd, #200, Glendale AZ 85305, USA

**Klett, Peter** — Guitarist (Candlebox)
Novi Entertainment, 201 N Robertson Blvd, #201, Beverly Hills CA 90211, USA

**Klever, Victor K (Rocky)** — Football Player
3829 W 42nd St, Anchorage AK 99517, USA

**Kley, Chaney** — Actor
Paradigm Agency, 360 N Crescent Dr, North Building, Beverly Hills CA 90210 USA

**Klibanoff, Hank** — Journalist, Historian
Emory University, Journalism Dept, 201 Dowman Drive, Atlanta GA 30322, USA

**Klim, Michael** — Swimmer
177 Bridge Road, Richmond VIC 3121, Australia

**Klima** — Singer, Songwriter (Klima)
Klimamusik Mgmt, Abt-Farcher-Weg 2, 83370 Seeon, Germany

**Klima, Petr** — Ice Hockey Player
1001 Forest Lane, Bloomfield Hills MI 48301, USA

**Klimchock, Louis S (Lou)** — Baseball Player
8876 S Myrtle Ave, Tempe AZ 85284, USA

**Klimisch, Dick** — Inventor (Auto Catalytic Converter)
43 Fairfold Road, Grosse Pointe Shores MI 48236, USA

**Klimke, Ingrid** — Equestrian
Kanalstr 340, 48159 Munster, Germany

**Klimke, Reiner** — Equestrian
Krumme Str 3, 48143 Munster, Germany

# K

**Klimov, Fedor A** — Figure Skater
Figure Skating Federation, Luzhnetskaya Nab 8, 119991 Moscow, Russia

**Klimova, Marina V** — Ice Dancer
Sharks Ice, 1500 S 10th St, San Jose CA 95112, USA

**Klimuk, Pyotr I** — Cosmonaut, Air Force General
Cosmonaut Training Center, Star City, 141160 Zvezdny Gorodok, Moscow Oblast, Russia

**Kline, J Robert (Bobby)** — Baseball Player
6656 31st Way S, Saint Petersburg FL 33712, USA

**Kline, Jeff** — Writer, Producer
Creative Artists Agency, 2000 Ave of Stars, #100, Los Angeles CA 90067 USA

**Kline, Kevin D** — Actor
1636 3rd Ave, #309, New York NY 10128, USA

**Kline, Richard** — Actor
Harden-Curtis Co, 214 W 29th St, #1203, New York NY 10001, USA

**Kline, Richard H** — Cinematographer
1001 Tiverton Ave, #2141, Los Angeles CA 90024, USA

**Kline-Randall, Maxine** — Baseball Player
105 Nottingham Road, Bloomsberg PA 17815, USA

**Kling, Anja** — Actress
Agentur Margarita Kling, Amselweg 6, 14557 Wilhelmhorst, Germany

**Kling, Gerit** — Actress
Pegasus Theater & Medienverlag, Bleibtustr 38/39 10623 Berlin, Germany

**Klingbeil, Charles (Chuck)** — Football Player
47921 US Highway 41, Houghton MI 49931, USA

**Klingenbeck, Scott E** — Baseball Player
6230 Kincora Court, Cincinnati OH 45233, USA

**Klingensmith, Michael J** — Publisher
Entertainment Weekly, Rockefeller Center, New York NY 10020, USA

**Klingler, David R** — Football Player
Dallas Theological Seminary, 6000 Dale Carnegie Lane, Houston TX 77036, USA

**Klinsmann, Jurgen** — Soccer Player, Coach
F C Bayern Munich, Postfach 900451, 81504 Munich, Germany

**Klishina, Darya I** — Track Athlete, Model
C S K A, Leningrad Prospect 39, 125167 Moscow A167, Russia

**Klitschko, Vitali V** — Boxer
Klitschko Management Group, Grosse Elbstr 275, 22767 Hamburg, Germany

**Klitschko, Wladimir** — Boxer
Klitschko Management Group, Grosse Elbstr 275, 22767 Hamburg, Germany

**Klocke, Piet** — Actor, Comedian
Agentur Alexia Agathos, Leostr 11, 50823 Cologne, Germany

**Klooparens, Beth** — Architect
Klooparens Inc, 250 5th Ave, New York NY 10001, USA

**Klop, Cody** — Actor
Curtis Talent Management, 9607 Arby Dr, Beverly Hills CA 90210, USA

**Klose, Miroslav** — Soccer Player
A S B W Sport Marketing, Hubertusstr 8, 65549 Limburg, Germany

**Kloser, Harald** — Composer
Gorfaine/Schwartz, 4111 W Alameda Ave, #509, Burbank CA 91505 USA

**Kloss, Karlie E** — Model
Next Model Mgmt, 23 Watts St, New York NY 10013 USA

**Klotz, Frank G** — Air Force General
Commander, Air Global Strike Force Command, Barksdale Air Force Base LA 71110, USA

**Klotz, Irving M** — Chemist, Biochemist
1500 Sheridan Road, #7D, Wilmette IL 60091, USA

**Klotz, John S (Jack)** — Football Player
729 E 25th St, Chester PA 19013, USA

**Klous, Patricia** — Actress
2539 Benedict Canyon Dr, Beverly Hills CA 90210, USA

**Kloves, Steve** — Director, Writer
Creative Artists Agency, 2000 Ave of Stars, #100, Los Angeles CA 90067 USA

**Klueh, Duane** — Basketball Player, Coach
200 Francis Avenue Court, #211, Terre Haute IN 47804, USA

**Klug, Aaron** — Nobel Chemistry Laureate
70 Cavendish Ave, Cambridge CB1 4OT, England

**Klug, Chris** — Snowboard Skier
Chris Klug Foundation, 182 Riverdown Dr, Aspen CO 81611, USA

**Kluger, Richard** — Writer
Random House, 1745 Broadway, #1800, New York NY 10019 USA

**Klugh, Earl** — Jazz Guitarist
I C M Partners, 10250 Constellation Blvd, #900, Los Angeles CA 90067 USA

**Klum, Heidi** — Model, Actress
W M E Entertainment, 9601 Wilshire Blvd, #300, Beverly Hills CA 90210 USA

**Klum, Mattias** — Photographer
Svanliden, Hammarskog, 755 91 Uppsala, Sweden

**Klunk, William E** — Neurologist
Alzheimer's Disease Laboratory, 200 Lothrop St, Pittsburgh PA 15213, USA

**Klutts, Gene E (Mickey)** — Baseball Player
6136 Maple Ave, Lake Isabella CA 93240, USA

**Kluttz, Lonnie** — Basketball Player
183 Greenwing Lane, Saint Matthews SC 29135, USA

**Kluwe, Christopher J (Chris)** — Football Player
13026 Ottawa Dr, Savage MN 55378, USA

**K'Maro** — Singer, Rap Artist, Songwriter
Warner Music, Alter Wandrahm 14, 20457 Hamburg, Germany

**K'Naan** — Rap Artist, Singer, Guitarist
Paquin Entertainment, 206B-219 Dufferin St, Toronto ON M6K 3J1, Canada

**Knackert, Brent B** — Baseball Player
16802 Leafwood Circle, Huntington Beach CA 92647, USA

**Knafelc, Gary** — Football Player
2147 Burley Ave, Clermont FL 34711, USA

**Knaifel, Alexander A** — Composer
Skobelevski Pr 5, #130, 194214 Saint Petersburg, Russia

**Knape Lindberg, Ulrike** — Diver
Drostvagen 7, 691 33 Karlskoga, Sweden

**Knapkova, Miroslava** — Rowing Athlete
V K Slavia Prague, Nabrezni 87, 15000 Prague 5, Czech Republic

**Knapp, Alexis** — Actress
Creative Artists Agency, 2000 Ave of Stars, #100, Los Angeles CA 90067 USA
**Knapp, Charles B** — Educator
120 Brookview Circle N, Atlanta GA 30339, USA
**Knapp, Cleon T** — Publisher
Talewood Corp, 8939 S Sepulveda Blvd, #110, Los Angeles CA 90045, USA
**Knapp, Jennifer L** — Singer
Maximum Artist Mgmt, 1305 Clinton St, #200-A, Nashville TN 37203, USA
**Knapp, John W** — Educator, Army General
Virginia Military Institute, Superintendent's Office, Lexington VA 24450, USA
**Knapp, R Christian (Chris)** — Baseball Player
788 Rich Dr, Oviedo FL 32765, USA
**Knapp, Steven** — Educator
George Washington University, President's Office, Washington DC 20052, USA
**Knaus, Chad A** — Auto Racing Crew Chief
149 Pin Oak Lane, Mooresville NC 28117, USA
**Knaus, William A** — Physician, Medical Activist
University of Virginia Medical School, Public Health Service Dept, Charlottesville VA 22908, USA
**Knauss, Hans** — Alpine Skier
Fastenberg 60, 8970 Schladming, Austria
**Knauss, Melania** — Model
T Mgmt, 91 5th Ave, #300, New York NY 10003 USA
**Kneale, R Bryan C** — Sculptor
10A Muswell Road, London N10 2BG, England
**Knebel, John A** — Secretary, Agriculture
1418 Laburnum St, McLean VA 22101, USA
**Knepper, Robert** — Actor
Innovative Artists, 1505 10th St, Santa Monica CA 90401 USA
**Knepper, Robert W (Bob)** — Baseball Player
5704 Callcott Way, #E, Alexandria VA 22312, USA
**Kness, Richard M** — Opera Singer
240 Central Park South, #16M, New York NY 10019, USA
**Kneuer, Cameo** — Physical Fitness Expert
Starshape by Cameo, 2554 Lincoln Blvd, #640, Venice CA 90291, USA
**Knezevic, Milena** — Handball Player
Z R K Buducnost, Ivana Milutinovica BB, 81000 Podgorica, Montenegro
**Knibb, Sean** — Landscape Architect
Knibb Design, 141 S Barrington Ave, Los Angeles CA 90049, USA
**Knicely, Alan L** — Baseball Player
PO Box 433, Dayton VA 22821, USA
**Knickman, Roy** — Cyclist
436 Fallbrook Ave, Newbury Park CA 91320, USA
**Knight, Beverly** — Singer, Songwriter
D W L, 53 Goodge St, #200, London W1T 1TG, England
**Knight, Brandon M** — Baseball Player
191 S Pacific Ave, #B, Ventura CA 93001, USA
**Knight, Brevin** — Basketball Player
3226 Bedford Lane, Germantown TN 38139, USA
**Knight, C Ray** — Baseball Player, Manager
PO Box 129, Auburn AL 36831, USA
**Knight, Charles F** — Businessman
Emerson Electric Co, 8000 W Florissant Ave, Box 41000, Saint Louis MO 63136, USA
**Knight, Chris** — Singer, Songwriter
Rick Alter Mgmt, 1018 17th Ave S, #12, Nashville TN 37212, USA
**Knight, Christopher** — Actor
Identity Talent Agency, 9107 Wilshire Blvd, #450, Beverly Hills CA 90210 USA
**Knight, David R** — Football Player
2600 Farm Road, Alexandria VA 22302, USA
**Knight, Gladys** — Singer
Shakeji, 3221 La Mirada Ave, Las Vegas NV 89120, USA
**Knight, Hilary A** — Ice Hockey Player
USA Hockey, 1775 Bob Johnson Dr, Colorado Springs CO 80906 USA
**Knight, Jean** — Singer
Acts Nashville, 1103 Bell Grimes Lane, Nashville TN 37207, USA
**Knight, Jonathan** — Singer (New Kids on the Block)
90 Apple St, Essex MA 01929, USA
**Knight, Jordan** — Singer (New Kids on the Block)
Supreme Entertainment Artists, PO Box 15601, Boston MA 02115, USA
**Knight, Keith** — Cartoonist (K Chronicles)
PO Box 341862, Los Angeles CA 90034, USA
**Knight, L Curtis (Curt), Jr** — Football Player
7230 Rio Flora Place, Downey CA 90241, USA
**Knight, Negele** — Basketball Player
18624 N 4th Ave, Phoenix AZ 85027, USA
**Knight, Philip H** — Businessman
Nike Inc, 1 SW Bowerman Dr, Beaverton OR 97005, USA
**Knight, Robert M (Bobby)** — Basketball Coach
8003 County Road 6910, Lubbock TX 79407, USA
**Knight, Shirley** — Actress
Diamond Mgmt, 31 Percy St, London W1T 2DD, England
**Knight, Sterling** — Actor
Greene Assoc, 1901 Ave of Stars, #130, Los Angeles CA 90067 USA
**Knight, Steven** — Writer
Creative Artists Agency, 2000 Ave of Stars, #100, Los Angeles CA 90067 USA
**Knight, T R** — Actor
Innovative Artists, 1505 10th St, Santa Monica CA 90401 USA
**Knight, Thomas L (Tommy)** — Football Player
70 Overington Ave, Marlton NJ 08053, USA
**Knight, Travis J** — Basketball Player
3159 Millcreek Road, Pleasant Grove UT 84062, USA
**Knight, Tuesday** — Actress
Stephany Hurkos Mgmt, 11935 Kling St, #10, Valley Village CA 91607 USA
**Knight, Wayne** — Actor, Comedian
Brillstein Entertainment Partners, 9150 Wilshire Blvd, #350, Beverly Hills CA 90212 USA
**Knight, William R (Billy)** — Basketball Player, Executive
1051 Bluffhaven Way NE, Atlanta GA 30319, USA

**Knightley, Keira** — Actress
United Agents, 12-26 Lexington St, London W1F 0LE, England

**Knighton, Zachary** — Actor
United Talent Agency, U T A Plaza, 9336 Civic Center Dr, Beverly Hills CA 90210 USA

**Knight-Pulliam, Keshia** — Actress
PO Box 866, Teaneck NJ 07666, USA

**Knights, Dave** — Bassist (Procol Harum)
195 Sandycombe Road, Kew TW9 2EW, England

**Knisley, Sam** — Basketball Player
14808 Hanover Pike, Upperco MD 21155, USA

**Knizka, Roman** — Actor
Girke Mgmt, Nymphenburgerstr 4, 10825 Berlin, Germany

**Knoblauch, E Charles (Chuck)** — Baseball Player
11702 Forest Glen St, Houston TX 77024, USA

**Knochenhauer, Agnes** — Curling Athlete
Curling Association, Idrottshuser, Marbackagatan 19, 123 43 Farsta, Sweden

**Knoff, Kurt** — Football Player
11121 Bluestem Lane, Eden Prairie MN 55347, USA

**Knol, Monique** — Cyclist
Draarlier 6, 3766 Soest ET, Netherlands

**Knoll, Andrew H** — Paleontologist
Harvard University, Botanical Museum, 26 Oxford St, Cambridge MA 02138, USA

**Knoll, Jozsef** — Pharmacologist
Semmelweis Medical University, Pharmacology Dept, 1445 Budapest, Hungary

**Knoop, Robert F (Bobby)** — Baseball Player
2543 E Mountain Sky Ave, Phoenix AZ 85048, USA

**Knopf, Sascha** — Actress, Model
Stone Manners Salners, 6100 Wilshire Blvd, #1500, Los Angeles CA 90035 USA

**Knopfler, David** — Guitarist (Dire Straits)
Damage Mgmt, 16 Lambton Place, London W11 2SH, England

**Knopfler, Mark** — Singer, Guitarist (Dire Straits)
Paul Crockford Mgmt, 272 Latimer Road, London W10 6QY, England

**Knorr, Randy D** — Baseball Player
3200 Arville St, #279, Las Vegas NV 89102, USA

**Knowles, Beyonce** — Singer, Actress, Model
1412 Broadway, #2400, New York NY 10018, USA

**Knowles, Darold D** — Baseball Player
1515 Whisper Wind Lane, Oldsmar FL 34677, USA

**Knowles, Michael R** — Medical Researcher
University of North Carolina Medical School, Pulmonary & Critical Care Dept, Chapel Hill NC 27599, USA

**Knowles, Rodney** — Basketball Player
3592 Island Dr, North Topsail Beach NC 28460, USA

**Knowles, Sabrina** — Artist
3824 SW Morgan St, Seattle WA 98126, USA

**Knowles, Solange** — Actress, Singer
I C M Partners, 10250 Constellation Blvd, #900, Los Angeles CA 90067 USA

**Knowlson, Elizabeth** — Writer
Bloomsbury Publishing, 50 Bedford Square, London WC1B 3DP, England

**Knowlson, James R** — Writer
Bloomsbury Publishing, 50 Bedford Square, London WC1B 3DP, England

**Knowlton, Steve R** — Skier
Palmer Yeager Assoc, 6600 E Hampden Ave, #210, Denver CO 80224, USA

**Knox, Charles R (Chuck)** — Football Coach
48711 San Vicente St, La Quinta CA 92253, USA

**Knox, Deborah** — Curling Athlete
Curling Association, 14 Donnelly Dr, Bedford, Bedfordshire MK4 9TU, England

**Knox, Heather** — Model
Playboy Promotions, 9346 Civic Center Dr, #200, Beverly Hills CA 90210 USA

**Knox, Kenny** — Golfer
3813 Dills Road, Monticello FL 32344, USA

**Knox, Ruth A** — Educator
Wesleyan College, President's Office, 4760 Forsyth Road, Macon GA 31210, USA

**Knox, Taylor** — Surfer
Pro Surfing Mgmt, 320 High Tide Dr, #101, Saint Augustine FL 32080 USA

**Knox, Terence** — Actor
House of Representatives, 1434 6th St, #1, Santa Monica CA 90401 USA

**Knox-Johnston, W R P (Robin)** — Yachtsman
26 Sefton St, Putney, London SW15, England

**Knoxville, Johnny** — Actor, Comedian
Creative Artists Agency, 2000 Ave of Stars, #100, Los Angeles CA 90067 USA

**Knuble, Michael (Mike)** — Ice Hockey Player
2107 San Lu Rae Dr SE, Grand Rapids MI 49506, USA

**Knudsen, Erik** — Actor
Fountainhead Talent, 131 Davenport Road, Toronto ON M5R 1H8, Canada

**Knudsen, Lars** — Producer
United Talent Agency, U T A Plaza, 9336 Civic Center Dr, Beverly Hills CA 90210 USA

**Knudson, Alfred G, Jr** — Geneticist
Institute for Cancer Research, 7701 Burholme Ave, Philadelphia PA 19111, USA

**Knudson, Mark R** — Baseball Player
881 W 100th Ave, Northglenn CO 80260, USA

**Knudson, Thomas J** — Journalist
Sacramento Bee, Editorial Dept, 21st & Q Sts, Sacramento CA 95852, USA

**Knuppe, Franziska** — Model
Model Mgmt, Hartungstr 5, 20146 Hamburg, Germany

**Knussen, S Oliver** — Conductor, Composer
BBC Symphony Orchestra, BBC Maida Vale Studios, Delaware Road, London W9 2LG, England

**Knuth, Donald E** — Computer Scientist; Kyoto Laureate
Stanford University, Computer Science Dept, Gates Building, Stanford CA 94305, USA

**Knuth, Shay** — Model
Playboy Promotions, 9346 Civic Center Dr, #200, Beverly Hills CA 90210 USA

**Ko Gi-Hyun** — Speed Skater
Skating Union, 88 Bangyee-Dong, Songpaku, Seoul 138 749, South Korea

**Ko Un** — Writer
Anseong, Gyeonggi-do 456 600, South Korea

**Ko, Lydia** — Golfer
Gulf Harbour Country Club, 180 Gulf Harbour Drive, Whangaparaoa 0943, New Zealand

**Koback, Nicholas N (Nick)**
71 Hopmeadow St, #9A-1, Weatogue CT 06089, USA — Baseball Player
**Kobayashi, Makoto**
High Energy Accelerator Research, 1-1 Oho, Tsukuba 305 0801, Japan — Nobel Physics Laureate
**Kobel, Kevin R**
7650 E Williams Dr, #1072, Scottsdale AZ 85255, USA — Baseball Player
**Kober, Amelie**
Meet Success AG, Heilmannstr 19, 81479 Munich, Germany — Snowboard Skier
**Kober, Jeff**
4544 Ethel Ave, Studio City CA 91604, USA — Actor
**Kobilka, Brian K**
Stanford University Medical School, 450 Serra Mall, 300 Pasteur Drive, Palo Alto CA 94305, USA — Nobel Chemistry Laureate
**Koblik, Steven**
Huntington Library & Art Gallery, 1151 Oxford Road, San Marino CA 91108, USA — Museum Executive, Educator
**Kobrin, Alex**
I M G Artists, Hogarth Business Park, Chiswick, London W4 2TH, England — Concert Pianist
**Kobylt, John**
248 Oceano Dr, Los Angeles CA 90049, USA — Entertainer
**Koch, Alan G**
1714 Pebble Creek Dr, Prattville AL 36066, USA — Baseball Player
**Koch, Alexander**
United Talent Agency, U T A Plaza, 9336 Civic Center Dr, Beverly Hills CA 90210 USA — Actor
**Koch, Carin**
2000 Auburn Dr, #330, Beachwood OH 44122, USA — Golfer
**Koch, Charles G**
Koch Industries, PO Box 2256, Wichita KS 67201, USA — Businessman
**Koch, Christopher (Chris)**
United Talent Agency, U T A Plaza, 9336 Civic Center Dr, Beverly Hills CA 90210 USA — Director
**Koch, David H**
Koch Industries, PO Box 2256, Wichita KS 67201, USA — Businessman
**Koch, Edwin**
1211 NW Ogden Ave, Bend OR 97701, USA — Artist
**Koch, Gary D**
2934 W Lawn Ave, Tampa FL 33611, USA — Golfer
**Koch, Gregory M (Greg)**
34 Valley Oaks Circle, Spring TX 77382, USA — Football Player
**Koch, James V**
Old Dominion University, Economics Dept, Norfolk VA 23529, USA — Educator, Economist
**Koch, Kurt Cardinal**
Pontifical Council for Promoting Christian Unity, Via della Conciliazione, 00193 Vatican City — Religious Leader
**Koch, Marianne**
Am Hohenberg 27, 82327 Tutzing, Germany — Actress
**Koch, Peter A (Pete)**
866 W 16th St, Newport Beach CA 92663, USA — Football Player
**Koch, Sebastian**
Die Agenten Beate Wolgast, Ackerstra 11B, 10115 Berlin, Germany — Actor
**Koch, Sophie**
I M G Artists, Hogarth Business Park, Chiswick, London W4 2TH, England — Opera Singer
**Koch, William (Bill)**
PO Box 115, Ashland OR 97520, USA — Nordic Skier
**Koch, William C (Billy)**
3160 Tusket Ave, North Port FL 34286, USA — Baseball Player
**Koch, William I (Bill)**
Oxbow Corp, 1601 Forum Place, West Palm Beach FL 33401, USA — Yachtsman, Businessman
**Kocherga, Anatoli I**
Gogolevskaho 37 Korp 2, #47, 254053 Kiev, Ukraine — Opera Singer
**Kocherry, Thomas**
Kerala Swatantra Matsyathozhilali Federation, Kerala 69508, India — Social Activist
**Kochi, Jay K**
4372 Faculty Lane, Houston TX 77004, USA — Chemist
**Kocsis, Zoltan**
Ringlo Utica 60/A, 1116 Budapest, Hungary — Concert Pianist, Composer
**Kocur, Joey**
2830 Vero Dr, Highland MI 48356, USA — Ice Hockey Player
**Kodes, Jan**
I C L T K Tennis Club, Ostrov Stvanice, 17000 Prague 7, Czech Republic — Tennis Player
**Kodjoe, Boris**
Untitled Entertainment, 350 S Beverly Dr, #200, Beverly Hills CA 90212 USA — Model, Actor
**Koechner, David**
Creative Artists Agency, 2000 Ave of Stars, #100, Los Angeles CA 90067 USA — Actor
**Koelle, George B**
3300 Darby Road, #3310, Haverford PA 19041, USA — Pharmacologist
**Koelling, Brian W**
20230 Augusta Dr, Lawrenceburg IN 47025, USA — Baseball Player
**Koen, Karleen**
Random House, 1745 Broadway, #1800, New York NY 10019 USA — Writer
**Koenekamp, Fred**
9222 Corbin Ave, #402, Northridge CA 91324, USA — Cinematographer
**Koenig, Ezra**
L B I Entertainment, 2000 Ave of Stars, Los Angeles CA 90067, USA — Singer, Guitarist (Vampire Weekend)
**Koenig, Walter**
PO Box 4395, Valley Village CA 91617, USA — Actor
**Koepp, David**
Creative Artists Agency, 2000 Ave of Stars, #100, Los Angeles CA 90067 USA — Director, Writer
**Koester, Helmut H K E**
12 Flintlock Road, Lexington MA 02420, USA — Theologian
**Koffigoh, Joseph Kokou**
Regional Integration Ministry, Lome, Togo — Prime Minister, Togo
**Kofler, Andreas**
A-Sponsoring, Spengergasse 37/3, 1050 Vienna, Austria — Ski Jumper
**Kofoed, Bart**
10161 Foxhall Dr, Charlotte NC 28210, USA — Basketball Player
**Kofoed, Seana**
Greene Assoc, 1901 Ave of Stars, #130, Los Angeles CA 90067 USA — Actress
**Kogan, Pavel L**
Bryusov Per 8/10, #19, 103009 Moscow, Russia — Concert Violinist, Conductor

**Kogan, Theo** — Singer (Lunachicks), Actress
Wilhelmina Creative Mgmt, 300 Park Ave S, #200, New York NY 10010, USA

**Kogen, Jay K** — Producer, Writer, Actor
Paradigm Agency, 360 N Crescent Dr, North Building, Beverly Hills CA 90210 USA

**Koh, Terence** — Artist
Galerie Thaddaeus Ropac, 7 Rue Debelleyme, 75003 Paris, France

**Kohan, David** — Producer
KoMut Entertainment, 300 Television Plaza, Building 140, Burbank CA 91505, USA

**Kohde-Kilsch, Claudia** — Tennis Player
Elsa-Brandstrom-Str 22, 66119 Saarbrucken, Germany

**Kohl, Ernest** — Singer
Nene Musik Productions, 1460 SW Santiago Ave, Port Saint Lucie FL 34953 USA

**Kohl, Helmut** — Chancellor, Germany
Buro Bundeskanzler H Kohl, Deutscher Bundestag, Unter den Linden 71, 10117 Berlin, Germany

**Kohlberg, Jerome, Jr** — Financier
155 Crow Hill Road, Mount Kisco NY 10549, USA

**Kohlbrand, Joseph (Joe)** — Football Player
480 Greenview Road, Merritt Island FL 32952, USA

**Kohler, Juliane** — Actress
Players Agentur Mgmt, Sophienstr 21, 10178 Berlin, Germany

**Kohler, Jurgen** — Soccer Player
V f R Aalen, Gmunder Str 16, 73430 Aalen, Germany

**Kohler, Kara** — Rowing Athlete
297 Mountain Parkway, Clayton CA 94517, USA

**Kohler, Sheila** — Writer
Margaret Hanbury, 27 Walcott Square, London SE11 4UB, England

**Kohlmeier, Ryan** — Baseball Player
301 Vine St, Cottonwood Falls KS 66845, USA

**Kohls, Kris** — Drummer (Adema)
Novi Entertainment, PO Box 17077, Beverly Hills CA 90209, USA

**Kohlsaat, Peter** — Cartoonist (Single Slices)
420 N 5th St, #707, Minneapolis MN 55401, USA

**Kohn, A Eugene** — Architect
Kohn Pedersen Fox Assoc, 111 W 57th St, #300, New York NY 10019, USA

**Kohn, Joseph J** — Mathematician
32 Sturges Way, Princeton NJ 08540, USA

**Kohn, Mike** — Bobsled Athlete
Bobsled & Skeleton Federation, 1631 Mesa Ave, #A, Colorado Springs CO 80906 USA

**Kohn, Walter** — Nobel Chemistry Laureate
236 La Vista Grande, Santa Barbara CA 93103, USA

**Kohner, Susan** — Actress
John Weitz Inc, 3 E 66th St, #2C, New York NY 10065, USA

**Kohoutek, Lubos** — Astronomer
Corthumstr 5, 21029 Hamburg, Germany

**Kohrs, Robert H (Bob)** — Football Player
2910 E Nance St, Mesa AZ 85213, USA

**Koivu, Mikko S** — Ice Hockey Player
Minnesota Wild, XCel Energy Arena, 1275 Saint Antoine W, Saint Paul MN 55104 USA

**Koivu, Saku A** — Ice Hockey Player
2200-201 Portage Ave, Winnipeg MB R3B 3L3, Canada

**Kojac, George** — Swimmer
33 Arboles del Norte, Fort Pierce FL 34951, USA

**Kojima, Ariko** — Beauty Queen
Miss Universe Organization, 1370 Ave of Americas, #1600, New York NY 10019 USA

**Kojis, Donald R (Don)** — Basketball Player
8186 Commercial St, La Mesa CA 91942, USA

**Kojovic, Lora** — Actress
Craig Wyckoff Assoc, 11350 Ventura Blvd, #100, Studio City CA 91604, USA

**Kok Oudegeest, Mary** — Swimmer
Escuela Nacional de Natacion, Izarra, Alava, Spain

**Kok, Willem (Wim)** — Prime Minister, Netherlands
Dijsselhofplantsoen 12, 1077, Amersterdam BL, Netherlands

**Kokeny, Roland** — Canoeing Athlete
Esztergomi Kajak-Kenu Sportegyesulet, Erzsebet Kiralyne U 2, 2500 Esztergom, Hungary

**Kokesh, Chris** — Singer, Fiddle Player (Misty River)
1111B NW 131st Way, Vancouver WA 98685, USA

**Kokonin, Vladimir** — Opera, Ballet Executive
Bolshoi Theater, Teatralnaya Pl 1, 103009 Moscow, Russia

**Kolander, Steve** — Singer, Guitarist, Songwriter
Sussman Assoc, 1222 16th Ave S, #300, Nashville TN 37212, USA

**Kolb Thomas, Claudia A** — Swimmer, Coach
Stanford University, Athletic Dept, Stanford CA 94305, USA

**Kolb, Brandon** — Baseball Player
2043 Pine Oak Place, Danville CA 94506, USA

**Kolb, Edward W (Rocky)** — Cosmologist
Fermi National Accelerator Laboratory, PO Box 500, Batavia IL 60510 USA

**Kolb, Gary A** — Baseball Player
5143 Hopewell Dr, Charleston WV 25313, USA

**Kolb, Jon P** — Football Player
1775 McDowell St, Sharon PA 16146, USA

**Kolbe, James T (Jim)** — Representative, AZ
German Marshall Fund, 1744 R St NW, Washington DC 20009, USA

**Kolber, Suzy** — Sportscaster
ESPN-TV, Sports Dept, ESPN Plaza, 935 Middle St, Bristol CT 06010 USA

**Kolbert, Kathryn** — Attorney
Center for Reproductive Law & Policy, 120 Wall St, New York NY 10005, USA

**Kolden, Scott C** — Actor
1515 E Trenton Ave, Orange CA 92867, USA

**Kole, Kelly** — Actress, Model
PO Box 226, Hartsdale NY 10530, USA

**Kole, Warren** — Actor
Paul Kohner, 9300 Wilshire Blvd, #555, Beverly Hills CA 90212 USA

**Kolehmaisen, Mikko** — Canoeing Athlete
Poppelitie 18, 50130 Mikkeli, Finland

**Kolen, J Michael (Mike)** — Football Player
1613 Manchester Lane, Birmingham AL 35243, USA

**Kolirin, Eran** — Director
I C M Partners, 10250 Constellation Blvd, #900, Los Angeles CA 90067 USA
**Kolius, John** — Yachtsman
PO Box 2113, Pearland TX 77588, USA
**Kollar, Trudi Eberle** — Gymnast
Pozsar's Gymnastics Academy, 2709 El Camino Ave, Sacramento CA 95821, USA
**Koller, Arnold** — President, Switzerland
Steinegg, Gschwendes 8, 9050 Appenzell, Switzerland
**Kollhoff, Hans** — Architect
Kurfursendamm 178-179, 10707 Berlin, Germany
**Kollner, Eberhard** — Cosmonaut, East Germany
An der Trainierbahn 7, 11536 Neuenhagen, Germany
**Kollo, Rene** — Opera Singer
Pran Event Gmbh, Ralf Sellelberg, An der Brucke 18, 26180 Rastede, Germany
**Kolm, Henry V** — Electrical Engineer (Magnetic Train)
Weir Meadow Road, Wayland MA 01778, USA
**Kolodner, Richard D** — Biochemist, Cancer Researcher
Dana-Farber Cancer Institute, 44 Binney St, Boston MA 02115, USA
**Kolodziej, Ross A** — Football Player
329 Scarlet Circle, Wexford PA 15090, USA
**Koloskov, Alex** — Photographer
2320 Rose Walk Dr, Alpharetta GA 30005, USA
**Kolpakova, Irina A** — Ballerina
American Ballet Theatre, 890 Broadway, #300, New York NY 10003 USA
**Kolstad, Dean** — Ice Hockey Player
15492 Brooklodge Road, Hickory Corners MI 49060, USA
**Kolstad, Harold E (Hal)** — Baseball Player
15149 Bel Escou Dr, San Jose CA 95124, USA
**Kolsti, Paul** — Editorial Cartoonist
Dallas News, Editorial Dept, Communications Center, Dallas TX 75265, USA
**Koltai, Lajos** — Cinematographer, Director
Gersh Agency, 9465 Wilshire Blvd, #600, Beverly Hills CA 90212 USA
**Kolvenbach, Peter-Hans** — Religious Leader
Borgo Santo Spirito 5, CP 6139, 00195 Rome, Italy
**Kolzig, Olaf** — Ice Hockey Player
1510 Clarendon Blvd, #819, Arlington VA 22209, USA
**Koma, Matthew** — Singer, Songwriter
Cherrytree Records, 256 Santa Monica Pier, Santa Monica CA 90401, USA
**Koman, Jacek** — Actor
R G M Artists, 8-12 Ann Street, Surry Hills NSW 2010, Australia
**Koman, William J (Bill)** — Football Player
5 Upper Ladue Road, Saint Louis MO 63124, USA
**Komar, Vitaly** — Artist
55 Lisspenard St, New York NY 10013, USA
**Komarov, Leo A** — Ice Hockey Player
H C Moscow Dynamo, Vostochnaya St 2/2, 115280 Moscow, Russia
**Komarova, Stanislava S** — Swimmer
Swiss Swimming Training Base, Haus des Sports, 3000 Bern 12, Switzerland
**Komenich, Kim** — Photojournalist
111 Cornelia Ave, Mill Valley CA 94941, USA
**Kometani, Pam** — Golfer
4342 Kilauea Ave, Honolulu HI 96816, USA
**Komleva, Gabriela T** — Ballerina
Fontanka Nab 116, #34, 198005 Saint Petersburg, Russia
**Komlos, Peter** — Concert Violinist
Sport-U 6, 2083 Solymar, Hungary
**Komminski, Brad L** — Baseball Player
688 Fallside Lane, Westerville OH 43081, USA
**Komorowska, Liliana** — Actress
Martinez Creative Mgmt, 6856 Saint-Laurent Blvd, #205, Montreal QC H2S 3C7, Canada
**Komorowski, Bronislaw M** — President, Poland
Palac Prezydencki, Ul Krakowskie Przedmiescie 48, 00071 Warsaw, Poland
**Komsic, Zeljko** — President, Bosnia & Herzegovina
President's Office, Marsala Titz 7, 71000 Sarajevo, Bosnia & Herzegovina
**Komunyakaa, Yusef** — Writer
900 W State St, Trenton NJ 08618, USA
**Kon Artis** — Rap Artist (D-12)
Coast to Coast Talent, 3350 Barham Blvd, Los Angeles CA 90068 USA
**Koncak, Jon** — Basketball Player
PO Box 10040, Jackson WY 83002, USA
**Koncar, Mark** — Football Player
447 N Alpine Blvd, Alpine UT 84004, USA
**Konchalovsky, Andrei** — Director
Weissmann Wolff Bergman, 9665 Wilshire Blvd, #900, Beverly Hills CA 90212, USA
**Kondakova, Elena V** — Cosmonaut
Scientific Industrial Assn, Utica Lenina 4A, 141070 Kaliningrad, Russia
**Kondla, Thomas A (Tom)** — Basketball Player
3517 Cleveland Ave, Brookfield IL 60513, USA
**Kondo, Jun** — Theoretical Physicist
A I S T, Tsukuba Central 2, Tsukuba, Ibaraki 305 8568, Japan
**Kondrattyeva, Marina V** — Ballerina
Bolshoi Theater, Teatralnaya Pl 1, 103009 Moscow, Russia
**Kondratyev, Dmitri Y** — Cosmonaut
Cosmonaut Training Center, Star City, 141160 Zvezdny Gorodok, Moscow Oblast, Russia
**Konerko, Paul H** — Baseball Player
8053 E Leaning Rock Road, Scottsdale AZ 85266, USA
**Kong, Venice** — Model, Actress
Playboy Promotions, 9346 Civic Center Dr, #200, Beverly Hills CA 90210 USA
**Konieczny, Douglas J (Doug)** — Baseball Player
9503 Dundalk St, Spring TX 77379, USA
**Konik, George** — Ice Hockey Player
1027 Savannah Road, Saint Paul MN 55123, USA
**Konitz, Lee** — Jazz Saxophonist
Bennett Morgan, 1022 RR 376, #3, Wappinger Falls NY 12590 USA
**Konkol, Mark** — Journalist
Chicago Sun-Times, Editorial Dept, 401 N Wabash Ave, Chicago IL 60611 USA

Kolirin - Konkol

**Konner, Jennifer (Jenni)** — Producer
United Talent Agency, U T A Plaza, 9336 Civic Center Dr, Beverly Hills CA 90210 USA
**Kono, Tamio (Tommy)** — Weightlifter
98-2025 Hapaki St, Aiea HI 96701, USA
**Kononenko, Oleg D** — Cosmonaut
Cosmonaut Training Center, Star City, 141160 Zvezdny Gorodok, Moscow Oblast, Russia
**Konrad, Cathy** — Producer
Tree Line Films, 1708 Berkeley St, Santa Monica CA 90404, USA
**Konrad, Robert L (Rob), Jr** — Football Player
11884 Windmill Lake Dr, Boynton Beach FL 33473, USA
**Konstantinov, Vladimir** — Ice Hockey Player
6782 Enclave, West Bloomfield MI 48322, USA
**Kont, Paul** — Composer
Doblinger Music, Dorotheergasse 10, 1011 Vienna, Austria
**Kontides, Pavlos** — Yachtsman
Limassol Nautical Club, Georgiou A 1004, Limassol, Cyprus
**Kontiola, Petri** — Ice Hockey Player
H C Traktor Chelyabinsk, Ul Savina 1, 454007 Chelyabinsk, Russia
**Kontos, Christopher (Chris)** — Ice Hockey Player
40 Beck Blvd, Penetanguishene ON L9M 1E1, Canada
**Konyukhov, Fedor F** — Explorer
Tourism/Sports Union, Studeniy Proyezd 7, 129282 Moscow, Russia
**Koo Ja-Cheol** — Soccer Player
VfL Wolfsburg, In den Allerwiesen 1, 38446 Wolfsburg, Germany
**Kool Moe Dee** — Rap Artist
Universal Attractions, 135 W 26th St, #1200, New York NY 10001 USA
**Koolhaas, Rem** — Architect
Metropolitan Architecture, Heer Bokelweg 149, 3032 Rotterdam AD, Netherlands
**Koolman, Olindo** — Governor, Aruba
Governor's Office, L G Smith Blvd 76, Oranjestad, Aruba
**Koonce, George E, Jr** — Football Player
925 E Wells St, #217, Milwaukee WI 53202, USA
**Koonce, Graham** — Baseball Player
2474 Pimlico Place, Alpine CA 91901, USA
**Koons, Jeff** — Artist, Sculptor
Jeff Koons Productions, 601 W 29th St, New York NY 10001, USA
**Koontz, Dean R** — Writer
PO Box 9529, Newport Beach CA 92658, USA
**Kooper, Al** — Singer, Guitarist
Second Octave Talent, 720 S Pointe Blvd, #A200, Petaluma CA 94954, USA
**Koopman, A Ton G M** — Conductor, Concert Keyboardist
Meerweg 23, 1405 Bussu BC, Netherlands
**Koopmans-Kint, Cor** — Swimmer
Pacific Sands C'Van Park, Nambucca Heads NSW 2448, Australia
**Kooser, Ted** — Writer
1820 Branched Oak Road, Garland NE 68360, USA
**Koosman, Jerry M** — Baseball Player
2483 State Road 35, Osceola WI 54020, USA
**Kopacz, Ewa B** — Prime Minister, Poland
Ul Ursad Rady Ministrow, Ul Wiejska 4/8, 00583 Warsaw, Poland
**Kopatchinskaja, Patricia** — Concert Violinist
Maren Borchers, Schlüterstrasse 36, 10629 Berlin, Germany
**Kopay, David M (Dave)** — Football Player
100 W Highland Dr, #102, Seattle WA 98119, USA
**Kopecky, Tomas** — Ice Hockey Player
4401 N Federal Highway, #201, Boca Raton FL 33431, USA
**Kopell, Bernard M (Bernie)** — Actor
Amsel Eisenstadt Frazier, 5055 Wilshire Blvd, #865, Los Angeles CA 90036 USA
**Kopelson, Arnold** — Producer
Kopelson Entertainment, 8560 Sunset Blvd, West Hollywood CA 90069, USA
**Koper, Herbert L (Bud)** — Basketball Player
1225 Lakeshore Dr, #118, Edmond OK 73013, USA
**Kopervas, Gary** — Cartoonist (Out on a Limb)
King Features Syndicate, 300 W 57th St, #1500, New York NY 10019 USA
**Kopicki, Joseph G (Joe)** — Basketball Player
47608 Cheryl Court, Shelby Township MI 48315, USA
**Kopins, Karen** — Actress
Sutton-Barth Vennari, 5900 Wilshire Blvd, #700, Los Angeles CA 90036 USA
**Kopit, Arthur** — Writer
207 W 106th St, #7D, New York NY 10025, USA
**Koplan, Jeffrey** — Medical Administrator
Emory University, Academic Health Affairs Dept, Atlanta GA 30322, USA
**Koplitz, Howard D (Howie)** — Baseball Player
623 Boyd St, Oshkosh WI 54901, USA
**Koplitz, Lynne** — Actress
Paradigm Agency, 360 N Crescent Dr, North Building, Beverly Hills CA 90210 USA
**Kopljar, Marko** — Handball Player
Paris Saint Germain Handball, 82 Ave Georges Lafont, 75016 Paris, France
**Koplove, Michael P (Mike)** — Baseball Player
3235 Chaucer St, Philadelphia PA 19145, USA
**Kopp, Jeffrey B (Jeff)** — Football Player
13752 Deer Chase Place, Jacksonville FL 32224, USA
**Kopp, Wendy** — Association Executive
Teach for America Foundation, 315 W 36th St, #700, New York NY 10018, USA
**Koppe, Erwin** — Gymnast
Th-Rener-Str 70, 07747 Jena, Germany
**Koppel, Ted** — Commentator
3505 Belfont Dr, Ellicot City MD 21043, USA
**Koppelman, Brian** — Director, Writer
Creative Artists Agency, 2000 Ave of Stars, #100, Los Angeles CA 90067 USA
**Koppelman, Chaim** — Artist
141 Wooster St, #6C, New York NY 10012, USA
**Koppen, Daniel (Dan)** — Football Player
1807 Old Bridge Lane, Bellingham MA 02019, USA
**Kopper, Hilmar** — Financier
DaimlerChrysler AG, Mercedestr 137, 70237 Stuttgart, Germany

**Kopperud, Gunnar** — Writer
Bloomsbury Publishing, 50 Bedford Square, London WC1B 3DP, England
**Koppes, Peter** — Guitarist (Church)
M O B Agency, 6404 Wilshire Blvd, #505, Los Angeles CA 90048 USA
**Kopple, Barbara J** — Director
Inphenate, 9701 Wilshire Blvd, #1000, Beverly Hills CA 90212 USA
**Kopra, Timothy L** — Astronaut
4912 Cross Creek Lane, League City TX 77573, USA
**Koptchak, Sergei** — Opera Singer
Robert Lombardo Assoc, Harkness Plaza, 61 W 62nd St, #6F, New York NY 10023 USA
**Korab, Jamie** — Curling Athlete
Curling Association, 1660 Vimont Court, Cumberland ON K4A 4J4, Canada
**Korab, Jerry** — Ice Hockey Player
Korab Inc, 960 N Weigel Ave, Elmhurst IL 60126, USA
**Koralek, Paul G** — Architect
7 Chalcot Road, #1, London NW1 8LH, England
**Korbut, Olga V** — Gymnast
16356 N Thompson Peak Parkway, #2024, Scottsdale AZ 85260, USA
**Korcheck, Stephen J (Steve)** — Baseball Player
6424 98th St E, Bradenton FL 34202, USA
**Korcia, Laurent** — Concert Violinist
E M I Records, 18 Rue de la Convention, 75-15 Paris, France
**Kord, Kazimierz** — Conductor
Ul Nadarzynska 37A, 05 805 Kanie-Otrebusy, Poland
**Korda, Jessica** — Golfer
4909 61st Ave Dr W, Bradenton FL 34210, USA
**Korda, Michael V** — Writer
Simon & Schuster, 1230 Ave of Americas, Concourse 1, New York NY 10020, USA
**Korda, Petr** — Tennis Player
4909 61st Ave Dr W, Bradenton FL 34210, USA
**Korder, Howard** — Writer
I C M Partners, 10250 Constellation Blvd, #900, Los Angeles CA 90067 USA
**Korec, Jan Chryzostom Cardinal** — Religious Leader
Diocese of Nitra, PP 46A, 95050 Nitra, Slovakia
**Korecky, Robert J (Bobby)** — Baseball Player
209 Culver Road, Monmouth Junction NJ 08852, USA
**Koreeda, Hirokazu** — Director, Producer
TV Man Union, 5-53-67 Jingumae, Shibuya, Tokyo 150 0001, Japan
**Koren, Christine (Chris)** — Model
Playboy Promotions, 9346 Civic Center Dr, #200, Beverly Hills CA 90210 USA
**Koren, Edward B** — Cartoonist
PO Box 464, Brookfield VT 05036, USA
**Koren, Steve** — Writer, Producer
Creative Artists Agency, 2000 Ave of Stars, #100, Los Angeles CA 90067 USA
**Koretsky, Kenny** — Drag Racing Driver, Builder
K P K Development Corp, 149 Newbold Road, Fairless Hills PA 19030, USA
**Korf, Mia** — Actress
Fran Saperstein Organization, 919 Victoria Ave, Venice CA 90291, USA
**Korie, Michael** — Librettist
I C M Partners, 10250 Constellation Blvd, #900, Los Angeles CA 90067 USA
**Kormakur, Baltasar** — Director, Producer, Actor
Blueeyes Productions, Seljaveg 2, 101 Reykjavik, Iceland
**Korman, Maxime Carlot** — Prime Minister, Vanuatu
PO Box 698, Port Vila, Vanuatu
**Kormann, Manuela** — Curling Athlete
Curling Association, PO Box 606, 3000 Bern, Switzerland
**Korn, Jim** — Ice Hockey Player
19679 Sweetwater Curve, Excelsior MN 55331, USA
**Korn, Lester B** — Businessman
466 Lexington Ave, #237, New York NY 10017, USA
**Kornberg, Roger D** — Nobel Chemistry Laureate
345 Walsh Road, Atherton CA 94027, USA
**Kornfeld, Stuart A** — Hematologist
Washington University Medical School, Clinical Science Dept, Saint Louis MO 63110, USA
**Kornheiser, Anthony I (Tony)** — Sportswriter, Sportscaster
ESPN-TV, Sports Dept, ESPN Plaza, 935 Middle St, Bristol CT 06010 USA
**Koroll, Cliff** — Ice Hockey Player
23W569 Glendale Terrace, Roselle IL 60172, USA
**Koroma, Ernest Bai** — President, Sierra Leone
President's Office, State House, Independence Ave, Freetown, Sierra Leone
**Koronka, John** — Baseball Player
1403 10th St, Clermont FL 34711, USA
**Korot, Alla** — Actress
Synergy Talent, 13251 Ventura Blvd, Studio City CA 91604, USA
**Kors, Michael** — Fashion Designer
11 W 42nd St, #2000, New York NY 10036, USA
**Korte, Steven J (Steve)** — Football Player
137 Dunleith Lane, Mandeville LA 70471, USA
**Korver, Kyle E** — Basketball Player
1483 Wesleys Run, Gladwyne PA 19035, USA
**Korver, Paul** — Actor
Gersh Agency, 9465 Wilshire Blvd, #600, Beverly Hills CA 90212 USA
**Korzeniowski, Abel** — Composer
Evolution Music Partners, 1680 N Vine St, #500, Los Angeles CA 90028 90028, USA
**Korzun, Valery G** — Cosmonaut
Cosmonaut Training Center, Star City, 141160 Zvezdny Gorodok, Moscow Oblast, Russia
**Kosar, Bernie J, Jr** — Football Player
PO Box 8, Nashport OH 43830, USA
**Kosar, Scott** — Writer
Gotham Group, 9255 Sunset Blvd, #515. Los Angeles, CA 90069, USA
**Kosco, Andrew J (Andy)** — Baseball Player
10324 Springfield Road, Youngstown OH 44514, USA
**Koshalek, Richard** — Museum Executive
Museum of Contemporary Art, 250 S Grand Ave, Los Angeles CA 90012, USA
**Koshansky, Joseph S (Joe)** — Baseball Player
13314 Point Pleasant Dr, Fairfax VA 22033, USA

**Koshiba, Masatoshi** — Nobel Physics Laureate
University of Tokyo, 7-3-1 Hongo, Nunkyoku, Tokyo 113 8654, Japan

**Koshiro, Matsumoto, IV** — Kabuki Actor, Dancer
Kabukiza Theatre, 12-15-4 Ginza, Chuoku, Tokyo 104 0061, Japan

**Koshlyakov, Valery N** — Artist
Kolodzei Art Foundation, 123 S Adelaide Ave, #1N, Highland Park NJ 08904, USA

**Kosier, Kyle B** — Football Player
8943 E Calle del Palo Verde, Scottsdale AZ 85255, USA

**Kosinski, Joseph** — Director
Verve Talent & Literary Agency, 96310 San Vicente Blvd, #100, Los Angeles CA 90048 USA

**Koskie, Cordel L (Corey)** — Baseball Player
161 Primrose Lane, Hamel MN 55340, USA

**Koskinen, John A** — Government Official
Internal Revenue Service, Commissioner's Office, 12th St & Pennsylvania Ave NW, Washington DC 20004, USA

**Koslow, Lauren** — Actress
Michael Bruno, 13576 Cheltenham Dr, Sherman Oaks CA 91423, USA

**Kosmalski, Lenonard J (Len)** — Basketball Player
404 Washington Ave, #PH 8, Miami Beach FL 33139, USA

**Kosminsky, Peter** — Director
United Agents, 12-26 Lexington St, London W1F 0LE, England

**Koss, Alan** — Actor
I C M Partners, 10250 Constellation Blvd, #900, Los Angeles CA 90067 USA

**Koss, Johann Olav** — Speed Skater
Dagaliveien 21, 0387 Oslo, Norway

**Koss, John C** — Inventor
Koss Corp, 4129 N Port Washington Ave, Milwaukee WI 53212, USA

**Kostabi, Mark** — Artist, Sculptor, Composer
Kostabi World, 514 W 24th St, New York NY 10011, USA

**Kostadinova, Stefka** — Track Athlete
Rue Anghel Kantchev 4, 1000 Sofia, Bulgaria

**Kostelecki, David** — Marksman
Palackeho 127, 66461 Holasice, Czech Republic

**Kostelic, Ivica** — Alpine Skier
Skiing Federation, Trg Sportova 11, 10000 Zagreb, Croatia

**Kostelic, Janica** — Alpine Skier
Medvedgradsken 45A, 10000 Zagreb, Croatia

**Koster, Gaby** — Actress
Management Tone Stallmeyer, Pleisermuhlenweg 194, 48157 Munster, Germany

**Koster, Steven J** — Cinematographer
26881 Goya Circle, Mission Viejo CA 92691, USA

**Kostic, Goran** — Actor
Agence Christine Parat 9 Rue de Maubeuge 75009 Paris France

**Kostner, Carolina** — Figure Skater
Mancini Group, Via Vallugana 9, 36033 Isola Vicentina (VI), Italy

**Kostomarov, Roman** — Ice Dancer
Skating Federation, Luchnesksaia Nab 8, 119871 Moscow, Russia

**Kostov, Ivan** — Prime Minister, Bulgaria
Blvd Rakovski 134, 1000 Sofia, Bulgaria

**Kostova, Elizabeth J** — Writer
Little Brown, 3 Center Plaza, #100, Boston MA 02108 USA

**Kostro, Frederick C (Frank)** — Baseball Player
3161 S Jasmine Way, Denver CO 80222, USA

**Kosugi, Kane** — Actor
Sun Music, 4-28 Yotsuya, Shinjuku, Tokyo 160 8501, Japan

**Kosuth, Joseph** — Artist
Spruth Magers Gallery, Oranienburger Stra 18, 10178 Berlin, Germany

**Koszelak, Stanley N** — Biochemist
1125 Mendocino Way, Redlands CA 92374, USA

**Kotalik, Ales** — Ice Hockey Player
17681 Hackberry Court, Eden Prairie MN 55347, USA

**Kotb, Hoda** — Commentator
NBC-TV, News Dept, 30 Rockefeller Plaza, #270E, New York NY 10112 USA

**Kotcheff, W Theodore (Ted)** — Director
Baumgarten Management & Productions, 406 Wilshire Blvd, Santa Monica CA 90401, USA

**Kotchman, Casey J** — Baseball Player
8442 125th Court, Seminole FL 33776, USA

**Koteas, Elias** — Actor
United Talent Agency, U T A Plaza, 9336 Civic Center Dr, Beverly Hills CA 90210 USA

**Kotelnik, Andreas** — Boxer
Universum Boxing Promotion, Am Stadtrand 27, 22047 Hamburg, Germany

**Koterba, Jeff** — Sports, Editorial Cartoonist
Omaha World Herald, Editorial Dept, 14th & Dodge St, Omaha NE 68102, USA

**Kotite, Richard E (Rich)** — Football Player, Coach
241 Fanning St, Staten Island NY 10314, USA

**Kotlarek, Gene** — Skier
4910 Walking Horse Point, Colorado Springs CO 80923, USA

**Kotlayakov, Vladimir M** — Geographer, Glacierologist
Profsoyuznaya St 43-1-80, 117420 Moscow, Russia

**Kotov, Oleg V** — Cosmonaut
Cosmonaut Training Center, Star City, 141160 Zvezdny Gorodok, Moscow Oblast, Russia

**Kotova, Nina** — Concert Cellist
I M G Artists, Hogarth Business Park, Chiswick, London W4 2TH, England

**Kotsay, Mark S** — Baseball Player
6659 Calle Ponte Bella, Rancho Santa Fe CA 92091, USA

**Kotsenburg, Sage** — Snowboard Athlete
Ski & Snowboard Association, 1 Victory Lane, Box 100, Park City UT 84060, USA

**Kottaras, George** — Baseball Player
167 Cartmel Dr, Markham ON L3S 1W6, Canada

**Kottke, Leo** — Singer, Songwriter, Guitarist
A E G Live, 930 W 7th Ave, Denver CO 80204, USA

**Kotto, Yaphet F** — Actor
Rival Agency, 9157 Sunset Blvd, #212, West Hollywood CA 90069, USA

**Kotulak, Ronald** — Editor
Chicago Tribune, Editorial Dept, 435 N Michigan Ave, #1, Chicago IL 60611, USA

**Kotzky, Alex S** — Cartoonist (Apartment 3-G)
25 Highfield Road, Glen Cove NY 11542, USA

**Koubessi, Mohamad Z** — Neurologist
George Washington University, Neurology Dept, 2150 Pennsylvania Ave NW, #700, Washington DC 20037, USA

**Kouchner, Bernard** — Physician; Government Official, France
L'Action d'Humanitaire, 8 Ave de Segur, 75350 Paris, France

**Koudelka, Josef** — Photographer
Magnum Photos, 19 Rue Hegesippe Moneau, 75018 Paris, France

**Koufax, Sanford (Sandy)** — Baseball Player
Los Angeles Dodgers, Stadium, 1000 Elysian Park Ave, Los Angeles CA 90090 USA

**Koufos, Konstantine D (Kosta)** — Basketball Player
Denver Nuggets, Pepsi Center, 1000 Chopper Circle, Denver CO 80204 USA

**Kounrouzan, Karen** — Model
Playboy Promotions, 9346 Civic Center Dr, #200, Beverly Hills CA 90210 USA

**Kournikova, Anna** — Tennis Player, Model
2345 Lake Ave, Sunset Isle 3, Miami Beach FL 33140, USA

**Koutouvides, Niko S** — Football Player
129 9th Lane, Kirkland WA 98033, USA

**Kouwenhoven, Leo P** — Physicist
University of Delft, Van Leeuwenhoek Laboratory, Van der Waalsweg 14, 2628 Delft CH, Netherlands

**Kouzmanoff, Kevin** — Baseball Player
28606 Evergreen Manor Dr, Evergreen CO 80439, USA

**Kovacevich, Stephen** — Concert Pianist, Conductor
C M Artists, 127 W 96th St, #13B, New York NY 10025 USA

**Kovach, Bill** — Editor, Foundation Executive
Harvard University, Nieman Fellows Program, Cambridge MA 02138, USA

**Kovacic, Ernst** — Concert Violinist
Im Muehlfeld 3, 2102 Bisamberg, Austria

**Kovacs, Andras** — Director
Magyar Jakobinusok Ter 2/3, 1122 Budapest, Hungary

**Kovacs, Denes** — Concert Violinist
Iranyi Utca 12, 1053 Budapest V, Hungary

**Kovacs, Istvan (Koko)** — Boxer
Box Utca, Bajcsy Zs, Ut 21, 1065 Budapest, Hungary

**Kovacs, Katalin** — Canoeing Athlete
Domino-Honved, Dozsa Gyorgy Ut 53, 1134 Budapest XIII, Hungary

**Kovalainen, Heikki J** — Auto Racing Driver
Caterham Motorsport Kennet Road Dartford Kent DA1 4QN, England

**Kovalenko, Andrei** — Ice Hockey Player
Kontinental Hockey League, 20/2 Ovchinnikovskaya, 115035 Moscow, Russia

**Kovalenok, Vladimir S** — Cosmonaut, Air Force General
3 Hovanskaya St, #22, 129515 Moscow, Russia

**Kovalev, Alexei V** — Ice Hockey Player
676 Riversville Road, Greenwich CT 6831, USA

**Kovalevsky, Jean** — Astronomer
Villa La Padovane, 8 Rue Saint Michel, Saint-Antoine, 06130 Grasse, France

**Kovatchev, Julian** — Conductor
I M G Artists, Hogarth Business Park, Chiswick, London W4 2TH, England

**Kove, Martin** — Actor
Rogues Gallery, 9107 Wilshire Blvd, #450, Beverly Hills CA 90210, USA

**Kowal, Charles T** — Astronomer
Space Telescope Science Institute, Homewood Campus, Baltimore MD 21218, USA

**Kowal, Kristian A (Kristy)** — Swimmer
128 Laurel Court, #128B, Reading PA 19610, USA

**Kowalczyk, Ed** — Singer, Guitarist (Live)
Monterey Peninsula Artists, 404 W Franklin St, Monterey CA 93940 USA

**Kowalczyk, Jozef** — Religious Leader
Metropolitan Curia, Ul Kanclerza Jana Laskiego 7, 62200 Gniezno, Poland

**Kowalczyk, Justyna** — Cross Country Skier
Budynek Poiskiego Radia, Ul Karkonoska 10, 53015 Wroclaw, Poland

**Kowalczyk, Walter J (Walt)** — Football Player
144 W Maryknoll Road, Rochester Hills CA 48309, USA

**Kowalewicz, Ben** — Singer (Billy Talent)
Big Machine Media, 579 Lexington Ave, #400, New York NY 10022, USA

**Kowalik, Trent** — Actor
Gersh Agency, 41 Madison Ave, #3301, New York NY 10010 USA

**Kowalkowski, Scott T** — Football Player
3995 Kelsey Road, Lake Orion MI 48360, USA

**Kowalski, James M** — Air Force General
Commander, Air Force Global Strike Command, Barksdale Air Force Base LA 71110 USA

**Kowitz, Brian M** — Baseball Player
1657 Bullock Circle, Owings Mills MD 21117, USA

**Koy, Ernest M (Ernie), Jr** — Football Player
PO Box 6, Kenney TX 77452, USA

**Koy, J Theo (Ted)** — Football Player
1225 County Road 155, Georgetown TX 78626, USA

**Koy, Jo** — Actor, Comedian, Writer
Creative Artists Agency, 2000 Ave of Stars, #100, Los Angeles CA 90067 USA

**Koyagialo, Louis Alphonse** — Premier, Congo Democratic Republic
Prime Minister's Office, Kinshasa, Congo Democratic Republic

**Koyama, Debbie** — Golfer
118 Tranquila Dr, Camarillo CA 93012, USA

**Koyamada, Shin** — Actor
Shannon Murphy, 8224A Santa Monica Blvd, #721, West Hollywood CA 90046, USA

**Koz, Dave** — Jazz Saxophonist, Flutist, Actor
W F Leopold Mgmt, 4425 Riverside Dr, #102, Burbank CA 91505, USA

**Kozak, Danuta** — Canoeing Athlete
Domino-Honved, Dozsa Gyorgy Ut 53, 1134 Budapest XIII, Hungary

**Kozak, Donald (Don)** — Ice Hockey Player
1028 N Columbus Dr, Gilbert AZ 85234, USA

**Kozak, Harley Jane** — Actress
TalentWorks, 3500 W Olive Ave, #1400, Burbank CA 91505 USA

**Kozak, Scott A** — Football Player
18617 S Grasle Road, Oregon City OR 97045, USA

**Kozar, Heather** — Model, Actress
C E S D, 10635 Santa Monica Blvd, #130, Los Angeles CA 90025 USA

**Kozeev, Konstantin M** — Cosmonaut
Cosmonaut Training Center, Star City, 141160 Zvezdny Gorodok, Moscow Oblast, Russia

Koubessi - Kozeev

**K**

**Kozelko, Thomas W (Tom)** — Basketball Player
6200 Peninsula Dr, Traverse City MI 49686, USA
**Kozena, Magdalena** — Opera Singer
Narodni Divadlo, Dvorakova 11, 60000 Brno, Czech Republic
**Kozerski, Bruce** — Football Player
3088 Waterbury Court, Edgewood KY 41017, USA
**Kozinski, Alex** — Judge
US Court of Appeals, 125 S Grand Ave, Pasadena CA 91105, USA
**Koziol, John C** — Air Force General
Deputy CinC, Intelligence & Surveillance, HgUSAF, Pentagon, Washington DC 20330 USA
**Kozlicki, Ronald F (Ron)** — Basketball Player
5002 Hidden Branches Dr, Atlanta GA 30338, USA
**Kozlov, Viktor N** — Ice Hockey Player
363 Merlin Way, Plantation FL 33324, USA
**Kozlov, Vyacheslav A** — Ice Hockey Player
4934 Powers Ferry Road, Atlanta GA 30327, USA
**Kozlova, Valentina** — Ballerina
New York City Ballet, Lincoln Center Plaza, New York NY 10023 USA
**Kozlowski, Brian S** — Football Player
61 E Shore Dr, Niantic CT 06357, USA
**Kozlowski, Glen A** — Football Player
455 Belmont Place, #262, Provo UT 84606, USA
**Kozlowski, Linda** — Actress
Bedford & Pearce, 19 Abbotsford Road, Katoomba NSW 2780, Australia
**Kozlowski, Michael J (Mike)** — Football Player
932 NW 110th Ave, Plantation FL 33324, USA
**Kozmus, Primoz** — Track Athlete
Hostel Primoz Kozmus, Solska Cesta 1, 8280 Brestanica, Slovenia
**Koznick, Kristina** — Alpine Skier
PO Box 85, Wolcott CO 81655, USA
**Kozol, Jonathan** — Writer
PO Box 145, Byfield MA 01922, USA
**Kraatz, Victor** — Figure Skater
Connecticut Skating Center, 300 Alumni Road, Newington CT 06111, USA
**Kraayeveld, Cathrine H** — Basketball Player
Atlanta Dream, 83 Walton St NW, #400, Atlanta, GA 30303 USA
**Krabbe, Jeroen** — Actor
Conway Van Gelder Grant, 8-12 Broadwick St, #300, London W1F 8HW, England
**Krabbe, Tim** — Writer
Bloomsbury Publishing, 50 Bedford Square, London WC1B 3DP, England
**Krabbe-Zimmermann, Katrin** — Track Athlete
Dorfstr 9, 17091 Pinnow, Germany
**Krackow, Jurgen** — Businessman
Schumannstr 100, 40237 Dusseldorf, Germany
**Kraemer, Harry J** — Businessman
Baxter International, 1 Baxter Parkway, Deerfield IL 60015, USA
**Kraemer, Joseph W (Joe)** — Baseball Player
3212 NE 401st Circle, La Center WA 98629, USA
**Kraft, Christopher C (Chris), Jr** — Space Administrator
14919 Village Elm St, Houston TX 77062, USA
**Kraft, Craig A** — Artist, Sculptor
931 R St NW, Washington DC 20001, USA
**Kraft, Greg** — Golfer
14820 Rue de Bayonne, #302, Clearwater FL 33762, USA
**Kraft, Robert** — Composer
4722 Noeline Ave, Encino CA 91436, USA
**Kraft, Robert P** — Astrophysicist
University of California, Lick Observatory, Santa Cruz CA 95064, USA
**Kragen, Greg** — Football Player
1447 Boulevard Way, Walnut Creek CA 94595, USA
**Kraggerud, Henning** — Concert Violinist
I M G Artists, Hogarth Business Park, Chiswick, London W4 2TH, England
**Kragthorpe, Steve** — Football Coach
University of Louisville, Athletic Dept, Louisville KY 40292, USA
**Kraguly, Radovan** — Artist
Llwyngarth Fawr, Comin Coch, Builth Wells, Powys LD2 3PP, Wales
**Krajicek, Richard** — Tennis Player
Krajicek Foundation, Olympisch Stadion 3, 1076 Amsterdam DE, Netherlands
**Krakau, Mervin F (Merv)** — Football Player
706 Prairie St, Guthrie Center IA 50115, USA
**Krakoff, Reed** — Fashion Designer
831 Madison Ave, New York NY 10021, USA
**Krakoski, Joseph A (Joe)** — Football Player
560 Village Blvd, #37, Incline Village NV 89451, USA
**Krakowski, Jane** — Actress, Singer
United Talent Agency, U T A Plaza, 9336 Civic Center Dr, Beverly Hills CA 90210 USA
**Krall, Diana** — Singer, Pianist, Songwriter
S L Feldman Mgmt, 1505 W 2nd Ave, #200, Vancouver BC V6H 3Y4, Canada
**Kraly, Steven C (Steve)** — Baseball Player
12 Davis Ave, Johnson City NY 13790, USA
**Kramarenko, Sergei M** — WW II, Korean War Russian Air Hero
Association of Heroes, Ulitsa Novyy Arbat 21, 119019 Moscow, Russia
**Kramarsky, David** — Director
1630 Berkeley St, #1, Santa Monica CA 90404, USA
**Kramek, Robert E** — Coast Guard Admiral
43 Firefall Court, Spring TX 77380, USA
**Kramer, Barry D** — Basketball Player
101 Deanna Court, Schenectady NY 12309, USA
**Kramer, Billy J** — Singer (Billy J Kramer & the Dakotas)
Lustig Talent, PO Box 770850, Orlando FL 32877 USA
**Kramer, Brad** — Harness Racing Driver
2455 Tittabawassee St, Alger MI 48610, USA
**Kramer, Chris** — Actor
Lucas Talent, 100 W Pender St, #700, Vancouver BC V6B 1RB, Canada
**Kramer, Clare** — Actress
S M S Talent, 8383 Wilshire Blvd, #230, Beverly Hills CA 90211 USA

Kozelko - Kramer

**Kramer, Eric Allen** — Actor
Stone Manners Salners, 6100 Wilshire Blvd, #1500, Los Angeles CA 90035 USA
**Kramer, Gerald L (Jerry)** — Football Player
11768 W Chinden Blvd, Garden City ID 83714, USA
**Kramer, Jeffrey** — Director, Writer
Innovative Artists, 1505 10th St, Santa Monica CA 90401 USA
**Kramer, Jim** — Writer
I C M Partners, 10250 Constellation Blvd, #900, Los Angeles CA 90067 USA
**Kramer, Joel B** — Basketball Player
3817 E Highland Ave, Phoenix AZ 85018, USA
**Kramer, Joseph M (Joey)** — Drummer (Aerosmith)
Front Line Mgmt, 1100 Glendon Ave, #2000, Los Angeles CA 90024 USA
**Kramer, Kent D** — Football Player
200 Troon Road, McKinney TX 75070, USA
**Kramer, Larry** — Social Activist, Writer
Gay Men's Health Crisis, 119 W 24th St, Lobby 1, New York NY 10011, USA
**Kramer, Randall J (Randy)** — Baseball Player
143 Camino Pacifico, Aptos CA 95003, USA
**Kramer, Stepfanie** — Actress
Teitelbaum Artists Group, 8840 Wilshire Blvd, #200, Beverly Hills CA 90211, USA
**Kramer, Sven** — Speed Skater
Grindweg 204/A, 8483 Scherpenzeel JL, Netherlands
**Kramer, Thomas F  (Tommy)** — Football Player
806 Emerald Bay, San Antonio TX 78260, USA
**Kramer, Thomas J (Tom)** — Baseball Player
10665 Hamilton Ave, Cincinnati OH 45231, USA
**Kramer, W Erik** — Football Player
5950 Kingham Court, Agoura Hills CA 91301, USA
**Kramer, Wayne** — Director
W M E Entertainment, 9601 Wilshire Blvd, #300, Beverly Hills CA 90210 USA
**Kramer, Wayne** — Jazz Guitarist (Was Not Was, MC5)
I C M Partners, 730 5th Ave, New York NY 10019 USA
**Kramlich, Richard S** — Marine Corps General
Deputy CofS, Installations & Logistics, HqUSMC, Navy St, Washington DC 20380 USA
**Kramnik, Vladimir** — Chess Player
Russian Chess Federation, Luchnetskaya 8, 119270 Moscow, Russia
**Kranepool, Edward E (Ed)** — Baseball Player
M E Promotions, 177 High Pond Dr, Jericho NY 11753, USA
**Krantz, Judith T** — Writer
166 Groverton Place, Los Angeles CA 90077, USA
**Kranz, Eugene (Gene)** — Space Scientist
1108 Shady Oak Lane, Dickinson TX 77539, USA
**Kranz, Fran** — Actor
United Talent Agency, U T A Plaza, 9336 Civic Center Dr, Beverly Hills CA 90210 USA
**Krapek, Karl** — Businessman
United Technologies Corp, United Technologies Building, Hartford CT 06101, USA
**Krasinski, John** — Actor, Comedian
W M E Entertainment, 9601 Wilshire Blvd, #300, Beverly Hills CA 90210 USA
**Krasniqi, Luan** — Boxer
Oschleweg 10, 78628 Rottweil, Germany
**Krasnoff, Eric** — Businessman
Pall Corp, 25 Harbor Park Dr, Port Washington NY 11050, USA
**Krasny, Yuri** — Artist
Sloane Gallery, Oxford Office Building, 1612 17th St, Denver CO 80202, USA
**Kratch, Robert A (Bob)** — Football Player
10685 County Road 24, Watertown MN 55388, USA
**Kratochvilova, Jarmila** — Track Athlete
Pod Vysehradem 207, 58282 Golcuv Jenikov, Czech Republic
**Kratschmer, Guido** — Track Athlete
Am Obstmarkt 41, 55126 Mainz, Germany
**Kratzert, William A (Bill)** — Golfer
8130 Merganser Dr, Ponte Vedra Beach FL 32082, USA
**Kraulis, Andrew** — Actor
Rosenthal Agency, 204-14 Prince Arthur Ave, Toronto ON M5R 1A9, Canada
**Kraupp, Sebastian** — Curling Athlete
Curling Association, Idrottshuser, Marbackagatan 19, 123 43 Farsta, Sweden
**Kraus, Alanna** — Speed Skater
Speed Skating Canada, 2781 Lancaster Road, #402, Ottawa ON K1B 1A7, Canada
**Kraus, Daniel J (Dan)** — Basketball Player
10101 Governor Warfield Parkway, #222, Columbia MD 21044, USA
**Kraus, Nicola** — Writer
Atria Books, 1230 Ave of Americas, New York NY 10020 USA
**Kraus, Peter** — Singer, Actor
Fechter Mgmt, Sieveringerstr 194, 1190 Vienna, Austria
**Krause, Brian** — Actor, Director, Producer
Sovereign Talent Group, 8421 Wilshire Blvd, #200, Beverly Hills CA 90211, USA
**Krause, Chester L** — Publisher
Krause Publications, 700 E State St, Iola WI 54990, USA
**Krause, Paul J** — Football Player
Pinewood Golf Course, Real Estate Dept, 18150 Waco St NW, Elk River MN 55330, USA
**Krause, Peter** — Actor
Creative Artists Agency, 2000 Ave of Stars, #100, Los Angeles CA 90067 USA
**Krause, Richard M** — Immunologist
4000 Cathedral Ave NW, #134B, Washington DC 20016, USA
**Kraushaar-Pielach, Silke** — Luge Athlete
Gorkistr 22, 96515 Sonneberg, Germany
**Krauss, Alison** — Singer, Fiddler
Arcieri Assoc, 305 Madison Ave, #2315, New York NY 10165 USA
**Krauss, Barry** — Football Player
5346 Creekbend Dr, Carmel IN 46033, USA
**Krauss, Lawrence M (Larry)** — Astrophysicist
Case Western Reserve University, Physics Dept, Cleveland OH 44106, USA
**Krauss, Nicole** — Writer
W W Norton, 500 5th Ave, #600, New York NY 10110 USA
**Krauss, Robert M** — Psychologist
Columbia University, Psychology Dept, Schermerhorn Hall, New York NY 10027, USA

K

Kramer - Krauss

**K**

**Krausse - Kreuk**

| | |
|---|---|
| **Krausse, Lewis B (Lew), Jr**<br>12811 NE 186th St, Holt MO 64048, USA | Baseball Player |
| **Krausse, Stefan**<br>Karl-Zink-Str 2, 96883 Ilmenau, Germany | Luge Athlete |
| **Krauthammer, Charles**<br>Washington Post Writers Group, 1150 15th St NW, Washington DC 20071, USA | Columnist |
| **Kravchuk, Igor A**<br>Harrington College, Athletic Dept, 300 Riviere Rouge, Harrington QC J8G 2S7, Canada | Ice Hockey Player |
| **Kravchuk, Leonid M**<br>Verkhovna Rada, M Hrushevskoho 5, 252019 Kiev, Ukraine | President, Ukraine |
| **Kravec, Kenneth P (Ken)**<br>6752 Taeda Dr, Sarasota FL 34241, USA | Baseball Player |
| **Kravitz, Lee**<br>Parade, Editorial Dept, 711 3rd Ave, New York NY 10017, USA | Editor |
| **Kravitz, Lenny**<br>Creative Artists Agency, 2000 Ave of Stars, #100, Los Angeles CA 90067 USA | Singer, Songwriter, Musician |
| **Krawczyk, Raymond A (Ray)**<br>67 Cloudcrest, Aliso Viejo CA 92656, USA | Baseball Player |
| **Krayer, Otto H**<br>4140 E Cooper St, Tucson AZ 85711, USA | Pharmacologist |
| **Krayzelburg, Lenny**<br>55 Oceana Dr E, #5H, Brooklyn NY 11235, USA | Swimmer |
| **Krayzie Bone**<br>Life Entertainment, 15441 Red Hill Ave, #G, Tustin CA 92780, USA | Rap Artist (Bone Thugs-N-Harmony) |
| **Kreamer, Ann**<br>W M E Entertainment, 9601 Wilshire Blvd, #300, Beverly Hills CA 90210 USA | Writer |
| **Krebbs, John**<br>Diamond Ridge, 3232 Amoruso Way, Roseville CA 95747, USA | Auto Racing Driver |
| **Krebs, Robert D**<br>Burlington North/Santa Fe, 2650 Lou Menk Dr, Fort Worth TX 76131, USA | Businessman |
| **Krebs, Susan**<br>6019 Buffalo Ave, #A, Van Nuys CA 91401, USA | Actress |
| **Kredel, Elmar Maria**<br>Obere Karolinenstra 5, 96033 Bamber, Germany | Religious Leader |
| **Kregel, Kevin R**<br>2601 Bay Shore Dr, Seabrook TX 77586, USA | Astronaut |
| **Kreider, Steve K**<br>350 Harrow Lane, Blue Bell PA 19422, USA | Football Player |
| **Kreis, Jason**<br>Real Salt Lake, 9256 S State St, Sandy UT 84070 USA | Soccer Player, Coach |
| **Kreitling, Richard A (Rich)**<br>24017 Trout Lake Road, Bovey MN 55709, USA | Football Player |
| **Kreklow, Wayne**<br>4001 S Old Mill Creek Road, Columbia MO 65203, USA | Basketball Player |
| **Krementz, Jill**<br>620 Sagaponack Main St, Southampton NY 11968, USA | Photographer |
| **Kremer, Andrea**<br>NBC-TV, Sports Dept, 30 Rockefeller Plaza, #270E, New York NY 10112 USA | Sportscaster |
| **Kremer, Arthur**<br>+1 Management/Public Relations, 242 Wythe Ave, #6, Brooklyn NY 11211, USA | Drummer (Stellarstarr*) |
| **Kremer, Gidon**<br>Opus 3 Artists, 470 Park Ave S, #900N, New York NY 10016 USA | Concert Violinist |
| **Kremer, J Kendall (Ken)**<br>6116 Double Eagle Court, Kansas City MO 64152, USA | Football Player |
| **Kremers, James E (Jimmy)**<br>6209 W Orlando St, Broken Arrow OK 74011, USA | Baseball Player |
| **Kremmel, James L (Jim)**<br>524 W 18th Ave, Spokane WA 99203, USA | Baseball Player |
| **Krens, Thomas**<br>Solomon R Guggenheim Museum, 1071 5th Ave, New York NY 10128, USA | Museum Executive |
| **Krentz, Jayne Ann (Amanda Quick)**<br>Axelrod Agency, 66 Church St, Lenox MA 01240, USA | Writer |
| **Krenz, Jan**<br>Al J Ch Szucha 16, 00 582 Warsaw, Poland | Conductor, Composer |
| **Krepfle, Keith R**<br>82 E Butler Dr, Drums PA 18222, USA | Football Player |
| **Kreps, David M**<br>Stanford University, Graduate Business School, Stanford CA 94305, USA | Economist |
| **Kresa, Kent**<br>General Motors Corp, 100 Renaissance Center, Detroit MI 48243, USA | Businessman |
| **Kresge, Chris**<br>834 Trailwood Dr, Apopka FL 32712, USA | Golfer |
| **Kreskin**<br>444 2nd St, Pitcairn PA 15140, USA | Illusionist |
| **Kress, Charles S (Charlie)**<br>1705 Pine St, #104, Sandpoint ID 83864, USA | Baseball Player |
| **Kress, Nathan**<br>A P A Talent & Literary Agency, 405 S Beverly Dr, #300, Beverly Hills CA 90212 USA | Actor |
| **Kressley, Carson**<br>Untitled Entertainment, 350 S Beverly Dr, #200, Beverly Hills CA 90212 USA | Entertainer |
| **Kretchmer, Arthur**<br>Playboy, Editorial Dept, 680 N Lake Shore Dr, Chicago IL 60611, USA | Editor |
| **Kretschmann, Thomas**<br>Hoestermann Mgmt, Gneisenaustr 94, 10961 Berlin, Germany | Actor |
| **Kretschmann, Winfried**<br>Haus der Abgeordneten, Konrad-Adenauer Str 12, 70173 Stuttgart, Germany | Government Official, Germany |
| **Kretschmer, Peter**<br>Kanu Club Potsdam, Am Luftschiffhafen 2, 14471 Potsdam, Germany | Canoeing Athlete |
| **Kretzschmar, Stefan**<br>Love & Power Mgmt, Scharfestr 10, 14169 Berlin, Germany | Handball Player |
| **Kretzschmar, Waltraud**<br>Berlinerstr 65, 81925 Munich, Germany | Handball Player |
| **Kreuger, Richard A (Rick)**<br>4664 Sheldon Court, Hudsonville MI 49426, USA | Baseball Player |
| **Kreuk, Kristin L**<br>Gersh Agency, 9465 Wilshire Blvd, #600, Beverly Hills CA 90212 USA | Actress |

Kreuter, Chadden M (Chad)                                          Baseball Player
6737 SW 77th Terrace, South Miami FL 33143, USA
Kreutz, Olin G                                                      Football Player
750 S Southmeadow Lane, Lake Forest IL 60045, USA
Kreutzberger, Mario                              Actor, Comedian, Writer, Producer
W M E Entertainment, 9601 Wilshire Blvd, #300, Beverly Hills CA 90210 USA
Kreutzer, Franklin J (Frank)                                       Baseball Player
921 Windwhisper Lane, Annapolis MD 21403, USA
Kreutzmann, Bill                                           Drummer (Grateful Dead)
Oliver & Sabec, 50 Balmy Alley, San Francisco CA 94110, USA
Kreviazuk, Chantal                                    Singer, Pianist, Songwriter
Characters Talent Mgmt, 8 Elm St, Toronto ON M5G 1G7, Canada
Kribel, Joel                                                              Golfer
26254 N 46th St, Phoenix AZ 85050, USA
Krick, Jaynie                                                      Baseball Player
1522 Azalea Dr, Arlington TX 76013, USA
Krickstein, Aaron                                                  Tennis Player
7559 Fairmont Court, Boca Raton FL 33496, USA
Krieg, Arthur M                                                     Immunologist
University of Iowa Medical College, Immunology Dept, Iowa City IA 52242, USA
Krieg, David M (Dave)                                              Football Player
2439 E Desert Willow Dr, Phoenix AZ 85048, USA
Krieger, Ellie                                            Dietician, Entertainer
Flutie Entertainment, 9320 Wilshire Blvd, #202, Beverly Hills CA 90212, USA
Krieger, Lee Toland                                                    Director
72nd Street Productions, 1041 N Formosa Ave, West Hollywood CA 90046, USA
Krieger, Robby                                      Guitarist (Doors), Songwriter
Doors Music, 8899 Beverly Blvd, #812, Los Angeles CA 90048, USA
Krier, Leon                                                          Architect
8 Rue des Chapeliers, 83830 Claviers, France
Kriewaldt, Clint                                                   Football Player
W3189 Center Valley Road, Freedom WI 54165, USA
Krige, Alice                                                          Actress
Diamond Mgmt, 31 Percy St, London W1T 2DD, England
Krikalev, Sergei K                                                   Cosmonaut
Cosmonaut Training Center, Star City, 141160 Zvezdny Gorodok, Moscow Oblast, Russia
Krim, Mathilde                                    Philanthropist, Medical Activist
AmfAR Foundation for AIDS Research, 5900 Wilshire Blvd, Los Angeles CA 90036, USA
Kring, Tim                                                    Writer, Producer
W M E Entertainment, 9601 Wilshire Blvd, #300, Beverly Hills CA 90210 USA
Krinsky, Yehuda                                         Religious Leader, Rabbi
Chabad-Lubavitch, 841 Ocean Parkway, Brooklyn NY 11230, USA
Kripke, Eric                                          Writer, Director, Producer
Principato-Young, 9465 Wilshire Blvd, #880, Beverly Hills CA 90212 USA
Kripke, Saul A                                                     Philosopher
Princeton University, Philosophy Dept, Princeton NJ 08544, USA
Krisar, Anders                                          Sculptor, Photographer
Staley-Wise Gallery, 560 Broadway, New York NY 10012, USA
Krislov, Marvin                                                       Educator
Oberlin College, President's Office, 70 N Professor St, Oberlin OH 44074, USA
Kriss, Gerard A                                                     Astronomer
Johns Hopkins University, Astronomy Dept, Baltimore MD 21218, USA
Kristen, Marta                                                        Actress
475 Mesa Dr, Santa Monica CA 90402, USA
Kristensen, Tom                                             Auto Racing Driver
Autosport International, Broom Road, Teddington Middlesex TW11 9BE, England
Kristiansen, Ingrid                                              Track Athlete
Nils Collett Vogts Vei 51B, 0765 Oslo, Norway
Kristiansen, Kjeld Kirk                              Businessman, Educator
Lego Group, 7190 Billund, Denmark
Kristine W                                                            Singer
Spectrum Talent, 1650 Broadway, #1105, New York NY 10019, USA
Kristjansson, Thor                                                     Actor
Creative Artists Agency, 2000 Ave of Stars, #100, Los Angeles CA 90067 USA
Kristmanson, Kyrie                                         Singer, Songwriter
Agency Group Ltd, 142 W 57th St, #600, New York NY 10019 USA
Kristof, Emory                                                    Photographer
National Geographic, Editorial Dept, 1145 17th St NW, Washington DC 20036 USA
Kristof, Joe                                                          Bowler
4290 Meadowview Court, Columbus OH 43224, USA
Kristof, Kathy M                                                    Columnist
Los Angeles Times, Editorial Dept, 202 W 1st St, Los Angeles CA 90012 USA
Kristof, Nicholas D                                                 Journalist
New York Times, Editorial Dept, 229 W 43rd St, New York NY 10036, USA
Kristoff, Alexander                                                   Cyclist
Alexander Kristoff Limited, Emmausv 1, 4015 Stavanger, Norway
Kristofferson, Kris                                  Singer, Songwriter, Actor
I C M Partners, 10250 Constellation Blvd, #900, Los Angeles CA 90067 USA
Kriukov, Nikita V                                        Cross Country Skier
Ski Association, Luzhnetskaya Nab 8, 119270 Moscow, Russia
Krivda, Rick M                                                     Baseball Player
112 Dolores Dr, Irwin PA 15642, USA
Krivokrasov, Sergei V                                       Ice Hockey Player
16500 Collins Ave, #1556, Sunny Island Beach FL 33160, USA
Kriwet, Heinz                                                     Businessman
Thyssen AG, August-Thyssen-Str 1, 40211 Dusseldorf, Germany
Krmpotich, David                                             Rowing Athlete
128 Archbishop Dr, Conshocken PA 19428, USA
Kroeger, Chad R                              Singer, Guitarist (Nickelback)
Union Entertainment Group, 1323 Newbury Road, #104, Newbury Park CA 91320, USA
Kroeger, Gary                                              Actor, Comedian
10474 Santa Monica Blvd, #380, Los Angeles CA 90025, USA
Kroeger, Josh                                                     Baseball Player
1007 Wildlife Road, San Diego CA 92131, USA
Kroeger, Michael D H (Mike)                             Bassist (Nickelback)
Union Entertainment Group, 1323 Newbury Road, #104, Newbury Park CA 91320, USA

**Kroemer, Herbert** — Nobel Physics Laureate
University of California, Electrical Engineering Dept, Santa Barbara CA 93106, USA

**Kroenig, Brad** — Model
Ford Models Inc, 111 5th Ave, #900, New York NY 10003 USA

**Kroes, Doutzen** — Model
D N A Model Mgmt, 555 W 25th St, #600, New York NY 10001, USA

**Kroes, Neelie** — Government Official, Netherlands
European Commission, 200 Rue de la Loi, 1049 Brussels, Belgium

**Kroesen, Frederick J, Jr** — US Army General
Military Professional Resources Inc, 2863 Duke St, Alexandria VA 22314, USA

**Krofft, Marty** — Puppeteer
700 Greentree Road, Pacific Palisades CA 90272, USA

**Krofft, Sid** — Puppeteer
7710 Woodrow Wilson Dr, Los Angeles CA 90046, USA

**Kroft, Steve** — Commentator
CBS-TV, News Dept, 51 W 52nd St, New York NY 10019 USA

**Kroger, Uwe** — Singer
Fechter Mgmt, Sieveringer Str 194, 1190 Vienna, Austria

**Krokidas, John** — Director
United Talent Agency, U T A Plaza, 9336 Civic Center Dr, Beverly Hills CA 90210 USA

**Krol, Joachim** — Actor
Barbarella Entertainment, Aachener Str 26, 50674 Cologne, Germany

**Kroll, Alexander S (Alex)** — Football Player, Businessman
581 Whalley Road, Charlotte VT 05445, USA

**Kroll, Lucien** — Architect
Ave Louis Berlaimont 20, Boite 9, 1160 Brussels, Belgium

**Kroll, Nick** — Actor, Comedian
Mosiac Media Group, 9200 W Sunset Blvd, #1000, Los Angeles CA 90069 USA

**Kromm, Richard (Rich)** — Ice Hockey Player
1935 Cheyenne Dr, Evansville IN 47715, USA

**Kromowidjojo, Ranomi** — Swimmer
Lindenlaan 29, 5653 Eindhoven KB, Netherlands

**Kron, Elizabeth S (Lisa)** — Actress
Joyce Ketay Agency, 930 9th Ave, #706, New York NY 10036, USA

**Kronberger, Petra** — Alpine Skier
Ellmautal 37, 5452 Pfarrwerfen, Austria

**Krone, Julie** — Thoroughbred Racing Jockey
7305 Marine Place, Carlsbad CA 92011, USA

**Kronwall, H Niklas** — Ice Hockey Player
22235 Picadilly Circle, Novi MI 48375, USA

**Kropf, Susan** — Businesswoman
Avon Products, 1251 Ave of Americas, #C2-63, New York NY 10020, USA

**Kropfeld, Jim** — Boat Racing Driver
Hydroplanes Inc, 9117 Zoellner Dr, Cincinnati OH 45251, USA

**Kropfelder, Nicholas** — Soccer Player
13803 Lighthouse Ave, Ocean City MD 21842, USA

**Kropp, Tom** — Basketball Player
1811 W 41st St, Kearney NE 68845, USA

**Kross, David** — Actor
Julian Belfrage Assoc, 9 Argyll St, #300, London W1F 7TG, England

**Kross, Kayden** — Actress
Media Artists Group, 8222 Melrose Ave, #203, Los Angeles CA 90048 USA

**Kroszner, Randall** — Government Official, Economist
Federal Reserve Board, 20th St & Constitution Ave NW, Washington DC 20551, USA

**Krot, Alexander N** — Astrobiologist, Cosmochemist
University of Hawaii-Manoa, Geophysics Institute, 1680 East-West Road, #602, Honolulu HI 96822, USA

**Kroto, Harold W** — Nobel Chemistry Laureate
Sussex University, Chemistry Dept, Falmer, Brighton BN1 9QJ, England

**Krsnich, Rocco P (Rocky)** — Baseball Player
5701 W 92nd St, Overland Park KS 66207, USA

**KRS-One** — Rap Artist
Richard Walters, PO Box 2789, Toluca Lake CA 91610 USA

**Krstic, Nenad** — Basketball Player
Boston Celtics, 226 Causeway St, #4, Boston MA 02114 USA

**Kruczek, Michael (Mike)** — Football Player
4028 Gilder Rose Place, Winter Park FL 32792, USA

**Krueck, Ronald** — Architect
Krueck & Sexton Architects, 221 W Erie, Chicago IL 60654, USA

**Krueger, Alan B** — Government Official, Economist
White House, 1600 Pennsylvania Ave NW, Washington DC 20500 USA

**Krueger, Anne O** — Economist
Stanford University, Economics Dept, Stanford CA 94305, USA

**Krueger, Charles A (Charlie)** — Football Player
44 Regency Dr, Clayton CA 94517, USA

**Krueger, James G** — Dermatologist
Rockefeller University Medical Center, Dermatology Dept, 1230 York Ave, New York NY 10065, USA

**Krueger, Ralph** — Ice Hockey Coach
Edmonton Oilers, 11230 110th St, Edmonton AB T5G 3H7, Canada

**Krueger, Robert C (Bob)** — Senator, TX; Diplomat
PO Box 311717, New Braunfels TX 78131, USA

**Krueger, Rolf F** — Football Player
22811 Rainbow Bend Lane, Katy TX 77450, USA

**Krueger, William C (Bill)** — Baseball Player
30132 SE Redmond Fall City Road, Fall City WA 98024, USA

**Kruger, Barbara** — Artist
Mary Boone Gallery, 745 5th Ave New York NY 10151, USA

**Kruger, Diane** — Actress, Model
U B B A, 6 Rue de Braque, 75003 Paris, France

**Kruger, Hardy** — Actor
Agence Elizabeth Simpson, 62 Blvd du Montparnasse, 75015 Paris, France

**Kruger, Kelly** — Actress
Amanda Rosenthal, 543 Richmond St W, Ste 123, PO Box 205, Toronto ON M5V 1Y6, Canada

**Kruger, Lon** — Basketball Coach
University of Oklahoma, Athletic Dept, Norman OK 73019, USA

**Kruger, Marcus** — Ice Hockey Player
Chicago Blackhawks, United Center, 1901 W Madison St, Chicago IL 60612 USA

**Kruger, Mike** — Actor, Comedian, Singer
Management Tone Stallmeyer, Pleister-Muhlenweg 194, 48157 Munster, Germany
**Kruger, Paul** — Football Player
Cleveland Browns, 76 Lou Groza Blvd, Berea OH 44017 USA
**Krugman, Paul R** — Nobel Economics Laureate
70 Lambert Dr, Princeton NJ 08540, USA
**Kruikov, Nikita** — Cross Country Skier
Ski Association, Luzhnetskaya Nab 8, 119270 Moscow, Russia
**Kruk, John M** — Baseball Player, Sportscaster
PO Box 7847, Naples FL 34101, USA
**Krukow, Michael E (Mike)** — Baseball Player
6094 Madbury Court, San Luis Obispo CA 93401, USA
**Krulak, Charles C** — Marine Corps General
4801 Bonita Bay Blvd, Bonita Springs FL 34134, USA
**Krulwich, Robert** — Commentator
CBS-TV, News Dept, 524 W 57th St, New York NY 10019, USA
**Krumholtz, David** — Actor
Maydew & Golenberg, 8383 Wilshire Blvd, #1050, Beverly Hills CA 90211, USA
**Krumrie, Timothy A (Tim)** — Football Player
21215 Bucking Way, Oak Creek CO 80467, USA
**Krupa, Joanna** — Model, Actress
Major Model Mgmt, 419 Park Ave, #1201, New York NY 10016, USA
**Krupp, Uwe** — Ice Hockey Player
3716 Strand, Manhattan Beach CA 90266, USA
**Krushelnyski, Mike** — Ice Hockey Player
7080 Holiday Dr, Bloomfield Hills MI 48301, USA
**Kruspe, Richard Z** — Guitarist (Rammstein)
Pilgrim Mgmt, PO Box 540101, 10042 Berlin, Germany
**Krylova, Angelika** — Ice Dancer
Skating Assn, Luchnesksaia Nab 8, 119871 Moscow, Russia
**Krynzel, Dave** — Baseball Player
951 Derringer Lane, Henderson NV 89014, USA
**Krypreos, Nick** — Ice Hockey Player
9209 Copenhaven Dr, Potomac MD 20854, USA
**Krystkowiak, Larry B** — Basketball Player, Coach
2343 S Dallin St, Salt Lake City UT 84109, USA
**Krzyzewski, Michael W (Mike)** — Basketball Coach
4406 W Cornwallis Road, Durham NC 27705, USA
**K's Choice** — Rock Musical Group
Sharpe's Entertainment Services, 683 Palmera Ave, Pacific Palisades CA 90272, USA
**Kuba, Filip** — Ice Hockey Player
17216 Emerald Chase Dr, Tampa FL 33647, USA
**Kuban, Bob** — Singer, Drummer
17626 Lasiandra Dr, Chesterfield MO 63005, USA
**Kubek, Anthony C (Tony)** — Baseball Player, Sportscaster
121 E Water St, #120, Appleton WI 54911, USA
**Kubel, Jason J** — Baseball Player
21031 Ventura Blvd, #1000, Woodland Hills CA 91364, USA
**Kube-McDowell, Michael P** — Writer
4403 Cherry Hill Dr, Okemos MI 48864, USA
**Kubenka, Jeffrey S (Jeff)** — Baseball Player
6935 FM 957, Schulenburg TX 78956, USA
**Kuberski, Robert K (Bob), Jr** — Football Player
13 Forwood Dr, Garnet Valley PA 19060, USA
**Kuberski, Stephen P (Steve)** — Basketball Player
91 Lawson Road, Winchester MA 01890, USA
**Kubiak, Gary** — Football Player, Coach
PO Box 350, Plantersville TX 77363, USA
**Kubiak, Leo** — Basketball Player
2638 N Prestwick Way, Lecanto FL 34461, USA
**Kubiak, Teresa M** — Opera Singer
Indiana University, Jacobs Music School, Bloomington IN 47405, USA
**Kubiak, Theodore R (Ted)** — Baseball Player
11956 Bernando Plaza Dr, San Diego CA 92128, USA
**Kubilius, Andrius** — Prime Minister, Lithuania
Prime Minister's Office, Tumo-Vaizganto 2, 01511 Vilnius, Lithuania
**Kubina, Pavel** — Ice Hockey Player
1145 81st St S, Saint Petersburg FL 33707, USA
**Kubski, Gilbert T (Gil)** — Baseball Player
4542 Scenario Dr, Huntington Beach CA 92649, USA
**Kucek, John A C (Jack)** — Baseball Player
8220 Blue Heron Lane, Canfield OH 44406, USA
**Kucera, Frantisek** — Ice Hockey Player
Sportovni, Tupolevova Ui 669, 19900 Prague Letnany 9, Czech Republic
**Kuchar, Matthew G (Matt)** — Golfer
1909 Dixon Lann, Saint Simons Island GA 31522, USA
**Kuchinskaya, Natalya A** — Gymnast
International Gymnastics Gym, 520 Business Center Dr, Mount Prospect IL 60056, USA
**Kuchma, Leonid D** — President, Ukraine
Koncha-Zaspa, Stolychne Shose, 08711 Kiev, Ukraine
**Kucinich, Dennis J** — Representative, OH; Mayor, Cleveland
14518 Drake Road, Strongsville OH 44136, USA
**Kuczenski, Bruce J** — Basketball Player
135 Southshire Dr, Southington CT 06489, USA
**Kuczynski Godard, Pedro-Pablo** — Prime Minister, Peru
Premier's Office, Urb Corpac, Calle 1 Oeste, San Isidro, Lima 27, Peru
**Kuczynski, Betty** — Bowler
4515 Prescott Ave, Lyons IL 60534, USA
**Kudelka, James A** — Ballet Choreographer, Dancer
National Ballet of Canada, 470 Queens Quay W, Toronto ON M5V 3K4, Canada
**Kudelski, Bob** — Ice Hockey Player
93 Copperleaf Dr, Cody WY 82414, USA
**Kuder, Mary** — Artist
Kuder Art Studio, 539 Navahopi Road, Sedona AZ 86336, USA
**Kudlow, Lawrence E** — Government Official, Economist
Kudlow Co, 301 Tahmore Dr, Fairfield CT 06825, USA

**Kudrna, Julius** — Canoeing Athlete
Sekaninova 36, 12000 Prague 2, Czech Republic

**Kudrow, Lisa** — Actress
Is or Isn't Entertainment, 8391 Beverly Blvd, #125, Los Angeles CA 90048, USA

**Kuebler, David** — Opera Singer
Haydn Rawstron, 36 Station Road, London SE20 7BQ, England

**Kuechenberg, Robert J (Bob)** — Football Player
2519 Arbor Dr, Fort Lauderdale FL 33312, USA

**Kuechenberg, Rudolph B (Rudy)** — Football Player
2928 SE 20th Ave, Cape Coral FL 33904, USA

**Kuehn, Enrico** — Bobsled Athlete
B S D, An der Schiessstatte 4, 83471 Berchtesgaden, Germany

**Kuehne, Hank** — Golfer
11117 Green Bayberry Dr, Palm Beach Gardens FL 33418, USA

**Kuehne, Kelli** — Golfer
245 Kings Peak Court, Heber City UT 84032, USA

**Kuerten, Gustavo** — Tennis Player
Octagon Worldwide, 1751 Pinnacle Dr, #1500, McLean VA 22102 USA

**Kuerti, Julian** — Conductor
I M G Artists, Hogarth Business Park, Chiswick, London W4 2TH, England

**Kuester, John D, Jr** — Basketball Player, Coach
105 Carnoustie Way, Media PA 19063, USA

**Kufeldt, James** — Businessman
Winn-Dixie Stores, 5050 Edgewood Court, Jacksonville FL 32254, USA

**Kuffner, Andreas** — Rowing Athlete
Berlin Ruder-Club, Bismarckstr 4, 14109 Berlin, Germany

**Kufuor, John Agyekum** — President, Ghana
President's Office, Golden Jubilee House, PO Box 1627, Accra, Ghana

**Kugler, Pete D** — Football Player
33 Peach Court, Marco Island FL 34145, USA

**Kuhaulua, Jesse** — Sumo Wrestler
Azumazeki Stable, 4-6-4 Higashi Komagata, Ryogoku, Tokyo 130 0005, Japan

**Kuhl, Patrick** — Swimmer
Sudring 2, 76532 Baden-Baden, Germany

**Kuhlman, Arkadi** — Financier
I N G Direct, PO Box 80, Saint Cloud MN 56302, USA

**Kuhlman, Ron** — Actor
5738 Willis Ave, Van Nuys CA 91411, USA

**Kuhlmann, Kathleen M** — Opera Singer
International Management Group, 54 Ave Marceau, 75008 Paris, France

**Kuhlmann-Wilsdorf, Doris** — Physicist
University of Virginia, Materials Science Dept, Charlottesville VA 22901, USA

**Kuhn, David E** — Animator
Plum TV, 419 Lafayette St, #700, New York NY 10003, USA

**Kuhn, Gustav** — Conductor
Winkel 25, 6343 Ere, Austria

**Kuhn, John A** — Football Player
Green Bay Packers, 1265 Lombardi Ave, Green Bay WI 54304 USA

**Kuhn, Mona** — Photographer
M+B Gallery, 612 N Almont Drive, Los Angeles CA 90069, USA

**Kuhn, Stephen L (Steve)** — Jazz Pianist, Composer
Berkeley Agency, 2608 9th St, #301, Berkeley CA 94710 USA

**Kuhne-Schiemann, Rita** — Track Athlete
Rosenweg 8, 14542 Werder/Havel, Germany

**Kuiper, Duane E** — Baseball Player
3665 Deer Trail Dr, Danville CA 94506, USA

**Kuipers, Andre** — Astronaut, Netherlands
European Space Centre, 8-10 Rue Mario Nikis, 75738 Paris Cedex, France

**Kuisma, Antti** — Nordic Combined Skier
Olympic Committee, Radiokatu 20, 00240 Helsinki, Finland

**Kukla, Yolane** — Swimmer
Saint Peters Western Swimming Club, PO Box 598, Indooroopilly QLD 4068, Australia

**Kukoc, Toni** — Basketball Player
1850 Hybernia Dr, Highland Park IL 60035, USA

**Kula, Irwin** — Religious Leader, Rabbi, Writer
Center for Learning & Leadership, 440 Park Ave S, #400, New York NY 10016, USA

**Kuleshov, Valery** — Concert Pianist
Musicians Corporate Mgmt, PO Box 825, Highland NY 12528, USA

**Kulhavy, Jaroslav** — Cyclist
Pivovarska 424, 56203 Ussti Nad Orlici, Czech Republic

**Kulich, Vladimir** — Actor
Jeff Goldberg Mgmt, 817 Monte Leon Dr, Beverly Hills CA 90210, USA

**Kulick, Bruce H** — Guitarist (Kiss)
60 Cycle Media, PO Box 3743, Santa Monica CA 90408, USA

**Kulick, Kelly** — Bowler
Professional Bowlers Association, 719 2nd Ave, #701, Seattle WA 98104 USA

**Kulifai, Tamas** — Canoeing Athlete
M T K Budapest, Salgotarjani Ut 12, 1087 Budapest, Hungary

**Kulik, Ilia A** — Figure Skater
Celebrity Consultants, 3340 Ocean Park Blvd, #1005, Santa Monica CA 90405 USA

**Kulka, Konstanty A** — Concert Violinist
Filharmonia Narodowa, Ul Jasna 5, 00007 Warsaw, Poland

**Kulkarni, Shrinivas R** — Astronomer
California Institute of Technology, Astronomy Dept, Pasadena CA 91125, USA

**Kullberg, Duane R** — Businessman
6444 N 79th St, Scottsdale AZ 85250, USA

**Kullman, Ellen** — Businesswoman
E I DuPont de Nemours, 1007 Market St, Wilmington DE 19895, USA

**Kulov, Feliks S** — Prime Minister, Kyrgyzstan
Prime Minister's Office, Ul Perromayskaya 57, 720003 Bishkek, Kyrgyzstan

**Kuma, Kengo** — Architect
Kengo Kuma Assoc, 2-12-12, Minamiaoyama, Minatoku, Tokyo 107 0062, Japan

**Kumagai, Saki** — Soccer Player
Olympique Lyon Feminin, 350 Ave Jean-Jaures, 69361 Lyon, France

**Kumanyika, Shiriki K** — Nutritionist
University of Illinois, Nutrition & Dietetics Dept, Chicago IL 60607, USA

**Kumar, Akshay** — Actor
Benzer Lokhandwala Complex Andheri (W), 203A Wing, Mumbai MS 400053, India

**Kumar, Dilip** — Actor
34/B Palli Hill, Nargis Dutt Road Bndra (W), Mumbai MS 400050, India

**Kumar, Manoj** — Actor, Director, Producer
Lakshmi Villa Grount, Tagore Road Santacruz (W), Mumbai MS 400050, India

**Kumbernuss, Astrid** — Track Athlete
Max Adrian Str 1, 17034 Neubrandenburg, Germany

**Kumble, Roger** — Director, Actor, Writer
United Talent Agency, U T A Plaza, 9336 Civic Center Dr, Beverly Hills CA 90210 USA

**Kume, John M** — Baseball Player
6810 Woodard Road, Andover OH 44003, USA

**Kummer, Glenn F** — Businessman
Fleetwood Enterprises, 3125 Myers St, Riverside CA 92503, USA

**Kummert, Andreas** — Singer, Songwriter
A2K-Media & Music, Ziegelwasenstr 17/1, 72661 Grafenberg, Germany

**Kundera, Milan** — Writer
Gallimard, 5 Rue Sebastien-Bottin, 75007 Paris, France

**Kundert, Kenneth S** — Engineer
Designers' Guide Consulting, 101 1st St, #150, Los Altos CA 94022, USA

**Kundla, John A** — Basketball Coach
909 Main St NE, #208, Minneapolis MN 55413, USA

**Kunerth, Mark J** — Writer, Producer
Broder Webb Chervin Silbermann, 9242 Beverly Blvd, Beverly Hills CA 90210 USA

**Kunes, Ellen** — Editor
Oprah Magazine, Editor's Office, 224 W 57th St, #900, New York NY 10019, USA

**Kung, Candie** — Golfer
Ladies Pro Golf Assn, 100 International Golf Dr, Daytona Beach FL 32124 USA

**Kung, Hans** — Theologian
Waldhauserstr 23, 72076 Tubingen, Germany

**Kung, Patrick C** — Pharmacologist
T Cell Sciences, 119 4th Ave, Needham MA 02494, USA

**Kunin, Madeline M** — Governor, VT
60 Southwind Dr, Burlington VT 05401, USA

**Kunis, Mila** — Actress
Creative Artists Agency, 2000 Ave of Stars, #100, Los Angeles CA 90067 USA

**Kunitz, Christopher (Chris)** — Ice Hockey Player
Pittsburgh Penguins, Consol Energy Center, 1001 5th Ave, Pittsburgh PA 15219 USA

**Kunitz, Matt** — Producer
Endemol Entertainment, 9255 W Sunset Blvd, #1100, Los Angeles CA 90069, USA

**Kunkel, Jeffrey W (Jeff)** — Baseball Player
4921 County Road 605, Burleson TX 76028, USA

**Kunkel, Louis M** — Pediatrician
Children's Hospital, 300 Longwood Ave, Boston MA 02115, USA

**Kunkle, John F** — Religious Leader
Evangelical Methodist Church, 3000 W Kellogg Dr, Wichita KS 67213, USA

**Kunnert, Kevin R** — Basketball Player
8286 SW Wilderland Court, Portland OR 97224, USA

**Kunstler, Morton** — Artist, Illustrator
137 Cove Neck Road, Oyster Bay NY 11771, USA

**Kuntz, Russell J (Rusty)** — Baseball Player
10102 W 152nd Terrace, Overland Park KS 66221, USA

**Kunz, George J** — Football Player
8215 S Bermuda Road, Las Vegas NV 89123, USA

**Kunze, Terry D** — Basketball Player
6931 Halifax Ave N, Minneapolis MN 55429, USA

**Kunzru, Hari** — Writer
E P Dutton, 375 Hudson St, New York NY 10014 USA

**Kupchak, Mitchell (Mitch)** — Basketball Player
361 Fordyce Road, Los Angeles CA 90049, USA

**Kupcinet, Kari** — Actress
1660 Mill Trail, Highland Park IL 60035, USA

**Kupec, Charles J** — Basketball Player
6448 River Run, Columbia MD 21044, USA

**Kupets, Courtney** — Gymnast
133 Falling Shoals Dr, Athens GA 30605, USA

**Kupfer, Abraham (Avi)** — Immunologist
Johns Hopkins University Medical School, Immunobiology Dept, 733 N Broadway, Baltimore MD 21205, USA

**Kupfer, Carl** — Ophthalmologist
National Institutes of Health, 10 Center Dr, Bethesda MD 20892, USA

**Kupfer, Harry** — Director
Komische Oper, Behrenstr 55-57, 10117 Berlin, Germany

**Kupferberg, Sabine** — Ballerina
Dans Theater 3, Scheldoekshaven 60, 2511 Gravenhage EN, Netherlands

**Kupp, Jacob R (Jake)** — Football Player
4801 Snowmountain Road, Yakima WA 98908, USA

**Kupper, Ernst-Joachim** — Swimmer
Lepiershof 8, 44649 Herne, Germany

**Kupperman, Joel J** — Philosopher
115 E 9th St, #15E, New York NY 10003, USA

**Kurant, Willy** — Cinematographer
Lyons Sheldon Agency, 800 S Robertson Blvd, #6, Los Angeles CA 90035, USA

**Kuras, Ellen M** — Cinematographer
54 Summit St, Nyack NY 10960, USA

**Kureishi, Hanif** — Writer
Rogers Coleridge White, 20 Powis Mews, London W11 1JN, England

**Kurek, Ralph E** — Football Player
1311 Lime Pond Road, South Royalton VT 05068, USA

**Kurita, Toyomichi** — Cinematographer
Sandra Marsh Assoc, 9150 Wilshire Blvd, #220, Beverly Hills CA 90212 USA

**Kurkova Emmons, Katerina** — Markswoman
Olympic Committee, 1 Olympic Plaza, Building 6, Colorado Springs CO 80909 USA

**Kurkova, Karolina I** — Model, Actress
One Mgmt, 42 Bond St, #200, New York NY 10012 USA

**Kurlander, Tom** — Actor
Independent Artists Agency, 9601 Wilshire Blvd, #750, Beverly Hills CA 90210, USA

**K**

**Kumar - Kurlander**

**Kuroda, Emily** — Actress
Stone Manners Salners, 6100 Wilshire Blvd, #1500, Los Angeles CA 90035 USA
**Kuroda, Hiroki** — Baseball Player
New York Yankees, Yankee Stadium, E 161st St & River Ave, Bronx NY 10451 USA
**Kurosaki, Ryan Y** — Baseball Player
3324 Huelani Dr, Honolulu HI 96822, USA
**Kurrat, Klaus-Dieter** — Track Athlete
Zeisigsteg 5, 14532 Stahnsdorf, Germany
**Kurri, Jari P** — Ice Hockey Player
Hockey Hall of Fame, B C E Place, 30 Yonge St, Toronto ON M5E 1X8, Canada
**Kursinski, Anne** — Equestrian
107 Spring Hill Road, Frenchtown NJ 08825, USA
**Kurstin, Gregory A (Greg)** — Keyboardist (Bird & the Bee)
Blue Note Records, 6920 W Sunset Blvd, Los Angeles CA 90028 USA
**Kurtag, Gyorgy** — Composer
Lihego V3, 2621 Veroce, Hungary
**Kurtenbach, Orland J** — Ice Hockey Player
14066 29A Ave, Surrey BC V4P 2J8, Canada
**Kurth, Wallace (Wally)** — Actor, Singer
C E S D, 10635 Santa Monica Blvd, #130, Los Angeles CA 90025 USA
**Kurtha, Akbar** — Actor
United Agents, 12-26 Lexington St, London W1F 0LE, England
**Kurtis, Bill** — Commentator
Kurtis Productions, 400 W Erie St, #500, Chicago IL 60654, USA
**Kurtis, Darlene** — Model, Actress
Playboy Promotions, 9346 Civic Center Dr, #200, Beverly Hills CA 90210 USA
**Kurtova, Karolina** — Model
D N A Model Mgmt, 555 W 25th St, #600, New York NY 10001 USA
**Kurtovic, Amanda** — Handball Player
Viborg H K, Tingvej 7, 8800 Viborg, Denmark
**Kurtz, Harold J (Hal)** — Baseball Player
511 Flat Iron Square Road, Church Hill MD 21623, USA
**Kurtz, Swoosie** — Actress, Singer
Innovative Artists, 1505 10th St, Santa Monica CA 90401 USA
**Kurtze, Andrew** — Businessman
Sprint P C S Group, 6391 Sprint Parkway, Overland Park KS 66251, USA
**Kurtzig, Sandra L** — Businesswoman
E-Benefits, 2420 Sand Hill Road, #201, Menlo Park CA 94025, USA
**Kurtzman, Alex** — Writer, Producer
Kurtzman Orci Paper Products, 100 Universal Plaza, Building 5171, Universal City CA 91608, USA
**Kurupt** — Rap Artist, Songwriter, Actor
Likwit Entertainment, PO Box 360713, Los Angeles CA 90036, USA
**Kurvers, Tom** — Ice Hockey Player
10146 Birch Grove Road, Brainerd MN 56401, USA
**Kurylenko, Olga** — Actress, Model
Tavistock Wood Mgmt, 45 Conduit St, London W1S 2YN, England
**Kurzak, Aleksandra** — Opera Singer
I M G Artists, Hogarth Business Park, Chiswick, London W4 2TH, England
**Kurzel, Justin** — Director
H L A Management, PO Box 1536, Strawberry Hills, NSW 2012, Australia
**Kurzweil, Raymond** — Inventor (Computer-Generated Voice)
Capel & Land, 29 Wardour St, London W1D 6PS, England
**Kusama, Karyn** — Director
I C M Partners, 10250 Constellation Blvd, #900, Los Angeles CA 90067 USA
**Kusama, Yayoi** — Artist
Gagosian Gallery, 980 Madison Ave, New York NY 10075 USA
**Kusatsu, Clyde** — Actor
Stone Manners Salners, 6100 Wilshire Blvd, #1500, Los Angeles CA 90035 USA
**Kuschak, Metropolitan Andrei** — Religious Leader
Ukranian Orthodox Church in America, 3 Davenport Ave, New Rochelle NY 10805, USA
**Kuschela, Kurt** — Canoeing Athlete
Kanu Club Potsdam, Am Luftschiffhafen 2, 14471 Potsdam, Germany
**Kush, Rod R** — Football Player
10111 S 177th St, Omaha NE 68136, USA
**Kushboo** — Actress
20/1 Arch Bishop, Mathiyas Ave, Boat Club Road, Chennai TN 600028, India
**Kushell, Lisa** — Actress
Abrams Artists, 9200 W Sunset Blvd, #1125, West Hollywood CA 90069 USA
**Kushner, Harold S** — Religious Leader, Rabbi, Writer
Temple Israel, 145 Hartford St, Natick MA 01760, USA
**Kushner, Robert E** — Artist
D C Moore Gallery, 724 5th Ave, #800, New York NY 10019, USA
**Kushner, Tony** — Writer
Steve Barclay Agency, 12 Western Ave, Petaluma CA 94952, USA
**Kuske, Kevin** — Bobsled Athlete
K-Solution, Lindstedter Str 13B, 14469 Potsdam, Germany
**Kusnyer, Arthur W (Art)** — Baseball Player
6598 Taeda Dr, Sarasota FL 34241, USA
**Kustra, Robert W** — Educator
Boise State University, President's Office, Boise ID 83725, USA
**Kusturica, Emir** — Director, Writer, Actor
Fondazione Cultural Edison, Largo VIII Marzo 9, 43100 Parma, Italy
**Kutcher, Ashton** — Actor
Katalyst Films, 6806 Lexington Ave, Los Angeles CA 90038, USA
**Kutcher, Randy S** — Baseball Player
3016 Purple Sage Lane, Palmdale CA 93550, USA
**Kuttner, Stephan G** — Historian
2270 Le Conte Ave, #601, Berkeley CA 94709, USA
**Kutwa, Jean-Pierre Cardinal** — Religious Leader
Archdiocese of Abidjan, Av Jean Paul II, 01 BP 1287, Abidjan 01, Cote d'Ivoire
**Kutyna, Donald J** — Air Force General, Businessman
4818 Kenyon Court, Colorado Springs CO 80917, USA
**Kutyna, Marion J (Marty)** — Baseball Player
2255 NW 14th St, Delray Beach FL 33445, USA
**Kutzler, Jerry S** — Baseball Player
9500 81st St, #311, Pleasant Prairie WI 53158, USA

| | |
|---|---|
| **Kuusela, Armi H** <br> 6241 Waverly Ave, La Jolla CA 92037, USA | Beauty Queen |
| **Kuykendall, Fulton G** <br> 1497 Rucker Circle, Woodstock GA 30188, USA | Football Player |
| **Kuzava, Robert L (Bob)** <br> 1118 Vinewood St, Wyandotte MI 48192, USA | Baseball Player |
| **Kuziel, Robert C (Bob)** <br> 3375 Walnut Dr, Ellicott City MD 21043, USA | Football Player |
| **Kuzmina, Anastasiya V** <br> Biathlon Assn, Partizaska Cesta 71, 974 01 Banska Bystrica, Slovakia | Biathlete |
| **Kuznetsoff, Alexei** <br> Columbia Artists Mgmt Inc, 5 Columbus Circle, 1790 Broadway, #1600, New York NY 10019 USA | Concert Pianist |
| **Kuznetsova, Svetlana A** <br> Women's Tennis Assn, 1 Progress Plaza, #1500, Saint Petersburg FL 33701 USA | Tennis Player |
| **Kuznetsoya, Dina** <br> Harrison/Parrott, 5-6 Albion Court, London W6 0QT, England | Opera Singer |
| **Kuzyk, Mimi** <br> Characters Talent Mgmt, 8 Elm St, Toronto ON M5G 1G7, Canada | Actress |
| **Kvapil, Radoslav** <br> Hradecka 5, 13000 Prague 3, Czech Republic | Concert Pianist |
| **Kvapil, Travis** <br> 141 Silverleaf Lane, Mooresville NC 28115, USA | Auto, Truck Racing Driver |
| **Kvasha, Oleg V** <br> 22 Bluff Road, Glen Cove NY 11542, USA | Ice Hockey Player |
| **Kvitova, Petra** <br> T K Agrofert Prostejev, Za Kestleckou 51, 79640 Prostejov, Czech Republic | Tennis Player |
| **Kwak Yoon-Gy** <br> Skating Union, 88 Bangyee-Dong, Songpaku, Seoul 138 749, South Korea | Speed Skater |
| **Kwalick, Thaddeus J (Ted)** <br> 755 Purdue Court, Santa Clara CA 95051, USA | Football Player |
| **Kwan, Jennie** <br> Innovative Artists, 1505 10th St, Santa Monica CA 90401 USA | Actress |
| **Kwan, Michelle W** <br> Tufts University, Fletcher Law & Diplomacy School, Medford MA 02155, USA | Figure Skater |
| **Kwan, Nancy** <br> Marlin, 252 7th Ave, #9P, New York NY 10001, USA | Actress |
| **Kwanten, Ryan** <br> Orly Adelson Productions, 2900 Olympic Blvd, Los Angeles CA 90404, USA | Actor |
| **Kwapis, Ken** <br> United Talent Agency, U T A Plaza, 9336 Civic Center Dr, Beverly Hills CA 90210 USA | Director, Producer, Actor |
| **Kwasniewski, Aleksander** <br> Kancelaria Prezydenta RP, Ul Wiejska 4/8, 00 902 Warsaw, Poland | President, Poland |
| **Kweli, Talib** <br> Creative Artists Agency, 2000 Ave of Stars, #100, Los Angeles CA 90067 USA | Rap Artist (Black Star), Songwriter |
| **Kweller, Ben** <br> Big Hassle, 44 Wall St, #2200, New York NY 10005, USA | Singer, Songwriter |
| **Kwiatkowski, Joel** <br> 2020 Tall Pines Dr SE, Grand Rapids MI 49546, USA | Ice Hockey Player |
| **Kwoh, Yik San** <br> Hi-Tech Medical Systems, 17155 Newhope St, Fountain Valley CA 92708, USA | Electrical Engineer, Inventor |
| **Kwouk, Burt** <br> QVoice, Holborn Hall, 193-197 High Holborn, London WC1V 7BD, England | Actor |
| **Kyd, Gerald** <br> Artists Partnership, 101 Finsbury Pavement, London EC2A 1RS, England | Actor |
| **Kydland, Finn E** <br> 169 Noble Lane, Worthington PA 16262, USA | Nobel Economics Laureate |
| **Kyle, Aaron D** <br> 14420 Ballantyne Lake Road, #313, Charlotte NC 28277, USA | Football Player |
| **Kyle, David L** <br> O N E O K Inc, 100 W 5th St, PO Box 871, Tulsa OK 74102, USA | Businessman |
| **Kyle, Jason C** <br> 19109 W Catawba Ave, #200, Cornelius NC 28031, USA | Football Player |
| **Kyle, Kaylyn M** <br> Boston Breakers, 214 Lincoln St, #304, Allston MA 02134, USA | Soccer Player |
| **Kylian, Jiri** <br> Netherlands Dance Theater, Schedeldoekshaven 60, 2501 The Haag CH, Netherlands | Ballet Dancer |
| **Kyllonen, Anne** <br> Suksihionta, Sormelantie 77, 38800 Jamijarvi, Finland | Cross Country Skier |
| **Kynard, Erik, Jr** <br> 4860 Catalina Dr, Toledo OH 43615, USA | Track Athlete |
| **Kynaston, Nicholas** <br> 25 High Park Road, Richmond-upon-Thames, Surrey TW9 4BH, England | Concert Organist |
| **Kyo, Machiko** <br> Olimpia Copu, 6-35 Jingumae, Shibuyaku, Tokyo 151 0001, Japan | Actress |
| **Kyrillos, Jean-Paul** <br> Food & Wine, Publisher's Office, 1120 Ave of Americas, New York NY 10036, USA | Publisher |
| **Kyson Lee, James** <br> Prestige Talent Agency, 9250 Wilshire Blvd, #208, Beverly Hills CA 90212 90212, USA | Actor |
| **Kyte, Jim** <br> 226 Sherwood Dr, Ottawa ON K1Y 3V8, Canada | Ice Hockey Player |

**Laage, Gerhart** — Architect
Schulterblatt 36, 20357 Hamburg, Germany

**Laaksonen, Antti** — Ice Hockey Player
9225 Red Oak Dr, Victoria MN 55386, USA

**Laaveg, Paul M** — Football Player
PO Box 406, Berryville VA 22611, USA

**LaBar, Jeffrey P (Jeff)** — Singer, Guitarist (Cinderella)
Union Entertainment Group, 1323 Newbury Road, #104, Thousand Oaks CA 91320, USA

**Labarthe, Samuel** — Actor
Cineart, 28 Rue Mogador, 78009 Paris, France

**LaBelle, Patti** — Singer
Resolution, 1801 Century Park E, #2300, Los Angeles CA 90067 USA

**Labelle, Rob** — Actor, Producer, Director
Foundation Features, 88 E Pender St, #515, Vancouver BC V6A 3X3, Canada

**LaBeouf, Shia S** — Actor
John Crosby Mgmt, 1310 N Spaulding Ave, Los Angeles CA 90046 USA

**Labeque, Katia** — Concert Pianist
Askonas Holt, Lincoln House, 300 High Holborn, London WC1V 7JH, England

**Labeque, Marielle** — Concert Pianist
Askonas Holt, Lincoln House, 300 High Holborn, London WC1V 7JH, England

**Labine, Tyler** — Actor
Creative Artists Agency, 2000 Ave of Stars, #100, Los Angeles CA 90067 USA

**Labis, Attilo** — Ballet Dancer, Choreographer
13 Ave Rubens, 78400 Chateau, France

**Labonte, Charline (Charlie)** — Ice Hockey Player
Hockey Canada, 151 Canada Olympic Road SW, #201, Calgary AB T3B 6B7, Canada

**Labonte, Justin** — Auto Racing Driver
PO Box 843, Trinity NC 27370, USA

**Labonte, Robert A (Bobby)** — Auto Racing Driver
Bobby Labonte Racing, PO Box 358, Trinity NC 27370, USA

**Labonte, Terrance L (Terry)** — Auto, Truck Racing Driver
PO Box 370, Trinity NC 27370, USA

**Labounty, Matthew J (Matt)** — Football Player
360 W 17th Ave, Eugene OR 97401, USA

**LaBour, Fred (Too Slim)** — Singer, Bassist (Riders in the Sky)
New Frontier Mgmt, 1921 Broadway, Nashville TN 37203, USA

**Labourier, Dominique** — Actress
Agence Elisabeth Simpson, 62 Blvd du Montparnasse, 75015 Paris, France

**LaBoy, Travis J** — Football Player
2709 Arnoldson Ave, San Diego CA 92122, USA

**Labre, Yvon** — Ice Hockey Player
7812 Tilmont Ave, Parkville MD 21234, USA

**Labrinth** — Singer, Songwriter
W M E Entertainment, Centrepoint Tower, 103 New Oxford St, London WC1A 1DD, England

**LaBute, Neil** — Director, Writer
Contemptible Entertainment, 1202 Poinsettia Drive, West Hollywood CA 90046, USA

**Labyorteaux, Matthew** — Actor
167 W 72nd St, #3R, New York NY 10023, USA

**Labyorteaux, Patrick** — Actor
C E S D, 10635 Santa Monica Blvd, #130, Los Angeles CA 90025 USA

**Lacasse, Genevieve** — Ice Hockey Player
Hockey Canada, 151 Canada Olympic Road SW, #201, Calgary AB T3B 6B7, Canada

**Lace, Jerry E** — Figure Skating Executive
10214 Pine Glade Dr, Colorado Springs CO 80920, USA

**Lacey, Deborah** — Actress
A K A Talent, 6310 San Vicente Blvd, #200, Los Angeles CA 90048 USA

**Lacey, Jesse T** — Singer (Taking Back Sunday, Brand New)
Stunt Company Media, 20 Jay St, #208, Brooklyn NY 11201, USA

**Lacey, Robert J (Bob)** — Baseball Player
1717 20th St NW, #308, Washington DC 20009, USA

**Lach, Elmer J** — Ice Hockey Player
89 Bayview Ave, Pointe Claire QC H9S 5C4, Canada

**Lachance, Michel (Mike)** — Harness Racing Driver
183 Sweetmans Lane, Millstone Township NJ 08535, USA

**LaChance, Scott** — Ice Hockey Player
15 Meadow View Lane, Andover MA 01810, USA

**LaChapelle, David** — Photographer
Creative Exchange Agency, 45 W 25th St, #1900, New York NY 10001, USA

**Lachemann, Marcel E** — Baseball Player, Manager
PO Box 1967, Nipomo CA 93444, USA

**Lachemann, Rene G** — Baseball Player, Manager
7500 E Boulders Parkway, #68, Scottsdale AZ 85266, USA

**Lacher, Blaine** — Ice Hockey Player
29 Shannon Crescent SE, Medicine Hat AB T1B 4C2, Canada

**Lachey, Andrew J (Drew)** — Singer (98 Degrees), Actor
Core Entertainment, 14742 Ventura Blvd, #PH, Sherman Oaks CA 91403, USA

**Lachey, James M (Jim)** — Football Player
1445 Roxbury Road, Columbus OH 43212, USA

**Lachey, Nicholas S (Nick)** — Singer (98 Degrees)
I C M Partners, 10250 Constellation Blvd, #900, Los Angeles CA 90067 USA

**LaChiusa, Michael John** — Composer, Librettist
Abrams Artists, 9200 W Sunset Blvd, #1125, West Hollywood CA 90069 USA

**Lachman, Dichen** — Actress
Gersh Agency, 9465 Wilshire Blvd, #600, Beverly Hills CA 90212 USA

**Lachman, Gary Valentine** — Writer, Musician
Tarcher/Penguin Books, 375 Hudson St, Basement 1, New York NY 10014, USA

**Lacina, Corbin** — Football Player
130 Otis Ave, Saint Paul MN 55104, USA

**Lack, Andrew** — Businessman
Sony/BMG Music Entertainment, 550 Madison Ave, #600, New York NY 10022, USA

**Lackberg, Camilla** — Writer
Nordin Agency, Gotgatan 58, 102 61 Stockholm, Sweden

**Lacke, Elizabeth (Beth)** — Actress
Aria Model & Talent Mgmt, 1017 W Washington, #2C, Chicago IL 60607, USA

**Lacker, Jeffrey** — Financier, Government Official
Federal Reserve Board, 701 E Byrd St, #200, Richmond VA 23219, USA

**Lackey, Elizabeth (Lisa)** — Actress
Marquee Mgmt, Gate House, 188 Oxford St, Paddington NSW 2021, Australia

**Lackey, John D** — Baseball Player
15176 NW 100th Avenue Road, Reddick FL 32686, USA

**Lackovic, Blazenko** — Handball Player
H S V Handball Betriebsgesellschaft, Hellgrundweg 50, 22525 Hamburg, Germany

**Laclavere, Georges** — Geophysicist
53 Ave de Breteuil, 70075 Paris, France

**Laclotte, Michel R** — Museum Executive
10 Bis Rue du Pre-aux-Clerc, 75007 Paris, France

**Lacock, R Pierre (Pete)** — Baseball Player
10019 Mackey Circle, Overland Park KS 66212, USA

**Lacombe, Francois** — Ice Hockey Player
Webster Hockey Academy, 22 Hampton Gardens, Point Claire QC H9S 5B8, Canada

**Lacombe, Henri** — Oceanographer
20 Bis Ave de Lattre de Tassigny, 92340 Bourg la Reine, France

**Lacorte, Frank J** — Baseball Player
1667 El Dorado Dr, Gilroy CA 95020, USA

**Lacoste, Catherine** — Golfer
Calle B6, #4, El Soto de la Moraleja Alcobendas, Madrid, Spain

**Lacroix, Andre J** — Ice Hockey Player
115 S Franklin St, Chagrin Falls OH 44022, USA

**Lacroix, Christian M M** — Fashion Designer
73 Rue du Faubourg Saint Honore, 75008 Paris, France

**Lacroix, Daniel** — Ice Hockey Player
New York Rangers, Madison Square Garden, 2 Penn Plaza, New York NY 10121 USA

**Lacroix, Gerald Cyprien Cardinal** — Religious Leader
Archdiocese of Quebec, 1073 Boul Rene-Levesque Ouest, Sillery QC G1S 4R5, Canada

**Lacy, Alan** — Businessman
Sears Roebuck Co, 3333 Beverly Blvd, Hoffman Estates IL 60179, USA

**Lacy, Edgar E** — Basketball Player
215 6th St, #D, West Sacramento CA 95605, USA

**Lacy, Jake** — Actor
Creative Artists Agency, 2000 Ave of Stars, #100, Los Angeles CA 90067 USA

**Lacy, Jeffrey S (Jeff)** — Boxer
5718 Eaglemount Dr, Lithia FL 33547, USA

**Lacy, Jerry** — Actor
Sutton-Barth Vennari, 5900 Wilshire Blvd, #700, Los Angeles CA 90036 USA

**Lacy, Leondaus (Lee)** — Baseball Player
6130 Nevada Ave, #E420, Woodland Hills CA 91367, USA

**Ladd, Alan W, Jr** — Producer
706 N Arden Dr, Beverly Hills CA 90210, USA

**Ladd, Andrew** — Ice Hockey Player
550 N Saint Clair St, #2403, Chicago IL 60611, USA

**Ladd, Cheryl** — Actress
Don Buchwald Talent Agency, 6500 Wilshire Blvd, #2200, Los Angeles CA 90048 USA

**Ladd, David** — Actor, Producer
David Ladd Films, 9465 Wilshire Blvd, Beverly Hills CA 90212, USA

**Ladd, Diane** — Actress
Scott Hart Mgmt, 14622 Ventura Blvd, #746, Sherman Oaks CA 91403, USA

**Ladd, Peter L (Pete)** — Baseball Player
239 Town Farm Road, New Gloucester ME 04260, USA

**Laderman, Ezra** — Composer
Yale University, Music School, New Haven CT 06520, USA

**Ladin, Eric** — Actor
Innovative Artists, 1505 10th St, Santa Monica CA 90401 USA

**Ladner, Benjamin** — Educator
American University, President's Office, Washington DC 20016, USA

**Ladouceur, Randy** — Ice Hockey Player
12116 Mabledon Court, Raleigh NC 27613, USA

**Lady Gaga** — Singer, Songwriter
40 Central Park S, #PHD, New York NY 10019, USA

**Lady Rizo** — Singer, Comedienne
Yonas Media, 1625 Broadway, Oakland CA 94612, USA

**Lady Sovereign** — Rap Artist
Paradigm Agency, 360 N Crescent Dr, North Building, Beverly Hills CA 90210 USA

**Laettner, Christian D** — Basketball Player
1041 Ponte Vedra Blvd, Ponte Vedra Beach FL 32082, USA

**LaFalce, John J** — Representative, NY
191 Bering Ave, Buffalo NY 14223, USA

**Lafayette, John** — Actor
Greene Assoc, 1901 Ave of Stars, #130, Los Angeles CA 90067 USA

**Lafayette, Nathan** — Ice Hockey Player
Travel Guard Canada, 145 Wellington St W, Toronto ON M5J 1H8, Canada

**Laffer, Arthur B** — Economist
24255 Pacific Coast Highway, Malibu CA 90263, USA

**Lafferty, James** — Actor, Director, Producer
Paradigm Agency, 360 N Crescent Dr, North Building, Beverly Hills CA 90210 USA

**Laffey, Aaron S** — Baseball Player
1545 N Lakewood Dr, Ridgeley WV 26753, USA

**Lafforgue, Laurent** — Mathematician
I H E S, Mathematics Dept, 91440 Bures sur Yvette, France

**LaFlamme, David** — Violinist (It's a Beautiful Day)
Tabletop Productions, PO Box 698, Carson City NV 89702, USA

**Lafleur, Gregory L (Greg)** — Football Player
PO Box 612, Baton Rouge LA 70821, USA

**Lafleur, Guy D** — Ice Hockey Player
14 Place du Moulin, L'Ile Bizard QC H9E 1N2, Canada

**Lafley, Alan G** — Businessman
Procter & Gamble Co, 1 Procter & Gamble Plaza, Cincinnati OH 45202, USA

**Laflin, Bonnie-Jill** — Model, Entertainer
C E S D, 10635 Santa Monica Blvd, #130, Los Angeles CA 90025 USA

**LaFontaine, Patrick (Pat)** — Ice Hockey Player
3 Beach Dr, Lloyd Harbor NY 11743, USA

**Laforet, Marie** — Actress
Agents Associes, 201 Rue du Faubourg Saint Honore, 75008 Paris, France

**L**

| | |
|---|---|
| **LaForgia, Michael** Tampa Bay Times, Editorial Dept, 401 Channelside Dr, Tampa FL 33602 USA | Journalist |
| **Lafrance, Noemie** 148 Classon Ave, Brooklyn NY 11205, USA | Choreographer |
| **Lafreniere, Roger** 110 Eugene Road, North Bay ON P1B 8B7, Canada | Ice Hockey Player |
| **LaFrentz, Raef A** PO Box 88, Decorah IA 52101, USA | Basketball Player |
| **Laga, Michael R (Mike)** 148 Maple Ridge Road, Florence MA 01062, USA | Baseball Player |
| **Lagarde, Christine** International Monetary Fund, 700 19th Ave NW, Washington DC 20431, USA | Financier |
| **LaGarde, Thomas J (Tom)** 3809 E Greensboro Chapel Hill Road, Snow Camp NC 27349, USA | Basketball Player |
| **Lagardere, Arnaud** Airbus Industrie, Ronde Point Maucie Bellont 1, 31707 Blagnac, France | Businessman |
| **Lagasse, Emeril** 829 Saint Charles Ave, New Orleans LA 70130, USA | Chef, Restauranteur |
| **Lagat, Bernard** 9121 E Cottonwood Court, Tucson AZ 85749, USA | Track Athlete |
| **Lagattuta, Bill** CBS-TV, News Dept, 7800 Beverly Blvd, Los Angeles CA 90036, USA | Commentator |
| **Lageman, Jeffrey D (Jeff)** PO Box 364, Basye VA 22810, USA | Football Player |
| **Lagerberg, Bengt F A** Talent Tust, Kungsgaten 9C, 411 19 Gothenburg, Sweden | Drummer (Cardigans) |
| **Lagerfeld, Karl** 31 Blvd de la Maubourg, 75007 Paris, France | Fashion Designer, Photographer |
| **Lago, Clara** Kuranda Mgmt, Santo Angel 84, 28043 Madrid, Spain | Actress |
| **Lagoo, Shreeram** 3 Gold Mist, 36 Carter Road, Bandra, Mumbai MS 400050, India | Actor |
| **Lagos Escobar, Ricardo** Club de Madrid, C/Goya 5-7, Pasaje 2, 28001 Madrid, Spain | President, Chile |
| **LaGravenese, Richard** Creative Artists Agency, 2000 Ave of Stars, #100, Los Angeles CA 90067 USA | Director, Writer |
| **LaGrossa, Stephanie** 42 Caldwell Dr, Toms River NJ 08757, USA | Actress |
| **Lagrow, Lerrin H** 12271 E Turquoise Ave, Scottsdale AZ 85259, USA | Baseball Player |
| **LaHaie, Dick** Kalitta Motorsports, 1010 James L Hart Parkway, Ypsilanti MI 48197, USA | Drag Racing Driver |
| **LaHaye, Tim** Tyndale House Publishers, 351 Executive Dr, PO Box 80, Wheaton IL 60187, USA | Writer |
| **Lahbib, Simone** Artists Partnership, 101 Finsbury Pavement, London EC2A 1RS, England | Actress, Producer |
| **Lahiri, Jhumpa** Knopf Publishers, 1745 Broadway, New York NY 10019 USA | Writer |
| **Lahm, Philipp** Rinab Grill, Rathausstr 39, 83734 Hausham, Germany | Soccer Player |
| **LaHood, Ray** Transportation Department, 400 7th St SW, Washington DC 20590 USA | Secretary, Transporation |
| **Lahoud, Joseph M (Joe)** 90 Tinker Hill Road, New Preston Marble Dale CT 06777, USA | Baseball Player |
| **Lahti, Christine** Management 360, 9111 Wilshire Blvd, Beverly Hills CA 90210 USA | Actress, Director |
| **Lahti, Jeffrey A (Jeff)** 4632 Tyler Dr, Hood River OR 97031, USA | Baseball Player |
| **Lai, Francis** 23 Rue Franklin, 75016 Paris, France | Composer |
| **Laidig, William R** 26455 S Tamiami Trail, #3108, Bonita Springs FL 34134, USA | Businessman |
| **Laidlaw, R Scott** 2286 Franklin Pike, Lewisburg TN 37091, USA | Football Player |
| **Laidlaw, Tom** Laidlaw Sports Mgmt, 32 Ridge Blvd, Port Chester NY 10573, USA | Ice Hockey Player |
| **Laimbeer, William (Bill)** 470 Gray Court, Marco Island FL 34145, USA | Basketball Player |
| **Laine, Cleo** Old Rectory, Wavendon, Milton Keynes MK1 8LT, England | Singer |
| **Laine, Denny** I C M Partners, 10250 Constellation Blvd, #900, Los Angeles CA 90067 USA | Singer, Guitarist (Moody Blues) |
| **Laing, Richard** Artists Partnership, 101 Finsbury Pavement, London EC2A 1RS, England | Actor |
| **Laingen, L Bruce** 9707 Old Georgetown Road, #2112, Bethesda MD 20814, USA | Diplomat |
| **Laird, Bruce A** 1405 Margarette Ave, Towson MD 21286, USA | Football Player |
| **Laird, Gerald L, III** 13735 E Yucca St, Scottsdale AZ 85259, USA | Baseball Player |
| **Laird, Martin** Professional Golfers Association, 100 Ave of Champions, Palm Beach Gardens FL 33418 USA | Golfer |
| **Laird, Melvin R** 1730 Rhode Island Ave NW, #406, Washington DC 20036, USA | Secretary, Defense; Businessman |
| **Laird, Peter** PO Box 417, Haydenville MA 01039, USA | Cartoonist (Ninja Turtles) |
| **Laird, Ronald (Ron)** 4706 Diane Dr, Ashtabula OH 44004, USA | Track Athlete |
| **Laitman, Jeffrey** Mount Sinai Medical Center, Anatomy Dept, 1 Levy Place, New York NY 10029, USA | Anatomist |
| **Lajoie, Jonathan** United Talent Agency, U T A Plaza, 9336 Civic Center Dr, Beverly Hills CA 90210 USA | Actor, Writer |
| **LaJoie, Randall (Randy)** PO Box 3478, Westport CT 06880, USA | Auto Racing Driver |
| **Lajolo, Giovanni Cardinal** Pontifical Commission for Vatican City State, Governatorate, 00120 Vatican City | Religious Leader |

**Lake, Antwan T** — Football Player
1032 Bluebell Dr, Dacula GA 30019, USA
**Lake, Carnell A** — Football Player
PO Box 55048, Irvine CA 92619, USA
**Lake, Don** — Actor, Writer
Divine Mgmt, 3822 Latrobe Ave, Los Angeles CA 90031, USA
**Lake, Gregory (Greg)** — Singer, Bassist (Emerson Lake Palmer)
Bruce Pilato Mgmt, PO Box 17775, Rochester NY 14617, USA
**Lake, James A** — Molecular Biologist
University of California, Molecular Biology Institute, Los Angeles CA 90024, USA
**Lake, Oliver E** — Jazz Saxophonist, Synthesizer Player
D L Media, 124 N Highland Ave, Bala Cynwyd PA 19004, USA
**Lake, Ricki** — Actress
W M E Entertainment, 9601 Wilshire Blvd, #300, Beverly Hills CA 90210 USA
**Lake, Sanoe** — Actress
Luber Rocklin Entertainment, 5815 Sunset Blvd, #206, Los Angeles CA 90028 USA
**Lake, Stephen M (Steve)** — Baseball Player
7402 N 177th Ave, Waddel AZ 85355, USA
**Laker, Jim** — Cricketer
Oak End, 9 Portinscale Road, Putney, London SW15, England
**Laker, Timothy J (Tim)** — Baseball Player
673 Azure Hills Dr, Simi Valley CA 93065, USA
**Lakes, Gary** — Opera Singer
I C M Artists, 40 W 57th St, #1800, New York NY 10019 USA
**Lake-Tack, Louise A** — Governor General, Antigua & Barbuda
Governor General's Office, Government House, Saint John's, Antigua & Barbuda
**Lakin, Christine** — Actress
Don Buchwald Talent Agency, 6500 Wilshire Blvd, #2200, Los Angeles CA 90048 USA
**Lakner, Yehoshua** — Composer
Postfach 7851, 6000 Lucerne 7, Switzerland
**Lakshmi, Padma** — Actress, Model, Writer
Baker Winokur Ryder Public Relations, 9100 Wilshire Blvd, #500W, Beverly Hills CA 90212 USA
**Lal, Devendra** — Oceanographer
4445 Via Precipicio, San Diego CA 92122, USA
**LaLande, Hector (Hec)** — Ice Hockey Player
848 McIntyre St E, North Bay ON P1B 1G1, Canada
**Lalas, Alexi** — Soccer Player, Executive, Sportscaster
1007 Maybrook Dr, Beverly Hills CA 90210, USA
**Laliberte, Guy** — Businessman, Circus Executive, Astronaut
Cirque du Soleil, 8400 2nd Ave, Montreal QC H1Z 4M6, Canada
**LaLiberte, Nicole** — Model
Click Model Mgmt, 881 7th Ave, New York NY 10019 USA
**Laliberte-Bourque, Andree** — Museum Executive
Musee du Quebec, 1 Ave Wolfe-Montcalm, Quebec QC G1R 5H3, Canada
**Lalime, Patrick** — Ice Hockey Player
70 Rive du Golf, Grand Mere QC G9T 5K4, Canada
**Lalla Salma** — Princess Consort, Morocco
Palais Royal, Le Mechouar, Rabat, Morocco
**Lalonde, R Lawrence (Larry)** — Guitarist (Primus)
Creative Artists Agency, 2000 Ave of Stars, #100, Los Angeles CA 90067 USA
**Lalonde, Robert P (Bobby)** — Ice Hockey Player
523 Broadgreen St, Pickering ON L1W 3E8, Canada
**Lam, Derek** — Fashion Designer
Jeffrey Lam Co, 446 W 13th St, New York NY 10014, USA
**Lam, Mei-Ling** — Model
Playboy Promotions, 9346 Civic Center Dr, #200, Beverly Hills CA 90210 USA
**Lam, Sal Kit** — Virologist
Malaysia University, Microbiolgy Dept, 50603 Kuala Lumpur, Malaysia
**Lamar, Dwight (Bo)** — Basketball Player
103 Claire St, Lafayette LA 70507, USA
**Lamar, Kendrick** — Rap Artist, R&B Singer
I C M Partners, 10250 Constellation Blvd, #900, Los Angeles CA 90067 USA
**LaMarr, Phil** — Actor, Comedian
TalentWorks, 3500 W Olive Ave, #1400, Burbank CA 91505 USA
**Lamas, Lorenzo** — Actor
Mavrick Artists Agency, 6100 Wilshire Blvd, #550, Los Angeles CA 90048, USA
**Lamb, Allan J** — Cricketer
Lamb Assoc, 4 Saint Giles St, #400, Northampton NN1 1JB, England
**Lamb, Brian P** — Businessman
C-Span Network, 400 N Capitol St NW, #650, Washington DC 20001, USA
**Lamb, Dennis** — Diplomat
19 Rue de Franqueville, 75016 Paris, France
**Lamb, Jeremy** — Basketball Player
Oklahoma City Thunder, 211 N Robinson Ave. #300, Oklahoma City OK 73102 USA
**Lamb, Larry** — Actor
MacFarlane Chard Assoc, 33 Percy St, London W1T 2DF, England
**Lamb, Michael** — Guitarist (Confederate Railroad)
Bobby Roberts, 3050 Business Park Circle, #303, Goodlettsville TN 37221 USA
**Lamb, Michael R (Mike)** — Baseball Player
17 Meadow Wood Dr, Trabuco Canyon CA 92679, USA
**Lamb, Raymond R (Ray)** — Baseball Player
3 Corte Tallista, San Clemente CA 92673, USA
**Lamberg, Adam M** — Actor
Innovative Artists, 1505 10th St, Santa Monica CA 90401 USA
**Lambert, Adam M** — Singer, Songwriter
19 Music & Mgmt, 35-37 Parkgate Road, London SW11 4NP, England
**Lambert, Chloe** — Actress
Artmedia, 20 Ave Rapp, 75007 Paris, France
**Lambert, Christopher** — Actor
A P A Talent & Literary Agency, 405 S Beverly Dr, #300, Beverly Hills CA 90212 USA
**Lambert, David** — Actor
Osbrink Talent Agency, 4343 Lankershim Blvd, #100, North Hollywood CA 91602 USA
**Lambert, John E** — Basketball Player
884 Dolphin Dr, Danville CA 94526, USA
**Lambert, John H (Jack)** — Football Player
PO Box 512, Worthington PA 16262, USA

**Lambert, Lane** — Ice Hockey Player, Coach
258 E Washington St, Jefferson WI 53549, USA

**Lambert, Mary M** — Director
Don Buchwald Talent Agency, 6500 Wilshire Blvd, #2200, Los Angeles CA 90048 USA

**Lambert, Miranda** — Singer, Guitarist, Songwriter
W M E Entertainment, 1600 Division St, #300, Nashville TN 37203 USA

**Lambert, Nathalie** — Speed Skater
Speed Skating Canada, 2781 Lancaster Road, #402, Ottawa ON K1B 1A7, Canada

**Lambert, Phyllis** — Architect
Centre d'Architecture, 1920 Rue Baile, Montreal QC H3H 2S6, Canada

**Lambiel, Stephane** — Figure Skater
Route de Praz Berard 3A, 1844 Villeneuve, Switzerland

**Lambo, T Adeoye** — Psychiatrist
Lambo Foundation, 11 Olatunsbosun St, Ikeja, Lagos State, Nigeria

**Lambrecht, Dietrich R** — Electrical Engineer
Rathenaustr 11, 45470 Mulheim an der Ruhr, Germany

**Lambrecht, Yves** — Actor
Artmedia, 20 Ave Rapp, 75007 Paris, France

**Lambro, Phillip** — Composer, Pianist
Trigram Music, 1888 Century Park East, #10, Los Angeles CA 90067, USA

**Lamm, Norman** — Educator, Religious Leader, Rabbi
Eicharen Theological Seminary, 2540 Amsterdam Ave, New York NY 10033, USA

**Lamm, Richard D** — Governor, CO
University of Denver, Public Policy Center, Denver CO 80208, USA

**Lamm, Robert W** — Singer, Keyboardist (Chicago)
Front Line Mgmt, 1100 Glendon Ave, #2000, Los Angeles CA 90024 USA

**Lamm, Tonya** — Singer (Tres Chicas)
Conqueroo, 11271 Ventura Blvd, #522, Studio City CA 91604 USA

**Lammers, Esmee** — Director, Writer
Features Creative Mgmt, Entrepotdok 76A, 1018 Amsterdam AD, Netherlands

**Lammers, Kim** — Field Hockey Player
Larensche Mixed Hockey Club, Postbus 105, 1250 Laren AC, Netherlands

**Lamonica, Daryle P** — Football Player
All Star Warehouse, 2860 S East Ave, Fresno CA 93725, USA

**Lamont, Gene W** — Baseball Player, Manager
5194 Siesta Woods Dr, Sarasota FL 34242, USA

**Lamont, Norman S H** — Government Official, England
Balli Group PLC, 5 Stanhope Gate, London W1Y 5LA, England

**Lamontagne, Ray** — Singer, Songwriter
Mick Mgmt, 35 Washington St, Brooklyn NY 11201 USA

**Lamoreaux, L Scott** — Navy Aviator
46 Harmony Lane, Port Angeles WA 98362, USA

**Lamoriello, Louis (Lou)** — Ice Hockey Executive, Coach
New Jersey Devils, Arena, 50 State Route 120, East Rutherford NJ 07073 USA

**Lamott, Anne** — Writer
Wylie Agency, 250 W 57th St, #2114, New York NY 10107 USA

**LaMotta, Jake** — Boxer
3598 Yacht Club Dr, #503, Miami FL 33180, USA

**Lamoureux, Jocelyne** — Ice Hockey Player
USA Hockey, 1775 Bob Johnson Dr, Colorado Springs CO 80906 USA

**Lamoureux-Kolls, Monique** — Ice Hockey Player
USA Hockey, 1775 Bob Johnson Dr, Colorado Springs CO 80906 USA

**Lamp, Dennis P** — Baseball Player
2 Enterprise, #6311, Aliso Viejo CA 92656, USA

**Lamp, Jeffrey A (Jeff)** — Basketball Player
4971 Credit River Dr, Savage MN 55378, USA

**Lampanelli, Lisa** — Actress, Comedienne
Parallel Artists Mgmt, 9420 Wilshire Blvd, #250, Beverly Hills CA 90212, USA

**Lampard, C Keith** — Baseball Player
6124 Highway 6 N, Houston TX 77084, USA

**Lamparski, Richard** — Writer
4202 Calle Real, #245, Santa Barbara CA 93110, USA

**Lampert, Edward S (Eddie)** — Businessman
E S L Investments, 1170 Kane Concourse, #200, Bay Harbour FL 33154, USA

**Lampert, Zohra** — Actress
Don Buchwald Talent Agency, 6500 Wilshire Blvd, #2200, Los Angeles CA 90048 USA

**Lampkin, Thomas M (Tom)** — Baseball Player
3810 SE 153rd Court, Vancouver WA 98683, USA

**Lampley, James (Jim)** — Sportscaster
3325 Caminito Daniella, Del Mar CA 92014, USA

**Lamprey, Zane** — Actor, Comedian
W M E Entertainment, 9601 Wilshire Blvd, #300, Beverly Hills CA 90210 USA

**Lampson, Butler W** — Computer Engineer
Microsoft Corp, 1 Microsoft Way, Redmond WA 98052, USA

**Lampton, Michael** — Astronaut
University of California, Space Science Laboratory, Berkeley CA 94720, USA

**Lamsma, Simone** — Concert Violinist
I M G Artists, Hogarth Business Park, Chiswick, London W4 2TH, England

**Lamy, Pascal L F** — Government Official, France
World Trade Organization, Rue Lausanne 154, 1211 Geneva 21, Switzerland

**LaNasa, Katherine** — Actress
Anderson Group Public Relations, 8060 Melrose Ave, #400, Los Angeles CA 90046, USA

**Lancaster, Lester W (Les)** — Baseball Player
PO Box 1105, Dothan AL 36302, USA

**Lancaster, Mark** — Artist
Cunningham Dance Foundation, 55 Bethune St, New York NY 10014, USA

**Lancaster, Neal** — Golfer
6 Quail Run, Smithfield NC 27577, USA

**Lancaster, Sarah** — Actress
United Talent Agency, U T A Plaza, 9336 Civic Center Dr, Beverly Hills CA 90210 USA

**Lance, Dirk** — Bassist (Incubus)
Variety Artists, 1924 Spring St, Paso Robles CA 93446 USA

**Lancelotti, Richard A (Rick)** — Baseball Player
5190 Thompson Road, Clarence NY 14031, USA

**Landau, Jon** — Producer
Lightstorm Entertainment, 91600 Rosecrans Ave, Manhattan Beach CA 90266, USA

**Landau, Juliet** — Actress
Miss Juliet Productions, PO Box 2792, Los Angeles CA 90078, USA
**Landau, Martin** — Actor
PO Box 10959, Beverly Hills CA 90213, USA
**Landau, Russ** — Composer
Evolution Music Partners, 1680 Vine St, #500, Los Angeles CA 90028 USA
**Landau, Tina** — Director
I C M Partners, 10250 Constellation Blvd, #900, Los Angeles CA 90067 USA
**Landeau, Alexia** — Actress, Writer
Tavistock Wood Mgmt, 45 Conduit St, London W1S 2YN, England
**Landecker, Amy** — Actress
Brillstein Entertainment Partners, 9150 Wilshire Blvd, #350, Beverly Hills CA 90212 USA
**Lander, David L** — Actor
918 S Tremaine Ave, Los Angeles CA 90019, USA
**Lander, Eric S** — Mathematician, Biologist
Massachusetts Institute of Technology, Broad Institute, 320 Charles Ave, Cambridge MA 02139, USA
**Landers, Andy** — Basketball Coach
University of Georgia, Athletic Dept, Athens GA 30602, USA
**Landers, Audrey** — Actress, Singer
Landers Productions, 4048 Las Palmas Dr, Sarasota FL 34238, USA
**Landers, Judy** — Actress
Landers Productions, 4048 Las Palmas Dr, Sarasota FL 34238, USA
**Landers, Larry** — Golfer
PO Box 497, Azle TX 76098, USA
**Landers, Paul H** — Guitarist (Rammstein)
Pilgrim Mgmt, PO Box 540101, 10042 Berlin, Germany
**Landertinger, Dominik** — Biathlete
Feistenau 34, 6395 Hochfilzen, Austria
**Landes, Michael** — Actor
Artists Partnership, 101 Finsbury Pavement, London EC2A 1RS, England
**Landeskog, Gabriel I J** — Ice Hockey Player
Colorado Avalanche, Pepsi Center, 1000 Chopper Circle, Denver CO 80204 USA
**Landestoy, Rafael** — Baseball Player
PO Box 940755, Miami FL 33194, USA
**Landeta, Sean E** — Football Player
137 Powerhouse Road, #7W, Roslyn Heights NY 11577, USA
**Landgrebe, Gudrun** — Actress
Above the Line, Theresienstr 31, 80333 Munich, Germany
**Landis, Floyd** — Cyclist
4632 Felton St, #2, San Diego CA 92116, USA
**Landis, James H (Jim)** — Baseball Player
203 Alchemy Way, Napa CA 94558, USA
**Landis, John D** — Director
Intellectual Artists Management, 10585 Santa Monica Blvd, #135, Los Angeles CA 90025, USA
**Landis, William H (Bill)** — Baseball Player
525 E Sycamore Dr, Hanford CA 93230, USA
**Lando, Joe** — Actor
Jay D Schwartz & Assoc, 6767 Forest Lawn Dr, #211, Los Angeles CA 90068, USA
**Landon, Jennifer** — Actress
Innovative Artists, 1505 10th St, Santa Monica CA 90401 USA
**Landon, Laurene** — Actress
Grant Savic Kopaloff, 6399 Wilshire Blvd, #415, Los Angeles CA 90048, USA
**Landon, Michael, Jr** — Director
Believe Pictures, 2 Saint Elias, Dove Canyon CA 92679, USA
**Landreaux, Kenneth F (Ken)** — Baseball Player
1510 N Siesta Ave, La Puente CA 91746, USA
**Landress, Ilene S** — Producer
Creative Artists Agency, 2000 Ave of Stars, #100, Los Angeles CA 90067 USA
**Landrieu, Moon** — Secretary, Housing & Urban Development
4301 S Prieur St, New Orleans LA 70125, USA
**Landrum, T William (Bill)** — Baseball Player
840 Silver Point Road, Chapin SC 29036, USA
**Landrum, Terry L (Tito)** — Baseball Player
428 E 50th St, Garden, New York NY 10022, USA
**Landry, Dawan F** — Football Player
309 Kennedy St, Ama LA 70031, USA
**Landry, Gregory P (Greg)** — Football Player, Coach
133 Melanie Lane, Troy MI 48098, USA
**Landry, Karen** — Actress
Don Buchwald Talent Agency, 6500 Wilshire Blvd, #2200, Los Angeles CA 90048 USA
**Landsberger, Mark W** — Basketball Player
1702 8th Ave SE, Saint Cloud MN 56304, USA
**Landsbergis, Vytautas** — President, Lithuania
European Parliament, Bat Altiero Spinelli, Wiertzstraat 60, 1047 Brussels, Belgium
**Landsburg, Valerie** — Actress
PO Box 1617, Topanga CA 90290, USA
**Landshamer, Christina** — Opera Singer
Kunstler Sekretariat am Gasteig, Rosenheimer Str 52, 81669 Munich, Germany
**Landsman, Mark** — Producer, Director
Hirsch Wallerstein Hayum, 10100 Santa Monica Blvd, #1700, Los Angeles CA 90067 USA
**Landy, Bernard** — Government Official, Canada
Gouvement du Quebec, 885 Grand Allee Est, Quebec QC GLA 1A2, Canada
**Lane, Abbe** — Singer, Actress
500 Bel Air Road, Los Angeles CA 90077, USA
**Lane, Akira** — Model
PO Box 8052, Laguna Hills CA 92654, USA
**Lane, Cristy** — Singer
L S Records, PO Box 654, Madison TN 37116, USA
**Lane, David P** — Oncologist
Dundee Medical Center, Molecular Research Dept, Dundee DD1 9SY, Scotland
**Lane, Diane** — Actress
W M E Entertainment, 9601 Wilshire Blvd, #300, Beverly Hills CA 90210 USA
**Lane, Gord** — Ice Hockey Player
8 Magnolia Dr, Brandon MB R7A 0Y9, Canada
**Lane, John R (Jack)** — Museum Executive
San Francisco Museum of Modern Art, 151 3rd St, San Francisco CA 94103, USA

**Lane, Kenneth Jay** — Fashion Designer
Kenneth Jay Lane Inc, 20 W 37th St, #900, New York NY 10018, USA

**Lane, Lilas** — Actress
TalentWorks, 3500 W Olive Ave, #1400, Burbank CA 91505 USA

**Lane, MacArthur** — Football Player
3238 Knowland Ave, Oakland CA 94619, USA

**Lane, Malcolm D** — Biological Chemist
717 Maiden Choice Lane, #525, Catonsville MD 21228, USA

**Lane, Marvin (Marv)** — Baseball Player
40164 Gulliver Dr, Sterling Heights MI 48310, USA

**Lane, Matthew** — Golfer
Links Mgmt, 5068 W Plano Parkway, #256, Plano TX 75093, USA

**Lane, Max A** — Football Player
16 Strong St, Newburyport MA 1950, USA

**Lane, Mike** — Editorial Cartoonist
Baltimore Sun, Editorial Dept, 501 N Calvert St, Baltimore MD 21278, USA

**Lane, Nathan** — Actor, Singer
I C M Partners, 10250 Constellation Blvd, #900, Los Angeles CA 90067 USA

**Lane, Richard H (Dick)** — Baseball Player
2717 Legend Dr, Las Vegas NV 89134, USA

**Lane, Robert W** — Businessman
Deere Co, 1 John Deere Place, Moline IL 61265, USA

**Lane, Robin** — Dancer, Choreographer
Do Jump Co, Echo Theater, 1515 SE 37th Ave, Portland OR 97214, USA

**Lanegan, Mark** — Singer, Guitarist (Queens of Stone Age)
Steve Stewart Mgmt, 10 Universal City Plaza, 2000, Universal City CA 91608, USA

**Laneuville, Eric** — Actor, Director
5138 W Slauson Ave, Los Angeles CA 90056, USA

**Laney, James T** — Educator, Diplomat
2015 Grand Prix Dr NE, Atlanta GA 30345, USA

**Laney, Sandra E** — Businesswoman
201 E 5th St, #1800, Cincinnati OH 45202, USA

**Lang Lang** — Concert Pianist
Columbia Artists Mgmt Inc, 5 Columbus Circle, 1790 Broadway, #1600, New York NY 10019 USA

**Lang, Antonio M** — Basketball Player
2255 Barretts Lane, Mobile AL 36617, USA

**Lang, Belinda** — Actress
Rabbit Vocal Mgmt, 94 Strand on the Green, London W4 3NN, England

**Lang, Brittany** — Golfer
Gaylord Sports Mgmt, 13845 N Northsight Blvd, #200, Scottsdale AZ 85260 USA

**Lang, David** — Composer
Red Poppy Music, 66 Greene St, #500, New York NY 10012, USA

**Lang, Gene E** — Football Player
11526 Azalea Trace, Gulfport MS 39503, USA

**Lang, Helmut** — Fashion Designer
Michele Morgan, 184 Rue Saint-Maur, 75010 Paris, France

**Lang, Jack M E** — Government Official, France
Mairie, 41000 Blois, France

**Lang, Jonny** — Singer, Guitarist
A B C Public Relations, 4570 Van Nuys Blvd, #320, Sherman Oaks CA 91403, USA

**lang, k d** — Singer, Actress
Paradigm Agency, 360 N Crescent Dr, North Building, Beverly Hills CA 90210 USA

**Lang, Katherine Kelly** — Actress, Model
Edmonds Entertainment Group, 1635 N Cahuenga Blvd, Los Angeles CA 90028, USA

**Lang, Kenard D** — Football Player
1781 Oakbrook Dr, Longwood FL 32779, USA

**Lang, Michelle** — Actress
Susan Nathe, 8281 Melrose Ave, #200, Los Angeles CA 90046 USA

**Lang, Perry** — Actor
A P A Talent & Literary Agency, 405 S Beverly Dr, #300, Beverly Hills CA 90212 USA

**Lang, Peter** — Yachtsman
Danish Sailing Assn, Idraettens Hus, 2605 Broendby, Denmark

**Lang, Robert** — Ice Hockey Player
PO Box 633, Diablo CA 94528, USA

**Lang, Stephen** — Actor, Director, Writer
Innovative Artists, 1505 10th St, Santa Monica CA 90401 USA

**Langan, Kevin** — Opera Singer
Columbia Artists Mgmt Inc, 5 Columbus Circle, 1790 Broadway, #1600, New York NY 10019 USA

**Langbein, John H** — Attorney, Educator
Yale University, Law School, 127 Wall St, New Haven CT 06511, USA

**Langbo, Arnold G** — Businessman
Kellogg Co, 1 Kellogg Square, PO Box 3599, Battle Creek MI 49016, USA

**Langdon, Darren** — Ice Hockey Player
1 Oake's Road, Deer Lake NF A8K 1X5, Canada

**Langdon, Harry** — Photographer
501 Center St, #6, El Segundo CA 90245, USA

**Lange, Allison** — Actress
Element Talent Agency, 120 S Vignes St, Los Angeles CA 90012, USA

**Lange, Andre** — Bobsled Athlete
Team Andre Lange, Robert-Schumann-Str 14B, 98529 Suhl, Germany

**Lange, Eric** — Actor
Domain Talent, 9229 W Sunset Blvd, #710, West Hollywood CA 90069 USA

**Lange, Jessica** — Actress
Untitled Entertainment, 350 S Beverly Dr, #200, Beverly Hills CA 90212 USA

**Lange, Marita** — Track Athlete
Moskauer Str 7, 06128 Halle, Germany

**Lange, Niklaus** — Actor
A P A Talent & Literary Agency, 405 S Beverly Dr, #300, Beverly Hills CA 90212 USA

**Lange, Otto L** — Botanist
Leitengraben 37, 97084 Wuerzburg, Germany

**Lange, Richard O (Dick)** — Baseball Player
39744 Salvatore Dr, Sterling Heights MI 48313, USA

**Lange, Ted** — Actor
House of Representatives, 1434 6th St, #1, Santa Monica CA 90401 USA

**Lange, Thomas** — Rowing Athlete
Ratzeburger Ruderclub, Domhof 57, 23909 Ratzburg, Germany

**Langehanenberg, Helen** — Equestrian
Schonebeck 21, 48329 Havixbeck, Germany

**Langella, Frank** — Actor
Paradigm Agency, 360 N Crescent Dr, North Building, Beverly Hills CA 90210 USA

**Langen, Christoph** — Bobsled Athlete
B C Unterhaching, Ottobrunner Str 16, 82008 Unterhaching, Germany

**Langenbrunner, Jaime** — Ice Hockey Player
94096 Warloe Shore Lane, Moose Lake MN 55767, USA

**Langer, A J** — Actress
Valeo Entertainment, 8265 Sunset Blvd, #103, Los Angeles CA 90046, USA

**Langer, Alois A** — Inventor (Implantable Defibrillator)
111 Saddlebrook Dr, Harrison City PA 15636, USA

**Langer, Bernhard** — Golfer
3667 Princeton Place, Boca Raton FL 33496, USA

**Langer, James J (Jim)** — Football Player
14280 Wolfram St NW, Anoka MN 55303, USA

**Langer, James S** — Physicist
1130 Las Canoas Lane, Santa Barbara CA 93105, USA

**Langer, Robert S, Jr** — Inventor (Controlled Drug Delivery)
Massachusetts Institute of Technolgy, Langer Laboratory, Cambridge MA 02139, USA

**Langerhans, Ryan D** — Baseball Player
PO Box 1026, Round Rock TX 78680, USA

**Langevin, David (Dave)** — Ice Hockey Player
1090 W Circle Court, Saint Paul MN 55118, USA

**Langfield, Camille** — Actress
PO Box 254, Carmel by the Sea CA 93921, USA

**Langford, J Rick** — Baseball Player
8330 9th Avenue Terrace NW, Bradenton FL 34209, USA

**Langham, C Antonio** — Football Player
PO Box 232, Town Creek AL 35672, USA

**Langham, Franklin** — Golfer
PO Box 3428, Peachtree City GA 30269, USA

**Langham, Wallace** — Actor
Imperium 7 Talent, 5455 Wilshire Blvd, #1706, Los Angeles CA 90036, USA

**Langhorne, Reginald D (Reggie)** — Football Player
12260 Smiths Neck Road, Carrollton VA 23314, USA

**Langkow, Daymond R** — Ice Hockey Player
11549 E Cochise Dr, Scottsdale AZ 85259, USA

**Langlands, Robert P** — Mathematician
60 Battle Road, Princeton NJ 08540, USA

**Lang-Lessing, Sebastian** — Conductor
I M G Artists, Hogarth Business Park, Chiswick, London W4 2TH, England

**Langlois, Albert, Jr** — Ice Hockey Player
2473 Crest View Dr, Los Angeles CA 90046, USA

**Langlois, Chibly Cardinal** — Religious Leader
Diocese of Les Cayes, BP 43, Rue Toussaint-Louverture, Les Cayes, Haiti

**Langlois, Paul** — Guitarist (Tragically Hip)
Bobby Breen Mgmt, 13 Blackburn St, #300, Toronto ON M4M 2B3, Canada

**Langmaid, Ben** — Singer, Songwriter (La Roux)
Beatnik Public Relations, 5 Little Portland St, London W1W 7JD, England

**Langmann, Thomas** — Producer, Actor
La Petite Reine, 20 Rue de Saint-Petersburg, 75008 Paris, France

**Langridge, Matthew** — Rowing Athlete
Leander Rowing Club, Henley on Thames, Leander Oxfordshire RG9 2LP, England

**Langston, J William** — Neurologist
Parkinson's Foundation, 2444 Moorpark Ave, San Jose CA 95128, USA

**Langston, Mark E** — Baseball Player
56 Golden Eagle, Irvine CA 92603, USA

**Langston, Murray** — Actor, Comedian
Entertainment Alliance, PO Box 4734, Santa Rosa CA 95402, USA

**Langton, Brooke** — Actress
Gersh Agency, 9465 Wilshire Blvd, #600, Beverly Hills CA 90212 USA

**Langway, Rod C** — Ice Hockey Player
8260 Powhickery Dr, Mechanicsville VA 23116, USA

**Lanier, Cathy L** — Law Enforcement Official
Metropolitan Police Dept, 300 Indiana Ave NW, Washington DC 20001, USA

**Lanier, Harold C (Hal)** — Baseball Player, Manager
3270 Countryside View Dr, Saint Cloud FL 34772, USA

**Lanier, Jaron Z** — Computer Engineer (Virtual Reality)
University of Southern California, Annenberg Center, Los Angeles CA 90089, USA

**Lanier, Kenneth W (Ken)** — Football Player
21923 E Ridge Trail Circle, Aurora CO 80016, USA

**Lanier, Robert J (Bob), Jr** — Basketball Player, Coach
13027 E Saddlehorn Trail, Scottsdale AZ 85259, USA

**Lanier, Willie E** — Football Player
2911 E Brigstock Road, Midlothian VA 23113, USA

**Lanig, Hans-Peter** — Alpine Skier
Omachstr 11, 87541 Hindelang, Germany

**Lankford, Frank G** — Baseball Player
104 Lakeview Ave NE, Atlanta GA 30305, USA

**Lankford, Kim** — Actress
House of Representatives, 1434 6th St, #1, Santa Monica CA 90401 USA

**Lankford, Paul J** — Football Player
3838 Biggin Church Road W, Jacksonville FL 32224, USA

**Lankford, Raymond L (Ray)** — Baseball Player
1520 Lake Whitney Dr, Windermere FL 34786, USA

**Lanners, Bouli** — Actor
Voyez Mon Agent, 20 Ave Rapp, 75007 Paris, France

**Lanois, Daniel** — Singer, Musician, Songwriter
Monterey Peninsula Artists, 404 W Franklin St, Monterey CA 93940 USA

**Lanoue, Virginie** — Actress
Artmedia, 20 Ave Rapp, 75007 Paris, France

**Lansbury, Angela** — Actress, Singer
Mavrick Artists Agency, 6100 Wilshire Blvd, #550, Los Angeles CA 90048, USA

**Lansbury, David** — Actor
Don Buchwald Talent Agency, 6500 Wilshire Blvd, #2200, Los Angeles CA 90048 USA

**Lansdale, Joe R** — Writer
199 County Road 508, Nacogdoches TX 75961, USA

**Lansford, Alex J (Buck)** — Football Player
PO Box 905, Lampasas TX 76550, USA

**Lansford, Carney R** — Baseball Player
43736 Pocahontas Road, Baker City OR 97814, USA

**Lansford, Michael J (Mike)** — Football Player
6200 E Canyon Rim Road, #205, Grants Pass OR 97526, USA

**Lansing, Michael T (Mike)** — Baseball Player
9691 S Sun Meadow St, Littleton CO 80129, USA

**Lansing, P J** — Model
Playboy Promotions, 9346 Civic Center Dr, #200, Beverly Hills CA 90210 USA

**Lansing, Sherry L** — Producer
10741 Levico Way, Los Angeles CA 90077, USA

**Lanter, Matt** — Actor
Emerald Talent Group, 15260 Ventura Blvd, #1200, Sherman Oaks CA 91403

**Lantz, Stuart B (Stu)** — Basketball Player
5270 Mount Burnham Dr, San Diego CA 92111, USA

**Lanvin, Bernard** — Fashion Designer
22 Rue du Faubourg Saint Honore, 70008 Paris, France

**Lanvin, Gerard** — Actor, Writer
Voyez Mon Agent, 20 Ave Rapp, 75007 Paris, France

**Lanz, Markus** — Actor
M S C Promotion, Postfach 1324, 61403 Oberursel, Germany

**Lanz, Rick** — Ice Hockey Player
18962 20th Ave, Surrey BC V3S 9V2, Canada

**Lanza, Manuel** — Opera Singer
I C M Artists, 40 W 57th St, #1800, New York NY 10019 USA

**Lanza, Suzanne** — Model, Actress
Greater Visions Artists Talent Agency, 8981 W Sunset Blvd, #101, West Hollywood CA 90069 USA

**Laoretti, Larry** — Golfer
10567 SW Whooping Crane Way, Palm City FL 34990, USA

**LaPaglia, Anthony** — Actor
400 N Bristol Ave, Los Angeles CA 90049, USA

**LaPaglia, Jonathan** — Actor
Untitled Entertainment, 350 S Beverly Dr, #200, Beverly Hills CA 90212 USA

**Laperriere, Ian** — Ice Hockey Player
415 Washington Ave, Haddonfield NJ 8033, USA

**Laperriere, J Jacques H** — Ice Hockey Player
1490 Rue Bergeron, Quebec QC G3E 1G5, Canada

**Lapham, David A (Dave)** — Football Player
8254 Sunfish Lane, Maineville OH 45039, USA

**Lapham, Lewis H** — Editor
Harper's, Editorial Dept, 666 Broadway, New York NY 10012, USA

**LaPier, Darcy L** — Actress, Model
Double R Mgmt, 5424 Crebs Ave, Tarzana CA 91356, USA

**Lapierre, Dominique** — Historian
Les Bignoles, 83350 Ramatuelle, France

**LaPierre, Wayne** — Association Executive
National Rifle Assn, 11250 Waples Mill Road, Fairfax VA 22030, USA

**Lapine, James E** — Writer, Director
85 Mill River Road, South Salem NY 10590, USA

**Lapkus, Lauren** — Actress
Odenkirk Provissiero Entertainment, 1936 N Bronson Ave, Los Angeles CA 90069 USA

**LaPlaca, Alison** — Actress, Producer
Marshak/Zachary/Mills, 8840 Wilshire Blvd, #100, Beverly Hills CA 90211 USA

**LaPlanche, Rosemary** — Actress, Beauty Queen
13914 Hartsook St, Sherman Oaks CA 91423, USA

**LaPlant, Rob** — Producer
Lighthearted Entertainment, 4111 W Alameda Ave, #409, Burbank CA 91505, USA

**LaPlante, Lynda** — Writer, Actress
LaPlante Productions, 162-170 Wardour St, London W1V 3AT, England

**Lapoint, David J (Dave)** — Baseball Player
11704 Stonewood Gate Dr, Riverview FL 33579, USA

**Lapointe, Claude** — Ice Hockey Player
805 Stony Creek Court, Lansdale PA 19446, USA

**Lapointe, Guy G** — Ice Hockey Player
Minnesota Wild, XCel Energy Arena, 1275 Saint Antoine W, Saint Paul MN 55104 USA

**LaPorte, Danny** — Motorcycle Racing Rider
18033 S Santa Fe Ave, Compton CA 90221, USA

**LaPorte, Juan** — Boxer, Trainer
77 Front St, Brooklyn NY 11201, USA

**LaPorte, Leon J** — Army General
McLane Advanced Technologies, 4001 Central Pointe Parkway, Temple TX 76504, USA

**Laposata, Joseph S** — Army General
Battle Monuments Commission, 20 Massachusetts, Washington DC 20314, USA

**Lapotaire, Jane** — Actress
92 Oxford Gardens, #C, London W10, England

**Lappalainen, Markku** — Bassist (Hoobastank)
Island Def Jam Records, 8920 W Sunset Blvd, #200, West Hollywood CA 90069 USA

**Lappas, Steve** — Basketball Coach
Villanova University, Athletic Dept, Villanova PA 19085, USA

**LaPraed, Ronald (Ron)** — Bassist, Trumpeter (Commodores)
Management Assoc, 1920 Benson Ave, Saint Paul MN 55116, USA

**Laqueur, Walter** — Historian
Journal of Contemporary History, 4 Devonshire St, London W1N 2BH, England

**Lara, Alexandra Maria** — Actress
Players Agentur Mgmt, Sophienstra 21, 10178 Berlin-Mitte, Germany

**Lara, Brian C** — Cricketer
West Indies Cricket Club, PO Box 616, Saint John's, Antigua

**Lara, Joanne** — Actress
Abraxas Talent, 4260 Troost Ave, #1, Studio City CA 91604, USA

**Laragh, John H** — Physician
435 E 70th St, New York NY 10021, USA

**Lardner, George, Jr** — Journalist
American University, Investigative Reporting Workshop, 3201 New Mexico Ave, Washington DC 20016, USA

| | |
|---|---|
| **Lardo, Vincent** <br> G P Putnam's Sons, 375 Hudson St, New York NY 10014 USA | Writer |
| **Laredo, Jaime** <br> Cleveland Institute of Music, 11021 East Blvd, Cleveland OH 44106, USA | Concert Violinist, Conductor |
| **Laresca, Vincent** <br> TalentWorks, 3500 W Olive Ave, #1400, Burbank CA 91505 USA | Actor |
| **Larese, York B** <br> 30 Revere Beach Parkway, #702, Medford MA 02155, USA | Basketball Player, Coach |
| **Large, Bonnie** <br> Playboy Promotions, 9346 Civic Center Dr, #200, Beverly Hills CA 90210 USA | Actress, Model |
| **Large, Corey** <br> Tunnel Post, 233 Wilshire Blvd, #100, Santa Monica CA 90401, USA | Actor, Producer, Writer |
| **Large, David C** <br> Montana State University, History Dept, Bozeman MT 59715, USA | Historian |
| **Largent, Steve M** <br> 3835 N Randolph Court, Arlington VA 22207, USA | Football Player; Representative, OK |
| **Larholm, Jonas** <br> Aalborg Handbold, Willy Brandts Vej 31, 9220 Aalborg Ost, Denmark | Handball Player |
| **Larimore, Stephanie** <br> Playboy Promotions, 9346 Civic Center Dr, #200, Beverly Hills CA 90210 USA | Model |
| **Larionov, Igor N** <br> 2025 Quarton Road, Bloomfield Hills MI 48301, USA | Ice Hockey Player |
| **Lariviere, Richard W** <br> Field Museum of Natural History, 1400 S Lake Shore Dr, Chicago IL 60605, USA | Museum Executive, Educator |
| **Lark, Maria** <br> Abrams Artists, 9200 W Sunset Blvd, #1125, West Hollywood CA 90069 USA | Actress |
| **Larkin, Barry L** <br> 5410 Osprey Isle Lane, Orlando FL 32819, USA | Baseball Player |
| **Larkin, Christopher (Chris)** <br> Lou Coulson Assoc, 37 Berwick St, London W1V 8RS, England | Actor |
| **Larkin, DeShane (Shane)** <br> Dallas Mavericks, Pavilion, 2909 Taylor Street, Dallas TX 75226 USA | Basketball Player |
| **Larkin, Eugene T (Gene)** <br> 9496 Abbott Court, Eden Prairie MN 55347, USA | Baseball Player |
| **Larmer, Steve** <br> 1664 Poplar Point Road, RR 4, Peterborough ON K9J 6X5, Canada | Ice Hockey Player |
| **Larmore, Jennifer** <br> I M G Artists, Carnegie Hall Tower, 152 W 57th St, #500, New York NY 10019 USA | Opera Singer |
| **Laro, David** <br> US Tax Court, 400 2nd St NW, Washington DC 20217, USA | Judge |
| **LaRoche, Andrews C (Andy)** <br> 842 195th St, Fort Scott KS 66701, USA | Baseball Player |
| **LaRoche, David E (Dave)** <br> 815 W 18th St, Fort Scott KS 66701, USA | Baseball Player |
| **LaRocque, Gene R** <br> 5015 Macomb St NW, Washington DC 20016, USA | Government Official, Navy Admiral |
| **Larocque, Jocelyne D M** <br> Hockey Canada, 151 Canada Olympic Road SW, #201, Calgary AB T3B 6B7, Canada | Ice Hockey Player |
| **Laroque, Michele** <br> Agents Associes, 201 Faubourg Saint Honore, 75008 Paris, France | Actress |
| **LaRosa, Julius** <br> 67 Sycamore Lane, Irvington NY 10533, USA | Singer |
| **LaRosa, Paul** <br> I M G Artists, Hogarth Business Park, Chiswick, London W4 2TH, England | Opera Singer |
| **Larose, Claude D** <br> 5060 NW 54th St, Coconut Creek FL 33073, USA | Ice Hockey Player |
| **LaRose, M Daniel (Danny)** <br> 4873 N Raymond Road, Luther MI 49656, USA | Football Player |
| **LaRouche, Lyndon H, Jr** <br> 18520 Round Top Lane, Round Hill VA 20141, USA | Political Activist |
| **Larouche, Pierre R** <br> 1005 Cherry Hill Dr, Presto PA 15142, USA | Ice Hockey Player |
| **Larrabee, Martin G** <br> 11630 Glen Arm Road, #V54, Glen Arm MD 21057, USA | Biophysicist |
| **Larrain, Pablo** <br> Fabula, Holanda 3017, Nunoa, Santiago 7770057, Chile | Director, Producer, Writer |
| **Larrieux, Amel** <br> Blisslife Records, 725 River Road, #32-215, Edgewater NJ 07020, USA | Singer |
| **Larroquette, John** <br> Brillstein Entertainment Partners, 9150 Wilshire Blvd, #350, Beverly Hills CA 90212 USA | Actor |
| **Larry the Cable Guy** <br> Parallel Entertainment, 9420 Wilshire Blvd, #250, Beverly Hills CA 90212 USA | Actor, Comedian |
| **Larry, Wendy** <br> Old Dominion University, Institutional Advancement Office, Norfolk VA 23529, USA | Basketball Coach |
| **Larsen, Blaine** <br> Morris Management Group, 818 19th Ave S, Nashville TN 37203, USA | Singer, Songwriter |
| **Larsen, Don J** <br> C M G Worldwide, 10500 Crosspoint Blvd, Indianapolis IN 46256, USA | Baseball Player |
| **Larsen, Gary L** <br> 4317 San Juan St NE, Olympia WA 98516, USA | Football Player |
| **Larsen, Jack Lenor** <br> LongHouse Reserve, 133 Hands Creek Road, East Hampton NY 11937, USA | Textile Designer |
| **Larsen, Libby** <br> 2205 Kenwood Parkway, Minneapolis MN 55405, USA | Composer |
| **Larsen, Marit** <br> United Stage, Box 11029, 100 61 Stockholm, Sweden | Singer, Songwriter (M-2-M) |
| **Larsen, Ralph S** <br> 100 Albany St, #200, New Brunswick NJ 08901, USA | Businessman |
| **Larsen, Terrance A** <br> 75 Bryn Mawr Ave, Lansdowne PA 19050, USA | Financier |
| **Larson, Breeja** <br> 922 S Lesueur, Mesa AZ 85204, USA | Swimmer |
| **Larson, Brie** <br> Authentic Talent Mgmt, 20 Jay St, #M17, Brooklyn NY 11201 USA | Actress |
| **Larson, Daniel J (Dan)** <br> 797 Oxen St, Paso Robles CA 93446, USA | Baseball Player |

**Larson, Edward J (Ed)** — Historian
24346 Baxter Dr, Malibu CA 90265, USA
**Larson, Erik** — Writer
Crown Publishing Group, 1745 Broadway, #1300, New York NY 10019 USA
**Larson, Gary** — Cartoonist (Far Side)
FarWorks, 601 Union St, #620, Seattle WA 98101, USA
**Larson, Gregory K (Greg)** — Football Player
PO Box 393, Nisswa MN 56468, USA
**Larson, Jack E** — Actor
449 N Skyewiay Road, Los Angeles CA 90049, USA
**Larson, Jill** — Actress
Innovative Artists, 1505 10th St, Santa Monica CA 90401 USA
**Larson, Jordan Q** — Volleyball Player
USA Volleyball, 4065 Sinton Road, #200, Colorado Springs CO 80907, USA
**Larson, Lance** — Swimmer
1131 La Limonar Road, Santa Ana CA 92705, USA
**Larson, Peter N** — Businessman
Brunswick Corp, 1 N Field Court, Lake Forest IL 60045, USA
**Larson, Reed** — Ice Hockey Player
14334 Fairway Dr, Eden Prairie MN 55344, USA
**Larson, Wolf** — Actor, Producer, Writer
Kazarian/Measures/Ruskin, 11969 Ventura Blvd, #300, Studio City CA 91604 USA
**Larsson, Dean** — Golfer
Advantage International, 1025 Thomas Jefferson NW, #450, Washington DC 20007 USA
**Larter, Ali** — Actress, Model
Water Street Anthem Entertainment, 5225 Wilshire Blvd, #615, Los Angeles CA 90036, USA
**LaRue, Eva** — Actress
A P A Talent & Literary Agency, 405 S Beverly Dr, #300, Beverly Hills CA 90212 USA
**LaRue, Florence** — Singer (Fifth Dimension), Actress
W M E Entertainment, 1325 Ave of Americas, New York NY 10019 USA
**Larue, M Jason (Dusty)** — Baseball Player
35 Jones Cemetary Road, Kendalia TX 78027, USA
**LaRussa, Anthony (Tony), Jr** — Baseball Player, Manager
338 Golden Meadow Place, Alamo CA 94507, USA
**LaRusso, Vincent** — Actor
419 Park Ave S, #1009, New York NY 10016, USA
**Lary, Frank S** — Baseball Player
11813 Baseball Dr, Northport AL 35475, USA
**Lary, R Yale** — Football Player
6366 Lansdale Road, Fort Worth TX 76116, USA
**LaSala, James** — Labor Leader
Amalgamated Transit Union, 5025 Wisconsin Ave NW, Washington DC 20016, USA
**LaSalle, Eriq** — Actor, Director
Principato-Young, 9465 Wilshire Blvd, #880, Beverly Hills CA 90212 USA
**Lascarro, Juanita** — Opera Singer
Harrison/Parrott, 5-6 Albion Court, London W6 0QT, England
**Laschenova, Natalia V** — Gymnast
450 Poppy Lane, Marysville OH 43040, USA
**Lascher, David** — Actor
Acumen Entertainment Partners, 15915 Ventura Blvd, #304, Encino CA 91436, USA
**Lash, Bill** — Skier
17438 Bothell Way NE, #C305, Bothell WA 98011, USA
**Lash, James V (Jim)** — Football Player
597 Van Everett Ave, Akron OH 44306, USA
**Lasher, Frederick W (Fred)** — Baseball Player
N9596 Highway K, Merrillan WI 54754, USA
**Laskey, William A (Bill)** — Baseball Player
PO Box 1556, Burlingame CA 94011, USA
**Laskey, William G (Bill)** — Football Player
PO Box 734, 3257 N Manitou Trail, Leland MS 49654, USA
**Laskin, Larissa** — Actress
Noble Caplan Abrams, 1260 Yonge St, #200, Toronto ON M4T 1W6, Canada
**Lasko, Michal** — Volleyball Player
Klub Sportwy Jastrzebski Wegiel, Ul Reja 20, 44 335 Jastrzebie Zdroj, Poland
**Laslavic, James E (Jim)** — Football Player
648 A Ave, Coronado CA 92118, USA
**LaSorda, Thomas** — Businessman
Daimler-Chrysler Group, 100 Chrysler Dr, Auburn Hills MI 48326, USA
**Lasorda, Thomas C (Tommy)** — Baseball Player, Manager, Executive
1473 W Maxzim Ave, Fullerton CA 92833, USA
**Lassally, Walter** — Cinematographer
6 Ladbroke Gardens, London W11 2PT, England
**Lasse, Richard S (Dick)** — Football Player
111 Windcrest Court, Beaver Falls PA 15010, USA
**Lasser, Louise** — Actress, Comedienne
200 E 71st St, #20C, New York NY 10021, USA
**Lasseter, John** — Director, Animator
Pixar Animation, 1200 Park Ave, Emeryville CA 94608, USA
**Lassetter, Donald O (Don)** — Baseball Player
379 Old Carrollton Road, Newnan GA 30263, USA
**Lassez, Sarah** — Actress
Untitled Entertainment, 350 S Beverly Dr, #200, Beverly Hills CA 90212 USA
**Lassila, Lydia** — Freestyle Aerials Skier
Team Buller Riders, PO Box 33, Mount Buller, VIC 3723, Australia
**Lassiter, Isaac T (Ike)** — Football Player
2812 Rawson St, Oakland CA 94619, USA
**Lassiter, Kwamie** — Football Player
122 W Sunrise Place, Chandler AZ 85248, USA
**Last, James** — Orchestra Leader
Semmel Concerts, Am Muhlengraben 70, 95445 Bayreuth, Germany
**Laster, Danny B** — Animal Research Scientist
Hruska Meat Animal Research Center, PO Box 166, Clay Center NE 68933, USA
**Lastra, Pilar** — Model, Actress
Playboy Promotions, 9346 Civic Center Dr, #200, Beverly Hills CA 90210 USA
**Latana, Valerie** — Editor
Shape, Editorial Dept, 1 Park Ave, New York NY 10016, USA

**Latham, Louise** — Actress
300 Hot Springs Road, Santa Barbara CA 93108, USA
**Lathan, Sanaa** — Actress
John Carrabino Mgmt, 5900 Wilshire Blvd, #406, Los Angeles CA 90036 USA
**Lathan, Stan** — Director, Producer, Writer
Simmons Latham Media Group, 6100 Wilshire Blvd, #1111, Los Angeles CA 90048, USA
**Latimer, Don B** — Football Player
562 S Kalispell Way, Aurora CO 80017, USA
**Latimore** — Singer, Keyboardist
Rodgers Redding, PO Box 4603, Macon GA 31208 USA
**Latimore, Jacob** — Actor
Creative Artists Agency, 2000 Ave of Stars, #100, Los Angeles CA 90067 USA
**Latimore, Joseph** — Actor
J E Talent, 323 Geary St, #302, San Francisco CA 94102, USA
**Latman, A Barry** — Baseball Player
2726 Shelter Island Dr, PO Box 519, San Diego CA 92106, USA
**Lattimore, Kenny** — Singer
Mauldin Brand Agency, 1280 W Peachtree St, #300, Atlanta GA 30309, USA
**Lattin, David (Big Daddy)** — Basketball Player
8230 Twin Tree Lane, Houston TX 77071, USA
**Lattisaw, Stacy** — Singer
Walt Reeder Productions, 93 Old York Road, #1-604, Jenkintown PA 19046, USA
**Lattner, John J (Johnny)** — Football Player
1700 Riverwoods Dr, #503, Melrose Park IL 60160, USA
**Laub, Larry** — Bowler
5380 W Eaglestone Loop, Tucson AZ 85742, USA
**Lauby, Chantal** — Actress
Voyez Mon Agent, 20 Ave Rapp, 75007 Paris, France
**Lauda, Andreas-Nikolaus (Niki)** — Auto Racing Driver
N I K I Luftfahrt, Office Park I, #B-03, Vienna-Flughafen, Austria
**Lauder, Leonard A** — Businessman
Estee Lauder Companies, 767 5th Ave, Basement 1, New York NY 10153, USA
**Lauder, Ronald S** — Businessman, Diplomat
Estee Lauder Companies, 767 5th Ave, Basement 1, New York NY 10153, USA
**Lauderdale, Jim** — Singer, Songwriter
Rosebud Agency, PO Box 170429, San Francisco CA 94117 USA
**Laudner, Timothy J (Tim)** — Baseball Player
PO Box 10, Hamel MN 55340, USA
**Laudrup, Brian** — Soccer Player
2960 Rungsted Kyst, Denmark
**Lauer, Andrew** — Actor
Motive Entertainment, 1149 3rd St, Santa Monica CA 90403, USA
**Lauer, Bonnie** — Golfer
525 Via Laguna Vista, San Luis Obispo CA 93405, USA
**Lauer, Martin** — Track Athlete
D L V, Alsfeder Str 17, 64289 Darmstadt, Germany
**Lauer, Matt** — Commentator
2301 Deerfield Road, Sag Harbor NY 11963, USA
**Lauer, Tod R** — Astronomer
6471 N Tierra de Las Catalina, Tucson AZ 85718, USA
**Laughlin, John** — Actor
Laughlin Enterprises, 13116 Albers St, Sherman Oaks CA 91401, USA
**Laughlin, Robert B** — Nobel Physics Laureate
960 Mears Court, Stanford CA 94305, USA
**Laukkanen, Janne K** — Ice Hockey Player
Tampa Bay Lightning, 401 Channelside Dr, Tampa FL 33602 USA
**Lauper, Cyndi** — Singer, Songwriter
So What Mgmt, 890 W End Ave, #1A, New York NY 10025, USA
**Laurance, Dale R** — Businessman
Occidental Petroleum, 10889 Wilshire Blvd, #1000, Los Angeles CA 90024, USA
**Laurance, Matthew W** — Actor
1951 Hillcrest Road, Los Angeles CA 90068, USA
**Laure, Carole** — Singer, Actress
Voyez Mon Agent, 20 Ave Rapp, 75007 Paris, France
**Laurel, Richard (Rich)** — Basketball Player
706 Antelope Way, Kissimmee FL 34759, USA
**Lauren, Carly** — Model
Playboy Promotions, 9346 Civic Center Dr, #200, Beverly Hills CA 90210 USA
**Lauren, Joy** — Actress
Paradigm Agency, 360 N Crescent Dr, North Building, Beverly Hills CA 90210 USA
**Lauren, Ralph** — Fashion Designer
867 Madison Ave, New York NY 10021, USA
**Lauren, Tammy** — Actress
Glick Agency, 347 5th Ave, #1404, New York NY 10016 USA
**Lauren, Val** — Actor, Writer, Director
Underground, 447 S Highland Ave, Los Angeles CA 90036, USA
**Laurence, Ashley** — Actress
International Talent Agency, 9701 Wilshire Blvd, Beverly Hills CA 90212, USA
**Laurens, Camille** — Writer
Bloomsbury Publishing, 50 Bedford Square, London WC1B 3DP, England
**Laurent, Melanie** — Actress
U B B A, 6 Rue de Braque, 75003 Paris, France
**Laurer, Joanie (Chyna)** — Professional Wrestler, Model
Esterman Entertainment, 12333 Pretoria Dr, Silver Spring MD 20904 USA
**Lauria, Dan** — Actor
Jeff Berger Mgmt, 301 W 53rd St, #10J, New York NY 10019, USA
**Lauria, Matt** — Actor, Writer
W M E Entertainment, 9601 Wilshire Blvd, #300, Beverly Hills CA 90210 USA
**Lauridsen, Morten** — Composer, Musician
University of Southern California, Music Dept, Los Angeles CA 90089, USA
**Laurie, Hugh** — Actor, Comedian, Writer
Hamilton Hodell, 20 Golden Square, London W1F 9JL, England
**Laurie, Miracle** — Actress
Pantheon Talent, 1801 Century Park E, #1910, Los Angeles CA 90067, USA
**Laurie, Piper** — Actress
Marion Rosenberg, PO Box 69826, West Hollywood CA 90212 USA

**Laurinaitis, James R** — Football Player
Saint Louis Rams, 901 N Broadway, Saint Louis MO 63101 USA

**Laursen, Jeppe (Senior)** — Singer, Keyboardist (Junior Senior)
Festival Network Mgmt, 30 Irving Place, #600, New York NY 10003, USA

**Lauterbach, Robert E** — Businessman
118 Dowling Dr, Pittsburgh PA 15215, USA

**Lautner, Taylor D** — Actor
Management 360, 9111 Wilshire Blvd, Beverly Hills CA 90210 USA

**Lavadour, James** — Artist
Umatilla Indian Reservation Confederated Tribles, Pendleton OR 97801, USA

**Lavalliere, Michael E (Mike)** — Baseball Player
216 81st St W, Bradenton FL 34209, USA

**Lavanant, Dominique** — Actress
Voyez Mon Agent, 20 Ave Rapp, 75007 Paris, France

**Lavant, Denis** — Actor
U B B A, 6 Rue de Braque, 75003 Paris, France

**Lave, Lester B** — Economist
1008 Devonshire Road, Pittsburgh PA 15213, USA

**Laveikin, Aleksandr I** — Cosmonaut
Cosmonaut Training Center, Star City, 141160 Zvezdny Gorodok, Moscow Oblast, Russia

**Lavelle, Gary R** — Baseball Player
1100 Worthington Court, Virginia Beach VA 23464, USA

**Lavender, Jay** — Producer, Director, Writer
Verve Talent, 9696 Culver Blvd, #301, Culver City CA 90232, USA

**Lavender, Joseph (Joe)** — Football Player
1929 W Erie Ave, Philadelphia PA 19140, USA

**Laventhol, Henry L (Hank)** — Artist
445 Heritage Hills, #F, Somers NY 10589, USA

**Laver, Rodney G (Rod)** — Tennis Player
3009 Via Conquistador, Carlsbad CA 92009, USA

**Lavergne, Didier** — Makeup Artist
Mirisch Agency, 1025 Colorado Ave, #B, Santa Monica CA 90211 USA

**Laverick, Elise** — Rowing Athlete
Thames Rowing Club, Putney Embankment, London SW15 1LB, England

**Lavery, Sean** — Ballet Dancer, Choreographer
New York City Ballet, Lincoln Center Plaza, New York NY 10023 USA

**LaVette, Bettye** — Singer
Rosebud Agency, PO Box 170429, San Francisco CA 94117 USA

**Lavi, Daliah** — Actress
134 W Wainman Ave, Asheboro NC 27203, USA

**Lavia, Gabriele** — Actor
Carol Levi Mgmt, Via Giuseppe Pisanelli 2, 00196 Rome, Italy

**Lavigne, Avril** — Singer, Songwriter
Azoff Music Mgmt, 1100 Glendon Ave, #2000, Los Angeles CA 90024, USA

**Lavillenie, Renaud** — Track Athlete
37 Chemin des Horts, 63170 Perignat Les Sarlieve, France

**Lavin, Leonard H** — Businessman
Alberto-Culver, 2525 Armitage Ave, Melrose Park IL 60160, USA

**Lavin, Linda** — Actress, Singer
PO Box 1887, Wilmington NC 28402, USA

**Laviolette, Peter** — Ice Hockey Player, Coach
7000 Firehouse Road, Longboat Key FL 34228, USA

**LaVorgna, Adam** — Actor
Hartig-Hilepo Agency, 54 W 21st St, #610, New York NY 10010 USA

**Lavoy, Robert W (Bob)** — Basketball Player
4902 Bayshore Blvd, #605, Tampa FL 33611, USA

**Lavrosky, Mikhail L** — Ballet Dancer
Voznesesenky Per 16/4, #7, 103009 Moscow, Russia

**Lavrsen, Helena Blach** — Curling Athlete
Curling Association, Idraettens Hus, 2605 Brondby, Denmark

**Law, Bernard F Cardinal** — Religious Leader
Basilica di Santa Maria Maggiore, Via Liberiana 27, 00185 Rome, Italy

**Law, Bob** — Artist, Sculptor
Warehouse, 18 Bread St, Penzance, Cornwall TR18 2EG, England

**Law, Jude** — Actor
Julian Belfrage Assoc, 9 Argyll St, #300, London W1F 7TG, England

**Law, Kelley** — Curling Athlete
Curling Association, 1660 Vimont Court, Cumberland ON K4A 4J4, Canada

**Law, Tajuan E (Ty)** — Football Player
10862 Hawks Vista St, Plantation FL 33324, USA

**Law, Vance A** — Baseball Player
1547 W 1970 N, Provo UT 84604, USA

**Law, Vernon S (Vern)** — Baseball Player
Bace Sports, 5699 Kanan Road, #157, Agoura Hills CA 91301, USA

**Lawanson, Ruth M** — Volleyball Player
8081 Highland Flume Circle, Reno NV 89523, USA

**Lawes, Kaitlyn** — Curling Athlete
Team Jennifer Jones, 246 Jacques Ave, Winnipeg MB R3W 1S9, Canada

**Lawler, Jerry** — Professional Wrestler, Sportscaster
415 Saint Nick Dr, Memphis TN 38117, USA

**Lawler, John (King)** — Professional Wrestler
415 Saint Nick Dr, Memphis TN 38117, USA

**Lawless, Blackie** — Singer, Guitarist (WASP)
Chipster, 100 Village Square Crossing, Palm Beach Gardens FL 33410 USA

**Lawless, Lucy** — Actress
Valeo Entertainment, 8265 Sunset Blvd, #103, Los Angeles CA 90046, USA

**Lawless, Paul** — Ice Hockey Player
4231 N Winfield Scott Plaza, #1, Scottsdale AZ 85251, USA

**Lawless, R Burton** — Football Player
2035 Oak Glen Dr, McGregor TX 76657, USA

**Lawless, Robert W** — Educator
University of Tulsa, President's Office, Tulsa OK 74104, USA

**Lawless, Thomas J (Tom)** — Baseball Player
1238 Laura St, Casselberry FL 32707, USA

**Lawrence, Andrew (Andy)** — Actor
Rebel Entertainment Partners, 5700 Wilshire Blvd, #456, Los Angeles CA 90036, USA

**Lawrence, Bill**
I C M Partners, 10250 Constellation Blvd, #900, Los Angeles CA 90067 USA — Producer, Director

**Lawrence, Carol**
Unified Mgmt, 4231 National Ave, Burbank CA 91505, USA — Actress, Singer

**Lawrence, Carolyn**
W M E Entertainment, 9601 Wilshire Blvd, #300, Beverly Hills CA 90210 USA — Actress

**Lawrence, Henry**
401 17th St W, Palmetto FL 34221, USA — Football Player

**Lawrence, James (Loz)**
PO Box 33, Pontypool, Gwent NP4 6YU, England — Guitarist (Strawberry Blondes)

**Lawrence, James R (Jim)**
225 Haddington St, Caledonia ON N3W 1G1, Canada — Baseball Player

**Lawrence, Jennifer**
Creative Artists Agency, 2000 Ave of Stars, #100, Los Angeles CA 90067 USA — Actress

**Lawrence, Joseph (Joey)**
United Talent Agency, U T A Plaza, 9336 Civic Center Dr, Beverly Hills CA 90210 USA — Actor

**Lawrence, Josie**
International Artists, 193-97 High Holborn, London WC1V 7BD, England — Actress

**Lawrence, Marc**
United Talent Agency, U T A Plaza, 9336 Civic Center Dr, Beverly Hills CA 90210 USA — Director, Producer, Writer

**Lawrence, Martin F**
Collective, 8383 Wilshire Blvd, #1050, Beverly Hills CA 90211 USA — Actor, Comedian

**Lawrence, Matthew W**
TalentWorks, 3500 W Olive Ave, #1400, Burbank CA 91505 USA — Actor

**Lawrence, Maya**
1091 Anna St, Teaneck NJ 07666, USA — Fencer

**Lawrence, Nina**
W Magazine, Publisher's Office, 3500 Piedmont Road, #505, Atlanta GA 30305, USA — Publisher

**Lawrence, Rebecca**
I C M Partners, 10250 Constellation Blvd, #900, Los Angeles CA 90067 USA — Actress

**Lawrence, Richard D**
7301 Valburn Dr, Austin TX 78731, USA — Army General

**Lawrence, Robert S**
4100 N Charles St, #311, Baltimore MD 21218, USA — Physician

**Lawrence, Robert Z**
Harvard University, Kennedy Government School, Cambridge MA 02138, USA — Government Official, Economist

**Lawrence, Rolland D**
317 Sugarcreek Dr, Franklin PA 16323, USA — Football Player

**Lawrence, Scott**
Ellis Talent Group, 4705 Laurel Canyon Blvd, #300, Valley Village CA 91607, USA — Actor

**Lawrence, Sean C**
336 S Poplar Ave, Elmhurst IL 60126, USA — Baseball Player

**Lawrence, Sharon**
A P A Talent & Literary Agency, 405 S Beverly Dr, #300, Beverly Hills CA 90212 USA — Actress

**Lawrence, Steve**
944 Pinehurst Dr, Las Vegas NV 89109, USA — Singer

**Lawrence, Steven Anthony**
Axiom Mgmt, 10701 Wilshire Blvd, #1202, Los Angeles CA 90024, USA — Actor

**Lawrence, Vicki**
6000 Lido Ave, Long Beach CA 90803, USA — Actress, Comedienne, Singer

**Lawrence, Wendy B**
National Reconnaissance Office, 14675 Lee Road, Chantilly VA 20151, USA — Astronaut

**Lawrie, Nathan E (Nate)**
1157 Melville Ave, Fairfield CT 06825, USA — Football Player

**Lawrie, Paul S**
Code:4 Sports Ltd, Milton Gate, 60 Chiswell St, London EC1Y 4AG, England — Golfer

**Lawson of Blaby, Nigel**
32 Sutherland Walk, London SE17, England — Government Official, England

**Lawson, Ben**
Untitled Entertainment, 350 S Beverly Dr, #200, Beverly Hills CA 90212 USA — Actor

**Lawson, Bianca**
Don Buchwald Talent Agency, 6500 Wilshire Blvd, #2200, Los Angeles CA 90048 USA — Actress

**Lawson, Denis**
Independent Talent Group, 40 Whitfield St, London W1T 2RH, England — Actor

**Lawson, Doyle**
Sugar Hill Records, 3322 West End Ave, #1100, Nashville TN 37203 USA — Mandolinist

**Lawson, Joshua (Josh)**
Management 360, 9111 Wilshire Blvd, Beverly Hills CA 90210 USA — Actor

**Lawson, Kara M**
Wasserman Media Group, 10960 Wilshire Blvd, #2200, Los Angeles CA 90024, USA — Basketball Player

**Lawson, Leigh**
CornerStone Talent Agency, 37 W 20th St, #1107, New York NY 10011, USA — Actor

**Lawson, Maggie**
Gersh Agency, 9465 Wilshire Blvd, #600, Beverly Hills CA 90212 USA — Actress

**Lawson, Michael**
C E S D, 10635 Santa Monica Blvd, #130, Los Angeles CA 90025 USA — Writer

**Lawson, Nigella**
Creative Artists Agency, 2000 Ave of Stars, #100, Los Angeles CA 90067 USA — Chef, Writer

**Lawson, Richard**
A M T Artists, 15260 Ventura Blvd, #1200, Sherman Oaks CA 91403, USA — Actor

**Lawson, Richard L**
6910 Clifton Road, Clifton VA 20124, USA — Air Force General

**Lawson, Sonia**
Royal Academy, Burlington House, Piccadilly, London W1V 0DS, England — Artist

**Lawson, Tywon R (Ty)**
Denver Nuggets, Pepsi Center, 1000 Chopper Circle, Denver CO 80204 USA — Basketball Player

**Lawson-Wade, Edwige**
Federation de Basketball, 117 Rue du Chateau des Rentiers, 75013 Paris, France — Basketball Player

**Lawton, Brian R**
5012 Oak Bend Lane, Minneapolis MN 55436, USA — Ice Hockey Player

**Lawton, Mary**
Chronicle Features, 901 Mission St, San Francisco CA 94103, USA — Cartoonist (Nowhere to Hide)

**Lawton, Matthew (Matt), III**
27264 Highway 67, Saucier MS 39574, USA — Baseball Player

**Lax, Benjamin**
Massachusetts Institute of Technology, Physics Dept, Cambridge MA 02139, USA — Physicist

# L

|  |  |
|---|---|
| **Lax, Peter D**<br>Courant Math Institute, 251 Mercer St, #910, New York NY 10012, USA | Abel Mathematics Laureate |
| **Laxalt, Paul D**<br>Paul Laxalt Group, 245 E Liberty St, #510, Reno NV 89501, USA | Governor, Senator, NV |
| **Laxton, William H (Bill)**<br>261 Mansion Ave, Audubon NJ 08106, USA | Baseball Player |
| **Laybourne, Geraldine (Gerry)**<br>Oxygen Media, 75 9th Ave, #700, New York NY 10011, USA | Businessman |
| **Layer, Friedemann**<br>I M G Artists, Hogarth Business Park, Chiswick, London W4 2TH, England | Conductor |
| **Layton, Dennis (Mo)**<br>872 S 14th St, Newark NJ 07108, USA | Basketball Player |
| **Layton, Donald H**<br>Federal Home Loan Mortgage Corp, 8100 Jones Branch Dr, McLean VA 22102, USA | Financier |
| **Layton, Peter**<br>London Glassblowing, 7 Leather Market, Weston St, London SE1 3ER, England | Artist |
| **Layzie Bone**<br>Green Light Talent Agency, PO Box 3172, Beverly Hills CA 90212 USA | Rap Artist (Bone Thugs-N-Harmony) |
| **Lazar, Aaron**<br>Abrams Artists, 9200 W Sunset Blvd, #1125, West Hollywood CA 90069 USA | Actor |
| **Lazar, J Dan (Danny)**<br>8444 Oakwood Ave, Munster IN 46321, USA | Baseball Player |
| **Lazar, Shira**<br>Innovative Artists, 1505 10th St, Santa Monica CA 90401 USA | Actress, Producer |
| **Lazare, Mylene**<br>A A S S Sarcelles Natation, Centre Nelson Mandela, Ave Paul Langevin, 95200 Sarcelles, France | Swimmer |
| **Lazarev, Alexander N**<br>Christopher Tennant Artists, 39 Tadema Road, #2, London SW10 0PY, England | Conductor |
| **Lazarus, Mell**<br>Creators Syndicate, 737 3rd St, Hermosa Beach CA 90254 USA | Cartoonist (Miss Peach, Momma) |
| **Lazarus, Rochelle B (Shelly)**<br>106 E 78th St, New York NY 10075, USA | Businesswoman |
| **Lazear, Edward P**<br>277 Old Spanish Trail, Portola Valley CA 94028, USA | Government Official, Economist |
| **Lazenby, George**<br>Hervey/Grimes Talent, 10561 Missouri Ave, #2, Los Angeles CA 90025 USA | Actor |
| **Lazetich, Peter G (Pete)**<br>185 Martin St, Reno NV 89509, USA | Football Player |
| **Lazier, Robert (Buddy)**<br>386 Hanson Ranch Road, Vail CO 81657, USA | Auto Racing Driver |
| **Lazlo, Viktor**<br>56 Rue de Lisbonne, 75008 Paris, France | Actress, Singer |
| **Lazorko, Jack T**<br>1360 Meandering Way, Rockwall TX 75087, USA | Baseball Player |
| **Lazovic, Suzana**<br>Z R K Buducnost, Ivana Nilutinovica B B, 81000 Podgorica, Montenegro | Handball Player |
| **Lazuktin, Alexander I**<br>Cosmonaut Training Center, Star City, 141160 Zvezdny Gorodok, Moscow Oblast, Russia | Cosmonaut |
| **Lazure, Gabrielle**<br>A C T 1, 83 Rue Saint Honore, 75001 Paris, France | Actress |
| **Le Toya**<br>Creative Artists Agency, 2000 Ave of Stars, #100, Los Angeles CA 90067 USA | Singer (Destiny's Child) |
| **Lea, Nicholas**<br>Global Artists Agency, 6253 Hollywood Blvd, #508, Los Angeles CA 90028 USA | Actor |
| **Leach, Michael C (Mike)**<br>Washington State University, Athleltic Dept, Pullman WA 99164, USA | Football Coach |
| **Leach, Penelope**<br>3 Tanza Lane, London NW3 2UA, England | Child Psychologist |
| **Leach, Reginald J (Reggie)**<br>263 Thomas Jefferson Terrace, Elkton MD 21921, USA | Ice Hockey Player |
| **Leach, Richard M (Rick)**<br>593 Layman Creek Circle, Grand Blanc MI 48439, USA | Baseball Player |
| **Leach, Robin**<br>Media Artists Group, 8222 Melrose Ave, #200, Los Angeles CA 90046, USA | Producer, Entertainer |
| **Leach, Rosemary**<br>Felix de Wolfe, 51 Maida Vale, London W9 1SD, England | Actress |
| **Leach, Sheryl**<br>Lyons Group, 300 E Bethany Road, Allen TX 75002, USA | Animator (Barney) |
| **Leach, Stephen (Steve)**<br>197 South St, Reading MA 01867, USA | Ice Hockey Player |
| **Leach, T Vonta**<br>5409 White Oak Dr, Lumberton NC 28358, USA | Football Player |
| **Leach, Terry H**<br>2135 SW Locks Road, Stuart FL 34997, USA | Baseball Player |
| **Leachman, Cloris**<br>410 S Barrington Ave, #307, Los Angeles CA 90049, USA | Actress |
| **Leader, Tom**<br>537 Golden Gate Ave, Richmond CA 94801, USA | Architect |
| **Leadon, Bernie**<br>Northstar Entertainment, 501 S Reino Road, #1-380, Thousand Oaks CA 91320, USA | Singer, Guitarist (Eagles) |
| **League, Brandon P**<br>2385 Lake Heather Heights Court, Dunedin FL 34698, USA | Baseball Player |
| **Leah, Rachelle**<br>W M E Entertainment, 9601 Wilshire Blvd, #300, Beverly Hills CA 90210 USA | Model, Actress |
| **Leahy, Patrick J (Pat)**<br>717 Chamblee Lane, Saint Louis MO 63141, USA | Football Player |
| **Leak, Jennifer**<br>James D'Auria Assoc, PO Box 2219, Amagansett NY 11930, USA | Actress |
| **Leak, Justice**<br>S M S Talent, 8383 Wilshire Blvd, #230, Beverly Hills CA 90211 USA | Actor |
| **Leakes, Nene**<br>Guttman Assoc, 118 S Beverly Dr, #201, Beverly Hills CA 90212 USA | Actress |
| **Leakey, Meave G**<br>PO Box 24926, Nairobi 00502, Kenya | Paleontologist |
| **Leakey, Richard E F**<br>PO Box 24926, Nairobi 00502, Kenya | Paleonotolgist |

**Leaks, Emanuel (Manny), Jr** — Basketball Player
9912 North Blvd, Cleveland OH 44108, USA

**Leaks, Roosevelt, Jr** — Football Player
Roosevelt Leaks Properties, 11525 Glen Falloch Court, Austin TX 78754, USA

**Leal, Sharon** — Actress, Singer
I F A Talent Agency, 8730 W Sunset Blvd, #490, West Hollywood CA 90069 USA

**Leali, Richard L, Sr** — Financier
1761 W Hillsboro Blvd, #104, Deerfield Beach FL 33442, USA

**Leanderson, Matthew** — Rowing Athlete
1301 N Highlands Parkway, #110, Tacoma WA 98406, USA

**Leandro Alfonso de Borbon** — Infante, Spain
Ediciones Martinez Rocca, Paseo de Recoletos 4, 28001 Madrid, Spain

**Leandro, Damiao** — Soccer Player
Santos Futebol Clube, Rua Jose de Alencar, Vila Belmiro 11975 580, Brazil

**Lear, Amanda** — Singer
Tony Denton Promotions, Charter House, 157-159 High St, London N14 6BP, England

**Lear, Harold C (Hal)** — Basketball Player
11321 E Sunnyside Dr, Scottsdale AZ 85259, USA

**Lear, Norman M** — Producer, Director
Act III Communications, 100 N Crescent Dr, #250, Beverly Hills CA 90210, USA

**Learned, Michael** — Actress
A M T Artists, 15260 Ventura Blvd, #1200, Sherman Oaks CA 91403, USA

**Leary, Denis** — Actor, Comedian, Producer
Apostle, 568 Broadway, #301, New York NY 10012, USA

**Leary, Paul** — Guitarist, Singer (Butthole Surfers)
Kork Agency, 1880 Century Park E, #711, Los Angeles CA 90067, USA

**Leary, Timothy J (Tim)** — Baseball Player
2461 Santa Monica Blvd, Santa Monica CA 90404, USA

**Leaud, Jean-Pierre** — Actor
Artmedia, 20 Ave Rapp, 75007 Paris, France

**Leavell, Alan F** — Basketball Player
7007 Windy Pines Dr, Spring TX 77379, USA

**Leavenworth, Scott** — Actor
Curtis Talent Mgmt, 9607 Arby Dr, Beverly Hills CA 90210, USA

**Leavitt, Judith W** — Historian
University of Wisconsin, Medical History Dept, Madison WI 53706, USA

**Leavitt, Phil** — Singer (Diamonds)
Lustig Talent, PO Box 770850, Orlando FL 32877 USA

**Leavy, Edward** — Judge
US Court of Appeals, Pioneer Courthouse, 555 SW Yamhill St, Portland OR 97204, USA

**Lebadang** — Artist
Circle Gallery, 303 E Wacker Dr, Chicago IL 60601, USA

**LeBar, Joshua** — Actor, Director, Writer
Talent House LA, 3000 Olympic Blvd, #2226, Santa Monica CA 90404, USA

**LeBaron, Edward W (Eddie), Jr** — Football Player
7524 Pineridge Lane, Fair Oaks CA 95628, USA

**LeBeau, C Richard (Dick)** — Football Player, Coach
10405 Stone Court, Cincinnati OH 45242, USA

**LeBeau, Patrick-Michael** — Ice Hockey Player
610 Vanier, Saint Jerome QC J7Z 6B4, Canada

**LeBeauf, Sabrina** — Actress
11 Asbury Road, Asheville NC 28804, USA

**Lebedev, Valentin V** — Cosmonaut
Cosmonaut Training Center, Star City, 141160 Zvezdny Gorodok, Moscow Oblast, Russia

**LeBel, B Harper** — Football Player
3379 Scadlock Lane, Sherman Oaks CA 91403, USA

**Leber, Ben** — Football Player
4457 35th Ave S, Minneapolis MN 55406, USA

**LeBlanc, Christian** — Actor
Alexander White Agency, 2316 Valley Brook Way, Atlanta GA 30319, USA

**Leblanc, Jean-Paul (J P)** — Ice Hockey Player
120 Gadwall Lane, Manlius NY 13104, USA

**LeBlanc, Karina C** — Soccer Player
Chicago Red Stars, 7300 W 71st St, Bridgeview IL 60455, USA

**LeBlanc, Matt** — Actor
W M E Entertainment, 9601 Wilshire Blvd, #300, Beverly Hills CA 90210 USA

**LeBlanc, Sherri** — Ballerina
New York City Ballet, Lincoln Center Plaza, New York NY 10023 USA

**LeBlanc-Boucher, Anouk** — Speed Skater
Speed Skating Canada, 2781 Lancaster Road, #402, Ottawa ON K1B 1A7, Canada

**Lebo, Jeffrey B (Jeff)** — Basketball Player, Coach
500 Hidden Lake Way, Santa Rosa Beach FL 32459, USA

**Leboeuf, Laurence** — Actress
K I Benzakein Talent, 1155 Rene-Levesque Blvd W, #2500, Montreal QC H3B 2K4, Canada

**LeBoeuf, Raymond W** — Businessman
P P G Industries, 1 P P G Place, Pittsburgh PA 15272, USA

**LeBon, Simon** — Singer, Songwriter (Duran Duran)
D D Productions, 93A Westbourne Park Villas, London W2 5ED, England

**LeBon, Yasmin** — Model
Place Model Mgmt, Am Feld 29, 22765 Hamburg, Germany

**LeBor, Adam** — Journalist, Writer
Bloomsbury Publishing, 50 Bedford Square, London WC1B 3DP, England

**Lebovitz, Nolan** — Director, Writer
Paradigm Agency, 360 N Crescent Dr, North Building, Beverly Hills CA 90210 USA

**Lebowitz, Fran** — Actress, Producer, Writer
Random House, 1745 Broadway, #1800, New York NY 10019 USA

**Lebowitz, Joel L** — Mathematician
Rutgers University, Math Sciences Center, New Brunswick NJ 08903, USA

**Leboyer, Frederick** — Physician
Georges Borchardt, 136 E 57th St, #1400, New York NY 10022, USA

**LeBrock, Kelly** — Actress, Model
Kaplan-Stahler Agency, 8383 Wilshire Blvd, #923, Beverly Hills CA 90211, USA

**LeBrun, Christopher M** — Artist
Marlborough Fine Art, 6 Albermarle St, London W1X 4BY, England

**LeBrun, Denis** — Cartoonist (Blondie)
King Features Syndicate, 300 W 57th St, #1500, New York NY 10019 USA

| | |
|---|---|
| **LeCarre, John** | Writer |
| 9 Gainsborough Gardens, London NW3 1BJ, England | |
| **LeCause, Carl D** | Harness Racing Driver, Owner |
| 124 Ashbury Ave, Freehold NJ 07728, USA | |
| **Lecavalier, Vincent** | Ice Hockey Player |
| 401 Channelside Dr, Tampa FL 33602, USA | |
| **Lechleiter, John** | Businessman |
| Eli Lilly Co, Lilly Corporate Center, Indianapolis IN 46285, USA | |
| **Lechler, E Shane** | Football Player |
| 4608 Sandyford Court, Dublin CA 94568, USA | |
| **Lechter, Sharon L** | Writer |
| Cashflow Technologies, 4330 N Civic Center Plaza, #100, Scottsdale AZ 85251, USA | |
| **Lechtman, Heather N** | Historian |
| Massachusetts Institute of Technology, History Dept, Cambridge MA 02139, USA | |
| **Leckey, Nicholas N (Nick)** | Football Player |
| 1056 E Windsor Dr, Gilbert AZ 85296, USA | |
| **Leckie, Mike** | Sculptor |
| PO Box 5718, Eugene OR 97405, USA | |
| **Leckner, Eric** | Basketball Player |
| 608 27th St, Manhattan Beach CA 90266, USA | |
| **LeClair, James M (Jim)** | Football Player |
| 32 4th Ave NE, Mayville ND 58257, USA | |
| **LeClair, John C** | Ice Hockey Player |
| 108 Tunbridge Circle, Haverford PA 19041, USA | |
| **LeClerc, Jean** | Actor |
| 19 W 44th St, #1500, New York NY 10036, USA | |
| **LeClerc, Mike** | Ice Hockey Player |
| 473 Abbie Way, Costa Mesa CA 92627, USA | |
| **LeClerc, Paul** | Librarian |
| New York Public Library, 5th Ave & 42nd St, New York NY 10018, USA | |
| **Leclerc, Roger A** | Football Player |
| 257 Elm St, Agawam MA 01001, USA | |
| **LeClezio, Jean-Marie Gustave** | Nobel Literature Laureate |
| Editions Gallimard, 5 Rue Sebastien-Bottin, 75007 Paris Cedex 07, France | |
| **LeClos, Chad G B** | Swimmer |
| Seagulls Swimming Club, 59 Stapleton Road, Durban, Pinetown, South Africa | |
| **Lecomte, Benoit** | Swimmer |
| Cross Atlantic Swimming Challenge, 3005 S Lamar, #D109-353, Austin TX 78704, USA | |
| **Leconte, Henri** | Tennis Player |
| International Mangement Group, Pier House, Chiswick, London W4M 3NN, England | |
| **Leconte, Patrice** | Director |
| Artmedia, 20 Ave Rapp, 75007 Paris, France | |
| **Lecount, Terry J** | Football Player |
| 1288 Branchfield Court, Riverdale GA 30296, USA | |
| **LeCroy, Matt** | Baseball Player |
| 11314 Cedar Pointe Dr N, Hopkins MN 55305, USA | |
| **L'Ecuyer, John** | Director |
| Paradigm Agency, 360 N Crescent Dr, North Building, Beverly Hills CA 90210 USA | |
| **Ledbetter, Lilly** | Social Activist |
| PO Box 72, Jacksonville AL 36265, USA | |
| **Ledecky, Kathleen G (Katie)** | Swimmer |
| 5395 Elliott Road, Bethesda MD 20816, USA | |
| **Ledee, Ricardo  A (Ricky)** | Baseball Player |
| D29 Calle Antonio Ledee Rivera, Extension Carmen, Salinas PR 00751, USA | |
| **Leder, Mimi** | Director |
| Creative Artists Agency, 2000 Ave of Stars, #100, Los Angeles CA 90067 USA | |
| **Leder, Philip** | Geneticist |
| Harvard Medical School, Genetics Dept, 77 Ave Louis Pasteur, Boston MA 02115, USA | |
| **Leder, Steven** | Religious Leader, Rabbi |
| Wilshire Boulevard Temple, 3663 Wilshire Blvd, Los Angeles CA 90010, USA | |
| **Lederman, Leon M** | Nobel Physics Laureate |
| 2163 Mount Davidson Dr, Driggs ID 83422, USA | |
| **Ledesma, Aaron D** | Baseball Player |
| 247 Los Prados Dr, Safety Harbor FL 34695, USA | |
| **Ledford, Brandy** | Actress, Model |
| Ellis Talent Group, 4705 Laurel Canyon Blvd, #300, Valley Village CA 91607, USA | |
| **Ledford, Frank F, Jr** | Army General, Physician |
| Southwest Biomed Research Foundation, PO Box 760549, San Antonio TX 78245, USA | |
| **Ledisi** | Singer, Songwriter |
| I C M Partners, 10250 Constellation Blvd, #900, Los Angeles CA 90067 USA | |
| **Ledoyen, Virginie** | Actress, Model |
| 80 Ave Gen Charles de Gaulle, 92200 Neuilly, France | |
| **Ledyard, Grant** | Ice Hockey Player |
| 5072 Old Goodrich Road, Clarence NY 14031, USA | |
| **Lee Beom-Young** | Soccer Player |
| Football Association, 1-131 Sinmunno, 2-Ga Jongno-Gu, Seoul 110 062, South Korea | |
| **Lee Byung-Chun** | Veternarian |
| National University, San 56-1, Shillim-Dong, Seoul 151 742, South Korea | |
| **Lee Hong-Koo** | Prime Minister, South Korea |
| Club de Madrid, C/Goya 5-7, Pasaje 2, 28001 Madrid, Spain | |
| **Lee Ho-Suk** | Speed Skater |
| Skating Union, 88 Bangyee-Dong, Songpaku, Seoul 138 749, South Korea | |
| **Lee Hsien Loong** | Prime Minister, Singapore |
| Premier's Office, Istana Annexe, Istana, 238823 Singapore, Singapore | |
| **Lee Sang-Hwa** | Speed Skater |
| Skating Union, 88 Bangyee-Dong, Songpaku, Seoul 138 749, South Korea | |
| **Lee Seung-Hoon** | Speed Skater |
| Skating Union, 88 Bangyee-Dong, Songpaku, Seoul 138 749, South Korea | |
| **Lee Ufan** | Artist, Sculptor |
| Pace Gallery, 32 E 57th St, New York NY 10022, USA | |
| **Lee, Adruitha** | Makeup & Hairstyling Artist |
| iTalent, 5023 N Parkway Calabasas, Calabasas CA 91302, USA | |
| **Lee, Alexandra** | Actress |
| Sanders/Armstrong/Caserta Mgmt, 2120 Colorado Ave, #120, Santa Monica CA 90404 USA | |
| **Lee, Amos** | Singer, Songwriter |
| Red Light Mgmt, 44 Wall St, #2200, New York NY 10005, USA | |

|  |  |
|---|---|
| **Lee, Amy**<br>Dennis Rider Mgmt, 931 Hilldale Ave, West Hollywood CA 90069, USA | Singer, Musician (Evanescence) |
| **Lee, Andrew P (Andy)**<br>San Francisco 49ers, 4949 Centennial Blvd, Santa Clara CA 95054 USA | Football Player |
| **Lee, Ang**<br>Creative Artists Agency, 2000 Ave of Stars, #100, Los Angeles CA 90067 USA | Director |
| **Lee, Anthonia W (Amp)**<br>990 Brickyard Road, Chipley FL 32428, USA | Football Player |
| **Lee, Ben**<br>Gold Village Entertainment, 72 Madison Ave, #800, New York NY 90016, USA | Singer (Luna), Songwriter |
| **Lee, Beverly**<br>Bevi Corp, PO Box 100, Clifton NJ 07015, USA | Singer (Shirelles) |
| **Lee, Bobby**<br>Creative Artists Agency, 2000 Ave of Stars, #100, Los Angeles CA 90067 USA | Actor |
| **Lee, Brenda**<br>5941 Ramirez Canyon Road, Malibu CA 90265, USA | Singer |
| **Lee, Brook A M**<br>A K A Talent, 6310 San Vicente Blvd, #200, Los Angeles CA 90048 USA | Beauty Queen, Actress |
| **Lee, Carl, III**<br>1 Stonegate Dr, Hurricane WV 25526, USA | Football Player |
| **Lee, Carlos N**<br>1400 N 11th Ave, Melrose Park IL 60160, USA | Baseball Player |
| **Lee, Catherine J**<br>3242 SE Taylor St, Portland OR 97214, USA | Artist |
| **Lee, Change Rae**<br>Princeton University, Creative Writing Dept, Princeton NJ 08544, USA | Writer |
| **Lee, Charles R**<br>Marathon Petroleum Corp, 539 S Main St, Findlay OH 45840, USA | Businessman |
| **Lee, Charles S (C S)**<br>Peter Strain, 5455 Wilshire Blvd, #1812, Los Angeles CA 90036 USA | Actor |
| **Lee, Christopher F C**<br>5 Sandown House, Wheat Field Terrace, London W4, England | Actor |
| **Lee, Clifton P (Cliff)**<br>5706 Riviera Dr, Benton AR 72019, USA | Baseball Player |
| **Lee, Clyde W**<br>1118 Crater Hill Dr, Nashville TN 37215, USA | Basketball Player |
| **Lee, Corey W**<br>278 Lancashire Run, Smithfield NC 27577, USA | Baseball Player |
| **Lee, Courtney**<br>Memphis Grizzlies, 191 Beale St, Memphis TN 38103 USA | Basketball Player |
| **Lee, David**<br>Grub Street Productions, 5555 Melrose Ave, #101, Los Angeles CA 90038, USA | Director, Writer |
| **Lee, David**<br>Golden State Warriors, 1011 Broadway, Oakland CA 94605 USA | Basketball Player |
| **Lee, David A**<br>2518 N Waverly Dr, Bossier City LA 71111, USA | Football Player |
| **Lee, David E**<br>56 Terrace Dr, Pittsburgh PA 15205, USA | Baseball Player |
| **Lee, David G (Dave)**<br>2580 Rampart Terrace, Reno NV 89519, USA | Basketball Player |
| **Lee, David H**<br>Plenum Publishing Group, 233 Spring St, #600, New York NY 10013, USA | Astronomer |
| **Lee, David L**<br>Global Crossing Ltd, Wessex House, 45 Reid St, Hamilton HM 12, Bermuda | Businessman |
| **Lee, David M**<br>Cornell University, Physics Dept, Clark Hall, Ithaca NY 14853, USA | Nobel Physics Laureate |
| **Lee, Dennis**<br>I C M Partners, 10250 Constellation Blvd, #900, Los Angeles CA 90067 USA | Director |
| **Lee, Derrek L**<br>3576 Brittany Way, El Dorado Hills CA 95762, USA | Baseball Player |
| **Lee, Dickey**<br>Cape Entertainment, 4799 Coconut Creek Parkway, Coconut Grove FL 33063, USA | Singer |
| **Lee, Don**<br>Ploughshares, Emerson College, 120 Boylston St, #414, Boston MA 02116, USA | Writer |
| **Lee, Donald E (Don)**<br>9101 E Palm Tree Dr, Tucson AZ 85710, USA | Baseball Player |
| **Lee, Doug**<br>10770 Procyon St, Las Vegas NV 89141, USA | Basketball Player |
| **Lee, Gary L**<br>Gary Lee Partners, 360 W Superior, #1, Chicago IL 60654, USA | Interior Designer |
| **Lee, Geddy**<br>S L Feldman Mgmt, 1505 W 2nd Ave, #200, Vancouver BC V6H 3Y4, Canada | Singer, Bassist (Rush) |
| **Lee, Grandma**<br>Lee Strong, 626 Staffordshire Dr, Jacksonville FL 32225, USA | Actress, Comedienne |
| **Lee, Gregory S (Greg)**<br>8077 Wild Flower Way, San Diego CA 92120, USA | Basketball Player |
| **Lee, Harper**<br>PO Box 278, Monroeville AL 36461, USA | Writer |
| **Lee, Ho Wang**<br>Life Sciences Institute, 388 Poongnap-Dong, Seoul 138 736, South Korea | Virologist |
| **Lee, Howard V**<br>529 King Arthur Dr, Virginia Beach VA 23464, USA | Vietnam War Marine Corps Hero (CMH) |
| **Lee, Jack R (Jacky)**<br>6306 Mid Pines Dr, Houston TX 77069, USA | Football Player |
| **Lee, Janice Y K**<br>Park Literary Group, 270 Lafayette St, #1504, New York NY 10012, USA | Writer |
| **Lee, Jared B**<br>Jared B Lee Studio, 2942 Hamilton Road, Lebanon OH 45036, USA | Cartoonist |
| **Lee, Jason**<br>Ribisi Entertainment Group, 3278 Wilshire Blvd, #702, Los Angeles CA 90010, USA | Actor |
| **Lee, Jason Scott**<br>Untitled Entertainment, 350 S Beverly Dr, #200, Beverly Hills CA 90212 USA | Actor |
| **Lee, Jeanette**<br>Octagon Worldwide, 1751 Pinnacle Dr, #1500, McLean VA 22102 USA | Billards Player |
| **Lee, Jennifer**<br>Creative Artists Agency, 2000 Ave of Stars, #100, Los Angeles CA 90067 USA | Writer, Director, Animator |

**Lee, Jieho**
United Talent Agency, U T A Plaza, 9336 Civic Center Dr, Beverly Hills CA 90210 USA — Director, Writer

**Lee, Jim**
Nicelle Beauchene Gallery, 327 Broome St, New York NY 10002, USA — Artist

**Lee, Jim**
Wildstorm Productions, 888 Prospect St, #240, La Jolla CA 92037, USA — Cartoonist

**Lee, Joe**
Darden Restaurants, 1000 Darden Center Dr, Orlando FL 32837, USA — Businessman

**Lee, Johnny**
Red 11 Music, 2110 S Lamar Blvd, Austin TX 78704, USA — Singer, Guitarist, Songwriter

**Lee, Jonathan (Jon)**
Elinor Hilton Assoc, 1 Goodwins Court, London WC2N 4LL, England — Actor, Singer (S Club 7)

**Lee, Jonna**
8721 W Sunset Blvd, #103, West Hollywood CA 90069, USA — Actress

**Lee, Keith D**
11653 Metz Place, Eads TN 38028, USA — Basketball Player

**Lee, Kristin**
I C M Artists, 40 W 57th St, #1800, New York NY 10019 USA — Concert Violinist

**Lee, Kurk**
2745 Scarborough Circle, Windsor Mill MD 21244, USA — Basketball Player

**Lee, Larry D**
PO Box 3889, Highland Park MI 48203, USA — Football Player

**Lee, Laura**
Lee Magid, 15414 Ridgewood Dr, Sonora CA 95370, USA — Singer

**Lee, Lela**
S M S Talent, 8383 Wilshire Blvd, #230, Beverly Hills CA 90211 USA — Actress

**Lee, Leron**
8150 Warren Court, Granite Bay CA 95746, USA — Baseball Player

**Lee, Luanne**
Playboy Promotions, 9346 Civic Center Dr, #200, Beverly Hills CA 90210 USA — Actress, Model

**Lee, Malcolm D**
Resolution, 1801 Century Park E, #2300, Los Angeles CA 90067 USA — Director

**Lee, Manuel L (Manny)**
321 NW 31st St, Miami FL 33127, USA — Baseball Player

**Lee, Mark**
Shanahan Mgmt, Berman House, 91 Campbell St, #300, Surry Hills NSW 2010, Australia — Actor, Director, Producer

**Lee, Mark D**
Creative Trust, 5141 Virginia Way, #320, Brentwood TN 37027, USA — Guitarist (Third Day), Songwriter

**Lee, Mark A**
3610 208th St SE, Bothell WA 98021, USA — Football Player

**Lee, Mark C**
79 S Player Crest Circle, Spring TX 77382, USA — Astronaut

**Lee, Marqise**
Jacksonville Jaguars, 1 AllTel Stadium Place, Jacksonville FL 32202 USA — Football Player

**Lee, Michele**
Michele Lee Productions, 10866 Wilshire Blvd, #1100, Los Angeles CA 90024, USA — Actress, Singer

**Lee, Minkyu**
United Talent Agency, U T A Plaza, 9336 Civic Center Dr, Beverly Hills CA 90210 USA — Animator, Director, Writer

**Lee, Nikki S**
Sikkema Jenkins Co, 530 W 22nd St, New York NY 10011, USA — Photographer

**Lee, Nina**
David Rowe Artists, 24 Beesom St, #2, Marblehead MA 01945, USA — Concert Cellist

**Lee, Patrick**
Links Mgmt, 5068 W Plano Parkway, #256, Plano TX 75093, USA — Golfer

**Lee, Rachel**
I M G Artists, Carnegie Hall Tower, 152 W 57th St, #500, New York NY 10019 USA — Concert Violinist

**Lee, Rex**
A P A Talent & Literary Agency, 405 S Beverly Dr, #300, Beverly Hills CA 90212 USA — Actor

**Lee, Robert D (Bob)**
PO Box 1589, Lake Havasu City AZ 86405, USA — Baseball Player

**Lee, Robert M (Bob)**
363 Parker Ave, San Francisco CA 94118, USA — Football Player

**Lee, Robinne**
Abrams Artists, 9200 W Sunset Blvd, #1125, West Hollywood CA 90069 USA — Actress

**Lee, Rock A**
4616 Blackfoot Ave, San Diego CA 92117, USA — Basketball Player

**Lee, Ronald V (Ronnie)**
139 Shady Trail, McGregor TX 76657, USA — Football Player

**Lee, RonReaco**
Principato-Young, 9465 Wilshire Blvd, #880, Beverly Hills CA 90212 USA — Actor

**Lee, Russell E**
1457 Smokehouse Lane, Stone Mountain GA 30088, USA — Basketball Player

**Lee, Ruta**
2623 Laurel Canyon Road, Los Angeles CA 90046, USA — Actress

**Lee, Samuel (Sammy)**
16537 Harbour Lane, Huntington Beach CA 92649, USA — Diver, Coach

**Lee, Sandra**
W M E Entertainment, 9601 Wilshire Blvd, #300, Beverly Hills CA 90210 USA — Style Expert

**Lee, Sandra**
Food Network, 1180 Ave of Americas, #1200, New York NY 10036 USA — Chef, Writer

**Lee, Seon-Hwa**
Ladies Pro Golf Assn, 100 International Golf Dr, Daytona Beach FL 32124 USA — Golfer

**Lee, Shannon E**
Innovative Artists, 1505 10th St, Santa Monica CA 90401 USA — Actress

**Lee, Sheryl**
Brillstein Entertainment Partners, 9150 Wilshire Blvd, #350, Beverly Hills CA 90212 USA — Actress

**Lee, Spike**
Forty Acres & A Mule Filmworks, 75 S Elliott Place, Brooklyn NY 11217, USA — Director

**Lee, Stan**
Pow Entertainment, 9440 Santa Monica Blvd, #620, Beverly Hills CA 90210, USA — Publisher, Cartoonist

**Lee, Terry J**
4650 Wendover St, Eugene OR 97404, USA — Baseball Player

**Lee, Tommy**
Vox Inc, 6420 Wilshire Blvd, #1080, Los Angeles CA 90048 USA — Drummer, Singer (Motley Crue)

**Lee, Travis R**
PO Box 1572, Rancho Santa Fe CA 92067, USA — Baseball Player

**L**

|  |  |
|---|---|
| **Lee, Tsung-Dao**<br>512 Clinton St, Brooklyn NY 11231, USA | Nobel Physics Laureate |
| **Lee, Wayne**<br>Jet Propulsion Laboratory, 4800 Oak Grove Dr, Pasadena CA 91109 USA | Space Engineer |
| **Lee, Will Yun**<br>A P A Talent & Literary Agency, 405 S Beverly Dr, #300, Beverly Hills CA 90212 USA | Actor |
| **Lee, William F (Bill)**<br>305 Common View Dr, Craftsbury VT 05826, USA | Baseball Player |
| **Lee, William Gregory**<br>Berneman Mgmt, 5820 Wilshire Blvd, #200, Los Angeles CA 90036, USA | Actor |
| **Lee, Yuan T**<br>19 Las Piedras, Orinda CA 94563, USA | Nobel Chemistry Laureate |
| **Leebron, David W**<br>Rice University, President's Office, Houston TX 77005, USA | Educator |
| **Leech, Allen**<br>Troika, 74 Clerkenwell Road, #300, London EC1M 5QA, England | Actor |
| **Leech, Beverly**<br>House of Representatives, 1434 6th St, #1, Santa Monica CA 90401 USA | Actress |
| **Leech, Kenneth**<br>Centrepoint, Central House, 25 Camperdown St, London E1 8DZ, England | Theologian, Social Activist |
| **Leech, Richard**<br>Thea Dispeker Artists, 59 E 54th St, New York NY 10022 USA | Opera Singer |
| **Leede, Ed**<br>307 Roca Place, Castle Rock CO 80108, USA | Basketball Player |
| **Leek, Eugene H (Gene)**<br>2722 E Parker Court, Visalia CA 93292, USA | Baseball Player |
| **Leeman, Gary**<br>15 Willow Fern Dr, Barrie ON L4N 0Z9, Canada | Ice Hockey Player |
| **Leemans, Kimberly**<br>Rothman/Andres Entertainment, 4400 Coldwater Canyon Ave, #125, Studio City CA 91604, USA | Model, Actress |
| **Leen, Bill**<br>W M E Entertainment, 1600 Division St, #300, Nashville TN 37203 USA | Bassist (Gin Blossoms) |
| **Leenstra, Marrit**<br>K N S B, Postbus 1120, 3800 Arnesfoort BC, Netherlands | Speed Skater |
| **Leeper, David D (Dave)**<br>23997 Kaleb Dr, Corona CA 92883, USA | Baseball Player |
| **Leerhuber, Brian**<br>I M G Artists, Hogarth Business Park, Chiswick, London W4 2TH, England | Opera Singer |
| **Leese, Howard**<br>1770 N Highland Ave, #H-482, Los Angeles CA 90028, USA | Guitarist, Keyboardist (Heart) |
| **Leestma, David C**<br>4314 Lake Grove Dr, Seabrook TX 77586, USA | Astronaut |
| **Leetch, Brian J**<br>40 Battery St, #PH 12, Boston MA 02109, USA | Ice Hockey Player |
| **Leeuwenburg, Jay R**<br>6268 S Coventry Lane W, Littleton CO 80123, USA | Football Player |
| **Leeves, Jane**<br>23501 Malibu Colony Road, Malibu CA 90265, USA | Actress |
| **Lefcourt, Gerald**<br>211 Central Park W, New York NY 10024, USA | Attorney |
| **Lefcourt, Peter**<br>Creative Artists Agency, 2000 Ave of Stars, #100, Los Angeles CA 90067 USA | Actor |
| **LeFebure, Estelle**<br>Cineart, 28 Rue Mogador, 78009 Paris, France | Model, Actress |
| **Lefebvre, James K (Jim)**<br>10160 E Whispering Wind Dr, Scottsdale AZ 85255, USA | Baseball Player, Manager |
| **Lefebvre, Joseph H (Joe)**<br>PO Box 16658, Hooksett NH 03106, USA | Baseball Player |
| **Lefebvre, Sylvain**<br>Colorado Avalanche, Pepsi Center, 1000 Chopper Circle, Denver CO 80204 USA | Ice Hockey Player |
| **Lefevre, Rachelle**<br>W M E Entertainment, 9601 Wilshire Blvd, #300, Beverly Hills CA 90210 USA | Actress |
| **Lefferts, Craig L**<br>40820 N Laurel Valley Way, Anthem AZ 85086, USA | Baseball Player |
| **Lefkofsky, Eric**<br>Groupon Inc, 600 W Chicago Ave, #620, Chicago IL 60654, USA | Businessman |
| **Lefkovitz, Keili**<br>Metropolitan Talent Agency, 5405 Wilshire Blvd, #218, Los Angeles CA 90036 USA | Actress |
| **Lefkowitz, Robert J**<br>Duke University Medical Center, Chemistry Dept, PO Box 3821, Durham NC 27710, USA | Nobel Chemistry Laureate |
| **Lefley, Chuck**<br>PO Box 65, Grosses Isle MB R0C 1G0, Canada | Ice Hockey Player |
| **Leflore, Ronald (Ron)**<br>6263 93rd Terrace, #4200, Pinellas Park FL 33782, USA | Baseball Player |
| **Leftwich, Byron A**<br>1322 Charter Court E, Jacksonville FL 32225, USA | Football Player |
| **Leftwich, Phillip D (Phil)**<br>15819 S 31st St, Phoenix AZ 85048, USA | Baseball Player |
| **Legace, Emmanuel F (Manny)**<br>40708 Village Oaks, Novi MI 48375, USA | Ice Hockey Player |
| **Legace, Jean-Guy**<br>126 Casa Grande Lane, Santa Rosa Beach FL 32459, USA | Ice Hockey Player |
| **Legato, Robert (Rob)**<br>W M E Entertainment, 9601 Wilshire Blvd, #300, Beverly Hills CA 90210 USA | Visual Effects Artist |
| **Legend, John**<br>Creative Artists Agency, 2000 Ave of Stars, #100, Los Angeles CA 90067 USA | Singer, Pianist, Songwriter, Actor |
| **Legere, John J**<br>T-Mobile USA, 12920 SE 38th St, Bellevue WA 98006, USA | Businessman |
| **Legette, Tyrone C**<br>1304 Hancock St, Columbia SC 29205, USA | Football Player |
| **Leggatt, Ian D**<br>101 Ginkgo Trail, Chapel Hill NC 27516, USA | Golfer |
| **Leggero, Natasha**<br>Brillstein Entertainment Partners, 9150 Wilshire Blvd, #350, Beverly Hills CA 90212 USA | Actress, Comedienne, Writer |
| **Leggett, Anthony J**<br>607 W Pennsylvania Ave, Urbana IL 61801, USA | Nobel Physics Laureate |

V.I.P. Address Book    571

**Lee - Leggett**

# L

**Legien, Waldemar** — Judo Athlete
Ul Grottgera 10, 41902 Bytom, Poland
**Legler, Timothy E (Tim)** — Basketball Player
20 W Woodland Ave, Cape May Court House NJ 08210, USA
**Legrand, Michel** — Composer, Conductor, Concert Pianist
Kraft-Engel Mgmt, 15233 Ventura Blvd, #200, Sherman Oaks CA 91403 USA
**Legrand, Ugo** — Judo Athlete
U S Orleans Judo, Rue Fernand Pellouier, BP 608, 45000 Orleans, France
**Legrande, Larry E, Sr** — Baseball Player
1331 Leon St NW, Roanoke VA 24017, USA
**Legree, Lance** — Football Player
25 Ardmore Ave, Clifton NJ 07012, USA
**Legris, Manuel C** — Ballet Dancer
National Theater of Paris Opera, 8 Rue Scribe, 75009 Paris, France
**LeGros, James** — Actor
Paradigm Agency, 360 N Crescent Dr, North Building, Beverly Hills CA 90210 USA
**LeGuin, Ursula K** — Writer
3321 NW Thurman St, Portland OR 97210, USA
**Leguizamo, John** — Actor, Comedian
United Talent Agency, U T A Plaza, 9336 Civic Center Dr, Beverly Hills CA 90210 USA
**Legwand, David** — Ice Hockey Player
26310 S Offshore Dr, Harrison Township MI 48045, USA
**Lehan, Michael** — Football Player
418 Madison Ave S, Hopkins MN 55343, USA
**Lehane, Dennis** — Writer
341 Kerrville South Dr, Kerrville TX 78028, USA
**Lehew, James A (Jim)** — Baseball Player
3086 Fairview Road, Grantsville MD 21536, USA
**Lehman, I Robert** — Biochemist
895 Cedro Way, Stanford CA 94305, USA
**Lehman, Kristin** — Actress, Dancer
Oscars Abrams Zimel, 438 Queen St E, Toronto ON M5A 1T4, Canada
**Lehman, Thomas E L (Tom)** — Golfer
9820 E Thompson Peak Parkway, #704, Scottsdale AZ 85255, USA
**Lehmann, Edie** — Actress
24844 Malibu Road, Malibu CA 90265, USA
**Lehmann, Jens** — Cyclist
V f B Stuttgart, Mercedesstr 109, 70372 Stuttgart, Germany
**Lehmann, Jens** — Soccer Player
Rosenthaler Str 40-41, Hackesche Hofe, 10179 Berlin, Germany
**Lehmann, Karl Cardinal** — Religious Leader
Bischofliches Ordinariat, Postfach 1560, Bischofsplatz 2, 55116 Mainz, Germany
**Lehmann, Michael** — Director
Industry Entertainment, 955 Carillo Dr, #300, Los Angeles CA 90048 USA
**Lehman-Smith, Debra** — Interior Designer
Lehman-Smith & McLeish, 1212 Banks St NW, Washington DC 20007, USA
**Lehmberg, Stanford E** — Historian
1005 Calle Largo, Santa Fe NM 87501, USA
**Lehn, Jean-Marie P** — Nobel Chemistry Laureate
6 Rue des Pontonniers, 67000 Strasbourg, France
**Lehne, Fredric** — Actor
Bauman Assoc, 250 W 57th St, #2223, New York NY 10107 USA
**Lehninger, Albert L** — Biochemist
15020 Tanyard Road, Sparks MD 21152, USA
**Lehr, Charles L (Justin)** — Baseball Player
6015 Nagel St, La Mesa CA 91942, USA
**Lehr, John** — Actor, Writer
Grade A Entertainment, 149 S Barrington Ave, #719, Los Angeles CA 90049, USA
**Lehrer, James C (Jim)** — Commentator, Writer
News Hour Show, 2700 S Quincy St, #250, Arlington VA 22206, USA
**Lehrer, Scott** — Sound Designer
I C M Partners, 10250 Constellation Blvd, #900, Los Angeles CA 90067 USA
**Lehrer, Thomas A (Tom)** — Pianist, Comedian
11 Sparks St, Cambridge MA 02138, USA
**Lehtera, Jori** — Ice Hockey Player
Ice Hockey Association, Veturitie 13H, 00240 Helsinki, Finland
**Lehtinen, Dexter** — Attorney, Government Official
US Attorney's Office, Justice Dept, 155 S Miami Ave, Miami FL 33130, USA
**Lehtinen, Jere K** — Ice Hockey Player
622 Stratford Lane, Coppell TX 75019, USA
**Lehtinen, Silja** — Yachtswoman
Nylandska Jaktklubben, Bjorkholmen Sodra, 00200 Helsingfors, Finland
**Lehtonen, Kari** — Ice Hockey Player
6331 Deloache Ave, Dallas TX 75225, USA
**Leibman, Ron** — Actor
27 W 87th St, #2, New York NY 10024, USA
**Leibovitz, Annie** — Photographer
68 River Road, Rhinebeck NY 12572, USA
**Leibovitz, Mitchell G** — Businessman
Pep Boys-Manny Moe & Jack, 3111 W Allegheny Ave, Philadelphia PA 19132, USA
**Leibrandt, Charles L (Charlie), Jr** — Baseball Player
1235 Stuart Ridge, Alpharetta GA 30022, USA
**Leick, Hudson** — Actress
Imperium 7 Artists, 5455 Wilshire Blvd, #1706, Los Angeles CA 90036 USA
**Leifer, Carol** — Actress, Comedienne
A P A Talent & Literary Agency, 405 S Beverly Dr, #300, Beverly Hills CA 90212 USA
**Leifer, Neil** — Photographer
235 W 56th St, #21B, New York NY 10019, USA
**Leiferkus, Sergei P** — Opera Singer
5 The Paddocks, Abberbury Road, Iffley, Oxford OX4 4ET, England
**Leifheit, Sylvia** — Model, Actress
L A P Services, Erika Mann Str 21, 80636 Munich, Germany
**Leigh, Chyler** — Actress
Burstein Co, 15304 W Sunset Blvd, #208, Pacific Palisades CA 90272 USA
**Leigh, Danni** — Singer
Cramden Coach Corp, PO Box 463, Austin TX 78767, USA

**Legien - Leigh**

**Leigh, Doug** — Figure Skating Coach
Mariposa Skating School, PO Box 444, Barrie ON L4M 4T7, Canada

**Leigh, Jennifer Jason** — Actress
Untitled Entertainment, 350 S Beverly Dr, #200, Beverly Hills CA 90212 USA

**Leigh, Mike** — Director
United Agents, 12-26 Lexington St, London W1F 0LE, England

**Leigh, Nikki** — Model
Playboy Promotions, 9346 Civic Center Dr, #200, Beverly Hills CA 90210 USA

**Leigh, Regina** — Singer (Regina Regina)
Buddy Lee Attractions, 38 Music Square E, #300, Nashville TN 37203 USA

**Leigh, Vince** — Actor
Artists Partnership, 101 Finsbury Pavement, London EC2A 1RS, England

**Leighton, Laura** — Actress
A P A Talent & Literary Agency, 405 S Beverly Dr, #300, Beverly Hills CA 90212 USA

**Leija, James (Jesse)** — Boxer
116 Cas Hills Dr, San Antonio TX 78213, USA

**Leiker, Anthony W (Tony)** — Football Player
411 E 21st St, Hays KS 67601, USA

**Leimkuehler, Paul** — Amputee Skier, Businessman
351 Darbys Run, Bay Village OH 44140, USA

**Leinart, Matthew S (Matt)** — Football Player
22 E Oakwood Hills Dr, Chandler AZ 85248, USA

**Leiner, Danny** — Director, Producer, Writer
Creative Artists Agency, 2000 Ave of Stars, #100, Los Angeles CA 90067 USA

**Leiper, David P (Dave)** — Baseball Player
3312 E Glenrosa Ave, Phoenix AZ 85018, USA

**Leipheimer, Levi** — Cyclist
1755 Crystal Springs Court, Santa Rosa CA 95404, USA

**Leishman, Marc** — Golfer
Professional Golfers Association, 100 Ave of Champions, Palm Beach Gardens FL 33418 USA

**Leiss, Ramona** — Actress
C F S Salecker & Wieser Consulting, Muhlenstr 10, 85567 Grafing bei Munich, Germany

**Leiss, Ramona** — Singer
M R Mgmt, Gleichmannstr 7, 81241 Munich, Germany

**Leisure, David** — Actor
TalentWorks, 3500 W Olive Ave, #1400, Burbank CA 91505 USA

**Leiter, Alois T (Al)** — Baseball Player
181 E 90th St, #9B, New York NY 10128, USA

**Leiter, Mark E** — Baseball Player
121 Carriage Way, Forked River NJ 8731, USA

**Leiter, Michael E** — Government Official
National Counterterrorism Center, 1505 Tysons McLean Blvd, McLean VA 22102, USA

**Leiter, Robert E (Bob)** — Ice Hockey Player
1921 Shorepoint Village, Gimli BC R0C 1B0, Canada

**Leith, Prudence M** — Food Expert
94 Kensington Park Road, London W11 2PN, England

**Leithauser, Hamilton** — Singer, Guitarist (Walkmen)
Mick Mgmt, 35 Washington St, Brooklyn NY 11201 USA

**Leitner, Patric-Fritz** — Luge Athlete
Gesprachsstoff Marketing, Scholssstr 9B, 82140 Olching, Germany

**Leitso, Tyron** — Actor
Lucas Talent, 6-1238 Homer St, Vancouver BC V6B 2YB, Canada

**Leitzel, Joan** — Educator
University of Nebraska, President's Office, Lincoln NE 68588, USA

**Leius, Scott T** — Baseball Player
12620 42nd Place N, Minneapolis MN 55442, USA

**Lekang, Anton** — Ski Jumper
47 Pratt St, Winsted CT 06098, USA

**Lekman, Jens** — Singer, Songwriter
Agency Group Ltd, 142 W 57th St, #600, New York NY 10019 USA

**Leland, David** — Director
Creative Artists Agency, 2000 Ave of Stars, #100, Los Angeles CA 90067 USA

**Lelie, Ashley J** — Football Player
501 Hahaione St, #13H, Honolulu HI 96825, USA

**Lelliott, Jeremy** — Actor
Joan Green Mgmt, 1836 Courtney Terrace, Los Angeles CA 90046, USA

**Lellouche, Gilles** — Actor
U B B A, 6 Rue de Braque, 75003 Paris, France

**Lelong, Pierre J** — Mathematician
9 Place de Rungis, 75013 Paris, France

**Lelouch, Claude** — Director
15 Ave Hoche, 75008 Paris, France

**Lelouch, Salome** — Actress
Artmedia, 20 Ave Rapp, 75007 Paris, France

**Lelyveld, Joseph** — Editor
Wylie Agency, 250 W 57th St, #2114, New York NY 10107 USA

**LeMaho, Yvon** — Ecologist
Centre for Ecological & Evolutionary Synthesis, PO Box 1066 Blindern, 0316 Oslo, Norway

**Lemaire, Jacques G** — Ice Hockey Player, Coach
PO Box 1207, Palmetto FL 34220, USA

**Lemanczyk, David L (Dave)** — Baseball Player
24 Lehigh Court, Rockville Centre NY 11570, USA

**LeMarche, Maurice** — Actor
Danis Panaro Nist Talent, 9201 W Olympic Blvd, Beverly Hills CA 90212 USA

**Lemaster, Denver C (Denny)** — Baseball Player
4833 Carlene Way SE, Lilburn GA 30047, USA

**LeMaster, Frank P** — Football Player
PO Box 159, Birchrunville PA 19421, USA

**Lemaster, Johnnie L** — Baseball Player
PO Box 943, Paintsville KY 41240, USA

**Lemasters, Braden** — Actor
Marnie Cooper Mgmt, 12801 Bloomfield St, Studio City CA 91604, USA

**LeMat, Paul** — Actor
6300 Wilshire Blvd, #1460, Los Angeles CA 90048, USA

**Lematta, Wes** — Auto Racing Executive
PacWest Racing Group, PO Box 1717, Bellevue WA 98009, USA

**Lemay, Richard P (Dick)** — Baseball Player
1741 Holland Lane, Wichita KS 67212, USA
**LeMay-Doan, Catriona A** — Speed Skater
Landmark Sport Group, 277 Richmond St W, Toronto ON M54 1X1, Canada
**Lembeck, Michael** — Director, Actor
Principato-Young, 9465 Wilshire Blvd, #880, Beverly Hills CA 90212 USA
**Lembo, Joseph** — Interior Designer
220 Riverside Blvd, #16V, New York NY 10069, USA
**Leme, Sebastiao Carvalho** — Photographer
Av Pedro de Toledo 1114, Banzato Marilia, Sao Paulo 17509 021, Brazil
**Lemelin, Reggie** — Ice Hockey Player
10 Benevenuto Circle, Peabody MA 01960, USA
**Lemelin, Stephanie** — Actress
Paradigm Agency, 360 N Crescent Dr, North Building, Beverly Hills CA 90210 USA
**Lemercier, Valerie** — Actress
Artmedia, 20 Ave Rapp, 75007 Paris, France
**Lemieux, Claude P** — Ice Hockey Player
720 Manhattan Ave, Manhattan Beach CA 90266, USA
**LeMieux, George S** — Senator, FL
Gunster Yoakley, 450 E Las Olas Blvd, Fort Lauderdale FL 30301, USA
**Lemieux, Jocelyn** — Ice Hockey Player
2004 E Glenn Dr, Phoenix AZ 85020, USA
**Lemieux, Joseph H** — Businessman
Owens-Illinois Inc, 1 Sea Gate, Toledo OH 43666, USA
**Lemieux, Laurence** — Dancer
Coleman Lemieux Compagnie, 304 Parliament St, Toronto ON M5A 3A4, Canada
**Lemieux, Mario** — Ice Hockey Player
630 Academy St, Sewickley PA 15143, USA
**Lemieux, Raymond U** — Chemist
7602 119th St, Edmonton AB T6G 1W3, Canada
**Lemke, Mark A** — Baseball Player
3 Olena Dr, Whitesboro NY 13492, USA
**Lemme, Steve** — Actor, Comedian, Writer, Producer
United Talent Agency, U T A Plaza, 9336 Civic Center Dr, Beverly Hills CA 90210 USA
**Lemmon, Chris** — Actor
80 Murray St, South Glastonbury CT 06073, USA
**Lemmons, Kasi** — Director, Writer, Actress
Gersh Agency, 9465 Wilshire Blvd, #600, Beverly Hills CA 90212 USA
**Lemon, Chester E (Chet)** — Baseball Player
38150 Timberlane Dr, Umatilla FL 32784, USA
**Lemon, George (Meadowlark), III** — Basketball Player
6501 E Greenway Parkway, #1206, Scottsdale AZ 85254, USA
**Lemon, Peter C** — Vietnam War Army Hero (CMH)
Lemco Enterprises, PO Box 49025, Colorado Springs CO 80949, USA
**LeMond, Gregory J (Greg)** — Cyclist
3000 Willow Dr, Hamel MN 55340, USA
**Lemonds, David L (Dave)** — Baseball Player
1501 Aringill Lane, Matthews NC 28104, USA
**Lemper, Ute** — Singer, Actress, Dancer
Boris Orlob Mgmt, Jagerstr 7, 10117 Berlin, Germany
**Lenahan, Edward P** — Publisher
Fortune, Publisher's Office, Rockefeller Center, New York NY 10020, USA
**Lenard, Michael B** — Olympics Executive
Olympic Committee, 1 Olympic Plaza, Building 6, Colorado Springs CO 80909 USA
**Lenard, Voshon K** — Basketball Player
22694 Nottingham Lane, Southfield MI 48033, USA
**Lenchewski, Andrew** — Producer, Writer
Creative Artists Agency, 2000 Ave of Stars, #100, Los Angeles CA 90067 USA
**Lendl, Ivan** — Tennis Player
400 5 1/2 Mile Road, Goshen CT 06756, USA
**Lenehan, Nancy** — Actress
Meghan Schumacher Mgmt, 12551D Riverside Dr, #387, Sherman Oaks CA 91423, USA
**Lenfant, Claude J M** — Physician
PO Box 65278, Vancouver WA 98665, USA
**Lengies, Vanessa** — Actress
Gersh Agency, 9465 Wilshire Blvd, #600, Beverly Hills CA 90212 USA
**Lenk, Hans** — Rowing Athlete, Philosopher
Neubrunnenschlag 15, 76337 Waldbronn, Germany
**Lenk, Thomas** — Sculptor
Gemeinde Braunsbach, 74542 Schloss Tierberg, Germany
**Lenk, Tom** — Actor, Writer, Producer
Vanguard Management Group, 8060 Melrose Ave, #400, Los Angeles CA 90046, USA
**Lenka** — Singer, Songwriter
Eon Shapiro Mgmt, 56 W 22nd St, #600, New York NY 10010, USA
**Lenkaitis, William E (Bill)** — Football Player
26 Rose Court Way, East Walpole MA 02032, USA
**Lenkov, Peter M** — Producer, Writer
Creative Artists Agency, 2000 Ave of Stars, #100, Los Angeles CA 90067 USA
**Lenkus, Linnea** — Photographer
820 Gladys Ave, Long Beach CA 90804, USA
**Lennertz, Christopher** — Composer
Kraft-Engel Mgmt, 15233 Ventura Blvd, #200, Sherman Oaks CA 91403 USA
**Lennix, Harry J** — Actor
Brookside Artist Mgmt, 250 W 57th St, #2303, New York NY 10107, USA
**Lennon, Diane** — Singer (Lennon Sisters)
1984 State Highway 165, Branson MO 65616, USA
**Lennon, Janet** — Singer (Lennon Sisters)
1984 State Highway 165, Branson MO 65616, USA
**Lennon, Julian** — Singer, Songwriter
Man from Another Room, 20 Bulstrode St, London W1M 5FR, England
**Lennon, Kathy** — Singer (Lennon Sisters)
Overlook Dr, #10, Branson MO 65616, USA
**Lennon, Patrick O** — Baseball Player
60 Meister Blvd, Freeport NY 11520, USA
**Lennon, Peggy** — Singer (Lennon Sisters)
1984 State Highway 165, Branson MO 65616, USA

**Lennon, Richard G** — Religious Leader
Archdiocese of Boston, 66 Brooks Dr, Braintree MA 02184, USA

**Lennon, Sean** — Singer, Actor
KillerMoxie Mgmt, 5890 W Jefferson Blvd, #J, Los Angeles CA 90016, USA

**Lennon, Thomas (Tom)** — Actor, Comedian
Creative Artists Agency, 2000 Ave of Stars, #100, Los Angeles CA 90067 USA

**Lennox, Annie** — Singer (Eurythmics), Songwriter
19 Music & Mgmt, 35-37 Parkgate Road, London SW11 4NP, England

**Lennox, Kai** — Actor
TalentWorks, 3500 W Olive Ave, #1400, Burbank CA 91505 USA

**Lennox, William J, Jr** — Army General, Educator
University of Nevada, President's Office, Las Vegas NV 89154, USA

**Leno, Jay** — Actor, Comedian
I C M Partners, 10250 Constellation Blvd, #900, Los Angeles CA 90067 USA

**Lenoir, Noemie** — Model
U B B A, 6 Rue de Braque, 75003 Paris, France

**Lenon, Paris M** — Football Player
1505 Taylor St, Lynchburg VA 24504, USA

**Lenormand, Marie** — Opera Singer
Columbia Artists Mgmt Inc, 5 Columbus Circle, 1790 Broadway, #1600, New York NY 10019 USA

**Lenox, Jack, Jr** — WW II Army Air Corps Hero
1550 Killingsworth Way, #309, The Villages FL 32162, USA

**Lenska, Rula** — Model, Actress
David Daley Assoc, 586A Kings Road, London SW6 2DX, England

**Lentine, James M (Jim)** — Baseball Player
1066 Calle del Cerro, #1411, San Clemente CA 92672, USA

**Lentz, Larry L (Leary)** — Basketball Player
1309 Whispering Pines Dr, Houston TX 77055, USA

**Lenz, Kay** — Actress
B R S / Gage Talent Agency, 5757 Wilshire Blvd, #659, Los Angeles CA 90036 USA

**Lenz, Kim** — Singer, Songwriter
Mark Pucia Media, 5000 Oak Bluff Court, Atlanta GA 30350, USA

**Lenz, Rick** — Actor
12955 Calvert St, Van Nuys CA 91401, USA

**Leo, Melissa C** — Actress
Creative Artists Agency, 2000 Ave of Stars, #100, Los Angeles CA 90067 USA

**Leon** — Actor, Singer (Young Lions)
Stone Manners Salners, 6100 Wilshire Blvd, #1500, Los Angeles CA 90035 USA

**Leon, Adam** — Director
United Talent Agency, U T A Plaza, 9336 Civic Center Dr, Beverly Hills CA 90210 USA

**Leon, Eduardo A (Eddie)** — Baseball Player
5285 N Strada de Rubino, Tucson AZ 85750, USA

**Leon, Kenny** — Director
W M E Entertainment, 1325 Ave of Americas, New York NY 10019 USA

**Leon, Richard J** — Judge
US District Court, 333 Constitution Ave NW, Washington DC 20001, USA

**Leon, Valerie** — Actress
Essanay Ltd, 2 Conduit St, London W1R 9TG, England

**Leonard, Isabel** — Opera Singer
I M G Artists, Hogarth Business Park, Chiswick, London W4 2TH, England

**Leonard, Bob** — Basketball Player
1241 Hillcrest Dr, Carmel IN 46033, USA

**Leonard, Brett** — Director, Producer, Writer
Quattro Media, 171 Pier Ave, #328, Santa Monica CA 90405, USA

**Leonard, Brian** — Football Player
20 Countryside Court Dr, Gouverneur NY 13642, USA

**Leonard, Dennis P** — Baseball Player
4102 SW Evergreen Lane, Blue Springs MO 64015, USA

**Leonard, Gary** — Basketball Player
2406 Ridgefield Road, Columbia MO 65203, USA

**Leonard, J Wayne** — Businessman
Entergy Corp, 10055 Grogans Mill Road, #150, Spring TX 77380, USA

**Leonard, James F (Jim)** — Football Player
119 Cress Road, Santa Cruz CA 95060, USA

**Leonard, Joanne** — Photographer
University of Michigan, Art Dept, Ann Arbor MI 48109, USA

**Leonard, Joe** — Motorcycle Racing Rider, Auto Driver
PO Box 194, Gasoline Alley, Indianapolis IN 46222, USA

**Leonard, Joshua** — Actor
Silver Lining Entertainment, 421 S Beverly Drive, #700, Beverly Hills CA 90212 USA

**Leonard, Justin** — Golfer
3700 Euclid Ave, Dallas TX 75205, USA

**Leonard, Kawhi** — Basketball Player
San Antonio Spurs, Alamodome, 1 AT&T Center Parkway, San Antonio TX 78219 USA

**Leonard, Mark D** — Baseball Player
22042 Hibiscus Dr, Cupertino CA 95014, USA

**Leonard, Myers** — Basketball Player
Portland Trail Blazers, Rose Garden, 1 N Center Court St, Portland OR 97227 USA

**Leonard, Ray C (Sugar Ray)** — Boxer
PO Box 1433, Pacific Palisades CA 90272, USA

**Leonard, Robert Sean** — Actor
W M E Entertainment, 9601 Wilshire Blvd, #300, Beverly Hills CA 90210 USA

**Leonard, William R (Slick)** — Basketball Player, Coach
5398 Baltimore Court, Carmel IN 46033, USA

**Leonard, Zoe** — Photographer
Paula Cooper Gallery, 534 W 21st St, New York NY 10011, USA

**Leonardini, Jean-Pierre** — Actor
U B B A, 6 Rue de Braque, 75003 Paris, France

**Leonardis, Tom** — Producer
Whoop/One Ho Productions, 333 W 52nd St, #600, New York NY 10019, USA

**Leone, Marianne** — Actress
Paradigm Agency, 360 N Crescent Dr, North Building, Beverly Hills CA 90210 USA

**Leone, Sunny** — Model, Actress, Director
SunLust Pictures, 7336 Santa Monica Blvd, #31, West Hollywood CA 90046, USA

**Leonetti, John R** — Cinematographer
Montana Artists Agency, 9150 Wilshire Blvd, #100, Beverly Hills CA 0212, USA

**Leonetti, Matthew F, Jr** — Cinematographer
1362 Bella Oceana Vista, Pacific Palisades CA 90272, USA

**Leong, Page** — Actress
C N A Assoc, 1875 Century Park East, #2250, Los Angeles CA 90067 USA

**Leonhard, David P (Dave)** — Baseball Player
87 Corning St, Beverly MA 01915, USA

**Leonhardt, Carolin** — Canoeing Athlete
Wassersportverein Mannheim-Sandhofen, Riedspitze 11, 68307 Mannheim, Germany

**Leonhardt, David** — Journalist
New York Times, Editorial Dept, 229 W 43rd St, New York NY 10036 USA

**Leonhardt, Ulf** — Theoretical Physicist
Saint Andrews University, Physics Dept, Fife KY16 9AJ, Scotland

**Leonhart, William** — Diplomat
119 Oak Terrace, Lake Bluff IL 60044, USA

**Leoni, Tea** — Actress
United Talent Agency, U T A Plaza, 9336 Civic Center Dr, Beverly Hills CA 90210 USA

**Leonov, Aleksei A** — Cosmonaut, Air Force General
Alfa Capital, Masha Porivaeva UI 11, 107078 Moscow, Russia

**Leonskaja, Elisabeth** — Concert Pianist
I M G Artists, Hogarth Business Park, Chiswick, London W4 2TH, England

**Leonti, Nikki** — Singer
W M E Entertainment, 9601 Wilshire Blvd, #300, Beverly Hills CA 90210 USA

**Leopardi, Chauncey** — Actor
Abrams Artists, 9200 W Sunset Blvd, #1125, West Hollywood CA 90069 USA

**Leopold, Jordan** — Ice Hockey Player
10988 Mississippi Dr N, Champlin MN 55316, USA

**Leopold, Leroy J (Bobby)** — Football Player
4221 W Spruce St, #1404, Tampa FL 33607, USA

**Leopold, Tom** — Actor, Comedian, Producer
Gersh Agency, 9465 Wilshire Blvd, #600, Beverly Hills CA 90212 USA

**Lepage, Robert** — Actor, Director
103 Dalhousie, Quebec City QC G1K 4B9, Canada

**Lepcio, Thaddeus S (Ted)** — Baseball Player
263 Greenlodge St, Dedham MA 02026, USA

**LePeilbet, Amy L** — Soccer Player
Andrew LePeilbet, 1145 Reese Way, Reno NV 89521, USA

**LePelley, Guernsey** — Editorial Cartoonist
35 Saint Germain St, Boston MA 02115, USA

**LePen, Marine** — Government Official, France
National Front, 76-78 Rue des Suisses, 92000 Nanterre, France

**LePichon, Xavier** — Geologist
Ecole Normale Superieure, 24 Rue Lhomond, 75005 Paris Cedex 05, France

**Lepore, Nanette** — Fashion Designer
225 W 35th St, #1700, New York NY 10001, USA

**Lepore, Tatiana** — Actress
Carol Levi Mgmt, Via Giuseppe Pisanelli 2, 00196 Rome, Italy

**Leppard, Raymond J** — Conductor
Indianapolis Symphony, 32 E Washington St, #600, Indianapolis IN 46204, USA

**LePrevost, Nicholas** — Actor
Artists Partnership, 101 Finsbury Pavement, London EC2A 1RS, England

**Lepsis, Matthew S (Matt)** — Football Player
1833 Broken Bend Dr, Westlake TX 76262, USA

**Lerach, William (Bill)** — Attorney
Milberg Weiss Hynes Lerach, 1600 W Broadway, #1800, San Diego CA 92101, USA

**Lerch, Randy L** — Baseball Player
19490 Monterey St, Morgan Hill CA 95037, USA

**Lerche, Sondre** — Singer, Guitarist, Songwriter
Zeitgeist Artist Mgmt, 660 York Ave, #216, San Francisco CA 94110, USA

**Lerman, Logan** — Actor
Creative Artists Agency, 2000 Ave of Stars, #100, Los Angeles CA 90067 USA

**Lerner, Dan** — Director
Paradigm Agency, 360 N Crescent Dr, North Building, Beverly Hills CA 90210 USA

**Lerner, Michael** — Religious Leader, Rabbi
Tikkun, 2342 Shattuck Ave, #1200, Berkeley CA 94704, USA

**Lerner, Michael** — Actor
Abrams Artists, 9200 W Sunset Blvd, #1125, West Hollywood CA 90069 USA

**Leroux, Francois** — Ice Hockey Player
507 Hickory Grade Road, Bridgeville PA 15017, USA

**LeRoux, Francois** — Opera Singer
I M G Artists, Burlington Lane, Chiswick, London W4 2TH, England

**Leroux, Sydney R** — Soccer Player
Seattle Reign, 3216 Sierra Dr S, Seattle WA 98144 USA

**LeRoy, Gloria** — Actress
TalentWorks, 3500 W Olive Ave, #1400, Burbank CA 91505 USA

**Les, James A (Jim)** — Basketball Player, Coach
4030 Shadybrook Court, Granite Bay CA 95746, USA

**Lesar, David** — Businessman
Halliburton Co, Lincoln Plaza, 500 N Akard St, Dallas TX 75201, USA

**LeSaunier, Jacqueline** — Actress
Angentur Retzlaff, Kurfuerstenstra 34, 10785 Berlin, Germany

**Lesch, James R** — Businessman
15840 Malibu E, Willis TX 77318, USA

**Leschin, Luisa** — Actress, Writer, Producer
W M E Entertainment, 9601 Wilshire Blvd, #300, Beverly Hills CA 90210 USA

**Leschyshyn, Curtis** — Ice Hockey Player
40 Laurel Mountain Dr, Littleton CO 80127, USA

**Lescroart, John T** — Writer
Penguin Books, 375 Hudson St, Basement 1, New York NY 10014 USA

**Lesh, Phil** — Bassist (Grateful Dead)
Paradigm Agency, 360 N Crescent Dr, North Building, Beverly Hills CA 90210 USA

**LeShana, David C** — Educator
8246 E Hoverland Road, Scottsdale AZ 85255, USA

**Lesher, Brian H** — Baseball Player
217 Vassar Dr, Newark DE 19711, USA

**LeSieur, Michael** — Producer, Writer
Kaplan/Perrone Entertainment, 9744 Wilshire Blvd, #300, Beverly Hills CA 90212, USA

**Leskanic, Curtis J (Curt)** — Baseball Player
2032 Alagua Dr, Longwood FL 32779, USA
**Leskanich, Katrina** — Singer (Katrina & the Waves)
Barry Collins, PO Box 2112, Hockley, Essex SS4 4WD, England
**Leslie, A Ryan** — Singer, Songwriter, Producer
Laine Mgmt, 131 Victoria Road, Salford M6 8LF, England
**Leslie, Fred W** — Astronaut
2038 Springhouse Road SE, Huntsville AL 35802, USA
**Leslie, Joan** — Actress
2228 N Catalina St, Los Angeles CA 90027, USA
**Leslie, Lisa** — Basketball Player, Model
PO Box 452447, Los Angeles CA 90045, USA
**Leslie, Rose** — Actress
United Talent Agency, U T A Plaza, 9336 Civic Center Dr, Beverly Hills CA 90210 USA
**Leslie, Ryan** — Rap Artist
W M E Entertainment, 9601 Wilshire Blvd, #300, Beverly Hills CA 90210 USA
**LeSourd, Philippe** — Cinematographer
Skouras Agency, 1149 3rd St, #300, Santa Monica CA 90403 USA
**Lespert, Jalil** — Actor
Artmedia, 20 Ave Rapp, 75007 Paris, France
**Lessac, Michael** — Director
Creative Artists Agency, 2000 Ave of Stars, #100, Los Angeles CA 90067 USA
**Lessard, Stefan** — Bassist (Dave Matthews Band), Songwriter
Red Light Mgmt, PO Box 520, Crozet VA 22932, USA
**Lesser, Erik** — Biathlete
Y E S Sport Marketing, Stefanusstr 4, 82166 Graefelfing, Germany
**Lessin, Robert H** — Financier
Smith Barney Inc, 590 Madison Ave, #1100, New York NY 10022, USA
**Lester of Herne Hill, Anthony P** — Attorney
Blackstone Chambers, Blackstone House, Temple, London EC4Y 9BW, England
**Lester, Adrian** — Actor
More/Medavoy Mgmt, 10203 Santa Monica Blvd, #400, Los Angeles CA 90067 USA
**Lester, Jonathan T (Jon)** — Baseball Player
Oakland Athletics, McAfee Coliseum, 7000 Coliseum Way, #3, Oakland CA 94621 USA
**Lester, Joseph (Joe)** — Keyboardist (Silversun Pickups)
Ink Tank Public Relations, 1824 W Sunset Blvd, #102, Los Angeles CA 90026, USA
**Lester, Ketty** — Actress, Singer
5931 Comey Ave, Los Angeles CA 90034, USA
**Lester, Mark L** — Director
American World Pictures, 21700 Oxnard St, #1770, Woodland Hills CA 91367, USA
**Lester, Richard (Dick)** — Director
Petersham Lodge, River Lane, Richmond Surrey TW10 7AG, England
**Lester, Ronnie** — Basketball Player, Executive
4841 NW 16th Terrace, Boca Raton FL 33431, USA
**Lester, Timothy L (Tim)** — Football Player
1160 Bream Dr, Alpharetta GA 30004, USA
**Lester, Tom** — Actor
PO Box 363, Laurel MS 39441, USA
**Lesuk, Bill** — Ice Hockey Player
40 Bracken Ave, East Saint Paul MB R2E 0K2, Canada
**Lesure, James** — Actor
Wolman Wealth Mgmt, 10640 Rochester Ave, Los Angeles CA 90024, USA
**Letarte, Pierre** — Cinematographer
551 W Pinacle, Abercorn QC J0E 1B0, Canada
**Letarte, Steve** — Auto Racing Mechanic
18420 Nantz Road, Cornelius NC 28031, USA
**Letbetter, R Steve** — Businessman
Reliant Energy, 1111 Louisiana, Houston TX 77002, USA
**Leterrier, Louis** — Director
Management 360, 9111 Wilshire Blvd, Beverly Hills CA 90210 USA
**Lethem, Jonathan** — Writer
McSweeney's Books, 372 5th Ave, Brooklyn NY 11215, USA
**Letheren, Mark** — Actor
Artists Partnership, 101 Finsbury Pavement, London EC2A 1RS, England
**Letherman, Lindze L** — Actress
Lovett Mgmt, 1327 Brinkley Ave, Los Angeles CA 90049, USA
**Letizia** — Queen, Spain
Palacio de la Zarzuela, 28080 Madrid, Spain
**Leto, Jared** — Actor
Untitled Entertainment, 350 S Beverly Dr, #200, Beverly Hills CA 90212 USA
**Letowski, Trevor** — Ice Hockey Player
3612 Lion Ridge Court, Raleigh NC 27612, USA
**Letscher, Matthew (Matt)** — Actor
Sanders/Armstrong/Caserta Mgmt, 2120 Colorado Ave, #120, Santa Monica CA 90404 USA
**Letsie III** — King, Lesotho
Royal Palace, PO Box 524, Maseru, Lesotho
**Letsinger, Robert L** — Chemist
8711 25th Ave NE, Seattle WA 98115, USA
**Lett, Clifford** — Basketball Player
7067 Rampart Way, Pensacola FL 32505, USA
**Lett, Leon, Jr** — Football Player
2 Longleaf Circle, Fairhope AL 36532, USA
**Letteri, Joseph (Joe)** — Special Effects Designer
Weta Digital, 9-11 Manuka St, Miramar, Wellington 6022, New Zealand
**Letterman, David** — Entertainer, Comedian
Worldwide Pants, 1697 Broadway, #3000, New York NY 10019, USA
**Letts, Tracy** — Writer, Actor
1756 W School St, Chicago IL 60657, USA
**Leung Chiu Wai, Tony** — Actor
W M E Entertainment, 9601 Wilshire Blvd, #300, Beverly Hills CA 90210 USA
**Leung, Ken** — Actor
Hartig-Hilepo Agency, 54 W 21st St, #610, New York NY 10010 USA
**Leuthard, Doris** — President, Switzerland
Federal Chancellery, Bundeshaus-W, Bundesgasse, 3033 Berne, Switzerland
**Leuwerik, Ruth** — Actress
Zuccalistr 31, 80639 Munich, Germany

**Levada, William J Cardinal** — Religious Leader
Doctrine of Faith Congregation, Palazzo del Uffizio 11, 00193 Rome, Italy
**Leval, Pierre N** — Judge
US Court of Appeals, Moynihan Courthouse, 500 Pearl St, New York NY 10007, USA
**Levane, Andrew J** — Basketball Player, Coach
14 Northstone Court, Irmo SC 29063, USA
**Levant, Brian** — Director
W M E Entertainment, 9601 Wilshire Blvd, #300, Beverly Hills CA 90210 USA
**LeVay, Simon** — Neuroscientist
970 Palm Ave, West Hollywood CA 90069, USA
**Leveaux, Amaury** — Swimmer
Federation de Natation, 148 Ave Gambetta, 75020 Paris, France
**Leveaux, David** — Director
Simpson Fox Assoc, 52 Shaftesbury Ave, London W1V 7DE, England
**Leven, Jeremy** — Director, Writer
Paradigm Agency, 360 N Crescent Dr, North Building, Beverly Hills CA 90210 USA
**Levene, Ben** — Artist
Royal Academy of Arts, Piccadilly, London W1V 0DS, England
**Levens, H Dorsey** — Football Player
4249 Olde Mille Lane NE, Atlanta GA 30342, USA
**Leveque, Michel** — Minister of State, Monaco
57 Rue de l'Universite, 75007 Paris, France
**Lever, Don** — Ice Hockey Player
247 Quail Hollow Lane, East Amherst NY 14051, USA
**Lever, Lafayette (Fat)** — Basketball Player
50 Regency Park Circle, #12107, Sacramento CA 95835, USA
**Leverenz, Caitlin** — Swimmer
9010 E 9th St, Tucson AZ 85710, USA
**Levering, Kate** — Actress
Paradigm Agency, 360 N Crescent Dr, North Building, Beverly Hills CA 90210 USA
**LeVert, Edward (Eddie)** — Singer (O'Jays)
Pyramid Entertainment Group, 377 Rector Place, #21A, New York NY 10280 USA
**Leverton, Irene** — Astronaut Candidate
1100 Willow Park Road, Prescott AZ 86301, USA
**Levesque, Joanna (JoJo)** — Singer, Actress
I C M Partners, 10250 Constellation Blvd, #900, Los Angeles CA 90067 USA
**Levet, Thomas** — Golfer
108 Via Quantera, Palm Beach Gardens FL 33418, USA
**Levi, Wayne** — Golfer
17 Ironwood Road, New Hartford NY 13413, USA
**Levi, Zachary** — Actor
Creative Artists Agency, 2000 Ave of Stars, #100, Los Angeles CA 90067 USA
**LeVias, Jerry** — Football Player
1626 Park St, Houston TX 77019, USA
**Levien, David** — Director, Writer
Creative Artists Agency, 2000 Ave of Stars, #100, Los Angeles CA 90067 USA
**Levieva, Margarita** — Actress
United Talent Agency, U T A Plaza, 9336 Civic Center Dr, Beverly Hills CA 90210 USA
**Levin, A Leo** — Attorney, Educator
University of Pennsylvania, Law School, 3400 Chestnut, Philadelphia PA 19104, USA
**Levin, Andres** — Composer, Musician
First Artists Mgmt, 4764 Park Granada, #210, Calabasas CA 91302 USA
**Levin, Jerry W** — Businessman
151 E 58th St, #43F, New York NY 10022, USA
**Levin, Marc** — Director, Producer
Blowback Productions, 601 W 26 St, #1776, New York NY 10001, USA
**Levin, Mark** — Entertainer, Writer
WPLJ-FM Radio, 2 Pennsylvania Plaza, #1700, New York NY 10121, USA
**Levin, Richard C** — Educator
Yale University, President's Office, New Haven CT 06520, USA
**Levin, Robert D** — Musicologist, Pianist, Composer
Harvard University, Music Dept, Cambridge MA 02138, USA
**Levine, Adam** — Singer (Maroon 5), Actor
Career Artists Mgmt, 203-207 W Hastings St, Vancouver BC V6B 1H7, Canada
**Levine, Alan B (Al)** — Baseball Player
10916 E Paradise Dr, Scottsdale AZ 85259, USA
**Levine, Alex** — Bassist (Gaslight Anthem)
Esther Creative Group, 27 W 24th St, #404, New York NY 10010, USA
**Levine, Arnold** — Molecular Biologist, Educator
Rockefeller University, President's Office, 1230 York Ave, New York NY 10065, USA
**Levine, James** — Conductor
Columbia Artists Mgmt Inc, 5 Columbus Circle, 1790 Broadway, #1600, New York NY 10019 USA
**Levine, Jerry** — Actor, Director
Rain Mgmt, 1801 Stanford St, Santa Monica CA 90404, USA
**Levine, Jonathan** — Director, Writer
Creative Artists Agency, 2000 Ave of Stars, #100, Los Angeles CA 90067 USA
**Levine, Philip** — Writer
4549 N Van Ness Blvd, Fresno CA 93704, USA
**Levine, Rachmiel** — Endocrinologist
614 Walnut St, Newton MA 02460, USA
**Levine, S Robert** — Businessman
Cabletron Systems, 50 Minuteman Road, Andover MA 01810, USA
**Levine, Samm** — Actor
A P A Talent & Literary Agency, 405 S Beverly Dr, #300, Beverly Hills CA 90212 USA
**Levine, Seymour** — Psychobiologist
1515 Shasta Dr, #3103, Davis CA 95616, USA
**Levine, Ted** — Actor
Kass Management, 501 Santa Monica Blvd, #604, Los Angeles CA 90401, USA
**Levingstone, Ken** — Government Official, England
House of Commons, Westminster, London SW1A 0AA, England
**Levinsohn, Gary** — Producer
Mutual Film Co, 150 S Rodeo Dr, #120, Beverly Hills CA 90212, USA
**Levinson, Arthur D** — Businessman
Genentech Inc, 400 Point San Bruno Blvd S, South San Francisco CA 94080, USA
**Levinson, Barry L** — Director
Baltimore Pictures, 8306 Wilshire Blvd, PMB 1012, Beverly Hills CA 90211, USA

**Levinson, Chris** — Producer, Writer
W M E Entertainment, 9601 Wilshire Blvd, #300, Beverly Hills CA 90210 USA

**Levinson, Sanford V** — Attorney, Educator
3410 Windsor Road, Austin TX 78703, USA

**Levinson, Stephen** — Producer
Leverage Mgmt, 3030 Pennsylvania Ave, Santa Monica CA 90404 USA

**Levinthal, David L** — Photographer
32 W 20th St, New York NY 10011, USA

**Levis, Jesse** — Baseball Player
1219 Highland Ave, Fort Washington PA 19034, USA

**Levis, Patrick** — Actor, Singer
Least of Three, PO Box 902652, Sylmar CA 91392, USA

**Levit, Igor** — Concert Pianist
Harrison/Parrott, 5-6 Albion Court, London W6 0QT, England

**Levitan, Steven (Steve)** — Director, Producer
United Talent Agency, U T A Plaza, 9336 Civic Center Dr, Beverly Hills CA 90210 USA

**Levitas, Andrew** — Actor
Creative Artists Agency, 2000 Ave of Stars, #100, Los Angeles CA 90067 USA

**Levitin, Daniel J** — Psychologist, Neuroscientist
McGill University, Psychology Dept, Montreal QC H3A 2T5, Canada

**Levitt, Arthur, Jr** — Government Official, Financier
Carlyle Group, 1001 Pennsylvania Ave NW, #220S, Washington DC 20004, USA

**Levitt, George** — Chemist
82 Via Del Corso, Palm Beach Gardens FL 33418, USA

**Levitt, Michael** — Nobel Chemistry Laureate
Stanford University Medical School, Structural Biology Dept, Stanford CA 94305, USA

**Levitt, Steven D** — Economist, Writer
University of Chicago, Economics Dept, Chicago IL 60637, USA

**LeVox, Gary** — Singer (Rascal Flatts)
Turner & Nichols, 49 Music Square W, #500, Nashville TN 37203, USA

**Levrault, Allen** — Baseball Player
5 Granada Dr, Westport MA 02790, USA

**Levrone, Kevin** — Body Builder, Actor
Beacon Talent, 170 Apple Ridge Road, Woodcliff Lake NJ 07677, USA

**Levy, Barrington A** — Singer
Solid Agency, 7 Dumbarton Ave, Kingston 10, Jamaica

**Levy, Bernard-Henri** — Philosopher
Editions Grasset/Fasquelle, 61 Rue des Saint-Peres, 75006 Paris, France

**Levy, Clifford J** — Journalist
New York Times, Editorial Dept, 229 W 43rd St, New York NY 10036 USA

**Levy, Dan** — Actor, Comedian
Great North Artists Mgmt, 350 Dupont St, Toronto ON M5R 1V9, Canada

**Levy, David H** — Astronomer
Mount Palomar Observatory, 35899 Canfield Road, Palomar Mountain CA 92060, USA

**Levy, Eugene** — Actor, Comedian, Director
Anonymous Content, 3532 Hayden Ave, Culver City CA 90232 USA

**Levy, Jane** — Actress
Suskin Management, 2 Charlton St, #5K, New York NY 10014, USA

**Levy, Jean-Bernard** — Businessman
Vivendi, 42 Ave de Friedland, 75380 Paris Cedex 08, France

**Levy, Marvin D (Marv)** — Football Coach
National Pro Athletes Organization, 1806 Watermere Lane, Windermere FL 34786, USA

**Levy, Marvin David** — Composer
Sheldon Sofer Mgmt, 130 W 56th St, New York NY 10019, USA

**Levy, Maximilian** — Cyclist
Rauber Jeschonek, August-Bebel-Str 10, 16321 Bernau bei Berlin, Germany

**Levy, Naomi** — Religious Leader, Rabbi
Academy of Jewish Religion, 574 Hilgard Ave, Los Angeles CA 90024, USA

**Levy, Peter** — Cinematographer
I C M Partners, 10250 Constellation Blvd, #900, Los Angeles CA 90067 USA

**Levy, Shawn** — Director
21 Laps Entertainment, 10201 W Pico Blvd, Building 41, Los Angeles CA 90035, USA

**Levy, William** — Actor
Creative Artists Agency, 2000 Ave of Stars, #100, Los Angeles CA 90067 USA

**Lew, Jacob J (Jack)** — Government Official
White House, 1600 Pennsylvania Ave NW, Washington DC 20500 USA

**Lew, Scott** — Director
Principato-Young, 9465 Wilshire Blvd, #880, Beverly Hills CA 90212 USA

**Lewan, Taylor** — Football Player
Tennessee Titans, 460 Great Circle Road, Nashville TN 37228 USA

**Lewin, Gene** — Drummer, Singer (GrooveLily)
GrooveLily, PO Box 11570, Glendale CA 91226, USA

**Lewin, Josh** — Sportscaster
601 N Park Blvd, #508, Grapevine TX 76051, USA

**Lewis, Albert R** — Football Player
3532 Macedonia Road, Centreville MS 39631, USA

**Lewis, Ananda** — Actress
Britto Agency, 234 W 56th St, #PH, New York NY 10019, USA

**Lewis, Andrew L (Drew)** — Secretary, Transportation; Businessman
PO Box 70, Lederach PA 19450, USA

**Lewis, Barbara** — Singer
American Mgmt, 19948 Mayall St, Chatsworth CA 91311, USA

**Lewis, Bernard** — Historian
Princeton University, Near Eastern Studies Dept, Princeton NJ 08544, USA

**Lewis, Blake C** — Singer, Songwriter
PO Box 806, Lynnwood WA 98046, USA

**Lewis, Bob** — Basketball Player
63910 E Squash Blossom Lane, Tucson AZ 85739, USA

**Lewis, Bobby** — Singer
Lustig Talent, PO Box 770850, Orlando FL 32877 USA

**Lewis, Charlotte** — Basketball Player
2814 N Sheridan Road, Peoria IL 61604, USA

**Lewis, Clea** — Actress
Innovative Artists, 1505 10th St, Santa Monica CA 90401 USA

**Lewis, Colby P** — Baseball Player
14800 Orchard Crest Ave, Bakersfield CA 93314, USA

**Lewis, Crystal** — Singer, Rap Artist
Creative Artists Agency, 2000 Ave of Stars, #100, Los Angeles CA 90067 USA
**Lewis, Cynthia R** — Publisher
Harper's Bazaar, Publisher's Office, 1770 Broadway, New York NY 10019, USA
**Lewis, Damaris** — Model
Elite Model Mgmt, 404 Park Ave S, #900, New York NY 10016 USA
**Lewis, Damian** — Actor
Markham Froggatt Irwin, Julian House, 4 Windmill St, London W1P 1HF, England
**Lewis, Damione R** — Football Player
9601 Gato del Sol Court, Waxhaw NC 28173, USA
**Lewis, Daniel N (Dan)** — Football Player
460 S Park St, Detroit MI 48215, USA
**Lewis, Darren J** — Baseball Player
2212 Rosemount Lane, San Ramon CA 94582, USA
**Lewis, Dave** — Ice Hockey Player, Coach
2040 Ranch Road, Holly MI 48442, USA
**Lewis, David** — Industrial Designer
Bang & Olufsen A/S, Peter Bangs Vej 15, PO Box 40, 7600 Stuer, Denmark
**Lewis, David Levering** — Writer
Rutgers University, History Dept, East Rutherford NJ 07073, USA
**Lewis, David R (Dave)** — Football Player
406 142nd St, Ocean City MD 21842, USA
**Lewis, Dawnn** — Actress
Stone Manners Salners, 6100 Wilshire Blvd, #1500, Los Angeles CA 90035 USA
**Lewis, De'Andre D (D D)** — Football Player
10230 125th Ave NE, Kirkland WA 98033, USA
**Lewis, Denise** — Heptathlete
Outside Organization, 177-8 Tottenham Court Road, London W1T 7NY, England
**Lewis, Dwight D (D D)** — Football Player
P C S Sales, 1624 Northcrest Dr, Plano TX 75075, USA
**Lewis, Emmanuel** — Actor
Orange Grove Group, 12178 Ventura Blvd, #205, Studio City CA 91604, USA
**Lewis, F Carlton (Carl)** — Track Athlete
Arluck Promotions, 9812 Falls Road, #114-305, Potomac MD 20854, USA
**Lewis, Frank D** — Football Player
118 Presque Isle Dr, Houma LA 70363, USA
**Lewis, Frederick L (Fritz)** — Basketball Player
4122 Illinois Ave NW, Washington DC 20011, USA
**Lewis, Gary** — Singer (Gary Lewis & the Playboys)
701 Balin Court, Nashville TN 37221, USA
**Lewis, Geoffrey** — Actor
5210 Collier Place, Woodland Hills CA 91364, USA
**Lewis, Herschell Gordon** — Director
Lewis Enterprises, 451 Heritage Dr, #215, Pompano Beach FL 33060, USA
**Lewis, Huey** — Singer, Actor
Hulex Corp, PO Box 819, Mill Valley CA 94942, USA
**Lewis, J L** — Golfer
2504 Orleans Dr, Cedar Park TX 78613, USA
**Lewis, Jamal L** — Football Player
10614 Lee Ave, Cleveland OH 44106, USA
**Lewis, Jasmine** — Actress
Evolution Entertainment, 901 N Highland Ave, Los Angeles CA 90038 USA
**Lewis, Jason** — Actor
Resolution, 1801 Century Park E, #2300, Los Angeles CA 90067 USA
**Lewis, Jenifer** — Actress, Singer
Innovative Artists, 1505 10th St, Santa Monica CA 90401 USA
**Lewis, Jennifer D (Jenny)** — Singer, Songwriter
5259 Vesper Ave, Sherman Oaks CA 91411, USA
**Lewis, Jermaine E** — Football Player
4919 Pleasant Grove Road, Reisterstown MD 21136, USA
**Lewis, Jerry** — Actor, Comedian, Director
Jerry Lewis Films, 3160 W Sahara Ave, #C16, Las Vegas NV 89102, USA
**Lewis, Jerry Lee** — Singer, Pianist, Composer
PO Box 206, Old Hickory TN 37138, USA
**Lewis, Jim** — Composer
I C M Partners, 10250 Constellation Blvd, #900, Los Angeles CA 90067 USA
**Lewis, Jonathan Guy** — Actor
Artists Partnership, 101 Finsbury Pavement, London EC2A 1RS, England
**Lewis, Juliette** — Actress
Troika, 74 Clerkenwell Road, #300, London EC1M 5QA, England
**Lewis, Karen** — Writer
Sarnoff Co, 10 Universal City Plaza, #2000, Universal City CA 91608, USA
**Lewis, Kevin** — Football Player
4417 Roy St, Orlando FL 32812, USA
**Lewis, Lennox** — Boxer
Gainsborough House, 81 Oxford St, #206, London W1D 2EU, England
**Lewis, Leo, III** — Football Player
10116 Ivywood Court, Eden Prairie MN 55347, USA
**Lewis, Lisa** — Boxer
7242 N Wheeler Ave, Fresno CA 93722, USA
**Lewis, Marcedes A** — Football Player
3725 Bouton Dr, Lakewood CA 90712, USA
**Lewis, Mark D** — Baseball Player
1246 Cleveland Ave, Hamilton OH 45013, USA
**Lewis, Marvin** — Football Coach
Cincinnati Bengals, 1 Paul Brown Stadium, Cincinnati OH 45202 USA
**Lewis, Michael** — Writer
Creative Artists Agency, 2000 Ave of Stars, #100, Los Angeles CA 90067 USA
**Lewis, Michael H (Mike)** — Football Player
3350 Blodgett St, Houston TX 77004, USA
**Lewis, Mike** — Basketball Player
490 Windsor Park Road, Kernersville NC 27284, USA
**Lewis, Monica** — Singer, Actress
Lang, 1100 Alta Loma Road, #16A, West Hollywood CA 90069, USA
**Lewis, Morris C (Mo)** — Football Player
22012 Gardner Dr, Alpharetta GA 30009, USA

**Lewis, Neville** — Interior Designer
Ted Moudis Assoc, 79 Madison Ave, #1000, New York NY 10016, USA
**Lewis, Phill** — Actor
L I N K Entertainment, 11872 La Grange Ave, Los Angeles CA 90025 USA
**Lewis, Ramsey E, Jr** — Jazz Pianist, Composer
7655 N Sheridan Road, Chicago IL 60626, USA
**Lewis, Rashard Q** — Basketball Player
9 E Rivercrest Dr, Houston TX 77042, USA
**Lewis, Ray A** — Football Player
2401 Tufton Ave, Reisterstown MD 21136, USA
**Lewis, Richard** — Actor, Comedian
Bauman Redanty Shaul Agency, 5757 Wilshire Blvd, #473, Los Angeles CA 90036 USA
**Lewis, Richie T** — Baseball Player
13209 E Country Road 700 S, Losantville IN 47354, USA
**Lewis, Robert Lloyd** — Producer
Gersh Agency, 9465 Wilshire Blvd, #600, Beverly Hills CA 90212 USA
**Lewis, Russell T** — Businessman, Publisher
New York Times Co, Publisher's Office, 229 W 43rd St, New York NY 10036, USA
**Lewis, Ryan** — Music Producer (Thrift Shop)
Artist Brand Alliance, 11 E 86th St, #900, New York NY 10028, USA
**Lewis, Sally Sirkin** — Interior Designer
502 N Oak St, Inglewood CA 90302, USA
**Lewis, Sherman** — Football Player, Coach
45822 Bristol Circle, Novi MI 48377, USA
**Lewis, Stacy** — Golfer
Sterling Sports Mgmt, 7650 Rivers Edge Dr, Columbus OH 43235, USA
**Lewis, Stephani** — Costume Deisgner
Sheldon Prosnit Agency, 800 S Robertson Blvd, #6, Los Angeles CA 90035, USA
**Lewis, T** — Cartoonist (Over the Hedge)
United Feature Syndicate, PO Box 5610, Cincinnati OH 45201 USA
**Lewis, Tom** — Singer
I C M Partners, 10250 Constellation Blvd, #900, Los Angeles CA 90067 USA
**Lewis, Vaughan A** — Prime Minister, Saint Lucia
West Indies University, International Relations Institute, Saint Augustine, Trinidad & Tobago
**Lewis, Vicki** — Actress, Comedienne
Stone Manners Salners, 6100 Wilshire Blvd, #1500, Los Angeles CA 90035 USA
**Lewis, Victor** — Jazz Drummer
Joanne Klein, 130 W 28th St, New York NY 10001, USA
**Lewis, Walter** — Ethnobotanist
7915 Park Dr, Saint Louis MO 63117, USA
**Lewis, William J (Bill)** — Football Coach
University of Notre Dame, Athletic Dept, Notre Dame IN 46556, USA
**Lewiston, Denis C** — Cinematographer
13700 Tahiti Way, #24, Marina del Rey CA 90292, USA
**Leyden, Paul** — Actor
Paradigm Agency, 360 N Crescent Dr, North Building, Beverly Hills CA 90210 USA
**Leygue, Louis Georges** — Sculptor
6 Rue de Docteur Blanche, 75016 Paris, France
**Leyla** — Model, Actress
Model Management Group, 1024 6th Ave, #201, New York NY 10018, USA
**Leyland, James R (Jim)** — Baseball Manager
261 Tech Road, Pittsburgh PA 15205, USA
**Leyritz, James J (Jim)** — Baseball Player
11060 Cameron Court, #304, Davie FL 33324, USA
**Leyton, John** — Actor, Singer
53 Keyes House, Dolphin Square, London SW1V 3NA, England
**Leyva, Danell J** — Gymnast
Yin E Alvarez, 11497 SW 235th St, Homestead FL 33032, USA
**Leyva, Nicholas T (Nick)** — Baseball Manager
1098 Tilghman Road, Chesterbrook PA 19087, USA
**Lezak, Jason E** — Swimmer
3 Galena, Irvine CA 92602, USA
**Lezcano, Sixto J** — Baseball Player
7828 Bardmoor Chill Circle, Orlando FL 32835, USA
**Lhuillier, Monique** — Fashion Designer
8485 Melrose Place, Los Angeles CA 90069, USA
**Li Hongzhi** — Religious Leader
Universe Publishing, PO Box 193, Gillette NJ 07933, USA
**Li Jiajun** — Speed Skater
Skating Association, 56 Zhonguancun South St, Beijing 100044, China
**Li Ka Shing** — Businessman
70/F Cheung Kong Center, 2 Queen's Road, Cental Region, Hong Kong, China
**Li Keyu** — Fashion Designer
21 Gong-Jian Hutong, Di An-Men, Beijing 100009, China
**Li Lanqing** — Government Official, China
Communist Party Central Committee, Zhonganahai, Beijing 100017, China
**Li Na** — Tennis Player
Women's Tennis Assn, 1 Progress Plaza, #1500, Saint Petersburg FL 33701 USA
**Li Peng** — Premier, China
Communist Party Central Committee, Zhonganahai, Beijing 100017, China
**Li, Frederick** — Molecular Biologist
Dana-Farber Cancer Institute, 44 Binney St, Boston MA 02115, USA
**Liagigre, Christian** — Interior Designer
122 Rue de Grenelle, 75007 Paris, France
**Liakhovich, Sergei** — Boxer
Central Boxing Gym, 1755 W Van Buren St, Phoenix AZ 85007, USA
**Liano, Jennifer** — Model
Playboy Promotions, 9346 Civic Center Dr, #200, Beverly Hills CA 90210 USA
**Liao, Sheri Xiaoyi** — Environmental Activist
Global Village, 86 Bei Yuan Road, Jiaming District, Beijing 100101, China
**Libano Christo, Carlos A** — Social Activist, Writer
Escola Dominicana de Teologia, Rua Atibaia 420, Sao Paulo SP 01235 010, Brazil
**Libatique, Matthew J** — Cinematographer
4524 Ambrose Ave, Los Angeles CA 90027, USA
**Libby, Wendy B** — Educator
Stetson University, President's Office, 421 N Woodland Blvd, DeLand FL 32723, USA

**L**

**Lewis - Libby**

# L

**Liberato, Liana** — Actress
Creative Artists Agency, 2000 Ave of Stars, #100, Los Angeles CA 90067 USA

**Liberman, Avigdor** — Government Official, Israel
Knesset, Kiryat Ben Gurion, Israel 91950, Israel

**Libertini, Richard** — Actor
House of Representatives, 1434 6th St, #1, Santa Monica CA 90401 USA

**Libeskind, Daniel** — Architect
Studio Daniel Libeskind, Windscheidstr 18, 10627 Berlin, Germany

**Libett, Nick** — Ice Hockey Player
4272 N McNay Court, West Bloomfield MI 48323, USA

**Libman, Leslie** — Director, Writer
I C M Partners, 10250 Constellation Blvd, #900, Los Angeles CA 90067 USA

**Liboiron, Landon** — Actor
Baker Winokur Ryder Public Relations, 9100 Wilshire Blvd, #500W, Beverly Hills CA 90212 USA

**Libor, Christiane** — Opera Singer
I M G Artists, Hogarth Business Park, Chiswick, London W4 2TH, England

**Libutti, Frank** — Marine Corps General, Police Official
New York City Deputy Commissioner's Office, 1 Police Plaza, New York NY 10038, USA

**Licht, Jeremy** — Actor
4355 Clybourn Ave, Toluca Lake CA 91602, USA

**Licht, Louis** — Environmental Scientist
Ecoltree, 3017 Valley View Lane NE, North Liberty IA 52317, USA

**Lichtblau, Eric** — Journalist
New York Times, Editorial Dept, 229 W 43rd St, New York NY 10036 USA

**Lichtenberg, Byron K** — Astronaut
5701 Impala South Road, Athens TX 75752, USA

**Lichtenberger, H W** — Businessman
Praxair Inc, 39 Old Ridgebury Road, #7, Danbury CT 06810, USA

**Lichtenstein, Harvey** — Music Executive
Brooklyn Academy of Music, 30 Lafayette Ave, Brooklyn NY 11217, USA

**Lichti, Todd S** — Basketball Player
2331 Holly View Dr, Martinez CA 94553, USA

**Lick, Dale W** — Mathematician, Computer Scientist
348 Remington Run Loop, Tallahassee FL 32312, USA

**Lick, Dennis A** — Football Player
6140 S Knox Ave, Chicago IL 60629, USA

**Lickliter, Frank, II** — Golfer
846 S Main St, Franklin OH 45005, USA

**Lickliter, Todd** — Basketball Coach
Marian University, Athletic Dept, 3200 Cold Spring Road, Indianapolis IN 46222, USA

**Licon, Jeffrey (Jeff)** — Director, Actor
Innovative Artists, 1505 10th St, Santa Monica CA 90401 USA

**Lidback, Jenny** — Golfer
1130 Graystone Crossing, Alpharetta GA 30005, USA

**Lidberg, Jimmy** — Greco-Roman Wrestler
Vikingagatan 1, 113 42 Stockholm, Sweden

**Liddell, Chuck** — Wrestler, Mixed Martial Athlete
Zinkin Entertainment, 5 E River Park Place W, #203, Fresno CA 93720, USA

**Liddy, G Gordon** — Watergate Figure, Actor
9112 Riverside Dr, Fort Washington MD 20744, USA

**Lidell, Jamie** — Singer
Windish Agency, 1658 N Milwaukee Ave, #211, Chicago IL 60647 USA

**Lidge, Bradley T (Brad)** — Baseball Player
4833 Front St, Castle Rock CO 80104, USA

**Lidov, Arthur** — Artist
Pleasant Ridge Road, Poughquag NY 12570, USA

**Lidster, J Douglas A (Doug)** — Ice Hockey Player
3000 Colonial Parkway, #3202, Cedar Park TX 78613, USA

**Lidstrom, Nicklas E** — Ice Hockey Player
47725 Bellagio Dr, Northville MI 48167, USA

**Lieber, Charles M** — Chemist
Harvard University, Chemistry Dept, Cambridge MA 02138, USA

**Lieber, Jonathan R (Jon)** — Baseball Player
3060 Isle of Palms Dr W, Mobile AL 36695, USA

**Lieber, Larry** — Cartoonist (Amazing Spider-Man)
King Features Syndicate, 300 W 57th St, #1500, New York NY 10019 USA

**Lieber, Mimi** — Actress
TalentWorks, 3500 W Olive Ave, #1400, Burbank CA 91505 USA

**Lieber, Rob** — Writer, Actor
Anonymous Content, 3532 Hayden Ave, Culver City CA 90232 USA

**Lieberman, Myron** — Educator
910 17th St NW, #800, Washington DC 20006, USA

**Lieberman, Robert** — Director
A P A Talent & Literary Agency, 405 S Beverly Dr, #300, Beverly Hills CA 90212 USA

**Lieberman, Todd** — Producer
Mandeville Films, 500 S Buena Vista St, Animation Building 2G, Burbank CA 91521, USA

**Lieberman-Cline, Nancy** — Basketball Player
2636 Creekway Dr, Carrollton TX 75010, USA

**Lieberstein, Paul B** — Actor, Comedian, Writer, Producer
Creative Artists Agency, 2000 Ave of Stars, #100, Los Angeles CA 90067 USA

**Liebert, Ottmar** — Guitarist, Composer
Segue Entertainment, PO Box A12, Santa Rosa CA 95403, USA

**Lieberthal, Michael S (Mike)** — Baseball Player
1740 Larkfield Ave, Westlake Village CA 91362, USA

**Liebeskind, John** — Brain Surgeon, Psychologist
University of California Medical Center, Surgery Dept, Los Angeles CA 90024, USA

**Liebesman, Jonathan** — Director
Principato-Young, 9465 Wilshire Blvd, #880, Beverly Hills CA 90212 USA

**Liebman, David** — Jazz Saxophonist
2206 Brislin Road, Stroudsburg PA 18360, USA

**Liebman, Wendy** — Actress, Comedienne
Art/Work Entertainment, 6100 Wilshire Blvd, #575, Los Angeles CA 90048, USA

**Liebowitz, Ronald D, Jr** — Educator
Middlebury College, President's Office, 9 Old Chapel Road, Middlebury VT 05753, USA

**Liechty, Mike** — Bassist (Neon Trees)
Creative Artists Agency, 2000 Ave of Stars, #100, Los Angeles CA 90067 USA

Liberato - Liechty

**Liefeld, Rob** — Cartoonist (Youngblood)
1440 N Harbor Blvd, #305, Fullerton CA 92835, USA

**Liefer, Jeff** — Baseball Player
1116 W Bay Ave, Newport Beach CA 92661, USA

**Liekens, Koen** — Drummer (K's Choice)
Sharpe Entertainment Services, 683 Palmera Ave, Pacific Palisades CA 90272, USA

**Lien, Jennifer** — Actress
Abrams Artists, 9200 W Sunset Blvd, #1125, West Hollywood CA 90069 USA

**Lienhard, William B (Bill)** — Basketball Player
1320 Lawrence Ave, Lawrence KS 66049, USA

**Liepa, Andris** — Ballet Dancer
Bryusov Per 17, #13, 103009 Moscow, Russia

**Liepa, Ilsa** — Ballerina
Bryusov Per 17, #12, 103009 Moscow, Russia

**Liepmann, Hans W** — Aeronautical Engineer, Physicist
55 Haverstock Road, La Canada Flintridge CA 91011, USA

**Lietzke, Bruce** — Golfer
PO Box 177, Larue TX 75770, USA

**Lifeson, Alex** — Guitarist (Rush)
S L Feldman Mgmt, 1505 W 2nd Ave, #200, Vancouver BC V6H 3Y4, Canada

**Ligety, Ted** — Alpine Skier
Park City Ski Resort, Ski Director's Office, 1345 Lowell Ave, Park City UT 84060, USA

**Light, John** — Actor
Markham Froggatt Irwin, Julian House, 4 Windmill St, London W1P 1HF, England

**Light, Judith** — Actress
2934 N Beverly Glen Circle, Los Angeles CA 90077, USA

**Light, Matthew C (Matt)** — Football Player
261 East St, Foxboro MA 02035, USA

**Lightbody, Gary** — Singer, Songwriter (Snow Patrol)
Big Life Mgmt, 67-69 Charlton St, London NW1 1HY, England

**Lightfoot, Edwin N** — Chemical, Biological Engineer
University of Wisconsin, Chemical Engineering Dept, 1415 Engineering Dr, Madison WI 53706, USA

**Lightfoot, Gordon** — Singer, Guitarist, Songwriter
ICON Performing Arts, 1557 Westwood Blvd, #242, Los Angeles CA 90024, USA

**Lightman, Alan P** — Physicist, Writer
Harvard University, Humanities Dept, Cambridge MA 02138, USA

**Lightman, Toby** — Singer, Songwriter
Creative Artists Agency, 2000 Ave of Stars, #100, Los Angeles CA 90067 USA

**Lightner, Candace L (Candy)** — Social Activist
1216 Portner Road, Alexandria VA 22314, USA

**Ligon, Bill** — Basketball Player
PO Box 1432, Gallatin TN 37066, USA

**Ligouri, James A** — Educator
Iona College, President's Office, New Rochelle NY 10801, USA

**Ligtenberg, Kerry** — Baseball Player
9274 Albright Court, Inver Grove Heights MN 55077, USA

**Lijn, Liliane** — Sculptor
99 Camden Mews, London NW1 9BU, England

**Likens, Gene E** — Ecologist, Biologist
Ecosystem Studies Institute, PO Box AB, Millbrook NY 12545, USA

**Lil Bow Wow** — Rap Artist
Central Entertainment Group, 251 W 39st, #700, New York NY 10018, USA

**Lil' Fame** — Rap Artist (MOP)
Pyramid Entertainment Group, 377 Rector Place, #21A, New York NY 10280 USA

**Lil' J** — Rap Artist
Thruline Entertainment, 9250 Wilshire Blvd, #100, Beverly Hills CA 90212 USA

**Lil' JJ** — Actor, Comedian
W M E Entertainment, 9601 Wilshire Blvd, #300, Beverly Hills CA 90210 USA

**Lil' Jon** — Rap Artist, Songwriter
FilmEngine, 345 Maple Dr, #222, Beverly Hills CA 90210, USA

**Lil' Kim** — Rap Artist
Universal Media Artists, 8222 Melrose Ave, #203, Los Angeles CA 90048, USA

**Lil Mama** — Rap Artist
F Y I Public Relations, 45 E 20th St, #5B, New York NY 10003, USA

**Lil' Wayne** — Rap Artist (Hot Boys), Actor
Bryant Mgmt, 800 Brickell Ave, #550, Miami FL 33131, USA

**Liles, John-Michael** — Ice Hockey Player
1540 E Shore Dr, Culver IN 46511, USA

**Liles, Robert L** — WW II Army Air Corps Hero
19520 Tiber Court, Montgomery Village MD 20886, USA

**Lilienfeld, Abraham M** — Epidemiologist
3203 Old Post Dr, Pikesville MD 21208, USA

**Lilja, Andreas** — Ice Hockey Player
6501 N Federal Highway, #2, Boca Raton FL 33487, USA

**Lilja, George V** — Football Player
8 Driftwood Dr, Warren PA 16365, USA

**Lill, Dennis** — Actor
Artists Partnership, 101 Finsbury Pavement, London EC2A 1RS, England

**Lillard, Bill** — Bowler
5418 Imogene St, Houston TX 77096, USA

**Lillard, Damian** — Basketball Player
Portland Trail Blazers, Rose Garden, 1 N Center Court St, Portland OR 97227 USA

**Lillard, Matthew** — Actor
Paradigm Agency, 360 N Crescent Dr, North Building, Beverly Hills CA 90210 USA

**Lillee, Dennis K** — Cricketer
Swan Sport, PO Box 158, Byron Bay NSW 2481, Australia

**Lilley, Chris** — Producer, Writer, Actor
Princess Pictures, 11 Princes St, Saint Kilda VIC 3182, Australia

**Lilley, James R** — Diplomat
2801 New Mexico Ave NW, #407, Washington DC 20007, USA

**Lillibridge, Brent S** — Baseball Player
14631 43rd Dr SE, Snohomish WA 98296, USA

**Lilliquist, Derek J** — Baseball Player
226 10th Ave, Vero Beach FL 32962, USA

**Lillis, Robert P (Bob)** — Baseball Player, Manager
5107 Cherry Tree Lane, Orlando FL 32819, USA

**Lilly, Evangeline** — Actress, Model
Silver Lining Entertainment, 421 S Beverly Drive, #7, Beverly Hills CA 90212, USA

**Lilly, Kristine** — Soccer Player
10 Bradford Terrace, #2, Brookline MA 02446, USA

**Lilly, Robert L (Bob)** — Football Player
3310 Drexel Dr, Dallas TX 75205, USA

**Lilly, Theodore R (Ted), III** — Baseball Player
1305 W Waveland Ave, Chicago IL 60613, USA

**Lim Chwen Jeng** — Architect
Bartlett Architecture School, 22 Gordon St, London WC1H 0QB, England

**Lim Siew Ai** — Golfer
304 Morning Sun Dr, Birmingham AL 35242, USA

**Lim, H J** — Concert Pianist
Harrison/Parrott, 5-6 Albion Court, London W6 0QT, England

**Lima, Adriana** — Model
Marilyn Agency, 4 Rue de la Paix, 75002 Paris, France

**Lima, Devin** — Singer, Rap Artist (Lyte Funky Ones)
LFO/BMG Records, 8750 Wilshire Blvd, Beverly Hills CA 90211, USA

**Lima, Kevin** — Director, Producer
W M E Entertainment, 9601 Wilshire Blvd, #300, Beverly Hills CA 90210 USA

**Liman, Doug** — Director
Resolution, 1801 Century Park E, #2300, Los Angeles CA 90067 USA

**Limbaugh, Rush** — Entertainer
PO Box 2795, Palm Beach FL 33480, USA

**Limbert, Deborah (Deb)** — Explorer, Speleologist
British Cave Research Assn, Old Methodist Chapel, Great Hucklow, Buxton SK17 8RG, England

**Limbert, Howard** — Explorer, Speleologist
British Cave Research Assn, Old Methodist Chapel, Great Hucklow, Buxton SK17 8RG, England

**Lime-Fedderson, Yvonne** — Actress
15757 N 78th St, Scottsdale AZ 85260, USA

**Lin, Cho-Liang** — Concert Violinist
Julliard School, 60 Lincoln Center Plaza, New York NY 10023, USA

**Lin, Jeremy S** — Basketball Player
Los Angeles Lakers, Staples Center, 1111 S Figueroa St, Los Angeles CA 90015 USA

**Lin, Junhao** — Electronic, Nanotechnology Engineer
Vanderbilt University, Physics & Astronomy Dept, Nashville TN 37240, USA

**Lin, Justin** — Director
Trailing Johnson Productions, 2100 Sawtell Blvd, Los Angeles CA 90025, USA

**Lin, Maya Ying** — Architect, Sculptor
Sidney Janis Gallery, 120 E 75th St, #6A, New York NY 10021, USA

**Lin, Yu Ping** — Golfer
Jerry Wong, 1450 Subtropic Dr, La Habra Heights CA 90631, USA

**Lincecum, Timothy L (Tim)** — Baseball Player
16062 SE 4th St, Belluvue WA 98008, USA

**Lincicome, Brittany G** — Golfer
7971 Idlewild Lane, Seminole FL 33777, USA

**Lincoln, Andrew** — Actor
Markham Froggatt Irwin, Julian House, 4 Windmill St, London W1P 1HF, England

**Lincoln, Craig** — Diver
20930 Almazan Road, Woodland Hills CA 91364, USA

**Lincoln, Jeremy A** — Football Player
3411 W Lincolnshire Blvd, Toledo OH 43606, USA

**Lincoln, Keith P** — Football Player
550 SE Crestview St, Pullman WA 99163, USA

**Lincoln, Lar Park** — Actress
Premiere Artists Agency, 1875 Century Park E, #2250, Los Angeles CA 90067 USA

**Lincoln, Michael G (Mike)** — Baseball Player
8269 Moss Oak Ave, Citrus Heights CA 95610, USA

**Lincoln, Todd** — Director, Writer
Creative Artists Agency, 2000 Ave of Stars, #100, Los Angeles CA 90067 USA

**Lind, Adam A** — Baseball Player
6520 Turf Way, Anderson IN 46013, USA

**Lind, Caroline** — Rowing Athlete
U S Rowing Assn, 2 Wall St, Princeton NJ 08540, USA

**Lind, Don L** — Astronaut
51 N 376 E, Smithfield UT 84335, USA

**Lind, Heather** — Actress
I C M Partners, 10250 Constellation Blvd, #900, Los Angeles CA 90067 USA

**Lind, Joan** — Rowing Athlete
240 Euclid Ave, Long Beach CA 90803, USA

**Lind, Jose** — Baseball Player
18 Brisas del Plata, Dorado PR 00646, USA

**Lind, Juha P** — Ice Hockey Player
Montreal Canadiens, 1275 Saint Antoine St W, Montreal QC H3C 5L2, Canada

**Lind, Marshall L** — Educator
University of Alaska, Chancellor's Office, Fairbanks AK 99775, USA

**Lind, Zach** — Drummer (Jimmy Eat World)
S A M, 722 Seward St, Los Angeles CA 90038, USA

**Lindahl, Cathrine** — Curling Athlete
Curling Association, Idrottshuser, Marbackagatan 19, 123 43 Farsta, Sweden

**Lindahl, George, III** — Businessman
Anadarko Petroleum Corp, 1201 Lake Robbins Dr, Spring TX 77380, USA

**Lindahl, Margaretha** — Curling Athlete
Curling Association, Idrottshuser, Marbackagatan 19, 123 43 Farsta, Sweden

**Lindbeck, Assar** — Economist
50 Ostermalmsgatan, 114 26 Stockholm, Sweden

**Lindbeck, George A** — Theologian
Yale University, Divinity School, New Haven CT 06520, USA

**Lindberg, Athena** — Model
Playboy Promotions, 9346 Civic Center Dr, #200, Beverly Hills CA 90210 USA

**Lindberg, Chad** — Actor
Creative Partners Group, 1522 2nd St, Santa Monica CA 90401, USA

**Lindbergh, Peter** — Photographer
12 Rue de Savoie, 75006 Paris, France

**Linde, Andrei D** — Astronomer
Stanford University, Astronomy Dept, Stanford CA 94305, USA

Lindelind, Liv — Model
PO Box 1029, Frazier Park CA 93225, USA

Lindell, Rian D — Football Player
1226 E Cumberland Ave, #315, Tampa FL 33602, USA

Lindeman, James W (Jim) — Baseball Player
2278 S Scott St, Des Plaines IL 60018, USA

Lindemann, Til — Singer (Rammstein)
Pilgrim Mgmt, PO Box 540101, 10042 Berlin, Germany

Linden, Eugene — Writer
Penguin Books, 375 Hudson St, Basement 1, New York NY 10014 USA

Linden, Hal — Actor
Stone Manners Salners, 6100 Wilshire Blvd, #1500, Los Angeles CA 90035 USA

Linden, Jamie — Director, Writer
Paradigm Agency, 360 N Crescent Dr, North Building, Beverly Hills CA 90210 USA

Linden, Todd — Baseball Player
7825 NW Anderson Hill Road, Silverdale WA 98383, USA

Linden, Trevor — Ice Hockey Player
1362 23rd St SE, Medicine Hat AB T1A 2C9, Canada

Lindenlaub, Karl W — Cinematographer
3021 Nichols Canyon Road, Los Angeles CA 90046, USA

Linder, Kate — Actress
Siegal Co, 9025 Wilshire Blvd, #400, Beverly Hills CA 90211, USA

Linderman, Earl W — Artist
5005 E Camelback Road, Phoenix AZ 85018, USA

Lindes, Hal — Guitarist (Dire Straits)
Damage Mgmt, 16 Lambton Place, London W11 2SH, England

Lindh, Hilary — Alpine Skier
PO Box 33036, Juneau AK 99803, USA

Lindholm, Ingvar N — Composer
Hringe Hages Vag 33, 144 00 Ronninge, Sweden

Lindholm, Tobias — Director
W M E Entertainment, 9601 Wilshire Blvd, #300, Beverly Hills CA 90210 USA

Lindhome, Riki — Actress
Principato-Young, 9465 Wilshire Blvd, #880, Beverly Hills CA 90212 USA

Lindig, Bill M — Businessman
Sysco Corp, 1390 Enclave Parkway, Houston TX 77077, USA

Lindley, Christina — Model, Actress
Esterman Entertainment, 12333 Pretoria Dr, Silver Spring MD 20904, USA

Lindley, David — Guitarist
Rosebud Agency, PO Box 170429, San Francisco CA 94117 USA

Lindley, John W — Cinematographer
PO Box 351, 15332 Antioch St, Pacific Palisades CA 90272, USA

Lindman, Karl — Model
Wilhelmina Models, 300 Park Ave S, #200, New York NY 10010 USA

Lindner, Deiter — Track Athlete
Moritz Hill Str 36, 06667 Weissenfels, Germany

Lindner, Patrick — Singer
Postfach 140212, 80469 Munich, Germany

Lindner, William G — Labor Leader
Transport Workers Union, 80 W End Ave, New York NY 10023, USA

Lindo, Delroy — Actor
A P A Talent & Literary Agency, 405 S Beverly Dr, #300, Beverly Hills CA 90212 USA

Lindquist, Barbara M (Barb) — Triathlete
215 Targhee Towne Road, Alta WY 83414, USA

Lindquist, Susan L — Biologist
Whitehead Institute, 9 Cambridge Circle, Cambridge MA 02142, USA

Lindqvist, David — Bassist (Caesars)
Paradigm Agency, 360 Park Ave, #1600, New York NY 10022 USA

Lindros, Eric B — Ice Hockey Player
1 Morton Square, #6BE, New York NY 10014, USA

Lindroth, Eric — Water Polo Player
13151 Dufresne Place, San Diego CA 92129, USA

Lindsay, Bill — Ice Hockey Player
700 NW 7th Ave, Boca Raton FL 33486, USA

Lindsay, Elvin (Lin) — WW II Navy Air Force Hero
6220 E Broadway Road, #347, Mesa AZ 85206, USA

Lindsay, Everett E — Football Player
5191 Bald Eagle Ave, Saint Paul MN 55110, USA

Lindsay, James J — Army General
676 Azalea Dr, Vass NC 28394, USA

Lindsay, Mark — Singer, Songwriter
Lustig Talent, PO Box 770850, Orlando FL 32877 USA

Lindsay, R B Theodore (Ted) — Ice Hockey Player
2598 Invitational Dr, Oakland MI 48363, USA

Lindsay, Robert — Actor, Singer
Hamilton Hodell, 20 Golden Square, London W1F 9JL, England

Lindsay-Abaire, David — Writer
W M E Entertainment, 9601 Wilshire Blvd, #300, Beverly Hills CA 90210 USA

Lindsey, James E (Jim) — Football Player
1165 E Joyce Blvd, Fayetteville AR 72703, USA

Lindsey, P Dale — Football Player
4020 Murphy Canyon Road, San Diego CA 92123, USA

Lindsey, Steven W — Astronaut
3217 W Yarrow Circle, Superior CO 80027, USA

Lindsey, Tracy — Actress
651B N Kilkea Dr, Los Angeles CA 90048, USA

Lindskog, Par — Opera Singer
Maxine Robertson Mgmt, 14 Forge Dr, Claygate KT10 0HR, England

Lindsley, Blake — Actress
Shelter Entertainment, 9255 Sunset Blvd, #300, Los Angeles CA 90069 USA

Lindstrand, Per — Balloonist
Thunder & Colt, Maesbury Road, Oswestry, Shropshire SY10 8HA, England

Lindstrom Breer, Murle — Golfer
7008 Sand Road, Savannah GA 31410, USA

Lindstrom, David A (Dave) — Football Player
11562 Hardy St, Overland Park KS 66210, USA

**Lindstrom, Jack** — Cartoonist (Executive Suite)
United Feature Syndicate, PO Box 5610, Cincinnati OH 45201 USA

**Lindstrom, Jon** — Actor, Writer, Producer
Jailbreak Films, 4341 Birch St, Newport Beach CA 92660, USA

**Lindstrom, Matthew J (Matt)** — Baseball Player
316 Mohawk Ave, Rexburg ID 83440, USA

**Lindvall, Angela** — Model, Actress
Rogue Entertainment, 10900 Wilshire Blvd, #1400, Los Angeles CA 90024, USA

**Lineback, Richard** — Actor
S M S Talent, 8383 Wilshire Blvd, #230, Beverly Hills CA 90211 USA

**Linebrink, Scott** — Baseball Player
2100 County Road 156, Granger TX 76530, USA

**Linehan, Marsha M** — Psychologist
University of Washington, Behavioral Research & Therapy Clinic, Seattle WA 98195, USA

**Linehan, Scott** — Football Coach
Detroit Lions, 222 Republic Dr, Allen Park MI 48101 USA

**Lineker, Gary W** — Soccer Player
Markee UK, 6 Saint George St, Nottingham NG1 3BE, England

**Linenger, Jerry M** — Astronaut
550 S Stoney Point Road, Suttons Bay MI 49682, USA

**Lines, Aaron** — Singer
Mark Jones Mgmt, 54 Music Square E, #200, Nashville TN 37203, USA

**Lines, Richard G (Dick)** — Baseball Player
1716 Pebble Beach Lane, Lady Lake FL 32159, USA

**Ling** — Model
I M G Models, 304 Park Ave S, #PH N, New York NY 10010 USA

**Ling, Jahja** — Conductor
Opus 3 Artists, 470 Park Ave S, #900N, New York NY 10016 USA

**Ling, Lisa** — Commentator
CNN-TV, News Dept, 820 1st St NE, #1000, Washington DC 20002 USA

**Ling, Sergei S** — Prime Minister, Belarus
Belarus Mission, United Nations, 136 E 67th St, New York NY 10065, USA

**Ling, Victor** — Biophysicist
5671 Trafalgar St, Vancouver BC V6N 1C2, Canada

**Lingenfelter, Steven R (Steve)** — Basketball Player
17378 Ithaca Court, Lakeville MN 55044, USA

**Linger, Andreas** — Luge Athlete
Bettelwurfsiedlung 9, 6067 Absam, Austria

**Linger, Wolfgang** — Luge Athlete
Bettelwurfsiedlung 9, 6067 Absam, Austria

**Lingner, Adam J** — Football Player
8395 Norwood Lane N, Maple Grove MN 55369, USA

**Linhart, Carl J** — Baseball Player
2647 Delmar Ave, Granite City IL 62040, USA

**Lini, Ham** — Prime Minister, Vanuatu
Prime Minister's Office, PO Box 053, Port Vila, Vanuatu

**Liniak, Cole E** — Baseball Player
PO Box 235625, Encinitas CA 92023, USA

**Linichuk, Natalia** — Ice Dancer, Coach
146 Dallam Road, Newark DE 19711, USA

**Link, Caroline** — Director, Writer
Just Publicity, Erhardtstr 8, 80469 Munich, Germany

**Link, Charlotte** — Writer
Verkagsgruppe Random House, Neumarkter Str 28, 81673 Munich, Germany

**Linker, Amy** — Actress
Lemack Co, 508 Gerona Ave, San Gabriel CA 91775, USA

**Linklater, Hamish** — Actor, Writer
I C M Partners, 10250 Constellation Blvd, #900, Los Angeles CA 90067 USA

**Linklater, Richard** — Director, Writer
Creative Artists Agency, 2000 Ave of Stars, #100, Los Angeles CA 90067 USA

**Linkletter, Nicole** — Model
Elite Model Mgmt, 404 Park Ave S, #900, New York NY 10016 USA

**Linley, Cody** — Actor
C E S D, 10635 Santa Monica Blvd, #130, Los Angeles CA 90025 USA

**Linn, Bambi** — Actress, Dancer, Choreographer
45 Compo Road S, Westport CT 06880, USA

**Linn, Britt** — Model
Playboy Promotions, 9346 Civic Center Dr, #200, Beverly Hills CA 90210 USA

**Linn, Rex** — Actor
Vox Inc, 6420 Wilshire Blvd, #1080, Los Angeles CA 90048 USA

**Linn, Richard** — Judge
US Court of Appeals, 717 Madison Place NW, Washington DC 20439, USA

**Linn, Teri Ann** — Actress
Sutton-Barth Vennari, 5900 Wilshire Blvd, #700, Los Angeles CA 90036 USA

**Linn-Baker, Mark** — Actor
27702 Fairweather St, Canyon Country CA 91351, USA

**Linnehan, Richard M** — Astronaut
16802 Hartwood Way, Houston TX 77058, USA

**Linney, Laura** — Actress
Brillstein Entertainment Partners, 9150 Wilshire Blvd, #350, Beverly Hills CA 90212 USA

**Linseman, Ken** — Ice Hockey Player
1070 Ocean Blvd, Hampton NH 03842, USA

**Linson, Art** — Director, Producer
I C M Partners, 10250 Constellation Blvd, #900, Los Angeles CA 90067 USA

**Lintel, Michelle** — Actress
Kazarian/Measures/Ruskin, 11969 Ventura Blvd, #300, Studio City CA 91604 USA

**Linteris, Gregory T** — Astronaut
US Commerce Dept, Fire Science Division, Gaithersburg MD 20899, USA

**Linton, Douglas W (Doug)** — Baseball Player
201 Ellison St, Rochester NY 14609, USA

**Linton, Tom** — Guitarist (Jimmy Eat World)
S A M, 722 Seward St, Los Angeles CA 90038, USA

**Lintu, Hannu** — Conductor
Tampere Philharmonic Orchestra, PL 16, 33101 Tampere, Finland

**Lintz, Larry** — Baseball Player
8529 Sun Sprite Way, Elk Grove CA 95624, USA

**Linville, Joanne** — Actress
Special Artists Agency, 9200 Sunset Blvd, #410, West Hollywood CA 90069 USA

**Linz, Alex D** — Actor
Innovative Artists, 1505 10th St, Santa Monica CA 90401 USA

**Linzy, Frank A** — Baseball Player
38947 E 151st St S, Coweta OK 74429, USA

**Lioeanjie, Rene** — Labor Leader
National Maritime Union, 1150 17th St NW, Washington DC 20036, USA

**Lionetti, Donald M** — Army General
4517 W Rosemere Road, Tampa FL 33609, USA

**Lions, Pierre-Louis** — Mathematician
Paris University, Mathematics Dept, Place Marechal Lattre-de-Tessigny, 75775 Paris, France

**Liotta, Ray** — Actor
United Talent Agency, U T A Plaza, 9336 Civic Center Dr, Beverly Hills CA 90210 USA

**Lipa, Elisabeta O** — Rowing Athlete
Str Reconstructiei 1, #78, 040547 Bucharest, Romania

**Lipes, Jody Lee** — Cinematographer
Sheldon Prosnit Agency, 800 S Robertson Blvd, Los Angeles CA 90035, USA

**Lipetri, N Angelo** — Baseball Player
150 Yoakum Ave, Farmingdale NY 11735, USA

**Lipez, Kermit V** — Judge
US Court of Appeals, 537 Congress St, Portland ME 04101, USA

**Lipinski, Ann Marie** — Journalist
Chicago Tribune, Editorial Dept, 435 N Michigan Ave, #1, Chicago IL 60611, USA

**Lipinski, Tara** — Figure Skater, Actress
Thumbs Up Enterprises, PO Box 1487, Sugar Land TX 77487, USA

**Lipman, Elinor** — Writer
Houghton Mifflin Harcourt, 215 Park Ave S, #1200, New York NY 10003 USA

**Lipman, Maureen** — Actress
Talking Concepts, 19 Bird St, Lichfield, Straffordshire WS13 6PW, England

**Lipnicki, Jonathan** — Actor
Greene Assoc, 1901 Ave of Stars, #130, Los Angeles CA 90067 USA

**Lipnitskaia, Julia V** — Figure Skater
Figure Skating Federation, Luzhnetskaya Nab 8, 119991 Moscow, Russia

**Lipovsek, Marjana** — Opera Singer
Kunstleragentur Raab & Bohm, Plankengasse 7, 1010 Vienna, Austria

**Lippard, Stephen J** — Chemist
975 Memorial Dr, #602, Cambridge MA 02138, USA

**Lippett, Ronald G (Ronnie)** — Football Player
610 Foundry St, South Easton MA 02375, USA

**Lippincott, Philip E** — Businessman
Campbell Soup Co, Campbell Place, Camden NJ 08103, USA

**Lipps, Louis A** — Football Player
17 Brilliant Ave, #100, Pittsburgh PA 15215, USA

**Lipscomb, Steve** — Poker Executive
World Poker Tour Enterprises, 5700 Wilshire Blvd, #350, Los Angeles CA 90036 USA

**Lipski, Robert P (Bob)** — Baseball Player
1 Snook St, Scranton PA 18505, USA

**Lipton, Martin** — Attorney
Wachtell Lipton Rosen Katz, 51 W 52nd St, New York NY 10019, USA

**Lipton, Peggy** — Actress
Saint Martin's Press, 175 5th Ave, #400, New York NY 10010 USA

**Liquori, Martin (Marty)** — Track Athlete, Sportscaster
2915 NW 58th Blvd, Gainesville FL 32606, USA

**Liriano, Nelson A** — Baseball Player
Burlington Royals, PO Box 1143, Burlington NC 27216, USA

**Lisa Lisa** — Singer (Lisa Lisa & Cult Jam)
Green Light Talent Agency, PO Box 3172, Beverly Hills CA 90212 USA

**LisaRaye** — Actress
C E S D, 10635 Santa Monica Blvd, #130, Los Angeles CA 90025 USA

**Lisbe, Mike** — Writer, Producer
I C M Partners, 10250 Constellation Blvd, #900, Los Angeles CA 90067 USA

**Lisch, Russell J (Rusty)** — Football Player
206 Country Club Lane, Belleville IL 62223, USA

**Liscio, Anthony F (Tony)** — Football Player
10348 Trailcliff Dr, Dallas TX 75238, USA

**Lisi, Ricardo P E (Rick)** — Baseball Player
1207 N Wren Dr, Rogers AR 72756, USA

**Lisi, Virna** — Actress
Voyez Mon Agent, 20 Ave Rapp, 75007 Paris, France

**Lisicki, Sabine** — Tennis Player
5500 34th St W, Bradenton FL 34210, USA

**Lisiecki, Jan** — Concert Pianist
I M G Artists. Hogarth Business Park, Chiswick, London W4 2TH, England

**Lisiewicz, Klaus** — Soccer Player
Blucherstr 5, 37441 Bad Sachsa, Germany

**Lisitsa, Valentina** — Concert Pianist
Columbia Artists Mgmt Inc, 5 Columbus Circle, 1790 Broadway, #1600, New York NY 10019 USA

**Liske, Peter A (Pete)** — Football Player
116 E Mountain Brook Lane, Wenatchee WA 98801, USA

**Liskevych, Taras** — Volleyball Player, Coach
Oregon State University, Athletic Dept, Corvallis OR 97331, USA

**Liskov, Barbara H** — Computer Engineer
Massachusetts Institute of Technology, Computer Science Laboratory, Cambridge MA 02139, USA

**Lissack, Russell D** — Guitarist (Bloc Party)
Coalition Mgmt, 12 Barley Mow Passage, London W4 4PH, England

**Lissner, Stephane M** — Director
Theatre du Chatelet, 2 Rue Edouuard Colonne, 75001 Paris, France

**Lissoni, Piero** — Interior Designer
Lissoni Assoc, Via Goito 9, 20121 Milan, Italy

**List, Peyton** — Actress
Innovative Artists, 1505 10th St, Santa Monica CA 90401 USA

**List, Peyton R** — Actress, Model
United Talent Agency, U T A Plaza, 9336 Civic Center Dr, Beverly Hills CA 90210 USA

**List, Robert F** — Governor, NV
1660 Catalpa Lane, Reno NV 89511, USA

**List, Spencer** — Actor
Untitled Entertainment, 350 S Beverly Dr, #200, Beverly Hills CA 90212 USA
**Listach, Patrick A (Pat)** — Baseball Player
6030 Durande Dr, Baton Rouge LA 70820, USA
**Lister, Alton L** — Basketball Player
5413 Kirkridge Place, Garland TX 75044, USA
**Lister, Tommy (Tiny)** — Actor, Wrestler
Abrams Artists, 9200 W Sunset Blvd, #1125, West Hollywood CA 90069 USA
**Liston, Ian** — Actor
Coolwaters Productions, 10061 Riverside Dr, Box 531, Toluca Lake CA 91602 USA
**Liteky, Angelo J (Charles)** — Vietnam War Army Chaplain (CMH)
Medal of Honor Society, 40 Patriots Point Road, Mount Pleasant SC 29464, USA
**Lithgow, John** — Actor, Singer
W M E Entertainment, 9601 Wilshire Blvd, #300, Beverly Hills CA 90210 USA
**Litsch, Jesse A** — Baseball Player
6948 80th Terrace, Pinellas Park FL 33781, USA
**Littell, Jonathan** — Writer
Harper Collins Publishers, 10 E 53rd St, Cellar 1, New York NY 10022 USA
**Littell, Mark A** — Baseball Player
21001 N Tatum Blvd, #1630511, Phoenix AZ 85050, USA
**Littell, Robert** — Writer
Simon & Schuster, 1230 Ave of Americas, Concourse 1, New York NY 10020 USA
**Littenberg, Barbara** — Architect
Peterson/Littenberg Architecture, 13 E 66th St, New York NY 10065, USA
**Little Anthony** — Singer
Dassinger Creative, 172 2nd Ave, Little Falls NJ 07424, USA
**Little Richard** — Singer
Hyatt Sunset Hotel, 8401 W Sunset Blvd, West Hollywood CA 90069, USA
**Little Steven** — Singer, Musician, Actor
Premier Talent, 3 E 54th St, #1100, New York NY 10022 USA
**Little, Carole** — Fashion Designer
Carole Little Inc, PO Box 77917, Los Angeles CA 90007, USA
**Little, Chad** — Auto Racing Driver
8718 Statesville Road, Charlotte NC 28269, USA
**Little, Charles L** — Labor Leader
United Transportation Union, 24950 Country Club Blvd, North Olmsted OH 44070, USA
**Little, D Jeffrey (Jeff)** — Baseball Player
5711 W Camper Road, Genoa OH 43430, USA
**Little, Dwight H** — Director
A P A Talent & Literary Agency, 405 S Beverly Dr, #300, Beverly Hills CA 90212 USA
**Little, Floyd D** — Football Player
34505 5th Place SW, Federal Way WA 98023, USA
**Little, Larry C** — Football Player, Coach
14761 SW 169th Lane, Miami FL 33187, USA
**Little, Leonard A** — Football Player
4 Rainier Pointe Court, Saint Charles MO 63301, USA
**Little, Natasha** — Actress
Hamilton Hodell, 20 Golden Square, London W1F 9JL, England
**Little, Rich** — Actor, Comedian
C E S D, 10635 Santa Monica Blvd, #130, Los Angeles CA 90025 USA
**Little, Robert A** — Chef
49 Firth St, London W1V 5TE, England
**Little, Sally** — Golfer
3210 S Ocean Blvd, #702, Highland Beach FL 33487, USA
**Little, Steve** — Actor
Odenkirk Provissiero Entertainment, 650 N Bronson Ave, #B145, Los Angeles, CA 90004, USA
**Little, Tasmin E** — Concert Violinist
Chamber Music Society, 70 Lincoln Center Plaza, Front 2, New York NY 10023, USA
**Little, Tawny Godin** — Entertainer, Beauty Queen
17941 Sky Park Circle, #F, Irvine CA 92614, USA
**Little, W Grady** — Baseball Manager
13115 Odell Heights Dr, Mint Hill NC 28227, USA
**Littlefield, John A** — Baseball Player
1935 Ramar Road, Bullhead City AZ 86442, USA
**Littlefield, Warren** — Businessman, Producer
Littlefield Co, 500 S Buena Vista St, #1835, Burbank CA 91521, USA
**Littleford, Beth** — Actress, Comedienne
Domain Talent, 9229 W Sunset Blvd, #710, West Hollywood CA 90069 USA
**Littlejohn, Dennis G** — Baseball Player
6813 Klamath Way, #D, Bakersfield CA 93309, USA
**Littler, Gene A** — Golfer
PO Box 1949, Rancho Santa Fe CA 92067, USA
**Littles, Eugene S (Gene)** — Basketball Player, Coach
6421 E Beck Lane, Scottsdale AZ 85254, USA
**Littleton, Cynthia** — Editor
Variety 11175 Santa Monica Blvd, Los Angeles CA 90025, USA
**Littman, Jonathan** — Producer
Jerry Bruckheimer Films, 1631 10th St, Santa Monica CA 90404, USA
**Litton, Andrew** — Conductor
I M G Artists, Burlington Lane, Chiswick, London W4 2TH, England
**Litton, Bruce** — Auto Racing Driver
10184 E US Highway 136, Clermont IN 46234, USA
**Litton, Drew** — Editorial Cartoonist
Rocky Mountain News, Editorial Dept, 101 W Colfax Ave, #500, Denver CO 80202, USA
**Litton, J Gregory (Greg)** — Baseball Player
785 Farmington Road, Pensacola FL 32504, USA
**Littrell, Brian T** — Singer (Backstreet Boys)
Wright Entertainment Group, PO Box 590009, Orlando FL 32859, USA
**Littrell, Gary L** — Vietnam War Army Hero (CMH)
4302 Belle Vista Dr, Saint Pete Beach FL 33706, USA
**Litwack, Leon F** — Historian
University of California, History Dept, Berkeley CA 94720, USA
**Liu Boming** — Taikonaut
Satellite Launch Center, Jiuquan, Guangzhou Province, China
**Liu Chao Shiuan** — Prime Minister, Taiwan
Premier's Office, 1 Chunghsiao East Road, Section 1, Taipei, Taiwan

|  |  |
|---|---|
| **Liu Chunhong**<br>9 Tiyuguan Road, Beijing 100763, China | Weightlifter |
| **Liu Yang**<br>Satellite Launch Center, Jiuquan, Guangzhou Province, China | Taikonaut |
| **Liu, Dyana**<br>Velocity Entertainment Partners, 5455 Wilshire Blvd, #802, Los Angeles CA 90036, USA | Actress |
| **Liu, Lucy**<br>United Talent Agency, U T A Plaza, 9336 Civic Center Dr, Beverly Hills CA 90210 USA | Actress, Model |
| **Liukin, Nastia**<br>World Olympic Gymnastics Academy, 1937 W Parker Road, Plano TX 75023, USA | Gymnast |
| **Liukin, Valeri**<br>World Olympic Gymnastics Academy, 1937 W Parker Road, Plano TX 75023, USA | Gymnast, Coach |
| **Liut, Michael D (Mike)**<br>26011 German Mill Road, Franklin MI 48025, USA | Ice Hockey Player |
| **Livadiotti, Massimo**<br>Piazza Vittorio Emanuele II, #31, 00185 Rome, Italy | Artist |
| **Livage, Jacques**<br>College de France, 11 Place M Berthelot, 75231 Paris Cedex 05, France | Chemist |
| **Lively, Blake**<br>Management 360, 9111 Wilshire Blvd, Beverly Hills CA 90210 USA | Actress |
| **Lively, Everett A (Bud)**<br>8605 Esslinger Court SE, Huntsville AL 35802, USA | Baseball Player |
| **Lively, Penelope M**<br>Duck End, Great Rollright, Chipping, Northern Oxfordshire OX7 5SB, England | Writer |
| **Lively, Pierce**<br>US Court of Appeals, PO Box 1226, Danville KY 40423, USA | Judge |
| **Lively, Robyn**<br>Mavrick Artists Agency, 6100 Wilshire Blvd, #550, Los Angeles CA 90048, USA | Actress |
| **Livengood, Ed**<br>Vamp Music Source, 902 W Franklin Ave, #15, Minneapolis MN 55405, USA | Drummer (Jucifer) |
| **Liveris, Andrew N**<br>Dow Chemical, 2030 Dow Center, Midland MI 48674, USA | Businessman |
| **Livermore, Ann**<br>Hewlett-Packard Co, 300 Hanover St, Palo Alto CA 94304, USA | Businesswoman |
| **Livermore, Brooks**<br>Associated International Mgmt, 7 Hatton Garden, #400, London EC1N 8AD, England | Actor |
| **Liverpool, Nicholas J O**<br>President's Office, Morne Bruce, Victoria St, Rouseau, Dominica | President, Dominica |
| **Livers, Virgil C, Jr**<br>313 Clearview Ave, Bowling Green KY 42101, USA | Football Player |
| **Livier, Ruth**<br>C E S D, 10635 Santa Monica Blvd, #130, Los Angeles CA 90025 USA | Actress |
| **Livingston, Andrew L (Andy)**<br>650 E Century Ave, Gilbert AZ 85296, USA | Football Player |
| **Livingston, Barry**<br>T G M D Agency, 6267 Forest Lawn Dr, #101, Los Angeles CA 90068, USA | Actor |
| **Livingston, David M**<br>Dana-Farber Cancer Institute, 44 Binney St, Boston MA 02115 USA | Internist |
| **Livingston, James E**<br>365 Cooper River Dr, Mount Pleasant SC 29464, USA | Vietnam Marine Hero (CMH), General |
| **Livingston, John**<br>Defining Artists, 10 Universal City Plaza, #2000, Universal City CA 91608, USA | Actor |
| **Livingston, Michael P (Mike)**<br>8181 Monrovia St, Lenexa KS 66215, USA | Football Player |
| **Livingston, Robert L, Jr**<br>Livingston Group, 499 S Capitol St SW, #600, Washington DC 20003, USA | Representative, LA |
| **Livingston, Ron**<br>United Talent Agency, U T A Plaza, 9336 Civic Center Dr, Beverly Hills CA 90210 USA | Actor |
| **Livingston, Shaun P**<br>7334 Trask Ave, Playa del Rey CA 90293, USA | Basketball Player |
| **Livingston, Stanley**<br>PO Box 1782, Studio City CA 91614, USA | Actor |
| **Livingston, Warren**<br>308 E Malibu Dr, Tempe AZ 85282, USA | Football Player |
| **Livingstone, Scott L**<br>3504 Sunrise Ranch Road, Southlake TX 76092, USA | Baseball Player |
| **Livio, Mario**<br>Hubble Space Technology Institute, 3700 San Martin Dr, Baltimore MD 21218, USA | Astrophysicist |
| **Livni, Tzipi**<br>Foreign Ministry, 9 Yitzhak Rubin Road, Jerusalem 91035, Israel | Acting Prime Minister, Israel |
| **Livsey, William J**<br>230 Carriage Chase, Fayetteville GA 30214, USA | Army General |
| **Liwienski, Chris**<br>6721 Pointe Lake Lucy, Chanhassen MN 55317, USA | Football Player |
| **Lizer, Kari**<br>Jackoway Tyerman Wertheimer, 1925 Century Park E, #2200, Los Angeles CA 90067 USA | Actress, Producer |
| **Ljungberg, K Fredrik (Freddie)**<br>Seattle Sounders, 12 Seahawks Way, Renton WA 98056 USA | Model, Soccer Player |
| **Ljungberg, Lasse 'Leari'**<br>Live Nation, Linnegatan 89, Box 21451, 104 51 Stockholm, Sweden | Bassist (The Ark) |
| **Ljungqvist, Ida**<br>Playboy Promotions, 9346 Civic Center Dr, #200, Beverly Hills CA 90210 USA | Model |
| **LL Cool J**<br>Alchemy Entertainment, 7024 Melrose Ave, #420, Los Angeles CA 90038 USA | Rap Artist, Actor |
| **Llamosa, Carlos**<br>13803 Via Lido, #300, Newport Beach CA 92663, USA | Soccer Player |
| **Llewellyn, John A**<br>University of South Florida, Chemical & Biomedical Engineering Dept, 4202 E Fowler Ave, Tampa FL 33620, USA | Astronaut |
| **Llewellyn, Robert**<br>United Agents, 12-26 Lexington St, London W1F 0LE, England | Actor, Writer |
| **Llewelyn, Doug**<br>Rebel Entertainment Partners, 5700 Wilshire Blvd, #456, Los Angeles CA 90036, USA | Actor |
| **Llodra, Michael**<br>Lagadere Paris Racing, 5 Rue Eble, 75007 Paris, France | Tennis Player |
| **Llorenna, Kelly**<br>Mission Control, City Business Center, Lower Road, London SE16 2XB, England | Singer |

**L**

**Liu Chunhong - Llorenna**

| | |
|---|---|
| **Lloyd** | Singer, Songwriter |
| Island Records, 925 8th St, New York NY 10019 USA | |
| **Lloyd Webber, Andrew** | Composer |
| Really Useful Group, 19/22 Tower St, London WC2H 9TW, England | |
| **Lloyd Webber, Julian** | Concert Cellist |
| I M G Artists, Burlington Lane, Chiswick, London W4 2TH, England | |
| **Lloyd, Brandon M** | Football Player |
| 5112 NW Downing St, Blue Springs MO 64015, USA | |
| **Lloyd, Carli A** | Soccer Player |
| Western New York Flash, 7070 Seneca St, Elma NY 14059, USA | |
| **Lloyd, Charles** | Jazz Saxophonist, Composer |
| Joel Chriss Co, 300 Mercer St, #3J, New York NY 10003 USA | |
| **Lloyd, Cher** | Singer, Songwriter |
| Syco Music, Bedford House, 69-79 Fulham High St, London SW6 3JW, England | |
| **Lloyd, Clive H** | Cricketer |
| Harefield, Harefield Dr, Wilmslow, Cheshire SK9 1NJ, England | |
| **Lloyd, David A (Dave)** | Football Player |
| 24432 County Road 3107, Gladewater TX 75647, USA | |
| **Lloyd, Earl F** | Basketball Player, Coach |
| 15 Pineridge Court, Crossville TN 38558, USA | |
| **Lloyd, Emily** | Actress |
| Rights House, Drury House, 34-43 Russell St, London WC2B 5HA, England | |
| **Lloyd, Eric** | Actor |
| Osbrink Talent Agency, 4343 Lankershim Blvd, #100, North Hollywood CA 91602 USA | |
| **Lloyd, Geoffrey E R** | Philosopher |
| 2 Prospect Row, Cambridge CB1 1DU, England | |
| **Lloyd, Georgina** | Writer |
| Bantam Books, 1745 Broadway, New York NY 10019 USA | |
| **Lloyd, Graeme J** | Baseball Player |
| 455 Oceanview Ave, Palm Harbor FL 34683, USA | |
| **Lloyd, Gregory L (Greg)** | Football Player |
| 805 Glynn St, #127, Box 305, Fayetteville GA 30214, USA | |
| **Lloyd, Jake** | Actor |
| Osbrink Talent, 4343 Lankershim Blvd, #100, North Hollywood CA 91602, USA | |
| **Lloyd, James** | Keyboardist (Pieces of a Dream) |
| 23309 Commerce Park Road, Cleveland OH 44122, USA | |
| **Lloyd, Lewis K** | Basketball Player |
| 1038 N Pallas St, Philadelphia PA 19104, USA | |
| **Lloyd, Madison** | Actress |
| Osbrink Talent Agency, 4343 Lankershim Blvd, #100, North Hollywood CA 91602 USA | |
| **Lloyd, Norman** | Actor |
| 1813 Old Ranch Road, Los Angeles CA 90049, USA | |
| **Lloyd, Phyllida** | Director |
| Annette Stone Assoc, 97 Mortimer St, London W1W 7SU, England | |
| **Lloyd, Robert A** | Opera Singer |
| 67B Fortis Green, London SE1 9HL, England | |
| **Lloyd, Sabrina** | Actress |
| Don Buchwald Talent Agency, 6500 Wilshire Blvd, #2200, Los Angeles CA 90048 USA | |
| **Lloyd, Sam** | Actor |
| Sloat Entertainment, 27631 Belmonte, Mission Viejo CA 92692, USA | |
| **Lloyd, Scott G** | Basketball Player |
| 6838 Alexander Dr, Dallas TX 75214, USA | |
| **Lloyd, Walt** | Cinematographer |
| 22287 Mulholland Highway, #393, Calabasas CA 91302, USA | |
| **Lloyd-Jones, David M** | Conductor |
| 94 Whitelands House, Cheltenham Terrace, London SW3 4RA, England | |
| **Llull Melia, Sergio** | Basketball Player |
| Valle de Tena 16, 28669 Urbanizaciones Noroeste, Spain | |
| **Lo, Ismael** | Singer, Composer |
| Mad Minute Music, 5-7 Rue Paul Bert, 93400 Saint Ouen, France | |
| **Loach, Kenneth (Ken)** | Director |
| Sixteen Films, 187 Wardour St, #200, London W1F 8ZB, England | |
| **Loach, Lonnie** | Ice Hockey Player |
| 1263 Colby Dr, Saint Peters MO 63376, USA | |
| **Loader, Danyon J** | Swimmer |
| 9 Prince Albert Road, Saint Kilda, Dunedin 9012, New Zealand | |
| **Loaiza Veyna, Esteban A** | Baseball Player |
| 2871 Gate Three Place, Chula Vista CA 91914, USA | |
| **Lobacheva, Irina** | Ice Dancer |
| Skating Federation, Luchnesksaia Nab 8, 119871 Moscow, Russia | |
| **Lobdell, Frank** | Artist |
| 2754 Octavia, San Francisco CA 94123, USA | |
| **Lobel, Anita** | Writer |
| Greenwillow/William Morrow, 1350 Ave of Americas, New York NY 10019, USA | |
| **Lobert, Jonathan** | Yachtsman |
| Sport Nautique de l'Ouest, Port Breton, 444470 Carquefou, France | |
| **LoBianco, Tony** | Actor |
| David Shapira Assoc, 193 N Robertson Blvd, Beverly Hills CA 90211 USA | |
| **Lobkowicz, Nicholas** | Philosopher |
| Am Kirchberg 6, 91804 Mornsheim, Germany | |
| **Lobo** | Singer, Songwriter |
| 14432 Clubhouse Dr, Bokeelia FL 33922, USA | |
| **Lobo Sosa, Porfirio** | President, Honduras |
| Casa Presidencial, Blvd Juan Pablo II, Tegucigalpa MDC, Honduras | |
| **Lobo, Rebecca** | Basketball Player |
| PO Box 734, Granby CT 06035, USA | |
| **Loca, Jean-Louie** | Actor |
| Jean-François Pignard de Marthod, 11 Rue Chanez, 75781 Paris Cedex 16, France | |
| **Locane, Amy** | Actress |
| McCabe Group, 3211 Cahuenga Blvd W, #104, Los Angeles CA 90068, USA | |
| **LoCascio, Luigi** | Actor |
| Media Art Mgmt, BaRbara de Braganza 11, #4 Derecha, 28004 Madrid, Spain | |
| **Loceff, Michael** | Producer |
| Paradigm Agency, 360 N Crescent Dr, North Building, Beverly Hills CA 90210 USA | |
| **Loch, Felix** | Luge Athlete |
| Am Bergheim 1, 83471 Schonau am Konigssee, Germany | |

**Locher, Richard (Dick)** — Editorial Cartoonist
Chicago Tribune, Editorial Dept, 435 N Michigan Ave, #1, Chicago IL 60611, USA
**Lochner, Philip R, Jr** — Government Official, Businessman
Time Warner Inc, 1 Time Warner Center, New York NY 10019, USA
**Lochner, Rudolf (Rudi)** — Bobsled Athlete
Hofreiterstr 15, 83471 Schonau/Konigsee, Germany
**Lochte, Ryan** — Swimmer
2701 NW 23rd Blvd, #FF219, Gainesville FL 32605, USA
**Lock, Donald W (Don)** — Baseball Player
11725 W Alderny Court, #42, Wichita KS 67212, USA
**Lockbaum, Gordon C (Gordie)** — Football Player
35 Brookshire Road, Worcester MA 01609, USA
**Locke, Bruce** — Actor
Vox Inc, 6420 Wilshire Blvd, #1080, Los Angeles CA 90048 USA
**Locke, Charles E (Chuck)** — Baseball Player
1560 Haven Hills Road, Poplar Bluff MO 63901, USA
**Locke, Gary F** — Secretary, Commerce; Governor, WA
Commerce Department, 14th St & Constitution Ave NW, Washington DC 20230 USA
**Locke, Lawrence D (Bobby)** — Baseball Player
194 Eight 80 Acres Road, Dunbar PA 15431, USA
**Locke, Sondra** — Actress, Director
7465 Hillside Ave, Los Angeles CA 90046, USA
**Locke, Spencer** — Actress
A P A Talent & Literary Agency, 405 S Beverly Dr, #300, Beverly Hills CA 90212 USA
**Locker, Jacob C (Jake)** — Football Player
Tennessee Titans, 460 Great Circle Road, Nashville TN 37228 USA
**Locker, Robert A (Bob)** — Baseball Player
1561 Rancho View Road, Lafayette CA 94549, USA
**Lockhart, Anne** — Actress
Linda McAlister Talent, 530 S Lake Ave, #435, Pasadena CA 91101, USA
**Lockhart, Dennis** — Government Official, Financier
Federal Reserve Bank, 1000 Peachtree St NE, Atlanta GA 30309, USA
**Lockhart, Eugene, Jr** — Football Player
2215 High Country Dr, Carrollton TX 75007, USA
**Lockhart, Ian** — Basketball Player
Q25 Calle Excelsa Villas del Cafetal II, Yauco PR 00698, USA
**Lockhart, James** — Conductor
105 Woodcock Hill, Harrow, Middlesex HA3 0JJ, England
**Lockhart, June** — Actress
PO Box 3207, Will Rogers Unit 261, Santa Monica CA 90408, USA
**Lockhart, Keith** — Conductor
Boston Pops Orchestra, Symphony Hall, 301 Massachusetts Ave, Boston MA 02115, USA
**Lockhart, Keith V** — Baseball Player
3330 McKinley Point Dr, Dacula GA 30019, USA
**Lockhart, Paul S** — Astronaut
8605 Cross View, Fairfax Station VA 22039, USA
**Lockhart, Sharon** — Photographer, Filmmaker
Barbara Gladstone Gallery, 515 W 24th St, New York NY 10011, USA
**Lockington, David** — Conductor
C M Artists, 127 W 96th St, #13B, New York NY 10025 USA
**Locklear, Gene** — Baseball Player
1811 Penasco Road, El Cajon CA 92019, USA
**Locklear, Heather** — Actress, Model
Gersh Agency, 9465 Wilshire Blvd, #600, Beverly Hills CA 90212 USA
**Locklear, Samuel J, III** — Navy Admiral
Commander, Pacific Command, 250 Makalapa Dr, Pearl Harbor HI 96860 USA
**Locklear, Sean H** — Football Player
New York Giants, Meadowlands Stadium, 102 Route 120, East Rutherford NJ 07073 USA
**Lockwood, Claude E (Skip), Jr** — Baseball Player
47 John Druce Lane, Wrentham MA 02093, USA
**Lockwood, Gary** — Actor
3083 1/2 Rambla Pacifica, Malibu CA 90265, USA
**Locorriere, Dennis** — Singer, Guitarist (Dr Hook)
John Taylor Mgmt, PO Box 272, London N2O O2Y, England
**Loder, Kevin** — Basketball Player
505 W 4th St, Mishawaka IN 46544, USA
**Lodge, David J** — Writer
University of Birmingham, English Dept, Birmingham B15 2TT, England
**Lodge, Roger** — Entertainer
Paradigm Agency, 360 N Crescent Dr, North Building, Beverly Hills CA 90210 USA
**Lodish, Harvey F** — Biologist
195 Fisher Ave, Brookline MA 02445, USA
**Lodish, Michael T (Mike)** — Football Player
171 E Lincoln St, Birmingham MI 48009, USA
**LoDuca, Joseph** — Composer
1117 Isabel St, Burbank CA 91506, USA
**LoDuca, Paul** — Baseball Player
3227 Medaris Lane, San Antonio TX 78258, USA
**Lodwick, Todd** — Nordic Combined Skier
Winter Sports Club, 845 Howelsen Hill Parkway, Steamboat Springs CO 84077, USA
**Loe, Harald A** — Dentist
National Dental Research Institute, 9000 Rockville Pike, Bethesda MD 20892, USA
**Loe, Kameron D** — Baseball Player
2323 N Houston St, #312, Dallas TX 75219, USA
**Loeb, Abraham (Avi)** — Theoretical Physicist
Harvard University, Theory & Computation Institute, Cambridge MA 02138, USA
**Loeb, Allan** — Writer
Scarlet Fire Entertainment, 561 28th Ave, Venice CA 90291, USA
**Loeb, Caroline** — Actress
A A C Agence Artistique, 10 Ave George V, 75009 Paris, France
**Loeb, Damian** — Artist
49 Lispenard St, New York NY 10013, USA
**Loeb, Jerome T** — Businessman
May Department Stores, 611 Olive St, #2076, Saint Louis MO 63101, USA
**Loeb, John L, Jr** — Diplomat, Financier
John L Loeb Jr Assoc, 50 Broad St, #1137, New York NY 10004, USA

**Loeb, Lisa** — Singer, Songwriter, Actress
Atlas Talent Agency, 15 E 32nd St, #600, New York NY 10016, USA

**Loeb, Marshall R** — Editor, Writer, Columnist
41 E 72nd St, New York NY 10021, USA

**Loeb, Sebastien** — Auto Racing Driver
I S C, 6 Saint Catherine's Mews, Milner St, London SW3 2PX, England

**Loeffler, Pete** — Singer, Guitarist (Chevelle)
In De Goot Entertainment, 119 W 23rd St, #609, New York NY 10011, USA

**Loeffler, Sam** — Drummer (Chevelle)
In De Goot Entertainment, 119 W 23rd St, #609, New York NY 10011, USA

**Loeillet, Sylvie** — Actress
Agence Laurence Bagoe, 11 Rue Delambre, 75014 Paris, France

**Loengard, John** — Photographer
20 W 86th St, New York NY 10024, USA

**Loescher, Peter** — Businessman
Siemens AG, Wittelsbacherplatz 2, 80333 Munich, Germany

**Loewen, Darcy** — Ice Hockey Player
11605 Cabo Del Verde Ave, Las Vegas NV 89138, USA

**Loewen, James W** — Historian
Catholic University, History Dept, Washington DC 20064, USA

**Loewer, Carlton E** — Baseball Player
PO Box 3590, Alpine WY 83128, USA

**Loffler, Horst** — Swimmer
Hugo-Bartsch-Str 44, 72459 Albstadt, Germany

**Lofgren, Esther** — Rowing Athlete
715 S Washington St, #C36, Alexandria VA 22314, USA

**Lofgren, Nils** — Singer, Guitarist, Songwriter
7422 E Berridge Lane, Scottsdale AZ 85250, USA

**Loftin, R Bowen** — Educator
Texas A&M University, President's Office, College Station TX 77843, USA

**Lofton, Curtis T** — Football Player
New Orleans Saints, 5800 Airline Highway, Metairie LA 70003 USA

**Lofton, Fred C** — Religious Leader
Progressive National Baptist Convention, 601 50th St NE, Washington DC 20019, USA

**Lofton, James** — Baseball Player
14103 Cerise Ave, #18, Hawthorne CA 90250, USA

**Lofton, James D** — Football Player
13177 Via Mesa Dr, San Diego CA 92129, USA

**Lofton, Kenneth (Kenny)** — Baseball Player
PO Box 68473, Tucson AZ 85737, USA

**Loftus, Aisling** — Actress
W M E Entertainment, 1325 Ave of Americas, New York NY 10019 USA

**Lofven, K Stefan** — Prime Minister, Sweden
Prime Minister's Office, Rosenbad 4, 103 33 Stockholm, Sweden

**Logan, David R** — Football Player
5875 S Dry Creek Court, Greenwood Village CO 80121, USA

**Logan, Eleanor (Elle)** — Rowing Athlete
261 Samoset Road, Boothbay Harbor ME 04538, USA

**Logan, Ernest E (Ernie)** — Football Player
609 Francis Court, Spring Lake NC 28390, USA

**Logan, Exavier (Nook)** — Baseball Player
19410 Creek Bend Dr, Spring TX 77388, USA

**Logan, Jack** — Singer
W M E Entertainment, 1325 Ave of Americas, New York NY 10019 USA

**Logan, James K** — Judge
US Court of Appeals, PO Box 790, 1 Patrons Plaza, Olathe KS 66061, USA

**Logan, Jerry D** — Football Player
1624 Hillcrest Dr, Graham TX 76450, USA

**Logan, John** — Writer, Producer
Creative Artists Agency, 2000 Ave of Stars, #100, Los Angeles CA 90067 USA

**Logan, Johnny** — Singer
Telamo Music, Lucile-Grahn-Str 41, 81675 Munich, Germany

**Logan, Lara** — Commentator
CBS-TV, News Dept, 51 W 52nd St, New York NY 10019 USA

**Logan, Marc A** — Football Player
2501 Glascow Lane, Lexington KY 40511, USA

**Logan, Melissa** — Singer (Chicks in Speed)
K Records, 924 Jefferson St SE, #101, Olympia WA 98501, USA

**Logan, Phyllis** — Actress
47 Courtfield Road, #9, London SW7 4DB, England

**Logan, Randolph (Randy)** — Football Player
330 W Fornance St, Norristown PA 19401, USA

**Logan, Samuel, Jr** — Religious Leader
World Reformed Fellowship, 430 Montier Road, Glenside PA 19038, USA

**Logano, Joseph T (Joey)** — Auto Racing Driver
Joe Gibbs Racing, 13415 Reese Blvd W, Huntersville NC 28078, USA

**Loges, Stephan** — Opera Singer
Hazard Chase, 72 Charlotte St, London W1T 4QQ, England

**Logevall, Fredrik** — Historian
Cornell University, Einaudi International Studies Center, Ithaca NY 14853, USA

**Logg, Charles P, Jr** — Rowing Athlete
3634 Shady Oak Trail, Gainesville GA 30506, USA

**Loggia, Robert** — Actor
3770 Highland Ave, #201, Manhattan Beach CA 90266, USA

**Logue, Antonia** — Writer
Bloomsbury Publishing, 50 Bedford Square, London WC1B 3DP, England

**Logue, Donal** — Actor
Kipperman Mgmt, 420 W End Ave, #1G, New York NY 10024 USA

**Logunov, Anatoly A** — Physicist
High Energy Research Center, 142281 Protvino, Moscow Region, Russia

**Loh, John M (Mike)** — Air Force General
125 Captain Graves, Williamsburg VA 23185, USA

**Loh, Sandra Tsing** — Entertainer, Writer, Activist
Crown Publishing Group, 1745 Broadway, #1300, New York NY 10019 USA

**Loh, Wallace D** — Educator
University of Maryland, President's Office, College Park MD 20742, USA

**Lohan, Aliana D (Ali)** — Singer
Baker Winokur Ryder Public Relations, 9100 Wilshire Blvd, #500W, Beverly Hills CA 90212 USA
**Lohan, Lindsay** — Actress, Singer, Model
Untitled Entertainment, 350 S Beverly Dr, #200, Beverly Hills CA 90212 USA
**Lohan, Sinead** — Singer, Songwriter
Pat Egan Sound, Merchant's Court, 24 Merchant's Quay, Dublin 8, Ireland
**Lohaus, Brad A** — Basketball Player
55 Tartan Dr, North Liberty IA 52317, USA
**Lohfink, Gina Lisa** — Model
Alex Sinner Artist Mgmt, Postach 1247, 64319 Pfungstadt, Germany
**Lohman, Alison** — Actress
Principato-Young, 9465 Wilshire Blvd, #880, Beverly Hills CA 90212 USA
**Lohmiller, John M (Chip)** — Football Player
PO Box 810, Crosslake MN 56442, USA
**Lohr, Bob** — Golfer
8225 Breeze Cove Lane, Orlando FL 32819, USA
**Lohse, Kyle M** — Baseball Player
8613 E Artisan Pass, Scottsdale AZ 85266, USA
**Loiola, Jose G** — Volleyball Player
1141 2nd St, Manhattan Beach CA 90266, USA
**Loiret, Anne** — Actress
Agence Artiste Adequat, 108 Rue Reaumur, 75002 Paris, France
**Loiseau, Sebastien** — Actor
Cineart, 28 Rue Mogador, 78009 Paris, France
**Loiselle, Claude** — Ice Hockey Player
3 Warren St, Hudson Falls NY 12839, USA
**Loiselle, Richard F (Rich)** — Baseball Player
560 Timber Dr, Harvard IL 60033, USA
**Loke, Heidi** — Handball Player
Gyori Audi E T O, Kiskutliget Magvassy Mihaly Sportcsarnok, 9027 Gyor, Hungary
**Loken, James B** — Judge
US Court of Appeals, 300 S 4th St, Minneapolis MN 55415, USA
**Loken, Kristanna** — Actress, Model
Levity Entertainment Group, 6701 Center Drive W, #1111, Los Angeles CA 90045, USA
**Lolene** — Singer, Songwriter
Red Light Mgmt, 44 Wall St, #2200, New York NY 10005, USA
**Lolich, Michael S (Mickey)** — Baseball Player
6252 Robin Hill, Washington MI 48094, USA
**Lollobrigida, Gina** — Actress
Via Appia Antica 223, 00179 Rome, Italy
**Lomas, Barbara Joyce** — Singer (BT Express)
Star-Vest Mgmt, 102 Ryders Lane, East Brunswick NJ 08816, USA
**Lomas, Mark A** — Football Player
PO Box 17781, Irvine CA 92623, USA
**Lomax, Michael** — Foundation Executive, Educator
United Negro Fund, 500 E 62nd St, New York NY 10065, USA
**Lomax, Neil V** — Football Player
5855 SW Blackberry Lane, Tualatin OR 97062, USA
**Lomax, Noah** — Actor
Amsel Eisenstadt Frazier, 5055 Wilshire Blvd, #865, Los Angeles CA 90036 USA
**Lombard, George P** — Baseball Player
2275 Rhinehill Road NE, Atlanta GA 30315, USA
**Lombard, Karina** — Actress, Model
Cineart, 28 Rue Mogador, 78009 Paris, France
**Lombard, Louise** — Actress
Paradigm Agency, 360 N Crescent Dr, North Building, Beverly Hills CA 90210 USA
**Lombardi, Louis** — Actor, Director, Writer
Stone Manners Salners, 6100 Wilshire Blvd, #1500, Los Angeles CA 90035 USA
**Lombardi, Michael (Mike)** — Actor
Paul Kohner, 9300 Wilshire Blvd, #555, Beverly Hills CA 90212 USA
**Lombardi, Pietro** — Singer
Xtrasystem, Durener Str 221, 50931 Cologne, Germany
**Lombardozzi, Domenick** — Actor
Gersh Agency, 9465 Wilshire Blvd, #600, Beverly Hills CA 90212 USA
**Lombardozzi, Stephen P (Steve), Sr** — Baseball Player
12404 Hall Shop Road, Fulton MD 20759, USA
**Lombreglio, Ralph** — Writer
Doubleday Press, 1540 Broadway, New York NY 10036, USA
**Lomonaco, Michael** — Restauranteur, Chef
Porter House, Time Warner Center, 10 Columbus Circle, #400, New York NY 10019, USA
**Lomotey, Lofi** — Educator
Southern University, Chancellor's Office, Baton Rouge LA 70813, USA
**Lonard, Peter** — Golfer
Links Sports, PO Box 6111, Lake Munmorah NSW 2259, Australia
**Lonborg, James R (Jim)** — Baseball Player
498 First Parish Road, Scituate MA 02066, USA
**Loncar, Amanda** — Actress
Gersh Agency, 9465 Wilshire Blvd, #600, Beverly Hills CA 90212 USA
**Lonchakov, Yuri V** — Cosmonaut
Cosmonaut Training Center, Star City, 141160 Zvezdny Gorodok, Moscow Oblast, Russia
**London, Alexandra** — Actress
Artmedia, 20 Ave Rapp, 75007 Paris, France
**London, Antonio M** — Football Player
404 SW Atlantic St, Tullahoma TN 37388, USA
**London, Daniel** — Actor
Paradigm Agency, 360 N Crescent Dr, North Building, Beverly Hills CA 90210 USA
**London, Irving M** — Physician
Harvard-M I T Health Sciences, 77 Massachusetts Ave, Cambridge MA 02139, USA
**London, Jeremy** — Actor
Media Artists Group, 8222 Melrose Ave, #203, Los Angeles CA 90048 USA
**London, Jonathan** — Writer
Chronicle Books, 680 2nd St, San Francisco CA 94107 USA
**London, Lauren** — Actress
John Carrabino Mgmt, 5900 Wilshire Blvd, #406, Los Angeles CA 90036 USA
**London, Lisa** — Actress, Model
Brooke Dunn Oliver, 9169 W Sunset Blvd, #202, West Hollywood CA 90069 USA

**London, Rick** — Cartoonist
Artistic Licensing Agency, 126 Oriole St, #516, Hot Springs AR 71901, USA

**Lone, John** — Actor
Sussman Assoc, 1222 16th Ave S, #300, Nashville TN 37212, USA

**Lonergan, Kenneth** — Director, Writer, Actor
Creative Artists Agency, 2000 Ave of Stars, #100, Los Angeles CA 90067 USA

**Loney, James A** — Baseball Player
4926 Birdsong Lane, Missouri City TX 77459, USA

**Loney, Troy** — Ice Hockey Player
4245 Glasgow Road, Valencia PA 16059, USA

**Long, Anthony A** — Educator
1088 Telvin St, Albany CA 94706, USA

**Long, Barry** — Ice Hockey Player
San Jose Sharks, San Jose Arena, 525 W Santa Clara St, San Jose CA 95113 USA

**Long, Charles F (Chuck), II** — Football Player, Coach
2504 Walnut Road, Norman OK 73072, USA

**Long, Dallas** — Track Athlete
PO Box 355, Whitefish MT 59937, USA

**Long, David F (Dave)** — Football Player
177 E Kaibab Way, Cochise AZ 85606, USA

**Long, Grant A** — Basketball Player
8501 Morton Taylor Road, Belleville MI 48111, USA

**Long, Howie** — Football Player, Sportscaster, Actor
I C M Partners, 10250 Constellation Blvd, #900, Los Angeles CA 90067 USA

**Long, Jodi** — Actress
Innovative Artists, 1505 10th St, Santa Monica CA 90401 USA

**Long, John E (Johnny)** — Basketball Player
11976 Hunt St, Romulus MI 48174, USA

**Long, Justin** — Actor
I C M Partners, 10250 Constellation Blvd, #900, Los Angeles CA 90067 USA

**Long, Kathy** — Actress
Cavaleri Assoc, 3500 W Olive Ave, #300, Burbank CA 91505, USA

**Long, Matthew (Matt)** — Actor
United Talent Agency, U T A Plaza, 9336 Civic Center Dr, Beverly Hills CA 90210 USA

**Long, Melvin (Mel), Sr** — Football Player
837 Imani Circle, Toledo OH 43604, USA

**Long, Nia** — Actress
Global Artists Agency, 6253 Hollywood Blvd, #508, Los Angeles CA 90028 USA

**Long, Robert A J (Bob)** — Football Player
3695 Stonebrook Court, Brookfield WI 53005, USA

**Long, Robert E (Bob)** — Baseball Player
3648 Willow Lake Circle, Chattanooga TN 37419, USA

**Long, Robert M** — Businessman
Longs Drug Stores, 1 C V S Dr, Woonsocket RI 02895, USA

**Long, Robert W (Bob)** — Football Player
1413 W Via de la Gloria, Green Valley AZ 85622, USA

**Long, Shelley** — Actress, Comedienne
Stone Manners Salners, 6100 Wilshire Blvd, #1500, Los Angeles CA 90035 USA

**Long, Terrence D** — Baseball Player
4208 Abrams Dr, Millbrook AL 36054, USA

**Long, William Ivey** — Costume Designer
I C M Partners, 730 5th Ave, New York NY 10019 USA

**Longet, Claudine** — Actress
Ronald D Austin, 6000 E Hopkins, Aspen CO 81611, USA

**Longley, Lucien J (Luc)** — Basketball Player
500 Marquette Ave NW, #400, Albuquerque NM 87102, USA

**Longo, Jeannie Ciprelli-** — Cyclist
Federation de Cyclisme, 5 Rue de Rome, 93561 Rosny-sous-Bois, France

**Longo, Lenny** — Singer (Box Tops)
Texas Sounds, PO Box 1644, Dickinson TX 77539, USA

**Longo, Robert** — Artist, Sculptor
Longo Studio, 224 Center St, New York NY 10013, USA

**Longo, Tony** — Actor
310 Tahiti Way, #209, Marina del Rey CA 90292, USA

**Longoria, Eva** — Actress, Model, Producer
UnbeliEVAble Entertainment, 7095 Hollywood Blvd, #797, Hollywood CA 90028, USA

**Longoria, Evan M** — Baseball Player
1211 E Cumberland Ave, #1403, Tampa FL 33602, USA

**Longwell, Ryan W** — Football Player
9748 Green Island Cove, Windermere FL 34786, USA

**Lonich, Yogi** — Guitarist (Buckcherry)
10th Street Mgmt, 700 N San Vicente Blvd, #G410, West Hollywood CA 90069, USA

**Lonnett, Joseph D (Joe)** — Baseball Player
126 Duncan Circle, Beaver PA 15009, USA

**Lonow, Claudia** — Actress, Comedienne, Producer
W M E Entertainment, 9601 Wilshire Blvd, #300, Beverly Hills CA 90210 USA

**Lonsdale, Gordon C** — Cinematographer
4513 W 10600 N, Highland UT 84003, USA

**Lonsdale, Michael** — Actor
Agence Aartis, 13 Rue de L'Epee de Bois, 75005 Paris, France

**Loob, P Hakan** — Ice Hockey Player
Farjestads BK, Box 318, 65108 Karlstad, Sweden

**Loof, M E Fredrik** — Yachtsman
K S S S, Royal Swedish Yacht Club, Hotellvagen 9, 133 35 Saltsjobaden, Sweden

**Look, Dean Z** — Baseball, Football Player
80 Victorian Hills Dr, Okemos MI 48864, USA

**Looker, Dane A** — Football Player
7213 41st Avenue Court E, Tacoma WA 98443, USA

**Lookinland, Mike** — Actor
PO Box 9968, Salt Lake City UT 84109, USA

**Lookstein, Haskel** — Religious Leader, Rabbi
Congregation Kehilath Jeshurun, Ramaz School, 60 E 78th St, New York NY 10075, USA

**Loomer, Lisa** — Writer
Abrams Artists, 9200 W Sunset Blvd, #1125, West Hollywood CA 90069 USA

**Loomis, Rick** — Journalist
Los Angeles Times, Editorial Dept, 202 W 1st St, Los Angeles CA 90012 USA

**Looney, Brian J** — Baseball Player
188 Romulus Road, Cheshire CT 06410, USA

**Looney, Shelley** — Ice Hockey Player
31 Beaman Lane, North Falmouth MA 02556, USA

**Looney, William R, III** — Air Force General
Trident University, 5757 Plaza Drive, #100, Cypress CA 22182, USA

**Looper, Braden L** — Baseball Player
16253 Wynncrest Ridge Court, Chesterfield MO 63005, USA

**Loose, Michael K** — Navy Admiral
Deputy CNO, Fleet Readiness & Logistics, HqUSN, Pentagon, Washington DC 20350 USA

**Lopardo, Frank** — Opera Singer
7 Suzanne B Court, Massapequa NY 11758, USA

**Lopata, Stanley E (Stan)** — Baseball Player
2239 Leisure World, Mesa AZ 85206, USA

**Loper, Daniel R** — Football Player
1115 Stillwater Trail, Hendersonville TN 37075, USA

**Lopert, Tanya** — Actress
Cineart, 28 Rue Mogador, 78000 Paris, France

**Lopes, David E (Davey)** — Baseball Player, Manager
309 San Elijo St, San Diego CA 92106, USA

**Lopes, Leila** — Beauty Queen
Miss Universe Organization, 1370 Ave of Americas, #1600, New York NY 10019 USA

**Lopez de Ayala, Pilar** — Actress
Media Art Mgmt, BaRbara de Braganza 11, #4 Derecha, 28004 Madrid, Spain

**Lopez Lujan, Leonardo** — Archaeologist
Museo del Templo Mayor, 8 Seminario Ave, Mexico City DF 06060, Mexico

**Lopez Molist, Raul** — Basketball Player
Bilbao Basket, Zona C/ Henao, 17 48009 Bilbao, Spain

**Lopez Rodriguez, Nicolas de J Cardinal** — Religious Leader
Archdiocese of Santo Domingo, Calle Isabel la Catolica 55, #186, Santo Domingo, Dominican Republic

**Lopez, Albert A (Albie)** — Baseball Player
2887 E Palo Verde Court, Gilbert AZ 85296, USA

**Lopez, Barry H** — Writer
PO Box 389, Blue River OR 97413, USA

**Lopez, Brook R** — Basketball Player
Brooklyn Nets, 15 Metro Tech Center, #1100, Brooklyn NY 11201 USA

**Lopez, Danny (Little Red)** — Boxer
16531 Aquamarine Court, Chino Hills CA 91709, USA

**Lopez, Felipe** — Baseball Player
2414 Hassonite St, Kissimmee FL 34744, USA

**Lopez, George** — Actor, Comedian
Creative Artists Agency, 2000 Ave of Stars, #100, Los Angeles CA 90067 USA

**Lopez, Gerry** — Surfer, Executive
PO Box 1202, Bend OR 97709, USA

**Lopez, Javier A** — Baseball Player
4824 Quaker Lane, Golden CO 80403, USA

**Lopez, Jennifer** — Actress, Singer, Model
Nuyorican Productions, 1100 Glendon Ave, #920, Los Angeles CA 90024, USA

**Lopez, Juan Manuel** — Boxer
P R Best Promotions, Cond Santa Juanita L58, Bayamon PR 00956, USA

**Lopez, Lourdes** — Ballerina, Ballet Executive
Miami City Ballet, Roca Center, 2200 Liberty Ave, Miami Beach FL 33139, USA

**Lopez, Luis S** — Baseball Player
1701 Pleasant Run Road, Carrollton TX 75006, USA

**Lopez, Mario** — Actor, Producer
3 Arts Entertainment, 9460 Wilshire Blvd, #700, Beverly Hills CA 90212 USA

**Lopez, Mickey** — Baseball Player
17430 SW 117th Ave, Miami FL 33177, USA

**Lopez, Nancy** — Golfer
2308 Tara Dr, Albany GA 31721, USA

**Lopez, Nano** — Sculptor
96 Frontage Road, Walla Walla WA 99362, USA

**Lopez, Oscar** — Guitar Player
Agency Group Ltd, 1880 Century Park E, #711, Los Angeles CA 90067 USA

**Lopez, Priscilla** — Actress
Stone Manners Salners, 6100 Wilshire Blvd, #1500, Los Angeles CA 90035 USA

**Lopez, Robert S** — Historian
41 Richmond Ave, New Haven CT 06515, USA

**Lopez, Robin B** — Basketball Player
Portland Trail Blazers, Rose Garden, 1 N Center Court St, Portland OR 97227 USA

**Lopez, Sal** — Actor
DePaz Mgmt, 2011 N Vermont Ave, Los Angeles CA 90027, USA

**Lopez, Sandra** — Opera Singer
Columbia Artists Mgmt Inc, 5 Columbus Circle, 1790 Broadway, #1600, New York NY 10019 USA

**Lopez, Sergi** — Actor
Artmedia, 20 Ave Rapp, 75007 Paris, France

**Lopez, Steve** — Writer
G P Putnam's Sons, 375 Hudson St, New York NY 10014 USA

**Lopez, Steven** — Taekwondo Athlete
Elite Taekwondo Center, 9707 S Highway 6, Sugar Land TX 77498, USA

**Lopez, T Joseph** — Navy Admiral
C N A Solutions, 3003 Washington Blvd, Arlington VA 22201, USA

**Lopez, Tim G** — Bassist (Plain White T's)
One Moment Mgmt, PO Box 55156, Sherman Oaks CA 91413 USA

**Lopez, Tony (Tiger)** — Boxer
3221 Sweet Maple Way, Sacramento CA 95833, USA

**Lopez, Trini** — Singer, Actor, Orchestra Leader
1139 Abrigo Road, Palm Springs CA 92262, USA

**Lopez-Alegria, Michael E** — Astronaut
1919 Tangle Press Court, Houston TX 77062, USA

**Lopez-Cobos, Jesus** — Conductor
8 Chemin de Bellerive, 1007 Lausanne, Switzerland

**Lopez-Gallego, Gonzalo** — Director
I C M Partners, 10250 Constellation Blvd, #900, Los Angeles CA 90067 USA

**Lopez-Garcia, Antonio** — Artist
Galeria Marlborough, Orfila 5, 28010 Madrid, Spain

# L

**Loquasto, Santo** — Lighting, Costume Designer
Paradigm Agency, 360 N Crescent Dr, North Building, Beverly Hills CA 90210 USA
**Lorain, Sophie** — Actress, Producer, Director
Maxine Vanasse Agency, 1009, Ave Laurier Ouest, Outremont QC H2V 2L1, Canada
**Lorca, Daniel** — Bassist (Nada Surf)
M-Square Mgmt, 201 W 72nd St, #12G, New York NY 10023, USA
**Lorch, George A** — Businessman
Armstrong World, 313 W Liberty St, Lancaster PA 17603, USA
**Lorch, Karl P, Jr** — Football Player
92-861 Palailai St, Kapolei HI 96707, USA
**Lorcy, Julian** — Boxer
BoBoxe, 68 Blvd Henri Barbusse, 78800 Houilles, France
**Lord, Albert L** — Businessman
S L M Corp, 12061 Bluemont Dr, Reston VA 20190, USA
**Lord, M G** — Editorial Cartoonist
Janklow & Nesbit Assoc, 445 Park Ave, #1300, New York NY 10022 USA
**Lord, Marjorie** — Actress
1110 Maytor Place, Beverly Hills CA 90210, USA
**Lord, Mary Lou** — Singer, Guitarist
Combat Jack Mgmt, 110-120 Brookline St, Cambridge MA 02139, USA
**Lord, Peter** — Animator, Director
Aardman Animations, Gas Ferry Road, Bristol BS1 6UN, England
**Lord, Winston** — Diplomat
740 Park Ave, New York NY 10021, USA
**Lorde** — Singer, Songwriter
Emma Banks, 3 Shortlands, #500, London W6 8DA, England
**Lordi, Mr** — Singer (Lordi)
Le Kepi Rouge, PL 285, 02601 Espoo, Finland
**Lordkipanidze, David O** — Anthropologist, Archaeologist
Georgian National Museum, 11 Shota Rustaveli Ave, 0108 Tbilisi, Georgia
**Loreen** — Singer
Mr Radar Music Group, Kungsgatan 5, #500, 111 43 Stockholm, Sweden
**Loren, Josie** — Actress
Ellen Meyer Mgmt, 8899 Beverly Blvd, #612, West Hollywood CA 90048, USA
**Loren, Natalie** — DJ Musician, Model
Leni's Model Mgmt, 55E Hatton Garden, London EC1N 8HP, England
**Loren, Sophia** — Actress
Casa Postale 430, 1211 Geneva 12, Switzerland
**Lorensson, Jalle** — Harmonica Player (Wilmer X)
United Stage Artists, Asogatan 142, Box 11029, 100 61 Stockholm, Sweden
**Lorentz, Jim** — Ice Hockey Player
2555 Staley Road, Grand Island NY 14072, USA
**Lorenz, Christian (Flake)** — Keyboardist (Rammstein)
Pilgrim Mgmt, PO Box 540101, 10042 Berlin, Germany
**Lorenz, Ericka** — Water Polo Player
2604 Fulton St, Berkeley CA 94704, USA
**Lorenz, Lee** — Cartoonist
PO Box 131, Easton CT 06612, USA
**Lorenzen, Fred** — Auto Racing Driver
64 E Elm St, #4, Chicago IL 60611, USA
**Lorenzo, Blas** — Actor
PO Box 2127, Los Angeles CA 90078, USA
**Lorenzoni, Andrea** — Astronaut, Italy
Via B Vergine del Carmelo 168, 00144 Rome, Italy
**Loretta, Mark D** — Baseball Player
7844 Sendora Angelica, San Diego CA 92127, USA
**Loria, Christopher J (Gus)** — Astronaut
102 Sea Mist Dr, League City TX 77573, USA
**Lorick, W Anthony (Tony)** — Football Player
349 Burney Lane, Kerrville TX 78028, USA
**Lorimer, Bob** — Ice Hockey Player
24 Cranberry Lane, Aurora ON L4G 5Y3, Canada
**Lorincz, Tamas** — Greco-Roman Wrestler
Kinizsi Uca 20, 2700 Cegled, Hungary
**Loring, Gloria** — Singer, Songwriter, Actress
R M C Mgmt, PO Box 1308, Pacific Palisades CA 90272, USA
**Loring, John R** — Artist
621 Avon Road, West Palm Beach FL 33401, USA
**Loring, Lynn** — Actress, Producer
Lynn Loring Assoc, 2313 Canyonback Road, Los Angeles CA 90049, USA
**Lorius, Claude** — Glaciologist
Glaciologies Laboratoire, Rue Moliere, 38402 Saint-Martin d'Heres, France
**Lorraine, Andrew J** — Baseball Player
14609 N 103rd Way, Scottsdale AZ 85255, USA
**Lorre, Chuck** — Producer
I C M Partners, 10250 Constellation Blvd, #900, Los Angeles CA 90067 USA
**Lortie, Louis** — Concert Pianist
Seldy Cramer Artists, 3436 Springhill Road, Lafayette CA 94549, USA
**Lortkipanidze, Vazha G** — Minister of State, Georgia
Government House, Ingorokva 7, 380034 Tbilisi, Georgia
**Losada, Isabel** — Writer
Curtis Brown Group, 28-29 Haymarket St, #500, London SW1Y 4SP, England
**LoSchiavo, Francesca** — Set Decorator
Via delle Querce 51, 47842 San Giovanni in Marignano, Italy
**Loscutoff, James (Jim)** — Basketball Player, Coach
166 Jenkins Road, Andover MA 01810, USA
**Losert, Venio** — Handball Player
K S Vive Targi Kielce, Ul Robotnicza 5, 25662 Kielce, Croatia
**Losick, Richard M** — Molecular Biologist
Harvard Medical School, 25 Shattuck St, Boston MA 02115, USA
**Losier, Michele** — Opera Singer
I M G Artists, Hogarth Business Park, Chiswick, London W4 2TH, England
**Losman, Jonathan P (J P)** — Football Player
70 Oakland Place, Buffalo NY 14222, USA
**Loss, Harold** — Religious Leader, Rabbi
Temple Israel, 5725 Walnut Lake Road, West Bloomfield MI 48323, USA

**Loquasto - Loss**

| | |
|---|---|
| **Lotan, Jonah** Gersh Agency, 9465 Wilshire Blvd, #600, Beverly Hills CA 90212 USA | Actor |
| **Lothamer, Edward D (Ed)** 14545 W 183rd St, Olathe KS 66062, USA | Football Player |
| **LoTruglio, Joe** United Talent Agency, U T A Plaza, 9336 Civic Center Dr, Beverly Hills CA 90210 USA | Actor |
| **Lott, Felicity A** Augstein & Hahn, Tal 28, 80331 Munich, Germany | Opera Singer |
| **Lott, Ronald M (Ronnie)** 2965 Woodside Road, Woodside CA 94062, USA | Football Player, Sportscaster |
| **Lotti, Helmut** Bevrijdinstraat 39, 2300 Turnhout, Belgium | Singer, Songwriter |
| **Lotton, Gerald** Lotton Glass, 24760 Country Lane, Crete IL 60417, USA | Artist |
| **Lotz, Anne Graham** AnGeL Ministries, 515 Hollyridge Dr, Raleigh NC 27612, USA | Religious Leader |
| **Lotz, Dick** 2058 Riesling Way, Shingle Springs CA 95682, USA | Golfer |
| **Lotz, Sarah** Little, Brown & Company, 237 Park Ave, New York NY 10017, USA | Writer |
| **Louboutin, Christian** 19 Rue Jean-Jacques Rousseau, 75001 Paris, France | Footwear Designer |
| **Loucks, Scott G** 1801 Viola Dr, Sierra Vista AZ 85635, USA | Baseball Player |
| **Loucks, Vernon R, Jr** Baxter Healthcare Corp, 1450 Waukegan Road, Waukegan IL 60085, USA | Businessman |
| **Louderback, Thomas F (Tom)** 15 Leopard Road, #1G, Berwyn PA 19312, USA | Football Player |
| **Loudon, Aarnout A** Rembrandt Kaan 16, 6881 Velp CS, Netherlands | Businessman |
| **Loudon, Rodney** 3 Gaston St, East Bergholt, Colchester, Essex CO7 6SD, England | Theoretical Physicist |
| **Loueke, Lionel** Blue Note Records, 6920 W Sunset Blvd, Los Angeles CA 90028 USA | Jazz Guitarist |
| **Louganis, Gregory E (Greg)** Premier Management Group, 115 Crescent Commons, #250, Cary, NC 27518 USA | Diver |
| **Loughery, Kevin M (Murph)** 4474 Club Dr NE, Atlanta GA 30319, USA | Basketball Player, Coach, Executive |
| **Loughlin, Lori** United Talent Agency, U T A Plaza, 9336 Civic Center Dr, Beverly Hills CA 90210 USA | Actress, Singer |
| **Loughlin, Mary Anne** WTBS-TV, News Dept, 1050 Techwood Dr NW, Atlanta GA 30318, USA | Commentator |
| **Loughnane, Lee David** Front Line Mgmt, 1100 Glendon Ave, #2000, Los Angeles CA 90024 USA | Trumpeter (Chicago), Songwriter |
| **Loughran, James** 34 Cleveden Dr, Glasgow G12 0RX, Scotland | Conductor |
| **Louis C K** 3 Arts Entertainment, 9460 Wilshire Blvd, #700, Beverly Hills CA 90212 USA | Director, Producer, Writer, Actor |
| **Louis, Justin** Lucas Talent, 1238 Homer St, #6, Vancouver BC V6B 2Y5, Canada | Actor |
| **Louis, Murray** Nikolais/Louis Foundation, 375 W Broadway, New York NY 10012, USA | Dancer, Choreographer |
| **Louisa, Maria** Next Model Mgmt, 23 Watts St, New York NY 10013 USA | Model |
| **Louisa-Godett, Mima** Premier's Office, Fort Amsterdam 17, Willemstad, Netherlands Antilles | Premier, Netherlands Antilles |
| **Louis-Dreyfus, Julia** Creative Artists Agency, 2000 Ave of Stars, #100, Los Angeles CA 90067 USA | Actress, Comedienne |
| **Louise, Tina** 310 E 46th St, #24G, New York NY 10017, USA | Actress, Singer |
| **Louiso, Todd** Anonymous Content, 3532 Hayden Ave, Culver City CA 90232 USA | Actor, Director, Writer |
| **Louisy, C Pearlette** Governor General's Office, Government House, Box 216, Morne Fortune, Castries, Saint Lucia | Governor General, Saint Lucia |
| **Loukos, Yorgos** Lyon Opera Ballet, Place de la Comédie, 69001 Lyon, France | Ballet Executive |
| **Louloudis, Constantine M** Leander Rowing Club, Henle-on-Thames, Oxfordshire RG9 2LP, England | Rowing Athlete |
| **Loun, Donald N (Don)** 9095 Wexford Dr, Vienna VA 22182, USA | Baseball Player |
| **Lourie, Alan D** US Court of Appeals, 717 Madison Place NW, Washington DC 20439, USA | Judge |
| **Louris, Gary** Sussman Assoc, 1222 16th Ave S, #300, Nashville TN 37212, USA | Singer, Songwriter (Jayhawks) |
| **Lousma, Jack R** 310 Twin Springs Road N, Kerrville TX 78028, USA | Astronaut |
| **Loutfi, Ali Mahmoud** 29 Ahmed Heshmat St, Zamalek, Cairo, Egypt | Prime Minister, Egypt |
| **Louvier, Alain** 53 Ave Victor Hugo, 92100 Boulogne-Billancourt, France | Composer |
| **Louwerse, Mirusia** PO Box 3169, Birkdale QLD 4159, Australia | Opera, Concert Singer |
| **Loux, Shane A** 4134 E Cherrywood Place, Chandler AZ 85249, USA | Baseball Player |
| **Lovano, Joe** 66 Beaver Brook Road, New Windsor NY 12553, USA | Jazz Saxophonist, Composer |
| **Lovato, Demi** Creative Artists Agency, 2000 Ave of Stars, #100, Los Angeles CA 90067 USA | Actress, Singer |
| **Love, Courtney** Resolution, 1801 Century Park E, #2300, Los Angeles CA 90067 USA | Singer (Hole), Actress, Songwriter |
| **Love, Darlene** Rainbow High Entertainment, 3500 W Olive Ave, #300, Burbank CA 91505, USA | Singer, Actress |
| **Love, Darris** H G Entertainment, 1734 N Frederic St, Burbank CA 91505, USA | Actor |
| **Love, Davis, III** Love Golf Design, 100 Brunswick Ave, Saint Simons Island GA 31522, USA | Golfer |

L

Lotan - Love

**Love, Duval L** — Football Player
8985 Yuba River Ave, Fountain Valley CA 92708, USA
**Love, Faizon** — Actor, Comedian, Writer, Director
Resolution, 1801 Century Park E, #2300, Los Angeles CA 90067 USA
**Love, Gerald** — Bassist (Teenage Fanclub)
High Road Touring, 751 Bridgeway, #200, Sausalito CA 94965 USA
**Love, Kevin W** — Basketball Player
Cleveland Cavaliers, Gund Arena, 1 Center Court, Cleveland OH 44115 USA
**Love, Loni** — Actress, Comedienne
United Talent Agency, U T A Plaza, 9336 Civic Center Dr, Beverly Hills CA 90210 USA
**Love, Michael D (Mike)** — Singer (Beach Boys)
24563 Ebelden Ave, Newhall CA 91321, USA
**Love, Randy** — Football Player
2202 Fairlands Dr, Garland TX 75040, USA
**Love, Stanley G** — Astronaut
4315 Indian Sunrise Court, Houston TX 77059, USA
**Love, Stanley S (Stan)** — Basketball Player
1950 Egan Way, Lake Oswego OR 97034, USA
**Love, Terence P** — Educator
Curtin University, Design Dept, GPO Box U1987, Perth WA 6845, Australia
**Lovelace, James L** — Army General
Deputy Chief of Staff, Operations Plans, HqUSA, Pentagon, Washington DC 20310 USA
**Lovelace, Vance O** — Baseball Player
5608 12th Ave S, Tampa FL 33619, USA
**Loveless, Patty** — Singer, Songwriter
Flood Bumstead McCready McCarthy, 16 W 22nd St, #200, New York NY 10010 USA
**Lovell, Jacqueline** — Actress, Model
8707 Shirley Ave, Northridge CA 91324, USA
**Lovell, James A (Jim), Jr** — Astronaut
Lovell Communications, PO Box 49, Lake Forest IL 60045, USA
**Lovell, Robert R** — Space Scientist
Orbital Sciences Corp, 21839 Atlantic Blvd, Dulles VA 20166, USA
**Lovellette, Clyde E** — Basketball Player
8 Woodspoint Circle, North Manchester IN 46962, USA
**Lovelock, James E** — Chemist, Inventor
Coombe Mill, Saint Giles on Heath, Launceston, Cornwall PL15 9RY, England
**Lovely, Randy** — Editor
Arizona Republic, Editorial Dept, 200 E Van Buren St, Phoenix AZ 85004 USA
**Lover, Seth** — Inventor, Engineer (Humbucking Pickup)
4 Village Dr, Saint Louis MO 63146, USA
**Lovering, David** — Singer, Drummer (Pixies)
X-Ray Touring, 77-79 Great Eastern St, #A, London EC2A 3HU, England
**Loverne, David** — Football Player
2307 Amber Falls Dr, Rocklin CA 95765, USA
**LoVetere, John M** — Football Player
PO Box 2901, Lebanon TN 37088, USA
**Lovett, Lyle** — Singer, Songwriter
Vector Mgmt, 1100 Glendon Ave, #2000, Los Angeles CA 90024, USA
**Lovett, Ruby** — Singer
Myers Media, PO Box 378, Canton NY 13617, USA
**Loviglio, John P (Jay)** — Baseball Player
23 3rd Ave, East Islip NY 11730, USA
**Loville, Derek K** — Football Player
D B L Financial, 3020 E Camelback Road, #301, Phoenix AZ 85016, USA
**Loving, Candy** — Model, Actress
8560 W Sunset Blvd, #600, West Hollywood CA 90069, USA
**Lovins, Amory B** — Physicist
Hypercar Inc, 3768 Highway 82, #204, Glenwood Springs CO 81601, USA
**Lovitz, Jon** — Actor, Comedian
Binder & Assoc, 1465 Lindacrest Dr, Beverly Hills CA 90210 USA
**Lovland, Rolf** — Pianist (Secret Garden), Composer
Thranesgate 2B, 0175 Oslo, Norway
**Lovretta, Michelle A** — Producer, Writer
Alpern Group, 15645 Royal Oak Road, Encino CA 91436, USA
**Lovrich, Peter (Pete)** — Baseball Player
19626 Beechnut Dr, Mokena IL 60448, USA
**Lovullo, Salvatore A (Torey)** — Baseball Player
32108 Sailview Lane, Westlake Village CA 91361, USA
**Lowder, Kyle** — Actor
Kazarian/Measures/Ruskin, 11969 Ventura Blvd, #300, Studio City CA 91604 USA
**Lowdermilk, R Kirk** — Football Player
9475 Apollo Road NE, Kensington OH 44427, USA
**Lowe, Barry** — Writer
315 Audley St, London W1K 2PJ, England
**Lowe, Chad** — Actor
Anonymous Content, 3532 Hayden Ave, Culver City CA 90232 USA
**Lowe, Chan** — Editorial Cartoonist
Fort Lauderdale Sun-Sentinel, Editorial Dept, 200 E Las Olas Blvd, Fort Lauderdale FL 33301, USA
**Lowe, Christopher S (Chris)** — Keyboardist (Pet Shop Boys)
W M E Entertainment, 9601 Wilshire Blvd, #300, Beverly Hills CA 90210 USA
**Lowe, Derek C** — Baseball Player
12711 Terabella Way, Fort Myers FL 33912, USA
**Lowe, Gary R** — Football Player
16940 Lauderdale Ave, Beverly Hills MI 48025, USA
**Lowe, J Sean** — Baseball Player
802 Oak Dr, Mesquite TX 75149, USA
**Lowe, Kevin** — Ice Hockey Player, Coach, Executive
Edmonton Oilers, 11230 110th St, Edmonton AB T5G 3H7, Canada
**Lowe, Nicholas D (Nick)** — Singer, Songwriter, Guitarist
High Road Touring, 751 Bridgeway, #200, Sausalito CA 94965 USA
**Lowe, Paul E** — Football Player
5134 Logan Ave, San Diego CA 92114, USA
**Lowe, Rebecca** — Sportscaster
NBC-TV, Sports Dept, 30 Rockefeller Plaza, #270E, New York NY 10112 USA
**Lowe, Rob** — Actor
W M E Entertainment, 9601 Wilshire Blvd, #300, Beverly Hills CA 90210 USA

**Lowe, Sidney R** — Basketball Player, Coach
2631 Wallingford Road, Winston-Salem NC 27101, USA

**Lowe, Stephanie** — Golfer
2004 Delancey Dr, Norman OK 73071, USA

**Lowe, Woodrow** — Football Player, Coach
PO Box 988, Alabaster AL 35007, USA

**Lowell, Abbe D** — Attorney
Chadbourne & Parke, 30 Rockefeller Plaza, New York NY 10112, USA

**Lowell, Charles D (Charlie)** — Keyboardist (Jars of Clay)
Nettwerk Mgmt, 1650 W 2nd Ave, Vancouver BC V6J 4R3, Canada

**Lowell, Chris** — Actor
Thruline Entertainment, 9250 Wilshire Blvd, #100, Beverly Hills CA 90212 USA

**Lowell, Elizabeth** — Writer
Avon Books, 1350 Ave of Americas, New York NY 10019 USA

**Lowell, Michael A (Mike)** — Baseball Player
620 Santurce Ave, Coral Gables FL 33143, USA

**Lowell, Scott** — Actor
Evolution Entertainment, 901 N Highland Ave, Los Angeles CA 90038 USA

**Lowenstein, John L** — Baseball Player
7017 Via Locanda Ave, Las Vegas NV 89131, USA

**Lowery, Corey** — Bassist (Stereo Mud)
Agency Group Ltd, 142 W 57th St, #600, New York NY 10019 USA

**Lowery, David** — Director
W M E Entertainment, 9601 Wilshire Blvd, #300, Beverly Hills CA 90210 USA

**Lowery, David** — Singer, Guitarist (Cracker), Songwriter
Back Bay Mgmt, 397 Little Neck Road, #305, Virginia Beach VA 23452 USA

**Lowery, Dominic G (Nick)** — Football Player
8416 E Via de Jardin, Scottsdale AZ 85258, USA

**Lowery, Stephen B (Steve)** — Golfer
379 Woodward Court, Birmingham AL 35242, USA

**Lowes, Katie** — Actress
Innovative Artists, 1505 10th St, Santa Monica CA 90401 USA

**Lowman, Nate** — Artist
Carlson Gallery, 55 S Audley St, London W1K 2QH, England

**Lown, Bernard** — Cardiologist
Lown Cardiovascular Group, 21 Longwood Ave, Brookline MA 02446, USA

**Lown, Omar J (Turk)** — Baseball Player
1106 Van Buren St, Pueblo CO 81004, USA

**Lowndes, Jessica** — Actress
Creative Artists Agency, 2000 Ave of Stars, #100, Los Angeles CA 90067 USA

**Lowrie, Jed C** — Baseball Player
1895 Evergreen Ave NE, Salem OR 97301, USA

**Lowry, Glenn D** — Museum Executive
Museum of Modern Art, Director's Office, 11 W 53rd St, New York NY 10019, USA

**Lowry, Kyle** — Basketball Player
Toronto Raptors, Air Canada Center, 20 Bay St, Toronto ON M5J 2N8, Canada

**Lowry, Lois** — Writer
9 Whipple Farm Lane, Falmouth ME 04105, USA

**Lowry, Noah** — Baseball Player
2621 Matera Lane, San Diego CA 92108, USA

**Lowry, Shanti** — Actress
Don Buchwald Talent Agency, 6500 Wilshire Blvd, #2200, Los Angeles CA 90048 USA

**Loy, James M** — Coast Guard Admiral, Government Official
L-1 Identity Solutions, 177 Broad St, #1200, Stamford CT 06901, USA

**Loy, Rory J** — Soccer Player
Rangers F C, Ibrox Stadium, 150 Edmiston Dr, Glasgow G51 2XD, Scotland

**Loynd, Michael W (Mike)** — Baseball Player
19 Randall Dr, Short Hills NJ 07078, USA

**Lozano Barragan, Javier Cardinal** — Religious Leader
Health Care Workers Pastoral Assistance, Via della Conciliazione 3, 00193 Rome, Italy

**Lozano, Conrad** — Singer, Bassist (Los Lobos)
Gold Mountain, 3940 Laurel Canyon Blvd, #444, Studio City CA 91604 USA

**Lozano, Florencia** — Actress
Paradigm Agency, 360 N Crescent Dr, North Building, Beverly Hills CA 90210 USA

**Lozano, Silvia** — Choreographer, Dancer
Anuka Center, Carrer Breton de los Herreros, 17, 08012 Barcelona, Spain

**Lu Qihui** — Sculptor
100-301, 398 Xin-Pei Road, Xin-Zuan, Shanghai, China

**Lu, Edward T (Ed)** — Astronaut
18222 Bal Harbour Dr, Houston TX 77058, USA

**Lu, Marie** — Writer
Nelson Literary Agency, 1732 Wazee St, #207, Denver CO 80202, USA

**Luan Jujie** — Fencer
146 Shuang-Le Yuan, #301, Qin-Huai Region, Nanjing 210009, China

**Lubanski, Ed** — Bowler
5326 Christi Dr, Warren MI 48091, USA

**Lubatti, Henri** — Actor
S D B Partners, 315 S Beverly Dr, #411, Beverly Hills CA 90067 USA

**Lubbers, Rudolphus F M (Ruud)** — Prime Minister, Netherlands
Lambertweg 4, 3062 Rotterdam RA, Netherlands

**Lubchenco, Jane** — Marine Biologist, Zoologist
Oregon State University, Marine Biology Dept, Corvallis OR 97331, USA

**Lubezki, Emmanuel** — Cinematographer
I C M Partners, 10250 Constellation Blvd, #900, Los Angeles CA 90067 USA

**Lubich, Bronko** — Professional Wrestler
3146 Whitemarsh Circle, Dallas TX 75234, USA

**Lubin, Barry (Grandma)** — Clown
Big Apple Circus, 505 8th Ave, #1900, New York NY 10018 USA

**Lubin, Gilson** — Actor, Comedian
Law Talent Agency, 5 Ambleside Ave, Toronto ON M8Z 2H5, Canada

**Lubin, Steven** — Concert Pianist
State University of New York, School of Arts, Purchase NY 10577, USA

**Lubotsky, Mark** — Concert Violinist
Overtoom 329 III, 1054 Amsterdam JM, Netherlands

**Lubovitch, Lar** — Dancer, Choreographer
Lar Lubovitch Dance Co, 229 W 42nd St, #8, New York NY 10036, USA

# L

**Lubratich, Steven G (Steve)** — Baseball Player
24 Sackett Road, Lee NH 03861, USA
**Lubs, Herbert A** — Geneticist
5133 SW 71st Place, Miami FL 33155, USA
**Luby, Thia** — Writer, Yoga Instructor
2918 Marion Dr, Colorado Springs CO 80909, USA
**Luc, Tone** — Rap Artist, Actor
Headline Talent, 1650 Broadway, #401, New York NY 10313 USA
**Lucado, Max** — Writer
Oak Hills Church of Christ, 6929 Camp Bullis Road, San Antonio TX 78256, USA
**Lucas Moura** — Soccer Player
Paris Saint Germain, 24 Rue du Commandant Guilbaud, 75015 Paris, France
**Lucas, Adetokunbo Oulmide** — Physician
25 Adebajo St, Kongi, PO Box 30917, Sec Bo, Ibadan, Nigeria
**Lucas, Ben C** — Director, Producer, Writer
Creative Artists Agency, 2000 Ave of Stars, #100, Los Angeles CA 90067 USA
**Lucas, Craig** — Lyricist, Writer, Director

**Lucas, Gary P** — Baseball Player
1511 High St, Rice Lake WI 54868, USA
**Lucas, George** — Director, Producer
LucasFilm, 5858 Lucas Valley Road, Nicasio CA 94946, USA
**Lucas, Jerry R** — Basketball Player
Dr Memorabilia, 231 E 2nd St, Chillicothe OH 45601, USA
**Lucas, Jessica** — Actress
Thruline Entertainment, 9250 Wilshire Blvd, #100, Beverly Hills CA 90212 USA
**Lucas, John H, Jr** — Basketball Player, Coach, Executive
21 Pin Oak Estates, Bellaire TX 77401, USA
**Lucas, Jon** — Director, Writer
Creative Artists Agency, 2000 Ave of Stars, #100, Los Angeles CA 90067 USA
**Lucas, Josh** — Actor
Principato-Young, 9465 Wilshire Blvd, #880, Beverly Hills CA 90212 USA
**Lucas, Kenneth C (Ken)** — Football Player
404 Oakmont Lane, Waxhaw NC 28173, USA
**Lucas, Marne** — Photographer
Aalto Lounge, 3356 SE Belmont St, Portland OR 97214, USA
**Lucas, Matthew R (Matt)** — Actor
Troika, 74 Clerkenwell Road, #300, London EC1M 5QA, England
**Lucas, Richard J (Richie)** — Football Player
1269 Estate Dr, West Chester PA 19380, USA
**Lucas, Robert E, Jr** — Nobel Economics Laureate
5448 S East View Park, #3, Chicago IL 60615, USA
**Lucas, Sarah** — Artist
Sadie Coles, 35 Heddon St, London W1B 4BP, England
**Lucas, Timothy B (Tim)** — Football Player
5081 S Florence Dr, Greenwood Village CO 80111, USA
**Lucchesi, Bruno** — Sculptor
30 5th Ave, New York NY 10011, USA
**Lucchesi, Frank J** — Baseball Player, Manager
4703 Mill Creek Dr, Colleyville TX 76034, USA
**Lucchesini, Andrea** — Concert Pianist
Arts Manangement Group, 1133 Broadway, #1025, New York NY 10010, USA
**Lucci, Michael G (Mike)** — Football Player
3184 Middlebelt Road, West Bloomfield MI 48323, USA
**Lucci, Susan** — Actress
Rogers & Cowan, 8687 Melrose Ave, #G700, West Hollywood CA 90069 USA
**Luce, Derrel J** — Football Player
4112 Green Oak Dr, Waco TX 76710, USA
**Luce, Don** — Ice Hockey Player
67 Tartan Lane, Buffalo NY 14221, USA
**Luce, Richard N** — Governor, Gibraltar
House of Lords, Westminster, London SW1A 0PW, England
**Lucero, Carlos F** — Judge
US Court of Appeals, 1929 Stout St, Denver CO 80294, USA
**Lucey, Dorothy** — Actress, Entertainer
Ken Lindner Assoc, 2029 Century Park E, #1000, Los Angeles CA 90067, USA
**Luchko, Klara S** — Actress
Kotelmicheskaya Nab 1/15 Korp B, #308, 109240 Moscow, Russia
**Luchsinger, Susie** — Singer
Psalm Ministries, 406 W 10th St, Atoka OK 74525, USA
**Lucic, Zeljko** — Opera Singer
Barrett Vantage Artists, 505 8th Ave, #12A00, New York NY 10018, USA
**Lucid, Shannon W** — Astronaut, Biophysicist
1622 Gunwale Road, Houston TX 77062, USA
**Lucier, Louis J (Lou)** — Baseball Player
7 Jaclyn Rae Dr, Millbury MA 01527, USA
**Lucio, Shannon** — Actress
6232 Monterey Road, Los Angeles CA 90042, USA
**Luck, Andrew A** — Football Player
Indianapolis Colts, 7001 W 56th St, Indianapolis IN 46254 USA
**Luck, Frank** — Biathlete
Lerchenweg 9, 98587 Springstille, Germany
**Luck, Gary E** — Army General
S A A H Foundation, 1147 N Clark St, #2044, West Hollywood CA 90069, USA
**Luck, Ingolf** — Actor, Comedian
Buero Berge, Baroper Bergstr 23, 44227 Dortmund, Germany
**Luckett, LeToya** — Singer
Resolution, 1801 Century Park E, #2300, Los Angeles CA 90067, USA
**Luckey, Ken** — Actor
Greene Assoc, 1901 Ave of Stars, #130, Los Angeles CA 90067 USA
**Luckhurst, Michael C W (Mick)** — Football Player
2757 Dawsons Chase, Duluth GA 30097, USA
**Luckinbill, Lawrence** — Actor
3 Big Shop Lane, #4, Ridgefield CT 06877, USA
**Luckovich, Mike** — Editorial Cartoonist
Atlanta Constitution,Editorial Dept, 223 Perimeter Center Parkway NE, Atlanta GA 30346, USA

| | |
|---|---|
| **Lucy, Tom**<br>Leander Club, Henley on Thames, Leander RG9 2LP, England | Rowing Athlete |
| **Luczo, Stephen J**<br>Seagate Technology, 920 Disc Dr, Scotts Valley CA 95066, USA | Businessman |
| **Ludacris**<br>Creative Artists Agency, 2000 Ave of Stars, #100, Los Angeles CA 90067 USA | Rap Artist, Actor |
| **Luddington, Camilla**<br>United Talent Agency, U T A Plaza, 9336 Civic Center Dr, Beverly Hills CA 90210 USA | Actress |
| **Luder, Owen H**<br>Communication in Construction, 2 Smith Square, London SW1P 3HS, England | Architect |
| **Ludes, John T**<br>Fortune Brands Inc, 300 Tower Parkway, Lincolnshire IL 60069, USA | Businessman |
| **Luding-Rothenburger, Christa**<br>Dresdener Eisspot-Club, Pieschener Allee 1, 01067 Dresden, Germany | Speed Skater, Cyclist |
| **Ludington, Nancy**<br>PO Box 60, Surry ME 04684, USA | Figure Skater |
| **Ludington, Ronald (Ron)**<br>611 Thompson Station Road, Newark DE 19711, USA | Figure Skater |
| **Ludwick, Ryan A**<br>511 County Road 262, Georgetown TX 78633, USA | Baseball Player |
| **Ludwig, Alexander**<br>Baker Winokur Ryder Public Relations, 9100 Wilshire Blvd, #500W, Beverly Hills CA 90212 USA | Actor |
| **Ludwig, Christa**<br>1458 Ter, Chemin des Colles, 06740 Chateauneuf de Grasse, France | Opera Singer |
| **Ludwig, Craig**<br>421 River St, Eagle River WI 54521, USA | Ice Hockey Player |
| **Ludwig, George H**<br>University of Iowa, Physics & Astronomy Dept, Iowa City IA 52242, USA | Physicist |
| **Ludwig, Ken**<br>Gersh Agency, 9465 Wilshire Blvd, #600, Beverly Hills CA 90212 USA | Writer |
| **Lue, Tyronn J**<br>2926 Montessouri St, Las Vegas NV 89117, USA | Basketball Player |
| **Lueck, William M (Bill)**<br>409 E Bird Lane, Litchfield Park AZ 85340, USA | Football Player |
| **Luecken, Richard F (Rick)**<br>2902 Fontana Dr, East Providence RI 02915, USA | Baseball Player |
| **Lueders, Pierre**<br>Bobsled Canada, 140 Canada Olympic Road SW, Calgary AB T3B 5R5, Canada | Bobsled Athlete |
| **Luft, Lorna**<br>Stiletto Entertainment, 8295 S La Cienega Blvd, Inglewood CA 90301, USA | Actress, Singer |
| **Lugansky, Nicolai**<br>Harrison/Parrott, 5-6 Albion Court, London W6 0QT, England | Concert Pianist |
| **Lugbill, Jon**<br>2422 Grove Ave, Richmond VA 23220, USA | Canoeing Athlete |
| **Luger, Gery**<br>Hinterfeld 598, 6861 Alberschwende, Austria | Photographer |
| **Lugo, Julio**<br>1555 Gants Circle, Kissimmee FL 34744, USA | Baseball Player |
| **Luhrmann, Baz**<br>Bazmark Inq, PO Box 430, Kings Cross NSW 2011, Australia | Director |
| **Luisi, Fabio**<br>Zurich Opera House, Falkenstr 1, 8008 Zurich, Switzerland | Conductor |
| **Luisotti, Nicola**<br>I M G Artists, Hogarth Business Park, Chiswick, London W4 2TH, England | Conductor |
| **Lujack, John C (Johnny)**<br>6321 Crow Valley Dr, Bettendorf IA 52722, USA | Football Player |
| **Lujan, Manuel, Jr**<br>Manuel Lujan Agencies, PO Box 3727, Albuquerque NM 87190, USA | Secretary, Interior |
| **Lukachyk, Robert J**<br>100 High St, Woodbridge NJ 07095, USA | Baseball Player |
| **Lukas, D Wayne**<br>1034 Oak Canyon Lane, Glendora CA 91741, USA | Thoroughbred Racing Trainer |
| **Lukashenko, Aleksandr**<br>President's Office, Karl Marx Str 38, 220016 Minsk, Belarus | President, Belarus |
| **Lukasiewicz, Mark**<br>8035 Fir Dr, Clay NY 13041, USA | Baseball Player |
| **Lukather, Steve (Luke)**<br>Monterey International, 200 W Superior St, #202, Chicago IL 60654 USA | Musician (Toto) |
| **Luke, Derek**<br>W M E Entertainment, 9601 Wilshire Blvd, #300, Beverly Hills CA 90210 USA | Actor |
| **Luke, John A, Jr**<br>Westvaco Corp, 299 Park Ave, #1300, New York NY 10171, USA | Businessman |
| **Luke, Mathew C (Matt)**<br>5262 Eucalyptus Hill Road, Yorba Linda CA 92886, USA | Baseball Player |
| **Lukeba, Merveille**<br>Independent Talent Group, 40 Whitfield St, London W1T 2RH, England | Actor |
| **Luken, Thomas J (Tom)**<br>8036 Cast A Way, Mason OH 45040, USA | Football Player |
| **Lukens, Max L**<br>Baker Hughes Inc, PO Box 4740, Houston TX 77210, USA | Businessman |
| **Luker, Rebecca**<br>Paradigm Agency, 360 N Crescent Dr, North Building, Beverly Hills CA 90210 USA | Actress, Singer |
| **Luketic, Robert**<br>Mosiaic Media Group, 9200 W Sunset Blvd, #1000, Los Angeles CA 90069 USA | Director |
| **Lukin, Matt**<br>Legends of 21st Century, 7 Trinity Row, Florence MA 01062, USA | Bassist (Mudhoney) |
| **Lukin, Valery**<br>Arctic/Antarctic Research Institute, 38 Bering Str, 199397 Saint Petersburg, Russia | Oceanographer |
| **Lukis, Adrian**<br>Artists Partnership, 101 Finsbury Pavement, London EC2A 1RS, England | Actor |
| **Lukowich, Brad**<br>3400 Craig Dr, #721, McKinney TX 75070, USA | Ice Hockey Player |
| **Luksic, Igor**<br>Prime Minister's Office, Jovana Tomasevica BB, Podgorica, Montenegro | Prime Minister, Montenegro |
| **Lulu**<br>Concorde International, 101 Shepherds Bush Road, London W6 7LP, England | Singer, Actress |

V.I.P. Address Book

**Lum, Michael K (Mike)** — Baseball Player
3476 Cochise Dr SE, Atlanta GA 30339, USA

**Lumbly, Carl W** — Actor
Core Public Relations Group, 4401 Wilshire Blvd, #400, Los Angeles CA 90010 USA

**Lumidee** — Singer
Central Entertainment Group, 166 5th Ave, #400, New York NY 10010, USA

**Lumley, Dave** — Ice Hockey Player
PO Box 610, Murfreesboro AR 71958, USA

**Lumley, Joanna** — Actress
Independent Talent Group, 40 Whitfield St, London W1T 2RH, England

**Lumley, John L** — Physicist
743 Snyder Hill Road, Ithaca NY 14850, USA

**Lumme, Jyrki O** — Ice Hockey Player
9646 E Laurel Lane, Scottsdale AZ 85260, USA

**Lumpkin, Sean F** — Football Player
4708 Virginia Lane, Minneapolis MN 55424, USA

**Lumpp, Raymond G (Ray)** — Basketball Player
21 Hewlett Dr, East Williston NY 11596, USA

**Lumsden, David J** — Conductor, Concert Organist
Melton House, Soham, Cambridgeshire CB7 5DB, England

**Luna, Barbara** — Actress
18026 Rodarte Way, Encino CA 91316, USA

**Luna, Diego** — Actor
Canana Films, Zacatecas 142-A, Colonia Roma, Mexico City DF 06700, Mexico

**Lunar, Fernando** — Baseball Player
3125 Zuni Place, Alamogordo NM 88310, USA

**Lund, Corb** — Singer, Songwriter
R G K Entertainment Group, 2B Minto St, #6, Toronto ON M4L 1B6, Canada

**Lund, Deanna** — Actress
Fred Eichelman, 545 Howard Dr, Salem VA 24153, USA

**Lund, Eva** — Curling Athlete
Curling Association, Idrottshuser, Marbackagatan 19, 123 43 Farsta, Sweden

**Lund, Gordon T** — Baseball Player
1602 S Harvard Ave, Arlington Heights IL 60005, USA

**Lund, Katia** — Director
Gersh Agency, 9465 Wilshire Blvd, #600, Beverly Hills CA 90212 USA

**Lundaas, Terje** — Artist, Sculptor
Glass Art & Design, 7003 N Waterway Dr, #201, Miami FL 33133, USA

**Lundberg, Anders** — Physiologist
Goteberg University, Physiology Dept, Box 33031, 40 033 Goteborg, Sweden

**Lundberg, Athena** — Model
Playboy Promotions, 9346 Civic Center Dr, #200, Beverly Hills CA 90210 USA

**Lundberg, Fred Borre** — Nordic Combined Skier
Skogbrynet 11, 9250 Bardu, Norway

**Lunde-Borgersen, Kristine** — Handball Player
Vag Handball, Postboks 8071, 4675 Kristiansand, Norway

**Lunden, Joan** — Commentator
Celebrity Consultants, 3340 Ocean Park Blvd, #1005, Santa Monica CA 90405 USA

**Lundgren, Dolph** — Actor
Baumgarten Mgmt, 11925 Wilshire Blvd, #310, Los Angeles CA 90025, USA

**Lundgren, Terry** — Businessman
Federated Department Stores, 151 W 34th St, New York NY 10001, USA

**Lundholm, Johan (Bengt)** — Ice Hockey Player
Torsgatan 16, 113 62 Stockholm, Sweden

**Lundi, Monika** — Actress
Ortlindestr 2, 81927 Munich, Germany

**Lundquist, M Laverne (Verne), Jr** — Sportscaster
1710 Natches Way, Steamboat Springs CO 80487, USA

**Lundquist, Stephen (Steve)** — Swimmer
246 Northwest Dr, Stockbridge GA 30281, USA

**Lundqvist, Alex** — Model
Wilhelmina Models, 300 Park Ave S, #200, New York NY 10010 USA

**Lundqvist, B Henrik** — Ice Hockey Player
310 W 52nd St, #PHD, New York NY 10019, USA

**Lundstedt, Thomas R (Tom)** — Baseball Player
9813 Brookside Lane, Ephraim WI 54211, USA

**Lundstrom, Tord G** — Ice Hockey Player
Brynas Byggnads AB, 801 33 Gavle, Sweden

**Lundy, Carmen** — Singer
Abby Hoffer Enterprises, 223 1/2 E 48th St, New York NY 10017 USA

**Lundy, Jessica** — Actress
Metropolitan Talent Agency, 5405 Wilshire Blvd, #218, Los Angeles CA 90036 USA

**Lundy, Victor A** — Architect
Victor A Lundy Assoc, 701 Mulberry Lane, Bellaire TX 77401, USA

**Lunenfeld, Bruno** — Endocrinologist
7 Rav Ashi St, Tel Aviv 69395, Israel

**Luner, Jaime** — Actress
Berneman Mgmt, 5820 Wilshire Blvd, #200, Los Angeles CA 90036, USA

**Lunka, Zoltan** — Boxer
Weinheimer Str 2, 69198 Schriesheim, Germany

**Lunke, Hilary** — Golfer
11701 Broad Oaks Dr, Austin TX 78759, USA

**Lunney, Glenn** — Space Scientist
United Space Alliance, 1150 Gemini Dr, Houston TX 77058, USA

**Lunsford, Trey** — Baseball Player
3955 Nail Road, Southaven MS 38672, USA

**Luongo, Aldo** — Artist
883 Westbourne Ave, West Hollywood CA 90069, USA

**Luongo, Roberto** — Ice Hockey Player
7280 Lemon Grass Dr, Parkland FL 33076, USA

**Lupberger, Edwin A** — Businessman
Nesher Investments, 2010 NE 164th St, North Miami Beach FL 33162, USA

**Lupica, Mike** — Sportswriter
87 Bald Hill Road, New Canaan CT 06840, USA

**Lupien, Gilles** — Ice Hockey Player
Sports Prospects, 77 Rue de Bleury, Rosemere QC J7A 4L9, Canada

**Luplow, Alvin D (Al)** — Baseball Player
4250 Lakecress Dr E, Saginaw MI 48603, USA
**Lupo, Janet P** — Model
PO Box 6232, Hoboken NJ 07030, USA
**LuPone, Patti** — Singer, Actress
235 Park Ave S, #700, New York NY 10003, USA
**Lupu, Radu** — Concert Pianist
Opus 3 Artists, 470 Park Ave S, #900N, New York NY 10016 USA
**Lupus, Peter** — Actor, Bodybuilder, Model
Greene Assoc, 1901 Ave of Stars, #130, Los Angeles CA 90067 USA
**Lurie, Alison** — Writer
Cornell University, English Dept, Ithaca NY 14850, USA
**Lurie, Jeffrey** — Football Executive
312 Llanfair Road, Wynnewood PA 19096, USA
**Lurie, Ranan R** — Editorial Cartoonist
Cartoonnews International, 375 Park Ave, #1301, New York NY 10152, USA
**Lurtsema, Robert R (Bob)** — Football Player
16920 Judicial Road, Lakeville MN 55044, USA
**Lurz, Dagmar** — Figure Skater
International Skating Union, Chemin du Primerose 2, 1007 Lausanne, Switzerland
**Lurz, Thomas** — Swimmer
S V Wurzburg, Oberer Bogenweg 1, 97074 Wurzburg, Germany
**Lusader, Scott E** — Baseball Player
4169 Bold Meadows, Oakland Township MI 48306, USA
**Lusardi, Linda** — Model
E3 Artists, 56 Shorts Gardens, London WC2H 9AN, England
**Lush, Billy** — Actor
Mary Erickson Mgmt, 2126 N Commonwealth Ave, Los Angeles CA 90027, USA
**Lusis, Janis** — Track Athlete
Vesetas 8-3, 1013 Riga, Latvia
**Lussier, Sheila** — Actress
Wilson Assoc, 5418 Wilshire Blvd, #510, Los Angeles CA 90036, USA
**Lust, Reimar** — Physicist
Bellevue 49, 22301 Hamburg, Germany
**Lusteg, G Booth** — Football Player
1100 SW 111th Way, Davie FL 33324, USA
**Lustig, M Bruce** — Religious Leader, Rabbi
Washington Hebrew Congregation, 3935 Macomb St NW, Washington DC 20016, USA
**Lustig, William** — Producer, Director, Actor
15016 Marble Dr, Sherman Oaks CA 91403, USA
**Lusztig, George** — Mathematician
106 Grant Ave, Newton MA 02459, USA
**Lute, Douglas E** — Army General
White House, 1600 Pennsylvania Ave NW, Washington DC 20500 USA
**Luter, Fred, Jr** — Religious Leader
Franklin Avenue Baptist Church, 2515 Franklin Ave, New Orleans LA 70117, USA
**Lutes, Eric** — Actor
Special Artists Agency, 9200 Sunset Blvd, #410, West Hollywood CA 90069 USA
**Luther, Edward A (Ed)** — Football Player
30486 Le Port, Laguna Niguel CA 92677, USA
**Luttrell, Marcus** — Afghanistan War Navy Hero, Writer
Beefy Marketing, PO Box 699, Tomball TX 77377, USA
**Luttrell, Rachel Z** — Actress
King Talent, 303-228 E 4th Ave, Vancouver V5T 1G5, Canada
**Lutui, Taitusi (Deuce)** — Football Player
3829 N Stone Gully, Mesa AZ 85207, USA
**Lutz, Bob** — Tennis Player
101 Via Ensueno, San Clemente CA 92672, USA
**Lutz, Jessica** — Ice Hockey Player
Swiss Ice Hockey, Hagenholzstr 81, 8050 Zurich, Switzerland
**Lutz, Kellan** — Actor
Baker Winokur Ryder Public Relations, 9100 Wilshire Blvd, #500W, Beverly Hills CA 90212 USA
**Lutz, Lisa** — Writer
Levine Greenberg Literary Agency, 307 7th Ave, #2407, New York NY 10001, USA
**Lutz, Robert A** — Businessman
3966 Pleasant Lake Road, Ann Arbor MI 48103, USA
**Lux, Danny** — Composer
I C M Partners, 10250 Constellation Blvd, #900, Los Angeles CA 90067 USA
**Lux, Loretta** — Photographer
Yossi Milo Gallery, 555 W 24th St, New York NY 10011, USA
**Luxon, Benjamin M** — Opera Singer
Mazet, Relubbus Lane, Saint Hilary, Penzance, Cornwall TR20 9DS, England
**Luyendyk, Arie** — Auto Racing Driver
9915 N Copper Ridge Trail, Fountain Hills AZ 85268, USA
**Luyties, Ricci** — Volleyball Player
2215 Hartford St, San Diego CA 92110, USA
**Luzinski, Gregory M (Greg)** — Baseball Player
25680 Streamlet Court, Bonita Springs FL 34135, USA
**Luzuriaga, Katherine** — Immunologist
University of Massachusetts Medical Center, Immunology Dept, 55 Lake Ave N, Worcester MA 01655, USA
**Lwin, Annabella** — Singer (Bow Wow Wow)
M O B Agency, 6404 Wilshire Blvd, #505, Los Angeles CA 90048 USA
**Lyakhov, Vladimir A** — Cosmonaut
Cosmonaut Training Center, Star City, 141160 Zvezdny Gorodok, Moscow Oblast, Russia
**Lyall, John A** — Architect
John Lyall Architects, 13-19 Curtain Road, London EC2A 3LT, England
**Lyden, Mitchell S (Mitch)** — Baseball Player
227 Shore Court, Lauderdale by the Sea FL 33308, USA
**Lydman, Toni** — Ice Hockey Player
6035 Corinne Lane, Clarence Center NY 14032, USA
**Lydon, Alexa** — Actress
Silver Lining Entertainment, 421 S Beverly Drive, #700, Beverly Hills CA 90212 USA
**Lydon, James (Jimmy)** — Actor
3538 Lomacitas Lane, Bonita CA 91902, USA
**Lydon, John (Johnny Rotten)** — Singer, Musician (Sex Pistols)
31962 Pacific Coast Highway, Malibu CA 90265, USA

# L

**Lydon, Malcolm**
1429 Jaudon Road, Dover FL 33527, USA — Astronaut

**Lydy, D Scott**
4278 S Leoma Lane, Chandler AZ 85249, USA — Baseball Player

**Lye, Mark R**
4610 Via Cappello, Bonita Springs FL 34134, USA — Golfer

**Lyght, Todd W**
912 Camino Ibiza, San Clemente CA 92672, USA — Football Player

**Lyhs, Gunter**
Im Baukholt 7, 58566 Kierspe, Germany — Gymnast

**Lyle, Gary T**
222 Beach Dr NE, Saint Petersburg FL 33701, USA — Football Player

**Lyle, Kami**
D S Mgmt, 2814 12th Ave S, #202, Nashville TN 37204, USA — Singer, Trumpeter, Songwriter

**Lyle, Keith A**
9615 Maypan Place, Seminole FL 33777, USA — Football Player

**Lyle, Sandy**
4904 Duck Creek Lane, #450, Ponte Vedra Beach FL 32082, USA — Golfer

**Lyles, Lester E**
6315 14th St NW, Washington DC 20011, USA — Football Player

**Lyles, Lester L (Les)**
United Services Automobile Assn, U S A A Building, 9800 Fredericksburg Road, San Antonio TX 78288, USA — Air Force General

**Lyles, Robert D**
PO Box 1075, Jackson MS 39215, USA — Football Player

**Lyman, Dorothy**
Stone Manners Salners, 6100 Wilshire Blvd, #1500, Los Angeles CA 90035 USA — Actress

**Lyman, Dustin S**
501 W Spruce St, Louisville CO 80027, USA — Football Player

**Lyn, Nicole**
McGowan Mgmt, 8733 W Sunset Blvd, #103, West Hollywood CA 90069, USA — Actress

**Lynam, Jim**
Philadelphia 76ers, 1st Union Center, 3601 S Broad St, Philadelphia PA 19148 USA — Basketball Coach, Executive

**Lynch, Allen J**
438 Belle Plaine Ave, Gurnee IL 60031, USA — Vietnam War Army Hero (CMH)

**Lynch, Charles A**
24 Susan Gale Court, Menlo Park CA 94025, USA — Businessman

**Lynch, Claire**
369 Gillette Road, Nashville TN 37211, USA — Singer

**Lynch, Dan**
Fort Wayne Journal-Gazette, Editorial Dept, 600 W Main St, Fort Wayne IN 46802, USA — Editorial Cartoonist

**Lynch, David K**
David Lynch Foundation, 216 E 45th St, #1200, New York NY 10017, USA — Director

**Lynch, Edele**
Clintons, 55 Drury Lane, Covent Garden, London WC2B 5SQ, England — Singer (B*Witched)

**Lynch, Edward F (Ed)**
7832 E Parkview Lane, Scottsdale AZ 85255, USA — Baseball Player

**Lynch, Francis X (Fran)**
2553 Lake Vista Dr, Broomfield CO 80023, USA — Football Player

**Lynch, George D, III**
1000 Phils Creek Road, Chapel Hill NC 27516, USA — Basketball Player

**Lynch, Jair**
9207 Three Oaks Dr, Silver Spring MD 20901, USA — Gymnast

**Lynch, James E (Jim)**
1717 W 91st Place, Kansas City MO 64114, USA — Football Player

**Lynch, Jane**
Domain Talent, 9229 W Sunset Blvd, #710, West Hollywood CA 90069 USA — Actress, Comedienne

**Lynch, Jennifer Chambers**
Water Street Anthem Entertainment, 5225 Wilshire Blvd, #615, Los Angeles CA 90036 USA — Writer, Director

**Lynch, Jessica**
Gregory Lynch, RR 1, Palestine WV 26160, USA — Iraqi War Army Hero

**Lynch, John**
Markham Froggatt Irwin, Julian House, 4 Windmill St, London W1P 1HF, England — Actor

**Lynch, John Carroll**
Abrams Artists, 9200 W Sunset Blvd, #1125, West Hollywood CA 90069 USA — Actor

**Lynch, John T, Jr**
13 Sandy Lake Road, Englewood CO 80113, USA — Football Player

**Lynch, Keavy**
Clintons, 55 Drury Lane, Covent Garden, London WC2B 5SQ, England — Singer (B*Witched)

**Lynch, Kelly**
TalentWorks, 3500 W Olive Ave, #1400, Burbank CA 91505 USA — Model, Actress

**Lynch, Marshawn T**
2100 Lake Washington Blvd N, #C101, Renton WA 98056, USA — Football Player

**Lynch, Peter S**
27 State St, Boston MA 02109, USA — Financier

**Lynch, Raymond (Ray)**
Ray Lynch Productions, 10336 Loch Lomond Road, Middletown CA 95461, USA — Musician, Composer

**Lynch, Ross S**
Core Public Relations Group, 4401 Wilshire Blvd, #400, Los Angeles CA 90010 USA — Actor

**Lynch, Sandra L**
US Court of Appeals, 1 Courthouse Way, Boston MA 02210, USA — Judge

**Lynch, Shane**
Associated International Mgmt, 7 Hatton Garden, #400, London EC1N 8AD, England — Singer (Boyzone), Actor

**Lynch, Susan**
Troika, 74 Clerkenwell Road, #300, London EC1M 5QA, England — Actress

**Lynch, Thomas C**
751 Eagle Farm Road, Villanova PA 19085, USA — Navy Admiral

**Lynch, Thomas W (Tom)**
Tom Lynch Co, 1801 Ave of Stars, #710, Los Angeles CA 90067, USA — Producer

**Lynde, Janice**
Stage 9 Talent, 1249 Lodi Place, Los Angeles CA 90038, USA — Actress

**Lynden-Bell, Donald**
Institute of Astronomy, Madingley Road, Cambridge CB3 0HA, England — Astronomer

**Lydon, Frank**
Paramount Entertainment, PO Box 12, Far Hills NJ 07931 USA — Singer (Belmonts)

**Lynds, Roger**
Kitt Peak National Observatory, Tucson AZ 85726, USA — Astronomer

**Lyne, Adrian** — Director
W M E Entertainment, 9601 Wilshire Blvd, #300, Beverly Hills CA 90210 USA

**Lyngstad, Anni-Frida** — Singer (ABBA), Songwriter
Mono Music, Sodra Brobaeken 41A, 111 49 Stockholm, Sweden

**Lynn Salomon, Janet** — Figure Skater
PO Box 1026, Haymarket VA 20168, USA

**Lynn, Anthony R** — Football Player
512 Paddock Lane, Celina TX 75009, USA

**Lynn, Cheryl** — Singer, Actress
PO Box 667, Smithtown NY 11787, USA

**Lynn, Frederic M (Fred)** — Baseball Player
7336 El Fuerte St, Carlsbad CA 92009, USA

**Lynn, Greg** — Architect
University of California, Architecture School, Los Angeles CA 90024, USA

**Lynn, Johnny R** — Football Player
896 N Willow Ave, Rialto CA 92376, USA

**Lynn, Jonathan** — Director
United Agents, 12-26 Lexington St, London W1F 0LE, England

**Lynn, Loretta** — Singer, Guitarist, Songwriter
44 Hurricane Mills Road, Hurricane Mills TN 37078, USA

**Lynn, Meredith Scott** — Actress
Bauman Redanty Shaul Agency, 5757 Wilshire Blvd, #473, Los Angeles CA 90036 USA

**Lynn, Patricia L (Patty)** — Singer (Wind + Wave)
Triple 8 Mgmt, 5524 W Highway 290, Austin TX 78735, USA

**Lynn, Theresa** — Actress
1435 Winter Ave, Louisville KY 40204, USA

**Lynn, Vera** — Actress, Singer
Hampers Croft, Common Lane, Ditchling, East Sussex BN6 8TJ, England

**Lynne, Gillian B** — Dance Director, Choreographer
Lean Two Productions, 18 Rutland St, Knightsbridge, London SW7 1EF, England

**Lynne, Jeff** — Singer, Guitarist, Songwriter
Front Line Mgmt, 1100 Glendon Ave, #2000, Los Angeles CA 90024 USA

**Lynne, Rockie** — Singer, Songwriter
Music Works, PO Box 447, Center City MN 55012, USA

**Lynne, Shelby** — Singer, Fiddle Player, Songwriter
High Road, 751 Bridgeway, #200, Sausalito CA 94965, USA

**Lynskey, Melanie** — Actress
Johnson & Laird Mgmt, PO Box 78340, Grey Lynn Auckland 1245, New Zealand

**Lyon, Brandon J** — Baseball Player
4291 S Iowa St, Chandler AZ 85248, USA

**Lyon, Sue** — Actress
Rudman, 1317 N Whitnall Highway, Burbank CA 91505, USA

**Lyonne, Natasha** — Actress
Viewpoint, 8820 Wilshire Blvd, #220, Beverly Hills CA 90211 USA

**Lyons, Barry S** — Baseball Player
527 Front Beach Dr, #71, Ocean Springs MS 39564, USA

**Lyons, Ben** — Film Critic, Columnist
W M E Entertainment, 9601 Wilshire Blvd, #300, Beverly Hills CA 90210 USA

**Lyons, Curt R** — Baseball Player
124 Virginia Dr, Richmond KY 40475, USA

**Lyons, David** — Actor
Anonymous Content, 3532 Hayden Ave, Culver City CA 90232 USA

**Lyons, Elena** — Actress
Innovative Artists, 1505 10th St, Santa Monica CA 90401 USA

**Lyons, James A, Jr** — Navy Admiral
9481 Piney Mountain Road, Warrenton VA 20186, USA

**Lyons, Laura** — Actress, Model
Playboy Promotions, 9346 Civic Center Dr, #200, Beverly Hills CA 90210 USA

**Lyons, Martin A (Marty)** — Football Player
8 White Pine Court, Smithtown NY 11787, USA

**Lyons, Phyllis** — Actress
Bauman Redanty Shaul Agency, 5757 Wilshire Blvd, #473, Los Angeles CA 90036 USA

**Lyons, Robert F** — Actor
3810 Magnolia Blvd, PO Box 1292, Burbank CA 91507, USA

**Lyons, Stephen K (Steve)** — Baseball Player
8196 E Del Platino Dr, Scottsdale AZ 85258, USA

**Lyons, Thomas L (Tommy)** — Football Player
2814 Drummond Point SE, Atlanta GA 30339, USA

**Lysacek, Evan F** — Figure Skater
Toyota Sports Center, 555 N Nash St, El Segundo CA 90245, USA

**Lysenko, Tatiana F** — Gymnast
722 Quartz St, Redwood City CA 94061, USA

**Lysiak, Thomas J (Tom)** — Ice Hockey Player
1050 Cedar Grove Road, Buckhead GA 30625, USA

**Lyst, John H** — Editor
Indianapolis Newspapers Inc, PO Box 145, Indianapolis IN 46206, USA

**Lythgoe, Nigel** — Producer, Director, Writer
Nigel Lythgoe Productions, 8560 W Sunset Blvd, #900, West Hollywood CA 90069, USA

**Lyttle, James L (Jim)** — Baseball Player
751 Camino Lakes Circle, Boca Raton FL 33486, USA

**Lyttle, Kevin** — Singer
Nene Musik Productions, 1460 SW Santiago Ave, Port Saint Lucie FL 34953 USA

**Lyttle, Sancho** — Basketball Player
Atlanta Dream, 83 Walton St NW, #400, Atlanta, GA 30303 USA

**Lyubshin, Stanislav A** — Actor
Vernadskogo Prosp 123, #171, 117571 Moscow, Russia

**M I A** — Rap Artist
2:30 Publicity, 304 Hudson St, #700, New York NY 10013, USA
**M J G** — Rap Artist (8Ball & M J G)
J L Entertainment, 18653 Ventura Blvd, #340, Los Angeles CA 91356 USA
**Ma Ying Jeou** — President, Taiwan
President's Office, Chieshshou Hall, Chongcing S Road, Taipei 100, Taiwan
**Ma, Chi** — Mineralogist
California Institute of Technology, Geological & Planetary Sciences Division, Pasadena, CA 91125, USA
**Ma, Tzi** — Actor
A P A Talent & Literary Agency, 405 S Beverly Dr, #300, Beverly Hills CA 90212 USA
**Ma, Yo-Yo** — Concert Cellist, Composer
Musichall Ltd, Vicarage Way, Ringmer BN8 5LA, England
**Maas, Georg** — Director, Writer
Resolution, 1801 Century Park E, #2300, Los Angeles CA 90067, USA
**Maas, Kevin C** — Baseball Player
Charles Schwab Corp, 20980 Redwood Road, Castro Valley CA 94546, USA
**Maas, William T (Bill)** — Football Player, Sportscaster
653 N Shoreline Dr, Lees Summit MO 64064, USA
**Maatta, Olli** — Ice Hockey Player
Pittsburgh Penguins, Consol Energy Center, 1001 5th Ave, Pittsburgh PA 15219 USA
**Mabe, Ricky** — Actor
K L Benzakein Talent, 1155 Rene-Levesque Blvd W, #2500, Montreal QC H3B 2K4, Canada
**Mabeus, Chris** — Baseball Player
151 Shady Lane, Soldotna AK 99669, USA
**Mabius, Eric** — Actor
I C M Partners, 10250 Constellation Blvd, #900, Los Angeles CA 90067 USA
**Mabrey, Sunny** — Actress
Paradigm Agency, 360 N Crescent Dr, North Building, Beverly Hills CA 90210 USA
**Mabry, John S** — Baseball Player
715 Bellerive Manor Dr, Saint Louis MO 63141, USA
**Mabus, Raymond E, Jr** — Governor, MS
Secretary of Navy, HqUSN, Pentagon, Washington DC 20350, USA
**MacAfee, Kenneth A (Ken), II** — Football Player
154 South St, Needham MA 02492, USA
**Macal, Zdenek** — Conductor
Opus 3 Artists, 470 Park Ave S, #900N, New York NY 10016 USA
**Macarron Jaime, Ricardo** — Artist
Agustin de Bethencourt 7, 28003 Madrid, Spain
**MacArthur, Ellen** — Yachtswoman
Whitegates, Arctic Road, Cowes, Isle of Wight PO31 7PG, England
**MacArthur, Hayes** — Actor
Creative Artists Agency, 2000 Ave of Stars, #100, Los Angeles CA 90067 USA
**Macat, Julio G** — Cinematographer
Paradigm Agency, 360 N Crescent Dr, North Building, Beverly Hills CA 90210 USA
**Macaulay, Stewart** — Attorney, Educator
University of Wisconsin, Law School, 975 Bascom Mall, #6107, Madison WI 53706, USA
**MacAvoy, Paul W** — Economist
920 Indian Beach Dr, Sarasota FL 34234, USA
**Maccarinelli, Enzo** — Boxer
13 Hengoed Hall Dr, Cefn, Hengoed, Mid Glamorgan CF8 7JW, Wales
**Macchio, Ralph** — Actor
Don Buchwald Talent Agency, 6500 Wilshire Blvd, #2200, Los Angeles CA 90048 USA
**Maccioni, Sirio** — Restaurateur, Chef
Le Cirque 200, 151 E 58th St, Front 1, New York NY 10022, USA
**MacDermid, Paul** — Ice Hockey Player
81 Lakeland Dr, Sauble Beach ON N0H 2G0, Canada
**MacDermot, Galt** — Composer
MacDermot Assoc, 12 Silver Lake Road, Staten Island NY 10301, USA
**Macdissi, Peter** — Actor
United Talent Agency, U T A Plaza, 9336 Civic Center Dr, Beverly Hills CA 90210 USA
**MacDonald, Amy** — Singer, Songwriter
Melodramatic Records, PO Box 623, Weybridge KT13 3DE, England
**MacDonald, C Parker** — Ice Hockey Player
3 Miller Road, Northford CT 06472, USA
**MacDonald, Danielle** — Actress
Justice & Ponder, PO Box 480033, Los Angeles CA 90048, USA
**Macdonald, Hettie** — Director
Independent Talent Group, 40 Whitfield St, London W1T 2RH, England
**MacDonald, Julien** — Fashion Designer
Haydens Place, 447A Portobello Road, London W11 1LT, England
**Macdonald, Kelly** — Actress
Independent Talent Group, 40 Whitfield St, London W1T 2RH, England
**Macdonald, Kevin** — Director
United Agents, 12-26 Lexington St, London W1F 0LE, England
**MacDonald, Norm** — Actor, Comedian
Gersh Agency, 9465 Wilshire Blvd, #600, Beverly Hills CA 90212 USA
**MacDonald, Parker** — Ice Hockey Player
3 Miller Road, Northford CT 06472, USA
**MacDonald, Richard** — Sculptor
213 Galisteo St, Santa Fe NM 87501, USA
**Macdonald, Robert (Bob)** — Baseball Player
522 Harbor Grove Circle, Safety Harbor FL 34695, USA
**Macdonald, Shauna** — Actress
United Agents, 12-26 Lexington St, London W1F 0LE, England
**Macdougal, R Meiklejohn (Mike)** — Baseball Player
2429 N Travis St, Mesa AZ 85207, USA
**MacDowell, Andie** — Model, Actress
I M P R, 357 S Robertson Blvd, Beverly Hills CA 90211, USA
**MacEachern, David** — Bobsled Athlete
Bobsled Canada, 140 Canada Olympic Road SW, Calgary AB T3B 5R5, Canada
**Macek, Donald M (Don)** — Football Player
3615 Monte Real, Escondido CA 92029, USA
**Macer, Sterling, Jr** — Actor, Director, Writer
A M T Artists, 15260 Ventura Blvd, #1200, Sherman Oaks CA 91403, USA
**MacFadyen, Angus** — Actor
Alchemy Entertainment, 7024 Melrose Ave, #420, Los Angeles CA 90038 USA

**MacFadyen, Matthew** — Actor
Hamilton Hodell, 20 Golden Square, London W1F 9JL, England
**MacFarlane, Michael A (Mike)** — Baseball Player
7421 Woodside Ave, Stockton CA 95207, USA
**MacFarlane, Seth** — Animator, Producer, Writer, Composer
Fuzzy Door Productions, 5700 Wilshire Blvd, #325, Los Angeles CA 90036, USA
**MacGraw, Ali** — Actress
Relatively Mgmt, 8899 Beverly Blvd, #509, Los Angeles CA 90048, USA
**MacGregor, Bruce** — Ice Hockey Player
8112 NW 133rd St, Edmonton AB T5R 0B1, Canada
**MacGregor, Jeff** — Writer
ESPN-TV, Sports Dept, ESPN Plaza, 935 Middle St, Bristol CT 06010 USA
**MacGregor, Joanna C** — Concert, Jazz Pianist
SoundCircus Records, PO Box 57, Reading, Berkshire BG1 5TX, England
**MacGregor, Katherine** — Actress
23388 Mulholland Dr, #205, Woodland Hills CA 91364, USA
**Mach, David S** — Sculptor
64 Canonbie Road, Forest Hill, London SE23 3AG, England
**Macha, Kenneth E (Ken)** — Baseball Player, Manager
1118 Winnie Way, Latrobe PA 15650, USA
**Machada, Lesley Ann** — Actress
Principato-Young, 9465 Wilshire Blvd, #880, Beverly Hills CA 90212 USA
**Machado Fajardo, Alicia** — Beauty Queen, Actress, Model
Miss Universe Organization, 1370 Ave of Americas, #1600, New York NY 10019 USA
**Machado Ventura, Jose Ramon** — Vice President, Cuba
Palacio de Gobierno, Cibsejo de la Ravolucion, Havana, Cuba
**Machado, China** — Model
I M G Models, 304 Park Ave S, #PH N, New York NY 10010 USA
**Machado, Justina** — Actress
Allman/Rhea Mgmt, 141 S Barrington Ave, #E, Los Angeles CA 90049, USA
**Machado, Rodolfo** — Architect
Machado & Silvetti, 500 Harrison Ave, Boston MA 02118, USA
**Macharski, Franciszek Cardinal** — Religious Leader
Archdiocese, Ul Franciszkanska 3, 31004 Cracow, Poland
**Machen, J Bernard** — Educator
University of Florida, President's Office, Tigert Hall, Gainesville FL 32611, USA
**Machlis, Gail** — Cartoonist (Quality Time)
Gail Machlis Illustrations, 1 Arcade Ave, Berkeley CA 94708, USA
**Machover, Tod** — Composer
Massachusetts Institute of Technology, Media Laboratory, Cambridge MA 02139, USA
**Macht, Gabriel S** — Actor
I C M Partners, 10250 Constellation Blvd, #900, Los Angeles CA 90067 USA
**Macht, Stephen** — Actor
Greater Visions Artists Talent Agency, 8981 W Sunset Blvd, #101, West Hollywood CA 90069 USA
**Machungo, Mario F de Graca** — Prime Minister, Mozambique
Banco International, Avda Zedequias, Mananhela 478, Maputo, Mozambique
**Maclellan, Brian** — Ice Hockey Player
Washington Capitals, 627 N Glebe Road, #850, Arlington VA 22203 USA
**MacInnis, Allan (Al)** — Ice Hockey Player, Executive
1132 Highland Point Dr, Saint Louis MO 63131, USA
**MacInnis, Frank T** — Businessman
E M C O R Group, 301 Merritt Seven, #600, Norwalk CT 06851, USA
**MacIntosh, Craig** — Cartoonist (Sally Forth)
3403 W 28th St, Minneapolis MN 55416, USA
**Macintyre, Carter** — Actor
United Talent Agency, U T A Plaza, 9336 Civic Center Dr, Beverly Hills CA 90210 USA
**MacIntyre, G Michael (Mike)** — Football Coach
University of Colorado, Athletic Dept, Boulder CO 80309, USA
**MacIsaac, Ashley** — Violinist, Dancer
Talk's Cheap Mgmt, 141 Winona Dr, Toronto ON M6G 3T1, Canada
**MacIsaac, Martha** — Actress
A M I Artists Mgmt, 464 King St E, Toronto ON M5A 1L7, Canada
**MacIver, Norm** — Ice Hockey Player
2119 Ponderosa Circle, Duluth MN 55811, USA
**MacIvor, Daniel** — Actor
I C M Partners, 10250 Constellation Blvd, #900, Los Angeles CA 90067 USA
**Mack, Allison** — Actress
Industry Entertainment, 955 Carillo Dr, #300, Los Angeles CA 90048 USA
**Mack, Bill** — Sculptor
Erin Taylor Editions, 5222 W 78th St, Minneapolis MN 55435, USA
**Mack, Cedric M** — Football Player
116 Chestnut St, Lake Jackson TX 77566, USA
**Mack, Consuelo** — Commentator
WealthTrack, PO Box 20485, Dag Hammarskjold Convenience Center, New York NY 10017, USA
**Mack, J Kevin** — Football Player
29359 Hummingbird Circle, Westlake OH 44145, USA
**Mack, John J** — Financier
Morgan Stanley Co, 1585 Broadway, Lower B, New York NY 10036, USA
**Mack, Lonnie** — Singer, Guitarist
Concerted Efforts, PO Box 440326, Somerville MA 02144 USA
**Mack, Shane L** — Baseball Player
35324 Marsh Lane, Wildomar CA 92595, USA
**Mack, Thomas I (Tom)** — Football Player
52 Grand Miramar Dr, Henderson NV 89011, USA
**Mackall, Michelle** — Golfer
2057 Oxford Ave, Cardiff CA 92007, USA
**Mackanin, Peter (Pete), Jr** — Baseball Player, Manager
11563 E Bronco Trail, Scottsdale AZ 85255, USA
**Mackay, David** — Director, Producer
Gersh Agency, 9465 Wilshire Blvd, #600, Beverly Hills CA 90212 USA
**Mackay, Harvey** — Writer
Mackay Envelope Corp, 2100 Elm St SE, Minneapolis MN 55414, USA
**MacKay-Lyons, Brian** — Architect
MacKay-Lyons Architect Inc, 2188 Gottingen St, Halifax NS B3K 3B4, Canada
**Macke, Richard C** — Navy Admiral
1887 Alaweo St, Honolulu HI 96821, USA

# M

**Macken, Eoin** — Actor
I C M Partners, 10250 Constellation Blvd, #900, Los Angeles CA 90067 USA

**Mackenzie, Alastair** — Actor
Artists Partnership, 101 Finsbury Pavement, London EC2A 1RS, England

**MacKenzie, David** — Director
United Agents, 12-26 Lexington St, London W1F 0LE, England

**MacKenzie, J Barry** — Ice Hockey Player
Minnesota Wild, XCel Energy Arena, 1275 Saint Antoine W, Saint Paul MN 55104 USA

**MacKenzie, Kenneth P (Ken)** — Baseball Player
15 Fair St, Guilford CT 06437, USA

**MacKenzie, Peter** — Actor
Precision Entertainment, 6338 Wilshire Blvd, Los Angeles CA 90048, USA

**Mackey, Cindy** — Golfer
1190 Millstone Run, Bogart GA 30622, USA

**Mackey, Lance** — Dog Sled Racer
PO Box 75015, Fairbanks AK 99707, USA

**Mackey, Malcolm M** — Basketball Player
504 Hemphill Ave, Chattanooga TN 37411, USA

**Mackey, Rick** — Dog Sled Racer
5938 Four Mile Road, Nenana AK 99760, USA

**Mackie, Allison** — Actress
A P A Talent & Literary Agency, 405 S Beverly Dr, #300, Beverly Hills CA 90212 USA

**Mackie, Anthony** — Actor
Inspire Entertainment, 1517 S Bentley Ave, #202, Los Angeles CA 90025, USA

**Mackie, Robert G (Bob)** — Fashion Designer
Bob Mackie Ltd, 530 Fashion Ave, New York NY 10018, USA

**Mackin, Sean** — Violinist (Yellowcard)
Capitol Records, 1750 N Vine St, Los Angeles CA 90028 USA

**MacKinnon, Catherine** — Attorney, Social Activist
University of Michigan, Law School, 625 S State St, Ann Arbor MI 48109, USA

**MacKinnon, Roderick** — Nobel Chemistry Laureate
53 Winchester St, #2, Brookline MA 2446, USA

**MacKinnon, Simmone J** — Actress
Mark Morrissey Assoc, 45 Oxford St, Bondi Junction NSW 2022, Australia

**Mackintosh, Cameron A** — Producer
Cameron Mackintosh Ltd, 1 Bedford Square, London WC1B 3RA, England

**Mackintosh, Steven** — Actor
Independent Talent Group, 40 Whitfield St, London W1T 2RH, England

**Macklemore** — Lyricist, Singer (Thrift Shop)
PO Box 19784, Seattle WA 98109, USA

**Macklin, David** — Actor
Wilson, 5410 Wilshire Blvd, #510, Los Angeles CA 90036, USA

**Macknowski, John A** — Basketball Player
1902 Garnet Lane, Dandridge, TN 37225, USA

**Macknowski, Stephen** — Canoeing Athlete
462 Kimball Ave, Yonkers NY 10704, USA

**Mackowiak, Robert W (Rob)** — Baseball Player
2414 W Superior St, Chicago IL 60612, USA

**Mackrides, William (Bill)** — Football Player
1060 Beverly Lane, Newtown Square PA 19073, USA

**MacLachlan, Kyle** — Actor
Gersh Agency, 9465 Wilshire Blvd, #600, Beverly Hills CA 90212 USA

**Maclachlan, Patricia** — Writer
21 Unquomonk Road, Williamsburg MA 01096, USA

**MacLaine, Shirley** — Actress
I C M Partners, 10250 Constellation Blvd, #900, Los Angeles CA 90067 USA

**MacLean, Donald J (Don)** — Basketball Player
216 Los Padres Dr, Thousand Oaks CA 91361, USA

**MacLean, Doug** — Ice Hockey Coach
466 Notre Dame St, Summerside PE C1N 1T3, Canada

**MacLean, John** — Ice Hockey Player, Coach
44 Old Farm Road, Basking Ridge NJ 7920, USA

**MacLean, Steven G** — Astronaut, Canada
N A S A, Johnson Space Center, 2101 NASA Road, Houston TX 77058 USA

**MacLeish, Richard G (Rick)** — Ice Hockey Player
5612 Bay Ave, Ocean City NJ 08226, USA

**MacLellan, Brian J** — Ice Hockey Player, Executive
Washington Capitals, 627 N Glebe Road, #850, Arlington VA 22203 USA

**Macleod, Carla** — Ice Hockey Player
Team Canada, 2424 University Dr NW, Calgary AB T2N 3Y9, Canada

**MacLeod, Gavin** — Actor
70070 Frank Sinatra Dr, #7, Rancho Mirage CA 92270, USA

**MacLeod, John M** — Basketball Coach
4610 E Fanfol Dr, Phoenix AZ 85028, USA

**MacLeod, Kathleen** — Basketball Player
Dandenong Rangers, 270 Stud Road, Dandenong North VIC 3175, Australia

**Macleod, Thomas W (Tom)** — Football Player
15412 N Hazard Road, Spokane WA 99208, USA

**MacMaster, Natalie** — Fiddler
Columbia Artists Mgmt Inc, 5 Columbus Circle, 1790 Broadway, #1600, New York NY 10019 USA

**MacMillan, John S** — Ice Hockey Player
2672 W Conifer Dr, Eagle ID 83616, USA

**MacMillan, William S (Billy)** — Ice Hockey Player
Upper Meadowbank Road, RR 2, Cornwall PE C0A 1H0, Canada

**MacMurray, William** — Electrical Engineer
200 Deer Run Road, Schaghticoke NY 12154, USA

**Macnee, Patrick** — Actor
7 Mount Holyoke, Rancho Mirage CA 92270, USA

**MacNeil, Allister W (Al)** — Ice Hockey Player, Coach
151 Parkview Way SE, Calgary AB T2J 4N3, Canada

**MacNeil, Robert B W** — Commentator
2700 S Quincy St, Arlington VA 22206, USA

**MacNeille, Tress** — Actress
Sutton-Barth Vennari, 5900 Wilshire Blvd, #700, Los Angeles CA 90036 USA

**MacNicol, Peter** — Actor
Principato-Young, 9465 Wilshire Blvd, #880, Beverly Hills CA 90212 USA

**Macomber, Debbie** — Writer
PO Box 1458, Port Orchard WA 98366, USA

**Macomber, Dick** — Thoroughbred Racing Jockey
6720 NW 28th Terrace, Fort Lauderdale FL 33309, USA

**Macomber, George B N** — Skier
1 Design Center Place, #600, Boston MA 02210, USA

**Macoun, Jamie** — Ice Hockey Player
J M A C Drilling, 1313 10th St, Misku AB T3E 2X3, Canada

**MacPherson, Duncan I** — Editorial Cartoonist
Toronto Star, Editorial Dept, 1 Yonge St, Toronto ON M5E 1E6, Canada

**Macpherson, Elle** — Model
Mavrick Artists Agency, 6100 Wilshire Blvd, #550, Los Angeles CA 90048, USA

**Macpherson, Wendy** — Bowler
PO Box 93433, Henderson NV 89009, USA

**MacQuitty, Jonathan** — Inventor (Immunodeficient Mouse)
Abingworth Mgmt Inc, 3000 Sand Hill Road, #4-135, Menlo Park CA 94025, USA

**MacTaggart, Barry** — Businessman
180 N Shore Point, Vero Beach FL 32963, USA

**MacTavish, Craig** — Ice Hockey Player, Coach
3 Quail Hollow Court, Voorhees NJ 08043, USA

**Macurdy, John** — Opera Singer
Columbia Artists Mgmt Inc, 5 Columbus Circle, 1790 Broadway, #1600, New York NY 10019 USA

**MacWhorter, Keith** — Baseball Player
75 Martin St, Rehoboth MA 02769, USA

**Macy, Geoffrey W** — Astronomer
University of California, Integrative Planetary Center, Berkeley CA 94720, USA

**Macy, Kyle R** — Basketball Player, Coach
3320 Overbrook Dr, Lexington KY 40502, USA

**Macy, William H (Bill)** — Actor
W M E Entertainment, 9601 Wilshire Blvd, #300, Beverly Hills CA 90210 USA

**Madani, Tala** — Artist
Pilar Corrias Gallery, 54 Eastcastle St, London W1W 8EF, England

**Madden, Beezie** — Equestrian
3908 Stone Bridge Road, Cazenovia NY 13035, USA

**Madden, Benji L** — Singer, Guitarist (Good Charlotte)
A Fein Martini, 37 W 20th St, #1008, New York NY 10011, USA

**Madden, David** — Writer
Louisiana State University, US Civil War Center, Baton Rouge LA 70803, USA

**Madden, Joel R** — Singer (Good Charlotte)
Girlie Action, 59 W 19th St, #4B, New York NY 10011, USA

**Madden, John** — Ice Hockey Player
6 Briarcliff Road, Montville NJ 07045, USA

**Madden, John E** — Football Player, Coach, Sportscaster
5095 Coronado Blvd, Pleasanton CA 94588, USA

**Madden, John P** — Director
Casorotto Ramsay, Waverley House, 7-12 Noel St, London W1F 8GQ, England

**Madden, Michael A (Mike)** — Baseball Player
4733 Frankfort Way, Denver CO 80239, USA

**Madden, Mickey** — Bassist (Maroon 5)
J Records, 745 5th Ave, #600, New York NY 10151 USA

**Madden, Morris D** — Baseball Player
105 Jennings St, Laurens SC 29360, USA

**Madden, Richard** — Actor
Troika, 74 Clerkenwell Road, #300, London EC1M 5QA, England

**Maddin, Guy** — Director
Loeb & Loeb, 10100 Santa Monica Blvd, #2200, Los Angeles CA 90067, USA

**Maddon, Joseph J (Joe)** — Baseball Manager
2560 N Lindsay Road, #32, Mesa AZ 85213, USA

**Maddow, Rachel A** — Commentator
Napoli Mgmt, 8844 W Olympic Blvd, #100, Beverly Hills CA 90211, USA

**Maddox, David M** — Army General
2301 Fort Scott Dr, Arlington VA 22202, USA

**Maddox, Elliott** — Baseball Player
980 Coral Ridge Dr, #104, Coral Springs FL 33071, USA

**Maddox, Eva** — Interior Designer
Eva Maddox Assoc, 333 N Wabash Ave, #3600, Chicago IL 60611, USA

**Maddox, Jerry G** — Baseball Player
20647 Thundersky Circle, Riverside CA 92508, USA

**Maddox, Mark A** — Football Player
100 W Washington St, #1900, Phoenix AZ 85003, USA

**Maddox, Rachel** — Commentator
MSNBC, News Dept, 22 Fletcher Ave, Fort Lee NJ 07024, USA

**Maddox, Thomas A (Tommy)** — Football Player
210 Ridge View Lane, Roanoke TX 76262, USA

**Maddux, Gregory A (Greg)** — Baseball Player
36 Innisbrook Ave, Las Vegas NV 89113, USA

**Madeley, Anna** — Actress
Independent Talent Group, 40 Whitfield St, London W1T 2RH, England

**Mader, Rebecca** — Actress
Innovative Artists, 1505 10th St, Santa Monica CA 90401 USA

**Madfai, Kahtan al** — Architect
22 Vassileos Constantinou, 11635 Athens, Greece

**Madi, Hamada (Bolero)** — Prime Minister, Comoros
Prime Minister's Office, BP 421, Moroni, Comoros

**Madigan, Amy** — Actress
Industry Entertainment, 955 Carillo Dr, #300, Los Angeles CA 90048 USA

**Madigan, Kathleen** — Actress, Comedienne, Writer, Producer
Creative Artists Agency, 2000 Ave of Stars, #100, Los Angeles CA 90067 USA

**Madigan, Martha** — Photographer
730 Carpenter Lane, Philadelphia PA 19119, USA

**Madinier, Bruno** — Actor
Agence Artiste Adequat, 108 Rue Reaumur, 75002 Paris, France

**Madison, Bailee** — Actress
Coast to Coast Talent, 3350 Barham Blvd, Los Angeles CA 90068 USA

**Madison, C Scott (Scotty)** — Baseball Player
5397 Thornapple Lane NW, Acworth GA 30101, USA

# M

**Madison, Holly**
Entertainment Fusion Group, 8899 Beverly Blvd, #412, West Hollywood CA 90046, USA — Model, Actress

**Madison, Samuel A (Sam)**
13153 SW 25th Place, Davie FL 33325, USA — Football Player

**Madison, Tianna**
351 Oakdale Circle, Elyria OH 44035, USA — Track Athlete

**Madkins, Gerald**
528 W 8th St, Merced CA 95341, USA — Basketball Player

**Madlock, Bill, Jr**
1565 Calle del Estribo, Pacific Palisades CA 90272, USA — Baseball Player

**Madobe, Sheikh Adeb Mohamed Nor**
President's Office, People's Palace, Mogadishu, Somalia — President, Somalia

**Madonna**
Untitled Entertainment, 350 S Beverly Dr, #200, Beverly Hills CA 90212 USA — Singer, Actress

**Madrigal, Al**
Creative Artists Agency, 2000 Ave of Stars, #100, Los Angeles CA 90067 USA — Actor

**Madrigali, Jeff**
6212 Greenblower Lane, Clinton WA 98236, USA — Yachtsman

**Madritsch, Bobby**
8628 Linder Ave, Burbank IL 60459, USA — Baseball Player

**Madsen, Loren W**
428 Broome St, New York NY 10013, USA — Sculptor

**Madsen, Mark E**
4223 Vintage Circle, Provo UT 84604, USA — Basketball Player

**Madsen, Michael**
Madsen International Mgmt, 9000 Sunset Blvd, Los Angeles CA 90069, USA — Actor

**Madsen, Ole Christian**
Nimbus Film Productions, Hauchsvej 17, 1825 Frederiksberg, Denmark — Director

**Madsen, Virginia**
Untitled Entertainment, 350 S Beverly Dr, #200, Beverly Hills CA 90212 USA — Actress

**Maduro, Calvin G**
793 Springdale Dr, Millersville MD 21108, USA — Baseball Player

**Mae, Audra**
The Mangement Co, 4220 Lankershim Blvd, North Hollywood CA 91602, USA — Singer, Songwriter

**Maedizossian, Prelate Moushegh**
Armenian Apostolic Church, 4401 Russell Ave, Los Angeles CA 90027, USA — Religious Leader

**Maese, Joseph M (Joe)**
4738 W Krystal Way, Glendale AZ 85308, USA — Football Player

**Maestro, Mia**
I C M Partners, Marlborough House, 10 Earlham St, #300, London WC2H 9LNP, England — Actress

**Maffay, Peter**
Buro Peter Maffay, Klenzestr 1, 82327 Tutzing, Germany — Singer

**Maffei, Lamberto**
National Research Council, Piazzale Aldo Moro 7, 00185 Rome, Italy — Neurobiologist

**Maffett, Debra Sue (Debbie)**
1525 McGavock St, Nashville TN 37203, USA — Beauty Queen

**Maffia, Roma**
S M S Talent, 8383 Wilshire Blvd, #230, Beverly Hills CA 90211 USA — Actress

**Magadan, David J (Dave)**
3733 Johnathon Ave, Palm Harbor FL 34685, USA — Baseball Player

**Magariaf, Mohamed Yousef el-**
President's Office, Bab el Asiziya Barracks, Tripoli, Libya — President, Libya

**Magath, Felix**
F C Fulham, Craven Cottage, Stevenage Road, London SW6 6HH, England — Soccer Player, Coach

**Magaw, John W**
Transportation Security Administration, 400 7th St SW, Washington DC 20590, USA — Law Enforcement Official

**Magee, Dave**
5S350 Deer Ridge Path, Big Rock IL 60511, USA — Harness Racing Driver

**Magee, David**
Creative Artists Agency, 2000 Ave of Stars, #100, Los Angeles CA 90067 USA — Writer

**Magee, Herb**
PO Box 67, Southeastern PA 19399, USA — Basketball Coach

**Magee, Kenneth**
11491 Riverside Dr, Los Angeles CA 91602, USA — Actor

**Magee, Wendell E, Jr**
6500 Muskogee Cove, Leeds AL 35094, USA — Baseball Player

**Maggard, Dave**
University of Houston, Athletic Dept, Houston TX 77204, USA — Track Athlete, Sports Executive

**Maggenti, Maria**
Paradigm Agency, 360 N Crescent Dr, North Building, Beverly Hills CA 90210 USA — Director

**Maggert, Jeff**
62 W Bracebridge Circle, Spring TX 77382, USA — Golfer

**Maggs, Donald J (Don)**
26525 Amhearst Circle, #106, Beachwood OH 44122, USA — Football Player

**Magic Dick (Salwitz)**
Nick Ben-Meir, 652 N Doheny Dr, West Hollywood CA 90069, USA — Harmonica Player (J Geils Band)

**Magilton, Gerard E (Jerry)**
Martin Marietta Astro Space, 100 Campus Dr, Newtown PA 18940, USA — Astronaut

**Maginn, Matt**
Ground Control Touring, 20 Jay St, #826, Brooklyn NY 11201 USA — Bassist (Cursive)

**Maginnes, John**
612 Topwater Lane, Greensboro NC 27455, USA — Golfer

**Magloire, Jamaal D**
Toronto Raptors, Air Canada Center, 20 Bay St, Toronto ON M5J 2N8, Canada — Basketball Player

**Magnani, Olivia**
Agents Associes, 201 Rue du Faubourg Saint Honore, 75008 Paris, France — Actress

**Magnante, Michael A (Mike)**
5305 Via Quinto, Newbury Park CA 91320, USA — Baseball Player

**Magnanti, Brooke**
Orion Publishing, 5 Upper Saint Martin's Lane, London WC2H 9EA, England — Writer, Epidemiologist

**Magni, James**
Magni Design, Pacific Design Center, 8687 Melrose Ave, West Hollywood CA 90069, USA — Architect, Interior Designer

**Magnus, Edie**
NBC-TV, News Dept, 30 Rockefeller Plaza, #270E, New York NY 10112 USA — Commentator

**Magnus, Sandra H (Sandy)**
3477 Vinings North Trail SE, Smyrna GA 30080, USA — Astronaut

**Magnuson, Ann** — Actress
1317 Maltman Ave, Los Angeles CA 90026, USA
**Magnussen, James** — Swimmer
Aquatic Centre, Olympic Blvd, Sydney Olympic Park NSW 2127, Australia
**Magnussen-Ceila, Karen D** — Figure Skater
2852 Thorndiff Dr, North Vancouver BC V7R 285, Canada
**Magnusson, Kim** — Producer
Dansk Film Kompagni, Teglgaardsvej 21, 2920 Charlottenlund, Denmark
**Magowan, Kate** — Actress
United Agents, 12-26 Lexington St, London W1F 0LE, England
**Magrane, Joseph D (Joe)** — Baseball Player
705 Guisando de Avila, Tampa FL 33613, USA
**Magri, Charles G (Charlie)** — Boxer
345 Bethnal Green Road, Bethnal Green, London E2 6LG, England
**Magris, Claudio** — Writer, Journalist
Via Carpaccio 2, 34127 Trieste, Italy
**Magruder, Christopher J (Chris)** — Baseball Player
1740 Leisure Lane, Yakima WA 98908, USA
**Magsamen, Sandra** — Writer, Artist
Orchard Books/Scholastic, 557 Broadway, New York NY 10012, USA
**Maguire, Adrian E** — Thoroughbred Racing Jockey
17 Willes Close, Faringdon, Oxfordshire SN7 7DU, England
**Maguire, Albert M** — Surgeon
Children's Hospital, 34th St & Civic Center Blvd, Philadelphia PA 19104, USA
**Maguire, Emily** — Field Hockey Player
Reading Hockey Club, La Chenaie Western Ave, Woodley Reading RG4 6ST, England
**Maguire, Gregory** — Writer
W M E Entertainment, 9601 Wilshire Blvd, #300, Beverly Hills CA 90210 USA
**Maguire, Joseph** — Navy Admiral
National Counterterrorism Center, 1505 Tysons McLean Blvd, McLean VA 22102, USA
**Maguire, Les** — Pianist (Gerry & the Pacemakers)
Barry Collins, 21A Cliftown Road, Southend-on-Sea, Essex SS1 1AB, England
**Maguire, Michael** — Actor, Singer
Epstein-Wyckoff, 280 S Beverly Dr, #400, Beverly Hills CA 90212 USA
**Maguire, Paul L** — Sportscaster, Football Player
707 Ocean Blvd, Isle of Palms SC 29451, USA
**Maguire, Richard W** — Cinematographer
605 Summer Mesa Dr, Las Vegas NV 89144, USA
**Maguire, Sean** — Actor
Paul Kohner, 9300 Wilshire Blvd, #555, Beverly Hills CA 90212 USA
**Maguire, Sharon** — Director, Producer, Writer
United Talent Agency, U T A Plaza, 9336 Civic Center Dr, Beverly Hills CA 90210 USA
**Maguire, Tobey** — Actor
W M E Entertainment, 9601 Wilshire Blvd, #300, Beverly Hills CA 90210 USA
**Mahaffey, John D, Jr** — Golfer
594 Sawdust Road, #229, Spring TX 77380, USA
**Mahaffey, Randolph (Randy)** — Basketball Player
25 Berkeley Road, Avondale Estates GA 30002, USA
**Mahaffey, Valerie** — Actress
Innovative Artists, 1505 10th St, Santa Monica CA 90401 USA
**Mahaffrey, Arthur (Art)** — Baseball Player
PO Box 1212, Allentown PA 18105, USA
**Mahal, Taj** — Singer, Musician, Songwriter
Red Light Mgmt, 44 Wall St, #2200, New York NY 10005, USA
**Mahalanabis, Dilip** — Physician
Applied Studies Society, 108 Manicktata Main Road, Kolkata 700054, India
**Mahalic, Drew A** — Football Player
2114 W Sunset Dr, Portland OR 97239, USA
**Mahama, John D** — President, Ghana
President's Office, Golden Jubilee House, PO Box 1627, Accra, Ghana
**Mahan, Hunter M** — Golfer
3316 Snowmass Lane, McKinney TX 75070, USA
**Mahan, Lawrence (Larry)** — Rodeo Rider
PO Box 119, Sunset TX 76270, USA
**Mahan, Sean C** — Football Player
4202 E 116th Place, Tulsa OK 74137, USA
**Mahanthappa, Rudresh** — Jazz Saxophonist, Composer
48 S Park St, #210, Montclair NJ 07042, USA
**Mahar, Kevin** — Baseball Player
2506 E Wheeler St, Midland MI 48642, USA
**Maharidge, Dale D** — Writer
Stanford University, Communications Dept, Stanford CA 94305, USA
**Mahay, Ronald M (Ron)** — Baseball Player
13177 E Cochise Road, Scottsdale AZ 85259, USA
**Mahendru, Annet** — Actress
Paradigm Agency, 360 N Crescent Dr, North Building, Beverly Hills CA 90210 USA
**Maher, Ben** — Equestrian
Eisenham Stud, Fullers End, Bishop's Stortford, Hertsfordshire CM22 6EA, England
**Maher, Bill** — Commentator, Comedian
Creative Artists Agency, 2000 Ave of Stars, #100, Los Angeles CA 90067 USA
**Maher, Chris** — Photographer
PO Box 5, Lambertville MI 48144, USA
**Maher, Sean** — Actor
S D B Partners, 315 S Beverly Dr, #411, Beverly Hills CA 90067 USA
**Mahinmi, Ian** — Basketball Player
Indiana Pacers, Conseco Fieldhouse, 125 S Pennsylvania, Indianapolis IN 46204 USA
**Mahler, Michael J (Mickey)** — Baseball Player
7911 Quirt St, San Antonio TX 78227, USA
**Mahohato Mohato Seeiso** — Queen, Lesotho
Royal Palace, PO Box 524, Maseru 100, Lesotho
**Maholm, Paul G** — Baseball Player
518 Village Green Blvd W, Mars PA 16046, USA
**Mahon, Sean** — Actor
Principal Entertainment, 9255 Sunset Blvd, #500, Los Angeles CA 90069 USA
**Mahone, Austin** — Singer
PO Box 409009, Fort Lauderdale FL 33340, USA

**Mahone, Ed**
Marvin Millett, 6548 Whitney Ave, Saint Louis MO 63133, USA — Boxer

**Mahoney, Brian C**
96 Greystone Road, Rockville Center NY 11570, USA — Basketball Player

**Mahoney, James T (Jim)**
345 Hawthorne Ave, #2, Hawthorne NJ 07506, USA — Baseball Player

**Mahoney, John**
I C M Partners, 10250 Constellation Blvd, #900, Los Angeles CA 90067 USA — Actor

**Mahoney, Maureen**
Latham & Watkins, 555 7th St NW, Washington DC 20004, USA — Attorney

**Mahoney, Mike**
4412 98th St, Urbandale IA 50322, USA — Baseball Player

**Mahoney, Roger**
2 Sussex Cottages, Emsworth Common Road, Emsworth, Hampshire PO10 7PU, England — Cartoonist (Millie)

**Mahoney, Tim**
College Agency, 7907 Stafford Trail, Savage MN 55376, USA — Guitarist (311), Songwriter

**Mahony, Roger Cardinal**
Archdiocese of Los Angeles, 3424 Wilshire Blvd, Los Angeles CA 90010, USA — Religious Leader

**Mahorn, Derrick A (Rick)**
44 Gordon Lane, East Hartford CT 06118, USA — Basketball Player, Coach

**Mahovlich, Francis W (Frank)**
2-954 Ave Road, Toronto ON M5P 2K8, Canada — Ice Hockey Player

**Mahovlich, Peter J (Pete)**
116 Farr Lane, Queensbury NY 12804, USA — Ice Hockey Player

**Mahr, Joe**
Toledo Blade, Editorial Dept, 541 N Superior St, Toledo OH 43660, USA — Journalist

**Mahre, Phillip (Phil)**
Mahre Training Center, Deer Valley Resort, PO Box 739, Park City UT 84060, USA — Alpine Skier

**Mahre, Steve**
Mahre Training Center, Deer Valley Resort, PO Box 739, Park City UT 84060, USA — Alpine Skier

**Mahumdi, Baghadadi al-**
General Secretary's Office, Bab el Asiziya Barracks, Tripoli, Libya — General Secretary, Libya

**Maida, Adam J Cardinal**
Archdiocese of Detroit, 1234 Washington Blvd, #1, Detroit MI 48226, USA — Religious Leader

**Maiden-Naccarato, Jeanne**
1 N Stadium Way, #4, Tacoma WA 98403, USA — Bowler

**Maier, Hermann**
Im 8 ErJet, Unterbergasse, 5542 Flachau, Austria — Alpine Skier

**Maier, Mitchell W (Mitch)**
435 Amelia Circle, South Lyon MI 48178, USA — Baseball Player

**Maier, Sepp**
Agentur Roth Sportpromotion, Lindenstr 12, 85664 Hohenlinden, Germany — Soccer Player

**Maiga, Ousmane Issoufi**
Prime Minister's Office, BP 97, Bamako, Mali — Prime Minister, Mali

**Maikki, Susanna**
Ensemble Intercontemporain, 223 Ave Jean-Jaurès 75019 Paris, France — Conductor

**Mailhouse, Robert**
Stone Manners Salners, 6100 Wilshire Blvd, #1500, Los Angeles CA 90035 USA — Actor

**Maillard, Carol**
I C M Partners, 10250 Constellation Blvd, #900, Los Angeles CA 90067 USA — Singer (Sweet Honey in the Rock)

**Main, Frank**
Chicago Sun-Times, Editorial Dept, 401 N Wabash Ave, Chicago IL 60611 USA — Journalist

**Main, Ravinder**
Charing Cross Hospital, Saint Dunstan's Road, London W6 8RP, England — Rheumatologist

**Maine, John K**
129 Richards Ferry Road, Fredericksburg VA 22406, USA — Baseball Player

**Maines, Natalie**
Strategic Artist Mgmt, 1100 Glendon Ave, #1000, Los Angeles CA 90024, USA — Singer (Dixie Chicks)

**Maino**
Hustle Hard Records, 1290 Ave of Americas, Concourse 3, New York NY 10104, USA — Rap Artist

**Mair, Adam**
25 San Fernando Lane, East Amherst NY 14051, USA — Ice Hockey Player

**Mairena, Oswaldo**
160 E 6th Place, Mesa AZ 85201, USA — Baseball Player

**Maisel, Harvey**
University of Nebraska, Chancellor's Office, Lincoln NE 68588, USA — Educator

**Maisel, Jay**
190 Bowery, New York NY 10012, USA — Photographer

**Maisenberg, Olega**
In Der Gugl 9, 3400 Klosterneuburg, Austria — Concert Pianist

**Maisky, Mischa M**
138 Meerlaan, 1900 Overijse, Belgium — Concert Cellist

**Maisuradze, Badri**
I M G Artists, Hogarth Business Park, Chiswick, London W4 2TH, England — Opera Singer

**Maitland, Beth**
Epstein-Wyckoff, 280 S Beverly Dr, #400, Beverly Hills CA 90212 USA — Actress

**Maiwenn**
Agence Artiste Adequat, 108 Rue Reaumur, 75002 Paris, France — Actress, Director, Writer

**Majdarzavyn Ganzorig**
Academy of Sciences, Peace Ave 54B, Ulan Bator 51, Mongolia — Cosmonaut, Mongolia

**Majerle, Daniel L (Dan)**
4534 E Oregon Ave, Phoenix AZ 85018, USA — Basketball Player

**Majewski, Gary W**
1103 Chamboard Lane, Houston TX 77018, USA — Baseball Player

**Majewski, Janusz**
Ul Forteczna 1A, 01540 Warsaw, Poland — Director, Writer

**Majewski, Tomasz**
A Z S Warsaw, Ul Marymoncka 34, 01813 Warsaw, Poland — Track Athlete

**Majkowski, Donald V (Don)**
1593 Bayhill Dr, Duluth GA 30097, USA — Football Player

**Majoli, Iva**
International Mangement Group, 1 Erieview Plaza, 1360 E 9th St, #100, Cleveland OH 44114 USA — Tennis Player

**Major, Clarence L**
University of California, English Dept, Voorhies Hall, Davis CA 95616, USA — Writer

**Major, Jason**
Principato-Young, 9465 Wilshire Blvd, #880, Beverly Hills CA 90212 USA — Actor, Writer

**Mahone - Major**

**Major, John** — Prime Minister, England
8 Stukeley Road, Huntingdon, Cambridgeshire PE29 6HQ, England
**Major, Malvina L** — Opera Singer
PO Box 11-175, Manners St, Te Aero, Wellington 6011, New Zealand
**Major, Reema** — Singer
Agency Group Ltd, 142 W 57th St, #600, New York NY 10019 USA
**Majorino, Tina** — Actress
Leverage Mgmt, 3030 Pennsylvania Ave, Santa Monica CA 90404 USA
**Majors, John T (Johnny)** — Football Player, Coach
4207 Beechwood Road, Knoxville TN 37920, USA
**Majors, Lee** — Actor
1831 Rocking Horse Dr, Simi Valley CA 93065, USA
**Makarov, Askold A** — Ballet Dancer
Plutalova Str 18-4, 197136 Saint Petersburg, Russia
**Makarov, Sergei M** — Ice Hockey Player
4072 Teale Ave, San Jose CA 95117, USA
**Makarova, Natalia R** — Ballerina
American Ballet Theatre, 890 Broadway, #300, New York NY 10003 USA
**Makela, P Helena** — Immunologist
National Public Health Service, Mannerheimintie 166, 00271 Helsinki, Finland
**Makela, Wille** — Curling Athlete
Curling Association, Kalatorppa 2A62, 02230 Espoo, Finland
**Makela-Nummela, Satu** — Markswoman
Radiokatu 20, 00240 Helsinki, Finland
**Makerov, Julie** — Opera Singer
Columbia Artists Mgmt Inc, 5 Columbus Circle, 1790 Broadway, #1600, New York NY 10019 USA
**Makhalina, Yulia V** — Ballerina
Kirov Ballet Theater, 1 Pl Iskusstr, 190000 Saint Petersburg, Russia
**Maki, Chico** — Ice Hockey Player
Norfolk County Sports Hall of Fame, 95 Culver, Simcoe ON N3Y 2V5, Canada
**Maki, Fumihiko** — Pritzker Architectural Laureate
5-16-22 Higashi-Gotanda, Shinagawaku, Tokyo 141 0022, Japan
**Makings, Elizabeth** — Golfer
1500 N Markdale, #12, Mesa AZ 85201, USA
**Makkena, Wendy** — Actress
Schumachr Mgmt, 10323 Santa Monica Blvd, #101, Los Angeles CA 90025, USA
**Makoare, Lawrence** — Actor
Robert Bruce Agency, 218 Richmond Road, Grey Lynn, Auckland, New Zealand
**Maksimova, Yekaterina S** — Ballerina
Smolenskaya Naberezhnaya 5/13-62, 121099 Moscow, Russia
**Maksudian, Michael B (Mike)** — Baseball Player
12148 E San Simeon Dr, Scottsdale AZ 85259, USA
**Maksymiuk, Jerzy** — Conductor
Gdanska 2 m 14, 01633 Warsaw, Poland
**Maktoum, Mohammed bin Rashid Al** — Prime Minister, United Arab Emirates
Prime Minister's Office, Manhal Palace, Abu Dhabi, United Arab Emirates
**Malachi, Carolyn** — Singer
Clarke & Assoc, 2020 Pennsylvania Ave NW, #271, Washington DC 20006, USA
**Malahide, Patrick** — Actor
I C M Partners, Marlborough House, 10 Earlham St, #300, London WC2H 9LNP, England
**Malakhov, Vladimir I** — Ice Hockey Player
PO Box 420536, Kissimmee FL 34742, USA
**Malakian, Daron V** — Singer, Guitarist (System of a Down)
Velvet Hammer Music, 9014 Melrose Ave, West Hollywood CA 90069, USA
**Malala Yousafzai** — Nobel Peace Laureate
I Am Malala Fund, 1201 Connecticut Ave NW, #300, Washington DC 20036, USA
**Malamala, Siupeli** — Football Player
122 110th Ave SE, Bellevue WA 98004, USA
**Malandrino, Catherine** — Fashion Designer
468 Bromme St, New York NY 10013, USA
**Malarchuk, Clint** — Ice Hockey Player
1308 Myers Dr, Gardnerville NV 89410, USA
**Malaret Contreras, Marisol** — Beauty Queen, Actress
Miss Universe Organization, 1370 Ave of Americas, #1600, New York NY 10019 USA
**Malarkey, Donald G** — WW II Army Hero
2233 Juneau Court S, Salem OR 97302, USA
**Malaska, Mark** — Baseball Player
3823 Cumberland Dr, Youngstown OH 44515, USA
**Malchow, Tom** — Swimmer
10220 NW Edgewood Dr, Portland OR 97229, USA
**Malco, Romany** — Actor
Principato-Young, 9465 Wilshire Blvd, #880, Beverly Hills CA 90212 USA
**Malcom, Shirley M** — Association Executive
Science Advancement Assn, 1200 New York Ave NW, Washington DC 20005, USA
**Malcomson, Paula** — Actress
United Talent Agency, U T A Plaza, 9336 Civic Center Dr, Beverly Hills CA 90210 USA
**Maldacena, Juan** — Physicist
Harvard University, Physics Dept, Cambridge MA 02138, USA
**Maldini, Paolo** — Soccer Player
F C Milan, Via Filippo Turati 3, 20121 Milan, Italy
**Maldonado, Candido (Candy)** — Baseball Player
HC 2 Box 16800, Arecibo PR 00612, USA
**Maldonado, Pastor R** — Auto Racing Driver
Team Lotus, Whiteways Centre, Enstone, Chipping Norton, Oxfordshire OX7 4EE, England
**Malee, Chompoo** — Fashion Designer
Hino & Malee Inc, 3701 N Ravenswood Ave, Chicago IL 60613, USA
**Maleeva, Katerina** — Tennis Player
Mladostr 1, #45, NH 14, Sofia 1174, Bulgaria
**Maleeva-Fragniere, Manuela** — Tennis Player
Chemin des Vignes, 1814 La Tour de Peilz, Switzerland
**Malek, Rami** — Actor
W M E Entertainment, 9601 Wilshire Blvd, #300, Beverly Hills CA 90210 USA
**Malenchenko, Yuri I** — Cosmonaut
Cosmonaut Training Center, Star City, 141160 Zvezdny Gorodok, Moscow Oblast, Russia
**Maler, James M (Jim)** — Baseball Player
1758 NE 177th St, North Miami Beach FL 33162, USA

**Malerba, Franco E**
Italian Space Agency, Viale Liegi 26, 00198 Rome, Italy — Astronaut, Italy

**Malfitano, Catherine**
I M G Artists, Burlington Lane, Chiswick, London W4 2TH, England — Opera Singer

**Malgarini, Ryan**
Savage Agency, 6212 Banner Ave, Los Angeles CA 90038 USA — Actor

**Malhotra, Manny**
1210 Oakland Ave, Columbus OH 43212, USA — Ice Hockey Player

**Mali, Anais**
Ford Models Inc, 111 5th Ave, #900, New York NY 10003 USA — Model

**Malice**
American Talent Agency, 26 Finney Farm Road, Croton on Hudson NY 10520, USA — Rap Artist (Clipse)

**Malick, Terrence F**
Creative Artists Agency, 2000 Ave of Stars, #100, Los Angeles CA 90067 USA — Director, Writer

**Malick, Wendie**
Innovative Artists, 1505 10th St, Santa Monica CA 90401 USA — Actress, Model

**Malicki-Sanchez, Keram**
TalentWorks, 3500 W Olive Ave, #1400, Burbank CA 91505 USA — Actor

**Malielegaoi, Tuila'epa L Sa'ilele**
Prime Minister's Office, PO Box L1861, Vailima, Apia, Samoa — Prime Minister, Samoa

**Malignaggi, Paulie**
1620 80th St, Brooklyn NY 11214, USA — Boxer

**Malik, Art**
18 Sydney Mews, London SW3 6HL, England — Actor

**Malík, Marek**
919 Anchorage Road, Tampa FL 33602, USA — Ice Hockey Player

**Malina, Joshua**
I F A Talent Agency, 8730 W Sunset Blvd, #490, West Hollywood CA 90069 USA — Actor

**Malinchak, William J (Bill)**
6422 NW 65th Way, Parkland FL 33067, USA — Football Player

**Malini, Hema**
17 Jai Hind Society, 12th Road Juhu Scheme, Mumbai MS 400049, India — Actress

**Malinvaud, Edmond**
42 Ave de Saxe, 75007 Paris, France — Economist

**Maliponte, Adrianna**
Gorlinsky Promotions, 35 Darer, London W1, England — Opera Singer

**Malizia, Mike**
570 SE Southwood Trail, Stuart FL 34997, USA — Golfer

**Malkin, Evgeni**
Pittsburgh Penguins, Consol Energy Center, 1001 5th Ave, Pittsburgh PA 15219 USA — Ice Hockey Player

**Malkin, Max**
Skouras Agency, 1149 3rd St, #300, Santa Monica CA 90403, USA — Cinematographer

**Malkmus, Robert E (Bobby)**
400 Wallingford Terrace, Union NJ 07083, USA — Baseball Player

**Malkovich, John**
Mr Mudd, 137 N Larchmont, Box 113, Los Angeles CA 90004, USA — Actor

**Mallard, Wesly A**
6073 SW 67th Place, Portland OR 97223, USA — Football Player

**Mallary, Robert**
PO Box 97, Conway MA 01341, USA — Sculptor

**Mallet, Gregory**
C N Marseille, Extremite Blvd Charles Livon, 13007 Marseille, France — Swimmer

**Mallett, Tania**
Bondstars, Tranzaqua, Pinewood Studios, Iver Heath, Buckshire SL0 0NH, England — Actress

**Mallette, Alfred J**
7040 Quail Hill Road, Charlotte NC 28210, USA — Army General

**Malley, Kenneth C**
136 Riverside Road, Edgewater MD 21037, USA — Navy Admiral

**Malley, M Matthew (Matt)**
Direct Mgmt, 947 N La Cienega Blvd, #G, West Hollywood CA 90069, USA — Bassist (Counting Crowes), Songwriter

**Mallick, Don**
42045 N Tilton Dr, Lancaster CA 93536, USA — Test Pilot

**Mallicoat, Robbin D (Rob)**
2050 SE Larson Court, Hillsboro OR 97123, USA — Baseball Player

**Mallon, Meg**
219 Palm Trail, Delray Beach FL 33483, USA — Golfer

**Mallon, Thomas**
801 25th St NW, Washington DC 20037, USA — Writer

**Mallory, Brenda**
Julie Nelson Gallery, 1280 Iron Horse Dr, Park City UT 84060, USA — Artist

**Mallory, Carole**
Pocket Books, 1230 Ave of Americas, New York NY 10020 USA — Actress

**Mallory, Glynn C, Jr**
19221 Heather Forest, San Antonio TX 78258, USA — Army General

**Malloy, Edward A**
University of Notre Dame, President's Office, Notre Dame IN 46556, USA — Educator

**Malloy, Marti**
333 S 11th St, #2, San Jose CA 95112, USA — Judo Athlete

**Malloy, Tom**
Stone Manners Salners, 6100 Wilshire Blvd, #1500, Los Angeles CA 90035 USA — Actor, Writer

**Malo, Pia**
Postfach 1593, 75005 Bretten, Germany — Singer

**Malo, Raul**
Conqueroo, 11271 Ventura Blvd, #522, Studio City CA 91604 USA — Singer (Mavericks), Songwriter

**Malolepski, Olaf**
Die Flippers, August Lammle Str 14, 75438 Knittlingen, Germany — Singer (Die Flippers)

**Malone, Ben (Benny)**
49 E Broadway Road, Tempe AZ 85282, USA — Football Player

**Malone, Charles R (Chuck)**
310 Liberty St, Marked Tree AR 72365, USA — Baseball Player

**Malone, James W**
Catholic Bishops Conference, 1312 Massachusetts Ave NW, Washington DC 20005, USA — Religious Leader

**Malone, Jeffrey N (Jeff)**
415 Lee Road 313, Smiths Station AL 36877, USA — Basketball Player

**Malone, Jena**
Gersh Agency, 9465 Wilshire Blvd, #600, Beverly Hills CA 90212 USA — Actress

| | |
|---|---|
| **Malone, John C** <br> Liberty Media Corp, 12300 Liberty Blvd, Englewood CO 80112, USA | Businessman |
| **Malone, Karl** <br> 105 W Charter St, Farmerville LA 71241, USA | Basketball Player |
| **Malone, Kype** <br> D G C/Interscope Records, 2220 Colorado Ave, Santa Monica CA 90404, USA | Singer (TV on the Radio) |
| **Malone, Maicel** <br> 4064 Bothwell Terrace, Tallahassee FL 32317, USA | Track Athlete |
| **Malone, Mark M** <br> 9391 E Mark Lane, Scottsdale AZ 85262, USA | Football Player |
| **Malone, Moses E** <br> 310 S Keswick Court, Sugar Land TX 77478, USA | Basketball Player |
| **Malone, Patricia** <br> Bruno Magli USA, 75 Triangle Blvd, Carlstadt NJ 07072, USA | Businesswoman |
| **Malone, Ryan G** <br> 4908 Yacht Club Dr, Tampa FL 33616, USA | Ice Hockey Player |
| **Malone, Wallace D, Jr** <br> SouthTrust Corp, 420 20th St N, Birmingham AL 35203, USA | Financier |
| **Malone, William** <br> A P A Talent & Literary Agency, 405 S Beverly Dr, #300, Beverly Hills CA 90212 USA | Director |
| **Maloney, Dan** <br> Sutton Group Realty, 241 Minet's Point Road, Barrie ON L4N 4C4, Canada | Ice Hockey Player, Coach, Executive |
| **Maloney, David W (Dave)** <br> 122 Dolphin Cove Quay, Stamford CT 06902, USA | Ice Hockey Player |
| **Maloney, Donald M (Don)** <br> 21 Guilford Lane, Greenwich CT 06831, USA | Ice Hockey Player, Executive |
| **Maloney, James W (Jim)** <br> 7027 N Teilman Ave, #102, Fresno CA 93711, USA | Baseball Player |
| **Maloney, Michael** <br> Markham Froggatt Irwin, Julian House, 4 Windmill St, London W1P 1HF, England | Actor |
| **Maloney, William R** <br> Navy Mutual Aid Assn, Henderson Hall, 29 Carpenter Road, Arlington VA 22214, USA | Marine Corps General |
| **Malouf, David G J** <br> Mobbs, 35A Sutherland Crescent, Darling Point, Sydney NSW 2027, Australia | Writer |
| **Malsby, Lynn** <br> R D M J Entertainment Mgmt, 3619 Rose Ave, Long Beach CA 90807 USA | Keyboardist (Klymaxx) |
| **Maltais, Dominique** <br> Speed Skating Canada, 2781 Lancaster Road, #402, Ottawa ON K1B 1A7, Canada | Snowboard Skier |
| **Maltais, Valerie** <br> Skate Canada, 865 Shefford Road, Ottawa ON K1J 1H9, Canada | Speed Skater |
| **Maltbie, Roger** <br> 179 Longmeadow Dr, Los Gatos CA 95032, USA | Golfer, Sportscaster |
| **Maltby, Kirk** <br> 58 Putnam Place, Grosse Pointe Shores MI 48236, USA | Ice Hockey Player |
| **Maltby, Richard E, Jr** <br> 200 E 89th St, #16B, New York NY 10128, USA | Lyricist, Director |
| **Malter, Arnold S** <br> 301 N Lake Ave, #810, Pasadena CA 91101, USA | Attorney |
| **Malthouse, Matthew** <br> Gavin Barker Assoc, 2D Wimpole St, London W1G 0EB, England | Actor |
| **Maltin, Leonard** <br> 10424 Whipple St, Toluca Lake CA 91602, USA | Film, TV Critic, Producer |
| **Maltzan, Michael** <br> 2801 Hyperion Ave, Los Angeles CA 90027, USA | Architect |
| **Malyshev, Yuri V** <br> Cosmonaut Training Center, Star City, 141160 Zvezdny Gorodok, Moscow Oblast, Russia | Cosmonaut |
| **Malysz, Adam H** <br> K S Wisla Ustronianka, Ul Wyzwolenia 67, 43460 Wisla, Poland | Ski Jumper |
| **Malzone, Frank J** <br> 16 Aletha Road, Needham MA 02492, USA | Baseball Player |
| **Mamby, Saoul** <br> 20 W Mosholu Parkway S, #17, Bronx NY 10468, USA | Boxer |
| **Mamet, David A** <br> 2 Northfield Plaza, #200, Northfield IL 60093, USA | Writer, Director |
| **Mamet, Zosia** <br> United Talent Agency, U T A Plaza, 9336 Civic Center Dr, Beverly Hills CA 90210 USA | Actress |
| **Mamula, Michael B (Mike)** <br> 4 Ithan Woods Lane, Villanova PA 19085, USA | Football Player |
| **Manabe, Syukuro** <br> Princeton University, Atmospheric Sciences Dept, Princeton NJ 08540, USA | Meteorologist |
| **Manahan, George** <br> Columbia Artists Mgmt Inc, 5 Columbus Circle, 1790 Broadway, #1600, New York NY 10019 USA | Conductor |
| **Manakov, Gennadi M** <br> Cosmonaut Training Center, Star City, 141160 Zvezdny Gorodok, Moscow Oblast, Russia | Cosmonaut |
| **Manarov, Musa C** <br> Khovanskeya 3, 129515 Moscow, Russia | Cosmonaut |
| **Mance, R Joshua** <br> Southern California Trojans, 3501 Watt Way, Los Angeles CA 90089, USA | Track Athlete |
| **Mancham, James R M** <br> PO Box 29, Mahe, Seychelles | President, Seychelles |
| **Manchester, Melissa** <br> A V O Talent Agency, 5670 Wilshire Blvd, #1930, Los Angeles CA 90036, USA | Singer, Songwriter |
| **Manchevski, Milcho** <br> A P A Talent & Literary Agency, 405 S Beverly Dr, #300, Beverly Hills CA 90212 USA | Director |
| **Mancina, Mark** <br> Gorfaine/Schwartz, 4111 W Alameda Ave, #509, Burbank CA 91505 USA | Composer |
| **Mancini, Ray (Boom Boom)** <br> 12524 Indianapolis St, Los Angeles CA 90066, USA | Boxer, Actor |
| **Mancuso, Frank G** <br> 201 N Canon Dr, #328, Beverly Hills CA 90210, USA | Businessman |
| **Mancuso, Julia** <br> USA Ski Team, 1500 Kearns Blvd, #100, Park City UT 84060 USA | Alpine Skier |
| **Mancuso, Nick** <br> Law Talent Agency, 5 Ambleside Ave, Toronto ON M8Z 2H5, Canada | Actor |
| **Mandabach, Caryn** <br> Oxygen Media, 75 9th Ave, New York NY 10011, USA | Producer |

**Mandarich - Manilow**

| | |
|---|---|
| **Mandarich, Ante J (Tony)** | Football Player |
| 12767 E Altadena Dr, Scottsdale AZ 85259, USA | |
| **Mandel, Howie** | Actor |
| Alevy Productions, 23679 Calabasas Road, #180, Calabasas CA 91302, USA | |
| **Mandel, Johnny** | Composer |
| 2401 Main St, Santa Monica CA 90405, USA | |
| **Mandel, Robert C** | Director |
| I C M Partners, 10250 Constellation Blvd, #900, Los Angeles CA 90067 USA | |
| **Mandela, N Winnie Madikizela-** | Social Activist |
| Orlando West, Soweto, Johannesburg 1804, South Africa | |
| **Mandella, Richard E** | Thoroughbred Racing Trainer |
| 285 W Huntington Dr, Arcadia CA 91007, USA | |
| **Mandelstam, Stanley** | Physicist |
| 1800 Spruce St, Berkeley CA 94709, USA | |
| **Manderino, Joey** | Actor, Comedian, Writer |
| Creative Artists Agency, 2000 Ave of Stars, #100, Los Angeles CA 90067 USA | |
| **Manders, David F (Dave)** | Football Player |
| 1504 Silverlake Road, McKinney TX 75070, USA | |
| **Mandic, Milica** | Taekwondo Athlete |
| Taekwondo Club Galeb, Nikodima Milasa 17, 11000 Belgrade, Serbia | |
| **Mandler, George** | Psychologist |
| 1406 La Jolla Knoll, La Jolla CA 92037, USA | |
| **Mandler, Jean M** | Psychologist |
| 1406 La Jolla Knoll, La Jolla CA 92037, USA | |
| **Mandley, William H (Pete)** | Football Player |
| 103 E Smoke Tree Road, Gilbert AZ 85296, USA | |
| **Mandlikova, Hana** | Tennis Player |
| Octagon Worldwide, 1751 Pinnacle Dr, #1500, McLean VA 22102 USA | |
| **Mandoki, Luis** | Director |
| Paradigm Agency, 360 N Crescent Dr, North Building, Beverly Hills CA 90210 USA | |
| **Mandrell, Barbara** | Singer, Actress |
| 2020 Fieldstone Parkway, Franklin TN 37069, USA | |
| **Mandrell, Erline** | Singer |
| 544 W Main St, Gallatin TN 37066, USA | |
| **Mandrell, Louise** | Singer |
| Mandrell Inc, 1101 Hunters Lane, Ashland City TN 37015, USA | |
| **Mandvi, Aasif** | Actor, Writer |
| I C M Partners, 10250 Constellation Blvd, #900, Los Angeles CA 90067 USA | |
| **Mandylor, Costas** | Actor |
| Greater Vision Artists Talent Agency, 8981 Sunset Blvd, #101, Los Angeles CA 90069, USA | |
| **Mane, Gucci** | Rap Artist |
| Susan Blond Inc, 50 W 57th St, #1400, New York NY 10019 USA | |
| **Manea, Marius** | Opera Singer |
| I M G Artists, Hogarth Business Park, Chiswick, London W4 2TH, England | |
| **Manea, Norman** | Writer |
| 201 W 70th St, #101, New York NY 10023, USA | |
| **Manery, Randy N** | Ice Hockey Player |
| 14418 John Beck Dr, Charlotte NC 28273, USA | |
| **Manetti, Larry** | Actor |
| Epstein-Wyckoff, 280 S Beverly Dr, #400, Beverly Hills CA 90212 USA | |
| **Manfred, Robert D (Rob), Jr** | Baseball Executive |
| Major League Baseball, Commissioner's Office, 75 9th Ave, #500, New York NY 10011, USA | |
| **Manfredi, Michael** | Architect, Sculptor |
| Weiss/Manfredi, 130 W 29th St, #1200, New York NY 10001, USA | |
| **Manfredini, Harry** | Composer |
| Soundtrack Music, 2229 Cloverfield Blvd, Santa Monica CA 90405, USA | |
| **Manganiello, Joe** | Actor |
| Creative Artists Agency, 2000 Ave of Stars, #100, Los Angeles CA 90067 USA | |
| **Mangels, Andy** | Writer |
| PO Box 3226, Portland OR 97208, USA | |
| **Mangelsdorf, David** | Geneticist |
| Salk Institute, 10100 N Torrey Pines Road, La Jolla CA 92037 USA | |
| **Mangieri, Dino M** | Football Player |
| 108 Lamport Blvd, #3C, Staten Island NY 10305, USA | |
| **Mangione, Chuck** | Jazz Trumpeter, Composer |
| Gates Music, 99 Park Ave, New York NY 10019, USA | |
| **Mangold, James** | Director, Producer, Writer |
| Tree Line Films, 1708 Berkeley St, Santa Monica CA 90404, USA | |
| **Mangold, Nick** | Football Player |
| 361 Shunpike Road, Chatham NJ 07928, USA | |
| **Mangold, Sylvia P** | Artist |
| 1 Bull Road, Washingtonville NY 10992, USA | |
| **Mangrum, James L (Jim Dandy)** | Singer (Black Oak Arkansas) |
| Lustig Talent, PO Box 770850, Orlando FL 32877 USA | |
| **Mangual, Jose M (Pepe)** | Baseball Player |
| 2325 Calle Tabonuco, Ponce PR 00716, USA | |
| **Mangue Gonzalez, Marta** | Handball Player |
| Fleury Loiret Handball, 109 Ave Louis Gallouedec, 45400 Fleury les Aubrais, France | |
| **Mangum, John W, Jr** | Football Player |
| 150 Summerwood Dr, Pearl MS 39208, USA | |
| **Mangum, Kristofer T (Kris)** | Football Player |
| 16720 Krishna Lane, Charlotte NC 28277, USA | |
| **Manh, Nong Duc** | General Secretary, Vietnam |
| General's Secretary Office, Hoang Hoa Tham St, Hanoi, Vietnam | |
| **Manheim, Camryn** | Actress |
| United Talent Agency, U T A Plaza, 9336 Civic Center Dr, Beverly Hills CA 90210 USA | |
| **Maniago, Cesare** | Ice Hockey Player |
| 19-788 Citadel Dr, Port Coquitlam BC V3C 6G9, Canada | |
| **Maniatis, Thomas P** | Genetics Engineer, Molecular Biologist |
| Harvard University, Biochemistry Dept, 7 Divinity St, Cambridge MA 02138, USA | |
| **Manificat, Maurice** | Cross Country Skier |
| 50 Rue Marquisates, BP 2451, 74011 Annecy Cedex, France | |
| **Manigault-Stallworth, Omarosa** | Actress |
| Don Buchwald Talent Agency, 6500 Wilshire Blvd, #2200, Los Angeles CA 90048 USA | |
| **Manilow, Barry** | Singer, Songwriter |
| Stilleto Entertainment, 8295 S La Cienega Blvd, Inglewood CA 90301, USA | |

| | |
|---|---|
| **Manion, Daniel A**<br>US Court of Appeals, 204 S Main St, South Bend IN 46601, USA | Judge |
| **Maniscalco, Sebastian**<br>Levity Entertainment Group, 6701 Center Drive W, #1111, Los Angeles CA 90045, USA | Actor, Comedian |
| **Manji, Rizwan**<br>Don Buchwald Talent Agency, 6500 Wilshire Blvd, #2200, Los Angeles CA 90048 USA | Actor |
| **Mankell, Henning**<br>Leopard Forlag AB, Paulsgatan 11, 118 46 Stockholm, Sweden | Writer |
| **Mankins, Logan L**<br>1 Jeffrey Dr, North Attleboro MA 02760, USA | Football Player |
| **Mankiw, N Gregory**<br>45 Chestnut St, Wellesley MA 02481, USA | Government Official, Economist |
| **Mankoff, Robert**<br>New Yorker, Editorial Dept, 4 Times Square, Basement C1B, New York NY 10036 USA | Cartoonist |
| **Mankowski, Philip A (Phil)**<br>2280 Southwestern Blvd, Buffalo NY 14224, USA | Baseball Player |
| **Manley, Christopher**<br>Sheldon Prosnit Agency, 800 S Robertson Blvd, Los Angeles CA 90035, USA | Cinematographer |
| **Manley, Dexter**<br>2350 Atascocita Road, Humble TX 77396, USA | Football Player |
| **Manley, Elizabeth**<br>Marco Enterprises, 74830 Velie Dr, #A, Palm Desert CA 92260, USA | Figure Skater |
| **Manlove, William B (Bill), Jr**<br>Delaware Valley College, Athletic Dept, 700 E Butler Ave, Doylestown PA 18901, USA | Football Coach |
| **Mann, Aimee**<br>Michael Hausman Mgmt, 511 Ave of Americas, #197, New York NY 10011, USA | Singer ('Til Tuesday); Songwriter |
| **Mann, Barry**<br>1010 Laurel Way, Beverly Hills CA 90210, USA | Composer |
| **Mann, Byron**<br>Red Mgmt, Box 3, 415 W Esplanade, North Vancouver BC V7M, Canada | Actor |
| **Mann, Carol A**<br>6 Cape Chestnut Dr, Spring TX 77381, USA | Golfer |
| **Mann, Catherine**<br>PO Box 6065, Navarre FL 32566, USA | Writer |
| **Mann, Charles A**<br>40741 Carry Back Lane, Leesburg VA 20176, USA | Football Player |
| **Mann, Cuonzo**<br>111 Wiggins St, #8, West Lafayette IN 47906, USA | Basketball Player |
| **Mann, Danny**<br>Danis Panaro Nist Talent, 9201 W Olympic Blvd, Beverly Hills CA 90212 USA | Actor |
| **Mann, David W**<br>10550 S 200 W, Columbia City IN 46725, USA | Religious Leader |
| **Mann, Dick**<br>American Motorcycle Assn, 13515 Yarmouth Dr, Pickerington OH 43147 USA | Motorcycle Racing Rider |
| **Mann, Errol D**<br>5521 Bonanza Place, Missoula MT 59808, USA | Football Player |
| **Mann, Gabriel**<br>Resolution, 1801 Century Park E, #2300, Los Angeles CA 90067 USA | Actor, Model |
| **Mann, H Thompson**<br>34 Titcomb St, #2, Newburyport MA 1950, USA | Swimmer |
| **Mann, James (Jim)**<br>197 N Franklin St, Holbrook MA 02343, USA | Baseball Player |
| **Mann, John W**<br>Mosiac Media Group, 9200 W Sunset Blvd, #1000, Los Angeles CA 90069 USA | Actor |
| **Mann, Kelly J**<br>1335 Franklin St, #4, Santa Monica CA 90404, USA | Baseball Player |
| **Mann, Kristen C**<br>Washington Mystics, Verizon Center, 401 9th St NW, #750, Washington DC 20004 USA | Basketball Player |
| **Mann, Leslie**<br>Creative Artists Agency, 2000 Ave of Stars, #100, Los Angeles CA 90067 USA | Actress |
| **Mann, Manfred**<br>E M I Records, 43 Brook Green, London W6 7EF, England | Keyboardist |
| **Mann, Michael K**<br>Forward Pass, 12233 W Olympic Blvd, #340, Los Angeles CA 90064, USA | Producer, Director |
| **Mann, Nieko**<br>C E S D, 10635 Santa Monica Blvd, #130, Los Angeles CA 90025 USA | Actress |
| **Mann, Shelley I**<br>1301 S Scott St, #638S, Arlington VA 22204, USA | Swimmer |
| **Mann, Terrance V**<br>138 W 118th St, #2, New York NY 10026, USA | Actor, Director |
| **Mann, Thomas E**<br>Brookings Institute, 1775 Massachusetts Ave NW, Washington DC 20036 USA | Political Scientist |
| **Mannelly, J Patrick**<br>1128 Kildare Ave, Libertyville IL 60048, USA | Football Player |
| **Manning Mims, Madeline**<br>7477 E 48th St, #83-4, Tulsa OK 74145, USA | Track Athlete |
| **Manning, Daniel R (Danny)**<br>205 Running Ridge Road, Lawrence KS 66049, USA | Basketball Player |
| **Manning, Dennis J**<br>Guardian Life Insurance, 7 Hanover Square, New York NY 10004, USA | Businessman |
| **Manning, Donald**<br>Fast Lane International, 4856 Haygood Road, #200, Virginia Beach VA 23455, USA | Singer (Abyssinians) |
| **Manning, E Archie, III**<br>1420 1st St, New Orleans LA 70130, USA | Football Player, Sportscaster |
| **Manning, Elisha N (Eli)**<br>New York Giants, Meadowlands Stadium, 102 Route 120, East Rutherford NJ 07073 USA | Football Player |
| **Manning, James B (Jim)**<br>41 Fox Run Dr, Weaverville NC 28787, USA | Baseball Player |
| **Manning, Jane**<br>2 Wilton Square, London N1 3DL, England | Opera Singer |
| **Manning, Linford**<br>Fast Lane International, 4856 Haygood Road, #200, Virginia Beach VA 23455, USA | Singer (Abyssinians) |
| **Manning, Paul C**<br>British Cycling Centre, Stuart St, Manchester M11 4DQ, England | Cyclist |
| **Manning, Peyton W**<br>Denver Broncos, 13655 E Broncos Parkway, Englewood CO 80112 USA | Football Player |

# M

**Manning, Richard (Ricky), Jr** — Football Player
Oakland Raiders, 1220 Harbor Bay Parkway, Alameda CA 94502 USA

**Manning, Richard E (Rick)** — Baseball Player
22447 N 49th Place, Phoenix AZ 85054, USA

**Manning, Rob** — Space Engineer
Jet Propulsion Laboratory, 4800 Oak Grove Dr, Pasadena CA 91109 USA

**Manning, Taryn** — Singer (Boomkat), Actress
A P A Talent & Literary Agency, 405 S Beverly Dr, #300, Beverly Hills CA 90212 USA

**Manningham, Mario C** — Football Player
New York Giants, Meadowlands Stadium, 102 Route 120, East Rutherford NJ 07073 USA

**Mannion, Pace S** — Basketball Player
4190 Achilles Dr, Salt Lake City UT 84124, USA

**Manoff, Dinah** — Actress
TalentWorks, 3500 W Olive Ave, #1400, Burbank CA 91505 USA

**Manojlovic, Miki** — Actor
Artmedia, 20 Ave Rapp, 75007 Paris, France

**Manon, Julio** — Baseball Player
4726 15th Ave S, Saint Petersburg FL 33711, USA

**Manor, Brison** — Football Player
3 Campden Hill Road, Sherwood AR 72120, USA

**Manos, James, Jr** — Producer, Director, Writer
James Manos Jr Productions, 215 W 6th St, #PH-15, Los Angeles CA 90014, USA

**Manoux, J P** — Actor
Bauman Redanty Shaul Agency, 5757 Wilshire Blvd, #473, Los Angeles CA 90036 USA

**Mansell, Clinton D (Clint)** — Composer
First Artists, 4764 Park Granada, #210, Calabasas CA 91302 USA

**Mansell, Kevin** — Businessman
Kohl's Corp, N56W17000 Ridgewood Dr, Menomonee Falls WI 53051, USA

**Mansell, Nigel** — Auto Racing Driver
Old House Farm, North Dean, High Wycombe, Buckshire HP14 4NL, England

**Manser, Michael J** — Architect
Manser Practice, Hammersmith Bridge, London W6 9DA, England

**Mansfield, E Von** — Football Player
1711 Lynwood Court, Flossmoor IL 60422, USA

**Mansfield, Peter** — Nobel Medicine Laureate
Nottingham University, Physics Dept, Nottingham NG7 2RD, England

**Manson, Dave** — Ice Hockey Player
Dallas Stars, 2601 Ave of Stars, #100, Frisco TX 75034 USA

**Manson, Marilyn** — Singer (Marilyn Manson)
Creative Artists Agency, 2000 Ave of Stars, #100, Los Angeles CA 90067 USA

**Manson, Shirley** — Singer (Garbage), Actress
Untitled Entertainment, 350 S Beverly Dr, #200, Beverly Hills CA 90212 USA

**Mansour, Adly** — President, Egypt
Presidential Palace, Abdin, Qasr El-Nile St, Cairo CA002, Egypt

**Mantalis, George** — Singer (Four Coins)
309 Winners Circle, Canonsburg PA 15317, USA

**Mantegna, Joe** — Actor
I C M Partners, 10250 Constellation Blvd, #900, Los Angeles CA 90067 USA

**Mantei, Matthew B (Matt)** — Baseball Player
4709 Chicago Path, Stevensville MI 49127, USA

**Mantel, Hilary M** — Writer
A M Heath, 79 Saint Martin's Lane, London WC2N 4AA, England

**Mantello, Joe** — Director
Creative Artists Agency, 2000 Ave of Stars, #100, Los Angeles CA 90067 USA

**Mantha, Moe** — Ice Hockey Player
1538 Scio Ridge Road, Ann Arbor MI 48103, USA

**Mantilla, Felix** — Baseball Player
6973 N Tacoma St, Milwaukee WI 53224, USA

**Mantis, Nick** — Basketball Player
1344 Autumn Dr, Crown Point IN 46307, USA

**Mantle, Anthony Dod** — Cinematographer
Independent Talent Group, 40 Whitfield St, London W1T 2RH, England

**Manto, Jeffrey P (Jeff)** — Baseball Player
725 Radcliffe St, Bristol PA 19007, USA

**Mantooth, Randolph** — Actor
6210 Rodgerton Dr, Los Angeles CA 90068, USA

**Mantreola, Patricia** — Singer, Model, Actress
B M G, 1540 Broadway, #9E, New York NY 10036, USA

**Mantz, Michael** — Astronaut
1940 Elanita Dr, San Pedro CA 90732, USA

**Mantzoukas, Jason** — Actor, Writer
United Talent Agency, U T A Plaza, 9336 Civic Center Dr, Beverly Hills CA 90210 USA

**Manuel, Barry P** — Baseball Player
805 Oak St, Mamou LA 70554, USA

**Manuel, Charles F (Chuck)** — Baseball Player, Manager
1496 Mira Vista Circle, Weston FL 33327, USA

**Manuel, Jerry** — Baseball Player, Manager
5556 Ridge Park Dr, Loomis CA 95650, USA

**Manuel, Lionel** — Football Player
827 E Cedar Dr, Chandler AZ 85249, USA

**Manuelidis, Laura** — Neuropathologist
Yale University Medical School, Neuropathology Dept, New Haven CT 06520, USA

**Manuelle, Victor** — Singer, Songwriter
Latin Artists Group, 11271 Ventura Blvd, #151, Studio City CA 91604, USA

**Manumaleuna, Brandon M** — Football Player
335 E Albertoni St, #200, Carson CA 90746, USA

**Manuwai, Vince K** — Football Player
4495 Ecton Lane E, Jacksonville FL 32246, USA

**Manwaring, Kurt D** — Baseball Player
20 Prospect Ridge, Horseheads NY 14845, USA

**Manx, Harry** — Singer, Guitar Player
Roots Agency, 177 Woodland Ave, Westwood NJ 07675, USA

**Manz, Wolfgang** — Concert Pianist
Pasteuralle 55, 30655 Hanover, Germany

**Manzanero, Armando** — Singer, Composer
Pro Art, Av El Rosario 165, #201, Lima 27, Peru

| | |
|---|---|
| **Manzanillo, Josias (Jose)** | Baseball Player |
| 274 Kennebec St, Mattapan MA 02126, USA | |
| **Manzano, Leonel (Leo)** | Track Athlete |
| 602 Jessie St, Austin TX 78704, USA | |
| **Manzano, Sonia** | Actress, Writer |
| American Program Bureau, 313 Washington St, #225, Newton MA 02458, USA | |
| **Manzi, Catello** | Harness Racing Driver |
| 1 Hickory Lane, Freehold NJ 07728, USA | |
| **Manzie, Jim** | Composer |
| 649 Platt Circle, El Dorado Hills CA 95762, USA | |
| **Manziel, Johnathan P (Johnny)** | Football Player |
| Cleveland Browns, 76 Lou Groza Blvd, Berea OH 44017 USA | |
| **Manzini, Antonio** | Actor |
| Carol Levi Mgmt, Via Giuseppe Pisanelli 2, 00196 Rome, Italy | |
| **Manzoni, Giacomo** | Composer |
| Viale Papiniano 31, 20123 Milan, Italy | |
| **Maple, Edward R (Eddie)** | Thoroughbred Racing Jockey |
| Rose Hill Plantation Boarding Center, 1 Rose Hill Dr, Bluffton SC 29910, USA | |
| **Mara, Kate** | Actress |
| United Talent Agency, U T A Plaza, 9336 Civic Center Dr, Beverly Hills CA 90210 USA | |
| **Mara, Paul** | Ice Hockey Player |
| 500 Commercial St, #D, Boston MA 02109, USA | |
| **Mara, Rooney** | Actress |
| W M E Entertainment, 9601 Wilshire Blvd, #300, Beverly Hills CA 90210 USA | |
| **Marais, Jessica** | Actress |
| R G M Artists, 8-12 Ann Street, Surry Hills NSW 2010, Australia | |
| **Marak, Paul P** | Baseball Player |
| 1211 Comanche Trail, Alamogordo NM 88310, USA | |
| **Maramorosch, Karl** | Entomologist |
| 1050 George St, New Brunswick NJ 08901, USA | |
| **Maran, Josie** | Model, Actress |
| Global Creative, 1051 N Cole Ave, #B, Los Angeles CA 90038, USA | |
| **Maraniss, David** | Journalist |
| Washington Post, Editorial Dept, 1150 15th St NW, Washington DC 20071, USA | |
| **Maratos-Flier, Elftheria** | Geneticist |
| Joslin Diabetes Center, 1 Joslin Place, Boston MA 02215, USA | |
| **Marber, Patrick** | Writer |
| Judy Daish Assoc, 2 Saint Charles Place, London W10 6EG, England | |
| **Marble, Roy Devyn** | Basketball Player |
| Orlando Magic, 8701 Maitland Summit Blvd, Orlando FL 32810 USA | |
| **Marbley, Harlan** | Boxer |
| 6113 Parkview Lane, Clinton MD 20735, USA | |
| **Marboeuf, Julie** | Actress |
| Intertalent, 16 Rue Henri Barbusse, 75005 Paris, France | |
| **Marbury, Stephon X** | Basketball Player |
| PO Box 52469, Durham NC 27717, USA | |
| **Marc 7** | Rap Artist |
| Vision Entertainment Group, 1100 Glendon Ave, #1100, Los Angeles CA 90024, USA | |
| **Marc, Alessandra** | Opera Singer |
| Clarisse B Kampel Foundation, 330 E 63rd St, New York NY 10065, USA | |
| **Marceau, Sophie** | Actress |
| Special Artists Agency, 9200 Sunset Blvd, #410, West Hollywood CA 90069 USA | |
| **Marcell, Joseph** | Actor, Director |
| Margrit Polak Mgmt, 1920 Hillhurst, #405, Los Angeles CA 90027, USA | |
| **Marcello, Vince** | Director, Writer, Actor |
| Gersh Agency, 9465 Wilshire Blvd, #600, Beverly Hills CA 90212 USA | |
| **March, Forbes** | Actor |
| Kirk Talent Agencies, 196 W 3rd Ave, #102, Vancouver BC V5Y 1E9, Canada | |
| **March, Jane** | Actress, Model |
| International Talent Mgmt, 31 Harley St, London W1G 9QS, England | |
| **March, Peggy** | Singer |
| Peggy March Harris, 9236 NW 9th St, Plantation FL 33324, USA | |
| **March, Stephanie** | Actress |
| Gersh Agency, 9465 Wilshire Blvd, #600, Beverly Hills CA 90212 USA | |
| **Marchal, Olivier** | Actor, Director |
| Artmedia, 20 Ave Rapp, 75007 Paris, France | |
| **Marchand, Guy** | Actor |
| Voyez Mon Agent, 20 Ave Rapp, 75007 Paris, France | |
| **Marchant, Todd** | Ice Hockey Player |
| 10448 Caribou Way, Tustin CA 92782, USA | |
| **Marchetti, Gino J** | Football Player |
| 324 Devon Way, West Chester PA 19380, USA | |
| **Marchibroda, Theodore J (Ted)** | Football Player, Coach, Executive |
| 90 Orchard Point Dr, Weems VA 22576, USA | |
| **Marchionne, Sergio** | Businessman |
| Fiat SpA, Via Nizza 250, 10126 Turin, Italy | |
| **Marchlewski, Frank C** | Football Player |
| 428 Toledo Dr, New Kensington PA 15068, USA | |
| **Marchment, Bryan** | Ice Hockey Player |
| San Jose Sharks, San Jose Arena, 525 W Santa Clara St, San Jose CA 95113 USA | |
| **Marchuk, Guri I** | Applied Mathematician |
| Numerical Mathematics Institute, Gubkin Str 8, 117333 Moscow, Russia | |
| **Marchuk, Yevhen K** | Prime Minister, Ukraine; General |
| Verkovna Rada, M Hrushevskoho Str 5, 252008 Kiev, Ukraine | |
| **Marciano, David** | Actor |
| Don Buchwald Talent Agency, 6500 Wilshire Blvd, #2200, Los Angeles CA 90048 USA | |
| **Marcikic, Ivan** | Physicist, Inventor (Unbreakable Codes) |
| Geneva University, 24 Rue du General Dufour, 1211 Geneva 4, Switzerland | |
| **Marcil, Vanessa** | Actress |
| Paradigm Agency, 360 N Crescent Dr, North Building, Beverly Hills CA 90210 USA | |
| **Marcinkiewicz, Kazimierz** | Prime Minister, Poland |
| European Bank for Reconstruction/Development, 1 Exchange Square, London EC2A 2JN, England | |
| **Marcis, Dave** | Auto Racing Driver |
| Marcis Auto Racing, PO Box 645, Skyland NC 28776, USA | |
| **Marciulionis, R Sarunas** | Basketball Player |
| Hotel Sarunas, Raitininku St 4, 2051 Vilnius, Lithuania | |

**M**

Manzanillo - Marciulionis

# M

**Marclay, Christian E** — Artist, Composer
European Graduate School, Alter Kehr 20, 3953 Leuk-Stadt, Switzerland
**Marcol, Czeslaw C (Chester)** — Football Player
PO Box 94, Dollar Bay MI 49922, USA
**Marcon, Andre** — Actor
Artmedia, 20 Ave Rapp, 75007 Paris, France
**Marcos, Imelda R** — First Lady, Philippines
Leyte Providencia Dept, Tolosa Leyte, Philippines
**Marcotte, Don** — Ice Hockey Player
12 Cote St, Amesbury MA 01913, USA
**Marcovicci, Andrea** — Actress, Singer
Michael Mann Mgmt, 8838 Saturn St, Los Angeles CA 90035, USA
**Marcum, Art** — Writer
Creative Artists Agency, 2000 Ave of Stars, #100, Los Angeles CA 90067 USA
**Marcum, Joseph L** — Financier
609 Lake Dr, Vero Beach FL 32963, USA
**Marcum, Shaun M** — Baseball Player
1413 Jill Lane, Excelsior Springs MO 64024, USA
**Marcus Schaffer, Jackie** — Producer, Director, Writer
United Talent Agency, U T A Plaza, 9336 Civic Center Dr, Beverly Hills CA 90210 USA
**Marcus, Bernard** — Businessman
Home Depot Inc, 2455 Paces Ferry Road SE, Atlanta GA 30339, USA
**Marcus, Egerton** — Boxer
Atlas Boxing Centre, 849 Saint Clair Ave W, Toronto ON M6C 1C1, Canada
**Marcus, Jurgen** — Singer
Kunstlermanagement Uwe Kanthak, Postfach 113124, 29431 Hamburg, Germany
**Marcus, Ken** — Photographer
Ken Marcus Studio, 6916 Melrose Ave, Los Angeles CA 90038, USA
**Marcus, Rudolph A** — Nobel Chemistry Laureate
331 S Hill Ave, Pasadena CA 91106, USA
**Marcus, Stanley** — Judge
US Court of Appeals, 36 NE 1st St, #300, Miami FL 33132, USA
**Marcus, Trula M** — Actress
Artists Agency, 9430 Olympic Blvd, Beverly Hills CA 90212 USA
**Marcy, Geoffrey W (Geoff)** — Astronomer
University of California, Astronomy Dept, Berkeley CA 94720, USA
**Mardall, Cyril L** — Architect
5 Boyne Terrace Mews, London W11 3LR, England
**Marden, Brice** — Artist
6 Saint Lukes Place, New York NY 10014, USA
**Marden, Matthew** — Actor
Mosiac Media Group, 9200 W Sunset Blvd, #1000, Los Angeles CA 90069 USA
**Mardones, Benny** — Singer
Tony Cee Assoc, PO Box 410, Utica NY 13503, USA
**Mare, Olindo F** — Football Player
106 Wescoe Dr, Mooresville NC 28117, USA
**Maree, Sydney** — Track Athlete
2 Braxton Road, Bryn Mawr PA 19010, USA
**Maren, Jerry** — Actor
PO Box 90010, San Diego CA 92169, USA
**Maretska, Maria** — Sculptor
730 W 14th St, Medford OR 97501, USA
**Margaglio, Maurizio** — Ice Dancer
Ice Sports Federation, Via Piransi 44B, 20137 Milan, Italy
**Margarito Montiel, Antonio** — Boxer
Top Rank Inc, 3908 Howard Hughes Parkway, #580, Las Vegas NV 89169 USA
**Margera, Brandon C (Bam)** — Actor, Skateboarder
PO Box 671, Westtown PA 19395, USA
**Margerum, Kenneth (Ken)** — Football Player
494 Riverview Dr, Capitola CA 95010, USA
**Margiela, Martin** — Fashion Designer
Maison Martin Margiela, 163 Rue Saint Maur, 75011 Paris, France
**Margison, Richard** — Opera Singer
George Martynuk, 352 7th Ave, New York NY 10001, USA
**Margo, Philip** — Singer, Pianist, Drummer (Tokens)
American Mgmt, 19948 Mayall St, Chatsworth CA 91311, USA
**Margolin, Phillip M** — Writer, Actor
United Talent Agency, U T A Plaza, 9336 Civic Center Dr, Beverly Hills CA 90210 USA
**Margolin, Stuart** — Actor, Director, Writer
Great North Artists Mgmt, 350 Dupont St, Toronto ON M5R 1V9, Canada
**Margolis, Cindy** — Model, Actress
12711 Ventura Blvd, #400, Studio City CA 91604, USA
**Margolis, Laura** — Actress
Artists Mgmt, 1119 Colorado Ave, #12, Santa Monica CA 90401, USA
**Margolis, Lawrence S** — Judge
US Claims Court, 717 Madison Place NW, Washington DC 20439, USA
**Margolis, Mark** — Actor
Abrams Artists, 9200 W Sunset Blvd, #1125, West Hollywood CA 90069 USA
**Margolyes, Miriam** — Actress
United Agents, 12-26 Lexington St, London W1F 0LE, England
**Margon, Bruce H** — Astronomer
University of Washington, Astronomy Dept, PO Box 351580, Seattle WA 98195, USA
**Margoneri, Joseph E (Joe)** — Baseball Player
341 Turkeytown Road, West Newton PA 15089, USA
**Margoyles, Miriam** — Actress
Innovative Artists, 1505 10th St, Santa Monica CA 90401 USA
**Margrave, John L** — Chemist
4511 Vrone, Bellaire TX 77401, USA
**Margrethe II** — Queen, Denmark
Amalienborg Palace, 1257 Copenhagen K, Denmark
**Margulies, Donald** — Writer
Yale University, English Dept, New Haven CT 06520, USA
**Margulies, James H (Jimmy)** — Editorial Cartoonist
Hackensack Record, Editorial Dept, 150 River St, Hackensack NJ 07601, USA
**Margulies, Julianna L** — Actress
W M E Entertainment, 9601 Wilshire Blvd, #300, Beverly Hills CA 90210 USA

**Marclay - Margulies**

**Maria Teresa** — Grand Duchess Consort, Luxembourg
Palais Grand-Ducal, 17 Rue du Marche-aux-Herbes, 1728 Luxembourg-Ville, Luxembourg
**Mariam, Mengistu Haile** — President, Ethiopia; Army General
PO Box 1536, Gunhill Enclave, Harare, Zimbabwe
**Marianelli, Dario** — Composer
Air Edel, 18 Rodmarton St, London W1U 8BJ, England
**Mariani, Carlo M** — Artist
117 W 171st St, #12E, New York NY 10023, USA
**Mariano, Jarah** — Model
I M G Models, 304 Park Ave S, #PH N, New York NY 10010 USA
**Marichal, Juan A S** — Baseball Player
9458 NW 54th Doral Circle Lane, Doral FL 33178, USA
**Marie** — Princess, Liechtenstein
Schloss Vaduz, 9490 Vaduz, Liechtenstein
**Marie, Constance** — Actress
Innovative Artists, 1505 10th St, Santa Monica CA 90401 USA
**Marimow, William K** — Journalist
440 S Broad St, #1602, Philadelphia PA 19146, USA
**Marin, Carlos** — Singer (Il Divo)
Octagon, 81-83 Fulham High St, London SW6 3JW, England
**Marin, John W (Jack)** — Basketball Player
3909 Regent Road, Durham NC 27707, USA
**Marin, Maguy** — Choreographer
10 Blvd de Lattre de Tassigny, 69143 Rillieux-la-Pape Cedex, France
**Marin, Richard A (Cheech)** — Actor, Comedian (Cheech & Chong)
Chicano Collection, 923 E 3rd St, #203, Los Angeles CA 90013, USA
**Marinaro, Edward F (Ed)** — Actor, Football Player
Amsel Eisenstadt Frazier, 5055 Wilshire Blvd, #865, Los Angeles CA 90036 USA
**Marinca, Anamaria** — Actress
Conway Van Gelder Grant, 8-12 Broadwick St, #300, London W1F 8HW, England
**Marinelli, Rod** — Football Coach
Chicago Bears, 1000 Football Dr, Lake Forest IL 60045 USA
**Marini, Gilles** — Actor, Model
A P A Talent & Literary Agency, 405 S Beverly Dr, #300, Beverly Hills CA 90212 USA
**Marinin, Maxim V** — Figure Skater
Skating Federation, Luznetskaya Nabererhnya 8, 119871 Moscow, Russia
**Marino, Cathy** — Golfer
6313 Willowdale Dr, Plano TX 75093, USA
**Marino, Daniel C (Dan), Jr** — Football Player, Sportscaster
3415 Stallion Lane, Weston FL 33331, USA
**Marino, Ken** — Actor
Principato-Young, 9465 Wilshire Blvd, #880, Beverly Hills CA 90212 USA
**Marino, Peter** — Architect
150 E 58th St, #3600, New York NY 10155, USA
**Mario** — Singer, Actor
Creative Artists Agency, 2000 Ave of Stars, #100, Los Angeles CA 90067 USA
**Mario, Ernest** — Businessman, Pharmacist
PO Box 445, Chatham NJ 07928, USA
**Marion, Brock E** — Football Player
12431 SW 55th Place, Portland OR 97219, USA
**Marion, Fred D** — Football Player
10032 Oak Quarry Dr, Orlando FL 32832, USA
**Marion, Shawn D** — Basketball Player
5434 E Cannon Dr, Paradise Valley AZ 85253, USA
**Marisol** — Sculptor
427 Washington St, #700, New York NY 10013, USA
**Mariucci, Steve** — Football Coach, Sportscaster
15940 Romita Court, Monte Sereno CA 95030, USA
**Mariye, Lily** — Actress
C E S D, 10635 Santa Monica Blvd, #130, Los Angeles CA 90025 USA
**Mariza** — Singer
Mad Minute Music, 5-7 Rue Paul Bert, Saint Ouen 93400, France
**Marjan, Marie-Luise** — Actress
Z A V-Kunstlervermittlung Hamburg, Gotenstr 11, #4, 20097 Hamburg, Germany
**Mark, Hans M** — Government Official, Physicist, Educator
1715 Scenic Dr, Austin TX 78703, USA
**Mark, Heidi** — Actress, Model
8730 W Sunset Blvd, #270, West Hollywood CA 90069, USA
**Mark, Mary Ellen** — Photographer
Mary Ellen Mark Library, 134 Spring St, #502, New York NY 10012, USA
**Markakis, Nicholas W (Nick)** — Baseball Player
949 E Piney Hill Road, Monkton MD 21111, USA
**Markarian, Andranik N** — Prime Minister, Armenia
Prime Minister's Office, Ul Nalbandyyrna 32, 375010 Yerevan, Armenia
**Marker, Laurie** — Animal Activist, Biologist
Cheetah Conservation Fund, PO Box 1380, Ojai CA 93024, USA
**Marker, Steve** — Guitarist (Garbage)
Borman Entertainment, 1250 6th St, #401, Santa Monica CA 90401, USA
**Markey, Edward J** — Senator, Representative, MA
7 Townsend St, Malden MA 02148, USA
**Markey, James A** — Guitarist (Concrete Blonde)
Agency Group Ltd, 142 W 57th St, #600, New York NY 10019 USA
**Markey, Lucille P** — Thoroughbred Racing Breeder
18 La Gorce Circle Lane, La Gorce Island, Miami Beach FL 33141, USA
**Markgraf, Kate** — Soccer Player
Octagon Worldwide, 1751 Pinnacle Dr, #1500, McLean VA 22102 USA
**Markham, Monte** — Actor, Producer, Director
C R Mgmt, 22337 Pacific Coast Highway, #627, Malibu CA 90265, USA
**Markle, C Wilson** — Film Engineer
Colorization Inc, 26 Soho St, Toronto ON M5T 1Z7, Canada
**Markle, Peter F** — Director
Blue Line Productions, 212 26th St, #295, Santa Monica CA 90402, USA
**Marklund, E Elisabeth (Liza)** — Writer
Piratforlaget AB, Kaptensgatan 6, 114 57 Stockholm, Sweden
**Markov, Alexey** — Opera Singer
I M G Artists, Hogarth Business Park, Chiswick, London W4 2TH, England

# M

**Markov, Daniil (Danny)** — Ice Hockey Player
17875 Collins Ave, Sunny Isles Beach FL 33160, USA

**Markowitz, Barry** — Cinematographer
Paradigm Agency, 360 N Crescent Dr, North Building, Beverly Hills CA 90210 USA

**Markowitz, Harry M** — Nobel Economics Laureate
1010 Turquoise St, #245, San Diego CA 92109, USA

**Markowitz, Robert** — Director, Producer
Paradigm Agency, 360 N Crescent Dr, North Building, Beverly Hills CA 90210 USA

**Marks, Albert J** — Beauty Pageant Executive
Miss America Organization, 1370 Ave of Americas, #1600, New York NY 10019 USA

**Marks, Bruce** — Ballet Dancer, Artistic Director
Boston Ballet Co, 19 Clarendon St, Boston MA 02116, USA

**Marks, David J** — Architect
Marks Barfield Architects, 50 Bromells Road, London SW4 0BG, England

**Marks, John G** — Ice Hockey Player
2733 47th St S, #205, Fargo ND 58104, USA

**Marks, Michael E** — Businessman
Flextronics International, 2090 Fortune St, San Jose CA 95131, USA

**Marks, Miko** — Singer, Guitarist
Mirrome Records, 2923 Verde Vista Dr, #C, Santa Barbara CA 93105, USA

**Marks, Paul A** — Oncologist, Cell Biologist
25680 Military Road, Watertown NY 13601, USA

**Marks, Sean A** — Basketball Player
2702 Circle Dr, Newport Beach CA 92663, USA

**Markstein, Gary** — Editorial Cartoonist
Milwaukee Journal, Editorial Dept, 333 W State St, Milwaukee WI 53203, USA

**Markus, Hazel R** — Psychologist
Stanford University, Psychology Dept, Jordan Hall, Stanford CA 94305, USA

**Marleau, Patrick D** — Ice Hockey Player
12021 Magnolia Court, Saratoga CA 95070, USA

**Marley, Damian (Jr Gong)** — Singer, Songwriter
Headline Entertainment, 8 Haughton Ave, Kingston 10, Jamaica

**Marley, Ziggy** — Singer, Songwriter
Ziggy Marley Mgmt, 269 S Beverly Dr, #175, Beverly Hills CA 90212, USA

**Marlin, Sterling** — Auto Racing Driver
Phoenix Racing, 195 Jones Road, Spartanburg SC 29307, USA

**Marlind, Mans** — Director
Zero Gravity Mgmt, 1531 14th St, Santa Monica CA 90404 USA

**Marling, Brit** — Actress, Writer
Creative Artists Agency, 2000 Ave of Stars, #100, Los Angeles CA 90067 USA

**Marlohe, Berenice** — Actress
I C M Partners, 10250 Constellation Blvd, #900, Los Angeles CA 90067 USA

**Marlowe, Andrew W** — Producer, Screenwriter
Creative Artists Agency, 2000 Ave of Stars, #100, Los Angeles CA 90067 USA

**Marm, Walter J, Jr** — Vietnam War Army Hero (CMH)
PO Box 2017, Fremont NC 27830, USA

**Marmel, Steve** — Producer, Writer
Gersh Agency, 9465 Wilshire Blvd, #600, Beverly Hills CA 90212 USA

**Marmol, Carlos A** — Baseball Player
1500 Robin Circle, #218, Hoffman Estates IL 60169, USA

**Marmont, Louise** — Curling Athlete
Curling Association, Idrottshuser, Marbackagatan 19, 123 43 Farsta, Sweden

**Marnell, Anthony M, III** — Architect
Marnell Properties, 222 Via Marnell Way, Las Vegas NV 89119, USA

**Marno, Mozhan** — Actress
TalentWorks, 3500 W Olive Ave, #1400, Burbank CA 91505 USA

**Marohn, William D** — Businessman
Whirlpool Corp, 2000 N State St, RR 63, Benton Harbor MI 49022, USA

**Marois, Mario** — Ice Hockey Player
Chicago Blackhawks, United Center, 1901 W Madison St, Chicago IL 60612 USA

**Maron, Marc** — Actor
W M E Entertainment, 9601 Wilshire Blvd, #300, Beverly Hills CA 90210 USA

**Maroney, Laurence** — Football Player
12560 Grandview Forest Dr, Saint Louis MO 63127, USA

**Maroney, McKayla R** — Gymnast
Erin E Maroney, 28621 Murrelet Dr, Laguna Nigel CA 92677, USA

**Maroon, Paul** — Guitarist, Pianist (Walkmen)
Mick Mgmt, 35 Washington St, Brooklyn NY 11201 USA

**Marosi, Adam** — Modern Pentathlete
Budapest Honved Sport Egyesulet, Dozsa Gyorgy Ut 3, 1134 Budapest, Hungary

**Marosz, Tom** — Artist
Botanical Enclosures, 606 Concepion Ave, La Mesa CA 91941, USA

**Maroth, Michael W (Mike)** — Baseball Player
909 Johns Pointe Dr, Oakland FL 34787, USA

**Maroulis, Constantine** — Actor, Singer
Abrams Artists, 275 7th Ave, #2600, New York NY 10001 USA

**Marozsan, Erika** — Actress
Scenario Agentur, Rambergstr 5, 80799 Munich, Germany

**Marquardt, Darcy** — Rowing Athlete
414-6508 Denbigh Ave, Burnaby BC V5H 4W6, Canada

**Marquette, Christopher (Chris)** — Actor
Silver Lining Entertainment, 421 S Beverly Drive, #700, Beverly Hills CA 90212 USA

**Marquez, Alfonso** — Baseball Umpire
4103 S Skyline Court, Gilbert AZ 85297, USA

**Marquez, Juan Manuel** — Boxer
961 Everett St, Los Angeles CA 90026, USA

**Marquez, Martin** — Actor
United Agents, 12-26 Lexington St, London W1F 0LE, England

**Marquez, Rafael** — Boxer
Romanza Gym, Regina St 252, Deligacion, Colonia Iztacalco, Mexico City DF 07300, Mexico

**Marquez, Raul** — Boxer
729 Evanston St, Houston TX 77015, USA

**Marquis, Jason S** — Baseball Player
300 Vogel Ave, Staten Island NY 10309, USA

**Marriner, Neville** — Conductor
Academy Saint Martin in Fields, Raine St, London E1 9RG, England

| | |
|---|---|
| **Marriott, J Willard, Jr** | Businessman |
| Marriott International, 10400 Fernwood Road, Bethesda MD 20817, USA | |
| **Marriott, Richard E** | Businessman |
| Host Marriott Corp, 10400 Fernwood Road, Bethesda MD 20817, USA | |
| **Marron, Donald B** | Financier |
| U B S PaineWebber, 1285 6th Ave, New York NY 10019, USA | |
| **Marrone, Douglas C (Doug)** | Football Player, Coach |
| 6100 Waitsfield Dr S, Jamesville NY 13078, USA | |
| **Marrs, Audrey M** | Producer |
| Representational Pictures, 75 E 4th St, #83, New York NY 10003, USA | |
| **Mars, Bruno** | Singer, Songwriter |
| W M E Entertainment, 9601 Wilshire Blvd, #300, Beverly Hills CA 90210 USA | |
| **Mars, Chris** | Drummer (Replacements) |
| PO Box 24631, Minneapolis MN 55424, USA | |
| **Mars, Mick** | Guitarist (Motley Crue) |
| 14949 Yerba Buena Road, Malibu CA 90265, USA | |
| **Mars, Susannah** | Singer, Actress |
| L M L Music Records, PO Box 48081, Los Angeles CA 90048, USA | |
| **Marsalis, Branford** | Jazz Saxophonist, Composer |
| Wilkins Mgmt, 323 Broadway, Cambridge MA 02139, USA | |
| **Marsalis, Delfeayo** | Jazz Trombonist |
| Ted Kurland, 173 Brighton Ave, Boston MA 02134 USA | |
| **Marsalis, Ellis** | Jazz Pianist |
| Management Ark, 116 Village Blvd, #200, Princeton NJ 08540, USA | |
| **Marsalis, James (Jim)** | Football Player |
| 101 Royal Oak Lane, Kathleen GA 31047, USA | |
| **Marsalis, Wynton** | Jazz Trumpeter, Composer |
| Management Ark, 116 Village Blvd, #200, Princeton NJ 08540, USA | |
| **Marsan, Eddie** | Actor |
| Paradigm Agency, 360 N Crescent Dr, North Building, Beverly Hills CA 90210 USA | |
| **Marsden, Gerard (Gerry)** | Singer, Guitarist (Gerry & Pacemakers) |
| Chimes International Entertainment, PO Box 26312, Glasgow G76 7WX, Scotland | |
| **Marsden, James P** | Actor |
| W M E Entertainment, 9601 Wilshire Blvd, #300, Beverly Hills CA 90210 USA | |
| **Marsden, Roy** | Actor |
| Artists Partnership, 101 Finsbury Pavement, London EC2A 1RS, England | |
| **Marsden, Russell** | Singer, Guitarist (Band of Skulls) |
| Pias Entertainment Group, Trading Centre, 101 Farm Lane, #24, London SW6 1QJ, England | |
| **Marsh of Mannington, Richard W** | Government Official, England |
| House of Lords, Westminster, London SW1A 0PW, England | |
| **Marsh, Brad** | Ice Hockey Player |
| Ottawa Senators, Scotia Bank Place, Kanata ON K2V 1A5, Canada | |
| **Marsh, Doug** | Football Player |
| 629 Forest Ave, Saint Louis MO 63135, USA | |
| **Marsh, Graham** | Golfer |
| Marsh Golf Design, 29 Commerce Dr, Box 300, Robina QED 4226, Australia | |
| **Marsh, James** | Documentary Producer, Director |
| Independent Talent Group, 40 Whitfield St, London W1T 2RH, England | |
| **Marsh, Jean** | Actress |
| 52 Shaftesbury Ave, London W1V 7DE, England | |
| **Marsh, Jeff (Swampy)** | Producer, Animator |
| Disney Channel, Phineas & Ferb Show, 500 S Buena Vista St, Burbank, CA 91521, USA | |
| **Marsh, Jodie** | Model |
| News International, Editorial Dept, 1 Virginia St, London E98 1XY, England | |
| **Marsh, Kym** | Singer (Hear'say) |
| Safe Mgmt, 111 Guildford Road, Lightwater, Surrey GU18 5RA, England | |
| **Marsh, Linda** | Actress |
| 170 W End Ave, #22P, New York NY 10023, USA | |
| **Marsh, Michael (Mike)** | Track Athlete |
| 2425 Holly Hall St, #152, Houston TX 77054, USA | |
| **Marsh, Michelle** | Model |
| Neon Mgmt, 34 Clare Lane, London N1 3DB, England | |
| **Marsh, Miles L** | Businessman |
| Fort James Corp, 1919 S Broadway, Green Bay WI 54304, USA | |
| **Marsh, Robert T** | Air Force General, Businessman |
| 20550 Falcons Landing Circle, #5106, Sterling VA 20165, USA | |
| **Marsh, Terry** | Boxer |
| 69 Ingaway, Langdon Hills, Basildon SS16 5QJ, England | |
| **Marsh, Thomas O (Tom)** | Baseball Player |
| 9140 Summerfield Road, Temperance MI 48182, USA | |
| **Marshal, Lyndsey** | Actress |
| Troika, 74 Clerkenwell Road, #300, London EC1M 5QA, England | |
| **Marshall, Albert L (Bert)** | Ice Hockey Player |
| Calgary Flames, PO Box 1540, Station M, Calgary AB T2P 3B9, Canada | |
| **Marshall, Amanda L** | Singer, Actress |
| Creative Artists Agency, 2000 Ave of Stars, #100, Los Angeles CA 90067 USA | |
| **Marshall, Andrew R C** | Journalist |
| Thompson Reuters, U Chu Liang Building, #3600, 968 Rama IV Road, Bangkok 10500, Thailand | |
| **Marshall, Arthur J** | Football Player |
| 4821 Rocky Shoals Circle, Evans GA 30809, USA | |
| **Marshall, Barry J** | Nobel Medicine Laureate |
| Charles Gairdner Hospital, Verdun St, Nedlands WA 6009, Australia | |
| **Marshall, Brian A** | Bassist (Creed, Alter Bridge) |
| Agency Group Ltd, 142 W 57th St, #600, New York NY 10019 USA | |
| **Marshall, David L (Dave)** | Baseball Player |
| 4802 E Centralia St, Long Beach CA 90808, USA | |
| **Marshall, Donald R (Don)** | Ice Hockey Player |
| 5887 SE Riverboat Dr, Stuart FL 34997, USA | |
| **Marshall, Donny E** | Basketball Player |
| 410 N 63rd St, Seattle WA 98103, USA | |
| **Marshall, Donyell L** | Basketball Player |
| 55 Ridgecreek Trail, Chagrin Falls OH 44022, USA | |
| **Marshall, F Ray** | Secretary, Labor |
| PO Box Y, Austin TX 78713, USA | |
| **Marshall, Frank W** | Producer |
| Kennedy/Marshall Co, 619 Arizona Ave, Santa Monica CA 90401, USA | |

# M

**Marshall, Garry K** — Director, Actor
Rogers & Cowan, 8687 Melrose Ave, #G700, West Hollywood CA 90069 USA

**Marshall, Grant** — Ice Hockey Player
General Delivery, North Rustico PE C0A 1X0, Canada

**Marshall, Gregg** — Basketball Coach
Wichita State University, Athletic Dept, Wichita KS 67260, USA

**Marshall, Henry H** — Football Player
68-1745 Waikoloa Road, #101, Waikoloa HI 96738, USA

**Marshall, James** — Actor
Trajectory, 3201 Benedict Canyon Dr, Beverly Hills CA 90210 90210, USA

**Marshall, James L (Jim)** — Football Player
4241 Basswood Road, Minneapolis MN 55416, USA

**Marshall, Jason** — Ice Hockey Player
438 Begonia Ave, Corona del Mar CA 92625, USA

**Marshall, John** — Geologist
S E T I Institute, 515 N Whitman Road, Mountain View CA 94043, USA

**Marshall, Kris** — Actor
Wishlab, 2225A Hyperion Ave, Los Angeles CA 90027, USA

**Marshall, Leonard A** — Football Player
PO Box 272016, Boca Raton FL 33427, USA

**Marshall, Margaret A** — Opera Singer
Woodside, Main St, Gargunnock, Stirling FK5 3BP, Scotland

**Marshall, Megan** — Writer
Emerson College, Writing & Literature Dept, Ansin Hall, 120 Boylston St, Boston MA 02116, USA

**Marshall, Michael A (Mike)** — Baseball Player
1280 W Desert Sun Dr, Yuma AZ 85365, USA

**Marshall, Michael G (Mike)** — Baseball Player
38324 Jendral Ave, Zephyrhills FL 33542, USA

**Marshall, Neil** — Director
I C M Partners, 10250 Constellation Blvd, #900, Los Angeles CA 90067 USA

**Marshall, Paula** — Actress
Innovative Artists, 1505 10th St, Santa Monica CA 90401 USA

**Marshall, Penny** — Actress, Director, Producer
Shelter Entertainment, 9454 Wilshire Blvd, #715, Beverly Hills CA 90212, USA

**Marshall, Peter** — Actor
Kazarian/Measures/Ruskin, 11969 Ventura Blvd, #300, Studio City CA 91604 USA

**Marshall, R James (Jim)** — Baseball Player, Manager
19700 N 76th St, #1091, Scottsdale AZ 85255, USA

**Marshall, Ray** — Economist
University of Texas, L B Johnson Public Affairs School, Dallas TX 78713, USA

**Marshall, Richard** — Football Player
11232 Colonial Country Lane, Charlotte NC 28277, USA

**Marshall, Rob** — Director; Choreographer
Creative Artists Agency, 2000 Ave of Stars, #100, Los Angeles CA 90067 USA

**Marshall, Tom** — Publisher
Sunset, Publisher's Office, 80 Willow Road, Menlo Park CA 94025, USA

**Marshall, Tonie** — Director
Artmedia, 20 Ave Rapp, 75007 Paris, France

**Marshall, Tony** — Singer, Opera Singer
Kunstleermanagement Herbert Nold, Postfach 1862, 76408 Rastatt, Germany

**Marshall, W W (Bones)** — Air Force General, Hero
4389 Malia St, #429, Honolulu HI 96821, USA

**Marshall, Wilber B** — Football Player
3016 E Main St, Mims FL 32754, USA

**Marshall, Willie** — Ice Hockey Player
2110 Acorn Court, Lebanon PA 17042, USA

**Marshall-Green, Logan** — Actor
Creative Artists Agency, 2000 Ave of Stars, #100, Los Angeles CA 90067 USA

**Marshburn, Thomas H (Tom)** — Astronaut
N A S A, Johnson Space Center, 2101 NASA Road, Houston TX 77058 USA

**Marson, Louis G (Lou)** — Baseball Player
6631 E Wilshire Dr, Scottsdale AZ 85257, USA

**Marsters, James** — Actor
Amanda Howard, 74 Clerkenwell Road, London EC1M 5QA, England

**Marston, Joshua M** — Director, Writer
W M E Entertainment, 9601 Wilshire Blvd, #300, Beverly Hills CA 90210 USA

**Marta** — Soccer Player
F C Rosengard Malmo, Frolichs Road 2, 213 68 Malmo, Sweden

**Marte, Judy** — Actress
Jordan Lee Talent, 8424A Santa Monica Blvd, #706, Los Angeles CA 90069, USA

**Martel, Christiane** — Beauty Queen, Actress
Miss Universe Organization, 1370 Ave of Americas, #1600, New York NY 10019 USA

**Martel, Yann** — Writer
Houghton Mifflin Harcourt, 215 Park Ave S, #1200, New York NY 10003 USA

**Martell, Arthur E** — Chemist
4047 Martinshire Dr, Houston TX 77025, USA

**Martell, Donna** — Actress
PO Box 3335, Granada Hills CA 91394, USA

**Martella, Vincent** — Actor
C E S D, 10635 Santa Monica Blvd, #130, Los Angeles CA 90025 USA

**Martelli, Adrienne** — Rowing Athlete
8302 53rd Street Court W, University Place WA 98467, USA

**Martelly, J Michel (Sweet Micky)** — President, Haiti
President's Office, Palais Nacional, Champ de Mars, Port-au-Prince, Haiti

**Martha, J Paul** — Football Player
6464 Dwane Ave, San Diego CA 92120, USA

**Marthouret, Francois** — Actor
Artmedia, 20 Ave Rapp, 75007 Paris, France

**Martika** — Singer
Entertainment Artists, 2409 21st Ave S, #100, Nashville TN 10019 USA

**Martikan, Michal** — Canoeing Athlete
Nabr Janka Krala 4287/4, 03101 Liptovsky Mikulas, Slovakia

**Martin Berenguer, Carmen** — Handball Player
C S M Bucuresti, Calea Plevnei 141B, #6, 060011 Bucharest, Romania

**Martin Chase, Deborah (Debra)** — Producer
Martin Chase Productions, 500 S Buena Vista St, Burbank CA 91521, USA

**Martin, Aaron B**    Football Player
3605 Seth Court, Springdale MD 20774, USA
**Martin, Albert S (Al)**    Baseball Player
400N Cornado St, #1062, Chandler AZ 85224, USA
**Martin, Andrea**    Actress, Comedienne
Innovative Artists, 1505 10th St, Santa Monica CA 90401 USA
**Martin, Ann M**    Writer
Chronicle Books, 85 2nd St, San Francisco CA 94105, USA
**Martin, Anne-Marie**    Actress
Creative Artists Agency, 2000 Ave of Stars, #100, Los Angeles CA 90067 USA
**Martin, Anthony I (Amos)**    Football Player
11824 Duane Point Circle, #201, Louisville KY 40243, USA
**Martin, Billy**    Jazz Percussionist, Composer
Creative Artists Agency, 2000 Ave of Stars, #100, Los Angeles CA 90067 USA
**Martin, Boyce F, Jr**    Judge
US Court of Appeals, US Courthouse, 601 W Broadway, Louisville KY 40202, USA
**Martin, Brad**    Singer
I C M Partners, 10250 Constellation Blvd, #900, Los Angeles CA 90067 USA
**Martin, Brian**    Luge Athlete
1123 66th St, Emeryville CA 94608, USA
**Martin, Carolyn (Biddy)**    Educator
University of Wisconsin, Chancellor's Office, 500 Lincoln Dr, Madison WI 53706, USA
**Martin, Casey**    Golfer
University of Oregon, Athletic Dept, 2727 Harris Parkway, Eugene OR 97405, USA
**Martin, Catherine**    Scenic, Costume Designer
Bazmark Films, PO Box 430, Kings Cross NSW 1340, Australia
**Martin, Cedric**    Singer, Bassist (Con Funk Shun)
Thrill Entertainment Group, 9530 Hageman St, #B278, Bakersfield CA 93312 USA
**Martin, Chris William**    Actor
A P A Talent & Literary Agency, 405 S Beverly Dr, #300, Beverly Hills CA 90212 USA
**Martin, Christoper A J (Chris)**    Singer (Coldplay)
Paradigm Agency, 360 N Crescent Dr, North Building, Beverly Hills CA 90210 USA
**Martin, Christopher (Chris)**    Football Player
15760 Horton Court, Overland Park KS 66223, USA
**Martin, Christopher C**    Architect
A C Martin Inc, 444 S Flower St, #1200, Los Angeles CA 90071, USA
**Martin, Christy**    Boxer
2015 University Heights Lane, Charlotte NC 28213, USA
**Martin, Cuonzo L**    Basketball Player
University of California, Athletic Dept, Berkeley CA 94720, USA
**Martin, Curtis**    Football Player
100 Hilton Ave, #PH 1, Garden City NY 11530, USA
**Martin, D Renie**    Baseball Player
509 Little Eagle Court, Valrico FL 33594, USA
**Martin, Damir**    Rowing Athlete
Tresnjevka V K, Savska Cesta 183, 10000 Zagreb, Croatia
**Martin, Darnell**    Director, Producer, Writer
Paradigm Agency, 360 N Crescent Dr, North Building, Beverly Hills CA 90210 USA
**Martin, David**    Commentator
CBS-TV, News Dept, 2020 M St NW, Washington DC 20036 USA
**Martin, Demetri E**    Actor, Comedian, Producer
Creative Artists Agency, 2000 Ave of Stars, #100, Los Angeles CA 90067 USA
**Martin, Dewey**    Actor
1371 East Ave de los Arboles, Thousand Oaks CA 91360, USA
**Martin, Doug**    Football Player
Tampa Bay Buccaneers, 1 W Buccaneer Place, Tampa FL 33607 USA
**Martin, Doug**    Golfer
Golf Ranch, 5390 Limaburg Road, Burlington KY 41005, USA
**Martin, Duane**    Actor, Producer, Writer
Paul Kohner, 9300 Wilshire Blvd, #555, Beverly Hills CA 90212 USA
**Martin, Edward H**    Navy Admiral
729 Guadalupe Ave, Coronado CA 92118, USA
**Martin, Eric W**    Football Player
111 Windfall Place, Clinton MS 39056, USA
**Martin, G Steven**    Biochemist, Biologist
University of California, Biological Sciences Dept, Barker Hall, Berkeley CA 94720, USA
**Martin, G Wayne**    Football Player
408 Rue de la Rivere, Kenner LA 70065, USA
**Martin, George C**    Aeronautical Engineer
900 University St, #5P, Seattle WA 98101, USA
**Martin, George D**    Football Player
50 Cheshire Lane, Ringwood NJ 07456, USA
**Martin, George H**    Businessman, Lyricist
Lynhurst Road, Hampstead, London NW3 5NG, England
**Martin, George R R**    Writer
103 San Salvador, Santa Fe NM 87501, USA
**Martin, Gerald W**    Football Player
New Orleans Saints, 5800 Airline Highway, Metairie LA 70003 USA
**Martin, Graham Patrick**    Actor
TalentWorks, 3500 W Olive Ave, #1400, Burbank CA 91505 USA
**Martin, Greg**    Singer, Musician (Kentucky Headhunters)
Bobby Roberts, 3050 Business Park Circle, #303, Goodlettsville TN 37221 USA
**Martin, Harold**    President, New Caledonia
President's Office, Artillerie 8 Rt des Artfices, BP M2, 98849 Noumea Cedex, New Caledonia
**Martin, Henry R**    Cartoonist (Good News Bad News)
1382 Newtown Langhorne Road, #G206, Newtown PA 18940, USA
**Martin, J Michael (Mike)**    Baseball Player
7904 Waterfalls Ave, Las Vegas NV 89128, USA
**Martin, J William (Billy)**    Football Player
PO Box 2969, Cumming GA 30028, USA
**Martin, Jacques**    Ice Hockey Coach
Jacques Martin Hockey School, 198 Daventry Crescent, Nepean ON K2J 4N1, Canada
**Martin, James G**    Governor, NC
Carolinas Medical Center, PO Box 32861, Charlotte NC 28232, USA
**Martin, Jerry L**    Baseball Player
109 Chelton Court, Columbia SC 29212, USA

# M

| | |
|---|---|
| **Martin, Jesse L**<br>I C M Partners, 730 5th Ave, New York NY 10019 USA | Actor, Singer |
| **Martin, Joe**<br>King Features Syndicate, 300 W 57th St, #1500, New York NY 10019 USA | Cartoonist (Mister Boffo) |
| **Martin, John H**<br>J H M Corp, 3930 RCA Blvd, #3240, Palm Beach Gardens FL 33410, USA | Educator |
| **Martin, Joseph C (J C)**<br>112 Oakmont Court, Advance NC 27006, USA | Baseball Player |
| **Martin, Judith (Miss Manners)**<br>1651 Harvard St NW, Washington DC 20009, USA | Journalist |
| **Martin, Kellie**<br>Thruline Entertainment, 9250 Wilshire Blvd, #100, Beverly Hills CA 90212 USA | Actress, Producer |
| **Martin, Kelvin B**<br>44 Veranda Lane, Colleyville TX 76034, USA | Football Player |
| **Martin, Kenyon L**<br>23104 Dolorosa St, Woodland Hills CA 91367, USA | Basketball Player |
| **Martin, Kevin**<br>Curling Association, 1660 Vimont Court, Cumberland ON K4A 4J4, Canada | Curling Athlete |
| **Martin, Kevin**<br>Novi Entertainment, PO Box 17077, Beverly Hills CA 90209, USA | Singer, Guitarist (Candlebox) |
| **Martin, Kevin D, Jr**<br>Minnesota Timberwolves, Target Center, 600 1st Ave N, Minneapolis MN 55403 USA | Basketball Player |
| **Martin, Luci**<br>Lustig Talent, PO Box 770850, Orlando FL 32877 USA | Singer (Chic) |
| **Martin, Lynn M**<br>Harry Walker Agency, 355 Lexington Ave, #2100, New York NY 10017, USA | Secretary, Labor |
| **Martin, Madeleine**<br>I C M Partners, 10250 Constellation Blvd, #900, Los Angeles CA 90067 USA | Actress |
| **Martin, Marilyn**<br>Atlantic Records, 9229 W Sunset Blvd, #900, West Hollywood CA 90069 USA | Singer |
| **Martin, Mark A**<br>210 Cessna Blvd, #1, Port Orange FL 32128, USA | Auto Racing Driver |
| **Martin, Marsha P**<br>Farm Credit Administration, 1501 Farm Credit Dr, #3600, McLean VA 22102, USA | Government Official, Financier |
| **Martin, Millicent**<br>London Mgmt, 2-4 Noel St, London W1V 3RB, England | Actress, Singer |
| **Martin, Nicholas**<br>United Agents, 12-26 Lexington St, London W1F 0LE, England | Director |
| **Martin, Norberto E (Paco)**<br>5905 Ricker Road, Raleigh NC 27610, USA | Baseball Player |
| **Martin, Pamela Sue**<br>PO Box 2278, Hailey ID 83333, USA | Actress |
| **Martin, Paul**<br>3401 Annandale Dr, Presto PA 15142, USA | Ice Hockey Player |
| **Martin, Paul C (Jake)**<br>1529 33rd St, San Diego CA 92102, USA | Baseball Player |
| **Martin, Phillip R (Phil)**<br>6937 Vineridge Dr, Dallas TX 75248, USA | Basketball Player |
| **Martin, R Bruce**<br>University of Virginia, Chemistry Dept, Charlottesville VA 22903, USA | Chemist |
| **Martin, Ray**<br>11-05 Cadmus Place, Fair Lawn NJ 07410, USA | Billiards Player |
| **Martin, Raymond J (Ray)**<br>383 Adams St, Quincy MA 02169, USA | Baseball Player |
| **Martin, Rhona**<br>Curling Association, 14 Donnelly Dr, Bedford, Bedfordshire MK4 9TU, England | Curling Athlete |
| **Martin, Ricky**<br>Creative Artists Agency, 2000 Ave of Stars, #100, Los Angeles CA 90067 USA | Actor, Singer |
| **Martin, Roderick D (Rod)**<br>PO Box 23, Manhattan Beach CA 90267, USA | Football Player |
| **Martin, Rudolf**<br>Mary Erickson Management, 2126 N Commonwealth Ave, Los Angeles CA 90027, USA | Actor |
| **Martin, Sandy**<br>TalentWorks, 3500 W Olive Ave, #1400, Burbank CA 91505 USA | Actress |
| **Martin, Sarah**<br>Ground Control Touring, 20 Jay St, #826, Brooklyn NY 11201 USA | Singer, Violinist (Belle & Sebastian) |
| **Martin, Stacy**<br>Tavistock Wood Mgmt, 45 Conduit St, London W1S 2YN, England | Actress |
| **Martin, Steve**<br>Martin/Stein Co, 1528 N Curson Ave, Los Angeles CA 90046, USA | Actor, Comedian, Writer |
| **Martin, Sylvia Wene**<br>2701 Clark Towers Court, #125, Las Vegas NV 89102, USA | Bowler |
| **Martin, T J**<br>Principato-Young, 9465 Wilshire Blvd, #880, Beverly Hills CA 90212 USA | Producer |
| **Martin, Terry G**<br>184 Hampton Hill Dr, Buffalo NY 14221, USA | Ice Hockey Player |
| **Martin, Thomas E (Tom)**<br>8001 Surf Dr, Panama City FL 32408, USA | Baseball Player |
| **Martin, Todd C**<br>156 Coach Lamp Way, Ponte Vedra FL 32082, USA | Tennis Player |
| **Martin, Tony**<br>TeamSpirit, Riethstr 29A, 99089 Erfurt, Germany | Cyclist |
| **Martin, Tony D**<br>1198 B Green Road, Boston GA 31626, USA | Football Player |
| **Martin, Walter**<br>Mick Mgmt, 35 Washington St, Brooklyn NY 11201 USA | Organist, Bassist (Walkmen) |
| **Martin, Zachery E (Zack)**<br>Dallas Cowboys, 1 Cowboys Parkway, Irving TX 75063 USA | Football Player |
| **Martina, Mia**<br>C P Records, 3341 Bloor St W, #77, Toronto ON M8X 1E9, Canada | Singer |
| **Martindale, Margo**<br>Gersh Agency, 41 Madison Ave, #3301, New York NY 10010 USA | Actress |
| **Martindale, Wink**<br>5744 Newcastle Lane, Calabasas CA 91302, USA | Entertainer, Singer |
| **Martinek, Radek**<br>64 Hope Dr, Plainview NY 11803, USA | Ice Hockey Player |

**Martin - Martinek**

626

| | |
|---|---|
| **Martinelli Berrocal, Ricardo A** | President, Panama |
| Palacio Presidencial, Valija 50, Panama City 1, Panama | |
| **Martines, Alessandra** | Actress |
| Artmedia, 20 Ave Rapp, 75007 Paris, France | |
| **Martinez Sistach, Lluis Cardinal** | Religious Leader |
| Archdiocese of Barcelona, Carrer del Bisbe 5, 08002 Barcelona, Spain | |
| **Martinez Somalo, Eduardo Cardinal** | Religious Leader |
| Apostolic Chamber, Palazzo Apostolico, 00120 Vatican City | |
| **Martinez, A** | Actor |
| David Shapira Assoc, 193 N Robertson Blvd, Beverly Hills CA 90211 USA | |
| **Martinez, Alfredo (Fred)** | Baseball Player |
| 2346 Thomas St, Los Angeles CA 90031, USA | |
| **Martinez, Ana Maria** | Opera Singer |
| J F Mastroianni, 161 W 61st St, #17E, New York NY 10023, USA | |
| **Martinez, Angela** | Actress |
| Abrams Artists, 9200 W Sunset Blvd, #1125, West Hollywood CA 90069 USA | |
| **Martinez, Carmelo** | Baseball Player |
| 32 Brisas del Plata, Dorado PR 00646, USA | |
| **Martinez, Conchita** | Tennis Player |
| 511 Westminster Dr, Cardiff by the Sea CA 92007, USA | |
| **Martinez, Constantino (Tino)** | Baseball Player |
| 2705 W Kathleen St, Tampa FL 33607, USA | |
| **Martinez, Daniel J** | Artist |
| Robert Berman/B1 Gallery, 2525 Michigan Ave, Santa Monica CA 90404, USA | |
| **Martinez, David (Dave)** | Baseball Player |
| 3315 Enterprise Road E, Safety Harbor FL 34695, USA | |
| **Martinez, Douglas V (S A)** | Singer, DJ Musician (311), Songwriter |
| 311 Hive, 8904 Florence Dr, Omaha NE 68147, USA | |
| **Martinez, Edgar** | Baseball Player |
| 3036 249th Ave SE, Sammamish WA 98075, USA | |
| **Martinez, Felix A (Tippy)** | Baseball Player |
| 1524 Dellsway Road, Towson MD 21286, USA | |
| **Martinez, J Dennis** | Baseball Player |
| 9400 SW 63rd Court, Miami FL 33156, USA | |
| **Martinez, John A (Buck)** | Baseball Player, Manager |
| 10315 Long Beach Blvd, Long Beach Township NJ 08008, USA | |
| **Martinez, Melquiades R (Mel)** | Secretary, Housing & Urban Development |
| D L A Piper, 500 8th St NW, Washington DC 20004, USA | |
| **Martinez, Natalie** | Actress, Model |
| W M E Entertainment, 9601 Wilshire Blvd, #300, Beverly Hills CA 90210 USA | |
| **Martinez, Olivier** | Actor |
| Gersh Agency, 9465 Wilshire Blvd, #600, Beverly Hills CA 90212 USA | |
| **Martinez, Pedro J** | Baseball Player |
| 3029 Birkdale Dr, Weston FL 33332, USA | |
| **Martinez, Ramon E** | Baseball Player |
| 3029 Birkdale Dr, Weston FL 33332, USA | |
| **Martinez, Ramon J** | Baseball Player |
| 3029 Birkdale Dr, Weston FL 33332, USA | |
| **Martinez, Rene O** | Drummer (Intocable) |
| Serca Music, 2020 W Houston Ave, McAllen TX 78501, USA | |
| **Martinez, Robert (Bob)** | Government Official; Governor, FL |
| 4647 W San Jose St, Tampa FL 33629, USA | |
| **Martinez, Vincent** | Actor |
| Artmedia, 20 Ave Rapp, 75007 Paris, France | |
| **Martin-Green, Sonequa** | Actress |
| Gersh Agency, 9465 Wilshire Blvd, #600, Beverly Hills CA 90212 USA | |
| **Martini, Steve** | Writer |
| Plume/GP Putnam's Sons, 375 Hudson St, New York NY 10014, USA | |
| **Martinie, Ryan** | Bassist (Mudvayne) |
| Agency Group Ltd, 142 W 57th St, #600, New York NY 10019 USA | |
| **Martinkovic, John G** | Football Player |
| 1001 Ernst Dr, Green Bay WI 54304, USA | |
| **Martino, Pat** | Jazz Guitarist, Composer |
| Donofrio Productions, 607 W Shore Road, Brigatine NJ 08203, USA | |
| **Martino, Renato R Cardinal** | Religious Leader |
| Justice & Peace Curia, Piazza S Calisto 16, 00153 Rome, Italy | |
| **Martins, Jean-Pierre** | Actor |
| Sophie Lemaitre, 22 Rue Nollet, 75017 Paris, France | |
| **Martins, Peter** | Ballet Dancer, Artistic Director |
| New York City Ballet, Lincoln Center Plaza, New York NY 10023 USA | |
| **Martinson, Leslie H** | Director |
| 2288 Coldwater Canyon Dr, Beverly Hills CA 90210, USA | |
| **Marton, Eva** | Opera Singer |
| International Artists Group, 201 E 87th St, #21E, New York NY 10128 USA | |
| **Martorella, Mildred (Millie)** | Bowler |
| Professional Bowlers Association, 719 2nd Ave, #701, Seattle WA 98104 USA | |
| **Marts, Lonnie** | Football Player |
| 13459 Nottingham Knoll Court, Jacksonville FL 32225, USA | |
| **Marty, Julia** | Ice Hockey Player |
| Swiss Ice Hockey, Hagenholzstr 81, 8050 Zurich, Switzerland | |
| **Marty, Martin E** | Theologian |
| 175 E Delaware Place, #8508, Chicago IL 60611, USA | |
| **Marty, Stefany** | Ice Hockey Player |
| Swiss Ice Hockey, Hagenholzstr 81, 8050 Zurich, Switzerland | |
| **Martynas** | Accordian Player |
| Agency Group Ltd, 361-373 City Road, London EC1V 1PQ, England | |
| **Martzke, Rudy** | Sportswriter |
| USA Today, Editorial Dept, 1000 Wilson Blvd, Arlington VA 22209, USA | |
| **Maruk, Dennis** | Ice Hockey Player |
| 2624 Garfield Ave, Minneapolis MN 55408, USA | |
| **Marusha** | Techno Musician |
| Kaiser-Friedrich-Str 41, 10627 Berlin, Germany | |
| **Maruyama, Karen** | Actress |
| Rooster Films, 5225 Wilshire Blvd, #406, Los Angeles CA 90036, USA | |
| **Maruyama, Karina** | Soccer Player |
| Football Association, 3-10-15 Hongo, Bunkyoku, Tokyo 113 0033 Japan | |

**Maruyama, Shigeki** — Golfer
15210 Antelo Place, Los Angeles CA 90077, USA

**Marve, Eugene R** — Football Player
4510 S Cameron Ave, Tampa FL 33611, USA

**Marvel, Jonathan** — Architect
Rogers Marvel Architects, 145 Hudson St, #304, New York NY 10013, USA

**Marvin, Gisele (Gigi)** — Ice Hockey Player
USA Hockey, 1775 Bob Johnson Dr, Colorado Springs CO 80906 USA

**Marvin, Hank B** — Guitarist (Shadows)
Universal Music, 364-366 Kensington High St, London W14 8NS, England

**Marx, Gilda** — Fashion Designer
Gilda Marx Industries, 11755 Exposition Blvd, Los Angeles CA 90064, USA

**Marx, Jeffrey A** — Journalist
Lexington Herald-Leader, Editorial Dept, Main & Midland, Lexington KY 40507, USA

**Marx, Michael** — Fencer
Northwest Fencing Center, 4950 SW Western Ave, Beaverton OR 97005, USA

**Marx, Reinhard Cardinal** — Religious Leader
Archdiocese of Munich, Postfach 330360, Rochusstr 5-7, 80063 Munich, Germany

**Marx, Richard** — Singer, Songwriter
Union Entertainment Group, 1323 Newbury Road, #102, Thousand Oaks CA 91329, USA

**Marzich, Andy** — Bowler
25141 Whitespring, Mission Viejo CA 92692, USA

**Marzoli, Andrea** — Geologist
Berkeley Geochronolgy Center, 2455 Ridge Road, Berkeley CA 94709, USA

**Marzouki, Moncef** — President, Tunisia
Palais Presidentiel, Carthage, 2070 Tunis, Tunisia

**Masak, Ron** — Actor, Writer, Producer
Neal Public Relations, 3117 Hollycrest Dr, Los Angeles CA 90068, USA

**Masakayan, Liz** — Volleyball Player
2864 Palomino Circle, La Jolla CA 92037, USA

**Masako** — Crown Princess, Japan
Imperial Palace, 1-1 Chiyoda, Chiyodaku, Tokyo 100 0001, Japan

**Mascarenas, Andi** — Sculptor
1984 Nova Road, Pine CO 80470, USA

**Maschio, Robert** — Actor
Stone Manners Salners, 6100 Wilshire Blvd, #1500, Los Angeles CA 90035 USA

**Masco, Judit** — Model
S S & M Model Mgmt, C/Provenca 286-88, 08008 Barcelona, Spain

**Masekela, Hugh R** — Jazz Trumpeter, Singer
Ritmo Artists, PO Box 684705, Austin TX 78768, USA

**Mashburn, Jamal** — Basketball Player
5625 Pine Tree Dr, Miami Beach FL 33140, USA

**Mashburn, Jesse** — Track Athlete
8520 S Pennsylvania Ave, Oklahoma City OK 73159, USA

**Masire, Quett K J** — President, Botswana
PO Box 70, Gaborone, Botswana

**Masius, John** — Producer, Writer
11948 Saltair Terrace, Los Angeles CA 90049, USA

**Maskaev, Oleg** — Boxer
Gleason's Boxing Gym, 75 Front St, New York NY 10005, USA

**Maskawa, Toshihide** — Nobel Physics Laureate
Koyoto Sangyo University, Kamigamo, Kitaku, Kyoto City 603 8553, Japan

**Maske, Henry** — Boxer
Tocardo, Neuer Wamdrahm 1, Speicherstadt, 20457 Hamburg, Germany

**Maskin, Eric S** — Nobel Economics Laureate
232 Washington St, Belmont MA 02478, USA

**Maslansky, Paul** — Producer, Director
Bamberger Business, 10850 Wilshire Blvd, #575, Los Angeles CA 90024, USA

**Maslany, Tatiana** — Actress
Characters Talent Agency, 8 Elm St, Toronto ON M5G 1G7, Canada

**Maslin, Janet** — Writer, Journalist
New York Times, Editorial Dept, 229 W 43rd St, New York NY 10036 USA

**Maslow, James** — Actor
Brillstein Entertainment Partners, 9150 Wilshire Blvd, #350, Beverly Hills CA 90212 USA

**Masohn, Mercedes** — Actress
Greene Assoc, 1901 Ave of Stars, #130, Los Angeles CA 90067 USA

**Mason of Barnsley, Roy** — Government Official, England
12 Victoria Ave, Barnsley, South Yorks S70 2BH, England

**Mason, Anthony G D** — Basketball Player
9 Brownstone Way, #308, Englewood NJ 07631, USA

**Mason, B John** — Meteorologist
64 Christchurch Road, East Sheen, London SW14, England

**Mason, Birny, Jr** — Chemical Engineer
2208 Theall Road, Rye NY 10580, USA

**Mason, Bob** — Ice Hockey Player
9549 Yukon Ave S, Minneapolis MN 55438, USA

**Mason, Bobbie Ann** — Writer
PO Box 518, Lawrenceburg KY 40342, USA

**Mason, Brent** — Singer
Mercury Records, 401 Commerce St, #1100, Nashville TN 37219 USA

**Mason, Chris** — Ice Hockey Player
PO Box 12465, Saint Louis MO 63132, USA

**Mason, Connie** — Model, Actress
Playboy Promotions, 9346 Civic Center Dr, #200, Beverly Hills CA 90210 USA

**Mason, Connie** — Writer
2960 Tampa Road, #106, Palm Harbor FL 34684, USA

**Mason, Dave** — Singer, Guitarist (Traffic); Songwriter
Jensen Communications, 709 E Colorado Blvd, #220, Pasadena CA 91101, USA

**Mason, Derrick J** — Football Player
9640 Portofino Dr, Brentwood TN 37027, USA

**Mason, Desmond T** — Basketball Player
6440 N Lake Dr, Milwaukee WI 53217, USA

**Mason, Henry (Hank)** — Baseball Player
5004 W Leyburn Court, #102, Henrico VA 23228, USA

**Mason, Jackie** — Actor, Comedian, Writer
W M E Entertainment, 1325 Ave of Americas, New York NY 10019, USA

**Mason, James P (Jim)** — Baseball Player
11410 Queens Way, Theodore AL 36582, USA
**Mason, Larry B** — Vietnam War Air Force Hero
826 Cinebar Road, Cinebar WA 98533, USA
**Mason, Lawrence** — Actor
Kazarian/Measures/Ruskin, 11969 Ventura Blvd, #300, Studio City CA 91604 USA
**Mason, Lindsey M** — Football Player
8665 Ritchboro Road, District Heights MD 20747, USA
**Mason, Marlyn** — Actress, Singer
27 Glen Oak Court, Medford OR 97504, USA
**Mason, Marsha** — Actress
1444 S Saint Francis Dr, #A, Santa Fe NM 87505, USA
**Mason, Michael P (Mike)** — Baseball Player
2711 Piper Ridge Lane, Excelsior MN 55331, USA
**Mason, Mila** — Singer
Fat City Artists, 1906 Chet Atkins Place, #502, Nashville TN 37212 USA
**Mason, Molly** — Fiddler (Blue Rose, Mammals)
Mike Greene Assoc, 339 E Liberty St, #220, Ann Arbor MI 48104, USA
**Mason, Monica** — Ballerina, Ballet Director
Royal Opera House, Convent Garden, Bow St, London WC2, England
**Mason, Nick** — Drummer (Pink Floyd)
One Fifteen, Globe House, Middle Lane Mews, London N8 8PN, England
**Mason, Roger L** — Baseball Player
322 Park St, Bellaire MI 49615, USA
**Mason, Roger P, Jr** — Basketball Player
Sacramento Kings, Arco Arena, 1 Sports Parkway, Sacramento CA 95834 USA
**Mason, Sally** — Educator
University of Iowa, President's Office, Iowa City IA 52242, USA
**Mason, Thomas C (Tommy)** — Football Player
240 S Orange Acres Dr, Anaheim CA 92807, USA
**Mason, Tom** — Actor
Hartig-Hilepo Agency, 54 W 21st St, #610, New York NY 10010 USA
**Mason, Tre** — Football Player
Saint Louis Rams, 901 N Broadway, Saint Louis MO 63101 USA
**Mason, Valerie Denise** — Model
Playboy Promotions, 9346 Civic Center Dr, #200, Beverly Hills CA 90210 USA
**Mason, Vince** — Rap Artist (De La Soul)
Richard Walters, PO Box 2789, Toluca Lake CA 91610 USA
**Masopust, Josef** — Soccer Player
Koulova 11, 16000 Prague 6, Czech Republic
**Masri, Tahir Nashat al-** — Prime Minister, Jordan
PO Box 5550, Amman 11183, Jordan
**Mass, Chris** — Writer, Producer, Actor
Untitled Entertainment, 350 S Beverly Dr, #200, Beverly Hills CA 90212 USA
**Mass, Wayne** — Football Player
71 Eagle View, Durango CO 81303, USA
**Massa, Felipe** — Auto Racing Driver
Caixa Postal 19091, Sao Paulo SP 04505 970, Brazil
**Massard, Didier** — Photographer
Julie Saul Gallery, 535 W 22nd St, #6F, New York NY 10011, USA
**Massari, Lea** — Actress
Viale Parioli 59, 00197 Rome, Italy
**Massenburg, Tony A** — Basketball Player
8210 Crestwood Heights Dr, #629, McLean VA 22102, USA
**Massenburg, Walter B** — Navy Admiral
Commander, Naval Air Systems Command, Patuxent River MD 20670 USA
**Masset, Andrew** — Actor
People Store Talent Agency, 645 Lambert Dr, Atlanta GA 30324, USA
**Masset, Nicholas A (Nick)** — Baseball Player
14575 W Mountain View Blvd, #11107, Surprise AZ 85374, USA
**Massevitch, Alla G** — Astronomer
6 Pushkurev Per, #4, 103045 Moscow, Russia
**Massey, Athena** — Actress
3673 El Encanto Dr, Calabasas CA 91302, USA
**Massey, Chandler** — Actor
Ferrantino Entertainment, 139 S Beverly Dr, #312, Beverly Hills CA 90212, USA
**Massey, Debbie** — Golfer
PO Box 116, Cheboygan MI 49721, USA
**Massey, Kent** — Yachtsman
4085 Foothill Road, Carpinteria CA 93013, USA
**Massey, Robert L** — Football Player
9617 Worley Dr, Charlotte NC 28215, USA
**Massey, Walter E** — Educator, Physicist, Financier
Bank of America Corp, 100 N Tryon St, #220, Charlotte NC 28202, USA
**Massie, Robert K** — Writer
52 W Clinton Ave, Irvington NY 10533, USA
**Massimino, Michael J** — Astronaut
15814 Elk Park Lane, Houston TX 77062, USA
**Massimino, Rolland V (Rollie)** — Basketball Coach
18578 SE Ferland Court, Jupiter FL 33469, USA
**Massimov, Karim K** — Prime Minister, Kazakhstan
Dom Pravieelstva, Plaza im VI Lenina, 148008 Astana, Kazakhstan
**Massof, Robert W** — Inventor (Seeing Eye Apparatus)
Wilmer Ophthalmological Institute, 550 N Broadway, #600, Baltimore MD 21205, USA
**Massoglia, Chris** — Actor
Zero Gravity Mgmt, 1531 14th St, Santa Monica CA 90404, USA
**Massu, Nicolas A** — Tennis Player
Association of Tennis Professionals, 201 A T P Blvd, Ponte Vedra Beach FL 32082 USA
**Mast, Richard (Dick)** — Golfer
913 Johnson Road, Lynchburg VA 24502, USA
**Mast, Richard K (Rick)** — Auto Racing Driver
390 E Midland Trail, Lexington VA 24450, USA
**Masta Killa** — Rap Artist (Wu-Tang Clan)
A&M Entertainment, 13280 NE Freeway, #F328, Houston TX 77040, USA
**Mastalli, Chiara** — Actress
Agenzie Fabrizia Mancuso, Piazza Benedetto Cairoli 6, 00186 Rome, Italy

# M

**Master P** — Rap Artist, Actor, Producer
Silverstone Entertainment USA, 10 Universal City Plaza, #2400, Universal City CA 91608, USA

**Masters, Blake** — Writer, Producer, Director
Brant Rose Agency, 6671 Sunset Blvd, #1584B, Los Angeles CA 90028, USA

**Masters, William J (Billy)** — Football Player
501 SW Silver Spur Circle, Lees Summit MO 64081, USA

**Masterson, Chase** — Actress
Masterson Entertainment, 12400 Ventura Blvd, #1200, Studio City CA 91604, USA

**Masterson, Danny** — Actor
Masterson Mgmt, 1566 Hillcrest Ave, Glendale CA 91202, USA

**Masterson, Fay** — Actress
Industry Entertainment, 955 Carillo Dr, #300, Los Angeles CA 90048 USA

**Masterson, Mary Stuart** — Actress
356 W Kerley Comers Road, Tivoli NY 12583, USA

**Masterson, Peter** — Writer, Director, Producer
1165 5th Ave, #15A, New York NY 10029, USA

**Masterson, Valerie** — Opera Singer
Music International, 13 Ardilaun Road, London N5 2QR, England

**Maston, Le'Shai E** — Football Player
7856 Overridge Dr, Dallas TX 75232, USA

**Mastracchio, Richard A (Rick)** — Astronaut
1910 Hillside Oak Lane, Houston TX 77062, USA

**Mastracci, Natalie** — Rowing Athlete
Sainte Catherine's Rowing Club, 600 Ontario St, Sainte Catherine's ON L2N 7P8, Canada

**Mastrangelo, Carlo** — Singer (Dion & the Belmonts)
Paramount Entertainment, PO Box 12, Far Hills NJ 07931 USA

**Mastrantonio, Mary Elizabeth** — Actress, Singer
Lou Coulson Assoc, 37 Berwick St, London W1V 8RS, England

**Mastrogiacomo, Gina** — Actress
Pakula/King, 9229 W Sunset Blvd, #315, West Hollywood CA 90069 USA

**Mastroianni, Armand** — Director
Creative Artists Agency, 2000 Ave of Stars, #100, Los Angeles CA 90067 USA

**Mastroianni, Chiara** — Actress
Zelig Films, 57 Rue Reaumur, 75002 Paris, France

**Masui, Yoshio** — Zoologist
32 Overton Crescent, Don Mills, North York ON M3B 2V2, Canada

**Masur, Kurt** — Conductor
Masur Music, Ansonia, 790 Riverside Dr, #6N, New York NY 10032, USA

**Masur, Richard** — Actor
Leading Artists, 145 W 45th St, #1000, New York NY 10036, USA

**Masvidal, Paul A** — Singer, Guitarist (Cynic, Aeon Spoke)
Season of Mist Records, 111 Route de Valentinell, 13011 Marseille, France

**Mata, Victor J** — Baseball Player
New York Yankees, Yankee Stadium, E 161st St & River Ave, Bronx NY 10451 USA

**Matalin, Mary** — Political Consultant
325 Fishers Road, Maureltown VA 22644, USA

**Matalon, J Rolando (Roly)** — Religious Leader, Rabbi
Congregation B'nai Jeshurun, 2109 Broadway, #2034, New York NY 10023, USA

**Matane, Paulius N** — Governor General, Papua New Guinea
Governor General's Office, PO Box 79, Port Moresby 121, Papua New Guinea

**Matarazzo, Heather** — Actress
Don Buchwald Talent Agency, 10 E 44th St, New York NY 10017 USA

**Mataskelekele, Kalkot** — President, Vanuata; Judge
President's Office, Port Vila, Vanuatu

**Matchefts, John** — Ice Hockey Player
2415 Chelton Road, Colorado Springs CO 80909, USA

**Matchett, Kari** — Actress
Paradigm Agency, 360 N Crescent Dr, North Building, Beverly Hills CA 90210 USA

**Matchick, J Thomas (Tom)** — Baseball Player
7700 Pillod Road, Holland OH 43528, USA

**Matejka, Adrian** — Writer
University of Indiana, Master of Fine Arts Program, Bloomington IN 47405, USA

**Mateparae, Jeremiah (Jerry)** — Governor General, New Zealand
Governor General's Office, Government House, Private Bag 39995, Wellington 5045, New Zealand

**Matheny, Eric** — Actor
Don Buchwald Talent Agency, 6500 Wilshire Blvd, #2200, Los Angeles CA 90048 USA

**Matheny, Logan** — Drummer (Roman Candle)
Russell Carter Artist Mgmt, 567 Ralph Magill Blvd, Atlanta GA 30312 USA

**Matheny, Skip** — Singer, Guitarist (Roman Candle)
Russell Carter Artist Mgmt, 567 Ralph Magill Blvd, Atlanta GA 30312 USA

**Matheny, Timshel** — Organist (Roman Candle)
Russell Carter Artist Mgmt, 567 Ralph Magill Blvd, Atlanta GA 30312 USA

**Mather, John C** — Nobel Physics Laureate
3400 Rosemary Lane, Hyattsville MD 20782, USA

**Mathers, Jerry** — Actor
McInerney Business Mgmt, 26372 Calle Lucana, San Juan Capistrano CA 92675, USA

**Matheson, Diana** — Soccer Player
Washington Spirit, Maryland SoccerPlex, 18031 Central Park Circle, Boyds MD 20841, USA

**Matheson, Hans** — Actor
Lou Coulson Assoc, 37 Berwick St, London W1V 8RS, England

**Matheson, Tim** — Actor, Director
Generate Mgmt, 1545 26th St, #200, Santa Monica CA 90404, USA

**Mathew, Suleka (Sue)** — Actress
S D B Partners, 315 S Beverly Dr, #411, Beverly Hills CA 90067 USA

**Mathews, F David** — Secretary, Health Education & Welfare
6050 Mad River Road, Dayton OH 45459, USA

**Mathews, Gregory I (Greg)** — Baseball Player
11721 Old Ballas Road, #107, Saint Louis MO 63141, USA

**Mathews, Jessica T** — Foundation Executive
Carnegie International Peace Endowment, 1779 Massachusetts NW, Washington DC 20036, USA

**Mathews, Raymond D (Ray)** — Football Player
PO Box 108, Harrisville PA 16038, USA

**Mathews, Robin** — Makeup & Hairstyling Artist
iTalent, 5023 N Parkway Calabasas, Calabasas CA 91302, USA

**Mathews, Timothy J (T J)** — Baseball Player
839 Autumn Rise Lane, Columbia IL 62236, USA

**Master P - Mathews**

**Mathewson, Courtney** — Water Polo Player
Roger B Mathewson, 1298 N Andrea Lane, Anaheim CA 92807, USA
**Mathieson, John** — Cinematographer
Independent Talent Group, 40 Whitfield St, London W1T 2RH, England
**Mathieu, Marquis** — Ice Hockey Player
113 W Lake Shore Dr, Hallandale FL 33009, USA
**Mathieu, Philip** — Concert Guitarist
Lindy S Martin Mgmt, 1007 Lakewater Dr, Henrico VA 23229, USA
**Mathilde** — Queen, Belgium
Koninklijk Palace, Rue de Brederode, 1000 Brussels, Belgium
**Mathis, Rashean** — Football Player
26200 Marsh Landing Parkway, Ponte Vedra FL 32082, USA
**Mathis, Buster, Jr** — Boxer
4409 Carol Ave SW, Wyoming MI 49519, USA
**Mathis, Chester A** — Radiologist
University of Pittsburgh Medical Center, P E T Facility, Radiology Dept, Pittsburgh PA 15213, USA
**Mathis, Clint** — Soccer Player
Los Angeles Galaxy, Home Depot Center, 18400 Avalon Blvd, Carson CA 90746 USA
**Mathis, Evan B** — Football Player
11938 N 113th Place, Scottsdale AZ 85259, USA
**Mathis, Jeffrey S (Jeff)** — Baseball Player
4420 Spring Valley Dr, Marianna FL 32448, USA
**Mathis, Johnny** — Singer
1469 Stebbins Terrace, Los Angeles CA 90069, USA
**Mathis, Samantha** — Actress
Paradigm Agency, 360 N Crescent Dr, North Building, Beverly Hills CA 90210 USA
**Mathis, Terance** — Football Player
3415 Camellia Lane, Suwanee GA 30024, USA
**Mathis-Eddy, Darlene** — Writer
1409 W Cardinal St, Muncie IN 47303, USA
**Mathison, Cameron** — Actor
Innovative Artists, 1505 10th St, Santa Monica CA 90401 USA
**Matisi, John R** — Baseball Player
98-1616 Hoolauae St, Aiea HI 96701, USA
**Matisyahu** — Singer
Agency Group Ltd, 142 W 57th St, #600, New York NY 10019 USA
**Matkevich, Mark** — Actor
TalentWorks, 3500 W Olive Ave, #1400, Burbank CA 91505 USA
**Matlack, Jonathan T (Jon)** — Baseball Player
2495 Sawdust Road, #1101, Spring TX 77380, USA
**Matlin, Marlee** — Actress
Solo Productions, 8205 Santa Monica Blvd, #1279, West Hollywood CA 90046, USA
**Matlock, Glen** — Bassist (Sex Pistols)
Bruce Pilato Mgmt, PO Box 17775, Rochester NY 14617, USA
**Matlock, Jack F, Jr** — Diplomat
940 Princeton-Kingston Road, Princeton NJ 08540, USA
**Matola, Sharon** — Zoo Director, Conservationist
Belize Zoo & Tropical Education Center, PO Box 1787, Belize City, Belize
**Matorin, Vladimir A** — Opera Singer
Ulansky Per 21, Korp 1, #53, 103045 Moscow, Russia
**Matos, Eddie** — Actor
Schumacher Mgmt, 10323 Santa Monica Blvd, #101, Los Angeles CA 90024, USA
**Matos, Elisabete** — Opera Singer
Opera et Concert, 37 Rue de la Chaussee d'Antin, 75009 Paris, France
**Matranga, Jonah** — Singer, Songwriter
Agency Group Ltd, 142 W 57th St, #600, New York NY 10019 USA
**Matronic, Ana** — Singer (Scissors Sisters), Songwriter
Girlie Action, 59 W 19th St, #4B, New York NY 10011 USA
**Matshikiza, Pumeza** — Opera Singer
I M G Artists, Hogarth Business Park, Chiswick, London W4 2TH, England
**Matson, J Randel (Randy)** — Track Athlete
1002 Park Place, College Station TX 77840, USA
**Matsos, Emil G (Archie)** — Football Player
1410 Coventry Close St, East Lansing MI 48823, USA
**Matsui, Hideki** — Baseball Player
119 W 72nd St, #306, New York NY 10023, USA
**Matsui, Keiko** — Jazz Pianist
M P I Talent Agency, 9255 Sunset Blvd, #407, West Hollywood CA 90069, USA
**Matsuyama, Hideki** — Golfer
Professional Golfers Association, 100 Ave of Champions, Palm Beach Gardens FL 33418 USA
**Matsuzaka, Daisuke** — Baseball Player
Cleveland Indians, Jacobs Field, 2401 Ontario St, Cleveland OH 44115 USA
**Matsuzaki, Yuki** — Actor
Williams-Michael Relations, 3940 Laurel Canyon, #785, Studio City CA 91604, USA
**Matt, Mike** — Rodeo Rider
111 S 24th St W, #9125, Billings MT 59102, USA
**Matta, Thad** — Basketball Coach
Ohio State University, Athletic Dept, Columbus OH 43210, USA
**Matte, Thomas R (Tom)** — Football Player
11309 Old Carriage Road, Glen Arm MD 21057, USA
**Mattea, Kathy** — Singer, Guitarist
International Music Network, 278 Main St, #400, Gloucester MA 01930 USA
**Mattei, Frank** — Singer (Danny & the Juniors)
Joe Taylor Mgmt, PO Box 1017, Blackwood NJ 08012, USA
**Mattek-Sands, Bethany** — Tennis Player
1146 W MacKenzie Dr, Phoenix AZ 85013, USA
**Mattel, Coline** — Ski Jumper
Les Contamines Montjoie Ski Club, 74085 Les Contamines, France
**Mattes, Eva** — Actress
Agentur Carola Studlar, Agnesstr 47, 80798 Munich, Germany
**Mattes, Ronald A (Ron)** — Football Player
1718 Moreland Wood Trail NW, Concord NC 28027, USA
**Matteson, John** — Writer
W W Norton, 500 5th Ave, #600, New York NY 10110 USA
**Matteson, Troy** — Golfer
6518 Old Shadburn Ferry Road, Buford GA 30518, USA

M

# M

**Matthes, Roland** — Swimmer
Luitpoldstr 35A, 97828 Marktheidenfeld, Germany

**Matthes, Ulrich** — Actor
Bleibtreustr 8, 10623 Berlin, Germany

**Matthew, Catriona I** — Golfer
I M G, Pier House, Strand-on-Green, Chiswick, London W4 3NN, England

**Matthews, Alvin L (Al)** — Football Player
19451 Diablo Dr, Pflugerville TX 78660, USA

**Matthews, Bruce R** — Football Player
1565 Lost Hollow Dr, Brentwood TN 37027, USA

**Matthews, Cerys** — Singer (Catatonia)
Rough Trade Mgmt, 66 Golborne Road, London W10 5PS, England

**Matthews, Chris** — Commentator
9 E Kirke St, Chevy Chase MD 20815, USA

**Matthews, Dakin** — Actor
Geddes Agency, 8430 Santa Monica Blvd, #201, West Hollywood CA 90069 USA

**Matthews, Dave** — Singer, Guitarist (Dave Matthews Band)
Red Light Mgmt, PO Box 1467, Charlottesville VA 22902, USA

**Matthews, DeLane** — Actress
Don Buchwald Talent Agency, 6500 Wilshire Blvd, #2200, Los Angeles CA 90048 USA

**Matthews, Eric** — Singer, Songwriter
Chords of Fame, 3030 Glenmanor Place, Los Angeles CA 90039, USA

**Matthews, Gary N, Jr** — Baseball Player
Cincinnati Reds, Great American Ball Park, 100 Main St, Cincinnati OH 45202 USA

**Matthews, Gary N, Sr** — Baseball Player
1542 W Jackson Blvd, Chicago IL 60607, USA

**Matthews, Ian** — Singer, Guitarist
Geoffrey Blumenauer Artists, PO Box 343, Burbank CA 91503 USA

**Matthews, Keith** — Astronomer
California Institute of Technology, Astronomy Dept, Pasadena CA 91125, USA

**Matthews, Liesel** — Actress
Creative Artists Agency, 2000 Ave of Stars, #100, Los Angeles CA 90067 USA

**Matthews, Lisa** — Model, Actress
Playboy Promotions, 9346 Civic Center Dr, #200, Beverly Hills CA 90210 USA

**Matthews, Michael S (Mike)** — Baseball Player
3657 Winged Foot Circle, Green Cove Springs FL 32043, USA

**Matthews, Pat Stanley** — Actress
210 Stanton St, Walla Walla WA 99362, USA

**Matthews, Robert C O** — Economist
Clare College, Economics Dept, Cambridge CB2 1TL, England

**Matthews, Sally** — Opera Singer
Maxine Robertson Mgmt, 14 Forge Dr, Claygate KT1O 0HR, England

**Matthews, Shane** — Football Player
848 NW 136th St, Agoura Hills CA 91301, USA

**Matthews, Vincent (Vince)** — Track Athlete
6755 193rd Lane, Fresh Meadows NY 11365, USA

**Matthews, W Clay, III** — Football Player
Green Bay Packers, 1265 Lombardi Ave, Green Bay WI 54304 USA

**Matthews, W Clay, Jr** — Football Player
6068 Canterbury Dr, Agoura Hills CA 91301, USA

**Matthies, Nina** — Volleyball Player, Coach
Pepperdine University, Athletic Dept, Malibu CA 90265, USA

**Matthiesen, Mads** — Director, Writer
Paradigm Agency, 360 N Crescent Dr, North Building, Beverly Hills CA 90210 USA

**Mattiace, Len** — Golfer
12802 Hunt Club Road N, Jacksonville FL 32224, USA

**Mattila, Karita M** — Opera Singer
45B Croxley Road, London W9 3HJ, England

**Mattingly, Ashley** — Model
Playboy Promotions, 9346 Civic Center Dr, #200, Beverly Hills CA 90210 USA

**Mattingly, Donald A (Don)** — Baseball Player, Manager
7601 Newburgh Road, Evansville IN 47715, USA

**Mattingly, Mack F** — Senator, GA; Diplomat
4315 10th St, East Beach, Saint Simons Island GA 31522, USA

**Mattingly, Thomas K, II** — Astronaut, Navy Admiral
Systems Planning & Analysis, 2001 N Beauregard St, Alexandria VA 22311, USA

**Mattis, James N** — Marine Corps General
Commander, Central Command, 7115 S Boundary, MacDill Air Force Base FL 33621 USA

**Mattscherodt, Katrin** — Speed Skater
Sportclub Berlin, Weissenseer Weg 53, 13053 Berlin, Germany

**Mattson, Riley C** — Football Player
12 Coconut Grove Lane, Lahaina HI 96761, USA

**Mattson, Robin** — Actress
Stan Kamens Mgmt, 7772 Torreyson Dr, Los Angeles CA 90046, USA

**Matuszek, Leonard J (Len)** — Baseball Player
10326 Deerfield Road, Cincinnati OH 45242, USA

**Matvichuk, Richard** — Ice Hockey Player
PO Box 96225, Southlake TX 76092, USA

**Matz, Michael R** — Equestrian, Thoroughbred Racing Trainer
2953 Hurlinham Dr, Wellington FL 33414, USA

**Matzdorf, Pat** — Track Athlete
1252 Bainbridge Dr, Naperville IL 60563, USA

**Matzner, Jason** — Director
Paradigm Agency, 360 N Crescent Dr, North Building, Beverly Hills CA 90210 USA

**Mau, Bruce** — Multimedia Designer
197 Spadina Ave, #501, Toronto ON M5T 2C8, Canada

**Maualuga, Rey** — Football Player
Cincinnati Bengals, 1 Paul Brown Stadium, Cincinnati OH 45202 USA

**Mauboy, Jessica H** — Actress, Singer, Songwriter
R G M Artists, 8-12 Ann Street, Surry Hills NSW 2010, Australia

**Mauceri, John** — Conductor
I C M Artists, 40 W 57th St, #1800, New York NY 10019 USA

**Mauck, Carl F** — Football Player
2129 Winthrop Hill Road, Argyle TX 76226, USA

**Maudsley, Tony** — Actor
United Agents, 12-26 Lexington St, London W1F 0LE, England

**Matthes - Maudsley**

**Mauer, Joseph P (Joe)**    Baseball Player
671 Lexington Parkway N, Saint Paul MN 55104, USA

**Maultsby, Nancy**    Opera Singer
I M G Artists, Hogarth Business Park, Chiswick, London W4 2TH, England

**Mauney, Carl V**    Navy Admiral
Deputy Commander, US Strategic Command, Offutt Air Force Base NE 68113, USA

**Maupin, Armistead J, Jr**    Writer
Literary Bent, PO Box 4109990, #528, San Francisco CA 94141, USA

**Maura, Carmen**    Actress
Ramon Pilaces, C/Hortaleza 20, #1 Izqda, 28004 Madrid, Spain

**Maurel, Julien**    Actor
J F P M, 11 Rue Chanez, 75781 Paris Cedex 16, France

**Maurer, Andrew L (Andy)**    Football Player
30 Perrydale Ave, Medford OR 97501, USA

**Maurer, Ingo**    Inventor, Lighting Designer
Team Ingo Maurer, Kaiserstr 47, 80801 Munich, Germany

**Maurer, Robert D**    Inventor (Silica Optical Waveguide)
2572 W 28th Ave, Eugene OR 97405, USA

**Maurer, Robert J (Rob)**    Baseball Player
3114 E Gum St, Evansville IN 47714, USA

**Mauresmo, Amelie**    Tennis Player
Athleteline, 2 Rue du Chemin Vert, 92110 Clichy, France

**Maurice, Paul**    Ice Hockey Coach
Winnipeg Jets, 260 Hargrave St, Winnipeg MB R3C 5S5, Canada

**Mauriello, Tammy**    Boxer
1148 E 81st St, Brooklyn NY 11236, USA

**Maurier, Claire**    Actress
Anne Alvares Correa, 34 Rue Jouffroy d'Abbans, 75017 Paris, France

**Maurstad, Toralv**    Director, Actor
Thorleif, Hangsvei 20, 0712 Voksenkollen, Norway

**Mauser, Timothy E (Tim)**    Baseball Player
114 Shadow Creek Lane, Aledo TX 76008, USA

**Mauz, Henry H (Hank), Jr**    Navy Admiral
1608 Viscaine Road, Pebble Beach CA 93953, USA

**Maven, Max**    Illusionist
PO Box 1298, La Mesa CA 91944, USA

**Mawae, Kevin J**    Football Player, Labor Leader
19414 Old Perkins Road E, Baton Rouge LA 70810, USA

**Mawby, Russell G**    Foundation Executive
W K Kellogg Foundation, 1 Michigan Ave E, Battle Creek MI 49017, USA

**Max, Kevin**    Singer, Songwriter
Pitch Music, PO Box 235185, Encinitas CA 92023, USA

**Max, Peter**    Artist
118 Riverside Dr, New York NY 10024, USA

**Maxcy, D Brian**    Baseball Player
982 Cobble Creek Dr, Birmingham AL 35226, USA

**Maxi Jazz**    Rap Artist (Faithless)
Helter Skelter, 347-353 Chiswick High Road, London W4 4HS, England

**Maxie, Brett D**    Football Player
131 Guineveres Retreat, Franklin TN 37067, USA

**Maximova, Elena**    Opera Singer
I M G Artists, Hogarth Business Park, Chiswick, London W4 2TH, England

**Maxsom, Alvin E**    Football Player
3215 S Danube St, Aurora CO 80013, USA

**Maxvill, C Dalian (Dal)**    Baseball Player
1115 Eagle Creek Road, Chesterfield MO 63005, USA

**Maxwell**    Singer
W M E Entertainment, 9601 Wilshire Blvd, #300, Beverly Hills CA 90210 USA

**Maxwell, Arthur E**    Oceanographer
8200 Neely Dr, #260, Austin TX 78759, USA

**Maxwell, Brad**    Ice Hockey Player
27285 Natchez Ave, Elko MN 55020, USA

**Maxwell, Cedric B (Cornbread)**    Basketball Player
151 Tremont St, #25H, Boston MA 02111, USA

**Maxwell, Charles R (Charlie)**    Baseball Player
730 Mapleview Ave, Paw Paw MI 49079, USA

**Maxwell, Kevin F H**    Publisher
Moulsford Manor, Moulsford, Oxfordshire OX10 9HO, England

**Maxwell, Robert D**    WW II Army Hero (CMH)
1001 SE 15th St, #44, Bend OR 97702, USA

**Maxwell, Ronald F (Ron)**    Director, Writer
Weissmann Wolff Bergman, 9665 Wilshire Blvd, #900, Beverly Hills CA 90212, USA

**Maxwell, Thomas M (Tommy)**    Football Player
1634 Rockview Dr, Granbury TX 76049, USA

**Maxwell, Vernon**    Basketball Player
2601 NW 23rd Blvd, #170, Gainesville FL 32605, USA

**Maxwell, Vernon L**    Football Player
1955 E Citation Lane, Tempe AZ 85284, USA

**May of Oxford, Robert M M**    Biologist
Royal Society, 6 Carlton House Terrace, London SW1Y 5AG, England

**May, Antoinette**    Writer
William Morrow Publishers, 1350 Ave of Americas, New York NY 10019 USA

**May, Arthur**    Architect
Kohn Pedersen Fox Assoc, 111 W 57th St, #300, New York NY 10019, USA

**May, B Deems**    Football Player
3922 Ayscough Road, Charlotte NC 28211, USA

**May, Bob**    Golfer
420 Grand Augusta Lane, Las Vegas NV 89144, USA

**May, Brad**    Ice Hockey Player
9167 E Mountain Spring Road, Scottsdale AZ 85255, USA

**May, Brian**    Guitarist (Queen), Songwriter
Old Bakehouse, 16A High St, Barnes, London SW13, England

**May, Darrell K**    Baseball Player
747 Minthorne Road, Rogue River OR 97537, USA

**May, Deborah**    Actress
Artists Agency, 9430 Olympic Blvd, Beverly Hills CA 90212 USA

**May, Derrick B**
2 Jaymar Road, Newark DE 19702, USA — Baseball Player

**May, Donald J (Don)**
1128 Colwick Dr, Dayton OH 45420, USA — Basketball Player

**May, Elaine**
146 Central Park West, #5D, New York NY 10023, USA — Actress, Comedienne, Director

**May, Imelda**
Neil O'Brien Entertainment, 26 Eastcastle St, #300, London W1W 8DQ, England — Singer, Guitarist, Songwriter

**May, James**
Arlington Enterprises, 1-3 Charlotte St, London W1T 1RD, England — Actor

**May, Lee A**
2200 Manatee Ave W, Bradenton FL 34205, USA — Baseball Player

**May, Maggie**
Playboy Promotions, 9346 Civic Center Dr, #200, Beverly Hills CA 90210 USA — Model

**May, Mark E**
3557 E Minton St, Mesa AZ 85213, USA — Football Player, Sportscaster

**May, Mathilda**
Voyez Mon Agent, 20 Ave Rapp, 75007 Paris, France — Actress

**May, Milton S (Milt)**
2200 Manatee Ave W, Bradenton FL 34205, USA — Baseball Player

**May, Phillip (Phil)**
Talent Consultants International, 105 Shad Row, #B, Piermont NY 10968 USA — Singer (Pretty Things)

**May, Ralphie**
United Talent Agency, U T A Plaza, 9336 Civic Center Dr, Beverly Hills CA 90210 USA — Actor, Comedian, Producer

**May, Ray**
1921 Wellington Road, Los Angeles CA 90016, USA — Football Player

**May, Richard H**
3732 E Pasadena Ave, Phoenix AZ 85018, USA — WW II Navy Air Hero

**May, Rudolph (Rudy), Jr**
8090 N Augusta St, Fresno CA 93720, USA — Baseball Player

**May, Scott G**
2001 E Hillside Dr, Bloomington IN 47401, USA — Basketball Player

**May, Sean G**
2001 E Hillside Dr, Bloomington IN 47401, USA — Basketball Player

**May, Torsten**
Frankfurt Boxing Ring, Kieler Str 9, 15234 Frankfurt/Oder, Germany — Boxer

**Mayall, John**
30844 Grenoble Court, Westlake Village CA 91362, USA — Singer, Keyboardist, Composer

**Mayasich, John E**
77 E Missouri Ave Unit 45, Phoenix AZ 85012, USA — Ice Hockey Player

**Maybank, Anthuan**
171 N Porter St, Elgin IL 60120, USA — Track Athlete

**Mayberry, Jermane T**
2208 Court del Rey, Round Rock TX 78681, USA — Football Player

**Mayberry, John C**
11115 W 121st Terrace, Overland Park KS 66213, USA — Baseball Player

**Mayberry, O Lee**
4115 E 36th St N, Tulsa OK 74115, USA — Basketball Player

**Maybin, Cameron K**
85 Brompton Road, Arden NC 28704, USA — Baseball Player

**Mayer H, Jurgen**
Bleibtreystr 54, 10623 Berlin, Germany — Architect

**Mayer, Christian**
Siedlerweg 18, 9584 Finkelstein, Austria — Alpine Skier

**Mayer, Edwin D (Ed)**
440 Oakdale Ave, Corte Madera CA 94925, USA — Baseball Player

**Mayer, Gene**
115 South St, Glenn Dale MD 20769, USA — Tennis Player

**Mayer, H Robert**
US Court of Appeals, 717 Madison Place NW, Washington DC 20439, USA — Judge

**Mayer, John**
Prime, 9696 Culver Blvd, #102, Culver City CA 90232, USA — Singer, Songwriter

**Mayer, Joseph E**
2345 Via Siena, La Jolla CA 92037, USA — Chemical Physicist

**Mayer, Marissa**
Yahoo Inc, 701 1st Ave, Sunnyvale CA 94089, USA — Businesswoman

**Mayer, Matthias**
Angerweg 2, 9542 Afritz, Austria — Alpine Skier

**Mayer, Michael**
Creative Artists Agency, 2000 Ave of Stars, #100, Los Angeles CA 90067 USA — Director

**Mayer, Travis**
37050 Williams St, Steamboat Springs CO 80487, USA — Freestyle Skier

**Mayers, Jamal**
9 Terrace Gardens, Saint Louis MO 63131, USA — Ice Hockey Player

**Mayes, Rueben**
610 SE Edge Knoll Dr, Pullman WA 99163, USA — Football Player

**Mayfair, Billy**
PO Box 25490, Scottsdale AZ 85255, USA — Golfer

**Mayfield, Jeremy A**
Mayfield Motorsports, 2220 Highway 49 N, Harrisburg NC 28075, USA — Auto Racing Driver

**Mayhew of Twysden, Patrick B B**
House of Lords, Westminster, London SW1A 0PW, England — Government Official, England

**Mayhew, Lauren C**
Abrams Artists, 9200 W Sunset Blvd, #1125, West Hollywood CA 90069 USA — Singer, Actress

**Mayhew, Martin**
4035 Sonnet Dr, Tallahassee FL 32303, USA — Football Player

**Mayle, Peter**
Knopf Publishers, 201 E 50th St, New York NY 10022, USA — Writer

**Maynard, Bradley A (Brad)**
284 Milford Circle, Mooresville NC 28117, USA — Football Player

**Maynard, Mimi**
Schlowitz Connor, 1680 N Vine St, #1016, Los Angeles CA 90028 USA — Actress

**Mayne, Brent D**
1863 Parklgen Circle, Costa Mesa CA 92627, USA — Baseball Player

**Mayne, D Roger**
Colway Manor, Colway Lane, Lyme Regis, Dorset DT7 3HD, England — Photographer

**Mayne, Kenny**
ESPN-TV, Sports Dept, ESPN Plaza, 935 Middle St, Bristol CT 06010 USA — Sportscaster
**Mayne, Thomas**
Morphosis Architects, 3444 Wesley St, Culver City CA 90232, USA — Pritzker Architectual Laureate
**Maynor, Asa**
PO Box 1469, Beverly Hills CA 90213, USA — Actress
**Maynor, Eric**
Philadelphia 76ers, 1st Union Center, 3601 S Broad St, Philadelphia PA 19148 USA — Basketball Player
**Maynor, Stephanie**
5205 Bordeaux Cove, Ellicott City MD 21043, USA — Golfer
**Mayo, John L (Jackie)**
450 Boardman Poland Road, Youngstown OH 44512, USA — Baseball Player
**Mayo, O J**
3576 Golf Walk Circle, Memphis TN 38125, USA — Basketball Player
**Mayock, Michael F (Mike)**
607 Georges Lane, Ardmore PA 19003, USA — Sportscaster
**Mayopoulos, Timothy J**
Federal National Mortgage Association, 3900 Wisconsin Ave NW, Washington DC 20016, USA — Businessman, Government Official
**Mayor Zaragoza, Federico**
Ma Caribe 15, Interland, Majadahonda, 28220 Madrid, Spain — Government Official, Spain
**Mayor, Michel G E**
University of Geneva, Geneva Observatory, 1211 Geneva 4, Switzerland — Astronomer
**Mayotte, Timothy S (Tim)**
266 W 115th St, #4A, New York NY 10026, USA — Tennis Player
**Mayron, Melanie**
1435 N Ogden Dr, Los Angeles CA 90046, USA — Actress, Director
**Mays, Alvoid**
3903 Cape Vista Dr, Bradenton FL 34209, USA — Football Player
**Mays, Daniel**
Curtis Brown Group, 28-29 Haymarket St, #500, London SW1Y 4SP, England — Actor
**Mays, Jayma**
United Talent Agency, U T A Plaza, 9336 Civic Center Dr, Beverly Hills CA 90210 USA — Actress
**Mays, Joseph E (Joe)**
10314 Riverbank Terrace, Bradenton FL 34212, USA — Baseball Player
**Mays, Lyle**
Ted Kurland, 173 Brighton Ave, Boston MA 02134 USA — Jazz Pianist
**Mays, Melinda**
2221 Peachtree Road NE, #D440, Atlanta GA 30309, USA — Model
**Mays, Willie H**
51 Mount Vernon Lane, Atherton CA 94027, USA — Baseball Player
**May-Treanor, Misty**
2829 N Bellflower Blvd, #482, Long Beach CA 90815, USA — Volleyball Player
**Mayweather, Floyd, Jr**
4720 Laguna Vista St, Las Vegas NV 89147, USA — Boxer
**Mayweather, Roger**
2784 Trotwood Lane, Las Vegas NV 89108, USA — Boxer, Trainer
**Mazach, John J**
1137 Quail Roost Court, Virginia Beach VA 23451, USA — Navy Admiral
**Mazar, Debi**
Framework Entertainment, 9057 Nemo St, #C, West Hollywood CA 90069 USA — Actress
**Maze, Tina**
Pristava 29, 2393 Crua na Koroskem, Slovenia — Alpine Skier
**Mazelle, Kym**
Tony Denton Promotions, Charter House, 157-159 High St, London N14 6BP, England — Singer
**Mazer, Dan**
United Agents, 12-26 Lexington St, London W1F 0LE, England — Writer
**Mazeroski, William S (Bill)**
281 Walton Tea Room Road, Greensburg PA 15601, USA — Baseball Player
**Mazin, Craig**
Creative Artists Agency, 2000 Ave of Stars, #100, Los Angeles CA 90067 USA — Actor
**Mazor, Stanley (Stan)**
F T I/Teklicon, 3031 Tisch Way, San Jose CA 95128, USA — Inventor (Microprocessor)
**Mazur, Jay J**
Industrial Textile Employees Needletrades, 1710 Broadway, New York NY 10019, USA — Labor Leader
**Mazur, Monet**
Innovative Artists, 1505 10th St, Santa Monica CA 90401 USA — Actress
**Mazurok, Yuri A**
Bolshoi State Theater, Teatralnaya Pl 1, 103009 Moscow, Russia — Opera Singer
**Mazza, Marc**
S N Bellefaye, 30 Rue Saint Marc, 75002 Paris, France — Actor
**Mazza, Valeria**
Riccardo Ga, 8/10 Via Revere, 20123 Milan, Italy — Model
**Mazzante, Kelly**
New York Liberty, Madison Square Garden, 2 Penn Plaza, New York NY 10121 USA — Basketball Player
**Mazzanti, Jerry E**
1712 S Lakeshore Dr, Lake Village AR 71653, USA — Football Player
**Mazzara, Glen**
Creative Artists Agency, 2000 Ave of Stars, #100, Los Angeles CA 90067 USA — Producer, Writer
**Mazzello, Joseph**
J J M Productions, 9560 Wilshire Blvd, #500, Beverly Hills CA 90212, USA — Actor
**Mazzie, Marin**
Mitchell K Stubbs Assoc, 8695 W Washington Blvd, #204, Culver City CA 90232 USA — Actress, Singer
**Mazzilli, Lee L**
67 Stonehedge Dr S, Greenwich CT 06831, USA — Baseball Player, Manager
**Mazzo, Kay**
School of American Ballet, 70 Lincoln Center Plaza, New York NY 10012, USA — Ballerina
**Mazzucco, Raphael**
Micon, 270 W 17th St, #6D, New York NY 10011, USA — Photographer
**Mbah a Moute, Luc**
Philadelphia 76ers, 1st Union Center, 3601 S Broad St, Philadelphia PA 19148 USA — Basketball Player
**Mbatha-Raw, Gugu**
Curtis Brown Group, 28-29 Haymarket St, #500, London SW1Y 4SP, England — Actress
**Mbaye, Abdoul**
Prime Minister's Office, Ave Leopold Sedar Senghor, Dakar, Senegal — Prime Minister, Senegal
**Mbeki, Thabo M**
Postal Box X1000, Pretoria 0001, South Africa — President, South Africa

# M

**Mbenga, D J**      Basketball Player
6112 Winton St, Dallas TX 75214, USA
**Mbete, Baleka M**      President, South Africa
PO Box 15, Cape Town, South Africa
**M'Bow, Amadou-Mahtar**      Government Official, Senegal
BP 5276, Dakar-Fann, Senegal
**MC Lyte**      Rap Artist
C E S D, 10635 Santa Monica Blvd, #130, Los Angeles CA 90025 USA
**MC Ren**      Rap Artist
J L Entertainment, 18653 Ventura Blvd, #340, Los Angeles CA 91356 USA
**McAdam, Gary**      Ice Hockey Player
34 Meadow Lane, Portland ME 04103, USA
**McAdams, Rachel**      Actress
Magnolia Entertainment, 9595 Wilshire Blvd, #601, Beverly Hills CA 90212, USA
**McAdoo, Robert A (Bob)**      Basketball Player, Coach
16710 SW 82nd Ave, Village of Palmetto Bay FL 33157, USA
**McAfee, Stephanie**      Writer
New American Library, 1633 Broadway, New York NY 10019 USA
**McAlear, Nancy**      Actress
Fountainhead Talent, 121 Davenport Road, Toronto ON M5R 1HZ, Canada
**McAlister, Dulumus J (Deuce)**      Football Player
2177 Doc Webb Road, Lena MS 39094, USA
**McAlpine, Christopher W (Chris)**      Ice Hockey Player
4390 Reiland Lane, Saint Paul MN 55126, USA
**McAlpine, Donald M**      Cinematographer
377 Placer Creek Lane, Henderson NV 89014, USA
**McAnally, Mac**      Singer, Songwriter
T K O Artist Mgmt, 2302 21st Ave S, #300, Nashville TN 37212, USA
**McAnally, Ron**      Thoroughbred Racing Trainer
18653 Paso Nuevo Dr, Tarzana CA 91356, USA
**McAndrew, James C (Jim)**      Baseball Player
17917 N 93rd St, Scottsdale AZ 85255, USA
**McAndrew, Nell**      Model
1 The Stabling, Barnet Lane, Elstree, Borehamwood WD6 3HJ, England
**McAnuff, Des**      Director
W M E Entertainment, 9601 Wilshire Blvd, #300, Beverly Hills CA 90210 USA
**McAnulty, Paul**      Baseball Player
921 Palomar Way, Oxnard CA 93033, USA
**McArdle, Aidan**      Actor
42 Agency, 8 Flitcroft St, London WC2H 8DL, England
**McArdle, Andrea**      Actress, Singer
301 W 45th St, #4D, New York NY 10036, USA
**McArthur, Alex**      Actor
9443 Hillrose St, Sunland CA 91040, USA
**McArthur, Derek**      Photographer
73 Strathaven Road, Kirkmuirhill, Lanark ML11 9RW, Scotland
**McArthur, James D, Jr**      Navy Admiral
Commander, Network Warfare Command, 2465 Guadalcanal, Norfolk VA 23521, USA
**McArthur, John H**      Educator
8 Kettle Lane, Weston MA 2493, USA
**McArthur, K Megan**      Astronaut
N A S A, Johnson Space Center, 2101 NASA Road, Houston TX 77058 USA
**McArthur, William S (Bill), Jr**      Astronaut
2512 Mountain Falls Court, Friendswood TX 77546, USA
**McAslan, John R**      Architect
McAslan Partners, 202 Kensington Church St, London W8 4DP, England
**McAuliffe, Callan**      Actor
R G M Artists, 8-12 Ann Street, Surry Hills NSW 2010, Australia
**McAuliffe, Dennis P**      Army General
9160 Belvoir Woods Parkway, Fort Belvoir VA 22060, USA
**McAuliffe, Richard J (Dick)**      Baseball Player
32 Worthington Dr, Farmington CT 06032, USA
**McAvoy, James**      Actor
United Agents, 12-26 Lexington St, London W1F 0LE, England
**McAvoy, Thomas J (Tom)**      Baseball Player
2 Clinton Court, Stillwater NY 12170, USA
**McBain, Andrew**      Ice Hockey Player
87 Balsam Ave, Toronto ON M4E 3B8, Canada
**McBain, Fiona**      Singer, Guitarist, Songwriter
High Road Touring, 751 Bridgeway, #200, Sausalito CA 94965 USA
**McBain, Nicko**      Drummer (Iron Maiden)
Sanctuary Music Mgmt, 82 Bishop's Bridge Road, London W2 6BB, England
**McBath, Michael S (Mike)**      Football Player
5044 Sailwind Circle, Orlando FL 32810, USA
**McBean, Alvin O (Al)**      Baseball Player
PO Box 4475, Saint Thomas VI 00801, USA
**McBee, Rives**      Golfer
1504 Canyon Oaks Dr, Irving TX 75061, USA
**McBeth, Marcus A**      Baseball Player
42052 W Sunland Dr, Maricopa AZ 85138, USA
**McBrayer, Jack**      Actor, Comedian
United Talent Agency, U T A Plaza, 9336 Civic Center Dr, Beverly Hills CA 90210 USA
**McBriar, Mat**      Football Player
4020 Buena Vista St, Dallas TX 75204, USA
**McBride, Arnold R (Bake)**      Baseball Player
4077 Reliant Circle, Owensboro KY 42301, USA
**McBride, Brian**      Soccer Player
Chicago Fire, Toyota Park, 7000 S Harlem Ave, Bridgeview IL 60455 USA
**McBride, Chi**      Actor
United Talent Agency, U T A Plaza, 9336 Civic Center Dr, Beverly Hills CA 90210 USA
**McBride, Christian**      Jazz Bassist
Ted Kurland, 173 Brighton Ave, Boston MA 02134 USA
**McBride, Daniel F (Danny)**      Actor, Comedian
Rough House, 1722 Whitley Ave, Los Angeles CA 90028, USA
**McBride, Jeff**      Illusionist
Innovative Artists, 1505 10th St, Santa Monica CA 90401 USA

## Mbenga - McBride

**McClain Johnson, Katrina** — Basketball Player
1907 Carlton St, North Charleston SC 29405, USA
**McClain, Cady** — Actress, Producer
Jey Assoc, 1507 7th St, #210, Santa Monica CA 90401, USA
**McClain, Charly** — Singer
John D Lentz, PO Box 198888, Nashville TN 37219, USA
**McClain, China Anne** — Actress
Paradigm Agency, 360 N Crescent Dr, North Building, Beverly Hills CA 90210 USA
**McClain, Dewey L** — Football Player
1032 Flagg Way, Lawrenceville GA 30044, USA
**McClain, Johnathan** — Actor
Innovative Artists, 1505 10th St, Santa Monica CA 90401 USA
**McClain, Scott M** — Baseball Player
660 Golden Gate Point, #61, Sarasota FL 34236, USA
**McClain, Theodore (Ted)** — Basketball Player
104 Eaton Court, Nashville TN 37218, USA
**McClairen, Jack (Cy)** — Football Player, Basketball Coach
1337 Idlewild Dr, Daytona Beach FL 32114, USA
**McClamon, Zahn** — Actor
Amsel Eisenstadt Frazier, 5055 Wilshire Blvd., #865, Los Angeles CA 90036 USA
**McClanahan, Randall D (Randy)** — Football Player
8107 W Via del Sol, Peoria AZ 85383, USA
**McClanahan, Robert B (Rob)** — Ice Hockey Player
3310 Watertown Road, Long Lake MN 55356, USA
**McClary, Thomas (Tom)** — Guitarist, Singer (Commodores)
Management Assoc, 1920 Benson Ave, Saint Paul MN 55116, USA
**McClatchy, J D** — Writer, Editor
15 Grand St, Stonington CT 06378, USA
**McClean, Lalisha** — Singer (Allure)
Universal Attractions, 135 W 26th St, #1200, New York NY 10001 USA
**McClelland, Kevin** — Ice Hockey Player
2886 Keeley Cove, Southaven MS 38671, USA
**McClements, Robert, Jr** — Businessman
31 Cardinal Lane, Key Largo FL 33037, USA
**McClenathan, Cory** — Drag Racing Driver
1681 E Northfield Dr, Brownsburg IN 46112, USA
**McClendon, Lloyd G** — Baseball Player, Manager
1082 Mission Hills Court, Chesterton IN 46304, USA
**McClendon, Reiley** — Actor
Innovative Artists, 1505 10th St, Santa Monica CA 90401 USA
**McClendon-Covey, Wendi** — Actress
United Talent Agency, U T A Plaza, 9336 Civic Center Dr, Beverly Hills CA 90210 USA
**McCleon, Dexter K** — Football Player
1901 Post Oak Blvd, #509, Houston TX 77056, USA
**McClintock, Eddie** — Actor
I C M Partners, 10250 Constellation Blvd, #900, Los Angeles CA 90067 USA
**McClintock, Jessica** — Fashion Designer
2307 Broadway St, San Francisco CA 94115, USA
**McClintock, William** — Space Scientist
University of Colorado, Atmospheric/Space Physics Dept, Boulder CO 80309, USA
**McClinton, Curtis R** — Football Player
McClinton Development, 11714 Jefferson St, Kansas City MO 64114, USA
**McClinton, Delbert** — Singer, Musician, Songwriter
PO Box 159008, Nashville TN 37215, USA
**McCloskey, Jim** — Social Activist
221 Witherspoon St, Princeton NJ 08542, USA
**McCloskey, Paul N (Pete), Jr** — Representative, CA
580 Mountain Home Road, Woodside CA 94062, USA
**McCloskey, Robert J** — Diplomat
84 Old Black Point Road, Niantic CT 06357, USA
**McCloughan, Kent A** — Football Player
2241 Woody Creek Circle, Loveland CO 80538, USA
**McClover, Darrell A, II** — Football Player
6120 SW 19th St, Pompano Beach FL 33068, USA
**McClure, Larry** — Auto Racing Executive
Morgan-McClure Motorsports, 26502 Newbanks Road, Abingdon VA 24210, USA
**McClure, Marc** — Actor
Amsel Eisenstadt Frazier, 5055 Wilshire Blvd, #865, Los Angeles CA 90036 USA
**McClure, Robert C (Bob)** — Baseball Player
3834 SE Fairway E, Stuart FL 34997, USA
**McClure, Tane** — Actress
Don Gerler, 3349 Cahuenga Blvd W, #1, Los Angeles CA 90068 USA
**McClure, Wilbert (Skeeter)** — Boxer
1 Centennial Dr, #9, Norwood MA 02062, USA
**McClurg, Edie** — Actress
Peyrot Lagnese Mucci, 5750 Wilshire Blvd, #580, Los Angeles CA 90036, USA
**McClurkin, Donnie** — Singer
Sierra Mgmt, 1035 Bates Court, Hendersonville TN 37075, USA
**McColgan, Elizabeth (Liz)** — Track Athlete
Marquee UK, 6 George St, Nottingham NG1 3BE, England
**McColl, William F (Bill), Jr** — Football Player
5166 Chelsea St, La Jolla CA 92037, USA
**McCollough, Jack** — Fashion Designer
Proenza Schouler, 120 Walker St, #1600, New York NY 10013, USA
**McColluh, Thayne M** — Educator
Gonzaga University, President's Office, 502 E Boone Ave, Spokane WA 99258, USA
**McCollum, Andrew J (Andy)** — Football Player
3933 Autumn Farms Dr, Pacific MO 63069, USA
**McCollum, Rick** — Guitarist (Afghan Whigs)
Rascoff/Zysblat Organization, 250 W 57th St, New York NY 10107 USA
**McColm, Matt** — Actor
ReBar Mgmt, 10061 Riverside Dr, #722, Toluca Lake CA 91602, USA
**McComas, Brian** — Singer, Songwriter
Liz Gregory Talent, 9 Music Sqaure S, #357, Nashville TN 37203, USA
**McComb, Heather** — Actress
1 Mgmt, 9000 W Sunset Blvd, #1550, Los Angeles CA 90069 USA

**McComb, Jeremy** — Singer, Songwriter
Parallel Entertainment, 209th Ave S, #506, Nashville TN 37203, USA
**McComb, Joanne (Jo)** — Baseball Player
105 Nottingham Road, Bloomsburg PA 17815, USA
**McComb, William (Bill)** — Businessman
Liz Clairborne Inc, 1441 Broadway, New York NY 10018, USA
**McCombs, Davis** — Writer
University of Arkansas, Creative Writing Program, Fayetteville AR 72701, USA
**McConathy, John R** — Basketball Player
2320 Belmont Blvd, Bossier City LA 71111, USA
**McConaughey, Matthew** — Actor
Creative Artists Agency, 2000 Ave of Stars, #100, Los Angeles CA 90067 USA
**McConkey, Jim C** — Cinematographer
505 W 54th St, #PH 12, New York NY 10019, USA
**McConkey, Philip J (Phil)** — Football Player
1856 Viking Way, La Jolla CA 92037, USA
**McConnell, Denise** — Model
Playboy Promotions, 9346 Civic Center Dr, #200, Beverly Hills CA 90210 USA
**McConnell, Harden M** — Chemist
Stanford University, Chemistry Dept, Stanford CA 94305, USA
**McConnell, Michael W** — Judge
US Court of Appeals, 2480 Cowper St, Palo Alto CA 94301, USA
**McConnell, Page** — Keyboardist (Phish)
Paradigm Agency, 360 N Crescent Dr, North Building, Beverly Hills CA 90210 USA
**McConnell-Serio, Suzanne (Suzie)** — Basketball Player, Coach
2590 Rossmoore Dr, Pittsburgh PA 15241, USA
**McCoo, Marilyn** — Singer (Fifth Dimension), Actress
Brokaw Co, 9255 W Sunset Blvd, #804, West Hollywood CA 90069 USA
**McCook, John** — Actor
Abrams Artists, 9200 W Sunset Blvd, #1125, West Hollywood CA 90069 USA
**McCord, AnnaLynne** — Actress
Innovative Artists, 1505 10th St, Santa Monica CA 90401 USA
**McCord, Bob** — Ice Hockey Player
11540 N Donley Dr, Parker CO 80138, USA
**McCord, Gary D** — Golfer, Sportscaster
PO Box 1964, Edwards CO 81632, USA
**McCord, Joe Milton** — Biochemist
University of Colorado, Waring Institute, 4200 E 9th Ave, Denver CO 80262, USA
**McCord, Keith R** — Basketball Player
1609 Five Acre Road, Dolomite AL 35061, USA
**McCord, Kent** — Actor
1738 N Orange Grove Ave, Los Angeles CA 90046, USA
**McCormack, Catherine** — Actress
120 Riverside Dr, #7G, New York NY 10024, USA
**McCormack, Donald R (Don)** — Baseball Player
866 Glenfield Dr, Palm Harbor FL 34684, USA
**McCormack, Eric** — Actor
I C M Partners, 10250 Constellation Blvd, #900, Los Angeles CA 90067 USA
**McCormack, Kelly** — Actress, Writer, Producer
Oldfield Talent Mgmt, 26 Soho St, #320, Toronto ON M5T 1Z7, Canada
**McCormack, Mary** — Actress
Creative Artists Agency, 2000 Ave of Stars, #100, Los Angeles CA 90067 USA
**McCormack, Patty** — Actress, Model
Rothman Patino Andres, 4360 Tujunga Ave, Studio City CA 91604, USA
**McCormack, Will** — Actor, Writer
United Talent Agency, U T A Plaza, 9336 Civic Center Dr, Beverly Hills CA 90210 USA
**McCormick, Carolyn** — Actress
Talent Works, 505 8th Ave, #603, New York NY 10018, USA
**McCormick, Maureen** — Actress, Singer
Rebel Entertainment Partners, 5700 Wilshire Blvd, #456, Los Angeles CA 90036, USA
**McCormick, Michael F (Mike)** — Baseball Player
1600 Morganton Road, #U9, Pinehurst NC 28374, USA
**McCormick, Patricia J (Pat)** — Diver
92 Riversea Road, Seal Beach CA 90740, USA
**McCormick, Timothy D (Tim)** — Basketball Player
2500 Leroy Lane, West Bloomfield MI 48324, USA
**McCorory, Francena** — Track Athlete
20 E Walker Road, Hampton VA 23666, USA
**McCorvey, Bill** — Singer (Pirates of the Mississippi)
Third Coast Talent, PO Box 110225, Nashville TN 37222, USA
**McCorvey, Norma** — Legal Litigant
11343 Cactus Lane, Dallas TX 75238, USA
**McCouch, Grayson** — Actor
A P A Talent & Literary Agency, 405 S Beverly Dr, #300, Beverly Hills CA 90212 USA
**McCoughtry, Angel** — Basketball Player
Atlanta Dream, 83 Walton St NW, #400, Atlanta, GA 30303 USA
**McCourt, Frank** — Baseball Executive
22426 Pacific Coast Highway, Malibu CA 90265, USA
**McCoury, Del** — Singer, Guitarist (Del McCoury Band)
W M E Entertainment, 1600 Division St, #300, Nashville TN 37203 USA
**McCoury, Robbie** — Banjo Player (Del McCoury Band)
W M E Entertainment, 9601 Wilshire Blvd, #300, Beverly Hills CA 90210 USA
**McCoury, Ronnie** — Mandolin Player (Del McCoury Band)
Media Artists Group, 8222 Melrose Ave, #203, Los Angeles CA 90048 USA
**McCovey, Willie L** — Baseball Player
PO Box 620342, Redwood City CA 94062, USA
**McCowen, Alec** — Actor
Conway Van Gelder Grant, 8-12 Broadwick St, #300, London W1F 8HW, England
**McCown, Joshua T (Josh)** — Football Player
1312 Lookout Circle, Waxhaw NC 28173, USA
**McCown, Lucas P (Luke)** — Football Player
30963 US Highway 69 N, Rusk TX 75785, USA
**McCoy, Glenn** — Editorial Cartoonist
Belleville News-Democrat, Editorial Dept, 120 S Illinois, Bellville IL 62220, USA
**McCoy, Jason** — Singer, Songwriter
Agency Group Ltd, 142 W 57th St, #600, New York NY 10019 USA

**McCoy, Jennifer** — Photographer, Artist
Postmasters Gallery, 459 W 19th St, New York NY 10011, USA
**McCoy, Jordan** — Singer
Bad Boy Entertainment, 1440 Broadway, #16, New York NY 10018 USA
**McCoy, Kevin** — Photographer, Artist
New York University, Steinhardt Art School, New York NY 10003, USA
**McCoy, Larry S** — Baseball Umpire
5758 Highway 139, Greenway AR 72430, USA
**McCoy, Matt** — Actor, Producer
S M S Talent, 8383 Wilshire Blvd, #230, Beverly Hills CA 90211 USA
**McCoy, Michael C (Mike)** — Football Player
PO Box 464263, Lawrenceville GA 30042, USA
**McCoy, Michael P (Mike)** — Football Player
2224 Cotton Gin Row, Jefferson GA 30549, USA
**McCoy, Mike (Mouse)** — Director
Bandito Brothers, 3115 S La Cienega Blvd, Los Angeles CA 10016, USA
**McCoy, Neal** — Singer
Webster Assoc, PO Box 23015, Nashville TN 37202, USA
**McCoy, Sandra** — Actress
15216 Morrison St, Sherman Oaks CA 91403, USA
**McCoy, Sherilyn S** — Businesswoman
Avon Products, 1345 Ave of Americas, Basement Concourse 9, New York NY 10105, USA
**McCracken, Quinton A** — Baseball Player
27911 Walsh Crossing Dr, Katy TX 77494, USA
**McCrackin, Daisy** — Actress
Stone Manners Salners, 6100 Wilshire Blvd, #1500, Los Angeles CA 90035 USA
**McCrae, George** — Singer
International Artists Holland, PO Box 32, 5360 Grave AA, Netherlands
**McCrane, Paul** — Actor
United Talent Agency, U T A Plaza, 9336 Civic Center Dr, Beverly Hills CA 90210 USA
**McCraney, Tarell Alvin** — Writer
I C M Partners, 10250 Constellation Blvd, #900, Los Angeles CA 90067 USA
**McCrary, Darius** — Actor
Diverse Talent Group, 9911 W Pico Blvd, #350W, Los Angeles CA 90035, USA
**McCrary, Fred D** — Football Player
134 Grandmar Chase, Clermont FL 34711, USA
**McCrary, Joel** — Actor
C E S D, 10635 Santa Monica Blvd, #130, Los Angeles CA 90025 USA
**McCrary, Michael C** — Football Player
9907 Chase Hill Court, Vienna VA 22182, USA
**McCraw, Tommy L (Tom)** — Baseball Player
3142 SE Monte Vista Court, Port Saint Lucie FL 34952, USA
**McCray, Bobby L, Jr** — Football Player
14907 SW 52nd St, Miramar FL 33027, USA
**McCray, Nikki** — Basketball Player
4278 Fox Hills Dr, Louisville TN 37777, USA
**McCray, Prentice** — Football Player
2109 N Argonaut St, Stockton CA 95204, USA
**McCray, Rodney E** — Basketball Player
33 Bonita Vista Road, Mount Vernon NY 10552, USA
**McCrea, John** — Singer (Cake), Songwriter
Umbrella Group, 1 West St, #3506, New York NY 10004, USA
**McCready, Mike** — Guitarist (Pearl Jam)
Curtis Mgmt, 1900 S Corgiat Dr, Seattle WA 98108, USA
**McCreary, Bear** — Composer
3622 Clarington Ave, #5, Los Angeles CA 90034, USA
**McCreary, William (Bill), Sr** — Ice Hockey Player, Coach
4318 Highcrest Dr, #1, Brighton MI 48116, USA
**McCree, Marlon T** — Football Player
2109 N Argonaut St, Windermere FL 34786, USA
**McCrory, Glenn** — Boxer
Yetholm Place, Newiggin Hall, Newcastle upon Tyne NE5 4EB, England
**McCrory, Helen** — Actress
Independent Talent Group, 40 Whitfield St, London W1T 2RH, England
**McCrory, Milton (Milt)** — Boxer
Escot Boxing Enterprises, 19244 Bretton Dr, Detroit MI 48223, USA
**McCrory, Robert (Bob)** — Baseball Player
30 Rebecca Lane, Hattiesburg MS 39402, USA
**McCue, Anne** — Singer, Guitarist, Songwriter
Conqueroo, 11271 Ventura Blvd, #522, Studio City CA 91604 USA
**McCuigan, Paul** — Director
Fallout Entertainment, 3100 Airport Ave, Santa Monica CA 90405, USA
**McCullagh, Peter** — Mathematician, Statistician
University of Chicago, Statistics Dept, 5734 University Ave, Chicago IL 60637, USA
**McCullers, Lance G** — Baseball Player
3309 Hoedt Road, Tampa FL 33618, USA
**McCulley, Michael J** — Astronaut
365 Private Road 652, Bay City TX 77414, USA
**McCullin, Donald (Don)** — Photographer
Hamiltons Gallery, 13 Carlos Place, London W1, England
**McCulloch, Bruce** — Actor, Writer, Producer
United Talent Agency, U T A Plaza, 9336 Civic Center Dr, Beverly Hills CA 90210 USA
**McCulloch, Earl** — Football Player, Track Athlete
2108 Santa Fe Ave, #15, Long Beach CA 90810, USA
**McCulloch, Ed (Ace)** — Auto Racing Driver
1397 Cherry Tree Road, Avon IN 46123, USA
**McCullough, Bernard J (Barry), III** — Navy Admiral
Commander, Cyber Command & 10th Fleet, Fort George C Meade MD 20755, USA
**McCullough, Colleen** — Writer
PO Box 333, Norfolk Island NSW 2899, Australia
**McCullough, David** — Writer, Entertainer
Creative Artists Agency, 2000 Ave of Stars, #100, Los Angeles CA 90067 USA
**McCullough, Julie** — Model, Actress
8306 Wilshire Blvd, #438, Beverly Hills CA 90211, USA
**McCullough, Kimberly** — Actress, Singer, Dancer
Brillstein Entertainment Partners, 9150 Wilshire Blvd, #350, Beverly Hills CA 90212 USA

| | |
|---|---|
| **McCullough, Wayne** | Boxer |
| Sky Sports, Grants Way, Isleworth, Middlesex TW7 5QD, England | |
| **McCullum, Samuel C (Sam)** | Football Player |
| 7701 88th Place SE, Mercer Island WA 98040, USA | |
| **McCumber, Mark** | Golfer, Sportscaster |
| 527 Le Master Dr, Ponte Vedra Beach FL 32082, USA | |
| **McCune, Don** | Bowler |
| 3551 Coventry Gardens Dr, Las Vegas NV 89135, USA | |
| **McCurdy, Jennette** | Actress, Singer |
| Management 360, 9111 Wilshire Blvd, Beverly Hills CA 90210 USA | |
| **McCurry, Jeffrey D (Jeff)** | Baseball Player |
| 9015 Linkmeadow Lane, Houston TX 77025, USA | |
| **McCurry, Margaret** | Architect |
| Tigerman McCurry Architects, 444 N Wells St, #206, Chicago IL 60654, USA | |
| **McCurry, Mike** | Government Official, Journalist |
| CNN-TV, News Dept, 190 Marietta Ave SW, Atlanta GA 30303 USA | |
| **McCurry, Steve** | Photographer |
| 2 5th Ave, New York NY 10011, USA | |
| **McCusker, James B (Jim)** | Football Player |
| 209 N Main St, Jamestown NY 14701, USA | |
| **McCusker, Joan** | Curling Athlete |
| Curling Association, 1660 Vimont Court, Cumberland ON K4A 4J4, Canada | |
| **McCutchen, Andrew S** | Baseball Player |
| Pittsburgh Pirates, P N C Park, 115 Federal St, #115B, Pittsburgh PA 15212 USA | |
| **McCutcheon, Daylon** | Football Player |
| 4393 Hiwassee, Claremont CA 91711, USA | |
| **McCutcheon, Hugh** | Volleyball Coach |
| US Olympic Committee, 1 Olympia Plaza, Building 6, Colorado Springs CO 80909, USA | |
| **McCutcheon, Lawrence** | Football Player |
| 19981 Weems Lane, Huntington Beach CA 92646, USA | |
| **McCutcheon, Linda** | Publisher |
| A A R P Publications, Director's Office, 601 E St NW, Washington DC 20049, USA | |
| **McCutcheon, Martine** | Actress, Singer |
| Amanda Howard, 74 Clerkenwell Road, London EC1M 5QA, England | |
| **McCutcheon, Shaun** | Legal Litigant |
| Coalmont Electrical Development Corp, 22577 Highway 216, McCalla AL 35111, USA | |
| **McDaniel, Chris** | Keyboardist (Confederate Railroad) |
| Bobby Roberts, 3050 Business Park Circle, #303, Goodlettsville TN 37221 USA | |
| **McDaniel, Edward (Ed)** | Football Player |
| 13111 Brenwood Trail, Hopkins MN 55343, USA | |
| **McDaniel, James** | Actor |
| Innovative Artists, 1505 10th St, Santa Monica CA 90401 USA | |
| **McDaniel, John (Johnny)** | Football Player |
| 2108 Becky Lane, Cedar Hill TX 75104, USA | |
| **McDaniel, Lyndall D (Lindy)** | Baseball Player |
| 16641 E 1550 Road, Hollis OK 73550, USA | |
| **McDaniel, Randall C** | Football Player |
| 20405 Manor Road, Excelsior MN 55331, USA | |
| **McDaniel, Terence L (Terry)** | Football Player |
| 730 Shenandoah, Cedar Hill TX 75104, USA | |
| **McDaniel, Xavier M** | Basketball Player |
| 2 Oakmist Court, Blythewood SC 29016, USA | |
| **McDaniels, Darryl (Darryl M)** | Rap Artist (Run-DMC) |
| Tracy Miller Assoc, 2610 Fire Road, Egg Harbor Township NJ 08234, USA | |
| **McDaniels, James R (Jim)** | Basketball Player |
| 2549 Smallhouse Road, Bowling Green KY 42104, USA | |
| **McDaniels, Josh** | Football Coach |
| Saint Louis Rams, 901 N Broadway, Saint Louis MO 63101 USA | |
| **McDaniels, K J** | Basketball Player |
| Philadelphia 76ers, 1st Union Center, 3601 S Broad St, Philadelphia PA 19148 USA | |
| **McDaniels, Pellom** | Football Player |
| 186 Ridgeland Ave, Decatur GA 30030, USA | |
| **McDavid, Ray D** | Baseball Player |
| 1245 Market St, #1348, San Diego CA 92101, USA | |
| **McDavis, Roderick J** | Educator |
| Ohio University, President's Office, Athens OH 45701, USA | |
| **McDermott, Anne-Marie** | Concert Pianist |
| Opus 3 Artists, 470 Park Ave S, #900N, New York NY 10016 USA | |
| **McDermott, Charlie** | Actor |
| L I N K Entertainment, 11872 La Grange Ave, Los Angeles CA 90025 USA | |
| **McDermott, Colleen** | Actress |
| C E S D, 10635 Santa Monica Blvd, #130, Los Angeles CA 90025 USA | |
| **McDermott, Dean** | Actor, Writer, Producer |
| Flutie Entertainment, 9320 Wilshire Blvd, #202, Beverly Hills CA 90212 USA | |
| **McDermott, Dylan** | Actor |
| Schiff Co, 9220 Sunset Blvd, #106, West Hollywood CA 90069 USA | |
| **McDermott, John** | Singer, Songwriter |
| McDermott Entertainment, 30 Rowes Wharf, #470, Boston MA 02110, USA | |
| **McDermott, R Terrance (Terry)** | Speed Skater |
| 5078 Chainbridge Dr, Bloomfield Hills MI 48304, USA | |
| **McDermott, Terence K (Terry)** | Baseball Player |
| 7205 Sunlight Peak Dr NE, Rio Rancho NM 87144, USA | |
| **McDiarmid, Ian** | Actor |
| Independent Talent Group, 40 Whitfield St, London W1T 2RH, England | |
| **McDill, Alan** | Baseball Player |
| 244 Richwoods Road, Arkadelphia AR 71923, USA | |
| **McDivitt, James A (Jim)** | Astronaut, Air Force General |
| 3530 E Calle Puerta de Acero, Tucson AZ 85718, USA | |
| **McDole, Roland O (Ron)** | Football Player |
| 2083 Lockes Mill Road, Berryville VA 22611, USA | |
| **McDonagh, Martin** | Writer, Director |
| Creative Artists Agency, 2000 Ave of Stars, #100, Los Angeles CA 90067 USA | |
| **McDonald, Alvin B (Ab)** | Ice Hockey Player |
| 419 Thompson Dr, Winnipeg MB R3J 3E7, Canada | |
| **McDonald, Arthur B** | Physicist |
| Queen's University, Physics Dept, Kingston ON K7L 3N6, Canada | |

**McDonald, Audra**
W M E Entertainment, 1325 Ave of Americas, New York NY 10019 USA — Actress, Singer

**McDonald, Ben**
8780 Henderson Road, Denham Springs LA 70726, USA — Baseball Player

**McDonald, Bruce**
Vanguarde Artists Management, 262 Avenue Road, Toronto ON M4V 2G7, Canada — Director

**McDonald, Christopher**
Gersh Agency, 9465 Wilshire Blvd, #600, Beverly Hills CA 90212 USA — Actor

**McDonald, Country Joe**
Savoy Music, 1844 SW Troy St, Portland OR 97219, USA — Singer, Guitarist

**McDonald, James L (Jim)**
PO Box 995, Brea CA 92822, USA — Baseball Player

**McDonald, James Z**
Los Angeles Dodgers, Stadium, 1000 Elysian Park Ave, Los Angeles CA 90090 USA — Baseball Player

**McDonald, Jiggs**
8331 Arborfield Court, Fort Myers FL 33912, USA — Sportscaster

**McDonald, L Benard (Ben)**
8780 Henderson Road, Denham Springs LA 70726, USA — Baseball Player

**McDonald, Lanny**
23 Springside St, Calgary AB T3Z 3M1, Canada — Ice Hockey Player

**McDonald, Mackey J**
V F Corp, 628 Green Valley Road, Greensboro NC 27408, USA — Businessman

**McDonald, Michael**
Vector Mgmt, 1607 17th Ave S, Nashville TN 37212, USA — Singer, Songwriter

**McDonald, Miriam**
Innovative Artists, 1505 10th St, Santa Monica CA 90401 USA — Actress

**McDonald, Paul B**
1815 Tradewinds Lane, Newport Beach CA 92660, USA — Football Player

**McDonald, Richie**
W M E Entertainment, 9601 Wilshire Blvd, #300, Beverly Hills CA 90210 USA — Singer (Lonestar)

**McDonald, Robert M**
Veteran Affairs Department, 810 Vermont Ave NW, Washington DC 20420 USA — Secretary, Veterans Administration

**McDonald, Thomas F (Tommy)**
537 W Valley Forge Road, King of Prussia PA 19406, USA — Football Player

**McDonald, Timothy (Tim)**
208 Stone Creek Court, Whippany NJ 07981, USA — Football Player

**McDonell, Thomas**
W M E Entertainment, 9601 Wilshire Blvd, #300, Beverly Hills CA 90210 USA — Actor

**McDonnell, Dirk**
Throckmorton Fine Art, 145 E 57th St, #300, New York NY 10022, USA — Photographer

**McDonnell, John F**
McDonnell Douglas Corp, PO Box 516, Saint Louis MO 63166, USA — Businessman

**McDonnell, Mary**
Innovative Artists, 1505 10th St, Santa Monica CA 90401 USA — Actress

**McDonnell, Patrick**
King Features Syndicate, 300 W 57th St, #1500, New York NY 10019 USA — Cartoonist (Mutts)

**McDonough, Mary**
6858 Canteloupe Ave, Van Nuys CA 91405, USA — Actress

**McDonough, Matthew (Spag)**
Agency Group Ltd, 142 W 57th St, #600, New York NY 10019 USA — Drummer (Mudvayne)

**McDonough, Michael**
Sheldon Prosnit Agency, 800 S Robertson Blvd, Los Angeles CA 90035, USA — Cinematographer

**McDonough, Neal**
Paradigm Agency, 360 N Crescent Dr, North Building, Beverly Hills CA 90210 USA — Actor

**McDonough, Sean**
ABC-TV, Sports Dept, 77 W 66th St, New York NY 10023 USA — Sportscaster

**McDonough, William**
700 E Jefferson St, Charlottesville VA 22902, USA — Architect

**McDonough, William J**
Public Company Accounting Oversight Board, 1666 K NW, Washington DC 20006, USA — Government Official, Financier

**McDorman, Jake**
United Talent Agency, U T A Plaza, 9336 Civic Center Dr, Beverly Hills CA 90210 USA — Actor

**McDormand, Frances**
W M E Entertainment, 9601 Wilshire Blvd, #300, Beverly Hills CA 90210 USA — Actress

**McDougal, R Meiklejohn (Mike)**
Kansas City Royals, Kauffman Stadium, 1 Royal Way, Kansas City MO 64129 USA — Baseball Player

**McDougall, Charles**
United Agents, 12-26 Lexington St, London W1F 0LE, England — Director, Writer

**McDougall, Walter A**
University of Pennsylvania, History Dept, Philadelphia PA 19104, USA — Historian

**McDowell, Jack B**
1141 Lynbrook Dr, Charlotte NC 28211, USA — Baseball Player

**McDowell, Leonard (Bubba)**
6353 Richmond Ave, Houston TX 77057, USA — Football Player

**McDowell, Oddibe**
5240 SW 18th St, West Park FL 33023, USA — Baseball Player

**McDowell, Roger A**
2690 Pete Shaw Road, Marietta GA 30066, USA — Baseball Player

**McDowell, Ronnie**
PO Box 53, Portland TN 37148, USA — Singer, Guitarist

**McDowell, Samuel E (Sam)**
City of Legends, 1925 Don Wickham Dr, Clermont FL 34711, USA — Baseball Player

**McDuffie, Matthew**
Paradigm Agency, 360 N Crescent Dr, North Building, Beverly Hills CA 90210 USA — Writer

**McDuffie, Otis J (O J)**
1333 NW 121st Ave, Plantation FL 33323, USA — Football Player

**McDuffie, Robert**
Columbia Artists Mgmt Inc, 5 Columbus Circle, 1790 Broadway, #1600, New York NY 10019 USA — Concert Violinist, Conductor

**McDyess, Antonio K**
30 Cranbrook Road, Bloomfield Hills MI 48304, USA — Basketball Player

**McEachern, Shawn**
71 Beach St, Marblehead MA 01945, USA — Ice Hockey Player

**McEldowney, Brooke**
Pib Press, PO Box 942, Kennebunk ME 04043, USA — Cartoonist (9 Chickwood Lane, Pobgorn)

**McElhenny, Hugh E**
3013 Via Venezia, Henderson NV 89052, USA — Football Player

**McElhone, Natascha** — Actress
Paradigm Agency, 360 N Crescent Dr, North Building, Beverly Hills CA 90210 USA

**McElligott, Dominique** — Actress
Creative Artists Agency, 2000 Ave of Stars, #100, Los Angeles CA 90067 USA

**McElmury, James D (Jim)** — Ice Hockey Player
9122 78th Street S, Cottage Grove MN 55016, USA

**McElroy, Charles D (Chuck)** — Baseball Player
1049 Nederland Ave, Port Arthur TX 77640, USA

**McElroy, Reginald L (Reggie)** — Football Player
RR 1 Box 109A, Preston MO 65732, USA

**McElroy, Vann W** — Football Player
524 Private Road 4450, Uvalde TX 78801, USA

**McEnaney, William H (Will)** — Baseball Player
1055 SW 3rd St, Boca Raton FL 33486, USA

**McEnery, Peter R** — Actor
Richard Stone Partnership, De Walden Court, 85 New Cavendish St, London W1W 6XD, England

**McEnroe, John P, Jr** — Tennis Player, Sportscaster
1080 5th Ave, New York NY 10128, USA

**McEntire, Reba** — Singer, Actress
Starstruck Entertainment, 40 Music Square W, Nashville TN 37203, USA

**McEuen, John** — Musician (Nitty Gritty Dirt Band)
New Frontier Touring, 1503 17th Ave S, Nashville TN 37212, USA

**McEwan, Geraldine** — Actress
Independent Talent Group, 40 Whitfield St, London W1T 2RH, England

**McEwan, Ian R** — Writer
15 Park Town, Oxford OX2 6SN, England

**McEwen, Dawn Askin** — Curling Athlete
Team Jennifer Jones, 246 Jacques Ave, Winnipeg MB R3W 1S9, Canada

**McEwen, Mark** — Commentator
CBS-TV, News Dept, 51 W 52nd St, New York NY 10019 USA

**McEwen, Mike** — Ice Hockey Player
3712 N Peniel Ave, Bethany OK 73008, USA

**McEwen, Tom** — Drag Racing Driver
17368 Buttonwood St, Fountain Valley CA 92708, USA

**McEwing, Joseph E (Joe)** — Baseball Player
630 Deerbrook Dr, Yardley PA 19067, USA

**McFadden, Bryan N** — Singer, Pianist, Songwriter, Actor
Creative Artists Agency, 2000 Ave of Stars, #100, Los Angeles CA 90067 USA

**McFadden, Cynthia** — Commentator
ABC-TV, News Dept, 77 W 66th St, New York NY 10023 USA

**McFadden, Daniel L** — Nobel Economics Laureate
41 Southampton Ave, Berkeley CA 94707, USA

**McFadden, Darren** — Football Player
Oakland Raiders, 1220 Harbor Bay Parkway, Alameda CA 94502 USA

**McFadden, Gates** — Actress
S M S Talent, 8383 Wilshire Blvd, #230, Beverly Hills CA 90211 USA

**McFadden, Katy** — Sculptor, Ceramist
313 SW Maricara St, Portland OR 97219, USA

**McFadden, Leon** — Baseball Player
8617 S 10th Ave, Inglewood CA 90305, USA

**McFadden, Mary J** — Fashion Designer
525 E 72nd St, #2A, New York NY 10021, USA

**McFadden, Paul** — Football Player
7395 Christopher Dr, Youngstown OH 44514, USA

**McFadden, Robert D** — Journalist
New York Times, Editorial Dept, 229 W 43rd St, New York NY 10036, USA

**McFadden-Rusynyk, Betty Jean** — Baseball Player
7267 W 130th St, Cleveland OH 44130, USA

**McFadyen, Jack** — Artist
284 Globe Road, London E2 0NS, England

**McFarland, Anthony D** — Football Player
7733 Still Lakes Dr, Odessa FL 33556, USA

**McFarland, Dennis** — Writer
Henry Holt, 175 5th Ave, #400, New York NY 10010 USA

**McFarland, James D (Jim)** — Football Player
5102 S 90th St, Lincoln NE 68526, USA

**McFarland, Michael C** — Educator
Holy Cross University, President's Office, 1 College St, Worcester MA 01610, USA

**McFarland, R Kay** — Football Player
7394 Monaco St, Centennial CO 80112, USA

**McFarlane, Robert C** — Government Official
2010 Prospect St NW, Washington DC 20037, USA

**McFarlane, Todd** — Cartoonist (Spawn)
Todd McFarlane Entertainment, 1711 W Greentree Dr, Tempe AZ 85284, USA

**McFarling, Ursula Lee** — Journalist
Los Angeles Times, Editorial Dept, 202 W 1st St, Los Angeles CA 90012 USA

**McFaull, David** — Yachtsman
109 Poloke Place, Honolulu HI 96822, USA

**McFeely, William S** — Historian, Writer
35 Mill Hill Road, Wellfleet MA 02667, USA

**McFerrin, Bobby** — Singer, Songwriter
Original Artists, 826 Broadway, #400, New York NY 10003, USA

**McG** — Director
W M E Entertainment, 9601 Wilshire Blvd, #300, Beverly Hills CA 90210 USA

**McGaffigan, Andrew J (Andy)** — Baseball Player
6243 Forestwood Dr E, Lakeland FL 33811, USA

**McGahee, Willis A, III** — Football Player
225 NE Mizner Blvd, #685, Boca Raton FL 33432, USA

**McGahey Heinzler, Kathleen** — Field Hockey Player
7427 W 81st St, Los Angeles CA 90045, USA

**McGann, Michelle** — Golfer
1200 Singer Dr, West Palm Beach FL 33404, USA

**McGann, Paul** — Actor
Artists Partnership, 101 Finsbury Pavement, London EC2A 1RS, England

**McGann, Stephen** — Actor
Associated International Mgmt, 7 Hatton Garden, #400, London EC1N 8AD, England

**McGarrahan, J Scott**
4704 Monte Carmelo Place, Austin TX 78738, USA — Football Player

**McGarrigle, Anna**
Moneypenny Agency, Stables, Main St, North Dalton, Fiffield, East Yorkshire YO25 9XA, England — Singer, Songwriter

**McGarry, Steve**
United Feature Syndicate, PO Box 5610, Cincinnati OH 45201 USA — Cartoonist (Pop Culture)

**McGary, Mitchell N W (Mitch)**
Oklahoma City Thunder, 211 N Robinson Ave, #300, Oklahoma City OK 73102 USA — Basketball Player

**McGaughey, Claude R (Shug), III**
1927 Keene Road, Nicholasville KY 40356, USA — Thoroughbred Racing Trainer

**McGee, Benjamin (Ben)**
35 Castle Cove, Jackson MS 39212, USA — Football Player

**McGee, Marcus**
Rainbow High Entertainment, 3500 W Olive Ave, #300, Burbank CA 91505, USA — Actor

**McGee, Michael B (Mike)**
22710 Uncompahgre Road, Montrose CO 81403, USA — Football Player

**McGee, Pat**
Elevation Group, 1408 Encinal Ave, #A, Alameda CA 94501, USA — Singer, Guitarist, Songwriter

**McGee, Terrence**
160 Fairlawn Dr, Buffalo NY 14226, USA — Football Player

**McGee, Tony L**
7238 Regina Way, Orlando FL 32819, USA — Football Player

**McGee, Willie D**
2081 Lupine Road, Hercules CA 94547, USA — Baseball Player

**Mcgee-Davis, Trina**
Framework Entertainment, 9057 Nemo St, #C, West Hollywood CA 90069 USA — Actress

**McGegan, Nicholas**
Schwalbe Partners, 170 E 61st St, #500, New York NY 10065, USA — Conductor

**McGehee, Scott**
Oasis Media Group, 8730 W Sunset Blvd, #700, West Hollywood CA 90069, USA — Director, Producer

**McGeorge, Missie**
1836 Willow Springs Court, Haslet TX 76052, USA — Golfer

**McGeorge, Richard E (Rich)**
2200 Trail Wood Dr, Durham NC 27705, USA — Football Player

**McGerr, Jason**
Zeitgeist Artist Mgmt, 660 York St, #216, San Francisco CA 94110, USA — Drummer (Death Cab for Cutie)

**McGhee, Carla**
103 Indigo Chase, Columbia SC 29229, USA — Basketball Player

**McGhee, Kanavis**
Challenge Earl College High School, 5601 West Loop S, Houston TX 77081, USA — Football Player

**McGilberry, Randall K (Randy)**
2110 Foxford St, Cantonment FL 32533, USA — Baseball Player

**McGill, Anthony**
Metropolitan Opera Orchestra, Lincoln Center Plaza, New York NY 10023, USA — Concert Clarinetist

**McGill, Bob**
116 Oriole Dr, Holland Landing ON L9N 1H1, Canada — Ice Hockey Player

**McGill, Bruce**
Stone Manners Salners, 6100 Wilshire Blvd, #1500, Los Angeles CA 90035 USA — Actor

**McGill, C Leonard (Lenny)**
3516 W 125th Circle, Broomfield CO 80020, USA — Football Player

**McGill, Don**
W M E Entertainment, 9601 Wilshire Blvd, #300, Beverly Hills CA 90210 USA — Producer, Writer

**McGill, Michael (Mickey)**
Associated Booking Corp, 501 Madison Ave, #501, New York NY 10022 USA — Singer (Dells)

**McGill, Michael Patrick**
C E S D, 10635 Santa Monica Blvd, #130, Los Angeles CA 90025 USA — Actor, Comedian

**McGill, Michael R (Mike)**
8930 Louis Court, Saint John IN 46373, USA — Football Player

**McGillion, Paul**
Amanda Howard, 74 Clerkenwell Road, London EC1M 5QA, England — Actor

**McGillis, Dan**
9 Country Club Dr, Chatham NJ 07928, USA — Ice Hockey Player

**McGillis, Kelly**
David Williams Mgmt, 9614 Olympic Blvd, #F, Beverly Hills CA 90212, USA — Actress

**McGinest, William L (Willie)**
20382 Tramore Lane, Strongsville OH 44149, USA — Football Player

**McGinley, John C**
W M E Entertainment, 9601 Wilshire Blvd, #300, Beverly Hills CA 90210 USA — Actor

**McGinley, Raymond**
High Road Touring, 751 Bridgeway, #200, Sausalito CA 94965 USA — Guitarist (Teenage Fanclub)

**McGinley, Ted**
Innovative Artists, 1505 10th St, Santa Monica CA 90401 USA — Actor

**McGinn, Bernard J**
5702 Kenwood Ave, Chicago IL 60637, USA — Theologian

**McGinn, Colin**
2411 SW 62nd Ave, Miami FL 33155, USA — Philosopher

**McGinn, Daniel M (Dan)**
1309 S 189th Court, Omaha NE 68130, USA — Baseball Player

**McGinnis, Dave**
3526 E Equestrian Trail, Phoenix AZ 85044, USA — Football Coach

**McGinnis, George F**
11245 Marlin Road, Indianapolis IN 46239, USA — Basketball Player

**McGinnis, Joe, Jr**
I C M Partners, 10250 Constellation Blvd, #900, Los Angeles CA 90067 USA — Writer

**McGirt, James (Buddy), Jr**
Elite Youth Program, 104 Day Dr, Sebastian FL 32958, USA — Boxer, Manager

**McGiver, Boris**
Harden-Curtis Associates, 850 7th Ave, #903, New York NY 10019, USA — Actor

**McGlocklin, Jon P**
5281 State Road, #83, Hartland WI 53029, USA — Basketball Player

**McGlone, Mike**
Don Buchwald Talent Agency, 6500 Wilshire Blvd, #2200, Los Angeles CA 90048 USA — Actor

**McGlynn, Richard A (Dick)**
38 Rock Glen Road, Medford MA 02155, USA — Ice Hockey Player

**McGonagle, Marta**
Charles Sherman, 8306 Wilshire Blvd, #2017, Beverly Hills CA 90211, USA — Actress

**McGoon, Dwight C** — Surgeon
840 9th Ave SW, Rochester MN 55902, USA

**McGovern, Elizabeth** — Actress
Rights House, Drury House, 34-43 Russell St, London WC2B 5HA, England

**McGovern, James D (Jim)** — Golfer
900 Amaryllis Ave, Oradell NJ 07649, USA

**McGovern, Maureen** — Singer
M M Productions, 8530 Wilshire Blvd, #200, Beverly Hills CA 90211, USA

**McGowan, Patrick R (Pat)** — Golfer
PO Box 88, Southern Pines NC 28388, USA

**McGowan, Zach** — Actor
Innovative Artists, 1505 10th St, Santa Monica CA 90401 USA

**McGrady, Charles** — Environmentalist
Sierra Club, 85 2nd St, #200 San Francisco CA 94105, USA

**McGrady, Tracy L, Jr** — Basketball Player
23 Beacon Hill, Sugar Land TX 77479, USA

**McGrain, Peter** — Artist
207 Maple St, White Salmon WA 98672, USA

**McGrath, C Peter** — Educator
State University of New York, President's Office, 4400 Vestal Parkway E, Binghamton NY 13902, USA

**McGrath, Douglas** — Director, Actor, Writer
Creative Artists Agency, 2000 Ave of Stars, #100, Los Angeles CA 90067 USA

**McGrath, James** — Geneticist
Yale University, Genetics Dept, New Haven CT 06520, USA

**McGrath, Jeremy** — Motorcycle Racing Rider
J R Motorsports 801 SW Ordnance Road, Ankeny IA 50023, USA

**McGrath, Judy** — Businesswoman
MTV Networks, 1515 Broadway, New York NY 10036, USA

**McGrath, Katie** — Actress
Curtis Brown Group, 28-29 Haymarket St, #500, London SW1Y 4SP, England

**McGrath, Mark** — Singer (Sugar Ray), Entertainer
Pinnacle Entertainment, 30 Glenn St, White Plains NY 10603, USA

**McGrath, Mike** — Bowler
63 W Napa Dr, Petaluma CA 94954, USA

**McGrath, Robert E (Bob)** — Actor, Writer
Bob McGrath Productions, 295 Frances St, Teaneck NJ 07666, USA

**McGraw, Joseph** — WW II Navy Air Hero
416 Alissa Lane, Burlington WA 98233, USA

**McGraw, Melinda** — Actress
Domain Talent, 9229 W Sunset Blvd, #710, West Hollywood CA 90069 USA

**McGraw, Michael S (Mike)** — Football Player
PO Box 529, Medicine Bow WY 82329, USA

**McGraw, Muffet** — Basketball Coach
University of Notre Dame, Athletic Dept, Notre Dame IN 46556, USA

**McGraw, Phillip C (Dr Phil)** — Entertainer, Psychologist
1008 Lexington Road, Beverly Hills CA 90210, USA

**McGraw, Tim** — Singer
Red Light Mgmt, PO Box 1467, Charlottesville VA 22902, USA

**McGregor, Ewan** — Actor
United Agents, 12-26 Lexington St, London W1F 0LE, England

**McGregor, Freddie** — Singer
Solid Agency, 7 Dumbarton Ave, Kingston 10, Jamaica

**McGregor, Katherine Ann** — Actress, Producer
Iconoblast Talent Mgmt, 1335 N La Brea, #2148, Los Angeles CA 90028, USA

**McGregor, Scott H** — Baseball Player
1514 Providence Road, #A, Towson MD 21286, USA

**McGriff, Frederick S (Fred)** — Baseball Player
16314 Millan de Avila, Tampa FL 33613, USA

**McGriff, Hershel** — Auto Racing Driver
General Delivery, Green Valley AZ 85622, USA

**McGriff, Terence R (Terry)** — Baseball Player
2905 Langston Dr, Fort Pierce FL 34946, USA

**McGruder, Aaron** — Cartoonist (Boondocks)
Universal Press Syndicate, 4520 Main St, #700, Kansas City MO 64111 USA

**McGuane, Thomas F, III** — Writer
410 S 3rd Ave, Bozeman MT 59715, USA

**McGuckin, Aislin** — Actress
Artists Partnership, 101 Finsbury Pavement, London EC2A 1RS, England

**McGuigan, Paul** — Bassist (Oasis)
Ignition Mgmt, 54 Linhope St, London NW1 6HL, England

**McGuigan, Paul** — Director
Fallout Entertainment Group, 3100 Airport Ave, Santa Monica CA 90405, USA

**McGuinn, Roger** — Singer, Guitarist (Byrds), Songwriter
Miracle Artists, 26 Dorset St, London W1U 8AP, England

**McGuinness, James (Jay)** — Singer (Wanted)
Industry Music Group, 128 Regent Road, Hanley Stoke, Trent ST1 3AY, England

**McGuinness, Martin** — Government Official, Northern Ireland
Sinn Fein, 170 Falls Road, Belfast BT12 4PD, Northern Ireland

**McGuire, Betty** — Actress
H David Moss, 733 Seward St, #PH, Los Angeles CA 90038 USA

**McGuire, Christine** — Singer (McGuire Sisters)
100 Rancho Circle, Las Vegas NV 89107, USA

**McGuire, Jack** — Association Executive
American Red Cross, 431 18th St NW, Washington DC 20006, USA

**McGuire, M C Adolfus (Mickey)** — Baseball Player
1521 Middle Park Dr, Dayton OH 45414, USA

**McGuire, Patti** — Model
1962 E Valley Road, Santa Barbara CA 93108, USA

**McGuire, Phyllis** — Singer (McGuire Sisters)
100 Rancho Circle, Las Vegas NV 89107, USA

**McGuire, Ryan B** — Baseball Player
171 Great Lawn, Irvine CA 92620, USA

**McGuire, W Eugene (Gene)** — Football Player
3229 Country Club Dr, Lynn Haven FL 32444, USA

**McGuire, Willard H** — Labor Leader
National Education Assn, 1201 16th St NW, Washington DC 20036, USA

**McGwire, Mark D** — Baseball Player
PO Box 165, 4521 Campus Dr, East Irvine CA 92650, USA
**McHaffie Vidal, Deborah** — Golfer
Tony Criscuolo, 8425 NW 222nd Ave, Alachua FL 32615, USA
**McHale, Joel** — Actor, Comedian
W M E Entertainment, 9601 Wilshire Blvd, #300, Beverly Hills CA 90210 USA
**McHale, Kevin** — Actor
Greene Assoc, 1901 Ave of Stars, #130, Los Angeles CA 90067 USA
**McHale, Kevin E** — Basketball Player, Executive, Coach
20 Blue Jay Lane, Saint Paul MN 55127, USA
**McHattie, Stephen** — Actor
Christopher Wright Mgmt, 3207 Winnie Dr, Los Angeles CA 90068, USA
**McHenry, Donald F** — Diplomat
Georgetown University, Foreign Service School, Washington DC 20057, USA
**McHenry, Vance L** — Baseball Player
2396 Brown St, Durham CA 95938, USA
**McHugh, Heather** — Writer
University of Washington, English Dept, PO Box 354330, Seattle WA 98195, USA
**McHugh, John M** — Secretary, Army; Representative, NY
Secretary's Office, HqUSA, Pentagon, Washington DC 20310, USA
**McIlhenny, Donald B (Don)** — Football Player
8505 Edgemere Road, #101, Dallas TX 75225, USA
**McIlrath, Tim** — Singer, Guitarist (Rise Against)
Agency Group Ltd, 142 W 57th St, #600, New York NY 10019 USA
**McIlravy, Lincoln** — Freestyle Wrestler
4220 210th St NE, Solon IA 52333, USA
**McIlroy, Rory** — Golfer
Holywood Golf Club, Nuns Walk, Demesne Road, Holywood, County Down BT18 9LE, Northern Ireland
**McIlvaine, James M (Jim)** — Basketball Player
Camp Anokijig, W5639 Anokijig Lane, Plymouth WI 53073, USA
**McInally, Patrick J (Pat)** — Football Player
19321 Ocean Heights Lane, Huntington Beach CA 92648, USA
**McInerney, John B (Jay), Jr** — Writer
I C M Partners, 10250 Constellation Blvd, #900, Los Angeles CA 90067 USA
**McInnis, Jeff L** — Basketball Player
3404 Lazy Day Lane, Charlotte NC 28269, USA
**McInnis, Marty** — Ice Hockey Player
21 Peter Hobart Dr, Hingham MA 02043, USA
**McIntosh, Damion A** — Football Player
1221 SW Summit Crossing Dr, Lees Summit MO 64081, USA
**McIntosh, Timothy A (Tim)** — Baseball Player
1815 S Talbott Place, Waynesboro VA 22980, USA
**McIntyre, Guy M** — Football Player
257 Arrowhead Way, Hayward CA 94544, USA
**McIntyre, Joey** — Singer (New Kids on the Block)
Spectrum Talent, 1650 Broadway, #1105, New York NY 10019, USA
**McIntyre, Liam** — Actor
Independent Mgmt Company, 50 Holt St, #307, Surry Hills NSW 2010, Australia
**McIver, Everett A** — Football Player
1205 Avignon Dr SW, Conyers GA 30094, USA
**McIver, Rose** — Actress
Sue Barnett & Associates, 1/96 Albion St, Surry Hills NSW 2010, Australia
**McKagan, Duff** — Bassist (Guns N' Roses)
Sanctuary Artist Mgmt, 15301 Ventura Blvd, Building B, Sherman Oaks CA 91403, USA
**McKart, Bronco** — Boxer
Scott Beard, 11343 Telegraph Road, #A, Erie PA 48133, USA
**McKay, Adam** — Actor, Director, Writer
Gary Sanchez Productions, 729 Seward St, #200, Los Angeles CA 90038, USA
**McKay, Al** — Guitarist (Earth Wind Fire), Songwriter
Spirit Media, PO Box 43591, Phoenix AZ 85080, USA
**McKay, Ami** — Writer
PO Box 146, Canning NS B0P 1H0, Canada
**McKay, Caroline** — Drummer (Glasvegas)
Sony Music, 9 Derry St, London W8 5HY, England
**McKay, Christian** — Actor
Independent Talent Group, 40 Whitfield St, London W1T 2RH, England
**McKay, David L (Dave)** — Baseball Player
9702 W La Posada Circle, Scottsdale AZ 85255, USA
**McKay, Heather** — Squash, Racquetball Player
48 Nesbitt Dr, Toronto ON M4W 2G3, Canada
**McKay, Mhairi** — Golfer
898 W Ashbourne Dr, Eagle ID 83616, USA
**McKay, Monroe G** — Judge
US Court of Appeals, Federal Building, 125 S State St, Salt Lake City UT 84138, USA
**McKay, Nellie** — Singer, Pianist, Songwriter
Creative Artists Agency, 2000 Ave of Stars, #100, Los Angeles CA 90067 USA
**McKay, Randy** — Ice Hockey Player
44640 US Highway 41, Chassell MI 49916, USA
**McKay, Ritchie** — Basketball Coach
Liberty University, Athletic Dept, Lynchburg VA 24502, USA
**McKay, Robert C (Bob)** — Football Player
4110 Bluffridge Dr, Austin TX 78759, USA
**McKeague, David W** — Judge
US Appellate Court, 315 W Allegan St, Lansing MI 48933, USA
**McKean, James G (Jim)** — Baseball Umpire
740 Sand Pine Dr NE, Saint Petersburg FL 33703, USA
**McKean, Michael J** — Actor, Comedian
A P A Talent & Literary Agency, 405 S Beverly Dr, #300, Beverly Hills CA 90212 USA
**McKechnie, Walt** — Ice Hockey Player
McKeck's Place, PO Box 752, Haliburton ON K0M 1S0, Canada
**McKee, Frank S** — Labor Leader
United Steelworkers Union, 60 Blvd of Allies, #5, Pittsburgh PA 15222, USA
**McKee, Gina** — Actress
United Agents, 12-26 Lexington St, London W1F 0LE, England
**McKee, Jay** — Ice Hockey Player
1423 Topping Road, Saint Louis MO 63131, USA

**M**

**McKee, Maria** — Singer, Songwriter
Concerted Efforts, PO Box 440326, Somerville MA 02144 USA

**McKee, Theodore A** — Judge
US Appeals Court, US Courthouse, 601 Market St, #20614, Philadelphia PA 19106, USA

**McKee, Todd** — Actor
1155 Monument St, Pacific Palisades CA 90272, USA

**McKellar, Danica** — Actress
C E S D, 10635 Santa Monica Blvd, #130, Los Angeles CA 90025 USA

**McKellen, Ian** — Actor
2act, Mirza Co, 826 Garratt Lane, London SW17 0LZ, England

**McKeller, T Keith** — Football Player
1972 Waccamaw Path, Winston Salem NC 27127, USA

**McKelvey, Rob** — Golfer
1814 Duke Road, Atlanta GA 30341, USA

**McKenna, Alex** — Actress
Innovative Artists, 1505 10th St, Santa Monica CA 90401 USA

**McKenna, Chris** — Actor
Stone Manners Salners, 6100 Wilshire Blvd, #1500, Los Angeles CA 90035 USA

**McKenna, Kevin R** — Basketball Player
15387 Nicholas St, Omaha NE 68154, USA

**McKenna, Lori** — Singer, Songwriter
Rolling Thunder Artist Mgmt, 174 Allen Ave, Waban MA 02468, USA

**McKenna, Stephen F** — Artist
Crocknafeola, Killybegs, County Donegal, Ireland

**McKenna, Virginia** — Actress
Brunskill Management, 169 Queens Gate, #8A, London SW7 5HE, England

**McKenney, Donald H (Don)** — Ice Hockey Player
16 Edgewater Dr, Norton MA 02766, USA

**McKenzie Smith, Ian** — Artist
70 Hamilton Place, Aberdeen AB15 5BA, Scotland

**McKenzie, Benjamin (Ben)** — Actor
Management 360, 9111 Wilshire Blvd, Beverly Hills CA 90210 USA

**McKenzie, Bret** — Singer (Flight of the Conchords), Actor
Creative Artists Agency, 2000 Ave of Stars, #100, Los Angeles CA 90067 USA

**McKenzie, Dan P** — Geologist
Bullard Labs, Madingley Rise, Madingley Road, Cambridge CB3 0EZ, England

**McKenzie, Derrick** — Drummer (Jamiroquai)
Nettwerk Mgmt, 6525 W Sunset Blvd, #800, Los Angeles CA 90028 USA

**McKenzie, Forrest D W** — Basketball Player
2516 S Laurelwood, Santa Ana CA 92704, USA

**McKenzie, Jacqueline** — Actress, Director, Writer
S M S Talent, 8383 Wilshire Blvd, #230, Beverly Hills CA 90211 USA

**McKenzie, James P (Jim)** — Ice Hockey Player
9266 Chevoit Dr, Brentwood TN 37027, USA

**McKenzie, John** — Ice Hockey Player
10 Clearview Road, Stoneham MA 02180, USA

**McKenzie, Julia** — Actress
Artists Partnership, 101 Finsbury Pavement, London EC2A 1RS, England

**McKenzie, Kevin** — Ballet Dancer
American Ballet Theatre, 890 Broadway, #300, New York NY 10003 USA

**McKenzie, Raleigh** — Football Player
715 Huntsman Place, Herndon VA 20170, USA

**McKenzie, Reggie** — Football Player, Executive
411 Carta Road, Knoxville TN 37914, USA

**McKenzie, Reginald (Reggie)** — Football Player
1247 Sunrise Ridge Dr, Lafayette CA 94549, USA

**McKenzie, Stanley (Stan)** — Basketball Player
8316 Governor Grayson Way, Ellicott City MD 21043, USA

**McKeon, Doug** — Actor
4644 Arriba Dr, Tarzana CA 91356, USA

**McKeon, Joel J** — Baseball Player
1901 Pierce St, Hollywood FL 33020, USA

**McKeon, John A (Jack)** — Baseball Player, Manager
1529 Charleigh Court, Elon NC 27244, USA

**McKeon, Lindsey** — Actress
Amsel Eisenstadt Frazier, 5055 Wilshire Blvd, #865, Los Angeles CA 90036 USA

**McKeon, Nancy** — Actress
Stone Manners Salners, 6100 Wilshire Blvd, #1500, Los Angeles CA 90035 USA

**McKeown, Bob** — Commentator
CBS-TV, News Dept, 51 W 52nd St, New York NY 10019 USA

**McKeown, M Margaret** — Judge
2447 Ardath Road, La Jolla CA 92037, USA

**McKernan, John R, Jr** — Governor, ME
77 Sanderson Road, Cumberland Foreside ME 04110, USA

**McKey, Derrick W** — Basketball Player
8 Woodard Place, Zionsville IN 46077, USA

**McKidd, Kevin** — Actor
Shelter Public Relations, 9465 Wilshire Blvd, #700, Beverly Hills CA 90212 USA

**McKie, Aaron F** — Basketball Player
1400 Youngs Ford Road, Gladwyne PA 19035, USA

**McKie, Jason A** — Football Player
4431 W Lawn Ave, Waukegan IL 60085, USA

**McKinley, Alvin J** — Football Player
45274 W Miraflores St, Maricopa AZ 85139, USA

**McKinley, Craig R** — Air Force General
Chief, National Guard Bureau, HqUSAF, Pentagon, Washington DC 20330 USA

**McKinley, John** — Rowing Athlete
952 Bloomfield Village, Auburn Hills MI 48326, USA

**McKinley, John K** — Businessman
1 Canterbury Green, #800, Stamford CT 06901, USA

**McKinley, Robin** — Writer
Writer's House, 21 W 26th St, New York NY 10010, USA

**McKinley-Uselmann, Therese** — Baseball Player
1644 N Greenwood Ave, Park Ridge IL 60068, USA

**McKinnely, Philip B (Phil)** — Football Player
585 Edgehill Place, Alpharetta GA 30022, USA

**McKinney, C Richard (Rich)** — Baseball Player
2495 E Peterson Road, Troy OH 45373, USA

**McKinney, DeMetria** — Actress
Don Buchwald Talent Agency, 6500 Wilshire Blvd, #2200, Los Angeles CA 90048 USA

**McKinney, Kennedy** — Boxer
187 B & R Lane, Golden Meadow LA 70357, USA

**McKinney, Kurt** — Actor
5003 Tilden Ave, #206, Sherman Oaks CA 91423, USA

**McKinney, Mark** — Actor, Comedian, Writer
Oscars Abrams Zimel, 438 Queen St E, Toronto ON M5A 1T4, Canada

**McKinney, Odis, Jr** — Football Player
23126 Collins St, Woodland Hills CA 91367, USA

**McKinney, Richard (Rick)** — Archery Athlete
549 E Silver Creek Road, Gilbert AZ 85296, USA

**McKinney, Seth A** — Football Player
2403 Crown Court, College Station TX 77845, USA

**McKinney, Stephen M (Steve)** — Football Player
335 County Road 201, Centerville TX 75833, USA

**McKinney, Tamara** — Alpine Skier
4395 Parkers Mill Road, Lexington KY 40513, USA

**McKinnie, Bryant D** — Football Player
12535 Stoneway Court, Davie FL 33330, USA

**McKinnon, Bruce** — Editorial Cartoonist
Halifax Chronicle Herald, 1650 Argyle St, Halifax NS B3J 2T2, Canada

**McKinnon, Daniel D (Dan)** — Ice Hockey Player
610 Riverdale Dr NE, Warroad MN 56763, USA

**McKinnon, Dennis L** — Football Player
1016 Adams St, North Chicago IL 60064, USA

**McKinnon, Kate** — Comedian, Composer
United Talent Agency, U T A Plaza, 9336 Civic Center Dr, Beverly Hills CA 90210 USA

**McKinnon, Ray** — Actor
Creative Artists Agency, 2000 Ave of Stars, #100, Los Angeles CA 90067 USA

**McKinnon, Ronald (Ron)** — Football Player
1063 Grand Oaks Dr, Bessemer AL 35022, USA

**McKissack, Patricia** — Writer
Scholastic Press, 555 Broadway, New York NY 10012 USA

**McKissick, John** — Football Coach
Summerville High School, Athletic Dept, Summerville SC 29484, USA

**McKittrick, Rob** — Director, Writer
Creative Artists Agency, 2000 Ave of Stars, #100, Los Angeles CA 90067 USA

**McKnight, Anthony (Tony)** — Baseball Player
406 Dundee Road, Texarkana AR 71854, USA

**McKnight, Brian** — Singer, Songwriter
Universal Attractions, 135 W 26th St, #1200, New York NY 10001 USA

**McKnight, Clarence E, Jr** — Army General
1624 Linway Park Dr, McLean VA 22101, USA

**McKnight, Ira** — Baseball Player
608 S Summit Dr, #1, South Bend IN 46619, USA

**McKnight, James** — Football Player
16705 Berkshire Court, Southwest Ranches FL 33331, USA

**McKnight, Jefferson A (Jeff)** — Baseball Player
3296 Highway 92 W, Bee Branch AR 72013, USA

**McKnight, John** — Singer, Musician (Fishbone)
Silverback Mgmt, 9469 Jefferson Blvd, #101, Culver City CA 90232, USA

**McKnight, Steven L** — Molecular Biologist
8513 Swananoah Road, Dallas TX 75209, USA

**McKnight, Theodore R (Ted)** — Football Player
10236 Cedarbrooke Lane, Kansas City MO 64131, USA

**McKnight, Thomas F** — Artist
PO Box 98, Litchfield CT 06759, USA

**Mckown, Zack** — Interior Designer
Tsao-McKorn Design, 20 Vandam St, #1000, New York NY 10013, USA

**McKuen, Rod** — Singer, Songwiter, Writer
C E S D, 10635 Santa Monica Blvd, #130, Los Angeles CA 90025 USA

**McKyer, Timothy B (Tim)** — Football Player
11201 Golden Dr, Charlotte NC 28216, USA

**McLachlan, Craig D** — Actor, Singer
Stone Meyer Genow, 9665 Wilshire Blvd, #510, Beverly Hills CA 90212 USA

**McLachlan, Sarah** — Singer, Songwriter
Sarah McLachlan School of Music, 138 E 7th Ave, #200, Vancouver, BC V5T 1M6, Canada

**McLafferty, Fred W** — Chemist
103 Needham Place, Ithaca NY 14850, USA

**McLaglen, Andrew V** — Director
Stanmore Productions, PO Box 1056, Friday Harbor WA 98250, USA

**McLain, Dennis D (Denny)** — Baseball Player
4432 Golf View Dr, Brighton MI 48116, USA

**McLane, James P (Jimmy), Jr** — Swimmer
97 Mount Vernon St, #1, Boston MA 02108, USA

**McLaren, Brandon Jay** — Actor
Pakula/King, 9229 W Sunset Blvd, #315, West Hollywood CA 90069 USA

**McLaren, John L** — Baseball Manager
Washington Nationals, 1500 S Capitol St SE, Washington DC 20003 USA

**McLaren, Kyle E** — Ice Hockey Player
6582 Skyfarm Dr, San Jose CA 95120, USA

**McLaughlin, Ann Dore** — Secretary, Labor
Rand Corp, 1200 S Hayes St, #400, Arlington VA 22202, USA

**McLaughlin, Audrey** — Government Official, Canada
410 Hoge St, Whitehorse, Yukon Y1A 1W2, Canada

**McLaughlin, Brian** — Actor
Brooks Murphy Stevens, 5619 N Lankershim Blvd, North Hollywood CA 91601 USA

**McLaughlin, Brianne** — Ice Hockey Player
USA Hockey, 1775 Bob Johnson Dr, Colorado Springs CO 80906 USA

**McLaughlin, Byron S** — Baseball Player
7030 Alamitos Ave, San Diego CA 92154, USA

**McLaughlin, David** — Association Executive
American Red Cross, 431 18th St NW, Washington DC 20006, USA

**M**

**McLaughlin, Emma**
Atria Books, 1230 Ave of Americas, New York NY 10020 USA
Writer

**McLaughlin, Jake**
Paradigm Agency, 360 N Crescent Dr, North Building, Beverly Hills CA 90210 USA
Actor

**McLaughlin, Jim**
McLaughlin Assoc, PO Box 479, Sun Valley ID 83353, USA
Architect

**McLaughlin, Joey R**
1611 S Troost Ave, Tulsa OK 74120, USA
Baseball Player

**McLaughlin, John E**
Central Intelligence Agency, Deputy Director's Office, Washington DC 20505, USA
Government Official

**McLaughlin, John J**
McLaughlin Group, 1717 Rhode Island Ave NW, #640, Washington DC 20036, USA
Commentator

**McLaughlin, Joseph J (Joe)**
65 Pells Fishing Road, Brewster MA 02631, USA
Football Player

**McLaughlin, Michael (Mike)**
PO Box 45, Waterloo NY 13165, USA
Auto Racing Driver

**McLaughlin, Michael D (Bo)**
536 N Grand, Mesa AZ 85201, USA
Baseball Player

**McLean, A J**
Podwell Entertainment, 710 N Orlando Ave, #203, West Hollywood CA 90069, USA
Singer (Backstreet Boys), Actor

**McLean, Don**
Paradise Artists, PO Box 1821, Ojai CA 93024 USA
Singer, Songwriter

**McLean, Greg**
W M E Entertainment, 9601 Wilshire Blvd, #300, Beverly Hills CA 90210 USA
Director, Writer

**McLean, Hayley**
Agency Group Ltd, 142 W 57th St, #600, New York NY 10019 USA
Singer, Songwriter

**McLean, Jane**
Oscars Abrams Zimel, 438 Queen St E, Toronto ON M5A 1T4, Canada
Actress

**McLean, Kirk**
Burnaby Express, 3676 Kensington Ave, Burnaby BC V5B 4Z6, Canada
Ice Hockey Player

**McLean, Michelle**
McLean Children's Trust, PO Box 97428, Maerua Mall, Windhoek, Namibia
Beauty Queen

**McLean, Rene**
Brad Simon Organization, 445 E 80th St, #4C, New York NY 10075 USA
Jazz Saxophonist, Flutist

**McLean, Sally**
Salmac Mgmt, PO Box 526, Mount Martha VIC 3934, Australia
Actress, Producer

**McLean-Ross, Lucella**
401-5107 47th St, Lloydminster AB T9V 0G1, Canada
Baseball Player

**McLellan, Zoe**
Domain Talent, 9229 W Sunset Blvd, #710, West Hollywood CA 90069 USA
Actress

**McLemore, Dana**
125 Seagate Dr, San Mateo CA 94403, USA
Football Player

**McLemore, Elle**
Paradigm Agency, 360 N Crescent Dr, North Building, Beverly Hills CA 90210 USA
Actress

**McLemore, LaMonte**
Brokaw Co, 9255 W Sunset Blvd, #804, West Hollywood CA 90069 USA
Singer (Fifth Dimension)

**McLemore, Mark T**
533 S White Chapel Blvd, Southlake TX 76092, USA
Baseball Player

**McLendon-Covey, Wendi**
John Carrabino Management, 5900 Wilshire, #406, Los Angeles CA 90036, USA
Actress, Producer, Writer

**McLennan, Jamie**
Calgary Flames, PO Box 1540, Station M, Calgary AB T2P 3B9, Canada
Ice Hockey Player

**McLeod, Erin**
Canadian Soccer, Place Soccer Canada, 237 Metcalfe St, Ottawa ON K2P 1R2, Canada
Soccer Player

**McLeod, R J Jackie**
13 John Hair Court, Saskatoon SK S7J 2K6, Canada
Ice Hockey Player

**McLeod, Robert D (Bob)**
600 Spring Creek Road, Brenham TX 77833, USA
Football Player

**McLerie, Allyn Ann**
3344 Campanil Dr, Santa Barbara CA 93109, USA
Actress, Dancer

**McLish, Rachel**
Ron Samuels Entertainment, 100 Wilshire Blvd, #750, Santa Monica CA 90401, USA
Actress, Body Builder

**McLlwain, Dave**
Yacht Club Woods, Grand Bend ON N0M 1T0, Canada
Ice Hockey Player

**McLoughlin, Tom**
Paradigm Agency, 360 N Crescent Dr, North Building, Beverly Hills CA 90210 USA
Director

**McLouth, Nathan R (Nate)**
6116 W Fieldstone Hills Dr SE, Caldedonia MI 49316, USA
Baseball Player

**McLure, Charles E, Jr**
250 Yerba Santa Ana, Los Altos CA 94022, USA
Government Official

**McMahan, Jack W**
131 Forest View Circle, Hot Springs AR 71913, USA
Baseball Player

**McMahon, Andrew R**
A P A Talent & Literary Agency, 405 S Beverly Dr, #300, Beverly Hills CA 90212 USA
Singer, Pianist, Songwriter

**McMahon, Donald A**
63 W Wieuca Road NE, #1, Atlanta GA 30342, USA
Businessman

**McMahon, James R (Jim)**
22431 N Violetta Dr, Scottsdale AZ 85255, USA
Football Player

**McMahon, Julian**
W M E Entertainment, 9601 Wilshire Blvd, #300, Beverly Hills CA 90210 USA
Actor

**McMahon, Michael E (Mike)**
313 Oak Grove Court, Wexford PA 15090, USA
Football Player

**McMahon, Stacy**
White Tiger Modeling, PO Box 5298, South Melbourne VIC 3205, Australia
Model

**McMahon, Vincent K, Jr**
World Wrestling Entertainment, Titan Towers, 1241 E Main St, Stamford CT 06902 USA
Professional Wrestling Executive

**McMakin, John G**
608 Longview Ave, Anacortes WA 98221, USA
Football Player

**McManus, James M (Jim)**
2352 Hopkins Mill Road, Duluth GA 30096, USA
Baseball Player

**McManus, Michaela**
United Talent Agency, U T A Plaza, 9336 Civic Center Dr, Beverly Hills CA 90210 USA
Actress

**McMartin, John**
Artists Agency, 9430 Olympic Blvd, Beverly Hills CA 90212 USA
Actor, Singer

**McMath, Jimmy L**
3321 22nd St, Tuscaloosa AL 35401, USA
Baseball Player

**McMenamin, Mark A S** — Geologist
Mount Holyoke College, Geology Dept, South Hadley MA 01075, USA
**McMenamy, Kristen** — Model
D N A Model Mgmt, 555 W 25th St, #600, New York NY 10001 USA
**McMichael, Gregory W (Greg)** — Baseball Player
240 Parkside Club Court, Duluth GA 30097, USA
**McMichael, Randy H** — Football Player
361 17th St NW, Atlanta GA 30363, USA
**McMichael, Steve D** — Football Player
644 Wild Indigo Ave, Romeoville IL 60446, USA
**McMillan, Caroline Pierce** — Golfer
7625 E Phantom Way, Scottsdale AZ 85255, USA
**McMillan, Ernest C (Ernie)** — Football Player
14816 Sycamore Manor Court, Chesterfield MO 63017, USA
**McMillan, Lewis L (Randy)** — Football Player
6832 Hayley Ridge Way, Baltimore MD 21209, USA
**McMillan, Nathaniel (Nate)** — Basketball Player, Coach
1000 Venetian Court, Cary NC 27518, USA
**McMillan, Terry L** — Writer
PO Box 378, Pasadena CA 91102, USA
**McMillan, Thomas E (Tommy)** — Baseball Player
712 Spring Lake Road, Thomasville GA 31792, USA
**McMillan, William (Bill)** — Marksman
1930 Sandstone Vista, Encinitas CA 92024, USA
**McMillen, C Thomas (Tom)** — Representative, MD; Basketball Player
Homeland Security Capital Corp, 1005 N Glebe Road, #550, Arlington VA 22201, USA
**McMillen, Robert** — Track Athlete
5708 Golden West Ave, Temple City CA 91780, USA
**McMillian, Audray G** — Football Player
1230 Hahlo St, Houston TX 77020, USA
**McMillian, James M (Jim)** — Basketball Player
4804 Tara Dr, Greensboro NC 27410, USA
**McMillian, Michael** — Actor
Innovative Artists, 1505 10th St, Santa Monica CA 90401 USA
**McMillin, James R (Jim)** — Football Player
7985 Westview Dr, Lakewood CO 80214, USA
**McMillon, C Douglas (Doug)** — Businessman
Wal-Mart Stores  702 SW 8th St, Bentonville AR 72716, USA
**McMillon, William (Billy)** — Baseball Player
1516 Lost Creek Dr, Columbia SC 29212, USA
**McMonagle, Donald R** — Astronaut
7737 E Shadow Vista Court, Tucson AZ 85750, USA
**McMorris, Mark** — Snowboard Athlete
Sports Syndicate, 20411 Birch St, #350, Newport Beach CA 92660, USA
**McMorrow, James Vincent** — Singer, Songwriter
Agency Group Ltd, 142 W 57th St, #600, New York NY 10019 USA
**McMullen, Curtis T** — Mathematician
Harvard University, Science Center, Cambridge MA 02138, USA
**McMullen, Kenneth L (Ken)** — Baseball Player
10 Estaban Dr, Camarillo CA 93010, USA
**McMullian, Amos R** — Businessman
Flowers Industries, 200 US Highway 19 S, Thomasville GA 31792, USA
**McMullin, Ernan V** — Philosopher
University of Notre Dame, Philosophy Dept, Notre Dame IN 46556, USA
**McMurray, James C (Jamie)** — Auto Racing Driver
211 Milford Circle, Mooresville NC 28117, USA
**McMurtry, Gregory W (Greg)** — Football Player
755 Oak Point Lane, Madison Heights MI 48071, USA
**McMurtry, J Craig** — Baseball Player
2835 Bottoms East Road, Troy TX 76579, USA
**McMurtry, James** — Singer, Songwriter
High Road Touring, 751 Bridgeway, #200, Sausalito CA 94965 USA
**McMurtry, Larry** — Writer
PO Box 552, Archer City TX 76351, USA
**McMurtry, Tom** — Test Pilot
PO Box 273, Edwards CA 93523, USA
**McNab, Mercedes** — Actress, Model
Stone Manners Salners, 6100 Wilshire Blvd, #1500, Los Angeles CA 90035 USA
**McNab, Peter M** — Ice Hockey Player
10311 Rancho Montecito, Parker CO 80138, USA
**McNabb, Donovan** — Football Player
21800 Towncenter Plaza, #266A, Sterling VA 20164, USA
**McNabb, Duncan J** — Air Force General
Commander, US Transportation Command, Scott Air Force Base IL 62225, USA
**McNairy, Scoot** — Actor
Group Films, 800 S Robertson Blvd, #5, Los Angeles CA 90035, USA
**McNally, Andrew, IV** — Publisher
Rand McNally Co, 9855 Woods Dr, Skokie IL 60077, USA
**McNally, David (Dave)** — Director, Producer, Writer
W M E Entertainment, 9601 Wilshire Blvd, #300, Beverly Hills CA 90210 USA
**McNally, Kevin** — Actor
Hatton McEwan, 3 Chocolate Studios, 7 Shepherdess Place, London N1 7LJ, England
**McNally, Shannon M** — Singer, Songwriter
Impact Artists Mgmt, 356 W 123rd St, New York NY 10027, USA
**McNally, Stephen (Ste)** — Singer, Guitarist (BBMak)
Spirit Media, PO Box 43591, Phoenix AZ 85080, USA
**McNally, Terrence** — Writer, Actor
Gersh Agency, 9465 Wilshire Blvd, #600, Beverly Hills CA 90212 USA
**McNamara, Brian** — Actor
TalentWorks, 3500 W Olive Ave, #1400, Burbank CA 91505 USA
**McNamara, Eileen** — Journalist
Boston Globe, Editorial Dept, 135 William Morrissey Blvd, Dorchester MA 02125 USA
**McNamara, Gerry** — Ice Hockey Player
213-350 Mill Road, Etobicoke ON M9C 5R7, Canada
**McNamara, James P (Jim)** — Baseball Player
15317 Surrey House Way, Centreville VA 20120, USA

**M**

**McNamara, John F**
1206 Beech Hill Road, Brentwood TN 37027, USA — Baseball Player, Manager

**McNamara, Julianne L**
Todd Zeile, 5445 Via Nicola, Newbury Park CA 91320, USA — Gymnast, Actress

**McNamara, Katherine**
C E S D, 10635 Santa Monica Blvd, #130, Los Angeles CA 90025 USA — Actress

**McNamara, Mark R C**
PO Box 134, Strawberry CA 95375, USA — Basketball Player

**McNamara, Melissa**
7715 S Quebec Ave, Tulsa OK 74136, USA — Golfer

**McNamara, Robert M (Bob)**
4764 Dalea Place, Oceanside CA 92057, USA — Baseball Player

**McNamara, Sean**
A P A Talent & Literary Agency, 405 S Beverly Dr, #300, Beverly Hills CA 90212 USA — Director

**McNamara, William (Billy)**
Venture I A B, 3211 Cahuenga Blvd W, #104, Los Angeles CA 90068, USA — Actor

**McNamee, Jessica**
United Talent Agency, U T A Plaza, 9336 Civic Center Dr, Beverly Hills CA 90210 USA — Actress

**McNanie, Sean**
261 26th St, Del Mar CA 92014, USA — Football Player

**McNaught, Judith**
Random House, 1745 Broadway, #1800, New York NY 10019 USA — Writer

**McNaughton, John D**
Gersh Agency, 9465 Wilshire Blvd, #600, Beverly Hills CA 90212 USA — Director, Producer, Writer

**McNaughton, Robert F, Jr**
2511 15th St, Troy NY 12180, USA — Computer Scientist

**McNeal, Donald (Don)**
3311 Toledo Plaza, Coral Gables FL 33134, USA — Football Player

**McNeal, Travis**
4707 40th Place N, Birmingham AL 35217, USA — Football Player

**McNealy, Scott G**
Sun Microsystems, 4150 Network Circle, Santa Clara CA 95054, USA — Businessman

**McNeely, Jeffrey L (Jeff)**
405 Everette St, Monroe NC 28112, USA — Baseball Player

**McNeil, Clifton A**
1001 Westbury Dr, #98, Mobile AL 36609, USA — Football Player

**McNeil, Freeman**
PO Box 62, Greenlawn NY 11740, USA — Football Player

**McNeil, Kate**
1743 N Dillon St, Los Angeles CA 90026, USA — Actress

**McNeil, Lori**
International Mangement Group, 1 Erieview Plaza, 1360 E 9th St, #100, Cleveland OH 44114 USA — Tennis Player

**McNeil, Patrick (Pat)**
2117 US Highway 80 E, Mesquite TX 75150, USA — Football Player

**McNeil, Ryan D**
315 14th St NW, Atlanta GA 30318, USA — Football Player

**McNeill, Corbin A, Jr**
P E C O Energy Co, 2301 Market St, Philadelphia PA 19103, USA — Businessman

**McNeill, Dan K**
Logistics Co, 3400 Walsh Parkway, Fayetteville NC 28311, USA — Army General

**McNeill, Frederick A (Fred)**
3500 W Manchester Blvd, #320, Inglewood CA 90305, USA — Football Player

**McNeill, Robert Duncan**
Stone Meyer Genow, 9665 Wilshire Blvd, #510, Beverly Hills CA 90212 USA — Actor

**McNeill, Robert J (Bob)**
1318 Wooded Way, Bryn Mawr PA 19010, USA — Basketball Player

**McNeill, Thomas G (Tom)**
31019 Torrey Road, Waller TX 77484, USA — Football Player

**McNeill, W Donald (Don)**
2165 15th Ave, Vero Beach FL 32960, USA — Tennis Player

**McNerney, W James, Jr**
Boeing Co, 100 N Riverside, Chicago IL 60606, USA — Businessman

**McNertney, Gerald E (Jerry)**
1124 10th St, Nevada IA 50201, USA — Baseball Player

**McNichol, Kristy**
Good Guy Entertainment, 3733 Oakfield Dr, Sherman Oaks CA 91423, USA — Actress

**McNish, Allan**
C S S Stellar Mgmt, 34-43 Russell St, London WC2B 5HA, England — Auto Racing Driver

**McNiven, Julie**
Don Buchwald Talent Agency, 6500 Wilshire Blvd, #2200, Los Angeles CA 90048 USA — Actress

**McNorton, Bruce E**
PO Box 672, Bloomfield Hills MI 48303, USA — Football Player

**McNutt, Stephen F**
Innovative Artists, 1505 10th St, Santa Monica CA 90401 USA — Cinematographer

**McOmie, Maggie**
Arthouse Talent, 107 SE Washington St, #156, Portland OR 97214, USA — Actress

**M'Cormack, Adetokumboh**
Hofflund/Polone, 9465 Wilshire Blvd, #420, Beverly Hills CA 90212 USA — Actor

**McPartlin, Anthony (Ant)**
B/W/R, 292 Madison Ave, #900, New York NY 10017, USA — Actor, Producer

**McPartlin, Ryan**
Evolution Entertainment, 901 N Highland Ave, Los Angeles CA 90038 USA — Actor, Model

**McPeak, Merrill A (Tony)**
123 Furnace St, Lake Oswego OR 97034, USA — Air Force General

**McPhee, John A**
475 Drake's Corner Road, Princeton NJ 08540, USA — Writer

**McPhee, Jonathan**
PO Box 1425, Marblehead MA 01945, USA — Conductor

**McPhee, Katharine H**
Schiff Co, 9220 Sunset Blvd, #106, West Hollywood CA 90069 USA — Singer, Actress

**McPhee, Kodi Smit**
I C M Partners, 10250 Constellation Blvd, #900, Los Angeles CA 90067 USA — Actor

**McPhee, Martha**
Wylie Agency, 250 W 57th St, #2114, New York NY 10107 USA — Writer

**McPhee, Mike**
16 Brook Point Road, Tantallon NS B3Z 2R3, Canada — Ice Hockey Player

McNamara - McPhee

**McPherson, Charles** — Jazz Saxophonist
Joel Chriss Co, 300 Mercer St, #3J, New York NY 10003 USA
**McPherson, Dallas L** — Baseball Player
219 Gold Crest Dr, Braselton GA 30517, USA
**McPherson, Donald G (Don)** — Football Player
Sports Leadership Institute, Adelphi University, Garden City NY 11530, USA
**McPherson, James A** — Writer
Little Brown, 3 Center Plaza, #100, Boston MA 02108 USA
**McPherson, James M** — Historian
15 Randall Road, Princeton NJ 08540, USA
**McPherson, John** — Cartoonist (Close to Home)
Universal Press Syndicate, 4520 Main St, #700, Kansas City MO 64111 USA
**McPherson, Kristy** — Golfer
Ladies Pro Golf Assn, 100 International Golf Dr, Daytona Beach FL 32124 USA
**McQuarrie, Christopher** — Writer, Director, Producer
Invisible Ink, 9696 Culver Blvd, #203, Culver City CA 90232, USA
**McQuarters, Robert W (R W)** — Football Player
1548 E 54th St N, Tulsa OK 74126, USA
**McQueen, Chad** — Actor
8306 Wilshire Blvd, #438, Beverly Hills CA 90211, USA
**McQueen, Cozell** — Basketball Player
100 E Charing Cross, Cary NC 27513, USA
**McQueen, Michael R (Mike)** — Baseball Player
6623 Lost Horizon Dr, Austin TX 78759, USA
**McQueen, Steven R** — Actor
Schiff Co, 9220 Sunset Blvd, #106, West Hollywood CA 90069 USA
**McQueen, Steven R (Steve)** — Artist, Director, Producer
Casorotto Ramsay, Waverley House, 7-12 Noel St, London W1F 8GQ, England
**McQueen, Tanya** — Actress
Generate, 1545 26th St, #200, Santa Monica CA 90404, USA
**McQuilken, Kim E** — Football Player
360 Highgrove Dr, Fayetteville GA 30215, USA
**McQuistion, Patricia E** — Army General
Deputy Commanding General, US Army Material Command, 4400 Martin Road, Redstone Arsenal AL 35898, USA
**McRae, Basil** — Ice Hockey Player
759 Hyde Park Road, #252, London ON N6H 3S2, Canada
**McRae, Benjamin P (Bennie)** — Football Player
532 W 143rd St, #63, New York NY 10031, USA
**McRae, Charles E** — Football Player
PO Box 30527, Knoxville TN 37930, USA
**McRae, Harold O (Hal)** — Baseball Player, Manager
519 Sand Crane Court, Bradenton FL 34212, USA
**McRae, Jordan T** — Basketball Player
Philadelphia 76ers, 1st Union Center, 3601 S Broad St, Philadelphia PA 19148 USA
**McRae, Mo** — Actor
Creative Artists Agency, 2000 Ave of Stars, #100, Los Angeles CA 90067 USA
**McRae, Shane** — Actor
Gersh Agency, 9465 Wilshire Blvd, #600, Beverly Hills CA 90212 USA
**McRaney, Gerald** — Actor
217 Keller St, Bay Saint Louis MS 39520, USA
**McReynolds, Jesse L** — Singer, Mandolin Player (Jim & Jesse)
PO Box 304, Gallatin TN 37066, USA
**McReynolds, W Kevin** — Baseball Player
2 Country Place, Roland AR 72135, USA
**McRobbie, Michael A** — Educator
Indiana University, President's Office, 107 S Indiana, Bloomington IN 47405, USA
**McRobbie, Peter** — Actor
Abrams Artists, 9200 W Sunset Blvd, #1125, West Hollywood CA 90069 USA
**McRoberts, Joshua S (Josh)** — Basketball Player
Miami Heat, American Airlines Arena, 601 Biscayne Blvd, Miami FL 33132 USA
**McRoy, Robert L (Spike), Jr** — Golfer
742 Mira Vista Dr SE, Huntsville AL 35802, USA
**McShane, Ian** — Actor
McShane Productions, 30 New Bridge St, London EC4V 6BJ, England
**McShera, Sophie** — Actress
Curtis Brown Group, 28-29 Haymarket St, #500, London SW1Y 4SP, England
**McSorley, Gerard** — Actor
Insight Mgmt, 1134 S Cloverdale Ave, Los Angeles CA 90019 USA
**McSorley, Marty** — Ice Hockey Player
3301 The Strand, Hermosa Beach CA 90254, USA
**McSwain, Rodney (Rod)** — Football Player
5393 Stonewood Dr, Hickory NC 28602, USA
**McTavish, Graham** — Actor
Stone Manners Salners, 6100 Wilshire Blvd, #1500, Los Angeles CA 90035 USA
**McTeer, Janet** — Actress
Curtis Brown Group, 28-29 Haymarket St, #500, London SW1Y 4SP, England
**McTeigue, James** — Director
Nikki Weiss Co, 754 N La Jolla Ave, Los Angeles CA 90046, USA
**McTiernan, John** — Director
Paradigm Agency, 360 N Crescent Dr, North Building, Beverly Hills CA 90210 USA
**McVey, Robert P** — Ice Hockey Player
3333 NE 34th St, #1522, Fort Lauderdale FL 33308, USA
**McVicar, Daniel** — Actor
1704 Oak St S, Santa Monica CA 90405, USA
**McVie, Christine** — Singer (Fleetwood Mac), Songwriter
406 Poplar Dr, Wilmette IL 60091, USA
**McVie, John** — Bassist (Fleetwood Mac), Songwriter
4224 Waialae Ave, Honolulu HI 96816, USA
**McVie, Tom** — Ice Hockey Coach
5713 Willow Springs Highway, Ferndale WA 98248, USA
**McWhirter, Jillian** — Actress
PO Box 6308, Beverly Hills CA 90212, USA
**McWilliams, Brian** — Labor Leader
Longshoremen/Warehousemen Union, 1188 Franklin St, San Francisco CA 94109, USA
**McWilliams, Fleming** — Singer
Michael Dixon Mgmt, 119 Pebble Creek Road, Franklin TN 37064, USA

**McWilliams, Johnny** — Football Player
4540 E Blue Spruce Lane, Gilbert AZ 85298, USA
**McWilliams, Larry D** — Baseball Player
5113 Park Road 21, Cleburne TX 76033, USA
**McWilliams-Franklin, Taj** — Basketball Player
Washington Mystics, Verizon Center, 401 9th St NW, #750, Washington DC 20004 USA
**Meacham, Jon** — Writer
Random House, 1745 Broadway, #1800, New York NY 10019 USA
**Meacham, Mildred** — Baseball Player
6053 Wilora Lake Road, #301, Charlotte NC 28212, USA
**Meacham, Robert A (Bobby)** — Baseball Player
20610 Prince Creek Dr, Katy TX 77450, USA
**Meacham, Russell L (Rusty)** — Baseball Player
1906 Eden Glen Lane, Pearland TX 77581, USA
**Meachem, Robert** — Football Player
New Orleans Saints, 5800 Airline Highway, Metairie LA 70003 USA
**Mead, Chuck** — Guitarist (BR5-149)
Thirty Tigers, 1604 8th Ave S, #200, Nashville TN 37203, USA
**Mead, Courtland** — Actor
I C M Partners, 10250 Constellation Blvd, #900, Los Angeles CA 90067 USA
**Mead, Dana G** — Businessman
300 Boylston St, #1103, Boston MA 02116, USA
**Mead, Lee S** — Actor, Singer
Artist Rights Group, 4A Exmoor St, London W10 6BD, England
**Mead, Shepherd** — Writer
53 Rivermead Court, London SW6 3RY, England
**Meade, Angela** — Opera Singer
I M G Artists, Hogarth Business Park, Chiswick, London W4 2TH, England
**Meade, Carl J** — Astronaut
15013 Live Oak Springs Canyon Road, Canyon Country CA 91387, USA
**Meador, Eddie D (Ed)** — Football Player
1135 Padgett Hill Road, Natural Bridge VA 24578, USA
**Meadows, Brian** — Baseball Player
917 Butter & Egg Road, Troy AL 36081, USA
**Meadows, Jayne** — Actress
16185 Woodvale Road, Encino CA 91436, USA
**Meadows, Michael R (Louie)** — Baseball Player
110 Heavens Lane, Maysville NC 28555, USA
**Meadows, Shane** — Director
Casorotto Ramsay, Waverley House, 7-12 Noel St, London W1F 8GQ, England
**Meadows, Stephen** — Actor
1760 Courtney Ave, Los Angeles CA 90046, USA
**Meadows, Tim** — Actor, Comedian
A P A Talent & Literary Agency, 405 S Beverly Dr, #300, Beverly Hills CA 90212 USA
**Meadows, William H** — Association Executive
Wilderness Society, President's Office, 1615 M St NW, Washington DC 20036, USA
**Meads, D Donald (Don)** — Baseball Player
3220 Cypress Way, Santa Rosa CA 95405, USA
**Meads, Johnny s** — Football Player
9419 Pine Lilly Court, Navarre FL 32566, USA
**Meagher, Mary T** — Swimmer
404 Vanderwall, Peachtree City GA 30269, USA
**Meagher, Rick** — Ice Hockey Player
2698 Innisfil Road, Mississauga ON L5M 4J2, Canada
**Mealing, Amanda** — Actress
Curtis Brown Group, 28-29 Haymarket St, #500, London SW1Y 4SP, England
**Meaney, Colm** — Actor
Troika, 74 Clerkenwell Road, #300, London EC1M 5QA, England
**Meaney, Kevin** — Actor, Comedian, Writer
OmniPop Talent Group, 4605 Lankershim Blvd, #201, Toluca Lake CA 91602 USA
**Means, David** — Writer
Wylie Agency, 250 W 57th St, #2114, New York NY 10107 USA
**Means, Natrone J** — Football Player
14602 Greenpoint Lane, Huntersville NC 28078, USA
**Means, Winslow** — Basketball Player
1336 Arch St, Zanesville OH 43701, USA
**Meany, Colm** — Actor
Troika, 74 Clerkenwell Road, #300, London EC1M 5QA, England
**Meara, Anne** — Actress, Comedienne
118 Riverside Dr, #5A, New York NY 10024, USA
**Meares, Patrick J (Pat)** — Baseball Player
8405 E Bridlewood St, Wichita KS 67206, USA
**Mears, Casey J** — Auto Racing Driver
4300 Sharon Road, #222, Charlotte NC 28211, USA
**Mears, Derek** — Actor
Kazarian/Measures/Ruskin, 11969 Ventura Blvd, #300, Studio City CA 91604 USA
**Mears, F Gary** — Singer, Guitarist (Casuals)
12170 Country Road 215, Tyler TX 75707, USA
**Mears, Rick R** — Auto Racing Driver
1536 NW Buttonbush Circle, Palm City FL 34990, USA
**Mears, Roger, Sr** — Truck Racing Driver
PO Box 520, Terrell NC 28682, USA
**Mears, Walter R** — Journalist
Associated Press, Editorial Dept, 2021 K St NW, #600, Washington DC 20006, USA
**Meat Loaf** — Singer, Actor
Greene Assoc, 1901 Ave of Stars, #130, Los Angeles CA 90067 USA
**Mebane, Brandon J** — Football Player
2310 SE 2nd Court, Renton WA 98056, USA
**Mecchi, Irene** — Writer
Abrams Artists, 9200 W Sunset Blvd, #1125, West Hollywood CA 90069 USA
**Meche, Gilbert A (Gil)** — Baseball Player
6513 Ridge Road, Kansas City MO 64152, USA
**Mechler, Pia** — Actress
Spielkind, Zimmerstr 11, 10969 Berlin, Germany
**Mechlowicz, Scott** — Actor
Management 360, 9111 Wilshire Blvd, Beverly Hills CA 90210 USA

**Meciar, Vladimir** — Prime Minister, Slovakia
Urad Vlady SR, Nam Slobody 1, 81370 Bratislava, Slovakia
**Mecir, James M (Jim)** — Baseball Player
3679 Annis Circle, Pleasanton CA 94588, USA
**Mecklenburg, Karl B** — Football Player
6372 S Zenobia Court, Littleton CO 80123, USA
**Medak, Peter** — Director
Gersh Agency, 9465 Wilshire Blvd, #600, Beverly Hills CA 90212 USA
**Medavoy, Mike** — Businessman, Producer
Phoenix Pictures, 10203 Santa Monica Blvd, #400, Los Angeles CA 90067, USA
**Medders, Brandon E** — Baseball Player
9732 Charolais Dr, Tuscaloosa AL 35405, USA
**Meddick, Jim** — Cartoonist (Monty)
United Feature Syndicate, PO Box 5610, Cincinnati OH 45201 USA
**Medeiros, Glenn** — Singer
PO Box 8, Lawai HI 96765, USA
**Medford, Paul J** — Actor, Choreographer
Gavin Barker Assoc, 2D Wimpole St, London W1G 0EB, England
**Mediate, Rocco** — Golfer
2548 Medina Circle, Medina WA 98039, USA
**Medich, George F (Doc)** — Baseball Player
3007 Woodfield Dr, Aliquippa PA 15001, USA
**Medina Estevez, Jorge Arturo Cardinal** — Religious Leader
Divine Worship Congregation, Palazzo Congregazioni, Piazza Pio XII 10, 00193 Rome, Italy
**Medina Sanchez, Dasnilo** — President, Dominican Republic
Palacio Nacional, Calle Moises Garcia, Ave Mexico, Santo Domingo, Dominican Republic
**Medlen, Kristopher A (Kris)** — Baseball Player
2161 Technology Place, Long Beach CA 90810, USA
**Medley, Bill** — Singer (Righteous Brothers)
Barry Rillera, 9841 Hot Springs Dr, Huntington Beach CA 92646, USA
**Medoff, Mark H** — Writer
PO Box 3072, Las Cruces NM 88003, USA
**Medved, Aleksandr V** — Freestyle Wrestler
Belarussian State University, Sports Excellence Dept, 220030 Minsk, Belarus
**Medved, Ronald G (Ron)** — Football Player
6615 239th Ave E, Buckley WA 98321, USA
**Medvedenko, Stanislav (Slava)** — Basketball Player
1700 Ruhland Ave, Manhattan Beach CA 90266, USA
**Medvedev, Andrei** — Tennis Player
Association of Tennis Professionals, 201 A T P Blvd, Ponte Vedra Beach FL 32082 USA
**Medvedev, Dmitri A** — Prime Minister, Russia
Prime Minister's Office, Krasnopresnenskaya Nab 2, 103274 Moscow, Russia
**Medvedev, Zhores A** — Biologist
4 Osborn Gardens, London NW7 1DY, England
**Medvin, Scott H** — Baseball Player
673 Lynbrook Ave, Tonawanda NY 14150, USA
**Medway, Heather** — Actress
A P A Talent & Literary Agency, 405 S Beverly Dr, #300, Beverly Hills CA 90212 USA
**Medwin, Michael** — Actor
I C M Partners, Marlborough House, 10 Earlham St, #300, London WC2H 9LNP, England
**Mee, L Darnell** — Basketball Player
2005 Westland Dr SW, #1201, Cleveland TN 37311, USA
**Meehan, Gerald M (Gerry)** — Ice Hockey Player
2 Dafoe Court, Aurora ON L4G 7C8, Canada
**Meehan, Martin T (Marty)** — Educator; Representative, MA
University of Massachusetts, Chancellor's Office, Lowell MA 01854, USA
**Meeke, Brent** — Ice Hockey Player
11331 Whitetail Run St NW, Bolivar OH 44612, USA
**Meeker, Howie** — Ice Hockey Player, Coach, Sportscaster
979 Dickinson Way, Parksville BC V9P 1Z7, Canada
**Meeks, Jodie** — Basketball Player
Detroit Pistons, Palace, 4 Championship Dr, Auburn Hills MI 48326 USA
**Meeks, Robert E (Bob)** — Football Player
PO Box 29734, Denver CO 80229, USA
**Meeler, C Philip (Phil)** — Baseball Player
102 Pine St, Knightdale NC 27545, USA
**Meena** — Actress
58 2nd St, Venkatesh Nagar, Virugambakkam, Chennai TN 600092, India
**Meents, Scott** — Basketball Player
4231 155th Place SE, Bellevue WA 98006, USA
**Meese, Edwin, III** — Attorney General
1800 Old Meadow Road, #810, Mc Lean VA 22102, USA
**Meester, Bradley R (Brad)** — Football Player
7644 Chipwood Lane, Jacksonville FL 32256, USA
**Meester, Leighton** — Actress, Singer
W M E Entertainment, 9601 Wilshire Blvd, #300, Beverly Hills CA 90210 USA
**Meeuwsen, Terry A** — Beauty Queen, Singer, Entertainer
Pat Robertson's 700 Club, 977 Centerville Turnpike, Virginia Beach VA 23463, USA
**Megaton, Olivier** — Director
W M E Entertainment, 9601 Wilshire Blvd, #300, Beverly Hills CA 90210 USA
**Meggysey, David M (Dave)** — Football Player
2528 Benvenue Ave, Berkeley CA 94704, USA
**MeGrew, Mike** — Baseball Player
25 Karen Dr, Hope Valley RI 02832, USA
**Mehl, Lance A** — Football Player
44920 Kacsmar Estates Dr, Saint Clairsville OH 43950, USA
**Mehldau, Brad** — Jazz Pianist
International Music Network, 278 Main St, Gloucester MA 01930, USA
**Mehleb, Ibrahim** — Prime Minister, Egypt
Prime Minister's Office, PO Box 191, 1 Majlis El-Shaab St, Cairo CA104, Egypt
**Mehra, Smriti** — Golfer
4038 Greystone Dr, Clermont FL 34711, USA
**Mehring, Sona** — Social Activist
CaringBridge, PO Box 6032, Albert Lea MN 56007, USA
**Mehringer, David M** — Astronomer
University of Illinois, Astronomy Dept, Champaign IL 61820, USA

# M

**Mehta, Deepa** — Director, Writer
I C M Partners, 10250 Constellation Blvd, #900, Los Angeles CA 90067 USA
**Mehta, Sujata** — Actress
56 Dev Chhaya Tardeo Haji Ali Road, Tardeo, Mumbai MS 400034, India
**Mehta, Ved P** — Writer
139 E 79th St, New York NY 10075, USA
**Mehta, Zubin** — Conductor
27 Oakmont Dr, Los Angeles CA 90049, USA
**Meidani, Rexhep** — President, Albania
Club de Madrid, C/Goya 5-7, Pasaje 2, 28001 Madrid, Spain
**Meier, David K (Dave)** — Baseball Player
523 W Stuart Ave, Fresno CA 93704, USA
**Meier, Dieter** — Synthesizer Player (Yello)
Creative Artists Agency, 2000 Ave of Stars, #100, Los Angeles CA 90067 USA
**Meier, Raymond** — Photographer
Raymond Meier Photography, 532 Broadway, #800, New York NY 10012, USA
**Meier, Richard A** — Pritzker Architectural Laureate
Richard Meier Partners, 475 10th Ave, #600, New York NY 10018, USA
**Meier, Robert J D (Rob)** — Football Player
7551 Scarlet Ibis Lane, Jacksonville FL 32256, USA
**Meier, Shadley B (Shad)** — Football Player
4001 Skyline Dr, Nashville TN 37215, USA
**Meier, Waltraud** — Opera Singer
Hilbert Artists Mgmt, Maximilanstr 22, 80539 Munich, Germany
**Meieran, Andrew** — Director, Producer
W M E Entertainment, 9601 Wilshire Blvd, #300, Beverly Hills CA 90210 USA
**Meiers, Shallan A** — Model
Playboy Promotions, 9346 Civic Center Dr, #200, Beverly Hills CA 90210 USA
**Meighan, Tom** — Singer (Kasabian)
International Talent Booking, Ariel House, 74A Charlotte St, #100 London W1T 4QJ, England
**Meigs, Montgomery C** — Army General
Business Executives for National Security, 1030 15th St NW, #200 East, Washington DC 20005, USA
**Meili, Launi** — Markswoman
2001 Wagon Gap Trail, Monument CO 80132, USA
**Meilinger, Steven F (Steve)** — Football Player
719 Camino Road, Lexington KY 40502, USA
**Meindl, James D** — Electrical Engineer
Georgia Institute of Technology, Microelectronics Center, Atlanta GA 30332, USA
**Meine, Klaus** — Singer, Guitarist (Scorpions)
Scorpions Musikproductions, Bohlenweg 8, 30835 Langenhagen, Germany
**Meinwald, Jerrold** — Chemist
429 Warren Road, Ithaca NY 14850, USA
**Meirelles, Fernando** — Director
O2 Films, Rua Heliopolis 410, Vila Hamburguesa, Sao Paulo SP 05318 010, Brazil
**Meisel, Stephen** — Photographer
64 Wooster St, New York NY 10012, USA
**Meiselas, Susan** — Photographer
256 Mott St, New York NY 10012, USA
**Meisner, Gregory P (Greg)** — Football Player
229 Carr Dr, Ligonier PA 15658, USA
**Meisner, Joachim Cardinal** — Religious Leader
Archdiocese of Cologne, Marzellenstr 32, 50668 Cologne, Germany
**Meisner, Randy** — Bassist, Singer (Eagles, Poco)
Rick Alter Mgmt, 1018 17th Ave S, #12, Nashville TN 37212, USA
**Meister, Elisabeth** — Opera Singer
I M G Artists, Hogarth Business Park, Chiswick, London W4 2TH, England
**Meixler, Edward (Ed)** — Football Player
13812 Hastings Farm Road, Huntersville NC 28078, USA
**Meja** — Singer (Legacy of Sound), Composer
Basic Music Mgmt, Norrtullsgatan 51, 113 45 Stockholm, Sweden
**Mejia, Jorge Maria Cardinal** — Religious Leader
Vatican Secret Archives, Biblioteca Apostolica Vaticina, 00120 Vatican City
**Mejia, Paul R** — Ballet Dancer, Choreographer
Fort Worth Ballet, 6848 Green Oaks Road, Fort Worth TX 76116, USA
**Mejias, Roman G** — Baseball Player
27325 Terrytown Road, Sun City CA 92586, USA
**Mekhissi-Benabbad, Mahiedine** — Track Athlete
2 Place Georges Braque, 51100 Reims, France
**Mekka, Eddie** — Actor
9925 W Russell Road, #2106, Las Vegas NV 89148, USA
**Mekki, Smail** — Actor
Cineart, 28 Rue Mogador, 78009 Paris, France
**Melamed, Lisa** — Producer
Paradigm Agency, 360 N Crescent Dr, North Building, Beverly Hills CA 90210 USA
**Melamid, Aleksander** — Artist
53 Lisspenard St, New York NY 10013, USA
**Melancon, Charles J (Charlie)** — Representative, LA
International Franchise Assn, 1501 K St NW, #350, Washington DC 20005, USA
**Melancon, Mei** — Actress
Intellectual Artists Mgmt, 10585 Santa Monica Blvd, #135, Los Angeles CA 90025, USA
**Melanie** — Singer, Guitarist, Songwriter
53 Baymont St, #5, Clearwater Beach FL 33767, USA
**Melanson, Roland (Rollie)** — Ice Hockey Player
728 Rue Pierre Biard, Boucherville QC J4B 7R3, Canada
**Melbardis, Oskars** — Bobsled Athlete
Bobsled Federation, Roberta Feldmana 11, Riga 1014, Latvia
**Melcher, John** — Senator, MT
2519 Wylie Ave, Missoula MT 59802, USA
**Melchionni, Gary D** — Basketball Player
1040 Grandview Blvd, Lancaster PA 17601, USA
**Melchionni, William P (Bill)** — Basketball Player
115 Whitehall Blvd, Garden City NY 11530, USA
**Melchior, Ib** — Writer
8228 Marymount Lane, Los Angeles CA 90069, USA
**Mele, Sabath A (Sam)** — Baseball Player, Manager
340 Adams St, Quincy MA 02169, USA

**Mele-Mel** — Rap Artist
Groove Entertainment, 1005 N Alfred St, #2, West Hollywood CA 90069, USA

**Melendez, John (Stuttering)** — Actor, Comedian
Paradigm Agency, 360 N Crescent Dr, North Building, Beverly Hills CA 90210 USA

**Melendez, Lisette** — Singer
La' Entertainment Booking, 2834 Rosemeade Dr, Monroe NC 28110, USA

**Melendez, Ron** — Actor
Jay D Schwartz Assoc, 3151 Cahuenga Blvd W, #220, Los Angeles CA 90068, USA

**Melhuse, Adam M** — Baseball Player
6940 Avila Valley Dr, San Luis Obispo CA 93405, USA

**Melinda** — Illusionist
Miracle Mile Shops, 3663 Las Vegas Blvd S, #900, Las Vegas NV 89109, USA

**Melini, Angela** — Model, Actress
Playboy Promotions, 9346 Civic Center Dr, #200, Beverly Hills CA 90210 USA

**Mellanby, Scott** — Ice Hockey Player
2548 Town and Country Lane, Saint Louis MO 63131, USA

**Mellekas, John S** — Football Player
498 Broadway, Newport RI 02840, USA

**Mellencamp, John** — Singer, Songwriter
Belmont Mall Studio, 5087 Lower Schooner Road, Nashville IN 47448, USA

**Mello, Craig C** — Nobel Medicine Laureate
25 Fessenden Road, Barrington RI 02806, USA

**Mello, Tamara** — Actress
A P A Talent & Literary Agency, 405 S Beverly Dr, #300, Beverly Hills CA 90212 USA

**Mellons, Ken** — Singer, Guitarist, Songwriter
PO Box 8293, Hermitage TN 37076, USA

**Mellor, James R** — Businessman
23 Shreve Dr, Laguna Beach CA 92651, USA

**Mellor, Thomas R (Tom)** — Ice Hockey Player
63 Spoonhill Ave, Marlborough MA 01752, USA

**Melman, Jeffrey (Jeff)** — Director, Producer
I C M Partners, 10250 Constellation Blvd, #900, Los Angeles CA 90067 USA

**Melnick, Bruce E** — Astronaut
Boeing Aerospace, PO Box 21233, Kennedy Space Center, Orlando FL 32815, USA

**Melnick, Valeriya** — Model
Fashion Model Mgmt, Via Monterosa 80, 20149 Milan, Italy

**Melnyk, Larry** — Ice Hockey Player
1748 Sugarpine Court, Coquitlam BC V3E 3E4, Canada

**Melo, Brian** — Singer, Songwriter
Agency Group Ltd, 142 W 57th St, #600, New York NY 10019 USA

**Meloan, Jonathan M (Jon)** — Baseball Player
8017 Lichtenauer Dr, Lenexa KS 66219, USA

**Meloche, Gilles** — Ice Hockey Player
Pittsburgh Penguins, Consol Energy Center, 1001 5th Ave, Pittsburgh PA 15219 USA

**Meloni, Christopher** — Actor
Gersh Agency, 41 Madison Ave, #3301, New York NY 10010 USA

**Meloy, Colin P H** — Singer, Guitarist (Decemberists)
Big Hassle, 44 Wall St, #2200, New York NY 10005, USA

**Melrose, Barry J** — Ice Hockey Player, Coach
10 Windy Ridge, Glens Falls NY 12801, USA

**Melroy, Pamela A** — Astronaut
3605 14th St N, Arlington VA 22201, USA

**Melson, Sara** — Actress
Jerry Lembo Entertainment Group, 96 Linwood Plaza, #470, Fort Lee NJ 07024, USA

**Melton, Barry** — Singer (Country Joe & the Fish)
PO Box 890983, Sacramento CA 95798, USA

**Melton, William E (Bill)** — Baseball Player
333 E 35th St, Chicago IL 60616, USA

**Meltzer, Allan L** — Economist
Carnegie Mellon University, Economics Dept, Pittsburgh PA 15260, USA

**Meltzer, Brad** — Writer
20533 Biscayne Blvd, #371, Aventura FL 33180, USA

**Melua, Katie** — Singer, Songwriter
Dramatico Ltd, PO Box 214, Farnham, Surrey GU10 5AL, England

**Meluskey, Mitchell W (Mitch)** — Baseball Player
26 Meadowbrooke Road, Yakima WA 98903, USA

**Melvill, Michael W (Mike)** — Astronaut, Test Pilot
24120 Jacaranda Dr, Tehachapi CA 93561, USA

**Melvin, Leland D** — Astronaut
N A S A, Johnson Space Center, 2101 NASA Road, Houston TX 77058 USA

**Melvin, Robert P (Bob)** — Baseball Player, Manager
5637 E Canyon Ridge North Dr, Cave Creek AZ 85331, USA

**Melvoin, Wendy** — Singer, Guitarist
Girl Brothers, 9454 Wilshire Blvd, #711, Beverly Hills CA 90212, USA

**Melzack, Ronald** — Psychologist
51 Banstead Road, Montreal QC H4X 1P1, Canada

**Melzer, Jurgen** — Tennis Player
Champ Events, Werbe und Handelsges, Salmgasse 5/25, 1030 Vienna, Austria

**Memmel, Chellsie M** — Gymnast
171 W 57th St, #8A, New York NY 10019, USA

**Memory, Thara** — Jazz Trumpeter
American Music Program, 116 NE 29th Ave, Portland OR 97232, USA

**Memphis Bleek** — Rap Artist
Green Light Talent Agency, PO Box 3172, Beverly Hills CA 90212 USA

**Mena, Maria V** — Singer, Songwriter
United Talent Agency, U T A Plaza, 9336 Civic Center Dr, Beverly Hills CA 90210 USA

**Menand, Louis** — Historian
New Yorker, Editorial Dept, 4 Times Square, Basement C1B, New York NY 10036 USA

**Menard, Paul** — Auto Racing Driver
T R G Motorsports, 292 Rolling Hill Road, Mooresville NC 28117, USA

**Menaul, Christopher S** — Director
United Agents, 12-26 Lexington St, London W1F 0LE, England

**Mench, Kevin F** — Baseball Player
1305 Danbury Parks Dr, Keller TX 76248, USA

**Menchaca, Penelope** — Entertainer
Telemundo Network Group, 2470 W 8th Ave, Hialeah FL 33010 USA

**Mele-Mel - Menchaca**

**Menchu Tum, Rigoberta** — Nobel Peace Laureate
Av Simeon Canas 4-04 Zona 2, Ciudad de Guatemala, Guatemala

**Mencia, Carlos** — Actor, Comedian, Writer
Brillstein Entertainment Partners, 9150 Wilshire Blvd, #350, Beverly Hills CA 90212 USA

**Menczer, Pauline** — Surfer
6 Burra Burra CL, Ocean Shores NSW 2483, Australia

**Mendel, Gilles** — Fashion Designer
J Mendel, 463 Fashion Ave, #10, New York NY 10018, USA

**Mendel, Nathan G (Nate)** — Bassist (Foo Fighters)
S A M, 722 Seward St, Los Angeles CA 90038, USA

**Mendelsohn, Ben** — Actor
Creative Artists Agency, 2000 Ave of Stars, #100, Los Angeles CA 90067 USA

**Mendelsohn, Carol** — Producer, Writer
W M E Entertainment, 9601 Wilshire Blvd, #300, Beverly Hills CA 90210 USA

**Mendenhall, John R** — Football Player
PO Box 532, Cullen LA 71021, USA

**Mendenhall, Ken E** — Football Player
1708 S Rankin St, Edmond OK 73013, USA

**Mendes, Eva** — Actress, Model
Management 360, 9111 Wilshire Blvd, Beverly Hills CA 90210 USA

**Mendes, Sam** — Director
Creative Artists Agency, 2000 Ave of Stars, #100, Los Angeles CA 90067 USA

**Mendes, Sergio** — Pianist
W M E Entertainment, 9601 Wilshire Blvd, #300, Beverly Hills CA 90210 USA

**Mendez, Akissa** — Singer (Allure)
Universal Attractions, 135 W 26th St, #1200, New York NY 10001 USA

**Mendler, Bridgit** — Actress
Gersh Agency, 9465 Wilshire Blvd, #600, Beverly Hills CA 90212 USA

**Mendoza Moncada, Dayana S** — Beauty Queen, Model
Trump Model Agency, 91 5th Ave, #300, New York NY 10003 USA

**Mendoza, Linda** — Director, Producer
A P A Talent & Literary Agency, 405 S Beverly Dr, #300, Beverly Hills CA 90212 USA

**Mendoza, Mark (Animal)** — Singer, Bassist (Twisted Sister)
Rebellion Entertainment, 2440 Broadway, #111, New York NY 10024, USA

**Mendoza, Martha** — Journalist
Associated Press, Editorial Dept, 450 W 33rd St, #1500, New York NY 10001 USA

**Mendoza, Michael J (Mike)** — Baseball Player
14207 S 20th St, Phoenix AZ 85048, USA

**Mendoza, Natalie J** — Actress, Singer
R G M Artists, 8-12 Ann Street, Surry Hills NSW 2010, Australia

**Mendoza, Ramiro** — Baseball Player
PO Box 7027, Brandon FL 33508, USA

**Menechino, Frank** — Baseball Player
522 Arlene St, Staten Island NY 10314, USA

**Meneses, Alex** — Actress
Pakula/King, 9229 W Sunset Blvd, #315, West Hollywood CA 90069 USA

**Meneses, Antonio** — Concert Cellist
Concert/Spectacle Agency, 29 Rue Couloureniere, 1204 Geneva, Switzerland

**Meneve, Russ** — Actor, Comedian
C H Entertainment, 6 W 14th St, New York NY 10011, USA

**Menez, Bernard** — Actor, Singer
119 Blvd de Grenelle, 75015 Paris, France

**Menges, Chris** — Cinematographer, Director
Claire Best Assoc, 736 Seward St, Los Angeles CA 90038, USA

**Menhart, Paul G** — Baseball Player
725 Kelsall Dr, Richmond Hill GA 31324, USA

**Menichetti, Roberto** — Fashion Designer
Via Perugina 88, Gubbio (PG), Italy

**Menke, Denis J** — Baseball Player
1246 Berkshire Lane, Tarpon Springs FL 34688, USA

**Menken, Alan** — Composer
Mason Co, 1212 Ave of Americas, #1400, New York NY 10036, USA

**Mennell, Laura** — Actress
I C M Partners, 10250 Constellation Blvd, #900, Los Angeles CA 90067 USA

**Menon, Mambillikalathil G K** — Physicist
C63 Tarang Apts, Mother Dairy Road, Patparganj, Delhi 110092, India

**Menounos, Maria** — Actress, Model
W M E Entertainment, 9601 Wilshire Blvd, #300, Beverly Hills CA 90210 USA

**Mensah, Peter** — Actor
A V O Talent, 5670 Wilshire Blvd, #1930, Los Angeles CA 90036, USA

**Menshov, Vladimir V** — Actor, Director
3D Tverskaya-Yamskaya 52, #29, 125047 Moscow, Russia

**Mentzer, Ethan** — Bassist (Click Five)
Sharp & Focused Mgmt, 323 Broadway St, Cambridge MA 02139, USA

**Menuicucci, Pier Marino** — Co-Regent, San Marino
Co-Regent's Office, Government Palace, 47031 San Marino

**Menzel, Idina** — Actress, Singer
One Entertainment, 347 5th Ave, #1404, New York NY 10016 USA

**Menzel, Jiri** — Director
Divadlo na Vinchradech, Namesti Miru 7, 12000 Prague 2, Czech Republic

**Menzer, Ina** — Boxer
Spotlight Boxing, Am Stadtrand 27, 22047 Hamburg, Germany

**Menzies, Marvin** — Basketball Coach
New Mexico State University, Athletic Dept, Las Cruces NM 88003, USA

**Menzies, Peter G, Jr** — Cinematographer
903 Tahoe Blvd, #802, Incline Village NV 89451, USA

**Menzies, Tobias** — Actor
Paradigm Agency, 360 N Crescent Dr, North Building, Beverly Hills CA 90210 USA

**Menzies-Ulrich, Heather** — Actress
University of Michigan Comprehensive Cancer Center, Urich Sarcoma Research Fund, Ann Arbor MI 48109, USA

**Meola, Tony** — Soccer Player
488 Forest St, Kearny NJ 07032, USA

**Meoli, Rudolph B (Rudy)** — Baseball Player
1211 San Gabriel Ave, Henderson NV 89002, USA

**Meow, Meow** — Opera Singer
I M G Artists, Hogarth Business Park, Chiswick, London W4 2TH, England

**Meraz, Alex** — Actor
Innovative Artists, 1505 10th St, Santa Monica CA 90401 USA
**Merbold, Ulf** — Astronaut, Germany
Am Sonnenhang 4, 53721 Siegburg, Germany
**Mercader, Julio** — Archaeologist
University of Calgary, Archaeology Dept, Calgary AB T2N 1N4, Canada
**Mercado, Orlando L** — Baseball Player
12021 W Louise Court, Sun City AZ 85373, USA
**Merced Villanueva, Orlando L** — Baseball Player
PO Box 190494, San Juan PR 00919, USA
**Mercein, Charles S (Chuck)** — Football Player
59 Club Pointe Dr, White Plains NY 10605, USA
**Mercer, James R** — Singer, Guitarist (Shins)
Nasty Little Man, 110 Greene St, #605, New York NY 10012 USA
**Mercer, Kelvin** — Rap Artist (De La Soul)
Richard Walters, PO Box 2789, Toluca Lake CA 91610 USA
**Mercer, Michael (Mike)** — Football Player
64463 McGrath Road, Bend OR 97701, USA
**Mercer, Robert E** — Businessman
11 Island Estates Parkway, Palm Coast FL 32137, USA
**Mercer, Toby** — Artist
Mercer Studios, 316 E Reserve Dr, Kalispell MT 59901, USA
**Merchant, Larry** — Boxing Sportscaster
470 20th St, Santa Monica CA 90402, USA
**Merchant, Natalie** — Singer, Songwriter
Creative Artists Agency, 2000 Ave of Stars, #100, Los Angeles CA 90067 USA
**Merchant, Stephen** — Producer, Comedian, Actor
W M E Entertainment, 9601 Wilshire Blvd, #300, Beverly Hills CA 90210 USA
**Mercier, Michele** — Actress
Residence Cape di Monte, 06400 Cannes, France
**Mercilus, Whitney** — Football Player
Houston Texans, 2 Reliant Park, Houston TX 77054 USA
**Mercker, Kent H** — Baseball Player
5340 Muirfield Court, Dublin OH 43017, USA
**Merckx, Eddy** — Cyclist
S'Herenweg 11, 1860 Meise, Belgium
**Mercurio, Jed** — Writer
Simon & Schuster, 1230 Ave of Americas, Concourse 1, New York NY 10020 USA
**Mercurio, Paul** — Actor, Singer
Beyond Films, 53-55 Brisbane St, Sunnyhills, Sydney NSW 2010, Australia
**Meredith, O Claiborne (Cla), III** — Baseball Player
3807 Kensington Ave, Richmond VA 23221, USA
**Meredith, Richard O (Dick)** — Ice Hockey Player
26580 Hickory Blvd, Bonita Springs FL 34134, USA
**Meridith, Ronald K (Ron)** — Baseball Player
308 Via Promesa, San Clemente CA 92673, USA
**Meriwether, Elizabeth (Liz)** — Writer, Producer
W M E Entertainment, 9601 Wilshire Blvd, #300, Beverly Hills CA 90210 USA
**Meriwether, Lee** — Actress, Beauty Queen
12139 Jeanette Place, Granada Hills CA 91344, USA
**Merkel, Angela D** — Chancellor, Germany
Bundeskanzlerant, Willy-Brandt-Str 1, 10557 Berlin, Germany
**Merkens, Guido A** — Football Player
8101 Research Forest Dr, Spring TX 77382, USA
**Merkerson, S Epatha** — Actress, Singer
I C M Partners, 10250 Constellation Blvd, #900, Los Angeles CA 90067 USA
**Merkosky, Glenn** — Ice Hockey Player
113 Farr Lane, Queensbury NY 12804, USA
**Merle-Pellet, Carole H** — Alpine Skier
Chalet La Calette, 04400 Super-Sauze, France
**Merletti, Lewis C** — Law Enforcement Official
Cleveland Browns, 76 Lou Groza Blvd, Berea OH 44017 USA
**Merlin, Jan** — Actor
347 N California St, Burbank CA 91505, USA
**Merlo, James L (Jim)** — Football Player
1547 E Starpass Dr, Fresno CA 93730, USA
**Merloni, Louis W (Lou)** — Baseball Player
29 Wild Hunter Road, Dennis MA 02638, USA
**Mero, Rena (Sable)** — Wrestler, Model, Actress
Rena Productions, 760 Valley Stream Dr, Geneva FL 32732, USA
**Meron, Neil** — Producer
Storyline Entertainment, 8335 Sunset Blvd, #207, West Hollywood CA 90069, USA
**Merow, James F** — Judge
US Claims Court, 717 Madison Place NW, Washington DC 20439, USA
**Merrell, Barry** — Ice Hockey Player
253 Raquette St, Winnipeg MB R3K 1M9, Canada
**Merrells, Jason** — Actor
QVoice, 8 Kings St, London WC2E 8HN, England
**Merrick, Doris** — Actress
609 Desert West Dr, Rancho Mirage CA 92270, USA
**Merrick, Marge** — Bowler
Professional Bowlers Association, 719 2nd Ave, #701, Seattle WA 98104 USA
**Merrick, Robert** — Yachtsman
470 Sea Meadow Dr, Portsmouth RI 02871, USA
**Merrick, Wayne** — Ice Hockey Player
68 Chesham Court, London ON N6G 3T4, Canada
**Merrill, Catherine** — Artist
Old Church Pottery, 1456 Florida St, San Francisco CA 94110, USA
**Merrill, Dina** — Actress
TalentWorks, 3500 W Olive Ave, #1400, Burbank CA 91505 USA
**Merrill, Edward W** — Chemical Engineer
90 Somerset St, Belmont MA 02478, USA
**Merrill, Mark C** — Football Player
782 Mimosa Lane, Saint Paul MN 55112, USA
**Merrill, Robbie** — Bassist (Godsmack, Everclear)
Front Line Mgmt, 1100 Glendon Ave, #2000, Los Angeles CA 90024 USA

| | |
|---|---|
| **Merrill, Stephen E (Steve)**<br>562 Main St, Farmington NH 03835, USA | Governor, NH |
| **Merriman, Ryan**<br>A P A Talent & Literary Agency, 405 S Beverly Dr, #300, Beverly Hills CA 90212 USA | Actor |
| **Merriman, Shawne D**<br>27750 Cowdrey St, #105, Wesley Chapel FL 33544, USA | Football Player |
| **Merriott, Ronald**<br>1271 McDole Dr, Sugar Grove IL 60554, USA | Diver |
| **Merritt, Aries**<br>6104 Indian Wood Circle SE, Mableton GA 30126, USA | Track Athlete |
| **Merritt, Chris**<br>Askonas Holt, Lincoln House, 300 High Holborn, London WC1V 7JH, England | Opera Singer |
| **Merritt, Courtney**<br>Coast to Coast Talent, 3350 Barham Blvd, Los Angeles CA 90068 USA | Actress |
| **Merritt, Gilbert S**<br>US Court of Appeals, US Courthouse, 701 Broadway, Nashville TN 37203, USA | Judge |
| **Merritt, Jack N**<br>US Army Assn, 2425 Wilson Blvd, #100, Arlington VA 22201, USA | Army General |
| **Merritt, James J (Jim)**<br>2777 Blue Spruce Dr, Hemet CA 92545, USA | Baseball Player |
| **Merritt, LaShawn**<br>2617 Markham St, Portsmouth VA 23707, USA | Track Athlete |
| **Merritt, Stephin R**<br>Sacks Co, 427 W 14th St, #300, New York NY 10014, USA | Singer (Magnetic Fields), Songwriter |
| **Merriweather, Daniel P**<br>Roc Nation, 1411 Broadway, #3800, New York NY 10018, USA | Singer, Songwriter |
| **Merriweather, Michael L (Mike)**<br>PO Box 8351, Stockton CA 95208, USA | Football Player |
| **Merrow, Jeffrey C (Jeff)**<br>5989 Shadburn Ferry Road, Buford GA 30518, USA | Football Player |
| **Merrow, Susan**<br>Sierra Club, 85 2nd St, #200, San Francisco CA 94105, USA | Association Executive |
| **Merten, Alan G**<br>George Mason University, President's Office, 4400 University Dr, Fairfax VA 22030, USA | Educator |
| **Merten, Lauri**<br>1010 Del Harbour Dr, Delray Beach FL 33483, USA | Golfer |
| **Mertens, Alan**<br>PacWest Racing Group, PO Box 1717, Bellevue WA 98009, USA | Auto Racing Executive |
| **Mertens, Francois**<br>79 Bonnie Vue Lane, New Milford CT 06776, USA | Cyclist |
| **Mertens, Jerome W (Jerry)**<br>465 Woodside Dr, Woodside CA 94062, USA | Football Player |
| **Merton, Robert C**<br>75 Cambridge Parkway, #E1108, Cambridge MA 02142, USA | Nobel Economics Laureate |
| **Mertz, Edwin T**<br>1504 Via Della Scala, Henderson NV 89052, USA | Biochemist |
| **Mertz, Francis J**<br>54 Woodcrest Dr, Morristown NJ 07960, USA | Educator |
| **Merullo, Matthew B (Matt)**<br>8 Fox Run Road, Madison CT 06443, USA | Baseball Player |
| **Merwin, John D**<br>PO Box 1029, Hudson OH 44236, USA | Governor, VI |
| **Merwin, William Stanley (W S)**<br>Steven Barclay Agency, 12 Western Ave, Petaluma CA 94952, USA | Writer |
| **Merz, Curtis (Curt)**<br>1111 W Seminole St, Springfield MO 65807, USA | Football Player |
| **Merz, Suzanne (Sue)**<br>5 Douglas Dr, Greenwich CT 06831, USA | Ice Hockey Player |
| **Mesa, Jose R N**<br>13080 SW 52nd St, Miramar FL 33027, USA | Baseball Player |
| **Meschery, Thomas N (Tom)**<br>1216 Versailles Ave, Alameda CA 94501, USA | Basketball Player |
| **Meselson, Matthew S**<br>Harvard University, Fairchild Biochemistry Laboratories, Cambridge MA 02138, USA | Biochemist |
| **Mesereau, Thomas D**<br>1875 Century Park E, Los Angeles CA 90067, USA | Attorney |
| **Mesguich, Daniel**<br>Agence Monita Derrieux, 17-21 Rue Duret, 75116 Paris, France | Actor, Director |
| **Mesina Stanley, Dianne**<br>Paradigm Agency, 360 N Crescent Dr, North Building, Beverly Hills CA 90210 USA | Producer, Writer |
| **Mesquida, Roxane**<br>Agence Elisabeth Simpson, 62 Boulevard Du Montparnasse, 75015 Paris, France | Actress |
| **Messenger, Randall J (Randy)**<br>455 Market St, #2240, San Francisco CA 94105, USA | Baseball Player |
| **Messer, L Dale**<br>5449 N Brooks Ave, Fresno CA 93711, USA | Football Player |
| **Messerschmid, Ernst**<br>Universitat Stuttgart, Pfaffenwaldring 31, 70569 Stuttgart, Germany | Astronaut, Germany |
| **Messerschmidt, J Alexander (Andy)**<br>200 Lagunita Dr, Soquel CA 95073, USA | Baseball Player |
| **Messi, Lionel A (Leo)**<br>F C Barcelona, Aristides Maillo S/N, 08028 Barcelona, Spain | Soccer Player |
| **Messier, Eric**<br>9671 Timber Hawk Circle, #22, Littleton CO 80126, USA | Ice Hockey Player |
| **Messier, Mark D**<br>45 Birchwood Dr, Greenwich CT 06831, USA | Ice Hockey Player |
| **Messina, Chris**<br>Brillstein Entertainment Partners, 9150 Wilshire Blvd, #350, Beverly Hills CA 90212 USA | Actor |
| **Messina, James M (Jim)**<br>Direct Management Group, 947 N La Cienega Blvd, #G, West Hollywood CA 90069, USA | Singer, Songwriter |
| **Messina, Jo Dee**<br>Sanctuary Mgmt, 15301 Ventura Blvd, Building B, Sherman Oaks CA 91403, USA | Singer, Songwriter |
| **Messing, Debra**<br>3 Arts Entertainment, 9460 Wilshire Blvd, #700, Beverly Hills CA 90212 USA | Actress |
| **Messinger, Rina**<br>Miss Universe Organization, 1370 Ave of Americas, #1600, New York NY 10019 USA | Beauty Queen |

**Messner, Heinrich (Heini)** — Alpine Skier
Huebenweg 11, 6150 Steinach, Austria
**Messner, Johnny** — Actor
A P A Talent & Literary Agency, 405 S Beverly Dr, #300, Beverly Hills CA 90212 USA
**Messner, Reinhold** — Explorer, Mountaineer
Firmian, Sigmudskronerstr 53, 39100 Bozen, Italy
**Meszaros, Andrej** — Ice Hockey Player
Boston Bruins, 100 Legends Way, #250, Boston MA 02114 USA
**Meszaros, Marta** — Director
MalFilm Studio, Lumumba Utca 174, 1149 Budapest, Hungary
**Metcalf, Eric Q** — Football Player
6027 S Redwing St, Seattle WA 98118, USA
**Metcalf, John** — Writer
128 Lewis St, Ottawa ON K2P 0S7, Canada
**Metcalf, Laurie** — Actress
W M E Entertainment, 9601 Wilshire Blvd, #300, Beverly Hills CA 90210 USA
**Metcalf, Ryan** — Actor
Red Letter Entertainment, 437 W 48th St, #D, New York NY 10036, USA
**Metcalf, Terrance R (Terry)** — Football Player
5112 S Fountain St, Seattle WA 98178, USA
**Metcalf, Terrence O** — Football Player
1524 Jackson Ave E, #9, Oxford MS 38655, USA
**Metcalfe, Jesse** — Actor
Gersh Agency, 9465 Wilshire Blvd, #600, Beverly Hills CA 90212 USA
**Metcalfe, Robert M** — Inventor (Ethernet), Computer Scientist
Polaris Venture Partners, 1000 Winter St, #3350, Waltham MA 02451, USA
**Metcalf-Lindenburger, Dorothy M** — Astronaut
N A S A, Johnson Space Center, 2101 NASA Road, Houston TX 77058 USA
**Metheny, Patrick B (Pat)** — Jazz Guitarist, Composer
Ted Kurland, 173 Brighton Ave, Boston MA 02134 USA
**Method Man** — Rap Artist (Wu-Tang Clan), Actor
Smart Girl Productions, 8335 Sunset Blvd, #222, West Hollywood CA 90069, USA
**Metrano, Art** — Actor
C E S D, 10635 Santa Monica Blvd, #130, Los Angeles CA 90025 USA
**Metro, Charles (Charlie)** — Baseball Player, Manager
7890 Indiana St, Arvada CO 80007, USA
**Metropolit, Glen** — Ice Hockey Player
1070 Redwine Cove Road SW, Dalton GA 30720, USA
**Mette-Marit** — Princess, Norway
Det Kongelige, Slottet, Drammensvein 1, 0010 Oslo, Norway
**Mettifogo, Roberto** — Photographer
Via Montorio 54, 37131 Verona, Italy
**Metz, Thomas F** — Army General
A-T Solutions, 1934 Old Gallows Road, #500, Vienna VA 22182, USA
**Metzelaars, Peter H (Pete)** — Football Player
10640 Pine Valley Path, Indianapolis IN 46234, USA
**Metzger, Clarence E (Butch)** — Baseball Player
641 Rivergate Way, Sacramento CA 95831, USA
**Metzger, Henry** — Immunologist
PO Box 1641, Center Harbor NH 03226, USA
**Metzger, Roger H** — Baseball Player
3560 Bluebonnet Blvd, Brenham TX 77833, USA
**Metzger, Stephane** — Actor
Agence Artiste Adequat, 108 Rue Reaumur, 75002 Paris, France
**Metzner, Raven** — Producer, Writer
W M E Entertainment, 9601 Wilshire Blvd, #300, Beverly Hills CA 90210 USA
**Meuli, Daniela** — Snowboard Athlete
Muehlstra 26, 7260 Davos Dorf, Switzerland
**Meunier-Lebouc, Patricia** — Golfer
176 W Bay Cedar Circle, Jupiter FL 33458, USA
**Mew** — Keyboardist (Elastica)
C E O Mgmt, Ransomes Dock, 35-37 Parkgate Road, London SW11 4NP, England
**Mewes, Jason** — Actor
C E S D, 10635 Santa Monica Blvd, #130, Los Angeles CA 90025 USA
**Mey, Reinhard** — Singer
E M I Music, Postfach 300329, 50773 Cologne, Germany
**Mey, Uwe-Jens** — Speed Skater
Vulkanstr 22, 10367 Berlin, Germany
**Meyer Reyes, Deborah E (Debbie)** — Swimmer
PO Box 2076, Carmichael CA 95609, USA
**Meyer, Aaron** — Concert, Rock Violinist; Composer
PO Box 25486, Portland OR 97298, USA
**Meyer, Breckin** — Actor
I C M Partners, 10250 Constellation Blvd, #900, Los Angeles CA 90067 USA
**Meyer, Dakota L** — Afghanistan War Hero (CMH)
1384 Brockman Keltner Road, Greensburg KY 42743, USA
**Meyer, Daniel J** — Businessman
7655 Annesdale Dr, Cincinnati OH 45243, USA
**Meyer, Daniel L (Dan)** — Baseball Player
433 Cedar Lane, Mickleton NJ 08056, USA
**Meyer, Daniel T (Dan)** — Baseball Player
11540 Marsh Creek Road, Clayton CA 94517, USA
**Meyer, Dina** — Actress
Evolution Entertainment, 901 N Highland Ave, Los Angeles CA 90038 USA
**Meyer, Dirk** — Businessman
Advanced Micro Devices, 1 A M D Place, PO Box 3453, Sunnyvale CA 94088, USA
**Meyer, Edgar** — Concert Double Bassist, Composer
I M G Artists, Carnegie Hall Tower, 152 W 57th St, #500, New York NY 10019 USA
**Meyer, Edward C** — Army General
1101 S Arlington Ridge Road, #1116, Arlington VA 22202, USA
**Meyer, John** — Architect
Meyer/Gifford/Jones, 270 Lafayette St, New York NY 10012, USA
**Meyer, Laurence H** — Economist, Government Official
Federal Reserve Board, 20th St & Constitution Ave NW, Washington DC 20551, USA
**Meyer, Loren H** — Basketball Player
3577 330th St, Ruthven IA 51358, USA

## M

**Meyer, Nicholas** — Director, Writer
Creative Artists Agency, 2000 Ave of Stars, #100, Los Angeles CA 90067 USA
**Meyer, Philipp** — Writer
Ecco/Harper Collins Publishers, 10 E 53rd St, Cellar 1, New York NY 10022, USA
**Meyer, Ron** — Businessman
Universal Studios, 100 Universal City Plaza, Universal City CA 91608, USA
**Meyer, Stephenie** — Writer
Little Brown/Mysterious Press/Warner, 1271 Ave of Americas, New York NY 10020 USA
**Meyer, Urban** — Football Coach
8562 SW 12th Lane, Gainesville FL 32607, USA
**Meyer, Yves F** — Mathematician
Ecole Normale Superieure, 61 Ave President Wilson, 94235 Cachan, France
**Meyer-Landrut, Lena** — Singer, Songwriter
Brainpool, Schanzenstr 22, 51063 Cologne, Germany
**Meyerowitz, Joel** — Photographer
817 W End Ave, #11D, New York NY 10025, USA
**Meyerriecks, Jeffrey** — Concert Guitarist
Lindy Martin Mgmt, 1007 Lakewater Dr, Henrico VA 23229, USA
**Meyers Drysdale, Ann E** — Basketball Player, Sportscaster
235 W Main St, Los Gatos CA 95030, USA
**Meyers Tikalsky, Linda** — Skier
RR 5 Box 265T, Santa Fe NM 87506, USA
**Meyers, Anne Akiko** — Concert Violinist
Colbert Artists, 111 W 57th St, #1416, New York NY 10019 USA
**Meyers, Ari** — Actress
Holly Lebed Personal Mgmt, 10535 Wilshire Blvd, #808, Los Angeles CA 90024, USA
**Meyers, August (Augie)** — Singer, Organist (Sir Douglas Quintet)
Encore Talent, 6803 Crown Ridge, San Antonio TX 78239, USA
**Meyers, Chad W** — Baseball Player
7636 Leawood St, Papillion NE 68046, USA
**Meyers, David** — Director, Writer
Creative Artists Agency, 2000 Ave of Stars, #100, Los Angeles CA 90067 USA
**Meyers, David W (Dave)** — Basketball Player
40629 Carmelina Circle, Temecula CA 92591, USA
**Meyers, Elana** — Bobsled Athlete
Bobsled Federation, 1631 Mesa Ave, #A, Colorado Springs CO 80906, USA
**Meyers, Josh** — Actor, Comedian
Paul Kohner, 9300 Wilshire Blvd, #555, Beverly Hills CA 90212 USA
**Meyers, Nancy** — Director, Producer
Creative Artists Agency, 2000 Ave of Stars, #100, Los Angeles CA 90067 USA
**Meyers, Seth** — Actor, Comedian
Brillstein Entertainment Partners, 9150 Wilshire Blvd, #350, Beverly Hills CA 90212 USA
**Meyfarth, Ulrike Nasse-** — Track Athlete
Buschweg 53, 51519 Odenthal, Germany
**Meyjes, Menno** — Director, Writer
Casorotto Ramsay, Waverley House, 7-12 Noel St, London W1F 8GQ, England
**Meyrowitz, Carol M** — Businesswoman
T J X Companies, 770 Conchitate Road, Framingham MA 01701, USA
**Meyssignac, Emmanuelle** — Actress
Artmedia, 20 Ave Rapp, 75007 Paris, France
**Meyyappan, Meyya** — Nanotechnologist
Ames Research Center, Nanotechnology Center, Moffett Field CA 94035, USA
**Mezentseva, Galina** — Ballerina
Kirov Ballet Theater, 1 Pl Iskusstr, 190000 Saint Petersburg, Russia
**Mezlekia, Nega** — Writer
Picador USA Books, 175 5th Ave, New York NY 10010, USA
**Mezzogiorno, Giovanna** — Actress
Media Art Mgmt, BaRbara de Braganza 11, #4 Derecha, 28004 Madrid, Spain
**Mfume, Kweisi** — Association Executive
3000 Druid Park Dr, Baltimore MD 21215, USA
**MGMT** — Pop, Rock Music Duo
Paradigm Agency, 404 W Franklin St, Monterey CA 93940 USA
**Mhyre, Wencke S** — Singer, Actress
Im Vendia 22, 1315 Nesoya, Norway
**Mi Hyun Kim** — Golfer
Ladies Pro Golf Assn, 100 International Golf Dr, Daytona Beach FL 32124 USA
**Miano, Richard J (Rich)** — Football Player
Miano Sports Bar, 7168 Makaa St, Honolulu HI 96825, USA
**Miartusova, Nella** — Model
Club Nella, PO Box 25, 18200 Prague 8, Czech Republic
**Mica, Daniel L** — Representative, FL
Credit Union National Assn, 601 Pennsylvania NW, #600W, Washington DC 20004, USA
**Micarelli, Lucia** — Concert, Jazz Violinist
I M C, 1155 Boul Ree-Levesque Ouest, #2500, Montreal QC H3B 2K4, Canada
**Miceli, Daniel (Danny)** — Baseball Player
8520 Bowden Way, Windermere FL 34786, USA
**Miceli, Justine** — Actress
Paradigm Agency, 360 N Crescent Dr, North Building, Beverly Hills CA 90210 USA
**Michael** — King, Romania
Villa Serena, 77 Chemin Louis-Degallier, 1290 Versoix-Geneva, Switzerland
**Michael, Eugene R (Gene)** — Baseball Player, Manager, Executive
49 Union Ave, Upper Saddle River NJ 07458, USA
**Michael, George** — Singer, Guitarist, Songwriter
Lippman Entertainment, 23586 Calabasas Road, #208, Calabasas CA 91302, USA
**Michael, M Blane** — Judge
US Appeals Court, 300 Virginia St E, #7602, Charleston WV 25301, USA
**Michael, Richard J (Rich)** — Football Player
957 S Van Ness Ave, San Francisco CA 94110, USA
**Michaelis, Liane** — Handball Player
Gemeinschaftspraxis Hierse & Schmidy, Wintergartenstr 2, 04103 Leipzig, Germany
**Michaell, Monnae** — Actress
Geddes Agency, 8430 Santa Monica Blvd, #201, West Hollywood CA 90069 USA
**Michaels, Alan R (Al)** — Sportscaster
401 S Bristol Ave, Los Angeles CA 90049, USA
**Michaels, Bret** — Singer (Poison)
Agency for Performing Arts, 405 S Beverly Dr, #500, Beverly Hills CA 90212, USA

**Michaels, Ellen** — Model, Photographer
PO Box 1757, New York NY 10021, USA
**Michaels, Fern** — Writer
9 David Court, Edison NJ 08820, USA
**Michaels, Jason D** — Baseball Player
10317 Carroll Cove Place, Tampa FL 33612, USA
**Michaels, Julie** — Actress
PO Box 7304, #149, North Hollywood CA 91603, USA
**Michaels, Lorne** — Producer, Screenwriter
Broadway Video, 1619 Broadway, #900, New York NY 10019, USA
**Michaels, Louis A (Lou)** — Football Player
69 Grace St, Kingston PA 18704, USA
**Michaels, Marilyn** — Actress, Comedienne, Singer
Scotland/Kozak Artist Group, 157 E 57th St, #18B, New York NY 10022, USA
**Michaels, Walter (Walt)** — Football Player, Coach
12 Birch Ave, Wilkes Barre PA 18705, USA
**Michaelsen, Kari** — Actress
Silver Star AG Ltd, 3905 Auto Mall Dr, Westlake Village CA 91362, USA
**Michaels-Moore, Anthony** — Opera Singer
I M G Artists, Burlington Lane, Chiswick, London W4 2TH, England
**Michaelson, Ingrid** — Singer, Pianist/Songwriter
Paradigm Agency, 360 N Crescent Dr, North Building, Beverly Hills CA 90210 USA
**Michalak, Christian M (Chris)** — Baseball Player
1108 Mockingbird Lane, Keller TX 76248, USA
**Michaleczewski, Dariusz** — Boxer
Ul Rajska 4C, 80850 Gdansk, Poland
**Michalek, Zbynek** — Ice Hockey Player
3160 Annandale Dr, Presto PA 15142, USA
**Michalka, Alyson (Aly)** — Singer, Actress
Creative Artists Agency, 2000 Ave of Stars, #100, Los Angeles CA 90067 USA
**Michalka, Amanda J (A J)** — Singer, Actress, Songwriter
Prospect Park, 2049 Century Park E, #2550, Los Angeles CA 90067, USA
**Michals, Duane** — Photographer
109 E 19th St, New York NY 10003, USA
**Micheaux, Larry W** — Basketball Player
2914 Calendar Lake Dr, Missouri City TX 77459, USA
**Micheaux, Nikki** — Actress
Don Buchwald Talent Agency, 6500 Wilshire Blvd, #2200, Los Angeles CA 90048 USA
**Micheel, Shaun** — Golfer
1267 Dubray Lake Circle, Collierville TN 38017, USA
**Michel, Charles D** — Coast Guard Admiral
Deputy Commandant for Operations, USCG Headquarters, 2703 Martin Luther King Ave, Washington DC 20593, USA
**Michel, F Curtis** — Astronaut
2101 University Blvd, Houston TX 77030, USA
**Michel, Hartmut** — Nobel Chemistry Laureate
Max Planck Biophysics Institute, 60438 Frankfurt am Main, Germany
**Michel, James A** — President, Seychelles
President's Office, State House, PO Box 655, Victoria, Mahe, Seychelles
**Michel, Jean-Louis** — Underwater Scientist
I F R E M E R, Center de Toulon, 83500 La Seyne dur Mer, Toulon, France
**Michel, Paul R** — Judge
US Court of Appeals, 717 Madison Place NW, Washington DC 20439, USA
**Michel, Pras** — Rap Artist, Actor
Blue Train Entertainment, 9333 Wilshire Blvd, G Level, Beverly Hills CA 90210 USA
**Michele, Chrisette** — Singer, Songwriter
I C M Partners, 10250 Constellation Blvd, #900, Los Angeles CA 90067 USA
**Michele, Michael** — Actress
Innovative Artists, 1505 10th St, Santa Monica CA 90401 USA
**Micheler, Elisabeth** — Canoeing Athlete
Gruntenstr 45, 86163 Augsburg, Germany
**Micheletti Bain, Roberto** — President, Honduras
Casa Presidencial, Blvd Juan Pablo II, Tegucigalpa MDC, Honduras
**Michell, Keith** — Actor
Chatto & Linnit, 123A King's Road, London SW3 4PL, England
**Michell, Roger** — Director
Independent Talent Group, 40 Whitfield St, London W1T 2RH, England
**Michelle** — Singer, Actress
Kunstlemanagement Uwe Kanthak, Hopfenmarkt 31, 20457 Hamburg, Germany
**Michelle, Candice** — Model, Wrestler, Actress
Abraxas Talent, 4260 Troost Ave, #1, Studio City CA 91604, USA
**Michels, John J** — Football Player
504 Matterhorn Dr, Gatlinburg TN 37738, USA
**Michels, Stephanie** — Actress
C E S D, 10635 Santa Monica Blvd, #130, Los Angeles CA 90025 USA
**Michelson, Claudia** — Actress
Agentur Hoestermann, Gneisenaustr 94, 10961 Berlin, Germany
**Michie, David A R** — Artist
17 Gilmour Road, Edinburgh EH16 5NS, England
**Michiko** — Empress, Japan
Imperial Palace, 1-1 Chiyoda, Chiyodaku, Tokyo 100 0001, Japan
**Michod, David** — Director
Blue-Tongue Films, PO Box 873, Darlinghurst, Sydney NSW 1300, Australia
**Michos, Anastas N** — Cinematographer
I C M Partners, 10250 Constellation Blvd, #900, Los Angeles CA 90067 USA
**Mick** — Drummer (Dave Dee Dozy Beaky Mick Tich)
Gerd Kehren Mgmt, Postfach 1408, 41804 Erkelenz, Germany
**Mickell, Darren** — Football Player
9250 Chelsea Dr, Miramar FL 33025, USA
**Mickelson Cummins, Anna** — Rowing Athlete
Cummins Chiropractic & Wellness, 4122 Factoria Blvd SE #202 Bellevue WA 98006, USA
**Mickelson, Philip A (Phil)** — Golfer
Gaylord Sports Mgmt, 13845 N Northsight Blvd, #200, Scottsdale AZ 85260, USA
**Mickens, Terry K** — Football Player
1420 W McDermott Dr, #838, Allen TX 75013, USA
**Middendorf, Tracy** — Actress
Bauman Redanty Shaul Agency, 5757 Wilshire Blvd, #473, Los Angeles CA 90036 USA

**Middlebrooks, Willie F** — Football Player
18775 SW 78th Court, Cutler Bay FL 33157, USA

**Middleditch, Thomas** — Actor
W M E Entertainment, 9601 Wilshire Blvd, #300, Beverly Hills CA 90210 USA

**Middleton, Clark** — Actor
CornerStone Talent Agency, 37 W 20th St, #1007, New York NY 10011, USA

**Middleton, Darren** — Guitarist (Powderfinger)
Secret Service, PO Box 401, Fortitude Valley QLD 4006, Australia

**Middleton, Richard (Rick)** — Ice Hockey Player
PO Box 1161, Hampton NH 03843, USA

**Middleton, Terdell** — Football Player
1893 Prospect St, Memphis TN 38106, USA

**Middleton, Tuppence** — Actress
United Talent Agency, U T A Plaza, 9336 Civic Center Dr, Beverly Hills CA 90210 USA

**Midgley, John** — Sound Mixer
Creative Media Mgmt, Ealing Studio, Ealing Green, London W5 5EP, England

**Midkiff, Dale** — Actor
Amsel Eisenstadt Frazier, 5055 Wilshire Blvd, #865, Los Angeles CA 90036 USA

**Midler, Bette** — Singer, Actress
1838 2nd Ave, #120, New York NY 10128, USA

**Midori** — Concert Violinist
Midori Foundation, 850 7th Ave, #705, New York NY 10019, USA

**Miechur, Thomas F** — Labor Leader
Cement & Allied Workers Union, 2500 Brickdale, Elk Grove Village IL 60007, USA

**Miele, Rudolf** — Businessman
Miele & Cie, Carl-Miele-Str 29, 33332 Guterslh, Germany

**Mientkiewicz, Douglas A (Doug)** — Baseball Player
810 Lugo Ave, Coral Gables FL 33156, USA

**Miers, Harriet E** — Government Official, Attorney
Locke Liddell Sapp, 901 15th St NW, #900, Washington DC 20005, USA

**Mies, Richard W** — Navy Admiral
Navy Mutual Aid Assn, Directors Board, 29 Carpenter Road, Arlington VA 22214, USA

**Mieske, Matthew T (Matt)** — Baseball Player
2199 E Bombay Road, Midland MI 48642, USA

**Miettinen, Antti** — Ice Hockey Player
Tampa Bay Lightning, 401 Channelside Dr, Tampa FL 33602 USA

**Mifsud Bonnici, Ugo** — President, Malta
18 Erin Serracino Inglott Road, Cospicua, Malta

**Migay, Rudolph J (Rudy)** — Ice Hockey Player
485 Belrose Road, Thunder Bay ON P7G 1K1, Canada

**Migenes, Julia** — Opera Singer
Rainbow High Entertainment, 3500 W Olive Ave, #300, Burbank CA 91505, USA

**Miggins, Lawrence E (Larry)** — Baseball Player
2405 Kingston St, Houston TX 77019, USA

**Migliore, Richard** — Thoroughbred Racing Jockey
48 Killearn Road, Millbrook NY 12545, USA

**Mignola, Mike** — Cartoonist (Hellboy)
Dark Horse Publishing, 10956 SE Main St, Portland OR 97222 USA

**Miguel** — Singer, Songwriter, Producer
W M E Entertainment, 9601 Wilshire Blvd, #300, Beverly Hills CA 90210 USA

**Miguel, Luis** — Singer
Front Line Mgmt, 1100 Glendon Ave, #2000, Los Angeles CA 90024 USA

**Mihm, Christopher S (Chris)** — Basketball Player
4708 Peace Pipe Path, Austin TX 78746, USA

**Mihok, Dash** — Actor
Gersh Agency, 9465 Wilshire Blvd, #600, Beverly Hills CA 90212 USA

**Mijares, Cristian** — Boxer
DiBella Entertainment, 350 7th Ave, #800, New York NY 10001, USA

**Mika** — Singer, Songwriter
Champion Entertainment, 9 E 63rd St, New York NY 10065, USA

**Mikan, G Lawrence (Larry)** — Basketball Player
891 Carmona Court, Chula Vista CA 91910, USA

**Mikati, Najib A** — Prime Minister, Lebanon
Premier's Office, Serail, Place de l'Etoile, Beirut, Lebanon

**Mike-Mayer, Istvan (Steve)** — Football Player
681 Lincoln Ave, Glen Rock NJ 07452, USA

**Mike-Mayer, Nicholas (Nick)** — Football Player
681 Lincoln Ave, Glen Rock NJ 07452, USA

**Mikhalchenko, Alla A** — Ballerina
Malaya Gruzinskaya St 12/18, 123242 Moscow, Russia

**Mikhalkov, Nikita S** — Director
Maly Kozikhinsky Per 4, #16-17, 103001 Moscow, Russia

**Mikita, Stanley (Stan)** — Ice Hockey Player
57 Chesterfield Court, Burr Ridge IL 60527, USA

**Mikkelborg, Palle** — Jazz Trumpeter, Composer
Kjell Kalleklev Mgmt, Georgerne Verft 12, 5011 Bergen, Norway

**Mikkelsen, Lars** — Actor
Conway Van Gelder Grant, 8-12 Broadwick St, #300, London W1F 8HW, England

**Mikkelsen, Mads** — Actor
Arts Mgmt, Kronprinsensgade 9A, 1114 Copenhagen K, Denmark

**Mikkelson, William R (Bill)** — Ice Hockey Player
47 Glen Meadow Crescent, Saint Aliber AB T8N 3A2, Canada

**Mikkelson-Reid, Meaghan** — Ice Hockey Player
Ice Complex, Winter Park, 88 Canada Olympic Road SW, Calgary AB T3B 5R5, Canada

**Miko, Izabella** — Actress
Affirmative Entertainment, 425 N Robertson Blvd, Los Angeles CA 90048, USA

**Mikolaj, Aga** — Opera Singer
Künstleragentur Augstein & Hahn, Tal 28 80331 Munich, Germany

**Miksis, Alfonse K (Al)** — Basketball Player
522 E Algonquin Road, #203, Schaumburg IL 60173, USA

**Mikva, Abner J** — Judge
442 New Jersey Ave SE, Washington DC 20003, USA

**Milacki, Robert (Bob)** — Baseball Player
1873 Martinique Dr, Lake Havasu City AZ 86406, USA

**Milano, Alyssa** — Actress
Creative Artists Agency, 2000 Ave of Stars, #100, Los Angeles CA 90067 USA

**Milano, Dan** — Producer, Writer, Actor
Gersh Agency, 9465 Wilshire Blvd, #600, Beverly Hills CA 90212 USA

**Milanov, Rossen** — Conductor
Princeton Symphony Orchestra, 575 Ewing St, Princeton, NJ 08540, USA

**Milanovic, Zoran** — Prime Minister, Croatia
Prime Minister's Office, Radicev Trg 7, 41000 Zagreb, Croatia

**Milbern, David** — Actor
Regent Entertainment, 10940 Wilshire Blvd, #1600, Los Angeles CA 90024, USA

**Milbourne, Lawrence W (Larry)** — Baseball Player
747 Yale Terrace, Lake Havasu City AZ 86406, USA

**Milbrett, Tiffeny** — Soccer Player
1902 SW Broadleaf Dr, Portland OR 97219, USA

**Milburn, Brendan** — Pianist (GrooveLily), Songwriter
GrooveLily, PO Box 11570, Glendale CA 91226, USA

**Milburn, Glyn C** — Football Player
8815 S 2nd Ave, Inglewood CA 90305, USA

**Milburn, H Theodore** — Judge
440 Alexian Way, #37, Signal Mountain TN 37377, USA

**Milbury, Mike** — Ice Hockey Player, Coach
61 Edwardel Road, Needham MA 02492, USA

**Milch, David** — Producer, Writer
Red Board Productions, 3000 W Olympic Blvd, Building 4, Santa Monica CA 90404, USA

**Milchan, Arnon** — Producer
Regency Enterprises, 4000 Warner Blvd, #66, Burbank CA 91522, USA

**Miledi, Ricardo** — Neurobiologist
9 Gibbs Court, Irvine CA 92617, USA

**Miles, Aaron W** — Baseball Player
1716 San Jose Dr, Davenport IA 52807, USA

**Miles, Darius L** — Basketball Player
1906 Llewellyn Road, Bellevue IL 62223, USA

**Miles, Heather** — Singer, Songwriter
Rounder Records, 1 Rounder Way, Burlington MA 01803 USA

**Miles, Joanna** — Actress
Artists Agency, 9430 Olympic Blvd, Beverly Hills CA 90212 USA

**Miles, John R (Jack)** — Writer
3568 Mountain View Ave, Pasadena CA 91107, USA

**Miles, John W** — Geophysicist
1764 Overlook Lane, Santa Barbara CA 93103, USA

**Miles, Leslie E (Les)** — Football Coach
Lousiana State University, Athletic Dept, Baton Rouge LA 70803, USA

**Miles, Lynn** — Singer, Songwriter
LiveTourArtists, 1451 White Oaks Blvd, Oakville ON L6H 4R9, Canada

**Miles, Ron** — Jazz Trumpeter
Metropolitan State University, Jazz Studies Dept, 1201 5th St, Denver CO 80204, USA

**Miles, Sarah** — Actress
Chithurst Manor, Trotten near Petersfield, Hampshire GU31 5EU, England

**Miles, Sylvia** — Actress
A P A Talent & Literary Agency, 405 S Beverly Dr, #300, Beverly Hills CA 90212 USA

**Miles, Vera** — Actress
PO Box 1599, Palm Desert CA 92261, USA

**Miles-Clark, Jearl** — Track Athlete
J J Clark, University of Florida, Athletic Dept, Gainesville FL 32604, USA

**Milhazes, Beatriz** — Artist
Stephen Friedman Gallery, 25-28 Old Burlington St, London W1S 3AN, England

**Milhoan, Michael** — Actor
TalentWorks, 3500 W Olive Ave, #1400, Burbank CA 91505 USA

**Mili, Itula** — Football Player
4468 Glenmoor Hills Dr, South Jordan UT 84095, USA

**Milian, Christina** — Singer, Actress, Songwriter
Milian Mgmt, 16830 Ventura Blvd, #501, Encino CA 91436, USA

**Miliband, David W** — Government Official, England
House of Commons, Westminster, London SW1A 0AA, England

**Milicevic, Ivana** — Actress, Model
A P A Talent & Literary Agency, 405 S Beverly Dr, #300, Beverly Hills CA 90212 USA

**Milicic, Darko** — Basketball Player
5460 Whitehall Blvd, Oakland Township MI 48306, USA

**Miligulo, Nikolai P** — Gymnast
1691 7th St E, Saint Paul MN 55106, USA

**Milinchik, Joseph M (Joe)** — Football Player
653 Ryan Dr, Allentown PA 18103, USA

**Milinovich, Gia M** — Producer
Sue Rider Mgmt, PO Box 49175, London SW19 3WY, England

**Milioti, Cristin** — Actress
Gersh Agency, 9465 Wilshire Blvd, #600, Beverly Hills CA 90212 USA

**Militzok, Nathan (Nat)** — Basketball Player
78 Blue Lagoon, Laguna Beach CA 92651, USA

**Milius, John F** — Director, Writer
I C M Partners, 10250 Constellation Blvd, #900, Los Angeles CA 90067 USA

**Milk, Barry** — Educator
Bowdoin College, President's Office, Brunswick ME 04011, USA

**Milk, Chris** — Photographer
Anonymous Content, 3532 Hayden Ave, Culver City CA 90232 USA

**Milk, Mike** — DJ Musician
Future Music, Bayerstr 77A, 80335 Munich, Germany

**Milken, Michael R** — Financier, Philanthropist
4543 Tara Dr, Encino CA 91436, USA

**Milla, Roger** — Soccer Player
Federation de Football, BP 1116, Yaounde, Cameroon

**Millan, Amy** — Singer, Guitarist
High Road Touring, 751 Bridgeway, #200, Sausalito CA 94965 USA

**Millan, Cesar** — Psychologist
Dog Psychology Center, PO Box 1130, Canyon Country CA 91386, USA

**Millan, Felix B** — Baseball Player
G16 Calle Camarero Parq Ecusetre, Carolina PR 00987, USA

**Millar, Ian** — Equestrian
Landmark Sport Group, 1 City Centre Dr, #605, Mississauga ON L5B 1M2, Canada

| | |
|---|---|
| **Millar, Kevin C** | Baseball Player |
| 14200 Flat Top Ranch Road, Austin TX 78732, USA | |
| **Millar, Miles** | Producer, Writer |
| Millar/Gough Ink, 500 S Buena Vista St, Animations Building, Burbank CA 91521, USA | |
| **Millar, Will** | Singer, Musician (Irish Rovers) |
| Lyon Group, PO Box 2428, Agoura Hills CA 91376, USA | |
| **Millard, Bart** | Singer (MercyMe) |
| Brickhouse Entertainment, 106 Mission Court, #1202, Franklin TN 37067, USA | |
| **Millard, Bryan J** | Football Player |
| 507 Sabine St, #1001, Austin TX 78701, USA | |
| **Millard, Keith** | Football Player |
| 5685 Maymont Lane, Dublin CA 94568, USA | |
| **Millardet, Patricia** | Actress |
| Agents Associes, 201 Rue du Faubourg Saint Honore, 75008 Paris, France | |
| **Milledge, Lastings D** | Baseball Player |
| 11114 Sailbrooke Dr, Riverview FL 33579, USA | |
| **Millegan, Eric** | Actor |
| Don Buchwald Talent Agency, 6500 Wilshire Blvd, #2200, Los Angeles CA 90048 USA | |
| **Millen, Greg** | Ice Hockey Player |
| 980 Orch, Bridgenorth ON K0L 1H0, Canada | |
| **Millen, Hugh B** | Football Player |
| 6836 Cascade Ave SE, Snoqualmie WA 98065, USA | |
| **Millen, Matt G** | Football Player, Executive, Sportscaster |
| 862 Durham Road, Riegelsville PA 18077, USA | |
| **Miller, Aaron** | Ice Hockey Player |
| 147 Appletree Point Road, Burlington VT 05408, USA | |
| **Miller, Alan** | Journalist |
| Los Angeles Times, Editorial Dept, 202 W 1st St, Los Angeles CA 90012 USA | |
| **Miller, Alan R** | Football Player |
| 3118 Erie Dr, Orchard Lake MI 48324, USA | |
| **Miller, Alice** | Golfer |
| 2 Log Church Road, Wilmington DE 19807, USA | |
| **Miller, Allison** | Actress |
| Beth Goldstein Mgmt, 4433 Colbath Ave, #34, Sherman Oaks CA 91423, USA | |
| **Miller, Alyssa** | Model |
| Mous Model Mgmt, 117 N Robertson Blvd, Los Angeles CA 90048, USA | |
| **Miller, Amara** | Actress |
| United Talent Agency, U T A Plaza, 9336 Civic Center Dr, Beverly Hills CA 90210 USA | |
| **Miller, Andre L** | Basketball Player |
| Washington Wizards, M C I Centre, 601 F St NW, Washington DC 20004 USA | |
| **Miller, Andrea** | Choreographer, Dance Executive |
| Gallim Dance, 304 W 75th St, New York NY 10023, USA | |
| **Miller, Anthony** | Basketball Player |
| 1083 Superior St, Benton Harbor MI 49022, USA | |
| **Miller, Bebe** | Choreographer, Dancer |
| Bebe Miller Dance Co, 54 W 21st St, #502, New York NY 10010, USA | |
| **Miller, Bennett** | Director, Producer |
| Creative Artists Agency, 2000 Ave of Stars, #100, Los Angeles CA 90067 USA | |
| **Miller, Billy J** | Actor |
| Gersh Agency, 9465 Wilshire Blvd, #600, Beverly Hills CA 90212 USA | |
| **Miller, Billy R** | Football Player |
| 3957 Skelton Canyon Circle, Westlake Village CA 91362, USA | |
| **Miller, Bode** | Alpine Skier |
| 65 Easton Valley Road, Franconia, NH 03580, USA | |
| **Miller, Bradley A (Brad)** | Basketball Player |
| 2731 Marl Oak Dr, Highland Park IL 60035, USA | |
| **Miller, Bruce** | Producer |
| Jackoway Tyerman Wertheimer, 1925 Century Park E, #2200, Los Angeles CA 90067 USA | |
| **Miller, C Arden** | Pediatrician |
| 350 Carolina Meadows Villa, Chapel Hill NC 27517, USA | |
| **Miller, Carol** | Bowler |
| Professional Bowlers Association, 719 2nd Ave, #701, Seattle WA 98104 USA | |
| **Miller, Cheryl D** | Basketball Player, Coach |
| 3206 Ellington Dr, Los Angeles CA 90068, USA | |
| **Miller, Christa** | Actress |
| I C M Partners, 10250 Constellation Blvd, #900, Los Angeles CA 90067 USA | |
| **Miller, Christine Cook** | Judge |
| US Claims Court, 717 Madison Place NW, Washington DC 20439, USA | |
| **Miller, Christopher J (Chris)** | Football Player |
| 701 W Hackberry Dr, Chandler AZ 85248, USA | |
| **Miller, Cleophus (Cleo), Jr** | Football Player |
| 16613 Raymond St, Maple Heights OH 44137, USA | |
| **Miller, Colleen M (Coco)** | Basketball Player |
| Los Angeles Sparks, 888 S Figueroa St, #2010, Los Angeles CA 90017 USA | |
| **Miller, Corky A P** | Baseball Player |
| 1115 7th St, Calimesa CA 92320, USA | |
| **Miller, Damian D** | Baseball Player |
| N1276 Wuensch Road, La Crosse WI 54601, USA | |
| **Miller, Dan** | Singer (O-Town) |
| J Records, 745 5th Ave, #600, New York NY 10151 USA | |
| **Miller, Darrell K** | Baseball Player |
| 21159 Via Alisa, Yorba Linda CA 92887, USA | |
| **Miller, David** | Cartoonist (Dave) |
| Back 40 Design, PO Box 7985, Edmond OK 73083, USA | |
| **Miller, David Alan** | Conductor |
| Opus 3 Artists, 470 Park Ave S, #900N, New York NY 10016 USA | |
| **Miller, Dennis** | Actor, Comedian |
| Brillstein Entertainment Partners, 9150 Wilshire Blvd, #350, Beverly Hills CA 90212 USA | |
| **Miller, Derek** | Guitarist, Singer (Sleigh Bells) |
| Agency Group Ltd, 142 W 57th St, #600, New York NY 10019 USA | |
| **Miller, Dyar K** | Baseball Player |
| 8816 Admirals Bay Dr, Indianapolis IN 46236, USA | |
| **Miller, E Heath, Jr** | Football Player |
| 1304 Hidden Canyon Court, Sewickley PA 15143, USA | |
| **Miller, Edward L (Eddie)** | Baseball Player |
| 1819 Alfreda Blvd, San Pablo CA 94806, USA | |

**Miller, Everett** — Hero
13655 Ahwahnee Way, Poway CA 92064, USA

**Miller, Frank** — Actor, Writer
Shapiro-Lichtman, 8827 Beverly Blvd, Los Angeles CA 90048 USA

**Miller, Frank** — Cartoonist (Sin City, Dark Knight)
Dark Horse Publishing, 10956 SE Main St, Portland OR 97222 USA

**Miller, Fred D** — Football Player
1945 Hillary Dr, Westminster MD 21157, USA

**Miller, Fred J** — Football Player
7143 Sawmill Trail, Houston TX 77040, USA

**Miller, Gabrielle** — Actress
Oscars Abrams Zimel, 438 Queen St E, Toronto ON M5A 1T4, Canada

**Miller, George D** — Air Force General
20 Phillips Pond South, Natick MA 01760, USA

**Miller, George T (Kennedy)** — Director, Producer
30 Orwell St, King's Cross, Sydney NSW 2011, Australia

**Miller, Harland** — Artist, Writer
N9 Design, Century Quay, Sutton Harbour, Plymouth PL4 0EP, England

**Miller, Howard S** — Actor
Endurance Talent Mgmt, 2920 W Olive Ave, #202, Burbank CA 91505, USA

**Miller, James A** — Oncologist
1822 Masters Lane, Madison WI 53719, USA

**Miller, James C, III** — Government Official
Citizens for Sound Economy, 1250 H St NW, Washington DC 20005, USA

**Miller, James D (Jim)** — Football Player
9916 King Road, Davisburg MI 48350, USA

**Miller, James G (Jim)** — Football Player
PO Box 863, Ripley MS 38663, USA

**Miller, Jeff** — Bassist (Caedmon's Call)
Breen Agency, 25 Music Square W, Nashville TN 37203, USA

**Miller, Jeremy** — Actor
Acumen Entertainment Partners, 15915 Ventura Blvd, #304, Encino CA 91436, USA

**Miller, Jerry** — Navy Admiral
Smithsonian Institution Press, 750 9th St NW, #4300, Washington DC 20560, USA

**Miller, Jody** — Singer
PO Box 413, Blanchard OK 73010, USA

**Miller, Joel McKinnon** — Actor
Greene Assoc, 1901 Ave of Stars, #130, Los Angeles CA 90067 USA

**Miller, John** — Commentator
ABC-TV, News Dept, 77 W 66th St, New York NY 10023 USA

**Miller, John A** — Baseball Player
5105 River Ave, #A, Newport Beach CA 92663, USA

**Miller, John E** — Baseball Player
13443 Old Annapolis Road, Mount Airy MD 21771, USA

**Miller, John L (Johnny)** — Golfer, Sportscaster
Johnny Miller Enterprises, PO Box 2260, Napa CA 94558, USA

**Miller, John W** — Educator
Central Connecticut State University, President's Office, New Britain CT 06050, USA

**Miller, Jon** — Sportscaster, Baseball Player
ESPN-TV, Sports Dept, ESPN Plaza, 935 Middle St, Bristol CT 06010 USA

**Miller, Jonathan W** — Director
Royce Carlton, 866 United Nations Plaza, New York NY 10017, USA

**Miller, Jonny Lee** — Actor
Independent Talent Group, 40 Whitfield St, London W1T 2RH, England

**Miller, Joshua H (Josh)** — Football Player
572 Macleod Dr, Gibsonia PA 15044, USA

**Miller, Joshua J (Josh)** — Actor, Director, Writer
Gersh Agency, 9465 Wilshire Blvd, #600, Beverly Hills CA 90212 USA

**Miller, Julie** — Singer, Songwriter
Vector Mgmt, PO Box 120479, Nashville TN 37212 USA

**Miller, Justin M** — Football Player
Arizona Cardinals, PO Box 888, Phoenix AZ 85001 USA

**Miller, Keith A** — Baseball Player
190 Water St, #2, Milford MI 48381, USA

**Miller, Keith H** — Governor, AK
3705 Arctic Blvd, Anchorage AK 99503, USA

**Miller, Kelly** — Basketball Player
New York Liberty, Madison Square Garden, 2 Penn Plaza, New York NY 10121 USA

**Miller, Kelly D** — Ice Hockey Player
3783 Chippendale Circle, Okemos MI 48864, USA

**Miller, Kevin** — Drummer (Fuel)
Media Five Entertainment, 3005 Brodhead Road, #170, Bethlehem PA 18020, USA

**Miller, Kevin B** — Ice Hockey Player
4243 Redbud Trail, Williamston MI 48895, USA

**Miller, Kip C** — Ice Hockey Player
2558 Lupine Court, Okemos MI 48864, USA

**Miller, Kristen E** — Actress, Comedienne
TalentWorks, 3500 W Olive Ave, #1400, Burbank CA 91505 USA

**Miller, Kurt E** — Baseball Player
1511 Iroquois Circle, Carrollton TX 75007, USA

**Miller, L Anthony** — Football Player
325 S San Dimas Canyon Road, #108, San Dimas CA 91773, USA

**Miller, Lajos** — Opera Singer
Hegyalja Utca 32, 3232 Matrafured, Hungary

**Miller, Larry** — Actor, Comedian
Brillstein Entertainment Partners, 9150 Wilshire Blvd, #350, Beverly Hills CA 90212 USA

**Miller, Lawrence J (Larry)** — Basketball Player
311 Mulberry St, Catasauqua PA 18032, USA

**Miller, Linda Lael** — Writer
Harlequin Enterprises, 225 Duncan Mill Road, Don Mills ON MJB JK9, Canada

**Miller, Marcus** — Jazz Bassist, Composer
I C M Partners, 10250 Constellation Blvd, #900, Los Angeles CA 90067 USA

**Miller, Marisa** — Actress, Model
Cartel Mgmt, 665 N Lillian Way, Los Angeles CA 90004, USA

**Miller, Mark** — Singer (Sawyer Brown)
O-Seven Artist Mgmt, PO Box 210586, Nashville TN 37221, USA

| | |
|---|---|
| **Miller, Marlin**<br>I M G Artists, Hogarth Business Park, Chiswick, London W4 2TH, England | Opera Singer |
| **Miller, McKaley**<br>Osbrink Talent Agency, 4343 Lankershim Blvd, #100, North Hollywood CA 91602 USA | Actress |
| **Miller, Michael L (Mike)**<br>2869 Ladbrook Way, Thousand Oaks CA 91361, USA | Basketball Player |
| **Miller, Mildred**<br>PO Box 110108, Pittsburgh PA 15232, USA | Opera Singer |
| **Miller, N Keith**<br>1831 W Alamosa Dr, Terrell TX 75160, USA | Baseball Player |
| **Miller, Nancy (Ann)**<br>W M E Entertainment, 9601 Wilshire Blvd, #300, Beverly Hills CA 90210 USA | Writer, Producer |
| **Miller, Nate**<br>1943 N Uber St, Philadelphia PA 19121, USA | Boxer |
| **Miller, Nicole J**<br>780 Madison Ave, Front 1, New York NY 10065, USA | Fashion Designer |
| **Miller, Norman C (Norm)**<br>43 Columbia Crest Place, Spring TX 77382, USA | Baseball Player |
| **Miller, Oliver J**<br>2912 S Meadow Dr, Fort Worth TX 76133, USA | Basketball Player |
| **Miller, Omar Benson**<br>A P A Talent & Literary Agency, 405 S Beverly Dr, #300, Beverly Hills CA 90212 USA | Actor |
| **Miller, Paul**<br>Fountainhead Talent, 131 Davenport Road, Toronto ON M5R 1H8, Canada | Actor |
| **Miller, Paul D**<br>Teledyne Technologies, 1049 Camino Dos Rios, Thousand Oaks CA 91360, USA | Navy Admiral, Businessman |
| **Miller, Penelope Ann**<br>A P A Talent & Literary Agency, 405 S Beverly Dr, #300, Beverly Hills CA 90212 USA | Actress |
| **Miller, Peter North**<br>Quinneys, Camilla Dr, Westhumble, Dorking, Surrey RH5 6BU, England | Businessman |
| **Miller, Randall S (Randy)**<br>22523 Oak Mist Lane, Katy TX 77494, USA | Baseball Player |
| **Miller, Raymond R (Ray)**<br>PO Box 41, New Athens OH 43981, USA | Baseball Manager |
| **Miller, Rebecca**<br>Creative Artists Agency, 2000 Ave of Stars, #100, Los Angeles CA 90067 USA | Actress, Director, Writer |
| **Miller, Reginald W (Reggie)**<br>3785 Puerco Canyon Road, Malibu CA 90265, USA | Basketball Player, Sportscaster |
| **Miller, Rhett**<br>Paradigm Agency, 360 N Crescent Dr, North Building, Beverly Hills CA 90210 USA | Singer (Old 97's), Songwriter |
| **Miller, Richard A (Rick)**<br>12790 Silverthorn Court, Bonita Springs FL 34135, USA | Baseball Player |
| **Miller, Risa**<br>Saint Martin's Press, 175 5th Ave, #400, New York NY 10010 USA | Writer |
| **Miller, Robert (Steve)**<br>Delphi Automotive Systems, 5725 Delphi Dr, Troy MI 48098, USA | Businessman |
| **Miller, Robert Ellis**<br>1901 Ave of Stars, #1040, Los Angeles CA 90067, USA | Director |
| **Miller, Robert G**<br>Albertsons, 250 E Parkcenter Blvd, Boise ID 83706, USA | Businessman |
| **Miller, Robert G (Bob)**<br>1702 Keim Trail, Saint Charles IL 60174, USA | Baseball Player |
| **Miller, Robert J (Bob)**<br>1202 Andover Circle, Commerce Township MI 48390, USA | Baseball Player |
| **Miller, Robert J (Bob)**<br>Jones Vargas, 3773 S Howard Hughes Parkway, #300S, Las Vegas NV 89169, USA | Governor, NV |
| **Miller, Robert L**<br>937 Clydesdale Lane, Windsor CO 80550, USA | Football Player |
| **Miller, Ryan**<br>Nettwerk Mgmt, 345 7th Ave, #2400, New York NY 10001, USA | Singer, Guitarist (Guster) |
| **Miller, Ryan**<br>1360 Londonderry Place, Los Angeles CA 90069, USA | Ice Hockey Player |
| **Miller, Sam**<br>Independent Talent Group, 40 Whitfield St, London W1T 2RH, England | Director |
| **Miller, Scott P**<br>1570 NW 128th Dr, #306, Sunrise FL 33323, USA | Football Player |
| **Miller, Sean**<br>University of Arizona, Athletic Dept, Tucson AZ 85721, USA | Basketball Coach |
| **Miller, Selvia (Junior)**<br>3051 Agate Court, Lincoln NE 68516, USA | Football Player |
| **Miller, Shannon**<br>4311 Salisbury Road, Jacksonville FL 32216, USA | Gymnast |
| **Miller, Shawn V**<br>3070 W Old Highway Road, Morgan UT 84050, USA | Football Player |
| **Miller, Sienna A**<br>United Agents, 12-26 Lexington St, London W1F 0LE, England | Actress, Model |
| **Miller, Steve**<br>Randex Communications, 906 Jonathan Lane, Marlton NJ 08053, USA | Singer, Songwriter, Orchestra Leader |
| **Miller, Steven P (Buddy)**<br>Vector Mgmt, PO Box 120479, Nashville TN 37212 USA | Guitarist, Songwriter |
| **Miller, Stuart L (Stu)**<br>3701 Ocaso Court, Cameron Park CA 95682, USA | Baseball Player |
| **Miller, Susan**<br>Playboy Promotions, 9346 Civic Center Dr, #200, Beverly Hills CA 90210 USA | Model, Actress |
| **Miller, Tangi**<br>Olivia Entertainment, PO Box 19398, Los Angeles CA 90019, USA | Actress, Producer, Writer |
| **Miller, Taylor**<br>Innovative Artists, 1505 10th St, Santa Monica CA 90401 USA | Actress |
| **Miller, Travis E**<br>51 Whisper Way, Eaton OH 45320, USA | Baseball Player |
| **Miller, Trever D**<br>24155 Hideout Trail, Land O Lakes FL 34639, USA | Baseball Player |
| **Miller, Troy**<br>Dakota Pictures, 4133 Lankershim Blvd, North Hollywood CA 91602, USA | Producer, Director |
| **Miller, Valerie Rae**<br>United Talent Agency, U T A Plaza, 9336 Civic Center Dr, Beverly Hills CA 90210 USA | Actress |

| | |
|---|---|
| **Miller, Von**<br>Denver Broncos, 13655 E Broncos Parkway, Englewood CO 80112 USA | Football Player |
| **Miller, Wade T**<br>12 Woods Way, Reading PA 19610, USA | Baseball Player |
| **Miller, Webb**<br>Pennsylvania State University, Biology Dept, Wartik Laboratory, University Park PA 16802, USA | Biologist |
| **Miller, Wentworth**<br>I C M Partners, 10250 Constellation Blvd, #900, Los Angeles CA 90067 USA | Actor |
| **Miller, Wiley**<br>8 Granite Heights Road, Kennebunkport ME 04046, USA | Cartoonist (Non Sequitur/Us & Them) |
| **Miller, William J (Bill)**<br>701 Belden Court, Saint Augustine FL 32086, USA | Football Player |
| **Miller, Zachary P (Zach)**<br>Seattle Seahawks, 12 Seahawks Way, Renton WA 98056 USA | Football Player |
| **Miller-Lawrence, Christa**<br>I C M Partners, 10250 Constellation Blvd, #900, Los Angeles CA 90067 USA | Actress |
| **Millett, Kate**<br>20 Old Overlook Road, Poughkeepsie NY 12603, USA | Women's Activist, Writer |
| **Millett, Terroon**<br>6548 Whitney Ave, Saint Louis MO 63133, USA | Boxer |
| **Milley, Mark A**<br>Commanding General, III Corps & Fort Hood, Fort Hood TX 76544 USA | Army General |
| **Millhauser, Steven**<br>235 Caroline St, Saratoga Springs NY 12866, USA | Writer |
| **Millican, Clay**<br>545 Watson Road, Atoka TN 38004, USA | Auto Racing Driver |
| **Milligan, Dustin**<br>Red Mgmt, 415 W Esplanade, #3, North Vancouver BC V7M 1A6, Canada | Actor |
| **Milligan, Joseph**<br>Arson Media Group, 23 N Summerlin Ave, #200, Orlando FL 32801, USA | Guitarist (Anberlin) |
| **Milligan, Randy A**<br>6905 Real Princess Lane, Gwynn Oak MD 21207, USA | Baseball Player |
| **Milliken, Angie**<br>Polaris Entertainment, 8048 W 3rd St, #300, Los Angeles CA 90048, USA | Actress |
| **Milliken, James B**<br>University of Nebraska, President's Office, Lincoln NE 68588, USA | Educator |
| **Million, Mike**<br>Brucks/McDonald Entertainment, 1635 N Cahuenga Blvd, #400, Los Angeles CA 90028, USA | Director, Producer, Writer |
| **Millman, Gabriel**<br>Harvest Talent Mgmt, 124 W 80th St, #1, New York NY 10024, USA | Actor |
| **Millner, F Ann**<br>Weber State University, President's Office, 3848 Harrison Blvd, Ogden UT 84408, USA | Educator |
| **Millns, James G (Jim), Jr**<br>7603 Dunbridge Dr, Odessa FL 33556, USA | Ice Dancer |
| **Millo, Aprile E**<br>Columbia Artists Mgmt Inc, 5 Columbus Circle, 1790 Broadway, #1600, New York NY 10019 USA | Opera Singer |
| **Millon, Henry A**<br>6200 Oregon Ave NW, #370, Washington DC 20015, USA | Architectural Historian |
| **Milloy, Lawyer M**<br>57 Chapman Loop, Steilacoom WA 98388, USA | Football Player |
| **Mills, Alan B**<br>1811 Bellgrove St, Lakeland FL 33805, USA | Baseball Player |
| **Mills, Alley**<br>Stone Manners Salners, 6100 Wilshire Blvd, #1500, Los Angeles CA 90035 USA | Actress |
| **Mills, Barry**<br>Bowdoin College, President's Office, Brunswick ME 04011, USA | Educator |
| **Mills, Christopher (Chris)**<br>2223 Camden Ave, Los Angeles CA 90064, USA | Basketball Player |
| **Mills, Crispian**<br>Little Big Man, 39A Grammercy Park N, #1C, New York NY 10010, USA | Singer, Guitarist (Kula Shakur) |
| **Mills, Donna**<br>TalentWorks, 3500 W Olive Ave, #1400, Burbank CA 91505 USA | Actress |
| **Mills, Ernest L (Ernie)**<br>PO Box 2435, Dunnellon FL 34430, USA | Football Player |
| **Mills, Frank**<br>Rocklands Entertainment, PO Box 48216, Saint Petersburg FL 33743, USA | Pianist, Composer |
| **Mills, Hayley**<br>Chatto & Linnit, 123A King's Road, London SW3 4PL, England | Actress, Singer |
| **Mills, J Bradley (Brad)**<br>4746 W Buena Vista Court, Visalia CA 93291, USA | Baseball Player, Manager |
| **Mills, John Henry**<br>755 Bahia Circle, Ocala FL 34472, USA | Football Player |
| **Mills, Judson**<br>Dino May Mgmt, 11262 Ventura Blvd, #PH, Studio City CA 91604, USA | Actor |
| **Mills, Juliet**<br>Diamond Management, 31 Percy St, London W1T 2DD, England | Actress |
| **Mills, Mary**<br>310 S Ocean Blvd, #106, Boca Raton FL 33432, USA | Golfer |
| **Mills, Mary**<br>I M G Artists, Hogarth Business Park, Chiswick, London W4 2TH, England | Opera Singer |
| **Mills, Michael E (Mike)**<br>REM/Athens Ltd, PO Box 8032, Athens GA 30603, USA | Bassist (REM) |
| **Mills, Mike**<br>United Talent Agency, U T A Plaza, 9336 Civic Center Dr, Beverly Hills CA 90210 USA | Director |
| **Mills, Phoebe**<br>Harris Agency, 17814 Lillian St, Omaha NE 68136, USA | Gymnast |
| **Mills, Stephanie**<br>Wenig-LaMonica Assoc, 580 White Plains Road, #130, Tarrytown NY 10591, USA | Singer, Actress |
| **Mills, Terry R**<br>37840 Scott Pine Dr, New Boston MI 48164, USA | Basketball Player |
| **Mills, William H (Bill)**<br>4344 Commercial St, Port Charlotte FL 33953, USA | Baseball Player |
| **Mills, William M (Billy)**<br>7760 Winding Way, #722, Fair Oaks CA 95628, USA | Track Athlete |
| **Mills, Zach**<br>Paradigm Agency, 360 N Crescent Dr, North Building, Beverly Hills CA 90210 USA | Actor |

**M**

| | |
|---|---|
| **Millsap, Paul** | Basketball Player |
| Atlanta Hawks, Centennial Tower, 101 Marietta St NW, #1900, Atlanta GA 30303 USA | |
| **Millwood, Kamla** | Model |
| Impact Model Mgmt, 324-326 Regent St, #104, London W1B 3HH, England | |
| **Millwood, Kevin A** | Baseball Player |
| 1204 Suncast Lane, #2, El Dorado Hills CA 95762, USA | |
| **Milne, Brian F** | Football Player |
| 1411 Beacon St, Cincinnati OH 45230, USA | |
| **Milner, Anthony F D** | Composer |
| 147 Heythorp St, Southfields, London SW18 5BT, England | |
| **Milner, Brenda** | Neuroscientist |
| McGill University, Neurological Institute, 3801 Rue University, Montreal QC H3A 2B4, Canada | |
| **Milner, Edward J (Eddie)** | Baseball Player |
| 491 Stambaugh Ave, Columbus OH 43207, USA | |
| **Milner, Martin** | Actor |
| 3106 Azahar St, Carlsbad CA 92009, USA | |
| **Milnes, Sherrill E** | Opera Singer |
| Barrett Vantage Artists, 508 8th Ave, #12A00, New York NY 10018 USA | |
| **Milnor, John W** | Abel Mathematics Laureate |
| 3 Laurel Lane, Setauket NY 11733, USA | |
| **Milos, Sofia** | Actress |
| Rogers & Cowan, 8687 Melrose Ave, #G700, West Hollywood CA 90069 USA | |
| **Miloszewski, Steve** | Guitarist (Reveille) |
| David Levy Mgmt, 200 W 57th St, #308, New York NY 10019, USA | |
| **Milot, Richard P (Rich)** | Football Player |
| 15840 Hunton Lane, Haymarket PA 20169, USA | |
| **Milsap, Ronnie** | Singer, Pianist, Songwriter |
| Ronnie Milsap Enterprises, PO Box 40665, Nashville TN 37204, USA | |
| **Milsome, Douglas** | Cinematographer |
| Gems, Studio Five, Stangate House, Stanwell Road, Penarth CF64 2AA, England | |
| **Milstead, Roderick L (Rod), Jr** | Football Player |
| 6674 Fenwick Road, Bryans Road MD 20616, USA | |
| **Milton, Eric R** | Baseball Player |
| 1133 Asquith Dr, Arnold MD 21012, USA | |
| **Milton, Peter W** | Artist |
| 2 New Hampshire Turnpike S, Francestown NH 03043, USA | |
| **Milton-Jones, DeLisha** | Basketball Player |
| San Antonio Silver Stars, 1 AT&T Center, San Antonio TX 78219 USA | |
| **Milva** | Singer, Actress |
| N A R International, Via Lessona 2, 20157 Milan, Italy | |
| **Mimbs, Michael R (Mike)** | Baseball Player |
| 2761 Mimbs Road, Alamo GA 30411, USA | |
| **Mimica-Gezzan, Sergio** | Director, Producer |
| United Talent Agency, U T A Plaza, 9336 Civic Center Dr, Beverly Hills CA 90210 USA | |
| **Mimieux, Yvette** | Actress |
| Howard Ruby Photography, 2222 Corinth Ave, Los Angeles CA 90064, USA | |
| **Mims-Flowers, Tairia** | Softball Player |
| Amateur Softball, 2801 NE 50th St, Oklahoma City OK 73111, USA | |
| **Mina, Denise** | Writer |
| Little Brown, 3 Center Plaza, #100, Boston MA 02108 USA | |
| **Minaj, Nicki** | Rap Artist, Singer, Songwriter |
| Creative Artists Agency, 2000 Ave of Stars, #100, Los Angeles CA 90067 USA | |
| **Mincey, Jeremy L** | Football Player |
| Dallas Cowboys, 1 Cowboys Parkway, Irving TX 75063 USA | |
| **Mincy, Charles A** | Football Player |
| 2227 W 24th St, #7, Los Angeles CA 90018, USA | |
| **Mindel, Lee F** | Architect |
| Shelton Mindel Assoc, 56 W 22nd St, #1200, New York NY 10010, USA | |
| **Minear, Tim** | Writer, Producer |
| W M E Entertainment, 9601 Wilshire Blvd, #300, Beverly Hills CA 90210 USA | |
| **Minenkov, Andrei** | Ice Dancer |
| Skating Federation, Luchnesksaia Nab 8, 119871 Moscow, Russia | |
| **Miner, Rachel** | Actress |
| Untitled Entertainment, 350 S Beverly Dr, #200, Beverly Hills CA 90212 USA | |
| **Miner, Steve** | Director |
| Gersh Agency, 9465 Wilshire Blvd, #600, Beverly Hills CA 90212 USA | |
| **Ming Tsai** | Chef |
| Food Network, 1180 Ave of Americas, #1200, New York NY 10036 USA | |
| **Mingenbach, Louise** | Costume Designer |
| United Talent Agency, U T A Plaza, 9336 Civic Center Dr, Beverly Hills CA 90210 USA | |
| **Minghella, Max** | Actor |
| Creative Artists Agency, 2000 Ave of Stars, #100, Los Angeles CA 90067 USA | |
| **Mingiedi, Mawangu** | Percussionist, Likembe Player |
| Concerted Efforts, PO Box 440326, Somerville MA 02144 USA | |
| **Ming-Na Wen** | Actress |
| L I N K Entertainment, 11872 La Grange Ave, Los Angeles CA 90025 USA | |
| **Mingo, Eugene L (Gene)** | Football Player |
| 5701 E Colorado Ave, Denver CO 80224, USA | |
| **Minh Tran** | Dancer, Choreographer |
| 2014 NE 47th Ave, Portland OR 97213, USA | |
| **Miniefield, Kevin L** | Football Player |
| 11733 E Starflower Dr, Chandler AZ 85249, USA | |
| **Minkoff, Rob** | Director, Producer, Animator |
| Oasis Media Group, 8730 W Sunset Blvd, #700, West Hollywood CA 90069, USA | |
| **Minkowski, Marc** | Conductor |
| Deutsche Grammaphon Records, 810 7th Ave, New York NY 10019, USA | |
| **Minnelli, Liza** | Actress, Singer |
| 150 E 69th St, #21G, New York NY 10021, USA | |
| **Minnette, Dylan** | Actor |
| C E S D, 10635 Santa Monica Blvd, #130, Los Angeles CA 90025 USA | |
| **Minnifield, Dirk D** | Basketball Player |
| 10902 Little Gap Court, Sugar Land TX 77498, USA | |
| **Minnifield, Frank D** | Football Player |
| 4809 Chaffey Lane, Lexington KY 40515, USA | |
| **Minnillo, Vanessa** | Entertainer |
| Baker Winokur Ryder Public Relations, 9100 Wilshire Blvd, #500W, Beverly Hills CA 90212 USA | |

**Minns, Martyn** — Religious Leader
Truro Church, Rector's Office, 10520 Main St, Fairfax VA 22030, USA

**Minogue, Danii** — Singer
PO Box 46824, London SW1 3WS, England

**Minogue, Kylie** — Singer, Actress
Primary Talent International, 10-11 Jockey's Fields, London WC1R 4BN, England

**Minor, Blas, Jr** — Baseball Player
7139 N Dean St, Winton CA 95388, USA

**Minor, Greg M** — Basketball Player
6543 Merrick Landing Blvd, Windermere FL 34786, USA

**Minor, Jerry** — Actor
United Talent Agency, U T A Plaza, 9336 Civic Center Dr, Beverly Hills CA 90210 USA

**Minor, Shane** — Singer
E S P Mgmt, 838 N Doheny Dr, #302, West Hollywood CA 90069, USA

**Minor, Travis D** — Football Player
PO Box 1635, Hallandale FL 33008, USA

**Minoso, Saturino O A A (Minnie)** — Baseball Player
3700 N Lake Shore Dr, #303, Chicago IL 60613, USA

**Minot, Eliza** — Writer
Knopf Publishers, 1745 Broadway, New York NY 10019 USA

**Minot, Susan** — Writer
Knopf Publishers, 1745 Broadway, New York NY 10019 USA

**Minow, Newton N** — Government Official
179 E Lake Shore Dr, #15W, Chicago IL 60611, USA

**Minshall, James E (Jim)** — Baseball Player
615 Manatee Ave, Ellenton FL 34222, USA

**Minshew, Alicia** — Actress
Don Buchwald Talent Agency, 6500 Wilshire Blvd, #2200, Los Angeles CA 90048 USA

**Minsky, Charles D** — Cinematographer
202 Toro Canyon Road, Carpinteria CA 93013, USA

**Minsky, Marvin L** — Computer Scientist
Massachusetts Institute of Technology, Computer Science Dept, Cambridge MA 02139, USA

**Minter, Alan** — Boxer
Fighting Talk, 30 Peterborough Way, Fellgate, Jarrow NE32 4XD, Canada

**Minter, Barry A** — Football Player
2626 Garcitas Creek, Richmond TX 77406, USA

**Minter, Kristin** — Actress
Lovett Mgmt, 1327 Brinkley Ave, Los Angeles CA 90049, USA

**Minter, Michael C )Mike)** — Football Player
506 N East Ave, Kannapolis NC 28083, USA

**Minton, Gregory B (Greg)** — Baseball Player
690 N Muleshoe Road, Apache Junction AZ 85119, USA

**Minton, Yvonne F** — Opera Singer
Organisation International Artistique, 16 Ave F D Roosevelt, 75008 Paris, France

**Mintz, Beatrice** — Embryologist
Fox Chase Cancer Center, 333 Cottman Ave, Philadelphia PA 19111, USA

**Mintz, Daniel (Dan)** — Actor, Writer
Creative Artists Agency, 2000 Ave of Stars, #100, Los Angeles CA 90067 USA

**Mintz, Shlomo** — Concert Violinist, Conductor
Kunstleragentur Raab & Bohm, Plankengasse 7, 1010 Vienna, Austria

**Mintz-Plasse, Christopher** — Actor
United Talent Agency, U T A Plaza, 9336 Civic Center Dr, Beverly Hills CA 90210 USA

**Minucci, Chieli** — Guitarist, Composer
Axis Artists Mgmt, 9715 Belmar Ave, Northridge CA 91324, USA

**Minutelli, Gino M** — Baseball
3305 Foxtrot Court, Spring Hill TX 76639, USA

**Mio, Eddie** — Ice Hockey Player
PO Box 252745, West Bloomfield MI 48325, USA

**Miou-Miou** — Actress
U B B A, 6 Rue de Braque, 75003 Paris, France

**Mir, Isabelle** — Alpine Skier
65170 Saint-Lary, France

**Mira, George** — Football Player
19225 SW 128th Court, Miami FL 33177, USA

**Mirabella, Erin** — Cyclist
914 N Idaho St, La Habra CA 90631, USA

**Mirabella, Grace** — Editor, Publisher
Mirabella, Editor's Office, 200 Madison Ave, New York NY 10016, USA

**Mirabella, Paul T** — Baseball Player
125 Jenks Road, Morristown NJ 07960, USA

**Mirabelli, Douglas A (Doug)** — Baseball Player
9788 Edgewood Ave, Traverse City MI 49685, USA

**Miraldi, Dean M** — Football Player
14015 Live Oak Lane, Grass Valley CA 95945, USA

**Miranda, Claudio** — Cinematographer
Dattner Disposto, 10635 Santa Monica Blvd, #165, Los Angeles CA 90025, USA

**Miranda, Lin-Manuel** — Lyricist, Actor, Singer
W M E Entertainment, 9601 Wilshire Blvd, #300, Beverly Hills CA 90210 USA

**Miranda, Pia** — Actress
United Mgmt, 61 Marlborough St, #400-45, Surry Hills NSW 2010, Australia

**Mirchoff, Beau** — Actor
A P A Talent & Literary Agency, 405 S Beverly Dr, #300, Beverly Hills CA 90212 USA

**Mirer, Rick F** — Football Player
820 Braxton Court, Goshen IN 46526, USA

**Mirich, Rex L** — Football Player
620 W Yaqui Dr, Tucson AZ 85704, USA

**Miricioiu, Nelly** — Opera Singer
53 Midhurst Ave, Muswell Hill, London N10 3EP, England

**Mirikitani, Janice** — Writer
Celestial Arts Press, 6001 Shellmound St, #400, Emeryville CA 94608, USA

**Mirisch, Walter M** — Producer
647 Warner Ave, Los Angeles CA 90024, USA

**Mirkin, Chad A** — Chemist
Northwestern University, Mirkin Research Group, 2145 Sheridan Road, Evanston IL 60208, USA

**Mirkin, David** — Director, Producer, Writer
Gersh Agency, 9465 Wilshire Blvd, #600, Beverly Hills CA 90212 USA

**Mirman, Eugene** — Actor
I C M Partners, 10250 Constellation Blvd, #900, Los Angeles CA 90067 USA
**Mirmira, Raghavendra G** — Biochemist, Molecular Biologist
University of Virginia Medical School, Endocrinology & Metabolism Dept, Charlottesville VA 22903, USA
**Mironov, Boris O** — Ice Hockey Player
2911 Bayview Ave, North York ON M2K 1E8, Canada
**Mironov, Dmitri O** — Ice Hockey Player
2911 Bayview Ave, North York ON M2K 1E8, Canada
**Mirotic, Nikola** — Basketball Player
Chicago Bulls, United Center, 1901 W Madison St, Chicago IL 60612 USA
**Mirren, Helen** — Actress
Stan Rosenfield Assoc, 2029 Century Park E, #1190, Los Angeles CA 90067 USA
**Mirrione, Stephen** — Editor
I C M Partners, 10250 Constellation Blvd, #900, Los Angeles CA 90067 USA
**Mirrlees, James A** — Nobel Economics Laureate
Trinity College, Economics Dept, Cambridge CB2 1TQ, England
**Mirzakhani, Maryam** — Mathematician
Stanford University, Mathematics Dept, Stanford CA 94305, USA
**Mirziyoyev, Shavkat M** — Prime Minister, Uzbekistan
Prime Minister's Office, Mustarilik 5, 70008 Tashkent, Uzbekistan
**Miscavige, David** — Religious Leader
Scientology Religious Technology Center, 1710 Ivar St, #1100, Los Angeles CA 90028, USA
**Misch, Patrick T J** — Baseball Player
366 E Krista Way, Tempe AZ 85284, USA
**Mischer, Don** — Producer, Director, Writer
Don Mischer Productions, 8899 Beverly Blvd, #902, Los Angeles CA 90048, USA
**Mischka, James** — Fashion Designer
Badgley Mischka, 215 W 40th St, New York NY 10018, USA
**Misersky, Antje** — Biathlete
Grenzgraben 3A, 98714 Stutzerbach, Germany
**Mishkin, Frederic** — Government Official, Economist
Columbia University, Economics Dept, New York NY 10027, USA
**Misiano, Christopher (Chris)** — Director, Producer
Creative Artists Agency, 2000 Ave of Stars, #100, Los Angeles CA 90067 USA
**Misiano, Vincent** — Director
Creative Artists Agency, 2000 Ave of Stars, #100, Los Angeles CA 90067 USA
**Miskulin, Joey (Cowpolka King)** — Singer, Accordionist (Riders in the Sky)
New Frontier Mgmt, 1921 Broadway, Nashville TN 37203, USA
**Misner, Susan** — Actress
One Entertainment, 1321 7th St, #203, Santa Monica CA 90401 USA
**Misrach, Richard L** — Photographer
1420 45th St, Emeryville CA 94608, USA
**Missick, Dorian** — Actor
A P A Talent & Literary Agency, 405 S Beverly Dr, #300, Beverly Hills CA 90212 USA
**Mistry, Jimi** — Actor
Brillstein Entertainment Partners, 9150 Wilshire Blvd, #350, Beverly Hills CA 90212 USA
**Mistry, Kaizad** — Computer Chip Engineer
Intel Corp, 5200 NE Elam Parkway, Hillsboro OR 97124, USA
**Mitalipov, Shoukhrat** — Reproductive Biologist
3075 NW Overlook Dr, Hillsboro OR 97124, USA
**Mitchard, Jacquelyn** — Writer
Penguin Books, 375 Hudson St, Basement 1, New York NY 10014 USA
**Mitchell, Aidan D** — Actor
Stone Manners Salners, 6100 Wilshire Blvd, #1500, Los Angeles CA 90035 USA
**Mitchell, Andrea** — Commentator
2710 Chain Bridge Road NW, Washington DC 20016, USA
**Mitchell, Augie** — Guitarist (Intruders)
Billy Paul Mgmt, 8215 Winthrop St, Philadelphia PA 19136, USA
**Mitchell, Betsy** — Swimmer
Laurel High School, Athletic Dept, 1 Lyman Circle, Beachwood OH 44122, USA
**Mitchell, Bobby** — Golfer
435 Wimbish Dr, Danville VA 24541, USA
**Mitchell, Brandon P** — Football Player
806 Schlessinger St, Abbeville LA 70510, USA
**Mitchell, Brian K** — Football Player
5435 Chandley Farm Circle, Centreville VA 20120, USA
**Mitchell, Brian Stokes** — Actor, Singer
Paradigm Agency, 360 N Crescent Dr, North Building, Beverly Hills CA 90210 USA
**Mitchell, Bruce D (Waddie)** — Singer, Guitarist, Writer
Scott O'Malley Assoc, 433 E Cuchamas St, Colorado Springs CO 80903, USA
**Mitchell, Daryl M (Chill)** — Actor
United Talent Agency, U T A Plaza, 9336 Civic Center Dr, Beverly Hills CA 90210 USA
**Mitchell, Donald R** — Football Player
5620 Minner Dr, Beaumont TX 77708, USA
**Mitchell, Dryden** — Bassist, Pianist (Alien Ant Farm)
Creative Artists Agency, 2000 Ave of Stars, #100, Los Angeles CA 90067 USA
**Mitchell, Edgar D** — Astronaut
PO Box 540037, Greenacres FL 33454, USA
**Mitchell, Elizabeth** — Actress
L I N K Entertainment, 11872 La Grange Ave, Los Angeles CA 90025 USA
**Mitchell, Elizabeth R (Liz)** — Singer (Boney M)
International Artists, PO Box 100334, 47563 Goch, Germany
**Mitchell, Finesse** — Actor, Comedian
I C M Partners, 10250 Constellation Blvd, #900, Los Angeles CA 90067 USA
**Mitchell, George** — Guitarist (Intruders)
Billy Paul Mgmt, 8215 Winthrop St, Philadelphia PA 19136, USA
**Mitchell, George J** — Senator, ME
D L A Piper, 1251 Ave of Americas, #C2-75, New York NY 10020, USA
**Mitchell, George P** — Businessman, Philanthropist
Mitchell Energy & Development, PO Box 4000, The Woodlands TX 77387, USA
**Mitchell, James H (Jim)** — Football Player
120 Twin Creek Terrace, Forest VA 24551, USA
**Mitchell, Jessie J (Mitch)** — Baseball Player
1964 Cherry Ave, Birmingham AL 35214, USA
**Mitchell, John** — Baseball Player
1708 Castleberry Way, Birmingham AL 35214, USA

| | |
|---|---|
| **Mitchell, John Cameron**<br>Creative Artists Agency, 2000 Ave of Stars, #100, Los Angeles CA 90067 USA | Actor, Director, Writer |
| **Mitchell, John K**<br>5017 Hasty Dr, Nashville TN 37211, USA | Baseball Player |
| **Mitchell, Johnny**<br>7617 Courtyard Run W, Boca Raton FL 33433, USA | Football Player |
| **Mitchell, Joni**<br>624 Funchal Road, Los Angeles CA 90077, USA | Singer, Songwriter |
| **Mitchell, Kawika U**<br>971 N Lake Sybelia Dr, Maitland FL 32751, USA | Football Player |
| **Mitchell, Keith**<br>A P A Talent & Literary Agency, 405 S Beverly Dr, #300, Beverly Hills CA 90212 USA | Actor |
| **Mitchell, Keith A**<br>731 S 42nd St, San Diego CA 92113, USA | Baseball Player |
| **Mitchell, Kenneth**<br>Innovative Artists, 1505 10th St, Santa Monica CA 90401 USA | Actor |
| **Mitchell, Kevin D**<br>3869 Ocean View Blvd, San Diego CA 92113, USA | Baseball Player |
| **Mitchell, Kim**<br>41 Britain St, #305, Toronto ON M5A 1R, Canada | Singer |
| **Mitchell, Kirsty L**<br>Conway Van Gelder Grant, 8-12 Broadwick St, #300, London W1F 8HW, England | Actress |
| **Mitchell, Leona**<br>Columbia Artists Mgmt Inc, 5 Columbus Circle, 1790 Broadway, #1600, New York NY 10019 USA | Opera Singer |
| **Mitchell, Leroy**<br>6598 N Pinewood Dr, Parker CO 80134, USA | Football Player |
| **Mitchell, Lydell D**<br>702 Reservoir St, Baltimore MD 21217, USA | Football Player |
| **Mitchell, Lyvonia A (Stump)**<br>43091 Old Gallivan Terrace, Ashburn VA 20147, USA | Football Player, Coach |
| **Mitchell, Mack H**<br>PO Box 741, Diboll TX 75941, USA | Football Player |
| **Mitchell, Maia**<br>W M E Entertainment, 9601 Wilshire Blvd, #300, Beverly Hills CA 90210 USA | Actress |
| **Mitchell, Michael T (Mike)**<br>Pittsburgh Steelers, 3400 S Water St, Pittsburgh PA 15203 USA | Football Player |
| **Mitchell, Mike**<br>Creative Artists Agency, 2000 Ave of Stars, #100, Los Angeles CA 90067 USA | Director, Actor, Writer |
| **Mitchell, Paul M**<br>23 Carr Road, Berlin MA 01503, USA | Baseball Player |
| **Mitchell, Penelope**<br>A P A Talent & Literary Agency, 405 S Beverly Dr, #300, Beverly Hills CA 90212 USA | Actress |
| **Mitchell, Peter C (Pete)**<br>125 Sawbill Palm Dr, Ponte Vedra Beach FL 32082, USA | Football Player |
| **Mitchell, Radha**<br>Shanahan Mgmt, PO Box 1509, Darlinghurst NSW 1300, Australia | Actress |
| **Mitchell, Robert**<br>2009 Elmwood Ave, Tampa FL 33605, USA | Baseball Player |
| **Mitchell, Robert C (Bobby)**<br>36 Hollyberry Court, Rockville MD 20852, USA | Football Player, Executive |
| **Mitchell, Robert Vance (Bobby)**<br>8697 Tiogawoods Dr, Sacramento CA 95828, USA | Baseball Player |
| **Mitchell, Roland E**<br>PO Box 5701, Lake Charles LA 70606, USA | Football Player |
| **Mitchell, Roscoe E, Jr**<br>S R O Artists, 6629 University Ave, #206, Middleton WI 53562, USA | Jazz Reeds Player, Composer |
| **Mitchell, Samuel E (Sam), Jr**<br>73 Smokerise Point, Peachtree City GA 30269, USA | Basektball Player, Coach |
| **Mitchell, Shareen**<br>Independent Artists Agency, 9601 Wilshire Blvd, #750, Beverly Hills CA 90210, USA | Actress |
| **Mitchell, Sharmba**<br>819 Hayward Ave, Takoma Park MD 20912, USA | Boxer |
| **Mitchell, Shay**<br>A P A Talent & Literary Agency, 405 S Beverly Dr, #300, Beverly Hills CA 90212 USA | Actress |
| **Mitchell, Silas Weir**<br>Greene Assoc, 1901 Ave of Stars, #130, Los Angeles CA 90067 USA | Actor |
| **Mitchell, Steven Long (Steve)**<br>Imagiquest Entertainment, 10200 Riverside Dr, #201, Toluca Lake CA 91602, USA | Writer, Producer, Director |
| **Mitchell, Thomas G (Tom)**<br>1421 SW 49th Terrace, Cape Coral FL 33914, USA | Football Player |
| **Mitchell, Tony**<br>United Agents, 12-26 Lexington St, London W1F 0LE, England | Cinematographer, Director |
| **Mitchell, Vernessa**<br>Higher Ground Ministries, PO Box 72651, Newnan, GA 30271, USA | Singer |
| **Mitchell, W Scott**<br>2375 S State St, Springville UT 84663, USA | Football Player |
| **Mitchell, Warren**<br>Shanahan Mgmt, 91 Campbell St, #300, Surry Hills NSW 2010, Australia | Actor |
| **Mitchell, William R (Willie)**<br>Los Angeles Kings, Staples Center, 1111 S Figueroa St, Los Angeles CA 90015 USA | Ice Hockey Player |
| **Mitchell-Smith, Ilan**<br>10460 Queens Blvd, #10C, Forest Hills NY 11375, USA | Actor |
| **Mitchison, N Avrion**<br>14 Belitha Villas, London N1 1PD, England | Zoologist, Anatomist |
| **Miti, Carlotta**<br>Carol Levi Mgmt, Via Giuseppe Pisanelli 2, 00196 Rome, Italy | Actress |
| **Mitra, Rhona**<br>Untitled Entertainment, 350 S Beverly Dr, #200, Beverly Hills CA 90212 USA | Actress |
| **Mitre, Sergio A**<br>1443 Blairwood Ave, Chula Vista CA 91913, USA | Baseball Player |
| **Mitsotakis, Konstantinos**<br>1 Aravantinou St, 106 74 Athens, Greece | Prime Minister, Greece |
| **Mittal, Lakshmi N**<br>L N M Group, Hofplein 20, #1500, Rotterdam 3032, Netherlands | Businessman |
| **Mitte, R J**<br>Bauman Redanty Shaul Agency, 5757 Wilshire Blvd, #473, Los Angeles CA 90036 USA | Actor |

**Mittermaier-Neureuther, Rosemarie (Rosi)** — Alpine Skier
Winkelmoos-Alm, 83242 Reit Im Winkel, Germany
**Mittermayer, Tatjana** — Freestyle Moguls Skier
Bucha 2A, 83661 Lenggries, Germany
**Mitterrutzner, Martin** — Opera Singer
Kunstler Sekretariat am Gasteig, Rosenheimer Str 52, 81669 Munich, Germany
**Mitterwald, George E** — Baseball Player
1721 Murdock Blvd, Orlando FL 32825, USA
**Mittleman, Steve** — Actor, Comedian
A K A Talent, 6310 San Vicente Blvd, #200, Los Angeles CA 90048 USA
**Mitts, Heather** — Soccer Player, Sportscaster
Atlanta Beat, 1955 Vaughn Road, #209, Kennesaw GA 30144, USA
**Mitz, Alonzo L** — Football Player
2609 NE 4th St, #216, Renton WA 98056, USA
**Mivelaz, Betty** — Bowler
1543 Grand Ave, Medford OR 97504, USA
**Mix, Bryant L** — Football Player
37 Greenwood Plantation Road, Natchez MS 39120, USA
**Mix, Ronald J (Ron)** — Football Player
13796 Lyons Valley Road, Jamul CA 91935, USA
**Mix, Steven C (Steve)** — Basketball Player
25743 Willowbend Road, Perrysburg OH 43551, USA
**Mix, Timothy** — Opera Singer
I M G Artists, Hogarth Business Park, Chiswick, London W4 2TH, England
**Mixon, Katy** — Actress
W M E Entertainment, 9601 Wilshire Blvd, #300, Beverly Hills CA 90210 USA
**Mixon, Kenneth J (Kenny)** — Football Player
175 Bayridge Lane, Weston FL 33326, USA
**Mixson, J Wayne** — Governor, FL
2219 Demeron Road, Tallahassee FL 32308, USA
**Miyamoto, Shigeru** — Video Game Designer
Nintendo, 11-1 Kamitoba, Hokotatecho Minamiku, Kyoto 601 8501, Japan
**Miyamura, Hiroshi H** — Korean War Army Hero (CMH)
659 Kaimalino St, Kailua HI 96734, USA
**Miyazaki, Hayao** — Animator
Studio Ghibli, 1-4-25 Kajinocho, Koganeishi 184 0002, Japan
**Miyazato, Ai** — Golfer
Ladies Pro Golf Assn, 100 International Golf Dr, Daytona Beach FL 32124 USA
**Miyori, Kim** — Actress
8033 W Sunset Blvd, #770, West Hollywood CA 90046, USA
**Mize, John D** — Vietnam War Air Force Hero
112 Sunset Dr, Belmond IA 50421, USA
**Mize, Larry** — Golfer
106 Graystone Court, Columbus GA 31904, USA
**Mizerock, John J** — Baseball Player, Manager
1189 Leasure Run Road, Rochester Mills PA 15771, USA
**Mizota, Diane** — Actress
Paradise Group, PO Box 69451, West Hollywood CA 90069, USA
**Mizrahi, Isaac** — Fashion Designer
1516 S Canfield Ave, Los Angeles CA 90035, USA
**Mleczko-Griswold, Allison J (A J)** — Ice Hockey Player
3 Hinckley Lane, Nantucket MA 02554, USA
**Mlicki, David J (Dave)** — Baseball Player
5350 Reserve Dr, Dublin OH 43017, USA
**Mnookin, Robert H** — Attorney, Educator
10 Follen St, Cambridge MA 02138, USA
**Mnouchkine, Ariane** — Director
Theatre du Soleil, Cartoucherie, 75012 Paris, France
**Mo Yan** — Nobel Literature Laureate
Meutheun, 215 Vauxhall Bridge Road, London SW1V 1EJ, England
**Moakes, Gordon P** — Guitarist (Bloc Party)
Coalition Mgmt, 12 Barley Mow Passage, London W4 4PH, England
**Moakler, Shanna L** — Beauty Queen, Actress, Model
Global Artists Agency, 6253 Hollywood Blvd, #508, Los Angeles CA 90028 USA
**Moalem, Sharon** — Writer
Harper Collins Publishers, 10 E 53rd St, Cellar 1, New York NY 10022 USA
**Moates, David A (Dave)** — Baseball Player
7924 24th Ave W, Bradenton FL 34209, USA
**Moats, David** — Journalist
Rutland Herald, Editorial Dept, PO Box 668, Rutland VT 05702, USA
**Moats, Sanford K** — Air Force General, WW II Hero
59-635 Akanoho Place, Haleiwa HI 96712, USA
**Mobley, Cuttino R** — Basketball Player
PO Box 11319, Beverly Hills CA 90213, USA
**Mobley, John U** — Football Player
3512 Legacy Hills Court, Longwood FL 32779, USA
**Mobley, Mary Ann** — Actress, Beauty Queen
Corsa Agency, 11704 Wilshire Blvd, #204, Los Angeles CA 90025, USA
**Mobley, Orson O** — Football Player
400 S 24th Ave, Hattiesburg MS 39401, USA
**Mobley, William H** — Educator
513 Hearn St, Austin TX 78703, USA
**Moby** — Singer, Guitarist
Deutsch-Ebgkuscge Freundschaft, 51 Lonsdale Road, London NW6 6RA, England
**Moceanu, Dominique** — Gymnast
211 Walden Ridge Dr, Hinckley OH 44233, USA
**Mochrie, Colin** — Actor, Comedian
385 Adelaide St W, Toronto ON M5V 1S4, Canada
**Mock, Garrett L** — Baseball Player
13650 Maisemore Road, Houston TX 77015, USA
**Mockett, Cathy** — Golfer
1601 Antigua Way, Newport Beach CA 92660, USA
**Mocumbi, Pascoal M** — Prime Minister, Mozambique
1874 Ave Arnando Tivane, Maputo, Mozambique
**Modano, Michael (Mike)** — Ice Hockey Player
10453 Epping Lane, Dallas TX 75229, USA

**Modell, Frank** — Cartoonist
115 Three Mile Course, Guilford CT 06437, USA
**Moder, Danny** — Cinematographer
W M E Entertainment, 9601 Wilshire Blvd, #300, Beverly Hills CA 90210 USA
**Modi, Narendra D** — Prime Minister, India
Prime Minister's Office, South Block, Safdaejun Road, New Delhi 110011, India
**Modiano, Patrick** — Nobel Literature Laureate
Editions Gallimard, 5 Rue Gaston-Gallimard, 75328 Paris Cedex 07, France
**Modin, Fredrik** — Ice Hockey Player
8955 Dunn Curt, Dublin OH 43017, USA
**Modine, Matthew** — Actor
Untitled Entertainment, 350 S Beverly Dr, #200, Beverly Hills CA 90212 USA
**Modry, Jaroslav** — Ice Hockey Player
1724 Malvern Hill Place, Duluth GA 30097, USA
**Modrzejewski, Robert J** — Vietnam War Marine Corps Hero (CMH)
4725 Oporto Court, San Diego CA 92124, USA
**Modzelewski, Richard B (Dick)** — Football Player
1357 Fox Run Dr, #105, Willoughby OH 44094, USA
**Moe, Douglas E (Doug)** — Basketball Player, Coach
13 Arnold Palmer, San Antonio TX 78257, USA
**Moe, Thomas S (Tommy)** — Alpine Skier
1556 Hidden Lane, Anchorage AK 99501, USA
**Moegle, Richard L (Dicky)** — Football Player
4207 DeForest Ridge Circle, Katy TX 77494, USA
**Moehler, Brian M** — Baseball Player
269 Woodlawn Dr NE, Marietta GA 30067, USA
**Moehringer, J R** — Journalist
Los Angeles Times, Editorial Dept, 202 W 1st St, Los Angeles CA 90012 USA
**Moe-Humphreys, Karen** — Swimmer, Swimming Coach
505 Augusta Dr, Moraga CA 94556, USA
**Moeller, Chad E** — Baseball Player
11058 E Raintree Dr, Scottsdale AZ 85255, USA
**Moeller, Chet** — Football Player
Wilson Price Information Technology, 3815 Interstate Court, Montgomery AL 36109, USA
**Moeller, David** — Luge Athlete
Meet Success, Auf der Eierwiese 1, 82031 Gruenwald, Germany
**Moeller, Dennis L** — Inventor (Micro Computer System)
147 Florence Dr, Jupiter FL 33458, USA
**Moeller, Edward** — Basketball Player
1011 Kelton College Way, Morrisville NC 27560, USA
**Moeller, Joseph D (Joe)** — Baseball Player
1505 Avenida de Nogales, San Clemente CA 92672, USA
**Moeller, Robert T** — Navy Admiral
Deputy Commander, Military Operations, US Africa Command, APO AE 09751, USA
**Moellering, John H** — Army General
United Services Automobile Assn, USAA Building, 9800 Fredericksburg Road, San Antonio TX 78288, USA
**Moen, John** — Drummer (Decemberists)
Big Hassle, 44 Wall St, #2200, New York NY 10005, USA
**Moennig, Katherine** — Actress
Framework Entertainment, 9057 Nemo St, #C, West Hollywood CA 90069 USA
**Moerner, William E (W E)** — Chemist
Stanford University, Moerner Laboratory, Chemistry Dept, Stanford CA 94305, USA
**Moffatt, Henry K** — Mathematical Physicist
6 Banhams Close, Cambridge CB4 1HX, England
**Moffatt, Katy** — Singer, Guitarist, Songwriter
PO Box 334, O Fallon IL 62269, USA
**Moffett, D W** — Actor
Innovative Artists, 1505 10th St, Santa Monica CA 90401 USA
**Moffett, Donald** — Artist
Anthony Meier Fine Arts, 1969 California St, San Francisco CA 94109, USA
**Moffitt, John** — Track Athlete
Vector Sports Mgmt, 417 Keller Parkway, Keller TX 76248, USA
**Moffitt, Peggy** — Model, Actress
Browns, 23-27 S Moulton St, London W1K 5RD, England
**Moffitt, Randall J (Randy)** — Baseball Player
1725 Baltic Ave, Prescott AZ 86301, USA
**Mofford, Rose** — Governor, AZ
330 W Maryland Ave, #104, Phoenix AZ 85013, USA
**Mogenburg, Dietmar** — Track Athlete
Alter Garfen 34, 51371 Leverkusen, Germany
**Mogilny, Alexander G** — Ice Hockey Player
24146 Malibu Road, Malibu CA 90265, USA
**Mogis, Michael R (Mike)** — Musician (Bright Eyes)
Press Here, 138 W 25th St, #700, New York NY 10001, USA
**Mohacsi, Mary** — Bowler
15445 Sunset St, Livonia MI 48154, USA
**Mohamed Khouna, Cheikh El Avia Ould** — Prime Minister, Mauritania
Prime Minister's Office, Nouakchott, Mauritania
**Mohammed VI** — King, Morocco
Royal Palais, Dar Al Mahkzen, Rabat, Morocco
**Mohammed, Nazr T** — Basketball Player
Chicago Bulls, United Center, 1901 W Madison St, Chicago IL 60612 USA
**Mohapatra, Bibhu** — Fashion Designer
270 W 38th St, #1100, New York NY 10018, USA
**Mohler, Michael R (Mike)** — Baseball Player
1627 S Shirley Ave, Gonzales LA 70737, USA
**Mohoric, Dale R** — Baseball Player
15501 Rockside Road, Maple Heights OH 44137, USA
**Mohr, Christopher G (Chris)** — Football Player
3260 Surrey Road, Thomson GA 30824, USA
**Mohr, Dustan** — Baseball Player
103 Parkwood Dr, Hattiesburg MS 39402, USA
**Mohr, Jay** — Actor, Comedian
Giraffe Productions, 4406 Vantage Ave, Studio City CA 91604, USA
**Mohri, Mamoru** — Astronaut, Japan
Japanese Aerospace Exploration Agency, 2-1-1 Sengen, Tsukuba, Ibaraki 305 8505, Japan

**Mohseni, Saad** — Businessman
Moby Group, 3 Street 12, Wazir Akbar Khan, District 10, Kabul, Afghanistan
**Mohyeldin, Ayman** — Journalist
Al Jazeera, PO Box 23127, Doha, Qatar
**Moio, Ashton** — Actor
Innovative Artists, 1505 10th St, Santa Monica CA 90401 USA
**Moir, Richard** — Actor
Shanahan Mgmt, PO Box 1509, Darlinghurst NSW 1300, Australia
**Moir, Scott** — Ice Dancer
Arctic Edge Ice Arena, 46615 Michigan Ave, Canton MI 48188, USA
**Moiso, Jerome** — Basketball Player
Cleveland Cavaliers, Gund Arena, 1 Center Court, Cleveland OH 44115 USA
**Mojsiejenko, Ralf** — Football Player
11334 Baldwin Road, Bridgman MI 49106, USA
**Mok, Karen** — Actress
Creative Artists Agency, 2000 Ave of Stars, #100, Los Angeles CA 90067 USA
**Mokeski, Paul K** — Basketball Player
4004 Crestwood Dr, Carrolton TX 75007, USA
**Mokosak, Carl** — Ice Hockey Player
8073 Rum Creek Trail NE, Rockford MI 49341, USA
**Mokri, Amir M** — Cinematographer
Gersh Agency, 9465 Wilshire Blvd, #600, Beverly Hills CA 90212 USA
**Mol, Gretchen** — Actress
John Carrabino Mgmt, 5900 Wilshire Blvd, #406, Los Angeles CA 90036 USA
**Molale, Brandon** — Actor
Coolwaters Productions, 10061 Riverside Dr, Box 531, Toluca Lake CA 91602 USA
**Molaro, Sandrine** — Actress
TalentBox Cineart, 28 Rue de Mogador, 75009 Paris, France
**Molden, Alex M** — Football Player
2030 Wellington Dr, West Linn OR 97068, USA
**Moldovan, Diana** — Model
I M G Models, 304 Park Ave S, #PH N, New York NY 10010 USA
**Mole, Fenton L** — Baseball Player
738 Glen Eagle Court, Danville CA 94526, USA
**Molgg, Manfred** — Alpine Skier
Via Paracia 3/5, 39030 S Vigilio, Italy
**Molina Matta, Jose B** — Baseball Player
Tampa Bay Rays, 1 Tropicana Dr, Saint Petersburg FL 33705 USA
**Molina, Alfred** — Actor, Singer
Lou Coulson, 37 Berwick St, London W1V 3RF, England
**Molina, Angela** — Actress
Agents Associes, 201 Rue du Faubourg Saint Honore, 75008 Paris, France
**Molina, Benjamin J (Bengie)** — Baseball Player
6475 E Crantree Place, Yuma AZ 85365, USA
**Molina, Mario J** — Nobel Chemistry Laureate
PO Box 12406, La Jolla CA 92039, USA
**Molina, Yadier B** — Baseball Player
1005 Bluff Pointe Court, Caseyville IL 62232, USA
**Molinari, Anna** — Fashion Designer
Via G Ferraris 13/15/15/15A, 411012 Carpi (Modena), Italy
**Molinaro, Al** — Actor
1530 Arboles Dr, Glendale CA 91207, USA
**Molinaro, Robert J (Bob)** — Baseball Player
1 Harbourside Dr, #2312, Delray Beach FL 33483, USA
**Molitor, Paul L** — Baseball Player
6725 Iroquois Circle, Minneapolis MN 55439, USA
**Molko, Brian** — Singer, Guitarist (Placebo), Songwriter
Riverman Records, George House, Brecon Road, London W6 8PY, England
**Moll, John L** — Electronics Engineer
4111 Old Trace Road, Palo Alto CA 94306, USA
**Moll, Kurt** — Opera Singer
Gross Theaterstr 34, 20354 Hamburg, Germany
**Moll, Richard** — Actor
Studio Talent Group, 1328 12th St, Santa Monica CA 90401, USA
**Molla, Jordi** — Actor
Paradigm Agency, 360 N Crescent Dr, North Building, Beverly Hills CA 90210 USA
**Moller, David** — Luge Athlete
Blessbergstr 29, 96528 Schalkau/Truckenthal, Germany
**Moller, Paul** — Inventor (Sky Car), Engineer
Moller International, 1222 Research Park Dr, Davis CA 95618, USA
**Moller, Randy** — Ice Hockey Player
3950 NW 23rd Terrace, Boca Raton FL 33431, USA
**Moller-Gladisch, Silke** — Track Athlete
Lange Str 6, 18055 Rostock, Germany
**Mollo, John** — Costume Designer
Dower House, Church St, West Hanney, Wantage OX12 0LW, England
**Mollo-Christensen, Erik L** — Oceanographer
10 Barberry Road, Lexington MA 02421, USA
**Molloy, Irene** — Actress
Gersh Agency, 9465 Wilshire Blvd, #600, Beverly Hills CA 90212 USA
**Molloy, Matt** — Flutist (Chieftains)
Macklam/Feldman Mgmt, 1505 W 2nd Ave, #200, Vancouver BC V6H 3Y4, Canada
**Moloney, Janel** — Actress
Gersh Agency, 9465 Wilshire Blvd, #600, Beverly Hills CA 90212 USA
**Moloney, Paddy** — Singer (Chieftains)
Macklam/Feldman Mgmt, 1505 W 2nd Ave, #200, Vancouver BC V6H 3Y4, Canada
**Moloney, Richard H (Rich)** — Baseball Player
125 Mallard Way, Waltham MA 02452, USA
**Moltmann, Jurgen** — Theologian
Liebermeister Str 12, 72076 Tubingen, Germany
**Molyneux, Juan Pablo** — Architect
J P Molyneux Studio, 29 E 69th St, New York NY 10021, USA
**Mom Rajawong Sirikit Kitiyarara** — Queen, Thailand
Royal Residence, Chitralada Villa, 9 Rama VI Road, Soi 30, Bangkok 10400, Thailand
**Momaday, N Scott** — Writer
University of Arizona, English Dept, Tucson AZ 85721, USA

**Momesso, Sergio** — Ice Hockey Player
Momesso Caffe, 3669 Boul St Jean, Dollard les Ormeaux QC H9G 1X2, Canada
**Momoa, Jason** — Actor, Model
A P A Talent & Literary Agency, 405 S Beverly Dr, #300, Beverly Hills CA 90212 USA
**Momsen, Taylor** — Actress
Das Communications, 83 Riverside Dr, New York NY 10024, USA
**Monacelli, Amleto** — Bowler
Professional Bowlers Association, 719 2nd Ave, #701, Seattle WA 98104 USA
**Monaco, Kara** — Model
Dino May Mgmt, 11262 Ventura Blvd, #PH, Studio City CA 91604, USA
**Monaco, Kelly M** — Actress, Model, Dancer
W M E Entertainment, 9601 Wilshire Blvd, #300, Beverly Hills CA 90210 USA
**Monae, Janelle** — Singer
W M E Entertainment, 9601 Wilshire Blvd, #300, Beverly Hills CA 90210 USA
**Monaghan, Cameron** — Actor
C E S D, 10635 Santa Monica Blvd, #130, Los Angeles CA 90025 USA
**Monaghan, Dominic** — Actor, Producer
A P A Talent & Literary Agency, 405 S Beverly Dr, #300, Beverly Hills CA 90212 USA
**Monaghan, Kris** — Golfer
54 Golf Course Dr, Ranchos de Taos NM 87557, USA
**Monaghan, Michelle** — Actress
I C M Partners, 10250 Constellation Blvd, #900, Los Angeles CA 90067 USA
**Monahan, Dan** — Actor
Cuzzings Mgmt, 1425 N Detroit St, #304, Los Angeles CA 90046, USA
**Monahan, David H** — Actor, Director
Bauman Redanty Shaul Agency, 5757 Wilshire Blvd, #473, Los Angeles CA 90036 USA
**Monahan, Garry** — Ice Hockey Player
4665 Piccadilly N, West Vancouver BC V7W 1E3, Canada
**Monahan, Gretchen (Gretta)** — Entertainer
Food Network, 1180 Ave of Americas, #1200, New York NY 10036 USA
**Monahan, Pat** — Singer (Train)
Jon Landau, 150 Rowayton Ave, Norwalk CT 06853, USA
**Monahan, William** — Writer, Director
W M E Entertainment, 9601 Wilshire Blvd, #300, Beverly Hills CA 90210 USA
**Monastyrska, Liudmyla** — Opera Singer
I M G Artists, Hogarth Business Park, Chiswick, London W4 2TH, England
**Monbouquette, William C (Bill)** — Baseball Player
46 Doonan St, Medford MA 02155, USA
**Moncrief, Sidney A** — Basketball Player
9842 Audelia Road, #1109, Dallas TX 75238, USA
**Moncrieff, Karen** — Actress, Director, Writer
Anonymous Content, 3532 Hayden Ave, Culver City CA 90232 USA
**Mond, Josh** — Producer
United Talent Agency, U T A Plaza, 9336 Civic Center Dr, Beverly Hills CA 90210 USA
**Mondale, Walter F** — Vice President; Senator, MN
Dorsey & Whitney, 50 S 6th St, #1500, Minneapolis MN 55402, USA
**Monday, Kenneth D (Kenny)** — Freestyle Wrestler
4119 W Deer Crossing Dr, Stillwater OK 74074, USA
**Monday, Robert J (Rick)** — Baseball Player, Sportscaster
811 Gayfeather Lane, Vero Beach FL 32963, USA
**Mondey, Fawnia** — Actress, Model
631 N Stephanie St, #162, Henderson NV 89014, USA
**Mondlock, Buddy** — Singer, Guitarist, Songwriter
Stewart Mgmt, PO Box 27581, Denver CO 80227, USA
**Mondou, Pierre** — Ice Hockey Player
239 Rue Wildor Larochelle, Sorel Tracy QC J3P 6R2, Canada
**Mone, Michelle** — Fashion Designer
M J M International, 8 Redwood Crescent, Peel Park, Glasgow G74 5PA, Scotland
**Moneo, J Rafael** — Pritzker Architectural Laureate
Calle Mino 5, 28002 Madrid, Spain
**Monet, Daniella** — Actress
Paradigm Agency, 360 N Crescent Dr, North Building, Beverly Hills CA 90210 USA
**Money B** — Rap Music
L W 1, 9378 Wilshire Blvd, #310, Beverly Hills CA 90212, USA
**Money, Eddie** — Singer
I C M Partners, 730 5th Ave, New York NY 10019 USA
**Money, Eric V** — Basketball Player
457 S Harvard Ave, Tucson AZ 85710, USA
**Money, Ken** — Astronaut, Canada
D C I E M, 1133 Sheppard Ave W, #2000, Downsview ON M3M 3B9, Canada
**Monger, Christopher** — Director
I C M Partners, 10250 Constellation Blvd, #900, Los Angeles CA 90067 USA
**Monger, Matthew L (Matt)** — Football Player
10219 S Canton Ave, Tulsa OK 74137, USA
**Monheit, Jane** — Singer, Songwriter
American International Artists, 356 Pine Valley Road, Hoosick Falls NY 12090, USA
**Monica** — Singer
Spirit Media, PO Box 43591, Phoenix AZ 85080, USA
**Monifah** — Singer, Songwriter
Richard Walters, PO Box 2789, Toluca Lake CA 91610 USA
**Moning, Karen Marie** — Writer
Delacorte Press, 1540 Broadway, New York NY 10036 USA
**Mo'Nique** — Actress, Comedienne
Spectrum Talent Agency, 520 W 43rd St, New York NY 10036, USA
**Moniz, Ernest J** — Secretary, Energy; Physicist
Energy Department, 1000 Independence Ave SW, Washington DC 20585 USA
**Moniz, Wendy** — Actress
Innovative Artists, 1505 10th St, Santa Monica CA 90401 USA
**Monk, Arthur (Art)** — Football Player, Sportscaster
10896 Lake Windemere Dr, Great Falls VA 22066, USA
**Monk, Debra** — Actress, Singer
B R S / Gage Talent Agency, 1650 Broadway, #1410, New York NY 10019 USA
**Monk, Meredith J** — Choreographer, Composer
228 W Broadway, New York NY 10013, USA
**Monk, Sophie** — Singer, Actress
A P A Talent & Literary Agency, 405 S Beverly Dr, #300, Beverly Hills CA 90212 USA

**Monninger, Nikki** — Bassist, Singer (Silversun Pickups)
Ink Tank Public Relations, 1825 W Sunset Blvd, #102, Los Angeles CA 90026, USA
**Monoharova, Taitana** — Opera Singer
I M G Artists, Hogarth Business Park, Chiswick, London W4 2TH, England
**Monoson, Lawrence** — Actor
Ovation Mgmt, 12028 National Blvd, Los Angeles CA 90064, USA
**Monroe, Ashley** — Singer, Songwriter
Spalding Entertainment, 1025 16th Ave, #303, Nashville TN 30312, USA
**Monroe, Craig K** — Baseball Player
4123 Lynn Dr, Texarkana TX 75503, USA
**Monroe, Jordan** — Model
Playboy Promotions, 9346 Civic Center Dr, #200, Beverly Hills CA 90210 USA
**Monroe, Kimber** — Actress
1230 N Horn, #728, West Hollywood CA 90069, USA
**Monroe, Lawrence J (Larry)** — Baseball Player
725 N Hundley St, Hoffman Estates IL 60169, USA
**Monroe, Maika** — Actress
W M E Entertainment, 9601 Wilshire Blvd, #300, Beverly Hills CA 90210 USA
**Monroe, Meredith** — Actress
Abrams Artists, 9200 W Sunset Blvd, #1125, West Hollywood CA 90069 USA
**Monroe, Mircea** — Actress
Innovative Artists, 1505 10th St, Santa Monica CA 90401 USA
**Monroe, Steve** — Actor
House of Representatives, 1434 6th St, #1, Santa Monica CA 90401 USA
**Monroe, V Earl (Pearl)** — Basketball Player
1925 Adam Clayton Powell Jr Blvd, #6D, New York NY 10026, USA
**Monroe, Zachary C (Zach)** — Baseball Player
1 Sandalwood Lane, Bartonville IL 61607, USA
**Monsengwo Pasinya, Laurent Cardinal** — Religious Leader
Archeveche, Ave de l'Universite, BP 8431, Kinshasa 1, Congo Democratic Republic
**Monson, Dan** — Basketball Coach
California State University, Athletic Dept, Long Beach CA 90840, USA
**Monson, Thomas S** — Religious Leader
Church of Latter-Day Saints, 47 E South Temple, Salt Lake City UT 84150, USA
**Montador, Steve** — Ice Hockey Player
5857 NW 122nd Terrace, Coral Springs FL 33076, USA
**Montag, Heidi** — Actress, Singer, Model
Innovator Mgmt, 8899 Beverly Blvd, #622, Los Angeles CA 90048, USA
**Montagnier, Luc** — Nobel Medicine Laureate
World AIDS Research Foundation, Castello 4930, 30122 Venice, Italy
**Montague, Diana** — Opera Singer
91 Saint Martin's Lane, London WC2, England
**Montague, Emily** — Actress
TalentWorks, 3500 W Olive Ave, #1400, Burbank CA 91505 USA
**Montague, John E** — Baseball Player
52 Northshore Circle, Dadeville AL 36853, USA
**Montaigne, Lawrence** — Actor
1827 Morganton Dr, Henderson NV 89052, USA
**Montalbano, Chuck** — Golfer
4725 Farmdale Ave, North Hollywood CA 91602, USA
**Montana, Claude** — Fashion Designer
131 Rue Saint-Denis, 75001 Paris, France
**Montana, Joseph C (Joe), Jr** — Football Player
9010 Franz Valley Road, Calistoga CA 94515, USA
**Montana, Manny** — Actor
S D B Partners, 315 S Beverly Dr, #411, Beverly Hills CA 90067 USA
**Montanaro, Carlo** — Conductor
I M G Artists, Hogarth Business Park, Chiswick, London W4 2TH, England
**Montanez, Guillermo N (Willie)** — Baseball Player
HC 5 Box 52020, Caguas PR 00725, USA
**Montefusco, John J** — Baseball Player
1 Oakdale Dr, Middletown NJ 07748, USA
**MonteiroDeCastro, Manuel Cardinal** — Religious Leader
Apostolic Penitentiary, Palazzo della Cancelleria 1, 00186 Rome, Italy
**Monteith, Hank** — Ice Hockey Player
35 William St, Stratford ON N5A 4X9, Canada
**Monteith, Kelly** — Actor, Comedian
PO Box 11669, Knoxville TN 37939, USA
**Montelone, Richard (Rich)** — Baseball Player
441 Lucerne Ave, Tampa FL 33606, USA
**Monterey, Judi** — Model
Playboy Promotions, 9346 Civic Center Dr, #200, Beverly Hills CA 90210 USA
**Monterisi, Francesco Cardinal** — Religious Leader
Saint Paul Outside-the-Walls Basilica, Piazza Pio XII, #10, 00120 Rome, Italy
**Montero, Miguel A** — Baseball Player
Arizona Diamondbacks, Chase Field, 401 E Jefferson, Phoenix AZ 85003 USA
**Montero, Pablo** — Singer, Actor
Apodaca Promotions, 7171 E Tidwell Road, Houston TX 77022, USA
**Montes, Marisa** — Singer, Guitarist
E M I Records, 150 5th Ave, #700, New York NY 10011 USA
**Montevecchi, Liliane** — Singer, Actress, Dancer
Fifi Oscard, 110 W 40th St, #1601, New York NY 10018, USA
**Monteverde, Alejandro Gomez** — Writer, Director, Producer
Metanoia Films, 2950 Los Feliz Blvd, #204, Los Angeles CA 90039, USA
**Montez, Chris** — Singer
Utopia Artists, PO Box 1569, Jupiter FL 33468, USA
**Montgomerie, Colin S** — Golfer
International Mgmt Group, Pier House, Strand on the Green, London W4 3NN, England
**Montgomery, Alton** — Football Player
441 N 9th St, Griffin GA 30223, USA
**Montgomery, Anne** — Sportscaster
ESPN-TV, Sports Dept, ESPN Plaza, 935 Middle St, Bristol CT 06010 USA
**Montgomery, Belinda** — Actress
Epstein-Wyckoff, 280 S Beverly Dr, #400, Beverly Hills CA 90212 USA
**Montgomery, Chuck** — Actor
Don Buchwald Talent Agency, 6500 Wilshire Blvd, #2200, Los Angeles CA 90048 USA

**Montgomery, Cleotha (Cleo)** — Football Player
1801 Crape Myrtle Circle, Irving TX 75063, USA
**Montgomery, D Lamont (Monty)** — Football Player
3011 Pecan Way Court, Richmond TX 77406, USA
**Montgomery, Eddie** — Singer (Montgomery Gentry)
Parallel Entertainment, 209 10th Ave S, #506, Nashville TN 37203, USA
**Montgomery, Gregory H (Greg), Jr** — Football Player
2112 Brentwood Dr, Baton Rouge LA 70809, USA
**Montgomery, James P (Jim)** — Swimmer, Coach
1537 Bella Vista Dr, Dallas TX 75218, USA
**Montgomery, Janet** — Actress
Hamilton Hodell, 20 Golden Square, London W1F 9JL, England
**Montgomery, Jeffrey T (Jeff)** — Baseball Player
3701 W 140th St, Overland Park KS 66224, USA
**Montgomery, Jim** — Ice Hockey Player
Rensselaer Polytechnic Institute, Athletic Dept, 110 8th St, Troy NY 12180, USA
**Montgomery, John Michael** — Singer
Hallmark Direction, 713 18th Ave S, Nashville TN 37203, USA
**Montgomery, Kevin** — Actor
Brooks Murphy Stevens, 5619 N Lankershim Blvd, North Hollywood CA 91601 USA
**Montgomery, Marvin J (Marv)** — Football Player
1509 S Macon St, Aurora CO 80012, USA
**Montgomery, Melba** — Singer
Fat City Artists, 1906 Chet Atkins Place, #502, Nashville TN 37212 USA
**Montgomery, Poppy** — Actress
United Talent Agency, U T A Plaza, 9336 Civic Center Dr, Beverly Hills CA 90210 USA
**Montgomery, Robert A** — Surgeon
Johns Hopkins University Medical Center, Transplantation Center, Baltimore MD 21218, USA
**Montgomery, Robert E (Bob)** — Baseball Player
2 Parkway Dr, Saugus MA 01906, USA
**Montgomery, Steven L (Steve)** — Baseball Player
13731 Mercado Dr, Del Mar CA 92014, USA
**Montgomery, Sy** — Writer
Ballatine Books, 1745 Broadway, New York NY 10019 USA
**Montgomery, Wilbert N** — Football Player
5846 Pine Brook Farm Road, Sykesville MD 21784, USA
**Montiel, Dito** — Director, Writer
Underground Films & Mgmt, 447 S Highland Ave, Los Angeles CA 90036, USA
**Montler, Michael R (Mike)** — Football Player
479 Tiara Vista Dr, Grand Junction CO 81507, USA
**Montminy, Marc R** — Neurochemist
Salk Institute, 10100 N Torrey Pines Road, La Jolla CA 92037 USA
**Montoya, Craig** — Bassist (Everclear)
Pinnacle Entertainment, 30 Glenn St, White Plains NY 10603, USA
**Montoya, Henry (Coco)** — Guitarist
J B Mgmt, PO Box 25703, Chicago IL 60625, USA
**Montoya, Juan** — Interior Designer
330 E 59th St, #200, New York NY 10022, USA
**Montoya, Juan Pablo** — Auto Racing Driver
Earnhardt Ganassi Racing, 8500 Westmoreland Dr, Concord NC 28027, USA
**Montoya, Max, Jr** — Football Player
2110 Williams Road, Hebron KY 41048, USA
**Montoyo, Jose Carlos (Charlie)** — Baseball Player
438 Summer Sails Dr, Valrico FL 33594, USA
**Montross, Eric S** — Basketball Player
4668 S NC Highway 150, Lexington NC 27295, USA
**Montsho Este** — Rap Artist (Arrested Development)
Agency Group Ltd, 142 W 57th St, #600, New York NY 10019 USA
**Montvidas, Edgaras** — Opera Singer
Maxine Robertson Mgmt, 14 Forge Dr, Claygate KT1O 0HR, England
**Montville, Leigh** — Sportswriter
I C M Partners, 10250 Constellation Blvd, #900, Los Angeles CA 90067 USA
**Monty, Peter C (Pete)** — Football Player
PO Box 338, Wellington CO 80549, USA
**Moock, Joseph G (Joe)** — Baseball Player
12432 Pecos Ave, Greenwell Springs LA 70739, USA
**Moodie, Janice** — Golfer
19746 Woodchase Circle, Orlando FL 32836, USA
**Moody, Eric** — Baseball Player
336 Gleneagle Circle, Irmo SC 29063, USA
**Moody, Ivan L (Ghost)** — Singer (Five Finger Death Punch)
10th Street Entertainment, 568 Broadway, #608, New York NY 10012, USA
**Moody, Keith M** — Football Player
4632 Riverview Court, Tracy CA 95377, USA
**Moody, Lynne** — Actress
Gersh Agency, 9465 Wilshire Blvd, #600, Beverly Hills CA 90212 USA
**Moody, Ron** — Actor
Ingleside, 41 The Green, Southgate, London N14, England
**Moody-Luckhurst, Teri** — Golfer
103 Pierrepont Isle, Duluth GA 30097, USA
**Moog, Andy** — Ice Hockey Player
109 Sunrise Dr, Coppell TX 75019, USA
**Moomaw, Donn D** — Football Player
3124 Corda Dr, Los Angeles CA 90049, USA
**Moon, Elizabeth** — Writer
Jabberwocky Literary Agency, PO Box 4558, Sunnyside NY 11104, USA
**Moon, H Warren** — Football Player
Seattle Seahawks, 12 Seahawks Way, Renton WA 98056 USA
**Moon, Jamario R** — Basketball Player
Charlotte Hornets, 333 E Trade St, #A, Charlotte NC 28202 USA
**Moon, Philip** — Actor
Don Buchwald Talent Agency, 6500 Wilshire Blvd, #2200, Los Angeles CA 90048 USA
**Moon, Sheri** — Actress
Dimension Films, 345 Hudson St, #1300, New York NY 10014, USA
**Moon, Wallace W (Wally)** — Baseball Player
3801 E Crest Dr, #6401, Bryan TX 77802, USA

# M

|  |  |
|---|---|
| **Mooney, Beth E**<br>KeyCorp, 127 Public Square, Cleveland OH 44114, USA | Businesswoman |
| **Mooney, Debra**<br>Principal Entertainment, 9255 Sunset Blvd, #500, Los Angeles CA 90069 USA | Actress |
| **Mooney, Edward K (Ed)**<br>4105 63rd St, Lubbock TX 79413, USA | Football Player |
| **Mooney, John**<br>Intrepid Artists, Midtown Plaza, 1300 Baxter St, #405, Charlotte NC 28204, USA | Singer, Guitarist |
| **Mooney, John J**<br>85 Colgate Ave, Wyckoff NJ 07481, USA | Inventor (3-Way Catalytic Converter) |
| **Mooneyham, William C (Bill)**<br>5731 White Crane Road, Atwater CA 95301, USA | Baseball Player |
| **Moonves, Leslie**<br>Columbia Broadcasting System Inc, 7800 Beverly Blvd, Los Angeles CA 90036, USA | Businessman, Producer |
| **Moore, Abra**<br>Progressive Global Agency, PO Box 50294, Nashville TN 37205, USA | Singer |
| **Moore, Alan**<br>Top Shelf, PO Box 1282, Marietta GA 30061, USA | Cartoonist, Writer |
| **Moore, Alvin**<br>1111 W Lark Dr, Chandler AZ 85286, USA | Football Player |
| **Moore, Alvin E (Junior)**<br>3728 Wall Ave, Richmond CA 94804, USA | Baseball Player |
| **Moore, Andre M**<br>12137 S Justine St, Chicago IL 60643, USA | Basketball Player |
| **Moore, Angelo C**<br>Silverback Mgmt, 9469 Jefferson Blvd, #101, Culver City CA 90232, USA | Singer, Saxophonist (Fishbone) |
| **Moore, Ann S**<br>Time-Life, Chairwoman's Office, Time-Life Building, New York NY 10020, USA | Publisher |
| **Moore, Archie F**<br>201 Courtland Road, Indiana PA 15701, USA | Baseball Player |
| **Moore, Balor L**<br>6301 Almeda Road, #717, Houston TX 77021, USA | Baseball Player |
| **Moore, Barbara**<br>Playboy Promotions, 9346 Civic Center Dr, #200, Beverly Hills CA 90210 USA | Actress, Model |
| **Moore, Benjamin P**<br>3123 39th Place S, Seattle WA 98144, USA | Artist |
| **Moore, Billie**<br>2247 Meadow Lane, Fullerton CA 92831, USA | Basketball Coach |
| **Moore, Bradley A (Brad)**<br>3135 Challenger Point Dr, Loveland CO 80538, USA | Baseball Player |
| **Moore, Brandon**<br>Enter-Sports Mgmt, 5 Concourse Parkway, #3000, Atlanta GA 30328, USA | Football Player |
| **Moore, Calvin C**<br>1408 Eagle Pointe Court, Lafayette CA 94549, USA | Mathematician |
| **Moore, Chante**<br>Mauldin Brand Agency, 1280 W Peachtree St, #300, Atlanta GA 30309, USA | Singer, Songwriter |
| **Moore, Charles W (Charlie)**<br>342 County Road 276, Cullman AL 35057, USA | Baseball Player |
| **Moore, Charles, Jr**<br>10 Barclay St, #39C, New York NY 10007, USA | Track Athlete |
| **Moore, Chris**<br>Hansen Jacobson Teller, 450 N Roxbury Dr, #800, Beverly Hills CA 90210 USA | Producer, Director, Actor |
| **Moore, Christina**<br>C E S D, 10635 Santa Monica Blvd, #130, Los Angeles CA 90025 USA | Actress |
| **Moore, Clinton R (Mikki)**<br>Golden State Warriors, 1011 Broadway, Oakland CA 94605 USA | Basketball Player |
| **Moore, Corey A**<br>Cincinnati Bengals, 1 Paul Brown Stadium, Cincinnati OH 45202 USA | Football Player |
| **Moore, Corwin**<br>Creative Artists Agency, 2000 Ave of Stars, #100, Los Angeles CA 90067 USA | Writer, Actor |
| **Moore, David E (Dave)**<br>PO Box 174, Macon NC 27551, USA | Football Player |
| **Moore, Demi**<br>Creative Artists Agency, 2000 Ave of Stars, #100, Los Angeles CA 90067 USA | Actress |
| **Moore, Dick**<br>Dick Moore Assoc, 1560 Broadway, New York NY 10036, USA | Cartoonist (Our Gang) |
| **Moore, Dorothy**<br>Betty of Troy, 100 Lincoln Ave, #12D, Mineola NY 11501, USA | Singer |
| **Moore, Dylan**<br>Stone Manners Salners, 6100 Wilshire Blvd, #1500, Los Angeles CA 90035 USA | Actress |
| **Moore, E McNeil**<br>1212 Woodlawn Dr, Center TX 75935, USA | Football Player |
| **Moore, Eric P**<br>2225 Lindsay Lane, Florissant MO 63031, USA | Football Player |
| **Moore, Ezekiel (Zeke), Jr**<br>3422 Prudence Court, Houston TX 77045, USA | Football Player |
| **Moore, Gary D**<br>7985 Roundrock Road, Dallas TX 75248, USA | Baseball Player |
| **Moore, Geoff**<br>Breen Agency, 110 30th Ave N, #3, Nashville TN 37203, USA | Singer, Songwriter |
| **Moore, Gerald H (Jerry)**<br>Appalachian State University, Athletic Dept, Boone NC 28608, USA | Football Coach |
| **Moore, Harold G (Hal)**<br>585 Moores Mill Road, Auburn AL 36830, USA | Army General, Writer, Hero |
| **Moore, Herman J**<br>3160 Fallen Oaks Court, #605, Rochester Hills MI 48309, USA | Football Player |
| **Moore, Jackie**<br>T-Best Talent Agency, 508 Honey Lake Court, Danville CA 94506 USA | Singer |
| **Moore, Jackie S**<br>2721 Laurel Valley Lane, Arlington TX 76006, USA | Baseball Player, Manager |
| **Moore, James**<br>2624 Abner Place NW, Atlanta GA 30318, USA | Baseball Player |
| **Moore, James E, Jr**<br>18940 Joaquin Court, Salinas CA 93908, USA | Army General |
| **Moore, Jason**<br>W M E Entertainment, 9601 Wilshire Blvd, #300, Beverly Hills CA 90210 USA | Director |

**Mooney - Moore**

**Moore, Joel David** — Actor
I C M Partners, 10250 Constellation Blvd, #900, Los Angeles CA 90067 USA
**Moore, Jonathan Patrick** — Actor
Management 360, 9111 Wilshire Blvd, Beverly Hills CA 90210 USA
**Moore, Josh** — Keyboardist (Caedmon's Call)
Breen Agency, 25 Music Square W, Nashville TN 37203, USA
**Moore, Joshua Logan** — Actor
Innovative Artists, 1505 10th St, Santa Monica CA 90401 USA
**Moore, Julianne** — Actress, Model
Management 360, 9111 Wilshire Blvd, Beverly Hills CA 90210 USA
**Moore, Justin** — Singer
Big Machine Label Group, Valory Music, 1219 16th Ave S, Nashville TN 37212, USA
**Moore, Kellen** — Football Player
Detroit Lions, 222 Republic Dr, Allen Park MI 48101 USA
**Moore, Langston** — Football Player
1727 Quail Run Dr, Garland TX 75040, USA
**Moore, Leonard E (Lenny)** — Football Player
8815 Stonehaven Road, Randallstown MD 21133, USA
**Moore, Loree** — Basketball Player
New York Liberty, Madison Square Garden, 2 Penn Plaza, New York NY 10121 USA
**Moore, Lorrie** — Writer
University of Wisconsin, English Dept, Madison WI 53706, USA
**Moore, Lucille** — Baseball Player
6450 Miami Circle, South Bend IN 46614, USA
**Moore, Mandy** — Singer, Actress, Model
Untitled Entertainment, 350 S Beverly Dr, #200, Beverly Hills CA 90212 USA
**Moore, Mary** — Baseball Player
4225 Lake Grove Court, White Lake MI 48383, USA
**Moore, Mary Tyler** — Actress
510 E 86th St, #21A, New York NY 10028, USA
**Moore, Maulty J** — Football Player
806 Darby Lane, Brooksville FL 34601, USA
**Moore, Maya A** — Basketball Player
Minnesota Lynx, Target Center, 600 1st Ave N, Minneapolis MN 55403 USA
**Moore, Melanie Deanne** — Actress
James/Levy Mgmt, 3500 W Olive Ave, #1470, Burbank CA 91505 USA
**Moore, Melba** — Singer, Actress
Hanns Wolters International, 501 5th Ave, #2112A, New York NY 10017, USA
**Moore, Melissa Anne** — Actress
PO Box 55, Versailles KY 40383, USA
**Moore, Mewelde J C** — Football Player
6345 Riverine Dr, Baton Rouge LA 70820, USA
**Moore, Michael (Mike)** — Attorney
Attorney General's Office, PO Box 220, Jackson MS 39205, USA
**Moore, Michael F** — Director
Dog Eat Dog Films, 430 W 14th St, #401, New York NY 10014, USA
**Moore, Michael W (Mike)** — Baseball Player
1472 E Calle de Caballos, Tempe AZ 85284, USA
**Moore, Nathaniel (Nat)** — Football Player
Nat Moore Assoc, 16911 NE 6th Ave, North Miami Beach FL 33162, USA
**Moore, Patrick** — Golfer
4638 E Dartmouth St, Mesa AZ 85205, USA
**Moore, R Barry** — Baseball Player
6702 Conifer Circle, Indian Trail NC 28079, USA
**Moore, Red** — Baseball Player
2450 Perry Blvd NW, Atlanta GA 30318, USA
**Moore, Richard W (Dickie)** — Ice Hockey Player
4955 Chemin Saint Francois, Saint Laurent QC H4S 1P3, Canada
**Moore, Robert A** — Football Player
1906 E Gate Dr, Stone Mountain GA 30087, USA
**Moore, Robert D (Bob)** — Baseball Player
1641 Chelsea Road, Palos Verdes Estates CA 90274, USA
**Moore, Robert R (Bob)** — Football Player
20 Sally Ann Road, Orinda CA 94563, USA
**Moore, Robert S (Rob)** — Football Player
14239 S 8th St, Phoenix AZ 85048, USA
**Moore, Robert V (Bobby)** — Baseball Player
3703 Hyde Park Ave, Cincinnati OH 45209, USA
**Moore, Roger** — Actor
Diamond Mgmt, 31 Percy St, London W1T 2DD, England
**Moore, Ronald L (Ron)** — Football Player
5730 N Oakwood St, Spencer TX 73084, USA
**Moore, Ryan D** — Golfer
Gaylord Sports Mgmt, 13845 N Northsight Blvd, #200, Scottsdale AZ 85260 USA
**Moore, Samuel D (Sam)** — Singer (Sam & Dave)
I'ma Da Wife Enterprises, 7119 E Shea Blvd, #109-436, Scottsdale AZ 85254, USA
**Moore, Scott** — Director, Writer
Creative Artists Agency, 2000 Ave of Stars, #100, Los Angeles CA 90067 USA
**Moore, Scott A** — Baseball Player
Baltimore Orioles, Oriole Park, 333 W Camden St, Baltimore MD 21201 USA
**Moore, Shemar** — Actor
Innovative Artists, 1505 10th St, Santa Monica CA 90401 USA
**Moore, Stephen Campbell** — Actor
Untitled Entertainment, 350 S Beverly Dr, #200, Beverly Hills CA 90212 USA
**Moore, Thomas** — Writer
Harper/Collins Publishers, 10 E 53rd St, Cellar 1, New York NY 10022, USA
**Moore, Thomas M (Tom)** — Football Player
1038 Forest Harbor Dr, Hendersonville TN 37075, USA
**Moore, Thurston** — Singer, Guitarist (Sonic Youth)
Silva Artist Mgmt, 722 Seward St, Los Angeles CA 90038, USA
**Moore, Tracy L** — Basketball Player
12116 E 37th Place, Tulsa OK 74146, USA
**Moore, Trevor P** — Actor, Comedian, Writer, Director
Creative Artists Agency, 2000 Ave of Stars, #100, Los Angeles CA 90067 USA
**Moore, Tyler Jacob** — Actor
B R S/Gage Talent Agency, 5757 Wilshire Blvd, #659, Los Angeles CA 90036, USA

# M

## Moore - Moore

**Moore, Warren N (Trey)** — Baseball Player
5128 Bellerive Bend Dr, College Station TX 77845, USA
**Moorehead, Aaron M** — Football Player
1717 Trillium Lane, Blacksburg VA 24060, USA
**Moorehead, Emery M** — Football Player
1005 Sussex Dr, Northbrook IL 60062, USA
**Moorehead, Kindal J** — Football Player
10011 Montrose Dr, Charlotte NC 28269, USA
**Moorer, Allison** — Singer, Songwriter, Actress
Gold Village Entertainment, 72 Madison Ave, #800, New York NY 10016, USA
**Moore-Towers, Kirsten** — Figure Skater
Skate Canada, 865 Shefford Road, Ottawa ON K1J 1H9, Canada
**Moore-Warner, Eleanor** — Baseball Player
2172 Kinney Ave NW, Grand Rapids MI 49534, USA
**Moore-Watkins, Pauline** — Actress
4077 SW Sunset Dr, #202, Lake Oswego OR 97035, USA
**Moorhouse, Jocelyn** — Director, Producer, Writer
Creative Artists Agency, 2000 Ave of Stars, #100, Los Angeles CA 90067 USA
**Moorman, Brian D** — Football Player
1035 Eagle Point Dr, Saint Augustine FL 32092, USA
**Moorman, Maurice F (Mo), Jr** — Football Player
9641 Shelbyville Road, Simpsonville KY 40067, USA
**Mora Gramunt, Gabriel** — Architect
Mora-Sanvisens Arquitectes, 24 Herzegovina, Pal 1, 08006 Barcelona, Spain
**Mora, Gene** — Cartoonist (Graffiti)
United Feature Syndicate, PO Box 5610, Cincinnati OH 45201 USA
**Mora, James L (Jim), Jr** — Football Coach
University of California, Athletic Dept, Los Angeles CA 90024, USA
**Mora, Melvin** — Baseball Player
2316 Willow Vale Dr, Fallston MD 21047, USA
**Mora, Naima** — Model
Ford Models Inc, 111 5th Ave, #900, New York NY 10003 USA
**Morabito, Timothy R (Tim)** — Football Player
98 Myrtle Ave, Edgewater NJ 07020, USA
**Moraes, Adrian** — Rodeo Bull Rider
Professional Bull Riders Assn, 6 S Tejon St, #700, Colorado Springs CO 80903, USA
**Moraga, David** — Baseball Player
608 Peach Court, Fairfield CA 94534, USA
**Morahan, Christopher T** — Director
Highcombe, Devil's Punchbowl, Thursley, Godalming, Surrey GU8 6NS, England
**Morales Ayma, Juan Evo** — President, Bolivia
President's Office, Palacio de Gobierno, Plaza Murilla, La Paz, Bolivia
**Morales Elvira, Erik I** — Boxer
Miguel Diaz, 9483 Bondeno St, Las Vegas NV 89123, USA
**Morales Hernandez, Jose M** — Baseball Player
PO Box 770985, Winter Garden FL 34777, USA
**Morales, Esai** — Actor
Innovative Artists, 1505 10th St, Santa Monica CA 90401 USA
**Morales, Natalie** — Actress
United Talent Agency, U T A Plaza, 9336 Civic Center Dr, Beverly Hills CA 90210 USA
**Morales, P Pablo** — Swimmer
University of Nebraska, Athletic Dept, Lincoln NE 68588, USA
**Morales, Richard A (Rich)** — Baseball Player
1650 Rosita Road, Pacifica CA 94044, USA
**Morales-Rhodes, Natalie L** — Actress, Producer, Commentator
United Talent Agency, U T A Plaza, 9336 Civic Center Dr, Beverly Hills CA 90210 USA
**Moran, Erin** — Actress
The Agency, 3711 Ocean Front Walk, #1, Marina del Rey CA 90292 USA
**Moran, Ian P** — Ice Hockey Player
PO Box 1462, Duxbury MA 02331, USA
**Moran, J Kevin** — Navy Admiral
Investor Relations Group, 11 Stone St, #300, New York NY 10003, USA
**Moran, Jason** — Jazz Pianist
Vision Arts Mgmt, 16 Clint Finger Roads, Saugerties NY 12477, USA
**Moran, Julie** — Sportscaster, Actress
Creative Artists Agency, 2000 Ave of Stars, #100, Los Angeles CA 90067 USA
**Moran, Nick** — Actor, Director
Artists Partnership, 101 Finsbury Pavement, London EC2A 1RS, England
**Moran, R Alan (Al)** — Baseball Player
34134 Banbury St, Farmington Hills MI 48331, USA
**Moran, Richard J (Rich)** — Football Player
7252 Mimosa Dr, Carlsbad CA 92011, USA
**Moran, Sean F** — Football Player
13577 W 84th Dr, Arvada CO 80005, USA
**Moran, Terry** — Commentator
ABC-TV, News Dept, 77 W 66th St, New York NY 10023 USA
**Moran, Thomas L (Tommy)** — Producer, Writer
Creative Artists Agency, 2000 Ave of Stars, #100, Los Angeles CA 90067 USA
**Moran, William N (Billy)** — Baseball Player
PO Box 82, Luthersville GA 30251, USA
**Morandi, Piergiorgio** — Conductor
I M G Artists, Hogarth Business Park, Chiswick, London W4 2TH, England
**Morandini, Michael R (Mickey)** — Baseball Player
242 Crabapple Lane, Valparaiso IN 46383, USA
**Moranis, Rick** — Actor, Comedian
Bailey Brand Mgmt, 506 Santa Monica Blvd, #327, Santa Monica CA 90401, USA
**Morano Walker, Reed** — Cinematographer
Gersh Agency, 9465 Wilshire Blvd, #600, Beverly Hills CA 90212 USA
**Morante, Laura** — Actress, Director, Writer
Voyez Mon Agent, 20 Ave Rapp, 75007 Paris, France
**Morariu, Ana Caterina** — Actress
Cristiano Cucchini Mgmt, Lungotevere dei Mellini 10, 00193 Rome, Italy
**Morath, Max** — Singer
Producers Inc, 11806 N 56th St, Tampa FL 33617 USA
**Moravcik, Jozef** — Prime Minister, Slovakia
Primacialne Ham 1, Box 192, 81422 Bratislava, Slovakia

**Moravec, Ivan** — Concert Pianist
Pod Vyhidkou 520, 16000 Prague 6, Czech Republic
**Morawetz, Cathleen S** — Mathematician
251 Mercer St, New York NY 10012, USA
**Morbito, Paul** — Guitarist (Chesterfield Kings)
Agency Group Ltd, 142 W 57th St, #600, New York NY 10019 USA
**Morceli, Noureddine** — Track Athlete
Youth & Sports Ministry, 3 Rue Mohamed Belouizdad, Algiers, Algeria
**Mordecai, Michael H (Mike)** — Baseball Player
10 Cross Creek Lane, Dothan AL 36303, USA
**Mordente, Tony** — Actor, Dancer, Choreographer
31 Bay Harbor Dr, Bigfork MT 59911, USA
**Mordkovitch, Lydia** — Concert Violinist
25B Belsize Ave, London NW3 3BL, England
**More, Camilla** — Actress
Sharon Kemp, 477 S Robertson Blvd, #204, Beverly Hills CA 90211 USA
**More, Jayson** — Ice Hockey Player
9532 Thoroughbred Way, Brentwood TN 37027, USA
**More, Michelle** — Volleyball Player, Model
Association of Volleyball Professionals, 2183 Fairview Road, #222, Costa Mesa CA 92627 USA
**Moreau, Ethan B** — Ice Hockey Player
Columbus Blue Jackets, Arena, 200 W Nationwide Blvd, #1, Columbus OH 43215 USA
**Moreau, Jeanne** — Actress
Artmedia, 20 Ave Rapp, 75007 Paris, France
**Moreh, Dror** — Director, Producer, Cinematographer
United Talent Agency, U T A Plaza, 9336 Civic Center Dr, Beverly Hills CA 90210 USA
**Morehead, David M (Dave)** — Baseball Player
13872 Glenmere Dr, Santa Ana CA 92705, USA
**Moreira, Airto** — Jazz Percussionist
A Train Entertainment, 401 Grand Ave, #300, Oakland CA 94610, USA
**Morel, Eric** — Boxer
7119 Tree Lane, Madison WI 53717, USA
**Morel, Francois** — Composer, Conductor, Concert Pianist
Laval University, 1055 Av du Seminaire, Quebec QC G1V 0A6, Canada
**Morel, Pierre** — Director, Cinematographer
Sentient Entertainment, 8840 Wilshire Blvd, #200, Beverly Hills CA 90211, USA
**Moreland, B Keith** — Baseball Player
4209 Hidden Canyon Cove, Austin TX 78746, USA
**Morell, Michael J** — Government Official
Central Intelligence Agency, Director's Office, Washington DC 20505, USA
**Morello, Thomas B (Tom)** — Singer, Guitarist
G A S Entertainment, 722 Seward St, Los Angeles CA 90038, USA
**Moreno, Belita** — Actress
Paradigm Agency, 360 N Crescent Dr, North Building, Beverly Hills CA 90210 USA
**Moreno, Catalina Sandino** — Actress
United Talent Agency, U T A Plaza, 9336 Civic Center Dr, Beverly Hills CA 90210 USA
**Moreno, Chino** — Singer, Guitarist (Deftones)
Velvet Hammer Music, 9911 W Pico Blvd, #350, Los Angeles CA 90035, USA
**Moreno, Ezekiel A (Zeke)** — Football Player
1881 Harris Mill Ave, Chula Vista CA 91913, USA
**Moreno, Jorge** — Singer
Rogers & Cowan, 8687 Melrose Ave, #G700, West Hollywood CA 90069 USA
**Moreno, Luis Alberto** — Financier, Government Official
Inter-America Development Bank, 1300 New York Ave NW, Washington DC 20577, USA
**Moreno, Mario** — Bassist (Los Tucanes de Tijuana)
Tucanes Inc, 6055 E Washington Blvd, #455, Commerce CA 90040, USA
**Moreno, Orber** — Baseball Player
4833 Kingston Circle, Kissimmee FL 34746, USA
**Moreno, Rita** — Actress, Singer
David Belenzon Mgmt, PO Box 5000, PO Box 67, Rancho Santa Fe CA 92067, USA
**Moreno, Roberto** — Auto Racing Driver
252 Montclaire Circle, Weston FL 33326, USA
**Moreno-Ocampo, Luis** — Attorney
International Criminal Court, Maanweg 174, 2516 The Hague AB, Netherlands
**Morenstein, Harley** — Actor, Comedian
Gersh Agency, 9465 Wilshire Blvd, #600, Beverly Hills CA 90212 USA
**Moresco, Robert (Bobby)** — Producer, Director, Writer, Actor
Moresco Productions, 4231 W National Ave, Burbank CA 91505, USA
**Moret, Rogelio (Roger)** — Baseball Player
HC 1 Box 5225, Guaynabo PR 00971, USA
**Moretti, Fabrizio** — Drummer (Strokes)
M V O Ltd, 370 7th Ave, #807, New York NY 10001, USA
**Moretti, Tobias** — Actor
Agentur ContrAct, Infanteriestr 19, #5, 80797 Munich, Germany
**Moretz, Chloe Grace** — Actress
W M E Entertainment, 9601 Wilshire Blvd, #300, Beverly Hills CA 90210 USA
**Morey, Bill** — Actor
Kazarian/Measures/Ruskin, 11969 Ventura Blvd, #300, Studio City CA 91604 USA
**Morey, Sean J** — Football Player
63 McCosh Circle, Princeton NJ 8540, USA
**Morga, Tom** — Actor, Stuntman
Stuntmen Assn, 10660 Riverside Dr, #200E, Toluca Lake CA 91602, USA
**Morgan, Abi** — Writer
Creative Artists Agency, 2000 Ave of Stars, #100, Los Angeles CA 90067 USA
**Morgan, Alexandra P (Alex)** — Soccer Player, Model
Wasserman Media Group, 10960 Wilshire Blvd, #2200, Los Angeles CA 90024, USA
**Morgan, Anthony E** — Football Player
10306 Reno Ave, Cleveland OH 44105, USA
**Morgan, Barbara R** — Astronaut
2996 S Rookery Lane, Boise ID 83706, USA
**Morgan, Chad** — Actor
S M S Talent, 8383 Wilshire Blvd, #230, Beverly Hills CA 90211 USA
**Morgan, Craig** — Singer, Guitarist, Songwriter
Vector Mgmt, PO Box 120479, Nashville TN 37212 USA
**Morgan, Daniel T (Dan), Jr** — Football Player
1915 Funny Cide Dr, Waxhaw NC 28173, USA

Moravec - Morgan

**Morgan, Debbi** — Actress
Mitchell K Stubbs Assoc, 8695 W Washington Blvd, #204, Culver City CA 90232 USA
**Morgan, Debelah** — Singer, Songwriter
D A S Communications, 83 Riverside Dr, New York NY 10024, USA
**Morgan, Donald M** — Cinematographer
15826 Mayall St, North Hills CA 91343, USA
**Morgan, Gil** — Golfer
PO Box 806, Edmond OK 73083, USA
**Morgan, Glen** — Director, Producer, Writer
Creative Artists Agency, 2000 Ave of Stars, #100, Los Angeles CA 90067 USA
**Morgan, James N** — Economist
1200 Earhart Road, #500, Ann Arbor MI 48105, USA
**Morgan, Jane** — Singer
63 North St, Kennebunkport ME 04046, USA
**Morgan, Jaye P** — Singer, Actress
1185 La Grange Ave, Newbury Park CA 91320, USA
**Morgan, Jeffrey Dean** — Actor
United Talent Agency, U T A Plaza, 9336 Civic Center Dr, Beverly Hills CA 90210 USA
**Morgan, John G, Jr** — Navy Admiral
Deputy CNO, Operations Plans & Strategy, HqUSN, Pentagon, Washington DC 20350 USA
**Morgan, Joseph** — Actor
Richard Konigsberg Mgmt, 400 N Mansfield Ave, Los Angeles CA 90036, USA
**Morgan, Joseph L (Joe)** — Baseball Player
3523 Country Club Place, Danville CA 94506, USA
**Morgan, Joseph M (Joe)** — Baseball Player, Manager
15 Oak Hill Dr, Walpole MA 02081, USA
**Morgan, Kevin L** — Baseball Player
205 Yearling Road, #A, Duson LA 70529, USA
**Morgan, Lorrie** — Singer
Webster Assoc, PO Box 23015, Nashville TN 37202, USA
**Morgan, Marabel** — Writer
Total Woman Inc, 1300 NW 167th St, Miami FL 33169, USA
**Morgan, Meli'sa** — Singer
Orpheus, 630 9th Ave, #1101, New York NY 10036, USA
**Morgan, Michael** — Geneticist
Wellcome Trust, 183 Euston Road, London NW1 2BE, England
**Morgan, Michele** — Actress, Singer
Agents Associes Claudie Nolte, 201 Rue du Faubourg Saint Honore, 75001 Paris, France
**Morgan, Mike** — Baseball Player
PO Box 681130, Park City UT 84068, USA
**Morgan, Mike** — Cartoonist (For Heaven's Sake)
Trinity United Methodist Church, 814 West Ave, Cartersville GA 30120, USA
**Morgan, Peter** — Writer, Director
Independent Talent Group, 40 Whitfield St, London W1T 2RH, England
**Morgan, Piers** — Commentator
CNN-TV, News Dept, 820 1st St NE, #1000, Washington DC 20002 USA
**Morgan, Quincy D E** — Football Player
2715 Taylorcrest, Missouri City TX 77459, USA
**Morgan, Robert B** — Senator, NC
PO Box 377, Lillington NC 27546, USA
**Morgan, Robert M (Bobby)** — Baseball Player
3004 Stoneybrook Road, Oklahoma City OK 73120, USA
**Morgan, Robin E** — Editor, Writer
Ms Magazine, Editorial Dept, 230 Park Ave, New York NY 10169, USA
**Morgan, Stanley D** — Football Player
PO Box 383048, Germantown TN 38183, USA
**Morgan, Thomas R** — Marine Corps General
8105 Haddington Court, Fairfax Station VA 22039, USA
**Morgan, Tim** — Auto Racing Executive
Morgan-McClure Motorsports, 26502 Newbanks Road, Abingdon VA 24210, USA
**Morgan, Tracy** — Actor, Comedian
P M K-B N C, 8687 Melrose Ave, #800, Los Angeles CA 90069 USA
**Morgan, Trevor** — Actor
I F A Talent Agency, 8730 W Sunset Blvd, #490, West Hollywood CA 90069 USA
**Morgan, Walter** — Golfer
15536 Fishermans Rest Court, Cornelius NC 28031, USA
**Morgan, William N** — Architect
William Morgan Architects, 220 E Forsyth St, Jacksonville FL 32202, USA
**Morganna** — Entertainer, Model
PO Box 20281, Columbus OH 43220, USA
**Morgenson, Gretchen C** — Journalist
New York Times, Editorial Dept, 229 W 43rd St, New York NY 10036 USA
**Morgenstern, Joe** — Journalist
Wall Street Journal, Editorial Dept, 1 World Financial Center, New York NY 10281 USA
**Morgenstern, Julie** — Writer
Julie Morgenstern Enterprises, 850 7th Ave, New York NY 10019, USA
**Morgenstern, Thomas** — Ski Jumper
Eichenweg 15, 9851 Liserbrucke, Austria
**Morgenthau, Kramer** — Cinematographer
1632 Maltman Ave, Los Angeles CA 90026, USA
**Morgenthau, Robert M** — Attorney
1085 Park Ave, New York NY 10128, USA
**Morhardt, Meredith G (Moe)** — Baseball Player
219 Spencer Hill Road, Winsted CT 06098, USA
**Mori, Barbara** — Actress
Caliber Media, 9229 W Sunset Blvd, #705, West Hollywood CA 90069, USA
**Mori, Emanuel (Manny)** — President, Micronesia
President's Office, Palikir, Kolonia, Pohnpei FM 96941, Micronesia
**Mori, Hanae** — Fashion Designer
Veronique de Moussai, 5 Place de l'Alma, 75008 Paris, France
**Mori, Riyo** — Beauty Queen
Miss Universe Organization, 1370 Ave of Americas, #1600, New York NY 10019 USA
**Mori, Yoshiro** — Prime Minister, Japan
House of Representatives, 1-7-1 Nagatacho, Chiyodaku, Tokyo 100 0014, Japan
**Morial, Marc H** — Social Activist; Mayor, New Orleans
National Urban League, 120 Wall St, #700, New York NY 10005, USA

| | |
|---|---|
| **Moriarty, Erin** | Actress |
| Jordan Gill Dornbaum, 1133 Broadway, #623, New York NY 10010, USA | |
| **Moriarty, Laura** | Writer |
| University of Kansas, English Dept, Lawrence KS 66045, USA | |
| **Moriarty, Liane** | Writer |
| Curtis Brown Literary Agents, 2 Boundary St, Paddington NSW 2021, Australia | |
| **Moriarty, Michael** | Actor |
| Actors International, Via Fosso del Poggio 141, 00189 Rome, Italy | |
| **Moriarty, Mike** | Baseball Player |
| 5 E Oleander Dr, Mount Laurel NJ 08054, USA | |
| **Moriarty, Thomas (Tom), Jr** | Football Player |
| 28800 Fairmount Blvd, Cleveland OH 44124, USA | |
| **Moriarty-Gentile, Cathy** | Actress |
| Liebman Entertainment, 235 Park Ave S, #1000, New York NY 10003, USA | |
| **Moric, Nina** | Model, Singer |
| New York Model Mgmt, 596 Broadway, #701, New York NY 10012 USA | |
| **Morillon, Philippe** | Army General, France |
| Ministere de la Defense, 14 Rue Saint-Dominique, 75700 Paris, France | |
| **Morin, Catherine** | Actress |
| Artmedia, 20 Ave Rapp, 75007 Paris, France | |
| **Morin, James C (Jim)** | Editorial Cartoonist |
| Miami Herald, Editorial Dept, 1 Herald Plaza, Miami FL 33132 USA | |
| **Morin, Lee M E** | Astronaut |
| 10 Marys Creek Lane, Friendswood TX 77546, USA | |
| **Moringstar, Darren** | Basketball Player |
| 1515 W Ingomar Road, Pittsburgh PA 15237, USA | |
| **Morissette, Alanis** | Singer, Songwriter, Actress, Producer |
| Creative Artists Agency, 2000 Ave of Stars, #100, Los Angeles CA 90067 USA | |
| **Moritz, Louisa** | Actress |
| 405 S Cliftwood Ave, Los Angeles CA 90049, USA | |
| **Moriyama, Raymond** | Architect |
| 32 Davenport Road, Toronto ON M5R 1H3, Canada | |
| **Mork, Truis** | Concert Cellist |
| Harrison/Parrott, 5-6 Albion Court, London W6 0QT, England | |
| **Morkis, Dorothy** | Equestrian |
| 17 Farm St, Dover MA 02030, USA | |
| **Morlan, John G** | Baseball Player |
| 3290 Belgreen St, Grove City OH 43123, USA | |
| **Morland, David** | Golfer |
| 5531 Oxford Moor Blvd, Windermere FL 34786, USA | |
| **Morley, Joanne** | Golfer |
| I M G, Pier House, Strand-on-the-Green, Chiswick, London W4 3NN England | |
| **Morley, Lawrence W** | Geophysicist |
| 90 Hemlock St, Saint Thomas ON N5R 1X9, Canada | |
| **Morley, Malcolm** | Artist, Sculptor |
| Sperone Westwater, 415 W 13th St, #200, New York NY 10014, USA | |
| **Morman, Alvin** | Baseball Player |
| 117 Philadelphia Dr, Rockingham NC 28379, USA | |
| **Morman, Russell L (Russ)** | Baseball Player |
| 3209 S Mark Twain Ave, Blue Springs MO 64015, USA | |
| **Mornas, Pierre-Olivier** | Actor |
| Art 7, 11 Rue Du Bouloi, 75001 Paris, France | |
| **Morneau, Justin E G** | Baseball Player |
| 1829 Forestview Lane N, Minneapolis MN 55441, USA | |
| **Moroder, Giorgio** | Composer |
| Soundtrack Music Assoc, 1460 4th St, #308, Santa Monica CA 90401 USA | |
| **Moronko, Jeffrey R (Jeff)** | Baseball Player |
| 3903 Bartons Court, Sugar Land TX 77479, USA | |
| **Moroski, Michael H (Mike)** | Football Player |
| 1214 Pine Lane, Davis CA 95616, USA | |
| **Morozov, Akeksei A** | Ice Hockey Player |
| Pittsburgh Penguins, Consol Energy Center, 1001 5th Ave, Pittsburgh PA 15219 USA | |
| **Morozov, Vladimir M** | Opera Singer |
| Kirov Ballet Theater, 1 Pl Iskusstr, 190000 Saint Petersburg, Russia | |
| **Morrell, David** | Writer, Producer |
| United Talent Agency, U T A Plaza, 9336 Civic Center Dr, Beverly Hills CA 90210 USA | |
| **Morricone, Andrea** | Composer |
| W M E Entertainment, 9601 Wilshire Blvd, #300, Beverly Hills CA 90210 USA | |
| **Morricone, Ennio** | Composer |
| A R S Latina Film, Viale Pl Nervi, 04100 Latina, Italy | |
| **Morris, Betty** | Bowler |
| 2169 Donovan Dr, Lincoln CA 95648, USA | |
| **Morris, Byron (Bam)** | Football Player |
| 251 NE 4th St, Cooper TX 75432, USA | |
| **Morris, Carol** | Beauty Queen |
| Miss Universe Organization, 1370 Ave of Americas, #1600, New York NY 10019 USA | |
| **Morris, Christopher V (Chris)** | Basketball Player |
| 3097 Milford Chase SW, Marietta GA 30008, USA | |
| **Morris, Danny W** | Baseball Player |
| 802 E Main St, Petersburg IN 47567, USA | |
| **Morris, Derek** | Ice Hockey Player |
| 9820 E Thompson Peak Parkway, #718, Scottsdale AZ 85255, USA | |
| **Morris, Doug** | Businessman |
| Universal Music Group, 100 Universal City Plaza, Universal City CA 91608, USA | |
| **Morris, Edmund** | Writer, Educator |
| 222 Central Park S, #14A, New York NY 10019, USA | |
| **Morris, Errol** | Director |
| W M E Entertainment, 9601 Wilshire Blvd, #300, Beverly Hills CA 90210 USA | |
| **Morris, Eugene E (Mercury)** | Football Player |
| 11315 SW 243rd Terrace, Homestead FL 33032, USA | |
| **Morris, Garrett** | Actor, Singer |
| Don Buchwald Talent Agency, 10 E 44th St, New York NY 10017 USA | |
| **Morris, Gary** | Singer |
| Gurley & Co, 1204 Cedar Lane, #B, Nashville TN 37212 USA | |
| **Morris, Heather E** | Actress, Writer |
| A K A Talent, 6310 San Vicente Blvd, #200, Los Angeles CA 90048 USA | |

**Morris, Iain** — Writer
Creative Artists Agency, 2000 Ave of Stars, #100, Los Angeles CA 90067 USA
**Morris, James P** — Opera Singer
Columbia Artists Mgmt Inc, 5 Columbus Circle, 1790 Broadway, #1600, New York NY 10019 USA
**Morris, James S (Jim)** — Baseball Player
2216 Rock Creek Dr, Kerrville TX 78028, USA
**Morris, James T** — Government Official
World Food Programme, Via Cesare Giulio Viola 68, 00148 Rome, Italy
**Morris, Jan** — Writer
Trefan Morys, Llanystumdwy, Criccieth, Gwynedd LL52 0LP, Wales
**Morris, Jason N** — Judo Athlete
575 Swaggertown Road, Schenectady NY 12302, USA
**Morris, Jay Hunter** — Opera Singer
I M G Artists, Carnegie Hall Tower, 152 W 57th St, #500, New York NY 10019 USA
**Morris, Jennifer P (Jenny)** — Singer
Harbour Agency, 135 Forbes St, Woolloomooloo NSW 2011, Australia
**Morris, Jessica** — Actress
Prestige Talent Agency, 9250 Wilshire Blvd, #208, Beverly Hills CA 90212, USA
**Morris, John** — Curling Athlete
Curling Association, 1660 Vimont Court, Cumberland ON K4A 4J4, Canada
**Morris, John C** — Neurologist
Memory Diagnostic Center, 4488 Forest Park Ave, Saint Louis MO 63108, USA
**Morris, John D** — Baseball Player
2645 Elm Dr, North Bellmore NY 11710, USA
**Morris, John S (Jack)** — Baseball Player
7993 100th St N, Saint Paul MN 55110, USA
**Morris, Johnny E** — Football Player
753 Shoreline Road, Lake Barrington IL 60010, USA
**Morris, Jon** — Ice Hockey Player
16 Gail St, Chelmsford MA 01824, USA
**Morris, Jon N** — Football Player
10 Berkeley Court, Bluffton SC 29910, USA
**Morris, Joseph E (Joe)** — Football Player
307 Mark Twain Way, Mahway NJ 07430, USA
**Morris, Julian** — Actor
Brillstein Entertainment Partners, 9150 Wilshire Blvd, #350, Beverly Hills CA 90212 USA
**Morris, Kathryn** — Actress
Mosiac Media Group, 9200 W Sunset Blvd, #1000, Los Angeles CA 90069 USA
**Morris, Keith** — Singer (Black Flag, Circle Jerks)
Agency Group, 1880 Century Park E, #711, Los Angeles CA 90067, USA
**Morris, Larry** — Sculptor
105 N Union St, #4, Alexandria VA 22314, USA
**Morris, Mark W** — Choreographer, Dancer
Mark Morris Dance Group, 3 Lafayette Ave, #504, Brooklyn NY 11217, USA
**Morris, Matthew C (Matt)** — Baseball Player
397 Old Jupiter Beach Road, Jupiter FL 33477, USA
**Morris, Maurice A** — Football Player
772 Golden Eagle Dr, Conway SC 29527, USA
**Morris, Melvin** — Vietnam War Army Hero (CMH)
4600 Fay Blvd, Cocoa FL 32927, USA
**Morris, Michael S (Mike)** — Football Player
5421 Oriole Dr, Farmington MN 55024, USA
**Morris, Nathan** — Singer (Boyz II Men)
Selverne Co, 3450 Cahuenga Blvd W, #906, Los Angeles CA 90068, USA
**Morris, Phil** — Actor
Innovative Artists, 1505 10th St, Santa Monica CA 90401 USA
**Morris, Raheem** — Football Coach
Washington Redskins, 21300 Redskin Park Dr, Ashburn VA 20147 USA
**Morris, Redmond** — Producer
Independent Talent Group, 40 Whitfield St, London W1T 2RH, England
**Morris, Reginald H** — Cinematographer
255 Bambaugh Circle, #308, Scarborough ON M1W 3T6, Canada
**Morris, Robert** — Sculptor
PO Box 100, Gardiner NY 12525, USA
**Morris, Ronald (Ron)** — Track Athlete
330 S Reese Place, Burbank CA 91506, USA
**Morris, Sarah Jane** — Actress, Producer
Gersh Agency, 9465 Wilshire Blvd, #600, Beverly Hills CA 90212 USA
**Morris, Shellee** — Singer (Twister Alley)
6117 Highway 135, Lake City AR 72437, USA
**Morris, Trevor** — Film Composer
Trevor Morris Studios, 1550 18th St, Santa Monica CA 90404, USA
**Morris, W Harold (Hal)** — Baseball Player
6138 Payne Stewart Dr, Windermere FL 34786, USA
**Morris, Warren R** — Baseball Player
1215 Wilshire Dr, Alexandria LA 71303, USA
**Morris, Wayna** — Singer (Boyz II Men)
Wright Entertainment Group, PO Box 590009, Orlando FL 32859, USA
**Morris, Wayne L** — Football Player
5715 Old Ox Road, Dallas TX 75241, USA
**Morrison, Adam J** — Basketball Player
7301 Vista del Mar, #11, Playa del Rey CA 90293, USA
**Morrison, Christopher W (Mink)** — Director, Writer
I C M Partners, 10250 Constellation Blvd, #900, Los Angeles CA 90067 USA
**Morrison, Denise M** — Businesswoman
Campbell Soup Co, 1 Campbell Place, Camden NJ 08103, USA
**Morrison, Denny** — Speed Skater
Agenda Sport Marketing, 119-9A St NE, Calgary AL T2E 9C5, Canada
**Morrison, Don A** — Football Player
10191 FM 512, Wolfe City TX 75496, USA
**Morrison, Fred L** — Football Player
38189 Greywalls Dr, Murrieta CA 92562, USA
**Morrison, Grant** — Cartoonist
I C M Partners, 10250 Constellation Blvd, #900, Los Angeles CA 90067 USA
**Morrison, Ian (Scotty)** — Ice Hockey Executive, Referee
Kennisis Lake, RR 1 PO Box 314, Haliburton ON K0M 1S0, Canada

**Morrison, James** — Actor, Producer, Director
Mitch Clem Mgmt, 2600 W Olive Ave, #500, Burbank CA 91505, USA
**Morrison, James** — Singer, Songwriter
412 S Pueblo Ave, Ojai CA 93023, USA
**Morrison, James F (Jim)** — Baseball Player
8715 11th Ave Place NW, Bradenton FL 34209, USA
**Morrison, Jennifer** — Actress
John Carrabino Mgmt, 5900 Wilshire Blvd, #406, Los Angeles CA 90036 USA
**Morrison, Jim** — Ice Hockey Player
1 Potts Lane, Port Hope ON L1A 0A4, Canada
**Morrison, Kathryn** — Model
Playboy Promotions, 9346 Civic Center Dr, #200, Beverly Hills CA 90210 USA
**Morrison, Lew** — Ice Hockey Player
406 Souris St, Harntey MB R0M 0X0, Canada
**Morrison, Mark** — Singer
Atlantic Records, 1290 Ave of Americas, Concourse 3, New York NY 10104 USA
**Morrison, Matthew J** — Actor
Creative Artists Agency, 2000 Ave of Stars, #100, Los Angeles CA 90067 USA
**Morrison, Michael F (Mike)** — Basketball Player
113 Rivanna Lane, Greenville SC 29607, USA
**Morrison, Phil** — Director, Producer
Management 360, 9111 Wilshire Blvd, Beverly Hills CA 90210 USA
**Morrison, Shayne** — Bassist (Perfect Stranger)
Great American Talent, PO Box 2476, Hendersonville TN 37077, USA
**Morrison, Shelley** — Actress
Don Gerler, 3349 Cahuenga Blvd W, #1, Los Angeles CA 90068 USA
**Morrison, Steven C (Steve)** — Football Player
4485 Lake Forest Dr E, Ann Arbor MI 48108, USA
**Morrison, Temuera** — Actor
Robert Bruce Agency, 218 Richmond, Grey Lynn, Auckland 1021, New Zealand
**Morrison, Toni** — Nobel Literature Laureate
185 Nassau St, Princeton NJ 08542, USA
**Morrison, Van** — Singer, Guitarist, Songwriter
115A Glenthorne, Hammersmith, London W6 OLJ, England
**Morrison-Gamberdella, Esther** — Baseball Player
3179 Pleasant Creek Road, Rogue River OR 97537, USA
**Morriss, Guy W** — Football Player
3825 Cocanougher Road, Perryville KY 40468, USA
**Morrissey** — Singer, Songwriter
Paradigm Agency, 360 N Crescent Dr, North Building, Beverly Hills CA 90210 USA
**Morrissey, David** — Actor
Troika, 74 Clerkenwell Road, #300, London EC1M 5QA, England
**Morrissey, James M (Jim)** — Football Player
48 Fox Trail, Lincolnshire IL 60069, USA
**Morrissey, Neil** — Actor
Independent Talent Group, 40 Whitfield St, London W1T 2RH, England
**Morrone, Joe** — Soccer Coach
University of Connecticut, Athletic Dept, Storrs Mansfield CT 06269, USA
**Morrow, Bobby Joe** — Track Athlete
2022 Elmwood Dr, Harlingen TX 78550, USA
**Morrow, Brenden** — Ice Hockey Player
Pittsburgh Penguins, Consol Energy Center, 1001 5th Ave, Pittsburgh PA 15219 USA
**Morrow, Bruce (Cousin Brucie)** — Entertainer
CBS Radio Network, 51 W 52nd St, New York NY 10019, USA
**Morrow, Harold, Jr** — Football Player
126 Golden Isles Dr, #62A, Hallandale Beach FL 33009, USA
**Morrow, Joshua** — Actor
Marv Dauer Mgmt, 11661 San Vicente Blvd, #104, Los Angeles CA 90049, USA
**Morrow, Kenneth (Ken)** — Ice Hockey Player
6732 NW Monticello Dr, Kansas City MO 64152, USA
**Morrow, Mari** — Actress
C E S D, 10635 Santa Monica Blvd, #130, Los Angeles CA 90025 USA
**Morrow, Rob** — Actor
Hofflund/Polone, 9465 Wilshire Blvd, #420, Beverly Hills CA 90212 USA
**Morrow, Steve** — Soccer Coach
F C Dallas, 9200 World Cup Way, #202, Frisco TX 75034 USA
**Morse, C Jeremy** — Financier
102A Drayton Gardens, London SW10 9RJ, England
**Morse, Catherine C (Cathy)** — Golfer
6228 Celadon Circle, West Palm Beach FL 33418, USA
**Morse, David** — Guitarist (Air Supply)
PO Box 3367, Beverly Hills CA 90212, USA
**Morse, David** — Actor
United Talent Agency, U T A Plaza, 9336 Civic Center Dr, Beverly Hills CA 90210 USA
**Morse, David E** — Publisher
Christian Science Monitor, Publisher's Office, 1 Norway St, Boston MA 02136, USA
**Morse, F Bradford** — Representative, MA
411 E 53rd Ave, #18C, New York NY 10022, USA
**Morse, Helen** — Actress
International Casting Service, 218 Crown St, #2, Darlinghurst, NSW 2010, Australia
**Morse, John P** — Golfer
9291 17 Mile Road, Marshall MI 49068, USA
**Morse, Michael J (Mike)** — Baseball Player
417 NW 97th Ave, Plantation FL 33324, USA
**Morse, Robert** — Actor
Bauman Redanty Shaul Agency, 5757 Wilshire Blvd, #473, Los Angeles CA 90036 USA
**Morse, Steven J (Steve)** — Guitarist, Songwriter
Frank Solomon Mgmt, PO Box 639, Natick MA 01760, USA
**Mort, Cynthia** — Writer, Producer, Director
W M E Entertainment, 9601 Wilshire Blvd, #300, Beverly Hills CA 90210 USA
**Mortensen, Chris (Mort)** — Sportscaster
ESPN-TV, Sports Dept, ESPN Plaza, 935 Middle St, Bristol CT 06010 USA
**Mortensen, Daniel E (Dan)** — Rodeo Saddle Bronc Rider
945 Noblewood Dr, Billings MT 59101, USA
**Mortensen, Jesper (Junior)** — Singer, Guitarist (Junior Senior)
Festival Network Mgmt, 30 Irving Place, #600, New York NY 10003, USA

**Mortensen, Viggo** — Actor
Rawlings Co, 3933 Patrick Henry Place, Agoura Hills CA 91301, USA
**Mortier, Koen** — Director, Producer, Writer
New School Media, 9229 Sunset Blvd, #301, West Hollywood CA 90069, USA
**Mortimer Barrett, Angela** — Tennis Player
Oaks, Coombe Hill, Beverly Lane, Kingston on Thames, Surrey, England
**Mortimer, Emily** — Actress
Independent Talent Group, 40 Whitfield St, London W1T 2RH, England
**Morton, Chad A** — Football Player
50 State Route 120, East Rutherford NJ 07073, USA
**Morton, Euan** — Actor, Singer
Innovative Artists, 1505 10th St, Santa Monica CA 90401 USA
**Morton, Guy, Jr** — Baseball Player
567 Ferndale Ave, Vermillion OH 44089, USA
**Morton, Joe** — Actor
TalentWorks, 220 E 23rd St, #400, New York NY 10010, USA
**Morton, Johnnie J** — Football Player
2911 Oakwood Lane, Torrance CA 90505, USA
**Morton, Judee** — Actress
2386 Sunset Heights Dr, Los Angeles CA 90046, USA
**Morton, K Elaine** — Model, Actress
PO Box 965, Lahaina HI 96767, USA
**Morton, Kristopher (Colt)** — Baseball Player
3245 Santa Barbara Dr, Wellington FL 33414, USA
**Morton, L Craig** — Football Player
450 E Strawberry Dr, #1, Mill Valley CA 94941, USA
**Morton, Lewis** — Producer, Writer
Creative Artists Agency, 2000 Ave of Stars, #100, Los Angeles CA 90067 USA
**Morton, Margaret** — Curling Athlete
Curling Association, 14 Donnelly Dr, Bedford, Bedfordshire MK4 9TU, England
**Morton, Mark** — Guitarist (Lamb of God)
Entertainment Services, 1000 Main Street Plaza, #303, Voorhees NJ 08043, USA
**Morton, Michael D** — Football Player
5254 Strike the Gold Lane, Wesley Chapel FL 33544, USA
**Morton, Richard** — Basketball Player
1111 Gilman Ave, San Francisco CA 94124, USA
**Morton, Samantha** — Actress
Principato-Young, 9465 Wilshire Blvd, #880, Beverly Hills CA 90212 USA
**Mortson, Gus** — Ice Hockey Player
Central Gas Ontario, PO Box 1456, Timmins ON P4N 7X4, Canada
**Morukov, Boris V** — Cosmonaut
Cosmonaut Training Center, Star City, 141160 Zvezdny Gorodok, Moscow Oblast, Russia
**Mos Def** — Rap Artist, Actor, Producer
Brookside Artists Mgmt, 250 W 57th St, #2303, New York NY 10107, USA
**Mosaku, Wunmi** — Actress
Scott Marshall Partners, 15 Little Portland St, #200, London W1W 8BW, England
**Mosby, Bernice** — Basketball Player
Washington Mystics, Verizon Center, 401 9th St NW, #750, Washington DC 20004 USA
**Moschen, Michael** — Juggler
PO Box 178, Cornwall Bridge CT 06754, USA
**Moschenko, Sergei I** — Cosmonaut
Cosmonaut Training Center, Star City, 141160 Zvezdny Gorodok, Moscow Oblast, Russia
**Moschitto, Rosario A (Ross)** — Baseball Player
1633 SW Harbour Isles Circle, Port Saint Lucie FL 34986, USA
**Moscovitch, Dylan** — Figure Skater
Skate Canada, 865 Shefford Road, Ottawa ON K1J 1H9, Canada
**Moscow, David** — Actor
Robert Stein Mgmt, PO Box 3797, Beverly Hills CA 90212, USA
**Mosebar, Donald H (Don)** — Football Player
1713 Walnut Ave, Manhattan Beach CA 90266, USA
**Moseby, Lloyd A** — Baseball Player
9140 Los Lagos Circle S, Granite Bay CA 95746, USA
**Moseley, Bill** — Actor
Judy Fox Mgmt, 1525 1/2 S Beverly Dr, Los Angeles CA 90035, USA
**Moseley, Dustin A** — Baseball Player
1602 Line Ferry Road, Texarkana AR 71854, USA
**Moseley, Jonny** — Freestyle Moguls Skier
167 Trinidad Dr, Belvedere Tiburon CA 94920, USA
**Moseley, Mark D** — Football Player
7250 Middle Road, Middletown VA 22645, USA
**Moseley, William** — Actor
A P A Talent & Literary Agency, 405 S Beverly Dr, #300, Beverly Hills CA 90212 USA
**Moseley-Braun, Carol** — Senator, IL
Ambassador Organics, 1634 E 53rd St, #200, Chicago IL 60615, USA
**Moser, Barry** — Illustrator
155 Pantry Road, North Hatfield MA 01066, USA
**Moser, Edvard** — Nobel Medicine Laureate
Norwegian University of Science & Technology, Kavli Institute, Olav Kyrres, 7489 Trondheim, Norway
**Moser, Johannes** — Concert Cellist
I M G Artists, Hogarth Business Park, Chiswick, London W4 2TH, England
**Moser, May-Britt** — Nobel Medicine Laureate, Neuroscientist
Norwegian University of Science & Technology, Kavli Institute, Olav Kyrres, 7489 Trondheim, Norway
**Moser, Michele** — Curling Athlete
Curling Association, PO Box 606, 3000 Bern, Switzerland
**Moser, Richard A (Rick)** — Football Player
24040 Camino del Avion, Dana Point CA 92629, USA
**Moses, Albert** — Actor
15 Overstone Road, Harpenden, Hertfordshire AL5 5PN, England
**Moses, Edwin C** — Track Athlete
1184 Daventry Way NE, Atlanta GA 30319, USA
**Moses, Gerald B (Jerry)** — Baseball Player
PO Box 2153, Wolfeboro NH 03894, USA
**Moses, Haven C** — Football Player
1140 Cherokee St, #604, Denver CO 80204, USA
**Moses, Mark** — Actor
Innovative Artists, 1505 10th St, Santa Monica CA 90401 USA

| | |
|---|---|
| **Moses, Pablo**<br>Keep on Kicking Music, 330 84th St, #9, Miami Beach FL 33141, USA | Singer |
| **Moses, Rick**<br>Calder Agency, 19919 Redwing St, Woodland Hills CA 91364 USA | Actor, Singer |
| **Moses, Robert (Bob)**<br>99 Bishop Allen Dr, Cambridge MA 02139, USA | Educator, Social Activist |
| **Moses, William R**<br>Amsel Eisenstadt Frazier, 5055 Wilshire Blvd, #865, Los Angeles CA 90036 USA | Actor |
| **Moshe, Guy**<br>Creative Artists Agency, 2000 Ave of Stars, #100, Los Angeles CA 90067 USA | Director, Writer |
| **Mosher, Gregory D**<br>I C M Partners, 730 5th Ave, New York NY 10019 USA | Director, Producer |
| **Mosimann, Anton**<br>Mosimann's, 11B W Halkin St, London SW1X 8JL, England | Chef |
| **Moskau, Paul R**<br>5041 N Apache Hills Trail, Tucson AZ 85750, USA | Baseball Player |
| **Moskovitz, Dustin**<br>Asana Inc, 3180 18th St, San Francisco CA 94110, USA | Businessman |
| **Moskowitz, Robert S**<br>81 Leonard St, New York NY 10013, USA | Artist |
| **Mosley, Lacey N**<br>W M E Entertainment, 9601 Wilshire Blvd, #300, Beverly Hills CA 90210 USA | Singer (Flyleaf) |
| **Mosley, Max R**<br>International Automobile Federation, 8 Place de la Concorde, 75008 Paris, France | Auto Racing Executive |
| **Mosley, Roger E**<br>4470 W Sunset Blvd, #107-342, Los Angeles CA 90027, USA | Actor |
| **Mosley, Shane (Sugar)**<br>Chrome Enterprise, PO Box 1924, Pomona CA 91769, USA | Boxer |
| **Mosley, Walter**<br>37 Carmine St, #275, New York NY 10014, USA | Writer |
| **Mosquera, Julio A**<br>1419 Stone Creek Dr, Tarpon Springs FL 34689, USA | Baseball Player |
| **Moss, Cynthia**<br>African Wildlife Foundation, Mara Road, PO Box 48177, Nairobi, Kenya | Animal Conservationist |
| **Moss, Damian**<br>1877 Georgia Highway 19 South, Dublin GA 31021, USA | Baseball Player |
| **Moss, Eddie B**<br>15404 Eagle Estates Lane, Florissant MO 63034, USA | Football Player |
| **Moss, Elisabeth G**<br>Ribisi Entertainment Group, 3278 Wilshire Blvd, #702, Los Angeles CA 90010, USA | Actress |
| **Moss, Eric Owen**<br>8557 Higuera St, Culver City CA 90232, USA | Architect |
| **Moss, Geoffrey**<br>315 E 68th St, New York NY 10065, USA | Cartoonist, Illustrator |
| **Moss, J Lester (Les)**<br>420 Tullis Ave, Longwood FL 32750, USA | Baseball Player |
| **Moss, Kate**<br>Colegrave House, 70 Berners St, London W1T 3NL, England | Model |
| **Moss, P Buckley**<br>1 Popular Grove Lane, Mathews VA 23109, USA | Artist |
| **Moss, Paige**<br>Open Entertainment, 1051 N Cole Ave, #B, Los Angeles CA 90038, USA | Actress |
| **Moss, Perry**<br>5660 S Lakeshore Dr, #505, Shreveport LA 71119, USA | Golfer |
| **Moss, Perry L**<br>420 Caddie Dr, Debary FL 32713, USA | Football Player, Coach |
| **Moss, Perry V**<br>165 Columbia Dr, Amherst MA 01002, USA | Basketball Player |
| **Moss, Randy G**<br>Victory Christian Center, Athletic Dept, 7224 Old Pineville Road, Charlotte NC 28224, USA | Football Player |
| **Moss, Ronald M (Ronn)**<br>Harbour Agency, 135 Forbes St, Woolloomooloo NSW 2011, Australia | Actor, Bassist |
| **Moss, Santana T**<br>7262 SW 123rd Place, Miami FL 33183, USA | Football Player |
| **Moss, Shirley**<br>Moss Studios, PO Box 18104, Anaheim CA 92817, USA | Sculptor |
| **Moss, Sinorice T**<br>18619 SW 50th Court, Miramar FL 33029, USA | Football Player |
| **Moss, Stirling**<br>Stirling Moss Ltd, 46 Shephard St, Mayfair, London W1Y 8JN, England | Auto Racing Driver |
| **Moss, Winston N**<br>937 Thornberry Creek Dr, Oneida WI 54155, USA | Football Player |
| **Moss, Zefross P**<br>126 Kensington Dr, Madison AL 35758, USA | Football Player |
| **Moss-Bachrach, Ebon**<br>Innovative Artists, 1505 10th St, Santa Monica CA 90401 USA | Actor |
| **Mossbauer, Rudolf L**<br>Stumpflingstr 6A, 82031 Grunwald, Germany | Nobel Physics Laureate |
| **Mosser, Jonell**<br>A P A Talent & Literary Agency, 405 S Beverly Dr, #300, Beverly Hills CA 90212 USA | Singer |
| **Mosshart, Alison**<br>Third Man Records, 623 7th Ave S, Nashville TN 37203, USA | Singer, Guitarist (Kills), Songwriter |
| **Mossi, Donald L (Don)**<br>23250 Canyon Lane, Caldwell ID 83607, USA | Baseball Player |
| **Most, Donny**<br>724 North Valley Dr, Westlake Village CA 91362, USA | Actor |
| **Mostert, Dutch**<br>93696 Mallard Lane, North Bend OR 97459, USA | Artist |
| **Mostow, George D**<br>200 Leeder Hill Dr, #2412, Hamden CT 06517, USA | Mathematician |
| **Mostow, Jonathan**<br>W M E Entertainment, 9601 Wilshire Blvd, #300, Beverly Hills CA 90210 USA | Director |
| **Mota, Jose M**<br>19058 E La Crosse St, Glendora CA 91741, USA | Baseball Player |
| **Mota, Manuel R (Manny)**<br>PO Box 2820, Toluca Lake CA 91610, USA | Baseball Player |

**Mota, Rosa**
R Teatro 194, 4 Esq, 4100 Porto, Portugal — Track Athlete

**Mote, Bobby**
6510 SW King Lane, Culver OR 97734, USA — Rodeo Rider

**Mote, Kelley H**
75 Baldwin Ave, Point Lookout NY 11569, USA — Football Player

**Mothersbaugh, Mark A**
Mutato Muzika, 8760 W Sunset Blvd, West Hollywood CA 90069, USA — Singer, Keyboardist (Devo), Songwriter

**Motion, Andrew**
University of East Anglia, English Dept, Norwich NR4 7TJ, England — Writer

**Motlanthe, Kgalema P**
PO Box 61884, Marshalltown 2107, South Africa — President, South Africa

**Motley, Darryl D**
10800 W 65th St, Shawnee KS 66203, USA — Baseball Player

**Mott, Darwin**
11 Palenchuk Place, Meadow Lake SK S9X 1H2, Canada — Ice Hockey Player

**Mott, Morris K**
9 Elmdale Blvd, Brandon MB R7B 1B5, Canada — Ice Hockey Player

**Mott, W Stephen (Steve), III**
7108 N Highfield Dr, Birmingham AL 35242, USA — Football Player

**Mott, William I (Bill)**
WinStar Farms, 3301 Pisgah Pike, Versailles KY 40383, USA — Horse Tracing Trainer

**Motta, J Richard (Dick)**
423 Highway 89, Fish Haven ID 83287, USA — Basketball Coach

**Mottau, Mike**
57 Herring Weir Road, Duxbury MA 02332, USA — Ice Hockey Player

**Mottelson, Ben R**
Nordita, Blegdamsvej 17, 2100 Copenhagen 0, Denmark — Nobel Physics Laureate

**Mottola, Charles E (Chad)**
6479 Lake Pembroke Place, Orlando FL 32829, USA — Baseball Player

**Mottola, Greg**
United Talent Agency, U T A Plaza, 9336 Civic Center Dr, Beverly Hills CA 90210 USA — Director, Writer

**Mottola, Thomas D**
Casablanca Records, 8255 W Sunset Blvd, West Hollywood CA 90046, USA — Businessman

**Motz, Diana Gribbon**
US Appeals Court, 101 W Lombard St, #3625, Baltimore MD 21201, USA — Judge

**Mouawad, Jerry**
Imago Theater, PO Box 15182, Portland OR 97293, USA — Director

**Mouchawar, Alan E**
30982 Steeplechase Dr, San Juan Capistrano CA 92675, USA — Water Polo Player

**Mouglalis, Anna**
Intertalent, 16 Rue Henri Barbusse, 75005 Paris, France — Actress

**Moulay Hassan**
Royal Palace, Rabat, Morocco — Crown Prince, Morocco

**Mould, Robert A (Bob)**
Zeitgeist Artist Mgmt, 660 York Ave, #216, San Francisco CA 94110 — Singer, Guitarist, Songwriter

**Moulder-Brown, John**
Spotlight, 7 Leicester Place, London WC2H 7RJ, England — Actor

**Moulds, Eric S**
5199 Highway 63 S, Lucedale MS 39452, USA — Football Player

**Mouli**
12 Srinivasa Ave, Chennai TN 600028, India — Actress

**Moulton, Sara**
Sara Moulton Enterprises, 130 W 24th St, #3B, New York NY 10011, USA — Chef

**Mounce, Anthony D (Tony)**
237 Cotton Bayou Lane, Kenner LA 70065, USA — Baseball Player

**Mounsey, Tara**
22 Forge Pond, #B, Canton MA 02021, USA — Ice Hockey Player

**Mount, Anson**
Creative Artists Agency, 2000 Ave of Stars, #100, Los Angeles CA 90067 USA — Actor

**Mount, Richard C (Rick)**
904 Hopkins Road, Lebanon IN 46052, USA — Basketball Player

**Mountcastle, Vernon B, Jr**
6605 Walnutwood Circle, Baltimore MD 21212, USA — Neurophysiologist

**Moura, Wagner**
United Talent Agency, U T A Plaza, 9336 Civic Center Dr, Beverly Hills CA 90210 USA — Actor, Producer

**Mourinho, Jose**
F C Inter Milan, Via Durini 24, 20122 Milan, Italy — Soccer Player, Coach

**Mourning, Alonzo**
3525 Anchorage Way, Miami FL 33133, USA — Basketball Player

**Mouskouri, Nana J**
Les Visiteurs du Soir, 40 Rue De la Folie Regmault, 75011 Paris, France — Singer, Songwriter

**Moussa, Amre M**
Arab League, PO Box 11642, Tahrir Square, Cairo, Egypt — Government Official, Egypt

**Mouton, James R**
4710 Lakeside Meadow Court, Missouri City TX 77459, USA — Baseball Player

**Mouton, Lyle J**
4101 Auston Way, Palm Harbor FL 34685, USA — Baseball Player

**Movsessian-Lamoriello, Victoria (Viki)**
17 Webb St, Lexington MA 02420, USA — Ice Hockey Player

**Mowatt, Ezekial (Zeke)**
Mowatt Inc, 194 Passaic St, #2A, Hackensack NJ 07601, USA — Football Player

**Mowatt, Judy**
Judy M Music, 25 Wellington Dr, Kingston 6, Jamaica — Singer

**Mowers, Mark**
10 Pollock Dr, Middleton MA 01949, USA — Ice Hockey Player

**Mowerson, Robert**
2601 Kenzie Terrace, #324, Minneapolis MN 55418, USA — Swimmer

**Mowg**
W M E Entertainment, 9601 Wilshire Blvd, #300, Beverly Hills CA 90210 USA — Composer

**Mowins, Beth**
ESPN-TV, Sports Dept, ESPN Plaza, 935 Middle St, Bristol CT 06010 USA — Sportscaster

**Mowrey, Caitlin**
Innovative Artists, 1505 10th St, Santa Monica CA 90401 USA — Actress

**Mowrey, Dude**
Joe Taylor Artist Agency, 2802 Columbine Place, Nashville TN 37204 USA — Singer

| | |
|---|---|
| **Mowry, Tahj D** | Actor |
| Felker Toczak Gellman, 10880 Wilshire Blvd, #2070, Los Angeles CA 90024 USA | |
| **Mowry, Tia** | Actress |
| Abrams Artists, 9200 W Sunset Blvd, #1125, West Hollywood CA 90069 USA | |
| **Mowry-Housley, Tamera** | Actress |
| United Talent Agency, U T A Plaza, 9336 Civic Center Dr, Beverly Hills CA 90210 USA | |
| **Moxey, Jim** | Ice Hockey Player |
| 7 Blue Heron Dr, Orangeville ON L9W 5K6, Canada | |
| **Moxey, John Llewellyn** | Director |
| Shapiro-Lichtman, 8827 Beverly Blvd, Los Angeles CA 90048 USA | |
| **Moya, Carlos** | Tennis Player |
| Ave Diagonal 618 3D, 08021 Barcelona, Spain | |
| **Moyer, Jamie** | Baseball Player |
| 5500 34th St W, Badenton FL 34210, USA | |
| **Moyer, Kenneth W (Ken)** | Football Player |
| 3896 Magma Court, Mason OH 45040, USA | |
| **Moyer, Paul S** | Football Player |
| 9411 NE 32nd St, Clyde Hill WA 98004, USA | |
| **Moyer, Stephen** | Actor, Director |
| United Agents, 12-26 Lexington St, London W1F 0LE, England | |
| **Moyers, Bill D** | Commentator |
| 151 Central Park W, #5N, New York NY 10023, USA | |
| **Moyes, Jo Jo** | Writer |
| Curtis Brown Group, 28-29 Haymarket St, #500, London SW1Y 4SP, England | |
| **Moyle, Allan** | Director, Writer |
| Becsey Wisdom Kalajian, 849 S Wooster St, #7, Los Angeles CA 90035, USA | |
| **Moynahan, Bridget** | Actress, Model |
| Brillstein Entertainment Partners, 9150 Wilshire Blvd, #350, Beverly Hills CA 90212 USA | |
| **Moynihan, Bobby** | Actor, Comedian |
| United Talent Agency, U T A Plaza, 9336 Civic Center Dr, Beverly Hills CA 90210 USA | |
| **Moynihan, Christopher (Chris)** | Actor, Producer, Writer |
| Domain Talent, 9229 W Sunset Blvd, #710, West Hollywood CA 90069 USA | |
| **Moynihan, Colin B** | Government Official, England |
| Crown Reach, 16 Grosvenor Road, London SW1V 3JV, England | |
| **Moyse, Heather** | Bobsled Athlete |
| Alberta Bobsled, Niven Center, 140 Canada Olympic Road, Calgary AB T3B 5RS, Canada | |
| **Mr Cheeks** | Rap Artist (Lost Boyz) |
| Agency Group Ltd, 142 W 57th St, #600, New York NY 10019 USA | |
| **Mraz, Jason** | Singer, Songwriter |
| Bill Silva Mgmt, 8225 Santa Monica Blvd, West Hollywood CA 90046, USA | |
| **Mrazovich, Chuck** | Basketball Player |
| 7260 W 12th Ave, Hialeah FL 33014, USA | |
| **Mross, Stefan** | Singer, Trumpeter |
| Mross Media, PO Box 1111, 83246 Unterwoessen, Germany | |
| **Mroudjae, Ali** | Prime Minister, Comoros |
| BP 58, Rond Point Gobadjou, Moroni, Comoros | |
| **Mrozik, Rick** | Ice Hockey Player |
| 2234 Kelly Ave, Cloquet MN 55720, USA | |
| **Mruczkowski, Scott A** | Football Player |
| 10701 Mountview Ave, Cleveland OH 44125, USA | |
| **Msamati, Lucian** | Actor |
| Diamond Mgmt, 31 Percy St, London W1T 2DD, England | |
| **Mswati III, Makhosetive** | King, Swaziland |
| Lozitha Palace, PO Box 1, Mbabane, Swaziland | |
| **Muccino, Gabriele** | Director |
| Untitled Entertainment, 350 S Beverly Dr, #200, Beverly Hills CA 90212 USA | |
| **Muchlinski, Michael W (Mike)** | Baseball Umpire |
| 3004 183rd St SE, Bothell WA 98012, USA | |
| **Muckalt, Bill** | Ice Hockey Player |
| 3001 Civic Center Circle NE, Rio Rancho NM 87144, USA | |
| **Mucke, Manuela** | Canoeing Athlete |
| Charlottenstr 13, 10315 Berlin, Germany | |
| **Muckensturm, Jerry R** | Football Player |
| 4209 Hickory Lane, Jonesboro AR 72401, USA | |
| **Muckler, John** | Ice Hockey Executive, Coach |
| 387 Woods Acres Dr, East Amherst NY 14051, USA | |
| **Mudd, Daniel** | Government Official, Financier |
| Federal National Mortgage Assn, 3900 Wisconsin Ave NW, Washington DC 20016, USA | |
| **Mudd, Howard E** | Football Player, Coach |
| 2573 Leisure World, Mesa AZ 85206, USA | |
| **Mudd, Roger H** | Commentator |
| 7167 Old Dominion Dr, McLean VA 22101, USA | |
| **Mudge, Jennifer** | Actress |
| Group Entertainment, 115 W 29th St, #1102, New York NY 10001, USA | |
| **Mudra, Darrell** | Football Coach |
| 424 Tiger Hammock Road, Crawfordville FL 32327, USA | |
| **Muehe, Anna Maria** | Actress |
| Fitz & Skoglund, Linienstr 130, 10115 Berlin, Germany | |
| **Mueller, Edward** | Businessman |
| Qwest Communications, 1801 California St, #5200, Denver CO 80202, USA | |
| **Mueller, George E** | Electrical Engineer, Missile Scientist |
| Kistler Aerospace Corp, 3760 Carillon Point, Kirkland WA 98033, USA | |
| **Mueller, Gerd** | Soccer Player |
| Neuestr 21, 81479 Munich, Germany | |
| **Mueller, Gerhard Ludwig Cardinal** | Religious Leader |
| Congregation for Doctrine of Faith, Piazza del S Uffizio 11, 00193 Rome, Italy | |
| **Mueller, Leah Poulos** | Speed Skater |
| 11455 N Mulberry Dr, Mequon WI 53092, USA | |
| **Mueller, Lisel** | Writer |
| Louisiana State University Press, PO Box 25053, Baton Rouge LA 70894, USA | |
| **Mueller, Niels** | Director |
| W M E Entertainment, 9601 Wilshire Blvd, #300, Beverly Hills CA 90210 USA | |
| **Mueller, Vance A** | Football Player |
| 8141 Damico Dr, El Dorado Hills CA 95762, USA | |
| **Mueller, Willard L (Willie)** | Baseball Player |
| 2320 Tolbert Lane, West Bend WI 53090, USA | |

# M

**Mueller, William R (Bill)** — Baseball Player
570 W Canyon Way, Chandler AZ 85248, USA

**Mueller-Stahl, Armin** — Actor
I C M Partners, 10250 Constellation Blvd, #900, Los Angeles CA 90067 USA

**Muench, David** — Photographer
PO Box 30500, Santa Barbara CA 93130, USA

**Mugabe, Robert G** — President, Zimbabwe
President's Office, Munhumutapa Bldg, Samora Machel Ave, Harare, Zimbabwe

**Mugabi, John** — Boxer
PO Box 246, Main Beach, Gold Coast QLD, Australia

**Mughelli, Ovie P** — Football Player
3485 Moye Trail, Duluth GA 30097, USA

**Mugler, Thierry** — Fashion Designer
Patrick Alaux, 4 Rue Faubourg Saint Honore, 75008 Paris, France

**Muhammad, Eddie Mustafa** — Boxer
9030 W Sahara Blvd, Las Vegas NV 89117, USA

**Muhammad, Shabazz** — Basketball Player
Minnesota Timberwolves, Target Center, 600 1st Ave N, Minneapolis MN 55403 USA

**Muhelsen, Muhammed** — Photojournalist
Associated Press, Editorial Dept, 450 W 33rd St, #1500, New York NY 10001 USA

**Muhlbach, Donald L (Don), Jr** — Football Player
711 Pinetree Lane, Lufkin TX 75904, USA

**Muhtadee Billah al-** — Prince Heir Apparent, Brunei
Istana Nural Iman, Bandar Seri Begawan 1100, Brunei Darussalam, Brunei

**Muir, David** — Commentator
ABC-TV, News Dept, 77 W 66th St, New York NY 10023 USA

**Muirhead, Eve** — Curling Athlete
Curling Association, 14 Donnelly Dr, Bedford, Bedfordshire MK4 9TU, England

**Muirhead, Oliver** — Actor
Don Buchwald Talent Agency, 6500 Wilshire Blvd, #2200, Los Angeles CA 90048 USA

**Mujica, Jose Pepe** — President, Uruguay
Chacra El Paso de la Arena, Montevideo, Uruguay

**Mujurawar, Ali Mohammed** — Prime Minister, Republic of Yemen
Premier's Office, Street of 26th September, Sana'a, Yemen Arab Republic

**Mukai, Chiaki Naito-** — Astronaut, Japan
100 Cyberonics Blvd, #201, Houston TX 77058, USA

**Mukherjee, Bharati** — Writer
130 Rivoli St, San Francisco CA 94117, USA

**Mukherjee, Pranab K** — President, India
President's Office, Bharat Ka, Rashtrapti Bhavan, New Delhi 110004, India

**Mukherjee, Siddhartha** — Writer
Charles Scribner's Sons, 866 3rd Ave, New York NY 10022 USA

**Mukwege, Denis** — Gynecologist, Medical Activist
Panzi Hospital, Bukavu, South Kivu, Congo Democratic Republic

**Mula, Inva** — Opera Singer
Columbia Artists Mgmt Inc, 5 Columbus Circle, 1790 Broadway, #1600, New York NY 10019 USA

**Mulari, Tarja** — Speed Skier
Motion Oy, Vanhan Mankkaantie 33, 02180 Espoo, Finland

**Mularkey, Michael R (Mike)** — Football Player, Coach
4411 Meadow Club Dr, Suwanee GA 30024, USA

**Mulcahy, Kathleen** — Artist, Sculptor
260 Whittengale Road, Oakdale PA 15071, USA

**Mulcahy, Russell** — Director
A P A Talent & Literary Agency, 405 S Beverly Dr, #300, Beverly Hills CA 90212 USA

**Muldaur, Diana** — Actress
20 Cummings Way, Edgartown MA 02539, USA

**Muldaur, Geoff** — Singer, Guitarist
Nancy Fly Agency, PO Box 90306, Austin TX 78709, USA

**Muldaur, Maria** — Singer, Songwriter
Prime Time Entertainment, 2388 Research Dr, Livermore CA 94550, USA

**Mulder, Karen** — Model
Metropolitan Modeling Agency, 5 Union Square W, #500, New York NY 10003, USA

**Mulder, Mark** — Baseball Player
10295 E Cholla St, Scottsdale AZ 85260, USA

**Muldoon, Patrick** — Actor, Model
Eclectic Pictures, 7119 Sunset Blvd, #375, Los Angeles CA 90046, USA

**Muldoon, Paul B** — Writer
Princeton University, Creative Writing Progam, Princeton NJ 08544, USA

**Muldowney, Dominic J** — Composer
Carlin Music, 3 Bridge Approach, Chalk Farm, London NW1 8BD, England

**Muldowney, Shirley** — Auto Racing Driver
13765 Aldenbrook Dr, Huntersville NC 28078, USA

**Mulgrew, Kate** — Actress
Innovative Artists, 1505 10th St, Santa Monica CA 90401 USA

**Mulhern, Matt** — Actor
Don Buchwald Talent Agency, 6500 Wilshire Blvd, #2200, Los Angeles CA 90048 USA

**Mulhern, Richard** — Ice Hockey Player
397 Walpole Ave, Beaconsfield QC H9W 2G6, Canada

**Mulhern, Ryan** — Ice Hockey Player
42 Faculty Circle, Kingston RI 02881, USA

**Mulhern, Sinead** — Opera Singer
Guy Barzilay Artists, 420 W 25th St, #4F, New York NY 10001, USA

**Mulholland, John F** — Army General
Army Special Operations Command, 2929 Desert Storm Dr, Fort Bragg NC 28310, USA

**Mulholland, Terence J (Terry)** — Baseball Player
11655 N 18th Place, Phoenix AZ 85020, USA

**Mulitalo, Edwin M** — Football Player
12587 Moonlite Hill Court, Herriman UT 84096, USA

**Mulkerin, Ted** — Writer
Creative Artists Agency, 2000 Ave of Stars, #100, Los Angeles CA 90067 USA

**Mulkey, Chris** — Actor
Don Buchwald Talent Agency, 6500 Wilshire Blvd, #2200, Los Angeles CA 90048 USA

**Mulkey-Robertson, Kim** — Basketball Player, Coach
Baylor University, Athletic Dept, Waco TX 76798, USA

**Mull, Carter** — Photographer
Marc Foxx Gallery, 6150 Wilshire Blvd, #5, Los Angeles CA 90048, USA

**Mull, Martin** — Actor
Anonymous Content, 3532 Hayden Ave, Culver City CA 90232 USA
**Mullady, Thomas S (Tom)** — Football Player
2855 Crooked Oak Dr, Germantown TN 38138, USA
**Mullally, Megan** — Actress, Singer
United Talent Agency, U T A Plaza, 9336 Civic Center Dr, Beverly Hills CA 90210 USA
**Mullan, Carrie** — Actress
United Agents, 12-26 Lexington St, London W1F 0LE, England
**Mullan, Peter** — Actor, Director
Markham Froggatt Irwin, Julian House, 4 Windmill St, London W1P 1HF, England
**Mullane, Richard M (Mike)** — Astronaut
1301 Las Lomas Road NE, Albuquerque NM 87106, USA
**Mullaney, Mark A** — Football Player
17448 Frondell Court, Eden Prairie MN 55347, USA
**Mullavey, Greg** — Actor
31 Tiemann Place, #48, New York NY 10027, USA
**Mullen, Brian** — Ice Hockey Player
124 Berkeley Circle, Basking Ridge NJ 07920, USA
**Mullen, Joseph P (Joey)** — Ice Hockey Player
36 Friends Lane, South Dennis MA 02660, USA
**Mullen, Larry, Jr** — Drummer (U-2)
Principle Mgmt, 30-32 Sir John Rogerson Quay, Dublin 2, Ireland
**Mullen, M David** — Cinematographer
3930 Wade St, Los Angeles CA 90066, USA
**Mullen, Michael G (Mike)** — Navy Admiral
General Motors Co, PO Box 33170, Detroit MI 48232, USA
**Mullen, Nicole C** — Singer, Songwriter
Creative Artists Agency, 2000 Ave of Stars, #100, Los Angeles CA 90067 USA
**Mullen, Scott** — Baseball Player
73 Walling Grove Road, Beaufort SC 29907, USA
**Mullen, Thomas** — Writer
I C M Partners, 10250 Constellation Blvd, #900, Los Angeles CA 90067 USA
**Mullens, Byron J (B J)** — Basketball Player
Charlotte Hornets, 333 E Trade St, #A, Charlotte NC 28202 USA
**Muller, Alina** — Ice Hockey Player
Swiss Ice Hockey, Hagenholzstr 81, 8050 Zurich, Switzerland
**Muller, Egon** — Motorcycle Racing Rider
Dorfstr 17, 24247 Rodenbek/Kiel, Germany
**Muller, Gerd** — Soccer Player
Heinrich-Vogel-Str 10A, 81479 Munich, Germany
**Muller, Ina** — Singer, Actress
105 Music, Hopfensack 20, 20457 Hamburg, Germany
**Muller, Jorg** — Auto Racing Driver
Insert Motorsport, Fassoldshof 1, 95336 Mainleus, Germany
**Muller, K Alex** — Nobel Physics Laureate
Haldenstr 54, 8909 Hedingen, Switzerland
**Muller, Lillian** — Model, Actress
PO Box 20029-414, Encino CA 91416, USA
**Muller, Lisel** — Writer
Goddard College, Fine Arts Writing Program, 123 Pitkin Road, Plainfield VT 05667, USA
**Muller, Michel** — Actor
Artmedia, 20 Ave Rapp, 75007 Paris, France
**Muller, Peter** — Alpine Skier
Haldenstr 18, 8134 Adliswil, Switzerland
**Muller, Peter** — Architect
The Pier, 201/19 Hickson Road, Sydney NSW 2000, Australia
**Muller, Richard S** — Electrical, Microbiotics Engineer
University of California, Sensor/Actuator Center, Berkeley CA 94720, USA
**Muller-Brachmann, Hanno** — Opera Singer
Kunstler Sekretariat am Gasteig, Rosenheimer Str 52, 81669 Munich, Germany
**Muller-Schott, Daniel** — Concert Violist
Konzertdirektion Schmid, Konigstra 36, 30175 Hannover, Germany
**Muller-Westernhagen, Marius** — Singer, Actor
Motor Entertainment, Brunnenstr 24, 10119 Berlin, Germany
**Mulligan, Brian** — Opera Singer
I M G Artists, Hogarth Business Park, Chiswick, London W4 2TH, England
**Mulligan, Carey H** — Actress
Julian Belfrage Assoc, 9 Argyll St, #300, London W1F 7TG, England
**Mulligan, Deanna M** — Businesswoman
Guardian Life Insurance, 7 Hanover Square, New York NY 10004, USA
**Mulligan, Richard C** — Molecular Biologist, Geneticist
Children's Hospital, Genetics Dept, 320 Longwood Ave, Boston MA 02115, USA
**Mulligan, Sean P** — Baseball Player
24474 Eastgate Dr, Diamond Bar CA 91765, USA
**Mulligan, Wayne E** — Football Player
2410 The Haul Over, Johns Island SC 29455, USA
**Mullin, Christopher P (Chris)** — Basketball Player
116 Laurelwood Dr, Danville CA 94506, USA
**Mullin, Reed D** — Drummer (Corrosion of Conformity)
Chipster, 100 Village Square Crossing, Palm Beach Gardens FL 33410 USA
**Mulliniks, S Rance** — Baseball Player
2614 S Peppertree St, Visalia CA 93277, USA
**Mullins, Aimee** — Model, Athlete
Authentic Talent/Literary Mgmt, 45 Main St, #1004, Brooklyn NY 11201, USA
**Mullins, Gerald B (Gerry)** — Football Player
PO Box 523, Saxonburg PA 16056, USA
**Mullins, Gregory E (Greg)** — Baseball Player
PO Box 443, Florahome FL 32140, USA
**Mullins, Jeffrey V (Jeff)** — Basketball Player, Coach
8866 N Sea Oaks Way, #202, Vero Beach FL 32963, USA
**Mullins, Melinda** — Actress
Access Talent Voice Overs, 171 Madison Ave, #910, New York NY 0016, USA
**Mullins, Shawn** — Singer, Songwriter
Russell Carter Artist Mgmt, 567 Ralph Mcgill Blvd NE, Atlanta GA 30312, USA
**Mullis, Kary B** — Nobel Chemistry Laureate
2743 Hillview Dr, Newport Beach CA 92660, USA

# M

**Mullova, Viktoria Y** — Concert Violinist
Kunstler Sekretariat am Gasteig, Rosenheimer Str 52, 81669 Munich, Germany
**Mulloy, Gardner P** — Tennis Player
800 NW 9th Ave, Miami FL 33136, USA
**Muloin, Wayne** — Ice Hockey Player
2991 Hayes St, Avon OH 44011, USA
**Mulroney, Dermot** — Actor
W M E Entertainment, 9601 Wilshire Blvd, #300, Beverly Hills CA 90210 USA
**Mulroney, Kieran** — Actor, Writer
Management 360, 9111 Wilshire Blvd, Beverly Hills CA 90210 USA
**Mulroney, M Brian** — Prime Minister, Canada
47 Forden Crescent, Westmount QC H3Y 2Y5, Canada
**Mulrooney, Richard** — Soccer Player
Houston Dynamo, 1415 Louisiana, #3400, Houston TX 77002 USA
**Mulva, James J** — Businessman
ConocoPhillips Inc, 600 N Daisy Ashford, Houston TX 77079, USA
**Mulvey, Callan** — Actor
Creative Artists Agency, 2000 Ave of Stars, #100, Los Angeles CA 90067 USA
**Mulvey, Grant** — Ice Hockey Player
70 E Scott St, #706, Chicago IL 60610, USA
**Mulvey, Kevin** — Baseball Player
24 Eric Court, Parlin NJ 08859, USA
**Mulvey, Paul** — Ice Hockey Player
8009 Oak Hollow Lane, Fairfax Station VA 22039, USA
**Mulvihill, Robert** — Basketball Player
53 Pike Dr, #1C, Wayne NJ 07470, USA
**Mumba, Samantha** — Singer, Actress
Helter Skelter, 347-353 Chiswick High Road, London W4 4HS, England
**Mumford, Eloise** — Actress
Paradigm Agency, 360 N Crescent Dr, North Building, Beverly Hills CA 90210 USA
**Mumley, Nicholas (Nick)** — Football Player
1432 Audubon Dr, Columbus IN 47203, USA
**Mumphrey, Jerry W** — Baseball Player
7709 FM 850, Tyler TX 75705, USA
**Mumy, Billy** — Actor
PO Box 433, 11333 Moorpark St, North Hollywood CA 91603, USA
**Munchak, Michael A (Mike)** — Football Player, Coach
9155 Saddlebow Dr, Brentwood TN 37027, USA
**Muncrief, Kevin** — Golfer
939 S Flood Ave, Norman OK 73069, USA
**Mundae, Misty** — Actress
El Independent Cinema, PO Box 132, Butler NJ 07405, USA
**Mundell, Robert A** — Nobel Economics Laureate
35 Claremont Ave, New York NY 10027, USA
**Mundy, Chris** — Producer, Writer
United Talent Agency, U T A Plaza, 9336 Civic Center Dr, Beverly Hills CA 90210 USA
**Mundy, John H** — Historian
29 Claremont Ave, New York NY 10027, USA
**Mungle, Matthew W** — Make-Up Artist
Milton Agency, 6715 Hollywood Blvd, #206, Los Angeles CA 90028, USA
**Muni, Craig** — Ice Hockey Player
37 Greenbriar Dr, Lancaster NY 14086, USA
**Munitz, Barry** — Foundation Executive
J Paul Getty Trust, 1200 Getty Center Dr, #400, Los Angeles CA 90049, USA
**Muniz, Armando** — Boxer
6657 45th St, Riverside CA 92509, USA
**Muniz, Frankie** — Actor
Paradigm Agency, 360 N Crescent Dr, North Building, Beverly Hills CA 90210 USA
**Muniz, Vik** — Photographer
169 Bond St, Brooklyn NY 11217, USA
**Munk, Walter H** — Geophysicist
9530 La Jolla Shores Dr, La Jolla CA 92037, USA
**Munn, Allison** — Actress
Innovative Artists, 1505 10th St, Santa Monica CA 90401 USA
**Munninghoff, Scott A** — Baseball Player
866 Laverty Lane, Cincinnati OH 45230, USA
**Munns, Allen G** — Navy Admiral
Commander, Submarine Command Atlantic, 7958 Blandy Road, Norfolk VA 23511 USA
**Munoz, J Oscar** — Baseball Player
14161 Leaning Pine Dr, Hialeah FL 33014, USA
**Munoz, M Anthony** — Football Player, Sportscaster
7575 Rockeby Court, Cincinnati OH 45241, USA
**Munoz, Michael A (Mike)** — Baseball Player
1000 Carroll Meadows Court, Southlake TX 76092, USA
**Munoz, Ricardo J (Ricky)** — Singer, Accordian Player (Intocable)
Serca Music, 2020 W Houston Ave, McAllen TX 78501, USA
**Munoz, Roberto (Bobby)** — Baseball Player
9040 NW 20th St, Pembroke Pines FL 33024, USA
**Munro, Alice A** — Nobel Literature Laureate
PO Box 1133, Clinton ON N0M 1L0, Canada
**Munro, Caroline** — Actress
Jim Thompson Mgmt, Herricks, School Lane, West Sussex BN18 9DR, England
**Munro, Lochlyn** — Actor, Producer
Characters Talent Mgmt, 8 Elm St, Toronto ON M5G 1G7, Canada
**Munro, Peter D** — Baseball Player
4311 Westmoreland St, Little Neck NY 11363, USA
**Munroe, Odessa** — Actress
Carrier Talent Mgmt, 1080 Howe St, #705, Vancouver BC V6Z 2T1, Canada
**Munsel, Patrice** — Opera Singer
PO Box 472, Schroon Lake NY 12870, USA
**Munson, Eric W** — Baseball Player
2640 Becker Court, Dubuque IA 52001, USA
**Munson, Curtis** — Bassist (Semisonic)
Monterey Peninsula Artists, 404 W Franklin St, Monterey CA 93940 USA
**Munter, Leilani** — Auto Racing Driver, Social Activist
PO Box 3355, Mooresville NC 38117, USA

Mullova - Munter

| | |
|---|---|
| **Munter, Scott** | Baseball Player |
| 13024 Jessie Ave, Omaha NE 68164, USA | |
| **Muntyan, Mikhail** | Opera Singer |
| 16 N Iorga Str, #13, 277012 Chisnau, Moldova | |
| **Mura, Stephen A (Steve)** | Baseball Player |
| 31892 Old Oak Road, Trabuco Canyon CA 92679, USA | |
| **Murad, Ferid** | Nobel Medicine Laureate |
| 3409 Wilson Blvd, Arlington VA 22201, USA | |
| **Murakami, Haruki** | Writer |
| I C M Partners, 730 5th Ave, New York NY 10019 USA | |
| **Murakami, Masanori** | Baseball Player |
| 1-4-15-1506 Nisho Ohi Shinagawaku, Tokyo 140 0015, Japan | |
| **Murakami, Ryu** | Writer |
| Kodansha Books, 2-12-21 Otowa, Bunkyoku, Tokyo 112 8001, Japan | |
| **Murakami, Takashi** | Artist |
| Management 360, 9111 Wilshire Blvd, Beverly Hills CA 90210 USA | |
| **Murat, Bernard** | Actor, Director |
| Artmedia, 20 Ave Rapp, 75007 Paris, France | |
| **Murat, Stephanie** | Actress, Director, Writer |
| Artmedia, 20 Ave Rapp, 75007 Paris, France | |
| **Murayama, Makio** | Biochemist |
| 304 Midsummer Dr, Gaithersburg MD 20878, USA | |
| **Murayama, Tomiichi** | Prime Minister, Japan |
| 3-2-2 Chiyomachi, Oita, Oita 870, Japan | |
| **Murch, Walter** | Editor, Sound Effects Editor |
| Mirisch Agency, 1025 Colorado Ave, #B, Santa Monica CA 90211 USA | |
| **Murchison, Ira** | Track Athlete |
| 10113 S Sangamon St, Chicago IL 60643, USA | |
| **Murciano, Enrique** | Actor |
| Untitled Entertainment, 350 S Beverly Dr, #200, Beverly Hills CA 90212 USA | |
| **Murcutt, Glenn** | Pritzker Architectural Laureate |
| Neeson Murcutt Architects, 71 York St, #500, Sydney NSW 2000, Australia | |
| **Murdoch, Don** | Ice Hockey Player |
| Hockey in the Rockies School, PO Box 383, Cranbrook BC V1C 4H9, Canada | |
| **Murdoch, K Rupert** | Publisher |
| News America Publishing, 1211 Ave of Americas, #500, New York NY 10036, USA | |
| **Murdoch, Robert (Bob)** | Ice Hockey Player |
| 410 11th Ave S, Cranbrook BC V1C 2P9, Canada | |
| **Murdoch, Robert J (Bob)** | Ice Hockey Player, Coach |
| 1330 Angelo Dr, Beverly Hills CA 90210, USA | |
| **Murdoch, Stuart L** | Singer, Songwriter (Belle & Sebastian) |
| Ground Control Touring, 20 Jay St, #826, Brooklyn NY 11201 USA | |
| **Murdoch, William W** | Population Ecologist |
| University of California, Ecology Evolution Marine Biology Dept, Santa Barbara CA 93106, USA | |
| **Murdock, David H** | Businessman |
| 10900 Wilshire Blvd, #1600, Los Angeles CA 90024, USA | |
| **Murdock, George P** | Anthropologist |
| 107 E Wynnewood Road, Wynnewood PA 19096, USA | |
| **Murdock, Shirley** | Singer |
| PO Box 26249, Dayton OH 45426, USA | |
| **Muresan, Gheorghe** | Basketball Player, Actor |
| 10913 Burbank Dr, Potomac MD 20854, USA | |
| **Muresan, Lucian Cardinal** | Religious Leader |
| Archdiocese, Fagaras & Alba Iulia, Str Petro Pavel Aron 2, 515 400 Blaj AB, Romania | |
| **Muriel, Xavier** | Drummer (Buckcherry) |
| 10th Street Mgmt, 700 N San Vicente Blvd, #G410, West Hollywood CA 90069, USA | |
| **Murillo, Oscar** | Artist |
| David Zwirner Gallery, 537 W 20th St, New York NY 10011, USA | |
| **Murino, Caterina** | Actress |
| Soli Assoc, Viale Dei Parioli 44, 00197 Rome, Italy | |
| **Muris, Timothy J** | Government Official |
| George Mason University, Law School, Fairfax VA 22030, USA | |
| **Murkoff, Heidi** | Writer |
| What To Expect Foundation, 211 W 80th St, Lower Level, New York, NY 10024, USA | |
| **Murley, Matt** | Ice Hockey Player |
| 32 Hialeah Dr, Troy NY 12182, USA | |
| **Muro, J Michael** | Cinematographer |
| Gersh Agency, 9465 Wilshire Blvd, #600, Beverly Hills CA 90212 USA | |
| **Murofushi, Koji A** | Track Athlete |
| World Athletics Mgmt, Untersperr 4A, 4644 Scharnstein, Austria | |
| **Murphey, Christopher** | Producer, Writer |
| Rothman Brecher Agency, 920 Wilshire Blvd, #PH, Beverly Hills CA 90212, USA | |
| **Murphey, Michael Martin** | Singer, Songwriter |
| Artra Artists, 130 S Canal St, #211, Chicago IL 60606, USA | |
| **Murphy, Ben** | Actor |
| 2690 Rambla Pacifico St, Malibu CA 90265, USA | |
| **Murphy, Bob** | Golfer |
| 12005 Dunes Road, Boynton Beach FL 33436, USA | |
| **Murphy, Calvin J** | Basketball Player, Executive |
| 8218 Cliffshire Court, Houston TX 77083, USA | |
| **Murphy, Carolyn** | Model, Actress |
| W M E Entertainment, 9601 Wilshire Blvd, #300, Beverly Hills CA 90210 USA | |
| **Murphy, Caryle M** | Journalist |
| Washington Post, Editorial Dept, 1150 15th St NW, Washington DC 20071, USA | |
| **Murphy, Charles S** | Government Official |
| 100 Bluff View Dr, #503C, Belleair Bluffs FL 33770, USA | |
| **Murphy, Charlie Q** | Actor, Comedian |
| I C M Partners, 10250 Constellation Blvd, #900, Los Angeles CA 90067 USA | |
| **Murphy, Cillian** | Actor |
| Lisa Richards Agency, 108 Upper Leeson St, Dublin 4, Ireland | |
| **Murphy, Dale B** | Baseball Player |
| 467 Aspen Ridge Lane, Alpine UT 84004, USA | |
| **Murphy, Daniel F (Danny)** | Baseball Player |
| 5030 Champion Blvd, #6226, Boca Raton FL 33496, USA | |
| **Murphy, Daniel T** | Baseball Player |
| 2878 Dickie Court, Jacksonville FL 32216, USA | |

**Murphy, David Lee** — Singer
D Mgmt, PO Box 121682, Nashville TN 37212, USA

**Murphy, David M** — Baseball Player
3708 Sunrise Ranch Road, Southlake TX 76092, USA

**Murphy, Diana E** — Judge
US Court of Appeals, 300 S 4th St, #11E, Minneapolis MN 55415, USA

**Murphy, Donald** — Actor
PO Box 904, Ranchester WY 82839, USA

**Murphy, Donald R (Donnie)** — Baseball Player
10211 Willow Bend Circle, #18, Charlotte NC 28210, USA

**Murphy, Donna** — Actress, Singer, Dancer
Brookside Artists Mgmt, 250 W 57th St, #2303, New York NY 10107, USA

**Murphy, Dwayne K** — Baseball Player
1811 S Karen Dr, Chandler AZ 85286, USA

**Murphy, Eddie** — Actor, Comedian
Eddie Murphy Productions, 9601 Wilshire Blvd, #300, Beverly Hills CA 90210, USA

**Murphy, Erin** — Actress
Commercial Talent, 12711 Ventura Blvd, #285, Studio City CA 91604, USA

**Murphy, Glenn** — Businessman
Gap Inc, 2 Folsom St, San Francisco CA 94105, USA

**Murphy, Gord** — Ice Hockey Player
10041 Cartgate Court, Dublin OH 43017, USA

**Murphy, Joe** — Ice Hockey Player
10292 Horton Road, Goodrich MI 48438, USA

**Murphy, Jonathan M** — Actor, Producer, Writer
Framework Entertainment, 9057 Nemo St, #C, West Hollywood CA 90069 USA

**Murphy, Kevin** — Producer, Writer
W M E Entertainment, 9601 Wilshire Blvd, #300, Beverly Hills CA 90210 USA

**Murphy, Kevin M** — Economist
University of Chicago, Booth School of Economics, 5807 S Woodlawn Ave, Chicago IL 60637, USA

**Murphy, Kim** — Journalist
Los Angeles Times, Editorial Dept, 202 W 1st St, Los Angeles CA 90012 USA

**Murphy, Lawrence T (Larry)** — Ice Hockey Player
1167 Connaught Dr, Ennismore ON K0L 1T0, Canada

**Murphy, Mark H** — Football Player
935 N Broadway, DePere WI 54115, USA

**Murphy, Mark H** — Singer
Janlyn Public Relations, 106 Cabrini Blvd, #4-I, New York NY 10033, USA

**Murphy, Mark S** — Football Player
3699 Myersville Road, Uniontown OH 44685, USA

**Murphy, Michael** — Actor
Paul Kohner, 9300 Wilshire Blvd, #555, Beverly Hills CA 90212 USA

**Murphy, Michael R** — Judge
US Court of Appeals, Federal Building, 125 S State St, Salt Lake City UT 84138, USA

**Murphy, Mike** — Ice Hockey Player, Coach
National Hockey League, 50 Bay St, #1100, Toronto ON M5J 2X8, Canada

**Murphy, Nate** — Paleontologist
Judith River Dinosaur Institute, PO Box 51177, Billings MT 59105, USA

**Murphy, Nick** — Director, Producer, Writer
Independent Talent Group, 40 Whitfield St, London W1T 2RH, England

**Murphy, Peter J** — Singer (Bauhaus)
C E C Mgmt, 520 E Ave, New York NY 10018, USA

**Murphy, Reg** — Editor, Publisher
National Geographic Society, 1145 17th St NW, Washington DC 20036, USA

**Murphy, Rob** — Ice Hockey Player
Hockey Stall, 35 Mika St, Stittsville ON K2S 1K8, Canada

**Murphy, Robert A (Rob)** — Baseball Player
44 S Sewalls Point Road, Stuart FL 34996, USA

**Murphy, Ron** — Ice Hockey Player
1 Valley Road, Nanticoke ON N0H 1L0, Canada

**Murphy, Ronald T (Ronnie)** — Basketball Player
14800 Hanover Pike, Upperco MD 21155, USA

**Murphy, Ryan** — Director, Producer, Writer
Creative Artists Agency, 2000 Ave of Stars, #100, Los Angeles CA 90067 USA

**Murphy, Sean P** — Golfer
1004 June Place, Lovington NM 88260, USA

**Murphy, Thomas (Tom)** — Writer
4 Garville Road, Dublin 6, County Dublin, Ireland

**Murphy, Thomas A (Tom)** — Baseball Player
26561 Via Sacramento, Capistrano Beach CA 92624, USA

**Murphy, Thomas F (Tommy)** — Baseball Player
1824 Dunsford Road, Jacksonville FL 32207, USA

**Murphy, Thomas S** — Businessman
Capital Cities/ABC, 77 W 66th St, New York NY 10023, USA

**Murphy, Tod J** — Basketball Player
23 Parsons Hill Road, Wenham MA 01984, USA

**Murphy, Troy B** — Basketball Player
Dallas Mavericks, Pavilion, 2909 Taylor Street, Dallas TX 75226 USA

**Murphy, William E (Billy)** — Baseball Player
5309 66th Ave Court W, University Place WA 98467, USA

**Murphy, William P, Jr** — Inventor (Disposable Metal Trays)
25 SW 24th Road, Miami FL 33129, USA

**Murphy-O'Connor, Cormac Cardinal** — Religious Leader
Archbishop's House, Ambrosden Ave, Westminster, London SW1P 1QJ, England

**Murray, Andrew (Andy)** — Tennis Player
Ace Group, 13 Harwood Road, London NW6 4QP, England

**Murray, Andy** — Ice Hockey Coach
5765 232nd St W, Faribault MN 55021, USA

**Murray, Ann** — Opera Singer
Augstein & Hahn, Tal 28, 80331 Munich, Germany

**Murray, Anne** — Singer
Box 69030, 12 Sainte Claire Ave E, Toronto, ON M4T 1KO, Canada

**Murray, Bill** — Actor, Comedian
Ziffren Brittenham Branca, 1801 Century Park W, #700, Los Angeles CA 90067 USA

**Murray, Brian Doyle** — Actor
Abrams Artists, 9200 W Sunset Blvd, #1125, West Hollywood CA 90069 USA

| | |
|---|---|
| **Murray, Bryan C** | Ice Hockey Coach, Executive |
| 2215 NE 32nd Ave, Fort Lauderdale FL 33305, USA | |
| **Murray, Calvin D** | Baseball Player |
| 17434 Courtney Pine Circle, Spring TX 77379, USA | |
| **Murray, Chad Michael** | Actor, Model |
| Brillstein Entertainment Partners, 9150 Wilshire Blvd, #350, Beverly Hills CA 90212 USA | |
| **Murray, Cherry A** | Physicist |
| Lucent Technologies, 700 Mountain Ave, New Providence NJ 07974, USA | |
| **Murray, Chris** | Chemist |
| I B M Watson Research Center, PO Box 218, Yorktown Heights NY 10598 USA | |
| **Murray, Dale A** | Baseball Player |
| 5695 FM 2718, Yorktown TX 78164, USA | |
| **Murray, Dave** | Guitarist (Iron Maiden) |
| Sanctuary Music Mgmt, 82 Bishop's Bridge Road, London W2 6BB, England | |
| **Murray, David K** | Jazz Saxophonist, Orchestra Leader |
| Joel Chriss Co, 300 Mercer St, #3J, New York NY 10003 USA | |
| **Murray, Devon** | Actor |
| PO Box 814, Maynooth, County Kildare, Ireland | |
| **Murray, Don** | Actor |
| 1201 La Patera Canyon Road, Goleta CA 93117, USA | |
| **Murray, Doug** | Cartoonist ('Nam) |
| Marvel Comic Group, 10 E 40th St, #900, New York NY 10016, USA | |
| **Murray, Eddie C** | Baseball Player |
| 15609 Bronco Dr, Canyon Country CA 91387, USA | |
| **Murray, Edward P (Eddie)** | Football Player |
| 1070 Forest Bay Dr, Waterford MI 48328, USA | |
| **Murray, Glen** | Ice Hockey Player |
| 1320 10th St, Manhattan Beach CA 90266, USA | |
| **Murray, Hannah** | Actress |
| Troika, 74 Clerkenwell Road, #300, London EC1M 5QA, England | |
| **Murray, Iain** | Yachtsman |
| International Management Group, 75490 Fairway Dr, Indian Wells CA 92210, USA | |
| **Murray, James D** | Biologist |
| University of Washington, Applied Mathematics Dept, PO Box 352420, Seattle WA 98195, USA | |
| **Murray, Jennifer** | Aviatrix, Explorer |
| Polar First, Onslow Gardens, #2, London SW7 3LX, England | |
| **Murray, Jim** | Ice Hockey Player |
| 37 Viceroy Crescent, Brandon MB R7B 3R7, Canada | |
| **Murray, Joel** | Actor |
| Abrams Artists, 9200 W Sunset Blvd, #1125, West Hollywood CA 90069 USA | |
| **Murray, Jonathan** | Producer, Director, Writer |
| Bunim/Murray Productions, 6007 Sepulveda Blvd, Van Nuys CA 91411, USA | |
| **Murray, Keith** | Rap Artist |
| Green Light Talent Agency, PO Box 3172, Beverly Hills CA 90212 USA | |
| **Murray, Larry** | Baseball Player |
| 3200 Round Hill Dr, Hayward CA 94542, USA | |
| **Murray, Peg** | Actress |
| 800 Light House Road, Southold NY 11971, USA | |
| **Murray, Randy** | Ice Hockey Player |
| Royal Lepage Foothills, 50-805 5th Ave SW, Calgary AB T2P 0N6, Canada | |
| **Murray, Rob** | Ice Hockey Player |
| Providence Bruins, 1 La Salle Square, Providence RI 02903, USA | |
| **Murray, Robert (Bob)** | Ice Hockey Player, Executive |
| Anaheim Ducks, 2695 E Katella Ave, Anaheim CA 92806 USA | |
| **Murray, Ronald (Flip)** | Basketball Player |
| Atlanta Hawks, Centennial Tower, 101 Marietta St NW, #1900, Atlanta GA 30303 USA | |
| **Murray, Sean** | Actor |
| Unified Mgmt, 4231 National Ave, Burbank CA 91505, USA | |
| **Murray, Stuart** | Architect |
| Stuart Murray Assoc, 144 High St, North Sydney NSW 2060, Australia | |
| **Murray, Terence R (Terry)** | Ice Hockey Player, Coach |
| 11 Kirkwood Road, Scarborough ME 04074, USA | |
| **Murray, Terrence (Terry)** | Financier |
| Fleet Boston Corp, PO Box 55850, Boston MA 02205, USA | |
| **Murray, Tracy L** | Basketball Player |
| 2419 Tour Edition Dr, Henderson NV 89074, USA | |
| **Murray, Troy** | Ice Hockey Player |
| Chicago Blackhawks, United Center, 1901 W Madison St, Chicago IL 60612, USA | |
| **Murray, Ty** | Rodeo Rider |
| 1660 Private Road 1213, Stephenville TX 76401, USA | |
| **Murray-Leslie, Alex** | Singer (Chicks in Speed) |
| K Records, 924 Jefferson St SE, #101, Olympia WA 98501, USA | |
| **Murrell, Adrian** | Football Player |
| 19412 Laurel Glen Ave, Cornelius NC 28031, USA | |
| **Murrett, Robert B** | Navy Admiral |
| National Geospatial Intelligence Agency, 7500 Geoint Dr, Springfield VA 22150 USA | |
| **Murrey, Dorie S** | Basketball Player |
| 230 NE 178th St, Shoreline WA 98155, USA | |
| **Murro, Noam** | Director, Producer |
| Management 360, 9111 Wilshire Blvd, Beverly Hills CA 90210 USA | |
| **Murtagh, Kate** | Actress |
| 5104 Greenbush Ave, Sherman Oaks CA 91423, USA | |
| **Murton, Matthew H (Matt)** | Baseball Player |
| 2304 Silver Palm Dr, #302, Kissimmee FL 34747, USA | |
| **Murzyn, Dana** | Ice Hockey Player |
| 41 Sunset Way SE, Calgary AB T2X 3H6, Canada | |
| **Musabayev, Talgat A** | Cosmonaut |
| Cosmonaut Training Center, Star City, 141160 Zvezdny Gorodok, Moscow Oblast, Russia | |
| **Musburger, Brent W** | Sportscaster |
| 286 Locha Dr, Jupiter FL 33458, USA | |
| **Muse, Arizona** | Model, Actress |
| Next Model Mgmt, 23 Watts St, New York NY 10013 USA | |
| **Muser, Anthony J (Tony)** | Baseball Player, Manager |
| 1122 Martha Ann Dr, Los Alamitos CA 90720, USA | |
| **Museveni, Yoweri K** | President, Uganda; Army General |
| President's Office, PO Box 7108, Kampala, Uganda | |

**Musgrave, F Story**
8572 Sweetwater Trail, Kissimmee FL 34747, USA — Astronaut

**Musgrave, Mandy**
TalentWorks, 3500 W Olive Ave, #1400, Burbank CA 91505 USA — Actress

**Musgrave, R Kenton**
US Court of International Trade, 1 Federal Plaza, New York NY 10278, USA — Judge

**Musgrave, Ted**
Ultra Motorsports, 22 Raceway Dr, Mooresville NC 28115, USA — Auto, Truck Racing Driver

**Musgrave, Thea**
Novello Co, 8/9 Firth St, London W1V 5TZ, England — Composer, Conductor

**Musgrave, William S (Bill)**
4062 Leprechan Way, Duluth GA 30097, USA — Football Player

**Musil, Frantisek (Frank)**
Edmonton Oilers, 11230 110th St, Edmonton AB T5G 3H7, Canada — Ice Hockey Player

**Musiol, Bogdan**
Fitness-Studio, Talstr 50, 98544 Zella-Mehlis, Germany — Bobsled Athlete

**Musiq**
Island/Def Soul Records, 825 8th Ave, #2700, New York NY 10019, USA — Singer

**Musk, Elon**
SpaceX, 1 Rocket Road, Hawthorne CA 90250, USA — Businessman

**Musker, John**
Creative Artists Agency, 2000 Ave of Stars, #100, Los Angeles CA 90067 USA — Animator, Director, Writer

**Musselman, Jeffrey J (Jeff)**
1842 Port Tiffin Place, Newport Beach CA 92660, USA — Baseball Player

**Musselwhite, Charlie**
Rosebud Agency, PO Box 170429, San Francisco CA 94117 USA — Singer, Harmonica Player, Guitarist

**Mussenden, Isis**
Messina Baker Entertainment, 955 Carrillo Dr, #100, Los Angeles CA 90048 USA — Costume Designer

**Mussina, Michael C (Mike)**
737 White Church Road, Muncy PA 17756, USA — Baseball Player

**Musso, Mitchel T**
Principato-Young, 9465 Wilshire Blvd, #880, Beverly Hills CA 90212 USA — Actor

**Mustafaa, Najee**
4265 Jailette Road, Atlanta GA 30349, USA — Football Player

**Mustaine, David S (Dave)**
E S P Mgmt, 838 N Doheny Dr, #302, West Hollywood CA 90069, USA — Guitarist (Metallica, Megadeth)

**Mustard, Chad A**
6329 S 171st St, Omaha NE 68135, USA — Football Player

**Muster, Brad W**
2017 Stony Oak Court, Santa Rosa CA 95403, USA — Football Player

**Muster, Thomas**
370 Felter Ave, Hewlett NY 11557, USA — Tennis Player

**Mustin, Henry C**
2347 S Rolfe St, Arlington VA 22202, USA — Navy Admiral

**Mustonen, Olli**
Hazard Chase, 25 City Road, Cambridge CB1 1DP, England — Concert Pianist, Conductor, Composer

**Mutchnick, Max**
W M E Entertainment, 9601 Wilshire Blvd, #300, Beverly Hills CA 90210 USA — Producer

**Mutebi II, Ronald Muwenda**
Mengo Palace, PO Box 58, Kampala, Uganda — King, Uganda

**Muth, Rene**
Pennsylvania State University, Athletic Dept, University Park PA 16802, USA — Basketball Coach

**Mutharika, A Peter**
President's Office, State House, PO Box 40, Zomba, Malawi — President, Malawi

**Muti, Ornella**
Union Italy S R L, Piazzle di Porta Pia 116, 00198 Rome, Italy — Actress

**Muti, Riccardo**
Via Corti Alle Mura 25, 48100 Ravenna, Italy — Conductor

**Mutombo, Dikembe**
4787 Northside Dr NW, Atlanta GA 30327, USA — Basketball Player

**Mutscheller, James F (Jim)**
12350 Rosslare Ridge Road, #102, Lutherville Timonium MD 21093, USA — Football Player

**Mutter, Anne-Sophie**
Elektrastr 6, 81925 Munich, Germany — Concert Violinist

**Muxworthy, Jake**
Innovative Artists, 1505 10th St, Santa Monica CA 90401 USA — Actor

**Muzzatti, Jason**
4581 Dunmorrow Dr, Okemos MI 48864, USA — Ice Hockey Player

**Mwampembwa, Godfrey (Gado)**
Sasa Serna Productions, PO Box 13956, Nairobi, Kenya — Editorial Cartoonist

**Mya**
Media Artists Group, 8222 Melrose Ave, #203, Los Angeles CA 90048 USA — Singer, Actress, Songwriter

**Myasnikovich, Mikhail U**
Prime Minister's Office, Karl Marx Str 38, 220016 Minsk, Belarus — Prime Minister, Belarus

**Myers, Barton**
949 Toro Canyon Road, Santa Barbara CA 93108, USA — Architect

**Myers, Billie**
R J O Artist Relations & Mgmt, H S B C Bank, 101 W 14th St, New York NY 10011, USA — Singer, Actress

**Myers, Brett A**
385 Summerset Dr, Saint Johns FL 32259, USA — Baseball Player

**Myers, Chris**
Fox-TV, Sports Dept, 205 W 67th St, New York NY 10065 USA — Sportscaster

**Myers, Dale D**
Dale Myers Assoc, 7835 Rush Rose Dr, #214, Carlsbad CA 92009, USA — Space Engineer

**Myers, Danny**
Childress Racing, PO Box 1189, Industrial Dr, Welcome NC 27374, USA — Auto Racing Driver

**Myers, Gregory J (Greg)**
2915 S Deframe Way, Lakewood CO 80228, USA — Football Player

**Myers, Gregory R (Greg)**
7917 Brasado Way, Riverside CA 92508, USA — Baseball Player

**Myers, Jack D**
14 Prout Road, Freeport ME 04032, USA — Physician

**Myers, Joel Philip**
151 W Market St, Marietta PA 17547, USA — Glass Artist

**Myers, John M (Jack)**
25 Biltmore Lane, Menlo Park CA 94025, USA — Football Player

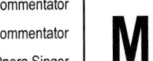

**Myers, Lisa**
NBC-TV, News Dept, 4001 Nebraska Ave NW, Washington DC 20016 USA
Commentator

**Myers, Margaret J (Dee Dee)**
Vanity Fair, Conde Nast Publications, 4 Times Square, New York NY 10036, USA
Government Official, Commentator

**Myers, Michael**
Opera et Concert, 37 Rue de la Chaussee d'Antin, 75009 Paris, France
Opera Singer

**Myers, Michael S (Mike)**
337 High Ridge Way, Castle Rock CO 80108, USA
Baseball Player

**Myers, Mike**
W M E Entertainment, 9601 Wilshire Blvd, #300, Beverly Hills CA 90210 USA
Actor, Comedian

**Myers, Norman**
Upper Meadow, Old Road, Headington, Oxford OX3 8SZ, England
Environmental Scientist, Conservationist

**Myers, Peter E (Pete)**
19W011 13th St, Lombard IL 60148, USA
Basketball Player

**Myers, Randall K (Randy)**
15525 NE Caples Road, Brush Prairie WA 98606, USA
Baseball Player

**Myers, Richard B (Dick)**
Kansas State University, History Dept, Manhattan KS 66506, USA
Air Force General

**Myers, Roderick D**
1816 S 3rd St, Conroe TX 77301, USA
Baseball Player

**Myers, Rodney L**
229 E Tanya Road, Phoenix AZ 85086, USA
Baseball Player

**Myers, Russell**
Tribune Media Services, 435 N Michigan Ave, #1500, Chicago IL 60611 USA
Cartoonist (Broom Hilda)

**Myers, Terry-Jo**
11592 Timberline Circle, Fort Myers FL 33966, USA
Golfer

**Myers, Thomas P (Tom)**
6015 Rapid Creek Court, Kingwood TX 77345, USA
Football Player

**Myerson, Bess**
453 7th St, Santa Monica CA 90402, USA
Beauty Queen, Actress, Consumer Activist

**Myerson, Mike**
Country Thunder Records, 1016 17th Ave S, Nashville TN 37212, USA
Guitarist (Heartland)

**Myerson, Roger B**
1219 Elmwood Ave, Wilmette IL 60091, USA
Nobel Economics Laureate

**Myers-Tikalsky, Linda**
RR 5 Box 2651, Santa Fe NM 87506, USA
Skier

**Myette, Aaron**
14277 101A Ave, Surry BC V0B 2G2, Canada
Baseball Player

**Mygind, Peter**
Elmer Dahl Agencies, Kanneworff Overgaard, Square 8B, 5600 Faabourg, Denmark
Actor

**Myhre, John**
Sandra Marsh & Associates, 9150 Wilshire Blvd, #220, Beverly Hills CA 90212, USA
Art Director, Production Designer

**Myhrvold, Nathan**
Intellectual Ventures, 3150 139th Ave SE, Building 4, Bellevue WA 98005, USA
Businessman

**Myles, Alannah**
Miracle Prestige, 1 Water Lane, Camden Town, London NW1 8N2, England
Singer, Guitarist, Songwriter

**Myles, Heather**
Heather Hotline, 5165 Brighton Dr, Riverside CA 92504, USA
Singer

**Myles, Sophia**
Gersh Agency, 9465 Wilshire Blvd, #600, Beverly Hills CA 90212 USA
Actress

**Myre, Philippe L (Phil)**
39270 Heatherbrook Dr, Farmington Hills MI 48331, USA
Ice Hockey Player

**Myrick, Daniel**
Media Talent Group, 9200 W Sunset Blvd, #550, West Hollywood CA 90069 USA
Director

**Myrtle, Charles J (Chip), Jr**
7500 E Quincy Ave, #E110, Denver CO 80237, USA
Football Player

**Myslinski, Thomas J (Tom), Jr**
1762 Dickens Cove, Germantown TN 38139, USA
Football Player

**Mystikal**
I C M Partners, 10250 Constellation Blvd, #900, Los Angeles CA 90067 USA
Rap Artist

# N

**Na, Kevin** — Golfer
Professional Golfers Association, 100 Ave of Champions, Palm Beach Gardens FL 33418 USA

**Naacke, Lisa** — Actress
Z B F Agentur, Friedrichstr 39, 10969 Berlin, Germany

**Naber, John P** — Swimmer
PO Box 50107, Pasadena CA 91115, USA

**Nabholz, Christopher W (Chris)** — Baseball Player
1 Cottage Hill W, Pottsville PA 17901, USA

**Nabokov, Evgeni V** — Ice Hockey Player
5763 Poppy Hills Place, San Jose CA 95138, USA

**Nabors, Jim** — Actor, Singer
PO Box 10364, Honolulu HI 96816, USA

**Nachamkin, Boris A** — Basketball Player
350 E 62nd St, #5J, New York NY 10065, USA

**Nachbaur, Donald K (Don)** — Ice Hockey Player
671 Clermont Dr, Richland WA 99352, USA

**Nachmanoff, Jeffrey** — Director, Writer
Creative Artists Agency, 2000 Ave of Stars, #100, Los Angeles CA 90067 USA

**Nachtwey, James** — Photojournalist
First Run/Icarus Films, 32 Court St, #2007, Brooklyn NY 11201, USA

**Nadal, Rafael (Rafa)** — Tennis Player
International Management Group, Via Augusta 200, 08021 Barcelona, Spain

**Nadeau, Gary** — Director
First Wave, 319 E 85th St, #200, New York NY 10028, USA

**Nadella, Satya** — Businessman
Microsoft Corp, 1 Microsoft Way, Redmond WA 98052, USA

**Nader, Laura** — Anthropologist
University of California, Anthropology Dept, Kroeber Hall, Berkeley CA 94720, USA

**Nader, Michael** — Actor
Paradigm Agency, 360 N Crescent Dr, North Building, Beverly Hills CA 90210 USA

**Nader, Ralph** — Consumer Activist
1600 20th St NW, Washington DC 20009, USA

**Nadig, Marie-Theres** — Alpine Skier
Haus Olympia, 8897 Flumserberg, Switzerland

**Nadingar, Emmanuel D** — Prime Minister, Chad
Prime Minister's Office, La Primature, Vale Royal, N'Djamena, Chad

**Nady, Xavier C, VI** — Baseball Player
11320 Wild Meadow Place, San Diego CA 92131, USA

**Naess, Leona K** — Singer, Songwriter
Paradigm Agency, 360 Park Ave S, #1600, New York NY 10010 USA

**Nafzger, Carl** — Thoroughbred Racing Trainer
General Delivery, Olton TX 79064, USA

**Nafziger, Dana A** — Football Player
251 El Dorado Way, Pismo Beach CA 93449, USA

**Nagalla, Srinivasa R** — Pediatrician
Oregon Health Science University, 3181 SW Jackson Park Dr, Portland OR 97239 USA

**Nagano, Kent G** — Conductor
Berkeley Symphony Orchestra, 1942 University Ave, #207, Berkeley CA 94704, USA

**Nagel, Sidney R** — Physicist
4913 S Kimbark Ave, Chicago IL 60615, USA

**Nagel, Thomas** — Philosopher
New York University, Law School, 40 Washington Square S, New York NY 10012, USA

**Nagerl, Hanns-Christoph** — Physicist
Institute for Experimental Physics, Technikerstra 25/4, 6020 Innsbruck, Austria

**Nagle, Browning** — Football Player
2281 Birchton Dr, Germantown TN 38139, USA

**Nagra, Parminder** — Actress
Rights House, Drury House, 34-43 Russell St, London WC2B 5HA, England

**Naguib, Antonios Cardinal** — Religious Leader
Patriarcat Copte Catholique, 34 Rue Ibn Sandar, 11712 Cairo, Egypt

**Nagy, Charles H** — Baseball Player
60 Robin Road, Westbury NY 11590, USA

**Nagy, Michael** — Opera Singer
Kunstler Sekretariat am Gasteig, Rosenheimer Str 52, 81669 Munich, Germany

**Nagy, Michael T (Mike)** — Baseball Player
8 Indian Trail, Bronx NY 10465, USA

**Naharin, Ohad** — Choreographer
Batsheva Dance Co, 6 Yechieli St, Tel-Aviv 65149, Israel

**Nahodha, Shamsi Vuai** — Chief Minister, Zanzibar
Chief Minister's Office, PO Box 239, Zanzibar, Tanzania

**Nahon, Chris** — Director
Hansen Jacobson Teller, 450 N Roxbury Dr, #800, Beverly Hills CA 90210, USA

**Nahorodny, William G (Bill)** — Baseball Player
1948 Rainbow Dr, Clearwater FL 33765, USA

**Nahyan, Khalifa bin Zayed Al** — President, United Arab Emirates
Manhal Palace, Abu Dhabi, United Arab Emirates

**Naidoo, Kumi** — Social Activist
Greenpeace International, Ottho Heldringstraat 5, 1066 Amsterdam AZ, Netherlands

**Naidu, Ajay** — Actor, Director, Writer
Global Artists Agency, 6253 Hollywood Blvd, #508, Los Angeles CA 90028 USA

**Naidus, Alex** — Bassist (Pains of Being Pure at Heart)
Slumberland Records, PO Box 19029, Oakland CA 94619, USA

**Naifeh, Steven W** — Writer
335 Sumter St SE, Aiken SC 29801, USA

**Nail, David** — Singer
Universal Music Group, 401 Commerce St, #1100, Nashville TN 37219 USA

**Nail, Jimmy** — Actor
Independent Talent Group, 40 Whitfield St, London W1T 2RH, England

**Nailatikau, Epeli** — President, Fiji; Brigadier General
President's Office, Government House, Berkeley Crescent, PO Box 2513, Suva, Viti Levu, Fiji

**Nails, Jamie M** — Football Player
PO Box 667291, Pompano Beach FL 33066, USA

**Naim, Yael** — Singer, Pianist, Songwriter
Partisan Arts, PO Box 5085, Larkspur CA 94977, USA

**Naima** — Model
Ford Models Inc, 111 5th Ave, #900, New York NY 10003 USA

**Naimoli, Vincent** — Baseball Executive
16616 Villalenda de Avila, Tampa FL 33613, USA
**Naipaul, V S** — Nobel Literature Laureate
Gillon Aitken Ltd, 29 Fernshaw Road, London SW10 0TG, England
**Nair, Mira** — Director
Lavin Agency, 222 3rd St, #1130, Cambridge MA 02142, USA
**Nairne, Robert C (Rob)** — Football Player
2611 Colt Road, Rancho Palos Verdes CA 90275, USA
**Naisbitt, John** — Writer
Spittelauer Platz 5A3A, 1090 Vienna, Austria
**Naish, Bronwen** — Concert Double Bass Player
Moelfre, Cwm Pennant, Garndolbenmaen, Gwunedd, North Wales LL5 9AX, Wales
**Najee** — Jazz Saxophonist
Red Entertainment Agency, 505 8th Ave, #1004, New York NY 10018, USA
**Najiib Tun Razak** — Prime Minister, Malaysia
Prime Minister's Office, Jalan Dato Onn, 50502 Kuala Lumpur, Malaysia
**Najimy, Kathy** — Actress
Abrams Artists, 9200 W Sunset Blvd, #1125, West Hollywood CA 90069 USA
**Najita, Tetsuo** — Historian
University of Chicago, History Dept, 1126 E 59th St, Chicago IL 60637, USA
**Nakache, Olivier** — Director
Creative Artists Agency, 2000 Ave of Stars, #100, Los Angeles CA 90067 USA
**Nakajima, Tadashi** — Astronomer
California Institute of Technology, Astronomy Dept, Pasadena CA 91125, USA
**Nakajima, Tsuneyuki (Tommy)** — Golfer
International Management Group, 7-18-18 Roppongi, Minatoku, Tokyo 106 0032 Japan
**Nakama, Keo** — Swimmer
1344 9th Ave, Honolulu HI 96816, USA
**Nakama, Yukie** — Actress, Singer
Production Ogi, 5-2-3-2F Shinjuku, Shinjuku, Tokyo 160 0022, Japan
**Nakamatsu, Jon** — Concert Pianist
Van Cliburn Foundation, 2525 Ridgmar Blvd, #307, Fort Worth TX 76116, USA
**Nakamura, Kuniwo** — President, Palau
Ta Belau Party, Oibill Era Kelulau, Koror PW 96940, Palau
**Nakamura, Shuji** — Nobel Physics Laureate
University of California, Engineering College, Santa Barbara CA 93106, USA
**Nakamura, Suzy** — Actress
Innovative Artists, 1505 10th St, Santa Monica CA 90401 USA
**Nakanishi, Koji** — Chemist
560 Riverside Dr, New York NY 10027, USA
**Nakata, Hideo** — Director
I C M Partners, 10250 Constellation Blvd, #900, Los Angeles CA 90067 USA
**Nakata, Hidetoshi** — Soccer Player
A C Parma, Viale Partigiani d'Italia, 43100 Parma, Italy
**Nakatani, Corey** — Thoroughbred Racing Jockey
PO Box 7673, Louisville KY 40257, USA
**Naked, Bif** — Singer, Songwriter
Crazed Mgmt, PO Box 356, Jamison PA 18929, USA
**Nakhirunkanok, Porntip (Bui)** — Beauty Queen
Angels Wings Foundation, 1482 E Valley Road, #428, Montecito CA 93108, USA
**Nalbandian, David** — Tennis Player
Asociacion de Tenis, Avda San Juan 1307, 1148 Buenos Aires, Argentina
**Nalder, Eric C** — Journalist
Seattle Times, Editorial Dept, 1000 Denny Way, Seattle WA 98109 USA
**Nalen, Thomas A (Tom)** — Football Player
4081 Preserve Parkway N, Greenwood Village CO 80121, USA
**Nalick, Anna** — Singer, Songwriter
Boulevard Mgmt, 21731 Ventura Blvd, #300, Woodland Hills CA 91364, USA
**Nalin, David R** — Pharmacologist
100 Luck Hill Road, West Chester PA 19382, USA
**Nall, Benita** — Actress
C E S D, 10635 Santa Monica Blvd, #130, Los Angeles CA 90025 USA
**Nall, N Anita** — Swimmer
PO Box 872505, Tempe AZ 85287, USA
**Nalluri, Bharat** — Director
Independent Talent Group, 40 Whitfield St, London W1T 2RH, England
**Nam Tae-Hee** — Soccer Player
Football Association, 1-131 Sinmunno, 2-Ga Jongno-Gu, Seoul 110 062, South Korea
**Nama, George A** — Artist, Sculptor
RR 1 Box 72, Montauk NY 11954, USA
**Namaliu, Rabbie L** — Prime Minister, Papua New Guinea
PO Box 6655, National Capital District, Boroko, Papua New Guinea
**Namath, Joseph W (Joe)** — Football Player, Actor
Namanco Productions, 300 E 51st St, #7D, New York NY 10022, USA
**Nambu, Yoichiro** — Nobel Physics Laureate
University of Chicago, Fermi Institute, 5640 S Ellis Ave, Chicago IL 60637, USA
**Nance, John J** — Writer
4512 8th Ave, Tacoma WA 98405, USA
**Nance, Todd** — Drummer (Widespread Panic)
Brown Cat Inc, 400 Foundry St, Athens GA 30601 USA
**Nanne, Louis V (Lou)** — Ice Hockey Player
6982 Tupa Dr, Minneapolis MN 55439, USA
**Nannini, Alessandro** — Auto Racing Driver
Via Massetana Romana 56, 53199 Siena, Italy
**Nannini, Gianna** — Singer, Songwriter
Cose di Musica, Via Plinio 15, 20129 Milan, Italy
**Nantis, Rich** — Ice Hockey Player
9585 Rue Jourdain, Quebec QC G2K 1K5, Canada
**Nanty, Isabelle** — Actress
Voyez Mon Agent, 20 Ave Rapp, 75007 Paris, France
**Nantz, James W (Jim), III** — Sportscaster
CBS-TV, Sports Dept, 51 W 52nd St, New York NY 10019 USA
**Napier, John** — Designer
M L R, Douglas House, 16-18 Douglas St, London SW1P 4PB, England
**Napier, Mark** — Ice Hockey Player, Executive
National Hockey League Alumni Assn, 170 Attwell Dr, #650, Toronto ON M9W 5Z5, Canada

**Napier, Shabazz B** — Basketball Player
Miami Heat, American Airlines Arena, 601 Biscayne Blvd, Miami FL 33132 USA

**Napier, Wilfrid F Cardinal** — Religious Leader
Archbishop's House, 154 Gordon Road, Durban 4001, KwaZulu-Natal, South Africa

**Napoles, Jose A** — Boxer
Cerrada Tizapan 9-303 Ediciov, Codigo Postel, Mexico City DF 06080, Mexico

**Napoli, Michael A (Mike)** — Baseball Player
2010 NW 118th Ave, Pembroke Pines FL 33026, USA

**Napolitano, Christopher** — Editor
Playboy, Editor's Office, 680 N Lake Shore Dr, Chicago IL 60611, USA

**Napolitano, Giorgio** — President, Italy
President's Office, Palazzo del Quirinale, Via Nazionale 190, 00184 Rome, Italy

**Napolitano, Janet** — Secretary, Homeland Security
University of California, President's Office, 1111 Franklin St, Oakland CA 9460, USA

**Napolitano, Johnette** — Singer (Concrete Blonde), Songwriter
Agency Group Ltd, 142 W 57th St, #600, New York NY 10019 USA

**Nara, Yoshitomo** — Artist
Stephen Friedman Gallery, 11 & 25-28 Old Burlington St, London W1S 3AN, England

**Naragon, Harold R (Hal)** — Baseball Player
1521 Hagey Dr, Barberton OH 44203, USA

**Narain, Nicole** — Model, Actress
8033 W Sunset Blvd, #224, West Hollywood CA 90046, USA

**Naranjo, Gerardo** — Director
Creative Artists Agency, 2000 Ave of Stars, #100, Los Angeles CA 90067 USA

**Narayen, Shantanu** — Businessman
Adobe Systems, 345 Park Ave, San Jose CA 95110, USA

**Narcisse, Daniel** — Handball Player
T H W Kiel Handball, Ziegelteich 30, 24103 Kiel, Germany

**Nardelli, Robert L** — Businessman
Chrysler Corp, 100 Chrysler Dr, Auburn Hills MI 48326, USA

**Narducci, Kathrine** — Actress
Greene Assoc, 1901 Ave of Stars, #130, Los Angeles CA 90067 USA

**Narducci, Tim** — Singer, Guitarist (Systematic)
Artist Group International, 9560 Wilshire Blvd, #400, Beverly Hills CA 90212 USA

**Nares, James** — Artist
Paul Kasmin Gallery, 511 W 27th St, New York NY 10001, USA

**Narita, Hiro** — Cinematographer
2262 Magnolia Ave, Petaluma CA 94952, USA

**Narleski, Raymond E (Ray)** — Baseball Player
1183 Chews Landing Road, Clementon NJ 08021, USA

**Narron, Jerry A** — Baseball Player, Manager
106 W Seeboth St, #809, Milwaukee WI 53204, USA

**Naruhito** — Crown Prince, Japan
Imperial Palace, 1-1 Chiyoda, Chiyodaku, Tokyo 100 0001, Japan

**Narvekar, Prabhakar R** — Government Official, Financier
4701 Willard Ave, Chevy Chase MD 20815, USA

**Narveson, Christopher G (Chris)** — Baseball Player
1804 Kenwyck Manor Way, Raleigh NC 27612, USA

**Nasar, Sylvia** — Writer
Columbia University, 2950 Broadway, Front 1, New York NY 10027, USA

**Nascimento, Milton** — Singer, Songwriter
Feinstein Mgmt, 8560 W Sunset Blvd, West Hollywood CA 90069, USA

**Nash Whitaker, Keisha** — Fashion Designer
344 E 59th St, New York NY 10022, USA

**Nash, Charles F (Cotton)** — Basketball, Baseball Player
600 Summershade Circle, Lexington KY 40502, USA

**Nash, David** — Sculptor
Capel Rhiw, Blanau, Ffestiniog, Gwynedd Wales LL41 3NT, Wales

**Nash, Graham W** — Singer, Songwriter
Creative Artists Agency, 2000 Ave of Stars, #100, Los Angeles CA 90067 USA

**Nash, James E (Jim)** — Baseball Player
4383 White Surrey Dr NW, Kennesaw GA 30144, USA

**Nash, Jamia S** — Actress, Singer
Carson-Adler Agency, 250 W 57 St, #2030, New York NY 10107, USA

**Nash, John F, Jr** — Nobel Economics Laureate
Princeton University, Economics Dept, Fine Hall, Princeton NJ 08544, USA

**Nash, Johnny** — Singer, Songwriter
I C M Partners, 730 5th Ave, New York NY 10019 USA

**Nash, Joseph A (Joe)** — Football Player
15 Colgate Road, Wellesley MA 02482, USA

**Nash, Kate** — Singer, Songwriter
High Road Touring, 751 Bridgeway, #200, Sausalito CA 94965 USA

**Nash, Kenny** — Singer
1336 NE 16th Terrace, Fort Lauderdale FL 33304, USA

**Nash, Leigh** — Singer (Sixpence None the Richer)
Nettwerk Mgmt, 1545 Wilcox Ave, #200, Los Angeles CA 90028, USA

**Nash, Niecy** — Actress, Comedienne
Principato-Young, 9465 Wilshire Blvd, #880, Beverly Hills CA 90212 USA

**Nash, Noreen** — Actress
719 N Maple Dr, Beverly Hills CA 90210, USA

**Nash, Richard** — Writer, Producer, Director
6024 Agapanthus Place, Woodland Hills CA 91367, USA

**Nash, Rick** — Ice Hockey Player
57 Deerfield Crescent, Brampton ON L6T 1K8, Canada

**Nash, Robert L (Bob)** — Basketball Player
659 Kahiau Loop, Honolulu HI 96821, USA

**Nash, Steven J (Steve)** — Basketball Player
6602 E Indian Bend Road, Paradise Valley AZ 85253, USA

**Nash, Tyson** — Ice Hockey Player
16895 SW 91st Ave, #17, Portland OR 97223, USA

**Naslund, Markus** — Ice Hockey Player
Mike Gillis Assoc, 154 Earl St, Kingston ON K7L 2H2, Canada

**Naslund, Mats T** — Ice Hockey Player
General Delivery, 6963 Pregassona, Switzerland

**Naslund, Ronald A (Ron)** — Ice Hockey Player
2600 Cheyenne Circle, Hopkins MN 55305, USA

| | |
|---|---|
| **Nasr, Seyyed Hossein**<br>George Washington University, Gelman Library, Washington DC 20052, USA | Theologian |
| **Nastase, Ilie**<br>Calea Plevnei 14, 1037 Bucharest, Hungary | Tennis Player |
| **Natal, Robert M (Bob)**<br>3913 Cockrill Dr, McKinney TX 75070, USA | Baseball Player |
| **Natali, Vincenzo**<br>Creative Artists Agency, 2000 Ave of Stars, #100, Los Angeles CA 90067 USA | Director, Writer |
| **Natalicio, Diana S**<br>University of Texas, President's Office, El Paso TX 79968, USA | Educator |
| **Natalie**<br>Supreme Entertainment Artists, PO Box 15601, Boston MA 02215, USA | Dancer, Choreographer, Singer |
| **Nater, Swen E**<br>4125 248th Court SE, Issaquah WA 98029, USA | Basketball Player |
| **Nathan, David G**<br>Dana-Farber Cancer Institute, 44 Binney St, Boston MA 02115, USA | Physician |
| **Nathan, Joseph A**<br>Compuware Corp, 1 Campus Martius, Detroit MI 48226, USA | Businessman |
| **Nathan, Joseph M (Joe)**<br>19066 Vogel Farm Road, Eden Prairie MN 55347, USA | Baseball Player |
| **Nathan, Sellapan Ramanathan (S R)**<br>President's Office, Orchard Road, Istana, 238823 Singapore, Singapore | President, Singapore |
| **Nathan, Tony C**<br>15110 Dunbarton Place, Hialeah FL 33016, USA | Football Player, Coach |
| **Nathaniel (Popp), Bishop**<br>Romanian Orthodox Episcopate, 2522 Grey Tower Road, Jackson MI 49201, USA | Religious Leader |
| **Nathanson, Jeff**<br>United Talent Agency, U T A Plaza, 9336 Civic Center Dr, Beverly Hills CA 90210 USA | Director, Producer, Writer |
| **Nathanson, Matt**<br>Zeitgeist Artist Mgmt, 660 York St, #216, San Francisco CA 94110, USA | Singer, Songwriter |
| **Nathman, John B**<br>C N A Solutions, 3003 Washington Blvd, Arlington VA 22201, USA | Navy Admiral |
| **Natonski, Richard F**<br>Commander, Marine Forces Command, 1468 Ingram St, Norfolk VA 23511 USA | Marine Corps General |
| **Natori, Josie C**<br>Natori Co, 40 E 34th St, New York NY 10016, USA | Fashion Designer |
| **Natsuki, Shizuko**<br>2-6-1 Ooile, Mini-amiku, Fukuokashi 815 0073, Japan | Writer |
| **Natt, Calvin L**<br>25201 E Indore Dr, Aurora CO 80016, USA | Basketball Player |
| **Natter, Robert J**<br>Robert J Natter Assoc, 507 Rutile Dr, Porte Vedre FL 32082, USA | Navy Admiral |
| **Nattiel, Ricky R**<br>835 NW 119th St, Gainesville FL 32606, USA | Football Player |
| **Nattress, Eric J (Ric)**<br>Stoney Creek Warriors, 467 Charlton Ave E, Hamilton ON L8W 2Z9, Canada | Ice Hockey Player |
| **Naughton, David**<br>14955 Dickens St, #208, Sherman Oaks CA 91403, USA | Actor |
| **Naughton, James**<br>Paradigm Agency, 360 N Crescent Dr, North Building, Beverly Hills CA 90210 USA | Actor, Singer |
| **Naughton, Naturi**<br>Innovative Artists, 1505 10th St, Santa Monica CA 90401 USA | Singer (3LW), Actress |
| **Naughty Boy**<br>Virgin/E M I Records, 364-366 Kensington High St, London W14 8NS, England | D J Musician, Songwriter |
| **Naulls, William D (Willie)**<br>511 S Carondelet St, #403, Los Angeles CA 90057, USA | Basketball Player |
| **Nault, Marie-Eve**<br>Canadian Soccer, Place Soccer Canada, 237 Metcalfe St, Ottawa ON K2P 1R2, Canada | Soccer Player |
| **Nauman, Bruce L**<br>HC 75, Box 82, Galisteo NM 87540, USA | Sculptor, Artist |
| **Nause, Martha**<br>13206 Patterson Trail, Minocqua WI 54548, USA | Golfer |
| **Nauta, Katie**<br>L A Talent, 7700 Sunset Blvd, Los Angeles CA 90046 USA | Actress, Singer, Model |
| **Nava, Michael**<br>California Supreme Court, 350 McAllister St, San Francisco CA 94102, USA | Writer |
| **Navarrete, Ximena**<br>Miss Universe Organization, 1370 Ave of Americas, #1600, New York NY 10019 USA | Beauty Queen, Model |
| **Navarro Cintron, Jaime**<br>8100 Oak Park Road, Orlando FL 32819, USA | Baseball Player |
| **Navarro Vivas, Dioner F**<br>13243 Pike Lake Dr, Riverview FL 33579, USA | Baseball Player |
| **Navarro, David M (Dave)**<br>Universal Media Artists, 8222 Melrose Ave, #203, Los Angeles CA 90048, USA | Guitarist, Pianist (Jane's Addiction) |
| **Navarro, Guillermo J**<br>Mirada, 4235 Redwood Ave, Los Angeles CA 90066, USA | Cinematographer |
| **Navarro, Juan Carlos**<br>19545 S Ashglen Circle, Collierville TN 38107, USA | Basketball Player |
| **Navies, Hannibal C**<br>1565 Briergate Dr, Duluth GA 30097, USA | Football Player |
| **Navka, Tatiana A**<br>Skating Federation, Luchnesksaia Nab 8, 119871 Moscow, Russia | Ice Dancer |
| **Navon, Itzhak**<br>39 Jabotinsky St, 94182 Jerusalem, Israel | President, Israel |
| **Navratilova, Martina**<br>Women's Tennis Assn, 1 Progress Plaza, #1500, Saint Petersburg FL 33701 USA | Tennis Player |
| **Naylor, Gloria**<br>One Way Productions, 638 2nd St, Brooklyn NY 11215, USA | Writer |
| **Naylor, Phyllis Reynolds**<br>401 Russell Ave, #713, Gaithersburg MD 20877, USA | Writer |
| **Naymark, Lola**<br>Agence Artiste Adequat, 108 Rue Reaumur, 75002 Paris, France | Actress |
| **Nayyar, Kunal**<br>Innovative Artists, 1505 10th St, Santa Monica CA 90401 USA | Actor, Comedian |
| **Nazarbayev, Nursultan A**<br>President's Office, 11 Beybitshilik St, 473000 Astana, Kazakhstan | President, Kazakhstan |

Naimoli - Nazarbayev

**Nazario, Ednita** — Singer, Songwriter
Angelo Medina Enterprises, PO Box 8319, Santyrce PR 00910, USA

**Nazario, Sonia** — Journalist
Los Angeles Times, Editorial Dept, 202 W 1st St, Los Angeles CA 90012 USA

**NdegeOcello, Me'Shell** — Singer, Bassist, Songwriter
Rosebud Agency, PO Box 170429, San Francisco CA 94117 USA

**N'Diaye, Mamadou** — Basketball Player
Georgia Institute of Technology, Athletic Dept, Atlanta GA 30332, USA

**N'Dour, Youssou** — Singer
International Music Network, 278 Main St, #400, Gloucester MA 01930 USA

**Neagle, Dennis E (Denny), Jr** — Baseball Player
16254 Sandstone Dr, Morrison CO 80465, USA

**Neal, Diane** — Actress
Socially Awkward Productions, 344 Grove St, #117, Jersey City NJ 07302, USA

**Neal, Dylan** — Actor
Metropolitan Talent Agency, 5405 Wilshire Blvd, #218, Los Angeles CA 90036 USA

**Neal, Elise** — Actress
A P A Talent & Literary Agency, 405 S Beverly Dr, #300, Beverly Hills CA 90212 USA

**Neal, Fred (Curly)** — Basketball Player
1639 Tiverton St, Winter Springs FL 32708, USA

**Neal, Lloyd** — Basketball Player
905 NE Mariners Loop, Portland OR 97211, USA

**Neal, Lorenzo L** — Football Player
10520 Waterbury Dr, Stockton CA 95209, USA

**Neal, Richard I** — Marine Corps General
Military Officers Assn, 201 N Washington St, Alexandria VA 22314, USA

**Neal, T Daniel (Dan)** — Football Player
711 Homestead Blvd, Louisville KY 40207, USA

**Neale, Harry** — Ice Hockey Coach
224 Quail Hollow Lane, East Amherst NY 14051, USA

**Nealon, Kevin** — Actor, Comedian
Gersh Agency, 41 Madison Ave, #3301, New York NY 10010 USA

**Nealy, Eddie C (Ed)** — Basketball Player
702 Lightstone Dr, San Antonio TX 78258, USA

**Neame, Christopher** — Actor
Brady Brannon Rich, 5670 Wilshire Blvd, #820, Los Angeles CA 90036 USA

**Neame, Gareth** — Producer
Carnival Film & Television, 55 New Oxford St, London WC1A 1BS, England

**Near, Holly** — Singer, Songwriter, Actress
PO Box 236, Ukiah CA 95482, USA

**Neary, Martin G J** — Concert Organist, Conductor
71 Clancarty Road, Fulham, London SW6 3BB, England

**Neaton, Patrick (Pat)** — Ice Hockey Player
3519 Olde Dominion Dr, #2, Brighton MI 48114, USA

**Neblett, Carol** — Opera Singer
Sardos Artists, 180 W End Ave, New York NY 10023, USA

**Nebout, Claire** — Actress
Artmedia, 20 Ave Rapp, 75007 Paris, France

**Necas, Petr** — Prime Minister, Czech Republic
Premier's Office, Nabrezi Edvarda Benese 4, 11801 Prague 1, Czech Republic

**Necciai, Ronald A (Ron)** — Baseball Player
6261 Overlook Lane, Belle Vernon PA 15012, USA

**Nece, Ryan C** — Football Player
4401 W Kennedy Blvd, #300, Tampa FL 33609, USA

**Nechita, Alexandra** — Artist
Wentworth Gallery, 1118 NW 159th Dr, Miami FL 33169, USA

**Neckar, Stanislav (Stan)** — Ice Hockey Player
10255 Waterside Oaks Dr, Tampa FL 33647, USA

**Nederlander, James M** — Producer
Nederlander Organization, 1450 Broadway, #2000, New York NY 10018, USA

**Nedjari, Al** — Actor
Grantham-Hazekdune, 5 Blenheim St, London W1S 1LD, England

**Nedney, Joseph T (Joe)** — Football Player
121 Lauren Circle, Scotts Valley CA 95066, USA

**Nedomansky, Vaclav** — Ice Hockey Player
32650 Nantasket Dr, #87, Rancho Palos Verdes CA 90275, USA

**Nedovic, Nemanja** — Basketball Player
Golden State Warriors, 1011 Broadway, Oakland CA 94605 USA

**Nedved, Pavel** — Soccer Player
F C Juventus, Corso Galilo Ferraris 32, 10128 Turin, Italy

**Nedved, Petr** — Ice Hockey Player
H C Bili Tygri Liberec, Tipsport Arena, Jeronymova 494/20, 46007 Liberec, Czech Republic

**Nee, Adam** — Actor
Brillstein Entertainment Partners, 9150 Wilshire Blvd, #350, Beverly Hills CA 90212 USA

**Needham, Connie** — Actress
26234 Kingsington Lane, Laguna Hills CA 92653, USA

**Needham, Tracey** — Actress
Stone Manners Salners, 6100 Wilshire Blvd, #1500, Los Angeles CA 90035 USA

**Needleman, Herbert L** — Cardiologist, Pharmacologist
Pittsburgh University Medical School, 3811 O'Hara St, Pittsburgh PA 15213, USA

**Needleman, Jacob** — Philosopher
841 Wawona Ave, Oakland CA 94610, USA

**Neel, Troy L** — Baseball Player
2613 Farleigh Lane, Cedar Park TX 78613, USA

**Neely, Cam** — Ice Hockey Player, Executive
76 Davison Dr, Lincoln MA 01773, USA

**Neely, Mark E, Jr** — Historian
Oxford University Press, 198 Madison Ave, #800, New York NY 10016, USA

**Neely, Ralph E** — Football Player
6943 Sperry St, Dallas TX 75214, USA

**Neeman, Calvin A (Cal)** — Baseball Player
93 Champagne Dr, Lake Saint Louis MO 63367, USA

**Neeson, Liam** — Actor
Artist Rights Group, 4A Exmoor St, London W10 6BD, England

**Nef, John U** — Historian
2726 N St NW, Washington DC 20007, USA

**Nef, Sonja** — Alpine Skier
Halten 345, 9035 Grub, Switzerland
**Neff, Garrett** — Model
Click Model Mgmt, 881 7th Ave, New York NY 10019 USA
**Neff, Lucas** — Actor
Untitled Entertainment, 350 S Beverly Dr, #200, Beverly Hills CA 90212 USA
**Neff, Steve** — Bowler
3655 S Suncoast Blvd, Homosassa FL 34448, USA
**Neffenger, Peter V** — Coast Guard Admiral
Vice Commandant, US Coast Guard, 2703 Martin Luther King Jr Ave SE, Washington DC 20020 USA
**Negahban, Navid** — Actor
House of Representatives, 1434 6th St, #1, Santa Monica CA 90401 USA
**Negay, Notah** — Golfer
Professional Golfers Association, 100 Ave of Champions, Palm Beach Gardens FL 33418 USA
**Negodaylo, Alexey A** — Bobsled Athlete
All-Russian Bobsled Federation, Luzhnetskaja Nab 8, 119992 Moscow, Russia
**Negray, Ronald A (Ron)** — Baseball Player
587 W Nimisila Road, Akron OH 44319, USA
**Negreanu, Daniel** — Poker Player
World Poker Tour Enterprises, 5700 Wilshire Blvd, #350, Los Angeles CA 90036 USA
**Negri Sembilan, Yang Di-Pertuan Besar** — Ruler, Malaysia
Yang Di-Pertuan Agong's Residence, Serembam, Malaysia
**Negron, Chuck** — Singer (Three Dog Night)
J-Bird Entertainment, 248 W Park Ave, #180, Long Beach NY 11561 USA
**Negron, Taylor** — Actor
Stone Manners Salners, 6100 Wilshire Blvd, #1500, Los Angeles CA 90035 USA
**Negroni, Daniele** — Singer
Postfach 45, 89276 Nersingen, Germany
**Negroponte, John D** — Government Official
Yale University, International Affairs Dept, New Haven CT 06520, USA
**Negroponte, Nicholas** — Computer Engineer
69 Mount Vernon St, Boston MA 02108, USA
**Nehamas, Alexander** — Philosopher
Princeton University, Philosophy Dept, Princeton NJ 08544, USA
**Nehberg, Rudiger** — Explorer, Adventurer
Target eV, Grossenseer Str 1A, 22929 Rausdorf, Germany
**Nehemiah, Renaldo** — Track Athlete, Football Player
15515 Owens Glen Terrace, North Potomac MD 20878, USA
**Neher, Erwin** — Nobel Medicine Laureate
Domane 11, 37120 Bovenden, Germany
**Nehmer, Meinhard** — Bobsled Athlete
Varnkevitz, 18556 Altenkirchen, Germany
**Nehy, Regine** — Actress
Innovative Artists, 1505 10th St, Santa Monica CA 90401 USA
**Neibauer, Gary W** — Baseball Player
146 Delta Ave, Bismarck ND 58504, USA
**Neid, Silvia** — Soccer Player
Betramstr 18, 60320 Frankfurt/Main, Germany
**Neidert, John T** — Football Player
4731 Placid Circle, Sarasota FL 34231, USA
**Neidich, Charles** — Conductor, Concert Clarinetist
Diane Saldick Mgmt, 225 E 36th St, New York NY 10016, USA
**Neil, Andrew F** — Editor
Glenburn Enterprises, PO Box 584, London SW7 3QY, England
**Neil, Dan** — Automobile Critic
Los Angeles Times, Editorial Dept, 202 W 1st St, Los Angeles CA 90012 USA
**Neil, Deanna** — Writer, Actress
EcoSeekers, PO Box 637, Nyack NY 10960, USA
**Neil, Hildegarde** — Actress
Associated International Mgmt, 7 Hatton Garden, #400, London EC1N 8AD, England
**Neill, Michael R (Mike)** — Baseball Player
17 Cape May Point, Greensboro NC 27455, USA
**Neill, Noel** — Actress
4421 N Bear Canyon Road, Tucson AZ 85749, USA
**Neill, Sam** — Actor
Rights House, Drury House, 34-43 Russell St, London WC2B 5HA, England
**Neils, Steven L (Steve)** — Football Player
1329 Waterford Road, Saint Paul MN 55125, USA
**Neilson, Jim** — Ice Hockey Player
907-525 Sainte Mary Ave, Winnipeg MB R3C 3X3, Canada
**Neilson-Bell, Sandra** — Swimmer
3101 Mistyglen Circle, Austin TX 78746, USA
**Neinas, Charles M (Chuck)** — Football Executive
5344 Westridge Dr, Boulder CO 80301, USA
**Neldel, Alexandra** — Actress, Model
Wasted Mgmt, Dieffenbachstr 33, 10967 Berlin, Germany
**Nelligan, Kate** — Actress
Innovative Artists, 235 Park Ave S, #1000, New York NY 10003 USA
**Nellis, M Duane** — Educator
University of Idaho, President's Office, Administration Building, Moscow ID 83844, USA
**Nellis, William J** — Physicist
Lawrence Livermore Laboratory, 7000 East Ave, Livermore CA 94550, USA
**Nelly** — Rap Artist (Saint Lunatics), Actor
ItGirl Public Relations, 5225 Wilshire Blvd, #718, Los Angeles CA 90036, USA
**Nelms, Michael (Mike)** — Football Player
11331 Fawn Lake Parkway, Spotsylvania VA 22551, USA
**Nelsen, William K (Bill)** — Football Player
13512 Dornoch Dr, Orlando FL 32828, USA
**Nelson, Alvin** — Rodeo Rider
1441 W Beicegel Creek Road, Grassy Butte ND 58634, USA
**Nelson, Azumah** — Boxer
Trustworthy Boxing, PO Box 939, Mamprobi, Accra, Ghana
**Nelson, Bob** — Writer, Actor
Creative Artists Agency, 2000 Ave of Stars, #100, Los Angeles CA 90067 USA
**Nelson, C Shane** — Football Player
115 Knoll Trail, Sandia TX 78383, USA

**Nelson, Cailin** — Astrophysicist
Lawrence Livermore Laboratory, 7000 East Ave, Livermore CA 94550, USA

**Nelson, Charles L (Chuck)** — Football Player
3028 162nd Place SE, Mill Creek WA 98012, USA

**Nelson, Colette** — Model, Bodybuilder
PO Box 1122, Seaford NY 11783, USA

**Nelson, Craig T** — Actor
Paradigm Agency, 360 N Crescent Dr, North Building, Beverly Hills CA 90210 USA

**Nelson, Cynthia (Cindy)** — Alpine Skier
PO Box 1699, 0171 Larkspur Lane, Vail CO 81658, USA

**Nelson, Darrin M** — Football Player
9116 1/2 S Manhattan Place, Los Angeles CA 90047, USA

**Nelson, David A** — Judge
US Court of Appeals, Courthouse Building, 425 Walnut St, Cincinnati OH 45202, USA

**Nelson, David E (Dave)** — Baseball Player
12213 Clubhouse Dr, Bradenton FL 34202, USA

**Nelson, Deborah** — Journalist
Seattle Times, Editorial Dept, 1000 Denny Way, Seattle WA 98109 USA

**Nelson, Dennis R** — Football Player
612 East St S, Kewanee IL 61443, USA

**Nelson, Diane** — Curling Athlete
Curling Association, 1660 Vimont Court, Cumberland ON K4A 4J4, Canada

**Nelson, Donald A (Nellie)** — Basketball Player, Coach, Executive
2284 S Kihei Road, Kihei HI 96753, USA

**Nelson, Dorothy W** — Judge
US Court of Appeals, 125 S Grand Ave, Pasadena CA 91105, USA

**Nelson, Edmund C (Ed)** — Football Player
1160 Billings Dr, Pittsburgh PA 15241, USA

**Nelson, George D** — Astronaut
A A A S Project, 1200 New York Ave NW, #100, Washington DC 20005, USA

**Nelson, Jameer** — Basketball Player
Orlando Magic, 8701 Maitland Summit Blvd, Orlando FL 32810 USA

**Nelson, James** — Singer (Celtic Tenors)
PO Box 32, Kells, County Meath, Ireland

**Nelson, James (Jim)** — Editor
Gentlemen's Quarterly, Editor's Office, 350 Madison Ave, New York NY 10017, USA

**Nelson, James E** — Religious Leader
Baha'i Faith, 536 Sheridan Road, Wilmette IL 60091, USA

**Nelson, Jeffrey A (Jeff)** — Baseball Player
8270 Stone Crop Dr, #N, Ellicott City MD 21043, USA

**Nelson, Jennifer Yuh** — Director, Animator
DreamWorks Animation, 1000 Flower St, Glendale CA 91201, USA

**Nelson, John** — Visual Effects Artist
I C M Partners, 10250 Constellation Blvd, #900, Los Angeles CA 90067 USA

**Nelson, John Allen** — Actor
4960 Fulton Ave, Sherman Oaks CA 91423, USA

**Nelson, John R** — Theologian
1111 Hermann Dr, #19A, Houston TX 77004, USA

**Nelson, Joseph G (Joe)** — Baseball Player
2407 Azure Circle, Highland CA 92346, USA

**Nelson, Judd** — Actor
Don Buchwald Talent Agency, 6500 Wilshire Blvd, #2200, Los Angeles CA 90048 USA

**Nelson, Judith** — Opera, Concert Singer
2600 Buena Vista Way, Berkeley CA 94708, USA

**Nelson, Keith E** — Guitarist (Buckcherry), Songwriter
10th Street Mgmt, 700 N San Vicente Blvd, #G410, West Hollywood CA 90069, USA

**Nelson, Larry G** — Golfer
438 Langley Oaks Dr SE, Marietta GA 30067, USA

**Nelson, Lars** — Cross Country Skier
Skiforbundet, Riksskistadion, 791 19 Falun, Sweden

**Nelson, Lauren** — Beauty Queen
Miss America Organization, 1370 Ave of Americas, #1600, New York NY 10019 USA

**Nelson, Lee M** — Football Player
23 Lindley Ave NW, Marietta GA 30064, USA

**Nelson, Liza** — Writer
G P Putnam's Sons, 375 Hudson St, New York NY 10014 USA

**Nelson, Marilyn Carlson** — Businesswoman
Carlson Companies, Carlson Parkway, PO Box 59159, Minneapolis MN 55459, USA

**Nelson, Mark** — Actor
TalentWorks, 3500 W Olive Ave, #1400, Burbank CA 91505 USA

**Nelson, Melvin F (Mel)** — Baseball Player
27420 Fisher St, Highland CA 92346, USA

**Nelson, Ralph A** — Nutritionist
Carle Foundation Hospital, 611 W Park St, #1, Urbana IL 61801, USA

**Nelson, Ricky L** — Baseball Player
2599 E Desert Broom Place, Chandler AZ 85286, USA

**Nelson, Robert A (Bob)** — Artist
125 Nelson, Lakeside OR 97449, USA

**Nelson, Robert A (Rob)** — Baseball Player
312 Alta Vista Ave, South Pasadena CA 91030, USA

**Nelson, Scott** — Baseball Umpire
800 Sara Dr, Coshocton OH 43812, USA

**Nelson, Sean C** — Singer, Keyboardist (Harvey Danger)
Barsuk Records, PO Box 22546, Seattle WA 98122, USA

**Nelson, Steven L (Steve)** — Football Player, Coach
143 Saddleworth Way, Middleboro MA 02346, USA

**Nelson, Terry L** — Football Player
3393 Highway 51 N, Arkadelphia AR 71923, USA

**Nelson, Tim Blake** — Actor, Director
Gateway Management, 860 Via de la Paz, #F10, Pacific Palisades CA 90272, USA

**Nelson, Todd** — Ice Hockey Player
Atlanta Thrashers, 101 Marietta St NW, #1900, Atlanta GA 30303 USA

**Nelson, Tracy** — Actress
Scott Carlson Entertainment, 5739 Bucknell Ave, Valley Village CA 91607, USA

**Nelson, W Eugene (Gene)** — Baseball Player
160 Habersham Landing Dr, Demorest GA 30535, USA

**Nelson, William H (Bill)** — Football Player
PO Box 9235, Pahrump NV 89060, USA

**Nelson, Willie** — Singer, Guitarist, Songwriter
Creative Artists Agency, 2000 Ave of Stars, #100, Los Angeles CA 90067 USA

**Nelson, Yvette** — Actress, Model
International Talent Agency, Beverly Hills Triangle, 9701 Wilshire Blvd, Beverly Hills CA 90212, USA

**Nemchinov, Sergei L** — Ice Hockey Player
14 Cornell Place, Rye NY 10580, USA

**Nemcova, Petra** — Model, Actress
Innovative Artists, 1505 10th St, Santa Monica CA 90401 USA

**Nemec, Corin** — Actor
Abrams Artists, 9200 W Sunset Blvd, #1125, West Hollywood CA 90069 USA

**Nemechek, Joseph F (Joe), III** — Auto, Truck Racing Driver
128 S Iredell Industrial Park Road, Mooresville NC 28115, USA

**Nemelka, Richard** — Basketball Player
6108 S 1300 E, Salt Lake City UT 84121, USA

**Nemeth, Miklos** — Prime Minister, Hungary
Keszi U 7, 1029 Budapest II, Hungary

**Nemov, Alexei** — Gymnast
Gymnastics Federation, Lujnetskaya Nabereynaya 8, 119270 Moscow, Russia

**Nen, Richard L (Dick)** — Baseball Player
48 Via Barcaza, Trabuca Canyon CA 92679, USA

**Nepomniaschy, Alex** — Cinematographer
Innovative Artists, 1505 10th St, Santa Monica CA 90401 USA

**Nerem, Robert M** — Mechanical Engineer
9435 Creekside Trail, Stone Mountain GA 30087, USA

**Neri Vela, Rodolfo** — Astronaut, Mexico
Playa Copacabana 131, Col Marte, Mexico City DF 08830, Mexico

**Neri, Francesca** — Actress
Blue Train Entertainment, 798 Brooktree Road, Pacific Palisades CA 90272, USA

**Neri, Manuel** — Sculptor
Charles Cowes Gallery, 210 11th Ave, #500, New York NY 10001, USA

**Nerlove, Marc L** — Economist
University of Maryland, Economics Research Dept, College Park MD 20742, USA

**Nero, Franco** — Actor
Muse Mgmt, 1541 Ocean Ave, #200, Santa Monica CA 90401, USA

**Nero, Peter** — Pianist, Conductor
202 Hidden Acres Lane, Media PA 19063, USA

**Nerud, John** — Thoroughbred Racing Executive, Trainer
19 Pound Hollow Road, Glen Head NY 11545, USA

**Nesbitt, Christine** — Speed Skater
13215 66th St NW, #36, Edmonton AB T5C 0B2, Canada

**Nesbitt, James** — Actor
Artist Rights Group, 4A Exmoor St, London W10 6BD, England

**Nesbitt, Mairead** — Fiddler, Violinist (Celtic Woman)
W M E Entertainment, 9601 Wilshire Blvd, #300, Beverly Hills CA 90210 USA

**Nesbo, Jo** — Writer
R W S G Agency, 1107 1/2 Glendon Ave, Los Angeles CA 90024

**Nesby, Ann** — Singer
Labor Force Mgmt, 1200 Highway 74 S, #103, Peachtree City GA 30269, USA

**Nesher, Avi** — Director, Producer, Writer
Gersh Agency, 9465 Wilshire Blvd, #600, Beverly Hills CA 90212 USA

**Nesic, Alex** — Actor
Principato-Young, 9465 Wilshire Blvd, #880, Beverly Hills CA 90212 USA

**Nesmith, Michael (Mike)** — Singer, Guitarist (Monkees)
Videoranch, 1793 Catalina St, Seaside CA 93955, USA

**Nespoli, Paolo A** — Astronaut, Italy
2011 Dawn Crest Court, Kemah TX 77565, USA

**Nespral, Jackie** — Commentator
NBC-TV, News Dept, 30 Rockefeller Plaza, #270E, New York NY 10112 USA

**Ness, Michael J (Mike)** — Singer, Guitarist (Social Distortion)
Relentless Artist Mgmt, 1922 Placentia, #A, Costa Mesa CA 92627, USA

**Ness, Rick** — Singer, Guitarist (Fig Dish)
Metropolitan Entertainment Group, 2 Penn Plaza, #1500, New York NY 10121, USA

**Nessen, Ronald H (Ron)** — Government Official, Journalist
6409 Walhonding Road, Bethesda MD 20816, USA

**Nessler, Brad** — Sportscaster
ABC-TV, Sports Dept, 77 W 66th St, New York NY 10023 USA

**Nesta, Alessandro** — Soccer Player
Lazio F C, Via di Santa Cornelia 14, 00060 Formello, Italy

**Nester, Eugene W** — Microbiologist
Washington University, Microbiology Dept, Seattle WA 98195, USA

**Nesterenko, Eric** — Ice Hockey Player
PO Box 1025, Vail CO 81658, USA

**Nesterenko, Yevgeny Y** — Opera Singer
Fruzenskaya Nab 24 Korp 1, #178, 119146 Moscow, Russia

**Nesterovic, Radoslav (Rasho)** — Basketball Player
11 Sanctuary Dr, San Antonio TX 78248, USA

**Nestico, Samuel A (Sammy)** — Composer, Arranger
1731 Blackbird Circle, Carlsbad CA 92011, USA

**Netanyahu, Benjamin** — Prime Minister, Israel
Prime Minister's Office, 3 Rehov Kaplan, Jerusalem 91919, Israel

**Netherland, Joseph H** — Businessman
F M C Corp, 200 E Randolph Dr, Chicago IL 60601, USA

**Netolicky, Robert (Bob)** — Basketball Player
PO Box 531, Carmel IN 46082, USA

**Netravali, Arun N** — Engineer
10 Byron Court, Westfield NJ 07090, USA

**Netrebko, Anna Y** — Opera Singer
Centre Stage Artist Mgmt, Stralauer Allee 1, 10245 Berlin, Germany

**Nettles, G Douglas (Doug)** — Football Player
13105 Quail Creek Court, Silver Spring MD 20904, USA

**Nettles, Graig** — Baseball Player
11217 Carmel Creek Road, #2, San Diego CA 92130, USA

**Nettles, James A (Jim)** — Football Player
3817 Mandeville Canyon Road, Los Angeles CA 90049, USA

**Nettles, James W (Jim)** — Baseball Player
4632 N Darien Dr, Tacoma WA 98407, USA
**Nettles, Jennifer** — Singer (Sugarland)
Supreme Entertainment Arists, PO Box 15601, Boston MA 02215, USA
**Nettles, John** — Actor
Saraband Assoc, 265 Liverpool Road, London N1 1NL, England
**Neu, Michael D (Mike)** — Baseball Player
406 Fraga Court, Martinez CA 94553, USA
**Neufeld, Elizabeth F** — Biochemist
University of California Medical School, Biology Dept, Los Angeles CA 90024, USA
**Neufeld, Ray** — Ice Hockey Player
Selkirk Steelers, 1011 Manitoba Ave, Selkirk MB R1A 3T7, Canada
**Neufeld, Sarah** — Violinist (Arcade Fire)
Billions Corp, 3522 W Armitage Ave, Chicago IL 60647 USA
**Neugebauer, Marcia** — Physicist
7519 S Elliot Lane, Tucson AZ 85747, USA
**Neugebauer, Nick** — Baseball Player
101 S Sahuaro Dr, Gilbert AZ 85233, USA
**Neuhauser, Duncan V B** — Epidemiologist
PO Box 932, Blue Hill ME 04614, USA
**Neuheisel, Richard (Rick)** — Football Player, Coach
3601 Winding Creek Road, Sacramento CA 95864, USA
**Neumann, Liselotte** — Golfer
11003 Muirfield Dr, Rancho Mirage CA 92270, USA
**Neumann, Randy** — Boxer, Referee
600 E Crescent Ave, #104, Upper Saddle River NJ 7458, USA
**Neumann, Wolfgang** — Opera Singer
Metropolitan Opera Assn, Lincoln Center Plaza, New York NY 10023 USA
**Neumannova, Katerina** — Cross Country Skier
Svantlova 1803, 39701 Pisek, Czech Republic
**Neumark, Julie** — Actress, Singer, Songwriter
Sterling Artists Mgmt, 11054 Ventura Blvd, #285, Studio City CA 91604, USA
**Neumeier, Daniel G (Dan)** — Baseball Player
N2635 County Road V, Lodi WI 53555, USA
**Neumeier, John** — Choreographer
Hamburg Ballet, 54 Caspar-Voght-Str, 20535 Hamburg, Germany
**Neuner, Magdalena** — Biathlete
Postfach 1354, 82145 Planegg, Germany
**Neuvic, Thierry** — Actor
Artmedia, 20 Ave Rapp, 75007 Paris, France
**Neuwelt, Edward A** — Neurologist
Oregon Health Sciences University, 3181 SW Jackson Park Dr, Portland OR 97201, USA
**Neuwirth, Bebe** — Actress, Dancer, Singer
I C M Partners, 10250 Constellation Blvd, #900, Los Angeles CA 90067 USA
**Nevarez, Alfred** — Singer (All-4-One)
Universal Attractions, 135 W 26th St, #1200, New York NY 10001 USA
**Neveldine, Mark** — Director, Writer
United Talent Agency, U T A Plaza, 9336 Civic Center Dr, Beverly Hills CA 90210 USA
**Neves, Jose Maria P** — Prime Minister, Cape Verde
Prime Minister's Office, Varzea CP 304, Cidade da Praia, Ilha de Santiago, Cape Verde
**Neville, Aaron** — Singer
Elevation Group, 1408 Encinal Ave, #A, Alameda CA 94501, USA
**Neville, Arthel** — Entertainer
1840 Victory Blvd, Glendale CA 91201, USA
**Neville, Bill** — Cartoonist (Tiny Toons)
511 Valleybrook Dr, Jamestown NC 27282, USA
**Neville, Robert C** — Theologian
Boston University, Theology School, Boston MA 02215, USA
**Neville, Thomas O (Tom), Jr** — Football Player
PO Box 11175, Montgomery AL 36111, USA
**Nevin, Bob** — Ice Hockey Player
61 River Court Blvd, East York ON M4K 3A3, Canada
**Nevin, Brooke** — Actress
TalentWorks, 3500 W Olive Ave, #1400, Burbank CA 91505 USA
**Nevin, Phil J** — Baseball Player
18795 Heritage Dr, Poway CA 92064, USA
**Nevins, Sheila** — Producer
H B O Documentary, 1100 Ave of Americas, New York NY 10036, USA
**Nevinson, Nancy** — Actress
23 Mill Close, Fishbourne, Chichester PO19 3JW, England
**Nevitt, Charles G (Chuck)** — Basketball Player
3124 Cartwright Dr, Raleigh NC 27612, USA
**Newacheck, Kyle** — Actor, Writer, Producer, Director
United Talent Agency, U T A Plaza, 9336 Civic Center Dr, Beverly Hills CA 90210 USA
**Newbern, George** — Actor
Leslie Allan-Rice Mgmt, 1007 Maybrook Dr, Beverly Hills CA 90210, USA
**Newberry, Jeremy D** — Football Player
1225 Almondwood Dr, Antioch VA 94509, USA
**Newberry, Thomas (Tom)** — Football Player
PO Box 9299, Tavernier FL 33070, USA
**Newborn, Ira** — Composer
Vangelos Mgmt, 15233 Ventura Blvd, #200, Sherman Oaks CA 91403 USA
**Newcombe, Donald (Don)** — Baseball Player
1448 Young St, #1108, Honolulu HI 96814, USA
**Newcombe, John D** — Tennis Player
Newcombe's Tennis Ranch, 325 Mission Valley Road, New Braunfels TX 78132, USA
**Newell, Catharine** — Sculptor
Bullseye Gallery, 300 NW 13th Ave, Portland OR 97209, USA
**Newell, Homer E** — Physicist
2567 Nicky Lane, Alexandria VA 22311, USA
**Newell, Mike** — Director, Producer, Actor
50 Canon Entertainment, Oxford House, 76 Oxford St, London W1D 1BS, England
**Newell, Thomas D (Tom)** — Baseball Player
9525 Cordoba Blvd, Sparks NV 89441, USA
**Newfield, Heidi** — Singer, Guitarist (Trick Pony)
McGhee Entertainment, 801 18th Ave S, Nashville TN 37203, USA

**Newfield, Marc A** — Baseball Player
5591 Selkirk Dr, Huntington Beach CA 92649, USA
**Newhart, Bob** — Actor, Comedian
420 Amapola Lane, Los Angeles CA 90077, USA
**Newhouse, Donald E** — Publisher
Advance Publications, 950 W Fingerboard Road, Staten Island NY 10305, USA
**Newhouse, Frederick (Fred)** — Track Athlete
3003 Pine Lake Trail, Houston TX 77068, USA
**Newhouse, Samuel I, Jr** — Publisher
Advance Publications, 950 W Fingerboard Road, Staten Island NY 10305, USA
**Newlin, Diandra** — Actress, Singer, Model
PO Box 29876, Henrico VA 23242, USA
**Newlin, Michael F (Mike)** — Basketball Player
1414 Horseshoe Dr, Sugar Land TX 77478, USA
**Newman, Alan C (A C)** — Singer (New Pornographers)
Billions Corp, 3522 W Armitage Ave, Chicago IL 60647 USA
**Newman, Albert D (Al)** — Baseball Player
1044 Laroda, Ontario CA 91762, USA
**Newman, Alec** — Actor
Markham Froggatt Irwin, Julian House, 4 Windmill St, London W1P 1HF, England
**Newman, Anthony** — Concert Harpsichordist, Conductor
Gami/Simonds, 42 County Road, Morris CT 06763, USA
**Newman, Barry** — Actor
N2N Entertainment, 1230 Montana Ave, #303, Santa Monica CA 90403 USA
**Newman, Dan** — Ice Hockey Player
192 E County Road 27, RR 1, Cottam ON N0R 1B0, Canada
**Newman, David** — Composer
First Artists Mgmt, 4764 Park Granada, #210, Calabasas CA 91302 USA
**Newman, Edward K (Ed)** — Football Player
10100 SW 140th St, Miami FL 33176, USA
**Newman, James** — Actor
Cassell-Levy Talent Agency, 843 N Sycamore Ave, Los Angeles CA 90038, USA
**Newman, James H** — Astronaut
18583 Martinique Dr, Houston TX 77058, USA
**Newman, Jeffrey L (Jeff)** — Baseball Player, Manager
10133 N 103rd St, Scottsdale AZ 85258, USA
**Newman, John W P** — Singer, Songwriter
Island Records, 364 Kensington High St, London W14 8NS, England
**Newman, Jon O** — Judge
US Court of Appeals, 450 Main St, #218, Hartford CT 06103, USA
**Newman, Kevin** — Commentator
ABC-TV, News Dept, 77 W 66th St, New York NY 10023 USA
**Newman, Kyle** — Director, Producer
Fire Thief Films, 15260 Ventura Blvd, #2100, Sherman Oaks CA 91403, USA
**Newman, Laraine** — Actress, Comedienne
TalentWorks, 3500 W Olive Ave, #1400, Burbank CA 91505 USA
**Newman, Nanette** — Actress
Seven Pines, Wentworth, Surrey GU25 4QP, England
**Newman, Oscar** — Architect, Urban Planner
Community Design Analysis Institute, 66 Clover Dr, Great Neck NY 11021, USA
**Newman, Pauline** — Judge
US Court of Appeals, 717 Madison Place NW, Washington DC 20439, USA
**Newman, Phyllis** — Actress, Singer
211 Central Park West, #19E, New York NY 10024, USA
**Newman, Randy** — Singer, Pianist, Composer
Cathy Kerr Mgmt, 9079 Nemo St, West Hollywood CA 90069, USA
**Newman, Ryan J** — Auto, Truck Racing Driver
Stewart-Haas Racing, 6001 Haas Way, Kannapolis NC 28081, USA
**Newman, Terence** — Football Player
2817 Park Bridge Court, Dallas TX 75219, USA
**Newman, Thomas M** — Composer
Gorfaine/Schwartz, 4111 W Alameda Ave, #509, Burbank CA 91505 USA
**Newman, Zeb** — Actor
Framework Entertainment, 9057 Nemo St, #C, West Hollywood CA 90069 USA
**Newmar, Julie** — Actress
204 S Carmelina Ave, Los Angeles CA 90049, USA
**Newmark, Craig A** — Businessman
Craigslist, PO Box 225159, San Francisco CA 94122, USA
**Newmark, Dave** — Basketball Player
545 Pierce St, #2301, Albany CA 94706, USA
**Newsom, David** — Actor
Thruline Entertainment, 9250 Wilshire Blvd, #100, Beverly Hills CA 90212 USA
**Newsom, Gavin E** — Mayor, San Francisco
Mayor's Office, 400 S Van Ness Ave, San Francisco CA 94103, USA
**Newsom, Joanna** — Singer, Harpist
Billions Corp, 3522 W Armitage Ave, Chicago IL 60647 USA
**Newsome, Harry K, Jr** — Football Player
213 Hawthorne Lane, Cheraw SC 29520, USA
**Newsome, Ozzie** — Football Player, Executive
6 Padonia Woods Court, Cockeysville MD 21030, USA
**Newsome, Timothy A (Timmy)** — Football Player
7005 Quartermile Lane, Dallas TX 75248, USA
**Newsome, Vincent K (Vince)** — Football Player
5308 Woodnote Lane, Columbia MD 21044, USA
**Newson, Warren D** — Baseball Player
13232 Padre Ave, Keller TX 76244, USA
**Newsted, Jason** — Bassist (Metallica)
205 Alamo View Place, Walnut Creek CA 94595, USA
**Newton, Becki** — Actress
United Talent Agency, U T A Plaza, 9336 Civic Center Dr, Beverly Hills CA 90210 USA
**Newton, Bill R** — Basketball Player
15 Brixworth Lane, #6, Nashville TN 37205, USA
**Newton, C M** — Basketball Coach, Administrator
524 Currie Way, Birmingham AL 35209, USA
**Newton, Cameron J (Cam)** — Football Player
Carolina Panthers, Ericsson Stadium, 800 S Mint St, Charlotte NC 28202 USA

**Newton, Chris** — Cyclist
National Cycling Centre, Stuart St, Manchester M11 4DQ, England

**Newton, Juice** — Singer, Guitarist, Songwriter
O J Mgmt, 4321 Reyes Dr, Tarzana CA 91356, USA

**Newton, Matthew** — Actor
Robyn Gardiner Mgmt, 397 Riley St, Surry Hills NSW 2010, Australia

**Newton, Nathaniel (Nate), Jr** — Football Player
1921 White Oak Clearing, Southlake TX 76092, USA

**Newton, Richard Y (Dick), III** — Air Force General
Deputy CofS, Manpower/Personnel, HqUSAF, Pentagon, Washington DC 20330, USA

**Newton, Robert L (Bob)** — Football Player
37701 Hollister Dr, Palm Desert CA 92211, USA

**Newton, Roger** — Medical Researcher
Esperion Therapeutics, 695 K M S Place, 3621 S State St, Ann Arbor MI 48108, USA

**Newton, Thandie** — Actress
Independent Talent Group, 40 Whitfield St, London W1T 2RH, England

**Newton, Thomas R (Tom)** — Football Player
169 Park Road, Rochester NY 14622, USA

**Newton, Wayne** — Singer, Actor
Wayne Newton Mgmt, 6730 S Pecos Road, Las Vegas NV 89120, USA

**Newton-John, Olivia** — Singer, Actress
104 Lighthouse Dr, Jupiter Inlet Colony FL 33469, USA

**Neyelova, Marina M** — Actress
Potapovsky Per 12, 117333 Moscow, Russia

**Neymar** — Soccer Player
Confederacion de Futebol, Rua Victor Civita 66, #1, Rio de Janeiro 22775 044, Brazil

**Ne-Yo** — Rap Artist, Singer, Songwriter
W M E Entertainment, 9601 Wilshire Blvd, #300, Beverly Hills CA 90210 USA

**Nezhat, Camran** — Endocrinologist
Fertility/Endocrinology Center, 5555 Peachtree Dunwoody Road NE, Atlanta GA 30342, USA

**Ngata, E Haloti** — Football Player
Baltimore Ravens, Ravens Stadium, 1 Winning Dr, Baltimore MD 21230 USA

**Nguyen Phu Trong** — General Secretary, Vietnam
General Secretary's Office, 1 Hoang Hoa Tham, Hanoi, Vietnam

**Nguyen Tan Dung** — Prime Minister, Vietnam
Prime Minister's Office, 1 Hoang Hoa Tham, Hanoi, Vietnam

**Nguyen, Dat T** — Football Player
115 Edge Creek, Boerne TX 78006, USA

**Nguyen, Dustin** — Actor
1051 S Dunsmuir Ave, Los Angeles CA 90019, USA

**Nguyen, Marcel** — Gymnast
PO Box 1307, 82003 Unterhaching, Germany

**Nguyen, Navia** — Model
Don Buchwald Talent Agency, 10 E 44th St, New York NY 10017 USA

**Nhamadjo, Manuel Serifo** — Acting President, Guinea-Bissau
President's Office, Palacio Presidential, Bissau, Guinea-Bissau

**Nibali, Vincenzo** — Cyclist
U C I Pro Team Astana, Gildo Pastor Center, 7 Rue du Gabian, 98000 Monaco

**Niblett, Emma (Scout)** — Singer, Songwriter
Puschen, Schleisische Str 38, 10997 Berlin, Germany

**Nichanian, Veronique** — Fashion Designer
Hermes, 24 Rue Faubourg Saint Honore, 75008 Paris, France

**Nichol, Gene R, Jr** — Educator
University of North Carolina, Law School, Chapel Hill NC 27599, USA

**Nichol, Scott B** — Ice Hockey Player
612 Ladyhawk Lane, Victor NY 14564, USA

**Nicholas, Alison** — Golfer
Pat Darby, Badgar Farm House, Badgar near Wolverhampton WV6 7LS, England

**Nicholas, Denise** — Actress
932 S Longwood Ave, Los Angeles CA 90019, USA

**Nicholas, Henry** — Labor Leader
Hospital & Health Care Union, 330 W 42nd St, #1905, New York NY 10036, USA

**Nicholas, J D** — Singer, Guitarist (Commodores)
Management Assoc, 1920 Benson Ave, Saint Paul MN 55116, USA

**Nicholas, Nicholas J, Jr** — Publisher
Pluggers Inc, 1000 SW Broadway, #1850, Portland OR 97205, USA

**Nicholas, Peter M** — Businessman
Boston Scientific Corp, 1 Boston Scientific Place, Natick MA 01760, USA

**Nicholas, Thomas Ian** — Actor
Innovative Artists, 1505 10th St, Santa Monica CA 90401 USA

**Nicholls, Bernie** — Ice Hockey Player
17101 Planters Row, Addison TX 75001, USA

**Nicholls, Craig** — Singer (Vines)
Winterman-Goldstein, 17 Holdsworth St, Newtown NSW 2042, Australia

**Nicholls, David A** — Writer
Curtis Brown Group, 28-29 Haymarket St, #500, London SW1Y 4SP, England

**Nichols, Austin** — Actor
United Talent Agency, U T A Plaza, 9336 Civic Center Dr, Beverly Hills CA 90210 USA

**Nichols, Carl E** — Baseball Player
901 E Artesia Blvd, Compton CA 90221, USA

**Nichols, David C, Jr** — Navy Admiral
Deputy Commander, US Central Command, MacDill Air Force Base, Tampa FL 33621, USA

**Nichols, Dorothy L** — Government Official, Financier
Farm Credit Administration, 1501 Farm Credit Dr, #3600, McLean VA 22102, USA

**Nichols, Gates** — Guitarist (Confederate Railroad)
Bobby Roberts, 3050 Business Park Circle, #303, Goodlettsville TN 37221 USA

**Nichols, Hamilton J, Jr** — Football Player
11015 Kirkmead Dr, Houston TX 77089, USA

**Nichols, Joe** — Singer
Alliance Media Relations, 3805 Rolland Road, Nashville TN 37205, USA

**Nichols, John** — Writer
New Press, 38 Greene St, #400, New York NY 10013, USA

**Nichols, Kenwood C** — Businessman
Champion International Corp, 1 Champion Plaza, Stamford CT 06921, USA

**Nichols, Kyra** — Ballerina
Peter Diggins Assoc, 133 W 71st St, New York NY 10023, USA

**Nichols, Larry** — Rubik Cube Designer
Moleculon Research Corp, 139 Main St, Cambridge MA 02142, USA
**Nichols, Lorrie** — Bowler
1251 Lexington Dr, Algonquin IL 60102, USA
**Nichols, Marisol** — Actress
Paradigm Agency, 360 N Crescent Dr, North Building, Beverly Hills CA 90210 USA
**Nichols, Mark S** — Football Player
5905 Penn Station Lane, Bakersfield CA 93311, USA
**Nichols, Michael (Nick)** — Photographer
National Geographic, Editorial Dept, 1145 17th St NW, Washington DC 20036 USA
**Nichols, Nichelle** — Actress
23281 Leonora Dr, Woodland Hills CA 91367, USA
**Nichols, Peter R** — Writer
Alan Brodie, 211 Piccadilly, London W1V 9LD, England
**Nichols, Rachel E** — Actress, Model, Producer
Management 360, 9111 Wilshire Blvd, Beverly Hills CA 90210 USA
**Nichols, Rachel M** — Sportscaster
CNN-TV, News Dept, 190 Marietta Ave SW, Atlanta GA 30303 USA
**Nichols, Robert H (Bobby)** — Golfer
8681 Glenlyon Court, Fort Myers FL 33912, USA
**Nichols, Rodney L (Rod)** — Baseball Player
1570 Elk Trail, Helena MT 59601, USA
**Nichols, Stephen** — Actor
PO Box 82231, Athens GA 30608, USA
**Nichols, T Reid** — Baseball Player
5473 Wild Cherry Circle, Milwaukee WI 53214, USA
**Nichols, Vincent G Cardinal** — Religious Leader
Archdiocese of Westminster, Ambrosden Avenue, Westminster, London SW1P 1QJ, England
**Nicholson, David L (Dave)** — Baseball Player
15316 Lakepoint Dr, Benton IL 62812, USA
**Nicholson, Jack** — Actor
Bresler Kelly Assoc, 11500 W Olympic Blvd, #400, Los Angeles CA 90064 USA
**Nicholson, Julianne** — Actress
Creative Artists Agency, 2000 Ave of Stars, #100, Los Angeles CA 90067 USA
**Nicholson, Scott** — Writer
1888 Bernard Bledsoe Lane, Todd NC 28684, USA
**Nichting, Christopher T (Chris)** — Baseball Player
7151 Gracely Dr, Cincinnati OH 45233, USA
**Nickel, Scott** — Cartoonist (Eek, Team Bob, His & Hers)
Paws Inc, 5440 E County Road 450, Albany IN 47320, USA
**Nickens, Tim** — Journalist
Tampa Bay Times, Editorial Dept, 490 1st Ave S, Saint Petersburg FL 33701, USA
**Nickerson, Donald A, Jr** — Religious Leader
Episcopal Church, 815 2nd Ave, Basement, New York NY 10017, USA
**Nickerson, Hardy O** — Football Player
1820 Melvin Road, Oakland CA 94602, USA
**Nickey, Donnie O** — Football Player
3491 General Hood Trail, Nashville TN 37204, USA
**Nicklaus, Jack W** — Golfer
Golf Podium, Infinity Sports, 5500 Military Trail, #22-294, Jupiter FL 33458, USA
**Nickle, Doug** — Baseball Player
19440 Victoria Court, #R2, Sonoma CA 95476, USA
**Nicks, Carl, Jr** — Football Player
Tampa Bay Buccaneers, 1 W Buccaneer Place, Tampa FL 33607 USA
**Nicks, Hakeem** — Football Player
Indianapolis Colts, 7001 W 56th St, Indianapolis IN 46254 USA
**Nicks, O Carl** — Basketball Player
10200 Yosemite Lane, Indianapolis IN 46234, USA
**Nicks, Regina** — Singer (Regina Regina)
Buddy Lee Attractions, 38 Music Square E, #300, Nashville TN 37203 USA
**Nicks, Stevie** — Singer, Songwriter
3929 E Clarendon Ave, Phoenix AZ 85018, USA
**Nickson, Julia** — Actress
Metropolitan Talent Agency, 5405 Wilshire Blvd, #218, Los Angeles CA 90036 USA
**Nickulas, Eric** — Ice Hockey Player
PO Box 507, West Barnstable MA 02668, USA
**Nicolaou, Kyriacos Costa** — Chemist
Scripps Research Institute, 10550 N Torrey Pines Road, La Jolla CA 92037 USA
**Nicole, Jasika** — Actress
Essay Management, 364 W 46th St, New York NY 10036, USA
**Nicole, Jayde** — Model
Playboy Promotions, 9346 Civic Center Dr, #200, Beverly Hills CA 90210 USA
**Nicole, Kristen** — Model
Playboy Promotions, 9346 Civic Center Dr, #200, Beverly Hills CA 90210 USA
**Nicolet, Danielle** — Actress
L I N K Entertainment, 11872 La Grange Ave, Los Angeles CA 90025 USA
**Nicol-Fox, Helen** — Baseball Player
432 E Cornell Dr, Tempe AZ 85283, USA
**Nicollier, Claude** — Astronaut, Switzerland
20 Leeward Lane, Houston TX 77058, USA
**Nicolodi, Daria** — Actress
Carol Levi Mgmt, Via Giuseppe Pisanelli 2, 00196 Rome, Italy
**Nicolson, Steve** — Actor
Artists Partnership, 101 Finsbury Pavement, London EC2A 1RS, England
**Nicora, Attilio Cardinal** — Religious Leader
Patrimony of Apostolic See, Palazzo Apostolico, 00120 Vatican City
**Nicosia, Steven R (Steve)** — Baseball Player
190 Northshore Crossing, Dallas GA 30157, USA
**Nidetch, Jean** — Businesswoman
Weight Watchers International, 3860 Crenshaw Blvd, Los Angeles CA 90008, USA
**Nie Haisheng** — Taikonaut
Satellite Launch Center, Jiuquan, Guangzhou Province, China
**Nieberg, Lars** — Equestrian
Gestit Waldershausen, 35315 Homberg, Germany
**Nied, David G** — Baseball Player
211 Masters Lane, Midlothian TX 76065, USA

| | |
|---|---|
| **Niedecken, Wolfgang** | Singer, Musician |
| Traveling Tunes Productions, Sternengasse 3, 50676 Cologne, Germany | |
| **Niedenfuer, Thomas E (Tom)** | Baseball Player |
| 3933 Losillias Dr, Sarasota FL 34238, USA | |
| **Nieder, William H (Bill)** | Track Athlete |
| PO Box 310, Mountain Ranch CA 95246, USA | |
| **Niederauer, Duncan** | Financier |
| N Y S E Euronext, 11 Wall St, New York NY 10005, USA | |
| **Niederhoffer, Victor** | Squash Player |
| Niederhoffer Cross Zeckhauser, 757 3rd Ave, New York NY 10017, USA | |
| **Niedermayer, Robert W (Rob)** | Ice Hockey Player |
| 49 Belcourt Dr, Newport Beach CA 92660, USA | |
| **Niedermayer, Scott** | Ice Hockey Player |
| 49 Belcourt Dr, Newport Beach CA 92660, USA | |
| **Niedernhuber, Barbara** | Luge Athlete |
| Schwarzeckstr 58, 83486 Ramsau, Germany | |
| **Niehaus, Leonard (Lennie)** | Composer, Jazz Saxophonist |
| Soundtrack Music Assoc, 1460 4th St, #308, Santa Monica CA 90401 USA | |
| **Niehoff, Robert T (Rob)** | Football Player |
| 4874 Sandalwood Court, Mason OH 45040, USA | |
| **Niekamp, Jim** | Ice Hockey Player |
| 3511 E Cochise Dr, Phoenix AZ 85028, USA | |
| **Niekro, Philip H (Phil)** | Baseball Player |
| 6382 Nichols Road, Flowery Branch GA 30542, USA | |
| **Nields, Nerissa** | Singer |
| Bulletproof Artist Mgmt, 241 Main St, Easthampton MA 01027, USA | |
| **Nielsen, Brian** | Boxer |
| Bettina Palle, 12 Skjulet, 2800 Bagsvend, Denmark | |
| **Nielsen, Brigitte** | Actress, Model |
| Almond Talent Mgmt, 8217 Beverly Blvd, #8, West Hollywood CA 90048, USA | |
| **Nielsen, Connie** | Actress |
| United Talent Agency, U T A Plaza, 9336 Civic Center Dr, Beverly Hills CA 90210 USA | |
| **Nielsen, Gerald A (Jerry)** | Baseball Player |
| 4631 Kewanee St, Fair Oaks CA 95628, USA | |
| **Nielsen, Jeffrey M (Jeff)** | Ice Hockey Player |
| 6113 Birchcrest Dr, Minneapolis MN 55436, USA | |
| **Nielsen, Rick** | Singer, Guitarist (Cheap Trick) |
| Oakie Dokie Mgmt, 6090 Central Ave, Saint Petersburg FL 33707, USA | |
| **Nielsen, S Gifford** | Football Player |
| 201 E South Temple, #416, Salt Lake City UT 84111, USA | |
| **Nielsen, William Johnk** | Actor |
| Panorama Agency, ApS Ryesgade 103B, 2100 Copenhagen, Denmark | |
| **Niemann, Jeffrey W (Jeff)** | Baseball Player |
| 5922 Jason St, Houston TX 77074, USA | |
| **Niemann, Randall H (Randy)** | Baseball Player |
| 1585 SW Harbour Isles Circle, Port Saint Lucie FL 34986, USA | |
| **Niemann, Richard W (Rich)** | Basketball Player |
| 7911 Stanford Ave, Saint Louis MO 63130, USA | |
| **Niemann-Stirnemann, Gunda** | Speed Skater |
| Postfach 503, 99010 Erfurt, Germany | |
| **Niemeyer, Paul V** | Judge |
| US Court of Appeals, 101 W Lombard St, #3625, Baltimore MD 21201, USA | |
| **Niemi Swayze, Lisa** | Actress |
| Wolf Kasteler Public Relations, 9350 Wilshire Blvd, #450, Beverly Hills CA 90212 USA | |
| **Niemi, Antti** | Ice Hockey Player |
| San Jose Sharks, San Jose Arena, 525 W Santa Clara St, San Jose CA 95113 USA | |
| **Nieminen, Minna** | Rowing Athlete |
| Vuoksen Soutajat Ry, Koskenparras 10, 55100 Imatra, Finland | |
| **Nieminen, Toni** | Ski Jumper |
| Landen Kanava 99, Vesijarvenkatu 74, 15140 Lahti, Finland | |
| **Nieminen, Ville** | Ice Hockey Player |
| Saint Louis Blues, Scottrade Center, 1401 Clark Ave, Saint Louis MO 63103 USA | |
| **Nierman, Leonardo** | Artist, Sculptor |
| Amsterdam 43 PH, Mexico City 11 DF, Mexico | |
| **Nies, Eric** | Actor, Model |
| Don Buchwald Talent Agency, 6500 Wilshire Blvd, #2200, Los Angeles CA 90048 USA | |
| **Nieto, Thomas A (Tom)** | Baseball Player |
| 22446 Eagles Watch Dr, Land O Lakes FL 34639, USA | |
| **Nieuwendyk, Joseph (Joe)** | Ice Hockey Player, Executive |
| 3204 Drexel Dr, Dallas TX 75205, USA | |
| **Nieuwenhuis, Hans** | Director |
| Columbia Artists Mgmt Inc, 5 Columbus Circle, 1790 Broadway, #1600, New York NY 10019 USA | |
| **Nieves, Joe** | Actor |
| Kazarian/Measures/Ruskin, 11969 Ventura Blvd, #300, Studio City CA 91604 USA | |
| **Nieves, Melvin R (Mel)** | Baseball Player |
| 6131 Seven Lakes W, West End NC 27376, USA | |
| **Nigam, Anjul** | Actor, Writer, Producer |
| Brittany House Pictures, 1680 N Vine St, #326, Los Angeles CA 90028, USA | |
| **Nigh, George P** | Governor, OK; Educator |
| University of Central Oklahoma, President's Office, Edmond OK 73034, USA | |
| **Nightingale, Maxine** | Singer |
| Utopia Artists, PO Box 1821, Ojai CA 93024, USA | |
| **Nighy, Bill** | Actor |
| W M E Entertainment, 9601 Wilshire Blvd, #300, Beverly Hills CA 90210 USA | |
| **Nighy, Jo-Anne** | Actress |
| Associated International Mgmt, 7 Hatton Garden, #400, London EC1N 8AD, England | |
| **Nigrelli, Ross F** | Pathologist |
| 29 Barracuda Road, East Quogue NY 11942, USA | |
| **Nihalani, Govind** | Director, Producer |
| 139 Aradhana, Bandra (E), Mumbai MS 400051, India | |
| **Niinimaa, Janne H** | Ice Hockey Player |
| 2200-201 Portage Ave, Winnipeg MB R3B 3L3, Canada | |
| **Niinisto, Sauli V** | President, Finland |
| President's Office, Mariankatu 2, 00170 Helsinki, Finland | |
| **Niittymaki, Antero** | Ice Hockey Player |
| 1751 Pinnacle Dr, #1500, McLean VA 22102, USA | |

| | |
|---|---|
| **Nikitina, Elena V** | Skeleton Athlete |
| All-Russian Skating Union, Luzhnetskaia Nab 8, 119992 Moscow, Russia | |
| **Niklason, Laura E** | Tissue Engineer |
| Duke University Medical School, Anesthesia Dept, Durham NC 27706, USA | |
| **Nikolas, Alexa** | Actress |
| Gersh Agency, 9465 Wilshire Blvd, #600, Beverly Hills CA 90212 USA | |
| **Nikolic, Tomislav** | Government Official, Serbia |
| President's Office, Nemanjina 11, 11000 Belgrade, Serbia | |
| **Nikolic, Tomislav** | Artist |
| Greenwood Street Project, 9 Greenwood St, Melbourne Abbotsford VIC 3067 Australia | |
| **Nikolishin, Andrei I** | Ice Hockey Player |
| 105 Bloomfield Ave, Hartford CT 06105, USA | |
| **Niksic, Nermin** | Prime Minister, Bosnia-Herzegovia |
| Prime Minister's Office, Alipasina 1, 71000 Sarajevo, Bosnia & Herzegovina | |
| **Nilan, Christopher J (Chris)** | Ice Hockey Player |
| 577 Adams St, #D, Milton MA 02186, USA | |
| **Niland, John H** | Football Player |
| 16058 Chalfont Court, Dallas TX 75248, USA | |
| **Niles, Prescott** | Bassist (Knack) |
| Edge Mgmt, 10850 Wilshire Blvd, #300, Los Angeles CA 90024, USA | |
| **Nill, Jim** | Ice Hockey Player |
| 20837 Dundee Dr, Novi MI 48375, USA | |
| **Nilsen, John** | Composer, Pianist |
| Magic Wing Music, PO Box 222, West Linn OR 97068, USA | |
| **Nilsen, Kurt E** | Singer, Guitarist, Songwriter |
| Playroom, Sandakerveien 24D, #F2, 0473 Oslo, Norway | |
| **Nilsmark, Catrin** | Golfer |
| 187 Commodore Dr, Jupiter FL 33477, USA | |
| **Nilsson, David W (Dave)** | Baseball Player |
| 34 Lawnhill Road, Nelang QLD 4211, Australia | |
| **Nilsson, Kent** | Ice Hockey Player |
| 9034 Crichton Woods Dr, Orlando FL 32819, USA | |
| **Nilsson, Lennart** | Photographer |
| Engelbrektsgatan 18, 114 32 Stockholm, Sweden | |
| **Nilsson, Sandra** | Model |
| Playboy Promotions, 9346 Civic Center Dr, #200, Beverly Hills CA 90210 USA | |
| **Nilsson, Ulf** | Ice Hockey Player |
| QBrick AB, Sodra Hamnvagen 22, Stockholm 11 541, Sweden | |
| **Nimoy, Leonard** | Actor, Director |
| Gersh Agency, 9465 Wilshire Blvd, #600, Beverly Hills CA 90212 USA | |
| **Nimphius, Kurt A** | Basketball Player |
| 750 Dry Creek Road, Sedona AZ 86336, USA | |
| **Nimri, Najwa** | Actress |
| Kuranda Mgmt, Santo Angel 84, 28043 Madrid, Spain | |
| **Ninowski, James (Jim), Jr** | Football Player |
| 2715 Melcombe Circle, #302, Troy MI 48084, USA | |
| **Nipar, Yvette** | Actress |
| Niad Mgmt, 15021 Ventura Blvd, #860, Sherman Oaks CA 91403, USA | |
| **Nipon, Albert** | Fashion Designer |
| Leslie Faye Co, Albert Nipon Div, 1400 Broadway, #1600, New York NY 10018, USA | |
| **Nipper, Albert S (Al)** | Baseball Player |
| 401 White Birch Valley Court, Chesterfield MO 63017, USA | |
| **Nirenberg, Louis** | Mathematician |
| 221 W 82nd St, New York NY 10024, USA | |
| **Nirmala, Sister** | Religious Leader |
| Missionaries of Charity, 54A Lower Circular Road, Kolkata 700016, India | |
| **Nisbet, Robert A** | Historian, Sociologist |
| 6131 Purple Aster Lane NE, Albuquerque NM 87111, USA | |
| **Nisbett, Richard E** | Psychologist |
| University of Michigan, Culture & Cognition Program, Ann Arbor MI 48109, USA | |
| **Nischwitz, Ronald L (Ron)** | Baseball Player |
| 17 S Saint Clair St, #330, Dayton OH 45402, USA | |
| **Nishani, Bujar F** | President, Albania |
| President's Office, Bulevardi Deshmoret E Kombit, Tirana, Albania | |
| **Nishizawa, Junichi** | Electronics Engineer, Inventor |
| Semiconductor Research Institute, Kawauchi, Aobaku, Sendai 980 0862, Japan | |
| **Nishizawa, Ryue** | Pritzker Architect Laureate |
| Sanaa Ltd, 2-2-35-6B Higashi-Shinagawa, Tokyo 140 0002, Japan | |
| **Nishizuka, Yasutomi** | Biochemist, Pharmacologist |
| Kobe University Medical School, Pharmacology Dept, 650 0017 Kobe, Japan | |
| **Nishkian, Byron** | Skier |
| 150 4th St, #PH, San Francisco CA 94103, USA | |
| **Nispel, Marcus** | Director |
| Stone Soup, 12200 W Olympic Blvd, #140, Los Angeles CA 90064, USA | |
| **Nissalke, Thomas E (Tom)** | Basketball Coach |
| 3075 Kennedy Dr, #406, Salt Lake City UT 84108, USA | |
| **Nissen, Steven E (Steve)** | Cardiologist |
| 2200 Devonshire Dr, Cleveland OH 44106, USA | |
| **Nistico, Louis (Lou)** | Ice Hockey Player |
| 404 Westbury Crescent, Thunder Bay ON P7C 4N4, Canada | |
| **Nitkowski, Christopher J (C J)** | Baseball Player |
| 205 Townsend Lane, Alpharetta GA 30004, USA | |
| **Nittmann, David** | Artist |
| PO Box 19065, Boulder CO 80308, USA | |
| **Nitzkowski, Monte** | Swimming Coach |
| 7041 Seal Circle, Huntington Beach CA 92648, USA | |
| **Nivea** | Singer |
| I C M Partners, 10250 Constellation Blvd, #900, Los Angeles CA 90067 USA | |
| **Niven, David, Jr** | Actor, Businessman |
| 1100 Alta Loma Road, West Hollywood CA 90069, USA | |
| **Niven, Kip** | Actor |
| 9000 W Sunset Blvd, #801, West Hollywood CA 90069, USA | |
| **Niven, Laurence V (Larry)** | Writer |
| 11874 Macoda Lane, Chatsworth CA 91311, USA | |
| **Nivola, Alessandro** | Actor |
| Management 360, 9111 Wilshire Blvd, Beverly Hills CA 90210 USA | |

**Niwa, Gail** — Concert Pianist
Siegel Artist Mgmt, 1416 Hinman Ave, Evanston IL 60201, USA

**Niwano, Nikkyo** — Religious Leader
Rissho Kosei-kai, 2-11-1 Wada Suginamiku, Tokyo 166 8537, Japan

**Niwatthamrong Boonsong Paisan** — Prime Minister, Thailand
Prime Minister's Office, Thanon Nakhon Patnom, Bangkok 10300, Thailand

**Nix, A Kent** — Football Player
2732 Colonial Parkway, Fort Worth TX 76109, USA

**Nix, Laynce M** — Baseball Player
1506 Princeton Ave, Midland TX 79701, USA

**Nix, Matthew E (Matt)** — Producer, Director, Writer
W M E Entertainment, 9601 Wilshire Blvd, #300, Beverly Hills CA 90210 USA

**Nix, Steve E** — Guitarist (Briefs)
Devil Dolls Booking, 3505 S Lamar Blvd, #1050, Austin TX 78704, USA

**Nix, William D** — Engineer
Stanford University, Materials Science/Engineering Dept, Stanford CA 94305, USA

**Nixo, Livinia H** — Actress
Laurel Bergman Mgmt, 389 Malvern Road, South Yarra VIC 3141, Australia

**Nixon, Agnes E** — Producer, Writer
774 Conestoga Road, Bryn Mawr PA 19010, USA

**Nixon, Amy** — Curling Athlete
Curling Association, 1660 Vimont Court, Cumberland ON K4A 4J4, Canada

**Nixon, C Trotman (Trot)** — Baseball Player
1023 Ocean Ridge Dr, Wilmington NC 28405, USA

**Nixon, Cynthia** — Actress
Innovative Artists, 1505 10th St, Santa Monica CA 90401 USA

**Nixon, Marni** — Singer, Actress
Harden-Curtis, 850 7th Ave, #903, New York NY 10019, USA

**Nixon, Nicholas** — Photographer
25 Waverly St, Brookline MA 02445, USA

**Nixon, Norman E (Norm)** — Basketball Player
607 Marguerita Ave, Santa Monica CA 90402, USA

**Nixon, Otis J, Jr** — Baseball Player
400 Bass Way NW, Kennesaw GA 30144, USA

**Nixon, Russell E (Russ)** — Baseball Player, Manager
4265 Tee Pee Lane, Las Vegas NV 89129, USA

**Nixon, Torran B (Tory)** — Football Player
PO Box 308, Colfax CA 95713, USA

**Niznik, Stephanie** — Actress
TalentWorks, 3500 W Olive Ave, #1400, Burbank CA 91505 USA

**Njue, John Cardinal** — Religious Leader
Archdiocese of Nairobi, PO Box 14231, Nairobi, Kenya

**Nkurunziza, Pierre** — President, Burundi
President's Office, Kiriri Presidential Palace, Bujumbura, Burundi

**Noah, Joakim** — Basketball Player
Chicago Bulls, United Center, 1901 W Madison St, Chicago IL 60612 USA

**Noah, John M** — Ice Hockey Player
3315 W Prairiewood Dr S, Fargo ND 58103, USA

**Noah, Max W** — Army General
820 Arcturus on the Potomac, Alexandria VA 22308, USA

**Noah, Trevor** — Actor, Comedian, Writer
Levity Entertainment Group, 6701 Center Drive W, #1111, Los Angeles CA 90045, USA

**Noah, Yannick** — Tennis Player, Coach
20 Rue Billancourt, 92100 Boulogne, France

**Nobacon, Danbent** — Singer, Keyboardist (Chumbawamba)
Doug Smith Assoc, PO Box 1151, London W3 8ZJ, England

**Nobilo, Frank** — Golfer
10209 Atterbury Court, Orlando FL 32827, USA

**Nobis, Thomas H (Tommy), Jr** — Football Player, Executive
40 S Battery Place NE, Atlanta GA 30342, USA

**Noble** — Guitarist, Pianist (British Sea Power)
Agency Group Ltd, 361-373 City Road, London EC1V 1PQ, England

**Noble, Adrian K** — Director
Askonas Holt, Lincoln House, 300 High Holborn, London WC1V 7JH, England

**Noble, Bailey** — Actress
C E S D, 10635 Santa Monica Blvd, #130, Los Angeles CA 90025 USA

**Noble, Brandon P** — Football Player
306 Lynne Place, Chester Springs PA 19425, USA

**Noble, Brian D** — Football Player
3664 Via Certaldo Ave, Henderson NV 89052, USA

**Noble, Charles E (Chuck)** — Basketball Player
3585 W Beechwood Ave, #106, Fresno CA 93711, USA

**Noble, Chelsea** — Actress
Insight Mgmt, 9818 Arkansas St, Bellflower CA 90706, USA

**Noble, Cheryl** — Curling Athlete
Curling Association, 1660 Vimont Court, Cumberland ON K4A 4J4, Canada

**Noble, James** — Actor
Paradigm Agency, 360 Park Ave S, #1600, New York NY 10010 USA

**Noble, John** — Actor
Coast to Coast Talent, 3350 Barham Blvd, Los Angeles CA 90068 USA

**Noble, Richard** — Auto Speed Racing Driver
Richard Noble Consulting, Hunters, Headley Road, Grayshott, Surrey GU26 6DL, England

**Noblitt, Niles L** — Businessman
Biomet Inc, Airport Industrial Park, PO Box 587, Warsaw IN 46581, USA

**Nobu** — Chef, Restaurateur
Nobu's, 105 Hudson St, New York NY 10013, USA

**Noce, Paul D** — Baseball Player
913 W Maumee St, Adrian MI 49221, USA

**Nocera, Daniel G** — Chemist
Massachusetts Institute of Technology, Chemistry Dept, Cambridge MA 02139, USA

**Nochlin, Linda** — Art Historian
New York University, Fine Arts Institute, New York NY 10012, USA

**Nocioni, Andres** — Basketball Player
2281 Royal Ridge Dr, Northbrook IL 60062, USA

**Nock, George V** — Football Player
1025 Nine North Dr, #H, Alpharetta GA 30004, USA

**Noda, Yoshihiko** — Prime Minister, Japan
Democratic Party of Japan, 1-11-1 Nagatacho, Chiyoda, Tokyo 100 0014, Japan

**Noddle, Jeffrey** — Businessman
SuperValu Inc, 11840 Valley View Parkway, Eden Prairie MN 55344, USA

**Noe, Gaspar** — Director
W M E Entertainment, 9601 Wilshire Blvd, #300, Beverly Hills CA 90210 USA

**Noel, Chris** — Vietnam Radio Personality, Actress
291 NE 19th Ave, Boynton Beach FL 33435, USA

**Noel, Monique** — Model, Actress
Playboy Promotions, 9346 Civic Center Dr, #200, Beverly Hills CA 90210 USA

**Noel, Nerlens** — Basketball Player
Philadelphia 76ers, 1st Union Center, 3601 S Broad St, Philadelphia PA 19148 USA

**Noel, Philip W** — Governor, RI
345 Channel View, #105, Warwick RI 02889, USA

**Noelle, Beyiana** — Model
Playboy Promotions, 9346 Civic Center Dr, #200, Beverly Hills CA 90210 USA

**Noghaideli, Zurab** — Prime Minister, Georgia
Prime Minister's Office, Government House, Ingorokva 7, 380034 Tbilsi, Georgia

**Noguchi, Soichi** — Astronaut
N A S A, Johnson Space Center, 2101 NASA Road, Houston TX 77058 USA

**Noguchi, Thomas T** — Pathologist
1110 Avoca Ave, Pasadena CA 91105, USA

**Nogueira, Lucas** — Basketball Player
Boston Celtics, 226 Causeway St, #4, Boston MA 02114 USA

**Nogulich, Natalia** — Actress
Green Vision Artists Talent, 8981 Sunset Blvd, #101, Los Angeles CA 90069, USA

**Noh Seung-Yul** — Golfer
Professional Golfers Association, 100 Ave of Champions, Palm Beach Gardens FL 33418 USA

**Noiega Gomez, Eduardo** — Actor, Writer
U B B A, 6 Rue de Braque, 75003 Paris, France

**Nojima, Minoru** — Concert Pianist
John Gingrich Mgmt, PO Box 515, New York NY 10023, USA

**Nokelainen, Petteri** — Ice Hockey Player
Montreal Canadiens, 1275 Saint Antoine St W, Montreal QC H3C 5L2, Canada

**Nokes, Matthew D (Matt)** — Baseball Player
2255 Oxford Ave, Cardiff by the Sea CA 92007, USA

**Nokio** — Singer (Dru Hill)
I C M Partners, 10250 Constellation Blvd, #900, Los Angeles CA 90067 USA

**Noko** — Musician (Apollo440)
X L Talent, Reverb House, Bennett St, London W4 2AH, England

**Nola, Britany** — Model
Playboy Promotions, 9346 Civic Center Dr, #200, Beverly Hills CA 90210 USA

**Nolan, Christopher** — Director, Writer
W M E Entertainment, 9601 Wilshire Blvd, #300, Beverly Hills CA 90210 USA

**Nolan, Faith** — Singer, Musician
PO Box 690, Station P, Toronto ON M5S 2Y4, Canada

**Nolan, Gary L** — Baseball Player
9025 Alpine Peaks Ave, Las Vegas NV 89147, USA

**Nolan, Graham** — Cartoonist
162 Godfrey Terrace, East Aurora NY 14052, USA

**Nolan, Jonathan** — Writer
W M E Entertainment, 9601 Wilshire Blvd, #300, Beverly Hills CA 90210 USA

**Nolan, Joseph W (Joe)** — Baseball Player
9515 Alix Dr, Saint Louis MO 63123, USA

**Nolan, Kathleen (Kathy)** — Actress
House of Representatives, 1434 6th St, #1, Santa Monica CA 90401 USA

**Nolan, Kenny** — Singer, Songwriter
Creative Artists Agency, 2000 Ave of Stars, #100, Los Angeles CA 90067 USA

**Nolan, Martin F** — Editor
Boston Globe, Editorial Dept, 135 W T Morrissey Blvd, Dorchester MA 02125, USA

**Nolan, Michelle** — Actress
Hofflund/Polone, 9465 Wilshire Blvd, #420, Beverly Hills CA 90212 USA

**Nolan, Mike** — Football Coach
Atlanta Falcons, 4400 Falcon Parkway, Flowery Branch GA 30542 USA

**Nolan, Norma B** — Beauty Queen
Miss Universe Organization, 1370 Ave of Americas, #1600, New York NY 10019 USA

**Nolan, Owen L** — Ice Hockey Player
3402 Crestmoor Dr, Saint Paul MN 55125, USA

**Nolan, Ted** — Ice Hockey Player, Coach
269 Queen St E, Sault Sainte Marie ON P6A 1Y9, Canada

**Nolan, Thomas B** — Geologist
2219 California St NW, Washington DC 20008, USA

**Nolan, Tom** — Actor
1335 N Ontario St, Burbank CA 91505, USA

**Noland, Robert L** — Businessman
5555 Eastlake Blvd, Washoe Valley NV 89704, USA

**Nolasco, Amaury** — Actor
Gersh Agency, 9465 Wilshire Blvd, #600, Beverly Hills CA 90212 USA

**Nolasco, C Enrique (Ricky)** — Baseball Player
824 Challenge Ave, Beaumont CA 92223, USA

**Noles, Dickie R** — Baseball Player
20 Dougherty Blvd, #I2, Glen Mills PA 19342, USA

**Nolet, Simon** — Ice Hockey Player
1342 Rue de la Belle Vue, Cap Rouge QC G1Y 2T1, Canada

**Nolfi, George** — Director, Producer, Writer
W M E Entertainment, 9601 Wilshire Blvd, #300, Beverly Hills CA 90210 USA

**Nolin, Gena Lee** — Actress, Model
Shandrew Public Relations, 1050 S Stanley Ave, Los Angeles CA 90019, USA

**Nolte, Claudia** — Government Official, Germany
Mulgarten 28, 98693 Ilmenau, Germany

**Nolte, Eric C** — Baseball Player
23885 Noelle Ave, Murrieta CA 92562, USA

**Nolte, Nick** — Actor
6714 Bonsall Dr, Malibu CA 90265, USA

**Nolting, Paul F** — Religious Leader
Church of Lutheran Confession, 620 E 50th St, Loveland CO 80538, USA

**Nomina, Thomas J (Tom)** — Football Player
20700 Park Place, Estero FL 33928, USA

**Nomura, Masayasu** — Molecular Biologist
74 Whitman Court, Irvine CA 92617, USA

**Nomvete, Pamela** — Actress
Artists Partnership, 101 Finsbury Pavement, London EC2A 1RS, England

**Nong Duc Manh** — General Secretary, Vietnam
General Secretary's Office, Hoang Hoa Tham St, Hanoi, Vietnam

**Nool, Erki** — Track Athlete
Regati 1, Tallinn 119871, Estonia

**Noonan, Brian** — Ice Hockey Player
262 W Eggleston Ave, Elmhurst IL 60126, USA

**Noonan, Chris** — Director
Creative Artists Agency, 2000 Ave of Stars, #100, Los Angeles CA 90067 USA

**Noonan, Daniel N (Danny)** — Football Player
19501 Woolworth Circle, Omaha NE 68130, USA

**Noonan, John T, Jr** — Judge
US Court of Appeals, Court Building, 95 7th St, San Francisco CA 94103, USA

**Noonan, Karl P** — Football Player
7149 Oxford Hunt Dr, Stanley NC 28164, USA

**Noonan, Pat** — Soccer Player
Los Angeles Galaxy, Home Depot Center, 18400 Avalon Blvd, Carson CA 90746 USA

**Noonan, Patrick F** — Association Executive, Conservationist
3553 Hamlet Place, Chevy Chase MD 20815, USA

**Noonan, Peggy** — Writer
Greater Talent Network, 437 5th Ave, #700, New York NY 10016, USA

**Noonan, Timothy J** — Businessman
Rite Aid Corp, 30 Hunter Lane, Camp Hill PA 17011, USA

**Noonan, Tom** — Actor
A K A Talent, 6310 San Vicente Blvd, #200, Los Angeles CA 90048 USA

**Noone, Kathleen** — Actress
130 W 42nd St, #1804, New York NY 10036, USA

**Noone, Nora Jane** — Actress
Creative Artists Mgmt, 55-59 Shaftesbury Ave, London W1D 6LD, England

**Noone, Peter** — Singer (Herman's Hermits), Actor
Creative Entertainment Assoc, 1950 Old Cuthbert Road, #J, Cherry Hill NJ 08034, USA

**Noor Al-Hussein** — Queen Mother, Jordan
Royal Hashemite Court, PO Box 5166, 11183 Amman, Jordan

**Nooteboom, Cees** — Writer
Suhrkamp Verlag, Linderstr 29, 60325 Frankfurt/Main, Germany

**Nooyi, Indra** — Businesswoman
PepsiCo, 700 Anderson Hill Road, Purchase NY 10577, USA

**Norberg, Anette** — Curling Athlete
Talaforum, Norr Malarstrand 6, 112 20 Stockholm, Sweden

**Norby, Caecilie** — Singer
Dansk Musikformidling, Tag Hammerskjolds Allee 42G, 2100 Copenhagen, Denmark

**Norcross, Clayton** — Actor
1327 Linda Way, Arcadia CA 91006, USA

**Nord, Kathleen** — Swimmer
28137 Turkey Branch Dr, Daphne AL 36526, USA

**Nordenberg, Mark A** — Educator
University of Pittsburgh, Chancellor's Office, Pittsburgh PA 15261, USA

**Nordenstrom, Bjorn** — Cancer Radiologist
Karolinska Institute, Radiology Dept, 171 77 Stockholm, Sweden

**Nordhaus, William D** — Economist
Yale University, Economics Dept, New Haven CT 06520, USA

**Nordli, Odvar** — Prime Minister, Norway
Snarveien 4, 2312 Ottestad, Norway

**Nordling, Jeffrey** — Actor
A P A Talent & Literary Agency, 405 S Beverly Dr, #300, Beverly Hills CA 90212 USA

**Nordquist, Mark A** — Football Player
3495 Seacrest Dr, Carlsbad CA 92008, USA

**Nordqvist, Anna** — Golfer
Ladies Pro Golf Assn, 100 International Golf Dr, Daytona Beach FL 32124 USA

**Nordsieck, Kenneth H** — Astronomer
University of California, Astronomy Dept, Santa Cruz CA 95060, USA

**Nordstrom, John E** — Composer
Gorfaine/Schwartz, 4111 W Alameda Ave, #509, Burbank CA 91505 USA

**Noren, Irving A (Irv)** — Baseball, Basketball Player
3154 Camino Crest Dr, Oceanside CA 92056, USA

**Noren, Lars** — Writer
Ostermalmsgatan 33, 114 26 Stockholm, Sweden

**Norgard, Erik C** — Football Player
60 Harbor View Dr, Sugar Land TX 77479, USA

**Noriega, Carlos I** — Astronaut
4630 Silhouette Dr, Katy TX 77493, USA

**Noris, Joe** — Ice Hockey Player
1111 Via Carolina, La Jolla CA 92037, USA

**Norman, Christopher W (Chris)** — Singer, Songwriter, Producer
K-Musix, Rahlstedter Str 92 A, 22149 Hamburg, Germany

**Norman, Daniel E (Dan)** — Baseball Player
430 McBroom Ave, Barstow CA 92311, USA

**Norman, Edie Jo** — Bowler
3544 Mariner Blvd, Spring Hill FL 34609, USA

**Norman, Gregory J (Greg)** — Golfer
Great White Shark Enterprises, 2041 Vista Parkway, #200, West Palm Beach FL 33411, USA

**Norman, Hayley Marie** — Actress
Underground Films & Mgmt, 447 S Highland Ave, Los Angeles CA 90036, USA

**Norman, Jessye** — Concert Singer
L'Orchidee, PO Box South, Crugers NY 10521, USA

**Norman, Kenneth D (Ken)** — Basketball Player
19020 Kedzie Ave, Homewood IL 60430, USA

**Norman, Marc** — Writer
I C M Partners, 10250 Constellation Blvd, #900, Los Angeles CA 90067 USA

**Norman, Marsha** — Writer
W M E Entertainment, 9601 Wilshire Blvd, #300, Beverly Hills CA 90210 USA

**Norman, Michael** — Astrophysicist
University of California, Astronomy Dept, La Jolla CA 90293, USA
**Norman, Monty** — Composer
P R S, 29/33 Berners St, London W1P 4AA, England
**Norman, Nelson A** — Baseball Player
6135 Long Key Lane, Boynton Beach FL 33472, USA
**Norman, Pettis B** — Football Player
1430 Bar Harbor Circle, Dallas TX 75232, USA
**Normandy, Jim** — Guitar Designer
Normandy Guitars, PO Box 3564, Salem OR 97302, USA
**Norodom Sihamoni** — King, Cambodia
Khemarind Palace, Phnom Penh, Cambodia
**Noronen, Mika** — Ice Hockey Player
65 S Autumn Dr, Rochester NY 14626, USA
**Norrena, Fredrik** — Ice Hockey Player
1750 Barrington Road, Columbus OH 43221, USA
**Norrington, Roger A C** — Conductor
Camerata Academica Salzburg, Bergstr 22, 5020 Salzburg, Austria
**Norrington, Stephen (Steve)** — Director
W M E Entertainment, 9601 Wilshire Blvd, #300, Beverly Hills CA 90210 USA
**Norris, Alan E** — Judge
US Court of Appeals, US Courthouse, 85 Marconi Blvd, Columbus OH 43215, USA
**Norris, Bruce** — Writer
Steppenwolf Theater, 758 W North Ave, #400, Chicago IL 60610, USA
**Norris, C Dwayne** — Ice Hockey Player
850 Eastlake Court, Oxford MI 48371, USA
**Norris, Carli** — Actress
Gavin Barker Assoc, 2D Wimpole St, London W1G 0EB, England
**Norris, Chuck** — Actor
L I N K Entertainment, 11872 La Grange Ave, Los Angeles CA 90025 USA
**Norris, David Owen** — Concert Pianist
17 Manor Road, Andover, Hantsfordshire SP10 3JS, England
**Norris, Dean J** — Actor
Industry Entertainment, 955 Carillo Dr, #300, Los Angeles CA 90048 USA
**Norris, Elwood G (Woody)** — Inventor (Hypersonic Sound Technology)
American Technology Corp, 13112 Evening Creek Dr S, San Diego CA 92128, USA
**Norris, Hermione** — Actress
Artist Rights Group, 4A Exmoor St, London W10 6BD, England
**Norris, Jack** — Ice Hockey Player
PO Box 332, Delisle SK S0L 0P0, Canada
**Norris, James F (Jim)** — Baseball Player
6375 Oak Hollow Dr, Burleson TX 76028, USA
**Norris, James R, Jr** — Chemist
University of Chicago, Chemistry Dept, 5735 S Ellis Ave, Chicago IL 60637, USA
**Norris, Lee** — Actor
Don Buchwald Talent Agency, 6500 Wilshire Blvd, #2200, Los Angeles CA 90048 USA
**Norris, Michael K (Mike)** — Baseball Player
6228 Ridgemont Dr, Oakland CA 94619, USA
**Norris, Michele** — Commentator
National Public Radio, 635 Massachusetts Ave NW, #1, Washington DC 20001, USA
**Norris, Patricia** — Costume Designer
Murtha Agency, 4240 Promenade Way, #232, Marina del Rey CA 90292, USA
**Norris, Paul J** — Businessman
W R Grace Co, 7500 Grace Dr, Columbia MD 21044, USA
**Norris, Terry** — Boxer
3668 Syracuse St, La Jolla CA 92122, USA
**Norris, Thomas R** — Vietnam War Navy Hero (CMH)
33593 E Hayden Lake Road, Hayden ID 83835, USA
**Norris, Tim** — Golfer
1604 Little Kitten Ave, Manhattan KS 66503, USA
**Norris, William A** — Judge
US Court of Appeals, 312 N Spring St, #G33, Los Angeles CA 90012, USA
**Norstrom, Mattias** — Ice Hockey Player
3516 Amherst Ave, Dallas TX 75225, USA
**Norsworthy, Lamar** — Businessman
2828 N Harwood St, #100, Dallas TX 75201, USA
**North, Andrew S (Andy)** — Golfer
3289 High Point Road, Madison WI 53719, USA
**North, Douglass C** — Nobel Economics Laureate
7569 Homestead Road, Benzonia MI 49616, USA
**North, Gary L** — Air Force General
Commander, Pacific Air Force, Hickam Air Force Base HI 96853 USA
**North, Jay** — Actor
290 NE 1st Ave, Lake Butler FL 32054, USA
**North, Nolan** — Actor, Comedian
Origin Talent, 4705 Laurel Canyon Blvd. #306, Studio City CA 91607, USA
**North, Oliver L** — Government Official, Marine Officer
Freedom Alliance, 22570 Markley Circle, #240, Sterling VA 20166, USA
**North, Peter** — Actor, Director, Producer
Vivid Entertainment, 3599 Cahuenga Blvd W, Los Angeles CA 90068, USA
**North, William A (Billy)** — Baseball Player
5523 106th Ave NE, Kirkland WA 98033, USA
**Northam, Jeremy** — Actor
Rights House, Drury House, 34-43 Russell St, London WC2B 5HA, England
**Northcutt, Dennis L** — Football Player
1 Park Plaza, #970, Irvine CA 92614, USA
**Northey, Scott R** — Baseball Player
9920 Bankside Dr, Roswell GA 30076, USA
**Northrop, Wayne** — Actor
37900 Road 800, Raymond CA 93653, USA
**Northrup, Anne M** — Representative, KY
Consumer Product Safety Commission, 4330 East West Highway, Bethesda MD 20814, USA
**Northway, Douglas (Doug)** — Swimmer
3239 E 3rd St, Tucson AZ 85716, USA
**Norton, Brad** — Ice Hockey Player
7 Great Road, Acton MA 01720, USA

**Norton, Edward** — Actor
W M E Entertainment, 9601 Wilshire Blvd, #300, Beverly Hills CA 90210 USA
**Norton, Graham** — Actor, Comedian
United Talent Agency, U T A Plaza, 9336 Civic Center Dr, Beverly Hills CA 90210 USA
**Norton, Gregory B (Greg)** — Baseball Player
11130 Eliot Court, Denver CO 80234, USA
**Norton, James** — Actor
Artists Partnership, 101 Finsbury Pavement, London EC2A 1RS, England
**Norton, James A (Jim)** — Football Player
2550 S Ellsworth Road, #13, Mesa AZ 85209, USA
**Norton, Jeff** — Ice Hockey Player
285 Saint George St, Duxbury MA 02332, USA
**Norton, Jerry R** — Football Player
6901 Chevy Chase Ave, Dallas TX 75225, USA
**Norton, Kenneth H (Ken), Jr** — Football Player, Sportscaster
135 Union Jack Mall, Marina del Rey CA 90292, USA
**Norton, Peter** — Computer Software Designer
225 Arizona Ave, #200W, Santa Monica CA 90401, USA
**Norton, Thomas J (Tom)** — Baseball Player
4900 Southwood Dr, Sheffield Lake OH 44054, USA
**Norton, Virginia** — Bowler
11706 Mindanao St, Cypress CA 90630, USA
**Norton-Taylor, Judy** — Actress, Model
Tisherman Agency, 6767 Forest Lawn Dr, #101, Los Angeles CA 90068 USA
**Norville, Deborah** — Commentator
PO Box 426, Mill Neck NY 11765, USA
**Norwich, Craig R** — Ice Hockey Player
11448 Welters Way, Eden Prairie MN 55347, USA
**Norwood, Daron** — Singer
Texas Artist Group, 6999 E Highway 80, Odessa TX 79762, USA
**Norwood, Dorothy** — Singer, Songwriter
Universal Attractions, 135 W 26th St, #1200, New York NY 10001 USA
**Norwood, Lee C** — Ice Hockey Player
28876 Olson St, Livonia MI 48150, USA
**Norwood, Scott A** — Football Player
41955 Blue Flag Terrace, Stone Ridge VA 20105, USA
**Norwood, Willie B** — Basketball Player
15710 Halldale Ave, #C, Gardena CA 90247, USA
**Noseworthy, Jack** — Actor
Oscars Abrams Zimel, 438 Queen St E, Toronto ON M5A 1T4, Canada
**Nossal, Gustav J V** — Immunologist, Pathologist
46 Fellows St, Kew VIC 3101, Australia
**Nosseck, Noel** — Director
1435 San Ysidro Dr, Beverly Hills CA 90210, USA
**Nossek, Joseph R (Joe)** — Baseball Player
630 Sunrise Dr, Amherst OH 44001, USA
**Nossiter, Jonathan** — Director, Producer, Writer
United Talent Agency, U T A Plaza, 9336 Civic Center Dr, Beverly Hills CA 90210 USA
**Notaro, Phyllis** — Bowler
11123 Maritime Court, Wellington FL 33449, USA
**Noth, Christopher** — Actor
Sanders/Armstrong/Caserta Mgmt, 2120 Colorado Ave, #120, Santa Monica CA 90404 USA
**Nothstein, Marty** — Cyclist
1019 Village Round, Allentown PA 18106, USA
**Notkin, Richard T** — Sculptor
PO Box 698, Helena MT 59624, USA
**Notkins, Abner L** — Virologist
National Institute of Dental Research, 9000 Rockville Pike, Bethesda MD 20892, USA
**Noto, Lucio A** — Businessman
Mobil Corp, 3225 Gallows Road, Fairfax VA 22037, USA
**Nott Cunningham, Tara** — Weightlifter
Olympic Training Center, 1 Olympic Plaza, Building 4, Colorado Springs CO 80909, USA
**Nott, John W F** — Government Official, England
31 Walpole St, London SW3 4QS, England
**Nottage, Lynn** — Writer
Gersh Agency, 9465 Wilshire Blvd, #600, Beverly Hills CA 90212 USA
**Nottebohm, Andreas** — Artist
17496 7th St E, Sonoma CA 95476, USA
**Nottingham, Donald R (Don)** — Football Player
5750 NE 36th Avenue Road, Ocala FL 34479, USA
**Nouri, Michael** — Actor
Burstein, 15304 W Sunset Blvd, #208, Pacific Palisades CA 90272, USA
**Noury, Alain** — Actor
Domaine de Hurlevents, 26400 Soyans Crest-Sud, France
**Nouvel, Jean** — Pritzker Architecture Laureate
Architectures Jean Nouvel, 10 Cite d'Angouleme, 75011 Paris, France
**Nova, Heather** — Singer
Free Trade Agency, 9 Chapel Place, Rivington St, London EC2A 3DQ, England
**Novacek, Jay M** — Football Player
PO Box 471490, Fort Worth TX 76147, USA
**Novack, K J** — Businessman
America Online, 22000 A O L Way, Sterling VA 20166, USA
**Novak Popper, Ilona** — Swimmer
Il Orso Utca 23, 1073 Budapest, Hungary
**Novak, Benjamin J (B J)** — Actor, Comedian, Writer
Baker Winokur Ryder Public Relations, 9100 Wilshire Blvd, #500W, Beverly Hills CA 90212 USA
**Novak, John R** — Inventor (Air Cleaning Radiator)
Engelhard Corp, Automotive Emissions Systems, 101 Wood Ave, Iselin NJ 08830, USA
**Novak, Kim** — Actress
Cameron Enterprises, 10100 Santa Monica Blvd, #1060, Los Angeles CA 90067, USA
**Novak, Michael** — Theologian
5050 Ave Maria Blvd, Ave Maria FL 34142, USA
**Novakovic, Bojana** — Actress
Creative Artists Agency, 2000 Ave of Stars, #100, Los Angeles CA 90067 USA
**Novaro, Jean-Claude** — Sculptor
32 Chemin Hautes Vignasses, 06410 Biot, France

**Novello, Antonia C** — Physician, Government Official
1110 SW Ivanhoe Blvd, #14, Orlando FL 32804, USA
**Novello, Don (Father Guido Sarducci)** — Actor, Comedian
Elizabeth Rush Agency, 82 Cumberland Ave, Verona NJ 07044, USA
**Noveskey, Matt** — Bassist (Blue October)
Rainmaker Artists, PO Box 551665, Dallas TX 75355, USA
**Novitsky, Oleg** — Cosmonaut
Cosmonaut Training Center, Star City, 141160 Zvezdny Gorodok, Moscow Oblast, Russia
**Novoa, Rafael** — Actor
Univision, 605 3rd Ave, #1200, New York NY 10158 USA
**Novoa, Rafael A** — Baseball Player
3420 N 47th Way, Phoenix AZ 85018, USA
**Novotna, Jana** — Tennis Player
7834 Montvale Way, McLean VA 22102, USA
**Novotny, Dave** — Bassist (Saliva)
Helter Skelter, 347-353 Chiswick High Road, London W4 4HS, England
**Nowak, Piotr (Peter)** — Soccer Player, Coach
Philadelphia Union, Union Field, Seaport Dr, Chester PA 19013 USA
**Nowatzke, Thomas M (Tom)** — Football Player
4335 Diuble Road, Ann Arbor MI 48103, USA
**Nowell, Peter C** — Pathologist, Biologist
9 Foxcroft Lane, Media PA 19063, USA
**Nowicki, Tom** — Actor
Davis Mgmt, 4111 Lankershim Blvd, North Hollywood CA 91602, USA
**Nowitzki, Dirk** — Basketball Player
10735 Strait Lane, Dallas TX 75229, USA
**Nowra, Louis** — Writer
Level 18, Plaza 11, 500 Oxford St, Bondi Junction NSW 2011, Australia
**Nowrasteh, Cyrus** — Director, Writer
Creative Artists Agency, 2000 Ave of Stars, #100, Los Angeles CA 90067 USA
**Noxon, Marti** — Producer, Writer
W M E Entertainment, 9601 Wilshire Blvd, #300, Beverly Hills CA 90210 USA
**Noyce, Phillip** — Director
United Talent Agency, U T A Plaza, 9336 Civic Center Dr, Beverly Hills CA 90210 USA
**Noyori, Ryoji** — Nobel Chemistry Laureate
135-417 Shinden, Umemoricho, Nisshin, Aichi 470 0132, Japan
**Nozieres, Philippe P G F** — Physicist
15 Route de Saint Nizier, 38180 Seyssins, France
**Nozuka, Justin** — Singer, Songwriter
Coalition Entertainment Mgmt, 10271 Yonge St, #302, Richmond Hill ON L4C 3B5, Canada
**Nsibambi, Apolo** — Prime Minister, Uganda
Premier's Office, Parliament Building, PO Box 341, Kampala, Uganda
**Ntombi** — Queen Regent, Swaziland
Royal Residence, PO Box 1, Lobamba, Swaziland
**Nuami, Sheikh Humaid IV ibin Rashid, Al** — Ruler, Ajman
Royal Palace, PO Box 1, Ajman, United Arab Emirates
**Nubiola, Esther** — Actress
Cineart, 28 Rue Mogador, 78009 Paris, France
**Nucci, Danny** — Actor
TalentWorks, 3500 W Olive Ave, #1400, Burbank CA 91505 USA
**Nucci, Leo** — Opera Singer
Ariosi Mgmt, Via al Lido, 9 6817 Maroggia, Switzerland
**Nuce, Ted** — Rodeo Bull Rider
12606 Victory Ave, Oakdale CA 95361, USA
**Nugent, Alecia** — Singer
Keith Case Assoc, 1025 17th Ave S, #200, Nashville TN 37212 USA
**Nugent, Michael (Mike)** — Football Player
Cincinnati Bengals, 1 Paul Brown Stadium, Cincinnati OH 45202 USA
**Nugent, Nelle** — Producer
Foxboro Entertainment, 133 E 58th St, #301, New York NY 10022, USA
**Nugent, Theodore A (Ted)** — Singer, Guitarist, Songwriter
Madhouse Mgmt, PO Box 130109, Ann Arbor MI 48113, USA
**Nugent-Hopkins, Ryan J** — Ice Hockey Player
Edmonton Oilers, 11230 110th St, Edmonton AB T5G 3H7, Canada
**Null, Jason** — Guitarist (Saving Abel), Songwriter
Virgin Records, 338 N Foothill Road, Beverly Hills CA 90210 USA
**Numan, Gary** — Singer, Songwriter
Kras Artists, Leernseesteenweg 168, 9800 Deinze, Belgium
**Nu-Mark** — Rap Artist
Vision Entertainment Group, 1100 Glendon Ave, #1100, Los Angeles CA 90024, USA
**Numbers, Ronald L** — Historian
University of Wisconsin, History of Science & Health Dept, Madison WI 53706, USA
**Numminen, Teppo K** — Ice Hockey Player
5975 Tipperary Manor, Clarence Center NY 14032, USA
**Nunez, Edwin** — Baseball Player
2618 E Locust Dr, Chandler AZ 85286, USA
**Nunez, Joseph (Joe)** — Actor
TalentWorks, 3500 W Olive Ave, #1400, Burbank CA 91505 USA
**Nunez, Miguel A, Jr** — Actor
TalentWorks, 3500 W Olive Ave, #1400, Burbank CA 91505 USA
**Nunez, Oscar** — Actor
Kazarian/Measures/Ruskin, 11969 Ventura Blvd, #300, Studio City CA 91604 USA
**Nunez, Victor** — Director
Gersh Agency, 9465 Wilshire Blvd, #600, Beverly Hills CA 90212 USA
**Nunley, Frank H** — Football Player
2131 Mulberry Circle, San Jose CA 95125, USA
**Nunn, Michael** — Boxer
314 E 13th St, #1, Davenport IA 52803, USA
**Nunn, Samuel A (Sam)** — Senator, GA
75 14th St NE, #4810, Atlanta GA 30309, USA
**Nunn, Terri** — Singer (Berlin)
M O B Agency, 6404 Wilshire Blvd, #505, Los Angeles CA 90048 USA
**Nunn, Trevor R** — Director
Royal National Theater, South Bank, London SE1 9PX, England
**Nunnally, Jonathan K (Jon)** — Baseball Player
36550 Chester Road, #504, Avon OH 44011, USA

**Nuo, Patrick** — Singer, Actor
Sundance Mgmt, Muhlenkamp 45, 22303 Hamburg, Germany

**Nurse, Paul M** — Nobel Medicine Laureate
Clare Hall Laboratories, Cell Cycle Control Laboratory, Hertsfordshire EN6 3LD, England

**Nussbaum, Danny** — Actor
Conway Van Gelder Grant, 8-12 Broadwick St, #300, London W1F 8HW, England

**Nussbaum, Karen** — Labor Activist
9-5 National Working Women Assn, 231 W Wisconsin, #900, Milwaukee WI 53203, USA

**Nussbaum, Martha C** — Philosopher
University of Chicago, Law School, 111 E 60th St, Chicago IL 60637, USA

**Nussle, James A (Jim)** — Government Official, Representative, IA
PO Box 445, Marion IA 52302, USA

**Nusslein-Volhard, Christiane** — Nobel Medicine Laureate
Klosttermuhle 15, 72074 Tubingen, Germany

**Nutini, Paolo** — Singer
Atlantic Records, 1290 Ave of Americas, Concourse 3, New York NY 10104 USA

**Nutt, Amy Ellis** — Journalist
Newark Star-Ledger, Editorial Dept, 1 Star-Ledger Plaza, Newark NJ 07102, USA

**Nutt, Jim** — Artist
1035 Greenwood Ave, Wilmette IL 60091, USA

**Nuttall, Amy** — Actress, Singer
Merlin Elite, 37 Lower Belgrave St, London SW1W 0LS, England

**Nutten, Thomas R (Tom)** — Football Player
431 S Creek Dr, Osprey FL 34229, USA

**Nutter, Alice** — Singer, Percussionist (Chumbawamba)
Doug Smith Assoc, PO Box 1151, London W3 8ZJ, England

**Nutter, David** — Director
W M E Entertainment, 9601 Wilshire Blvd, #300, Beverly Hills CA 90210 USA

**Nutting, Wallace H** — Army General
6 Schooner Way, Saco ME 04072, USA

**Nutzle, Futzie** — Artist, Cartoonist
PO Box 325, Aromas CA 95004, USA

**Nuveman, Stacey** — Softball Player
USA Softball, 2801 NE 50th St, Oklahoma City OK 73111, USA

**Nuwer, Hank** — Writer, Journalist, Educator
Franklin College, Shirk Hall, 1100 Branigin Blvd, Franklin IN 46131, USA

**Nuyen, France** — Actress
1800 Franklin Canyon Terrace, Beverly Hills CA 90210, USA

**Nuzorewa, Abel Tendekayi** — Prime Minister, Zimbabwe
United African National Council, 40 Charter Road, Harare, Zimbabwe

**Nyad, Diana** — Swimmer, Sportscaster
870 5th Ave, Los Angeles CA 90005, USA

**Nyberg, Frederik** — Alpine Skier
Kaptensgatan 2C, 832 00 Froson, Sweden

**Nyberg, Karen L** — Astronaut
1848 Lake Landing Dr, League City TX 77573, USA

**Nyberg, Katarina** — Curling Athlete
Curling Association, Idrottshuser, Marbackagatan 19, 123 43 Farsta, Sweden

**Nycz, Kazimierz Cardinal** — Religious Leader
Kuria Metropolital, Ul Miodow 17-19, 00246 Warsaw, Poland

**Nydal, Lymari** — Actress, Writer
Global Artists Agency, 6253 Hollywood Blvd, #508, Los Angeles CA 90028 USA

**Nye, Bill** — Actor
W M E Entertainment, 9601 Wilshire Blvd, #300, Beverly Hills CA 90210 USA

**Nye, Blaine F** — Football Player
1200 Bay Laurel Dr, Menlo Park CA 94025, USA

**Nye, Erle A** — Businessman
6924 Desco, Dallas TX 75225, USA

**Nye, Joseph S, Jr** — Political Scientist
Harvard University, John Kennedy Government School, Cambridge MA 02138, USA

**Nye, Richard R (Rich)** — Baseball Player
40W257 Seavey Road, Batavia IL 60510, USA

**Nye, Robert** — Writer
Thornfield, Kingsland, Ballinghassig, County Cork, Ireland

**Nyemiah Supreme** — Rap Artist
Mosley Music Group, 10395 SW 67th Ave, Miami FL 33156, USA

**Nyers, C Richard (Dick)** — Football Player
4055 N Riverside Dr, Columbus IN 47203, USA

**Nyers, Rezso** — Secretary General, Hungary
Ozgida Utca 22/A, 1025 Budapest, Hungary

**Nygaard, Richard L** — Judge
US Court of Appeals, 1st National Bank Building, 717 State St, Erie PA 16501, USA

**Nyland, William L** — Marine Corps General
2750 Semoran Circle, Pensacola FL 32503, USA

**Nylander, Michael** — Ice Hockey Player
8813 Mayberry Court, Potomac MD 20854, USA

**Nyman, Michael L** — Composer, Pianist
Michael Nyman Ltd, PO Box 430, High Wycombe HP13 5QT, England

**Nyong'o, Lupita** — Actress
Innovative Artists, 1505 10th St, Santa Monica CA 90401 USA

**Nyqvist, Michael** — Actor
W M E Entertainment, 9601 Wilshire Blvd, #300, Beverly Hills CA 90210 USA

**Nystad, Claudia Kunzel** — Cross Country Skier
D S V Skiverband, Hubertusstr 1, 82152 Planegg, Germany

**Nystedt, Knut** — Composer, Conductor
Det Norske Musikforlag A/S, Postbuks 1499 Bika, 0116 Oslo, Norway

**Nystrom, Eric** — Ice Hockey Player
475 Berry Road, Syosset NY 11791, USA

**Nystrom, Joakim** — Tennis Player
Torsgatan 194, 931 00 Skellefteaa, Sweden

**Nyswaner, Ronald L (Ron)** — Writer, Producer, Director
United Talent Agency, U T A Plaza, 9336 Civic Center Dr, Beverly Hills CA 90210 USA

**O, Karen** — Singer (Yeah Yeah Yeahs), Songwriter
Yeah Yeah Yeahs, 249 Metropolitan Ave, Brooklyn NY 11211, USA

**Oakenfold, Paul M** — DJ Musician
International Talent Booking, Ariel House, 74A Charlotte St, #100 London W1T 4QJ, England

**Oakes, W Warren** — Drummer (Against Me)
Boca Fiesta Restaurant, 232 SE 1st St, Gainesville FL 32601, USA

**Oakley, Charles** — Basketball Player
700 Park Regency Place NE, #1105, Atlanta GA 30326, USA

**Oates, Adam R** — Ice Hockey Player, Coach
204 N Shore Blvd, East Sandwich MA 02537, USA

**Oates, Bart S** — Football Player, Sportscaster
2 Silverbrook Road, Morristown NJ 07960, USA

**Oates, John** — Singer (Hall & Oates), Songwriter
Doyle-Kos Entertainment, 1 Penn Plaza, 2107, New York NY 10119, USA

**Oates, Joyce Carol** — Writer
McClelland & Stewart, 75 Sherbourne St, #500, Toronto ON M5A 2P9, Canada

**Oats, Carleton** — Football Player
10605 E Coralbell Ave, Mesa AZ 85208, USA

**Obama, Barack H, II** — President, USA; Nobel Peace Laureate
White House, 1600 Pennsylvania Ave NW, Washington DC 20500 USA

**Obama, Michelle** — Wife of US President
White House, 1600 Pennsylvania Ave NW, Washington DC 20500 USA

**Obando Bravo, Miguel Cardinal** — Religious Leader
Arzobispado, Apartado 3058, Managua, Nicaragua

**O'Bannon, Edward C (Ed)** — Basketball Player
1397 Minuet St, Henderson NV 89052, USA

**Obasanjo, Olusegun** — President, Nigeria; Army General
Obasanjo Farms Nigeria, PO Box 90, Otta, Ogun State, Nigeria

**Obato, Gyo** — Architect
100 N Broadway, Saint Louis MO 63102, USA

**Obeid, Atef M** — Prime Minister, Egypt
Arab International Bank, 35 Abdel Khalek Sarwat St, Cairo, Egypt

**Obeidat, Ahmad Abdul-Majeed** — Prime Minister, Jordan
Law & Arbitration Center, PO Box 926544, Amman, Jordan

**Oben, Roman D** — Football Player
11476 Creekstone Lane, San Diego CA 92128, USA

**Oberg, Margo** — Surfer
Margo Oberg Surf School, Poipu Beach, Koloa HI 96756, USA

**Obergfoll, Christina** — Track Athlete
Alsfelder Str 27, 64289 Darnstadt, Germany

**Oberholser, Arron** — Golfer
5901 E Via Los Caballos, Paradise Valley AZ 85253, USA

**Oberkfell, Kenneth R (Ken)** — Baseball Player
1335 W Welsford Dr, Spring TX 77386, USA

**Obermeyer, Klaus F** — Fashion Designer
Sport Obermeyer, 115 Atlantic Ave, Aspen CO 81611, USA

**Obermueller, Wesley M (Wes)** — Baseball Player
7031 27th Ave, Newhall IA 52315, USA

**Oberoi, Vivek** — Actor
5 Krta Kunj Golden Beach, Ruia Park Juhu, Mumbai MS 400049, India

**O'Berry, Carl G** — Air Force General
Boeing Co, PO Box 4921, 3370 Miraloma Ave, Anaheim CA 92806, USA

**O'Berry, P Michael (Mike)** — Baseball Player
5977 S Fork Dr, Hoover AL 35244, USA

**Oberst, Conor M** — Singer, Guitarist (Bright Eyes)
Team Love Records, 11 Church St, New Paltz NY 12561, USA

**Oberto, Fabricio R J** — Basketball Player
901 15th St, #1605, Arlington VA 22202, USA

**Obiang Nguema Mbasogo, Teodoro** — President, Equatorial Guinea
President's Office, Palacio de la Presidencia, Malabo, Equatorial Guinea

**O'Boyle, Maureen** — Entertainer
1600 Meadowood Lane, Charlotte NC 28211, USA

**Obradors, Jacqueline** — Actress
A P A Talent & Literary Agency, 405 S Beverly Dr, #300, Beverly Hills CA 90212 USA

**Obradovic, Paulo** — Water Polo Player
V K Primorje Rojeka, Podkoludricu, 51000 Rijeka, Croatia

**O'Bradovich, Edward (Ed)** — Football Player
235 N Smith St, #207, Palatine IL 60067, USA

**Obradovich, James R (Jim)** — Football Player
2601 Morningside Dr, Lomita CA 90717, USA

**Obraztsova, Elena V** — Opera Singer
Bolshoi Theater, Teatralnaya Pl 1, 103009 Moscow, Russia

**Obreht, Tea** — Writer
Random House, 1745 Broadway, #1800, New York NY 10019 USA

**O'Brian, Hugh** — Actor
O'Brian Youth Leadership, 31255 Cedar Valley, #327, Westlake Village CA 91362, USA

**O'Brien, Bill** — Football Coach
Houston Texans, 2 Reliant Park, Houston TX 77054 USA

**O'Brien, Carl (Cubby)** — Actor
39919 NE 127th Court, Amboy WA 98601, USA

**O'Brien, Cathy** — Track Athlete
19 Foss Farm Road, Durham NH 03824, USA

**O'Brien, Charles H (Charlie)** — Baseball Player
4932 E 38th Place, Tulsa OK 74135, USA

**O'Brien, Conan** — Writer, Producer, Actor
W M E Entertainment, 9601 Wilshire Blvd, #300, Beverly Hills CA 90210 USA

**O'Brien, Dan** — Track Athlete
8390 E Via de Ventura, #110, Scottsdale AZ 85258, USA

**O'Brien, Dennis** — Ice Hockey Player
31 Hope St N, Port Hope ON L1A 2N4, Canada

**O'Brien, Edna** — Writer
David Godwin Assoc, 55 Monmouth St, London WC2H 9DG, England

**O'Brien, Edwin F Cardinal** — Religious Leader
Equestrian Order of Holy Sepulchre of Jerusalem, 00120 Vatican City

**O'Brien, G Dennis** — Educator
PO Box 510, Middlebury VT 05753, USA

**O'Brien, Keith M P Cardinal** — Religious Leader
Diocesan Offices, Gillis Centre, 100 Strathearn Road, Edinburgh EH9 1BB, Scotland

**O'Brien, Kenneth J (Ken), Jr** — Football Player
201 Manhattan Ave, Manhattan Beach CA 90266, USA

**O'Brien, Margaret** — Actress
14840 Valerio St, Van Nuys CA 91405, USA

**O'Brien, Maureen** — Actress
United Agents, 12-26 Lexington St, London W1F 0LE, England

**O'Brien, Michael** — Labor Leader
Transport Workers Union, 1700 Broadway, #200, New York NY 10019, USA

**O'Brien, Pat** — Sportscaster, Entertainer
I C M Partners, 10250 Constellation Blvd, #900, Los Angeles CA 90067 USA

**O'Brien, Peter M (Pete)** — Baseball Player
5509 Montclair Dr, Colleyville TX 76034, USA

**O'Brien, Richard** — Composer, Lyricist
TimeWarp, 1 Elm Grove, Hildenborough, Tonbridge Kent TN11 9HE, England

**O'Brien, Ron** — Diving Coach
80450 Overseas Highway, #401, Islamorada FL 33036, USA

**O'Brien, Soledad** — Commentator
Starfish Media Group, 134 W 26th St, #1150, New York NY 10001, USA

**O'Brien, Terrence L** — Judge
US Court of Appeals, 2120 Capitol Ave, #2131, Cheyenne WY 82001, USA

**O'Brien, Tim** — Singer, Musician
W N S Group, 6 Rolyn Hills Dr, Orangeburg NY 10962, USA

**O'Brien, Tina** — Actress
Shepherd Mgmt, 45 Maddox St, #400, London W1S 2PE, England

**O'Brien, Tom** — Football Coach
North Carolina State University, Athletic Dept, Raleigh NC 27695, USA

**O'Bryan, Sean** — Actor
Domain Talent, 9229 W Sunset Blvd, #710, West Hollywood CA 90069 USA

**Obst, Lynda** — Producer, Writer
Lynda Obst Productions, 5555 Melrose Ave, Astaire Building, Los Angeles CA 90038, USA

**O'Byrne, Brian F** — Actor
Lisa Richards Agency, 108 Upper Leeson St, Dublin 4, Ireland

**O'Callaghan, Patricia M** — Singer
B C Fielder Mgmt, 53 Seton Park Road, Toronto ON M3C 3ZB, Canada

**O'Callahan, John (Jack)** — Ice Hockey Player
101 Linden Ave, Glencoe IL 60022, USA

**Ocampo Uria, Adriana C** — Geologist, Planetary Scientist
National Aeronautics/Space Administration, 300 E St SW, Washington DC 20546, USA

**Ocampo, Miguel** — Artist
Wood Street Gallery, 601 Wood St, Pittsburgh PA 15222, USA

**O'Caroll, Sinead** — Singer (B*Witched)
Clintons, 55 Drury Lane, Covent Garden, London WC2B 5SQ, England

**O'Carroll, Brendan** — Actor
Kaplan-Stahler Agency, 8383 Wilshire Blvd, #923, Beverly Hills CA 90211 USA

**Ocasek, Ric** — Singer, Guitarist (Cars); Songwriter
Lookout Mgmt, 1460 4th St, #300, Santa Monica CA 90401 USA

**Occhilupo, Mark** — Surfer
Billabong, 1 Billabong Place, Burleigh Heads QLD 4220, Australia

**Ocean, Billy** — Singer, Songwriter
Universal Attractions, 135 W 26th St, #1200, New York NY 10001 USA

**Ochiai, Masayuki** — Director
Director's Guild, Shibuya Goto Building, 3-2 Maruyama, #5, Shibuya, Tokyo 150 0044, Japan

**Ochiltree, Dianne** — Writer
716 Tropical Circle, Sarasota FL 34242, USA

**Ochirbat, Punsalmaagiin** — President, Mongolia
Tengeriin Tsag Co, Olympic St 14, Ulan Bator, Mongolia

**Ochman, Wieslaw** — Opera Singer
Ul Miaczynska 46B, 02-637 Warsaw, Poland

**Ochoa, Alex** — Baseball Player
14526 NW 83rd Passage, Hialeah FL 33016, USA

**Ochoa, Ellen** — Astronaut
4515 Sterling Wood Way, Houston TX 77059, USA

**Ochoa, Lorena** — Golfer
Ladies Pro Golf Assn, 100 International Golf Dr, Daytona Beach FL 32124 USA

**Ochowicz, James L (Jim)** — Cyclist
945 Hutchinson Ave, Palo Alto CA 94301, USA

**O'Connell, Brian** — Bassist
Junoon, Sidco Tower, #A-10/2, Strachen Road, Karachi 74200, Pakistan

**O'Connell, Carol** — Writer
Berkley Publishing Group, 375 Hudson St, Basement 1, New York NY 10014 USA

**O'Connell, Deirdre** — Actress
Innovative Artists, 1505 10th St, Santa Monica CA 90401 USA

**O'Connell, Jerry** — Actor, Director
3 Arts Entertainment, 9460 Wilshire Blvd, #700, Beverly Hills CA 90212 USA

**O'Connell, Maura** — Singer
Rubin Media, PO Box 158161, Nashville TN 37215, USA

**O'Connell, Mike** — Ice Hockey Player, Coach
17 Border St, Cohasset MA 02025, USA

**O'Connell, Robbie** — Singer, Songwriter
Producers Inc, 11806 N 56th St, Tampa FL 33617 USA

**O'Connor, Brian** — Baseball Player
3054 Inwood Dr, Cincinnati OH 45241, USA

**O'Connor, Bryan D** — Astronaut
1305 Lafayette Dr, Alexandria VA 22308, USA

**O'Connor, Christy, Jr** — Golfer
Gaylord Sports Mgmt, 13845 N Northsight Blvd, #200, Scottsdale AZ 85260 USA

**O'Connor, Derrick** — Actor
Markham Froggatt Irwin, Julian House, 4 Windmill St, London W1P 1HF, England

**O'Connor, Edmund F** — Army General
1169 Ironsides Ave, Melbourne FL 32940, USA

**O'Connor, Erin** — Model
2pm Model Mgmt, Norregade 2, 1165 Copenhagen K, Denmark

**O'Connor, Frances** — Actress
Gersh Agency, 9465 Wilshire Blvd, #600, Beverly Hills CA 90212 USA

**O'Connor, Gavin** — Actor, Director, Writer
Nikki Weiss & Co, 754 N La Jolla Ave, Los Angeles CA 90046, USA
**O'Connor, Glynnis** — Actress
Bauman Redanty Shaul Agency, 5757 Wilshire Blvd, #473, Los Angeles CA 90036 USA
**O'Connor, J Dennis** — Educator
Smithsonian Institution, Provost's Office, Washington DC 20560, USA
**O'Connor, Jack W** — Baseball Player
PO Box 430, Yucca Valley CA 92286, USA
**O'Connor, Jane** — Writer
Harper Collins Publishers, 10 E 53rd St, Cellar 1, New York NY 10022 USA
**O'Connor, Kelley** — Opera Singer
I M G Artists, Hogarth Business Park, Chiswick, London W4 2TH, England
**O'Connor, Kevin J** — Actor
Innovative Artists, 1505 10th St, Santa Monica CA 90401 USA
**O'Connor, Mark** — Fiddler, Violinist
Columbia Artists Mgmt Inc, 5 Columbus Circle, 1790 Broadway, #1600, New York NY 10019 USA
**O'Connor, Mary Anne** — Basketball Player
60 Romanock Place, Fairfield CT 06825, USA
**O'Connor, Michael** — Costume Designer
Dench Arnold Agency, 10 Newburgh St, London W1F 7RN, England
**O'Connor, Myles** — Ice Hockey Player
O'Connors Fine Footwear, 1415 1st St SW, Calgary AB T2R 0V9, Canada
**O'Connor, Patrick** — Actor
Paradigm Agency, 360 N Crescent Dr, North Building, Beverly Hills CA 90210 USA
**O'Connor, Patrick D (Pat)** — Director, Writer
United Agents, 12-26 Lexington St, London W1F 0LE, England
**O'Connor, Renee** — Actress
R O R Productions, 1601 N Sepulveda Blvd, #768, Manhattan Beach CA 90266, USA
**O'Connor, Sandra Day** — Supreme Court Justice, Educator
College of William & Mary, Chancellor's Office, Williamsburg VA 23187, USA
**O'Connor, Sinead** — Singer, Songwriter
Paradigm Agency, 360 N Crescent Dr, North Building, Beverly Hills CA 90210 USA
**O'Connor, Thom** — Artist
Moss Road, Voorheesville NY 12186, USA
**O'Connor, Timothy J (Tim)** — Actor
House of Representatives, 1434 6th St, #1, Santa Monica CA 90401 USA
**O'Connor, William F (Bill)** — Football Player
1905-40 Richview Road, Toronto ON M9A 5C1, Canada
**O'Conor, John** — Concert Pianist
Columbia Artists Mgmt Inc, 5 Columbus Circle, 1790 Broadway, #1600, New York NY 10019 USA
**Odadjian, Sharvarsh S (Shavo)** — Bassist (System of a Down)
Velmet Hammer Music, 9911 W Pico Blvd, #360W, Los Angeles CA 90035, USA
**Odar, Baran Bo** — Director, Producer, Writer
United Talent Agency, U T A Plaza, 9336 Civic Center Dr, Beverly Hills CA 90210 USA
**O'Dassey, Seregon** — Actress, Model, Producer
G & G Talent, 926C Lincoln Ave, New York NY 11741, USA
**O'Day, Aubrey M** — Singer (Danity Kane), Songwriter, Model
Artists International Mangement Talent, 333 E 43rd St, #115, New York NY 10017, USA
**O'Day, George** — Yachtsman
6 Turtle Lane, Dover MA 02030, USA
**Oddleifson, Christopher R (Chris)** — Ice Hockey Player
1950 Westover Road, North Vancouver BC V7J 3J3, Canada
**Odelein, Lyle** — Ice Hockey Player
12569 Winding Hollow Lane, Frisco TX 75033, USA
**Odelein, Selmar** — Ice Hockey Player
Farm, Quill Lake SK S0A 3E0, Canada
**Odell, Bob H** — Football Player, Coach
911 Stenton Place, Ocean City NJ 08226, USA
**O'Dell, Nancy** — Actress
W M E Entertainment, 9601 Wilshire Blvd, #300, Beverly Hills CA 90210 USA
**Odell, Tom** — Singer, Songwriter
Sony Music Entertainment, 9 Derry St, London W8 5HY, England
**O'Dell, Tony** — Actor
417 N Griffith Park Dr, Burbank CA 91506, USA
**O'Dell, William O (Billy)** — Baseball Player
225 O'Dell Road, Newberry SC 29108, USA
**Oden, Gregory W (Greg), Jr** — Basketball Player
Miami Heat, American Airlines Arena, 601 Biscayne Blvd, Miami FL 33132 USA
**Oden, McDonald** — Football Plater
480 Chimneytop Dr, Antioch TN 37013, USA
**Oden, Robert A, Jr** — Educator
Carleton College, President's Office, 1 N College St, Northfield MN 55057, USA
**Oden, Robert R** — Surgeon, Skiing Physician
PO Box 172, Captiva FL 33924, USA
**Odenkirk, Bob** — Actor
Odenkirk Provissiero Entertainment, 1936 N Bronson Ave, Los Angeles CA 90069 USA
**Odgers, Jeff** — Ice Hockey Player
Farm, Spy Hill SK S0A 3W0, Canada
**Odhiambo, David** — Writer
7 8th Ave, Lake Pleasant MA 01347, USA
**Odierno, Raymond T** — Army General
Chief of Staff, HqUSA, Pentagon, Washington DC 20310 USA
**Odjick, Gino** — Ice Hockey Player
Musquem Golf Academy, 3904 51st Ave W, Vancouver BC V6N 3W1, Canada
**Odjig, Daphne** — Artist
7841 Highway 97 North, #182, Kelowna BC V4V 1E7, Canada
**Odmark, Matthew T (Matt)** — Guitarist (Jars of Clay)
Nettwerk Mgmt, 1650 W 2nd Ave, Vancouver BC V6J 4R3, Canada
**Odom, Antwan** — Football Player
4562 Raynor Court, Mason OH 45040, USA
**Odom, Clifton L (Cliff)** — Football Player
6708 Marthas Vineyard Dr, Arlington TX 76001, USA
**Odom, Johnny Lee (Blue Moon)** — Baseball Player
10343 Slater Ave, #204, Fountain Valley CA 92708, USA
**Odom, Lamar J** — Basketball Player
21731 Ventura Blvd, #300, Woodland Hills CA 91364, USA

| | |
|---|---|
| **Odomes, Nathaniel B (Nate)** | Football Player |
| 900 Quail Creek Dr, Columbus GA 31907, USA | |
| **Odoms, Riley M** | Football Player |
| 16731 Quail Park Dr, Missouri City TX 77489, USA | |
| **O'Donnell, Andrew** | Basketball Player |
| 3310 Lincoln Ave, Allentown PA 18103, USA | |
| **O'Donnell, Annie** | Actress |
| Kazarian/Measures/Ruskin, 11969 Ventura Blvd, #300, Studio City CA 91604 USA | |
| **O'Donnell, Chris** | Actor |
| W M E Entertainment, 9601 Wilshire Blvd, #300, Beverly Hills CA 90210 USA | |
| **O'Donnell, Daniel** | Singer |
| Brockwell, 90B Lagan Road, Dublin Industrial Estate, Dublin 11, Ireland | |
| **O'Donnell, Fred** | Ice Hockey Player |
| 690 Carnaby St, Kingston ON K0H 2H0, Canada | |
| **O'Donnell, Joseph R (Joe)** | Football Player |
| 447 Bodley Crescent, Milan MI 48160, USA | |
| **O'Donnell, Keir** | Actor |
| United Talent Agency, U T A Plaza, 9336 Civic Center Dr, Beverly Hills CA 90210 USA | |
| **O'Donnell, Neil K** | Football Player |
| 5329 Stanford Dr, Nashville TN 37215, USA | |
| **O'Donnell, Rosie** | Actress |
| W M E Entertainment, 9601 Wilshire Blvd, #300, Beverly Hills CA 90210 USA | |
| **O'Donnell, Sean** | Ice Hockey Player |
| 1656 Manhattan Ave, Hermosa Beach CA 90254, USA | |
| **O'Donnell, William (Bill)** | Harness Racing Driver |
| 569 Penn Estate, East Stroudsburg PA 18301, USA | |
| **O'Donoghue, Colin** | Actor |
| Alchemy Entertainment, 7024 Melrose Ave, #420, Los Angeles CA 90038 USA | |
| **O'Donoghue, John E** | Baseball Player |
| 5246 Far Oak Circle, Sarasota FL 34238, USA | |
| **O'Donoghue, Neil** | Football Player |
| 1118 Flushing Ave, Clearwater FL 33764, USA | |
| **O'Donohue, John F** | Actor |
| Don Buchwald Talent Agency, 6500 Wilshire Blvd, #2200, Los Angeles CA 90048 USA | |
| **O'Dowd, Chris** | Actor |
| United Talent Agency, U T A Plaza, 9336 Civic Center Dr, Beverly Hills CA 90210 USA | |
| **Odrowski, Gerry** | Ice Hockey Player |
| PO Box 126, Trout Creek ON P0H 2L0, Canada | |
| **Oduber, Nelson O** | Prime Minister, Aruba |
| Prime Minister's Office, L G Smith Blvd 76, Oranjestad, Aruba | |
| **Oduye, Adepero** | Actress |
| Washington Square Arts, 1041 N Formosa Ave, Formosa Building, West Hollywood CA 90046, USA | |
| **O'Dwyer, Billy** | Ice Hockey Player |
| 11 Fox Hill Dr, Braintree MA 02184, USA | |
| **Oe, Kenzaburo** | Nobel Literature Laureate |
| 585 Seijo-Machi, Setagayaku, Tokyo 157 0066, Japan | |
| **Oedekerk, Steve** | Director |
| W M E Entertainment, 9601 Wilshire Blvd, #300, Beverly Hills CA 90210 USA | |
| **Oefelein, William A** | Astronaut |
| Adventure Write, PO Box 113074, Anchorage AK 99511, USA | |
| **Oelkers, Bryan A** | Baseball Player |
| 3404 Taylor Ave, Bridgeton MO 63044, USA | |
| **Oelze, Christiane** | Opera Singer |
| Augstein & Hahn, Tal 28, 80331 Munich, Germany | |
| **Oerding, Johannes** | Singer, Songwriter |
| Cruiser Entertainment, Neuer Pferdemarkt 1, 20359 Hamburg, Germany | |
| **Oester, Ronald J (Ron)** | Baseball Player |
| 3760 Nine Mile-Tobasco Road, Cincinnati OH 45255, USA | |
| **Oetiker, Phil** | Cinematographer |
| 422 10th St, Brooklyn NY 11215, USA | |
| **Oettinger, Anthony G** | Mathematician |
| 65 Elizabeth Road, Belmont MA 02478, USA | |
| **Offerdahl, John A** | Football Player |
| 2749 NE 37th Dr, Fort Lauderdale FL 33308, USA | |
| **Offerman, Jose A** | Baseball Player |
| 10720 Moorpark St, North Hollywood CA 91602, USA | |
| **Offerman, Nick** | Actor |
| United Talent Agency, U T A Plaza, 9336 Civic Center Dr, Beverly Hills CA 90210 USA | |
| **Office, Rowland J (Rollie)** | Baseball Player |
| 1028 Lake Glen Way, Sacramento CA 95822, USA | |
| **Officer, Jill** | Curling Athlete |
| Team Jennifer Jones, 246 Jacques Ave, Winnipeg MB R3W 1S9, Canada | |
| **Ofili, Chris** | Artist |
| Victoria Miro Gallery, 21 Cork St, London W1X 1HB, England | |
| **O'Flaherty, Gerry** | Ice Hockey Player |
| 5446 Cortez Crescent, North Vancouver BC V7R 4R4, Canada | |
| **Ogando, Alexi** | Baseball Player |
| Texas Rangers, Ameriquest Field, 1000 Ballpark Way, #306, Arlington TX 76011 USA | |
| **Ogato, Sadako** | Government Official, Japan |
| United Nations Office for Refugees, CP 2500, 1211 Geneva 2, Switzerland | |
| **Ogbogu, Eric O** | Football Player |
| 16814 Harbour Town Dr, Silver Spring MD 20905, USA | |
| **Ogden, Carlos (Bud)** | Basketball Player |
| 3324 S 4th St, Springfield IL 62703, USA | |
| **Ogden, Jonathan P (Jon)** | Football Player |
| 3330 Georgia Ave NW, Washington DC 20010, USA | |
| **Ogea, Chad W** | Baseball Player |
| 3233 Plantation Court, Baton Rouge LA 70820, USA | |
| **Ogi, Adolf** | President, Switzerland |
| United Nations, Palais des Nations, #C119, 1211 Geneva 10, Switzerland | |
| **Ogier, Bulle** | Actress, Writer |
| Artmedia, 20 Ave Rapp, 75007 Paris, France | |
| **Ogilvie, Brian H** | Ice Hockey Player |
| 4708 60th St, Red Deer AB T4N 7C7, Canada | |
| **Ogilvie, Lana** | Model |
| Company Models, 17 Little West 12th St, #333, New York NY 10014, USA | |

**Ogilvie, N Joseph (Joe)** — Golfer
10 Cicero Lane, Austin TX 78746, USA

**Ogilvy, Geoff C** — Golfer
8355 E Hartford Dr, #105, Scottsdale AZ 85255, USA

**Ogilvy, Ian** — Actor
B R S / Gage Talent Agency, 5757 Wilshire Blvd, #659, Los Angeles CA 90036 USA

**Ogimi, Yūki Nagasato** — Soccer Player
F F C Turbine Potsdam, Am Luftschiffhafen 2, #33, 14471 Potsdam, Germany

**Ogio, Michel** — Governor General, Papua New Guinea
Governor General's Office, PO Box 79, Port Moresby 121, Papua New Guinea

**Ogle, Brett** — Golfer
Advantage International, 1751 Pinnacle Dr, #1500, McLean VA 22102 USA

**Oglivie, Benjamin A (Ben)** — Baseball Player
1012 E Sandpiper Dr, Tempe AZ 85283, USA

**O'Grady, Gail** — Actress
Shelter Entertainment, 9255 Sunset Blvd, #300, Los Angeles CA 90069 USA

**O'Grady, Sean** — Boxer
5808 NW 117th Terrace, Oklahoma City OK 73162, USA

**Ogren, Jayce** — Conductor
I M G Artists, Carnegie Hall Tower, 152 W 57th St, #500, New York NY 10019 USA

**Ogrin, David** — Golfer
1074 Running River, New Braunfels TX 78130, USA

**Ogrodnick, John** — Ice Hockey Player
37034 Aldgate Court, Farmington Hills MI 48335, USA

**Ogunleye, Adewale** — Football Player
19113 NW 23rd Court, Pembroke Pines FL 33029, USA

**Ogwumike, Nnemkadi (Nnenka)** — Basketball Player
Los Angeles Sparks, 888 S Figueroa St, #2010, Los Angeles CA 90017 USA

**Oh Jae-Seok** — Soccer Player
Football Association, 1-131 Sinmunno, 2-Ga Jongno-Gu, Seoul 110 062, South Korea

**Oh, Sadaharu** — Baseball Player
Fukuoka Dome Daiei Hawks, 2-2-2 Jigyohama, Chuoku Fukuoka 810 0065, Japan

**Oh, Sandra** — Actress
Principal Entertainment, 9255 Sunset Blvd, #500, Los Angeles CA 90069 USA

**Oh, Soon Teck** — Actor
Lee Assoc, 8961 W Sunset Blvd, #V, West Hollywood CA 90069, USA

**O'Hair, Sean M** — Golfer
1312 Fieldpoint Dr, West Chester PA 19382, USA

**Ohakete, Ifeanyi** — Football Player
11912 Crosswind Court, Reston VA 20194, USA

**O'Hanlon, Francis B (Fran)** — Basketball Player
27 W Wayne Ave, Easton PA 18042, USA

**O'Hara, Catherine** — Actress, Comedienne
I C M Partners, 10250 Constellation Blvd, #900, Los Angeles CA 90067 USA

**O'Hara, Kelli** — Actress, Singer
Gersh Agency, 9465 Wilshire Blvd, #600, Beverly Hills CA 90212 USA

**O'Hara, M Kelley** — Soccer Player
Soccer Federation, 1801 S Prairie Ave, Chicago IL 60616 USA

**O'Hara, Maureen** — Actress
Hipnoggin Inc, PO Box 480200, Los Angeles CA 90048, USA

**O'Hare, Damian** — Actor
Innovative Artists, 1505 10th St, Santa Monica CA 90401 USA

**O'Hare, Denis** — Actor, Singer
Innovative Artists, 1505 10th St, Santa Monica CA 90401 USA

**O'Haver, Tommy** — Director, Writer, Actor
Media Talent Group, 9200 W Sunset Blvd, #550, West Hollywood CA 90069 USA

**O'Hea, Jenna** — Basketball Player
Seattle Storm, Key Arena, 351 Elliott Ave W, #500, Seattle WA 98119 USA

**O'Heir, Jim** — Actor
Stone Manners Salners, 6100 Wilshire Blvd, #1500, Los Angeles CA 90035 USA

**Oher, Michael J** — Football Player
Tennessee Titans, 460 Great Circle Road, Nashville TN 37228 USA

**Ohka, Tomokazu (Tomo)** — Baseball Player
Toronto Blue Jays, Skydome, 1 Blue Jay Way, Toronto ON M5V 1J1, Canada

**Ohl, Donald J (Don)** — Basketball Player
2 E Lockhaven Court, Edwardsville IL 62025, USA

**Ohlde, Nicole** — Basketball Player
Tulsa Shock, B O K Center, 200 S Denver, Tulsa OK 74103 USA

**Ohlendorf, C Ross** — Baseball Player
2300 Barton Creek Blvd, #40, Austin TX 78735, USA

**Ohlsson, Garrick** — Concert Pianist
Opus 3 Artists, 470 Park Ave S, #900N, New York NY 10016 USA

**Ohlund, K Mattias** — Ice Hockey Player
Tampa Bay Lightning, 401 Channelside Dr, Tampa FL 33602 USA

**Ohman, Jack** — Editorial Cartoonist (Mixed Media)
Portland Oregonian, Editorial Dept, 1320 SW Broadway, Portland OR 97201, USA

**Ohman, William M (Will)** — Baseball Player
8939 E Norwood Circle, Mesa AZ 85207, USA

**Ohnishi, Minoru** — Businessman
Fuji Photo Film, 26-30 Nishiazabu, Minatoku, Tokyo 106 8620, Japan

**Ohno, Apolo Anton** — Speed Skater
Dreams Inc, 2 S University Dr, #325, Plantation FL 33324 USA

**Ohno, Shinobu** — Soccer Player
Football Association, 3-10-15 Hongo, Bunkyoku, Tokyo 113 0033 Japan

**Ohno, Yumiko** — Singer, Bassist (Buffalo Daughter)
W M E Entertainment, 9601 Wilshire Blvd, #300, Beverly Hills CA 90210 USA

**Ohr, Fred** — WW II Army Air Corps Hero
6401 Newburg Road, #211, Rockford IL 61108, USA

**Ohrner, Tommy (Tommi)** — Actor, Producer
Pool Position Mgmt, Eifelstr 29, 50677 Cologne, Germany

**Ohta, Tomoko** — Geneticist
20-20 Hatsunedai, Mishimachi, Shizuokaken 411 0018, Japan

**Ohtani, Monshu Koshin** — Religious Leader
Horikawa-Dori, Hanayachosagaru, Shimogyoku, Kyoto 600 8501, Japan

**O'Hurley, John** — Actor
Marv Dauer Mgmt, 11661 San Vicente Blvd, #104, Los Angeles CA 90049, USA

# O

**Ohuruogu, Christine I** — Track Athlete
N & E Beagles, 281 Prince Regent Lane, London E13 8SD, England

**Oistrakh, Igor D** — Concert Violinist
Novolesnaya Str 3, Korp 2, #10, Moscow, Russia

**Ojala, Kirt S** — Baseball Player
1902 Forest Lake Dr SE, Grand Rapids MI 49546, USA

**Ojeda, Eddie** — Singer, Guitarist (Twisted Sister)
Rebellion Entertainment, 2440 Broadway, #111, New York NY 10024, USA

**Ojeda, O Augie** — Baseball Player
5351 W Morgan Place, Chandler AZ 85226, USA

**Ojeda, Robert M (Bob)** — Baseball Player
20 Somerset Dr, Rumson NJ 07760, USA

**Oka, Masi** — Actor
United Talent Agency, U T A Plaza, 9336 Civic Center Dr, Beverly Hills CA 90210 USA

**Oka, Takeshi** — Chemist
1463 E Park Place, Chicago IL 60637, USA

**Okabe, Noriaki** — Engineer, Architect
Noriaki Okabe, Architecture Network, 1-14-19-1F Minato Chuohku, Tokyo 104 0043, Japan

**Okafor, Chukwuemeka N (Emeka)** — Basketball Player
840 Tchoupitoulas St, #102, New Orleans LA 70130, USA

**Okajima, Hideki** — Baseball Player
303 3rd St, #704, Cambridge MA 2142, USA

**Okamoto, Ayako** — Golfer
22627 Ladeene Ave, Torrance CA 90505, USA

**Okamoto, Tao** — Actress
I C M Partners, 10250 Constellation Blvd, #900, Los Angeles CA 90067 USA

**O'Kane, Deirdre** — Actress
Lisa Richards Agency, 108 Upper Leeson St, Dublin 4, Ireland

**Oke, Janette** — Writer
Baker Publishing Group, PO Box 6287, Grand Rapids MI 49516, USA

**Okeafor, Chikezie R (Chike)** — Football Player
8340 N Ridgeview Dr, Paradise Valley AZ 85253, USA

**O'Keefe, Jeremiah J, Sr** — WW II Marine Corps Air Force Hero
202 White Blvd, Ocean Springs MS 39564, USA

**O'Keefe, Jodie Lyn** — Actress
Resolution, 1801 Century Park E, #2300, Los Angeles CA 90067 USA

**O'Keefe, John** — Nobel Medicine Laureate, Neuroscientist
Sainsbury Wellcome Centre, University College, Gower St, London WC1E 6BT, England

**O'Keefe, Laurence (Larry)** — Composer
I C M Partners, 10250 Constellation Blvd, #900, Los Angeles CA 90067 USA

**O'Keefe, Michael** — Actor
Paradigm Agency, 360 N Crescent Dr, North Building, Beverly Hills CA 90210 USA

**O'Keefe, Miles** — Actor
Sharp/Karrys, 117 N Orlando Ave, Los Angeles CA 90048, USA

**O'Keefe, Sean** — Educator, Governmemt Official
E A D S North America, 1616 N Fort Myer Dr, #1600, Arlington VA 22209, USA

**O'Keefe, Thomas V (Tommy)** — Basketball Player
1000 Potomac Lane, Alexandria VA 22308, USA

**Okeniyi, Dayo** — Actor
United Talent Agency, U T A Plaza, 9336 Civic Center Dr, Beverly Hills CA 90210 USA

**Okereke, Kelechukwu R (Kele)** — Singer, Guitarist (Bloc Party)
Coalition Mgmt, 12 Barley Mow Passage, London W4 4PH, England

**Okhotnikoff, Nikolai P** — Opera Singer
Canal Griboedova 109, #13, 190068 Saint Petersburg, Russia

**Okobi, Chukwunweze S (Chukky)** — Football Player
5516 Maple Heights Court, Pittsburgh PA 15232, USA

**Okogie, Anthony Olubunmi Cardinal** — Religious Leader
Archdiocese, PO Box 8, 19 Catholic Mission St, Lagos, Nigeria

**Okolowicz, Jeff** — Guitarist (Chesterfield Kings)
Agency Group Ltd, 142 W 57th St, #600, New York NY 10019 USA

**Okolowicz, Ted** — Guitarist (Chesterfield Kings)
Agency Group Ltd, 142 W 57th St, #600, New York NY 10019 USA

**Okonedo, Sophie** — Actress
Hamilton Hodell, 20 Golden Square, London W1F 9JL, England

**Okoniewski, J Stephen (Steve)** — Football Player
222 S Oakland Ave, Oconto Falls WI 54154, USA

**O'Koren, Michael F (Mike)** — Basketball Player
109 Quaker Road, Mickleton NJ 08056, USA

**Okoye, Christian E** — Football Player
10082 Big Pine Dr, Rancho Cucamonga CA 91737, USA

**Okrie, Leonard J (Len)** — Baseball Player
2636 Burke Lane, Fayetteville NC 28306, USA

**Okumoto, Yuji** — Actor
Kono Kitchen, 8501 5th Ave NE, Seattle WA 98115, USA

**Okumura, Tomohiro** — Concert Violinist
Jecklin Assoc, 2717 Nichols Lane, Davenport IA 52803, USA

**Okun, Daniel A** — Environmental Engineer
204 Carol Woods, 750 Weaver Dairy Road, Chapel Hill NC 27514, USA

**Okur, Mehmet** — Basketball Player
1387 Perrys Hollow Road, Salt Lake City UT 84103, USA

**Oladipo, Victor** — Basketball Player
Orlando Magic, 8701 Maitland Summit Blvd, Orlando FL 32810 USA

**Olafsson, Olafur Darri** — Actor
A P A Talent & Literary Agency, 405 S Beverly Dr, #300, Beverly Hills CA 90212 USA

**Olagundoye, Toks** — Actress
Glick Agency, 1321 7th St, #203, Santa Monica CA 90401 USA

**Olah, George A** — Nobel Chemistry Laureate
2252 Gloaming Way, Beverly Hills CA 90210, USA

**Olajuwon, Hakeem A** — Basketball Player
1305 N Horseshoe Dr, Sugar Land TX 77478, USA

**Oland Fabricius, Nanna (O Land)** — Singer, Actress
Paradigm Agency, 360 Park Ave S, #1600, New York NY 10010 USA

**Olander, James B (Jim)** — Baseball Player
8421 S Triangle R Ranch Place, Vail AZ 85641, USA

**Olander, Jimmy** — Guitarist (Diamond Rio)
Modern Mgmt, 1625 Broadway, #600, Nashville TN 37203, USA

**Ohuruogu - Olander**

726             V.I.P. Address Book

**Olandt, Ken** — Actor
601 Hampshire Road, #475, Westlake Village CA 91361, USA
**Olazabel, Jose Maria** — Golfer
Real Club Golf de San Sebastian, Baserritar Etorbidea 1, 20280 Hondarribia, Gipuzkoa, Spain
**Olberding, Mark A** — Basketball Player
403 Geddington, Shavano Park TX 78249, USA
**Olbermann, Keith T** — Sportscaster, Commentator
I C M Partners, 10250 Constellation Blvd, #900, Los Angeles CA 90067 USA
**Olczyk, Ed** — Ice Hockey Player, Coach
4581 Pamela Court, Long Grove IL 60047, USA
**Olden, Paul** — Sportscaster
244 Madison Ave, #3E, New York NY 10016, USA
**Oldenburg, Brandon** — Animator
Moonbot Studios, 2031 Kings Highway, #102, Shreveport LA 71103, USA
**Oldenburg, Claes T** — Sculptor
556 Broome St, New York NY 10013, USA
**Oldenburg, Richard E** — Museum Executive
447 E 57th St, New York NY 10022, USA
**Olderman, Murray** — Sportswriter
28 La Costa Dr, Rancho Mirage CA 92270, USA
**Oldershaw, Kelsey** — Actress
Darren Goldberg Mgmt, 5225 Wilshire Blvd, #419, Los Angeles CA 90036, USA
**Oldfield, Bruce** — Fashion Designer
27 Beauchamp Place, London SW3 1 NJ, England
**Oldfield, Mike** — Singer, Songwriter
PO Box 2031, Blandford DT11 9YB, England
**Oldfield, Sally** — Singer
Global Artists Mgmt, Willy-Brandt-Str 39, 50374 Erftstadt, Germany
**Oldham, Christopher M (Chris)** — Football Player
8701 E Wilshire Dr, Scottsdale AZ 85257, USA
**Oldham, John H** — Baseball Player
1845 Anne Way, San Jose CA 95124, USA
**Oldham, John O (Johnny)** — Basketball Player, Coach
2127 Sycamore Dr, Bowling Green KY 42104, USA
**Oldham, Todd** — Fashion Designer
120 Wooster St, New York NY 10012, USA
**Oldis, Robert C (Bob)** — Baseball Player
7414 Pohick Road, Lorton VA 22079, USA
**Oldman, Gary** — Actor, Director
A P A Talent & Literary Agency, 405 S Beverly Dr, #300, Beverly Hills CA 90212 USA
**Oldring, Peter** — Actor, Comedian
Schumacher Mgmt, 10323 Santa Monica Blvd, #101, Los Angeles CA 90024, USA
**Olds, Gabriel** — Actor
Stone Manners Salners, 6100 Wilshire Blvd, #1500, Los Angeles CA 90035 USA
**Olds, Sharon** — Writer
Knopf Publishers, 1745 Broadway, New York NY 10019 USA
**Oldstone, Michael B A** — Neuropharmacologist
Scripps Research Institute, Neuropharmacology Dept, La Jolla CA 92037, USA
**Olear, Doug** — Actor
Progressive Artists Agency, 9696 Culver Blvd, #110, Culver City CA 90232 USA
**O'Leary, Brian T** — Astronaut
Future Focus on Human Potential, 5136 E Karen Dr, Scottsdale AZ 85254, USA
**O'Leary, George J** — Football Player
Central Florida University, Athletic Dept, 4000 Central Florida Blvd, Orlando FL 32816, USA
**O'Leary, Hazel R** — Secretary, Energy; Educator
Fisk University, President's Office, 1000 17th Ave N, Nashville TN 37208, USA
**O'Leary, Matthew** — Actor
I C M Partners, 10250 Constellation Blvd, #900, Los Angeles CA 90067 USA
**O'Leary, Michael** — Actor
242 Bellevue Ave, Montclair NJ 07043, USA
**O'Leary, Troy F** — Baseball Player
1060 W Norwood St, Rialto CA 92377, USA
**Olejnik, Craig** — Actor
Robert Stein Mgmt, PO Box 3797, Beverly Hills CA 90212, USA
**Oleksy, Jozef** — Prime Minister, Poland
Sejm R P, Ul Wiejska 4/6/8, 00 902 Warsaw, Poland
**Ole-Moiyol, Onesmo** — Molecular Biologist, Immunologist
Insect Physiologist Centre, Nyayo Stadium, PO Box 30772, Nairobi, Kenya
**Olerud, John G** — Baseball Player
PO Box 606, Medina WA 98039, USA
**Olesz, Rostislav** — Ice Hockey Player
8687 Melrose Ave, #7, West Hollywood CA 90069, USA
**Olevsky, Julian** — Concert Violinist
68 Blue Hills Road, Amherst MA 01002, USA
**Oleynik, Larisa** — Actress
Savage Agency, 6212 Banner Ave, Los Angeles CA 90038 USA
**Olin, Ken** — Actor
Innovative Artists, 1505 10th St, Santa Monica CA 90401 USA
**Olin, Laurie** — Landscape Architect
227 S 6th St, Philadelphia PA 19106, USA
**Olin, Lena** — Actress
Paradigm Agency, 360 N Crescent Dr, North Building, Beverly Hills CA 90210 USA
**Oliphant, Patrick B (Pat)** — Editorial Cartoonist
Susan Conway Gallery, 1214 13th St, Washington DC 20005, USA
**Olitzky, Kerry M** — Religious Leader, Rabbi
Jewish Outreach Institute, 1270 Broadway, #609, New York NY 10001, USA
**Oliu, Ingrid** — Actress
Appletini Agency, 224 E Olive St, #209, Burbank CA 91502, USA
**Oliva, Pedro (Tony)** — Baseball Player
212 Spring Valley Dr, Minneapolis MN 55420, USA
**Olivares Palqu, Omar** — Baseball Player
PO Box 1328, San German PR 00683, USA
**Olivares, Ruben** — Boxer
Geno Productions, PO Box 113, Montebello CA 90640, USA
**Olivas, John D** — Astronaut
595 36th St, Manhattan Beach CA 90266, USA

**Olive, Jason** — Actor, Director, Producer
Liebman Entertainment, 12 E 46th St, #500, New York NY 10017, USA
**Olive, John** — Basketball Player
8652 Harjoan Ave, San Diego CA 92123, USA
**Oliveira, Elmar** — Concert Violinist
C M Artists, 127 W 96th St, #13B, New York NY 10025 USA
**Oliver, Albert (Al)** — Baseball Player
PO Box 1466, Portsmouth OH 45662, USA
**Oliver, Brian** — Producer
Creative Artists Agency, 2000 Ave of Stars, #100, Los Angeles CA 90067 USA
**Oliver, Christian** — Actor
House of Representatives, 1434 6th St, #1, Santa Monica CA 90401 USA
**Oliver, Clarence H (Clancy)** — Football Player
233 Springview, Irvine CA 92620, USA
**Oliver, Daniel T** — Navy Admiral
318 Prince St, #6, Alexandria VA 22314, USA
**Oliver, Darren C** — Baseball Player
1804 Larkspur Court, Southlake TX 76092, USA
**Oliver, Dean** — Rodeo Rider
21386 Notus Road, Greenleaf ID 83626, USA
**Oliver, Hubert (Hubie)** — Football Player
136 Blake St, Elyria OH 44035, USA
**Oliver, Jamie** — Chef
PO Box 51372, London N1 7WX, England
**Oliver, John** — Actor, Writer, Producer
W M E Entertainment, 9601 Wilshire Blvd, #300, Beverly Hills CA 90210 USA
**Oliver, Joseph M (Joe)** — Baseball Player
5223 Oak Island Road, Belle Isle FL 32809, USA
**Oliver, Louis, III** — Football Player
5082 SW 167th Ave, Miramar FL 33027, USA
**Oliver, Mary** — Writer
Molly Malone Cook Agency, PO Box 1071, Sweet Briar VA 24595, USA
**Oliver, Murray C** — Ice Hockey Player
5505 McGuire Road, Minneapolis MN 55439, USA
**Oliver, Nancy** — Producer, Writer
United Talent Agency, U T A Plaza, 9336 Civic Center Dr, Beverly Hills CA 90210 USA
**Oliver, Nathaniel (Nate)** — Baseball Player
4403 Oak Hill Road, Oakland CA 94605, USA
**Oliver, Pam** — Sportscaster
Ken Lindner Assoc, 2049 Century Park East, #1000, Los Angeles CA 90067, USA
**Oliver, Robert L (Bob)** — Baseball Player
1716 G St, Rio Linda CA 95673, USA
**Oliver, Winslow P** — Football Player
2027 Summerall Court, Richmond TX 77406, USA
**Olivero, Chris** — Actor
Innovative Artists, 1505 10th St, Santa Monica CA 90401 USA
**Olivia** — Artist, Illustrator
Ozone Productions, PO Box 4153 Point Dume Station, Malibu CA 90265, USA
**Olivier, Philip** — Actor
Associated International Mgmt, 7 Hatton Garden, #400, London EC1N 8AD, England
**Olivieri, Dawn** — Actress
A P A Talent & Literary Agency, 405 S Beverly Dr, #300, Beverly Hills CA 90212 USA
**Olivo, America** — Actress, Model
Northern Exposure Talent, 570 Granville St, #503, Vancouver BC V6C 3P1, Canada
**Olivo, Joey** — Boxer
9628 Poinciana St, Pico Rivera CA 90660, USA
**Olivo, Karen** — Actress, Dancer
Liebman Entertainment, 12 E 46th St, #500, New York NY 10017, USA
**Olivo, Miguel E** — Baseball Player
10004 Plaza de Oro Dr, Oakdale CA 95361, USA
**Olivor, Jane** — Singer
Ed Keane, 32 Saint Edwards Road, Boston MA 02128, USA
**Oliwa, Krzystof** — Ice Hockey Player
4 Meeker Dr, Florham Park NJ 07932, USA
**Olkewicz, Neal T** — Football Player
116 Topaz Dr, Gilbertsville PA 19525, USA
**Ollie, Kevin J** — Basketball Player, Coach
University of Connecticut, Athletic Dept, Storrs CT 06269, USA
**Ollila, Jorma J** — Businessman
Royal Dutch Shell, Carel v Bylandtlaan 16, 2596 The Haag HR, Netherlands
**Ollom, James D (Jim)** — Baseball Player
10916 27th Ave SE, Everett WA 98208, USA
**Olmedo, Alex** — Tennis Player
5067 Woodley Ave, Encino CA 91436, USA
**Olmert, Ehud** — Prime Minister, Israel
29 November Road, Jerusalem 92105, Israel
**Olmi, Paolo** — Conductor
I M G Artists, Hogarth Business Park, Chiswick, London W4 2TH, England
**Olmo, Luis F R (Jibaro)** — Baseball Player
620 Calle Jose Ramon Figueroa, San Juan PR 00907, USA
**Olmos, Edward James** — Actor
Olmos Productions, 500 S Buena Vista St, Old Animation Building, Burbank CA 91521, USA
**Olmstead, Alan R (Al)** — Baseball Player
1008 Pinecone Trail, Florissant MO 63031, USA
**Olmstead, M Bert** — Ice Hockey Player, Coach
2-1512 High Country Dr NW, High River AB T1V 1V9, Canada
**Olmstead, Matt** — Producer
W M E Entertainment, 9601 Wilshire Blvd, #300, Beverly Hills CA 90210 USA
**Olney, Claude W** — Educator
Olney 'A' Seminars, PO Box 686, Scottsdale AZ 85252, USA
**Olney, David C** — Singer, Songwriter
Mary Sack Mgmt, PO Box 330911, Nashville TN 37203, USA
**Olofsson-Zidek, Anna Carin** — Biathlete
Margareta Silver, Jamtlandsgatan 8, 842 32 Sveg, Sweden
**Olojede, Dele** — Journalist
New York Newsday, Editorial Dept, 235 Pinelawn Road, Melville NY 11747 USA

**O'Loughlin, Alex** — Actor
United Talent Agency, U T A Plaza, 9336 Civic Center Dr, Beverly Hills CA 90210 USA
**O'Loughlin, Gerald S** — Actor
23388 Mulholland Dr, #204, Woodland Hills CA 91364, USA
**O'Loughlin, Sean** — Conductor, Composer
I M G Artists, Carnegie Hall Tower, 152 W 57th St, #500, New York NY 10019 USA
**Olowokandi, Michael** — Basketball Player
10061 SW 60th Court, Miami FL 33156, USA
**Olsavsky, Jerome D (Jerry)** — Football Player
92 Lake Shore Dr, Youngstown OH 44511, USA
**Olsdal, Stefan A B** — Bassist, Guitarist (Placebo)
Riverman Records, George House, Brecon Road, London W6 8PY, England
**Olsen, Andrew H (Andy)** — Baseball Umpire
451 93rd Ave N, Saint Petersburg FL 33702, USA
**Olsen, Ashley** — Actress
DualStar Entertainment Group, 3760 Robertson Blvd, Los Angeles CA 90067, USA
**Olsen, Bud** — Basketball Player
1602 Gardiner Lane, #130, Louisville KY 40205, USA
**Olsen, Elizabeth** — Actress
Gersh Agency, 41 Madison Ave, #3301, New York NY 10010 USA
**Olsen, Eric Christian** — Actor
United Talent Agency, U T A Plaza, 9336 Civic Center Dr, Beverly Hills CA 90210 USA
**Olsen, Gregory (Greg)** — Tourist Cosmonaut
Sensors Unlimited, 3490 US Route 1, Building 12, Princeton NJ 08540, USA
**Olsen, Kevin** — Baseball Player
3353 Dales Dr, Norco CA 92860, USA
**Olsen, Kristina** — Singer, Songwriter
Emerging Music, Sarah's Cottage Horns Cross, Bideford, Devonshire EX39 5DW, England
**Olsen, Mark V** — Producer, Writer
Creative Artists Agency, 2000 Ave of Stars, #100, Los Angeles CA 90067 USA
**Olsen, Mary Kate** — Actress
DualStar Entertainment Group, 3760 Robertson Blvd, Los Angeles CA 90067, USA
**Olsen, Olaf** — Archaeologist
Strevelsjovedvej 2, Alro, 8300 Oder, Denmark
**Olsen, Paul E** — Geologist
Columbia University, Lamont-Doherty Geological Laboratory, New York NY 10027, USA
**Olsen, Phillip V (Phil)** — Football Player
112 Hitching Post Road, Bozeman MT 59715, USA
**Olsen, Scott M** — Baseball Player
2991 NE 185th St, #1701, Aventura FL 33180, USA
**Olsen, Stanford** — Opera Singer
Columbia Artists Mgmt Inc, 5 Columbus Circle, 1790 Broadway, #1600, New York NY 10019 USA
**Olshansky, Igor** — Football Player
PO Box 5000, Rancho Santa Fe CA 92067, USA
**Olshwanger, Ron** — Photojournalist
3821 Silver Ridge, Saint Peters MO 63376, USA
**Olson, Allen I** — Governor, ND
631 Broken Arrow Road, Chanhassen MN 55317, USA
**Olson, Benjamin D (Benji)** — Football Player
2211 Old Natchez Trace, Franklin TN 37069, USA
**Olson, Candice** — Interior Designer
Fusion Television, 145 Front St E, #L1, Toronto ON M5A 1E3, Canada
**Olson, Dennis** — Ice Hockey Player
521 1st Ave S, Kenora ON P9N 1W6, Canada
**Olson, Eric T** — Navy Admiral
Mission Essential, 6525 West Campus Oval, #101, New Albany OH 43054, USA
**Olson, Gale** — Model
Playboy Promotions, 9346 Civic Center Dr, #200, Beverly Hills CA 90210 USA
**Olson, Greggory W (Gregg)** — Baseball Player
1996 Port Nelson Place, Newport Beach CA 92660, USA
**Olson, Gregory W (Greg)** — Baseball Player
18592 Saint Mellion Place, Eden Prairie MN 55347, USA
**Olson, Harold V** — Football Player
1012 Keystone Lane, Clemson SC 29631, USA
**Olson, Heather** — Actress
T C M Model & Talent, 2200 6th Ave, #530, Seattle WA 98121, USA
**Olson, Hope** — Model
Playboy Promotions, 9346 Civic Center Dr, #200, Beverly Hills CA 90210 USA
**Olson, James** — Actor
29122 Cliffside Dr, Malibu CA 90265, USA
**Olson, Jeremy** — Journalist
Minneapolis Star Tribune, Editorial Dept, 425 Portland Ave S, Minneapolis MN 55488 USA
**Olson, Josh** — Writer, Director
BenderSpink, 8447 Wilshire Blvd, #250, Beverly Hills CA 90211 USA
**Olson, Kaitlin** — Actress
Creative Artists Agency, 2000 Ave of Stars, #100, Los Angeles CA 90067 USA
**Olson, Karl A** — Baseball Player
1417 Pin Oak Dr, Gardnerville NV 89410, USA
**Olson, Lisa** — Sportswriter
New York Daily News, Editorial Dept, 220 E 42nd St, New York NY 10017 USA
**Olson, Mancur** — Economist
4316 Claggett Pine Way, University Park MD 20782, USA
**Olson, Mark** — Singer, Songwriter (Jayhawks)
Red Ryder Entertainment, 1532 N Milwaukee Ave, #207, Chicago IL 60622, USA
**Olson, Mark W** — Government Official, Economist
Public Accounting Oversight Board, 1666 K St NW, #800, Washington DC 20006, USA
**Olson, Nancy** — Actress
945 N Alpine Dr, Beverly Hills CA 90210, USA
**Olson, Peter W** — Businessman, Publisher
Random House, 1745 Broadway, #1800, New York NY 10019 USA
**Olson, R Lute** — Basketball Coach
5831 E Finisterra, Tucson AZ 85750, USA
**Olson, Theodore B** — Government Official
Gibson Dunn Crutcher, 1050 Connecticut Ave NW, #300, Washington DC 20036, USA
**Olson, Timothy L (Tim)** — Baseball Player
5416 Pebble Court, McKinney TX 75070, USA

# O

**Olson, Weldon N (Weldy)** — Ice Hockey Player
2623 Goldenrod Lane, Findlay OH 45840, USA

**Olsson, Christian** — Track Athlete
F S D Internet Tjanster, Box 5026, 250 03 Helsinborg, Sweden

**Olsson, Curt G** — Financier
Skandinaviska Enskilda Banken, 106 40 Stockholm, Sweden

**Olsson, E Staffan** — Handball Player, Coach
Hammarby I F, Box 20056, 104 60 Stockholm, Sweden

**Olsson, Johan A** — Cross Country Skier
Asarna Idrottsklubb, Box 79, 840 31 Asarna, Sweden

**Olsson, Paul J (P J)** — Singer, Songwriter
Good Times Music, 506 Shelden Ave, Houghton MI 49931, USA

**Olszewski, Jan F** — Prime Minister, Poland
Biuro Poselskie, Al Ujazdowskie 13, 00567 Warsaw, Poland

**Olwine, Edward R (Ed)** — Baseball Player
223 Spanish Lakes Dr, Nokomis FL 34275, USA

**Olynyk, Kelly** — Basketball Player
Boston Celtics, 226 Causeway St, #4, Boston MA 02114 USA

**Olyphant, Timothy** — Actor
Brillstein Entertainment Partners, 9150 Wilshire Blvd, #350, Beverly Hills CA 90212 USA

**O'Malley, Bert W** — Biologist
Baylor College of Medicine, Molecular & Cellular Biology Dept, Baylor Plaza, Houston TX 77030, USA

**O'Malley, Kerry** — Actress
Professional Artists, 321 W 44th St, #605, New York NY 10036, USA

**O'Malley, Mike** — Actor
Creative Artists Agency, 2000 Ave of Stars, #100, Los Angeles CA 90067 USA

**O'Malley, Peter** — Baseball Executive
515 S Figueroa St, #1988, Los Angeles CA 90071, USA

**O'Malley, Robert E** — Vietnam War Marine Corps Hero (CMH)
PO Box 775, Goldthwaite TX 76844, USA

**O'Malley, Sean P Cardinal** — Religious Leader
Archdiocese of Boston, 66 Brooks Dr, Braintree MA 02184, USA

**O'Malley, Susan** — Basketball Executive
Washington Wizards, M C I Centre, 601 F St NW, Washington DC 20004 USA

**O'Malley, Thomas D** — Businessman
Tosco Corp, 1700 E Putnam Ave, #500, Old Greenwich CT 06870, USA

**O'Malley, Thomas P (Tom)** — Baseball Player
10 Carriage Square, Montoursville PA 17754, USA

**Omar, Don** — Singer
Relentless Agency, 261 E 134th St, #200, South Bronx NY 10454, USA

**O'Mara, Jason** — Actor
Independent Talent Group, 40 Whitfield St, London W1T 2RH, England

**O'Mara, Mark** — Harness Racing Driver, Trainer
6882 NW 65th Terrace, Parkland FL 33067, USA

**Omarion** — Singer (B2K), Songwriter, Actor
Pyramid Entertainment Group, 377 Rector Place, #21A, New York NY 10280 USA

**O'Meara, Mark F** — Golfer
2000 Auburn Dr, #330, Beachwood OH 44122, USA

**O'Meara, Peter** — Actor
Roar Mgmt, 9701 Wilshire Blvd, #800, Beverly Hills CA 90212 USA

**Omeyer, Thierry** — Handball Player
T H W Kiel Handball, Ziegelteich 30, 24103 Kiel, Germany

**Omidyar, Pierre M** — Businessman
Omidyar Network, 2145 Hamilton Ave, San Jose CA 95125, USA

**Omundson, Timothy** — Actor
Innovative Artists, 1505 10th St, Santa Monica CA 90401 USA

**Omura, Satoshi** — Organic Chemist
Kitasato Institute, 9-1-5 Shirokane, Tokyo 108 8641, Japan

**Onaiyekan, John O Cardinal** — Religious Leader
Archbishop's House, Area 3, Section 2, PO Box 286, Garki, Abuja FCT, Nigeria

**Ondaatje, Michael** — Writer
Glendon College, English Dept, 2275 Bayview, Toronto ON M4N 3M6, Canada

**Ondricek, Miroslav** — Cinematographer
Nad Pomnikem 1, 15200 Prague 5 Smichow, Czech Republic

**O'Neal, Alexander** — Singer, Songwriter
Green Light Talent Agency, PO Box 3172, Beverly Hills CA 90212 USA

**O'Neal, Carlton (Carol)** — Model
Playboy Promotions, 9346 Civic Center Dr, #200, Beverly Hills CA 90210 USA

**O'Neal, Deltha L, III** — Football Player
10225 Meadowknoll Dr, Loveland OH 45140, USA

**O'Neal, E Stanley** — Financier
Merrill Lynch Co, World Financial Center, 2 Vesey St, New York NY 10007, USA

**O'Neal, Griffin** — Actor
21368 Pacific Coast Highway, Malibu CA 90265, USA

**O'Neal, Jermaine** — Basketball Player
1500 Ocean Dr, #1206, Miami Beach FL 33139, USA

**O'Neal, Leslie C** — Football Player
8015 Hemingway Ave, San Diego CA 92120, USA

**O'Neal, Ralph T** — Chief Minister, British Virgin Islands
Chief Minister's Office, Road Town, Tortola, British Virgin Islands

**O'Neal, Randall J (Randy)** — Baseball Player
10015 Honey Tree Court, Orlando FL 32836, USA

**O'Neal, Ryan** — Actor, Producer
Scott Zimmerman Mgmt, 1644 Courtney Ave, Los Angeles CA 90046, USA

**O'Neal, Shaquille R** — Basketball Player
9927 Giffin Court, Windermere FL 34786, USA

**O'Neal, Steve** — Football Player
2914 Coronado Dr, College Station TX 77845, USA

**O'Neal, Tatum** — Actress
Mavrick Artists Agency, 6100 Wilshire Blvd, #550, Los Angeles CA 90048, USA

**O'Neil, Edward W (Ed)** — Football Player
6691 Aiken Road, Lockport NY 14094, USA

**O'Neil, Lillian** — Artist
The Commercial, 148 Abercrombie St, Redfern, Box 830, Strawberry Hills, Sydney NSW 2016, Australia

**O'Neil, Linda** — Actress, Model
C E S D, 10635 Santa Monica Blvd, #130, Los Angeles CA 90025 USA

Olson - O'Neil

**O'Neil, Melissa C** — Singer
19 Entertainment, 8560 W Sunset Blvd, #900, Los Angeles CA 90069 USA

**O'Neil, Robert M** — Educator
University of Virginia, Law School, Charlottesville VA 22903, USA

**O'Neil, Tricia** — Actress
David Shapira Assoc, 193 N Robertson Blvd, Beverly Hills CA 90211 USA

**O'Neill of Bengarve, O Sylvia** — Philosopher
Newham College, Philosophy Dept, Cambridge CB3 9DF, England

**O'Neill, Brian** — Ice Hockey Executive
2600-1800 McGill College Ave, Montreal QC H3A 3J6, Canada

**O'Neill, Dan** — Association Executive
Mercy Corps, 45 SW Ankeny St, Portland OR 97204, USA

**O'Neill, Dan** — Cartoonist (Odd Bodkins, O'Neill)
PO Box 1297, Nevada City CA 95959, USA

**O'Neill, Doug** — Thoroughbred Racing Trainer
Doug O'Neill Stable, Hollywood Park, 1050 S Prairie Ave, Inglewood CA 90301, USA

**O'Neill, Ed** — Actor
Paradigm Agency, 360 N Crescent Dr, North Building, Beverly Hills CA 90210 USA

**O'Neill, Eugene F** — Communications Engineer
394 Dogford Road, Etna NH 03750, USA

**O'Neill, Jennifer** — Actress, Model
Jennifer O'Neill Ministries, 30 Hillenglade Dr, Nashville TN 37207, USA

**O'Neill, Maggie** — Actress
Independent Talent Group, 40 Whitfield St, London W1T 2RH, England

**O'Neill, Michael E** — Financier
Citigroup Inc, 55 E 52nd St, New York NY 10055, USA

**O'Neill, Morgan** — Director, Writer, Actor
Paradigm Agency, 360 N Crescent Dr, North Building, Beverly Hills CA 90210 USA

**O'Neill, Paul A** — Baseball Player
7785 Hartford Hill Lane, Cincinnati OH 45242, USA

**O'Neill, Paul H** — Secretary, Treasury
3 Von Lent Place, Pittsburgh PA 15232, USA

**O'Neill, Susan (Susie)** — Swimmer
Elite Sports Properties, 326 Seaview Road, Henley Beach SA 5022, Australia

**Ong, John D** — Businessman, Diplomat
230 Aurora St, Hudson OH 44236, USA

**Onkotz, Dennis H** — Football Player
270 Walker Dr, State College PA 16801, USA

**Ono, Takashi** — Gymnast
Gymnastics Assn, Kishi Hall, 1-1 Jinnan Shibuyaku, Tokyo 150 8050, Japan

**Ono, Yoko** — Filmmaker, Singer, Artist
Dakota Hotel, 1 W 72nd St, #1, New York NY 10023, USA

**Onopka, Snejana** — Model
Women Model Mgmt, 199 Lafayette St, #700, New York NY 10012 USA

**O'Nora, Brian** — Baseball Umpire
5265 Nashua Dr, Youngstown OH 44515, USA

**Onorati, Peter** — Actor
Liberman-Zerman Mgmt, 252 N Larchmont Blvd, #200, Los Angeles CA 90004 USA

**Ontiveros, Steven (Steve)** — Baseball Player
9970 E Charter Oak Road, Scottsdale AZ 85260, USA

**Ontiveros, Steven R (Steve)** — Baseball Player
18061 N 87th Dr, #2127, Peoria AZ 85382, USA

**Ontkean, Michael** — Actor
PO Box 51, Kilauea HI 96754, USA

**Onufriyenko, Yuri I** — Cosmonaut
Cosmonaut Training Center, Star City, 141160 Zvezdny Gorodok, Moscow Oblast, Russia

**Onweagba, Oluchi** — Model
D N A Model Mgmt, 555 W 25th St, #600, New York NY 10001 USA

**Onyali, Mary** — Track Athlete
Kurt Varricchio, 23861 El Toro Road, #700, Lake Forest CA 92630, USA

**Oosterhuis, Peter** — Golfer
2823 Providence Road, #182, Charlotte NC 28211, USA

**Opacic, Paul** — Actor
Associated International Mgmt, 7 Hatton Garden, #400, London EC1N 8AD, England

**Opasik, Jim** — Artist
1914 Beverly Road, Catonsville MD 21228, USA

**Opertti Baddan, Didier** — Government Official, Uruguay
A L A D I, Calle Cebollati 1461, Montevideo CP 11200, Uruguay

**Ophuls, Marcel** — Director
10 Rue Ernest Deloison, 92200 Neuilly-sur-Seine, France

**Opie, Alan** — Opera Singer
I M G Artists, Hogarth Business Park, Chiswick, London W4 2TH, England

**Opik, Ernst J** — Astronomer
University of Maryland, Physics & Astronomy Dept, College Park MD 20742, USA

**Oplev, Niels Arden** — Director
I C M Partners, 10250 Constellation Blvd, #900, Los Angeles CA 90067 USA

**Oppegard, Peter** — Figure Skater
East West Ice Palace, 11446 Artesia Blvd, Artesia CA 90701, USA

**Oppenheim, Irwin** — Chemical Physicist
140 Upland Road, Cambridge MA 02140, USA

**Oppenheim-Barnes of Gloucester, Sally** — Government Official, England
Quietways, Highlands, Painswick, Gloustershire GL6 6SL, England

**Oppenheimer, Alan** — Actor
200 N Swall Dr, #405, Beverly Hills CA 90211, USA

**Oppenheimer, Benjamin R** — Astronomer
Columbia University, Astronomy Dept, New York NY 10027, USA

**Oppenheimer, Deborah** — Producer, Writer
N B C Universal, 100 Universal City Plaza, Universal City CA 91608, USA

**Oppewall, Jeannine Claudia** — Art Director
Gersh Agency, 9465 Wilshire Blvd, #600, Beverly Hills CA 90212 USA

**Oquendo, Jose M R G** — Baseball Player
13219 Selma Road, De Soto MO 63020, USA

**O'Quinn, Terry** — Actor
L B I Entertainment, 2000 Avenue of Stars, Century City CA 90067, USA

**Oquist, Michael L (Mike)** — Baseball Player
1910 Raton Ave, La Junta CO 81050, USA

**Ora, Rita** — Actress, Singer
Creative Artists Agency, 2000 Ave of Stars, #100, Los Angeles CA 90067 USA
**Orakpo, Brian N** — Football Player
Washington Redskins, 21300 Redskin Park Dr, Ashburn VA 20147 USA
**Oram, Tara** — Actress, Singer
R G K Entertainment Group, 2B Minto St,#6, Toronto ON M4L 1B6, Canada
**Oram, Tara** — Singer
Agency Group Ltd, 142 W 57th St, #600, New York NY 10019 USA
**Oramo, Sakari M** — Conductor
Royal Stockholm Symphony Orchestra, Konserthus, Hotorget 8, Box 7083, 103 87 Stockholm, Sweden
**Orange, Walter (Clyde)** — Singer, Drummer (Commodores)
Management Assoc, 1920 Benson Ave, Saint Paul MN 55116, USA
**Orbach, Raymond L** — Educator
4004 Petra Path, Austin TX 78731, USA
**Orban, Viktor** — Prime Minister, Hungary
Prime Minister's Office, Kossuth Lajos Ter 1-3, 1055 Budapest, Hungary
**Orbit, William** — Keyboardist, Songwriter, Actor
Creative Artists Agency, 2000 Ave of Stars, #100, Los Angeles CA 90067 USA
**Ord, Robert L (Bob), III** — Army General
3020 Ribera Road, Carmel CA 93923, USA
**Ordonez Delgado, Magglio J** — Baseball Player
181 Nurmi Dr, Fort Lauderdale FL 33301, USA
**Ordonez Pereira, Reynaldo (Rey)** — Baseball Player
16501 NW 84th Ave, Hialeah FL 33016, USA
**Ordovas, Jose M** — Nutritionist, Geneticist
Tufts University, Meyer Human Nutrition Research Center on Aging, Medford MA 02155, USA
**O'Ree, William E (Willie)** — Ice Hockey Player
7961 Anders Circle, La Mesa CA 91942, USA
**O'Reilly Werry, Heather A** — Soccer Player
Soccer Federation, 1801 S Prairie Ave, Chicago IL 60616 USA
**O'Reilly, Ahna** — Actress
W M E Entertainment, 9601 Wilshire Blvd, #300, Beverly Hills CA 90210 USA
**O'Reilly, Anthony J F** — Businessman, Publisher
H J Heinz Co, PO Box 57, Pittsburgh PA 15230, USA
**O'Reilly, Bill** — Commentator
O'Reilly Factor, Fox-TV, 1211 Ave of Americas, New York NY 10036, USA
**O'Reilly, David J** — Businessman
Chevron Corp, 6001 Bollinger Canyon Road, San Ramon CA 94583, USA
**O'Reilly, Genevieve** — Actress
R G M Artists, 8-12 Ann Street, Surry Hills NSW 2010, Australia
**O'Reilly, Ryan** — Hockey Player
Colorado Avalanche, Pepsi Center, 1000 Chopper Circle, Denver CO 80204 USA
**O'Reilly, Terry** — Ice Hockey Player
PO Box 5544, Salisbury MA 01952, USA
**O'Reilly, Tim** — Publisher, Businessman
O'Reilly Media, 1005 Gravenstein Highway N, Sebastopol CA 95472, USA
**Oremans, Miriam** — Tennis Player
Octagon Worldwide, 1751 Pinnacle Dr, #1500, McLean VA 22102 USA
**Orenstein, Andrew** — Producer, Writer
Paradigm Agency, 360 N Crescent Dr, North Building, Beverly Hills CA 90210 USA
**Oreskovich, Alesha** — Model
Playboy Promotions, 9346 Civic Center Dr, #200, Beverly Hills CA 90210 USA
**Orgeron, Ed** — Football Coach
University of Southern California, Athletic Dept, Los Angeles CA 90089, USA
**Origliasso, Jessica** — Singer (Vernoicas), Actress
Harbour Agency, 135 Forbes St, Woolloomooloo NSW 2011, Australia
**Origliasso, Lisa** — Singer (Veronicas), Actress
Harbour Agency, 135 Forbes St, Woolloomooloo NSW 2011, Australia
**O'Riordan, Dolores M E** — Singer (Cranberries), Songwriter
Creative Artists Agency, 2000 Ave of Stars, #100, Los Angeles CA 90067 USA
**Oritz, John** — Actor
Gersh Agency, 9465 Wilshire Blvd, #600, Beverly Hills CA 90212 USA
**Orkin, Stuart H** — Pediatrician, Oncologist
Harvard Stem Cell Institute, Holyoke Center, #727W, 1350 Massachusetts Ave, Cambridge MA 02138, USA
**Orland, Frank J** — Oral Microbiologist, Dentist
519 Jackson Blvd, Forest Park IL 60130, USA
**Orlandi, Daniel** — Costume Designer
W M E Entertainment, 9601 Wilshire Blvd, #300, Beverly Hills CA 90210 USA
**Orlandi, Luca** — Fashion Designer
Luca Luca, 19 W 36th St, #400, New York NY 10018, USA
**Orlando, Gates** — Ice Hockey Player
252 Bennington Hills Court, West Henrietta NY 14586, USA
**Orlando, Tony** — Singer
Brokaw Co, 9255 W Sunset Blvd, #804, West Hollywood CA 90069 USA
**Orlean, Susan** — Writer
New Yorker, Editorial Dept, 4 Times Square, Basement C1B, New York NY 10036 USA
**Orleans, Joan** — Singer
PO Box 2596, New York NY 10009, USA
**Orloff, John** — Producer, Writer
Creative Artists Agency, 2000 Ave of Stars, #100, Los Angeles CA 90067 USA
**Orlovsky, Daniel J (Dan)** — Football Player
2 Reliant Park, Houston TX 77054, USA
**Orman, Suze** — Writer
Suze Orman Financial Group, 2000 Powell St, #1605, Emeryville CA 94608, USA
**Ormond, Julia** — Actress
Gersh Agency, 9465 Wilshire Blvd, #600, Beverly Hills CA 90212 USA
**Orms, Barry D** — Basketball Player
3 Loudon Dr, #8, Fishkill NY 12524, USA
**Ornish, Dean** — Cardiologist
Preventive Medicine Research Institute, 900 Bridgeway, #2, Sausalito CA 94965, USA
**Ornstein, Norman J** — Political Scientist
2212 Wyoming Ave NW, Washington DC 20008, USA
**Orosco, Jesse R** — Baseball Player
16242 Winecreek Road, San Diego CA 92127, USA
**O'Ross, Ed** — Actor
Across the Board Talent Agency, 22543 Ventura Blvd, #225, Woodland Hills CA 91364, USA

| | |
|---|---|
| **O'Rourke, James P (Charlie)** | Baseball Player |
| 15612 N Little Spokane Dr, Spokane WA 99208, USA | |
| **O'Rourke, Tom** | Actor |
| TalentWorks, 3500 W Olive Ave, #1400, Burbank CA 91505 USA | |
| **Orozco, Gabriel** | Sculptor |
| Marian Goodman Gallery, 124 W 57th St, New York NY 10019, USA | |
| **Orozco-Estrada, Andres** | Conductor |
| I M G Artists, Hogarth Business Park, Chiswick, London W4 2TH, England | |
| **Orpik, R Brooks** | Ice Hockey Player |
| 2396 Hilltop Road, Presto PA 15142, USA | |
| **Orr, James F, III** | Businessman |
| U N U M Provident Corp, 2211 Congress St, Portland ME 04122, USA | |
| **Orr, Kay S** | Governor, NE |
| 1425 H St, Lincoln NE 68508, USA | |
| **Orr, Louis M** | Basketball Player, Coach |
| 1333 Pine Valley Dr, Bowling Green OH 43402, USA | |
| **Orr, Peterson T (Pete)** | Baseball Player |
| 400 Rannie Road, Newmarket ON L3X 2N3, Canada | |
| **Orr, Robert G (Bobby)** | Ice Hockey Player |
| Orr Hockey Group, PO Box 290836, Charlestown MA 02129, USA | |
| **Orr, Shantee D** | Football Player |
| PO Box 20301, Houston TX 77225, USA | |
| **Orr, Terrance F (Terry)** | Football Player |
| 2710 Kellogg Ave, Dallas TX 75216, USA | |
| **Orr, Terrence S** | Ballet Dancer, Executive |
| Pittsburgh Ballet Theater, 2900 Liberty Ave, Pittsburgh PA 15201, USA | |
| **Orrall, Robert Ellis** | Singer |
| 3 E 54th St, #1400, New York NY 10022, USA | |
| **Orr-Cahall, Christina** | Museum Director |
| Museum & Library Service Institute, 1800 M St NW, #900, Washington DC 20036, USA | |
| **Orrell, Thomas M** | Biologist |
| Smithsonian Natural History Museum, 10th & Constitution, Washington DC 20560, USA | |
| **Orr-Ewing, Hamish** | Businessman |
| Fox Mill, Purton near Swindon, Wilts SN5 9EF, England | |
| **Orrico, Stacie** | Singer, Actress |
| Creative Artists Agency, 2000 Ave of Stars, #100, Los Angeles CA 90067 USA | |
| **Orser, Brian** | Figure Skater |
| I M G Canada, 175 Bloor St E, #400S, Toronto ON M4W 3R8, Canada | |
| **Orser, Leland** | Actor, Director, Writer |
| Gersh Agency, 9465 Wilshire Blvd, #600, Beverly Hills CA 90212 USA | |
| **Orsini, Myrna J** | Sculptor |
| Orsini Studios, 4411 N 7th St, Tacoma WA 98406, USA | |
| **Orsino, John J** | Baseball Player |
| 6141 Terra Mere Circle, Boynton Beach FL 33437, USA | |
| **Orsulak, Joseph M (Joe)** | Baseball Player |
| 29 Keansburg Road, Parsippany NJ 07054, USA | |
| **Orszag, Peter R** | Economist, Government Official |
| Citigroup Inc, Financial Strategy & Solutions Group, 399 Park Ave, New York NY 10001, USA | |
| **Orta, Jorge** | Baseball Player |
| 1201 Heather Hill Crescent, Flossmoor IL 60422, USA | |
| **Ortega Gaona, Amancio** | Businessman |
| Inditex SA, Avenida de la Diputacion, 15142 Arteixo, La Coruna, Spain | |
| **Ortega Saavedra, J Daniel** | President, Nicaragua |
| President's Office, Casa de Gobierno, Barrio El Carmen, #2398, Managua, Nicaragua | |
| **Ortega y Alamino, Jaime L Cardinal** | Religious Leader |
| Archdiocese of San Cristobal de la Havana, Apartado 594, Calle Habana 152, Havana 10100, Cuba | |
| **Ortega, Bill** | Baseball Player |
| 4635 NW 95th Ave, Doral FL 33178, USA | |
| **Ortega, Chico P (Chick)** | Actor |
| Artmedia, 20 Ave Rapp, 75007 Paris, France | |
| **Ortega, Fernando** | Singer, Songwriter |
| Street Level Artist Agency, 107 E Centre St, Warsaw IN 46580, USA | |
| **Ortega, Kenny** | Director, Choreographer |
| Paradigm Agency, 360 N Crescent Dr, North Building, Beverly Hills CA 90210 USA | |
| **Ortega, Lindi** | Singer, Songwriter |
| Agency Group Ltd, 142 W 57th St, #600, New York NY 10019 USA | |
| **Ortenzio, Frank J** | Baseball Player |
| 2357 Oak Forest St, Jacksonville FL 32250, USA | |
| **Orth, Viviane** | Model |
| Louisa Models, Ebersbergerstr 9, 81679 Munich, Germany | |
| **Orth, Zak** | Actor |
| Gersh Agency, 9465 Wilshire Blvd, #600, Beverly Hills CA 90212 USA | |
| **Ortiz, Adalberto C (Junior)** | Baseball Player |
| 296 Strayer St, Johnstown PA 15906, USA | |
| **Ortiz, Ana** | Actress |
| G E F Entertainment, 611 N Cherokee Ave, Los Angeles CA 90004, USA | |
| **Ortiz, Carlos** | Boxer |
| 2050 Seward Ave, #3L, Bronx NY 10473, USA | |
| **Ortiz, Cristina** | Concert Pianist |
| Harrison/Parrott, 5-6 Albion Court, London W6 0QT, England | |
| **Ortiz, David A** | Baseball Player |
| 296 Strayer St, Johnstown PA 15906, USA | |
| **Ortiz, Domingo** | Percussionist (Widespread Panic) |
| Brown Cat Inc, 400 Foundry St, Athens GA 30601 USA | |
| **Ortiz, John** | Actor, Producer |
| Gersh Agency, 41 Madison Ave, #3301, New York NY 10010 USA | |
| **Ortiz, Russell R (Russ)** | Baseball Player |
| 4040 E McClellan Road, #13, Mesa AZ 85205, USA | |
| **Ortiz, Shalim** | Actor |
| C E S D, 10635 Santa Monica Blvd, #130, Los Angeles CA 90025 USA | |
| **Ortiz, Victor** | Boxer |
| Gersh Agency, 9465 Wilshire Blvd, #600, Beverly Hills CA 90212 USA | |
| **Ortlieb, Patrick** | Alpine Skier |
| Hotel Montana, Oberlech 588, 6764 Lech, Austria | |
| **Ortmeyer, Jed** | Ice Hockey Player |
| 1421 S 52nd St, Omaha NE 68106, USA | |

**O**

**O'Rourke - Ortmeyer**

**Ortner, Bev** — Bowler
PO Box 436, Odebolt IA 51458, USA
**Orton, Beth** — Singer
Paradigm Agency, 360 Park Ave S, #1600, New York NY 10010 USA
**Orton, John A** — Baseball Player
2929 E Dublin St, Gilbert AZ 85295, USA
**Orton, Kyle R** — Football Player
3114 Coates Crossing, Baton Rouge LA 70810, USA
**Oruche, Phina** — Actress
Markham Agency, 405 Strand, London WC2R 0NE, England
**Orvis, Herbert V (Herb)** — Football Player
1235 Autumn Court, Longmont CO 80504, USA
**Ory, Meghan** — Actress
Pacific Artists Mgmt, 112 E 3rd Ave, #210, Vancouver BC V5T 1C8, Canada
**Osborn, David V (Dave)** — Football Player
18067 Judicial Way N, Lakeville MN 55044, USA
**Osborn, John Jay, Jr** — Writer
14 Fair Oaks St, San Francisco CA 94110, USA
**Osborn, Kassidy** — Singer (SheDaisy)
L G B Media, 1228 Pineview Lane, Nashville TN 37211, USA
**Osborn, Kelsi** — Singer (SheDaisy)
L G B Media, 1228 Pineview Lane, Nashville TN 37211, USA
**Osborn, Kristyn** — Singer (SheDaisy), Songwriter
L G B Media, 1228 Pineview Lane, Nashville TN 37211, USA
**Osborne, Anders** — Singer, Guitarist, Songwriter
525 Worldwide Music, PO Box 957, Salem MA 01945, USA
**Osborne, Bobby** — Singer, Mandolinist (Osborne Brothers)
Lancer Agency, PO Box 160, Hendersonville TN 37077, USA
**Osborne, Donovan A** — Baseball Player
1851 Brightstone Court, Reno NV 89521, USA
**Osborne, James H (Jim)** — Football Player
4 Canyon Court, Algonquin IL 60102, USA
**Osborne, Jeffrey** — Singer, Songwriter
Wenig-LaMonica Associates, 580 White Plains Road, #130, Tarrytown NY 10591 USA
**Osborne, Joan** — Singer, Songwriter
Paradigm Agency, 360 N Crescent Dr, North Building, Beverly Hills CA 90210 USA
**Osborne, Keith** — Ice Hockey Player
Niagara Falls Hockey, 6570 Frederica St, Niagara Falls ON L2G 1C9, Canada
**Osborne, Kent** — Actor
Creative Management Entertainment Group, 2050 S Bundy Dr, #280, Los Angeles CA 90025, USA
**Osborne, Lawrence** — Writer
Farrar Straus Giroux, 18 W 18th St, #700, New York NY 10011 USA
**Osborne, Mark** — Ice Hockey Player
28 Princess Anne Crescent, Etobicoke ON M9A 2P1, Canada
**Osborne, Mark** — Director, Animator
W M E Entertainment, 9601 Wilshire Blvd, #300, Beverly Hills CA 90210 USA
**Osborne, Mary** — Surfer, Model
Patagonia, 8550 White Fir St, Reno NV 89523 USA
**Osborne, Mary Pope** — Writer
Random House, 1745 Broadway, #1800, New York NY 10019 USA
**Osborne, Thomas W (Tom)** — Football Coach; Representative, NE
5400 Trotter Road, Lincoln NE 68516, USA
**Osbourne, Jack** — Actor
W M E Entertainment, 9601 Wilshire Blvd, #300, Beverly Hills CA 90210 USA
**Osbourne, John M (Ozzy)** — Singer, Songwriter
Sharon Osbourne Mgmt, 8899 Beverly Blvd, #905, Los Angeles CA 90048, USA
**Osbourne, Kelly** — Singer, Actress
W M E Entertainment, 9601 Wilshire Blvd, #300, Beverly Hills CA 90210 USA
**Osbourne, Sharon** — Producer, Actress
Sharon Osbourne Mgmt, Regent House, 1 Pratt Mews, London NW1 0AD, England
**Osburn, Julie** — Actress
S M S Talent, 8383 Wilshire Blvd, #230, Beverly Hills CA 90211 USA
**Osburn, L Pat** — Baseball Player
208 64th Street Court NW, Bradenton FL 34209, USA
**Osby, Greg** — Jazz Saxophonist
Kavon Artist Mgmt, 295 E Swedesford Road, #161, Wayne PA 19087, USA
**O'Scannlain, Diarmuid F** — Judge
US Court of Appeals, Pioneer Courthouse, 555 SW Yamhill St, Portland OR 97204, USA
**Oscar, Carlos** — Actor, Comedian
Heidi Rotbart Management, 1810 Malcolm Ave, #207, Los Angeles CA 90025, USA
**Osgood, Charles** — Commentator
CBS-TV, News Dept, 524 W 57th St, New York NY 10019, USA
**Osgood, Charles E** — Psychologist
30 E Main St, Champaign IL 61820, USA
**Osgood, Chris** — Ice Hockey Player
1445 Penniman Ave, Plymouth MI 48170, USA
**Osgood, Kassim A** — Football Player, Actor
Gersh Agency, 9465 Wilshire Blvd, #600, Beverly Hills CA 90212 USA
**O'Shannon, Daniel T (Dan)** — Producer, Writer
Gendler & Kelly, 450 N Roxbury Dr, #1000, Beverly Hills CA 90210, USA
**O'Shea, Daniel P (Danny)** — Ice Hockey Player
7343 Colfax Ave S, Minneapolis MN 55423, USA
**O'Shea, Michael D** — Cinematographer
Murtha Agency, 1025 Colorado Ave, Santa Monica CA 90401, USA
**Osheroff, Douglas D** — Nobel Physics Laureate
75 Ranch Road, Woodside CA 94062, USA
**Oshima, Hiromi** — Model
Playboy Promotions, 9346 Civic Center Dr, #200, Beverly Hills CA 90210 USA
**Osik, Keith R** — Baseball Player
5 Pal Court, Shoreham NY 11786, USA
**Osin, Roman** — Cinematographer
Independent Talent Group, 40 Whitfield St, London W1T 2RH, England
**Osinski, Daniel (Dan)** — Baseball Player
9723 W Amber Trail, Sun City AZ 85351, USA
**Oslin, K T** — Singer
Consortium, 49 Music Square W, #210, Nashville TN 37203, USA

| | |
|---|---|
| **Osman, H P**<br>Deputy CofS, Manpower/Reserves, HqUSMC, 2 Navy St, Washington DC 20380, USA | Marine Corps General |
| **Osman, Mat**<br>Interceptor Enterprises, 98 White Lion St, London N1 9PF, England | Bassist (Suede) |
| **Osman, Osman Ahmed**<br>Osman Ahmed Osman Co, 34 Adly St, Cairo, Egypt | Civil Engineer |
| **Osmanski, Joy**<br>TalentWorks, 3500 W Olive Ave, #1400, Burbank CA 91505 USA | Actress |
| **Osmar, Dean**<br>PO Box 32, Clam Gulch AK 99568, USA | Dog Sled Racer |
| **Osment, Emily J**<br>Creative Artists Agency, 2000 Ave of Stars, #100, Los Angeles CA 90067 USA | Actress |
| **Osment, Haley Joel**<br>Resolution, 1801 Century Park E, #2300, Los Angeles CA 90067 USA | Actor |
| **Osmond, Alan**<br>Tony Denton Promotions, Charter House, 157-159 High St, London N14 6BP, England | Singer (Osmonds) |
| **Osmond, Donny**<br>Donny Osmond Entertainment, 1329 South 800 East, Orem UT 84097, USA | Singer |
| **Osmond, Jay**<br>Tony Denton Promotions, Charter House, 157-159 High St, London N14 6BP, England | Singer (Osmonds) |
| **Osmond, Kaetlyn**<br>Skate Canada, 865 Shefford Road, Ottawa ON K1J 1H9, Canada | Figure Skater |
| **Osmond, Ken**<br>9863 Wornom Ave, Sunland CA 91040, USA | Actor |
| **Osmond, Marie**<br>Rogers & Cowan, 8687 Melrose Ave, #G700, West Hollywood CA 90069 USA | Singer, Actress |
| **Osmond, Merrill**<br>Tony Denton Promotions, Charter House, 157-159 High St, London N14 6BP, England | Singer (Osmonds) |
| **Osmond, Wayne**<br>Tony Denton Promotions, Charter House, 157-159 High St, London N14 6BP, England | Singer (Osmonds) |
| **Osorio, Jorge Federico**<br>Columbia Artists Mgmt Inc, 5 Columbus Circle, 1790 Broadway, #1600, New York NY 10019 USA | Concert Pianist |
| **Osrin, Raymond H**<br>Cleveland Plain Dealer, Editorial Dept, 1801 Superior Ave, Cleveland OH 44114, USA | Editorial Cartoonist |
| **Oss, Arnold, Jr**<br>25601 N Abajo Dr, Rio Verde AZ 85263, USA | Ice Hockey Player |
| **Ossana, Diana**<br>Anonymous Content, 3532 Hayden Ave, Culver City CA 90232 USA | Writer, Producer |
| **Ost, Friedheim**<br>Vermogensberatungs AG, Querstr 1, 60322 Frankfurt/Main, Germany | Government Official, Germany |
| **Ostaseski, Frank**<br>Zen Hospice Project, 273 Page St, San Francisco CA 94102, USA | Hospice Director |
| **Osteen, Claude W**<br>2313 Duncan Perry Road, Grand Prairie TX 75050, USA | Baseball Player |
| **Osteen, Joel S H**<br>Lakewood Church, 3700 Southwest Freeway, Houston TX 77027, USA | Religious Leader |
| **Osterhage, Jeff**<br>C E S D, 10635 Santa Monica Blvd, #130, Los Angeles CA 90025 USA | Actor |
| **Osterkorn, Walter R (Wally)**<br>3202 E Medlock Dr, Phoenix AZ 85018, USA | Basketball Player |
| **Osterman, Catherine L (Cat)**<br>PO Box 77084, Houston TX 77084, USA | Softball Player |
| **Ostertag, Gregory D (Greg)**<br>8434 E Havasupai Dr, Scottsdale AZ 85255, USA | Basketball Player |
| **Ostheim, Michael**<br>Louisa Models, Ebersberger Str 9, 81679 Munich, Germany | Model |
| **Ostholt, Frank**<br>Vohren 31, 48231 Warendorf, Germany | Equestrian |
| **Ostin, Michael (Mo)**<br>DreamWorks SKG, 1000 Flower St, Glendale CA 91201, USA | Businessman |
| **Osting, Jimmy**<br>927 Lakeside Dr, Taylorsville KY 40071, USA | Baseball Player |
| **Ostman, Arnold**<br>Haydn Rawstron, 36 Station Road, London SE20 7BQ, England | Conductor |
| **Ostriker, Jeremiah P**<br>33 Philip Dr, Princeton NJ 08540, USA | Astrophysicist |
| **Ostroff, Dawn**<br>C W Television Network, 4000 Warner Blvd, Burbank CA 91522, USA | Businesswoman |
| **Ostroski, Gerald (Jerry), Jr**<br>6926 E 115th Place S, Bixby OK 74008, USA | Football Player |
| **Ostrosky, Beth**<br>Don Buchwald Talent Agency, 10 E 44th St, New York NY 10017 USA | Model, Actress |
| **Ostrosser, Brian L**<br>27 Chelsea Crescent, Stoney Creek ON L8E 5R7, Canada | Baseball Player |
| **Ostrum, Peter**<br>6065 Duncan Road, Glenfield NY 13343, USA | Actor |
| **O'Sullevan, Peter J**<br>37 Cranmer Court, London SW3 3HW, England | Sportswriter, Sportscaster |
| **O'Sullivan, Adele**<br>Health Care for the Homeless, 220 S 12th Ave, Phoenix AZ 85007, USA | Physician, Social Activist |
| **O'Sullivan, Chris**<br>114 Elmer Road, Dorchester Center MA 02124, USA | Ice Hockey Player |
| **O'Sullivan, Daniel J (Dan)**<br>33 Crescent Ave, Summit NJ 07901, USA | Basketball Player |
| **O'Sullivan, Gilbert**<br>Park Promotions, PO Box 651, Park Road, Oxford OX2 9RB, England | Singer, Songwriter |
| **O'Sullivan, Shawn**<br>Cabbagetown Boxing Club, 2 Lancaster Ave, Toronto ON M4X 1C1, Canada | Boxer |
| **O'Sullivan, Sonia**<br>Kim McDonald, 201 High St, Hampton Hill, Middlesex TW12 1NL, England | Track Athlete |
| **O'Sullivan, Terence**<br>Laborers International Union, 905 16th St NW, #600, Washington DC 20006, USA | Labor Leader |
| **Osuna, Alfonso (Al)**<br>8256 Via Rosa, Orlando FL 32836, USA | Baseball Player |
| **Osuna, P Antonio**<br>10345 W Olympic Blvd, Los Angeles CA 90064, USA | Baseball Player |

**Osvart, Andrea** — Actress, Producer
Innovative Artists, 1505 10th St, Santa Monica CA 90401 USA

**Oswald, Mark** — Opera Singer
Manhattan School of Music, 132 Claremont Ave, New York NY 10027, USA

**Oswald, Mark** — Drag Racing Driver
Don Schumacher Racing, 1681 E Northfield Dr, #A, Brownsburg IN 46112, USA

**Oswald, Stephen S** — Astronaut, Admiral
N A S A, Johnson Space Center, 2101 NASA Road, Houston TX 77058 USA

**Oswalt, Roy E** — Baseball Player
292 Jenny Penn Road, Crawford MS 39743, USA

**Oszajca, John** — Singer
Interscope Records, 2220 Colorado Ave, Santa Monica CA 90404 USA

**Otanez, Willis A** — Baseball Player
7904 March Brown Ave, Las Vegas NV 89149, USA

**Otellini, Paul S** — Businessman
Intel Corp, 2200 Mission College Blvd, Santa Clara CA 95054, USA

**Oteri, Cheri** — Actress, Comedienne
Mavrick Artists Agency, 6100 Wilshire Blvd, #550, Los Angeles CA 90048, USA

**Othenin-Girard, Dominque** — Director
327 S Church Lane, Los Angeles CA 90049, USA

**Otis, Amos J** — Baseball Player
8930 Tiger Shale Way, Las Vegas NV 89123, USA

**Otis, Carre** — Actress, Model
Dash Group, 550 N Larchmont Blvd, #201, Los Angeles CA 90004, USA

**Otis, James L (Jim)** — Football Player
14795 Greenleaf Valley Dr, Chesterfield MO 63017, USA

**O'Toole, Annette** — Actress
I C M Partners, 10250 Constellation Blvd, #900, Los Angeles CA 90067 USA

**O'Toole, James J (Jim)** — Baseball Player
1010 Lanette Dr, Cincinnati OH 45230, USA

**O'Toole, Shane** — Architect
68 Irishtown Road, Dublin 4, Ireland

**Otstott, Charles P** — Army General
6152 Pohick Station Dr, Fairfax Station VA 22039, USA

**Ott, Alice Sara** — Concert Pianist
Harrison/Parrott, 5-6 Albion Court, London W6 0QT, England

**Ott, Mirjam** — Curling Athlete
Curling Association, PO Box 606, 3000 Bern, Switzerland

**Ott, Mona Asuka** — Concert Pianist
Harrison/Parrott, 5-6 Albion Court, London W6 0QT, England

**Ott, Steve** — Ice Hockey Player
2758 Saint Clair, Pointe Aux Roches ON N0R 1N0, Canada

**Otten, James E (Jim)** — Baseball Player
1417 N Forest, Mesa AZ 85203, USA

**Ottenbrite, Anne** — Swimmer
Swimming Canada, 2197 Riverside Dr, #700, Ottawa ON K1H 7X3, Canada

**Ottey-Page, Merlene** — Track Athlete
Jamaican Olympic Committee, PO Box 544, Kingston 10, Jamaica

**Ottke, Sven** — Boxer
Public & Business Relations, Goethestr 25, 12207 Berlin, Germany

**Otto, August J (Gus)** — Football Player
8705 Leeward Dr, Las Vegas NV 89117, USA

**Otto, Bjorn** — Track Athlete
T S V Bayer Dormagen, Hohenberg 30, 41539 Dormagen, Germany

**Otto, David A (Dave)** — Baseball Player
1383 Shady Lane, Wheaton IL 60187, USA

**Otto, Frei P** — Architect, Structural Engineer
Berghalde 19, 7250 Leonberg, 71229 Warmbroun, Germany

**Otto, Gotz** — Actor
Z B F Agentur, Friedrichstr 39, 10969 Berlin, Germany

**Otto, James** — Singer, Songwriter
Red Light Mgmt, PO Box 159310, Nashville TN 37215, USA

**Otto, James E (Jim)** — Football Player
00 Estates Dr, Auburn CA 95602, USA

**Otto, Joel** — Ice Hockey Player
7144 Sues Dr, Pequot Lakes MN 56472, USA

**Otto, John E** — Drummer (Limp Bizkop)
Flip/Interscope Records, 8733 Sunset Blvd, #205, West Hollywood CA 90069, USA

**Otto, Kristin** — Swimmer
Z D F Sportedaktion, Postfach 4040, 55100 Mainz, Germany

**Otto, Michael** — Businessman
Wandsbeker Str 3-7, 22179 Hamburg, Germany

**Otto, Miranda** — Actress
United Agents, 12-26 Lexington St, London W1F 0LE, England

**Otto, Sylke** — Luge Athlete
Egersdorfer Str 3, 90513 Zirndorf, Germany

**Otunbayeva, Roza I** — President, Kyrgyzstan
Social Democratic Party, Ul Shabdan Baatyr, #D4B, 720003 Bishkek, Kyrgyzstan

**Ouattara, Alassane D** — President, Cote d'Ivoire; Financier
International Monetary Fund, 700 19th St NW, #12-300H, Washington DC 20431, USA

**Oubre, Louis B, III** — Football Player
12345 I 10 Service Road, #2403, New Orleans LA 70128, USA

**Ouchi, William G** — Educator
University of California, Graduate Management School, Los Angeles CA 90024, USA

**Oue, Eiji** — Conductor
I M G Artists, Hogarth Business Park, Chiswick, London W4 2TH, England

**Ouedraogo, Idrissa** — Director
01 BP 2524, Ouagadougou, Burkina Faso

**Ouedraogo, Philippe N Cardinal** — Religious Leader
Archdiocese of Ouagadougou, 01 BP 1472, Ouagadougou 01, Burkina Faso

**Ouellet, Marc Cardinal** — Religious Leader
Congregation for Bishops, Palazzo della Congregazioni, Piazza Pio XII 10, 00193 Rome, Italy

**Ouellette, Caroline** — Ice Hockey Player
Team Canada, 2424 University Dr NW, Calgary AB T2N 3Y9, Canada

**Ouellette, Philip R (Phil)** — Baseball Player
7421 Poppy St, Corona CA 92881, USA

**Oukach, Zineb**
Anthony Assoc, PO Box 910, New York NY 10108, USA — Actress
**Ouma, Kassim**
Peltz Boxing Promotions, 2501 Brown St, Philadelphia PA 19130, USA — Boxer
**Oumarou, Seyni**
Prime Minister's Office, State House, BP 353, Abuja, Niger — Prime Minister, Niger
**Oundjian, Peter**
Toronto Symphony Orchestra, 6-212 King St E, Toronto ON M58 1K5, Canada — Conductor
**Ousland, Borge**
Axel Huitfeldts V5, 1170 Oslo, Norway — Trans Polar Skier
**Ousset, Cecile**
Intermusica Artists Mgmt, 16 Duncan Terrace, London N1 8B7, England — Concert Pianist
**Outerbridge, Peter**
O A Z, 438 Queen St E, Toronto ON M5A 1T4, Canada — Actor
**Outhwaite, Tamzin**
Conway Van Gelder Grant, 8-12 Broadwick St, #300, London W1F 8HW, England — Actress
**Outlaw, Charles (Bo)**
Orlando Magic, 8701 Maitland Summit Blvd, Orlando FL 32810 USA — Basketball Player
**Outman, Joshua S (Josh)**
5273 Seasonbrooks Lane, Imperial MO 63052, USA — Baseball Player
**Outman, Tim**
2863 Lydick Way, Eugene OR 97401, USA — Sculptor
**Outtara, Alassane D**
President's Office, Presidential Palace, N'Gokro, Yamoussoukro, Cote d'Ivoire — President, Ivory Coast
**Ouyahia, Ahmed**
Prime Minister's Office, 32 Ave Souidani Boudiemad, Algiers, Algeria — Prime Minister, Algeria
**Ovchinikov, Vladimir P**
Manygate, 13 Cotswold Mews, 30 Battersea Square, London SW11 3RA, England — Concert Pianist
**Ovechkin, Alexander M**
6301 Osprey Terrace, Coconut Creek FL 33073, USA — Ice Hockey Player
**Overall, Park**
1374 Ripley Island Road, Afton TN 37616, USA — Actress
**Overath, Wolfgang**
Auf Dem Hummerich 5, 53721 Siegburg, Germany — Soccer Player
**Overbay, Lyle S**
107 Captain Lane, Centralia WA 98531, USA — Baseball Player
**Overbeck, Carla**
205 Zaoata Lane, Chapel Hill NC 27517, USA — Soccer Player
**Overbey, Kellie**
Stone Manners Salners, 6100 Wilshire Blvd, #1500, Los Angeles CA 90035 USA — Actress
**Overend, Ned**
Boure Bicycle Clothing, 98 Everett St, Durango CO 81303, USA — Cyclist
**Overgard, Robert M**
Church of Lutheran Brethren, PO Box 655, Fergus Falls MN 56538, USA — Religious Leader
**Overhauser, Albert W**
236 Pawnee Dr, West Lafayette IN 47906, USA — Physicist
**Overman, Ion**
Don Buchwald Talent Agency, 6500 Wilshire Blvd, #2200, Los Angeles CA 90048 USA — Actress
**Overman, Larry E**
University of California, Chemistry Dept, Irvine CA 92717, USA — Chemist
**Overmyer, Eric**
Creative Artists Agency, 2000 Ave of Stars, #100, Los Angeles CA 90067 USA — Writer, Producer
**Overstreet, Chord**
W M E Entertainment, 9601 Wilshire Blvd, #300, Beverly Hills CA 90210 USA — Actor
**Overstreet, Paul**
White Horse Enterprises, 475 Annex Ave, Nashville TN 37209, USA — Singer, Songwriter
**Overstreet, Tommy**
Capitol Mgmt Group, 1214 16th Ave S, Nashville TN 37212, USA — Singer, Songwriter
**Overton, David**
Cheesecake Factory Inc, 26901 Malibu Hills Road, Agoura Hills CA 91301, USA — Businessman, Restauranteur
**Overton, Kelly**
Management 360, 9111 Wilshire Blvd, Beverly Hills CA 90210 USA — Actress
**Overy, H Michael (Mike)**
3010 N 152nd Lane, Goodyear AZ 85395, USA — Baseball Player
**Ovitz, Michael S**
1234 Benedict Canyon Dr, Beverly Hills CA 90210, USA — Businessman
**Ovredal, Andre**
W M E Entertainment, 9601 Wilshire Blvd, #300, Beverly Hills CA 90210 USA — Director
**Ovsyannikov, Oleg**
Skating Assn, Luchnesksaia Nab 8, 119871 Moscow, Russia — Ice Dancer
**Owchar, Dennis**
154 Krieghoff Ave, Markham ON L3R 1W1, Canada — Ice Hockey Player
**Owchinko, Robert D (Bob)**
15111 N Hayden Road, #160-357, Scottsdale AZ 85260, USA — Baseball Player
**Owen, Beverly**
Tony Greco, 1435 Bellaire Place, Pittsburgh PA 15226, USA — Actress
**Owen, Chris**
J L A Talent Agency, 9151 Sunset Blvd, West Hollywood CA 90069, USA — Actor
**Owen, Clive**
42 West, 220 W 42nd St, #1200, New York NY 10036, USA — Actor
**Owen, Dave**
1921 FM 3136, Cleburne TX 76031, USA — Baseball Player
**Owen, David A L**
78 Narrow St, Limehouse, London E14 8BP, England — Government Official, Educator
**Owen, Gary**
I C M Partners, 10250 Constellation Blvd, #900, Los Angeles CA 90067 USA — Actor
**Owen, Jake**
R C A Records, 1400 18th Ave S, Nashville TN 37212 USA — Singer, Guitarist, Songwriter
**Owen, Joshua R (Jake)**
Morris Management Group, 818 19th Ave S, Nashville TN 37203, USA — Singer
**Owen, Lawrence T (Larry)**
804 White Pine St, New Carlisle OH 45344, USA — Baseball Player
**Owen, Lloyd**
Hamilton Hodell, 20 Golden Square, London W1F 9JL, England — Actor
**Owen, Michael**
Liverpool F C, Anfield Road, Liverpool L4 0TH, England — Soccer Player

# O

**Owen, Priscilla R** — Judge
US Court of Appeals, 903 San Jacinto Blvd, #400, Austin TX 78701, USA

**Owen, Randy Y** — Singer, Guitarist (Alabama)
Alabama Band Promotions, PO Box 680529, Fort Payne AL 35968, USA

**Owen, Spike D** — Baseball Player
11211 Musket Rim St, Austin TX 78738, USA

**Owen, W Thomas (Tom)** — Football Player
PO Box 3, Albany OK 74721, USA

**Owens, Billy E** — Basketball Player
608 Canary Dr, Carlisle PA 17013, USA

**Owens, C Burgess, Jr** — Football Player
1430 Telegraph Road, West Chester PA 19380, USA

**Owens, Daniel W (Dan)** — Football Player
280 Selkirk Lane, Duluth GA 30097, USA

**Owens, Edwin (Cotton)** — Auto Racing Driver, Owner
Cotton Owens Enterprises, 7921 Valley Falls Road, Spartanburg SC 29303, USA

**Owens, Eric B** — Baseball Player
22431 N 54th St, Phoenix AZ 85054, USA

**Owens, Gary** — Entertainer
I C M Partners, 10250 Constellation Blvd, #900, Los Angeles CA 90067 USA

**Owens, James P (Jim)** — Baseball Player
1426 Ramada Dr, Houston TX 77062, USA

**Owens, Joseph T (Joe)** — Football Player
2754 Highway 13 N, Columbia MS 39429, USA

**Owens, Loren E (Steve)** — Football Player
3700 W Robinson, #230, Norman OK 73072, USA

**Owens, Luke** — Football Player
3330 Warrensville Center Road, #502, Shaker Heights OH 44122, USA

**Owens, Mel T** — Football Player
13603 Marina Pointe Dr, #A612, Marina del Rey CA 90292, USA

**Owens, Morris L** — Football Player
4156 W Michigan Ave, Glendale AZ 85308, USA

**Owens, Rena** — Actress, Model
Ken Belling, PO Box 300471, Casselberry FL 32730, USA

**Owens, Robert G, Jr** — WW II Marine Corps Air Force Hero
730 Amicus Ave, Newport Beach CA 92610, USA

**Owens, Terrell E** — Football Player
5207 Sandy Shores Court, Lithonia GA 30038, USA

**Owens, Terry W** — Football Player
2524 Poovey Road SE, Decatur GA 35603, USA

**Owens, Thomas W (Tom)** — Basketball Player
19788 Wildwood Dr, West Linn OR 97068, USA

**Owens, Virginia L (Ginny)** — Singer
Street Level Artist Agency, 107 E Centre St, Warsaw IN 46580, USA

**Owings, Micah B** — Baseball Player
3208 Druid Hills Reserve Dr NE, Atlanta GA 30329, USA

**Owsley, Douglas** — Anthropologist
Smithsonian Institution, 17th & M Sts NW, Washington DC 20036, USA

**Oxenberg, Catherine** — Actress
Power Entertainment, 9100 Wilshire Blvd, Beverly Hills CA 90212, USA

**Oxford, Vern P** — Singer, Songwriter
Landmark Communications Group, 116 W Rockwood St, Rockwood TN 37854, USA

**Oxtoby, David W** — Educator
Pomona College, President's Office, 120 E Bonita, Claremont CA 91711, USA

**Oyakawa, Yoshinobu (Yoshi)** — Swimmer
4171 Hutchinson Road, Cincinnati OH 45248, USA

**Oyaya, Mary** — Actress
Coolwaters Productions, 10061 Riverside Dr, Box 531, Toluca Lake CA 91602 USA

**Oyelowo, David O** — Actor
Creative Artists Agency, 2000 Ave of Stars, #100, Los Angeles CA 90067 USA

**Oz, Amos** — Writer
Ben Gurion University, PO Box 653, 84105 Beersheva, Israel

**Oz, Frank R** — Puppeteer, Director
36 Herrick Road, Sharon CT 06069, USA

**Ozaki, Masashi** — Golfer
Bridgestone Sports, 14230 Lochridge Blvd, #G, Covington GA 30014, USA

**Ozaki, Satoshi** — Physicist
Brookhaven National Laboratory, Heavy Ion Collider, 2 Center St, Upton NY 11973, USA

**Ozawa, Ichiro** — Government Official, Japan
2-38 Fukuromachi, Mizusawashi, Iwateken 023-0814, Japan

**Ozawa, Maria** — Actress
T-Powers, 4-6-1-5F Naka Meguro, Meguro, Tokyo 153 0061, Japan

**Ozawa, Seiji** — Conductor
Vienna State Opera, Opernrig 2, 1010 Vienna, Austria

**Ozbek, Rifat** — Fashion Designer
Ozbek Ltd, 18 Haunch of Venison Yard, London W1Y 1AF, England

**Ozick, Cynthia** — Writer
34 Soundview St, New Rochelle NY 10805, USA

**Ozio, David** — Bowler
6110 Barrington Ave, Beaumont TX 77706, USA

**Ozolinsh, Sandis** — Ice Hockey Player
701 Golf Club Dr, Castle Rock CO 80108, USA

**Ozon, Francois** — Director
Films Talents, 34 Rue Du Louvre, 75001 Paris, France

**Ozuk, Charles, Jr** — WW II Army Air Corps Hero
5740 Churchill Lane, Libertyville IL 60048, USA

**Ozuna, Fritz** — Artist
6769 State Highway 27, Comfort TX 78013, USA

**Ozzie, Raymond (Ray)** — Computer Software Designer
50 Harbor St, Manchester MA 01944, USA

## Owen - Ozzie

**Paabo, Svante** — Zoo Executive
Evolutionary Anthropology Institute, Deutscher Platz 6, 04103 Leipzig, Germany

**Paasikivi, Lilli** — Opera Singer
Harrison/Parrott, 5-6 Albion Court, London W6 0QT, England

**Paavo, Jarvi** — Conductor
Cincinnati Symphony Orchestra, 1241 Elm St, Cincinnati OH 45202, USA

**Pabo, Carl O** — Biologist
Protean Futures, 475 Gate 5 Road, #210A, Sausalito CA 94965, USA

**Pabst, Augie** — Auto Racing Driver
Race Legends, 5410 Highway 73, Marshall WI 53559, USA

**Pacar, Johnny** — Actor
Innovative Artists, 1505 10th St, Santa Monica CA 90401 USA

**Pace, Betty D** — Molecular Chemist
University of Texas Medical Center, 900 W Campbell Road, Richardson TX 75080, USA

**Pace, Calvin L** — Football Player
4044 Lyon Blvd SW, Atlanta GA 30331, USA

**Pace, Darrell O** — Archery Athlete
4394 Princeton Road, Hamilton OH 45011, USA

**Pace, Dominic** — Actor
Shapiro-Lichtman, 8827 Beverly Blvd, Los Angeles CA 90048 USA

**Pace, Judy** — Actress
4139 Cloverdale Ave, Los Angeles CA 90008, USA

**Pace, Lee** — Actor
Management 360, 9111 Wilshire Blvd, Beverly Hills CA 90210 USA

**Pace, Norman R, Jr** — Microbiologist
University of Colorado, Molecular Cellular Dept, Boulder CO 80309, USA

**Pace, Orlando L** — Football Player
939 Tucker Lane, Saint Louis MO 63131, USA

**Pace, Stanley C** — Businessman
16561 Merrill Court, Chagrin Falls OH 44023, USA

**Pacella, John L** — Baseball Player
1500 Abbotsford Green Dr, Powell OH 43065, USA

**Pacey, Steven** — Actor
Artists Partnership, 101 Finsbury Pavement, London EC2A 1RS, England

**Pachal, Clayton** — Ice Hockey Player
230 Laycoe Crescent, Saskatoon SK S7S 1H5, Canada

**Pachauri, Rajendra K** — Climatologist
Tata Energy Reseach Institute, Habitat Place, New Delhi 110003, India

**Pacheco, Ferdie** — Sportscaster
4151 Gate Lane, Miami FL 33137, USA

**Pacheco, Johnny** — Musician, Composer
Universal Attractions, 135 W 26th St, #1200, New York NY 10001 USA

**Pacini, Sophie** — Concert Pianist
Komarova & Reinicke Artists, Ludwigkirchplatz 11, 10719 Berlin, Germany

**Pacino, Al** — Actor
I C M Partners, 730 5th Ave, New York NY 10019 USA

**Paciorek, James J (Jim)** — Baseball Player
9641 E Waters Edge Place, Tucson AZ 85749, USA

**Paciorek, Thomas M (Tom)** — Baseball Player
2389 Broad Creek Dr, Stone Mountain GA 30087, USA

**Packard, Kelly** — Actress, Model
21071 Placerita Canyon Road, Newhall CA 91321, USA

**Packer, A William (Billy)** — Sportscaster
Bazel Group, 115 Penn Warren Dr, #300, Brentwood TN 37027, USA

**Packer, Ann** — Writer
Random House, 1745 Broadway, #1800, New York NY 10019 USA

**Packer, David** — Actor
Creative Artists Agency, 2000 Ave of Stars, #100, Los Angeles CA 90067 USA

**Packham, Jenny** — Fashion Designer
Spectrum House, 32-34 Gordon House Road, #A, London NW5 1LP, England

**Packwood, Robert W (Bob)** — Senator, OR
Sunrise Research, 2201 Wisconsin Ave NW, #C120, Washington DC 20007, USA

**Pacquiano, Alberto D (Bobby)** — Boxer
Top Rank Inc, 3908 Howard Hughes Parkway, #580, Las Vegas NV 89169, USA

**Pacquiao, Emanuel D (Manny)** — Boxer
4th St, Seaview Heights, Lawaan, Talisay City, Cebu PH 6045, Philippines

**Pacula, Joanna** — Actress
Binder & Assoc, 1465 Lindacrest Dr, Beverly Hills CA 90210 USA

**Padalecki, Jared** — Actor
Industry Entertainment, 955 Carillo Dr, #300, Los Angeles CA 90048 USA

**Padalka, Gennady I** — Cosmonaut
Cosmonaut Training Center, Star City, 141160 Zvezdny Gorodok, Moscow Oblast, Russia

**Padberg, Eva** — Actress, Model
Performance Plus, Maximilianstr 20, 80539 Munich, Germany

**Padbury, Wendy** — Actress
Evans & Reiss, 100 Fawe Park Road, London SW15 2EA, England

**Paddio, Gerald** — Basketball Player
2801 Crystal Bay Dr, Las Vegas NV 89117, USA

**Paddock, John** — Ice Hockey Player, Coach, Executive
Philadelphia Flyers, 1st Union Center, 3601 S Broad St, Philadelphia PA 19148 USA

**Padgett, Jason** — Actor
G V A Talent Agency, 8981 W Sunset Blvd, #101, West Hollywood CA 90069, USA

**Padilha, Jose** — Director, Producer, Writer
Creative Artists Agency, 2000 Ave of Stars, #100, Los Angeles CA 90067 USA

**Padilla, Douglas (Doug)** — Track Athlete
182 N 555 W, Orem UT 84057, USA

**Padilla, Vicente D** — Baseball Player
1816 O'Henry Court, Arlington TX 76006, USA

**Padjean, Gary A** — Football Player
9314 Tower Bridge Road, Indianapolis IN 46240, USA

**Padma-Nathan, Harin** — Urologist
1245 16th St, #312, Santa Monica CA 90404, USA

**Padmore, Mark** — Opera Singer
Maxine Robertson Mgmt, 14 Forge Dr, Claygate KT10 0HR, England

**Padukone, Deepika** — Actress, Model
Katz Entertainment, Commerce Centre, Off Andheri Link Road, Andheri (W), Mumbai 400053, India

**P**

**Paabo - Padukone**

# P

**Paek, Jim** — Ice Hockey Player
119 Alexander Dr, Elyria OH 44035, USA

**Paerson, Anja** — Alpine Skier
Bjorkvagen 9, 920 64 Tarnaby, Sweden

**Paetkau, David** — Actor
Precision Entertainment, 6338 Wilshire Blvd, Los Angeles CA 90048, USA

**Paetz, Robert** — Space Scientist
7203 Macy Court, Riverside CA 92503, USA

**Paez, Jorge (Maromero)** — Boxer
Call G 650-4, Col Nueva, Mexicali 21100 , Baja, Mexico

**Paez, Richard A** — Judge
US Appellate Court, Court Building, 125 S Grand Ave, Pasadena CA 91105, USA

**Paez, Rodolfo (Fito)** — Pianist
Sony Records, 550 Madison Ave, #600, New York NY 10022 USA

**Pagan, David P (Dave)** — Baseball Player
504 10th Ave W, Nipawin SK S0E 1E0, Canada

**Pagan, Michael J** — Actor
Innovative Artists, 1505 10th St, Santa Monica CA 90401 USA

**Pagano,  Charles D (Chuck)** — Football Coach
Indianapolis Colts, 7001 W 56th St, Indianapolis IN 46254 USA

**Pagano, Lindsay** — Singer
Azoff Music, 1100 Glendon Ave, #2000, Los Angeles CA 90024, USA

**Pagano, Walter** — Actor
Artmedia, 20 Ave Rapp, 75007 Paris, France

**Page, Alan C** — Football Player, Judge
Page Education Foundation, PO Box 581254, Minneapolis MN 55458, USA

**Page, Anthony** — Director
I C M Partners, 10250 Constellation Blvd, #900, Los Angeles CA 90067 USA

**Page, Ashley** — Ballet Dancer, Choreographer
Scottish Ballet, Tramway, 25 Albert Dr, Glasgow G41 2PE, Scotland

**Page, David C** — Geneticist
Massachusetts Institute of Techonolgy, Genetics Dept, Cambridge MA 02139, USA

**Page, Ellen** — Actress
W M E Entertainment, 9601 Wilshire Blvd, #300, Beverly Hills CA 90210 USA

**Page, Erika** — Actress
Hines & Hunt Entertainment, 1213 W Magnolia Blvd, Burbank CA 91506, USA

**Page, Frank S** — Religious Leader
First Baptist Church, 200 W Main St, Taylors SC 29687, USA

**Page, Genevieve** — Actress
52 Rue de Vaugirard, 75006 Paris, France

**Page, Harrison** — Actor
S D B Partners, 315 S Beverly Dr, #411, Beverly Hills CA 90067 USA

**Page, Jimmy** — Singer (Yardbirds/Led Zeppelin)
International Talent Booking, Ariel House, 74A Charlotte St, #100 London W1T 4QJ, England

**Page, Joanna** — Actress
Independent Talent Group, 40 Whitfield St, London W1T 2RH, England

**Page, Larry** — Businessman, Computer Scientist
Google Inc, 1600 Amphitheatre Parkway, #41, Mountain View CA 94043, USA

**Page, Michael** — Equestrian
PO Box 229, North Salem NY 10560, USA

**Page, Michael R (Mike)** — Baseball Player
599 Briarcliff Dr, Woodruff SC 29388, USA

**Page, Michelle** — Actress
House of Representatives, 1434 6th St, #1, Santa Monica CA 90401 USA

**Page, Pierre** — Ice Hockey Coach
Anaheim Ducks, 2695 E Katella Ave, Anaheim CA 92806 USA

**Page, Sam** — Actor
Inphenate, 9701 Wilshire Blvd, #1000, Beverly Hills CA 90212 USA

**Page, Solomon** — Football Player
9302 Vista Circle, Irving TX 75063, USA

**Page, Steven** — Singer, Guitarist (Barenaked Ladies)
Paradigm Agency, 360 Park Ave S, #1600, New York NY 10010 USA

**Page, Tim** — Journalist
Washington Post, Editorial Dept, 1150 15th St NW, Washington DC 20071, USA

**Pagel, Karl D** — Baseball Player
2698 N Ellis St, Chandler AZ 85224, USA

**Pagel, Mike J** — Football Player
3263 Millstone Creek Road, Lancaster SC 29720, USA

**Pagels, Elaine H** — Theologian
Princeton University, Religion Dept, Princeton NJ 08544, USA

**Pagett, Nicola** — Actress
Art Work Entertainment, 5900 Wilshire Blvd, #2900, Los Angeles CA 90036, USA

**Paglia, Camille** — Writer, Educator
University of the Arts, Humanities Dept, 320 S Broad St, Philadelphia PA 19102, USA

**Pagliarulo, Michael T (Mike)** — Baseball Player
11 Fieldstone Dr, Winchester MA 01890, USA

**Pagonis, William G** — Army General
202 Smalstig Road, Evans City PA 16033, USA

**Pahang** — Sultan, Malaysia
Istana Abu Bakar, Pekan, Pahang, Malaysia

**Pahlavi, Fara Diba** — Empress, Iran
Kambiz Atabai, PO Box 2931, New York NY 10185, USA

**Pahlsson, O Samuel (Sammy)** — Ice Hockey Player
9429 Tartan Ridge Blvd, Dublin OH 43017, USA

**Pahud, Emmanuel** — Concert Flutist
Opus 3 Artists, 470 Park Ave S, #900N, New York NY 10016 USA

**Pahukoa, Jeff K** — Football Player
2612 79th Ave NE, Everett WA 98258, USA

**Paich, David F** — Singer, Keyboardist (Toto)
Monterey International, 200 W Superior St, #202, Chicago IL 60654 USA

**Paiement, Rosaire W** — Ice Hockey Player
3351 S Palm Aire Dr, #301, Pompano Beach FL 33069, USA

**Paiement, Wilf** — Ice Hockey Player
1064 Streambank Dr, Mississauga ON L5H 3Z1, Canada

**Paige Kent, Heather** — Actress
Paradigm Agency, 360 N Crescent Dr, North Building, Beverly Hills CA 90210 USA

**Paige, Amanda** — Model
Playboy Promotions, 9346 Civic Center Dr, #200, Beverly Hills CA 90210 USA
**Paige, Elaine** — Singer, Actress
Douglas Gorman Rothacker Wilhelm, 1501 Broadway, #703, New York NY 10036 USA
**Paige, Janis** — Actress
1700 Rising Glen Road, Los Angeles CA 90069, USA
**Paige, Jennifer** — Singer, Songwriter
Great Scott Productions, 4750 Lincoln Blvd, #229, Marina del Rey CA 90292, USA
**Paige, Peter** — Actor
Creative Artists Agency, 2000 Ave of Stars, #100, Los Angeles CA 90067 USA
**Paige, Stephone** — Football Player
8293 N Paula Ave, Fresno CA 93720, USA
**Paige, Tony** — Football Player
208 Mowbray Road, Silver Spring MD 20904, USA
**Paik Kun Woo** — Concert Pianist
Worldwide Artists, 12 Rosebery, Thornton Heath, Surrey CR7 8PT, England
**Pailes, William A** — Astronaut
411 S Cedar Ridge Circle, Robinson TX 76706, USA
**Paine, John** — Singer, Guitarist (Brothers Four)
Bob Flick Productions, 300 Vine St, #14, Seattle WA 98121, USA
**Painter, John Mark** — Musician (Fleming & John)
Michael Dixon Mgmt, 119 Pebblecreek Road, Franklin TN 37064, USA
**Painter, Lance T** — Baseball Player
3561 E Loma Vista St, Gilbert AZ 85295, USA
**Pais, Josh** — Actor
Innovative Artists, 1505 10th St, Santa Monica CA 90401 USA
**Paisley, Brad** — Singer
Schmidt Relations, 3012 Business Park Circle, #500, Goodlettsville TN 37072, USA
**Paisley, David** — Actor
Associated International Mgmt, 7 Hatton Garden, #400, London EC1N 8AD, England
**Pak, Charles** — Medical Researcher
University of Texas Southwestern Medical Center, 5323 Harry Hines Blvd, Dallas TX 75390 USA
**Pak, Se Ri** — Golfer
7926 Versilia Dr, Orlando FL 32836, USA
**Paksas, Rolandus** — President, Lithuania
Liberal Union, Radvilaites Gatve 1, #210, 01124 Vilnius, Lithuania
**Palahniuk, Chuck** — Writer, Actor
United Talent Agency, U T A Plaza, 9336 Civic Center Dr, Beverly Hills CA 90210 USA
**Palance, Holly** — Actress
98 Millstone Road, Brewster MA 02631, USA
**Palast, Greg** — Writer
E P Dutton, 375 Hudson St, New York NY 10014 USA
**Palastra, Joseph T, Jr** — Army General
RR 1 Box 267, Myrtle MO 65778, USA
**Palatas, Cameron** — Actor
New Wave Entertainment, 2660 W Olive Ave, Burbank CA 91505 USA
**Palau, Doug** — Producer, Writer
A P A Talent & Literary Agency, 405 S Beverly Dr, #300, Beverly Hills CA 90212 USA
**Palau, Luis** — Evangelist
Luis Palau Evangelistic Assn, 1500 NW 167th Place, Beaverton OR 97006, USA
**Palazzari, Doug** — Ice Hockey Player, Executive
4370 Dynasty Dr, Colorado Springs CO 80918, USA
**Palazzi, Togo A** — Basketball Player
84 Framingham Road, Southborough MA 01772, USA
**Palden Namgyal** — Prince, Sikkim
J P Morgan Chase, 270 Park Ave, #1200, New York NY 10017, USA
**Paleczny, Piotr** — Concert Pianist
Chopin Music Academy, Ul Okolnik 2, 00 368 Warsaw, Poland
**Palekar, Amol** — Actor, Director
Chire Bandee, 10th N S Road, J V P D Scheme, Mumbai MS 400049, India
**Palelei, Si'ulagi J (Lonnie)** — Football Player
1808 SW Chief Circle, Blue Springs MO 64015, USA
**Palermaa, Osku** — Bowler
Storm Products, 165 S 8th W, Brigham City UT 84302, USA
**Palermo, Stephen M (Steve)** — Baseball Umpire
5102 W 143rd Terrace, Overland Park KS 66224, USA
**Palesh, Shirley** — Baseball Player
120 Grand Ave, #307, Wausau WI 54403, USA
**Paley, Albert R** — Sculptor
Paley Studio, 25 N Washington St, Rochester NY 14614, USA
**Paley, Michael** — Religious Leader, Rabbi
Jewish Resource Center, 130 E 59th St, New York NY 10022, USA
**Palffy, Zigmund (Ziggy)** — Ice Hockey Player
H K 36 Skalica Clementisova 50, 90901 Skalica, Slovakia
**Palicki, Adrianne** — Actress
W M E Entertainment, 9601 Wilshire Blvd, #300, Beverly Hills CA 90210 USA
**Palin, Michael E** — Actor, Comedian, Writer (Monty Python)
Mayday Mgmt, 34 Tavistock St, London WC2E 7PB, England
**Palin, Sarah L H** — Governor, Alaska
Alive Communications, 7680 Goddard St, #200, Colorado Springs CO 80920, USA
**Palis, Jacob** — Mathematician
Instituto Matematica, Estrrada Castornina 110, Rio de Janeiro 22460 320 RJ, Brazil
**Palkiewicz, Jacek** — Explorer
Via Filzi 18, 36022 Cassola Vicenza, Italy
**Pall, Donn S** — Baseball Player
8001 Waterford Lakes Dr, #2311, Charlotte NC 28210, USA
**Pall, Olga Scarzezzini-** — Alpine Skier
Fahrenweg 28, 6060 Absam, Austria
**Palladino, Aleksa** — Actress, Singer
Gersh Agency, 9465 Wilshire Blvd, #600, Beverly Hills CA 90212 USA
**Palladino, Daniel** — Producer, Writer
Creative Artists Agency, 2000 Ave of Stars, #100, Los Angeles CA 90067 USA
**Palladino, Erik** — Actor, Producer, Writer
Coronel Group, 1100 Glendon Ave, #1700, Los Angeles CA 90046, USA
**Palladio, Sam** — Actor
W M E Entertainment, 9601 Wilshire Blvd, #300, Beverly Hills CA 90210 USA

Paige - Palladio

**Palleroni, Sergio** — Architect
University of Texas, Architecture School, Austin TX 78712, USA

**Palli, Anne-Marie** — Golfer
7477 E Cannon Dr, Scottsdale AZ 85258, USA

**Pallone, David M (Dave)** — Baseball Umpire
1610 Little Raven St, #515, Denver CO 80202, USA

**Pally, Adam** — Actor
Creative Artists Agency, 2000 Ave of Stars, #100, Los Angeles CA 90067 USA

**Palm, Richard P (Mike)** — Baseball Player
21 Riverview Place, Scituate MA 02066, USA

**Palm, Siegfried** — Concert Cellist
Gerhild Baron Mgmt, Dornbacher Str 41/III/3, 1170 Vienna, Austria

**Palmateer, Mike** — Ice Hockey Player
30 Simmons Crescent, Aurora ON L4G 6B5, Canada

**Palmaz, Julio C** — Inventor (Intravascular Stent)
University of Texas Health & Science Center, 7703 Floyd Curl Dr, San Antonio TX 78229, USA

**Palmeiro Corrales, Rafael C** — Baseball Player
5216 Reims Court, Colleyville TX 76034, USA

**Palmeiro, Orlando** — Baseball Player
11991 SW 103rd Terrace, Miami FL 33186, USA

**Palmer, Amanda** — Singer, Songwriter
Agency Group Ltd, 1880 Century Park E, #711, Los Angeles CA 90067 USA

**Palmer, Arnold D** — Golfer
9007 Bay Hill Blvd, Orlando FL 32819, USA

**Palmer, Betsy** — Actress
3 Glen Hill Road, #304, Danbury CT 6811, USA

**Palmer, Brad** — Ice Hockey Player
Box 544, Lake Cowichan BC V0R 2G0, Canada

**Palmer, Carl** — Drummer (Emerson Lake & Palmer, Asia)
Talent Consultants International, 105 Shad Row, #B, Piermont NY 10968 USA

**Palmer, Carson** — Football Player
25052 Adelanto Dr, Laguna Niguel CA 92677, USA

**Palmer, Chris** — Football Player, Coach
Houston Texans, 2 Reliant Park, Houston TX 77054 USA

**Palmer, Dave R** — Army General, Educator
4531 Blue Ridge Dr, Belton TX 76513, USA

**Palmer, David L** — Football Player
4301 Avenue Q, Birmingham AL 35208, USA

**Palmer, David W** — Baseball Player
61 Sherman Ave, Glens Falls NY 12801, USA

**Palmer, Dean W** — Baseball Player
3943 Old Mill Run, Tallahassee FL 32312, USA

**Palmer, Diana** — Writer
Harlequin Enterprises, 225 Duncan Mill Road, Don Mills ON MJB JK9, Canada

**Palmer, Geoffrey** — Actor
Marmont Mgmt, Langham House, 302/8 Regent St, London W1R 5AL, England

**Palmer, Geoffrey W R** — Prime Minister, New Zealand
63 Roxburgh St, Mount Victoria, Wellington 6011, New Zealand

**Palmer, Gregg** — Actor
5726 Graves Ave, Encino CA 91316, USA

**Palmer, James A (Jim)** — Baseball Player, Sportscaster
239 Sanford Ave, Palm Beach FL 33480, USA

**Palmer, Jeffrey D (Jeff)** — Molecular Biologist
Indiana University, Molecular Biology Dept, Bloomington IN 47405, USA

**Palmer, Jesse J** — Football Player, Sportscaster
8052 Hopkins Lane, Indianapolis IN 46250, USA

**Palmer, Patsy** — Actress
Qtalent, 161 Drury Lane, #300, London WC2B 5PN, England

**Palmer, Peter W** — Actor
PO Box 482, Simpsonville KY 40067, USA

**Palmer, Russell E** — Financier
Palmer Group, 3600 Market St, #530, Philadelphia PA 19104, USA

**Palmer, Ryan H** — Golfer
4909 Rockrimmon Court, Colleyville TX 76034, USA

**Palmer, Sandra** — Golfer
498 Peralta Ave, Long Beach CA 90803, USA

**Palmer, Teresa** — Actress
Management 360, 9111 Wilshire Blvd, Beverly Hills CA 90210 USA

**Palmer, Violet** — Basketball Referee
N B A Referees Assn, 1455 Pennsylvania Ave NW, #225, Washington DC 20004, USA

**Palmer, Walter** — Basketball Player
87 South St, Rockport MA 01966, USA

**Palmer, William R** — Publisher
Detroit News, Publisher's Office, 615 W Lafayette Blvd, Detroit MI 48226, USA

**Palmer, Zoie** — Actress
Characters Talent Mgmt, 8 Elm St, Toronto ON M5G 1G7, Canada

**Palmieri, Eddie** — Jazz Pianist, Singer
Universal Attractions, 135 W 26th St, #1200, New York NY 10001 USA

**Palminteri, Chazz** — Actor
W M E Entertainment, 1325 Ave of Americas, New York NY 10019 USA

**Palmisano, Samuel J** — Businessman
I B M Corp, 1 North Castle Dr, #2, Armonk NY 10504, USA

**Palombi, Ron** — Bowler
227 E 29th St, Erie PA 16504, USA

**Palomino, Carlos** — Boxer
4200 Longridge Ave, Studio City CA 91604, USA

**Palsson, Thorsteinn** — Prime Minister, Iceland
Hateigsvegur 40, 105 Reykjavik, Iceland

**Paltrow, Gwyneth** — Actress, Model, Singer
Brillstein Entertainment Partners, 9150 Wilshire Blvd, #350, Beverly Hills CA 90212 USA

**Paltrow, Jake** — Director
United Talent Agency, U T A Plaza, 9336 Civic Center Dr, Beverly Hills CA 90210 USA

**Palumba, Joseph C (Joe)** — Football Player
927 Old Garth Road, Charlottesville VA 22901, USA

**Pampling, Rodney (Rod)** — Golfer
9 Campbell Court, Lewisville TX 75077, USA

| | |
|---|---|
| **Pamuk, Orhan** | Nobel Literature Laureate |
| Purtelas Mah Beyoglu, Beyoglu Istanbul, Turkey | |
| **Pan Hong** | Actress |
| Omei Film Studio, Tonghui Menwai, Chengdu City, Sichuan Province, China | |
| **Panabaker, Danielle** | Actress |
| Management 360, 9111 Wilshire Blvd, Beverly Hills CA 90210 USA | |
| **Panabaker, Kay** | Actress |
| Sanders/Armstrong/Caserta Mgmt, 2120 Colorado Ave, #120, Santa Monica CA 90404 USA | |
| **Panafieu, Bernard L A Cardinal** | Religious Leader |
| Archdiocese, 14 Place du Colonel-Edon, 13284 Marseille Cedex 07, France | |
| **Pancake, Sam** | Actor |
| Pakula/King, 9229 W Sunset Blvd, #315, West Hollywood CA 90069 USA | |
| **Pandey, Chunky** | Actor |
| 1 A/B Monisha Apts, Saint Andrews Road, Bandra, Mumbai MS 400050, India | |
| **Pandolfo, Jay** | Ice Hockey Player |
| 3 Meadowcroft Road, Burlington MA 01803, USA | |
| **Pandor, Henk** | Artist |
| 3422 Harrison St SE, Portland OR 97214, USA | |
| **Panetta, Leon E** | Government Official; Representative, NY |
| Defense Department, Pentagon, Washington DC 20301 USA | |
| **Panettiere, Hayden** | Actress, Singer |
| Brookside Artists Mgmt, 250 W 57th St, #2303, New York NY 10107, USA | |
| **Panettiere, Jansen** | Actor |
| C E S D, 10635 Santa Monica Blvd, #130, Los Angeles CA 90025 USA | |
| **Pang Qing** | Figure Skater |
| Skating Association, 56 Zhonguancun South St, Beijing 100044, China | |
| **Pang, Darren R** | Ice Hockey Player |
| 7439 Washington Ave, Saint Louis MO 63130, USA | |
| **Panic, Milan** | Prime Minister, Yugoslavia; Businessman |
| I C N Pharmaceuticals, 3300 Hyland Ave, Costa Mesa CA 92626, USA | |
| **Panichas, George A** | Writer |
| PO Box AB, College Park MD 20741, USA | |
| **Panichgul, Thakoon** | Fashion Designer |
| 270 Lafayette St, #810, New York NY 10012, USA | |
| **Panikkar, Sean** | Opera Singer |
| I M G Artists, Hogarth Business Park, Chiswick, London W4 2TH, England | |
| **Panis, Olivier** | Auto Racing Driver |
| Bar Team, Box 5014, Brackley, Northhamptonshire NN13, England | |
| **Panish, Morton B** | Physical Chemist |
| 52 Baldwin Road, Freeport ME 04032, USA | |
| **Panjabi, Archana (Archie)** | Actress |
| Biscuit Boy Productions, PO Box 13467, London NW4 1WQ, England | |
| **Panke Reithofer, Norbert** | Businessman |
| Bayerische Motoren Werke, Petuelring 130, 80788 Munich, Germany | |
| **Pankey, Irvin L (Irv)** | Football Player |
| 348 Walker St, Aberdeen MD 21001, USA | |
| **Pankin, Stuart** | Actor |
| Abrams Artists, 9200 W Sunset Blvd, #1125, West Hollywood CA 90069 USA | |
| **Pankovits, James F (Jim)** | Baseball Player |
| 6014 Catalina Dr, #115, North Myrtle Beach SC 29582, USA | |
| **Pankow, James C** | Trombone Player (Chicago), Songwriter |
| 3826 Bowsprit Circle, Westlake Village CA 91361, USA | |
| **Pankow, John** | Actor |
| Gersh Agency, 9465 Wilshire Blvd, #600, Beverly Hills CA 90212 USA | |
| **Panni, Marcello** | Conductor, Composer |
| 3 Piazza Borghese, 00186 Rome, Italy | |
| **Panoff, Robert** | Nuclear Engineer |
| 1140 Connecticut Ave NW, Washington DC 20036, USA | |
| **Panos, Zois (Joe)** | Football Player |
| 360 Rustic Lane, Hartland WI 53029, USA | |
| **Panova, Elena** | Circus Aerialist |
| Cirque du Soleil, 8400 2nd Ave, Montreal QC H1Z 4M6, Canada | |
| **Panozzo, Chuck** | Bassist (Styx) |
| Alliance Artists, 1225 Northmeadow Parkway, #100, Roswell GA 30076, USA | |
| **Panteleev, Grigori** | Ice Hockey Player |
| 5 Commonwealth Road, Natick MA 01760, USA | |
| **Pantoliano, Joe** | Actor |
| Principal Entertainment, 130 W 42nd St, #614, New York NY 10036, USA | |
| **Panula, Jorma** | Conductor, Composer |
| Sibelius Academy, P Rautatiekatu 9, 00100 Helsinki 10, Finland | |
| **Paola** | Queen, Belgium |
| Koninklijk Palais, Rue de Brederode, 1000 Brussels, Belgium | |
| **Paoli, Cecile** | Actress |
| Agents Associes, 201 Rue du Faubourg Saint Honore, 75008 Paris, France | |
| **Paolini, Christopher** | Writer |
| Random House, 1745 Broadway, #1800, New York NY 10019 USA | |
| **Paolo, Connor** | Actor |
| Abrams Artists, 9200 W Sunset Blvd, #1125, West Hollywood CA 90069 USA | |
| **Papa, Bob** | Sportscaster |
| N F L Network, 10950 Washington Blvd, #100, Culver City CA 90232 USA | |
| **Papa, John P** | Baseball Player |
| 275 Mary Ave, Stratford CT 06614, USA | |
| **Papamichael, Phedon M** | Cinematographer |
| Innovative Artists, 1505 10th St, Santa Monica CA 90401 USA | |
| **Papas, Irene** | Actress |
| Anne Alvares Correa, 34 Rue Jouffroy d'Abbans, 75017 Paris, France | |
| **Papazian, Marty** | Actor |
| Chasen Agency, 8899 Beverly Blvd, #405, Los Angeles CA 90048 USA | |
| **Pape, Rene** | Opera, Concert Singer, Actor |
| Artists Mgmt, Dahlmannstra 9, 10629 Berlin, Germany | |
| **Papert, Seymour S** | Mathematician |
| Learning Barn, PO Box 387, Blue Hill ME 04614, USA | |
| **Papi, Stanley G (Stan)** | Baseball Player |
| 1111 W Sierra Madre Ave, Fresno CA 93705, USA | |
| **Papis, Massimiliano (Max)** | Auto Racing Driver |
| 10855 NW 33rd St, Miami FL 33172, USA | |

**P**

Pamuk - Papis

## P

**Papo, Brandon** — Actor
C E S D, 10635 Santa Monica Blvd, #130, Los Angeles CA 90025 USA

**Papoulias, Karolos** — President, Greece
President's Office, Presidential Palace, Herodes Atticus St, 10674 Athens, Greece

**Papp, Robert J, Jr** — Coast Guard Admiral
State Department, Special Representative for the Arctic Region, 2201 C St NW, Washington DC 20520, USA

**Pappalardi, Felix** — Singer, Bassist (Mountain)
Skyline Music, 2270 Maiden Lane SW, Roanoke VA 24015, USA

**Pappano, Antonio** — Conductor
I M G Artists, Hogarth Business Park, Chiswick, London W4 2TH, England

**Pappas, Deane** — Golfer
4409 Stoney Dr, Jonesboro AR 72404, USA

**Pappas, George** — Bowler
21108 Blakely Shores Dr, Cornelius NC 28031, USA

**Pappas, Milton S (Milt)** — Baseball Player
319 Aspen Dr, Beecher IL 60401, USA

**Pappin, James J (Jim)** — Ice Hockey Player
48947 Greasewood Lane, Palm Desert CA 92260, USA

**Paquette, Craig H** — Baseball Player
16626 S Magenta Road, Phoenix AZ 85048, USA

**Paquin, Anna** — Actress
W M E Entertainment, 9601 Wilshire Blvd, #300, Beverly Hills CA 90210 USA

**Paradis, Vanessa** — Model, Singer, Actress
Agence Artiste Adequat, 108 Rue Reaumur, 75002 Paris, France

**Paradise, Robert (Bob)** — Ice Hockey Player
1303 Beechwood Place, Saint Paul MN 55116, USA

**Parazaider, Walter** — Woodwind Musician (Chicago)
Front Line Mgmt, 1100 Glendon Ave, #2000, Los Angeles CA 90024 USA

**Parazynski, Scott E** — Astronaut
2015 Wroxton Road, Houston TX 77005, USA

**Parcells, Duane C (Bill)** — Football Coach, Executive
Miami Dolphins, 7500 SW 30th St, Davie FL 33314 USA

**Pardee, Arthur B** — Biochemist
987 Memorial Dr, #271, Cambridge MA 02138, USA

**Pardee, John** — Producer
Paradigm Agency, 360 N Crescent Dr, North Building, Beverly Hills CA 90210 USA

**Pardes, Herbert** — Psychiatrist
New York Presbyterian Hospital, 161 Fort Washington Ave, New York NY 10032, USA

**Pardo, Etela** — Actress
Gavin Barker Assoc, 2D Wimpole St, London W1G 0EB, England

**Pardo, J D** — Actor
Innovative Artists, 1505 10th St, Santa Monica CA 90401 USA

**Pardo, Jimmy** — Actor, Comedian, Writer
Gersh Agency, 9465 Wilshire Blvd, #600, Beverly Hills CA 90212 USA

**Pardue, Kip** — Actor
Roar Mgmt, 9701 Wilshire Blvd, #800, Beverly Hills CA 90212 USA

**Pardue, Mary-Lou** — Biologist
Massachusetts Institute of Technology, Biology Dept, Cambridge MA 02139, USA

**Pare, Jessica** — Actress
United Talent Agency, U T A Plaza, 9336 Civic Center Dr, Beverly Hills CA 90210 USA

**Pare, Michael** — Actor
Mavrick Artists Agency, 6100 Wilshire Blvd, #550, Los Angeles CA 90048, USA

**Pare, Richard** — Photographer
43 Brunswick Road, Montclair NJ 07042, USA

**Paredes, Marisa** — Actress
Alsire Garcia Maroto, Pl Espana 18, #15, 28008 Madrid, Spain

**Parekh, Asha** — Actress
Azad Road, Juhu, Mumbai MS 400049, India

**Paremski, Natasha** — Concert Pianist
I M G Artists, Hogarth Business Park, Chiswick, London W4 2TH, England

**Parent, Bernard M (Bernie)** — Ice Hockey Player
Schooner Island Marina, 5100 Lake Road, #H-01, Wildwood NJ 08260, USA

**Parent, Mark A** — Baseball Player
8829 Midview Dr, Palo Cedro CA 96073, USA

**Paret, Peter** — Historian
Institute for Advanced Studies, Historical Studies School, Princeton NJ 08540, USA

**Paretsky, Sara N** — Writer
5831 S Blackstone Ave, Chicago IL 60637, USA

**Parfit, Derek A** — Philosopher
All Souls College, Philosophy Dept, Oxford OX1 4AL, England

**Parfitt, Judy** — Actress
Conway Van Gelder Grant, 8-12 Broadwick St, #300, London W1F 8HW, England

**Pargo, Jannero** — Basketball Player
3280 Timberwood Lane, Riverwoods IL 60015, USA

**Parham, Lennon** — Producer, Writer, Actress
Mosiac Media Group, 9200 W Sunset Blvd, #1000, Los Angeles CA 90069 USA

**Parillaud, Anne** — Actress
Artmedia, 20 Ave Rapp, 75007 Paris, France

**Parilli, Vito (Babe)** — Football Player, Coach
8060 E Girard Ave, #218, Denver CO 80231, USA

**Paris, Jhevon** — Singer, Songwriter
Agency Group Ltd, 142 W 57th St, #600, New York NY 10019 USA

**Paris, Kelly J** — Baseball Player
42 Warwick Circle, #111, Clover SC 29710, USA

**Paris, Mica** — Singer
Richard Walters, PO Box 2789, Toluca Lake CA 91610 USA

**Paris, Myrna** — Opera Singer
Columbia Artists Mgmt Inc, 5 Columbus Circle, 1790 Broadway, #1600, New York NY 10019 USA

**Paris, Paulin** — Artist
13703 Cordary Ave, #6, Hawthorne CA 90250, USA

**Paris, Twila** — Singer, Songwriter
Proper Mgmt, PO Box 150867, Nashville TN 37215, USA

**Paris, William (Bubba)** — Football Player
225 S Sonrisa St, Tracy CA 95391, USA

**Parise, Jean-Paul (J P)** — Ice Hockey Player
3814 Raspberry Ridge Road NW, Prior Lake MN 55372, USA

**Papo - Parise**

**Parise, Vanessa** — Actress
Lara Rosenstock Mgmt, 8371 Blackburn Ave, #1, Los Angeles CA 90048, USA
**Parise, Zachary J (Zach)** — Ice Hockey Player
78 Blackburne Terrace, West Orange NJ 07052, USA
**Parish, Diane** — Actress
C A M, 111 Shoreditch High St, #400, London E1 6JN, England
**Parish, Robert L** — Basketball Player
6609 Virgo Dr, Shreveport LA 71119, USA
**Parish, Sarah** — Actress
Another Tongue, 10-11 D'Arblay St, London W1F 8DS, England
**Parisi, Angelo** — Judo Athlete
Judo Institute, 21-25 Ave de la Porte de Chatillon, 75680 Paris, France
**Parisse, Annie** — Actress
Gersh Agency, 9465 Wilshire Blvd, #600, Beverly Hills CA 90212 USA
**Parizeau, Michel G** — Ice Hockey Player
250 Rue Chauveau, Drummondville QC J2C 6L2, Canada
**Park Chan-Wook** — Director
Moho Films, 3002 S K M CITY, 869 Janghang-Dong, Ilsandong-Gu, Gyeonggi-Do 410 839, South Korea
**Park Chu-Young** — Soccer Player
Football Association, 1-131 Sinmunno, 2-Ga Jongno-Gu, Seoul 110 062, South Korea
**Park Geun-Hye** — President, South Korea
President's Office, Chong Wa Dae, 1 Sejong-no, Seoul 110 820, South Korea
**Park Hye-Won** — Speed Skater
Skating Union, 88 Bangyee-Dong, Songpaku, Seoul 138 749, South Korea
**Park Seung-Hi** — Speed Skater
Skating Union, 88 Bangyee-Dong, Songpaku, Seoul 138 749, South Korea
**Park, Chan Ho** — Baseball Player
10 Hallcrest Dr, Ladera Ranch CA 92694, USA
**Park, D Bradford (Brad)** — Ice Hockey Player
20 Stanley Road, Lynnfield MA 01940, USA
**Park, Ernest C (Ernie)** — Football Player
3160 Private Road 1101, Clyde TX 79510, USA
**Park, Grace** — Golfer
8298 E Tallfeather Dr, Scottsdale AZ 85255, USA
**Park, Grace** — Actress
Characters Talent Agency, 8 Elm St, Toronto ON M5G 1G7, Canada
**Park, Inbee** — Golfer
Ladies Pro Golf Assn, 100 International Golf Dr, Daytona Beach FL 32124 USA
**Park, James T** — Microbiologist
11 Bradford Road, Weston MA 02493, USA
**Park, Linda** — Actress
Seven Summits, 8906 W Olympic Blvd, Beverly Hills CA 90211, USA
**Park, Megan** — Actress
Paradigm Agency, 360 N Crescent Dr, North Building, Beverly Hills CA 90210 USA
**Park, Merle F** — Ballerina
Royal Ballet School, 144 Talgarth Road, London W14 9DE, England
**Park, Michael** — Actor
Innovative Artists, 1505 10th St, Santa Monica CA 90401 USA
**Park, Nicholas W (Nick)** — Animator, Director
Aardvark Animation, Gas Ferry Road, Bristol B51 6UN, England
**Park, Ray** — Actor
Priluck Co, 1230 Montana Ave, Santa Monica CA 90403, USA
**Park, Richard** — Ice Hockey Player
6416 Vista Pacifica, Rancho Palos Verdes CA 90275, USA
**Park, Steve** — Auto Racing Driver
261 Indian Trail Road, Mooresville NC 28117, USA
**Park, Sydney** — Actress
Silver Lining Entertainment, 421 S Beverly Drive, #700, Beverly Hills CA 90212, USA
**Parke, Dorothy** — Actress
A K A Talent Agency, 6310 San Vicente Blvd, #200, Los Angeles CA 90048, USA
**Parke, Evan** — Actor
Essential Talent, 6399 Wilshire Blvd, #400, Los Angeles CA 90048, USA
**Parkening, Christopher** — Concert Guitarist
I M G Artists, Carnegie Hall Tower, 152 W 57th St, #500, New York NY 10019 USA
**Parker Kennedy, Jessica** — Actress
Play Mgmt, 807 Powell St, #220, Vancouver BC V6A 1H7, Canada
**Parker, Alan W** — Director
United Talent Agency, U T A Plaza, 9336 Civic Center Dr, Beverly Hills CA 90210 USA
**Parker, Andrea** — Actress
A P A Talent & Literary Agency, 405 S Beverly Dr, #300, Beverly Hills CA 90212 USA
**Parker, B Frank** — Football Player
RR 4 Box 83-2, Broken Bow OK 74728, USA
**Parker, Barrington D, Jr** — Judge
US Court of Appeals, Moynihan Courthouse, 500 Pearl St, New York NY 10007, USA
**Parker, Candace** — Basketball Player
Los Angeles Sparks, 888 S Figueroa St, #2010, Los Angeles CA 90017 USA
**Parker, Caryl Mack** — Singer
Rancho Divine Productions, 9 Music Square S, #108, Nashville TN 37203, USA
**Parker, Christian** — Baseball Player
10101 Mesa Arriba Ave NE, Albuquerque NM 87111, USA
**Parker, Christopher** — Actor
I C M Partners, 10250 Constellation Blvd, #900, Los Angeles CA 90067 USA
**Parker, Craig** — Actor
Karen Kay Mgmt, PO Box 446, Auckland 1140, New Zealand
**Parker, David G (Dave)** — Baseball Player
Cobra Industries, 4038 Oak Tree Court, Loveland OH 45140, USA
**Parker, Denise** — Archery Athlete
2821 S Lakeview Dr, Salt Lake City UT 84109, USA
**Parker, Eugene N** — Physicist
1006 Gardner Road, Flossmoor IL 60422, USA
**Parker, Franklin** — Writer
Western Carolina University, Education & Psychology Dept, Cullowhee NC 28723, USA
**Parker, Glenn A** — Football Player, Sportscaster
5420 N Campbell Ave, Tucson AZ 85718, USA
**Parker, Graham** — Singer, Guitarist
Roots Agency, 177 Woodland Ave, Westwood NJ 07675, USA

**Parker, Harry W** — Baseball Player
7180 Ellerson Mill Circle, #B, Mechanicsville VA 23111, USA

**Parker, Jabari A** — Basketball Player
Milwaukee Bucks, Bradley Center, 1001 N 4th St, #2, Milwaukee WI 53203 USA

**Parker, Jameson** — Actor
1604 N Vista Ave, Los Angeles CA 90046, USA

**Parker, Jamie** — Actor
Rights House, Drury House, 34-43 Russell St, London WC2B 5HA, England

**Parker, Jeff** — Editorial Cartoonist
Florida Today, Editorial Dept, 1 Gannett Plaza, Melbourne FL 32940, USA

**Parker, Jo Ellen Johnson** — Educator
Sweet Briar College, President's Office, Sweet Briar VA 24595, USA

**Parker, Jon Kimura** — Concert Pianist
Opus 3 Artists, 470 Park Ave S, #900N, New York NY 10016 USA

**Parker, Juqua D** — Football Player
5182 Dungarvin Road, Warriors Mark PA 16877, USA

**Parker, Kelly** — Soccer Player
Canadian Soccer, Place Soccer Canada, 237 Metcalfe St, Ottawa ON K2P 1R2, Canada

**Parker, Kristal** — Golfer
5675 E Bent Tree Dr, Scottsdale AZ 85266, USA

**Parker, Lara** — Actress
PO Box 1254, Topanga CA 90290, USA

**Parker, Lucinda** — Artist
Laura Russo Gallery, 805 NW 21st St, Portland OR 97209, USA

**Parker, Maceo** — Jazz Saxophonist
Coda Agency, 229 Shoreditch High St, London E1 6PJ, England

**Parker, Mark** — Businessman
Nike Inc, 1 SW Bowerman Dr, Beaverton OR 97005, USA

**Parker, Mary-Louise** — Actress
W M E Entertainment, 1325 Ave of Americas, New York NY 10019 USA

**Parker, Molly** — Actress
Circle of Confusion, 315 S Beverly Dr, #201, Beverly Hills CA 90212, USA

**Parker, Nate** — Actor
W M E Entertainment, 9601 Wilshire Blvd, #300, Beverly Hills CA 90210 USA

**Parker, Nathaniel** — Actor
Independent Talent Group, 40 Whitfield St, London W1T 2RH, England

**Parker, Nicole Ari** — Actress
Gersh Agency, 41 Madison Ave, #3301, New York NY 10010 USA

**Parker, Noelle** — Actress
9300 Wilshire Blvd, #555, Beverly Hills CA 90212, USA

**Parker, Oliver** — Director, Actor
Independent Talent Group, 40 Whitfield St, London W1T 2RH, England

**Parker, Paula Jai** — Actress
Levity Entertainment, 6701 Center Drive W, #1111, Los Angeles CA 90045 USA

**Parker, Ray, Jr** — Singer, Guitarist
Paradise Artists, 2002 Hogback Road, Ann Arbor MI 48015, USA

**Parker, Richard A (Rick)** — Baseball Player
2641 NE 74th St, Kansas City MO 64119, USA

**Parker, Riddick T, Jr** — Football Player
11226 NE 68th St, #212B, Kirkland WA 98033, USA

**Parker, Robert** — Singer, Saxophonist
Jeff Hubbard, PO Box 26334, Indianapolis IN 46226, USA

**Parker, Robert A R** — Astronaut
N A S A, Johnson Space Center, 2101 NASA Road, Houston TX 77058 USA

**Parker, Sage** — Actress
Kazarian/Measures/Ruskin, 11969 Ventura Blvd, #300, Studio City CA 91604 USA

**Parker, Sarah Jessica** — Actress, Model
Pretty Matches Productions, 1100 Ave of Americas, #G26, New York NY 10026, USA

**Parker, Scott** — Motorcyle Racing Rider
6096 Grand Blanc Road, Swartz Creek MI 48473, USA

**Parker, Scott** — Ice Hockey Player
1950 W Wolfensberger Court, Castle Rock CO 80109, USA

**Parker, Sean** — Businessman
Founders Fund, Presidio of San Francisco, 1 Letterman Dr, San Francisco CA 94129, USA

**Parker, T Jefferson** — Writer
E P Dutton, 375 Hudson St, New York NY 10014 USA

**Parker, Thomas A (Tom)** — Singer, Guitarist (Wanted)
Industry Music Group, 128 Regent Road, Hanley Stoke, Trent ST1 3AY, England

**Parker, Trey, II** — Animator, Writer
Important Films, 12910 Culver Blvd, #A, Los Angeles CA 90066, USA

**Parker, Vaughn A** — Football Player
2500 6th Ave, #107, San Diego CA 92103, USA

**Parker, W Anthony (Tony)** — Basketball Player
11214 Anaqua Springs, Boerne TX 78006, USA

**Parker, W Douglas (Doug)** — Businessman
America West Airlines, 4000 E Sky Harbor Blvd, Phoenix AZ 85034, USA

**Parker, William** — Surgeon
Duke University Medical School, Surgery Dept, 201 Trent Dr, Durham NC 27710, USA

**Parker, William N (Willie)** — Football Player
9327 Kai Dr, Beach City TX 77523, USA

**Parker, Willie E** — Football Player
Washington Redskins, 21300 Redskin Park Dr, Ashburn VA 20147 USA

**Parker-Bowles, Camilla** — Duchess of Cornwall, England
Buckingham Palace, London SW1A 1AA, England

**Parkhill, Barry** — Basketball Player
3429 Cesford Grange, Keswick VA 22947, USA

**Parkhurst, Carolyn** — Writer
Little Brown, 3 Center Plaza, #100, Boston MA 02108 USA

**Parkhurst, Heather-Elizabeth** — Actress
8491 W Sunset Blvd, #440, West Hollywood CA 90069, USA

**Parkins, Barbara** — Actress
Bis Mgmt, 12115 San Vicente Blvd, #109, Los Angeles CA 90049, USA

**Parkinson, Bradford W** — Businessman, Inventor
2360 Camino Edna, San Luis Obispo CA 93401, USA

**Parkinson, Dian** — Entertainer, Model
Jo-Ann Geffem, 3151 Cahuenga Blvd, #235, Los Angeles CA 90068, USA

**Parkinson, Mark V**
American Health Care Assn, 1201 L St NW, Washington DC 20005, USA
Governor, KS

**Parkinson, Robert L, Jr**
Abbott Laboratories, 100 Abbott Park Road, North Chicago IL 60064, USA
Businessman

**Parks, Cherokee B**
PO Box 11525, Las Vegas NV 89111, USA
Basketball Player

**Parks, David W (Dave)**
12113 Palisades Parkway, Austin TX 78732, USA
Football Player

**Parks, Francine**
Playboy Promotions, 9346 Civic Center Dr, #200, Beverly Hills CA 90210 USA
Model

**Parks, Maxie**
4545 E Norwich Ave, Fresno CA 93726, USA
Track Athlete

**Parks, Michael**
1618 N Vine St, #614, Los Angeles CA 90028, USA
Actor

**Parks, Suzan-Lori**
Steven Barclay Agency, 12 Western Ave, Petaluma CA 94952, USA
Writer

**Parks, Van Dyke**
2141 Layton St, Pasadena CA 91104, USA
Singer, Composer

**Parks, Wole**
Abrams Artists, 9200 W Sunset Blvd, #1125, West Hollywood CA 90069 USA
Actor

**Parlow, Cindy**
3911 Tamarron Circle, #101, Memphis TN 38125, USA
Soccer Player

**Parmalee, Bernard A (Bernie)**
9208 158th St, Overland Park KS 66221, USA
Football Player

**Parmenter, Charles S**
Indiana University, Chemistry Dept, Bloomington IN 47405, USA
Chemist

**Parmet, Philip (Phil)**
Paradigm Agency, 360 N Crescent Dr, North Building, Beverly Hills CA 90210 USA
Cinematographer

**Parmitano, Luca**
European Space Center, Linder Hohe, Box 906096, 51127 Cologne, Germany
Cosmonaut, Italy

**Parnell, Chris**
Mosiac Media Group, 24 Music Square W, #100, Nashville TN 37203, USA
Actor, Comedian

**Parnell, Lee Roy**
A P A Talent/Literary Agency, 3017 Poston Ave, #200, Nashville TN 37203 USA
Singer, Guitarist

**Parnell, Robert A (Bobby)**
2265 Barger Road, Salisbury NC 28146, USA
Baseball Player

**Parnevik, Jesper**
17553 SE Conch Bar Ave, Jupiter FL 33469, USA
Golfer

**Parodi, Starr**
Evolution Music, 1680 Vine St, #500, Los Angeles CA 90028, USA
Composer

**Parol, Tina**
Motown Records, 6255 W Sunset Blvd, Los Angeles CA 90028 USA
Singer, Songwriter

**Parolin, Pietro Cardinal**
Secretariat of State, Palazzo Apostolico Vaticano, 00120 Vatican City
Religious Leader

**Paronto, Chad M**
617 Benedict Road, Pittsfield MA 01201, USA
Baseball Player

**Parque, James V (Jim)**
4109 Crystal Ridge Dr SE, Puyallup WA 98372, USA
Baseball Player

**Parr, Carolyn Miller**
US Tax Court, 400 2nd St NW, Washington DC 20217, USA
Judge

**Parr, Robert G**
701 Kenmore Road, Chapel Hill NC 27514, USA
Chemist

**Parra, Derek**
14927 Treseder St, Draper UT 84020, USA
Speed Skater

**Parra, Manuel A (Manny)**
3142 Halverson Way, Roseville CA 95661, USA
Baseball Player

**Parrella, John L**
8161 Regency Dr, Pleasanton CA 94588, USA
Football Player

**Parrett, Jeffrey D (Jeff)**
2765 Pinckard Pike, Versailles KY 40383, USA
Baseball Player

**Parrett, William**
Deloitte Touche Tohmatsu, 433 Country Club Road, New Canaan CT 06840, USA
Businessman

**Parrilla, Lana**
Paradigm Agency, 360 N Crescent Dr, North Building, Beverly Hills CA 90210 USA
Actress

**Parris, Fred**
First Class Entertainment, 483 Ridgewood Road, Maplewood NJ 07040, USA
Singer (Five Satins)

**Parris, Gary T**
5170 9th St, Vero Beach FL 32966, USA
Football Player

**Parris, Steven M (Steve)**
403 Rookery Court, Joliet IL 60431, USA
Baseball Player

**Parris, Teyonah**
A P A Talent & Literary Agency, 405 S Beverly Dr, #300, Beverly Hills CA 90212 USA
Actress

**Parrish, Bernard P (Bernie)**
4129 NW 32nd St, Gainesville FL 32605, USA
Football Player

**Parrish, Hunter**
Management 360, 9111 Wilshire Blvd, Beverly Hills CA 90210 USA
Actor

**Parrish, Janel**
Rough Diamond Management, 1424 N Kings Road, Los Angeles CA 90069, USA
Actress, Singer

**Parrish, John H**
325 Charles Road, Lancaster PA 17603, USA
Baseball Player

**Parrish, Lance M**
1101 Chateau Lane, Nashville TN 37215, USA
Baseball Player

**Parrish, Larry A**
234 Green Haven Lane W, Dundee FL 33838, USA
Baseball Player, Manager

**Parrish, Lemar R**
52 Brittany Way, Palmetto GA 30268, USA
Football Player

**Parros, Peter**
Amsel Eisenstadt Frazier, 5055 Wilshire Blvd, #865, Los Angeles CA 90036 USA
Actor

**Parros, Rick U**
15932 E Lehigh Circle, Aurora CO 80013, USA
Football Player

**Parrott, Andrew H**
Allied Artists, 42 Montpelier Square, London SW7 1JZ, England
Conductor

**Parrott, Michael E A (Mike)**
PO Box 1264, Lyons CO 80540, USA
Baseball Player

**Parry, Craig**
5139 Latrobe Dr, Windermere FL 34786, USA
Golfer

**Parry, Edward (Ed)** — Basketball Player
6152 Benoit Road, Clay MI 48001, USA
**Parry, Richard Reed** — Musician (Arcade Fire)
Billions Corp, 3522 W Armitage Ave, Chicago IL 60647 USA
**Parry, Robert T** — Government Official, Financier
11362 Barranca Road, Santa Rosa Valley CA 93012, USA
**Pars, Krisztian** — Track Athlete
Magyar Atletikai Szovetseg, Istvanmezei Ut 1-3, 1146 Budapest, Hungary
**Parseghian, Ara R** — Football Coach, Sportscaster
51767 Oakbrook Court, Granger IN 46530, USA
**Parshall, George W** — Chemist
2401 Pennsylvania Ave, #714, Wilmington DE 19806, USA
**Parsky, Gerald L** — Attorney
Aurora Capital Partners, 1800 Century Park East, Los Angeles CA 90067, USA
**Parsley, Ambrosia** — Singer (Shivaree)
Zoe/Rounder Records, 1 Rounder Way, Burlington MA 01803, USA
**Parsley, Clifford D (Cliff)** — Football Player
7601 E 134th Terrace, Grandview MO 64030, USA
**Parsons, Alan** — Musician
World Entertainment Assoc, 8815 Conroy Windermere Road, #407, Orlando FL 32835, USA
**Parsons, Chandler** — Basketball Player
Dallas Mavericks, Pavilion, 2909 Taylor Street, Dallas TX 75226 USA
**Parsons, Charles D** — Philosopher
22 Hancock St, Cambridge MA 02139, USA
**Parsons, David** — Choreographer
Parsons Dance Foundation, 476 Broadway, New York NY 10013, USA
**Parsons, David (Dave)** — Bassist (Bush)
Front Line Mgmt, 1100 Glendon Ave, #2000, Los Angeles CA 90024 USA
**Parsons, Estelle** — Actress
Paradigm Agency, 360 Park Ave S, #1600, New York NY 10010 USA
**Parsons, Jim** — Actor, Comedian
Creative Artists Agency, 2000 Ave of Stars, #100, Los Angeles CA 90067 USA
**Parsons, John T** — Inventor (Machine Numerical Control)
1456 Brigadoon Court, Traverse City MI 49686, USA
**Parsons, Karyn** — Actress
Lesher Entertainment, 1134 S Cloverdale Ave, Los Angeles CA 90019, USA
**Parsons, Nicholas** — Actor
Diamond Mgmt, 31 Percy St, London W1T 2DD, England
**Parsons, Phil** — Auto Racing Driver
18801 Coveside Lane, Cornelius NC 28031, USA
**Parsons, Robert H (Bob)** — Football Player
1098 Stanton Road, Lake Zurich IL 60047, USA
**Parsons, Robert K** — Astronaut
Jackson & Kelly, PO Box 553, Charleston WV 25322, USA
**Part, Arvo** — Composer
Universal Edition, 48 Great Marlborough St, London S1F 7BB, England
**Partee, Barbara H** — Educator
50 Hobart Lane, Amherst MA 01002, USA
**Partee, Dennis F** — Football Player
103 Denise Dr, Marshall TX 75672, USA
**Parten, Ty D** — Football Player
23217 N 71st Dr, Glendale AZ 85310, USA
**Parton, Dolly** — Singer, Actress, Songwriter
Dollywood Co, 2700 Dollywood Parks Blvd, Pigeon Forge TN 37863, USA
**Parton, Stella** — Singer
Attic Entertainment, PO Box 120871, Nashville TN 37212, USA
**Partridge, Alex** — Rowing Athlete
Leander Club, Henley on Thames, Leander RG9 2LP, England
**Partridge, John A** — Architect
Cudham Court, Cudham near Sevenoaks, Kent TN14 7QF, England
**Partridge, Leah** — Opera Singer
Columbia Artists Mgmt Inc, 5 Columbus Circle, 1790 Broadway, #1600, New York NY 10019 USA
**Partridge, Richard B (Rick)** — Football Player
707 Reeder Road, Paramus NJ 07652, USA
**Partridge, Wendy** — Costume Designer
Paradigm Agency, 360 N Crescent Dr, North Building, Beverly Hills CA 90210 USA
**Paruzzi, Gabriella** — Cross Country Skier
Via Cardorna 47, 33010 Fuzine UR, Italy
**Pasanella, Giovanni** — Architect
Pasanella & Klein, 330 W 42nd St, New York NY 10036, USA
**Pasanella, Marco** — Furniture Designer
Pasanella Co, 45 W 18th St, New York NY 10011, USA
**Pasarell, Charles** — Tennis Player
78200 Miles Ave, Indian Wells CA 92210, USA
**Pascal, Adam** — Actor, Singer
Innovative Artists, 1505 10th St, Santa Monica CA 90401 USA
**Pascal, Amy** — Businesswoman
Sony Pictures Entertainment, 10202 W Washington Blvd, Culver City CA 90232, USA
**Pascal, Olivia** — Actress
Opal Models, Franziska-Reindl-Platz 2, 81379 Munich, Germany
**Pascal, Pedro** — Actor
Innovative Artists, 235 Park Ave S, #1000, New York NY 10003 USA
**Pascal, Petra** — Singer
Johannes Muller, Buchschacherstr 17, 66292 Riegelsberg, Germany
**Pascal-Trouillot, Ertha** — President, Haiti
Christ Roi 21, Port-au-Prince, Haiti
**Paschall, William H (Bill)** — Baseball Player
7926 Windspray Dr, Summerfield NC 27358, USA
**Pasco, Richard** — Actor
Michael Whitehall, 125 Gloucester Road, London SW7 4TE, England
**Pascoal, Hermeto** — Jazz Musician, Composer
Eye for Eye Talent, 1139 San Carlos Ave, #310, San Carlos CA 94070, USA
**Pascual, Camilo A** — Baseball Player
7741 SW 32nd St, Miami FL 33155, USA
**Pascual, Luis** — Director
Theatre de l'Europe, 1 Place Paul Claudel, 75006 Paris, France

**Pascual, Mercedes** — Ecologist, Evolutionary Biologist
University of Michigan, Ecology & Biology Dept, Ann Arbor MI 48109, USA

**Pasdar, Adrian** — Actor
I C M Partners, 10250 Constellation Blvd, #900, Los Angeles CA 90067 USA

**Pasek, Justine** — Beauty Queen, Model
Physical Modelos, Edifica Parque Uracaca Av, Balboa, Panama City, Panama

**Pash, Jim** — Singer (Surfaris)
624 Sistine St, Las Vegas NV 89144, USA

**Pashnick, Larry J** — Baseball Player
506 Highland St, Wyandotte MI 48192, USA

**Pashos, Anthony G (Tony)** — Football Player
23 30th Ave, Jacksonville Beach FL 32250, USA

**Pasian, Karina** — Singer
Def Jam Records, 828 8th Ave, New York NY 10019 USA

**Pasillas, Jose A, II** — Drummer (Incubus)
Variety Artists, 1924 Spring St, Paso Robles CA 93446 USA

**Pasin, Dave** — Ice Hockey Player
787 Holly Oak Dr, Palo Alto CA 94303, USA

**Paskai, Laszlo Cardinal** — Religious Leader
Archdiocese of Esztergom-Budapest, Primasi Erseki Hivatal, Uri Utca 62, 1024 Budapest, Hungary

**Paslawski, Greg** — Ice Hockey Player
10 Topping Lane, Saint Louis MO 63131, USA

**Pasqua, Daniel A (Dan)** — Baseball Player
45 Silo Ridge Road E, Orland Park IL 60467, USA

**Pasquale, Steven** — Actor
I C M Partners, 10250 Constellation Blvd, #900, Los Angeles CA 90067 USA

**Pasqualino, Luke** — Actor
B W H Agency, 117 Shaftesbury Ave, London WC2H 8AD, England

**Pasqualoni, Paul** — Football Coach
University of Connecticut, Athletic Dept, Storrs CT 06269, USA

**Pasquette, Didier** — Circus Tightrope Walker
15 Ave du Stade, 10400 Trainelfrance, France

**Pasquin, John R** — Director, Producer
Paradox Productions, 801 Tarcuto Way, Los Angeles CA 90077, USA

**Pass, Patrick D** — Football Player
57 Revere Terrace, Attleboro MA 02703, USA

**Passarelli, Pasquale** — Greco-Roman Wrestler
Pfalzer Waldweg 5, 68753 Waghausel, Germany

**Passenger** — Singer, Songwriter
Paradigm Agency, 360 N Crescent Dr, North Building, Beverly Hills CA 90210 USA

**Passer, Ivan** — Director
Innovative Artists, 1505 10th St, Santa Monica CA 90401 USA

**Passmore, John A** — Philosopher
6 Jansz Crescent, Manuka ACT 2603, Australia

**Passmore, Matt** — Actor
W M E Entertainment, 9601 Wilshire Blvd, #300, Beverly Hills CA 90210 USA

**Passos Coelho, Pedro M M** — Prime Minister, Portugal
Prime Minister's Office, Rua do Imprensa a Estrela 8, 1249068 Lisbon, Portugal

**Pastan, Linda** — Writer
11710 Beall Mountain Road, Potomac MD 20854, USA

**Pastides, Harris** — Educator
University of South Carolina, President's Office, Osborne Building, Columbia SC 29208, USA

**Pastis, Stephan** — Cartoonist
1 Snoopy Place, Santa Rosa CA 95403, USA

**Pastner, Josh** — Basketball Coach
University of Memphis, Athletic Dept, 570 Normal St, Memphis TN 38152, USA

**Pastore, Vincent** — Actor
PO Box 207, Bronx NY 10464, USA

**Pastorini, Dante A (Dan), Jr** — Football Player
2323 McCue Road, #1909, Houston TX 77056, USA

**Pastrana, Al** — Football Player
1628 Ridout Road, Annapolis MD 21409, USA

**Patat, Frederic** — Spatinaut, France
Faculte de Medecine, 2 Bis Blvd Tonnelle, 37032 Tours Cedex, France

**Patch, Karen** — Costume Designer
United Talent Agency, U T A Plaza, 9336 Civic Center Dr, Beverly Hills CA 90210 USA

**Patchett, Ann** — Writer
Saint Martin's Press, 175 5th Ave, #400, New York NY 10010 USA

**Pate, Jerome K (Jerry)** — Golfer
5 Hyde Park Road, Pensacola FL 32503, USA

**Pate, Jonas** — Director, Writer
W M E Entertainment, 9601 Wilshire Blvd, #300, Beverly Hills CA 90210 USA

**Pate, Josh** — Director, Writer
W M E Entertainment, 9601 Wilshire Blvd, #300, Beverly Hills CA 90210 USA

**Pate, Steve** — Golfer
1034 Brookview Ave, Westlake Village CA 91361, USA

**Patek, Frederick J (Freddie)** — Baseball Player
5408 NE Wedgewood Lane, Lees Summit MO 64064, USA

**Patekar, Nana** — Actor
304 Sheetal Apna Ghar Soc, Samarth Nagar Andgeri, Mumbai MS 400058, India

**Patel, C Kumar N** — Inventor (Carbon Dioxide Laser)
1171 Roberto Lane, Los Angeles CA 90077, USA

**Patel, Dev** — Actor
Curtis Brown Group, 28-29 Haymarket St, #500, London SW1Y 4SP, England

**Patera, John A (Jack)** — Football Player, Coach
82 Osprey Dr, Cle Elum WA 98922, USA

**Patera, Ken** — Weightlifter
6932 Stratford Road, Saint Paul MN 55125, USA

**Paterson, Bill** — Actor
Gordon & French, 12-13 Poland St, London W1F 8QB, England

**Paterson, D Rick** — Ice Hockey Player, Executive
Anaheim Ducks, 2695 E Katella Ave, Anaheim CA 92806 USA

**Paterson, David A** — Governor, NY
WOR Radio, 111 Broadway, #300, New York NY 10006, USA

**Paterson, Jodi Ann** — Model
Playboy Promotions, 9346 Civic Center Dr, #200, Beverly Hills CA 90210 USA

**Paterson, Joseph A (Joe)** — Ice Hockey Player
49 Sullivan Place, Lake George NY 12845, USA

**Paterson, Katherine** — Writer
70 Wildersburg Common, Barre VT 05641, USA

**Patey, Larry J** — Ice Hockey Player
2713 Autumn Run Court, Chesterfield MO 63005, USA

**Pathon, Jerome** — Football Player
611 Carrotwood Terrace, Plantation FL 33324, USA

**Patil, Pratibha** — President, India
President's Office, Bharat Ka, Rashtrapti Bhavan, New Delhi 110004, India

**Patinkin, Mandy** — Actor, Singer
Paradigm Agency, 360 N Crescent Dr, North Building, Beverly Hills CA 90210 USA

**Patitz, Tatjana** — Model, Actress
Trump Model Agency, 91 5th Ave, #300, New York NY 10003 USA

**Patkau, John** — Architect
Patkau Architects, 560 Beaty St, #L110, Vancouver BC V6B 2L3, Canada

**Pato, Alexandre** — Soccer Player
F C Milan, Via Filippo Turati 3, 20121 Milan, Italy

**Patriarco, Earle** — Opera Singer
Askonas Holt, Lincoln House, 300 High Holborn, London WC1V 7JH, England

**Patric, Jason** — Actor
Gersh Agency, 9465 Wilshire Blvd, #600, Beverly Hills CA 90212 USA

**Patrick, Bill** — Sportscaster
NBC-TV, Sports Dept, 30 Rockefeller Plaza, #270E, New York NY 10112 USA

**Patrick, Butch** — Actor
15701 Redington Dr, Redington Beach FL 33708, USA

**Patrick, Craig** — Ice Hockey Player
113 Royston Road, Pittsburgh PA 15238, USA

**Patrick, Danica** — Auto Racing Driver, Model
Danica Racing, PO Box 155, Roscoe IL 61073, USA

**Patrick, James** — Ice Hockey Player
5024 Red Tail Run, Buffalo NY 14221, USA

**Patrick, Kyle** — Singer, Guitarist (Click Five)
Sharp & Focused Mgmt, 323 Broadway St, Cambridge MA 02139, USA

**Patrick, Mike** — Sportscaster
ESPN-TV, Sports Dept, ESPN Plaza, 935 Middle St, Bristol CT 06010 USA

**Patrick, Nicholas J M** — Astronaut
13708 NE 32nd Place, Bellevue WA 98005, USA

**Patrick, Robert** — Actor
Coronel Group, 1100 Glendon Ave, #1700, Los Angeles CA 90046, USA

**Patrick, Thomas M** — Businessman
Peoples Energy Corp, 130 E Randolph Dr, #300, Chicago IL 60601, USA

**Patridge, Audrina** — Actress
I C M Partners, 10250 Constellation Blvd, #900, Los Angeles CA 90067 USA

**Patsavas, Alexandra** — Music Supervisor, Producer
First Artists Mgmt, 4764 Park Granada, #210, Calabasas CA 91302 USA

**Patten of Barnes, Christopher F** — Governor General, Hong Kong; Educator
Oxford University, Chancellor's Office, Oxford OX1 2JD, England

**Patten, Cassandra** — Swimmer
Stockport Metro, 12 Grand Central Square, Stockport SK1 3TA, England

**Patten, David** — Football Player
761 Longtown Road W, Blythewood SC 29016, USA

**Patten, John L (Joel), II** — Football Player
13415 Marble Rock Dr, Chantilly VA 20151, USA

**Patterson, Berman** — Singer (Cleftones)
605 Universe Blvd, #T1212, Juno Beach FL 33408, USA

**Patterson, Christian** — Actor
Artists Partnership, 101 Finsbury Pavement, London EC2A 1RS, England

**Patterson, Colin** — Ice Hockey Player
Just in Case Fire, 11979 40th St SE, Calgary AB T2Z 4M3, Canada

**Patterson, D Corey** — Baseball Player
1115 Gordon Combs Road NW, Marietta GA 30064, USA

**Patterson, Daryl A** — Baseball Player
20145 Tollhouse Road, Clovis CA 93619, USA

**Patterson, Elvis V** — Football Player
8915 Allman Road, Lenexa KS 66219, USA

**Patterson, Francine G (Penny)** — Animal Psychologist (Koko Trainer)
Gorilla Foundation, PO Box 620640, Redwood City CA 94062, USA

**Patterson, Gary** — Cartoonist
Patterson International, 25208 Malibu Road, Malibu CA 90265, USA

**Patterson, Gary** — Football Coach
Texas Christian University, Athletic Dept, Fort Worth TX 76129, USA

**Patterson, James** — Writer, Businessman
10 Red Horse Hill Road, Sharon CT 06069, USA

**Patterson, James T** — Historian
Brown University, History Dept, Providence RI 02912, USA

**Patterson, John H** — Baseball Player
2709 Country Club Dr, Orange TX 77630, USA

**Patterson, John M** — Governor, AL
Court of Judiciary, PO Box 30155, Montgomery AL 36103, USA

**Patterson, K Shawn** — Football Player
15711 E Avenida del Ville Court, Chandler AZ 85249, USA

**Patterson, Kenneth B (Ken)** — Baseball Player
1202 Maverick Trail, McGregor TX 76657, USA

**Patterson, Lamar** — Basketball Player
Atlanta Hawks, Centennial Tower, 101 Marietta St NW, #1900, Atlanta GA 30303 USA

**Patterson, Lorna** — Actress
23852 Pacific Coast Highway, #355, Malibu CA 90265, USA

**Patterson, Merritt** — Actress
Play Management, 807 Powell St, #220, Vancouver BC V6A 1H7, Canada

**Patterson, Michael** — Financier
J P Morgan Chase, 270 Park Ave, #1200, New York NY 10017, USA

**Patterson, Richard North** — Writer
PO Box 183, West Tisbury MA 02575, USA

**Patterson, Robert C (Bob)** — Baseball Player
3106 47th Avenue Lane NE, Hickory NC 28601, USA

| | |
|---|---|
| **Patterson, Robert M**<br>907 Ironwood Dr, Henderson KY 42420, USA | Vietnam War Army Air Hero (CMH) |
| **Patterson, Ross**<br>Baker Winokur Ryder Public Relations, 9100 Wilshire Blvd, #500W, Beverly Hills CA 90212 USA | Actor |
| **Patterson, Scott**<br>Hofflund/Polone, 9465 Wilshire Blvd, #420, Beverly Hills CA 90212 USA | Actor |
| **Patterson, Scott R**<br>148 Tall Maple Court, Freeburg IL 62243, USA | Baseball Player |
| **Patterson-Caldwell, Carly R**<br>3401 Therondunn Dr, Plano TX 75023, USA | Gymnast, Singer, Actress |
| **Patti, Sandi**<br>PO Box 6, Pendleton IN 46064, USA | Singer, Pianist |
| **Patti, Thomas**<br>10 Federico Dr, Pittsfield MA 01201, USA | Artist |
| **Pattillo, Charles C**<br>11514 Little Bay Harbor Way, Spotsylvania VA 22551, USA | Air Force General, WW II Hero |
| **Pattillo, Cuthbert A (Bill).**<br>59 E Weaver Ave, Harrisonburg VA 22801, USA | WW II Army Air Corps Hero |
| **Pattillo, Linda**<br>CNN-TV, News Dept, 820 1st St NE, #1000, Washington DC 20002 USA | Commentator |
| **Pattin, Martin W (Marty)**<br>3401 Sweetgrass Court, Lawrence KS 66049, USA | Baseball Player |
| **Pattinson, Robert**<br>Curtis Brown Group, 28-29 Haymarket St, #500, London SW1Y 4SP, England | Actor |
| **Patton, Carl V**<br>Georgia State University, President's Office, Atlanta GA 30303, USA | Educator |
| **Patton, Marvcus R**<br>110 Gallatin St NW, Washington DC 20011, USA | Football Player |
| **Patton, Mike**<br>Ipecac Records, PO Box 1778, Orinda CA 94563, USA | Singer (Faith No More) |
| **Patton, Paula**<br>W M E Entertainment, 9601 Wilshire Blvd, #300, Beverly Hills CA 90210 USA | Actress |
| **Patton, Ricky R**<br>1454 Brookline Court SE, Mableton GA 30126, USA | Football Player |
| **Patton, Troy J**<br>33635 W Decker Dr, Magnolia TX 77355, USA | Baseball Player |
| **Patton, William C (Will)**<br>Paradigm Agency, 360 N Crescent Dr, North Building, Beverly Hills CA 90210 USA | Actor |
| **Patty, J Edward (Budge)**<br>La Marne, 14 Ave de Jurigoz, 1006 Lausanne, Switzerland | Tennis Player |
| **Patulski, Walter G (Walt)**<br>420 Kimber Road, Syracuse NY 13224, USA | Football Player |
| **Patzaichin, Ivan**<br>S C Sportiv Unirea Tricolor, Soseaua Stefan Cel Mare 9, 020121 Bucharest, Romania | Canoeing Athlete |
| **Patzakis, Michele**<br>Prappas Co, 9201 Wilshire Blvd, #204, Beverly Hills CA 90210, USA | Opera Singer |
| **Pau, Peter**<br>Gersh Agency, 9465 Wilshire Blvd, #600, Beverly Hills CA 90212 USA | Cinematographer |
| **Pauk, Gyorgy**<br>27 Armitage Road, London NW11 8QT, England | Concert Violinist |
| **Paul, Aaron M**<br>United Talent Agency, U T A Plaza, 9336 Civic Center Dr, Beverly Hills CA 90210 USA | Actor |
| **Paul, Adrian**<br>Filmblips, 4968 Yonge St, #2911, Toronto ON M2N 7G9, Canada | Actor |
| **Paul, Alexandra**<br>Forster Entertainment, 12533 Woodgreen St, Building B, Los Angeles CA 90036, USA | Actress |
| **Paul, Billy**<br>Billy Paul Mgmt, 8215 Winthrop St, Philadelphia PA 19136, USA | Singer |
| **Paul, Christi**<br>CNN-TV, News Dept, 190 Marietta Ave SW, Atlanta GA 30303 USA | Commentator |
| **Paul, Christiane**<br>Players Agentur Mgmt, Sophienstr 21, 10178 Berlin-Mille, Germany | Actress |
| **Paul, Christopher E (Chris)**<br>749 Fountain Brook Lane, Lewisville NC 27023, USA | Basketball Player |
| **Paul, Dana**<br>Dana Paul Productions, 9421 Live Oak Place, #101, Davie/Fort Lauderdale FL 33324, USA | Singer, Bassist (Cornerstone) |
| **Paul, Don Michael**<br>A P A Talent & Literary Agency, 405 S Beverly Dr, #300, Beverly Hills CA 90212 USA | Director, Writer, Actor |
| **Paul, Ellis**<br>Ralph Jaccodine Mgmt, PO Box 381982, Cambridge MA 02238, USA | Singer, Songwriter |
| **Paul, Frankie**<br>Keep on Kicking Music, 330 84th St, #9, Miami Beach FL 33141, USA | Singer |
| **Paul, Henry**<br>Debra McCloud Accounting, 1400 18th Ave S, #C3, Nashville TN 37212, USA | Singer (BlackHawk), Songwriter |
| **Paul, Jarrad**<br>Principato-Young, 9465 Wilshire Blvd, #880, Beverly Hills CA 90212 USA | Actor, Writer |
| **Paul, Joshua W (Josh)**<br>4126 Canoga Park Dr, Brandon FL 33511, USA | Baseball Player |
| **Paul, Kevin**<br>Jana Luker Agency, 1923 1/2 Westwood Blvd, #3, Los Angeles CA 90025, USA | Actor |
| **Paul, Markus D**<br>26 Reid Court, Mahwah NJ 07430, USA | Football Player |
| **Paul, Michael G (Mike)**<br>5121 N Circulo Sobrio, Tucson AZ 85718, USA | Baseball Player |
| **Paul, Robert**<br>10675 Rochester Ave, Los Angeles CA 90024, USA | Figure Skater |
| **Paul, Sean**<br>Headline Entertainment, 8 Haughton Ave, Kingston 10, Jamaica | Rap Artist (Youngbloodz) |
| **Paul, Tito J**<br>2394 Ness Court, Powell OH 43065, USA | Football Player |
| **Paul, Tommy**<br>3578 Village Green Dr, Sarasota FL 34239, USA | Boxer |
| **Paul, Vinnie**<br>Concrete Mgmt, 361 W Broadway, #200, New York NY 10013, USA | Drummer (Pantera) |
| **Paul, Whitney**<br>6802 Thornwild Road, Missouri City TX 77489, USA | Football Player |

**Paul, Wolfgang J** — Soccer Player
Postfach 1324, 59939 Olsberg-Bigge, Germany

**Paula, Alejandro F (Jandi)** — Prime Minister, Netherlands Antilles
Premier's Office, Fort Amsterdam 17, Willemstad, Netherlands Antilles

**Paulauskas, Arturas** — President, Lithuania
Seimas, Gedimino Pr 53, LT 2600 Vilnius, Lithuania

**Pauley, Jane** — Commentator
459 Columbus Ave, #113, New York NY 10024, USA

**Paulino, Ronny A** — Baseball Player
129 Cardinal Circle, Pittsburgh PA 15237, USA

**Pauls, Raymond** — Jazz Pianist, Composer
Veidenbaum Str 41/43, #26, 226001 Riga, Latvia

**Paulsen, Gary** — Writer
126 Bookout NE, Tularosa NM 88352, USA

**Paulsen, Robert (Rob)** — Actor
Sutton-Barth Vennari, 5900 Wilshire Blvd, #700, Los Angeles CA 90036 USA

**Paulsen, Tiffany** — Actress
Creative Artists Agency, 2000 Ave of Stars, #100, Los Angeles CA 90067 USA

**Paulson, Carl A** — Golfer
13221 Sunkiss Loop, Windermere FL 34786, USA

**Paulson, Dainard A** — Football Player
2904 Main St, Union Gap WA 98903, USA

**Paulson, Dennis J** — Golfer
1872 Shadetree Dr, San Marcos CA 92078, USA

**Paulson, Henry M (Hank), Jr** — Secretary, Treasury; Financier
401 N Michigan Ave, #3100, Chicago IL 60611, USA

**Paulson, Jay** — Actor
Ira Belgrade Mgmt, 5850E W 3rd St, Los Angeles CA 90036, USA

**Paulson, Kenneth** — Editor, Foundation Executive
Newseum, 555 Pennsylvania Ave NW, Washington DC 20001, USA

**Paulson, Richard L** — Businessman
Potlatch Corp, 601 W Riverside Ave, #1100, Spokane WA 99201, USA

**Paulson, Sarah** — Actress
United Talent Agency, U T A Plaza, 9336 Civic Center Dr, Beverly Hills CA 90210 USA

**Paultz, William E (Billy)** — Basketball Player
1914 Waters Edge Lane, Seabrook TX 77586, USA

**Paulus, Diane** — Director, Writer
Gersh Agency, 9465 Wilshire Blvd, #600, Beverly Hills CA 90212 USA

**Paulusma, Polly** — Singer, Guitarist, Songwriter
One Little Indian Records, 34 Trinity Crescent, London SW17 7AE, England

**Paup, Bryce E** — Football Player
3110 Pendleton Dr, Cedar Falls IA 50613, USA

**Pausini, Laura** — Singer, Songwriter
Gente Mgmt, Via Palermo 8, 20121 Milan, Italy

**Pavan, Marisa** — Actress
4 Allee des Brouillards, 75018 Paris, France

**Pavan, Sarah L** — Volleyball Player
University of Nebraska, Athletic Dept, Lincoln NE 68588, USA

**Pavano, Carl A** — Baseball Player
PO Box 1307, Thomasville GA 31799, USA

**Pavelich, Martin N (Marty)** — Ice Hockey Player
1709 Forest Lane, Bloomfield Hills MI 48301, USA

**Pavese, James P (Jim)** — Ice Hockey Player
65 Whittier Dr, Kings Park NY 11754, USA

**Pavia, Ria** — Actress
TalentWorks, 3500 W Olive Ave, #1400, Burbank CA 91505 USA

**Pavic, Josip** — Water Polo Player
H A V K Mladost, Jarunska 5, 10000 Zagreb, Croatia

**Pavin, Corey** — Golfer
4332 Gilbert Ave, Dallas TX 75219, USA

**Pavlas, David L** — Baseball Player
PO Box 1224, Shiner TX 77984, USA

**Pavletich, Donald S (Don)** — Baseball Player
13645 Adelaide Lane, Brookfield WI 53005, USA

**Pavlik, Kelly (Ghost)** — Boxer
949 Cornell Ave, Youngstown OH 44502, USA

**Pavlik, Roger A** — Baseball Player
622 Beaver Bend Road, Houston TX 77037, USA

**Pavlo** — Guitar Player
Agency Group Ltd, 142 W 57th St, #600, New York NY 10019 USA

**Pavlovic, Aleksandar (Sasha)** — Basketball Player
Boston Celtics, 226 Causeway St, #4, Boston MA 02114 USA

**Pawelczyk, James A (Jim)** — Astronaut
N A S A, Johnson Space Center, 2101 NASA Road, Houston TX 77058 USA

**Pawlak, Waldemar** — Prime Minister, Poland
Zarzad Glowny ZOSP RP, Ul Obozna 1, 00 340 Warsaw, Poland

**Pawlenty, Timothy J (Tim)** — Governor, MN
Financial Services Roundtable, 1001 Pennsylvania Ave NW, #500 South, Washington DC 20004, USA

**Pawlikowski, Pawel** — Director
Creative Artists Agency, 2000 Ave of Stars, #100, Los Angeles CA 90067 USA

**Pawlowski, John** — Baseball Player
257 Mill Branch Way, North Augusta SC 29860, USA

**Pawson, John** — Architect
70-78 York Way, #B, London N1 9AG, England

**Paxon, L William (Bill)** — Representative, NY
Akin Gump Strauss Hauer, 1333 New Hampshire NW, #400, Washington DC 20036, USA

**Paxson, John M** — Basketball Player, Executive
125 Boardman Court, Lake Bluff IL 60044, USA

**Paxton, Leonitas E (Lonie), III** — Football Player
2495 Oak Vista Court, Castle Rock CO 80104, USA

**Paxton, Michael D (Mike)** — Baseball Player
1145 S Indian Wells Dr, Collierville TN 38017, USA

**Paxton, Robert O** — Historian
460 Riverside Dr, #72, New York NY 10027, USA

**Paxton, Sara** — Actress
United Talent Agency, U T A Plaza, 9336 Civic Center Dr, Beverly Hills CA 90210 USA

**Paxton, Tom** — Singer, Songwriter
Fleming Artists, 543 N Main St, Ann Arbor MI 48104, USA
**Paxton, William A (Bill)** — Actor
W M E Entertainment, 9601 Wilshire Blvd, #300, Beverly Hills CA 90210 USA
**Payer, Serge** — Ice Hockey Player
2343 Lorraine St, RR 1, Rockland ON K4K 1K7, Canada
**Payette, Julie** — Astronaut, Canada
Space Agency, Rockliffe Base, Ottawa ON K1A 1A1, Canada
**Paymah, Karl** — Football Player
PO Box 4268, Culver City CA 90231, USA
**Paymer, David** — Actor
A P A Talent & Literary Agency, 405 S Beverly Dr, #300, Beverly Hills CA 90212 USA
**Payne, Adreian** — Basketball Player
Atlanta Hawks, Centennial Tower, 101 Marietta St NW, #1900, Atlanta GA 30303 USA
**Payne, Alexander** — Director, Producer, Writer
Ad Hominem Enterprises, 506 Santa Monica Blvd, #400, Santa Monica CA 90401, USA
**Payne, Allen** — Actor
Harrison Stokes, 8730 W Sunset Blvd, #270, West Hollywood CA 90069, USA
**Payne, Anthony E** — Composer
2 Wilton Square, London N1 3DL, England
**Payne, Bruce** — Actor
Gilbertson Entertainment, 1334 3rd Street Promenade, #201, Santa Monica CA 90401 USA
**Payne, C Ladell** — Educator
Randolph-Macon College, President's Office, Ashland VA 23005, USA
**Payne, David N** — Optical Fiber Engineer
Southampton University, Electronics Dept, Highfield, Southampton SO17 1BJ, England
**Payne, Dougie** — Bassist (Travis)
Wildlife Entertainment, 21 Heathmans Road, London SW6 4TJ, England
**Payne, Freda** — Singer, Actress
Scott Stander Assoc, 4533 Van Nuys Blvd, #401, Sherman Oaks CA 91403 USA
**Payne, Harry C** — Educator
Williams College, President's Office, Williamstown MA 01267, USA
**Payne, Henry** — Editorial Cartoonist
Detroit News, Editorial Dept, 615 W Lafayette, Detroit MI 48226, USA
**Payne, Julie** — Actress
Pakula/King, 9229 W Sunset Blvd, #315, West Hollywood CA 90069 USA
**Payne, Keith** — Vietnam War Australian Army Hero (VC)
2 Saint Bee's Ave, Bucasia QLD 4740, Australia
**Payne, Keri-Anne** — Swimmer
Stockport Metro, 12 Grand Central Square, Stockport SK1 3TA, England
**Payne, Roger S** — Biologist, Conservationist
191 Western Road, Lincoln MA 01773, USA
**Payne, Scherrie** — Singer
Starwil Talent, 433 N Camden Dr, #400, Beverly Hills CA 90210, USA
**Payne, Seth C** — Football Player
7908 Westwood Dr, Houston TX 77055, USA
**Payne, Steven J (Steve)** — Ice Hockey Player
N6497 County Road N, Beldenville WI 54003, USA
**Payne, Tom** — Actor
Paradigm Agency, 360 N Crescent Dr, North Building, Beverly Hills CA 90210 USA
**Payne, Waylon** — Singer, Actor
Nine Yards Entertainment, 8530 Wilshire Blvd, #500, Beverly Hills CA 90211 USA
**Pays, Amanda** — Actress
Origin Talent, 4705 Laurel Canyon Blvd, #306, Studio City CA 91607, USA
**Payton, Benjamin F** — Educator
20200 Chapel Trace, Estero FL 33928, USA
**Payton, Christian** — Actor
Grossman & Jack Talent, 33 W Grand Ave, #402, Chicago IL 60654, USA
**Payton, Edward (Eddie)** — Football Player
118 Woodland Hills Blvd, Madison MS 39110, USA
**Payton, Gary D** — Basketball Player
2745 S Monte Cristo Way, Las Vegas NV 89117, USA
**Payton, Gary E** — Astronaut
2367 Diamond Creek Dr, Colorado Springs CO 80921, USA
**Payton, Jason L (Jay)** — Baseball Player
3000 Cone Manor Lane, Raleigh NC 27613, USA
**Payton, Nicholas** — Jazz Trumpeter
Management Ark, 116 Village Blvd, #200, Princeton NJ 08540, USA
**Payton, Sean** — Football Player, Coach
830 Wagner Way, Lantana TX 76226, USA
**Pazienza, Vinny** — Boxer
54 Tivoli Court, Warwick RI 02886, USA
**Peaches** — Singer, Songwriter
Butterscotch Castle, 535 Geary St, #612, San Francisco CA 94102, USA
**Peacock, Alice** — Singer, Songwriter
Silverleaf Booking, 59 W 1st St, Boiling Springs PA 17007, USA
**Peacock, Andrew S** — Government Official, Australia
19 Queens Road, Melbourne VIC 3004, Australia
**Peacock, James L, III** — Anthropologist
University of North Carolina, Anthropology Dept, 301 Alumni Building, Chapel Hill NC 27599, USA
**Peake, Don** — Guitarist, Composer
Marcelli Co, 11333 Moorpark, #411, Studio City CA 91602, USA
**Peake, Pat** — Ice Hockey Player
327 Hecht Dr, Madison Heights MI 48071, USA
**Peake, Ryan A** — Singer, Guitarist (Nickelback)
Union Entertainment Group, 17737 Ventura Blvd, #208, Encino CA 91316, USA
**Peaker, E J** — Actress
4935 Densmore Ave, Encino CA 91436, USA
**Pear, David L (Dave)** — Football Player
3126 199th Ave SE, Sammamish WA 98075, USA
**Pearce, Guy** — Actor
Shanahan Mgmt, PO Box 1509, Darlinghurst NSW 1300, Australia
**Pearce, Jacqueline** — Actress
Rhubarb Personal Mgmt, 6 Langley St, #41, London WC2H 9JA, England
**Pearce, Oscar** — Actor
Artists Partnership, 101 Finsbury Pavement, London EC2A 1RS, England

**Pearce, Reynold** — Fashion Designer
Pearce Fionda, Loft, 27 Horsell Road, Highbury, London N5 1XL, England
**Pearce, Stephen** — Religious Leader, Rabbi
Congregation Emanuel, 2 Lake St, San Francisco CA 94118, USA
**Pearce, Steven W (Steve)** — Baseball Player
1928 E Gachet Blvd, Lakeland FL 33813, USA
**Pearcy, Stephen** — Singer (Ratt)
Tom Vitorino Mgmt, 11606 Vimy Road, Granada Hills CA 91344, USA
**Pearl, Barry** — Actor
Coolwaters Productions, 10061 Riverside Dr, Box 531, Toluca Lake CA 91602 USA
**Pearl, Bruce D-F** — Basketball Coach
Auburn University, Athletic Dept, Auburn AL 36849, USA
**Pearl, Judea** — Computer Scientist, Statistician
University of California, Computer Science Dept, Los Angeles CA 90024, USA
**Pearlstein, Philip** — Artist
361 W 36th St, New York NY 10018, USA
**Pearlstein, Randy** — Actor
Bleeker Street Entertainment, 853 Broadway, #1214, New York NY 10003, USA
**Pearlstein, Steven** — Journalist
Washington Post, Editorial Dept, 1150 15th St NW, Washington DC 20071 USA
**Pearlstine, Norman** — Editor
Carlyle Group, 1000 Pennsylvania Ave NW, Washington DC 20003, USA
**Pearman, F Alvin, Jr** — Football Player
5601 Chadfort Lane, Charlotte NC 28226, USA
**Pearson, Albert G (Albie)** — Baseball Player
55473 Oakhill, La Quinta CA 92253, USA
**Pearson, Allison** — Writer
Knopf Publishers, 1745 Broadway, New York NY 10019 USA
**Pearson, Becky** — Golfer
1630 SW 8th Ave, Boca Raton FL 33486, USA
**Pearson, David G** — Auto Racing Driver
290 Burnett Road, Boiling Springs SC 29316, USA
**Pearson, Drew** — Football Player
3721 Mount Vernon Way, Plano TX 75025, USA
**Pearson, Jayice (J C)** — Football Player
721 SW Winterhill Lane, Lees Summit MO 64081, USA
**Pearson, Keir** — Writer, Editor, Producer
Management 360, 9111 Wilshire Blvd, Beverly Hills CA 90210 USA
**Pearson, Larry** — Auto Racing Driver
Buckshot Racing, 182 Belue Road, Spartansburg SC 29303, USA
**Pearson, Mike Parker** — Archaeologist
Sheffield University, Archaeology Dept, Sheffield S1 4ET, England
**Pearson, Preston J** — Football Player
Pro Style Assoc, 9104 Moss Farm Lane, Dallas TX 75243, USA
**Pearson, Ralph G** — Chemist
715 Grove Lane, Santa Barbara CA 93105, USA
**Pearson, Ridley** — Writer
Dell Books, 1745 Broadway, New York NY 10019 USA
**Pearson, Robert G** — Ice Hockey Player
Beyond the Point, 467 Meadow St, Oshawa ON L1L 1B9, Canada
**Pearson, Scott** — Ice Hockey Player
Medassets Inc, 100 N Point Center E, #200, Alpharetta GA 30022, USA
**Pearson, T R** — Writer
Crown Publishing Group, 1745 Broadway, #1300, New York NY 10019 USA
**Peart, Neal** — Drummer (Rush)
S L Feldman Mgmt, 1505 W 2nd Ave, #200, Vancouver BC V6H 3Y4, Canada
**Pease, Patsy** — Actress
15432 Hartland St, Van Nuys CA 91406, USA
**Peavy, Jacob E (Jake)** — Baseball Player
PO Box 346, Catherine AL 36728, USA
**Peay, J H Binford (Binnie), III** — Army General, Educator
Virginia Military Institute, Superintendent's Office, Lexington VA 24450, USA
**Peca, Michael A (Mike)** — Ice Hockey Player
46 Golden Pheasant Dr, Getzville NY 14068, USA
**Pechstein, Claudia** — Speed Skater
Powerplay Mgmt, Seepromenade 53, 14476 Gross, Germany
**Peck, Austin** — Actor
Stone Manners Salners, 6100 Wilshire Blvd, #1500, Los Angeles CA 90035 USA
**Peck, Carolyn** — Basketball Player, Coach
University of Florida, Athletic Dept, Gainesville FL 32611, USA
**Peck, Cecilia** — Actress
Cabin Creek Films, 270 Lafayette St, #710, New York NY 10012, USA
**Peck, Ethan** — Actor
I C M Partners, 10250 Constellation Blvd, #900, Los Angeles CA 90067 USA
**Peck, J Eddie** — Actor
Element Talent Agency, 120 S Vignes, #202, Los Angeles CA 90012, USA
**Peck, Raoul** — Director, Producer, Writer
United Talent Agency, U T A Plaza, 9336 Civic Center Dr, Beverly Hills CA 90210 USA
**Peck, Richard E** — Educator, Writer
96 Homesteads Road, Placitas NM 87043, USA
**Peck, Robert Newton** — Writer
430 Village Place, #214, Longwood FL 32779, USA
**Peck, Tom** — Auto Racing Driver
417 E North St, McConnellsburg PA 17233, USA
**Pecker, David J** — Publisher
American Media, 600 S East Coast Ave, Lantana FL 33462, USA
**Pecker, Jean-Claude** — Astronomer
Pusat-Tasek, Les Corbeaux, 85350 L'Ile d'Yeu, France
**Peckovam Dagmar** — Opera Singer
Na Pankraci 101, 14000 Prague 4, Czech Republic
**Pecota, William J (Bill)** — Baseball Player
332 NE Warrington Court, Lees Summit MO 64064, USA
**Pecqueur, Mario** — Actor
Artmedia, 20 Ave Rapp, 75007 Paris, France
**Pedersen, Allen (Al)** — Ice Hockey Player
2261 Fieldcrest Dr, Colorado Springs CO 80921, USA

**Pedersen, William** — Architect
Kohn Pedersen Fox Assoc, 111 W 57th St, #300, New York NY 10019, USA
**Pedersen-Bieri, Maya** — Skeleton Athlete
Saeter, 3818 Oyer, Norway
**Pederson, Barry A** — Ice Hockey Player
18 Cutting Road, Swampscott MA 01907, USA
**Pederson, Denis E** — Ice Hockey Player
74 Cummings Circle, West Orange NJ 07052, USA
**Pederson, Douglas I (Doug)** — Football Player
12 Gladwynne Terrace, Moorestown NJ 08057, USA
**Pederson, Mark** — Ice Hockey Player
151 Equestrian Lane, Kalispell MT 59901, USA
**Pedregon, Cruz** — Drag Racing Driver
Cruz Pedregon Racing, 462 South Point Circle, #A, Brownsburg IN 46112, USA
**Pedregon, Frank** — Drag Racing Driver
Frank Pedregon Racing, 6174 Cabernet Place, Alta Loma CA 91766, USA
**Pedretti, Adam** — Drummer (Killing Heidi)
Harbour Agency, 135 Forbes St, Woolloomooloo NSW 2011, Australia
**Pedrique, Alfredo J (Al)** — Baseball Player
10382 E Oakbrook St, Tucson AZ 85747, USA
**Pedro, James A (Jimmy)** — Judo Athlete
52 Valley St, Wakefield MA 01880, USA
**Pedroia, Dustin L** — Baseball Player
4551 S Ethan Place, Chandler AZ 85248, USA
**Pedroni, Simone** — Concert Pianist
Pro Arte, Fosswinckelsgt 9, 5007 Bergen, Norway
**Pedroza, Mauricio** — Sportscaster
ESPN-TV, Sports Dept, ESPN Plaza, 935 Middle St, Bristol CT 06010 USA
**Peebles, Ann** — Singer
Universal Attractions, 135 W 26th St, #1200, New York NY 10001 USA
**Peebles, P James E** — Physicist, Educator
24 Markham Road, Princeton NJ 08540, USA
**Peek, Antwan M** — Football Player
19555 E Kerry Place, Strongsville OH 44149, USA
**Peele, Jordan** — Actor
Principato-Young, 9465 Wilshire Blvd, #880, Beverly Hills CA 90212 USA
**Peeler, Anthony E** — Basketball Player
4502 E 48th St, Kansas City MO 64130, USA
**Peelle, Justin M** — Football Player
14040 Iris Lane, Poway CA 92064, USA
**Peeples, George** — Basketball Player
1032 Loma Lisa Lane, Arcadia CA 91006, USA
**Peeples, Lewis** — Singer (Five Satins)
Paramount Entertainment, PO Box 12, Far Hills NJ 07931 USA
**Peeples, Nia** — Actress, Singer
C E S D, 10635 Santa Monica Blvd, #130, Los Angeles CA 90025 USA
**Peerce, Larry** — Director
225 W 34th St, #1012, New York NY 10122, USA
**Peers, Holly J** — Model
Samantha Bond Mgmt, Elysium Gate, 126-128 New Kings Road, London SW6 4LZ, England
**Peet, Amanda** — Actress
Management 360, 9111 Wilshire Blvd, Beverly Hills CA 90210 USA
**Peete, Calvin** — Golfer
128 Garden Gate Dr, Ponte Vedra Beach FL 32082, USA
**Peete, Rodney** — Football Player
11964 Crest Place, Beverly Hills CA 90210, USA
**Peeters, Pete** — Ice Hockey Player
Peeters Farm, Namao AB T0A 2N0, Canada
**Pegg, Simon** — Actor, Comedian, Writer
United Talent Agency, U T A Plaza, 9336 Civic Center Dr, Beverly Hills CA 90210 USA
**Pegram, Erric D** — Football Player
1485 Serrano Circle, Naples FL 34105, USA
**Pei, Ieoh Ming (I M)** — Pritzker Architectural Laureate
11 Sutton Place, New York NY 10022, USA
**Peinemann, Edith** — Concert Pianist
Pro Musicis, Ruetistr 38, 8032 Zurich, Switzerland
**Peirce, Kimberly** — Director, Producer, Writer
Creative Artists Agency, 2000 Ave of Stars, #100, Los Angeles CA 90067 USA
**Peirse, Sarah** — Actress
R G M Artists, 8-12 Ann Street, Surry Hills NSW 2010, Australia
**Peirsol, Aaron** — Swimmer
1748 Plaza Del Norte, Newport Beach CA 92661, USA
**Peirson, John** — Ice Hockey Player, Sportscaster
3 Steepletree Lane, Wayland MA 01778, USA
**Peizewat, Gwendal** — Ice Dancer
Sports de Glace Federation, 35 Rue Felicien David, 75016 Paris, France
**Pejman, Bob** — Artist
Pejman Gallery, 509 Millburn Ave, Short Hills NJ 07078, USA
**Pekarkova, Iva** — Writer
Farrar Straus Giroux, 18 W 18th St, #700, New York NY 10011 USA
**Pekovic, Nikola** — Basketball Player
Minnesota Timberwolves, Target Center, 600 1st Ave N, Minneapolis MN 55403 USA
**Peldon, Ashley** — Actress
Marshak/Zachary/Mills, 8840 Wilshire Blvd, #100, Beverly Hills CA 90211 USA
**Peldon, Courtney** — Actress
Aqua Talent Agency, 9000 Sunset Blvd, #700, Los Angeles CA 90069, USA
**Pele** — Soccer Player
Rua Riachuelo 121-3, Andar-Fones 34-1633/35, Santos SP 11010 911, Brazil
**Pelecanos, George P** — Writer
Little Brown, 3 Center Plaza, #100, Boston MA 02108 USA
**Pelen, Perrine** — Alpine Skier
31 Ave de l'Eygala, 38700 Corens Mont Fleury, France
**Pelfrey, Michael A (Mike)** — Baseball Player
1204 Suncast Lane, #2, El Dorado Hills CA 95762, USA
**Pelham, Moses** — Rap Artist
3-P Supporter Club, Postfach 180350, 60084 Frankfurt am Main, Germany

**Pelikan, Lisa** — Actress
Diamond Mgmt, 31 Percy St, London W1T 2DD, England
**Pelini, Mark (Bo)** — Football Coach
University of Nebraska, Athletic Dept, Lincoln NE 68588, USA
**Pell, George Cardinal** — Religious Leader
Archdiocese, Polding Centre, 133 Liverpool St, Sydney NSW 2000, Australia
**Pell, Paula** — Writer
W M E Entertainment, 9601 Wilshire Blvd, #300, Beverly Hills CA 90210 USA
**Pellea, Oana** — Actress
Artists Partnership, 101 Finsbury Pavement, London EC2A 1RS, England
**Pellegrino, Edmund D** — Physician
5610 Wisconsin Ave, Chevy Chase MD 20815, USA
**Pellegrino, Mark** — Actor
Framework Entertainment, 9057 Nemo St, #C, West Hollywood CA 90069 USA
**Pellerin, Scott** — Ice Hockey Player
10 Dunraven Road, Windham NH 03087, USA
**Pelletier, David J** — Ice Dancer
12116 NW 128th St, Edmonton AB T5L 1C3, Canada
**Pelletier, Marcel** — Ice Hockey Player
Boston Bruins, 100 Legends Way, #250, Boston MA 02114 USA
**Pelletreau, Robert H, Jr** — Diplomat
State Department, 2201 C St NW, Washington DC 20520 USA
**Pelley, Scott** — Commentator
CBS-TV, News Dept, 51 W 52nd St, New York NY 10019 USA
**Pelli, Cesar A** — Architect
Cesar Pelli Assoc, 1056 Chapel St, New Haven CT 06510, USA
**Pellington, Mark** — Director
Creative Artists Agency, 2000 Ave of Stars, #100, Los Angeles CA 90067 USA
**Pelluer, Steven C (Steve)** — Football Player
2632 W Lake Sammamish Parkway NE, Redmond WA 98052, USA
**Pelphrey, John** — Basketball Coach
University of Arkansas, Athletic Dept, Fayetteville AR 72701, USA
**Peltason, Jack W** — Educator
18 Whistler Court, Irvine CA 92617, USA
**Pelton, M Lee** — Educator
Willamette University, President's Office, 900 State St, Salem OR 97301, USA
**Peltonen, Ville** — Ice Hockey Player
Dynamo Minsk, Minsk Arena, Pr Pobeditelei 111, 220116 Minsk, Belarus
**Peltz, J Russell** — Boxing Promoter
Peltz Boxing Promotions, 2501 Brown St, Philadelphia PA 19130, USA
**Peltz, Nelson** — Businessman
Trian Companies, 900 3rd Ave, New York NY 10022, USA
**Peluce, Meeno** — Actor
PO Box 3743, Glendale CA 91221, USA
**Peluso, Lisa** — Actress
Shauna Sickenger, PO Box 301, Ramona CA 92065, USA
**Peluso, Michael D (Mike)** — Ice Hockey Player
3616 W Fuller St, Edina, MN 55410, USA
**Pelyk, Michael J (Mike)** — Ice Hockey Player
56-385 East Mall, Toronto ON M9B 6J4, Canada
**Pelzer, David J (Dave)** — Writer
PO Box 131, The Sea Ranch CA 95497, USA
**Pemberton, Johnny** — Actor
Principato-Young, 9465 Wilshire Blvd, #880, Beverly Hills CA 90212 USA
**Pena Martinez, Geronimo** — Baseball Player
KM 17 7 Pista Duarte, Los Alcarrizzos, Dominican Republic
**Pena Nieto, Enrique** — President, Mexico
Palacio Nacional, Los Pinos, Puerto 1, 11850 Mexico City DF, Mexico
**Pena Padilla, Antonio F (Tony)** — Baseball Player, Manager
New York Yankees, Yankee Stadium, E 161st St & River Ave, Bronx NY 10451 USA
**Pena Vasquez, Alejandro** — Baseball Player
PO Box 4414, Suwanee GA 30024, USA
**Pena, Anthony** — Actor
Sha'Lin Talent Mgmt, PO Box 11411, Burbank CA 91510, USA
**Pena, Carlos F** — Baseball Player
4248 Cascada Circle, Hollywood FL 33024, USA
**Pena, Federico F** — Secretary, Transportation, Energy
362 Detroit St, #A, Denver CO 80206, USA
**Pena, Jennifer M** — Singer
Apodaca Promotions, 717 E Tidwell Road, Houston TX 77022, USA
**Pena, Michael A** — Actor
Management 360, 9111 Wilshire Blvd, Beverly Hills CA 90210 USA
**Pena, Orlando G** — Baseball Player
1750 W 46th St, #416, Hialeah FL 33012, USA
**Pena, Paco** — Concert Guitarist, Composer
Wim Visser Ruysdaelkade 5, 1072 Amsterdam AG, Netherlands
**Pena, Wilfredo M (Wily Mo)** — Baseball Player
27250 Breakers Dr, Wesley Chapel FL 33544, USA
**Penacoli, Jerry** — Entertainer
I C M Partners, 10250 Constellation Blvd, #900, Los Angeles CA 90067 USA
**Penate, Jack** — Singer, Songwriter
United Agents, 12-26 Lexington St, London W1F 0LE, England
**Pence, Hunter A** — Baseball Player
10301 Wagon Road W, Austin TX 78736, USA
**Penchion, Robert E (Bob)** — Football Player
110 Elliott Ave, Muscle Shoals AL 35661, USA
**Pendatchanska, Alexandrina** — Opera Singer
Opera et Concert, 37 Rue de la Chaussee d'Antin, 75009 Paris, France
**Pender, Melvin (Mel)** — Track Athlete
2330 Goodwood Blvd SE, Smyrna GA 30080, USA
**Penderecki, Krzysztof E** — Composer, Conductor
Ul Cisowa 22, 30229 Cracow, Poland
**Pendergrass, Henry P** — Physician
Vanderbilt University Medical School, 1621 21st Ave S, Nashville TN 37212, USA
**Penders, Tom** — Basketball Coach
George Washington University, Athletic Dept, Washington DC 20052, USA

| | |
|---|---|
| **Pendleton, Moses** | Dancer, Choreographer |
| Momix, PO Box 35, Washington CT 06794, USA | |
| **Pendleton, Terry L** | Baseball Player |
| 332 Grassmeade Way, Snellville GA 30078, USA | |
| **Pendleton, Victoria** | Cyclist |
| Three60 Sports Mgmt, 158-160 N Gower St, London NW1 2ND, England | |
| **Pendry, John B** | Theoretical Physicist |
| Imperial College, Physics Dept, Prince Consort Road, London SW7 2AZ, England | |
| **Penghlis, Thaao** | Actor |
| Metropolitan Talent Agency, 5405 Wilshire Blvd, #218, Los Angeles CA 90036 USA | |
| **Pengily, Kirk** | Guitarist, Saxophonist, Singer (INXS) |
| 8 Hayes St, #1, Neutral Bay 2089 NSW, Australia | |
| **Pengo, Polycarp Cardinal** | Religious Leader |
| Archdiocese of Dar-es-Salaam, PO Box 167, Dar-es-Salaam, Tanzania | |
| **Penhall, Joe** | Director, Writer |
| Judy Daish Assoc, 2 Saint Charles Place, London W10 6EG, England | |
| **Penicheiro, Ticha** | Basketball Player |
| Los Angeles Sparks, 888 S Figueroa St, #2010, Los Angeles CA 90017 USA | |
| **Penick, Trevor** | Singer (O-Town) |
| Trans Continental Records, 127 W Church St, #350, Orlando FL 32801, USA | |
| **Penikett, Tahmoh** | Actor |
| Gersh Agency, 9465 Wilshire Blvd, #600, Beverly Hills CA 90212 USA | |
| **Peniston, Cecilia V (CeCe)** | Singer |
| 250 W 57th St, #821, New York NY 10107, USA | |
| **Penky, Joseph F** | Chemical Engineer |
| Purdue University, Chemical Engineering Dept, West Lafayette IN 47907, USA | |
| **Penn, (Jillette)** | Comedian, Illusionist (Penn & Teller) |
| A P A Talent & Literary Agency, 405 S Beverly Dr, #300, Beverly Hills CA 90212 USA | |
| **Penn, Christopher A (Chris)** | Football Player |
| PO Box 123, South Coffeyville OK 74072, USA | |
| **Penn, Kal** | Actor |
| Gersh Agency, 9465 Wilshire Blvd, #600, Beverly Hills CA 90212 USA | |
| **Penn, Michael** | Singer, Songwriter |
| Mark Spector, 100 5th Ave, #1100, New York NY 10011, USA | |
| **Penn, Sean** | Actor, Director |
| Creative Artists Agency, 2000 Ave of Stars, #100, Los Angeles CA 90067 USA | |
| **Penn, Zak** | Director, Producer, Writer, Actor |
| Zak Penn's Co, 6240 W 3rd St, #421, Los Angeles CA 90036, USA | |
| **Pennacchio, Len A** | Geneticist |
| Stanford University, Human Genome Center, Stanford CA 94305, USA | |
| **Penner, Dustin** | Ice Hockey Player |
| 117 E Balboa Blvd, Newport Beach, CA 92661, USA | |
| **Penner, Jonathan** | Actor |
| I C M Partners, 10250 Constellation Blvd, #900, Los Angeles CA 90067 USA | |
| **Penner, Stanford S** | Aeronautical Engineer |
| 5912 Avenida Chamnez, La Jolla CA 92037, USA | |
| **Penney, Steve** | Ice Hockey Player |
| 155 Rue Notre Dame, Saint Pereol des Neiges QC G0A 3R0, Canada | |
| **Pennie, Collins** | Actor |
| Untitled Entertainment, 350 S Beverly Dr, #200, Beverly Hills CA 90212 USA | |
| **Pennie, Michael W** | Sculptor |
| 117 Bradford Road, Atworth, Melksham, Wiltshire SN12 8HY, England | |
| **Pennington, Brad L** | Baseball Player |
| 7220 E State Road 160, Salem IN 47167, USA | |
| **Pennington, Clifford (Cliff)** | Ice Hockey Player |
| 9960 5th St N, #203, Saint Petersburg FL 33702, USA | |
| **Pennington, Clifton R (Cliff)** | Baseball Player |
| 23603 Hartwick Lane, San Antonio TX 78259, USA | |
| **Pennington, J Chad** | Football Player |
| 2421 Dry Ridge Road, Versailles KY 40383, USA | |
| **Pennington, Janice** | Model, Actress |
| PO Box 11402, Beverly Hills CA 90213, USA | |
| **Pennington, Julia** | Actress |
| Abrams Artists, 9200 W Sunset Blvd, #1125, West Hollywood CA 90069 USA | |
| **Pennington, Michael** | Actor |
| 41 Marlborough Hill, London NW8 0NG, England | |
| **Pennington, Ty** | Actor |
| Agency  S G H, 6525 Sunset Blvd, #900-PH, Los Angeles CA 90028, USA | |
| **Pennison, Jay L** | Football Player |
| 3007 W Autumn Run Circle, Sugar Land TX 77479, USA | |
| **Pennock of Norton, Raymond** | Businessman |
| Morgan Grenfell Group, 23 Great Winchester St, London EC2P 2AX, England | |
| **Pennock, Chris** | Actor |
| 25150 1/2 Malibu Road, Malibu CA 90265, USA | |
| **Penny, Bradley W (Brad)** | Baseball Player |
| 25071 Abercrombie Lane, Calabasas CA 91302, USA | |
| **Penny, Daniel** | Geoscientist |
| University of Sydney, Geoscience Dept, Sydney NSW 2006, Australia | |
| **Penny, Joe** | Actor |
| Shelter Entertainment, 9255 Sunset Blvd, #300, Los Angeles CA 90069 USA | |
| **Penny, Roger P** | Businessman |
| Bethlehem Steel, 1655 Valley Center Parkway, #200, Bethlehem PA 18017, USA | |
| **Penny, Sydney** | Actress |
| Stone Manners Salners, 6100 Wilshire Blvd, #1500, Los Angeles CA 90035 USA | |
| **Pennyfeather, William N (Will)** | Baseball Player |
| 333 Rector St, #6D, Perth Amboy NJ 08861, USA | |
| **Penot, Jacques** | Actor |
| 9 Rue de l'Isly, 75008 Paris, France | |
| **Penrose, Patricia (Tricia)** | Actress, Singer |
| International Artists, 193-197 High Holborn, London WC1V 7BD, England | |
| **Penry-Jones, Rupert** | Actor |
| Artist Rights Group, 4A Exmoor St, London W10 6BD, England | |
| **Penske, Jay** | Businessman |
| Penske Media Corporation, 16026 Royal Oak Rd, Encino CA 91436, USA | |
| **Penske, Roger S** | Auto Racing Driver, Executive |
| Penske Racing, Penske Plaza, 366 Riverfront, Reading PA 19602, USA | |

|  |  |
|---|---|
| **Pentecost, Del**<br>Paradigm Agency, 360 N Crescent Dr, North Building, Beverly Hills CA 90210 USA | Actor |
| **Pentland, Alex P**<br>Massachusetts Institute of Technology, Media Laboratory, Cambridge MA 02139, USA | Computer Scientist |
| **Penzias, Arno A**<br>New Enterprise Assoc, 2855 Sand Hill Road, Menlo Park CA 94025, USA | Nobel Physics Laureate |
| **Peoples, David**<br>2545 Cedarwood Dr, Germantown TN 38138, USA | Golfer |
| **Peoples, David Webb**<br>Creative Artists Agency, 2000 Ave of Stars, #100, Los Angeles CA 90067 USA | Director, Writer |
| **Peoples, John**<br>Fermi National Acceleration Laboratory, C D F Collaboration, PO Box 500, Batavia IL 60510, USA | Physicist |
| **Peper, Tim**<br>Paradigm Agency, 360 N Crescent Dr, North Building, Beverly Hills CA 90210 USA | Actor |
| **Pepitone, Joseph A (Joe)**<br>27 Roosevelt Blvd, Massapequa NY 11758, USA | Baseball Player |
| **Peplinski, Jim**<br>Peplinski Auto Leasing, 212 Meridian Road NE, Calgary AB T2A 2N6, Canada | Ice Hockey Player |
| **Peplowski, Ken**<br>Hot Jazz Mgmt, 116 E 27th St, New York NY 10016, USA | Jazz Saxophonist, Clarinetist |
| **Pepoy, Andrew**<br>Tribune Media Services, 435 N Michigan Ave, #1500, Chicago IL 60611 USA | Cartoonist (Annie) |
| **Pepper Mochrie, Dorothy (Dottie)**<br>PO Box 623, Saratoga Springs NY 12866, USA | Golfer |
| **Pepper, Barry**<br>Paul Kohner, 9300 Wilshire Blvd, #555, Beverly Hills CA 90212 USA | Actor |
| **Pepper, Beverly**<br>Torre Gentile, 06059 Todi (PG), Italy | Sculptor |
| **Pepper, Cynthia**<br>219 Friendly Court, Henderson NV 89052, USA | Actress |
| **Pepper, John E, Jr**<br>Walt Disney Co, 500 S Buena Vista St, Burbank CA 91521, USA | Businessman |
| **Pepperberg, Irene M**<br>Harper Collins Publishers, 10 E 53rd St, Cellar 1, New York NY 10022 USA | Writer |
| **Peppers, Julius F**<br>173 Rehoboth Lane, Mooresville NC 28117, USA | Football Player |
| **Peppler, Mary Jo**<br>Coast Volleyball Club, 11526 Sorrento Valley Road, San Diego CA 92121, USA | Volleyball Player |
| **Pera, Renee Reijo**<br>University of California Medical Center, 505 Parnassus, San Francisco CA 94122, USA | Human Reproductive Biologist |
| **Pera, Robert J**<br>Ubiquiti Networks, 2580 Orchard Parkway, San Jose CA 95131, USA | Businessman |
| **Perabo, Piper**<br>United Talent Agency, U T A Plaza, 9336 Civic Center Dr, Beverly Hills CA 90210 USA | Actress |
| **Perahia, Murray**<br>Askonas Holt, Lincoln House, 300 High Holborn, London WC1V 7JH, England | Concert Pianist |
| **Peralta Fabi, Ricardo**<br>Ciudad Universitaria, Instituto de Ingenieria, Circuito Escolar Sn, CP 04510, Mexico DF, Mexico | Astronaut, Mexico |
| **Peralta Morones, Oribe P**<br>Federacion de Futbol, Colima 373 Colonia Roma, Delegacion Cuauhtemoc, Mexico City DF 06700, Mexico | Soccer Player |
| **Peralta, Jhonny A**<br>27940 Berringer Run, Westlake OH 44145, USA | Baseball Player |
| **Percival, Brian**<br>Gotham Group, 9255 Sunset Blvd, #515, Los Angeles CA 90069, USA | Director |
| **Percival, Lance**<br>Rhubarb Agency, 1A Devonshire Road, #100, London W4 2EU, England | Actor |
| **Percival, Mac L**<br>6710 Flowermound Dr, Sugar Land TX 77479, USA | Football Player |
| **Percival, Troy E**<br>1090 Coronet Dr, Riverside CA 92506, USA | Baseball Player |
| **Perconte, John P (Jack)**<br>6197 Hinterlong Court, Lisle IL 60532, USA | Baseball Player |
| **Perdue, William E (Will)**<br>6310 Innisbrook Dr, Prospect KY 40059, USA | Basketball Player |
| **Perec, Marie-Jose**<br>H S International Sports Mgmt, 9871 Irvine Center Dr, Irvine CA 92618, USA | Track Athlete |
| **Peregrym, Missy**<br>Gersh Agency, 9465 Wilshire Blvd, #600, Beverly Hills CA 90212 USA | Actress |
| **Pereira, Mike**<br>National Football League, 280 Park Ave, #12W, New York NY 10017, USA | Football Executive, Sportscaster |
| **Perek, Lubos**<br>Kourimska 28, 13000 Prague 3, Czech Republic | Astronomer |
| **Perelman, Ronald O**<br>Revlon Group, 35 E 62nd St, New York NY 10065, USA | Businessman |
| **Perelman, Vadim**<br>Rumble Media, 1620 Broadway, Santa Monica CA 90403, USA | Director, Writer |
| **Perenyi, Miklos**<br>Liszt Academy of Music, PO Box 206, Liszt Ter 8, 1391 Budapest, Hungary | Concert Violinist |
| **Peress, Gilles**<br>48 Great Jones St, #2SE, New York NY 10012, USA | Photographer |
| **Peretokin, Mark**<br>Bolshoi Theater, Teatralnaya Pl 1, 103009 Moscow, Russia | Ballet Dancer |
| **Peretti, Chelsea**<br>Mosiac Media Group, 9200 W Sunset Blvd, #1000, Los Angeles CA 90069 USA | Actress |
| **Peretti, Lucia**<br>Federation of Ice Sports, Via Vitorchiano 113/117, 00189 Rome, Italy | Speed Skater |
| **Peretz, Jesse**<br>United Talent Agency, U T A Plaza, 9336 Civic Center Dr, Beverly Hills CA 90210 USA | Director |
| **Pereyra, Marianela**<br>Brady Brannon Rich, 5670 Wilshire Blvd, #820, Los Angeles CA 90036, USA | Actress |
| **Perez Batista, Manuel M (Manny)**<br>Don Buchwald Talent Agency, 6500 Wilshire Blvd, #2200, Los Angeles CA 90048 USA | Actor |
| **Perez de Cuellar, Javier**<br>Avenida Aurelio Miro Quesada 1071, San Isifro, Lima 2, Peru | Secretary General, United Nations |
| **Perez Esquivel, Adolfo**<br>Servicio Paz y Justicia, Piedras 730, 1070 Buenos Aires, Argentina | Nobel Peace Laureate |

**Perez Fernandez, Pedro** — Government Official, Spain
Partido Socialista Obrero Espanol, Ferraz 68 y 70, 28008 Madrid, Spain

**Perez Molina, Otto F** — President, Guatemala
President's Office, Palacio Nacional, 6 Avenida 419, Guatemala City, Guatemala

**Perez, Amanda** — Singer, Songwriter
Paradigm Agency, 360 N Crescent Dr, North Building, Beverly Hills CA 90210 USA

**Perez, Antonio M** — Businessman
Eastman Kodak Co, 343 State St, Rochester NY 14650, USA

**Perez, Atanasio R (Tony)** — Baseball Player, Manager
1717 N Bayshore Dr, #3246, Miami FL 33132, USA

**Perez, Carmen** — Actress
Evolution Entertainment, 901 N Highland Ave, Los Angeles CA 90038 USA

**Perez, Chris** — Guitarist, Orchestra Leader, Actor
Big F D Entertainment, 301 Arizona Ave, #200, Santa Monica CA 90401, USA

**Perez, Christopher R (Chris)** — Baseball Player
Los Angeles Dodgers, Stadium, 1000 Elysian Park Ave, Los Angeles CA 90090 USA

**Perez, Eduardo A** — Baseball Player
113 Calle Las Flores, San Juan PR 00911, USA

**Perez, Hugo E** — Soccer Player
22018 Newbridge Dr, Lake Forest CA 92630, USA

**Perez, Jossie** — Opera Singer
Columbia Artists Mgmt Inc, 5 Columbus Circle, 1790 Broadway, #1600, New York NY 10019 USA

**Perez, Luiz (Louie)** — Drummer, Singer (Los Lobos)
Gold Mountain, 3940 Laurel Canyon Blvd, #444, Studio City CA 91604 USA

**Perez, Manny** — Actor
Don Buchwald Talent Agency, 6500 Wilshire Blvd, #2200, Los Angeles CA 90048 USA

**Perez, Martin R (Marty), Jr** — Baseball Player
30 Willowick Dr, Decatur GA 30034, USA

**Perez, Melido T G** — Baseball Player
Nigua KM 21 1/2, Santo Domingo, Dominican Republic

**Perez, Rosie** — Actress, Singer
Silver Lining Entertainment, 421 S Beverly Drive, #700, Beverly Hills CA 90212 USA

**Perez, Timothy Paul** — Actor
Three Moons Entertainment, 5441 E Beverly Blvd, #G, Los Angeles CA 90022, USA

**Perez, Vincent** — Actor, Director
United Agents, 12-26 Lexington St, London W1F 0LE, England

**Pergine, John S** — Football Player
5 Jody Dr, Plymouth Meeting PA 19462, USA

**Perillo, Gregory** — Artist
2 Blackwell Road, Nesconset NY 11767, USA

**Perine, Kelly** — Actor, Comedian
Mark Holder Mgmt, 5225 Wilshire Blvd, #600, Los Angeles CA 90036 USA

**Perisho, Matthew A (Matt)** — Baseball Player
1462 W Cardinal Way, Chandler AZ 85286, USA

**Perkin, J D** — Sculptor
Laura Russo Gallery, 805 NW 21st St, Portland OR 97209, USA

**Perkins, Broderick P** — Baseball Player
5367 San Vicente Blvd, #237, Los Angeles CA 90019, USA

**Perkins, Carl C** — Representative, KY
1401 15th St, Huntington WV 25701, USA

**Perkins, Courtland D** — Aeronautical Engineer
400 Hilltop Terrace, Alexandria VA 22301, USA

**Perkins, David G** — Army General
Commanding General, Training & Doctrine Command, Fort Monroe VA 23651 USA

**Perkins, Donald A (Don)** — Football Player
808 Vassar Dr NE, Albuquerque NM 87106, USA

**Perkins, Edward J** — Diplomat
2801 New Mexico Ave NW, #1407, Washington DC 20007, USA

**Perkins, Elizabeth** — Actress
Gersh Agency, 9465 Wilshire Blvd, #600, Beverly Hills CA 90212 USA

**Perkins, Elvis** — Singer, Songwriter
Flatiron Borman Mgmt, 15 W 26th St, #1200, New York NY 10010, USA

**Perkins, Emily** — Actress
Wales University, Film Studies, Aberystwuth, Ceredigion SY23 3AJ, Wales

**Perkins, Glen W** — Baseball Player
19775 Jersey Ave, Lakeville MN 55044, USA

**Perkins, Gregory S (Tex)** — Singer, Songwriter
MajorBox Music, PO Box 1164, Windsor VIC 3181, Australia

**Perkins, Homer G** — Businessman
372 S Shore Road, Pascoag RI 02859, USA

**Perkins, Jack** — Commentator
A&E Network, News Dept, 235 E 45th St, New York NY 10017, USA

**Perkins, John M** — Civil Rights Activist
1655 Saint Charles St, Jackson MS 39209, USA

**Perkins, Kathleen Rose** — Actress
Trademark Talent, 144 S Beverly Dr, #404, Beverly Hills CA 90212, USA

**Perkins, Kendrick** — Basketball Player
137 Fox Road, Waltham MA 02451, USA

**Perkins, Kieren** — Swimmer
GPO Box 232, Brisbane QED 4001, Australia

**Perkins, Lawrence B, Jr** — Architect
4 Rectory Lane, Scarsdale NY 10583, USA

**Perkins, Lucian** — Photojournalist
3103 17th St NW, Washington DC 20010, USA

**Perkins, Millie** — Actress
2511 Canyon Dr, Los Angeles CA 90068, USA

**Perkins, Oz** — Actor
Greene Assoc, 1901 Ave of Stars, #130, Los Angeles CA 90067 USA

**Perkins, Polly** — Actress
Associated International Mgmt, 7 Hatton Garden, #400, London EC1N 8AD, England

**Perkins, Samuel B (Sam)** — Basketball Player
14901 Bellbrook Dr, Dallas TX 75254, USA

**Perkins, Stephen A** — Drummer (Jane's Addiction), Songwriter
DeMann Entertainment, 9465 Wilshire Blvd, #426, Beverly Hills CA 90212, USA

**Perkins, Susan Y** — Beauty Queen
23 Winsor Way, Weston MA 02493, USA

# P

**Perkins, Travis** — Actor
Abraxas Talent, 4260 Troost Ave, #1, Studio City CA 91604, USA

**Perkins, W Ray** — Football Player, Coach
57 Honors Lane, Hattiesburg MS 39402, USA

**Perkins, Warren C (Red)** — Basketball Player
717 Fairfield Ave, Gretna LA 70056, USA

**Perkowski, Harold W (Harry)** — Baseball Player
211 McGinnis St, Beckley WV 25801, USA

**Perks, Craig** — Golfer
321 Thibodeaux Dr, Lafayette LA 70503, USA

**Perl, Frank J** — Cinematographer
5020 Biloxi Ave, North Hollywood CA 91601, USA

**Perlich, Max** — Actor
Anthem Entertainment, 5225 Wilshire Blvd, #615, Los Angeles CA 90036, USA

**Perlinger, Sissi** — Singer, Actress
Kunstlerag Heidrun Abels, Gartenstr 9, 79211 Denzlingen, Germany

**Perlini, Fred** — Ice Hockey Player
409 Albert St W, Sault Sainte Marie ON P6A 1C2, Canada

**Perlman, Harvey** — Educator
University of Nebraska, Chancellor's Office, Lincoln NE 68588, USA

**Perlman, Itzhak** — Concert Violinist, Conductor
I M G Artists, Hogarth Business Park, Chiswick, London W4 2TH, England

**Perlman, Jonathan S (Jon)** — Baseball Player
3225 Bryn Mawr Dr, Dallas TX 75225, USA

**Perlman, Lawrence** — Businessman
Ceridian Corp, 3311 E Old Shakopee Road, Minneapolis MN 55425, USA

**Perlman, Navah** — Concert Pianist
I M G Artists, Hogarth Business Park, Chiswick, London W4 2TH, England

**Perlman, Rhea** — Actress
8665 Burton Way, #507, Los Angeles CA 90048, USA

**Perlman, Ron** — Actor
L I N K Entertainment, 11872 La Grange Ave, Los Angeles CA 90025 USA

**Perlmutter, Saul** — Nobel Physics Laureate
Lawrence Berkeley National Laboratory, 1 Cycloton Road, Berkeley CA 94720 USA

**Perlozzo, Samuel B (Sam)** — Baseball Player, Manager
18101 Emerald Bay St, Tampa FL 33647, USA

**Perls, Tom** — Physician
2 Harrington Lane, Weston MA 02493, USA

**Perman, Jay A** — Educator
University of Maryland, President's Office, 220 Arch St, Baltimore MD 21201, USA

**Pernel, Florence** — Actress
Artmedia, 20 Ave Rapp, 75007 Paris, France

**Pernice, Tom, Jr** — Golfer
38390 Shoal Creek Dr, Murrieta CA 92562, USA

**Pero, Anthony J (A J)** — Singer, Drummer (Twisted Sister)
Rebellion Entertainment, 2440 Broadway, #111, New York NY 10024, USA

**Peron, Carlos** — Synthesizer Player (Yello)
Creative Artists Agency, 2000 Ave of Stars, #100, Los Angeles CA 90067 USA

**Perot, Edward J (Petey)** — Football Player
2401 Hillside Road, Ruston LA 71270, USA

**Perot, H Ross** — Businessman, Presidential Candidate
Perot Systems, 2300 W Plano Parkway, Plano TX 75075, USA

**Perot, Henry Ross, Jr** — Aviator
Perot Group, Lakeside Square, 12377 Merit Dr, #1700, Dallas TX 75251, USA

**Perranoski, Ronald P (Ron)** — Baseball Player
3805 Indian River Dr, Vero Beach FL 32963, USA

**Perrault, Dominique** — Architect
Perrault Architecte, 26 Rue Brunneseau, 75629 Paris Cedex 13, France

**Perreau, Gigi** — Actress
18411 Hatteras St, #120, Tarzana CA 91356, USA

**Perreault, Annie** — Speed Skater
Speed Skating Canada, 2781 Lancaster Road, #402, Ottawa ON K1B 1A7, Canada

**Perreault, Gilbert (Gil)** — Ice Hockey Player
4 Rue de la Serenite, Victoriaville QC G6S 1J4, Canada

**Perreault, Yanic** — Ice Hockey Player
4303 E Cactus Road, #345, Phoenix AZ 85032, USA

**Perrella, James E** — Businessman
Ingersoll-Rand Co, PO Box 6820, Piscataway NJ 08855, USA

**Perren, Diego** — Curling Athlete
Curling Association, PO Box 606, 3000 Bern, Switzerland

**Perret, Craig** — Thoroughbred Racing Jockey
825 Antioch Road, Shelbyville KY 40065, USA

**Perretta, Ralph J** — Football Player
1305 Calle Scott, Encinitas CA 92024, USA

**Perrette, Pauley** — Actress
S D B Partners, 315 S Beverly Dr, #411, Beverly Hills CA 90067 USA

**Perri, Christina** — Singer, Songwriter
W M E Entertainment, 9601 Wilshire Blvd, #300, Beverly Hills CA 90210 USA

**Perri, Nicholas B (Nick)** — Guitarist, Songwriter, Producer
Perri Ink, PO Box 931509, Los Angeles CA 90093, USA

**Perrier, Mireille** — Actress
Jean-François Pignard de Marthod, 11 Rue Chanez, 75781 Paris Cedex 16, France

**Perriman, Brett R** — Football Player
PO Box 83337, Conyers GA 30013, USA

**Perrine, Valerie** — Actress
Bensky Entertainment, 15021 Ventura Blvd, #343, Sherman Oaks CA 91403, USA

**Perrineau, Harold, Jr** — Actor
A P A Talent & Literary Agency, 405 S Beverly Dr, #300, Beverly Hills CA 90212 USA

**Perrotta, Tom** — Writer
Saint Martin's Press, 175 5th Ave, #400, New York NY 10010 USA

**Perry, A Joseph (Joe)** — Guitarist (Aerosmith), Songwriter
Front Line Mgmt, 1100 Glendon Ave, #2000, Los Angeles CA 90024 USA

**Perry, Alex** — Fashion Designer
104/106 The Strand, 412-414 George St, Sydney NSW 2000, Australia

**Perry, Anne** — Writer
Tyrn Vawr, Seafield, Portmahomack, Rosshire IV20 1RE, Scotland

**Perry, Barry W** — Businessman
Engelhard Corp, 101 Wood Ave, Iselin NJ 08830, USA
**Perry, Bradley Steven** — Actor
Coast to Coast Talent, 3350 Barham Blvd, Los Angeles CA 90068 USA
**Perry, Curtis R** — Basketball Player
1222 I St NE, Washington DC 20002, USA
**Perry, Darren** — Football Player
801 Volvo Parkway, #109, Chesapeake VA 23320, USA
**Perry, Edward L (Ed)** — Football Player
1583 SW 161st Ave, Pembroke Pines FL 33027, USA
**Perry, Elliott L** — Basketball Player
3230 Scheibler Road, Memphis TN 38128, USA
**Perry, Felton** — Actor
Hollywood Book, 6562 Hollywood Blvd, Los Angeles CA 90028, USA
**Perry, Gaylord J** — Baseball Player
All Sports USA, PO Box 489, Spruce Pine NC 28777, USA
**Perry, Gerald** — Football Player
2940 Dell Dr, Columbia SC 29209, USA
**Perry, Gerald E** — Football Player
336 5th St, Manhattan Beach CA 90266, USA
**Perry, Gerald J** — Baseball Player
1348 Waterford Green Close, Marietta GA 30068, USA
**Perry, Herbert E (Herb), Jr** — Baseball Player
978 N Fletcher Ave, Mayo FL 32066, USA
**Perry, J Christopher (Chris)** — Golfer
170 Valley Run Dr, Powell OH 43065, USA
**Perry, J Kenneth (Kenny)** — Golfer
418 Quail Ridge Road, Franklin KY 42134, USA
**Perry, James E (Jim)** — Baseball Player
155 Porters Glen, New London NC 28127, USA
**Perry, Jeff** — Actor
Principal Entertainment, 9255 Sunset Blvd, #500, Los Angeles CA 90069 USA
**Perry, John R** — Philosopher
Stanford University, Language/Information Study Center, Stanford CA 94305, USA
**Perry, Katy** — Singer, Songwriter
Direct Management Group, 947 N La Cienega Blvd, #G, West Hollywood CA 90069, USA
**Perry, Keith** — Singer, Fiddler, Songwriter
Curb Records, 48 Music Square E, Nashville TN 37203 USA
**Perry, Kimberly M** — Singer, Guitarist, Pianist (Band Perry)
W M E Entertainment, 9601 Wilshire Blvd, #300, Beverly Hills CA 90210 USA
**Perry, Lee (Scratch)** — Singer (Upsetters)
Agency Group Ltd, 142 W 57th St, #600, New York NY 10019 USA
**Perry, Linda** — Singer (Four Non Blondes), Songwriter
W M E Entertainment, 9601 Wilshire Blvd, #300, Beverly Hills CA 90210 USA
**Perry, Luke** — Actor
Himber Entertainment, PO Box 950, South Orange NJ 07079 USA
**Perry, Matthew** — Actor
Creative Artists Agency, 2000 Ave of Stars, #100, Los Angeles CA 90067 USA
**Perry, Melvin G (Bob)** — Baseball Player
445 Fox Chase Village, New Bern NC 28562, USA
**Perry, Michael Dean** — Football Player
1029 Sedgewood Circle, Charlotte NC 28211, USA
**Perry, Michael R** — Writer, Producer
United Talent Agency, U T A Plaza, 9336 Civic Center Dr, Beverly Hills CA 90210 USA
**Perry, Michelle** — Concert French Horn Player
Columbia Artists Mgmt Inc, 5 Columbus Circle, 1790 Broadway, #1600, New York NY 10019 USA
**Perry, Neil** — Bassist (Band Perry)
W M E Entertainment, 9601 Wilshire Blvd, #300, Beverly Hills CA 90210 USA
**Perry, Phil** — Singer
Morey Management Group, 1100 Glendon Ave, #1100, Los Angeles CA 90024, USA
**Perry, Reid** — Drummer (Band Perry)
W M E Entertainment, 9601 Wilshire Blvd, #300, Beverly Hills CA 90210 USA
**Perry, Rodney C (Rod)** — Football Player
40 E Bloomfield Lane, Westfield IN 46074, USA
**Perry, Scott E** — Football Player
2807 Graysby Ave, San Pedro CA 90732, USA
**Perry, Stephen H (Steve)** — Singer (Cherry Poppin Daddies)
Paradise Artists, PO Box 1821, Ojai CA 93024 USA
**Perry, Stephen P (Steve)** — Singer (Journey), Songwriter
Perry S Oretzky, 10880 Wilshire Blvd, #920, Los Angeles CA 90024, USA
**Perry, Steve** — Writer
959 E Cinnamon Dr, Lemoore CA 93245, USA
**Perry, Todd J** — Football Player
13805 Brittle Road, Alpharetta GA 30004, USA
**Perry, Troy D** — Religious Leader
Metropolitan Churches Fellowship, 5300 Santa Monica Blvd, Los Angeles CA 90029, USA
**Perry, Tyler** — Actor, Director, Writer
34th Street Films, 8200 Wilshire Blvd, #300, Beverly Hills CA 90211, USA
**Perry, Vernon, Jr** — Football Player
PO Box 842201, Houston TX 77284, USA
**Perry, W Patrick (Pat)** — Baseball Player
1115 W Franklin St, Taylorville IL 62568, USA
**Perry, William A (Refrigerator)** — Football Player
2885 Old Camp Long Road, Aiken SC 29805, USA
**Perry, William J** — Secretary, Defense
11210 Hooper Lane, Los Altos Hills CA 94024, USA
**Perryman, Jill** — Actress
4 Hillside Crescent, Gooseberry Hill WA 6076, Australia
**Perryman, Robert L (Bob)** — Football Player
PO Box 8543, Haverhill MA 01835, USA
**Persad-Bissessar, Kamla** — Prime Minister, Trinidad & Tobago
Prime Minister's Office, Whitehall, Maraval Road, Port of Spain, Trinidad & Tobago
**Persaud, Deborah** — Pediatrician, Surgeon, Virologist
Johns Hopkins Children's Hospital, Surgery Dept, 1800 Orleans St, Baltimore MD 21287, USA
**Persbrandt, Mikael** — Actor
I C M Partners, 10250 Constellation Blvd, #900, Los Angeles CA 90067 USA

**P**

**Perry - Persbrandt**

# P

**Pershing, Jennifer**
Playboy Promotions, 9346 Civic Center Dr, #200, Beverly Hills CA 90210 USA — Model

**Persoff, Nehemiah**
5670 Moonstone Dr, Cambria CA 93428, USA — Actor

**Person, Chuck C**
2903 McKinley Dr, Opelika AL 36804, USA — Basketball Player

**Person, Houston**
Hot Jazz Mgmt, 116 E 27th St, New York NY 10016, USA — Jazz Saxophonist

**Person, Robert A**
25 Bellerive Acres, Saint Louis MO 63121, USA — Baseball Player

**Person, Wesley L**
PO Box 481, Brantley AL 36009, USA — Basketball Player

**Personen, Richard M**
765 Pine Hills Place, The Villages FL 32162, USA — Football Player

**Persons, Peter**
1153 Saint Andrews Dr, Macon GA 31210, USA — Golfer

**Persson, Elisabeth**
Curling Association, Idrottshuser, Marbackagatan 19, 123 43 Farsta, Sweden — Curling Athlete

**Persson, H Goran**
J K L Group, Sveavagen 24-26, 111 84 Stockholm, Sweden — Prime Minister, Sweden

**Persson, Jorgen**
Rydbolundsvagen 7, 185 31 Vaxholm, Sweden — Cinematographer

**Persson, Nina E**
Talent Trust, Kungsgatan 9C, 411 19 Gothenburg, Sweden — Singer (Cardigans), Songwriter

**Persson, Ricard**
2200-201 Portage Ave, Winnipeg MB R3B 3L3, Canada — Ice Hockey Player

**Persson, Stefan**
Hennes & Mauritz AB, Sverigekontoret, 106 38 Stockholm, Sweden — Businessman

**Persson, Torsten**
Stockholm University, International Economic Studies Institute, 106 91 Stockholm, Sweden — Economist

**Perzanowski, Stanley (Stan)**
PO Box 133, New Park PA 17352, USA — Baseball Player

**Pescatelli, Tammy**
Parallel Entertainment, 9420 Wilshire Blvd, #250, Beverly Hills CA 90212 USA — Actress, Comedienne

**Pesce, Gaetano**
543 Broadway, #5, New York NY 10012, USA — Interior Designer

**Pesch, Dorothee (Doro)**
Postfach 105313, 40044 Dusseldorf, Germany — Singer (Warlock)

**Pesci, Joe**
Jay Julien Mgmt, 1501 Broadway, #2600, New York NY 10036, USA — Actor

**Pescia, Lisa**
Coast to Coast Talent, 3350 Barham Blvd, Los Angeles CA 90068 USA — Actress

**Pescucci, Gabriella**
Sandra Marsh & Associates, 9150 Wilshire Blvd, #220, Beverly Hills CA 90212, USA — Costume Designer

**Pesek, Libor**
I M G Artists, Hogarth Business Park, Chiswick, London W4 2TH, England — Conductor

**Pesonen, Dick**
2032 Fairview Lane, The Villages FL 32162, USA — Football Player

**Pess, Katalin**
Names Model Mgmt, Via Savona 53, 20144 Milan, Italy — Model

**Pestka, Sidney**
Robert Wood Johnson Medical School, 675 Hoes Lane, Piscataway NJ 08854, USA — Molecular Geneticist

**Pestova, Daniela**
Next Model Mgmt, 9 Boul de la Madeleine, 75001 Paris, France — Model

**Pesut, George**
1008-415 Michigan St, Victoria BC V8V 1R8, Canada — Ice Hockey Player

**Petagine, Roberto A**
1123 Obispo Ave, Coral Gables FL 33134, USA — Baseball Player

**Peter, Valentine J**
Father Flanagan's Boys Town, 14100 Crawford St, Boys Town NE 68010, USA — Religious Leader, Social Worker

**Peterek, Jeffrey A (Jeff)**
8073 Elm Valley Road, Three Oaks MI 49128, USA — Baseball Player

**Peterle, Lozje**
Slovenian Christian Democrats, Beethovnova 4, 1000 Ljubljana, Slovenia — Prime Minister, Slovenia

**Peterman, D Brian**
Commander, US Coast Guard Atlantic, 4131 Crawford St, Portsmouth VA 23704 USA — Coast Guard Admiral

**Peterman, Melissa**
A P A Talent & Literary Agency, 405 S Beverly Dr, #300, Beverly Hills CA 90212 USA — Actress

**Peterman, Steven**
Jackoway Tyerman Wertheimer, 1925 Century Park E, #2200, Los Angeles CA 90067 USA — Producer

**Peters, Anthony L (Tony)**
2402 Boston St, Muskogee OK 74401, USA — Football Player

**Peters, Bernadette**
323 W 80th St, New York NY 10024, USA — Singer, Actress

**Peters, Bob**
Bemidji State University, Athletic Dept, Bemidji MN 56601, USA — Ice Hockey Coach

**Peters, Christopher M (Chris)**
613 Chessbriar Dr, Three Oaks MI 49128, USA — Baseball Player

**Peters, Clarke**
Stone Manners Salners, 6100 Wilshire Blvd, #1500, Los Angeles CA 90035 USA — Actor

**Peters, Clayre**
Playboy Promotions, 9346 Civic Center Dr, #200, Beverly Hills CA 90210 USA — Model

**Peters, Dan**
Legends of 21st Century, 7 Trinity Row, Florence MA 01062, USA — Drummer (Mudhoney)

**Peters, Devereaux**
Minnesota Lynx, Target Center, 600 1st Ave N, Minneapolis MN 55403 USA — Basketball Player

**Peters, Emmitt**
General Delivery, Ruby AK 99768, USA — Dog Sled Racer

**Peters, Evan**
Creative Artists Agency, 2000 Ave of Stars, #100, Los Angeles CA 90067 USA — Actor

**Peters, Garry**
3020 Eastview, Saskatoon SK S7J 3J2, Canada — Ice Hockey Player

**Peters, Gary C**
7121 N Serenoa Dr, Sarasota FL 34241, USA — Baseball Player

**Peters, Gretchen**
Val Denn Agency, 100 Congress Ave, #2000, Austin TX 78701, USA — Singer, Songwriter

| | |
|---|---|
| **Peters, Jan** | Singer |
| 959 7th St, Beaver PA 15009, USA | |
| **Peters, Jason R** | Football Player |
| 95 Stroughton Lane, Orchard Park NY 14127, USA | |
| **Peters, Jim, Jr** | Ice Hockey Player |
| Vermont Academy, PO Box 500, Saxtons River VT 05154, USA | |
| **Peters, Jon** | Producer |
| 9941 Tower Lane, Beverly Hills CA 90210, USA | |
| **Peters, Maria Liberia** | Prime Minister, Netherlands Antilles |
| Prime Minister's Office, Fort Amsterdam, Willemstad, Netherlands Antilles | |
| **Peters, Mary** | Track Athlete |
| Willowtree Cottage, River Road, Dunmurray, Belfast, Northern Ireland | |
| **Peters, Mike** | Editorial Cartoonist |
| PO Box 957, Bradenton FL 34206, USA | |
| **Peters, Ralph** | Writer |
| Trident Media Group, 41 Madison Ave, #3600, New York NY 10010 USA | |
| **Peters, Rick** | Actor |
| TalentWorks, 3500 W Olive Ave, #1400, Burbank CA 91505 USA | |
| **Peters, Roberta** | Opera Singer, Actress |
| 19356 Cedar Glen Dr, Boca Raton FL 33434, USA | |
| **Peters, Russell** | Actor, Comedian |
| Seven Summits Mgmt, 8906 W Olympic Blvd, Beverly Hills CA 90211 USA | |
| **Peters, Scott** | Producer, Writer |
| Rothman Brecher Agency, 9465 Wilshire Blvd, #840, Beverly Hills CA 90212 USA | |
| **Peters, Timothy** | Auto, Truck Racing Drivier |
| B H R, PO Box 1708, Mount Juliet TN 37121, USA | |
| **Peters, Tom** | Writer, Management Consultant |
| Tom Peters Group, 555 Hamilton Ave, Palo Alto CA 94301, USA | |
| **Peters, Vicki** | Model, Actress |
| Playboy Promotions, 9346 Civic Center Dr, #200, Beverly Hills CA 90210 USA | |
| **Peters, Volney M** | Football Player |
| 325 Lancaster Road, Walnut Creek CA 94595, USA | |
| **Petersen, Byron E** | Pathologist |
| University of Florida Medical School, PO Box 100275, Gainesville FL 32610, USA | |
| **Petersen, Chris** | Football Coach |
| University of Washington, Athletic Dept, Seattle WA 98195, USA | |
| **Petersen, Christopher R (Chris)** | Baseball Player |
| 242 Timberland Ave, Longwood FL 32750, USA | |
| **Petersen, Cole** | Actor |
| Simmons & Scott, 7942 Mulholland Dr, Los Angeles CA 90046, USA | |
| **Petersen, John D** | Educator |
| University of Tennessee, President's Office, Holt Tower, Knoxville TX 37996, USA | |
| **Petersen, Kurt D** | Football Player |
| 5520 Linmore Lane, Plano TX 75093, USA | |
| **Petersen, Paul** | Actor, Singer |
| A Minor Consideration, 14530 Denker Ave, Gardena CA 90247, USA | |
| **Petersen, Suzann** | Golfer |
| Gladengveien 3B, 0661 Oslo, Norway | |
| **Petersen, Theodore H (Ted)** | Football Player |
| 1195 N 17000E, Momence IL 60954, USA | |
| **Petersen, Toby** | Ice Hockey Player |
| 2529 Bryant Ave S, Minneapolis MN 55405, USA | |
| **Petersen, William L** | Actor |
| High Horse Films, 100 Universal City Plaza, Building 2128, Universal City CA 91608, USA | |
| **Petersen, Wolfgang** | Director |
| Paradigm Agency, 360 N Crescent Dr, North Building, Beverly Hills CA 90210 USA | |
| **Peterson, Adam C** | Baseball Player |
| 6401 NE 14th St, Vancouver WA 98665, USA | |
| **Peterson, Adrian L** | Football Player |
| 9212 Cold Stream Lane, Eden Prairie MN 55347, USA | |
| **Peterson, Adrian N** | Football Player |
| 558 W Daybreak Lane, Round Lake IL 60073, USA | |
| **Peterson, Anthony W (Tony)** | Football Player |
| 1124 Lakewood Circle, Naperville IL 60540, USA | |
| **Peterson, Bob** | Writer |
| Pixar, 1200 Park Ave, Emeryville CA 94608, USA | |
| **Peterson, Buzz** | Basketball Coach |
| University of Tennessee, Athletic Dept, Knoxville TN 37996, USA | |
| **Peterson, Calvin E (Cal)** | Football Player |
| 22646 Ingomar St, Canoga Park CA 91304, USA | |
| **Peterson, Chase N** | Educator |
| 910 S Donner Way, #201, Salt Lake City UT 84108, USA | |
| **Peterson, David C** | Photojournalist |
| 4805 Pinehurst Court, Pleasant Hill IA 50327, USA | |
| **Peterson, Debbi** | Singer, Drummer (Bangles) |
| Russell Carter Artist Mgmt, 567 Ralph Mcgill Blvd, Atlanta GA 30312, USA | |
| **Peterson, Donald H** | Astronaut |
| Aerospace Operations Consultants, 427 Pebblebrook Dr, Seabrook TX 77586, USA | |
| **Peterson, Fred I (Fritz)** | Baseball Player |
| PO Box 137, East Dubuque IL 61025, USA | |
| **Peterson, George P (Bud)** | Educator |
| Georgia Institute of Technology, President's Office, Atlanta GA 30332, USA | |
| **Peterson, J Todd** | Football Player |
| 135 Bellacree Road, Duluth GA 30097, USA | |
| **Peterson, John** | Freestyle Wrestler |
| 457 19th Ave, Comstock WI 54826, USA | |
| **Peterson, Julian T** | Football Player |
| 1750 Merton Road NE, Atlanta GA 30306, USA | |
| **Peterson, Melvin L (Mel)** | Basketball Player |
| 2896 Evergreen Lane, Aurora IL 60502, USA | |
| **Peterson, Michael J** | Singer |
| Dennis Mgmt, 1002 18th Ave S, Nashville TN 37212, USA | |
| **Peterson, Morris, Jr** | Basketball Player |
| 909 Lafayette St, #12, New Orleans LA 70113, USA | |
| **Peterson, Patrick D** | Football Player |
| Arizona Cardinals, PO Box 888, Phoenix AZ 85001 USA | |

| | |
|---|---|
| **Peterson, Peter G** | Secretary of Commerce, Financier |
| Blackstone Group, 345 Park Ave, Basement LB4, New York NY 10154, USA | |
| **Peterson, Seth** | Actor |
| 6125 Fulton Ave, #31, Van Nuys CA 91401, USA | |
| **Peterson, Steven** | Architect |
| Peterson/Littenberg Architecture, 131 E 66th St, #1B, New York NY 10065, USA | |
| **Peterson, Sylvia** | Singer (Chiffons) |
| Lustig Talent, PO Box 770850, Orlando FL 32877 USA | |
| **Peterson, Vicki** | Singer, Guitarist (Bangles) |
| Russell Carter Artist Mgmt, 567 Ralph Mcgill Blvd, Atlanta GA 30312, USA | |
| **Peterson, William W (Bill)** | Football Player |
| 13536 Mijo Lane, Lakeside CA 92040, USA | |
| **Petersson, Tom** | Singer, Bassist (Cheap Trick, Swag) |
| Oakie Dokie Mgmt, 6090 Central Ave, Saint Petersburg FL 33707, USA | |
| **Petey Pablo** | Rap Artist |
| Green Light Talent Agency, PO Box 3172, Beverly Hills CA 90212 USA | |
| **Petit, Michel** | Ice Hockey Player |
| 129 Latches Lane, Media PA 19063, USA | |
| **Petit, Philippe** | High Wire Walker |
| Cathedral of Saint John the Devine, 1047 Amsterdam Ave, New York NY 10025, USA | |
| **Petitbon, Richard A (Richie)** | Football Player, Coach |
| 9628 Percussion Way, Vienna VA 22182, USA | |
| **Petitgout, Lewis G (Luke)** | Football Player |
| 5221 S Nichol St, Tampa FL 33611, USA | |
| **Petke, Mike** | Soccer Player, Coach |
| Red Bulls New York, 600 Cape May St, Harrison, NJ 07029 USA | |
| **Petkovic, Andrea** | Tennis Player |
| Tannenweg 24, 64347 Griesheim, Germany | |
| **Peto, Richard** | Epidemiologist |
| Radcliffe Infirmary, Harkness Building, Oxford ON OX2 6HE, England | |
| **Petra, Yvon** | Tennis Player |
| Residence du Prieure, 78100 Saint Germain-en-Laye, France | |
| **Petraeus, David H** | Director, C I A; Army General |
| K K R Global Institute, 9 W 57th St, #4200, New York NY 10019, USA | |
| **Petraglia, John (Johnny)** | Bowler |
| 25 Turnbridge Court, Jackson NJ 08527, USA | |
| **Petralli, Eugene J (Geno)** | Baseball Player |
| 119 Laser Lane, Weatherford TX 76087, USA | |
| **Petrella, Robert (Bob)** | Football Player |
| 116 Aberdeen Way, Rio Grande NJ 08242, USA | |
| **Petrenko, Viktor V** | Figure Skater |
| Ice Vault Arena, 10 Nevins Road, Wayne NJ 07470, USA | |
| **Petri, Michala** | Concert Recorder Player |
| Nordskraenten 3, 2980 Kokkedal, Denmark | |
| **Petri, Nina** | Actress |
| Agentur Carola Studlar, Agnesstr 47, 80798 Munich, Germany | |
| **Petrich, Robert M (Bob)** | Football Player |
| 1391 Silverberry Court, El Cajon CA 92019, USA | |
| **Petrick, Benjamin W (Ben)** | Baseball Player |
| 1553 NE Jackson School Road, Hillsboro OR 97124, USA | |
| **Petrie, Daniel M, Jr** | Director |
| Enderby Entertainment, 18034 Ventura Blvd, #445, Encino CA 91316, USA | |
| **Petrie, Donald** | Director |
| Gersh Agency, 9465 Wilshire Blvd, #600, Beverly Hills CA 90212 USA | |
| **Petrie, Geoff M** | Basketball Player, Executive |
| 3675 Holly Hill Lane, Loomis CA 95650, USA | |
| **Petrino, Paul** | Football Player, Coach |
| University of Idaho, Athletic Dept, Moscow ID 83844, USA | |
| **Petrino, Robert P (Bobby)** | Football Coach |
| University of Louisville, Athletic Dept, Louisville KY 40208, USA | |
| **Petro, Johan** | Basketball Player |
| Brooklyn Nets, 15 Metro Tech Center, #1100, Brooklyn NY 11201 USA | |
| **Petrocelli, Americo P (Rico)** | Baseball Player |
| 37 Green Heron Lane, Nashua NH 03062, USA | |
| **Petrone, Shana** | Singer |
| Epic Records, 34 Music Square E, Nashville TN 37203, USA | |
| **Petroni, Michael** | Director, Writer, Actor |
| W M E Entertainment, 9601 Wilshire Blvd, #300, Beverly Hills CA 90210 USA | |
| **Petronio, Stephen** | Dancer, Choreographer |
| 95 Saint Marks Place, New York NY 10009, USA | |
| **Petroro, Marisa** | Actress |
| House of Representatives, 1434 6th St, #1, Santa Monica CA 90401 USA | |
| **Petroske, John E (Jack)** | Ice Hockey Player |
| PO Box 366, Side Lake MN 55781, USA | |
| **Petrov, Denis A** | Figure Skater |
| World Ice Arena, 1881th Bao'an Road, Luohu District, Shenzhen 518001, China | |
| **Petrova, Nadia** | Tennis Player |
| Women's Tennis Assn, 1 Progress Plaza, #1500, Saint Petersburg FL 33701 USA | |
| **Petrovic, Tim** | Golfer |
| 11602 Turtle Lane, Austin TX 78726, USA | |
| **Petrovicky, Ronald** | Ice Hockey Player |
| 3236 Birkdale Ave, Duluth, GA 30097, USA | |
| **Petrovics, Emil** | Composer |
| Attila Utca 29, 1013 Budapest, Hungary | |
| **Petruska, Richard** | Basketball Player |
| 4704 Pine Oak Park, #636, Houston TX 77081, USA | |
| **Petry, Daniel J (Dan)** | Baseball Player |
| 30715 Mystic Forest Dr, Farmington Hills MI 48331, USA | |
| **Petry, Leroy A** | Afghanistan War Army Hero (CMH) |
| Public Affairs Office, PO Box 339500, Joint Base Lewis-McChord WA 98433, USA | |
| **Petsko, Gregory A** | Chemist, Biochemist |
| 51 Hampshire St, West Newton MA 02465, USA | |
| **Pett, Joel** | Editorial Cartoonist |
| PO Box 174, Wilmore KY 40390, USA | |
| **Pettengill, Gordon H** | Planetary Physicist |
| Massachusetts Institute of Technology, Space Research Center, Cambridge MA 02139, USA | |

**Pettersen, Suzann** — Golfer
R&A Group Services, Beach House, Golf Place, Saint Andrews Fife KY16 9JA, Scotland
**Pettersson, Carl** — Golfer
1604 Dogwood View Lane, Raleigh NC 27614, USA
**Pettet, Joanna** — Actress
Paradigm Agency, 360 N Crescent Dr, North Building, Beverly Hills CA 90210 USA
**Pettie, Jim** — Ice Hockey Player
81 Kirk Road, Rochester NY 14612, USA
**Pettiford, Valerie** — Actress, Singer
TalentWorks, 3500 W Olive Ave, #1400, Burbank CA 91505 USA
**Pettigrew, Gary L** — Football Player
2707 E 27th Ave, #2B, Spokane WA 99223, USA
**Pettigrew, L Eudora** — Educator
State University of New York, President's Office, Old Westbury NY 11568, USA
**Pettine, Michael A (Mike), Jr** — Football Coach
Cleveland Browns, 76 Lou Groza Blvd, Berea OH 44017 USA
**Pettinger, Matt** — Ice Hockey Player
3075 Eastdowne Road, Victoria BC V8R 5S1, Canada
**Pettini, Joseph P (Joe)** — Baseball Player
112 Logan Court, Bethany WV 26032, USA
**Pettis, Gary G** — Baseball Player
3129 Crestline Court, Antioch CA 94531, USA
**Pettis, Madison** — Actress
Coast to Coast Talent, 3350 Barham Blvd, Los Angeles CA 90068 USA
**Pettit, Donald R** — Astronaut
2014 Country Ridge Dr, Houston TX 77062, USA
**Pettit, G W Paul** — Baseball Player
928 Sarazen St, Hemet CA 92543, USA
**Pettit, Robert E (Bob), Jr** — Basketball Player
7 Garden Lane, New Orleans LA 70124, USA
**Pettitte, Andrew E (Andy)** — Baseball Player
2222 W Lawther Dr, Deer Park TX 77536, USA
**Petty, J T** — Director, Writer
Creative Artists Agency, 2000 Ave of Stars, #100, Los Angeles CA 90067 USA
**Petty, Kyle E** — Auto Racing Driver
135 Longfield Dr, Mooresville NC 28115, USA
**Petty, Lori** — Actress
Intellectual Property Group, 10585 Santa Monica Blvd, #140, Los Angeles CA 90025, USA
**Petty, Richard L** — Auto Racing Driver
Richard Petty Motorsports, 7065 Zephyr Place, Concord NC 28027, USA
**Petty, Tom** — Singer, Guitarist, Songwriter
East End Mgmt, 13721 Ventura Blvd, #200, Sherman Oaks CA 91423, USA
**Pettyfer, Alex** — Actor
W M E Entertainment, 9601 Wilshire Blvd, #300, Beverly Hills CA 90210 USA
**Petzschner, Philipp** — Tennis Player
Global Sports Mgmt, Dirk Hordorff Assoc, Ludwigstr 12, 61348 Bad Homburg, Germany
**Peugeot, Roland** — Businessman
170 Ave Victor Hugo, 75116 Paris, France
**Peugnet, Herve** — Fashion Designer
32 Rue Jacob, 75006 Paris, France
**Pevec, Katja** — Actress
Greene Assoc, 1901 Ave of Stars, #130, Los Angeles CA 90067 USA
**Peyroux, Madeleine** — Singer, Songwriter
American International Artists, 356 Pine Valley Road, Hoosick Falls NY 12090, USA
**Peyser, Penny** — Actress
22039 Alizondo Dr, Woodland Hills CA 91364, USA
**Peyton, Brad** — Director
Characters Talent Mgmt, 8 Elm St, Toronto ON M5G 1G7, Canada
**Pfaff, Judy** — Sculptor
319 Greenwich St, #5L, New York NY 10013, USA
**Pfahl, John** — Photographer
Janet Borden, 560 Broadway, #601, New York NY 10012, USA
**Pfann, George R** — Football Player, Coach
120 Warwick Place, Ithaca NY 14850, USA
**Pfeiffer, Meg** — Singer
Kuka, Bolschestr 20, 12587 Berlin, Germany
**Pfeiffer, Michelle** — Actress
Management 360, 9111 Wilshire Blvd, Beverly Hills CA 90210 USA
**Pfeiffer, Norman** — Architect
Hardy Holzman Pfeiffer, 811 W 7th St, #430, Los Angeles CA 90017, USA
**Pfeil, Robert R (Bobby)** — Baseball Player
2358 Pheasant Run Circle, Stockton CA 95207, USA
**Pfell, Mark** — Golfer
2565 Chelsea Road, Palos Verdes Estates CA 90274, USA
**Pfister, Wally** — Cinematographer
2500 Jupiter Dr, Los Angeles CA 90046, USA
**Pflaume, Kai** — Actor
M S C Promotion, Aumuhlenstr 4, 61440 Oberursel, Germany
**Pflug, Jo Ann** — Actress
PO Box 3292, Jupiter FL 33469, USA
**Pfund, Leroy H (Lee)** — Baseball Player
130 Windsor Park Dr, #C214, Carol Stream IL 60188, USA
**Pfund, Randy** — Basketball Coach, Executive
50 S Pointe Dr, #608, Miami Beach FL 33139, USA
**Phair, Liz** — Singer, Songwriter, Actress
KillerMoxie Mgmt, 5890 W Jefferson Blvd, #J, Los Angeles CA 90016, USA
**Pham Minh Man, Jean-Baptiste Cardinal** — Religious Leader
Archdiocese, Toa Tong Giam Muc, 180 Nguyen Dink Chieu, Thanh-Pho Ho Chi Minh, Vietnam
**Pham Tuan** — Cosmonaut, Vietnam
4C-1000-Soc Son, Hanoi, Vietnam
**Phaneuf, Dion** — Ice Hockey Player
271 Heath Road NW, Edmonton AB T6R 1V3, Canada
**Pharr, Tommy L** — Football Player
314 Harrison Lane, Winder GA 30680, USA
**Phegley, Roger D** — Basketball Player
43 Timberlane Dr, Morton IL 61550, USA

**Phelan, James J (Jim)** — Basketball Player, Coach
16579 Old Emmitsburg Road, Emmitsburg MD 21727, USA

**Phelps, Doug** — Singer, Bassist (Kentucky Headhunters)
Webster & Assoc Public Relations, PO Box 23015, Nashville TN 37202, USA

**Phelps, Edmund S** — Nobel Economics Laureate
45 E 89th St, #28B, New York NY 10128, USA

**Phelps, James** — Actor
United Agents, 12-26 Lexington St, London W1F 0LE, England

**Phelps, Jaycie** — Gymnast
5041 N Fortville Pike, Greenfield IN 46140, USA

**Phelps, Joshua L (Josh)** — Baseball Player
1503 Regal Mist Loop, Trinity FL 34655, USA

**Phelps, Kelly Joe** — Singer, Guitarist, Songwriter
Different Strings, 30 Eldon Terrace, Windmill Hill Bristol BS3 4PA, England

**Phelps, Kenneth A (Ken)** — Baseball Player
6030 E Foothill Dr N, Paradise Valley AZ 85253, USA

**Phelps, Michael E** — Neuroscientist, Inventor
16720 Huerta Road, Encino CA 91436, USA

**Phelps, Michael F** — Swimmer
Octagon, 15 Lund Road, Saco ME 04072, USA

**Phelps, Oliver** — Actor
United Agents, 12-26 Lexington St, London W1F 0LE, England

**Phelps, Richard F (Digger)** — Basketball Coach, Sportscaster
Lordly & Dane, 1344 Main St, Waltham MA 02451, USA

**Phelps, Ricky Lee** — Singer, Musician (Kentucky Headhunters)
Webster & Assoc Public Relations, PO Box 23015, Nashville TN 37202, USA

**Phifer, Mekhi** — Actor
Facilitator Films, 4000 Warner Blvd, Building 17, Burbank CA 91522, USA

**Philaret, Patriarch** — Religious Leader
10 Osvobozdeniya St, 220004 Minsk, Belarus

**Philbin, Gerald J (Gerry)** — Football Player
9976 Marsala Way, Delray Beach FL 33446, USA

**Philbin, Joseph (Joe)** — Football Coach
Miami Dolphins, 7500 SW 30th St, Davie FL 33314 USA

**Philbin, Regis** — Entertainer
101 W 67th St, #51A, New York NY 10023, USA

**Philbrick, Denise** — Golfer
5364 Carnegie Loop, Livermore CA 94550, USA

**Philip** — Prince, England; Duke of Edinburgh
Buckingham Palace, Westminster, London SW1A 1AA, England

**Philip, George M** — Educator
State University of New York, President's Office, 1400 Washington Ave, Albany NY 12222, USA

**Philip, Primate** — Religious Leader
Antiochian Orthodox Christian Church, 358 Mountain Road, Englewood NJ 07631, USA

**Philippe** — King, Belgium
Koninklijk Palais, Rue de Brederode, 1000 Brussels, Belgium

**Philippoussis, Mark** — Tennis Player
Octagon Worldwide, 1751 Pinnacle Dr, #1500, McLean VA 22102 USA

**Philipps, Busy** — Actress
I C M Partners, 10250 Constellation Blvd, #900, Los Angeles CA 90067 USA

**Philipps, David N** — Journalist
Colorado Springs Gazette, Editorial Dept, 30 E Pikes Peak Ave, Colorado Springs CO 80903, USA

**Philips, Chuck** — Journalist
Los Angeles Times, Editorial Dept, 202 W 1st St, Los Angeles CA 90012 USA

**Philips, Gina** — Actress
Zero Gravity Mgmt, 1531 14th St, Santa Monica CA 90404 USA

**Phillipoff, Harold** — Ice Hockey Player
736 Georgia St SE, Albuquerque NM 87108, USA

**Phillippe, Ryan** — Actor
Schiff Co, 9220 Sunset Blvd, #106, West Hollywood CA 90069 USA

**Phillips, Andre L P** — Track Athlete
Edison High School, 1425 Center St, Stockton CA 95206, USA

**Phillips, Anthony** — Guitarist (Genesis), Songwriter
Solo Agency, 53-55 Fulham High St, #200, London SW6 3JJ, England

**Phillips, Arianne** — Costume Designer
United Talent Agency, U T A Plaza, 9336 Civic Center Dr, Beverly Hills CA 90210 USA

**Phillips, Bijou** — Singer, Model, Actress
Untitled Entertainment, 350 S Beverly Dr, #200, Beverly Hills CA 90212 USA

**Phillips, Bill** — Physical Fitness Expert
Muscle Media, 444 Corporate Circle, Golden CO 80401, USA

**Phillips, Bobbie** — Actress
Kelly Agency, 3001 Heavenly Ridge St, Thousand Oaks CA 91362, USA

**Phillips, Brandon E** — Baseball Player
586 Rowland Road, Stone Mountain GA 30083, USA

**Phillips, Britta** — Bassist (Luna, Dean & Britta)
Don Buchwald Talent Agency, 6500 Wilshire Blvd, #2200, Los Angeles CA 90048 USA

**Phillips, Caryl** — Writer
A P Watt Ltd, 20 John St, London WC1N 2DR, England

**Phillips, Charles W** — Football Player
915 N Holliston Ave, Pasadena CA 91104, USA

**Phillips, Chynna** — Singer, Actress
D S W Entertainment, 116 E 16th St, #900, New York NY 10003, USA

**Phillips, Clarence G (J R)** — Baseball Player
12210 N Rio Vista Dr, Sun City AZ 85351, USA

**Phillips, D Eugene (Gene)** — Basketball Player
11606 Whisper Willow St, San Antonio TX 78230, USA

**Phillips, Derek** — Actor
Evolution Entertainment, 901 N Highland Ave, Los Angeles CA 90038 USA

**Phillips, Dwight** — Track Athlete
USA Track & Field, RCA Dome, PO Box 140, Indianapolis IN 46225 USA

**Phillips, Eddie L** — Basketball Player
800 McCary St SW, Birmingham AL 35211, USA

**Phillips, Emo** — Actor, Comedian
Harbour Agency, 63 William St, #300, East Sydney NSW 1022, Australia

**Phillips, Erin V** — Basketball Player
Phoenix Mercury, American West Arena, 201 E Jefferson St, Phoenix AZ 85004 USA

**Phillips, Ethan** — Actor
TalentWorks, 3500 W Olive Ave, #1400, Burbank CA 91505 USA
**Phillips, G Andrew (Andy)** — Baseball Player
12744 Frog Ridge Road, Buhl AL 35446, USA
**Phillips, Gersha** — Costume Designer
Paradigm Agency, 360 N Crescent Dr, North Building, Beverly Hills CA 90210 USA
**Phillips, Grant-Lee** — Singer, Guitarist, Songwriter, Actor
Umbrella Group, 20 West St, #30E, New York NY 10002, USA
**Phillips, J Dixon, Jr** — Judge
US Court of Appeals, 100 Europa Dr, Chapel Hill NC 27517, USA
**Phillips, James J (Red)** — Football Player
67 Lakeview Dr, #10D, Alexander City AL 35010, USA
**Phillips, Jason H** — Football Player
6350 W Mystic Meadow, Houston TX 77021, USA
**Phillips, Jason L** — Baseball Player
1777 Tara Way, San Marcos CA 92078, USA
**Phillips, Jay** — Actor
I C M Partners, 10250 Constellation Blvd, #900, Los Angeles CA 90067 USA
**Phillips, Jermaine** — Football Player
11802 Derbyshire Dr, Tampa FL 33626, USA
**Phillips, John** — Basketball Coach
University of Tulsa, Athletic Dept, Tulsa OK 74104, USA
**Phillips, John L** — Astronaut
154 Canoe Cove Lane, Sandpoint ID 83864, USA
**Phillips, Joseph C** — Actor
Don Buchwald Talent Agency, 6500 Wilshire Blvd, #2200, Los Angeles CA 90048 USA
**Phillips, Joseph G (Joe)** — Football Player
4080 SE 39th Circle, Ocala FL 34480, USA
**Phillips, Judith** — Landscape Architect
1840 Zearing Ave NW, Albuquerque NM 87104, USA
**Phillips, Julianne** — Actress
3 Arts Entertainment, 9460 Wilshire Blvd, #700, Beverly Hills CA 90212 USA
**Phillips, K Anthony (Tony)** — Baseball Player
13341 E Cochise Road, Scottsdale AZ 85259, USA
**Phillips, Kate** — Writer
Houghton Mifflin Harcourt, 215 Park Ave S, #1200, New York NY 10003 USA
**Phillips, Kevin** — Actor
A P A Talent & Literary Agency, 405 S Beverly Dr, #300, Beverly Hills CA 90212 USA
**Phillips, Kevin P** — Political Analyst
Grand Central Publishing, 237 Park Ave, #1300, New York NY 10017, USA
**Phillips, Kimberly** — Model
Playboy Promotions, 9346 Civic Center Dr, #200, Beverly Hills CA 90210 USA
**Phillips, Kristie** — Gymnast
610 1st Ave, Asbury Park NJ 07712, USA
**Phillips, Lawrence L** — Football Player
9527 Langdon Ave, North Hills CA 91343, USA
**Phillips, Leslie S** — Actor
78 Maida Vale, London W9 1PR, England
**Phillips, Lisa Ann** — Actress
Don Buchwald Talent Agency, 6500 Wilshire Blvd, #2200, Los Angeles CA 90048 USA
**Phillips, Lou Diamond** — Actor
Global Artists Agency, 6253 Hollywood Blvd, #508, Los Angeles CA 90028, USA
**Phillips, Loyd W** — Football Player
739 Sands Road, Cave Springs AR 72718, USA
**Phillips, Mackenzie** — Actress
S D B Partners, 315 S Beverly Dr, #411, Beverly Hills CA 90067 USA
**Phillips, Melvin (Mel), Jr** — Football Player
6368 Milk Wagon Lane, Hialeah FL 33014, USA
**Phillips, Michael D (Mike)** — Baseball Player
3322 Ridgefield St, Irving TX 75062, USA
**Phillips, Michelle** — Singer (Mamas & Papas), Actress
Rebel Entertainment Partners, 5700 Wilshire Blvd, #456, Los Angeles CA 90036, USA
**Phillips, Nathan** — Actor
Principato-Young, 9465 Wilshire Blvd, #880, Beverly Hills CA 90212 USA
**Phillips, Norma** — Social Activist
Mothers Against Drunk Driving, PO Box 819100, Dallas TX 75381, USA
**Phillips, Owen M** — Geophysical Engineer
462 Heron Point, Chestertown MD 21620, USA
**Phillips, Paul A** — Baseball Player
507 N Main Ave, Demopolis AL 36732, USA
**Phillips, Peter C B** — Economist
PO Box 208281, New Haven CT 06520, USA
**Phillips, Phil** — Singer, Songwriter
PO Box 105, Jennings LA 70546, USA
**Phillips, Preston T** — Architect
Preston T Phillips Architect, PO Box 3037, Bridgehampton NY 11932, USA
**Phillips, Reginald K** — Football Player
8300 W Airport Blvd, #906, Houston TX 77071, USA
**Phillips, Richard** — Captain, Maersk Alabama Cargo Ship
211 River Road, Underhill VT 05489, USA
**Phillips, Sam** — Singer, Songwriter
High Road Touring, 751 Bridgeway, #200, Sausalito CA 94965 USA
**Phillips, Sean** — Cartoonist
153 Petherton Road, Highbury, London N5 2RS, England
**Phillips, Sian** — Actress
Dalzell & Beresford, 55 Charterhouse St, Paddock Suite, London EC1M 6HA, England
**Phillips, Susanna** — Opera Singer
I M G Artists, Hogarth Business Park, Chiswick, London W4 2TH, England
**Phillips, Todd** — Director, Writer
Green Hat Productions, 4000 Warner Blvd, Building 66, Burbank CA 91522, USA
**Phillips, W Taylor (Tay)** — Baseball Player
594 Mein Mitchell Road, Hiram GA 30141, USA
**Phillips, Wade** — Football Coach
6115 Norway Road, Dallas TX 75230, USA
**Phillips, Warren H** — Publisher
Bridge Works Publications, PO Box 1798, Bridgehampton NY 11932, USA

**Phillips, Wendy**  — Actress
Stone Manners Salners, 6100 Wilshire Blvd, #1500, Los Angeles CA 90035 USA
**Phillips, William D** — Nobel Physics Laureate
13409 Chestnut Oak Dr, Gaithersburg MD 20878, USA
**Phillips, Zara A E** — Princess, England; Equestrian
Gatecombe Park, Hampton Fields, Minchinhampton, Gloucestershire GL6 9AT, England
**Phillipson, Don** — Soccer Executive
5014 Gladiola Way, Golden CO 80403, USA
**Philo, Phoebe** — Fashion Designer
Chloe, 54-56 Rue du Faubourg Saint Honore, 75008 Paris, France
**Philp, Tom** — Journalist
Sacramento Bee, Editorial Dept, 2100 Q St, Sacramento CA 95816 USA
**Phinney, Davis** — Cyclist, Sportscaster
470 Juniper Ave, Boulder CO 80304, USA
**Phipps, Michael E (Mike)** — Football Player
2748 NE 25th St, Lighthouse Point FL 33064, USA
**Phipps, William E** — Actor
Commercial Talent, 9255 Sunset Blvd, #505, Los Angeles CA 90069, USA
**Phoebus, Thomas H (Tom)** — Baseball Player
2822 SW Lakemont Place, Palm City FL 34990, USA
**Phoenix, Joaquin R** — Actor, Singer, Guitarist
W M E Entertainment, 9601 Wilshire Blvd, #300, Beverly Hills CA 90210 USA
**Piacenza, Mauro Cardinal** — Religious Leader
Apostolic Penitentiary, Palazzo della Cancelleria, Piazza della Cancelleria 1, 00186 Rome, Italy
**Piano, Renzo** — Pritzker Architectural Laureate
Renzo Piano Building Workshop, Via Rubens 29, 16158 Genoa, Italy
**Piat, Jean** — Actor
Artmedia, 20 Ave Rapp, 75007 Paris, France
**Piatkowski, Eric T** — Basketball Player
2125 S 189th Circle, Omaha NE 68130, USA
**Piau, Sandrine** — Opera Singer
I M G Artists, Hogarth Business Park, Chiswick, London W4 2TH, England
**Piazza, Michale J (Mike)** — Baseball Player
1000 S Pointe Dr, #3101, Miami Beach FL 33139, USA
**Piazza, Rod** — Singer, Harmonica Player
Blue Mountain Artists, 810 Tyvola Road, #114, Charlotte NC 28217, USA
**Piazza, Vincent** — Actor
Gersh Agency, 9465 Wilshire Blvd, #600, Beverly Hills CA 90212 USA
**Picard, Geoffrey** — Rowing Athlete
2020 W Lake Blvd, Tahoe City CA 96145, USA
**Picard, J Noel** — Ice Hockey Player
3636 Wilmington Ave, Saint Louis MO 63116, USA
**Picard, Robert R J** — Ice Hockey Player
4718 Grand Cypress Circle N, Coconut Creek FL 33073, USA
**Picardo, Robert** — Actor
Sovereign Talent Group, 8421 Wilshire Blvd, #200, Beverly Hills CA 90211, USA
**Picasso, Paloma** — Jewelry Designer, Actress
Quintana Ron Ltd, 291A Brompton Road, London SW3 2DY, England
**Picatto, Alexandra** — Actress
Abrams Artists, 9200 W Sunset Blvd, #1125, West Hollywood CA 90069 USA
**Piccard, Bertrand** — Balloonist
Winds of Hope, Ave de Florimont 20, 1006 Lausanne, Switzerland
**Picciolo, Robert M (Rob)** — Baseball Player
11773 Invierno Dr, San Diego CA 92124, USA
**Piccoli, Michel** — Actor
11 Rue des Lions Saint Paul, 75004 Paris, France
**Piccolo, Ottavia** — Actress
Anne Alvares Correa, 34 Rue Jouffroy d'Abbans, 75017 Paris, France
**Piccolo, Rina** — Cartoonist (Six Chix, Tina's Groove)
King Features Syndicate, 300 W 57th St, #1500, New York NY 10019 USA
**Piccone, Louis J (Lou)** — Football Player
325 N Forest Road, Buffalo NY 14221, USA
**Piccone, Robin** — Fashion Designer
Piccone Apparel Corp, 1424 Washington Blvd, Venice CA 90291, USA
**Pichardo, Hipolito** — Baseball Player
21218 Saint Andrews Blvd, #305, Boca Raton FL 33433, USA
**Pichette, Dave** — Ice Hockey Player
4751 Rue Escoffier, Quebec QC G1Y 3J4, Canada
**Pick, Amelie** — Actress
Artmedia, 20 Ave Rapp, 75007 Paris, France
**Pickard, Nancy** — Writer
4020 W 94th Terrace, #211, Prairie Village KS 66207, USA
**Pickel, William G (Bill)** — Football Player
9 Autumn Ridge Road, South Salem NY 10590, USA
**Pickens, Carl M** — Football Player
3085 Sugarloaf Club Dr, Duluth GA 30097, USA
**Pickens, James, Jr** — Actor
Wright Entertainment, 3207 Winnier Dr, Los Angeles CA 90068, USA
**Pickens, Jo Ann** — Opera Singer
Norman McCann Artists, 56 Lawrie Park Gardens, London SE26 6XJ, England
**Pickens, T Boone, Jr** — Businessman
B P Capital, 8117 Preston Road, #260, Dallas TX 75225, USA
**Pickering, Jeff** — Cartoonist (Spats)
King Features Syndicate, 300 W 57th St, #1500, New York NY 10019 USA
**Pickering, Thomas R** — Diplomat, Businessman
2318 Kimbro St, Alexandria VA 22307, USA
**Pickett, Cecil L (Ricky)** — Baseball Player
1017 Wood Ridge Dr, Azle TX 76020, USA
**Pickett, Cindy** — Actress
Shelter Entertainment, 9255 Sunset Blvd, #300, Los Angeles CA 90069 USA
**Pickett, Rex** — Director, Writer
A P A Talent & Literary Agency, 405 S Beverly Dr, #300, Beverly Hills CA 90212 USA
**Pickford, Kevin P** — Baseball Player
6006 N Harcourt Dr, Coeur D'Alene ID 83815, USA
**Pickitt, John L** — Air Force General
38 Sunrise Point Road, Clover SC 29710, USA

**Pickler, Kellie** — Singer, Songwriter
Fitzgerald Hartley, 1908 Wedgewood Ave, Nashville TN 37212, USA
**Pickles, Christina** — Actress
Domain Talent, 9229 W Sunset Blvd, #710, West Hollywood CA 90069 USA
**Pickup, Ronald** — Actor
54 Crouch Hall Road, London N8 8HG, England
**Picolotti, Romina** — Social Activist
Human Rights Center, Gen Paz 186, 10 Mo Pisa A, Cordoba 5000, Argentina
**Picoult, Jodi** — Writer
PO Box 508, Etna NH 03750, USA
**Pictor, Bruce** — Drummer (Association)
Variety Artists, 1924 Spring St, Paso Robles CA 93446 USA
**Piddock, Jim** — Actor
Amsel Eisenstadt Frazier, 5055 Wilshire Blvd, #865, Los Angeles CA 90036 USA
**Pidgeon, Rebecca** — Actress, Singer
Artists Partnership, 101 Finsbury Pavement, London EC2A 1RS, England
**Pidhirny, Harry** — Ice Hockey Player
1880 Valley Farm Road, Pickering ON L1V 6B3, Canada
**Pidhrushna, Olena** — Biathlete
Biathlon Federation, Vul Dimitrova 5, 03680 Kiev, Ukraine
**Piech, Ferdinand** — Businessman
Volkswagenwerk AG, 38436 Wolfsburg, Germany
**Piedmont, Matt** — Director, Producer, Writer
Creative Artists Agency, 2000 Ave of Stars, #100, Los Angeles CA 90067 USA
**Piedra, Jorge** — Baseball Player
2208 Vaquero Estates Blvd, Westlake TX 76262, USA
**Pielmeier, John** — Writer, Actor, Producer
Creative Artists Agency, 2000 Ave of Stars, #100, Los Angeles CA 90067 USA
**Pienaar, Jacobus F** — Rugby Player
Rugby Football Union, PO Box 99, Newlands 7725, South Africa
**Pier, Christina** — Opera Singer
I M G Artists, Hogarth Business Park, Chiswick, London W4 2TH, England
**Pierce, Allison** — Singer, Guitarist (Pierces)
Paradigm Agency, 360 N Crescent Dr, North Building, Beverly Hills CA 90210 USA
**Pierce, Catherine** — Singer (Pierces)
Paradigm Agency, 360 N Crescent Dr, North Building, Beverly Hills CA 90210 USA
**Pierce, Chester M** — Psychiatrist
17 Prince St, Jamaica Plain MA 02130, USA
**Pierce, David Hyde** — Actor, Singer
2400 Inverness Ave, Los Angeles CA 90027, USA
**Pierce, Donald R (Don)** — Thoroughbred Racing Jockey
340 Neptune Ave, Encinitas CA 92024, USA
**Pierce, Edward J (Ed)** — Baseball Player
702 E Laurel Ave, Glendora CA 91741, USA
**Pierce, Jeffrey C (Jeff)** — Baseball Player
1046 Lantern Lanes, Circle Pines MN 55014, USA
**Pierce, Jill** — Actress
Extreme Team Productions, 15941 S Harlem, #319, Tinley Park IL 60477, USA
**Pierce, Jonathan** — Singer
Bob Doyle Assoc, 1111 17th Ave S, Nashville TN 37212, USA
**Pierce, Kirstin** — Actress
Don Buchwald Talent Agency, 6500 Wilshire Blvd, #2200, Los Angeles CA 90048 USA
**Pierce, L Jack** — Baseball Player
1002 Cortez St, Laredo TX 78040, USA
**Pierce, Lincoln** — Cartoonist (Big Nate)
United Feature Syndicate, PO Box 5610, Cincinnati OH 45201 USA
**Pierce, Mary** — Tennis Player
Women's Tennis Assn, 1 Progress Plaza, #1500, Saint Petersburg FL 33701 USA
**Pierce, Paul A** — Basketball Player
25201 Prado del Misterio, Calabasas CA 91302, USA
**Pierce, Randy** — Ice Hockey Player
178 Five Arches Dr, RR 2, Pakenham ON K0A 2X0, Canada
**Pierce, Ron** — Harness Racing Driver
PO Box 361, Clarksburg NJ 08510, USA
**Pierce, Tamora** — Writer
Random House, 1745 Broadway, #1800, New York NY 10019 USA
**Pierce, W William (Billy)** — Baseball Player
1321 Baileys Crossing Dr, Lemont IL 60439, USA
**Pierce, Wendell** — Actor
Paradigm Agency, 360 N Crescent Dr, North Building, Beverly Hills CA 90210 USA
**Pierce-Roberts, Tony** — Cinematographer
1 Princes Gardens, London W5 1SD, England
**Piercy, Marge** — Writer
PO Box 1473, Wellfleet MA 02667, USA
**Piercy, Scott** — Golfer
Professional Golfers Association, 100 Ave of Champions, Palm Beach Gardens FL 33418 USA
**Pierpoint, Eric** — Actor
2199 Topanga Skyline Dr, Topanga CA 90290, USA
**Pierre, Juan D** — Baseball Player
6148 NW 65th Terrace, Parkland FL 33067, USA
**Pierre-Paul, Jason** — Football Player
New York Giants, Meadowlands Stadium, 102 Route 120, East Rutherford NJ 07073 USA
**Piers, Julie** — Golfer
Ladies Pro Golf Assn, 100 International Golf Dr, Daytona Beach FL 32124 USA
**Piersall, James A (Jimmy)** — Baseball Player
1105 Oakview Dr, Wheaton IL 60187, USA
**Pierson, Emma** — Actress
Independent Talent Group, 40 Whitfield St, London W1T 2RH, England
**Pierson, Geoffrey** — Actor
Stone Manners Salners, 6100 Wilshire Blvd, #1500, Los Angeles CA 90035 USA
**Pierson, Jack** — Photographer, Sculptor
Cheim & Read, 547 W 25th St, New York NY 10001, USA
**Pierson, Kate** — Singer, Organist (B-52's)
Lazy Meadow Motel, 5191 Route 28, Mount Tremper NY 12457, USA
**Pierson, Markus** — Artist, Sculptor
OutWest, 7216 Washington St NE, #A, Albuquerque NM 87109, USA

P

Pickler - Pierson

**Pierson, Peter S (Pete)** — Football Player
17646 Jamestown Way, #D, Lutz FL 33558, USA
**Pierson, Plenette** — Basketball Player
New York Liberty, Madison Square Garden, 2 Penn Plaza, New York NY 10121 USA
**Pierson, Reggie L** — Football Player
17566 Elderberry Circle, Carson CA 90746, USA
**Pierzynski, Anthony J (A J)** — Baseball Player
9313 Tibet Pointe Circle, Windermere FL 34786, USA
**Pieterse, Sasha** — Actress, Singer
W M E Entertainment, 9601 Wilshire Blvd, #300, Beverly Hills CA 90210 USA
**Pietkiewicz, Stanley T (Stan)** — Basketball Player
2213 Venetian Way, Winter Park FL 32789, USA
**Pietrangeli, Nicola (Nicky)** — Tennis Player
Via Eustachio Manfredi 15, 00197 Rome, Italy
**Pietrangelo, Alexander (Alex)** — Ice Hockey Player
Saint Louis Blues, Scottrade Center, 1401 Clark Ave, Saint Louis MO 63103 USA
**Pietrangelo, Frank** — Ice Hockey Player
6371 Moretta Dr, Niagara Falls ON L2E 4H7, Canada
**Pietrus, Mickael** — Basketball Player
PO Box 2874, Windermere FL 34786, USA
**Pietruski, John M, Jr** — Businessman
27 E Corsica Court, Farmingdale NJ 07727, USA
**Pietrzak, James M (Jim)** — Football Player
8807 Citrus Village Dr, #108, Tampa FL 33626, USA
**Pietz, Amy** — Actress
Innovative Artists, 1505 10th St, Santa Monica CA 90401 USA
**Pifferini, Robert M (Bob), Jr** — Football Player
1731 Granite Hill Road, Placerville CA 95667, USA
**Pigford, Eva** — Model, Actress
Ford Models Inc, 111 5th Ave, #900, New York NY 10003 USA
**Pigg, Landon** — Singer, Songwriter
R C A Records, 8750 Wilshire Blvd, Beverly Hills CA 90211 USA
**Piggott, Lester K** — Thoroughbred Racing Jockey
Beech Tree House, Tostock, Bury Saint Edmonds, Suffolk 1P30 9NY, England
**Piggott, Marcus** — Photographer
Art Partner, 155 6th Ave, #1500, New York NY 10013, USA
**Pignatano, Joseph B (Joe)** — Baseball Player
150 78th St, Brooklyn NY 11209, USA
**Pigott-Smith, Tim** — Actor
Conway Van Gelder Grant, 8-12 Broadwick St, #300, London W1F 8HW, England
**Pihlman, Tuomas** — Ice Hockey Player
105 Spit Brook Road, Nashua NH 03062, USA
**Pihlstrom, Antti** — Ice Hockey Player
Salavat Yulaev Ufa, 450000 Ufa, Bashkortostan, Russia
**Pike, Gary** — Singer (Lettermen)
10031 Benares Place, Sun Valley CA 91352, USA
**Pike, Jim** — Singer (Lettermen)
M P I Talent Agency, 1801 Ave of Stars, #1420, Los Angeles CA 90067, USA
**Pike, Mike H (Mark)** — Football Player
508 Marywood Court, Edgewood KY 41017, USA
**Pike, Nicholas** — Composer
First Artists Mgmt, 4764 Park Granada, #210, Calabasas CA 91302 USA
**Pike, Rosamund** — Actress
United Agents, 12-26 Lexington St, London W1F 0LE, England
**Pilarczyk, Daniel E** — Religious Leader
100 E 8th St, #800, Cincinnati OH 45202, USA
**Pilati, Stefano** — Fashion Designer
Yves Saint Laurent, 7 Ave George V, 75008 Paris, France
**Pileggi, Mitch** — Actor
Pakula/King, 9229 W Sunset Blvd, #315, West Hollywood CA 90069 USA
**Pileggi, Nicholas** — Writer, Producer
Bloom Hergott Diemer, 150 S Rodeo Dr, #300, Beverly Hills CA 90212 USA
**Pilger, John R** — Journalist, Filmmaker, Environmentalist
57 Hambatt Road, London SW4 9EQ, England
**Pilgrim, Evan B** — Football Player
1787 Cobblestone Dr, Provo UT 84604, USA
**Piligian, Craig** — Producer
Pilgrim Films, 12020 Chandler Blvd, #200, North Hollywood CA 91607, USA
**Pilkington, Lorraine** — Actress
Another Tongue, 10-11 D'Arbay St, London W1F 8DS, England
**Pill, Alison** — Actress
Burstein Co, 15304 W Sunset Blvd, #208, Pacific Palisades CA 90272 USA
**Pilla, Anthony M** — Religious Leader
Catholic Bishops National Conference, 3211 4th St, Washington DC 20017, USA
**Pillari, Ross** — Businessman
B P America Inc, 535 Madison Ave, #200, New York NY 10022, USA
**Piller Cottrer, Pietro** — Cross Country Skier
Borgo Gran Villa 76, 32047 Sappada, Italy
**Pilfer, Zachery P (Zach)** — Football Player
23 Colonel Winstead Dr, Brentwood TN 37027, USA
**Pillers, Lawrence D** — Football Player
140 David Clemons Road, Quincy FL 32352, USA
**Pilliod, Charles J, Jr** — Diplomat, Businessman
49 Twin Oaks Road, #2, Akron OH 44313, USA
**Pillitteri, Lynn J** — Biologist
Western Washington University, Biology Dept, 516 High St, Bellingham WA 98225, USA
**Pillow, Ray** — Singer, Songwriter
Joe Taylor Artist Agency, 2802 Columbine Place, Nashville TN 37204 USA
**Pilote, Pierre P** — Ice Hockey Player
PO Box 247, Wyevale ON L0L 2T0, Canada
**Pinault, Francois** — Businessman
Artemis SA, 5 Blvd de Latour-Maubourg, 75007 Paris, France
**Pincay, Laffit, Jr** — Thoroughbred Racing Jockey
719 Carriage House Dr, Arcadia CA 91006, USA
**Pinchak, Jimmy (Jax)** — Actor
Stone Manners Salners, 6100 Wilshire Blvd, #1500, Los Angeles CA 90035 USA

**Pinchot, Bronson** — Actor
Amsel Eisenstadt Frazier, 5055 Wilshire Blvd, #865, Los Angeles CA 90036 USA

**Pinckney, Edward L (Ed)** — Basketball Player
3350 SW 27th Ave, #1004, Miami FL 33133, USA

**Pinckney, Sandra** — Chef
Food Network, 1180 Ave of Americas, #1200, New York NY 10036 USA

**Pincling, Andrew (Pinch)** — Drummer (Damned)
Leave Home Booking, 1400 S Foothill Dr, #34, Salt Lake City UT 84108, USA

**Pincus, Henry** — Director, Writer
Principato-Young, 9465 Wilshire Blvd, #880, Beverly Hills CA 90212 USA

**Pinda, Mizengo** — Prime Minister, Tanzania
Prime Minister's Office, PO Box 980, Dodoma, Tanzania

**Pinder, A Geraold (Gerry)** — Ice Hockey Player
320 39th Ave SW, Calgary AB T2S 0W7, Canada

**Pinder, Cyril C** — Football Player
7137 S Luella Ave, Chicago IL 60649, USA

**Pinder, Lucy K** — Model
Girl Mgmt, 22 Noel St, London W1F 8GS, England

**Pinder, Michael (Mike)** — Keyboardist (Moody Blues)
Moody Blues, 53-55 High St, Cobham, Surrey KT11 3DP, England

**Pine, Chris** — Actor
Creative Artists Agency, 2000 Ave of Stars, #100, Los Angeles CA 90067 USA

**Pine, Courtney** — Jazz Saxophonist
Free Trade Agency, 20-22 Curtain Road, London EC2A 3NF, England

**Pine, Linda** — Actress
Abrams-Rubaloff Lawrence, 8075 W 3rd St, #303, Los Angeles CA 90048 USA

**Pine, Robert** — Actor
4212 Ben Ave, Studio City CA 91604, USA

**Pineau-Valencienne, Didier** — Businessman
63 Rue de la Boetie, 75008 Paris, France

**Pineda, Daniella** — Actress
Innovative Artists, 1505 10th St, Santa Monica CA 90401 USA

**Pineda, Michael F** — Baseball Player
New York Yankees, Yankee Stadium, E 161st St & River Ave, Bronx NY 10451 USA

**Pineiro, Joel A** — Baseball Player
3410 Poinciana Ave, Miami FL 33133, USA

**Piñera Echenique, M J Sebastian** — President, Chile
President's Office, Palacio de la Monedo, Santiago, Chile

**Pinera, Mike** — Singer, Guitarist
Neal Hollander Agency, 9966 Majorca Place, Boca Raton FL 33434 USA

**Pines, Alexander** — Chemist
University of California, Chemistry Dept, Hildebrand Hall, Berkeley CA 94720, USA

**Pinger, Mark** — Swimmer
5201 Orduna Dr, #6, Coral Gables FL 33146, USA

**Pini, Daniela** — Opera Singer
I M G Artists, Hogarth Business Park, Chiswick, London W4 2TH, England

**Piniella, Louis V (Lou)** — Baseball Player, Manager
1005 Taray de Avila, Tampa FL 33613, USA

**Pink** — Singer, Songwriter
R D W M, 1158 26th St, #564, Santa Monica CA 90403, USA

**Pinkel, Donald P** — Pediatrician
275 Marlene Dr, San Luis Obispo CA 93405, USA

**Pinkel, Gary** — Football Coach
University of Missouri, Athletic Dept, Columbia MO 64211, USA

**Pinker, Steven A** — Psychologist
Harvard University, Psychology Dept, Cambridge MA 01238, USA

**Pinkett Smith, Jada** — Actress
Paradigm Agency, 360 N Crescent Dr, North Building, Beverly Hills CA 90210 USA

**Pinkett, Allen J** — Football Player
320 W 8th Place, Hobart IN 46342, USA

**Pinkins, Tonya** — Actress, Singer
Warren Cowan, 8899 Beverly Blvd, #918, Los Angeles CA 90048 USA

**Pinkney, V Reginald (Reggie)** — Football Player
518 Rock Canyon Dr, Fayetteville NC 28303, USA

**Pinkston, Rob** — Actor
Momentum Talent, 9401 Wilshire Blvd, #501, Beverly Hills CA 90212, USA

**Pinkston, Ryan** — Actor
A P A Talent & Literary Agency, 405 S Beverly Dr, #300, Beverly Hills CA 90212 USA

**Pinkwater, Julie** — Publisher
Ladies' Home Journal, Publisher's Office, 125 Park Ave, New York NY 10017, USA

**Pinner, Artose D** — Football Player
102 Big Blue Court, Hopkinsville KY 42240, USA

**Pinney, Raymond E (Ray)** — Football Player
6529 NE Windermere Road, #B, Seattle WA 98105, USA

**Pinnock, Trevor** — Conductor, Concert Harpsichordist
35 Gloucester Crescent, London NW1 7DL, England

**Pino, Danny** — Actor
G E F Entertainment, 611 N Cherokee Ave, Los Angeles CA 90004, USA

**Pino, Mario** — Thoroughbred Racing Jockey
8400 Serena Creek Ave, Boynton Beach FL 33473, USA

**Pinol, Jacqueline** — Actress
TalentWorks, 3500 W Olive Ave, #1400, Burbank CA 91505 USA

**Pinon, Dominique** — Actor
Agence Artiste Adequat, 108 Rue Reaumur, 75002 Paris, France

**Pinos, Carmen** — Architect
Av Diagonal 490, #3/2, 08026 Barcelona, Spain

**Pinsent, Gordon E** — Actor
Noble Caplan Abrams, 1260 Yonge St, #200, Toronto ON M4T 1W6, Canada

**Pinsent, Matthew** — Rowing Athlete
British International Rowing Office, 6 Lower Mall, London W6 9DJ, England

**Pinsky, Drew** — Actor, Producer
Dr Drew Productions, 14742 Ventura Blvd, #PH, Sherman Oaks CA 91403, USA

**Pinsky, Robert N** — Writer
Boston University, Creative Writing Dept, 236 Bay State Road, Boston MA 02215, USA

**Pinson, Bobby O** — Singer, Guitarist, Songwriter
Susan Niles Public Relations, 726 Bresslyn Road, Nashville TN 37205, USA

**P**

Pinchot - Pinson

**Pinson, Julie** — Actress
13576 Cheltenham Dr, Sherman Oaks CA 91423, USA

**Pintat Santolaria, Albert** — Head of Government, Andorra
President's Office, Casa de la Valle, Andorra la Vella, Andorra

**Pintauro, Danny** — Actor
Preston Entertainment, 8033 Sunset Blvd, #2750, Los Angeles CA 90046, USA

**Pinter, Mark** — Actor
Artist Agent, 13410 Magnolia Blvd, Sherman Oaks CA 91423, USA

**Pinto, Freida** — Actress, Model
Creative Artists Agency, 2000 Ave of Stars, #100, Los Angeles CA 90067 USA

**Pinto, Inbal** — Dancer, Choreographer
Inbal Pinto Dance Co, 5 Yechley St, Neve Tzedek, Tel-Aviv 65149, Israel

**Pinto, Mandie** — Singer
27660 Heather Ridge Way, Canyon Country CA 91351, USA

**Pinto, Maria** — Fashion Designer
133 N Jefferson St, #600, Chicago IL 60601, USA

**Pintscher, Matthias** — Composer, Conductor
Grenenau, Fischerweg 2, 34302 Guxhagen, Germany

**Pinturault, Alexis** — Alpine Skier
Hotel Annapurna, Route de l'Altiport, Courchevel 1850, 75116 Courchevel, France

**Piollet, Marc** — Conductor
Kunstler Sekretariat am Gasteig, Rosenheimer Str 52, 81669 Munich, Germany

**Piot, Peter** — Microbiologist
London School of Hygiene & Tropical Medicine, Keppel Street, London WC1E 7HT, England

**Piotrovsky, Mikhail B** — Museum Executive
State Hermitage Museum, 2 Dvortsovaya, 190000 Saint Petersburg, Russia

**Piotrowski, Tom** — Basketball Player
80 Clarks Landing Road, Port Republic, NJ 08241, USA

**Piovanelli, Silvano Cardinal** — Religious Leader
Archdiocese of Florence, Piazzi S Giovanni 3, 50129 Florence, Italy

**Piovani, Nicola** — Composer
Via G Veroese 103, 00146 Rome, Italy

**Piper, Billie P** — Singer, Actress
Rights House, Drury House, 34-43 Russell St, London WC2B 5HA, England

**Piper, Cherie** — Ice Hockey Player
Team Canada, 2424 University Dr NW, Calgary AB T2N 3Y9, Canada

**Piper, Jacki** — Actress
Rob Groves Mgmt, 33 Glasshouse St, Soho, London W1B 5DG, England

**Piper, Roddy** — Professional Wrestler, Actor
Super Artists, 2910 Main St, #200, Santa Monica CA 90405, USA

**Pipes, Leah** — Actress
Untitled Entertainment, 350 S Beverly Dr, #200, Beverly Hills CA 90212 USA

**Pipes, R Byron** — Educator
4509 Sugar Maple Dr, Lafayette IN 47905, USA

**Pipkin, Joyce C (J C)** — Football Player
1026 Stone Stack Dr, Bethlehem PA 18015, USA

**Pippen, Scottie** — Basketball Player
3393 Old Mill Road, Highland Park IL 60035, USA

**Pippig, Uta** — Track Athlete
Take the Magic Step, 777 NW 51st St, #309, Boca Raton FL 33431, USA

**Pippy, Katelyn** — Actress
A P A Talent & Literary Agency, 405 S Beverly Dr, #300, Beverly Hills CA 90212 USA

**Piquet, Nelson** — Auto Racing Driver
Autodromo, SEN/CDPM, Rua da Gasolina #01, Brasilia DF 7007 400, Brazil

**Piraro, Dan** — Cartoonist (Bizarro)
534 Wilcox Ave, Los Angeles CA 90004, USA

**Pires de Miranda, Pedro** — Government Official, Portugal
Avenida da India 10, 1300 Lisbon, Portugal

**Pires do Nascimento, Alexandre** — Singer
E M I Records, 150 5th Ave, #700, New York NY 10011 USA

**Pires, Cleo** — Actress
Ascend Entertainment, 950 10th St, #A, Santa Monica CA 90403, USA

**Pires, Maria Joao** — Concert Pianist
Deutsche Grammaphon Records, 810 7th Ave, New York NY 10019 USA

**Pirkis, Max** — Actor
I C M Partners, 10250 Constellation Blvd, #900, Los Angeles CA 90067 USA

**Pirkl, Gregory D (Greg)** — Baseball Player
6822 Emerald Bay Lane, Indianapolis IN 46237, USA

**Pirner, Dave** — Singer (Soul Asylum), Songwriter
Monterey Peninsula Artists, 404 W Franklin St, Monterey CA 93940 USA

**Piro, Stephanie** — Cartoonist (Six Chix)
PO Box 605, Hampton NH 03843, USA

**Pirtie, Gerald E (Gerry)** — Baseball Player
30306 E 59th St, Broken Arrow OK 74014, USA

**Pirus, Alex** — Ice Hockey Player
15W222 Concord St, Elmhurst IL 60126, USA

**Pisapia, Joe** — Singer, Bassist (Guster)
Nettwerk Mgmt, 345 7th Ave, #2400, New York NY 10001, USA

**Pisarcik, Joseph A (Joe)** — Football Player
27 Compass Circle, Mount Laurel NJ 08054, USA

**Pisarev, Andrei** — Concert Pianist
I M G Artists, Hogarth Business Park, Chiswick, London W4 2TH, England

**Pischetsrider, Bernd** — Businessman
Volkswagen AG, Brieffach 1849, 38436 Wolfsburg, Germany

**Pisciotta, Marc G** — Baseball Player
867 Village Green NW, Marietta GA 30064, USA

**Piscitelli, Sabitino C (Sabby), Jr** — Football Player
500 NW 15th Court, Boca Raton FL 33486, USA

**Piscopo, Joe** — Actor, Comedian
Amsel Eisenstadt Frazier, 5055 Wilshire Blvd, #865, Los Angeles CA 90036 USA

**Pister, Karl S** — Educator
University of California, Chancellor's Office, Santa Cruz CA 95064, USA

**Pistone, Tom** — Auto Racing Driver
7858 Old Concord Road, Charlotte NC 28213, USA

**Pistor, Ludger** — Actor
Stacey Castro Media, 4009 Leeward Ave, Los Angeles CA 90005 USA

**Pitbull** — Rap Artist
Media Artists Group, 8255 Sunset Blvd, Los Angeles CA 90046, USA

**Pitchford, Dean** — Lyricist, Writer
8491 W Sunset Blvd, PO Box 111, West Hollywood CA 90069, USA

**Pitcock, Joan** — Golfer
341 E Lester Ave, Fresno CA 93720, USA

**Pitel, Piyush** — Businessman
Cabletron Systems, 35 Industrial Way, Rochester NY 14614, USA

**Pithart, Petr** — Government Official, Czech Republic
Drazickeho Nam 10/65, 11800 Prague 1, Czech Republic

**Pitillo, Maria** — Actress
Karen Foreman Mgmt, 17547 Ventura Blvd, Encino CA 91316, USA

**Pitino, Richard (Rick)** — Basketball Coach
200 Pepperbush Road, Louisville KY 40207, USA

**Pitkamaki, Tero** — Track Athlete
P L 42, 60511 Hyllykallio, Finland

**Pitkanen, Joni** — Ice Hockey Player
1214 Cobble Creek Circle, Cherry Hill NJ 08003, USA

**Pitko, Alexander (Alex)** — Baseball Player
2689 Sports Village Loop, #12, Pinetop AZ 85935, USA

**Pitlick, Lance** — Ice Hockey Player
5010 Shenandoah Lane N, Minneapolis MN 55446, USA

**Pitlock, Lee E (Skip)** — Baseball Player
215 Prospect St, Seguin TX 78155, USA

**Pitman, Jennifer S** — Thoroughbred Racing Trainer
Owls Barn, Kintbury, Hungerford, Berkshire RG17 9XS, England

**Pitou Zimmerman, Penny** — Alpine Skier
560 Sanborn Road, Sanbornton NH 03269, USA

**Pitre, Louise** — Singer, Actress
Paquin Entertainment, 395 Notre Dame Ave, Winnipeg MB R3B 1R2, Canada

**Pitt, Brad** — Actor, Producer
Brillstein Entertainment Partners, 9150 Wilshire Blvd, #350, Beverly Hills CA 90212 USA

**Pitt, Eugene S** — Singer (Jive Five)
Neal Hollander Agency, 9966 Majorca Place, Boca Raton FL 33434 USA

**Pitt, Harvey L** — Government Official, Financier
Kalorama Partners, 1130 Connecticut Ave NW, #800, Washington DC 20036, USA

**Pitt, Michael** — Actor
W M E Entertainment, 9601 Wilshire Blvd, #300, Beverly Hills CA 90210 USA

**Pittas, Dimitri** — Opera Singer
Columbia Artists Mgmt Inc, 5 Columbus Circle, 1790 Broadway, #1600, New York NY 10019 USA

**Pittin, Alessandro** — Nordic Combined Skier
G S Fiamme Gialle, Via alle Coste 14, 38037 Predazzo (TN), Italy

**Pittman, Charles H** — Marine Corps General
Lexington Institute, 1600 Wilson Blvd, #900, Arlington VA 22209 USA

**Pittman, Danny R** — Football Player
2456 E Ficus Way, Gilbert AZ 85298, USA

**Pittman, James A, Jr** — Endocrinologist
5 Ridge Dr, Birmingham AL 35213, USA

**Pittman, Kavika C** — Football Player
3316 Mayfair Lane, Lewisville TX 75077, USA

**Pittman, Michael** — Football Player
21201 Kittridge St, #4202, Woodland Hills CA 91303, USA

**Pittman, Richard A** — Vietnam War Marine Corps Hero (CMH)
1217 Chaparral Way, Stockton CA 95209, USA

**Pitts, Frank H** — Football Player
8249 S Laredo Ave, Baton Rouge LA 70811, USA

**Pitts, Gaylen R** — Baseball Player
214 Rocky Bluff Lane, Mountain Home AR 72653, USA

**Pitts, Greg** — Actor
Innovative Artists, 1505 10th St, Santa Monica CA 90401 USA

**Pitts, Jacob** — Actor
Domain Talent, 9229 W Sunset Blvd, #710, West Hollywood CA 90069 USA

**Pitts, John M** — Football Player
3412 Stoneleigh Run Dr, Buford GA 30519, USA

**Pitts, Leonard, Jr** — Columnist
Miami Herald, Editorial Dept, 1 Herald Plaza, Miami FL 33132 USA

**Pitts, Robert (R C)** — Basketball Player
12655 E Milburn Ave, Baton Rouge LA 70815, USA

**Pitts, Ron** — Football Player, Sportscaster
3811 Davids Road, Agoura Hills CA 91301, USA

**Pitts, Ryan M** — Afghanistan War Army Hero (CMH)
23 Hawkshead Hollow, Nashua NH 03063, USA

**Pittsley, James M (Jim)** — Baseball Player
102 Dixon Ave, DuBois PA 15801, USA

**Piven, Jeremy** — Actor
Creative Artists Agency, 2000 Ave of Stars, #100, Los Angeles CA 90067 USA

**Pivonka, Michal** — Ice Hockey Player
8312 Grand Estuary Trail, #102, Bradenton FL 34212, USA

**Piznarski, Mark** — Director
W M E Entertainment, 9601 Wilshire Blvd, #300, Beverly Hills CA 90210 USA

**Pizzarelli, John P (Bucky), Sr** — Jazz Guitarist
Abby Hoffer Enterprises, 223 1/2 E 48th St, New York NY 10017 USA

**Pizzarelli, John, Jr** — Singer, Jazz Guitarist
Vector Mgmt, PO Box 120479, Nashville TN 37212 USA

**Pizzaro, Juan C** — Baseball Player
2262 Ave Borinquen, San Juan PR 00915, USA

**Pizzolatto, Nic** — Producer, Writer
Anonymous Content, 3532 Hayden Ave, Culver City CA 90232 USA

**Pizzorno, Sergio** — Guitarist (Kasabian), Songwriter
International Talent Booking, Ariel House, 74A Charlotte St, #100 London W1T 4QJ, England

**Place, Marcella** — Field Hockey Player
141 Meadow View Road, Orinda CA 94563, USA

**Place, Mary Kay** — Actress
Gersh Agency, 9465 Wilshire Blvd, #600, Beverly Hills CA 90212 USA

**Placido, Violante** — Actress, Singer
Via dela Farnesina 240, 00194 Rome, Italy

**Pladson, Gordon C** — Baseball Player
19087 87th Ave, Surrey BC V4N 3G5, Canada

**Plager, Robert B (Bob)** — Ice Hockey Player
362 Branchport Dr, Chesterfield MO 63017, USA

**Plager, S Jay** — Judge
US Court of Appeals, 717 Madison Place NW, Washington DC 20439, USA

**Plakson, Suzie** — Actress
302 N La Brea Ave, #363, Los Angeles CA 90036, USA

**Plamondon, Gerard (Gerry)** — Ice Hockey Player
450 Rue de Montreal, Sherbrooke QC J1H 1E5, Canada

**Plan B** — Rap Artist
679 Artists, 21 Carnaby St, London W1F 7DA, England

**Plana, Tony** — Actor
A P A Talent & Literary Agency, 405 S Beverly Dr, #300, Beverly Hills CA 90212 USA

**Plank, Douglas M (Doug)** — Football Player
12622 E Paradise Dr, Scottsdale AZ 85259, USA

**Plank, Edward A (Eddie)** — Baseball Player
1353 Leawood Road, Englewood FL 34223, USA

**Plank, Julie** — Basketball Coach
Washington Mystics, Verizon Center, 401 9th St NW, #750, Washington DC 20004 USA

**Plank, Raymond** — Businessman
Apache Corp, 2000 Post Oak Blvd, #100, Houston TX 77056, USA

**Plano, Richard J** — Physicist
10 Longwood Dr, #533, Westwood MA 02090, USA

**Plant, Robert** — Singer, Songwriter
High Road Touring, 751 Bridgeway, #200, Sausalito CA 94965 USA

**Plante, Bruce** — Editorial Cartoonist
Chattanooga Times, Editorial Dept, 100 E 11th St, #400, Chattanooga TN 37402, USA

**Plante, Derek J** — Ice Hockey Player
6829 Meadow Grass Lane S, Cottage Grove MN 55016, USA

**Plante, Pierre R** — Ice Hockey Player
129 Rue Rapin, Salaberry-de-Valleyfield QC J6S 5M4, Canada

**Plante, William M** — Commentator
CBS-TV, News Dept, 2020 M St NW, Washington DC 20036 USA

**Plantenberg, Erik J** — Baseball Player
1846 Creekside Dr NE, Owatonna MN 55060, USA

**Plantier, Phillip A (Phil)** — Baseball Player
16001 Martincoit Road, Poway CA 92064, USA

**Plantu** — Editorial Cartoonist
Le Monde, Editorial Dept, 21 Bis Rue Claude Bernard, 75005 Paris, France

**Plaskett, Thomas G** — Businessman
5215 N O'Connor Blvd, #1070, Irving TX 75039, USA

**Platanias, Dimitri** — Opera Singer
I M G Artists, Hogarth Business Park, Chiswick, London W4 2TH, England

**Plate, Peter** — Singer, Songwriter, Keyboardist
Pop Out Musik Mgmt, Forster Str 5, 10999 Berlin, Germany

**Plater-Zyberk, Elizabeth M** — Architect
Duany & Plater-Zyberk Architects, 1023 SW 25th Ave, Miami FL 33135, USA

**Platini, Michel** — Soccer Player
Union of Euopean Football Associations, Route de Geneve 46, 1260 Nyon 2, Switzerland

**Platov, Evgeni** — Ice Dancer
Princeton Sports Center, PO Box 155, Blawenburg NJ 08504, USA

**Platt, Campion A** — Architect
Campion A Platt Architect, 152 Madison Ave, #900, New York NY 10016, USA

**Platt, Howard** — Actor
Shirley Hamilton, 333 E Ontario, #302, Chicago IL 60611, USA

**Platt, Marc E** — Producer
Marc Platt Productions, 100 Universal City Plaza, Bungalow 5163, Universal City CA 91608, USA

**Platt, Oliver** — Actor
W M E Entertainment, 9601 Wilshire Blvd, #300, Beverly Hills CA 90210 USA

**Player, Gary J** — Golfer
Blair Atholl Farm, Lanseria, Fourways near Johannesburg, Gauteng 2068, South Africa

**Player, Scott D** — Football Player
115 Averley Way, Saint Johns FL 32259, USA

**Playfair, James (Jim)** — Ice Hockey Player, Coach
200-99 Station St, Saint John NB E2L 4X4, Canada

**Playfair, Larry** — Ice Hockey Player
724 Ransom Road, Grand Island NY 14072, USA

**Plaza, Aubrey** — Actress, Comedienne
Creative Artists Agency, 2000 Ave of Stars, #100, Los Angeles CA 90067 USA

**Pleasant, Anthony D** — Football Player
17249 Connor Quay Court, Cornelius NC 28031, USA

**Pleasant, Marquis A** — Football Player
3549 Rio Grande Circle, Dallas TX 75233, USA

**Pleau, Lawrence W (Larry)** — Ice Hockey Player, Executive
650 Spyglass Summit Dr, Chesterfield MO 63017, USA

**Plec, Julie** — Producer, Writer
W M E Entertainment, 9601 Wilshire Blvd, #300, Beverly Hills CA 90210 USA

**Pleis, William (Bill)** — Baseball Player
16744 4th Ave NE, Bradenton FL 34212, USA

**Plemons, Jesse** — Actor
TalentWorks, 3500 W Olive Ave, #1400, Burbank CA 91505 USA

**Plesac, Daniel T (Dan)** — Baseball Player
245 White Thorne Lane, Valpariso IN 46383, USA

**Pleshette, John** — Actor, Director
2643 Creston Dr, Los Angeles CA 90068, USA

**Pless, Rance** — Baseball Player
5528 Asheville Highway, Greenville TN 37743, USA

**Pletcher, Todd A** — Thoroughbred Racing Trainer
Todd Pletcher Racing Stables, PO Box 30066, Elmont NY 11003, USA

**Pletnev, Mikhail V** — Conductor, Concert Pianist
Russian National Orchestra, Garibaldi 19, 117335 Moscow, Russia

**Plett, Willi** — Ice Hockey Player
Willi Plett Sports Park, 1248 Harris Commons Place, Roswell GA 30076, USA

**Plevneliev, Rosen A** — President, Bulgaria
President's Office, 2 Dondukov Blvd, 1123 Sofia, Bulgaria

**Plews, Herbert E (Herb)** — Baseball Player
350 Ponca Place, Boulder CO 80303, USA

**Pliego, Cesar** — Bassist (Kinky)
Marcella C Public Relations, 646 S Barrington Ave, #206, Brentwood CA 90049, USA

**Plies** — Rap Artist
Multi Entertainment, 4044 W Lake Mary Blvd, #104-324, Lake Mary FL 32746, USA

**Plimpton, Martha** — Actress
Innovative Artists, 1505 10th St, Santa Monica CA 90401 USA

**Plisetskaya, Maya M** — Ballerina
Tverskaya 25/9, #31, 103050 Moscow, Russia

**Pliska, Paul** — Opera Singer
George M Martynuk, 352 7th Ave, New York NY 10001, USA

**Plitmann, Hila** — Opera Singer
I M G Artists, Hogarth Business Park, Chiswick, London W4 2TH, England

**Plodinec, Timothy A (Tim)** — Baseball Player
23251 Gilmore St, West Hills CA 91307, USA

**Ploeger, Kurt A** — Football Player
6451 E Nance St, Mesa AZ 85215, USA

**Ploenchit, Saen Sor** — Boxer
Songchai Co, 71/23 Setsiri Road, Sams Payathai, Bangkok 10400, Thailand

**Ploszek, Pete** — Actor
Gersh Agency, 9465 Wilshire Blvd, #600, Beverly Hills CA 90212 USA

**Plotkin, Stanley A** — Virologist
3940 Delancey St, Philadelphia PA 19104, USA

**Plotnick, Jack** — Actor
Stone Manners Salners, 6100 Wilshire Blvd, #1500, Los Angeles CA 90035 USA

**Plott, Charles R** — Economist
881 El Campo Dr, Pasadena CA 91107, USA

**Plowden, David** — Writer, Photographer
609 Cherry St, Winnetka IL 60093, USA

**Plowright, Joan A** — Actress
Malthouse, Horsham Road, Ashurst, Steyning, West Sussex BN44 3AR, England

**Plowright, Rosalind A** — Opera Singer
83 Saint Mark's Ave, Salisbury, Wiltshire SP1 3DW, England

**Pluhar, Erika** — Actress
Huschkgasse 5, 1190 Vienna, Austria

**Plum, Milton R (Milt)** — Football Player
1104 Oakside Court, Raleigh NC 27609, USA

**Plumb** — Singer
FlatRock Mgmt, 2021 21st Ave S, #B104, Nashville TN 37212, USA

**Plumb, C Henry** — Government Official
Dairy Farm, Maxstoke, Coleshill, Warwicks B46 2QJ, England

**Plumb, Eve** — Actress
Clear Talent Group, 325 W 38th St, #1203, New York NY 10018, USA

**Plumb, Ron** — Ice Hockey Player
975 Auden Park Dr, Kingston ON K7M 7T9, Canada

**Plumer, Patricia (PattiSue)** — Track Athlete
USA Track & Field, 4341 Starlight Dr, Indianapolis IN 46239 USA

**Plumlee, Mason A** — Basketball Player
Brooklyn Nets, 15 Metro Tech Center, #1100, Brooklyn NY 11201 USA

**Plumlee, Miles C** — Basketball Player
Phoenix Suns, 201 E Jefferson St, Phoenix AZ 85004 USA

**Plummer, Ahmed K** — Football Player
PO Box 30147, Columbus OH 43230, USA

**Plummer, Amanda** — Actress
Artist Group, 1650 Broadway, #1105, New York NY 10019, USA

**Plummer, Bruce E** — Football Player
1047 Apalachee Run Trail, Dacula GA 30019, USA

**Plummer, Christopher** — Actor, Singer
49 Wampum Hill Road, Weston CT 06883, USA

**Plummer, Gary L** — Football Player
10374 Rue Chamberry, San Diego CA 92131, USA

**Plummer, Glenn** — Actor
Innovative Artists, 1505 10th St, Santa Monica CA 90401 USA

**Plummer, Jason S (Jake)** — Football Player
282 Winterberry Way, Sandpoint ID 83864, USA

**Plummer, William F (Bill)** — Baseball Player, Manager
8504 Oak Terrace Lane, Millville CA 96062, USA

**Plunk, Eric V** — Baseball Player
9520 Pats Point Dr, Corona CA 92883, USA

**Plunkett, Arthur S (Art)** — Football Player
332 Santa Monica Dr, Henderson NV 89014, USA

**Plunkett, Gerard** — Actor
M A Mgmt, 1947 Pendrell St, #106, Vancouver BC V6G 1T5, Canada

**Plunkett, James W (Jim), Jr** — Football Player
51 Kilroy Way, Atherton CA 94027, USA

**Plunkett, Marcella** — Actress
Lisa Richards Agency, 108 Upper Leeson St, Dublin 4, Ireland

**Plunkett, Maryann** — Actress
Davis Spylios Mgmt, 244 W 54th St, #707, New York NY 10019, USA

**Plushenko, Evgeny** — Figure Skater
Flashlight Artists Agency, Via Enrico Fermi 18, 39100 Bolzano (BZ), Italy

**Ply, Robert V (Bobby)** — Football Player
8616 Ash Ave, Raytown MO 64138, USA

**Plympton, Jeffrey H (Jeff)** — Baseball Player
8 Robin St, Plainville MA 02762, USA

**Plyushch, Ivan S** — Head of State, Ukraine
Verkhovna Rada, M Hrushevskoho 5, 252019 Kiev, Ukraine

**P-Nut** — Bassist (311)
311 Hive, 8904 Florence Dr, Omaha NE 68147, USA

**Poapst, Steve** — Ice Hockey Player
502 Kelly Court, Lombard IL 60148, USA

**Pocklington, Peter H** — Ice Hockey Executive
Edmonton Oilers, 11230 110th St, Edmonton AB T5G 3H7, Canada

**Pocoroba, Biff B** — Baseball Player
2700 Forest Dr, Melbourne FL 32901, USA

**Pocza, Harvie** — Ice Hockey Player
135 Sun Harbour Close Road, Calgary AB T2X 3C4, Canada
**Podalydes, Denis** — Actor, Writer
Zelig, 52 Rue ReAumur, 75002 Paris, France
**Podein, Shjon** — Ice Hockey Player
4350 Browndale Ave, Minneapolis MN 55424, USA
**Podell, Eyal** — Actor
Paul Kohner, 9300 Wilshire Blvd, #555, Beverly Hills CA 90212 USA
**Podesta, John D** — Government Official
3743 Brandywine St, Washington DC 20016, USA
**Podeswa, Jeremy** — Director
Rebelfilms, 317 Manning Ave, Toronto ON M6J 2K8, Canada
**Podewell, Cathy** — Actress
17328 S Crest Dr, Los Angeles CA 90035, USA
**Podhoretz, Norman** — Editor, Writer
Commentary, Editor's Office, 165 E 56th St, New York NY 10022, USA
**Podlesh, Adam** — Football Player
1500 Calming Water Dr, #3003, Fleming Island FL 32003, USA
**Podloski, Ray** — Ice Hockey Player
13323 118th St NW, Edmonton AB T5E 5L6, Canada
**Podolak, Edward J (Ed)** — Football Player
2227 Emma Road, Basalt CO 81621, USA
**Podolski, Lukas J** — Soccer Player
Player Mgmt, Berta-Morena-Weg 9, 83700 Rottach Egern, Germany
**Podowski, Debbie** — Actress
Red Mgmt, Box 3, 415 W Esplanade, North Vancouver BC V7M 1A6, Canada
**Podsednik, Scott E** — Baseball Player
6613 Herbert Road, Colleyville TX 76034, USA
**Poe, Dontari** — Football Player
Kansas City Chiefs, 1 Arrowhead Dr, Kansas City KS 64129 USA
**Poe, Johnnie E** — Football Player
1102 Colas Ave, East Saint Louis IL 62207, USA
**Poehler, Amy** — Actress, Comedienne
W M E Entertainment, 9601 Wilshire Blvd, #300, Beverly Hills CA 90210 USA
**Poelvoorde, Benoit** — Actor
Voyez Mon Agent, 20 Ave Rapp, 75007 Paris, France
**Poepping, Michael H (Mike)** — Baseball Player
13791 250th Ave, Pierz MN 56364, USA
**Poesy, Clemence** — Actress, Model
Agence Elizabeth Simpson, 62 Blvd du Montparnasse, 75015 Paris, France
**Poff, John W** — Baseball Player
2786 Mishler Road, Mio MI 48647, USA
**Poggioli, Sylvia** — Commentator
National Public Radio, 635 Massachusetts Ave NW, #1, Washington DC 20001, USA
**Pogorelich, Ivo** — Concert Pianist
Columbia Artists Mgmt Inc, 5 Columbus Circle, 1790 Broadway, #1600, New York NY 10019 USA
**Pogostkina, Alina** — Concert Violinist
Harrison/Parrott, 5-6 Albion Court, London W6 0QT, England
**Pogrebin, Letty Cottin** — Editor, Writer, Social Activist
33 W 67th St, New York NY 10023, USA
**Pogue, Donald W** — Judge
US Court of International Trade, 1 Federal Plaza, New York NY 10278, USA
**Pohamba, Hifikepunye L** — President, Namibia
President's Office, State House, Mugabe Ave, Windhoek 9000, Namibia
**Pohl, Don** — Golfer
903 E Bellows St, Mount Pleasant MI 48858, USA
**Pohl, John (Johnny)** — Ice Hockey Player
2382 Clover Lane, Red Wing MN 55066, USA
**Pohlman, Jenny** — Artist
3824 SW Morgan St, Seattle WA 98126, USA
**Poile, David R** — Ice Hockey Executive
Nashville Predators, 501 Broadway, Nashville TN 37203 USA
**Poile, Don** — Ice Hockey Player
165 Woodford Dr SW, Calgary AB T2W 4C2, Canada
**Poinar, George O, Jr** — Entomologist
Oregon State University, Entomology Dept, Corvallis OR 97331, USA
**Poindexter, Buster** — Singer
Agency Group Ltd, 142 W 57th St, #600, New York NY 10019 USA
**Poindexter, John M** — Navy Admiral, Government Official
10 Barrington Fare, Rockville MD 20850, USA
**Poindexter, Larry** — Actor
TalentWorks, 3500 W Olive Ave, #1400, Burbank CA 91505 USA
**Pointer, Aaron E** — Baseball Player
4902 N Scenic View Lane, Tacoma WA 98407, USA
**Pointer, Anita** — Singer (Pointer Sisters)
12060 Crest Court, Beverly Hills CA 90210, USA
**Pointer, Bonnie** — Singer (Pointer Sisters)
T-Best Talent Agency, 508 Honey Lake Court, Danville CA 94506 USA
**Pointer, Noel** — Jazz Violinist
Headline Talent, 1650 Broadway, #401, New York NY 10313 USA
**Pointer, Priscilla** — Singer (Pointer Sisters)
213 16th St, Santa Monica CA 90402, USA
**Pointer, Ruth** — Singer (Pointer Sisters)
Morey Management Group, 1100 Glendon Ave, #1100, Los Angeles CA 90024 USA
**Poirot, Pierre** — Actor
Artmedia, 20 Ave Rapp, 75007 Paris, France
**Poisel, Philipp** — Singer
Holunder Records, Waldhornlestr 18, 72072 Tuebingen, Germany
**Poison Ivy** — Bassist (Cramps), Songwriter
Leave Home Booking, 10 W Broadway, #608, Salt Lake City UT 84101, USA
**Poitier, Sidney** — Actor
Creative Artists Agency, 2000 Ave of Stars, #100, Los Angeles CA 90067 USA
**Poitier, Sydney Tamiia** — Actress
I C M Partners, 10250 Constellation Blvd, #900, Los Angeles CA 90067 USA
**Polaha, Kristoffer** — Actor
More/Medavoy Mgmt, 10203 Santa Monica Blvd, #400, Los Angeles CA 90067 USA

**Polamalu, Troy A**
1761 Colgate Circle, La Jolla CA 92037, USA — Football Player

**Polanco, Dascha**
Gersh Agency, 9465 Wilshire Blvd, #600, Beverly Hills CA 90212 USA — Actress

**Polanco, Placido E**
8950 SW 63rd Court, Miami FL 33156, USA — Baseball Player

**Polanski, Roman**
Chalet Milky Way, 3780 Gstaad, Switzerland — Director, Writer

**Polansky, Mark L**
2010 Hillside Oak Lane, Houston TX 77062, USA — Astronaut

**Polanyi, John C**
University of Toronto, Chemistry Dept, Toronto ON M5S 3H6, Canada — Nobel Chemistry Laureate

**Polchinski, Joseph G**
University of California, Physics Institute, Santa Barbara CA 93106, USA — Physicist

**Pole, Richard H (Dick)**
5124 Marsh Field Lane, Sarasota FL 34235, USA — Baseball Player

**Polee, Dwayne L**
1169 E 60th St, Los Angeles CA 90001, USA — Basketball Player

**Polegato, Brett**
International Mgmt Group, Pier House, Strand on the Green, London W4 3NN, England — Opera, Concert Singer

**Polese, Kim**
Marimba Inc, 440 Clyde Ave, Mountain View CA 94043, USA — Businesswoman

**Poleshchuk, Alexander F**
Cosmonaut Training Center, Star City, 141160 Zvezdny Gorodok, Moscow Oblast, Russia — Cosmonaut

**Poletiek, Noah**
Don Buchwald Talent Agency, 6500 Wilshire Blvd, #2200, Los Angeles CA 90048 USA — Actor

**Poletto, Severino Cardinal**
Archdiocese of Turin, Via Val della Torre 3, 10149 Turin, Italy — Religious Leader

**Poleway, Christopher J**
Fortune Group, Time & Life Building, Rockefeller Center, New York NY 10020, USA — Businessman

**Poli, Mario Aurelio Cardinal**
Archdiocese, Rivadavia 415, Buenos Aires C1002 AAC, Argentina — Religious Leader

**Polich, Mike**
825 3rd St NE, Osseo MN 55369, USA — Ice Hockey Player

**Polinsky, Alexander**
C E S D, 10635 Santa Monica Blvd, #130, Los Angeles CA 90025 USA — Actor

**Polish, Mark**
United Talent Agency, U T A Plaza, 9336 Civic Center Dr, Beverly Hills CA 90210 USA — Actor, Producer, Writer

**Polish, Michael**
Creative Artists Agency, 2000 Ave of Stars, #100, Los Angeles CA 90067 USA — Director, Producer, Writer

**Polito, Jon**
Domain Talent, 9229 W Sunset Blvd, #710, West Hollywood CA 90069 USA — Actor

**Politte, Clifford A (Cliff)**
6306 Sprig Oak Court, #C, Saint Louis MO 63128, USA — Baseball Player

**Politzer, H David**
1145 Linda Vista Ave, Pasadena CA 91103, USA — Nobel Physics Laurete

**Polizzi, Nicole (Snooki)**
Neon Entertainment, 3577 Harlem Road, Buffalo NY 14225, USA — Actress, Writer, Producer

**Polk, Carlos D**
18121 Diamond Cove Court, Tampa FL 33647, USA — Football Player

**Polk, DaShon L**
3503 Cornwall Court, Missouri City TX 77459, USA — Football Player

**Polk, Steven R**
Inspector General, HqUSAF, Pentagon, Washington DC 20330 USA — Air Force General

**Polkinghorne, John C**
Queen's College, Cambridge University, Cambridge CB3 9ET, England — Theologian, Templeton Laureate

**Poll, Jon**
Gersh Agency, 9465 Wilshire Blvd, #600, Beverly Hills CA 90212 USA — Director, Producer

**Polla, Dennis L**
University of Minnesota, Electrical Engineering Dept, Minneapolis MN 55455, USA — Microbiotics Engineer

**Pollack, Andrea**
S S V, Postfach 420140, 34070 Kassel, Germany — Swimmer

**Pollack, Daniel**
University of Southern California, Music Dept, Los Angeles CA 90089, USA — Concert Pianist

**Pollack, Frank**
907 Hillcrest Trail, Southlake TX 76092, USA — Football Player

**Pollack, Jeffrey N**
Federated Sports & Gaming, Palms Casino & Resort, 4301 W Flamingo Road, Las Vegas NV 89103, USA — Poker Executive

**Pollack, Kevin**
Don Buchwald Talent Agency, 6500 Wilshire Blvd, #2200, Los Angeles CA 90048 USA — Actor

**Pollak, Avshalom**
Inbal Pinto Dance Co, 5 Yechley St, Neve Tzedek, Tel-Aviv 65149, Israel — Dancer, Choreographer

**Pollak, Cheryl A**
PO Box 761460, Los Angeles CA 90076, USA — Actress

**Pollak, Kevin**
Red Bird Cinema, 11601 Wilshire Blvd, #2200, Los Angeles CA 90025, USA — Actor, Comedian

**Pollak, Lisa**
Baltimore Sun, Editorial Dept, 501 N Calvert St, Baltimore MD 21278, USA — Journalist

**Pollak, Michael D (Mike)**
Carolina Panthers, Ericsson Stadium, 800 S Mint St, Charlotte NC 28202 USA — Football Player

**Pollan, Tracy**
Gersh Agency, 9465 Wilshire Blvd, #600, Beverly Hills CA 90212 USA — Actress

**Pollard, Bernard K**
5605 Fairhaven Ave, Woodland Hills CA 91367, USA — Football Player

**Pollard, Frank D, Jr**
113 L C R 474, Mexia TX 76667, USA — Football Player

**Pollard, Marcus L**
673 Meadow Lakes Dr, Pine Mountain GA 31822, USA — Football Player

**Pollard, Michael J**
520 S Burnside Ave, #12A, Los Angeles CA 90036, USA — Actor

**Pollard, Robert**
Manage This, PO Box 256, Old Chelsea Station, New York NY 10113, USA — Singer, Musician, Songwriter

**Pollard, Robert L (Bob)**
8987 Washington Blvd, Beaumont TX 77707, USA — Football Player

**Pollard, Scot**
730 New Hampshire St, #5D, Lawrence KS 66044, USA — Basketball Player

## P

**Pollari, Joey** — Actor
United Talent Agency, U T A Plaza, 9336 Civic Center Dr, Beverly Hills CA 90210 USA

**Pollen, Arabella R H** — Fashion Designer
Canham Mews, #8, Canham Road, London W3 7SR, England

**Polley, Sarah** — Actress, Director
10 Mary St, #308, Toronto ON M4Y 1P9, Canada

**Pollini, Armando** — Fashion Designer
Via Gambolina 51/6, 27029 Vigevano (PV), Italy

**Pollini, Maurizio** — Concert Pianist
R E S I A, Via Manzoni 31, 20120 Milan, Italy

**Pollock, Adam Jackson** — Lighting Designer
Fire Farm Lighting, PO Box 458, 104 1st St SW, Elkander IA 52043, USA

**Pollock, Alex J** — Government Official, Financier
Federal Home Loan Bank, 111 E Wacker Dr, #800, Chicago IL 60601, USA

**Pollock, David M** — Football Player
Cincinnati Bengals, 1 Paul Brown Stadium, Cincinnati OH 45202 USA

**Pollock, Griselda** — Artist
Leeds University, Fine Arts Dept, Leeds LS2 9JT, England

**Pollock, J C** — Writer
I C M Partners, 10250 Constellation Blvd, #900, Los Angeles CA 90067 USA

**Pollock, Tom** — Producer
Cold Spring Pictures, 9465 Wilshire Blvd, #920, Los Angeles CA 90212, USA

**Polo, Ana Maria** — Commentator
Telemundo Network Group, 2470 W 8th Ave, Hialeah FL 33010 USA

**Polo, Joseph (Joe)** — Curling Athlete
Curling Association, 5525 Clem's Way, Stevens Point WI 54482 USA

**Polo, Teri** — Actress, Model
Gersh Agency, 9465 Wilshire Blvd, #600, Beverly Hills CA 90212 USA

**Polone, Gavin** — Actor, Producer
Pariah, 9229 W Sunset Blvd, #208, West Hollywood CA 90069, USA

**Poloni, John P** — Baseball Player
1714 Polo Club Dr, Tarpon Springs FL 34689, USA

**Polonich, Dennis** — Ice Hockey Player
70 Varsity Estates Close NW, Calgary AB T3B 5J1, Canada

**Poloujadoff, Michel E** — Electrical Engineer
8 Rue Roches, 77760 Buthiers, France

**Polshak, James Stewart** — Architect
Polshak Partnership, 320 W 134th St, #800, New York NY 10030, USA

**Polson, John** — Actor, Director, Producer
Creative Artists Agency, 2000 Ave of Stars, #100, Los Angeles CA 90067 USA

**Polson, Ralph M** — Basketball Player
3846 S Eagle Lane, Spokane WA 99206, USA

**Polyakov, Valeri V** — Cosmonaut
Health Ministry, Choroshevskoye Chaussee 76A, 123007 Moscow, Russia

**Polynice, Olden** — Basketball Player
PO Box 220339, Newhall CA 91322, USA

**Pomakov, Robert** — Opera Singer
I M G Artists, Hogarth Business Park, Chiswick, London W4 2TH, England

**Pomeroy, Earl R** — Representative, ND
Alston & Bird LLP, 950 F St NW, Washington DC 20004, USA

**Pomers, Scarlett** — Actress, Singer
D M G Talent, 4804 Laurel Canyon Blvd, Valley Village CA 91607, USA

**Pominville, Jason J** — Ice Hockey Player
5333 Halifax Ave S, Minneapolis MN 55424, USA

**Pommier, Jean-Bernard** — Concert Pianist, Conductor
Musike Academies, 12 Rte Praz Gilliard, 1000 Lausanne, Switzerland

**Pomodora, Arnaldo** — Sculptor
Via Vigevano 5, 20144 Milan, Italy

**Pompeo, Ellen** — Actress
John Carrabino Mgmt, 5900 Wilshire Blvd, #406, Los Angeles CA 90036 USA

**Pomplun, Raquel** — Model
PO Box 9235, Glendale CA 91226, USA

**Ponazecki, Joe** — Actor
Don Buchwald Talent Agency, 10 E 44th St, New York NY 10017 USA

**Ponce Enrile, Juan** — Government Official, Philippines
2305 Morado St, Dasmarinas Village, Makati, Metro Manila, Philippines

**Ponce, Carlos** — Singer, Actor
Luber Rocklin Entertainment, 5815 Sunset Blvd, #206, Los Angeles CA 90028 USA

**Ponce, Miguel A** — Soccer Player
Federacion de Futbol, Colima 373 Colonia Roma, Delegacion Cuauhtemoc, Mexico City DF 06700, Mexico

**Ponce, Walter** — Concert Pianist
University of California, Music Dept, Los Angeles CA 90024, USA

**Poncia, Vincent (Vinnie), Jr** — Singer, Songwriter
Joel Faden, 250 W 57th St, New York NY 10107, USA

**Ponder, David E (Dave)** — Football Player
1818 Sandalwood Lane, Grapevine TX 76051, USA

**Ponder, Moana** — Sculptor
Art Inc, 9401 San Pedro, San Antonio TX 78216, USA

**Pondexter, Cappie** — Basketball Player
New York Liberty, Madison Square Garden, 2 Penn Plaza, New York NY 10121 USA

**Pondexter, Clifton (Cliff)** — Basketball Player
1135 W Stuart Ave, Fresno CA 93711, USA

**Ponomarenko, Sergei V** — Ice Dancer
Sharks Ice, 1500 S 10th St, San Jose CA 95112, USA

**Pons, B Stanley** — Chemist
University of Utah, Chemistry Dept, Eyring Building, Salt Lake City UT 84112, USA

**Ponsoldt, James** — Director
United Talent Agency, U T A Plaza, 9336 Civic Center Dr, Beverly Hills CA 90210 USA

**Ponson, Sidney A** — Baseball Player
2541 NE 35th Dr, Fort Lauderdale FL 33308, USA

**Ponta, Victor-Viorel (Vic)** — Prime Minister, Romania
Prime Minister's Office, Piata Vicotriei 1, 71201 Bucharest, Romania

**Pontbriand, Ryan D** — Football Player
3044 Forest Lake Dr, Westlake OH 44145, USA

**Pontes, Marcos C** — Astronaut, Brazil
Cosmonaut Training Center, Star City, 141160 Zvezdny Gorodok, Moscow Oblast, Russia

**Ponti, Michael** — Concert Pianist
Heubergstr 32, 83565 Eschenlohe, Germany
**Pontius, Chris** — Actor
Untitled Entertainment, 350 S Beverly Dr, #200, Beverly Hills CA 90212 USA
**Pontois, Noella-Chantal** — Ballerina
25 Rue de Maubeuge, 75009 Paris, France
**Ponty, Jean-Luc** — Jazz Violinist, Composer
10340 Santa Monica Blvd, Los Angeles CA 90025, USA
**Pook, Christopher R (Chris)** — Auto Racing Executive
Championship Auto Racing, 5350 Lakeview Parkway S Dr, Indianapolis IN 46268 USA
**Pook, Jocelyn** — Composer
Kraft-Engel Mgmt, 15233 Ventura Blvd, #200, Sherman Oaks CA 91403 USA
**Pool, David A** — Football Player
8120 Walcot Lane, #D, Cincinnati OH 45249, USA
**Pool, James L** — Pharmacologist
Baylor Medical Center, 1200 Moursand Ave, Houston TX 77030 USA
**Pool, Kenneth R (Bud)** — WW II Army Air Corps Hero
6840 Kilimanjaro Dr, Evergreen CO 80439, USA
**Pool, Tilman E** — WW II Navy Air Force Hero
232 Warrenton Dr, Houston TX 77024, USA
**Poole, Brian** — Singer (Tremeloes)
Jason West Agency, Gables House, Saddlebow, Kings Lynn PE34 3AR, England
**Poole, David J** — Artist
Royal Portrait Painters Society, 17 Carlton House Terrace, London SW1Y 5BD, England
**Poole, James R (Jim)** — Baseball Player
605 Falls Lake Dr, Alpharetta GA 30022, USA
**Poole, Keith R S** — Football Player
4100 S Arizona Ave, #4, Chandler AZ 85248, USA
**Poole, Nathan L** — Football Player
8686 Longwood St, San Diego CA 92126, USA
**Poole, Tyrone** — Football Player
3415 Rivers Call Blvd, Atlanta GA 30339, USA
**Poole, William** — Government Official, Economist
Federal Reserve Bank, PO Box 442, Saint Louis MO 63166, USA
**Pooler, Rosemary S** — Judge
US Court of Appeals, Lee Courthouse, 100 S Clinton St, Syracuse NY 13202, USA
**Pooley, Don** — Golfer
5251 N Camino Sumo, Tucson AZ 85718, USA
**Pooley, Emma** — Cyclist
Bigla Cycling Team, Bahnhofstr 4, 3507 Biglen, Switzerland
**Poons, Larry** — Artist
Salander O'Reilly Galleries, 20 E 79th St, New York NY 10075, USA
**Poots, Imogen** — Actress
Independent Talent Group, 40 Whitfield St, London W1T 2RH, England
**Pop, Iggy** — Singer, Songwriter, Actor
Susan Blond Inc, 50 W 57th St, #1400, New York NY 10019 USA
**Popa Chubby** — Singer, Guitarist
Concerted Efforts, PO Box 440326, Somerville MA 02144 USA
**Popcorn, Faith** — Businesswoman
Brain Reserve, 1 Dag Hammarskjold Plaza, #1600, New York NY 10017, USA
**Pope, Carly** — Actress
L I N K Entertainment, 11872 La Grange Ave, Los Angeles CA 90025 USA
**Pope, Charles (Charlies)** — Singer (Tams)
Richard De La Font Agency, 4845 S Sheridan Road, #505, Tulsa OK 74145 USA
**Pope, Clarence C, Jr** — Religious Leader
Fort Worth Episcopal Church Diocese, 6300 Ridlea Place, Fort Worth TX 76116, USA
**Pope, Dick** — Cinematographer
Independent Talent Group, 40 Whitfield St, London W1T 2RH, England
**Pope, Edwin** — Sportswriter
Miami Herald, Editorial Dept, 1 Herald Plaza, Miami FL 33132 USA
**Pope, Jeff** — Producer, Writer
United Agents, 12-26 Lexington St, London W1F 0LE, England
**Pope, Manley** — Actor
Albewanin, 156 5th Ave, #904, New York NY 10010 10010, USA
**Pope, Marquez P** — Football Player
PO Box 470487, San Francisco CA 94147, USA
**Pope, Odeon** — Jazz Saxophonist, Orchestra Leader
MarsJazz Booking, 1006 Ashby Place, Charlottesville VA 22901, USA
**Pope, Tim** — Director
I C M Partners, 10250 Constellation Blvd, #900, Los Angeles CA 90067 USA
**Popein, Larry** — Ice Hockey Player
80-650 Harrington Road, Kamloops BC V2B 6T7, Canada
**Popfinger, Bill** — Harness Racing Driver
6205 Bay Club Dr, #1, Fort Lauderdale FL 33308, USA
**Popiel, Jan V** — Ice Hockey Player
2501 Peppermill Ridge Dr, Chesterfield MO 63005, USA
**Popiel, Poul P** — Ice Hockey Player
2501 Peppermill Ridge Dr, Chesterfield MO 63005, USA
**Popoff, A Jay** — Singer (Lit)
Sepeyts Entertainment, 5543 Edmondson Pike, #8A, Nashville TN 37211, USA
**Popoff, Frank P** — Businessman
Indiana University, Kelly Business School, 1309 East St, Bloomington IN 47405, USA
**Popoff, Jeremy A** — Guitarist (Lit)
Sepetys Entertainment, 5543 Edmondson Pike, #8A, Nashville TN 37211, USA
**Popov, Aleksandr** — Swimmer
International Olympic Committee, Chateau de Vidy, 1007 Lausanne, Switzerland
**Popov, Dmytro** — Opera Singer
I M G Artists, Hogarth Business Park, Chiswick, London W4 2TH, England
**Popov, Leonid I** — Cosmonaut
Cosmonaut Training Center, Star City, 141160 Zvezdny Gorodok, Moscow Oblast, Russia
**Popovac, Gwynn** — Artist, Sculptor
17270 Robin Ridge, Sonora CA 95370, USA
**Popovic, Bojana Petrovic** — Handball Player
Z R K Buducnost T-Mobile, Ivan Milutinovic B B, 81000 Podgorica, Montenegro
**Popovic, Mark** — Ice Hockey Player
30 New Mountain Road, Stoney Creek ON L8G 2R7, Canada

# P

| | |
|---|---|
| **Popovich, Gregg** <br> 41 Vineyard Dr, San Antonio TX 78257, USA | Basketball Executive, Coach |
| **Popovich, Gregory** <br> Planet Hollywood Theater Resort, 3667 Las Vegas Blvd S, Las Vegas NV 89109, USA | Animal Trainer, Comedian |
| **Popovich, Paul E** <br> 2604 Woodlawn Road, Northbrook IL 60062, USA | Baseball Player |
| **Poppen, Christoph** <br> Deutsche Radio Philharmonie, Saint Johanner Markt 27, 66111 Saarbrücken, Germany | Conductor |
| **Popper, John** <br> Hard Head Productions, PO Box 651, New York NY 10014, USA | Singer, Musician (Blues Traveler) |
| **Popplewell, Anna** <br> I C M Partners, 10250 Constellation Blvd, #900, Los Angeles CA 90067 USA | Actress |
| **Popson, David G (Dave)** <br> 82 Fall St, Ashley PA 18706, USA | Basketball Player |
| **Poquette, Benedict J (Ben)** <br> 17917 N Shore Estates Road, Spring Lake MI 49456, USA | Basketball Player |
| **Poquette, Thomas A (Tom)** <br> 3411 Ridgeway Dr, Eau Claire WI 54701, USA | Baseball Player |
| **Poranski, Jason** <br> Ba Da Bing Records, 181 Clermont Ave, #403, Brooklyn NY 11205, USA | Guitarist, Mandolin Player (Beirut) |
| **Porcaro, Steven M (Steve)** <br> 13596 Contour Dr, Sherman Oaks CA 91423, USA | Composer, Keyboardist (Toto) |
| **Porcellino, John** <br> PO Box 881, Elgin IL 60121, USA | Cartoonist (King-Cat) |
| **Porcello, Frederick A (Rick), III** <br> PO Box 27, Oldwick NJ 08858, USA | Baseball Player |
| **Porch, Colleen** <br> Amsel Eisenstadt Frazier, 5055 Wilshire Blvd, #865, Los Angeles CA 90036 USA | Actress |
| **Porch, Michelle** <br> Vincent Cirrincione Assoc, 1516 N Fairfax Ave, Los Angeles CA 90046 USA | Actress |
| **Porcher, Robert** <br> PO Box 691464, Orlando FL 32869, USA | Football Player |
| **Porfilio, John C** <br> US Court of Appeals, 1919 Stout St, Denver CO 80294, USA | Judge |
| **Porizkova, Paulina** <br> One Entertainment, 347 5th Ave, #1404, New York NY 10016 USA | Model, Actress |
| **Poroshenko, Petro O** <br> President's Office, Bankova Str 11, 01220 Kiev, Ukraine | President, Ukraine |
| **Porretta, Matthew** <br> A K A Talent, 6310 San Vicente Blvd, #200, Los Angeles CA 90048 USA | Actor |
| **Port, Christopher C (Chris)** <br> 432 Walnut St, New Orleans LA 70118, USA | Football Player |
| **Port, Whitney** <br> Creative Artists Agency, 2000 Ave of Stars, #100, Los Angeles CA 90067 USA | Producer, Actress |
| **Portenoy, Russell K** <br> Beth Israel Medical Center, Pain Medicine Dept, 1st Ave & 16th St, New York NY 10003, USA | Neurologist |
| **Porter, Andrew (Andy)** <br> 2502 W 117th St, Hawthorne CA 90250, USA | Baseball Player |
| **Porter, Billy** <br> Industry Entertainment, 955 Carillo Dr, #300, Los Angeles CA 90048 USA | Singer, Actor |
| **Porter, Charles W (Chuck)** <br> 9321 Snyder Lane, Perry Hall MD 21128, USA | Baseball Player |
| **Porter, Daniel E (Dan)** <br> 7360 Cowles Mountain Road, San Diego CA 92119, USA | Baseball Player |
| **Porter, Daryl M** <br> 9053 W Sunrise Blvd, Plantation FL 33322, USA | Football Player |
| **Porter, David H** <br> Skidmore College, President's Office, Saratoga Springs NY 12866, USA | Educator |
| **Porter, Gary** <br> Milwaukee Journal Sentinel, Editorial Dept, PO Box 371, Milwaukee WI 53201 USA | Journalist |
| **Porter, Gayle** <br> Gaston-Porter Health Improvement Center, 8612 Timber Hill, Potomac MD 20854, USA | Psychologist, Social Activist |
| **Porter, Greg** <br> God's Katrina Kitchen, 554 Camp Ave, Gulfport MS 39501, USA | Social Activist |
| **Porter, Gregory** <br> Maria Matias Music, 316 Mid Valley Center, #203, Carmel CA 93923, USA | Singer, Songwriter |
| **Porter, J W (Jay)** <br> 9677 Heather Circle W, Palm Beach Gardens FL 33410, USA | Baseball Player |
| **Porter, James W (Jim), II** <br> National Rifle Association, 11250 Waples Mill Road, Fairfax VA 22030, USA | Association Executive |
| **Porter, Jody** <br> Big Hassle, 157 Chambers St, #1200, New York NY 10007, USA | Singer (Fountains of Wayne), Guitarist |
| **Porter, John E** <br> Hogan & Hartson, 555 13th Ave NW, #800E, Washington DC 20004, USA | Representative, IL |
| **Porter, Joseph E (Joey)** <br> 9523 Laramie Ave, Bakersfield CA 93314, USA | Football Player |
| **Porter, Kalan** <br> Agency Group Ltd, 142 W 57th St, #600, New York NY 10019 USA | Singer, Songwriter |
| **Porter, Kevin J** <br> 20 Savannah Dr, Senoia GA 30276, USA | Football Player |
| **Porter, Lee** <br> 1604 Birch Lane, Greensboro NC 27408, USA | Golfer |
| **Porter, Lorena** <br> R D M J Entertainment Mgmt, 3619 Rose Ave, Long Beach CA 90807 USA | Singer (Klymaxx) |
| **Porter, Marquis D (Bo)** <br> 1226 N Teal Estates Circle, Fresno TX 77545, USA | Baseball Player, Manager |
| **Porter, Otto, Jr** <br> Washington Wizards, M C I Centre, 601 F St NW, Washington DC 20004 USA | Basketball Player |
| **Porter, R Kalan** <br> B M G Canada, 190 Liberty St, #100, Toronto ON M6K 3L5, Canada | Singer |
| **Porter, Randy** <br> Laughlin Racing, 113 Pride Dr, Simpsonville SC 29681, USA | Auto Racing Driver |
| **Porter, Richard A (Ricky)** <br> 24 Wyegate Court, Owings Mills MD 21117, USA | Football Player |
| **Porter, Robert L (Bob)** <br> 771 Pueblo Ave, Napa CA 94558, USA | Baseball Player |

**Pounds, Darryl L** — Football Player
4613 Lambert Place, Alexandria VA 22311, USA
**Poundstone, Paula** — Actress, Comedienne
A P A Talent & Literary Agency, 405 S Beverly Dr, #300, Beverly Hills CA 90212 USA
**Poupard, Paul Cardinal** — Religious Leader
Pontifical Council for Culture, Via della Conciliazione 5, 00193 Rome, Italy
**Poupaud, Pierre** — Actor
Artmedia, 20 Ave Rapp, 75007 Paris, France
**Pournelle, Jerry E** — Writer
12051 Laurel Terrace, Studio City CA 91604, USA
**Pousette, Lena** — Actress
Atkins Assoc, 8040 Ventura Canyon Ave, Panorama City CA 91402 USA
**Poussaint, Alvin F** — Psychiatrist
Judge Baker Guidance Center, 53 Parker Hill Ave, Roxbury Crossing MA 02120, USA
**Poust, Tracy** — Producer, Writer
W M E Entertainment, 9601 Wilshire Blvd, #300, Beverly Hills CA 90210 USA
**Povenmire, Daniel K (Dan)** — Producer, Animator
Disney Channel, Phineas & Ferb Show, 500 S Buena Vista St, Burbank, CA 91521, USA
**Povetkin, Aleksandr V** — Boxer
Sauerland Event, Hanns-Braun-Str, 14053 Berlin, Germany
**Povich, Maury R** — Commentator, Entertainer
Creative Artists Agency, 2000 Ave of Stars, #100, Los Angeles CA 90067 USA
**Povinelli, Mark** — Actor
Kazarian/Measures/Ruskin, 11969 Ventura Blvd, #300, Studio City CA 91604 USA
**Powe, Leon, Jr** — Basketball Player
45 Kings Way, Waltham MA 02451, USA
**Powell, A J Philip** — Architect
16 Little Boltons, London SW10 9LP, England
**Powell, Alonzo S** — Baseball Player
220 N Patterson Blvd, Dayton OH 45402, USA
**Powell, Arthur L (Art)** — Football Player
1304 City Lights Dr, Aliso Viejo CA 92656, USA
**Powell, Brittney** — Actress, Model
Amsel Eisenstadt Frazier, 5055 Wilshire Blvd, #865, Los Angeles CA 90036 USA
**Powell, Cecil** — Test Pilot
220 Villa Verde Dr SE, Rio Rancho NM 87124, USA
**Powell, Cincinnatus (Cincy)** — Basketball Player
2541 Brookside Dr, Irving TX 75063, USA
**Powell, Clifton** — Actor
Opus Entertainment, 5225 Wilshire Blvd, #905, Los Angeles CA 90036, USA
**Powell, Colin L** — Army General, Secretary of State
1317 Ballantrae Farm Dr, McLean VA 22101, USA
**Powell, D Dwane, Jr** — Editorial Cartoonist
Raleigh News Observer, Editorial Dept, 215 S McDowell, Raleigh NC 27601, USA
**Powell, Dennis C** — Baseball Player
1743 Eastgate Ave, Upland CA 91784, USA
**Powell, Donald D** — Interior Designer
Powell Kleinschmidt, PO Box 1130, Libertyville IL 60048, USA
**Powell, Dwight** — Basketball Player
Charlotte Hornets, 333 E Trade St, #A, Charlotte NC 28202 USA
**Powell, Earl A (Rusty), III** — Museum Executive
National Gallery of Art, Constitution Ave & 4th St NW, Washington DC 20565, USA
**Powell, Eric** — Cartoonist (Goon)
2401 Cairo Bend Road, Lebanon TN 37087, USA
**Powell, Esteban** — Actor, Producer
C E S D, 10635 Santa Monica Blvd, #130, Los Angeles CA 90025 USA
**Powell, Glen** — Actor
Resolution, 1801 Century Park E, #2300, Los Angeles CA 90067 USA
**Powell, Hosken** — Baseball Player
1289 Tamara St, Pensacola FL 32504, USA
**Powell, J Mac** — Singer, Guitarist (Third Day)
Creative Trust, 5141 Virginia Way, #320, Brentwood TN 37027, USA
**Powell, James R** — Inventor (Magnetic Levitation Train)
Plus Ultra Technologies, 180 Harbor Road, Stony Brook NY 11790, USA
**Powell, James W (Jay)** — Baseball Player
155 Butler Dr, Ridgeland MS 39157, USA
**Powell, Jane** — Singer, Actress
150 W End Ave, #26C, New York NY 10023, USA
**Powell, Jeremy R** — Baseball Player
3022 W Summit Walk Court, Anthem AZ 85086, USA
**Powell, Jerome (Jay)** — Government Leader, Financier
Federal Reserve System, 20th St & Constitution Ave NW, Washington DC 20551, USA
**Powell, Jesse** — Singer, Songwriter
Universal Attractions, 135 W 26th St, #1200, New York NY 10001 USA
**Powell, Jimmy** — Golfer
49895 Lago Dr, La Quinta CA 92253, USA
**Powell, John** — Composer
Kraft-Engel Mgmt, 15233 Ventura Blvd, #200, Sherman Oaks CA 91403 USA
**Powell, John G** — Track Athlete
5545 Sobb Ave, Las Vegas NV 89118, USA
**Powell, John W (Boog)** — Baseball Player
Boog's Barbeque, 333 W Camden St, Baltimore MD 21201, USA
**Powell, Josh** — Basketball Player
Atlanta Hawks, Centennial Tower, 101 Marietta St NW, #1900, Atlanta GA 30303 USA
**Powell, L Dante** — Baseball Player
5715 W Walton St, Long Beach CA 90815, USA
**Powell, Luke** — Football Player
Indiana State University, Athletic Dept, 401 N 4th St, Terre Haute IN 47809, USA
**Powell, Marvin, Jr** — Football Player
5441 8th Ave, Los Angeles CA 90043, USA
**Powell, Michael (Mike)** — Track Athlete
7676 N Fresno St, #27, Fresno CA 93720, USA
**Powell, Michael K** — Government Official
College of William & Mary, PO Box 8795, Williamsburg VA 23187, USA
**Powell, Monroe** — Singer (Platters)
Personality Presents, 880 E Sahara Ave, #101, Las Vegas NV 89104, USA

**Powell, Nicole K** — Basketball Player
Tulsa Shock, B O K Center, 200 S Denver, Tulsa OK 74103 USA
**Powell, Renee** — Golfer
PO Box 30196, East Canton OH 44730, USA
**Powell, Robert** — Actor
Diamond Mgmt, 31 Percy St, London W1T 2DD, England
**Powell, Sandy** — Costume Designer
Independent Talent Group, 40 Whitfield St, London W1T 2RH, England
**Powell, Susan** — Actress
6333 Bryn Mawr Dr, Los Angeles CA 90068, USA
**Power, Cat** — Singer, Pianist, Guitarist
Ground Control, 108 E Main St, #8, Carrboro NC 27510, USA
**Power, Dave** — Actor
Allegory Creative Mgmt, 13261 Moorpark St, #103, Sherman Oaks CA 91423, USA
**Power, J D (Dave)** — Businessman
J D Power Associates, 2625 Townsgate Road, Westlake Village CA 91361, USA
**Power, Lawrence** — Concert Viola Player
Ingpen & Williams, 131 Putney Bridge Road, London SW15 2PA, England
**Power, Samantha** — Diplomat, Writer, Social Activist
US Mission, United Nations Plaza, New York NY 10017, USA
**Power, Susan** — Writer
G P Putnam's Sons, 375 Hudson St, New York NY 10014 USA
**Power, Ted H** — Baseball Player
1165 Tahiti Parkway, Sarasota FL 34236, USA
**Power, Udana** — Actress, Writer
Iatia Well Inc, 1050 S Hayworth Ave, Los Angeles CA 90035, USA
**Power, Will** — Auto Racing Driver
Penske Racing, Penske Plaza, 366 Riverfront, Reading PA 19602, USA
**Power, Will** — Writer, Composer, Actor
I C M Partners, 10250 Constellation Blvd, #900, Los Angeles CA 90067 USA
**Powers, Clyde J** — Football Player
6020 NW Williams Ave, Lawton OK 73505, USA
**Powers, James B** — Religious Leader
American Baptist Assn, 4605 N State Line, Texarkana TX 75503, USA
**Powers, Richard** — Writer
University of Illinois, English Dept, Champaign IL 61820, USA
**Powers, Ross** — Snowboard Skier
PO Box 186, Londonderry VT 05148, USA
**Powers, Stefanie** — Actress
PO Box 5087, Sherman Oaks CA 91413, USA
**Powers, Warren A** — Football Player
14742 Thornbird Manor Parkway, Chesterfield MO 63017, USA
**Powers, Williams, Jr** — Educator
University of Texas, President's Office, Austin TX 78712, USA
**Powis, Lynn** — Ice Hockey Player
2669 S Columbine St, Denver CO 80210, USA
**Powter, Daniel P** — Singer, Pianist, Songwriter
Gary Stamler Mgmt, 3055 Overland Ave, #200, Los Angeles CA 90034, USA
**Powter, Susan** — Physical Fitness Expert, Writer
Stop the Insanity, 6250 Ridgewood Road, Saint Cloud MN 56395, USA
**Poynter, Dougie** — Bassist (McFly), Songwriter
Helter Skelter, 347-353 Chiswick High Road, London W4 4HS, England
**Poza, Jorge** — Actor
Televisa, Blvd A Lopez Mateos 232, Colonia San Angel, Mexico City DF 01060 CP, Mexico
**Pozsgay, Imre** — Government Official, Hungary
Parliament Buildings, Kossuth Lajos Ter 1, 1055 Budapest, Hungary
**Prabaya, Adrian** — Conductor
Harrison/Parrott, 5-6 Albion Court, London W6 0QT, England
**Prabhakar, Arati** — Financier
US Venture Partners, 2735 Sand Hill Road, Menlo Park CA 94025, USA
**Prada, Miuccia** — Fashion Designer
Galleria Vittorio Emanuele 60-65, 20121 Milan, Italy
**Prado, Edgar** — Thoroughbred Racing Jockey
1519 Shoreline Way, Hollywood FL 33019, USA
**Prado, Edward C** — Judge
US Court of Appeals, 755 E Mulberry Ave, San Antonio TX 78212, USA
**Prady, Bill** — Producer, Writer, Actor
Rothman Brecher Agency, 9250 Wilshire Blvd, #PH, Beverly Hills CA 90212, USA
**Prammanasudh, Stacy** — Golfer
5016 S Toledo Ave, #18-O, Tulsa OK 74135, USA
**Prance, Ghillean T** — Botanist
Old Vicarage, Silver St, Lyme Regis, Dorset DT7 3HS, England
**Prantera, Amanda** — Writer
Bloomsbury Publishing, 50 Bedford Square, London WC1B 3DP, England
**Pras** — Rap Artist (Fugees)
I C M Partners, 10250 Constellation Blvd, #900, Los Angeles CA 90067 USA
**Prasad, Sunand** — Architect
Penoyre & Prasad, 28-42 Banner St, London EC1Y 8QE, England
**Prasad, Udayan** — Director, Actor
United Talent Agency, U T A Plaza, 9336 Civic Center Dr, Beverly Hills CA 90210 USA
**Prasong Tuchinda** — Pediatrician
Phya-Thai II Hospital, 943 Phaholythin, Phayatha Bangkok 10400, Thailand
**Pratchett, Terry** — Writer
Colin Smythe, PO Box 6, Gerrards Cross, Buckshire SL9 8XA, England
**Prather, Joan** — Actress
Brady Brannon Rich, 5670 Wilshire Blvd, #820, Los Angeles CA 90036 USA
**Pratiwi Sudarmono P** — Astronaut, Indonesia
Universitas Indonesia, Microbiology Dept, Salemba Raya, Jakarta 10430, Indonesia
**Pratt, Awadagin** — Concert Pianist
C M Artists, 127 W 96th St, #13B, New York NY 10025 USA
**Pratt, Chris** — Actor
Creative Artists Agency, 2000 Ave of Stars, #100, Los Angeles CA 90067 USA
**Pratt, Deborah** — Actress
Bruce Clute, 8205 Santa Monica Blvd, #1-299, West Hollywood CA 90046, USA
**Pratt, George C** — Judge
55 Sugar Tom Ridge, East Norwich NY 11732, USA

**Pratt, Judson**
2585 N Fountain Arbor Way, Orange CA 92867, USA — Actor
**Pratt, Kelly**
Ba Da Bing Records, 181 Clermont Ave, #403, Brooklyn NY 11205, USA — Trumpeter (Beirut)
**Pratt, Kelly**
23 Lombard Crescent, Saint Albert AB T8N 3N1, Canada — Ice Hockey Player
**Pratt, Keri Lynn**
Innovative Artists, 1505 10th St, Santa Monica CA 90401 USA — Actress
**Pratt, Michael P (Mike)**
14603 Landon Court, Louisville KY 40245, USA — Basketball Player
**Pratt, Robert H (Bob), Jr**
4322 Monument Park, Richmond VA 23230, USA — Football Player
**Pratt, Roger**
10 Nightingale Lane, Hornsey, London N8 7QU, England — Cinematographer
**Pratt, Todd A**
5950 Dorset Bridge Road, Douglasville GA 30135, USA — Baseball Player
**Pratt, Tracy**
1705-15038 101st Ave, Surrey BC V3R 0N2, Canada — Ice Hockey Player
**Pratt, Victoria**
Don Buchwald Talent Agency, 6500 Wilshire Blvd, #2200, Los Angeles CA 90048 USA — Actress
**Praver, Tori**
I M G Models, 304 Park Ave S, #PH N, New York NY 10010 USA — Model
**Prayuth Chan-Ocha**
Prime Minister's Office, Thanon Nakhon Patnom, Bangkok 10300, Thailand — Prime Minister, Thailand, Army General
**Preate, Ernest D, Jr**
Attorney General's Office, 4th & Walnut, Harrisburg PA 17120, USA — Attorney, Government Official
**Prebble, Lucy**
Rod Hall Agency, 7 Mallow St, London EC1Y 8RQ, England — Producer, Writer
**Precourt, Charles J**
1960 Shoshone Dr, Ogden UT 84403, USA — Astronaut
**Predock, Antoine**
Antoine Predock Architect, 300 12th St, Albuquerque NM 87102, USA — Architect
**Preece, Steven P (Steve)**
2723 NW Monte Vista Terrace, Portland OR 97210, USA — Football Player
**Pregerson, Harry**
US Court of Appeals, 21800 Oxnard St, Woodland Hills CA 91367, USA — Judge
**Preisler, Gary**
I C M Partners, 10250 Constellation Blvd, #900, Los Angeles CA 90067 USA — Director
**Preissing, Thomas J (Tom)**
1824 Anglers Dr, Steamboat Springs CO 80487, USA — Ice Hockey Player
**Prejean, Patrick**
Agence Babette Pouget, 36 Rue de Ponthieu, 75008 Paris, France — Actor
**Prejean, Sister Helen**
3009 Grand Route Saint John, #6, New Orleans LA 70119, USA — Social Activist, Writer
**Prelutsky, Jack**
PO Box 366, 7683 SE 27th St, Mercer Island WA 98040, USA — Writer
**Premji, Azim**
Wipro Ltd, Doddakannelli, Sarjapur Road, Bangalore 560035, India — Businessman, Philanthropist
**Prentice, Dean S**
350 Doon Valley Dr, Kitchener ON N2P 2M9, Canada — Ice Hockey Player
**Prepon, Laura**
Gersh Agency, 9465 Wilshire Blvd, #600, Beverly Hills CA 90212 USA — Actress
**Prescott, Edward C**
2308 Lake Place, Minneapolis MN 55405, USA — Nobel Economics Laureate
**Prescott, John L**
365 Saltshouse Road, Sutton on Hull, North Humberside, England — Government Official, England
**Prescott, Jon**
Abrams Artists, 9200 W Sunset Blvd, #1125, West Hollywood CA 90069 USA — Actor
**Prescott, Kathryn**
Curtis Brown Group, 28-29 Haymarket St, #500, London SW1Y 4SP, England — Actress
**Prescott, Robert T**
Innovative Artists, 1505 10th St, Santa Monica CA 90401 USA — Actor
**Presko, Joseph E (Joe)**
1612 NE 77th Terrace, Kansas City MO 64118, USA — Baseball Player
**Presle, Micheline**
6 Rue Antoine Dubois, 75006 Paris, France — Actress
**Presley, Angaleena**
Ten Ten Music Group, 33 Music Square W, #110, Nashville TN 37203, USA — Singer/Songwriter
**Presley, Brian**
I/D Public Relations, 7060 Hollywood Blvd, #800, Los Angeles CA 90028 USA — Actor
**Presley, James A (Jim)**
2449 Bonanza Dr, Cantonment FL 32533, USA — Baseball Player
**Presley, Lisa Marie**
International Talent Agency, Beverly Hills Triangle, 9701 Wilshire Blvd, Beverly Hills CA 90212, USA — Actress, Singer
**Presley, Priscilla**
1167 Summit Dr, Beverly Hills CA 90210, USA — Actress
**Presley, Richard**
W M E Entertainment, 9601 Wilshire Blvd, #300, Beverly Hills CA 90210 USA — Guitarist (Breeders)
**Presley, Wayne**
1339 Kingsway Dr, Highland MI 48356, USA — Ice Hockey Player
**Press, Bill**
CNN-TV, News Dept, 190 Marietta Ave SW, Atlanta GA 30303 USA — Commentator
**Press, Frank**
2500 Virginia Ave, #616 South, Washington DC 20037, USA — Geophysicist
**Press, Natalie**
United Agents, 12-26 Lexington St, London W1F 0LE, England — Actress
**Pressel, Morgan**
3111 Clint Moore Road, #101, Boca Raton FL 33496, USA — Golfer
**Pressey, Paul M**
782 Haddonstone Circle, Lake Mary FL 32746, USA — Basketball Player, Coach
**Pressler, H Paul**
3711 San Felipe St, #9J, Houston TX 77027, USA — Attorney, Judge
**Pressler, Larry L**
1666 K St NW, #500, Washington DC 20006, USA — Senator, SD
**Pressler, Menahem M J**
Melvin Kaplan, 115 College St, #4, Burlington VT 05401, USA — Concert Pianist

# P

**Pressley, Dominic I**
1406 Whooping Court, Upper Marlboro MD 20774, USA — Basketball Player

**Pressley, Harold**
6470 Matheny Way, Citrus Heights CA 95621, USA — Basketball Player

**Pressley, Robert**
6 Forestdale Dr, Asheville NC 28803, USA — Auto, Truck Racing Driver

**Pressman, Edward R**
Edward R Pressman Films, 1639 11th St, #251, Santa Monica CA 90404, USA — Producer

**Pressman, Lawrence**
15033 Encanto Dr, Sherman Oaks CA 91403, USA — Actor

**Pressman, Sally**
United Talent Agency, U T A Plaza, 9336 Civic Center Dr, Beverly Hills CA 90210 USA — Actress

**Prestel, James F (Jim)**
6150 N Hurricane Court, Parker CO 80134, USA — Football Player

**Prestia, Francis (Rocco)**
Air Tight Mgmt, PO Box 113, Winchester Center CT 06094, USA — Bassist (Tower of Power)

**Preston, Carrie**
Innovative Artists, 1505 10th St, Santa Monica CA 90401 USA — Actress

**Preston, Douglas**
Editions L'Archipel, 34 Rue des Bourdonnais, 75001 Paris, France — Writer

**Preston, Duncan**
46 Hilltop House, Hornsey Lane, London N6 5NW, England — Actor

**Preston, J A**
Paradigm Agency, 360 N Crescent Dr, North Building, Beverly Hills CA 90210 USA — Actor

**Preston, Kelly**
Creative Artists Agency, 2000 Ave of Stars, #100, Los Angeles CA 90067 USA — Actress, Model

**Preston, Mike**
House of Representatives, 1434 6th St, #1, Santa Monica CA 90401 USA — Actor

**Preston, R David (Dave)**
PO Box 16511, Golden CO 80402, USA — Football Player

**Preston, Raymond N (Ray), Jr**
820 Regulo Place, #1811, Chula Vista CA 91910, USA — Football Player

**Preston, Simon J**
Little Hardwick, Langton Green, Tunbridge Wells, Kent TN3 0EY, England — Concert Organist, Choirmaster

**Preston, Steven C**
Small Business Administration, 409 3rd St SW, Washington DC 20024, USA — Secretary of Housing & Urban Development

**Prestridge, Luke E**
17802 Island Spring Lane, Tomball TX 77377, USA — Football Player

**Pretre, Georges**
Chateau de Vaudricourt, A Naves, 81100 Par Castres, France — Conductor

**Prettyman, Tristan**
High Road Touring, 751 Bridgeway, #200, Sausalito CA 94965 USA — Singer, Songwriter

**Preus, David W**
2481 Como Ave, Saint Paul MN 55108, USA — Religious Leader

**Prevc, Peter**
Skating Union, Celovska 25, 1000 Ljubljana, Slovenia — Ski Jumper

**Previn, Andre G**
180 W 80th St, #206, New York NY 10024, USA — Conductor, Composer, Jazz Pianist

**Prevost, Greg**
Agency Group Ltd, 142 W 57th St, #600, New York NY 10019 USA — Singer, Musician (Chesterfield Kings)

**Prevost, Josette**
Levin Agency, 8484 Wilshire Blvd, #745, Beverly Hills CA 90211, USA — Actress

**Prew, William A**
30600 Telegraph Road, #3110, Bingham Farms MI 48025, USA — Swimmer, Businessman

**Preziosi, Alessandro**
Carol Levi Mgmt, Via Giuseppe Pisanelli 2, 00196 Rome, Italy — Actor

**Price, Alan**
Barry Collings Entertainments, PO Box 1151, Saint Albans, Herthshire AL1 9WB, England — Singer, Organist (Animals), Songwriter

**Price, Antony**
17 Langton St, London SW10 0JL, England — Fashion Designer

**Price, Armintie A**
Atlanta Dream, 83 Walton St NW, #400, Atlanta, GA 30303 USA — Basketball Player

**Price, Bryan R**
Cincinnati Reds, Great American Ball Park, 100 Main St, Cincinnati OH 45202 USA — Baseball Manager

**Price, Carey**
Montreal Canadiens, 1275 Saint Antoine St W, Montreal QC H3C 5L2, Canada — Ice Hockey Player

**Price, Elex D**
2833 J B Mance Ave, Jackson MS 39213, USA — Football Player

**Price, Ferne**
40 Jackson Blvd, Greencastle IN 46135, USA — Baseball Player

**Price, Frank**
Price Entertainment, 527 Spoleto Dr, Pacific Palisades CA 90272, USA — Film Executive

**Price, H Brent**
1111 W Wynona Ave, Enid OK 73703, USA — Basketball Player

**Price, Hilary**
221 Pine St, #414, Florence MA 01062, USA — Cartoonist (Rhymes with Orange)

**Price, Jack**
39 Waterloo St S, Goderich ON N7A 3P1, Canada — Ice Hockey Player

**Price, James G**
12205 Mohawk Road, Leawood KS 66209, USA — Physician, Columnist

**Price, Jimmie W (Jim)**
57152 Willow Way, Washington MI 48094, USA — Baseball Player

**Price, Joseph W (Joe)**
1874 Arabian Court, Hebron KY 41048, USA — Baseball Player

**Price, Katie (Jordan)**
Volition, Raleigh Studios, 1600 Rosecrans Ave, #400, Manhattan Beach CA 90266, USA — Model, Singer

**Price, Kelly**
J L Entertainment, 18653 Ventura Blvd, #340, Tarzana CA 91356, USA — Singer

**Price, Larry C**
930 S Garfield St, Denver CO 80209, USA — Photojournalist

**Price, Lia Scott**
Lia Scott Price Productions, 4455 Torrance Blvd, #866, Torrance CA 90503, USA — Actress, Producer, Writer

**Price, Lindsay**
Management 360, 9111 Wilshire Blvd, Beverly Hills CA 90210 USA — Actress

**Price, Lloyd**
95 Horseshoe Hill Road, Pound Ridge NY 10576, USA — Singer, Pianist, Songwriter

| | |
|---|---|
| **Price, M V Leontyne**<br>9 Vandam St, New York NY 10013, USA | Opera Singer |
| **Price, Marc**<br>8444 Magnolia Dr, Los Angeles CA 90046, USA | Actor |
| **Price, Megyn**<br>A P A Talent & Literary Agency, 405 S Beverly Dr, #300, Beverly Hills CA 90212 USA | Actress |
| **Price, Michael F**<br>Franklin Mutual Advisors, 57 John F Kennedy Parkway, Short Hills NJ 07078, USA | Financier |
| **Price, Mike**<br>4415 Thorleigh Dr, Indianapolis IN 46226, USA | Basketball Player |
| **Price, Mitchell L**<br>9944 Candlestick Lane, Pensacola FL 32514, USA | Football Player |
| **Price, Molly**<br>Gersh Agency, 9465 Wilshire Blvd, #600, Beverly Hills CA 90212 USA | Actress |
| **Price, Nichoas R L (Nick)**<br>Nick Price Group, 900 S US Highway 1, #105, Jupiter FL 33477, USA | Golfer |
| **Price, Noel**<br>21 Windeyer Crescent, Kanata ON K2K 2P6, Canada | Ice Hockey Player |
| **Price, Pat**<br>PO Box 3, Robson BC V0G 1X0, Canada | Ice Hockey Player |
| **Price, Paul B**<br>1056 Overlook Road, Berkeley CA 94708, USA | Physicist |
| **Price, Peerless L**<br>5658 Legends Club Circle, Braselton GA 30517, USA | Football Player |
| **Price, Phoebe**<br>P Mgmt, 11666 Montana Ave, Los Angeles CA 90049, USA | Actress |
| **Price, Rachael**<br>Claire Vision Productions, 515 N Flagler Dr, #808, West Palm Beach FL 33401, USA | Singer, Guitarist (Lake Street Dive) |
| **Price, Richard**<br>Creative Artists Agency, 2000 Ave of Stars, Los Angeles CA 90067, USA | Writer |
| **Price, Rick**<br>Harbour Agency, 135 Forbes St, Woolloomooloo NSW 2011, Australia | Singer, Musician, Songwriter |
| **Price, Steven**<br>Gorfaine/Schwartz, 4111 W Alameda Ave, #509, Burbank CA 91505 USA | Composer |
| **Price, Willard D**<br>PO Box 2783, Laguna Hills CA 92654, USA | Explorer |
| **Price-Francis, Amy**<br>A M I Artists Mgmt, 464 King St E, Toronto ON M5A 1L7, Canada | Actress |
| **Priddy, Nancy**<br>11223 Sunshine Terrace, Studio City CA 91604, USA | Actress |
| **Priddy, Robert S (Bob)**<br>136 Shingiss St, #214, McKees Rocks PA 15136, USA | Baseball Player |
| **Pride, Charley**<br>C E C C A Productions, 3198 Royal Lane, #200, Dallas TX 75229, USA | Singer, Guitarist, Baseball Player |
| **Pride, Curtis J**<br>Gallaudet University, Athletic Dept, 800 Florida Ave NE, Washington DC 20002, USA | Baseball Player |
| **Pride, Richard F (Dicky), III**<br>1214 Belleaire Circle, Orlando FL 32804, USA | Golfer |
| **Pridemore, L Thomas (Tom), Jr**<br>3935 Poplar Springs Road, Gainesville GA 30507, USA | Football Player |
| **Priesand, Sally J**<br>32 Fernwood Dr, Asbury Park NJ 07712, USA | Religious Leader |
| **Priest, Eddie Lee (Ed), Jr**<br>445 Ballard Road, Altoona AL 35952, USA | Baseball Player |
| **Priest, Maxi**<br>Virgin Records, 150 5th Ave, Front 3, New York NY 10011 USA | Singer |
| **Priest, Steve**<br>D C M International, 296 Nether St, Finchley, London N3 1RJ, England | Singer, Bassist (Sweet) |
| **Priestlay, Ken**<br>5438 Crescent Dr, Delta BC V4K 2C9, Canada | Ice Hockey Player |
| **Priestley, Jason**<br>A P A Talent & Literary Agency, 405 S Beverly Dr, #300, Beverly Hills CA 90212 USA | Actor |
| **Priestley, Thomas (Tom), Jr**<br>Paradigm Agency, 360 N Crescent Dr, North Building, Beverly Hills CA 90210 USA | Director |
| **Prieto, Ariel**<br>15325 SW 53rd St, Miami FL 33185, USA | Baseball Player |
| **Prieto, Rodrigo**<br>PO Box 3338, Beverly Hills CA 90212, USA | Cinematographer |
| **Prigioni, Pablo**<br>New York Knicks, Madison Square Garden, 2 Penn Plaza, New York, NY 10121 USA | Basketball Player |
| **Primack, Joel R**<br>University of California, Astronomy Dept, Santa Cruz CA 95064, USA | Astronomer |
| **Primakov, Yevgeny M**<br>Federation Chamber of Commerce, Ilyinka Str 6, 103684 Moscow, Russia | Prime Minister, Russia |
| **Primeau, Keith**<br>2 Danforth Dr, Voorhees NJ 08043, USA | Ice Hockey Player |
| **Primeau, Wayne**<br>Toronto Maple Leafs, AirCanada Center, 40 Bay St, Toronto ON M5J 2K2, Canada | Ice Hockey Player |
| **Primes, Robert**<br>Innovative Artists, 1505 10th St, Santa Monica CA 90401 USA | Cinematographer |
| **Primrose, Neil**<br>Wildlife Entertainment, 21 Heathmans Road, London SW6 4TJ, England | Drummer (Travis) |
| **Prince**<br>Paisley Park Enterprises, 7801 Audubon Road, Chanhassen MN 55317, USA | Singer, Guitarist, Songwriter |
| **Prince Kay One**<br>Gartenstr 67, 88212 Ravensburg, Germany | Rap Artist |
| **Prince Paul**<br>Agency Group Ltd, 142 W 57th St, #600, New York NY 10019 USA | Rap Artist, DJ Musician, Producer |
| **Prince Royce**<br>Sony Records, 2100 Colorado Ave, Santa Monica CA 90404 USA | Singer, Songwriter |
| **Prince, Bart**<br>3501 Monte Vista NE, Albuquerque NM 87106, USA | Architect |
| **Prince, Donald M (Don)**<br>11143 James B White Highway S, Whiteville NC 28472, USA | Baseball Player |
| **Prince, Faith**<br>Hart Mgmt, 1900 Ave of Stars, #1800, Los Angeles CA 90067, USA | Actress, Singer |

**Prince, Harold S (Hal)**
Directors Company, 311 W 43rd St, #307, New York NY 10036, USA — Producer, Director

**Prince, Jonathan**
723 N Elm Dr, Beverly Hills CA 90210, USA — Actor, Producer, Writer

**Prince, Larry L**
Genuine Parts Co, 2999 Circle 75 Parkway, Atlanta GA 30339, USA — Businessman

**Prince, Peter**
Bloomsbury Publishing, 50 Bedford Square, London WC1B 3DP, England — Writer

**Prince, Richard**
57 E 78th St, New York NY 10001, USA — Artist, Photographer

**Prince, Tayshaun D**
8866 Prestancia Cove S, Memphis TN 38125, USA — Basketball Player

**Prince, Thomas A (Tom)**
6816 10th Ave NW, Bradenton FL 34209, USA — Baseball Player

**Prince-Bythewood, Gina**
Creative Artists Agency, 2000 Ave of Stars, #100, Los Angeles CA 90067 USA — Writer, Director, Producer

**Princess Superstar**
SuperVision Management Group, 59-65 Worship St, London EC2A 2DU, England — Rap Artist, Singer, Songwriter

**Principal, Victoria**
23852 Pacific Coast Highway, #785, Malibu CA 90265, USA — Actress

**Principe, Joe**
Agency Group Ltd, 142 W 57th St, #600, New York NY 10019 USA — Bassist (Rise Against)

**Prine, Andrew**
361 17th St NW, #2601, Atlanta GA 30363, USA — Actor

**Prine, John**
Al Bunetta Mgmt, 33 Music Square W, #102B, Nashville TN 37203, USA — Singer, Songwriter

**Pringle, Joan**
TalentWorks, 3500 W Olive Ave, #1400, Burbank CA 91505 USA — Actress

**Prinosil, David**
T C Wolfsberg, Am Schanzl 3, 92224 Amberg, Germany — Tennis Player

**Prinsloo, Behati**
Women Model Mgmt, 199 Lafayette St, #700, New York NY 10012 USA — Model

**Printup, Marcus**
Universal Attractions, 135 W 26th St, #1200, New York NY 10001 USA — Jazz Trumpeter

**Prinz, Bret R**
15471 N 88th Ave, Peoria AZ 85382, USA — Baseball Player

**Prinze, Freddie, Jr**
Gersh Agency, 9465 Wilshire Blvd, #600, Beverly Hills CA 90212 USA — Actor

**Prinzi, Frank**
571 W 113th St, #24, New York NY 10025, USA — Cinematographer

**Prioleau, Pierson O**
2221 Santee River Road, Saint Stephen SC 29479, USA — Football Player

**Prior of Brampton, James M L**
36 Morpeth Mansions, London SW1P 1ER, England — Government Official, England

**Prior, Anthony E**
3529 Holding St, Riverside CA 92501, USA — Football Player

**Prior, Madeleine E (Maddy)**
Park Promotions, PO Box 651, Park Road, Oxford OX2 9RB, England — Singer

**Prior, Mark W**
10284 Waddell Circle, San Diego CA 92124, USA — Baseball Player

**Prior, Michael R (Mike)**
14511 Quail Pointe Dr, Carmel IN 46032, USA — Football Player

**Prior, Susan**
ArtWork Entertainment, 6100 Wilshire Blvd, #575, Los Angeles CA 90048, USA — Actress

**Priory, Richard B**
Duke Energy Co, 526 S Church St, Charlotte NC 28202, USA — Businessman

**Pritchard, Barry**
Lustig Talent, PO Box 770850, Orlando FL 32877 USA — Singer, Guitarist (Fortunes)

**Pritchard, Connor**
I C M Partners, 10250 Constellation Blvd, #900, Los Angeles CA 90067 USA — Producer, Writer

**Pritchard, David E**
Massachusetts Institute of Technology, Physics Dept, Cambridge MA 02139, USA — Physicist

**Pritchard, Kevin L**
141 S Meridian St, #402, Indianapolis IN 46225, USA — Basketball Player

**Pritchard, Michael R (Mike)**
PO Box 93114, Las Vegas NV 89193, USA — Football Player

**Pritchard, Ronald D ((Ron)**
495 E Coconino Dr, Chandler AZ 85249, USA — Football Player

**Pritchett, Christopher D (Chris)**
959 Fir Tree Place, Carlsbad CA 92011, USA — Baseball Player

**Pritchett, Kelvin B**
46679 Pinehurst Circle, Stone Mountain GA 30087, USA — Football Player

**Pritchett, Matthew (Matt)**
London Daily Telegraph, 181 Marsh Wall, London E14 9SR, England — Cartoonist (Matt)

**Pritchett, Stanley J**
523 Monteagle Trace, Stone Mountain GA 30087, USA — Football Player

**Pritko, Steven (Steve)**
328 Chanticlair Dr, Apex NC 27502, USA — Football Player

**Probst, Lawrence F (Larry), III**
Olympic Committee, 1 Olympic Plaza, Building 6, Colorado Springs CO 80909 USA — Businessman

**Prochaska, Andreas**
Spielkind-Mattias Frik, Zimmerstr 11, 10969 Berlin, Germany — Director

**Prochazka, Martin**
H C Kladno, Petra Bezruc 2531, 27280 Kladno, Czech Republic — Ice Hockey Player

**Prochnow, Jurgen**
Maximilian Lautenbacher Mgmt, Rumfordstr 35, 80469 Munich, Germany — Actor

**Prock, Markus**
Tyrolean Luge Assn, Olympia World, Olympiastr 10, 6020 Innsbruck, Austria — Luge Athlete

**Procter, Emily**
Paradigm Agency, 360 N Crescent Dr, North Building, Beverly Hills CA 90210 USA — Actress, Model

**Proctor, James A (Jim)**
2 Westmoreland Place, Saint Louis MO 63108, USA — Baseball Player

**Proctor, Phillip**
C E S D, 10635 Santa Monica Blvd, #130, Los Angeles CA 90025 USA — Actor

**Proctor, Robert N**
Stanford University, History Dept, Stanford CA 94305, USA — Scientific Historian

**Proctor, Scott C** — Baseball Player
428 NE Bayberry Lane, Jensen Beach FL 34957, USA
**Prodi, Romano** — Prime Minister, Italy
Prime Minister's Office, Palazzo Chigi, Piazza Colonna 370, 00187 Rome, Italy
**Proehl, Richard S (Ricky)** — Football Player
3504 Bromley Wood Lane, Greensboro NC 27410, USA
**Proenza, William (Bill)** — Climatologist, Government Official
US National Weather Service, 11691 SW 17th St, Miami FL 33165, USA
**Professor Griff** — Rap Artist (Public Enemy)
Brookes Co, 3710 S Robertson Blvd, #100, Culver City CA 90232, USA
**Prohgress** — Singer (Far East Movement)
Stampede Mgmt, 12530 Beatrice St, Los Angeles CA 90066, USA
**Prokop, Joseph M (Joe)** — Football Player
1042 N Mountain Ave, Upland CA 91786, USA
**Prokop, Matt** — Actor
Management 360, 9111 Wilshire Blvd, Beverly Hills CA 90210 USA
**Proly, Michael J (Mike)** — Baseball Player
21 Hollander Dr, Taylors SC 29687, USA
**Promuto, Vincent L (Vince)** — Football Player
9 Island Dr, Norwalk CT 06855, USA
**Pronger, Christopher R (Chris)** — Ice Hockey Player
345 S Hinchman Ave, Haddonfield NJ 08033, USA
**Pronger, Sean J** — Ice Hockey Player
1229 Firwood Dr, Pittsburgh PA 15243, USA
**Pronovost, Andre J A** — Ice Hockey Player
1412 46E Rue, Shawinigan QC G9N 5B8, Canada
**Pronovost, J Jean D** — Ice Hockey Player, Coach
Hockey Ministries, 1100 La Gauchetiere St W, Montreal QC H3B 2S2, Canada
**Pronovost, R Marcel** — Ice Hockey Player
4620 Dali Court, Windsor ON N9G 2M8, Canada
**Propes, Duane** — Guitarist (Little Texas)
Splash Public Relations, 1520 16th Ave S, #2, Nashville TN 37212, USA
**Prophet, Billy** — Singer (Jive Five)
Paramount Entertainment, PO Box 12, Far Hills NJ 07931 USA
**Prophet, Ronald L V (Ronnie)** — Singer
1227 Saxon Dr, Nashville TN 37215, USA
**Propp, Brian** — Ice Hockey Player
2320 Riverton Road, Cinnaminson NJ 08077, USA
**Prose, Francine** — Writer
P E N American Center, 588 Broadway, #303, New York NY 10012, USA
**Prospal, Vaclav** — Ice Hockey Player
17 S Treasure Dr, Tampa FL 33609, USA
**Prosser, James** — Singer
Refugee Mgmt, 209 10th Ave S, #347, Cummins Station, Nashville TN 37203, USA
**Prosser, Robert** — Religious Leader
Cumberland Presbyterian Church, 1978 Union Ave, Memphis TN 38104, USA
**Prost, Alain M P** — Auto Racing Driver
11 Ave de la Gare, 1260 Nyon, Switzerland
**Prost, Sharon** — Judge
US Court of Appeals, 717 Madison Place NW, Washington DC 20439, USA
**Protopopov, Oleg A** — Figure Skater
Chalet Hubel, 3818 Grindelwald, Switzerland
**Proulx, Brooklynn** — Actress
Global Creative, 1051 N Cole Ave, #B, Los Angeles CA 90038, USA
**Proulx, E Annie** — Writer
2030 290th Ave NE, Carnation WA 98014, USA
**Prout, Brian** — Drummer (Diamond Rio)
Modern Mgmt, 1625 Broadway, #600, Nashville TN 37203, USA
**Prout, Kirsten** — Actress
Alchemy Entertainment, 7024 Melrose Ave, #420, Los Angeles CA 90038 USA
**Proval, David** — Actor
Greater Vision Artists Talent Agency, 8981 Sunset Blvd, #101, Los Angeles CA 90069, USA
**Provence, Andrew C** — Football Player
224 Providence Road, Fayetteville GA 30215, USA
**Provenza, Paul** — Actor, Director
Metropolitan Talent Agency, 5405 Wilshire Blvd, #218, Los Angeles CA 90036 USA
**Provost, Jon** — Actor
627 Montclair Ave, Santa Rosa CA 95409, USA
**Prowse, David** — Actor
Spotlight, 7 Leicester Place, London WC2H 7BP, England
**Proyas, Alex** — Director, Producer, Writer
Creative Artists Agency, 2000 Ave of Stars, #100, Los Angeles CA 90067 USA
**Prpic, Joel** — Ice Hockey Player
2586 S Shore Road, Sudbury ON P3G 1M3, Canada
**Prucha, Petr** — Ice Hockey Player
6122 S Cypress Point Dr, Chandler AZ 85249, USA
**Prudhomme, Christian** — Cycling Executive
A S O, 2 Rue Rouget de l'Isle, 92130 Issy Les Mouoimeaux, France
**Prudhomme, Don** — Drag Racing Driver
Don Prudhomme Racing, 1232 Distribution Way, Vista CA 92081, USA
**Prudhomme, Paul** — Chef
2424 Chartres St, New Orleans LA 70117, USA
**Pruett, Jeanne** — Singer, Songwriter
Joe Taylor Artist Agency, 2802 Columbine Place, Nashville TN 37204 USA
**Pruett, Scott** — Auto Racing Driver
PO Box 814, Star ID 83669, USA
**Pruetz, Jill** — Primatologist, Anthropologist
Iowa State University, Anthropology Dept, Ames IA 50011, USA
**Pruitt, Gregory D (Greg)** — Football Player
13851 Larchmere Blvd, Cleveland OH 44120, USA
**Pruitt, James B** — Football Player
PO Box 432301, Miami FL 33243, USA
**Pruitt, Jordan L** — Singer
Black Angel Records, PO Box 54, Fairview TN 37862, USA
**Pruitt, Michael L (Mike)** — Football Player
20568 Kelsey Lane, Strongsville OH 44149, USA

**Pruitt, Mickey A**
15647 Dante Dr, South Holland IL 60473, USA — Football Player

**Pruitt, Ronald R (Ron)**
3632 Turnberry Dr, Medina OH 44256, USA — Baseball Player

**Prunariu, Dumitru D**
Str Sf Spiridon 12, #4, 70231 Bucharest, Romania — Cosmonaut, Romania

**Prunskiene, Kazimiera D**
Kriviu 53A-13, 2007 Vilnius, Lithuania — Prime Minister, Lithuania

**Prusiner, Stanley B**
University of California, Biochemistry Dept, San Francisco CA 94143, USA — Nobel Medicine Laureate

**Pruzansky, Mark E**
975 Park Ave, New York NY 10028, USA — Orthopedic Surgeon

**Pryce, Jonathan**
Julian Belfrage Assoc, 9 Argyll St, #300, London W1F 7TG, England — Actor, Singer

**Pryce, Malcolm**
Bloomsbury Publishing, 50 Bedford Square, London WC1B 3DP, England — Writer

**Pryce, Trevor W**
12057 Open Run Road, Ellicott City MD 21042, USA — Football Player

**Prydz, Eric**
Ministry of Sound, 103 Gaunt St, London SE1 6DP, England — DJ Musician

**Prynoski, Chris**
Titmouse, 6616 Lexington Ave, Los Angeles CA 90038, USA — Animator, Producer

**Pryor, Aaron**
5311 Lees Crossing Dr, #10, Cincinnati OH 45239, USA — Boxer

**Pryor, Calvin**
New York Jets, 1 Jets Dr, Florham Park NJ 07932 USA — Football Player

**Pryor, Christopher M (Chris)**
6877 Macbeth Court, Saint Paul MN 55125, USA — Ice Hockey Player

**Pryor, David H**
507 N 11th St, Paragould AR 72450, USA — Senator, Governor, AR

**Pryor, Gregory R (Greg)**
9726 W 115th Terrace, Overland Park KS 66210, USA — Baseball Player

**Pryor, Nicholas**
S D B Partners, 315 S Beverly Dr, #411, Beverly Hills CA 90067 USA — Actor

**Prysirr, Geoff**
10921 Whipple St, #406, North Hollywood CA 91602, USA — Actor

**Prytz, Maria**
Skelleftea Curling Club, Mossgatan 27, 931 70 Skelleftea, Sweden — Curling Athlete

**Przybilla, Joel A**
3815 N Brookfield Road, #104, Brookfield WI 53045, USA — Basketball Player

**Psycho Les**
Agency Group Ltd, 142 W 57th St, #600, New York NY 10019 USA — Rap Artist (Beatnuts)

**Ptacek, Louis J**
University of California Medical Center, Fu & Ptacek Laboratories, 1550 4th St, San Francisco CA 94158, USA — Geneticist

**Ptashne, Mark S**
Harvard University, Biochemistry Dept, Cambridge MA 02138, USA — Biochemist

**Pucci, Josephine**
USA Hockey, 1775 Bob Johnson Dr, Colorado Springs CO 80906 USA — Ice Hockey Player

**Pucci, Lou Taylor**
United Talent Agency, U T A Plaza, 9336 Civic Center Dr, Beverly Hills CA 90210 USA — Actor

**Pucillo, Michael (Mike)**
9402 Council Rock Court, Riverview FL 33578, USA — Football Player

**Puck, Wolfgang**
805 N Sierra Dr, Beverly Hills CA 90210, USA — Chef

**Puckett, Gary**
10710 Seminole Blvd, #3, Largo FL 33778, USA — Singer, Songwriter

**Pudi, Danny**
United Talent Agency, U T A Plaza, 9336 Civic Center Dr, Beverly Hills CA 90210 USA — Actor, Writer

**Puenzo, Luis A**
Cinematografia Nacional Instituto, Lima 319, 1073 Buenos Aires, Argentina — Director

**Puerta, Joe**
Lustig Talent, PO Box 770850, Orlando FL 32877 USA — Singer, Guitarist (Ambrosia)

**Puett, Tommy**
16621 Cerulean Court, Chino Hills CA 91709, USA — Actor

**Puetz, Garry S**
1779 Robinson Road, Dahlonega GA 30533, USA — Football Player

**Puffer, Brandon**
1546 Haynie Bend, Round Rock TX 78665, USA — Baseball Player

**Pugacheva, Alla B**
State Variety Theater, Bersenevskaya Nab 20/2, 109072 Moscow, Russia — Singer

**Puget, Jade E**
S A M, 722 Seward St, Los Angeles CA 90038, USA — Guitarist (AFI)

**Puget, Jean-Loup**
Institut d'Astrophysique Spatiale, Paris-Sud, 91898 Orsay Cedex, France — Astrophysicist

**Pugh, Gareth**
Mandi Lennard Publicity, 2 Hoxton St, London N1 6NG, England — Fashion Designer

**Pugh, Jethro, Jr**
Gifts Inc, 329 E Colorado Blvd, #505, Dallas TX 75203, USA — Football Player

**Pugh, Larry**
RR 4, New Castle PA 16101, USA — Football Player

**Pugh, Timothy D (Tim)**
8015 N 187th East Ave, Owasso OK 74055, USA — Baseball Player

**Pugsley, Don**
Gar Lester Agency, 4130 Cahuenga Blvd, #108, Universal City CA 91602, USA — Actor

**Puhl, Terrance S (Terry)**
918 Gondola St, Sugar Land TX 77478, USA — Baseball Player

**Pujats, Janis Cardinal**
Metropolijas Kurija, Maza Pils Iela 2/A, 1050 Riga, Latvia — Religious Leader

**Pujol, Laetitia**
Paris Opera Ballet, Place de l'Opera, 75009 Paris, France — Ballerina

**Pujols Alcantara, J Albert**
102 Grand Meridien Forest, Chesterfield MO 63005, USA — Baseball Player

**Pujols, Luis B**
3867 Jonathans Way, Boynton Beach FL 33436, USA — Baseball Player, Manager

**Puleo, Charles M (Charlie)**
3202 Miser Station Road, Louisville TN 37777, USA — Baseball Player

**Puleston-Davies, Ian** — Actor
Artists Partnership, 101 Finsbury Pavement, London EC2A 1RS, England

**Pulford, Robert J (Bob)** — Ice Hockey Player, Coach
78 Coventry Road, Northfield IL 60093, USA

**Pulgram, William** — Interior Designer
3747 Peachtree Road NE, #1425, Atlanta GA 30319, USA

**Pulido, Roberto (Bobby), Jr** — Singer
Texas Sounds Entertainment, 957 NASA Parkway, #542, Houston TX 77058, USA

**Puljic, Vinko Cardinal** — Religious Leader
Nadbiskupski Ordinarijat, Kaptol 7, 71000 Sarajevo, Bosnia & Herzegovina

**Pulkkinen, David** — Ice Hockey Player
5095 Croatia Road, Sudbury ON P3G 1L5, Canada

**Pullen, Melanie Clark** — Actress
Julian Belfrage Assoc, 9 Argyll St, #300, London W1F 7TG, England

**Pulliam, Harvey J** — Baseball Player
2009 Mount Hamilton Dr, Antioch CA 94531, USA

**Pulliam, Keshia Knight** — Actress
A P A Talent & Literary Agency, 405 S Beverly Dr, #300, Beverly Hills CA 90212 USA

**Pullman, Bill** — Actor
I C M Partners, 10250 Constellation Blvd, #900, Los Angeles CA 90067 USA

**Pullman, Philip** — Writer
24 Templar Road, Oxford OX2 8LT, England

**Pulsford, K H Nigel** — Singer, Guitarist (Bush)
Front Line Mgmt, 1100 Glendon Ave, #2000, Los Angeles CA 90024 USA

**Pulsipher, Lindsay** — Actress
I C M Partners, 10250 Constellation Blvd, #900, Los Angeles CA 90067 USA

**Pulsipher, William T (Bill)** — Baseball Player
1986 SW Certosa Road, Port Saint Lucie FL 34953, USA

**Pulver, Lara** — Actress
Independent Talent Group, 40 Whitfield St, London W1T 2RH, England

**Pulver, Liselotte** — Actress
Villa Bip, Route Suisse 21, 1166 Perroy VD, Switzerland

**Pulz, Penny** — Golfer
10315 W Winninger Circle, Sun City AZ 85351, USA

**Puna, Henry T** — Prime Minister, Cook Islands
Prime Minister's Office, Avarua, Rarotonga, Cook Islands

**Punch, Lucy** — Actress
United Agents, 12-26 Lexington St, London W1F 0LE, England

**Punsalan Swallow, Elizabeth** — Ice Dancer, Coach
Detroit Skating Club, 888 Denison Court, Bloomfield Hills MI 48302, USA

**Punto, Nicholas P (Nick)** — Baseball Player
19550 N Grayhawk Dr, #1122, Scottsdale AZ 85255, USA

**Puppa, Daren** — Ice Hockey Player
4526 Cheval Blvd, Lutz FL 33558, USA

**Pupunu, Alfred S (Al)** — Football Player
415 Conestoga Road, Moscow ID 83843, USA

**Purcell, Dominic** — Actor
Untitled Entertainment, 350 S Beverly Dr, #200, Beverly Hills CA 90212 USA

**Purcell, James N** — Government Official
5113 W Running Brook Road, Columbia MD 21044, USA

**Purcell, Lee** — Actress
Coast to Coast Talent, 3350 Barham Blvd, Los Angeles CA 90068 USA

**Purcell, Patrick B** — Publisher
Boston Herald, Publisher's Office, 1 Herald St, Boston MA 02118, USA

**Purcell, Sarah** — Actress
4437 Alla Road, #6, Marina del Rey CA 90292, USA

**Purcell, William** — Astrophysicist
Northwestern University, Astrophysics Dept, Evanston IL 60208, USA

**Purdee, Nathan** — Actor
Irv Schechter, 9460 Wilshire Blvd, #300, Beverly Hills CA 90212 USA

**Purdie, Bernard (Pretty)** — Jazz Drummer
Benay Enterprises, 62 E Starrs Plain Road, Danbury CT 06810, USA

**Purdy, Alfred** — Writer
Harbour Publishing, PO Box 219, Madeira Park BC V0N 2H0, Canada

**Purdy, Joe** — Singer, Songwriter
Agency Group Ltd, 142 W 57th St, #600, New York NY 10019 USA

**Purdy, Jolene** — Actress
Innovative Artists, 1505 10th St, Santa Monica CA 90401 USA

**Purdy, Robert** — Actor
Associated International Mgmt, 7 Hatton Garden, #400, London EC1N 8AD, England

**Purdy, Ted** — Golfer
14259 N 2nd Ave, Phoenix AZ 85023, USA

**Purefoy, James** — Actor
Independent Talent Group, 40 Whitfield St, London W1T 2RH, England

**Puri, Om** — Actor
Conway Van Gelder Grant, 8-12 Broadwick St, #300, London W1F 8HW, England

**Purify, Robert L (Bobby)** — Singer
Conqueroo, 11271 Ventura Blvd, #522, Studio City CA 91604 USA

**Purim, Flora** — Singer
A Train Mgmt, 401 Grand Ave, #300, Oakland CA 94610, USA

**Purinton, Dale** — Ice Hockey Player
2045 Cowichan Bay Road, Cowichan Bay BC V0R 1N1, Canada

**Purl, Linda** — Actress
820 Vista Grande Dr, Colorado Springs CO 80906, USA

**Purtzer, Tom** — Golfer
10529 N 106th Place, Scottsdale AZ 85258, USA

**Purvanov, Georgi** — President, Bulgaria
President's Office, 2 Dondukov Blvd, 1123 Sofia, Bulgaria

**Purves, William** — Financier
100 Ebury Mews, London SW1 9NX, England

**Purvis, Jeffrey (Jeff)** — Auto Racing Driver
1157 Dunbar Cove Road, Clarksville TN 37043, USA

**Purvis, Neal** — Writer, Producer
United Talent Agency, U T A Plaza, 9336 Civic Center Dr, Beverly Hills CA 90210 USA

**Puryear, Martin** — Sculptor
Drysdale Gallery, 700 New Hampshire Ave NW, #917, Washington DC 20037, USA

**P**

Puleston-Davies - Puryear

**P**

| | |
|---|---|
| **Puscau, Alina**<br>I M G Models, 304 Park Ave S, #PH N, New York NY 10010 USA | Model, Singer, Actress |
| **Pusch, Alexander**<br>Lindenweg 39, 97941 Tauberbischofsheim, Germany | Fencer |
| **Pusey, Chris**<br>287 Brantwood Park Road, Brantford ON N3P 1H6, Canada | Ice Hockey Player |
| **Pusha T**<br>American Talent Agency, 26 Finney Farm Road, Croton on Hudson NY 10520, USA | Rap Artist (Clipse) |
| **Pushelberg, Glenn**<br>Yabu Pushelberg, 138 Spring St, #400, New York NY 10012, USA | Architect, Interior Designer |
| **Pushelberg, Glenn**<br>Yabu Pushelberg, 88 Prince St, #200F, New York NY | Architect, Interior Designer |
| **Pushor, Jamie**<br>29 Jay Road W, Lake George NY 12845, USA | Ice Hockey Player |
| **Puskaric, Ljubomir**<br>I M G Artists, Hogarth Business Park, Chiswick, London W4 2TH, England | Opera Singer |
| **Putch, John**<br>I C M Partners, 10250 Constellation Blvd, #900, Los Angeles CA 90067 USA | Actor |
| **Putilin, Nikolai G**<br>Mariinsky Theater, Teatralnaya Square 1, 190000 Saint Petersburg, Russia | Opera Singer |
| **Putin, Vladimir V**<br>President's Office, Kremlin, Staraya Pl 4, 103132 Moscow, Russia | President, Russia |
| **Putman, P Edward (Ed)**<br>PO Box 3366, Mesquite NV 89024, USA | Baseball Player |
| **Putnam, Ashley**<br>Maurice Mayer, 201 W 54th St, #1C, New York NY 10019, USA | Opera Singer |
| **Putnam, C Duane**<br>1545 Magnolia Ave, Ontario CA 91762, USA | Football Player |
| **Putnam, Hilary W**<br>31 Cleveland St, Arlington MA 02474, USA | Philosopher |
| **Putnam, Patrick E (Pat)**<br>4040 Staley Road, Fort Myers FL 33905, USA | Baseball Player |
| **Putnis, Andrew**<br>University of Munster, Mineralogy Institute, Corrensstr 24, 48149 Munster, Germany | Mineralogist |
| **Putnis, Christine V**<br>University of Munster, Mineralogy Institute, Corrensstr 24, 48149 Munster, Germany | Mineralogist |
| **Putterman, Seth J**<br>University of California, Physics & Astronomy Dept, Knudson Hall, Los Angeles CA 90024, USA | Physicist |
| **Puttnam, David T**<br>Enigma Productions, 29A Tufton St, London SW1P 3QL, England | Producer |
| **Putz, Joseph J (J J)**<br>7818 N Sherri Lane, Paradise Valley AZ 85253, USA | Baseball Player |
| **Putze, Martin**<br>Hainstr 4, 99518 Bad Sulza, Germany | Bobsled Athlete |
| **Putzier, Jebediah L (Jeb)**<br>2641 W 131st Terrace, Leawood KS 66209, USA | Football Player |
| **Putzulu, Bruno**<br>Voyez Mon Agent, 20 Ave Rapp, 75007 Paris, France | Actor |
| **Pyatt, F Nelson**<br>1680 Arthur St W, Thunder Bay ON P7K 1A8, Canada | Ice Hockey Player |
| **Pyavko, Vladislav I**<br>Bryusov Per 2/14, #27, 103009 Moscow, Russia | Opera Singer |
| **Pye, R Edward (Eddie)**<br>307 Polk St, Columbia TN 38401, USA | Baseball Player |
| **Pyfrom, Shawn C**<br>Podwall Entertainment, 710 N Orlando Ave, #203, West Hollywood CA 90069, USA | Actor |
| **Pygram, Wayne**<br>Peachtree Services, 1805 134th Ave SE, #27, Bellevue WA 98005, USA | Actor |
| **Pyle, Andy**<br>Larry Page, 29 Ruston Mews, London W11 1RB, England | Bassist (Kinks) |
| **Pyle, Chuck**<br>Terri Stewart Management & Booking, PO Box 27581, Denver CO 80227, USA | Singer, Guitarist, Songwriter |
| **Pyle, Michael J (Mike)**<br>2436 Saranac Court, Glenview IL 60026, USA | Football Player |
| **Pyle, Missi**<br>McKeon-Myrones Mgmt, 3500 Olive Ave, #770, Burbank CA 91505 USA | Actress |
| **Pyle, Thomas D (Artimus)**<br>Lustig Talent, PO Box 770850, Orlando FL 32877 USA | Drummer (Lynyrd Skynyrd) |
| **Pyle, W Palmer**<br>14808 N Olympic Way, Fountain Hills AZ 85268, USA | Football Player |
| **Pynchon, Thomas**<br>Henry Holt, 175 5th Ave, #400, New York NY 10010 USA | Writer |
| **Pyne, Natasha**<br>Kate Feast, Primrose Hill Studios, Fitzroy Road, London NW1 8TR, England | Actress |
| **Pyne, Stephen J**<br>Arizona State University, History Dept, Tempe AZ 85287, USA | Historian |

**Puscau - Pyne**

**Q**
Def Jam Records, 828 8th Ave, New York NY 10019 USA — Singer (112)

**Q, Maggie**
Creative Artists Agency, 2000 Ave of Stars, #100, Los Angeles CA 90067 USA — Actress, Model

**Qabus ibin Sa'id al Sa'id**
Diwan, PO Box 632, Muscat 113, Oman — Sultan, Oman

**Qasimi, Sheikh Dr Sultan ibn Muhammad Al**
Ruler's Palace, Sharjah, United Arab Emirates — Ruler, Sharjah

**Qasimi, Sheikh Saqr ibn Muhammad Al**
Ruler's Palace, Ras Al Khaimah, United Arab Emirates — Ruler, Ras Al Khaimah

**Qawi, Dwight Muhammad**
Lighthouse, 5034 Atlantic Ave, Mays Landing NJ 08330, USA — Boxer

**Q-Tip**
Creative Artists Agency, 2000 Ave of Stars, #100, Los Angeles CA 90067 USA — Rap Artist

**Quagmire, Joshua**
PO Box 2221, Los Angeles CA 90078, USA — Cartoonist (Cutey Bunny)

**Quaid, Dennis**
W M E Entertainment, 9601 Wilshire Blvd, #300, Beverly Hills CA 90210 USA — Actor

**Quaid, Jack**
United Talent Agency, U T A Plaza, 9336 Civic Center Dr, Beverly Hills CA 90210 USA — Actor

**Quaid, Randy**
Quaid Films, Box 156 Station F, 50 Charles St, Toronto ON M4Y 2L5, Canada — Actor, Producer

**Quaintance, Rachel**
Greater Visions Artists Talent Agency, 8981 W Sunset Blvd, #101, West Hollywood CA 90069 USA — Actress, Comedienne

**Qualls, Chad M**
8416 Big View Dr, Austin TX 78730, USA — Baseball Player

**Qualls, D J**
Paul Kohner, 9300 Wilshire Blvd, #555, Beverly Hills CA 90212 USA — Actor

**Qualls, James R (Jim)**
410 N Country Road 950, Sutter IL 62373, USA — Baseball Player

**Quance, Kristine**
1320 Moncado Dr, Glendale CA 91207, USA — Swimmer

**Quann Jendrick, Megan**
11602 135th Street Court E, Puyallup WA 98374, USA — Swimmer

**Quant, Mary**
Mary Quant Ltd, 7 Montpelier St, Knightsbridge, London SW7 1EX, England — Fashion Designer

**Quantrill, Paul J**
334 E Lake Road, Palm Harbor FL 34685, USA — Baseball Player

**Quarles, Shelton E**
17019 Candeleda de Avila, Tampa FL 33613, USA — Football Player

**Quarrie, Donald (Don)**
Jamaican Amateur Athletic Assn, PO Box 272, Kingston 5, Jamaica — Track Athlete

**Quast, Anne**
1261 Parkside Dr E, Seattle WA 98112, USA — Golfer

**Quasthoff, Thomas**
C M Artists, 127 W 96th St, #13B, New York NY 10025 USA — Concert Singer

**Quatro, Suzi**
Cape Entertainment, 8432 NW 31st Court, Fort Lauderdale FL 33351, USA — Singer, Songwriter, Actress

**Quaye, Finley**
Paquin Entertainment, 468 Stradbrook Ave, Winnipeg MB R3L 0J9, Canada — Singer

**Quayle, Anna**
C D A, 167-169 Kensington High St, London W8 6SH, England — Actress

**Quayle, J Danforth (Dan)**
Laura Mintner, 7001 N Scottsdale Road, Scottsdale AZ 85253, USA — Vice President

**Quayle, Steven**
Gersh Agency, 9465 Wilshire Blvd, #600, Beverly Hills CA 90212 USA — Director

**Queen Ida**
Traditional Arts Services, 3661 Albion Place N, #2, Seattle WA 98103, USA — Singer, Accordian Player

**Queen Latifah**
Flavor Unit Entertainment, 119 Washington Ave, #400, Miami Beach FL 33139, USA — Rap Artist, Actress, Model

**Queen, Jeffrey R (Jeff)**
4765 Canterbury Court, Oceanside CA 92056, USA — Football Player

**Queffelec, Anne**
15 Ave Corneille, 78600 Maisons-Laffitte, France — Concert Pianist

**Queler, Eve**
Opera Orchestra of New York, 344 E 63rd St, #B1, New York NY 10065, USA — Conductor

**Quenneville, Joel N**
835 S Park Ave, Hinsdale IL 60521, USA — Ice Hockey Player, Coach

**Querim, Molly**
CBS-TV, Sports Dept, 51 W 52nd St, New York NY 10019 USA — Sportscaster

**Query, Jeff L**
93 Woodlilly Place, Spring TX 77382, USA — Football Player

**Questlove**
Paradigm Agency, 360 N Crescent Dr, North Building, Beverly Hills CA 90210 USA — Drummer (Roots), DJ

**Questrom, Allen I**
J C Penney Co, 6501 Legacy Dr, Plano TX 75024, USA — Businessman

**Quevedo, Orlando B Cardinal**
Archdiocese of Cotabato, PO Box 186, 158 Sinsuat Ave, 9600 Cotobato City, Philippines — Religious Leader

**Quezada, Milly**
Alpha Artists , 261 E 134th St, #200, Bronx NY 10454, USA — Singer

**Quick, Diana**
Independent Talent Group, 40 Whitfield St, London W1T 2RH, England — Actress

**Quick, James E (Jim)**
6061 Keeble Lane, Camino CA 95709, USA — Baseball Umpire

**Quick, Jonathan D (Jon)**
Los Angeles Kings, Staples Center, 1111 S Figueroa St, Los Angeles CA 90015 USA — Ice Hockey Player

**Quick, Michael A (Mike)**
13 Slab Branch Road, Marlton NJ 08053, USA — Football Player

**Quie, Albert H (Al)**
4209 Christy Lane, Minnetonka MN 55345, USA — Governor, MN

**Quigley, Dana C**
2670 Tecumseh Dr, West Palm Beach FL 33409, USA — Golfer

**Quigley, Laura**
1111B NW 131st Way, Vancouver WA 98685, USA — Singer, Bassist (Misty River)

**Quigley, Linnea**
Purrfect Productions, PO Box 1771, Pompano Beach, FL 33061 USA — Actress

**Quilici, Frank R**
3413 E 126th St, Burnsville MN 55337, USA — Baseball Player, Manager

**Quill, Timothy E**
University of Rochester, Medical & Dentistry School, Rochester NY 14642, USA — Social Activist, Internist

**Quillan, Frederick D (Fred)**
2924 Bailey Lane, Eugene OR 97401, USA — Football Player

**Quin, Sara K**
Paquin Entertainment, 468 Stradbrooke Ave, Winnipeg MB R3L 0J9, Canada — Singer (Tegan & Sara), Songwriter

**Quince, Dolvett**
Rogers & Cowan, 8687 Melrose Ave, #G700, West Hollywood CA 90069 USA — Physical Fitness Instructor, Actor

**Quindlen, Anna M**
I C M Partners, 10250 Constellation Blvd, #900, Los Angeles CA 90067 USA — Columnist

**Quinlan, Kathleen**
Mavrick Artists Agency, 6100 Wilshire Blvd, #550, Los Angeles CA 90048, USA — Actress

**Quinlan, Thomas R (Tom)**
1061 Sterling St S, Saint Paul MN 55119, USA — Baseball Player

**Quinlan, William D (Bill)**
393 Mount Vernon St, Lawrence MA 01843, USA — Football Player

**Quinn, Aidan**
Paradigm Agency, 360 N Crescent Dr, North Building, Beverly Hills CA 90210 USA — Actor

**Quinn, Aileen**
12747 Riverside Dr, #208, Valley Village CA 91607, USA — Actress

**Quinn, Brayden T (Brady)**
5889 Connolly Court, Dublin OH 43016, USA — Football Player

**Quinn, Brian**
Brian Quinn Soccer School, 9606 Aero Dr, #3500, San Diego CA 92123, USA — Soccer Player, Coach

**Quinn, Carmel**
Producers Inc, 11806 N 56th St, Tampa FL 33617 USA — Singer

**Quinn, Colin**
Brillstein Entertainment Partners, 9150 Wilshire Blvd, #350, Beverly Hills CA 90212 USA — Actor, Comedian

**Quinn, Cynthia**
Momix, PO Box 35, Washington CT 06794, USA — Dancer

**Quinn, DeClan**
22 Cherry Ave, Cornwall on Hudson NY 12520, USA — Cinematographer

**Quinn, Ed**
I C M Partners, 10250 Constellation Blvd, #900, Los Angeles CA 90067 USA — Actor

**Quinn, Freddy**
Bear Family Records, Achtern Dahl 30, 27729 Vollersode, Germany — Actor, Singer, Composer

**Quinn, J B Patrick (Pat)**
Edmonton Oilers, 11230 110th St, Edmonton AB T5G 3H7, Canada — Ice Hockey Player, Coach

**Quinn, Jane Bryant**
Newsweek, Editorial Dept, 251 W 57th St, New York NY 10019, USA — Columnist

**Quinn, Jonathan G (Jonny)**
Big Life Mgmt, 67-69 Charlton St, London NW1 1HY, England — Drummer (Snow Patrol)

**Quinn, Jonathan R**
132 Strathmore Way, Hendersonville TN 37075, USA — Football Player

**Quinn, Kimberly**
Don Buchwald Talent Agency, 6500 Wilshire Blvd, #2200, Los Angeles CA 90048 USA — Actress

**Quinn, Martha**
Kazarian/Measures/Ruskin, 11969 Ventura Blvd, #300, Studio City CA 91604 USA — Actress, Model

**Quinn, Michael P (Mike)**
10703 Del Monte Dr, Houston TX 77042, USA — Football Player

**Quinn, Molly C**
Ellen Meyer Mgmt, 8899 Beverly Blvd, #612, West Hollywood CA 90048, USA — Actress

**Quinn, Noelle**
Washington Mystics, Verizon Center, 401 9th St NW, #750, Washington DC 20004 USA — Basketball Player

**Quinn, Patricia**
Jonathan Altaras Assoc, 11 Garrick St, London WC2E 9AR, England — Actress

**Quinn, Sally**
3014 N St NW, Washington DC 20007, USA — Journalist

**Quinones August, Denise M**
Untitled Entertainment, 350 S Beverly Dr, #200, Beverly Hills CA 90212 USA — Beauty Queen, Actress

**Quinones Torruellas, Luis R**
5821 Calle San Bruno Urb Santa Teresita, Ponce PR 00730, USA — Baseball Player

**Quinones, John**
ABC-TV, News Dept, 77 W 66th St, New York NY 10023 USA — Commentator

**Quint, Deron T**
13 Littlehale Road, Durham NH 03824, USA — Ice Hockey Player

**Quintal, Stephane**
1356A Rue La Fontaine, Montreal QC H2L 1T5, Canada — Ice Hockey Player

**Quintana, Carlos**
DiBella Entertainment, 350 7th Ave, #800, New York NY 10001, USA — Boxer

**Quinto, Zachary**
Creative Artists Agency, 2000 Ave of Stars, #100, Los Angeles CA 90067 USA — Actor

**Quinto, Zachary**
Shelter Public Relations, 9465 Wilshire Blvd, #700, Beverly Hills CA 90212 USA — Actor

**Quirk, James P (Jamie)**
310 W 123rd Terrace, Kansas City MO 64145, USA — Baseball Player

**Quirk, Matthew**
Hatchette Book Group, 3 Center Plaza, Boston MA 02108, USA — Writer

**Quiroga, Elena**
Agencia Balcells, Diagonal 580, 08021 Barcelona, Spain — Writer

**Quist, Janet**
13446 Poway Road, #239, Poway CA 92064, USA — Model

**Quivar, Florence**
Columbia Artists Mgmt Inc, 5 Columbus Circle, 1790 Broadway, #1600, New York NY 10019 USA — Opera Singer

**Quivers, Robin O**
Sirius Satellite Radio, 1221 Ave of Americas, New York NY 10020, USA — Entertainer

**Quock, Audrey**
New York Model Mgmt, 596 Broadway, #701, New York NY 10012 USA — Model, Actress

**Quon, Xian**
Otto Models, 2901 W Coast Highway, #350, Newport Beach CA 92663, USA — Model

**Qureshi, Aisam**
Octagon Worldwide, 1751 Pinnacle Dr, #1500, McLean VA 22102 USA — Tennis Player

**Raabe, Max** — Opera Singer
Max Raabe & Partner, Meinekestr 6, 10719 Berlin, Germany
**Rabach, Casey E** — Football Player
5707 Bay Shore Dr, Sturgeon Bay WI 54235, USA
**Rabal, Liberto** — Actor
Anne Alvares Correa, 34 Rue Jouffroy d'Abbans, 75017 Paris, France
**Raban, Jonathan** — Writer
Pantheon Books, 1745 Broadway, New York NY 10019, USA
**Rabe, Charles H (Charlie)** — Baseball Player
6059 E Sierra Blanca St, Mesa AZ 85215, USA
**Rabe, David W** — Writer
Creative Artists Agency, 2000 Ave of Stars, #100, Los Angeles CA 90067 USA
**Rabe, Lily** — Actress
Framework Entertainment, 9057 Nemo St, #C, West Hollywood CA 90069 USA
**Rabemananjara, Charles** — Prime Minister, Madagascar
Premier's Office, BP 248, Mahazoarivo, 101 Antananarivo, Madagascar
**Rabin, Trevor** — Composer
Kraft-Engel Mgmt, 15233 Ventura Blvd, #200, Sherman Oaks CA 91403 USA
**Rabinovitch, B Seymour** — Chemist
116 Fairview Ave N, #832, Seattle WA 98109, USA
**Rabinowitz, David L** — Astronomer
Yale University, Astronomy & Astrophysics Dept, New Haven CT 06520, USA
**Rabinowitz, Dorothy** — Journalist
Wall Street Journal, Editorial Dept, 1 World Financial Center, New York NY 10281 USA
**Rabinowitz, Jesse C** — Biochemist
University of California, Molecular & Cell Biology Dept, Berkeley CA 94720, USA
**Rabinyan, Dorit** — Writer
Bloomsbury Publishing, 50 Bedford Square, London WC1B 3DP, England
**Rabkin, Mitchell T** — Physician
Beth Israel Deaconess Medical Center, 330 Brookline Ave, Boston MA 02215, USA
**Raboteau, Albert J** — Religious Historian
Princeton University, Religion School, Princeton NJ 08544, USA
**Rabourdin, Olivier** — Actor
J F P M, 11 Rue Chavez, 75781 Paris Cedex 16, France
**Raboy, Marcus** — Director
Modus Entertaiment, 8730 W Sunset Blvd, #290, West Hollywood CA 90069, USA
**Raburn, Ryan N** — Baseball Player
6612 Ike Smith Road, Plant City FL 33565, USA
**Raby, Stuart** — Physicist
Ohio State University, Physics Dept, Columbus OH 43210, USA
**Race, Harley L** — Professional Wrestler
198 Cherry Blossom Way, Troy MO 63379, USA
**Racette, Patricia** — Opera Singer
Opus 3 Artists, 470 Park Ave S, #900N, New York NY 10016 USA
**Rachel, Allyn** — Actress
Creative Artists Agency, 2000 Ave of Stars, #100, Los Angeles CA 90067 USA
**Rachel, Leah** — Actress, Writer
W M E Entertainment, 9601 Wilshire Blvd, #300, Beverly Hills CA 90210 USA
**Rachins, Alan** — Actor
TalentWorks, 3500 W Olive Ave, #1400, Burbank CA 91505 USA
**Rachlin, Julian** — Concert Violinist
Askonas Holt, Lincoln House, 300 High Holborn, London WC1V 7JH, England
**Racicot, Marc F** — Governor, MT
28013 Swan Cove Dr, Bigfork MT 59911, USA
**Racine, Yves** — Ice Hockey Player
Arizona Capital Inc, 1515 Ave Saint Jean Baptiste, Quebec QC G2E 5E2, Canada
**Rackers, Neil W** — Football Player
12374 Whitworth Terrace Court, Saint Louis MO 63141, USA
**Raczka, Michael (Mike)** — Baseball Player
72 Foley Dr, Southington CT 06489, USA
**Radachowsky, George J, Jr** — Football Player
63 Lake Place N, Danbury CT 06810, USA
**Radcliffe, Daniel** — Actor
Artist Rights Group, 4A Exmoor St, London W10 6BD, England
**Rade, John A** — Football Player
611 Deertrail Dr, Hailey ID 83333, USA
**Rademacher, Ingo** — Actor
S D B Partners, 315 S Beverly Dr, #411, Beverly Hills CA 90067 USA
**Rademacher, T Peter (Pete)** — Boxer
5585 River Styx Road, Medina OH 44256, USA
**Rademacher, William S (Bill)** — Football Player
5409 Maple Ridge, Haslett MI 48840, USA
**Rader, David M (Dave)** — Baseball Player
14413 Westdale Dr, Bakersfield CA 93314, USA
**Rader, Dotson C** — Writer
Parade Magazine, Editorial Dept, 750 3rd Ave, New York NY 10017, USA
**Rader, Douglas L (Doug)** — Baseball Player, Manager
3332 SE Court Dr, Stuart FL 34997, USA
**Rader, Paul A** — Religious Leader, Educator
Ashbury College, President's Office, 1 Macklem Dr, Wilmore KY 40390, USA
**Rader, Randall R** — Judge
US Appeals Court, 717 Madison Place NW, Washington DC 20439, USA
**Rader-Shieber, Chas** — Director
Columbia Artists Mgmt Inc, 5 Columbus Circle, 1790 Broadway, #1600, New York NY 10019 USA
**Radford, Eric** — Figure Skater
Skate Canada, 865 Shefford Road, Ottawa ON K1J 1H9, Canada
**Radford, Mark J** — Basketball Player
3423 NE 22nd Ave, Portland OR 97212, USA
**Radford, Michael** — Director
Intellectual Artists Mgmt, 10585 Santa Monica Blvd, #135, Los Angeles CA 90025, USA
**Radigan, Terry** — Singer, Songwriter
S C Entertainment, 360 W 22nd St, #9A, New York NY 10011, USA
**Radin, Joshua** — Singer, Songwriter, Actor
Wilspro Mgmt, PO Box 9, Point Pleasant NJ 08742, USA
**Radinsky, Scott D** — Baseball Player
2974 Santiago St, Westlake Village CA 91362, USA

**Radke, Brad W**
125 18th St, Belleair Beach FL 33786, USA — Baseball Player

**Radko, Christopher**
PO Box 536, Elmsford NY 10523, USA — Artist

**Radloff, Wayne R**
60 S Sea Pines Dr, Hilton Head Island SC 29928, USA — Football Player

**Radmanovic, Nebojsa**
President's Office, Marsala Titz 7, 71000 Sarajevo, Bosnia & Herzegovina — President, Bosnia & Herzegovina

**Radmanovic, Vladimir**
Chicago Bulls, United Center, 1901 W Madison St, Chicago IL 60612 USA — Basketball Player

**Radner, Roy**
30711 Overlook Run, Buena Vista CO 81211, USA — Economist

**Radnor, Josh**
United Talent Agency, U T A Plaza, 9336 Civic Center Dr, Beverly Hills CA 90210 USA — Actor

**Radojevic, Danilo**
American Ballet Theatre, 890 Broadway, #300, New York NY 10003 USA — Ballet Dancer

**Radovich, Frank R**
121 Lakewood Dr, Statesboro GA 30458, USA — Basketball Player

**Radtke, Ed**
Parseghian/Planco, 388 2nd Ave, #506, New York, NY 10010 USA — Director, Writer

**Radulov, Alexander**
2600 Hillsboro Pike, #322, Nashville TN 37212, USA — Ice Hockey Player

**Radvanovsky, Sondra**
I M G Artists, Hogarth Business Park, Chiswick, London W4 2TH, England — Opera Singer

**Radwanska, Agnieszka**
Women's Tennis Assn, 1 Progress Plaza, #1500, Saint Petersburg FL 33701 USA — Tennis Player, Model

**Rady, Michael**
Gersh Agency, 9465 Wilshire Blvd, #600, Beverly Hills CA 90212 USA — Actor

**Rae, Brenda**
Columbia Artists Mgmt Inc, 5 Columbus Circle, 1790 Broadway, #1600, New York NY 10019 USA — Opera Singer

**Rae, Charlotte**
C E S D, 10635 Santa Monica Blvd, #130, Los Angeles CA 90025 USA — Actress

**Rae, Corinne Bailey**
Creative Artists Agency, 2000 Ave of Stars, #100, Los Angeles CA 90067 USA — Singer, Songwriter

**Rae, Patricia**
Rebel Entertainment Partners, 5701 Wilshire Blvd, #456, Los Angeles CA 90036, USA — Actress

**Raether, Harold H (Hal)**
6105 Lincoln Dr, #133, Minneapolis MN 55436, USA — Baseball Player

**Rafalski, Brian C**
615 Lighthouse Way, Sanibel FL 33957, USA — Ice Hockey Player

**Rafelson, Bob**
1543 Dog Team Road, New Haven VT 05472, USA — Director

**Raffarin, Jean-Pierre**
7 Route de Saint-Georges, 86360 Chasseneuil-du-Poitou, France — Prime Minister, France

**Rafferty, Thomas M (Tom)**
1526 Mount Gilead Road, Roanoke TX 76262, USA — Football Player

**Rafikov, Mars Z**
Ul M Gorkova 59, KV 44, 480 002 Almaty, Kazakhstan — Cosmonaut

**Rafman, Jon**
Zach Feuer Gallery, 548 W 22nd St, New York NY 10011, USA — Photographer

**Rafsanjani, Hojatoleslam H**
Expediency Council of Islamic Order, Majilis, Teheran, Iran — President, Iran

**Rafter, Patrick**
Cherish the Children Foundation, 108 King William St, #800, Adelaide SA 5000, Australia — Tennis Player

**Ragan, David**
Roush Fenway Racing, 4600 Roush Place, Concord NC 28027, USA — Auto Racing Driver

**Ragin, John S**
5706 Briarcliff Road, Los Angeles CA 90068, USA — Actor

**Ragnarsson, Marcus**
Hallonstigen 2, Bjorklinge 74 030, Sweden — Ice Hockey Player

**Rago, Joseph**
Wall Street Journal, Editorial Dept, 1 World Financial Center, New York NY 10281 USA — Journalist

**Ragogna, Mike**
PO Box 2331, Fairfield IA 52556, USA — Singer, Guitarist, Songwriter

**Ragonese, Isabella**
Officine Artistiche, Via Francesco Domenico Guerrazzi 7, 00152 Rome, Italy — Actress

**Ragsdale, William**
Stone Manners Salners, 6100 Wilshire Blvd, #1500, Los Angeles CA 90035 USA — Actor

**Rahal, Robert W (Bobby)**
Team Rahal Racing, 4601 Lyman Dr, Hilliard OH 43026, USA — Auto Racing Driver, Owner

**Rahim, Tahar**
Agence Artiste Adequat, 108 Rue Reaumur, 75002 Paris, France — Actor

**Rahlves, Daron**
11655 Mount Rose View Dr, Truckee CA 96161, USA — Alpine Skier

**Rahm, Kevin**
Gersh Agency, 9465 Wilshire Blvd, #600, Beverly Hills CA 90212 USA — Actor

**Rahman Khan, Ataur**
Bangladesh Jatiya League, 500A Dhanmondi R/A, Road 7, Dhaka, Bangladesh — Prime Minister, Bangladesh

**Rahman, Allah Rakkha (A R)**
Panchthan Recording Inn, 5 4th St, Dr Subbaraya Nagar, Kodambakkam, Chennai 24, India — Composer

**Rahzel**
Agency Group Ltd, 142 W 57th St, #600, New York NY 10019 USA — Rap Artist, Percussionist (Roots)

**Rai Bachchan, Aishwarya**
A B Corp, 13 North South Road, Juhu, Mumbai 400 049, India — Beauty Queen, Actress

**Rai, Rajeev**
22 Sonmarg Nepean Sea Road, Mumbai MS 400 006, India — Director, Producer

**Raible, Steve C**
18 W Raye St, Seattle WA 98119, USA — Football Player

**Raich, Eric J**
3963 Edward Dr, Brunswick OH 44212, USA — Baseball Player

**Raichle, Marcus E**
Washington University Medical School, Radiology Dept, Saint Louis MO 63110, USA — Neurologist, Radiologist

**Raikkonen, Kimi**
Obere Rebhalde, 6340 Baar, Switzerland — Auto Racing Driver

**Railsback, Steve**
11684 Ventura Blvd, #581, Studio City CA 91604, USA — Actor

**Raimey, David E (Dave)**  Football Player
2212 W 2nd St, Dayton OH 45417, USA
**Raimi, Sam**  Director, Producer, Actor
Stars Road Entertainment, 10202 W Washington Blvd, Lean Building, Culver City CA 90232, USA
**Raimi, Ted**  Actor
Liberman-Zerman Mgmt, 252 N Larchmont Blvd, #200, Los Angeles CA 90004 USA
**Raimond, Jean-Bernard**  Government Official, France
12 Rue des Poissonniers, 92200 Neuilly-sur-Seine, France
**Raimondi, Ruggero**  Opera Singer
M Gromof, 140 Bis Rue Lecourbe, 75015 Paris, France
**Raine, Craig A**  Writer
New College, English Dept, Oxford OX1 3BN, England
**Rainer, Luise**  Actress
34 Eaton Mews North, London SW1 XAS, England
**Rainer, Wali R**  Football Player
8119 Braidstone Terrace, Chesterfield VA 23838, USA
**Raines, F Anthony (Tony)**  Auto, Truck Racing Driver
Front Row Motorsports, 3536 Denver Dr, Denver NC 28037, USA
**Raines, Shirley C**  Educator
University of Memphis, President's Office, Administration Building, Memphis TN 38152, USA
**Raines, Timothy (Tim)**  Baseball Player
1242 Saint Albans Loop, Lake Mary FL 32746, USA
**Rainey, Charles D (Chuck)**  Baseball Player
6484 Del Cerro Blvd, San Diego CA 92120, USA
**Rainey, James**  Pianist (Stamps Quartet)
PO Box 1471, Brentwood TN 37024, USA
**Rainey, Matt**  Photojournalist
Star-Ledger, Editorial Dept, 1 Star-Ledger Plaza, Newark NJ 07102, USA
**Rainford, Rob**  Chef
Agency Group, 1100 Century Park E, #711, Los Angeles CA 90067 USA
**Rains, Traver**  Fashion Designer
Heatherette, 111 E 7th St, New York NY 10009, USA
**Rainwater, Keech**  Drummer (Lonestar)
Borman Entertainment, 4322 Harding Pike, #429, Nashville TN 37205, USA
**Raiola, Dominic**  Football Player
7940 Barnsbury Ave, West Bloomfield MI 48324, USA
**Raisa, Francia**  Actress
Abrams Artists, 9200 W Sunset Blvd, #1125, West Hollywood CA 90069 USA
**Raisman, Alexandra R (Aly)**  Gymnast
Octagon Worldwide, 1751 Pinnacle Dr, #1500, McLean VA 22102 USA
**Raison, Miranda**  Actress
Artists Partnership, 101 Finsbury Pavement, London EC2A 1RS, England
**Raitt, Bonnie L**  Singer, Songwriter
Gold Mountain, 3940 Laurel Canyon Blvd, #444, Studio City CA 91604 USA
**Raja Permaisuri Agong XIII**  Sultana, Malaysia
Sultan's Palace, Istana Bukit Serene, 50502 Kuala Lumpur, Malaysia
**Rajapakse, Mahinda**  President, Sri Lanka
President's Office, Republic Square, Sri Jayewardenepura Kotte, Sri Lanka
**Rajasulochana**  Actress
70 G N Chetty Road, T Nagar, Chennai TN 600017, India
**Rajat, Kapoor**  Actor, Director
140 Andheri Indl Est, Andheri (W), Mumbai MS 400053, India
**Rajna, Thomas**  Concert Pianist, Composer
10 Wyndover Road, Claremont, Cape Town, West Cape 7708, South Africa
**Rajoelina, Audray**  President, Madagascar
President's Office, 11 Oktomvri BB, 101 Antananarivo, Madagascar
**Rajoy, Mariano**  Prime Minister, Spain
Prime Minister's Office, Complejo de las Moncloa, 28071 Madrid, Spain
**Rajskub, Mary Lynn**  Actress
Innovative Artists, 1505 10th St, Santa Monica CA 90401 USA
**Rakaa Iriscience**  Rap Artist (Dilated Peoples)
Zzonked, Stratford Workshops, Burford Road, London E15 2SP, England
**Rakers, Jason P**  Baseball Player
547 Hickory Hollow Dr, Canfield OH 44406, USA
**Rakhmonov, Imomali S**  President, Tajikistan
President's Office, Rudaki Prospect 80, 734051 Dusanabe, Tajikistan
**Rakim**  Rap Artist (Eric B & Rakim)
Padell Nadell Fine Wineberger, 59 Maiden Lane, #2700, New York NY 10038 USA
**Rakoczy, Gregg A**  Football Player
2679 NW 42nd St, Boca Raton FL 33434, USA
**Rakove, Jack N**  Historian, Writer
Stanford University, History Dept, Stanford CA 94305, USA
**Rales, Steven M**  Businessman
Danaher Corp, 1250 24th St NW, Washington DC 20037, USA
**Rall, J Edward**  Physician
9901 Longs Mill Road, Rocky Ridge MD 21778, USA
**Rall, Ted**  Editorial Cartoonist
Chronicle Features, 901 Mission St, San Francisco CA 94103 USA
**Ralph, Richard P**  Governor, Falkland Islands
Governor's Office, Government House, Stanley, Falkland Islands
**Ralph, Sheryl Lee**  Actress, Singer
S M S Talent, 8383 Wilshire Blvd, #230, Beverly Hills CA 90211 USA
**Ralston, Dennis**  Tennis Player
203 Wellwood Lane, Conroe TX 77304, USA
**Ralston, John R**  Football Player, Coach
8245 Claret Court, San Jose CA 95135, USA
**Ralston, Steve**  Soccer Player
New England Revolution, 1 Patriot Place, Foxboro MA 02035 USA
**Ram, C Venkata**  Physician
Texas Southwestern Medical Center, 5323 Harry Hines Blvd, Dallas TX 75390, USA
**Rama IX**  King, Thailand
Chitralada Villa, Bangkok, Thailand
**Ramachandran, Vilayanur S**  Neuroscientist
University of California San Diego, Brian/Cognition Center, 9500 Gilman Drive, La Jolla CA 92093, USA
**Ramage, Rob**  Ice Hockey Player
16127 Wilson Manor Dr, Chesterfield MO 63005, USA

**Ramahatra, Victor**
PO Box 6004, 101 Antananarivo, Madagascar — Prime Minister, Madagascar; Army General

**Ramakrishnan, Venkatraman**
M R C Molecular Biology Laboratory, Hills Road, Cambridge CB2 0QH, England — Nobel Chemistry Laureate

**Ramamurthy, Sendhil**
Levine Okwu Erickson, 6363 Wilshire Blvd, #300, Los Angeles CA 90048, USA — Actor

**Ramazzotti, Eros L W**
Trident Mgmt, Corso Europa 13, 20122 Milan, Italy — Singer, Songwriter

**Rambahadur Limbu**
Box 420, Bandar Seri Begawan, Negara Brunei Darussalam, Brunei — Vietnam War Borneo Army Hero (VC)

**Rambin, Leven**
Creative Artists Agency, 2000 Ave of Stars, #100, Los Angeles CA 90067 USA — Actress

**Rambis, D Kurt**
20 Chatham, Manhattan Beach CA 90266, USA — Basketball Player, Coach

**Ramenofsky Wingfield, Marilyn**
1240 NW 116th St, Seattle WA 98177, USA — Swimmer

**Ramey, Samuel E**
320 Central Park West, New York NY 10025, USA — Opera Singer

**Ramgoolam, Navinchandra**
Prime Minister's Office, Government Center, Port Louis, Mauritius — Prime Minister, Mauritius

**Ramirez Vazquez, Pedro**
Avenida de la Fuentes 170, Mexico City 01900 DF, Mexico — Architect

**Ramirez, Aramis N**
1440 N Lake Shore Dr, #10EG, Chicago IL 60610, USA — Baseball Player

**Ramirez, Cear**
Brooklyn Fare Restaurant, 200 Schermerhorn St, Brooklyn NY 11201, USA — Chef

**Ramirez, Cierra**
Corsa Agency, 11704 Wilshire Blvd, #204, Los Angeles CA 90025, USA — Actress

**Ramirez, Dania**
I C M Partners, 10250 Constellation Blvd, #900, Los Angeles CA 90067 USA — Actress

**Ramirez, Edgar**
Creative Artists Agency, 2000 Ave of Stars, #100, Los Angeles CA 90067 USA — Actor

**Ramirez, Efren**
Clear Talent Group, 10950 Ventura Blvd, Studio City, CA 91604, USA — Actor

**Ramirez, Hanley**
2903 Lake Ridge Lane, Weston FL 33332, USA — Baseball Player

**Ramirez, Hector**
17219 Midwood Drive, Granada Hills CA 91344, USA — Cinematographer

**Ramirez, Horacio**
850 Cox Road, Roswell GA 30075, USA — Baseball Player

**Ramirez, Manuel A (Manny)**
13737 NW 18th Court, Pembroke Pines FL 33028, USA — Baseball Player

**Ramirez, Marisa**
Harrison Stokes, 8730 W Sunset Blvd, #270, West Hollywood CA 90069, USA — Actress

**Ramirez, Michael P (Mike)**
Investor's Business Daily, 19 W 44th St, #1804, New York NY 10036, USA — Editorial Cartoonist

**Ramirez, Pedro J**
El Mundo, Editor's Office, Calle Pradillo 42, 28002 Madrid, Spain — Editor

**Ramirez, Raul**
Avenida Ruiz, 65 Sur Ensenada, Baja California, Mexico — Tennis Player

**Ramirez, Sara**
Mitchell K Stubbs Assoc, 8695 W Washington Blvd, #204, Culver City CA 90232 USA — Actress

**Ramo, Simon**
1221 Ocean Ave, #1003, Santa Monica CA 90401, USA — Businessman

**Ramon, Haim**
Knesset, Kiryat Ben-Gurion, Jerusalem 91950, Israel — Government Official, Israel

**Ramos Guerra, Pedro G (Pete)**
6637 W 22nd Lane, Hialeah FL 33016, USA — Baseball Player

**Ramos Ricciardi, Tabare R (Tab)**
Tab Ramos Soccer Programs, 17 Blair Road, Aberdeen NJ 07747, USA — Soccer Player

**Ramos, Constance (Connie)**
Paradigm Agency, 360 N Crescent Dr, North Building, Beverly Hills CA 90210 USA — Actress

**Ramos, Del**
Variety Artists, 1924 Spring St, Paso Robles CA 93446 USA — Singer (Association)

**Ramos, Domingo A**
Carr Duarte KM 8 1/2, Ucey al Medio, Santiago, Dominican Republic — Baseball Player

**Ramos, Fidel V**
120 Maria Cristina St, AAVA Muntinlupa City, Philippines — President, Philippines; Army General

**Ramos, Hilario (Larry), Jr**
Variety Artists, 1924 Spring St, Paso Robles CA 93446 USA — Singer, Guitarist (Association)

**Ramos, Melvin J (Mel)**
5941 Ocean View Dr, Oakland CA 94618, USA — Artist

**Ramos, Patrick**
Ground Control Touring, 20 Jay St, #838, Brooklyn NY 11201, USA — Drummer (Versus)

**Ramos, Roberto (Bobby)**
8945 Lake Irma Point, Orlando FL 32817, USA — Baseball Player

**Ramos, Rudy**
Craig Wyckoff Mgmt, 11300 Ventura Blvd, #100, Studio City CA 91604, USA — Actor, Singer

**Ramos, Sarah**
I C M Partners, 10250 Constellation Blvd, #900, Los Angeles CA 90067 USA — Actress, Director, Writer

**Ramos-Horta, Jose**
President's Office, Dili, Timor-Leste — Nobel Laureate; President, Timor-Leste

**Ramotar, Donald**
President's Office, Brickham, New Garden & South Sts, Georgetown, Guyana — President, Guyana

**Ramphele, Mamphela A**
International Bank of Reconstruction/Development, 1818 H St NW, Washington DC 20433, USA — Educator

**Rampling, Charlotte**
Diamond Mgmt, 31 Percy St, London W1T 2DD, England — Actress

**Ramsay, Anne**
A P A Talent & Literary Agency, 405 S Beverly Dr, #300, Beverly Hills CA 90212 USA — Actress

**Ramsay, Craig**
10602 Plantation Bay Dr, Tampa FL 33647, USA — Ice Hockey Player, Coach

**Ramsay, Gordon**
One Potato Two Potato, 1950 Sawtelle Blvd, #346, Los Angeles CA 90025, USA — Chef, Entertainer

**Ramsay, Laymon**
2417 Princeton Ave SW, Birmingham AL 35211, USA — Baseball Player

**Ramsay, Lynne**
W M E Entertainment, 9601 Wilshire Blvd, #300, Beverly Hills CA 90210 USA — Director, Writer

**Ramsay, Marshall**
Copley News Service, 123 Camino de la Reina, San Diego CA 92108, USA — Cartoonist

**Ramsey, Anessa**
Mitchell K Stubbs Assoc, 8695 W Washington Blvd, #204, Culver City CA 90232 USA — Actress

**Ramsey, Calvin (Cal)**
New York University, Alumni Office, 181 Mercer St, New York NY 10012, USA — Basketball Player

**Ramsey, David**
A P A Talent & Literary Agency, 405 S Beverly Dr, #300, Beverly Hills CA 90212 USA — Actor

**Ramsey, Derrick K**
C M R 445 Box 23, APO AE 09046, USA — Football Player

**Ramsey, Fernando D**
2501 Sandy Trail, Keller TX 76248, USA — Baseball Player

**Ramsey, Frank V, Jr**
PO Box 363, Madisonville KY 42431, USA — Basketball Player, Coach

**Ramsey, James R**
University of Louisville, President's Office, Louisville KY 40292, USA — Educator

**Ramsey, Laura**
Luber Rocklin Entertainment, 5815 Sunset Blvd, #206, Los Angeles CA 90028 USA — Actress

**Ramsey, Lowell W (Chuck), Jr**
17519 Martel Road, Lenoir City TN 37772, USA — Football Player

**Ramsey, Mary**
Geffen Records, 10900 Wilshire Blvd, #1000, Los Angeles CA 90024 USA — Singer (10000 Maniacs)

**Ramsey, Michael**
2120 Welch St, Houston TX 77019, USA — Attorney

**Ramsey, Michael (Mike)**
Ramsey's Gold Medal Sports, 445 W 79th St, Chanhassen MN 55317, USA — Ice Hockey Player

**Ramsey, Michael Jeffrey (Mike)**
11564 92nd Way N, Largo FL 33773, USA — Baseball Player

**Ramsey, Nathan L (Nate)**
1938 Cambridge St, Philadelphia PA 19130, USA — Football Player

**Ramsey, Patrick A**
515 Toma Lodge Dr, Ruston LA 71270, USA — Football Player

**Ramsey, Wesley (Wes)**
Abrams Artists, 9200 W Sunset Blvd, #1125, West Hollywood CA 90069 USA — Actor

**Ramsey, William E**
825 Bayshore Dr, Pensacola FL 32507, USA — Navy Admiral

**Ramsfjell, Bent Aanund**
Curling Assn, Sognsveien 75, Serviceboks 1, 0840 Oslo, Norway — Curling Athlete

**Ramson, Eason L**
3526 Bayberry Dr, Walnut Creek CA 94598, USA — Football Player

**Ramstein, Marco**
Curling Association, PO Box 606, 3000 Bern, Switzerland — Curling Athlete

**Ran, Shulamit**
University of Chicago, Music Dept, 5845 S Ellis Ave, Chicago IL 60637, USA — Composer

**Ranaldo, Lee**
Silva Artist Mgmt, 722 Steward St, Los Angeles CA 90038, USA — Guitarist (Sonic Youth)

**Rancic, Bill**
W M E Entertainment, 9601 Wilshire Blvd, #300, Beverly Hills CA 90210 USA — Actor, Producer, Writer

**Rancic, Giuliana**
W M E Entertainment, 9601 Wilshire Blvd, #300, Beverly Hills CA 90210 USA — Producer, Actress, Writer

**Rand Reese, Mary**
6650 Los Gatos, Atascadero CA 93422, USA — Track Athlete

**Rand, Robert W**
Good Samaritan Hospital, Neurosciences Institute, Los Angeles CA 90017, USA — Neurosurgeon, Educator

**Randa, Joseph G (Joe)**
6436 Ensley Lane, Mission Hills KS 66208, USA — Baseball Player

**Randall, Alice**
McCormick & Williams, 37 W 20th St, New York NY 10011, USA — Writer, Songwriter

**Randall, Anne**
10526 W Tropicana Circle, Sun City AZ 85351, USA — Actress, Model

**Randall, Carolyn D**
US Court of Appeals, 515 Rusk St, #12015, Houston TX 77002, USA — Judge

**Randall, Claire**
9965 W Royal Oak Road, #1214, Sun City AZ 85351, USA — Religious Leader

**Randall, Frankie**
1210 Ashwood Dr, Jefferson City TN 37760, USA — Boxer

**Randall, James O (Sap)**
158 Heather Lane, Ruston LA 71270, USA — Baseball Player

**Randall, Jon**
Joe's Garage, 4405 Belmont Park Terrace, Nashville TN 37215, USA — Singer, Songwriter

**Randall, Josh**
I F A Talent Agency, 8730 W Sunset Blvd, #490, West Hollywood CA 90069 USA — Actor

**Randall, Lisa**
Harvard University, Physics Dept, Cambridge MA 02138, USA — Physicist

**Randall, Semeka C**
Michigan State University, Athletic Dept, East Lansing MI 48824, USA — Basketball Player, Coach

**Randazzo, Mike**
585 Gatewood Dr, Greenwood IN 46143, USA — Actor

**Randi, James**
201 SE 12th St, Fort Lauderdale FL 33316, USA — Illusionist

**Randle El, Antwaan**
PO Box 3247, Leesburg VA 20177, USA — Football Player

**Randle, John A**
375 Calamus Circle, Hamel MN 55340, USA — Football Player

**Randle, Julius**
Los Angeles Lakers, Staples Center, 1111 S Figueroa St, Los Angeles CA 90015 USA — Basketball Player

**Randle, Leonard S (Lenny)**
39461 Cozumel Court, Murrieta CA 92563, USA — Baseball Player

**Randle, Theresa**
Agency Group, 1100 Century Park E, #711, Los Angeles CA 90067 USA — Actress

**Randle, Tom**
I M G Artists, Hogarth Business Park, Chiswick, London W4 2TH, England — Opera Singer

**Randolph, A Raymond**
US Court of Appeals, 333 Constitution NW, #4400, Washington DC 20001, USA — Judge

**Randolph, Alvin C (Al)** — Football Player
319 Roble Ave, Redwood City CA 94061, USA

**Randolph, Joyce** — Actress
295 Central Park West, #18A, New York NY 10024, USA

**Randolph, Leo** — Boxer
17020 20th Ave E, Spanaway WA 98387, USA

**Randolph, Robert** — Guitarist
Red Light Mgmt, 44 Wall St, #2200, New York NY 10005, USA

**Randolph, Sam** — Golfer
5285 Heightsview Lane E, #322, Fort Worth TX 76132, USA

**Randolph, Stephen** — Baseball Player
3706 Apache Forest Dr, Austin TX 78739, USA

**Randolph, Willie I** — Baseball Player, Manager
715 Jenney Trail, Franklin Lakes NJ 07417, USA

**Randolph, Zachary (Zach)** — Basketball Player
Memphis Grizzlies, 191 Beale St, Memphis TN 38103 USA

**Randrup, Michael** — Test Pilot
10 Fairlawn Road, Lythamst, Annes, Lancashire FY8 5PT, England

**Rands, Bernard** — Composer, Conductor
Harvard University, Music Dept, Cambridge MA 02138, USA

**Raney, Sue** — Singer
5114 Ranchito Ave, Sherman Oaks CA 91423, USA

**Ranford, William (Bill)** — Ice Hockey Player
670 Vista Lago Circle N, Palm Desert CA 92211, USA

**Ranglin, Ernest** — Guitarist, Composer
Universal Attractions, 135 W 26th St, #1200, New York NY 10001 USA

**Ranheim, Paul S** — Ice Hockey Player
12128 N Reflection Ridge Dr, Oro Valley AZ 85755, USA

**Rania al-Abdullah** — Queen, Jordan
Royal Palace, Royal Hashemite Court, Amman, Jordan

**Raniere, Sandro** — Soccer Player
Confederacion de Futebol, Rua Victor Civita 66, #1, Rio de Janeiro 22775 044, Brazil

**Ranieri, Luisa** — Actress
Media Art Mgmt, BaRbara de Braganza 11, #4 Derecha, 28004 Madrid, Spain

**Ranken, Andrew** — Drummer (Pogues)
Agency Group Ltd, 361-373 City Road, London EC1V 1PQ, England

**Ranki, Dezso** — Concert Pianist
Ordogorom Lejto 11/B, 1112 Budapest, Hungary

**Rankin, Alfred M, Jr** — Businessman
N A C C O Industries, 5875 Landerbrook Dr, #300, Cleveland OH 44124, USA

**Rankin, Chris** — Actor
Marlowes Agency, HMS President, Victoria Embankment, Blackfriars, London EC4Y 0HJ, England

**Rankin, Judy** — Golfer
2715 Racquet Club Dr, Midland TX 79705, USA

**Rankin, Kevin** — Actor
Abrams Artists, 9200 W Sunset Blvd, #1125, West Hollywood CA 90069 USA

**Rankine, Terry** — Architect
Cambridge Seven Assoc, 1050 Massachusetts Ave, Cambridge MA 02138, USA

**Ranks, Shabba** — Singer
Sony Records, 2100 Colorado Ave, Santa Monica CA 90404 USA

**Rannazzisi, Stephen** — Actor
Brillstein Entertainment Partners, 9150 Wilshire Blvd, #350, Beverly Hills CA 90212 USA

**Rannells, Andrew** — Actor
United Talent Agency, U T A Plaza, 9336 Civic Center Dr, Beverly Hills CA 90210 USA

**Ransey, Kelvin** — Basketball Player
3195 Monterey Dr, Tupelo MS 38801, USA

**Ransom, B Cody** — Baseball Player
2168 E Maplewood St, Gilbert AZ 85297, USA

**Ransom, Derrick W, Jr** — Football Player
505 Sawgrass Dr, Akron OH 44333, USA

**Ransom, Jeffrey D (Jeff)** — Baseball Player
2131 Curtis St, Berkeley CA 94702, USA

**Ransone, James (P J)** — Actor
Management 360, 9111 Wilshire Blvd, Beverly Hills CA 90210 USA

**Rao, C N Ramachandra** — Chemist
J N C President's House, Indian Science Institute, Bangalor 560012, India

**Rao, Calyampudi R** — Mathematician, Statistician
29 Old Orchard St, Buffalo NY 14221, USA

**Rao, Michael** — Educator
Virginia Commonwealth University, President's Office, Richmond VA 23284, USA

**Rapace, Noomi** — Actress
Agentfirman Planthaber/Kilden, Drottninggatan 55, 111 21 Stockholm, Sweden

**Rapada, Clayton A (Clay)** — Baseball Player
2737 Fenway Ave, Chesapeake VA 23323, USA

**Rapaport, Michael** — Actor
Paradigm Agency, 360 N Crescent Dr, North Building, Beverly Hills CA 90210 USA

**Raphael** — Singer, Actor
Los Rosales #7, Monteprincipe, 28668 Boadilla del Monte, Madrid, Spain

**Raphael, Fredric M** — Writer, Director
Steve Kenis Co, 95 Barkston Gardens, London SW5 0EU, England

**Raphael, June Diane** — Actress
United Talent Agency, U T A Plaza, 9336 Civic Center Dr, Beverly Hills CA 90210 USA

**Raphael, Sally Jessy** — Entertainer, Actress
249 Quaker Hill Road, Pawling NY 12564, USA

**Rapinoe, Megan A** — Soccer Player
Seattle Sounders, 12 Seahawks Way, Renton WA 98056 USA

**Rapoport, Ellen** — Writer, Producer
Creative Artists Agency, 2000 Ave of Stars, #100, Los Angeles CA 90067 USA

**Rapp, Adam** — Writer, Director
United Talent Agency, U T A Plaza, 9336 Civic Center Dr, Beverly Hills CA 90210 USA

**Rapp, Anthony D** — Actor, Singer
Untitled Entertainment, 435 Hudson St, #900, New York NY 10014 USA

**Rapp, Patrick L (Pat)** — Baseball Player
2554 Pete Seay Road, Sulphur LA 70663, USA

**Rapp, Vernon F (Vern)** — Baseball Player, Manager
1559 Redwing Lane, Broomfield CO 80020, USA

**Rappaport, Ben** — Actor
Gersh Agency, 9465 Wilshire Blvd, #600, Beverly Hills CA 90212 USA
**Rappeneau, Jean-Paul** — Director, Writer
24 Rue Henri Barbusse, 75005 Paris, France
**Rapping 4-Tay** — Rap Artist
Richard Walters, PO Box 2789, Toluca Lake CA 91610 USA
**Rapsody** — Rap Artist
Jamla Records, 984 Trinity Road, Raleigh NC 27607, USA
**Rarick, Cindy** — Golfer
PO Box 30001, Tucson AZ 85751, USA
**Rasby, Walter H** — Football Player
6413 Brookbury Court, Charlotte NC 28226, USA
**Rasche, David** — Actor
Innovative Artists, 1505 10th St, Santa Monica CA 90401 USA
**Rascoe, Robert B (Bobby)** — Basketball Player
523 Sumpter Ave, Bowling Green KY 42101, USA
**Rascoff, Spencer M** — Businessman
Zillow Inc, Russell Investment Center, 1301 2nd Ave, #3100, Seattle WA 98101, USA
**Rascon, Alfred V** — Vietnam War Army Hero (CMH)
10397 Derby Dr, Laurel MD 20723, USA
**Raselli, Evelina** — Ice Hockey Player
Swiss Ice Hockey, Hagenholzstr 81, 8050 Zurich, Switzerland
**Rash, Jim** — Actor, Writer
Innovative Artists, 1505 10th St, Santa Monica CA 90401 USA
**Rash, Ron** — Writer
320 Princess Grace Ave, Clemson SC 29631, USA
**Rash, Steve** — Director
Gersh Agency, 9465 Wilshire Blvd, #600, Beverly Hills CA 90212 USA
**Rashad, Ahmad** — Football Player, Sportscaster
13220 Verdun Dr, Palm Beach Gardens FL 33410, USA
**Rashad, Phylicia** — Actress
Parseghian/Planco, 388 2nd Ave, #506, New York, NY 10010 USA
**Rasheeda** — Rap Artist
I C M Partners, 10250 Constellation Blvd, #900, Los Angeles CA 90067 USA
**Rashid, Karim** — Furniture Designer
428 W 54th St, New York NY 10019, USA
**Rasizade, Artur T** — Prime Minister, Azerbaijan
Prime Minister's Office, Lermontov Str 68, 370066 Baku, Azerbaijan
**Rask, Tuukka M** — Ice Hockey Player
Boston Bruins, 100 Legends Way, #250, Boston MA 02114 USA
**Raskin, Alex** — Journalist
Los Angeles Times, Editorial Dept, 202 W 1st St, Los Angeles CA 90012 USA
**Rasley, Rocky** — Football Player
1747 W Harbor Dr, Isleton CA 95641, USA
**Rasmussen, Anders Fogh** — Prime Minister, Denmark
Prins Jorgens Gard 11, 1218 Copenhagen K, Denmark
**Rasmussen, Blair A** — Basketball Player
9810 SE 35th Place, Mercer Island WA 98040, USA
**Rasmussen, Dennis L** — Baseball Player
PO Box 547341, Orlando FL 32854, USA
**Rasmussen, Eric R** — Baseball Player
237 SW 45th St, Cape Coral FL 33914, USA
**Rasmussen, Erik** — Ice Hockey Player
5124 Clear Spring Court, Minnetonka MN 55345, USA
**Rasmussen, Gerry B** — Cartoonist (Bub Slug, Betty)
10716 69th Ave NW, Edmonton AB T6H 2E1, Canada
**Rasmussen, Poul Nyrup** — Prime Minister, Denmark
Allegade 6A, 2000 Frederiksberg, Denmark
**Rasmussen, Randall L (Randy)** — Football Player
81 Grumman Hill Road, Wilton CT 06897, USA
**Rasmussen, Randy R** — Football Player
3990 114th Lane NW, Minneapolis MN 55433, USA
**Rasmussen, Rie** — Actress, Director
McCue Sussmane Zapfel, 521 5th Ave, #2800, New York NY 10175, USA
**Rasmussen, Wayne F** — Football Player
PO Box 756, Brandon SD 57005, USA
**Raspberry, Larry** — Singer (Gentrys)
Craig Nowag Attractions, 2095 Exeter Road, Germantown TN 38138, USA
**Rasuk, Victor** — Actor
Gersh Agency, 9465 Wilshire Blvd, #600, Beverly Hills CA 90212 USA
**Ratajkowski, Emily** — Actress, Model
Innovative Artists, 1505 10th St, Santa Monica CA 90401 USA
**Ratchford, Jeremy** — Actor
A K A Talent, 6310 San Vicente Blvd, #200, Los Angeles CA 90048 USA
**Ratcliffe, John A** — Radio Astronomer
193 Huntingdon Road, Cambridge CB3 0DL, England
**Ratelle, J G Y Jean** — Ice Hockey Player
1200 Salem St, #111, Lynnfield MA 01940, USA
**Rath, A Gary** — Baseball Player
202 James Dr, Long Beach MS 39560, USA
**Rath, Meaghan** — Actress
Rain Mgmt, 1800 Stanford St, Santa Monica CA 90404, USA
**Rathbone, Jackson** — Actor
Cutler Mgmt, 165 Little Park Lane, Los Angeles CA 90049, USA
**Rather, Dan** — Commentator
45 E 80th St, #26A, New York NY 10075, USA
**Rather, David E (Bo)** — Football Player
4050 W Centre Ave, #215, Portage MI 49024, USA
**Rathje, Mike** — Ice Hockey Player
14850 Blossom Hill Road, Los Gatos CA 95032, USA
**Rathke, Henrich K M H** — Religious Leader
Schleifmuhlenweg 11, 19061 Schwering, Germany
**Rathman, Thomas D (Tom)** — Football Player
2762 Bloomfield Crossing, Bloomfield Hills MI 48304, USA
**Rathmann, Miriam** — Model
Playboy Promotions, 9346 Civic Center Dr, #200, Beverly Hills CA 90210 USA

**Ratleff, W Edward (Ed)** — Basketball Player
4202 Paseo de Oro, Cypress CA 90630, USA

**Ratley, Sarah Lee** — Astronaut Candidate
PO Box 6973, Leawood KS 66206, USA

**Ratliff, Paul H** — Baseball Player
78 Campton Place, Laguna Niguel CA 92677, USA

**Ratliff, Theo C** — Basketball Player
1180 Mount Paran Road NW, Atlanta GA 30327, USA

**Ratliffe, Lisa** — Model
New York Model Mgmt, 596 Broadway, #701, New York NY 10012 USA

**Ratner, Brett** — Director
Rat Entertainment, 100 Universal City Plaza, Bungalow 5196, Universal City CA 91608, USA

**Ratner, Marina** — Mathematician
University of California, Mathematics Dept, Berkeley CA 94720, USA

**Ratner, Mark A** — Chemist
615 Greenleaf Ave, Glencoe IL 60022, USA

**Ratser, Dmitri** — Concert Pianist
Naxim Gershunoff, 1401 NE 9th St, #38, Fort Lauderdale FL 33304, USA

**Rattay, Timothy F (Tim)** — Football Player
2556 W Princeville Dr, Anthem AZ 85086, USA

**Rattle, Simon D** — Conductor
Askonas Holt, Lincoln House, 300 High Holborn, London WC1V 7JH, England

**Ratushinskaya, Irina B** — Writer
Vargius Publishing House, Kazakova Str 18, 107005 Moscow, Russia

**Ratzenberger, John** — Actor
Management Squared, 10900 Wilshire Blvd, #1400, Los Angeles CA 90024, USA

**Rau, Douglas J (Doug)** — Baseball Player
RR 1 Box 154A, Columbus TX 78934, USA

**Rauch, Jasen** — Guitarist, Composer (Red)
Paradigm Agency, 404 W Franklin St, Monterey CA 93940 USA

**Rauch, Jon** — Baseball Player
14081 N Old Forest Trail, Oro Valley AZ 85755, USA

**Rauch, Melissa** — Actress
W M E Entertainment, 9601 Wilshire Blvd, #300, Beverly Hills CA 90210 USA

**Rauch, Siegfried** — Actor
Alexander Agentur, Lamontstr 9, 81679, Munich, Germany

**Raup, David M** — Paleontologist
423 Johnson Dr, Washington Island WI 54246, USA

**Rausse, Errol** — Ice Hockey Player
338 Rosslare Dr, Arnold MD 21012, USA

**Rautins, Leo R** — Basketball Player
202 Litchfield Dr, Syracuse NY 13224, USA

**Rautzhan, Clarence G (Lance)** — Baseball Player
2472 Covington Dr, Myrtle Beach SC 29579, USA

**Ravanello, Rick** — Actor
Greene Assoc, 1901 Ave of Stars, #130, Los Angeles CA 90067 USA

**Ravasi, Gianfranco Cardinal** — Religious Leader
Pontifical Council for Culture, Via della Conciliazione 5, 00193 Rome, Italy

**Raven, Eddy** — Singer, Guitarist, Songwriter
Birds of a Feather, PO Box 2476, Hendersonville TN 37077, USA

**Raven, Marion** — Singer (M-2-M), Songwriter
10th Street Mgmt, 700 N San Vicente Blvd, #G410, West Hollywood CA 90069, USA

**Raven, Peter H** — Botanist
Missouri Botanical Garden, 4355 Shaw Blvd, Saint Louis MO 63110, USA

**Raven-Symone** — Actress, Singer
United Talent Agency, U T A Plaza, 9336 Civic Center Dr, Beverly Hills CA 90210 USA

**Raver, Kim** — Actress
Mosiac Media Group, 9200 W Sunset Blvd, #1000, Los Angeles CA 90069 USA

**Ravera, Gina** — Actress
Rookery, 8200 Wilshire Blvd, #100, Beverly Hills CA 90212, USA

**Ravich, Rand** — Director, Producer, Writer
Creative Artists Agency, 2000 Ave of Stars, #100, Los Angeles CA 90067 USA

**Ravitch, Diane S** — Historian
New York University, Press Building, Washington Place, New York NY 10003, USA

**Ravlich, Matt** — Ice Hockey Player
15 Appletree Lane, Dalton MA 01226, USA

**Ravony, Francisque** — Prime Minister, Madagascar
Union des Forces Vivas Democratiques, Antananarivo, Madagascar

**Rawat, Navi** — Actress
Innovative Artists, 1505 10th St, Santa Monica CA 90401 USA

**Rawi, Raad** — Actor
Artists Partnership, 101 Finsbury Pavement, London EC2A 1RS, England

**Rawle, Matt** — Actor
Eamonn Bedfor Agency, 80-81 Saint Martin's Lane, #400, London WC2N 4AA, England

**Rawles, James Wesley** — Writer
Trident Media Group, 41 Madison Ave, #3600, New York NY 10010 USA

**Rawley, Shane W** — Baseball Player
4587 Cherrybark Court, Sarasota FL 34241, USA

**Rawlings, David T** — Singer, Guitarist, Songwriter
D S Mgmt, 2814 12th Ave S, #202, Nashville TN 37204, USA

**Rawlings, Donnell** — Actor, Writer, Director
Innovative Artists, 1505 10th St, Santa Monica CA 90401 USA

**Rawlings, Florence** — Singer, Songwriter
Agency Group Ltd, 361-373 City Road, London EC1V 1PQ, England

**Rawlins, Adrian** — Actor
Artists Partnership, 101 Finsbury Pavement, London EC2A 1RS, England

**Rawlinson, Johnnie B** — Judge
US Court of Appeals, US Courthouse, 333 Las Vegas Blvd S, Las Vegas NV 89101, USA

**Rawls, Elizabeth E (Betsy)** — Golfer
101 Lynthwaite Farm Lane, Wilmington DE 19803, USA

**Rawls, Sam** — Cartoonist (Pops Place)
King Features Syndicate, 300 W 57th St, #1500, New York NY 10019 USA

**Ray J** — Singer, Songwriter, Actor
Norwood & Norwood, 22817 Ventura Blvd, #432, Woodland Hills CA 91364, USA

**Ray, Amy** — Singer (Indigo Girls), Songwriter
Russell Carter Artist Mgmt, 567 Ralph Mcgill Blvd, Atlanta GA 30312, USA

**Ray, Billy**
Management 360, 9111 Wilshire Blvd, Beverly Hills CA 90210 USA — Director, Writer

**Ray, Chris**
15311 Winding Creek Dr, Tampa FL 33613, USA — Baseball Player

**Ray, Clifford (Cliff)**
Boston Celtics, 226 Causeway St, #4, Boston MA 02114 USA — Basketball Player, Coach

**Ray, Darrol A**
13000 Doriath Way, Oklahoma City OK 73170, USA — Football Player

**Ray, Edward B (Eddie)**
219 W Oak Lane, Lake Charles LA 70605, USA — Football Player

**Ray, Edward J**
Oregon State University, President's Office, Corvallis OR 97331, USA — Educator

**Ray, J Earl**
446 N Lowell St, Casper WY 82601, USA — Basketball Player

**Ray, Jimmy**
Epic Records, 9830 Wilshire Blvd, Beverly Hills CA 90212 USA — Singer

**Ray, John**
Gucci Group, 1 Amstelplein, 1096 Amsterdam HA, Netherlands — Fashion Designer

**Ray, John C (Johnny)**
12470 S 432, Chouteau OK 74337, USA — Baseball Player

**Ray, Lisa**
Brunskill Mgmt, 169 Queens Gate, #8A, London SW7 5HE, England — Actress

**Ray, Rachael**
W M E Entertainment, 1325 Ave of Americas, New York NY 10019 USA — Chef

**Ray, Rob**
289 Sausalito Dr, East Amherst NY 14051, USA — Ice Hockey Player

**Ray, Robert D**
Blue Cross/Blue Shield of Iowa, 636 Grand Ave, Des Moines IA 50309, USA — Governor, IA

**Ray, Ronald E**
117 Planters Row E, Ponte Vedra Beach FL 32082, USA — Vietnam War Army Hero (CMH)

**Ray, Terry**
42559 Angel Wing Way, Ashburn WA 20148, USA — Football Player

**Raybon, Marty**
Bobby Roberts, 3050 Business Park Circle, #303, Goodlettsville TN 37221 USA — Singer, Songwriter

**Raycroft, Andrew**
Vancouver Canucks, 800 Griffiths Way, Vancouver BC V6B 6G1, Canada — Ice Hockey Player

**Raye, Collin**
Flood Bumstead McCready McCarthy, 16 W 22nd St, #200, New York NY 10010 USA — Singer

**Rayford, Floyd K**
1621 NE Waldo Road # 56, Gainesville FL 32609, USA — Baseball Player

**Rayl, James R (Jim)**
201 W Boulevard, Kokomo IN 46902, USA — Basketball Player

**Raymer, Cory G**
13554 Mountain Road, Lovettsville VA 20180, USA — Football Player

**Raymo, Maureen**
Boston University, Geology Dept, Boston MA 02215, USA — Geologist

**Raymond, Corey**
106 Carter St, New Iberia LA 70560, USA — Football Player

**Raymond, J Claude**
3 De la Citiere, #911, Saint Luc QC J0J 2A0, Canada — Baseball Player

**Raymond, Janice**
Playboy Promotions, 9346 Civic Center Dr, #200, Beverly Hills CA 90210 USA — Model

**Raymond, Lisa**
5 Diemer Dr, Media PA 19063, USA — Tennis Player

**Raymond, Ralph**
USA Softball, 1 Olympia Plaza, Colorado Springs CO 80909, USA — Softball Coach

**Raymonde, Tania**
A P A Talent & Literary Agency, 405 S Beverly Dr, #300, Beverly Hills CA 90212 USA — Actress

**Raymond-James, Michael**
TalentWorks, 3500 W Olive Ave, #1400, Burbank CA 91505 USA — Actor

**Raymund, Monica**
Gersh Agency, 9465 Wilshire Blvd, #600, Beverly Hills CA 90212 USA — Actress

**Raymund, Steven A**
Tech Data Corp, 5350 Tech Data Dr, Clearwater FL 33760, USA — Businessman

**Raynaud, Jean-Pierre**
12 Ave Rhin et Danube, 92250 La Gareene Colombes, France — Sculptor

**Rayner, Adam**
Innovative Artists, 1505 10th St, Santa Monica CA 90401 USA — Actor

**Raynor, Bruce**
Unite, 275 7th Ave, #1100, New York NY 10001, USA — Labor Leader

**Raz, Joseph**
Oxford University, Balliol College, Oxford OX1 3BJ, England — Philosopher

**Raz, Kavi**
Dale Garrick, 1017 N La Cienega Blvd, #109, West Hollywood CA 90069 USA — Actor

**Razah**
Def Jam Records, 828 8th Ave, New York NY 10019 USA — Singer, Songwriter

**Raz-B**
Pyramid Entertainment Group, 377 Rector Place, #21A, New York NY 10280 USA — Singer (B2K)

**Razborov, A A**
Princeton University, Mathematics Dept, Princeton NJ 08540, USA — Mathematician

**Raziano, Barry J**
1315 4th St, Kenner LA 70062, USA — Baseball Player

**Re, Giovanni Battisti Cardinal**
Congregation for Bishops, Palazzo delle Congregazioni, Piazza Pio XII, #10, 00193 Rome, Italy — Religious Leader

**Rea, Chris**
Richard De La Font Agency, 4845 S Sheridan Road, #505, Tulsa OK 74145 USA — Singer, Guitarist, Songwriter

**Rea, Connie M**
13 Marina Dr, Winter Haven FL 33881, USA — Basketball Player

**Rea, Stephen**
Barking Dog Entertainment, 609 Greenwich St, #600, New York NY 10014, USA — Actor

**Read, Dolly**
30765 Pacific Coast Highway, #103, Malibu CA 90265, USA — Model, Actress

**Read, James**
Pakula/King, 9229 W Sunset Blvd, #315, West Hollywood CA 90069 USA — Actor

**Read, Richard**
Portland Oregonian, Editorial Dept, 1320 SW Broadway, Portland OR 97201, USA — Journalist

**Read, Sister Joel** — Educator
Alverno College, President's Office, PO Box 343922, Milwaukee WI 53234, USA
**Readdy, William F (Bill)** — Astronaut
N A S A, Johnson Space Center, 2101 NASA Road, Houston TX 77058 USA
**Reader, Ted** — Chef
Agency Group, 1100 Century Park E, #711, Los Angeles CA 90067 USA
**Readman, Andrew** — Actor
Artists Partnership, 101 Finsbury Pavement, London EC2A 1RS, England
**Ready, Randy M** — Baseball Player
4410 Enfield Dr, Dallas TX 75220, USA
**Reagan, Nancy D** — Wife of US President, Actress
10880 Wilshire Blvd, #870, Los Angeles CA 90024, USA
**Reagon, Bernice Johnson** — Singer (Sweet Honey in the Rock)
American University, History Dept, Washington DC 20016, USA
**Reagon, Toshi** — Singer, Guitarist
M R A Records, PO Box 8322, Silver Spring MD 20907, USA
**Reagor, W Montae** — Football Player
2328 Sunset Ridge Circle, Cedar Hill TX 75104, USA
**Reale, Willie** — Writer, Lyricist
Creative Artists Agency, 2000 Ave of Stars, #100, Los Angeles CA 90067 USA
**Reality, Maxim** — Singer, Emcee (Prodigy)
Midi Mgmt, Jenkins Lane, Great Hallinsbury, Essex CM22 7QL, England
**Reardon, Jeffrey J (Jeff)** — Baseball Player
5 Marlwood Lane, Palm Beach Gardens FL 33418, USA
**Reaser, Elizabeth** — Actress
United Talent Agency, U T A Plaza, 9336 Civic Center Dr, Beverly Hills CA 90210 USA
**Reason, Rex** — Actor
Roadside Productions, 20105 Rhapsody Road, Walnut Creek CA 91789, USA
**Reasoner, Marty** — Ice Hockey Player
9427 Crystal Beach Road, Hammondsport NY 14840, USA
**Reasons, Gary P** — Football Player
805 Glendevon Dr, McKinney TX 75071, USA
**Reaume, Marc A** — Ice Hockey Player
299 Laurier Dr, LaSalle ON N9J 1L7, Canada
**Reaves, Kenneth M (Ken)** — Football Player
413 Oakside Dr SW, Atlanta GA 30331, USA
**Reaves, T Johnson (John)** — Football Player
4825 W San Miguel St, Tampa FL 33629, USA
**Reavie, Chez** — Golfer
Gaylord Sports Mgmt, 13845 N Northsight Blvd, #200, Scottsdale AZ 85260 USA
**Reavis, David C (Dave)** — Football Player
5495 S Newport Circle, Greenwich Village CO 80111, USA
**Reavley, Thomas M** — Judge
3830 Wickersham Lane, Houston TX 77027, USA
**Rebek, Julius, Jr** — Chemist
2330 Calle de Oro, La Jolla CA 92037, USA
**Rebekah** — Singer
International Talent Booking, Ariel House, 74A Charlotte St, #100 London W1T 4QJ, England
**Rebensburg, Viktoria** — Alpine Skier
Hirschbergweg 1, 83708 Kreuth, Germany
**Reboulet, Jeffrey A (Jeff)** — Baseball Player
3776 Grand Oak Trail, Dayton OH 45440, USA
**Rebraca, Zeljko** — Basketball Player
1550 8th St, Manhattan Beach CA 90266, USA
**Recari, Beatriz** — Golfer
Ladies Pro Golf Assn, 100 International Golf Dr, Daytona Beach FL 32124 USA
**Recasner, Eldridge D** — Basketball Player
6159 164th Ave SE, Bellevue WA 98006, USA
**Recchi, Mark** — Ice Hockey Player
114 Fairway Lane, Pittsburgh PA 15238, USA
**Rechichar, Albert D (Bert)** — Football Player
141 W McClain Road, Belle Vernon PA 15012, USA
**Reckell, Peter** — Actor
Mattie Mgmt, 415 N Camden Dr, #203, Beverly Hills CA 90210, USA
**Reckermann, Jonas** — Volleyball Player
Vitesse Karcher GmbH, Karolingerstra 41, 70736 Fellbach, Germany
**Rector, Jeff** — Actor
10748 Aqua Vista St, North Hollywood CA 91602, USA
**Redahl, Gordon (Gord)** — Ice Hockey Player
201 Milton St, Flin Flon MB R8A 0H8, Canada
**Redbone, Leon** — Singer, Guitarist
Pathfinder Mgmt, 1009 16th Ave S, Nashville TN 37212, USA
**Redd, Glenn H** — Football Player
4526 W 1500 N, Ogden UT 84404, USA
**Redd, Michael W** — Basketball Player
2 Crescent Pond, New Albany OH 43054, USA
**Redden, Barry D** — Football Player
PO Box 6501, Katy TX 77491, USA
**Redden, Wade** — Ice Hockey Player
Boston Bruins, 100 Legends Way, #250, Boston MA 02114 USA
**Reddick, Cat** — Soccer Player
2620 Altadena Road, Birmingham AL 35243, USA
**Reddick, Jaret R** — Singer, Guitarist (Bowling for Soup)
Rainmaker Artists, PO Box 551665, Dallas TX 75355, USA
**Reddick, Lance** — Actor
Innovative Artists, 1505 10th St, Santa Monica CA 90401 USA
**Redding, Timothy J (Tim)** — Baseball Player
1801 E Palm Valley Blvd, Round Rock TX 78664, USA
**Reddout, Franklin P (Frank)** — Basketball Player
379 Niblick Circle, Winter Haven FL 33881, USA
**Reddy, D Raj** — Computer Scientist
Robotics Institute, Carnegie-Mellon University, Pittsburgh PA 15213, USA
**Reddy, Helen** — Singer, Actress
Stacey Testro International, 8265 W Sunset Blvd, #102, West Hollywood CA 90046, USA
**Redeker, Quinn** — Actor
8075 3rd Ave, #303, Los Angeles CA 90048, USA

**Redfern, Peter I (Pete)** — Baseball Player
12516 Haddon Ave, Sylmar CA 91342, USA
**Redford, Amy Hart** — Actress
Paradigm Agency, 360 N Crescent Dr, North Building, Beverly Hills CA 90210 USA
**Redford, J A C** — Composer
Gorfaine/Schwartz, 4111 W Alameda Ave, #509, Burbank CA 91505 USA
**Redford, Paul** — Writer, Producer
W M E Entertainment, 9601 Wilshire Blvd, #300, Beverly Hills CA 90210 USA
**Redford, Robert** — Actor, Director
Sundance Institute, 5900 Wilshire Blvd, #800, Los Angeles CA 90036, USA
**Redgrave, Jemma** — Actress
Conway Van Gelder Grant, 8-12 Broadwick St, #300, London W1F 8HW, England
**Redgrave, Steven G** — Rowing Athlete
Athole Still Mgmt, 25-27 Westow St, London SE19 3RY, England
**Redgrave, Vanessa** — Actress, Singer
Gavin Barker Assoc, 2D Wimpole St, London W1G 0EB, England
**Redick, Jonathan Clay (J J)** — Basketball Player
2919 Toro Canyon Road, Austin TX 78746, USA
**Reding, Juli** — Actress, Model
PO Box 1806, Beverly Hills CA 90213, USA
**Redman** — Rap Artist
One Entertainment, 347 5th Ave, #1404, New York NY 10016 USA
**Redman, Amanda** — Actress
Lip Service Casting, 60-66 Wardour St, London W1F 0TA, England
**Redman, Chris J** — Football Player
15410 Beckley Crossing Dr, Louisville KY 40245, USA
**Redman, Joshua** — Jazz Saxophonist, Composer
Wilkins Mgmt, 323 Broadway, Cambridge MA 02139, USA
**Redman, Julian (Tike)** — Baseball Player
1109 Lauren Way NW, Acworth GA 30101, USA
**Redman, Magdalen (Mamie)** — Baseball Player
N7780 Vicksburg Way, #D, Oconomowoc WI 53066, USA
**Redman, Michele** — Golfer
3410 Queensland Lane N, Minneapolis MN 55447, USA
**Redman, Richard C (Rick)** — Football Player
8953 Windham Court NE, Lacey WA 98516, USA
**Redman, Susie** — Golfer
30442 Wayside Dr, Spanish Fort AL 36527, USA
**Redmann, Teal** — Actress
Innovative Artists, 1505 10th St, Santa Monica CA 90401 USA
**Redmayne, Eddie** — Actor
United Agents, 12-26 Lexington St, London W1F 0LE, England
**Redmond, H Wayne** — Baseball Player
18061 Sussex St, Detroit MI 48235, USA
**Redmond, Markus** — Actor
Stagecoach Entertainment, 1223 Wilshire Blvd, #1560, Santa Monica CA 90403, USA
**Redmond, Marlon B** — Basketball Player
441 Oak St, San Francisco CA 94102, USA
**Redmond, Michael E (Mickey)** — Ice Hockey Player
30699 Harlincin Court, Franklin MI 48025, USA
**Redmond, Michael P (Mike)** — Baseball Player
13506 S Bluegrouse Lane, Spokane WA 99224, USA
**Redquest, Greg** — Ice Hockey Player
139 Springdale Dr, Barrie ON L4M 4Y1, Canada
**Redstone, Sumner M** — Businessman
98 Baldpate Hill Road, Newton MA 02459, USA
**Redus, Gary E** — Baseball Player
2202 Mallard Lane SE, Decatur AL 35601, USA
**Redzepi, Rene** — Chef, Restauranteur
Noma Restaurant, Strandgade 93, 1401 Copenhagen K, Denmark
**Reece, Beasley** — Football Player, Sportscaster
17 Stirling Way, Lumberton NJ 08048, USA
**Reece, Daniel L (Danny)** — Football Player
5519 S Corning Ave, Los Angeles CA 90056, USA
**Reece, Gabrielle (Gabby)** — Volleyball Player, Model
PO Box 2227, Malibu CA 90265, USA
**Reece, Maynard** — Artist
5315 Robertson Dr, Des Moines IA 50312, USA
**Reed Lorsch, Kira** — Actress, Producer, Writer
Michael Zanuck Agency, 4929 Wilshire Blvd, #808, Los Angeles CA 90010, USA
**Reed, Alvin D** — Football Player
3910 Abbeywood Dr, Pearland TX 77584, USA
**Reed, Alyson** — Actress, Singer, Dancer
Opus Entertainment, 5225 Wilshire Blvd, #905, Los Angeles CA 90036, USA
**Reed, Andre D** — Football Player
1058 America Way, Del Mar CA 92014, USA
**Reed, Anthony W (Tony)** — Football Player
14068 Mount Tabor Road, Odessa MO 64076, USA
**Reed, Brandy** — Basketball Player
Los Angeles Sparks, 888 S Figueroa St, #2010, Los Angeles CA 90017 USA
**Reed, Brian** — Guitarist (EvinRudes), Songwriter
Turner Management Group, 9200 W Sunset Blvd, #600, West Hollywood CA 90069, USA
**Reed, Darren D** — Baseball Player
8101 Santa Ana Road, Ventura CA 93001, USA
**Reed, Edward E (Ed), Jr** — Football Player
4703 Avatar Lane, Owings Mills MD 21117, USA
**Reed, Eric** — Jazz Pianist
Ellora Mgmt, PO Box 755, Lakeville CT 06039, USA
**Reed, Frank R** — Football Player
6989 Windstone Lane, Stone Mountain GA 30087, USA
**Reed, Hubert F (Hub)** — Basketball Player
46601 Garretts Lake Road, Shawnee OK 74804, USA
**Reed, Ishmael S** — Writer
1446 6th St, #C, Berkeley CA 94710, USA
**Reed, Jeff S** — Baseball Player
259 Sunrise Dr, Elizabethton TN 37643, USA

| | |
|---|---|
| **Reed, Jeffrey M (Jeff)**<br>1702 S Shore Court, Pittsburgh PA 15203, USA | Football Player |
| **Reed, Jerry M**<br>13964 106th Ave, Largo FL 33774, USA | Baseball Player |
| **Reed, Jody E**<br>3539 Lake Padgett Dr, Land O'Lakes FL 34639, USA | Baseball Player |
| **Reed, John Shedd**<br>Citigroup Inc, 55 E 52nd St, New York NY 10055, USA | Financier |
| **Reed, Johnny**<br>Jackson Artists, 7251 Lowell Dr, #200, Overland Park KS 66204, USA | Singer (Orioles) |
| **Reed, Joseph B (Joe)**<br>106 Whitechapel Court, Cedar Park TX 78613, USA | Football Player |
| **Reed, Joshua B (Josh)**<br>7333 Camelia Way Court, Baton Rouge LA 70808, USA | Football Player |
| **Reed, Mark A**<br>Syracuse University, Engineering/Applied Science Dept, Syracuse NY 13244, USA | Physicist |
| **Reed, Mitchell**<br>Rosebud Agency, PO Box 170429, San Francisco CA 94117 USA | Bassist, Fiddle Player (BeauSoleil) |
| **Reed, Nikki**<br>Thruline Entertainment, 9250 Wilshire Blvd, #100, Beverly Hills CA 90212 USA | Actress, Writer |
| **Reed, Oscar L**<br>700 Elizabeth Lane, Minneapolis MN 55411, USA | Football Player |
| **Reed, Pamela**<br>Innovative Artists, 1505 10th St, Santa Monica CA 90401 USA | Actress |
| **Reed, Patrick**<br>White Pine Pictures, 822 Richmond St W, #301, Toronto ON M6J 1C9, Canada | Director |
| **Reed, Patrick N**<br>Professional Golfers Association, 100 Ave of Champions, Palm Beach Gardens FL 33418 USA | Golfer |
| **Reed, Peter (Pete)**<br>Leander Club, Henley on Thames, Leander RG9 2LP, England | Rowing Athlete |
| **Reed, Peyton**<br>W M E Entertainment, 9601 Wilshire Blvd, #300, Beverly Hills CA 90210 USA | Director, Producer, Writer, Actor |
| **Reed, Ralph**<br>1801 Sarah Dr, #L, Chesapeake VA 23320, USA | Religious Leader |
| **Reed, Rex T**<br>Dakota Hotel, 1 W 72nd St, #86, New York NY 10023, USA | Film Critic |
| **Reed, Richard A (Rick)**<br>9604 County Road 107, #7, Proctorville OH 45669, USA | Baseball Player |
| **Reed, Ronald L (Ron)**<br>2613 Cliffview Dr, Lilburn GA 30047, USA | Baseball, Basketball Player |
| **Reed, Shanna**<br>1327 Brinkley Ave, Los Angeles CA 90049, USA | Actress |
| **Reed, Stephen V (Steve)**<br>5335 Pine Ridge Road, Golden CO 80403, USA | Baseball Player |
| **Reed, Thomas C**<br>Quaker Hill Development Corp, PO Box 2240, Healdsburg CA 95448, USA | Government Official |
| **Reed, W Jake**<br>PO Box 1848, Frisco TX 75034, USA | Football Player |
| **Reed, Willis, Jr**<br>PO Box 1779, Ruston LA 71273, USA | Basketball Player, Coach, Executive |
| **Reeder, Serena**<br>Hess Entertainment, 250 S Beverly Dr, #201, Beverly Hills CA 90212, USA | Actress |
| **Reeds, Mark**<br>7823 Cardinal Ridge Court, Saint Louis MO 63119, USA | Ice Hockey Player |
| **Reedus, Norman**<br>Brillstein Entertainment Partners, 9150 Wilshire Blvd, #350, Beverly Hills CA 90212 USA | Actor, Model |
| **Reekie, Joe**<br>622 Sean Dr, Annapolis MD 21401, USA | Ice Hockey Player |
| **Reep, Jon**<br>Gersh Agency, 9465 Wilshire Blvd, #600, Beverly Hills CA 90212 USA | Actor, Comedian |
| **Rees, Andrew**<br>Musichall Ltd, Vicarage Way, Ringmer BN8 5LA, England | Opera Singer |
| **Rees, Clifford H (Ted), Jr**<br>1620 Mayflower Court, #B414, Winter Park FL 32792, USA | Air Force General |
| **Rees, Dai**<br>6 Blackstock Mews, Blackstock Road, London N4 2BT, England | Fashion Designer |
| **Rees, Eberhard**<br>69 Revere Way, Huntsville AL 35801, USA | Physicist |
| **Rees, Jed**<br>Paradigm Agency, 360 N Crescent Dr, North Building, Beverly Hills CA 90210 USA | Musician, Actor |
| **Rees, John W**<br>Fish Creek, Gippsland VIC 3959, Australia | Bassist (Men at Work) |
| **Rees, Martin J**<br>King's College, Astronomy Institute, Cambridge CB2 1ST, England | Astronomer |
| **Rees, Mina**<br>301 E 66th St, New York NY 10065, USA | Mathematician |
| **Rees, Roger**<br>Innovative Artists, 1505 10th St, Santa Monica CA 90401 USA | Actor |
| **Reese, Calvin (Pokey)**<br>12416 Sylvan Oak Way, Charlotte NC 28273, USA | Baseball Player |
| **Reese, Della**<br>Lett-Reese International Promotions, 1910 Bel Air Road, Los Angeles CA 90077, USA | Singer, Actress |
| **Reese, Eddie**<br>908 E 3rd St, Fort Worth TX 76102, USA | Swimming Coach |
| **Reese, Izell**<br>10270 Willeo Creek Trace, Roswell GA 30075, USA | Football Player |
| **Reese, Jeffrey K (Jeff)**<br>856 Longwood Circle, Haddonfield NJ 08033, USA | Ice Hockey Player |
| **Reese, Kevin P**<br>1221 Willow St, San Diego CA 92106, USA | Baseball Player |
| **Reese, Mason**<br>Nowbar, 22 7th Ave S, New York NY 10014, USA | Actor |
| **Reese, Richard B (Rich)**<br>PO Box 2339, Carefree AZ 85377, USA | Baseball Player |
| **Reese, Tracy**<br>T R Designs, 260 W 39th St, #1900, New York NY 10018, USA | Fashion Designer |

**Reeser, Autumn** — Actress
L I N K Entertainment, 11872 La Grange Ave, Los Angeles CA 90025 USA
**Reeser, Morgan** — Yachtsman
1948 Coral Gardens Dr, Wilton Manors FL 33306, USA
**Reeves, Bryant** — Basketball Player
11648 S 4710 Road, Muldrow OK 74948, USA
**Reeves, Daniel E (Dan)** — Football Player, Coach; Sportscaster
785 W Conway Dr SW, Atlanta GA 30327, USA
**Reeves, Dianne** — Singer
Depth of Field Mgmt, 1501 Broadway, #1304, New York NY 10036, USA
**Reeves, Jacques D** — Football Player
619 Scenic Dr, Irving TX 75039, USA
**Reeves, Julie** — Singer
PO Box 300, Russell KY 41169, USA
**Reeves, Keanu** — Actor
P M K-B N C, 8687 Melrose Ave, #800, Los Angeles CA 90069 USA
**Reeves, Khalid** — Basketball Player
11519 140th St, Jamaica NY 11436, USA
**Reeves, Martha** — Singer (Martha & the Vandellas)
Ideal Entertainment, 1674 Broadway, #300, New York NY 10019, USA
**Reeves, Matt** — Director, Producer, Writer
Creative Artists Agency, 2000 Ave of Stars, #100, Los Angeles CA 90067 USA
**Reeves, Perrey** — Actress
Paradigm Agency, 360 N Crescent Dr, North Building, Beverly Hills CA 90210 USA
**Reeves, Richard** — Columnist
Universal Press Syndicate, 4520 Main St, #700, Kansas City MO 64111 USA
**Reeves, Robert (Bobby)** — Singer (Adema)
Novi Entertainment, PO Box 17077, Beverly Hills CA 90209, USA
**Reeves, Saskia** — Actress
Markham Froggatt Irwin, Julian House, 4 Windmill St, London W1P 1HF, England
**Reeves, Scott** — Actor, Singer (Blue County)
House of Representatives, 1434 6th St, #1, Santa Monica CA 90401 USA
**Reeves, Shirley Alston** — Singer
Universal Attractions, 135 W 26th St, #1200, New York NY 10001 USA
**Reeves, Walter J** — Football Player
PO Box 16171, Fort Worth TX 76162, USA
**Refaeli, Bar** — Model
One Mgmt, 42 Bond St, #200, New York NY 10012 USA
**Refn, Nicolas Winding** — Director
W M E Entertainment, 9601 Wilshire Blvd, #300, Beverly Hills CA 90210 USA
**Regalado, Rudolph V (Rudy)** — Baseball Player
PO Box 475, Borrego Springs CA 92004, USA
**Regalado, Victor** — Golfer
Tijuana Country Club, 2630 E Point Beyer Blvd, #106, San Ysidro CA 92703, USA
**Regalbuto, Joe** — Actor
Intellectual Artists Mgmt, 10585 Santa Monica Blvd, #135, Los Angeles CA 90025, USA
**Regan, Brian** — Actor, Comedian, Writer, Producer
Gersh Agency, 9465 Wilshire Blvd, #600, Beverly Hills CA 90212 USA
**Regan, Bridget** — Actress
United Talent Agency, U T A Plaza, 9336 Civic Center Dr, Beverly Hills CA 90210 USA
**Regan, Fionn** — Singer, Songwriter
Coalition Mgmt, 3A Brackenbury Road, London W6 0BE, England
**Regan, Judith** — Writer, Entertainer
New Enterprises, 1211 Ave of Americas, Lower C31, New York NY 10036, USA
**Regan, Philip R (Phil)** — Baseball Player, Manager
1375 108th St, Byron Center MI 49315, USA
**Regbo, Toby** — Actor
B W H Agency, 35 Soho Square, #500, London W1D 3QX, England
**Regehr, Duncan P** — Actor
Oscars Abrams Zimel, 438 Queen St E, Toronto ON M5A 1T4, Canada
**Regen, Elizabeth** — Actress
Don Buchwald Talent Agency, 6500 Wilshire Blvd, #2200, Los Angeles CA 90048 USA
**Reger, Nate** — Writer
I C M Partners, 10250 Constellation Blvd, #900, Los Angeles CA 90067 USA
**Regilio, Nicholas D (Nick)** — Baseball Player
6505 Raham Court, Port Orange FL 32128, USA
**Regina Lee** — Singer
Brothers Management Assoc, 141 Dunbar Ave, Fords NJ 08863 USA
**Regis, John** — Track Athlete
67 Fairby Road, London SE12 8JP, England
**Regner, Thomas E (Tom)** — Football Player
2231 Big Trail Circle, Reno NV 89521, USA
**Regni, John F** — Air Force General, Educator
Vantage Mobility International, 5202 S 28th Place, Phoenix AZ 85040, USA
**Regnier, Charles** — Actor, Director
Neherstr 7, 81675 Munich, Germany
**Rehberg, Scott J** — Football Player
1153 Thistle Lane, Lebanon OH 45036, USA
**Reherman, Lee** — Actor
Ellis Talent Group, 4705 Laurel Canyon Blvd, #300, Valley Village CA 91607, USA
**Rehm, Fred** — Basketball Player
19340 W Stonehedge Dr, #A, Brookfield WI 53045, USA
**Rehm, Jack D** — Publisher
19 Neponset Ave, #9A, Old Saybrook CT 06475, USA
**Rehr, Frank** — Cartoonist (Ferd'nand)
United Feature Syndicate, PO Box 5610, Cincinnati OH 45201 USA
**Reibsten, Janet** — Psychologist
Bloomsbury Publishing, 50 Bedford Square, London WC1B 3DP, England
**Reich, Charles A** — Attorney, Educator, Writer
Crown Publishing Group, 1745 Broadway, #1300, New York NY 10019 USA
**Reich, Frank M** — Football Player
7591 Pennycroft Dr, Indianapolis IN 46236, USA
**Reich, Robert B** — Secretary, Labor
1230 Bonita Ave, Berkeley CA 94709, USA
**Reich, Stephen M (Steve)** — Composer
Howard Stokar Mgmt, 870 W End Ave, New York NY 10025, USA

**Reichardt, Frederic C (Rick)** — Baseball Player
2404 NW 63rd Terrace, Gainesville FL 32606, USA
**Reichardt, Louis F (Lou)** — Mountaineer, Physiologist
Simons Foundation Autism Research Initiative, 160 5th Ave, #700, New York NY 10010, USA
**Reichel, Robert** — Ice Hockey Player
Toronto Maple Leafs, AirCanada Center, 40 Bay St, Toronto ON M5J 2K2, Canada
**Reichenbach, J Michael (Mike)** — Football Player
2230 Cloverly Circle, Jamison PA 18929, USA
**Reichert, Daniel R (Dan)** — Baseball Player
445 Cornell Dr, Turlock CA 95382, USA
**Reichert, David G (Dave)** — Law Enforcement Official, Representative
PO Box 53322, Bellevue WA 98015, USA
**Reichert, Jack F** — Businessman, Bowling Executive
580 Douglas Dr, Lake Forest IL 60045, USA
**Reichert, Tanja** — Actress
Pacific Artists, 1404-510 W Hastings St, Vancouver BC V6B 1L8, Canada
**Reichl, Ruth M** — Editor, Columnist
Gourmet, Editorial Dept, 4 Times Square, New York NY 10036, USA
**Reichle, Luke** — Costume Designer
Innovative Artists, 1505 10th St, Santa Monica CA 90401 USA
**Reichow, Garet N (Jerry)** — Football Player
9 Meredith Dr, Santa Fe NM 87506, USA
**Reichs, Kathleen (Kathy)** — Writer, Anthropologist
University of North Carolina, English Dept, Charlotte NC 28223, USA
**Reid, Andrew W (Andy)** — Football Player, Coach
Kansas City Chiefs, 1 Arrowhead Dr, Kansas City KS 64129 USA
**Reid, Clifford A** — Research Scientist, Businessman
Complete Genomics, 2071 Stierlin Court, Mountain View CA 94043, USA
**Reid, Dale** — Golfer
Ladies European Tour, Denham Court Drive, Denham, Buckinghamshire UB9 5PG, England
**Reid, Daphne Maxwell** — Actress, Producer
Tim Reid Productions, 1 New Millennium Dr, Petersburg VA 23805, USA
**Reid, Dave** — Ice Hockey Player
1522 Hawkswood Dr, RR 1, Ennismore ON K0L 1T0, Canada
**Reid, Delroy (Junior)** — Singer (Black Uhuru)
Caribbean Entertainment, PO Box 1115, Miami FL 33160, USA
**Reid, Don S** — Singer (Statler Brothers), Songwriter
American Major Talent, 8747 Highway 304, Hernando MS 38632, USA
**Reid, Harold W** — Singer (Statler Brothers), Songwriter
American Major Talent, 8747 Highway 304, Hernando MS 38632, USA
**Reid, Herman (J R)** — Basketball Player
121 Cemetary St, Chester SC 29706, USA
**Reid, Jim** — Singer, Guitarist (Jesus & Mary Chain)
Paradise Artists, PO Box 1821, Ojai CA 93024 USA
**Reid, Michael B (Mike)** — Football Player, Composer
825 Overton Lane, Nashville TN 37220, USA
**Reid, Mike** — Golfer
1220 Chadwick Dr, Westminster MD 21158, USA
**Reid, Ogden R** — Journalist, Diplomat
Ophir Hill, Purchase NY 10577, USA
**Reid, Richard** — Actor
TalentWorks, 3500 W Olive Ave, #1400, Burbank CA 91505 USA
**Reid, Robert K** — Basketball Player, Coach
Washington Wizards, M C I Centre, 601 F St NW, Washington DC 20004 USA
**Reid, Sebastian (Sam)** — Actor
Rights House, Drury House, 34-43 Russell St, London WC2B 5HA, England
**Reid, Shauna** — Writer
Harper Collins Publishers, 10 E 53rd St, Cellar 1, New York NY 10022 USA
**Reid, Tanya** — Actress
Edna Talent Mgmt, 318 Dundas St W, Toronto ON M5T 1G5, Canada
**Reid, Tara** — Actress, Model
Prestige Talent Agency, 9250 Wilshire Blvd, #208, Beverly Hills CA 90212, USA
**Reid, Terry** — Singer
Geoffrey Blumenauer Artists, PO Box 343, Burbank CA 91503 USA
**Reid, Tim** — Actor, Director, Producer
Tim Reid Productions, 1 New Millennium Dr, Petersburg VA 23805, USA
**Reid, Tom** — Ice Hockey Player
603 Hawthorne Woods Dr, Saint Paul MN 55123, USA
**Reid, William** — Singer, Guitarist (Jesus & Mary Chain)
Paradise Artists, PO Box 1821, Ojai CA 93024 USA
**Reiff, Ethan** — Writer, Director
United Talent Agency, U T A Plaza, 9336 Civic Center Dr, Beverly Hills CA 90210 USA
**Reifsnyder, Robert H (Bob)** — Football Player
681 Ocean Parkway, Berlin MD 21811, USA
**Reightler, Kenneth S, Jr** — Astronaut
1602 Honeysuckle Ridge Court, Annapolis MD 21401, USA
**Reihner, George A** — Football Player
1010 Electric St, Scranton PA 18509, USA
**Reilly, Gabrielle** — Model, Commentator
14117 W 53rd Terrace, Shawnee KS 66216, USA
**Reilly, James F, II** — Astronaut
15903 Lake Lodge Dr, Houston TX 77062, USA
**Reilly, John** — Actor
1944 N Normandie Ave, Los Angeles CA 90027, USA
**Reilly, John C** — Actor
Framework Entertainment, 9057 Nemo St, #C, West Hollywood CA 90069 USA
**Reilly, Kelly** — Actress
I C M Partners, 10250 Constellation Blvd, #900, Los Angeles CA 90067 USA
**Reilly, Michael E (Mike)** — Baseball Umpire
131 Smithfield Road, Battle Creek MI 49015, USA
**Reilly, William K** — Government Official
Stanford University, International Studies Institute, Stanford CA 94305, USA
**Reimann, Aribert** — Composer, Concert Pianist
Hohenzollerndamm 97, 10717 Berlin, Germany
**Reimer, Dennis J (Denny)** — Army General
2602 N Brandywine St, Arlington VA 22207, USA

**Reimers, Bruce M** — Football Player
2206 W River Dr, Humboldt IA 50548, USA
**Rein, Andrew** — Freestyle Wrestler
31 Acorn Dr, Hawthorn Woods IL 60047, USA
**Reina** — Singer, Songwriter
T-Best Talent Agency, 508 Honey Lake Court, Danville CA 94506 USA
**Reinders, Kate** — Singer, Actress
Paradigm Agency, 360 N Crescent Dr, North Building, Beverly Hills CA 90210 USA
**Reineck, Thomas** — Canoeing Athlete
Graf-Bernadotte-Str 4, 45133 Essen, Germany
**Reineke, Chad** — Baseball Player
1904 Tanglewood Dr, Defiance OH 43512, USA
**Reinemund, Steven S** — Businessman
PepsiCo Inc, 700 Anderson Hill Road, Purchase NY 10577, USA
**Reiner, Alysia** — Actress, Producer, Writer
Luber Rocklin Entertainment, 5815 Sunset Blvd, #206, Los Angeles CA 90028 USA
**Reiner, Carl** — Actor, Writer, Director
714 N Rodeo Dr, Beverly Hills CA 90210, USA
**Reiner, Rob** — Director, Producer, Actor
Castle Rock Entertainment, 9169 W Sunset Blvd, West Hollywood CA 90069, USA
**Reinfeldt, Michael R (Mike)** — Football Player
1204 Waterstone Blvd, Franklin TN 37069, USA
**Reinhardt, John E** — Diplomat
3154 Gracefield Road, #417, Silver Spring MD 20904, USA
**Reinhardt, Nicole** — Canoeing Athlete
Agentur Koster, Alsterdorfer Str 208, 22297 Hamburg, Germany
**Reinhardt, Stephen R** — Judge
US Court of Appeals, 312 N Spring St, #G33, Los Angeles CA 90012, USA
**Reinhart, Gregory** — Opera Singer
I M G Artists, Hogarth Business Park, Chiswick, London W4 2TH, England
**Reinhart, Haley** — Singer
19 Entertainment, 8560 W Sunset Blvd, #900, Los Angeles CA 90069 USA
**Reinhart, Paul** — Ice Hockey Player
2911 Altamont Crescent, West Vancouver BC V7V 3B9, Canada
**Reinharz, Jehuda** — Educator
131 Sewall Ave, #71, Brookline MA 2446, USA
**Reinhold, Judge** — Actor, Director
Hirsch Wallerstein Hayum, 10100 Santa Monica Blvd, #1700, Los Angeles CA 90067 USA
**Reinking, Ann** — Actress, Dancer, Choreographer, Director
5912 E Sapphire Lane, Phoenix AZ 85253, USA
**Reinprecht, Steven E** — Ice Hockey Player
45 S Garfield St, Denver CO 80209, USA
**Reirden, Todd** — Ice Hockey Player
17 Herons Bill Dr, Bluffton SC 29909, USA
**Reiser, Jerry** — Architect
28 S Washington Ave, Dobbs Ferry NY 10522, USA
**Reiser, Paul** — Actor, Writer
Nuance Productions, 4049 Radford Ave, Studio City CA 91604, USA
**Reisman, Garrett E** — Astronaut
1715 Hedgecroft Dr, Seabrook TX 77586, USA
**Reiss, Albert J, Jr** — Sociologist
600 Prospect St, #7A, New Haven CT 06511, USA
**Reiss, Howard** — Chemist
16656 Oldham St, Encino CA 91436, USA
**Reiss, Tom** — Writer
Crown Publishing Group, 1745 Broadway, #1300, New York NY 10019 USA
**Reisz, Michael** — Actor
Mosiac Media Group, 9200 W Sunset Blvd, #1000, Los Angeles CA 90069 USA
**Reiter, Mario** — Alpine Skier
Hauselweg 5, 6830 Rankweil, Austria
**Reiter, Sabrina** — Actress
Daniela Stibitz Mgmt, Himmelstr 11/6, 1190 Vienna, Austria
**Reiter, Stanley** — Economist
425 Davis St, #425, Evanston IL 60201, USA
**Reiter, Thomas** — Astronaut, Germany
European Space Center, Linder Hohe, Box 906096, 51127 Cologne, Germany
**Reithmayer, Nina** — Luge Athlete
An der Lan Str 22, 6020 Innsbruck, Austria
**Reitman, Ivan** — Director, Producer
Montecito Picture Co, 1482 E Valley Road, #477, Montecito CA 93108, USA
**Reitman, Jason** — Director, Writer
W M E Entertainment, 9601 Wilshire Blvd, #300, Beverly Hills CA 90210 USA
**Reitman, Joseph D (Joe)** — Actor
TalentWorks, 3500 W Olive Ave, #1400, Burbank CA 91505 USA
**Reitsma, Chris** — Baseball Player
6050 Jim Davis Road, Parrish FL 34219, USA
**Reitz, Bruce A** — Cardiac Surgeon
Falk CV Research Center, 300 Pasteur Dr, Stanford CA 94305, USA
**Reitz, Kenneth J (Ken)** — Baseball Player
2833 Fairways Circle, Lutz FL 33558, USA
**Reklow, Jesse** — Cartoonist (Slow Wave)
2415 College Ave, #20, Berkeley CA 94704, USA
**Relaford, Desmond L (Desi)** — Baseball Player
12483 Highview Dr, Jacksonville FL 32225, USA
**Rellford, Richard A** — Basketball Player
28 Balfour Road W, Palm Beach Gardens FL 33418, USA
**Relyea, John** — Singer
Opus 3 Artists, 470 Park Ave S, #900N, New York NY 10016 USA
**Remar, James** — Actor
Gersh Agency, 9465 Wilshire Blvd, #600, Beverly Hills CA 90212 USA
**Rembert, John L (Johnny)** — Football Player
2564 Willow Creek Dr, Orange Park FL 32003, USA
**Remedios, Alberto T** — Opera Singer
Stuart Trotter, 21 Lanhill Road, London W9 2BS, England
**Remek, Vladimir** — Cosmonaut, Czech Republic
European Parliament, Batiment Altiero Spinelli, Rue Wiertz 60, 1047 Brussels, Belgium

**Remigino, Lindy** — Track Athlete
22 Paris Lane, Newington CT 06111, USA
**Remini, Leah M** — Actress
A P A Talent & Literary Agency, 405 S Beverly Dr, #300, Beverly Hills CA 90212 USA
**Remlinger, Michael J (Mike)** — Baseball Player
18331 N 93rd Way, Scottsdale AZ 85255, USA
**Remnick, David J** — Writer, Editor
257 W 86th St, #11A, New York NY 10024, USA
**Rempe, Jim** — Billiards Player
60 George Dr, Jefferson Township PA 18436, USA
**Remy, Gerald P (Jerry)** — Baseball Player
1403 Wisteria Way, Wayland MA 01778, USA
**Renaud, Line** — Singer, Actress
5 Rue de Bois de Boulogne, 75016 Paris, France
**Renaud, Mark** — Ice Hockey Player
11788 Tecumseh Road E, Windsor ON N8N 1L7, Canada
**Renault, Dennis** — Editorial Cartoonist
Sacramento Bee, Editorial Dept, 21st & Q Sts, Sacramento CA 95852, USA
**Renbourn, John** — Guitarist (Pentangle), Songwriter
Folklore Inc, 1671 Appian Way, Santa Monica CA 90401, USA
**Rendall, Mark** — Actor
TalentWorks, 3500 W Olive Ave, #1400, Burbank CA 91505 USA
**Rendell of Barbergh, Ruth B** — Writer
26 Cornwall Terrace Mews, London NW1 5LL, England
**Rendell, Edward G (Ed)** — Governor, PA
Ballard Spahr, 1755 Market St, #5100, Philadelphia PA 19103, USA
**Rendell, Marjorie O** — Judge
US Court of Appeals, US Courthouse, 601 Market St, Philadelphia PA 19106, USA
**Renee, Leah** — Actress
InVision Artists Talent Management, 344 Bloor St W, #304, Toronto ON M5S 3A7, Canada
**Renee, Lyne** — Actress
Don Buchwald Talent Agency, 6500 Wilshire Blvd, #2200, Los Angeles CA 90048 USA
**Renes, Lawrence** — Conductor
Harrison/Parrott, 5-6 Albion Court, London W6 0QT, England
**Renfrew of Kaimsthorn, Andrew C** — Archaeologist
McDonald Archaeological Institute, Downing St, Cambridge CB2 3ER, England
**Renfro, Melvin L (Mel)** — Football Player
Renfro Bridge Foundation, 8211 Hunnicut Road, Dallas TX 75228, USA
**Renfro, Mike R** — Football Player
PO Box 93073, Southlake TX 76092, USA
**Renfroe, Cohen W (Laddie)** — Baseball Player
236 Hickory Lane, Batesville MS 38606, USA
**Renfroe, Jeff** — Director
Characters Talent Agency, 1505 W 2nd Ave, #200, Vancouver BC V6H 3Y4, Canada
**Renick, W Richard (Rick)** — Baseball Player
7320 Hawkins Road, Sarasota FL 34241, USA
**Renier, Jeremie** — Actor
A C T 1, 83 Rue Saint Honore, 75001 Paris, France
**Renko, Steven (Steve)** — Baseball Player
15812 W 136th St, Olathe KS 66062, USA
**Renne, Paul** — Geologist
Berkeley Geochronology Center, 2445 Ridge Road, Berkeley CA 94709, USA
**Renner, Jeremy** — Actor
Creative Artists Agency, 2000 Ave of Stars, #100, Los Angeles CA 90067 USA
**Rennert, Laurence H (Dutch)** — Baseball Umpire
2560 46th Road, Vero Beach FL 32966, USA
**Rennert, Wolfgang** — Conductor
Holbeinstr 58, 12203 Berlin, Germany
**Renney, Tom** — Ice Hockey Coach
Detroit Red Wings, Joe Louis Arena, 600 Civic Center Dr, Detroit MI 48226 USA
**Rennie, Callum Keith** — Actor
A P A Talent & Literary Agency, 405 S Beverly Dr, #300, Beverly Hills CA 90212 USA
**Reno, Janet** — Attorney General
11200 N Kendall Dr, Miami FL 33176, USA
**Reno, Jean** — Actor
I C M Partners, 10250 Constellation Blvd, #900, Los Angeles CA 90067 USA
**Reno, Loren M** — Air Force General
Deputy CofS, Logistics & Installations, HqUSAF, Pentagon, Washington DC 20330 USA
**Reno, William H** — Army General
2706 S Ives St, Arlington VA 22202, USA
**Renoth, Heidi** — Snowboard Skier
Lercheckerweg 23, 83471 Berchtesgaden, Germany
**Rensberger, Scott** — Journalist
914 7th St NE, Washington DC 20002, USA
**Rense Noland, Paige** — Editor
Architectural Digest, Editorial Dept, 5900 Wilshire Blvd, Los Angeles CA 90036, USA
**Renshaw, Jeannine** — Actress, Producer
United Talent Agency, U T A Plaza, 9336 Civic Center Dr, Beverly Hills CA 90210 USA
**Renteria, Richard A (Rich)** — Baseball Player, Manager
43310 Calle Nacido, Temecula CA 92592, USA
**Rentmeester, Co** — Photographer
PO Box 1562, Westhampton Beach NY 11978, USA
**Renton of Mount Harry, R Timothy** — Government Official, England
Mount Harry House, Offham, Lewes, East Sussex BN7 3QW, England
**Rentzel, T Lance** — Football Player
12014 Monument Dr, #354, Fairfax VA 22033, USA
**Rentzepis, Peter M** — Chemist
University of California, Chemistry Dept, Irvine CA 92717, USA
**Renuart, V Eugene (Gene), Jr** — Air Force General
Commander, US Northern Command, Peterson Air Force Base CO 80914 USA
**Renzetti, Donato** — Conductor
Columbia Artists Mgmt Inc, 5 Columbus Circle, 1790 Broadway, #1600, New York NY 10019 USA
**Renzi, Andrea** — Actor
Carol Levi Mgmt, Via Giuseppe Pisanelli 2, 00196 Rome, Italy
**Repin, Vadim V** — Concert Violinist
Eckholdtweg 2A, 23566 Lubeck, Germany

**Repko, Jason E** — Baseball Player
93005 E Chelsea Road, Kennewick WA 99338, USA
**Requa, John** — Writer, Director
W M E Entertainment, 9601 Wilshire Blvd, #300, Beverly Hills CA 90210 USA
**Rerych, Stephen (Steve)** — Swimmer
1142 Ridgewood Dr, Point Pleasant WV 25550, USA
**Res** — Singer
Padell Nadell Fine Wineberger, 59 Maiden Lane, #2700, New York NY 10038 USA
**Resch, Alexander** — Luge Athlete
Gesprachsstoff Marketing, Scholssstr 9B, 82140 Olching, Germany
**Resch, Glenn A (Chico)** — Ice Hockey Player
607 8th St, Lyndhurst NJ 07071, USA
**Rescher, Nicholas** — Philosopher
1033 Milton St, Pittsburgh PA 15218, USA
**Reske, Hans-Joachim** — Track Athlete
Sinshimer Str 18, 69226 Nussloch, Germany
**Reskin, Barbara** — Sociologist
University of Washington, Sociology Dept, Seattle WA 98195, USA
**Resnick, Marcia** — Photographer
2 Grove St, #1F, New York NY 10014, USA
**Resop, Christopher P (Chris)** — Baseball Player
2152 Harlans Run, Naples FL 34105, USA
**Resor, Helen** — Ice Hockey Player
22 N Stanwich Road, Greenwich CT 06831, USA
**Ressler, Glenn E** — Football Player
1524 Woodcreek Dr, Mechanicsburg PA 17055, USA
**Restani, Jane A** — Judge
US Court of International Trade, 1 Federal Plaza, New York NY 10278, USA
**Restovich, Michael** — Baseball Player
710 11th St SW, Rochester MN 55902, USA
**Resweber, Carroll C** — Motorcycle Racing Rider
2440 Imhoff Ave, Port Arthur TX 77642, USA
**Reswick, James B** — Engineer
PO Box 549, Crozet VA 22932, USA
**Retondo, Mike** — Guitarist (Plain White T's)
One Moment Mgmt, PO Box 55156, Sherman Oaks CA 91413 USA
**Retore, Guy** — Theater Executive
Theatre de l'Est Parisien, 159 Ave Gambetta, 75020 Paris, France
**Retta** — Actress
United Talent Agency, U T A Plaza, 9336 Civic Center Dr, Beverly Hills CA 90210 USA
**Rettenmund, Mervin W (Merv)** — Baseball Player
1860 San Carlos Ave, San Carlos CA 94070, USA
**Retton, Mary Lou** — Gymnast
254 Maple Ridge Dr, Canonsburg PA 15317, USA
**Retzer, Kenneth L (Ken)** — Baseball Player
746 Harvard Dr, Edwardsville IL 62025, USA
**Retzer, Otto W** — Director
Justinus-Kerner-Str 10, 80686 Munich, Germany
**Retzlaff, Palmer (Pete)** — Football Player
669 New Road, Gilbertsville PA 19525, USA
**Reuben, David R** — Psychiatrist
Scott Meredith, 1675 Broadway, New York NY 10019, USA
**Reuben, Gloria** — Actress
Great Northern Artists, 350 Dupont St, Toronto ON M5R 1V9, Canada
**Reubens, Paul** — Comedian, Actor
W M E Entertainment, 9601 Wilshire Blvd, #300, Beverly Hills CA 90210 USA
**Reuschel, Ricky E (Rick)** — Baseball Player
PO Box 143, Renfrew PA 16053, USA
**Reuss, Jerry** — Baseball Player
1 Line Dr, Des Moines IA 50309, USA
**Reuten, Thekla** — Actress
Innovative Artists, 1505 10th St, Santa Monica CA 90401 USA
**Reutimann, David** — Auto Racing Driver
Tommy Baldwin Racing, 296 Cayuga Road, Mooresville NC 28117, USA
**Reutter, Katherine** — Speed Skater
Q Sports Marketing, 534 W Evergreen St, Wheaton IL 60187, USA
**Reveiz, Fuad Y** — Football Player
PO Box 22430, Knoxville TN 37933, USA
**Revell, Graeme** — Composer
Kraft-Engel Mgmt, 15233 Ventura Blvd, #200, Sherman Oaks CA 91403 USA
**Reverho, Christine** — Actress
Artmedia, 20 Ave Rapp, 75007 Paris, France
**Revering, David A (Dave)** — Baseball Player
1063 Crows Wing Way, Ivins UT 84738, USA
**Revill, Clive** — Actor
Arlene Thornton & Associates, 12711 Ventura Blvd, #490, Studio City CA 91604, USA
**Revin, Sergei N** — Cosmonaut
Cosmonaut Training Center, Star City, 141160 Zvezdny Gorodok, Moscow Oblast, Russia
**Rex, Simon** — Actor, Producer
Luber Rocklin Entertainment, 5815 Sunset Blvd, #206, Los Angeles CA 90028 USA
**Rey, Antonia** — Actress
Alvarado Rey Agency, 7906 Santa Monica Blvd, #205, West Hollywood CA 90046, USA
**Rey, Reynaldo** — Actor, Comedian, Writer
Starwil Talent Agency, 433 N Camden Dr, #400, Beverly Hills CA 90210, USA
**Reyes Rosales, Diego Antonio** — Soccer Player
Federacion de Futbol, Colima 373 Colonia Roma, Delegacion Cuauhtemoc, Mexico City DF 06700, Mexico
**Reyes, Anthony L** — Baseball Player
8929 Watson Ave, Whittier CA 90605, USA
**Reyes, Carlos A** — Baseball Player
23811 Butterfly Landing Dr, Land O'Lakes FL 34638, USA
**Reyes, Eddie** — Guitarist
Helter Skelter, 347-353 Chiswick High Road, London W4 4HS, England
**Reyes, Jose B** — Baseball Player
24 Stone Hill Dr S, Manhasset NY 11030, USA
**Reyes, Joseph A (Jo-Jo)** — Baseball Player
9554 Paradise Place, Riverside CA 92508, USA

**Reyes, Judy** — Actress
TalentWorks, 3500 W Olive Ave, #1400, Burbank CA 91505 USA
**Reynolds Booth, Nancy** — Skier
3197 Padaro Lane, Carpinteria CA 93013, USA
**Reynolds, Archie E** — Baseball Player
1828 Pinecrest Dr, Tyler TX 75701, USA
**Reynolds, Burt** — Actor
Innovative Artists, 1505 10th St, Santa Monica CA 90401 USA
**Reynolds, Carolyn** — Artist
1440 Catalina, Laguna Beach CA 92651, USA
**Reynolds, Corey** — Actor
New Wave Entertainment, 2660 W Olive Ave, Burbank, CA 91505, USA
**Reynolds, Dean** — Commentator
ABC-TV, News Dept, 5010 Creston St, Hyattsville MD 20781 USA
**Reynolds, Debbie** — Actress, Singer
6514 Lankershim Blvd, North Hollywood CA 91606, USA
**Reynolds, Derrick S (Ricky)** — Football Player
37540 Church Ave, Dade City FL 33525, USA
**Reynolds, Donald E (Don)** — Baseball Player
6035 NE 35th Place, Portland OR 97211, USA
**Reynolds, Edward (Ed)** — Football Player
2387 Country Side Dr, Fleming Isle FL 32003, USA
**Reynolds, G Craig** — Baseball Player
4210 Hidden Links Court, Kingwood TX 77339, USA
**Reynolds, Gene** — Actor, Producer
2034 Castillian Dr, Los Angeles CA 90068, USA
**Reynolds, Glenn F** — Inventor (Proscar Drug)
242 Edgewood Ave, Westfield NJ 07090, USA
**Reynolds, Harold C** — Baseball Player, Sportscaster
2890 NW Angelica Dr, Corvallis OR 97330, USA
**Reynolds, James** — Actor
1925 Hanscom Dr, South Pasadena CA 91030, USA
**Reynolds, James N (Jim), IV** — Baseball Umpire
708 Highpoint Dr, Rocky Hill CT 06067, USA
**Reynolds, Jerry O** — Basketball Coach, Executive
Sacramento Kings, Arco Arena, 1 Sports Parkway, Sacramento CA 95834 USA
**Reynolds, John Brently** — Actor
Hansen Jacobson Teller, 450 N Roxbury Dr, #800, Beverly Hills CA 90210 USA
**Reynolds, John H** — Physicist, Educator
University of California, Physics Dept, Berkeley CA 94720, USA
**Reynolds, John S (Jack)** — Football Player
11480 SW 102nd St, Miami FL 33176, USA
**Reynolds, Kenneth L (Ken)** — Baseball Player
182 Greenwood St, Marlborough MA 01752, USA
**Reynolds, Kevin** — Director
W M E Entertainment, 9601 Wilshire Blvd, #300, Beverly Hills CA 90210 USA
**Reynolds, Patrick** — Actor, Social Activist
260 S Rodeo Dr, Beverly Hills CA 90212, USA
**Reynolds, R Shane** — Baseball Player
129 E Shore Road, Monroe LA 71203, USA
**Reynolds, Robert** — Bassist (Mavericks, Swag)
AristoMedia, 1620 16th Ave S, Nashville TN 37212, USA
**Reynolds, Robert A (Bob)** — Baseball Player
952 SW Campus Dr, #2603, Federal Way WA 98023, USA
**Reynolds, Roger L** — Composer
University of California, Music Department, La Jolla CA 92093, USA
**Reynolds, Ronn D** — Baseball Player
1410 N Armour St, Wichita KS 67206, USA
**Reynolds, Ryan** — Actor
Dark Trick Films, PO Box 10605, Beverly Hills CA 90213, USA
**Reynolds, Sheldon** — Guitarist (Earth Wind & Fire)
Great Scott Productions, 4750 Lincoln Blvd, #229, Marina del Rey CA 90292, USA
**Reynolds, Thomas A, Jr** — Attorney
Winston & Strawn, 1 First National Plaza, 45 W Wacker Dr, Chicago IL 60601, USA
**Reynolds, Thomas D (Tommie)** — Baseball Player
640 Jinks Crossing Road, Bainbridge GA 39819, USA
**Reynolds, Tim** — Instrumentalist
Blue Mountain Artists, 810 Tyvola Road, #114, Charlotte NC 28217, USA
**Reynolds, W Ann** — Educator
University of Alabama, Outreach Development Center, Birmingham AL 35294, USA
**Reynor, Jack** — Actor
W M E Entertainment, 9601 Wilshire Blvd, #300, Beverly Hills CA 90210 USA
**Reynoso, Armando R** — Baseball Player
PO Box 442, Scottsdale AZ 85252, USA
**Reza, Yasmina** — Writer, Actresss, Comedienne
Gersh Agency, 9465 Wilshire Blvd, #600, Beverly Hills CA 90212 USA
**Reznikoff, William S** — Biochemist
University of Wisconsin, Biochemistry Dept, 433 Babcock Dr, Madison WI 53706, USA
**Reznor, M Trent** — Singer (Nine Inch Nails)
W M E Entertainment, 9601 Wilshire Blvd, #300, Beverly Hills CA 90210 USA
**Rhames, Ving** — Actor
Kramer Management, 10 Universal City Plaza, Universal City CA 91608, USA
**Rhea, Caroline** — Actress, Comedienne
Kipperman Mgmt, 420 W End Ave, #1G, New York NY 10024 USA
**Rheaume, Manon** — Ice Hockey Player
50499 Laurel Ridge Court, Northville MI 48168, USA
**Rheims, Bettina** — Photographer
Grand Large, 54 Mercer St, New York NY 10013, USA
**Rhett, Errict U** — Football Player
6 NW 108th Terrace, Plantation FL 33324, USA
**Rhett, Thomas** — Singer, Songwriter
Big Machine Record Group, Valory Music, 1219 16th Ave S, Nashville TN 37212, USA
**Rhey, Ashley** — Actress, Model
1220 Airport Freeway, #G456, Bedford TX 76022, USA
**Rhimes, Shonda** — Writer, Producer
I C M Partners, 10250 Constellation Blvd, #900, Los Angeles CA 90067 USA

**Rhine, Kendall L, Sr** — Basketball Player
6240 State Route 127 N, Alto Pass IL 62905, USA
**Rhines, Peter B** — Oceanographer
5753 61st Ave NE, Seattle WA 98105, USA
**Rhoads, James B** — Archivist
17803 Mandi Lane, Weston MO 64098, USA
**Rhoads, Paul** — Football Coach
Iowa State University, Athletic Dept, 1800 S 4th St, Ames IA 50011, USA
**Rhoda, Hilary** — Model
I M G Models, 304 Park Ave S, #PH N, New York NY 10010 USA
**Rhoden, Richard A (Rick)** — Baseball Player
8009 Whisper Lake Lane E, Ponte Vedra FL 32082, USA
**Rhodes, Arthur L, Jr** — Baseball Player
14114 Phoenix Road, Phoenix MD 21131, USA
**Rhodes, Cynthia** — Actress, Dancer
15260 Ventura Blvd, #2100, Sherman Oaks CA 91403, USA
**Rhodes, Damian (Dusty)** — Ice Hockey Player
8595 Sanctuary Dr, Mentor OH 44060, USA
**Rhodes, Donnelly** — Actor
Northern Exposure Talent Management Group, 570 Granville St, Vancouver BC V6C 3P1, Canada
**Rhodes, Eugene S (Gene)** — Basketball Player
132 N Peterson Ave, #8, Louisville KY 40206, USA
**Rhodes, Frank H T** — Geologist, Educator
Cornell University, Geology Dept, Snee Hall, Ithaca NY 14853, USA
**Rhodes, Jewell Parker** — Writer
Arizona State University, English Dept, Tempe AZ 85287, USA
**Rhodes, Karl D (Dusty)** — Baseball Player
4230 Cedar Bend Dr, Missouri City TX 77459, USA
**Rhodes, Kim** — Actress
Kerner Management Associates, 311 N Robertson Blvd, #288, Beverly Hills CA 90211, USA
**Rhodes, Nick** — Keyboardist (Duran Duran)
D D Productions, 93A Westbourne Park Villas, London W2 5ED, England
**Rhodes, Philip** — Drummer (Gin Blossoms, Pharaohs)
W M E Entertainment, 1600 Division St, #300, Nashville TN 37203 USA
**Rhodes, Ray** — Football Player, Coach
1507 Juliet Dr, Allen TX 75013, USA
**Rhodes, Richard L** — Writer
Janklow & Nesbit, 445 Park Ave, #1300, New York NY 10022, USA
**Rhodes, Robert** — Architect
Robert Rhodes Associates Architects, 330 W 42nd St, New York NY 10036, USA
**Rhodes, Rodrick** — Basketball Player
PO Box 17704, Sugar Land TX 77496, USA
**Rhodes, Tom** — Actor, Comedian
OmniPop Talent Group, 4605 Lankershim Blvd, #201, Toluca Lake CA 91602 USA
**Rhodes, Zandra L** — Fashion Designer
79-85 Bermondsey St, London SE1 3XF, England
**Rhodri, Steffan** — Actor
Artists Partnership, 101 Finsbury Pavement, London EC2A 1RS, England
**Rhomberg, Kevin J** — Baseball Player
9692 Executive Court, Mentor OH 44060, USA
**Rhome, Gerald B (Jerry)** — Football Player, Coach
3883 Morning Meadow Lane, Buford GA 30519, USA
**Rhone, Earnest C (Earnie)** — Football Player
3603 Potomac Ave, Texarkana TX 75503, USA
**Rhone, Sylvia** — Businesswoman
Epic Records, 9830 Wilshire Blvd, Beverly Hills CA 90212 USA
**Rhyan, Dick** — Golfer
111 Camp Dr, Georgetown TX 78633, USA
**Rhymes, Busta** — Rap Artist, Actor
T C A/Jed Root, 9220 Sunset Blvd, #315, Los Angeles CA 90069, USA
**Rhys Meyers, Jonathan** — Actor
Brillstein Entertainment Partners, 9150 Wilshire Blvd, #350, Beverly Hills CA 90212 USA
**Rhys, Matthew** — Actor
W M E Entertainment, 9601 Wilshire Blvd, #300, Beverly Hills CA 90210 USA
**Rhys, Phillip** — Actor
Independent Talent Group, 40 Whitfield St, London W1T 2RH, England
**Rhys-Davies, John** — Actor
Johnson & Laird Mgmt, PO Box 78340, Grey Lynn Auckland 1245, New Zealand
**Ribant, Dennis J** — Baseball Player
46 Sidra Cove, Newport Coast CA 92657, USA
**Ribble, Pat** — Ice Hockey Player
23 Cheyenne Court, Leamington ON N8H 5E2, Canada
**Ribbs, Willy T** — Auto Racing Driver
2343 Ribbs Lane, San Jose CA 95116, USA
**Ribeau, Sidney A** — Educator
Howard University, President's Office, Washington DC 20059, USA
**Ribeiro, Alfonso** — Actor
Creative Talent Group, 1900 Ave of Stars, #2475, Los Angeles CA 90067, USA
**Ribeiro, Ignacio** — Fashion Designer
Clements Ribeiro Ltd, 48 S Molton St, London W1X 1HE, England
**Ribeiro, Michael T (Mike)** — Ice Hockey Player
5609 Monterey Dr, Frisco TX 75034, USA
**Ribes, Jean-Michel** — Actor, Director, Writer
Artmedia, 20 Ave Rapp, 75007 Paris, France
**Ribisi, Giovanni** — Actor
Management 360, 9111 Wilshire Blvd, Beverly Hills CA 90210 USA
**Ribisi, Marissa** — Actress
United Talent Agency, U T A Plaza, 9336 Civic Center Dr, Beverly Hills CA 90210 USA
**Ricard, Adrian** — Actress
Amsel Eisenstadt Frazier, 5055 Wilshire Blvd, #865, Los Angeles CA 90036 USA
**Ricard, Alan C** — Football Player
10306 Ripple Lake Dr, Houston TX 77065, USA
**Ricard, Jean-Pierre B Cardinal** — Religious Leader
Archeveche of Bordeaux, 183 Cours de la Somme, CS 21386, 33077 Bordeaux Cedex, France
**Ricardo, Benito C (Benny)** — Football Player, Actor, Comedian
3012 Harding Way, Costa Mesa CA 92626, USA

**Ricci, Christina** — Actress
Management 360, 9111 Wilshire Blvd, Beverly Hills CA 90210 USA
**Ricci, Italia** — Actress
Coast to Coast Talent, 3350 Barham Blvd, Los Angeles CA 90068 USA
**Ricci, Mike** — Ice Hockey Player
286 Mountain Laurel Lane, Los Gatos CA 95032, USA
**Ricciardo, Daniel** — Auto Racing Driver
Red Bull, Am Brunnen 1, 5330 Fuschl am See, Austria
**Rice, Andrew (Andy)** — Football Player
801 N Main St, Hallettsville TX 77964, USA
**Rice, Anne** — Writer
9 Monte Carlo Dr, Kenner LA 70065, USA
**Rice, Bobby G** — Singer
505 Canton Pass, Madison TN 37115, USA
**Rice, Buddy** — Auto Racing Driver
Panther Racing, 5740 Decatur Blvd, Indianapolis IN 46241, USA
**Rice, Chris** — Singer, Pianist, Songwriter
Hardly Entertainment, 1650 Murfreesboro Road, #133, Franklin TN 37067, USA
**Rice, Condoleezza** — Secretary, State
Stanford University, Hoover Institution, Stanford CA 94305, USA
**Rice, Damien** — Singer, Guitarist, Songwriter
13 Artists, 11-14 Kensington St, Brighton BN1 4AJ, England
**Rice, Gigi** — Actress
Bamboo Mgmt, 17 Buccaneer St, Marina Del Rey CA 90292, USA
**Rice, Glen A** — Basketball Player
8920 SW 162nd Terrace, Palmetto Bay FL 33157, USA
**Rice, James E (Jim)** — Baseball Player
35 Bobby Jones Dr, Andover MA 01810, USA
**Rice, James R** — Geophysicist
Harvard University, Applied Science Division, Cambridge MA 02138, USA
**Rice, Jerry L** — Football Player
3223 Paseo, Grand Prairie TX 75054, USA
**Rice, Luanne** — Writer
I C M Partners, 10250 Constellation Blvd, #900, Los Angeles CA 90067 USA
**Rice, Ronald W (Ron)** — Football Player
22880 Twyckingham Ave, Southfield MI 48034, USA
**Rice, Simeon J** — Football Player
371 Channelside Walkway, #301, Tampa FL 33602, USA
**Rice, Stephanie** — Swimmer
Saint Peters Swim Club, Box 598, Indooroopilly QLD 4068, Australia
**Rice, Steven (Steve)** — Ice Hockey Player
99 Duncairn Ave, Kitchener ON N2M 4S5, Canada
**Rice, Stuart A** — Chemist
5517 S Kimbark Ave, Chicago IL 60637, USA
**Rice, Susan E** — Government Official, Diplomat
US Mission, United Nations Plaza, New York NY 10017, USA
**Rice, Thomas M** — Theoretical Physicist
Theoretische Physik, ETH-Honggerberg, 8093 Zurich, Switzerland
**Rice, Timothy M B (Tim)** — Lyricist
Chilterns, France-Hill Dr, Camberley, Surrey GU153 30A, England
**Rich, Adam** — Actor
Jeff Ballard Public Relations 4814 Lemona Ave, Sherman Oaks CA 91403, USA
**Rich, Alexander** — Molecular Biologist
2 Walnut Ave, Cambridge MA 02140, USA
**Rich, Allan** — Actor
Greater Vision Agency, 9229 W Sunset Blvd, #320, West Hollywood CA 90069, USA
**Rich, Christopher** — Actor, Director, Producer
Stone Manners Salners, 6100 Wilshire Blvd, #1500, Los Angeles CA 90035 USA
**Rich, David Lowell** — Director
721 Royal Anne Lane, #201, Raleigh NC 27615, USA
**Rich, Frank H** — Drama Critic, Columnist
New York Times, Editorial Dept, 229 W 43rd St, New York NY 10036 USA
**Rich, John** — Singer, Guitarist, Songwriter
Morris Management Group, 818 19th Ave S, Nashville TN 37203, USA
**Rich, Katie** — Actress
10100 Santa Monica Blvd, #2490, Los Angeles CA 90067, USA
**Rich, Tommy** — Basketball Player
1348 Clubview Court, Venice FL 34292, USA
**Rich, Tony** — Singer, Keyboardist, Songwriter
Prestige, 220 E 23rd St, #303, New York NY 10010, USA
**Richard of Ammanford, Ivor S** — Government Official, England
11 South Square, Gray's Inn, London WC1R 5EU, England
**Richard, Cecile** — Association Executive
Planned Parenthood Federation, 434 W 33rd St, New York NY 10001, USA
**Richard, Chris** — Baseball Player
11389 Ironwood Road, San Diego CA 92131, USA
**Richard, Cliff** — Singer
Harley House, Portsmouth Road, Box 46C, Esher, Surrey KT10 0RB, England
**Richard, Dawn** — Model, Actress
Playboy Promotions, 9346 Civic Center Dr, #200, Beverly Hills CA 90210 USA
**Richard, Dawn A** — Singer (Danity Kane)
Bad Boy Entertainment, 1440 Broadway, #16, New York NY 10018 USA
**Richard, Deb** — Golfer
736 Port Charlotte Dr, Ponte Vedra FL 32081, USA
**Richard, Henri** — Ice Hockey Player
905-4300 Place de Cageux, Ile Paton Laval QC H7W 4Z3, Canada
**Richard, James Rodney (J R)** — Baseball Player
Mary Olive Baptist Church, 2804 McGowan St, Houston TX 77004, USA
**Richard, Lee E (Bee Bee)** — Baseball Player
1621 14th St, Port Arthur TX 77640, USA
**Richard, Nathalie** — Actress
Voyez Mon Agent, 20 Ave Rapp, 75007 Paris, France
**Richard, Pierre** — Actor
Artmedia, 20 Ave Rapp, 75007 Paris, France
**Richards of Herstmonceux, Baron David J** — Army General, England
International Strategic Studies Institute, 13 Arundel St, Temple Place, London WC2R 3DX, England

**Richards, Ariana** — Actress
Don Buchwald Talent Agency, 6500 Wilshire Blvd, #2200, Los Angeles CA 90048 USA
**Richards, Bradley G (Brad)** — Ice Hockey Player
101 Warren St, #3150, New York NY 10007, USA
**Richards, Brooke** — Model
Playboy Promotions, 9346 Civic Center Dr, #200, Beverly Hills CA 90210 USA
**Richards, Dakota Blue** — Actress
Artist Rights Group, 4A Exmoor St, London W10 6BD, England
**Richards, David R (Dave)** — Football Player
4209 San Carlos St, Dallas TX 75205, USA
**Richards, Denise** — Actress, Model
Model Management Group, 1024 6th Ave, #201, New York NY 10018, USA
**Richards, Emilie** — Writer
PO Box 228, Chautauqua NY 14722, USA
**Richards, Eugene** — Photographer, Filmmaker
Many Voices, 472 13th St, Brooklyn NY 11215, USA
**Richards, George Maxwell** — President, Trinidad & Tobago
President's House, Botanical Garden Area, Port of Spain, Trinidad & Tobago
**Richards, J August (Jamie)** — Actor
Greenlight Mgmt, 13848 Valleyheart Dr, Sherman Oaks CA 91423, USA
**Richards, J Golden** — Football Player
7274 Winesap Court, Salt Lake City UT 84121, USA
**Richards, J R** — Singer (Dishwalla)
W M E Entertainment, 1325 Ave of Americas, New York NY 10019 USA
**Richards, Keith** — Singer (Rolling Stones), Songwriter
25 Walden Woods Lane, Weston CT 06883, USA
**Richards, Kim** — Actress
10326 Orton Ave, Los Angeles CA 90064, USA
**Richards, Lucille** — Baseball Player
17 Stonemeadow Dr, Bridgewater MA 2324, USA
**Richards, Mark** — Surfer
Mark Richards Surfboards, 755 Hunter St, Newcastle NSW 2302, Australia
**Richards, Michael** — Actor, Comedian
Abrams Artists, 275 7th Ave, #2600, New York NY 10001 USA
**Richards, Paul L** — Physicist
University of California, Physics Dept, LeConte Hall, Berkeley CA 94720, USA
**Richards, Paul W** — Astronaut
N A S A, Johnson Space Center, 2101 NASA Road, Houston TX 77058 USA
**Richards, Renee** — Tennis Player
1604 Union St, San Francisco CA 94123, USA
**Richards, Rex E** — Chemist
13 Woodstock Close, Oxford OX2 8DB, England
**Richards, Richard N** — Astronaut
N A S A, Johnson Space Center, 2101 NASA Road, Houston TX 77058 USA
**Richards, Robert E (Bob)** — Track Athlete
76782 Interstate 20, Gordon TX 76453, USA
**Richards, Robert G (Bobby)** — Football Player
2881 Fairplay Road, Rutledge GA 30663, USA
**Richards, Russell E (Rusty)** — Baseball Player
1193 Spring Sage St, Henderson NV 89011, USA
**Richards, Stephanie** — Actress
H David Moss, 733 Seward St, #PH, Los Angeles CA 90038 USA
**Richards, Todd M** — Ice Hockey Player, Coach
Columbus Blue Jackets, Arena, 200 W Nationwide Blvd, #1, Columbus OH 43215 USA
**Richards, Warren J** — Writer
9075 S 700 E, #109, Sandy UT 84070, USA
**Richardson Joyner, Donna** — Physical Fitness Expert
Word Network, 20733 W 10 Mile Road, Southfield MI 48075, USA
**Richardson, Alpette (Al)** — Football Player
PO Box 371105, Decatur GA 30037, USA
**Richardson, Anna C** — Entertainer, Writer, Producer
Yakety Yak, 7A Bloomsbury Square, London WC1A 2LP, England
**Richardson, Ashley** — Model
Jason Weinberg Assoc, 451 Greenwich St, New York NY 10013, USA
**Richardson, Ben** — Cinematographer
Gersh Agency, 9465 Wilshire Blvd, #600, Beverly Hills CA 90212 USA
**Richardson, Calvin** — Singer, Songwriter
Primary Wave Music, 116 E 16th St, #900, New York NY 10003, USA
**Richardson, Cameron** — Model, Actress
Paradigm Agency, 360 N Crescent Dr, North Building, Beverly Hills CA 90210 USA
**Richardson, Charles C** — Biochemist
Harvard Medical School, 25 Shattuck St, Boston MA 02115, USA
**Richardson, Clint D** — Basketball Player
1207 9th Ave NW, Puyallup WA 98371, USA
**Richardson, Damien A** — Football Player
1300 E Cromwell Ave, Fresno CA 93720, USA
**Richardson, Dave** — Ice Hockey Player
62 Agassie Dr, Winnipeg MB R3T 2K7, Canada
**Richardson, Derek** — Actor
I C M Partners, 10250 Constellation Blvd, #900, Los Angeles CA 90067 USA
**Richardson, Dorothy (Dot)** — Softball Player
1120 W Lakeshore Dr, Clermont FL 34711, USA
**Richardson, Emma** — Singer, Bassist (Band of Skulls)
Pias Entertainment Group, Trading Centre, 101 Farm Lane, #24, London SW6 1QJ, England
**Richardson, Gloster V** — Football Player
9143 S Euclid Ave, Chicago IL 60617, USA
**Richardson, Greg** — Boxer
382 Camden Ave, Youngstown OH 44505, USA
**Richardson, J O Daniel** — Cross Country Skier
Skiforbundet, Riksskistadion, 791 19 Falun, Sweden
**Richardson, Jack** — Artist
12171 Sunset Ave, Grass Valley CA 95945, USA
**Richardson, Jacob M (Jake)** — Actor
Coast to Coast Talent, 3350 Barham Blvd, Los Angeles CA 90068 USA
**Richardson, Jason A** — Basketball Player
75 Dahlia St, Denver CO 80220, USA

**Richardson, Jeffrey S (Jeff)** — Baseball Player
11779 W Fordson Dr, Marana AZ 85653, USA
**Richardson, Jerome (Pooh)** — Basketball Player
23434 Sherman Way, West Hills CA 91307, USA
**Richardson, Joely** — Actress
Artists Partnership, 101 Finsbury Pavement, London EC2A 1RS, England
**Richardson, John E** — Football Player
3053 Eagles Claw Ave, Thousand Oaks CA 91362, USA
**Richardson, John M** — Navy Admiral
Director, Naval Nuclear Propulsion Program, Navy Yard, Washington DC 20374 USA
**Richardson, Ken** — Ice Hockey Player
Hockey Heritage, 400 Government Road W, Kirkland Lake ON P2N 3M6, Canada
**Richardson, Ken** — Chemist, Inventor
Pfizer Laboratories, Ramsgate Road, Sandwich Kent CT13 9NJ, England
**Richardson, Kevin Michael** — Actor
C E S D, 10635 Santa Monica Blvd, #130, Los Angeles CA 90025 USA
**Richardson, Kevin S** — Singer (Backstreet Boys)
Vox Inc, 6420 Wilshire Blvd, #1080, Los Angeles CA 90048 USA
**Richardson, Kyle D** — Football Player
3516 Balmar Mews Road, Baltimore MD 21211, USA
**Richardson, LaTanya** — Actress
Framework Entertainment, 9057 Nemo St, #C, West Hollywood CA 90069 USA
**Richardson, Linda** — Opera Singer
Musichall Ltd, Vicarage Way, Ringmer BN8 5LA, England
**Richardson, Mark** — Drummer (Skunk Anansie)
13 Artists, 11-14 Kensington St, Brighton BN1 4AJ, England
**Richardson, Michael C (Mike)** — Football Player
723 Owen Ave, #C, Huntington Beach CA 92648, USA
**Richardson, Micheal Ray** — Basketball Player
5012 SW Oxford Place, Lawton OK 73505, USA
**Richardson, Mike** — Publisher
Dark Horse Publishing, 10956 SE Main St, Portland OR 97222 USA
**Richardson, Miranda** — Actress
Independent Talent Group, 40 Whitfield St, London W1T 2RH, England
**Richardson, Nolan** — Basketball Coach
4057 N Hughmount Road, Fayetteville AR 72704, USA
**Richardson, Patricia** — Actress
Innovative Artists, 1505 10th St, Santa Monica CA 90401 USA
**Richardson, Robert B** — Cinematographer
Skouras Agency, 1149 3rd St, #300, Santa Monica CA 90403 USA
**Richardson, Robert C (Bobby)** — Baseball Player
47 Adams Ave, Sumter SC 29150, USA
**Richardson, Robert, Jr** — Auto Racing Driver
PO Box 523, McKinney TX 75070, USA
**Richardson, Sam** — Sculptor
4121 Sequoyah Road, Oakland CA 94605, USA
**Richardson, Terry** — Ice Hockey Player
3598 Rosemary Heights Crescent, Surrey BC V3S 0P2, Canada
**Richardson, Trent** — Football Player
Indianapolis Colts, 7001 W 56th St, Indianapolis IN 46254 USA
**Richardson, William B (Bill)** — Secretary, Energy; Governor, NM
A P C O Worldwide, Global Strategies Division, 700 12th St NW, #800, Washington DC 20005, USA
**Richardson, William C** — Foundation Executive, Educator
W K Kellogg Foundation, 1 Michigan Ave E, Battle Creek MI 49017, USA
**Richardson, William R** — Army General
8612 Dixie Place, McLean VA 22102, USA
**Richardson, Willie L** — Football Player
5928 Waverly Dr, Jackson MS 39206, USA
**Richardson-Whitfield, Salli** — Actress
Innovative Artists, 1505 10th St, Santa Monica CA 90401 USA
**Richards-Ross, Sanya (Sandie)** — Track Athlete
Octagon Worldwide, 1751 Pinnacle Dr, #1500, McLean VA 22102 USA
**Richen, John M** — Sculptor
Contemporary Fine Arts Gallery, 7946 Ivanhoe Ave, La Jolla CA 92037, USA
**Richer, Stephane** — Ice Hockey Player
Club de Golf Montpelier, 440 Ave S Richaer, Montpelier QC J0V 1M0, Canada
**Richert, Peter G (Pete)** — Baseball Player
80 La Cerra Dr, Rancho Mirage CA 92270, USA
**Richey, Cliff** — Tennis Player
2936 Cumberland Dr, San Angelo TX 76904, USA
**Richey, Jennifer** — Actress
C E S D, 10635 Santa Monica Blvd, #130, Los Angeles CA 90025 USA
**Richey, Kim** — Singer, Songwriter
Flood Bumstead McCready McCarthy, 1700 Hayes St, #304, Nashville TN 37203 USA
**Richey, Wade E** — Football Player
207 Bayonne Dr, Lafayette LA 70507, USA
**Richie, Lionel** — Singer, Songwriter
Creative Artists Agency, 2000 Ave of Stars, #100, Los Angeles CA 90067 USA
**Richie, Nicole** — Actress, Producer
Paradigm Agency, 360 N Crescent Dr, North Building, Beverly Hills CA 90210 USA
**Richie, Robert E (Bob)** — Baseball Player
1835 Meadowvale Way, Sparks NV 89431, USA
**Richie, Shane** — Singer, Actor
International Artistes, 193-197 High Holborn, London WC1V 7BD, England
**Richling, Greg** — Singer, Bassist (Wallflowers)
B K Entertainment Group, 15300 Ventura Blvd, #203, Sherman Oaks CA 91403, USA
**Richman, Caryn** — Actress
1805 Via Arriba, Palos Verdes Estates CA 90274, USA
**Richman, Jason** — Producer, Writer
W M E Entertainment, 9601 Wilshire Blvd, #300, Beverly Hills CA 90210 USA
**Richman, Jonathan** — Singer, Guitarist (Modern Lovers), Actor
High Road Touring, 751 Bridgeway, #200, Sausalito CA 94965 USA
**Richman, Peter Mark** — Actor
5114 Del Moreno Dr, Woodland Hills CA 91364, USA
**Richmond, Anthony B** — Cinematograhper
United Talent Agency, U T A Plaza, 9336 Civic Center Dr, Beverly Hills CA 90210 USA

**Richmond, Deon** — Actor
Innovative Artists, 1505 10th St, Santa Monica CA 90401 USA
**Richmond, Geri** — Chemist
University of Oregon, Chemistry Dept, Eugene OR 97403, USA
**Richmond, Mitchell J (Mitch)** — Basketball Player
25374 Prado de la Felicidad, Calabasas CA 91302, USA
**Richmond, Steve** — Ice Hockey Player
21290 W Pepper Dr, Lake Zurich IL 60047, USA
**Richt, Mark** — Football Coach
University of Georgia, Athletic Dept, PO Box 1472, Athens GA 30603, USA
**Richter, Allen G (Al)** — Baseball Player
3810 Atlantic Ave, #703, Virginia Beach VA 23451, USA
**Richter, Andy** — Actor, Comedian
Creative Artists Agency, 2000 Ave of Stars, #100, Los Angeles CA 90067 USA
**Richter, Barry** — Ice Hockey Player
7202 Timberwood Dr, Madison WI 53719, USA
**Richter, Burton** — Nobel Physics Laureate
620 Sand Hill Road, #206C, Palo Alto CA 94304, USA
**Richter, Gerhard** — Artist
Bismarckstr 50, 50672 Cologne, Germany
**Richter, Jason James** — Actor
Aqua Talent, 9000 Sunset Blvd, #700, Los Angeles CA 90069, USA
**Richter, John F** — Basketball Player
2740 Narcissa Road, Plymouth Meeting PA 19462, USA
**Richter, Michael T (Mike)** — Ice Hockey Player
61 Cutler Road, Greenwich CT 06831, USA
**Richter, Pat V** — Football Player, Administrator
11111 Bardon Road, Woodruff WI 54568, USA
**Richwine, Maria** — Actress
Acme Talent Agency, 4727 Wilshire Blvd, #333, Los Angeles CA 90010 USA
**Rickard, Joe** — Drummer (Red)
Paradigm Agency, 404 W Franklin St, Monterey CA 93940 USA
**Rickard, Robbie** — Bowler
Professional Bowlers Association, 719 2nd Ave, #701, Seattle WA 98104 USA
**Rickards, Ashley** — Actress
United Talent Agency, U T A Plaza, 9336 Civic Center Dr, Beverly Hills CA 90210 USA
**Ricker, Maelle D** — Snowboarding Skier
Agenda Sport Marketing, 318 11th Ave SE, #340, Calgary AB T2G 0Y2 Canada T2G
**Ricketts, Thomas G (Tom), Jr** — Football Player
720 Warrendale Bayne Road, Wexford PA 15090, USA
**Rickhards, Dominic** — Actor
Gavin Barker Assoc, 2D Wimpole St, London W1G 0EB, England
**Rickles, Don** — Actor, Comedian
1440 Fielder St, Ashland OR 97520, USA
**Rickman, Alan** — Actor
Independent Talent Group, 40 Whitfield St, London W1T 2RH, England
**Ricks, Christopher B** — Writer, Educator
Lasborough Park near Tetbury, Gloucestershire GL8 8UF, England
**Ricks, Mikhael R** — Football Player
5024 Lincoln St, Hollywood FL 33021, USA
**Rickter, Alicia** — Model, Actress
Innovative Artists, 1505 10th St, Santa Monica CA 90401 USA
**Rico, Alfredo C (Fred)** — Baseball Player
7720 Ensign Ave, Sun Valley CA 91352, USA
**Rida, Flo** — Rap Artist
Susan Blond Inc, 50 W 57th St, #1400, New York NY 10019 USA
**Riddell, Derek** — Actor
Hamilton Hodell, 20 Golden Square, London W1F 9JL, England
**Riddick, Frank A, Jr** — Physician
150 Broadway St, #709, New Orleans LA 70118, USA
**Riddick, Robbert L (Robb)** — Football Player
111 Lilli Lane, Woodstock GA 30188, USA
**Riddick, Steven (Steve)** — Track Athlete
PO Box 1892, Norfolk VA 23501, USA
**Riddiford, Lynn M** — Zoologist
40733 Manor House Road, Leesburg VA 20175, USA
**Riddleberger, Dennis M (Denny)** — Baseball Player
35785 Hunter Ave, Westland MI 48185, USA
**Riddles, Libby** — Dog Sled Racer
PO Box 15253, Fritz Creek AK 99603, USA
**Riddoch, Gregory L (Greg)** — Baseball Player, Manager
703 Windflower Dr, Longmont CO 80504, USA
**Rider, Isaiah (J R)** — Basketball Player
PO Box 121R, Montchanin DE 19710, USA
**Ridge, Thomas J (Tom)** — Secretary, Home Security; Governor, PA
Westwood Estate Dr, Erie PA 16506, USA
**Ridgeley, Andrew** — Singer, Guitarist (Wham!)
8800 W Sunset Blvd, #401, West Hollywood CA 90069, USA
**Ridgeway, Angie** — Golfer
419 Glen Crest Dr, Moore SC 29369, USA
**Ridgeway, Frank** — Cartoonist (Mr Abernathy)
King Features Syndicate, 300 W 57th St, #1500, New York NY 10019 USA
**Ridgway, Jeff** — Baseball Player
9041 Parlor Dr, Ladson SC 29456, USA
**Ridgway, Stanard (Stan)** — Singer, Songwriter
Conqueroo, 11271 Ventura Blvd, #522, Studio City CA 91604 USA
**Ridker, Paul** — Cardiologist
Brigham & Women's Hospital, 75 Francis St, Boston MA 02115, USA
**Ridley, John** — Writer, Director, Producer
Creative Artists Agency, 2000 Ave of Stars, #100, Los Angeles CA 90067 USA
**Ridley, Michael O G (Mike)** — Ice Hockey Player
Home Run Sports, 1005 Sainte Mary's Road, Winnipeg MB R2M 3S4, Canada
**Ridlon, James A (Jim)** — Football Player
4468 E Lake Road, Cazenovia NY 13035, USA
**Ridnour, Lukas R (Luke)** — Basketball Player
Charlotte Hornets, 333 E Trade St, #A, Charlotte NC 28202 USA

**R**

Richmond - Ridnour

# R

**Riedel, Lars** — Track Athlete
Albus Sportmangement oHG, Hospitalstr 7, 69115 Heidelberg, Germany
**Riedel, Oliver (Ollie)** — Bassist (Rammstein)
Pilgrim Mgmt, PO Box 540101, 10042 Berlin, Germany
**Riedlbauch, Vaclav** — Composer
Revolucni 6, 11000 Prague 1, Czech Republic
**Riedling, John** — Baseball Player
2118 Homestead Lane, Franklin TN 37064, USA
**Riegelhuth Koren, Linn-Kristin** — Handball Player
Paulines vei 5B, 3244 Sandefjord, Norway
**Riegert, Peter** — Actor
Don Buchwald Talent Agency, 10 E 44th St, New York NY 10017 USA
**Riegger, John** — Golfer
768 Tossa de Mar Ave, Henderson NV 89002, USA
**Riegle, Gene** — Harness Racing Driver, Trainer
818 Chestnut Circle, Greenville OH 45331, USA
**Riehle, Richard** — Actor
Stone Manners Salners, 6100 Wilshire Blvd, #1500, Los Angeles CA 90035 USA
**Riemersma, A Jay** — Football Player
3067 Regency Parkway, Zeeland MI 49464, USA
**Riendeau, Vincent** — Ice Hockey Player
Harrington College, Che Riviere Rouge, Harrington QC JBG 2S7, Canada
**Rienstra, John W** — Football Player
PO Box 2447, Frisco CO 80443, USA
**Ries, Christopher D** — Artist
Keelersburg Road, Tunkhannock PA 18657, USA
**Riesch, Maria Hoefl-** — Alpine Skier
Wildenauer Str 22, 82467 Garmisch-Partenkirchen, Germany
**Riesco, Armando** — Actor
Liebman Entertainment, 12 E 46th St, #500, New York NY 10017, USA
**Riesenberg, Douglas J (Doug)** — Football Player
25068 Starr Creek Road, Corvallis OR 97333, USA
**Riesgo, D Nikco** — Baseball Player
29625 Bermuda Lane, Southfield MI 48076, USA
**Riesgraf, Beth** — Actress, Director, Writer
Hansen Jacobson Teller, 450 N Roxbury Dr, #800, Beverly Hills CA 90210 USA
**Riess, Adam G** — Nobel Physics Laureate
Space Telescope Science Institute, 3700 San Martin Dr, Baltimore MD 21218, USA
**Riessen, Marty** — Tennis Player
PO Box 5444, Santa Barbara CA 93150, USA
**Riessle, Fabian** — Nordic Combined Skier
Felling 4, 79274 Saint Margen, Germany
**Rieu, Andre L M N** — Concert Violinist, Conductor, Composer
Andre Rieu Productions, Postfach 1329, 6201 Maastricht BH, Netherlands
**Riffenburgh, Beau** — Historian
Bloomsbury Publishing, 50 Bedford Square, London WC1B 3DP, England
**Rifkin, Arnold** — Producer
Cheyenne Enterprises, 406 Wilshire Blvd, Santa Monica CA 90401, USA
**Rifkin, Jeremy** — Writer, Social Activist
1660 L St NW, #216, Washington DC 20036, USA
**Rifkin, Joshua** — Concert Pianist, Conductor
100 Montgomery St, Cambridge MA 02140, USA
**Rifkin, Ron** — Actor, Singer
Innovative Artists, 235 Park Ave S, #1000, New York NY 10003 USA
**Rifkind, Malcolm L** — Government Official, England
Intelligence & Security Committee, 35 Great Smith St, London SW1P 3BQ, England
**Rigali, Justin F Cardinal** — Religious Leader
Archdiocese, 222 N 17th St, Philadelphia PA 19103, USA
**Rigazio, Donald** — Ice Hockey Player
8514 Cheffield Dr, Louisville KY 40222, USA
**Rigby McCoy, Cathleen R (Cathy)** — Gymnast, Actress
McCoy Rigby Entertainment, 22601 La Palma Ave, #105, Yorba Linda CA 92887, USA
**Rigby, Amy** — Singer, Songwriter
Public Emily, 56 Main St, #206, Northampton MA 01060, USA
**Rigby, Jean P** — Opera Singer
John Coast Mgmt, Manfield House, 3769 Strand, London WC1, England
**Rigby, Randall L, Jr** — Army General
869 Oak Hill Road, Lake Barrington IL 60010, USA
**Rigg, Diana** — Actress
Dalzell & Beresford, 55 Charterhouse St, Paddock Suite, London EC1M 6HA, England
**Riggi, Chris** — Actor
Gersh Agency, 9465 Wilshire Blvd, #600, Beverly Hills CA 90212 USA
**Riggin, Patrick M (Pat)** — Ice Hockey Player
112 Fairlane Ave, London ON N6K 3E6, Canada
**Riggins, John** — Football Player, Sportscaster
8000 Riverside Dr, Cabin John MD 20818, USA
**Riggle, Rob** — Actor, Comedian
Principato-Young, 9465 Wilshire Blvd, #880, Beverly Hills CA 90212 USA
**Riggleman, James D (Jim)** — Baseball Player, Manager
14950 Gulf Blvd, #1003, Madeira Beach FL 33708, USA
**Riggs, Adam D** — Baseball Player
26 Pebble Hollow Court, Spring TX 77381, USA
**Riggs, Chandler** — Actor
I C M Partners, 10250 Constellation Blvd, #900, Los Angeles CA 90067 USA
**Riggs, Gerald** — Football Player
566 Elizabeth Crest Road, Chattanooga TN 37421, USA
**Riggs, Lorrin A** — Psychologist
80 Lyme Road, #104, Hanover NH 03755, USA
**Riggs, R Scott** — Auto, Truck Racing Driver
216 Preston Andrews Road, Bahama NC 27503, USA
**Riggs, Ransom** — Writer
Paradigm Agency, 360 N Crescent Dr, North Building, Beverly Hills CA 90210 USA
**Righetti, Amanda** — Actress
United Talent Agency, U T A Plaza, 9336 Civic Center Dr, Beverly Hills CA 90210 USA
**Righetti, David A (Dave)** — Baseball Player
552 Magdalena Ave, Los Altos Hills CA 94024, USA

**Rigoni, Benito** — Bobsled Athlete
Olympic Committee, Foro Italico, Largo Lauro de Bosis 15, 00135 Rome, Italy
**Rihanna** — Singer
Roc Nation, 1411 Broadway, #3800, New York NY 10018, USA
**Riis, Bjarne L** — Cyclist
Riis Cycling, Firskowej 36, 2800 KGS Lyngby, Denmark
**Rijker, Lucia** — Boxer, Kickboxer, Actress
Sports Placement Service, 6671 W Sunset Blvd, #1521, Los Angeles CA 90028, USA
**Rijo, Jose A** — Baseball Player
2127 Brickell Ave, #2101, Miami FL 33129, USA
**Rikaart, Greg** — Actor
S D B Partners, 315 S Beverly Dr, #411, Beverly Hills CA 90067 USA
**Riker, Albert J** — Plant Pathologist
2760 E 8th St, Tucson AZ 85716, USA
**Riker, Robin** — Actress
Stone Manners Salners, 6100 Wilshire Blvd, #1500, Los Angeles CA 90035 USA
**Riker, Thomas E (Tom)** — Basketball Player
600 Fines Creek Road, Clyde NC 28721, USA
**Riklis, Meshulam** — Businessman
Riklis Family Corp, 2901 Las Vegas Blvd S, Las Vegas NV 89109, USA
**Riles, Ernest** — Baseball Player
221 Asante Dr, Ellenwood GA 30294, USA
**Riley, Amber** — Actress
P M K-B N C, 8687 Melrose Ave, #800, Los Angeles CA 90069 USA
**Riley, Bridget L** — Artist
Karsten Schubert, 47 Lexington St, London W1R 3LG, England
**Riley, Chris J** — Golfer
2625 Barbaradale Circle, Las Vegas NV 89146, USA
**Riley, E Theodore (Teddy)** — Songwriter, Singer (Blackstreet)
Richard Walters, PO Box 2789, Toluca Lake CA 91610 USA
**Riley, Elaine** — Actress
405 N Bay Front, Newport Beach CA 92662, USA
**Riley, Eric** — Basketball Player
6601 Sands Point Dr, #4, Houston TX 77074, USA
**Riley, Gerald (Jerry)** — Dog Sled Racer
General Delivery, Nenana AK 99760, USA
**Riley, Jack** — Actor
C E S D, 10635 Santa Monica Blvd, #130, Los Angeles CA 90025 USA
**Riley, James C** — Army General
Commanding General, V Corps, APO AE 09079 USA
**Riley, James G (Jim)** — Football Player
2201 Cardinal Dr, Edmond OK 73013, USA
**Riley, Jeannie C** — Singer
906 Granville Road, Franklin TN 37064, USA
**Riley, John P (Jack), Jr** — Ice Hockey Player, Coach
PO Box 1302, Marstons Mills MA 02648, USA
**Riley, Kenneth J (Ken)** — Football Player
1035 Carver Ave, Bartow FL 33830, USA
**Riley, Madison** — Actress
Emerald Talent Group, 15260 Ventura Blvd, #1200, Sherman Oaks CA 91403, USA
**Riley, Matthew P (Matt)** — Baseball Player
17169 W Ironwood St, Surprise AZ 85388, USA
**Riley, Michael** — Actor
Gary Goodard Agency, 149 Chuch St, #200, Toronto ON M5B 1Y4, Canada
**Riley, Mike** — Football Coach
Oregon State University, Athletic Dept, Corvallis OR 97331, USA
**Riley, Patrick J (Pat)** — Basketball Player, Coach, Executive
180 Arvida Parkway, Miami FL 33156, USA
**Riley, Richard D** — Association Executive
16 Boathouse Road, Laconia NH 03246, USA
**Riley, Richard W** — Secretary, Education; Governor, SC
Nelson Mullins Riley Scarborough, 104 S Main St, #900, Greenville SC 29601, USA
**Riley, Ruth** — Basketball Player
Metis Sports Management, 132 N Old Woodward Ave, Birmingham MI 48009
**Riley, Sam** — Actor
Creative Artists Agency, 2000 Ave of Stars, #100, Los Angeles CA 90067 USA
**Riley, Steve B** — Football Player
7 Via Cancion, San Clemente CA 92673, USA
**Riley, Talulah** — Actress
Independent Talent Group, 40 Whitfield St, London W1T 2RH, England
**Riley, Tarrus** — Singer
Agency Group Ltd, 142 W 57th St, #600, New York NY 10019 USA
**Riley, Terry M** — Composer, Pianist
Shri Moonshine Ranch, 13699 Moonshine Road, Camptonville CA 95922, USA
**Riley, Tom** — Actor
I C M Partners, 10250 Constellation Blvd, #900, Los Angeles CA 90067 USA
**Riley, Victor A** — Football Player
1430 Bavand Circle, #107, Rock Hill SC 29732, USA
**Riley, Victor J, Jr** — Financier
100 Elm St, Williamstown MA 01267, USA
**Riley, William (Bill)** — Ice Hockey Player
286 Buckingham Ave, Riverview NB E1B 2P2, Canada
**Riley, William J** — Judge
US Court of Appeals, Federal Building, PO Box 307, Omaha NE 68101, USA
**Rilling, Helmuth** — Conductor, Concert Organist
Opus 3 Artists, 470 Park Ave S, #900N, New York NY 10016 USA
**Rimer, Jeff** — Sportscaster
5454 Waxen Dr, Dublin OH 43016, USA
**Rimes, LeAnn** — Singer
PO Box 150667, Nashville TN 37215, USA
**Rimington, Dave B** — Football Player
125 W 110th St, #5A, New York NY 10026, USA
**Rimington, Stella** — Government Official, England
PO Box 1604, London SW1P 1XB, England
**Rimmel, James E** — Religious Leader
Evangelical Presbyterian Church, 26049 Five Mile Road, Redford MI 48239, USA

**Rinaldi, Kathy** — Tennis Player
Advantage International, 1025 Thomas Jefferson NW, #450, Washington DC 20007 USA
**Rinaldi, Richard P (Rich)** — Basketball Player
1117 Perry Lane, Collegeville PA 19426, USA
**Rincon, Juan M** — Baseball Player
5150 Lincoln Dr, Minneapolis MN 55436, USA
**Rinehart, Kenneth** — Chemist
University of Illinois, Chemistry Dept, Urbana IL 61801, USA
**Ring, R Royce** — Baseball Player
PO Box 2184, El Cajon CA 92021, USA
**Ring, Timothy M** — Businessman
C F Bard Co, 730 Central Ave, Murray Hill NJ 07974, USA
**Ringenberg, Jason** — Singer (Jason & the Scorchers)
Roughneck Music, 7553 Gannon Ave, Saint Louis MO 63130, USA
**Ringer, Jennifer** — Ballerina
New York City Ballet, Lincoln Center Plaza, New York NY 10023 USA
**Ringer, Noah** — Actor
Creative Artists Agency, 2000 Ave of Stars, #100, Los Angeles CA 90067 USA
**Ringgold, Faith** — Writer, Artist
Simon & Schuster, 1230 Ave of Americas, Concourse 1, New York NY 10020 USA
**Ringle, William M** — Anthropologist
Davidson College, Anthropolgy Dept, Chambers Hall, Davidson NC 28035, USA
**Ringwald, Molly** — Actress
Untitled Entertainment, 350 S Beverly Dr, #200, Beverly Hills CA 90212 USA
**Rinker, Laurie A** — Golfer
PO Box 550, Jensen Beach FL 34958, USA
**Rinker, Lee C** — Golfer
1151 Egret Circle S, #380, Jupiter FL 33458, USA
**Rinna, Lisa** — Actress, Model
Paradigm Agency, 360 N Crescent Dr, North Building, Beverly Hills CA 90210 USA
**Rinne, Pekka** — Ice Hockey Player
Nashville Predators, 501 Broadway, Nashville TN 37203 USA
**Rinsch, Carl** — Director, Producer, Writer
Brillstein Entertainment Partners, 9150 Wilshire Blvd, #350, Beverly Hills CA 90212 USA
**Rintoul, David** — Actor
Artists Partnership, 101 Finsbury Pavement, London EC2A 1RS, England
**Rintoul, Steve** — Golfer
17506 Osprey Manor Way, Lithia FL 33547, USA
**Rintzler, Marius A** — Opera Singer
Friedingstr 18, 40625 Dusseldorf, Germany
**Rinzler, Lisa** — Cinematographer
Gersh Agency, 9465 Wilshire Blvd, #600, Beverly Hills CA 90212 USA
**Riordan, Michael W (Mike)** — Basketball Player
140 Inwood Road, Stevensville MD 21666, USA
**Riordan, Richard J** — Mayor, Los Angeles
141 N Bristol Ave, Los Angeles CA 90049, USA
**Rios, Alberto** — Writer
Arizona State University, English Dept, Tempe AZ 85287, USA
**Rios, Armando** — Baseball Player
790 Ridenhour Circle, Orlando FL 32809, USA
**Rios, Brandon L** — Boxer
Top Rank Inc, 3908 Howard Hughes Parkway, #580, Las Vegas NV 89169 USA
**Rios, Daniel (Danny)** — Baseball Player
2523 W 9th Lane, Hialeah FL 33010, USA
**Rios, Emily** — Actress
Kass Management, 501 Santa Monica Blvd, #604, Los Angeles CA 90401, USA
**Rios, Marcelo** — Tennis Player
International Mgmt Group, Via Augusta 200, #400, 08021 Barcelona, Spain
**Rios, Mark** — Architect
Rios Clementi Hale Studios, 639 N Larchmont Blvd, #101, Los Angeles CA 90004, USA
**Rios, Susan** — Artist
Try Art Galleries, 3100 Porter St, Soquel CA 95073, USA
**Riotta, Vincent** — Actor
Untitled Entertainment, 350 S Beverly Dr, #200, Beverly Hills CA 90212 USA
**Rioux, Gerry** — Ice Hockey Player
213 Grosvenor, Ironquois Falls ON P0K 1G0, Canada
**Ripa, Kelly** — Actress, Model
Milojo Productions, 270 Lafayette St, #702, New York NY 10012, USA
**Ripert, Eric** — Chef
Le Bernardin, 787 7th Ave, Concourse 1, New York NY 10019, USA
**Ripken, Calvin E (Cal), Jr** — Baseball Player
1427 Clarkview Road, #100, Baltimore MD 21209, USA
**Ripken, William O (Bill)** — Baseball Player
900 Mount Soma Court, Fallston MD 21047, USA
**Ripley, Alice** — Actress, Singer
Thruline Entertainment, 9250 Wilshire Blvd, #100, Beverly Hills CA 90212 USA
**Rippey, Rodney Allan** — Actor
3941 Veselich Ave, #4-251, Los Angeles CA 90039, USA
**Ripple, Kenneth F** — Judge
US Court of Appeals, 204 S Main St, South Bend IN 46601, USA
**Rippy, Leon** — Actor
Greene Assoc, 1901 Ave of Stars, #130, Los Angeles CA 90067 USA
**Rippy, Nicolas** — Model
Wilhelmina Models, 300 Park Ave S, #200, New York NY 10010 USA
**Ris, Hans** — Zoologist
2116 Madison St, Madison WI 53711, USA
**RisCassi, Robert W** — Army General
Spectrum Group, 11 Canal Center Plaza, #103, Alexandria VA 22314, USA
**Riseborough, Andrea** — Actress
Independent Talent Group, 40 Whitfield St, London W1T 2RH, England
**Risebrough, Douglas J (Doug)** — Ice Hockey Player, Coach
77928 Grey Wolf Trail, La Quinta CA 92253, USA
**Risen, James** — Journalist
New York Times, Editorial Dept, 229 W 43rd St, New York NY 10036 USA
**Risien, Cody L** — Football Player
505 Bulian Lane, Austin TX 78746, USA

**Risley, William C (Bill)** — Baseball Player
1160 Prim Rose Circle, Greenwood AR 72936, USA

**Rison, Andre P** — Football Player
6293 N Jennings Road, Mount Morris MI 48458, USA

**Rispoli, Michael** — Actor
Principal Entertainment, 9255 Sunset Blvd, #500, Los Angeles CA 90069 USA

**Rissling, Gary** — Ice Hockey Player
7905 Tilmont Ave, Parkville MD 21234, USA

**Riszdorfer, Michal** — Canoeing Athlete
Bratislava Ul M Scho SKP, Trnasvkeho 2/A, 84446 Bratislava, Slovakia

**Riszdorfer, Richard** — Canoeing Athlete
Bratislava Ul M Scho SKP, Trnasvkeho 2/A, 84446 Bratislava, Slovakia

**Ritcher, James A (Jim)** — Football Player
8620 Bournemouth Dr, Raleigh NC 27615, USA

**Ritchie, Brian** — Bassist (Violent Femmes)
Good Feelings Artist Mgmt, PO Box 6632, Minneapolis MN 55406, USA

**Ritchie, Darren** — Actor
A P A Talent & Literary Agency, 405 S Beverly Dr, #300, Beverly Hills CA 90212 USA

**Ritchie, Guy** — Director
Creative Artists Agency, 2000 Ave of Stars, #100, Los Angeles CA 90067 USA

**Ritchie, Ian** — Architect
110 Three Colt St, London E14 8A2, England

**Ritchie, Jay S** — Baseball Player
8275 Highway 52, Rockwell NC 28138, USA

**Ritchie, Jean** — Singer, Dulcimer Player, Songwriter
Music Tree Artist Mgmt, 1414 Philadelphia Ave, Pittsburgh PA 15233, USA

**Ritchie, Jill** — Actress
Wallman Public Relations, 10323 Santa Monica Blvd, #109, Los Angeles CA 90025, USA

**Ritchie, Jim** — Sculptor
Adelson Galleries, Mark Hotel, 19 E 82nd St, New York NY 10028, USA

**Ritchie, John H** — Architect
Mount, Heswall, Wirral L60 4RD, England

**Ritchie, Jon D** — Football Player
6135 Log Cabin Trail, Enola PA 17025, USA

**Ritchie, Richard Stephen (Steve)** — Vietnam War Air Force Hero
4479 163rd Place SE, Bellevue WA 98006, USA

**Ritchie, Todd E** — Baseball Player
114 Hulan Dr, Kerens TX 75144, USA

**Ritchson, Alan** — Actor, Writer, Producer
AlleyCat Entertainment, 3400 Cahuenga Blvd W, Universal City CA 90068, USA

**Ritenour, Lee M** — Jazz Guitarist, Singer, Composer
11808 Dorothy St, #108, Los Angeles CA 90049, USA

**Ritger, Dick** — Bowler
804 Valley View Dr, River Falls WI 54022, USA

**Ritson, Blake** — Actor
Curtis Brown Group, 28-29 Haymarket St, #500, London SW1Y 4SP, England

**Rittenhouse, Lenore** — Golfer
295 Bellhaven Dr, Carthage NC 28327, USA

**Ritter, C Dowd** — Financier
AmSouth Bancorp, AmSouth Sonat Tower, 1900 5th Ave N, Birmingham AL 35203, USA

**Ritter, Jason** — Actor
I C M Partners, 730 5th Ave, New York NY 10019 USA

**Ritter, Josh** — Singer, Songwriter
Concerted Efforts, PO Box 440326, Somerville MA 02144 USA

**Ritter, Krysten** — Actress
Group Entertainment, 115 West 29th St, #1102, New York NY 10001, USA

**Ritter, Reggie B** — Baseball Player
1564 Estep Road, Donaldson AR 71941, USA

**Ritter, Tyson J** — Singer, Bassist (All-American Rejects)
Creative Artists Agency, 2000 Ave of Stars, #100, Los Angeles CA 90067 USA

**Rittinger, Al** — Ice Hockey Player
5423 Wallace Ave, Delta BC V4M 3V4, Canada

**Ritts, Jim** — Golf Executive
Ladies Pro Golf Assn, 100 International Golf Dr, Daytona Beach FL 32124 USA

**Ritz, Kevin D** — Baseball Player
68559 8th Street Road, Cambridge OH 43725, USA

**Ritzman, Alice** — Golfer
614 S Foys Lake Dr, Kalispell MT 59901, USA

**Riva, Diana-Maria** — Actress
Jonas Public Relations, 240 26th St, #3, Santa Monica CA 90402 USA

**Riva, Emmanuelle** — Actress, Photographer
Anne Alvares Correa, 34 Rue Jouffroy d'Abbans, 75017 Paris, France

**Rivaldo** — Soccer Player
F C Milan, Via Filippo Turati 3, 20121 Milan, Italy

**Rivas, Daniel Louis** — Actor, Producer
Pantheon Talent, 1801 Century Park E, #1910, Los Angeles CA 90067, USA

**Rivera Carrera, Norberto Cardinal** — Religious Leader
Archdiocese of Mexico, Apartado Postal 24-433, Durango 90, Col Roma, 06700 Mexico, DF, Mexico

**Rivera Mendoza, Zuleyka J** — Beauty Queen
Miss Universe Organization, 1370 Ave of Americas, #1600, New York NY 10019 USA

**Rivera Pedraza, Luis A** — Baseball Player
16 Calle Lazaro Ramos, Cidra PR 00739, USA

**Rivera, Ana Liz** — Actress
Televisa, Blvd A Lopez Mateos 232, Colonia San Angel, Mexico City DF 01060 CP, Mexico

**Rivera, Chita** — Actress, Singer, Dancer
Shopiro & Lobel, 220 W 42nd St, #1900, New York NY 10036, USA

**Rivera, Geraldo** — Entertainer
17 Annett Ave, Edgewater NJ 07020, USA

**Rivera, Jerry** — Singer
Alpha Artists International, 261 E 134th St, #200, Bronx NY 10454, USA

**Rivera, Jessica** — Opera Singer
I M G Artists, Hogarth Business Park, Chiswick, London W4 2TH, England

**Rivera, Jose** — Writer, Producer
I C M Partners, 10250 Constellation Blvd, #900, Los Angeles CA 90067 USA

**Rivera, Jose Antonio** — Boxer
7 Rodi Circle, Worcester MA 01603, USA

**Rivera, Manuel J (Jim)** — Baseball Player
2311 Abbey Dr, #7, Fort Wayne IN 46835, USA
**Rivera, Marco A** — Football Player
1854 Rue de Isabelle, Flower Mound TX 75022, USA
**Rivera, Mariano** — Baseball Player
147 Anderson Hill Road, Purchase NY 10577, USA
**Rivera, Michael** — Actor
Innovative Artists, 1505 10th St, Santa Monica CA 90401 USA
**Rivera, Michael R (Mike)** — Baseball Player
2814 Harwood Court, Kissimmee FL 34744, USA
**Rivera, Naya** — Actress
United Talent Agency, U T A Plaza, 9336 Civic Center Dr, Beverly Hills CA 90210 USA
**Rivera, Robert** — Artist
21 Sandia Lane, Placitas NM 87043, USA
**Rivera, Ronald E (Ron)** — Football Player, Coach
14420 Rancho del Prado Trail, San Diego CA 92127, USA
**Rivero, Jorge** — Actor
H David Moss, 733 Seward St, #PH, Los Angeles CA 90038 USA
**Rivers, Austin J** — Basketball Player
New Orleans Pelicans, 1250 Poydras St, #101, New Orleans LA 70113 USA
**Rivers, Glenn A (Doc)** — Basketball Player, Coach
5 Isle Of Sicily, Winter Park FL 32789, USA
**Rivers, J Milton (Mickey)** — Baseball Player
350 NW 48th St, Miami FL 33127, USA
**Rivers, Jamie A** — Football Player
40 Waterman Place, Saint Louis MO 63112, USA
**Rivers, Johnny** — Singer, Songwriter
3141 Coldwater Canyon Lane, Beverly Hills CA 90210, USA
**Rivers, Keith** — Football Player
Buffalo Bills, 1 Bills Dr, Orchard Park NY 14127 USA
**Rivers, Marcellus** — Football Player
12003 Eden Lane, Frisco TX 75034, USA
**Rivers, Melissa** — Actress, Producer
Larry Thompson Organization, 9663 Santa Monica Blvd, #801, Beverly Hills CA 90210, USA
**Rivers, Philip** — Football Player
San Diego Chargers, 4020 Murphy Canyon Road, San Diego CA 92123 USA
**Rivers, Reginald C (Reggie)** — Football Player
407 Corona St, Denver CO 80218, USA
**Rivers, Samuel R (Sam)** — Bassist (Limp Bizkit)
Flip/Interscope Records, 8733 Sunset Blvd, #205, West Hollywood CA 90069, USA
**Rivers, Wayne** — Ice Hockey Player
7736 Cedar Lake Ave, San Diego CA 92119, USA
**Rives, Donald E (Don)** — Football Player
4910 Oldfield Dr, Arlington TX 76016, USA
**Rivest, Ronald L** — Computer Scientist
Massachusetts Institute of Technology, Electrical Engineering Dept, Cambridge MA 02139, USA
**Riviere, Jean-Max** — Composer
6 Rue Choron, 75009 Paris, France
**Rivlin, Alice M** — Government Official
2842 Chesterfield Place, Washington DC 20008, USA
**Rivlin, Reuven (Ruvi)** — President, Israel
President's Office, Beit Hanassi, 3 Hanassi St, Jerusalem 92188, Israel
**Rix, J Simon** — Bassist (Kaiser Chiefs)
Red Light Mgmt, 8439 Sunset Blvd, West Hollywood CA 90069, USA
**Rizzi, Darren** — Football Player, Coach
University of Rhode Island, Athletic Dept, Kingston RI 02881, USA
**Rizzo, Joseph V (Joe)** — Football Player
6131 Dorsett Place, Wilmington NC 28403, USA
**Rizzo, Michael (Mike)** — DJ Musician
T-Best Talent Agency, 508 Honey Lake Court, Danville CA 94506 USA
**Rizzo, Patrice (Patti)** — Golfer
1033 NE 17th Way, #2004, Fort Lauderdale FL 33304, USA
**Rizzo, Todd M** — Baseball Player
7 Williamsburg Court, Sewell NJ 08080, USA
**Rizzo, Willy** — Photographer, Furniture Designer
Paul Smith Gallery, 9 Albermarle St, London W1S 4BL, England
**Rizzotti, Jennifer** — Basketball Player, Coach
University of Hartford, Athletic Dept, West Hartford CT 06117, USA
**Rizzuto, Garth** — Ice Hockey Player
109 13th Ave S, Cranbrook BC B1C 2V6, Canada
**Roa, Joseph R (Joe)** — Baseball Player
677 E Brickley Ave, Hazel Park MI 48030, USA
**Roach, Jay** — Director
Everyman Pictures, 1512 16th St, #3, Santa Monica CA 90404, USA
**Roach, John G** — Football Player
4101 San Carlos St, Dallas TX 75205, USA
**Roach, Melvin E (Mel)** — Baseball Player
4131 Southhaven Road, Richmond VA 23235, USA
**Roach, Steve** — Musician
Hearts of Space, PO Box 5916, Sausalito CA 94966, USA
**Roache, Linus** — Actor
I C M Partners, 10250 Constellation Blvd, #900, Los Angeles CA 90067 USA
**Roaches, Carl E** — Football Player
1314 Twining Oaks Lane, Missouri City. TX 77489, USA
**Roaf, William L (Willie)** — Football Player
208 Cypress Bayou Lane, Kenner LA 70065, USA
**Roan, Michael P** — Football Player
11275 Green Valley Road, Sebastopol CA 95472, USA
**Roark, Terry P** — Educator
1752 Edward Dr, Laramie WY 82072, USA
**Roarke, Michael T (Mike)** — Baseball Player
940 Quaker Lane, #2302, East Greenwich RI 02818, USA
**Robards, Jake** — Actor
Don Buchwald Talent Agency, 10 E 44th St, New York NY 10017 USA
**Robards, Karen** — Writer
Pocket Books, 1230 Ave of Americas, New York NY 10020 USA

| | |
|---|---|
| **Robards, Sam** | Actor |
| Paradigm Agency, 360 N Crescent Dr, North Building, Beverly Hills CA 90210 USA | |
| **Robb, AnnaSophia** | Actress |
| Creative Artists Agency, 2000 Ave of Stars, #100, Los Angeles CA 90067 USA | |
| **Robb, Charles S** | Governor, Senator, VA |
| George Mason University, Law School, 3301 N Fairfax Dr, Arlington VA 22201, USA | |
| **Robb, David** | Actor |
| Hobson's International, 62 Chiswick High Road, London W4 1SY, England | |
| **Robb, Douglas (Doug)** | Singer (Hoobastank) |
| Creative Artists Agency, 2000 Ave of Stars, #100, Los Angeles CA 90067 USA | |
| **Robb, Peter** | Writer |
| Bloomsbury Publishing, 50 Bedford Square, London WC1B 3DP, England | |
| **Robb, Walter L** | Businessman, Inventor |
| 1358 Ruffner Road, Schenectady NY 12309, USA | |
| **Robbie, Margot** | Actress |
| Creative Artists Agency, 2000 Ave of Stars, #100, Los Angeles CA 90067 USA | |
| **Robbins, Austin D** | Football Player |
| 4627 Hilltop Terrace SE, Washington DC 20019, USA | |
| **Robbins, Barret G** | Football Player |
| 27246 Valderrama Dr, Valencia CA 91381, USA | |
| **Robbins, Brian** | Director, Producer, Actor |
| Varsity Pictures, 1040 N Las Palmas Ave, Building 2, Los Angeles CA 90038, USA | |
| **Robbins, Deanna** | Actress |
| 630 N Keystone St, Burbank CA 91506, USA | |
| **Robbins, Jake** | Baseball Player |
| 14208 Castle Abbey Lane, Charlotte NC 28277, USA | |
| **Robbins, James E (Tootie)** | Football Player |
| 3600 W Ray Road, #1031, Chandler AZ 85226, USA | |
| **Robbins, Jane** | Actress |
| Scott Marshall Mgmt, 44 Perry Road, London W3 7NA, England | |
| **Robbins, Kelly** | Golfer |
| 1025 Lincoln Dr, Weidman MI 48893, USA | |
| **Robbins, Randy** | Football Player |
| 583 E Palo Verde St, Casa Grande AZ 85122, USA | |
| **Robbins, Tim** | Actor, Director |
| Actor's Gang, 9070 Venice Blvd, Culver City CA 90232, USA | |
| **Robbins, Tom** | Writer |
| PO Box 338, La Conner WA 98257, USA | |
| **Robelot, Jane** | Commentator |
| CBS-TV, News Dept, 51 W 52nd St, New York NY 10019 USA | |
| **Roberge, Bertrand R (Bert)** | Baseball Player |
| 267 Sunderland Dr, Auburn ME 04210, USA | |
| **Roberge, Kalyna** | Speed Skater |
| Speed Skating Canada, 2781 Lancaster Road, #402, Ottawa ON K1B 1A7, Canada | |
| **Roberson, Antoinette** | Singer, Songwriter, Record Producer |
| Diva Central, 7510 W Sunset Blvd, #1445, Los Angeles CA 90046 USA | |
| **Roberson, James W** | Cinematographer |
| PO Box 121013, Big Bear Lake CA 92315, USA | |
| **Roberson, Rick** | Basketball Player |
| 635 W West Ave, Fullerton CA 92832, USA | |
| **Robert, Alain (Spiderman)** | Rock, Urban Climber |
| Maverick House Publishing, Dunboyne Business Park, Dunboyne, County Meath, Ireland | |
| **Robert, Jacques F** | Attorney, Educator |
| 14 Villa Saint-Georges, 92160 Antony, France | |
| **Robert, Rene P** | Ice Hockey Player |
| 8-5490 Glen Erin Dr, Mississauga ON L5M 5R4, Canada | |
| **Roberto, Phillip J (Phil)** | Ice Hockey Player |
| 5238 Ottawa Ave, Niagara Falls ON L2E 4Y8, Canada | |
| **Roberts, Alfredo** | Football Player |
| 4001 Tolbert Place, Carmel IN 46074, USA | |
| **Roberts, Ashley** | Singer (Pussycat Dolls), Actress |
| A K A Talent, 6310 San Vicente Blvd, #200, Los Angeles CA 90048 USA | |
| **Roberts, Bernard** | Concert Pianist |
| Uwchlaw'r Coed, Llanbedr, Gwynedd LL45 2NA, Wales | |
| **Roberts, Bradley K (Brad)** | Singer, Guitarist (Crash Test Dummies) |
| Agency Group Ltd, 142 W 57th St, #600, New York NY 10019 USA | |
| **Roberts, Brian L** | Businessman |
| Comcast Corp, 1500 Market St, #800W, Philadelphia PA 19102, USA | |
| **Roberts, Brian M** | Baseball Player |
| 11326 E Mimosa Dr, Scottsdale AZ 85262, USA | |
| **Roberts, Bruce** | Singer, Songwriter |
| Gorfaine/Schwartz, 4111 W Alameda Ave, #509, Burbank CA 91505 USA | |
| **Roberts, Cecil** | Labor Leader |
| United Mine Workers, 8315 Lee Highway, #500, Fairfax VA 22031, USA | |
| **Roberts, Chris** | Singer, Actor |
| C R Promotion, Postfach 1254, 51582 Numbrecht, Germany | |
| **Roberts, Corrine (Cookie)** | Commentator |
| 5315 Bradley Blvd, Bethesda MD 20814, USA | |
| **Roberts, Craig** | Actor |
| W M E Entertainment, 9601 Wilshire Blvd, #300, Beverly Hills CA 90210 USA | |
| **Roberts, Dallas** | Actor |
| United Talent Agency, U T A Plaza, 9336 Civic Center Dr, Beverly Hills CA 90210 USA | |
| **Roberts, Dan** | Bassist (Crash Test Dummies) |
| Agency Group Ltd, 142 W 57th St, #600, New York NY 10019 USA | |
| **Roberts, David (Dave)** | Track Athlete |
| 14310 SW 73rd Ave, Archer FL 32618, USA | |
| **Roberts, David L (Dave)** | Ice Hockey Player |
| 43690 Algonquin Dr, #26, Novi MI 48375, USA | |
| **Roberts, David L (Dave)** | Baseball Player |
| 9705 Sam Bass Trail, Keller TX 76244, USA | |
| **Roberts, David R (Dave)** | Baseball Player |
| 1208 Crestview Dr, Cardiff by the Sea CA 92007, USA | |
| **Roberts, David W (Dave)** | Baseball Player |
| 6937 Laurel Valley Dr, Fort Worth TX 76132, USA | |
| **Roberts, Dee** | Artist |
| 2012 N 19th St, Boise ID 83702, USA | |

**R**

**Robards - Roberts**

**Roberts, Doris** — Actress
6225 Quebec Dr, Los Angeles CA 90068, USA

**Roberts, Emma R** — Actress, Singer
Sweeney Entertainment, 6253 Hollywood Blvd, #201, Los Angeles CA 90028, USA

**Roberts, Eric A** — Actor
Sovereign Talent Group, 8421 Wilshire Blvd, #200, Beverly Hills CA 90211, USA

**Roberts, Eugene L (Gene), Jr** — Editor, Historian
University of Maryland, Journalism Dept, College Park MD 20742, USA

**Roberts, Eugene L, Jr** — Editor
New York Times, Editorial Dept, 229 W 43rd St, New York NY 10036, USA

**Roberts, Frederick C (Fred)** — Basketball Player
463 Knight Circle, Alpine UT 84004, USA

**Roberts, Gary** — Ice Hockey Player
2095 Lake Shore Blvd, Toronto ON M8V 4G4, Canada

**Roberts, Gordon R** — Vietnam War Army Hero (CMH)
445 Ward-Koebel Road, Oregonia OH 45054, USA

**Roberts, Ian** — Actor
W M E Entertainment, 9601 Wilshire Blvd, #300, Beverly Hills CA 90210 USA

**Roberts, Jake (The Snake)** — Professional Wrestler
Prince Marketing Group, 18 Carillon Circle, Livingston NJ 07039 USA

**Roberts, James A (Jim)** — Ice Hockey Player, Coach
137 Ridgecrest Dr, Chesterfield MO 63017, USA

**Roberts, John** — Director
Creative Artists Agency, 2000 Ave of Stars, #100, Los Angeles CA 90067 USA

**Roberts, John** — Chief Justice, Supreme Court
US Supreme Court, 1st St NE, Washington DC 20543, USA

**Roberts, John** — Commentator
CBS-TV, News Dept, 51 W 52nd St, New York NY 10019 USA

**Roberts, John D** — Chemist
California Institute of Technology, Crellin Laboratory, Pasadena CA 91125, USA

**Roberts, John D (J D)** — Football Player, Coach
6708 Trevi Court, Oklahoma City OK 73116, USA

**Roberts, Jonathan** — Dancer
Abrams Artists, 9200 W Sunset Blvd, #1125, West Hollywood CA 90069 USA

**Roberts, Jordan** — Director, Writer, Actor
Creative Artists Agency, 2000 Ave of Stars, #100, Los Angeles CA 90067 USA

**Roberts, Joseph (Joe)** — Basketball Player
10975 Elvessa St, Oakland CA 94605, USA

**Roberts, Julia** — Actress
Creative Artists Agency, 2000 Ave of Stars, #100, Los Angeles CA 90067 USA

**Roberts, Julie** — Singer
Ron Shapiro Mgmt, 56 W 22nd St, #600S, New York NY 10010, USA

**Roberts, Kenny** — Motorcycle Racing Rider
K R Marketing, 419 Medina Road, Medina OH 44256, USA

**Roberts, Kevin J** — Businessman
Saatchi & Saatchi Worldwide, 375 Hudson St, Basement 3, New York NY 10014, USA

**Roberts, Larry** — Sculptor
PO Box 663, Bandon OR 97411, USA

**Roberts, Lawrence G** — Computer Scientist, Engineer
Caspian Networks, 170 Baytech Dr, San Jose CA 95134, USA

**Roberts, Leon J (Bip)** — Baseball Player
PO Box 170299, Arlington TX 76003, USA

**Roberts, Leon K** — Baseball Player
4711 Chapel Springs Court, Arlington TX 76017, USA

**Roberts, Leonard** — Actor
Luber Rocklin Entertainment, 5815 Sunset Blvd, #206, Los Angeles CA 90028 USA

**Roberts, Loren** — Golfer
8429 Orchard Hill Dr, Germantown TN 38138, USA

**Roberts, Lynn** — Singer, Actress
42 Vespers Way, Okatie SC 29909, USA

**Roberts, M Brigitte** — Writer
Gillon Atkin, 29 Fernshaw Road, London SW10 0TG, England

**Roberts, Marcus** — Jazz Pianist
R C A Records, 8750 Wilshire Blvd, Beverly Hills CA 90211 USA

**Roberts, Marvin J (Marv)** — Basketball Player
6202 Carriage Gate Lane SE, Mableton GA 30126, USA

**Roberts, Michele** — Writer
Henry Holt, 175 5th Ave, #400, New York NY 10010 USA

**Roberts, Nicola M** — Singer (Girls Aloud)
Concorde International, 101 Shepherds Bush Road, London W6 7LP, England

**Roberts, Nora** — Writer
19239 Burnside Bridge Road, Keedysville MD 21756, USA

**Roberts, Patricia (Trish)** — Basketball Player
218 Carver Dr, Monroe GA 30655, USA

**Roberts, Paul H** — Mathematician
PO Box 951567, Los Angeles CA 90095, USA

**Roberts, R Michael** — Animal Scientist
2213 Hominy Branch Court, Columbia MO 65201, USA

**Roberts, R Ray, Jr** — Football Player
2040 Via Florence Road, Charlottesville VA 22911, USA

**Roberts, Richard J** — Nobel Medicine Laureate
New England Biolabs, 240 County Road, Ipswich MA 01938, USA

**Roberts, Richard L** — Educator
Oral Roberts University, President's Office, 7777 S Lewis Ave, Tulsa OK 74171, USA

**Roberts, Rick** — Actor
Gary Goddard Agency, 10 Sainte Mary's St, #305, Toronto ON M4Y 5QD, Canada

**Roberts, Robin** — Sportscaster, Commentator
ESPN-TV, Sports Dept, ESPN Plaza, 935 Middle St, Bristol CT 06010 USA

**Roberts, Ryan A** — Baseball Player
6017 Avalon St, North Richland Hills TX 76180, USA

**Roberts, Sam** — Singer
Agency Group Ltd, 142 W 57th St, #600, New York NY 10019 USA

**Roberts, Shawn** — Actor
Gersh Agency, 9465 Wilshire Blvd, #600, Beverly Hills CA 90212 USA

**Roberts, Stanley C** — Basketball Player
1192 Congaree Road, Hopkins SC 29061, USA

**Roberts, Stephen**                                          Opera Singer
I M G Artists, Hogarth Business Park, Chiswick, London W4 2TH, England
**Roberts, Tanya**                                                  Actress
Good Guy Entertainment, 3733 Oakfield Dr, Sherman Oaks CA 91423, USA
**Roberts, Tiffany**                                          Soccer Player
2772 Ascot Dr, San Ramon CA 94583, USA
**Roberts, Tony**                                                     Actor
970 Park Ave, #8N, New York NY 10028, USA
**Roberts, Walter (Walt)**                                Football Player
268 Kenbrook Circle, San Jose CA 95111, USA
**Roberts, William H (Bill)**                              Football Player
18520 NW 67th Ave, #141, Hialeah FL 33015, USA
**Roberts, Willis A**                                       Baseball Player
11501 Harts Road, Jacksonville FL 32218, USA
**Roberts, Xavier**                              Businessman, Doll Designer
PO Box 1438, Cleveland GA 30528, USA
**Robertson of Port Ellen, George I M**          Government Official, England
House of Lords, Westminster, London SW1A 0PW, England
**Robertson, Alvin C**                                    Basketball Player
2919 Biering Peak, San Antonio TX 78247, USA
**Robertson, Andre L**                                      Baseball Player
2229 Cross Lane, Orange TX 77630, USA
**Robertson, Belinda**                                    Fashion Designer
B R Cashmere, 22 Palmerston Place, Edinburgh EH12 5AL, Scotland
**Robertson, Brittany (Britt)**                                    Actress
Innovative Artists, 1505 10th St, Santa Monica CA 90401 USA
**Robertson, Daryl B**                                      Baseball Player
52 Princeton Dr, Midvale UT 84047, USA
**Robertson, David**                                             Conductor
Opus 3 Artists, 470 Park Ave S, #900N, New York NY 10016 USA
**Robertson, David A**                                      Baseball Player
New York Yankees, Yankee Stadium, E 161st St & River Ave, Bronx NY 10451 USA
**Robertson, Davis**                                                 Dancer
Joffrey Ballet, 70 E Lake St, #1300, Chicago IL 60601, USA
**Robertson, DeWayne**                                      Football Player
26 Green St, Newbury MA 01951, USA
**Robertson, Donald A (Don)**                               Baseball Player
5715 W Monte Vista Road, Phoenix AZ 85035, USA
**Robertson, Ed**                        Guitarist (Barenaked Ladies), Songwriter
Nettwerk Mgmt, 6525 W Sunset Blvd, #800, Los Angeles CA 90028 USA
**Robertson, Finlay**                                                 Actor
Independent Talent Group, 40 Whitfield St, London W1T 2RH, England
**Robertson, Geordie**                                     Ice Hockey Player
1 Scarborough Park, Rochester NY 14625, USA
**Robertson, Isiah B**                                      Football Player
8005 Saint Fillans Lane, Rowlett TX 75089, USA
**Robertson, Jenny**                                                Actress
Shelter Entertainment, 9255 Sunset Blvd, #300, Los Angeles CA 90069 USA
**Robertson, Joseph E, Jr**                       Ophthalmologist, Educator
Oregon Health Science University, President's Office, Portland OR 97201, USA
**Robertson, Kathleen**                                            Actress
Noble Caplan Abrams, 1260 Yonge St, #200, Toronto ON M4T 1W6, Canada
**Robertson, Kimmy**                                               Actress
Innovative Artists, 1505 10th St, Santa Monica CA 90401 USA
**Robertson, Leslie E**                                 Structural Engineer
100 Riverside Blvd, #18D, New York NY 10069, USA
**Robertson, M G (Pat)**                                        Evangelist
Christian Broadcast Network, 100 Centerville Turnpike, Virginia Beach VA 23463, USA
**Robertson, Marcus A**                                     Football Player
39534 Danielle Dr, Northville MI 48167, USA
**Robertson, Mike**                                     Snowboarding Athlete
Snowboard Federation, 301-333 Terminal Ave, Vancouver BC V6A 4C1, Canada
**Robertson, Nathan D (Nate)**                              Baseball Player
7918 W 53rd St N, Maize KS 67101, USA
**Robertson, Oscar P**                                     Basketball Player
621 Tusculum Ave, Cincinnati OH 45226, USA
**Robertson, Richard P (Rich)**                             Baseball Player
1201 Crescent Terrace, Sunnyvale CA 94087, USA
**Robertson, Richard W (Rich)**                             Baseball Player
32202 Sandwedge Dr, Waller TX 77484, USA
**Robertson, Robbie**                    Singer, Guitarist (Band); Songwriter
Special Artists Agency, 9200 Sunset Blvd, #410, West Hollywood CA 90069 USA
**Robertson, Robert E (Bob)**                               Baseball Player
10015 Shinnamon Dr SW, Cumberland MD 21502, USA
**Robertson, Ruth**                                     Artist, Photographer
22804 Goldsborough Terrace, Ashburn VA 20148, USA
**Robertson, Shirley A**                                       Yachtswoman
Lynx Sports Mgmt, Lymington Road, Lymington, Hampshire SO41 5S5, England
**Roberts-Smith, Benjamin**                     Afghanistan War Air Hero (VC)
Victoria Cross Assn, Old Admiralty Building, London SW1A 2BL, England
**Robes, Ernest C (Bill)**                                        Ski Jumper
3 Mile Road, Etna NH 03750, USA
**Robey, Frederick R (Rick)**                             Basketball Player
2108 Club Vista Place, Louisville KY 40245, USA
**Robidoux, William J (Billy Joe)**                         Baseball Player
2 King George Dr, Ware MA 01082, USA
**Robillard, Michael J (Duke)**                  Guitarist, Orchestra Leader
Rosebud Agency, PO Box 170429, San Francisco CA 94117 USA
**Robin, Cynthia**                                            Archaeologist
Northwestern University, Anthropology Dept, 1812 Hillman, Evanston IL 60208, USA
**Robin, Janet**                                          Singer, Guitarist
Little Sister Records, PO Box 351715, Los Angeles CA 90035, USA
**Robin, Muriel**                                                  Actress
Voyez Mon Agent, 20 Ave Rapp, 75007 Paris, France
**Robins, Craig**                                             Businessman
Dacra Development Corp, 3841 NE 2nd Ave, #400, Miami FL 33137, USA

V.I.P. Address Book

R

Roberts - Robins

# R

| | |
|---|---|
| **Robins, Laila**<br>Paradigm Agency, 360 N Crescent Dr, North Building, Beverly Hills CA 90210 USA | Actress |
| **Robinson Peete, Holly**<br>Innovative Artists, 1505 10th St, Santa Monica CA 90401 USA | Actress |
| **Robinson, Adam M, Jr**<br>C N A Solutions, 3003 Washington Blvd, Arlington VA 22201, USA | Navy Admiral, Surgeon |
| **Robinson, Alex J**<br>Agency Group Ltd, 142 W 57th St, #600, New York NY 10019 USA | Singer, Songwriter |
| **Robinson, Alexia**<br>Heylee Winters Assoc, 8491 W Sunset Blvd, #268, West Hollywood CA 90069, USA | Actress |
| **Robinson, Andrew J**<br>2671 Byron Place, Los Angeles CA 90046, USA | Actor |
| **Robinson, Ann**<br>1357 Elysian Park Dr, Los Angeles CA 90026, USA | Actress |
| **Robinson, Anne**<br>Penrose Media, 19 Victoria Grove, London W8 5RW, England | Entertainer |
| **Robinson, Brooks C**<br>9210 Baltimore National Pike, Ellicot MD 21042, USA | Baseball Player |
| **Robinson, Bruce**<br>Paradigm Agency, 360 N Crescent Dr, North Building, Beverly Hills CA 90210 USA | Writer, Actor, Director |
| **Robinson, Bruce P**<br>1310 Dellcrest Lane, La Jolla CA 92037, USA | Baseball Player |
| **Robinson, Charles**<br>Stone Manners Salners, 6100 Wilshire Blvd, #1500, Los Angeles CA 90035 USA | Actor |
| **Robinson, Chip**<br>3034 Lake Forest Dr, Augusta GA 30909, USA | Auto Racing Driver |
| **Robinson, Chris**<br>Daniel Hoff Agency, 5455 Wilshire Blvd, #1100, Los Angeles CA 90036, USA | Actor |
| **Robinson, Christopher M (Chris)**<br>Paradigm Agency, 404 W Franklin St, Monterey CA 93940, USA | Singer, Guitarist (Black Crowes) |
| **Robinson, Clarence (Arnie)**<br>2904 Ocean View Blvd, San Diego CA 92113, USA | Track Athlete |
| **Robinson, Clifford R**<br>702 Sandia Place, Franklin Lakes NJ 07417, USA | Basketball Player |
| **Robinson, Clifford T (Cliff)**<br>98 S Bardsbrook Circle, Spring TX 77382, USA | Basketball Player |
| **Robinson, Craig**<br>3 Arts Entertainment, 9460 Wilshire Blvd, #700, Beverly Hills CA 90212 USA | Actor, Comedian |
| **Robinson, Craig G**<br>648 Picketts Mill Dr, Shreveport LA 71115, USA | Baseball Player |
| **Robinson, David M**<br>PO Box 691207, San Antonio TX 78269, USA | Basketball Player |
| **Robinson, Dawn S**<br>Creative Artists Agency, 2000 Ave of Stars, #100, Los Angeles CA 90067 USA | Singer (En Vogue, Lucy Pearl) |
| **Robinson, Don A**<br>1215 86th Court NW, Bradenton FL 34209, USA | Baseball Player |
| **Robinson, Doug**<br>6 Tiffany Court, Saint Catherines ON L2M 7N3, Canada | Ice Hockey Player |
| **Robinson, E Rafael**<br>4312 Forest Hill Circle, Forest Hill TX 76140, USA | Football Player |
| **Robinson, Eddie J**<br>6315 E Mystic Meadow, Houston TX 77021, USA | Football Player |
| **Robinson, Emily Erwin**<br>Strategic Artists Mgmt, 1100 Glendon Ave, #1100, Los Angeles CA 90024, USA | Singer (Dixie Chicks); Songwriter |
| **Robinson, Fatima**<br>PO Box 833, 8306 Wilshire Blvd, Beverly Hills CA 90213, USA | Dancer, Choreographer, Video Director |
| **Robinson, Floyd A**<br>PO Box 152419, San Diego CA 92195, USA | Baseball Player |
| **Robinson, Frank**<br>15557 Aqua Verde Dr, Los Angeles CA 90077, USA | Baseball Player, Manager |
| **Robinson, Fred C**<br>Yale University, English Dept, New Haven CT 06520, USA | Educator |
| **Robinson, Gerald**<br>4708 Scarborough Place, Stone Mountain GA 30087, USA | Football Player |
| **Robinson, Glenn**<br>Franklin & Marshall College, Athletic Dept, Lancaster PA 17604, USA | Basketball Coach |
| **Robinson, Glenn A, III**<br>Minnesota Timberwolves, Target Center, 600 1st Ave N, Minneapolis MN 55403 USA | Basketball Player |
| **Robinson, Greg**<br>Saint Louis Rams, 901 N Broadway, Saint Louis MO 63101 USA | Football Player |
| **Robinson, Ivan**<br>140 W Roselyn St, Philadelphia PA 19120, USA | Boxer |
| **Robinson, Jackie**<br>130 W Harcourt St, Long Beach CA 90805, USA | Basketball Player |
| **Robinson, James P (Jimmy)**<br>4326 Fox Hollow Court, Oneida WI 54155, USA | Football Player |
| **Robinson, Janice**<br>Nene Musik Productions, 1460 SW Santiago Ave, Port Saint Lucie FL 34953 USA | Singer (Livin' Joy) |
| **Robinson, Jeffrey D (Jeff)**<br>27 Weber Lane, Trabuco Canyon CA 92679, USA | Baseball Player |
| **Robinson, Jeffrey W (Jeff)**<br>1020 W Ruffner St, Seattle WA 98119, USA | Football Player |
| **Robinson, Jerry D**<br>2398 Julio Lane, Santa Rosa CA 95401, USA | Football Player |
| **Robinson, John**<br>Paradigm Agency, 360 N Crescent Dr, North Building, Beverly Hills CA 90210 USA | Actor |
| **Robinson, John A**<br>1513 Village View Road, Encinitas CA 92024, USA | Football Coach |
| **Robinson, Johnny N**<br>3209 S Grand St, Monroe LA 71202, USA | Football Player |
| **Robinson, Keith D**<br>A P A Talent & Literary Agency, 405 S Beverly Dr, #300, Beverly Hills CA 90212 USA | Actor, Singer |
| **Robinson, Ken**<br>Washington Speakers Bureau, 1663 Prince St, Alexandria VA 22314, USA | Educator |
| **Robinson, Kerry K**<br>133 Vlasis Dr, Ballwin MO 63011, USA | Baseball Player |

**Robins - Robinson**

826

| | |
|---|---|
| **Robinson, Koren** | Football Player |
| 6735 Middleboro Dr, Raleigh NC 27612, USA | |
| **Robinson, Larry** | Ice Hockey Player, Coach |
| 10709 Winding Stream Way, Bradenton FL 34212, USA | |
| **Robinson, Larry C (Bumper), II** | Actor |
| Mathews Management, 8730 Sunset Blvd, #200, Los Angeles CA 90069, USA | |
| **Robinson, Laura** | Actress |
| Henderson/Hogan, 850 7th Ave, #1003, New York NY 10019 USA | |
| **Robinson, Marcus A** | Football Player |
| PO Box 1924, Fort Valley GA 31030, USA | |
| **Robinson, Marilynne** | Writer |
| University of Iowa, Iowa Writers' Workshop, Dey House, Iowa City IA 52242, USA | |
| **Robinson, Mark L** | Football Player |
| 303 Pennsylvania Ave, Palm Harbor FL 34683, USA | |
| **Robinson, Mark R** | Singer, Guitarist (Unrest, Grenadine) |
| Go Ahead Booking, PO Box 5068, Hoboken NJ 07030, USA | |
| **Robinson, Mary T W** | President, Ireland |
| Aras an Uachtarain, Phoenix Park, Dublin 8, Ireland | |
| **Robinson, Matthew (Matt)** | Director, Producer |
| M C S Agency, 47 Dean St, London W1D 5BE, England | |
| **Robinson, Matthew G (Matt)** | Football Player |
| 12374 Mandarin Road, Jacksonville FL 32223, USA | |
| **Robinson, Melvin D (Bo)** | Football Player |
| PO Box 2323, Coppell TX 75019, USA | |
| **Robinson, Morris** | Singer |
| Opus 3 Artists, 470 Park Ave S, #900N, New York NY 10016 USA | |
| **Robinson, Nathaniel C (Nate)** | Basketball Player |
| Chicago Bulls, United Center, 1901 W Madison St, Chicago IL 60612 USA | |
| **Robinson, Nick** | Actor |
| Savage Agency, 6212 Banner Ave, Los Angeles CA 90038 USA | |
| **Robinson, Nicole** | Actress |
| Stone Manners Salners, 6100 Wilshire Blvd, #1500, Los Angeles CA 90035 USA | |
| **Robinson, Oliver L** | Basketball Player |
| 9640 Eastpointe Circle, Birmingham AL 35217, USA | |
| **Robinson, Patrick** | Fashion Designer |
| Gap Inc, 2 Folsom St, San Francisco CA 94105, USA | |
| **Robinson, Patrick** | Writer |
| Harper Collins Publishers, 10 E 53rd St, Cellar 1, New York NY 10022 USA | |
| **Robinson, Paul H** | Football Player |
| 1303 W 26th St, Safford AZ 85546, USA | |
| **Robinson, Phil Alden** | Director, Writer |
| Academy of Motion Picture Arts & Sciences, 8949 Wilshire Blvd, Beverly Hills CA 90211, USA | |
| **Robinson, R David (Dave)** | Football Player |
| 406 S Rose Blvd, Akron OH 44320, USA | |
| **Robinson, Randall** | Social Activist, Writer |
| African American Registry, PO Box 19441, Minneapolis MN 55419, USA | |
| **Robinson, Richard S (Rich)** | Guitarist (Black Crowes), Songwriter |
| Monterey International, 200 W Superior St, #202, Chicago IL 60654 USA | |
| **Robinson, Rob** | Ice Hockey Player |
| 23466 Greening Dr, Novi MI 48375, USA | |
| **Robinson, Ronald D (Ron)** | Baseball Player |
| 3128 E Race Ave, Visalia CA 93292, USA | |
| **Robinson, Ronnie** | Basketball Player |
| 4169 S Germantown Road, Memphis TN 38125, USA | |
| **Robinson, Shawna** | Auto, Truck Racing Driver |
| Performance One, 545 Pitts School Road NW, #C, Concord NC 28027, USA | |
| **Robinson, Shelton D** | Football Player |
| 18725 20th Dr SE, Bothell WA 98012, USA | |
| **Robinson, Smokey** | Singer, Songwriter |
| Podwall Entertainment, 710 N Orlando Ave, #203, West Hollywood CA 90069, USA | |
| **Robinson, Stephen K** | Astronaut |
| 286 Cottage Circle, Davis CA 95616, USA | |
| **Robinson, Thomas E** | Basketball Player |
| Portland Trail Blazers, Rose Garden, 1 N Center Court St, Portland OR 97227 USA | |
| **Robinson, Todd** | Director, Producer, Writer |
| Paradigm Agency, 360 N Crescent Dr, North Building, Beverly Hills CA 90210 USA | |
| **Robinson, Twyla** | Opera Singer |
| Columbia Artists Mgmt Inc, 5 Columbus Circle, 1790 Broadway, #1600, New York NY 10019 USA | |
| **Robinson, V Gene** | Religious Leader |
| Diocesan House, 63 Green St, Concord NH 03301, USA | |
| **Robinson, W Dunta** | Football Player |
| 485 Vincent Dr, Athens GA 30607, USA | |
| **Robinson, W Edward (Eddie)** | Baseball Player |
| 6104 Cholla Dr, Fort Worth TX 76112, USA | |
| **Robinson, Wayne L** | Football Player |
| 2341 Main Highway, Breaux Bridge LA 70517, USA | |
| **Robinson, Wendy Raquel** | Actress |
| TalentWorks, 3500 W Olive Ave, #1400, Burbank CA 91505 USA | |
| **Robinson, Zuleikha** | Actress |
| Gersh Agency, 41 Madison Ave, #3301, New York NY 10010 USA | |
| **Robisch, David G (Dave)** | Basketball Player |
| 1401 Guemes Court, Springfield IL 62702, USA | |
| **Robiskie, Terry J** | Football Player, Coach |
| 2802 Tree Park Circle, Flowery Branch GA 30542, USA | |
| **Robison, Charles F (Charlie)** | Singer, Songwriter |
| S H O Artists, 864 Pinnacle Hill Road, Kingston Springs TN 37082, USA | |
| **Robison, Paula** | Concert Flutist |
| Musicians Corporate Mgmt, PO Box 825, Highland NY 12528, USA | |
| **Robitaille, Luc** | Ice Hockey Player, Executive |
| 1750 14th St, #D, Santa Monica CA 90404, USA | |
| **Robitaille, Mike** | Ice Hockey Player |
| 121 Ransom Oaks Dr, East Amherst NY 14051, USA | |
| **Robitaille, Pat** | Singer, Songwriter |
| Agency Group Ltd, 142 W 57th St, #600, New York NY 10019 USA | |
| **Robitaille, Randy** | Ice Hockey Player |
| 632 Seyton Dr, Nepean ON K2H 7X5, Canada | |

**Robles Ortega, Francisco Cardinal** — Religious Leader
Archbishop of Guadalajara, Apartado 1-331, Calle Liceo 17, 44100 Guadalajara, Jalisco, Mexico

**Robles, Marisa** — Concert Harpist
38 Luttrell Ave, London SW15 6PE, England

**Robles, Mike** — Actor, Comedian, Producer
I C M Partners, 10250 Constellation Blvd, #900, Los Angeles CA 90067 USA

**Robson, Bryan** — Soccer Player
Middlesbrough F C, Riverside Stadium, Middlebrough TS3 6RS, England

**Robson, Thomas J (Tom)** — Baseball Player
7331 W Morrow Dr, Glendale AZ 85308, USA

**Robuchon, Joel** — Chef
Societe de Gestion Culinaire, 67 Blvd Gen M Valin, 75015 Paris, France

**Roby, Bradley** — Football Player
Denver Broncos, 13655 E Broncos Parkway, Englewood CO 80112 USA

**Robyn** — Singer
D E F Mgmt, 51 Lonsdale Road, Queens Park, London NW6 6RA, England

**Rocard, Michel L L** — Prime Minister, France
Hotel de Ville, 63 Rue M Berteaux, 78700 Conflans-Sainte-Honorine, France

**Rocca, Constantino** — Golfer
Golf Products International, 5719 Lake Lindero Dr, Agoura Hills CA 91301, USA

**Rocca, Maurice A (Mo)** — Actor, Comedian, Writer
Gersh Agency, 9465 Wilshire Blvd, #600, Beverly Hills CA 90212 USA

**Rocca, Patrick** — Actor
Artmedia, 20 Ave Rapp, 75007 Paris, France

**Rocca, Peter** — Swimmer
534 Hazel Ave, San Bruno CA 94066, USA

**Rocchigiani, Ralf** — Boxer
Rocky's Gym, Grabenstr 200A, 47057 Duisburg, Germany

**Rocco Yim** — Architect
38/F A I A Tower, 183 Electric Road, North Point, Hong Kong SAR, China

**Rocco, Alex** — Actor
Sovereign Talent Group, 10474 S Santa Monica Blvd, #301, Los Angeles CA 90025, USA

**Rocha, John** — Fashion Designer
12-13 Temple Lane, Dublin 2, Ireland

**Roche, Alden S, Jr** — Football Player
1082 Farragut St, New Orleans LA 70114, USA

**Roche, Anthony D (Tony)** — Tennis Player
5 Kapiti St, Saint Ives NSW 2075, Australia

**Roche, E Kevin** — Pritzker Architectural Laureate
Roche Dinkeloo Assoc, 20 Davis St, Hamden CT 06517, USA

**Roche, John M** — Basketball Player
191 Clayton Lane, #303, Denver CO 80206, USA

**Rochefort, Jean** — Actress
Le Chene Rogneaux, 078125 Grosvre, France

**Rochefort, Julien** — Actor
Artmedia, 20 Ave Rapp, 75007 Paris, France

**Rochefort, Leon J F** — Ice Hockey Player
1661 Rue Notre Dame, Sainte Marthe du Cap QC G8T 4J9, Canada

**Rochefort, Normand** — Ice Hockey Player
1530 Burgos Dr, Sarasota FL 34238, USA

**Rochelle, Michael D** — Army General
Deputy CofS Manpower & Personnel, HqUSA, Pentagon, Washington DC 20310, USA

**Rocher, Guy** — Sociologist
4911 Chemin de la Cote-des-Neiges, #409, Montreal QC H3V 1H7, Canada

**Rochester, Paul G** — Football Player
9209 Sweet Berry Dr, Jacksonville FL 32256, USA

**Rochford, Michael J (Mike)** — Baseball Player
5185 Cougars Prowl, Lake Worth FL 33449, USA

**Rochon, Lela** — Actress
Brillstein Entertainment Partners, 9150 Wilshire Blvd, #350, Beverly Hills CA 90212 USA

**Rock, Angela** — Volleyball Player
4771 Vista Lane, San Diego CA 92116, USA

**Rock, Antonio (Tony)** — Actor, Comedian
Bleu Entertainment, 4935 Whitsett Ave, #8, Valley Village CA 91607, USA

**Rock, Chris** — Actor, Comedian, Director
I C M Partners, 10250 Constellation Blvd, #900, Los Angeles CA 90067 USA

**Rock, Pete** — Rap Artist, DJ Musician
Agency Group Ltd, 142 W 57th St, #600, New York NY 10019 USA

**Rock, Walter W (Walt)** — Football Player
1030 Highams Court, Woodbridge VA 22191, USA

**Rockburne, Dorothea G** — Artist, Sculptor
140 Grand St, #2WF, New York NY 10013, USA

**Rockefeller, David** — Financier
1 Chase Manhattan Plaza, New York NY 10005, USA

**Rockefeller, James S** — Financier
425 Park Ave, New York NY 10022, USA

**Rockell** — Singer, Songwriter
T-Best Talent Agency, 508 Honey Lake Court, Danville CA 94506 USA

**Rocker, John L** — Baseball Player
1223 Manor Oaks Court, Atlanta GA 30338, USA

**Rocker, Lee** — Bassist (Stray Cats)
LiveTourArtists, 1451 White Oaks Blvd, Oakville ON L6H 4R9, Canada

**Rocker, Tracy Q** — Football Player
1792 Northumberland Dr, Brentwood TN 37027, USA

**Rockett, Patrick E (Pat)** — Baseball Player
17107 Eagle Hollow Dr, San Antonio TX 78248, USA

**Rockett, Richard A (Rikki)** — Drummer (Poison)
Front Line Mgmt, 1100 Glendon Ave, #2000, Los Angeles CA 90024 USA

**Rockette, Joannie** — Figure Skater
International Management Group, 767 5th Ave, #4500, New York NY 10153, USA

**Rockwell, David** — Architect
Rockwell Group, 5 Union Square W, New York NY 10003, USA

**Rockwell, Sam** — Actor
Arcieri Assoc, 305 Madison Ave, #2315, New York NY 10165 USA

**Rodan, Jay** — Actor
Entertainment Creative Interface, 9200 W Sunset Blvd, #434, West Hollywood CA 90069, USA

**Rodas, Richard M (Rick)** — Baseball Player
6877 Bergano Place, Rancho Cucamonga CA 91701, USA
**Rodat, Robert** — Producer, Writer
Gersh Agency, 9465 Wilshire Blvd, #600, Beverly Hills CA 90212 USA
**Roday, James** — Actor
Principal Entertainment, 9255 Sunset Blvd, #500, Los Angeles CA 90069 USA
**Rodd, Marcia** — Actress
12315 Tiara St, Valley Village CA 91607, USA
**Roddam, Francis G (Franc)** — Director
Independent Talent Group, 40 Whitfield St, London W1T 2RH, England
**Roddick, Andrew S (Andy)** — Tennis Player
140 Shermans Mill Dr, Ingram TX 78025, USA
**Rode, Franc Cardinal** — Religious Leader
Consecrated Life Institutes, Palazzo della Congregazioni, Piazza Pio XII 3, 00193 Rome, Italy
**Rodela, Jose** — Vietnam War Army Hero (CMH)
3523 Antigua, San Antonio TX 78259, USA
**Roden, Karel** — Actor
W M E Entertainment, 9601 Wilshire Blvd, #300, Beverly Hills CA 90210 USA
**Rodenhauser, Mark T** — Football Player
1451 Charlotte Highway, York SC 29745, USA
**Rodenheiser, Richard P (Dick)** — Ice Hockey Player
186 State St, Framingham MA 01702, USA
**Roderick, Brande** — Model, Actress
Prince Marketing Group, 18 Carillon Circle, Livingston NJ 07039 USA
**Rodger, Kate** — Actress, Model
J K A Talent Agency, 12725 Ventura Blvd, #H, Studio City CA 91604, USA
**Rodgers of Quarry Bank, William T** — Government Official, England
43 North Road, London N6 4BE, England
**Rodgers, Aaron C** — Football Player
2360 Crown Pointe Blvd, Suamico WI 54173, USA
**Rodgers, Derrick A** — Football Player
15222 SW 52nd St, Miramar FL 33027, USA
**Rodgers, Jimmie** — Singer, Songwriter
42230 Sandy Bay Road, Bermuda Dunes CA 92203, USA
**Rodgers, Joan** — Opera Singer
113 Sotheby Road, London N5 2UT, England
**Rodgers, John S (Johnny)** — Football Player
PO Box 11172, Omaha NE 68111, USA
**Rodgers, Michael E** — Actor
Innovative Artists, 1505 10th St, Santa Monica CA 90401 USA
**Rodgers, Nile G** — Guitarist (Chic), Businessman
Lustig Talent, PO Box 770850, Orlando FL 32877 USA
**Rodgers, Paul** — Singer (Free, Bad Company), Songwriter
Work Hard, 19D Pinhold Road, London SW16 5GD, England
**Rodgers, Phil** — Golfer
Grand Del Mar, 5200 Grand Del Mar Way, San Diego CA 92130, USA
**Rodgers, Robert L (Buck)** — Baseball Player, Manager
5181 West Knoll Dr, Yorba Linda CA 92886, USA
**Rodgers, William H (Bill)** — Track Athlete
Bill Rodgers Running Center, 1 N Market St, #353, Boston MA 02109, USA
**Rodgers-Cromartie, Dominique R** — Football Player
New York Giants, Meadowlands Stadium, 102 Route 120, East Rutherford NJ 07073 USA
**Rodiger, Alexander** — Bobsled Athlete
Schlossstr 10, 99831 Scherbda, Germany
**Rodl, Henrik** — Basketball Player
A L B A Berlin, Olympischer Platz 4, 14053 Berlin, Germany
**Rodman, Dennis K** — Basketball Player, Actor
Rodman Group, 4910 Campus Dr, Newport Beach CA 92660, USA
**Rodney, Fernando** — Baseball Player
Seattle Mariners, Safeco Field, PO Box 4100, Seattle WA 98194 USA
**Rodnina, Irina** — Figure Skater
7415 W 80th St, Los Angeles CA 90045, USA
**Rodowsky, Colby F** — Writer
3114 Gracefield Road, #401, Silver Spring MD 20904, USA
**Rodrigue, George** — Journalist
Dallas News, Editorial Dept, 508 Young St, Dallas TX 75202, USA
**Rodrigues, Charlie** — Cartoonist (Charlie)
Tribune Media Services, 435 N Michigan Ave, #1500, Chicago IL 60611 USA
**Rodriguez** — Singer, Songwriter
Agency Group Ltd, 142 W 57th St, #600, New York NY 10019 USA
**Rodriguez Madariaga, Oscar A Cardinal** — Religious Leader
Arzobispado, Colonia Palcartagua, Apartado 106, 3A y 2A Ave 1113, Tegucigalpa, Honduras
**Rodriguez Romero, Jose Antonio** — Soccer Player
Federacion de Futbol, Colima 373 Colonia Roma, Delegacion Cuauhtemoc, Mexico City DF 06700, Mexico
**Rodriguez Zapatero, Jose Luis** — Prime Minister, Spain
Council of State, C/Mayor 79, 28013 Madrid, Spain
**Rodriguez, Adam** — Actor
United Talent Agency, U T A Plaza, 9336 Civic Center Dr, Beverly Hills CA 90210 USA
**Rodriguez, Alexander E (Alex)** — Baseball Player
171 E Sunrise Ave, Coral Gables FL 33133, USA
**Rodriguez, Alfredo** — Concert Pianist
I M G Artists, Hogarth Business Park, Chiswick, London W4 2TH, England
**Rodriguez, Amy J** — Soccer Player
Philadelphia Independence, Union Field, Seaport Dr, Chester PA 19013 USA
**Rodriguez, Anthony** — Golfer
13602 Summer Glen Dr, San Antonio TX 78247, USA
**Rodriguez, Arturo S** — Labor Leader
United Farm Workers, 29700 Woodford Tehachapi Road, Keene CA 93531, USA
**Rodriguez, Carlos** — Baseball Player
10139 Snyder Church Road, Baltimore OH 43105, USA
**Rodriguez, Carrie** — Singer, Fiddle Player, Songwriter
Rosebud Agency, PO Box 170429, San Francisco CA 94117 USA
**Rodriguez, Daniel** — Opera Singer
Performers of the World, 5657 Wilshire Blvd, #280, Los Angeles CA 90036 USA
**Rodriguez, David M** — Army General
Commander, US Africa Command, APO AE 09751 USA

**Rodriguez, Davinia** — Opera Singer
I M G Artists, Hogarth Business Park, Chiswick, London W4 2TH, England

**Rodriguez, Edwin** — Baseball Player, Manager
7901 30th Ave N, Saint Petersburg FL 33710, USA

**Rodriguez, Freddy** — Actor, Producer
3 Arts Entertainment, 9460 Wilshire Blvd, #700, Beverly Hills CA 90212 USA

**Rodriguez, Genesis** — Actress
I C M Partners, 10250 Constellation Blvd, #900, Los Angeles CA 90067 USA

**Rodriguez, Gina** — Actress
A P A Talent & Literary Agency, 405 S Beverly Dr, #300, Beverly Hills CA 90212 USA

**Rodriguez, Ivan (Pudge)** — Baseball Player
15530 SW 70th Terrace, Miami FL 33193, USA

**Rodriguez, Jai** — Actor
Michael Einfeld Mgmt, 10630 Moorpark Ave, #101, Toluca Lake CA 91602, USA

**Rodriguez, Jennifer (Jen)** — Speed Skater
Q Sports Marketing, 534 W Evergreen St, Wheaton IL 60187 USA

**Rodriguez, Johnny** — Singer, Guitarist, Songwriter
240 S Wilson Blvd, Nashville TN 37205, USA

**Rodriguez, Jose Luis** — Actor
T G A Voice, 100 Lincoln Road, #928, Miami Beach FL 33178, USA

**Rodriguez, Juan (Chi Chi)** — Golfer
Chi Chi Rodriguez Academy, 3030 N McMullen Booth Road, Clearwater FL 33761, USA

**Rodriguez, Marco** — Actor
Ellis Talent Group, 4705 Laurel Canyon Blvd, #300 Valley Village CA 91607, USA

**Rodriguez, Michelle** — Actress
Untitled Entertainment, 350 S Beverly Dr, #200, Beverly Hills CA 90212 USA

**Rodriguez, Narciso** — Fashion Designer
50 Bond St, #700, New York NY 10012, USA

**Rodriguez, Paul** — Actor, Comedian, Producer
Rodriguez Entertainment, 3940 Laurel Canyon Blvd, #1159, Studio City CA 91604, USA

**Rodriguez, Ramon** — Actor
Viewpoint, 8820 Wilshire Blvd, #220, Beverly Hills CA 90211 USA

**Rodriguez, Raul** — Float Designer
Fiesta Floats, 9362 Lower Azusa Road, Temple City CA 91780, USA

**Rodriguez, Richard A (Rich)** — Football Coach, Sportscaster
University of Arizona, Athletic Dept, Tucson AZ 85721, USA

**Rodriguez, Richard A (Rich)** — Baseball Player
14578 Corkwood Dr, Moorpark CA 93021, USA

**Rodriguez, Rico** — Actor
Clear Talent Group, 10950 Ventura Blvd, Studio City CA 91604, USA

**Rodriguez, Rita M** — Financier
Academy for Educational Development, 1825 Connecticut Ave NW, Washington DC 20006, USA

**Rodriguez, Robert** — Director
Trouble Maker Studios, 4900 Old Manor Road, Austin TX 78723, USA

**Rodriguez, Sergio** — Basketball Player
New York Knicks, Madison Square Garden, 2 Penn Plaza, New York, NY 10121 USA

**Rodriguez, Valente** — Actor
TalentWorks, 3500 W Olive Ave, #1400, Burbank CA 91505 USA

**Rodriguez-Lopez, Omar** — Guitarist (Mars Volta), Composer
Agency Group Ltd, 142 W 57th St, #600, New York NY 10019 USA

**Roe, Alex** — Actor
Associated International Mgmt, 7 Hatton Garden, #400, London EC1N 8AD, England

**Roe, Allison P** — Track Athlete
34 Martin Crescent, Northcote, Auckland 0627, New Zealand

**Roe, John H** — Businessman
Bemis Co, Northstar Center, 222 S 9th St, Minneapolis MN 55402, USA

**Roe, Marty** — Singer, Guitarist (Diamond Rio)
Modern Mgmt, 1625 Broadway, #600, Nashville TN 37203, USA

**Roe, Tommy** — Singer, Songwriter
Horizon Talent Agency, PO Box 26037, Minneapolis MN 55426, USA

**Roebuck, Daniel** — Actor
Leslie Allen-Rice Mgmt, 1007 Maybrook Dr, Beverly Hills CA 90210, USA

**Roebuck, Edward J (Ed)** — Baseball Player
3434 Warwood Road, Lakewood CA 90712, USA

**Roeder, Robert G** — Biochemist
504 E 63rd St, #33P, New York NY 10065, USA

**Roeg, Nicolas J** — Director
Luc Roeg Artists, 32 Tavustick St, London WC2, England

**Roehm, Carolyn J** — Fashion Designer
Carolyn Roehm Inc, 257 W 39th St, #400, New York NY 10018, USA

**Roelandts, Willem P** — Businessman
Xilinx, PO Box 240010, San Jose CA 95154, USA

**Roelofs, Wendell L** — Biochemist, Entomologist
4 Crescence Dr, Geneva NY 14456, USA

**Roemer, John E** — Economist
University of California, Economics Dept, Davis CA 95616, USA

**Roemer, Sarah** — Actress
Luber Rocklin Entertainment, 5815 Sunset Blvd, #206, Los Angeles CA 90028 USA

**Roenick, Jeremy** — Ice Hockey Player
8525 E Dixileta Dr, Scottsdale AZ 85266, USA

**Roenicke, Gary S** — Baseball Player
11023 Rough and Ready Road, Rough and Ready CA 95975, USA

**Roenicke, Ronald J (Ron)** — Baseball Player, Manager
2212 Avenida Las Ramblas, Chino Hills CA 91709, USA

**Roenning, Joachim** — Director
Roenbergfilm, Pilestredet 75C, 0354 Oslo, Norway

**Roerig, Zach** — Actor
Innovative Artists, 1505 10th St, Santa Monica CA 90401 USA

**Roesch, Michael** — Biathlete
Im Kohlhau 6, 01773 Zinwald, Germany

**Roesky, Herbert W** — Chemist
Gottingen University, Inorganic Chemistry Dept, 37077 Gottingen, Germany

**Roethlisberger, Ben** — Football Player
200 Fernwood Dr, Clinton PA 15026, USA

**Roethlisberger, Nadia** — Curling Athlete
Curling Association, PO Box 606, 3000 Bern, Switzerland

**Roffe-Steinrotter, Diann**　　　　　　　　　　　　　Alpine Skier
248 N 29th St, Camp Hill PA 17011, USA
**Rogan, Joe**　　　　　　　　　　　　　　　　Actor, Comedian
W M E Entertainment, 9601 Wilshire Blvd, #300, Beverly Hills CA 90210 USA
**Roge, Pascal**　　　　　　　　　　　　　　　Concert Pianist
17 Ave des Cavaliers, 1224 Geneva, Switzerland
**Rogen, Seth**　　　　　　　Actor, Comedian, Writer, Producer
Principal Entertainment, 9255 Sunset Blvd, #500, Los Angeles CA 90069 USA
**Rogers of Riverside, Richard G**　　Pritzker Architectural Laureate
Rogers Partnership, Thames Wharf, Rainville Road, London W6 9HA, England
**Rogers, Carlos C**　　　　　　　　　　　　　Football Player
San Francisco 49ers, 4949 Centennial Blvd, Santa Clara CA 95054 USA
**Rogers, Carlos D**　　　　　　　　　　　　Basketball Player
Indiana Pacers, Conseco Fieldhouse, 125 S Pennsylvania, Indianapolis IN 46204 USA
**Rogers, Erik**　　　　　　　　　　　　Singer (Stereo Mud)
Agency Group Ltd, 142 W 57th St, #600, New York NY 10019 USA
**Rogers, Garnet**　　　　　　Singer, Songwriter, Guitarist
Fleming Artists, 543 N Main St, Ann Arbor MI 48104, USA
**Rogers, George W, Jr**　　　　　　　　　　　Football Player
1007 Lofty Pine Dr, Columbia SC 29212, USA
**Rogers, Gil**　　　　　　　　　　　　　　　　　Actor
Don Buchwald Talent Agency, 10 E 44th St, New York NY 10017 USA
**Rogers, Ingrid**　　　　　　　　　　　　　　　Actress
Flick Commercials, 9057 Nemo St, #A, West Hollywood, CA 90069, USA
**Rogers, James B (J B)**　　　　　　　　　　　　Director
Reflection Pictures, 2001 Wilshire Blvd, #250, Santa Monica CA 90403, USA
**Rogers, James E**　　　　　　　　　　　　　Businessman
Duke Energy, 212 S Tryon St, #400, Charlotte NC 28281, USA
**Rogers, John A**　　　　　　　Chemist, Materials Scientist
University of Illinois, Seitz Materials Research Laboratory, 104 S Goodwin Ave, Urbana IL 61801, USA
**Rogers, John M**　　　　　　　　　　　　　　　Judge
US Court of Appeals, US Courthouse, 100 E 5th St, #3100, Cincinnati OH 45202, USA
**Rogers, Judith W**　　　　　　　　　　　　　　Judge
US Court of Appeals, 333 Constitution NW, #4400, Washington DC 20001, USA
**Rogers, June Scobee**　　　　　　　　　　　　　Writer
Challenger Center, 1250 N Pitt St, #1, Alexandria VA 22314, USA
**Rogers, Kenneth A (Kenny)**　　　　　　　　Baseball Player
1730 Ottinger Road, Roanoke TX 76262, USA
**Rogers, Laura**　　　Singer (Secret Sisters), Songwriter
Universal Republic Records, 1755 Broadway, #800, New York NY 10019 USA
**Rogers, Lydia**　　　　　　　　　　Singer (Secret Sisters)
Universal Republic Records, 1755 Broadway, #800, New York NY 10019 USA
**Rogers, Lynn L**　　　　　　　Wildlife Biologist, Ecologist
145 W Conan St, Ely MN 55731, USA
**Rogers, Melody**　　　　　　　　　　　　　　Actress
C E S D, 10635 Santa Monica Blvd, #130, Los Angeles CA 90025 USA
**Rogers, Melvin N**　　　　　　　　　　　　Football Player
3113 S Manitoba Dr, Santa Ana CA 92704, USA
**Rogers, Michael S**　　　　　　　　　　　　Navy Admiral
Director, National Security Agency, Fort George G Meade MD 20755, USA
**Rogers, Michele**　　　　　　　　　　　　　　Model
Playboy Promotions, 9346 Civic Center Dr, #200, Beverly Hills CA 90210 USA
**Rogers, Mimi**　　　　　　　　　　　　　　　Actress
Paradigm Agency, 360 N Crescent Dr, North Building, Beverly Hills CA 90210 USA
**Rogers, Nick**　　　　　　　　　　　　　　Yachtsman
Royal Yachting Squadron, Castle Cowles, Isle of Wight PO31 7QT, England
**Rogers, Randy**　　　　　　　　　　Singer, Band Leader
36D Mgmt, 36 Natta Circle, New Braunfels TX 78132, USA
**Rogers, Rob**　　　　　　　　　　　Editorial Cartoonist
Pittsburgh Post-Gazette, Editorial Dept, 23 Blvd Allies, Pittsburgh PA 15222, USA
**Rogers, Robert**　　　　　　　　　　　　　　Architect
Rogers Marvel Architects, 145 Hudson St, #304, New York NY 10013, USA
**Rogers, Rodney R**　　　　　　　　　　　Basketball Player
Jazzie's Trucking LLC, 333 Shady Grove Dr, Timberlake NC 27583, USA
**Rogers, Rosemary**　　　　　　　　　　　　　Writer
Avon Books, 959 8th Ave, New York NY 10019, USA
**Rogers, Stephen D (Steve)**　　　　　　　　Baseball Player
2 Lenape Lane, Princeton Junction NJ 08550, USA
**Rogers, Tracy D**　　　　　　　　　　　　Football Player
1011 Tam O'Shanter Dr, Bakersfield CA 93309, USA
**Rogers, Tristan**　　　　　　　　　　　　　　　Actor
C E S D, 10635 Santa Monica Blvd, #130, Los Angeles CA 90025 USA
**Rogers, Wayne**　　　　　　　　　　　　　　　Actor
11828 La Grange Ave, Los Angeles CA 90025, USA
**Rogers, William C (Bill)**　　　　　　　　　　　Golfer
123 Eaton St, #104, San Antonio TX 78209, USA
**Roggenburk, Garry E**　　　　　　　　　　Baseball Player
33550 Streamview Dr, Avon OH 44011, USA
**Rogoff, Ilan**　　　　　　　　　　　　　Concert Pianist
Apdo 1098, 07080 Palma de Mallorca, Spain
**Rogoff, Kenneth S**　　　　　　　　　　　　Economist
11 Hillside Ave, Cambridge MA 02140, USA
**Rogombe, Rose Francine**　　　　　　　President, Gabon
Senate President's Office, BP 546, Libreville, Gabon
**Rohbock, Shauna**　　　　　　　　　　　Bobsled Athlete
Q Sports Marketing, 534 W Evergreen St, Wheaton IL 60187 USA
**Rohde, David**　　　　　　　　　　　　　　Journalist
Christian Science Monitor, Editorial Dept, 1 Norway St, Boston MA 02136 USA
**Rohde, Hillary**　　　　　　　　　　　　Fashion Designer
Hillary Rohde Cashmere, 22 Moray Place, Edinburgh EH3 6DB, Scotland
**Rohde, Leonard E (Len)**　　　　　　　　　　Football Player
324 Alta Vista Ave, Los Altos Hills CA 94022, USA
**Rohde, Lisa**　　　　　　　　　　　　　Rowing Athlete
9807 Whitehorn Dr, Charlotte NC 28277, USA
**Rohlander, Uta**　　　　　　　　　　　　Track Athlete
Liebigstr 9, 06237 Leuna, Germany

# R

**Rohlf, F James** — Biometrician
State University of New York, Ecology & Evolution Dept, Stony Brook NY 11794, USA

**Rohm, Elisabeth** — Actress
A P A Talent & Literary Agency, 405 S Beverly Dr, #300, Beverly Hills CA 90212 USA

**Rohner, Clayton** — Actor
620 S Oakland Ave, Pasadena CA 91106, USA

**Rohr, James E** — Financier
P N C Bank Corp, 1 P N C Plaza, 249 5th Ave, Pittsburgh PA 15222, USA

**Rohrbach, Kelly** — Actress, Model
Untitled Entertainment, 350 S Beverly Dr, #200, Beverly Hills CA 90212 USA

**Rohrer, Katherine** — Opera Singer
Columbia Artists Mgmt Inc, 5 Columbus Circle, 1790 Broadway, #1600, New York NY 10019 USA

**Rohrl, Walter** — Auto Racing Driver
Eckhard Eybl, Porschplatz 1, 70335 Stuttgart-Zuffenhausen, Germany

**Roiphe, Anne** — Writer
Bloomsbury Publishing, 50 Bedford Square, London WC1B 3DP, England

**Roiz, Sasha** — Actress
Domain Talent, 9229 W Sunset Blvd, #710, West Hollywood CA 90069 USA

**Roizman, Bernard** — Virologist
5555 S Everett Ave, Chicago IL 60637, USA

**Roizman, Owen** — Cinematographer
17533 Magnolia Blvd, Encino CA 91316, USA

**Rojas Medrano, Melquiades (Mel)** — Baseball Player
15645 Collins Ave, #802, North Miami Beach FL 33160, USA

**Rojas Rivas, Octavio R (Cookie)** — Baseball Player, Manager
19195 Mystic Pointe Dr, #3002, Aventura FL 33180, USA

**Rojas, Tito (El Gallo)** — Singer, Orchestra Leader
Alpha Artists International, 261 E 134th St, #200, Bronx NY 10454, USA

**Rojcewicz, Susan (Sue)** — Basketball Player
30 Via Encina, Monterey CA 93940, USA

**Roje, Zoran** — Water Polo Player
Ivana Milcetica 12, 51000 Rijeka, Croatia

**Rojeski, Shawn** — Curling Athlete
510 11th St NW, Chisholm MN 55719, USA

**Roker, Al** — Entertainer
W M E Entertainment, 1325 Ave of Americas, New York NY 10019 USA

**Rokke, Ervin J** — Air Force General
810 Dolan Dr, Monument CO 80132, USA

**Rokker, Heinz** — WW II German Luftwaffe Hero
Zietenstr 21, 26131 Oldenburg, Germany

**Roland, Edgar E (Ed), Jr** — Singer (Collective Soul), Songwriter
Creative Artists Agency, 2000 Ave of Stars, #100, Los Angeles CA 90067 USA

**Roland, Johnny E** — Football Player, Coach
10339 Corbell Dr, #C, Saint Louis MO 63146, USA

**Roland, M Dean** — Guitarist, Keyboardist (Collective Soul)
Creative Artists Agency, 2000 Ave of Stars, #100, Los Angeles CA 90067 USA

**Rolandi, Gianna** — Opera Singer
New York City Opera, Lincoln Center Plaza, New York NY 10023, USA

**Rolen, Scott B** — Baseball Player
11711 N Pennsylvania St, #250, Carmel IN 46032, USA

**Roles-Williams, Barbara** — Figure Skater
3790 Leisure Lane, Las Vegas NV 89103, USA

**Rolfe Johnson, Anthony** — Opera Singer
Ulf Tornqvist, Sankt Eriksgatan 100, 113 31 Stockholm, Sweden

**Rolfe, Dale** — Ice Hockey Player
365 Hughson St, Gravenhurst ON P1P 1G8, Canada

**Rolie, Gregg** — Singer, Keyboardist (Santana)
Tabletop Productions, PO Box 698, Carson City NV 89702, USA

**Roll, Dean M** — Wrestler
Shark Stuff, PO Box 752073, Dayton OH 45475, USA

**Rolle** — Musician (Fearless)
Helter Skelter, 347-353 Chiswick High Road, London W4 4HS, England

**Rolle, Antrel R** — Football Player
28232 SW 158th Court, Homestead FL 33033, USA

**Rolle, Donald D (Butch)** — Football Player
17822 NW 15th St, Pembroke Pines FL 33029, USA

**Rolle, Samari T** — Football Player
16201 Quiet Vista Circle, Delray Beach FL 33446, USA

**Rolling, Henry L** — Football Player
6885 W Lone Mountain Road, #260, Las Vegas NV 89108, USA

**Rollins, Edward J (Ed)** — Political Consultant
Dilenschneider Group, 200 Park Ave, MetLife Building, New York NY 10166, USA

**Rollins, Henry** — Singer, Songwriter, Actor
Rollins Mgmt, 7510 Sunset Blvd, #602, Los Angeles CA 90046, USA

**Rollins, James C (Jimmy)** — Baseball Player
120 Fox Chase Court, Swedesboro NJ 08085, USA

**Rollins, John** — Golfer
5501 Montclair Dr, Colleyville TX 76034, USA

**Rollins, Richard J (Rich)** — Baseball Player
4146 Evergreen Lane, Richfield OH 44286, USA

**Rollins, Theodore W (Sonny)** — Jazz Saxophonist, Composer
Ted Kurland, 173 Brighton Ave, Boston MA 02134 USA

**Rollins, Wayne M (Tree)** — Basketball Player, Coach
PO Box 681971, Orlando FL 32868, USA

**Rolston, Brian** — Ice Hockey Player
1604 Stanley Blvd, Birmingham MI 48009, USA

**Rolston, Holmes III** — Philosopher, Templeton Religion Laureate
1712 Concord Dr, Fort Collins CO 80526, USA

**Roman, Freddie** — Actor, Comedian
Dick Hall Productions, 889 S Brentwood Blvd, #201, Saint Louis MO 63105, USA

**Roman, John G** — Football Player
27 Duffryn Ave, Malvern PA 19355, USA

**Roman, Joseph** — Actor
888 N West Knoll Dr, #105, West Hollywood CA 90069, USA

**Roman, Lauren E** — Actress
8330 Grand Ave NE, Bainbridge Island WA 98110, USA

**Roman, Petre** — Prime Minister, Romania
Str Nikolai Gogol 2, Sector 1, 012017 Bucharest, Romania
**Romanchych, Larry** — Ice Hockey Player
3989 206A St, Langley BC V3A 7A8, Canada
**Romanek, Mark** — Director, Writer
Creative Artists Agency, 2000 Ave of Stars, #100, Los Angeles CA 90067 USA
**Romanenko, Roman Y** — Cosmonaut
Cosmonaut Training Center, Star City, 141160 Zvezdny Gorodok, Moscow Oblast, Russia
**Romanenko, Yuri V** — Cosmonaut
Cosmonaut Training Center, Star City, 141160 Zvezdny Gorodok, Moscow Oblast, Russia
**Romano, Chris** — Actor, Writer, Producer
United Talent Agency, U T A Plaza, 9336 Civic Center Dr, Beverly Hills CA 90210 USA
**Romano, Christy Carlson** — Actress, Singer
Rebel Entertainment Partners, 5700 Wilshire Blvd, #456, Los Angeles CA 90036, USA
**Romano, Jason A** — Baseball Player
1411 Willow Oak Circle, Bradenton FL 34209, USA
**Romano, John A (Johnny), Jr** — Baseball Player
160 W Pago Pago Dr, Naples FL 34113, USA
**Romano, Larry** — Actor
C E S D, 10635 Santa Monica Blvd, #130, Los Angeles CA 90025 USA
**Romano, Pete** — Cinematographer
HydroFlex Inc, 301 E El Segundo Blvd, El Segundo CA 90245, USA
**Romano, Ray** — Actor, Comedian, Producer
I C M Partners, 10250 Constellation Blvd, #900, Los Angeles CA 90067 USA
**Romano, Rino** — Actor
6931 Paseo del Serra, Los Angeles CA 90068, USA
**Romano, Roberto** — Ice Hockey Player
5865 Rue Brossard, Saint-Leonard QC H1T 3R6, Canada
**Romanov, Pyotr V** — Government Official, Russia
Pr Mira 108, 660017 Krasnoyarsk, Russia
**Romanov, Stephanie** — Actress
Untitled Entertainment, 350 S Beverly Dr, #200, Beverly Hills CA 90212 USA
**Romanowski, William T (Bill)** — Football Player
390 Hampton Road, Piedmont CA 94611, USA
**Romans, Ben** — Keyboardist (Click Five)
Soundtrack Music, 1460 4th St, #308, Santa Monica CA 90401, USA
**Romanus, Richard** — Actor
14011 Ventura Blvd, #213, Sherman Oaks CA 91403, USA
**Romar, Lorenzo** — Basketball Player, Coach
4408 164th Lane SE, Issaquah WA 98027, USA
**Romario** — Soccer Player
Adelaide F C, PO Box 620, Hindmarsh SA 5007, Australia
**Romashin, Anatoliy V** — Actor
Vspolny Per 16 Korp 1, #60, 103101 Moscow, Russia
**Romatowski, Jenny** — Softball, Baseball Player
3116 Highlands Blvd, Palm Harbor FL 34684, USA
**Rombolo, Tony** — Guitarist (Godsmack)
Front Line Mgmt, 1100 Glendon Ave, #2000, Los Angeles CA 90024 USA
**Rome, Jim** — Actor, Writer
Creative Artists Agency, 2000 Ave of Stars, #100, Los Angeles CA 90067 USA
**Rome, Sydne** — Actress
Isabella Gull Assoc, Vicolo del Buon Consiglio, 00184 Rome, Italy
**Romeike, Hinrich** — Equestrian
Moholzu, 24809 Nubbel, Germany
**Romensky, Anka** — Model
PO Box 3897, Hallandale FL 33008, USA
**Romeo** — Singer (Immature), Actor
Don Buchwald Talent Agency, 6500 Wilshire Blvd, #2200, Los Angeles CA 90048 USA
**Romeo, Paolo Cardinal** — Religious Leader
Archdiocese of Palermo, Corso Vittorio Emanuele 461, 90134 Palermo, Italy
**Romeo, Robin** — Bowler
Professional Bowlers Association, 719 2nd Ave, #701, Seattle WA 98104 USA
**Romer, Christina D** — Government Official, Economist
University of California, Economics Dept, Evans Hall, Berkeley CA 94720, USA
**Romer, Roy R** — Governor, CO; Educator
Los Angeles School District, 333 S Beaudry Ave, #209, Los Angeles CA 90017, USA
**Romero, Anders** — Golfer
Professional Golfers Association, 100 Ave of Champions, Palm Beach Gardens FL 33418 USA
**Romero, Angel** — Concert Guitarist
Richard Gilkerson, 1737 Whitley Ave, #200, Los Angeles CA 90028, USA
**Romero, Celino** — Concert Guitarist
Columbia Artists Mgmt Inc, 5 Columbus Circle, 1790 Broadway, #1600, New York NY 10019 USA
**Romero, Danny, Jr** — Boxer
800 Salida Sandia SW, Albuquerque NM 87105, USA
**Romero, Edgardo (Ed)** — Baseball Player
1380 Wood Row Way, Wellington FL 33414, USA
**Romero, George A** — Director
Gersh Agency, 9465 Wilshire Blvd, #600, Beverly Hills CA 90212 USA
**Romero, Ned** — Actor
249 Vista Royale Circle W, Palm Desert CA 92211, USA
**Romero, Pepe** — Concert Guitarist
Columbia Artists Mgmt Inc, 5 Columbus Circle, 1790 Broadway, #1600, New York NY 10019 USA
**Romero, Randy P** — Thoroughbred Racing Jockey
7124 Louisiana Highway 343, Kaplan LA 70548, USA
**Romero, Rebecca J** — Cyclist, Rowing Athlete
National Cycling Centre, Stewart St, Manchester M11 4DQ, England
**Rometty, Virginia M** — Businesswoman
I B M Corp, 1 North Castle Dr, #2, Armonk NY 10504, USA
**Romig, Joseph H (Joe)** — Football Player
1300 Plaza Court N, Lafayette CO 80026, USA
**Romijn, Rebecca** — Model, Actress
United Talent Agency, U T A Plaza, 9336 Civic Center Dr, Beverly Hills CA 90210 USA
**Romine, Kevin A** — Baseball Player
8750 Rogue River Ave, Fountain Valley CA 92708, USA
**Rominger, Kent V** — Astronaut
2714 Bridgeport Ave, Salt Lake City UT 84121, USA

# R

**Romney, Hervin A R** — Architect
1556 San Benito Ave, Coral Gables FL 33134, USA

**Romo, Antonio R (Tony)** — Football Player
Dallas Cowboys, 1 Cowboys Parkway, Irving TX 75063 USA

**Romo, Daniela** — Actress
Televisa, Blvd A Lopez Mateos 232, Colonia San Angel, Mexico City DF 01060 CP, Mexico

**Romulo** — Soccer Player
Confederacion de Futebol, Rua Victor Civita 66, #1, Rio de Janeiro 22775 044, Brazil

**Ronaldinho** — Soccer Player
F C Milan, Via Filippo Turati 3, 20121 Milan, Italy

**Ronaldo** — Soccer Player
S C Corinthians Paulista, Rua Sao Jorge 777, Tatuape 03087 000, Sao Paulo SP, Brazil

**Ronaldo, Christiano** — Soccer Player
Gestifute, Oceans 3/15/02 #D, 2 Office, United Park, 1990-197 Lisbon, Portugal

**Ronan, Edward (Ed)** — Ice Hockey Player
70 Jefferson Road, Franklin MA 02038, USA

**Ronan, Saoirse** — Actress
Macfarlane Chard, 7 Adelaide St, Dun Laoghaire, County Dublin, Ireland

**Rondo, Rajon P** — Basketball Player
9 Fridolin Hill, Lincoln MA 01773, USA

**Roney, Wallace** — Jazz Trumpeter
BookArts Co, 6404 Wilshire Blvd, #1750, Los Angeles CA 90048, USA

**Ronney, Paul D** — Astronaut
613 Ranchito Road, Monrovia CA 91016, USA

**Ronning, Clifford J (Cliff)** — Ice Hockey Player
7130 Kitchener St, Burnaby BC V5A 1L3, Canada

**Ronning, Joachim** — Director
Roenbergfilm, Pilestredet 75C, 0354 Oslo, Norway

**Ronningen, Jon** — Greco-Roman Wrestler
Mellomasveien 132, 1414 Trollasen, Norway

**Rono, Peter** — Track Athlete
Mount Saint Mary's College, Athletic Dept, Emmitsburg MD 21727, USA

**Ronson, Leonard K (Len)** — Ice Hockey Player
2006 SW Eastwood Ave, Gresham OR 97080, USA

**Ronson, Samatha** — Singer, Songwriter
Creative Artists Agency, 2000 Ave of Stars, #100, Los Angeles CA 90067 USA

**Ronstadt, Linda M** — Singer
Trident Media Group, 41 Madison Ave, #3600, New York NY 10010, USA

**Ronty, Paul** — Ice Hockey Player
2300 Commonwealth Ave, #3-4, Auburndale MA 02466, USA

**Roof, Phillip A (Phil)** — Baseball Player
1301 Pillar Chase, Paducah KY 42001, USA

**Rook, Susan** — Commentator
CNN-TV, News Dept, 190 Marietta Ave SW, Atlanta GA 30303 USA

**Rooker, James P (Jim)** — Baseball Player
2378 Windchime Dr, Jacksonville FL 32224, USA

**Rooker, Michael** — Actor
L I N K Entertainment, 11872 La Grange Ave, Los Angeles CA 90025 USA

**Rooney** — Rock Music Group
Agency Group Ltd, 1880 Century Park E, #711, Los Angeles CA 90067 USA

**Rooney, Daniel M (Dan)** — Football Executive, Diplomat
940 N Lincoln Ave, Pittsburgh PA 15233, USA

**Rooney, Joe Don** — Singer, Guitarist (Rascal Flatts)
Turner & Nichols, 49 Music Square W, #500, Nashville TN 37203, USA

**Rooney, Kathleen** — Writer
University of Arkansas Press, 105 N McIlroy Ave, Fayetteville AR 72701, USA

**Rooney, Kevin** — Actor
Emptage Hallett, 14 Rathbone Place, London W1T 1HT, England

**Rooney, Mercy** — Model, Actress
Playboy Promotions, 9346 Civic Center Dr, #200, Beverly Hills CA 90210 USA

**Rooney, Patrick E (Pat)** — Baseball Player
4825 Lighthouse Dr, Racine WI 53402, USA

**Rooney, Steven P (Steve)** — Ice Hockey Player
5 Helen Dr, Canton MA 02021, USA

**Roop, Jeff** — Actor
Ambition Talent, 487 Adelaide St W, #202, Toronto ON M5V 1T4, Canada

**Roos, Don** — Director, Writer
Is or Isn't Entertainment, 8391 Beverly Blvd, #125, Los Angeles CA 90048, USA

**Roos, Mary** — Singer, Actress
Buro Mary Roos, Dorfstr 36, 25551 Schlotfeld, Germany

**Roos, Michael (Mike)** — Football Player
500 Madison Ave, #103, Nashville TN 37208, USA

**Root, Amanda** — Actress
I C M Partners, 10250 Constellation Blvd, #900, Los Angeles CA 90067 USA

**Root, Stephen** — Actor
Gersh Agency, 9465 Wilshire Blvd, #600, Beverly Hills CA 90212 USA

**Root, William J (Bill)** — Ice Hockey Player
33 Hamilton Hall Dr, Markham ON L3P 3L5, Canada

**Roper, Dee Dee (Spinderella)** — Rap Artist (Salt'N'Pepa)
Next Plateau Records, 1650 Broadway, #1103, New York NY 10019, USA

**Roper, John A** — Football Player
4213 Alice St, Houston TX 77021, USA

**Roponun, Riitta-Liise** — Cross Country Skier
Oulu Ski Club, Sammonkatu 6, 90570 Oulu, Finland

**Rorem, Ned** — Composer, Writer
PO Box 764, Nantucket MA 02554, USA

**Rosa, Angela Alvarado** — Actress
Marshak/Zachary/Mills, 8840 Wilshire Blvd, #100, Beverly Hills CA 90211 USA

**Rosa, John W, Jr** — Air Force General, Educator
Citadel, President's Office, Charleston SC 29409, USA

**Rosa, Robi Draco (Robby)** — Singer, Producer, Composer
Creative Artists Agency, 2000 Ave of Stars, #100, Los Angeles CA 90067 USA

**Rosado, Eduardo** — Opera Singer
Calle 3, Ave Cupules 112A, Col G Giberes, Menda, Yucatan 97070, Mexico

**Rosales, Gaudencio B Cardinal** — Religious Leader
Archdiocese of Manila, 121 Arzobispo St, PO Box 132, 1099 Manila, Philippines

**Rosales, Jennifer (Jenny)** — Golfer
265 S Vine St, Anaheim CA 92805, USA
**Rosamilia, Alex** — Guitarist (Gaslight Anthem)
Esther Creative Group, 27 W 24th St, #404, New York NY 10010, USA
**Rosario** — Singer, Actress, Songwriter
Mega Music Productions, 16950 North Bay Road, #1706, Sunny Isles Beach FL 33160, USA
**Rosario, Joann** — Singer
Universal Attractions, 135 W 26th St, #1200, New York NY 10001 USA
**Rosas, Cesar** — Singer, Songwriter (Los Lobos)
Gold Mountain, 3940 Laurel Canyon Blvd, #444, Studio City CA 91604 USA
**Rosato, Genesia** — Ballerina
Royal Ballet, Covent Garden, Bow St, London WC2E 9DD, England
**Rosberg, Keke E** — Auto Racing Driver
7 Rue Gabian, 9800 Monte Carlo, Monaco
**Rosberg, Nico E** — Auto Racing Driver
Le Gildo Pastor Center, 7 Rue du Gabian, 98000 Monaco, Monaco
**Rosborough, Patty** — Actress, Comedienne
OmniPop Talent Group, 4605 Lankershim Blvd, #201, Toluca Lake CA 91602 USA
**Roschkov, Victor** — Editorial Cartoonist
Toronto Star, Editorial Dept, 1 Yonge St, Toronto ON M5E 1E5, Canada 90068, USA
**Rose Marie** — Actress, Singer
6916 Chisholm Ave, Van Nuys CA 91406, USA
**Rose, Adam** — Actor
Stone Manners Salners, 6100 Wilshire Blvd, #1500, Los Angeles CA 90035 USA
**Rose, Andrew** — Composer
1620 Ashland Ave, Santa Monica CA 90405, USA
**Rose, Anika Noni** — Actress, Singer
David Williams Mgmt, 9614 Olympic Blvd, #F, Beverly Hills CA 90212, USA
**Rose, Axl** — Singer (Guns N' Roses), Songwriter
5055 Latigo Canyon Road, Malibu CA 90265, USA
**Rose, Bernard** — Director, Writer, Cinematographer
Casorotto Ramsay, Waverley House, 7-12 Noel St, London W1F 8GQ, England
**Rose, Brian** — Baseball Player
5 Ashland St, South Dartmouth MA 02748, USA
**Rose, Charles (Charlie)** — Commentator, Producer, Actor
Rose Communications, 499 Park Ave, #1500, New York NY 10022, USA
**Rose, Chris** — Sportscaster
Fox-TV, Sports Dept, PO Box 900, Beverly Hills CA 90213 USA
**Rose, Clarence** — Golfer
106 Harding Place, Goldsboro NC 27534, USA
**Rose, Cristine** — Actress
S M S Talent, 8383 Wilshire Blvd, #230, Beverly Hills CA 90211 USA
**Rose, Derrick M** — Basketball Player
Chicago Bulls, United Center, 1901 W Madison St, Chicago IL 60612 USA
**Rose, Donovan J** — Football Player
103 Lenox Court, Yorktown VA 23693, USA
**Rose, Emily** — Actress
Domain Talent, 9229 W Sunset Blvd, #710, West Hollywood CA 90069 USA
**Rose, Irwin** — Nobel Chemistry Laureate
3 McClelland Farm Road, Deerfield MA 01342, USA
**Rose, Jalen** — Basketball Player
Three Tier Entertainment, 645 W 9th St, #406, Los Angeles CA 90015, USA
**Rose, Jamie** — Actress
Marshak/Zachary/Mills, 8840 Wilshire Blvd, #100, Beverly Hills CA 90211 USA
**Rose, Jessica** — Actress
Hirsch Wallerstein Hayum, 10100 Santa Monica Blvd, #1700, Los Angeles CA 90067 USA
**Rose, John** — Cartoonist (Snuffy Smith)
King Features Syndicate, 300 W 57th St, #1500, New York NY 10019 USA
**Rose, Joseph H (Joe)** — Football Player
3293 SW 138th Way, Davie FL 33330, USA
**Rose, Justin R** — Golfer
4sports & Entertainment, 8 Celbridge Mews, London W2 6EU, England
**Rose, Kenny F (Ken)** — Football Player
1736 Bronzewood Court, Newbury Park CA 91320, USA
**Rose, Lee** — Director, Producer
Broder Webb Chervin Silbermann, 9242 Beverly Blvd, Beverly Hills CA 90210 USA
**Rose, Lela** — Fashion Designer
224 W 30th St, #1400, New York NY 10001, USA
**Rose, Mervyn G** — Tennis Player
PO Box 6177, Coffs Harbour Plaza NSW 2450, Australia
**Rose, Michael** — Singer (Black Uhuru)
Ultima Talent, 858 Westbourne Dr, #3, West Hollywood CA 90069, USA
**Rose, Pam** — Singer (Kennedy Rose)
PO Box 50362, Nashville TN 37205, USA
**Rose, Peter E (Pete)** — Baseball Player, Manager
13348 Chandler Blvd, Sherman Oaks CA 91401, USA
**Rose, Peter E (Pete), Jr** — Baseball Player
3921 Legendary Ridge Lane, Cleves OH 45002, USA
**Rose, Sherrie** — Actress, Model
1758 Laurel Canyon Blvd, Los Angeles CA 90046, USA
**Roseau, Maurice E D** — Mechanical Engineer
144 Bis Ave du General Leclerc, 92330 Sceaux, France
**Roselle, David P** — Educator
14 Laurel Ridge Road, Wilmington DE 19807, USA
**Rosello Rodriguez, David (Dave)** — Baseball Player
HC 1 Box 8125, Hormigueros PR 00660, USA
**Rosemont, Romy** — Actress
Main Title Mgmt, 8383 Wilshire Blvd, #408, Beverly Hills CA 90211 USA
**Rosen, Albert L (Al)** — Baseball Player, Executive
15 Mayfair Dr, Rancho Mirage CA 92270, USA
**Rosen, Beatrice** — Actress
Cinetalent, 18 Rue Seguier, 75006 Paris, France
**Rosen, Dan** — Director
Modus Entertainment, 8569 Holloway Dr, #1, West Hollywood CA 90069, USA
**Rosen, Harold A** — Engineer, Inventor
Rosen Electrical Equipment, 8401 Slauson Ave, Pico Rivera CA 90660, USA

# R

|  |  |
|---|---|
| **Rosen, Milton W**<br>5610 Alta Vista Road, Bethesda MD 20817, USA | Engineer, Physicist |
| **Rosen, Nathaniel**<br>3273 SW Avalon Way, #B, Seattle WA 98126, USA | Concert Cellist |
| **Rosenbaum, Edward E**<br>333 NW 23rd St, Portland OR 97210, USA | Physician |
| **Rosenbaum, Michael**<br>A P A Talent & Literary Agency, 405 S Beverly Dr, #300, Beverly Hills CA 90212 USA | Actor |
| **Rosenberg, Alan**<br>Innovative Artists, 1505 10th St, Santa Monica CA 90401 USA | Actor |
| **Rosenberg, Howard**<br>5859 Larboard Lane, Agoura Hills CA 91301, USA | Music Critic |
| **Rosenberg, Marianne**<br>Public Image, Bulowstr 49, 10783 Berlin, Germany | Singer, Songwriter |
| **Rosenberg, Pierre M**<br>Musee du Louvre, 34-36 Quai du Louvre, 75068 Paris, France | Museum Executive |
| **Rosenberg, Scott**<br>W M E Entertainment, 9601 Wilshire Blvd, #300, Beverly Hills CA 90210 USA | Writer |
| **Rosenberg, Steven A**<br>National Cancer Institute, 31 Center Dr, Building 10, Bethesda MD 20892, USA | Oncologist, Surgeon |
| **Rosenberg, Tina**<br>New School for Social Research, World Policy Institute, New York NY 10011, USA | Writer |
| **Rosenblath, Marshall N**<br>2311 Via Siena, La Jolla CA 92037, USA | Physicist |
| **Rosenblatt, Dana**<br>39 Cleveland Road, Chestnut Hill MA 02467, USA | Boxer |
| **Rosenbluth, Leonard R (Lennie)**<br>124 Meadowmont Village Circle, Chapel Hill NC 27517, USA | Basketball Player |
| **Rosenburg, Saul A**<br>Stanford University Medical School, Oncology Division, 300 Pasteur Dr, Stanford CA 94305, USA | Oncologist |
| **Rosendahl, Heidemarie (Heide) Ecker-**<br>Burscheider Str 426, 51381 Leverkusen, Germany | Track Athlete |
| **Rosenfeld, Isadore**<br>Warner Books, 1271 Ave of Americas, New York NY 10020 USA | Clinical Physician |
| **Rosenfels, Sage J**<br>19651 Hickory St, Omaha NE 68130, USA | Football Player |
| **Rosenfelt, David**<br>Warner Books, 1271 Ave of Americas, New York NY 10020 USA | Writer |
| **Rosenfield, Ben**<br>United Talent Agency, U T A Plaza, 9336 Civic Center Dr, Beverly Hills CA 90210 USA | Actor |
| **Rosenfield, John Max**<br>75 State St, #1800, Boston MA 02109, USA | Educator |
| **Rosengrant, John**<br>Legacy Effects, 340 Parkside Dr, San Fernando CA 91340, USA | Visual Effects Designer |
| **Rosengren, Eric**<br>Federal Reserve Bank, 500 Atlantic Ave, Boston MA 02210, USA | Government Official, Financier |
| **Rosenquist, James A**<br>1334 Osowaw Blvd, Spring Hill FL 34607, USA | Artist |
| **Rosenstein, Samuel M**<br>US Court of International Trade, 2200 S Ocean Lane, Fort Lauderdale FL 33316, USA | Judge |
| **Rosenthal, Amy Krouse**<br>Harper Collins Publishers, 10 E 53rd St, Cellar 1, New York NY 10022 USA | Writer |
| **Rosenthal, Jacob (Jack)**<br>New York Times, Editorial Dept, 229 W 43rd St, New York NY 10036, USA | Journalist |
| **Rosenthal, Jody Anschutz**<br>18938 E McDowell Mountain Dr, Rio Verde AZ 85263, USA | Golfer |
| **Rosenthal, Mark D**<br>Verve Talent, 9696 Culver Blvd, #301, Culver City CA 90232, USA | Director, Producer, Writer |
| **Rosenthal, Philip**<br>Creative Artists Agency, 2000 Ave of Stars, #100, Los Angeles CA 90067 USA | Producer, Writer, Actor |
| **Rosenthal, Rachel**<br>2847 S Robertson Blvd, Los Angeles CA 90034, USA | Performance Artist |
| **Rosenthal, Rick**<br>Whitewater Films, 11264 La Grange Ave, Los Angeles CA 90025, USA | Director |
| **Rosenthal, Robert J**<br>Philadelphia Inquirer, Editorial Dept, 400 N Broad St, Philadelphia PA 19130, USA | Editor |
| **Rosenzweig, Barney**<br>2311 Fisher Island Dr, Miami Beach FL 33109, USA | Producer |
| **Rosenzweig, Robert M**<br>1462 Dana Ave, Palo Alto CA 94301, USA | Educator |
| **Roses, Allen D**<br>Glaxo Wellcome, 5 Moore Dr, Durham NC 27709, USA | Neurologist |
| **Rosewall, Ken**<br>Turramurra, 111 Pentacost Ave, Sydney NSW 2074, Australia | Tennis Player |
| **Roshan, Hrithik**<br>Filmkraft Mayur, Tilak Road, Santa Cruz (W), Mumbai MS 400054, India | Actor |
| **Roshan, Rakesh**<br>Kavita 10th Road, J V P D Scheme, Mumbai MS 400049, India | Director, Producer, Actor |
| **Rosin, Dino**<br>Arte Studio, Fondamento Manin 40, 30141 Murano, Italy | Sculptor |
| **Rosinski, Edward J**<br>1308 Kellogg Ave, Utica NY 13502, USA | Inventor (Zeolite Catalytic Cracking) |
| **Rosman, Mark**<br>Paradigm Agency, 360 N Crescent Dr, North Building, Beverly Hills CA 90210 USA | Director |
| **Rosner, Robert**<br>4950 S Greenwood Ave, Chicago IL 60615, USA | Astrophysicist |
| **Rosnes, Renee**<br>Integrity Talent, 1 Westcroft Court, Cockeysville MD 21030 USA | Jazz Pianist |
| **Rosovsky, Henry**<br>130 Mount Auburn St, #506, Cambridge MA 02138, USA | Economist |
| **Ross Fairbanks, Anne**<br>995 Lombardy Lane, Denver CO 80215, USA | Swimmer |
| **Ross, Aaron J**<br>13001 Bay Hill Dr, Beltsville MD 20705, USA | Football Player |
| **Ross, Annie**<br>Abby Hoffer Enterprises, 223 1/2 E 48th St, New York NY 10017 USA | Actress, Singer |

**Ross, Atticus** — Composer
Costa Communications, 8265 Sunset Blvd, #101, Los Angeles CA 90046, USA
**Ross, Ben** — Director
Brillstein Entertainment Partners, 9150 Wilshire Blvd, #350, Beverly Hills CA 90212 USA
**Ross, Betsy** — Sportscaster
ESPN-TV, Sports Dept, ESPN Plaza, 935 Middle St, Bristol CT 06010 USA
**Ross, Charlotte** — Actress
Untitled Entertainment, 350 S Beverly Dr, #200, Beverly Hills CA 90212 USA
**Ross, Chris** — Bassist, Keyboardist (Wolfmother)
John Watson Mgmt, PO Box 281, Surry Hills NSW 2010, Australia
**Ross, Christopher** — Cinematographer
Independent Talent Group, 40 Whitfield St, London W1T 2RH, England
**Ross, Cody J** — Baseball Player
21469 N 83rd St, Scottsdale AZ 85255, USA
**Ross, David A** — Museum Director
Whitney Museum of American Art, 945 Madison Ave, New York NY 10021, USA
**Ross, David W (Dave)** — Baseball Player
2768 Millstone Plantation Road, Tallahassee FL 32312, USA
**Ross, Diana** — Singer, Actress
Sunshine Sachs Assoc, 149 5th Ave, #700, New York NY 10010, USA
**Ross, Don** — Body Builder
PO Box 981, Venice CA 90294, USA
**Ross, Evan** — Actor
L I N K Entertainment, 11872 La Grange Ave, Los Angeles CA 90025 USA
**Ross, F Robert (Bob)** — Baseball Player
862 Bergamo Ave, San Jacinto CA 92583, USA
**Ross, Gary** — Director, Writer
Creative Artists Agency, 2000 Ave of Stars, #100, Los Angeles CA 90067 USA
**Ross, Gary D** — Baseball Player
1729 Cuadro Vista, San Marcus CA 92078, USA
**Ross, Jeffrey (Jeff)** — Actor, Comedian
Thruline Entertainment, 9250 Wilshire Blvd, #100, Beverly Hills CA 90212 USA
**Ross, Jerry L** — Astronaut
N A S A, Johnson Space Center, 2101 NASA Road, Houston TX 77058 USA
**Ross, John** — Chemist
620 Sand Hill Road, #402B, Palo Alto CA 94304, USA
**Ross, Jonathan** — Actor
Off the Kerb Productions, 22 Thornhill Crescent, London N1 1BJ, England
**Ross, Karie** — Sportscaster
ESPN-TV, Sports Dept, ESPN Plaza, 935 Middle St, Bristol CT 06010 USA
**Ross, Katharine** — Actress
33050 Pacific Coast Highway, Malibu CA 90265, USA
**Ross, Kevin L** — Football Player
537 Beacon St, Camden NJ 08105, USA
**Ross, Kyla B** — Gymnast
Gym-Max Academy, 2969 Century Place, Costa Mesa CA 92626, USA
**Ross, Liberty** — Model
Storm Model Agency, 5 Jubilee Place, Chelsea, London SW3 3TD, England
**Ross, Lonny** — Actor, Comedian
Thruline Entertainment, 9250 Wilshire Blvd, #100, Beverly Hills CA 90212 USA
**Ross, Marion** — Actress
C E S D, 10635 Santa Monica Blvd, #130, Los Angeles CA 90025 USA
**Ross, Mark J** — Baseball Player
1747 N Wild Hyacinth Dr, Tucson AZ 85715, USA
**Ross, Marv** — Guitarist (Quarterflash)
Pacific Talent Agency, PO Box 19145, Portland OR 97280, USA
**Ross, Matt** — Actor
W M E Entertainment, 9601 Wilshire Blvd, #300, Beverly Hills CA 90210 USA
**Ross, Rick** — Rap Artist, Songwriter
Multi Entertainment Group, 4044 W Lake Mary Blvd, #104-324, Lake Mary FL 32746, USA
**Ross, Ricky** — Singer (Deacon Blue)
Impressive Public Relations, 9 Jeffreys Place, London NW1 9PP, England
**Ross, Rindy** — Singer, Saxophonist (Quarterflash)
Pacific Talent Agency, PO Box 19145, Portland OR 97280, USA
**Ross, Terrence** — Basketball Player
Toronto Raptors, Air Canada Center, 20 Bay St, Toronto ON M5J 2N8, Canada
**Ross, Thomas W, Sr** — Educator
University of North Carolina, President's Office, 910 Raleigh Road, Chapel Hill NC 27514, USA
**Ross, Tracee Ellis** — Actress
I C M Partners, 10250 Constellation Blvd, #900, Los Angeles CA 90067 USA
**Ross, Wilburn K** — WW II Army Hero (CMH)
819 Haskell St, Dupont WA 98327, USA
**Ross, William** — Composer
Gorfaine/Schwartz, 4111 W Alameda Ave, #509, Burbank CA 91505 USA
**Rossant, Colette** — Writer
Bloomsbury Publishing, 50 Bedford Square, London WC1B 3DP, England
**Rossdale, Gavin M** — Singer, Songwriter (Bush); Actor
Creative Artists Agency, 2000 Ave of Stars, #100, Los Angeles CA 90067 USA
**Rossellini, Isabella** — Model, Actress
Ancieri Assoc, 345 Madison Ave, #2315, New York NY 10165, USA
**Rossen, Carol** — Actress
15450 Longbow Dr, Sherman Oaks CA 91403, USA
**Rosser, Ronald E** — WW II Army Hero (CMH)
36 James St, Roseville OH 43777, USA
**Rosset, Marc** — Tennis Player
Michel Rosset, Rue Albert Gos 16, 1206 Geneva, Switzerland
**Rossi, Anni** — Violist
Agency Group Ltd, 142 W 57th St, #600, New York NY 10019 USA
**Rossi, Derrick J** — Pathologist
Harvard University, Stem Cell Institute, 124 Mount Auburn St, Cambridge MA 02138, USA
**Rossi, Paolo** — Soccer Player
F C Juventus, Corso Galilo Ferraris 32, 10128 Turin, Italy
**Rossi, Semino** — Singer
Paul Promotion, Uhlandstr 49, 41238 Monchengladbach, Germany
**Rossi, Theo** — Actor
Greene Assoc, 1901 Ave of Stars, #130, Los Angeles CA 90067 USA

| | |
|---|---|
| **Rossi, Valentino** | Motorcycle Racing Rider |
| Via Boceaceo 20, 81100 Pesaro, Italy | |
| **Rossier, Bernard** | Pharmacologist |
| University of Lausanne, Biology Dept, Rue du Bugnon 27, 1005 Lausanne, Switzerland | |
| **Rossington, Gary R** | Guitarist (Lynyrd Skynyrd) |
| Vector Mgmt, PO Box 120479, Nashville TN 37212 USA | |
| **Rossini, Bianca** | Actress |
| Arlene Thornton, 12001 Ventura Blvd, #201, Studio City CA 91604, USA | |
| **Rossio, Terry** | Writer, Producer |
| Creative Artists Agency, 2000 Ave of Stars, #100, Los Angeles CA 90067 USA | |
| **Rossiter, Martin** | Singer, Pianist (Gene) |
| Agency Group Ltd, 361-373 City Road, London EC1V 1PQ, England | |
| **Rossiter, Robert E** | Businessman |
| Lear Corp, 21557 Telegraph Road, Southfield MI 48033, USA | |
| **Rosskopf, Joerg** | Table Tennis Player |
| Wiesenstr 13, 76833 Siebeldingen, Germany | |
| **Rossman, Michael G** | Biochemist |
| 1208 Wiley Dr, West Lafayette IN 47906, USA | |
| **Rosso, Louis T** | Businessman |
| 4300 N Harbor Blvd, Fullerton CA 92835, USA | |
| **Rossouw, Jacques** | Physician |
| National Institutes of Health, Women's Health Initiative, 6701 Rockledge Dr, Bethesda MD 20817, USA | |
| **Rossovich, Rick** | Actor |
| Schumacher Mgmt, 10323 Santa Monica Blvd, #101, Los Angeles CA 90024, USA | |
| **Rossovich, Timothy J (Tim)** | Football Player, Actor |
| 19811 Wildwood West Dr, Penn Valley CA 95946, USA | |
| **Rossum, Allen B L** | Football Player |
| 5669 Legends Club Circle, Braselton GA 30517, USA | |
| **Rossum, Emmy** | Actress, Singer |
| Schiff Co, 9220 Sunset Blvd, #106, West Hollywood CA 90069 USA | |
| **Rossy, Elam J (Rico)** | Baseball Player |
| A7 Calle Atenas, Repto Flamingo, Ext Forest Hills, Bayamon PR 00959, USA | |
| **Rost, Andrea** | Opera Singer |
| Nefelejes U 27, Budaors 2040, Hungary | |
| **Roszak, Thomas** | Architect |
| Roszak/A D C, PO Box 8528, Northfield IL 60093, USA | |
| **Rota, Darcy** | Ice Hockey Player |
| 2510 Ashurst Ave, Coquitlam BC V3K 5T4, Canada | |
| **Rotas, Nikiphoros G** | Composer |
| 15 Astydamantos St, Athens 116 34, Greece | |
| **Roth, Andrea** | Actress |
| Domain Talent, 9229 W Sunset Blvd, #710, West Hollywood CA 90069 USA | |
| **Roth, Ann** | Costume Designer |
| Road 3, Box 3124, Bangor PA 18013, USA | |
| **Roth, Arnold** | Cartoonist (Poor Arnold's Almanac) |
| National Cartoonists Society, 9 Ebony Court, Brooklyn NY 11229, USA | |
| **Roth, David Lee** | Singer (Van Halen), Songwriter |
| Rhino Entertainment, 3400 W Olive Ave, Burbank CA 91505, USA | |
| **Roth, Doug** | Basketball Player |
| 9975 Spillway Circle, #201, Cordova TN 38016, USA | |
| **Roth, Eli** | Actor, Director, Writer |
| Creative Artists Agency, 2000 Ave of Stars, #100, Los Angeles CA 90067 USA | |
| **Roth, Jack A** | Molecular Biologist |
| M D Anderson Medical Center, 1515 Holcombe Blvd, #207, Houston TX 77030 USA | |
| **Roth, Jane R** | Judge |
| US Court of Appeals, 333 Constitution Ave NW, #3128, Washington DC 20001, USA | |
| **Roth, Jesse** | Endocrinologist |
| National Institute of Arthritis, 9000 Rockville Pike, Bethesda MD 20892, USA | |
| **Roth, Joe** | Businessman |
| Creative Artists Agency, 2000 Ave of Stars, #100, Los Angeles CA 90067 USA | |
| **Roth, John A** | Businessman |
| Nortel Networks Corp, 8200 Dixie Road, Brampton ON L6T 5P6, Canada | |
| **Roth, Klaus F** | Mathematician |
| Colbost, 16A Drummond Road, Iverness IV2 4NB, Scotland | |
| **Roth, Mark S** | Bowler |
| 13 Wellesley Road, Montclair NJ 07043, USA | |
| **Roth, Matt** | Actor |
| Bauman Redanty Shaul Agency, 5757 Wilshire Blvd, #473, Los Angeles CA 90036 USA | |
| **Roth, Matthew M (Matt)** | Football Player |
| 14081 SW 54th St, Miramar FL 33027, USA | |
| **Roth, Michael S** | Educator |
| Wesleyan University, President's Office, Wesleyan Station, Middletown CT 06459, USA | |
| **Roth, Philip** | Writer |
| Wylie Agency, 250 W 57th St, #2114, New York NY 10107, USA | |
| **Roth, Rachel** | Actress |
| Amsel Eisenstadt Frazier, 5055 Wilshire Blvd, #865, Los Angeles CA 90036 USA | |
| **Roth, Tim** | Actor, Director |
| Markham Froggatt Irwin, Julian House, 4 Windmill St, London W1P 1HF, England | |
| **Roth, Veronica** | Writer |
| Katherine Tegen Books, Harper Collins Publishers, 10 E 53rd St, Cellar 1, New York NY 10022, USA | |
| **Rothberg, Patti** | Singer, Songwriter |
| Marquee Mgmt, 240 Madison Ave, #800, New York NY 10016, USA | |
| **Rothenberg, Adam** | Actor |
| United Talent Agency, U T A Plaza, 9336 Civic Center Dr, Beverly Hills CA 90210 USA | |
| **Rothhaar, Will** | Actor |
| Innovative Artists, 1505 10th St, Santa Monica CA 90401 USA | |
| **Rothman, James E** | Nobel Medicine Laureate |
| Yale University, Chemistry Dept, 225 Prospect St, Box 208107, New Haven CT 06520, USA | |
| **Rothman, John** | Actor |
| Don Buchwald Talent Agency, 10 E 44th St, New York NY 10017 USA | |
| **Rothman, Les** | Basketball Player |
| 11854 Fountainside Circle, Boynton Beach FL 33437, USA | |
| **Rothman, Stephanie** | Director |
| 11925 Mayfield Ave, #4, Los Angeles CA 90049, USA | |
| **Rothrock, Cynthia** | Actress |
| 561 Calle Arroyo, Thousand Oaks CA 91360, USA | |

| | |
|---|---|
| **Rothschild, Lawrence L (Larry)**<br>4508 W Culbreath Ave, Tampa FL 33609, USA | Baseball Player, Manager |
| **Rothstein, Ronald (Ron)**<br>60 Edgewater Dr, #4E, Coral Gables FL 33133, USA | Basketball Coach |
| **Rotimi**<br>Category 5 Entertainment, 1601 Cloverfield Blvd, South Tower #200, Santa Monica CA 90404, USA | Singer, Songwriter, Actor |
| **Rottenberg, Linda**<br>Endeavor Global, 900 Broadway, #301, New York NY 10003, USA | Non-Profit Executive |
| **Rotter, Stephen A**<br>Paradigm Agency, 360 N Crescent Dr, North Building, Beverly Hills CA 90210 USA | Editor |
| **Rottet, Lauren**<br>D M J M/Rottet, 515 S Flower St, 800, Los Angeles CA 90071, USA | Interior Designer |
| **Rottino, Vincent A (Vinny)**<br>4939 Crystal Spring, Racine WI 53406, USA | Baseball Player |
| **Rottner, Marvin (Mickey)**<br>5757 N Sheridan Road, #88, Chicago IL 60660, USA | Basketball Player |
| **Rouco Varela, Antonio Maria Cardinal**<br>Archdiocese of Madrid, Bailen 8, 28071 Madrid, Spain | Religious Leader |
| **Rouen, Thomas F (Tom), Jr**<br>20343 N Hayden Road, #105, Scottsdale AZ 85255, USA | Football Player |
| **Rougeau, Laurianne**<br>Hockey Canada, 151 Canada Olympic Road SW, #201, Calgary AB  T3B 6B7, Canada | Ice Hockey Player |
| **Roughead, Gary**<br>Stanford University, Hoover Institution, Stanford CA 94305, USA | Navy Admiral |
| **Roughgarden, Joan E**<br>Stanford University, Biological Sciences Dept, Stanford CA 94305, USA | Ecologist, Evolutionary Biologist |
| **Rouhani, Hassan**<br>President's Office, Pastor Ave, Teheran, Iran | President, Iran |
| **Rouleau, Joseph-Alfred**<br>32 Lakeshore Road, Beaconsfield QC H9W 4H3, England | Opera Singer |
| **Roulston, Tom**<br>6814 E 25th St, #N, Wichita KS 67226, USA | Ice Hockey Player |
| **Roundtree, Raleigh C**<br>2001 Roosevelt Dr, Augusta GA 30904, USA | Football Player |
| **Roundtree, Richard**<br>4441 Cahuenga Blvd, #A, Toluca Lake CA 91602, USA | Actor |
| **Roundtree, Saudia**<br>University of Central Florida, Athletic Dept, 4000 Central Florida Blvd, Orlando FL 32816, USA | Basketball Player, Coach |
| **Rounsaville, V Gene**<br>537 Red Rome Lane, Brentwood CA 94513, USA | Baseball Player |
| **Rourke, James P (Jim)**<br>466 Plymouth St, Abington MA 02351, USA | Football Player |
| **Rourke, Mickey**<br>Edelstein Laird Sobel, 9255 W Sunset Blvd, #800, Los Angeles CA 90069 USA | Actor |
| **Rouse, Bob**<br>19135 74th Ave, RR 15, Surrey BC V4N 3G5, Canada | Ice Hockey Player |
| **Rouse, Christopher**<br>University of Rochester, Eastman Music School, 26 Gibbs St, Rochester NY 14604, USA | Composer |
| **Rouse, Christopher**<br>Levin Law, 8060 Melrose Ave, #205, Los Angeles CA 90046, USA | Editor |
| **Rouse, Irving**<br>509 Rockavon Road, Narberth PA 19072, USA | Anthropologist |
| **Rouse, Jeffrey (Jeff)**<br>600 Sharon Park Dr, #B208, Menlo Park CA 94025, USA | Swimmer |
| **Rouse, Mitch**<br>Paradigm Agency, 360 N Crescent Dr, North Building, Beverly Hills CA 90210 USA | Actor, Director, Writer |
| **Rousey, Ronda J (Rowdy)**<br>Hayastan M M A Academy, 7229 Atoll Ave, North Hollywood CA 91601, USA | Judo Athlete, Mixed Martial Fighter |
| **Roush, Jack**<br>Roush Racing, 4600 Roush Place, Concord NC 28027, USA | Auto Racing Executive |
| **Rouson, C Lee**<br>20 Main St, Flanders NJ 07836, USA | Football Player |
| **Rousseau, J J Robert (Bobby)**<br>Golf Club, PO Box 222 Suc Bureau Chef, Louiseville QC J5V 2L6, Canada | Ice Hockey Player |
| **Rousseff, Dilma V**<br>Palacio do Planalto, Praca 3 Poderas, 70 150 Brasilia DF, Brazil | President, Brazil |
| **Roussel, Dominic**<br>Success Hockey, 1717 Rue Fleetwood, Laval QC H7N 4B2, Canada | Ice Hockey Player |
| **Roussel, Nathalie**<br>Artmedia, 20 Ave Rapp, 75007 Paris, France | Actress |
| **Roussel, Thomas J (Tom)**<br>13 Heron Lane, Mandeville LA 70471, USA | Football Player |
| **Rousselot, Philippe**<br>Gersh Agency, 9465 Wilshire Blvd, #600, Beverly Hills CA 90212 USA | Cinematographer |
| **Route, Ronald A**<br>Inspector General, HqUSN, Pentagon, Washington DC 20350 USA | Navy Admiral |
| **Routh, Brandon**<br>Main Title Mgmt, 8383 Wilshire Blvd, #408, Beverly Hills CA 90211 USA | Actor |
| **Routledge, Alison**<br>Marmont Mgmt, Langham House, 302/8 Regent St, London W1R 5AL, England | Actress |
| **Routledge, Patricia**<br>Marmont Mgmt, Langham House, 302/8 Regent St, London W1R 5AL, England | Actress |
| **Routt, Stanford B**<br>Kansas City Chiefs, 1 Arrowhead Dr, Kansas City KS 64129 USA | Football Player |
| **Rouvali, Santtu-Matias**<br>Tapiola Sinfonietta, PO Box 3262, 02070 City of Espoo, Finland | Conductor |
| **Rouve, Jean-Paul**<br>U B B A, 6 Rue de Braque, 75003 Paris, France | Actor |
| **Rouvel, Catherine**<br>Artmedia, 20 Ave Rapp, 75007 Paris, France | Actress |
| **Rouviere, Koby**<br>C E S D, 10635 Santa Monica Blvd, #130, Los Angeles CA 90025 USA | Actor |
| **Rouw, Roxanne (Roxy)**<br>Association of Surfing Professionals, 300 Pacific Coast Highway, #114, Huntington Beach CA 92648 USA | Surfer, Model, Actress |
| **Roux, Albert H**<br>Le Gavroche, 43 Upper Brook St, London W1Y 1PF, England | Chef, Restaurateur |

**Rothschild - Roux**

**Roux, Michel A, Sr** — Chef, Restaurateur
Waterside Inn, Ferry Road, Bray, Berkshire SL6 2AT, England
**Rove, Karl C** — Government Official
1333 New Hampshire Ave NW, #600, Washington DC 20036, USA
**Roven, Charles (Chuck)** — Producer
Atlas Entertainment, 9200 Sunset Blvd, #1000, Los Angeles CA 90069, USA
**Rovero, Jennifer** — Model
Playboy Promotions, 9346 Civic Center Dr, #200, Beverly Hills CA 90210 USA
**Rovner, Ilana D** — Judge
US Court of Appeals, 219 S Dearborn St, Chicago IL 60604, USA
**Rovner, Michael** — Photographer, Artist
640 Broadway, #7E, New York NY 10012, USA
**Rowan, Kelly** — Actress
Untitled Entertainment, 350 S Beverly Dr, #200, Beverly Hills CA 90212 USA
**Rowan, Peter** — Singer, Guitarist
A-Train Entertainment, 401 Grand Ave, #300, Oakland CA 94610, USA
**Rowand, Aaron R** — Baseball Player
34 Meadowhawk Lane, Las Vegas NV 89135, USA
**Rowbotham, Stephen** — Rowing Athlete
Leander Club, Henley on Thames, Leander RG9 2LP, England
**Rowden, William H** — Navy Admiral
55 Pinewood Court, Lancaster VA 22503, USA
**Rowdon, Wade L** — Baseball Player
230 Crooked Tree Trail, Deland FL 32724, USA
**Rowe, Brad** — Actor
Domain Talent, 9229 W Sunset Blvd, #710, West Hollywood CA 90069 USA
**Rowe, Charlie** — Actor
United Talent Agency, U T A Plaza, 9336 Civic Center Dr, Beverly Hills CA 90210 USA
**Rowe, David H (Dave)** — Football Player
980 Sherwood Ave, Asheboro NC 27205, USA
**Rowe, Jack** — Writer
Pocket Books, 1230 Ave of Americas, New York NY 10020 USA
**Rowe, John W** — Businessman
Exelon Corp, 10 S Dearborn St, #4800, Chicago IL 60603, USA
**Rowe, Misty** — Actress, Model
2193 River Road, Egg Harbor Cay NJ 08215, USA
**Rowe, Nicholas** — Actor
Julian Belfrage Assoc, 9 Argyll St, #300, London W1F 7TG, England
**Rowe, Robert B (Bob)** — Football Player
1754 Highview Circle Court, Ballwin MO 63021, USA
**Rowe, Sandra M** — Editor
Portland Oregonian, Editorial Dept, 1320 SW Broadway, Portland OR 97201, USA
**Rowe, Thomas J (Tom)** — Ice Hockey Player
1121 Park West Blvd, Mount Pleasant SC 29466, USA
**Rowell, Victoria** — Actress
Third Hill Entertainment, 195 S Beverly Dr, #400, Beverly Hills CA 90212, USA
**Rowland, Dave** — Singer (Dave & Sugar)
PO Box 121089, Nashville TN 37212, USA
**Rowland, Derrick** — Basketball Player
3 Island View Road, Cohoes NY 12047, USA
**Rowland, J David** — Businessman
6 Danbury St, London N1 8JU, England
**Rowland, James Anthony** — Governor General, Australia; Marshal
17 Pindari Ave, Mosman NSW 2088, Australia
**Rowland, Kelly** — Singer (Destiny's Child), Actress
I C M Partners, 10250 Constellation Blvd, #900, Los Angeles CA 90067 USA
**Rowland, Landon H** — Businessman
Kansas City Southern, PO Box 219335, Kansas City MO 64121, USA
**Rowland, Mark** — Track Athlete, Coach
Oregon Track Club, PO Box 11364, Eugene OR 97440, USA
**Rowland, Richard G (Rich)** — Baseball Player
593 E 1st St, Cloverdale CA 95425, USA
**Rowlands, Gena** — Actress
7917 Woodrow Wilson Dr, Los Angeles CA 90046, USA
**Rowlands, Tom** — Singer, Musician (Chemical Brothers)
9PR, 65-69 White Lion St, London N1 9PR, England
**Rowley, Cynthia** — Fashion Designer
W M E Entertainment, 9601 Wilshire Blvd, #300, Beverly Hills CA 90210 USA
**Rowling, J K (Jo)** — Writer
PO Box 27036, Edinburgh EH10 5WB, Scotland
**Rowlinson, John S** — Chemist
12 Pullens Field, Headington OX3 0BU, England
**Rowny, Edward L** — Army General
6200 Oregon Ave NW, #345, Washington DC 20015, USA
**Rowser, John F** — Football Player
17564 Alta Vista Dr, Southfield MI 48075, USA
**Roxburgh, Richard** — Actor
United Agents, 12-26 Lexington St, London W1F 0LE, England
**Roy** — Animal Illusionist (Siegfried & Roy)
Kirvin Doak Communications, 7935 W Sahara Ave, #201, Las Vegas NV 89117, USA
**Roy C** — Singer, Songwriter
Carolina Record Distributors, 229 Augusta Highway, Allendale SC 29810, USA
**Roy, Alfred** — Songwriter, Lyricist
2708 Range Road, Los Angeles CA 90065, USA
**Roy, Andre** — Ice Hockey Player
Calgary Flames, PO Box 1540, Station M, Calgary AB T2P 3B9, Canada
**Roy, Aruna** — Political, Social Activist
Mazdoor Kisan Shakti Sangathan, Village Devdoongri, Post Brar, Rajsamand, Rajasthan, India
**Roy, Arundhati** — Writer
India Ink Publishing, C1 Soami Nagar, New Delhi 110 017, India
**Roy, Brandon** — Basketball Player
19807 183rd Way SE, Renton WA 98058, USA
**Roy, Derek** — Ice Hockey Player
100 Rivermist Dr, Buffalo NY 14202, USA
**Roy, Drew** — Actor
United Talent Agency, U T A Plaza, 9336 Civic Center Dr, Beverly Hills CA 90210 USA

|  |  |
|---|---|
| **Roy, John**<br>Galloways One, 15 Lexham Mews, London W8 6JW, England | Actor, Comedian |
| **Roy, Jonathan**<br>Agency Group Ltd, 142 W 57th St, #600, New York NY 10019 USA | Singer |
| **Roy, Lesley**<br>Jive Records, 137-39 W 25th St, #1100, New York NY 10001 USA | Singer |
| **Roy, Loriene**<br>American Library Assn, 50 E Huron, Chicago IL 60611, USA | Association Executive, Librarian |
| **Roy, Patrick**<br>201 Chemin de la Plage Saint Laurent, Quebec QC G1Y 1W6, Canada | Ice Hockey Player |
| **Roy, Rachel**<br>Mavrick Artists Agency, 6100 Wilshire Blvd, #550, Los Angeles CA 90048, USA | Fashion Designer |
| **Roy, Reena**<br>Pam Villa D'Monte Park Road, Bandra, Mumbai MS 400050, India | Actress |
| **Royal, Bert V**<br>Paradigm Agency, 360 N Crescent Dr, North Building, Beverly Hills CA 90210 USA | Producer, Writer |
| **Royal, Billy Joe**<br>Bobby Roberts, 3050 Business Park Circle, #303, Goodlettsville TN 37221 USA | Singer; Songwriter |
| **Royal, Lauren**<br>PO Box 52932, Irvine CA 92619, USA | Writer |
| **Royal, Segolene**<br>Parti Socialiste, 10 Rue de Solferino, 75333 Paris, France | Government Official, France |
| **Royals, Mark A**<br>4035 Courtside Way, Tampa FL 33618, USA | Football Player |
| **Royce Da 5'9"**<br>I C M Partners, 10250 Constellation Blvd, #900, Los Angeles CA 90067 USA | Rap Artist |
| **Roye, Orpheus M**<br>12955 NW 18th Manor, Pembroke Pines FL 33028, USA | Football Player |
| **Royer, Stanley D (Stan)**<br>9301 Christopher Lake Dr, Columbia IL 62236, USA | Baseball |
| **Royo Sanchez, Aristides**<br>Morgan & Morgan, PO Box 1824, Panama City 1, Panama | President, Panama |
| **Royo, Andre**<br>Don Buchwald Talent Agency, 6500 Wilshire Blvd, #2200, Los Angeles CA 90048 USA | Actor |
| **Royo, Jose**<br>Triad Art Group, 44 E Belmont Dr, Romeoville IL 60446, USA | Artist |
| **Royo-Torres, Rafael**<br>Teruel-Dinopolis Museum, Poligono de los Planos, 44002 Teruel, Spain | Paleontologist |
| **Royster, Jeron K (Jerry)**<br>1 Brewers Way, Milwaukee WI 53214, USA | Baseball Player, Manager |
| **Royster, Willie A**<br>229 55th St NE, Washington DC 20019, USA | Baseball Player |
| **Rozalla**<br>Mission Control, City Business Center, Lower Road, London SE16 2XB, England | Singer |
| **Rozanov, Evgeny G**<br>International Architecture Academy, 2nd Brestskaya Str 4, 103104 Moscow, Russia | Architect |
| **Rozbruch, S Robert**<br>Cornell University Weill Medical College, 519 E 72nd St, New York NY 10021, USA | Orthopedic Surgeon |
| **Rozema, David S (Dave)**<br>1560 N Renaud Road, Grosse Pointe Woods MI 48236, USA | Baseball Player |
| **Rozema, Patricia**<br>Creative Artists Agency, 2000 Ave of Stars, #100, Los Angeles CA 90067 USA | Director |
| **Rozhdestvensky, Gennady N**<br>Victor Hochhauser Ltd, 4 Oak Hill Way, London NW3, England | Conductor |
| **Rozier, Clifford G**<br>PO Box 1194, Palmetto FL 34220, USA | Basketball Player |
| **Rozier, Michael M (Mike)**<br>9 Hidden Hollow Lane, Sicklerville NJ 08081, USA | Football Player |
| **Roznovsky, Victor S (Vic)**<br>266 W Bluff Ave, Fresno CA 93711, USA | Baseball Player |
| **Rozsival, Michal**<br>6751 N Sunset Blvd, Glendale AZ 85305, USA | Ice Hockey Player |
| **Ruah, Daniela**<br>Gersh Agency, 9465 Wilshire Blvd, #600, Beverly Hills CA 90212 USA | Actress |
| **Ruais, Brie**<br>Nicole Klagsbrun Gallery, 532 W 24th St, New York NY 10001, USA | Ceramist |
| **Ruano Pascual, Virginia**<br>Women's Tennis Assn, 1 Progress Plaza, #1500, Saint Petersburg FL 33701 USA | Tennis Player |
| **Rubalcaba, Gonzalo**<br>Joel Chriss Co, 300 Mercer St, #3J, New York NY 10003 USA | Jazz Pianist, Composer |
| **Rubbia, Carlo**<br>C E R N, Particle Physics Laboratory, 1211 Geneva 23, Switzerland | Nobel Physics Laureate |
| **Ruben, Joseph P (Joe)**<br>Paradigm Agency, 360 N Crescent Dr, North Building, Beverly Hills CA 90210 USA | Director |
| **Rubens, Sibylla**<br>Kunstler Sekretariat am Gasteig, Rosenheimer Str 52, 81669 Munich, Germany | Opera Singer |
| **Rubenstein, Ann**<br>NBC-TV, News Dept, 30 Rockefeller Plaza, #270E, New York NY 10112 USA | Commentator |
| **Rubenstein, Edward**<br>Stanford University Medical School, Surgery Dept, Stanford CA 94305, USA | Physician |
| **Rubiano Saenz, Pedro Cardinal**<br>Archdiocese of Bogota, Carrera 7A, #10-20, Santa Fe de Bogota DC 1, Colombia | Religious Leader |
| **Rubick, Robin J (Rob)**<br>PO Box 63, Curtis MI 49820, USA | Football Player |
| **Rubik, Erno**<br>Rubik Studio, Varosmajor Utca 74, 1122 Budapest, Hungary | Inventor (Rubik Cube) |
| **Rubin, Amy**<br>Hervey/Grimes Talent, 10561 Missouri Ave, #2, Los Angeles CA 90025 USA | Actress |
| **Rubin, Chandra**<br>708 S Saint Antoine St, Lafayette LA 70501, USA | Tennis Player |
| **Rubin, Gloria**<br>I C M Partners, 10250 Constellation Blvd, #900, Los Angeles CA 90067 USA | Actress |
| **Rubin, Harry**<br>University of California, Molecular Biology Dept, Berkeley CA 94720, USA | Biologist |
| **Rubin, Jennifer**<br>Charles Riley Public Relations, 7122 Beverly Blvd, #F, Los Angeles CA 90036, USA | Actress, Model |

# R

**Rubin, Leigh** — Cartoonist (Rubes)
Creators Syndicate, 737 3rd St, Hermosa Beach CA 90254 USA

**Rubin, Richard** — Actor, Musician
Metropolitan Talent Agency, 5405 Wilshire Blvd, #218, Los Angeles CA 90036 USA

**Rubin, Robert** — Medical Researcher
Massachusetts General Hospital, 32 Fruit St, Boston MA 02114, USA

**Rubin, Robert E** — Secretary, Treasury; Financier
Citigroup Inc, 55 E 52nd St, New York NY 10055, USA

**Rubin, Tibor (Ted)** — Korean War Army Hero (CMH)
5442 Marietta Ave, Garden Grove CA 92845, USA

**Rubin, Vanessa** — Singer
Joel Chriss Co, 300 Mercer St, #3J, New York NY 10003 USA

**Rubin, Vera C** — Astronomer
Carnegie Institution, 5241 Broad Branch Road NW, Washington DC 20015, USA

**Rubinek, Saul** — Actor, Director, Producer
Great Northern Artists Mgmt, 350 Dupont St, Toronto ON M5R 1V9, Canada

**Rubino, Frank A** — Attorney
1001 Brickell Bay Dr, #2206, Miami FL 33131, USA

**Rubinoff, Ira** — Biologist
Smithsonian Tropical Research Institute, Roosevelt Ave, Building 401, Balboa, Ancon, Panama

**Rubinstein, John A** — Actor
4417 Leydon Ave, Woodland Hills CA 91364, USA

**Rubinstein, Jonathan J (Jon)** — Businessman, Computer Scientist
Palm Inc, 950 W Maude Ave, Sunnyvale CA 94085, USA

**Rubinstein, Peter J** — Religious Leader, Rabbi
Central Synagogue, 123 E 55th St, New York NY 10022, USA

**Rubin-Vega, Daphne** — Actress, Singer
Paradigm Agency, 360 N Crescent Dr, North Building, Beverly Hills CA 90210 USA

**Rubio, Paulina** — Singer
Sanctuary Artist Mgmt, 15301 Ventura Blvd, #400 Building B, Sherman Oaks CA 91403, USA

**Rubio, Ricard (Ricky)** — Basketball Player
Minnesota Timberwolves, Target Center, 600 1st Ave N, Minneapolis MN 55403 USA

**Ruby, Sterling** — Artist
Xavier Hufkens, 6-8 Rue Saint-Georges, 1050 Brussels, Belgium

**Rucchin, Steve** — Ice Hockey Player
614 Acacia Ave, Corona del Mar CA 92625, USA

**Rucci, Ralph** — Fashion Designer, Artist
151 W 26th St, #200, New York NY 10001, USA

**Rucci, Todd L** — Football Player
5 Southview Lane, Lititz PA 17543, USA

**Ruccolo, Richard** — Actor
A P A Talent & Literary Agency, 405 S Beverly Dr, #300, Beverly Hills CA 90212 USA

**Rucinski, Artur** — Opera Singer
I M G Artists, Hogarth Business Park, Chiswick, London W4 2TH, England

**Rucinsky, Martin** — Ice Hockey Player
8025 Bonhomme Ave, Saint Louis MO 63105, USA

**Ruck, Alan** — Actor
Innovative Artists, 1505 10th St, Santa Monica CA 90401 USA

**Ruckelshaus, William D** — Businessman, Government Official
999 3rd Ave, #3400, Seattle WA 98104, USA

**Ruckenstein, Eli** — Chemical Engineer
755 Renaissance Dr, #203, Buffalo NY 14221, USA

**Rucker, Anja** — Track Athlete
T U S Jena, Wollnitzer Str 42, 07749 Jena, Germany

**Rucker, Darius** — Singer (Hootie & the Blowfish)
McGhee Entertainment, 801 18th Ave S, Nashville TN 37203, USA

**Rucker, David M (Dave)** — Baseball Player
18602 Piper Place, Yorba Linda CA 92886, USA

**Rucker, Michael D (Mike)** — Football Player
5971 Rolling Ridge Dr, Kannapolis NC 28081, USA

**Rucker, Reginald J (Reggie)** — Football Player
4517 Saint Germain Blvd, Cleveland OH 44128, USA

**Rudakova, Natalya** — Actress
Don Buchwald Talent Agency, 10 E 44th St, New York NY 10017 USA

**Rudbottom, Roy R, Jr** — Diplomat
7831 Park Lane, #213A, Dallas TX 75225, USA

**Rudd, Delaney** — Basketball Player
422 Chesham Dr, Kernersville NC 27284, USA

**Rudd, Dwayne D** — Football Player
22 Williams Road, Trenton SC 29847, USA

**Rudd, John** — Basketball Player
4440 Sweet Bay Dr, Lake Charles LA 70611, USA

**Rudd, Paul** — Actor
United Talent Agency, U T A Plaza, 9336 Civic Center Dr, Beverly Hills CA 90210 USA

**Rudd, Phillip H N (Phil)** — Drummer (AC/DC)
Alberts Music, 9 Rangers Road, Neutral Bay, Sydney NSW 2089, Australia

**Rudd, Ricky** — Auto Racing Driver
Entertainment Marketing, 124 Summerville Dr, Mooresville NC 28115, USA

**Rudd, Xavier** — Singer, Songwriter
Creative Artists Agency, 1 Beadon Road, #400 London W6 0EA, England

**Ruddy, Timothy D (Tim)** — Football Player
3885 Vale View Lane, Mead CO 80542, USA

**Rudenstine, Neil L** — Educator
A W Mellon Foundation, 140 E 62nd St, New York NY 10065, USA

**Rudi, Joseph O (Joe)** — Baseball Player
17667 Deer Park Loop, Baker City OR 97814, USA

**Rudin, Scott** — Producer
Scott Rudin Productions, 120 W 45th St, #1001, New York NY 10036, USA

**Rudisha, David L** — Track Athlete
Saint Patrick's High School, PO Box 310, 30700 Iten, Keiyo District, Rift Valley Province, Kenya

**Rudnay, John C (Jack)** — Football Player
7219 Whipperwill Road, Versailles MO 65084, USA

**Rudner, Rita** — Actress, Comedienne, Writer
2877 Paradise Dr, #1605, Los Angeles CA 90032, USA

**Rudnick, Paul** — Writer
Creative Artists Agency, 2000 Ave of Stars, #100, Los Angeles CA 90067 USA

**Rubin - Rudnick**

**Rudolf, Kevin** — Singer, Musician, Songwriter
Cash Money/Motown Records, 6255 W Sunset Blvd, Los Angeles CA 90028, USA
**Rudolph, Alan S** — Director
William J Goldstein, 15760 Ventura Blvd, #1600, Encino CA 91436, USA
**Rudolph, Benjamin (Ben)** — Football Player
561 E General Gorgas Dr, Mobile AL 36617, USA
**Rudolph, Council, Jr** — Football Player
8310 Lago Vista Dr, Tampa FL 33614, USA
**Rudolph, John L (Jack)** — Football Player
2211 Glynndale Dr, Valdosta GA 31602, USA
**Rudolph, Kenneth V (Ken)** — Baseball Player
9969 E Bayview Dr, Scottsdale AZ 85258, USA
**Rudolph, Lars** — Actor
Gunda Kniggendorff Mgmt, Postfach 440414, 12004 Berlin, Germany
**Rudolph, Maya** — Actress, Comedienne
3 Arts Entertainment, 9460 Wilshire Blvd, #700, Beverly Hills CA 90212 USA
**Rudometkin, John** — Basketball Player
6181 Wise Road, Newcastle CA 95658, USA
**Rudorffer, Erich** — WW II German Luftwaffe Hero
Bismarkstr 3A, 23677 Bad Schwarteau, Germany
**Rudzinski, Witold** — Composer
Ul Narbutta 50 m 6, 02541 Warsaw, Poland
**Rue, Sara** — Actress, Comedienne
Alan David Mgmt, 8840 Wilshire Blvd, #200, Beverly Hills CA 90211, USA
**Ruebell, Matthew A (Matt)** — Baseball Player
7509 W Augusta Blvd, Yorktown IN 47396, USA
**Ruegamer, C Grey** — Football Player
7380 E Eastern Ave, #124, Las Vegas NV 89123, USA
**Ruehl, Mercedes** — Actress
Innovative Artists, 1505 10th St, Santa Monica CA 90401 USA
**Ruel, Claude** — Ice Hockey Coach
102-1450 Rue Beauhamois, Longueuil QC J4M 1X2, Canada
**Ruelas, Gabriel (Gabe)** — Boxer
1119 S Hudson Ave, Los Angeles CA 90019, USA
**Ruell, Aaron** — Actor, Director, Writer
Universal Media Artists, 8222 Melrose Ave, #203, Los Angeles CA 90048, USA
**Ruelle, David P** — Mathematician
1 Ave Charles-Comar, 91440 Bures-sur-Yvette, France
**Ruess, Nathaniel J (Nate)** — Singer (Fun, Format), Songwriter
Nettwerk Management Group, 1650 W 2nd Ave, Vancouver BC V6J 4R3, Canada
**Rueter, Kirk W** — Baseball Player
46 Pheasant Ridge Court, Nashville IL 62263, USA
**Ruether, Mike A** — Football Player
23014 Gardner Dr, Alpharetta GA 30009, USA
**Ruether, Rosemary R** — Theologian
530 Mayflower Road, Claremont CA 91711, USA
**Ruettgers, Kenneth F (Ken)** — Football Player
16897 Golden Stone Dr, Sisters OR 97759, USA
**Ruettiger, Daniel E (Rudy)** — Football Player
293 Goldstar St, Henderson NV 89012, USA
**Ruff, Howard J** — Financial Analyst, Writer
PO Box 441, Orem UT 84059, USA
**Ruff, Lindy** — Ice Hockey Player, Coach
5006 Winding Lane, Clarence NY 14031, USA
**Ruff, Matt** — Writer
Harper Collins Publishers, 10 E 53rd St, Cellar 1, New York NY 10022 USA
**Ruff, Orlando B** — Football Player
202 S Raymond Ave, #304, Pasadena CA 91105, USA
**Ruffalo, Mark** — Actor
Brillstein Entertainment Partners, 9150 Wilshire Blvd, #350, Beverly Hills CA 90212 USA
**Ruffcorn, Scott P** — Baseball Player
2137 Barton Hills Dr, Austin TX 78704, USA
**Ruffin, Bruce W** — Baseball Player
4808 Pyrenees Pass, Austin TX 78738, USA
**Ruffin, Johnny R** — Baseball Player
4229 Trumpworth Court, Valrico FL 33596, USA
**Ruffner, Paul** — Basketball Player
3352 N 100 E, #210, Provo UT 84604, USA
**Ruge, John A** — Cartoonist
240 Bronxville Road, #B4, Bronxville NY 10708, USA
**Ruge, Nina** — Commentator, Actress, Writer
Postfach 860611, 81633 Munich, Germany
**Rugers, Martin** — Astronomer
University of Washington, Astronomy Dept, Seattle WA 98195, USA
**Ruggiano, Justin M** — Baseball Player
8711 Tallwood Dr, Austin TX 78759, USA
**Ruggiero, Angela** — Ice Hockey Player
171 W 57th St, #8A, New York NY 10019, USA
**Ruhe, Martin** — Cinematographer
Independent Talent Group, 40 Whitfield St, London W1T 2RH, England
**Ruhl, Sarah** — Writer
Bret Adams Artists Agency, 448 W 44th St, New York NY 10036, USA
**Ruhnke, Kent** — Ice Hockey Player
Felsenrainstr 11, Zurich 8052, Switzerland
**Ruhsam, John W** — WW II Marine Corps Air Force Hero
1010 American Eagle Blvd, #346, Sun City Center FL 33573, USA
**Ruini, Camillo Cardinal** — Religious Leader
Diocese of Rome, Apostolic Palace, 00120 Vatican City
**Ruivivar, Anthony M** — Actor
Gersh Agency, 9465 Wilshire Blvd, #600, Beverly Hills CA 90212 USA
**Ruiz, Hector** — Businessman
Advanced Micro Devices, 1 A M D Place, PO Box 3453, Sunnyvale CA 94088, USA
**Ruiz, John** — Boxer
11009 Salford Dr, Las Vegas NV 89144, USA
**Ruiz, Manuel (Chico)** — Baseball Player
267 Calle Tapia, San Juan PR 00912, USA

**Ruiz-Corforte, Tracie L** — Synchronized Swimmer
B T O Foundation, 312 Sweet Cherry Court, Hollidaysburg PA 16648, USA
**Rukajarvi, Enni** — Slopestyle Skier
Red Bull, 1740 Stewart St, Santa Monica CA 90404, USA
**Rukeyser, William S** — Publisher
1509 Rudder Lane, Knoxville TN 37919, USA
**Rule, Ann** — Writer
PO Box 98846, Seattle WA 98198, USA
**Rule, Bobby F (Bob)** — Basketball Player
4303 Kansas Ave, Riverside CA 92507, USA
**Ruley, Amy** — Basketball Coach
North Dakota State University, Athletic Dept, Fargo ND 58105, USA
**Rulin, Olesya** — Actress
Paul Kohner, 9300 Wilshire Blvd, #555, Beverly Hills CA 90212 USA
**Rullo, Gerenoso C (Jerry)** — Basketball Player
300 Brookline Blvd, Havertown PA 19083, USA
**Rumer** — Singer, Songwriter
Agency Group Ltd, 361-373 City Road, London EC1V 1PQ, England
**Rummells, Dave** — Golfer
1820 Harbor Blvd, Kissimmee FL 34744, USA
**Rummenigge, Karl-Heinz** — Soccer Player
Eichleite 4, 80231 Grunwald, Germany
**Rumph, Michael J (Mike)** — Football Player
4686 SW 179th Way, Miramar FL 33029, USA
**Rumsfeld, Donald H** — Secretary, Defense; Businessman
1718 M St NW, #366, Washington DC 20036, USA
**Runager, Max C** — Football Player
109 Roger Smith, Williamsburg VA 23185, USA
**Runcie, James** — Writer
David Godwin Assoc, 55 Monument St, London WC2H 9DG, England
**Runco, Mario, Jr** — Astronaut
207 Lakeshore Dr, Seabrook TX 77586, USA
**Rundgren, Todd** — Singer, Songwriter
Panacea Entertainment, 13587 Andalusia Dr, Santa Rosa Valley CA 93102, USA
**Runge, Brian** — Baseball Umpire
8225 E County Dr, El Cajon CA 92021, USA
**Runge, Paul W** — Baseball Player
1719 W Community Dr, Jupiter FL 33458, USA
**Runnells, Thomas W (Tom)** — Baseball Player, Manager
6045 Settlers Ridge Circle, Sylvania OH 43560, USA
**Runnicles, Donald** — Conductor
Opus 3 Artists, 470 Park Ave S, #900N, New York NY 10016 USA
**Running, Steve** — Ecologist
1419 Khanabad Dr, Missoula MT 59802, USA
**Runyan, Joe** — Dog Sled Racer
Rt 1, 314.5 Parks Highway, Nenana AK 99760, USA
**Runyan, Jon D** — Football Player
262 Mount Laurel Road, #1, Mount Laurel NJ 08054, USA
**Runyan, Marla** — Track Athlete
42 Royal St, Watertown MA 02472, USA
**Runyan, Sean D** — Baseball Player
1958 Bermuda Pointe Dr, Haines City FL 33844, USA
**Runyon, Edwin** — Religious Leader
General Baptists Assn, 100 Stinson Dr, Poplar Bluff MO 63901, USA
**Ruotsalainen, Reijo J** — Ice Hockey Player
Jukurit Mikkeli Raviradantie 1, 50100 Mikkeli, Finland
**RuPaul** — Actor, Producer, Singer
RuCo, 332 Bleeker St, #F22, New York NY 10014, USA
**Rupe, Joshua M (Josh)** — Baseball Player
225 Arrowfield Road, Virginia Beach VA 23454, USA
**Rupe, Ryan K** — Baseball Player
2 Windflower Place, Spring TX 77381, USA
**Rupert, Michael** — Actor, Composer, Director
Don Buchwald Talent Agency, 10 E 44th St, New York NY 10017 USA
**Rupp, Debra Jo** — Actress
Stone Manners Salners, 6100 Wilshire Blvd, #1500, Los Angeles CA 90035 USA
**Rupp, Duane** — Ice Hockey Player
2446 McMonagle Ave, Pittsburgh PA 15216, USA
**Rupp, Galen** — Track Athlete
5406 NW 146th Ave, Portland OR 97229, USA
**Rupp, Michael (Mike)** — Ice Hockey Player
3936 Medford Square, Hilliard OH 43026, USA
**Ruppel, Adam** — Guitarist (Systematic)
Artist Group International, 9560 Wilshire Blvd, #400, Beverly Hills CA 90212 USA
**Rupprath, Thomas** — Swimmer
City Mobel, Industriestr 10, 18069 Rostock, Germany
**Ruprecht, Tom** — Writer
United Talent Agency, U T A Plaza, 9336 Civic Center Dr, Beverly Hills CA 90210 USA
**Rusby, Kate A** — Singer, Songwriter
Pure Records & Mgmt, PO Box 174, Penistone S36 8XB, England
**Rusch, Glendon J** — Baseball Player
6428 Chaffee St, Tujunga CA 91042, USA
**Rusch, Kristine Kathryn** — Writer
PO Box 479, Lincoln City OR 97367, USA
**Ruscha, Edward J** — Artist
5920-24 Blackwelder St, Culver City CA 90232, USA
**Ruscio, Kenneth** — Educator
Washington & Lee University, President's Office, Lexington VA 24450, USA
**Ruse, Michael** — Philosopher
651 E 6th Ave, Tallahassee FL 32303, USA
**Rusedski, Greg** — Tennis Player
Association of Tennis Professionals, 201 A T P Blvd, Ponte Vedra Beach FL 32082 USA
**Rusesabagina, Paul** — Humanitarian
Baron Albert d'Huartlaan 124, 1950 Kraainem, Belgium
**Rush, Barbara** — Actress
House of Representatives, 1434 6th St, #1, Santa Monica CA 90401 USA

**Rush, Bobby** — Singer, Musician, Songwriter
Wenig-LaMonica Associates, 580 White Plains Rd, #130, Tarrytown NY 10591, USA

**Rush, Brandon L** — Basketball Player
Golden State Warriors, 1011 Broadway, Oakland CA 94605 USA

**Rush, Cathy** — Basketball Coach
Future Stars Camps, 546 Bedford Road, Armonk NY 10504, USA

**Rush, Deborah** — Actress
Gersh Agency, 9465 Wilshire Blvd, #600, Beverly Hills CA 90212 USA

**Rush, Geoffrey** — Actor
Shanahan Mgmt, Berman House, 91 Campbell St, #300, Surry Hills NSW 2010, Australia

**Rush, Gerald M (Jerry)** — Football Player
17536 Oak Dr, Detroit MI 48221, USA

**Rush, Jennifer** — Singer
Michow Concerts, Postfach 20264, 29216 Hamburg, Germany

**Rush, Kareem L** — Basketball Player
2805 E 62nd St, Kansas City MO 64130, USA

**Rush, Merrilee** — Singer, Songwriter
Cape Entertainment, 4799 Coconut Creek Parkway, #258, Coconut Creek FL 33063 USA

**Rush, Odeya** — Actress
Creative Artists Agency, 2000 Ave of Stars, #100, Los Angeles CA 90067 USA

**Rush, Otis** — Singer, Guitarist
J W Entertainment, PO Box 78904, Atlanta GA 30357 USA

**Rush, Richard W** — Director, Producer
821 Stradella Road, Los Angeles CA 90077, USA

**Rush, Robert J (Bob)** — Football Player
420 Mary Lane, Auburn AL 36830, USA

**Rush, Robert R (Bob)** — Baseball Player
444 S Higley Road, #116, Mesa AZ 85206, USA

**Rushbrook, Claire** — Actress
Troika, 74 Clerkenwell Road, #300, London EC1M 5QA, England

**Rushdie, A Salman** — Writer
United Talent Agency, U T A Plaza, 9336 Civic Center Dr, Beverly Hills CA 90210 USA

**Rushen, Patrice L** — Singer, Songwriter
Groove Entertainment, 1005 N Alfred St, #2, West Hollywood CA 90069, USA

**Rushlow, Timothy A (Tim)** — Singer, Guitarist (Rushlow Harris)
K M G Records, 3631 W End Ave, Nashville TN 37205, USA

**Ruskowski, Terry W (Rosco)** — Ice Hockey Player
7000 Langmuir Dr, McKinney TX 75071, USA

**Russ, Tim** — Actor
C E S D, 10635 Santa Monica Blvd, #130, Los Angeles CA 90025 USA

**Russ, William** — Actor
26500 Agoura Road, Calabasas CA 91302, USA

**Russell Beale, Simon** — Actor
Richard Stone Partnership, De Walden Court, 85 New Cavendish St, London W1W 6XD, England

**Russell, Adam W** — Baseball Player
627 Mariner Village, Huron OH 44839, USA

**Russell, Allison** — Singer (Po' Girl)
Emerging Music, Horns Cross, Bidesford, Devon EX39 5DW, England

**Russell, Betsy** — Actress
Marshak/Zachary/Mills, 8840 Wilshire Blvd, #100, Beverly Hills CA 90211 USA

**Russell, Brenda** — Singer, Songwriter, Keyboardist
S K M Artist Mgmt, PO Box 25906, Los Angeles CA 90025, USA

**Russell, Bryon D** — Basketball Player
22451 Cass Ave, Woodland Hills CA 91364, USA

**Russell, C Andrew (Andy)** — Football Player
230 Glen Abbey Court, Presto PA 15142, USA

**Russell, Catherine** — Actress
Rights House, Drury House, 34-43 Russell St, London WC2B 5HA, England

**Russell, Cazzie L** — Basketball Player
Savannah College of Art & Design, Athletic Dept, Savannah GA 31402, USA

**Russell, Charles O (Chuck)** — Director
Gersh Agency, 9465 Wilshire Blvd, #600, Beverly Hills CA 90212 USA

**Russell, Christopher T** — Geophysicist
University of California, Institute of Geophysics & Planetary Physics, Los Angeles CA 90024, USA

**Russell, Clive** — Actor
Shepherd Mgmt, 45 Maddox St, #400, London W1S 2PC, England

**Russell, Craig** — Actor, Writer, Producer
Langford Assoc, 17 Westfields Ave, Barnes, London SW13 0AT, England

**Russell, David O** — Director, Writer
Creative Artists Agency, 2000 Ave of Stars, #100, Los Angeles CA 90067 USA

**Russell, Graham C** — Singer (Air Supply)
PO Box 3367, Beverly Hills CA 90212, USA

**Russell, Hugh** — Opera Singer
Columbia Artists Mgmt Inc, 5 Columbus Circle, 1790 Broadway, #1600, New York NY 10019 USA

**Russell, JaMarcus** — Football Player
13111 Skyline Road, Oakland CA 94619, USA

**Russell, James T** — Inventor
14589 51st St, Bellevue WA 98006, USA

**Russell, Jay** — Director
A P A Talent & Literary Agency, 405 S Beverly Dr, #300, Beverly Hills CA 90212 USA

**Russell, Jeffrey L (Jeff)** — Baseball Player
2325 Oak Knoll Dr, Colleyville TX 76034, USA

**Russell, Jena** — Actress, Singer
United Agents, 12-26 Lexington St, London W1F 0LE, England

**Russell, John W** — Baseball Player, Manager
1709 NE Woodland Shores Court, Lees Summit MO 64086, USA

**Russell, Keri** — Actress, Model
Burstein Co, 15304 W Sunset Blvd, #208, Pacific Palisades CA 90272 USA

**Russell, Kimberly** — Actress
14622 Ventura Blvd, Sherman Oaks CA 91403, USA

**Russell, Kurt** — Actor
Go Mav Productions, 229 E Gainsborough Road, Thousand Oaks CA 91360, USA

**Russell, Leon** — Singer, Pianist, Songwriter
PO Box 24455, New Orleans LA 70184, USA

**Russell, Liane B** — Geneticist
130 Tabor Road, Oak Ridge TN 37830, USA

# R

| | |
|---|---|
| **Russell, Lucy**<br>Hamilton Hodell, 20 Golden Square, London W1F 9JL, England | Actress, Model |
| **Russell, M Campanella (Campy)**<br>66 Earlmoor Blvd, Pontiac MI 48341, USA | Basketball Player |
| **Russell, Margaret A**<br>Architectural Digest, Editorial Dept, 5900 Wilshire Blvd, Los Angeles CA 90036, USA | Editor |
| **Russell, Mark**<br>PO Box 9904, Washington DC 20016, USA | Actor, Comedian |
| **Russell, Phil**<br>590 Wind Drift Lane, Spring Lake MI 49456, USA | Ice Hockey Player |
| **Russell, Sharman Apt**<br>Western New Mexico State University, English Dept, Silver City NM 88062, USA | Writer |
| **Russell, Steven J**<br>Massachusetts General Hospital, Diabetes Center, 50 Staniford St, #301, Boston MA 02114, USA | Endocinologist |
| **Russell, Theresa**<br>Scott Zimmerman Mgmt, 1644 Courtney Ave, Los Angeles CA 90046, USA | Actress |
| **Russell, Tom**<br>Val Denn Agency, 100 Congress Ave, #2000, Austin TX 78701, USA | Singer, Songwriter |
| **Russell, Twan S**<br>212 Lakeside Circle, Sunrise FL 33326, USA | Football Player |
| **Russell, William E (Bill)**<br>27982 Red Pine Court, Valencia CA 91354, USA | Baseball Player, Manager |
| **Russell, William F (Bill)**<br>9415 SE 52nd St, Mercer Island WA 98040, USA | Basketball Player, Coach |
| **Russell, Willy**<br>Casorotto Ramsay, Waverley House, 7-12 Noel St, London W1F 8GQ, England | Writer |
| **Russell, Wyatt**<br>United Talent Agency, U T A Plaza, 9336 Civic Center Dr, Beverly Hills CA 90210 USA | Actor |
| **Russi, Bernhard**<br>Postfach 107, 5620 Bremgarten, Switzerland | Alpine Skier |
| **Russo Adamo, Pat**<br>Playboy Promotions, 9346 Civic Center Dr, #200, Beverly Hills CA 90210 USA | Model |
| **Russo, Daniel**<br>Agents Associes, 201 Rue du Faubourg Saint Honore, 75008 Paris, France | Actor |
| **Russo, David**<br>Rugolo Entertainment, 195 S Beverly Drive, #400, Beverly Hills CA 90212, USA | Director, Writer, Actor |
| **Russo, Dominic**<br>I C M Partners, 10250 Constellation Blvd, #900, Los Angeles CA 90067 USA | Producer, Writer |
| **Russo, Gianni**<br>Sanders Agency, 9014 Melrose Ave, West Hollywood CA 90069, USA | Actor |
| **Russo, James**<br>8306 Wilshire Blvd, #438, Beverly Hills CA 90211, USA | Actor, Writer |
| **Russo, John**<br>216 Euclid Ave, Glassport PA 15045, USA | Writer |
| **Russo, Martin A**<br>Cassidy & Assoc, 700 13th Ave NW, #400, Washington DC 20005, USA | Representative, IL |
| **Russo, Rene**<br>John Crosby Mgmt, 1357 N Spaulding Ave, Los Angeles CA 90046, USA | Actress, Model |
| **Russo, Richard**<br>Knopf Publishers, 1745 Broadway, New York NY 10019 USA | Writer |
| **Rut, Tomasz**<br>1909 Tigertail Blvd, Dania Beach FL 33004, USA | Artist |
| **Rutan, Elbert L (Burt)**<br>14329 Rutan Road, Mojave CA 93501, USA | Airplane Designer |
| **Rutan, Richard G (Dick)**<br>2833 Delmar Ave, Mojave CA 93501, USA | Experimental Airplane Pilot, Designer |
| **Rutgens, Joseph C (Joe)**<br>227 W Devlin St, Spring Valley IL 61362, USA | Football Player |
| **Ruth, Daniel**<br>Tampa Bay Times, Editorial Dept, 490 1st Ave S, Saint Petersburg FL 33701, USA | Journalist |
| **Ruth, Lauren**<br>PO Box 200206, New Haven CT 06520, USA | Cartoonist |
| **Ruth, Michael J (Mike)**<br>8222 Kirkbride Dr, Danvers MA 01923, USA | Football Player |
| **Rutherford, Emily**<br>Paradigm Agency, 360 N Crescent Dr, North Building, Beverly Hills CA 90210 USA | Actress |
| **Rutherford, James E (Jim)**<br>2542 Village Manor Way, Raleigh NC 27614, USA | Ice Hockey Player |
| **Rutherford, John S (Johnny), III**<br>4919 Black Oak Lane, River Oaks TX 76114, USA | Auto Racing Driver |
| **Rutherford, Kelly**<br>Luber Rocklin Entertainment, 5815 Sunset Blvd, #206, Los Angeles CA 90028 USA | Actress |
| **Rutherford, Mike**<br>Solo Agency, 53-55 Fulham High St, #200, London SW6 3JJ, England | Guitarist (Genesis) |
| **Rutherfurd, Emily**<br>Paradigm Agency, 360 N Crescent Dr, North Building, Beverly Hills CA 90210 USA | Actress |
| **Ruthven, Richard D (Dick)**<br>13480 Providence Lake Dr, Alpharetta GA 30004, USA | Baseball Player |
| **Rutigliano, Sam**<br>9671 Metcalf Road, Willoughby OH 44094, USA | Football Coach |
| **Rutkowski, Edward J A (Ed)**<br>47 Brenton Lane, Hamburg NY 14075, USA | Football Player |
| **Rutland, Robert A**<br>Tulsa University, History Dept, Tulsa OK 74101, USA | Historian |
| **Rutledge, Jeffrey R (Jeff)**<br>6102 W Gary Dr, Chandler AZ 85226, USA | Football Player, Coach |
| **Rutledge, Johnny B, Jr**<br>756 SW 10th St, Belle Glade FL 33430, USA | Football Player |
| **Rutledge, Justin**<br>Six Shooter Mgmt, PO Box 98038, 970 Queen St E, Toronto ON M5V 1V2, Canada | Singer, Songwriter |
| **Rutledge, Roderick A (Rod)**<br>1254 4th Way, Pleasant Grove AL 35127, USA | Football Player |
| **Rutschman, Adolph (Ad)**<br>2142 NW Pinehurst Dr, McMinnville OR 97128, USA | Football Coach |
| **Rutschow-Stomporowski, Katrin**<br>Rosenthaler Str 34-35, 10178 Berlin, Germany | Rowing Athlete |

**Russell - Rutschow-Stomporowski**

**Ruttan, Susan**
TalentWorks, 3500 W Olive Ave, #1400, Burbank CA 91505 USA — Actress
**Rutter, John M**
Old Lacey's, Saint John's St, Duxford, Cambridge CB2 4RA, England — Composer, Conductor
**Ruttman, Joe**
1221 Night Wind Terrace, North Port FL 34291, USA — Truck Racing Driver
**Ruud, Barrett J**
1821 S 33rd St, Lincoln NE 68506, USA — Football Player
**Ruud, Thomas R (Tom)**
1821 S 33rd St, Lincoln NE 68506, USA — Football Player
**Ruuska Percy, Sylvia**
4216 College View Way, Carmichael CA 95608, USA — Swimmer
**Ruusuvuori, Aarno E**
Annankatu 15 B 10, 00120 Helsinki 12, Finland — Architect
**Ruuttu, Christian**
Arizona Coyotes, 6751 N Sunset Blvd, #200, Glendale AZ 85305 USA — Ice Hockey Player
**Ruutu, Jarko**
Ottawa Senators, Scotia Bank Place, Kanata ON K2V 1A5, Canada — Ice Hockey Player
**Ruutu, Tuomo I**
New Jersey Devils, Arena, 50 State Route 120, East Rutherford NJ 07073 USA — Ice Hockey Player
**Rux, Carl Hancock**
Music & Art Mgmt, 9 W Walnut St, #2D, Asheville NC 28801, USA — Rap Artist
**Ruzek, Roger B**
6404 Penina Trail, Denton TX 76210, USA — Football Player
**Ruzici, Virginia**
9 Boul Chateau, 92200 Neuilly sur Seine, France — Tennis Player
**Ruzowitsky, Stefan**
United Agents, 12-26 Lexington St, London W1F 0LE, England — Director
**Ryal, Mark D**
PO Box 1107, Henryetta OK 74437, USA — Baseball Player
**Ryan, Amy**
Gersh Agency, 9465 Wilshire Blvd, #600, Beverly Hills CA 90212 USA — Actress
**Ryan, Bob**
Boston Globe, Editorial Dept, 135 William Morrissey Blvd, Dorchester MA 02125 USA — Sportswriter
**Ryan, Cathy Cahlin**
Sovereign Talent Group, 8421 Wilshire Blvd, #200, Beverly Hills CA 90211 USA — Actress
**Ryan, Debbie**
University of Virginia, Athletic Dept, PO Box 400827, Charlottesville VA 22904, USA — Basketball Coach
**Ryan, Ed**
PO Box 6249, Freehold NJ 07728, USA — Harness Racing Executive
**Ryan, Frank B**
PO Box 185, Grafton VT 05146, USA — Football Player
**Ryan, Heather**
Playboy Promotions, 9346 Civic Center Dr, #200, Beverly Hills CA 90210 USA — Model
**Ryan, James D (Buddy)**
819 Abingdon Lane, Shelbyville KY 40065, USA — Football Coach
**Ryan, James J (Jim)**
1726 C St NE, Washington DC 20002, USA — Football Player
**Ryan, James L**
US Court of Appeals, US Courthouse, 231 W Lafayette Blvd, Detroit MI 48226, USA — Judge
**Ryan, Jay**
United Talent Agency, U T A Plaza, 9336 Civic Center Dr, Beverly Hills CA 90210 USA — Actor
**Ryan, Jeri L**
I C M Partners, 10250 Constellation Blvd, #900, Los Angeles CA 90067 USA — Actress
**Ryan, Kay**
College of Marin, English Dept, 835 College Ave, Kentfield CA 94904, USA — Writer
**Ryan, Kenneth E (Ken)**
45 Tanager Road, Seekonk MA 02771, USA — Baseball Player
**Ryan, Kevin J**
42, 8 Flitcroft St, London WC2H 8DC, England — Actor
**Ryan, Kwame**
Orchestre National Bordeaux Aquataine, Place de Comédie, BP 90095, 33025 Bordeaux Cedex, France — Conductor
**Ryan, L Nolan, Jr**
237 Escalera Parkway, Georgetown TX 78628, USA — Baseball Player
**Ryan, Lee**
Independent Talent Group, 40 Whitfield St, London W1T 2RH, England — Singer, Songwriter, Actor
**Ryan, Lisa Dean**
1327 Brinkley Ave, Los Angeles CA 90049, USA — Actress
**Ryan, Matt**
Julian Belfrage Assoc, 9 Argyll St, #300, London W1F 7TG, England — Actor, Producer
**Ryan, Matthew T (Matt)**
3268 Bransley Way, Duluth GA 30097, USA — Football Player
**Ryan, Max**
L I N K Entertainment, 11872 La Grange Ave, Los Angeles CA 90025 USA — Actor, Producer
**Ryan, Meg**
I C M Partners, 10250 Constellation Blvd, #900, Los Angeles CA 90067 USA — Actress
**Ryan, Michael E (Mike)**
United Services Automobile Assn, 9800 Fredericksburg Road, San Antonio TX 78288, USA — Air Force General
**Ryan, Michael J (Mike)**
592 Stoneham Road, Wolfeboro NH 03894, USA — Baseball Player
**Ryan, Michael S**
521 Water St, Indiana PA 15701, USA — Baseball Player
**Ryan, Michelle**
Independent Talent Group, 40 Whitfield St, London W1T 2RH, England — Actress
**Ryan, Mitchell**
C E S D, 10635 Santa Monica Blvd, #130, Los Angeles CA 90025 USA — Actor
**Ryan, Norbert R, Jr**
Military Officers Assn, 201 N Washington St, Alexandria VA 22314, USA — Navy Admiral
**Ryan, Patrick L (Pat)**
6930 Old Kent Dr, Knoxville TN 37919, USA — Football Player
**Ryan, Rebecca**
United Agents, 12-26 Lexington St, London W1F 0LE, England — Model, Actress
**Ryan, Rex**
New York Jets, 1 Jets Dr, Florham Park NJ 07932 USA — Football Coach
**Ryan, Robert V (B J), Jr**
1211 Perdenalas Trail, Westlake TX 76262, USA — Baseball Player

# R

**Ryan, Roz**
B R S / Gage Talent Agency, 1650 Broadway, #1410, New York NY 10019 USA — Actress

**Ryan, Shawn**
MiddKid Productions, 10201 W Pico Blvd, Los Angeles CA 90035, USA — Producer, Writer

**Ryan, Thomas M**
C V S/Caremark Corp, 1 C V S/Caremark Dr, Woonsocket RI 02895, USA — Businessman

**Ryan, Tim**
S M S Talent, 8383 Wilshire Blvd, #230, Beverly Hills CA 90211 USA — Actor

**Ryan, Tom K**
North American Syndicate, 235 E 45th St, New York NY 10017 USA — Cartoonist (Tumbleweeds)

**Ryans, DeMeco**
Philadelphia Eagles, 1 Novacare Way, Philadelphia PA 19145 USA — Football Player

**Ryazanov, Eldar A**
Bolshoi Tishinski Per 12, #70, 123557 Moscow, Russia — Director

**Ryazansky, Sergey**
Cosmonaut Training Center, Star City, 141160 Zvezdny Gorodok, Moscow Oblast, Russia — Cosmonaut

**Rybczynski, Witold**
Charles Scribner's Sons, 866 3rd Ave, New York NY 10022 USA — Writer

**Rybkin, Ivan P**
Administration of President, Staraya Pl 4, 103132 Moscow, Russia — Government Official, Russia

**Rychel, Warren**
Windsor Spitfires, 334 Wyandotte St E, Windsor ON N9A 3H6, Canada — Ice Hockey Player

**Rychlec, Thomas R (Tom)**
71 Round Hill Road, Southington CT 06489, USA — Football Player

**Rycroft Strickland, Melissa K**
W M E Entertainment, 9601 Wilshire Blvd, #300, Beverly Hills CA 90210 USA — Actress

**Rycroft, Carter**
Curling Association, 1660 Vimont Court, Cumberland ON K4A 4J4, Canada — Curling Athlete

**Ryczek, Daniel S (Dan)**
3714 Monitor Place, Olney MD 20832, USA — Football Player

**Ryczek, Paul A**
9335 Scott Road, Roswell GA 30076, USA — Football Player

**Rydal, Emma**
Rights House, Drury House, 34-43 Russell St, London WC2B 5HA, England — Actress

**Rydalch, Ronald J (Ron)**
500 E Durfee St, Grantsville UT 84029, USA — Football Player

**Rydell, Bobby**
917 Bryn Mawr Ave, Penn Valley PA 19072, USA — Singer, Actor

**Rydell, Christopher**
911 N Sweetzer, #C, West Hollywood CA 90069, USA — Actor

**Rydell, Mark**
Concourse Productions, 435 N Oakhurst Dr, #602, Beverly Hills CA 90210, USA — Director

**Ryder, Lisa**
Red Mgmt, 415 W Esplanade, Box 3, North Vancouver BC V7M 1A6, Canada — Actress

**Ryder, Mitch**
Utopia Artists, 108 E Matilja St, #1821, Ojai CA 93023, USA — Singer, Guitarist, Band Leader

**Ryder, Norman B**
Princeton University, Sociology Dept, Princeton NJ 08544, USA — Sociologist

**Ryder, Thomas O**
Reader's Digest Assn, Publisher's Office, PO Box 100, Pleasantville NY 10570, USA — Publisher

**Ryder, Winona**
Gersh Agency, 9465 Wilshire Blvd, #600, Beverly Hills CA 90212 USA — Actress

**Ryding, Yvonne A**
Letsfaceit A B, Saint Erik Way 63, 112 34 Stockholm, Sweden — Beauty Queen

**Rydze, Richard**
383 Kane Blvd, Pittsburgh PA 15243, USA — Diver

**Rydzek, Johannes**
Im Steinach 6, 87561 Oberstdorf, Germany — Nordic Combined Skier

**Ryerson, Ann**
Abrams Artists, 9200 W Sunset Blvd, #1125, West Hollywood CA 90069 USA — Actress

**Rykiel, Sonia F**
175 Blvd Saint Germain, 75006 Paris, France — Fashion Designer

**Rylance, Georgina**
Markham Froggatt Irwin, Julian House, 4 Windmill St, London W1P 1HF, England — Actress

**Rylance, Mark**
Hamilton Hodell, 20 Golden Square, London W1F 9JL, England — Director, Actor

**Rylko, Stanislaw Cardinal**
Pontifical Council for Laity, Piazza S Calisto 16, 00153 Rome, Italy — Religious Leader

**Ryman, Robert T**
17 W 16th St, New York NY 10011, USA — Artist

**Rymer, Charlie**
225 Magnolia St, Windermere FL 34786, USA — Golfer, Sportscaster

**Rynkiewicz, Mariusz**
12401 Alexander Road, Everett WA 98204, USA — Sculptor

**Rypdal, Terje**
Kjell Kalleklev Mgmt, Georgemes Verft 12, 5011 Bergen, Norway — Guitarist, Flutist, Composer

**Rypien, Mark R**
8817 N Warren St, Spokane WA 99208, USA — Football Player

**Ryu So-Yeon**
Ladies Pro Golf Assn, 100 International Golf Dr, Daytona Beach FL 32124 USA — Golfer

**Ryumin, Valery V**
Cosmonaut Training Center, Star City, 141160 Zvezdny Gorodok, Moscow Oblast, Russia — Cosmonaut

**Ryun, James R (Jim)**
132 D St SE, Washington DC 20003, USA — Track Athlete; Representative, KS

**Ryzhkov, Nikolai I**
Federation Council, Bolshaya Dmitrovka Str 26, 103009 Moscow, Russia — Premier, Russia

**RZA**
Creative Artists Agency, 2000 Ave of Stars, #100, Los Angeles CA 90067 USA — Rap Artist (Wu-Tang Clan), Actor

## Ryan - RZA

| | |
|---|---|
| **Saadiq, Raphael**<br>Universal Attractions, 135 W 26th St, #1200, New York NY 10001 USA | Singer, Songwriter |
| **Saarinen, Aino-Kalsa**<br>Suomen Hiihtoliitto, Radiokatu 20, 00093 Slu, Finland | Cross Country Skier |
| **Saarinen, Tero**<br>Tero Saarinen Co, Bulevardi 23-27, 00180 Helsinki, Finland | Dancer, Choreographer |
| **Saatchi, Charles**<br>36 Golden Square, London W1R 4EE, England | Businessman |
| **Saatchi, Maurice**<br>36 Golden Square, London W1R 4EE, England | Businessman |
| **Sabah IV, Sheikh Ahmad Jabar al-Sabah**<br>Darwa Salwa Palace, Amiry Diwan, Kuwait City, Kuwait | Emir, Kuwait |
| **Sabah, Sheikh Nasser Al Mohammed al-**<br>Prime Minister's Office, PO Box 4, Safat 13001, Kuwait City, Kuwait | Prime Minister, Kuwait |
| **Saban, Louis H (Lou)**<br>2087 Appalachee Circle, Tavares FL 32778, USA | Football Player, Coach |
| **Saban, Nicholas L (Nick), Jr**<br>University of Alabama, Athletic Dept, Tuscaloosa AL 35487, USA | Football Coach |
| **Sabara, Daryl**<br>A P A Talent & Literary Agency, 405 S Beverly Dr, #300, Beverly Hills CA 90212 USA | Actor |
| **Sabates, Felix**<br>Ganassi Racing, 600 E Laburnum Ave, Richmond VA 23222, USA | Auto Racing Executive |
| **Sabathia, Carsten C (C C)**<br>PO Box 30, Alpine NJ 07620, USA | Baseball Player |
| **Sabatini, David D**<br>New York University, Cell Biology & Biochemistry Dept, New York NY 10012, USA | Cell Biologist, Biochemist |
| **Sabatini, Gabriela**<br>35/35 Grosvenor St, London W1K 4QX, England | Tennis Player |
| **Sabatino, Joe**<br>Wayne Agency, 1617 N El Centro Ave, #7, Los Angeles CA 90028, USA | Actor |
| **Sabatino, Michael**<br>13538 Valleyheart Dr, Sherman Oaks CA 91423, USA | Actor, Model |
| **Sabato, Antonio, Jr**<br>Global Artists Agency, 6253 Hollywood Blvd, #508, Los Angeles CA 90028 USA | Actor |
| **Sabbah, Sam**<br>Premier Talent Group, 4370 Tujunga Ave, #110, Studio City CA 91604, USA | Golfer |
| **Sabbatini, Rory**<br>2939 Crockett St, #348, Fort Worth TX 76107, USA | Singer, Songwriter |
| **Sabelle**<br>Sarmast Entertainment, 241 W 36th St, #2R, New York NY 10018, USA | Baseball Player |
| **Saberhagen, Bret W**<br>Bret Saberhagen Make a Difference Foundation, 22817 Ventura Blvd, #474, Woodland Hills CA 91364, USA | Speed Skater |
| **Sablikova, Martina**<br>Nowis Team, V Zahradach 755, 261 51 Velky Osek, Czech Republic | Baseball Player |
| **Sabo, Christopher A (Chris)**<br>7455 Stonemeadow Lane, Cincinnati OH 45242, USA | Producer, Filmmaker |
| **Sabol, Edward E (Ed)**<br>N F L Films, 330 Fellowship Road, Mount Laurel NJ 08054, USA | Ice Hockey Player |
| **Sabourin, Gary B**<br>54 Holland Ave, Chatham ON N7M 2C7, Canada | Football Player |
| **Sacca, Anthony J (Tony)**<br>11 Heather Glen Lane, Riverside NJ 08075, USA | Cartoonist |
| **Sacco, Joe**<br>305 SE Ankeny St, Portland OR 97233, USA | Ice Hockey Player, Coach |
| **Sacco, Joe W**<br>95 Roxbury Park, East Amherst NY 14051, USA | Writer |
| **Sachar, Louis**<br>Delacorte Press, 1540 Broadway, New York NY 10036 USA | Ice Hockey Player |
| **Sacharuk, Lawrence W (Larry)**<br>HG Tiroler Wasserkraft, Olumpiastr 10, 6020 Innsbruck, Austria | Actress |
| **Sachdev, Asha**<br>18B Sunset Heights, 59 Pali Hill Bandra, Mumbai MS 400050, India | Cross Country Skier |
| **Sachenbacher-Stehle, Evi**<br>Birnbacher Str 1, 83242 Reit im Winkl, Germany | Actor |
| **Sachs, Andrew**<br>Lynda Ronan Personal Mgmt, Hunters House, 1 Redcliffe Road, London SW10 9NR, England | Director, Writer |
| **Sachs, Ira**<br>Marie Therese Guirgis Mgmt, 125 Riverside Dr, #8C, New York NY 10024, USA | Economist |
| **Sachs, Jeffrey D**<br>Harvard University, International Development Institute, Cambridge MA 02138, USA | Director |
| **Sachs, William**<br>Greenwald Mayfield Vigil, 400 Continental Blvd, #600, El Segundo CA 90245, USA | Journalist |
| **Sack, Kevin**<br>Los Angeles Times, Editorial Dept, 202 W 1st St, Los Angeles CA 90012 USA | Judge |
| **Sack, Robert D**<br>US Court of Appeals, Moynihan Courthouse, 500 Pearl St, New York NY 10007, USA | Editorial Cartoonist |
| **Sack, Steve**<br>Minneapolis Star-Tribune, 425 Portland Ave, Minneapolis MN 55488, USA | Director |
| **Sackheim, Daniel**<br>Creative Artists Agency, 2000 Ave of Stars, #100, Los Angeles CA 90067 USA | Actress |
| **Sackhoff, Katee**<br>Bleu Entertainment, 5225 Wilshire Blvd, #336, Los Angeles CA 90036, USA | Prime Minister, Mali |
| **Sacko, Soumana**<br>Villa 14 Bis 48, Sema Gexco, Bamako, Mali | Auto Racing Driver |
| **Sacks, Greg**<br>6092 Sabal Creek Blvd, Port Orange FL 32128, USA | Religious Leader |
| **Sacks, Jonathan H**<br>735 High Road, London N12 0US, England | Writer, Physician, Neurologist |
| **Sacks, Oliver W**<br>2 Horatio St, #3G, New York NY 10014, USA | Gymnast |
| **Sacramone, Alicia M**<br>Frederick Sacramone, 41 Hastings Road, Winchester MA 01890, USA | Social Activist |
| **Sadat, Jehan El-**<br>University of Maryland, International Development Center, College Park MD 20742, USA | Singer, Songwriter |
| **Sade**<br>Marshall Arts, Utopia Village, 7 Chalcot Road, London NW1 8LH, England | |

**Sadecki, Raymond M (Ray)**
4237 E Clovis Ave, Mesa AZ 85206, USA — Baseball Player

**Sadier, Laetitia**
Duophonic Records, PO Box 3787, London SE22 9DZ, England — Singer, Musician (Stereolab)

**Sadik, Nafis**
300 E 56th St, #9J, New York NY 10022, USA — Government Official, Pakistan

**Sadiq Al-Mahedi**
Club de Madrid, C/Goya 5-7, Pasaje 2, 28001 Madrid, Spain — Prime Minister, Sudan

**Sadler, Benjamin**
Agentur Carola Studlar, Agnesstr 47, 80798 Munich, Germany — Actor

**Sadler, Donnie L**
802 Sadler Road, Valley Mills TX 76689, USA — Baseball Player

**Sadler, Elliott W B**
108 Conway Court, Mooresville NC 28117, USA — Auto, Truck Racing Driver

**Sadler, Herman M (Hermie), III**
PO Box 32, Emporia VA 23847, USA — Auto Racing Driver

**Sadoski, Thomas**
United Talent Agency, U T A Plaza, 9336 Civic Center Dr, Beverly Hills CA 90210 USA — Actor

**Sadoyan, Isabelle**
Artmedia, 20 Ave Rapp, 75007 Paris, France — Actress

**Saenz, Olmedo**
4300 W Ford City Dr, #1002, Chicago IL 60652, USA — Baseball Player

**Saez Conde, Inez L**
Miss Universe Organization, 1370 Ave of Americas, #1600, New York NY 10019 USA — Beauty Queen

**Safdie, Moshe**
100 Rev Nazareno Properzi Way, Somerville MA 02143, USA — Architect

**Safer, Morley**
CBS-TV, News Dept, 524 W 57th St, New York NY 10019, USA — Commentator

**Saffiotti, Umberto**
5114 Wissioming Road, Bethesda MD 20816, USA — Pathologist

**Saffo, Paul**
Institute for the Future, 27740 Sand Hill Road, Menlo Park CA 94025, USA — Non-Profit Executive, Journalist

**Saffold, Rodger, III**
Saint Louis Rams, 901 N Broadway, Saint Louis MO 63101 USA — Football Player

**Saffron, Inga**
Philadelphia Inquirer, Editorial Dept, 1830 Town Center Dr, Langhorne PA 19047 USA — Journalist

**Safin, Marat M**
T C Weiden am Postkeller, Schirmitzer Weg, 92637 Weiden, Germany — Tennis Player

**Safina, Carl**
Blue Spring Institute, 250 Lawrence Hill Road, Cold Spring Harbor NY 11724, USA — Marine Biologist

**Safina, Dinara M**
Women's Tennis Assn, 1 Progress Plaza, #1500, Saint Petersburg FL 33701 USA — Tennis Player

**Safiq, Ahmed M**
Prime Minister's Office, PO Box 191, 1 Majlis El-Shaab St, Cairo CA104, Egypt — Prime Minister, Egypt

**Safran, Joshua**
United Talent Agency, U T A Plaza, 9336 Civic Center Dr, Beverly Hills CA 90210 USA — Director, Writer

**Safuto, Dominick (Randy)**
Brothers Management Assoc, 141 Dunbar Ave, Fords NJ 08863 USA — Singer (Randy & the Rainbows)

**Safuto, Frank**
Brothers Management Assoc, 141 Dunbar Ave, Fords NJ 08863 USA — Singer (Randy & the Rainbows)

**Sagal, Katey**
B & B Mgmt, 1041 N Formosa Ave, West Hollywood CA 90046, USA — Actress

**Saganiuk, Rocky**
13252 Lake Mary Dr, Plainfield IL 60585, USA — Ice Hockey Player

**Sagdeev, Roald Z**
University of Maryland, East-West Space Center, College Park MD 20742, USA — Physicist

**Sage, Bill**
Don Buchwald Talent Agency, 6500 Wilshire Blvd, #2200, Los Angeles CA 90048 USA — Actor

**Sage, Peter D (Pete)**
AirForce1.TV Music, Alte Schonhauser Str 44, 10119 Berlin, Germany — Singer, Violinist (Santiano)

**Sage, William (Bill)**
Don Buchwald Talent Agency, 6500 Wilshire Blvd, #2200, Los Angeles CA 90048 USA — Actor

**Sagebrecht, Marianne**
Agentur Olivia Reinecke, Kirchenleite 16, 82057 Icking bei Munich, Germany — Actress

**Sagemiller, Melissa**
Paradigm Agency, 360 N Crescent Dr, North Building, Beverly Hills CA 90210 USA — Actress

**Sager, Anthony J (A J)**
10310 Belmont Meadows Lane, Perrysburg OH 43551, USA — Baseball Player

**Sager, Carole Bayer**
10779 Bellagio Road, Los Angeles CA 90077, USA — Singer, Songwriter

**Sager, Craig**
Jock Jill & Frankie's Sports Grill, 5600 Roswell Road NE, #M3, Atlanta GA 30342, USA — Sportscaster

**Saget, Robert L (Bob)**
Brillstein Entertainment Partners, 9150 Wilshire Blvd, #350, Beverly Hills CA 90212 USA — Actor, Comedian

**Sagnier, Ludivine**
Agence Elisabeth Simpson, 62 Blvd du Montparnasse, 75015 Paris, France — Actress

**Sagripanti, Giacomo**
I M G Artists, Hogarth Business Park, Chiswick, London W4 2TH, England — Conductor

**Sahagun, Elena**
Artists Agency, 9430 Olympic Blvd, Beverly Hills CA 90212 USA — Actress

**Sahakyan, Bako**
President's Office, Nagorno-Karabakh, Stepanakert, Nahorni, Azerbaijan — President, Nagorno-Karabakh

**Sahanaja, Darian**
Paradise Artists, PO Box 1821, Ojai CA 93024 USA — Keyboardist (Wondermints)

**Sahay, Vikram (Vik)**
Don Buchwald Talent Agency, 6500 Wilshire Blvd, #2200, Los Angeles CA 90048 USA — Actor

**Sahin, Ramazan**
Istanbul Buyukşehir Belediyesi, Ataturk Bulvary Cebeci Spor Kompleksi, Istanbul, Turkey — Freestyle Wrestler

**Sahl, Mort**
1441 3rd Ave, #12C, New York NY 10028, USA — Actor, Comedian

**Said, Ali Ahmad (Adonis)**
Green Inter Books, 6022 Wilshire Blvd, #200A, Los Angeles CA 90036, USA — Writer

**Said, Boris**
15 Avalon Road, Martin GA 30557, USA — Auto, Truck Racing Driver

**Sailors, Kenneth L (Ken)**
2119 E Grand Ave, #6, Laramie WY 82070, USA — Basketball Player

**Saini, Rajiv** — Architect, Interior Designer
Rajiv Saini Assoc, 9 Jer Mansion, Bandra (W), Mumbai 400050, India

**Sainsbury of Preston Candover, John D** — Businessman
J Sainsbury PLC, 33 Holborn, London EC1N 2HT, England

**Sainsbury of Turville, David J** — Businessman
Eagle House, 110 Jermyn St, London SW1Y 6EE, England

**Sainsbury, R Mark** — Philosopher
King's College, Philosophy Dept, London WC2R 2LS, England

**Saint Claire, Randy A** — Baseball Player
7117 State Route 8, Brant Lake NY 12815, USA

**Saint James, Susan** — Actress
174 West St, #54, Litchfield CT 06759, USA

**Saint, Crosbie E** — Army General
1116 N Pitt St, Alexandria VA 22314, USA

**Saint, Eva Marie** — Actress
Glick Agency, 347 5th Ave, #1404, New York NY 10016 USA

**Sainte-Marie, Buffy** — Singer, Guitarist, Songwriter
RR 1 Box 368, Kapaa HI 96746, USA

**Saint-Subber, Arnold** — Producer
116 E 64th St, New York NY 10065, USA

**Sainz Gall de Perez, Ines** — Journalist
TV Azteca, Periferico 4121, Colonia Fuentes Pedregal, DF CP 14141, Mexico

**Sainz, Salvador** — Actor, Director
Ave Prat de la Riba 43, 43201 Reus (Tarragona), Spain

**Saipaia, Blaine** — Football Player
1603 Holly Way, Fort Collins CO 80526, USA

**Saipe, Mike E** — Baseball Player
4191 Combe Way, San Diego CA 92122, USA

**Sajak, Pat** — Entertainer
Wheel of Fortune Show, 3400 Riverside Dr, #201, Burbank CA 91505, USA

**Sajko, Kristina** — Model
D N A Model Mgmt, 555 W 25th St, #600, New York NY 10001 USA

**Sakaguchi, Mizuho** — Soccer Player
Football Association, 3-10-15 Hongo, Bunkyoku, Tokyo 113 0033 Japan

**Sakamoto, Ryoichi** — Composer, Musician
K A B America, 302A W 12th St, #181, New York NY 10014, USA

**Sakamura, Ken** — Computer Scientist, Inventor
University of Tokyo, Information Science Dept, 7-3-1 Hongo, Bunkyoku, Tokyo 113 0033, Japan

**Sakata, Lenn H** — Baseball Player
2490 2nd Ave, Merced CA 95340, USA

**Sakato, George T** — WW II Army Hero (CMH)
8369 Katherine Way, Denver CO 80221, USA

**Sakharov, Alik** — Cinematographer
Global Artists Agency, 6253 Hollywood Blvd, #508, Los Angeles CA 90028 USA

**Sakic, Joseph S (Joe)** — Ice Hockey Player
4785 S Franklin St, Englewood CO 80113, USA

**Sakmann, Bert** — Nobel Medicine Laureate
Max Planck Institute, Jahnstr 39, 69120 Heidelberg, Germany

**Saks, Gene** — Director, Actor
I C M Partners, 730 5th Ave, New York NY 10019 USA

**Sakshaug, Eugene C** — Electrical Engineer
18 Grove Ave, Pittsfield MA 01201, USA

**Sala, Edoardo** — Actor
Agenzia Paola Bonelli, Via Parioli 50, 00197 Rome, Italy

**Sala, Richard** — Cartoonist (Peculia)
3131 College Ave, Berkeley CA 94705, USA

**Sala, Sharon** — Writer
Mira/Harlequin, 225 Duncan Mill Road, Don Mills ON MJB JK9, Canada

**Salaam, Ephraim M** — Football Player
8868 Chadbury Place, Elk Grove CA 95758, USA

**Salaam, Rashaan I** — Football Player
8132 Brookhaven Road, San Diego CA 92114, USA

**Saladino, John F** — Interior Designer
Saladino Group, 200 Lexington Ave, #1600, New York NY 10016, USA

**Salans, Lester B** — Physician
Sandoz Research Institute, RR 10, East Hanover NJ 07936, USA

**Salas, Mark B** — Baseball Player
1302 6th St SE, Ruskin FL 33570, USA

**Salazar Gomez, Jesus R Cardinal** — Religious Leader
Archdiocese of Bogota, Carrera 7A, #10-20, Bogota DC 1, Colombia

**Salazar, Alberto** — Track Athlete
Nike Inc, 1 SW Bowerman Dr, Beaverton OR 97005, USA

**Salazar, Angel** — Actor, Comedian
Roger Paul, 1650 Broadway, #304, New York NY 10019, USA

**Salazar, Kenneth L (Ken)** — Secretary, Interior; Senator, CO
Interior Department, 1849 C St NW, Washington DC 20240 USA

**Salazar, Luis E** — Baseball Player
20808 Cabrillo Way, Boca Raton FL 33428, USA

**Salazar, Rosa** — Actress
Paradigm Agency, 360 N Crescent Dr, North Building, Beverly Hills CA 90210 USA

**Salcido Flores, Carlos A** — Soccer Player
Federacion de Futbol, Colima 373 Colonia Roma, Delegacion Cuauhtemoc, Mexico City DF 06700, Mexico

**Saldana, Theresa** — Actress
I C M Partners, 10250 Constellation Blvd, #900, Los Angeles CA 90067 USA

**Saldana, Zoe** — Actress
I C M Partners, 10250 Constellation Blvd, #900, Los Angeles CA 90067 USA

**Saldanha, Carlos** — Animator, Director
W M E Entertainment, 9601 Wilshire Blvd, #300, Beverly Hills CA 90210 USA

**Saldi, J Jay, IV** — Football Player
303 Donley Court, Southlake TX 76092, USA

**Saldivar, Lou** — Graphic Artist
Milwaukee Journal Sentinel, Editorial Dept, PO Box 371, Milwaukee WI 53201 USA

**Sale, Jamie R** — Ice Dancer
12116 NW 128th St, Edmonton AB T5L 1C3, Canada

**Saleaumua, R Daniel (Dan)** — Football Player
1603 Morning Breeze Lane, National City CA 91950, USA

**Saleh, Karim**
Artists Partnership, 101 Finsbury Pavement, London EC2A 1RS, England — Actor

**Salem, Dahlia**
Precision Entertainment, 6338 Wilshire Blvd, Los Angeles CA 90048, USA — Actress

**Salem, Harvey M**
25 Menlo Place, Berkeley CA 94707, USA — Football Player

**Salem, Kario**
Creative Artists Agency, 2000 Ave of Stars, #100, Los Angeles CA 90067 USA — Writer, Actor

**Salenger, Meredith**
Genesis Entertainment Partners, 4145 Garden Ave, Los Angeles CA 90039, USA — Actress

**Salerno-Sonnenberg, Nadja**
Opus 3 Artists, 470 Park Ave S, #900N, New York NY 10016 USA — Concert Violinist

**Sales, Nykesha**
Connecticut Sun, 1 Mohegan Sun Blvd, Uncasville CT 06382 USA — Basketball Player

**Saleski, Don**
1800 N Ridley Creek Road, Media PA 19063, USA — Ice Hockey Player

**Salfati, Pierre-Henri**
Artmedia, 20 Ave Rapp, 75007 Paris, France — Actor, Director, Writer

**Salgado, Curtis**
Pacific Talent, PO Box 19145, Portland OR 97280, USA — Singer, Harmonica Player

**Salgado, Michael**
Management Plus, PO Box 132, Seguin TX 78155, USA — Singer, Accordionist

**Salgado, Sebastiano R, Jr**
Instituto Terra, Bulcao Farm Land Institute, PO Box 005, 35200 000 Aimores MG, Brazil — Photographer

**Saliers, Emily**
Russell Carter Artist Mgmt, 567 Ralph Mcgill Blvd, Atlanta GA 30312, USA — Singer (Indigo Girls), Songwriter

**Salim, Salim Ahmed**
Organization of African Unity, PO Box 3243, Addis Ababa, Ethiopia — Prime Minister, Tanzania

**Salisbury, Laney**
Random House, 1745 Broadway, #1800, New York NY 10019 USA — Writer

**Salisbury, R Sean**
5823 Brushy Creek Trail, Dallas TX 75252, USA — Football Player

**Sall, Macky**
President's Office, Ave Roume, BP 168, Dakar, Senegal — Prime Minister, Senegal

**Sallah, Michael D**
Toledo Blade, Editorial Dept, 541 N Superior St, Toledo OH 43660, USA — Journalist

**Salle, David**
Deitch-Boone Gallery, 541 W 24th St, New York NY 10011, USA — Artist

**Salles, Walter, Jr**
VideoFilmes, Rua Do Russel 270 - Gloria, Rio de Janeiro RJ 22210 110, Brazil — Director

**Salley, John T**
4619 Caritina Dr, Tarzana CA 91356, USA — Basketball Player, Sportscaster, Actor

**Sallinen, Aulis H**
Teosto, Lauttasaarentie 1, 00200 Helsinki 20, Finland — Composer

**Sallis, Peter**
Jonathan Altaras Assoc, 11 Garrick St, London WC2E 9AR, England — Actor

**Sally, Jerome E**
4107 Roxbury Court, Columbia MO 65203, USA — Football Player

**Salminen, Matti**
Mariedi Anders Artists, 3030 Baker St, San Francisco CA 94123 USA — Opera Singer

**Salming, Borje**
Box 45438, 104 31 Stockholm, Sweden — Ice Hockey Player

**Salmoiraghi, Franco**
PO Box 61708, Honolulu HI 96839, USA — Photographer

**Salmon, Timothy J (Tim)**
6061 E Sunnyside Dr, Scottsdale AZ 85254, USA — Baseball Player

**Salmons, John R**
909 Waverly Road, Bryn Mawr PA 19010, USA — Basketball Player

**Salmons, Stephen (Steve)**
1717 N El Dorado Ave, Ontario CA 91764, USA — Volleyball Player

**Salo, Mika J**
Sauber Racing, Wildbachstr 9, 8340 Hinwil, Switzerland — Auto Racing Driver

**Salo, Ola**
Live Nation, Linnegatan 89, Box 21451, 104 51 Stockholm, Sweden — Singer, Guitarist, Pianist (The Ark)

**Salo, Sami S**
Tampa Bay Lightning, 401 Channelside Dr, Tampa FL 33602 USA — Ice Hockey Player

**Salo, Teemu**
Curling Association, Kalatorppa 2A62, 02230 Espoo, Finland — Curling Athlete

**Salo, Tommy M**
Lefksands I F, Box 118, 793 23 Leksand, Sweden — Ice Hockey Player

**Salome, Jean-Paul**
Voyez Mon Agent, 20 Ave Rapp, 75007 Paris, France — Director

**Salomon, Leon E (Lee)**
2795 Kipps Colony Dr S, Saint Petersburg FL 33707, USA — Army General

**Salomon, Mikael**
Creative Artists Agency, 2000 Ave of Stars, #100, Los Angeles CA 90067 USA — Director, Cinematographer

**Salonen, Esa-Pekka**
Cathy Nelson, Court House, Dorstone, Herefordshire HR3 6AW, England — Conductor, Composer

**Salonga, Lea**
David Belenzon Mgmt, PO Box 5000, PMB 67, Rancho Santa Fe CA 92067, USA — Singer, Actress

**Salopek, Paul**
Chicago Tribune, Editorial Dept, 350 N Orleans St, Chicago IL 60654 USA — Journalist

**Salt, Jennifer**
3742 Sheridge Dr, Sherman Oaks CA 91403, USA — Actress

**Saltalamacchia, Jarrod S**
2095 Windsock Way, Wellington FL 33414, USA — Baseball Player

**Salter, Bryant J**
16810 SW 88th Court, Village of Palmetto Bay FL 33157, USA — Football Player

**Salter, James**
Knopf Publishers, 1745 Broadway, New York NY 10019 USA — Writer

**Salter, Russell D**
University of Pittsburgh Medical School, Immunology Dept, Pittsburgh PA 15260, USA — Immunologist

**Saltykov, Aleksey A**
Institute Mosfilmovsky Per 4A, #104, 119285 Moscow, Russia — Director

**Saltykov, Boris G**
Russian Technologies, Bryusov Per 11, 103009 Moscow, Russia — Economist; Government Official, Russia

**Salva, Victor** — Director
Resolution, 1801 Century Park E, #2300, Los Angeles CA 90067 USA

**Salvador, Bryce** — Ice Hockey Player
422 Lenox Ave, Westfield NJ 07090, USA

**Salvadori, Al** — Basketball Player
1204 Lenox Dr, Bethel Park PA 15102, USA

**Salvatore, Robert A (R A)** — Writer
Tom Doherty Assoc, 175 5th Ave, New York NY 10010, USA

**Salvay, Bennett** — Composer
Gorfaine/Schwartz, 4111 W Alameda Ave, #509, Burbank CA 91505 USA

**Salvino, Carmen** — Bowler
65 Stevens Dr, Schaumburg IL 60173, USA

**Salzman, Mark** — Writer
Random House, 1745 Broadway, #1800, New York NY 10019 USA

**Sam the Sham** — Singer
6123 Old Brunswick Road, Arlington TN 38002, USA

**Samaras, Antonis** — Prime Minister, Greece
Prime Minister's Office, Maximos Mansion, 19 Irodou Attikou St, 10674 Athens, Greece

**Samaras, Lucas** — Sculptor, Photographer
Pace Wildenstein Gallery, 32 E 57th St, #400, New York NY 10022, USA

**Samardzija, Jeff** — Baseball Player
3351 N Southport Ave, Chicago IL 60657, USA

**Samba-Panza, Catherine** — President, Central African Republic
Palais de la Renaissance, Bangui, Central African Republic

**Samberg, Andy** — Actor
United Talent Agency, U T A Plaza, 9336 Civic Center Dr, Beverly Hills CA 90210 USA

**Samberg, D Andrew (Andy)** — Actor, Comedian
Mosiac Media Group, 9200 W Sunset Blvd, #1000, Los Angeles CA 90069 USA

**Sambito, Joseph C (Joe)** — Baseball Player
23 Modesto, Irvine CA 92602, USA

**Sambora, Richard S (Richie)** — Singer, Songwriter (Bon Jovi)
Bon Jovi Mgmt, 809 Elder Circle, Austin TX 78733, USA

**Samcoff, Edward W (Ed)** — Baseball Player
8153 Maderia Port Lane, Fair Oaks CA 95628, USA

**Sameshima, Aya** — Soccer Player
Football Association, 3-10-15 Hongo, Bunkyoku, Tokyo 113 0033 Japan

**Samet, Jonathan M** — Epidemiologist
Johns Hopkins University, Bloomberg Public Health School, Baltimore MD 21205, USA

**Samie, Catherine** — Actress
Artmedia, 20 Ave Rapp, 75007 Paris, France

**Samios, Nicholas P** — Science Administrator, Physicist
Brookhaven National Laboratory, Director's Office, 2 Center St, Upton NY 11973, USA

**Sammons, Mary F** — Businesswoman
Rite Aid Corp, 30 Hunter Lane, Camp Hill PA 17011, USA

**Samms, Emma** — Actress
2934 1/2 N Beverly Glen Circle, #417, Los Angeles CA 90077, USA

**Samokutyayev, Alexandr M** — Cosmonaut
Cosmonaut Training Center, Star City, 141160 Zvezdny Gorodok, Moscow Oblast, Russia

**Sampen, William A (Bill)** — Baseball Player
11 Carnaby Court, Brownsburg IN 46112, USA

**Sampey, Angelle** — Motorcycle Racing Rider, Auto Driver
Star Racing, PO Box 1241, Americus GA 31709, USA

**Sample, Steven B** — Educator
211 S Orange Grove Blvd, #14, Pasadena CA 91105, USA

**Sample, William A (Billy)** — Baseball Player
10 Pascack Road, Township of Washington NJ 07676, USA

**Sampler, Philece** — Actress
Vox Inc, 6420 Wilshire Blvd, #1080, Los Angeles CA 90048 USA

**Samples, Keith** — Writer
Characters Talent Mgmt, 8 Elm St, Toronto ON M5G 1G7, Canada

**Sampleton, Lawrence** — Football Player
2900 Bunny Run, Austin TX 78746, USA

**Sampras, Peter (Pete)** — Tennis Player
2552 Via Anita, Palos Verdes Estates CA 90274, USA

**Sampson, Benjamin D (Benji)** — Baseball Player
8312 Flat Rock Court, North Richland Hills TX 76182, USA

**Sampson, Gary** — Ice Hockey Player
Alaska Sportsman's Lodge, PO Box 231985, Anchorage AK 99523, USA

**Sampson, Kelvin M** — Basketball Coach
University of Houston, Athletic Dept, Houston TX 77204, USA

**Sampson, R Gregory (Greg)** — Football Player
3286 Highland Dr, Carlsbad CA 92008, USA

**Sampson, Ralph L, Jr** — Basketball Player, Coach
530 Myrtle St, Harrisonburg VA 22802, USA

**Sams, Dean** — Keyboardist (Lonestar)
Borman Entertainment, 4322 Harding Pike, #429, Nashville TN 37205, USA

**Sams, Jeremy** — Composer
Faber Music, 3 Queen Square, London WC1N 3AU, England

**Sams, Russell** — Actor
TalentWorks, 3500 W Olive Ave, #1400, Burbank CA 91505 USA

**Samsonov, Sergei V** — Ice Hockey Player
2896 Croftshire Court, Rochester MI 48306, USA

**Samuel, Asante T** — Football Player
4130 Triple Crown Court, Davie FL 33330, USA

**Samuel, Juan M** — Baseball Player
777 S Eden St, Baltimore MD 21231, USA

**Samuel, Xavier** — Actor
Shanahan Mgmt, Berman House, 91 Campbell St, #300, Surry Hills NSW 2010, Australia

**Samuels, Chris** — Football Player
University of Alabama, Athletic Dept, Tuscaloosa AL 35487, USA

**Samuels, Roger N** — Baseball Player
4865 Tampico Way, San Jose CA 95118, USA

**Samuelsson, Bengt I** — Nobel Medicine Laureate
Karolinska Institute, Chemistry Dept, 171 77 Stockholm, Sweden

**Samuelsson, K Mikael** — Ice Hockey Player
44751 Roundview Dr, Novi MI 48375, USA

**Samuelsson, Kjell** — Ice Hockey Player
5 Simsbury Dr, Voorhees NJ 08043, USA

**Samuelsson, Ulf** — Ice Hockey Player, Coach
6783 Onyx Place, Carlsbad CA 92009, USA

**Sanada, Hiroyuki** — Actor
Lighthouse Entertainment, 9220 W Sunset Blvd, #200, West Hollywood CA 90069 USA

**Sanborn, David** — Jazz Saxophonist, Composer
Patrick Rains Assoc, 1255 5th Ave, #7J, New York NY 10029, USA

**Sanches, Brian L** — Baseball Player
9020 Taylor Circle, Orange TX 77630, USA

**Sanches, Stacy** — Model, Actress
Playboy Promotions, 9346 Civic Center Dr, #200, Beverly Hills CA 90210 USA

**Sanchez Azuara, Rocio** — Actress
TV Azteca, Periferico 4121, Colonia Fuentes Pedregal, DF CP 14141, Mexico

**Sanchez Ceren, Salvador** — President, El Salvador
Casa Presidencial, Calle Dario Gonzales 806, San Salvador, El Salvador

**Sanchez Vicario, Arantxa** — Tennis Player
Sabino de Arana 28, #6-1A, 08028 Barcelona, Spain

**Sanchez, Alejandro A (Alex)** — Baseball Player
1400 Mellissa Circle, Antioch CA 94509, USA

**Sanchez, Ana Maria** — Opera Singer
Opera et Concert, 37 Rue de la Chaussee d'Antin, 75009 Paris, France

**Sanchez, David** — Saxophonist
Addeo Music International, 37 W 26th St, #315, New York NY 10010, USA

**Sanchez, Duaner** — Baseball Player
56748 Eastvue Dr, Osceola IN 46561, USA

**Sanchez, Eduardo** — Director, Producer, Writer
Haxan Films, PO Box 261370, Encino CA 91426, USA

**Sanchez, Frederick P (Freddy), Jr** — Baseball Player
2494 E Cloud Dr, Chandler AZ 85249, USA

**Sanchez, Gabriel (Gaby)** — Baseball Player
5621 SW 130th Place, Miami FL 33183, USA

**Sanchez, Keram Malicki** — Actor
Nine Yards Entertainment, 8530 Wilshire Blvd, #500, Beverly Hills CA 90211 USA

**Sanchez, Kiele** — Actress
Industry Entertainment, 955 Carillo Dr, #300, Los Angeles CA 90048 USA

**Sanchez, Marco** — Actor
Stone Manners Salners, 6100 Wilshire Blvd, #1500, Los Angeles CA 90035 USA

**Sanchez, Mark D** — Football Player
Philadelphia Eagles, 1 Novacare Way, Philadelphia PA 19145 USA

**Sanchez, Pedro** — Soil Scientist
Columbia University, Earth Institute, New York NY 10027, USA

**Sanchez, Poncho** — Jazz Drummer
Regime Mgmt, 150 W Alameda Ave, #230, Burbank CA 91502, USA

**Sanchez, Rey F** — Baseball Player
788 Calle Pampero, Urb Country Club, San Juan PR 00924, USA

**Sanchez, Roselyn** — Actress
A P A Talent & Literary Agency, 405 S Beverly Dr, #300, Beverly Hills CA 90212 USA

**Sanchez, Samuel** — Cyclist
Euskadi-Fundacio Ciolista, C/Iparragirre 46-1, 48010 Bilboa, Spain

**Sanchez, Sergio G** — Writer
United Talent Agency, U T A Plaza, 9336 Civic Center Dr, Beverly Hills CA 90210 USA

**Sanchez-Gijon, Aitana** — Actress
Alsira Garcia Maroto, Gran Via 63, #3 Izda, 28013 Madrid, Spain

**Sanchez-Vilella, Roberto** — Governor, Puerto Rico
414 Ave Munoz Rivera, #7A, Stop 31-1/2, San Juan PR 00918, USA

**Sand, Paul** — Actor
Paradigm Agency, 360 N Crescent Dr, North Building, Beverly Hills CA 90210 USA

**Sand, Todd** — Figure Skater
2973 Harbor Blvd, #468, Costa Mesa CA 92626, USA

**Sanda, Dominique** — Actress
Agence Metropolitan Paris, 23 Blvd des Capucines, 75002 Paris, France

**Sandberg of Passfield, Michael G R** — Financier
Waterside, Passfield, Liphook, Hampshire GU30 7RT, England

**Sandberg, Espen** — Director
Roenbergfilm, Pilestredet 75C, 0354 Oslo, Norway

**Sandberg, Ryne D** — Baseball Player, Manager
26 Biltmore Estates, Phoenix AZ 85016, USA

**Sande, Emeli** — Singer, Musician, Songwriter
Virgin Records, Kensal House, 533-79 Harrow Road, London W10 4RH, England

**Sandelin, Scott** — Ice Hockey Player, Coach
4880 Adrian Lane, Hermantown MN 55811, USA

**Sandeman, William S (Bill)** — Football Player
PO Box 203, Homewood CA 96141, USA

**Sandeno, Kaitlin** — Swimmer
356 Rochester St, #B, Costa Mesa CA 92627, USA

**Sander, Casey** — Actor
Leavitt Talent Group, 11500 W Olympic Blvd, #400, Los Angeles CA 90064, USA

**Sander, Ian** — Producer, Director, Actor
Sander/Moses Productions, 500 S Buena Vista St, Burbank CA 91521, USA

**Sander, Jil** — Fashion Designer
Osterfeldstr 32-34, 22529 Hamburg, Germany

**Sander, Judith M** — Artist
25218 Oak Lane, Philomath OR 97370, USA

**Sanders, Anthony M** — Baseball Player
7881 E McGee Mountain Road, Tucson AZ 85750, USA

**Sanders, Barry D** — Football Player
PO Box 81336, Rochester MI 48308, USA

**Sanders, Beverly** — Actress
12218 Morrison St, Valley Village CA 91607, USA

**Sanders, Bill** — Cartoonist
PO Box 661, Milwaukee WI 53201, USA

**Sanders, C J** — Actor
Abrams Artists, 9200 W Sunset Blvd, #1125, West Hollywood CA 90069 USA

**Sanders, Charles A (Charlie)** — Football Player, Coach
3418 Palm Aire Court, Rochester Hills MI 48309, USA

**Sanders, Chris** — Director, Actor
W M E Entertainment, 9601 Wilshire Blvd, #300, Beverly Hills CA 90210 USA
**Sanders, David A** — Baseball Player
10411 S Ellen St, Mulvane KS 67110, USA
**Sanders, Deion L** — Football, Baseball Player, Sportscaster
1280 N Preston Road, Prosper TX 75078, USA
**Sanders, Doug** — Golfer
1311 Nantucket Dr, Houston TX 77057, USA
**Sanders, Eric D** — Football Player
9325 Tailey Circle, Duluth GA 30097, USA
**Sanders, Erin** — Actress
C E S D, 10635 Santa Monica Blvd, #130, Los Angeles CA 90025 USA
**Sanders, Frank V** — Football Player
4551 E Desert Trumpet Road, Phoenix AZ 85044, USA
**Sanders, Franklyn B (Frank)** — Ice Hockey Player
613 Lake View Dr, Saint Paul MN 55129, USA
**Sanders, James B** — Football Player
Arizona Cardinals, PO Box 888, Phoenix AZ 85001 USA
**Sanders, Jay O** — Actor
Innovative Artists, 1505 10th St, Santa Monica CA 90401 USA
**Sanders, Jeff** — Basketball Player
PO Box 374, South Holland IL 60473, USA
**Sanders, John F** — Baseball Player
3004 Cheshire Court, Woodstock GA 30189, USA
**Sanders, Jonathan (Jon)** — Yachtsman
Riverview Gardens, 20 Dean St, #95, Claremont, Perth WA 6010, Australia
**Sanders, Kenneth G (Ken)** — Baseball Player
12141 Parkview Lane, Hales Corners WI 53130, USA
**Sanders, Kenneth R (Ken)** — Football Player
3067 FM 217, Valley Mills TX 76689, USA
**Sanders, Marlene** — Commentator
175 Riverside Dr, New York NY 10024, USA
**Sanders, Pharoah** — Jazz Saxophonist
Joel Chriss Co, 300 Mercer St, #3J, New York NY 10003 USA
**Sanders, Reginald L (Reggie)** — Baseball Player
122 Vista Del Mar Lane, #102, Myrtle Beach SC 29572, USA
**Sanders, Richard** — Actor
4954 Strohm Ave, North Hollywood CA 91601, USA
**Sanders, Ricky W** — Football Player
4822 Rockwood Dr, Houston TX 77004, USA
**Sanders, Rupert** — Director
Independent Talent Group, 40 Whitfield St, London W1T 2RH, England
**Sanders, Scott G** — Baseball Player
315 Belmont Dr, Thibodaux LA 70301, USA
**Sanders, Summer** — Swimmer, Sportscaster
731 Martingale Lane, Park City UT 84098, USA
**Sanders, Susan (Sue)** — Golfer
3888 Cheyenne Place, Sedalia CO 80135, USA
**Sanders, Thomas D** — Football Player
2030 Appleton Dr, Missouri City TX 77489, USA
**Sanders, Thomas E (Satch)** — Basketball Player, Executive
114 Fenway, Boston MA 02115, USA
**Sanders, Troy** — Singer, Bassist (Mastodon)
Pinnacle Entertainment, 30 Glenn St, White Plains NY 10603, USA
**Sanders, W J (Jerry), III** — Businessman
Advanced Micro Devices, 1 A M D Place, PO Box 3453, Sunnyvale CA 94088, USA
**Sanderson, Cael S** — Freestyle Wrestler
Pennsylvania State University, Athletic Dept, University Park PA 16802, USA
**Sanderson, Derek M** — Ice Hockey Player
Howland Capital Mgmt, 75 Federal St, Boston MA 02110, USA
**Sanderson, Geoff M** — Ice Hockey Player
Philadelphia Flyers, 1st Union Center, 3601 S Broad St, Philadelphia PA 19148 USA
**Sanderson, Peter** — Artist
1105 Shell Gate Plaza, Alameda CA 94501, USA
**Sanderson, Scott D** — Baseball Player
945 Newcastle Dr, Lake Forest IL 60045, USA
**Sanderson, Theresa (Tessa)** — Track Athlete
Performing Artistes, 24A High St, Cobham KT11 3EB, England
**Sanderson, William** — Actor
401 Bonnymead Ave, Harrisburg PA 17111, USA
**Sandeson, William S** — Editorial Cartoonist
2230 Muskoday Pass, Fort Wayne IN 46809, USA
**Sandford, Ed** — Ice Hockey Player
18 Clearwater Road, Winchester MA 01890, USA
**Sandford, John** — Writer, Journalist
G P Putnam's Sons, 375 Hudson St, New York NY 10014 USA
**Sandiford, L Erskine** — Prime Minister, Barbados
Hillvista, Porters, Saint James, Barbados
**Sandin, Daniel J** — Inventor (Cave Electronic Visualization)
University of Illinois, Electronic Visualization Laboratory, 842 W Taylor St, Chicago IL 60607, USA
**Sandlak, Jim** — Ice Hockey Player
74 Green Hedge Lane, London ON N6H 5A6, Canada
**Sandler, Adam** — Actor, Comedian
Brillstein Entertainment Partners, 9150 Wilshire Blvd, #350, Beverly Hills CA 90212 USA
**Sandler, Herbert M** — Financier
Sandler Foundation, 121 Steuart St, San Francisco CA 94105, USA
**Sandler, Tony** — Singer (Sandler & Young)
Producers Inc, 11806 N 56th St, Tampa FL 33617 USA
**Sandlock, Michael J (Mike)** — Baseball Player
81 Bible St, Cos Cob CT 06807, USA
**Sandlund, Debra** — Actress
Innovative Artists, 1505 10th St, Santa Monica CA 90401 USA
**Sandoval Iniguez, Juan Cardinal** — Religious Leader
Archdiocese of Guadalajara, Calle Liceo 17, #1-331, 44100 Guadalajara, Jalisco, Mexico
**Sandoval, Arturo** — Jazz Trumpeter, Pianist
PO Box 143936, Coral Gables FL 33114, USA

**Sandoval, Eugene** — Architect
Zimmer Gunner Frasca Partnership, 320 SW Oak St, #500, Portland OR 97204, USA

**Sandoval, Hope** — Singer (Mazzy Star, Going Home)
High Road Touring, 751 Bridgeway, #200, Sausalito CA 94965 USA

**Sandoval, Miguel** — Actor
Innovative Artists, 1505 10th St, Santa Monica CA 90401 USA

**Sandoval, Sonny** — Singer (POD)
Atlantic Records, 9229 W Sunset Blvd, #900, West Hollywood CA 90069 USA

**Sandow, Nicholas J (Nick)** — Actor
Stone Manners Salners, 6100 Wilshire Blvd, #1500, Los Angeles CA 90035 USA

**Sandrelli, Stefania** — Actress
T N A, Viale Parioli 41, 00197 Rome, Italy

**Sandri, Leonardo Cardinal** — Religious Leader
Oriental Churches Congregation, Palazzo del Bramante, Via Conciliazione 34, 00193 Rome, Italy

**Sandrich, Jay H** — Director
Creative Artists Agency, 2000 Ave of Stars, #100, Los Angeles CA 90067 USA

**Sands, Charles D (Charlie)** — Baseball Player
28940 Bermuda Pointe Circle, #103, Bonita Springs FL 34134, USA

**Sands, Julian** — Actor
S D B Partners, 315 S Beverly Dr, #411, Beverly Hills CA 90067 USA

**Sands, Stark** — Actor
Management 360, 9111 Wilshire Blvd, Beverly Hills CA 90210 USA

**Sands, Terdell D** — Football Player
PO Box 2217, Chattanooga TN 37409, USA

**Sands, Tommy** — Singer, Actor
Lustig Talent, PO Box 770850, Orlando FL 32877 USA

**Sandt, Thomas J (Tom)** — Baseball Player
15265 Boones Way, Lake Oswego OR 97035, USA

**Sandusky, Alexander B (Alex)** — Football Player
22 Floral Ave, Key West FL 33040, USA

**Sandusky, Michael G (Mike)** — Football Player
2786 Amberwood Court, Naples FL 34120, USA

**Sandvig, Jake** — Actor
Innovative Artists, 1505 10th St, Santa Monica CA 90401 USA

**Sandy B** — Singer
T-Best Talent Agency, 508 Honey Lake Court, Danville CA 94506 USA

**Sandy, Gary** — Actor
PO Box 818, Cynthiana KY 41031, USA

**Sane, Justin** — Singer, Songwriter
Agency Group Ltd, 142 W 57th St, #600, New York NY 10019 USA

**Sanejouand, Jean Michel** — Artist
Belle-Ville, 49150 Vaulandry, France

**Sanford, Arlene** — Director, Producer, Writer
Anonymous Content, 3532 Hayden Ave, Culver City CA 90232 USA

**Sanford, Chance S** — Baseball Player
15028 Bardwell Lane, Frisco TX 75035, USA

**Sanford, Ed** — Ice Hockey Player
18 Clearwater Road, Winchester MA 01890, USA

**Sanford, J Frederick (Fred)** — Baseball Player
1046 W 600 N, Salt Lake City UT 84116, USA

**Sanford, Lucius M** — Football Player
1350 Allegheny St SW, Atlanta GA 30310, USA

**Sanford, Meredith L (Mo)** — Baseball Player
2800 Highway 389, Starkville MS 39759, USA

**Sanford, O'Leo** — Football Player
3044 Gorton Road, Columbia MD 21046, USA

**Sanford, Ron** — Basketball Player
3129 Santana Lane, Plano TX 75023, USA

**Sang Hun Choe** — Journalist
Associated Press, Editorial Dept, 450 W 33rd St, #1500, New York NY 10001 USA

**Sangare, Oumou** — Singer
Concerted Efforts, PO Box 440326, Somerville MA 02144 USA

**Sangay, Lonsang** — Prime Minister, Tibet Exile Government
Tibet Government in Exile, Kashag, Dharmsala 176205 H P, India

**Sanger, Mark** — Editor
Worldwide Production Agency, 144 N Robertson Blvd, #200, West Hollywood CA 90048, USA

**Sangheli, Andrei** — Prime Minister, Moldova
Parliament House, Prosp 105, 277073 Kishineau, Moldova

**SanGiacomo, Laura** — Actress
Imperium 7 Artists, 5455 Wilshire Blvd, #1706, Los Angeles CA 90036 USA

**Sangster, Thomas** — Actor
Curtis Brown Group, 28-29 Haymarket St, #500, London SW1Y 4SP, England

**Sanguillen, Manny** — Baseball Player
2838 SW 4th St, Boynton Beach FL 33435, USA

**Sanguinetti Coirolo, Julio Maria** — President, Uruguay
Partido Colorado, Andres Martinez Trueba 1271, Montevideo, Uruguay

**SanMiguel, Renay** — Commentator
CNN-TV, News Dept, 190 Marietta Ave SW, Atlanta GA 30303 USA

**Sano, Roy I** — Religious Leader
United Methodist Church, 100 Maryland Ave NE, #300, Washington DC 20002, USA

**Sansa, Maya** — Actress
Markham Froggatt Irwin, Julian House, 4 Windmill St, London W1P 1HF, England

**Sansom Harris, Harriet** — Actress
B R S / Gage Talent Agency, 5757 Wilshire Blvd, #659, Los Angeles CA 90036 USA

**Sansom, Chip** — Cartoonist (Born Loser)
204 Long Beach Road, Centerville MA 02632, USA

**Sansweet, Steven J** — Writer
PO Box 2009, San Rafael CA 94912, USA

**Sant, Alfred** — Prime Minister, Malta
National Labor Center, Mills End Road, Hanrum, Malta

**Santa Rosa, Gilberto** — Singer
Universal Attractions, 135 W 26th St, #1200, New York NY 10001 USA

**Santana Araque, Johan A** — Baseball Player
10471 Via Lombardia Court, Miromar Lakes FL 33913, USA

**Santana, Carlos** — Guitarist, Singer, Songwriter
Santana Mgmt, 121 Jordan St, San Rafael CA 94901, USA

**Santana, Ervin R**
Atlanta Braves, Turner Field, 755 Hank Aaron Dr, Atlanta GA 30315 USA — Baseball Player

**Santana, Manuel M**
Manolo Santana Racquets Club, Carretera Ds Carretera Istan, 2, 29602 Marbella, Malaga, Spain — Tennis Player

**Santangelo, Frank P (F P)**
3602 Rocky Ridge Way, El Dorado Hills CA 95762, USA — Baseball Player

**Santaolalla, Gustavo**
First Artists, 4764 Park Granada, #210, Calabasas CA 91302 USA — Guitarist, Composer

**Santer, Jacques**
69 Rue J P Huberty, 1742 Luxembourg-Ville, Luxembourg — Prime Minister, Luxembourg

**Santiago, Benito R**
PO Box 5759, Lighthouse Point FL 33074, USA — Baseball Player

**Santiago, Christina L**
Playboy Promotions, 9346 Civic Center Dr, #200, Beverly Hills CA 90210 USA — Model

**Santiago, Eddie**
Pozo International Promotions, 170 E 116th St, New York NY 10029, USA — Singer

**Santiago, Jose**
690 Calle Cesar Gonzalez, #2108, San Juan PR 00918, USA — Baseball Player

**Santiago, Joseph A (Joey)**
X-Ray Touring, 77-79 Great Eastern St, #A, London EC2A 3HU, England — Guitarist (Pixies)

**Santiago, Lina**
Richard Walters, PO Box 2789, Toluca Lake CA 91610 USA — Singer

**Santiago, Otis J (O J)**
8780 NW 37th Place, Hollywood FL 33024, USA — Football Player

**Santiago, Ray**
Innovative Artists, 1505 10th St, Santa Monica CA 90401 USA — Actor

**Santiago, Saundra**
C E S D, 257 Park Ave S, #950, New York NY 10010 USA — Actress

**Santiago-Hudson, Ruben**
Vincent Cirrincione Assoc, 1516 N Fairfax Ave, Los Angeles CA 90046 USA — Actor

**Santigold**
Roc Nation Mgmt, 1411 Broadway New York NY 10018, USA — Singer, Songwriter

**Santilli, Ivana D**
The Agency Group, 2 Berkeley St, #202, Toronto ON M5A 4J5, Canada — Singer, Songwriter, Keyboardist

**SantoDomingo, Rafael**
PO Box 21, Orocovis PR 00720, USA — Baseball Player

**Santoni, Reni**
Geddes Agency, 8430 Santa Monica Blvd, #201, West Hollywood CA 90069 USA — Actor

**Santora, Nick**
W M E Entertainment, 9601 Wilshire Blvd, #300, Beverly Hills CA 90210 USA — Producer

**Santorelli, Frank**
Bleecker Street Entertainment, 853 Broadway, #1214, New York NY 10003, USA — Actor

**Santorini, Alan J (Al)**
100 Wescott Dr, Clemson SC 29631, USA — Baseball Player

**Santoro, Rodrigo**
I C M Partners, 10250 Constellation Blvd, #900, Los Angeles CA 90067 USA — Actor

**Santos Ordonez, Elvin E**
Casa Presidencial, Blvd Juan Pablo II, Tegucigalpa MDC, Honduras — President, Honduras

**Santos, Anthony (Romeo)**
Sony Music Miami, 605 Lincoln Road Road, #700, Miami Beach FL 33139 USA — Singer, Songwriter

**Santos, Joe**
Amsel Eisenstadt Frazier, 5055 Wilshire Blvd, #865, Los Angeles CA 90036 USA — Actor

**Santos, Jose**
620 SW 99th Ave, Pembroke Pines FL 33025, USA — Thoroughbred Racing Jockey

**Santos, Juan Manuel**
Palacio de Narino, Plaza de Bolivar, Santa Fe, Bogota DE, Colombia — President, Colombia

**Santos, Rick**
S&S Automotive, 14127 Washington Ave, San Leandro CA 94578, USA — Drag Racing Driver

**SantosDeOliveira, Alessandra**
Washington Mystics, Verizon Center, 401 9th St NW, #750, Washington DC 20004 USA — Basketball Player

**Santovenia, Nelson G**
14642 SW 141st Court, Miami FL 33186, USA — Baseball Player

**Sanz, Alejandro**
R L M International, Puerto de Santa Maria 65, 28043 Madrid, Spain — Singer, Songwriter

**Sanz, Horatio**
United Talent Agency, U T A Plaza, 9336 Civic Center Dr, Beverly Hills CA 90210 USA — Actor, Comedian

**Saperstein, David**
Religious Action Center, 2027 Massachusetts Ave NW, Washington DC 20036, USA — Religious Leader, Rabbi, Writer

**Sapienza, Al**
S D B Partners, 315 S Beverly Dr, #411, Beverly Hills CA 90067 USA — Actor

**Sapolu, M Jesse**
1123 Buckingham Dr, #B, Costa Mesa CA 92626, USA — Football Player

**Sapp, Marvin**
Sony Records, 2100 Colorado Ave, Santa Monica CA 90404 USA — Singer

**Sapp, Theron C**
892 N Belair Road, Augusta GA 30909, USA — Football Player

**Sapp, Warren H**
PO Box 585, Windermere FL 34786, USA — Football Player, Sportscaster

**Sapphire**
Viking Press, 375 Hudson St, New York NY 10014 USA — Writer

**Saprykin, Oleg V**
15802 N 71st St, #451, Scottsdale AZ 85254, USA — Ice Hockey Player

**Sara, Mia**
Gersh Agency, 9465 Wilshire Blvd, #600, Beverly Hills CA 90212 USA — Actress

**Sarafyan, Angela**
Innovative Artists, 1505 10th St, Santa Monica CA 90401 USA — Actress

**Sarah, Robert Cardinal**
Pontifical Council Cor Unum, Palazzo San Pio X, Via della Conciliazione 5, 00193 Rome, Italy — Religious Leader

**Saraiva Martins, Jose Cardinal**
Causes of Saints Congregation, Palazzo delle Congregazioni, Piazza Pio XII 10, 00193 Rome, Italy — Religious Leader

**Saralegui, Cristina**
T G A Voice, 100 Lincoln Road, #928, Miami Beach FL 33178, USA — Commentator

**Sarandon, Chris**
Stone Manners Salners, 6100 Wilshire Blvd, #1500, Los Angeles CA 90035 USA — Actor

**Saraste, Jukka-Pekka**
Columbia Artists Mgmt Inc, 5 Columbus Circle, 1790 Broadway, #1600, New York NY 10019 USA — Conductor

**S**

**Sarasvuo, Virpi Kuitunen**
Ilmarisentie 26B, 03100 Nummela, Finland — Senator, MD

**Sarbanes, Paul S**
320 Suffolk Road, Baltimore MD 21218, USA — Religious Leader

**Sardi, Paolo Cardinal**
Apostolic Chamber, Palazzo Apostolico, 00120 Vatican City — Baseball Player

**Sardinha, Dane**
156 Kuuhei Road, Kailua HI 96734, USA — Producer, Writer

**Sardo, Michael**
Creative Artists Agency, 2000 Ave of Stars, #100, Los Angeles CA 90067 USA — Singer

**Sardou, Michel**
Artmedia, 20 Ave Rapp, 75007 Paris, France — Actress

**Sarelle, Leilani**
Affinity Artists Agency, 5724 W 3rd St, #511, Los Angeles CA 90036, USA — Architect

**Sarfati, Alain**
43 Rue Maurice Ripoche, 75014 Paris, France — Editorial Cartoonist

**Sargent, Ben**
Austin American-Statesman, 166 E Riverside Dr, Austin TX 78704, USA — Producer, Director

**Sargent, Joseph D**
27432 Latigo Bay View Dr, Malibu CA 90265, USA — President, Armenia

**Sargsyan, Serzh A**
President's Office, Marshal Bagramian Prosp 19, 375010 Yerevan, Armenia — Ice Hockey Player

**Sarich, Cory**
19322 Autumn Woods Ave, Tampa FL 33647, USA — Football Player, Coach

**Sarkisian, Steve**
University of Southern California, Athletic Dept, Los Angeles CA 90089, USA — Fashion Designer

**Sarne, Tanya**
Ghost Ltd, The Chapel, 263 Kensal Road, London W10 5DB, England — Ice Hockey Player

**Sarner, Craig B**
3607 E Gillespie Lane, Odessa TX 79765, USA — Writer

**Sarno, Joe**
5941 W Irving Park Road, Chicago IL 60634, USA — Producer, Writer

**Sarnoff, Elizabeth (Liz)**
W M E Entertainment, 9601 Wilshire Blvd, #300, Beverly Hills CA 90210 USA — Religious Leader

**Sarr, Theodore-Adrien Cardinal**
Archdiocese of Dakar, BP 1908, Avenue Jean XXIII, Dakar, Senegal — Actor

**Sarsgaard, Peter**
Creative Artists Agency, 2000 Ave of Stars, #100, Los Angeles CA 90067 USA — Singer, Songwriter

**Sartain, Dan**
Agency Group Ltd, 142 W 57th St, #600, New York NY 10019 USA — Baseball Player

**Sasaki, Kazuhiro**
Seattle Mariners, Safeco Field, PO Box 4100, Seattle WA 98194 USA — Actress, Model

**Sasaki, Kokone**
Cel World Entertainment, 8-12-15-B1 Akasaka, Minato, Tokyo 107 0052, Japan — Ice Hockey Player

**Saskamoose, Fred**
PO Box 225, Shell Lake SK S0J 2G0, Canada — Journalist

**Saslow, Eli**
Washington Post, Editorial Dept, 1150 15th St NW, Washington DC 20071 USA — Actor

**Sasse, Joshua**
Olivia Bell Management, 193 Wardour St, London W1F 8ZF, England — Astronomer

**Sasselov, Dimitar**
Harvard-Smithsonian Astrophysics Center, 60 Garden St, Cambridge MA 02138, USA — Vietnam War Army Hero (CMH)

**Sasser, Clarence E**
13414 FM 521, Rosharon TX 77583, USA — Ice Hockey Player

**Sasser, Grant**
1949 SE Orient Dr, Gresham OR 97080, USA — Senator, TN; Diplomat

**Sasser, James R (Jim)**
601 Mainstream Dr, Nashville TN 37228, USA — Baseball Player

**Sasser, Mack D (Mackey)**
19 Harrington Lane, Dothan AL 36305, USA — Actor, Comedian

**Sasso, Will**
Paradigm Agency, 360 N Crescent Dr, North Building, Beverly Hills CA 90210 USA — Opera, Pop Singer

**Sasson, Deborah**
Erlenhaupstr 10, 64625 Bensheim, Germany — Model

**Sassoon, Beverly**
2533 Benedict Canyon Dr, Beverly Hills CA 90210, USA — Fashion Designer

**Sassoon, David**
Bellville Sassoon, 18 Culford Gardens, London SW3 2ST, England — President, Congo People's Republic

**Sassou-Nguesso, Denis**
Palais du Peuple, Quartier Plateau, Brazzaville, Congo Republic — Cyclist

**Sastre Candil, Carlos**
Team Geox, Via Feltrina Centro 16, 31044 Biadene de Montebelluna, Italy — Model, Actress

**Sastre, Ines**
Paradigm Agency, 360 N Crescent Dr, North Building, Beverly Hills CA 90210 USA — Ice Hockey Player

**Satan, Miroslav**
46 Kettlepond Road, Jericho NY 11753, USA — Navy Admiral, Government Official

**Satcher, David M**
Morehouse College Medical School, Atlanta GA 30314, USA — Astronaut

**Satcher, Robert L (Bobby), Jr**
N A S A, Johnson Space Center, 2101 NASA Road, Houston TX 77058 USA — Lyricist, Writer, Producer

**Sater, Steven**
Creative Artists Agency, 2000 Ave of Stars, #100, Los Angeles CA 90067 USA — Ice Hockey Player, Executive

**Sather, Glen C**
77380 Vista Rosa, La Quinta CA 92253, USA — Actress

**Satine, Elena**
I C M Partners, 10250 Constellation Blvd, #900, Los Angeles CA 90067 USA — Economist

**Sato, Kazuo**
300 E 71st St, #15H, New York NY 10021, USA — Figure Skater

**Sato, Yuka**
Detroit Figure Skating Club, 888 Denison Court, Bloomfield Hills MI 48302, USA — Actress

**Satra, Sonia**
C E S D, 257 Park Ave S, #950, New York NY 10010 USA — Writer, Director, Actress

**Satrapi, Marjane**
United Talent Agency, U T A Plaza, 9336 Civic Center Dr, Beverly Hills CA 90210 USA — Singer, Guitarist

**Satriani, Joe**
Entourage Talent Assoc, 236 W 27th St, #800, New York NY 10001, USA

**Sarasvuo - Satriani**

**Satriano, Thomas V (Tom)** — Baseball Player
5320 Otis Ave, Tarzana CA 91356, USA

**Satterfield, Paul** — Actor
8323 W 1st St, Los Angeles CA 90048, USA

**Saturno, William** — Archaeologist
University of New Hampshire, Anthropology Dept, Durham NH 03824, USA

**Saturova, Simona** — Opera Singer
Kunstler Sekretariat am Gasteig, Rosenheimer Str 52, 81669 Munich, Germany

**Satyarthi, Kailash** — Nobel Peace Laureate
Bachpan Bachao Andolan, L-6 Kalkaji, New Delhi 110019, India

**Saucier, Kevin A** — Baseball Player
2316 Silversides Loop, Pensacola FL 32526, USA

**Saud, Prince Sultan Bin Abdulaziz al** — Government Official, Saudi Arabia
Defense Ministry, PO Box 26731, Airport Road, Riyadh 11165, Saudi Arabia

**Saudek, Jan** — Photographer
Blodkova 6, 13000 Prague 3, Czech Republic

**Sauer, Craig C** — Football Player
6926 Pagenkopf Road, Maple Plain MN 55359, USA

**Sauer, Louis** — Architect
3472 Marlowe St, Montreal QC H4A 3L7, Canada

**Sauer, Richard J** — Educator, Association Executive
National 4-H Council, 7100 Connecticut Ave, Chevy Chase MD 20815, USA

**Sauerbeck, Scott W** — Baseball Player
1818 4th St W, Palmetto FL 34221, USA

**Sauerbrun, Todd S** — Football Player
8201 N Oleander Ave, Niles IL 60714, USA

**Sauerbrunn, Rebecca E (Becky)** — Soccer Player
D C United, R F K Stadium, 2400 E Capitol St SE, Washington DC 20003 USA

**Sauerlander, Willibald P W** — Art Historian
Victoriastr II, 80803 Munich, Germany

**Sauers, Gene** — Golfer
9 Judsons Court, Savannah GA 31410, USA

**Saul, David J** — Prime Minister, Bermuda
Rocky Ledge, 18 Devonshire Bay Road, DV 07, Bermuda

**Saul, John W, III** — Writer
Grade A Entertainment, 149 S Barrington Ave, #719, Los Angeles CA 90049, USA

**Saul, Ralph S** — Businessman
1400 Waverly Road, #B037, Gladwyne PA 19035, USA

**Saul, Ronald R (Ron)** — Football Player
78 Sleepy Hollow Circle, Charles Town WV 25414, USA

**Saul, Stephanie** — Journalist
Newsday, Editorial Dept, 235 Pinelawn Road, Melville NY 11747, USA

**Saulters, Glynn** — Basketball Player
240 Country Lane, Quitman LA 71268, USA

**Saum, Sherri M** — Actress
Abrams Artists, 9200 W Sunset Blvd, #1125, West Hollywood CA 90069 USA

**Saunders, Bernie** — Ice Hockey Player
150 Pinecrest Dr, Hastings on Hudson NY 10706, USA

**Saunders, George** — Writer
Random House, 1745 Broadway, #1800, New York NY 10019 USA

**Saunders, Jennifer** — Actress
United Agents, 12-26 Lexington St, London W1F 0LE, England

**Saunders, John** — Sportscaster
ESPN-TV, Sports Dept, ESPN Plaza, 935 Middle St, Bristol CT 06010 USA

**Saunders, John R** — Auto Racing Executive
Watkins Glen Speedway, PO Box 500F, Watkins Glen NY 14891, USA

**Saunders, Joseph F (Joe)** — Baseball Player
1415 E Grand Canyon Dr, Chandler AZ 85249, USA

**Saunders, Pamela** — Model, Actress
Playboy Promotions, 9346 Civic Center Dr, #200, Beverly Hills CA 90210 USA

**Saunders, Phillip (Flip)** — Basketball Coach
Minnesota Timberwolves, Target Center, 600 1st Ave N, Minneapolis MN 55403 USA

**Saunders, Tony** — Baseball Player
PO Box 434, Severna Park MD 21146, USA

**Saunders, Townsend** — Freestyle Wrestler
733 Chantilly Dr, Sierra Vista AZ 85635, USA

**Saura, Carlos** — Director
Antonio Duran, Calle Arturo Soria 52, #Edif 2, 1-5A, 28027 Madrid, Spain

**Sauter, Johnathan J (Johnny)** — Auto, Truck Racing Driver
779 S Washburn St, #8, Oshkosh WI 54904, USA

**Sauve, Robert (Bob)** — Ice Hockey Player
Jandec Inc, 803-3080 Boul le Carrefour, Laval QC H7T 2R5, Canada

**Sauveur, Richard D (Rich)** — Baseball Player
3312 47th Ave E, Bradenton FL 34203, USA

**Savage, Ben** — Actor
Abrams Artists, 9200 W Sunset Blvd, #1125, West Hollywood CA 90069 USA

**Savage, Chantay** — Singer
Universal Attractions, 135 W 26th St, #1200, New York NY 10001 USA

**Savage, Charlie** — Journalist
Boston Globe, Editorial Dept, 135 William Morrissey Blvd, Dorchester MA 02125 USA

**Savage, Don** — Basketball Player
53 Park Edge, #1E, Berkeley Heights NJ 07922, USA

**Savage, Fred** — Actor, Director
Creative Artists Agency, 2000 Ave of Stars, #100, Los Angeles CA 90067 USA

**Savage, John** — Actor
5584 Bonneville Road, Hidden Hills CA 91302, USA

**Savage, John J (Jack)** — Baseball Player
9920 White Blossom Blvd, Louisville KY 40241, USA

**Savage, Martin** — Actor
United Agents, 12-26 Lexington St, London W1F 0LE, England

**Savage, Michael (Mike)** — Actor, Writer
Hilda Phisick Agency, 78 Temple Sheen Road, London SW14 7RR, England

**Savage, Paul** — Curling Athlete
Curling Association, 1660 Vimont Court, Cumberland ON K4A 4J4, Canada

**Savage, Rick** — Bassist (Def Leppard)
Front Line Mgmt, 1100 Glendon Ave, #2000, Los Angeles CA 90024 USA

**Savage, Stephanie** — Producer
W M E Entertainment, 9601 Wilshire Blvd, #300, Beverly Hills CA 90210 USA

**Savage, Theodore E (Ted)** — Baseball Player
1510 Mallard Landing Court, Chesterfield MO 63017, USA

**Savage-Rumbaugh, Susan** — Primatologist
Great Ape Trust, 4200 SE 44th Ave, Des Moines IA 50320, USA

**Saval, Dany** — Actress
131 Rue de l'Universite, 75007 Paris, France

**Savant, Doug** — Actor
Paradigm Agency, 360 N Crescent Dr, North Building, Beverly Hills CA 90210 USA

**Savard, Andre** — Ice Hockey Player
Pittsburgh Penguins, Consol Energy Center, 1001 5th Ave, Pittsburgh PA 15219 USA

**Savard, Denis** — Ice Hockey Player, Coach
8307 Regency Court, Willow Springs IL 60480, USA

**Savard, Marc** — Ice Hockey Player
197 8th St, #511, Charlestown MA 02129, USA

**Savard, Serge A** — Ice Hockey Player, Executive
1790 Champs du Golf, RR 1, Saint Bruno QC J3V 4P6, Canada

**Savary, Jerome** — Director
Opera Comique, 5 Rue Favart, 75002 Paris, France

**Savchenko, Aliona** — Figure Skater
Deutsche Eislauf-Union, Menzinger Str 68, 80992 Munich, Germany

**Savchenko, Arkadiy M** — Opera Singer
8-358 Storozhovskaya Str, 220002 Minsk, Belarus

**Saverin, Eduardo L** — Businessman
Facebook, 156 University Ave, #200, Palo Alto CA 94301, USA

**Saverine, Robert P (Bob)** — Baseball Player
228 Slice Dr, Stamford CT 06907, USA

**Savery, Uffe** — Percussion Musician (Safri Duo)
P D H Music, Dag Hammarskjold Alle 42 G, 2100 Copenhagen 0, Denmark

**Savic, Maja** — Handball Player
Z R K Buducnost T-Mobile, Ivan Milutinovic B B, 81000 Podgorica, Montenegro

**Savident, John** — Actor
Granada Television, Quay St, Manchester M60 9EA, England

**Savidge, Jennifer** — Actress
TalentWorks, 3500 W Olive Ave, #1400, Burbank CA 91505 USA

**Saville, Curtis** — Long Distance Rower, Explorer
RFD Box 44, West Charleston VT 05872, USA

**Saville, Kathleen** — Long Distance Rower, Explorer
RFD Box 44, West Charleston VT 05872, USA

**Saville, Matthew** — Director
R G M Artists, 8-12 Ann Street, Surry Hills NSW 2010, Australia

**Savini, Tom** — Actor, Special Effects Artist
311 Taylor St, Pittsburgh PA 15224, USA

**Savinykh, Viktor P** — Cosmonaut
Moscow State University, Aerophotogrammetry Institute, Gorokhovskiy 4, 103064 Moscow, Russia

**Saviola, Camille** — Actress
Kazarian/Measures/Ruskin, 11969 Ventura Blvd, #300, Studio City CA 91604 USA

**Savitskaya, Svetlana Y** — Cosmonaut
Russian Association, Khovanskaya Str 3, 129515 Moscow, Russia

**Savitt, Richard (Dick)** — Tennis Player
19 E 80th St, New York NY 10075, USA

**Savoy, Guy** — Chef
101 Blvd Pereire, 75017 Paris, France

**Savransky, Morris (Moe)** — Baseball Player
128 Dorset Dr, Boca Raton FL 33434, USA

**Savre, Danielle** — Actress, Singer
TalentWorks, 3500 W Olive Ave, #1400, Burbank CA 91505 USA

**Sawa, Devon** — Actor
Gersh Agency, 9465 Wilshire Blvd, #600, Beverly Hills CA 90212 USA

**Sawa, Homare** — Soccer Player
Football Association, 3-10-15 Hongo, Bunkyoku, Tokyo 113 0033 Japan

**Sawajiri, Erika** — Actress, Model, Musician
Avex Mgmt, 3-1-30-7F, Minami Aoyama, Minato, Tokyo 107 0062, Japan

**Sawalha, Julia** — Actress
Artists Partnership, 101 Finsbury Pavement, London EC2A 1RS, England

**Sawalha, Nadim** — Actor
Associated International Mgmt, 7 Hatton Garden, #400, London EC1N 8AD, England

**Sawallisch, Wolfgang** — Conductor, Concert Pianist
Hinterm Bichl 2, 83224 Grassau, Germany

**Sawyer, Alan L** — Basketball Player
117 San Juan Dr, Sequim WA 98382, USA

**Sawyer, Diane** — Commentator
147 Columbus Ave, #300, New York NY 10023, USA

**Sawyer, Forrest** — Commentator
NBC-TV, News Dept, 30 Rockefeller Plaza, #270E, New York NY 10112 USA

**Sawyer, John W** — Football Player
23637 Sunnyside Lane, Zachary LA 70791, USA

**Sawyer, Kevin** — Ice Hockey Player
5118 N Ivy Court, Spokane Valley WA 99206, USA

**Sawyer, Ray** — Singer, Guitarist (Dr Hook)
Artists International Mgmt, 9850 Sandalfoot Blvd, #458, Boca Raton FL 33428, USA

**Sawyer, Talance M** — Football Player
6150 Brookhaven Dr, Bastrop LA 71220, USA

**Sawyers, Charles L** — Oncologist
Memorial Sloan Kettering Cancer Center, 1275 York Ave, New York NY 10065 USA

**Sax, David J (Dave)** — Baseball Player
3352 Eaton Dr, Roseville CA 95661, USA

**Sax, Geoffrey** — Director
I C M Partners, 10250 Constellation Blvd, #900, Los Angeles CA 90067 USA

**Sax, Stephen L (Steve)** — Baseball Player
201 Wesley Court, Roseville CA 95661, USA

**Saxe, Adrian A** — Artist
4835 N Figueroa St, Los Angeles CA 90042, USA

**Saxon, Edward** — Producer
Edward Saxon Productions, 1526 14th St, #105, Santa Monica CA 90404, USA

**Saxon, James E** — Football Player
28500 Fox Hollow Dr, Hayward CA 94542, USA
**Saxon, John** — Actor
Beacon Talent, 9250 Sunset Blvd, #727, Los Angeles CA 90069, USA
**Saxon, Michael E (Mike)** — Football Player
211 Winding Hollow Lane, Coppell TX 75019, USA
**Saxton, Charlie** — Actor
Creative Artists Agency, 2000 Ave of Stars, #100, Los Angeles CA 90067 USA
**Sayako** — Princess, Japan
Imperial Palace, 1-1 Chiyoda, Chiyodaku, Tokyo 100 0001, Japan
**Sayalero Fernandez, Maritza** — Beauty Queen
Aveida Ruiz, 65 Sun Ensenada, Baja California, Mexico
**Sayed, Mostafa Amr El** — Chemist
579 Westover Dr NW, Atlanta GA 30305, USA
**Sayer, Leo** — Singer, Songwriter
Harbour Agency, 135 Forbes St, Woolloomooloo NSW 2011, Australia
**Sayers, Gale E** — Football Player
1313 N Ritchie Court, #407, Chicago IL 60610, USA
**Saykally, Richard J** — Chemist
University of California, Chemistry Dept, Latimer Hall, Berkeley CA 94720, USA
**Sayles, John T** — Director
210 13th St, Hoboken NJ 07030, USA
**Saylor, Edward J** — WW II Army Air Corps Hero
41802 207th Ave SE, Enumclaw WA 98022, USA
**Saylor, Morgan** — Actress
United Talent Agency, U T A Plaza, 9336 Civic Center Dr, Beverly Hills CA 90210 USA
**Scacchi, Greta** — Actress
A P A Talent & Literary Agency, 405 S Beverly Dr, #300, Beverly Hills CA 90212 USA
**Scaggs, William R (Boz)** — Singer, Songwriter
Front Line Mgmt, 1100 Glendon Ave, #2000, Los Angeles CA 90024 USA
**Scaglione, Josefina** — Actress, Singer
Untitled Entertainment, 350 S Beverly Dr, #200, Beverly Hills CA 90212 USA
**Scagliotti, Allison** — Actress
Schiff Co, 9220 Sunset Blvd, #106, West Hollywood CA 90069 USA
**Scaife, Oliver L (Bo), III** — Football Player
6505 Banbury Crossing, Brentwood TN 37027, USA
**Scala, Tina** — Actress
Jack Scagneti Talent, 5118 Vineland Ave, #101, North Hollywood CA 91601, USA
**Scalabrine, Brian D** — Basketball Player
176 Vernal Dr, Alamo CA 94507, USA
**Scalapino, Douglas J** — Physicist
University of California, Physics Dept, Santa Barbara CA 93106, USA
**Scales, Dwight A** — Football Player
6112 Roosevelt Circle NW, Huntsville AL 35810, USA
**Scales, Prunella M** — Actress
Conway Van Gelder Grant, 8-12 Broadwick St, #300, London W1F 8HW, England
**Scalia, Antonin** — Supreme Court Justice
US Supreme Court, 1 1st St NE, Washington DC 20543 USA
**Scalia, Jack** — Actor
16260 Ventura Blvd, Encino CA 91436, USA
**Scallions, Bret** — Singer, Guitarist (Fuel)
Media Five Entertainment, 3005 Brodhead Road, #170, Bethlehem PA 18020, USA
**Scalzo, Tony** — Singer, Bassist (Fastball)
Russell Carter Artists, 315 Ponce de Leon Blvd, #755, Decatur GA 30030, USA
**Scamarcio, Riccardo** — Actor
Cineart, 28 Rue Mogador, 78009 Paris, France
**Scaminace, Joseph M** — Businessman
Sherwin-Williams Co, 101 W Prospect Ave, #1020, Cleveland OH 44115, USA
**Scamurra, Peter (Pete)** — Ice Hockey Player
15 Guinevere Court, Getzville NY 14068, USA
**Scancarelli, Jim** — Cartoonist (Gasoline Alley)
Mark J Cohen, PO Box 1892, Santa Rosa CA 95402, USA
**Scandiuzzi, Roberto** — Opera Singer
Atelier Fedelli, Via Casekke 76, 40068 San Lazzaro Savena (Bo), Italy
**Scanlan, Robert G (Bob). Jr** — Baseball Player
12400 Montecito Road, #315, Seal Beach CA 90740, USA
**Scanlan, Teresa** — Beauty Queen
Miss America Organization, 1370 Ave of Americas, #1600, New York NY 10019 USA
**Scanlon, J Patrick (Pat)** — Baseball Player
7400 Portland Ave S, Minneapolis MN 55423, USA
**Scanlon, Thomas M, Jr** — Philosopher
Harvard University, Philosophy Dept, Cambridge MA 02138, USA
**Scannell, Susan** — Actress
247 S Beverly Dr, #102, Beverly Hills CA 90212, USA
**Scaparrotti, Curtis M (Mike)** — Army General
Commander, United Nations Command & US Forces Korea, Unit 15327, APO AP 96218 USA
**Scarabelli, Michele** — Actress
Characters Talent Agency, 8 Elm St, Toronto ON M5G 1G7, Canada
**Scarbath, John C (Jack)** — Football Player
736 Calvert Road, Rising Sun MD 21911, USA
**Scarbery, Randy J** — Baseball Player
5010 E Lewis Ave, Fresno CA 93727, USA
**Scarborough, C Joseph (Joe)** — Commentator; Representative, FL
MSNBC-TV, News Dept, 900 Sylvan Ave, Englewood Cliffs NJ 07632, USA
**Scarce, G McCurdy (Mac)** — Baseball Player
1010 Richmond Glen Circle, Alpharetta GA 30004, USA
**Scardapane, Dario** — Producer, Writer
Management 360, 9111 Wilshire Blvd, Beverly Hills CA 90210 USA
**Scardelletti, Robert A** — Labor Leader
Transportation Communications Union, 3 Research Place, Rockville MD 20850, USA
**Scardino, Don** — Director
Creative Artists Agency, 2000 Ave of Stars, #100, Los Angeles CA 90067 USA
**Scarf, Herbert E** — Economist
200 Leeder Hill Dr, #2711, Hamden CT 06517, USA
**Scarface** — Rap Artist (Geto Boys)
J L Entertainment, 18653 Ventura Blvd, #340, Los Angeles CA 91356 USA

**Scarfe, Gerald A** — Cartoonist
Jane Asher Party Cakes, 22-24 Cale St, London SW3 3QU, England

**Scarfe, Jonathan** — Actor
Gary Goddard Agency, 10 Saint Mary's St, #305, Toronto ON M4Y 1P9, Canada

**Scargill, Arthur** — Labor Leader
National Union of Mineworkers, 2 Huddersfield Road, Barnsley, England

**Scarimbolo, Adam** — Actor
C E S D, 10635 Santa Monica Blvd, #130, Los Angeles CA 90025 USA

**Scarpati, Joseph H (Joe), Jr** — Football Player
32 Lexington Circle, Marlton NJ 08053, USA

**Scarr, Sandra W** — Psychologist
77-6222 Kaunmakumalu Dr, Holualoa HI 96725, USA

**Scarry, Elaine** — Educator
Harvard University, English Dept, Cambridge MA 02138, USA

**Scarsone, Steven W (Steve)** — Baseball Player
3935 E Rough Rider Road, #1158, Phoenix AZ 85050, USA

**Scarwid, Diana E** — Actress
Committed Artists Entertainment, 2600 W Olive Ave, #500, Burbank CA 91505, USA

**Scatchard, Dave** — Ice Hockey Player
8312 N 50th St, Paradise Valley AZ 85253, USA

**Scates, Allen E** — Volleyball Coach
8433 Apple Hill Court, Las Vegas NV 89128, USA

**Scattini, Monica** — Actress
Carol Levi Mgmt, Via Giuseppe Pisanelli 2, 00196 Rome, Italy

**Scelzi, Gary** — Drag Racing Driver
Alan Johnson Racing, 2772 S Cherry Ave, Fresno CA 93706, USA

**Scerbo, Cassie** — Actress
Abrams Artists, 9200 W Sunset Blvd, #1125, West Hollywood CA 90069 USA

**Schaaf-Behle, Petra** — Biathlete
Am Rodeland 22, 34508 Willingen, Germany

**Schaal, Kristen** — Actress, Writer
Avalon Mgmt, 4A Exmoor St, London W10 6BD, England

**Schaal, Paul** — Baseball Player
68-1962 Puu Nui St, Waikoloa HI 96738, USA

**Schaal, Wendy** — Actress
B R S / Gage Talent Agency, 5757 Wilshire Blvd, #659, Los Angeles CA 90036 USA

**Schacher, Mel** — Bassist (Grand Funk Railroad)
Lustig Talent, PO Box 770850, Orlando FL 32877 USA

**Schachman, Howard K** — Molecular Biochemist
University of California, Molecular Biology Dept, Berkeley CA 94720, USA

**Schacht, Henry B** — Businessman
Lucent Technologies Inc, 600 Mountain Ave, New Providence NJ 07974, USA

**Schacker, Harold (Hal)** — Baseball Player
4609 N Matanzas Ave, Tampa FL 33614, USA

**Schacter, Beth** — Director, Writer
Anonymous Content, 3532 Hayden Ave, Culver City CA 90232 USA

**Schacter-Shalomi, Zalman** — Religious Leader
Spiritual Eldering Institute, 535 W S Boulder Road, Lafayette CO 80026, USA

**Schade, Frank** — Basketball Player
826 Nicolet Ave, Oshkosh WI 54901, USA

**Schaden, Rick** — Businessman
Quiznos, 1975 Lawrence St, #400, Denver CO 80202, USA

**Schadler, Bernard R (Ben)** — Basketball Player
808 Bauer Dr, San Carlos CA 94070, USA

**Schadler, Jay** — Commentator
ABC-TV, News Dept, 77 W 66th St, New York NY 10023 USA

**Schaech, Jonathan** — Actor
A P A Talent & Literary Agency, 405 S Beverly Dr, #300, Beverly Hills CA 90212 USA

**Schaefer, Henry F, III** — Chemist
University of Georgia, Computational Quantum Chemistry Center, Athens GA 30602, USA

**Schaefer, Jeffrey S (Jeff)** — Baseball Player
2110 Woodbend Trail, Fort Mill SC 29708, USA

**Schaefer, Roberto** — Cinematographer
Innovative Artists, 1505 10th St, Santa Monica CA 90401 USA

**Schaeffer, Eric** — Actor, Director, Producer
Paradigm Agency, 360 N Crescent Dr, North Building, Beverly Hills CA 90210 USA

**Schaeffer, Frank** — Writer
Carroll & Graf, 245 W 17th St, #1100, New York NY 10011, USA

**Schaeffer, Leonard** — Businessman
WellPoint Health Networks, 1 Wellpoint Way, Westlake Village CA 91362, USA

**Schaeffer, Mark P** — Baseball Player
18261 Parthenia St, Northridge CA 91325, USA

**Schaeffer, William** — Hero
1865 Paseo de Oro, Colorado Springs CO 80904, USA

**Schaetzel, John R** — Writer
3050 Military Road NW, #555, Washington DC 20015, USA

**Schafer, Christine** — Opera Singer
Columbia Artists Mgmt Inc, 5 Columbus Circle, 1790 Broadway, #1600, New York NY 10019 USA

**Schafer, Edward T (Ed)** — Secretary, Agriculture; Governor, ND
1131 N 4th St, Bismarck ND 58501, USA

**Schafer, Hans** — Soccer Player
D F B, Postfach 710265, 60492 Frankfurt, Germany

**Schafer, Jordan J** — Baseball Player
80 Pine Forest Dr, Haines City FL 33844, USA

**Schafer, Susanne** — Actress
Agentur Carola Studlar, Agnesstr 47, 80798 Munich, Germany

**Schaffer, Eric** — Concert Executive
Kennedy Center for Performing Arts, 2700 F St NW, Washington DC 20566, USA

**Schaffer, Jimmie R (Jim)** — Baseball Player
655 Birch Terrace, Coopersburg PA 18036, USA

**Schafrath, Richard P (Dick)** — Football Player
704 Ashland Road, Mansfield OH 44905, USA

**Schaible, Michael** — Interior Designer
Bray-Schnaible Design, 80 W 40th St, #800, New York NY 10018, USA

**Schaitber, Harold A** — Labor Leader
International Fire Fighters, 1750 New York Ave NW, #300, Washington DC 20006, USA

**Schajris Rodriguez, Noel** — Singer, Guitarist (Sin Bandera)
Westwood Mgmt, Maria de Teresa 250, San Angel, Mexico City 01040, Mexico

**Schall, Alvin A** — Judge
US Appeals Court, 717 Madison Place NW, Washington DC 20439, USA

**Schaller, George B** — Zoologist
90 Sentry Hill Road, Roxbury CT 06783, USA

**Schaller, Willie** — Soccer Player
3283 S Indiana St, Lakewood CO 80228, USA

**Schallert, William** — Actor
14920 Ramos Place, Pacific Palisades CA 90272, USA

**Schallock, Arthur L (Art)** — Baseball Player
749 Crocus Dr, Sonoma CA 95476, USA

**Schally, Andrew V** — Nobel Medicine Laureate
3801 Collins Ave, Miami Beach FL 33140, USA

**Schama, Simon M** — Historian, Writer
Columbia University, Art History Dept, Fairweather Hall, Cambridge MA 02138, USA

**Schamehorn, Kevin** — Ice Hockey Player
5536 Stoney Brook Road, Kalamazoo MI 49009, USA

**Schamus, James** — Director, Producer
Creative Artists Agency, 2000 Ave of Stars, #100, Los Angeles CA 90067 USA

**Schanberg, Sydney H** — Journalist
PO Box 236, Rifton NY 12471, USA

**Schankweiler, Scott B** — Football Player
11 Bartley Court, Nottingham MD 21236, USA

**Schanley, Tom** — Actor
Maverick Artists, 6100 Wilshire Blvd, #550, Los Angeles CA 90048, USA

**Schapiro, Mary L** — Financier, Government Official
Promontory Financial Group, 801 17th St NW, #1100, Washington DC 20006, USA

**Schapker, Alison** — Producer, Writer
W M E Entertainment, 9601 Wilshire Blvd, #300, Beverly Hills CA 90210 USA

**Schapp, Dick** — Sportscaster
ESPN-TV, Sports Dept, ESPN Plaza, 935 Middle St, Bristol CT 06010 USA

**Scharansky, Natan** — Social Activist, Computer Scientist
Shalem Center, 13 Yehoshua Bin-Nun St, Jersalem 93145, Israel

**Scharer, Erich** — Bobsled Athlete
Grutstra 63, 8074 Herrliberg, Switzerland

**Scharping, Rudolf** — Government Official, Germany
Wilhelmstr 5, 56112 Lahnstein, Germany

**Schattinger, Jeffrey C (Jeff)** — Baseball Player
PO Box 134, Lake Arrowhead CA 92352, USA

**Schatz, Howard** — Photographer
435 W Broadway, #200, New York NY 10012, USA

**Schatz, Mark** — Bassist (Nickel Creek)
Q-Prime South, 131 S 11th St, Nashville TN 37206 USA

**Schatzeder, Daniel E (Dan)** — Baseball Player
186 River Mist Dr, Oswego IL 60543, USA

**Schatzman, Evry** — Astrophysicist
11 Rue de l'Eglise, Dompierre, 60420 Maignelay-Montigny, France

**Schaub, Matthew R (Matt)** — Football Player
3300 Irvine Ave, #300, Newport Beach CA 92660, USA

**Schaudt, Martin** — Equestrian
Gerhardstr 10/2, 72461 Albstadt, Germany

**Schauer, Frederick F** — Attorney, Educator
Harvard University, Kennedy Government School, Cambridge MA 02138, USA

**Schaufuss, Peter** — Ballet Dancer, Director
Papoutsis Representation, 18 Sundial Ave, London SE25 4BX, England

**Schaukowith, Carl** — Football Player
11700 Bishops Content Road, Bowie MD 20721, USA

**Schaus, Molly** — Ice Hockey Player
USA Hockey, 1775 Bob Johnson Dr, Colorado Springs CO 80906 USA

**Schayes, Adolph (Dolph)** — Basketball Player, Coach
PO Box 156, Syracuse NY 13214, USA

**Schayes, Daniel L (Danny)** — Basketball Player
8586 E Krail St, Scottsdale AZ 85250, USA

**Schazad, Graziella** — Singer
Warner Music Group, Alter Wandraham 14, 20457 Hamburg, Germany

**Schechtman, Daniel** — Nobel Chemistry Laureate
Technion Institute of Technology, Haifa 32000, Israel

**Scheck, Barry** — Attorney, Educator
Yeshiva University, Law School, 55 5th Ave, #600, New York NY 10003, USA

**Scheckter, Jody D** — Auto Racing Driver
Home Farm, Laverstoke Park, Overton, Hampshire RG25 3DR, England

**Schedeen, Anne** — Actress
Metropolitan Talent Agency, 5405 Wilshire Blvd, #218, Los Angeles CA 90036 USA

**Schedwill, Sybille J** — Actress
Funke & Stertz, Schulterblatt 58, 20357 Hamburg, Germany

**Scheel, Walter** — President, West Germany
Buro Walter Scheel, Basler Str 30, 79189 Bad Krozingen, Germany

**Scheer, Paul** — Actor, Comedian, Writer
Principato-Young, 9465 Wilshire Blvd, #880, Beverly Hills CA 90212 USA

**Scheffer, Will** — Producer, Writer
Creative Artists Agency, 2000 Ave of Stars, #100, Los Angeles CA 90067 USA

**Schefter, Adam** — Sportscaster
ESPN-TV, Sports Dept, ESPN Plaza, 935 Middle St, Bristol CT 06010 USA

**Scheib, Carl A** — Baseball Player
2922 Old Ranch Road, San Antonio TX 78217, USA

**Scheibel, Arnold B** — Psychiatrist
100 Bay Place, #804, Oakland CA 94610, USA

**Scheid, Eusebio Oscar Cardinal** — Religious Leader
Curia Metropolitana, Rua Benjamin Constant 23, Gloria, 20241 150 Rio de Janeiro RJ, Brazil

**Scheider, Timo** — Auto Racing Driver
W W P Group, Lustenauerstra 64, 6850 Dornbirn, Austria

**Schein, Philip S** — Internist
Schein Group, 2805 SE Dune Dr, Stuart FL 34996, USA

**Scheinblum, Richard A (Richie)** — Baseball Player
1308 Woodstock Dr, Palm Harbor FL 34684, USA

**Schekman, Randy W** — Nobel Medicine Laureate
University of California Medical School, Molecular & Cell Biology Dept, Berkeley CA 94720, USA

**Schell, Catherine** — Actress
Postfach 800504, 51005 Cologne, Germany

**Schellhase, David G (Dave)** — Basketball Player
862 Walnut Ridge E, Logansport IN 46947, USA

**Schelling, Florence** — Ice Hockey Player
Swiss Ice Hockey, Hagenholzstr 81, 8050 Zurich, Switzerland

**Schelling, Thomas C** — Nobel Economics Laureate
8300 Burdette Road, #222, Bethesda MD 20817, USA

**Schellman, John A** — Chemist
65 W 30th Ave, #508, Eugene OR 97405, USA

**Schelmerding, Kirk** — Auto Racing Mechanic
Childress Racing, PO Box 1189, Industrial Dr, Welcome NC 27374, USA

**Schelotto, Guillermo Barros** — Soccer Player
Columbus Crew, 1 Black & Gold Blvd, Columbus OH 43211 USA

**Schemansky, Norbert** — Weightlifter
24826 New York St, Dearborn MI 48124, USA

**Schenkenberg, Markus** — Model, Actor
Kuhlmann Beauty Consulting, Kaiserstr 51, 63065 Offenbach, Germany

**Schenker, Michael** — Guitarist (UFO, Scorpions)
Artists Worldwide, 3921 Wilshire Blvd, #619, Los Angeles CA 90010, USA

**Schenker, Rudolf** — Guitarist (Scorpions)
Und Verlags, Bohlenweg 8, 30835, Germany

**Schenkkan, Robert F, Jr** — Writer, Actor
W M E Entertainment, 9601 Wilshire Blvd, #300, Beverly Hills CA 90210 USA

**Schenkman, Eric** — Musician (Spin Doctors)
D A S Communications, 83 Riverside Dr, New York NY 10024 USA

**Schepisi, Frederic A (Fred)** — Director
Echo Lake Productions, 421 S Beverly Dr, #800, Beverly Hills CA 90212, USA

**Scheraga, Harold A** — Chemist
223 Savage Farm Dr, Ithaca NY 14850, USA

**Scherbachenko, Ekaterina** — Opera Singer
I M G Artists, Hogarth Business Park, Chiswick, London W4 2TH, England

**Scherbo, Vitaly V** — Gymnast
3250 N Bronco St, Las Vegas NV 89108, USA

**Scherer, Frederic M** — Economist
53 Standish St, #2, Cambridge MA 02138, USA

**Scherer, Odilo P Cardinal** — Religious Leader
Curia Metropolitana, Ave Higienopolis 890, 01238 000 Sao Paulo SP, Brazil

**Scherman, Frederick J (Fred)** — Baseball Player
7454 S Tipp Cowlesville Road, Tipp City OH 45371, USA

**Scherman, Nossom** — Religious Leader, Rabbi, Editor
ArtScroll/Mesorah Publications, 4514 11th Ave, Brooklyn NY 11219, USA

**Scherrer, Tom** — Golfer
2608 Drommore Lane, Raleigh NC 27614, USA

**Scherrer, William J (Bill)** — Baseball Player
222 Fareway Lane, Grand Island NY 14072, USA

**Scherzinger, Nicole** — Singer (Eden's Crush, Pussycat Dolls)
W M E Entertainment, 9601 Wilshire Blvd, #300, Beverly Hills CA 90210 USA

**Scheuer, Paul J** — Chemist
3217 Melemele Place, Honolulu HI 96822, USA

**Schiavo, Mary** — Government Official, Social Activist
Ohio State University, Public Policy Dept, Columbus OH 43210, USA

**Schiavo, Richard J** — Thoroughbred Racing Executive
I E A H Stables, 595 Stewart Ave, #450, Garden City NY 11530, USA

**Schiavone, Francesca** — Tennis Player
Via Teano 21, 20161 Milan, Italy

**Schickel, Richard** — Writer, Film Critic
9051 Dicks St, West Hollywood CA 90069, USA

**Schickele, Peter** — Composer, Comedian
Opus 3 Artists, 470 Park Ave S, #900N, New York NY 10016 USA

**Schiebold, Hans** — Artist
13705 SW 118th Court, Portland OR 97223, USA

**Schieffer, Bob** — Commentator
CBS-TV, News Dept, 2020 M St NW, Washington DC 20036 USA

**Schierholtz, Nathan J (Nate)** — Baseball Player
7500 E Deer Valley Road, #118, Scottsdale AZ 85255, USA

**Schiff, Andras** — Concert Pianist
Terry Harrison Mgmt, Market St, Charlbury, Oxfordshire OX7 3PJ, England

**Schiff, Heinrich** — Concert Cellist, Conductor
Astrid Schoerke, Monckegergallee 41, 30453 Hanover, Germany

**Schiff, Mark** — Actor, Comedian
Gail Stocker Presents, 1025 N Kings Road, #113, West Hollywood CA 90069, USA

**Schiff, Richard** — Actor
I F A Talent Agency, 8730 W Sunset Blvd, #490, West Hollywood CA 90069 USA

**Schiff, Stacy** — Writer
Little Brown, 1271 Ave of Americas, New York NY 10020, USA

**Schiffer, Claudia** — Model, Actress
Aussenwall 94, 47495 Rheinberg, Germany

**Schiffer, Michael** — Writer, Producer
Ballpark Pictures, PO Box 508, Venice CA 90294, USA

**Schiffman, Guillaume** — Cinematographer
20 Rue Saulnier, 75009 Paris, France

**Schiffman, Mark** — Physician, Epidemiologist
National Cancer Institute, 6120 Executive Blvd, Bethesda MD 20892, USA

**Schiffman, Michael** — Actor
Harvest Mgmt, PO Box 279, Jefferson Valley NY 10535, USA

**Schifrin, Lalo** — Composer
710 N Hillcrest Road, Beverly Hills CA 90210, USA

**Schild, Marlies** — Alpine Skier
Weikersbach 9, 5760 Saalfelden, Austria

**Schiller, Lawrence J** — Producer, Director, Writer
60 W 57th St, #19B, New York NY 10019, USA

**Schiller, Rob** — Director
Evolution Entertainment, 901 N Highland Ave, Los Angeles CA 90038 USA

**Schiller, Robert J** — Nobel Economics Laureate
Cowles Foundation, Box 208281, New Haven CT 06511, USA
**Schilling, Curtis M (Curt)** — Baseball Player
7 Woodridge Road, Medfield MA 02052, USA
**Schilling, Taylor** — Actress
Gersh Agency, 9465 Wilshire Blvd, #600, Beverly Hills CA 90212 USA
**Schimberni, Mario** — Businessman
Armando Curcio Editore SpA, Via IV Novembre, 00187 Rome, Italy
**Schimmel, Paul R** — Biologist, Biochemist
Scripps Research Institute, 10550 N Torrey Pines Road, La Jolla CA 92037, USA
**Schindelholz, Lorenz** — Bobsled Athlete
Hardstr 184, 4715 Herbetswil, Switzerland
**Schinkel, Kenneth (Ken)** — Ice Hockey Player
19927 Beaulieu Court, Fort Myers FL 33908, USA
**Schipper, Jessicah** — Swimmer
Swimming Australia, 12/7 Beissel St, Belconnen ACT 2617, Australia
**Schirripa, Steve R** — Actor
Innovative Artists, 1505 10th St, Santa Monica CA 90401 USA
**Schisgal, Murray J** — Writer
I C M Partners, 730 5th Ave, New York NY 10019 USA
**Schissler, Les** — Bowler
3060 E Bridge St, #20, Brighton CO 80601, USA
**Schlafly, Phyllis S** — Women's Activist
68 Fairmount Ave, Alton IL 62002, USA
**Schlamme, Thomas (Tommy)** — Director
Creative Artists Agency, 2000 Ave of Stars, #100, Los Angeles CA 90067 USA
**Schlatter, Charlie** — Actor
Sutton-Barth Vennari, 5900 Wilshire Blvd, #700, Los Angeles CA 90036 USA
**Schleeh, Russ** — Test Pilot
21634 Paseo Maravia, Mission Viejo CA 92692, USA
**Schlegel, Hans W** — Astronaut, Germany
European Space Center, Linder Hohe, Box 906096, 51127 Cologne, Germany
**Schlegel, Sylvester** — Drummer (The Ark)
Live Nation, Linnegatan 89, Box 21451, 104 51 Stockholm, Sweden
**Schleper, Anne** — Ice Hockey Player
USA Hockey, 1775 Bob Johnson Dr, Colorado Springs CO 80906 USA
**Schlereth, Mark F** — Football Player
9479 S Shadow Hill Circle, Lone Tree CO 80124, USA
**Schlesinger, Adam** — Singer (Fountains of Wayne), Songwriter
Big Hassle, 157 Chambers St, #1200, New York NY 10007, USA
**Schlesinger, Cory M** — Football Player
36 Bradford Court, Dearborn MI 48126, USA
**Schlessinger, Laura** — Radio Psychologist, Physiologist
3201 Campanil Dr, Santa Barbara CA 93109, USA
**Schlichtmann, Jan** — Attorney
359 Hale St, Beverly Farms MA 01915, USA
**Schlierenzauer, Gregor** — Ski Jumper
Red Bull GmbH, Am Brunnen 1, 5330 Fuschl am See, Austria
**Schlink, Bernhard** — Writer
Heilbronner Str 3, 10779 Berlin, Germany
**Schlitt, John W** — Singer (Petra, Head East)
112 Glen Haven Lane, Franklin TN 37069, USA
**Schlondorff, Volker O** — Director
Studio Babelsberg, Postfach 900361, 14439 Potsdam, Germany
**Schloredt, Robert S (Bob)** — Football Player
Nestle-Beich, 1827 N 167th St, Shoreline WA 98133, USA
**Schlossberg, Hayden** — Director, Writer
Creative Artists Agency, 2000 Ave of Stars, #100, Los Angeles CA 90067 USA
**Schlosser, Eric M** — Historian
Steven Barclay Agency, 12 Western Ave, Petaluma CA 94952, USA
**Schluter, Poul H** — Prime Minister, Denmark
Frederiksberg Allee 66, 1820 Frederiksberg C, Denmark
**Schmautz, Robert J (Bobby)** — Ice Hockey Player
19866 N 90th Ave, Peoria AZ 85382, USA
**Schmeichel, Peter** — Soccer Player
Aston Villa, Villa Park, Trinity Road, Birmingham B6 6HE, England
**Schmelz, Alan G (Al)** — Baseball Player
7406 E Camino Rayo de Luz, Scottsdale AZ 85266, USA
**Schmemann, Serge** — Journalist
New York Times, Editorial Dept, 229 W 43rd St, New York NY 10036, USA
**Schmid, Benjamin** — Concert, Jazz Violinist
Harrison/Parrott, Lucile-Grahn-Stra 37, 81675 Munich, Germany
**Schmid, Daniel J (Dan)** — Bassist (Cherry Poppin' Daddies)
Paradise Artists, PO Box 1821, Ojai CA 93024 USA
**Schmid, Harald** — Track Athlete
Schulstr 11, 63594 Hasselroth, Germany
**Schmid, Kyle** — Actor
Don Buchwald Talent Agency, 10 E 44th St, New York NY 10017 USA
**Schmid, Sigi** — Soccer Coach
Seattle Sounders, 12 Seahawks Way, Renton WA 98056 USA
**Schmidgall-Potter, Jennifer L** — Ice Hockey Player
3640 Wooddale Ave S, #103, Minneapolis MN 55416, USA
**Schmidly, David J** — Educator
University of New Mexico, President's Office, Albuquerque NM 87131, USA
**Schmidt, Andreas** — Opera Singer
Fossredder 51, 22359 Hamburg, Germany
**Schmidt, Benno C, Jr** — Educator
Edison Project, 375 Park Ave, New York NY 10152, USA
**Schmidt, Brian P** — Nobel Physics Laureate
Australian National University, Mount Stromlo Observatory, Canberra ACT 0200, Australia
**Schmidt, David J (Dave)** — Baseball Player
7172 N Serenoa Dr, Sarasota FL 34241, USA
**Schmidt, Eric E** — Businessman, Computer Engineer
Google Inc, 1600 Amphitheatre Parkway, #41, Mountain View CA 94043, USA
**Schmidt, Helmut** — Chancellor, West Germany
Neuberger Weg 80/82, 22419 Hamburg, Germany

| | |
|---|---|
| **Schmidt, Henry J (Hank)**<br>4641 Mission Bell Lane, La Mesa CA 91941, USA | Football Player |
| **Schmidt, Jason D**<br>2909 Roosevelt Ave, Enumclaw WA 98022, USA | Baseball Player |
| **Schmidt, Joseph P (Joe)**<br>226 Norcliff Dr, Bloomfield Hills MI 48302, USA | Football Player |
| **Schmidt, Kathryn (Kate)**<br>1008 Dexter St, Los Angeles CA 90042, USA | Track Athlete |
| **Schmidt, Kenneth**<br>Coast to Coast Talent, 3350 Barham Blvd, Los Angeles CA 90068 USA | Actor |
| **Schmidt, Klaus**<br>German Archaeological Institute, Inonu Caddesi 10, 34437 Istanbul, Turkey | Archeologist |
| **Schmidt, Maarten**<br>California Institute of Technology, Astronomy Dept, Pasadena CA 91125, USA | Astronomer |
| **Schmidt, Michael J (Mike)**<br>373 Eagle Dr, Jupiter FL 33477, USA | Baseball Player |
| **Schmidt, Milton C (Milt)**<br>10 Longwood Dr, #376, Westwood MA 02090, USA | Ice Hockey Player |
| **Schmidt, Rob**<br>Gersh Agency, 9465 Wilshire Blvd, #600, Beverly Hills CA 90212 USA | Director |
| **Schmidt, Robert B (Bob)**<br>9 Hardwood Dr, Saint Charles MO 63303, USA | Baseball Player |
| **Schmidt, Robert M (Bob)**<br>10005 Sky View Way, #2106, Fort Myers FL 33913, USA | Football Player |
| **Schmidt, Sam**<br>Sam Schmidt Racing, 6803 Coffman Road, Indianapolis IN 46208, USA | Auto Racing Driver |
| **Schmidt, Sophie**<br>Canadian Soccer, Place Soccer Canada, 237 Metcalfe St, Ottawa ON K2P 1R2, Canada | Soccer Player |
| **Schmidt, Susan**<br>Washington Post, Editorial Dept, 1150 15th St NW, Washington DC 20071 USA | Journalist |
| **Schmidt, Terry R**<br>2 Stone River Dr, Asheville NC 28804, USA | Football Player |
| **Schmidt, Walter**<br>Wilhelm Raabe Weg 23, 38110 Brauschweig, Germany | Track Athlete |
| **Schmidt, Wolfgang**<br>Birkheckenstr 116B, 70599 Stuttgart, Germany | Track Athlete |
| **Schmidt, Wrenn**<br>I C M Partners, 10250 Constellation Blvd, #900, Los Angeles CA 90067 USA | Actress |
| **Schmiegel, Klaus K**<br>4507 Staughton Dr, Indianapolis IN 46226, USA | Inventor (Prozac) |
| **Schmiesing, Joseph F (Joe)**<br>19460 County Road 2, Sauk Centre MN 56378, USA | Football Player |
| **Schmirler, Sandra**<br>Curling Association, 1660 Vimont Court, Cumberland ON K4A 4J4, Canada | Curling Athlete |
| **Schmit, Timothy B**<br>W M E Entertainment, 1325 Ave of Americas, New York NY 10019 USA | Singer, Bassist (Eagles) |
| **Schmitt, Arnd**<br>Rheinuferweg 59B, 47495 Bornheim, Germany | Fencer |
| **Schmitt, Harrison H (Jack)**<br>PO Box 90730, Albuquerque NM 87199, USA | Senator, NM; Astronaut |
| **Schmitt, Janis**<br>Playboy Promotions, 9346 Civic Center Dr, #200, Beverly Hills CA 90210 USA | Model |
| **Schmitt, John C**<br>2 Mayflower Road, Glen Head NY 11545, USA | Football Player |
| **Schmitt, Martin**<br>Weirather Wenzel Partner, Lustennauerstr 64, 6850 Dornbirn, Austria | Ski Jumper |
| **Schmitt, Maximilian**<br>Kunstler Sekretariat am Gasteig, Rosenheimer Str 52, 81669 Munich, Germany | Opera Singer |
| **Schmitz, Bruna**<br>International Surfing Association, 5580 La Jolla Blvd, #145, La Jolla CA 92037 USA | Surfer, Model |
| **Schmitz, Oliver**<br>Above the Line, Wielandstr 5, 10625 Berlin, Germany | Director, Writer |
| **Schmock, Jonathan**<br>A P A Talent & Literary Agency, 405 S Beverly Dr, #300, Beverly Hills CA 90212 USA | Actor, Director |
| **Schmoeller, David**<br>3910 Woodhill Ave, Las Vegas NV 89121, USA | Director |
| **Schmoll, Steve**<br>4758 Chastain Dr, Melbourne FL 32940, USA | Baseball Player |
| **Schmolzer, August**<br>Agentur Carola Studlar, Agnesstr 47, 80798 Munich, Germany | Actor, Writer |
| **Schnabel, Julian**<br>Creative Artists Agency, 2000 Ave of Stars, #100, Los Angeles CA 90067 USA | Artist, Director |
| **Schnackenberg, Roy L**<br>731 W 18th St, #1RW, Chicago IL 60616, USA | Artist, Sculptor |
| **Schnarre, Monika**<br>Alex Stevens, 137 N Larchmont, #259, Los Angeles CA 90004, USA | Model, Actress |
| **Schnebel, Dieter**<br>Hektorstr 15, 10711 Berlin, Germany | Composer |
| **Schnebli, Dolf**<br>Sudstr 45, 8008 Zurich, Switzerland | Architect |
| **Schneck, David L (Dave)**<br>3891 Lehigh Dr, Northampton PA 18067, USA | Baseball Player |
| **Schneck, Michael L (Mike)**<br>2006 Condor Lane, Gibsonia PA 15044, USA | Football Player |
| **Schneeberger, Gisela**<br>Agentur Carola Studlar, Agnesstr 47, 80798 Munich, Germany | Actress |
| **Schneerson, Rachel**<br>National Institutes of Health, 9000 Rockville Pike, Bethesda MD 20892, USA | Immunologist |
| **Schneider, Aaron**<br>Anonymous Content, 3532 Hayden Ave, Culver City CA 90232 USA | Cinematographer |
| **Schneider, Bob**<br>Agency Group Ltd, 142 W 57th St, #600, New York NY 10019 USA | Singer, Songwriter |
| **Schneider, Brian D**<br>130 Playa Rienta Way, Palm Beach Gardens FL 33418, USA | Baseball Player |
| **Schneider, Christoph (Doom)**<br>Pilgrim Mgmt, PO Box 54101, 10042 Berlin, Germany | Drummer (Rammstein) |

**Schneider, Cory** — Ice Hockey Player
Vancouver Canucks, 800 Griffiths Way, Vancouver BC V6B 6G1, Canada
**Schneider, Daniel J (Dan)** — Actor, Director, Producer
W M E Entertainment, 9601 Wilshire Blvd, #300, Beverly Hills CA 90210 USA
**Schneider, Daniel L (Dan)** — Baseball Player
PO Box 30940, Tucson AZ 85751, USA
**Schneider, Eliza** — Actress
W M E Entertainment, 9601 Wilshire Blvd, #300, Beverly Hills CA 90210 USA
**Schneider, Fred** — Singer, Songwriter (B-52s)
Direct Management Group, 947 N La Cienega Blvd, #G, West Hollywood CA 90069, USA
**Schneider, Helge** — Actor, Comedian, Jazz Musician
Meine Supermaus, Wallstr 3A, 45468 Mulheim an der Ruhr, Germany
**Schneider, Jeffrey T (Jeff)** — Baseball Player
268 Pin Oak Dr, Geneseo IL 61254, USA
**Schneider, John** — Actor, Singer
Trail's End, 4607 Lakeview Canyon Road, #569, Westlake Village CA 91361, USA
**Schneider, Lew** — Producer, Writer, Actor
United Talent Agency, U T A Plaza, 9336 Civic Center Dr, Beverly Hills CA 90210 USA
**Schneider, Mathieu** — Ice Hockey Player
1311 6th St, Manhattan Beach CA 90266, USA
**Schneider, Max** — Actor
W M E Entertainment, 9601 Wilshire Blvd, #300, Beverly Hills CA 90210 USA
**Schneider, Paul** — Writer
MacMillan, 175 5th Ave, New York NY 10010 USA
**Schneider, Paul A** — Actor
Creative Artists Agency, 2000 Ave of Stars, #100, Los Angeles CA 90067 USA
**Schneider, Rob** — Actor, Comedian
Gersh Agency, 9465 Wilshire Blvd, #600, Beverly Hills CA 90212 USA
**Schneider, Robert** — Singer, Guitarist (Apples in Stereo)
Billions Corp, 3522 W Armitage Ave, Chicago IL 60647 USA
**Schneider, Siegfried** — Volleyball Player
Haydnstr 4, 04107 Leipzig, Germany
**Schneider, Verena (Vreni)** — Alpine Skier
An der Matt, 8767 Elm, Switzerland
**Schneider, William C (Buzz)** — Ice Hockey Player
5656 Turtle Lake Road, Saint Paul MN 55126, USA
**Schneiderman, David A** — Publisher, Editor
I C M Partners, 10250 Constellation Blvd, #900, Los Angeles CA 90067 USA
**Schneier, Arthur** — Religious Leader, Association Executive
Appeal of Conscience Foundation, 119 W 57th St, #820, New York NY 10019, USA
**Schnelker, Robert B (Bob)** — Football Player
85 Silver Oaks Circle, Naples FL 34119, USA
**Schnell, Matthais J** — Microbiologist
Thomas Jefferson University, Microbiology Dept, 233 S 10th St, Philadelphia PA 19107, USA
**Schnelldorfer, Manfred** — Figure Skater
Seydlitzstr 55, 80993 Munich, Germany
**Schnellenberger, Howard** — Football Coach
118 SE 25th Ave, Boynton Beach FL 33435, USA
**Schnetzer, Stephen** — Actor
Liebman Entertainment, 25 E 21st St, #PH, New York NY 10010, USA
**Schnieders, Richard** — Businessman
Sysco Corp, 1390 Enclave Parkway, Houston TX 77077, USA
**Schnitker, J Michael (Mike)** — Football Player
PO Box 968, Conifer CO 80433, USA
**Schnittker, Richard D (Dick)** — Basketball Player
2303 E Las Granadas, Green Valley AZ 85614, USA
**Schnitzer, Morris** — Organic Chemist
6035 Murray St, Niagara Falls ON L2G 2K4, Canada
**Schnoeink, Birte** — Actress
Sandra Rudorff Artist Agency, On Oak, #8, 22549 Hamburg, Germany
**Schobel, Aaron R** — Football Player
1024 Yaupon Creek Estuary, Columbus TX 78934, USA
**Schobel, Frank** — Singer
Artist Management Uwe Kanthak, Postfach 113124, 20431 Hamburg, Germany
**Schobel, Matthew T (Matt)** — Football Player
PO Box 1276, Columbus TX 78934, USA
**Schoch, Philipp** — Snowboarding Athlete
Waldheim, 8496 Steg, Switzerland
**Schochet, Bob** — Cartoonist
6 Sunset Road, Highland Mills NY 10930, USA
**Schock, Gina** — Singer, Drummer (Go-Go's)
Direct Managment Group, 947 N La Cienega Blvd, #G, West Hollywood CA 90069, USA
**Schock, Ron** — Ice Hockey Player
1360 Whalen Road, Penfield NY 14526, USA
**Schockemohle, Alwin** — Equestrian
Kreis Diepholz/Niedersachsen, 49453 Muhlen, Germany
**Schoen, Gerald T (Gerry)** — Baseball Player
110 Mark Twain Dr, #21, New Orleans LA 70123, USA
**Schoen, Max H** — Dentist
123 Wellfleet Circle, Folsom CA 95630, USA
**Schoenaerts, Matthias** — Actor
Lisa Richards Agency, 108 Upper Leeson St, Dublin 4, Ireland
**Schoenbaechler, Andreas** — Aerials Skier
Muhlrutistr 2, 8910 Affoltern a A, Switzerland
**Schoendienst, Albert F (Red)** — Baseball Player, Manager
1105 Jo Carr Dr, Town and Country MO 63017, USA
**Schoene, Russell (Russ)** — Basketball Player
6319 189th Place NE, #103, Redmond WA 98052, USA
**Schoeneweis, Scott D** — Baseball Player
14420 E Kern Court, Fountain Hills AZ 85268, USA
**Schoenfeld, Jim** — Ice Hockey Player, Coach
45 W 60th St, #18D, New York NY 10023, USA
**Schoenfield, Al** — Swimming Executive
75 Santa Rosa St, San Luis Obispo CA 93405, USA
**Schoenke, Raymond F (Ray), Jr** — Football Player
21151 Woodfield Road, Gaithersburg MD 20882, USA

**Schofield, David** — Actor
Artists Partnership, 101 Finsbury Pavement, London EC2A 1RS, England
**Schofield, Dwight** — Ice Hockey Player
9024 Cardinal Terrace, Saint Louis MO 63144, USA
**Schofield, J Richard (Dick)** — Baseball Player
138 Circle Dr, Springfield IL 62703, USA
**Schofield, John** — Jazz Guitarist, Composer
International Music Network, 278 Main St, Gloucester MA 01930, USA
**Schofield, Oscar** — Oceanographer
Marine Biology/Ocean Optics Center, 71 Dudley Road, New Brunswick NJ 08901, USA
**Schofield, Richard C (Dick)** — Baseball Player
17703 Gardenview Place Court, Glencoe MO 63038, USA
**Scholes, Myron S** — Nobel Economics Laureate
34 Stern Lane, Atherton CA 94027, USA
**Scholl, Andreas** — Opera Singer
I M G Artists, Hogarth Business Park, Chiswick, London W4 2TH, England
**Schollander, Donald A (Don)** — Swimmer
3576 Lakeview Blvd, Lake Oswego OR 97035, USA
**Scholten, Jim** — Singer, Bassist (Sawyer Brown)
O-Seven Artist Mgmt, PO Box 210586, Nashville TN 37221, USA
**Scholtz, Bruce D** — Football Player
6636 W William Cannon Dr, #834, Austin TX 78735, USA
**Scholtz, Robert J (Bob)** — Football Player
6721 S 71st East Ave, Tulsa OK 74133, USA
**Scholz, Walter** — Trumpeter
Bert-Brecht-Str 58, 77855 Achern, Germany
**Schomberg, A Thomas** — Sculptor
4923 S Snowberry Lane, Evergreen CO 80439, USA
**Schon, Jan Hendrik** — Inventor (Molecule Transistor)
Lucent Technology Bell Laboratory, 600 Mountain Ave, New Providence NJ 07974, USA
**Schon, Kyra** — Actress
930 N Sheridan Ave, Pittsburgh PA 15206, USA
**Schon, Neal J** — Guitarist (Journey)
Front Line Mgmt, 1100 Glendon Ave, #2000, Los Angeles CA 90024 USA
**Schonberg, Claude-Michel** — Composer
Cameron Mackintosh Ltd, 1 Bedford Square, London WC1B 3RA, England
**Schonborn, Christoph Cardinal** — Religious Leader
Archdiocese of Vienna, Wollzeile 2, 1010 Vienna, Austria
**Schonert, Turk L** — Football Player
7 Sugar Mill Court, Lancaster NY 14086, USA
**Schonherr, Ivonne** — Actress
Sascha Wunsch Artists Mgmt, Stubenrauchstr 57, 12161 Berlin, Germany
**Schonhuber, Franz** — Commentator
Europaburo, Fraunhoferstr 23, 80469 Munich, Germany
**Schonrock-Ermisch, Sybille** — Swimmer
Merseburger Str 93, 06112 Halle/Saale, Germany
**Schoofs, Mark** — Journalist
Village Voice, Editorial Dept, 32 Cooper Square, New York NY 10003, USA
**Schoolboy Q** — Rap Artist
Interscope Records, 2220 Colorado Ave, Santa Monica CA 90404 USA
**Schooler, Michael R (Mike)** — Baseball Player
519 N Buttonwood St, Anaheim CA 92805, USA
**Schoolnik, Gary** — Microbiologist
Stanford University Medical School, Microbiology Dept, Stanford CA 94305, USA
**Schools, Dave** — Bassist (Widespread Panic)
Brown Cat Inc, 400 Foundry St, Athens GA 30601 USA
**Schoomaker, Peter J (Pete)** — Army General
Special Operations Warrior Foundation, PO Box 13483, Tampa FL 33681, USA
**Schopf, J William** — Paleobiologist
University of California, Study of Evolution Center, Los Angeles CA 90024, USA
**Schorer, Jane** — Journalist
Des Moines Register, Editorial Dept, PO Box 957, Des Moines IA 50306, USA
**Schorr, Bill** — Cartoonist (Phoebe's Place, Grizzwells)
Cagle Cartoons, PO Box 22342, Santa Barbara CA 93121 USA
**Schorske, Carl E** — Historian, Writer
112 Sunnyside Road, Silver Spring MD 20910, USA
**Schott, Ben** — Photographer, Writer
Rogers Coleridge White, 20 Powis Mews, London W11 1JN, England
**Schottenheimer, Martin E (Marty)** — Football Coach, Sportscaster
19825 Northcove Road, #B, Cornelius NC 28031, USA
**Schourek, Peter A (Pete)** — Baseball Player
13761 Balmoral Greens Ave, Clifton VA 20124, USA
**Schrade, Brad** — Journalist
Minneapolis Star Tribune, Editorial Dept, 425 Portland Ave S, Minneapolis MN 55488 USA
**Schrader, Kenneth (Ken)** — Auto, Truck Racing Driver
Ken Schrader Racing, 4403 Stough Road, Concord NC 28027, USA
**Schrader, Maria** — Actress
Davien Littlefield Mgmt, 477 Madison Ave, New York NY 10022, USA
**Schrader, Paul J** — Director, Writer
Parseghian/Planco, 388 2nd Ave, #506, New York, NY 10010 USA
**Schram, Bitty** — Actress
Sovereign Talent Group, 8421 Wilshire Blvd, #200, Beverly Hills CA 90211, USA
**Schramka, Paul E** — Baseball Player
W180N9923 Riversbend Circle W, Germantown WI 53022, USA
**Schramm, David** — Actor
Gersh Agency, 9465 Wilshire Blvd, #600, Beverly Hills CA 90212 USA
**Schranz, Karl** — Alpine Skier
Hotel Garni, 6580 Saint Anton, Austria
**Schreiber, Lawrence A (Larry)** — Football Player
388 Albion Ave, Woodside CA 94062, USA
**Schreiber, Liev** — Actor, Director
United Talent Agency, U T A Plaza, 9336 Civic Center Dr, Beverly Hills CA 90210 USA
**Schreiber, Martin J** — Governor, WI
2700 S Shore Dr, #B, Milwaukee WI 53207, USA
**Schreiber, Pablo** — Actor
I C M Partners, 10250 Constellation Blvd, #900, Los Angeles CA 90067 USA

| | |
|---|---|
| **Schreiber, Stuart L** | Chemist |
| Harvard University, Chemistry Dept, Cambridge MA 02138, USA | |
| **Schreiber, Theodore H (Ted)** | Baseball Player |
| 116 Nantucket Isle, Centerville GA 31028, USA | |
| **Schreier, Peter** | Opera Singer, Conductor |
| Peter McCann Ltd, 56 Lawrie Park Gardens, London SE26 6XY, England | |
| **Schremp, Rob** | Ice Hockey Player |
| 303 Phillips St, Fulton NY 13069, USA | |
| **Schrempf, Detlef** | Basketball Player |
| 9735 NE 1st St, Bellevue WA 98004, USA | |
| **Schrempp, Jurgen E** | Businessman |
| Daimler-Chrysler AG, Plieningerstra, 70546 Stuttgart, Germany | |
| **Schreyer, Cynthia (Cindy)** | Golfer |
| 208 Brushy Hill Road, Danbury CT 06810, USA | |
| **Schreyer, Edward R** | Governor General, Canada |
| 250 Wellington Crescent, #401, Winnipeg MB R3M 0B3, Canada | |
| **Schrieber, Paul W** | Baseball Umpire |
| 9179 N 102nd St, Scottsdale AZ 85258, USA | |
| **Schrieffer, John R** | Nobel Physics Laureate |
| 22465 Tuna Place, Boca Raton FL 33428, USA | |
| **Schrimshaw, Nevin S** | Nutritionist |
| Sandwich Notch Farm, Thornton NH 03223, USA | |
| **Schrock, Richard R** | Nobel Chemistry Laureate |
| 15 Cabot St, Winchester MA 01890, USA | |
| **Schroder, Ernst A** | Actor |
| Podere Montalto, Castellina In Chianti, 53011 Siena, Italy | |
| **Schroder, Rick** | Actor, Director |
| Hofflund/Polone, 9465 Wilshire Blvd, #420, Beverly Hills CA 90212 USA | |
| **Schroeder, A William (Bill)** | Baseball Player |
| 4760 S Providence Dr, New Berlin WI 53146, USA | |
| **Schroeder, Barbet G** | Director, Producer |
| Creative Artists Agency, 2000 Ave of Stars, #100, Los Angeles CA 90067 USA | |
| **Schroeder, Carly** | Actress |
| Innovative Artists, 1505 10th St, Santa Monica CA 90401 USA | |
| **Schroeder, Eugene W (Gene)** | Football Player |
| 918 Aaron Court, Crown Point IN 46307, USA | |
| **Schroeder, Gerhard** | Chancellor, Germany |
| Buro Bundeskanzler, Unter den Linden 50, 10117 Berlin, Germany | |
| **Schroeder, Jay B** | Football Player |
| 1849 S Paragon Dr, Saint George UT 84790, USA | |
| **Schroeder, Jim** | Bowler |
| 3 Greenhaven Terrace, Tonawanda NY 14150, USA | |
| **Schroeder, John H** | Educator |
| University of Wisconsin, Chancellor's Office, Milwaukee WI 53211, USA | |
| **Schroeder, Manfred R** | Physicist |
| Rieswartenweg 8, 37077 Gottingen, Germany | |
| **Schroeder, Mary M** | Judge |
| US Court of Appeals, 230 N 1st Ave, #101, Phoenix AZ 85003, USA | |
| **Schroeder, Patricia S** | Representative, CO |
| 621 Nadina Place, Kissimmee FL 34747, USA | |
| **Schroeder, Paul W** | Historian |
| 604 S Western Ave, Champaign IL 61821, USA | |
| **Schroeder, Steven A** | Foundation Executive, Physician |
| 10 Paseo Mirasol, Belvedere Tiburon CA 94920, USA | |
| **Schroeder, Terry** | Water Polo Player, Coach |
| 30200 Agoura Road, #130, Agoura Hills CA 91301, USA | |
| **Schroeder, William F (Bill)** | Football Player |
| 2176 Shady Lane, Green Bay WI 54313, USA | |
| **Schrom, Kenneth M (Ken)** | Baseball Player |
| 1002 Black Diamond Court, Portland TX 78374, USA | |
| **Schroy, Kenneth M (Ken)** | Football Player |
| 79 Russell Road, Garden City NY 11530, USA | |
| **Schroyer, Heath** | Basketball Coach |
| University of Wyoming, Athletic Dept, Laramie WY 82071, USA | |
| **Schruefer, John J** | Gynecologist |
| 3800 Reservoir Road NW, Washington DC 20007, USA | |
| **Schu, Richard S (Rick)** | Baseball Player |
| 2013 Driftwood Circle, El Dorado Hills CA 95762, USA | |
| **Schuba, Beatrice (Trixi)** | Figure Skater |
| Zenker Public Relations, Am Neubau 70, 2104 Spillern, Austria | |
| **Schubert, Christoph** | Ice Hockey Player |
| Atlanta Thrashers, 101 Marietta St NW, #1900, Atlanta GA 30303 USA | |
| **Schubert, Richard F** | Association Executive |
| 6615 Madison-McLean Dr, McLean VA 22101, USA | |
| **Schubert, Steven W (Steve)** | Football Player |
| 7 Douglas Dr, Candia NH 03034, USA | |
| **Schuck, Anett** | Canoeing Athlete |
| Defoestry 6A, 04159 Leipzig, Germany | |
| **Schuck, John** | Actor |
| Douglas Gorman Rothacker Wilhelm, 1501 Broadway, #703, New York NY 10036, USA | |
| **Schuck, Walter** | WW II German Luftwaffe Hero |
| Tekstr 55, 66424 Homburg/Saar, Germany | |
| **Schueler, Ronald R (Ron)** | Baseball Player |
| 3201 E Camino Sin Nombre, Paradise Valley AZ 85253, USA | |
| **Schuffenhauer, Bill** | Bobsled Athlete |
| 2888 Marilyn Dr, Ogden UT 84403, USA | |
| **Schuh, Jeffrey J (Jeff)** | Football Player |
| 5550 Vagabond Lane N, Minneapolis MN 55446, USA | |
| **Schuhl, Jean Jacques** | Writer |
| Editions Gallimard, 5 Rue Sebastien Bottin, 75007 Paris, France | |
| **Schul, Robert (Bob)** | Track Athlete |
| 320 Wisteria Dr, Dayton OH 45419, USA | |
| **Schuldt, Travis** | Actor |
| Stone Manners Salners, 6100 Wilshire Blvd, #1500, Los Angeles CA 90035 USA | |
| **Schuler, Carolyn J** | Swimmer |
| 26552 Via del Sol, Mission Viejo CA 92691, USA | |

**Schull, Amanda** — Ballerina, Actress
San Francisco Ballet, 455 Franklin St, San Francisco CA 94102, USA

**Schull, Rebecca** — Actress
Stewart Talent, 318 W 53rd St, #201, New York NY 10019, USA

**Schuller, Grete** — Sculptor
8 Barstow Road, #7G, Great Neck NY 11021, USA

**Schuller, Gunther** — Composer, Conductor
Margun Music, 167 Dudley Road, Newton Center MA 02459, USA

**Schuller, Robert H** — Evangelist
464 S Esplanade St, Orange CA 92869, USA

**Schult, Arthur W (Art)** — Baseball Player
9255 SW 90th St, Ocala FL 34481, USA

**Schult, Jurgen** — Track Athlete
Drosselweg 6, 19069 Leuna, Germany

**Schulters, Lance A** — Football Player
594 Grant Ave, Roselle NJ 07203, USA

**Schultz, C Budd (Buddy)** — Baseball Player
14639 N 55th Place, Scottsdale AZ 85254, USA

**Schultz, Carl** — Director
I C M Partners, 10250 Constellation Blvd, #900, Los Angeles CA 90067 USA

**Schultz, Connie** — Journalist
Cleveland Plain Dealer, Editorial Dept, 801 Superior Ave, Cleveland OH 44113 USA

**Schultz, Dave** — Ice Hockey Player
1001 Harbour Cove, Somers Point NJ 08244, USA

**Schultz, Dean** — Government Official, Financier
Federal Home Loan Bank, 1079 Hutchinson Road, Walnut Creek CA 94598, USA

**Schultz, Dwight** — Actor
Media Partners, 8306 Wilshire Blvd, #337, Beverly Hills CA 90211, USA

**Schultz, George W (Barney)** — Baseball Player
400 Fern Brook Lane, #218, Mount Laurel NJ 08054, USA

**Schultz, Howard** — Businessman
Starbucks Corp, 2401 Utah Ave S, #800, Seattle WA 98134, USA

**Schultz, John** — Director, Producer, Writer
Creative Artists Agency, 2000 Ave of Stars, #100, Los Angeles CA 90067 USA

**Schultz, Mark** — Singer
Lucid Artists Mgmt, 54 Music Square E, #200, Nashville TN 37203, USA

**Schultz, Michael A** — Director
Chrystalite Productions, PO Box 1940, Santa Monica CA 90406, USA

**Schultz, Nick** — Ice Hockey Player
201 Downey St, Strasbourg SK S9G 4V0, Canada

**Schultz, Peter C** — Inventor (Silica Optical Waveguide)
Heraeus Amersil Inc, 3473 Satellite Blvd, #300, Duluth GA 30096, USA

**Schultz, Peter G** — Chemist
Salk Research Institute, 10550 N Torrey Pine Road, La Jolla CA 92037, USA

**Schultz, Philip** — Writer
Houghton Mifflin Harcourt, 215 Park Ave S, #1200, New York NY 10003 USA

**Schultz, Richard D** — Association Executive
Olympic Committee, 1 Olympic Plaza, Building 6, Colorado Springs CO 80909 USA

**Schultz, Stanley G** — Physiologist
4955 Heatherglen Dr, Houston TX 77096, USA

**Schultz, William (Bill)** — Football Player
9954 Hidden Falls Circle, Fishers IN 46037, USA

**Schultze, Charles L** — Government Official, Economist
8100 Connecticut Ave, #1204, Chevy Chase MD 20815, USA

**Schulweis, Harold M** — Religious Leader, Rabbi
Congregation Valley Beth Shalom, 15739 Ventura Blvd, Encino CA 91436, USA

**Schulz, Axel** — Boxer
Bliss Media, Nuhrenstr 23, 15234 Frankfurt, Germany

**Schulz, Jeffrey A (Jeff)** — Baseball Player
1167 N Stockwell Road, Evansville IN 47715, USA

**Schulz, Jody J** — Football Player
222 Schulz Lane, Chester MD 21619, USA

**Schulz, Kurt E** — Football Player
5130 Rockledge Dr, Clarence NY 14031, USA

**Schulz, Ted** — Golfer
94 Persimmon Ridge Dr, Louisville KY 40245, USA

**Schulze, Donald A (Don)** — Baseball Player
20558 Geer Ave, Hilmar CA 95324, USA

**Schulze, Paul** — Actor
Kyle Friz Mgmt, 6325 Heather Dr, Los Angeles CA 90068, USA

**Schulze, Richard M** — Businessman
Best Buy Co, 7601 Penn Ave S, Minneapolis MN 55423, USA

**Schumacher, Joel** — Director
Joel Schumacher Productions, 10960 Wilshire Blvd, #1900, Los Angeles CA 90024, USA

**Schumacher, Michael** — Auto Racing Driver
Postfach 308, 1234 Vufflens-le-Chateau, Switzerland

**Schumacher, Ralf** — Auto Racing Driver
Williams B M W, Grove Wantage, Oxfordshire OX12 0DQ, England

**Schumacher, Tony** — Drag Racing Driver
Schumacher Racing, 1681 E Northfield Dr, #A, Brownsburg IN 46112, USA

**Schumacher, William (Billy)** — Boat Racing Driver
U-37 Racing Team, 2819 20th Ave W, Seattle, WA 98199, USA

**Schumaker, Jared M (Skip)** — Baseball Player
8877 Tulare Dr, #310B, Huntington Beach CA 92646, USA

**Schumann, Jochen** — Yachtsman
Birkenstr 88, 48336 Penzberg, Germany

**Schumann, Ralf** — Marksman
Steomach 22, 97640 Stockheim, Germany

**Schumer, Amy** — Actress, Comedienne, Writer, Producer
Mosiac Media Group, 9200 W Sunset Blvd, #1000, Los Angeles CA 90069 USA

**Schur, Michael** — Producer, Writer, Actor
United Talent Agency, U T A Plaza, 9336 Civic Center Dr, Beverly Hills CA 90210 USA

**Schurman, Maynard F** — Ice Hockey Player
301 Beaver St, Summerside PE C1N 2A2, Canada

**Schurmann, Petra** — Swimmer
Max-Emanuel-Str 7, 82319 Starnberg, Germany

**Schurr, Harry W** — Vietnam War Air Force Hero
1544 Yellow Rose Court, Fairborn OH 45324, USA
**Schurr, Wayne A** — Baseball Player
10030 W 500 S, Hudson IN 46747, USA
**Schussler Fiorenza, Elisabeth** — Writer, Theologian
Notre Dame University, Theology Dept, Notre Dame IN 46556, USA
**Schutz, Carl J** — Baseball Player
PO Box 162, French Settlement LA 70733, USA
**Schutz, Dana** — Artist
Friedrich Petzel Gallery, 456 W 18th St, New York NY 10011, USA
**Schutz, Susan Polis** — Writer
Blue Mountain Arts Inc, PO Box 4549, Boulder CO 80306, USA
**Schutz, William N (Bill)** — Football Player
9954 Hidden Falls Circle, Fishers IN 46037, USA
**Schutze, Jim** — Writer, Journalist
Avon Books, 1350 Ave of Americas, New York NY 10019, USA
**Schuur, Diane** — Singer
Stiletto Entertainment, 8295 S La Cienega Blvd, Inglewood CA 90301, USA
**Schwab, Charles R** — Financier
Charles Schwab Co, 101 Montgomery St, #200, San Francisco CA 94104, USA
**Schwab, Corey** — Ice Hockey Player
20633 76th Ave SE, Snohomish WA 98296, USA
**Schwabe, Michael S (Mike)** — Baseball Player
304 36th St, Newport Beach CA 92663, USA
**Schwahn, Mark** — Producer, Writer
W M E Entertainment, 9601 Wilshire Blvd, #300, Beverly Hills CA 90210 USA
**Schwall, Donald B (Don)** — Baseball Player
2000 Lake Marshall Dr, Gibsonia PA 15044, USA
**Schwaller, Andreas** — Curling Athlete
Curling Association, PO Box 606, 3000 Bern, Switzerland
**Schwaller, Christof** — Curling Athlete
Curling Association, PO Box 606, 3000 Bern, Switzerland
**Schwantz, James W (Jim)** — Football Player
1047 W Chatham Dr, Palatine IL 60067, USA
**Schwantz, Kevin** — Motorcycle Racing Rider
Kevin Schwantz School, 3446 Winder Highway, #M234, Flowery Branch GA 30542, USA
**Schwarthoff, Florian** — Track Athlete
Fischweiher 51, 64646 Heppenheim, Germany
**Schwartz, Alan** — Financier
Guggenheim Partners, 330 Madison Ave, New York NY 10017, USA
**Schwartz, Ben** — Actor, Comedian, Writer
W M E Entertainment, 9601 Wilshire Blvd, #300, Beverly Hills CA 90210 USA
**Schwartz, Bryan L** — Football Player
14805 Silver Feather Circle, Broomfield CO 80023, USA
**Schwartz, D Randall (Randy)** — Baseball Player
757 El Rancho Dr, El Cajon CA 92019, USA
**Schwartz, Josh** — Writer, Producer
W M E Entertainment, 9601 Wilshire Blvd, #300, Beverly Hills CA 90210 USA
**Schwartz, Lloyd** — Journalist
27 Pennsylvania Ave, Somerville MA 02145, USA
**Schwartz, Maite** — Actress
TalentWorks, 3500 W Olive Ave, #1400, Burbank CA 91505 USA
**Schwartz, Martha** — Landscape Architect
Martha Schwartz Partners, 147 Sherman St, #200A, Cambridge MA 02140, USA
**Schwartz, Maxime** — Medical Administrator
Institut Pasteur, 25-28 Rue du Docteur-Roux, 75724 Paris Cedex 15, France
**Schwartz, Neena B** — Endocrinologist
450 Davis St, Evanston IL 60201, USA
**Schwartz, Norton A** — Air Force General
Business Executives for National Security, 1030 15th St NW, #200 East, Washington DC 20005, USA
**Schwartz, Scott** — Actor
19111 Arminta St, Reseda CA 91335, USA
**Schwartz, Stephen L** — Composer, Lyricist, Singer
Andrew Freedman Public Relations, 9127 Thrasher Ave, Los Angeles CA 90069, USA
**Schwartz, Thomas A** — Army General
Military Child Education Coalition, PO Box 2519, Harker Heights TX 76548, USA
**Schwartzbach, Gerald** — Attorney
655 Redwood Highway, #277, Mill Valley CA 94941, USA
**Schwartzel, Charl A J L** — Golfer
International Sports Mgmt, Cherry Tree Farm, Rostherne, Cheshire WA14 3RZ, England
**Schwartzman, John** — Cinematographer, Director
Murtha Agency, 1025 Colorado Ave, Santa Monica CA 90401, USA
**Schwartzman, Robert** — Actor
I C M Partners, 10250 Constellation Blvd, #900, Los Angeles CA 90067 USA
**Schwary, Ronald L** — Actor, Producer, Director
W M E Entertainment, 9601 Wilshire Blvd, #300, Beverly Hills CA 90210 USA
**Schwarz, Gerard R** — Conductor
Royal Liverpool Orchestra, Hope St, Liverpool L1 9BP, England
**Schwarz, Hanna** — Opera Singer
Opera et Concert, 37 Rue de la Chaussee d'Antin, 75009 Paris, France
**Schwarz, Julian** — Concert Cellist
C M Artists, 127 W 96th St, #13B, New York NY 10025 USA
**Schwarzbein, Diana** — Physician, Writer
Health Communications, 3201 SW 15th St, Deerfield Beach FL 33442, USA
**Schwarzenegger, Arnold A** — Body Builder, Actor; Governor, CA
Creative Artists Agency, 2000 Ave of Stars, #100, Los Angeles CA 90067 USA
**Schwarzman, Stephen A** — Financier
Blackstone Group, 345 Park Ave, Basement Lobby B4, New York NY 10154, USA
**Schwarz-Schilling, Christian** — Government Official, Germany
Am Dohlberg 10, 63564 Budingen, Germany
**Schweickart, Russell L** — Astronaut
B612 Foundation, 2440 W El Camino Real, #300, Mountain View CA 94040, USA
**Schweiger, Til** — Actor
Barefoot Films, Saarbrueckerstra 36, 10405 Berlin, Germany
**Schweigert, Stuart E** — Football Player
4825 Gratiot Road, Saginaw MI 48638, USA

**Schweighofer, Matthias** — Actor, Producer, Director
Agentur Players, Sophiestr 21, 10178 Berlin, Germany
**Schweiker, Richard S (Dick)** — Secretary, Health & Human Services
8890 Windy Ridge Way, McLean VA 22102, USA
**Schweikher, Paul** — Architect
3222 E Missouri Ave, Phoenix AZ 85018, USA
**Schweitz, John E** — Basketball Player
813 Smith Dr, Florence SC 29501, USA
**Schwentke, Robert** — Director
Creative Artists Agency, 2000 Ave of Stars, #100, Los Angeles CA 90067 USA
**Schwer, William (Billy)** — Boxer
5 Grange Ave, Luton LU4 9AS, England
**Schwertsik, Kurt** — Composer
Penzinger Str 26, 1140 Vienna, Austria
**Schwery, Henri Cardinal** — Religious Leader
CP 2334, 1950 Sion 2, Switzerland
**Schwimmer, Rusty** — Actress
Meghan Schumacher Mgmt, 13351D Riverside Dr, #387, Sherman Oaks CA 91423, USA
**Schwinden, Ted** — Governor, MT
401 N Fee St, Helena MT 59601, USA
**Schwitters, Roy F** — Physicist
1718 Cromwell Hill, Austin TX 78703, USA
**Schygulla, Hanna** — Actress
Agents Associes Marie Chen, 201 Rue Faubourg Saint Honore, 75008 Paris, France
**Schypinski, Gerald A (Jerry)** — Baseball Player
28014 Shadowwood Lane, Harrison Township MI 48045, USA
**Scialfa, Patty** — Singer (E Street Band)
1224 Benedict Canyon, Beverly Hills CA 90210, USA
**Sciarra, John M** — Football Player
404 Morning Star Lane, Newport Beach CA 92660, USA
**Scifres, Michael T (Mike)** — Football Player
13100 Dear Canyon Court, San Diego CA 92131, USA
**Scio, Yvonne** — Actress, Model
Artmedia, 20 Ave Rapp, 75007 Paris, France
**Scioli, Brad E** — Football Player
106 Steinbright Dr, Collegeville PA 19426, USA
**Sciorra, Annabella** — Actress
A P A Talent & Literary Agency, 405 S Beverly Dr, #300, Beverly Hills CA 90212 USA
**Scioscia, Michael L (Mike)** — Baseball Player, Manager
1915 Falling Star Ave, Westlake Village CA 91362, USA
**Scirica, Anthony J** — Judge
US Court of Appeals, 601 Market St, #22614, Philadelphia PA 19106, USA
**Sclisizzi, Enio** — Ice Hockey Player
100 Millside Dr, Milton ON L9T 5E2, Canada
**Scobee, Joshua T (Josh)** — Football Player
11686 Blackstone River Dr, Jacksonville FL 32256, USA
**Scodelario, Kaya** — Actress
Curtis Brown Group, 28-29 Haymarket St, #500, London SW1Y 4SP, England
**Scofidio, Ricardo** — Architect
Diller Scofidio Renfro, 601 W 26th St, #1815, New York NY 10001, USA
**Scofield, John** — Jazz Guitarist
International Music Network, 278 Main St, Gloucester MA 01930, USA
**Scofield, Richard M (Dick)** — Air Force General
3251 Country Club Parkway, Castle Rock CO 80108, USA
**Scoggins, Matt** — Diving Coach
4900 Calhoun Canyon Loop, Austin TX 78735, USA
**Scoggins, Tracy** — Actress
Metropolitan Talent Agency, 5405 Wilshire Blvd, #218, Los Angeles CA 90036 USA
**Scola Balvoa, Luis A** — Basketball Player
11801 Sea Shadow Bend, Pearland TX 77584, USA
**Scola, Angelo Cardinal** — Religious Leader
Archdiocese, Palazzo Arcivescovile, Piazza Fontana 2, 20122 Milan, Italy
**Scola, Ettore** — Director
Via Bertoloni 1/E, 00197 Rome, Italy
**Scolari, Peter** — Actor
C E S D, 10635 Santa Monica Blvd, #130, Los Angeles CA 90025 USA
**Scolnick, Edward M** — Geneticist, Virologist
1201 Magnolia Dr, Wayland MA 01778, USA
**Sconiers, Daryl A** — Baseball Player
16775 S Paine St, #1, Fontana CA 92336, USA
**Score, Michael (Mike)** — Singer, Keyboardist (Flock of Seagulls)
Lustig Talent, PO Box 770850, Orlando FL 32877 USA
**Scorpio** — Rap Artist (Furious Five)
Universal Attractions, 135 W 26th St, #1200, New York NY 10001 USA
**Scorsese, Martin** — Director
Sikelia Productions, 110 W 57th St, #500, New York NY 10019, USA
**Scorupco, Izabella** — Actress, Singer, Model
Mikas Stockholm, Bredgrand 2, 111 30 Stockholm, Sweden
**Scott Brown, Denise** — Architect
Venturi Scott Brown Assoc, 4236 Main St, Philadelphia PA 19127, USA
**Scott Thomas, Kristin A** — Actress
Agence Artiste Adequat, 108 Rue Reaumur, 75002 Paris, France
**Scott, Adam** — Golfer
Professional Golfers Association, 100 Ave of Champions, Palm Beach Gardens FL 33418 USA
**Scott, Adam** — Actor
W M E Entertainment, 9601 Wilshire Blvd, #300, Beverly Hills CA 90210 USA
**Scott, Alvin L** — Basketball Player
5786 W Townley Ave, Glendale AZ 85302, USA
**Scott, Andy** — Guitarist (Sweet)
D C M International, 296 Nether St, Finchley, London N3 1RJ, England
**Scott, Anthony (Tony)** — Baseball Player
120 Seay St, Spartanburg SC 29306, USA
**Scott, April** — Actress
C E S D, 10635 Santa Monica Blvd, #130, Los Angeles CA 90025 USA
**Scott, Bartholomew E (Bart)** — Football Player
6 Kings Court, Morristown NJ 07960, USA

**Scott, Brian** — Truck Racing Driver
Joe Gibbs Racing, 6001 Haas Way, Kannapolis NC 28127, USA
**Scott, Byron A** — Basketball Player, Coach
7505 Hannum Ave, Culver City CA 90230, USA
**Scott, Camilla** — Actress
Characters Talent Mgmt, 8 Elm St, Toronto ON M5G 1G7, Canada
**Scott, Campbell** — Actor, Producer, Director
Paradigm Agency, 360 N Crescent Dr, North Building, Beverly Hills CA 90210 USA
**Scott, Chad O** — Football Player
18526 Reliant Dr, Gaithersburg MD 20879, USA
**Scott, Charles T (Charlie)** — Basketball Player
300 Chastain Manor Dr, Norcross GA 30071, USA
**Scott, Clarence R, Jr** — Football Player
216 Sisson Ave NE, Atlanta GA 30317, USA
**Scott, Clyde L (Smackover)** — Football Player, Track Athlete
12840 Rivercrest Dr, Little Rock AR 72212, USA
**Scott, Darnay** — Football Player
18551 Patton St, Detroit MI 48219, USA
**Scott, Darrell** — Singer, Songwriter
New Frontier Touring, 1503 17th Ave S, Nashville TN 37212, USA
**Scott, Dave** — Triathlete, Coach
3080 Valmont Road, #242, Boulder CO 80301, USA
**Scott, David R** — Astronaut
Merces, V C Johnson, 30 Hackamore Lane, #1, Bell Canyon CA 91307, USA
**Scott, Deborah Lynn** — Costume Designer
Innovative Artists, 1505 10th St, Santa Monica CA 90401 USA
**Scott, Dennis E** — Basketball Player
5425 Palm Lake Circle, Orlando FL 32819, USA
**Scott, DeQuincy** — Football Player
PO Box 5746, Pearl MS 39288, USA
**Scott, Desiree R M** — Soccer Player
Canadian Soccer, Place Soccer Canada, 237 Metcalfe St, Ottawa ON K2P 1R2, Canada
**Scott, Donald M (Donnie)** — Baseball Player
6042 114th Terrace N, Pinellas Park FL 33782, USA
**Scott, Donovan** — Actor
Red Baron Mgmt, 1600 Rosecrans Ave, Building 7 #400, Manhattan Beach CA 90266
**Scott, Doug** — Mountaineer
Warwick Mill Center, Weck Bridge, Carlisle Cumbria CA4 8RR, England
**Scott, Dougray** — Actor
W M E Entertainment, 9601 Wilshire Blvd, #300, Beverly Hills CA 90210 USA
**Scott, E C** — Singer
Jay Reil Assoc, 3430 Bayberry Dr, Northbrook IL 60062, USA
**Scott, Freddie L** — Football Player
PO Box 197, Coahoma MS 38617, USA
**Scott, Gary T** — Baseball Player
25 W Elm St, #47, Greenwich CT 06830, USA
**Scott, Gloria Dean Randle** — Educator
Bennett College, President's Office, Greensboro NC 27401, USA
**Scott, Herbert C, Jr** — Football Player
605 Rawhide Court, Plano TX 75023, USA
**Scott, Hillary** — Singer, Songwriter (Lady Antebellum)
Capitol Records, 810 7th Ave, New York NY 10019 USA
**Scott, Irene F** — Judge
US Tax Court, 400 2nd St NW, Washington DC 20217, USA
**Scott, J Raymond (Ray)** — Basketball Player, Coach
5318 Indian Trail, Ypsilanti MI 48197, USA
**Scott, Jack** — Singer, Songwriter
34039 Coachwood Dr, Sterling Heights MI 48312, USA
**Scott, Jacob E (Jake), Jr** — Football Player
32 Seaside South Court, Key West FL 33040, USA
**Scott, Jacqueline** — Actress
Lichtman/Salners, 15865 Royal Haven Place, Sherman Oaks CA 91403 USA
**Scott, Jake** — Singer, Guitarist
PO Box 18106, Encino CA 91416, USA
**Scott, Jake** — Director
Black Dog Films, 42-44 Beak St, London W1F 9RH, England
**Scott, Janette** — Actress
Old Loft, 21 Leinster Mews, Lancaster Gate, London W2 3EX, England
**Scott, Jason Shane** — Actor
Aqua Talent Agency, 9000 Sunset Blvd, #700, Los Angeles CA 90069, USA
**Scott, Jean Bruce** — Actress
Pinnacle Commercial Talent, 5055 Wilshire Blvd, #865, Los Angeles CA 90036, USA
**Scott, Jerry** — Cartoonist (Baby Blues, Zits)
Creators Syndicate, 737 3rd St, Hermosa Beach CA 90254 USA
**Scott, Jill** — Singer, Songwriter, Actress
Creative Artists Agency, 2000 Ave of Stars, #100, Los Angeles CA 90067 USA
**Scott, Josey** — Singer (Saliva)
Helter Skelter, 347-353 Chiswick High Road, London W4 4HS, England
**Scott, Kathryn Leigh** — Actress
3236 Bennett Dr, Los Angeles CA 90068, USA
**Scott, Klea** — Actress
Sovereign Talent Group, 8421 Wilshire Blvd, #200, Beverly Hills CA 90211, USA
**Scott, LaToucha** — Singer (Xscape)
Richard Walters, PO Box 2789, Toluca Lake CA 91610 USA
**Scott, Lizabeth** — Actress
8277 Hollywood Blvd, Los Angeles CA 90069, USA
**Scott, Luke B** — Baseball Player
1111 Saxon Blvd, Orange City FL 32763, USA
**Scott, Manda** — Writer
Delacorte Press, 1540 Broadway, New York NY 10036 USA
**Scott, Mark (Gus)** — Drummer (Trixter)
Global Star Productions, 103 Godwin Ave, #225, Midland Park NJ 07432, USA
**Scott, Matthew P** — Developmental Biologist
Stanford University, Clark Center, 318 Campus Dr, Stanford CA 94305, USA
**Scott, Melody Thomas** — Actress
12068 Crest Court, Beverly Hills CA 90210, USA

| | |
|---|---|
| **Scott, Michael W (Mike)** | Baseball Player |
| 28355 Chat Dr, Laguna Niguel CA 92677, USA | |
| **Scott, Mike** | Singer (Waterboys), Songwriter |
| Agency Group Ltd, 142 W 57th St, #600, New York NY 10019 USA | |
| **Scott, Nitty** | Rap Artist |
| Boombox Family Entertainment, 14235 84th Drive, Jamaica NY 11435, USA | |
| **Scott, Patricia (Pat)** | Baseball Player |
| 1901 Tanners Cove Road, Hebron KY 41048, USA | |
| **Scott, Pippa** | Actress |
| 10 Ocean Park Blvd, #1, Santa Monica CA 90405, USA | |
| **Scott, Randolph C (Randy)** | Football Player |
| 1440 Woodland Lake Dr, Snellville GA 30078, USA | |
| **Scott, Ray** | Singer |
| Hallmark Direction, 713 18th Ave S, Nashville TN 37203, USA | |
| **Scott, Reid** | Actor |
| Impression Entertainment, 9229 W Sunset Blvd, #700, Los Angeles CA 90069, USA | |
| **Scott, Richard U (Dick)** | Football Player |
| 3369 Upland Court, Adamstown MD 21710, USA | |
| **Scott, Ridley** | Director |
| Scott Free Productions, 614 N La Peer Dr, Los Angeles CA 90069, USA | |
| **Scott, Robert B (Bobby)** | Football Player |
| 801 McKinley Pointe Lane, Knoxville TN 37934, USA | |
| **Scott, Rodney** | Actor |
| Domain Talent, 9229 W Sunset Blvd, #710, West Hollywood CA 90069 USA | |
| **Scott, Rodney D** | Baseball Player |
| 4206 Priscilla Ave, Indianapolis IN 46226, USA | |
| **Scott, Seann William** | Actor |
| Elephant Pictures, 200 N Elizabeth St, #200C, Chicago IL 60607, USA | |
| **Scott, Sherie Rene** | Actress, Singer |
| Principal Entertainment, 9255 Sunset Blvd, #500, Los Angeles CA 90069 USA | |
| **Scott, Spencer** | Model |
| PO Box 461177, Los Angeles CA 90046, USA | |
| **Scott, Stephen** | Jazz Pianist |
| Bridge Agency, 35 Clark St, #A5, Brooklyn Heights NY 11201, USA | |
| **Scott, Stuart** | Sportscaster |
| ESPN-TV, Sports Dept, ESPN Plaza, 935 Middle St, Bristol CT 06010 USA | |
| **Scott, Tamika** | Singer (Xscape) |
| Richard Walters, PO Box 2789, Toluca Lake CA 91610 USA | |
| **Scott, Thomas C (Tom)** | Football Player |
| 3259 Kirkwood Court, Keswick VA 22947, USA | |
| **Scott, Timothy** | Sculptor |
| 50 Clare Court, Judd St, London WC1H 9QW, England | |
| **Scott, Timothy D (Tim)** | Baseball Player |
| 956 W Julia Way, Hanford CA 93230, USA | |
| **Scott, Todd C** | Football Player |
| 5605 Avenue P, Galveston TX 77551, USA | |
| **Scott, Tom** | Jazz Saxophonist, Composer |
| Performers of the World, 5657 Wilshire Blvd, #280, Los Angeles CA 90036 USA | |
| **Scott, Tom Everett** | Actor |
| Paradigm Agency, 360 N Crescent Dr, North Building, Beverly Hills CA 90210 USA | |
| **Scott, Walter B** | Football Player |
| 1991 Edgefield Road, Trenton SC 29847, USA | |
| **Scott, Willard H, Jr** | Entertainer |
| NBC-TV, News Dept, 30 Rockefeller Plaza, #270E, New York NY 10112 USA | |
| **Scott, Willie L, Jr** | Football Player |
| 1123 Long St, Newberry SC 29108, USA | |
| **Scott, Winston E** | Astronaut |
| PO Box 1192, Cape Canaveral FL 32920, USA | |
| **Scotti, Benjamin J (Ben)** | Football Player |
| 715 N Beverly Dr, Beverly Hills CA 90210, USA | |
| **Scotti, Nick** | Actor, Singer |
| Untitled Entertainment, 350 S Beverly Dr, #200, Beverly Hills CA 90212 USA | |
| **Scotto, Renata** | Opera Singer |
| 3 Stone Hallow Way, Armonk NY 10504, USA | |
| **Scottoline, Lisa** | Writer |
| Harper Collins Publishers, 10 E 53rd St, Cellar 1, New York NY 10022 USA | |
| **Scotty, Ludwig** | President, Nauru |
| President's Office, Government Offices, Yaren, Nauru | |
| **Scovell, Nell** | Producer |
| Paradigm Agency, 360 N Crescent Dr, North Building, Beverly Hills CA 90210 USA | |
| **Scowcroft, Brent** | Government Official, Air Force General |
| 900 17th St NW, #500, Washington DC 20006, USA | |
| **Scrafford, Kirk T** | Football Player |
| 19400 US Highway 93 N, Florence MT 59833, USA | |
| **Scranton, James D (Jim)** | Baseball Player |
| 27519 Hammack Ave, Perris CA 92570, USA | |
| **Scranton, Nancy** | Golfer |
| 1816 Forest Glen Way, Saint Augustine FL 32092, USA | |
| **Scribner, William C (Bucky)** | Football Player |
| 246 Porter Mill Bend Dr, Camdenton MO 65020, USA | |
| **Scrimm, Angus** | Actor |
| PO Box 5193, North Hollywood CA 91616, USA | |
| **Scrivener, Wayne A (Chuck)** | Baseball Player |
| 1766 Hazel St, Birmingham AL 48009, USA | |
| **Scroggins, Tracy L** | Football Player |
| 6001 N Ocean Dr, #707, Hollywood FL 33019, USA | |
| **Scruggs, Anthony R (Tony)** | Baseball Player |
| 11621 Braddock Dr, #17, Culver City CA 90230, USA | |
| **Scruggs, Randy** | Singer, Songwriter |
| Creative Artists Agency, 3310 W End Ave, #500, Nashville TN 37203 USA | |
| **Scudamore, Peter** | Steeplechase Racing Jockey |
| Mucky Cottage, Grangehill, Naunton, Cheltenham, Glos GL54 3AY, England | |
| **Scudder, W Scott** | Baseball Player |
| 38 Fernwood Dr, Texarkana TX 75503, USA | |
| **Scuderi, Robert J (Rob)** | Ice Hockey Player |
| 16 Old Colony Dr, Dover MA 02030, USA | |

**Scudero, Joseph A (Joe)**  Football Player
2534 N Railroad Way, Hernando FL 34442, USA
**Scullion, Mary**  Social Activist
Project Home, 1515 Fairmount Ave, Philadelphia PA 19130, USA
**Scully, John F, Jr**  Football Player
3500 Bankview Dr, Joliet IL 60431, USA
**Scully, Sean P**  Artist
Brooke Alexander Gallery, 59 Wooster St, New York NY 10012, USA
**Scully, Vincent E (Vin)**  Sportscaster
25090 Jim Bridger Road, Hidden Hills CA 91302, USA
**Scully-Power, Paul D**  Astronaut
US Navy Underwater Systems Laboratory, 33A Code, New London CT 06320, USA
**Scurlock, Clifton T (Kliph)**  Drummer (Flaming Lips)
World's Fair Mgmt, 1208 Chowing Ave, Edmond OK 73034, USA
**Scurry, Briana**  Soccer Player
11610 137th Ave N, Dayton MN 55327, USA
**Scurti, John**  Actor
C E S D, 257 Park Ave S, #950, New York NY 10010 USA
**Scutaro, Marcos H (Marco)**  Baseball Player
19877 E Country Club Dr, #3503, Miami FL 33180, USA
**Seacrest, Ryan**  Entertainer
Creative Artists Agency, 2000 Ave of Stars, #100, Los Angeles CA 90067 USA
**Seaforth-Hayes, Susan**  Actress
Hayforth Enterprises, 11333 Moorpark St, #368, Studio City CA 91602, USA
**Seaga, Edward P G**  Prime Minister, Jamaica
24-26 Grenada Crescent, New Kingston, Kingston 5, Jamaica
**Seagal, Steven**  Actor
Red Entertainment Agency, 505 8th Ave, #1004, New York NY 10018, USA
**Seagrave, Jocelyn**  Actress
Perspective Film, 15030 Ventura Blvd, Sherman Oaks CA 91403, USA
**Seagren, Robert L (Bob)**  Track Athlete, Actor
24710 Palermo Dr, Calabasas CA 91302, USA
**Seagrove, Jenny**  Actress
Rights House, Drury House, 34-43 Russell St, London WC2B 5HA, England
**Seal**  Singer, Songwriter
Creative Artists Agency, 2000 Ave of Stars, #100, Los Angeles CA 90067 USA
**Seal, Mark**  Writer
Viking Press, 375 Hudson St, New York NY 10014 USA
**Seal, Paul N**  Football Player
21599 Hidden Rivers Dr N, Southfield MI 48075, USA
**Seale, Bobby**  Political Activist (Black Panthers)
Cafe Society, 302 W Chelton Ave, Philadelphia PA 19144, USA
**Seale, John C**  Cinematographer
Mirisch Agency, 1801 Century Park E, Los Angeles CA 90067, USA
**Seale, Samuel R (Sam)**  Football Player
1818 Da Gama Court, Escondido CA 92026, USA
**Seals, Bruce A**  Basketball Player
29 2nd St, Malden MA 02148, USA
**Seals, George E**  Football Player
1101 1st St, #204, Coronado CA 92118, USA
**Seals, James**  Singer, Songwriter (Seals & Crofts)
Star Entertainment, 1675 York Ave, #32C, New York NY 10128, USA
**Seals, Raymond B (Ray)**  Football Player
664 NW Shaw Glen, Lake City FL 32055, USA
**Seaman, Christopher**  Conductor
Symphony Australia, 1 Oxford Street, #5-2, Darlinghurst NSW 2010, Australia
**Seaman, David**  Soccer Player
Arsenal London, Avenell Road, Highbury, London N5 1BU, England
**Searage, Raymond M (Ray)**  Baseball Player
9737 Pine Lake Trail, Saint Petersburg FL 33708, USA
**Searcy, Leon, Jr**  Football Player
3841 Biggin Church Road, Jacksonville FL 32224, USA
**Searcy, Nick**  Actor
Evolution Entertainment, 901 N Highland Ave, Los Angeles CA 90038 USA
**Searcy, W Stephen (Steve)**  Baseball Player
5112 Gouffon Road, Knoxville TN 37918, USA
**Searfoss, Richard A**  Astronaut
24480 Silver Creek Way, Tehachapi CA 93561, USA
**Sears, Joe**  Actor
Gersh Agency, 9465 Wilshire Blvd, #600, Beverly Hills CA 90212 USA
**Sears, Kenneth R (Ken)**  Basketball Player
40 Cutter Dr, Watsonville CA 95076, USA
**Sears, Paul B**  Ecologist
17 Las Milpas, Taos NM 87571, USA
**Sears, Teddy**  Actor
A P A Talent & Literary Agency, 405 S Beverly Dr, #300, Beverly Hills CA 90212 USA
**Seasick Steve**  Singer, Songwriter
Agency Group Ltd, 1880 Century Park E, #711, Los Angeles CA 90067 USA
**Seaver, G Thomas (Tom)**  Baseball Player
1761 Diamond Mountain Road, Calistoga CA 94515, USA
**Seavey, David**  Editorial Cartoonist
USA Today, Editorial Dept, 1000 Wilson Blvd, Arlington VA 22209, USA
**Seay, Robert M (Bobby)**  Baseball Player
1591 Oak Circle N, Sarasota FL 34232, USA
**Sebaldt, Maria**  Actress
Agentur Lentz, Herzogstr 66, 80803 Munich, Germany
**Sebastian, Cuthbert M**  Governor General, Saint Kitts & Nevis
Governor General's House, 6 Canyon St, Basseterre, Saint Kitts & Nevis
**Sebastian, John**  Singer, Songwriter
2431 Briarcrest Road, Beverly Hills CA 90210, USA
**Sebastiani, Sergio Cardinal**  Religious Leader
Economic Affairs Prefecture, Congregazioni Palazzo, Lardo Colonnato 3, 00193 Rome, Italy
**Sebestyen, Marta**  Singer, Flutist
Konzertagentur Berthold Seliger, Nonnengasse 15, 36037 Fulda, Germany
**Sebold, Alice**  Writer
Dunow Carlson Lerner Literary Agency, 27 W 20th St, #1107, New York NY 10011, USA

**Sebra, Robert B (Bob)** — Baseball Player
20 Misners Trail, Ormond Beach FL 32174, USA

**Secada, Jon** — Singer, Songwriter
Bridge Mgmt, 427 NE 107th St, Miami FL 33161, USA

**Seckel, Danny** — Actor, Comedian
OmniPop Talent Group, 4605 Lankershim Blvd, #201, Toluca Lake CA 91602 USA

**Secor, Kyle** — Actor
Brillstein Entertainment Partners, 9150 Wilshire Blvd, #350, Beverly Hills CA 90212 USA

**Secord, Al** — Ice Hockey Player
950 Ginger Court, Southlake TX 76092, USA

**Secord, John** — Singer, Guitarist, Songwriter
Making Texas Music, Old Putnam Bank Building, PO Box 1013, Putnam TX 76469, USA

**Secord, Richard V** — Army General
Computerized Thermal Imaging, 1719 W 2800 S, Ogden UT 84401, USA

**Secrest, Meryle** — Writer
Bloomsbury Publishing, 50 Bedford Square, London WC1B 3DP, England

**Secrest, Wayne** — Bassist (Confederate Railroad)
Bobby Roberts, 3050 Business Park Circle, #303, Goodlettsville TN 37221 USA

**Seda, Jon** — Actor
I C M Partners, 10250 Constellation Blvd, #900, Los Angeles CA 90067 USA

**Sedaka, Neil** — Singer, Pianist, Songwriter
Neal Sedaka Music, 730 5th Ave, #950, New York NY 10019, USA

**Sedaris, Amy** — Actress, Comedienne
Paradigm Agency, 360 N Crescent Dr, North Building, Beverly Hills CA 90210 USA

**Sedaris, David** — Writer
64 Thompson St, New York NY 10012, USA

**Seddon, Margaret Rhea** — Astronaut
1709 Shagbark Trail, Murfreesboro TN 37130, USA

**Sedelmaier, J Josef (Joe)** — Director; Animator
Sedelmaier Film Productions, 858 W Armitage Ave, #267, Chicago IL 60614, USA

**Sedgman, Frank A** — Tennis Player
28 Bolton Ave, Hampton VIC 3188, Australia

**Sedgwick, Kyra** — Actress
Impression Entertainment, 9229 W Sunset Blvd, #700, Los Angeles CA 90069, USA

**Sedin, Daniel** — Ice Hockey Player
1233 Nanton Ave, Vancouver BC V6H 2C7, Canada

**Sedin, Henrik** — Ice Hockey Player
C A A Hockey, 822 11th Ave SW, #204, Calgary AB T2R 0E5, Canada

**Sedlbauer, Ronald A (Ron)** — Ice Hockey Player
4231 Lakeshore Road, Burlington ON L7L 1A5, Canada

**Sedney, Jules** — Prime Minister, Suriname
May St 34, Paramaribo, Suriname

**Sedykh, Yuri G** — Track Athlete
Light Athletics Federation, Luzhnetskaya Nab 8, 119270 Moscow, Russia

**See, Carolyn** — Writer
930 3rd St, #203, Santa Monica CA 90403, USA

**See, Lisa** — Writer
El Pueblo Monument Authority, 125 Paseo de Plaza, #400, Los Angeles CA 90012, USA

**See, Marshall** — Basketball Player
1138 S Canal Circle, Camp Verde AZ 86322, USA

**See, R Laurence (Larry)** — Baseball Player
1913 W Remington Dr, Chandler AZ 85286, USA

**Seear, Beatrice N S** — Government Official, England
189B Kennington Road, London SE11 6ST, England

**Seear, Noot** — Model, Actress
Innovative Artists, 1505 10th St, Santa Monica CA 90401 USA

**Seedorf, Clarence** — Soccer Player
F C Milan, Via Filippo Turati 3, 20121 Milan, Italy

**Seeger, Anthony** — Ethnomusicologist
University of California, Music Dept, Los Angeles CA 90024, USA

**Seeger, Peggy** — Singer, Songwriter
Real People Music, 520 S Clinton Ave, Oak Park IL 60304, USA

**Seehofer, Horst L** — President, Germany
Bundeskanzlerant, Schlossplatz 1, 10178 Berlin, Germany

**Seehorn, Rhea** — Actress
Untitled Entertainment, 350 S Beverly Dr, #200, Beverly Hills CA 90212 USA

**Seelbach, Charles F (Chuck)** — Baseball Player
13800 Fairhill Road, #501, Cleveland OH 44120, USA

**Seeler, Uwe** — Soccer Player
H S V, Rothenbaumchaussee 125, 20149 Hamburg, Germany

**Seeley, Andrew M E (Drew)** — Actor, Singer, Songwriter
PO Box 250, 522 S Hunt Club Blvd, Apopka FL 32704, USA

**Seeley, Thomas D** — Biologist
Cornell University, Biological Sciences Division, Ithaca NY 14853, USA

**Seeling, Angelle** — Motorcycle Racing Rider
G Smith Motorsports, 10567 Airline Dr, Saint Rose LA 70087, USA

**Seely, Jeannie** — Singer, Songwriter
Tessier-Marsh Talent, 2825 Blue Book Dr, Nashville TN 37214 USA

**Seeman, Nadrian C (Ned)** — Chemist, Nanotechnologist
New York University, Chemistry Dept, New York NY 10003, USA

**Seezer, Maurice** — Singer, Composer
Bloomsbury Publishing, 50 Bedford Square, London WC1B 3DP, England

**Sefcki, Kevin J** — Baseball Player
16921 Steeplechase Parkway, Orland Park IL 60467, USA

**Seffrin, John R** — Association Executive
American Cancer Society, 1599 Clifton Road NE, Atlanta GA 30329, USA

**Sefolosha, Thabo** — Basketball Player
910 Colony Dr, Salisbury MD 21804, USA

**Sega, Ronald M** — Astronaut, Electrical Engineer
711A Massey Lane, Alexandria VA 22314, USA

**Segal, Fred** — Fashion Designer
Fred Segal Jeans, 8100 Melrose Ave, Los Angeles CA 90046, USA

**Segal, George** — Actor
A Mgmt, 12001 Ventura Place, #340, Studio City CA 91604 USA

**Segal, Peter** — Director, Producer, Writer
Creative Artists Agency, 2000 Ave of Stars, #100, Los Angeles CA 90067 USA

**Segal, Uri** — Conductor
M A Artists Mgmt, 28 Sheffield Terrace, London W8 7NA, England

**Segan, Noah** — Actor, Producer
United Talent Agency, U T A Plaza, 9336 Civic Center Dr, Beverly Hills CA 90210 USA

**Segel, Jason** — Actor
W M E Entertainment, 9601 Wilshire Blvd, #300, Beverly Hills CA 90210 USA

**Seger, Bob** — Singer, Songwriter
3841 LaPlaya Lane, Orchard Lake MI 48324, USA

**Seger, Shea** — Singer
Helter Skelter, 347-353 Chiswick High Road, London W4 4HS, England

**Segerstam, Leif S** — Composer, Conductor
Garvey & Ivor, 59 Lansdowne Place, Hove BN3 1FL, England

**Segui, Diego P** — Baseball Player
7520 King St, #J, Overland Park KS 66214, USA

**Seguin, Tyler P** — Ice Hockey Player
Dallas Stars, 2601 Ave of Stars, #100, Frisco TX 75034 USA

**Segura, Francisco (Pancho)** — Tennis Player
Rancho La Costa Hotel & Spa, 7690 Camino Real, Carlsbad CA 92009, USA

**Seguso, Robert** — Tennis Player
3405 54th Dr W, Bradenton FL 34210, USA

**Sehorn, Jason H** — Football Player, Sportscaster
1901 Wild Holly Lane, Charlotte NC 28226, USA

**Seibel, Anne** — Production Designer, Art Director
Sheldon Prosnit Agency, 800 S Robertson Blvd, #6, Los Angeles CA 90035, USA

**Seibert, Kurt E** — Baseball Player
95 Amberwood Circle, Irmo SC 29063, USA

**Seidel, Guenter** — Equestrian
2108 Oxford Ave, Cardiff-by-the-Sea CA 92007, USA

**Seidel, Martie** — Singer (Dixie Chicks)
Strategic Artists Mgmt, 1100 Glendon Ave, #1100, Los Angeles CA 90024, USA

**Seidelman, Susan** — Director
Michael Shedler, 350 5th Ave, New York NY 10118, USA

**Seidenberg, Dennis** — Ice Hockey Player
20073 N 85th Place, Scottsdale AZ 85255, USA

**Seidenberg, Ivan G** — Businessman
Verizon Communications, 1095 Ave of Americas, New York NY 10036, USA

**Seidler, David** — Writer
Independent Talent Group, 40 Whitfield St, London W1T 2RH, England

**Seidler, Helga** — Track Athlete
Bersarinstr 42, 09130 Chemnitz, Germany

**Seifert, George G** — Football Coach, Sportscaster
1276 Estate Dr, Los Altos Hills CA 94024, USA

**Seiffert, Lisa** — Model
Elite Model Mgmt, 404 Park Ave S, #900, New York NY 10016 USA

**Seigenthaler, John M** — Commentator
Al Jazeera America, Editorial Dept, 311 W 34th St, New York NY 10001 USA

**Seigner, Emmanuelle** — Actress
Agence Artiste Adequat, 108 Rue Reaumur, 75002 Paris, France

**Seigner, Mathilde** — Actress
Artmedia, 20 Ave Rapp, 75007 Paris, France

**Seikaly, Ronald F (Rony)** — Basketball Player
2060 N Bay Road, Miami Beach FL 33140, USA

**Seiling, Richard J (Ric)** — Ice Hockey Player
71 Christina Dr, North Chili NY 14514, USA

**Seiling, Rodney A (Rod)** — Ice Hockey Player
Toronto Hotel Assn, 590-207 Queens Quay W, Toronto ON M5J 1A7, Canada

**Seimetz, Amy** — Actress
One Entertainment, 347 5th Ave, #1404, New York NY 10016 USA

**Seinfeld, Evan** — Actor, Director, Writer
Larger Than Life Mgmt, 12119 Morrison St, Valley Village CA 91607, USA

**Seinfeld, Jerry** — Actor, Comedian
Shapiro/West Assoc, 141 El Camino, #205, Beverly Hills CA 90212, USA

**Seinfeld, John H** — Chemical Engineer
363 Patrician Way, Pasadena CA 91105, USA

**Seiple, Larry R** — Football Player
1361 W Golfview Dr, Pembroke Pines FL 33026, USA

**Seipp, Michelle** — Actress
Chateau/Billings Talent Agency, 8489 W 3rd St, #1032, Los Angeles CA 90048, USA

**Seitzer, Kevin L** — Baseball Player
2845 W 137th Terrace, Overland Park KS 66224, USA

**Seiwald, Robert J** — Inventor (Fluorescent Dye)
59 Burnside Ave, San Francisco CA 94131, USA

**Seixas, E Victor (Vic), Jr** — Tennis Player
8 Harbor Point Dr, #207, Mill Valley CA 94941, USA

**Seizinger, Katja** — Alpine Skier
Rudolf-Epp-Str 48, 69412 Eberbach, Germany

**Sejima, Kazuyo** — Pritzker Architect Laureate
Sanaa Ltd, 2-2-35-6B Higashi-Shinagawa, 140 0002 Tokyo, Japan

**Seki, Syuzo** — Chemist
Osaka University, Chemistry Dept, 1-1 Yamadaoka, Suitashi, Osaka 565-0871, Japan

**Sekler, Eduard F** — Educator, Architect
Harvard University, Graduate Design School, Gund Hall, Cambridge MA 02138, USA

**Sela, Michael** — Immunologist, Chemist
Weizmann Science Institute, Immunology Dept, Rehovot 76100, Israel

**Selander, Robert K** — Biologist
Pennsylvania State University, Biology Dept, University Park PA 16802, USA

**Selanne, Teemu I** — Ice Hockey Player
31731 Madre Selva Lane, Trabuco Canyon CA 92679, USA

**Selby, David** — Actor
S M S Talent, 8383 Wilshire Blvd, #230, Beverly Hills CA 90211 USA

**Selby, Hubert, Jr** — Writer
Bloomsbury Publishing, 50 Bedford Square, London WC1B 3DP, England

**Selby, R Briton (Brit)** — Ice Hockey Player
174 Divadale Dr, East York ON M4G 2P6, Canada

**Selby, William F (Bill)** — Baseball Player
4468 Misty Oaks Lane, Nesbit MS 38651, USA

**Seldin, Donald W** — Physician
Texas Southwestern Medical Center, 5323 Harry Hines Blvd, Dallas TX 75390, USA
**Seldon, Bruce** — Boxer
Rocco DePersia, 35 Kings Highway E, #102, Haddonfield NJ 08033, USA
**Sele, Aaron H** — Baseball Player
4 Oak Tree Dr, Newport Beach CA 92660, USA
**Seles, Monica** — Tennis Player
2895 Dick Wilson Dr, Sarasota FL 34240, USA
**Self, Bill** — Basketball Coach
University of Kansas, Athletic Dept, Allen Fieldhouse, Lawrence KS 66045, USA
**Self, Clarence E** — Football Player
43W689 Willow Creek Court, Elburn IL 60119, USA
**Self, Todd** — Baseball Player
10238 Cardiff Dr, Keithville LA 71047, USA
**Selfridge, Andrew P (Andy)** — Football Player
3400 Dunscroft Court, Keswick VA 22947, USA
**Selick, Henry** — Director
Laika Entertainment, 1400 NW 22nd Ave, Portland OR 97210, USA
**Selig, Franz-Josef** — Opera Singer
I M G Artists, Hogarth Business Park, Chiswick, London W4 2TH, England
**Selim, Ali** — Director, Writer
I C M Partners, 10250 Constellation Blvd, #900, Los Angeles CA 90067 USA
**Selivanov, Alexander** — Ice Hockey Player
4003 W Tacon St, Tampa FL 33629, USA
**Sellar JoAnne** — Producer
United Talent Agency, U T A Plaza, 9336 Civic Center Dr, Beverly Hills CA 90210 USA
**Sellars, Peter** — Director
American National Theater, Kennedy Center, 2700 F St NW, Washington DC 20566, USA
**Selldorf, Annabelle** — Architect
Selldorf Architects, 860 Broadway, #200, New York NY 10003, USA
**Selleca, Connie** — Actress
Binder Assoc, 1465 Lindacrest Dr, Beverly Hills CA 90210, USA
**Selleck, Tom** — Actor
PO Box 1029, Penrose CO 81240, USA
**Seller, Peg** — Synchronized Swimmer, Coach
72 Monkswood Crescent, Newmarket ON L3Y 2K1, Canada
**Sellers, Bradley D (Brad)** — Basketball Player
682 Arbor Way, Aurora OH 44202, USA
**Sellers, Franklin** — Religious Leader
Reformed Episcopal Church, 2001 Frederick Road, Catonsville MD 21228, USA
**Sellers, Jeffrey D (Jeff)** — Baseball Player
266 Raines Road, Easley NC 29640, USA
**Sellers, Piers J** — Astronaut
16011 Craighurst Dr, Houston TX 77059, USA
**Sellers, Ron F** — Football Player
1111 Green Bayberry Dr, Palm Beach Gardens FL 33418, USA
**Sellers, Rosabell Laurenti** — Actress
Studio Emme, Via Leonardo Greppi 130, 00149 Rome, Italy
**Sells, David W (Dave)** — Baseball Player
700 Blue Ridge Lane, Vacaville CA 95688, USA
**Selmon, Dewey W** — Football Player
2725 S Berry Road, Norman OK 73072, USA
**Selten, Reinhard** — Nobel Economics Laureate
Hardtweg 23, 53639 Konigswinter, Germany
**Seltmann, Sally** — Singer, Songwriter
Agency Group Ltd, 142 W 57th St, #600, New York NY 10019 USA
**Seltz, Rolland A** — Basketball Player
3328 Oswego Heights Road, Saint Paul MN 55126, USA
**Seltzer, David** — Director, Writer
I C M Partners, 10250 Constellation Blvd, #900, Los Angeles CA 90067 USA
**Selverstone, Katy** — Actress
Agency Group, 1100 Century Park E, #711, Los Angeles CA 90067 USA
**Selvy, Franklin D (Frank)** — Basketball Player
18 Oglethorpe Lane, Hilton Head SC 29926, USA
**Selway, Philip J (Phil)** — Drummer (Radiohead)
Courtyard, 21 Nursery, Sutton Courtenay, Abingdon, Oxon OX14 4UA, England
**Selwood, Brad** — Ice Hockey Player
77 Colonel Wayling Blvd, Sharon ON L0G 1V0, Canada
**Selya, Bruce M** — Judge
US Court of Appeals, US Courthouse, Pastore Building, Kennedy Plaza, Providence RI 02903, USA
**Selzer, Richard** — Writer, Surgeon
88 Notch Hill Road, #154, North Branford CT 06471, USA
**Selznick, Brian** — Writer, Illustrator
Scholastic Press, 555 Broadway, New York NY 10012 USA
**Semak, Michael W** — Photographer
1796 Spruce Hill Road, Pickering ON L1V 1S4, Canada
**Sember, Michael D (Mike)** — Baseball Player
285 S Country Club Blvd, Boca Raton FL 33487, USA
**Semel, David** — Director, Producer
W M E Entertainment, 9601 Wilshire Blvd, #300, Beverly Hills CA 90210 USA
**Semel, Terry S** — Businessman
Windsor Media Investments, 10877 Wilshire Blvd, Los Angeles CA 90024, USA
**Semenchuk, Ekaterina** — Opera Singer
I M G Artists, Hogarth Business Park, Chiswick, London W4 2TH, England
**Semenov, Anatoli A** — Ice Hockey Player
4015 Royal Vista Circle, Corona CA 92881, USA
**Semenova, Juliana** — Basketball Player
Zalalela 4-35, Riga 1010, Latvia
**Semerenko, Valentyna (Valya)** — Biathlete
Biathlon Federation, Vul Dimitrova 5, 03680 Kiev, Ukraine
**Semerenko, Vita O** — Biathlete
Biathlon Federation, Vul Dimitrova 5, 03680 Kiev, Ukraine
**Seminara, Frank P** — Baseball Player
8029 Harbor View Terrace, Brooklyn NY 11209, USA
**Semiz, Teata** — Bowler
27 Burnside Place, Haskell NJ 07420, USA

| | |
|---|---|
| **Semizorova, Nina L** <br> Bolshoi Theater, Teatralnaya Pl 1, 103009 Moscow, Russia | Ballerina |
| **Semkow, Jerzy G** <br> Opus 3 Artists, 470 Park Ave S, #900N, New York NY 10016 USA | Conductor |
| **Semler, Dean** <br> 4260 Arcola Ave, Toluca Lake CA 91602, USA | Cinematographer, Director |
| **Semmelrogge, Martin** <br> Jondral Künstlermanagement, Schanzenstr 39, Gebaude E1, 51063 Cologne, Germany | Actor |
| **Sempe, Jean-Jacques** <br> 4 Rue du Moulin-Vert, 75014 Paris, France | Cartoonist |
| **Semple Thompson, Carol** <br> 2045 Henry Road, Sewickley PA 15143, USA | Golfer |
| **Semple, Maria** <br> Little Brown, 3 Center Plaza, #100, Boston MA 02108 USA | Writer, Producer |
| **Semple, Robert B, Jr** <br> New York Times, Editorial Dept, 229 W 43rd St, New York NY 10036 USA | Journalist |
| **Semproch, Roman A (Ray)** <br> 4220 Buechner Ave, Cleveland OH 44109, USA | Baseball Player |
| **Semyonov, Vladilen G** <br> 15/17-504 Roubinshteina St, 191002 Saint Petersburg, Russia | Ballet Dancer |
| **Sen, Amartya K** <br> Trinity College, Economics Dept, Cambridge CB2 1TQ, England | Nobel Economics Laureate |
| **Sen, Nandana** <br> Prinicipal Entertainment,130 W 42nd St, #614, New York NY 10036, USA | Actress |
| **Sen, Riya** <br> 62B Ruia Park, Huhu, Mumbai MS 400049, India | Actress, Model |
| **Sen, Sushmita** <br> Beach Queen, #600 Rd, Versova Andheri (W), Mumbai MS 400061, India | Beauty Queen, Actress |
| **Sena, Dominic** <br> W M E Entertainment, 9601 Wilshire Blvd, #300, Beverly Hills CA 90210 USA | Director |
| **Sendel, Peter** <br> Zallaer Str 9, 98599 Oberhof, Germany | Biathlete |
| **Senderens, Alain** <br> Restaurant Lucas Carton, 9 Place de la Madeleine, 75008 Paris, France | Chef |
| **Sendlein, Robin B** <br> 5645 Friars Road, #379, San Diego CA 92110, USA | Football Player |
| **Senior, Peter** <br> International Mangement Group, 1 Erieview Plaza, 1360 E 9th St, #100, Cleveland OH 44114 USA | Golfer |
| **Senna, Bruno** <br> Williams F1, Grove, Wantage, Oxfordshire OX12 0DQ, England | Auto Racing Driver |
| **Sennewald, Robert W** <br> 311 S Lee St, Alexandria VA 22314, USA | Army General |
| **Sensabaugh, Gerald L** <br> 12251 Heron Cove Court, Jacksonville FL 32218, USA | Football Player |
| **Sensibaugh, J Michael (Mike)** <br> 18414 Woodlands Terrace Dr, Glencoe MO 63038, USA | Football Player |
| **Sentelle, David B** <br> US Court of Appeals, 333 Constitution Ave NW, #4400, Washington DC 20001, USA | Judge |
| **Sepe, Crescenzio Cardinal** <br> Archdiocese of Naples, Largo Donnaregina 22, 80138 Naples, Italy | Religious Leader |
| **Sepulveda, Charlie** <br> Ralph Mercado Mgmt, 568 Broadway, #608, New York NY 10012, USA | Jazz Trumpeter |
| **Serafini, Daniel J (Dan)** <br> 4380 Garratt Circle, Sparks NV 89436, USA | Baseball Player |
| **Serafinowicz, Peter** <br> Troika, 74 Clerkenwell Road, #300, London EC1M 5QA, England | Actor, Comedian |
| **Seraphine, Oliver J** <br> 44 Green's Lane, Goodwill, Dominica | Prime Minister, Dominica |
| **Serbedzija, Rade** <br> United Agents, 12-26 Lexington St, London W1F 0LE, England | Actor |
| **Sereba, Nico** <br> Warner Bros Records, 3300 Warner Blvd, Burbank CA 91505 USA | Rap Artist, Singer (Nico & Vinz) |
| **Serebrier, Jose** <br> 20 Queensgate Gardens, London SW7 5LZ, England | Conductor, Composer |
| **Seredova, Alena** <br> Riccardo Gay Model Mgmt, Corso Vercelli 40, 20145 Milan, Italy | Model, Actress |
| **Sereno, Paul** <br> University of Chicago, Paleontology Dept, Chicago IL 60537, USA | Paleontologist |
| **Seres, Fiona** <br> Independent Talent Group, 40 Whitfield St, London W1T 2RH, England | Writer, Actress |
| **Seresin, Michael** <br> 59 N Wharf Road, London W2 1LA, England | Cinematographer |
| **Sereys, Jacques** <br> 84 Blvd Malesherbes, 75008 Paris, France | Actor |
| **Sergeant, Peta** <br> Principato-Young, 9465 Wilshire Blvd, #880, Beverly Hills CA 90212 USA | Actress, Director, Writer |
| **Sergei, Ivan** <br> McKeon-Myrones Mgmt, 3500 Olive Ave, #770, Burbank CA 91505 USA | Actor |
| **Serig, Jennifer** <br> Perception Public Relations, 13333 Ventura Blvd, #203, Sherman Oaks CA 91423, USA | Fashion Designer |
| **Serkin, Peter A** <br> C M Artists, 127 W 96th St, #13B, New York NY 10025 USA | Concert Pianist |
| **Serkis, Andy** <br> Lou Coulson Assoc, 37 Berwick St, London W1V 8RS, England | Actor |
| **Serlemitsos, Peter J** <br> B B X R T Project, Goddard Space Flight Center, Greenbelt MD 20771, USA | Astronomer |
| **Serlenga, Nikki** <br> 1489 Hawthorne Ave NW, Atlanta GA 30309, USA | Soccer Player |
| **Sermet, Huseyin** <br> Harrison/Parrott, 5-6 Albion Court, London W6 0QT, England | Composer, Concert Pianist |
| **Sermon, Erick** <br> I C M Partners, 10250 Constellation Blvd, #900, Los Angeles CA 90067 USA | Rap Artist (EPMD) |
| **Serna, Assumpta** <br> 8306 Wilshire Blvd, #438, Beverly Hills CA 90211, USA | Actress |
| **Serna, Pepe** <br> Jeffrey Leavitt Agency, 11500 W Olympic Blvd, #400, Los Angeles CA 90064, USA | Actor |

| | |
|---|---|
| **Serniz, Teata** <br> Professional Bowlers Association, 719 2nd Ave, #701, Seattle WA 98104 USA | Bowler |
| **Serota, Nicholas A** <br> Tate Britain, Millbank, London SW1P 4RG, England | Museum Executive |
| **Serowik, Jeff** <br> 371 Davisville Road, East Falmouth MA 02536, USA | Ice Hockey Player |
| **Serpico, Terry** <br> Don Buchwald Talent Agency, 6500 Wilshire Blvd, #2200, Los Angeles CA 90048 USA | Actor |
| **Serra, Eduardo** <br> United Agents, 12-26 Lexington St, London W1F 0LE, England | Cinematographer |
| **Serra, Richard** <br> 173 Duane St, New York NY 10013, USA | Sculptor |
| **Serralles, Jeanine** <br> Don Buchwald Talent Agency, 6500 Wilshire Blvd, #2200, Los Angeles CA 90048 USA | Actress |
| **Serrano, Jimmy** <br> 2943 E Erika Court, Grand Junction CO 81504, USA | Baseball Player |
| **Serrano, Nestor** <br> D2 Mgmt, 9255 Sunset Blvd, #600, West Hollywood CA 90069, USA | Actor |
| **Serratos, Christian** <br> Global Artists Agency, 6253 Hollywood Blvd, #508, Los Angeles CA 90028 USA | Actress |
| **Serre, Jean-Pierre** <br> 6 Ave de Montespan, 75116 Paris, France | Abel Mathematics Laureate |
| **Serreau, Coline** <br> Artmedia, 20 Ave Rapp, 75007 Paris, France | Director, Writer, Actress |
| **Servais, Scott D** <br> 4409 Triple Eagle Trail, Larkspur CO 80118, USA | Baseball Player |
| **Servan-Schreiber, Jean-Claude** <br> 147 Bis Rue d'Alesia, 75014 Paris, France | Journalist |
| **Server, Josh** <br> Amsel Eisenstadt Frazier, 5055 Wilshire Blvd, #865, Los Angeles CA 90036 USA | Actor |
| **Service, Scott D** <br> 9920 Prechtel Road, Cincinnati OH 45252, USA | Baseball Player |
| **Servis, John C** <br> 2649 Woodsview Dr, Bensalem PA 19020, USA | Thoroughbred Racing Trainer |
| **Servitto, Matt** <br> Abrams Artists, 275 7th Ave, #2600, New York NY 10001 USA | Actor |
| **Seshadri, Vijay** <br> Sarah Lawrence College, Writing Dept, 1 Mead Way, Bronxville/Yonkers NY 10708, USA | Writer |
| **Sesselmann, Lauren** <br> Canadian Soccer, Place Soccer Canada, 237 Metcalfe St, Ottawa ON K2P 1R2, Canada | Soccer Player |
| **Sessions, John** <br> Markham Froggatt Irwin, Julian House, 4 Windmill St, London W1P 1HF, England | Actor, Writer |
| **Sessions, Ramon** <br> Sacramento Kings, Arco Arena, 1 Sports Parkway, Sacramento CA 95834 USA | Basketball Player |
| **Sessions, Ronnie** <br> PO Box 242, Horseshoe Bend AR 72536, USA | Singer, Guitarist, Songwriter |
| **Sessions, William S** <br> 112 E Pecan St, #2900, San Antonio TX 78205, USA | Law Enforcement Official, Judge |
| **Sessler, Gerhard M** <br> Fichtenstra 30B, 64285 Darmstadt, Germany | Inventor (Telephone Microphone) |
| **Seth, Vikram** <br> Curtis Brown, 37 Queensferry St, Edinburgh EH2 4QS, Scotland | Writer |
| **Settani, Sandra** <br> Playboy Promotions, 9346 Civic Center Dr, #200, Beverly Hills CA 90210 USA | Model |
| **Settle, Matthew** <br> A P A Talent & Literary Agency, 405 S Beverly Dr, #300, Beverly Hills CA 90212 USA | Actor |
| **Setton, Amanda** <br> CornerStone Talent Agency, 37 W 20th St, #1107, New York NY 10011, USA | Actress |
| **Setzer, Brian** <br> W M E Entertainment, 9601 Wilshire Blvd, #300, Beverly Hills CA 90210 USA | Singer, Guitarist |
| **Setzer, Dennis** <br> Saint Paul's Church Road, #47A, Asheville NC 28803, USA | Auto, Truck Racing Driver |
| **Setzer, Philip** <br> I M G Artists, Burlington Lane, Chiswick, London W4 2TH, England | Violinist (Emerson String Quartet) |
| **Setziol-Phillips, Monica** <br> 542 NE Hill St, Sheridan OR 97378, USA | Sculptor |
| **Seubert, Richard A (Rich)** <br> 35 Oak Lane, Wayne NJ 07470, USA | Football Player |
| **Sevcik, Jaroslav** <br> Dalhousie Memorial Arena, 6185 South St, Halifax NS B3H 1T7, Canada | Ice Hockey Player |
| **Sevele, Feleti V** <br> Prime Minister's Office, PO Box 62, Taufa'ahau Road, Nuku'alofa, Tonga | Prime Minister, Tonga |
| **Severance, Joan** <br> PO Box 282, Carbondale CO 81623, USA | Model, Actress |
| **Severin, G Timothy (Tim)** <br> Inchybridge, Timoleague, County Cork, Ireland | Explorer |
| **Severinsen, Carl H (Doc)** <br> 11812 San Vicente Blvd, #200, Los Angeles CA 90049, USA | Jazz Trumpeter, Conductor |
| **Severinson, Albert H (Al)** <br> 133 Warren Ave, Mystic CT 06355, USA | Baseball Player |
| **Severson, Jeffrey K (Jeff)** <br> 216 College Park Dr, Seal Beach CA 90740, USA | Football Player |
| **Severson, John** <br> PO Box 10699, Lahaina HI 96761, USA | Publisher |
| **Severson, Kimberly (Kim)** <br> 631 Dobby Creek Road, Scottsville VA 24590, USA | Equestrian |
| **Severson, Richard A (Rich)** <br> 1036 N 145th Circle, Omaha NE 68154, USA | Baseball Player |
| **Severyn, Brent** <br> 4521 Avebury Dr, Plano TX 75024, USA | Ice Hockey Player |
| **Sevier, Corey** <br> Innovative Artists, 1505 10th St, Santa Monica CA 90401 USA | Actor |
| **Sevigny, Chloe** <br> W M E Entertainment, 9601 Wilshire Blvd, #300, Beverly Hills CA 90210 USA | Actress |
| **Seward, Adam H** <br> 8905 Coast Walk Circle, Las Vegas NV 89117, USA | Football Player |

**Sewell, Rufus**
Julian Belfrage Assoc, 9 Argyll St, #300, London W1F 7TG, England — Actor

**Sewell, Steven E (Steve)**
15918 E Crestridge Place, Centennial CO 80015, USA — Football Player

**Seweryn, Andrzej**
Comedie Francaise, Place Colette, 75001 Paris, France — Actor

**Sexsmith, Ron**
S L Feldman Mgmt, 1505 W 2nd Ave, #200, Vancouver BC V6H 3Y4, Canada — Singer, Songwriter

**Sexson, Richmond L (Richie)**
2828 NW Lakemont Dr, Bend OR 97701, USA — Baseball Player

**Sexton, Brendan, III**
Innovative Artists, 1505 10th St, Santa Monica CA 90401 USA — Actor

**Sexton, Brent**
Greene Assoc, 1901 Ave of Stars, #130, Los Angeles CA 90067 USA — Actor

**Sexton, Chad R**
311 Hive, 8904 Florence Dr, Omaha NE 68147, USA — Drummer (311)

**Sexton, Charlie**
Don Buchwald Talent Agency, 6500 Wilshire Blvd, #2200, Los Angeles CA 90048 USA — Actor

**Sexton, Jimmy D**
2680 Baxter Road, Wilmer AL 36587, USA — Baseball Player

**Sexton, John**
New York University, President's Office, Washington Square, New York NY 10012, USA — Educator

**Sexton, John W**
2217 Miner St, Costa Mesa CA 92627, USA — Photographer

**Sexton, Martin**
Red Light Mgmt, 925 W 7th Ave, Denver CO 80204, USA — Singer, Songwriter

**Sexton, Michael R (Mike)**
World Poker Tour Enterprises, 1920 Main St, #1150, Irvine CA 92615, USA — Poker Player

**Seydoux, Geraldine**
Johns Hopkins University, Molecular Biology Dept, Baltimore MD 21218, USA — Molecular Biologist, Geneticist

**Seydoux, Lea**
Creative Artists Agency, 2000 Ave of Stars, #100, Los Angeles CA 90067 USA — Actress

**Seyferth, Dietmar**
Massachusetts Institute of Technology, Chemistry Dept, Cambridge MA 02139, USA — Chemist

**Seyfried, Amanda**
Innovative Artists, 1505 10th St, Santa Monica CA 90401 USA — Actress

**Seyfried, Gordon C**
56428 Lowe Ave, Yucca Valley CA 92284, USA — Baseball Player

**Seymour, Cara**
Artists Partnership, 101 Finsbury Pavement, London EC2A 1RS, England — Actress

**Seymour, Jane**
Catfish Productions, 22631 Pacific Coast Highway, #313, Malibu CA 90265, USA — Actress

**Seymour, John**
239 S Helix Ave, #26, Solana Beach CA 92075, USA — Senator, CA

**Seymour, Lynn**
Artistes in Action, 16 Balderton St, London W1Y 1TF, England — Ballerina

**Seymour, Mark**
Loud & Clear Mgmt, PO Box 276, Albert Park VIC 3206, Australia — Singer, Songwriter

**Seymour, Paul C**
4188 Shoals Dr, Okemos MI 48864, USA — Football Player

**Seymour, Richard V**
862 Chattooga Trace, Suwanee GA 30024, USA — Football Player

**Seymour, Stephanie**
4180 Ruffin Road, #235, San Diego CA 92123, USA — Model

**Seymour, Stephanie K**
US Court of Appeals, US Courthouse, 333 W 4th St, #411, Tulsa OK 74103, USA — Judge

**Sezer, Ahmet Necdet**
Milli Savunma Bakanligi, 06100 Ankara, Turkey — President, Turkey

**Sfeir, Nasrallah Pierre Cardinal**
Patriarcat Maronite, Bkerke, Lebanon — Religious Leader

**Sgouros, Dimitris**
Tompazi 28 Str, Piraeus 18537, Greece — Concert Pianist

**Sgreccia, Elio Cardinal**
Sant'Angelo in Pescheria, Via della Tribuna di Campitelli 6, 00186 Rome, Lazio, Italy — Religious Leader

**Shaara, Jeff**
Ballatine Books, 1745 Broadway, New York NY 10019 USA — Writer

**Shaback, Nicholas (Nick)**
3019 49th St, Astoria NY 11103, USA — Basketball Player

**Shack, Edward S P (Eddie)**
508 Fairlawn Ave, North York ON M5M 1V2, Canada — Ice Hockey Player

**Shackelford, Ted**
12305 Valley Heart Dr, Studio City CA 91604, USA — Actor

**Shackleford, Charles E**
107 E Peyton Ave, Kinston NC 28501, USA — Basketball Player

**Shacochis, Bob**
Florida State University, Creative Writing Dept, Tallahassee FL 32306, USA — Writer

**Shadyac, Tom**
W M E Entertainment, 9601 Wilshire Blvd, #300, Beverly Hills CA 90210 USA — Director

**Shaeffer, William F**
12105 Ambassador Dr, #352, Colorado Springs CO 80921, USA — WW II, Korean War Air Force Hero

**Shafer, Martin**
Castle Rock Entertainment, 9169 W Sunset Blvd, West Hollywood CA 90069, USA — Producer, Writer

**Shaffer, Atticus**
Osbrink Talent Agency, 4343 Lankershim Blvd, #100, North Hollywood CA 91602 USA — Actor

**Shaffer, Kevin C**
5779 Legends Club Circle, Braselton GA 30517, USA — Football Player

**Shaffer, Lee P, II**
3822 Nottaway Road, Durham NC 27707, USA — Basketball Player

**Shaffer, Paul**
Panacea Entertainment, 13587 Andalusia Dr E, Camarillo CA 93012, USA — Orchestra Leader, Keyboardist

**Shaffer, Peter L**
Lantz, 888 7th Ave, #2500, New York NY 10106, USA — Writer

**Shagan, Steve**
10375 Wilshire Blvd, #10E, Los Angeles CA 90024, USA — Writer

**Shagari, A Shehu U A**
22 Shehu Crescent, PO Box 162, Adarawa, Sokoto State, Nigeria — President, Nigeria

**Shaggy**
Scikron Entertainment, PO Box 297350, Pembroke Pines FL 33029, USA — Singer

**Shagimuratova, Albina**
I M G Artists, Hogarth Business Park, Chiswick, London W4 2TH, England — Opera Singer

**Shaguch, Marina**
Columbia Artists Mgmt Inc, 5 Columbus Circle, 1790 Broadway, #1600, New York NY 10019 USA — Opera, Concert Singer

**Shah, Idries**
A P Watt Ltd, 26/28 Bedford Row, London WC1R 4HL, England — Writer

**Shah, Satish**
30A Anand Nagar, Forjeet St, Mumbai MS 400036, India — Actor, Comedian

**Shah, Sonal**
Don Buchwald Talent Agency, 6500 Wilshire Blvd, #2200, Los Angeles CA 90048 USA — Actress, Singer

**Shaham, Gil**
Canary Classics, Knifedge Ltd, 4 Margaret St, London W1W 8RF, England — Concert Violinist

**Shaham, Orli**
Opus 3 Artists, 470 Park Ave S, #900N, New York NY 10016 USA — Concert Pianist

**Shahi, Sarah**
McKeon-Myones Mgmt, 3500 W Olive Ave, #770, Burbank CA 91505, USA — Actress, Model

**Shaiman, Marc**
8476 Brier Dr, Los Angeles CA 90046, USA — Composer, Lyricist

**Shain, Irving**
8301 Old Sauk Road, #221, Middleton WI 53562, USA — Educator

**Shake, Christi**
Starr Entertainment, 2518 Lodge Forest Dr, Sparrows Point MD 21219, USA — Model

**Shakes, Paul**
RR 4 PO, Slayner ON L0M 1S0, Canada — Ice Hockey Player

**Shakespeare, Frank J, Jr**
303 Coast Blvd, La Jolla CA 92037, USA — Businessman, Diplomat

**Shakin' Stevens**
Agency Group Ltd, 142 W 57th St, #600, New York NY 10019 USA — Singer, Songwriter

**Shakira**
Creative Artists Agency, 2000 Ave of Stars, #100, Los Angeles CA 90067 USA — Singer, Songwriter

**Shakman, Matt**
W M E Entertainment, 9601 Wilshire Blvd, #300, Beverly Hills CA 90210 USA — Actor, Director

**Shalala, Donna E**
University of Miami, President's Office, Coral Gables FL 33124, USA — Secretary, Health & Human Services

**Shales, Thomas W**
Washington Post, Editorial Dept, 1150 15th St NW, Washington DC 20071, USA — Journalist

**Shalhoub, Tony**
I C M Partners, 10250 Constellation Blvd, #900, Los Angeles CA 90067 USA — Actor

**Shalit, Gene**
NBC-TV, News Dept, 30 Rockefeller Plaza, #270E, New York NY 10112 USA — Film Critic

**Sham, Brad M**
Dallas Cowboys, 1 Cowboys Parkway, Irving TX 75063 USA — Sportscaster

**Shamblin, Allen**
Built On Rock Music, PO Box 417, Franklin TN 37065, USA — Songwriter

**Shamsky, Art**
PO Box 1400, New York NY 10163, USA — Baseball Player

**Shanahan, Brendan F**
47 Saquatucket Bluffs Road, Harwich Port MA 02646, USA — Ice Hockey Player

**Shanahan, Michael E (Mike)**
20 Cherry Hills Farm Dr, Englewood CO 80113, USA — Football Coach

**Shand, David (Dave)**
307 N Harris St, Saline MI 48176, USA — Ice Hockey Player

**Shand, Remy**
S L Feldman Mgmt, 1505 W 2nd Ave, #200, Vancouver BC V6H 3Y4, Canada — Singer, Songwriter

**Shandling, Garry**
Creative Artists Agency, 2000 Ave of Stars, #100, Los Angeles CA 90067 USA — Actor, Comedian

**Shandrowsky, Alex**
Marine Engineer Beneficial Assn, 444 N Capitol St NW, Washington DC 20001, USA — Labor Leader

**Shane, Bob**
Fuji Productions, PO Box 34397, San Diego CA 92163, USA — Singer (Kingston Trio)

**Shange, Ntozake**
Saint Martin's Press, 175 5th Ave, #400, New York NY 10010, USA — Writer

**Shanice**
Performers of the World, 5657 Wilshire Blvd, #280, Los Angeles CA 90036 USA — Singer, Songwriter

**Shankar, Anoushka**
Opus 3 Artists, 470 Park Ave S, #900N, New York NY 10016 USA — Sitar Player, Singer, Composer

**Shankar, Naren**
Rothman Brecher Agency, 9465 Wilshire Blvd, #840, Beverly Hills CA 90212, USA — Producer, Writer

**Shankle, Joel**
16181 Berryvale Lane, Culpepper VA 22701, USA — Track Athlete

**Shankman, Adam**
United Talent Agency, U T A Plaza, 9336 Civic Center Dr, Beverly Hills CA 90210 USA — Director

**Shanks, Michael**
Don Buchwald Talent Agency, 6500 Wilshire Blvd, #2200, Los Angeles CA 90048 USA — Actor, Writer, Director

**Shanle, Scott**
3736 Loyola Dr, #263, Kenner LA 70065, USA — Football Player

**Shanley, John Patrick**
Creative Artists Agency, 2000 Ave of Stars, #100, Los Angeles CA 90067 USA — Writer

**Shannon, Carver B**
6005 S La Cienega Blvd, Los Angeles CA 90056, USA — Football Player

**Shannon, Colleen**
Identity Talent Agency, 9107 Wilshire Blvd, #450, Beverly Hills CA 90210 USA — Model

**Shannon, Darryl**
18 Landings Dr, Buffalo NY 14228, USA — Ice Hockey Player

**Shannon, Howard P (Howie)**
4009 Valdez Court, Plano TX 75074, USA — Basketball Player, Coach

**Shannon, Karissa**
Playboy Promotions, 9346 Civic Center Dr, #200, Beverly Hills CA 90210 USA — Model

**Shannon, Kristina**
Playboy Promotions, 9346 Civic Center Dr, #200, Beverly Hills CA 90210 USA — Model

**Shannon, Mem**
Miasma Mgmt, 1048 Hesper Ave, Metairie LA 70005, USA — Singer, Guitarist, Songwriter

**Shannon, Michael**
Creative Artists Agency, 2000 Ave of Stars, #100, Los Angeles CA 90067 USA — Actor

**Shelton, Lonnie J (L J)** — Football Player
6034 W Trovita Place, Chandler AZ 85226, USA

**Shelton, Lynn** — Director
United Talent Agency, U T A Plaza, 9336 Civic Center Dr, Beverly Hills CA 90210 USA

**Shelton, Marley C** — Actress
Untitled Entertainment, 350 S Beverly Dr, #200, Beverly Hills CA 90212 USA

**Shelton, Richard E** — Football Player
6367 Raw Hyde Trail N, Jacksonville FL 32210, USA

**Shelton, Ricky Van** — Singer, Guitarist, Songwriter
PO Box 111, Woodlawn VA 24381, USA

**Shelton, Robert N** — Educator
University of Arizona, President's Office, Tucson AZ 85721, USA

**Shelton, Ronald W (Ron)** — Director
Oasis Media Group, 8730 W Sunset Blvd, #PHW, Los Angeles CA 90069, USA

**Shelton, Samantha** — Actress
Untitled Entertainment, 350 S Beverly Dr, #200, Beverly Hills CA 90212 USA

**Shelton, Uriah** — Actor
Coronet Mgmt, 1438 N Gower St, Box 67, Los Angeles CA 90068, USA

**Shemi, Calman** — Artist
Jacques Soussana Graphics, 37 Pierre Koenig St, Jerusalem 91401, Israel

**Shen Wei** — Choreographer
Shen Wei Dance Arts, 520 8th Ave, #303, New York NY 10018, USA

**Shen Xue** — Figure Skater
Skating Association, 56 Zhonguancun South St, Beijing 100044, China

**Shen, Parry** — Actor
Stone Manners Salners, 6100 Wilshire Blvd, #1500, Los Angeles CA 90035 USA

**Shenandoh, Joanne** — Singer, Songwriter, Actress
Oneida Nation Territory, PO Box 450, Oneida NY 13421, USA

**Shengelaia, Eldar N** — Director, Writer
Ioseliani St 37, #58, 380091 Tbilisi, Georgia

**Shengelaia, Georgy N** — Director
Kekelidze St 16, #12, 380091 Tbilisi, Georgia

**Shenk, Thomas E** — Molecular Biologist
Princeton University, Molecular Biology Dept, Princeton NJ 08544, USA

**Shenkman, Ben** — Actor
Suskin Mgmt, 2 Charlton St, #5K, New York NY 10014, USA

**Shenton, Ann** — Synthesizer Player (Add N to X)
Kork Agency, 1880 Century Park E, #711, Los Angeles CA 90067 USA

**Shepard, Dax** — Actor
Creative Artists Agency, 2000 Ave of Stars, #100, Los Angeles CA 90067 USA

**Shepard, Devon** — Writer, Producer
I C M Partners, 10250 Constellation Blvd, #900, Los Angeles CA 90067 USA

**Shepard, Jean** — Singer
Midnight Special Productions, PO Box 916, Hendersonville TN 37077, USA

**Shepard, Jewel** — Actress, Model
A P A Talent & Literary Agency, 405 S Beverly Dr, #300, Beverly Hills CA 90212 USA

**Shepard, Jules** — Social Activist
7120 Minstrel Way, #206, Columbia MD 21045, USA

**Shepard, Richard** — Director, Writer
W M E Entertainment, 9601 Wilshire Blvd, #300, Beverly Hills CA 90210 USA

**Shepard, Roger N** — Psychologist
6041 Fair Oaks Blvd, Carmichael CA 95608, USA

**Shepard, Samuel K (Sam)** — Writer, Actor
I C M Partners, 730 5th Ave, New York NY 10019 USA

**Shepard, Vonda** — Singer, Songwriter
Marleah Leslie Assoc, 1645 Vine St, #712, Los Angeles CA 90028, USA

**Shepherd, Ben** — Bassist (Soundgarden)
Susan Silver Mgmt, 6523 California Ave SW, #348, Seattle WA 98136, USA

**Shepherd, Cybill** — Actress, Model
Don Buchwald Talent Agency, 6500 Wilshire Blvd, #2200, Los Angeles CA 90048 USA

**Shepherd, Elizabeth** — Actress
London Mgmt, 2-4 Noel St, London W1V 3RB, England

**Shepherd, Kenny Wayne** — Guitarist
Shepherd Entertainment, 1085 Crouch Road, Benton LA 71006, USA

**Shepherd, Morgan** — Auto, Truck Racing Driver
Shepherd Racing Ventures, 4905 Jeffrey Lane, Conover NC 28613, USA

**Shepherd, Neferteri** — Model
Amsel Eisenstadt Frazier, 5055 Wilshire Blvd, #865, Los Angeles CA 90036 USA

**Shepherd, Ronald W (Ron)** — Baseball Player
5821 FM 349, Kilgore TX 75662, USA

**Shepherd, Sherri** — Actress
Darris Hatch Management, 9538 Brighton Way, #308, Beverly Hills CA 90210 90210, USA

**Shepherd, Sherrie** — Cartoonist (Francie)
United Feature Syndicate, PO Box 5610, Cincinnati OH 45201 USA

**Shepherd, William M** — Astronaut
18623 Prince William Lane, Houston TX 77058, USA

**Sheppard, Anna** — Costume Designer
I C M Partners, 10250 Constellation Blvd, #900, Los Angeles CA 90067 USA

**Sheppard, Delia** — Actress, Model
Kazarian/Measures/Ruskin, 11969 Ventura Blvd, #300, Studio City CA 91604 USA

**Sheppard, Gregg** — Ice Hockey Player
2521 Blue Jay Crescent, North Battleford SK S9A 3Z3, Canada

**Sheppard, Henry F, Jr** — Football Player
313 Waterstone, Victoria TX 77901, USA

**Sheppard, Jonathan E** — Steeplechase Racing Trainer
287 Lamborn Town Road, West Grove PA 19390, USA

**Sheppard, Lito D** — Football Player
11001 Apple Blossom Trail E, Jacksonville FL 32218, USA

**Sheppard, Mark** — Actor
Artists Partnership, 101 Finsbury Pavement, London EC2A 1RS, England

**Sheppard, Ray** — Ice Hockey Player
19110 Fox Landing Dr, Boca Raton FL 33434, USA

**Sheppard, Scott S** — Astronomer
Carnegie Institution for Science, 1530 P St NW, Washington, DC 20005, USA

**Sheppard, T G** — Singer, Guitarist
R J Kaltenbach Personal Mgmt, PO Box 550, Harvard IL 60033, USA

**Sher, Antony** — Actor
I C M Partners, Marlborough House, 10 Earlham St, #300, London WC2H 9LNP, England

**Sher, Bartlett** — Director
Creative Artists Agency, 2000 Ave of Stars, #100, Los Angeles CA 90067 USA

**Sher, Eden** — Actress
A P A Talent & Literary Agency, 405 S Beverly Dr, #300, Beverly Hills CA 90212 USA

**Sher, Stacey** — Producer
Double Feature Films, 9320 Wilshire Blvd, #200, Beverly Hills CA 90212, USA

**Shera, Mark** — Actor
PO Box 15717, Beverly Hills CA 90209, USA

**Sherbedgia, Rade** — Actor
United Agents, 12-26 Lexington St, London W1F 0LE, England

**Sherffius, John** — Editorial Cartoonist
Saint Louis Post Dispatch, Editorial Dept, 900 N Tucker, Saint Louis MO 63101, USA

**Sheridan, Bonnie Bramlett** — Singer (Delaney & Bonnie), Actress
18011 Martha St, Encino CA 91316, USA

**Sheridan, Howard M** — Radiologist, Businessman
4020 Sheridan St, #B, Hollywood FL 33021, USA

**Sheridan, James P (Jamey)** — Actor
Brillstein Entertainment Partners, 9150 Wilshire Blvd, #350, Beverly Hills CA 90212 USA

**Sheridan, Jim** — Director, Producer
Hell's Kitchen International, 21 Mespil Road, Dublin 4, Ireland

**Sheridan, Liz** — Actress
Synergy Talent, 13251 Ventura Blvd, Studio City CA 91604, USA

**Sheridan, Nicolette** — Actress
Baker Winokur Ryder Public Relations, 9100 Wilshire Blvd, #500W, Beverly Hills CA 90212 USA

**Sheridan, Patrick A (Pat)** — Baseball Player
31654 Taft St, Wayne MI 48184, USA

**Sheridan, Ryan** — Singer, Guitarist, Songwriter
Sabrina Sheehan Mission Public Relations, 12-14 College Green, Dublin 2, Ireland

**Sheridan, Tayler** — Actress
Evolution Entertainment, 901 N Highland Ave, Los Angeles CA 90038 USA

**Sheridan, Tye** — Actor
Mosiac Media Group, 9200 W Sunset Blvd, #1000, Los Angeles CA 90069 USA

**Sherk, Jerry M** — Football Player
1518 Orangeview Dr, Encinitas CA 92024, USA

**Sherk, Kathy** — Golfer
1333 Dorval Dr, Oakville ON L6M 4G2, Canada

**Sherlock, Nancy J** — Astronaut
N A S A, Johnson Space Center, 2101 NASA Road, Houston TX 77058 USA

**Sherman, Alex (Allie)** — Football Player, Coach
136 E 55th St, #12H, New York NY 10022, USA

**Sherman, Bobby** — Singer, Actor
1870 Sunset Plaza Dr, Los Angeles CA 90069, USA

**Sherman, Cindy M** — Photographer
9 Debrosses St, #520A, New York NY 10032, USA

**Sherman, Heath B** — Football Player
PO Box 54, Glen Flora TX 77443, USA

**Sherman, Michael (Mickey)** — Attorney
Sherman & Richichi, 27 5th St, Stamford CT 06905, USA

**Sherman, Michael F (Mike)** — Football Coach
3337 Arapaho Ridge Dr, College Station TX 77845, USA

**Sherman, Patsy O** — Chemist, Inventor (Scotchgard)
1451 Highview Ave, Saint Paul MN 55121, USA

**Sherman, Richard K** — Football Player
Seattle Seahawks, 12 Seahawks Way, Renton WA 98056 USA

**Sherman, Richard M** — Composer, Lyricist
Cowans DeBaets Abrahams, 41 Madison Ave, 3400, New York NY 10010, USA

**Sherman, Rodney J (Rod)** — Football Player
PO Box 4551, Incline Village NV 89450, USA

**Sherman-Palladino, Amy** — Producer, Director, Writer
Creative Artists Agency, 2000 Ave of Stars, #100, Los Angeles CA 90067 USA

**Sherod, Edmund (Ed)** — Basketball Player
519 Montvale Ave, Richmond VA 23222, USA

**Sherrard, Michael W (Mike)** — Football Player
PO Box 992, Agoura Hills CA 91376, USA

**Sherrill, Betty** — Interior Designer
McMillen Inc, 155 E 56th St, #500, New York NY 10022, USA

**Sherrill, George F** — Baseball Player
1432 Villa Paloma Blvd, Little Elm TX 75068, USA

**Sherrington, Georgina** — Actress
J G M, 15 Lexham Mews, London W8 6JW, England

**Sherry, Fionnuala** — Violinist (Secret Garden)
Thranesgate 2B, Oslo 473, Norway

**Sherry, Norman B (Norm)** — Baseball Player, Manager
4383 Nobel Dr, #89, San Diego CA 92122, USA

**Sherven, Gord** — Ice Hockey Player
184 Hampshire Grove NW, Calgary AB T3A 5B3, Canada

**Sherwin, Timothy T (Tim)** — Football Player
6 Mill Road, Latham NY 12110, USA

**Sherwood, Alison** — Journalist
Milwaukee Journal Sentinel, Editorial Dept, PO Box 371, Milwaukee WI 53201 USA

**Sherwood, Brad** — Actor, Comedian
C E S D, 10635 Santa Monica Blvd, #130, Los Angeles CA 90025 USA

**Shesol, Jeff** — Cartoonist (Thatch)
Creators Syndicate, 737 3rd St, Hermosa Beach CA 90254 USA

**Sheth, Sheetal** — Actress
Defining Artists Agency, 10 Universal City Plaza, #2000, Universal City CA 91608, USA

**Shetty, Reshma** — Actress
Station 3 Entertainment, 300 W 55th St, #5L, New York NY 10019, USA

**Shetty, Sunil** — Actor
18/B Prithvi Apartments, Altamont Road, Mumbai MS 400026, India

**Shevchenki, Andriy** — Soccer Player
F C Milan, Via Filippo Turati 3, 20121 Milan, Italy

**Shi, David E** — Educator
Furman University, President's Office, Greenville SC 29613, USA

| | |
|---|---|
| **Shiancoe, Visanthe**<br>2316 City Place, Edgewater NJ 07020, USA | Football Player |
| **Shicoff, Neil**<br>Opera et Concert, 37 Rue de la Chaussee d'Antin, 75009 Paris, France | Opera Singer |
| **Shields, Ashley**<br>Atlanta Dream, 83 Walton St NW, #400, Atlanta, GA 30303 USA | Basketball Player |
| **Shields, Ben**<br>Abrams Artists, 9200 W Sunset Blvd, #1125, West Hollywood CA 90069 USA | Actor |
| **Shields, Blake**<br>Pakula/King, 9229 W Sunset Blvd, #315, West Hollywood CA 90069 USA | Actor |
| **Shields, Brooke**<br>United Talent Agency, U T A Plaza, 9336 Civic Center Dr, Beverly Hills CA 90210 USA | Model, Actress |
| **Shields, Perry**<br>US Tax Court, 400 2nd St NW, Washington DC 20217, USA | Judge |
| **Shields, R Scot**<br>16139 Pine Valley Dr, Northville MI 48168, USA | Baseball Player |
| **Shields, Robert**<br>Robert Shields Designs, PO Box 3161, Cottonwood AZ 86326, USA | Mime (Shields & Yarnell), Artist |
| **Shields, Stephen C (Steve)**<br>123 E Balboa Blvd, Newport Beach CA 92661, USA | Ice Hockey Player |
| **Shields, Stephen M (Steve)**<br>4969 Leonard Dr, Gadsden AL 35903, USA | Baseball Player |
| **Shields, Will H**<br>13125 W 127th Place, Overland Park KS 66213, USA | Football Player |
| **Shields, William D (Billy)**<br>12701 Treeridge Terrace, Poway CA 92064, USA | Football Player |
| **Shields, Willow**<br>I C M Partners, 10250 Constellation Blvd, #900, Los Angeles CA 90067 USA | Actress |
| **Shifflett, Steven E (Steve)**<br>24004 E 172nd St, Pleasant Hill MO 64080, USA | Baseball Player |
| **Shiffrin, Mikaela**<br>Jeffrey S Shiffrin, PO Box 6439, Vail CO 81658, USA | Alpine Skier |
| **Shiflett, Chris**<br>Silva Artists Mgmt, 722 Seward St, Los Angeles CA 90038, USA | Guitarist (Foo Fighters, Dead Peasants) |
| **Shifrin, David**<br>C M Artists, 127 W 96th St, #13B, New York NY 10025 USA | Concert Clarinetist |
| **Shifty Shellshock**<br>Q Prime, 729 7th Ave, #1600, New York NY 10019, USA | Rap Artist, Lyricist (Crazy Town) |
| **Shikler, Aaron**<br>Meredith Long Co, 2323 San Felipe St, Houston TX 77019, USA | Artist |
| **Shiller, Robert J**<br>Yale University, Cowles Foundation, PO Box 208281, New Haven CT 06520, USA | Economist |
| **Shima, Masatoshi**<br>Shima Co, 260 Tsurumaki, Omika Haramachishi, Fukushima 975 0049, Japan | Electronics Engineer |
| **Shimabukuro, Jake**<br>A P A Talent & Literary Agency, 405 S Beverly Dr, #300, Beverly Hills CA 90212 USA | Singer, Ukulele Player |
| **Shimell, William**<br>I M G Artists, Hogarth Business Park, Chiswick, London W4 2TH, England | Opera Singer |
| **Shimer, Brian**<br>2613 Lakeview Dr, Naples FL 34112, USA | Bobsled Athlete |
| **Shimerman, Armin**<br>Stone Manners Salners, 6100 Wilshire Blvd, #1500, Los Angeles CA 90035 USA | Actor |
| **Shimizu, Jenny**<br>Elite Model Mgmt, 404 Park Ave S, #900, New York NY 10016 USA | Model, Actress |
| **Shimkus, Joanna**<br>Creative Artists Agency, 2000 Ave of Stars, #100, Los Angeles CA 90067 USA | Actress |
| **Shimomura, Osamu**<br>324 Sippewissett Road, Falmouth MA 02540, USA | Nobel Chemistry Laureate |
| **Shimono, Sab**<br>12711 Ventura Blvd, #440, Studio City CA 91604, USA | Actor |
| **Shimony, Abner E**<br>16 Claflin Road, #2, Brookline MA 02445, USA | Physicist |
| **Shin Sang-Ho**<br>Hong-ik University, Sangsu Dong, Ma Po Gu, Seoul 121 791, South Korea | Sculptor |
| **Shin Yong-Moon**<br>National University, Sillimdong, Gwanakgu, Seoul 151 742, South Korea | Geneticist |
| **Shin, Jiyai**<br>Ladies Pro Golf Assn, 100 International Golf Dr, Daytona Beach FL 32124 USA | Golfer |
| **Shinabarger, Tim**<br>Legacy Gallery, 75 N Cache Ave, Box 4977, Jackson WY 83001, USA | Sculptor |
| **Shinall, Zakary S (Zak)**<br>16605 Sell Circle, Huntington Beach CA 92649, USA | Baseball Player |
| **Shindle, Katherine (Kate)**<br>Stewart Talent, 500 Bishop St NW, #A-2, Atlanta GA 30318, USA | Beauty Queen, Actress |
| **Shine, Michael (Mike)**<br>508 Royal Road, State College PA 16801, USA | Track Athlete |
| **Shiner, Richard E (Dick), Jr**<br>19 Fox Trail, Gettysburg PA 17325, USA | Football Player |
| **Shinji, Aoyama**<br>Beacon Alliance, 4-22-7-5F Ebidu, Shibuya, Tokyo 150 0013, Japan | Director, Writer, Composer |
| **Shinkoda, Peter**<br>Characters Talent Mgmt, 8 Elm St, Toronto ON M5G 1G7, Canada | Actor |
| **Shinners, J John T**<br>N120W14985 Freistadt Road, Germantown WI 53022, USA | Football Player |
| **Shinoda, Mike**<br>Gorfaine/Schwartz, 4111 W Alameda Ave, #509, Burbank CA 91505 USA | Singer (Linkin Park) |
| **Shinya, Hiromi**<br>Beth Israel Medical Center, Endoscopy Unit, 1st Ave & 16th St, New York NY 10461, USA | Gastroenterologist |
| **Shipka, Kiernan**<br>42 West, 11400 W Olympic Blvd, #1100, Los Angeles CA 90064 USA | Actress |
| **Shipler, David K**<br>4005 Thornapple St, Chevy Chase MD 20815, USA | Journalist |
| **Shipley, Craig B**<br>Boston Red Sox, Fenway Park, 4 Yawkey Way, Boston MA 02215 USA | Baseball Player |
| **Shipley, Jennifer M**<br>Club de Madrid, C/Goya 5-7, Pasaje 2, 28001 Madrid, Spain | Prime Minister, New Zealand |

**Shipley, Walter V** — Financier
Chase Manhattan Corp, 270 Park Ave, New York NY 10017, USA

**Shipman, Claire** — Commentator
ABC-TV, News Dept, 77 W 66th St, New York NY 10023 USA

**Shipp, Alexandra** — Actress
Osbrink Talent Agency, 4343 Lankershim Blvd, #100, North Hollywood CA 91602 USA

**Shipp, E R** — Columnist
New York Daily News, Editorial Dept, 220 E 42nd St, New York NY 10017, USA

**Shipp, Jerry** — Basketball Player
PO Box 370, Kingston OK 73439, USA

**Shipp, John Wesley** — Actor
Stewart Talent, 500 Bishop St NW, #A-2, Atlanta GA 30318, USA

**Shirakawa, Hideki** — Nobel Chemistry Laureate
University of Tsukuba, Chemistry Dept, Sakura-Mura, Ibaraki 000 305, Japan

**Shiraki, Ryan** — Director, Writer, Actor
A P A Talent & Literary Agency, 405 S Beverly Dr, #300, Beverly Hills CA 90212 USA

**Shire, David L** — Composer
250 Piermont Ave, Piermont NY 10968, USA

**Shire, Talia** — Actress, Director
10730 Bellagio Road, Los Angeles CA 90077, USA

**Shirk, Gary L** — Football Player
PO Box 287, Laporte PA 18626, USA

**Shirley, Barton A (Bart)** — Baseball Player
6538 Orangetip Dr, Corpus Christi TX 78414, USA

**Shirley, Danny** — Singer (Confederate Railroad)
Bobby Roberts, 3050 Business Park Circle, #303, Goodlettsville TN 37221 USA

**Shirley, George I** — Opera Singer
University of Michigan, Music School, Ann Arbor MI 48109, USA

**Shirley, John** — Writer
Tarcher/Penguin Press, 375 Hudson St, Basement 3, New York NY 10014, USA

**Shirley, Robert C (Bob)** — Baseball Player
761 W 13th St, Tulsa OK 74127, USA

**Shirreffs, John A** — Thoroughbred Racing Trainer
Hollywood Park Race Track, Barn 55 S, PO Box 369, Inglewood CA 90306, USA

**Shiver, Sanders T** — Football Player
16507 Ariel Court, Bowie MD 20716, USA

**Shivers, Chris** — Rodeo Bull Rider
192 Shivers Road, Jonesville LA 71343, USA

**Shivers, Roy L** — Football Player
2067 Hidden Hollow Lane, Henderson NV 89012, USA

**Shkaplerov, Anton N** — Cosmonaut
Cosmonaut Training Center, Star City, 141160 Zvezdny Gorodok, Moscow Oblast, Russia

**Shnapir, Simon** — Figure Skater
Skating Club of Boston, 1240 Soldiers Field Road, Brighton MA 02135, USA

**Shoals, Roger R** — Football Player
365 Righters Mill Road, Gladwyne PA 19035, USA

**Shobert, Don W (Bubba)** — Motorcycle Racing Rider
8905 153rd St, Wolfforth TX 79382, USA

**Shock G** — Rap Artist, Producer
Entertainment Artists, 2409 21st Ave S, #100, Nashville TN 10019 USA

**Shocked, Michelle** — Singer, Guitarist, Songwriter
Conqueroo, 11271 Ventura Blvd, #522, Studio City CA 91604 USA

**Shockley, J Costen** — Baseball Player
493 Wilson St, Georgetown DE 19947, USA

**Shockley, Jeremy C** — Football Player
1330 West Ave, #3601, Miami Beach FL 33139, USA

**Shockley, William** — Actor
JKA Talent Agency, 12725 Ventura Blvd, #H, Studio City CA 91604, USA

**Shoebottom, Bruce** — Ice Hockey Player
40 Woodfield Dr, Scarborough ME 04074, USA

**Shoecraft, John A** — Balloonist
Shoecraft Contracting Co, 7430 E Stetson Dr, Scottsdale AZ 85251, USA

**Shoemaker, Carolyn S** — Geologist, Astronomer
US Geological Survey, 2255 N Gemini Dr, Flagstaff AZ 86001, USA

**Shoemaker, Craig** — Actor, Comedian
Levity Entertainment Group, 6701 Center Drive W, #1111, Los Angeles CA 90045, USA

**Shoemaker, Robert M** — Army General
PO Box 768, Belton TX 76513, USA

**Shofner, Delbert M (Del)** — Football Player
1665 Del Mar Ave, San Marino CA 91108, USA

**Shofner, James (Jim)** — Football Player, Coach
9620 Champions Dr, Granbury TX 76049, USA

**Shoji, Dave** — Volleyball Coach
University of Hawaii, Athletic Dept, Hilo HI 96720, USA

**Shoji, Tadashi** — Fashion Designer
Tadashi Shoji Assoc, 3016 E 44th St, Vernon CA 90058, USA

**Shonekan, Ernest A O** — President, Nigeria
12 Alexander Ave, Ikoyi, Lagos, Nigeria

**Shonin, Georgi S** — Cosmonaut, Air Force General
Cosmonaut Training Center, Star City, 141160 Zvezdny Gorodok, Moscow Oblast, Russia

**Shonta, Charles J (Chuck)** — Football Player
17435 Ava Court, New Boston MI 48164, USA

**Shontelle** — Singer, Songwriter
Creative Artists Agency, 2000 Ave of Stars, #100, Los Angeles CA 90067 USA

**Shooter, Eric M** — Neurobiologist
370 Golden Oak Dr, Portola Valley CA 94028, USA

**Shopay, Thomas M (Tom)** — Baseball Player
10145 NW 19th St, Doral FL 33172, USA

**Shope, Allan** — Architect
Shope Reno Wharton, 18 Marshall St, #114, Norwalk CT 06854, USA

**Shoppach, Kelly B** — Baseball Player
6117 Forest River Dr, Fort Worth TX 76112, USA

**Shor, Miriam** — Actress
Impression Entertainment, 9229 W Sunset Blvd, #700, Los Angeles CA 90069, USA

**Shor, Peter W** — Applied Mathematician
47 Manor Ave, Wellesley MA 02482, USA

**Shore, David** — Writer, Producer
Shore Z Productions, 9100 Wilshire Blvd, #400W, Beverly Hills CA 90212, USA
**Shore, Gary** — Director, Producer
Anonymous Content, 3532 Hayden Ave, Culver City CA 90232 USA
**Shore, Howard** — Composer
Columbia Artists Mgmt Inc, 5 Columbus Circle, 1790 Broadway, #1600, New York NY 10019 USA
**Shore, Pauly** — Actor, Comedian
Innovative Artists, 1505 10th St, Santa Monica CA 90401 USA
**Shore, Roberta** — Actress
PO Box 71639, Salt Lake City UT 84171, USA
**Shore, Stephen** — Photographer
Bard College, Photography Dept, Annandale-on-Hudson NY 12504, USA
**Shores, Del** — Producer, Writer
Del Shores Productions, 8581 Santa Monica Blvd, #560, West Hollywood CA 90069, USA
**Shorr, Lonnie** — Actor, Comedian
W B A Entertainment, PO Box 281802, Nashville TN 37229, USA
**Short, Brandon D** — Football Player
6700 Fairview Road, #430, Charlotte NC 28210, USA
**Short, Columbus** — Actor
Brillstein Entertainment Partners, 9150 Wilshire Blvd, #350, Beverly Hills CA 90212 USA
**Short, Eugene** — Basketball Player
8111 Fondren Lake Dr, Houston TX 77071, USA
**Short, Margaret E** — Artist
105 Garibaldi St, Lake Oswego OR 97035, USA
**Short, Martin** — Actor, Comedian, Singer
Brillstein Entertainment Partners, 9150 Wilshire Blvd, #350, Beverly Hills CA 90212 USA
**Short, Purvis** — Basketball Player
8111 Fondren Lake Dr, Houston TX 77071, USA
**Short, Rick** — Baseball Player
3021 Forsythe Court, Peoria IL 61614, USA
**Short, Roger V** — Biologist
18 Gwingana Crescent, Glen Waverley VIC 3150, Australia
**Short, Wes** — Golfer
11128 Sea Hero Lane, Austin TX 78748, USA
**Short, William R (Bill)** — Baseball Player
2975 57th St, Sarasota FL 34243, USA
**Shorter, Frank** — Track Athlete
558 Utica Court, Boulder CO 80304, USA
**Shorter, Wayne** — Jazz Saxophonist, Composer
Universal Attractions, 135 W 26th St, #1200, New York NY 10001 USA
**Shorthill, Richard W** — Engineer
University of Utah, Mechanical Engineering Dept, Salt Lake City UT 84112, USA
**Shortridge, George** — Golfer
13896 Ironstone Trail NW, Anoka MN 55303, USA
**Shortridge, Kennedy F** — Microbiologist
University of Auckland, Medical Dept, PB 92019, Auckland, New Zealand
**Shortridge, Stephen C** — Actor, Artist
223 E Sherman Ave, Coeur D'Alene ID 83814, USA
**Shortz, Will** — Columnist
New York Times, Editorial Dept, 229 W 43rd St, New York NY 10036 USA
**Shostakovich, Maxim D** — Conductor, Concert Pianist
Columbia Artists Mgmt Inc, 5 Columbus Circle, 1790 Broadway, #1600, New York NY 10019 USA
**Shouse, Brian D** — Baseball Player
3121 W Summerbend Court, Peoria IL 61615, USA
**Shouse, Dexter** — Basketball Player
4523 E Rhonda Dr, Phoenix AZ 85018, USA
**Show Tha Product** — Rap Artist, Singer
Atlantic Records, 1290 Ave of Americas, Concourse 3, New York NY 10104 USA
**Show, Grant** — Actor
Innovative Artists, 1505 10th St, Santa Monica CA 90401 USA
**Showalter, Michael** — Actor, Producer, Writer
United Talent Agency, U T A Plaza, 9336 Civic Center Dr, Beverly Hills CA 90210 USA
**Showalter, William N (Buck), III** — Baseball Manager
9736 Hathaway St, Dallas TX 75220, USA
**Shower, Kathy** — Model, Actress
Playboy Promotions, 9346 Civic Center Dr, #200, Beverly Hills CA 90210 USA
**Shreve, Anita** — Writer
Little Brown, 3 Center Plaza, #100, Boston MA 02108 USA
**Shreve, Susan R** — Writer
3506 35th St NW, Washington DC 20016, USA
**Shribman, David M** — Journalist, Cartoonist
Boston Globe, Editorial Dept, 135 William Morrissey Blvd, Dorchester MA 02125 USA
**Shrimpton, Jean** — Model, Actress
Abbey Hotel, Penzance, Cornwall TR18 4AR, England
**Shriner, Kin** — Actor
63 Cavalry Road, Weston CT 06883, USA
**Shriner, Wil** — Entertainer, Director
5313 Quakertown Ave, Woodland Hills CA 91364, USA
**Shriver, Loren J** — Astronaut
2513 Nimbus Dr, Estes Park CO 80517, USA
**Shriver, Maria O** — Commentator
Hyperion Books, 114 5th Ave, New York NY 10011 USA
**Shriver, Pamela H (Pam)** — Tennis Player
8743 Mylander Lane, #R, Towson MD 21286, USA
**Shroff, Jackie** — Actor
1302 Le Pepeyon, Mount Mary Road, Bandra, Mumbai MS 400050, India
**Shrontz, Frank A** — Businessman
2949 81st Place, #P, Mercer Island WA 98040, USA
**Shtalenkov, Mikhail A** — Ice Hockey Player
7 Faenza, Newport Coast CA 92657, USA
**Shtokolov, Boris T** — Opera Singer
Kirov Ballet Theater, 1 Pl Iskusstr, 190000 Saint Petersburg, Russia
**Shu Qi** — Actress, Model
I M G Models, 8 Rue Danielle Casanova, 75002 Paris, France
**Shu, Yiqian** — Artist
30 SW 167th Ave, Beaverton OR 97006, USA

| | |
|---|---|
| **Shuchuk, Gary**<br>5713 Lancashier Court, Fitchburg WI 53711, USA | Ice Hockey Player |
| **Shue, Andrew**<br>Creative Artists Agency, 2000 Ave of Stars, #100, Los Angeles CA 90067 USA | Actor |
| **Shue, Elisabeth**<br>Management 360, 9111 Wilshire Blvd, Beverly Hills CA 90210 USA | Actress |
| **Shue, Eugene W (Gene)**<br>4338 Redwood Ave, #303, Marina del Rey CA 90292, USA | Basketball Coach, Executive |
| **Shuey, Paul K**<br>5252 Mill Dam Road, Wake Forest NC 27587, USA | Baseball Player |
| **Shuffield, Joey**<br>Russell Carter Artists, 567 Ralph Mcgill Blvd NE, Atlanta GA 30312, USA | Drummer (Fastball) |
| **Shui, Lan**<br>Singapore Symphony, 4 Battery Road #20-01, 049908 Singapore | Conductor |
| **Shukor, Sheikh Muszaphar**<br>Cosmonaut Training Center, Star City, 141160 Zvezdny Gorodok, Moscow Oblast, Russia | Cosmonaut |
| **Shula, David D (Dave)**<br>10805 Indian Trail, Cooper City FL 33328, USA | Football Coach |
| **Shula, Donald F (Don)**<br>16 Indian Creek Island Road, Indian Creek Village FL 33154, USA | Football Player, Coach |
| **Shula, Mike**<br>19140 Peninsula Club Dr, Cornelius NC 28031, USA | Football Player, Coach |
| **Shuler, Ellie G (Buck), Jr**<br>32 Willow Way W, Alexander City AL 35010, USA | Air Force General |
| **Shuler, Mickey C, Sr**<br>332 Belle Vista Dr, Marysville PA 17053, USA | Football Player |
| **Shulman, Douglas H**<br>Internal Revenue Service, 1111 Constitution Ave NW, Washington DC 20224, USA | Government Official |
| **Shulman, Julius**<br>314 E Arrellaga St, Santa Barbara CA 93101, USA | Interior Designer |
| **Shultz, George P**<br>776 Dolores St, Stanford CA 94305, USA | Secretary, State, Treasury & Labor |
| **Shum, Harry, Jr**<br>Innovative Artists, 1505 10th St, Santa Monica CA 90401 USA | Actor, Dancer |
| **Shumate, John H**<br>16406 S 12th Place, Phoenix AZ 85048, USA | Basketball Player, Coach |
| **Shumeyko Hegre, Luba**<br>Ocinum, Rua das Hortas, 9050-024 Funchal Madeira, Portugal | Model |
| **Shumpert, Terrance D (Terry)**<br>8432 Fairview Court, Lone Tree CO 80124, USA | Baseball Player |
| **Shure, Aaron**<br>Katz Golden Sullivan Rosenman, 2001 Wilshire Blvd, #400, Santa Monica CA 90403, USA | Writer, Producer |
| **Shuster, John**<br>Curling Association, 5525 Clem's Way, Stevens Point WI 54482 USA | Curling Athlete |
| **Shutler, Philip D**<br>8917 Braeburn Dr, Annandale VA 22003, USA | Marine Corps General |
| **Shutt, Stephen J (Steve)**<br>7814 Heritage Grand Place, Bradenton FL 34212, USA | Ice Hockey Player |
| **Shuttleworth, Mark**<br>H B D Venture Capital, PO Box 1159, Durbanville 7551, South Africa | Tourist Cosmonaut |
| **Shvachka, Anzhelina**<br>I M G Artists, Hogarth Business Park, Chiswick, London W4 2TH, England | Opera Singer |
| **Shved, Alexey V**<br>Philadelphia 76ers, 1st Union Center, 3601 S Broad St, Philadelphia PA 19148 USA | Basketball Player |
| **Shy, Leslie F (Les)**<br>512 N McClurg Court, #3611, Chicago IL 60611, USA | Football Player |
| **Shyamalan, M Night**<br>W M E Entertainment, 9601 Wilshire Blvd, #300, Beverly Hills CA 90210 USA | Director, Writer |
| **Shyne**<br>Entertainment Artists, 2409 21st Ave S, #100, Nashville TN 10019 USA | Rap Artist |
| **Sia, Beau**<br>Creative Artists Agency, 2000 Ave of Stars, #100, Los Angeles CA 90067 USA | Actor |
| **Siana**<br>2113 Cocoa Circle, Virginia Beach VA 23454, USA | Model |
| **Siani, Michael J (Mike)**<br>3601 W Broadway, #25-102, Columbia MO 65203, USA | Football Player |
| **Siaosi Tupov V**<br>Royal Palace, PO Box 6, Nuku'alofa, Tonga | King, Tonga |
| **Sibbett, Jane**<br>Mitchell K Stubbs Assoc, 8695 W Washington Blvd, #204, Culver City CA 90232 USA | Actress |
| **Siberry, Jane**<br>Sheeba Records, 238 Davenport Road, #291, Toronto ON M5R 1J6, Canada | Singer, Songwriter |
| **Sibley, Antoinette**<br>Royal Dancing Academy, 36 Battersea Square, London SW11 3LT, England | Ballerina |
| **Sichting, Jerry L**<br>3190 Country Club Road, Martinsville IN 46151, USA | Basketball Player, Executive |
| **Siddall, Joseph C (Joe)**<br>2785 Sierra Dr, Windsor ON N9E 2Y9, Canada | Baseball Player |
| **Siddig, Alexander**<br>Markham Froggatt Irwin, Julian House, 4 Windmill St, London W1P 1HF, England | Actor |
| **Siddons, Anne R**<br>767 Vermont Road, Atlanta GA 30319, USA | Writer |
| **Sidibe, Gabourey**<br>United Talent Agency, U T A Plaza, 9336 Civic Center Dr, Beverly Hills CA 90210 USA | Actress |
| **Sidibe, Modibo**<br>Prime Minister's Office, BP 97, Bamako, Mali | Prime Minister, Mali |
| **Sidlin, Murray**<br>Catholic University, Music School, Washington DC 20064, USA | Conductor |
| **Sidney, Dainon T**<br>605 Lakemeade Point, Old Hickory TN 37138, USA | Football Player |
| **Sido**<br>Aggro Berlin, Postfach 613134, 10942 Berlin, Germany | Rap Artist |
| **Sidora, Drew**<br>I C M Partners, 10250 Constellation Blvd, #900, Los Angeles CA 90067 USA | Actress |
| **Sidorenko, Wladimir**<br>Universum Boxing Promotion, Am Stadtrand 27, 22047 Hamburg, Germany | Boxer |

**Sidorkiewicz, Peter** — Ice Hockey Player
1056 Swiss Heights, Oshawa ON L1K 3B4, Canada
**Sidorski, Sergei S** — Prime Minister, Belarus
Prime Minister's Office, Pl Nezavisimosti, 220010 Minsk, Belarus
**Sidran, Ben** — Jazz Entertainer, Composer
Blue Moon/Go Jazz Records, PO Box 2023, Madison WI 53701, USA
**Siebels, Jonathan L (Jon)** — Guitarist (Eve 6)
Agency Group Ltd, 1880 Century Park E, #711, Los Angeles CA 90067 USA
**Siebern, Norman L (Norm)** — Baseball Player
4181 5th Ave NW, Naples FL 34119, USA
**Siebert, Wilfred C (Sonny)** — Baseball Player
2583 Brush Creek Road, Saint Louis MO 63129, USA
**Siebler, Dwight L** — Baseball Player
11565 S 204th St, Gretna NE 68028, USA
**Sieg, Derek** — Director, Writer
United Agents, 12-26 Lexington St, London W1F 0LE, England
**Siega, Marcos** — Director
Creative Artists Agency, 2000 Ave of Stars, #100, Los Angeles CA 90067 USA
**Siegal, John W (Johnny)** — Football Player
PO Box 47, Harvey's Lake PA 18618, USA
**Siegel, Barry** — Journalist
Los Angeles Times, Editorial Dept, 202 W 1st St, Los Angeles CA 90012 USA
**Siegel, Bernard S (Bernie)** — Surgeon, Writer
61 Oxbow Lane, Woodbridge CT 06525, USA
**Siegel, Dan** — Pianist, Composer
Central Entertainment Group, 251 W 39th St, New York NY 10018, USA
**Siegel, David** — Director, Producer, Writer
W M E Entertainment, 9601 Wilshire Blvd, #300, Beverly Hills CA 90210 USA
**Siegel, Eric** — Actor
I C M Partners, 10250 Constellation Blvd, #900, Los Angeles CA 90067 USA
**Siegel, Herbert J** — Businessman
Chris-Craft Industries, 55 E 59th St, #22B, New York NY 10022, USA
**Siegel, Janis** — Singer (Manhattan Transfer)
I C M Partners, 730 5th Ave, New York NY 10019 USA
**Siegel, Jay** — Singer, Guitarist (Tokens)
Brothers Management Assoc, 141 Dunbar Ave, Fords NJ 08863 USA
**Siegel, Mike** — Actor, Comedian
Parallel Entertainment, 9420 Wilshire Blvd, #250, Beverly Hills CA 90212 USA
**Siegel, Randolph** — Publisher
Parade, Publisher's Office, 711 3rd Ave, New York NY 10017, USA
**Siegel, Robert** — Architect
Gwathmey-Siegel Architects, 475 10th Ave, #300, New York NY 10018, USA
**Siegel, Robert C** — Commentator
National Public Radio, 635 Massachusetts Ave NW, #1, Washington DC 20001, USA
**Siegfried** — Animal Illusionist (Siegfried & Roy)
Kirvin Doak Communications, 7935 W Sahara Ave, #201, Las Vegas NV 89117, USA
**Siekevitz, Philip** — Cell Biologist
290 W End Ave, New York NY 10023, USA
**Siemaszko, Casey** — Actor
Abrams Artists, 9200 W Sunset Blvd, #1125, West Hollywood CA 90069 USA
**Siemaszko, Nina** — Actress
Vanguard Management Group, 8060 Melrose Ave, #400, Los Angeles CA 90046, USA
**Sieminski, Charles L (Chuck)** — Football Player
5000 Village Way, #406, Marcus Hook PA 19061, USA
**Siemionow, Maria** — Reconstructive Surgeon
Cleveland Clinic, 9500 Euclid Ave, Cleveland OH 44195 USA
**Siemon, Jeffrey G (Jeff)** — Football Player
5401 Londonderry Road, Minneapolis MN 55436, USA
**Siena, James** — Artist
83 Canal St, #508, New York NY 10002, USA
**Siering, Laura G (Lauri)** — Swimmer
PO Box 1352, Tres Pinos CA 95075, USA
**Sierra, Gregory** — Actor
3374 Punta Alta, #C, Laguna Woods CA 92637, USA
**Sierra, Ruben A** — Baseball Player
12355 SW 51st St, Miami Fl 33175, USA
**Siers, Kevin** — Editorial Cartoonist
Charlotte Observer, Editorial Dept, 600 S Tryon St, Charlotte NC 28202, USA
**Sievers, Eric** — Football Player
11550 Great Falls Way, Great Falls VA 22066, USA
**Sievers, Roy E** — Baseball Player
11505 Bellefontaine Road, Saint Louis MO 63138, USA
**Sievwright, Ebe** — Actor
Associated International Mgmt, 7 Hatton Garden, #400, London EC1N 8AD, England
**Siew, Vincent C** — Prime Minister, Taiwan
Kuomintang, #232-234, Sec 2, BaDe Road, Zhongshan District, Taipei, Taiwan
**Siff, Maggie** — Actress
Paradigm Agency, 360 N Crescent Dr, North Building, Beverly Hills CA 90210 USA
**Sifford, Charlie** — Golfer
7540 Sanctuary Circle, Brecksville OH 44141, USA
**Sigel, Beanie** — Rap Artist, Actor, Composer
Big Bloc Entertainment, 2 Bala Plaza, #300, Bala Cynwyd PA 19004, USA
**Sigel, Jay** — Golfer
1284 Farm Road, Berwyn PA 19312, USA
**Sigel, N Thomas (Tom)** — Cinematographer
I C M Partners, 10250 Constellation Blvd, #900, Los Angeles CA 90067 USA
**Sigfridsson, Margaretha** — Curling Athlete
Skelleftea Curling Club, Mossgatan 27, 931 70 Skelleftea, Sweden
**Sights, Shay** — Actress
15030 Ventura Blvd, #556, Sherman Oaks CA 91403, USA
**Siglar, Ricky A** — Football Player
13901 Newton St, #406, Overland Park KS 66223, USA
**Sigler, Jamie-Lynn** — Actress, Singer
Paradigm Agency, 360 N Crescent Dr, North Building, Beverly Hills CA 90210 USA
**Sigler, John C** — Association Executive
National Rifle Association, 11250 Waples Mill Road, Fairfax VA 22030, USA

| | |
|---|---|
| **Sigman, Stan**<br>Cingular Wireless, 5565 Glenridge Connector, Atlanta GA 30342, USA | Businessman |
| **Sigman, Stephanie**<br>I C M Partners, 10250 Constellation Blvd, #900, Los Angeles CA 90067 USA | Actress |
| **Sihol, Caroline**<br>Artmedia, 20 Ave Rapp, 75007 Paris, France | Actress |
| **Siilasvuo, Ensio**<br>Castrenikatu 6A17, 00530 Helsinki 53, Finland | Army General, Finland |
| **Siimann, Mart**<br>Riigikugu, Lossi Plats 1A, Tallinn 0100, Estonia | Prime Minister, Estonia |
| **Sikahema, Vai**<br>28 Abington Road, Mount Laurel NJ 08054, USA | Football Player |
| **Sikander, Shahzia**<br>Deitch Projs, 76 Grand St, New York NY 10013, USA | Artist |
| **Sikes, Cynthia**<br>Defining Artists Agency, 4370 Tujunga Ave, #120, Studio City CA 91604, USA | Actress |
| **Sikharulidze, Anton T**<br>Skating Federation, Luznetskaya Nab 8, 119871 Moscow, Russia | Figure Skater |
| **Sikking, James B**<br>258 S Carmelina Ave, Los Angeles CA 90049, USA | Actor |
| **Sikma, Jack W**<br>9125 NE 21st Place, Clyde Hill WA 98004, USA | Basketball Player |
| **Sikorski, Brian**<br>17930 Wexford St, Roseville MI 48066, USA | Baseball Player |
| **Sikovetsky, Dimitry**<br>I M G Artists, Hogarth Business Park, Chiswick, London W4 2TH, England | Conductor, Concert Violinist |
| **Silajdzic, Haris**<br>President's Office, Marsala Titz 7, 71000 Sarajevo, Bosnia & Herzegovina | Co-Prime Minister, Bosnia & Herzegovina |
| **Silas, James E**<br>6800 Thistle Hill Way, Austin TX 78754, USA | Basketball Player |
| **Silas, Paul T**<br>2463 Peninsula Shores Court, Denver NC 28037, USA | Basketball Player, Coach |
| **Silas, Samuel L (Sam)**<br>PO Box 308, Hawthorne NJ 07507, USA | Football Player |
| **Silatolu, Ratu Timoci**<br>Prime Minister's Office, New Government Buildings, 6 Berkeley Crescent, Suva, Viti Levu, Fiji | Prime Minister, Fiji |
| **Silberling, Bradley (Brad)**<br>United Talent Agency, U T A Plaza, 9336 Civic Center Dr, Beverly Hills CA 90210 USA | Director, Writer |
| **Silberman, Laurence H**<br>US Court of Appeals, 333 Constitution Ave NW, #4400, Washington DC 20001, USA | Judge, Diplomat |
| **Silberstein, Diane Wichard**<br>Playboy, Publisher's Office, 680 N Lake Shore Dr, Chicago IL 60611, USA | Publisher |
| **Silbey, Robert J**<br>Massachusetts Institute of Technology, Chemistry Dept, Cambridge MA 02139, USA | Chemist |
| **Siler, Eugene E, Jr**<br>403 Sycamore St, #1, Williamsburg KY 40769, USA | Judge |
| **Silfverberg, Jakob**<br>Anaheim Ducks, 2695 E Katella Ave, Anaheim CA 92806 USA | Ice Hockey Player |
| **Silja, Anja**<br>Artists Mgmt, Rutistr 52, 8044 Zurich, Switzerland | Opera Singer |
| **Silk, Alexandria**<br>396 Bethany St, Thousand Oaks CA 91360, USA | Exotic Dancer, Model |
| **Silk, Anna**<br>K G Talent, 55-1/2 Sumach St, Toronto, ON M5A 3J6, Canada | Actress |
| **Silk, David M (Dave)**<br>PO Box 130, Minot MA 02055, USA | Ice Hockey Player |
| **Sill, Aleta**<br>Professional Bowlers Association, 719 2nd Ave, #701, Seattle WA 98104 USA | Bowler |
| **Silla, Felix**<br>5313 Magenta Court, Las Vegas NV 89108, USA | Actor |
| **Sillas, Karen**<br>PO Box 725, Wading River NY 11792, USA | Actress |
| **Silliman, Ron**<br>262 Orchard Road, Paoli PA 19301, USA | Writer |
| **Sillinger, Mike**<br>Edmonton Oilers, 11230 110th St, Edmonton AB T5G 3H7, Canada | Ice Hockey Player, Executive |
| **Sillman, Amy**<br>705 Driggs Ave, Brooklyn NY 11211, USA | Artist |
| **Sills, Douglas (Doug)**<br>TalentWorks, 3500 W Olive Ave, #1400, Burbank CA 91505 USA | Actor, Singer |
| **Sills, Stephen**<br>Sills Huniford Assoc, 30 E 67th St, #300, New York NY 10065, USA | Architect, Interior Designer |
| **Silpa, Mitch**<br>OmniPop Talent Group, 4605 Lankershim Blvd, #201, Toluca Lake CA 91602 USA | Actor, Comedian |
| **Siltala, Michael (Mike)**<br>1693 Ruscombe Close, Mississauga ON L5J 1Y4, Canada | Ice Hockey Player |
| **Silva, Alan Jones**<br>Cirque du Soleil, 8400 2nd Ave, Montreal QC H1Z 4M6, Canada | Circus Tightrope Walker |
| **Silva, Anibal Antonio Cavaco**<br>President's Office, Palacio de Belem, Calcada da Ajuda 11, 1349022 Lisbon, Portugal | President, Portugal |
| **Silva, Carlos**<br>280 Bergamot Dr, Hamel MN 55340, USA | Baseball Player |
| **Silva, Daniel**<br>3512 Winfield Lane NW, Washington DC 20007, USA | Writer |
| **Silva, Henry**<br>8747 Clifton Way, #305, Beverly Hills CA 90211, USA | Actor |
| **Silva, Jose L**<br>401 Pappan Dr, Imperial PA 15126, USA | Baseball Player |
| **Silva, Thiago E**<br>Confederacion de Futebol, Rua Victor Civita 66, #1, Rio de Janeiro 22775 044, Brazil | Soccer Player |
| **Silver, Adam**<br>National Basketball Association, 645 5th Ave, #1800, New York NY 10022 USA | Basketball Executive |
| **Silver, Joan Micklin**<br>Silverfilm Productions, 510 Park Ave, #9B, New York NY 10022, USA | Director, Producer, Writer |
| **Silver, Joel**<br>Silver Pictures, 4000 Warner Blvd, Burbank CA 91522, USA | Producer |

**Silver, Joshua D** — Inventor (Adjustable Corrective Glasses)
Clarendon Laboratory, Parks Road, Oxford OX1 3PU, England
**Silver, Nathaniel A (Nate)** — Statistician
New York Times, FiveThirtyEight, Editorial Dept, 229 W 43rd St, New York NY 10036, USA
**Silver, Nicky** — Writer
W M E Entertainment, 9601 Wilshire Blvd, #300, Beverly Hills CA 90210 USA
**Silver, Noah** — Actor
Artists Partnership, 101 Finsbury Pavement, London EC2A 1RS, England
**Silver, Scott** — Director, Writer
Creative Artists Agency, 2000 Ave of Stars, #100, Los Angeles CA 90067 USA
**Silvera, Charles A R (Charlie)** — Baseball Player
1240 Manzanita Dr, Millbrae CA 94030, USA
**Silverberg, Robert** — Writer
PO Box 13160, Station E, Oakland CA 94661, USA
**Silveri, Scott** — Producer, Writer
W M E Entertainment, 9601 Wilshire Blvd, #300, Beverly Hills CA 90210 USA
**Silverio, Luis P** — Baseball Player
9600 NW 58th Court, Parkland FL 33076, USA
**Silverman, Barry G** — Judge
US Court of Appeals, 230 N 1st St, Phoenix AZ 85004, USA
**Silverman, Henry R** — Businessman
Cendant Corp, 9 W 57th St, New York NY 10019, USA
**Silverman, Jerry** — Harness Racing Trainer
540 Christina Dr, #106, Wellington FL 33414, USA
**Silverman, Jonathan** — Actor
Untitled Entertainment, 350 S Beverly Dr, #200, Beverly Hills CA 90212 USA
**Silverman, Kenneth E** — Writer, Educator
New York University, English Dept, 19 University Place, New York NY 10003, USA
**Silverman, Peter** — Writer
Paradigm Agency, 360 N Crescent Dr, North Building, Beverly Hills CA 90210 USA
**Silverman, Sarah** — Actress, Comedienne, Producer
Creative Artists Agency, 2000 Ave of Stars, #100, Los Angeles CA 90067 USA
**Silvers, Robert** — Artist
Henry Holt, 175 5th Ave, #400, New York NY 10010 USA
**Silverstein, Craig** — Producer, Writer
W M E Entertainment, 9601 Wilshire Blvd, #300, Beverly Hills CA 90210 USA
**Silverstein, Joseph H** — Conductor, Concert Violinist
Utah Symphony Orchestra, 123 W South Temple, Salt Lake City UT 84101, USA
**Silverstone, Alicia** — Actress
United Talent Agency, U T A Plaza, 9336 Civic Center Dr, Beverly Hills CA 90210 USA
**Silvestri, Alan A** — Composer
Gorfaine/Schwartz, 4111 W Alameda Ave, #509, Burbank CA 91505 USA
**Silvestri, David J (Dave)** — Baseball Player
15511 Country Mill Court, Chesterfield MO 63017, USA
**Silvestrini, Achille Cardinal** — Religious Leader
San Benedetto Fuori Porta S Paolo, Via del Gazometro 23, 00186 Rome, Lazio, Italy
**Silvetti, Jorge** — Architect
Machado & Silvetti, 500 Harrison Ave, Boston MA 02118, USA
**Silvia** — Queen Consort, Sweden
Kungliga Slottet, Stottsbacken, 111 30 Stockholm, Sweden
**Silvstedt, Victoria** — Model, Actress
Abrams Artists, 9200 W Sunset Blvd, #1125, West Hollywood CA 90069 USA
**Sim, Jonathan (Jon)** — Ice Hockey Player
104 Willow Ave, New Glasgow NS B2H 1Z5, Canada
**Sim, Keong** — Actor
A K A Talent, 6310 San Vicente Blvd, #200, Los Angeles CA 90048 USA
**Sima, Raymond Ndong** — Prime Minister, Gabon
Prime Minister's Office, BP 91, Immeuble du 2 Decembre, Libreville, Gabon
**Simanek, Robert E** — Korean War Marine Corps Hero (CMH)
25194 Westmoreland Dr, Farmington Hills MI 48336, USA
**Simas, William A (Bill)** — Baseball Player
6084 Millerton Road, Friant CA 93626, USA
**Simbomana, Adrien** — Prime Minister, Burundi
PO Box 2251, Vugizo, Bujumbura, Burundi
**Sime, David W (Dave)** — Track Athlete, Physician
9140 Bay Dr, Surfside FL 33154, USA
**Simenc, Zlatko** — Water Polo Player
Loparska 3, 10000 Zagreb, Croatia
**Simeone, Diane M** — Oncologist
University of Michigan Comprehensive Cancer Center, 1500 E Medical Center Dr, Ann Arbor MI 48109, USA
**Simeoni, Sara** — Track Athlete
Via di Castello, Veronese 32, 37010 Rivoli Verona, Italy
**Simes, John W (Jack), II** — Cyclist
7753 Probst Hill Road, New Tripoli PA 18066, USA
**Simic, Charles** — Writer
PO Box 192, Strafford NH 03884, USA
**Simien, Tracy A** — Football Player
409 N Martin Luther King St, Sweeny TX 77480, USA
**Simitis, Konstantinos (Kostas)** — Prime Minister, Greece
Maximus Mansion, Herodou Atticou 19, 10674 Athens, Greece
**Simmer, Charlie** — Ice Hockey Player
70 Coulee View SW, Calgary AB T3H 5J6, Canada
**Simmonds, Kennedy A** — Prime Minister, Saint Kitts & Nevis
PO Box 167, Earle Morne Development, Basseterre, Saint Kitts & Nevis
**Simmonds, Kim** — Guitarist (Savoy Brown)
Ozark Talent, 718 Schwarz Road, Lawrence KS 66049, USA
**Simmons, Adele S** — Foundation Executive, Educator
Catherine T MacArthur Foundation, 140 S Dearborn St, #1000, Chicago IL 60603, USA
**Simmons, Bill** — Sportscaster
ESPN-TV, Sports Dept, ESPN Plaza, 935 Middle St, Bristol CT 06010 USA
**Simmons, Brian E** — Football Player
6417 Lake Burden Way Dr, Windermere FL 34786, USA
**Simmons, Brian L** — Baseball Player
226 Village Dr, Canonsburg PA 15317, USA
**Simmons, Chelan** — Actress
Intellectual Artists Mgmt, 10585 Santa Monica Blvd, #135, Los Angeles CA 90025, USA

| | |
|---|---|
| **Simmons, Clyde, Jr**<br>3948 3rd St S, #344, Jacksonville Beach FL 32250, USA | Football Player |
| **Simmons, Curtis T (Curt)**<br>200 Park Road, Ambler PA 19002, USA | Baseball Player |
| **Simmons, Dan**<br>Baror International, PO Box 868, Armonk NY 10504, USA | Writer |
| **Simmons, Don**<br>4998 Skerkston Road, RR 1, Ridgway ON L0S 1N9, Canada | Ice Hockey Player |
| **Simmons, Gene**<br>Gene Simmons Co, PO Box 16075, Beverly Hills CA 90209, USA | Singer, Bassist (Kiss) |
| **Simmons, H A Kendall**<br>1725 Altamont Court, Auburn AL 36830, USA | Football Player |
| **Simmons, Harris H**<br>Zions Bancorp, 1 S Main St, Salt Lake City UT 84133, USA | Financier |
| **Simmons, Henry**<br>Principato-Young, 9465 Wilshire Blvd, #880, Beverly Hills CA 90212 USA | Actor |
| **Simmons, J K**<br>Gersh Agency, 41 Madison Ave, #3301, New York NY 10010 USA | Actor |
| **Simmons, Jerry B**<br>30227 Avenida Selecta, Rancho Palos Verdes CA 90275, USA | Football Player |
| **Simmons, Johnny**<br>I C M Partners, 10250 Constellation Blvd, #900, Los Angeles CA 90067 USA | Actor |
| **Simmons, Joseph**<br>Richard Walters, PO Box 2789, Toluca Lake CA 91610 USA | Rap Artist (Run-DMC) |
| **Simmons, Kimora Lee**<br>Phat Fashions, 512 Fashion Ave, #4300, New York NY 10018, USA | Model, Fashion Designer |
| **Simmons, Lili**<br>I C M Partners, 10250 Constellation Blvd, #900, Los Angeles CA 90067 USA | Actress, Model |
| **Simmons, Lionel J**<br>108 Wellesley Court, Mount Laurel NJ 08054, USA | Basketball Player |
| **Simmons, Nelson B**<br>4445 Rosebud Lane, #B, La Mesa CA 91941, USA | Baseball Player |
| **Simmons, Richard**<br>Celebrities Plus, 8899 Beverly Blvd, #811, Los Angeles CA 90048, USA | Physical Fitness Instructor, Producer |
| **Simmons, Robert G (Bob)**<br>16040 Chalfont Circle, Dallas TX 75248, USA | Football Player |
| **Simmons, Rudd**<br>Claire Best Assoc, 736 Seward St, Los Angeles CA 90038, USA | Producer |
| **Simmons, Russell**<br>Simmons-Lathan Media Group, 6100 Wilshire Blvd, #1111, Los Angeles CA 90048, USA | Music Producer, Fashion Designer |
| **Simmons, Ruth J**<br>Brown University, President's Office, Providence RI 02912, USA | Educator |
| **Simmons, Tabitha**<br>Tabitha Simmons Accessories, 601 W 26th St, #309, New York, NY 10001, USA | Stylist, Shoe Designer |
| **Simmons, Ted L**<br>PO Box 26, Chesterfield MO 63006, USA | Baseball Player |
| **Simms, Christopher D (Chris)**<br>811 Lynnbrook Road, Nashville TN 37215, USA | Football Player |
| **Simms, Larry**<br>3441 Lewis Ave, Long Beach CA 90807, USA | Actor |
| **Simms, Michael E (Mike)**<br>PO Box 96011, Southlake TX 76092, USA | Baseball Player |
| **Simms, Philip (Phil)**<br>930 Old Mill Road, Franklin Lakes NJ 07417, USA | Football Player, Sportscaster |
| **Simms, Travis**<br>28 Martin Luther King, #43, South Norwalk CT 06854, USA | Boxer |
| **Simollardes, Drew**<br>David Levin Mgmt, 200 W 57th St, #308, New York NY 10019, USA | Singer (Reveille) |
| **Simon, Alfredo S**<br>Cincinnati Reds, Great American Ball Park, 100 Main St, Cincinnati OH 45202 USA | Baseball Player |
| **Simon, Arndt**<br>Max Planck Institute, Solid State Institute, Heisenberg Str 1, 70569 Stuttgart, Germany | Chemist |
| **Simon, Bob**<br>CBS-TV, News Dept, 2020 M St NW, Washington DC 20036 USA | Commentator |
| **Simon, Carly**<br>Ciancia Mgmt, 1 William Morris Place, Beverly Hills CA 90212, USA | Singer, Songwriter |
| **Simon, Chris**<br>PO Box 1, Wawa ON P0S 1K0, Canada | Ice Hockey Player |
| **Simon, Corey J**<br>3081 Obrien Dr, Tallahassee FL 32309, USA | Football Player |
| **Simon, David**<br>Creative Artists Agency, 2000 Ave of Stars, #100, Los Angeles CA 90067 USA | Producer, Writer, Actor |
| **Simon, Dick**<br>24896 SeaCrest Dr, Dana Point CA 92829, USA | Auto Racing Executive |
| **Simon, George W**<br>PO Box 62, Sunspot NM 88349, USA | Astronaut |
| **Simon, Hugh**<br>Artists Partnership, 101 Finsbury Pavement, London EC2A 1RS, England | Actor |
| **Simon, James E (Jim)**<br>8501 SW 103rd Ave, Gainesville FL 32608, USA | Football Player |
| **Simon, John I**<br>New York Magazine, Editorial Dept, 444 Madison Ave, #1400, New York NY 10022, USA | Film, Drama Critic |
| **Simon, Josette**<br>Conway Van Gelder Grant, 8-12 Broadwick St, #300, London W1F 8HW, England | Actress |
| **Simon, Leon M**<br>Stanford University, Mathematics Dept, Stanford CA 94305, USA | Mathematician |
| **Simon, Lou Anna**<br>Michigan State University, President's Office, East Lansing MI 48824, USA | Educator |
| **Simon, Melvin I**<br>California Institute of Technology, Biology Dept, Pasadena CA 91125, USA | Biologist |
| **Simon, Neil**<br>350 Park Ave, #1600, New York NY 10022, USA | Writer |
| **Simon, Paul**<br>Paul Simon Music, 1619 Broadway, #500, New York NY 10019, USA | Singer, Guitarist, Songwriter |
| **Simon, Sam**<br>Paradigm Agency, 360 N Crescent Dr, North Building, Beverly Hills CA 90210 USA | Producer, Writer, Animator |

**Simon, Scott**
NBC-TV, News Dept, 30 Rockefeller Plaza, #270E, New York NY 10112 USA — Commentator, Writer
**Simonds, Charles F**
26 E 22nd St, New York NY 10010, USA — Sculptor, Architect
**Simone, Hannah**
Alpita Patel Management, 7336 Santa Monica Blvd, #745, West Hollywood CA 90046, USA — Actress
**Simoneau, Mark L**
1018 Park Ave, Rose Hill KS 67133, USA — Football Player
**Simoneau, Yves**
W M E Entertainment, 9601 Wilshire Blvd, #300, Beverly Hills CA 90210 USA — Director
**Simonini, Edward C (Ed)**
3825 E 66th St, Tulsa OK 74136, USA — Football Player
**Simonis, Adrianus J Cardinal**
Aartsbisdom, BP 14019, Maliebaan, 3508 Utrecht SB, Netherlands — Religious Leader
**Simonischek, Maximilian**
Agentur Carola Studlar, Agnesstr 47, 80798 Munich, Germany — Actor
**Simonov, Yuriy I**
Moscow Symphony Orchestra, Gorky Park, 9 Krymsky Val, 119049 Moscow, Russia — Conductor
**Simons, Douglas E (Doug)**
1988 Mount Olive Road, Lookout Mountain GA 30750, USA — Baseball Player
**Simons, Ed**
9PR, 65-69 White Lion St, London N1 9PR, England — Singer, Musician (Chemical Brothers)
**Simons, Elwyn L**
Duke University, Primate Center, 3705 Erwin Road, Durham NC 27705, USA — Anthropologist
**Simons, Kai L**
Max-Planck-Molekulare Zellbiologie-Institut, 01307 Dresden, Germany — Biochemist
**Simons, Raf**
House of Dior, 30 Ave Montaigne, 75008 Paris, France — Fashion Designer
**Simons, Timothy (Tim)**
United Talent Agency, U T A Plaza, 9336 Civic Center Dr, Beverly Hills CA 90210 USA — Actor
**Simonyan, Mikhail**
I M G Artists, Carnegie Hall Tower, 152 W 57th St, #500, New York NY 10019 USA — Concert Violinist
**Simonyi, Charles**
International Software Corp, 2821 Northup Way, #250, Bellevue WA 98004, USA — Tourist Cosmonaut
**Simpkins, L Dixon (Dickey)**
6104 Saint Andrews Way, Hixson TN 37343, USA — Basketball Player
**Simpson, Alan**
Yellow Gate Farm, Little Compton RI 02837, USA — Educator
**Simpson, Alan K**
1201 Sunshine Ave, PO Box 270, Cody WY 82414, USA — Senator, WY
**Simpson, Ashlee**
Creative Artists Agency, 2000 Ave of Stars, #100, Los Angeles CA 90067 USA — Singer, Songwriter, Actress
**Simpson, Bill**
Simpson Performance Products, 328 FM 306, New Braunfels TX 78130, USA — Auto Racing Executive
**Simpson, Bobby**
4779 Limestone Lane NW, Acworth GA 30102, USA — Ice Hockey Player
**Simpson, Carl W**
2507 Brentwood Road, Decatur GA 30032, USA — Football Player
**Simpson, Carole**
ABC-TV, News Dept, 77 W 66th St, New York NY 10023 USA — Commentator
**Simpson, Charles R**
US Tax Court, 400 2nd St NW, Washington DC 20217, USA — Judge
**Simpson, Claire**
Independent Talent Group, 40 Whitfield St, London W1T 2RH, England — Film Editor
**Simpson, Cody**
PO Box 1766, Studio City CA 91614, USA — Singer, Songwriter
**Simpson, Craig**
CBC-TV, PO Box 500, Station A, Toronto ON M5W 1E6, Canada — Ice Hockey Player
**Simpson, Daryl**
PO Box 32, Kells, County Meath, Ireland — Singer (Celtic Tenors)
**Simpson, Derrick (Duckie)**
Agency Group, 1100 Century Park E, #711, Los Angeles CA 90067 USA — Singer (Black Uhuru)
**Simpson, Geoffrey**
PO Box 3194, Bellevue Hills NSW 2023, Australia — Cinematographer
**Simpson, J F Webb**
Professional Golfers Association, 100 Ave of Champions, Palm Beach Gardens FL 33418 USA — Golfer
**Simpson, Jessica**
J T Entertaiment, 14804 Greenleaf St, Sherman Oaks CA 91403, USA — Singer, Songwriter, Actress, Model
**Simpson, Jimmi**
W M E Entertainment, 9601 Wilshire Blvd, #300, Beverly Hills CA 90210 USA — Actor
**Simpson, Joe A**
4681 Jefferson Township Lane, Marietta GA 30066, USA — Baseball Player
**Simpson, Josh**
Frank Williams Road, Shelburne Falls MA 01370, USA — Artist
**Simpson, Juliene Brazinski**
PO Box 1267, Stroudsburg PA 18360, USA — Basketball Player
**Simpson, Martin**
Moneypenny Agency, Stables, Main St, North Dalton, Driffield East Yorkshire YO25 9XA, England — Guitarist
**Simpson, Orenthal James (O J)**
Lovelock Correctional Center, #1027820, 1200 Prison Road, Lovelock NV 89419, USA — Football Player, Actor, Sportscaster
**Simpson, Ralph D**
7578 S Duquesne Way, Aurora CO 80016, USA — Basketball Player
**Simpson, Richard C (Dick)**
PO Box 3593, Culver City CA 90231, USA — Baseball Player
**Simpson, Scott**
15778 Paseo Hermosa, Poway CA 92064, USA — Golfer
**Simpson, Suzi**
24338 El Toro Road, #E315, Laguna Woods CA 92637, USA — Model, Actress
**Simpson, Timothy J (Tim)**
1061 Spy Glass Hill, Greensboro GA 30642, USA — Golfer
**Simpson, Tom**
Big Life Mgmt, 67-69 Charlton St, London NW1 1HY, England — Keyboardist (Snow Patrol)
**Simpson, Valerie**
Spirit Media, PO Box 43591, Phoenix AZ 85080, USA — Singer (Ashford & Simpson), Songwriter
**Simpson, Wayne K**
330 E Collamer Dr, Carson CA 90746, USA — Baseball Player

**Simpson, William (Will)**
PO Box 211957, Royal Palm Beach FL 33421, USA — Equestrian

**Simpson, William T (Bill)**
5732 Huntley Ave, Garden Grove CA 92845, USA — Football Player

**Simpson-Miller, Portia L**
Prime Minister's Office, 1 Devon Road, PO Box 272, Kingston 6, Jamaica — Prime Minister, Jamaica

**Sims, Allan E (Al)**
4215 Winding Way Dr, Fort Wayne IN 46835, USA — Ice Hockey Player

**Sims, Barry A**
369 Golden Grass Dr, Alamo CA 94507, USA — Football Player

**Sims, Billy R**
PO Box 3147, Coppell TX 75019, USA — Football Player

**Sims, Christopher A (Chris)**
Princeton University, Economics Dept, Princeton NJ 08544, USA — Economist

**Sims, Darryl**
University of Wisconsin, Athletic Dept, Kolf Sports Center, Oshkosh WI 54901, USA — Football Player

**Sims, Duane B (Duke)**
10509 Shoalhaven Dr, Las Vegas NV 89134, USA — Baseball Player

**Sims, Jocko**
Benedetti Management, 13101 W Washington Blvd, #234, Culver City CA 90066, USA — Actor

**Sims, Keith A**
1522 SW 37th St, Fort Lauderdale FL 33312, USA — Football Player

**Sims, Kenneth W (Ken)**
PO Box 236, Kosse TX 76653, USA — Football Player

**Sims, Molly**
W M E Entertainment, 9601 Wilshire Blvd, #300, Beverly Hills CA 90210 USA — Model, Actress

**Sims, Neil**
Paradigm Agency, 360 Park Ave, #1600, New York NY 10022 USA — Drummer (Catherine Wheel)

**Sims, Robert A (Bob)**
915 Highland Ave, #3, Duarte CA 91010, USA — Basketball Player

**Sims, Ryan O**
311 Yellow Poplar Terrace, Spartanburg SC 29306, USA — Football Player

**Sinatra, Christina (Tina)**
30966 Broach Beach Road, Malibu CA 90265, USA — Actress, Writer

**Sinatra, Frank, Jr**
Universal Attractions, 135 W 26th St, #1200, New York NY 10001 USA — Singer, Actor

**Sinatra, Nancy**
Universal Attractions, 135 W 26th St, #1200, New York NY 10001 USA — Singer, Actress

**Sinatro, Matthew S (Matt)**
2619 239th Ave SE, Sammamish WA 98075, USA — Baseball Player

**Sinbad**
A P A Talent & Literary Agency, 405 S Beverly Dr, #300, Beverly Hills CA 90212 USA — Actor, Comedian

**Sinclair, Christine M**
Western New York Flash, Sahlen Sports Park, 7070 Seneca St, Elma NY 14059, USA — Soccer Player

**Sinclair, Claire**
Playboy Promotions, 9346 Civic Center Dr, #200, Beverly Hills CA 90210 USA — Model, Actress

**Sinclair, Clive M**
Sinclair Research, 7 York Central, 70 York Way, London N1 9AG, England — Inventor (Pocket Calculator)

**Sinclair, Michael G (Mike)**
1914 Pannell St, Houston TX 77020, USA — Football Player

**Sinclair, Nancy**
Studio Talent Group, 1328 12th St, Santa Monica CA 90401, USA — Actress

**Sindelar, Joey**
18 Prospect Ridge, Horseheads NY 14845, USA — Golfer

**Sinden, Harold J (Harry)**
9 Olde Village Dr, Winchester MA 01890, USA — Ice Hockey Player, Coach, Executive

**Sinegal, James D**
Costco Wholesale Corp, 999 Lake Dr, #200, Issaquah WA 98027, USA — Businessman

**Singer, Bryan**
Bad Hat Productions, 10201 W Pico Blvd, Building 50, Los Angeles CA 90064, USA — Director, Producer

**Singer, Eric W**
E D M Productions, 11684 Ventura Blvd, #408, Studio City CA 91604, USA — Drummer (Kiss, Alice Cooper)

**Singer, Eric Warren**
Creative Artists Agency, 2000 Ave of Stars, #100, Los Angeles CA 90067 USA — Writer, Producer, Actor

**Singer, Isadore M**
Massachusetts Institute of Technology, Mathematics Dept, Cambridge MA 02139, USA — Abel Mathematics Laureate

**Singer, Jerome L**
Yale University, Zigler Center, New Haven CT 06520, USA — Psychologist

**Singer, Lori**
Jackoway Tyerman Wertheimer, 1925 Century Park E, #2200, Los Angeles CA 90067 USA — Actress

**Singer, Marc**
David Shapira Assoc, 193 N Robertson Blvd, Beverly Hills CA 90211 USA — Actor

**Singer, Maxine F**
5410 39th St NW, Washington DC 20015, USA — Educator, Molecular Biochemist

**Singer, Peter A D**
Princeton University, Human Values Center, Princeton NJ 08544, USA — Philosopher, Ethicist

**Singer, Rachel**
Bauman Assoc, 250 W 57th St, #2223, New York NY 10107 USA — Actress

**Singer, William R (Bill)**
1119 Mallard Marsh Dr, Osprey FL 34229, USA — Baseball Player

**Singh, Amrita**
Lokhandwala Complex, #5, Andheri Link Road, Mumbai MS 400058, India — Actress

**Singh, Bipin**
Manipuri Nartanalaya, 15A Bipin Pal Road, Kolkata 700026, India — Dancer, Choreographer

**Singh, Tjinder**
Zzonked Public Relations, Burford Road, London E15 2SP, England — Singer (Cornershop)

**Singh, Vijay**
210 N Serenata Dr, #532, Ponte Vedra Beach FL 32082, USA — Golfer

**Singletary, Daryle**
Bobby Roberts, 3050 Business Park Circle, #303, Goodlettsville TN 37221 USA — Singer

**Singletary, Michael (Mike)**
18601 Turnbridge Dr, Dallas TX 75252, USA — Football Player, Coach

**Singletary, Tony**
A P A Talent & Literary Agency, 405 S Beverly Dr, #300, Beverly Hills CA 90212 USA — Director

**Singleton, Chris**
6025 Carol St, San Diego CA 92115, USA — Football Player

Singleton, Christopher V (Chris)                                    Baseball Player
2038 Town Manor Court, Dacula GA 30019, USA
Singleton, Isaac                                                           Actor
Coolwaters Productions, 10061 Riverside Dr, Box 531, Toluca Lake CA 91602 USA
Singleton, Kenneth W (Kenny)                                       Baseball Player
10 Sparks Farm Road, Sparks MD 21152, USA
Singleton, Margie                                                          Singer
Country Music Spectacular, PO Box 567, Hendersonville TN 37077, USA
Singleton, William D                                                      Publisher
MediaNews Group, 101 W Colfax Ave, Denver CO 80202, USA
Sinha, Mala                                                                Actress
8 Turner Road, Bandra, Mumbai MS 400050, India
Sinha, Shatrughan                                                          Actor
104 Green Star Apts, Sherly Rajan Road, Bandra, Mumbai MS 400050, India
Sinisalo, Ikka                                                     Ice Hockey Player
6221 Main St, Voorhees NJ 08043, USA
Sinise, Gary                                                               Actor
Polaris Productions, 8135 W 4th St, #200, Los Angeles CA 90048, USA
Sinise, Moira                                                             Actress
Creative Artists Agency, 2000 Ave of Stars, #100, Los Angeles CA 90067 USA
Sinkford, William                                                  Religious Leader
Unitarian Universalist Assn, President's Office, 25 Beacon St, Boston MA 02108, USA
Sinn, Pearl                                                               Golfer
132 21st Place, Manhattan Beach CA 90266, USA
Sinner, George A                                                    Governor, ND
6218 14th St S, Fargo ND 58104, USA
Sinsheimer, Robert L                                             Biologist, Educator
4606 Via Cavente, Santa Barbara CA 93110, USA
Sinyavskaya, Tamara I                                              Opera Singer
Kunstleragentur Raab & Bohm, Plankengasse 7, 1010 Vienna, Austria
Siorpaes, Gildo                                                   Bobsled Athlete
Olympic Committee, Foro Italico, Largo Lauro de Bosis 15, 00135 Rome, Italy
Siouxsie Sioux                                        Singer (Siouxsie & the Banshees)
Helter Skelter, 347-353 Chiswick High Road, London W4 4HS, England
Sipchen, Bob                                                             Journalist
Los Angeles Times, Editorial Dept, 202 W 1st St, Los Angeles CA 90012 USA
Sipe, Brian W                                                     Football Player
1630 Luneta Dr, Del Mar CA 92014, USA
Sipinen, Arto K                                                         Architect
Munkkiniemenranta 39, 00330 Helsinki, Finland
Sipos, Shaun                                                              Actor
Innovative Artists, 1505 10th St, Santa Monica CA 90401 USA
Sir Mix-A-Lot                                                           Rap Artist
Entertainment Artists, 2409 21st Ave S, #100, Nashville TN 10019 USA
Siraguso, Tony                                          Football Player, Sportscaster
15 Annabelle Lane, Florham Park NJ 07932, USA
Sircar, Tiya                                                             Actress
John Carrabino Mgmt, 5900 Wilshire Blvd, #406, Los Angeles CA 90036, USA
Siren, Heikki                                                           Architect
Tiirasaarentie 35, 00200 Helsinki, Finland
Siren, Katri A H                                                        Architect
Tiirasaarentie 35, 00200 Helsinki, Finland
Siren, Ville                                                       Ice Hockey Player
Saint Louis Blues, Scottrade Center, 1401 Clark Ave, Saint Louis MO 63103 USA
Sirgo, Otto                                                        Actor, Director
Televisa, Blvd A Lopez Mateos 232, Colonia San Angel, Mexico City DF 01060 CP, Mexico
Siri Singh Sahib                                                   Religious Leader
Sikh, PO Box 351149, Los Angeles CA 90035, USA
Sirico, Tony                                                              Actor
McGowan Mgmt, 8733 W Sunset Blvd, #103, West Hollywood CA 90069 USA
Sirikit                                                           Queen, Thailand
Royal Residence, Chitralada Villa, 9 Rama VI Road, Soi 30, Bangkok 10400, Thailand
Sirindhorn                                                       Princess, Thailand
Royal Residence, Chitralada Villa, 9 Rama VI Road, Soi 30, Bangkok 10400, Thailand
Sirleaf, Ellen Johnson                       President, Liberia; Nobel Peace Laureate
President's Office, Executive Mansion, Capitol Hill, Monrovia, Liberia
Sirmon, Peter A                                                   Football Player
5729 Sterling Oaks Dr, Brentwood TN 37027, USA
Sirola, Joseph A                                                          Actor
T G M D Talent, 6767 Forest Lawn Dr, #101, Los Angeles CA 90068, USA
Sirtis, Marina                                                            Actress
Polaris Entertainment, 8048 W 3rd St, #300, Los Angeles CA 90048 USA
Sisemore, Jerald G (Jerry)                                       Football Player
17301 Whippoorwill Trail, Leander TX 78645, USA
Sisi, Abdel Fattah al-                              President, Army General, Egypt
Presidential Palace, Abdin, Qasr El-Nile St, Cairo CA002, Egypt
Sisk, Douglas R (Doug)                                            Baseball Player
3610 42nd Ave NE, Tacoma WA 98422, USA
Sisk, Tommie W                                                    Baseball Player
164 E 4635 N, Provo UT 84604, USA
Siska, Adam T                                                  Bassist (Academy Is)
Decaydance Records, 9229 W Sunset Blvd, #900, West Hollywood CA 90069, USA
Siskin, Paul                                                     Interior Designer
Siskin Valls Inc, 21 W 58th St, #2B, New York NY 10019, USA
Sislen, Myrna                                                   Concert Guitarist
Lindy Martin Mgmt, 1007 Lakewater Dr, Henrico VA 23229, USA
Sisley, Tomer                                             Actor, Director, Writer
Cineart, 28 Rue Mogador, 78009 Paris, France
Sisqo                                                          Singer (Dru Hill)
Davis Shapiro Lewit Hayes, 150 S Rodeo Dr, #200, Beverly Hills CA 90212, USA
Sissel                                                                    Singer
Continental A/s, PO Box 143, 2051 Jessheim, Norway
Sister Bliss                                                  Musician (Faithless)
Helter Skelter, 347-353 Chiswick High Road, London W4 4HS, England
Sister Max                                                       Fashion Designer
Mount Everest Centre for Buddhist Studies, Katmandu, Nepal

**Sisto, Jeremy** — Actor
Gersh Agency, 9465 Wilshire Blvd, #600, Beverly Hills CA 90212 USA

**Sistrunk, Manuel (Manny)** — Football Player
3856 Williams Road, Montgomery AL 36110, USA

**Sistrunk, Otis** — Football Player
PO Box 372, Dupont WA 98327, USA

**Sitbon, Martine** — Fashion Designer
6 Rue de Braque, 75003 Paris, France

**Sites, Brian** — Actor
Innovative Artists, 1505 10th St, Santa Monica CA 90401 USA

**Sitkovetsky, Dmitry** — Concert Violinist, Conductor
Kunstleragentur Raab & Bohm, Plankengasse 7, 1010 Vienna, Austria

**Sittenfeld, Curtis** — Writer
Random House, 1745 Broadway, #1800, New York NY 10019 USA

**Sittler, Darryl G** — Ice Hockey Player
18 Jedburgh Road, Toronto ON M5M 3J6, Canada

**Sittler, Walter** — Actor
Agentur Heppeler, Seinstr 54, 81667 Munich, Germany

**Sitton, Charles E (Charlie)** — Basketball Player
3035 SW Homesteader Road, West Linn OR 97068, USA

**Sivad, Darryl** — Actor
Commercial Talent, 12711 Ventura Blvd, #285, Studio City CA 91604, USA

**Siwy, James G (Jim)** — Baseball Player
6919 April Wind Ave, Las Vegas NV 89131, USA

**Siza, Alvaro** — Pritzker Architectural Laureate
Oporto University, Architecture School, 4150 755 Oporto, Portugal

**Sizemore, Grady, III** — Baseball Player
1951 W 26th St, #512, Cleveland OH 44113, USA

**Sizemore, Ted C** — Baseball Player
14030 Conway Road, Chesterfield MO 63017, USA

**Sizemore, Tom** — Actor
Global Artists Agency, 6253 Hollywood Blvd, #508, Los Angeles CA 90028 USA

**Sizova, Alla I** — Ballerina
Universal Ballet School, 4301 Harewood Road NE, Washington DC 20017, USA

**Sjoberg, Patrik** — Track Athlete
Hokegatan 17, 416 66 Goteberg, Sweden

**Sjoland, Patrik** — Golfer
PGA European Tour, Wentworth Drive, Virginia Water Surrey GU25 4LX, England

**Sjooblom, Lenna** — Model
Playboy Promotions, 9346 Civic Center Dr, #200, Beverly Hills CA 90210 USA

**Sjostrom, Fredrik** — Ice Hockey Player
18362 N 94th Place, Scottsdale AZ 85255, USA

**Skabo, Paul** — Test Pilot
529 Nevada St, Sausalito CA 94965, USA

**Skaggs, David L (Dave)** — Baseball Player
11131 Arlington Ave, Riverside CA 92505, USA

**Skaggs, James L (Jimmie)** — Football Player
421 Falcon Ridge Road, Ellensburg WA 98926, USA

**Skaggs, Ricky** — Singer, Guitarist
380 Forest Retreat, Hendersonville TN 37075, USA

**Skah, Khalid** — Track Athlete
Boite Postale 2577, Fez, Morocco

**Skalde, Jarrod** — Ice Hockey Player
305 1/2 E Front St, Bloomington IL 61701, USA

**Skalski, Joseph D (Joe)** — Baseball Player
15546 Drexel Ave, Dolton IL 60419, USA

**Skansi, Paul A** — Football Player
23795 Brixton Place, Poulsbo WA 98370, USA

**Skarda, Randy** — Ice Hockey Player
26885 Noble Road, Excelsior MN 55331, USA

**Skaricic, Marija** — Actress
Croatian Audiovisual Center, Nova Ves 18, 10 000 Zacreb, Croatia

**Skarmeta, Antonio** — Writer
Mohrenstr 42, 10117 Berlin, Germany

**Skarsgard, Alexander J H** — Actor
Creative Artists Agency, 2000 Ave of Stars, #100, Los Angeles CA 90067 USA

**Skarsgard, Bill** — Actor
Agentfirman Planthaber/Kildén, Drottninggatan 55, 111 21 Stockholm, Sweden

**Skarsten, Rachel** — Actress
Creative Drive Artists, 66 King St E, #400, Toronto ON M5A 1J3, Canada

**Skaugstad, David W (Dave)** — Baseball Player
16222 Monterey Lane, #274, Huntington Beach CA 92649, USA

**Skeggs, Leonard T, Jr** — Biochemist
10212 Blair Lane, Willoughby OH 44094, USA

**Skelin, Niksa** — Rowing Athlete
Put Plokita 89, 21000 Split, Croatia

**Skelin, Sinisa** — Rowing Athlete
Domovinskog Rata 27C, 21000 Split, Croatia

**Skelly, James** — Singer (Coral)
S J M Mgmt, St Matthews, Liverpool Road, Manchester M3 4NQ, England

**Skelton, Richard K (Rich), Jr** — Rodeo Rider
1139 County Road 312, Llano TX 78643, USA

**Skelton, Stuart** — Opera Singer
I M G Artists, Hogarth Business Park, Chiswick, London W4 2TH, England

**Skerrit, Roosevelt** — Prime Minister, Dominica
Premier's Office, Government Headquarters, Kennedy Ave, Roseau, Dominica

**Skerritt, Tom** — Actor
Pitt Group, 9465 Wilshire Blvd, #420, Beverly Hills CA 90212, USA

**Skiba, Matthew T (Matt)** — Singer, Guitarist (Alkaline Trio)
X-Ray Touring, 77-79 Great Eastern St, London EC2A 3HU, England

**Skibbie, Lawrence F** — Army General
2309 S Queen St, Arlington VA 22202, USA

**Skidmore, R Roe** — Baseball Player
964 E Martin Dr, Decature IL 62521, USA

**Skiles, Scott A** — Basketball Player, Coach
3975 S Inverness Farm Road, Bloomington IN 47401, USA

**Skillings, Muzz**
Entertainment Artists, 2409 21st Ave S, #100, Nashville TN 10019 USA — Bassist (Living Colour)
**Skin**
13 Artists, 11-14 Kensington St, Brighton BN1 4AJ, England — Singer (Skunk Anansie)
**Skinner, Albert L (Al)**
145 Great Plain Ave, Wellesley MA 02482, USA — Basketball Player, Coach
**Skinner, Claire**
Markham Froggatt Irwin, Julian House, 4 Windmill St, London W1P 1HF, England — Actress
**Skinner, Joel P**
275 Pamilla Circle, Avon Lake OH 44012, USA — Baseball Player
**Skinner, John A (Jonty)**
University of Alabama, Athletic Dept, Tuscaloosa AL 35487, USA — Swimmer, Coach
**Skinner, Julie**
Curling Association, 1660 Vimont Court, Cumberland ON K4A 4J4, Canada — Curling Athlete
**Skinner, Michael K**
Washington State University, Skinner Laboratory, PO Box 644234, Pullman WA 99164, USA — Biologist
**Skinner, Mike**
Mike Skinner Enterprises, 201 Cessna Blvd, #4, Port Orange FL 32128, USA — Auto, Truck Racing Driver
**Skinner, Robert R (Bob)**
1576 Diamond St, San Diego CA 92109, USA — Baseball Player, Manager
**Skinner, Samuel K**
Commonwealth Edison, 1 First National Plaza, PO Box 767, Chicago IL 60690, USA — Secretary, Transportation; Businessman
**Skinner, Sonny**
114 Northlake Dr, Sylvester GA 31791, USA — Golfer
**Skinner, Val**
44 Bridge Ave, Bay Head NJ 08742, USA — Golfer
**Skizas, Louis P (Lou)**
2101 W White St, #118, Champaign IL 61821, USA — Baseball Player
**Skjelbreid, Ann-Elen**
5640 Eikelandsosen, Norway — Biathlete
**Skjvorecky, Josef**
Erindale College, English Dept, Toronto ON M5S 1A5, Canada — Writer
**Skladany, Thomas E (Tom)**
6666 Highland Lakes Place, Westerville OH 43082, USA — Football Player
**Skloff, Michael**
Gorfaine/Schwartz, 4111 W Alameda Ave, #509, Burbank CA 91505 USA — Composer
**Skoglund, Sandy**
Janet Borden, 560 Broadway, #601, New York NY 10012, USA — Photographer, Sculptor
**Skok, Craig R**
981 Slash Pine Way, Lawrenceville GA 30043, USA — Baseball Player
**Skolimowski, Jerzy**
Film Polski, Ul Mazowiecka 6/8, 00048 Warsaw, Poland — Director, Actor
**Skolnick, Mark H**
University of Utah Medical Center, Genetics Dept, Salt Lake City UT 84112, USA — Geneticist
**Skolnikoff, Eugene B**
1010 Waltham St, #542, Lexington MA 2421, USA — Political Scientist
**Skoog, Meyer U (Whitey)**
1302 W Traverse Road, #203, Saint Peter MN 56082, USA — Basketball Player, Coach
**Skorodenski, Warren**
161 MacEwan Ridge Circle NW, Calgary AB T3K 3W3, Canada — Ice Hockey Player
**Skoronski, Robert F (Bob)**
3807 Signature Dr, Middletown WI 53562, USA — Football Player
**Skorton, David J**
Cornell University, President's Office, Ithaca NY 14853, USA — Educator
**Skorupan, John P**
142 Crossing Ridge Trail, Cranberry Township PA 16066, USA — Football Player
**Skotheim, Robert A**
2120 Place Road, Port Angeles WA 98363, USA — Museum Executive
**Skou, Jens C**
Rislundvej 9, Risskov 8240, Denmark — Nobel Chemistry Laureate
**Skoula, Martin**
2441 Sheridan Ave S, Minneapolis MN 55405, USA — Ice Hockey Player
**Skouras, Thanos**
8 Chlois St, 14562 Athens, Greece — Economist
**Skovhus, Bo**
Balmer & Dixon Mgmt, Granitweg 2, 8006 Zurich, Switzerland — Opera Singer
**Skow, James J (Jim)**
748 Knollview Blvd, Ormond Beach FL 32174, USA — Football Player
**Skream**
Columbia Records, 9 Derry St, London W8 5HY, England — Electronic Musician (Magnetic Man)
**Skrebneski, Victor**
1350 N LaSalle Dr, Chicago IL 60610, USA — Photographer
**Skrepenak, Gregory A (Greg)**
Hyders Total Fitness Center, 420 Middle Road, Nanticoke PA 18634, USA — Football Player
**Skride, Baiba**
Konzertdirektion Schmid, Konigstra 36, 30175 Hannover, Germany — Concert Violinist
**Skriko, Petri**
Kirjatyontekijankatu 4 A 3, 00170 Helsinki, Finland — Ice Hockey Player
**Skripochka, Oleg I**
Cosmonaut Training Center, Star City, 141160 Zvezdny Gorodok, Moscow Oblast, Russia — Cosmonaut
**Skrmetta, Matt**
827 Poinsetta Dr, Indian Harbour Beach FL 32937, USA — Baseball Player
**Skrovan, Steve**
W M E Entertainment, 9601 Wilshire Blvd, #300, Beverly Hills CA 90210 USA — Actor, Comedian, Producer
**Skrowaczewski, Stanislaw**
Minnesota Symphony, 1111 Nicollet Mall, Minneapolis MN 55403, USA — Conductor, Composer
**Skrudland, Brian**
Argo Sales, 717 7th Ave SW, #1300, Calgary AB T2P 0Z3, Canada — Ice Hockey Player
**Skube, Robert J (Bob)**
4153 W Charlotte Dr, Glendale AZ 85310, USA — Baseball Player
**Skvortsov, Alexander A**
Cosmonaut Training Center, Star City, 141160 Zvezdny Gorodok, Moscow Oblast, Russia — Cosmonaut
**Sky, Alison**
60 Greene St, New York NY 10012, USA — Environmental Artist
**Sky, Amy**
LiveTourArtists, 1451 White Oaks Blvd, Oakville ON L6H 4R9, Canada — Singer, Songwriter

**Sky, Jennifer** — Actress
Dunham Literary, 110 William St, #2202, New York NY 10038 10038, USA

**Sky, Patrick** — Singer, Songwriter
Ossian Records, 118 Beck Road, Loudon NH 03307, USA

**Skye, Azura** — Actress
Baker Winokur Ryder Public Relations, 9100 Wilshire Blvd, #500W, Beverly Hills CA 90212 USA

**Skye, Ione** — Actress
Concrete Entertainment, 468 N Camden Dr, #200, Beverly Hills CA 90210, USA

**Skyrms, Brian** — Philosopher
University of California, Philosophy Dept, Irvine CA 92697, USA

**Slack, Reggie** — Football Player
5973 Queen St, Milton FL 32570, USA

**Slade, Bernard N** — Writer
345 N Saltair Ave, Los Angeles CA 90049, USA

**Slade, Chris** — Drummer (AC/DC)
11 Leominster Road, Morden, Surrey SA4 6HN, England

**Slade, Christopher C (Chris)** — Football Player
4163 Onslow Place SE, Smyrna GA 30080, USA

**Slade, David** — Actor, Comedian, Director
Anonymous Content, 3532 Hayden Ave, Culver City CA 90232 USA

**Slade, Isaac** — Singer, Pianist (Fray)
A2 Mgmt, 624 Davis St, #200, Evanston IL 60201, USA

**Slade, Jeff** — Basketball Player
5354 Farmington Road, Toledo OH 43623, USA

**Slade, Mark** — Actor
38 Joppa Road, Worcester MA 01602, USA

**Slade, Roy** — Artist, Museum Executive
31 Island Way, #801, Clearwater FL 33767, USA

**Slagle, James R** — Computer Scientist
Massachusetts Institute of Technology, Mathematics Dept, Cambridge MA 02139, USA

**Slagle, Roger L** — Baseball Player
536 W 3rd St, Larned KS 67550, USA

**Slaney, John** — Ice Hockey Player
96 Mullen Dr, Sicklerville NJ 08081, USA

**Slaney, Mary Decker** — Track Athlete
87141 Kellmore St, Eugene OR 97402, USA

**Slash** — Singer, Guitarist (Guns N' Roses)
First Artists Mgmt, 4764 Park Granada, #210, Calabasas CA 91302 USA

**Slate, Jenny** — Actress, Comedianne
W M E Entertainment, 9601 Wilshire Blvd, #300, Beverly Hills CA 90210 USA

**Slaten, Douglas (Doug)** — Baseball Player
233 Rennie Ave, Venice CA 90291, USA

**Slater, Christian** — Actor
United Talent Agency, U T A Plaza, 9336 Civic Center Dr, Beverly Hills CA 90210 USA

**Slater, Helen** — Actress
DeSante Frank Co, 10061 Riverside Dr, #377, Toluca Lake CA 91602, USA

**Slater, Jackie R** — Football Player
PO Box 6411, Orange CA 92863, USA

**Slater, Kelly** — Surfer, Actor
Quicksilver, 15202 Graham St, Huntington Beach CA 92649, USA

**Slater, Mark W** — Football Player
10545 Rome Ave, Young America MN 55397, USA

**Slater, Reggie** — Basketball Player
8 Saint Christopher Court, Sugar Land TX 77479, USA

**Slater, Rodney E** — Secretary, Transportation
Paton Boggs, 2050 M St NW, Washington DC 20036, USA

**Slatkin, Leonard E** — Conductor
Detroit Symphony, 3711 Woodward Ave, Detroit MI 48201, USA

**Slaton, Anthony T (Tony)** — Football Player
122 E Childs Ave, Merced CA 95341, USA

**Slaton, James M (Jim)** — Baseball Player
4082 N Arbor Lane, Buckeye AZ 85396, USA

**Slattery, Anthony D J (Tony)** — Actor
Belfield & Ward, 80-81 Saint Martin's Lane, London WC2N 4AA, England

**Slattery, John M, Jr** — Actor
Gersh Agency, 9465 Wilshire Blvd, #600, Beverly Hills CA 90212 USA

**Slattvik, Simon** — Nordic Combined Athlete
Bankgata 22, 2600 Lillehammer, Norway

**Slaught, Donald M (Don)** — Baseball Player
27 Middleridge Lane S, Rolling Hills CA 90274, USA

**Slaughter, Alvin** — Singer, Songwriter
Alvin Slaughter Ministries, 3221 Southwestern Blvd, #311, Orchard Park NY 14127, USA

**Slaughter, Karin** — Writer
Delacorte Press, 1540 Broadway, New York NY 10036 USA

**Slaughter, Webster M** — Football Player
3706 Rory Court, Missouri City TX 77459, USA

**Slavin, Jonathan** — Actor
Coronel Group, 1100 Glendon Ave, #1700, Los Angeles CA 90046, USA

**Slavin, Neal** — Photographer
62 Green St, New York NY 10012, USA

**Slavitt, David R** — Writer
35 West St, #5, Cambridge MA 02139, USA

**Slay, Brandon** — Freestyle Wrestler
6155 Lehman Dr, Colorado Springs CO 80918, USA

**Slayback, William G (Bill)** — Baseball Player
25710 Armstrong Circle, #E, Stevenson Ranch CA 91381, USA

**Slayton, Maurice W** — Financier
Conning Corp, City Place II, 185 Asylum St, #1500, Hartford CT 06103, USA

**Slean, Sarah** — Singer, Songwriter
Agency Group, 2 Berkeley St, #202, Toronto ON M5A 4J5, Canada

**Sledge, Joni** — Singer (Sister Sledge)
Nationwide Entertainment, 2756 N Green Valley Parkway, Henderson NV 89014 USA

**Sledge, Kathy** — Singer (Sister Sledge)
491 York Road, Jenkintown PA 19046, USA

**Sledge, Percy** — Singer
PO Box 220082, Great Neck NY 11022, USA

|  |  |
|---|---|
| **Sleiman, Haaz**<br>Gersh Agency, 9465 Wilshire Blvd, #600, Beverly Hills CA 90212 USA | Actor |
| **Slezak, Erika**<br>I C M Partners, 730 5th Ave, New York NY 10019 USA | Actress |
| **Slichter, Charles P**<br>61 Chestnut Court, Champaign IL 61822, USA | Physicist |
| **Slick Rick**<br>Entertainment Artists, 2409 21st Ave S, #100, Nashville TN 10019 USA | Rap Artist |
| **Slick, Grace**<br>Mission Control, 15030 Ventura Blvd, #541, Sherman Oaks CA 91403, USA | Singer (Jefferson Airplane), Songwriter |
| **Slim Helu, Carlos**<br>Telmex, Porque Via 198, Cuauhtemoc CP, 06599 Mexico City DF, Mexico | Businessman |
| **Sliwinska, Edyta**<br>Bloc Talent Agency, 5651 Wilshire Blvd, #C, Los Angeles CA 90036, USA | Dancer |
| **Sloan, Anna**<br>Curling Association, 14 Donnelly Dr, Bedford, Bedfordshire MK4 9TU, England | Curling Athlete |
| **Sloan, Bridget**<br>USA Gymnastics, 201 S Capital Ave, #300, Indianapolis IN 46275 USA | Gymnast |
| **Sloan, David L**<br>3833 Cummins St, #1128, Houston TX 77027, USA | Football Player |
| **Sloan, Edward J (Ed)**<br>216 Lincoln St, West Columbia SC 29170, USA | Singer, Guitarist (Crossfade) |
| **Sloan, Eliot**<br>Union Artists Group, 214 Woodhavens, Union SC 29379, USA | Singer (Blessid Union of Souls) |
| **Sloan, Gerald E (Jerry)**<br>5583 W 13680 S, Herriman UT 84096, USA | Basketball Player, Coach |
| **Sloan, John**<br>Innovative Artists, 1505 10th St, Santa Monica CA 90401 USA | Actor |
| **Sloan, P F**<br>All the Best, PO Box 164, Cedarhurst NY 11516, USA | Singer, Songwriter |
| **Sloan, Stephen C (Steve)**<br>6312 Masters Blvd, Orlando FL 32819, USA | Football Player, Coach, Administrator |
| **Sloan, Tod**<br>11 Hedge Road, RR 2, Sutton West ON L0E 1R0, Canada | Ice Hockey Player |
| **Sloane, Carol**<br>Bennett Morgan, 1022 RR 376, #3, Wappinger Falls NY 12590 USA | Singer |
| **Sloane, Lindsay**<br>Gersh Agency, 9465 Wilshire Blvd, #600, Beverly Hills CA 90212 USA | Actress |
| **Slocombe, Douglas**<br>London Mgmt, 2-4 Noel St, London W1V 3RB, England | Cinematographer |
| **Slocum, Heath**<br>5640 Keystone Road, Pensacola FL 32504, USA | Golfer |
| **Slocum, Matt**<br>Nettwerk Mgmt, 1201 Villa Place, #206, Nashville TN 37212 USA | Instrumentalist (Sixpence), Songwriter |
| **Slocumb, Heathcliff (Heath)**<br>1045 Arthur St, Uniondale NY 11553, USA | Baseball Player |
| **Slon, Steven**<br>Saturday Evening Post, 1100 Waterway Blvd, Indianapolis IN 46202, USA | Editor |
| **Slonimski, Piotr**<br>Le Haut Chantemesle, 72150 Courdemanche, France | Biologist |
| **Slonimsky, Sergey M**<br>9 Kanal Griboedova, #97, 191186 Saint Petersburg, Russia | Composer |
| **Slotnick, Joey**<br>Gersh Agency, 9465 Wilshire Blvd, #600, Beverly Hills CA 90212 USA | Actor |
| **Slotnick, Mortimer H**<br>43 Amherst Dr, New Rochelle NY 10804, USA | Artist |
| **Sloves, Marvin**<br>31 San Juan Ranch Road, Santa Fe NM 87506, USA | Businessman |
| **Sloviter, Dolores K**<br>US Court of Appeals, Courthouse, 601 Market St, #18614, Philadelphia PA 19106, USA | Judge |
| **Slowery, Kevin M**<br>1478 Quigg Dr, Pittsburgh PA 15241, USA | Baseball Player |
| **Sloyan, James**<br>920 Kagawa St, Pacific Palisades CA 90272, USA | Actor |
| **Sluby, Tom**<br>39 Poplar St, Ramsey NJ 07446, USA | Basketball Player |
| **Slug**<br>Progressive Global Agency, 103 W Tyne Dr, Nashville TN 37205, USA | Drummer (Marvelous 3) |
| **Sluman, Jeffrey G (Jeff)**<br>939 Cleveland Road, Hinsdale IL 60521, USA | Golfer |
| **Slusarski, Joseph A (Joe)**<br>11 Rodelle Woods Dr, Weldon Spring MO 63304, USA | Baseball Player |
| **Slutskaya, Irina E**<br>Skating Federation, Luznetskaya Nabererhnya 8, 11987 Moscow, Russia | Figure Skater |
| **Smail, Doug**<br>PO Box 573, Blum TX 76627, USA | Ice Hockey Player |
| **Smale, Stephen**<br>68 Highgate Road, Kensington CA 94707, USA | Mathematician |
| **Small, Aaron J**<br>775 Loudon Road, Loudon TN 37774, USA | Baseball Player |
| **Small, Mary**<br>PO Box 765, Rozelle NSW 2039, Australia | Writer, Illustrator |
| **Small, Torrance R**<br>66 Chateau Mouton Dr, Kenner LA 70065, USA | Football Player |
| **Small, William N**<br>1605 Bluecher Court, Virginia Beach VA 23454, USA | Navy Admiral |
| **Smalley, Roy F, III**<br>6319 Timber Trail, Minneapolis MN 55439, USA | Baseball Player |
| **Smallwood, Dwana**<br>Alvin Ailey American Dance Foundation, 405 W 55th St, New York NY 10019, USA | Dancer |
| **Smallwood, Richard**<br>Sierra Mgmt, 1035 Bates Court, Hendersonville TN 37075, USA | Singer, Composer |
| **Smart, Amy**<br>Gersh Agency, 9465 Wilshire Blvd, #600, Beverly Hills CA 90212 USA | Actress |
| **Smart, Erinn**<br>343 Gold St, #3405, Brooklyn NY 11201, USA | Fencer |

| | |
|---|---|
| **Smart, J Keith** | Basketball Player, Coach |
| 6071 Round Hill Dr, Dublin CA 94568, USA | |
| **Smart, Jean** | Actress |
| 17351 Rancho St, Encino CA 91316, USA | |
| **Smart, Keeth** | Fencer |
| 15 Washington Place, #1F, New York NY 10003, USA | |
| **Smart, Shaka** | Basketball Coach |
| Virginia Commonwealth, Athletic Dept, Richmond VA 23284, USA | |
| **Smatresek, Neal J** | Educator |
| University of Nevada, President's Office, 4505 S Maryland Parkway, Las Vegas NV 89154, USA | |
| **Smeal, Eleanor C** | Women's Activist |
| Feminist Majority Foundation, 1600 Wilson Blvd, #8014, Arlington VA 22209, USA | |
| **Smedile, Anthony** | Drummer (Dig) |
| Overland Productions, 156 W 56th St, #500, New York NY 10019, USA | |
| **Smedsmo, Dale** | Ice Hockey Player |
| 609 3rd St NE, Roseau MN 56751, USA | |
| **Smedvig, Rolf** | Concert Trumpeter |
| Columbia Artists Mgmt Inc, 5 Columbus Circle, 1790 Broadway, #1600, New York NY 10019 USA | |
| **Smee, Sebastian** | Journalist |
| Boston Globe, Editorial Dept, 135 William Morrissey Blvd, Dorchester MA 02125 USA | |
| **Smehlik, Richard** | Ice Hockey Player |
| 8824 Hearthstone Dr, East Amherst NY 14051, USA | |
| **Smerlas, Frederick C (Fred)** | Football Player |
| 23 Farwell St, Newtonville MA 02460, USA | |
| **Smigel, Robert** | Actor, Comedian |
| Creative Artists Agency, 2000 Ave of Stars, #100, Los Angeles CA 90067 USA | |
| **Smigelsky, David W (Dave)** | Football Player |
| 4332 Nesting Place, Oakwood GA 30566, USA | |
| **Smiley, Jane G** | Writer |
| 235 El Caminto Road, Carmel Valley CA 93924, USA | |
| **Smiley, John P** | Baseball Player |
| 208 W 3rd Ave, Collegeville PA 19426, USA | |
| **Smiley, Justin** | Football Player |
| 721 Baldwin Palm Ave, Plantation FL 33324, USA | |
| **Smiley, Tava** | Actress |
| P M K-B N C, 8687 Melrose Ave, #800, Los Angeles CA 90069 USA | |
| **Smiley, Tavis** | Entertainer |
| Smiley Group, 4434 Crenshaw Blvd, Los Angeles CA 90043, USA | |
| **Smirnoff, Karina** | Dancer |
| Karina Smirnoff Dance, 21270 Ventura Blvd, Woodland Hills CA 91364, USA | |
| **Smirnoff, Yakov** | Actor, Comedian |
| Comrade Entertainment, 3750 W 76 Country Blvd, Branson MO 65616, USA | |
| **Smirnov, Igor N** | President, Transnistria |
| President's Office, 25 October Str, Tiraspol, Transnistria, Moldova | |
| **Smisek, Jeff** | Businessman |
| United-Continental Airlines, 77 W Wacker Dr, Mezzanine, Chicago IL 60601, USA | |
| **Smit, Johannes H M (Jantje)** | Singer |
| Vollendam Music, B Van Baarstraat 4, 1131 Volendam WT, Netherlands | |
| **Smith Court, Margaret** | Tennis Player |
| 21 Lowanna Way, City Beach, Perth WA 6010, Australia | |
| **Smith, Aaron D** | Football Player |
| 4900 S Ulster St, #8-106, Denver CO 80237, USA | |
| **Smith, Adrian D** | Architect |
| 1100 W Summerfield Dr, Lake Forest IL 60045, USA | |
| **Smith, Adrian F** | Guitarist (Iron Maiden) |
| Chipster, 100 Village Square Crossing, Palm Beach Gardens FL 33410 USA | |
| **Smith, Adrian H** | Basketball Player |
| 2829 Saddleback Dr, Cincinnati OH 45244, USA | |
| **Smith, Al F** | Football Player |
| 15 Pembroke St, Sugar Land TX 77479, USA | |
| **Smith, Alan E** | Molecular Biologist |
| Genzyme Corp, 500 Kendall St, Cambridge MA 02142, USA | |
| **Smith, Alexander D (Alex)** | Football Player |
| 4665 Gaviota Court, Bonita CA 91902, USA | |
| **Smith, Alexander McCall** | Writer |
| Pantheon Books, 1745 Broadway, New York NY 10019 USA | |
| **Smith, Alexis** | Artist |
| 1625 Shell Ave, Venice CA 90291, USA | |
| **Smith, Allison** | Actress |
| Barry Freed, 2040 Ave of Stars, #400, Los Angeles CA 90067 USA | |
| **Smith, Amber** | Model, Actress |
| Elite Model Mgmt, 119 Washington Ave, #501, Miami Beach FL 33139, USA | |
| **Smith, Andre D, Jr** | Football Player |
| Cincinnati Bengals, 1 Paul Brown Stadium, Cincinnati OH 45202 USA | |
| **Smith, Andrea B** | Artist |
| 1590 Lokia St, Lahaina HI 96761, USA | |
| **Smith, Anna Deavere** | Actress |
| Creative Artists Agency, 2000 Ave of Stars, #100, Los Angeles CA 90067 USA | |
| **Smith, Anne** | Tennis Player |
| Bew Ravs, 3737 Cole Ave, #110, Dallas TX 75204, USA | |
| **Smith, Anthony W** | Football Player |
| PO Box 573, Fontana CA 92334, USA | |
| **Smith, Antonio D** | Football Player |
| 2015 Grand River Dr, Richmond TX 77406, USA | |
| **Smith, Antonique** | Actress, Singer |
| P M K-B N C, 8687 Melrose Ave, #800, Los Angeles CA 90069 USA | |
| **Smith, Antowain D** | Football Player |
| 2121 Hepburn St, #917, Houston TX 77054, USA | |
| **Smith, April** | Writer |
| 427 7th St, Santa Monica CA 90402, USA | |
| **Smith, Arlene** | Singer (Chantels) |
| Veta Gardner, 1661 SE Goucho Ave, Port Saint Lucie FL 34952, USA | |
| **Smith, Arthur K, Jr** | Educator |
| 45 Wexford Club Dr, Hilton Head SC 29928, USA | |
| **Smith, Artie E** | Football Player |
| 3809 W 68th St, Stillwater OK 74074, USA | |

**Smith, B** — Model, Publisher, Restauranteur
B Smith with Style, 168 Park Ave, Harrison NY 10528, USA
**Smith, Barbara Herrnstein** — Educator
Duke University, Science & Cultural Theory Center, Durham NC 27708, USA
**Smith, Barry** — Synthesizer Player (Add N to X)
Kork Agency, 1880 Century Park E, #711, Los Angeles CA 90067 USA
**Smith, Barton E (Barty)** — Football Player
2290 Dabney Road, Richmond VA 23230, USA
**Smith, Beau** — Cartoonist
Flying Fist Ranch, PO Box 706, Ceredo WV 25507, USA
**Smith, Ben** — Ice Hockey Coach
47 Norwood Heights, Gloucester MA 01930, USA
**Smith, Ben** — Cartoonist (Ratz)
King Features Syndicate, 300 W 57th St, #1500, New York NY 10019 USA
**Smith, Benjamin J (Ben)** — Football Player
211 Cobblestone Trail, Avondale Estates GA 30002, USA
**Smith, Billy E** — Baseball Player
9246 Mare Country, San Antonio TX 78254, USA
**Smith, Billy Ray, Jr** — Football Player
14755 Caminito Porta Delgada, Del Mar CA 92014, USA
**Smith, Blake** — Guitarist (Fig Dish)
Metropolitan Entertainment Group, 2 Penn Plaza, #1500, New York NY 10121, USA
**Smith, Bob** — Golfer
PO Box 6511, Ventura CA 93006, USA
**Smith, Bobby** — Ice Hockey Player
10800 E Cactus Road, #46, Scottsdale AZ 85259, USA
**Smith, Bobby Gene** — Baseball Player
1267 Tucker Road, #15, Hood River OR 97031, USA
**Smith, Bradley A (Brad)** — Ice Hockey Player
Colorado Avalanche, Pepsi Center, 1000 Chopper Circle, Denver CO 80204 USA
**Smith, Brady** — Actor
Schachter Entertainment, 1157 S Beverly Dr, #200, Los Angeles CA 90035 USA
**Smith, Brady M** — Football Player
3555 Move Trail, Duluth GA 30097, USA
**Smith, Brent M** — Football Player
258 Ridgewood Dr, Pontotoc MS 38863, USA
**Smith, Bruce A** — Businessman
Tesoro Petroleum Corp, 300 Concord Plaza Dr, San Antonio TX 78216, USA
**Smith, Bruce B** — Football Player
1640 Spring House Trail, Virginia Beach VA 23455, USA
**Smith, Byther** — Singer, Guitarist, Bassist
J Reil Assoc, 3430 Bayberry Dr, Northbrook IL 60062, USA
**Smith, C Douglas (Doug)** — Football Player
25661 Pacific Crest Dr, Mission Viejo CA 92692, USA
**Smith, C Reginald (Reggie)** — Baseball Player
Reggie Smith Baseball Center, 16161 Ventura Blvd, #775, Encino CA 91436, USA
**Smith, Calvin** — Track Athlete
16703 Sheffield Park Dr, Lutz FL 33549, USA
**Smith, Carl R** — Air Force General
2345 S Queen St, Arlington VA 22202, USA
**Smith, Carter** — Director
Cinetic Mgmt, 555 W 25th St, #400, New York NY 10001 USA
**Smith, Cedric D** — Football Player
14808 Benson St, Overland Park KS 66221, USA
**Smith, Chadwick G (Chad)** — Drummer (Red Hot Chili Peppers)
Q Prime, 729 7th Ave, #1600, New York NY 10019 USA
**Smith, Charles D** — Basketball Player
PO Box 190, Cedar Grove NJ 07009, USA
**Smith, Charles E (Charlie)** — Football Player
1906 Crescent Dr, Monroe LA 71202, USA
**Smith, Charles H (Charlie)** — Football Player
14074 Skyline Blvd, Oakland CA 94619, USA
**Smith, Charles Martin** — Actor, Director
A P A Talent & Literary Agency, 405 S Beverly Dr, #300, Beverly Hills CA 90212 USA
**Smith, Chelsi** — Beauty Queen, Singer, Actress
335 E San Augustine St, Deer Park TX 77536, USA
**Smith, Chris** — Golfer
208 S Bellerive Dr, Peru IN 46970, USA
**Smith, Christina** — Model
Playboy Promotions, 9346 Civic Center Dr, #200, Beverly Hills CA 90210 USA
**Smith, Christine** — Model
Playboy Promotions, 9346 Civic Center Dr, #200, Beverly Hills CA 90210 USA
**Smith, Christoper W (Chris)** — Baseball Player
4206 Dawn Lane, Oceanside CA 92056, USA
**Smith, Christopher** — Physiologist, Pharmacologist
King's College, Strand, London WC2R 2LS, England
**Smith, Christopher** — Director, Writer
United Agents, 12-26 Lexington St, London W1F 0LE, England
**Smith, Chuck** — Baseball Player
1300 Saint Charles Place, #810, Pembroke Pines FL 33026, USA
**Smith, Clifford V, Jr** — Educator, Foundation Executive
1205 NW Kline Place, Corvallis OR 97330, USA
**Smith, Colin** — Rowing Athlete
Leander Club, Henley on Thames, Leander RG9 2LP, England
**Smith, Connie** — Singer
TG2 Artists, 201 Rainbow Dr, Carrboro NC 27510, USA
**Smith, Cotter** — Actor
Innovative Artists, 1505 10th St, Santa Monica CA 90401 USA
**Smith, D Brooks** — Judge
US Court of Appeals, Allegheny Center, Old Route 22 W, Duncansville PA 16635, USA
**Smith, Dallas** — Ice Hockey Player
4390 SW 107th Ave, #4, Beaverton OR 97005, USA
**Smith, Dan F** — Businessman
Lyondell Petrochemical Co, 1221 McKinney St, #700, Houston TX 77010, USA
**Smith, Daniel C (Dan), Jr** — Baseball Player
4411 Adonis Dr, Salt Lake City UT 84124, USA

**Smith, Danny**  
Roger A Pliakas, 9720 Wilshire Blvd, #700, Beverly Hills CA 90212, USA — Actor, Producer, Writer

**Smith, Darden**  
Eastern Star Productions, 2625 Alcatraz Ave, #302, Berkeley CA 94705, USA — Singer, Guitarist, Songwriter

**Smith, Darrin A**  
7274 NW 19th Court, Pembroke Pines FL 33024, USA — Football Player

**Smith, Daryl C**  
3 Sunny Hills Court, Randallstown MD 21133, USA — Baseball Player

**Smith, David Lee**  
Chaotic Mgmt, 4221 Wilshire Blvd, #395, Los Angeles CA 90010, USA — Actor

**Smith, David R**  
Duke University, Electrical Engineering Dept, Durham NC 27708, USA — Electrical Engineer

**Smith, David W (Dave)**  
3709 E Meadowview Dr, Gilbert AZ 85298, USA — Football Player

**Smith, Dean E**  
University of North Carolina, Athletic Dept, PO Box 2126, Chapel Hill NC 27515, USA — Basketball Coach

**Smith, Dennis**  
2450 Achilles Dr, Los Angeles CA 90046, USA — Football Player

**Smith, Derek**  
201 Bramblewood Lane, East Amherst NY 14051, USA — Ice Hockey Player

**Smith, Derek M**  
3352 Adams Run, Encinitas CA 92024, USA — Football Player

**Smith, Derrick**  
Durham Fury, 595 Wentworth St E, Oshawa ON L1H 3V8, Canada — Ice Hockey Player

**Smith, Detron N**  
6390 Saddle Rock Trail S, Aurora CO 80016, USA — Football Player

**Smith, Dick**  
PO Box 1831, Dewey AZ 86327, USA — Diving Coach

**Smith, Donald L (Don)**  
3338 Pineview Dr, Holiday FL 34691, USA — Football Player

**Smith, Doug**  
25661 Pacifc Crest Dr, Mission Viejo CA 92692, USA — Football Player, Coach

**Smith, Douglas (Doug)**  
25482 Pennsylvania Ave, Novi MI 48375, USA — Basketball Player

**Smith, Douglas (Doug)**  
More/Medavoy Mgmt, 10203 Santa Monica Blvd, #400, Los Angeles CA 90067 USA — Actor

**Smith, Dylan**  
TalentWorks, 3500 W Olive Ave, #1400, Burbank CA 91505 USA — Actor

**Smith, E Alexander (Alex)**  
10514 Broadland Pass, Thonotosassa FL 33592, USA — Football Player

**Smith, E Perry**  
14251 E Wyoming Place, Aurora CO 80012, USA — Football Player

**Smith, E Z**  
2036 N Farris Ave, Fresno CA 93704, USA — Photogapher

**Smith, Earl J (J R), III**  
New York Knicks, Madison Square Garden, 2 Penn Plaza, New York, NY 10121 USA — Basketball Player

**Smith, Elliott A**  
850 N Jefferson St, #A205, Jackson MS 39202, USA — Football Player

**Smith, Elmore**  
PO Box 241475, Cleveland OH 44124, USA — Basketball Player

**Smith, Emmitt J, III**  
15001 Winnwood Road, Dallas TX 75254, USA — Football Player, Sportscaster

**Smith, Erik Scott**  
Leverage Mgmt, 3030 Pennsylvania Ave, Santa Monica CA 90404 USA — Actor, Singer

**Smith, Eugene C (Geno), III**  
New York Jets, 1 Jets Dr, Florham Park NJ 07932 USA — Football Player

**Smith, F Dean**  
PO Box 71, Breckenridge TX 76424, USA — Track Athlete

**Smith, Faryl**  
Agency Group Ltd, 361-373 City Road, London EC1V 1PQ, England — Singer

**Smith, Floyd**  
138 Stonehenge Dr, Orchard Park NY 14127, USA — Ice Hockey Player

**Smith, Frankie L**  
620 N Grayson St, Groesbeck TX 76642, USA — Football Player

**Smith, Frederick W**  
F D X Corp, 942 S Shady Grove Road, Memphis TN 38120, USA — Businessman

**Smith, G Seth**  
76 Sunline Dr, Brandon MS 39042, USA — Baseball Player

**Smith, Gary**  
Colorado Rapids, 1000 Chopper Circle, Denver CO 80204 USA — Soccer Coach

**Smith, Geoff**  
42-1525 Westside Road S, Kelowna BC V1Z 3Y3, Canada — Ice Hockey Player

**Smith, George**  
Universal Press Syndicate, 4520 Main St, #700, Kansas City MO 64111 USA — Cartoonist (Smith Family)

**Smith, George E**  
Bell Laboratories, 600 Mountain Ave, Murray Hill NJ 07974, USA — Nobel Physics Laureate

**Smith, George E (G E)**  
Boston Event Works, PO Box 180, Medford MA 02155, USA — Guitarist/Orchestra Leader

**Smith, Gerard**  
World Tennis Assn, 133 1st St NE, Saint Petersburg FL 33701, USA — Publisher, Tennis Executive

**Smith, Gordon C**  
14227 Kellywood Lane, Houston TX 77079, USA — Football Player

**Smith, Gordon H**  
116 S Main St, #3, Pendleton OR 97801, USA — Senator, OR

**Smith, Gordon J (Gord)**  
6 Carriage Dr, West Haven CT 06516, USA — Ice Hockey Player

**Smith, Gregory**  
Paradigm Agency, 360 N Crescent Dr, North Building, Beverly Hills CA 90210 USA — Actor

**Smith, Gregory D (Greg)**  
9930 SW Lumbee Lane, Tualatin OR 97062, USA — Basketball Player

**Smith, Hamilton O**  
13607 Hanover Pike, Reisterstown MD 21136, USA — Nobel Medicine Laureate

**Smith, Harry**  
580 E Cuyahoga Falls Ave, Akron OH 44310, USA — Bowler

**Smith, Harry**  
CBS-TV, News Dept, 51 W 52nd St, New York NY 10019 USA — Commentator

| | |
|---|---|
| **Smith, Hedrick L**<br>6935 Wisconsin Ave, #208, Chevy Chase MD 20815, USA | Journalist |
| **Smith, Hunter D**<br>9601 E 300 S, Zionesville IN 46077, USA | Football Player |
| **Smith, Ian Michael**<br>C E S D, 10635 Santa Monica Blvd, #130, Los Angeles CA 90025 USA | Actor |
| **Smith, Irvin M (Irv)**<br>11552 W Green Dr, Youngtown AZ 85363, USA | Football Player |
| **Smith, J D, Jr**<br>3332 Florida St, Oakland CA 94602, USA | Football Player |
| **Smith, J Dwight**<br>PO Box 98, Varnville SC 29944, USA | Baseball Player |
| **Smith, Jackie L**<br>1566 Walpole Dr, Chesterfield MO 63017, USA | Football Player |
| **Smith, Jaclyn**<br>10398 Sunset Blvd, #1200, Los Angeles CA 90077, USA | Actress |
| **Smith, Jaden**<br>W M E Entertainment, 9601 Wilshire Blvd, #300, Beverly Hills CA 90210 USA | Actor |
| **Smith, James (Bonecrusher)**<br>6850 Blue Heron Blvd, #302, Myrtle Beach SC 29588, USA | Boxer |
| **Smith, James A (Jim)**<br>3805 Chimney Rock Dr, Flower Mound TX 75022, USA | Football Player |
| **Smith, James L (Jimmy)**<br>1730 S Arroyo Lane, Gilbert AZ 85295, USA | Baseball Player |
| **Smith, James Ray (Jim Ray)**<br>7049 Cliffbrook Dr, Dallas TX 75254, USA | Football Player |
| **Smith, Jason M**<br>Pro-Rep Entertainment, 113-276 Midpark Way SE, Calgary AB T2X 1J6, Canada | Ice Hockey Player |
| **Smith, Jason Matthew**<br>Greene Assoc, 1901 Ave of Stars, #130, Los Angeles CA 90067 USA | Actor |
| **Smith, Jason W**<br>6350 Golden Acres Dr, Cottondale AL 35453, USA | Baseball Player |
| **Smith, Jean Kennedy**<br>4 Sutton Place, New York NY 10022, USA | Diplomat, Foundation Executive |
| **Smith, Jerry E**<br>US Court of Appeals, 515 Rusk Ave, #12015, Houston TX 77002, USA | Judge |
| **Smith, Jimmy Lee, Jr**<br>105 Long Leaf Place, Madison MS 39110, USA | Football Player |
| **Smith, John F (Jack), Jr**<br>Delta Airlines, Board of Directors, PO Box 20706, Atlanta GA 30320, USA | Businessman |
| **Smith, John M**<br>184 Centre St, Dover MA 02030, USA | Football Player |
| **Smith, John Thomas (J T)**<br>1904 Chasewood Circle, Arlington TX 76011, USA | Football Player |
| **Smith, John W**<br>5315 S Sangre Road, Stillwater OK 74074, USA | Freestyle Wrestler, Coach |
| **Smith, Jonathan Z**<br>University of Chicago, History of Religion Dept, Chicago IL 60637, USA | Historian, Religion Educator |
| **Smith, Joseph L (Joe)**<br>7639 Leafwood Dr, Norfolk VA 23518, USA | Basketball Player |
| **Smith, Joshua (Josh)**<br>Detroit Pistons, Palace, 4 Championship Dr, Auburn Hills MI 48326 USA | Basketball Player |
| **Smith, Justin**<br>2222 Terra Nova Lane, San Jose CA 95121, USA | Football Player |
| **Smith, Kathy**<br>42080 State St, Palm Desert CA 92211, USA | Physical Fitness Instructor |
| **Smith, Katie**<br>2494 Farleigh Road, Columbus OH 43221, USA | Basketball Player |
| **Smith, Keely Shaye**<br>W M E Entertainment, 9601 Wilshire Blvd, #300, Beverly Hills CA 90210 USA | Entertainer, Writer |
| **Smith, Keith L**<br>5823 13th St E, Bradenton FL 34203, USA | Baseball Player |
| **Smith, Kellita**<br>Stone Manners Salners, 6100 Wilshire Blvd, #1500, Los Angeles CA 90035 USA | Actress |
| **Smith, Ken**<br>80 Warren St, #28, New York NY 10007, USA | Landscape Architect |
| **Smith, Kenneth (Kenny)**<br>Octagon Worldwide, 1751 Pinnacle Dr, #1500, McLean VA 22102 USA | Basketball Player, Sportscaster |
| **Smith, Kenneth E (Ken)**<br>100 Lansdowne Blvd, Youngstown OH 44506, USA | Baseball Player |
| **Smith, Kerr**<br>Gersh Agency, 9465 Wilshire Blvd, #600, Beverly Hills CA 90212 USA | Actor |
| **Smith, Kevin**<br>View Askew Productions, PO Box 93339, Los Angeles CA 90093, USA | Director, Writer |
| **Smith, Kevin Max (see Kevin Max)**<br>True Artist Mgmt, 227 3rd Ave N, Franklin TN 37064, USA | Singer (DC Talk), Songwriter |
| **Smith, Kurtwood L**<br>Progressive Artists Agency, 9696 Culver Blvd, #110, Culver City CA 90232 USA | Actor |
| **Smith, Lacey B**<br>Northwestern University, History Dept, Evanston IL 60208, USA | Historian |
| **Smith, Lance**<br>4600 Nobility Court, Charlotte NC 28269, USA | Football Player |
| **Smith, Lanty L**<br>Wachovia Corp, 301 S College St, #4000, Charlotte NC 28202, USA | Financier |
| **Smith, Larry**<br>1767 Lakeside Dr, Vicksburg MS 39180, USA | Basketball Player |
| **Smith, Lauren Lee**<br>Gersh Agency, 9465 Wilshire Blvd, #600, Beverly Hills CA 90212 USA | Actress |
| **Smith, Lavay**<br>Berkeley Agency, 2608 9th St, #301, Berkeley CA 94710 USA | Singer |
| **Smith, Lavenski R**<br>11 Twin Pine Place, Little Rock AR 72210, USA | Judge |
| **Smith, Lee**<br>219 N Churton St, Hillsborough NC 27278, USA | Writer |
| **Smith, Lee A**<br>PO Box 399, Castor LA 71016, USA | Baseball Player |

Smith - Smith

| | |
|---|---|
| **Smith, Leslie C**<br>1700 Tice Valley Blvd, #221, Walnut Creek CA 94595, USA | WW II Army Air Corps Hero |
| **Smith, Lois**<br>A K A Talent, 6310 San Vicente Blvd, #200, Los Angeles CA 90048 USA | Actress |
| **Smith, Lonnie**<br>145 Wesley Forest Dr, Fayetteville GA 30214, USA | Baseball Player |
| **Smith, Lonnie Liston, Jr**<br>Universal Attractions, 135 W 26th St, #1200, New York NY 10001 USA | Jazz Keyboardist |
| **Smith, Louis**<br>Huntingdon Gymnastic Club, Claytons Way, Huntingdon PE29 1UT, England | Gymnast |
| **Smith, M Elizabeth (Liz)**<br>160 E 38th St, #33C, New York NY 10016, USA | Columnist |
| **Smith, Madeline**<br>Joan Gray, Sunbury Island, Sunbury on Thames, Middlesex, England | Actress |
| **Smith, Maggie**<br>Independent Talent Group, 40 Whitfield St, London W1T 2RH, England | Actress |
| **Smith, Margo**<br>Tri-Star Enterprises, PO Box 3367 Brentwood TN 37024, USA | Singer, Songwriter |
| **Smith, Marilynn**<br>3784 N 162nd Lane, Goodyear AZ 85395, USA | Golfer |
| **Smith, Mark E**<br>1312 Elmhurst Lane, Flower Mound TX 75028, USA | Baseball Player |
| **Smith, Marquis T**<br>843 51st St, San Diego CA 92114, USA | Football Player |
| **Smith, Martha**<br>Maggie Smith Management, 3365 Paseo Del Sol, Calabasas CA 91302, USA | Actress, Model |
| **Smith, Marvel A**<br>30 Waterfront Dr, Pittsburgh PA 15222, USA | Football Player |
| **Smith, Marvin (Smitty)**<br>Joel Chriss Co, 300 Mercer St, #3J, New York NY 10003 USA | Jazz Drummer |
| **Smith, Matt**<br>Troika, 74 Clerkenwell Road, #300, London EC1M 5QA, England | Actor |
| **Smith, Michael**<br>Artists of Note, PO Box 11, Kaneville IL 60144, USA | Singer, Songwriter |
| **Smith, Michael A (Mike)**<br>3226 Livingston Road, Jackson MS 39213, USA | Baseball Player |
| **Smith, Michael W**<br>Creative Artists Agency, 2000 Ave of Stars, #100, Los Angeles CA 90067 USA | Singer, Keyboardist, Songwriter |
| **Smith, Michael W (Mike)**<br>619 Feamster Dr, Houston TX 77022, USA | Football Player, Coach |
| **Smith, Mike**<br>Las Vegas Sun, Editorial Dept, 2275 Corporate Circle, #300, Henderson NV 89074, USA | Editorial Cartoonist |
| **Smith, Mike**<br>3445 NE 210th St, Miami FL 33180, USA | Thoroughbred Racing Jockey |
| **Smith, Mike**<br>Arizona Coyotes, 6751 N Sunset Blvd, #200, Glendale AZ 85305 USA | Ice Hockey Player |
| **Smith, Mike**<br>Atlanta Falcons, 4400 Falcon Parkway, Flowery Branch GA 30542 USA | Football Player, Coach |
| **Smith, Mindy**<br>Monterey International, 200 W Superior St, #202, Chicago IL 60654 USA | Singer, Songwriter |
| **Smith, Musa**<br>229 Anniversary Lane, Acworth GA 30102, USA | Football Player |
| **Smith, Nathaniel B (Nate)**<br>6365 Tahoe Dr, Atlanta GA 30349, USA | Baseball Player |
| **Smith, Neal**<br>Maxine Harvard, 7942 W Bell Road, #C5, Glendale AZ 85308 USA | Drummer (Alice Cooper) |
| **Smith, Neil**<br>9423 Nall Ave, Overland Park KS 66207, USA | Football Player |
| **Smith, Nicholas**<br>Michelle Braidman, 10/11 Lower John St, London W1R 3PE, England | Actor |
| **Smith, O Guinn**<br>2 Hawthorne Place, #3P, Boston MA 02114, USA | Track Athlete |
| **Smith, Onterrio P**<br>PO Box 38252, Sacramento CA 95838, USA | Football Player |
| **Smith, Orlando (Tubby)**<br>Texas Tech University, Athletic Dept, Lubbock TX 79409, USA | Basketball Coach |
| **Smith, Osborne E (Ozzie)**<br>201 Kendall Bluff Court, Chesterfield MO 63017, USA | Baseball Player, Sportscaster |
| **Smith, Otis F**<br>607 Applewood Ave, Altamonte Springs Fl 32714, USA | Basketball Player |
| **Smith, Parrish**<br>I C M Partners, 10250 Constellation Blvd, #900, Los Angeles CA 90067 USA | Rap Artist (EPMD) |
| **Smith, Patti**<br>High Road Touring, 751 Bridgeway, #200, Sausalito CA 94965 USA | Singer, Songwriter |
| **Smith, Peter J (Pete)**<br>10030 Halstead Dr, Suwanee GA 30024, USA | Baseball Player |
| **Smith, Peter L (Pete)**<br>3512 Dixon Lane, The Villages FL 32162, USA | Baseball Player |
| **Smith, R Jackson**<br>122 Palmers Hill Road, #3101, Stamford CT 06902, USA | Diver |
| **Smith, R Jeffrey**<br>Washington Post, Editorial Dept, 1150 15th St NW, Washington DC 20071 USA | Journalist |
| **Smith, Raonall A**<br>1609 119th Street Court NW, Gig Harbor WA 98332, USA | Football Player |
| **Smith, Raymond E (Ray)**<br>17183 Poblado Court, San Diego CA 92127, USA | Baseball Player |
| **Smith, Renee Felice**<br>Don Buchwald Talent Agency, 6500 Wilshire Blvd, #2200, Los Angeles CA 90048 USA | Actress |
| **Smith, Rex**<br>Re/Max Realtors, 6695 E Pacific Coast Highway, #150, Long Beach CA 90803, USA | Actor |
| **Smith, Richard H (Dick)**<br>1926 Norwood Lane, State College PA 16803, USA | Baseball Player |
| **Smith, Rick**<br>RR 1, Perth Road Village ON K0H 2L0, Canada | Ice Hockey Player |
| **Smith, Riley**<br>Gersh Agency, 9465 Wilshire Blvd, #600, Beverly Hills CA 90212 USA | Actor |

**Smith, Robaire F** — Football Player
4002 Silver Ridge Blvd, Missouri City TX 77459, USA

**Smith, Robert** — Singer, Guitarist (Cure)
Primary Talent International, 10-11 Jockey's Fields, London WC1R 4BN, England

**Smith, Robert C (Bob)** — Senator, NH
9012 Rocky Lake Court, Sarasota FL 34238, USA

**Smith, Robert E (Bobby)** — Baseball Player
2822 60th Ave, Oakland CA 94605, USA

**Smith, Robert Gray (Graysmith)** — Editorial Cartoonist
San Francisco Chronicle, 901 Mission St, San Francisco CA 94103, USA

**Smith, Robert H** — Financier
1277 Parkview Ave, Pasadena CA 91103, USA

**Smith, Robert Lee** — Singer (Tams)
Speer Entertainment Services, PO Box 2620, McDonough GA 30253, USA

**Smith, Robert S** — Football Player
2202 Spring Lake Park Lane, Spring TX 77386, USA

**Smith, Robyn** — Thoroughbred Racing Jockey
1155 San Ysidro Dr, Beverly Hills CA 90210, USA

**Smith, Roderick (Rod)** — Football Player
6304 Charrington Dr, Englewood CO 80111, USA

**Smith, Roger** — Actor
2707 Benedict Canyon Dr, Beverly Hills CA 90210, USA

**Smith, Rolland** — Commentator
CBS-TV, News Dept, 524 W 57th St, New York NY 10019, USA

**Smith, Ron** — Drag Racing Driver
14933 165th Place SE, Renton WA 98059, USA

**Smith, Russell** — Singer (Amazing Rhythm Aces), Songwriter
Gen-X Entertainment, PO Box 128164, Nashville TN 37212, USA

**Smith, Sam** — Actor
Lorraine Brennan Mgmt, Greenmount Industrial Estate, #22, Harold's Cross, Dublin 6, Ireland

**Smith, Sam** — Basketball Player
246 Calvary Colony Road, Memphis TN 38127, USA

**Smith, Samuel F (Sam)** — Singer, Songwriter
Capitol Records, 810 7th Ave, New York NY 10019 USA

**Smith, Scott B** — Writer
Lynne Pleshette Agency, 2700 N Beachwood Dr, Los Angeles CA 90068, USA

**Smith, Shawnee** — Actress
L I N K Entertainment, 11872 La Grange Ave, Los Angeles CA 90025 USA

**Smith, Shelley** — Actress, Model
4184 Colfax Ave, Studio City CA 91604, USA

**Smith, Sheridan** — Actress
Independent Talent Group, 40 Whitfield St, London W1T 2RH, England

**Smith, Sherman L** — Football Player
1032 N 41st Place, Renton WA 98056, USA

**Smith, Sinjin** — Volleyball Player, Model
Beach Volleyball Camps, PO Box 1714, Pacific Palisades CA 90272, USA

**Smith, Stanley R (Stan)** — Tennis Player
2 Widewater Road, Hilton Head SC 29926, USA

**Smith, Stephanie** — Singer
Select Artist Group, PO Box 1418, La Vergne TN 37086, USA

**Smith, Stephen C (Steve)** — Football Player
1104 Lake Shore Dr, Barrington IL 60010, USA

**Smith, Steve** — Basketball Coach
Oak Hill Academy, Atheltic Dept, 2635 Oak Hill Road, Mouth of Wilson VA 24363, USA

**Smith, Steve** — Ice Hockey Player
5712 NW 118th St, Oklahoma City OK 73162, USA

**Smith, Steve (T J Tatters)** — Clown
Big Apple Circus, 505 8th Ave, #1900, New York NY 10018 USA

**Smith, Steven** — Labor Leader
National Rural Letter Carriers Assn, 1630 Duke St, #200, Alexandria VA 22314, USA

**Smith, Steven A (Steve)** — Football Player
2717 Millwood Dr, Richardson TX 75082, USA

**Smith, Steven D (Steve)** — Basketball Player
755 Heards Ferry Road NW, Atlanta GA 30328, USA

**Smith, Steven L** — Astronaut
N A S A, Johnson Space Center, 2101 NASA Road, Houston TX 77058 USA

**Smith, Steven W** — Inventor (Whole Body Scanner)
Tek84 Engineering Group, 10907 Technology Place, San Diego CA 92127, USA

**Smith, Stevonne L (Steve)** — Football Player
Baltimore Ravens, Ravens Stadium, 1 Winning Dr, Baltimore MD 21230 USA

**Smith, Susan M** — Model
Playboy Promotions, 9346 Civic Center Dr, #200, Beverly Hills CA 90210 USA

**Smith, Tangela N** — Basketball Player
San Antonio Silver Stars, 1 AT&T Center, San Antonio TX 78219 USA

**Smith, Tasha** — Actress
A P A Talent & Literary Agency, 405 S Beverly Dr, #300, Beverly Hills CA 90212 USA

**Smith, Taylor** — Golfer
1157 Sandlake Road, Saint Augustine FL 32092, USA

**Smith, Thomas L, Jr** — Football Player
360 N C Highway 37 N, Gates NC 27937, USA

**Smith, Tommie** — Track Athlete, Football Player
1800 Lilburn Stone Mountain Road, Stone Mountain GA 30087, USA

**Smith, Tony** — Basketball Player
2645 N 40th St, Milwaukee WI 53210, USA

**Smith, Travian D** — Football Player
13841 County Road 2167D, Tatum TX 75691, USA

**Smith, Travis W** — Baseball Player
1865 Cherry St, Clarkston WA 99403, USA

**Smith, Vernice C** — Football Player
4347 Arajo Court, Orlando FL 32812, USA

**Smith, Vernon L** — Nobel Economics Laureate
336 N Lemon St, Orange CA 92866, USA

**Smith, Vince** — Singer, Songwriter
Process Talent Mgmt, 439 Wiley Ave, Franklin PA 16323, USA

**Smith, Vinson R** — Football Player
807 Alexander St, #807, Statesville NC 28677, USA

**Smith, Wadada Leo** — Jazz Trumpeter, Composer
California Institute of the Arts, Music Dept, 24700 McBean Parkway, Valencia CA 91355, USA

**Smith, Wallace B** — Religious Leader
1817 NW Rose Court, Lees Summit MO 64081, USA

**Smith, Walter** — Computer Software Designer
Microsoft Corp, 1 Microsoft Way, Redmond WA 98052, USA

**Smith, Walter H F** — Oceanographer, Cartologist
National Oceanic/Atmospheric Admin, 14th St & Constitution Ave, Washington DC 20230, USA

**Smith, Wayne L** — Football Player
7730 S Bishop St, Chicago IL 60620, USA

**Smith, Wendy** — Singer, Guitarist (Prefab Sprout)
Paradigm Agency, 360 N Crescent Dr, North Building, Beverly Hills CA 90210 USA

**Smith, Wilbur A** — Writer
Charles Pick Consultancy, 21 Dagmar Terrace, London N1 2BN, England

**Smith, Will** — Actor, Singer, Rap Artist
Overbrook Entertainment, 10202 W Washington Blvd, Poitier Building, Culver City CA 90232, USA

**Smith, William** — Actor
Spotlight, 7 Leicester Place, London WC2H 7RJ, England

**Smith, William (Bill), Jr** — Swimmer
45-090 Namoku St, #E2, Kaneohe HI 96744, USA

**Smith, William (Will), III** — Football Player
New England Patriots, 1 Patriot Place, Foxboro MA 02035 USA

**Smith, William D** — Navy Admiral
7452 Spring Village Dr, #309, Springfield VA 22150, USA

**Smith, William J (Billy)** — Ice Hockey Player
8356 Quail Meadow Way, West Palm Beach FL 33412, USA

**Smith, William Jay** — Writer
62 Luther Shaw Road, RR 1 Box 151, Cummington MA 01026, USA

**Smith, William Y** — Army General
6541 Brooks Place, Falls Church VA 22044, USA

**Smith, Willie E** — Baseball Player
1330 E 68th St, Savannah GA 31404, USA

**Smith, Willow** — Actress, Singer
Overbrook Entertainment, 450 N Roxbury Dr, #400, Beverly Hills CA 90210, USA

**Smith, Wyatt** — Actor
Coast to Coast Talent, 3350 Barham Blvd, Los Angeles CA 90068 USA

**Smith, Yeardley** — Actress
A P A Talent & Literary Agency, 405 S Beverly Dr, #300, Beverly Hills CA 90212 USA

**Smith, Zadie** — Writer
A P Watt, 20 John St, London WC1N 2DR, England

**Smith, Zane W** — Baseball Player
420 Windship Place NW, Atlanta GA 30327, USA

**Smith-Cameron, J** — Actress
Gersh Agency, 9465 Wilshire Blvd, #600, Beverly Hills CA 90212 USA

**Smither, Chris** — Singer, Guitarist, Songwriter
Young/Hunter Mgmt, PO Box 3219, Amherst MA 01004, USA

**Smitherman, Stephen** — Baseball Player
PO Box 1890, McAlester OK 74502, USA

**Smithers, William** — Actor
2202 Anacapa St, Santa Barbara CA 93105, USA

**Smithies, Oliver** — Nobel Medicine Laureate
318 Umstead Dr, Chapel Hill NC 27516, USA

**Smithson, W Michael (Mike)** — Baseball Player
25405 Swan Creek Road, Centerville TN 37033, USA

**Smit-McPhee, Kodi** — Actor
I C M Partners, 10250 Constellation Blvd, #900, Los Angeles CA 90067 USA

**Smit-McPhee, Sianoa** — Actress
Intellectual Artists Mgmt, 10585 Santa Monica Blvd, #135, Los Angeles CA 90025, USA

**Smitrovich, Bill** — Actor
3512 Crownridge Dr, Sherman Oaks CA 91403, USA

**Smits, Jimmy** — Actor
United Talent Agency, U T A Plaza, 9336 Civic Center Dr, Beverly Hills CA 90210 USA

**Smits, Rik** — Basketball Player
8346 E 550 S, Zionsville IN 46077, USA

**Smiun, Dick** — Basketball Player
2073 Donegal Circle, Salt Lake City UT 84109, USA

**Smoke** — Rap Artist (Field Mob)
Geffen Records, 10900 Wilshire Blvd, #1000, Los Angeles CA 90024, USA

**Smolan, Rick** — Photographer
Workman Publishers, 225 Varick St, #900, New York NY 10014, USA

**Smolinski, Bryan A** — Ice Hockey Player
4869 Stoneleigh Road, Bloomfield Hills MI 48302, USA

**Smolinski, Mark W** — Football Player
3300 Country Club Road, Petoskey MI 49770, USA

**Smolka, James W** — Test Pilot
PO Box 2123, Lancaster CA 93539, USA

**Smollett, Jurnee** — Actress
I C M Partners, 10250 Constellation Blvd, #900, Los Angeles CA 90067 USA

**Smoltz, John A** — Baseball Player
700 Foxhollow Run, Alpharetta GA 30004, USA

**Smoot, George F, III** — Nobel Physics Laureate
Lawrence Berkeley Laboratory, 1 Cyclotron Road, Berkeley CA 94720, USA

**Smoove, J B** — Actor, Comedian, Writer
W M E Entertainment, 9601 Wilshire Blvd, #300, Beverly Hills CA 90210 USA

**Smothers, Dick** — Actor, Comedian (Smothers Brothers)
Smothers Winery, PO Box 219, Kenwood CA 95452, USA

**Smothers, Tom** — Actor, Comedian (Smothers Brothers)
Smothers Winery, PO Box 219, Kenwood CA 95452, USA

**Smulders, Cobie** — Actress
United Talent Agency, U T A Plaza, 9336 Civic Center Dr, Beverly Hills CA 90210 USA

**Smurfit, Victoria** — Actress
United Agents, 12-26 Lexington St, London W1F 0LE, England

**Smyl, Stanley P (Stan)** — Ice Hockey Player
Vancouver Canucks, 800 Griffiths Way, Vancouver BC V6B 6G1, Canada

**Smyth, Greg** — Ice Hockey Player
62 Carrick Dr, Saint John's NF A1A 4N7, Canada

| | |
|---|---|
| **Smyth, Joe**<br>O-Seven Artist Mgmt, PO Box 210586, Nashville TN 37221, USA | Singer, Drummer (Sawyer Brown) |
| **Smyth, Patty**<br>23712 Malibu Colony Road, Malibu CA 90265, USA | Singer, Songwriter |
| **Smyth, Randy**<br>17136 Bluewater Lane, Huntington Beach CA 92649, USA | Yachtsman |
| **Smyth, Ryan A G**<br>Chance Restaurant, 2550-10155 102nd St NW, Edmonton ON T5J 4G8, Canada | Ice Hockey Player |
| **Smyth, Steve**<br>44005 Northgate Ave, Temecula CA 92592, USA | Baseball Player |
| **Smythe, Danny**<br>Horizon Mgmt, PO Box 8770, Endwell NY 13762, USA | Singer, Drummer (Box Tops) |
| **Snead, Esix**<br>1332 42nd St, Orlando FL 32839, USA | Baseball Player |
| **Snead, Jesse Caryle (J C)**<br>11815 SE Plandome Dr, Hobe Sound FL 33455, USA | Golfer |
| **Snead, Norman B (Norm)**<br>6311 Courthouse Road, Providence Forge VA 23140, USA | Football Player |
| **Snead, W T, Sr**<br>Baptist Convention Missionary, PO Box 1602, Los Angeles CA 90001, USA | Religious Leader |
| **Snedden, Stephen**<br>Marshak/Zachary/Mills, 8840 Wilshire Blvd, #100, Beverly Hills CA 90211 USA | Actor |
| **Snedeker, Brandt**<br>2509 Iron Gate Court, Franklin TN 37069, USA | Golfer |
| **Snee, Christopher (Chris)**<br>1049 Clark Road, Franklin Lake NJ 07417, USA | Football Player |
| **Sneed, Ed**<br>4155 Nottinghill Gate Road, Columbus OH 43220, USA | Golfer |
| **Sneed, Floyd**<br>Creative Artists Agency, 2000 Ave of Stars, #100, Los Angeles CA 90067 USA | Drummer (Three Dog Night) |
| **Snegur, Mircea Ion**<br>62A Puschin Str, Chsinev, Moldova | President, Moldova |
| **Snell, Ian D**<br>15612 Lemon Fish Dr, Bradenton FL 34202, USA | Baseball Player |
| **Snell, Matthews (Matt)**<br>Snell Construction, 175 Clendenny Ave, Jersey City NJ 07304, USA | Football Player |
| **Snell, Nathaniel (Nate)**<br>272 Hampton Dr, Orangeburg SC 29118, USA | Baseball Player |
| **Snell, Peter**<br>6452 Dunston Lane, Dallas TX 75214, USA | Track Athlete |
| **Snell, Ray M**<br>1411 W Linebaugh Ave, Tampa FL 33612, USA | Football Player |
| **Snelling, Chris**<br>PO Box 184, Sumner WA 98390, USA | Baseball Player |
| **Snelson, Kenneth D**<br>37 W 12th St, New York NY 10011, USA | Sculptor, Artist |
| **Snepsts, Harold**<br>5623 Highfield Dr, Burnaby BC V5B 1E4, Canada | Ice Hockey Player |
| **Sneva, Tom**<br>3301 E Valley Vista Lane, Paradise Valley AZ 85253, USA | Auto Racing Driver |
| **Sniadecki, James B (Jim)**<br>3267 Congressional Circle, Fairfield CA 94534, USA | Football Player |
| **Snicket, Lemony**<br>Harper Collins Publishers, 10 E 53rd St, Cellar 1, New York NY 10022 USA | Writer |
| **Snider, David D (Dee)**<br>Coallier Entertainment, 48 W 56th St, #5A, New York NY 10019, USA | Singer (Twisted Sister) |
| **Snider, Edward M (Ed)**<br>PO Box 25088, Philadelphia PA 19147, USA | Ice Hockey Executive |
| **Snider, Malcolm P**<br>3997 Orchard Heights Road NW, Salem OR 97304, USA | Football Player |
| **Snider, Mike**<br>PO Box 610, Gleason TN 38229, USA | Banjo Player, Comedian |
| **Snider, R Michael**<br>Pfizer Pharmaceuticals, Eastern Point Road, Groton CT 06340, USA | Medical Researcher |
| **Snider, Todd**<br>Gold Mountain, 3940 Laurel Canyon Blvd, #444, Studio City CA 91604 USA | Singer, Songwriter |
| **Snider, Van V**<br>1615 Windsor Dr, Cleveland OH 44124, USA | Baseball Player |
| **Snipes, Wesley**<br>Snell & Wilmer, 600 Anton Ave, #1400, Costa Mesa CA 92626, USA | Actor |
| **Snitzler, Larry**<br>Lindy Martin Mgmt, 1007 Lakewater Dr, Henrico VA 23229, USA | Concert Guitarist |
| **Snook, Frank W**<br>2580 Elysium Ave, Eugene OR 97401, USA | Baseball Player |
| **Snook, Sarah**<br>United Talent Agency, U T A Plaza, 9336 Civic Center Dr, Beverly Hills CA 90210 USA | Actress |
| **Snoop Dogg-Lion**<br>Stampede Mgmt, 12530 Beatrice St, Los Angeles CA 90066, USA | Rap Artist |
| **Snopek, Christopher S (Chris)**<br>101 Ashton Park Blvd, Madison WS 39110, USA | Baseball Player |
| **Snow**<br>Agency Group Ltd, 142 W 57th St, #600, New York NY 10019 USA | Singer, Songwriter |
| **Snow, Brittany**<br>I C M Partners, 10250 Constellation Blvd, #900, Los Angeles CA 90067 USA | Actress |
| **Snow, D J (Michelle)**<br>Washington Mystics, Verizon Center, 401 9th St NW, #750, Washington DC 20004 USA | Basketball Player |
| **Snow, Eric**<br>3115 Manor Bridge Dr, Alpharetta GA 30004, USA | Basketball Player |
| **Snow, Garth**<br>4 Weeping Willow Court, Glen Head NY 11545, USA | Ice Hockey Player |
| **Snow, Jack T (J T)**<br>750 W California Way, Woodside CA 94062, USA | Baseball Player |
| **Snow, John W**<br>Cerberus Capital Mgmt, 299 Park Ave, #2300, New York NY 10171, USA | Secretary, Treasury; Businessman |
| **Snow, Justin W**<br>1826 Milford St, Carmel IN 46032, USA | Football Player |

**Snow, Mark** — Composer
Robert Urband Assoc, 8981 W Sunset Blvd, #311, West Hollywood CA 90069, USA
**Snowden, James J (Jim)** — Football Player
8647 Point of Woods Dr, Manassas VA 20110, USA
**Snowden, M L** — Sculptor
Masterpiece Publishing, 5 Watson, Irvine CA 92618, USA
**Snowdon, Earl of (A C R Armstrong-Jones)** — Photographer
22 Launceston Place, London W8 5RL, England
**Snowdon, Lisa** — Model, Actress
Creative Mgmt Entertainment Group, 2050 South Bundy Dr, #280, Los Angeles CA 90025, USA
**Snuggerud, Dave** — Ice Hockey Player
4529 Saddlewood Dr, Minnetonka MN 55345, USA
**Snyder, Allan W** — Optical Scientist
National University, Optical Science Center, Canberra ACT 2601, Australia
**Snyder, Barbara** — Educator
Case Western University, President's Office, Aldebert Hall, Cleveland OH 44106, USA
**Snyder, Bill** — Football Coach
Kansas State University, Athletic Dept, Manhattan KS 66506, USA
**Snyder, Christoper R (Chris)** — Baseball Player
4921 W Electra Lane, Glendale AZ 85310, USA
**Snyder, Evan** — Neurologist
Harvard Medical School, 25 Shattuck St, Boston MA 02115, USA
**Snyder, Gary S** — Writer
18442 MacNab Cypress Road, Nevada City CA 95959, USA
**Snyder, Gerald G (Jerry)** — Baseball Player
2553 Wild Oak Forest Lane, Seabrook TX 77586, USA
**Snyder, J Cory** — Baseball Player
468 N Loafer Dr, Payson UT 84651, USA
**Snyder, James R (Jimmy)** — Baseball Player, Manager
7516 Dunbridge Dr, Odessa FL 33556, USA
**Snyder, Joey, III** — Golfer
8811 E Riviera Dr, Scottsdale AZ 85260, USA
**Snyder, Kyle E** — Baseball Player
1869 Upper Cove Terrace, Sarasota FL 34231, USA
**Snyder, Liza** — Actress
Greene Assoc, 1901 Ave of Stars, #130, Los Angeles CA 90067 USA
**Snyder, Richard J (Dick)** — Basketball Player
4621 E Mockingbird Lane, Paradise Valley AZ 85253, USA
**Snyder, Russell H (Russ)** — Baseball Player
PO Box 264, Nelson NE 68961, USA
**Snyder, Solomon H** — Psychiatrist, Pharmacologist
3801 Canterbury Road, #1001, Baltimore MD 21218, USA
**Snyder, Suzanne** — Actress
Premiere Artists Agency, 1875 Century Park E, #2250, Los Angeles CA 90067 USA
**Snyder, William D** — Photojournalist
Rochester Institute of Technology, Photojournalism Dept, Rochester NY 14623, USA
**Snyder, Zack** — Director, Writer
Cruel & Unusual Films, 4000 Warner Blvd, Building 90, Burbank CA 91522, USA
**Snyderman, Nancy** — Surgeon, Entertainer
ABC-TV, News Dept, 77 W 66th St, New York NY 10023 USA
**So Ywon Ryu** — Golfer
Ladies Pro Golf Assn, 100 International Golf Dr, Daytona Beach FL 32124 USA
**So, Perry** — Conductor
Harrison/Parrott, 5-6 Albion Court, London W6 0QT, England
**Soares, Mario A N L** — President, Portugal
Rua Dr Joao Soares #2-3, 1600 Lisbon, Portugal
**Sobchuk, Dennis J** — Ice Hockey Player
PO Box 2541, Carefree AZ 85377, USA
**Sobel, Dava** — Writer
Walker Co, 435 Hudson St, New York NY 10014, USA
**Sobers, Ricky B** — Basketball Player
6530 Annie Oakley Dr, #1414, Henderson NV 89014, USA
**Sobieski, Leelee** — Actress
Mosiac Media Group, 9200 W Sunset Blvd, #1000, Los Angeles CA 90069 USA
**Sobrero Markgraf, Kate** — Soccer Player
5055 N Cumberland Blvd, Milwaukee WI 53217, USA
**Sobrino-Stearns, Michelle** — Publisher
Variety 11175 Santa Monica Blvd, Los Angeles CA 90025, USA
**Sobule, Jill** — Singer, Songwriter
Fleming Artists, 543 N Main St, Ann Arbor MI 48104, USA
**Sochor, James (Jim)** — Football Coach
1018 Kent Dr, Davis CA 95616, USA
**Sodano, Angelo Cardinal** — Religious Leader
Santa Maria Nuova, Piazza di Santa Francesca Romana 4, 00186 Rome, Lazio, Italy
**Soderbergh, Steven A** — Director
Anonymous Content, 3532 Hayden Ave, Culver City CA 90232 USA
**Soderholm, Eric T** — Baseball Player
10S360 Hampshire Lane W, Willowbrook IL 60527, USA
**Soderqvist, Johan** — Composer
First Artists, 4764 Park Granada, #210, Calabasas CA 91302 USA
**Sodowski, Clint R** — Baseball Player
351 Whippoorwill Road, Ponca City OK 74604, USA
**Soedergren, Anders** — Cross Country Skier
Hinderstigen 4, 831 32 Ostersund, Sweden
**Soell, Stefan** — Photographer
Fotodesign Stefan Soell, Gewerbepark, Fallenbrunner 17, 88045 Friedrichshafen, Germany
**Soetaert, Douglas H (Doug)** — Ice Hockey Player
13006 66th Ave SE, Snohomish WA 98296, USA
**Sofaer, Abraham D** — Attorney
1200 Bryant St, Palo Alto CA 94301, USA
**Sofer, Rena** — Actress
Framework Entertainment, 9057 Nemo St, #C, West Hollywood CA 90069 USA
**Soffer, Jesse Lee** — Actor
Innovative Artists, 1505 10th St, Santa Monica CA 90401 USA
**Sofield, William** — Interior Designer, Artist
Studio Sofield, 380 Lafayette St, #300, New York NY 10003, USA

| | |
|---|---|
| **Softley, Iain** | Director |
| 32A Carnaby St, London W1V 1PA, England | |
| **Sogaard, Ole S** | Epidemiologist |
| Aarhus Universiy Hospital, Skejby, Brendstrupgardsvej 100, 8000 Aarhus N, Denmark | |
| **Sogliuzzo, Andre** | Actor |
| W M E Entertainment, 9601 Wilshire Blvd, #300, Beverly Hills CA 90210 USA | |
| **Sohn, Kurt F** | Football Player |
| 6 Paine Commons, Yaphank NY 11980, USA | |
| **Sohn, Sonja** | Actress |
| A P A Talent/Literary Agency, 250 W 57th St, #1701, New York NY 10107 USA | |
| **Sojo, Luis B** | Baseball Player |
| 19250 Wood Sage Dr, Tampa FL 33647, USA | |
| **Soklosky, Bing** | Cinematographer |
| 4654 Cartwright Ave, North Hollywood CA 91602, USA | |
| **Soko** | Singer, Actress |
| Agence Artiste Adequat, 108 Rue Reaumur, 75002 Paris, France | |
| **Sokoloff, Marla** | Actress |
| A P A Talent & Literary Agency, 405 S Beverly Dr, #300, Beverly Hills CA 90212 USA | |
| **Sokolov, Grigory L** | Concert Pianist |
| Konzertdirektion Schmid, Konigstra 36, 30175 Hannover, Germany | |
| **Sokolov, Valeriy** | Concert Violinist |
| Harrison/Parrott, 5-6 Albion Court, London W6 0QT, England | |
| **Sokomanu, A George** | President, Vanuatu |
| Mele Village, PO Box 1319, Port Vila, Vanuatu | |
| **Sokurov, Alexander N** | Director |
| Smolenskaya Nab 4, #222, 199048 Saint Petersburg, Russia | |
| **Solana Madariaga, Javier** | Government Official, Spain |
| European Union Foreign Office, Rue de la Loi, 1048 Brussels, Belgium | |
| **Solberg, Erna** | Prime Minister, Norway |
| Prime Minister's Office, Akersgaten 42, Ploensgt 8, 0030 Oslo, Norway | |
| **Solberg, Magnar** | Biathlete |
| Stabellvn 60, 7000 Trondheim, Norway | |
| **Soleil, Stella** | Singer |
| Kurfirst/Blackwell, 601 W 26th St, #11, New York NY 10001, USA | |
| **Soles, P J** | Actress |
| Paradigm Agency, 360 N Crescent Dr, North Building, Beverly Hills CA 90210 USA | |
| **Solich, Frank** | Football Coach |
| Ohio University, Athletic Dept, Athens OH 45701, USA | |
| **Solinger, Bob** | Ice Hockey Player |
| 65-101 Grove Dr, Spruce Grove AB T7X 3H7, Canada | |
| **Solis, Alex** | Thoroughbred Racing Jockey |
| 2241 Redwood Dr, Glendora CA 91741, USA | |
| **Soljacic, Marin** | Physicist |
| Massachusetts Institute of Technology, Physics Dept, Cambridge MA 02139, USA | |
| **Sollee, Ben** | Cellist, Singer, Songwriter |
| High Road Touring, 751 Bridgeway, #200, Sausalito CA 94965 USA | |
| **Sollett, Peter** | Director |
| W M E Entertainment, 9601 Wilshire Blvd, #300, Beverly Hills CA 90210 USA | |
| **Sollscher, Goran** | Concert Guitarist |
| Barrett Vantage Artists, 508 8th Ave, #12A00, New York NY 10018 USA | |
| **Solo, Hope A** | Soccer Player |
| Seattle Reign, 3216 Sierra Dr S, Seattle WA 98144 USA | |
| **Solo, Ksenia** | Actress |
| Abrams Artists, 9200 W Sunset Blvd, #1125, West Hollywood CA 90069 USA | |
| **Soloff, Lew** | Trumpeter (Blood Sweat & Tears) |
| Abby Hoffer Enterprises, 223 1/2 E 48th St, New York NY 10017 USA | |
| **Soloman, Sean C** | Space Scientist |
| Carnegie Institution, Terrestrial Magnetism Dept, Washington DC 20015, USA | |
| **Solomon, Ariel E** | Football Player |
| 5045 51st St, Boulder CO 80301, USA | |
| **Solomon, Bruce** | Actor |
| Hollander, 14011 Ventura Blvd, #202W, Sherman Oaks CA 91423, USA | |
| **Solomon, Jesse W** | Football Player |
| 401 SW Bunker St, Madison FL 32340, USA | |
| **Solomon, Susan** | Atmospheric Chemist |
| National Oceanic/Atmospheric Admin, 325 Broadway, Boulder CO 80305, USA | |
| **Solondz, Todd** | Director, Writer |
| W M E Entertainment, 9601 Wilshire Blvd, #300, Beverly Hills CA 90210 USA | |
| **Solovay, Robert M** | Mathematician |
| University of California, Mathematics Dept, Berkeley CA 94720, USA | |
| **Soloviev, Dmitri V** | Figure Skater |
| Figure Skating Federation, Luzhnetskaya Nab 8, 119991 Moscow, Russia | |
| **Soloviyev, Vladimir A** | Cosmonaut |
| Khovanskaya Ul D 3, Kv 28, 129515 Moscow, Russia | |
| **Solovyev, Anatoly Y** | Cosmonaut |
| Cosmonaut Training Center, Star City, 141160 Zvezdny Gorodok, Moscow Oblast, Russia | |
| **Solow, Robert M** | Nobel Economics Laureate |
| 1010 Waltham St, #328, Lexington MA 02421, USA | |
| **Solt, Ronald M (Ron)** | Football Player |
| 1200 Thornhurst Road, Bear Creek Township PA 18702, USA | |
| **Soltan, Jerzy** | Architect |
| 148 Boylston St, Watertown MA 02472, USA | |
| **Solvay, Jacques E** | Businessman |
| Solvay & Cie SA, Rue du Prince Albert 33, 1050 Brussels, Belgium | |
| **Solzhenitsyn, Ignat** | Concert Pianist |
| Columbia Artists Mgmt Inc, 5 Columbus Circle, 1790 Broadway, #1600, New York NY 10019 USA | |
| **Som, Peter** | Fashion Designer |
| Peter Som Inc, 215 W 40th St, New York NY 10018, USA | |
| **Somare, Michael T** | Prime Minister, Papua New Guinea |
| Prime Minister's Office, Parliament House, Waigani 131 N D, Papua New Guinea | |
| **Somerhalder, Ian** | Actor |
| I C M Partners, 10250 Constellation Blvd, #900, Los Angeles CA 90067 USA | |
| **Somers, Gwen** | Actress, Model |
| Alice Fries Agency, 1927 Vista Del Mar Ave, Los Angeles CA 90068, USA | |
| **Somers, Suzanne** | Actress |
| Port Carling Productions, 23961 Craftsman Road, Calabasas CA 91302, USA | |

**Somerset, Williard F (Willie)** — Basketball Player
6441 Oak View Dr, Harrisburg PA 17112, USA

**Somerville, Bonnie** — Actress, Singer
McKeon-Myrones Mgmt, 3500 Olive Ave, #770, Burbank CA 91505 USA

**Somerville, David (Dave)** — Singer (Diamonds)
10061 Riverside Dr, #114, Toluca Lake CA 91602, USA

**Somerville, Phyllis** — Actress
Hartig-Hilepo Agency, 54 W 21st St, #610, New York NY 10010 USA

**Somerville, Robert E** — Religion Educator
Columbia University, Religion Dept, Claremont Hall, New York NY 10027, USA

**Sommaruga, Cornelio** — Association Executive
16 Chemin des Crets-de-Champel, 1206 Geneva, Switzerland

**Sommer, Alfred** — Epidemiologist
Johns Hopkins University, Hygiene & Public Health School, Baltimore MD 21218, USA

**Sommer, Elke** — Actress, Model
Literature Unlimited, 1850 N Whitley Ave, #1020, Los Angeles CA 90028, USA

**Sommer, Josef** — Actor
Don Buchwald Talent Agency, 6500 Wilshire Blvd, #2200, Los Angeles CA 90048 USA

**Sommer, Richard O (Rich), II** — Actor
A P A Talent & Literary Agency, 405 S Beverly Dr, #300, Beverly Hills CA 90212 USA

**Sommer, Ron** — Businessman
Deutsche Telekom, Friedrich-Ebert-Allee 140, 53113 Bonn, Germany

**Sommer, Roy** — Ice Hockey Player
65 Roman Dr, Shrewsbury MA 01545, USA

**Sommer-Bodenbu, Angela** — Writer, Artist
PO Box 834, Silver City NM 88062, USA

**Sommers, Joanie** — Singer
Xentel, 101 NE 3rd Ave, #203, Fort Lauderdale FL 33301, USA

**Sommore, Laura Rambough** — Actress, Comedienne
Universal Attractions, 135 W 26th St, #1200, New York NY 10001 USA

**Somorjai, Gabor A** — Chemist
665 San Luis Road, Berkeley CA 94707, USA

**Son, Masayoshi** — Inventor (Pocket Electronic Translator)
24-1 Nihonbash, Hakozakicho, Chuoku, Tokyo 103 8501, Japan

**Sondeckis, Saulis** — Conductor
Saint Petersburg Hermitage Orchestra, Mikhailovskaya Str 2, 191186 Saint Petersburg, Russia

**Sondheim, Stephen J** — Composer, Lyricist
265 Wollaton Vale, Wollato, Nottingham NG8 2PX, England

**Sonefeld, Jim** — Drummer (Hootie & the Blowfish)
FishCo Mgmt, 2519 Devine Street  Columbia SC 29205, USA

**Song, Brenda** — Actress
United Talent Agency, U T A Plaza, 9336 Civic Center Dr, Beverly Hills CA 90210 USA

**Songaila, Antoinette** — Astronomer
University of Hawaii, Astronomy Dept, Honolulu HI 96822, USA

**Songaila, Darius** — Basketball Player
141 S Longfellow Lane, Mooresville NC 28117, USA

**Soni, Karan** — Actor
Michael Zanuck's Agency, 28035 Dorothy Dr, #120, Agoura Hills CA 91301, USA

**Soni, Rebecca** — Swimmer
University of Southern California, Trojan Swim Club, Athletic Dept, Los Angeles CA 90089, USA

**Sonique** — Singer, Synthesizer Player
Ultra D J Mgmt, 2 City Business Centre, Lower Road, London SE16 2XB, England

**Sonja** — Queen, Norway
Det Kongelige Slott, Drammensveien 1, 0010 Oslo, Norway

**Sonnanstine, Andrews M (Andy)** — Baseball Player
526 Reimer Road, Wadsworth OH 44281, USA

**Sonnenfeld, Barry** — Director
W M E Entertainment, 9601 Wilshire Blvd, #300, Beverly Hills CA 90210 USA

**Sonnenschein, Hugo F** — Educator, Economist
1126 E 59th St, Chicago IL 60637, USA

**Sonnichsen, Matt** — Volleyball Player
Newberry College, Athletic Dept, Newberry SC 29108, USA

**Sonnier, Jo-El** — Singer, Guitarist
Fat City Artists, 1906 Chet Atkins Place, #502, Nashville TN 37212 USA

**Sonzero, Jim** — Director, Writer
United Talent Agency, U T A Plaza, 9336 Civic Center Dr, Beverly Hills CA 90210 USA

**Soo Yun Kang** — Golfer
Ladies Pro Golf Assn, 100 International Golf Dr, Daytona Beach FL 32124 USA

**Soomekh, Bahar** — Actress
McClure Assoc, 5225 Wilshire Blvd, #909, Los Angeles CA 90036, USA

**Sope Mautamata, Barak T** — Prime Minister, Vanuatu
Melanesian Progressive Pati (MPP), PO Box 39, Port Vila, Vanuatu

**Sophia** — Queen Consort, Spain
Palacio de la Zarzuela, 28071 Madrid, Spain

**Sophie** — Hereditary Princess, Liechtenstein
Heriditary Princess's Residence, Schloss Vaduz, 9490 Vaduz, Liechtenstein

**Sorbo, Kevin** — Actor
914 Westwood Blvd, #584, Los Angeles CA 90024, USA

**Sorel, Edward** — Artist, Illustrator
156 Franklin St, New York NY 10013, USA

**Sorel, Jean** — Actor
Agents Associes, 201 Rue du Faubourg Saint Honore, 75008 Paris, France

**Sorel, Louise** — Actress
20 E 74th St, #3F, New York NY 10021, USA

**Sorensen, Andrew A** — Educator
Greenville Hospital System, 701 Grove Road, Greenville SC 29605, USA

**Sorensen, Holly B** — Producer, Writer, Actress
United Talent Agency, U T A Plaza, 9336 Civic Center Dr, Beverly Hills CA 90210 USA

**Sorensen, Jacki F** — Physical Fitness Expert
Jacki's Inc, 129 1/2 N Woodland Blvd, #5, Deland FL 32720, USA

**Sorensen, Lary A** — Baseball Player
42515 Northville Place Dr, #406, Northville MI 48167, USA

**Sorensen, Marco L (Rocco)** — Auto Racing Driver
Zinksvej 59, 8006 Zurich, Switzerland

**Sorensen, Nicholas C (Nick)** — Football Player
305 Grandview Dr, Blacksburg VA 24060, USA

| | |
|---|---|
| **Sorenson, B Reed** | Auto Racing Driver |
| 4623 Rivers Edge Village, #6508, Ponce Inlet FL 32127, USA | |
| **Sorenson, Garrett** | Opera Singer |
| I M G Artists, Hogarth Business Park, Chiswick, London W4 2TH, England | |
| **Sorenstam, Annika** | Golfer |
| International Mangement Group, 1 Erieview Plaza, 1360 E 9th St, #100, Cleveland OH 44114 USA | |
| **Sorenstam, Charlotta** | Golfer |
| 1411 W Whitman Court, Anthem AZ 85086, USA | |
| **Sorey, Revie C, II** | Football Player |
| 10 E Delaware Place, #31C, Chicago IL 60611, USA | |
| **Sorgi, James (Jim)** | Football Player |
| 28 Hollaway Blvd, Brownsburg IN 46112, USA | |
| **Soriano, Alfonso G** | Baseball Player |
| 21 E Huron St, #3301, Chicago IL 60611, USA | |
| **Soriano, Edward** | Army General |
| Northrop Grumman, 1840 Century Park E, Los Angeles CA 90067, USA | |
| **Soriano, Rafael** | Baseball Player |
| 7601 60th Dr NE, #A, Marysville WA 98270, USA | |
| **Sorkin, Aaron B** | Producer, Writer |
| W M E Entertainment, 9601 Wilshire Blvd, #300, Beverly Hills CA 90210 USA | |
| **Sorkin, Andrew Ross** | Actor |
| Creative Artists Agency, 2000 Ave of Stars, #100, Los Angeles CA 90067 USA | |
| **Sorkin, Arleen** | Actress |
| Creative Artists Agency, 2000 Ave of Stars, #100, Los Angeles CA 90067 USA | |
| **Sorlie, Donald M** | Test Pilot |
| 6947 Wagner Way NW, #A, Gig Harbor WA 98335, USA | |
| **Sorokin, Peter P** | Physicist |
| 5 Ashwood Road, South Salem NY 10590, USA | |
| **Soros, George** | Financier |
| Soros Fund Mgmt, 888 7th Ave, #2900, New York NY 10106, USA | |
| **Sorrell, Henry T** | Football Player |
| 404 Oak St, Talladega AL 35160, USA | |
| **Sorrell, John W** | Fashion Designer |
| Lawns, 16 South Grove, London N6 6BJ, England | |
| **Sorrell, Martin** | Businessman |
| Ogilvy & Mather Worldwide, 1 Soldiers Field Park, #413, Boston MA 02163, USA | |
| **Sorrenti, Mario** | Photographer |
| Art Partner, 155 6th Ave, #1500, New York NY 10013, USA | |
| **Sorrentino, Paolo** | Director, Writer |
| United Talent Agency, U T A Plaza, 9336 Civic Center Dr, Beverly Hills CA 90210 USA | |
| **Sortun, Henrik M (Rick)** | Football Player |
| 6708 16th Ave NW, Seattle WA 98117, USA | |
| **Sorum, Matt** | Drummer (Velvet Revolver) |
| Sanctuary Mgmt, 15301 Ventura Blvd, Building B, Sherman Oaks CA 91403, USA | |
| **Sorvino, Mira K** | Actress |
| Untitled Entertainment, 350 S Beverly Dr, #200, Beverly Hills CA 90212 USA | |
| **Sorvino, Paul** | Actor |
| Innovative Artists, 1505 10th St, Santa Monica CA 90401 USA | |
| **Sosa, Elias M** | Baseball Player |
| 333 Red Barn Trail, Matthews NC 28104, USA | |
| **Sosa, Ernest** | Philosopher |
| Brown University, Philosophy Dept, Providence RI 02912, USA | |
| **Sosa, Samuel (Sammy)** | Baseball Player |
| 505 N Lake Shore Dr, #5500, Chicago IL 60611, USA | |
| **Sosnovska, Olga** | Actress |
| Innovative Artists, 1505 10th St, Santa Monica CA 90401 USA | |
| **Sossamon, Shannyn** | Actress |
| A P A Talent & Literary Agency, 405 S Beverly Dr, #300, Beverly Hills CA 90212 USA | |
| **Sostorics, Colleen** | Ice Hockey Player |
| Team Canada, 2424 University Dr NW, Calgary AB T2N 3Y9, Canada | |
| **Sotillo, Nolan A** | Actor |
| United Talent Agency, U T A Plaza, 9336 Civic Center Dr, Beverly Hills CA 90210 USA | |
| **Sotin, Hans** | Opera Singer |
| Schulheide 10, 21227 Bendestorf, Germany | |
| **Sotkilava, Zurab L** | Opera Singer |
| Bolshoi Theater, Teatralnaya Pl 1, 103009 Moscow, Russia | |
| **Soto, Blanca** | Actress |
| Latin World Entertainment, 3470 NW 82nd Ave, #670, Miami FL 33122, USA | |
| **Soto, Geovany** | Baseball Player |
| 6319 Perch Creek Dr, Houston TX 77049, USA | |
| **Soto, Jock** | Ballet Dancer |
| New York City Ballet, Lincoln Center Plaza, New York NY 10023 USA | |
| **Soto, Mario M** | Baseball Player |
| Cincinnati Reds, Great American Ball Park, 100 Main St, Cincinnati OH 45202 USA | |
| **Soto, Talisa** | Actress, Model |
| Framework Entertainment, 9057 Nemo St, #C, West Hollywood CA 90069 USA | |
| **Sotomayor Sanabria, Javier** | Track Athlete |
| International Mangement Group, 1 Erieview Plaza, 1360 E 9th St, #100, Cleveland OH 44114 USA | |
| **Sotomayor, Antonio** | Artist |
| 3 LeRoy Place, San Francisco CA 94109, USA | |
| **Sotomayor, Sonia M** | Supreme Court Justice |
| US Supreme Court, 1 1st St NE, Washington DC 20543 USA | |
| **Soualem, Zinedine** | Actor |
| Voyez Mon Agent, 20 Ave Rapp, 75007 Paris, France | |
| **Souare, Ahmed Tidiane** | Prime Minister, Guinea |
| Prime Minister's Office, PO Box 5141, Cite des Nations, Conakry, Guinea | |
| **Souchon, Alain** | Singer |
| Voyez Mon Agent, 20 Ave Rapp, 75007 Paris, France | |
| **Soukalova, Gabriela** | Biathlete |
| K B L SG, Liberecky Krog, 46601 Jablonec Nad Nisou, Czech Republic | |
| **Soukupova, Hana** | Model |
| Mega Model Agency, Kaiser-Wilhelm-Str 93, 20355 Hamburg, Germany | |
| **Soul, David** | Actor, Singer |
| Diamond Mgmt, 31 Percy St, London W1T 2DD, England | |
| **Soulja Boy** | Rap Artist |
| Soulja Boy Music, 113 Shadow Lane, Batesville MS 38606, USA | |

**Soumare, Cheikh Hadjibou** — Prime Minister, Senegal
Prime Minister's Office, Ave Leopold Sedar Senghor, Dakar, Senegal
**Soumyanath, Amala** — Neurologist
Oregon Health Science University, 3181 SW Jackson Park Dr, Portland OR 97239 USA
**Souray, Sheldon S** — Ice Hockey Player
4124 Madella Ave, Sherman Oaks CA 91403, USA
**Sourouzian, Hourig** — Archaeologist
31 Abu El Reda, 11211 Cairo-Zamalek, Egypt
**Soutar, Dave** — Bowler
6910 Chickasaw Bayou Road, Bradenton FL 34203, USA
**Soutar, Judy** — Bowler
6910 Chickasaw Bayou Road, Bradenton FL 34203, USA
**Soutendijk, Renee** — Actress
Mover Shaker, De Lairessestraat 141, 1075 Amsterdam HJ, Netherlands
**Souter, David H** — Supreme Court Justice
214 Hopkins Green Road, Contoocook NH 03229, USA
**Southam, James** — Cross Counry Skier
18230 Norway Dr, Anchorage AK 99516, USA
**Souther, J D** — Singer, Guitarist, Songwriter
Paul Hanan Mgmt, 7775 Sunset Blvd, #118, Los Angeles CA 90046, USA
**Southern, Edwin M** — Biochemist
Oxford University, Wellington Square, Oxford OX1 2JD, England
**Southern, Silas (Eddie)** — Track Athlete
2006 Custer Parkway, Richardson TX 75080, USA
**Southern, Taryn** — Actress, Singer
I C M Partners, 10250 Constellation Blvd, #900, Los Angeles CA 90067 USA
**Southwick, Leslie H** — Judge
US Court of Appeals, Eastland Courthouse, 245 E Capitol St, Jackson MS 39201, USA
**Southworth, William F (Bill)** — Baseball Player
320 Dobbins Road, Saint Louis MO 63119, USA
**Souto de Moura, Eduardo** — Pritzker Architectual Laureate
University of Oporto, Architecture Faculty, Praca Gomes Teixeira, 4099 002 Oporto, Portugal
**Souza, K Mark** — Baseball Player
1120 Dumas Way, Roseville CA 95747, USA
**Souza, Luciana** — Singer, Composer
Vision Arts Mgmt, 16 Clint Fingers Road, Saugerties NY 12477, USA
**Sova, Peter M** — Cinematographer
1492 Roses Brook Road, South Kortright NY 13842, USA
**Sovern, Michael I** — Educator, Attorney
Columbia University, Law School, 435 W 116th St, New York NY 10027, USA
**Sovran, Gino** — Basketball Player
2669 Cheswick Dr, Troy MI 48084, USA
**Sowell, Arnold (Arnie)** — Track Athlete
1647 Waterstone Lane, #1, Charlotte NC 28262, USA
**Sowell, Jerald M** — Football Player
201 Stockton Dr, Southlake TX 76092, USA
**Sowell, Thomas** — Economist
Stanford University, Hoover Institution, Stanford CA 94305, USA
**Sowells, Richard A (Rich)** — Football Player
16718 Chewton Glen St, Tomball TX 77377, USA
**Soyer, Ferdi Sabit** — Prime Minister, Turkish Northern Cypress
Prime Minister's Office, Via Mersin 10, Lefkosa, Turkish Northern Cypress
**Soyinka, Wole** — Nobel Literature Laureate
University of Nevada, Creative Writing Dept, Las Vegas NV 89154, USA
**Soyster, Harry E** — Army General
56 Lakeview Ave, #14, New Canaan CT 06840, USA
**Sozen, Melisa** — Actress
Id Iletisim Mgmt, Guvercin Sok, #28/3, Levent, Istanbul, Turkey
**Sozzi, Sebastian** — Actor
Harvest Talent Mgmt, 121 W 80th St, #1, New York NY 10024, USA
**Spaak, Ruth** — Artist
20 Sandfield Road, Stratford upon Avon, Warwickshire CV37 9AG, England
**Spacek, Jaroslav** — Ice Hockey Player
5944 Corinne Lane, Clarence Center NY 14032, USA
**Spacek, Sissy** — Actress
PO Box 22, #640, Cobham VA 22947, USA
**Spacey, Kevin** — Actor
Joanne Horowitz Mgmt, 9350 Wilshire Blvd, #224, Beverly Hills CA 90212, USA
**Spacks, Patricia M** — Educator
249 E Jefferson St, Charlottesville VA 22902, USA
**Spade, David** — Actor, Comedian
W M E Entertainment, 9601 Wilshire Blvd, #300, Beverly Hills CA 90210 USA
**Spade, Kate** — Fashion Designer
48 W 25th St, #400, New York NY 10010, USA
**Spader, James T** — Actor
I C M Partners, 10250 Constellation Blvd, #900, Los Angeles CA 90067 USA
**Spaelty, Valeria** — Curling Athlete
Curling Association, PO Box 606, 3000 Bern, Switzerland
**Spagnola, John S** — Football Player
414 Hillbrook Road, Bryn Mawr PA 19010, USA
**Spagnuolo, Steve J** — Football Coach
New Orleans Saints, 5800 Airline Highway, Metairie LA 70003 USA
**Spain, Douglas** — Actor
L I N K Entertainment, 11872 La Grange Ave, Los Angeles CA 90025 USA
**Spalding, Esperanza** — Singer, Bassist, Composer
Montuno Producciones, Calle Rosello 246, #5-2, 08008 Barcelona, Spain
**Spalding, Leslie** — Golfer
1055 O'Malley Dr, Billings MT 59102, USA
**Spall, Timothy** — Actor
Markham Froggatt Irwin, Julian House, 4 Windmill St, London W1P 1HF, England
**Spampinato, Joey** — Bassist (NRBQ)
Skyline Music, 2270 Maiden Lane SW, Roanoke VA 24015, USA
**Spampinato, Johnny** — Guitarist (NRBQ)
Skyline Music, 2270 Maiden Lane SW, Roanoke VA 24015, USA
**Span, K Denard** — Baseball Player
Washington Nationals, 1500 S Capitol St SE, Washington DC 20003 USA

**Spanbauer, Tom**          Writer
Houghton Mifflin Harcourt, 215 Park Ave S, #1200, New York NY 10003 USA
**Spander, Art**          Sportswriter
San Francisco Examiner, Editorial Dept, 110 5th Ave, San Francisco CA 94118, USA
**Spangler, Albert D (Al)**          Baseball Player
27202 Afton Way, Huffman TX 77336, USA
**Spani, Gary L**          Football Player
3920 NE Sequoia St, Lees Summit MO 64064, USA
**Spano, Joe**          Actor
Sutton-Barth Vennari, 5900 Wilshire Blvd, #700, Los Angeles CA 90036 USA
**Spano, Robert**          Conductor
Opus 3 Artists, 470 Park Ave S, #900N, New York NY 10016 USA
**Spano, Vincent**          Actor
Kincaid Mgmt, 849 S Broadway, #902, Los Angeles CA 90014, USA
**Spanswick, Willaim H (Bill)**          Baseball Player
1200 Commonwealth Circle, #202, Naples FL 34116, USA
**Sparks, Dana**          Actress
Regenerate Films, 1408 E Thousand Oaks Blvd, Thousand Oaks CA 91362, USA
**Sparks, Daniel E (Dan)**          Basketball Player, Coach
2396 N Bruceville Road, Vincennes IN 47591, USA
**Sparks, Hal**          Actor, Singer, Comedian
Innovative Artists, 1505 10th St, Santa Monica CA 90401 USA
**Sparks, J Jeffrey (Jeff)**          Baseball Player
714 W 42nd St, Houston TX 77018, USA
**Sparks, Jordin**          Singer, Actress
Varela Media, 14 E 77th St, #3F, New York NY 10075, USA
**Sparks, Larry**          Singer
Larry Sparks Show, PO Box 505, Greensburg IN 47240, USA
**Sparks, Nicholas C**          Writer
United Talent Agency, U T A Plaza, 9336 Civic Center Dr, Beverly Hills CA 90210 USA
**Sparks, Paul**          Actor
Gersh Agency, 41 Madison Ave, #3301, New York NY 10010 USA
**Sparks, Phillippi D**          Football Player
4812 W Avenida del Rey, Phoenix AZ 85083, USA
**Sparks, Stephanie**          Golfer
48 Redwood Lane, Wheeling WV 26003, USA
**Sparks, Steven W (Steve)**          Baseball Player
4019 Colony Oaks Dr, Sugar Land TX 77479, USA
**Sparrow, Rory D**          Basketball Player
111 Valley Road, Montclair NJ 07042, USA
**Sparv, Camilla**          Actress
1460 Ocean Dr, #311, Miami Beach FL 33139, USA
**Sparxxx, Bubba**          Rap Artist
Esterman Entertainment, 12333 Pretoria Dr, Silver Spring MD 20904 USA
**Speake, Robert C (Bob)**          Baseball Player
4742 SW Urish Road, Topeka KS 66610, USA
**Speakes, Stephen M**          Army General
Deputy CofStaff, Resourcing/Programs, HqUSA, Pentagon, Washington DC 20310, USA
**Speakman-Pitt, William**          Korean War South African Army Hero (VC)
Victoria Cross Assn, Old Admiralty Building, London SW1A 2BL, England
**Spear, Laurinda H**          Architect
Arquitectonica International, 801 Brickell Ave, #1100, Miami FL 33131, USA
**Spearin, Charles**          Musician
Agency Group Ltd, 142 W 57th St, #600, New York NY 10019 USA
**Spearritt, Hannah**          Actress, Singer, Model
Curtis Brown Group, 28-29 Haymarket St, #500, London SW1Y 4SP, England
**Spears, Abigail M**          Tennis Player
15552 Cool Valley Road, Valley Center CA 92082, USA
**Spears, Aries**          Actor, Comedian, Writer, Producer
J K A Talent, 12725 Ventura Blvd, #H, Studio City CA 91604, USA
**Spears, Britney**          Singer, Actress, Model
Creative Artists Agency, 2000 Ave of Stars, #100, Los Angeles CA 90067 USA
**Spears, Eddie**          Actor
N A S S Talent Management, 2212 Lea Ave, Bozeman MT 59715, USA
**Spears, Glen F**          Air Force General
Commander, 12th Air Force, Davis-Monthan Air Force Base AZ 85707 USA
**Spears, Jamie Lynn**          Actress
Tri Star Sports & Entertainment, 450 N Roxbury Dr, #602, Beverly Hills CA 90210, USA
**Spears, Marcus D**          Football Player
18634 Cypress Lake Village Dr, Cypress TX 77429, USA
**Spears, Marcus R**          Football Player
3649 Shady Creek Court, Frisco TX 75033, USA
**Spears, Stephen**          Sculptor
2021 County Road 33, Fair Hope AL 36532, USA
**Special Ed**          Rap Artist
Entertainment Artists, 2409 21st Ave S, #100, Nashville TN 10019 USA
**Speck, Fred**          Ice Hockey Player
2165 Country Club Dr, #23, Burlington ON L7M 4H4, Canada
**Speck, Will**          Director
Management 360, 9111 Wilshire Blvd, Beverly Hills CA 90210 USA
**Specter, Rachel**          Actress
Luber Rocklin Entertainment, 5815 Sunset Blvd, #206, Los Angeles CA 90028 USA
**Spector, Ronnie**          Singer
Universal Attractions, 135 W 26th St, #1200, New York NY 10001 USA
**Speech**          Rap Artist (Arrested Development)
Agency Group Ltd, 142 W 57th St, #600, New York NY 10019 USA
**Speeckaert, Glynn**          Cinematographer
Dattner Dispoto, 10635 Santa Monica Blvd, #165, Los Angeles CA 90025, USA
**Speed, Horace A**          Baseball Player
6821 State Boulevard Extension, Meridian MS 39305, USA
**Speed, Lake C**          Auto Racing Driver
Bud Moore Engineering, 400 N Fairview St, Spartanburg SC 29303, USA
**Speed, Scott A**          Auto, Truck Racing Driver
Red Bull Racing, 136 Knob Hill Road, Mooresville NC 28117, USA
**Speed, U Grant**          Sculptor
139 S 400 E, Lindon UT 84042, USA

**Speedman, Scott** — Actor
Gary Goddard Agency, 10 Sainte Mary St, #305, Toronto, ON M4Y 1P9, Canada
**Speer, Hugo** — Actor
Independent Talent Group, 40 Whitfield St, London W1T 2RH, England
**Speers, Ted** — Ice Hockey Player
61515 Brookway Dr, South Lyon MI 48178, USA
**Spehr, Timothy J (Tim)** — Baseball Player
8524 Briargrove Dr, Woodway TX 76712, USA
**Speidel, Jutta** — Actress
Postfach 650022, 81213 Munich, Germany
**Speier, Chris E** — Baseball Player
3614 El Encarto Dr, Calabasas CA 91302, USA
**Speight, Lester (Rasta)** — Actor, Producer
T C A/Jed Root, 9220 Sunset Blvd, #315, Los Angeles CA 90069, USA
**Speigner, Levale** — Baseball Player
1041 Bond St, Thomasville GA 31757, USA
**Speir, Dona** — Model, Actress
Playboy Promotions, 9346 Civic Center Dr, #200, Beverly Hills CA 90210 USA
**Speiser, Jerry** — Drummer (Men at Work)
T P A, PO Box 124, Round Corner NSW, Australia
**Spektor, Regina** — Singer, Pianist, Songwriter
Ron Shapiro Mgmt, 56 W 22nd St, #601, New York NY 10010, USA
**Spelke, Elizabeth S** — Psychologist
Harvard University, Psychology Dept, Cambridge MA 02138, USA
**Spelling, Randy** — Actor
United Talent Agency, U T A Plaza, 9336 Civic Center Dr, Beverly Hills CA 90210 USA
**Spelling, Tori** — Actress
594 S Mapleton Dr, Los Angeles CA 90024, USA
**Spellman, Alonzo R** — Football Player
1201 W Queen St, Tulsa OK 74127, USA
**Spellman, John D** — Governor, WA
7048 51st Ave NE, Seattle WA 98115, USA
**Spence, A Michael** — Nobel Economics Laureate
899 Northgate Dr, #301, San Rafael CA 94903, USA
**Spence, Bruce** — Actor
Johnson & Laird Management, PO Box 78340, Grey Lynn Auckland 1245, New Zealand
**Spence, Gerry** — Attorney
3325 N University Ave, #200B, Provo UT 84604, USA
**Spence, J Robert (Bob)** — Baseball Player
3081 Bonita Woods Dr, Bonita CA 91902, USA
**Spence, Nicky** — Opera Singer
I M G Artists, Carnegie Hall Tower, 152 W 57th St, #500, New York NY 10019 USA
**Spence, Sebastian** — Actor
Kirk Talent Agencies, 196 W 3rd Ave, #102, Vancouver BC V5Y 1E9, Canada
**Spencer, Abigail** — Actress
I C M Partners, 10250 Constellation Blvd, #900, Los Angeles CA 90067 USA
**Spencer, Andre** — Basketball Player
1315 W Gage Ave, Los Angeles CA 90044, USA
**Spencer, Baldwin** — Prime Minister, Antigua & Barbuda
Prime Minister's Office, Factory Road, Saint John's, Antigua & Barbuda
**Spencer, Bud** — Actor
European Film GmbH, Invalidenstr 99, 10115 Berlin, Germany
**Spencer, Chaske** — Actor
Josselyne Herman Assoc, 345 E 56th St, #3B, New York NY 10022, USA
**Spencer, Chris** — Actor, Comedian
Parallel Entertainment, 9420 Wilshire Blvd, #250, Beverly Hills CA 90212 USA
**Spencer, Daryl D** — Baseball Player
2740 S Larkin St, Wichita KS 67216, USA
**Spencer, Des** — Artist
Sheraton Mirage, Davidson St, Port Douglas 4871 QLD, Australia
**Spencer, Elizabeth** — Writer
402 Longleaf Dr, Chapel Hill NC 27517, USA
**Spencer, Elmore** — Basketball Player
2770 Foxlair Trail, Atlanta GA 30349, USA
**Spencer, Felton L** — Basketball Player
4102 Nicholas Roy Court, Prospect KY 40059, USA
**Spencer, Freddie** — Motorcycle Racing Rider
7055 Speedway Blvd, #E106, Las Vegas NV 89115, USA
**Spencer, George E** — Baseball Player
8160 Hickory Ave, Galena OH 43021, USA
**Spencer, J Robert** — Actor, Singer
Polaris Entertainment, 8048 W 3rd St, #300, Los Angeles CA 90048, USA
**Spencer, James A (Jimmy), Jr** — Football Player, Coach
5331 Talavera Place, Parker CO 80134, USA
**Spencer, Jeremy** — Drummer (Five Finger Death Punch)
10th Street Entertainment, 568 Broadway, #608, New York NY 10012, USA
**Spencer, Jesse** — Actor, Musician
Management 360, 9111 Wilshire Blvd, Beverly Hills CA 90210 USA
**Spencer, Jimmy** — Auto Racing Driver
597 Kenway Loop, Mooresville NC 28117, USA
**Spencer, Jon** — Singer, Guitarist (Pussy Galore)
Rascoff/Zysblat Organization, 250 W 57th St, New York NY 10107 USA
**Spencer, Lara** — Actress
W M E Entertainment, 9601 Wilshire Blvd, #300, Beverly Hills CA 90210 USA
**Spencer, LaVryle** — Writer
Berkley Publishing Group, 375 Hudson St, Basement 1, New York NY 10014 USA
**Spencer, M Shane** — Baseball Player
2858 Manzanita View Road, Alpine CA 91901, USA
**Spencer, Octavia** — Actress
W M E Entertainment, 9601 Wilshire Blvd, #300, Beverly Hills CA 90210 USA
**Spencer, Scott** — Writer
Harper Collins Publishers, 10 E 53rd St, Cellar 1, New York NY 10022 USA
**Spencer, Sean** — Baseball Player
3584 E Calistoga Court, Port Orchard WA 98366, USA
**Spencer, Shawntae** — Football Player
3714 Henley Dr, Pittsburgh PA 15235, USA

| | |
|---|---|
| **Spencer, Sidney** | Basketball Player |
| New York Liberty, Madison Square Garden, 2 Penn Plaza, New York NY 10121 USA | |
| **Spencer, Stanley R (Stan)** | Baseball Player |
| 3100 NE 188th St, Ridgefield WA 98642, USA | |
| **Spencer, Timothy A (Tim)** | Football Player |
| 1675 N Pebble Beach Way, Vernon Hills IL 60061, USA | |
| **Spencer, Tracie** | Singer |
| Richard Walters, PO Box 2789, Toluca Lake CA 91610 USA | |
| **Spencer-Devlin, Muffin** | Golfer |
| 1278 Glenneyre St, #155, Laguna Beach CA 92651, USA | |
| **Spenn, Frederick C (Fred)** | Baseball Umpire |
| 105 Heather Lane, Parrish FL 34219, USA | |
| **Sperber Carter, Paula** | Bowler |
| 10331 SW 102nd Ave, Miami FL 33176, USA | |
| **Sperber, Jonathan** | Writer |
| University of Missouri, History Dept, Read Hall, Columbia MO 65211, USA | |
| **Sperl, Natalie Denise** | Actress |
| C E S D, 10635 Santa Monica Blvd, #130, Los Angeles CA 90025 USA | |
| **Sperring, Robert W (Rob)** | Baseball Player |
| 13302 Chriswood Dr, Cypress TX 77429, USA | |
| **Speth, James G** | Government Official |
| 986 Forest Road, New Haven CT 06515, USA | |
| **Spezialy, Tom** | Producer, Writer |
| Jackoway Tyerman Wertheimer, 1925 Century Park E, #2200, Los Angeles CA 90067 USA | |
| **Spezza, Jason A R** | Ice Hockey Player |
| 26 Edenvale Dr, Kanata ON K2K 3L4, Canada | |
| **Spheeris, Penelope** | Director |
| Spheeris Films, 3940 Laurel Canyon Blvd, #18, Studio City CA 91604, USA | |
| **Spice 1** | Rap Artist |
| Richard Walters, PO Box 2789, Toluca Lake CA 91610 USA | |
| **Spicer, Kimberly** | Model |
| Playboy Promotions, 9346 Civic Center Dr, #200, Beverly Hills CA 90210 USA | |
| **Spicer, Paul** | Football Player |
| 12868 Old Saint Augustine Road, Jacksonville FL 32258, USA | |
| **Spicer, Robert O (Bob)** | Baseball Player |
| 423 McPhee Dr, Fayetteville NC 28305, USA | |
| **Spicer, William E, III** | Physicist |
| 620 Sand Hill Road, #305E, Palo Alto CA 94304, USA | |
| **Spiegel, Scott** | Director |
| A P A Talent & Literary Agency, 405 S Beverly Dr, #300, Beverly Hills CA 90212 USA | |
| **Spiegelman, Art** | Illustrator, Writer |
| Raw Books & Graphics, 27 Greene St, New York NY 10013, USA | |
| **Spielberg, David** | Actor |
| 10537 Cushdon Ave, Los Angeles CA 90064, USA | |
| **Spielberg, Robin** | Pianist, Composer |
| Roots Agency, 108 Glenray Court, New Freedom PA 17349, USA | |
| **Spielberg, Steven** | Director |
| Amblin Entertainment, 100 Universal City Plaza, #477, Universal City CA 91608, USA | |
| **Spielman, C Christopher (Chris)** | Football Player, Sportscaster |
| 2481 Stonehaven Place, Columbus OH 43220, USA | |
| **Spierig, Michael** | Director |
| W M E Entertainment, 9601 Wilshire Blvd, #300, Beverly Hills CA 90210 USA | |
| **Spierig, Peter** | Director |
| W M E Entertainment, 9601 Wilshire Blvd, #300, Beverly Hills CA 90210 USA | |
| **Spiers, Ronald I** | Diplomat |
| 1329 Middletown Road, South Londonderry VT 05155, USA | |
| **Spiers, William J (Bill)** | Baseball Player |
| 9233 Old State Road, Cameron SC 29030, USA | |
| **Spieth, Jordan** | Golfer |
| Professional Golfers Association, 100 Ave of Champions, Palm Beach Gardens FL 33418 USA | |
| **Spiezio, Edward W (Ed)** | Baseball Player |
| 2027 Taller Road, Morris IL 60450, USA | |
| **Spiezio, Scott E** | Baseball Player |
| 7615 Saratoga Road, Morris IL 60450, USA | |
| **Spikes, Brandon** | Football Player |
| Buffalo Bills, 1 Bills Dr, Orchard Park NY 14127 USA | |
| **Spikes, Cameron W** | Football Player |
| 35 Raven Dr, Bryan TX 77808, USA | |
| **Spikes, Jack E** | Football Player |
| 9537 Highland View Dr, Dallas TX 75238, USA | |
| **Spikes, L Charles (Charlie)** | Baseball Player |
| 531 N Border Dr, Bogalusa LA 70427, USA | |
| **Spikes, Takeo G** | Football Player |
| 5005 Heatherwood Court, Roswell GA 30075, USA | |
| **Spilborghs, Ryan A** | Baseball Player |
| 1204 Suncast Lane, #2, El Dorado Hills CA 95762, USA | |
| **Spiller, Michael A** | Cinematographer |
| 2418 Roscomare Road, Los Angeles CA 90077, USA | |
| **Spillner, Daniel R (Dan)** | Baseball Player |
| 18505 SE Newport Way, #C113, Issaquah WA 98027, USA | |
| **Spindler, Marc R** | Football Player |
| 6993 Bond Trail, Clarkston MI 48348, USA | |
| **Spindt, Capp** | Inventor (Field Emission Display Screen) |
| S R I International, 333 Ravenswood Ave, Menlo Park CA 94025, USA | |
| **Spinella, Stephen** | Actor |
| Innovative Artists, 1505 10th St, Santa Monica CA 90401 USA | |
| **Spinelli, Jerry** | Writer |
| 331 Melvin Road, Phoenixville PA 19460, USA | |
| **Spiner, Brent** | Actor |
| Innovative Artists, 1505 10th St, Santa Monica CA 90401 USA | |
| **Spinetta, Jean-Cyril** | Businessman |
| Groupe Air France, 45 Rue de Paris, 95747 Roissy CDG Cedex, France | |
| **Spinks, Cory** | Boxer |
| 6167 Tennessee St, Saint Louis MO 63111, USA | |
| **Spinks, Leon** | Boxer |
| 209 Jones St, Hollister MO 65672, USA | |

**Spencer - Spinks**

**Spinks, Michael** — Boxer
925 Centre Road, Wilmington DE 19807, USA

**Spinks, Scipio R** — Baseball Player
11422 Rock Bridge Lane, Sugar Land TX 77498, USA

**Spinotti, Dante** — Cinematographer
334 14th St, Santa Monica CA 90402, USA

**Spires, Gregory T (Greg)** — Football Player
26202 Ridgefield Park Lane, Cypress TX 77433, USA

**Spiridakos, Tracy** — Actress
Gersh Agency, 9465 Wilshire Blvd, #600, Beverly Hills CA 90212 USA

**Spiro, Jordana** — Actress
I C M Partners, 10250 Constellation Blvd, #900, Los Angeles CA 90067 USA

**Spirtas, Kevin** — Actor
Stone Manners Salners, 6100 Wilshire Blvd, #1500, Los Angeles CA 90035 USA

**Spitz, Mark A** — Swimmer
383 Dalehurst Ave, Los Angeles CA 90024, USA

**Spitz, Sabine** — Cyclist
Sabine Spitz Sport Pro, Ralf Schaeuble, Diegeringerstr 17, 79730 Murg, Germany

**Spitzer, Eliot L** — Governor, NY
Current TV, Viewpoint Show, 435 Hudson St, #400, New York NY 10014, USA

**Spitzer, Robert** — Psychiatrist
Columbia University, Psychiatry School, New York NY 10027, USA

**Spitzer, Toby** — Religious Leader, Rabbi
Congregation Dorshei Tzedek, 60 Highland St, West Newton MA 02465, USA

**Spivakov, Vladimir T** — Conductor, Concert Violinist
Kosmodamianskaya Embankment 52, #301, 115054 Moscow, Russia

**Spivey, Ernest L (Junior), Jr** — Baseball Player
4140 S Ambrosia Dr, Chandler AZ 85248, USA

**Spizzirri, Angelo** — Actor
Don Buchwald Talent Agency, 6500 Wilshire Blvd, #2200, Los Angeles CA 90048 USA

**Splatt, Rachelle** — Drag Racing Driver
Rachelle Splatt Racing, 37 MacQuarie Drive, Thomastown VIC 3074, Australia

**Spoelstra, Erik** — Basketball Coach
Miami Heat, American Airlines Arena, 601 Biscayne Blvd, Miami FL 33132 USA

**Spoljaric, Paul N** — Baseball Player
545 Gramiak Road, Kelowna BC V1X 1K4, Canada

**Sponable, Jess M** — Astronaut
7786 Willow Point Dr, Falls Church VA 22042, USA

**Spong, John S** — Religious Leader
24 Puddingstone Road, Morris Plains NJ 07950, USA

**Spooner, Natalie** — Ice Hockey Player
Hockey Canada, 151 Canada Olympic Road SW, #201, Calgary AB  T3B 6B7, Canada

**Spooneybarger, Tim** — Baseball Player
7815 Eight Mile Creek Road, Pensacola FL 32526, USA

**Spork, Shirley** — Golfer
73010 Somera Road, Palm Desert CA 92260, USA

**Sporkin, Stanley** — Government Official, Judge
US District Court, Courthouse, 3rd St & Constitution Ave NW, Washington DC 20001, USA

**Sporleder, Gregory** — Actor
Brian Wilkins Mgmt, 10585 Santa Monica Blvd, #120, Los Angeles CA 90025, USA

**Sposa, Mike** — Golfer
11678 Sunrise View Lane, Wellington FL 33449, USA

**Spose** — Rap Artist
Agency Group Ltd, 142 W 57th St, #600, New York NY 10019 USA

**Spotakova, Barbora** — Track Athlete
A S C Dukla Prague, Oddil Aletiky, PS 59, 16044 Prague 6, Czech Republic

**Spottiswoode, Roger** — Director
9696 Culver Blvd, #203, Culver City CA 90232, USA

**Spound, Michael** — Actor
Kazarian/Measures/Ruskin, 11969 Ventura Blvd, #300, Studio City CA 91604 USA

**Spowart, Ruby** — Photographer
PO Box 779, North Sydney NSW 2066, Australia

**Spradlin, Danny R** — Football Player
1011 Laurie St, Maryville TN 37803, USA

**Spragan, Donald (Donnie), Jr** — Football Player
312 Riviera Dr, Union City CA 94587, USA

**Sprague, Edward N (Ed), Jr** — Baseball Player
4677 Pine Valley Circle, Stockton CA 95219, USA

**Sprague, Edward N (Ed), Sr** — Baseball Player
19015 N Davis Road, Lodi CA 95242, USA

**Sprague, Jack** — Truck Racing Driver
X-Press Motorsports, 610 Performance Road, Mooresville NC 28117, USA

**Spratlan, Lewis** — Composer
Amherst College, Music Dept, Amherst MA 01002, USA

**Sprayberry, Dylan** — Actor
United Talent Agency, U T A Plaza, 9336 Civic Center Dr, Beverly Hills CA 90210 USA

**Sprayberry, James M** — Vietnam War Army Hero
426 Holiday Dr, Titus AL 36080, USA

**Sprecher, Jill** — Director, Producer, Writer
Paradigm Agency, 360 N Crescent Dr, North Building, Beverly Hills CA 90210 USA

**Sprecher, Karen** — Director, Producer, Writer
Paradigm Agency, 360 N Crescent Dr, North Building, Beverly Hills CA 90210 USA

**Spreitler, Taylor** — Actress
Coast to Coast Talent, 3350 Barham Blvd, Los Angeles CA 90068 USA

**Sprewell, Latrell F** — Basketball Player
1120 E Pleasant St, Milwaukee WI 53202, USA

**Spriggs, George H** — Baseball Player
77A W Bay Front Road, Lothian MD 20711, USA

**Spriggs, Larry M** — Basketball Player
23900 Cancuna Court, Huson MT 59846, USA

**Spring, Frank** — Ice Hockey Player
638 Upper Ottawa St, Hamilton ON L8T 3T5, Canada

**Spring, Jack R** — Baseball Player
PO Box 118, Colbert WA 99005, USA

**Spring, Justin E** — Gymnast
University of Illinois, Athletic Dept, Champaign IL 61820, USA

**Spring, Sherwood C** — Astronaut
2104 McDonough Lane, San Diego CA 92106, USA

**Springer, Dennis L** — Baseball Player
537 Sherwood Court, Hanford CA 93230, USA

**Springer, Jerry** — Entertainer; Mayor, Cincinnati
Coast to Coast Talent, 3350 Barham Blvd, Los Angeles CA 90068 USA

**Springer, Michael (Mike)** — Golfer
1482 E Forest Oaks Dr, Fresno CA 93730, USA

**Springer, Robert C** — Astronaut
202 Village Circle, Sheffield AL 35660, USA

**Springer, Russell P (Russ)** — Baseball Player
PO Box 185, 4357 Highway 8, Pollock LA 71467, USA

**Springer, Steven M (Steve)** — Baseball Player
6962 Carla Circle, Huntington Beach CA 92647, USA

**Springfield, Rick** — Singer, Actor
Doyle-Kos Entertainment, 1 Penn Plaza, #2107, New York NY 10119, USA

**Springs, Alice** — Photographer
Residence Saint-Roman, 7 Ave Saint-Ramon, #T1008, Monte Carlo, Monaco

**Springs, Kirk E** — Football Player
3220 Oakley Station Blvd, #112, Cincinnati OH 45209, USA

**Springs, Shawn** — Football Player
19892 Naples Lakes Terrace, Ashburn VA 20147, USA

**Springsteen, Bruce** — Singer, Songwriter
2 Cross Road, Colts Neck NJ 07722, USA

**Springsteen, Jay R** — Motorcycle Racing Rider
3774 S Shore Dr, Lapeer MI 48446, USA

**Sproles, Darren L** — Football Player
Philadelphia Eagles, 1 Novacare Way, Philadelphia PA 19145 USA

**Sprouse, Cole** — Actor
I/D Public Relations, 7060 Hollywood Blvd, #800, Los Angeles CA 90028 USA

**Sprouse, Dylan** — Actor
I/D Public Relations, 7060 Hollywood Blvd, #800, Los Angeles CA 90028 USA

**Spruce, Andrew (Andy)** — Ice Hockey Player
1223 Kantora Road, Lively ON P3Y 1H8, Canada

**Spurgeon, Jay** — Baseball Player
212 Hartsdale Road, Rochester NY 14622, USA

**Spurlock, Morgan** — Actor, Director
Arlook Group, 205 S Beverly Dr, #209, Beverly Hills CA 90212, USA

**Spurrier, Stephen O (Steve)** — Football Player, Coach
126 Beaver Ridge Dr, Elgin SC 29045, USA

**Spuzich, Sandra** — Golfer
Ladies Pro Golf Assn, 100 International Golf Dr, Daytona Beach FL 32124 USA

**Squibb, June** — Actress
B R S / Gage Talent Agency, 5757 Wilshire Blvd, #659, Los Angeles CA 90036 USA

**Squier, Billy** — Singer, Guitarist, Songwriter
Paradise Artists, PO Box 1821, Ojai CA 93024 USA

**Squier, Ken** — Sportscaster
Ken Squier Productions, 9 Stowe St, Waterbury VT 05676, USA

**Squire, Chris** — Bassist (Yes)
Sun Artists, 9 Hillgate St, London W8 7SP, England

**Squirek, Jack S** — Football Player
4051 Vezbar Dr, Seven Hills OH 44131, USA

**Squires, Michael L (Mike)** — Baseball Player
9548 Autumnwood Circle, Kalamazoo MI 49009, USA

**Squyres, Steven W** — Space Scientist
Cornell University, Planetary Science Dept, Ithaca NY 14853, USA

**Srinivasan, Rangaswamy** — Inventor (Excimer Laser)
UVTech Assoc, 98 Cedar Lane, Ossining NY 10562, USA

**Srinivasan, Skikanth (Sri)** — Judge
US Court of Appeals, 333 Constitution Ave NW, #4400, Washington DC 20001, USA

**St Clair, Jessica** — Actress, Comedienne
United Talent Agency, U T A Plaza, 9336 Civic Center Dr, Beverly Hills CA 90210 USA

**St Clair, R Michael (Mike)** — Football Player
1606 Birchwood Ave, Cincinnati OH 45224, USA

**St Clair, Robert B (Bob)** — Football Player
3312 Parker Hill Road, Santa Rosa CA 95404, USA

**St Croix, Rick** — Ice Hockey Player
27 Brigantine Bay, Winnipeg MB R3P 1R1, Canada

**St Esprit, Patrick** — Actor
Abrams Artists, 9200 W Sunset Blvd, #1125, West Hollywood CA 90069 USA

**St George, William R** — Navy Admiral
862 San Antonio Place, San Diego CA 92106, USA

**St James, Lyn** — Auto Racing Driver
L S J Racing, 57 Gasoline Alley, #D, Indianapolis IN 46222, USA

**St James, Rebecca** — Singer
Smallbone Mgmt, PO Box 1524, Franklin TN 37065, USA

**St Jean, Leonard W (Len).** — Football Player
32 Ledgebrook Ave, Stoughton MA 02072, USA

**St John, Jill** — Actress
3271 Melrose Ave, #110, Los Angeles CA 90046, USA

**St John, Kristoff** — Actor, Producer
21781 Ventura Blvd, Woodland Hills CA 91364, USA

**St John, Lara** — Concert Violinist
Barrett Vantage Artists, 505 8th Ave, #601, New York NY 10018, USA

**St John, Scott** — Concert Violinist, Viola Player
Frank Salomon, 121 W 27th St, #703, New York NY 10001 USA

**St John, Trevor** — Actor
Innovative Artists, 1505 10th St, Santa Monica CA 90401 USA

**St Laurent, Andre** — Ice Hockey Player
947 Rue Riverview, Otterburn Park QC J3H 1Z1, Canada

**St Laurent, Dollard H** — Ice Hockey Player
Les Tour Angrignons, 1500 Angrignon Blvd, LaSalle QC H8N 3H8, Canada

**St Louis, Frantz** — Actor
Artists Agency, 9430 Olympic Blvd, Beverly Hills CA 90212 USA

**St Louis, Martin** — Ice Hockey Player
22 Pilot Rock Lane, Riverside CT 06878, USA

**St Patrick, Mathew** — Actor
Ace Media, 9200 W Sunset Blvd, #1000, Los Angeles CA 90069, USA

**St Pier, Natasha** — Singer
Guy Cloutier, 446 Blvd Saint Lautenbur 900, Montreal QC H2W 1Z5, Canada

**St Pierre, Brian** — Football Player
Carolina Panthers, Ericsson Stadium, 800 S Mint St, Charlotte NC 28202 USA

**St Pierre, Monique** — Model, Actress
Playboy Promotions, 9346 Civic Center Dr, #200, Beverly Hills CA 90210 USA

**Staab, Rebecca** — Actress
Stone Manners Salners, 6100 Wilshire Blvd, #1500, Los Angeles CA 90035 USA

**Staal, Eric C** — Ice Hockey Player
6009 Over Hadden Court, Raleigh NC 27614, USA

**Staal, Jordan** — Ice Hockey Player
Candy Mountain Road, RR 6, Thunder Bay ON P7C 5N5, Canada

**Stabile, Nick** — Actor
Raw Talent Mgmt, 9615 Brighton Way, #300, Beverly Hills CA 90210 USA

**Stabiner, Karen** — Writer
Voice/Hyperion Books, 77 W 66th St, #1100, New York NY 10023, USA

**Stablein, Brian P** — Football Player
2023 Woodland Hall Dr, Delaware OH 43015, USA

**Stablein, George C** — Baseball Player
2903 Penman, Tustin CA 92782, USA

**Stabler, Ken M (Kenny)** — Football Player
7311 Bay Road, #A, Mobile AL 36605, USA

**Stacey Q** — Singer, Actress, Songwriter
641 S Palm St, #D, La Habra CA 90631, USA

**Stacey, John** — Actor
Gavin Barker Assoc, 2D Wimpole St, London W1G 0EB, England

**Stackhouse, Jerry D** — Basketball Player
5266 Settles Bridge Road, Suwanee GA 30024, USA

**Stackhouse, Ron** — Ice Hockey Player
RR 2, Haliburton ON K0M 1S0, Canada

**Stackpole, H C (Hank)** — Marine Corps General
Asia-Pacific Security Studies Center, 2058 Maluhia Road, Honolulu HI 96815, USA

**Stackpole, Michael A** — Writer
PO Box 60333, Phoenix AZ 85082, USA

**Stacomb, Kevin M** — Basketball Player
14 Florida Ave, Jamestown RI 02835, USA

**Stacy, Billy M** — Football Player
400 Colonial Circle, Starkville MS 39759, USA

**Stacy, Hollis** — Golfer
405 74th St, Holmes Beach FL 34217, USA

**Stacy, Peter (Spider)** — Singer (Pogues)
Agency Group Ltd, 361-373 City Road, London EC1V 1PQ, England

**Stadlen, Lewis J** — Actor
B R S / Gage Talent Agency, 1650 Broadway, #1410, New York NY 10019 USA

**Stadler, Craig R** — Golfer
113 Elk Crossing, Evergreen CO 80439, USA

**Stadler, Kevin** — Golfer
Professional Golfers Association, 100 Ave of Champions, Palm Beach Gardens FL 33418 USA

**Stadler, Sergei V** — Concert Violinist, Conductor
Kaiserstr 43, 80801 Munich, Germany

**Stadtman, Thressa C** — Biochemist
16907 Redland Road, Derwood MD 20855, USA

**Staehle, Marvin G (Marv)** — Baseball Player
19421 Cromwell Court, #208, Fort Myers FL 33912, USA

**Stafford, J Matthew** — Football Player
Detroit Lions, 222 Republic Dr, Allen Park MI 48101 USA

**Stafford, James Francis Cardinal** — Religious Leader
Pontifical Council for the Laity, Piazza S Calisto 16, 00153 Rome, Italy

**Stafford, James W (Jim)** — Singer, Songwriter
Dick Hall Productions, 1767 Lakewood Ranch Blvd, Bradenton FL 34211, USA

**Stafford, Jimmy** — Guitarist (Train)
Jon Landau, 150 Rowayton Ave, Norwalk CT 06853, USA

**Stafford, Michelle** — Actress
Glick Agency, 347 5th Ave, #1404, New York NY 10016 USA

**Stafford, Nancy** — Actress
PO Box 3353, Westlake Village CA 91359, USA

**Stafford, Thomas P** — Astronaut, Air Force General
A V D, PO Box 604, Glenn Dale MD 20769, USA

**Stafford-Clark, Max** — Director, Actor
Royal Court Theatre, Sloane Square, London SW1 8AS, England

**Stager, Gus** — Swimming Coach
University of Michigan, Athletic Dept, Ann Arbor MI 48104, USA

**Staggers, Jonathan L (Jon), Jr** — Football Player
3835 Oakes Dr, Hayward CA 94542, USA

**Staggs, Jeffrey H (Jeff)** — Football Player
4641 Jeri Way, El Cajon CA 92020, USA

**Stahl, Georgia** — Actress
Sokoll & Friends Eventmanagement, Im Husarenlager 12A, 76187 Karlsruhe, Germany

**Stahl, Larry F** — Baseball Player
1506 E Main St, #A, Belleville IL 62221, USA

**Stahl, Lesley R** — Commentator
CBS-TV, News Dept, 51 W 52nd St, New York NY 10019 USA

**Stahl, Lisa** — Actress
Peak Models & Talent, 25852 McBean Parkway, #190, Valencia CA 91355, USA

**Stahl, Nick** — Actor
L I N K Entertainment, 11872 La Grange Ave, Los Angeles CA 90025 USA

**Stahl, Norman H** — Judge
US Court of Appeals, 1 Courthouse Way, Boston MA 02210, USA

**Stahl-David, Michael** — Actor
Baker Winokur Ryder Public Relations, 9100 Wilshire Blvd, #500W, Beverly Hills CA 90212 USA

**Stahle, Louise** — Golfer
Gaylord Sports Mgmt, 13845 N Northsight Blvd, #200, Scottsdale AZ 85260 USA

**Stähler, Jeff** — Editorial Cartoonist
United Feature Syndicate, PO Box 5610, Cincinnati OH 45201 USA

| | |
|---|---|
| **Stahoviak, Scott E** | Baseball Player |
| 507 Balmoral Court, Grayslake IL 60030, USA | |
| **Stai, Brenden M** | Football Player |
| 5333 New Castle Road, Lincoln NE 68516, USA | |
| **Staiano-Coico, Lisa** | Educator |
| City College of New York, President's Office, 160 Convent Ave, New York NY 10031, USA | |
| **Staiger, Roy J** | Baseball Player |
| 1233 Tyler Dr, Lebanon MO 65536, USA | |
| **Staios, Steve** | Ice Hockey Player |
| 1213 Newbridge Trace NE, Atlanta GA 30319, USA | |
| **Stairs, Matthew W (Matt)** | Baseball Player |
| 79 Skyline Road, Bangor ME 04401, USA | |
| **Staite, Jewel** | Actress |
| Elements Entertainment, 1635 N Cahuenga Blvd, #500, Los Angeles CA 90028, USA | |
| **Stajan, Matthew (Matt)** | Ice Hockey Player |
| 1369 Victor Ave, Mississauga ON L5G 3A2, Canada | |
| **Stalder, Keith J** | Marine Corps General |
| Commanding General, 2nd Marine Expeditionary Force, Camp Lejeune NC 28542 USA | |
| **Stalder, Lara** | Ice Hockey Player |
| Swiss Ice Hockey, Hagenholzstr 81, 8050 Zurich, Switzerland | |
| **Staley, Dawn M** | Basketball Player, Coach |
| Dawn Staley Foundation, 1224 Glenwood Road, Columbia SC 29204, USA | |
| **Staley, Duce** | Football Player |
| 150 N 9th St, West Columbia SC 29169, USA | |
| **Staley, Joan** | Actress, Model |
| 24516 Windsor Dr, #B, Valencia CA 91355, USA | |
| **Staley, William P (Bill)** | Football Player |
| 9210 Todd Road, Potter Valley CA 95469, USA | |
| **Stallard, E Tracy** | Baseball Player |
| PO Box 905, Wise VA 24293, USA | |
| **Stallard, Tom** | Rowing Athlete |
| Leander Club, Henley on Thames, Leander RG9 2LP, England | |
| **Stallings, Eugene C (Gene), Jr** | Football Coach |
| 6508 County Road 43200, Powderly TX 75473, USA | |
| **Stallings, George** | Religious Leader |
| African American Catholic Congregation, 1015 I St NE, Washington DC 20002, USA | |
| **Stallings, Larry J** | Football Player |
| 555 Town Hall Court, Saint Louis MO 63141, USA | |
| **Stallings, Scott** | Golfer |
| Brad Rose, Willow Tree Golf Club, 12003 Kingston Pike, Knoxville TN 37934, USA | |
| **Stallone, Sylvester** | Actor, Director, Writer |
| W M E Entertainment, 9601 Wilshire Blvd, #300, Beverly Hills CA 90210 USA | |
| **Stalls, David M** | Football Player |
| 2800 Forest St, Denver CO 80207, USA | |
| **Stallworth, David A (Dave)** | Basketball Player |
| 4400 N Rushwood St, Wichita KS 67226, USA | |
| **Stallworth, Donte' L** | Football Player |
| 6601 53rd St, Sacramento CA 95823, USA | |
| **Stallworth, Issac (Bud)** | Basketball Player |
| 14 Westwood Road, Lawrence KS 66044, USA | |
| **Stallworth, Johnny L (John)** | Football Player |
| 302 Osman Dr, Madison AL 35756, USA | |
| **Stam, Jessica** | Model |
| International Model Mgmt, 25 Dunlop St E, Barrie ON L4M 1A2, Canada | |
| **Stam, Katie** | Beauty Queen |
| Miss America Organization, 1370 Ave of Americas, #1600, New York NY 10019 USA | |
| **Stamberg, Josh** | Actor |
| Abrams Artists, 9200 W Sunset Blvd, #1125, West Hollywood CA 90069 USA | |
| **Stamberg, Peter** | Interior Designer |
| Stamberg Aferiat Assoc, 126 5th Ave, #13A, New York NY | |
| **Stamer, Joshua L (Josh)** | Football Player |
| 202 Oxford Creek Road, Cary NC 27519, USA | |
| **Stamey, Christopher C (Chris)** | Singer, Guitarist, Songwriter |
| Conqueroo, 11271 Ventura Blvd, #522, Studio City CA 91604 USA | |
| **Stamile, Lauren** | Actress |
| Schumacher Mgmt, 10323 Santa Monica Blvd, #101, Los Angeles CA 90024, USA | |
| **Stamkos, Steven** | Ice Hockey Player |
| Tampa Bay Lightning, 401 Channelside Dr, Tampa FL 33602 USA | |
| **Stamm, Daniel** | Director, Writer |
| Creative Artists Agency, 2000 Ave of Stars, #100, Los Angeles CA 90067 USA | |
| **Stamm, Michael E (Mike)** | Swimmer |
| 3929 Everett Ave, Oakland CA 94602, USA | |
| **Stamos, John** | Actor |
| Brillstein Entertainment Partners, 9150 Wilshire Blvd, #350, Beverly Hills CA 90212 USA | |
| **Stamp, Terence** | Actor |
| Untitled Entertainment, 350 S Beverly Dr, #200, Beverly Hills CA 90212 USA | |
| **Stampley, Joe** | Singer, Songwriter |
| Joe Taylor Artist Agency, 2802 Columbine Place, Nashville TN 37204 USA | |
| **Stamps, Sylvester** | Football Player |
| 1831 Eisenhower Dr, Vicksburg MS 39180, USA | |
| **Stams, Frank M** | Football Player |
| 2870 Marcia Blvd, Cuyahoga Falls OH 44223, USA | |
| **Stan, Sebastian** | Actor |
| W M E Entertainment, 9601 Wilshire Blvd, #300, Beverly Hills CA 90210 USA | |
| **Stanat, Dug** | Sculptor, Animator |
| 46828 Bradley St, Fremont CA 94539, USA | |
| **Stanback, Haskell L** | Football Player |
| 1523 Windward Dr, Locust Grove GA 30248, USA | |
| **Stanbury, John B** | Pharmacologist |
| 10 Longwood Dr, #106, Westwood MA 02090, USA | |
| **Stanchfield, Darby** | Actress |
| Principal Entertainment, 9255 Sunset Blvd, #500, Los Angeles CA 90069 USA | |
| **Standhardt, Kenneth** | Artist |
| 55 W 27th Ave, Eugene OR 97405, USA | |
| **Standiford, Les** | Writer |
| Harper/Collins, 10 E 53rd St, Cellar 1, New York NY 10022, USA | |

**Standing, George** — Ice Hockey Player
34 Cliff Ave, Huntsville ON P1H 1G1, Canada

**Standing, John** — Actor
United Agents, 12-26 Lexington St, London W1F 0LE, England

**Standridge, Jason** — Baseball Player
6228 Cardinal Dr, Pinson AL 35126, USA

**Stanek, Al** — Baseball Player
96 Allyn St, Holyoke MA 01040, USA

**Stanfel, Richard (Dick)** — Football Player, Coach
1104 Juniper Parkway, Libertyville IL 60048, USA

**Stanfield, Frederic W (Fred)** — Ice Hockey Player
59 Cheshire Lane, East Amherst NY 14051, USA

**Stanfield, Kevin B** — Baseball Player
7565 Newcomb St, San Bernardino CA 92410, USA

**Stanfill, William T (Bill)** — Football Player
3117 Wisteria Court, Albany GA 31721, USA

**Stanford, Aaron** — Actor
Management 360, 9111 Wilshire Blvd, Beverly Hills CA 90210 USA

**Stanford, Angela** — Golfer
6225 Pecan Orchard Court, Fort Worth TX 76179, USA

**Stanford, Jason** — Baseball Player
4505 W Mesquital del Oro, Tucson AZ 85742, USA

**Stang, Peter J** — Organic Chemist
University of Utah, Chemistry Dept, Salt Lake City UT 84112, USA

**Stangassinger, Thomas** — Alpine Skier
Hofgasse 19, 5422 Durenberg-Hallein, Austria

**Stange, A Lee** — Baseball Player
436 Dolphin St, Melbourne Beach FL 32951, USA

**Stange, Maya** — Actress
L M C M, 99 Spring St, #100, Bondi Junction NSW 2022, Australia

**Stanhope, Douglas G (Doug)** — Actor, Comedian
Gersh Agency, 9465 Wilshire Blvd, #600, Beverly Hills CA 90212 USA

**Stanhope, Mark** — Navy Admiral, England
Worshipful Company of Upholders, 162 Tonbridge Road, Hildenborough Kent TN11 9HP, England

**Stanhouse, Donald J (Don)** — Baseball Player
4 Creekmere Dr, Roanoke TX 76262, USA

**Stanich, George** — Track Athlete, Basketball Player
15816 Marigold Ave, Gardena CA 90249, USA

**Stankalla, Stefan** — Alpine Skier
Furstenstr 14, 82467 Garmisch-Partenkirchen, Germany

**Stankiewicz, Andrew N (Andy)** — Baseball Player
9729 Wren Bluff Dr, San Diego CA 92127, USA

**Stankiewicz, Myron** — Ice Hockey Player
53 Tynedale Ave, London ON N6H 5P6, Canada

**Stankovic, Borislav (Boris)** — Basketball Executive
PO Box 7005, 81479 Munich, Germany

**Stankowski, Paul** — Golfer
4713 Rangewood Dr, Flower Mound TX 75028, USA

**Stanley, B Chadwick (Chad)** — Football Player
21451 Merlot Lane, Tyler TX 75703, USA

**Stanley, Christopher** — Actor
A P A Talent & Literary Agency, 405 S Beverly Dr, #300, Beverly Hills CA 90212 USA

**Stanley, Daryl** — Ice Hockey Player
PO Box 164, Balmoral MB R0C 0H0, Canada

**Stanley, Frederick B (Fred)** — Baseball Player
2109 Winthrop Hill Road, Argyle TX 76226, USA

**Stanley, James C (Jim)** — Producer, Writer
Paradigm Agency, 360 N Crescent Dr, North Building, Beverly Hills CA 90210 USA

**Stanley, Marianne Crawford** — Basketball Coach
Los Angeles Sparks, 888 S Figueroa St, #2010, Los Angeles CA 90017 USA

**Stanley, Mitchell J (Mickey)** — Baseball Player
6370 Cunningham Lake Road, Brighton MI 48116, USA

**Stanley, P Stephen** — Navy Admiral
Director, Force Structure Resources, Joint Staff, Pentagon, Washington DC 20318 USA

**Stanley, Paul** — Singer, Guitarist (Kiss)
McGhee Entertainment, 8730 W Sunset Blvd, #200, West Hollywood CA 90069, USA

**Stanley, R Michael (Mike)** — Baseball Player
1108 NE 10th Ave, Fort Lauderdale FL 33304, USA

**Stanley, Ralph** — Guitarist, Singer
7455 Dr Ralph Stanley Highway, Coeburn WA 24230, USA

**Stanley, Ralph, II** — Singer, Guitarist
Class Act Entertainment, PO Box 160236, Nashville TN 37216, USA

**Stanley, Robert W (Bob)** — Baseball Player
30 Tansy Ave, Stratham NH 03885, USA

**Stanley, Samuel L, Jr** — Educator
State University of New York, President's Office, Stony Brook NY 11784, USA

**Stanley, Steven M** — Paleobiologist
4308 Folly Quarter Road, Ellicott City MD 21042, USA

**Stanley, Walter** — Football Player
23977 E Alamo Place, Aurora CO 80016, USA

**Stanowski, Wally** — Ice Hockey Player
227 Mill Road, Toronto ON M9C 1Y3, Canada

**Stansfield Smith, Colin** — Architect
Three Ministers House, 76 High St, Winchester, Hantforshire SO23 8UL, England

**Stansfield, Lisa** — Singer, Songwriter
PO Box 59, Ashwell, Hertsfordshire SG7 5NG, England

**Stansky, Peter D L** — Historian
375 Pinehill Road, Hillsborough CA 94010, USA

**Stantis, Scott** — Editorial Cartoonist (Buckets)
Birmingham News, Editorial Dept, 2200 4th Ave N, Birmingham AL 35203, USA

**Stanton, Andrew** — Animator, Director, Writer
Pixar Animation, 1200 Park Ave, Emeryville CA 94608, USA

**Stanton, Doug** — Writer
Charles Scribner's Sons, 866 3rd Ave, New York NY 10022 USA

**Stanton, Harry Dean** — Actor
14527 Mulholland Dr, Los Angeles CA 90077, USA

**Stanton, Jeff** — Motorcycle Racing Rider
1137 Athens Road, Sherwood MI 49089, USA
**Stanton, Leroy B** — Baseball Player
1751 N Norwood Lane, Florence SC 29506, USA
**Stanton, Michael T (Mike)** — Baseball Player
PO Box 1154, Woodinville WA 98072, USA
**Stanton, Molly** — Actress
Luber Rocklin Entertainment, 5815 Sunset Blvd, #206, Los Angeles CA 90028 USA
**Stanton, Paul** — Ice Hockey Player
2061 Snook Dr, Naples FL 34102, USA
**Stanton, Phil** — Entertainer (Blue Man Group)
Blue Man Group Productions, 411 Lafayette St, #300, New York NY 10003, USA
**Stanton, W Michael (Mike)** — Baseball Player
19602 Indigo Lake Dr, Magnolia TX 77355, USA
**Stanton-Ogulnick, Alysa** — Religious Leader, Rabbi
Congregation Bayt Shalom, 4351 E 10th St, Greenville NC 27858, USA
**Stanz, Phoebe** — Ice Hockey Player
Swiss Ice Hockey, Hagenholzstr 81, 8050 Zurich, Switzerland
**Stanzler, Wendey** — Director, Producer
Verve Talent & Literary Agency, 96310 San Vicente Blvd, #100, Los Angeles CA 90048 USA
**Stapinski, Helene** — Writer
Saint Martin's Press, 175 5th Ave, #400, New York NY 10010 USA
**Staple, Neville E** — Singer, Percussionist (Specials)
1st 4 UK Artists, 4 Spencer Walk, Tilbury RM18 8XJ, England
**Staples, Mavis** — Singer (Staple Singers)
PO Box 498360, Chicago IL 60649, USA
**Stapleton, David L** — Baseball Player
51 N Bayview Ave, Fairhope AL 36532, USA
**Stapleton, Kevin** — Actor
Roth Assoc, 250 W 85th St, New York NY 10024, USA
**Stapleton, Mike** — Ice Hockey Player
7719 Cottage Dr, Bellaire MI 49615, USA
**Stapleton, Oliver** — Cinematographer
Independent Talent Group, 40 Whitfield St, London W1T 2RH, England
**Stapleton, Pat** — Ice Hockey Player
623 Saulsberry St, Strathroy ON N7G 3R4, Canada
**Stapleton, Sullivan** — Actor
W M E Entertainment, 9601 Wilshire Blvd, #300, Beverly Hills CA 90210 USA
**Stapleton, Walter K** — Judge
US Court of Appeals, Federal Building, 844 N King St, Wilmington DE 19801, USA
**Stapp, Scott** — Singer (Creed), Lyricist
W M E Entertainment, 9601 Wilshire Blvd, #300, Beverly Hills CA 90210 USA
**Star, Darren W** — Director, Producer
Darren Star Productions, 9200 Sunset Blvd, #430, Los Angeles CA 90069, USA
**Star, Ryan** — Singer, Songwriter
Creative Artists Agency, 2000 Ave of Stars, #100, Los Angeles CA 90067 USA
**Starbird, Kate** — Basketball Player
Indiana Fever, Conseco Fieldhouse, 125 S Pennsylvania, Indianapolis IN 46204 USA
**Starbuck, Jo Jo** — Figure Skater
33 Pomeroy Road, Madison NJ 07940, USA
**Starck, Philippe** — Architect, Industrial Designer
Starck-Ubix, 27 Rue Pierre Poli, 92130 Issey-le-Mooulineaux, France
**Starfield, Barbara H** — Physician
Johns Hopkins University, Hygiene School, 624 N Broadway, Baltimore MD 21205, USA
**Stargell, Tony L** — Football Player
131 Jenny Road, Grantville GA 30220, USA
**Starikov, Sergei V** — Ice Hockey Player
209 Greenbrook Road, Green Brook NJ 08812, USA
**Stark, Dennis J (Denny)** — Baseball Player
213 N Elm St, Edgerton OH 43517, USA
**Stark, Jonathan** — Tennis Player
11593 NW Blackhawk Dr, Portland OR 97229, USA
**Stark, Koo** — Actress
Rebecca Blond, 69A King's Road, London SW3 4NX, England
**Stark, Matthew S (Matt)** — Baseball Player
3203 E Birchwood Place, Chandler AZ 85249, USA
**Stark, Melissa** — Sportscaster, Commentator
NBC-TV, News Dept, 30 Rockefeller Plaza, #270E, New York NY 10112 USA
**Stark, Nathan J** — Attorney
4000 Cathedral Ave NW, #132, Washington DC 20016, USA
**Stark, Rohn T** — Football Player
PO Box 10067, Lahaina HI 96761, USA
**Starke, Anthony** — Actor
Geddes Agency, 8430 Santa Monica Blvd, #201, West Hollywood CA 90069 USA
**Starke, George L** — Football Player
1406 Corcoran St NW, #A, Washington DC 20009, USA
**Starks, Duane L** — Football Player
12495 Stoneway Court, Davie FL 33330, USA
**Starks, John L** — Basketball Player
PO Box 8146, Stamford CT 06905, USA
**Starks, Randolph (Randy), Jr** — Football Player
2535 SW 105th Terrace, Davie FL 33324, USA
**Starks, Scott D** — Football Player
1006 Briarcreek Road, Jacksonville FL 32225, USA
**Starkweather, Gary K** — Optical Engineer
10274 Parkwood Dr, #7, Cupertino CA 95014, USA
**Starling, H Denby** — Navy Admiral
Commander, Naval Cyber Command, 2465 Guadalcanal, Little Creek VA 23521, USA
**Starling, James D** — Army General
3581 Joshua Road, Shingle Springs CA 95682, USA
**Starling, John** — Singer, Guitarist
M Hitchcock Mgmt, 1204 Talon Way, Franklin TN 37069, USA
**Starling, Marlon** — Boxer
235 Main St, #9C1, West Hartford CT 06106, USA
**Starn, Douglas** — Photographer
Stux Gallery, 163 Mercer St, #1, New York NY 10012, USA

**Starn, Mike** — Photographer
Stux Gallery, 163 Mercer St, #1, New York NY 10012, USA

**Starner, Shelby** — Singer
Morebarn Music, 30 Hillcrest Ave, Morristown NJ 07960, USA

**Starnes, James R** — WW II Army Air Corps Hero
16001 Lakeshore Villa Dr, #330, Tampa FL 33613, USA

**Starnes, Vaughn A** — Cardiac, Lung Surgeon
Stanford University Medical Center, Heart & Lung Transplant Dept, Stanford CA 94305, USA

**Starobinsky, Alexei A** — Physicist
Landau Theroetical Physics Institute, Kosygina St 2, 119334 Moscow, Russia

**Starr, Albert** — Cardiac Surgeon
1792 SW Montgomery Dr, Portland OR 97201, USA

**Starr, B Bartlett (Bart)** — Football Player, Coach
2065 Royal Fern Lane, Birmingham AL 35244, USA

**Starr, Blaze** — Exotic Dancer
HC 70, Box 1477, Wilsonville WV 25699, USA

**Starr, Brenda K** — Singer
Brothers Management Assoc, 141 Dunbar Ave, Fords NJ 08863 USA

**Starr, David** — Auto, Truck Racing Driver
Boys Will Be Boys Racing, 610 Performance Road, Mooresville NC 28115, USA

**Starr, Kay** — Singer
Ira Okun Entertainment, 1459 Lauren Court, Encinitas CA 92024, USA

**Starr, Kenneth W** — Government Official, Judge
Baylor University, President's Office, Waco TX 76798, USA

**Starr, Martin** — Actor
United Talent Agency, U T A Plaza, 9336 Civic Center Dr, Beverly Hills CA 90210 USA

**Starr, Paul E** — Sociologist
Princeton University, Sociology Dept, Green Hall, Princeton NJ 08544, USA

**Starr, Randy** — Singer (Insiders), Songwriter
D D S, 230 Park Ave, New York NY 10169, USA

**Starr, Richard E (Dick)** — Baseball Player
613 N Crescent Dr, Kittanning PA 16201, USA

**Starr, Ringo** — Singer, Drummer (Beatles)
Rocca Bella, 90 Jermyn St, #100, London SW1Y 6JD, England

**Starrette, Herman P (Herm)** — Baseball Player
103 Howard Pond Loop, Statesville NC 28625, USA

**Starring, Stephen D** — Football Player
9035 S Tenaya Way, Las Vegas NV 89113, USA

**Starzewski, Tomasz** — Fashion Designer
House of Tomasz Starzewski, 15-17 Pont St, London SW1X 9EH, England

**Starzl, Thomas E** — Surgeon
University of Pittsburgh Medical School, Surgery Dept, Pittsburgh PA 15261, USA

**Stashower, Daniel** — Writer
E P Dutton, 375 Hudson St, New York NY 10014 USA

**Stashwick, Todd** — Actor
A P A Talent & Literary Agency, 405 S Beverly Dr, #300, Beverly Hills CA 90212 USA

**Stasiuk, Victor J (Vic)** — Ice Hockey Player
7 Canyon Gardens W, Leftbridge AB T1K 6V1, Canada

**Stassforth, Bowen** — Swimmer
26203 Birchfield Ave, Rancho Palos Verdes CA 90275, USA

**Stastny, Anton** — Ice Hockey Player
Route de Broye 45, 1008 Prilli, Swtizerland

**Stastny, Paul** — Ice Hockey Player
Colorado Avalanche, Pepsi Center, 1000 Chopper Circle, Denver CO 80204 USA

**Stastny, Peter** — Ice Hockey Player
465 S Mason Road, Saint Louis MO 63141, USA

**Staten, Vince** — Writer
9323 Loch Lea Lane, Louisville KY 40291, USA

**Statham, Harry** — Basketball Coach
McKendree College, Athletic Dept, Lebanon IL 62254, USA

**Statham, Jason** — Actor
Current Entertainment, 9378 Wilshire Blvd, #210, Beverly Hills CA 90212, USA

**Station, Larry W, Jr** — Football Player
PO Box 471, Seale AL 36875, USA

**Statman, Andy** — Mandolinist
C M Mgmt, 5749 Larryan Dr, Woodland Hills CA 91367, USA

**Staton, Aaron** — Actor
I C M Partners, 10250 Constellation Blvd, #900, Los Angeles CA 90067 USA

**Staton, Candi** — Singer
Celebrity Talent Agency, 111 E 14th St, #249, New York NY 10003, USA

**Staub, Daniel J (Rusty)** — Baseball Player
403 S Sapodilla Ave, #214, West Palm Beach FL 33401, USA

**Staubach, Roger T** — Football Player
5242 Ravine Dr, Dallas TX 75220, USA

**Stauber, Liz** — Actress
Blue Ridge, 535 W 23rd St, #S10A, New York NY 10011, USA

**Stauber, Robb** — Ice Hockey Player
Stauber's Goal Crease, 7401A Washington Ave S, Minneapolis MN 55439, USA

**Stauffer, Timothy J(Tim)** — Baseball Player
1464 Summit Ave, Cardiff CA 92007, USA

**Stauffer, William A (Bill)** — Basketball Player
13808 Sheridan Ave, Urbandale IA 50323, USA

**Staunton, Imelda** — Actress
Conway Van Gelder Grant, 8-12 Broadwick St, #300, London W1F 8HW, England

**Staurovsky, Jason C** — Football Player
4822 E 87th Place, Tulsa OK 74137, USA

**Stavridis, James G** — Navy Admiral
Tufts University, Fletcher Law & Diplomacy School, 160 Packard Ave, Medford MA 02155, USA

**Stayskal, Wayne** — Editorial Cartoonist
Tampa Tribune, Editorial Dept, 200 S Parker St, Tampa FL 33606, USA

**Staysniak, Joseph A (Joe)** — Football Player
4094 Forest Dr, Brownsburg IN 46112, USA

**Stead, Erin E** — Illustrator
MacMillan, 175 5th Ave, New York NY 10010 USA

**Stead, Philip** — Writer
MacMillan, 175 5th Ave, New York NY 10010 USA

**Steadman, Alison** — Actress
Artist Rights Group, 4A Exmoor St, London W10 6BD, England

**Steadman, J Richard** — Sports Orthopedic Surgeon
Steadman Hawkins Clinic, 181 W Meadows Dr, #400, Vail CO 81657, USA

**Steadman, Mark** — Writer
450 Pin-du-Lac Dr, Central SC 29630, USA

**Steadman, Ralph I** — Cartoonist, Illustrator
Old Loose Court, Loose Valley, Maidstone, Kent ME15 9SE, England

**Steadman, Robert L** — Cinematographer
15925 Temecula St, Pacific Palisades CA 90272, USA

**Steagall, Russell (Red)** — Singer, Guitarist
PO Box 136639, Fort Worth TX 76136, USA

**Stearns, Cheryl** — Skydiver
613 Saddlebred Lane, Raeford NC 28376, USA

**Stearns, Jeff** — Actor
Abrams Artists, 9200 W Sunset Blvd, #1125, West Hollywood CA 90069 USA

**Stearns, John H** — Baseball Player
2251 Shell Beach Road, #36, Pismo Beach CA 93449, USA

**Stebbins, Richard V** — Track Athlete
9305 Bahia Track Way, Ocala FL 34472, USA

**Stebbins, Theodore Ellis, Jr** — Art Historian
Harvard University, Fogg Art Museum, Cambridge MA 02138, USA

**Steber, Christopher L** — Actor
Gavin Barker Assoc, 2D Wimpole St, London W1G 0EB, England

**Stecher, Mario** — Nordic Combined Skier
Leins 103, 6471 Arzi im Pitztal, Austria

**Stecher, Renate Meissner-** — Track Athlete
Haydnstr 11, #526/38, 07749 Jena, Germany

**Stecher, Theodore P** — Astronomer
U I T Project, Goddard Space Flight Center, Greenbelt MD 20771, USA

**Stechschulte, Gene** — Baseball Player
206 Wellington Place, Findlay OH 45840, USA

**Steckel, Les** — Football Player, Coach
195 Blew Court, East Brunswick NJ 08816, USA

**Stecker, Aaron** — Football Player
26 Vernal Spring, Irvine CA 92603, USA

**Stecklein, Lee** — Ice Hockey Player
USA Hockey, 1775 Bob Johnson Dr, Colorado Springs CO 80906 USA

**Ste-Croix, Gilles** — Circus Executive
Cirque du Soleil, 8400 2nd Ave, Montreal QC H1Z 4M6, Canada

**Steding, Katy** — Basketball Player, Coach
21625 SW 100th Dr, Tualatin OR 97062, USA

**Steed, Joel E** — Football Player
12607 Blanco Terrace Lane, Houston TX 77041, USA

**Steeger, Ingrid** — Actress
Marlies Prinz, Rathelbeckstr 246, 40627 Dusseldorf, Germany

**Steel of Aikwood, David M S** — Government Official, England
Aikwood Tower, Ettrick Bridge, Selkirkshire Sel TD7 5HJ, Scotland

**Steel, Amy** — Actress
Imperium 7 Artists, 5455 Wilshire Blvd, #1706, Los Angeles CA 90036 USA

**Steel, Danielle F** — Writer
PO Box 470130, San Francisco CA 94147, USA

**Steel, John** — Drummer (Animals)
Lustig Talent, PO Box 770850, Orlando FL 32877 USA

**Steele, Allan M, Jr** — Writer
1640 S Sepulveda Blvd, #218, Los Angeles CA 90025, USA

**Steele, Barbara** — Actress
2460 Benedict Canyon Dr, Beverly Hills CA 90210, USA

**Steele, Dan** — Bobsled Athlete
Bobsled & Skeleton Federation, 1631 Mesa Ave, #A, Colorado Springs CO 80906 USA

**Steele, George (Animal)** — Professional Wrestler, Actor
PO Box 321343, Cocoa Beach FL 32932, USA

**Steele, J Lendale (Glen), Jr** — Football Player
188 Marshdale Ave SW, Concord NC 28025, USA

**Steele, Jeffrey** — Singer, Songwriter
Lofton Creek Records, 13751 Lebanon Road, Old Hickory TN 37138, USA

**Steele, Larry N** — Basketball Player
PO Box 372, Vernonia OR 97064, USA

**Steele, Michael** — Singer, Bassist (Bangles)
Bangles Mall, PO Box 180, 1341 W Fullerton Ave, Chicago IL 60614, USA

**Steele, Richard** — Boxing Referee
2438 Antler Point Dr, Henderson NV 89074, USA

**Steele, Sarah** — Actress
Gersh Agency, 41 Madison Ave, #3301, New York NY 10010 USA

**Steele, Shelby** — Writer
San Jose State University, English Dept, San Jose CA 95192, USA

**Steele, Tim** — Auto Racing Driver
11433 24th Ave, Marne MI 49435, USA

**Steele, Tommy** — Singer, Actor
International Management Group, 3 Burlington Lane, London W4 2TH, England

**Steele-Perkins, Christopher H** — Photographer
49 Saint Francis Road, London SE22 8DE, England

**Steels, James E (Jim)** — Baseball Player
1654 Via Rico, Santa Maria CA 93454, USA

**Steen, Cassandra** — Singer, Songwriter
A S S Concerts & Promotion, Rahlstedter Str 92A, 22149 Hamburg, Germany

**Steen, Jessica** — Actress
Bauman Redanty Shaul Agency, 5757 Wilshire Blvd, #473, Los Angeles CA 90036 USA

**Steen, Paprika** — Actress, Director
Agentfirman Planthaber/Kilden, Drottninggatan 112, 113 60 Stockholm, Sweden

**Steenburgen, Mary** — Actress
Management 360, 9111 Wilshire Blvd, Beverly Hills CA 90210 USA

**Steenland, Douglas** — Businessman
Northwest Airlines, 2700 Lone Oak Parkway, Saint Paul MN 55121, USA

**Steenstra, Kenneth G (Ken)** — Baseball Player
1228 Pheasant Court, Liberty MO 64068, USA

**S**

| | | |
|---|---|---|
| **Steeples, Eddie** | | Actor |
| Innovative Artists, 1505 10th St, Santa Monica CA 90401 USA | | |
| **Steers, Burr** | | Director |
| Creative Artists Agency, 2000 Ave of Stars, #100, Los Angeles CA 90067 USA | | |
| **Steevens, Morris D (Morrie)** | | Baseball Player |
| 14465 Cadillac Dr, San Antonio TX 78248, USA | | |
| **Stefan, Gregory S** | | Ice Hockey Player |
| 10810 Emerald Club Court, #203, Raleigh NC 27617, USA | | |
| **Stefan, Patrik** | | Ice Hockey Player |
| 1450 Bluebird Canyon Dr, Laguna Beach CA 92651, USA | | |
| **Stefani, Gwen** | | Singer (No Doubt), Songwriter |
| Schiff Co, 9220 Sunset Blvd, #106, West Hollywood CA 90069 USA | | |
| **Stefanich, Jim** | | Bowler |
| 1444 Coral Bell Dr, Joliet IL 60435, USA | | |
| **Stefanik, Mike** | | Auto Racing Driver |
| 106 Pierremount Ave, New Britain CT 06053, USA | | |
| **Stefaniuk, Robert** | | Actor, Director |
| Loeb & Loeb, 10100 Santa Monica Blvd, #2200, Los Angeles CA 90067 USA | | |
| **Stefanovich, Tamara** | | Concert Pianist |
| Harrison/Parrott, 5-6 Albion Court, London W6 0QT, England | | |
| **Stefanski, Bud** | | Ice Hockey Player |
| RR 1, Buckhorn ON K0L 1J0, Canada | | |
| **Stefanson, Leslie** | | Actress |
| I C M Partners, 10250 Constellation Blvd, #900, Los Angeles CA 90067 USA | | |
| **Stefanyshyn-Piper, Heidemarie M** | | Astronaut |
| 3722 W Pine Brook Way, Houston TX 77059, USA | | |
| **Stefecekova, Zuzana** | | Markswoman |
| Jurkovicova 1, 94911 Nitra, Slovakia | | |
| **Stefero, John R** | | Baseball Player |
| 6239 Chestnut Oak Lane, Linthicum Heights MD 21090, USA | | |
| **Steffen, Britta** | | Swimmer |
| Regine Eichhorn, Bizestr 1, 13088 Berlin, Germany | | |
| **Steffen, James W (Jim)** | | Football Player |
| 1440 Westway, Arnold MD 21012, USA | | |
| **Steffes, Kent** | | Volleyball Player |
| 14675 Titus St, Panorama City CA 91402, USA | | |
| **Steger, Michael** | | Actor |
| Stone Manners Salners, 6100 Wilshire Blvd, #1500, Los Angeles CA 90035 USA | | |
| **Stegman, David W (Dave)** | | Baseball Player |
| 3234 Simmons Dr, Grove City OH 43123, USA | | |
| **Steiger, Ueli** | | Cinematographer |
| 2222 Kenilworth Ave, Los Angeles CA 90039, USA | | |
| **Steigerwalt, Gary** | | Concert Pianist |
| Pro Musicus Foundation, 1351 Ocean Front Walk, #203, Santa Monica CA 90401, USA | | |
| **Stein, Ben** | | Actor, Comedian |
| Innovative Artists, 1505 10th St, Santa Monica CA 90401 USA | | |
| **Stein, Chris** | | Guitarist (Blondie) |
| Agency Group Ltd, 142 W 57th St, #600, New York NY 10019 USA | | |
| **Stein, Ed** | | Editorial Cartoonist |
| Rocky Mountain News, Editorial Dept, 101 W Colfax Ave, #500, Denver CO 80202, USA | | |
| **Stein, Elias M** | | Mathematician |
| 132 Dodds Lane, Princeton NJ 08540, USA | | |
| **Stein, Gilbert (Gil)** | | Ice Hockey Executive |
| National Hockey League, 650 5th Ave, #3300, New York NY 10019, USA | | |
| **Stein, Jeremy C** | | Government Leader, Economist |
| Federal Reserve System, 20th St & Constitution Ave NW, Washington DC 20551, USA | | |
| **Stein, Mark** | | Singer, Organist (Vanilla Fudge) |
| Future Vision, 280 Riverside Dr, #12L, New York NY 10025, USA | | |
| **Stein, Uli** | | Cartoonist |
| Catprint Media, Postfach 101969, 30840 Langenhagen, Germany | | |
| **Stein, W Blake** | | Baseball Player |
| 115 Bonne Vie Dr, Brandon MS 39047, USA | | |
| **Stein, William A (Bill)** | | Baseball Player |
| 10421 Grayhawk Lane, Fort Worth TX 76244, USA | | |
| **Steinbach, Alice** | | Journalist |
| Baltimore Sun, Editorial Dept, 501 N Calvert St, Baltimore MD 21278, USA | | |
| **Steinbach, Eric** | | Football Player |
| 2043 W Fletcher St, Chicago IL 60618, USA | | |
| **Steinbach, Terry L** | | Baseball Player |
| Terry Steinbach Scholarship Fund, PO Box 181, Hamel MN 55340, USA | | |
| **Steinbacher, Arabella** | | Concert Violinist |
| I M G Artists, Bandelstrasse 35, 30171 Hannover, Germany | | |
| **Steinbauer, Ben** | | Director, Producer |
| United Talent Agency, U T A Plaza, 9336 Civic Center Dr, Beverly Hills CA 90210 USA | | |
| **Steinberg, Daniel** | | Physician |
| University of California Medical School, 9500 Gilman Dr, La Jolla CA 92093, USA | | |
| **Steinberg, David** | | Actor, Comedian, Director |
| Coolwaters Productions, 10061 Riverside Dr, Box 531, Toluca Lake CA 91602 USA | | |
| **Steinberg, Jon** | | Producer, Writer |
| W M E Entertainment, 9601 Wilshire Blvd, #300, Beverly Hills CA 90210 USA | | |
| **Steinberg, Mark** | | Concert Violinist |
| Mannes College of Music, 150 W 85th St, New York NY 10024, USA | | |
| **Steinberg, Paul** | | Cartoonist |
| New Yorker, Editorial Dept, 4 Times Square, Basement C1B, New York NY 10036 USA | | |
| **Steinberg, William (Billy)** | | Lyricist |
| McDaniel Entertainment, 1311 Broadway, Santa Monica CA 90404, USA | | |
| **Steinberger, Jack** | | Nobel Physics Laureate |
| 25 Chemin des Merles, 1213 Onex, Geneva, Switzerland | | |
| **Steindorff, Scott** | | Producer, Writer |
| Stone Village, 1036 Carol Dr, West Hollywood CA 90069, USA | | |
| **Steinem, Gloria** | | Women's Activist, Editor |
| 118 E 73rd St, New York NY 10021, USA | | |
| **Steiner, F George** | | Writer |
| 32 Barrow Road, Cambridge, England | | |
| **Steiner, Melvin J (Mel)** | | Baseball Umpire |
| 27217 White Alder Court, Murrieta CA 92562, USA | | |

**Steiner, Michael** — Sculptor, Artist
704 Broadway, New York NY 10003, USA
**Steiner, Paul** — Editorial Cartoonist
Washington Times, Editorial Dept, 3600 New York Ave NE, Washington DC 20002, USA
**Steiner, Peter** — Cartoonist
New Yorker, Editorial Dept, 4 Times Square, Basement C1B, New York NY 10036 USA
**Steiner, Tommy Shane** — Singer
Collinsworth Bright, 209 10th Ave S, #216, Nashville TN 37203, USA
**Steinfeld, Hailee** — Actress
I C M Partners, 10250 Constellation Blvd, #900, Los Angeles CA 90067 USA
**Steinfeld, Jake** — Actor, Body Builder
622 Toyopa Dr, Pacific Palisades CA 90272, USA
**Steinfort, Frederick W (Fred)** — Football Player
PO Box 24981, Denver CO 80224, USA
**Steinhardt, Arnold** — Violinist (Guarneri String Quartet)
Barrett Vantage Artists, 508 8th Ave, #12A00, New York NY 10018 USA
**Steinhardt, Paul J** — Physicist
1000 Cedargrove Road, Wynnewood PA 19096, USA
**Steinhardt, Richard** — Biologist
University of California, Biology Dept, Berkeley CA 94720, USA
**Steinhauer, Sherri** — Golfer
5010 Hammersley Road, Madison WI 53711, USA
**Steinkraus, William (Bill)** — Equestrian
40 Great Island, Darien CT 06820, USA
**Steinkuhler, Dean E** — Football Player
8041 S 37th St, Lincoln NE 68516, USA
**Steinman, James R (Jim)** — Composer, Songwriter
D A S Communications, 83 Riverside Dr, New York NY 10024, USA
**Steinmetz, Richard** — Actor
Melanie Greene Mgmt, 425 N Robertson Blvd, West Hollywood CA 90048 USA
**Steinseifer Bates, Carolyn L (Carrie)** — Swimmer
9309 Benzon Dr, Pleasanton CA 94588, USA
**Steinwedell, Nicole** — Actress
I C M Partners, 10250 Constellation Blvd, #900, Los Angeles CA 90067 USA
**Steir, Pat** — Artist
601 W 26th St, #1207, New York NY 10001, USA
**Steirer, Ricky F** — Baseball Player
1015 Haverhill Road, Baltimore MD 21229, USA
**Steitz, Joan A** — Biochemist
45 Prospect Hill Road, Branford CT 06405, USA
**Steitz, Thomas A** — Nobel Chemistry Laureate
Yale University, Molecular Biophysics Dept, New Haven CT 06520, USA
**Stelfox, Shirley** — Actress
Associated International Mgmt, 7 Hatton Garden, #400, London EC1N 8AD, England
**Stella, Beniamino Cardinal** — Religious Leader
Congregation for Clergy, Palazzo delle Congregazioni, Piazza Pio XII 3, 00193 Rome, Italy
**Stella, Frank P** — Artist, Sculptor
17 Jones St, New York NY 10014, USA
**Stelle, Kellogg S** — Physicist
Imperial College, Prince Consort Road, London SW7 2BZ, England
**Steltzner, Adam** — Space Engineer
Jet Propulsion Laboratory, 4800 Oak Grove Dr, Pasadena CA 91109 USA
**Stemkowski, Peter D (Pete)** — Ice Hockey Player
146 Albany Blvd, #21C, Atlantic Beach NY 11509, USA
**Stempniak, Lee** — Ice Hockey Player
4469 Clinton St, Buffalo NY 14224, USA
**Stemrick, Gregory E (Greg), Sr** — Football Player
1012 Matthews Dr, Cincinnati OH 45215, USA
**Sten, Sanna** — Rowing Athlete
Helsingin Soutuklubi Ry, Kousatie 17 E 10, 00430 Helsinki, Finland
**Stenerud, Jan** — Football Player
6955 Overhill Road, Mission Hills KS 66208, USA
**Stengade, Stine** — Actress
Jonathan Arun, 2.06 Clerkenwell Workshops, 31 Clerkenwell Close, London EC1R 0AU, England
**Stenger, Brian F** — Football Player
7921 Kellogg Creek Dr, Mentor OH 44060, USA
**Stenhouse, Michael S (Mike)** — Baseball Player
70 Woodbury Road, Cranston RI 02905, USA
**Stenmark, Ingemar** — Alpine Skier
Karlsuddsvagen 58B, 185 93 Vaxholm, Sweden
**Stenner, Charles E, Jr** — Air Force General
Chief, Air Force Reserve, HqUSAF, Pentagon, Washington DC 20310 USA
**Stennett, Renaldo A (Rennie)** — Baseball Player
6519 Boticelli Dr, Lake Worth FL 33467, USA
**Stensrud, Michael I (Mike)** — Football Player
304 S Winnebago St, Lake Mills IA 50450, USA
**Stepanek, Ondrej** — Canoeing Athlete
S K Neumanna 386, 25001 Brandy's Nad Labem, Tschenchien, Czech Republic
**Stepanova, Maria** — Basketball Player
Phoenix Mercury, American West Arena, 201 E Jefferson St, Phoenix AZ 85004 USA
**Stepanovich, Aleksandar (Alex)** — Football Player
939 W 29th St, Lorain OH 44052, USA
**Stepashin, Sergei V** — Prime Minister, Russia; Army General
Accounts Chamber, Zubovskaya Pl 2, 119992 Moscow, Russia
**Stephanie** — Princess, Monaco
Palais Grimaldi, 2 Blvd du Moulins, 98015 Monte Carlo, Monaco
**Stephanopoulos, George R** — Journalist, Government Official
474 W 238th St, #2B, Bronx NY 10463, USA
**Stephanson, Ken** — Ice Hockey Player
6 Heron Road, Box 1491, Siglavik MB R0C 1B0, Canada
**Stephen, Louis R (Buzz)** — Baseball Player
15512 Sycamore St, Porterville CA 93257, USA
**Stephen, Marcus** — President, Nauru
President's Office, Government Offices, Yaren, Nauru
**Stephen, Scott D** — Football Player
4132 Palm Tree Court, La Mesa CA 91941, USA

**Stephens, Aaron** — Actor
Michael Bruno Group, 13576 Cheltenham Dr, Sherman Oaks CA 91423, USA

**Stephens, Bret L** — Journalist
Wall Street Journal, Editorial Dept, 1 World Financial Center, New York NY 10281 USA

**Stephens, G Eugene (Gene)** — Baseball Player
602 Erin Ave, Monroe LA 71201, USA

**Stephens, Jamain** — Football Player
105 W 6th St, Tabor City NC 28463, USA

**Stephens, John M** — Baseball Player
1325 Oak Point Court, Venice FL 34292, USA

**Stephens, Louanne** — Actress
Mary Collins Agency, 2909 Cole Ave, #250, Dallas TX 75204, USA

**Stephens, Stanley G (Stan)** — Governor, MT
4 Capitol Court, Helena MT 59601, USA

**Stephens, Thomas G (Tom)** — Football Player
69 Orchard Road, Swampscott MA 01907, USA

**Stephens, Toby** — Actor
United Agents, 12-26 Lexington St, London W1F 0LE, England

**Stephenson, C Earl** — Baseball Player
4043 Zacks Mill Road, Angier NC 27501, USA

**Stephenson, Debra** — Actress, Comedienne
Independent Talent Group, 40 Whitfield St, London W1T 2RH, England

**Stephenson, Dwight E** — Football Player
6241 N Dixie Highway, Fort Lauderdale FL 33334, USA

**Stephenson, Garrett C** — Baseball Player
947 W State St, Eagle ID 83616, USA

**Stephenson, Gordon** — Architect
55/14 Albert St, Claremont WA 6010, Australia

**Stephenson, Jan L** — Golfer
500 Rugby St, Orlando FL 32804, USA

**Stephenson, John H (Johnny)** — Baseball Player
7 Mauroner Dr, Hammond LA 70401, USA

**Stephenson, Lance, Jr** — Basketball Player
Charlotte Hornets, 333 E Trade St, #A, Charlotte NC 28202 USA

**Stephenson, Neal T** — Writer
Avon Books, 1350 Ave of Americas, New York NY 10019 USA

**Stephenson, Randall** — Businessman
A T & T Inc, 175 E Houston St, San Antonio TX 78205, USA

**Stephens-Tysland, Kelly** — Ice Hockey Player
Experience Momentum, 4720 200th St SW, Lynnwood WA 98036, USA

**Stepnoski, Mark M** — Football Player
1131 Meadow Creek Dr, #C1108, Irving TX 75038, USA

**Steppe, M Holbrook (Brook)** — Basketball Player
3486 Clare Cottage Terrace, Palm Desert CA 92211, USA

**Steranka, Joe** — Golf Executive
Professional Golfers Association, 100 Ave of Champions, Palm Beach Gardens FL 33418 USA

**Steranko, Jim** — Cartoonist
PO Box 974, Reading PA 19603, USA

**Sterban, Richard A** — Singer (Oak Ridge Boys)
329 Rockland Road, Hendersonville TN 37075, USA

**Sterkel, Jill** — Swimmer
2206 Heritage Well Lane, Pflugerville TX 78660, USA

**Sterling, Annette B** — Singer (Martha & Vandellas)
Soundedge Personal Mgmt, 332 Southdown Road, Huntington NY 11743, USA

**Sterling, Maury** — Actor
Innovative Artists, 1505 10th St, Santa Monica CA 90401 USA

**Sterling, Mindy** — Actress
Groundlings, 7307 Melrose Ave, Los Angeles CA 90046, USA

**Sterling, Randall W (Randy)** — Baseball Player
2516 Linda Ave, Key West FL 33040, USA

**Sterling, Tisha** — Actress
PO Box 235, Ketchum ID 83340, USA

**Stern, Daniel** — Actor
C E S D, 10635 Santa Monica Blvd, #130, Los Angeles CA 90025 USA

**Stern, David** — Religious Leader, Rabbi
8500 Hillcrest Ave, Dallas TX 75225, USA

**Stern, David J** — Basketball Executive
National Basketball Association, 645 5th Ave, #1800, New York NY 10022 USA

**Stern, David J** — Conductor
I M G Artists, Hogarth Business Park, Chiswick, London W4 2TH, England

**Stern, Fritz R** — Historian
15 Claremont Ave, New York NY 10027, USA

**Stern, Gardner** — Writer, Producer
Paradigm Agency, 360 N Crescent Dr, North Building, Beverly Hills CA 90210 USA

**Stern, Gary H** — Government Official, Financier
Federal Reserve Bank, PO Box 291, Minneapolis MN 55480, USA

**Stern, Gerald** — Writer
W W Norton, 500 5th Ave, #600, New York NY 10110 USA

**Stern, Howard A** — Entertainer
Don Buchwald Talent Agency, 10 E 44th St, New York NY 10017 USA

**Stern, Joseph** — Actor, Producer
Creative Artists Agency, 2000 Ave of Stars, #100, Los Angeles CA 90067 USA

**Stern, Marcus** — Journalist
San Diego Union-Tribune, Editorial Dept, 350 Camino Reina, San Diego CA 92108 USA

**Stern, Melvin E** — Oceanographer
Florida State University, Oceanography Dept, Tallahassee FL 32306, USA

**Stern, Michael (Mike)** — Jazz Guitarist
Universal Attractions, 135 W 26th St, #1200, New York NY 10001 USA

**Stern, Robert A M** — Architect
Robert A M Stern Architects, 460 W 34th St, #1800, New York NY 10001, USA

**Stern, Ronnie** — Ice Hockey Player
224 Oakwood Blvd, Hustisford WI 53034, USA

**Stern, Shoshannah** — Actress
C E S D, 257 Park Ave S, #950, New York NY 10010 USA

**Stern, Thomas E (Tom)** — Cinematographer
I C M Partners, 10250 Constellation Blvd, #900, Los Angeles CA 90067 USA

**Sternberg, Robert J** — Psychologist
64 Reach Run, Ithaca NY 14850, USA

**Sternberg, Sigmund** — Religous Leader, Templeton Laureate
80 East End Road, London N3 2SY, England

**Sternberg, Thomas** — Businessman
Staples Inc, PO Box 9265, Framingham MA 01701, USA

**Sternecky, Neal** — Cartoonist (Pogo)
52 Bluebird Lane, Naperville IL 60565, USA

**Sternhagen, Frances** — Actress
152 Sutton Manor Road, New Rochelle NY 10801, USA

**Sternin, Joshua** — Producer, Writer
Morris Yorn Barnes, 2000 Ave of Stars, #300N, Los Angeles CA 90067 USA

**Sternlicht, Barry** — Interior Designer
Starwood Capital Group, 591 W Putnam Ave, Greenwich CT 06830, USA

**Sterrett, Samuel B** — Judge
US Tax Court, 400 2nd St NW, Washington DC 20217, USA

**Stetter, Karl O** — Microbiologist
Universtat Regensburg, Universitats Str 31, 93053 Regensburg, Germany

**Stetter, Mitch B** — Baseball Player
4135 N Olcott Ave, Norridge IL 60706, USA

**Stettner, Louis** — Photographer
172 W 79th St, #6G, New York NY 10024, USA

**Stettner, Patrick** — Director
United Talent Agency, U T A Plaza, 9336 Civic Center Dr, Beverly Hills CA 90210 USA

**Steuer, Ingo** — Figure Skater
Liebigstr 9, 09113 Chemnitz, Germany

**Steussie, Todd E** — Football Player
59 Clermont Lane, Saint Louis MO 63124, USA

**Stevenin, Robinson** — Actor
Artmedia, 20 Ave Rapp, 75007 Paris, France

**Stevens, Amber** — Actress
I C M Partners, 10250 Constellation Blvd, #900, Los Angeles CA 90067 USA

**Stevens, Andrew** — Actor
CineTel Films, 8255 Sunset Blvd, Los Angeles CA 90046, USA

**Stevens, April** — Singer
19530 Superior St, Northridge CA 91324, USA

**Stevens, Brad** — Basketball Coach
Boston Celtics, 226 Causeway St, #4, Boston MA 02114 USA

**Stevens, Brinke** — Actress
PO Box 7112, Van Nuys CA 91409, USA

**Stevens, Carrie** — Model, Actress
C A Talent, 25 Palatine, #437, Irvine CA 92612, USA

**Stevens, Charles A (Chuck)** — Baseball Player
12591 George Reyburn Road, Garden Grove CA 92845, USA

**Stevens, Chuck** — Photographer
PO Box 422782, San Francisco CA 94142, USA

**Stevens, Connie** — Singer, Actress
Brogan Agency, 1517 Park Row Dr, Venice CA 90291, USA

**Stevens, D Lee** — Baseball Player
940 Graland Place, Highlands Ranch CO 80126, USA

**Stevens, Dan** — Actor
Julian Belfrage Assoc, 9 Argyll St, #300, London W1F 7TG, England

**Stevens, Dana** — Director, Writer, Actress
United Talent Agency, U T A Plaza, 9336 Civic Center Dr, Beverly Hills CA 90210 USA

**Stevens, David J (Dave)** — Baseball Player
2630 Candlewood Way, La Habra CA 90631, USA

**Stevens, Dorit** — Actress, Model
22425 Ventura Blvd, #118, Woodland Hills CA 91364, USA

**Stevens, Eileen** — Social Activist
126 Marion St, Sayville NY 11782, USA

**Stevens, Eric Sheffer** — Actor
A P A Talent & Literary Agency, 405 S Beverly Dr, #300, Beverly Hills CA 90212 USA

**Stevens, Fisher** — Actor
Paradigm Agency, 360 N Crescent Dr, North Building, Beverly Hills CA 90210 USA

**Stevens, Gary** — Thoroughbred Racing Jockey
136 W Carter Ave, Sierra Madre CA 91024, USA

**Stevens, George, Jr** — Producer
C E S D, 10635 Santa Monica Blvd, #130, Los Angeles CA 90025 USA

**Stevens, Howard M, Jr** — Football Player
235 Cedarhurst Lane, Franklinton NC 27525, USA

**Stevens, Jan** — Composer
Gorfaine/Schwartz, 4111 W Alameda Ave, #509, Burbank CA 91505 USA

**Stevens, Jeffrey A (Jeff)** — Baseball Player
Chicago Cubs, Wrigley Field, 1060 W Addison St, Chicago IL 60613 USA

**Stevens, Jerramy** — Football Player
10047 Main St, #515, Bellevue WA 98004, USA

**Stevens, John A** — Ice Hockey Player, Coach
Los Angeles Kings, Staples Center, 1111 S Figueroa St, Los Angeles CA 90015 USA

**Stevens, John Paul** — Supreme Court Justice
US Supreme Court, 1 1st St NE, Washington DC 20543 USA

**Stevens, Kenneth N** — Electrical Engineer
15298 SE Oregon Trail Dr, Clackamas OR 97015, USA

**Stevens, Kevin M** — Ice Hockey Player
70 Onion Hill Road, Duxbury MA 02332, USA

**Stevens, Louis D** — Inventor (Disk Storage Device)
421 Coates Dr, Aptos CA 95003, USA

**Stevens, Mark** — Writer
New York Times, Editorial Dept, 229 W 43rd St, New York NY 10036 USA

**Stevens, Mick** — Cartoonist
New Yorker, Editorial Dept, 4 Times Square, Basement C1B, New York NY 10036 USA

**Stevens, Rachel L** — Actress, Singer (S Club 7), Model
Artist Rights Group, 4A Exmoor St, London W10 6BD, England

**Stevens, Ray** — Singer, Songwriter
Bobby Roberts Co, PO Box 1547, Goodlettsville TN 37070, USA

**Stevens, Richard G (Dick)** — Football Player
4100 Cimmaron Trail, Granbury TX 76049, USA

**Stevens, Robert J** — Businessman
Lockheed Martin Corp, 6801 Rockledge Dr, Bethesda MD 20817, USA
**Stevens, Robert M** — Cinematographer
1920 S Beverly Glen Blvd, #106, Los Angeles CA 90025, USA
**Stevens, Rogers** — Guitarist (Blind Melon)
Shapiro Co, 9229 W Sunset Blvd, #607, West Hollywood CA 90069 USA
**Stevens, Rosemary A** — Political Scientist, Historian
171 W 71st St, #3C, New York NY 10023, USA
**Stevens, Scott** — Ice Hockey Player
280 Spook Hollow Road, Far Hills NJ 07931, USA
**Stevens, Shadoe** — Actor, Entertainer
James Kellem Assoc, 8033 Sunset Blvd, #115, Los Angeles CA 90046, USA
**Stevens, Shakin'** — Singer, Songwriter
Mgmt Gerd Kehren, Postfach 1455, 41804 Erkelenz, Germany
**Stevens, Stella** — Actress, Model
2180 Coldwater Canyon Dr, Beverly Hills CA 90210, USA
**Stevens, Sufjan** — Singer, Songwriter
Billions Corp, 3522 W Armitage Ave, Chicago IL 60647 USA
**Stevens, Taylor** — Writer
Crown Publishing Group, 1745 Broadway, #1300, New York NY 10019 USA
**Stevens, Tony** — Bassist (Foghat)
J-Bird Entertainment, 248 W Park Ave, #180, Long Beach NY 11561 USA
**Stevens, Wass** — Actor
A T A Management, 12 Desbrosses St, New York NY 10013, USA
**Stevenson, Adlai E, III** — Senator, IL
20 N Clark St, #750, Chicago IL 60602, USA
**Stevenson, DeShawn** — Basketball Player
1348 Lake Whitney Dr, Windermere FL 34786, USA
**Stevenson, G Raymond (Ray)** — Actor
Conway Van Gelder Grant, 8-12 Broadwick St, #300, London W1F 8HW, England
**Stevenson, Jeremy** — Ice Hockey Player
7899 W 6 Mile Road, Brimley MI 49715, USA
**Stevenson, John** — Animator
I/D Public Relations, 7060 Hollywood Blvd, #800, Los Angeles CA 90028 USA
**Stevenson, Juliet** — Actress
68 Pall Mall, London SW1Y 5ES, England
**Stevenson, Miriam J** — Beauty Queen
Miss Universe Organization, 1370 Ave of Americas, #1600, New York NY 10019 USA
**Stevenson, Parker** — Actor
A K A Talent, 6310 San Vicente Blvd, #200, Los Angeles CA 90048 USA
**Stevenson, Turner** — Ice Hockey Player
4530 251st Way NE, Redmond WA 98053, USA
**Stevenson, Venetia** — Actress
4827 Riverton Ave, North Hollywood CA 91601, USA
**Steverson, Todd A** — Baseball Player
109 W Glenhaven Dr, Phoenix AZ 85045, USA
**Stevie B** — Singer, Songwriter
Paramount Entertainment, PO Box 12, Far Hills NJ 07931 USA
**Stew** — Singer, Songwriter, Actor
Paradigm Agency, 360 Park Ave S, #1600, New York NY 10010 USA
**Steward, John** — Drummer (Fishbone)
Silverback Mgmt, 9469 Jefferson Blvd, #101, Culver City CA 90232, USA
**Stewart, A Ewan** — Actor
Lou Coulson Assoc, 37 Berwick St, London W1V 8RS, England
**Stewart, Al** — Singer, Guitarist, Songwriter
Chapman & Co Mgmt, 14011 Ventura Blvd, #405, Sherman Oaks CA 91423, USA
**Stewart, Alana** — Actress
Boulevard Mgmt, 21731 Ventura Blvd, #300, Woodland Hills CA 91364, USA
**Stewart, Alec** — Cricketer
Surrey County Cricket Club, Kennington Oval, London SE11 5SS, England
**Stewart, Amy** — Actress
Amsel Eisenstadt Frazier, 5055 Wilshire Blvd, #865, Los Angeles CA 90036 USA
**Stewart, Andrew D (Andy)** — Baseball Player
641 Geddes St, Wilmington DE 19805, USA
**Stewart, Anthony W (Tony)** — Auto Racing Driver
Stewart-Haas Racing, 6001 Haas Way, Kannapolis NC 28081, USA
**Stewart, Bill** — Jazz Drummer
Blue Note Records, 6920 W Sunset Blvd, Los Angeles CA 90028 USA
**Stewart, Blair J** — Ice Hockey Player
1604 Cottenham Lane, Virginia Beach VA 23454, USA
**Stewart, Booboo** — Actor
Platform Public Relations, 2666 N Beachwood Dr, Los Angeles CA 90068, USA
**Stewart, Cameron G (Cam)** — Ice Hockey Player
2929 Buffalo Speedway, #218, Houston TX 77098, USA
**Stewart, Carl E** — Judge
US Court of Appeals, 300 Fannin St, Shreveport LA 71101, USA
**Stewart, Catherine Mary** — Actress
Don Buchwald Talent Agency, 6500 Wilshire Blvd, #2200, Los Angeles CA 90048 USA
**Stewart, Charlotte** — Actress
E J C Mgmt, 6562 Hollywood Blvd, Los Angeles CA 90028, USA
**Stewart, Chelsea** — Soccer Player
Canadian Soccer, Place Soccer Canada, 237 Metcalfe St, Ottawa ON K2P 1R2, Canada
**Stewart, David A (Dave)** — Keyboardist, Guitarist (Eurythmics)
I C M Partners, 10250 Constellation Blvd, #900, Los Angeles CA 90067 USA
**Stewart, David A (Dave)** — Composer
Weapons of Mass Entertainment, 6253 Hollywood Blvd, #1104, Los Angeles CA 90028, USA
**Stewart, David K (Dave)** — Baseball Player
17762 Vineyard Lane, Poway CA 92064, USA
**Stewart, Donald L (Don)** — Televangelist
Don Stewart Ministries, PO Box 2960, Phoenix AZ 85062, USA
**Stewart, French** — Actor
Innovative Artists, 1505 10th St, Santa Monica CA 90401 USA
**Stewart, Garry** — Dancer
Australian Dance Theatre, 126 Belair Road, Hawthorn SA 5062 Australia
**Stewart, Ian** — Government Official, England
House of Commons, Westminster, London SW1A 0AA, England

**Stewart, Ian K** — Baseball Player
125 Rainbow Lane, Candler NC 28715, USA

**Stewart, James B** — Journalist
Wall Street Journal, Editorial Dept, 1 World Financial Center, New York NY 10281, USA

**Stewart, James O** — Football Player
4610 34th Ave, Vero Beach FL 32967, USA

**Stewart, Jim** — Ice Hockey Player
57 Lincoln St, Spencer MA 01562, USA

**Stewart, John Y (Jackie)** — Auto Racing Driver
Clayton House, Butler Cross, Ellesborough, Buckinghamshire HP17 0UR, England

**Stewart, Jon** — Actor, Comedian, Writer, Director
Busboy Productions, 375 Greenwich St, New York NY 10013, USA

**Stewart, Kimberly** — Actress, Model, Producer
Amsel Eisenstadt Frazier, 5055 Wilshire Blvd, #865, Los Angeles CA 90036 USA

**Stewart, Kordell** — Football Player
Robinson Griege Theole, 5950 Sherry Lane, #700, Dallas TX 75225, USA

**Stewart, Kristen** — Actress
Gersh Agency, 9465 Wilshire Blvd, #600, Beverly Hills CA 90212 USA

**Stewart, Larry** — Singer, Guitarist
Fitzgerald-Hartley, 1908 Wedgewood Ave, Nashville TN 37212, USA

**Stewart, Lisa** — Singer
Friedman & LaRosa, 1344 Lexington Ave, New York NY 10128, USA

**Stewart, Martha H** — Businesswoman, Entertainer, Publisher
Martha Stewart Living Omnimedia, 11 W 42nd St, #2500, New York NY 10036, USA

**Stewart, Matt** — Football Player
4389 Village Club Dr, Powell OH 43065, USA

**Stewart, Melvin, Jr** — Swimmer
7308 Seneca Falls Loop, Austin TX 78739, USA

**Stewart, Michael A** — Football Player
103 Los Padres Dr, Thousand Oaks CA 91361, USA

**Stewart, Natalie** — Singer (Floetry), Songwriter
DreamWorks Records, 1000 Flower St, Glendale CA 91201 USA

**Stewart, Patrick** — Actor
Independent Talent Group, 40 Whitfield St, London W1T 2RH, England

**Stewart, Paul** — Ice Hockey Player
16 Bridgeview Circle, Walpole MA 02081, USA

**Stewart, Pete** — Singer, Guitarist (Tait)
True Artist Mgmt, 227 3rd Ave N, Franklin TN 37064, USA

**Stewart, Philip J** — Ecologist
Oxford University, Plant Sciences Dept, Oxford OX1 2JD, England

**Stewart, Potter** — Judge
US Court of Appeals, US Courthouse, 100 E 5th St, #317, Cincinnati OH 45202, USA

**Stewart, R J** — Writer, Producer
A P A Talent & Literary Agency, 405 S Beverly Dr, #300, Beverly Hills CA 90212 USA

**Stewart, Ralph** — Ice Hockey Player
175 Sherwood Dr, Thunder Bay ON P7B 6L1, Canada

**Stewart, Ray** — Golfer
2777 DeHavilland Place, Abbotsford BC V2T 5E2, Canada

**Stewart, Robert H (Bob)** — Ice Hockey Player
16756 Kehrs Mill Estates Dr, Chesterfield MO 63005, USA

**Stewart, Robert L** — Astronaut, Army General
2303 Covemont Dr SE, Huntsville AL 35801, USA

**Stewart, Roderick D (Rod)** — Singer, Songwriter
Artists Group International, 150 E 58th, New York NY 10155, USA

**Stewart, Ryan E** — Football Player
2715 Owens Ave SW, Marietta GA 30064, USA

**Stewart, Sara** — Actress
Roxane Vacca Mgmt, 61 Judd St, London WC1H 9QT, England

**Stewart, Shannon H** — Baseball Player
14348 SW 156th Ave, Miami FL 33196, USA

**Stewart, Tommy** — Drummer (Godsmack)
Front Line Mgmt, 1100 Glendon Ave, #2000, Los Angeles CA 90024 USA

**Stewart, Tonea** — Actress
Alabama State University, Theater Arts Dept, Montgomery AL 36101, USA

**Stewart, Tyler** — Drummer (Barenaked Ladies)
Nettwerk Mgmt, 6525 W Sunset Blvd, #800, Los Angeles CA 90028 USA

**Stewart, Will Foster** — Actor
8730 Santa Monica Blvd, #1, West Hollywood CA 90069, USA

**Stewart, William W (Bill)** — Baseball Player
44842 Aspen Ridge Dr, Northville MI 48168, USA

**Stewart-Wilson, Belinda** — Actress
Amanda Howard Assoc, 74 Clerkenwell Road, London EC1M 5QA, England

**Steyer, Andre** — Singer
Dynasty Mgmt, Puchheimer Str 13, 82194 Grobenzell, Germany

**Stezer, Philip** — Violinist (Emerson String Quartet)
I M G Artists, Burlington Lane, Chiswick, London W4 2TH, England

**St-Gelais, Marianne** — Speed Skater
Speed Skating Canada, 2781 Lancaster Road, #402, Ottawa ON K1B 1A7, Canada

**Stice, Eric** — Psychologist
Oregon Research Institute, 1715 Franklin Blvd, Eugene OR 97403, USA

**Stich, Michael** — Tennis Player
Ernst-Barlach-Str 44, 25336 Elmshorn, Germany

**Stich, Stephen P** — Philosopher
55 Liberty St, #8A, New York NY 10005, USA

**Sticht, J Paul** — Businessman
11732 Lake House Court, North Palm Beach FL 33408, USA

**Stickles, Edward (Ted)** — Swimmer
1142 Sharynwood Dr, Baton Rouge LA 70808, USA

**Stickney, Timothy D** — Actor
TalentWorks, 3500 W Olive Ave, #1400, Burbank CA 91505 USA

**Sticky Fingaz** — Rap Artist (Onyx), Actor
I C M Partners, 10250 Constellation Blvd, #900, Los Angeles CA 90067 USA

**Stieb, David A (Dave)** — Baseball Player
3375 Cory Dr, Reno NV 89509, USA

**Stieber, Tamar** — Journalist
Albuquerque Journal, Editorial Dept, 7777 Jefferson NE, Albuquerque NM 87109, USA

| | |
|---|---|
| **Stiefel, Anja** | Ice Hockey Player |
| Swiss Ice Hockey, Hagenholzstr 81, 8050 Zurich, Switzerland | |
| **Stiefel, Ethan** | Ballet Dancer |
| American Ballet Theatre, 890 Broadway, #300, New York NY 10003 USA | |
| **Stiegler, Josef (Pepi)** | Alpine Skier |
| PO Box 290, Teton Village WY 83025, USA | |
| **Stielike, Ulrich (Uli)** | Soccer Player, Manager |
| Casa Postale 78, 2000 Neuchatel, Switzerland | |
| **Stienburg, Trevor** | Ice Hockey Player |
| 2376 Connaught Ave, Halifax NS B3L 2Z4, Canada | |
| **Stienke, James L (Jim)** | Football Player |
| 4707 Interlachen Lane, Austin TX 78747, USA | |
| **Stiers, David Ogden** | Actor |
| Mitchell K Stubbs Assoc, 8695 W Washington Blvd, #204, Culver City CA 90232 USA | |
| **Stieve, Terry A** | Football Player |
| 1407 Vail Place, Saint Louis MO 63104, USA | |
| **Stigers, Curtis** | Singer, Saxophonist |
| Bennett Morgan, 1022 RR 376, #3, Wappinger Falls NY 12590 USA | |
| **Stiglitz, Joseph E** | Nobel Economics Laureate |
| Columbia University, Economics Dept, New York NY 10027, USA | |
| **Stigman, Richard L (Dick)** | Baseball Player |
| 12914 5th Ave S, Burnsville MN 55337, USA | |
| **Stigwood, Robert C** | Producer |
| Barton Manor, Whippingham, East Cowes, Isle of Wight PO32 6LB, England | |
| **Stiles, Darron** | Golfer |
| 130 Wild Turkey Run, Pinehurst NC 28374, USA | |
| **Stiles, Jackie** | Basketball Player |
| Patrick J Stiles, 115 E Hamilton, Claflin KS 67525, USA | |
| **Stiles, Julia** | Actress |
| Untitled Entertainment, 350 S Beverly Dr, #200, Beverly Hills CA 90212 USA | |
| **Stiles, Ryan** | Actor, Comedian |
| A P A Talent & Literary Agency, 405 S Beverly Dr, #300, Beverly Hills CA 90212 USA | |
| **Stilgoe, Richard** | Lyricist |
| Noel Gray Artists, 24 Denmark St, London WC2H 8NJ, England | |
| **Still, Arthur B (Art)** | Football Player |
| 9813 Betsy Ross Court, Liberty MO 64068, USA | |
| **Still, Ken** | Golfer |
| 1210 Princeton St, Fircrest WA 98466, USA | |
| **Still, Susan L** | Astronaut |
| N A S A, Johnson Space Center, 2101 NASA Road, Houston TX 77058 USA | |
| **Still, Valerie** | Basketball Player |
| Valerie Still Foundation, PO Box 452, Powell OH 43065, USA | |
| **Still, William C, Jr** | Chemist |
| Columbia University, Chemistry Dept, New York NY 10027, USA | |
| **Stiller, Ben** | Actor, Comedian, Director |
| Red Hour Films, 629 N La Brea Ave, Los Angeles CA 90036, USA | |
| **Stiller, Jerry** | Actor, Comedian |
| 118 Riverside Dr, #5A, New York NY 10024, USA | |
| **Stillman, Cory** | Ice Hockey Player |
| 397 Sweet Bay Ave, Plantation FL 33324, USA | |
| **Stillman, Royle E** | Baseball Player |
| 580 J B Court, Glenwood Springs CO 81601, USA | |
| **Stillman, Whit** | Director |
| Mosiac Media Group, 9200 W Sunset Blvd, #1000, Los Angeles CA 90069 USA | |
| **Stills, Kenneth L (Ken)** | Football Player |
| 647 Michael St, Oceanside CA 92057, USA | |
| **Stills, Stephen** | Singer, Guitarist (Crosby Stills Nash) |
| I C M Partners, 10250 Constellation Blvd, #900, Los Angeles CA 90067 USA | |
| **Stillwagon, Jim R** | Football Player |
| 3999 Parkway Lane, Hilliard OH 43026, USA | |
| **Stillwell, Kurt A** | Baseball Player |
| 1105 Lassen View Dr, Westwood CA 96137, USA | |
| **Stilwell, Richard D** | Opera Singer |
| Columbia Artists Mgmt Inc, 5 Columbus Circle, 1790 Broadway, #1600, New York NY 10019 USA | |
| **Stilwell, Victoria** | Actress |
| W M E Entertainment, Centrepoint Tower, 103 New Oxford St, London WC1A 1DD, England | |
| **Stinchcomb, Jonathan (Jon)** | Football Player |
| 1010 Chateau Lafitte Dr W, Kenner LA 70065, USA | |
| **Stinchcomb, Matthew D (Matt)** | Football Player |
| 301 Anderson Road, Alameda CA 94502, USA | |
| **Stine, Richard** | Editorial Cartoonist |
| PO Box 348, Hansville WA 98340, USA | |
| **Stine, Robert L (R L)** | Writer |
| 225 W 71st St, New York NY 10023, USA | |
| **Stiner, Carl W** | Army General |
| Special Operations Warrior Foundation, PO Box 13483, Tampa FL 33681, USA | |
| **Sting** | Singer, Actor, Bassist, Songwriter |
| Kathryn Shenker Mgmt, 1776 Broadway, #2205, New York NY 10019, USA | |
| **Stinnett, Kelly L** | Baseball Player |
| 845 N Harris Dr, Mesa AZ 85203, USA | |
| **Stinson, G Robert (Bob)** | Baseball Player |
| 1309 Bando Lane, The Villages FL 32162, USA | |
| **Stinson, Lemuel D** | Football Player |
| 7629 Grassland Dr, Fort Worth TX 76133, USA | |
| **Stinson, Thomas E (Tommy)** | Bassist (Replacement, Guns 'N' Roses) |
| Agency Group Ltd, 142 W 57th St, #600, New York NY 10019 USA | |
| **Stipanovich, Stephen E (Steve)** | Basketball Player |
| 14 Ridgecreek, Saint Louis MO 63141, USA | |
| **Stipe, J Michael** | Singer (REM), Songwriter |
| REM/Athens Ltd, 170 College Ave, Athens GA 30601, USA | |
| **Stirling, Lindsey** | Rap Violinist, Dancer |
| I C M Partners, 10250 Constellation Blvd, #900, Los Angeles CA 90067 USA | |
| **Stirling, Rachel** | Actress |
| United Agents, 12-26 Lexington St, London W1F 0LE, England | |
| **Stirratt, John** | Bassist (Uncle Tupelo, Wilco) |
| Tom Margherita Mgmt, 2200 W Foster Ave, #2, Chicago IL 60625, USA | |

**Stirrup of Marylebone, Graham E (Jock)** — Air Force Marshal, England
House of Lords, Westminster, London SW1A 0PW, England

**Stitch, Stephen P** — Philosopher
Rutgers University, Philosophy Dept, New Brunswick NJ 08901, USA

**Stith, Bryant L** — Basketball Player
20697 Governor Harrison Parkway, Freeman VA 23856, USA

**Stits, William D (Bill)** — Football Player
1177 Eolus Ave, Encinitas CA 92024, USA

**Stivrins, Alex F** — Basketball Player
11330 Sundown Dr, Scottsdale AZ 85260, USA

**Stix-Brunell, Beatriz** — Ballerina
Morphoses/Wheeldon Co, 800 5th Ave, #18F, New York NY 10065, USA

**Stock, Barbara** — Actress
7329 Capistrano Ave, West Hills CA 91307, USA

**Stock, Mark A** — Football Player
16549 Levade Dr, Leesburg VA 20176, USA

**Stock, P J** — Ice Hockey Player
Team 990, 1310 Greene Ave, #300, Montreal QC H3Z 2B5, Canada

**Stock, Wesley G (Wes)** — Baseball Player
PO Box 1309, Allyn WA 98524, USA

**Stockard, Aaron** — Writer
W M E Entertainment, 9601 Wilshire Blvd, #300, Beverly Hills CA 90210 USA

**Stockdale, Andrew** — Singer, Guitarist (Wolfmother)
John Watson Mgmt, PO Box 281, Surry Hills NSW 2010, Australia

**Stockdale, Gretchen** — Actress
Don Buchwald Talent Agency, 6500 Wilshire Blvd, #2200, Los Angeles CA 90048 USA

**Stocker, Kevin D** — Baseball Player
1204 N Murray Lane, Liberty Lake WA 99019, USA

**Stockett, Kathryn** — Writer
Don Congdon Assoc, 110 William St, New York NY 10038, USA

**Stockman, Shawn** — Singer (Boyz II Men)
Creative Talent Management Group, 433 N Camden Dr, #600, Beverly Hills CA 90210, USA

**Stockmayer, Walter H** — Physical Chemist
Willey Hill, Norwich VT 05055, USA

**Stockton, Dave K** — Golfer
30378 Copper Hill Court, Redlands CA 92373, USA

**Stockton, David** — Cinematographer
Dattner Dispoto, 10635 Santa Monica Blvd, #165, Los Angeles CA 90025, USA

**Stockton, David, Jr** — Golfer
10 Carrera Dr, Redlands CA 92373, USA

**Stockton, Dick** — Sportscaster
2470 NW 63rd St, Boca Raton FL 33496, USA

**Stockton, John H** — Basketball Player
538 W Sumner Ave, Spokane WA 99204, USA

**Stockton, Richard L (Dick)** — Tennis Player
715 Stadium Dr, San Antonio TX 78212, USA

**Stockwell, Dean** — Actor
Imperium 7 Artists, 5455 Wilshire Blvd, #1706, Los Angeles CA 90036 USA

**Stockwell, Jeff** — Writer, Producer
United Talent Agency, U T A Plaza, 9336 Civic Center Dr, Beverly Hills CA 90210 USA

**Stockwell, John** — Actor, Director
I C M Partners, 10250 Constellation Blvd, #900, Los Angeles CA 90067 USA

**Stoddard, Jack** — Ice Hockey Player
27-4275 Millcroft Park Dr, Burlington ON L7M 4L9, Canada

**Stoddard, Robert L (Bob)** — Baseball Player
15760 Sunnyside Ave, Morgan Hill CA 95037, USA

**Stoddard, Timothy P (Tim)** — Baseball Player
4545 Gettysburg Dr, Rolling Meadows IL 60008, USA

**Stoermer, Mark** — Bassist (Killers)
W M E Entertainment, 9601 Wilshire Blvd, #300, Beverly Hills CA 90210 USA

**Stofa, John C** — Football Player
5893 Falling Brook Dr, Mason OH 45040, USA

**Stogner, Patrick** — Actor
C E S D, 10635 Santa Monica Blvd, #130, Los Angeles CA 90025 USA

**Stoicheff, Boris P** — Physicist
66 Collier St, #6B, Toronto ON M4W 1L9, Canada

**Stojakovic, Predrag (Peja)** — Basketball Player
501 Gibson Dr, #424, Roseville CA 95678, USA

**Stojko, Elvis** — Figure Skater
Mentor Marketing, 2 Saint Clair Ave E, Toronto ON M4T 2T, Canada

**Stok, Barbara** — Cartoonist (Barbaraal)
PO Box 1012, 9701 Groningen BA, Netherlands

**Stoker, Michael G P** — Virologist
3 Barrington House, Southacre Dr, Cambridge CB2 2TY, England

**Stoker, Richard** — Composer
Ricordi Co, 210 New King's Road, London SW6 4NZ, England

**Stokes, Brian** — Baseball Player
12140 66th Ave, Seminole FL 33772, USA

**Stokes, Gregory L (Greg)** — Basketball Player
2505 Plymouth St, Marion IA 52302, USA

**Stokes, John** — WW II Navy Air Force Hero
351 Windermere Blvd, #411, Alexandria LA 71303, USA

**Stokes, L Fred** — Football Player
2132 Alameda St, Orlando FL 32804, USA

**Stokes, Patrick T** — Businessman
Anheuser-Busch Co, 1 Busch Place, Saint Louis MO 63118, USA

**Stokkan, Bill** — Auto Racing Executive
Championship Auto Racing, 5350 Lakeview Parkway S Dr, Indianapolis IN 46268 USA

**Stokley, Brandon** — Football Player
1029 Anaconda Dr, Castle Rock CO 80108, USA

**Stoklos, Randy** — Volleyball Player
Beach Volleyball Camps, PO Box 1714, Pacific Palisades CA 90272, USA

**Stolbova, Ksenia A** — Figure Skater
Figure Skating Federation, Luzhnetskaya Nab 8, 119991 Moscow, Russia

**Stole, Mink** — Actress
635 Colorado Ave, #3B, Baltimore MD 21210, USA

**S**

Stirrup of Marylebone - Stole

| | |
|---|---|
| **Stolhanske, Eric** | Actor, Comedian, Writer, Producer |
| United Talent Agency, U T A Plaza, 9336 Civic Center Dr, Beverly Hills CA 90210 USA | |
| **Stoll, Corey** | Actor |
| Suskin Mgmt, 2 Charlton St, #5K, New York NY 10014, USA | |
| **Stolle, Frederick S** | Tennis Player |
| Turnberry Isle Yacht & Racquet Club, 19735 Turnberry Way, Miami FL 33180, USA | |
| **Stoller, Fred** | Actor |
| Amsel Eisenstadt Frazier, 5055 Wilshire Blvd, #865, Los Angeles CA 90036 USA | |
| **Stoller, Mike** | Composer |
| PO Box 11267, Marina del Rey CA 90295, USA | |
| **Stolley, Paul D** | Epidemiologist, Pharmacologist |
| 10205 Wincopin Circle, #312, Columbia MD 21044, USA | |
| **Stolper, Pinchas** | Religious Leader |
| Orthodox Jewish Congregations Union, 11 Broadway, New York NY 10004, USA | |
| **Stoltenberg, Jens** | Prime Minister, Norway |
| N A T O, Secretary General's Office, Blvd Leopold III, 1110 Brussels, Belgium | |
| **Stoltz, Eric** | Actor, Director, Producer |
| United Talent Agency, U T A Plaza, 9336 Civic Center Dr, Beverly Hills CA 90210 USA | |
| **Stoltz, Kelley** | Singer, Songwriter |
| Goldstar Public Relations, PO Box 130, Ross on Wye HR9 6WY, England | |
| **Stoltz, Roland** | Ice Hockey Player |
| Lilgatan 16, Skelleftea 93 154, Sweden | |
| **Stoltzman, Richard L** | Concert Clarinetist |
| Frank Salomon, 121 W 27th St, #703, New York NY 10001 USA | |
| **Stolze, Lena** | Actress |
| Agentur Carola Studlar, Neuroeder Str 1C, 82152 Planegg, Germany | |
| **Stone, Angie** | Singer, Songwriter |
| J Erving Group, 154 Krog St, #130, Atlanta GA 30307, USA | |
| **Stone, Charles, III** | Director, Actor |
| United Talent Agency, U T A Plaza, 9336 Civic Center Dr, Beverly Hills CA 90210 USA | |
| **Stone, Curtis** | Chef |
| Creative Artists Agency, 2000 Ave of Stars, #100, Los Angeles CA 90067 USA | |
| **Stone, D Dean** | Baseball Player |
| 1451 20th Ave, #204, East Moline IL 61244, USA | |
| **Stone, Doug** | Singer, Songwriter |
| PO Box 943, Springfield TN 37172, USA | |
| **Stone, Dwight** | Football Player |
| 1128 Deep Hollow Court, Waxhaw NC 28173, USA | |
| **Stone, E Donald (Donnie)** | Football Player |
| 101 W H St, Jenks OK 74037, USA | |
| **Stone, Edward C, Jr** | Space Scientist, Physicist |
| PO Box 40747, Pasadena CA 91114, USA | |
| **Stone, Emma** | Actress |
| Anonymous Content, 3532 Hayden Ave, Culver City CA 90232 USA | |
| **Stone, Eugene D (Gene)** | Baseball Player |
| 6897 Highway 262 SE, Othello WA 99344, USA | |
| **Stone, Fred** | Artist |
| Equinart Inc, 5911 Colodny Dr, Agoura Hills CA 91301, USA | |
| **Stone, George H** | Baseball Player |
| 1206 Eastland Ave, Ruston LA 71270, USA | |
| **Stone, H Ronald (Ron)** | Baseball Player |
| 11720 NW Lovejoy St, Portland OR 97229, USA | |
| **Stone, Isaac (Biz)** | Businessman |
| Twitter Inc, 795 Folsom St, #600, San Francisco CA 94107, USA | |
| **Stone, Jeffrey G (Jeff)** | Baseball Player |
| RR 1 Box 392, Portageville MO 63873, USA | |
| **Stone, Jennifer** | Actress |
| United Talent Agency, U T A Plaza, 9336 Civic Center Dr, Beverly Hills CA 90210 USA | |
| **Stone, Jessica** | Actress |
| Paradigm Agency, 360 N Crescent Dr, North Building, Beverly Hills CA 90210 USA | |
| **Stone, Joss** | Singer, Songwriter, Actress |
| Mavrick Artists Agency, 6100 Wilshire Blvd, #550, Los Angeles CA 90048, USA | |
| **Stone, Kenneth B (Ken), Jr** | Football Player |
| 16 W Riverside Dr, Jupiter FL 33469, USA | |
| **Stone, Lara C** | Model |
| I M G Models, 304 Park Ave S, #PH N, New York NY 10010 USA | |
| **Stone, Matt** | Animator, Writer |
| Morris Yorn Barnes, 2000 Ave of Stars, #300N, Los Angeles CA 90067 USA | |
| **Stone, Michael A** | Football Player |
| 23162 Coventry Woods Lane, Southfield MI 48034, USA | |
| **Stone, Nicole L (Nikki)** | Freestyle Aerials Skier |
| 5272 Heather Lane, Park City UT 84098, USA | |
| **Stone, Oliver W** | Director, Writer |
| Ixtlan Corp, 12233 W Olympic Blvd, #322, Los Angeles CA 90064, USA | |
| **Stone, Ricky** | Baseball Player |
| 6494 Lakeview Court, Hamilton OH 45011, USA | |
| **Stone, Robert A** | Writer |
| PO Box 967, Block Island RI 02807, USA | |
| **Stone, Sharon** | Actress, Model |
| Binder & Assoc, 1465 Lindacrest Dr, Beverly Hills CA 90210 USA | |
| **Stone, Skyler** | Actor, Comedian |
| Don Buchwald Talent Agency, 10 E 44th St, New York NY 10017 USA | |
| **Stone, Sly** | Singer, Keyboardist, Songwriter |
| Richard Walters, PO Box 2789, Toluca Lake CA 91610 USA | |
| **Stone, Steven M (Steve)** | Baseball Player, Sportscaster |
| 9261 N 128th Way, Scottsdale AZ 85259, USA | |
| **Stonebarger Barnes, Suzanne** | Volleyball Player, Model |
| Association of Volleyball Professionals, 2183 Fairview Road, #222, Costa Mesa CA 92627 USA | |
| **Stoneman, William H (Bill)** | Baseball Player, Executive |
| 2519 N San Miguel Dr, Orange CA 92867, USA | |
| **Stoner, Alyson R** | Actress, Dancer |
| Paradigm Agency, 360 N Crescent Dr, North Building, Beverly Hills CA 90210 USA | |
| **Stoner, Casey** | Motorcycle Racing Rider |
| Ducati Moto G P, Via C Ducati 3, 40132 Bologna, Italy | |
| **Stones, Dwight E** | Track Athlete |
| 4790 Irvine Blvd, #105, Irvine CA 92620, USA | |

**Stonesipher, Donald H (Don)** — Football Player
1502 Canberry Court, Wheeling IL 60090, USA

**Stonestreet, Eric** — Actor
I C M Partners, 10250 Constellation Blvd, #900, Los Angeles CA 90067 USA

**Stookey, Paul** — Singer (Peter Paul & Mary), Songwriter
Fritz/Byers Mgmt, 1455 N Doheny Dr, Los Angeles CA 90069, USA

**Stoops, Mark** — Football Coach
University of Kentucky, Athletic Dept, Lexington KY 40506, USA

**Stoops, Robert A (Bob)** — Football Coach
University of Oklahoma, Athletic Dept, 108 E Brooks St, Norman OK 73069, USA

**Stoppard, Tom S** — Writer
United Agents, 12-26 Lexington St, London W1F 0LE, England

**Storaro, Vittorio** — Cinematographer
Via Divino Amore 2, 00040 Frattocchie Merino, Italy

**Storch, Larry** — Actor, Comedian
330 W End Ave, #17F, New York NY 10023, USA

**Storey, Awvee** — Basketball Player
Edge Sports Int'l, 3649 W Chase St, #100, Skokie IL 60076, USA

**Storey, David M** — Writer
2 Lyndhurst Gardens, London NW3, England

**Stork, Jeffrey (Jeff)** — Volleyball Player
Pepperdine University, Athletic Dept, 24255 Pacific Coast Highway, Malibu CA 90263, USA

**Storke, Adam** — Actor
Don Buchwald Talent Agency, 6500 Wilshire Blvd, #2200, Los Angeles CA 90048 USA

**Storl, David** — Track Athlete
L C Erdgas Chemnitz, Reichenhainer Str 154, 09125 Chemnitz, Germany

**Storm, Gregory** — Actor
Paradigm Agency, 360 N Crescent Dr, North Building, Beverly Hills CA 90210 USA

**Storm, Hannah** — Commentator, Sportscaster
ESPN-TV, Sports Dept, ESPN Plaza, 935 Middle St, Bristol CT 06010 USA

**Storm, Jim** — Ice Hockey Player
2609 Harvest Hills Dr, Brighton MI 48114, USA

**Storm, Tempest** — Exotic Dancer
3905 Cambridge St, #3, Las Vegas NV 89119, USA

**Stormare, Peter** — Actor
Silver Lining Entertainment, 421 S Beverly Drive, #700, Beverly Hills CA 90212 USA

**Stormer, Horst L** — Nobel Physics Laureate
20 E 9th St, #14P, New York NY 10003, USA

**Storms, Kirsten** — Actress
Paradigm Agency, 360 N Crescent Dr, North Building, Beverly Hills CA 90210 USA

**Storr, Jamie** — Ice Hockey Player
Jamie Storr Goalie School, 650 N Sepulveda Blvd, Los Angeles CA 90049, USA

**Story, Karl** — Illustrator (Nightwing)
D C Comics, 1700 Broadway, #400, New York NY 10019 USA

**Story, Liz** — Pianist, Songwriter
S R O Artists, PO Box 9532, Madison WI 53715, USA

**Story, Tim** — Director, Producer
United Talent Agency, U T A Plaza, 9336 Civic Center Dr, Beverly Hills CA 90210 USA

**Stosberg, Axel** — Singer, Harmonica Player (Santiano)
AirForce1.TV Music, Alte Schonhauser Str 44, 10119 Berlin, Germany

**Stossel, John** — Commentator
Beresford Apartments, 211 Central Park West, #15K, New York NY 10024, USA

**Stosur, Samatha J (Sam)** — Tennis Player
Tennis Australia, Melbourne Park, Batman Avenue, Melbourne VIC 3121, Australia

**Stothers, Mike** — Ice Hockey Player
Grand Rapids Griffins, 130 Fulton St W, #111, Grand Rapids MI 49503, USA

**Stott, Kathryn L** — Concert Pianist
Jane Ward, 38 Townfield, Rickmansworth, Hertfordshire WD3 2DD, England

**Stott, Ken** — Actor
Rights House, Drury House, 34-43 Russell St, London WC2B 5HA, England

**Stott, Nicole M P** — Astronaut
N A S A, Johnson Space Center, 2101 NASA Road, Houston TX 77058 USA

**Stottlemyre, Melvin L (Mel)** — Baseball Player
26004 SE 27th St, Sammamish WA 98075, USA

**Stottlemyre, Todd V** — Baseball Player
10839 E Gold Dust Ave, Scottsdale AZ 85259, USA

**Stotts, Terry** — Basketball Coach
Portland Trail Blazers, Rose Garden, 1 N Center Court St, Portland OR 97227 USA

**Stoudamire, Damon L** — Basketball Player
8325 Broadway St, #202, Pearland TX 77581, USA

**Stoudemire, Amar'e** — Basketball Player
346 E Tuckey Lane, Phoenix AZ 85012, USA

**Stouder, Sharon M** — Swimmer
144 Loucks Ave, Los Altos CA 94022, USA

**Stoudt, Bud** — Bowler
431 Lehman St, Lebanon PA 17046, USA

**Stoudt, Clifford L (Cliff)** — Football Player
5348 Drumcally Lane, Dublin OH 43017, USA

**Stouffer, Kelly W** — Football Player
7430 370th Trail, Rushville NE 69360, USA

**Stoughton, Blaine** — Ice Hockey Player
267th Ave SW, Dauphin MB R7N 1W5, Canada

**Stoutmire, Omar A** — Football Player
PO Box 85, Prosper TX 75078, USA

**Stovall, Dale E** — Vietnam War Air Force Hero
7440 Arroyo Lane, Missoula MT 59808, USA

**Stovall, DaRond** — Baseball Player
1107 Goelz Dr, East Saint Louis IL 62203, USA

**Stovall, Jerry L** — Football Player
7948 Wrenwood Blvd, #C, Baton Rouge LA 70809, USA

**Stovall, Maurice A, Jr** — Football Player
4406 Kendal Court, Valrico FL 33596, USA

**Stover Irwin Russ, Juno** — Diver
512 Lanai Circle, Union City CA 94587, USA

**Stover, George** — Actor
PO Box 10005, Baltimore MD 21285, USA

**Stover, J Matthew (Matt)** — Football Player
15 Ivy Reach Court, Cockeysville MD 21030, USA

**Stover, Jeffrey O (Jeff)** — Football Player
260 Cohasset Road, #190, Chico CA 95926, USA

**Stover, Stewart L (Smokey)** — Football Player
140 Ridgela Circle, Duson LA 70529, USA

**Stowe, David H, Jr** — Businessman
435 L'Ambiance Dr, #308 Longboat Key FL 34228, USA

**Stowe, Harold R (Hal)** — Baseball Player
1361 Union New Hope Road, Gastonia NC 28056, USA

**Stowe, Madeleine** — Actress
Brillstein Entertainment Partners, 9150 Wilshire Blvd, #350, Beverly Hills CA 90212 USA

**Stowe, Tyronne K** — Football Player
PO Box 164, Chandler AZ 85244, USA

**Stowell, Austin** — Actor
Creative Artists Agency, 2000 Ave of Stars, #100, Los Angeles CA 90067 USA

**Stowers, Christopher J (Chris)** — Baseball Player
3773 Wakefield Hall Square SE, Smyrna GA 30080, USA

**Stowers, Saleisha** — Model
Elite Model Mgmt, 404 Park Ave S, #900, New York NY 10016 USA

**Stoya** — Actress
Media Artists Group, 333 E 43rd St, #115, New York NY 10017, USA

**Stoyanov, Krasimir M** — Cosmonaut, Bulgaria
Cosmonaut Training Center, Star City, 141160 Zvezdny Gorodok, Moscow Oblast, Russia

**Stoyanovich, Peter (Pete)** — Football Player
18185 Parkshore Dr, Northville MI 48168, USA

**St-Pierre, Kim** — Ice Hockey Player
Team Canada, 2424 University Dr NW, Calgary AB T2N 3Y9, Canada

**Stracey, John H** — Boxer
8 Serpentine Road, Wallasey CH44 0AX, England

**Strachan, Michael D (Mike)** — Football Player
105 Yellowstone St, Kenner LA 70065, USA

**Strachan, Rodney (Rod)** — Swimmer
3250 Cabrillo Highway, Harmony CA 93435, USA

**Strachan, Stephen M (Steve)** — Football Player
161 Old Post Road, Mooresville NC 28117, USA

**Strader, Cam** — Auto Racing Driver
J R Motorsports, 349 Cayuga Dr, Mooresville NC 28117, USA

**Stradford, Troy E** — Football Player
James Crystal Radio Group, 6600 N Andrews Ave, #160, Fort Lauderdale FL 33309, USA

**Stradlin, Izzy** — Guitarist (Guns N' Roses)
Front Line Mgmt, 1100 Glendon Ave, #2000, Los Angeles CA 90024 USA

**Stradling, Harry A, Jr** — Cinematographer
3664 Avenida Callada, Calabasas CA 91302, USA

**Strahan, Michael A** — Football Player, Actor, Sportscaster
23679 Calabasas Road, Calabasas CA 91302, USA

**Strahler, Michael W (Mike)** — Baseball Player
8 Canyon Draw, Alamogordo NM 88310, USA

**Strahovski, Yvonne** — Actress
McKeon-Myrones Mgmt, 3500 Olive Ave, #770, Burbank CA 91505 USA

**Straight, Susan** — Writer
Hyperion Books, 114 5th Ave, New York NY 10011 USA

**Strain, Joseph A (Joe)** — Baseball Player
8668 E Otero Circle, Centennial CO 80112, USA

**Strain, Julie** — Actress, Model
J S Inc, 8491 Sunset Blvd, #1850, West Hollywood CA 90069, USA

**Strain, Sammy** — Singer (O'Jays)
Associated Booking Corp, 501 Madison Ave, #501, New York NY 10022 USA

**Strait, Donald** — WW II Army Air Corps Hero
6 Burning Tree Place, Jackson Springs NC 27281, USA

**Strait, George** — Singer, Guitarist
Erv Woolsey Co, 1000 18th Ave S, Nashville TN 37212, USA

**Strait, Steven** — Actor, Singer
R G M Artists, 8-12 Ann Street, Surry Hills NSW 2010, Australia

**Straka, Martin** — Ice Hockey Player
HC Pizen Stefanikovo, Namesti 1, 30133 Pizen, Czech Republic

**Strampe, Bob** — Bowler
31029 Louise Court, Warren MI 48088, USA

**Strampe, Robert E (Bob)** — Baseball Player
19210 W Lance Hill Road, Cheney WA 99004, USA

**Strand, Mark** — Writer
5825 S Dorchester Ave, #9W, Chicago IL 60637, USA

**Strand, Robin** — Actor
4083 Camellia Ave, Studio City CA 91604, USA

**Strane, John** — WW II Navy Air Force Hero
18230 Mirasol Dr, San Diego CA 92128, USA

**Strang, Deborah** — Actress
McCabe Group, 3211 Cahuenga Blvd W, #104, Los Angeles CA 90068, USA

**Strang, William G** — Mathematician
7 Southgate Road, Wellesley MA 02482, USA

**Strange, Curtis N** — Golfer, Sportscaster
147 S Spooners St, Morehead City NC 28557, USA

**Strange, J Douglas (Doug)** — Baseball Player
435 Heights Dr, Gibsonia PA 15044, USA

**Strange, Pat** — Baseball Player
156 Mill St, Springfield MA 01108, USA

**Strange, Sarah** — Actress
Elizabeth Hodgson Mgmt. 1536 W 12th Ave, #5, Vancouver BC V6J 2E1, Canada

**Strassen, Volker** — Mathematician
Oskar-Pletsch-Str 12, 01324 Dresden, Germany

**Strasser, Robin** — Actress
Innovative Artists, 235 Park Ave S, #1000, New York NY 10003 USA

**Strasser, Todd** — Writer
PO Box 859, Larchmont NY 10538, USA

**Stratas, Teresa** — Opera Singer
Vincent Farrell Assoc, 481 8th Ave, #340, New York NY 10001, USA

**Strathairn, David** — Actor
I C M Partners, 10250 Constellation Blvd, #900, Los Angeles CA 90067 USA

**Stratham, Jason** — Actor
Creative Artists Agency, 2000 Ave of Stars, #100, Los Angeles CA 90067 USA

**Stratton, Arthur (Art)** — Ice Hockey Player
General Delivery, Succ Main, Saint Adolphie MB R5A 1A3, Canada

**Stratton, Charlie** — Actor
Judi Farkas Mgmt, 116 N Mansfield Ave, Los Angeles CA 90036, USA

**Stratton, D Michael (Mike)** — Football Player
2611 Shore Lane Dr, Knoxville TN 37932, USA

**Stratton, Dennis** — Guitarist (Iron Maiden)
Sanctuary Music Mgmt, 82 Bishop's Bridge Road, London W2 6BB, England

**Straub, Chester J** — Judge
US Court of Appeals, Moynihan Courthouse, 500 Pearl St, New York NY 10007, USA

**Straub, Peter F** — Writer
53 W 85th St, New York NY 10024, USA

**Straughan, Peter** — Writer
Casorotto Ramsay, Waverley House, 7-12 Noel St, London W1F 8GQ, England

**Straus, Robert** — Behavioral Scientist
690 Mason Headley Road, #312, Lexington KY 40504, USA

**Strause, Colin** — Visual Effects Producer, Director
Hydraulx, 12901 W Jefferson Blvd, Los Angeles CA 90066, USA

**Strause, Greg** — Visual Effects Producer, Director
Hydraulx, 12901 W Jefferson Blvd, Los Angeles CA 90066, USA

**Strauss, Neil** — Writer
Anderson Group Public Relations, 8060 Melrose Ave, #400, Los Angeles CA 90046, USA

**Strauss, Peter** — Actor
Stone Manners Salners, 6100 Wilshire Blvd, #1500, Los Angeles CA 90035 USA

**Straw, John W (Jack)** — Government Official, England
House of Commons, Westminster, London SW1A 0AA, England

**Strawberry, Darryl E** — Baseball Player
1802 Sterling Oaks Dr, Saint Peters MO 63376, USA

**Strawbridge, George W, Jr** — Throughbred, Steeplechase Racing Owner
Augustin Stables, Greenlawn Road, Cochranville PA 19330, USA

**Strawder, Joe** — Basketball Player
3037 SW Taylors Ferry Road, Portland OR 97219, USA

**Streck, Ron** — Golfer
7527 S 84th East Ave, Tulsa OK 74133, USA

**Streck, Ronald J** — Association Executive
Healthcare Distribution Mgmt Assn, 1821 Michael Faraday Dr, Reston VA 20190, USA

**Streep, Meryl** — Actress
Creative Artists Agency, 2000 Ave of Stars, #100, Los Angeles CA 90067 USA

**Street, Elliott** — Actor
Atlanta Models & Talent, 309 Maple Dr, #201, Atlanta GA 30354, USA

**Street, Huston L** — Baseball Player
8300 Big View Dr, Austin TX 78730, USA

**Street, Picabo** — Alpine Skier
Park City Ski Resort, Director of Skiing, 1345 Lowell Ave, Park City UT 84060, USA

**Street, Rebecca** — Actress
255 Cabrini Blvd, #7G, New York NY 10040, USA

**Streets, Tai** — Football Player
16134 Hillcrest Circle, Orland Park IL 60467, USA

**Streets, The** — Rap Artist
Coalition Mgmt, 12 Barley Mow Passage, London W4 4PH, England

**Streisand, Barbra** — Singer, Actress, Director
160 W 96th St, New York NY 10025, USA

**Streit, Kurt** — Opera Singer
I M G Artists, Hogarth Business Park, Chiswick, London W4 2TH, England

**Streitenfeld, Marc** — Composer
First Artists, 4764 Park Granada, #210, Calabasas CA 91302 USA

**Strekalov, Gennady M** — Cosmonaut
Federation Peace Committee, 36 Mira Prospekt, 129090 Moscow, Russia

**Strel, Martin** — Swimmer
Marathon Swim Mgmt Group, 227 H St, #207, Salt Lake City UT 84103, USA

**Strenga, Janis** — Bobsled Athlete
Bobsled Federation, Roberta Feldmana 11, 1014 Riga, Latvia

**Strenger, Richard G (Rich)** — Football Player
1064 Arborak Way, Lake Orion MI 48362, USA

**Stresi, Alexia** — Actress
Artmedia, 20 Ave Rapp, 75007 Paris, France

**Streuli, Walter H (Walt)** — Baseball Player
1107 Westminster Dr, Greensboro NC 27410, USA

**Strianese, Michael** — Businessman
L-3 Communications, 600 3rd Ave, New York NY 10016, USA

**Stricker, Steven C (Steve)** — Golfer
5804 N Sherman Ave, Madison WI 53704, USA

**Stricker, Williams L (Bill)** — Basketball Player
2930 Driftwood Place, #70, Stockton CA 95219, USA

**Strickland, Donald D** — Football Player
1110 Gilman Ave, San Francisco CA 94124, USA

**Strickland, Gail** — Actress
14732 Oracle Place, Pacific Palisades CA 90272, USA

**Strickland, James M (Jim)** — Baseball Player
2139 Equestrian Road, Paso Robles CA 93446, USA

**Strickland, KaDee** — Actress
Anonymous Content, 3532 Hayden Ave, Culver City CA 90232 USA

**Strickland, Keith** — Drummer (B-52's)
Direct Management Group, 947 N La Cienega Blvd, #G, West Hollywood CA 90069, USA

**Strickland, Rodney (Rod)** — Basketball Player
226 Wind Haven Dr, Nicholasville KY 40356, USA

**Strickland, Scott M** — Baseball Player
415 Enchanted River Dr, Spring TX 77388, USA

**Strickland, Ted, III** — Governor, Representative, OH
Midwest Gateway Partners, 35 N 4th St, #340, Columbus OH 43215, USA

**Strickson, Mark** — Actor
Evans & Reiss, 100 Fawe Park Road, London SW15 2EA, England

**Strieber, Whitney** — Writer, Producer, Actor
Gersh Agency, 9465 Wilshire Blvd, #600, Beverly Hills CA 90212 USA

**Strief, Zachary D (Zach)** — Football Player
5480 Carterway Dr, Milford OH 45150, USA

**Strigl, Dennis F (Denny)** — Businessman
Verizon Communications, 140 West St, New York NY 10007, USA

**Strik, Reshad** — Actor
Baker Winokur Ryder Public Relations, 9100 Wilshire Blvd, #500W, Beverly Hills CA 90212 USA

**Striker, Gisela** — Philosopher
Harvard University, Philosophy Dept, Cambridge MA 02138, USA

**Stringer, Arthur (Art)** — Football Player
12680 Royal Shores Dr, Conroe TX 77303, USA

**Stringer, C Vivian** — Basketball Coach
Rutgers University, Athletic Dept, New Brunswick NJ 08903, USA

**Stringer, Howard** — Businessman
186 Riverside Dr, New York NY 10024, USA

**Stringert, Harold L (Hal)** — Football Player
1711 Dole St, #603, Honolulu HI 96822, USA

**Stringfellow, Ken** — Musician (Posies), Songwriter
Entourage Talent Assoc, 236 W 27th St, #800, New York NY 10001, USA

**Stringfield, Sherry** — Actress
Imperium 7 Artists, 5455 Wilshire Blvd, #1706, Los Angeles CA 90036 USA

**Strobel, Eric M** — Ice Hockey Player
6617 129th St W, Saint Paul MN 55124, USA

**Strobel, Heidi** — Illusionist, Model
RR 1 Box 274A, Long Lane MO 65590, USA

**Stroble, Bobby** — Golfer
526 W 2nd Ave, Albany GA 31701, USA

**Strock, Donald J (Don)** — Football Player, Coach
1512 Passion Vine Circle, Weston FL 33326, USA

**Strode, Haley** — Actress
Paradigm Agency, 360 N Crescent Dr, North Building, Beverly Hills CA 90210 USA

**Strohmayer, John E** — Baseball Player
1825 Crosby Lane, Redding CA 96003, USA

**Strohmayer, Tod** — Astronomer
Goddard Space Flight Center, NASA/GSFC, Greenbelt MD 20771, USA

**Strollsteimer, Jason E** — Singer, Guitarist (VonBondies)
Tsunami Entertainment, 2525 Hyperion Ave, Los Angeles CA 90027, USA

**Strolz, Hubert** — Alpine Skier
6767 Warth 19, Austria

**Strom, Brent T** — Baseball Player
2202 N Catalina Vista Loop, Tucson AZ 85749, USA

**Strom, Brock T** — Football Player
4301 W 110th St, Leawood KS 66211, USA

**Strom, Richard J (Rick)** — Football Player
8905 Moor Park Run, Duluth GA 30097, USA

**Strom, Sally** — Artist
2388 SW Vermont St, #36, Portland OR 97219, USA

**Stroman, Susan** — Choreographer, Director
42 West, 220 W 42nd St, #1200, New York NY 10036 USA

**Stromberg, Robert** — Art Director, Production Designer
United Talent Agency, U T A Plaza, 9336 Civic Center Dr, Beverly Hills CA 90210 USA

**Strominger, Jack L** — Biochemist
Dana Faber Cancer Institute, Biochemistry Dept, 44 Binney St, Boston MA 02115, USA

**Strong, Barrett** — Singer, Songwriter
Motown Records, 6255 W Sunset Blvd, Los Angeles CA 90028 USA

**Strong, Brenda** — Actress
Liberman-Zerman Mgmt, 252 N Larchmont Blvd, #200, Los Angeles CA 90004 USA

**Strong, Charles R (Charlie)** — Football Coach
University of Texas, Athletic Dept, Austin TX 78712, USA

**Strong, Daniel W (Danny)** — Actor, Writer
Sweeney Entertainment, 6253 Hollywood Blvd, #201, Los Angeles CA 90028, USA

**Strong, Joe** — Baseball Player
1340 Corcoran St, Vallejo CA 94589, USA

**Strong, Ken** — Ice Hockey Player
1773 Grosvenor Place, Mississauga ON L5L 3V8, Canada

**Strong, Mack C** — Football Player
14343 SE 92nd St, Newcastle WA 98059, USA

**Strong, Mark** — Actor
Markham Froggatt Irwin, Julian House, 4 Windmill St, London W1P 1HF, England

**Strong, Mary** — Sportscaster
N F L Network, 10950 Washington Blvd, #100, Culver City CA 90232 USA

**Strong, Maurice F** — Government Official, Canada
S3 Holdings, 150 Isabella St, #100, Ottawa ON K15 1V7, Canada

**Strong, Rider** — Actor
United Talent Agency, U T A Plaza, 9336 Civic Center Dr, Beverly Hills CA 90210 USA

**Stroock, Daniel W** — Mathematician
55 Frost St, Cambridge MA 02140, USA

**Strossen, Nadine** — Attorney, Association Executive
450 Riverside Dr, #51, New York NY 10027, USA

**Stroucken, Albert** — Businessman
Owens-Illinois Inc, 1 Michael Owens Way, Perrysburg OH 43551, USA

**Stroud, Don** — Actor
500 Lunalilo Home Road, #16A, Honolulu HI 96825, USA

**Stroud, Edwin M (Ed)** — Baseball Player
1696 Oak St SW, Warren OH 44485, USA

**Stroud, Marcus L** — Football Player
964 Detroit St, Jacksonville FL 32254, USA

**Stroughter, Stephen L (Steve)** — Baseball Player
323 NE 2nd Ave, Visalia CA 93291, USA

**Stroup, Jessica** — Actress
I C M Partners, 10250 Constellation Blvd, #900, Los Angeles CA 90067 USA

**Stroup, Theodore G (Ted), Jr** — Army General
2085 Hopewood Dr, Falls Church VA 22043, USA

**Strouse, Charles** — Composer
171 W 57th St, New York NY 10019, USA

**Strout, Elizabeth** — Writer
Random House, 1745 Broadway, #1800, New York NY 10019 USA
**Strube, Juergen F** — Businessman
B A S F Corp, Aktiengesellschaft, 67056 Ludwigshafen, Germany
**Strudwick, Suzanne** — Golfer
5525 Crestwood Dr, Knoxville TN 37914, USA
**Struever, Stuart M** — Anthropologist
2000 Sheridan Road, Evanston IL 60208, USA
**Strug, Kerri** — Gymnast
2611 N Santa Lucia Dr, Tucson AZ 85715, USA
**Struth, Thomas** — Photographer
Achenbachstr 74, 40237 Dusseldorf, Germany
**Struthers, Sally** — Actress
Vincent Cirrincione Assoc, 1516 N Fairfax Ave, Los Angeles CA 90046 USA
**Struycken, Carel** — Actor
PO Box 1365, Avalon CA 90704, USA
**Stuart, Bradley (Brad)** — Ice Hockey Player
131 Pinta Court, Los Gatos CA 95030, USA
**Stuart, Freundel J** — Prime Minister, Barbados
Prime Minister's Office, Bay St, Saint Michael, Bridgetown, Barbados
**Stuart, James Patrick** — Actor
Stone Manners Salners, 6100 Wilshire Blvd, #1500, Los Angeles CA 90035 USA
**Stuart, Jason** — Actor, Comedian
Ideal Talent Agency, 10806 Ventura Blvd, #2, Studio City CA 91604, USA
**Stuart, Jill** — Fashion Designer
550 Fashion Ave, #2400, New York NY 10018, USA
**Stuart, Katie** — Actress
Pacific Artists Mgmt, 1285 W Broadway, #685, Vancouver BC V6H 3X8, Canada
**Stuart, Marty** — Singer, Mandolin Player, Songwriter
Green Room, 1100 16th Ave S, Nashville TN 37212, USA
**Stubblefield, Dana W** — Football Player
2464 Cottle Ave, San Jose CA 95125, USA
**Stubblefield, Mickey** — Baseball Player
4870 Seldon Way SE, Smyrna GA 30080, USA
**Stubbs, Franklin L** — Baseball Player
PO Box 325, Goshen KY 40026, USA
**Stubbs, Imogen M** — Actress
Nick Hern Books, Glasshouse, 49A Goldhawk Road, London W12 8QP, England
**Stubing, Lawrence G (Moose)** — Baseball Player, Manager
10821 Laconia Dr, Villa Park CA 92861, USA
**Stucchio, Emil** — Singer
LaGuardia Associates Entertainment, 271 Grove Ave, #E, Verona NJ 07044, USA
**Stuck, Hans-Joachim** — Auto Racing Driver
Harmstatt 3, 6352 Ellmau/Tirol, Austria
**Stuckey, Henry L** — Football Player
3615 Winchester Ave, Atlantic City NJ 08401, USA
**Stuckey, James D (Jim)** — Football Player
1314 Headquarters Plantation Dr, Johns Island SC 29455, USA
**Stuckey, Rodney N** — Basketball Player
2740 Castlemartin Court, Oakland Township MI 48306, USA
**Stuckey, Sophie L** — Actress
United Agents, 12-26 Lexington St, London W1F 0LE, England
**Studdard, David D (Dave)** — Football Player
4490 S Clarkson St, Englewood CO 80113, USA
**Studdard, Ruben** — Singer
19 Music & Mgmt, 35-37 Parkgate Road, London SW11 4NP, England
**Studer, Cheryl** — Opera Singer
International Performing Artists, 125 Crowfield Dr, Knoxville TN 37922, USA
**Studin, Jan** — Publisher
Better Homes & Gardens, Publisher's Office, 1716 Locust, Des Moines IA 50309, USA
**Studney, Dan** — Actor
Paradigm Agency, 360 N Crescent Dr, North Building, Beverly Hills CA 90210 USA
**Studstill, Patrick L (Pat)** — Football Player
2235 Linda Flora Dr, Los Angeles CA 90077, USA
**Studt, Amy** — Singer, Pianist
19 Music & Mgmt, 35-37 Parkgate Road, London SW11 4NP, England
**Studwell, J Scott** — Football Player
10415 Brown Farm Circle, Eden Prairie MN 55347, USA
**Stufflebeem, John** — Navy Admiral
Director, Navy Staff, HqUSN, Pentagon, Washington DC 20350 USA
**Stuhlbarg, Michael** — Actor
Viking Entertainment, 445 W 23rd St, #1A, New York NY 10011, USA
**Stuhr, Jerzy** — Actor, Director
Graffiti Ltd, Ul SW Gertrudy 5, 31107 Cracow, Poland
**Stukes, Charles (Charlie)** — Football Player
4020 Cedar Grove Crest, Chesapeake VA 23321, USA
**Stulce, Michael D (Mike)** — Track Athlete
5711 Hunters Chase Court, Lithonia GA 30038, USA
**Stults, Eric W** — Baseball Player
13810 Ranier Dr, Middlebury, IN 46540, USA
**Stults, George S** — Actor, Model
Bleu Entertainment, 5225 Wilshire Blvd, #401, Los Angeles CA 90036, USA
**Stultz, Geoffrey S (Geoff)** — Actor
United Talent Agency, U T A Plaza, 9336 Civic Center Dr, Beverly Hills CA 90210 USA
**Stultz, Jack C** — Army General
Chief, Army Reserve, HqUSA, Pentagon, Washington DC 20310, USA
**Stump, David** — Cinematographer
H F W D Creative Representation, 394 E Glaucus St, Encinitas CA 92024, USA
**Stump, James G (Jim)** — Baseball Player
7432 Creekside Dr, Lansing MI 48917, USA
**Stump, Patrick** — Singer, Guitarist (Fall Out Boy)
PO Box 219, 1187 Wilmette Ave, Wilmette IL 60091, USA
**Stumpel, Jozef** — Ice Hockey Player
6301 Osprey Terrace, Coconut Creek FL 33073, USA
**Stumpf, John** — Financier
Wells Fargo, 420 Montgomery St, San Francisco CA 94104, USA

**Stumpf, Kenneth E**
16528 State Highway 131, Tomah WI 54660, USA
Vietnam War Army Hero (CMH)

**Stumpf, Paul K**
1515 Shasta Dr, #2219, Davis CA 95616, USA
Biochemist

**Stunyo-Korpak, Jeanne G**
1435 Almagre Peak Dr, Colorado Springs CO 80921, USA
Diver

**Stuper, John A**
38 Lake St, Hamden CT 06517, USA
Baseball Player

**Stupnitsky, Gene**
W M E Entertainment, 9601 Wilshire Blvd, #300, Beverly Hills CA 90210 USA
Actor, Comedian, Writer

**Stupp, Samuel I**
Northwestern University, Engineering Dept, Evanston IL 60208, USA
Engineer

**Stupples, Karen L**
9409 Silver Buttonwood St, Orlando FL 32832, USA
Golfer

**Sturckow, Frederick W (Rick)**
RR 2 Box 14, Dickinson TX 77539, USA
Astronaut

**Sturgeon, Peter**
23 Millwood Road, Erin ON N0B 1T0, Canada
Ice Hockey Player

**Sturges, Shannon**
Precision Entertainment, 6338 Wilshire Blvd, Los Angeles CA 90048, USA
Actress

**Sturgess, Jim**
Garricks, Angel House, 76 Mallinson Road, London SW11 1BN, England
Actor

**Sturm, Felix**
Sturm Box-Promotion, Bonner Wall 122, 50677 Cologne, Germany
Boxer

**Sturm, Jerry G**
1900 E Girard Place, #1503, Englewood CO 80113, USA
Football Player

**Sturm, Marco J**
500 Atlantic Ave, #14P, Boston MA 02210, USA
Ice Hockey Player

**Sturm, Yfke**
I M G Models, 304 Park Ave S, #PH N, New York NY 10010 USA
Model

**Sturman, Eugene**
190 Loma Metisse St, Malibu CA 90265, USA
Sculptor, Artist

**Sturr, James W (Jimmy), Jr**
United Polka Artists, PO Box 1, Florida NY 10921, USA
Orchestra Leader

**Sturridge, Charles**
United Agents, 12-26 Lexington St, London W1F 0LE, England
Director

**Sturt, Frederick N (Fred)**
120 N Berkey Southern Road, Swanton OH 43558, USA
Football Player

**Sturtze, Tanyon J**
501 Knights Run Ave, #2316, Tampa FL 33602, USA
Baseball Player

**Sturzaker, David**
Artists Partnership, 101 Finsbury Pavement, London EC2A 1RS, England
Actor

**Styler, Trudie**
Maven Pictures, 380 Lafayette St, #202, New York NY 10003, USA
Actress, Producer

**Styles P**
J Erving Group, 154 Krog St, #130, Atlanta GA 30307, USA
Rap Artist (Lox)

**Styles, Lorenzo C**
10276 Oxford Dr, Lewiston ID 83501, USA
Football Player

**Stynes, Christopher D (Chris)**
1980 NE 7th St, #106, Deerfield Beach FL 33441, USA
Baseball Player

**Styron, Alexandra**
Little Brown, 3 Center Plaza, #100, Boston MA 02108 USA
Writer

**Suarez Navarro, Carla**
Saragossa 145, 08006 Barcelona, Spain
Tennis Player

**Suarez, Anne**
U B B A, 6 Rue de Braque, 75003 Paris, France
Actress

**Suarez, Daniel**
Joe Gibbs Racing, 13415 Reese Blvd W, Huntersville NC 28078, USA
Auto Racing Driver

**Suarez, Jeremy**
Innovative Artists, 1505 10th St, Santa Monica CA 90401 USA
Actor

**Suarez, Kenneth R (Ken)**
6000 Forest Lane, Fort Worth TX 76112, USA
Baseball Player

**Suau, Anthony**
Denver Post, Editorial Dept, PO Box 1709, Denver CO 80201, USA
Photojournalist

**Subban, Pernell K (P K)**
Montreal Canadiens, 1275 Saint Antoine St W, Montreal QC H3C 5L2, Canada
Ice Hockey Player

**Subkoff, Tara**
I C M Partners, 10250 Constellation Blvd, #900, Los Angeles CA 90067 USA
Actress

**Subotnick, Morton L**
301 E 87th St, #23B, New York NY 10128, USA
Composer

**Substance, Markee**
Moksha Mgmt, PO Box 102, London E15 2HH, England
Keyboardist (Kosheen)

**Such, Richard S (Dick)**
7614 Divot Dr, Sanford NC 27332, USA
Baseball Player

**Sucharetza, Marla**
Abrams Artists, 9200 W Sunset Blvd, #1125, West Hollywood CA 90069 USA
Actress

**Suchecka, Rysia**
N B B J Architecture/Design, 111 S Jackson St, Seattle WA 98104, USA
Interior Designer

**Suchet, David**
Artists Partnership, 101 Finsbury Pavement, London EC2A 1RS, England
Actor

**Suchocka, Hanna**
Urzad Rady Ministrow, Al Ujazdowskie 1/3, 00567 Warsaw, Poland
Prime Minister, Poland

**Suchy, Radoslav**
7801 N 54th St, Paradise Valley AZ 85253, USA
Ice Hockey Player

**Sud, Veena**
Felker Toczak Gellman, 10880 Wilshire Blvd, #2070, Los Angeles CA 90024 USA
Producer

**Sudakis, William P (Bill)**
44054 Elkhorn Trail, Indian Wells CA 92210, USA
Baseball Player

**Sudan, Madhu**
519 Pleasant St, Belmont MA 02478, USA
Computer Scientist

**Sudano, Brooklyn**
A P A Talent & Literary Agency, 405 S Beverly Dr, #300, Beverly Hills CA 90212 USA
Actress, Singer

**Sudduth, Skipp**
One Entertainment, 347 5th Ave, #1404, New York NY 10016 USA
Actor, Director

**Sudduth-Smith, Jill**
9917 Calabasas Ave, Las Vegas NV 89117, USA
Synchronized Swimmer

**Sudeikis, Jason** — Actor, Comedian
Creative Artists Agency, 2000 Ave of Stars, #100, Los Angeles CA 90067 USA
**Suedhof, Thomas C** — Nobel Medicine Laureate
Stanford University Medical School, Molecular Physiology Dept, Stanford CA 94305, USA
**Sugar, Leo T** — Football Player
7161 Golden Eagle Court, #1012, Fort Myers FL 33912, USA
**Sugar, Steve** — DJ Musician (Mike & Sugar)
Future Music, Bayerstr 77A, 80335 Munich, Germany
**Sugarman, Burt** — Producer
9440 Santa Monica Blvd, #407, Beverly Hills CA 90210, USA
**Sugg, B Alan** — Educator
University of Arkansas, President's Office, Fayetteville AR 72701, USA
**Sugg, Diana K** — Journalist
Baltimore Sun, Editorial Dept, 501 N Calvert St, Baltimore MD 21278, USA
**Suggs, M Louise** — Golfer
424 Royal Crescent Court, Saint Augustine FL 32092, USA
**Suggs, Terrell R** — Football Player
281 N Brookside St, Chandler AZ 85225, USA
**Suh, Ndamukong** — Football Player
Detroit Lions, 222 Republic Dr, Allen Park MI 48101 USA
**Suh, Yeree** — Opera Singer
I M G Artists, Hogarth Business Park, Chiswick, London W4 2TH, England
**Suhey, Matthew J (Matt)** — Football Player
550 Carriage Way, Deerfield IL 60015, USA
**Suhl, Harry** — Physicist
University of California, Physics Dept, 9500 Gilman Dr, La Jolla CA 92093, USA
**Suhonen, Alpo** — Ice Hockey Coach
Chicago Blackhawks, United Center, 1901 W Madison St, Chicago IL 60612 USA
**Suhr, Jennifer Stuczynski (Jenn)** — Track Athlete
730 Jenkins Road, Churchville NY 14428, USA
**Suhrheinrich, Richard F** — Judge
US Court of Appeals, 315 W Allegan St, #210, Lansing MI 48933, USA
**Suhrstedt, Timothy (Tim)** — Cinematographer
Innovative Artists, 1505 10th St, Santa Monica CA 90401 USA
**Sui, Anna** — Fashion Designer
113 Greene St, Front A, New York NY 10012, USA
**Suits, Julia** — Editorial Cartoonist
Creators Syndicate, 737 3rd St, Hermosa Beach CA 90254 USA
**Sukarnoputri, D F Megawati** — President, Indonesia
Dewan Perwakilan Rakyat, Jalan Gatot Subroto 16, Jakarta, Indonesia
**Sukla, Edward A (Ed)** — Baseball Player
16 Perch, Irvine CA 92604, USA
**Sukova, Helena** — Tennis Player
1 Ave Grande Bretagne, Monte Carlo, Monaco
**Sukowa, Barbara** — Actress
Artmedia, 20 Ave Rapp, 75007 Paris, France
**Sularz, Guy P** — Baseball Player
10818 N 83rd St, Scottsdale AZ 85260, USA
**Suleiman, Michel** — President, Lebanon; General
President's Office, Palais de Baebda, Beirut, Lebanon
**Sulfsted, Alex F** — Football Player
7300 Sanderson Place, Cincinnati OH 45243, USA
**Suliman, Ali** — Actor
Paradigm Agency, 360 N Crescent Dr, North Building, Beverly Hills CA 90210 USA
**Sulkin, Gregg** — Actor
D2 Mgmt, 9255 Sunset Blvd, #600, West Hollywood CA 90069, USA
**Sullanmaa, Jani** — Curling Athlete
Curling Association, Kalatorppa 2A62, 02230 Espoo, Finland
**Sullenberger, Chesley B (Sully)** — Airline Pilot Hero
General Delivery, Danville CA 94526, USA
**Sulliman, S Douglas (Doug)** — Ice Hockey Player
PO Box 28964, Scottsdale AZ 85255, USA
**Sullinger, Jared** — Basketball Player
Boston Celtics, 226 Causeway St, #4, Boston MA 02114 USA
**Sullivan, Brian** — Ice Hockey Player
392 E Beach Road, Charlestown RI 02813, USA
**Sullivan, Camille** — Actress
Red Mgmt, Box 3, 415 W Esplanade, North Vancouver BC V7M 1A6, Canada
**Sullivan, Chip** — Golfer
49 Homestead Circle, Troutville VA 24175, USA
**Sullivan, Christopher P (Chris)** — Football Player
64 Wagon Wheel Road, North Attleboro MA 02760, USA
**Sullivan, Cory** — Baseball Player
405 Overlook Court, Evanston WY 82930, USA
**Sullivan, Daniel J (Dan)** — Football Player
25 Algonquin Ave, Andover MA 01810, USA
**Sullivan, Danny** — Auto Racing Driver
PO Box 34290, Louisville KY 40232, USA
**Sullivan, David** — Actor
Intellectual Artists Mgmt, 10585 Santa Monica Blvd, #135, Los Angeles CA 90025, USA
**Sullivan, Erik Per** — Actor
Suzanne Smith, 451 Greenwich St, #500, New York NY 10103, USA
**Sullivan, Franklin L (Frank)** — Baseball Player
2715 Apapane St, Lihue HI 96766, USA
**Sullivan, George (Red)** — Ice Hockey Player
RR 2, Indian River ON K0L 2B0, Canada
**Sullivan, Gordon R** — Army General
Strategic Studies Institute, War College, 122 Forbes Ave, Carlisle PA 17013, USA
**Sullivan, Jazmine** — Singer, Songwriter
Creative Artists Agency, 2000 Ave of Stars, #100, Los Angeles CA 90067 USA
**Sullivan, Kathryn D** — Astronaut
795 Old Oak Trace, Columbus OH 43235, USA
**Sullivan, Kevin** — Journalist
Washington Post, Editorial Dept, 1150 15th St NW, Washington DC 20071 USA
**Sullivan, Kyle R** — Actor
Abrams Artists, 9200 W Sunset Blvd, #1125, West Hollywood CA 90069 USA

**Sullivan, Laura** — Pianist, Composer
Robin Samora, PO Box 66, Readville MA 02137, USA

**Sullivan, Liam K** — Actor, Comedian
Kazarian/Measures/Ruskin, 11969 Ventura Blvd, #300, Studio City CA 91604 USA

**Sullivan, Louis W** — Secretary, Health & Human Services
223 Chestnut St, Atlanta GA 30314, USA

**Sullivan, Marc C** — Baseball Player
2038 W 1st S, #100, Fort Myers FL 33901, USA

**Sullivan, Michael J (Mike)** — Governor, WY; Diplomat
1124 S Durbin St, Casper WY 82601, USA

**Sullivan, Michael J (Mike)** — Golfer
Mike Sullivan Golf School, 5715 Fayetteville Road, Raleigh NC 27603, USA

**Sullivan, Mike** — Ice Hockey Player, Coach
275 Elm St, Duxbury MA 02332, USA

**Sullivan, Nicole** — Actress
Innovative Artists, 1505 10th St, Santa Monica CA 90401 USA

**Sullivan, Patrick J (Pat)** — Football Player, Coach
1717 Indian Creek Dr, Birmingham AL 35243, USA

**Sullivan, Paul E** — Navy Admiral
Commander, Naval Sea Systems, 1333 Isaac Hull Ave SE, Washington Navy Yard DC 20376 USA

**Sullivan, Peter** — Ice Hockey Player
316 Fairway Road, Regina SK S4Y 1J5, Canada

**Sullivan, Russell G M (Russ)** — Baseball Player
1701 Hill 'n' Dale St, Fredericksburg VA 22405, USA

**Sullivan, Sean** — Actor
Caldwell Jeffrey, 943 Queen St E, #200, Toronto ON M4M 1J6, Canada

**Sullivan, Stacy** — Actress
Cassell Levy Talent Agency, 843 N Sycamore Ave, Los Angeles CA 90038, USA

**Sullivan, Steve** — Ice Hockey Player
5536 Iron Gate Dr, Franklin TN 37069, USA

**Sullivan, Susan** — Actress
15355 Mulholland Dr, Los Angeles CA 90077, USA

**Sullivan, Tom** — Actor
Paradigm Agency, 360 N Crescent Dr, North Building, Beverly Hills CA 90210 USA

**Sullivan, W Scott** — Baseball Player
1649 Mayfair Court, Auburn AL 36830, USA

**Sullivan, William D** — Navy Admiral
US Representative, NATO Military Committee, PSC 80, Box 300, APO AE 09724 USA

**Sulston, John E** — Nobel Medicine Laureate
39 Mingle Lane, Stapleford, Cambridge CB2 5BG, England

**Sultan Salman Abdulaziz Al-Saud** — Astronaut, Saudi Arabia
Tourism/Antiquities Commission, PO Box 66680, Riyadh 11586, Saudi Arabia

**Sultan, Altoon** — Artist
PO Box 2, Groton VT 05046, USA

**Sultan, Donald K** — Artist
19 E 70th St, New York NY 10021, USA

**Sulzberger, Arthur O, Jr** — Publisher, Businessman
New York Times Co, Publisher's Office, 229 W 43rd St, New York NY 10036, USA

**Sumann, Christoph** — Biathlete
Skiing Skiverband, Olympiastra 10, 6020 Innsbruck, Austria

**Sumika, Aya** — Actress
I C M Partners, 10250 Constellation Blvd, #900, Los Angeles CA 90067 USA

**Sumlin, Kevin** — Football Coach
Texas A&M University, Athletic Dept, College Station TX 77843, USA

**Summar, Trent** — Singer (New Row Mob)
Grassroots Media, 1005 S Orlando Ave, Los Angeles CA 90035, USA

**Summe, Gregory L** — Businessman
PerkinElmer Inc, 45 William St, Wellesley MA 02481, USA

**Summer, Cree** — Actress, Singer
W M E Entertainment, 9601 Wilshire Blvd, #300, Beverly Hills CA 90210 USA

**Summerhays, Bruce P** — Golfer
2 Condie Circle, Farmington UT 84025, USA

**Summers, Andrew (Andy)** — Singer, Guitarist (Police)
21A Noel St, London W1V 3PD, England

**Summers, Carol** — Artist
2817 Smith Grade, Santa Cruz CA 95060, USA

**Summers, Dana** — Cartoonist (Lug Nuts, Bound & Gagged)
Orlando Sentinel, Editorial Dept, 633 N Orange Ave, Lobby, Orlando FL 32801, USA

**Summers, Jerry** — Singer (Dovells)
American Promotions, 2011 Ferry Ave, #U19, Camden NJ 08104, USA

**Summers, Kennedy** — Model
Playboy Promotions, 9346 Civic Center Dr, #200, Beverly Hills CA 90210 USA

**Summers, Lawrence H (Larry)** — Educator; Secretary, Treasury
National Economic Council, 1600 Pennsylvania Ave NW, Washington DC 20502, USA

**Summers, Linda** — Model
Playboy Promotions, 9346 Civic Center Dr, #200, Beverly Hills CA 90210 USA

**Summers, Marc** — Entertainer
Rebel Entertainment Partners, 5700 Wilshire Blvd, #456, Los Angeles CA 90036, USA

**Summers, Tara** — Actress
I C M Partners, 10250 Constellation Blvd, #900, Los Angeles CA 90067 USA

**Summerville, Trish** — Costume Designer
W M E Entertainment, 9601 Wilshire Blvd, #300, Beverly Hills CA 90210 USA

**Summitt, Pat S Head** — Basketball Player, Coach
3720 River Trace Lane, Knoxville TN 37920, USA

**Sumner, Charles (Charlie)** — Football Player, Coach
PO Box 11621, Lahaina HI 96761, USA

**Sumner, Mickey** — Actress
I C M Partners, 10250 Constellation Blvd, #900, Los Angeles CA 90067 USA

**Sumner, Peter** — Actor
Morrissey Mgmt, 77 Glebe Point Road, Glebe NSW 2037, Australia

**Sumner, Walter H (Walt)** — Football Player
PO Box 112, Ocilla GA 31774, USA

**Sumners, Rosalyn D** — Figure Skater
13314 NE 86th Place, Redmond WA 98052, USA

**Sumpter, Jeremy** — Actor
Innovative Artists, 1505 10th St, Santa Monica CA 90401 USA

**Sumpter, Tika** — Actress
C E S D, 10635 Santa Monica Blvd, #130, Los Angeles CA 90025 USA
**Sun Dandan** — Speed Skater
Skating Association, 56 Zhonguancun South St, Beijing 100044, China
**Sundaresh, S (Sundi)** — Businessman
Adeptec Inc, 691 S Milpitas Blvd, Milpitas CA 95035, USA
**Sunday, Gabriel** — Actor
Abrams Artists, 9200 W Sunset Blvd, #1125, West Hollywood CA 90069 USA
**Sundberg, James H (Jim)** — Baseball Player
2308 Newforest Court, Arlington TX 76017, USA
**Sunde, Milton J (Milt)** — Football Player
6008 W 104th St, Minneapolis MN 55438, USA
**Sundhage, Pia** — Soccer Player, Coach
US Women's Soccer, 1801 S Prairie Ave, Chicago IL 60616, USA
**Sundin, Gordon V (Gordie)** — Baseball Player
15600 Old 41 N, Naples FL 34110, USA
**Sundin, Mats J** — Ice Hockey Player
International Management Group, 801 6th St SW, Calgary AB T2P 3V8, Canada
**Sundvold, Jon T** — Basketball Player
2700 Westbrook Way, Columbia MO 65203, USA
**Sung Kang** — Actor
W M E Entertainment, 9601 Wilshire Blvd, #300, Beverly Hills CA 90210 USA
**Sung, Elizabeth** — Actress
G V A Talent, 9229 W Sunset Blvd, #320, West Hollywood CA 90069, USA
**Sung, Shi Yeon** — Conductor
I M G Artists, Hogarth Business Park, Chiswick, London W4 2TH, England
**Sunjata, Daniel** — Actor
United Talent Agency, U T A Plaza, 9336 Civic Center Dr, Beverly Hills CA 90210 USA
**Sunny, Tehmina** — Actress
Don Buchwald Talent Agency, 6500 Wilshire Blvd, #2200, Los Angeles CA 90048 USA
**Sunohara, Vicky** — Ice Hockey Player
Team Canada, 2424 University Dr NW, Calgary AB T2N 3Y9, Canada
**Sununu, John H** — Governor, NH; Government Official
49 Linden Road, Hampton Falls NH 03844, USA
**Sunyayev, Rashid A** — Astronomer
Space Studies Institute, Profsoyuznaya Str 84/32, 117910 Moscow, Russia
**Supernaw, Douglas A (Doug)** — Singer, Songwriter
Maximus Entertainment Booking, PO Box 27517, Austin TX 78755, USA
**Suplee, Ethan** — Actor
Don Buchwald Talent Agency, 6500 Wilshire Blvd, #2200, Los Angeles CA 90048 USA
**Suppan, Jeffrey S (Jeff)** — Baseball Player
17836 Sidwell St, Granada Hills CA 91344, USA
**Surayev, Maksim V** — Cosmonaut
Cosmonaut Training Center, Star City, 141160 Zvezdny Gorodok, Moscow Oblast, Russia
**Sure!, Al B** — Singer, Songwriter
I C M Partners, 10250 Constellation Blvd, #900, Los Angeles CA 90067 USA
**Surhoff, William J (B J)** — Baseball Player
5 Fenton St, Rye NY 10580, USA
**Surin, Bruny** — Track Athlete
PO Box 2, Succ Saint Michel, Montreal QC H2A 3L8, Canada
**Surmelis, Angelo** — Actor
Paradise Group, PO Box 69451, West Hollywood CA 90069, USA
**Surnow, Joel** — Producer
Paradigm Agency, 360 N Crescent Dr, North Building, Beverly Hills CA 90210 USA
**Sursok, Tammin** — Actress
Charlie Baby Productions, 8391 Beverly Blvd, #283, Los Angeles CA 90048, USA
**Surtain, Patrick F** — Football Player
2704 Boot Lane, Weston FL 33331, USA
**Surtees, John** — Auto Racing Driver
Team Surtees, Fircroft Way, Edenbridge, Kent TN8 6EJ, England
**Suschitzky, J Peter** — Cinematographer
13 Priory Road, London NW6 4NN, England
**Suschitzky, Wolfgang** — Cinematographer
Douglas House, 6 Maida Ave, #11, London W2 1TG, England
**Suskind, Patrick** — Writer
Diogenes Verlag AG, Sprecherstr 8, 8032 Zurich, Switzerland
**Suslick, Kenneth S** — Chemist
University of Illinois, Chemistry Dept, Champaign IL 61820, USA
**Susman, Todd** — Actor
Luedtke Agency, 1674 Broadway, #7A, New York NY 10019, USA
**Susser, Craig** — Actor
I C M Partners, 10250 Constellation Blvd, #900, Los Angeles CA 90067 USA
**Sussman, Adam** — Writer, Producer
Brian Lutz Mgmt, 6464 Sunset Blvd, #860, Los Angeles CA 90028, USA
**Sussman, Kevin** — Actor
C E S D, 257 Park Ave S, #950, New York NY 10010 USA
**Sussman, Susan** — Writer
A P A Talent & Literary Agency, 405 S Beverly Dr, #300, Beverly Hills CA 90212 USA
**Sutcliffe, David** — Actor
Noble-Caplan Agency, 1260 Yonge St, #200, Toronto ON M4T 1W6, Canada
**Sutcliffe, Richard L (Rick)** — Baseball Player
616 NE Seabrook Court, Lees Summit MO 64064, USA
**Suter, Gary** — Ice Hockey Player
2128 County Road D, Lac du Flambu WI 54538, USA
**Suter, Ryan** — Ice Hockey Player
1554 Shining Ore Dr, Brentwood TN 37027, USA
**Sutherland, David** — Golfer
5431 Tree Side Dr, Carmichael CA 95608, USA
**Sutherland, Donald** — Actor
Creative Artists Agency, 2000 Ave of Stars, #100, Los Angeles CA 90067 USA
**Sutherland, Douglas A (Doug)** — Football Player
511 Kenilworth Ave, Duluth MN 55803, USA
**Sutherland, Gary L** — Baseball Player
338 Oakcliff Road, Monrovia CA 91016, USA
**Sutherland, Ivan E** — Computer Scientist
California Institute of Technology, Computer Science Dept, Pasadena CA 91125, USA

**S**

**Sutherland - Svendsen**

**Sutherland, Kevin** — Golfer
1230 Carter Road, Sacramento CA 95864, USA
**Sutherland, Kiefer** — Actor
Management 360, 9111 Wilshire Blvd, Beverly Hills CA 90210 USA
**Sutherland, Kristine** — Actress
S M S Talent, 8383 Wilshire Blvd, #230, Beverly Hills CA 90211 USA
**Sutherland, Leonardo C (Leo)** — Baseball Player
12082 Nieta Dr, Garden Grove CA 92840, USA
**Sutherland, Peter D** — Government Official, Ireland
68 Eglinton Road, Dublin 4, Ireland
**Sutherland, Sarah** — Actress
Gersh Agency, 9465 Wilshire Blvd, #600, Beverly Hills CA 90212 USA
**Sutherland, William F (Bill)** — Ice Hockey Player
305-2425 Main St, Winnipeg MB R2V 3N4, Canada
**Sutko, Glenn E** — Baseball Player
1403 River Green Dr NW, Atlanta GA 30327, USA
**Sutley, Nancy** — Government Official
White House, 1600 Pennsylvania Ave NW, Washington DC 20500, USA
**Sutor, George** — Basketball Player
29840 State Highway 27, Holcombe WI 54745, USA
**Sutorius, James** — Actor
A M T Artists, 15260 Ventura Blvd, #1200, Sherman Oaks CA 91403, USA
**Sutta, Jessica** — Singer (Pussycat Dolls), Actress
Almond Talent Agency, 8217 Beverly Blvd, #8, West Hollywood CA 90048, USA
**Sutter, Brent** — Ice Hockey Player, Coach
PO Box 545, Viking AB T0B 4N0, Canada
**Sutter, Brian** — Ice Hockey Player, Coach
Red Deer Rebels, C-4847 19th St, Red Deer AB T4R 2N7, Canada
**Sutter, Duane** — Ice Hockey Player, Coach
Calgary Flames, PO Box 1540, Station M, Calgary AB T2P 3B9, Canada
**Sutter, Edward L (Eddie)** — Football Player
5104 N Bevalon Place, Peoria IL 61614, USA
**Sutter, H Bruce** — Baseball Player
59 Waterside Dr SE, Cartersville GA 30121, USA
**Sutter, Kurt** — Producer, Writer
W M E Entertainment, 9601 Wilshire Blvd, #300, Beverly Hills CA 90210 USA
**Sutter, Richard G (Rich)** — Ice Hockey Player
Sutter Ice, 1920 17th St, Cooldale AB T1M 1M1, Canada
**Sutter, Ronald (Ron)** — Ice Hockey Player
44 Chaparral Cove SE, Calgary AB T2X 3L4, Canada
**Suttle, Dane L** — Basketball Player
138 W 69th St, Los Angeles CA 90003, USA
**Sutton, Donald H (Don)** — Baseball Player, Sportscaster
120 Calle de las Rosas, Rancho Mirage CA 92270, USA
**Sutton, Greg** — Basketball Player
PO Box 8101, Edmond OK 73083, USA
**Sutton, Hal E** — Golfer
40 Duck Haven Point, Bossier City LA 71111, USA
**Sutton, Larry J** — Baseball Player
14209 Woodward St, Overland Park KS 66223, USA
**Sutton, Michael** — Actor
Somers Teitelbaum David, 8840 Wilshire Blvd, #200, Beverly Hills CA 90211 USA
**Sutton, Tierney** — Singer
Terry M Hill, 41910 Boardwalk, #A2, Palm Desert CA 92211 USA
**Sutton, William (Will)** — Football Player
Chicago Bears, 1000 Football Dr, Lake Forest IL 60045 USA
**Suvalatsumi** — Actress
39 M G Chakrapani St, Sathya Garden, Saligrammam, Chennai TN 600093, India
**Suvari, Mena A** — Actress
Alchemy Entertainment, 7024 Melrose Ave, #420, Los Angeles CA 90038 USA
**Suwa, Gen** — Anthropologist
University of California, Human Evolutionary Science Laboratory, Berkeley CA 94720, USA
**Suwanai, Akiko** — Concert Violinist
Harrison/Parrott, 5-6 Albion Court, London W6 0QT, England
**Suyderhoud, Mike** — Water Skier
PO Box 492052, Redding CA 96049, USA
**Suzman, Janet** — Actress
Steve Kenis Co, 95 Barkston Gardens, London SW5 0EU, England
**Suzor, Mark J** — Ice Hockey Player
1639 Hillcrest Dr, Sheridan WY 82801, USA
**Suzuki, David T** — Commentator, Geneticist, Enviromentalist
David Suzuki Foundation, 2221 W 4th Ave, Vancouver BC V6K 4S2, Canada
**Suzuki, Ichiro** — Baseball Player
New York Yankees, Yankee Stadium, E 161st St & River Ave, Bronx NY 10451 USA
**Suzuki, Kurt K** — Baseball Player
Washington Nationals, 1500 S Capitol St SE, Washington DC 20003 USA
**Suzuki, Masaaki** — Concert Organist, Harpsichord Player
Frank Salomon, 121 W 27th St, #703, New York NY 10001 USA
**Suzuki, Pat** — Actress, Singer
343 E 30th St, New York NY 10016, USA
**Suzuki, Robert** — Educator
California State University, President's Office, Bakersfield CA 93311, USA
**Suzy** — Columnist
18 E 68th St, #1B, New York NY 10065, USA
**Svala** — Singer, Songwriter
Tonaljos Music, Box 520, Rejkavikurvegur 38, Hafnafjordur 220, Iceland
**Svankmajer, Jan** — Director
Cerninska 5, 11800 Prague 1, Czech Republic
**Svare, Harland** — Football Player, Coach
6127 Paseo Jaquita, Carlsbad CA 92009, USA
**Svehla, Robert** — Ice Hockey Player
Dukla Trencin Hockey, Povazska 34, 91101 Trencin, Slovakia
**Svenden, Birgitta** — Concert Singer
Ulf Tornqvist, Sankt Eriksgatan 100, 113 31 Stockholm, Sweden
**Svendsen, Emil Hegle** — Biathlete
Strindheim I L, Postboks 1406, 7444 Trondheim, Norway

|  |  |
|---|---|
| **Svendsen, Louise A**<br>16 Park Ave, New York NY 10016, USA | Museum Executive |
| **Sveningsson, Magnus J**<br>Talent Trust, Kungsgatan 9C, 411 19 Gothenburg, Sweden | Bassist (Cardigans) |
| **Svenson, Bo**<br>Feldman Bailey Mgmt, 21781 Ventura Blvd, Woodland Hills CA 91364, USA | Actor |
| **Svensson, Leif**<br>Lisselbyvagan 39, 793 33 Leksand, Sweden | Ice Hockey Player |
| **Sverak, Jan**<br>PO Box 33, 15500 Prague 515, Czech Republic | Director |
| **Sveum, Dale C**<br>13483 E Estrella Ave, Scottsdale AZ 85259, USA | Baseball Player |
| **Svihus, Robert C (Bob)**<br>23000 Guidotti Dr, Salinas CA 93908, USA | Football Player |
| **Svoboda, Jiri**<br>Performing Arts Academy, Malostranske Nam 12, 11800 Prague 1, Czech Republic | Director |
| **Svoboda, Petr**<br>Sportrust Assoc, 818 18th St, #F, Santa Monica CA 90403, USA | Ice Hockey Player |
| **Swaby, Donn**<br>C E S D, 10635 Santa Monica Blvd, #130, Los Angeles CA 90025 USA | Actor |
| **Swados, Elizabeth A**<br>360 Central Park West, #16G, New York NY 10025, USA | Writer, Composer |
| **Swagerty, Jane**<br>9128 N 70th St, Paradise Valley AZ 85253, USA | Swimmer |
| **Swagerty, Keith M**<br>22232 17th Ave SE, #205, Bothell WA 98021, USA | Basketball Player |
| **Swaggart, Jimmy L**<br>PO Box 262550, Baton Rouge LA 70826, USA | Evangelist |
| **Swaggerty, William D (Bill)**<br>116 S Forney Ave, Hanover PA 17331, USA | Baseball Player |
| **Swail, Julie**<br>University of California, Athletic Dept, Irvine CA 92697, USA | Water Polo Player, Coach |
| **Swain, Dominique**<br>Don Buchwald Talent Agency, 6500 Wilshire Blvd, #2200, Los Angeles CA 90048 USA | Actress |
| **Swain, John W**<br>409 E 135th St, Burnsville MN 55337, USA | Football Player |
| **Swain, Michael L (Mike)**<br>128 W Campbell Ave, Campbell CA 95008, USA | Judo Athlete |
| **Swallow, Jerod**<br>Detroit Skating Club, 888 Denison Court, Bloomfield Hills MI 48302, USA | Ice Dancer, Coach |
| **Swaminathan, Monkombu S**<br>M S Swaminathan Foundation, 3 Cross St, Taramani, Madras 600113, India | Geneticist |
| **Swan, Billy**<br>Geoffrey Blumenauer Artists, PO Box 343, Burbank CA 91503 USA | Singer, Songwriter |
| **Swan, Craig S**<br>16704 Bobcat Dr, Fort Myers FL 33908, USA | Baseball Player |
| **Swan, John W D**<br>11 Grape Bay Dr, Paget PG 06, Bermuda | Prime Minister, Bermuda |
| **Swan, Michael**<br>13576 Cheltenham Dr, Sherman Oaks CA 91423, USA | Actor |
| **Swan, Richard G**<br>700 Melrose Ave, #M3, Winter Park FL 32789, USA | Mathematician |
| **Swan, Robert**<br>2041, 561 Keystone Ave, PM Box 640, Reno NV 89503, USA | Explorer |
| **Swan, Serinda**<br>Performers Mgmt, #2-636 Clyde Ave, West Vancouver BC V7T 1E1, Canada | Actress |
| **Swanberg, Joe**<br>Creative Artists Agency, 2000 Ave of Stars, #100, Los Angeles CA 90067 USA | Director, Actor |
| **Swanepoel, Candice**<br>I M G Models, 304 Park Ave S, #PH N, New York NY 10010 USA | Model |
| **Swank, Hilary**<br>M R C, 8530 Wilshire Blvd, #420, Beverly Hills CA 90211, USA | Actress |
| **Swann, Charles D**<br>5815 Vinings Retreat Court SW, Mableton GA 30126, USA | Football Player |
| **Swann, Eric J**<br>2321 Carex Court, Elk Grove CA 95757, USA | Football Player |
| **Swann, Lynn C**<br>506 Hegner Way, #2, Sewickley PA 15143, USA | Football Player, Sportscaster |
| **Swanson, Arthur L (Red)**<br>1139 Chippenham Dr, Baton Rouge LA 70808, USA | Baseball Player |
| **Swanson, August G**<br>3146 Portage Bay Place E, #H, Seattle WA 98102, USA | Physician |
| **Swanson, Jackie**<br>C E S D, 10635 Santa Monica Blvd, #130, Los Angeles CA 90025 USA | Actress |
| **Swanson, Judith**<br>Persona Mgmt, 40 E 9th St, New York NY 10003, USA | Actress |
| **Swanson, Kristy**<br>Inphenate, 9701 Wilshire Blvd, #1000, Beverly Hills CA 90212 USA | Actress, Model |
| **Swanson, Stanley L (Stan)**<br>1705 E Whaley St, Longview TX 75601, USA | Baseball Player |
| **Swanson, Steven R**<br>1414 Blueberry Lane, Friendswood TX 77546, USA | Astronaut |
| **Swanson, William H**<br>Raytheon Co, 870 Winter St, Waltham MA 02451, USA | Businessman |
| **Swaray, Estelle**<br>Atlantic Records, 1290 Ave of Americas, Concourse 4, New York NY 10104, USA | Singer, Rap Artist |
| **Sward, Anne**<br>Talent Management Group, 339 E 3900 S, #210, Salt Lake City UT 84107, USA | Actress |
| **Swardson, Nick**<br>Brillstein Entertainment Partners, 9150 Wilshire Blvd, #350, Beverly Hills CA 90212 USA | Actor, Comedian, Writer, Producer |
| **Swartzbaugh, David T (Dave)**<br>113 Orchard St, Middletown OH 45044, USA | Baseball Player |
| **Swatek, Barret**<br>Harrison Stokes, 8730 W Sunset Blvd, #270, West Hollywood CA 90069, USA | Actress |
| **Sway**<br>Bloom Effect, 112 S Portland Ave, #3A, Brooklyn NY 11217, USA | Entertainer |

**Swayne, Harry V** — Football Player
2702 Baubitz Road, Reistertown MD 21136, USA

**Swayze, Don** — Actor
Baron Entertainment, 13848 Ventura Blvd, #A, Sherman Oaks CA 91423, USA

**Swead, Stephen** — Government Official, Financier
Fannie Mae, 3900 Wisconsin Ave NW, Washington DC 20016, USA

**Sweat, Keith** — Singer, Songwriter
Red Entertainment Agency, 505 8th Ave, #1004, New York NY 10018, USA

**Sweat, Lynn** — Artist
17 Good Hill Road, Weston CT 06883, USA

**Swedberg, Heidi** — Actress
Frontline Mgmt, 8265 Sunset Blvd, #209, West Hollywood CA 90046, USA

**Swedberg, Jaclyn** — Model, Actress
Playboy Promotions, 9346 Civic Center Dr, #200, Beverly Hills CA 90210 USA

**Swedlin, Rosalie** — Producer
Anonymous Content, 3532 Hayden Ave, Culver City CA 90232 USA

**Sweeney, Alison** — Actress, Director, Producer
United Talent Agency, U T A Plaza, 9336 Civic Center Dr, Beverly Hills CA 90210 USA

**Sweeney, Bob** — Ice Hockey Player
110 Brookview Dr, North Andover MA 01845, USA

**Sweeney, Brian E** — Baseball Player
199 Morsemere Ave, Yonkers NY 10703, USA

**Sweeney, Calvin E** — Football Player
4120 Olympiad Dr, Los Angeles CA 90043, USA

**Sweeney, D B** — Actor
Rain Management Group, 1631 21st St, Santa Monica CA 90404, USA

**Sweeney, Donald C (Don)** — Ice Hockey Player, Executive
5 Shady Nook Lane, Lynnfield MA 01940, USA

**Sweeney, I Anne** — Businesswoman
Disney Media Network, 3800 W Alameda Ave, #B, Burbank CA 91505, USA

**Sweeney, James J (Jim)** — Football Player
119 Justabout Road, Venetia PA 15367, USA

**Sweeney, John E** — Representative, NY
1 Stratford Dr, Clifton Park NY 12065, USA

**Sweeney, John J** — Labor Leader
AFL-CIO, 1750 New York Ave NW, Lobby 1, Washington DC 20006, USA

**Sweeney, Julia** — Actress, Comedienne
W M E Entertainment, 9601 Wilshire Blvd, #300, Beverly Hills CA 90210 USA

**Sweeney, Mark P** — Baseball Player
6394 W Dublin Lane, Chandler AZ 85226, USA

**Sweeney, Michael J (Mike)** — Baseball Player
PO Box 1193, Rancho Santa Fe CA 92067, USA

**Sweeney, Pepper** — Actor
B R S / Gage Talent Agency, 5757 Wilshire Blvd, #659, Los Angeles CA 90036 USA

**Sweeney, Ryan J** — Baseball Player
1212 Millet St, Naperville IL 60563, USA

**Sweeney, Sunny M** — Singer, Songwriter, Guitarist
Republic Nashville Records, 1219 16th Ave S, Nashville TN 37212, USA

**Sweeney, Terry** — Actress, Comedienne
Creative Artists Agency, 2000 Ave of Stars, #100, Los Angeles CA 90067 USA

**Sweeney, Tim** — Ice Hockey Player
47 Ledgewood Dr, Hanover MA 02339, USA

**Sweet, Joseph L (Joe)** — Football Player
1530 NE 89th Court, Vancouver WA 98664, USA

**Sweet, Matthew** — Singer, Songwriter
Russell Carter Artists Mgmt, 567 Ralph Mcgill Blvd NE, Atlanta GA 30312, USA

**Sweet, Richard J (Rick)** — Baseball Player
1503 NE 89th Court, Vancouver WA 98664, USA

**Sweet, Sharon** — Opera Singer
Kunstleragentur Raab & Bohm, Plankengasse 7, 1010 Vienna, Austria

**Sweeten, Madylin** — Actress
Innovative Artists, 1505 10th St, Santa Monica CA 90401 USA

**Sweetland, Brad** — Animator
Pixar Animation, 1200 Park Ave, Emeryville CA 94608, USA

**Sweetnam, Skye** — Singer, Songwriter
Creative Artists Agency, 3310 W End Ave, #500, Nashville TN 37203 USA

**Swensen, Joseph A** — Conductor, Composer
Malmo Opera, Ronneholmsv 20, 200 10 Malmo, Sweden

**Swenson, Inga** — Actress, Singer
3351 Halderman St, Los Angeles CA 90066, USA

**Swenson, Jesse** — Actor
Innovative Artists, 1505 10th St, Santa Monica CA 90401 USA

**Swenson, Rick** — Dog Sled Racer
PO Box 16205, Two Rivers AK 99716, USA

**Swenson, Robert C (Bob)** — Football Player
PO Box 403, Erie CO 80516, USA

**Swenson, Ruth Ann** — Opera Singer
Metropolitan Opera Assn, Lincoln Center Plaza, New York NY 10023 USA

**Swenson, William D** — Afghanistan War Army Hero (CMH)
PO Box 4647, Rollingbay WA 98061, USA

**Swensson, Earl S** — Architect
Earl Swensson Assoc, 2100 W End Ave, #1200, Nashville TN 37203, USA

**Swiczinsky, Helmut** — Architect
Coop Himmelblau, Seilerstatte 16/11A, 1010 Vienna, Austria

**Swienton, Gregory T** — Businessman
Ryder System Inc, 11690 NW 105th St, Medley FL 33178, USA

**Swift** — Rap Artist (D-12)
Coast to Coast Talent, 3350 Barham Blvd, Los Angeles CA 90068 USA

**Swift, Clive** — Actor
Roxane Vacca Mgmt, 8 Silver Place, London W1R 3LJ, England

**Swift, Douglas A (Doug)** — Football Player
265 S 25th St, Philadelphia PA 19103, USA

**Swift, Graham C** — Writer
A P Watt, 20 John St, London WC1N 2DR, England

**Swift, Harley E (Skeeter)** — Basketball Player
4987 Highway 11 W, Kingsport TN 37660, USA

**Swift, Hewson H** — Biologist
University of Chicago, Cell Biology Dept, Chicago IL 60637, USA
**Swift, Jeremy** — Actor
Independent Talent Group, 40 Whitfield St, London W1T 2RH, England
**Swift, Scott H** — Navy Admiral
Commander, 7th Fleet Yokosuka Japan, FPO AP 96601 USA
**Swift, Stephen J** — Judge
US Tax Court, 400 2nd St NW, Washington DC 20217, USA
**Swift, Stromile** — Basketball Player
3256 S Silverwind Cove, Memphis TN 38125, USA
**Swift, Taylor** — Singer, Guitarist, Songwriter
Taylor Swift Enterprises, 242 W Main St, PM Box 412, Hendersonville TN 37075, USA
**Swift, William C (Bill)** — Baseball Player
5880 E Sapphire Lane, Paradise Valley AZ 85253, USA
**Swilley, Dennis N** — Football Player
1020 Gruene River Dr, New Braunfels TX 78132, USA
**Swilling, Patrick T (Pat)** — Football Player
4425 Plum Orchard Ave, New Orleans LA 70126, USA
**Swinburne, Clare** — Actress
Associated International Mgmt, 7 Hatton Garden, #400, London EC1N 8AD, England
**Swindell, Colden R (Cole)** — Singer, Songwriter
Warner Bros Records, 3300 Warner Blvd, Burbank CA 91505 USA
**Swindells, William, Jr** — Businessman
Willamette Industries, 1300 SW 5th Ave, #500, Portland OR 97201, USA
**Swindle, Orson** — Government Official
500 University Ave, #309, Honolulu HI 96826, USA
**Swindoll, Charles R** — Evangelist, Writer
Insight for Living, 211 Imperial Highway, Fullerton CA 92835, USA
**Swingle, Paul C** — Baseball Player
6844 S Whetstone Place, Chandler AZ 85249, USA
**Swingley, Douglas L (Doug)** — Dog Sled Racer
PO Box 672, Lincoln MT 59639, USA
**Swink, James E (Jim)** — Football Player
723 Euclid Ave, Rusk TX 75785, USA
**Swinny, Wayne** — Guitarist (Saliva)
Helter Skelter, 347-353 Chiswick High Road, London W4 4HS, England
**Swinson, Aaron** — Basketball Player
1004 Longley Cove, Heathrow FL 32746, USA
**Swinton, Reginald T (Reggie)** — Football Player
14200 Wimbledon Loop, Little Rock AR 72210, USA
**Swinton, Tilda** — Actress
Hamilton Hodell, 20 Golden Square, London W1F 9JL, England
**Swisher, Carl C** — Anthropologist
Institute of Human Origins, 1288 9th St, Berkeley CA 94710, USA
**Swisher, Nicholas T (Nick)** — Baseball Player
6803 E Main St, #6601, Scottsdale AZ 85251, USA
**Swisher, Steven E (Steve)** — Baseball Player
432 60th St, Vienna WV 26105, USA
**Swisten, Amanda** — Actress
Xposure Public Relations, 8271 Melrose Ave, #110, Los Angeles CA 90046, USA
**Swit, Loretta** — Actress
Malibu Business/Shipping Center, 23852 Pacific Coast Highway, Malibu CA 90265, USA
**Switzer, Barry** — Football Player, Coach
700 W Timberdell Road, Norman OK 73072, USA
**Switzer, Jon M** — Baseball Player
2110 Paramount Ave, Austin TX 78704, USA
**Switzer, Louis** — Interior Designer
Switzer Group, 535 5th Ave, #1100, New York NY 10017, USA
**Swizz Beatz** — Rap Artist, Music Producer
5W Public Relations, 888 7th Ave, #1200, New York NY 10106, USA
**Swoboda, Ronald A (Ron)** — Baseball Player
315 Alonzo St, New Orleans LA 70115, USA
**Swoopes, Sheryl** — Basketball Player
2020 Eldridge Parkway, #4605, Houston TX 77077, USA
**Sy, Omar** — Actor
Agence Artiste Adequat, 108 Rue Reaumur, 75002 Paris, France
**Syal, Meera** — Actress, Comedienne, Writer
United Agents, 12-26 Lexington St, London W1F 0LE, England
**Syberberg, Hans-Jurgen** — Director
Genter Str 15A, 80805 Munich, Germany
**Sybil** — Singer
Tony Denton Promotions, Charter House, 157-159 High St, London N14 6BP, England
**Sydney, Harry F** — Football Player
1558 Cardinal Lane, Green Bay WI 54313, USA
**Sydnor, Charles W, Jr** — Businessman, Educator
Commonwealth Public Broadcasting Corp, 23 Sesame St, Richmond VA 23235, USA
**Sydor, Darryl** — Ice Hockey Player
3358 Windmill Curve, Saint Paul MN 55129, USA
**Syed Sirajuddin Syed Putra Jamalullail** — Head of State, Malaysia
Sultan's Palace, Istana Bukit Serene, 50502 Kuala Lumpur, Malaysia
**Sykes, Eugene C (Gene)** — Football Player
15809 Council Ave, Baton Rouge LA 70817, USA
**Sykes, Jesse** — Singer, Songwriter
Barsuk Records, PO Box 22546, Seattle WA 98122, USA
**Sykes, Lynn R** — Geologist
100 Washington Spring Road, RR 1 Box 248, Palisades NY 10964, USA
**Sykes, Nathan J** — Singer (Wanted)
Industry Music Group, 128 Regent Road, Hanley Stoke, Trent ST1 3AY, England
**Sykes, Peter** — Director
International Talent Booking, Ariel House, 74A Charlotte St, #100 London W1T 4QJ, England
**Sykes, Phil** — Ice Hockey Player
1486 Brooke Court, Hastings MN 55033, USA
**Sykes, Richard B** — Businessman, Microbiologist
Imperial College, Exhibition Road, London SW7 2AZ, England
**Sykes, Robert J (Bob)** — Baseball
1451 County Road 900 E, Carmi IL 62821, USA

V.I.P. Address Book

**Sykes, Wanda** — Actress, Comedienne
W M E Entertainment, 9601 Wilshire Blvd, #300, Beverly Hills CA 90210 USA

**Sykora, Petr** — Ice Hockey Player
2548 Appletree Dr, Pittsburgh PA 15241, USA

**Sylbert, Anthea** — Costume Designer
13949 Ventura Blvd, #309, Sherman Oaks CA 91423, USA

**Sylvester, Charles (Chuck)** — Harness Racing Trainer
PO Box 1066, Williamstown NJ 08094, USA

**Sylvester, Dean** — Ice Hockey Player
51 Upland Road, Plympton MA 02367, USA

**Sylvester, George H** — Air Force General
4571 Conicville Road, Mount Jackson VA 22842, USA

**Sylvester, Harold** — Actor
A M T Artists, 15260 Ventura Blvd, #1200, Sherman Oaks CA 91403, USA

**Sylvester, Michael** — Opera Singer
Columbia Artists Mgmt Inc, 5 Columbus Circle, 1790 Broadway, #1600, New York NY 10019 USA

**Sylvester, Steven P (Steve)** — Football Player
10425 Londonderry Court, Cincinnati OH 45242, USA

**Sylvestri, Don** — Ice Hockey Player
1610 Redfern St, Sudbury ON P3A 3S9, Canada

**Sylvian, David** — Singer, Guitarist (Japan)
Opium Arts, 49 Portland Road, London W11 4LJ, England

**Symington, J Fife, III** — Governor, AZ
1700 W Washington St, Phoenix AZ 85007, USA

**Symms, Steven D** — Senator, ID
127 S Fairfax St, #137, Alexandria VA 22314, USA

**Symon, Michael** — Chef, Restauranteur
Lola Restaurant, 2058 E 4th St, Cleveland OH 44115, USA

**Symone, Raven** — Actress, Singer
United Talent Agency, U T A Plaza, 9336 Civic Center Dr, Beverly Hills CA 90210 USA

**Syms, Sylvia** — Actress
Barry Brown, 47 West Square, London SE11 4SP, England

**Synek, Ondrej** — Rowing Athlete
A S C Dukla Prague, Oddil Aletiky, PS 59, 16044 Prague 6, Czech Republic

**Sypek, Richard** — Actor
Paradigm Agency, 360 N Crescent Dr, North Building, Beverly Hills CA 90210 USA

**Syracuse, Joe** — Writer, Actor, Director
United Talent Agency, U T A Plaza, 9336 Civic Center Dr, Beverly Hills CA 90210 USA

**Syron, Richard F** — Financier, Government Official
Federal Home Loan Mortgage, 8200 Jones Branch Dr, McLean VA 22102, USA

**Szabados, Shannon** — Ice Hockey Player
Team Canada, 2424 University Dr NW, Calgary AB T2N 3Y9, Canada

**Szabo, Istvan** — Director
Vaci 6, 1132 Budapest, Hungary

**Szaro, Richard J (Rich)** — Football Player
171 Metropolitan Ave, Brooklyn NY 11211, USA

**Szasz, Janos** — Director, Writer, Actor
Hunnia Filmstudio, Rona Utca 174, Budapest 1145, Hungary

**Szczerbiak, Walter R (Wally)** — Basketball Player, Sportscaster
26 Peabody Road, Cold Spring Harbor NY 11724, USA

**Szekely, Eva** — Swimmer
Szepvolgyi Utca 4/B, 1025 Budapest, Hungary

**Szekessy, Karen** — Photographer
Haynstr 2, 20249 Hamburg, Germany

**Szemborski, Stanley R** — Navy Admiral
Northrup Grumman Corp, Strategy Dept, 2980 Fairview Park Drive, Falls Church VA 22042, USA

**Szemeredi, Endre** — Mathematician
Rutgers State University, Mathematics Dept, New Brunswick NJ 08903, USA

**Szep, Jason** — Journalist
Thompson Reuters, Editorial Dept, 1333 H St NW, Washington DC 20005, USA

**Szep, Paul M** — Editorial Cartoonist
10610 Andrew Lane, Seminole FL 33777, USA

**Szewczenko, Tanja** — Figure Skater, Model, Actress
Korallenweg 1, 44267 Dortmund, Germany

**Szigmond, Vilmos** — Cinematographer
PO Box 2230, Los Angeles CA 90078, USA

**Szmanda, Eric** — Actor
A P A Talent & Literary Agency, 405 S Beverly Dr, #300, Beverly Hills CA 90212 USA

**Szohr, Jessica** — Actress
I C M Partners, 10250 Constellation Blvd, #900, Los Angeles CA 90067 USA

**Szolkowy, Robin** — Figure Skater
Deutsche Eislauf-Union, Menzinger Str 68, 80992 Munich, Germany

**Szostak, Jack W** — Nobel Medicine Laureate
Simches Research Center, 185 Cambridge St, Boston MA 02114, USA

**Szostak, Stephanie** — Actress
United Talent Agency, U T A Plaza, 9336 Civic Center Dr, Beverly Hills CA 90210 USA

**Szot, Paulo** — Actor, Opera Singer
Opera et Concert, 37 Rue de la Chaussee d'Antin, 75009 Paris, France

**Szott, David A (Dave)** — Football Player
11 Manor Dr, Morristown NJ 07960, USA

**Szulc, Radoslaw** — Conductor
Harrison/Parrott, 5-6 Albion Court, London W6 0QT, England

**Szuminski, Jason E** — Baseball Player
680 Serra St, #W402, Stanford CA 94305, USA

**Szymanski, James P (Jim)** — Football Player
541 Riverwalk Dr, Mason MI 48854, USA

**Szymanski, Richard F (Dick)** — Football Player
5270 Forest Edge Court, Sanford FL 32771, USA

**T Hooft, Gerardus** — Nobel Physics Laureate
Leuvenlaan 4, Postbus 80.195, 3508 Utrecht TD, Netherlands

**T, Mr** — Actor
15203 La Maida St, Sherman Oaks CA 91403, USA

**Tabachnik, Michel** — Composer, Conductor
Garvey & Ivor, 59 Lansdowne Place, Hove BN3 1FL, England

**Tabackin, Lewis B (Lew)** — Jazz Flutist, Saxophonist
38 W 94th St, New York NY 10025, USA

**Tabai, Ieremia T** — President, Kiribati
Foreign Affairs Ministry, PO Box 68, Bairiki, Tarawa, Kiribati

**Tabak, Zan** — Basketball Player
Mihanoviceva 37C, 21000 Split, Croatia

**Tabaka, Jeffrey J (Jeff)** — Baseball Player
1481 Norview Dr, Clinton OH 44216, USA

**Tabaksblat, Morris** — Businessman
Reed Elsevier, Sara Burgerhartstr 25, 1055 Amsterdam KV, Netherlands

**Tabaracci, Rick** — Ice Hockey Player
PO Box 982001, Park City UT 84098, USA

**Tabata, Maki** — Speed Skater
Skating Federation, 1-1-1 Jinnan, #414, Shibuyaku, Tokyo 150 8050, Japan

**Tabin, Clifford S** — Geneticist, Molecular Biologist
Harvard Medical School, 240 Longwood Ave, Boston MA 02115, USA

**Tabitha 'Masentle** — Princess, Lesotho
Royal Palace, PO Box 524, Maseru, Lesotho

**Tabler, Patrick S (Pat)** — Baseball Player
8715 Blome Road, Cincinnati OH 45243, USA

**Taboo** — Rap Artist (Elephunk, Black Eyed Peas)
Paradigm Agency, 404 W Franklin St, Monterey CA 93940 USA

**Tabor, June** — Singer
Headline Agency, 39 Churchffields, Milltown, Dublin 14, Ireland

**Tabor, Philip M (Phil)** — Football Player
519 E Harrison Ave, Wheaton IL 60187, USA

**Tabora, Roy Gonzalez** — Artist
Tabora Gallery, 2005 Kalia Road, Honolulu HI 96815, USA

**Tabori, Kristoffer** — Actor
International Artistes, 235 Regent St, London W1R 8AX, England

**Tabori, Laszlo** — Track Athlete
2221 W Olive Ave, Burbank CA 91506, USA

**Tacha, Deanell R** — Judge
US Court of Appeals, 4830 W 15th St, Lawrence KS 66049, USA

**Tadic, Boris** — President, Serbia
President's Office, Nemanjina 11, 11000 Belgrade, Serbia

**Taff, Russ** — Singer
Glickman Entertainment Group, PO Box 570815, Tarzana CA 91357, USA

**Taffe, Jeff** — Ice Hockey Player
1455 Truax Circle, Hastings MN 55033, USA

**Tafoya, Joseph P (Joe)** — Football Player
14341 189th Way NE, Woodinville WA 98072, USA

**Tafoya, Michele** — Sportscaster
NBC-TV, Sports Dept, 30 Rockefeller Plaza, #270E, New York NY 10112 USA

**Taft, John** — Ice Hockey Player
5224 Oaklawn Ave, Minneapolis MN 55424, USA

**Taft, William H, IV** — Diplomat
Fried Frank Assoc, 1001 Pennsylvania Ave NW, #800, Washington DC 20004, USA

**Tagawa, Cary-Hiroyuki** — Actor
Abrams Artists, 9200 W Sunset Blvd, #1125, West Hollywood CA 90069 USA

**Tagg, Barclay** — Thoroughbred Racing Trainer
86 Geranium Ave, Floral Park NY 11001, USA

**Taghmaoui, Said** — Actor
Innovative Artists, 1505 10th St, Santa Monica CA 90401 USA

**Tagle, Luis Antonio G Cardinal** — Religious Leader
Archdiocese, 121 Arzobispo St, Intramuros, PO Box 132, 1099 Manila, Philippines

**Tagliabue, Paul J** — Football Executive
4149 Parkglen Court NW, Washington DC 20007, USA

**Taglianetti, Peter A** — Ice Hockey Player
PO Box 120, Lawrence PA 15055, USA

**Taglioni, Alice** — Actress
Agence Artiste Adequat, 108 Rue Reaumur, 75002 Paris, France

**Taguchi, So** — Baseball Player
12931 Twin Meadows Court, Saint Louis MO 63146, USA

**Tahir, Faran** — Actor
Greene Assoc, 1901 Ave of Stars, #130, Los Angeles CA 90067 USA

**Taillibert, Roger** — Architect
Agence Roger Taillibert, 163 Rue de la Pompe, 75116 Paris, France

**Taillibert, Roger R** — Architect
163 Rue de la Pompe, 75116 Paris, France

**Taimak** — Actor
Media Artists Group, 8222 Melrose Ave, #203, Los Angeles CA 90048 USA

**Tait, John B** — Football Player
3408 Echo Springs Road, Lafayette CA 94549, USA

**Tait, Michael D** — Singer (DC Talk, Tait, Newsboys)
True Artist Mgmt, 227 3rd Ave N, Franklin TN 37064, USA

**Taittinger, Claude** — Businessman
9 Place Saint-Nicaise, BP 2741, 51061 Reims Cedex, France

**Tajbert, Vitali** — Boxer
Spotlight Boxing, Am Stadtrand 27, 22047 Hamburg, Germany

**Takac, Robby** — Bassist (Goo Goo Dolls)
Atlas/Third Rail Entertainment, 9200 W Sunset Blvd, West Hollywood CA 90069, USA

**Takacs, Tibor** — Director
A P A Talent & Literary Agency, 405 S Beverly Dr, #300, Beverly Hills CA 90212 USA

**Takacs-Nagy, Gabor** — Concert Violinist
Case Postale 186, 1245 Collonge-Bellerive, Switzerland

**Takagi, Toranosuke** — Auto Racing Driver
Nakajima Planning, 1-3-10 Higushi, Shivuyaku, Tokyo 150 0011, Japan

**Takahashi, Daisuke** — Figure Skater
Kansai University Skate Club, 3-3-35 Yamatecho, Suitashi, Osaka 564 8680 Japan

**Takahashi, Joseph S** — Neuroscientist
Northwestern University, Neurobiology Dept, 2153 Campus Dr, Evanston IL 60208, USA
**Takahashi, Naoko** — Track Athlete
Sekisui Chemical Co, 4-4-2 Nishitenma, Kitaku, Osaka 530 8565, Japan
**Takase, Megumi** — Soccer Player
Football Association, 3-10-15 Hongo, Bunkyoku, Tokyo 113 0033 Japan
**Takei, George** — Actor
Cole Kitchenn Personal Management, ROAR House, 46 Charlotte St, London W1T 2GS, England
**Takezawa, Kyoko** — Concert Violinist
Opus 3 Artists, 470 Park Ave S, #900N, New York NY 10016 USA
**Takko, Kari** — Ice Hockey Player
Dallas Stars, 2601 Ave of Stars, #100, Frisco TX 75034 USA
**Tal, Alona** — Actress
Innovative Artists, 1505 10th St, Santa Monica CA 90401 USA
**Tal, Shiraz** — Model
Women Mgmt, 199 Lafayette St, New York NY 10012, USA
**Talaba, Marian** — Opera Singer
I M G Artists, Hogarth Business Park, Chiswick, London W4 2TH, England
**Talafous, Dean** — Ice Hockey Player
2418 Foxglove Circle, Hudson WI 54016, USA
**Talagi, Toke T** — Premier, Niue
Premier's Office, PO Box 40, Alofi, Niue Island
**Talalay, Paul** — Pharmacologist
5512 Boxhill Lane, Baltimore MD 21210, USA
**Talalay, Rachel** — Director
A P A Talent & Literary Agency, 405 S Beverly Dr, #300, Beverly Hills CA 90212 USA
**Talamini, Robert G (Bob)** — Football Player
3577 Cave Creek Manor, Las Cruces NM 88011, USA
**Talancon, Ana Claudia** — Actress
Gold Levin, 8424-A Santa Monica Blvd, #706, Los Angeles CA 90069, USA
**Talat, Mehmet Ali** — President, Turkish Northern Cyprus
President's Office, Turkish North Cypress, Via Mersin 10, Lefkosa, Turkey
**Talavera, Tracee** — Gymnast
106 Mandala Court, Walnut Creek CA 94596, USA
**Talbert, David E** — Director, Producer, Writer
Brillstein Entertainment Partners, 9150 Wilshire Blvd, #350, Beverly Hills CA 90212 USA
**Talbert, Diron V** — Football Player
PO Box 388, Rosenberg TX 77471, USA
**Talbot, Don** — Swimming Coach
Sports Federation, 333 River Road, Vanier, Ottawa ON K1L 8B9, Canada
**Talbot, Frederick L (Fred)** — Baseball Player
7701 Lunceford Lane, Falls Church VA 22043, USA
**Talbot, Jena-Guy** — Ice Hockey Player
4248 Notre Dame Quest St, Trois-Rivieres QC G9A 4Z5, Canada
**Talbot, Maxime (Max)** — Ice Hockey Player
111 Bellevue Ave, Pittsburgh PA 15229, USA
**Talbot, Nita** — Actress
3420 Merrimac Road, Los Angeles CA 90049, USA
**Talbot, Stephen H** — Actor, Producer
University of California, Graduate Journalism School, Berkeley CA 94720, USA
**Talbot, Susan** — Actress
Media Artists Group, 8222 Melrose Ave, #203, Los Angeles CA 90048 USA
**Talbott, Michael** — Actor, Director
231A Tano Road, Santa Fe NM 87506, USA
**Talbott, N Strobridge (Strobe), III** — Journalist, Association Executive
Brookings Institution, 1775 Massachusetts Ave NW, Washington DC 20036, USA
**Talese, Gay** — Writer
154 E Atlantic Blvd, Ocean City NJ 08226, USA
**Tali, Anu** — Conductor
Tali Management, Kohtu 3, 10130 Tallinn, Estonia
**Taliaferro, George** — Football Player
2708 Olcott Blvd, Bloomington IN 47401, USA
**Taliaferro, Myron E (Mike)** — Football Player
7332 Oakbluff Dr, Dallas TX 75254, USA
**Tallas, Rob** — Ice Hockey Player
1884 Classic Dr, Coral Springs FL 33071, USA
**Tallet, Brian C** — Baseball Player
3167 McClendon Court, Baton Rouge LA 70810, USA
**Talley, Darryl V** — Football Player
7517 Clementine Way, Orlando FL 32819, USA
**Talley, Gary** — Singer, Guitarist (Box Tops)
Horizon Mgmt, PO Box 8770, Endwell NJ 13762, USA
**Talley, Joel E** — Vietnam War Air Force Hero
20 Lakeshore Dr, Shalimar FL 32579, USA
**Tallinder, Henrik** — Ice Hockey Player
Buffalo Sabres, 1 Seymour Knox Plaza, #1, Buffalo NY 14203 USA
**Tallman, Bob** — Rodeo Sportscaster
3401 Lone Star Road, Poolville TX 76487, USA
**Tallman, Patricia** — Actress
Innovative Artists, 1505 10th St, Santa Monica CA 90401 USA
**Tallman, Richard C** — Judge
US Court of Appeals, US Courthouse, 1010 5th Ave, Seattle WA 98104, USA
**Tallon, Dale** — Ice Hockey Player
1533 W Everett Road, Lake Forest IL 60045, USA
**Tally, Ted** — Writer
Creative Artists Agency, 2000 Ave of Stars, #100, Los Angeles CA 90067 USA
**Talon, Amelia** — Model
Playboy Promotions, 9346 Civic Center Dr, #200, Beverly Hills CA 90210 USA
**Talton, Marion L (Tim)** — Baseball Player
130 Hardy Talton Road, Pikeville NC 27863, USA
**Talwalkar, Abhijit Y** — Businessman
L S I Logic Corp, 1621 Barber Lane, Milpitas CA 95035, USA
**Tam, Jeffrey E (Jeff)** — Baseball Player
5255 Pina Vista Dr, Melbourne FL 32934, USA
**Tam, Vivienne** — Fashion Designer
550 Fashion Ave, #2000, New York NY 10018, USA

**Tamahori, Lee** — Director
W M E Entertainment, 9601 Wilshire Blvd, #300, Beverly Hills CA 90210 USA
**Tamaian, Ion** — Artist
Sibiu, Str Stadionului, 557260 Selimbar, Romania
**Tamargo, John F** — Baseball Player
19018 Fern Meadow Loop, Lutz FL 33558, USA
**Tamaro, Janet** — Producer, Writer
Creative Artists Agency, 2000 Ave of Stars, #100, Los Angeles CA 90067 USA
**Tamaryn** — Singer
Agency Group Ltd, 142 W 57th St, #600, New York NY 10019 USA
**Tamayo Mendez, Arnaldo** — Cosmonaut, Cuba
Calle 16, #504, C/5A y 7MA, Miramar, Ciudad Havana 11300, Cuba
**Tambellini, Roger** — Golfer
32513 N Scottsdale Road, #105, Scottsdale AZ 85266, USA
**Tambellini, Steve** — Ice Hockey Player
9 Laurel Place, Port Moody BC 33H 4N1, Canada
**Tambiah, Stanley J** — Anthropologist
Harvard University, Anthropology Dept, Cambridge MA 02138, USA
**Tamblyn, Amber** — Actress
United Talent Agency, U T A Plaza, 9336 Civic Center Dr, Beverly Hills CA 90210 USA
**Tamblyn, Russell I (Russ)** — Actor, Dancer
Hyler Mgmt, 20 Ocean Park Blvd, #25, Santa Monica CA 90405 USA
**Tambor, Jeffrey** — Actor
Burstein Co, 15304 W Sunset Blvd, #208, Pacific Palisades CA 90272 USA
**Tambosi, Fabiana** — Model
Way Model Mgmt, Av Rebucos 3642, Jardim Paulistano, Sao Paulo CEP 01457 30, Brazil
**Tamburello, Benjamin A (Ben), Jr** — Football Player
4385 Milner Road W, Birmingham AL 35242, USA
**Tamer, Chris** — Ice Hockey Player
4215 Cornwell Lane, Whitmore Lake MI 48189, USA
**Tamia** — Singer, Songwriter, Actress
Chris Smith Mgmt, 21 Camden St, #500, Toronto ON M5V 1V2, Canada
**Tamm, Ralph E** — Football Player
942 Lake Gulch Road, Castle Rock CO 80104, USA
**Tan Dun** — Composer
Columbia Artists Mgmt Inc, 5 Columbus Circle, 1790 Broadway, #1600, New York NY 10019 USA
**Tan, Amy R** — Writer
I C M Partners, 10250 Constellation Blvd, #900, Los Angeles CA 90067 USA
**Tan, Melvyn** — Concert Pianist
Valerie Barber Mgmt, 4 Winsley St, #305, London W1N 7AR, England
**Tanabe, David** — Ice Hockey Player
2321 Fieldstone Curve, Saint Paul MN 55129, USA
**Tanaka, Asuna** — Soccer Player
Football Association, 3-10-15 Hongo, Bunkyoku, Tokyo 113 0033 Japan
**Tanaka, Koichi** — Nobel Chemistry Laureate
Shimadzu Corp, 1 Nishinokyo-Kuwabaracho, Nakagoku, Kyoto 604 8511, Japan
**Tanaka, Masahiro** — Baseball Player
New York Yankees, Yankee Stadium, E 161st St & River Ave, Bronx NY 10451 USA
**Tanaka, Shoji** — Physicist
Superconductivity Laboratory, 1-10-13 Shinonome, Kotoku, Tokyo 135 0062, Japan
**Tanana, Frank D** — Baseball Player
28492 S Harwich Dr, Farmington Hills MI 48334, USA
**Tancill, Chris** — Ice Hockey Player
14 Kingswood Circle, Verona WI 53593, USA
**Tancredi, Melissa P J** — Soccer Player
Canadian Soccer, Place Soccer Canada, 237 Metcalfe St, Ottawa ON K2P 1R2, Canada
**Tandja, Mamadou** — President, Niger
President's Office, State House, Aso Villa, Abuja, Niger
**Tanen, Sloane** — Writer
Bloomsbury Publishing, 50 Bedford Square, London WC1B 3DP, England
**Tanenbaum, Robert K** — Writer
Robert K Tanenbaum Law Offices, 708 N Roxbury Dr, Beverly Hills CA 90210, USA
**Tang Fei** — Prime Minister, Taiwan
Kuomintang, 11 Chang Shan South Road, Taipei 100, Taiwan
**Tang Wei** — Actress
Creative Artists Agency, 2000 Ave of Stars, #100, Los Angeles CA 90067 USA
**Tang, David** — Fashion Designer
Shanghai Tang, 148 Connaught Road Central, #2300, Hong Kong, China
**Tang, Muhai** — Conductor
I M G Artists, Hogarth Business Park, Chiswick, London W4 2TH, England
**Tanguay, Alex** — Ice Hockey Player
78 Jackson St, #1, Denver CO 80206, USA
**Tani, Daniel M** — Astronaut
PO Box 1453, Great Falls VA 22066, USA
**Taniguchi, Tadatsugu** — Molecular Biologist
University of Tokyo Medical Center, 7-3-1, Hongo, Bunkyoku, Tokyo 113 0033 Japan
**Tank** — Singer, Songwriter
J L Entertainment, 511 Ave of Americas, #230, New York NY 10011, USA
**Tankersley, Taylor M** — Baseball Player
853 Chartier Court, Asheboro NC 27205, USA
**Tankian, Serj** — Singer, Musician (System of a Down)
Velvet Hammer Music, 9014 Melrose Ave, West Hollywood CA 90069, USA
**Tanksley, Rick** — Singer
Teerajay Music, PO Box 183, White House TN 37188, USA
**Tanksley, Steven D** — Plant Geneticist
Cornell University, Plant Genetics Dept, Emerson Hall, Ithaca NY 14853, USA
**Tannahill, Don** — Ice Hockey Player
10113 Lakeview Dr, Rancho Mirage CA 92270, USA
**Tannehill, Ryan T** — Football Player
Miami Dolphins, 7500 SW 30th St, Davie FL 33314 USA
**Tannen, Deborah F** — Writer
Georgetown University, Linguistics Dept, Washington DC 20057, USA
**Tannen, Steven O (Steve)** — Football Player
735 N Niagara St, Burbank CA 91505, USA
**Tannenwald, Theodore, Jr** — Judge
US Tax Court, 400 2nd St NW, Washington DC 20217, USA

**Tanner, Alain** — Director
Chemin Point-du-Jour 12, 1202 Geneva, Switzerland
**Tanner, Antwon** — Actor
TalentWorks, 3500 W Olive Ave, #1400, Burbank CA 91505 USA
**Tanner, Barron K** — Football Player
7556 W Oregon Ave, Glendale AZ 85303, USA
**Tanner, Bruce M** — Baseball Player
324 Hearthstone Dr, New Castle PA 16105, USA
**Tanner, John P** — Ice Hockey Player
Hewlett Packard, 5150 Spectrum Way, Mississauga ON L4W 5G1, Canada
**Tanner, John S** — Representative, TN
Prime Policy Group LLP, 1110 Vermont Ave NW, #1000, Washington DC 20005, USA
**Tanner, Joseph R (Joe)** — Astronaut
800 Nelson Park Lane, Longmont CO 80503, USA
**Tanner, Roscoe** — Tennis Player
1109 Gnome Trail, Lookout Mountain TN 37350, USA
**Tannous, Afif I** — Government Official
6912 Oak Court, Annandale VA 22003, USA
**Tanon Ortiz, Olga T** — Singer, Composer
Universal Attractions, 135 W 26th St, #1200, New York NY 10001 USA
**Tanovic, Danis** — Director, Writer, Composer
Creative Artists Agency, 2000 Ave of Stars, #100, Los Angeles CA 90067 USA
**Tanti, Tony** — Ice Hockey Player
Tanti Interiors, 121-2323 Boundray Road, Vancouver BC V5M 4V8, Canada
**Tanuja** — Actress
14 Usha Kiran 15, M L Dhahanukar Marg, Mumbai MS 400026, India
**Tanuvasa, Maa J** — Football Player
PO Box 893309, Mililani HI 96789, USA
**Tanzi, Vito** — Economist
5912 Walhondine Road, Bethesda MD 20816, USA
**Tao, Conrad** — Concert Pianist
I M G Artists, Hogarth Business Park, Chiswick, London W4 2TH, England
**Tao, Terence** — Mathematician
University of California, Mathematics Dept, Los Angeles CA 90024, USA
**Taormina, Sheila** — Swimmer, Triathlete
172 Nautica Mile Dr, Clermont FL 34711, USA
**Tapani, Kevin R** — Baseball Player
781 Ferndale Road N, Wayzata MN 55391, USA
**Tape, Gerald F** — Physicist
90 Camino Espejo, Santa Fe NM 87507, USA
**Taplitz, Daniel** — Director
United Talent Agency, U T A Plaza, 9336 Civic Center Dr, Beverly Hills CA 90210 USA
**Tapp, Darryl A** — Football Player
203 Catalpa Court, Suffolk VA 23435, USA
**Tapper, Zoe** — Actress
Independent Talent Group, 40 Whitfield St, London W1T 2RH, England
**Tapping, Amanda** — Actress, Producer, Director
Play Mgmt, 220-807 Powell St, Vancouver BC V6A 1H7, Canada
**Tarabay, Nick E** — Actor
Medavoy Mgmt, 10203 Santa Monica Blvd, #400, Los Angeles CA 90067, USA
**Tarand, Andres** — Prime Minister
Riigikogu, Lossi Plats 1A, Tallinn 10130, Estonia
**Tarantino, Quentin** — Director
W M E Entertainment, 9601 Wilshire Blvd, #300, Beverly Hills CA 90210 USA
**Taranu, Cornel** — Composer, Conductor
Gh Dima Music Academy, IIC Bratianu Str 25, 3400 Cluj, Romania
**Tarasco, Anthony G (Tony)** — Baseball Player
3528 Maplewood Ave, Los Angeles CA 90066, USA
**Tarasova, Tatiana** — Figure Skating Coach
Connecticut Skating Center, 300 Alumni Road, Newington CT 06111, USA
**Tarasovic, George K** — Football Player
1503 Michael Dr, Pittsburgh PA 15227, USA
**Tarbuck, Jimmy (Tarby)** — Actor, Comedian
118 Beaufort St, London SW3 6BU, England
**Tardif, Marc** — Ice Hockey Player
Charlesbourg Toyota, 16070 Henri-Bourassa, Charlesbourg QC G1G 3Z8, Canada
**Tardio, Chris** — Actor
Framework Entertainment, 9057 Nemo St, #C, West Hollywood CA 90069 USA
**Tarelkin, Yevgeny I** — Cosmonaut
Cosmonaut Training Center, Star City, 141160 Zvezdny Gorodok, Moscow Oblast, Russia
**Tarjan, Robert E** — Mathematician
4 Constitution Hill E, Princeton NJ 08540, USA
**Tarkan** — Singer
International Creative Talent Agency, Mualim Cad 17, Orta Koy, 2007 Istanbul, Turkey
**Tarkanian, Jerry** — Basketball Coach
4767 Ocean Blvd, #1005, San Diego CA 92109, USA
**Tarkenton, Francis A (Fran)** — Football Player, Businessman
Tarkenton Co, 3340 Peachtree Road NE, #2570, Atlanta GA 30326, USA
**Tarpley, Roy J** — Basketball Player
819 Foxridge Dr, Arlington TX 76017, USA
**Tarr, Juraj** — Canoeing Athlete
Topolova 7, 94501 Komarno, Slovakia
**Tarses, Jamie** — Producer
W M E Entertainment, 9601 Wilshire Blvd, #300, Beverly Hills CA 90210 USA
**Tartabull Guzman, Jose M** — Baseball Player
1658 W 72nd St, Hialeah FL 33014, USA
**Tartabull Mora, Danilio (Danny)** — Baseball Player
27337 Garza Dr, Santa Clarita CA 91350, USA
**Tartaglia, Antonio** — Bobsled Athlete
Olympic Committee, Foro Italico, Largo Lauro de Bosis 15, 00135 Rome, Italy
**Tartakovsky, Genndy** — Producer, Director
W M E Entertainment, 9601 Wilshire Blvd, #300, Beverly Hills CA 90210 USA
**Tarter, Jill** — Astrophysicist
Seti Institute Research Center, 2035 Mountain View, Mountain View CA 94043, USA
**Tartt, Donna** — Writer
Rogers Coleridge White, 20 Powis Mews, London W11 1JN, England

**Tarver, Antonio D** — Boxer
4701 Rue Bordeaux, Lutz FL 33558, USA

**Tarzier, Carol** — Sculptor
1217 32nd St, Emeryville CA 94608, USA

**Tasby, Willie, Jr** — Baseball Player
1210 E Renfro St, Plant City FL 33563, USA

**Tash** — Rap Artist
Likwit Entertainment, PO Box 360713, Los Angeles CA 90036, USA

**Tashian, Barry** — Singer, Guitarist, Songwriter
Tashian Music, PO Box 150921, Nashville TN 37215, USA

**Tashima, A Wallace** — Judge
US Court of Appeals, 125 S Grand Ave, Pasadena CA 91105, USA

**Tasker, Steven J (Steve)** — Football Player, Sportscaster
16 Gypsy Lane, East Aurora NY 14052, USA

**Tatarek, Robert F (Bob)** — Football Player
5829 Southhall Road, Birmingham AL 35213, USA

**Tataryn, Dave** — Ice Hockey Player
27 Fairway Court, Horseshoe Valley ON L0K 1N0, Canada

**Tataurangi, Phillip M (Phil)** — Golfer
PO Box 15325, Irvine CA 92623, USA

**Tate, Bruce** — Singer (Penguins)
David Harris Enterprises, 24210 E Fork Road, #9, Azusa CA 91702, USA

**Tate, Catherine** — Actress
United Talent Agency, U T A Plaza, 9336 Civic Center Dr, Beverly Hills CA 90210 USA

**Tate, David F** — Football Player
3481 S Blackhawk Way, Aurora CO 80014, USA

**Tate, Frank** — Boxer
9560 Deering Dr, #18, Houston TX 77036, USA

**Tate, Geoffrey W (Geoff)** — Singer (Queensryche), Songwriter
Monterey International, 200 W Superior St, #202, Chicago IL 60654 USA

**Tate, Grady** — Jazz Drummer, Singer
Abby Hoffer Enterprises, 223 1/2 E 48th St, New York NY 10017 USA

**Tate, James V** — Writer
PO Box 9668, North Amherst MA 01059, USA

**Tate, Jeffrey P** — Conductor
Columbia Artists Mgmt Inc, 5 Columbus Circle, 1790 Broadway, #1600, New York NY 10019 USA

**Tate, Larenz** — Actor
A P A Talent & Literary Agency, 405 S Beverly Dr, #300, Beverly Hills CA 90212 USA

**Tate, Randy** — Religious Leader, Representative, WA
Christian Coalition, 100 Centerville Turnpike, Virginia Beach VA 23463, USA

**Tate, Stuart D (Stu)** — Baseball Player
695 Liberty Hill Road, Toney AL 35773, USA

**Tatel, David S** — Judge
US Court of Appeals, 333 Constitution Ave NW, #4400, Washington DC 20001, USA

**Tatham, Chuck** — Actor, Writer
Collective, 8383 Wilshire Blvd, #1050, Beverly Hills CA 90211 USA

**Tatopolous, Patrick** — Special Effects Director
I C M Partners, 10250 Constellation Blvd, #900, Los Angeles CA 90067 USA

**Tattersall, David** — Cinematographer
Lucasfilm, PO Box 2459, San Rafael CA 94912, USA

**Tatulli, Mark** — Cartoonist (Heart of the City)
Universal Press Syndicate, 4520 Main St, #700, Kansas City MO 64111 USA

**Tatum, Bradford** — Actor, Director, Writer
B R S/Gage Talent, 5757 Wilshire Blvd, #659, Los Angeles CA 90036, USA

**Tatum, Channing** — Actor, Model
Management 360, 9111 Wilshire Blvd, Beverly Hills CA 90210 USA

**Tatum, Kenneth R (Ken)** — Baseball Player
19 Oakdale Dr, Montevallo AL 35115, USA

**Tatum, W Earl** — Basketball Player
7916 W Heather Ave, Milwaukee WI 53223, USA

**Tatupu, M Mea'alofa (Lofa)** — Football Player
PO Box 1053, Bellevue WA 98009, USA

**Taubensee, Edward K (Eddie)** — Baseball Player
2582 S Maguire Road, #287, Ocoee FL 34761, USA

**Taubman, A Alfred** — Businessman
Taubman Co, 200 E Long Lake Road, #300, Bloomfield Hills MI 48304, USA

**Taubman, Anatole** — Actor
United Agents, 12-26 Lexington St, London W1F 0LE, England

**Taubman, Anatole** — Actor, Producer
Agentur Charade Kunstler, Joseph-Hayden-Str 1, 10557 Berlin, Germany

**Taubman, William** — Writer
Amherst College, Political Science Dept, Amherst MA 01002, USA

**Taupin, Bernie** — Singer, Songwriter
2905 Roundup Road, Santa Ynez CA 93460, USA

**Tauran, Jean-Louis Cardinal** — Religious Leader
Palazzo Apostolico, 00120 Vatican City

**Taurasi, Diana** — Basketball Player
Phoenix Mercury, American West Arena, 201 E Jefferson St, Phoenix AZ 85004 USA

**Tauriello, Dena** — Drummer (Antigone Rising)
W Mgmt, 266 Elizabeth St, #1A, New York NY 10012, USA

**Tausch, Terry W** — Football Player
2804 Ryder Court, Plano TX 75093, USA

**Tauscher, Hansjorg** — Alpine Skier
Schwand 7, 87561 Oberstdorf, Germany

**Tauscher, Mark G** — Football Player
2964 Nessie Lane, Sun Prairie WI 53590, USA

**Taussig, Donald F (Don)** — Baseball Player
1111 Ocean Dunes Circle, Jupiter FL 33477, USA

**Tautolo, Terry L** — Football Player
5713 E Huntdale St, Long Beach CA 90808, USA

**Tautou, Audrey** — Actress
Artmedia, 20 Ave Rapp, 75007 Paris, France

**Tauziat, Nathalie** — Tennis Player
Federation de Tennis, 1 Ave Gordon Bennett, 75016 Paris, France

**Tauzin, Wilbert J (Billy)** — Association Official; Representative, LA
Pharmaceutical Research, 1100 15th St NW, #900, Washington DC 20005, USA

**Tavare, Jay**
Paul Greenstone, 3008 Sorrelwood Dr, San Ramon CA 94582, USA — Actor

**Tavares, John**
New York Islanders, 1255 Hempstead Turnpike, Uniondale NY 11553 USA — Ice Hockey Player

**Tavares, John**
Buffalo Bandits, H S B C Arena, 1 Knox Place, Buffalo NY 14216, USA — Lacrosse Player

**Tavares, Sara**
Columbia Artists Mgmt Inc, 5 Columbus Circle, 1790 Broadway, #1600, New York NY 10019 USA — Singer, Songwriter

**Tavarez Carmen, Julian**
1108 Fireside Trail, Broadview Heights OH 44147, USA — Baseball Player

**Taverner, Sonia**
PO Box 2039, Stony Plain AB T7Z 1X6, Canada — Ballerina

**Tavernier, Bertrand R M**
I C M Partners, Marlborough House, 10 Earlham St, #300, London WC2H 9LNP, England — Director

**Tawan, Serria**
Playboy Promotions, 9346 Civic Center Dr, #200, Beverly Hills CA 90210 USA — Model

**Taye, John**
1412 E Jefferson St, Boise ID 83712, USA — Sculptor

**Taylor, Aaron**
278 Black Amber Way, Brentwood CA 94513, USA — Football Player

**Taylor, Alan**
Knopf Publishers, 1745 Broadway, New York NY 10019 USA — Historian

**Taylor, Andy**
D D Productions, 93A Westbourne Park Villas, London W2 5ED, England — Guitarist (Duran Duran)

**Taylor, Angel**
A2 Mgmt, 2336 W Belmont Ave, Chicago IL 60618, USA — Singer, Songwriter

**Taylor, Angelo F**
Vector Sports Mgmt, 417 Keller Parkway, Keller TX 76248, USA — Track Athlete

**Taylor, Anna Diggs**
US District Court, US Courthouse, 231 W Lafayette Blvd, #827, Detroit MI 48226, USA — Judge

**Taylor, Anthony P**
5300 Parkview Dr, #1093, Lake Oswego OR 97035, USA — Basketball Player

**Taylor, Antonio (Tony)**
8415 NW 165th Terrace, Hialeah FL 33016, USA — Baseball Player

**Taylor, April**
Thompson Entertainment Group, 1300 Division St, #207, Nashville TN 37203, USA — Singer

**Taylor, Ben**
W M E Entertainment, 9601 Wilshire Blvd, #300, Beverly Hills CA 90210 USA — Singer, Songwriter

**Taylor, Benedict**
Rhubarb, 1a Devonshire Road, Chiswick, London W4 2EU, England — Actor

**Taylor, Bobby (Chief)**
3912 Americana Dr, Tampa FL 33634, USA — Ice Hockey Player

**Taylor, Brian**
United Talent Agency, U T A Plaza, 9336 Civic Center Dr, Beverly Hills CA 90210 USA — Director, Writer

**Taylor, Brian D**
3622 Green Vista Dr, Encino CA 91436, USA — Basketball Player

**Taylor, Bruce B**
8 Highland Park Road, Rutland MA 01543, USA — Baseball Player

**Taylor, Bruce L**
10324 Pontofino Circle, Trinity FL 34655, USA — Football Player

**Taylor, Buck**
Linda McAlister Talent, 30 N Raymond, #409, Pasadena CA 91103, USA — Actor

**Taylor, Cecil P**
Abby Hoffer Enterprises, 223 1/2 E 48th St, New York NY 10017 USA — Jazz Pianist, Composer

**Taylor, Charles**
6603 Jeanne Mance, Montreal QC H2V 4LI, Canada — Philosopher, Templeton Religion Laureate

**Taylor, Charles G (Chuck)**
1535 Georgetown Lane, Murfreesboro TN 37129, USA — Baseball Player

**Taylor, Charles R (Charley)**
12032 Canter Lane, Reston VA 20191, USA — Football Player, Executive

**Taylor, Chester L**
29006 Burning Tree Lane, Romulus MI 48174, USA — Football Player

**Taylor, Christian**
3700 SW 27th St, #1B, Gainesville FL 32608, USA — Track Athlete

**Taylor, Christian M**
Creative Artists Agency, 2000 Ave of Stars, #100, Los Angeles CA 90067 USA — Producer, Director, Writer

**Taylor, Christine**
United Talent Agency, U T A Plaza, 9336 Civic Center Dr, Beverly Hills CA 90210 USA — Actress

**Taylor, Christy**
10990 Massachusetts Ave, #3, Los Angeles CA 90024, USA — Actress

**Taylor, Daren**
Island Def Jam Records, 8920 W Sunset Blvd, #200, West Hollywood CA 90069 USA — Drummer (Airborne Toxic Event)

**Taylor, Dave**
Dallas Stars, 2601 Ave of Stars, #100, Frisco TX 75034 USA — Ice Hockey Player, Executive

**Taylor, David M**
82 Manchester St, Glen Rock PA 17327, USA — Football Player

**Taylor, Doris A**
University of Minnesota Medical School, Stem Cell Dept, Minneapolis MN 55455, USA — Cardiovascular Repair Researcher

**Taylor, Dwight B**
5163 Queen Mary Lane, Jackson MS 39209, USA — Baseball Player

**Taylor, Dylan**
Thruline Entertainment, 9250 Wilshire Blvd, #100, Beverly Hills CA 90212 USA — Actor

**Taylor, Edwin W**
University of Chicago, Biophysics Dept, 920 E 58th St, Chicago IL 60637, USA — Biophysicist, Molecular Geneticist

**Taylor, Eric**
Virgin Records, 338 N Foothill Road, Beverly Hills CA 90210 USA — Bassist (Saving Abel)

**Taylor, Everett E (Ed)**
2901 Clarke Road, Memphis TN 38115, USA — Football Player

**Taylor, Femi**
Coolwaters Productions, 10061 Riverside Dr, Box 531, Toluca Lake CA 91602 USA — Actress, Dancer

**Taylor, Finn**
Creative Artists Agency, 2000 Ave of Stars, #100, Los Angeles CA 90067 USA — Director, Writer, Actor

**Taylor, Frederick**
Jane Turnbull Agency, 58 Elgin Crescent, London W11 2JJ, England — Writer

**Taylor, Gwendoline**
Auckland Actors, P O Box 56460, Dominion Road, Auckland 1446, New Zealand — Actress

| | |
|---|---|
| **Taylor, Harry E**<br>2125 Cooks Lane, Fort Worth TX 76120, USA | Baseball Player |
| **Taylor, Henry S**<br>1120 Aqua Vista Dr NW, Gig Harbor WA 98335, USA | Writer |
| **Taylor, Holland**<br>Gersh Agency, 9465 Wilshire Blvd, #600, Beverly Hills CA 90212 USA | Actress |
| **Taylor, Ivan (Ike)**<br>4206 Lenox Oval, Pittsburgh PA 15237, USA | Football Player |
| **Taylor, J Herbert**<br>110 Wood Road, #H210, Los Gatos CA 95030, USA | Botanist |
| **Taylor, James**<br>Kunstler Sekretariat am Gasteig, Rosenheimer Str 52, 81669 Munich, Germany | Opera Singer |
| **Taylor, James**<br>2238 Dundas St W, PO Box 59039, Toronto ON, M6R 3B5, Canada | Singer, Songwriter |
| **Taylor, James (J T)**<br>Brothers Management Assoc, 141 Dunbar Ave, Fords NJ 08863 USA | Singer (Kool & the Gang) |
| **Taylor, James A**<br>PO Box 284, Trinity Center CA 96091, USA | Vietnam War Army Hero (CMH) |
| **Taylor, James Arnold**<br>19360 Rinaldi St, #501, Porter Ranch CA 91326, USA | Actor |
| **Taylor, James C (Jim)**<br>7840 Walden Road, Baton Rouge LA 70808, USA | Football Player |
| **Taylor, Jason P**<br>2980 Paddock Road, Weston FL 33331, USA | Football Player |
| **Taylor, Jennifer B**<br>Stone Meyer Genow, 9665 Wilshire Blvd, #510, Beverly Hills CA 90212 USA | Model, Actress |
| **Taylor, Jermaine**<br>PO Box 3456, Little Rock AR 72203, USA | Boxer |
| **Taylor, Jill**<br>Playboy Promotions, 9346 Civic Center Dr, #200, Beverly Hills CA 90210 USA | Model |
| **Taylor, Jill Bolte**<br>University of Indiana Medical School, Neuroanatomy Dept, Bloomington IN 47405, USA | Neuroanatomist |
| **Taylor, Jim**<br>Ad Hominem Enterprises, 506 Santa Monica Blvd, #400, Santa Monica CA 90401, USA | Producer |
| **Taylor, John**<br>D D Productions, 93A Westbourne Park Villas, London W2 5ED, England | Bassist (Duran Duran) |
| **Taylor, John G**<br>PO Box 326, Fresno CA 93708, USA | Football Player |
| **Taylor, Jonathan**<br>I C M Partners, 10250 Constellation Blvd, #900, Los Angeles CA 90067 USA | Producer, Director |
| **Taylor, Joseph H, Jr**<br>272 Hartley St, Princeton NJ 08540, USA | Nobel Physics Laureate |
| **Taylor, Kathleen**<br>Four Seasons Hotels, 1165 Leslie St, Toronto ON M3C 2K8, Canada | Businesswoman |
| **Taylor, Kitrick L**<br>25975 Hacienda Court, Moreno Valley CA 92551, USA | Football Player |
| **Taylor, Lawrence J**<br>5796 Devon St, Port Orange FL 32127, USA | Football Player |
| **Taylor, Lili**<br>A P A Talent & Literary Agency, 405 S Beverly Dr, #300, Beverly Hills CA 90212 USA | Actress |
| **Taylor, Lionel**<br>201 Pinnacle Dr SE, #3614, Rio Rancho NM 87124, USA | Football Player, Coach |
| **Taylor, Livingston**<br>11806 N 56th St, Tampa FL 33617 USA | Singer, Songwriter |
| **Taylor, Louise**<br>Producers Inc, Signature Sounds, PO Box 106, Whately MA 01093, USA | Singer, Songwriter |
| **Taylor, Marianne**<br>Harve Bennett Productions, PO Box 825, Culver City CA 90232, USA | Actress |
| **Taylor, Mark C**<br>Cyclone Taylor Hockey, 10386 Nordel Court, Delta BC V4G 1J7, Canada | Ice Hockey Player |
| **Taylor, Mark L**<br>S D B Partners, 315 S Beverly Dr, #411, Beverly Hills CA 90067 USA | Actor |
| **Taylor, Martin**<br>P3 Music, Seabraes, 2 Perth Road, Dundee DD1 4LA, Scotand | Jazz Guitarist |
| **Taylor, Meldrick**<br>2917 N 4th St, Philadelphia PA 19133, USA | Boxer |
| **Taylor, Mick**<br>Jacobson & Colin, 60 Madison Ave, #1026, New York NY 10010, USA | Guitarist (Rolling Stones) |
| **Taylor, Nicole R (Niki)**<br>Actors Clearinghouse, 501 N IH-35, Austin TX 78702, USA | Model, Actress |
| **Taylor, Noah**<br>Linsten Morris Mgmt, 3 Gladstone St, #301, Newtown NSW 2042, Australia | Actor |
| **Taylor, Otis**<br>Conqueroo, 11271 Ventura Blvd, #522, Studio City CA 91604 USA | Singer, Musician |
| **Taylor, Otis, Jr**<br>6608 Woodson Road, Raytown MO 64133, USA | Football Player |
| **Taylor, Paul B**<br>Paul Taylor Dance Co, 551 Grand St, Lobby A, New York NY 10002, USA | Dancer, Choreographer |
| **Taylor, Penny**<br>Phoenix Mercury, American West Arena, 201 E Jefferson St, Phoenix AZ 85004 USA | Basketball Player |
| **Taylor, R Scott**<br>925 Indian Bridge Lane, Defiance OH 43512, USA | Baseball Player |
| **Taylor, Rachael**<br>Marquee Mgmt, Gate House, 188 Oxford St, Paddington NSW 2021, Australia | Actress |
| **Taylor, Reggie**<br>828 Havird St, Newberry SC 29108, USA | Baseball Player |
| **Taylor, Regina**<br>Innovative Artists, 1505 10th St, Santa Monica CA 90401 USA | Actress |
| **Taylor, Renee**<br>B R S / Gage Talent Agency, 5757 Wilshire Blvd, #659, Los Angeles CA 90036 USA | Actress |
| **Taylor, Richard C (Dick)**<br>Talent Consultants International, 105 Shad Row, #B, Piermont NY 10968 USA | Guitarist (Pretty Things) |
| **Taylor, Richard E**<br>757 Mayfield Ave, Stanford CA 94305, USA | Nobel Physics Laureate |
| **Taylor, Richard L**<br>Weta Workshop, PO Box 15208, Miramar, Wellington, New Zealand | Costume & Special Effects Designer |

**Taylor, Rip** — Actor, Comedian
1133 N Clark Dr, Los Angeles CA 90035, USA

**Taylor, Robert** — Actor
Marquee Mgmt, The Gatehouse, 188 Oxford St, #B, Paddington NSW 2021, Australia

**Taylor, Robert D (Hawk)** — Baseball Player
136 Skyway Dr, Murray KY 42071, USA

**Taylor, Robert E (Rob)** — Football Player
1820 Rebecca Road, Lutz FL 33548, USA

**Taylor, Robert L (Bob)** — Baseball Player
27 Sunnybrook Road, Springfield MA 01119, USA

**Taylor, Robert W** — Computer Engineer
1 Stadler Dr, Woodside CA 94062, USA

**Taylor, Rod** — Actor
Contemporary Artists, 610 Santa Monica Blvd, #202, Santa Monica CA 90401 USA

**Taylor, Roger** — Tennis Player
Salterswell Farm, Moreton-in-the-Marsh, Gloucester GL53 7HN, England

**Taylor, Roger A** — Drummer (Duran Duran)
D D Productions, 93A Westbourne Park Villas, London W2 5ED, England

**Taylor, Roger M** — Drummer (Queen)
Neal Levin, 15260 Ventura Blvd, #1700, Sherman Oaks CA 91403, USA

**Taylor, Roland M (Fatty)** — Basketball Player
3812 Homewood Ave, Ashtabula OH 44004, USA

**Taylor, Ronald W (Ron)** — Baseball Player
19 Alvin Ave, Toronto ON M4T 2A7, Canada

**Taylor, Roosevelt (Rosey)** — Football Player
7331 Ebbtide Dr, New Orleans LA 70126, USA

**Taylor, Samuel D (Sammy)** — Baseball Player
PO Box 152, Woodruff SC 29388, USA

**Taylor, Sandra** — Actress, Model
I P A Network, 231 E Alessandro Blvd, #A355, Riverside CA 92508, USA

**Taylor, Shane** — Actor
Emptage Hallett, 14 Rathbone Place, London W1T 1HT, England

**Taylor, Tamara** — Actress
Greene Assoc, 1901 Ave of Stars, #130, Los Angeles CA 90067 USA

**Taylor, Tate** — Actor, Director
W M E Entertainment, 9601 Wilshire Blvd, #300, Beverly Hills CA 90210 USA

**Taylor, Ted** — Ice Hockey Player
PO Box 244, Oak Lake MB R0M 1P0, Canada

**Taylor, Teresa** — Drummer (Butthole Surfers)
Kork Agency, 1880 Century Park E, #711, Los Angeles CA 90067, USA

**Taylor, Terry D** — Baseball Player
743 W Walnut Ave, Crestview FL 32536, USA

**Taylor, Teyana** — Rap Artist
Star Trak/Interscope Records, 2220 Colorado Ave, Santa Monica CA 90404, USA

**Taylor, Tiffany** — Model, Actress
PO Box 4511, West Hills CA 91308, USA

**Taylor, Tim** — Ice Hockey Player
9119 Woodridge Run Dr, Tampa FL 33647, USA

**Taylor, Travis L** — Football Player
13114 Tom Morris Dr, Jacksonville FL 32224, USA

**Taylor, Vanessa** — Actress, Model
Management 360, 9111 Wilshire Blvd, Beverly Hills CA 90210 USA

**Taylor, Vaughn** — Golfer
2536 Queens Court, Grovetown GA 30813, USA

**Taylor, William H (Billy)** — Baseball Player
201 Washington Place, Thomasville GA 31792, USA

**Taylor, William M (Bill)** — Baseball Player
PO Box 146, Acton CA 93510, USA

**Taylor, William T (Billy)** — Football Player
3 Greenwich Dr, #86, Jersey City NJ 07305, USA

**Taylor-Compton, Scout** — Actress
Gersh Agency, 9465 Wilshire Blvd, #600, Beverly Hills CA 90212 USA

**Taylor-Gordon, Hannah** — Actress
Independent Talent Group, 40 Whitfield St, London W1T 2RH, England

**Taylor-Johnson, Aaron** — Actor
Hamilton Hodell, 20 Golden Square, London W1F 9JL, England

**Taylor-Taylor, Courtney** — Singer, Guitarist (Dandy Warhols)
Monqui Records, PO Box 5908, Portland OR 97228, USA

**Taylor-Young, Leigh** — Actress
11300 W Olympic Blvd, #610, Los Angeles CA 90064, USA

**Taymor, Julie** — Director, Lyricist
Cinetic Mgmt, 555 W 25th St, #400, New York NY 10001 USA

**Tazel, Erica** — Actress
Management 360, 9111 Wilshire Blvd, Beverly Hills CA 90210 USA

**Tazoi, Jim Y** — WW II Army Hero
13360 N 600 W, Garland UT 84312, USA

**Tcherezov, Ivan Y** — Biathlete
Biathlon Union, Luzhnetskaja Nab 8, 119270 Moscow, Russia

**Tchongo Domingos, Salvador** — Government Official, Guinea-Bisseau
Assembleia Nacional Popular, Bisseau, Guinea-Bisseau

**Tchoudov, Maxim A** — Biathlete
Biathlon Union, Luzhnetskaja Nab 8, 119270 Moscow, Russia

**Te Kanawa, Kiri** — Opera Singer
Michael Storrs Music, 211 Piccadilly, London W1J 9HF, England

**Teacher, Brian D** — Tennis Player
Tennis Academy, Arroyo Seco Racquet Club, 920 Lohman Lane, South Pasadena CA 91030, USA

**Teachout, John** — Body Builder
3470 Sears Road, Horton MI 49246, USA

**Teaff, Grant G** — Football Coach, Executive
8265 Forest Ridge Dr, Waco TX 76712, USA

**Teagarden, Taylor H** — Baseball Player
2007 Blestem Lane, Carrollton TX 75007, USA

**Teagle, Terry M** — Basketball Player
2111 Heatherwood Dr, Missouri City TX 77489, USA

**Teague, Fred E (Trey), III** — Football Player
862 Ashport Road, Jackson TN 38305, USA

**Teague, George T** — Football Player
6561 Meadow Lark Dr, Montgomery AL 36116, USA

**Teague, Jeffrey D (Jeff)** — Basketball Player
Atlanta Hawks, Centennial Tower, 101 Marietta St NW, #1900, Atlanta GA 30303 USA

**Teague, Lewis** — Director
Gersh Agency, 9465 Wilshire Blvd, #600, Beverly Hills CA 90212 USA

**Teague, Marquis** — Basketball Player
Brooklyn Nets, 15 Metro Tech Center, #1100, Brooklyn NY 11201 USA

**Teague, Marshall** — Actor
Linda McAlister Talent, 30 N Raymond, #409, Pasadena CA 91103, USA

**Teahen, Mark T** — Baseball Player
8610 E Via Del Sol Dr, Scottsdale AZ 85255, USA

**Teal, Clare** — Singer
Agency Group Ltd, 142 W 57th St, #600, New York NY 10019 USA

**Teal, Willie, Jr** — Football Player
1322 Westchester Dr, Baton Rouge LA 70810, USA

**Teale, Owen** — Actor
Markham Froggatt Irwin, Julian House, 4 Windmill St, London W1P 1HF, England

**Teasley, Nikki** — Basketball Player
Tulsa Shock, B O K Center, 200 S Denver, Tulsa OK 74103 USA

**Teasley, Ronald (Ron)** — Baseball Player
19317 Coyle St, Detroit MI 48235, USA

**Tebbit of Chingford, Norman B** — Government Official, England
House of Lords, Westminster, London SW1A 0PW, England

**Tebow, Timothy R (Tim)** — Football Player
Creative Artists Agency, 2000 Ave of Stars, #100, Los Angeles CA 90067 USA

**Tech N9ne** — Rap Artist
Strange Music, PO Box 1114, Blue Springs MO 64013, USA

**Tedeschi, David** — Editor
Innovative Artists, 1505 10th St, Santa Monica CA 90401 USA

**Tedeschi, Susan** — Singer
S L Feldman Mgmt, 1505 W 2nd Ave, #200, Vancouver BC V6H 3Y4, Canada

**Tedford, Jeffrey R (Jeff)** — Football Coach
Green Bay Packers, 1265 Lombardi Ave, Green Bay WI 54304 USA

**Tee, Brian** — Actor
Bauman Redanty Shaul Agency, 5757 Wilshire Blvd, #473, Los Angeles CA 90036 USA

**Tee, Hayden** — Actor, Singer
Lambert House Enterprises, PO Box 226, Collaroy Beach NSW 2097, Australia

**Teegarden, Aimee** — Actress
Innovative Artists, 1505 10th St, Santa Monica CA 90401 USA

**Teevens, Eugene F (Buddy)** — Football Coach
Dartmouth College, Athletic Dept, Hanover NH 03755, USA

**Tefkin, Blair** — Actress, Singer, Songwriter
Bossyroots Records, 8033 W Sunset Blvd, #850, Los Angeles CA 90046, USA

**Teich, Malvin C** — Electrical Engineer
Boston University, Electrical & Computer Engineering Dept, Boston MA 02215, USA

**Teichman, Axel** — Cross Country Skier
Neue Str 8, 98559 Oberhof, Germany

**Teitel, Robert** — Actor, Producer
Creative Artists Agency, 2000 Ave of Stars, #100, Los Angeles CA 90067 USA

**Teitelbaum, Bill** — Cartoonist (Bottom Liners)
Tribune Media Services, 435 N Michigan Ave, #1500, Chicago IL 60611 USA

**Teitelbaum, Eric** — Cartoonist (Bottom Liners)
Tribune Media Services, 435 N Michigan Ave, #1500, Chicago IL 60611 USA

**Teitelbaum, Zalman** — Religious Leader, Rabbi
Satmar Hasidic, 87 Morton St, Brooklyn NY 11211, USA

**Teitell, Conrad L** — Attorney
Cummings & Lockwood, 6 Landmark Square, Stamford CT 06901, USA

**Teixeira, Mark C (Tex)** — Baseball Player
2220 King Fisher Dr, Westlake TX 76262, USA

**Tejada, Miguel O M** — Baseball Player
3013 NE 20th Court, Fort Lauderdale FL 33305, USA

**Tekulve, Kenton C (Kent)** — Baseball Player
1531 Sequoia Dr, Pittsburgh PA 15241, USA

**Tela** — Rap Artist
American Talent Agency, 26 Finney Farm Road, Croton on Hudson NY 10520, USA

**Telavi, Willy** — Prime Minister, Tuvalu
Prime Minister's Office, Vaiaku, Funafuti, Tuvalu

**Telfair, Sebastian** — Basketball Player
Toronto Raptors, Air Canada Center, 20 Bay St, Toronto ON M5J 2N8, Canada

**Telfer, Paul** — Actor
Don Buchwald Talent Agency, 6500 Wilshire Blvd, #2200, Los Angeles CA 90048 USA

**Telford, Anthony C** — Baseball Player
9109 Cypress Keep Lane, Odessa FL 33556, USA

**Telito, Filoimea** — Governor General, Tuvalu
Governor General's Office, Government House, Vaiaku, Funafuti, Tuvalu

**Tellefsen, Christopher** — Editor
Claire Best Assoc, 736 Seward St, Los Angeles CA 90038, USA

**Teller** — Comedian, Illusionist (Penn & Teller)
A P A Talent & Literary Agency, 405 S Beverly Dr, #300, Beverly Hills CA 90212 USA

**Teller, Juergen** — Photographer
1 Telford Road, London W10 5SH, England

**Teller, Miles** — Actor
Creative Artists Agency, 2000 Ave of Stars, #100, Los Angeles CA 90067 USA

**Tellmann, Thomas J (Tom)** — Baseball Player
1021 Yankee Bush Road, Warren PA 16365, USA

**Tellqvist, K Mikael** — Ice Hockey Player
7932 E Feathersong Lane, Scottsdale AZ 85255, USA

**Telnaes, Ann C** — Editorial Cartoonist
Tribune Media Services, 435 N Michigan Ave, #1500, Chicago IL 60611 USA

**Teltscher, Eliot** — Tennis Player, Coach
Pepperdine University, Athletic Dept, Malibu CA 90265, USA

**Teltscher, Kate** — Historian
Bloomsbury Publishing, 50 Bedford Square, London WC1B 3DP, England

**Telushkin, Joseph** — Religious Leader, Rabbi, Writer
Center for Learning & Leadership, 440 Park Ave S, #400, New York NY 10016, USA

**T**

**Temchen, Sybil** — Actress
Untitled Entertainment, 350 S Beverly Dr, #200, Beverly Hills CA 90212 USA

**Temerlin, J Liener** — Businessman
201 E John Carpenter Freeway, Irving TX 75062, USA

**Temesvari, Andrea** — Tennis Player
ProServe, 1101 Woodrow Wilson Blvd, #1800, Arlington VA 22209 USA

**Temirkanov, Yuri K** — Conductor
State Philharmonia, Mikhailovskaya 2, 191186 Saint Petersburg, Russia

**Tempesta, Orani Joao Cardinal** — Religious Leader
Archdiocese of Rio de Janeiro, Rua Benjamin Constant 23, 20241 150 Rio de Janeiro RJ, Brazil

**Temple, Collis** — Basketball Player
2614 Dalrymple Dr, Baton Rouge LA 70808, USA

**Temple, Juno V** — Actress
United Talent Agency, U T A Plaza, 9336 Civic Center Dr, Beverly Hills CA 90210 USA

**Temple, Peter** — Writer
Text Publishing, 22 William St, Melbourne VIC 3000, Australia

**Templeman, Simon** — Actor
A P A Talent & Literary Agency, 405 S Beverly Dr, #300, Beverly Hills CA 90212 USA

**Templeton, Ben** — Cartoonist (Motley's Crew)
Tribune Media Services, 2 Perry St, Cortlandt Manor NY 10567, USA

**Templeton, Garry L** — Baseball Player
13552 Del Poniente Road, Poway CA 92064, USA

**Tena, Natalia** — Actress
Curtis Brown Group, 28-29 Haymarket, #500, London SW1Y 4SP, England

**Tenace, F Gene** — Baseball Player, Manager
2650 Cliff Hawk Court, Redmond OR 97756, USA

**Tendulkar, Sachin R** — Cricketer
7 Uskakkal, Sahitya Sahawas Colony, Bandra East, Mumbai 400051, India

**Tenet, George J** — Government Official
Allen & Co, 711 5th Ave, New York NY 10022, USA

**Teng, Vienna** — Singer, Pianist, Songwriter
Deep South Entertainment, PO Box 17737, Raleigh NC 27619, USA

**Tenison, Renee** — Model, Actress
Tenison Group, 171 Pier Ave, #403, Santa Monica CA 90405, USA

**Tennant, Andy** — Director, Writer
Creative Artists Agency, 2000 Ave of Stars, #100, Los Angeles CA 90067 USA

**Tennant, David** — Actor, Director
Independent Talent Group, 40 Whitfield St, London W1T 2RH, England

**Tennant, Neil F** — Singer (Pet Shop Boys)
W M E Entertainment, 9601 Wilshire Blvd, #300, Beverly Hills CA 90210 USA

**Tennant, Scott** — Guitarist (LAGQ)
University of Southern California, Thornton Music School, Los Angeles CA 90089, USA

**Tennant, Stella** — Model
Select Model Mgmt, 17 Ferdinand St, London NW1 8EU, England

**Tennant, Veronica** — Ballerina
National Ballet of Canada, 157 King St E, Toronto ON M5C 1G9, Canada

**Tennant, Victoria** — Actress
Glick Agency, 347 5th Ave, #1404, New York NY 10016 USA

**Tenneson, Joyce** — Photographer
PO Box 228, Rockport ME 04856, USA

**Tenney, Jon** — Actor
L I N K Entertainment, 11872 La Grange Ave, Los Angeles CA 90025 USA

**Tennille, Toni** — Singer (Captain & Tennille)
1040 Sun Wood Dr, Las Vegas NV 89145, USA

**Tennison, Chalee** — Singer
Buddy Lee Attractions, 38 Music Square E, #300, Nashville TN 37203 USA

**Tensi, Stephen M (Steve)** — Football Player
300 Flannery Fork Road, Blowing Rock NC 28605, USA

**Tent, Kevin** — Editor
Eastern Talent Agency, 849 S Broadway, #811, Los Angeles CA 90014, USA

**Tenuta, Judy** — Actress, Comedienne
13504 Contour Dr, Sherman Oaks CA 91423, USA

**Tepedino, Frank R** — Baseball Player
2 Pear Court, Saint James NY 11780, USA

**Teplitzky, Jonathan** — Director
Cameron Creswell Agency, 61 Marlborough St, #700, Surry Hills NSW 2010, Australia

**Tequila, Tila** — Singer, Model
8033 Sunset Blvd, #1029, West Hollywood CA 90046, USA

**Teraoka, Masami** — Artist
41-048 Kaulu St, Waimanalo HI 96795, USA

**Terbenche, Paul F** — Ice Hockey Player
238 Victoria St N, Port Hope ON L1A 3N4, Canada

**Terborgh, John W** — Ecologist, Environmentalist
Duke University, Tropical Conservation Center, PO Box 90381, Durham NC 27708, USA

**Terebey, Susan** — Astronomer
California State University, Physics & Astronomy Dept, Los Angeles CA 90032, USA

**Terentieva, Nina N** — Opera Singer
Bolshoi Theater, Teatralnaya Pl 1, 103009 Moscow, Russia

**Tereshchenko, Sergei A** — Prime Minister, Kazakhstan
121-18 Kounaev Str, 480100 Almaty, Kazakhstan

**Tereshkova, Valentina V** — Cosmonaut
International Co-operation Association, Vozdvizhenka Str 14-18, 103885 Moscow, Russia

**Terfel Jones, Bryn** — Opera Singer
Harlequin Agency, 203 Fidlas Road, Cardiff CF4 5NA, Wales

**Tergesen, Lee** — Actor
Industry Entertainment, 955 Carillo Dr, #300, Los Angeles CA 90048 USA

**Terminator X** — Rap Artist (Public Enemy)
Brookes Co, 8223 Gulana Ave, Playa del Rey CA 90293, USA

**TerMors, Jorien** — Speed Skater
K N S B, Postbus 1120, 3800 Arnesfoort BC, Netherlands

**Ter-Petrossian, Levon A** — President, Armenia
Marshal Baghramian Prospect 19, 375016 Yerevan, Armenia

**Terra, Scott** — Actor
Abrams Artists, 9200 W Sunset Blvd, #1125, West Hollywood CA 90069 USA

**Terracciano, Anthony P** — Financier
S L M Corp, 12061 Bluemont Way, Reston VA 20190, USA

Temchen - Terracciano

**Terrace, Herbert S** — Anthropologist, Primatologist
17 Campfire Road, Chappaqua NY 10514, USA

**Terranova, Joe** — Singer (Danny and the Juniors)
Joe Taylor Artist Agency, 2802 Columbine Place, Nashville TN 37204 USA

**Terrasson, Jacques-Laurent (Jacky)** — Jazz Pianist
Joel Chriss Co, 300 Mercer St, #3J, New York NY 10003 USA

**Terrazas Sandoval, Julio Cardinal** — Religious Leader
Arzobispado, Casilla 25, Calle Ingavi 49, Santa Cruz de la Sierra, Bolivia

**Terrell, C Walter (Walt)** — Baseball Player
1304 Oxley Court, Union KY 41091, USA

**Terrell, David W (Dave)** — Football Player
43628 Cather Court, Ashburn VA 20147, USA

**Terrell, Ernie** — Boxer
11136 S Parnell, Chicago IL 60628, USA

**Terrell, Patrick C (Pat)** — Football Player
2490 Madrid Way S, Saint Petersburg FL 33712, USA

**Terreri, Christopher A (Chris)** — Ice Hockey Player
120 Lake Dr, Mountain Lakes NJ 07046, USA

**Terrile, Richard** — Astronomer
2121 E Woodlyn Road, Pasadena CA 91104, USA

**Terrio, Christopher (Chris)** — Writer
W M E Entertainment, 9601 Wilshire Blvd, #300, Beverly Hills CA 90210 USA

**Terrion, Greg** — Ice Hockey Player
Terrion Esso Service, PO Box 428, Marmoro ON K0K 2M0, Canada

**Terris, Malcolm** — Actor
14 England's Lane, London NW3, England

**Terry, Christopher A (Chris)** — Football Player
8209 Marshall Brae Dr, Raleigh NC 27616, USA

**Terry, Clark** — Jazz Trumpeter, Singer
4720 S Beech St, Pine Bluff AR 71603, USA

**Terry, Claude L** — Basketball Player
4437 E Palmdale Lane, Gilbert AZ 85298, USA

**Terry, James L** — Army General
Commanding General, US Army Central, 7115 S Boundary Blvd, MacDill Air Force Base FL 33621, USA

**Terry, Jason E** — Basketball Player
105 Kingston Minor NE, Atlanta GA 30342, USA

**Terry, John** — Actor
1 Mgmt, 9000 W Sunset Blvd, #1550, Los Angeles CA 90069 USA

**Terry, John** — Soccer Player
Chelsea F C, Stamford Bridge, Fulham Road, London SW6 1HS, England

**Terry, John Q** — Architect
Old Exchange, Dedham, Colchester, Essex CO7 6HA, England

**Terry, Megan D** — Writer
2309 Hanscom Blvd, Omaha NE 68105, USA

**Terry, Nigel** — Actor
PO Box 1116, Belfast BT2 7AJ, Northern Ireland

**Terry, Ralph W** — Baseball Player
801 Park St, Larned KS 67550, USA

**Terry, Randall A** — Social Activist
Operation Rescue National, PO Box 360221, Melbourne FL 32936, USA

**Terry, Ruth** — Singer, Actress
622 Hospitality Dr, Rancho Mirage CA 92270, USA

**Terry, Scott R** — Baseball Player
4943 Montford Dr, Saint Louis MO 63128, USA

**Terry, Tony** — Singer
Green Light Talent Agency, PO Box 3172, Beverly Hills CA 90212 USA

**Terwilliger, W Wayne** — Baseball Player
1909 Clear Creek Dr, Weatherford TX 76087, USA

**Terzic, Adnan** — Prime Minister, Bosnia & Herzegovina
Prime Minister's Office, Alipasina 1, 71000 Sarajevo, Bosnia & Herzegovina

**Terzopoulos, Dmitri** — Computer Scientist
University of California, Computer Science Dept, Los Angeles CA 90024, USA

**Tesh, John** — Composer, Pianist, Entertainer
TeshMedia Group, 13245 Riverside Dr, #305, Sherman Oaks CA 91423, USA

**Teske, Rachel** — Golfer
Gaylord Sports Mgmt, 13845 N Northsight Blvd, #200, Scottsdale AZ 85260 USA

**Tesori, Jeanine** — Composer
W M E Entertainment, 9601 Wilshire Blvd, #300, Beverly Hills CA 90210 USA

**Tessaro, Kathleen** — Writer
William Morrow, 1350 Ave of Americas, New York NY 10019, USA

**Tessier, John** — Opera Singer
I M G Artists, Hogarth Business Park, Chiswick, London W4 2TH, England

**Tessier, Orval** — Ice Hockey Player
411 McDonell Crescent, Cornwall ON K6H 5N7, Canada

**Tessier-Lavigne, Marc** — Neurobiologist
255 Selby Lane, Atherton CA 94027, USA

**Tessmer, Jay W** — Baseball Player
7861 Red Mahogany Road, Boynton Beach FL 33437, USA

**Testa, Franco** — Cyclist
Via Calvi 15, 32021 Mogliano, Italy

**Testa, Mary** — Actress, Singer
B R S / Gage Talent Agency, 1650 Broadway, #1410, New York NY 10019 USA

**Testa, Sylvio** — Photographer
Les Jardines du Golf, 06210 Mandelieu, Alpes Maritimes, France

**Testaverde, Vincent F (Vinny)** — Football Player
17122 Gunn Highway, Odessa FL 33556, USA

**Testi, Fabio** — Actor
Via Siacci 38, 00197 Rome, Italy

**Testino, Mario** — Photographer
Art Partner, 12 Oval Road, London NW1 7DH, England

**Teteak, Deral D** — Football Player
8067 Palomino Dr, Naples FL 34113, USA

**Teter, Hannah** — Snowboard Athlete, Model
1554 Plumas Circle, South Lake Tahoe CA 96150, USA

**Teton, John** — Social Activist
Earthlight Pictures, 791 4th St, Lake Oswego OR 97034, USA

**Tetriani, Lina** — Opera Singer
I M G Artists, Hogarth Business Park, Chiswick, London W4 2TH, England

**Tettamanzi, Dionigi Cardinal** — Religious Leader
Curia Vescovile, Piazza S Ambrogio 14, 27029 Vigevano (Pavia), Italy

**Tettleton, Mickey L** — Baseball Player
3500 Hollister Trail, Norman OK 73071, USA

**Tetzlaff, Christian** — Concert Violinist
Shuman Assoc, 120 W 58th St, #8D, New York NY 10019, USA

**Teufel, Timothy S (Tim)** — Baseball Player, Manager
PO Box 3517, Jupiter FL 33469, USA

**Teukolsky, Saul A** — Astrophysicist
Cornell University, Physics & Astronomy Dept, Ithaca NY 14853, USA

**Teut, Nate** — Baseball Player
2010 Sugar Creek Dr, Waukee IA 50263, USA

**Tewell, Doug** — Golfer
15216 Fairview Farm Road, Edmond OK 73013, USA

**Tewes, Lauren** — Actress
Actor's Group Talent and Literary Agency, 9703 SW 246th St, Vashon WA 98070 98070, USA

**Tewkesbury, Joan F** — Director, Writer
Creative Artists Agency, 2000 Ave of Stars, #100, Los Angeles CA 90067 USA

**Tewksbury, Robert A (Bob)** — Baseball Player
63 Ridge Road, Concord NH 03301, USA

**Tews, Andreas** — Boxer
Pflaumenbaum, Brunnenstr 32, 19053 Schwerin, Germany

**Texada, Tia** — Actress
Power & Twersky Business Mgmt, 13801 Ventura Blvd, Sherman Oaks CA 91423, USA

**Tezel, Ayse** — Actress
Encompass Mgmt, 19A Boundary St, #508, Rushcutters Bay NSW 2011, Australia

**Thabane, Thomas M** — Prime Minister, Lesotho
Chairman's Office, Military Council, PO Box 527, Maseru 100, Lesotho

**Thabeet, Hasheem** — Basketball Player
Oklahoma City Thunder, 211 N Robinson Ave, #300, Oklahoma City OK 73102 USA

**Thaborik, Marian** — Ice Hockey Player
301 Kenwood Parkway, #401, Minneapolis MN 55403, USA

**Thaci, Hashim** — Prime Minister, Kosovo
Prime Minister's Office, Assembly, Mother Theresa St, 10000 Pristina, Kosovo

**Thacker, Brian M** — Vietnam War Army Hero (CMH)
11413 Monterey Dr, Silver Spring MD 20902, USA

**Thacker, Charles P** — Computer Engineer
543 Tennyson Ave, Palo Alto CA 94301, USA

**Thacker, Thomas P (Tom)** — Basketball Player
3655 Dogwood Lane, Cincinnati OH 45213, USA

**Thackery, Jimmy** — Singer, Guitarist (Nighthawks)
Thunderbird Management Group, 133 Industrial Park Road, Larose LA 70373, USA

**Thagard, Norman E** — Astronaut, Physician
502 N Ride, Tallahassee FL 32303, USA

**Thain, John A** — Financier
C I T Group, 505 5th Ave, New York NY 10017, USA

**Thaler, Richard H** — Economist
University of Chicago, Booth Business School, Chicago IL 60637, USA

**Thalia** — Singer, Actress
Doyle-Kos Entertainment, 1 Penn Plaza, #2107, New York NY 10119, USA

**Thalmann, Melchior** — Gymnast
Kreuzbuhlstr 43, 8600 Dubendorf, Switzerland

**Thalmann, Sandra** — Ice Hockey Player
Swiss Ice Hockey, Hagenholzstr 81, 8050 Zurich, Switzerland

**Thames, Marcus M** — Baseball Player
101 Mount Moriah Circle, Louisville MS 39339, USA

**Thames, Xavier R** — Basketball Player
Brooklyn Nets, 15 Metro Tech Center, #1100, Brooklyn NY 11201 USA

**Thani, Abdullah Nasser Khalifa al-** — Prime Minister, Qatar
Prime Minister's Office, PO Box 923, Dohar, Qatar

**Thani, Tamim bin Hamad al-** — Emir, Qatar
Royal Palace, PO Box 923, Doha, Qatar

**Thapa, Surya Bahadur** — Prime Minister, Nepal
Tangal, Kathmandu, Bagmati 44601, Nepal

**Tharp, Twyla** — Dancer, Choreographer
Twyla Tharp Productions, 336 Central Park West, #17B, New York NY 10025, USA

**Tharpe, Larry J** — Football Player
3665 Greenbriar Road E, Macon GA 31204, USA

**Thatcher, David J** — WW II Army Air Corps Hero
440 Dearborn Ave, Missoula MT 59801, USA

**Thatcher, Joseph (Joe)** — Baseball Player
310 Ruddell Dr, Kokomo IN 46901, USA

**Thatcher, Karen** — Ice Hockey Player
USA Hockey, 1775 Bob Johnson Dr, Colorado Springs CO 80906 USA

**Thatcher, Roland C, IV** — Golfer
18 Floweruff Court, Spring TX 77380, USA

**Thaxton, James I (Jim)** — Football Player
4319 Deergrove Road, Memphis TN 38141, USA

**Thayer, Bill** — Explorer
PO Box 233, Snohomish WA 98291, USA

**Thayer, Brynn** — Actress
PO Box 15006, Beverly Hills CA 90209, USA

**Thayer, Gregory A (Greg)** — Baseball Player
1000 3rd St N, Sauk Rapids MN 56379, USA

**Thayer, Helen** — Explorer, Skier
PO Box 233, Snohomish WA 98291, USA

**Thayer, Maria** — Actress
A P A Talent & Literary Agency, 405 S Beverly Dr, #300, Beverly Hills CA 90212 USA

**Thayer, Thomas A (Tom)** — Football Player
50 Nohea Kai Dr, #I303, Lahaina HI 96761, USA

**Thayer, Thomas C (Tommy)** — Guitarist (Kiss), Songwriter
PO Box 7147, Thousand Oaks CA 91359, USA

**Thayer, W Paul** — Government Official, Businessman
10200 Hollow Way, Dallas TX 75229, USA

**Theberge, Greg** — Ice Hockey Player
31 Edgar, Sundridge ON P0A 1Z0, Canada
**Theile, David** — Swimmer
84 Woodville St, Hendea, Brisbane QLD 4011, Australia
**Thein Sein** — President, Myanmar; General
President's Office, Zaw Gyi St, Mayangon Tsp, Yangon, Myanmar
**Theismann, Joseph R (Joe)** — Football Player, Sportscaster
PO Box 186, Leesburg VA 20178, USA
**Theiss, Brooke** — Actress
Characters Talent Agency, 8 Elm St, Toronto ON M5G 1G7, Canada
**Theiss, Duane C** — Baseball Player
66 Juniper Ave, Westerville OH 43081, USA
**Thelan, Jodi** — Actress
8428 Melrose Place, #C, West Hollywood CA 90069, USA
**Thelen, Eduard** — Field Hockey Player
Ruhrstr 11, 50937 Cologne, Germany
**Theler, Derek** — Actor
Paradigm Agency, 360 N Crescent Dr, North Building, Beverly Hills CA 90210 USA
**Theobald, Ronald M (Ron)** — Baseball Player
319 Jacaranda Place, Fullerton CA 92832, USA
**Theodorakis, Mikis** — Composer
Epifanous 1, Akropolis, Athens, Greece
**Theodore, Jose** — Ice Hockey Player
238 S Maya Palm Dr, Boca Raton FL 33432, USA
**Theodorescu, Monica** — Equestrian
Gestit Lindenhof, 48336 Sassenberg, Germany
**Theodosakis, Jason** — Physician, Writer
Saint Martin's Press, 175 5th Ave, #400, New York NY 10010 USA
**Theodosius, Primate Metropolitan** — Religious Leader
Orthodox Church in America, PO Box 675 RR 25A, Syosset NY 11791, USA
**Therien, Christopher B (Chris)** — Ice Hockey Player
15 Milford Dr, Marlton NJ 08053, USA
**Theriot, Ryan S** — Baseball Player
87 Woodchuck Hill Road, Savannah GA 31405, USA
**Theron, Charlize** — Actress, Model
W M E Entertainment, 9601 Wilshire Blvd, #300, Beverly Hills CA 90210 USA
**Theroux, Justin** — Actor, Director
Creative Artists Agency, 2000 Ave of Stars, #100, Los Angeles CA 90067 USA
**Theroux, Paul E** — Writer
35 Elsynge Road, London SW18 2NR, England
**Therrien, Michel** — Ice Hockey Player, Coach
118 Carriage Dr, McKnight PA 15237, USA
**Theus, Reggie W** — Basketball Player, Coach
4259 Enoro Dr, Los Angeles CA 90008, USA
**Theusner, Ulrike** — Model
Take 2 Model Mgmt, 6 Willow St, London EC2 4BH, England
**Thewlis, David** — Actor
Artists Partnership, 101 Finsbury Pavement, London EC2A 1RS, England
**Theys, Didier** — Auto Racing Driver
5773 N 78th Place, Scottsdale AZ 85259, USA
**Thibaudet, Jean-Yves** — Concert Pianist
M L Falcone, 55 W 68th St, #1114, New York NY 10023, USA
**Thibault, Charles** — Physiologist
4 Place Jussieu, 75005 Paris, France
**Thibault, Jocelyn** — Ice Hockey Player
550 Ch du Domaine, RR 5, Saint-Denis-de-Brompton QC J0B 2P0, Canada
**Thibault, Mike F** — Basketball Coach
Washington Mystics, Verizon Center, 401 9th St NW, #750, Washington DC 20004 USA
**Thibiant, Aida** — Fashion Consultant
Institut de Beaute, 449 N Canon Dr, Beverly Hills CA 90210, USA
**Thibodeaux, Keith** — Actor
5372 Jamaica Dr, Jackson MS 39211, USA
**Thich Quang Do** — Religious Activist
Thanh Zinh Zen Monastery, Ho Chi Minh City, Vietnam
**Thicke, Alan** — Actor
7110 Gobernador Canyon Road, Carpinteria CA 93013, USA
**Thicke, Chris** — Mandolin Player
Nonesuch Records, 75 Rockefeller Plaza, #800, New York NY 10019 USA
**Thicke, Robin A** — Singer
Creative Artists Agency, 2000 Ave of Stars, #100, Los Angeles CA 90067 USA
**Thiedemann, Fritz** — Equestrian
Ostreherweg 28, 25746 Heide, Germany
**Thiele, Gerhard P J** — Astronaut, Germany
European Space Center, Linder Hohe, Box 906096, 51127 Cologne, Germany
**Thielemann, Ray C (R C)** — Football Player
210 Rose Meadow Lane, Alpharetta GA 30005, USA
**Thielemans, Jean B (Toots)** — Jazz Harmonica Player, Guitarist
Uncle Jazz Productions, Fluitberg St 66, #5, 2900 Schoten, Belgium
**Thielen, Gunter** — Businessman
Bertelsmann AG, Carl-Bertelsmann-Str 270, 33311 Guetersloh, Germany
**Thiemens, Mark H** — Chemist
University of California, Chemistry Dept, 9500 Gilman Dr, La Jolla CA 92093, USA
**Thieriot, Max** — Actor
Gersh Agency, 9465 Wilshire Blvd, #600, Beverly Hills CA 90212 USA
**Thierry, John F** — Football Player
6884 Arias Way, Painesville OH 44077, USA
**Thiessen, Tiffani** — Actress
Paradigm Agency, 360 N Crescent Dr, North Building, Beverly Hills CA 90210 USA
**Thiffault, Leo** — Ice Hockey Player
1340 Marble Dr, Columbus OH 43227, USA
**Thigpen, Robert T (Bobby)** — Baseball Player
1857 Brightwaters Blvd NE, Saint Petersburg FL 33704, USA
**Thigpen, Yancey D** — Football Player
7210 Yellowhorn Trail, Waxhaw NC 28173, USA
**Thile, Christopher S (Chris)** — Mandolinist, Guitarist (Nickel Creek)
Creative Artists Agency, 2000 Ave of Stars, #100, Los Angeles CA 90067 USA

**Thinnes, Roy** — Actor
163 Amsterdam Ave, #307, New York NY 10023, USA

**Thirlby, Olivia** — Actress
Management 360, 9111 Wilshire Blvd, Beverly Hills CA 90210 USA

**Thirlwell, J G** — Singer, Songwriter
Agency Group Ltd, 142 W 57th St, #600, New York NY 10019 USA

**Thirsk, Robert B (Bob)** — Astronaut, Canada
N A S A, Johnson Space Center, 2101 NASA Road, Houston TX 77058 USA

**Thistlethwaite, Anthony** — Musician (Waterboys)
Agency Group Ltd, 142 W 57th St, #600, New York NY 10019 USA

**Thobele, Dingaan B** — Boxer
1202 Chiwelo, PO Chiwelo, Soweto 1818, South Africa

**Thoen, Skip** — Basketball Player
330 Buckland Trace, Louisville KY 40245, USA

**Thoenen, Richard C (Dick)** — Baseball Player
862 Smith St, Harrisburg OR 97446, USA

**Thom, Bing W** — Architect
1430 Burrad St, Vancouver BC V6Z 2A3, Canada

**Thoma, Georg** — Nordic Combined Athlete
Bisten 6, 79856 Hinterzarten, Germany

**Thomas Grossman, Robin** — Actor
B R S / Gage Talent Agency, 5757 Wilshire Blvd, #659, Los Angeles CA 90036, USA

**Thomas, Aaron N** — Football Player
3793 NW Sparrow Place, Corvallis OR 97330, USA

**Thomas, Adalius D** — Football Player
195 Highway 9, Kellyton AL 35089, USA

**Thomas, Andrew S W (Andy)** — Astronaut
N A S A, Johnson Space Center, 2101 NASA Road, Houston TX 77058 USA

**Thomas, Aurelius** — Football Player
PO Box 91157, Columbus OH 43209, USA

**Thomas, B Clendon** — Football Player
7508 Rumsey Road, Oklahoma City OK 73132, USA

**Thomas, B J** — Singer, Songwriter
Honeyman Music, PO Box 120003, Arlington TX 76012, USA

**Thomas, Barbara S** — Government Official
News International, 1 Virginia St, London E1 9XY, England

**Thomas, Benjamin (Ben), Jr** — Football Player
2155 Herndon St, Auburn AL 36830, USA

**Thomas, Betty** — Actress, Director
Dominant Pictures, 1438 N Gower St, Building 35, Los Angeles CA 90028, USA

**Thomas, Billy M** — Army General
626 Sweetbrush, San Antonio TX 78258, USA

**Thomas, Broderick L** — Football Player
12004 Opal Creek Dr, Pearland TX 77584, USA

**Thomas, Cal** — Actor
Creative Artists Agency, 2000 Ave of Stars, #100, Los Angeles CA 90067 USA

**Thomas, Calvin L** — Football Player
908 Manchester Ave, Westchester IL 60154, USA

**Thomas, Carl** — Singer (Faith Evans)
Universal Attractions, 135 W 26th St, #1200, New York NY 10001 USA

**Thomas, Carla** — Singer
Rodgers Redding, PO Box 4603, Macon GA 31208 USA

**Thomas, Charles** — Baseball Player
137 Black Oak Dr, Asheville NC 28804, USA

**Thomas, Charles G (Chuck)** — Football Player
2201 Purple Majesty Court, Las Vegas NV 89117, USA

**Thomas, Clarence** — Supreme Court Justice
US Supreme Court, 1 1st St NE, Washington DC 20543 USA

**Thomas, Craig** — Actor, Producer
United Talent Agency, U T A Plaza, 9336 Civic Center Dr, Beverly Hills CA 90210 USA

**Thomas, D Etan** — Basketball Player
2147 Vittoria Court, Bowie MD 20721, USA

**Thomas, Damien** — Actor
Curtis Brown Group, 28-29 Haymarket St, #500, London SW1Y 4SP, England

**Thomas, Dave G** — Football Player
2115 Salt Myrtle Lane, Orange Park FL 32003, USA

**Thomas, David** — Concert Singer
Allied Artists, 42 Montpelier Square, London SE10 8HP, England

**Thomas, David (Dave)** — Actor, Comedian
M B S T Entertainment, 345 N Maple Dr, #200, Beverly Hills CA 90210 USA

**Thomas, David Clayton** — Singer (Blood Sweat & Tears)
Music Avenue Inc, 43 Washington St, Groveland MA 01834, USA

**Thomas, David L** — Singer (Pere Ubu)
Billions Corp, 3522 W Armitage Ave, Chicago IL 60647 USA

**Thomas, Debra J (Debi)** — Figure Skater
2601 Windward Blvd, Champaign IL 61821, USA

**Thomas, Demaryius A** — Football Player
Denver Broncos, 13655 E Broncos Parkway, Englewood CO 80112 USA

**Thomas, Dennis (Dee Tee)** — Saxophonist (Kool & the Gang)
Spirit Media, PO Box 43591, Phoenix AZ 85080 USA

**Thomas, Derrel O** — Baseball Player
112 Juniperhill Lane, Riverside CA 92506, USA

**Thomas, Donald A** — Astronaut
1029 Hart Road, Towson MD 21286, USA

**Thomas, Donald Michael (D M)** — Writer
Coach House, Rashleigh Vale, Tregolls Road, Truro, Cornwall TR1 1TJ, England

**Thomas, Dontarrious D** — Football Player
9132 Creek Way, Savage MN 55378, USA

**Thomas, Earl L** — Football Player
4202 Clearwater City, Missouri City TX 77459, USA

**Thomas, Eddie Kaye** — Actor
Gersh Agency, 9465 Wilshire Blvd, #600, Beverly Hills CA 90212 USA

**Thomas, Elizabeth Marshall** — Anthropologist, Environmentalist, Writer
80 E Mountain Road, Peterborough NH 03458, USA

**Thomas, Emma** — Producer
Bloom Hergott Diemer, 150 S Rodeo Dr, #300, Beverly Hills CA 90212 USA

| | |
|---|---|
| **Thomas, Emmitt E** | Football Player, Coach |
| 4603 NE Dick Howser Circle, Lees Summit MO 64064, USA | |
| **Thomas, Frank E, Jr** | Baseball Player |
| 1515 Sunnyview Road, Libertyville IL 60048, USA | |
| **Thomas, Frank J** | Baseball Player |
| 118 Doray Dr, Pittsburgh PA 15237, USA | |
| **Thomas, Gareth** | Actor |
| Emptage Hall, 14 Rathbone Place, London W1T 1HT, England | |
| **Thomas, Gareth** | Engineer |
| University of California, Materials Science Dept, Berkeley CA 94720, USA | |
| **Thomas, George E, Jr** | Baseball Player |
| 5804 Ivrea Dr, Sarasota FL 34238, USA | |
| **Thomas, Geraint** | Cyclist |
| Team Barolworld, Trav Via Provinciale 1/C, 25030 Adro (BS), Italy | |
| **Thomas, Heather** | Actress |
| Innovative Artists, 1505 10th St, Santa Monica CA 90401 USA | |
| **Thomas, Henry** | Actor |
| Brillstein Entertainment Partners, 9150 Wilshire Blvd, #350, Beverly Hills CA 90212 USA | |
| **Thomas, Henry L, Jr** | Football Player |
| 16811 Southern Oaks Dr, Houston TX 77068, USA | |
| **Thomas, Henry W** | Writer |
| 3214 Warder St NW, Washington DC 20010, USA | |
| **Thomas, Hollis** | Baseball Player |
| 9163 SE 48th Court Road, Ocala FL 34480, USA | |
| **Thomas, Hollis, Jr** | Football Player |
| 5957 McLeod Dr, Las Vegas NV 89120, USA | |
| **Thomas, Ian** | Singer, Songwriter |
| Anthem Entertainment, 189 Carlton St, Toronto ON M5A 2K7, Canada | |
| **Thomas, Irma** | Singer |
| Irma Thomas Inc, PO Box 26126, New Orleans LA 70186, USA | |
| **Thomas, Isiah L, III** | Basketball Player, Executive, Coach |
| Florida International University, Athletic Dept, Miami FL 33199, USA | |
| **Thomas, J Gorman** | Baseball Player |
| 5 Reef Club, Hilton Head Island SC 29926, USA | |
| **Thomas, J Leroy (Lee)** | Baseball Player |
| 14260 Manderleigh Woods Dr, Chesterfield MO 63017, USA | |
| **Thomas, J Michael (Mickey)** | Singer (Starship) |
| That's Entertainment International, PO Box 2230, Folsom CA 95763, USA | |
| **Thomas, Jake** | Actor |
| Stan Rogow Productions, 3000 Olympic Blvd, Santa Monica CA 90404, USA | |
| **Thomas, James (J T)** | Football Player |
| 408 Arden Dr, Monroeville PA 15146, USA | |
| **Thomas, James E (Jim), Jr** | Basketball Player |
| 4499 Willow Hill Road, Portal GA 30450, USA | |
| **Thomas, Jay** | Actor |
| Don Buchwald Talent Agency, 6500 Wilshire Blvd, #2200, Los Angeles CA 90048 USA | |
| **Thomas, Joe** | Football Player |
| 2276 Stones Throw, Westlake OH 44145, USA | |
| **Thomas, John M** | Chemist |
| Royal Institution, 21 Albemarle St, London W1X 4BS, England | |
| **Thomas, John T (Bud)** | Baseball Player |
| 2475 Woodland Dr, Sedalia MO 65301, USA | |
| **Thomas, Johnny, Jr** | Football Player |
| 1818 Darby Lane, Fresno TX 77545, USA | |
| **Thomas, Jonathan Taylor** | Actor |
| Innovative Artists, 1505 10th St, Santa Monica CA 90401 USA | |
| **Thomas, Julian** | Archaeologist |
| Manchester University, Archaeology Dept, Manchester M13 9PL, England | |
| **Thomas, Keith V** | Historian |
| Broad Gate, Broad St, Ludlow, Shropshire SY8 1NJ, England | |
| **Thomas, Keni** | Singer, Songwriter |
| W M E Entertainment, 1600 Division St, #300, Nashville TN 37203 USA | |
| **Thomas, Kenny** | Singer, Songwriter |
| Lou Coulson Assoc, 37 Berwick St, London W1V 8RS, England | |
| **Thomas, Khleo** | Actor |
| Creative Partners Group, 1522 2nd St, Santa Monica CA 90401, USA | |
| **Thomas, Kiwaukee S** | Football Player |
| 901 W Pinedale Dr, Plant City FL 33563, USA | |
| **Thomas, Kurt** | Gymnast |
| 4421 Hidden Hill Road, Norman OK 73072, USA | |
| **Thomas, Kurt V** | Basketball Player |
| 1826 Brook Terrace Trail, Dallas TX 75232, USA | |
| **Thomas, Lamar N** | Football Player |
| 10524 NW 13th Lane, Gainesville FL 32606, USA | |
| **Thomas, Larry** | Actor, Director |
| Synergy Talent, 13251 Ventura Blvd, Studio City CA 91604, USA | |
| **Thomas, Larry W** | Baseball Player |
| 3825 Graham Lane, Eight Mile AL 36613, USA | |
| **Thomas, Lavale A** | Football Player |
| 7602 Antlers Lane, Charlotte NC 28210, USA | |
| **Thomas, Linn** | Model, Actress |
| 80 5th Avenue, #908, Box 21, New York NY 10011, USA | |
| **Thomas, Mark A** | Football Player |
| 556 Hillsboro St, Monticello GA 31064, USA | |
| **Thomas, Marlo** | Actress |
| 420 E 54th St, #28G, New York NY 10022, USA | |
| **Thomas, Mary** | Singer (Crystals) |
| American Mgmt, 19948 Mayall St, Chatsworth CA 91311, USA | |
| **Thomas, Michael Tilson** | Conductor, Concert Pianist |
| San Francisco Symphony, Davies Symphony Hall, San Francisco CA 94102, USA | |
| **Thomas, Norris L** | Football Player |
| 3202 Boston Ave, Pascagoula MS 39581, USA | |
| **Thomas, Patrick S (Pat)** | Football Player |
| 612 Middle Cove Dr, Plano TX 75023, USA | |
| **Thomas, Peter** | Composer |
| Via Riviera 28, 6976 Castagnola/Lugano, Switzerland | |

Thomas - Thomas

| | |
|---|---|
| **Thomas, Philip Michael**<br>PO Box 23714, Brooklyn NY 11202, USA | Actor |
| **Thomas, Pinklon**<br>2045 Wild Tamarind Blvd, Orlando FL 32828, USA | Boxer |
| **Thomas, Randy**<br>2254 Nelms Dr SW, Atlanta GA 30315, USA | Football Player |
| **Thomas, Ray**<br>Insight Mgmt, 1222 16th Ave S, #300, Nashville TN 37212, USA | Flutist, Singer (Moody Blues) |
| **Thomas, Rebecca**<br>Paradigm Agency, 360 N Crescent Dr, North Building, Beverly Hills CA 90210 USA | Director |
| **Thomas, Reg**<br>7245 Colonel Talbot Road, London ON N6L 1H9, Canada | Ice Hockey Player |
| **Thomas, Richard**<br>1419 Clearfork N, Morehead KY 40351, USA | Actor |
| **Thomas, Rob**<br>Lippman Entertainment, 23586 Calabasas Road, #208, Calabasas CA 91302, USA | Singer (Matchbox 20), Songwriter |
| **Thomas, Robb W**<br>179 NW Outlook Vista Dr, Bend OR 97701, USA | Football Player |
| **Thomas, Robert D**<br>223 Mariomi Road, New Canaan, CT 06840 | Publisher |
| **Thomas, Robert R (Bob)**<br>259 Linden St, Glen Ellyn IL 60137, USA | Football Player |
| **Thomas, Roy J**<br>6881 SW 167th Place, Beaverton OR 97007, USA | Baseball Player |
| **Thomas, Rozonda (Chilli)**<br>Diggit Entertainment, 6 W 18th St, #800, New York NY 10011, USA | Rap Artist (TLC), Actress |
| **Thomas, Scott**<br>49 Redspire Way, East Amherst NY 14051, USA | Ice Hockey Player |
| **Thomas, Sean**<br>Bloomsbury Publishing, 50 Bedford Square, London WC1B 3DP, England | Writer |
| **Thomas, Sean Patrick**<br>Innovative Artists, 1505 10th St, Santa Monica CA 90401 USA | Actor |
| **Thomas, Serena Scott**<br>S M S Talent, 8383 Wilshire Blvd, #230, Beverly Hills CA 90211 USA | Actress |
| **Thomas, Sidney R**<br>US Court of Appeals, 316 N 26th St, #5405, Billings MT 59101, USA | Judge |
| **Thomas, Stanley B (Stan)**<br>10827 159th Court NE, Redmond WA 98052, USA | Baseball Player |
| **Thomas, Steve**<br>'This Old House' Show, PO Box 2284, South Burlington VT 05407, USA | Entertainer |
| **Thomas, Steve**<br>Plain & Simple, 289 Bering Ave, Toronto ON M8Z 3A5, Canada | Ice Hockey Player |
| **Thomas, Tamara Craig**<br>Independent Artists Agency, 9601 Wilshire Blvd, #750, Beverly Hills CA 90210, USA | Actress |
| **Thomas, Thurman L**<br>7562 Eddy Road, Colden NY 14033, USA | Football Player |
| **Thomas, Tillman J**<br>Prime Minister's Office, Botanical Gardens, Tanteen, Saint George's, Grenada | Prime Minister, Grenada |
| **Thomas, Timothy J (Tim), Jr**<br>29 James Ave, Middleton MA 01949, USA | Ice Hockey Player |
| **Thomas, Timothy M (Tim)**<br>Dallas Mavericks, Pavilion, 2909 Taylor Street, Dallas TX 75226 USA | Basketball Player |
| **Thomas, Tommy**<br>Ivett Stone Agency, W292N6910 Dorn Road, Hartland WI 53029, USA | Singer |
| **Thomas, Tony**<br>Creative Artists Agency, 2000 Ave of Stars, #100, Los Angeles CA 90067 USA | Producer, Writer, Actor |
| **Thomas, Wayne**<br>San Jose Sharks, San Jose Arena, 525 W Santa Clara St, San Jose CA 95113 USA | Ice Hockey Player |
| **Thomas, William (Tra), III**<br>17 Elderberry Dr, Medford NJ 08055, USA | Football Player |
| **Thomas, Zachary M (Zach)**<br>PO Box 491631, Charlotte NC 28269, USA | Football Player |
| **Thomas-Graham, Pamela**<br>Liz Claiborne Inc, 1441 Broadway, New York NY 10018, USA | Businesswoman |
| **Thomason, C J**<br>Peter Strain, 5455 Wilshire Blvd, #1812, Los Angeles CA 90036 USA | Actor |
| **Thomason, Harry Z**<br>10732 Riverside Dr, North Hollywood CA 91602, USA | Producer |
| **Thomason, Marsha**<br>Artist Rights Group, 4A Exmoor St, London W10 6BD, England | Actress |
| **Thomassin, Florence**<br>Artmedia, 20 Ave Rapp, 75007 Paris, France | Actress |
| **Thomasson, Gary L**<br>263 Carriage Lane, Auburn CA 95603, USA | Baseball Player |
| **Thome, James H (Jim)**<br>125 E 8th St, Hinsdale IL 60521, USA | Baseball Player |
| **Thomerson, Tim**<br>Innovative Artists, 1505 10th St, Santa Monica CA 90401 USA | Actor |
| **Thomese, P F**<br>Bloomsbury Publishing, 50 Bedford Square, London WC1B 3DP, England | Writer |
| **Thomopoulos, Anthony D**<br>5357 Long Shadow Court, Westlake Village CA 91362, USA | Businessman |
| **Thompkins, Russell, Jr**<br>Wenig-LaMonica Associates, 580 White Plains Road, #130, Tarrytown NY 10591 USA | Singer (Stylistics) |
| **Thompson, Al**<br>S M S Talent, 8383 Wilshire Blvd, #230, Beverly Hills CA 90211 USA | Actor, Producer, Director |
| **Thompson, Alexis (Lexi)**<br>Ladies Pro Golf Assn, 100 International Golf Dr, Daytona Beach FL 32124 USA | Golfer |
| **Thompson, Andrea**<br>Sovereign Talent Group, 8421 Wilshire Blvd, #200, Beverly Hills CA 90211 USA | Actress |
| **Thompson, Andrew J (Andy)**<br>1405 Bayshore Blvd, Tampa FL 33606, USA | Baseball Player |
| **Thompson, Anthony**<br>5035 E DeAnn Dr, Bloomington IN 47404, USA | Football Player, Coach |
| **Thompson, April Yvette**<br>SimonSez Entertainment, 12 Desbrosses St, New York NY 10013, USA | Actress |

| | |
|---|---|
| **Thompson, Arland L**<br>6692 S Routt St, Littleton CO 80127, USA | Football Player |
| **Thompson, Aundra**<br>12060 Galva Dr, Dallas TX 75243, USA | Football Player |
| **Thompson, Barbara**<br>1721 Edgebrook Dr, Rockford IL 61107, USA | Baseball Player |
| **Thompson, Bennie**<br>10157 Placid Lake Court, Columbia MD 21044, USA | Football Player |
| **Thompson, Bobb'e J**<br>I C M Partners, 10250 Constellation Blvd, #900, Los Angeles CA 90067 USA | Rap Artist, Actor |
| **Thompson, Bobby L**<br>7006 Hunters Glen Dr, Charlotte NC 28214, USA | Baseball Player |
| **Thompson, Brent K**<br>New York Islanders, 1255 Hempstead Turnpike, Uniondale NY 11553 USA | Ice Hockey Player |
| **Thompson, Brian**<br>David Shapira Assoc, 193 N Robertson Blvd, Beverly Hills CA 90211 USA | Actor, Director, Writer |
| **Thompson, Brooke**<br>10515 Mersham Hill Dr, Bakersfield CA 93311, USA | Actress |
| **Thompson, Brooks J**<br>29222 Oakview Ridge, Boerne TX 78015, USA | Basketball Player |
| **Thompson, Caroline W**<br>I C M Partners, 10250 Constellation Blvd, #900, Los Angeles CA 90067 USA | Writer, Director |
| **Thompson, Charissa**<br>Fox-TV, Sports Dept, 205 W 67th St, New York NY 10065 USA | Sportscaster |
| **Thompson, Charles L (Tim)**<br>536 Summit Dr, Lewistown PA 17044, USA | Baseball Player |
| **Thompson, Chaun T**<br>10514 Huffines Dr, Rowlett TX 75089, USA | Football Player |
| **Thompson, Chris**<br>Rothman Brecher Agency, 9465 Wilshire Blvd, #840, Beverly Hills CA 90212 USA | Producer, Writer |
| **Thompson, Christopher**<br>University of North Carolina, Astrophysics Dept, Chapel Hill NC 27599, USA | Astrophysicist |
| **Thompson, Christopher**<br>Artmedia, 20 Ave Rapp, 75007 Paris, France | Actor |
| **Thompson, Cornelius A (Corny)**<br>207 Lamentation Dr, Berlin CT 06037, USA | Basketball Player |
| **Thompson, Darrell A**<br>4220 Oakview Lane N, Minneapolis MN 55442, USA | Football Player |
| **Thompson, David O**<br>5114 Berkeley Creek Lane, Charlotte NC 28277, USA | Basketball Player, Executive |
| **Thompson, David W**<br>Orbital Science Corp, 21839 Atlantic Blvd, Dulles VA 20166, USA | Space Scientist, Businessman |
| **Thompson, Derek**<br>3212 Pine Shadow Dr, Land O'Lakes FL 34639, USA | Baseball Player |
| **Thompson, Derrius D**<br>3810 Vitruvian Way, #504, Addison TX 75001, USA | Football Player |
| **Thompson, Don**<br>McDonald's Corp, McDonald's Plaza, 1 Kroc Dr, Oak Brook IL 60523, USA | Businessman |
| **Thompson, Edward T**<br>11 Cotswold Dr, North Salem NY 10560, USA | Editor |
| **Thompson, Emma**<br>Hamilton Hodell, 20 Golden Square, London W1F 9JL, England | Actress |
| **Thompson, Ernest**<br>RR 1 Box 3240, Ashland NH 03217, USA | Writer |
| **Thompson, Errol**<br>PO Box 58, Station Main, Summerside PE C1N 4P6, Canada | Ice Hockey Player |
| **Thompson, F M (Daley)**<br>Olympic Assn, 1 Wadsworth Plain, London SW18 1EH, England | Track Athlete |
| **Thompson, Fred Dalton**<br>Paradigm Agency, 360 Park Ave S, #1600, New York NY 10010 USA | Senator, TN; Actor |
| **Thompson, G Ralph**<br>Seventh-Day Adventists, 12501 Old Columbia Pike, Silver Spring MD 20904, USA | Religious Leader |
| **Thompson, Gary**<br>2531 Park Vista Circle, Ames IA 50014, USA | Basketball Player |
| **Thompson, Gerald**<br>I M G Artists, Hogarth Business Park, Chiswick, London W4 2TH, England | Opera Singer |
| **Thompson, Gina**<br>Richard Walters, PO Box 2789, Toluca Lake CA 91610 USA | Singer |
| **Thompson, Hilary**<br>13202 Weddington St, Sherman Oaks CA 91401, USA | Actress |
| **Thompson, Hugh D (Rocky)**<br>2608 Chamberlain Dr, Plano TX 75023, USA | Golfer |
| **Thompson, Hugh L**<br>752 Bayside Dr, #402, Cape Canaveral FL 32920, USA | Educator |
| **Thompson, Ian**<br>Bloomsbury Publishing, 50 Bedford Square, London WC1B 3DP, England | Landscape Architect |
| **Thompson, Jack**<br>June Cann Mgmt, 118 Oxford St, Woollahra NSW 2025, Australia | Actor |
| **Thompson, Jack B**<br>10439 7th Ave SW, Seattle WA 98146, USA | Football Player |
| **Thompson, James A (Jamie)**<br>University of Wisconsin, Morgridge Research Institute, 330 N Orchard St, Madison WI 53715, USA | Stem Cell Biologist |
| **Thompson, James R (Jim), Jr**<br>Winston & Strawn, 35 W Wacker Dr, #2800, Chicago IL 60601, USA | Governor, IL |
| **Thompson, James R, Jr**<br>5046 Somerby Dr SE, Huntsville AL 35802, USA | Space Administrator |
| **Thompson, Jason**<br>Sacramento Kings, Arco Arena, 1 Sports Parkway, Sacramento CA 95834 USA | Basketball Player |
| **Thompson, Jason C**<br>Wishlab, 2225 Hyperion Ave, #A, Los Angeles CA 90027, USA | Actor |
| **Thompson, Jason D**<br>Jason Thompson Baseball, 1827 N Squirrel Road, Auburn Hills MI 48326, USA | Baseball Player |
| **Thompson, Jason M**<br>10535 Oak Terrace Ave, Las Vegas NV 89149, USA | Baseball Player |
| **Thompson, Jennifer (Jenny)**<br>6 Evans Dr, Dover NH 03820, USA | Swimmer |

**Thompson, Jill** — Cartoonist
D C Comics, 1700 Broadway, #400, New York NY 10019 USA

**Thompson, Jody** — Actress
Characters Talent, 200-1505 W 2nd Ave, Vancouver BC V6H 3Y4, Canada

**Thompson, John Griggs** — Abel Mathematics Laureate
University of Florida, Mathematics Dept, PO Box 118105, Gainesville FL 32611, USA

**Thompson, John R** — Basketball Player, Coach, Sportscaster
3636 16th St NW, #B1161, Washington DC 20010, USA

**Thompson, Justin W** — Baseball Player
32807 Clearwater Court, Magnolia TX 77354, USA

**Thompson, Kenan** — Actor
United Talent Agency, U T A Plaza, 9336 Civic Center Dr, Beverly Hills CA 90210 USA

**Thompson, Kenneth L** — Computer Scientist
A T & T Bell Lucent Laboratory, 600 Mountain Ave, New Providence NJ 07974 USA

**Thompson, Klay A** — Basketball Player
Golden State Warriors, 1011 Broadway, Oakland CA 94605 USA

**Thompson, L Donnell** — Football Player
7503 Kepley Road, Chapel Hill NC 27517, USA

**Thompson, Lamont D** — Football Player
1320 Wildwing Lane, Vallejo CA 94591, USA

**Thompson, Larry D** — Government Official
PepsiCo, 700 Anderson Hill Road, Purchase NY 10577, USA

**Thompson, LaSalle** — Basketball Player
3805 Northcliff Lane, Roseville CA 95747, USA

**Thompson, Lea** — Actress
Innovative Artists, 1505 10th St, Santa Monica CA 90401 USA

**Thompson, Lee (Kix)** — Singer, Saxophonist (Madness)
I T F, Ariel House, 74A Charlotte St, London W1T 4QJ, England

**Thompson, Leonard I** — Football Player
5534 W Glenrosa Ave, Phoenix AZ 85031, USA

**Thompson, Leonard S** — Golfer
9010 Marsh View Court, Ponte Vedra FL 32082, USA

**Thompson, Linda** — Actress, Songwriter
6342 Sycamore Meadows Dr, Malibu CA 90265, USA

**Thompson, Linda** — Singer, Songwriter
Shore Fire Media, 32 Court St, #1600, Brooklyn NY 11201 USA

**Thompson, Lonnie** — Glaciologist
Ohio State University, Geology Dept, Columbus OH 43210, USA

**Thompson, Mark R** — Baseball Player
1122 Lord Murphy Way, Bowling Green KY 42104, USA

**Thompson, Mike** — Editorial Cartoonist
Detroit Free Press, Editorial Dept, 600 W Fort St, Detroit MI 48226 USA

**Thompson, Milton B (Milt)** — Baseball Player
PO Box 663, Williamstown NJ 08094, USA

**Thompson, Mychal G** — Basketball Player
11 Paverstone Lane, Laderna Ranch CA 92694, USA

**Thompson, Norman J (Norm)** — Football Player
PO Box 4552, Hayward CA 94540, USA

**Thompson, Obadele** — Track Athlete
Amateur Athletics Assn, PO Box 46, Bridgetown, Barbados

**Thompson, Paul R J N** — Drummer (Franz Ferdinand)
M A M A Group, 57-65 Worship Ave, London EC2A 2DU, England

**Thompson, Reece** — Actor
Play Mgmt, 807 Powell St, #220, Vancouver BC V6A 1H7, Canada

**Thompson, Reyna O** — Football Player
1502 NW 183rd Terrace, Pembroke Pines FL 33029, USA

**Thompson, Richard** — Cartoonist (Cul de Sac)
Universal Press Syndicate, 4520 Main St, #700, Kansas City MO 64111 USA

**Thompson, Richard** — Singer, Songwriter, Guitarist
High Road Touring, 751 Bridgeway, #200, Sausalito CA 94965 USA

**Thompson, Richard G** — Baseball Player
Oakland Athletics, McAfee Coliseum, 7000 Coliseum Way, #3, Oakland CA 94621 USA

**Thompson, Richard N (Rich)** — Baseball Player
7 Chambers Court, Huntington Station NY 11746, USA

**Thompson, Ricky D** — Football Player
1277 Brazos Bluff Dr, China Spring TX 76633, USA

**Thompson, Robert R (Robby)** — Baseball Player
4438 Gun Club Road, West Palm Beach FL 33406, USA

**Thompson, Rocky L** — Ice Hockey Player
Oklahoma City Barons, 501 N Walker, #140, Oklahoma City OK 73102, USA

**Thompson, Ryan O** — Baseball Player
2153 Fullerton Dr, Indianapolis IN 46214, USA

**Thompson, Sarah** — Actress
Brillstein Entertainment Partners, 9150 Wilshire Blvd, #350, Beverly Hills CA 90212 USA

**Thompson, Scott** — Actor, Singer, Writer, Producer
Glickman Alexander Talent Mgmt, 204 Saint George St, #20, Toronto ON M5R 2N6, Canada

**Thompson, Scott** — Businessman
ShopRunner, 225 Washington St, #300, Conshohocken PA 19428, USA

**Thompson, Sophie** — Actress
Saint James Mgmt, 22 Groom Place, London SW1, England

**Thompson, Steve M** — Football Player
Victory Foursquare Gospel Church, 11911 State Ave, Marysville WA 98271, USA

**Thompson, Sue** — Singer, Guitarist
Curb Entertainment, 3907 W Alameda Ave, #200, Burbank CA 91505, USA

**Thompson, Susanna** — Actress
Weissenbach Mgmt, 5951 Airdrome St, Los Angeles CA 90035, USA

**Thompson, Taylor Ann** — Actress
A P A Talent & Literary Agency, 405 S Beverly Dr, #300, Beverly Hills CA 90212 USA

**Thompson, Ted C** — Football Player
222 Nicolet Place, De Pere WI 54115, USA

**Thompson, Teddy** — Singer, Songwriter
Gold Village Entertainment, 72 Madison Ave, #800, New York NY 10016, USA

**Thompson, Teri** — Actress
Red Talent, 9595 Wilshire Blvd, #900, Beverly Hills CA 90212, USA

**Thompson, Tessa** — Actress
Greene Assoc, 1901 Ave of Stars, #130, Los Angeles CA 90067 USA

**Thompson, Tina M** — Basketball Player
Los Angeles Sparks, 888 S Figueroa St, #2010, Los Angeles CA 90017 USA

**Thompson, Tommy G** — Secretary, Health & Human Services
1313 Manassas Trail, Madison WI 53718, USA

**Thompson, Tristan T J** — Basketball Player
Cleveland Cavaliers, Gund Arena, 1 Center Court, Cleveland OH 44115 USA

**Thompson, U Leroy** — Football Player
5005 Princess Anne Court, Knoxville TN 37918, USA

**Thompson, V Scot** — Baseball Player
330 Dodds Road, Butler PA 16002, USA

**Thompson, Verlon** — Singer, Guitarist, Songwriter
V N S Records, 9 Music Square S, #148, Nashville TN 37203, USA

**Thompson, William A (Billy)** — Football Player
6522 Jackson Court, Littleton CO 80130, USA

**Thompson, William T (Billy)** — Basketball Player
19678 Palm Spring Dr, Boca Raton FL 33428, USA

**Thompson, Willis H (Weegie)** — Football Player
14501 Felbridge Way, Midlothian VA 23113, USA

**Thoms, Arthur W (Art), Jr** — Football Player
90 Goodfellow Dr, Moraga CA 94556, USA

**Thoms, Tracie** — Actress
Gersh Agency, 41 Madison Ave, #3301, New York NY 10010 USA

**Thomsen, Martha E** — Actress, Model
Playboy Promotions, 9346 Civic Center Dr, #200, Beverly Hills CA 90210 USA

**Thomsen, Ulrich** — Actor
Greene Assoc, 1901 Ave of Stars, #130, Los Angeles CA 90067 USA

**Thomson of Fleet, David** — Businessman
Thomson Newspapers, 65 Queen St W, Toronto ON M5H 2M8, Canada

**Thomson, Brian E** — Designer
5 Little Dowling St, Paddington NSW 2021, Australia

**Thomson, Erik** — Actor
R G M Artists, 8-12 Ann Street, Surry Hills NSW 2010, Australia

**Thomson, Floyd** — Ice Hockey Player
General Delivery, Dunchurch ON P0A 1G0, Canada

**Thomson, Gordon** — Actor
A M T Artists, 15260 Ventura Blvd, #1200, Sherman Oaks CA 91403, USA

**Thomson, Gordon** — Actor
Gage Group, 14724 Ventura Blvd, #505, Sherman Oaks CA 91403 USA

**Thomson, H C (Hank)** — Harness Racing Official
PO Box 38, Mullett Lake MI 49761, USA

**Thomson, James A** — Biologist
University of Wisconsin, Morgridge Research Institute, Madison WI 53706, USA

**Thomson, John C** — Baseball Player
1414 E Kent St, Sulphur LA 70663, USA

**Thomson, Judith J** — Philosopher, Metaphysician
Massachusetts Institute of Technology, Philosophy Dept, Cambridge MA 02139, USA

**Thomson, June** — Commentator
KNBC-TV, News Dept, 3000 W Alameda Ave, Burbank CA 91523, USA

**Thomson, Kim** — Actress
C D A, 167-169 Kensington High St, London W8 6SH, England

**Thomson, Kristen** — Actress
LaFeaver Talent Mgmt, 162 John St, #300, Toronto ON M5V 2E5, Canada

**Thomson, Peter W** — Golfer
Carmel House, 44 Mathoura Road, Toorak VIC 3142, Australia

**Thomson, Rupert** — Writer
Bloomsbury Publishing, 50 Bedford Square, London WC1B 3DP, England

**Thon, Olaf** — Soccer Player
Rosenthaler Str 40-41, Hackesche Hofe, 10178 Berlin, Germany

**Thon, Richard W (Dickie)** — Baseball Player
C17 Calle Lirio del Mar, Urb Dorado del Mar, Dorado PR 00646, USA

**Thone, Charles** — Governor, NE
Erickson & Sederstrom, 301 S 13th St, #400, Lincoln NE 68508, USA

**Thoni, Gustav** — Alpine Skier, Coach
39026 Prato Allo Stelvio-Prao BZ, Italy

**Thor, Brad** — Writer
Pocket Books, 1230 Ave of Americas, New York NY 10020 USA

**Thora** — Actress
C E S D, 10635 Santa Monica Blvd, #130, Los Angeles CA 90025 USA

**Thorburn, Clifford C D (Cliff)** — Snooker Player
31 West Side Dr, Markham ON L3P 7J5, Canada

**Thorell, Clarke** — Actor
Paradigm Agency, 360 N Crescent Dr, North Building, Beverly Hills CA 90210 USA

**Thoresen, Jan** — Curling Athlete
Curling Assn, Sognsveien 75, Serviceboks 1, 0840 Oslo, Norway

**Thorin, Donald E, Sr** — Cinematographer
15260 Ventura Blvd, #1040, Sherman Oaks CA 91403, USA

**Thorkildsen, Andreas** — Track Athlete
Rore Hageby 5, 4886 Grimstad, Norway

**Thormodsgard, Paul G** — Baseball Player
7752 E Rose Lane, Scottsdale AZ 85250, USA

**Thorn, Christopher** — Guitarist (Blind Melon)
Shapiro Co, 9229 W Sunset Blvd, #607, West Hollywood CA 90069 USA

**Thorn, Paul** — Singer, Songwriter
New Frontier Touring, 1503 17th Ave S, Nashville TN 37212, USA

**Thorn, Rodney K (Rod)** — Basketball Player, Executive
17008 Treviso Way, Naples FL 34110, USA

**Thorn, Tracey** — Singer (Everything But the Girl)
J F D Mgmt, Acklam Workshops, 10 Acklam Road, London W10 5QZ, England

**Thornburgh, Richard L (Dick)** — Attorney General; Governor, PA
Kirkpatrick & Lockhart, 210 6th Ave, #1100, Pittsburgh PA 15222, USA

**Thorne, Bella** — Actress
W M E Entertainment, 9601 Wilshire Blvd, #300, Beverly Hills CA 90210 USA

**Thorne, Callie** — Actress
Gersh Agency, 41 Madison Ave, #3301, New York NY 10010 USA

**Thorne, Frank** — Cartoonist (Moonshine McJuggs)
1967 Grenville Road, Scotch Plains NJ 07076, USA

# T

|  |  |
|---|---|
| **Thorne, Gary**<br>55 W Chops Point Road, Bath ME 04530, USA | Commentator |
| **Thorne, Kip S**<br>California Institute of Technology, Physics Dept, Pasadena CA 91125, USA | Physicist |
| **Thornell, Jack R**<br>3421 Tennessee Ave, Kenner LA 70065, USA | Photojournalist |
| **Thorne-Smith, Courtney**<br>W M E Entertainment, 9601 Wilshire Blvd, #300, Beverly Hills CA 90210 USA | Actress, Model |
| **Thornhill, Lisa**<br>Glick Agency, 347 5th Ave, #1404, New York NY 10016 USA | Actress |
| **Thorning-Schmidt, Helle**<br>Christiansborg Palace, Prins Jorgens Gard 11, 1218 Copenhagen K, Denmark | Prime Minister, Denmark |
| **Thornton, Al**<br>Golden State Warriors, 1011 Broadway, Oakland CA 94605 USA | Basketball Player |
| **Thornton, Billy Bob**<br>Media Talent Group, 9200 W Sunset Blvd, #550, West Hollywood CA 90069 USA | Actor, Director, Writer |
| **Thornton, James M**<br>1010 Fuller Road, Gurnee IL 60031, USA | Football Player |
| **Thornton, Joseph E (Joe)**<br>20121 Hill Ave, Saratoga CA 95070, USA | Ice Hockey Player |
| **Thornton, Kathryn C**<br>100 Bedford Place, Charlottesville VA 22903, USA | Astronaut |
| **Thornton, Kevin**<br>J-Bird Entertainment, 4905 S Atlantic Ave, Ponce Inlet FL 32127 USA | Singer (Color Me Badd) |
| **Thornton, Louis (Lou)**<br>725 Henderson Road, Hope Hull AL 36043, USA | Baseball Player |
| **Thornton, Matthew J (Matt)**<br>9820 W Eagle Talon Trail, Peoria AZ 85383, USA | Baseball Player |
| **Thornton, Melody**<br>J H Mgmt, 420 Lexington Ave, #331, New York NY 10170 USA | Singer (Pussycat Dolls), Actress |
| **Thornton, Michael E**<br>17040 W FM 1097 Road, #6101, Montgomery TX 77356, USA | Vietnam War Navy Air Hero (CMH) |
| **Thornton, Otis B**<br>4312 Ave L, Birmingham AL 35208, USA | Baseball Player |
| **Thornton, Robert G (Bob)**<br>27865 Espinoza, Mission Viejo CA 92692, USA | Basketball Player |
| **Thornton, Scott C**<br>624 30th St, Manhattan Beach CA 90266, USA | Ice Hockey Player |
| **Thornton, Shawn**<br>12 Sackville St, #2, Charlestown MA 02129, USA | Ice Hockey Player |
| **Thornton, Sidney**<br>8537 Parkdale Dr, Shreveport LA 71108, USA | Football Player |
| **Thornton, Sigrid**<br>Australian Film Institute, 236 Dorcas St, South Melbourne VIC 3205, Australia | Actress |
| **Thornton, Tiffany**<br>C E S D, 10635 Santa Monica Blvd, #130, Los Angeles CA 90025 USA | Actress |
| **Thornton, William E**<br>7640 Pimilco Lane, Boerne TX 78015, USA | Astronaut |
| **Thornton, Zach**<br>Club Deportivo Chivas, 18400 Avalon Blvd, #500, Carson CA 90746 USA | Soccer Player |
| **Thorogood, George**<br>Monterey International, 200 W Superior St, #202, Chicago IL 60654 USA | Singer, Guitarist |
| **Thorp, H Holden**<br>University of North Carolina, Chancellor's Office, South Building, Chapel Hill NC 27599, USA | Educator |
| **Thorpe, Harriet**<br>Gavin Barker Assoc, 2D Wimpole St, London W1G 0EB, England | Actress |
| **Thorpe, Ian**<br>Sports & Entertainment, 243 Liverpool St, #300, East Sydney NSW 2010, Australia | Swimmer |
| **Thorpe, J Jeremy**<br>2 Orme Square, Bayswater, London W2 4RS, England | Government Official, England |
| **Thorpe, Jason**<br>Independent Talent Group, 40 Whitfield St, London W1T 2RH, England | Actor |
| **Thorpe, Jimmy L (Jim)**<br>1612 Kersley Circle, Lake Mary FL 32746, USA | Golfer |
| **Thorpe, Otis H**<br>PO Box 400, Canfield OH 44406, USA | Basketball Player |
| **Thorsness, Leo K**<br>239 Watterson Way, Madison AL 35756, USA | Vietnam Air Force Hero (CMH) |
| **Thorson, Linda**<br>Noble Caplan Abrams, 1260 Yonge St, #200, Toronto ON M4T 1W6, Canada | Actress |
| **Thoss, Regina**<br>Grunheider Weg 165, 12589 Berlin, Germany | Singer |
| **Thost, Nicola**<br>German Competitors Assn, Kuppenheimstr 15, 75179 Pforzheim, Germany | Snowboard Skier |
| **Thottunkal, Baselios Cleemis Cardinal**<br>Major Archbishop's House, Pattom, Thiruvananthapuram, Kerala 695004, India | Religious Leader |
| **Thouless, David James**<br>University of Washington, Physics Dept, Seattle WA 98195, USA | Physicist |
| **Thrash, James**<br>16005 Hampton Road, Hamilton VA 20158, USA | Football Player |
| **Thrash, William G**<br>8 Hadley Lane, Hilton Head Island SC 29926, USA | Marine Corps General |
| **Threadgill, Henry L**<br>Joel Chriss Co, 300 Mercer St, #3J, New York NY 10003 USA | Jazz Saxophonist, Composer |
| **Threatt, Sedale E**<br>PO Box 1085, Alabaster AL 35007, USA | Basketball Player |
| **Threets, Erick**<br>2080 Vintage Lane, Livermore CA 94550, USA | Baseball Player |
| **Threlfall, David**<br>James Sharkey, 34 Kingly Court, London W1R 5LE, England | Actor |
| **Thrift, Clifford R (Cliff)**<br>705 Trisha Lane, Norman OK 73072, USA | Football Player |
| **Throop, George L**<br>239 Windwood Lane, Sierra Madre CA 91024, USA | Baseball Player |
| **Thrower, James M (Jim)**<br>17421 Pontchartrain Blvd, Detroit MI 48203, USA | Football Player |

| | |
|---|---|
| **Thrower, Robin L** <br> ImOnlineMusic, David Maida, PO Box 21176, Philadelphia PA 19114, USA | Singer, Guitarist |
| **Thuillier, Luc** <br> Artmedia, 20 Ave Rapp, 75007 Paris, France | Actor |
| **Thumann, Chad** <br> United Talent Agency, U T A Plaza, 9336 Civic Center Dr, Beverly Hills CA 90210 USA | Writer, Actor |
| **Thun, Matteo** <br> 9 Via Appiani, 20121 Milan, Italy | Interior Designer |
| **Thune, Nick** <br> 3 Arts Entertainment, 9460 Wilshire Blvd, #700, Beverly Hills CA 90212 USA | Actor, Comedian |
| **Thunman, Nils R** <br> 1516 S Willemore Ave, Springfield IL 62704, USA | Navy Admiral |
| **Thuot, Pierre J** <br> 22897 Thornbury Dr, Hollywood MD 20636, USA | Astronaut |
| **Thurber, Rawson Marshall** <br> Creative Artists Agency, 2000 Ave of Stars, #100, Los Angeles CA 90067 USA | Director, Writer, Actor |
| **Thurier, Blaine** <br> Skrzyniarz & Mallean, 9229 Sunset Blvd, #525, Los Angeles CA 90069, USA | Singer, Director |
| **Thurlow, Stephen C (Steve)** <br> 198 Shore Road, Old Greenwich CT 06870, USA | Football Player |
| **Thurman, Dennis L** <br> New York Jets, 1 Jets Dr, Florham Park NJ 07932, USA | Football Player |
| **Thurman, Gary M** <br> 225 W 32nd St, Indianapolis IN 46208, USA | Baseball Player |
| **Thurman, Michael R (Mike)** <br> 1360 7th St, West Linn OR 97068, USA | Baseball Player |
| **Thurman, Uma** <br> Untitled Entertainment, 350 S Beverly Dr, #200, Beverly Hills CA 90212 USA | Actress, Model |
| **Thurman, William E** <br> 10 Firestone Dr, Pinehurst NC 28374, USA | Air Force General |
| **Thurmond, Mark A** <br> 1614 Kings Castle Dr, Katy TX 77450, USA | Baseball Player |
| **Thurmond, Nathaniel (Nate)** <br> 5094 Diamond Heights Blvd, #B, San Francisco CA 94131, USA | Basketball Player, Executive |
| **Thurow, Lester C** <br> Massachusetts Institute of Technology, Economics Dept, Cambridge MA 02139, USA | Economist |
| **Thurston, Frederick C (Fuzzy)** <br> E1462 Grandview Road, Waupaca WI 54981, USA | Football Player |
| **Thurston, Joseph W (Joe)** <br> 9024 Paso Robles Way, Elk Grove CA 95758, USA | Baseball Player |
| **Thwaites, Brenton** <br> W M E Entertainment, 9601 Wilshire Blvd, #300, Beverly Hills CA 90210 USA | Actor |
| **Thyer, Mario** <br> 170 Silver Road, Bangor ME 04401, USA | Ice Hockey Player |
| **Thyne, T J** <br> Greene Assoc, 1901 Ave of Stars, #130, Los Angeles CA 90067 USA | Actor |
| **Thyssen, Greta** <br> 444 E 82nd St, New York NY 10028, USA | Actress |
| **Tian, Valerie** <br> Argent Talent Management, 332 Water St, #130, Vancouver BC V6B 1B6, Canada | Actress |
| **Tiangaye, Nicolas** <br> Prime Minister's Office, Primature, Bangui, Central African Republic | Prime Minister, Central African Republic |
| **Tiant, Luis C** <br> 392 Clubhouse Road, Wells ME 04090, USA | Baseball Player |
| **Tiao, Luc-Adolphe** <br> Prime Minister's Office, 03 BP 7027, Ouagadougou 03, Burkina Faso | Prime Minister, Burkina Faso |
| **Tibbetts, Billy** <br> 79 Jericho Road, Scituate MA 02066, USA | Ice Hockey Player |
| **Tibbs, Jay L** <br> 1100 Stonebrook Lane, Oneonta AL 35121, USA | Baseball Player |
| **Ticci, Stefano** <br> Olympic Committee, Foro Italico, Largo Lauro de Bosis 15, 00135 Rome, Italy | Bobsled Athlete |
| **Tice, George A** <br> 581 Kings Highway E, Atlantic Hills NJ 07716, USA | Photographer |
| **Tice, John K** <br> 1004 Bartlett Loop, West Point NY 10996, USA | Football Player |
| **Tice, Michael P (Mike)** <br> 1213 Ashbury Lane, Libertyville IL 60048, USA | Football Player, Coach |
| **Tich** <br> Gerd Kehren Mgmt, Postfach 1408, 41804 Erkelenz, Germany | Musician (Dave Dee Dozy Beaky Mick Tich) |
| **Tichy, Milan** <br> 2413 NW 7th St, Boynton Beach FL 33426, USA | Ice Hockey Player |
| **Tickner, Charles (Charlie)** <br> 5410 Sunset Dr, Littleton CO 80123, USA | Figure Skater |
| **Ticotin, Rachel** <br> Stone Manners Salners, 6100 Wilshire Blvd, #1500, Los Angeles CA 90035 USA | Actress |
| **Tidrow, Richard W (Dick)** <br> 324 NE Warrington Court, Lees Summit MO 64064, USA | Baseball Player |
| **Tidwell, Moody R, III** <br> US Claims Court, 717 Madison Place NW, Washington DC 20439, USA | Judge |
| **Tiefenthaler, Verle M** <br> 1852 Quint Ave, Carroll IA 51401, USA | Baseball Player |
| **Tiegs, Cheryl** <br> 809 Nimes, Los Angeles CA 90077, USA | Model |
| **Tierney, Garrett** <br> Stunt Company Media, 20 Jay St, #208, Brooklyn NY 11201, USA | Bassist (Brand New) |
| **Tierney, Maura** <br> Untitled Entertainment, 350 S Beverly Dr, #200, Beverly Hills CA 90212 USA | Actress, Producer |
| **Tierney, William (Bill)** <br> Denver University, Athletic Dept, Peter Barton Stadium, Denver CO 80210, USA | Lacrosse Coach |
| **Tiffany** <br> Almond Talent Agency, 8217 Beverly Blvd, #8, West Hollywood CA 90048, USA | Singer, Model |
| **Tiffany, John** <br> Casorotto Ramsay, Waverley House, 7-12 Noel St, London W1F 8GQ, England | Director |
| **Tiffee, Terry R** <br> 4 Epernay Circle, Little Rock AR 72223, USA | Baseball Player |

**Tiffin, Pamela** — Actress
15 W 67th St, New York NY 10023, USA
**Tigah** — Rap Artist
Columbia Records, 9830 Wilshire Blvd, Beverly Hills CA 90212 USA
**Tigar, Kenneth** — Actor
B R S / Gage Talent Agency, 5757 Wilshire Blvd, #659, Los Angeles CA 90036 USA
**Tigelaar, Liz** — Producer, Writer
W M E Entertainment, 9601 Wilshire Blvd, #300, Beverly Hills CA 90210 USA
**Tiger, Lionel** — Anthropologist, Social Scientist
248 W 23rd St, #400, New York NY 10011, USA
**Tigerman, Stanley** — Architect
910 N Lakeshore Dr, #2916, Chicago IL 60611, USA
**Tighe, Kevin** — Actor
Domain Talent, 9229 W Sunset Blvd, #710, West Hollywood CA 90069 USA
**Tijan, Robert** — Biochemist, Molecular Biologist
Howard Hughes Medical Institution, 4000 Jones Bridge Road, Chevy Chase MD 20815, USA
**Tikaram, Ramon** — Actor
Curtis Brown Group, 28-29 Haymarket St, #500, London SW1Y 4SP, England
**Tilbrook, Glenn** — Singer, Guitarist (Squeeze)
Quioxtic Records/Stress Mgmt, PO Box 27947, London SE7 8WN, England
**Tilelli, John H, Jr** — Army General
Stanford University, International Studies Dept, Stanford CA 94305, USA
**Tilghman, Kelly** — Sportscaster
Golf Channel, 7580 Commerce Center Dr, Orlando FL 32819, USA
**Tilghman, Shirley M C** — Educator, Molecular Biologist
Princeton University, President's Office, Princeton NJ 08544, USA
**Tiliakos, Dimitris** — Opera Singer
I M G Artists, Hogarth Business Park, Chiswick, London W4 2TH, England
**Till, James E** — Biophysicist, Cell Biologist
182 Briar Hill Ave, Toronto ON M4R 1H9, Canada
**Tilleman, Michael J (Mike)** — Football Player
180 Country Road 800 NW, Havre MT 59501, USA
**Tiller, Nadja** — Actress
Via Tamporiva 26, 6976 Castagnola, Switzerland
**Tillerson, Rex W** — Businessman
ExxonMobil Corp, 5959 Las Colinas Blvd, Irving TX 75039, USA
**Tillery, Linda** — Singer, Percussionist (Loading Zone)
Berkeley Agency, 2608 9th St, #301, Berkeley CA 94710 USA
**Tilley, Jacob** — Guitarist (Young the Giant)
Foundations Artists Mgmt, 628 Broadway, #503, New York NY 10012, USA
**Tilley, Patrick L (Pat)** — Football Player, Coach
PO Box 4523, Shreveport LA 71134, USA
**Tilley, Tom** — Ice Hockey Player
14724 Maple St, Overland Park KS 66223, USA
**Tilling, Camilla** — Opera, Concert Singer
Harrison/Parrott, 5-6 Albion Court, London W6 0QT, England
**Tillis, Mel** — Singer, Guitarist, Songwriter
Mel Tillis Enterprises, PO Box 305, Silver Springs FL 34489, USA
**Tillis, Pam** — Singer, Songwriter
PO Box 128575, Nashville TN 37212, USA
**Tillman, Charles** — Football Player
31227 Sage Court, Libertyville IL 60048, USA
**Tillman, George, Jr** — Director, Producer, Writer
State Street Pictures, 9255 W Sunset Blvd, #528, Los Angeles CA 90069, USA
**Tillman, Kerry J (Rusty)** — Baseball Player
8711 Newton Road, #61, Jacksonville FL 32216, USA
**Tillman, Lewis D** — Football Player
PO Box 166, Madison MS 39130, USA
**Tillman, Robert L** — Businessman
Lowe's Companies, 1605 Curtis Bridge Road, Wilkesboro NC 28697, USA
**Tillman, Spencer A** — Football Player
19 Lake Mist Court, Sugar Land TX 77479, USA
**Tillman, Travares A** — Football Player
3720 Tanglewood Dr SE, Atlanta GA 30339, USA
**Tillmans, Wolfgang** — Artist, Photographer
Maureen Paley Interim Art, 21 Herald St, London E 6JT, England
**Tillotson, Johnny** — Singer
American Mgmt, 19948 Mayall St, Chatsworth CA 91311, USA
**Tilly, Jennifer** — Actress
Innovative Artists, 1505 10th St, Santa Monica CA 90401 USA
**Tilly, Meg** — Actress
I F A Talent Agency, 8730 W Sunset Blvd, #490, West Hollywood CA 90069 USA
**Tilson, Joseph (Joe)** — Artist
2 Brook Street Mansions, 41 Davies St, London W1Y 1FJ, England
**Tilton, Charlene** — Actress, Model
Premier Talent Group, 4370 Tujunga Ave, #110, Studio City CA 91604, USA
**Tilton, Robert** — Evangelist
Robert Tilton Ministries, PO Box 819000, Dallas TX 75381, USA
**Timbaland** — Rap Artist, Music Producer
W M E Entertainment, 9601 Wilshire Blvd, #300, Beverly Hills CA 90210 USA
**Timberlake, Gary D** — Baseball Player
14016 Waters Edge Dr, Louisville KY 40245, USA
**Timberlake, Justin** — Singer ('N Sync), Actor
W M E Entertainment, 9601 Wilshire Blvd, #300, Beverly Hills CA 90210 USA
**Timchal, Cindy** — Lacrosse Coach
University of Maryland, Athletic Dept, College Park MD 20742, USA
**Timken, William R, Jr** — Businessman, Diplomat
State Department, 2201 C St NW, Washington DC 20520 USA
**Timko, Brittany** — Soccer Player
Vancouver Whitecaps, The Landing, 375 Water St, Vancouver BC V6B 5C6, Canada
**Timlin, Addison** — Actress
Gersh Agency, 9465 Wilshire Blvd, #600, Beverly Hills CA 90212 USA
**Timlin, Michael A (Mike)** — Baseball Player
355 High Ridge Way, Castle Rock CO 80108, USA
**Timm, Hans Hinrichsen (Timmes)** — Singer, Guitarist (Santiano)
AirForce1.TV Music, Alte Schonhauser Str 44, 10119 Berlin, Germany

| | |
|---|---|
| **Timmer, Marianne**<br>K N S B, Postbus 1120, 3800 Amersfoort BC, Netherlands | Speed Skater |
| **Timmerman, Adam L**<br>1635 585th St, Cherokee IA 51012, USA | Football Player |
| **Timmermann, Thomas H (Tom)**<br>197 Coyote Court, Pinckney MI 48169, USA | Baseball Player |
| **Timmermann, Ulf**<br>Conrad Blenkle Str 34, 13055 Berlin, Germany | Track Athlete |
| **Timmins, Margo**<br>S L Feldman Mgmt, 1505 W 2nd Ave, #200, Vancouver BC V6H 3Y4, Canada | Singer (Cowboy Junkies) |
| **Timmins, Michael**<br>S L Feldman Mgmt, 1505 W 2nd Ave, #200, Vancouver BC V6H 3Y4, Canada | Guitarist (Cowboy Junkies), Songwriter |
| **Timmins, Peter**<br>S L Feldman Mgmt, 1505 W 2nd Ave, #200, Vancouver BC V6H 3Y4, Canada | Drummer (Cowboy Junkies) |
| **Timmons, Jeffrey B (Jeff)**<br>Marsellie Mgmt, 6228 Fallbrook Ave, Woodland Hills CA 91367, USA | Singer (98 Degrees) |
| **Timmons, Osborne L (Ozzie)**<br>4901 S 83rd St, Tampa FL 33619, USA | Baseball Player |
| **Timms, Michele**<br>Phoenix Mercury, American West Arena, 201 E Jefferson St, Phoenix AZ 85004 USA | Basketball Player |
| **Timms, Sally**<br>Billions Corp, 3522 W Armitage Ave, Chicago IL 60647 USA | Singer (Pine Valley Cosmonauts) |
| **Timmy T**<br>Richard Walters, PO Box 2789, Toluca Lake CA 91610 USA | Singer, Rap Artist, Musician |
| **Timofeyeva, Nina V**<br>Bolshoi Theater, Teatralnaya Pl 1, 103009 Moscow, Russia | Ballerina |
| **Timofti, Nicolae**<br>Presidential Palace, 23 Nicolae Iorge Str, 227033 Chishinev, Moldova | President, Moldova |
| **Timonen, Kimmo S (Kime)**<br>125 Upland Way, Haddonfield NJ 08033, USA | Ice Hockey Player |
| **Timoney, John F**<br>Miami Police Department, 400 NW 2nd Ave, Miami FL 33128, USA | Law Enforcement Official |
| **Timpson, Michael D**<br>1823 Derby Glen Dr, Orlando FL 32837, USA | Football Player |
| **Timsit, Patrick**<br>Artmedia, 20 Ave Rapp, 75007 Paris, France | Actor |
| **Tinashe**<br>Type One Mgmt, PO Box 957, New York NY 10021, USA | Singer, Songwriter, Actress |
| **Tindemans, Leonard C (Leo)**<br>Jan Verbertlei 24, 2650 Edegem, Belgium | Prime Minister, Belgium |
| **Tindle, David**<br>Via Giovanni Pacchini 118B, S Maria del Giudice, 55058 Lucca, Italy | Artist |
| **Ting, Alice**<br>Massachusetts Institute of Technology, Chemistry Dept, Cambridge MA 02139, USA | Chemist |
| **Ting, Samuel C C**<br>2 Eliot Place, Jamaica Plain MA 02130, USA | Nobel Physics Laureate |
| **Tinglehoff, H Michael (Mick)**<br>20517 Kalmeadow Court, Lakeview MN 55044, USA | Football Player |
| **Tingley, Ronald I (Ron)**<br>349 Omni Dr, Sparks NV 89441, USA | Baseball Player |
| **Tinker, Grant A**<br>541 Perugia Way, Los Angeles CA 90077, USA | Businessman |
| **Tinkham, Michael**<br>6126 SE Grant St, Portland OR 97215, USA | Physicist |
| **Tinoisamoa, Pisa D**<br>636 California Oak Dr, Vista CA 92081, USA | Football Player |
| **Tinordi, Mark**<br>545 Devonshire Court, Severna Park MD 21146, USA | Ice Hockey Player |
| **Tinsley, Bruce**<br>King Features Syndicate, 300 W 57th St, #1500, New York NY 10019 USA | Editorial Cartoonist |
| **Tinsley, Jackson B (Jack)**<br>Fort Worth Star-Telegram, Editorial Dept, PO Box 1870, Fort Worth TX 76101 USA | Editor |
| **Tinsley, Jamaal L**<br>12122 Ellingwood Dr, Auburndale FL 33823, USA | Basketball Player |
| **Tinsley, Jeremy**<br>World Poker Tour, 1041 N Formosa Blvd, #PH 2, West Hollywood CA 90046, USA | Poker Player |
| **Tinsley, Lee O**<br>237 Tenor St, Shelbyville KY 40065, USA | Baseball Player |
| **Tinsley, Michael**<br>3426 Guadalajara St, Round Rock TX 78665, USA | Track Athlete |
| **Tippett, Andre B**<br>17 Knob Hill St, Sharon MA 02067, USA | Football Player |
| **Tippett, David (Dave)**<br>10287 E Diamond Rim Dr, Scottsdale AZ 85255, USA | Ice Hockey Player, Coach, Executive |
| **Tippett, Phil**<br>Tippett Studio, 2741 10th St, Berkeley CA 94710, USA | Animator |
| **Tippin, Aaron**<br>Tip Top Entertainment, PO Box 41689, Nashville TN 37204, USA | Singer, Songwriter |
| **Tippins, Kenny (Ken)**<br>524 Renaissance Way, Conyers GA 30012, USA | Football Player |
| **Tipton, Analeigh**<br>Creative Artists Agency, 2000 Ave of Stars, #100, Los Angeles CA 90067 USA | Actress |
| **Tipton, Dave L**<br>915 Bonneville Ave, Sunnyvale CA 94087, USA | Football Player, Coach |
| **Tipton, Glenn R**<br>Trinfold Mgmt, 12 Oval Road, #300, Camden, London NW1 7D4, England | Guitarist (Judas Priest) |
| **Tiriac, Ion**<br>Ion Tiriac/T V Enterprises, 251 E 49th St, New York NY 10017, USA | Tennis Player, Coach |
| **Tirico, Michael J (Mike)**<br>ESPN-TV, Sports Dept, ESPN Plaza, 935 Middle St, Bristol CT 06010 USA | Sportscaster |
| **Tirimo, Martino**<br>1 Romeyn Road, London SW16 2NU, England | Concert Pianist, Conductor |
| **Tirio, Dave**<br>One Moment Mgmt, PO Box 55156, Sherman Oaks CA 91413 USA | Guitarist (Plain White T's) |
| **Tirole, Jean M**<br>Toulouse University, Advanced Study Institute, 15 Rue des Lois, 31013 Toulouse Cedex 6, France | Nobel Economics Laureate |

**T**

**Timmer - Tirole**

**Tisby, Dexter** — Singer (Penguins)
David Harris Enterprises, 24210 E Fork Road, #9, Azusa CA 91702, USA

**Tisch, James S** — Businessman
Loews Corp, 667 Madison Ave, #700, New York NY 10065, USA

**Tisch, Steve** — Writer
1162 Tower Road, Beverly Hills CA 90210, USA

**Tischinski, Thomas A (Tom)** — Baseball Player
9905 N Donnelly Ave, Kansas City MO 64157, USA

**Tisdale, Ashley** — Actress, Singer, Songwriter
Blondie Girl Productions, 1040 N Las Palmas, Building 40, Los Angeles CA 90038, USA

**Tishby, Noa** — Actress
Burstein Co, 15304 W Sunset Blvd, #208, Pacific Palisades CA 90272 USA

**Titanic, Morris** — Ice Hockey Player
146 Delta Road, Buffalo NY 14226, USA

**Titensor, Glen W** — Football Player
729 Montrose Court, Flower Mound TX 75022, USA

**Title, Stacy** — Director
I C M Partners, 10250 Constellation Blvd, #900, Los Angeles CA 90067 USA

**Titmuss, Abi** — Model, Entertainer
Money Mgmt, 42A Berwick St, London W1F 8RE, England

**Tito, Dennis A** — Tourist Cosmonaut
1800 Alta Mura Road, Pacific Palisades CA 90272, USA

**Titov, German M** — Ice Hockey Player
9 Aspen Ridge Gate SW, Calgary AB T3H 5V4, Canada

**Titov, Vladimir G** — Cosmonaut
3 Hovanskaya Str 8, 129515 Moscow, Russia

**Titov, Yuri E** — Gymnast
Kolokolnikov Per 6, #19, 103045 Moscow, Russia

**Tits, Jacques L** — Abel Mathematics Laureate
12 Rue du Moulin des Pres, 75013 Paris, France

**Tittle, Yelberton A (Y A)** — Football Player
168 Elana Ave, Atherton CA 94027, USA

**Titus, Christopher** — Actor, Comedian, Writer
Gersh Agency, 9465 Wilshire Blvd, #600, Beverly Hills CA 90212 USA

**Tizard, Catherine A** — Governor General, New Zealand
1/12A Wallace St, Herne Bay, Auckland 1011, New Zealand

**Tizon, Albert** — Journalist
Seattle Times, Editorial Dept, 1000 Denny Way, Seattle WA 98109 USA

**Tjarnqvist, C Daniel** — Ice Hockey Player
Colorado Avalanche, Pepsi Center, 1000 Chopper Circle, Denver CO 80204 USA

**Tjeknavorian, Loris-Zare** — Composer, Conductor
State Philharmonia, Mashtots Prospekt 46, 0002 Yerevan, Armenia

**Tjoflat, Gerald B** — Judge
US Court of Appeals, 311 W Monroe St, Jacksonville FL 32202, USA

**Tkachuk, Keith** — Ice Hockey Player
11243 Hunters Pond Road, Saint Louis MO 63141, USA

**Tkaczuk, Walter R (Walt)** — Ice Hockey Player
River Valley Golf & Country Club, RR 3, Sainte Mary's ON N0M 2G0, Canada

**To, Johnnie** — Director
Milky Way Image, Milky Way Building, #1F, 77 Hung To Road, Kwun Tong, Hong Kong, China

**Toback, James** — Director, Writer
Resolution, 1801 Century Park E, #2300, Los Angeles CA 90067, USA

**Tobeck, Robert L (Robbie)** — Football Player
6620 320th St E, Eatonville WA 98328, USA

**Tober, Barbara D** — Editor
620 Park Ave, New York NY 10065, USA

**Tobey, James** — Actor
Paradigm Agency, 360 N Crescent Dr, North Building, Beverly Hills CA 90210 USA

**Tobian, Gary M** — Diver
9171 Belted Kingfisher Road, Blaine WA 98230, USA

**Tobias, Andrew** — Writer, Columnist
146 Central Park W, New York NY 10023, USA

**Tobias, Oliver** — Actor
Agentur Lentz, Barestr 48, 80799 Munich, Germany

**Tobias, Randall L** — Businessman, Diplomat
State Department, 2201 C St NW, Washington DC 20520 USA

**Tobias, Robert M** — Labor Leader
American University, Public Affairs School, Washington DC 20057, USA

**Tobik, David V (Dave)** — Baseball Player
848 Chancellor Heights Dr, Ballwin MO 63011, USA

**Tobin, Don** — Cartoonist (Little Woman)
12312 Ranchwood Road, Santa Ana CA 92705, USA

**Tobin, James R** — Businessman
Baxter Scientific, 1 Boston Scientific Place, Natick MA 01760, USA

**Tobin, Robert G** — Businessman
Ahold USA, 1385 Hancock St, Quincy MA 02169, USA

**Tobin, Vince** — Football Coach
15997 W Monterey Way, Goodyear AZ 85395, USA

**Tobolowsky, Stephen** — Actor
Innovative Artists, 1505 10th St, Santa Monica CA 90401 USA

**TobyMac** — Singer, Rap Artist (DC Talk)
True Artist Mgmt, 227 3rd Ave B, Franklin TN 37064, USA

**Toca, Jorge L** — Baseball Player
7940 NW 167th Terrace, Hialeah FL 33016, USA

**Tocchet, Rick** — Ice Hockey Player, Coach
PO Box 13563, Pittsburgh PA 15243, USA

**Tochi, Brian** — Actor
247 S Beverly Dr, #102, Beverly Hills CA 90212, USA

**Toczyska, Stefania** — Opera Singer
Stafford Law, 6 Barham Close, Weybridge, Surrey KT13 9PR, England

**Toda, Erika** — Actress
Flame, Minami Aoyama, Shibuya, Tokyo 106 0032, Japan

**Todd, Ann E** — Actress
2419 Oregon St, Berkeley CA 94705, USA

**Todd, Brendan** — Golfer
Professional Golfers Association, 100 Ave of Champions, Palm Beach Gardens FL 33418 USA

| | |
|---|---|
| **Todd, C Richard**<br>PO Box 478, Florence AL 35631, USA | Football Player |
| **Todd, Hallie**<br>In-House Media, 13636 Ventura Blvd, #298, Sherman Oaks CA 91423, USA | Actress |
| **Todd, Harry W**<br>Carlisle Enterprises, 777 Fay Ave, La Jolla CA 92037, USA | Businessman |
| **Todd, James R (Jim), Jr**<br>21639 Hill Gail Way, Parker CO 80138, USA | Baseball Player |
| **Todd, Josh**<br>Agency Group Ltd, 142 W 57th St, #600, New York NY 10019 USA | Singer (Buckcherry) |
| **Todd, Kevin**<br>15 Narla Lane, Utica NY 13501, USA | Ice Hockey Player |
| **Todd, Lani**<br>Playboy Promotions, 9346 Civic Center Dr, #200, Beverly Hills CA 90210 USA | Model |
| **Todd, Lee**<br>University of Kentucky, President's Office, Lexington KY 40506, USA | Educator |
| **Todd, Mark J**<br>Mark Todd Eventing, Badgerstown, Foxhill, Swindon Wiltshire SN4 0DR, England | Equestrian |
| **Todd, Mia Doi**<br>Fanatic Promotion, 322 Bleecker St, #G7, New York NY 10014, USA | Singer, Guitarist, Songwriter |
| **Todd, Tony**<br>Innovative Artists, 1505 10th St, Santa Monica CA 90401 USA | Actor |
| **Todd, Virgil H**<br>3095 E Glengarry Road, Memphis TN 38128, USA | Religious Leader, Educator |
| **Toennies, Jan Peter**<br>Ewaldstr 7, 37075 Gottingen, Germany | Physicist |
| **Toews, Jeffrey M (Jeff)**<br>11924 Silver Oak Dr, Davie FL 33330, USA | Football Player |
| **Toews, Jonathan B**<br>Chicago Blackhawks, United Center, 1901 W Madison St, Chicago IL 60612 USA | Ice Hockey Player |
| **Toews, Loren J**<br>165 Hawthorne Ave, Los Altos Hills CA 94022, USA | Football Player |
| **Tofani, Loretta A**<br>Philadelphia Inquirer, Editorial Dept, 400 N Broad St, Philadelphia PA 19130, USA | Journalist |
| **Toffler, Alvin**<br>Random House, 1745 Broadway, #1800, New York NY 10019 USA | Writer, Futurist |
| **Toft, Rod**<br>11350 12th St N, Lake Elmo MN 55042, USA | Bowler |
| **Tognini, Michel**<br>European Space Center, Linder Hohe, Box 906096, 51127 Cologne, Germany | Cosmonaut, France; Air Force General |
| **Tognoni, Gina**<br>Innovative Artists, 1505 10th St, Santa Monica CA 90401 USA | Actress |
| **Togo, Jonathan**<br>C E S D, 10635 Santa Monica Blvd, #130, Los Angeles CA 90025 USA | Actor |
| **Togunde, Victor**<br>Greater Visions Artists Talent Agency, 8981 W Sunset Blvd, #101, West Hollywood CA 90069 USA | Actor |
| **Toibin, Colm**<br>23 Carnew St, Arbour Hill, Dublin 7, County Dublin, Ireland | Writer |
| **Tokarev, Valery I**<br>Cosmonaut Training Center, Star City, 141160 Zvezdny Gorodok, Moscow Oblast, Russia | Cosmonaut |
| **Tokes, Laszlo**<br>Craivei Str 1, 3700 Oradea, Romania | Religious Leader, Political Activist |
| **Tokody, Ilona**<br>Hungarian State Opera, Andrassy Utca 22, 1062 Budapest, Hungary | Opera Singer |
| **Tokombayeva, Aysulu A**<br>Usenbaev Str 37, #33, 720021 Bishkek, Kyrgystan | Ballerina |
| **Tolan, Peter**<br>Fedora Entertainment, 15300 Ventura Blvd, Sherman Oaks CA 91403, USA | Actor, Director, Producer |
| **Tolan, Robert (Bobby)**<br>2213 Signal Hill Dr, Pearland TX 77584, USA | Baseball Player |
| **Tolbert, B Thomas (Tom)**<br>368 Creedon Circle, Alameda CA 94502, USA | Basketball Player |
| **Tolbert, Berlinda**<br>Isaacman Kaufman & Painter, 10250 Constellation Blvd, #2900, Los Angeles CA 90067, USA | Actress |
| **Tolbert, L James (Jim)**<br>2435 Corinna Court, San Diego CA 92105, USA | Football Player |
| **Tolbert, Mike**<br>Carolina Panthers, Ericsson Stadium, 800 S Mint St, Charlotte NC 28202 USA | Football Player |
| **Tolbert, Raymond L (Ray)**<br>2205 Crestwood Dr, Anderson IN 46016, USA | Basketball Player |
| **Tolbert, Tony L**<br>475 S White Chapel Blvd, Southlake TX 76092, USA | Football Player |
| **Tolcher, Michael**<br>Elevation Group, 1408 Encinal Ave, #A, Alameda CA 94501, USA | Singer, Guitarist, Songwriter |
| **Toledano, Eric**<br>Creative Artists Agency, 2000 Ave of Stars, #100, Los Angeles CA 90067 USA | Director |
| **Toledo, Esteban**<br>61 Rockport, Irvine CA 92602, USA | Golfer |
| **Toledo, Francisco**<br>Vorpal Gallery, 1 Front St, #1550, San Francisco CA 94111, USA | Artist |
| **Toledo, Isabel**<br>277 5th Ave, New York NY 10016, USA | Fashion Designer |
| **Toledo, Rafael**<br>Culbertson Group, 8430 Santa Monica Blvd, #210, West Hollywood CA 90069, USA | Actor |
| **Tolentino, Jose F**<br>26711 Caceres Circle, Mission Viejo CA 92691, USA | Baseball Player |
| **Toles, Thomas G (Tom)**<br>4625 46th St NW, Washington DC 20016, USA | Editorial Cartoonist |
| **Tolhurst, Lol**<br>Primary Talent International, 10-11 Jockey's Fields, London WC1R 4BN, England | Drummer (Cure) |
| **Toliver, Freddie L (Fred)**<br>674 Medical Center Dr, San Bernardino CA 92411, USA | Baseball Player |
| **Toliver, Kristi**<br>Chicago Sky, 20 W Kinzie St, #1010, Chicago IL 60654 USA | Basketball Player |
| **Tolkan, James**<br>Paradigm Agency, 360 N Crescent Dr, North Building, Beverly Hills CA 90210 USA | Actor |

Todd - Tolkan

**Toll, Joanne** — Producer
W M E Entertainment, 9601 Wilshire Blvd, #300, Beverly Hills CA 90210 USA

**Toll, Robert I** — Businessman
Toll Brothers, 250 Gibraltar Road, Horsham PA 19044, USA

**Tollberg, Brian** — Baseball Player
2104 39th St W, Bradenton FL 34205, USA

**Tolles, Tommy** — Golfer
233 Park Dr, Hendersonville NC 28739, USA

**Tolleson, J Wayne** — Baseball Player
313 Mossycup Oak Court, Spartanburg SC 29306, USA

**Tolliver, Billy Joe** — Football Player
9837 Neesonwood Dr, Shreveport LA 71106, USA

**Tolman, Allison** — Actress
Odenkirk Provissiero Entertainment, 1936 N Bronson Ave, Los Angeles CA 90069 USA

**Tolman, Timothy L (Tim)** — Baseball Player
11425 N Ingot Loop, Tucson AZ 85737, USA

**Tolsky, Susan** — Actress
10815 Acama St, North Hollywood CA 91602, USA

**Tom, Heather** — Actress
Luedtke Agency, 1674 Broadway, #7A, New York NY 10019, USA

**Tom, Kiana** — Physical Fitness Expert, Model
PO Box 1111, Sunset Beach CA 90742, USA

**Tom, Lauren** — Actress
Pop Art Mgmt, PO Box 55363, Sherman Oaks CA 91413, USA

**Tom, Logan M L** — Volleyball Player
2001 E 21st St, #136, Signal Hill CA 90755, USA

**Tom, Nicholle** — Actress
TalentWorks, 3500 W Olive Ave, #1400, Burbank CA 91505 USA

**Toma, David** — Writer
PO Box 854, Rahway NJ 07065, USA

**Tomalty, Glenn** — Ice Hockey Player
5423 Boomerang Way, RR 6, Fernie BC V0B 1M6, Canada

**Tomanek, Richard C (Dick)** — Baseball Player
165 Duff Dr, Avon Lake OH 44012, USA

**Tomanova, Renata** — Tennis Player
T C Gauting, Leutstettener Str 52-54, 82131 Gauting, Germany

**Tomasevicz, Curtis (Curt)** — Bobsled Athlete
2 Jarecki Lake, Columbus NE 68601, USA

**Tomasson, Helgi** — Ballet Dancer, Director
San Francisco Ballet, 455 Franklin St, San Francisco CA 94102, USA

**Tomba, Alberto** — Alpine Skier
Via Pambarola 7, 40068 S Lazzaro Di Savana, Italy

**Tomberlin, Andy L** — Baseball Player
7411 Crooked Creek Church Road, Monroe NC 28110, USA

**Tombs, Tina M** — Golfer
5502 E Rockridge Road, Phoenix AZ 85018, USA

**Tomczak, Michael J (Mike)** — Football Player
139 Witherow Road, Sewickley PA 15143, USA

**Tomei, Concetta** — Actress
Innovative Artists, 1505 10th St, Santa Monica CA 90401 USA

**Tomei, Marisa** — Actress
Creative Artists Agency, 2000 Ave of Stars, #100, Los Angeles CA 90067 USA

**Tomi, Vicente Ehate** — Prime Minister, Equatorial Guinea
Prime Minister's Office, Malabo, Equatorial Guinea

**Tomich, Jared J** — Football Player
2222 Red River Dr, Schererville IN 46375, USA

**Tomita, Stan** — Photographer
2439 Saint Louis Dr, Honolulu HI 96816, USA

**Tomita, Tamlyn** — Actress
Geddes Agency, 8430 Santa Monica Blvd, #201, West Hollywood CA 90069 USA

**Tomjanovich, Rudolph (Rudy)** — Basketball Player, Coach
19 West Lane, Houston TX 77019, USA

**Tomko, Brett D** — Baseball Player
14008 Lake Poway Road, Poway CA 92064, USA

**Tomko, Jozef Cardinal** — Religious Leader
Committee for International Eucharistic Congresses, Palazzo San Calisto, 00120 Vatican City

**Tomlak, Mike** — Ice Hockey Player
2200 Bordeaux Crescent, Thunder Bay ON P7K 1C2, Canada

**Tomlin, Chris** — Singer, Songwriter
Creative Artists Agency, 2000 Ave of Stars, #100, Los Angeles CA 90067 USA

**Tomlin, David A (Dave)** — Baseball Player
2020 Clayton Pike, Manchester OH 45144, USA

**Tomlin, Lily** — Actress, Comedienne
W M E Entertainment, 9601 Wilshire Blvd, #300, Beverly Hills CA 90210 USA

**Tomlin, Mike** — Football Coach
1224 Shady Ave, Pittsburgh PA 15232, USA

**Tomlin, Randy L** — Baseball Player
153 Ridgeview Lane, Madison Heights VA 24572, USA

**Tomlinson, Charles** — Writer
Bristol University, English Dept, Bristol BS8 1TH, England

**Tomlinson, Derek J (Ray)** — Computer Scientist, Inventor
B B & N Technologies, 10 Moulton St, Cambridge MA 02138, USA

**Tomlinson, Eleanor** — Actress
Conway Van Gelder Grant, 8-12 Broadwick St, #300, London W1F 8HW, England

**Tomlinson, John** — Opera Singer
Music International, 13 Ardilaun Road, Highbury, London N5 2QR, England

**Tomlinson, LaDainian** — Football Player
18755 Heritage Dr, Poway CA 92064, USA

**Tomlinson, Mel A** — Ballet Dancer
790 Riverside Dr, #6B, New York NY 10032, USA

**Tompkins, Paul F** — Actor
Avalon Mgmt, 4a Exmoor St, London W10 6BD, England

**Tompkins, Ronald E (Ron)** — Baseball Player
25072 Leucadia St, #G, Laguna Niguel CA 92677, USA

**Tompkins, Susie** — Fashion Designer
2500 Steiner St, #PH, San Francisco CA 94115, USA

**Toms, David**
6606 Gilbert Dr, Shreveport LA 71106, USA — Golfer
**Toms, Thomas H (Tommy)**
126 Leadbetter Road, Wayne ME 04284, USA — Baseball Player
**Tomsco, George**
Fireballs Entertainment, 1224 Cottonwood, Raton NM 87740, USA — Musician (Fireballs)
**Tomsic, Dubravka**
Hazard Chase, Richmond House, 16-20 Regent St, Cambridge BB2 1DB, England — Concert Pianist
**Tomsic, Ronald P (Ron)**
22 Twilight Bluff, Newport Beach CA 92657, USA — Basketball Player
**Tomson, Christopher W**
L B I Entertainment, 2000 Ave of Stars, Los Angeles CA 90067, USA — Drummer, Percussionist (Vampire Weekend)
**Tomson, Shaun**
Solitude Clothing, 1206 Coast Village Circle, Santa Barbara CA 93108, USA — Surfer
**Tonchi, Stefano**
W, Editorial Dept, 1166 Ave of Americas, #1500, New York NY 10036, USA — Editor
**Toneff, Robert (Bob)**
18 Dutch Valley Lane, San Anselmo CA 94960, USA — Football Player
**Tonegawa, Susumu**
101 Chestnut Hill Road, Chestnut Hill MA 02467, USA — Nobel Medicine Laureate
**Tonelli, John**
4 Vincent Lane, Armonk NY 10504, USA — Ice Hockey Player
**Toner, Mike**
Atlanta Journal-Constitution, Editorial Dept, 223 Perimeter Center Parkway, Atlanta GA 30346, USA — Journalist
**Toney, Andrew**
1613 14th Ave N, Birmingham AL 35204, USA — Basketball Player
**Toney, Anthony**
632 Donner Way, Salinas CA 93906, USA — Football Player
**Toney, Sedric A**
3831 Sweetwater Dr, Brecksville OH 44141, USA — Basketball Player
**Tong Hon, John Cardinal**
Catholic Diocese Center, 12F, 16 Caine Road, Hong Kong, China — Religious Leader
**Tong Jian**
Skating Association, 56 Zhonguancun South St, Beijing 100044, China — Figure Skater
**Tong, Anote**
President's Office, PO Box 68, Bairiki, Tarawa Atoll, Kiribati — President, Kiribati
**Tong, Matthew C H (Matt)**
Coalition Mgmt, 12 Barley Mow Passage, London W4 4PH, England — Drummer (Bloc Party)
**Tong, Stanley**
Innovative Artists, 1505 10th St, Santa Monica CA 90401 USA — Director
**Tongue, Reginal C (Reggie)**
1353 Saint Albans Dr, Baton Rouge LA 70810, USA — Football Player
**Tonioli, Bruno**
Independent Talent Group, 40 Whitfield St, London W1T 2RH, England — Dance Judge
**Tonis, Mike**
9231 Bella Vista Place, Elk Grove CA 95624, USA — Baseball Player
**Tonkin, Peter F**
Tonkin Zulaikha Greer, 2 Liverpool Lane, East Sydney NSW 2010, Australia — Architect
**Tonkin, Phoebe**
I C M Partners, 10250 Constellation Blvd, #900, Los Angeles CA 90067 USA — Actress
**Tonnesen, Bill**
105 E 15th St, Tempe AZ 85281, USA — Landscape Architect
**Tookey, Tim**
21008 W Ridge Road, Buckeye AZ 85396, USA — Ice Hockey Player
**Toolson, Andrew K (Andy)**
722 Ranch Circle, Alpine UT 84004, USA — Basketball Player
**Toom, Tanel**
W M E Entertainment, 9601 Wilshire Blvd, #300, Beverly Hills CA 90210 USA — Director
**Toomay, Patrick J (Pat)**
221 Tornasol Lane NE, Albuquerque NM 87113, USA — Football Player
**Toomer, Amani A**
25 Regency Place, Weehawken NJ 07086, USA — Football Player
**Toomey, Sean**
1741 Saunders Ave, Saint Paul MN 55116, USA — Ice Hockey Player
**Toomey, William A (Bill)**
4360 Park Terrace Dr, #160, Westlake Village CA 91361, USA — Track Athlete
**Toomin, Amy**
United Talent Agency, U T A Plaza, 9336 Civic Center Dr, Beverly Hills CA 90210 USA — Writer, Producer
**Toon, Al L, Jr**
PO Box 620770, Middleton WI 53562, USA — Football Player
**Tootoo, Jordin J K**
2600 Hillsboro Pike, #359, Nashville TN 37212, USA — Ice Hockey Player
**Toparovsky, Simon**
5760 W Adams Blvd, Los Angeles CA 90016, USA — Sculptor
**Topol, Chaim**
22 Vale Court, Maidville, London W9 1RT, England — Actor
**Topol, Richard**
Bret Adams Agency, 448 W 44th St, New York NY 10036, USA — Actor
**Topolsky, Ken**
A P A Talent & Literary Agency, 405 S Beverly Dr, #300, Beverly Hills CA 90212 USA — Director
**Topper, John**
Monterey Peninsula Artists, 404 W Franklin St, Monterey CA 93940 USA — Singer (Blues Traveler)
**Toppin, Ruperto (Rupe)**
PO Box 25724, Miami FL 33102, USA — Baseball Player
**Toppo, Telesphore P Cardinal**
Archdiocese, PO Box 5, Dr Camil Bulcke Path, Ranchi, Jharkland 834001, India — Religious Leader
**Toradze, Alexander**
Columbia Artists Mgmt Inc, 5 Columbus Circle, 1790 Broadway, #1600, New York NY 10019 USA — Concert Pianist
**Torbert, Stephanie**
3824 Harriet Ave, Minneapolis MN 55409, USA — Photographer
**Torborg, Jeffrey A (Jeff)**
47 Railroad Ave, Manahawkin NJ 08050, USA — Baseball Player, Manager
**Torcato, Anthony D (Tony)**
1547 SW Clay St, Dallas OR 97338, USA — Baseball Player
**Torchetti, John**
14 Crows Nest Lane, Marshfield MA 2050, USA — Ice Hockey Coach

| | |
|---|---|
| **Torczon, Laverne J** <br> 6472 Country Club Dr, Columbus NE 68601, USA | Football Player |
| **Torenstra, Waldemar** <br> Mover Shaker, De Lairessestraat 141, Amsterdam 1075 HJ, Netherlands | Actor |
| **Torgeson, LaVern E** <br> 17672 Gainsford Lane, Huntington Beach CA 92649, USA | Football Player |
| **Torii, Keiko U** <br> Washington University, Torii Laboratory, Biology Dept, Box 355325, Seattle WA 98195, USA | Biologist |
| **Tork, Peter** <br> Alan Cottam Agency, 19 Charles St, Lancashire Wigan WN1 2BP, England | Singer, Bassist (Monkees) |
| **Torke, Michael** <br> Columbia Artists Mgmt Inc, 5 Columbus Circle, 1790 Broadway, #1600, New York NY 10019 USA | Composer |
| **Torkelson, Eric G** <br> 1196 Pleasant Valley Dr, Oneida WI 54155, USA | Football Player |
| **Tormis, Veljo** <br> Estonian Academy of Music, Ravala Pst 16, Tallinn 10143, Estonia | Composer |
| **Tormohlen, Gene** <br> 2248 Walker Dr, Lawrenceville GA 30043, USA | Basketball Player |
| **Torn, Rip** <br> Sovereign Talent Group, 8421 Wilshire Blvd, #200, Beverly Hills CA 90211 USA | Actor |
| **Torng, Hwa C** <br> Cornell University, Electrical Engineering Dept, Ithaca NY 14853, USA | Inventor (Computer Processor) |
| **Torok, Mitchell** <br> 5100 Weaver Road, #702, Lake Charles LA 70605, USA | Singer, Guitarist, Songwriter |
| **Torp, Niels A** <br> Industrigaten 59, PO Box 5387, 0304 Oslo, Norway | Architect |
| **Torrance, Ingrid** <br> Lucas Talent, 100 W Pender St, #700, Vancouver BC V6B 1RB, Canada | Actress |
| **Torrance, Sam** <br> Parallel Murray Mgmt, 56 Ennismore Gardens, London SW7 1AJ, England | Golfer |
| **Torre, Joseph P (Joe)** <br> 20 Lawrence Lane, Harrison NY 10528, USA | Baseball Player, Manager |
| **Torrealba, Yorvit A** <br> 3801 S Ocean Dr, #15F, Hollywood FL 33019, USA | Baseball Player |
| **Torrence, Dean** <br> 18932 Gregory Lane, Huntington Beach CA 92646, USA | Singer (Jan & Dean), Songwriter |
| **Torrence, Gwendolyn (Gwen)** <br> Gold Medal Mgmt, 1750 14th St, Boulder CO 80302, USA | Track Athlete |
| **Torrence, Nate** <br> Messina Baker Entertainment, 955 Carrillo Dr, #100, Los Angeles CA 90048 USA | Actor |
| **Torres Delgado, Dayanara** <br> Univision, 605 3rd Ave, #1200, New York NY 10158 USA | Beauty Queen, Actress |
| **Torres, Dara** <br> 47 Wilsondale St, Dover MA 02030, USA | Swimmer, Model |
| **Torres, Diego** <br> Mega Music Productions, 16950 North Bay Road, #1706, Sunny Isles Beach FL 33160, USA | Singer |
| **Torres, Eve** <br> World Wrestling Entertainment, Titan Towers, 1241 E Main St, Stamford CT 06902 USA | Dancer, Model, Wrestler |
| **Torres, Felix** <br> HC 1 Box 6424, Santa Isabel PR 00757, USA | Baseball Player |
| **Torres, Fina** <br> I C M Partners, 10250 Constellation Blvd, #900, Los Angeles CA 90067 USA | Director |
| **Torres, Gina** <br> Framework Entertainment, 9057 Nemo St, #C, West Hollywood CA 90069 USA | Actress |
| **Torres, Harold** <br> PO Box 5357, Spring Hill FL 34611, USA | Singer (Crests) |
| **Torres, Hector E** <br> 662 Lexington St, Dunedin FL 34698, USA | Baseball Player |
| **Torres, Hector S J (Tico)** <br> Bon Jovi Mgmt, 809 Elder Circle, Austin TX 78733, USA | Drummer (Bon Jovi) |
| **Torres, Oscar Orlando** <br> Caliber Media, 9229 W Sunset Blvd, #705, West Hollywood CA 90069, USA | Actor, Writer, Producer |
| **Torres, Raffi** <br> 118 Church St, Markham ON L3P 2M4, Canada | Ice Hockey Player |
| **Torres, Rosendo (Rusty)** <br> 250 N Cedar St, Massapequa NY 11758, USA | Baseball Player |
| **Torres, Salomon R** <br> 101 Crimson Dr, Pittsburgh PA 15237, USA | Baseball Player |
| **Torres, Tommy** <br> A-PR Media, 8334 Lefferts Blvd, #3C, Kew Gardens NY 11415, USA | Singer, Songwriter |
| **Torressani, Alessandra** <br> United Talent Agency, U T A Plaza, 9336 Civic Center Dr, Beverly Hills CA 90210 USA | Actress |
| **Torreton, Philippe** <br> Artmedia, 20 Ave Rapp, 75007 Paris, France | Actor |
| **Torretta, Gino L** <br> 7830 SW 48th Court, Miami FL 33143, USA | Football Player |
| **Torrey, Bill** <br> 2740 Clubhouse Pointe, West Palm Beach FL 33409, USA | Ice Hockey Player, Executive |
| **Torrey, Rich** <br> King Features Syndicate, 300 W 57th St, #1500, New York NY 10019 USA | Cartoonist (Hartland) |
| **Torrez, Michael A (Mike)** <br> 1015 Frances Court, Naperville IL 60563, USA | Baseball Player |
| **Torriero, Talan** <br> I C M Partners, 10250 Constellation Blvd, #900, Los Angeles CA 90067 USA | Actor |
| **Torrijos Espino, Martin E** <br> Palacio Presidencial, Valija 50, Panama City 1, Panama | President, Panama |
| **Torrini, Emiliana** <br> International Talent Booking, Ariel House, 74A Charlotte St, #100 London W1T 4QJ, England | Singer, Songwriter |
| **Torrissen, Birger** <br> PO Box 216, Lakeville CT 06039, USA | Nordic Skier |
| **Torruella, Juan R** <br> US Court of Appeals, 150 Ave Carlos Chardon, #119, San Juan PR 00918, USA | Judge |
| **Torry, Guy** <br> Barry Katz Entertainment, 10100 Santa Monica Blvd, #2400, Los Angeles CA 90067, USA | Actor, Comedian |
| **Torry, Joe** <br> Proclaim Talent Agency, PO Box 23158, New Orleans LA 70183, USA | Actor, Comedian |

**Tortelier, Yan Pascal** — Conductor, Concert Violinist
M A de Valmalete, Building Gaceau, 11 Ave Delcasse, 75635 Paris, France
**Torti, Robert** — Actor
Sovereign Talent Group, 8421 Wilshire Blvd, #200, Beverly Hills CA 90211 USA
**Tortorella, John** — Ice Hockey Coach
108 3rd Ave, Saint Pete Beach FL 33706, USA
**Tortorella, Nico** — Actor
Gersh Agency, 9465 Wilshire Blvd, #600, Beverly Hills CA 90212 USA
**Torv, Anna** — Actress
United Mgmt, Marlborough House, 61 Marlborough St, #400-45, Surry Hills NSW 2010, Australia
**Torvalds, Linus** — Computer Software Designer
Open Source Development Laboratories, 12725 SW Millikan Way, Beaverton OR 97005, USA
**Torvbraaten, Tore** — Curling Athlete
Curling Assn, Sognsveien 75, Serviceboks 1, 0840 Oslo, Norway
**Torve, Kelvin C** — Baseball Player
18701 Hammock Lane, Davidson NC 28036, USA
**Torvill, Jayne** — Ice Dancer
Sue Young, PO Box 32, Heathfield, East Sussex TN21 0BW, England
**Tory, Anna** — Actress
Conway Van Gelder Grant, 8-12 Broadwick St, #300, London W1F 8HW, England
**Tosca, Carlos** — Baseball Manager
PO Box 3623, Brandon FL 33509, USA
**Toscano, Harry** — Golfer
231 Rose Hill Dr, New Castle PA 16105, USA
**Tosh, Daniel** — Actor, Comedian
W M E Entertainment, 9601 Wilshire Blvd, #300, Beverly Hills CA 90210 USA
**Toskala, Vesa** — Ice Hockey Player
Calgary Flames, PO Box 1540, Station M, Calgary AB T2P 3B9, Canada
**Toski, Bob** — Golfer
20914 Hamaca Court, Boca Raton FL 33433, USA
**Totenberg, Nina** — Commentator
National Public Radio, 635 Massachusetts Ave NW, #1, Washington DC 20001, USA
**Toth, Melissa** — Costume Designer
Gersh Agency, 9465 Wilshire Blvd, #600, Beverly Hills CA 90212 USA
**Toth, Thomas J (Tom)** — Football Player
13723 Lindsay Dr, Orland Park IL 60462, USA
**Toth, Tiffany** — Model
Playboy Promotions, 9346 Civic Center Dr, #200, Beverly Hills CA 90210 USA
**Totmianina, Tatiana** — Figure Skater
Skating Federation, Luznetskaya Nabererhnya 8, 119871 Moscow, Russia
**Totten, Robert** — Director
PO Box 7180, Big Bear Lake CA 92315, USA
**Totushek, John B** — Navy Admiral
Military Officers Assn, 201 N Washington St, Alexandria VA 22314, USA
**Toub, Shaun** — Actor
818 N Doheny Dr, #605, Los Angeles CA 90069, USA
**Tough, Kelly** — Model, Actress
Playboy Promotions, 9346 Civic Center Dr, #200, Beverly Hills CA 90210 USA
**Toulouse, Gerard** — Physicist
Laboratoire de Physique d'E N S, 24 Rue Lhomond, 75231 Paris, France
**Tountas, Pete** — Bowler
10100 N Calle del Carnero, Tucson AZ 85737, USA
**Toups, Fontaine** — Bassist, Guitarist, Singer (Versus)
Ground Control Touring, 20 Jay St, #838, Brooklyn NY 11201, USA
**Touraine, Jean-Louis** — Immunologist
Edouard-Herriot Hopital, Place d'Arsonval, 69437 Lyons Cedex 03, France
**Toure, Daby** — Singer, Songwriter
Rosebud Agency, PO Box 170429, San Francisco CA 94117 USA
**Toure, Younoussi** — Prime Minister, Mali
Union Economique/Monetaire, 01 BP 543, Ouagadougou 01, Burkina Faso
**Tournet, Scott** — Guitarist (Grace Potter & Nocturnals)
Paradigm Agency, 404 W Franklin St, Monterey CA 93940 USA
**Tournier, Michel** — Writer
Le Presbytere, Choisel, 78460 Chevreuse, France
**Toussaint, Allen** — Jazz Singer, Pianist, Composer
272 Abalon Court, New Orleans LA 70114, USA
**Toussaint, Beth** — Actress
Innovative Artists, 1505 10th St, Santa Monica CA 90401 USA
**Toussaint, Lorraine** — Actress
Innovative Artists, 1505 10th St, Santa Monica CA 90401 USA
**Tov, Emanuel** — Theologian
Hebrew University of Jerusalem, Bible Dept, Rabin Building, Jerusalem 91905, Israel
**Tovar, Steven E (Steve)** — Football Player
5607 Wagstaff Dr, Lawrence KS 66049, USA
**Tovey, Bramwell** — Conductor
I M G Artists, Hogarth Business Park, Chiswick, London W4 2TH, England
**Tovey, Russell** — Actor
Independent Talent Group, 40 Whitfield St, London W1T 2RH, England
**Tovoli, Luciano** — Cinematographer
United Talent Agency, U T A Plaza, 9336 Civic Center Dr, Beverly Hills CA 90210 USA
**Towe, Monte C** — Basketball Player, Coach
4952 SW 91st Way, Gainesville FL 32608, USA
**Tower, Joan P** — Composer
Bard College, Music Dept, Annandale on Hudson NY 12504, USA
**Tower, Keith R** — Basketball Player
12530 Aldershot Lane, Windermere FL 34786, USA
**Towers, Constance** — Actress
Cassell-Levy, 843 N Sycamore Ave, Los Angeles CA 90038, USA
**Towers, Joshua E (Josh)** — Baseball Player
1033 Crescent Falls St, Henderson NV 89011, USA
**Towery, William C (Blackie)** — Basketball Player
314 W Carlisle St, Marion KY 42064, USA
**Towle, Stephen R (Steve)** — Football Player
609 NE Lake Pointe Dr, Lees Summit MO 64064, USA
**Towles, Justin R (J R)** — Baseball Player
13806 Lowell Ave, Tomball TX 77377, USA

**Towne, Robert** — Director, Writer
1417 San Remo Dr, Pacific Palisades CA 90272, USA
**Townend, Peter** — Surfer, Publisher
820 Geneva Ave, #A, Huntington Beach CA 92648, USA
**Towner, Ralph N** — Jazz Guitarist, Pianist
Ted Kurland, 173 Brighton Ave, Boston MA 02134 USA
**Townes, Charles H** — Nobel Physics, Templeton Prize Laureate
5016 Wallingford Ave N, Seattle WA 98103, USA
**Townes, Linton R** — Basketball Player
PO Box 254, Luray VA 22835, USA
**Towns, Lester, III** — Football Player
2225 Hawkins St, #131, Charlotte NC 28203, USA
**Townsell, Joseph R (Jo Jo)** — Football Player
PO Box 606, Gardnerville NV 89410, USA
**Townsend, Andre** — Football Player
6206 Providence Club Dr, Mableton GA 30126, USA
**Townsend, Colleen** — Actress
National Presbyterian Church, 4101 Nebraska Ave NW, Washington DC 20016, USA
**Townsend, Heath** — Model
I M G Models, 304 Park Ave S, #PH N, New York NY 10010 USA
**Townsend, Jill Perry** — Artist, Sculptor
Skob Knob Studios, 1936 NE 63rd St, Lincoln City OR 97367, USA
**Townsend, John W, Jr** — Space Scientist
6532 79th St, Cabin John MD 20818, USA
**Townsend, Milon** — Artist
Blue Moon Press, 262 Moul Road, Hilton NY 14468, USA
**Townsend, Raymond** — Basketball Player
5160 Cribari Knolls, San Jose CA 95135, USA
**Townsend, Robert** — Actor, Director
A P A Talent & Literary Agency, 405 S Beverly Dr, #300, Beverly Hills CA 90212 USA
**Townsend, T Deshea** — Football Player
3208 Lenox Oval, Pittsburgh PA 15237, USA
**Townsend, Tammy** — Actress, Singer
Kass Management, 501 Santa Monica Blvd, #604, Los Angeles CA 90401, USA
**Townshend, Graeme S** — Ice Hockey Player
PO Box 1231, Saco ME 04072, USA
**Townshend, Peter D B** — Singer, Guitarist (Who), Songwriter
4 Friars Lane, Richmond, Surrey TW9 1NL, England
**Toy, Camden** — Actor
Coolwaters Productions, 10061 Riverside Dr, Box 531, Toluca Lake CA 91602 USA
**Toynton, Ian** — Director, Producer
Creative Artists Agency, 2000 Ave of Stars, #100, Los Angeles CA 90067 USA
**Toyoda, Akio** — Businessman
Toyota Motor Corp, 1 Toyotacho, Toyota City, Aichi Pref 471 8701, Japan
**Toyoda, Shoichiro** — Businessman
Keidanren Kaikan Building, 1-9-4 Ohtemachi, Chuyodaku, Tokyo 100 8188, Japan
**Tozer, Faye L** — Singer, Actress
Concorde International Artistes, 101 Shepherds Bush Road, London W6 7LP, England
**Tozzi, Umberto** — Singer, Songwriter
Momy Records, Le Vallespir, 25 Blvd Du, 98000 Monaco, Monaco
**T-Pain** — Singer, Rap Artist, Songwriter, Actor
American Talent Agency, 248 W 35th St, # 501  New York NY 10001, USA
**Traa** — Bassist (POD)
Atlantic Records, 9229 W Sunset Blvd, #900, West Hollywood CA 90069 USA
**Traber, William H (Billy), Jr** — Baseball Player
836 Lomita St, El Segundo CA 90245, USA
**Trabert, M Anthony (Tony)** — Tennis Player
115 Knotty Pine Trail, Ponte Vedra Beach FL 32082, USA
**Tracewski, Richard J (Dick)** — Baseball Player, Manager
5 Flora Dr, Peckville PA 18452, USA
**Trachsel, Stephen P (Steve)** — Baseball Player
18750 Heritage Dr, Poway CA 92064, USA
**Trachta, Jeff** — Actor
590 S Indian Trail, Palm Springs CA 92264, USA
**Trachtenberg, Michelle** — Actress
Gersh Agency, 9465 Wilshire Blvd, #600, Beverly Hills CA 90212 USA
**Tracy, Andrew M (Andy)** — Baseball Player
2226 Park Circle, Lewis Center OH 43035, USA
**Tracy, Chad A** — Baseball Player
9422 Sir Huon Lane, Waxhaw NC 28173, USA
**Tracy, James E (Jim)** — Baseball Player, Manager
7112 Woodhall Court, Presto PA 15142, USA
**Tracy, Jeanie** — Singer
T-Best Talent Agency, 508 Honey Lake Court, Danville CA 94506 USA
**Tracy, Keegan Connor** — Actress
S M S Talent, 8383 Wilshire Blvd, #230, Beverly Hills CA 90211 USA
**Tracy, Paul** — Auto Racing Driver
10524 Allthorn Ave, Las Vegas NV 89144, USA
**Trager, Milton** — Physical Therapist
Trager Institute, 3800 Park East Dr, #100, Beachwood OH 44122, USA
**Trahan, Donald R (D J), Jr** — Golfer
32 Eastlake Road, Mount Pleasant SC 29464, USA
**Train, Harry D, II** — Navy Admiral
401 College Place, #10, Norfolk VA 23510, USA
**Train, Kristina** — Singer, Songwriter
Michael Hausman Artist Mgmt, 511 Ave of Americas, #197, New York NY 10011, USA
**Trainor, Bernard E** — Marine Corps General
46874 Grissom St, Sterling VA 20165, USA
**Trainor, Kevin** — Actor
Artists Partnership, 101 Finsbury Pavement, London EC2A 1RS, England
**Trainor, Mary Ellen** — Actress
Full Empire Promotions, 1034 2nd Ave, Croydon PA 19021, USA
**Trainor, Meghan E** — Singer, Songwriter
Epic Records, 550 Madison Ave, #600, New York NY 10022 USA
**Trammell, Alan S** — Baseball Player, Manager
191 22nd St, Del Mar CA 92014, USA

**Trammell, Sam** — Actor
Innovative Artists, 1505 10th St, Santa Monica CA 90401 USA
**Trammell, Terry** — Sports Orthopedic Surgeon
Orthopedics-Indianapolis, 1801 N Senate Blvd, #200, Indianapolis IN 46202, USA
**Trammell, Thomas J (Bubba)** — Baseball Player
4672 NW 114th St, #310, Doral FL 33178, USA
**Tran, Claire** — Actress
Elizabeth Simpson Agency, 62 Blvd du Montparnasse, 75015 Paris, France
**Trank, Josh** — Director
W M E Entertainment, 9601 Wilshire Blvd, #300, Beverly Hills CA 90210 USA
**Trankov, Maxim L** — Figure Skater
Figure Skating Federation, Luzhnetskaya Nab 8, 119991 Moscow, Russia
**Transtromer, Tomas G** — Nobel Literature Laureate
Stadahuset, 421 87 Vasteras, Sweden
**Traore, Diouncounda** — Acting President, Mali
President's Office, BP 1463, Bamako, Mali
**Trapp, John Q** — Basketball Player
4785 Primavera St, Las Vegas NV 89122, USA
**Traub, Charles H** — Photographer
39 E 10th St, New York NY 10003, USA
**Traub, Sophie** — Actress
Characters Talent Mgmt, 8 Elm St, Toronto ON M5G 1G7, Canada
**Traub, Yaron** — Conductor
Opus 3 Artists, 470 Park Ave S, #900N, New York NY 10016 USA
**Traue, Antje** — Actress
United Talent Agency, U T A Plaza, 9336 Civic Center Dr, Beverly Hills CA 90210 USA
**Trautmann, Richard** — Judo Athlete
Horemansstr 29, 80636 Munich, Germany
**Trautwig, Al** — Sportscaster
NBC-TV, Sports Dept, 30 Rockefeller Plaza, #270E, New York NY 10112 USA
**Travanti, Daniel J** — Actor
1077 Melody Road, Lake Forest IL 60045, USA
**Travers, Patrick H (Pat)** — Singer, Guitarist
Hook Entertainment, 26033 Mulholland Highway, Malibu CA 91302, USA
**Travers, William E (Bill)** — Baseball Player
10 Shoreline Dr, Foxboro MA 02035, USA
**Travis, Dale** — Opera Singer
Columbia Artists Mgmt Inc, 5 Columbus Circle, 1790 Broadway, #1600, New York NY 10019 USA
**Travis, Kylie** — Model, Actress
Hartig-Hilepo Agency, 54 W 21st St, #610, New York NY 10010 USA
**Travis, Nancy** — Actress
A P A Talent & Literary Agency, 405 S Beverly Dr, #300, Beverly Hills CA 90212 USA
**Travis, Pete** — Director
W M E Entertainment, 9601 Wilshire Blvd, #300, Beverly Hills CA 90210 USA
**Travis, Randy** — Singer, Guitarist, Songwriter
Pure Fix Entertainment, 15333 N Pima Road, #145, Scottsdale AZ 85258, USA
**Travis, Scott** — Drummer (Judas Priest)
Trinifold Mgmt, 12 Oval Road, #300, Camden, London NW1 7DH, England
**Travis, Stacey** — Actress
Essential Talent Mgmt, 6399 Wilshire Blvd, #400, Los Angeles CA 90048, USA
**Traviss, Karen** — Writer
Scovil Chichak Galen, 276 5th Ave, #708, New York NY 10001, USA
**Travolta, Ellen** — Actress
6470 E Sunnyside Road, Coeur D'Alene ID 83814, USA
**Travolta, Joey** — Singer, Director
23634 Tiara St, Woodland Hills CA 91367, USA
**Travolta, John** — Actor
1504 Live Oak Lane, Santa Barbara CA 93105, USA
**Traxler, William B, Jr** — Judge
US Court of Appeals, Powell Courthouse, 1100 E Main St, Richmond VA 23219, USA
**Traya, Misti** — Actress
Abrams Artists, 9200 W Sunset Blvd, #1125, West Hollywood CA 90069 USA
**Traylor, B Keith** — Football Player
508 E Shreveport St, Broken Arrow OK 74011, USA
**Traylor, Susan** — Actress
Abrams Artists, 275 7th Ave, #2600, New York NY 10001 USA
**Traynor, J Michael** — Attorney
3131 Eton Ave, Berkeley CA 94705, USA
**Traynowicz, Mark J** — Football Player
1668 Sioux St, Lincoln NE 68502, USA
**Trcic, Michael** — Sculptor
175 Goodrow Lane, Sedona AZ 86336, USA
**Treach** — Rap Artist (Naughty By Nature)
Don Buchwald Talent Agency, 6500 Wilshire Blvd, #2200, Los Angeles CA 90048 USA
**Treacy, Philip** — Fashion Designer
Philip Treacy Ltd, 69 Elizabeth St, London SW1W 9PJ, England
**Treadaway, Luke** — Actor
Hamilton Hodell, 20 Golden Square, London W1F 9JL, England
**Treadell, Victoria M (Vicki)** — High Commissioner, New Zealand
High Commissioner's Office, 44 Hill St, Wellington 6011, New Zealand
**Treadway, H Jeffrey (Jeff)** — Baseball Player
8812 Estes Road, Macon GA 31220, USA
**Treadway, James C, Jr** — Government Official
Laurel Ledge Farm, Croton Lake Road, RR 4, Mount Kisco NY 10549, USA
**Treadwell, David M** — Football Player
553 Rita Place, Castle Pines CO 80108, USA
**Treanor, Matthew A (Matt)** — Baseball Player
460 NW 115th Way, Coral Springs FL 33071, USA
**Trebek, Alex** — Entertainer
3405 Fryman Road, Studio City CA 91604, USA
**Trebelhorn, Thomas L (Tom)** — Baseball Player, Manager
7753 E Montebello Ave, Scottsdale AZ 85250, USA
**Trebil, Dan** — Ice Hockey Player
8551 Big Woods Lane, Eden Prairie MN 55347, USA
**Trebunskaya, Anna** — Dancer
Kazarian/Measures/Ruskin, 11969 Ventura Blvd, #300, Studio City CA 91604 USA

| | |
|---|---|
| **Tree, Michael** | Violist (Guarneri String Quartet) |
| 45 E 89th St, New York NY 10128, USA | |
| **Tregear, Lucy** | Actress |
| Gavin Barker Assoc, 2D Wimpole St, London W1G 0EB, England | |
| **Treisman, Anne M** | Psychologist |
| Princeton University, Psychology Dept, Princeton NJ 08544, USA | |
| **Treitler, Leo** | Musicologist |
| City University of New York, Graduate Center, 365 5th Ave, #8204, New York NY 10016, USA | |
| **Trejo, Danny** | Actor |
| Amsel Eisenstadt Frazier, 5055 Wilshire Blvd, #865, Los Angeles CA 90036 USA | |
| **Tremblay, Francois-Louis** | Speed Skater |
| C P V Quebec, Arena Duberger, Duberger Park, 3050 Boul Central, Quebec QC G1P3N9, Canada | |
| **Tremblay, Gilles** | Ice Hockey Player |
| 104-218 Rue Notre-Dame, Repentigny QC P1B 7R5, Canada | |
| **Tremblay, Mario** | Ice Hockey Player, Coach |
| 743 Passaic Ave, #412, Clifton NJ 07012, USA | |
| **Tremblay, Michel** | Writer |
| 294 Carre Saint Louis, #5E, Montreal QC H2X 1A4, Canada | |
| **Tremblay, Yannick** | Ice Hockey Player |
| 9911 Carrington Lane, Alpharetta GA 30022, USA | |
| **Tremel, William L (Bill)** | Baseball Player |
| 315 E 23rd Ace, Altoona PA 16601, USA | |
| **Tremie, Christopher J (Chris)** | Baseball Player |
| 484 Marion Lane, New Waverly TX 77358, USA | |
| **Tremonti, Mark T** | Guitarist (Creed, Alter Bridge) |
| Agency Group, 1776 Broadway, #430, New York NY 10019, USA | |
| **Trenary, Jill** | Figure Skater |
| 4445 Governors Point, Colorado Springs CO 80906, USA | |
| **Trent, Gary D** | Basketball Player |
| 1150 Northwood Circle, New Albany OH 43054, USA | |
| **Trentini, Caroline** | Model |
| Why Not Model Mgmt, Via Zenale 9, 20123 Milan, Italy | |
| **Trento, Joseph** | Writer |
| Public Education Center, 1830 Connecticut Ave NW, #3, Washington DC 20009, USA | |
| **Trepagnier, Jeffrey (Jeff)** | Basketball Player |
| 1414 N McDivitt Ave, Compton CA 90221, USA | |
| **Treschev, Sergei Y** | Cosmonaut |
| Cosmonaut Training Center, Star City, 141160 Zvezdny Gorodok, Moscow Oblast, Russia | |
| **Tress, Arthur** | Photographer |
| 2705 Marlborough Lane, Cambria CA 93428, USA | |
| **Tressel, James P (Jim)** | Football Coach |
| Indianapolis Colts, 7001 W 56th St, Indianapolis IN 46254 USA | |
| **Trestman, Marc** | Football Coach |
| 576 Maple St, Winnetka IL 60093, USA | |
| **Tresvant, John B** | Basketball Player |
| 14814 61st Dr SE, Snohomish WA 98296, USA | |
| **Trethewey, Natasha** | Writer |
| Emory University, Creative Writing Program, 201 Dowman Drive, Atlanta GA 30322, USA | |
| **Tretiak, Vladislav** | Ice Hockey Player |
| Hockey Federation, Luzhnetskaia Naberezhnaia 8, 119992 Moscow, Russia | |
| **Tretiakov, Alexander V** | Skeleton Athlete |
| Ski Association, Luzhnetskaya Nab 8, 119270 Moscow, Russia | |
| **Tretyakov, Victor V** | Concert Violinist |
| Berlin Konzeragentur Monika Ott, Dramburger Str 46, 12683 Berlin, Germany | |
| **Treu, Adam R** | Football Player |
| 3176 NW Shevlin Meadows Dr, Bend OR 97701, USA | |
| **Trever, John** | Editorial Cartoonist |
| Albuquerque Journal, Editorial Dept, 717 Silver Ave SW, Albuquerque NM 87102, USA | |
| **Trevi, Gloria** | Singer, Songwriter, Actress |
| Westwood Entertainment, J M de Teresa 250, Col Tlacopc San Miguel, Mexico City 01040, Mexico | |
| **Trevino, Alejandro (Alex)** | Baseball Player |
| PO Box 288, Houston TX 77001, USA | |
| **Trevino, Lee B** | Golfer |
| 4906 Park Lane, Dallas TX 75220, USA | |
| **Trevino, Michael** | Actor |
| Greene Assoc, 1901 Ave of Stars, #130, Los Angeles CA 90067 USA | |
| **Trevino, Rick** | Singer |
| Texas Boogie Productions, 1 Bis Chemin Aman, 64370 Orthez, France | |
| **Trevor, William** | Writer |
| Viking Press, 375 Hudson St, New York NY 10014, USA | |
| **Trey Songz** | Singer, Songwriter |
| Atlantic Records, 1290 Ave of Americas, Concourse 3, New York NY 10104 USA | |
| **Trezeguet, David N** | Soccer Player |
| F C Juventus, Corso Galilo Ferraris 32, 10128 Turin, Italy | |
| **Triano, Jay** | Basketball Coach |
| Toronto Raptors, Air Canada Center, 20 Bay St, Toronto ON M5J 2N8, Canada | |
| **Trias, Jasmine S** | Singer |
| Universal Records, 70 Universal City Plaza, Universal City CA 91608 USA | |
| **Tribbett, Greg (Gurgg)** | Guitarist (Mudvayne) |
| Agency Group Ltd, 142 W 57th St, #600, New York NY 10019 USA | |
| **Tribe, Laurence H** | Attorney, Educator |
| Harvard University, Law School, Griswold Hall, Cambridge MA 02138, USA | |
| **Trible, Paul S, Jr** | Senator, VA; Educator |
| Christopher Newport University, President's Office, 50 University Place, Newport News VA 23606, USA | |
| **Trice, Obie** | Rap Artist |
| J L Entertainment, 18653 Ventura Blvd, #340, Los Angeles CA 91356 USA | |
| **Trichet, Jean-Claude** | Financier |
| 5 Rue de Beaujolais, 75001 Paris, France | |
| **Trick Daddy** | Rap Artist |
| Nene Musik Productions, 1460 SW Santiago Ave, Port Saint Lucie FL 34953 USA | |
| **Trickett, Lisbeth (Libby) C** | Swimmer |
| Swimming Australia, 12/7 Beissel St, Bekonnen ACT 2617, Australia | |
| **Tricky** | Rap Artist, Songwriter |
| Crown Music, Matrix Complex, 91 Peterborough Road, London SW6 3BU, England | |
| **Trier, Joachim** | Director |
| Casorotto Ramsay, Waverley House, 7-12 Noel St, London W1F 8GQ, England | |

**Triffle, Carol** — Director
Imago Theater, PO Box 15182, Portland OR 97293, USA
**Trigger, Sarah** — Actress
Forward Entertainment, 9255 Sunset Blvd, #805, Los Angeles CA 90069, USA
**Triggs Hodge, Andrew** — Rowing Athlete
Molesey Boat Club, Barge Walk, East Molesey, Surrey KT8 9AJ, England
**Trillin, Calvin M** — Writer
New Yorker, Editorial Dept, 4 Times Square, Basement C1B, New York NY 10036 USA
**Trillo, J Manuel (Manny)** — Baseball Player
7309 W Coyle Ave, Chicago IL 60631, USA
**Trimble, David W** — Nobel Peace Laureate
2 Queen St, Lurgan, County Armagh BT66 8BQ, Northern Ireland
**Trimble, Vance H** — Editor
25 Oakhurst St, Wewoka OK 74884, USA
**Trimble, Vivian** — Keyboardist (Luscious Jackson)
Metropolitan Entertainment, 2 Penn Plaza, #2600, New York NY 10121, USA
**Trimmer, H William** — Macrobiotics Engineer
1345 McLaurin Road, Siler City NC 27344, USA
**Trimper, Tim** — Ice Hockey Player
1028 Broughton Lane, Newmarket ON L3X 2L7, Canada
**Trina** — Rap Artist
Pyramid Entertainment Group, 377 Rector Place, #21A, New York NY 10280 USA
**Trinca, Jasmine** — Actress
Tavistock Wood Mgmt, 45 Conduit St, London W1S 2YN, England
**Trinh, Eugene** — Astronaut
N A S A Headquarters, 300 E St SW, Washington DC 20546, USA
**Trinidad, Felix (Tito)** — Boxer
RR 6 Box 11479, San Juan PR 00926, USA
**Trinkaus, Erik** — Paleontologist
Washington University, Paleontolgy Dept, PO Box 1214, Saint Louis MO 63188, USA
**Trinneer, Connor** — Actor
Abrams Artists, 9200 W Sunset Blvd, #1125, West Hollywood CA 90069 USA
**Trintignant, Jean-Louis** — Actor
Artmedia, 20 Ave Rapp, 75007 Paris, France
**Triplett, Kirk** — Golfer
4527 N 61st Place, Scottsdale AZ 85251, USA
**Triplett, William C (Bill)** — Football Player
222 Beechwood Dr, Youngstown OH 44506, USA
**Trippe, Thomas G** — Physicist
Lawrence Livermore Laboratory, 7000 East Ave, Livermore CA 94550 USA
**Trippi, Charles L (Charlie)** — Football Player
125 Riverhill Court, Athens GA 30606, USA
**Tripplehorn, Jeanne** — Actress
Gersh Agency, 9465 Wilshire Blvd, #600, Beverly Hills CA 90212 USA
**Tripplett, Larry C J** — Football Player
4065 Ambergate Place, Dublin CA 94568, USA
**Tripucka, P Kelly** — Basketball Player
14 Devon Road, Boonton NJ 07005, USA
**Trischka, Tony** — Banjoist
Blue Mountain Artists, 810 Tyvola Road, #114, Charlotte NC 28217, USA
**Tristan, Dorothy** — Actress
Film Acres, 2622 E 850 N, La Porte IN 46350, USA
**Trlicek, Richard A (Ricky)** — Baseball Player
PO Box 1109, La Grange TX 78945, USA
**Troccoli, Kathleen C (Kathy)** — Singer, Songwriter
K T Designs, 5543 Edmondson Pike, #7A, Nashville TN 37211, USA
**Troche, Celeste** — Golfer
560 Perry St, #108, Auburn AL 36830, USA
**Troche, Rose** — Actress, Writer, Director, Producer
Gersh Agency, 9465 Wilshire Blvd, #600, Beverly Hills CA 90212 USA
**Trocheck, Kathy H** — Writer
Harper Collins Publishers, 10 E 53rd St, Cellar 1, New York NY 10022 USA
**Troe, Jurgen** — Chemist
Universitat Gottingen, Tammannstr 6, 37077 Gottingen, Germany
**Troedson, Richard L (Rich)** — Baseball Player
899 Bowen Ave, San Jose CA 95123, USA
**Troger, Christian-Alexander** — Swimmer
I Muncher Swim Club, Josefstr 26, 82941 Deisenhofen, Germany
**Trohman, Joe** — Guitarist (Fall Out Boy)
PO Box 219, 1187 Wilmette Ave, Wilmette IL 60091, USA
**Troisgros, Pierre E R** — Chef, Restauranteur
20 Route de Commelle, 42120 Le Coteau, France
**Trollope, Joanna** — Writer
Crossworld Publishing, 61-63 Uxbridge Road, London W5 5SA, England
**Trombetta, Monica** — Actress
I C M Partners, 730 5th Ave, New York NY 10019 USA
**Trombley, Michael S (Mike)** — Baseball Player
2 Hilltop Park, Wilbraham MA 01095, USA
**Trombone Shorty** — Jazz Trombonist, Band Leader
Rosebud Agency, PO Box 170429, San Francisco CA 94117 USA
**Tronnier, Ellen** — Baseball Player
328 Anemone Ave, Palmyra WI 53156, USA
**Troost, Ernest** — Singer, Songwriter
First Artists Mgmt, 4764 Park Granada, #210, Calabasas CA 91302 USA
**Troska, Zdenek** — Director
Hostice u Volyne 77, 38701 Volyne, Czech Republic
**Trosper, Jennifer Harris** — Space Scientist
Jet Propulsion Laboratory, 4800 Oak Grove Dr, Pasadena CA 91109 USA
**Trost, Barry M** — Chemist
24510 Amigos Court, Los Altos Hills CA 94024, USA
**Trost, Carlisle A H** — Navy Admiral
7101 River Crescent Dr, Annapolis MD 21401, USA
**Trott, Stephen S** — Judge, Singer (Highwaymen)
US Court of Appeals, US Courthouse, 550 W Fort St, Boise ID 83724, USA
**Trotter, De'Hashia T (Deedee)** — Track Athlete
9900 Brannigan Circle, Knoxville TN 37923, USA

| | |
|---|---|
| **Trotter, Jeremiah**<br>6863 F M 1398, Parkton MD 21120, USA | Football Player |
| **Trottier, Bryan J**<br>528 Brookfield Court, Canonsburg PA 15317, USA | Ice Hockey Player, Coach |
| **Trotz, Barry**<br>9001 Demery Court, Brentwood TN 37027, USA | Ice Hockey Coach |
| **Trouble Valli**<br>Q Prime, 729 7th Ave, #1600, New York NY 10019, USA | Guitarist (Crazy Town) |
| **Troughton, Sam**<br>Markham Froggatt Irwin, Julian House, 4 Windmill St, London W1P 1HF, England | Actor |
| **Trounson, Alan**<br>Monash University, Immunology & Stem Cell Laboratory, Monash VIC 3800, Australia | Biologist |
| **Troup, P William (Bill), III**<br>4 Quail Wood Court, Parkton MD 21120, USA | Football Player |
| **Troupe, Benjamin L (Ben)**<br>1105 Rannoch Place, Nashville TN 37220, USA | Football Player |
| **Troupe, Tom**<br>8829 Ashcroft Ave, West Hollywood CA 90048, USA | Actor, Writer |
| **Trout, Michael N (Mike)**<br>Los Angeles Angels, Angel Stadium, 2000 E Gene Autry Way, Anaheim CA 92806 USA | Baseball Player |
| **Trout, Steven R (Steve)**<br>PO Box 1155, Tinley Park IL 60477, USA | Baseball Player |
| **Trout, Walter**<br>Fish-Net Productions, 5840 W Craig Road, #120-228, Las Vegas NV 89130, USA | Singer, Guitarist, Songwriter |
| **Trower, Robin**<br>Stardust Enterprises, 4600 Franklin Ave, Los Angeles CA 90027, USA | Singer, Guitarist (Procol Harum) |
| **Troxel, Gary**<br>11471 Earle Dr, Mount Vernon WA 98273, USA | Singer (Fleetwoods) |
| **Troxel, Melanie**<br>PO Box 637, Brownsburg IN 46112, USA | Auto Racing Driver |
| **Troy, Michael F (Mike)**<br>21187 E Alyssa Road, Queen Creek AZ 85142, USA | Swimmer |
| **Troyer, Verne**<br>12400 Ventura Blvd, #630, Studio City CA 91604, USA | Actor |
| **Trpceski, Simon**<br>Kirshbaum Demler Assoc, 711 W End Avenue, #5KN, New York, NY 10025, USA | Concert Pianist |
| **Truax, William F (Billy)**<br>735 Ruth Ave, Gulfport MS 39501, USA | Football Player |
| **Truby, Chris**<br>12244 Silverado Dr, Fishers IN 46037, USA | Baseball Player |
| **Trucco, Michael**<br>McKeon-Myrones Mgmt, 3500 Olive Ave, #770, Burbank CA 91505 USA | Actor, Director |
| **Trucks, Derek**<br>Monterey International, 200 W Superior St, #202, Chicago IL 60654 USA | Orchestra Leader, Guitarist |
| **Trucks, Toni**<br>Greene Assoc, 1901 Ave of Stars, #130, Los Angeles CA 90067 USA | Actress |
| **Trudeau, Garry B**<br>459 Columbus Ave, #200, New York NY 10024, USA | Cartoonist (Doonesbury) |
| **Trudeau, Jack F**<br>PO Box 375, Zionsville IN 46077, USA | Football Player |
| **True, Rachel**<br>L I N K Entertainment, 11872 La Grange Ave, Los Angeles CA 90025 USA | Actress |
| **Trueba, Fernando**<br>Creative Artists Agency, 2000 Ave of Stars, #100, Los Angeles CA 90067 USA | Animator, Producer, Writer |
| **Trueblood, Jeremy T**<br>10603 Keswick Place, Tampa FL 33626, USA | Football Player |
| **True-Frost, Jim**<br>Paradigm Agency, 360 N Crescent Dr, North Building, Beverly Hills CA 90210 USA | Actor |
| **Truesdale, Yanic**<br>Nancy Iannios Public Relations, PO Box 430, Signal Mountain TN 37377 USA | Actor |
| **Truex, Lambertson**<br>I C Insight Communications, Piazzale Baiamonti 4, 20154 Milan, Italy | Fashion Designer |
| **Truex, Martin L, Jr**<br>172 Tennessee Circle, Mooresville NC 28117, USA | Auto Racing Driver |
| **Trufant, Marcus L**<br>15504 SE 79th Place, Newcastle WA 98059, USA | Football Player |
| **Truglio, Joe Lo**<br>United Talent Agency, U T A Plaza, 9336 Civic Center Dr, Beverly Hills CA 90210 USA | Actor |
| **Truhill, Geraldine Sloan (Jerri)**<br>1431 Lamp Post Lane, Richardson TX 75080, USA | Astronaut Candidate |
| **Truitt, Olanda R**<br>1901 16th Way N, Bessemer AL 35020, USA | Football Player |
| **Trujillo, Chadwick A (Chad)**<br>Gemini Observatory, 670 N A'ohoku Place, Hilo HI 96720, USA | Astronomer |
| **Trujillo, Michael A (Mike)**<br>16373 6475 Road, Montrose CO 81403, USA | Baseball Player |
| **Trujillo, Robert**<br>Q Prime, 729 7th Ave, #1600, New York NY 10019 USA | Bassist (Ozzy Osborne, Metallica) |
| **Trujillo, Solomon D**<br>Qwest Communications, 700 Qwest Tower, 1801 California St, Denver CO 80202, USA | Businessman |
| **Trull, Donald D (Don)**<br>8706 Bloomfield Turn, Missouri City TX 77459, USA | Football Player |
| **Trulli, Jarno**<br>Casa del Muschna, 7513 Silvaplana, Switzerland | Auto Racing Driver |
| **Trulsen, Paal**<br>Curling Assn, Sognsveien 75, Serviceboks 1, 0840 Oslo, Norway | Curling Athlete |
| **Truluck, R-Kal K**<br>418 McDonough St, Saint Charles MO 63301, USA | Football Player |
| **Truly, Richard H**<br>2340 Juniper Court, Golden CO 80401, USA | Astronaut, Space Administrator, Admiral |
| **Truman, Dan**<br>Modern Mgmt, 1625 Broadway, #600, Nashville TN 37203, USA | Pianist, Keyboardist (Diamond Rio) |
| **Truman, James**<br>Conde Nast Publications, Editorial Office, 4 Times Square, New York NY 10036, USA | Editor |
| **Trumka, Richard L**<br>AFL-CIO, 1750 New York Ave NW, Lobby 1, Washington DC 20006, USA | Labor Leader |

|  |  |
|---|---|
| **Trump, Donald J**<br>Trump Organization, 725 5th Ave, Basement, New York NY 10022, USA | Businessman, Actor |
| **Trump, Ivana**<br>10 E 64th St, New York NY 10065, USA | Businesswoman, Model |
| **Trump, Ivanka**<br>W M E Entertainment, 9601 Wilshire Blvd, #300, Beverly Hills CA 90210 USA | Model |
| **Trumpy, Robert T (Bob), Jr**<br>75 Oak St, Cincinnati OH 45246, USA | Football Player, Sportscaster |
| **Trundy, Natalie**<br>2109 S Wilbur Ave, Walla Walla WA 99362, USA | Actress |
| **Trunenkov, Dmitry V**<br>All-Russian Bobsled Federation, Luzhnetskaja Nab 8, 119992 Moscow, Russia | Bobsled Athlete |
| **Truong Tan Sang**<br>President's Palace, 1 Hoang Hoa Tham, Hanoi, Vietnam | President, Vietnam |
| **Truscott, Lucian K, IV**<br>Avon/William Morrow, 1350 Ave of Americas, #200, New York NY 10019 USA | Writer |
| **Trusnik, Jason**<br>Cleveland Browns, 76 Lou Groza Blvd, Berea OH 44017 USA | Football Player |
| **Truth Hurts**<br>Aftermath/Interscope Records, 2220 Colorado Ave, Santa Monica CA 90404, USA | Singer, Songwriter, Actress |
| **Tryba, Ted**<br>6321 Cheryl St, Orlando FL 32819, USA | Golfer |
| **Tryggvason, Bjarni V**<br>Space Agency, 6767 Route de Aeroport, Saint Hubert QC J3Y 8Y9, Canada | Astronaut, Canada |
| **Trynin, Jennifer**<br>Vector Mgmt, PO Box 120479, Nashville TN 37212 USA | Singer, Songwriter, Guitarist |
| **Tryon, W Augustus (Ty), IV**<br>8713 Esplanade, #1, Orlando FL 32836, USA | Golfer |
| **Tsakalidis, Iakovos (Jake)**<br>6940 E Doubletree Ranch Road, Paradise Valley AZ 85253, USA | Basketball Player |
| **Tsallagova, Elena**<br>I M G Artists, Hogarth Business Park, Chiswick, London W4 2TH, England | Opera Singer |
| **Tsamis, George A**<br>12 Sweetbriar Court, Colchester CT 06415, USA | Baseball Player |
| **Tsantiris, Len**<br>University of Connecticut, Athletic Dept, Storrs CT 06239, USA | Soccer Coach |
| **Tsao, I Fu**<br>University of Michigan, Chemical Engineering Dept, Ann Arbor MI 48109, USA | Chemical Engineer |
| **Tscharnke, Tim**<br>Ulf Tscharnke, Simmersbergstra 55, 98666 Masserberg Ortsteil Schnett, Germany | Cross Country Skier |
| **Tschauner, Oliver**<br>University of Nevada, Geoscience Dept, 4505 S Maryland Parkway, Las Vegas NV 89154, USA | Mineralogist |
| **Tschetter, Kris**<br>13 Culpepper St, Warrenton VA 20186, USA | Golfer |
| **Tschogl, John M**<br>295 Shirley St, Chula Vista CA 91910, USA | Basketball Player |
| **Tschumi, Bernard**<br>7 Rue Pecquay, 75004 Paris, France | Architect |
| **Tschutscher, Klaus**<br>Prime Minister's Office, Peter-Kaiser-Platz 1, 9490 Vaduz, Liechtenstein | Prime Minister, Liechtenstein |
| **Tseng, Z Jack**<br>University of California, Palaeontology Dept, Berkeley CA 94720, USA | Palaeontologist |
| **Tsereteli, Zurab K**<br>21 Prechistenka St, 119034 Moscow, Russia | Sculptor |
| **Tsia, Ming**<br>Blue Ginger, 583 Washington St, Wellesley MA 02482, USA | Chef |
| **Tsibliyev, Vasili V**<br>Cosmonaut Training Center, Star City, 141160 Zvezdny Gorodok, Moscow Oblast, Russia | Cosmonaut |
| **Tsien, Billie**<br>Tod Williams Billie Tsien Architects, 222 Central Park S, New York NY 10019, USA | Interior Designer |
| **Tsien, Richard W**<br>29 Washington Square W, #15A, New York NY 10011, USA | Neurobiologist |
| **Tsien, Roger Y**<br>University of California, Chemistry Dept, 9500 Gilman Dr, La Jolla CA 92093, USA | Nobel Chemistry Laureate |
| **Tsitouris, John P**<br>5207 Austin Road, Monroe NC 28112, USA | Baseball Player |
| **Tsonga, Jo-Wilfried**<br>Association of Tennis Professionals, 201 A T P Blvd, Ponte Vedra Beach FL 32082 USA | Tennis Player |
| **Tsopei, Kiriaki (Corinna)**<br>Miss Universe Organization, 1370 Ave of Americas, #1600, New York NY 10019 USA | Beauty Queen, Actress |
| **Tsou, Cece**<br>C E S D, 10635 Santa Monica Blvd, #130, Los Angeles CA 90025 USA | Actress, Producer, Writer |
| **Tsoucalas, Nicholas**<br>US Court of International Trade, 1 Federal Plaza, New York NY 10278, USA | Judge |
| **Tsu, Irene**<br>House of Representatives, 1434 6th St, #1, Santa Monica CA 90401 USA | Actress |
| **Tsugibara, Kana**<br>Fitone, 4-32-12-4F, Jingumae, Shibuya, Tokyo 150 0001, Japan | Actress, Model |
| **Tsui, Daniel C**<br>53 College Road W, Princeton NJ 08540, USA | Nobel Physics Laureate |
| **Tsui, Lap-Chee**<br>Hong Kong University, Vice Chancellor's Office, Pokfulam Road, Hong Kong, China | Molecular Geneticist, Educator |
| **Tsujihara, Kevin**<br>Warner Bros, 4000 Warner Blvd, Burbank CA 91522, USA | Businessman |
| **Tsujii, Nobuyuki**<br>I M G Artists, Hogarth Business Park, Chiswick, London W4 2TH, England | Concert Pianist |
| **Tsuno, Yoshikazu**<br>Imperial Palace, 1-1 Chiyoda, Chiyodaku, Tokyo 100 0001, Japan | Prime Minister, Japan |
| **Tsvangirai, Morgan R**<br>Prime Minister's Office, Private Bag 7700, Causeway, Harare, Zimbabwe | Prime Minister, Zimbabwe |
| **Tua, David**<br>Gotham Boxing, 1414 Ave of Americas, #404, New York NY 10019, USA | Boxer |
| **Tuan, Nguyan**<br>Masterpiece Publishing, 5 Watson, Irvine CA 92618, USA | Sculptor |
| **Tuan, Yi-Fu**<br>University of Wisconsin, Geography Dept, Madison WI 53706, USA | Humanistic Geographer |

**Tubbs, Gregory A (Greg)** — Baseball Player
833 Clay Ave, Cookeville TN 38501, USA

**Tubbs, Tony** — Boxer
913 Alcorn Lane, Muscatine IA 52761, USA

**Tubbs, Winfred O** — Football Player
4212 Debbie Dr, Grand Prairie TX 75052, USA

**Tuberville, Thomas H (Tommy)** — Football Coach
Cincinnati University, Athletic Dept, 2600 Clifton Ave, Cincinnati OH 45221, USA

**Tucci, Michael** — Actor
1425 Irving Ave, Glendale CA 91201, USA

**Tucci, Roberto Cardinal** — Religious Leader
Sant Ignazio di Loyola a Campo Marzio, Via del Caravita 8/A, 00186 Rome, Lazio, Italy

**Tucci, Stanley** — Actor, Director
Olive Productions, 161 Ave of Americas, #1100, New York NY 10013, USA

**Tuccillo, Liz** — Writer, Producer
United Talent Agency, U T A Plaza, 9336 Civic Center Dr, Beverly Hills CA 90210 USA

**Tuchman, Maurice** — Museum Curator
150 E 57th St, #PH 1A, New York NY 10022, USA

**Tuck, Jessica** — Actress
Greene Assoc, 1901 Ave of Stars, #130, Los Angeles CA 90067 USA

**Tuck, Justin L** — Football Player
Oakland Raiders, 1220 Harbor Bay Parkway, Alameda CA 94502 USA

**Tucker, Anand** — Director
United Talent Agency, U T A Plaza, 9336 Civic Center Dr, Beverly Hills CA 90210 USA

**Tucker, Barbara** — Singer
Nene Musik Productions, 1460 SW Santiago Ave, Port Saint Lucie FL 34953 USA

**Tucker, Bill** — Bowler
26126 Meadowcrest Blvd, Huntington Woods MI 48070, USA

**Tucker, Chad** — Actor
W M E Entertainment, 9601 Wilshire Blvd, #300, Beverly Hills CA 90210 USA

**Tucker, Chris** — Actor, Comedian
W M E Entertainment, 9601 Wilshire Blvd, #300, Beverly Hills CA 90210 USA

**Tucker, Darcy** — Ice Hockey Player
8754 Crooked Stick Court, Lone Tree CO 80124, USA

**Tucker, Duncan** — Director, Writer
Brillstein Entertainment Partners, 9150 Wilshire Blvd, #350, Beverly Hills CA 90212 USA

**Tucker, John** — Ice Hockey Player
19833 Michigan Ave, Odessa FL 33556, USA

**Tucker, Jonathan** — Actor
United Talent Agency, U T A Plaza, 9336 Civic Center Dr, Beverly Hills CA 90210 USA

**Tucker, Lisa** — Actress, Singer
Creative Artists Agency, 2000 Ave of Stars, #100, Los Angeles CA 90067 USA

**Tucker, Michael** — Actor
Stone Manners Salners, 6100 Wilshire Blvd, #1500, Los Angeles CA 90035 USA

**Tucker, Michael A** — Fertility Biologist
Reproductive Biology, 5505 Peachtree Dunwoody Road NE, Atlanta GA 30342, USA

**Tucker, Michael A** — Baseball Player
407 Maple Ave N, Lehigh Acres FL 33972, USA

**Tucker, Robert L (Bob), Jr** — Football Player
8 Hunter Road, Hazleton PA 18201, USA

**Tucker, Ryan H** — Football Player
24752 Eagle Pointe, Columbia Station OH 44028, USA

**Tucker, Tanya** — Singer
A P A Talent & Literary Agency, 405 S Beverly Dr, #300, Beverly Hills CA 90212 USA

**Tucker, Thomas J (T J)** — Baseball Player
6616 Ridge Top Dr, New Port Richey FL 34655, USA

**Tucker, Tony** — Boxer
Club Prana, 1619 7th Ave, Ybor City, Tampa FL 33605, USA

**Tucker, Trent** — Basketball Player
433 River St, Minneapolis MN 55401, USA

**Tucker, Y Arnold** — Football Player
PO Box 514, Hilbert WI 54129, USA

**Tuckwell, Barry E** — Concert French Horn Player, Conductor
Gallo & Giordano, 76 W 86th St, New York NY 10024, USA

**Tudor, John T** — Baseball Player
5 Nathan Lane, Middleton MA 01949, USA

**Tudor, Rob A** — Ice Hockey Player
69 Cimarron Meadows Way, Okotoks AB T1S 1V9, Canada

**Tudyk, Alan** — Actor
Gersh Agency, 9465 Wilshire Blvd, #600, Beverly Hills CA 90212 USA

**Tuer, Al** — Ice Hockey Player
Calgary Flames, PO Box 1540, Station M, Calgary AB T2P 3B9, Canada

**Tueting, Sarah** — Ice Hockey Player
PO Box 980608, Park City UT 84098, USA

**Tufts, Robert M (Bob)** — Baseball Player
6738 108th St, #A27, Forest Hills NY 11375, USA

**Tufuga Efi, Tupuola Taisi** — Head of State, Samoa
Head of State's Office, Government House, Vailima, Apia, Samoa

**Tuggle, Anthony I** — Football Player
12345 Plymouth Dr, Baton Rouge LA 70807, USA

**Tuggle, Jessie L** — Football Player
540 Avala Court, Alpharetta GA 30022, USA

**Tugnutt, Ronald F B (Ron)** — Ice Hockey Player
10 Beech Grove Gardens, Stittsville ON K2S 1W5, Canada

**Tuiasosopo, Manu A** — Football Player
14616 NE 184th Place, Woodinville WA 98072, USA

**Tuilaepa Sailele Maljelegaio** — Prime Minister, Samoa
Prime Minister's Office, PO Box 193, Apia, Samoa

**Tuitert, Mark** — Speed Skater
Mauritslaan 34, 8448 Heerenveen PE, Netherlands

**Tu'ivakano, Lord** — Prime Minister, Tonga
Prime Minister's Office, PO Box 62, Taufa'ahau Road, Nuku'alofa, Tonga

**Tuke, Blair** — Yachtsman
Kerikeri Cruising Club, 346 Opito Bay Road, R D 1, Kerikeri 0294, Bay of Islands, New Zealand

**Tukur, Ulrich** — Actor
Anne Alvares Correa, 34 Rue Jouffroy d'Abbans, 75017 Paris, France

**Tullis, William J (Willie)** — Football Player
10018 Knoboak Dr, #4, Houston TX 77080, USA
**Tulloch, Elizabeth (Bitsie)** — Actress, Producer
W M E Entertainment, 9601 Wilshire Blvd, #300, Beverly Hills CA 90210 USA
**Tulloch, Stephen M** — Football Player
629 Palisades Court, Brentwood TN 37027, USA
**Tully, Caitlin** — Concert Violinist
I M G Artists, Hogarth Business Park, Chiswick, London W4 2TH, England
**Tulowitzki, Troy T** — Baseball Player
Colorado Rockies Foundation, 2001 Blake St, Denver CO 80205, USA
**Tulving, Endel** — Psychologist
45 Baby Point Crescent, York ON M6S 2B7, Canada
**Tuman, Jerame D** — Football Player
1303 Hidden Canyon Court, Sewickley PA 15143, USA
**Tumi, Christian W Cardinal** — Religious Leader
Archveche, BP 179, Douala, Cameroon
**Tune, Thomas J (Tommy)** — Dancer, Actor, Choreographer
I C M Partners, 10250 Constellation Blvd, #900, Los Angeles CA 90067 USA
**Tung Chee Hwa** — Chief Executive, Hong Kong
Emeritus Chief Executive's Office, 28 Kennedy Road, Hong Kong, China
**Tunie, Tamara** — Actress
Paradigm Agency, 360 N Crescent Dr, North Building, Beverly Hills CA 90210 USA
**Tunnell, B Lee** — Baseball Player
6000 Kingsbridge Dr, Oklahoma City OK 73162, USA
**Tunney, Jim** — Football Referee
PO Box 1440, Pebble Beach CA 93953, USA
**Tunney, John V** — Senator, CA
304 Chautauqua Blvd, Pacific Palisades CA 90272, USA
**Tunney, Robin** — Actress
Creative Artists Agency, 2000 Ave of Stars, #100, Los Angeles CA 90067 USA
**Tunnicliffe, Anna** — Yachtswoman
New York Yacht Club, 37 W 44th St, New York NY 10036, USA
**Tunstall, Kate V (K T)** — Singer, Guitarist, Songwriter
Creative Artists Agency, 2000 Ave of Stars, #100, Los Angeles CA 90067 USA
**Tuohy, Kat** — Actress, Comedienne
OmniPop Talent Group, 4605 Lankershim Blvd, #201, Toluca Lake CA 91602 USA
**Tupa, Thomas J (Tom)** — Football Player
6761 Rivercrest Dr, Brecksville OH 44141, USA
**Tupman, Matt** — Baseball Player
3 Lincoln St, Concord NH 03301, USA
**Tupov VI** — King, Tonga
Royal Palace, PO Box 6, Nuku'alofa, Tonga
**Tupper, James** — Actor
I C M Partners, 10250 Constellation Blvd, #900, Los Angeles CA 90067 USA
**Tur, Arlene** — Actress, Comedienne
Gersh Agency, 9465 Wilshire Blvd, #600, Beverly Hills CA 90212 USA
**Turang, Brian C** — Baseball Player
3014 McNab Ave, Long Beach CA 90808, USA
**Turchynov, Oleksandr V** — President, Prime Minister, Ukraine
President's Office, Bankova Str 11, 01220 Kiev, Ukraine
**Turco, Marty V** — Ice Hockey Player
3207 Drexel Dr, Highland Park TX 75205, USA
**Turco, Paige** — Actress
Gersh Agency, 9465 Wilshire Blvd, #600, Beverly Hills CA 90212 USA
**Turcotte, Alfie** — Ice Hockey Player
816 Hawk Dr, Wolverine Lake MI 48390, USA
**Turcotte, Darren** — Ice Hockey Player
North Bay Skyhawks, 100 Chippewa W, North Bay ON P1B 6G2, Canada
**Turcotte, Donald L (Don)** — Geophysicist
27104 Middle Golf Dr, El Macero CA 95618, USA
**Turcotte, Jean-Claude Cardinal** — Religious Leader
1071 Rue de la Cathedrale, Montreal QC H2B 2V4, Canada
**Turcotte, Mathieu** — Speed Skater
Speed Skating Canada, 2781 Lancaster Road, #402, Ottawa ON K1B 1A7, Canada
**Turcotte, Ron J M** — Thoroughbred Racing Jockey
82 Seattle Slew Dr, Howell NJ 07731, USA
**Turek, Roman** — Ice Hockey Player
Sports Corp, 10088 102nd Ave, Edmonton AB T5J 2Z1, Canada
**Turgeon, Mark** — Basketball Coach
University of Maryland, Athletic Dept, College Park MD 20742, USA
**Turgeon, Pierre** — Ice Hockey Player
2930 E Iliff Ave, Denver CO 80210, USA
**Turgoose, Thomas** — Actor
Troika, 74 Clerkenwell Road, #300, London EC1M 5QA, England
**Turk, Danilo** — President, Slovenia
President's Office, Erjavceva 17, 61000 Ljubljana, Slovenia
**Turk, Matt E** — Football Player
54 Old Woods Passage, Missouri City TX 77459, USA
**Turkel, Ann** — Actress, Model
10701 Wilshire Blvd, #2001, Los Angeles CA 90024, USA
**Turkoglu, Hidayet (Hedo)** — Basketball Player
322 E Central Blvd, #1203, Orlando FL 32801, USA
**Turkson, Peter K A Cardinal** — Religious Leader
Pontifical Council for Justice & Peace, Piazza S Calisto 16, 00120 Vatican City
**Turley, Kyle D** — Football Player
7548 Kingdom Dr, Riverside CA 92506, USA
**Turlington, Christy** — Model, Director
United Talent Agency, U T A Plaza, 9336 Civic Center Dr, Beverly Hills CA 90210 USA
**Turman, Glynn R** — Actor
Elkins Mgmt, 8306 Wilshire Blvd, #3643, Beverly Hills CA 90211, USA
**Turnage, Mark-Anthony** — Composer
Cathy Nelson, Court House, Dorstone, Herefordshire HR3 6AW, England
**Turnball, Ian** — Ice Hockey Player
23930 Ocean Ave, #154, Torrance CA 90505, USA
**Turnbloom, Lucas** — Editorial Cartoonist
Southern Cross, Editorial Dept, 3888 Paducah Dr, San Diego CA 92117, USA

V.I.P. Address Book

987

| | |
|---|---|
| **Turnbow, T Derrick**<br>2224 Brienz Valley Dr, Franklin TN 37064, USA | Baseball Player |
| **Turnbull, Perry**<br>2186 Cedar Forest Court, Chesterfield MO 63017, USA | Ice Hockey Player |
| **Turnbull, Renaldo A**<br>9507 Chanson Place, Matthews NC 28105, USA | Football Player |
| **Turnbull, Wendy**<br>822 Boylston Dt, #203, Chestnut Hill MA 02467, USA | Tennis Player |
| **Turner, Aidan**<br>Creative Artists Agency, 2000 Ave of Stars, #100, Los Angeles CA 90067 USA | Actor |
| **Turner, Alexander D (Alex)**<br>Wildlife Entertainment, 21 Heathman's Road, London SW6 4TJ, England | Singer, Guitarist (Arctic Monkeys) |
| **Turner, Andy**<br>Windish Agency, 1658 N Milwaukee Ave, #211, Chicago IL 60647, USA | Musician (Plaid) |
| **Turner, Brad**<br>A P A Talent & Literary Agency, 405 S Beverly Dr, #300, Beverly Hills CA 90212 USA | Director, Producer |
| **Turner, Bree N**<br>Brillstein Entertainment Partners, 9150 Wilshire Blvd, #350, Beverly Hills CA 90212 USA | Actress |
| **Turner, Cathy**<br>251 East Ave, Hilton NY 14468, USA | Speed Skater |
| **Turner, Cecil A**<br>2717 Dog Leg Trail, McKinney TX 75069, USA | Football Player |
| **Turner, Christopher W (Chris)**<br>28553 N Quarry Dr, Elberta AL 36530, USA | Baseball Player |
| **Turner, Craig**<br>Hardin-Simmons University, President's Office, Abilene TX 79698, USA | Educator |
| **Turner, Dean**<br>26900 Captains Lane, Franklin MI 48025, USA | Ice Hockey Player |
| **Turner, Dylan**<br>Hatton McEwan, 3 Chocolate Studios, 7 Shepherdess Place, London N1 7LJ, England | Actor |
| **Turner, Edwin L**<br>Princeton University, Astrophysical Sciences Dept, Princeton NJ 08544, USA | Astrophysicist |
| **Turner, Elston H**<br>23 Commanders Cove, Missouri City TX 77459, USA | Basketball Player |
| **Turner, Evan N**<br>Indiana Pacers, Conseco Fieldhouse, 125 S Pennsylvania, Indianapolis IN 46204 USA | Basketball Player |
| **Turner, Floyd, Jr**<br>9626 Garden Row Dr, Sugar Land TX 77498, USA | Football Player |
| **Turner, Gideon**<br>Artists Partnership, 101 Finsbury Pavement, London EC2A 1RS, England | Actor |
| **Turner, Guinevere**<br>Jaret Entertainment, 6973 Birdview Ave, Malibu CA 90265, USA | Actress |
| **Turner, James A (Jim)**<br>14155 W 59th Place, Arvada CO 80004, USA | Football Player |
| **Turner, James T**<br>US Claims Court, 717 Madison Place NW, Washington DC 20439, USA | Judge |
| **Turner, James, Jr**<br>General Dynamics, 2941 Fairview Park Dr, #100, Falls Church VA 22042, USA | Businessman |
| **Turner, Janine**<br>Linda McAlister Talent, 530 S Lake Ave, #435, Pasadena CA 91101, USA | Actress, Model |
| **Turner, Jeffrey S (Jeff)**<br>1590 Woodland Ave, Winter Park FL 32789, USA | Basketball Player |
| **Turner, John N W**<br>59 Oriole Road, Toronto ON M4V 2E9, Canada | Prime Minister, Canada |
| **Turner, John W (Jerry)**<br>1935 18th St, #B, Santa Monica CA 90404, USA | Baseball Player |
| **Turner, John, Jr**<br>3217 Cedar Ave S, Minneapolis MN 55407, USA | Football Player |
| **Turner, Josh**<br>Modern Mgmt, 1625 Broadway, #600, Nashville TN 37203, USA | Singer, Guitarist |
| **Turner, Karri**<br>Premiere Artists Agency, 1875 Century Park E, #2250, Los Angeles CA 90067 USA | Actress |
| **Turner, Kathleen**<br>Don Buchwald Talent Agency, 6500 Wilshire Blvd, #2200, Los Angeles CA 90048 USA | Actress |
| **Turner, Keena**<br>8200 W Erb Way, Tracy CA 95304, USA | Football Player, Coach |
| **Turner, Kevin**<br>Microsoft Corp, 1 Microsoft Way, Redmond WA 98052, USA | Businessman |
| **Turner, Marcus J**<br>5032 Meadow Wood Ave, Lakewood CA 90712, USA | Football Player |
| **Turner, Michael**<br>912 Chattanooga Trace, Suwanee GA 30024, USA | Football Player |
| **Turner, Morgan**<br>I C M Partners, 10250 Constellation Blvd, #900, Los Angeles CA 90067 USA | Actress |
| **Turner, Nicholas (Nik)**<br>Money Talks Mgmt, PO Box 5, Whitland Dyfed SA34 0WA, Wales | Singer, Saxophonist (Hawkwind) |
| **Turner, Norv**<br>PO Box 400, Del Mar CA 92014, USA | Football Coach |
| **Turner, Odessa**<br>177 Cortland Terrace, Teaneck NJ 07666, USA | Football Player |
| **Turner, P Kevin**<br>215 Liberty Lake Dr, Vestavia AL 35242, USA | Football Player |
| **Turner, R E (Ted), III**<br>Turner Foundation, 133 Luckie St NW, #200, Atlanta GA 30303, USA | Sports Executive, Yachtsman, Businessman |
| **Turner, R Gerald**<br>Southern Methodist University, President's Office, Dallas TX 75275, USA | Educator |
| **Turner, Robert H (Bake)**<br>PO Box 277, Alpine TX 79831, USA | Football Player |
| **Turner, Ronald L**<br>Ceridian Corp, 3311 E Old Shakopee Road, Minneapolis MN 55425, USA | Businessman |
| **Turner, Shane L**<br>3032 Van Reed Road, Reading PA 19608, USA | Baseball Player |
| **Turner, Sherri**<br>5 Alpine St, Carbondale CO 81623, USA | Golfer |
| **Turner, Sophie**<br>Independent Talent Group, 40 Whitfield St, London W1T 2RH, England | Actress |

| | |
|---|---|
| **Turner, Stansfield**<br>600 New Hampshire Ave NW, #800, Washington DC 20037, USA | Navy Admiral, Government Official |
| **Turner, Steve**<br>Legends of 21st Century, 7 Trinity Row, Florence MA 01062, USA | Guitarist (Green River, Mudhoney) |
| **Turner, Tina**<br>L M A Productions, 998C Old Country Road, #409, Plainview NY 11803, USA | Singer, Actress |
| **Turner, Tyrin**<br>Williams Talent Agency, 1438 N Gower St, Building 35, Los Angeles CA 90028, USA | Actor |
| **Turner, Vernon M**<br>86 Crosshill St, Staten Island NY 10301, USA | Football Player |
| **Turner, W Matthew (Matt)**<br>829 Della Dr, Lexington KY 40504, USA | Baseball Player |
| **Turner, William (Bill)**<br>3271 Wisteria Tree St, Las Vegas NV 89135, USA | Basketball Player |
| **Turner, William H (Billy), Jr**<br>230 Nassau Blvd, Garden City NY 11530, USA | Thoroughbred Racing Trainer |
| **Turnesa, Marc**<br>Professional Golfers Association, 100 Ave of Champions, Palm Beach Gardens FL 33418 USA | Golfer |
| **Turnley, David C**<br>34 Rue des Frances Bourgeois, 75003 Paris, France | Photojournalist |
| **Turnovsky, Martin**<br>Gerhild Baron, Dornbacher Str 41/III/2, 1170 Vienna, Austria | Conductor |
| **Turow, Scott F**<br>233 S Wacker Dr, #8000, Chicago IL 60606, USA | Writer |
| **Turre, Steve**<br>Brad Simon Organization, 445 E 80th St, #4C, New York NY 10075 USA | Jazz Trombonist |
| **Turrell, James A**<br>Skystone Foundation, PO Box 220, Flagstaff AZ 86002, USA | Artist |
| **Turteltaub, Jon**<br>Junction Entertainment, 500 S Buena Vista St, Animation Building, Burbank CA 91521, USA | Director |
| **Turturro, Aida**<br>Framework Entertainment, 9057 Nemo St, #C, West Hollywood CA 90069 USA | Actress |
| **Turturro, John**<br>I C M Partners, 10250 Constellation Blvd, #900, Los Angeles CA 90067 USA | Actor, Director |
| **Turturro, Nicholas**<br>L I N K Entertainment, 11872 La Grange Ave, Los Angeles CA 90025 USA | Actor, Director |
| **Turunen, Tarja**<br>N E M S Enterprises, Av Rivadavia 4686, 14 Capital Federal, Argentina | Singer, Songwriter |
| **Tushingham, Rita**<br>Lip Service, 4 Kingly St, London W1R 5LF, England | Actress |
| **Tuten, Melvin E, Jr**<br>13779 Mottlestone Dr, Pickerington OH 43147, USA | Football Player |
| **Tuten, Richard L (Rick)**<br>1146 SE 15th St, Ocala FL 34471, USA | Football Player |
| **Tutone, Tommy**<br>Hook Entertainment, 26033 Mulholland Highway, Malibu CA 91302, USA | Singer, Dancer |
| **Tutor, Ronald N**<br>Tutor Perini Corp, 15901 Olden St, Sylmar CA 91342, USA | Producer, Businessman |
| **Tuttle, Jerry O**<br>J O T Enterprises, 5875 Trinity Parkway, #130, Centreville VA 20120, USA | Navy Admiral |
| **Tuttle, Steve**<br>928 Belfair Road, Bellevue WA 98004, USA | Ice Hockey Player |
| **Tuttle, William G T, Jr**<br>9707 Ceralene Dr, Fairfax VA 22032, USA | Army General |
| **Tutu, Desmond M**<br>PO Box 1092, Milnerton, 7435 Cape Town, South Africa | Nobel Peace Laureate, Religious Leader |
| **Tuur, Regilio**<br>New York Boxing Club, 1616 Whitestone Expressway, Whitestone NY 11357, USA | Boxer |
| **Tuzzolino, Tony**<br>75 Chasewood Lane, East Amherst NY 14051, USA | Ice Hockey Player |
| **Tveit, Aaron**<br>Creative Artists Agency, 2000 Ave of Stars, #100, Los Angeles CA 90067 USA | Actor |
| **Tverdovsky, Oleg I**<br>17832 Margate St, #6, Encino CA 91316, USA | Ice Hockey Player |
| **Twaalfhoven, Merlijn**<br>La Vie Sur Terre, Palamedesstr 9-1, 1054 Amsterdam HS, Netherlands | Composer |
| **Twain, Shania**<br>Special Artists Agency, 9200 Sunset Blvd, #410, West Hollywood CA 90069 USA | Singer, Songwriter, Model |
| **Twardzik, Dave J**<br>PO Box 6351, Norfolk VA 23508, USA | Basketball Player, Executive |
| **Tway, Bob**<br>6405 Oak Tree Circle, Edmond OK 73025, USA | Golfer |
| **Tweed, Shannon**<br>Characters Talent Mgmt, 8 Elm St, Toronto ON M5G 1G7, Canada | Actress, Model |
| **Tweedy, Cheryl**<br>Polydor Records, 364-366 Kensington High St, London W14 8NS, England | Singer (Girls Aloud) |
| **Tweedy, Jeff S**<br>Tom Margherita Mgmt, 2200 W Foster Ave, #2, Chicago IL 60625, USA | Singer, Guitarist (Uncle Tupelo, Wilco) |
| **Tweet**<br>Creative Artists Agency, 2000 Ave of Stars, #100, Los Angeles CA 90067 USA | Singer, Songwriter |
| **Twellman, Taylor**<br>ESPN-TV, Sports Dept, ESPN Plaza, 935 Middle St, Bristol CT 06010 USA | Soccer Player, Sportscaster |
| **Twigg, Rebecca**<br>7001 Old Redmond Road, #E318, Redmond WA 98052, USA | Cyclist |
| **Twiggs, Gregory W (Greg)**<br>PO Box 5293, Carefree AZ 85377, USA | Golfer |
| **Twiggy**<br>4 Saint Georges House, Hanover Square, London W1R 9AJ, England | Model, Actress |
| **Twilley, Dwight**<br>Paramour Group, 10002 Hewlett St, Neillsville WI 54456, USA | Singer, Keyboardist, Songwriter |
| **Twilley, Howard J, Jr**<br>7040 Hill Forest Dr, Dallas TX 75230, USA | Football Player |
| **Twist, Tony**<br>63 Nordic Lane, Defiance MO 63341, USA | Ice Hockey Player |
| **Twista**<br>Courtney Barnes Group, 1680 N Vine St, #1119, Los Angeles CA 90028, USA | Rap Artist |

**Twitty, Howard** — Golfer
8007 E Mercer Lane, Scottsdale AZ 85260, USA

**Twitty, Jeffrey D (Jeff)** — Baseball Player
812 Willow Cove Road, Chapin SC 29036, USA

**Twohy, David** — Director
603 Ocean Ave, #3, Santa Monica CA 90402, USA

**Twohy, Mike** — Cartoonist
605 Beloit Ave, Kensington CA 94708, USA

**Twohy, Robert** — Cartoonist
New Yorker, Editorial Dept, 4 Times Square, Basement C1B, New York NY 10036 USA

**Twomey, Steve** — Journalist
City University of New York, Graduate Journalism School, 219 W 40th St, New York NY 10018, USA

**Tydings, Joseph D** — Senator, MD
2705 Pocock Road, Monkton MD 21111, USA

**Tyers, Kathy** — Writer
Martha Millard Agency, 204 Park Ave, Madison NJ 07940, USA

**Tykwer, Tom** — Director, Writer, Actor
X-Film Creative Pool, Kurfenstenstr 57, 10785 Berlin, Germany

**Tyler, Aisha** — Actress, Comedienne
United Talent Agency, U T A Plaza, 9336 Civic Center Dr, Beverly Hills CA 90210 USA

**Tyler, Anne** — Writer
8 Roland Gardens, Baltimore MD 21210, USA

**Tyler, Bonnie** — Singer, Songwriter
International Artists, PO Box 32, 5360 Grave AA, Netherlands

**Tyler, Brian** — Composer
Chasen Agency, 8899 Beverly Blvd, #405, Los Angeles CA 90048 USA

**Tyler, James Michael** — Actor
A K A Talent, 6310 San Vicente Blvd, #200, Los Angeles CA 90048, USA

**Tyler, Judy** — Model
Playboy Promotions, 9346 Civic Center Dr, #200, Beverly Hills CA 90210 USA

**Tyler, Liv** — Actress, Model
Untitled Entertainment, 350 S Beverly Dr, #200, Beverly Hills CA 90212 USA

**Tyler, Maurice M** — Football Player
7066 Whitfield Dr, Riverdale GA 30296, USA

**Tyler, Richard** — Fashion Designer
Richard Tyler Couture, 727 Washington St, New York NY 10014, USA

**Tyler, Robert** — Actor
Don Buchwald Talent Agency, 10 E 44th St, New York NY 10017 USA

**Tyler, Steven V** — Singer (Aerosmith), Songwriter
Front Line Mgmt, 1100 Glendon Ave, #2000, Los Angeles CA 90024 USA

**Tyler, Terry C** — Basketball Player
6500 Tauton Road NW, Albuquerque NM 87120, USA

**Tyler, Wendell A** — Football Player
44143 20th St W, Lancaster CA 93534, USA

**Tylo, Hunter** — Actress, Model
11684 Ventura Blvd, #910, Studio City CA 91604, USA

**Tylo, Michael** — Actor
11684 Ventura Blvd, #910, Studio City CA 91604, USA

**Tylski, Richard L (Rich)** — Football Player
5456 Tierra Verde Lane, Jacksonville FL 32258, USA

**Tyminski, Daniel J (Dan)** — Singer, Guitarist (Union Station)
Keith Case Assoc, 1025 17th Ave S, #200, Nashville TN 37212 USA

**Tyner, Jason R** — Baseball Player
5535 Sul Ross, Beaumont TX 77706, USA

**Tyner, McCoy** — Jazz Pianist, Composer
Blue Note Management Group, 131 W 3rd St, New York NY 10012, USA

**Tyree, David M** — Football Player
38 Poplar Road, Piscataway NJ 08854, USA

**Tyrell, Steve** — Singer
Oscar Music Agency, 14 Inchmurrin Dr, Glasgow G73 5RT, Scotland

**Tyrrell, Timothy G (Tim)** — Football Player
17 Fallstone Dr, Streamwood IL 60107, USA

**Tyson, Cicely** — Actress
315 W 70th St, New York NY 10023, USA

**Tyson, Ian** — Singer, Songwriter
Richard Flohil Assoc, 60 McGill St, Toronto ON M5B 1H2, Canada

**Tyson, John H** — Businessman
Tyson Foods Inc, 2200 W Don Tyson Parkway, Springdale AR 72762, USA

**Tyson, Laura D** — Government Official, Economist
London Business School, Sussex Place, Regent Park, London NW1 4SA, England

**Tyson, Michael G (Mike)** — Boxer
Krupp Kommunications, 636 Ave of Americas, #4C, New York NY 10011, USA

**Tyson, Michael R (Mike)** — Baseball Player
479 Thunderhead Canyon Dr, Ballwin MO 63011, USA

**Tyson, Neil de Grasse** — Astrophysicist
Hayden Planetarium, 81 Central Park W, New York NY 10024, USA

**Tyson, Richard** — Actor
C E S D, 10635 Santa Monica Blvd, #130, Los Angeles CA 90025 USA

**Tyson, Sylvia** — Singer, Songwriter
Jensen Music International, PO Box 3445, Charlottetown PE C1A 8W5, Canada

**Tyurin, Mikhail V** — Cosmonaut
Cosmonaut Training Center, Star City, 141160 Zvezdny Gorodok, Moscow Oblast, Russia

| | |
|---|---|
| **Ubach, Alanna**<br>Margrit Polak Mgmt, 1920 Hillhurst, #405, Los Angeles CA 90027, USA | Actress |
| **Uchan, Philippe**<br>Artmedia, 20 Ave Rapp, 75007 Paris, France | Actor, Director |
| **Uchida, Mitsuko**<br>Victoria Rowsell Artist Mgmt, 34 Addington Square, London SE5 7LB, England | Concert Pianist |
| **Ude, Filip**<br>Gimnasticki Klub Majan Zadravec Macan, Tome Masaryka 24, 40000 Cakovec, Croatia | Gymnast |
| **Udenio, Fabiana**<br>House of Representatives, 1434 6th St, #1, Santa Monica CA 90401 USA | Actress |
| **Uderzo, Albert**<br>Les Editions Albert Rene, 26 Ave Victor Hugo, 75016 Paris, France | Cartoonist |
| **Udeze, Kenechi N**<br>Seattle Seahawks, 12 Seahawks Way, Renton WA 98056 USA | Football Player |
| **Udoka, Ime S**<br>1654 N Simpson St, Portland OR 97217, USA | Basketball Player |
| **Udovenko, Hennadiy Y**<br>Desyatynna Str 10, #2, 01025 Kiev, Ukraine | Government Official, Ukraine |
| **Udrih, Beno**<br>46 Arnold Palmer, San Antonio TX 78257, USA | Basketball Player |
| **Udvar-Hazy, Steven F**<br>67 Beverly Park, Beverly Hills CA 90210, USA | Businessman, Philanthropist |
| **Udy, Helene**<br>Society Entertainment, 15303 Ventura Blvd, Building C, Sherman Oaks CA 91403, USA | Actress |
| **Ueberroth, Peter V**<br>184 Emerald Bay, Laguna Beach CA 92651, USA | Baseball, Olympics Executive |
| **Uecker, Gunther**<br>Kaiserstr 10, 40221 Dusseldorf, Germany | Artist |
| **Uecker, R Keith**<br>169 Dorchester Road, Akron OH 44313, USA | Football Player |
| **Uecker, Robert G (Bob)**<br>W131N7867 N Country Club Court, Menomonee Falls WI 53051, USA | Actor, Baseball Player, Sportscaster |
| **Uelses, John**<br>30660 Rolling Hills Dr, Valley Center CA 92082, USA | Track Athlete |
| **Uelsmann, Jerry N**<br>5701 SW 17th Dr, Gainesville FL 32608, USA | Photographer |
| **Ueto, Aya**<br>Oscar Promotion, 3-6-7-5F Kita Aoyama, Minato, Tokyo 107 0061, Japan | Actress, Singer, Model |
| **Ufland, Len**<br>16900 NE 19th Ave, North Miami Beach FL 33162, USA | Actor, Director |
| **Uggams, Leslie**<br>B R S / Gage Talent Agency, 1650 Broadway, #1410, New York NY 10019 USA | Singer, Actress |
| **Uggla, Dan**<br>2004 Lincoln Road, Spring Hill TN 37174, USA | Baseball Player |
| **Ughi, Uto**<br>Cannareggio 4990/E, 30121 Venice, Italy | Concert Violinist |
| **U-God**<br>A&M Entertainment, 13280 NE Freeway, #F328, Houston TX 77040, USA | Rap Artist (Wu-Tang Clan) |
| **Ugueto, Luis E**<br>6009 188th Lane NE, #201, Redmond WA 98052, USA | Baseball Player |
| **Uhalt, Alfred H**<br>2533 Shalmar Dr, Colorado Springs CO 80915, USA | Astronaut |
| **Uhl, George R**<br>Johns Hopkins University Medical Center, Genetics Dept, Baltimore MD 21218, USA | Geneticist |
| **Uhl, Petr**<br>Pravo, Slezska 13, 12150 Prague, Czech Republic | Human Rights Activist |
| **Uhlenbeck, Karen K**<br>University of Texas, Mathematics Dept, Austin TX 78712, USA | Mathematician |
| **Uhlenhake, Jeffrey A (Jeff)**<br>1304 Normandy Dr, Newark OH 43055, USA | Football Player |
| **Uhrmann, Michael**<br>Harslemstr 2, 94139 Breitenberg, Germany | Ski Jumper |
| **Uhry, Alfred F**<br>Marshall Purdy, 226 W 47th St, #900, New York NY 10036, USA | Writer |
| **Ulbrich, Jeffrey W (Jeff)**<br>2316 88th Place NE, Clyde Hill WA 98004, USA | Football Player |
| **Ulene, Arthur L**<br>6511 Moore Dr, Los Angeles CA 90048, USA | Physician, Entertainer |
| **Ulevich, Neal H**<br>11954 Glencoe Dr, Denver CO 80233, USA | Photojournalist |
| **Ulion-Silverman, Gretchen**<br>640 Pleasant St, Framingham MA 01701, USA | Ice Hockey Player |
| **Ullman, Myron E, III**<br>Jackson Hole Group, 100 Spear St, #935, San Francisco CA 94105, USA | Businessman |
| **Ullman, Norman V A (Norm)**<br>819-25 Austin Dr, Markham ON L3R 8H4, Canada | Ice Hockey Player |
| **Ullman, Ricky**<br>Gersh Agency, 41 Madison Ave, #3301, New York NY 10010 USA | Actor |
| **Ullman, Tracey**<br>Special Artists Agency, 9200 Sunset Blvd, #410, West Hollywood CA 90069 USA | Actress, Comedienne, Singer |
| **Ullmann, Liv J**<br>Diamond Management, 31 Percy St, London W1T 2DD, England | Actress |
| **Ullrich, Jan**<br>Burgunderweg 10, 79291 Merdingen, Germany | Cyclist |
| **Ulmer, C Arthur (Artie)**<br>2200 Enclave Mill Dr, Dacula GA 30019, USA | Football Player |
| **Ulmer, Frances (Fran)**<br>University of Alaska, Chancellor's Office, 3211 Providence Dr, Anchorage AK 99508, USA | Educator |
| **Ulmer, James (Blood)**<br>J W Entertainment, PO Box 78904, Atlanta GA 30357 USA | Jazz Guitarist, Singer |
| **Ulmer, Kristen**<br>3734 Thousand Oaks Circle, Salt Lake City UT 84124, USA | Extreme Athlete |
| **Ulrich, Eugene C**<br>University of Notre Dame, Theology Dept, Notre Dame IN 46556, USA | Theologian |
| **Ulrich, Henry G (Harry), III**<br>A-T Solutions, 1934 Old Gallows Road, #500, Vienna VA 22182, USA | Navy Admiral |

**Ulrich, Lars** — Drummer (Metallica)
Q Prime, 729 7th Ave, #1600, New York NY 10019 USA

**Ulrich, Skeet** — Actor
Brillstein Entertainment Partners, 9150 Wilshire Blvd, #350, Beverly Hills CA 90212 USA

**Ulrich, Thomas** — Boxer
Brunsbutteler Damm 29, 13581 Berlin, Germany

**Ultra Nate** — Singer
Peach Bisquit, 963 Kent Ave, Brooklyn NY 11205, USA

**Ulvaeus, Bjorn** — Singer (ABBA), Composer
Mono Music, Sodra Brobanken 41A, Skeppsjolmen, 111 49 Stockholm, Sweden

**Ulvang, Vegard** — Cross Country Skier
Fjellveien 53, 9900 Kirkenes, Norway

**Umbarger, James H (Jim)** — Baseball Player
3909 W Harmont Dr, Phoenix AZ 85051, USA

**Umberger, Richard A (R J), Jr** — Ice Hockey Player
835 Rose Mary Hill Dr, Pittsburgh PA 15239, USA

**Umbers, Mark** — Actor
Paradigm Agency, 360 N Crescent Dr, North Building, Beverly Hills CA 90210 USA

**Umemoto, Nanako** — Architect
118 E 59th St, #402, New York NY 10022, USA

**Umhoefer, David** — Journalist
Journal Sentinal, Editorial Dept, 6525 W Bluemound Road, Milwaukee WI 53213, USA

**Umphlett, Thomas M (Tommy)** — Baseball Player
104 Berkley Road, Ahoskie NC 27910, USA

**Unanue, Emil R** — Immunopathologist
Washington University Medical School, Pathology Dept, Saint Louis MO 63110, USA

**Underwood, Blair** — Actor
I C M Partners, 10250 Constellation Blvd, #900, Los Angeles CA 90067 USA

**Underwood, Carrie** — Singer, Songwriter
8 Wentworth Place, Brentwood TN 37027, USA

**Underwood, Jacob** — Singer (O-Town)
Trans Continental Records, 127 W Church St, #350, Orlando FL 32801, USA

**Underwood, Jay** — Actor
6100 Wilshire Blvd, #1170, Los Angeles CA 90048, USA

**Underwood, Olen U** — Football Player
PO Box 2514, Conroe TX 77305, USA

**Underwood, Patrick J (Pat)** — Baseball Player
708 Riverview Dr, Kokomo IN 46901, USA

**Underwood, Sara Jean** — Model, Actress
I A G Entertainment, 5189 Argonne Court, San Diego CA 92117, USA

**Underwood, Scott** — Drummer (Train)
Jon Landau, 150 Rowayton Ave, Norwalk CT 06853, USA

**Unel, Birol** — Actor
Agentur Drews, Schumannstr 16, 10117 Berlin, Germany

**Uner, Idil** — Actress
Neue Schonhauser Str 16, 10178 Berlin, Germany

**Ungar, Jay** — Musician, Songwriter
Mike Greene Assoc, 339 E Liberty St, #220, Ann Arbor MI 48104, USA

**Ungaro, Emanuel M** — Fashion Designer
2 Ave Montaigne, 75008 Paris, France

**Unger, Brian** — Actor, Producer
Global Artists Agency, 6253 Hollywood Blvd, #508, Los Angeles CA 90028 USA

**Unger, Deborah Kara** — Actress
Seven Summits Mgmt, 8906 W Olympic Blvd, Beverly Hills CA 90211 USA

**Unger, Garry D** — Ice Hockey Player
Banff Hockey Academy, Box 2422, Banff AB T1L 1B9, Canada

**Unger, Joe** — Actor
718 N Kings, #30, West Hollywood CA 90069, USA

**Unger, Kay** — Fashion Designer
Saint Gillian Sportswear, 498 Fashion Ave, New York NY 10018, USA

**Unger, Lutz** — Swimmer
Gensler Str 31, 13055 Berlin, Germany

**Unger, Roger H** — Internist
Texas Southwestern Medical Center, 5323 Harry Hines Blvd, Dallas TX 75390, USA

**Union, Gabrielle** — Actress
Intellectual Artists Mgmt, 10585 Santa Monica Blvd, #135, Los Angeles CA 90025, USA

**Unroe, Timothy Brian (Tim)** — Baseball Player
2719 S Joplin, Mesa AZ 85209, USA

**Unruh, James A** — Businessman
5426 E Morrison Lane, Paradise Valley AZ 85253, USA

**Unseld, Westley S (Wes)** — Basketball Player, Coach, Executive
2210 Cedar Circle Dr, Catonsville MD 21228, USA

**Unser, Alfred (Al), Jr** — Auto Racing Driver
PO Box 56696, Albuquerque NM 87187, USA

**Unser, Alfred (Al), Sr** — Auto Racing Driver
7625 Central Ave NW, Albuquerque NM 87121, USA

**Unser, Delbert E (Del)** — Baseball Player
33516 N 79th Way, Scottsdale AZ 85266, USA

**Unser, Robbie** — Auto Racing Driver
806 Laguayra Dr NE, Albuquerque NM 87108, USA

**Unser, Robert W (Bobby)** — Auto Racing Driver
7617 Frederick Lane SW, Albuquerque NM 87121, USA

**Unutoa, Morris T** — Football Player
2158 W 2180 N, Lehi UT 84043, USA

**Upatnieks, Juris** — Optical Engineer
Applied Optics, 2662 Valley Dr, Ann Arbor MI 48103, USA

**Upchurch, Richard (Rick)** — Football Player
4104 SE 20th Place, #B2, Cape Coral FL 33904, USA

**Upham, John L** — Baseball Player
1502 Pierre Ave, Windsor ON N9C 2K7, Canada

**Uphoff, Nicole** — Equestrian
Turnierstall Nicole Uphoff, Auf dem Bremmenkamp 1B, 47199 Duisburg, Germany

**Upshaw, Dawn** — Opera Singer
Nonesuch Records, 75 Rockefeller Plaza, #800, New York NY 10019 USA

**Upshaw, Marvin A (Marv)** — Football Player
3851 Madrone Ave, Oakland CA 94619, USA

**Upshaw, Willie C** — Baseball Player
3250 Fairfield Ave, #211, Bridgeport CT 06605, USA
**Upton, Kate** — Model, Actress
I M G Models, 304 Park Ave S, #PH N, New York NY 10010 USA
**Upton, Melvin E (B J)** — Baseball Player
1428 Harbour Walk Road, Tampa FL 33602, USA
**Upton, Pat** — Singer (Spiral Staircase)
Lustig Talent, PO Box 770850, Orlando FL 32877 USA
**Urango, Juan** — Boxer
Groupe Yvon Michel, 10172 Saint-Laurent, Montreal QC H3L 2N8, Canada
**Urb, Johann** — Actor
A P A Talent & Literary Agency, 405 S Beverly Dr, #300, Beverly Hills CA 90212 USA
**Urb, Johann** — Model, Actor
Innovative Artists, 1505 10th St, Santa Monica CA 90401 USA
**Urban, Jerheme W** — Football Player
217 Fleetwood Dr, San Antonio TX 78232, USA
**Urban, Karl L** — Actor
Principato-Young, 9465 Wilshire Blvd, #880, Beverly Hills CA 90212 USA
**Urban, Keith** — Singer
Borman Entertainment, 1222 16th Ave S, #23, Nashville TN 37212, USA
**Urbano, Michael (Mike)** — Drummer (Smash Mouth)
Creative Artists Agency, 2000 Ave of Stars, #100, Los Angeles CA 90067 USA
**Urbanski, Douglas** — Producer, Writer
Douglas Management Group, PO Box 691763, West Hollywood CA 90069, USA
**Urbanski, Krzysztof** — Conductor
Indianapolis Symphony, 32 E Washington St., #600, Indianapolis, IN 46204, USA
**Urdang, Leslie** — Producer
Olympus Pictures, 12424 Wilshire Blvd, #1120, Los Angeles CA 90025, USA
**Ure, Midge** — Singer, Guitarist
Tony Denton Promotions, Charter House, 157-159 High St, London N14 6BP, England
**Uresti, Omar** — Golfer
7005 Mitra Dr, Austin TX 78739, USA
**Uribe, Juan C** — Baseball Player
425 Shoreline Road, Lake Barrington IL 60010, USA
**Urich, Justin** — Actor
Talent Group, 5670 Wilshire Blvd, #820, Los Angeles CA 90036, USA
**Urie, Brendon B** — Singer, Guitarist (Panic at the Disco)
Crush Music Mgmt, 60-62 E 11th St, #700, New York NY 10002, USA
**Urie, Michael** — Actor
Paradigm Agency, 360 N Crescent Dr, North Building, Beverly Hills CA 90210 USA
**Urin, Vladimir** — Ballet Executive
Bolshoi Theater, Teatralnaya Pl 1, 103009 Moscow, Russia
**Urkal, Oktay** — Boxer
Frank Bleydorn, Goethestr 25, 12207 Berlin, Germany
**Urlacher, Brian K** — Football Player
15044 W Little Saint Marys Road, Libertyville IL 60048, USA
**Urmanov, Aleksei** — Figure Skater
Union of Skaters, Luzhnetskaya Nab 8, 119871 Moscow, Russia
**Urosa Savino, Jorge L Cardinal** — Religious Leader
Archdiocese, Plaza Bolivar, #954, Caracas 1010A, Venezuela
**Urquhart, Brian E** — Diplomat
Howard Farms, Jerusalem Road, Tyringham MA 01264, USA
**Urzi, Daniela** — Model
Trump Model Agency, 91 5th Ave, #300, New York NY 10003 USA
**Usachyov, Yury V** — Cosmonaut
Cosmonaut Training Center, Star City, 141160 Zvezdny Gorodok, Moscow Oblast, Russia
**Usery, Willie J, Jr** — Secretary, Labor
1101 S Arlington Ridge Road, Arlington VA 22202, USA
**Usher** — Rap Artist, Actor
W M E Entertainment, 9601 Wilshire Blvd, #300, Beverly Hills CA 90210 USA
**Usher, Robert R (Bob)** — Baseball Player
1022 N 5th St, San Jose CA 95112, USA
**Usher, Thomas J** — Businessman
U S X Corp, 600 Grant St, #450, Pittsburgh PA 15219, USA
**Usova, Maya** — Ice Dancer
Igloo Skating Rink, 3033 Fostertown, Mount Laurel NJ 08054, USA
**Ut, Nick** — Photographer
Associated Press, Photo Dept, 221 S Figueroa St, #300, Los Angeles CA 90012, USA
**Utay, William** — Actor
Arlene Thornton, 12711 Ventura Blvd, #490, Studio City CA 91604, USA
**Utkina, Sveta** — Model
I M G Models, 304 Park Ave S, #PH N, New York NY 10010 USA
**Utley, Chase C** — Baseball Player
210 W Washington Square, #125W, Philadelphia PA 19106, USA
**Utley, Michel G (Mike)** — Football Player
PO Box 349, Orondo WA 98843, USA
**Utley, Stanley F (Stan)** — Golfer
20701 N Scottsdale Road, #107-619, Scottsdale AZ 85255, USA
**Utt, Benjamin M (Ben)** — Football Player
143 Blackland Road NW, Atlanta GA 30342, USA
**Uvarov, Andrei I** — Ballet Dancer
Bolshoi Theater, Teatralnaya Pl 1, 103009 Moscow, Russia
**Uvini, Bruno** — Soccer Player
Confederacion de Futebol, Rua Victor Civita 66, #1, Rio de Janeiro 22775 044, Brazil
**Uzawa, Hirofumi** — Economist
Kamiyamacho 20-23, Shibuyaku, Tokyo 150 0047, Japan
**Uzumcu, Ahmet** — Government Official, Turkey
Prohibition of Chemical Weapons Organization, Johan de Wittlaan 32, 2517 Hague JR, Netherlands

**V, Bobby** — Singer, Songwriter, Pianist
Agency for Artists, 244 5th Ave, #H230, New York NY 10001, USA

**Vaananen, Ossi** — Ice Hockey Player
Jokerit, Helsinki Halli Oy Areenankuja 1, 00240 Helsinki, Finland

**Vacanti, Charles A** — Surgeon
Massachusetts University Medical Center, Anesthesiology Dept, Worcester MA 02139, USA

**Vacariou, Nicolae** — President, Romania
Romanian Senate, Piata Revolutiei, 71243 Bucharest, Romania

**Vaccariello, Liz** — Editor
Reader's Digest, 750 3rd Ave, #400, New York NY 10017, USA

**Vaccarino, Chad** — Singer, Composer (Great Big World)
Epic Records, 9830 Wilshire Blvd, Beverly Hills CA 90212 USA

**Vaccaro, Brenda** — Actress
I C M Partners, 10250 Constellation Blvd, #900, Los Angeles CA 90067 USA

**Vachon, Rogatien R (Rogie)** — Ice Hockey Player
648 Oxford Ave, Venice CA 90291, USA

**Vachss, Andrew H** — Writer
106-23 Metro Ave, Forest Hills NY 11375, USA

**Vactor, Theodore F (Ted)** — Football Player
11504 Channing Dr, Silver Spring MD 20902, USA

**Vadim, Christian** — Actor
Artmedia, 20 Ave Rapp, 75007 Paris, France

**Vaduva, Leontina** — Opera Singer
Stafford Law, 6 Barham Close, Weybridge, Surrey KT13 9PR, England

**Vagelos, P Roy** — Businessman, Biochemist
82 Mosle Road, Far Hills NJ 07931, USA

**Vagnorius, Gediminas** — Prime Minister, Lithuania
Parliament, Prospekt Gedimino 53, 2002 Vilnius, Lithuania

**Vago, Constant** — Pathologist
Chemin Serre de Laurian, 30100 Ales, France

**Vagt, Robert F** — Foundation Executive, Educator
Heinz Endowments, 30 Dominion Tower, 625 Liberty Ave, Pittsburgh PA 15222, USA

**Vahala, Elina** — Concert Violinist
Sublime Music Agency, Ruusulankatu 14, 00250 Helsinki, Finland

**Vahi, Tiit** — Prime Minister, Estonia
Coalition Eesti Koonderakond, Raekoja Plats 16, 10146 Tallinn, Estonia

**Vai, Steve** — Guitarist (Alcatrazz, Whitesnake)
Septys Entertainment Group, 5543 Edmondson Park, #8A, Nashville TN 37211, USA

**Vail Evans, Justina** — Actress
651 N Kilkea Dr, Los Angeles CA 90048, USA

**Vail, Eric** — Ice Hockey Player
10055 Piney Ridge Walk, Alpharetta GA 30022, USA

**Vail, Michael L (Mike)** — Baseball Player
7946 San Jose Road, El Paso TX 79915, USA

**Vail, Thomas** — Editor
29225 Chagrin Blvd, #200, Beachwood OH 44122, USA

**Vaillancourt, Sarah M** — Ice Hockey Player
Team Canada, 2424 University Dr NW, Calgary AB T2N 3Y9, Canada

**Vaive, Richard C (Rick)** — Ice Hockey Player
Toronto Maple Leafs, AirCanada Center, 40 Bay St, Toronto ON M5J 2K2, Canada

**Vajiralongkorn** — Crown Prince, Thailand
Royal Residence, Chitralada Villa, 9 Rama VI Road, Soi 30, Bangkok 10400, Thailand

**Vajna, Andrew G** — Producer
Cinergi Productions, 2308 Broadway, Santa Monica CA 90404, USA

**Vajpayee, Atal Behari** — Prime Minister, India
7 Race Course Road, New Delhi 110011, India

**Valabik, Boris** — Ice Hockey Player
Boston Bruins, 100 Legends Way, #250, Boston MA 02114 USA

**Valaitis, Lena** — Singer
E P O S Medien & Marketing, Leonhardplatz 8, 82256 Furstenfeldbruck, Germany

**Valance, Holly** — Singer, Actress
Curtis Brown Group, 28-29 Haymarket St, #500, London SW1Y 4SP, England

**Valar, Paul** — Skier
34 Hubertus Ring, Franconia NH 03580, USA

**Valbusa, Fulvio** — Cross Country Skier
Biancaneve 7, 37021 Bosco Chiesanuova, Italy

**Valcepina, Martina** — Speed Skater
Federation of Ice Sports, Via Vitorchiano 113/117, 00189 Rome, Italy

**Valderrama Palacio, Carlos A** — Soccer Player
Colorado Rapids, 1000 Chopper Circle, Denver CO 80204 USA

**Valderrama, Wilmer** — Actor
United Talent Agency, U T A Plaza, 9336 Civic Center Dr, Beverly Hills CA 90210 USA

**Valdes, Ismael V** — Baseball Player
4001 26th St, Vero Beach FL 32960, USA

**Valdes, Jesus (Chucho)** — Jazz Pianist
D L Media, 124 N Highland Ave, Bala Cynwyd PA 19004 USA

**Valdes, Marc C** — Baseball Player
7519 Paula Dr, Tampa FL 33615, USA

**Valdes, Maximiano** — Conductor
C M Artists, 127 W 96th St, #13B, New York NY 10025 USA

**Valdespino, Hilario (Sandy)** — Baseball Player
3937 Lilac Haze St, Las Vegas NV 89147, USA

**Valdez, Luis** — Writer
El Teatro Capesino, 705 4th St, San Juan Bautista CA 95045, USA

**Valdivielso Lopez, Jose L** — Baseball Player
14 Rita Dr, Mount Sinai NY 11766, USA

**Valdivieso Sarmiento, Alfonso** — Government Official, Colombia
Foreign Affairs Ministry, Palacio San Carlos, Santa Fe, Bogota, Colombia

**Valek, Vladimir** — Conductor
Cesky Rozhlas, Vinohradska 12, 12000 Prague 2, Czech Republic

**Valen, Nancy** — Actress
Commercial Talent, 12711 Ventura Blvd, #285, Studio City CA 91604, USA

**Valensi, Nick** — Guitarist (Strokes)
M V O Ltd, 370 7th Ave, #807, New York NY 10001, USA

**Valent, Eric** — Baseball Player
102 Harvard Blvd, Reading PA 19609, USA

**Valente, Benita** — Opera Singer
Maurice Mayer, 201 W 54th St, #1C, New York NY 10019, USA
**Valente, Catarina** — Singer, Guitarist, Actress
Villa Corallo, Via ai Ronci 12, 6816 Bissone, Switzerland
**Valenti, James** — Opera Singer
I M G Artists, Hogarth Business Park, Chiswick, London W4 2TH, England
**Valentin Rosario, Jose A** — Baseball Player
3714 E Park Ave, Phoenix AZ 85044, USA
**Valentin, Dave** — Jazz Flutist
Abby Hoffer Enterprises, 223 1/2 E 48th St, New York NY 10017 USA
**Valentin, John W** — Baseball Player
37 Golden Lane, Hazlet NJ 07730, USA
**Valentine, Amber** — Singer, Guitarist (Jucifer)
Vamp Music Source, 902 W Franklin Ave, #15, Minneapolis MN 55405, USA
**Valentine, Brooke** — Singer, Songwriter, Model, Actress
Virgin Records, 338 N Foothill Road, Beverly Hills CA 90210 USA
**Valentine, Christopher W (Chris)** — Ice Hockey Player
Bell Sensplex, 1565 Maple Grove Road, Kanata ON K2V 1A3, Canada
**Valentine, Dan** — Businessman
C-Cube Microsystems, 1551 McCarthy Blvd, Milpitas CA 95035, USA
**Valentine, Darnell T** — Basketball Player
7546 SW Ashford St, Portland OR 97224, USA
**Valentine, Dean** — Businessman
Symbolic Action, 11601 Wilshire Blvd, #750, Los Angeles CA 90025, USA
**Valentine, DeWain** — Artist
17921 S Western Ave, Gardena CA 90248, USA
**Valentine, Ellis C** — Baseball Player
2708 Bridgemarker Dr, Grand Prairie TX 75054, USA
**Valentine, Gary** — Actor, Comedian
Legacy Talent, 1300 Baxter St, #100A, Charlotte NC 28204, USA
**Valentine, Greg** — Professional Wrestler
13045 Farmington Trail, Seminole FL 33776, USA
**Valentine, Hilton** — Guitarist (Animals)
Patty Mgmts, PO Box 605, Wallingford CT 06492, USA
**Valentine, Jacqui** — Singer, Bassist (Civet)
Kirky Organization, 9200 Sunset Blvd, #600, Los Angeles CA 90069, USA
**Valentine, James** — Guitarist (Maroon 5)
J Records, 745 5th Ave, #600, New York NY 10151 USA
**Valentine, James W** — Paleobiologist
2235 Sacramento St, #208, Berkeley CA 94702, USA
**Valentine, Joseph J (Joe)** — Baseball Player
4168 Chiffon Lane, North Port FL 34287, USA
**Valentine, Karen** — Actress
PO Box 1295, Washington CT 06793, USA
**Valentine, Kathy** — Singer, Guitarist, Bassist (Go-Go's)
Rajiworld Tour Consultants, 800 W 3rd St, #2306, Austin TX 78701, USA
**Valentine, Raymond C** — Agronomist
University of California, Plant Growth Laboratory, Davis CA 95616, USA
**Valentine, Robert J (Bobby)** — Baseball Player, Manager, Sportscaster
71 Wynnewood Lane, Stamford CT 06903, USA
**Valentine, Scott E** — Actor
David Shapira Assoc, 193 N Robertson Blvd, Beverly Hills CA 90211 USA
**Valentine, Steve** — Actor, Writer, Producer
Greater Visions Artists Talent Agency, 8981 W Sunset Blvd, #101, West Hollywood CA 90069 USA
**Valentine, Zachary B (Zack)** — Football Player
162 Harvest Road, Swedesboro NJ 08085, USA
**Valentinetti, Vito J** — Baseball Player
271 Summit Ave, Mount Vernon NY 10552, USA
**Valentino** — Fashion Designer
Palazzo Mignanelli, Piazza Mignanelli 22, 00187 Rome, Italy
**Valentino, Jim** — Cartoonist
Image Comics, 1071 N Batavia St, #A, Orange CA 92867, USA
**Valentino, Victoria** — Model
Playboy Promotions, 9346 Civic Center Dr, #200, Beverly Hills CA 90210 USA
**Valenza, Tasia** — Actress
Danis Panaro Nist Talent, 9201 W Olympic Blvd, Beverly Hills CA 90212 USA
**Valenzuela, Fernando** — Baseball Player
2123 N Beachwood Dr, Los Angeles CA 90068, USA
**Valeriani, Richard G** — Commentator
23 Island View Dr, Sherman CT 06784, USA
**Valiant, Leslie G** — Computer Scientist
50 Tyler Road, Belmont MA 02478, USA
**Valiquette, John J (Jack)** — Ice Hockey Player
28 Peacock Lane, Barrie ON L4N 3R8, Canada
**Valk, Garry** — Ice Hockey Player
681 Baycrest Dr, North Vancouver BC V7G 1N7, Canada
**Vall, Ely Ould Mohamed** — President, Mauritania; Army Officer
President's Office, Cabinet Building, PO Box 2, Majuro, Marshall Islands
**Valle, David (Dave)** — Baseball Player
2260 95th Ave NE, Clyde Hill WA 98004, USA
**Vallee, Jean-Marc** — Director
Sloane Offer Weber, 9601 Wilshire Blvd, #500, Beverly Hills CA 90210 USA
**Vallee, Roy** — Businessman
Avnet Inc, 2211 S 47th St, Phoenix AZ 85034, USA
**Vallely, James (Jim)** — Writer
Brillstein Entertainment Partners, 9150 Wilshire Blvd, #350, Beverly Hills CA 90212 USA
**Valletta, Amber E** — Model, Actress
Creative Artists Agency, 2000 Ave of Stars, #100, Los Angeles CA 90067 USA
**Valley, Mark** — Actor
Vox Inc, 6420 Wilshire Blvd, #1080, Los Angeles CA 90048 USA
**Valli, Frankie** — Singer, Guitarist
I C M Partners, 10250 Constellation Blvd, #900, Los Angeles CA 90067 USA
**Valli, Giambattista** — Fashion Designer
30 Rue Boissy de'Anglais, 75008 Paris, France
**Vallien, Bertil** — Artist
Roleks Vall, 621 93 Visby, Sweden

V

Valente - Vallien

**Vallini, Agostino Cardinal** — Religious Leader
Vica General's Office, Diocese of Rome, Apostolic Palace, 00120 Vatican City

**Valls, Manuel C** — Prime Minister, France
Prime Minister's Office, Hotel Matignon, 57 Rue de Varenne, 75700 Paris, France

**Valmon, Andrew** — Track Athlete
16403 Danforth Circle, Rockville MD 20853, USA

**Valory, Ross L** — Bassist (Journey)
Front Line Mgmt, 1100 Glendon Ave, #2000, Los Angeles CA 90024 USA

**Valuev, Nikolai** — Boxer
Box-Way, Zaharyevskaya Ul 12, 191123 Saint Petersburg, Russia

**Valverde, Maria** — Actress
Tavistock Wood Mgmt, 45 Conduit St, London W1S 2YN, England

**Van, Lindsey** — Ski Jumper
1600 Pinebrook Blvd, #H3, Park City UT 84098, USA

**VanAcker, Drew** — Actor
Greene Assoc, 1901 Ave of Stars, #130, Los Angeles CA 90067 USA

**VanAllsburg, Chris** — Artist, Writer
Scholastic Press, 555 Broadway, New York NY 10012 USA

**VanAlmsick, Franziska (Franzi)** — Swimmer
FvA, Postfach 1280, 68755 Hockenheim, Germany

**VanAlstine, John** — Sculptor
PO Box 526, Wells NY 12190, USA

**VanAmerongen, Jerry** — Cartoonist (Neighborhood)
10926 Owensmouth Ave, Chatsworth CA 91311, USA

**VanAmstel, Louis** — Dancer, Choreographer
Jay D Schwartz Assoc, 3151 Cahuenga Blvd, #220, Los Angeles CA 90068, USA

**VanArk, Joan** — Actress
Don Buchwald Talent Agency, 6500 Wilshire Blvd, #2200, Los Angeles CA 90048 USA

**VanArsdale, Richard A (Dick)** — Basketball Player, Executive
5434 E Lincoln Dr, Paradise Valley AZ 85253, USA

**VanArsdale, Thomas A (Tom)** — Basketball Player
7510 N Eucalyptus Dr, Paradise Valley AZ 85253, USA

**Vanasse, Karine** — Actress
W M E Entertainment, 9601 Wilshire Blvd, #300, Beverly Hills CA 90210 USA

**VanBeek, Lotte** — Speed Skater
K N S B, Postbus 1120, 3800 Arnesfoort BC, Netherlands

**VanBenschoten, John** — Baseball Player
5918 Milburne Dr, Milford OH 45150, USA

**VanBerg, John C (Jack)** — Thoroughbred Racing Trainer
420 Fair Hill Dr, #1, Elkton MD 21921, USA

**VanBerkel, Bernard F (Ben)** — Architect
U N Studio, Stradhouderskade 113, 1073 Amsterdam AX, Netherlands

**Vanbiesbrouck, John** — Ice Hockey Player
15467 Oak Ridge Dr, Spring Lake MI 49456, USA

**VanBoxmeer, John M** — Ice Hockey Player
8033 E Santa Cruz Ave, Orange CA 92869, USA

**VanBrabant, C Oscar (Ozzie)** — Baseball Player
5389 William Dr, Lexington MI 48450, USA

**VanBreda Kolff, Jan M** — Basketball Player, Coach
1102 French Town Lane, Franklin TN 37067, USA

**VanCamp, Emily** — Actress
Thruline Entertainment, 9250 Wilshire Blvd, #100, Beverly Hills CA 90212 USA

**Vance, Courtney B** — Actor
Lighthouse Entertainment, 9220 Sunset Blvd, #200, West Hollywood CA 90069, USA

**Vance, Eric D** — Football Player
PO Box 278202, Miramar FL 33027, USA

**Vance, G Christopher (Chris)** — Actor
Paradigm Agency, 360 N Crescent Dr, North Building, Beverly Hills CA 90210 USA

**Vance, Gene C (Sandy)** — Baseball Player
5863 Chelton Dr, Oakland CA 94611, USA

**Vance, Kenny** — Singer (Jay & the Americans)
Perfect Impressions Entertainment, 154 Seminole Dr, Springfield IL 62704, USA

**VanCitters, Robert L** — Physiologist, Biophysicist
University of Washington Medical School, Physiology Dept, Seattle WA 98815, USA

**VanClief, D G** — Thoroughbred Racing Executive
Breeders' Cup Ltd, 2525 Harrodsburg Road, #500, Lexington KY 40504, USA

**Van-Culin, Samuel** — Religious Leader
16A Burgate, Canterbury CT1 2HG, England

**VanDam, Jose** — Opera Singer
Zurich Artists, Rutistr 52, 8044 Zurich-Gockhausen, Switzerland

**VandeBerg, Edward J (Ed)** — Baseball Player
4903 S Meadows Place, Chandler AZ 85248, USA

**VandenBerg, Lodewijk** — Astronaut
Constellation Technology Corp, 7887 Bryan Dairy Road, #100, Seminole FL 33777, USA

**VandenBergh, Maarten A** — Businessman
Lloyds T S B Group, 71 Lombard St, London EC3P 3BS, England

**VandenBosch, Kyle D** — Football Player
2331 E Cedar Place, Chandler AZ 85249, USA

**Vandenbussche, Ryan** — Ice Hockey Player
RE/Max Erie Shores Realty, 103 Queensway East, Simco ON N3Y 4M5, Canada

**VanDenHeuvel, Carlien** — Field Hockey Player
Stichtsche Cricket-en Hockeyclub, Postbus 72, 3720 Bilthoven BA, Netherlands

**VanDenHoogenband, Pieter** — Swimmer
PO Box 302, 6800 Arnhem AH, Netherlands

**Vander, Musetta** — Actress
David Shapira Assoc, 193 N Robertson Blvd, Beverly Hills CA 90211 USA

**VanderArk, Brad** — Bassist (Verve Pipe)
Artist in Mind, 14100 Dickens St, #2, Sherman Oaks CA 91423, USA

**VanderArk, Brian** — Singer, Guitarist (Verve Pipe)
Artist in Mind, 14100 Dickens St, #2, Sherman Oaks CA 91423, USA

**VanDerBeek, James** — Actor
Paradigm Agency, 360 N Crescent Dr, North Building, Beverly Hills CA 90210 USA

**Vanderbeek, Matthew J (Matt)** — Football Player
54 Endless Vista, Aliso Viejo CA 92656, USA

**Vanderberg Shaw, Helen** — Synchronized Swimming Coach
Heaven's Fitness, 301 14th St NW, Calgary AB T2N 2A1, Canada

| | |
|---|---|
| **VanderBerge, Camille** | Sculptor |
| Solomon Dubnick Gallery, 1017 25th St, Sacramento CA 95816, USA | |
| **Vanderbundt, William G (Skip)** | Football Player |
| 4225 Los Coches Way, Sacramento CA 95864, USA | |
| **VanDerGroen, Guido** | Virologist |
| Institute of Tropical Medicine, Nationalestraat 155, 2000 Antwerp, Belgium | |
| **Vanderham, Joanna** | Actress |
| W M E Entertainment, 9601 Wilshire Blvd, #300, Beverly Hills CA 90210 USA | |
| **VanDerham, Katarina** | Model |
| PO Box 64666, Los Angeles CA 90064, USA | |
| **Vanderhoef, Larry N** | Educator |
| 615 Francisco Place, Davis CA 95616, USA | |
| **Vanderjagt, Michael J (Mike)** | Football Player |
| 631 Lewis Court, Marco Island FL 34145, USA | |
| **Vanderkaay, Peter** | Swimmer |
| 292 W Woodland St, Ferndale MI 48220, USA | |
| **Vanderkelen, Ronald (Ron)** | Football Player |
| 5300 Vernon Ave S, #307, Minneapolis MN 55436, USA | |
| **Vanderloo, Mark** | Model |
| Wilhelmina Models, 300 Park Ave S, #200, New York NY 10010 USA | |
| **Vandermeersch, Bernard** | Anthropologist |
| University of Bordeaux, Anthropology Dept, 33800 Bordeaux, France | |
| **VanderPoel, J Mark** | Football Player |
| 14760 Ave 208, Tulare CA 93274, USA | |
| **VanDerPol, Anneliese** | Actress |
| Kazarian/Measures/Ruskin, 11969 Ventura Blvd, #300, Studio City CA 91604 USA | |
| **Vanderpool, Clare** | Writer |
| Random House, 1745 Broadway, #1800, New York NY 10019 USA | |
| **VanDerRym, Sim** | Architect, Designer |
| Ecological Design Institute, PO Box 858, Inverness CA 94937, USA | |
| **Vanderveen, Loet** | Sculptor |
| Lime Creek 5, Big Sur CA 93920, USA | |
| **VanDerveer, Tara** | Basketball Coach |
| 1036 Cascade Dr, Menlo Park CA 94025, USA | |
| **VanDerWal, Frederique** | Model |
| Innovative Artists, 1505 10th St, Santa Monica CA 90401 USA | |
| **VanderWal, John H** | Baseball Player |
| 5142 Abbeydale Dr SW, Grand Rapids MI 49546, USA | |
| **VanDerWee, Herman F A** | Historian |
| Ettingestraat 10, 9170 Saint-Pauwels, Belgium | |
| **Vanderzalm, Bas** | Association Executive |
| Medical Teams International, 14150 SW Milton Court, Portland OR 97224, USA | |
| **VandeSande, Theo A** | Cinematographer |
| Innovative Artists, 1505 10th St, Santa Monica CA 90401 USA | |
| **VandeVen, Monique** | Actress, Director |
| 9255 W Sunset Blvd, #505, West Hollywood CA 90069, USA | |
| **VandeWeghe, Albert** | Swimmer |
| 7712 W Skyline Dr, Tulsa OK 74107, USA | |
| **Vandeweghe, Ernest M (Kiki)** | Basketball Player, Coach, Executive |
| PO Box 3006, Englewood CO 80155, USA | |
| **VandeWetering, John E** | Educator |
| 29 Brickstone Circle, Rochester NY 14620, USA | |
| **VanDien, Casper** | Actor |
| A P A Talent & Literary Agency, 405 S Beverly Dr, #300, Beverly Hills CA 90212 USA | |
| **VanDoren, Mamie** | Actress, Dancer, Model |
| 3419 Via Lido, #184, Newport Beach CA 92663, USA | |
| **VanDorp, Wayne** | Ice Hockey Player |
| 380 Laurentian Crescent, Coquitlam BC V3K 1Y5, Canada | |
| **VanDusen, Frederick W (Fred)** | Baseball Player |
| 331 Gillette Dr, Franklin TN 37069, USA | |
| **VanDusen, Granville** | Actor |
| 10974 Alta View Dr, Studio City CA 91604, USA | |
| **VanDyke, Bruce R** | Football Player |
| 143 Lakeview Dr, Canonsburg PA 15317, USA | |
| **VanDyke, Dick** | Actor |
| 23215 Mariposa de Oro, Malibu CA 90265, USA | |
| **VanDyke, F Alexander (Alex)** | Football Player |
| 8338 Sea Island Court, Elk Grove CA 95758, USA | |
| **VanDyke, Jerry** | Actor, Comedian |
| J Cast Productions, 2550 Greenvalley Road, Los Angeles CA 90046, USA | |
| **VanDyke, Leroy F** | Singer |
| Leroy Van Dyke Enterprises, 29000 Highway V, Smithton MO 65350, USA | |
| **VanDyke, Milton D** | Aeronautical Engineer |
| Stanford University, Applied Mechanics Dept, Stanford CA 94305, USA | |
| **VanDyke, Philip** | Actor |
| 1464 Madera Road, #108N, Simi Valley CA 93065, USA | |
| **VanDyke, William G** | Businessman |
| Donaldson Co, 1400 W 94th St, Minneapolis MN 55431, USA | |
| **VanDyken Rouen, Amy** | Swimmer, Sportscaster |
| 20343 N Hayden Road, #105, Scottsdale AZ 85255, USA | |
| **VanEeghen, Mark K** | Football Player |
| 90 Woodstock Lane, Cranston RI 02920, USA | |
| **VanEgmond, Timothy L (Tim)** | Baseball Player |
| 8839 Callaway Road, Gay GA 30218, USA | |
| **Vanek, John** | Basketball Referee |
| 9th St, RD 1, Nesquehoning PA 18240, USA | |
| **Vanek, Thomas** | Ice Hockey Player |
| 9131 Curry Lane, Clarence Center NY 14032, USA | |
| **Vaness, Carol** | Opera Singer |
| I C M Artists, 40 W 57th St, #1800, New York NY 10019 USA | |
| **Vanessa-Mae** | Singer, Concert Violinist |
| PO Box 363, Bournemouth, Dorset BH7 6LA, England | |
| **VanEtten, Sharon** | Singer, Songwriter |
| Jagjaguwar Records, 1499 W 2nd St, Bloomington IN 47403, USA | |
| **VanEvery, John** | Baseball Player |
| 555 Dixon Dr, Brandon MS 39047, USA | |

|  |  |
|------|-----------|
| **VanExcel, Nicky M (Nick)** | Basketball Player |
| 3102 Noble Lakes Lane, Houston TX 77082, USA | |
| **VanFraasen, Bastiaan C** | Philosopher |
| 1347 Curtis St, Berkeley CA 94702, USA | |
| **VanGaalen, Chad** | Musician |
| Agency Group Ltd, 142 W 57th St, #600, New York NY 10019 USA | |
| **Vangelis** | Composer |
| Robert Urband Assoc, 8981 W Sunset Blvd, #311, West Hollywood CA 90069, USA | |
| **Vangen, Scott D** | Astronaut |
| N A S A, Johnson Space Center, 2101 NASA Road, Houston TX 77058 USA | |
| **Vangorder, David T (Dave)** | Baseball Player |
| 212 Black Eagle Ave, Henderson NV 89002, USA | |
| **VanGorkum, Harry** | Actor |
| Insight Mgmt, 5300 Melrose Ave, #412D, Los Angeles CA 90036, USA | |
| **VanGorp, Michele** | Basketball Player |
| Minnesota Lynx, Target Center, 600 1st Ave N, Minneapolis MN 55403 USA | |
| **VanGrunsven, Theodora E G (Anky)** | Equestrian |
| Bonengang 1, 5421 Gemert BZ, Netherlands | |
| **Vangsness, Kirsten** | Actress |
| Abrams Artists, 9200 W Sunset Blvd, #1125, West Hollywood CA 90069 USA | |
| **VanGundy, Jeff** | Basketball Coach, Sportscaster |
| W M E Entertainment, 9601 Wilshire Blvd, #300, Beverly Hills CA 90210 USA | |
| **VanGundy, Stanley A (Stan)** | Basketball Coach, Executive |
| Detroit Pistons, Palace, 4 Championship Dr, Auburn Hills MI 48326 USA | |
| **VanHalen, Alex** | Drummer (Van Halen) |
| 12024 Summit Circle, Beverly Hills CA 90210, USA | |
| **VanHalen, Eddie** | Singer, Guitarist (Van Halen) |
| 20411 Chapter Dr, Woodland Hills CA 91364, USA | |
| **VanHalen, Wolfgang** | Singer, Guitarist |
| Jackoway Tyerman Wertheimer, 1925 Century Park E, #2200, Los Angeles CA 90067 USA | |
| **VanHamel, Martine** | Ballerina |
| 290 Riverside Dr, New York NY 10025, USA | |
| **VanHeek, Margaret** | Chemist |
| Schering-Plough Research, 2000 Galloping Hill Road, Kenilworth NJ 07033, USA | |
| **VanHelden, Armand** | Music Producer |
| Ministry of Sound, 103 Grant St, London SE1 6DP, England | |
| **VanHellmond, Andy** | Ice Hockey Referee |
| 71 Hyde Road, Stratford ON N5A 7Z3, Canada | |
| **VanHeusen, William P (Billy)** | Football Player |
| 835 Hudson St, Denver CO 80220, USA | |
| **VanHoften, James C D A** | Astronaut |
| Bechtel National Inc, 50 Beale St, San Francisco CA 94105, USA | |
| **VanHolde, Kensal E** | Biochemist |
| 2800 NW 29th St, #17, Corvallis OR 97330, USA | |
| **VanHolt, Brian** | Actor |
| Paradigm Agency, 360 N Crescent Dr, North Building, Beverly Hills CA 90210 USA | |
| **VanHorn, Buddy** | Director |
| 4409 Ponca Ave, Toluca Lake CA 91602, USA | |
| **VanHorn, Christian** | Opera Singer |
| Opus 3 Artists, 470 Park Ave S, #900N, New York NY 10016 USA | |
| **VanHorn, Douglas C (Doug)** | Football Player |
| 149 Feronia Way, Rutherford NJ 07070, USA | |
| **VanHorn, Patrick** | Actor |
| Brillstein Entertainment Partners, 9150 Wilshire Blvd, #350, Beverly Hills CA 90212 USA | |
| **VanHorne, Keith** | Football Player |
| 680 Thornmeadow Road, Riverwoods IL 60015, USA | |
| **VanHouten, Carice** | Actress |
| Troika, 74 Clerkenwell Road, #300, London EC1M 5QA, England | |
| **VanHoy, Jay** | Producer |
| Parts & Labor, 177 N 10th St, #F, Brooklyn NY 11211, USA | |
| **Vanhoye, Albert Cardinal** | Religious Leader |
| S Maria della Mercede e S Adriano a Villa Albani, Via Basento 100, 00198 Rome, Italy | |
| **Vanian, David (Dave)** | Singer (Damned) |
| Leave Home Booking, 10 W Broadway, #608, Salt Lake City UT 84101, USA | |
| **Vanilla Ice** | Rap Artist, Actor |
| T Q Mgmt, 2412 Piedra Dr, Plano TX 75023, USA | |
| **VanImpe, Ed C** | Ice Hockey Player |
| 849 Streams Dr, West Chester PA 19382, USA | |
| **Vanity** | Singer, Actress, Model |
| 39279 Paseo Padre Parkway, #214, Fremont CA 94538, USA | |
| **VanKooten, Katie** | Opera Singer |
| I M G Artists, Hogarth Business Park, Chiswick, London W4 2TH, England | |
| **VanLandingham, William J** | Baseball Player |
| 3023 Old Hillsboro Road, Franklin TN 37064, USA | |
| **VanLiere, Donna** | Writer |
| Saint Martin's Press, 175 5th Ave, #400, New York NY 10010 USA | |
| **VanLyck, Henry** | Actor |
| Z B F Agentur, Friedrichstr 39, 10969 Berlin, Germany | |
| **VanMontfork, Roos** | Model |
| Playboy Promotions, 9346 Civic Center Dr, #200, Beverly Hills CA 90210 USA | |
| **Vannelli, Gino** | Singer, Songwriter |
| McLachlan Management International, 2821 Bransford Ave, Nashville TN 37204, USA | |
| **VanNistelrooy, Ruud** | Soccer Player |
| F C Real Madrid, Avda Concha Espana 1, 28036 Madrid, Spain | |
| **Vannoni, Dina Marue** | Model |
| PO Box 473, Chino CA 91708, USA | |
| **VanNote, Jeffrey A (Jeff)** | Football Player |
| 345 Hollyberry Dr, Roswell GA 30076, USA | |
| **Vannucci, Ronnie, Jr** | Drummer (Killers) |
| W M E Entertainment, 9601 Wilshire Blvd, #300, Beverly Hills CA 90210 USA | |
| **Vanocur, Sander** | Commentator |
| C E S D, 10635 Santa Monica Blvd, #130, Los Angeles CA 90025 USA | |
| **Vanous, Lucky** | Model, Actor |
| 28345 La Calenta, Mission Viejo CA 92692, USA | |
| **VanOuten, Denise** | Actress |
| Artist Rights Group, 4A Exmoor St, London W10 6BD, England | |

**Vanover, Larry W**
3037 Sterling Court, Owensboro KY 42303, USA
Baseball Umpire

**Vanover, Tamarick T**
703 NW Wilson St, Lake City FL 32055, USA
Football Player

**VanPatten, Dick**
13920 Magnolia Blvd, Sherman Oaks CA 91423, USA
Actor

**VanPatten, Joyce**
S M S Talent, 8383 Wilshire Blvd, #230, Beverly Hills CA 90211 USA
Actress

**VanPatten, Nels**
12439 Magnolia Blvd, #197, Valley Village CA 91607, USA
Actor

**VanPatten, Timothy**
Creative Artists Agency, 2000 Ave of Stars, #100, Los Angeles CA 90067 USA
Actor, Director

**VanPatten, Vincent**
Michael Slessinger, 8730 W Sunset Blvd, #220W, West Hollywood CA 90069 USA
Actor

**VanPeebles, Mario**
Don Buchwald Talent Agency, 6500 Wilshire Blvd, #2200, Los Angeles CA 90048 USA
Actor, Director

**VanPeebles, Melvin**
353 W 56th St, #10F, New York NY 10019, USA
Director, Writer

**VanPelt, Bo**
3025 Backmeyer Road, Richmond IN 47374, USA
Golfer

**VanPelt, G Alexander (Alex)**
2080 Shady Lane, Green Bay WI 54313, USA
Football Player

**VanPoppel, Todd M**
340 Springfield Bend, Argyle TX 76226, USA
Baseball Player

**VanPraagh, James**
Special Artists Agency, 9200 Sunset Blvd, #410, West Hollywood CA 90069 USA
Actor, Producer

**VanRensselaer, Miles**
1352-54 River Road, Lopatcong NJ 08865, USA
Artist

**VanRiper, Paul K**
Marine Corps Heritage Foundation, PO Box 998, 307 5th Ave, Quantico VA 22134, USA
Marine Corps General

**VanRompuy, Herman A**
European Council, Rue de la Loi 175, 1048 Brussels, Belgium
Prime Minister, Belgium

**VanRyn, Benjamin A (Ben)**
8911 Saddle Trail, San Antonio TX 78255, USA
Baseball Player

**VanRyn, Mike**
17681 SW 54th St, Southwest Ranches FL 33331, USA
Ice Hockey Player

**VanSant, Gus G, Jr**
W M E Entertainment, 9601 Wilshire Blvd, #300, Beverly Hills CA 90210 USA
Director

**VanSanten, Shantel**
Leverage Mgmt, 3030 Pennsylvania Ave, Santa Monica CA 90404 USA
Actress, Model

**VanScott, Eugene J**
3 Hidden Lane, Abington PA 19001, USA
Dermatologist

**VanSickle, Craig W**
Paradigm Agency, 360 N Crescent Dr, North Building, Beverly Hills CA 90210 USA
Writer, Producer, Director

**Vanska, Osmo**
Minnesota Symphony, Orchestra Hall, 1111 Nicollet Mall, Minneapolis MN 55403, USA
Conductor

**VanSlyke, Andrew J (Andy)**
710 S Price Road, Saint Louis MO 63124, USA
Baseball Player

**VanSprang, Alan**
Artists Representation, 1147 S Big Island Road, RR 1, Demorestville ON K0K 1W0, Canada
Actor

**Vanstone, Ellen**
Alpern Group, 15645 Royal Oak Road, Encino CA 91436, USA
Producer

**VanSusteren, Greta**
Fox-TV, News Dept, 5151 Wisconsin Ave NW, #100, Washington DC 20016 USA
Commentator

**VanUmmerson, Claire A**
Cleveland State University, President's Office, Cleveland OH 44115, USA
Educator

**VanValkenburgh, Deborah**
Beth Stein Assoc, 920 Abbot Kinney Blvd, Venice CA 90291, USA
Actress

**VanVooren, Monique**
165 E 66th St, New York NY 10065, USA
Actress

**VanWachem, Loedwijk C**
Royal Dutch Petroleum, 30 Van Bylandtaan, 2596 The Hague HR, Netherlands
Businessman

**VanWageningen, Yorick**
Conway Van Gelder Grant, 8-12 Broadwick St, #300, London W1F 8HW, England
Actor

**VanWagner, James P (Jimmy)**
5246 N Royal Dr, Traverse City MI 49684, USA
Football Player

**VanWinkle, Travis**
Stone Manners Salners, 6100 Wilshire Blvd, #1500, Los Angeles CA 90035 USA
Actor

**VanWormer, Steve**
Vox Inc, 6420 Wilshire Blvd, #1080, Los Angeles CA 90048 USA
Actor

**VanWyngarden, Andrew**
Paradigm Agency, 404 W Franklin St, Monterey CA 93940 USA
Singer, Guitarist, Pianist (MGMT)

**VanZandt, Steven**
Renegade Nation Holdings, 434 Ave of Americas, #6R, New York NY 10011, USA
Guitarist, Actor

**VanZant, Donnie**
Vector Mgmt, PO Box 120479, Nashville TN 37212 USA
Singer (Lynyrd Skynyrd, .38 Special)

**VanZant, Johnny**
Vector Mgmt, PO Box 120479, Nashville TN 37212 USA
Singer (Lynyrd Skynyrd), Songwriter

**VanZweden, Jaap**
I M G Artists, Hogarth Business Park, Chiswick, London W4 2TH, England
Conductor

**Varad'a, Vaclav**
9042 Stonebriar Dr, Clarence Center NY 14032, USA
Ice Hockey Player

**Varadhan, Srinivasa S R**
New York University, Courant Institute, 251 Mercer St, New York NY 10012, USA
Abel Mathematics Laureate

**Varady, Julia**
Hanns Eisler Musik Hochschule, Charlottenstra 55, 10117 Berlin, Germany
Opera Singer

**Varda, Agnes**
Cine-Tamaris, 86-88 Rue Daguerre, 75014 Paris, France
Director

**Vardalos, Nia**
Untitled Entertainment, 350 S Beverly Dr, #200, Beverly Hills CA 90212 USA
Actress, Writer

**Vardell, Thomas A (Tommy)**
2424 E Ruby Hill Dr, Pleasanton CA 94566, USA
Football Player

**Varejao, Anderson F**
Cleveland Cavaliers, Gund Arena, 1 Center Court, Cleveland OH 44115 USA
Basketball Player

**Varekova, Veronica**
Next Model Mgmt, 9 Boul de la Madeleine, 75001 Paris, France
Model

# V

**Varela, Fernando** — Singer
Mascioli Entertainment, 2202 Curry Ford Road, #E, Orlando FL 32806, USA
**Varela, Leonor** — Actress
L I N K Entertainment, 11872 La Grange Ave, Los Angeles CA 90025 USA
**Varga, Imre** — Sculptor
Bartha Utca 1, 1126 Budapest XII, Hungary
**Vargas Llosa, Mario** — Nobel Literature Laureate
Las Magnolias 295, 6 Piso, Barranco, Lima 4, Peru
**Vargas, Devin** — Boxer
Star Boxing, 991 Morris Park Ave, Bronx NY 10462, USA
**Vargas, Elizabeth** — Commentator
ABC-TV, News Dept, 77 W 66th St, New York NY 10023 USA
**Vargas, Fernando** — Boxer
1695 Mesa Verde Ave, #220, Ventura CA 93003, USA
**Vargas, Ieda Maria** — Beauty Queen
Miss Universe Organization, 1370 Ave of Americas, #1600, New York NY 10019 USA
**Vargas, Jacob** — Actor
Paradigm Agency, 360 N Crescent Dr, North Building, Beverly Hills CA 90210 USA
**Vargas, Jason M** — Baseball Player
14775 Keota Lane, Apple Valley CA 92307, USA
**Vargas, Jay R** — Vietnam War Marine Corps Hero (CMH)
12466 Thornbush Court, San Diego CA 92131, USA
**Vargo, Tim** — Businessman
AutoZone Inc, 123 S Front St, Memphis TN 38103, USA
**Varitek, Jason A** — Baseball Player
PO Box 669, Suwanee GA 30024, USA
**Varlamarv, Sergei** — Ice Hockey Player
213 Germain St, Saint John NB E2L 2G5, Canada
**Varma, Indira** — Actress
Gordon & French, 12-13 Poland St, London W1F 8QB, England
**Varmus, Harold E** — Nobel Medicine Laureate
1 Gracie Square, #1E, New York NY 10028, USA
**Varney, Carleton B, Jr** — Interior Designer
Dorothy Draper Co, 60 E 56th St, #1000, New York NY 10022, USA
**Varney, Richard F (Pete)** — Baseball Player
14 Juniper Ridge Road, Acton MA 01720, USA
**Varo, Marton G** — Sculptor
111 Baypointe Dr, Newport Beach CA 92660, USA
**Varon, Lisa Marie** — Model
131 Promenade Court, Louisville KY 40223, USA
**Varrichone, Frank J** — Football Player
26 Coffin Brook Road, Alton NH 03809, USA
**Varshavsky, Alexander** — Cell Biologist
California Institute of Technology, Cell Biology Dept, Pasadena CA 91125, USA
**Varsho, Gary A** — Baseball Player, Manager
11921 Starr Road, Chili WI 54420, USA
**Vartan, Michael** — Actor
Thruline Entertainment, 9250 Wilshire Blvd, #100, Beverly Hills CA 90212 USA
**Vartan, Sylvie** — Singer
Charley Marouani, 176 Avenue Charles de Gaulle, 92200 Neuilly sur Seine, France
**Varvatos, John** — Fashion Designer
2346 E Pacifica Place, Rancho Dominguez CA 90220, USA
**Varvel, Gary** — Editorial Cartoonist
PO Box 1121, Brownsburg IN 46112, USA
**Vasary, Tamas** — Concert Pianist, Conductor
Magyar Radio Zenekari Iroda, Brody Sandor Utica 5, 1800 Budapest, Hungary
**Vasconcellos Ferreira, Gabriel** — Soccer Player
F C Milan, Via Filippo Turati 3, 20121 Milan, Italy
**Vasconcellos, Martha M C** — Beauty Queen
2 Oak Terrace, #4, Somerville MA 02143, USA
**Vasgersian, Matt** — Sportscaster
7211 Eads Ave, La Jolla CA 92037, USA
**Vasher, Nathaniel D (Nathan)** — Football Player
1850 N Sawgrass St, Vernon Hills IL 60061, USA
**Vasilyev, Vladimir V** — Ballet Dancer, Executive
Smolenskaya Naberezhnaya 5/13 62, 121099 Moscow, Russia
**Vaske, Dennis J** — Ice Hockey Player
9750 Crescent Park Circle, #119, Orland Park IL 60462, USA
**Vasquez Rana, Mario** — Publisher
El Sol de Mexico, Guillermo Prieto 7, Cuauhtemoc DF 06470, Mexico
**Vasquez Rodriguez, Greivis J** — Basketball Player
Sacramento Kings, Arco Arena, 1 Sports Parkway, Sacramento CA 95834 USA
**Vasquez, Jacinto** — Thoroughbred Racing Jockey
4449 18th Terrace, Ocala FL 34479, USA
**Vasquez, Wilfredo** — Boxer
Call 1 D-3, Urb San Fernando, Bayamon PR 00957, USA
**Vassar, Phil** — Singer, Songwriter
Red Light Mgmt, PO Box 159310, Nashville TN 37215, USA
**Vasser, Jimmy** — Auto Racing Driver
8605 Robinson Ridge Dr, Las Vegas NV 89117, USA
**Vassilieva, Sofia** — Actress
Brillstein Entertainment Partners, 9150 Wilshire Blvd, #350, Beverly Hills CA 90212 USA
**Vassiliou, George V** — President, Cyprus
PO Box 874, 21 Academiou Ave, Aglandjia, Nicosia, Cyprus
**Vassy** — Singer, Songwriter
Peace Bisquit, 963 Kent Ave, Brooklyn NY 11205, USA
**Vasyutin, Vladimir V** — Cosmonaut
Cosmonaut Training Center, Star City, 141160 Zvezdny Gorodok, Moscow Oblast, Russia
**Vataha, Randel E (Randy)** — Football Player
36 Longmeadow Road, Lincoln MA 01773, USA
**Vatanen, Sami** — Ice Hockey Player
Anaheim Ducks, 2695 E Katella Ave, Anaheim CA 92806 USA
**Vatcher, James E (Jim)** — Baseball Player
16039 Northfield St, Pacific Palisades CA 90272, USA
**Vatchkov, Deyan** — Opera Singer
I M G Artists, Hogarth Business Park, Chiswick, London W4 2TH, England

**Vaughan, Greg** — Actor
Abrams Artists, 9200 W Sunset Blvd, #1125, West Hollywood CA 90069 USA
**Vaughan, Jimmie L** — Guitarist (Fabulous Thunderbirds)
Luther Wolf Agency, PO Box 685138, Austin TX 78768, USA
**Vaughan, Martha** — Biochemist
11351 Woodglen Dr, #501, Rockville MD 20852, USA
**Vaughan, Peter** — Actor
Independent Talent Group, 40 Whitfield St, London W1T 2RH, England
**Vaughan, Tom** — Director, Writer
United Agents, 12-26 Lexington St, London W1F 0LE, England
**Vaughn, Ben** — Singer, Songwriter, Guitarist
Cross Road Mgmt, 45 W 11th St, #7B, New York NY 10011, USA
**Vaughn, Bruce** — Golfer
5615 N Monroe St, Hutchinson KS 67502, USA
**Vaughn, Clyde** — Army General
Director, Army National Guard, HqUSA, Pentagon, Washington DC 20310, USA
**Vaughn, Gregory L (Greg)** — Baseball Player
10830 Sheldon Woods Way, Elk Grove CA 95624, USA
**Vaughn, Jacque** — Basketball Player, Coach
715 Coving Court, Lawrence KS 66049, USA
**Vaughn, Jimmie** — Guitarist
Artemis Records, 130 5th Ave, #7, New York NY 10011, USA
**Vaughn, Matthew** — Director, Producer, Actor
Independent Talent Group, 40 Whitfield St, London W1T 2RH, England
**Vaughn, Maurice John** — Singer, Guitarist, Saxophonist
Jay Reil Assoc, 3430 Bayberry Dr, Northbrook IL 60062, USA
**Vaughn, Maurice S (Mo)** — Baseball Player
5455 Rings Road, #100, Dublin OH 43017, USA
**Vaughn, Ned** — Actor
James/Levy Mgmt, 3500 W Olive Ave, #1470, Burbank CA 91505 USA
**Vaughn, Robert** — Actor
68 Salem View Dr, Ridgefield CT 06877, USA
**Vaughn, Thomas R (Tom)** — Football Player
860 E Linda Lane, Gilbert AZ 85234, USA
**Vaughn, Tichina** — Opera Singer
I M G Artists, Hogarth Business Park, Chiswick, London W4 2TH, England
**Vaughn, Vince** — Actor
Wild West Picture Show Productions, 1210 N La Brea Ave, West Hollywood CA 90038, USA
**Vaught, Loy S** — Basketball Player
838 Andover Court SE, Grand Rapids MI 49508, USA
**Vaugier, Emmanuelle** — Actress
A P A Talent & Literary Agency, 405 S Beverly Dr, #300, Beverly Hills CA 90212 USA
**Vaupen, Drew** — Producer, Writer
I C M Partners, 10250 Constellation Blvd, #900, Los Angeles CA 90067 USA
**Vavakin, Leonid V** — Architect
Academy of Architecture, Dmitrova Str 24, 103874 Moscow, Russia
**Vavasseur, Sophie** — Actress
Troika, 74 Clerkenwell Road, #300, London EC1M 5QA, England
**Vayda, Brandon Michael** — Actor
Stone Manners Salners, 6100 Wilshire Blvd, #1500, Los Angeles CA 90035 USA
**Vaydik, Gregory (Greg)** — Ice Hockey Player
6041 Village Bend Dr, #1007, Dallas TX 75206, USA
**Vazquez Rosas, Tabare R** — President, Uruguay
Chacra El Paso de la Arena, Montevideo, Uruguay
**Veal, Orville I (Coot)** — Baseball Player
238 Stone Gables Dr, Gray GA 31032, USA
**Veale, Robert A (Bob)** — Baseball Player
2833 Bush Blvd, Birmingham AL 35208, USA
**Veals, Elton A** — Football Player
2981 Joyce Dr, Baton Rouge LA 70814, USA
**Veasey, Josephine** — Opera Singer
5 Meadow View, Whitechurch, Hantsfordshire RG28 7BL, England
**Veber, Francis P** — Director
Artmedia, 20 Ave Rapp, 75007 Paris, France
**Vecchione, Mike** — Marine Scientist
National Oceanic/Atmospheric Admin, 14th St & Constitution Ave, Washington DC 20230, USA
**Vecsey, George S** — Sportswriter
New York Times, Editorial Dept, 229 W 43rd St, New York NY 10036, USA
**Vedder, Ed (Eddie)** — Singer (Pearl Jam), Songwriter
Curtis Mgmt, 1900 S Corgiat Dr, Seattle WA 98108, USA
**Vedernikov, Alexander** — Conductor
Askonas Holt, Lincoln House, 300 High Holborn, London WC1V 7JH, England
**Vee, Bobby** — Singer, Songwriter
Rockhouse Mgmt, PO Box 757, Saint Joseph MN 56374, USA
**Vega Polanco, Amelia** — Beauty Queen, Actress
Trump Model Agency, 91 5th Ave, #300, New York NY 10003 USA
**Vega, Alan** — Singer (Suicide)
International Booking Dept, Bodenseestr 91, 81243 Munich, Germany
**Vega, Alexa** — Actress
John Carrabino Mgmt, 5900 Wilshire Blvd, #406, Los Angeles CA 90036 USA
**Vega, Makenzie** — Actress
Hansen Jacobson Teller, 450 N Roxbury Dr, #800, Beverly Hills CA 90210 USA
**Vega, Paz** — Actress
Baker Winokur Ryder Public Relations, 9100 Wilshire Blvd, #500W, Beverly Hills CA 90212 USA
**Vega, Suzanne N** — Singer, Songwriter
Windish Agency, 1658 N Milwaukee Ave, #211, Chicago IL 60647, USA
**Vega, Tata** — Singer
Universal Attractions, 135 W 26th St, #1200, New York NY 10001 USA
**Vegas, Jhonattan** — Golfer
Professional Golfers Association, 100 Ave of Champions, Palm Beach Gardens FL 33418 USA
**Veglio, Antonio M Cardinal** — Religious Leader
Pastoral Care of Migrants & Itinerant People, Piazza S Calisto 16, 00120 Vatican City
**Veiga, Carlos A Wahnon de C** — Prime Minister, Cape Verde
W V Consultants, CP43A Praia, Santiago, Cape Verde
**Veigel, Allen F (Al)** — Baseball Player
1907 Dover Ave, Dover OH 44622, USA

**Veihmeyer, John B** — Businessman
K P M G, 345 Park Ave, New York NY 10154, USA

**Veil, Simone** — Government Official, France
11 Place Vauban, 75007 Paris, France

**Veingard, Allen S** — Football Player
1940 NW 180th Way, Pembroke Pines FL 33029, USA

**Veirs, Laura** — Singer, Songwriter
Primary Talent International, 10-11 Jockey's Fields, London WC1R 4BN, England

**Veisor, Michael D (Mike)** — Ice Hockey Player
16091 W Lakepoint Court, Prairieville LA 70769, USA

**Veitch, Darren W** — Ice Hockey Player
3410 Maricopa Highway, Ojai CA 93023, USA

**Veitch, John M** — Thoroughbred Racing Trainer
Kentucky Horse Racing Authority, 4063 Ironwood Turnpike, Lexington KY 40511, USA

**Veitch, Tom** — Writer
PO Box 479, Lincoln City OR 97367, USA

**Vejar, Chico** — Boxer
8103 N Hollow, #313, San Antonio TX 78240, USA

**Vejtasa, Stanley W (Swede)** — WW II Navy Air Force Hero
1649 Summit Lane, Escondido CA 92025, USA

**Velard, Julian** — Singer, Songwriter, Pianist
Agency Group Ltd, 142 W 57th St, #600, New York NY 10019 USA

**Velarde, Randy L** — Baseball Player
4902 Thames Court, Midland TX 79705, USA

**Velasquez, Jacquelyn D (Jaci)** — Singer
Breen Agency, 110 30th Ave N, #3, Nashville TN 37203, USA

**Velasquez, Jorge L, Jr** — Thoroughbred Racing Jockey
2701 Valentine Ave, #407, Bronx NY 14058, USA

**Velasquez, Patricia** — Model, Actress
A P A Talent & Literary Agency, 405 S Beverly Dr, #300, Beverly Hills CA 90212 USA

**Velazquez, Frederico A (Freddie)** — Baseball Player
Jose Amado Solier #70, Santo Domingo, Dominican Republic

**Velazquez, John R** — Thoroughbred Racing Jockey
133 Avon Place, West Hempstead NY 11552, USA

**Velazquez, Nadine** — Actress
Much & House Public Relations, 8075 W 3rd St, #500, Los Angeles CA 90048 USA

**Veldheer, Jared** — Football Player
Arizona Cardinals, PO Box 888, Phoenix AZ 85001 USA

**Veldhuis, Magdalena J M (Marleen)** — Swimmer
Eiffel Swimming PSV, Het Lover 40, 5501 Veldhoven CR, Netherlands

**Velez, Eddie** — Actor
Stone Manners Salners, 6100 Wilshire Blvd, #1500, Los Angeles CA 90035 USA

**Velez, Lauren** — Actress
T M T Entertainment Group, 648 Broadway, #1002, New York NY 10012, USA

**Velez, Natalia** — Model
Mega Models Miami, 420 Lincoln Road, Miami Beach FL 33139, USA

**Velgos, Alicia** — Actress
Advance L A, 77904 Santa Monica Blvd, #200, Los Angeles CA 90046, USA

**Velikhov, Yevgeni P** — Physicist
Kurchatovskiy Institute, Kurchatova Pl 1, 123182 Moscow, Russia

**Velischek, Randy** — Ice Hockey Player
22 Hemlock Lane, Kinnelon NJ 07405, USA

**Veljohnson, Reginald** — Actor, Writer
22309 Haynes St, Woodland Hills CA 91303, USA

**Vella, John A** — Football Player
1890 Saint George Road, Danville CA 94526, USA

**Vellucci, Mike** — Ice Hockey Player
17302 Cameron Dr, Northville MI 48168, USA

**Veloso, Moreno** — Singer, Songwriter
Luaka Bop, 195 Chrystie St, #901F, New York NY 10002, USA

**Veloz, David** — Director, Producer, Writer
Creative Artists Agency, 2000 Ave of Stars, #100, Los Angeles CA 90067 USA

**Velten, Andreas** — Optical Physicist
Morgridge Research Institute, PO Box 7667, Madison WI 53707, USA

**Veltman, Jim (Scoop)** — Lacrosse Player
Agincort Collegiate Institute, Athletic Dept, Toronto ON M1S 1R6, Canada

**Veltman, Martinus J G** — Nobel Physics Laureate
University of Michigan, Randall Laboratory, Ann Arbor MI 48109, USA

**Veltri, Rachel** — Actress, Model
Luber Rocklin Entertainment, 5815 Sunset Blvd, #206, Los Angeles CA 90028 USA

**Venable, W McKinley (Mac)** — Baseball Player
107 Clark St, San Rafael CA 94901, USA

**Venables, Terry F** — Soccer Coach
Terry Venables Holdings, 213 Putney Bridge Road, London SW15 2NY, England

**Venafro, Michael R (Mike)** — Baseball Player
15151 Whimbrel Court, Fort Myers FL 33908, USA

**Venasky, Vic** — Ice Hockey Player
4307 W 234th Place, Torrance CA 90505, USA

**Vendela** — Model
T R Management Group, 11740 Wilshire Blvd, #A2109, Los Angeles CA 90025, USA

**Vendler, Helen H** — Educator, Writer
54 Trowbridge St, #2, Cambridge MA 02138, USA

**Vendt, Erik** — Swimmer
17 Amberwood Court, Buzzards Bay MA 02532, USA

**Venegas, Julieta** — Singer, Songwriter, Actress
United Talent Agency, U T A Plaza, 9336 Civic Center Dr, Beverly Hills CA 90210 USA

**Veneruzzo, Gary** — Ice Hockey Player
185 Fanshaw St, Thunder Bay ON P7C 5T7, Canada

**Venet, Bernar** — Sculptor, Artist
145 Ave of Americas, #5C, New York NY 10013, USA

**Venetiaan, R Ronald** — President, Suriname
Presidential Palace, Onafhankelikheidsplein 1, Paramaribo, Suriname

**Vengerov, Maxim** — Concert Violinist
Columbia Artists Mgmt Inc, 5 Columbus Circle, 1790 Broadway, #1600, New York NY 10019 USA

**Venito, Lenny** — Actor
Paradigm Agency, 360 N Crescent Dr, North Building, Beverly Hills CA 90210 USA

| | |
|---|---|
| **Venlet, David J** | Navy Admiral |
| Commander, Naval Air Systems Command, Patuxent River MD 20670 USA | |
| **Venora, Diane** | Actress |
| Don Buchwald Talent Agency, 6500 Wilshire Blvd, #2200, Los Angeles CA 90048 USA | |
| **Venter, J Craig** | Molecular Biologist |
| 11210 S Glen Road, Potomac MD 20854, USA | |
| **Venters, Jonathan W (Jonny)** | Baseball Player |
| Atlanta Braves, Turner Field, 755 Hank Aaron Dr, Atlanta GA 30315 USA | |
| **Ventimiglia, John** | Actor |
| Paul Kohner, 9300 Wilshire Blvd, #555, Beverly Hills CA 90212 USA | |
| **Ventimiglia, Milo** | Actor |
| Creative Artists Agency, 2000 Ave of Stars, #100, Los Angeles CA 90067 USA | |
| **Ventresca, Vincent** | Actor |
| Abrams Artists, 9200 W Sunset Blvd, #1125, West Hollywood CA 90069 USA | |
| **Ventura, Robin M** | Baseball Player |
| 1088 Newsom Springs Road, Arroyo Grande CA 93420, USA | |
| **Venturi, Rick** | Football Coach |
| 910 Banbury Road, Noblesville IN 46062, USA | |
| **Venturi, Robert** | Pritzker Architectural Laureate |
| Venturi Scott Brown Assoc, 4236 Main St, Philadelphia PA 19127, USA | |
| **Venturini, Tisha** | Soccer Player |
| 7101 Del Rio Ave, Modesto CA 95356, USA | |
| **Venzago, Mario** | Conductor |
| Indianapolis Symphony, 32 E Washington St, #600, Indianapolis IN 46204, USA | |
| **Vera, Billy** | Singer, Songwriter, Actor |
| Sutton-Barth Vennari, 5900 Wilshire Blvd, #700, Los Angeles CA 90036 USA | |
| **Veras, Jose E** | Baseball Player |
| Chicago Cubs, Wrigley Field, 1060 W Addison St, Chicago IL 60613 USA | |
| **Veras, Quilvio A P** | Baseball Player |
| 4244 Vineyard Circle, Weston FL 33332, USA | |
| **Verba, Ross R** | Football Player |
| 3066 Arden Place, Saint Paul MN 55129, USA | |
| **Verbeek, Lotte** | Actress |
| Innovative Artists, 1505 10th St, Santa Monica CA 90401 USA | |
| **Verbeek, Pat** | Ice Hockey Player |
| Verbeek Farm, RR 1, Wyoming ON N0N 1T0, Canada | |
| **Verbinski, Gregor (Gore)** | Director, Writer, Animator |
| Anonymous Content, 3532 Hayden Ave, Culver City CA 90232 USA | |
| **Verchota, Philip J (Phil)** | Ice Hockey Player |
| PO Box 1181, Bemidji MN 56619, USA | |
| **Verdi, Bob** | Sportswriter |
| Chicago Tribune, Editorial Dept, 435 N Michigan Ave, #1, Chicago IL 60611, USA | |
| **Verdi, Maria** | Actress |
| Artmedia, 20 Ave Rapp, 75007 Paris, France | |
| **Verdin, Clarence** | Football Player |
| 6221 Eastover Dr, New Orleans LA 70128, USA | |
| **Verdugo, Elena** | Actress |
| PO Box 2048, Chula Vista CA 91912, USA | |
| **Verdy, Violette** | Ballerina |
| 2000 Broadway, #2B, New York NY 10023, USA | |
| **Vereen, Ben** | Actor, Dancer, Singer |
| TalentWorks, 3500 W Olive Ave, #1400, Burbank CA 91505 USA | |
| **Veres, David S (Dave)** | Baseball Player |
| 871 Diamond Ridge Circle, Castle Rock CO 80108, USA | |
| **Veres, Randolph R (Randy)** | Baseball Player |
| 9213 W Frank Ave, Peoria AZ 85382, USA | |
| **Vergara, Sofia** | Singer, Actress, Model |
| Creative Artists Agency, 2000 Ave of Stars, #100, Los Angeles CA 90067 USA | |
| **Verhagen, Eduard** | Pediatrician |
| Groningen University Medical Center, Pediatrics Dept, Hanzeplein 1, 9700 Groningen RB, Netherlands | |
| **Verhoeven, Lis** | Actress |
| Agentur Doris Mattes, 14 Merzstr, 81679 Munich, Germany | |
| **Verhoeven, Paul** | Director |
| Marion Rosenberg, PO Box 69826, West Hollywood CA 90212 USA | |
| **Verhoeven, Peter G (Pete)** | Basketball Player |
| 12722 Fargo Ave, Hanford CA 93230, USA | |
| **Verica, Tom** | Actor |
| 20 Ironsides St, #18, Marina del Rey CA 90292, USA | |
| **Veris, Garin L** | Football Player |
| 2 Christine Dr, Atkinson NH 03811, USA | |
| **Verkaik, Petra** | Actress, Model |
| Playboy Promotions, 9346 Civic Center Dr, #200, Beverly Hills CA 90210 USA | |
| **Verlaine, Tom** | Singer, Bassist (Television) |
| High Road Touring, 751 Bridgeway, #200, Sausalito CA 94965 USA | |
| **Verlander, Justin B** | Baseball Player |
| 3928 Fairfax Dr, Troy MI 48083, USA | |
| **Verma, Inder M** | Molecular Biologist |
| Salk Institute, 10100 N Torrey Pines Road, La Jolla CA 92037, USA | |
| **Vermeij, Geerat J** | Evolutionary Biologist, Paleontologist |
| University of California, Geology Dept, Davis CA 95616, USA | |
| **Vermeil, Richard A (Dick)** | Football Coach, Sportscaster |
| 775 Fairview Road, Coatesville PA 19320, USA | |
| **Vermes, Peter** | Soccer Player, Manager |
| Sporting Kansas City, 210 W 19th Terrace, #200, Kansas City MO 64108 USA | |
| **Vermilyea, Jamie** | Baseball Player |
| 7051 E Calle Arandas, Tucson AZ 85750, USA | |
| **Vernarsky, Kris** | Ice Hockey Player |
| 13192 Hunt Road, Riley MI 48041, USA | |
| **Vernon, Annie** | Rowing Athlete |
| Marlow Rowing Club, 17 Elizabeth Road, Marlow SL7 1RH, England | |
| **Vernon, Conrad** | Director, Writer, Actor |
| United Talent Agency, U T A Plaza, 9336 Civic Center Dr, Beverly Hills CA 90210 USA | |
| **Vernon, Kate** | Actress |
| Shelter Entertainment, 9255 Sunset Blvd, #300, Los Angeles CA 90069 USA | |
| **Vernon, Mike** | Ice Hockey Player |
| Bear Mountain, 208-2800 Bryn Mawr Road, Victoria BC V9B 3T4, Canada | |

|  |  |
|---|---|
| **Vernonesi, Alberto**<br>I M G Artists, Hogarth Business Park, Chiswick, London W4 2TH, England | Conductor |
| **Veroni, Craig**<br>Muse Artists, 401-207 W Hastings St, Vancouver BC V6B 1H7, Canada | Actor |
| **Veronica**<br>Nene Musik Productions, 1460 SW Santiago Ave, Port Saint Lucie FL 34953 USA | Singer, Actress |
| **Veronica, Mayra**<br>Parallel Entertainment, 9420 Wilshire Blvd, #250, Beverly Hills CA 90212 USA | Model, Beauty Queen |
| **Veronis, John J, Jr**<br>Veronis Suhler Stevenson, 350 Park Ave, New York NY 10022, USA | Publisher |
| **Verplank, Scott**<br>1850 W Waterloo Road, Edmond OK 73025, USA | Golfer |
| **Verraros, James C (Jim)**<br>Stiletto Entertainment, 8295 S La Cienega Blvd, Inglewood CA 90301, USA | Singer, Actor |
| **Verrell, Cec**<br>Michael Slessinger, 8730 W Sunset Blvd, #220W, West Hollywood CA 90069 USA | Actress |
| **Verrett, Jason**<br>San Diego Chargers, 4020 Murphy Canyon Road, San Diego CA 92123 USA | Football Player |
| **Versace, Dick**<br>Memphis Grizzlies, 191 Beale St, Memphis TN 38103 USA | Basketball Coach |
| **Versace, Donatella**<br>Gianni Versace SpA, Via Manzoni 38, 20121 Milan, Italy | Fashion Designer |
| **Versaldi, Giuseppe Cardinal**<br>Economic Affairs Prefecture, Palazzo della Congregazioni, Largo del Colonnato 3, 00193 Rome, Italy | Religious Leader |
| **Verser, David**<br>21 Bellemonte Ave, Lakeside Park KY 41017, USA | Football Player |
| **Versini, Marie**<br>23 Residence Elysses, 78170 La Celle-Saint Cloud, France | Actress |
| **Verveen, Arie**<br>Global Artists Agency, 6253 Hollywood Blvd, #508, Los Angeles CA 90028, USA | Actor |
| **Ververgaert, Dennis A**<br>34484 Stoneleigh Ave, Abbotsford BC V2S 8N5, Canada | Ice Hockey Player |
| **Verwaayen, Ben**<br>Alcatel-Lucent, 54 Rue le Boetie, 75006 Paris, France | Businessman |
| **Verweij, Koen**<br>K N S B, Postbus 1120, 3800 Arnesfoort BC, Netherlands | Speed Skater |
| **Verwey, Bob**<br>International Mangement Group, 1 Erieview Plaza, 1360 E 9th St, #100, Cleveland OH 44114 USA | Golfer |
| **Very, Charlotte**<br>Cineart, 28 Rue Mogador, 78009 Paris, France | Actress |
| **Vesey, Jim**<br>11 Ellwood St, Charlestown MA 02129, USA | Ice Hockey Player |
| **Vesser, Dale A**<br>1313 Merchant Lane, McLean VA 22101, USA | Army General |
| **Vessey, John W, Jr**<br>27650 Little Whitefish Road, Garrison MN 56450, USA | Army General |
| **Vessey, Tricia**<br>Jackoway Tyerman Wertheimer, 1925 Century Park E, #2200, Los Angeles CA 90067 USA | Actress, Director, Producer |
| **Vest, Jake**<br>PO Box 350757, Grand Island FL 32735, USA | Cartoonist (That's Jake) |
| **Vesterbacka, Peter**<br>Rovio Mobile Ltd, Keilaranta 17, 02150 Espoo, Finland | Video Game Designer |
| **Vestiel, Franck**<br>Paradigm Agency, 360 N Crescent Dr, North Building, Beverly Hills CA 90210 USA | Director, Writer |
| **Vetri, Victoria**<br>610 N Van Ness Ave, Los Angeles CA 90004, USA | Actress |
| **Vetrov, Aleksandr**<br>Bolshoi Theater, Teatralnaya Pl 1, 103009 Moscow, Russia | Ballet Dancer |
| **Vettel, Sebastian**<br>Postfach 1479, 64632 Heppenheim, Germany | Auto Racing Driver |
| **Vetter, Jessi**<br>USA Hockey, 1775 Bob Johnson Dr, Colorado Springs CO 80906 USA | Ice Hockey Player |
| **Vettori, Ernst**<br>Fohrenweg 1, 6060 Absam-Eichat, Austria | Ski Jumper |
| **Vevers, Stuart**<br>Mulberry Ltd, Kilver Court, Shepton Mallet, Somerset BA4 5NF, England | Fashion Designer |
| **Veysey, Sid**<br>178 Ridgevale Dr, Bedford NS B4A 3S7, Canada | Ice Hockey Player |
| **Vezzoli, Francesco**<br>Gagosian Gallery, 980 Madison Ave, New York NY 10075 USA | Artist |
| **Via, Dennis L**<br>Commanding General, Army Material Command, Alexandria VA 22333, USA | Army General |
| **Viator, John A**<br>University of Missouri, Life Sciences Center, Columbia MO 65211, USA | Biological Engineer |
| **Vicent, Tania**<br>Speed Skating Canada, 2781 Lancaster Road, #402, Ottawa ON K1B 1A7, Canada | Speed Skater |
| **Vicius, Nicole**<br>Innovative Artists, 1505 10th St, Santa Monica CA 90401 USA | Actress |
| **Vick, Michael D**<br>21 Haywagon Trail, Hampton VA 23669, USA | Football Player |
| **Vickaryous, Jake**<br>University of Oregon, Chemistry Dept, Eugene OR 97403, USA | Chemist |
| **Vickers, Brian L**<br>27 High Tech Blvd, Thomasville NC 27360, USA | Auto Racing Driver |
| **Vickers, Jonathan S (Jon)**<br>Collingtree, 18 Riddells Bay Road, Warwick WK 04, Bermuda | Opera Singer |
| **Vickers, Kipp E**<br>PO Box 78365, Indianapolis IN 46278, USA | Football Player |
| **Vickers, Mike**<br>E M I Records, 43 Brook Green, London W6 7EF, England | Guitarist (Manfred Mann) |
| **Vickers, Steve**<br>238 Zokol Dr, Aurora ON L4G 0C2, Canada | Ice Hockey Player |
| **Vickrey, Dan**<br>Creative Artists Agency, 2000 Ave of Stars, #100, Los Angeles CA 90067 USA | Singer, Guitarist (Counting Crowes) |
| **Vico C**<br>A R Entertainment, 3400 Coral Way, #404, Miami FL 33145, USA | Rap, Reggae Artist |

Victor, James — Actor
H David Moss, 733 Seward St, #PH, Los Angeles CA 90038 USA

Victor, Renee — Actress
Independent Artists, 9601 Wilshire Blvd, #750, Beverly Hills CA 90210, USA

Victoria — Crown Princess, Sweden
Royal Palace, Kung Slottet, Stottsbacken, 111 30 Stockholm, Sweden

Victorino, Shane P — Baseball Player
1997 Alcova Ridge Dr, Las Vegas NV 89135, USA

Vidal, Cesar — Singer, Guitarist (Caesars)
Paradigm Agency, 360 Park Ave, #1600, New York NY 10022 USA

Vidal, Christina — Actress
McGowan Mgmt, 8733 W Sunset Blvd, #103, West Hollywood CA 90069 USA

Vidal, Deborah — Golfer
2033 Paramount Dr, Los Angeles CA 90068, USA

Vidal, Jean-Pierre — Alpine Skier
Ski Federation, 50 Rue de Marquisats, BP 51, 74011 Annecy Cedex, France

Vidal, Lisa — Actress
Don Buchwald Talent Agency, 6500 Wilshire Blvd, #2200, Los Angeles CA 90048 USA

Vidal, Ricardo J Cardinal — Religious Leader
Chancery, D Jakosalem Str, PO Box 52, Corner P Gomez & P Burgos Sts, Cebu City 6000, Philippines

Vidal, Tanya — Actress
McGowan Mgmt, 8733 W Sunset Blvd, #103, West Hollywood CA 90069 USA

Vidmar, Peter — Gymnast
455 Camino Flora Vista, San Clemente CA 92673, USA

Vidrio Serrano, Nestor V — Soccer Player
Federacion de Futbol, Colima 373 Colonia Roma, Delegacion Cuauhtemoc, Mexico City DF 06700, Mexico

Vidro, Jose A C — Baseball Player
159 Wentworth Ave, Brockton MA 02301, USA

Viehboeck, Franz A — Cosmonaut, Austria
Hauptstr 102/Top 3, 1140 Vienna, Austria

Vieillard, Roger — Artist
7 Rue de l'Estrapade, 75005 Paris, France

Vieira, Jelon — Choreographer
Pentocle/Danceworks, 246 W 38th St, #800, New York NY 10018, USA

Vieira, Marcelo — Soccer Player
F C Real Madrid, Avda Concha Espana 1, 28036 Madrid, Spain

Vieira, Meredith — Commentator
Meredith Vieira Productions, 888 7th Ave, #503, New York NY 10106, USA

Vieira, Patrick — Soccer Player
F C Juventus, Corso Galilo Ferraris 32, 10128 Turin, Italy

Viellard, Eric — Actor
Artmedia, 20 Ave Rapp, 75007 Paris, France

Viener, John — Actor, Writer
United Talent Agency, U T A Plaza, 9336 Civic Center Dr, Beverly Hills CA 90210 USA

Viesturs, Ed — Mountaineer
4462 NE Mill Heights Circle, Bainbridge Island WA 98110, USA

Vieth, Michelle — Actress, Model
Televisa, Blvd A Lopez Mateos 232, Colonia San Angel, Mexico City DF 01060 CP, Mexico

Vig, Butch — Drummer (Garbage), Record Producer
Creative Artists Agency, 2000 Ave of Stars, #100, Los Angeles CA 90067 USA

Vigil, Frederico — Artist
National Hispanic Cultural Center, 1701 4th St SW, Albuquerque NM 87102, USA

Vigman, Gillian — Actress, Comedienne
Brillstein Entertainment Partners, 9150 Wilshire Blvd, #350, Beverly Hills CA 90212 USA

Vigna, Marino — Cyclist
Via Bruno Buozzi 130, 20089 Rozzano, Italy

Vigneault, Alain — Ice Hockey Player, Coach
New York Rangers, Madison Square Garden, 2 Penn Plaza, New York NY 10121 USA

Vignelli, Lella — Interior Designer
Vignelli Assoc, 130 E 67th St, New York NY 10065, USA

Vigneron, Thierry G — Track Athlete
Adidas USA, 685 Cedar Crest Road, Spartanburg SC 29301, USA

Vigoda, Abe — Actor
3 Zircon Way, #D1, Woodland Park NJ 07424, USA

Vigoda, Valerie — Singer, Violinist (GrooveLily)
GrooveLily, PO Box 11570, Glendale CA 91226, USA

Vikander, Alicia — Actress
Actors in Scandanavia, Jaakarinkatu 10, 00150 Helsinki, Finland

Viktorenko, Aleksandr S — Cosmonaut
Cosmonaut Training Center, Star City, 141160 Zvezdny Gorodok, Moscow Oblast, Russia

Vila, Bob — Entertainer, Writer
115 Kingston St, #300, Boston MA 02111, USA

Vilar, Tracy — Actress
Raw Talent Mgmt, 9615 Brighton Way, #300, Beverly Hills CA 90210 USA

Vilaro, Eduardo — Dancer, Choreographer
Ballet Hispanico, 167 W 89th St, New York NY 10024, USA

Vilas, Guillermo — Tennis Player
Ave Foch 86, 75016 Paris, France

Vilasuso, Jordi — Actor
Artistry Mgmt, 340 N Camden Dr, #302, Beverly Hills CA 90210, USA

Vilenkin, Alex — Physicist, Astronomer
Tufts University, Physics & Astronomy Dept, Medford MA 02155, USA

Viletta, Sandro — Alpine Skier
House of Skiing, Worbstr 52, PO Box 252, 3074 Mori bei Bern, Switzerland

Vilkaste, Arvis — Bobsled Athlete
Bobsled Federation, Roberta Feldmana 11, 1014 Riga, Latvia

Villa Sanchez David — Soccer Player
New York City Soccer, Yankee Stadium, 1 E 161st St, Bronx NY 10451 USA

Villa, Carlos — Artist
San Francisco Art Institute, 800 Chestnut St, San Francisco CA 94133, USA

Villafuerte, Brandon — Baseball Player
PO Box 188, North Bridgton ME 04057, USA

Villanueva, Charlie — Basketball Player
Detroit Pistons, Palace, 4 Championship Dr, Auburn Hills MI 48326 USA

Villapiano, Philip J (Phil) — Football Player
21 Riverside Dr, Rumson NJ 07760, USA

**Villaraigosa, Antonio** — Mayor, Los Angeles
Mayor's Office, City Hall, 200 N Spring St, Los Angeles CA 90012, USA

**Villari, Guy** — Singer (Regents)
293 Airport Road, Liberty NY 12754, USA

**Villarrial, Christopher H (Chris)** — Football Player
7234 Bibbs Road, Little Valley NY 14755, USA

**Villarroel, Vernoica** — Opera Singer
Columbia Artists Mgmt Inc, 5 Columbus Circle, 1790 Broadway, #1600, New York NY 10019 USA

**Villasenor, Diego** — Architect
Gob Tiburcio Montiel 96, Col S M Chapultepec, Mexico City DF 11850, Mexico

**Villazon, Rolando** — Opera Singer
Centre Stage Artist Mgmt, Stralauer Allee 1, 10245 Berlin, Gerany

**Villegas, Camilo** — Golfer
318 W Riverside Dr, Tequesta FL 33469, USA

**Villella, Edward J** — Ballet Dancer, Choreographer
Miami City Ballet, Roca Center, 2200 Liberty Ave, Miami Beach FL 33139, USA

**Villeneuve, Denis** — Director, Writer
Claude Girard, 5230 Boul Saint-Laurent, Montreal QC H2T 1S1, Canada

**Villeneuve, Gilles** — Ice Hockey Player
38 Grey Lane, Levittown NY 11756, USA

**Villeneuve, Jacques** — Auto Racing Driver
B A R Team, PO Box 5014, Brackley, Northamptonshire NN13 7YY, England

**Villiers, Christopher** — Actor
Hillman Trelfall, 33 Brookfield, Highgate W Hill, London N6 6AT, England

**Villone, Ronald T (Ron), Jr** — Baseball Player
855 NE Mulberry Dr, Boca Raton FL 33487, USA

**Vilma, Jonathan P** — Football Player
1331 Brickell Bay Dr, #2709, Miami FL 33131, USA

**Viloria, Brian** — Boxer
Gary Gittlesohn, 14372 Mulholland Dr, Los Angeles CA 90077, USA

**Vilsack, Thomas (Tom)** — Secretary, Agriculture; Governor, IA
Agriculture Department, 14th St & Independence Ave SW, Washington DC 20250 USA

**Vimond, Paul M** — Architect
91 Ave Niel, 75017 Paris, France

**Vin Rock** — Rap Artist (Naughty By Nature)
Evolution Talent Agency, 1501 Broadway, #1301, New York NY 10036 USA

**Vina, Fernando** — Baseball Player
9464 Clementine Way, Elk Grove CA 95758, USA

**Vinatieri, Adam M** — Football Player
11595 Ditch Road, Carmel IN 46032, USA

**Vince, Pruitt Taylor** — Actor
Burstein Co, 15304 Sunset Blvd, #208, Pacific Palisades CA 90272, USA

**Vincelette, Dan** — Ice Hockey Player
1345 Rue Bernier, RR 3, Acton Vale QC J0H 1A0, Canada

**Vincent of Coleshill, Baron Richard F** — Army Field Marshal, England
House of Lords, Westminster, London SW1A 0PW, England

**Vincent, Amy** — Cinematographer
5932 Graciosa Dr, Los Angeles CA 90068, USA

**Vincent, Brian** — Actor
Imperium 7, 5455 Wilshire Blvd, #1706, Los Angeles CA 90036, USA

**Vincent, Cerina** — Actress
Brillstein Entertainment Partners, 9150 Wilshire Blvd, #350, Beverly Hills CA 90212 USA

**Vincent, Francis T (Fay), Jr** — Baseball Executive
290 Harbor Dr, Stamford CT 06902, USA

**Vincent, J Samuel (Sam)** — Basketball Player, Coach
PO Box 27459, Lansing MI 48909, USA

**Vincent, James F (Jim), Jr** — Choreographer, Dance Executive
Netherlands Dance Theater, Schedeldoekshaven 60, 2501 The Haag CH, Netherlands

**Vincent, Jan-Michael** — Actor
Freeman & Sutton, 8961 W Sunset Blvd, #200, West Hollywood CA 90069, USA

**Vincent, Jay F** — Basketball Player
PO Box 27459, Lansing MI 48909, USA

**Vincent, Keydrick T** — Football Player
1769 Derby Glen Dr, Orlando FL 32837, USA

**Vincent, Rhonda** — Singer
Upper Mgmt, 1036 Tulip Grove Road, Nashville TN 37076, USA

**Vincent, Rick** — Singer, Songwriter
Carter Career Mgmt, 1028 18th Ave S, #B, Nashville TN 37212 USA

**Vincent, Troy D** — Football Player
18900 Longhouse Place, Leesburg VA 20176, USA

**Vincent, Virginia** — Actress
4738 Works Place, San Diego CA 92116, USA

**Vincentelli, Francois** — Actor
Artmedia, 20 Ave Rapp, 75007 Paris, France

**Vincenzi, Penny** — Writer
Overlook Press, 141 Wooster St, #4B, New York NY 10012, USA

**Vinci, Roberta** — Tennis Player
Via Taranto 89, 74015 Martina Franca (TA), Italy

**Vincz, Melanie** — Actress
2212 Earle Court, Redondo Beach CA 90278, USA

**Vineyard, David K (Dave)** — Baseball Player
1850 Tariff Road, Left Hand WV 25251, USA

**Vingt-Trois, Andre A Cardinal** — Religious Leader
Ordinary of France, 7 Rue Saint Vincent, 75018 Paris Cedex 08, France

**Vining, David** — Gastroenterologist
2210 Bellefontaine St, #D, Houston TX 77030, USA

**Vinogradov, Pavel V** — Cosmonaut
Cosmonaut Training Center, Star City, 141160 Zvezdny Gorodok, Moscow Oblast, Russia

**Vinokourov, Alexandre N** — Cyclist
U C I Pro Team Astana, Gildo Pastor Center, 7 Rue du Gabian, 98000 Monaco

**Vinoly, Rafael** — Architect
50 Vandam St, New York NY 10013, USA

**Vinson, Charles A (Charlie)** — Baseball Player
3821 Walters Lane, District Heights MD 20747, USA

**Vinson, Sharni** — Actress, Model, Dancer
Flutie Entertainment, 9320 Wilshire Blvd, #202, Beverly Hills CA 90212 USA

**Vint, Jesse Lee, III** — Actor
Film Artists, 13563 1/2 Ventura Blvd, #200, Sherman Oaks CA 91423 USA

**Vinton, Bobby** — Singer
M P I Talent Agency, 9255 W Sunset Blvd, #407, West Hollywood CA 90069, USA

**Vinton, Will** — Animator, Director, Producer
Creative Artists Agency, 2000 Ave of Stars, #100, Los Angeles CA 90067 USA

**Viola, Bill** — Sculptor, Video Artist
282 Granada Ave, Long Beach CA 90803, USA

**Viola, Frank J, Jr** — Baseball Player
9868 Kilgore Road, Orlando FL 32836, USA

**Viola, Lisa** — Dancer
Paul Taylor Dance Co, 551 Grand St, Lobby A, New York NY 10002, USA

**Violette, Banks** — Artist
Blum & Poe Gallery, 2727 S La Cienega Blvd, Los Angeles CA 90034, USA

**Virata, Cesar E** — Prime Minister, Philippines
Rizal Banking, 333 Sen Gil Puyat Ave, Makati City, Metro Manila, Philippines

**Virden, Claude** — Basketball Player
337 Fernwood Dr, Akron OH 44320, USA

**Virdon, William C (Bill)** — Baseball Player, Manager
1311 E River Road, Springfield MO 65804, USA

**Viren, Lasse** — Track Athlete
Suomen Urheilulitto Ry, Box 25202, 00250 Helsinki 25, Finland

**Virgil, Osvaldo J (Ozzie), Jr** — Baseball Player
5444 W Credance Blvd, Glendale AZ 85310, USA

**Virgil, Osvaldo J (Ozzie), Sr** — Baseball Player
4316 W Mescal St, Glendale AZ 85304, USA

**Virsaladze, Eliso K** — Concert Pianist
Moscow Conservatory, Bolshaya Nikitskaya Str 13/6, 125009 Moscow, Russia

**Virts, Terry W, Jr** — Astronaut
1904 Edgewater Court, Friendswood TX 77546, USA

**Virtue, Tessa** — Ice Dancer
Arctic Edge Ice Arena, 46615 Michigan Ave, Canton MI 48188, USA

**Virtue, Tom** — Actor
A M T Artists, 15260 Ventura Blvd, #1200, Sherman Oaks CA 91403, USA

**Viscuso, Sal** — Actor
Imperium 7 Talent, 5455 Wilshire Blvd, #1706, Los Angeles CA 90036, USA

**Vise, David A** — Journalist
Washington Post, Editorial Dept, 1150 15th St NW, Washington DC 20071, USA

**Vishnevski, Vitaly** — Ice Hockey Player
Internatioanl Sports Advisors, 878 Ridge View Way, Franklin Lakes NJ 07417, USA

**Vishnyova, Diana V** — Ballerina
Marinsky Theater, Teatralnaya Square 1, 190000 Saint Petersburg, Russia

**Visitor, Nana** — Actress
Pantheon Talent, 1801 Century Park E, #1910, Los Angeles CA 90067, USA

**Visnjic, Goran** — Actor
Management 360, 9111 Wilshire Blvd, Beverly Hills CA 90210 USA

**Visnovsky, Lubomir** — Ice Hockey Player
1531 9th St, Manhattan Beach CA 90266, USA

**Viso, Michel** — Spatinaut, France
7 Domaine Chateau-Gaillard, 94700 Maisons-d'Alfort, France

**Visser, Angela** — Beauty Queen, Actress
4127 Crisp Canyon Road, Sherman Oaks CA 91403, USA

**Visser, Douwe** — Religious Leader
World Reformed Churches, 150 Rt de Ferney, 1211 Geneva 2, Switzerland

**Visser, Lesley** — Sportscaster
CBS-TV, Sports Dept, 51 W 52nd St, New York NY 10019 USA

**Vissi, Anna** — Singer
Confidential Talent Agency, 745 5th Ave, #800, New York NY 10151, USA

**Vitale, Dick** — Sportscaster, Basketball Coach
7810 Mathern Court, Bradenton FL 34202, USA

**Vitali, Massimo** — Photographer
Brancolini Grimaldi Gallery, 43-44 Albemarle St, London W1S 4JJ, England

**Vitamin C** — Singer, Actress
I C M Partners, 10250 Constellation Blvd, #900, Los Angeles CA 90067 USA

**Vitez, Michael** — Journalist
Philadelphia Inquirer, Editorial Dept, 400 N Broad St, Philadelphia PA 19130, USA

**Vitiello, Joseph D (Joe)** — Baseball Player
13615 Old El Camino Real, San Diego CA 92130, USA

**Vitkova, Veronika** — Biathlete
United Sports Partners, Ovenecka 9, 17000 Prague 7, Czech Republic

**Vito, Robert D** — Actor
Strong Management, 9350 Wilshire Blvd, #224, Beverly Hills CA 90212, USA

**Vitolo, Dennis** — Auto Racing Driver
2130 Intracoastal Dr, Fort Lauderdale FL 33305, USA

**Vitorgan, Emmanuil** — Actor, Director
Maly Kislovsky Per 7, #26, 103009 Moscow, Russia

**Vitousek, Peter M** — Botanist, Ecologist
Stanford University, Biological Science Dept, Stanford CT 94305, USA

**Vittadini, Adrienne** — Fashion Designer
Adrienne Vittadini Inc, 575 Fashion Ave, New York NY 10018, USA

**Vitti, Monica** — Actress
I P C, Via Francesco Siacci 38, 00197 Rome, Italy

**Vittori, Roberto** — Astronaut
European Space Center, Linder Hohe, Box 906096, 51127 Cologne, Germany

**Vitukhnovskaya, Alina A** — Writer
Leningradskoye Shosse 80, #89, 125565 Moscow, Russia

**Vivas, Miguel A** — Director, Writer, Actor
United Talent Agency, U T A Plaza, 9336 Civic Center Dr, Beverly Hills CA 90210 USA

**Vivek** — Actor, Comedian
9 Subhiksha Apts, 5 Tank St, U I Colony, Chennai TN 600024, India

**Vives I Silva, Joan E** — Co-Prince, Andorra; Religious Leader
Bisbat D'Urgell, Pati Palau 1-5, La Seu d'Urgell, Lleida, 25700 Andorra

**Vivian, Cody T (C T)** — Religious Leader, Writer, Activist
C T Vivian Leadership Institute, 355 Dix-Lee-On Drive, Fairburn GA 30213, USA

**Viviani, Elena** — Speed Skater
Federation of Ice Sports, Via Vitorchiano 113/117, 00189 Rome, Italy

**Viviani, Gabriele** — Opera Singer
I M G Artists, Hogarth Business Park, Chiswick, London W4 2TH, England

**Vizquel Gonzalez, Omar E** — Baseball Player
2704 212th Ave SE, Sammamish WA 98075, USA

**Vlady, Marina** — Actress
10 Ave de Marivaux, 78800 Mission Lafitte, France

**Vlasic, Blanka** — Track Athlete
Hrvatski Atletski Savez, Krizaniceva 5, 10000 Zagreb, Croatia

**Vlasic, Marc-Edouard** — Ice Hockey Player
San Jose Sharks, San Jose Arena, 525 W Santa Clara St, San Jose CA 95113 USA

**Vlk, Miloslav Cardinal** — Religious Leader
Arcibiskupstvi, Hradcanske Nam 16/56, 11902 Prague 1, Czech Republic

**Voda, Jan K** — Surgeon
608 NW 9th St, Oklahoma City OK 73102, USA

**Vodianova, Natalia** — Model
D N A Model Mgmt, 555 W 25th St, #600, New York NY 10001 USA

**Vodopyanova, Natalia** — Basketball Player
Seattle Storm, Key Arena, 351 Elliott Ave W, #500, Seattle WA 98119 USA

**Voegele, Kate** — Singer, Songwriter, Actress
Wilspro Mgmt, PO Box 9, Point Pleasant NJ 08742, USA

**Voelker, Sabine** — Speed Skater
Rube Marketing, Maximilian-Welsch Str 7, 99084 Erfurt, Germany

**Voevodsky, Vladimir** — Mathematician
35 Stonehouse Dr, Princeton NJ 08540, USA

**Vogel, Darlene** — Actress
Venture I A B, 3211 Cahuenga Blvd W, #104, Los Angeles CA 90068, USA

**Vogel, Frank** — Basketball Coach
Indiana Pacers, Conseco Fieldhouse, 125 S Pennsylvania, Indianapolis IN 46204 USA

**Vogel, Mike** — Actor
W M E Entertainment, 9601 Wilshire Blvd, #300, Beverly Hills CA 90210 USA

**Vogel, Paula** — Writer
Gersh Agency, 9465 Wilshire Blvd, #600, Beverly Hills CA 90212 USA

**Vogel, Robert L (Bob)** — Football Player
2065 N Galena Road, Sunbury OH 43074, USA

**Vogelsong, Ryan A** — Baseball Player
637 W Jardin Dr, Casa Grande AZ 85122, USA

**Vogelstein, Bert** — Geneticist, Oncologist
Howard Hughes Medical Institute, 4000 Jones Bridge Road, Chevy Chase MD 20815, USA

**Vogler, Jan** — Concert Cellist
Moira Johnson Consulting, 180 Metcalfe St, #404, Ottawa ON K2P 1P5, Canada

**Vogler, Timothy (Tim)** — Football Player
6710 Woodland Dr, Hamburg NY 14075, USA

**Vogt, Carina** — Ski Jumper
Rechbachweg 6, 73550 Waldsteten, Germany

**Vogt, Peter K** — Virologist
Scripps Institute, Oncovirology Dept, 10550 N Torrey Pines, La Jolla CA 92037, USA

**Vogts, Hans-Hubert (Berti)** — Soccer Player
Football Assoc, 2208 Nobel Ave, 1025 Baku, Azerbaijan

**Vohor, Serge** — Prime Minister, Vanuatu
Moderate Parties Union, PO Box 698, Port Via, Vanuatu

**Voie, Angelica** — Opera Singer
Harrison/Parrott, 5-6 Albion Court, London W6 0QT, England

**Voight, Jon** — Actor
Artists Only Management, 10203 Santa Monica Blvd, #500, Los Angeles CA 90067, USA

**Voight, Karen** — Physical Fitness Expert
Entertaining Fitness, 827 Chautauqua Blvd, Pacific Palisades CA 90272, USA

**Voight, Stuart A (Stu)** — Football Player
8832 Hunters Way, Saint Paul MN 55124, USA

**Voigt, Deborah** — Opera Singer
Columbia Artists Mgmt Inc, 5 Columbus Circle, 1790 Broadway, #1600, New York NY 10019 USA

**Voigt, John D (Jack)** — Baseball Player
1759 Bayshore Road, Nokomis FL 34275, USA

**Voisine, Roch** — Singer, Songwriter
Don Jones Productions, 550 Wellington St, London ON N6A 3P9, Canada

**Vokoun, Tomas** — Ice Hockey Player
6685 NW 122nd Ave, Parkland FL 33076, USA

**Volberding, Paul A** — Oncologist
General Hospital, AIDS Activities Dept, 995 Protrero, San Francisco CA 94110, USA

**Volchenkov, Anton** — Ice Hockey Player
New Jersey Devils, Arena, 50 State Route 120, East Rutherford NJ 07073 USA

**Volcker, Paul A** — Government Official, Financier
151 E 79th St, New York NY 10075, USA

**Volek, David** — Ice Hockey Player
5 Blue Sky Court, Huntington NY 11743, USA

**Volek, J William (Billy)** — Football Player
12487 Valley Vista Lane, Fresno CA 93730, USA

**Volf, Jaroslav** — Canoeing Athlete
S K Neumanna 386, 25001 Brandys Nad Labem, Czech Republic

**Volibracht, Michaele** — Fashion Designer, Artist
Bill Blass Ltd, 236 5th Ave, #800, New York NY 10001, USA

**Volk, Igor P** — Cosmonaut
G N C-R F L II, Zhukovskiy 2, 140160 Moscow, Russia

**Volk, Patricia** — Writer
Gloria Loomis, 133 E 35th St, New York NY 10016, USA

**Volk, Richard R (Rick)** — Football Player
15860 Irish Ave, Monkton MD 21111, USA

**Volkaert, Redd** — Guitarist (Twangbangers)
Nancy Fly Agency, PO Box 90306, Austin TX 78709, USA

**Volkert, Stephan** — Rowing Athlete
Semmelweisstr 42, 51061 Cologne, Germany

**Volkmann, Elisabeth** — Opera Singer
Sonnenstr 20, 80331 Munich, Germany

**Volkov, Aleksandr A** — Cosmonaut
Cosmonaut Training Center, Star City, 141160 Zvezdny Gorodok, Moscow Oblast, Russia

**Volkov, Sergei A** — Cosmonaut
Cosmonaut Training Center, Star City, 141160 Zvezdny Gorodok, Moscow Oblast, Russia

| | |
|---|---|
| **Volkow, Nora D** | Physician |
| National Drug Abuse Institute, 6001 Executive Blvd, Bethesda MD 20892, USA | |
| **Vollbracht, Michaele** | Fashion Designer, Artist |
| General Delivery, Safety Harbor FL 34695, USA | |
| **Volle, Michael** | Opera Singer |
| I M G Artists, Hogarth Business Park, Chiswick, London W4 2TH, England | |
| **Vollenweider, Andreas** | Concert Harpist |
| Sempacher Str 16, 8032 Zurich, Switzerland | |
| **Vollman, William T** | Writer |
| 2090 8th Ave, Sacramento CA 95818, USA | |
| **Vollmer, Dana W** | Swimmer |
| 4002 Laramie Dr, Granbury TX 76049, USA | |
| **Volmar, Douglas (Doug)** | Ice Hockey Player |
| 120 Royal Oak Dr, #L, Bel Air MD 21015, USA | |
| **Volmer, Arvo** | Conductor |
| Estonia National Opera, Estonia Ave 4, 10148 Tallinn, Estonia | |
| **Volodos, Arcadi** | Concert Pianist |
| Columbia Artists Mgmt Inc, 5 Columbus Circle, 1790 Broadway, #1600, New York NY 10019 USA | |
| **Voloshin, Valeri** | Cosmonaut |
| Cosmonaut Training Center, Star City, 141160 Zvezdny Gorodok, Moscow Oblast, Russia | |
| **Volosozhar, Tatiana A** | Figure Skater |
| Figure Skating Federation, Luzhnetskaya Nab 8, 119991 Moscow, Russia | |
| **Volstad, Christopher K (Chris)** | Baseball Player |
| 11774 Hemlock St, Palm Beach Gardens FL 33410, USA | |
| **Volynov, Boris V** | Cosmonaut |
| Cosmonaut Training Center, Star City, 141160 Zvezdny Gorodok, Moscow Oblast, Russia | |
| **VonAroldingen, Karin** | Ballerina |
| New York City Ballet, Lincoln Center Plaza, New York NY 10023 USA | |
| **VonDaniken, Erich** | Writer |
| Postfach, 3803 Beatenberg, Switzerland | |
| **VonDetten, Erik T** | Actor |
| Innovative Artists, 1505 10th St, Santa Monica CA 90401 USA | |
| **VonDohnanyi, Christoph** | Conductor |
| Cleveland Orchestra, Severance Hall, Cleveland OH 44106, USA | |
| **VonDonnersmarck, Florian H** | Director |
| United Talent Agency, U T A Plaza, 9336 Civic Center Dr, Beverly Hills CA 90210 USA | |
| **Vondracek, Lukas** | Concert Pianist |
| Harrison/Parrott, Lucile-Grahn-Str 37, 81675 Munich, Germany | |
| **VonEschenbach, Andrew** | Surgeon, Government Official |
| US Food & Drug Administration, 5600 Fishers Lane, Rockville MD 20857, USA | |
| **VonEsmarch, Nick** | Actor |
| TalentWorks, 3500 W Olive Ave, #1400, Burbank CA 91505 USA | |
| **VonFurstenberg, Betsy** | Actress |
| 230 Central Park West, #16A, New York NY 10024, USA | |
| **VonFurstenberg, Diane** | Fashion Designer |
| 444 W 14th St, New York NY 10014, USA | |
| **VonGarnier, Katja** | Director, Writer |
| Above the Line, Theresienstr 31, 80333 Munich, Germany | |
| **Vongerichten, Jean-Georges** | Chef |
| Jean-Georges Restaurant, 19 Greene St, New York NY 10013, USA | |
| **VonGerkan, Manon** | Model |
| Trump Model Mgmt, 91 5th Ave, #300, New York NY 10003, USA | |
| **VonGrunigen, Michael** | Alpine Skier |
| Chalet Sunneblick, 3778 Schonried, Switzerland | |
| **VonHagens, Gunther** | Anatomist |
| Institute for Plastination, Rathausstr 11, 69126 Heidelberg, Germany | |
| **VonHoff, Bruce F** | Baseball Player |
| 423 S River Hills Dr, Tampa FL 33617, USA | |
| **VonHohenzollern, Furst** | Heir, House of Hohenzollern-Sigmaringen |
| Landhaus Josefslust, 72488 Sigmaringen, Germany | |
| **VonKlitzing, Klaus** | Nobel Physics Laureate |
| Max Planck Institute, Heisenbergstr 1, 70506 Stuttgart, Germany | |
| **Vonleh, Noah** | Basketball Player |
| Charlotte Hornets, 333 E Trade St, #A, Charlotte NC 28202 USA | |
| **Vonn, Lindsey K** | Alpine Skier |
| I M G Worldwide, 200 5th Ave, #700, New York NY 10010, USA | |
| **VonOelhoffen, Kimo K** | Football Player |
| 402 Adams St, Richland WA 99352, USA | |
| **VonOhlen, David (Dave)** | Baseball Player |
| 653 Windmill Ave, West Babylon NY 11704, USA | |
| **VonOtter, Anne Sofie** | Opera Singer |
| Opus 3 Artists, 470 Park Ave S, #900N, New York NY 10016 USA | |
| **VonQuast, Veronika** | Actress |
| Agentur Ebisch, Schellingstra 124, 80798 Munich, Germany | |
| **VonRingelheim, Paul H** | Sculptor |
| 9 Great Jones St, New York NY 10012, USA | |
| **VonSaltza Olmstead, S Christine (Chris)** | Swimmer |
| 520 Crocker Road, Sacramento CA 95864, USA | |
| **VonSchamann, Uwe D W** | Football Player |
| 1236 Loma Dr, Norman OK 73072, USA | |
| **VonStade, Frederica** | Opera Singer |
| 333 Kennedy St, Oakland CA 94606, USA | |
| **VonSydow, Max** | Actor |
| Diamond Mgmt, 31 Percy St, London W1T 2DD, England | |
| **VonTeese, Dita** | Model, Actress, Dancer |
| Dishell Multimedia Group, 8306 Wilshire Blvd, #833, Beverly Hills CA 90211, USA | |
| **VonThurn und Taxis, Albert** | Businessman |
| Emmeramsplatz 5, 93047 Regensburg, Germany | |
| **VonThurn und Taxis, Gloria** | Princess, House of Thurn und Taxis |
| Emmeramsplatz 5, 93047 Regensburg, Germany | |
| **VonTrier, Lars** | Director |
| Zentropa Entertainments, Filmbyen 22, 2650 Hvidovre, Denmark | |
| **VonTrotta, Margarethe** | Director |
| Above The Line, Wielandstr 5, 10625 Berlin, Germany | |
| **VonWeizsacker, Richard** | President, Germany |
| Am Kupfergraben 7, 10117 Berlin, Germany | |

**Voog, Ana**
M C A Records, 1755 Broadway, New York NY 10019 USA — Singer, Songwriter

**Voorhees, John J**
3965 Waldenwood Dr, Ann Arbor MI 48105, USA — Dermatologist

**Voorhies, Lark**
Cyrus & Cyrus, 9935 S Santa Monica Blvd, Beverly Hills CA 90212, USA — Actress

**Voorman, Klaus**
K & K Galleries, Grindelalla 182, 20144 Hamburg, Germany — Artist

**Voris, Cyrus**
United Talent Agency, U T A Plaza, 9336 Civic Center Dr, Beverly Hills CA 90210 USA — Writer, Producer, Actor

**Voronin, Vladimir N**
Presidential Palace, 23 Nicolae Iorge Str, 227033 Chishinev, Moldova — President, Moldova

**Vorontsov, Nikolai N**
Koltsov Biology Institute, Vavilova Str 26, 117334 Moscow, Russia — Geneticist, Zoologist

**Voros, Christina**
Gersh Agency, 9465 Wilshire Blvd, #600, Beverly Hills CA 90212 USA — Director, Cinematographer

**Voroshilo, Aleksander S**
Bolshoi Theater, Teatralnaya Pl 1, 103009 Moscow, Russia — Opera Singer

**Vosberg, Edward J (Ed)**
7839 E Marquise Dr, Tucson AZ 85715, USA — Baseball Player

**Vosloo, Arnold**
A P A Talent & Literary Agency, 405 S Beverly Dr, #300, Beverly Hills CA 90212 USA — Actor

**Voss, Brian**
6115 Abbotts Bridge Road, #111, Duluth GA 30097, USA — Bowler

**Voss, James S**
4207 Indian Sunrise Court, Houston TX 77059, USA — Astronaut

**Voss, John**
University of California, Biochemistry Dept, Davis CA 95616, USA — Biochemist

**Voss, Torsten**
Dunkirchener Str 74, 47839 Krefeld, Germany — Track Athlete

**Voss, William E (Bill)**
10625 E Oak Creek Trail, Cornville AZ 86325, USA — Baseball Player

**VosSavant, Marilyn**
Parade Publications, 711 3rd Ave, New York NY 10017, USA — Writer

**Vostell, Wolf**
Giesebrechstr 12, 10629 Berlin, Germany — Video Artist

**Votaw, Ty**
Ladies Pro Golf Assn, 100 International Golf Dr, Daytona Beach FL 32124 USA — Golf Executive

**Votel, Joseph L**
Commander, US Special Operations Command, MacDill Air Force Base FL 33621 USA — Army General

**Voth, Julia**
C E S D, 10635 Santa Monica Blvd, #130, Los Angeles CA 90025 USA — Actress

**Votolato, Rocky**
Undertow Music Collective, 1124 W Daniel, Champaign IL 61822, USA — Singer, Guitarist

**Votsis, Gloria**
T M T Entertainment Group, 648 Broadway, #912, New York, NY 10012, USA — Actress

**Votto, Joseph D (Joey)**
4 Nantucket Crescent, Brampton ON L6S 3X5, Canada — Baseball Player

**Voyagis, Yorgo**
Anne Alvares Correa, 34 Rue Jouffroy d'Abbans, 75017 Paris, France — Actor

**Voyce, Inez**
PO Box 4284, Sunland CA 91041, USA — Baseball Player

**Voyles, Brad**
314 East Ave, Casco WI 54205, USA — Baseball Player

**Vraa, Sanna**
Irv Schechter, 9460 Wilshire Blvd, #300, Beverly Hills CA 90212 USA — Model, Actress

**Vrabel, Michael G (Mike)**
777 W Orange Road, Delaware OH 43015, USA — Football Player

**Vraciu, Alexander (Alex)**
2829 Cascade Place, Davis CA 95618, USA — WW II Navy Air Force Hero

**Vranes, Daniel L (Danny)**
6480 Canyon Ranch Road, Salt Lake City UT 84121, USA — Basketball Player

**Vratogna, Marco**
I M G Artists, Hogarth Business Park, Chiswick, London W4 2TH, England — Opera Singer

**Vreeman, Rachel C**
Indiana University Medical School, Pediatrics Dept, 410 W 10th St, Indianapolis IN 46202, USA — Pediatrician

**Vuarnet, Jean**
Chalet Squaw Peak, 74110 Auoriaz, France — Alpine Skier

**Vucevic, Nikola**
Orlando Magic, 8701 Maitland Summit Blvd, Orlando FL 32810 USA — Basketball Player

**Vuckovich, Peter D (Pete)**
86 Leonard St, Johnstown PA 15902, USA — Baseball Player

**Vujanovic, Filip**
Presidential Palace, Cetinje, Montenegro — President, Montenegro

**Vukoto, Mick**
PO Box 3213, 7 Peases Point Road, Edgartown MA 02539, USA — Ice Hockey Player

**Vukovich, George S**
305 W Calle Gota, Sahuarita AZ 85629, USA — Baseball Player

**Vuolo, Lindsey**
Playboy Promotions, 9346 Civic Center Dr, #200, Beverly Hills CA 90210 USA — Model

**Vuono, Carl E**
5796 Westchester St, Alexandria VA 22310, USA — Army General

**Vyborny, David**
4075 Blendon Grove Way, Columbus OH 43230, USA — Ice Hockey Player

**Vyent, Louise**
Louise Vyent Photography, 13 Mountainview Place, Montclair NJ 07042, USA — Model, Photographer

**Vylegzhanin, Maxim M**
Ski Association, Luzhnetskaya Nab 8, 119270 Moscow, Russia — Cross Country Skier

**Waakataar-Savoy, Paul** — Singer, Guitarist (A-Ha), Songwriter
Agency Group Ltd, 361-373 City Road, London EC1V 1PQ, England

**Wachowski, Andy** — Director
Circle of Confusion, 107-23 71st Road, #300, Forest Hills NY 11375, USA

**Wachowski, Laurence (Lana)** — Director
Circle of Confusion, 107-23 71st Road, #300, Forest Hills NY 11375, USA

**Wachs, Caitlin** — Actress
I C M Partners, 10250 Constellation Blvd, #900, Los Angeles CA 90067 USA

**Wachtel, Christine** — Track Athlete
Rostock Sports Club, Rostock, 17033 Mecklenburg-Vorpommoern, Germany

**Wachter, Anita** — Alpine Skier
Gantschierstr 579, 6780 Schruns, Austria

**Wackerman, Brooks** — Drummer (Bad Religion)
Goldstar Mgmt, PO Box 130, Ross on Wye HR9 6WY, England

**Wada, Tsuyoshi** — Baseball Player
Baltimore Orioles, Oriole Park, 333 W Camden St, Baltimore MD 21201 USA

**Waddell, Chris** — Model, Skier
Athletes for Hope, 3 Bethesda Metro Center, #450, Bethesda MD 20814, USA

**Waddell, Ernest** — Actor
Stone Manners Salners, 6100 Wilshire Blvd, #1500, Los Angeles CA 90035 USA

**Waddell, John Henry** — Artist
10050 E Waddell Road, Cornville AZ 86325, USA

**Waddell, Justine** — Actress
United Agents, 12-26 Lexington St, London W1F 0LE, England

**Waddell, Thomas D (Tom)** — Baseball Player
10171 E Achi St, Tucson AZ 85748, USA

**Waddington of Read, David** — Governor General, Bermuda
39 Chester Way, #4, London SE11 4UR, England

**Waddington, Steven** — Actor
Julian Belfrage Assoc, 9 Argyll St, #300, London W1F 7TG, England

**Waddle, Thomas (Tom)** — Football Player, Sportscaster
8190 Tollbridge Dr, West Chester OH 45069, USA

**Waddy, William D (Billy)** — Football Player
2838 Highway 88, Minneapolis MN 55418, USA

**Wade, Adam** — Singer
C E S D, 257 Park Ave S, #950, New York NY 10010 USA

**Wade, Chrissie** — Musician (Alien Sex Fiend)
Mission Control, City Business Center, Lower Road, London SE16 2XB, England

**Wade, Dwyane T** — Basketball Player
9330 SW 59th Place, Miami FL 33156, USA

**Wade, Jason M** — Singer, Guitarist (Lifehouse)
Universal/Geffen Records, 2220 Colorado Ave, Santa Monica CA 90404, USA

**Wade, Justin** — Actor
TalentWorks, 3500 W Olive Ave, #1400, Burbank CA 91505 USA

**Wade, Nik** — Musician (Alien Sex Fiend)
Mission Control, City Business Center, Lower Road, London SE16 2XB, England

**Wade, R John** — Football Player
3540 Traveler Road, Harrisonburg VA 22801, USA

**Wade, S Virginia** — Tennis Player
International Mangement Group, Pier House, Chiswick, London W4M 3NN, England

**Wade, William J (Bill), Jr** — Football Player
PO Box 210124, Nashville TN 37221, USA

**Wader, Hannes** — Singer, Songwriter
Scala, Parkstr 2, 60322 Frankfurt am Maim, Germany

**Wadham, Julian** — Actor
Artists Partnership, 101 Finsbury Pavement, London EC2A 1RS, England

**Wadhams, Wayne** — Singer, Keyboardist (Fifth Estate)
73 Hemenway, Boston MA 02115, USA

**Wadkins, Bobby** — Golfer
204 Kinloch Road, Manakin Sabot VA 23103, USA

**Wadkins, J Langston (Lanny), Jr** — Golfer, Sportscaster
5200 Keller Springs Road, #1217, Dallas TX 75248, USA

**Wadlow, Jeff** — Director, Writer
W M E Entertainment, 9601 Wilshire Blvd, #300, Beverly Hills CA 90210 USA

**Wadsworth, Charles W** — Concert Pianist
PO Box 157, Charleston SC 29402, USA

**Wadsworth, Fred** — Golfer
823 Bryon Road, Columbia SC 29205, USA

**Waechter, Douglas M (Doug)** — Baseball Player
4590 13th Way NE, Saint Petersburg FL 33703, USA

**Waena, Nathaniel** — Governor General, Solomon Islands
Governor General's House, Box 252, Honiara, Guadacanal, Solomon Islands

**Wafer, Vakeaton Q (Von)** — Basketball Player
2503 Dallas St, Houston TX 77003, USA

**Wages, Harmon L** — Football Player
1846 Margaret St, #3C, Jacksonville FL 32204, USA

**Wages, William** — Cinematographer
Innovative Artists, 1505 10th St, Santa Monica CA 90401 USA

**Waggoner, Brooke** — Singer, Songwriter
Agency Group Ltd, 142 W 57th St, #600, New York NY 10019 USA

**Waggoner, Lyle** — Actor
1124 Oak Mirage Place, Westlake Village CA 91362, USA

**Waggoner, Paul E** — Agronomist
100 Crockett St, #312, Seattle WA 98109, USA

**Wagner, Allison** — Swimmer
912 NW 45th Terrace, Gainesville FL 32605, USA

**Wagner, Amber** — Opera Singer
I M G Artists, Hogarth Business Park, Chiswick, London W4 2TH, England

**Wagner, Ashley** — Figure Skater
27444 Camden, #9L, Mission Viejo CA 92692, USA

**Wagner, Barbara A** — Figure Skater
Alpharetta Family Skate Center, 10800 Davis Dr, Alpharetta GA 30009, USA

**Wagner, Bryan J** — Football Player
6020 Arlyne Lane, Medina OH 44256, USA

**Wagner, Catherine** — Photographer
308 Precita Ave, San Francisco CA 94110, USA

**Wagner, Chuck** — Actor, Singer
1200 Maldonado Dr, Pensacola Beach FL 32561, USA

**Wagner, Dajuan M** — Basketball Player
Golden State Warriors, 1011 Broadway, Oakland CA 94605 USA

**Wagner, Fred** — Cartoonist (Grin & Bear It)
King Features Syndicate, 300 W 57th St, #1500, New York NY 10019 USA

**Wagner, Gary E** — Baseball Player
1707 Northbrook Court, Seymour IN 47274, USA

**Wagner, Harold A** — Businessman
4031 Savannah Trail, Santa Rosa CA 95404, USA

**Wagner, Jill** — Model, Actress
United Talent Agency, U T A Plaza, 9336 Civic Center Dr, Beverly Hills CA 90210 USA

**Wagner, Johnson** — Golfer
Professional Golfers Association, 100 Ave of Champions, Palm Beach Gardens FL 33418 USA

**Wagner, Katie** — Actress
Creative Managment Entertainment, 2050 S Bundy Dr, #280, Los Angeles CA 90025, USA

**Wagner, Kurt** — Singer (Lambchop)
High Road Touring, 751 Bridgeway, #200, Sausalito CA 94965 USA

**Wagner, Lindsay** — Model
Playboy Promotions, 9346 Civic Center Dr, #200, Beverly Hills CA 90210 USA

**Wagner, Lindsay** — Actress
22817 Ventura Blvd, #888, Woodland Hills CA 91364, USA

**Wagner, Lisa** — Bowler
Professional Bowlers Association, 719 2nd Ave, #701, Seattle WA 98104 USA

**Wagner, Lou** — Actor
Amsel Eisenstadt Frazier, 5055 Wilshire Blvd, #865, Los Angeles CA 90036 USA

**Wagner, Louis C, Jr** — Army General
6336 Manchester Way, Alexandria VA 22304, USA

**Wagner, Mark D** — Baseball Player
1838 Willow Arms Dr, Ashtabula OH 44004, USA

**Wagner, Matthew (Matt)** — Cartoonist
4340 Horton Road, West Linn OR 97068, USA

**Wagner, Melinda** — Composer
Theodore Presser, 588 N Gulph Road, #B, King of Prussia PA 19406, USA

**Wagner, Michael R (Mike)** — Football Player
203 E Wild Cherry Dr, Mars PA 16046, USA

**Wagner, P Jack, Jr** — Actor, Singer
Shelter Entertainment, 9255 Sunset Blvd, #300, Los Angeles CA 90069 USA

**Wagner, Paul A** — Baseball Player
27081 State Highway 3, Kirksville MO 63501, USA

**Wagner, Philip M** — Columnist
32 Montgomery St, Boston MA 02116, USA

**Wagner, Robert** — Actor
Binder & Assoc, 1465 Lindacrest Dr, Beverly Hills CA 90210 USA

**Wagner, Robert W** — Army General
Commander, Joint Forces Command, Norfolk VA 23551, USA

**Wagner, Robin S A** — Stage, Set Designer
Robin Wagner Studio, 890 Broadway, New York NY 10003, USA

**Wagner, Ryan S** — Baseball Player
59 County Road 311, Yoakum TX 77995, USA

**Wagner, Sune Rose** — Singer, Guitarist (Ravenonettes)
Orchard, 100 Park Ave, #200, New York NY 10017, USA

**Wagner, William E (Billy)** — Baseball Player
5066 Jones Mill Road, Crozet VA 22932, USA

**Wagner-Augustin, Katrin** — Canoeing Athlete
Kaastaienallee 35, 14471 Potsdam, Germany

**Wagoner, Dan** — Dancer, Choreographer
Contemporary Dance Theater, 17 Duke's Road, London WC1H 9AB, England

**Wagoner, David R** — Writer
5416 154th Place SW, Edmonds WA 98026, USA

**Wagoner, Harold E** — Architect
331 Lindsey Dr, Berwyn PA 19312, USA

**Wahl, Ken** — Actor
9654 W 131st St, #206, Palos Park IL 60464, USA

**Wahlberg, Donnie** — Singer, Actor
16815 Bircher St, Granada Hills CA 91344, USA

**Wahlberg, Mark** — Actor, Singer, Model
Closest to the Hole, 3030 Pennsylvania Ave, Santa Monica CA 90404, USA

**Wahle, Michael J (Mike)** — Football Player
6210 Avenida Cresta, La Jolla CA 92037, USA

**Wahlgren, Olof G C** — Editor
Nicoloviusgatan 5B, 217 57 Malmo, Sweden

**Wahlstrom, Jarl H** — Religious Leader
Borgstrominkuja 1A10, 00840 Helsinki 84, Finland

**Waidacher, Nina** — Ice Hockey Player
Swiss Ice Hockey, Hagenholzstr 81, 8050 Zurich, Switzerland

**Waigel, Theodor** — Government Official, Germany
Oberrohr, 86513 Ursberg, Germany

**Waihee, John D, III** — Governor, HI
745 Fort Street Mall, #600, Honolulu HI 96813, USA

**Wailer, Bunny** — Singer (Bob Marley & the Wailers)
Wenig-LaMonica Associates, 580 White Plains Road, #130, Tarrytown NY 10591 USA

**Wain, Bea** — Singer
Society of Singers, 15456 Ventura Blvd, #304, Sherman Oaks CA 91403, USA

**Wain, David B** — Director
Principato-Young, 9465 Wilshire Blvd, #880, Beverly Hills CA 90212 USA

**Wainhouse, David P (Dave)** — Baseball Player
6101 85th Place SE, Mercer Island WA 98040, USA

**Wainwright, Adam P** — Baseball Player
2100 Brook Hill Court, Chesterfield MO 63017, USA

**Wainwright, Angel M** — Actress
Amatruda Benson Assoc, 9107 Wilshire Blvd, #500, Beverly Hills CA 90210, USA

**Wainwright, Loudon, III** — Singer, Songwriter
Rosebud Agency, PO Box 170429, San Francisco CA 94117 USA

**Wainwright, Rufus M** — Singer, Songwriter
M C T Mgmt, 520 8th Ave, #2001, New York NY 10018, USA

**Wainwright, Rupert** — Director, Actor, Writer
Luber Rocklin Entertainment, 5815 Sunset Blvd, #206, Los Angeles CA 90028 USA

**Waite, Alison** — Model
Playboy Promotions, 9346 Civic Center Dr, #200, Beverly Hills CA 90210 USA

**Waite, Grant** — Golfer
1615 SE 73rd Place, Ocala FL 34480, USA

**Waite, John** — Singer (Babys, Bad English), Songwriter
Rounder Records, 1 Rounder Way, Burlington MA 01803 USA

**Waite, Terence H (Terry)** — Religious Leader
Wheelrights, Green Harvest, Bury Saint Edmunds, Suffolk IP29 4DH, England

**Waiters, Granville S** — Basketball Player
PO Box 91361, Columbus OH 43209, USA

**Waiters, Van A** — Football Player
6021 NW 201st Lane, Hialeah FL 33015, USA

**Waits, M Richard (Rick)** — Baseball Player
PO Box 1001, Patagonia AZ 85624, USA

**Waits, Tom** — Singer, Pianist, Songwriter
W M E Entertainment, 9601 Wilshire Blvd, #300, Beverly Hills CA 90210 USA

**Waitt, Theodore W (Ted)** — Businessman
Gateway Inc, 7565 Irvine Center Dr, Irvine CA 92618, USA

**Waitz, Richard H** — Cinematographer
405 Zenith Ave, Lafayette CO 80026, USA

**Wajda, Andrzej** — Director
Japanese/Technology Center, Ul Konopnickiej 26, 30 302 Cracow, Poland

**Wakamatsu, W Donald (Don)** — Baseball Player, Manager
8740 Ramblewood Court, Keller TX 76248, USA

**Wakata, Koichi** — Astronaut, Japan
Japanese Aerospace Exploration Agency, 2-1-1 Sengen, Tsukuba, Ibaraki 305 8505, Japan

**Waked, Amr** — Actor
Artists Partnership, 101 Finsbury Pavement, London EC2A 1RS, England

**Wakefield, Charity** — Actress
I C M Partners, 10250 Constellation Blvd, #900, Los Angeles CA 90067 USA

**Wakefield, Jennifer (Jenn)** — Ice Hockey Player
Hockey Canada, 151 Canada Olympic Road SW, #201, Calgary AB  T3B 6B7, Canada

**Wakefield, Rhys** — Actor
R G M Artists, 8-12 Ann Street, Surry Hills NSW 2010, Australia

**Wakefield, Timothy S (Tim)** — Baseball Player
241 Lansing Island Dr, Indian Harbour Beach FL 32937, USA

**Wakeham of Maldon, John** — Government Official, England
House of Lords, Westminster, London SW1A 0PW, England

**Wakeland, Chris** — Baseball Player
60997 Luttrell Lane, Saint Helens OR 97051, USA

**Wakeley, Amanda** — Fashion Designer
7 Old Park Lane, London W1K 1QR, England

**Wakelin, Cara** — Model, Actress
Playboy Promotions, 9346 Civic Center Dr, #200, Beverly Hills CA 90210 USA

**Wakeling, Dave** — Singer (General Public, English Beat)
Arcadia Group Mgmt, 11400 W Olympic Blvd, #200, Los Angeles CA 90064, USA

**Wakely, Ernie** — Ice Hockey Player
11052 E Roundup Dr, Dewey AZ 86327, USA

**Wakeman, Rick** — Keyboardist, Songwriter
I C M Partners, Marlborough House, 10 Earlham St, #300, London WC2H 9LNP, England

**Wakoski, Diane** — Writer
607 Division St, East Lansing MI 48823, USA

**Walbeck, Matthew L (Matt)** — Baseball Player
8216 Olive Ave, Fair Oaks CA 95628, USA

**Walchuk, Don** — Curling Athlete
Curling Association, 1660 Vimont Court, Cumberland ON K4A 4J4, Canada

**Walcott, Derek A** — Nobel Literature Laureate
PO Box GM 926, Castries, Saint Lucia, West Indies

**Walcott, Gregory** — Actor
22246 Saticoy St, Canoga Park CA 91303, USA

**Walcott, Jennifer** — Model, Actress
O'Grady Entertainment Group, 4550 Via Marina, #305, Marina del Rey CA 90292, USA

**Wald, Patricia M** — Judge
Open Society Justice Initiative, 224 W 57th St, New York NY 10019, USA

**Waldau, Nicolaj Coster** — Actor
Lindberg Mgmt, Lavendelstre De 5-7, Baghuset 4 Sal, 1462 Copenhagen K, Denmark

**Waldegrave of North Hill, William** — Government Official, England
66 Palace Gardens Terrace, London W8 4RR, England

**Waldemore, Stanley A (Stan)** — Football Player
PO Box 611, New Vernon NJ 07976, USA

**Walden, Jordan C** — Baseball Player
Atlanta Braves, Turner Field, 755 Hank Aaron Dr, Atlanta GA 30315 USA

**Walden, Lynette** — Actress
Metropolitan Talent Agency, 5405 Wilshire Blvd, #218, Los Angeles CA 90036 USA

**Walden, Robert** — Actor, Director, Writer
Bret Adams Agency, 448 W 44th St, New York NY 10036, USA

**Walden, Robert E (Bobby)** — Football Player
107 Springfield Dr, Bainbridge GA 39819, USA

**Walden, W G (Snuffy)** — Composer
Gorfaine/Schwartz, 4111 W Alameda Ave, #509, Burbank CA 91505 USA

**Waldhauser, Thomas D** — Marine Corps General
Commander, Central Command, 7115 S Boundary, MacDill Air Force Base FL 33621 USA

**Waldie, Marc R** — Volleyball Player
14020 E Ayesbury Circle, Wichita KS 67228, USA

**Waldner, Jan-Ove** — Table Tennis Player
Banda, Skjulstagatan 10, 632 29 Eskilstuna, Sweden

**Waldo, Janet** — Actress
C E S D, 10635 Santa Monica Blvd, #130, Los Angeles CA 90025 USA

**Waldorf, James J (Duffy), Jr** — Golfer
18510 Brymer St, Porter Ranch CA 91326, USA

**Waldron, Jeffrey** — Cinematographer
United Talent Agency, U T A Plaza, 9336 Civic Center Dr, Beverly Hills CA 90210 USA

**Waldron, Jeremy J** — Educator, Attorney
1061 Keith Ave, Berkeley CA 94708, USA

| | |
|---|---|
| **Waldrop, Alex** | Thoroughbred Racing Executive |
| National Thoroughbred Racing, 2525 Harrodsburg Road, #500, Lexington KY 40504, USA | |
| **Wales, Jimmy D (Jimbo)** | Internet Encyclopedia Designer |
| Wikipedia Foundation, 200 2nd Ave S, #358, Saint Petersburg FL 33701, USA | |
| **Wales, Ross** | Swimmer |
| 2233 Eastern Ave, #1B, Cincinnati OH 45202, USA | |
| **Walesa, Lech** | Nobel Peace Laureate; President, Poland |
| Ul Dlugi Targ 24, 80828 Gdansk, Poland | |
| **Walewander, James (Jim)** | Baseball Player |
| 5023 Albridal Way, San Ramon CA 94582, USA | |
| **Walger, Sonya** | Actress |
| Gersh Agency, 9465 Wilshire Blvd, #600, Beverly Hills CA 90212 USA | |
| **Walheim, Rex J** | Astronaut |
| 142 Hidden Lake Dr, League City TX 77573, USA | |
| **Walia, Sonu** | Actress |
| 20 Anchorage, Juhu-Versova Link Road, Andheri (W), Mumbai MS 400058, India | |
| **Walk, Neal** | Basketball Player |
| 6030 N 11th Ave, Phoenix AZ 85013, USA | |
| **Walk, Robert V (Bob)** | Baseball Player |
| 2494 Shadowbrook Dr, Wexford PA 15090, USA | |
| **Walken, Christopher** | Actor |
| I C M Partners, 10250 Constellation Blvd, #900, Los Angeles CA 90067 USA | |
| **Walker, Adam C** | Football Player |
| 923 Bucknell Ave, Johnstown PA 15905, USA | |
| **Walker, Alan C** | Anthropologist |
| Pennsylvania State University, Anthropology Dept, Pittsburgh PA 16802, USA | |
| **Walker, Alice M** | Writer, Social Activist |
| PO Box 378, Philo CA 95466, USA | |
| **Walker, Ally** | Actress |
| Luber Rocklin Entertainment, 5815 Sunset Blvd, #206, Los Angeles CA 90028 USA | |
| **Walker, Andrew Kevin** | Actor, Writer |
| Kennedy/Miller Productions, 30 Orwell St, Sydney NSW 2011, Australia | |
| **Walker, Andrew W** | Actor |
| Amanda Rosenthal Talent, 1255 University St, #502, Montreal QC H3B 3V8, Canada | |
| **Walker, Anthony B (Tony)** | Baseball Player |
| 2724 Morgan Dr, San Ramon CA 94583, USA | |
| **Walker, Antoine D** | Basketball Player |
| 450 W Huron St, Chicago IL 60654, USA | |
| **Walker, Arnetia** | Actress |
| 1040 4th St, #406, Santa Monica CA 90403, USA | |
| **Walker, Benjamin** | Actor |
| Inspire Entertainment, 2332 Cotner Ave, #302, Los Angeles CA 90064, USA | |
| **Walker, Bracy W** | Football Player |
| 5683 Notting Hill Road, Gurnee IL 60031, USA | |
| **Walker, Bradley G (Butch)** | Singer, Guitarist (Marvelous 3) |
| Crush Mgmt, 60-62 E 11th St, #700, New York NY 10003 USA | |
| **Walker, Brian** | Cartoonist (Hi & Lois) |
| King Features Syndicate, 300 W 57th St, #1500, New York NY 10019 USA | |
| **Walker, Bruce R** | Football Player |
| 279 Eastlawn St, Detroit MI 48215, USA | |
| **Walker, Charles D** | Astronaut |
| Boeing Co, 1200 Wilson Blvd, MC RS00, Arlington VA 22209, USA | |
| **Walker, Charles D (Chuck)** | Football Player |
| 1613 Tradd Court, Chesterfield MO 63017, USA | |
| **Walker, Charls E** | Economist |
| 19207 Racine Court, Montgomery Village MD 20886, USA | |
| **Walker, Chester (Chet)** | Basketball Player |
| 124 Fleet St, Marina del Rey CA 90292, USA | |
| **Walker, Chris** | Actor |
| Rolf Kruger, 121 Gloucester Place, London W1H 3PJ, England | |
| **Walker, Clay** | Singer |
| W M E Entertainment, 1600 Division St, #300, Nashville TN 37203 USA | |
| **Walker, Cleotha (Chico)** | Baseball Player |
| 450 W Huron St, Chicago IL 60654, USA | |
| **Walker, Clint** | Actor |
| 101 W McKnight Way, #B303, Grass Valley CA 95949, USA | |
| **Walker, Darnell R** | Football Player |
| 501 N 44th St, Muskogee OK 74401, USA | |
| **Walker, Darrell** | Basketball Player, Coach |
| 16122 Patriot Dr, Little Rock AR 72212, USA | |
| **Walker, David M** | Government Official |
| Comeback America Initiative, 211 State St, #401, Bridgeport CT 06604, USA | |
| **Walker, Denard A** | Football Player |
| 1221 Mackey St, Garland TX 75040, USA | |
| **Walker, Derek** | Architect |
| 2 General Sage Dr, Santa Fe NM 87505, USA | |
| **Walker, Derrick** | Auto Racing Executive |
| Walker Racing, 4035 Championship Dr, Indianapolis IN 46268, USA | |
| **Walker, DeWayne** | Football Coach |
| New Mexico State University, Athletic Dept, Box 30001, Las Cruces NM 88003, USA | |
| **Walker, Dreama** | Actress |
| Gersh Agency, 9465 Wilshire Blvd, #600, Beverly Hills CA 90212 USA | |
| **Walker, Duane A** | Baseball Player |
| 2509 Georgia Ave, Deer Park TX 77536, USA | |
| **Walker, Eamonn** | Actor |
| I C M Partners, 10250 Constellation Blvd, #900, Los Angeles CA 90067 USA | |
| **Walker, Fiona** | Actress |
| 13 Despard Road, London N19 5NP, England | |
| **Walker, G Mickey** | Football Player |
| 22828 S Maple Point Road, Pickford MI 49774, USA | |
| **Walker, George T, Jr** | Composer |
| 323 Grove St, Montclair NJ 07042, USA | |
| **Walker, Greg** | Cartoonist (Hi & Lois) |
| King Features Syndicate, 300 W 57th St, #1500, New York NY 10019 USA | |
| **Walker, Greg T** | Singer, Bassist (Blackfoot) |
| Artists International Mgmt, 9850 Sandalfoot Blvd, #458, Boca Raton FL 33428 USA | |

**Walker, Gregory L (Greg)**
530 N Lake Shore Dr, #1009, Chicago IL 60611, USA — Baseball Player

**Walker, Herschel J**
2210 King Fisher Dr, Westlake TX 76262, USA — Football Player

**Walker, Hezekiah X, Jr**
Love Fellowship Tabernacle, 464 Liberty Ave, Brooklyn NY 11207, USA — Singer, Choir Director, Religious Leader

**Walker, I Kenyatta**
14813 Tudor Chase Dr, Tampa FL 33626, USA — Football Player

**Walker, James T (Jamie)**
11450 W 187th St, Spring Hill KS 66083, USA — Baseball Player

**Walker, Javon L**
59 Wincrest Falls Dr, Cypress TX 77429, USA — Football Player

**Walker, Jerry Jeff**
Goodknight Music, PO Box 39, Austin TX 78767, USA — Singer, Guitarist, Songwriter

**Walker, Jimmie (J J)**
Roger Paul, 1650 Broadway, New York NY 10019, USA — Actor, Comedian

**Walker, Jimmy**
Professional Golfers Association, 100 Ave of Champions, Palm Beach Gardens FL 33418 USA — Golfer

**Walker, Joe Louis**
Oceanside Talent, 124 Virginia Place, #3, Costa Mesa CA 92627, USA — Singer, Guitarist

**Walker, John E**
M R C Molecular Biology Laboratory, Hills Road, Cambridge CB2 2QH, England — Nobel Chemistry Laureate

**Walker, John G**
Jeffs Road, RD Papatoetoe, Aukland 2016, New Zealand — Track Athlete

**Walker, John M, Jr**
US Court of Appeals, Moynihan Courthouse, 500 Pearl St, New York NY 10007, USA — Judge

**Walker, Jon Patrick**
Paradigm Agency, 360 N Crescent Dr, North Building, Beverly Hills CA 90210 USA — Actor

**Walker, Kelly**
321 W Madison St, Baltimore MD 21201, USA — Artist

**Walker, Kemba H**
Charlotte Hornets, 333 E Trade St, #A, Charlotte NC 28202 USA — Basketball Player

**Walker, Kenneth (Kenny)**
2252 Terrace Woods Park, Lexington KY 40513, USA — Basketball Player

**Walker, Kenneth H**
Future Brand, 300 Park Ave S, #700, New York NY 10010, USA — Interior Designer

**Walker, Kevin (Geordie)**
Agency Group, 1100 Century Park E, #711, Los Angeles CA 90067 USA — Guitarist (Killing Joke)

**Walker, Kevin M**
759 Chestnut Ave, Holtville CA 92250, USA — Baseball Player

**Walker, Kurt**
1951 N Wesley Chapel Road, Eatonton GA 31024, USA — Ice Hockey Player

**Walker, Langston B**
1281 Alder Creek Circle, San Leandro CA 94577, USA — Football Player

**Walker, Larry K R**
1667 Flagler Parkway, West Palm Beach FL 33411, USA — Baseball Player

**Walker, Leonore**
Nova Southeastern University, Psychology Dept, Fort Lauderdale FL 33308, USA — Psychologist

**Walker, Little Toby**
PO Box 219, Wantagh NY 11793, USA — Singer

**Walker, Liza**
Jonathan Altaras Assoc, 11 Garrick St, London WC2E 9AR, England — Actress

**Walker, Lucy**
Circle of Confusion, 8548 Washington Blvd, Culver City CA 90232, USA — Director, Producer, Actress

**Walker, Mack**
Johns Hopkins University, History Dept, Baltimore MD 21218, USA — Historian

**Walker, Malcolm E, Jr**
7140 Winterwood Lane, Dallas TX 75248, USA — Football Player

**Walker, Marcy**
Leslie Bader, 2686 Lakewood Place, Westlake Village CA 91361, USA — Actress

**Walker, Marquis R**
11576 Cherrylawn St, Detroit MI 48221, USA — Football Player

**Walker, Michael C (Mike)**
23195 Tankerley Road, Brooksville FL 34601, USA — Baseball Player

**Walker, Michael Patrick**
W M E Entertainment, 1325 Ave of Americas, New York NY 10019 USA — Composer, Lyricist

**Walker, Mort**
61 Studio Road, Stamford CT 06903, USA — Cartoonist (Beetle Bailey, Sarge)

**Walker, Peter**
Peter Walker Partners, 739 Allston Way, Berkeley CA 94710, USA — Landscape Architect

**Walker, Peter**
23 Bentinck St, London W1U 2E8, England — Director

**Walker, Peter B (Pete)**
2 White Oak Lane, Quaker Hill CT 06375, USA — Baseball Player

**Walker, Phillip (Phil) B**
720 E Phil Ellena St, Philadelphia PA 19119, USA — Basketball Player

**Walker, Polly**
Hamilton Hodell, 20 Golden Square, London W1F 9JL, England — Actress

**Walker, R Thomas (Tom)**
817 Whippoorwill Hill Road, Gibsonia PA 15044, USA — Baseball Player

**Walker, Rebecca**
W M E Entertainment, 9601 Wilshire Blvd, #300, Beverly Hills CA 90210 USA — Writer

**Walker, Rick**
906 Winstead St, Great Falls VA 22066, USA — Football Player

**Walker, Sarah E B**
152 Inchmery Road, London SE6 1DF, England — Opera Singer

**Walker, Scott**
301 Bailey Ridge Dr, Morrisville NC 27560, USA — Ice Hockey Player

**Walker, Scott**
Negus-Fancy Co, 78 Portland Road, London W11 4LQ, England — Singer

**Walker, Tim**
Art & Commerce, 531 W 25th St, #400, New York NY 10001, USA — Photographer

**Walker, Tonja**
Tonja Walker Productions, 404 E 76th St, #15C, New York NY 10021, USA — Actress

**Walker, Tyler L**
45 Via del Sol, Nicasio CA 94946, USA — Baseball Player

Walker - Walker

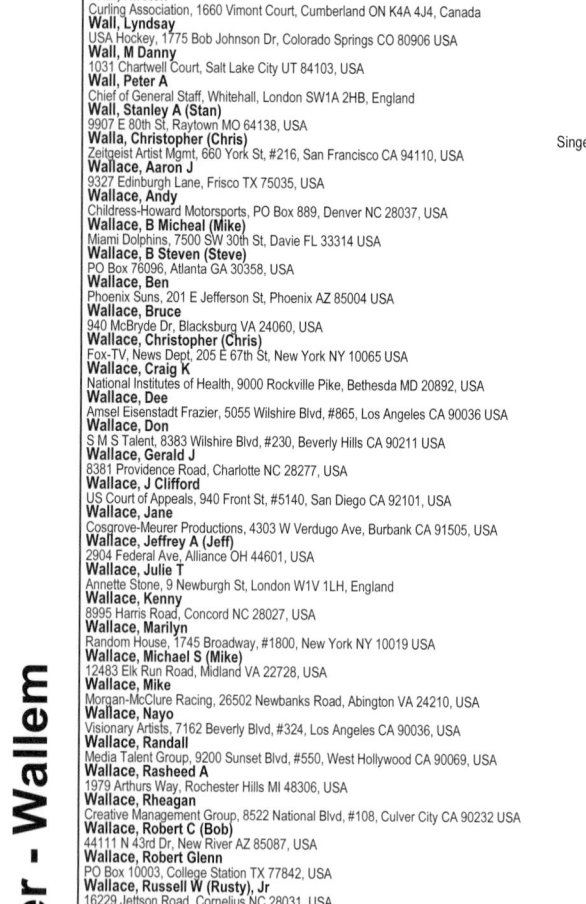

**Walker, Val J** — Football Player
3857 S Versailles Ave, Dallas TX 75209, USA

**Walker, Walter F (Wally)** — Basketball Player
154 Lombard St, #58, San Francisco CA 94111, USA

**Walker, Wayne H** — Football Player
2033 S White Pine Lane, Boise ID 83706, USA

**Walker, Wesley D** — Football Player
5841 Edmond Ave, Huntington Station NY 11746, USA

**Wall, Angus** — Editor
Creative Artists Agency, 2000 Ave of Stars, #100, Los Angeles CA 90067 USA

**Wall, Brian A** — Sculptor
306 Lombard St, San Francisco CA 94133, USA

**Wall, Donnell L (Donne)** — Baseball Player
116 River Breeze Way, Saint Louis MO 63129, USA

**Wall, Erin** — Opera Singer
Columbia Artists Mgmt Inc, 5 Columbus Circle, 1790 Broadway, #1600, New York NY 10019 USA

**Wall, Frederick T** — Physical Chemist
2044 Kerwood Ave, Los Angeles CA 90025, USA

**Wall, John F** — Army General
507 Hanover St, Fredericksburg VA 22401, USA

**Wall, Jordan** — Actor
Level Talent Group, 12807 W Hillsborough Ave, #L, Tampa FL 33635, USA

**Wall, Kirsten** — Curling Athlete
Curling Association, 1660 Vimont Court, Cumberland ON K4A 4J4, Canada

**Wall, Lyndsay** — Ice Hockey Player
USA Hockey, 1775 Bob Johnson Dr, Colorado Springs CO 80906 USA

**Wall, M Danny** — Financier
1031 Chartwell Court, Salt Lake City UT 84103, USA

**Wall, Peter A** — Army General, England
Chief of General Staff, Whitehall, London SW1A 2HB, England

**Wall, Stanley A (Stan)** — Baseball Player
9907 E 80th St, Raytown MO 64138, USA

**Walla, Christopher (Chris)** — Singer, Guitarist (Death Cab for Cutie)
Zeitgeist Artist Mgmt, 660 York St, #216, San Francisco CA 94110, USA

**Wallace, Aaron J** — Football Player
9327 Edinburgh Lane, Frisco TX 75035, USA

**Wallace, Andy** — Auto Racing Driver
Childress-Howard Motorsports, PO Box 889, Denver NC 28037, USA

**Wallace, B Micheal (Mike)** — Football Player
Miami Dolphins, 7500 SW 30th St, Davie FL 33314 USA

**Wallace, B Steven (Steve)** — Football Player
PO Box 76096, Atlanta GA 30358, USA

**Wallace, Ben** — Basketball Player
Phoenix Suns, 201 E Jefferson St, Phoenix AZ 85004 USA

**Wallace, Bruce** — Geneticist
940 McBryde Dr, Blacksburg VA 24060, USA

**Wallace, Christopher (Chris)** — Commentator
Fox-TV, News Dept, 205 E 67th St, New York NY 10065 USA

**Wallace, Craig K** — Physician
National Institutes of Health, 9000 Rockville Pike, Bethesda MD 20892, USA

**Wallace, Dee** — Actress
Amsel Eisenstadt Frazier, 5055 Wilshire Blvd, #865, Los Angeles CA 90036 USA

**Wallace, Don** — Actor
S M S Talent, 8383 Wilshire Blvd, #230, Beverly Hills CA 90211 USA

**Wallace, Gerald J** — Basketball Player
8381 Providence Road, Charlotte NC 28277, USA

**Wallace, J Clifford** — Judge
US Court of Appeals, 940 Front St, #5140, San Diego CA 92101, USA

**Wallace, Jane** — Entertainer
Cosgrove-Meurer Productions, 4303 W Verdugo Ave, Burbank CA 91505, USA

**Wallace, Jeffrey A (Jeff)** — Baseball Player
2904 Federal Ave, Alliance OH 44601, USA

**Wallace, Julie T** — Actress
Annette Stone, 9 Newburgh St, London W1V 1LH, England

**Wallace, Kenny** — Auto Racing Driver
8995 Harris Road, Concord NC 28027, USA

**Wallace, Marilyn** — Writer
Random House, 1745 Broadway, #1800, New York NY 10019 USA

**Wallace, Michael S (Mike)** — Baseball Player
12483 Elk Run Road, Midland VA 22728, USA

**Wallace, Mike** — Auto Racing Driver
Morgan-McClure Racing, 26502 Newbanks Road, Abington VA 24210, USA

**Wallace, Nayo** — Actress
Visionary Artists, 7162 Beverly Blvd, #324, Los Angeles CA 90036, USA

**Wallace, Randall** — Director
Media Talent Group, 9200 Sunset Blvd, #550, West Hollywood CA 90069, USA

**Wallace, Rasheed A** — Basketball Player
1979 Arthurs Way, Rochester Hills MI 48306, USA

**Wallace, Rheagan** — Actress
Creative Management Group, 8522 National Blvd, #108, Culver City CA 90232 USA

**Wallace, Robert C (Bob)** — Football Player
44111 N 43rd Dr, New River AZ 85087, USA

**Wallace, Robert Glenn** — Businessman
PO Box 10003, College Station TX 77842, USA

**Wallace, Russell W (Rusty), Jr** — Auto Racing Driver
16229 Jettson Road, Cornelius NC 28031, USA

**Wallach, Evan J** — Judge
US International Trade Court, 1 Federal Plaza, New York NY 10278, USA

**Wallach, Timothy C (Tim)** — Baseball Player
21750 Deveron Cove, Yorba Linda CA 92887, USA

**Wallack, Melisa** — Writer, Director
Resolution, 1801 Century Park E, #2300, Los Angeles CA 90067, USA

**Wallberg, Heinz** — Conductor
Stocksiepen, 45133 Essen, Germany

**Wallem, Linda** — Producer
Jackoway Tyerman Wertheimer, 1925 Century Park E, #2200, Los Angeles CA 90067 USA

| | |
|---|---|
| **Wallenda, Delilah**<br>3650 Henrietta Place, Sarasota FL 34234, USA | Circus Tightrope Walker |
| **Wallenda, Nikolas (Nik)**<br>Wallenda Enterprises, PO Box 52551, Sarasota FL 34232, USA | Circus Tightrope Walker |
| **Wallenda, Tino**<br>3650 Henrietta Place, Sarasota FL 34234, USA | Circus Tightrope Walker |
| **Wallenstein, Andrew**<br>Variety 11175 Santa Monica Blvd, Los Angeles CA 90025, USA | Editor |
| **Waller, Anthony**<br>Seven Arts Pictures, 6121 W Sunset Blvd, #512, Los Angeles CA 90028, USA | Director |
| **Waller, Robert James**<br>12 Old Harper Road, Harper TX 78631, USA | Writer |
| **Waller, Ronald B (Ron)**<br>8773 Concord Road, Seaford DE 19973, USA | Football Player |
| **Wallerstein, Ralph G**<br>3447 Clay St, San Francisco CA 94118, USA | Hematologist |
| **Wallfisch, Raphael**<br>Ikon Artists Mgmt, 52 Upper St, #111B, London N1 0QH, England | Concert Cellist |
| **Williams, David**<br>Troika, 74 Clekrenwell St, London EC1M 5QA, England | Actor |
| **Wallin, Niclas**<br>244 Johnson Ave, Los Gatos CA 95030, USA | Ice Hockey Player |
| **Walling, Camryn**<br>Abrams Artists, 9200 W Sunset Blvd, #1125, West Hollywood CA 90069 USA | Actor |
| **Walling, Dennis (Denny)**<br>PO Box 1312, Waynesboro VA 22980, USA | Baseball Player |
| **Wallinger, Karl**<br>Agency Group Ltd, 142 W 57th St, #600, New York NY 10019 USA | Keyboardist, Songwriter |
| **Wallis, Annabelle**<br>I C M Partners, 10250 Constellation Blvd, #900, Los Angeles CA 90067 USA | Actress |
| **Wallis, H Joseph (Joe)**<br>PO Box 659, Chesterfield MO 63006, USA | Baseball Player |
| **Wallis, Michael**<br>Perfect Impressions, 154 Seminole Dr, Springfield IL 62704, USA | Writer |
| **Wallis, Shani**<br>2119 Via Puerta, #Q, Laguna Woods CA 92637, USA | Actress, Singer |
| **Walliser, Maria**<br>Selfwingert, 7208 Malans, Switzerland | Alpine Skier |
| **Walls, C Wesley**<br>8711 Lake Challis Lane, Charlotte NC 28226, USA | Football Player |
| **Walls, Denise (Nee-C)**<br>2113 South Ave, Youngstown OH 44502, USA | Singer (Annointed), Songwriter |
| **Walls, Everson C**<br>1925 Antwerp Ave, Plano TX 75025, USA | Football Player |
| **Walls, Jeannette**<br>Charles Scribner's Sons, 866 3rd Ave, New York NY 10022 USA | Writer |
| **Walls, Lenny B**<br>2800 Bush St, San Francisco CA 94115, USA | Football Player |
| **Walmsley, Jon**<br>Howard Talent West, 10657 Riverside Dr, Toluca Lake CA 91602, USA | Actor |
| **Walsch, Neale Donald**<br>Trident Media Group, 41 Madison Ave, #3600, New York NY 10010 USA | Writer |
| **Walser, Derrick**<br>592 Lorne St, New Glasgow NS B2H 4L3, Canada | Ice Hockey Player |
| **Walser, Martin**<br>Zum Hecht 36, 88662 Uberlingen-Nussdorf, Germany | Writer |
| **Walsh Jennings, Kerri L**<br>PO Box 33053, Los Gatos CA 95031, USA | Volleyball Player |
| **Walsh, Amanda**<br>I C M Partners, 10250 Constellation Blvd, #900, Los Angeles CA 90067 USA | Actress |
| **Walsh, Baillie**<br>Independent Talent Group, 40 Whitfield St, London W1T 2RH, England | Director |
| **Walsh, David M**<br>Gersh Agency, 9465 Wilshire Blvd, #600, Beverly Hills CA 90212 USA | Cinematographer |
| **Walsh, David P (Dave)**<br>500 Concord Lane, Edmond OK 73003, USA | Baseball Player |
| **Walsh, Diana Chapman**<br>Wellesley College, President's Office, Wellesley MA 02181, USA | Educator |
| **Walsh, Don**<br>International Maritime Inc, 14758 Sitkum Lane, Myrtle Point OR 97458, USA | Underwater Explorer |
| **Walsh, Donnie**<br>Indiana Pacers, Conseco Fieldhouse, 125 S Pennsylvania, Indianapolis IN 46204 USA | Basketball Coach, Executive |
| **Walsh, Dylan**<br>Gersh Agency, 9465 Wilshire Blvd, #600, Beverly Hills CA 90212 USA | Actor |
| **Walsh, Gwynyth**<br>Allman/Rea Mgmt, 141 Barrington Ave, Los Angeles CA 90049, USA | Actress |
| **Walsh, Joe**<br>Front Line Mgmt, 1100 Glendon Ave, #2000, Los Angeles CA 90024 USA | Singer, Guitarist (Eagles); Songwriter |
| **Walsh, John**<br>3111 S Dixie Highway, #244, West Palm Beach FL 33405, USA | Producer, Director, Actor |
| **Walsh, John, Jr**<br>J Paul Getty Museum, Getty Center, 1200 Getty Center Dr, Los Angeles CA 90049, USA | Museum Executive |
| **Walsh, Kate**<br>Creative Artists Agency, 2000 Ave of Stars, #100, Los Angeles CA 90067 USA | Actress |
| **Walsh, Kimberly J**<br>Concorde International, 101 Shepherds Bush Road, London W6 7LP, England | Singer (Girls Aloud) |
| **Walsh, M Emmet**<br>S L J Mgmt, 833 N Edinburgh Ave, PH 11, Los Angeles CA 90046, USA | Actor |
| **Walsh, Maiara**<br>A P A Talent & Literary Agency, 405 S Beverly Dr, #300, Beverly Hills CA 90212 USA | Actress |
| **Walsh, Martin**<br>National Organization on Disability, 910 16th NW, #400, Washington DC 20006, USA | Association Executive |
| **Walsh, Martin**<br>Independent Talent Group, 40 Whitfield St, London W1T 2RH, England | Editor |
| **Walsh, Matt**<br>Creative Artists Agency, 2000 Ave of Stars, #100, Los Angeles CA 90067 USA | Actor, Comedian, Producer |

# W

## Wallenda - Walsh

# W

**Walsh, Patrick C** — Urologist
Johns Hopkins University, Brady Urological Institute, Baltimore MD 21205, USA
**Walsh, Peter** — Actor
Paradigm Agency, 360 N Crescent Dr, North Building, Beverly Hills CA 90210 USA
**Walsh, Stephen J (Steve)** — Football Player
8801 Wellington View Dr, West Palm Beach FL 33411, USA
**Walsh, Sydney** — Actress
Connor Ankrum Assoc, 1680 Vine St, #1016, Los Angeles CA 90028, USA
**Walsh, Tom** — Sculptor
PO Box 133, Philomath OR 97370, USA
**Walsh, Willie** — Businessman
British Airways, Waterside, PO Box 365, Harmondsworth UB7 0GB, England
**Walsman, Leanna** — Actress
I C M Partners, 10250 Constellation Blvd, #900, Los Angeles CA 90067 USA
**Walter, Anders** — Producer
Independent Talent Group, 40 Whitfield St, London W1T 2RH, England
**Walter, Gene W** — Baseball Player
1901 Fairway Dr, LaGrange KY 40031, USA
**Walter, Jessica** — Actress
Innovative Artists, 1505 10th St, Santa Monica CA 90401 USA
**Walter, Joseph F (Joe), Jr** — Football Player
4136 Binley Dr, Richardson TX 75082, USA
**Walter, Lisa Ann** — Actress, Comedienne, Writer, Producer
Abrams Artists, 9200 W Sunset Blvd, #1125, West Hollywood CA 90069 USA
**Walter, Michael D (Mike)** — Football Player
6900 SW Knollwood St, Tualatin OR 97062, USA
**Walter, Robert D** — Businessman
Cardinal Health, 7000 Cardinal Place, Dublin OH 43017, USA
**Walter, Ryan** — Ice Hockey Player
Vancouver Canucks, 800 Griffiths Way, Vancouver BC V6B 6G1, Canada
**Walter, Tracey** — Actress
Stone Manners Salners, 6100 Wilshire Blvd, #1500, Los Angeles CA 90035 USA
**Walter, Ulrich** — Astronaut, Germany
I B M Germany, Schonaicherstr 220, 71032 Boblingen, Germany
**Walters, Barbara** — Commentator
944 5th Ave, #6, New York NY 10021, USA
**Walters, Charles L (Charlie)** — Baseball Player
1717 Sutton Lane, Saint Paul MN 55118, USA
**Walters, Dale** — Boxer
Ringside Fitness, 4 Bentall Centre, #49271, Vancouver BC V5Y 1C7, Canada
**Walters, David** — Swimmer
Premier Management Group, 115 Crescent Commons, #250, Cary, NC 27518 USA
**Walters, David L** — Governor, OK
RR 2, Watts OK 74964, USA
**Walters, Harry N** — Government Official
D H C Holdings Corp, 125 Thomas Dale, Williamsburg VA 23185, USA
**Walters, Jamie** — Actor, Singer
Atlantic Records, 9229 W Sunset Blvd, #900, West Hollywood CA 90069 USA
**Walters, Julie** — Actress
153 Petherton Road, London N5 2RS, England
**Walters, Kirk** — Editorial Cartoonist
Toledo Blade, Editorial Dept, 541 N Superior St, Toledo OH 43660, USA
**Walters, Lisa** — Golfer
211 S Westland Ave, #2, Tampa FL 33606, USA
**Walters, Melora** — Actress
More/Medavoy Mgmt, 10203 Santa Monica Blvd, #400, Los Angeles CA 90067 USA
**Walters, Michael C (Mike)** — Baseball Player
79070 Desert Stream Dr, La Quinta CA 92253, USA
**Walters, Minette** — Writer
Panmacmillan, 20 New Wharf Road, London N1 9RR, England
**Walters, Peter I** — Businessman
22 Hill St, London W1X 7FU, England
**Walters, Rex A** — Basketball Player
690 45th Ave, San Francisco CA 94121, USA
**Walters, Ron** — Ice Hockey Player
8 Garrison Crescent, Sherwood Park AB T8A 2S8, Canada
**Walters, Stanley P (Stan)** — Football Player
2021 W Wesley Road NW, Atlanta GA 30327, USA
**Walters, Susan** — Actress
Allman/Rea Mgmt, 9255 Sunset Blvd, #600, Los Angeles CA 90069, USA
**Walterscheid, Leonard W (Len)** — Football Player
2312 I Road, Grand Junction CO 81505, USA
**Walthall, Romy** — Actress
Defining Artists Agency, 4370 Tujunga Ave, #120, Studio City CA 91604 USA
**Walthan, John** — Baseball Manager
1354 NE Todd George Road, Lees Summit MO 64086, USA
**Walther, Herbert** — Physicist
Egenhoferstr 7A, 81243 Munich, Germany
**Walther, Paul G** — Basketball Player
6555 Riverside Dr NW, Atlanta GA 30328, USA
**Walther, Philip** — Physicist
University of Vienna, Physics Dept, Boltzmanngasse 5, 1090 Vienna, Austria
**Walton, Anthony J (Tony)** — Scenic Designer, Illustrator
I C M Partners, 730 5th Ave, New York NY 10019 USA
**Walton, Anthony J (Tony)** — Costume, Set Designer
Costume Design Guild, 11969 Ventura Blvd, #100, Studio City CA 91604, USA
**Walton, Bruce K** — Baseball Player
10704 Sunset Canyon Dr, Bakersfield CA 93311, USA
**Walton, Christy R** — Businesswoman
Wal-Mart Stores, 702 SW 8th St, Bentonville AR 72712, USA
**Walton, Daniel J (Danny)** — Baseball Player
PO Box 296, Huntsville UT 84317, USA
**Walton, David** — Actor
One Set One Rep Productions, 839 N Gardner St, Los Angeles CA 90046, USA
**Walton, Jim C** — Businessman
CNN-TV, News Dept, 190 Marietta Ave SW, Atlanta GA 30303 USA

**Walsh - Walton**

**Walton, Joseph (Joe)** — Football Player, Coach
8 Windycrest Dr, Beaver Falls PA 15010, USA
**Walton, Kendall L** — Philosopher
University of Michigan, Philosophy Dept, Ann Arbor MI 48109, USA
**Walton, Lawrence J (Larry)** — Football Player
PO Box 32204, Phoenix AZ 85064, USA
**Walton, Luke T** — Basketball Player
1613 Gates Ave, Manhattan Beach CA 90266, USA
**Walton, Mike** — Ice Hockey Player
Re/Max Professionals, 200-270 Kingsway, Etobicoke ON M9A 3T7, Canada
**Walton, S Robson (Rob)** — Businessman
Wal-Mart Stores, 702 SW 8th St, Bentonville AR 72716, USA
**Walton, William T (Bill), III** — Basketball Player, Sportscaster
1010 Myrtle Way, San Diego CA 92103, USA
**Waltrip, Darrell L** — Auto, Truck Racing Driver
Michael Waltrip Racing, 20310 Chartwell Center Dr, Cornelius NC 28031, USA
**Waltrip, Michael C (Mike)** — Auto Racing Driver
Michael Waltrip Racing, 20310 Chartwell Center Dr, Cornelius NC 28031, USA
**Waltz, Christoph** — Actor
Players Agentur Mgmt, Sophienstra 21, 10178 Berlin-Mitte, Germany
**Waltz, Lisa** — Actress
Stone Manners Salners, 6100 Wilshire Blvd, #1500, Los Angeles CA 90035 USA
**Waluska, Nick** — Guitarist (Wondermints)
Paradise Artists, PO Box 1821, Ojai CA 93024 USA
**Walz, Carl E** — Astronaut
15506 Eagle Tavern Lane, Centreville VA 20120, USA
**Walz, Kevin** — Interior Designer
Walz Design, 12 Vestry St, New York NY 10013, USA
**Walz, Wesley (Wes)** — Ice Hockey Player
10435 Raleigh Road, Saint Paul MN 55129, USA
**Wamala, Emmanuel Cardinal** — Religious Leader
Archbishop's House, PO Box 14125, Mengo-Kampala, Uganda
**Wambach, M Abigail (Abby)** — Soccer Player
Powerplay Consultants, 1600 Parkwood Circle SE, #600, Atlanta GA 30339, USA
**Wambaugh, Joseph** — Writer
3520 Kellogg Way, San Diego CA 92106, USA
**Wamsley, Rick** — Ice Hockey Player
Saint Louis Blues, Scottrade Center, 1401 Clark Ave, Saint Louis MO 63103 USA
**Wan Li** — Government Official, China
State Council, People's Congress, Tiananmen Square, Beijing 100006, China
**Wanamaker, Zoe** — Actress
Conway Van Gelder Grant, 8-12 Broadwick St, #300, London W1F 8HW, England
**Wand, Seth P** — Football Player
5515 NW 93rd St, Kansas City MO 64154, USA
**Wandmacher, Michael** — Composer
First Artists Mgmt, 4764 Park Granada, #210, Calabasas CA 91302 USA
**Wandrey, Ralph H** — WW II Army Air Corps Hero
1113 SW 15th Place, Cape Coral FL 33991, USA
**Wang Chunlu** — Speed Skater
Skating Association, 56 Zhonguancun South St, Beijing 100044, China
**Wang Jida** — Sculptor
7612 35th Ave, #3E, Jackson Heights NY 11372, USA
**Wang Jin** — Artist
Chinese Contemporary Gallery, Studio House, 7/9 Edith Grove, London SW 10 0JZ, England
**Wang Junxia** — Track Athlete
Athletic Assn, 9 Tiyuguan Road, Chongwen District, Beijing 100061, China
**Wang Meng** — Speed Skater
Skating Association, 56 Zhonguancun South St, Beijing 100044, China
**Wang Tian Ren** — Sculptor
Shaanxi Sculpture Institute, Longshoucun, Xi'am, Shaanxi 710016, China
**Wang Zhi Zhi** — Basketball Player
Miami Heat, American Airlines Arena, 601 Biscayne Blvd, Miami FL 33132 USA
**Wang, Chien-Ming** — Baseball Player
New York Yankees, Yankee Stadium, E 161st St & River Ave, Bronx NY 10451 USA
**Wang, Garrett** — Actor
501 E Del Mar Blvd, #310, Pasadena CA 91101, USA
**Wang, Henry Y** — Chemical Engineer
University of Michigan, Chemical Engineering Dept, Ann Arbor MI 48109, USA
**Wang, Lai-Sheng** — Physical Chemist
Brown University, Chemistry Dept, 324 Brook St, Providence RI 02912, USA
**Wang, Peggy** — Singer (Pains of Being Pure at Heart)
Slumberland Records, PO Box 19029, Oakland CA 94619, USA
**Wang, Taylor G** — Astronaut, Physicist
1224 Arno Dr, Sierra Madre CA 91024, USA
**Wang, Vera** — Fashion Designer
Vera Wang Bridal House, 225 W 39th St, #900, New York NY 10018, USA
**Wang, Wayne** — Director
I C M Partners, 10250 Constellation Blvd, #900, Los Angeles CA 90067 USA
**Wang, Zhong L** — Nanotechnologist
Georgia Institute of Technology, Nanostructure Center, Atlanta GA 30332, USA
**Wangchuck, Jigme Khesar Namgyal** — King, Bhutan
Royal Palace, Tashichhodzong, Thimphu, Bhutan
**Wangchuck, Lyonpo Khandu** — Prime Minister, Bhutan
Jangsa, Shari Geog, Paro, Bhutan
**Wangchuk, Jigme Singye** — King, Bhutan
Royal Palace, Tashichhodzong, Thimphu, Bhutan
**Wank, Andreas** — Ski Jumper
Fohrwald-Jungholz 16, 79874 Breitnau, Germany
**Wanner, H Eric** — Foundation Executive
Russell Sage Foundation, 112 E 64th St, New York NY 10065, USA
**Wannstedt, David R (Dave)** — Football Coach
151 Rock Haven Lane, Pittsburgh PA 15228, USA
**Wansel, Dexter G** — Keyboardist, Pianist
Walt Reeder Productions, 93 Old Yorke Road, #1-604, Jenkintown PA 19046, USA
**Wanzer, Robert F (Bobby)** — Basketball Player
28 Greenwood Park, Pittsford NY 14534, USA

**Waples, Keith** — Harness Racing Driver
PO Box 632, Durham ON N0G 1R0, Canada

**Waples, Ronald (Ron)** — Harness Racing Driver, Trainer
7 Mill Run W, Hightstown NJ 08520, USA

**Wapner, Joseph A** — Entertainer, Judge
C E S D, 10635 Santa Monica Blvd, #130, Los Angeles CA 90025 USA

**Wapnick, Steven L (Steve)** — Baseball Player
5934 Woodcliffe Dr, Windsor CO 80550, USA

**Wappel, Gord** — Ice Hockey Player
5544 Kartusch Place, Regina SK S4X 4K1, Canada

**Warbeck, Stephen** — Composer
United Agents, 12-26 Lexington St, London W1F 0LE, England

**Warburton, Patrick** — Actor
Sutton-Barth Vennari, 5900 Wilshire Blvd, #700, Los Angeles CA 90036 USA

**Warby, Kenneth P (Ken)** — Boat Racing Driver
7432 State Route 128, Miamitown OH 45041, USA

**Warchus, Matthew** — Director
Hamilton Hodell, 20 Golden Square, London W1F 9JL, England

**Ward, Aaron** — Ice Hockey Player
112 Ronsard Lane, Cary NC 27511, USA

**Ward, Andre** — Boxer
Prince Boxing Gym, 3030 Jensen Dr, Houston TX 77026, USA

**Ward, Andre** — Jazz Saxophonist
Celebrity Talent Agency, 111 E 14th St, #249, New York NY 10003 USA

**Ward, Anita** — Singer
Richard Walters, PO Box 2789, Toluca Lake CA 91610 USA

**Ward, Bryan A** — Baseball Player
140 Bannock Court, East Dundee IL 60118, USA

**Ward, Burt** — Actor
Gentle Giants & Adoptions, PO Box 6005, Norco CA 92860, USA

**Ward, Burton** — Auto Racing Driver
Bill Davis Racing, 301 Old Thomasville Road, Winston Salem NC 27107, USA

**Ward, Cameron (Cam)** — Ice Hockey Player
1608 Shambrook Court, Raleigh NC 27614, USA

**Ward, Carlos N** — Jazz Saxophonist (B T Express)
Star-Vest Mgmt, 102 Ryders Lane, East Brunswick NJ 08816, USA

**Ward, Catherine** — Ice Hockey Player
Hockey Canada, 151 Canada Olympic Road SW, #201, Calgary AB  T3B 6B7, Canada

**Ward, Charlie** — Football, Basketball Player
2611 Dunsinane Road, Pensacola FL 32503, USA

**Ward, Christian** — Artist
Max Wigram Gallery,  106 New Bond St, London W1S 1DN, England

**Ward, Christopher L J (Chris)** — Football Player
PO Box 1365, Inglewood CA 90308, USA

**Ward, Colin N** — Baseball Player
1045 S Amandes, Mesa AZ 85208, USA

**Ward, Dale** — Singer (Crescendo)
A Crosse the World, PO Box 23066, London W11 3FR, England

**Ward, David** — Opera Singer
1 Kennedy Crescent, Lake Wanaka, New Zealand

**Ward, David S** — Director, Writer
I C M Partners, 10250 Constellation Blvd, #900, Los Angeles CA 90067 USA

**Ward, Dedric L** — Football Player
3435 N 45th St, Phoenix AZ 85018, USA

**Ward, Dixon** — Ice Hockey Player
Okanagan Hockey School, 201-851 Eckhardt W, Penticton BC V2A 9C4, Canada

**Ward, Douglas Turner** — Actor, Writer
Negro Ensemble Co, 303 W 42nd St, #501, New York NY 10036, USA

**Ward, Edward J (Ed)** — Ice Hockey Player
9150 Weathervane Trail, Galesburg MI 49053, USA

**Ward, Fred** — Actor
A P A Talent & Literary Agency, 405 S Beverly Dr, #300, Beverly Hills CA 90212 USA

**Ward, Gemma** — Model
Creative Artists Agency, 2000 Ave of Stars, #100, Los Angeles CA 90067 USA

**Ward, Hines E, Jr** — Football Player
155 Fairfax Road, Pittsburgh PA 15221, USA

**Ward, Jacky** — Singer
821 19th Ave S, Nashville TN 37203, USA

**Ward, Jeff** — Motorcycle Racing Rider
Speed Technologies, 9716 S Virginia St, Reno NV 89511, USA

**Ward, Jimmie** — Football Player
San Francisco 49ers, 4949 Centennial Blvd, Santa Clara CA 95054 USA

**Ward, JoAnn** — Actress, Producer
Creative Artists Agency, 2000 Ave of Stars, #100, Los Angeles CA 90067 USA

**Ward, John T, Jr** — Thoroughbred Racing Trainer
573 Clay Kiser Road, Paris KY 40361, USA

**Ward, Jonathan** — Actor
Auckland Actors, PO Box 56460, Dominion Road, Auckland 1030, New Zealand

**Ward, Kevin M** — Baseball Player
160 F Ave, Coronado CA 92118, USA

**Ward, M** — Singer (She & Him), Songwriter
Ground Control Touring, 420 W Main St, Carrboro NC 27510, USA

**Ward, Maitland** — Actress
Perlman Management Group, PO Box 2939, Beverly Hills CA 90209, USA

**Ward, Mickey (Irish)** — Boxer
132 Upham St, Lowell MA 01851, USA

**Ward, Pam** — Sportscaster
ESPN-TV, Sports Dept, ESPN Plaza, 935 Middle St, Bristol CT 06010 USA

**Ward, Preston M** — Baseball Player
4371 De Silva Place, Las Vegas NV 89121, USA

**Ward, Rachel** — Actress, Director
Himber Entertainment, PO Box 950, South Orange NJ 07079 USA

**Ward, Rebecca** — Fencer
Oregon Fencing Alliance, 4840 SW Western Ave, #80, Beaverton OR 97005, USA

**Ward, Robert R (Bob)** — Football Player
515 N Academy St, Greensboro MD 21639, USA

**Ward, Ronald (Scooter)** — Singer (Cold)
Front Line Mgmt, 1100 Glendon Ave, #2000, Los Angeles CA 90024 USA
**Ward, Ronald L (Ron)** — Ice Hockey Player
3178 W 140th St, Cleveland OH 44111, USA
**Ward, Sela** — Actress
Management 360, 9111 Wilshire Blvd, Beverly Hills CA 90210 USA
**Ward, Susan** — Actress, Model
Pakula/King, 9229 W Sunset Blvd, #315, West Hollywood CA 90069 USA
**Ward, Tom** — Actor
Independent Talent Group, 40 Whitfield St, London W1T 2RH, England
**Ward, Turner M** — Baseball Player
232 Autumn Dr, Saraland AL 36571, USA
**Ward, Vincent** — Director, Writer, Actor
United Talent Agency, U T A Plaza, 9336 Civic Center Dr, Beverly Hills CA 90210 USA
**Ward, Wendy** — Golfer
12850 Sassin Station Road N, Edwall WA 99008, USA
**Ward, William T (Bill)** — Singer, Drummer (Black Sabbath)
Sharon Osborne Mgmt, 8899 Beverly Blvd, #905, West Hollywood CA 90048, USA
**Ward, Zach** — Actor
Muse Artist Management, 708 Denman St, #200, Vancouver BC V6G 2L5, Canada
**Warden, John** — Attorney
Sullivan & Cromwell 125 Broad St, New York NY 10004, USA
**Warden, Jonathan E (Jon)** — Baseball Player
6575 Oasis Dr, Loveland OH 45140, USA
**Warden, Rick** — Actor
Independent Talent Group, 40 Whitfield St, London W1T 2RH, England
**Wardlaw, Kim McLane** — Judge
US Court of Appeals, 125 S Grand Ave, Pasadena CA 91105, USA
**Wardle, Curtis J (Curt)** — Baseball Player
13900 Pheasant Knoll Lane, Moreno Valley CA 92553, USA
**Ware, Andre** — Football Player, Sportscaster
3910 Wood Park, Sugar Land TX 77479, USA
**Ware, Billy** — Percussionist (BeauSoleil)
Rosebud Agency, PO Box 170429, San Francisco CA 94117 USA
**Ware, Chris** — Cartoonist
Fantagraphics Books, 7563 Lake City Way NE, Seattle WA 98115, USA
**Ware, DeMarcus** — Football Player
690 Rockingham Court, Colleyville TX 76034, USA
**Ware, Derek G** — Football Player
2315 W Shannon St, Chandler AZ 85224, USA
**Ware, Hannah** — Actress
Independent Talent Group, 40 Whitfield St, London W1T 2RH, England
**Ware, Jeffrey A (Jeff)** — Baseball Player
2560 Mulberry Loop, Virginia Beach VA 23456, USA
**Ware, Justin** — Writer, Actor
Gersh Agency, 9465 Wilshire Blvd, #600, Beverly Hills CA 90212 USA
**Ware, Leon** — Singer, Pianist, Songwriter
13700 Tahiti Way, #147, Marina del Rey CA 90292, USA
**Warfield, Paul D** — Football Player
16 Normandy Way, Rancho Mirage CA 92270, USA
**Warfield, Sonja** — Writer
Creative Artists Agency, 2000 Ave of Stars, #100, Los Angeles CA 90067 USA
**Wargo, Tom** — Golfer
2801 Putter Dr, Centralia IL 62801, USA
**Warhola, James** — Writer, Illustrator
56 Walkers Hill, Tivoli NY 12583, USA
**Wariner, Steve** — Singer, Guitarist, Songwriter
Steve Wariner Productions, PO Box 1647, Franklin TN 37065, USA
**Waring, Todd** — Actor
145 W 45th St, #1204, New York NY 10036, USA
**Warkentin, Thomas (Tom)** — Cartoonist (Flash Gordon)
King Features Syndicate, 300 W 57th St, #1500, New York NY 10019 USA
**Warlock, Billy** — Actor
Abrams Artists, 9200 W Sunset Blvd, #1125, West Hollywood CA 90069 USA
**Warmack, Chance** — Football Player
Tennessee Titans, 460 Great Circle Road, Nashville TN 37228 USA
**Warmenhoven, Daniel J** — Businessman
Network Appliance Inc, 495 E Java Dr, Sunnyvale CA 94089, USA
**Warnecke, Mark** — Swimmer
Am Schichtmeister 100, 58453 Witten, Germany
**Warner, Amelia** — Actress
Authentic Talent Mgmt, 20 Jay St, #M17, Brooklyn NY 11201 USA
**Warner, Chris** — Cartoonist (Black Cross)
Dark Horse Publishing, 10956 SE Main St, Portland OR 97222 USA
**Warner, Cornell** — Basketball Player
2479 Glen Meadow Lane, Escondido CA 92027, USA
**Warner, Curtis E (Curt)** — Football Player
2843 NW Lacamas Dr, Camas WA 98607, USA
**Warner, David** — Actor
Julian Belfrage Assoc, 9 Argyll St, #300, London W1F 7TG, England
**Warner, Douglas A, III** — Financier
J P Morgan Chase, 270 Park Ave, #1200, New York NY 10017, USA
**Warner, Jack D** — Baseball Player
5938 W Calle Lejos, Glendale AZ 85310, USA
**Warner, Jack Lionel** — Architect
Warner Group Architects, 1250 Coast Village Road, #J, Santa Barbara CA 93108, USA
**Warner, Jane** — Model
166 Ditching Road, Brighton Essex BN1 6JA, England
**Warner, Jim** — Ice Hockey Player
2011 Upper Saint Dennis Road, Saint Paul MN 55116, USA
**Warner, John J (Jackie)** — Baseball Player
19136 Highway 18 N, Apple Valley CA 92307, USA
**Warner, John W** — Senator, VA
Atoka Farm, PO Box 1320, Middleburg VA 20118, USA
**Warner, Julie** — Actress
Innovative Artists, 1505 10th St, Santa Monica CA 90401 USA

# W

| | |
|---|---|
| **Warner, Kurtis E (Kurt)** | Football Player |
| 6712 E Cheney Dr, Paradise Valley AZ 85253, USA | |
| **Warner, Malcolm-Jamal** | Actor |
| Abrams Artists, 9200 W Sunset Blvd, #1125, West Hollywood CA 90069 USA | |
| **Warner, Margaret** | Commentator |
| News Hour Show, 2700 S Quincy St, #250, Arlington VA 22206, USA | |
| **Warner, T C** | Actress |
| S D B Partners, 315 S Beverly Dr, #411, Beverly Hills CA 90067 USA | |
| **Warner, Todd** | Sculptor |
| 155 NW 11th St, Boca Raton FL 33432, USA | |
| **Warner, Tom** | Producer |
| Carsey-Warner Productions, 4024 Radford Ave, Building 3, Studio City CA 91604, USA | |
| **Warner, Ty** | Toy Designer |
| Ty Inc, PO Box 5377, Hinsdale IL 60522, USA | |
| **Warner, Volney F** | Army General |
| V F Warner Assoc, 6832 Old Dominion Dr, #206, McLean VA 22101, USA | |
| **Warnes, Jennifer** | Singer, Songwriter |
| Donald Miller, 12746 Kling St, Studio City CA 91604, USA | |
| **Warnock, John E** | Businessman |
| Adobe Systems, 375 Park Ave, San Jose CA 95110, USA | |
| **Warren G** | Rap Artist |
| Progressive Global Agency, PO Box 50294, Nashville TN 37025, USA | |
| **Warren, Anthony (T J), Jr** | Basketball Player |
| Phoenix Suns, 201 E Jefferson St, Phoenix AZ 85004 USA | |
| **Warren, Christoper (Chris), Jr** | Actor |
| Innovative Artists, 1505 10th St, Santa Monica CA 90401 USA | |
| **Warren, Christopher C (Chris), Jr** | Football Player |
| 13707 Black Spruce Way, Chantilly VA 20151, USA | |
| **Warren, Cicero** | Baseball Player |
| 119 Brookwood St, East Orange NJ 07018, USA | |
| **Warren, Diane** | Songwriter |
| 1896 Rising Glen Road, Los Angeles CA 90069, USA | |
| **Warren, Donald J (Don)** | Football Player |
| 13507 Wilder Court, Clifton VA 20124, USA | |
| **Warren, Estella** | Model, Actress |
| Don Buchwald Talent Agency, 6500 Wilshire Blvd, #2200, Los Angeles CA 90048 USA | |
| **Warren, Frederick M** | Architect |
| 65 Cambridge Terrace, Christchurch 80013, New Zealand | |
| **Warren, Gerard T** | Football Player |
| 13786 NE 222nd Place, Raiford FL 32083, USA | |
| **Warren, Gloria** | Singer, Actress |
| 16872 Bosque Dr, Encino CA 91436, USA | |
| **Warren, Gregory R (Greg)** | Football Player |
| 14 S 18th St, Pittsburgh PA 15203, USA | |
| **Warren, J Robin** | Nobel Medicine Laureate |
| 178 Lake St, Perth WA 6000, Australia | |
| **Warren, Jennifer** | Actress |
| 1675 Old Oak Road, Los Angeles CA 90049, USA | |
| **Warren, Kenneth S** | Immunologist |
| Picower Medical Research Institute, 350 Community Dr, Manhasset NY 11030, USA | |
| **Warren, Kiersten** | Actress |
| Gallagher Stewart Agency, 955 Carrillo Dr, #100, Los Angeles CA 90048, USA | |
| **Warren, Lamont A** | Football Player |
| 17735 Sorrel Ridge Dr, Spring TX 77388, USA | |
| **Warren, Lesley Ann** | Actress |
| Innovative Artists, 1505 10th St, Santa Monica CA 90401 USA | |
| **Warren, Marc** | Actor |
| Artists Partnership, 101 Finsbury Pavement, London EC2A 1RS, England | |
| **Warren, Michael (Mike)** | Actor, Basketball Player |
| 21216 Escondido St, Woodland Hills CA 91364, USA | |
| **Warren, Richard D (Rick)** | Evangelist, Writer |
| Saddleback Church, 1 Saddleback Parkway, Lake Forest CA 92630, USA | |
| **Warren, Robert G (Bobby)** | Basketball Player |
| 989 Hardin Wadesboro Road, Hardin KY 42048, USA | |
| **Warren, Ron** | Baseball Player |
| 4025 Paddock Road, #401, Cincinnati OH 45229, USA | |
| **Warren, Rosanna** | Writer |
| 11 Robinwood Ave, Needham MA 02492, USA | |
| **Warren, Thomas L** | Association Executive |
| National Wildlife Federation, 11100 Wildlife Center Dr, Reston VA 20190, USA | |
| **Warren, Tom** | Triathlete |
| 2393 La Marque St, San Diego CA 92109, USA | |
| **Warren, Ty'ron M (Ty)** | Football Player |
| 22 Ronald C Meyer Dr, North Attleboro MA 02760, USA | |
| **Warren, William M, Jr** | Businessman |
| Energen Corp, 605 Richard Arrington Jr Blvd N, Birmingham AL 35203, USA | |
| **Warrener, Rhett** | Ice Hockey Player |
| 761 W Ferry St, Buffalo NY 14222, USA | |
| **Warren-Green, Christopher** | Conductor, Concert Violinist |
| Charlotte Symphony Orchestra, 301 S Tryon St, #1700, Charlotte, NC 28282, USA | |
| **Warrick, Hakim H** | Basketball Player |
| Orlando Magic, 8701 Maitland Summit Blvd, Orlando FL 32810 USA | |
| **Warrick, Peter** | Football Player |
| 1508 11th Ave E, Palmetto FL 34221, USA | |
| **Warshel, Arieh** | Nobel Chemistry Laureate |
| University of Southern California, Chemistry Dept, Los Angeles CA 90089, USA | |
| **Warwick, Carl W** | Baseball Player |
| 14102 Bonney Brier Circle, Houston TX 77069, USA | |
| **Warwick, Dionne** | Singer |
| Red Entertainment Agency, 505 8th Ave, #1004, New York NY 10018, USA | |
| **Warwick, Lonnie P** | Football Player |
| 828 Main St, Mount Hope WV 25880, USA | |
| **Wasdin, John T** | Baseball Player |
| 2676 Riverport Dr S, Jacksonville FL 32223, USA | |
| **Wash, Martha** | Singer |
| Mike Church Entertainment, 1100 Osborn Road, #335, Phoenix AZ 85014, USA | |

**Warner - Wash**

**Washburn, Abigail** — Banjo Player, Singer
A C Entertainment, 507 S Gay St, Knoxville TN 37902, USA
**Washburn, Barbara** — Cartographer
1010 Waltham St, #D327, Lexington MA 02421, USA
**Washburn, Beverly** — Actress
2561 Olivia Heights Ave, Henderson NV 89052, USA
**Washburn, Jarrod M** — Baseball Player
10003 Olinger Road, Webster WI 54893, USA
**Washburn, Ray C** — Baseball Player
1103 N 49th St, Seattle WA 98103, USA
**Washed Out** — Electronica Musician
Constant Artists, 3780 Wilshire Blvd, #500, Los Angeles CA 90010, USA
**Washington Tashiana** — Actress
Shirley Grant Management, 1333 Wellington Ave, Teaneck NJ 07666, USA
**Washington, Alonzo** — Cartoonist (Omega Man)
Omega 7, PO Box 171046, Kansas City KS 66117, USA
**Washington, Christopher (Chris)** — Football Player
PO Box 17823, San Diego CA 92177, USA
**Washington, Claudell** — Baseball Player
4081 Clayton Road, #227, Concord CA 94521, USA
**Washington, Denzel** — Actor
Rogers & Cowan, 8687 Melrose Ave, #G700, West Hollywood CA 90069 USA
**Washington, Eugene (Gene)** — Football Player
2725 N Jewell Lane, Minneapolis MN 55447, USA
**Washington, Gene A** — Football Player
10521 Bellagio Road, Los Angeles CA 90077, USA
**Washington, Hayma** — Producer
A P A Talent & Literary Agency, 405 S Beverly Dr, #300, Beverly Hills CA 90212 USA
**Washington, Herbert (Herb) L** — Baseball Player
640 Saddlebrook Dr, Youngstown OH 44512, USA
**Washington, Isaiah** — Actor
Anderson & Smith, 7322 Southwest Freeway, #2010, Houston TX 77074, USA
**Washington, James H (Jim)** — Basketball Player
1108 Cardinal Way SW, Atlanta GA 30311, USA
**Washington, Joe D** — Football Player
Meadow Lark, 4 Treadwell Court, Lutherville Timonium MD 21093, USA
**Washington, Justin (Baby)** — Singer, Pianist
Headline Talent, 1650 Broadway, #401, New York NY 10313 USA
**Washington, Keith** — Singer
Associated Booking Corp, 501 Madison Ave, #501, New York NY 10022 USA
**Washington, Keith L** — Football Player
548 Parkview Dr, Grand Prairie TX 75052, USA
**Washington, Kermit A** — Basketball Player
7208 NE Hazel Dell Ave, Vancouver WA 98665, USA
**Washington, Kerry** — Actress
Creative Artists Agency, 2000 Ave of Stars, #100, Los Angeles CA 90067 USA
**Washington, Lionel** — Football Player
5 Gleneagles Dr, La Place LA 70068, USA
**Washington, MaliVai** — Tennis Player
5 S Roscoe Blvd, Ponte Vedra Beach FL 32082, USA
**Washington, Marcus C** — Football Player
18263 Mullfield Village Terrace, Leesburg VA 20176, USA
**Washington, Mickey L** — Football Player
12302 Bayport Dr, Pearland TX 77584, USA
**Washington, Richard L** — Basketball Player
4606 SE Logus Road, Portland OR 97222, USA
**Washington, Rico** — Baseball Player
2050 Old Clinton Road, Macon GA 31211, USA
**Washington, Ronald (Ron)** — Baseball Player, Manager
1400 S Clearview Parkway, New Orleans LA 70123, USA
**Washington, Russell E (Russ)** — Football Player
4375 Florida St, #4, San Diego CA 92104, USA
**Washington, Theodore (Ted), Jr** — Football Player
2715 Joust St, North Las Vegas NV 89030, USA
**Washington, U L** — Baseball Player
PO Box 164, Stringtown OK 74569, USA
**Washington, Wilson** — Basketball Player
2625 Mapleton Ave, Norfolk VA 23504, USA
**Wasif, Imaad** — Singer, Songwriter
Agency Group Ltd, 142 W 57th St, #600, New York NY 10019 USA
**Wasikowska, Mia** — Actress
W M E Entertainment, 9601 Wilshire Blvd, #300, Beverly Hills CA 90210 USA
**Waslewski, Gary L** — Baseball Player
1799 E Terrestrial Place, Tucson AZ 85737, USA
**Wasmeier, Markus** — Alpine Skier
Breitensteinstr 14D, 83727 Schliersee-Neuhaus, Germany
**Wasmuth, Conny** — Canoing Athlete
S C Magdeburg, Friedrich-Ebert-Str 68, 39114 Magdeburg, Germany
**Wass, Ted** — Actor, Director, Producer
I C M Partners, 10250 Constellation Blvd, #900, Los Angeles CA 90067 USA
**Wasserburg, Gerald J** — Geophysicist
PO Box 2959, Florence OR 97439, USA
**Wasserman, Dan** — Editorial Cartoonist
Boston Globe, Editorial Dept, 135 William Morrissey Blvd, Dorchester MA 02125, USA
**Wasserman, Robert H** — Physiologist, Veterinarian
358 Savage Farm Dr, Ithaca NY 14850, USA
**Wasson, Erin** — Model
I M G Models, 304 Park Ave S, #PH N, New York NY 10010 USA
**Watanabe, Gedde** — Actor
Opus Entertainment, 5225 Wilshire Blvd, #905, Los Angeles CA 90036, USA
**Watanabe, Katsuaki** — Businessman
Toyota Motor Corp, 1 Toyotacho, Toyota City, Aichi Pref 471 8701, Japan
**Watanabe, Kazuhide** — Businessman
Mazda Motor Co, 3-1 Shinchi, Fuchucho, Akigun, Hiroshima 730 8670, Japan
**Watanabe, Ken** — Actor, Producer, Director
K-Dash, 2-7-10-5F Higashi, Shibuya, Tokyo 150 0011, Japan

**Watanabe, Sadao** — Jazz Saxophonist
International Music Network, 278 Main St, #400, Gloucester MA 01930 USA
**Watanabe, Shigeo** — Businessman
Bridgestone Corp, 10-1-1 Kyobashi, Chuoku, Tokyo 104 8340, Japan
**Watchorn, Tara** — Ice Hockey Player
Hockey Canada, 151 Canada Olympic Road SW, #201, Calgary AB  T3B 6B7, Canada
**Waterbury, Steven C (Steve)** — Baseball Player
710 N Garfield St, Marion IL 62959, USA
**Waterhouse, Gabriel M (Gai)** — Thoroughbred Racing Trainer
Gai Waterhouse Racing, PO Box 834, Kensington NSW 1465, Australia
**Waterman, Dennis** — Actor
Associated International Mgmt, 7 Hatton Garden, #400, London EC1N 8AD, England
**Waterman, Hannah** — Actress
Smith & Jones Mgmt, 74-78 Wentworth Ave, Sydney NSW 2000, Australia
**Waterman, Michael S** — Mathematician
University of Southern California, Mathematics Dept, Los Angeles CA 90089, USA
**Waterman, Pete** — Actor
Fremantle Media, 2700 Colorado Ave, #450, Santa Monica CA 90404 USA
**Waterman, Robert H** — Writer
Enterprise Media, 91 Harvey St, Cambridge MA 02140, USA
**Waters, Alice** — Chef
Chez Panisse, 1517 Shattuck Ave, Berkeley CA 94709, USA
**Waters, Brian D** — Football Player
6911 W 138th Terrace, Overland Park KS 66223, USA
**Waters, Charles T (Charlie)** — Football Player, Coach
9305 Moss Trail, Dallas TX 75231, USA
**Waters, Crystal** — Singer
AM/PM Entertainment Concepts, 415 63rd St, #200, Brooklyn NY 11220, USA
**Waters, Derek** — Actor
United Talent Agency, U T A Plaza, 9336 Civic Center Dr, Beverly Hills CA 90210 USA
**Waters, Dina** — Actress
Gersh Agency, 9465 Wilshire Blvd, #600, Beverly Hills CA 90212 USA
**Waters, Drew** — Actor, Model
A P A Talent & Literary Agency, 405 S Beverly Dr, #300, Beverly Hills CA 90212 USA
**Waters, John** — Director, Writer, Actor
United Talent Agency, U T A Plaza, 9336 Civic Center Dr, Beverly Hills CA 90210 USA
**Waters, John B** — Government Official
405 Burridge Waters Edge, Sevierville TN 37862, USA
**Waters, Lou** — Commentator
CNN-TV, News Dept, 190 Marietta Ave SW, Atlanta GA 30303 USA
**Waters, Mark** — Director, Producer, Writer
Creative Artists Agency, 2000 Ave of Stars, #100, Los Angeles CA 90067 USA
**Waters, Richard** — Publisher
13919 Woods Run Court, Centreville VA 20121, USA
**Waters, Roger** — Singer, Bassist (Pink Floyd)
One Fifteen, Globe House, Middle Lane Mews, London N8 8PN, England
**Waterston, Katherine** — Actress
United Talent Agency, U T A Plaza, 9336 Civic Center Dr, Beverly Hills CA 90210 USA
**Waterston, Sam** — Actor
Gersh Agency, 9465 Wilshire Blvd, #600, Beverly Hills CA 90212 USA
**Wathan, John D** — Baseball Player, Manager
1354 NE Todd George Road, Lees Summit MO 64086, USA
**Watkins, Calvert W** — Educator
University of California, Classics Dept, Los Angeles CA 90024, USA
**Watkins, Carlene** — Actress
Bresler Kelly Assoc, 11500 W Olympic Blvd, #400, Los Angeles CA 90064 USA
**Watkins, David R (Dave)** — Baseball Player
506 Ridgewood Road, Louisville KY 40207, USA
**Watkins, Dean A** — Inventor (Electron Tubes), Businessman
Watkins-Johnson Co, 401 River Oaks Parkway, San Jose CA 95134, USA
**Watkins, Hays T, Jr** — Businessman
2111 Cedarfield Lane, Henrico VA 23233, USA
**Watkins, Michael W** — Director, Producer
A P A Talent & Literary Agency, 405 S Beverly Dr, #300, Beverly Hills CA 90212 USA
**Watkins, Michaela S** — Actress, Comedienne, Producer
Evolution Entertainment, 901 N Highland Ave, Los Angeles CA 90038 USA
**Watkins, Michelle** — Actress
Capital Artists, 6404 Wilshire Blvd, #950, Los Angeles CA 90048, USA
**Watkins, Robert C (Bob)** — Baseball Player
4417 W 58th Place, Los Angeles CA 90043, USA
**Watkins, Robert L (Bobby)** — Football Player
1112 Devonshire Dr, DeSoto TX 75115, USA
**Watkins, Sammy** — Football Player
Buffalo Bills, 1 Bills Dr, Orchard Park NY 14127 USA
**Watkins, Sara U** — Singer, Fiddler (Nickel Creek)
Nonesuch Records, 75 Rockefeller Plaza, #800, New York NY 10019 USA
**Watkins, Scott A** — Baseball Player
14660 W 18th St, Sand Springs OK 74063, USA
**Watkins, Sean C** — Guitarist (Nickel Creek)
Q-Prime South, 131 S 11th St, Nashville TN 37206 USA
**Watkins, Simon C** — Immunologist
University of Pittsburgh Medical School, Immunology Dept, Pittsburgh PA 15260, USA
**Watkins, Steve** — Baseball Player
3408 Evanston Ave, Lubbock TX 79407, USA
**Watkins, Tionne (T-Boz)** — Rap Artist (TLC)
Venture I A B, 3211 Cahuenga Blvd W, #104, Los Angeles CA 90068, USA
**Watkins, Tuc** — Actor
Stone Manners Salners, 6100 Wilshire Blvd, #1500, Los Angeles CA 90035 USA
**Watley, Jody** — Singer
T C I, 1560 Broadway, #1308, New York NY 10036, USA
**Watling, Leonor** — Actress
A6 Cinema, Almirante 4, #3B, 28004 Madrid, Spain
**Watlington, J Neal** — Baseball Player
PO Box 418, Yanceyville NC 27379, USA
**Watney, Nicholas A (Nick)** — Golfer
816 Veramar Court, Henderson NV 89052, USA

| | |
|---|---|
| **Watrous, Cynthia** | Actress |
| Principal Entertainment, 9255 Sunset Blvd, #500, Los Angeles CA 90069 USA | |
| **Watrous, William R (Bill), Jr** | Jazz Trombonist |
| Thomas Cassidy, PO Box 1311, Tucson AZ 85702 USA | |
| **Watson Richardson, Lillian (Pokey)** | Swimmer |
| 4960 Maunalani Circle, Honolulu HI 96816, USA | |
| **Watson, Adrienne** | Actress, Comedienne |
| OmniPop Talent Group, 4605 Lankershim Blvd, #201, Toluca Lake CA 91602 USA | |
| **Watson, Albert M** | Photographer |
| 44 Laight St, #1A, New York NY 10013, USA | |
| **Watson, Alberta** | Actress |
| Gary Goddard Assoc, 10 Saint Mary St, #305, Toronto ON M4Y 1P9, Canada | |
| **Watson, Alexander F** | Diplomat |
| Nature Conservancy International, 4245 Fairfax Dr, #100, Arlington VA 22203, USA | |
| **Watson, Allen K** | Baseball Player |
| 6144 65th St, Middle Village NY 11379, USA | |
| **Watson, Barry** | Actor |
| Innovative Artists, 1505 10th St, Santa Monica CA 90401 USA | |
| **Watson, Benjamin S (Ben)** | Football Player |
| 12397 Steeplechase Lane, Strongsville OH 44149, USA | |
| **Watson, Bryan J** | Ice Hockey Player |
| 400 Madison St, Alexandria VA 22314, USA | |
| **Watson, Cecil J** | Physician |
| Abbott Northwestern Hospital, 2727 Chicago Ave, Minneapolis MN 55407, USA | |
| **Watson, Dale** | Singer |
| Davis McLarty Agency, 708 S Lamar Blvd, #D, Austin TX 78704, USA | |
| **Watson, Denis** | Golfer |
| 142 Segovia Way, Jupiter FL 33458, USA | |
| **Watson, E Bruce** | Environmentalist |
| Rensselaer Polytechnic Institute, Earth & Environmental Dept, Troy NY 12180, USA | |
| **Watson, Earl J** | Basketball Player |
| 4310 N Holly Court, Kansas City MO 64116, USA | |
| **Watson, Elizabeth M** | Law Enforcement Official |
| Houston Police Department, Chief's Office, 1200 Travis St, Houston TX 77002, USA | |
| **Watson, Emily** | Actress |
| Independent Talent Group, 40 Whitfield St, London W1T 2RH, England | |
| **Watson, Emma** | Actress, Model |
| Markham Froggatt Irwin, Julian House, 4 Windmill St, London W1P 1HF, England | |
| **Watson, Gene** | Singer, Guitarist |
| Lytle Management Group, PO Box 128228, Nashville TN 37212, USA | |
| **Watson, Gerry L (Bubba), Jr** | Golfer |
| Professional Golfers Association, 100 Ave of Champions, Palm Beach Gardens FL 33418 USA | |
| **Watson, Jack H, Jr** | Government Official |
| Long Aldridge Norman, 1900 K St NW, Washington DC 20006, USA | |
| **Watson, James A (Jim)** | Ice Hockey Player |
| 1702 Coventry Lane, Glen Mills PA 19342, USA | |
| **Watson, James D** | Nobel Medicine Laureate |
| Bungtown Road, Cold Spring Harbor NY 11724, USA | |
| **Watson, Jamie L** | Basketball Player |
| PO Box 761, Elm City NC 27822, USA | |
| **Watson, Jill** | Figure Skater |
| Desert Schools Coyote Center, 15829 N 83rd Ave, Peoria AZ 85382, USA | |
| **Watson, Kenneth M** | Physicist, Oceanographer |
| 8515 Costa Verde Blvd, #2008, San Diego CA 92122, USA | |
| **Watson, Lillian** | Opera Singer |
| I M G Artists, Hogarth Business Park, Chiswick, London W4 2TH, England | |
| **Watson, Mark** | Baseball Player |
| 555 Spender Trace, Atlanta GA 30350, USA | |
| **Watson, Martha** | Track Athlete |
| 5509 Royal Vista Lane, Las Vegas NV 89149, USA | |
| **Watson, Mills** | Actor |
| PO Box 600, Talent OR 97540, USA | |
| **Watson, Patrick** | Singer, Songwriter |
| Agency Group, 2 Berkeley St, #202, Toronto ON M5A 4J5, Canada | |
| **Watson, Patty Jo** | Anthropologist |
| Washington University, Anthropology Dept, PO Box 1114, Saint Louis MO 63188, USA | |
| **Watson, Paul** | Environmental Activist |
| Sea Shepherd Conservation Society, PO Box 2670, Malibu CA 90265, USA | |
| **Watson, Paul** | Photojournalist |
| Toronto Star, Editorial Dept, 1 Yonge St, Toronto ON M5E 1E6, Canada | |
| **Watson, Richard Jesse** | Illustrator |
| 2305 Ivy St, Port Townsend WA 98368, USA | |
| **Watson, Robert E (Bobby)** | Basketball Player |
| 1625 Sherwood Dr, Owensboro KY 42301, USA | |
| **Watson, Robert J (Bob)** | Baseball Player |
| 18103 Darling Point Court, Cypress TX 77429, USA | |
| **Watson, Robert M (Bobby), Jr** | Jazz Saxophonist |
| Hot Jazz Mgmt, 328 W 43rd St, #4FW, New York NY 10036, USA | |
| **Watson, Russell** | Singer |
| Sanctuary Artist Mgmt, 45-53 Sinclair Road, London W14 0NS, England | |
| **Watson, Stephen E** | Businessman |
| Dayton Hudson, 1000 Nicollet Mall, Minneapolis MN 55403, USA | |
| **Watson, Stephen R (Steve)** | Football Player |
| 4675 S Vine Way, Englewood CO 80113, USA | |
| **Watson, Thomas S (Tom)** | Golfer |
| 16104 Riggs Road, Stilwell KS 66085, USA | |
| **Watson, Tuc** | Actor, Producer |
| Stone Manners Salners, 6100 Wilshire Blvd, #1500, Los Angeles CA 90035 USA | |
| **Watson, Wayne** | Singer |
| T B A Artist Mgmt, 300 10th Ave S, Nashville TN 37203, USA | |
| **Watson, William C (Bill)** | Ice Hockey Player |
| 1725 Vermillon Road, Duluth MN 55803, USA | |
| **Watson-Johnson, Vernee** | Actress |
| C E S D, 10635 Santa Monica Blvd, #130, Los Angeles CA 90025 USA | |
| **Watt, Ben** | Guitarist, Singer, Songwriter |
| J F D Mgmt, Acklam Workshops, 10 Acklam Road, London W10 5QZ, England | |

**W**

**Watrous - Watt**

# W

**Watt, Edward D (Eddie)**  Baseball Player
940 Locust St, North Bend NE 68649, USA
**Watt, James G**  Secretary, Interior
PO Box 3705, Jackson Hole WY 83001, USA
**Watt, Michael D (Mike)**  Singer, Bassist (Porno for Pyros)
Agency Group Ltd, 142 W 57th St, #600, New York NY 10019 USA
**Watt, Tom**  Ice Hockey Coach
Calgary Flames, PO Box 1540, Station M, Calgary AB T2P 3B9, Canada
**Watt-Cloutier, Sheila**  Social Activist
Inuit Circumpolar, 170 Laurier Ave, #504, Ottawa ON K1P 5V5, Canada
**Wattelet, Frank L**  Football Player
4 Deer Run Dr, Joplin MO 64804, USA
**Wattenberg, Ben J**  Demographer
American Enterprise Institute, 1150 17th St NW, Washington DC 20036, USA
**Watters, Mark**  Composer, Conductor
Air Edel, 9100 Wilshire Blvd, #350E, Beverly Hills CA 90212 USA
**Watters, Richard J (Rickie)**  Football Player
6263 Cypress Chase Dr, Windermere FL 34786, USA
**Watters, Sam**  Singer (Color Me Badd)
J-Bird Entertainment, 4905 S Atlantic Ave, Ponce Inlet FL 32127 USA
**Watters, Tim**  Ice Hockey Player
2390 E Camelback Road, #100, Phoenix AZ 85016, USA
**Wattleton, A Faye**  Association Executive
Center for Advancement of Women, 165 W 46th St, #512, New York NY 10036, USA
**Watts, Andre**  Concert Pianist
C M Artists, 127 W 96th St, #13B, New York NY 10025 USA
**Watts, Charles E (Billy)**  WW II Navy Air Force Hero
4500 Alamance St, Baytown TX 77521, USA
**Watts, Charles R (Charlie)**  Drummer (Rolling Stones)
Rosebud Agency, PO Box 170429, San Francisco CA 94117 USA
**Watts, Daniele**  Actress
Anonymous Content, 3532 Hayden Ave, Culver City CA 90232 USA
**Watts, Donald E (Slick)**  Basketball Player
5015 256th Ave NE, Redmond WA 98053, USA
**Watts, Elizabeth**  Opera Singer
Ingpen & Williams, 131 Putney Bridge Road, London SW15 2PA, England
**Watts, Ernest J (Ernie)**  Jazz Saxophonist
Bates Meyer, PO Box 2821, Big Bear Lake CA 92315, USA
**Watts, Ernie**  Art Director, Stage Designer
I C M Partners, 730 5th Ave, New York NY 10019 USA
**Watts, Heather**  Ballerina
New York City Ballet, Lincoln Center Plaza, New York NY 10023 USA
**Watts, Julius Caesar (J C), Jr**  Representative, OK; Football Player
J C Watts Companies, 600 13th St NW, #790, Washington DC 20005, USA
**Watts, Lou**  Singer (Chumbawamba)
Doug Smith Assoc, PO Box 1151, London W3 8ZJ, England
**Watts, Naomi**  Actress
Untitled Entertainment, 350 S Beverly Dr, #200, Beverly Hills CA 90212 USA
**Watts, Quincy**  Track Athlete
H S International Sports Mgmt, 9871 Irvine Center Dr, Irvine CA 92618, USA
**Watts, Ronald M (Ron)**  Basketball Player
875 Grace St, #101, Herndon VA 20170, USA
**Waugh, Scott**  Director
W M E Entertainment, 9601 Wilshire Blvd, #300, Beverly Hills CA 90210 USA
**Waugh, Stephen R (Steve)**  Cricketer
Team-Duet, 3 Winnie St, Cremone NSW 2090, Australia
**Wauters, Ann H W**  Basketball Player
Seattle Storm, Key Arena, 351 Elliott Ave W, #500, Seattle WA 98119 USA
**Wax, Ruby**  Actress, Comedienne
United Agents, 12-26 Lexington St, London W1F 0LE, England
**Waxman, Seth P**  Government Official, Attorney
Wilmer Hale, 1875 Pennsylvania Ave NW, Washington DC 20006, USA
**Wayans, Damon**  Actor, Comedian, Writer, Producer
I C M Partners, 10250 Constellation Blvd, #900, Los Angeles CA 90067 USA
**Wayans, Damon, Jr**  Actor, Writer
Mosiac Media Group, 9200 W Sunset Blvd, #1000, Los Angeles CA 90069 USA
**Wayans, Dwayne**  Actor
16405 Mulholland Dr, Los Angeles CA 90049, USA
**Wayans, Keenen Ivory**  Actor, Director
Wayans Brothers Entertainment, 8730 W Sunset Blvd, #290, Los Angeles CA 90069, USA
**Wayans, Kim**  Actress, Writer, Director
A P A Talent & Literary Agency, 405 S Beverly Dr, #300, Beverly Hills CA 90212 USA
**Wayans, Marlon**  Actor, Comedian
Wayans Brothers Entertainment, 8730 W Sunset Blvd, #290, Los Angeles CA 90069, USA
**Wayans, Shawn**  Actor
Wayans Brothers Entertainment, 8730 W Sunset Blvd, #290, Los Angeles CA 90069, USA
**Wayda, Stephen**  Photographer
Celebrity Pictures, 5757 Wilshire Blvd, Beverly Hills CA 90210, USA
**Wayne, Gary A**  Baseball Player
5762 W Ashbury Place, Lakewood CO 80227, USA
**Wayne, Jimmy**  Singer, Songwriter
W M E Entertainment, 1600 Division St, #300, Nashville TN 37203 USA
**Wayne, John Ethan**  Actor
Wayne Enterprises, 210 62nd St, Newport Beach CA 92663, USA
**Wayne, Nathaniel (Nate), Jr**  Football Player
2878 Grey Moss Pass, Duluth GA 30097, USA
**Wayne, Patrick J**  Actor
10502 Whipple St, Toluca Lake CA 91602, USA
**Wayne, Reggie**  Football Player
17000 Berkshire Court, Southwest Ranches FL 33331, USA
**Wearing, Gillian**  Artist
Maureen Paley Interim Art, 21 Herald St, London E2 6JT, England
**Weary, J Fredrick (Fred)**  Football Player
11315 Sailwing Creek Court, Pearland TX 77584, USA
**Weatherall, David J**  Hematologist
8 Cumnor Rise Road, Cumnor Hill, Oxford OX2 9HD, England

|  |  |
|---|---|
| **Weatherly, Michael**<br>Anonymous Content, 3532 Hayden Ave, Culver City CA 90232 USA | Actor |
| **Weatherly, Shawn N**<br>Connor Ankrum Assoc, 1680 Vine St, #1016, Los Angeles CA 90028, USA | Actress, Beauty Queen |
| **Weatherman, Woodroe (Woody)**<br>Chipster, 100 Village Square Crossing, Palm Beach Gardens FL 33410 USA | Guitarist (Corrosion of Conformity) |
| **Weathers, Carl**<br>2228 Walnut Ave, Venice CA 90291, USA | Actor, Football Player |
| **Weathers, J David (Dave)**<br>979 Lexington Highway, Loretto TN 38469, USA | Baseball Player |
| **Weatherspoon, Clarence**<br>PO Box 117, Crawford MS 39743, USA | Basketball Player |
| **Weatherspoon, Teresa G**<br>Los Angeles Sparks, 888 S Figueroa St, #2010, Los Angeles CA 90017 USA | Basketball Player |
| **Weatherston, Katie**<br>Team Canada, 2424 University Dr NW, Calgary AB T2N 3Y9, Canada | Ice Hockey Player |
| **Weaver, Al**<br>Julian Belfrage Assoc, 9 Argyll St, #300, London W1F 7TG, England | Actor |
| **Weaver, Charles E (Charlie)**<br>309 W Muncie Ave, Fresno CA 93711, USA | Football Player |
| **Weaver, DeWitt**<br>Weaver Golf Solutions, 5640 Golf Club Dr, Braselton GA 30517, USA | Golfer |
| **Weaver, Fritz**<br>161 W 75th St, #15A, New York NY 10023, USA | Actor |
| **Weaver, Gary L**<br>3496 Arden Road, Hayward CA 94545, USA | Football Player |
| **Weaver, J Eric**<br>2641 Weaver Road, Illiopolis IL 62539, USA | Baseball Player |
| **Weaver, James**<br>3438 Admiralty Lane, Indianapolis IN 46240, USA | Cartoonist |
| **Weaver, Jason**<br>Luber Rocklin Entertainment, 5815 Sunset Blvd, #206, Los Angeles CA 90028 USA | Actor |
| **Weaver, Jered D**<br>1204 Suncast Lane, #2, El Dorado Hills CA 95762, USA | Baseball Player |
| **Weaver, Michael**<br>Brillstein Entertainment Partners, 9150 Wilshire Blvd, #350, Beverly Hills CA 90212 USA | Actor |
| **Weaver, Reg**<br>National Education Assn, 1201 16th St NW, Washington DC 20036, USA | Labor Leader |
| **Weaver, Roger E**<br>65 Moyer St, Canajoharie NY 13317, USA | Baseball Player |
| **Weaver, Sigourney**<br>Arcieri Assoc, 305 Madison Ave, #2315, New York NY 10165 USA | Actress |
| **Weaver, T Jed**<br>39725 Layng Creek Road, Dorena OR 97434, USA | Football Player |
| **Weaver, W Herman**<br>8105 Hamilton Mill Dr, Chattanooga TN 37421, USA | Football Player |
| **Weaver, Warren E**<br>7607 Horsepen Road, Richmond VA 23229, USA | Chemist |
| **Weaving, Hugo**<br>Shanahan Mgmt, 91 Campbell St, #300, Surry Hills NSW 2010, Australia | Actor |
| **Webb, Alexander D (Alex)**<br>151 W 25th St, New York NY 10001, USA | Photographer |
| **Webb, Anthony J (Spud)**<br>1453 Mosslake Dr, DeSoto TX 75115, USA | Basketball Player |
| **Webb, Brandon T**<br>8814 E Ann Way, Scottsdale AZ 85260, USA | Baseball Player |
| **Webb, Chloe**<br>PO Box 2824, Venice CA 90294, USA | Actress |
| **Webb, Christiaan**<br>SuperVision Mgmt, 109B Regents Park Road, London NW1 8UR, England | Singer, Musician, Songwriter |
| **Webb, Derek W**<br>Dryve Artist Mgmt, 510A E Iris Dr, Nashville TN 37204, USA | Singer, Guitarist (Caedmon's Call) |
| **Webb, Donald W (Don)**<br>906 Roland Court, Jefferson City MO 65101, USA | Football Player |
| **Webb, Henry G (Hank)**<br>4527 Lake Valencia Blvd W, Palm Harbor FL 34684, USA | Baseball Player |
| **Webb, James R (Jimmy)**<br>1319 S Prairie Flower Road, Turlock CA 95380, USA | Football Player |
| **Webb, Jimmy**<br>1560 N Laurel Ave, #109, Los Angeles CA 90046, USA | Singer, Songwriter |
| **Webb, Justin**<br>SuperVision Mgmt, 109B Regents Park Road, London NW1 8UR, England | Singer, Musician, Songwriter |
| **Webb, Karrie**<br>725 Presidential Dr, Boynton Beach FL 33435, USA | Golfer |
| **Webb, Lardarius**<br>Baltimore Ravens, Ravens Stadium, 1 Winning Dr, Baltimore MD 21230 USA | Football Playeer |
| **Webb, Lee**<br>700 Club, 977 Centerville Turnpike, Virginia Beach VA 23463, USA | Evangelist, Commentator |
| **Webb, Marc**<br>Creative Artists Agency, 2000 Ave of Stars, #100, Los Angeles CA 90067 USA | Director |
| **Webb, Richmond J**<br>4120 Humphrey Dr, Dallas TX 75216, USA | Football Player |
| **Webb, Russell (Russ)**<br>611 Knob Hill Ave, Redondo Beach CA 90277, USA | Water Polo Player |
| **Webb, Sarah K**<br>Lynx Sports Mgmt, Lymington Road, Lymington, Hampshire SO41 5S5, England | Yachtswoman |
| **Webb, Steve**<br>27 Barberry Lane, Center Moriches NY 11934, USA | Ice Hockey Player |
| **Webb, Tamilee**<br>1770 Haydn Dr, Cardiff By The Sea CA 92007, USA | Physical Fitness Instructor |
| **Webb, Veronica**<br>Don Buchwald Talent Agency, 10 E 44th St, New York NY 10017 USA | Model, Actress |
| **Webb, Watt W**<br>Cornell University, BioPhysics Program, Ithaca NY 14853, USA | Applied Physicist |
| **Webb, Wayne**<br>5850 Freeport Blvd, Sacramento CA 95822, USA | Bowler |

**W**

| | |
|---|---|
| **Webber, Julian Lloyd**<br>I M G Artists, Hogarth Business Park, Chiswick, London W4 2TH, England | Concert Cellist |
| **Webber, Mark**<br>W M E Entertainment, 9601 Wilshire Blvd, #300, Beverly Hills CA 90210 USA | Actor, Producer, Writer |
| **Webber, Mark A**<br>Octagon, Royal Naval House, 32 Grosvenor St, Rocks, Sydney NSW 2000, Australia | Auto Racing Driver |
| **Webber, Peter**<br>United Agents, 12-26 Lexington St, London W1F 0LE, England | Director |
| **Webber, Tristan**<br>Brower Lewis Public Relations, 74 Gloucester Place, London W1H 3HN, England | Fashion Designer |
| **Weber, Arnold R**<br>Northwestern University, Chancellor's Office, Evanston IL 60208, USA | Educator |
| **Weber, Ben**<br>5550 Baird St, Groves TX 77619, USA | Baseball Player |
| **Weber, Ben, Jr**<br>King Features Syndicate, 300 W 57th St, #1500, New York NY 10019 USA | Cartoonist |
| **Weber, Bernard**<br>New7Wonders Foundation, PO Box 1212, 8034 Zurich, Switzerland | Explorer, Filmmaker |
| **Weber, Bruce**<br>Little Bear, 135 Watts St, #5, New York NY 10013, USA | Photographer |
| **Weber, Bruce**<br>University of Illinois, Athletic Dept, Assembly Hall, Champaign IL 61820, USA | Basketball Coach |
| **Weber, Charles F (Chuck), Jr**<br>12740 Cobblestone Creek Road, Poway CA 92064, USA | Football Player |
| **Weber, Charlie**<br>Warren Cowan Assoc, 8899 Beverly Blvd, #918, Los Angeles CA 90048, USA | Actor |
| **Weber, Eberhard**<br>Ted Kurland, 173 Brighton Ave, Boston MA 02134 USA | Jazz Bassist, Cellist, Composer |
| **Weber, Emmanuelle**<br>Artmedia, 20 Ave Rapp, 75007 Paris, France | Actress |
| **Weber, George B**<br>Chemin Moise-Duboule 19, 1209 Geneva, Switzerland | Association Executive |
| **Weber, Holly**<br>Webland Entertainment, 1235 W Balboa Blvd, Newport Beach CA 92661, USA | Actress, Model |
| **Weber, J Vincent (Vin)**<br>Clark & Weinstock, 601 13th St NW, #410S, Washington DC 20005, USA | Representative, MN |
| **Weber, Jack**<br>C E S D, 10635 Santa Monica Blvd, #130, Los Angeles CA 90025 USA | Actor |
| **Weber, Jacques**<br>U B B A, 6 Rue de Braque, 75003 Paris, France | Actor, Director, Writer |
| **Weber, Jake**<br>Paradigm Agency, 360 N Crescent Dr, North Building, Beverly Hills CA 90210 USA | Actor |
| **Weber, Joseph F**<br>Commanding General, 3rd Marine Expeditionary Force Okinawa, FPO AP 96602 USA | Marine Corps General |
| **Weber, Mary E**<br>14 Hawkview St, Portola Valley CA 94028, USA | Astronaut |
| **Weber, Neil A**<br>1 Morning View, Irvine CA 92603, USA | Baseball Player |
| **Weber, Peter**<br>Hermsdorfer Str 112, 16552 Schildow, Germany | Gymnast |
| **Weber, Peter D (Pete)**<br>10500 Saint Xavier Lane, Saint Ann MO 63074, USA | Bowler |
| **Weber, Robert M (Bob)**<br>New Yorker, Editorial Dept, 4 Times Square, Basement C1B, New York NY 10036 USA | Cartoonist |
| **Weber, Shea M**<br>4527 Yancey Dr, Nashville TN 37215, USA | Ice Hockey Player |
| **Weber, Stephen L**<br>San Diego State University, President's Office, San Diego CA 92182, USA | Educator |
| **Weber, Steven**<br>Brillstein Entertainment Partners, 9150 Wilshire Blvd, #350, Beverly Hills CA 90212 USA | Actor |
| **Webre, Septime**<br>Washington Ballet, 3515 Wisconsin Ave NW, Washington DC 20016, USA | Choreographer |
| **Webster, Corey J**<br>66 Mallard Place, Secaucus NJ 07094, USA | Football Player |
| **Webster, James**<br>Cornell University, Music Dept, Ithaca NY 14853, USA | Musicologist |
| **Webster, Jeffrey T (Jeff)**<br>10405 SE 15th St, Oklahoma City OK 73130, USA | Basketball Player |
| **Webster, Larry M, Jr**<br>12 Oakridge Court, Elkton MD 21921, USA | Football Player |
| **Webster, Leonard N (Lenny)**<br>6211 Bridgeport Dr, Charlotte NC 28215, USA | Baseball Player |
| **Webster, Martell**<br>Washington Wizards, M C I Centre, 601 F St NW, Washington DC 20004 USA | Basketball Player |
| **Webster, Mitchell D (Mitch)**<br>3120 NE 91st Terrace, Kansas City MO 64156, USA | Baseball Player |
| **Webster, Robert D (Bob)**<br>269 Hacienda Carmel, Carmel CA 93923, USA | Diver |
| **Webster, Tom**<br>1750 Longfellow Dr, Canton MI 48187, USA | Ice Hockey Player |
| **Webster, Victor**<br>Innovative Artists, 1505 10th St, Santa Monica CA 90401 USA | Actor |
| **Webster, William G**<br>Commander, Army Central, Camp Arifjan Kuwait, APO AE 09306, USA | Army General |
| **Webster, William H**<br>4777 Dexter St NW, Washington DC 20007, USA | Law Enforcement Official |
| **Wechsler, Nick**<br>Defining Artists Agency, 4370 Tujunga Ave, #120, Studio City CA 91604 USA | Actor |
| **Wecker, Andreas**<br>Am Dorfplatz 1, 16766 Klein-Ziethen, Germany | Gymnast |
| **Wecker, Kendra**<br>San Antonio Silver Stars, 1 AT&T Center, San Antonio TX 78219 USA | Basketball Player |
| **Weddington, Michael W (Mike)**<br>237 Sycamore Grove St, Simi Valley CA 93065, USA | Football Player |
| **Weddington, Sarah R**<br>Weddington Center, 709 W 14th St, Austin TX 78701, USA | Attorney |

| | |
|---|---|
| **Wedel, Dieter** | Director |
| Nibelungenfestspiele, Von-Steuben-Str 5, 67549 Worms, Germany | |
| **Wedge, Chris** | Animator, Director, Producer |
| Blue Sky Studios, 1 American Lane, Greenwich CT 06831, USA | |
| **Wedge, Eric M** | Baseball Player, Manager |
| 25 Old Post Road, Lancaster NY 14086, USA | |
| **Wedgeworth, Ann** | Actress |
| 70 Riverside Dr, New York NY 10024, USA | |
| **Wedman, Scott D** | Basketball Player |
| 7912 NW Scenic Dr, Kansas City MO 64152, USA | |
| **Weed, Maurice James** | Composer |
| 308 Overlook Road, #55, Asheville NC 28803, USA | |
| **Weedman, Lauren** | Actress |
| United Talent Agency, U T A Plaza, 9336 Civic Center Dr, Beverly Hills CA 90210 USA | |
| **Weekes, Stephen K (Steve)** | Ice Hockey Player |
| 2883 Thurleston Lane, Duluth GA 30097, USA | |
| **Weekley, Thomas B (Boo)** | Golfer |
| 2555 New York St, Jay FL 32565, USA | |
| **Weeks, Ed** | Actor |
| W M E Entertainment, 9601 Wilshire Blvd, #300, Beverly Hills CA 90210 USA | |
| **Weeks, Honeysuckle** | Actress |
| Artists Partnership, 101 Finsbury Pavement, London EC2A 1RS, England | |
| **Weeks, Jared** | Singer (Saving Abel), Songwriter |
| Virgin Records, 338 N Foothill Road, Beverly Hills CA 90210 USA | |
| **Weeks, John D** | Chemist |
| 15301 Watergate Road, Silver Spring MD 20905, USA | |
| **Weeks, John R** | Architect |
| 39 Jackson's Lane, Highgate, London N6 5SR, England | |
| **Weeks, Kent R** | Archaeologist |
| American University, 113 Kar El Aini St, Cairo 11511, Egypt | |
| **Weeks, Perdita** | Actress |
| Troika, 74 Clerkenwell Road, #300, London EC1M 5QA, England | |
| **Weeks, Rickie D** | Baseball Player |
| 7473 Park Springs Circle, Orlando FL 32835, USA | |
| **Weeks, Wendell** | Businessman |
| Corning Inc, Houghton Park, Corning NY 14931, USA | |
| **Ween, Dean** | Singer, Guitarist (Ween) |
| High Road Touring, 751 Bridgeway, #200, Sausalito CA 94965 USA | |
| **Ween, Gene** | Singer, Guitarst (Ween) |
| High Road Touring, 751 Bridgeway, #200, Sausalito CA 94965 USA | |
| **Weese, Miranda** | Ballerina |
| New York City Ballet, Lincoln Center Plaza, New York NY 10023 USA | |
| **Weger, Michael R (Mike)** | Football Player |
| 825 Markwood Dr, Oxford MS 38655, USA | |
| **Wegman, William E (Bill)** | Baseball Player |
| 20521 Heather Court, Lawrenceburg IN 47025, USA | |
| **Wegman, William G** | Artist, Photographer |
| 239 W 18th St, New York NY 10011, USA | |
| **Wegner, Mark P** | Baseball Umpire |
| 1722 Open Field Loop, Brandon FL 33510, USA | |
| **Wegner, Paul D** | Sculptor |
| PO Box 603, Prather CA 93651, USA | |
| **Wegryn Gross, Halley** | Actress |
| Innovative Artists, 1505 10th St, Santa Monica CA 90401 USA | |
| **Wehling, Ulrich** | Nordic Combined Athlete |
| Skiverband, Hubertusstr 1, 81477 Munich, Germany | |
| **Wehner, John P** | Baseball Player |
| 105 Avery's Way, Cranberry Township PA 16066, USA | |
| **Wehrli, Roger R** | Football Player |
| 204 Fox Haven Court, O'Fallon MO 63368, USA | |
| **Wehrmeister, David T (Dave)** | Baseball Player |
| 115 Sharene Lane, #20, Walnut Creek CA 94596, USA | |
| **Wei Hui** | Writer |
| Pocket Books, 1230 Ave of Americas, New York NY 10020 USA | |
| **Wei, James** | Chemical Engineer |
| 571 Lake St, Princeton NJ 08540, USA | |
| **Weibel, Ewald R** | Biologist |
| University of Berne, Biology Dept, Hochshulstr 4, 3012 Berne, Switzerland | |
| **Weibel, Robert** | Pediatrician |
| University of Pennsylvania Medical School, Pediatrics Dept, Philadelphia PA 19104, USA | |
| **Weibring, D A** | Golfer |
| 5865 Versailles Ave, Frisco TX 75034, USA | |
| **Weicker, Lowell P, Jr** | Governor, Senator, CT |
| PO Box 877, Old Lyme CT 06371, USA | |
| **Weida, Johnny A** | Air Force General, Educator |
| Deputy Chief of Staff, Operations Plans, HqUSA, Pentagon, Washington DC 20310 USA | |
| **Weide, Robert B** | Director, Writer |
| Whyaduck Productions, 4804 Laurel Canyon Blvd, PMB 502, North Hollywood CA 91607, USA | |
| **Weidinger, Christine** | Opera Singer |
| Robert Lombardo Assoc, Harkness Plaza, 61 W 62nd St, #6F, New York NY 10023 USA | |
| **Weidner, Bert J** | Football Player |
| 517 NW 106th Ave, Plantation FL 33324, USA | |
| **Weidner, Brant** | Basketball Player |
| 1111 Colfax St, Evanston IL 60201, USA | |
| **Weigand, Cary Lathan** | Artist |
| 12715 Upper Smith River Road, Drain OR 97435, USA | |
| **Weigel, Teri** | Actress, Model |
| 6433 Topanga Canyon Blvd, #103, Woodland Hills CA 91303, USA | |
| **Weigert, Robin** | Actress |
| Innovative Artists, 1505 10th St, Santa Monica CA 90401 USA | |
| **Weight, Douglas D (Doug)** | Ice Hockey Player |
| 72 Feeks Lane, Locust Valley NY 11560, USA | |
| **Weihenmayer, Erik** | Mountaineer |
| 682 Partridge Circle, Golden CO 80403, USA | |
| **Weikl, Bernd** | Opera Singer |
| Opera et Concert, 37 Rue de la Chaussee d'Antin, 75009 Paris, France | |

**Weil, Andrew** — Physician
1670 N Kolb Road, #240, Tucson AZ 85715, USA

**Weil, Bruno** — Conductor, Composer
Ingpen & Williams, 131 Putney Bridge Road, London SW15 2PA, England

**Weil, Cynthia** — Songwriter
Gorfaine/Schwartz, 4111 W Alameda Ave, #509, Burbank CA 91505 USA

**Weil, Frank A** — Association Executive
Smithsonian Institution, 900 Jefferson Dr SW, Washington DC 20560, USA

**Weil, Liza** — Actress
Principal Entertainment, 9255 Sunset Blvd, #500, Los Angeles CA 90069 USA

**Weiland, John H** — Businessman
C F Bard Co, 730 Central Ave, Murray Hill NJ 07974, USA

**Weiland, Paul** — Director
I C M Partners, 10250 Constellation Blvd, #900, Los Angeles CA 90067 USA

**Weiland, Scott** — Singer (Stone Temple Pilots), Songwriter
Brillstein Entertainment Partners, 9150 Wilshire Blvd, #350, Beverly Hills CA 90212 USA

**Weilerstein, Alisa** — Concert Cellist
Opus 3 Artists, 470 Park Ave S, #900N, New York NY 10016 USA

**Weill, David (Dave)** — Track Athlete
120 Mountain Spring Ave, San Francisco CA 94114, USA

**Weill, Sanford I (Sandy)** — Businessman
Citigroup Inc, 55 E 52nd St, New York NY 10055, USA

**Wein, George** — Musical Producer
Festival Productions, 30 Irving Place, #600, New York NY 10003, USA

**Weinbach, Lawrence A** — Businessman
Unisys Corp, Unisys Way, Blue Bell PA 19424, USA

**Weinberg, Gerhard L** — Historian
1416 Mount Willing Road, Efland NC 27243, USA

**Weinberg, Max** — Drummer (E-Street Band)
2 Bayside Dr, Atlantic Highlands NJ 07716, USA

**Weinberg, Mike** — Actor
Innovative Artists, 1505 10th St, Santa Monica CA 90401 USA

**Weinberg, Robert A** — Cancer Researcher, Biochemist
Whitehead Institute, 9 Cambridge Center, Cambridge MA 02142, USA

**Weinberg, Steven** — Nobel Physics Laureate
University of Texas, Physics Dept, 2613 Wichita St, Austin TX 78712, USA

**Weinbrecht, Donna** — Freestyle Moguls Skier
177 High Crest Dr, West Milford NJ 07480, USA

**Weiner, Erik** — Writer, Producer, Commentator
Bleeker Street Entertainment, 853 Broadway, #1214, New York NY 10003, USA

**Weiner, Gerald (Gerry)** — Government Official, Canada
40 Fredmir St, Dollard-des-Ormeaux QC H9A 2R3, Canada

**Weiner, Jennifer** — Writer
BenderSpink, 8447 Wilshire Blvd, #250, Beverly Hills CA 90211 USA

**Weiner, Matthew** — Producer, Writer
Creative Artists Agency, 2000 Ave of Stars, #100, Los Angeles CA 90067 USA

**Weiner, Mel** — Artist
Silverlake Mosaics, 1809 San Jacinto St, Los Angeles CA 90026, USA

**Weiner, Timothy E (Tim)** — Journalist
New York Times, Editorial Dept, 1627 I St NW, #700, Washington DC 20006, USA

**Weingarten, David M** — Architect
332 2nd St, Oakland CA 94607, USA

**Weingarten, Gene** — Journalist
Washington Post, Editorial Dept, 1150 15th St NW, Washington DC 20071 USA

**Weingarten, Randi** — Labor Leader, Educator
American Federation of Teachers, 555 New Jersey Ave NW, Washington DC 20001, USA

**Weingarten, Reid H** — Attorney
Steptoe & Johnson, 1330 Connecticut Ave NW, Washington DC 20036, USA

**Weinger, Scott** — Actor, Producer, Writer
W M E Entertainment, 9601 Wilshire Blvd, #300, Beverly Hills CA 90210 USA

**Weinhold, Matt** — Actor, Comedian
OmniPop Talent Group, 4605 Lankershim Blvd, #201, Toluca Lake CA 91602 USA

**Weinke, Christopher J (Chris)** — Football Player
12504 Portmarnock Court, Charlotte NC 28277, USA

**Weinman, Rosalyn (Roz)** — Producer, Writer
United Talent Agency, U T A Plaza, 9336 Civic Center Dr, Beverly Hills CA 90210 USA

**Weinrich, Eric J** — Ice Hockey Player
337 Sea Meadows Lane, Yarmouth ME 04096, USA

**Weinstein, Diane Gilbert** — Judge
US Court of Claims, 717 Madison Place NW, Washington DC 20439, USA

**Weinstein, Harvey** — Producer
Weinstein Company, 345 Hudson St, #1300, New York NY 10014, USA

**Weinstein, Jack B** — Judge
US District Court, US Courthouse, 225 Cadman Plaza E, Brooklyn NY 11201, USA

**Weinstein, Paula** — Producer
Tribeca Enterprises, 375 Greenwich St, New York NY 10013, USA

**Weintraub, Jerry** — Producer
Jerry Weintraub Productions, 190 N Canon Dr, #204, Beverly Hills CA 90210, USA

**Weir, Alex** — Guitarist (Brothers Johnson)
Green Light Talent Agency, PO Box 3172, Beverly Hills CA 90212 USA

**Weir, Gillian C** — Concert Organist, Harpsichordist
Denny Lyster Artists, PO Box 155, Stanmore HA1 3WF, England

**Weir, John G (Johnny)** — Figure Skater
Global Artists Agency, 6253 Hollywood Blvd, #508, Los Angeles CA 90028 USA

**Weir, Judith** — Composer
Chester Music, 14-15 Berners St, London W1T 3LJ, England

**Weir, Mike** — Golfer
2960 Oberland Road, Sandy UT 84092, USA

**Weir, Peter L** — Director, Writer
Australian Director's Guild, PO Box 211, Rozelle, Sydney NSW 2039, Australia

**Weir, Stephinie C** — Actress, Comedienne
United Talent Agency, U T A Plaza, 9336 Civic Center Dr, Beverly Hills CA 90210 USA

**Weir, Wally** — Ice Hockey Player
448 Lakeshore Road, Beaconsfield QC H9W 4J5, Canada

**Weir, William F (Bill)** — Commentator
CNN-TV, News Dept, 820 1st St NE, #1000, Washington DC 20002 USA

**Weis, Albert J (Al)** — Baseball Player
902 S Poplar Ave, Elmhurst IL 60126, USA
**Weis, Charles J (Charlie)** — Football Coach
University of Kansas, Athletic Dept, Lawrence KS 66045, USA
**Weis, Heidelinde** — Actress
Agentur Alexander, Lamontstr 9, 81679 Munich, Germany
**Weisacosky, Edward L (Ed)** — Football Player
3291 2nd Ave SE, Naples FL 34117, USA
**Weisberg, Ruth E** — Artist
11452 W Washington Blvd, Los Angeles CA 90066, USA
**Weisberger, Lauren** — Writer, Actress
Simon & Schuster, 1230 Ave of Americas, Concourse 1, New York NY 10020 USA
**Weisel, Heidi** — Fashion Designer
Heidi Weisel Inc, 420 W 14th St, #4SE, New York NY 10014, USA
**Weishoff, Paula** — Volleyball Player
20021 Colgate Circle, Huntington Beach CA 92646, USA
**Weishuhn, Clayton C (Clay)** — Football Player
4521 Kropala Road, San Angelo TX 76905, USA
**Weiskopf, Tom** — Golfer
Weiskopf Designs, 20875 N Pima Road, #C4-173, Scottsdale AZ 85255, USA
**Weiskrantz, Lawrence** — Psychologist
Oxford University, Experimental Psychology Dept, Oxford OX1 3UD, England
**Weisman, Annie** — Actress, Producer, Writer
W M E Entertainment, 9601 Wilshire Blvd, #300, Beverly Hills CA 90210 USA
**Weisman, Sam** — Actor, Director, Producer
United Talent Agency, U T A Plaza, 9336 Civic Center Dr, Beverly Hills CA 90210 USA
**Weiss, Avi** — Religious Leader, Rabbi
Hebrew Institute of Riverdale, 3700 Henry Hudson Parkway, Bronx NY 10463, USA
**Weiss, Brian L** — Psychotherapist, Writer
Weiss Institute, PO Box 560788, Miami FL 33256, USA
**Weiss, Cole Evan** — Actor
Greene Assoc, 1901 Ave of Stars, #130, Los Angeles CA 90067 USA
**Weiss, Daniel B (D B)** — Producer, Writer
Creative Artists Agency, 2000 Ave of Stars, #100, Los Angeles CA 90067 USA
**Weiss, David (David Was)** — Musician (Was Not Was), Songwriter
United Talent Agency, U T A Plaza, 9336 Civic Center Dr, Beverly Hills CA 90210 USA
**Weiss, Janet** — Singer, Drummer (Sleater-Kinney)
High Road Touring, 751 Bridgeway, #200, Sausalito CA 94965 USA
**Weiss, Julie** — Costume Designer
I C M Partners, 10250 Constellation Blvd, #900, Los Angeles CA 90067 USA
**Weiss, Kenneth R** — Journalist
Los Angeles Times, Editorial Dept, 202 W 1st St, Los Angeles CA 90012 USA
**Weiss, Margaret** — Writer
T S R, PO Box 707, Renton WA 98057, USA
**Weiss, Marion** — Architect, Sculptor
Weiss/Manfredi, 130 W 29th St, #1200, New York NY 10001, USA
**Weiss, Mary** — Singer (Shangri-Las)
Norton Records, PO Box 646, Cooper Station, New York NY 10276, USA
**Weiss, Michael** — Figure Skater
5301 Wisconsin Ave NW, #425, Washington DC 20015, USA
**Weiss, Michael T** — Actor, Director
Robert Stein Mgmt, 1180 S Beverly Drive, #304, Los Angeles CA 90035, USA
**Weiss, Mitch** — Journalist
Toledo Blade, 541 N Superior St, Toledo OH 43660 USA
**Weiss, Orion** — Concert Pianist
I M G Artists, Hogarth Business Park, Chiswick, London W4 2TH, England
**Weiss, Rob** — Producer, Writer, Actor
United Talent Agency, U T A Plaza, 9336 Civic Center Dr, Beverly Hills CA 90210 USA
**Weiss, Robert W (Bob)** — Basketball Player, Coach
3309 E Saint Andrews Way, Seattle WA 98112, USA
**Weiss, Stephen** — Ice Hockey Player
1346 Washington Blvd, Birmingham MI 48009, USA
**Weiss, Walter W** — Baseball Player, Manager
1275 Castle Point Dr, Castle Rock CO 80104, USA
**Weissenbach, Jean** — Geneticist
Genoscope, 2 Rue Gaston Cremieur, 91006 Evry Cedex, France
**Weissensteiner, Gerda** — Luge, Bobsled Athlete
Olympic Committee, Foro Italico, Largo Lauro de Bosis 15, 00135 Rome, Italy
**Weissflog, Jens** — Ski Jumper
Agentur Koster, Lubecker Str 6A, 23909 Ratzeburg, Germany
**Weissman, Irving L** — Cancer Biologist, Pathologist
Stanford University, Pathology Dept, Beckman Center, Stanford CA 94305, USA
**Weissman, Robert** — Businessman
I M S Health Inc, 1499 Post Road, #12, Fairfield CT 06824, USA
**Weisz, Rachel** — Actress
Independent Talent Group, 40 Whitfield St, London W1T 2RH, England
**Weithaas, Antje** — Concert Violinist
C L B Mgmt, 28 Earlswood Road, London NW10 5QB, England
**Weithorn, Michael J** — Director, Writer
I C M Partners, 10250 Constellation Blvd, #900, Los Angeles CA 90067 USA
**Weitz, Bruce** — Actor
18826 Erwin St, Tarzana CA 91335, USA
**Weitz, Patricia** — Writer
Riverhead/Penguin Books, 375 Hudson St, Basement 1, New York NY 10014, USA
**Weitz, Paul** — Director, Producer, Actor
Depth of Field, 1724 Whitley Ave, Los Angeles CA
**Weitz, Paul J** — Astronaut
3086 N Tam O'Shanter Dr, Flagstaff AZ 86004, USA
**Weitzman, Howard L** — Attorney
2049 Central Park East, #1400, Los Angeles CA 90067, USA
**Weitzman, Matt** — Producer, Writer, Actor
Creative Artists Agency, 2000 Ave of Stars, #100, Los Angeles CA 90067 USA
**Weitzman, Richard L (Rick)** — Basketball Player
76 Birch St, Peabody MA 01960, USA
**Weitzman, Susan** — Writer, Psychotherapist
25 E Washington St, #2005, Chicago IL 60602, USA

Weis - Weitzman

**Weixler, Jess** — Actress, Writer
Gersh Agency, 9465 Wilshire Blvd, #600, Beverly Hills CA 90212 USA

**Weizenbaum, Zoe** — Actress
Innovative Artists, 1505 10th St, Santa Monica CA 90401 USA

**Welbourn, John R** — Football Player
3301 Palos Verdes Dr N, Palos Verdes Estates CA 90274, USA

**Welch, Florence** — Singer (Florence & the Machine)
Universal-Island Records, 22 Saint Peters Square, London W6 9NW, England

**Welch, Gillian** — Singer, Banjoist, Songwriter
Q Prime, 729 7th Ave, #1600, New York NY 10019 USA

**Welch, Herbert D (Herb), Jr** — Football Player
999 La Senda, Santa Barbara CA 93105, USA

**Welch, Jack** — Astronomer
University of California, Electrical Engineering Dept, Berkeley CA 94720, USA

**Welch, John F, Jr** — Businessman
3135 Easton Turnpike, Fairfield CT 06828, USA

**Welch, Justin** — Drummer (Elastica)
C M O Mgmt, Ransomes Dock, 35-37 Parkgate Road, London SW11 4NP, England

**Welch, Kevin** — Singer, Songwriter
Asgard Promotions, 125 Parkway, London NW1 7PS, England

**Welch, Larry D** — Air Force General
Henry L Stimson Center, 1111 19th St NW, #1200, Washington DC 20036, USA

**Welch, Lenny** — Singer
Lustig Talent, PO Box 770850, Orlando FL 32877 USA

**Welch, Lisa** — Model
Playboy Promotions, 9346 Civic Center Dr, #200, Beverly Hills CA 90210 USA

**Welch, Michael** — Actor
Curtis Talent Mgmt, 9607 Arby Dr, Beverly HIlls CA 90210, USA

**Welch, Raquel** — Actress
Innovative Artists, 1505 10th St, Santa Monica CA 90401 USA

**Welch, Robert W (Bo), III** — Production Designer, Director
United Talent Agency, U T A Plaza, 9336 Civic Center Dr, Beverly Hills CA 90210 USA

**Welch, Tahnee** — Actress, Model
John Doherity Mgmt, 125 Christopher St, #6C, New York NY 10014, USA

**Weld, Tuesday K** — Actress
711 W End Ave, #5KN, New York NY 10025, USA

**Weld, William F** — Governor, MA
Hale & Dorr, 60 State St, #25, Boston MA 02109, USA

**Weldon, Fay** — Writer
Casorotto Ramsay, Waverley House, 7-12 Noel St, London W1F 8GQ, England

**Weldon, Joan** — Actress
67 E 78th St, New York NY 10075, USA

**Weldon, W Casey** — Football Player
380 Castleton Ave, #5, Tallahassee FL 32312, USA

**Weldon, William C** — Businessman
Johnson & Johnson, 1 Johnson & Johnson Plaza, New Bruswick NJ 08933, USA

**Welker, Frank** — Actor
C E S D, 10635 Santa Monica Blvd, #130, Los Angeles CA 90025 USA

**Welker, Wesley C (Wes)** — Football Player
42 Commonwealth Ave, #5, Boston MA 02116, USA

**Welland, Colin** — Actor, Writer
United Agents, 12-26 Lexington St, London W1F 0LE, England

**Wellber, Omer Meir** — Conductor
I M G Artists, Hogarth Business Park, Chiswick, London W4 2TH, England

**Wellemeyer, Todd A** — Baseball Player
8402 Westover Dr, Prospect KY 40059, USA

**Weller, Freddy** — Singer, Songwriter
Ace Productions, PO Box 428, Portland TN 37148, USA

**Weller, Frederick (Fred)** — Actor, Writer, Director
Gersh Agency, 9465 Wilshire Blvd, #600, Beverly Hills CA 90212 USA

**Weller, Josh** — Singer, Songwriter
Agency Group Ltd, 142 W 57th St, #600, New York NY 10019 USA

**Weller, Michael** — Writer
Gersh Agency, 9465 Wilshire Blvd, #600, Beverly Hills CA 90212 USA

**Weller, Paul** — Singer, Musician (Jam), Songwriter
High Road Touring, 751 Bridgeway, #200, Sausalito CA 94965 USA

**Weller, Peter** — Actor
A P A Talent & Literary Agency, 405 S Beverly Dr, #300, Beverly Hills CA 90212 USA

**Weller, Walter** — Conductor, Concert Violinist
Harrison/Parrott, 5-6 Albion Court, London W6 0QT, England

**Welles, Terri** — Model, Actress
PO Box 2549, Del Mar CA 92014, USA

**Wellford, Harry W** — Judge
US Court of Appeals, Federal Building, 167 N Main St, Memphis TN 38103, USA

**Welling, Tom** — Actor, Model
Tom Welling Productions, 9350 Wilshire Blvd, #250, Beverly Hills CA 90212, USA

**Wellinger, Andreas** — Ski Jumper
Seelauerweg 29, 83458 Weissbach/Inzell, Germany

**Welliver, Titus** — Actor
Leverage Mgmt, 3030 Pennsylvania Ave, Santa Monica CA 90404, USA

**Wellman, Brad E** — Baseball Player
733 Graham Court, Danville CA 94526, USA

**Wellman, Gary J** — Football Player
1638 Wellington Place, Westlake Village CA 91361, USA

**Wellman, Mac** — Writer
Brooklyn College, Play Writing Dept, Brooklyn NY 11210, USA

**Wellman, William, Jr** — Actor
Angel City Talent, 8318 Kirkwood Drive, Los Angeles CA 90046, USA

**Wellner, Jon** — Actor
Greater Vision Artists Talent Agency, 8981 Sunset Blvd, #101, Los Angeles CA 90069, USA

**Wells, Albert P** — WW II Marine Corps Air Force Hero
903 Park Lane, Santa Barbara CA 93108, USA

**Wells, Audrey** — Writer, Director, Producer
Creative Artists Agency, 2000 Ave of Stars, #100, Los Angeles CA 90067 USA

**Wells, Chris** — Ice Hockey Player
7228 Ridge Way, Park City UT 84098, USA

**Wells, Cory** — Singer (Three Dog Night)
PO Box 96597, Las Vegas NV 89193, USA
**Wells, D Dean** — Football Player
1146 Copperfield Dr, Georgetown IN 47122, USA
**Wells, David L (Dave)** — Baseball Player
PO Box 8107, Rancho Santa Fe CA 92067, USA
**Wells, Dawn** — Actress
Scott Stander Assoc, 4533 Van Nuys Blvd, #401, Sherman Oaks CA 91403 USA
**Wells, Gawen D (Bonzi)** — Basketball Player
6416 N Bobtail Dr, Muncie IN 47304, USA
**Wells, Jay** — Ice Hockey Player
Hockey School, 990 Keg Lane, RR 22, Paris ON N3L 3E2, Canada
**Wells, Joel W** — Football Player
11 Flicker Point, Greenville SC 29609, USA
**Wells, John** — Producer, Director
John Wells Productions, 4000 Warner Blvd, Building 1, Burbank CA 91522, USA
**Wells, Kerry Anne** — Beauty Queen
Miss Universe Organization, 1370 Ave of Americas, #1600, New York NY 10019 USA
**Wells, Llewellyn** — Producer, Director
United Talent Agency, U T A Plaza, 9336 Civic Center Dr, Beverly Hills CA 90210 USA
**Wells, Mark R** — Ice Hockey Player
2341 Union Road, #132, West Seneca NY 14224, USA
**Wells, Matthew** — Rowing Athlete
Leander Club, Henley on Thames, Leander RG9 2LP, England
**Wells, Patricia** — Journalist
Harper Collins Publishers, 10 E 53rd St, Cellar 1, New York NY 10022 USA
**Wells, R Kip** — Baseball Player
12891 Westbrook Dr, Tyler TX 75704, USA
**Wells, Reggie A** — Football Player
114 Snyder Road, Venetia PA 15367, USA
**Wells, Robert L (Bob)** — Baseball Player
154 Wilcox Road, Cowiche WA 98923, USA
**Wells, Simon** — Director
Todd Smith Assoc, 11835 W Olympic Blvd, #640, Los Angeles CA 90064, USA
**Wells, Stephen G** — Educator
University of Nevada, President's Office, Reno NV 89511, USA
**Wells, Theodore V, Jr** — Attorney
Paul Weiss Rifkind Warton Garrison, 1285 Ave of Americas, New York NY 10019, USA
**Wells, Thomas B** — Judge
US Tax Court, 400 2nd St NW, Washington DC 20217, USA
**Wells, Vernon, III** — Baseball Player
2251 King Fisher Dr, Westlake TX 76262, USA
**Wells, Warren** — Football Player
1399 Pipkin St, Beaumont TX 77705, USA
**Wells, Wayne A** — Freestyle Wrestler
2010 S Broadway, Edmond OK 73013, USA
**Welp, Christian (Chris)** — Basketball Player
20618 38th Dr SE, Bothell WA 98021, USA
**Welser-Most, Franz** — Conductor
Cleveland Symphony, Severance Hall, 11001 Euclid Ave, Cleveland OH 44106, USA
**Welsh, Christopher C (Chris)** — Baseball Player
12640 Huey Lane, Walton KY 41094, USA
**Welsh, Darrell G** — Hero
102 El Rancho Way, San Antonio TX 78209, USA
**Welsh, David (Dave)** — Guitarist (Fray)
A2 Mgmt, 624 Davis St, #200, Evanston IL 60201, USA
**Welsh, Irvine** — Writer
Independent Talent Group, 40 Whitfield St, London W1T 2RH, England
**Welsh, Moray M** — Concert Cellist
28 Somerfield Ave, Queens Park, London NW6 6JY, England
**Welsh, Stephanie** — Photojournalist
PO Box 277, Wayne ME 04284, USA
**Welsman, Carol** — Singer, Pianist
Bennett Morgan, 1022 RR 376, #3, Wappinger Falls NY 12590 USA
**Welsome-Martin, Eileen** — Journalist
2040 Locust St, Denver CO 80207, USA
**Welteroth, Richard J (Dick)** — Baseball Player
122 Eldred St, Williamsport PA 17701, USA
**Welty, John D** — Educator
81060 Legends Way, La Quinta CA 92253, USA
**Wen Jiabao** — Premier, China
Premier's Office, Zhonganahai, Beijing 100017, China
**Wendell, Krissy** — Ice Hockey Player
325 9th St SE, Minneapolis MN 55414, USA
**Wendell, Steven J (Turk)** — Baseball Player
227 Hidden Valley Lane, Castle Rock CO 80108, USA
**Wendelstedt, H Hunter, III** — Baseball Umpire
3044 SW 98th Way, Gainesville FL 32608, USA
**Wenders, E Wilhelm (Wim)** — Director
Neue Road Movies, Meunzstr 15, 10178 Berlin, Germany
**Wendkos, Gina** — Writer
Industry Entertainment, 955 Carillo Dr, #300, Los Angeles CA 90048 USA
**Wendl, Ingrid Turkovic-** — Figure Skater
Parliament, Innere Stadt, Dr Karl-Renner Ring 3, 2004 Vienna, Austria
**Wendl, Tobias** — Luge Athlete
Oberschonauer Str 105, 83471 Schonau, Germany
**Wendorf, Edward G** — Hero
11588 Via Rancho San Diego, El Cajon CA 92019, USA
**Wendt, George** — Actor
B R S / Gage Talent Agency, 5757 Wilshire Blvd, #659, Los Angeles CA 90036 USA
**Wendt, Henry, III** — Businessman
560 Warbass Way, Friday Harbor WA 98250, USA
**Wengert, Donald P (Don)** — Baseball Player
13100 Cedarwood Ave, Clive IA 50325, USA
**Wengren, Mike** — Drummer (Disturbed)
Mitch Schneider Organization, 14724 Ventura Blvd, #500, Sherman Oaks CA 91403 USA

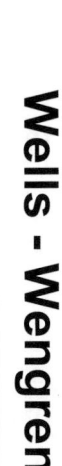

**Wenham, David** — Actor
Markham Froggatt Irwin, Julian House, 4 Windmill St, London W1P 1HF, England
**Wenner, Jann S** — Publisher, Producer
37 W 70th St, New York NY 10023, USA
**Wennerstrom, Maria** — Curling Athlete
Skelleftea Curling Club, Mossgatan 27, 93170 Skelleftea, Sweden
**Wennington, William P (Bill)** — Basketball Player
1985 Oak Grove Lane, Lake Forest IL 60045, USA
**Wensink, John** — Ice Hockey Player
29311 Bidwell Creek Road, Fredericktown MO 63645, USA
**Wenstrom, Matt** — Basketball Player
15714 Blanco Trails Lane, Cypress TX 77429, USA
**Went, Joseph J** — Marine Corps General
9204 Kristin Lane, Fairfax VA 22032, USA
**Wentworth, Alexandra** — Actress, Comedienne, Writer
Gersh Agency, 9465 Wilshire Blvd, #600, Beverly Hills CA 90212 USA
**Wentz, Pete** — Bassist (Fall Out Boy), Lyricist
PO Box 219, 1187 Wilmette Ave, Wilmette IL 60091, USA
**Wenz, Otto** — Cycling Executive
14230 W Armour Ave, New Berlin WI 53151, USA
**Wenzel, Hanni Weirather-** — Alpine Skier
Fanalwegle 4, 9494 Schaan, Liechtenstein
**Wenzel, Kurt** — Writer
Random House, 1745 Broadway, #1800, New York NY 10019 USA
**Wepner, Chuck** — Boxer
153 Ave E, Bayonne NJ 07002, USA
**Wepper, Elmar** — Actor
Agentur Alexander, Lamontstr 9, 81679 Munich, Germany
**Wepper, Fritz** — Actor
N D F, Joseph-Dollinger-Bogen 26, 80807 Munich, Germany
**Werbach, Adam** — Environmentalist
Sierra Club, 85 2nd St, #200, San Francisco CA 94105, USA
**Werbowy, Daria** — Model
I M G Models, 304 Park Ave S, #PH N, New York NY 10010 USA
**Werdann, Robert** — Basketball Player
4739 40th St, #5F, Sunnyside NY 11104, USA
**Werenka, Bradley J (Brad)** — Ice Hockey Player
PO Box 92030, Edgemont RPO, Calgary AB T3A 6L9, Canada
**Werkheiser, Devon** — Actor
Coast to Coast Talent, 3350 Barham Blvd, Los Angeles CA 90068, USA
**Werley, George W** — Baseball Player
15415 Elk Ridge Lane, Chesterfield MO 63017, USA
**Werner, Anna** — Commentator
KHOU-TV, News Department, 1945 Allan Parkway, Houston TX 77019, USA
**Werner, Bjoern** — Football Player
Indianapolis Colts, 7001 W 56th St, Indianapolis IN 46254 USA
**Werner, Carla** — Singer, Songwriter
PO Box 3241, Tamarama NSW 2026, Australia
**Werner, Clyde L** — Football Player
3009 Islandview Court, Gig Harbor WA 98335, USA
**Werner, Donald P (Don)** — Baseball Player
2204 Briarwood Blvd, Arlington TX 76013, USA
**Werner, Marianne** — Track Athlete
Gauseland 2A, 44227 Dortmund, Germany
**Werner, Peter** — Director
Paradigm Agency, 360 N Crescent Dr, North Building, Beverly Hills CA 90210 USA
**Werner, Roger L, Jr** — Businessman
Prime Sports Ventures, 10000 Santa Monica Blvd, Los Angeles CA 90067, USA
**Werner, Susan** — Singer, Songwriter
Roots Agency, 177 Woodland Ave, Westwood NJ 07675, USA
**Werner, Tom** — Producer
Good Humor Television, 9255 W Sunset Blvd, #1040, West Hollywood CA 90069, USA
**Wernick, Pete** — Singer, Banjoist (Hot Rize)
Keith Case Assoc, 1025 17th Ave S, #200, Nashville TN 37212 USA
**Wersching, Annie** — Actress
S M S Talent, 8383 Wilshire Blvd, #230, Beverly Hills CA 90211 USA
**Wersching, Raimund (Ray)** — Football Player
18 Buttercup Lane, San Carlos CA 94070, USA
**Wert, Donald R (Don)** — Baseball Player
341 Smithville Road, New Providence PA 17560, USA
**Werth, Isabell** — Equestrian
Winterswicker Feld 4, 47495 Rheinberg, Germany
**Werth, Jayson R** — Baseball Player
PO Box 13457, Springfield IL 62791, USA
**Wertheimer, Fredric M** — Public Policy Activist
3502 Macomb St NW, Washington DC 20016, USA
**Wertheimer, Linda** — Commentator
National Public Radio, 635 Massachusetts Ave NW, #1, Washington DC 20001, USA
**Wertmuller, Lina** — Director
Piazza Clotilde, 00196 Rome, Italy
**Wertmuller, Massimo** — Actor
Carol Levi Mgmt, Via Giuseppe Pisanelli 2, 00196 Rome, Italy
**Wertz, Matt** — Singer, Songwriter
Nettwerk Music Group, 1201 Villa Place, #206, Nashville TN 37212, USA
**Wertz, William C (Bill)** — Baseball Player
26514 Mingo Dr, Perrysburg OH 43551, USA
**Wescott, Seth B** — Snowboarding Athlete
Octagon Worldwide, 2 Union St, #300, Portland ME 04101 USA
**Wesker, Arnold** — Writer
Hay on Wye, Hereford HR3 5RJ, England
**Wesley, Dante J** — Football Player
104 Fawn Cove, White Hall AR 71602, USA
**Wesley, David B** — Basketball Player
721 Spring Thyme Dr, Belle Chasse LA 70037, USA
**Wesley, Fred** — Jazz Trombonist
Universal Attractions, 135 W 26th St, #1200, New York NY 10001 USA

Wenham - Wesley

| | |
|---|---|
| **Wesley, Glen E** | Ice Hockey Player |
| 5305 Newstead Manor Lane, Raleigh NC 27606, USA | |
| **Wesley, Gregory L (Greg)** | Football Player |
| 9752 Sunset Circle, Lenexa KS 66220, USA | |
| **Wesley, Norman H** | Businessman |
| Fortune Brands Inc, 520 Lake Cook Road, Deerfield IL 60015, USA | |
| **Wesley, Paul** | Actor, Producer |
| I C M Partners, 10250 Constellation Blvd, #900, Los Angeles CA 90067 USA | |
| **Wesley, Rutina** | Actress |
| Inspire Entertainment, 2332 Cotner Ave, #302, Los Angeles CA 90064, USA | |
| **Wesley, Trevor (Blake)** | Ice Hockey Player |
| Okanagan Hockey School, 101-697 Wade W, Penticton BC V2A 1V6, Canada | |
| **Wesley, Walter (Walt)** | Basketball Player |
| 6417 Scott Lane, Fort Myers FL 33966, USA | |
| **Wessel, Henry, Jr** | Photographer |
| PO Box 475, Richmond CA 94807, USA | |
| **Wesson, Barry** | Baseball Player |
| 36 Shore Dr NE, Brookhaven MS 39601, USA | |
| **West of Spithead, Baron Alan W J** | Navy Admiral, England |
| Solent University, Chancellor's Office, 157 Above Bar St, Southampton SO14 7NN, England | |
| **West, Adam** | Actor |
| Kazarian/Measures/Ruskin, 11969 Ventura Blvd, #300, Studio City CA 91604 USA | |
| **West, Billy** | Actor |
| Danis Panaro Nist Talent, 9201 W Olympic Blvd, Beverly Hills CA 90212 USA | |
| **West, Chandra** | Actress |
| Characters Talent Mgmt, 8 Elm St, Toronto ON M5G 1G7, Canada | |
| **West, Charles (Charlie)** | Football Player |
| 184 Laurel Ridge, South Salem NY 10590, USA | |
| **West, Cornel** | Theologian, Sociologist |
| Princeton University, Afro American Studies Program, Princeton NJ 08544, USA | |
| **West, David J** | Businessman |
| Hershey Co, 100 Crystal A Dr, PO Box 810, Hershey PA 17033, USA | |
| **West, David L** | Baseball Player |
| 1242 SW Seahawk Way, Palm City FL 34990, USA | |
| **West, David M** | Basketball Player |
| Indiana Pacers, Conseco Fieldhouse, 125 S Pennsylvania, Indianapolis IN 46204 USA | |
| **West, Delonte** | Basketball Player |
| 8805 Charm Court, Brandywine MD 20613, USA | |
| **West, Dominic** | Actor |
| W M E Entertainment, 9601 Wilshire Blvd, #300, Beverly Hills CA 90210 USA | |
| **West, Edward L (Ed), Jr** | Football Player |
| 1930 Ma Lee Dr, Moody AL 35004, USA | |
| **West, Ernest E** | Korean War Army Hero (CMH) |
| 912 Adams Ave, Greenup KY 41144, USA | |
| **West, Geoffrey** | Theoretical Physicist |
| Santa Fe Institute, 1399 Hyde Park Road, Santa Fe NM 87501, USA | |
| **West, Jacqueline** | Costume Designer |
| Gersh Agency, 9465 Wilshire Blvd, #600, Beverly Hills CA 90212 USA | |
| **West, James E** | Inventor (Telephone Microphone) |
| 724 Berkeley Ave, Plainfield NJ 07062, USA | |
| **West, Jason** | Video Games Developer |
| Respawn Entertainment, 5990 Sepulveda Blvd, Van Nuys CA 91411, USA | |
| **West, Jeffrey H (Jeff)** | Football Player |
| 12376 Adair Creek Way NE, Redmond WA 98053, USA | |
| **West, Jerome A (Jerry)** | Basketball Player, Coach, Executive |
| Golden State Warriors, 1011 Broadway, Oakland CA 94605 USA | |
| **West, Joel** | Model, Actor |
| Don Carroll Mgmt, 14211 Hatteras St, Sherman Oaks CA 91401, USA | |
| **West, Joseph H (Joe)** | Baseball Umpire |
| 17531 Cobblestone Lane, Clermont FL 34711, USA | |
| **West, Josh** | Rowing Athlete |
| 22 Cherwell St, Oxford OX 41BG, England | |
| **West, Kanye** | Rap Artist, Music Producer |
| 3200 Cherry Creek South Dr, #620, Denver CO 80209, USA | |
| **West, Keith** | Bassist, Singer (Heartland) |
| Country Thunder Records, 1016 17th Ave S, Nashville TN 37212, USA | |
| **West, Leslie** | Singer, Guitarist (Mountain) |
| Survival Mgmt, 30765 Pacific Coast Highway, #325, Malibu CA 90265, USA | |
| **West, Lizzie** | Singer |
| Warner Bros Records, 3300 Warner Blvd, Burbank CA 91505 USA | |
| **West, Mark A** | Basketball Player |
| 644 Old Wagner Road, Petersburg VA 23805, USA | |
| **West, Martin** | Actor |
| 427 N Canon Dr, Beverly Hills CA 90210, USA | |
| **West, Maura** | Actress |
| Innovative Artists, 1505 10th St, Santa Monica CA 90401 USA | |
| **West, Nathan** | Actor |
| United Talent Agency, U T A Plaza, 9336 Civic Center Dr, Beverly Hills CA 90210 USA | |
| **West, Paul** | Writer |
| Elaine Markson Agency, 44 Greenwich Ave, #300, New York NY 10011, USA | |
| **West, Roland D** | Basketball Player |
| 7464 Shaker Run Lane, West Chester OH 45069, USA | |
| **West, Samuel** | Actor |
| United Agents, 12-26 Lexington St, London W1F 0LE, England | |
| **West, Shelly** | Singer |
| Acts Nashville Talent, 1103 Bell Grimes Lane, Nashville TN 37207, USA | |
| **West, Simon** | Director, Producer, Writer |
| Simon West Productions, 3450 Cahuenga Blvd W, Building 609, Los Angeles CA 90068, USA | |
| **West, Stu** | Bassist (Damned) |
| Leave Home Booking, 10 W Broadway, #608, Salt Lake City UT 84101, USA | |
| **West, Timothy L** | Actor |
| Gavin Barker Assoc, 2D Wimpole St, London W1G 0EB, England | |
| **West, Togo D, Jr** | Secretary, Veterans Affairs |
| 922 N Cameron Ave, Winston Salem NC 27101, USA | |
| **Westbrook, Brian C** | Football Player |
| 6204 Blue Sage Lane, Upper Marlboro MD 20772, USA | |

Wesley - Westbrook

**Westbrook, Bryant A** — Football Player
28017 N 17th Dr, Phoenix AZ 85085, USA
**Westbrook, Dexter** — Basketball Player
200 E Church Lane, #405, Philadelphia PA 19144, USA
**Westbrook, Jacob C (Jake)** — Baseball Player
PO Box 574, Danielsville GA 30633, USA
**Westbrook, Michael D** — Football Player
2797 E Teakwood Place, Chandler AZ 85249, USA
**Westbrook, Peter** — Fencer
15 Washington Place, #1F, New York NY 10003, USA
**Westbrook, Russell** — Basketball Player
Oklahoma City Thunder, 211 N Robinson Ave, #300, Oklahoma City OK 73102 USA
**Westbrooks, Gregory M (Greg)** — Football Player
3832 10th Avenue Place, Moline IL 61265, USA
**Westenhiser, Jamie** — Model
Playboy Promotions, 9346 Civic Center Dr, #200, Beverly Hills CA 90210 USA
**Westenhofer, Bill** — Visual Effects Designer
Rhythm & Hues Studio, 2100 E Grand Ave, El Segundo CA 90245 90245, USA
**Westenra, Hayley** — Singer
Bandana Mgmt, 160 New Kings Road, London SW6 4LZ, England
**Westerberg, Paul** — Singer, Guitarist, Songwriter
Mitch Schneider Organization, 14724 Ventura Blvd, #500, Sherman Oaks CA 91403 USA
**Westerfield, Putney** — Publisher
501 Portola Road, #8021, Portola Valley CA 94028, USA
**Westfall, V Edward (Ed)** — Ice Hockey Player
699 Hillside Ave, New Hyde Park NY 11040, USA
**Westfeldt, Jennifer** — Actress
Innovative Artists, 1505 10th St, Santa Monica CA 90401 USA
**Westhead, Paul W** — Basketball Coach
University of Oregon, Athletic Dept, Eugene OR 97403, USA
**Westheimer, Gerald** — Optometrist
582 Santa Barbara Road, Berkeley CA 94707, USA
**Westheimer, Ruth S** — Sex Therapist, Psychologist, Producer
C E S D, 10635 Santa Monica Blvd, #130, Los Angeles CA 90025 USA
**Westin, Av** — Businessman, Journalist
King World Productions, 1700 Broadway, #3200, New York NY 10019, USA
**Westlake, Waldon T (Wally)** — Baseball Player
3800 61st St, Sacramento CA 95820, USA
**Westling, Jon** — Educator
285 Goddard Ave, Brookline MA 02445, USA
**Westmore, McKenzie K** — Actress, Singer
W M E Entertainment, 9601 Wilshire Blvd, #300, Beverly Hills CA 90210 USA
**Westmoreland, James** — Actor
52940 Avenida Navarro, La Quinta CA 92253, USA
**Westmoreland, Richard C (Dick)** — Football Player
5601 Sea Reef Place, San Diego CA 92154, USA
**Weston, Celia** — Actress
Innovative Artists, 235 Park Ave S, #1000, New York NY 10003 USA
**Weston, Ken** — Sound Mixer
I C M Partners, 10250 Constellation Blvd, #900, Los Angeles CA 90067 USA
**Weston, Kim** — Singer
Powerplay, PO Box 533, 5434 W Sample Road, Margate FL 33073, USA
**Weston, Michael** — Actor
Paradigm Agency, 360 N Crescent Dr, North Building, Beverly Hills CA 90210, USA
**Weston, Michael L (Mickey)** — Baseball Player
2702 Eisenhower Ave, Valparaiso IN 46383, USA
**Weston, Randolph (Randy)** — Jazz Pianist
PO Box 749, Maplewood NJ 07040, USA
**Weston, Stan** — Businessman
Leisure Concepts, 1414 Ave of Americas, New York NY 10019, USA
**Weston-Jones, Tom** — Actor
Markham Froggatt Irwin, Julian House, 4 Windmill St, London W1P 1HF, England
**Westphal, Paul D** — Basketball Player, Coach
1424 Granvia Altamira, Palos Verdes Estates CA 90274, USA
**Westwick, Edward G (Ed)** — Actor, Singer
Emptage Hallett, 14 Rathbone Place, London W1T 1HT, England
**Westwood, Joey** — Bassist (Red Jumpsuit Apparatus)
Virgin Records, 338 N Foothill Road, Beverly Hills CA 90210 USA
**Westwood, Vivienne** — Fashion Designer
Lanterns #3, Old School House, Bridge Lane, London SW11 3AD, England
**Wetherbee, James D (Jim)** — Astronaut
3818 Trailstone Lane, Katy TX 77494, USA
**Wetherby, Jeffrey B (Jeff)** — Baseball Player
28410 Great Bend Place, Fresno CA 93710, USA
**Wethington, Charles T, Jr** — Educator
2926 Four Pines Dr, Lexington KY 40502, USA
**Wetoska, Robert S (Bob)** — Football Player
1295 Forest Glen Dr S, Winnetka IL 60093, USA
**Wetteland, John K** — Baseball Player
352 Old Justin Road, Argyle TX 76226, USA
**Wetter, Friedrich Cardinal** — Religious Leader
Archdiocese of Munich & Fresing, Postfach 330360, Rochusstr 5-7, 80063 Munich, Germany
**Wetterich, Brett M** — Golfer
147 Castle Island Place, Jupiter FL 33458, USA
**Wettig, Patricia** — Actress
Innovative Artists, 1505 10th St, Santa Monica CA 90401 USA
**Wetton, John** — Singer, Bassist (Asia, UK)
Entourage Talent Assoc, 236 W 27th St, #800, New York NY 10001, USA
**Wetzel, Carl** — Ice Hockey Player
9401 James Ave S, #11, Minneapolis MN 55431, USA
**Wetzel, Donald C (Don)** — Inventor (Automated Teller Machine)
5706 Trail Meadow Dr, Dallas TX 75230, USA
**Wetzel, Gary G** — Vietnam War Army Hero (CMH)
PO Box 84, Oak Creek WI 53154, USA
**Wetzel, John F** — Basketball Player, Coach
13011 N Sunrise Canyon Lane, Marana AZ 85658, USA

| | |
|---|---|
| **Wetzel, Robert G** | Botanist |
| 16 Dunbrook, Tuscaloosa AL 35406, USA | |
| **Wetzel, Robert L** | Army General |
| 1425 Dartmouth Road, Columbus GA 31904, USA | |
| **Wever, Merritt** | Actress |
| Innovative Artists, 1505 10th St, Santa Monica CA 90401 USA | |
| **Wever, Stefan M** | Baseball Player |
| 7 Corte Los Sombras, Greenbrae CA 94904, USA | |
| **Wexler, Haskell** | Cinematographer |
| 1247 Lincoln Blvd, #585, Santa Monica CA 90401, USA | |
| **Wexler, Nancy S** | Clinical Psychologist |
| Hereditary Disease Foundation, 3960 Broadway, New York NY 10032, USA | |
| **Wexler, Robert** | Religious Leader, Rabbi, Educator |
| Brandeis-Bardin, 1101 Peppertree, Brandeis CA 93064, USA | |
| **Wexler, Robert F** | Representative, FL |
| Middle East Peace Center, 633 Pennsylvania NW, #500, Washington DC 20004, USA | |
| **Weyerhaeuser, George** | Businessman |
| Weyerhaeuser Co, 33663 32nd Ave S, Federal Way WA 98023, USA | |
| **Weymouth, Tina** | Bassist (Talking Heads, Tom Tom Club) |
| Premier Talent, 3 E 54th St, #1100, New York NY 10022 USA | |
| **Whalen, Laurence J** | Judge |
| US Tax Court, 400 2nd St NW, Washington DC 20217, USA | |
| **Whalen, Lindsay M** | Basketball Player |
| Minnesota Lynx, Target Center, 600 1st Ave N, Minneapolis MN 55403 USA | |
| **Whalen, Sara** | Soccer Player |
| 10 Francis Dr, Greenlawn NY 11740, USA | |
| **Whaley, Frank** | Actor |
| A P A Talent & Literary Agency, 405 S Beverly Dr, #300, Beverly Hills CA 90212 USA | |
| **Whaley, Suzi** | Golfer |
| 15 Whitehall Place, Farmington CT 06032, USA | |
| **Whalin, Justin G** | Actor |
| Deborah Miller, 9454 Wilshire Blvd, #715, Beverly Hills CA 90212, USA | |
| **Whalley, Joanne** | Actress |
| Markham Froggatt Irwin, Julian House, 4 Windmill St, London W1P 1HF, England | |
| **Whalum, Kirk** | Jazz Saxophonist |
| Cole Classic Mgmt, PO Box 231, Canoga Park CA 91305, USA | |
| **Whang, Suzanne** | Actress |
| I C M Partners, 10250 Constellation Blvd, #900, Los Angeles CA 90067 USA | |
| **Whannell, Leigh** | Actor |
| Paradigm Agency, 360 N Crescent Dr, North Building, Beverly Hills CA 90210 USA | |
| **Wharram, Ken** | Ice Hockey Player |
| 382 Aubrey St W, North Bay ON P1B 6H9, Canada | |
| **Wharton, Bernard** | Architect |
| Shope Reno Wharton, 18 Marshall St, #114, Norwalk CT 06854, USA | |
| **Wharton, G Travelle** | Football Player |
| 111 Stenhouse Road, Simpsonville SC 29680, USA | |
| **Whatley, Ennis** | Basketball Player |
| 42 Brinkwood Road, Brookeville MD 20833, USA | |
| **Whatmore, Sarah L** | Singer |
| Fremantle Media, 2700 Colorado Ave, #450, Santa Monica CA 90404 USA | |
| **Wheatcroft, Georgina** | Curling Athlete |
| Curling Association, 1660 Vimont Court, Cumberland ON K4A 4J4, Canada | |
| **Wheatley, Ben** | Director |
| W M E Entertainment, 9601 Wilshire Blvd, #300, Beverly Hills CA 90210 USA | |
| **Wheatley, Kevin** | Actor |
| Seven Summits Mgmt, 8906 W Olympic Blvd, Beverly Hills CA 90211 USA | |
| **Wheatley, Tyrone A** | Football Player |
| 32 Winterhall Road, Orchard Park NY 14127, USA | |
| **Wheaton, David** | Tennis Player |
| PO Box 401, Tonka Bay MN 55331, USA | |
| **Wheaton, Wil** | Actor |
| Opus Entertainment, 5225 Wilshire Blvd, #905, Los Angeles CA 90036, USA | |
| **Whedon, Joseph H (Joss)** | Actor, Director, Producer |
| Creative Artists Agency, 2000 Ave of Stars, #100, Los Angeles CA 90067 USA | |
| **Wheeldon, Christopher** | Choreographer, Ballet Dancer |
| Morphoses/Wheeldon Co, 800 5th Ave, #18F, New York NY 10065, USA | |
| **Wheeler, Adam** | Greco-Roman Wrestler |
| 4854 Jedediah Smith Road, Colorado Springs CO 80922, USA | |
| **Wheeler, Cheryl** | Singer, Songwriter |
| Morningstar Mgmt, PO Box 1770, Hendersonville TN 37077, USA | |
| **Wheeler, Clinton** | Basketball Player |
| 199 Scenic View Lane, Stone Mountain GA 30087, USA | |
| **Wheeler, Daniel M (Dan)** | Baseball Player |
| 215 Harrison Ave, Belleair Beach FL 33786, USA | |
| **Wheeler, Dwight** | Football Player |
| 2012 Sunnyslope Lane, Goodlettsville TN 37072, USA | |
| **Wheeler, Gary** | Interior Designer |
| Perkins & Will, 330 N Wabash Ave, #3600, Chicago IL 60611, USA | |
| **Wheeler, H Anthony** | Architect |
| South Inverleith Manor, 31/6 Kinnear Road, Edinburgh EH3 5PG, Scotland | |
| **Wheeler, Howard A (Humpy)** | Auto Racing Executive |
| Wheeler Co, PO Box 1327, Cornelius NC 28031, USA | |
| **Wheeler, John A** | Actor |
| 414 Troy Court, Claremont CA 91711, USA | |
| **Wheeler, Maggie** | Actress |
| Affirmative Entertainment, 425 N Robertson Blvd, Los Angeles CA 90048 USA | |
| **Wheeler, Mark A** | Football Player |
| 101 Meadowridge Cove, San Marcos TX 78666, USA | |
| **Wheeler, Nicholas D (Nick)** | Singer, Guitarist (All-American Rejects) |
| Creative Artists Agency, 2000 Ave of Stars, #100, Los Angeles CA 90067 USA | |
| **Wheeler-Nicholson, Dana** | Actress |
| Glick Agency, 347 5th Ave, #1404, New York NY 10016 USA | |
| **Wheelock, Douglas H** | Astronaut |
| PO Box 580408, Houston TX 77258, USA | |
| **Wheelock, Gary R** | Baseball Player |
| 3354 N Park St, Buckeye AZ 85396, USA | |

**W**

**Wetzel - Wheelock**

**W**

| | |
|---|---|
| **Whelan, Bill** <br> Sony Records, 2100 Colorado Ave, Santa Monica CA 90404 USA | Composer |
| **Whelan, Gary** <br> Artists Partnership, 101 Finsbury Pavement, London EC2A 1RS, England | Actor |
| **Whelan, Julia M** <br> Genesis Entertainment Partners, 4145 Garden Ave, Los Angeles CA 90039, USA | Actress |
| **Whelan, Nicky** <br> United Talent Agency, U T A Plaza, 9336 Civic Center Dr, Beverly Hills CA 90210 USA | Actress, Model |
| **Whelan, Peter** <br> Lemon Unna Durbridge, Holland Park, 24 Pottery Lane, London W11 4LZ, England | Writer |
| **Whelan, Wendy** <br> New York City Ballet, Lincoln Center Plaza, New York NY 10023 USA | Ballerina |
| **Whelchel, Lisa** <br> Arcieri Assoc, 305 Madison Ave, #2315, New York NY 10165 USA | Actress |
| **Wheless, Jamy** <br> 405 Fair St, Petaluma CA 94952, USA | Animator |
| **Whicker, Alan D** <br> Trinity, Jersey JE3 5BA, Channel Islands, England | Commentator |
| **Whigham, Larry J** <br> 33 Collins Road, Hattiesburg MS 39401, USA | Football Player |
| **Whigham, Shea** <br> Principal Entertainment, 9255 Sunset Blvd, #500, Los Angeles CA 90069 USA | Actor |
| **Whillock, Jack F** <br> 2118 River Ridge Road, Arlington TX 76017, USA | Baseball Player |
| **Whimper, Guy** <br> 1010 Main St, New Bern NC 28560, USA | Football Player |
| **Whirry, Shannon** <br> Ford/Robert Black Agency, 4032 N Miller Road, #104, Scottsdale AZ 95251, USA | Actress |
| **Whisenant, Matthew M (Matt)** <br> 1035 Fairview Dr, La Canada Flintridge CA 91011, USA | Baseball Player |
| **Whisenhunt, Kenneth M (Ken)** <br> 5 Oxmoor Court, Brentwood TN 37027, USA | Football Player, Coach |
| **Whishaw, Anthony** <br> 7A Albert Place, Victoria Road, London W8 5PD, England | Artist |
| **Whishaw, Ben** <br> Hamilton Hodell, 20 Golden Square, London W1F 9JL, England | Actor |
| **Whisler, J Steven** <br> Phelps Dodge Corp, 1 N Central Ave, #100, Phoenix AZ 85004, USA | Businessman |
| **Whiston, Donald (Don)** <br> 2 Jeffreys Neck Road, Ipswich MA 01938, USA | Ice Hockey Player |
| **Whitacre, Edward E, Jr** <br> General Motors Corp, 100 Renaissance Center, Detroit MI 48243, USA | Businessman |
| **Whitaker, Denzel** <br> Luber Rocklin Entertainment, 5815 Sunset Blvd, #206, Los Angeles CA 90028 USA | Actor |
| **Whitaker, Forest** <br> Spirit Dance Entertainment, 1023 N Orange Dr, Los Angeles CA 90038, USA | Actor, Director |
| **Whitaker, Jack** <br> 500 Berwyn Baptist Road, Devon PA 19333, USA | Sportscaster |
| **Whitaker, Jack** <br> International Golf Partners, 3300 PGA Blvd, #820, Palm Beach Gardens FL 33410, USA | Golfer |
| **Whitaker, Louis R (Lou), Jr** <br> 17 Brownstone Lane, Greensboro NC 27410, USA | Baseball Player |
| **Whitaker, Meade** <br> US Tax Court, 400 2nd St NW, Washington DC 20217, USA | Judge |
| **Whitaker, Pernell** <br> 1701 Rock Bridge Mews, #B, Chesapeake VA 23320, USA | Boxer |
| **Whitaker, Steve E** <br> 900 SE 6th Court, Fort Lauderdale FL 33301, USA | Baseball Player |
| **Whitbread, Fatima** <br> Javel-Inn, Mill Hill, Shenfield, Brentwood, Essex CM15 8EU, England | Track Athlete |
| **Whitcomb, Bob** <br> Whitcomb Racing, 9201 Garrison Road, Charlotte NC 28278, USA | Auto Racing Executive |
| **Whitcomb, Edgar D** <br> 15415 Rome Road, Rome IN 47574, USA | Governor, IN |
| **Whitcomb, Ian** <br> PO Box 451, Altadena CA 91003, USA | Singer, Songwriter |
| **White, Adrian D** <br> 688 Allen Lane, Orange Park FL 32073, USA | Football Player |
| **White, Alan, III** <br> Ignition Mgmt, 54 Linhope St, London NW1 6HL, England | Drummer (Yes, Oasis) |
| **White, Andrew N, III** <br> Vezco Productions, 163 Main St, Odessa ON K0H 2H0, Canada | Jazz Saxophonist |
| **White, Andrew R (Whitey)** <br> Red Light Mgmt, 8439 Sunset Blvd, West Hollywood CA 90069, USA | Guitarist (Kaiser Chiefs) |
| **White, Artie** <br> C A I Entertainment Agency, PO Box 9267, Jackson MS 39286, USA | Singer |
| **White, Betty M** <br> PO Box 491965, Los Angeles CA 90049, USA | Actress, Comedienne |
| **White, Brian** <br> 3 Gedick Road, Burlington MA 01803, USA | Ice Hockey Player |
| **White, Brian J, Jr** <br> Paradigm Agency, 360 N Crescent Dr, North Building, Beverly Hills CA 90210 USA | Actor |
| **White, Brooke** <br> Sanctuary Mgmt, 15301 Ventura Blvd, Building B, Sherman Oaks CA 91403, USA | Singer, Songwriter, Actress |
| **White, Bryan** <br> Loudmouth Public Relations, PO Box 128192, Nashville TN 37212, USA | Singer, Songwriter |
| **White, Charles R** <br> 31841 Via Faisan, Trabuco Canyon CA 92679, USA | Football Player, Administrator |
| **White, Charlie** <br> Arctic Edge Ice Skating Club, 46615 Michigan Ave, Canton MI 48188, USA | Ice Dancer |
| **White, Chris** <br> Lustig Talent, PO Box 770850, Orlando FL 32877 USA | Bassist (Zombies) |
| **White, Devon M** <br> 6440 E Sierra Vista Dr, Paradise Valley AZ 85253, USA | Baseball Player |
| **White, Dewayne (D J), Jr** <br> Charlotte Hornets, 333 E Trade St, #A, Charlotte NC 28202 USA | Basketball Player |

**Whelan - White**

| | |
|---|---|
| **White, Donna**<br>200 Caribe Court, Greenacres FL 33413, USA | Golfer |
| **White, Dwayne A**<br>2117 Pinehurst Way, Coral Springs FL 33071, USA | Football Player |
| **White, Edmund V**<br>I C M Partners, 10250 Constellation Blvd, #900, Los Angeles CA 90067 USA | Writer |
| **White, Edward A (Ed)**<br>PO Box 1437, Julian CA 92036, USA | Football Player |
| **White, G Edward**<br>University of Virginia, Law School, Charlottesville VA 22903, USA | Educator, Attorney |
| **White, Gabriel A (Gabe)**<br>1571 Lakeview Dr, Sebring FL 33870, USA | Baseball Player |
| **White, Gary C**<br>Water.org, 920 Main St, #1800, Kansas City MO 64105, USA | Biologist |
| **White, Harvey D**<br>Green Lane Hospital, Cardioloy Dept, PB 92189, Auckland 1030, New Zealand | Cardiologist |
| **White, Hubert L (Hubie)**<br>101 E Gowen Ave, Philadelphia PA 19119, USA | Basketball Player |
| **White, J Colin**<br>81 Western Ave, Morristown NJ 07960, USA | Ice Hockey Player |
| **White, J Melville (Mel)**<br>Soulforce, PO Box 2499, Abilene TX 79604, USA | Writer, Religious Activist |
| **White, J Michael (Mike)**<br>26438 S Jardin Dr, Sun Lakes AZ 85248, USA | Baseball Player |
| **White, Jack**<br>Monotone Mgmt, 820 Seward St, Los Angeles CA 90038, USA | Singer, Guitarist (White Stripes) |
| **White, Jaleel**<br>Mavrick Artists Agency, 6100 Wilshire Blvd, #550, Los Angeles CA 90048, USA | Actor |
| **White, James C (Jim)**<br>14430 Andrea Way Lane, Houston TX 77083, USA | Football Player |
| **White, James L**<br>I C M Partners, 10250 Constellation Blvd, #900, Los Angeles CA 90067 USA | Writer |
| **White, Jason**<br>3203 Stone Dr, Tuttle OK 73089, USA | Football Player |
| **White, Jeordie O**<br>Coast II Coast Entertainment, 8671 Wilshire Blvd, Beverly Hills CA 90211, USA | Bassist (Marilyn Manson, Perfect Circle) |
| **White, Jeris J**<br>15 N Wisner St, Frederick MD 21701, USA | Football Player |
| **White, Jerome C (Jerry)**<br>343 N Wildwood, Hercules CA 94547, USA | Baseball Player |
| **White, Jessica**<br>New York Model Mgmt, 596 Broadway, New York NY 10012, USA | Model |
| **White, John H**<br>Chicago Sun-Times, Editorial Dept, 401 N Wabash Ave, Chicago IL 60611 USA | Photojournalist |
| **White, John Patrick**<br>C E S D, 10635 Santa Monica Blvd, #130, Los Angeles CA 90025 USA | Actor |
| **White, Joseph H (Jo Jo)**<br>2 Mansfield Road, Middleton MA 01949, USA | Basketball Player |
| **White, Josh, Jr**<br>23625 Ripple Creek, Novi MI 48375, USA | Singer, Songwriter |
| **White, Joy Lynn**<br>J E G Mgmt, 72 Birch Grove, Slough, Berkshire SL2 1EP, England | Singer |
| **White, Katie**<br>Paradigm Agency, 404 W Franklin St, Monterey CA 93940 USA | Singer, Guitarist (Ting Tings) |
| **White, Kyle**<br>Royal Bank of Canada, 4720 Piedmont Row, Charlotte NC 28210, USA | Afghanistan War Army Hero (CMH) |
| **White, Lari**<br>R C A Records, 1400 18th Ave S, Nashville TN 37212 USA | Singer, Songwriter |
| **White, Lee A**<br>600 Langtry Dr, Las Vegas NV 89107, USA | Football Player |
| **White, Lenny, III**<br>Universal Attractions, 135 W 26th St, #1200, New York NY 10001 USA | Jazz Drummer |
| **White, Lillias**<br>TalentWorks, 3500 W Olive Ave, #1400, Burbank CA 91505 USA | Actress |
| **White, Lorenzo M**<br>2860 Somerset Dr, #111, Lauderdale Lakes FL 33311, USA | Football Player |
| **White, Marco P**<br>The Restaurant, 66 Knightsbridge, London SW1X 7LA, England | Chef |
| **White, Marilyn**<br>9605 6th Ave, Inglewood CA 90305, USA | Track Athlete |
| **White, Mark**<br>D A S Communications, 83 Riverside Dr, New York NY 10024 USA | Musician (Spin Doctors) |
| **White, Mary Anne**<br>30 Burnt Log Crescent, Etobicoke ON M9C 2J8, Canada | Chemist |
| **White, Matthew J (Matt)**<br>1853 Old Route 9, Windsor MA 01270, USA | Baseball Player |
| **White, Maurice**<br>Spirit Media, PO Box 43591, Phoenix AZ 85080, USA | Singer (Earth Wind & Fire), Songwriter |
| **White, Meg**<br>Monotone Mgmt, 820 Seward St, Los Angeles CA 90038, USA | Singer, Drummer (White Stripes) |
| **White, Michael D**<br>DirecTV, 2230 E Imperial Highway, El Segundo CA 90245, USA | Businessman |
| **White, Michael Jai**<br>24602 Garland Dr, Valencia CA 91355, USA | Actor, Producer |
| **White, Michael R**<br>11655 Blue Ridge Road, Newcomerstown OH 43832, USA | Mayor, Cleveland |
| **White, Michael S**<br>48 Dean St, London W1V 5HL, England | Producer |
| **White, Mike**<br>United Talent Agency, U T A Plaza, 9336 Civic Center Dr, Beverly Hills CA 90210 USA | Actor, Director, Writer |
| **White, Mike**<br>115 Grand Canal, Newport Beach CA 92662, USA | Football Coach |
| **White, Miles D**<br>Abbott Laboratories, 100 Abbott Park Road, North Chicago IL 60064, USA | Businessman |
| **White, Myron A**<br>3201 S Deegan Dr, Santa Ana CA 92704, USA | Baseball Player |

**W**

White - White

White, Nera D — Basketball Player
RR 3 Box 165, Lafayette TN 37083, USA

White, Persia — Singer, Songwriter, Actress
Stone Manners Salners, 6100 Wilshire Blvd, #1500, Los Angeles CA 90035 USA

White, Peter — Jazz Guitarist
Chapman Mgmt, 14011 Ventura Blvd, #405, Sherman Oaks CA 91423, USA

White, Peter — Actor
S M S Talent, 8383 Wilshire Blvd, #230, Beverly Hills CA 90211 USA

White, Randy L — Football Player
1360 E Frontier Parkway, Prosper TX 75078, USA

White, Raymond P, Jr — Oral Surgeon
1506 Velma Road, Chapel Hill NC 27514, USA

White, Rex — Auto Racing Driver
187 Rivers Road, #222, Fayetteville GA 30214, USA

White, Richard A (Rick) — Baseball Player
2860 Windy Ridge Dr, Springfield OH 45502, USA

White, Robert — Artist
380 Millwood Ave, Winchester VA 22601, USA

White, Robert M — Meteorologist
Somerset House II, 5610 Wisconsin Ave, #1506, Chevy Chase MD 20815, USA

White, Ron — Actor, Writer, Producer
A P A Talent & Literary Agency, 405 S Beverly Dr, #300, Beverly Hills CA 90212 USA

White, Rondell B — Baseball Player
407 Creekside Dr, Gray GA 31032, USA

White, Rory W — Basketball Player
5303 32nd St S, Fargo ND 58104, USA

White, Roy H — Baseball Player
534 Mill Pond Way, Eatontown NJ 07724, USA

White, Samuel (Sammy) — Football Player
102 Margaret Dr, Monroe LA 71203, USA

White, Sarah — Actress
Associated International Mgmt, 7 Hatton Garden, #400, London EC1N 8AD, England

White, Sharod L (Roddy) — Football Player
2540 Shumard Oak Dr, Braselton GA 30517, USA

White, Shaun — Snowboard, Skateboard Athlete
Burton Snowboards, 80 Industrial Parkway, Burlington VT 05401, USA

White, Sheldon D — Football Player
PO Box 622, Novi MI 48376, USA

White, Sherman E (Sherm) — Football Player
2710 Summerland Road, Aromas CA 95004, USA

White, Steven A — Navy Admiral, Businessman
Stone & Webster Engineering, 4 Mount Royal Ave, #420, Marlboro MA 01752, USA

White, Susanna — Director
United Talent Agency, U T A Plaza, 9336 Civic Center Dr, Beverly Hills CA 90210 USA

White, Sylvain — Director
United Talent Agency, U T A Plaza, 9336 Civic Center Dr, Beverly Hills CA 90210 USA

White, Timothy D — Anthropologist
University of California, Human Evolutionary Studies Laboratory, Berkeley CA 94720, USA

White, Timothy P — Educator
University of California, Chancellor's Office, 900 University Ave, Riverside CA 92521, USA

White, Tony Joe — Singer, Songwriter
Tony Joe White Music, PO Box 1292, Franklin TN 37065, USA

White, Vanna — Entertainer, Actress, Model
'Wheel of Fortune' Show, 10202 W Washington Blvd, #2000, Culver City CA 90232, USA

White, Verdine — Bassist (Earth Wind & Fire), Songwriter
Spirit Media, PO Box 43591, Phoenix AZ 85080, USA

White, W Daniel (Danny) — Football Player
902 E San Angelo Ave, Gilbert AZ 85234, USA

White, Willard W — Opera Singer
10 Montague Ave, London SE4 1YP, England

White, William B (Bill) — Baseball Player, Executive
8517 Barn Owl, San Antonio TX 78255, USA

White, William E — Football Player
2323 Woodland Hall Dr, Powell OH 43065, USA

Whited, Edward M (Ed) — Baseball Player
PO Box 34, Carmel IN 46082, USA

Whitehead, Axle — Actor
United Talent Agency, U T A Plaza, 9336 Civic Center Dr, Beverly Hills CA 90210 USA

Whitehead, Barb — Golfer
9820 E Thompson Peak Parkway, #707, Scottsdale AZ 85255, USA

Whitehead, Colson — Writer
Doubleday Press, 1745 Broadway, New York NY 10019 USA

Whitehead, Geoffrey — Actor
Bryan Drew, Quadrant House, 80-82 Regent St, London W1B 5AU, England

Whitehead, Jerome C — Basketball Player
PO Box 5932, Playa del Rey CA 90296, USA

Whitehead, John A — Physical Oceanographer
Woods Hole Oceanographic Institution, Physical Oceanography Dept, Woods Hole MA 02543, USA

Whitehead, John C — Foundation Executive, Financier
Goldman Sachs Foundation, 85 Broad St, Building 85, New York NY 10004, USA

Whitehead, Lorne A — Inventor (Prism Light Guide System)
T I R Systems, 77 Riverfront Gate, Burnaby BC V5J 5M4, Canada

Whitehead, Nicole — Model
Playboy Promotions, 9346 Civic Center Dr, #200, Beverly Hills CA 90210 USA

Whitehead, Paxton — Actor
Gary Goddard Agency, 10 Saint Mary's St, Toronto ON M4Y 1P9, Canada

Whitehead, Rachel — Sculptor
Luhring Augustine Gallery, 531 W 24th St, New York NY 10011, USA

Whitehead, Richard F — Navy Admiral
American Cage & Machine Co, 135 S LaSalle St, Chicago IL 60603, USA

Whitehurst, C David — Football Player
11010 Linbrook Lane, Duluth GA 30097, USA

Whitehurst, Walter R (Wally) — Baseball Player
102 Beverly Dr, Bay Saint Louis MS 39520, USA

Whitelaw, Billie — Actress
Rose Cottage, Plum St, Glensford, Suffolk C010 7PX, England

**Whiteman, Andrew** — Guitarist (Apostle of Hustle)
High Road Touring, 751 Bridgeway, #200, Sausalito CA 94965 USA
**Whitemore, Hugh** — Writer
Creative Artists Agency, 2000 Ave of Stars, #100, Los Angeles CA 90067 USA
**Whitemore, Willet F, Jr** — Cancer Researcher
2 Hawthorne Lane, Manhasset NY 11030, USA
**Whiten, Mark A** — Baseball Player
5810 Jefferson Park Dr, Tampa FL 33625, USA
**Whiteread, Rachel** — Sculptor
Anthony D'Offay, 22 Dering St, London W1R 9AA, England
**Whitesell, Emily** — Writer, Producer, Actress
United Talent Agency, U T A Plaza, 9336 Civic Center Dr, Beverly Hills CA 90210 USA
**Whitesell, John P** — Director
Luber Rocklin Entertainment, 5815 Sunset Blvd, #206, Los Angeles CA 90028 USA
**Whiteside, Matthew C (Matt)** — Baseball Player
255 Palisades Ridge Court, Eureka MO 63025, USA
**Whitesides, George M** — Chemist
124 Grasmere St, Newton MA 02458, USA
**Whitfield, Charles Malik** — Actor
Paradigm Agency, 360 N Crescent Dr, North Building, Beverly Hills CA 90210 USA
**Whitfield, Dondre** — Actor
Paul Kohner, 9300 Wilshire Blvd, #555, Beverly Hills CA 90212 USA
**Whitfield, Fred** — Rodeo Rider
17915 Becker Road, Hockley TX 77447, USA
**Whitfield, Lynn** — Actress
Pantheon Talent, 1801 Century Park E, #1910, Los Angeles CA 90067, USA
**Whitfield, Malvin G (Mal)** — Track Athlete
1322 28th St SE, Washington DC 20020, USA
**Whitfield, Mark** — Guitarist
Joel Chriss Co, 300 Mercer St, #3J, New York NY 10003 USA
**Whitfield, Simon** — Triathlete
Triathlon Canada, 4050 Wheelwright Crest, Mississauga ON L5L 2X5, Canada
**Whitfield, Terry B** — Baseball Player
849 Clearfield Dr, Millbrae CA 94030, USA
**Whitfield, Trent** — Ice Hockey Player
8781 Piney Orchard Parkway, Odenton MD 21113, USA
**Whitford, Bradley E (Brad)** — Guitarist (Aerosmith)
Front Line Mgmt, 1100 Glendon Ave, #2000, Los Angeles CA 90024 USA
**Whitham, Gerald B** — Mathematician
California Institute of Technology, Mathematics Dept, Pasadena CA 91125, USA
**Whiting, Lynn S** — Thoroughbred Racing Trainer
Lynn S Whiting Stable, 700 Central Ave, Louisville KY 40208, USA
**Whitley, Kym** — Actress
Innovative Artists, 1505 10th St, Santa Monica CA 90401 USA
**Whitlock, Isiah, Jr** — Actor
Liebman Entertainment, 25 E 21st St, #PH, New York NY 10010 USA
**Whitlow, Robert E (Bob)** — Football Player
2005 S Rogers St, #41, Bloomington IN 47403, USA
**Whitman, Kari** — Actress, Model
House of Representatives, 1434 6th St, #1, Santa Monica CA 90401 USA
**Whitman, Mae** — Actress
I C M Partners, 10250 Constellation Blvd, #900, Los Angeles CA 90067 USA
**Whitman, Margaret C (Meg)** — Businesswoman
Hewlett Packard Co, 3000 Hanover St, Palo Alto CA 94304, USA
**Whitman, Marina Von Neumann** — Economist, Government Official
University of Michigan, Public Policy School, Ann Arbor MI 48109, USA
**Whitman, Stuart** — Actor
749 San Ysidro Road, Santa Barbara CA 93108, USA
**Whitmore, James, Jr** — Actor
1284 La Brea St, Thousand Oaks CA 91362, USA
**Whitmore, Jon** — Educator
Texas Tech University, President's Office, Lubbock TX 79409, USA
**Whitmore, Kay** — Ice Hockey Player
National Hockey League, 50 Bay St, #1100, Toronto ON M5J 2X8, Canada
**Whitmore, Tamika** — Basketball Player
Connecticut Sun, 1 Mohegan Sun Blvd, Uncasville CT 06382 USA
**Whitner, Donte** — Football Player
Cleveland Browns, 76 Lou Groza Blvd, Berea OH 44017 USA
**Whitney, Ashley A** — Swimmer
124 Hearthstone Manor Circle, Brentwood TN 37027, USA
**Whitney, CeCe** — Actress
16857 San Fernando Mission Blvd, #46, Granada Hills CA 91344, USA
**Whitney, David** — Basketball Coach, Baseball Player
2178 Popps Ferry Road, Biloxi MS 39532, USA
**Whitney, Grace Lee** — Actress
PO Box 1869, Coarsegold CA 93614, USA
**Whitney, Raymond D (Ray)** — Ice Hockey Player
2908 Spaldwick Court, Raleigh NC 27613, USA
**Whitson, Eddie L (Ed)** — Baseball Player
10473 Mackenzie Way, Dublin OH 43017, USA
**Whitson, Elizabeth** — Actress
Sweeney Entertainment, 6253 Hollywood Blvd, #201, Los Angeles CA 90028, USA
**Whitson, Peggy A** — Astronaut
306 Lakeview Circle, Seabrook TX 77586, USA
**Whitt, Ernest L (Ernie)** — Baseball Player
37370 Moravian Dr, Clinton Township MI 48036, USA
**Whittaker, James (Jim)** — Mountaineer
2023 E Sims Way, #277, Port Townsend WA 98368, USA
**Whittaker, Jodie** — Actress
Independent Talent Group, 40 Whitfield St, London W1T 2RH, England
**Whittaker, Roger** — Singer, Songwriter
Howard Elson Promotions, 16 Penn Ave, Chesham Buckinghamshire HP5 2HS, England
**Whittenton, U Jesse** — Football Player
1748 Boulders Dr, Las Cruces NM 88011, USA
**Whittingham, Charles A** — Publisher
1 E 66th St, #13D, New York NY 10065, USA

W

Whiteman - Whittingham

**Whittington, Arthur L (Art)** — Football Player
6709 La Tijera Blvd, #190, Los Angeles CA 90045, USA
**Whittington, Bill** — Auto Racing Driver
1881 W State Road 84, Fort Lauderdale FL 33315, USA
**Whittington, Reginald (Don)** — Auto Racing Driver
1881 W State Road 54, Fort Lauderdale FL 33315, USA
**Whittle, Jason** — Football Player
PO Box 1980, Osage Beach MO 65065, USA
**Whittle, Ricky** — Actor
True Public Relations, 6725 Sunset Blvd, #470, Los Angeles CA 90028, USA
**Whitton, Margaret** — Actress, Producer, Director
Tashtego Films, 11 W 10th St, New York NY 10011, USA
**Whitwam, David R** — Businessman
Whirlpool Corp, 2000 N State St, RR 63, Benton Harbor MI 49022, USA
**Whitworth, Andrew J** — Football Player
903 Adams Crossing, #110, Cincinnati OH 45202, USA
**Whitworth, Johnny** — Actor, Producer
Greene Assoc, 1901 Ave of Stars, #130, Los Angeles CA 90067 USA
**Whitworth, Kathrynne A (Kathy)** — Golfer
1735 Mistletoe Dr, Flower Mound TX 75022, USA
**Whyte, Sandra** — Ice Hockey Player
81 Golden Hills Road, Saugus MA 01906, USA
**Wi, Charlie** — Golfer
9400 Burnet Ave, #109, North Hills CA 91343, USA
**Wiberg, Kenneth B** — Chemist
865 Central Ave, #A404, Needham MA 02492, USA
**Wiberg, Pernilla** — Alpine Skier
Margaretha Wiberg, Katterumsv 32, 602 10 Norrkoping, Sweden
**Wickander, Kevin D** — Baseball Player
4319 W Banff Lane, Glendale AZ 85306, USA
**Wickenheiser, Hayley** — Ice Hockey Player
Newport Sports Management, 201 City Centre Dr, Mississauga ON L5B 2T4, Canada
**Wickersham, David C (Dave)** — Baseball Player
9118 W 104th Terrace, Overland Park KS 66212, USA
**Wickersham, Emily** — Actress
Untitled Entertainment, 350 S Beverly Dr, #200, Beverly Hills CA 90212 USA
**Wickham, John A, Jr** — Army General
13500 N Rancho Vistoso Blvd, #519, Tucson AZ 85755, USA
**Wickham, Madeleine** — Writer
Thomas Dunne/Saint Martin's Press, 175 5th Ave, #400, New York NY 10010, USA
**Wicki-Fink, Agnes** — Actress
Weisgerberstr 2, 80805 Munich, Germany
**Wickman, Robert J (Bob)** — Baseball Player
6568 Cheyenne Dr, Abrams WI 54101, USA
**Wickner, Reed B** — Geneticist
National Institutes of Health, 9000 Rockville Pike, Bethesda MD 20892, USA
**Wickner, Sue H** — Molecular Biolgist
N C I Molecular Biology Laboratory, 37 Convent Dr, Bethesda MN 20892, USA
**Wicks, Ben** — Editorial Cartoonist
38 Yorkville Ave, Toronto ON M4W 1L5, Canada
**Wicks, Chuck** — Singer, Songwriter
W M E Entertainment, 1600 Division St, #300, Nashville TN 37203 USA
**Wicks, Ron** — Ice Hockey Referee
4 McLaughlin Road S, Brampton ON L6Y 3B2, Canada
**Wicks, Sidney** — Basketball Player
8650 Cashio St, #5, Los Angeles CA 90035, USA
**Wicks, Sue** — Basketball Player
Saint Francis College, Athletic Dept, 180 Remsen St, Brooklyn Heights NY 11201, USA
**Wickwire, Jim** — Mountaineer
1416 W Roy St, Seattle WA 98112, USA
**Wickwire, Maria** — Sculptor
PO Box 2911, Battle Creek WA 97604, USA
**Wicoff, Erika** — Golfer
7815 Four Leaf Dr, Greenville IN 47124, USA
**Widby, G Ronald (Ron)** — Football, Basketball Player
1521 Lesli Dr, Royse City TX 75189, USA
**Widdoes, Jamie** — Director, Producer, Actor
United Talent Agency, U T A Plaza, 9336 Civic Center Dr, Beverly Hills CA 90210 USA
**Widdoes, Kathleen** — Actress
24 E 11th St, New York NY 10003, USA
**Widdrington, Peter N T** — Businessman
Laidlaw Inc, 3221 N Service Road, Burlington ON L7R 3Y8, Canada
**Widell, David H (Dave)** — Football Player
13050 Wexford Hollow Road N, Jacksonville FL 32224, USA
**Widell, Douglas J (Doug)** — Football Player
4638 Pebble Brook Dr, Jacksonville FL 32224, USA
**Wideman, John Edgar** — Writer
University of Massachusetts, English Dept, Amherst MA 01003, USA
**Widger, Christopher J (Chris)** — Baseball Player
95 Fort Mott Road, Pennsville NJ 08070, USA
**Widman, Herbert (Herb)** — Water Polo Player
844 Monarch Circle, San Jose CA 95138, USA
**Widmann, Jorg** — Concert Clarinetist, Composer
Schott Music, Weihergarten 5, 55116 Mainz, Germany
**Widmer, Corey E** — Football Player
PO Box 1201, Manhattan MT 59741, USA
**Widmer-Schlumpf, Eveline** — President, Switzerland
Federal Chancellery, Bundeshaus-W, Bundesgasse, 3033 Berne, Switzerland
**Widodo, Joko (Jokowi)** — President, Indonesia
President's Office, 15 Jalam Merdeka Utara, Jarkata, Indonesia
**Widom, Benjamin** — Chemist
204 The Parkway, Ithaca NY 14850, USA
**Wie, Michelle** — Golfer
17217 Leal Ave, Cerritos CA 90703, USA
**Wiebe, Susanne** — Fashion Designer
Amalienstr 39, 80799 Munich, Germany

**Wiegert, Zachary A (Zach)** — Football Player
919 N 264th St, Waterloo NE 68069, USA
**Wieghaus, Thomas R (Tom)** — Baseball Player
9724 E 8000 Road, #N, Grant Park IL 60940, USA
**Wiegmann, Casey P** — Football Player
21010 W 60th Terrace, Shawnee KS 66218, USA
**Wiehl, Christopher** — Actor
A P A Talent & Literary Agency, 405 S Beverly Dr, #300, Beverly Hills CA 90212 USA
**Wielicki, Krzysztof J** — Mountaineer
Ul A Frycza Modrzewskiego 21, 43100 Tychy, Poland
**Wieman, Carl E** — Nobel Physics Laureate
University of Colorado, Physics Dept, Campus Box 440, Boulder CO 80309, USA
**Wiemer, Jason** — Ice Hockey Player
428-5201 Dalhousie Dr NW, Calgary AB T3A 5Y7, Canada
**Wiener, Jacques L, Jr** — Judge
US Court of Appeals, 600 Camp St, New Orleans LA 70130, USA
**Wier, Murray N** — Basketball Player, Coach
118 Goodwater St, Georgetown TX 78633, USA
**Wieringa, Jeffrey A** — Navy Admiral
Director, Defense Security Cooperation Agency, Pentagon, Washington DC 20301, USA
**Wieschaus, Eric F** — Nobel Medicine Laureate
11 Pelham St, Boston MA 02118, USA
**Wiese, John P** — Judge
US Claims Court, 717 Madison Place NW, Washington DC 20439, USA
**Wiesel, Elie** — Writer, Nobel Peace Laureate
10155 Collins Ave, #1502, Bal Harbor FL 33154, USA
**Wiesenhahn, Robert B (Bob)** — Basketball Player
3315 Hickorycreek Dr, Cincinnati OH 45244, USA
**Wiesler, Robert G (Bob)** — Baseball Player
2325 Indiancup Dr, Florissant MO 63033, USA
**Wiesner, Kenneth (Ken)** — Track Athlete
3601 Meta Lake Road, Eagle River WI 54521, USA
**Wiest, Dianne** — Actress
I C M Partners, 730 5th Ave, New York NY 10019 USA
**Wigger, Lones W, Jr** — Marksman
US Shooting Team, Olympic Training Center, 1 Olympic Plaza, Colorado Springs CO 80909, USA
**Wiggin, Paul** — Football Player, Coach
5013 Ridge Road, Minneapolis MN 55436, USA
**Wiggin, Tom** — Actor
Don Buchwald Talent Agency, 6500 Wilshire Blvd, #2200, Los Angeles CA 90048 USA
**Wiggins, Andrew C** — Basketball Player
Minnesota Timberwolves, Target Center, 600 1st Ave N, Minneapolis MN 55403 USA
**Wiggins, Audrey** — Singer
PO Box 121196, Nashville TN 37212, USA
**Wiggins, Bradley M** — Cyclist
Team High Road, 425 O'Connor Way, San Luis Obispo CA 93405, USA
**Wiggins, Candice** — Basketball Player
Los Angeles Sparks, 888 S Figueroa St, #2010, Los Angeles CA 90017 USA
**Wiggins, Jennifer** — Actress
D P N Talent, 9201 W Olympic Blvd, Beverly Hills CA 90212, USA
**Wiggins, Jermaine** — Football Player
35 King George Dr, Boxford MA 01921, USA
**Wiggins, John** — Singer
W M E Entertainment, 1600 Division St, #300, Nashville TN 37203 USA
**Wiggins, Laura Slade** — Actress
Don Buchwald Talent Agency, 6500 Wilshire Blvd, #2200, Los Angeles CA 90048 USA
**Wiggins, Mitchell L** — Basketball Player
PO Box 5072, Kinston NC 28503, USA
**Wiggins, Phil** — Singer, Harmonica Player, Songwriter
Blue Mountain Artists, 810 Tyvola Road, #114, Charlotte NC 28217, USA
**Wigginton, Ty A** — Baseball Player
605 Kenway Loop, Mooresville NC 28117, USA
**Wigglesworth, Marian McKean** — Alpine Skier
General Delivery, Wilson WY 83014, USA
**Wigglesworth, Mark** — Conductor
C M Artists, 127 W 96th St, #13B, New York NY 10025 USA
**Wigglesworth, Ryan** — Composer, Conductor
Konzertdirektion Schmid, Konigstra 36, 30175 Hannover, Germany
**Wiggs, Susan** — Writer
PO Box 4469, Rolling Bay WA 98061, USA
**Wightman, Arthur S** — Mathematician, Physicist
16 Balsam Lane, Princeton NJ 08540, USA
**Wihtol, Alexander A (Sandy)** — Baseball Player
1889 Anthony Court, Mountain View CA 94040, USA
**Wiig, Kristen C** — Actress, Comedienne, Writer
United Talent Agency, U T A Plaza, 9336 Civic Center Dr, Beverly Hills CA 90210 USA
**Wiik, Sven** — Skier
PO Box 774484, Steamboat Springs CO 80477, USA
**Wiita, Carrie** — Actress
OmniPop Talent Group, 4605 Lankershim Blvd, #201, Toluca Lake CA 91602 USA
**Wilander, Mats** — Tennis Player
104 Cove Creek Road, Hailey ID 83333, USA
**Wilbraham, John H G** — Concert Cornetist, Trumpeter
9 Cuthbert St, Wells, Somerset BA5 2AW, England
**Wilbur, Delbert Q (Del)** — Baseball Player
4378 Autumn Lane, Lewiston NY 14092, USA
**Wilbur, Richard C** — Judge
US Tax Court, 400 2nd St NW, Washington DC 20217, USA
**Wilbur, Richard P** — Writer
87 Dodswell Road, Cummington MA 01026, USA
**Wilbur, Richard S** — Physician, Association Executive
985 Hawthorne Place, Lake Forest IL 60045, USA
**Wilburn, Johnnie R (J R), Jr** — Football Player
2211 Chalkwell Dr, Midlothian VA 23113, USA
**Wilburn, Ken** — Basketball Player
17 E Meyran Ave, Somers Point NJ 08244, USA

**W**

# W

**Wilby, James** — Actor
Artist Rights Group, 4A Exmoor St, London W10 6BD, England

**Wilcher, Mary** — Actress
Levine Mgmt, 9028 W Sunset Blvd, #PH1, West Hollywood CA 90069, USA

**Wilcher, Michael D (Mike)** — Football Player
1501 Fairlakes Place, Bowie MD 20721, USA

**Wilcox, Barry** — Ice Hockey Player
18859 86th Ave, Surrey BC V4N 3G5, Canada

**Wilcox, Daniel** — Football Player
4119 Old Washington Blvd, Halethorpe MD 21227, USA

**Wilcox, David** — Singer, Songwriter, Guitarist
Concerted Efforts, PO Box 440326, Somerville MA 02144 USA

**Wilcox, David** — Producer, Writer
W M E Entertainment, 9601 Wilshire Blvd, #300, Beverly Hills CA 90210 USA

**Wilcox, David (Dave)** — Football Player
94471 Willamette Dr, Junction City OR 97448, USA

**Wilcox, Larry** — Actor
6763 Daryn Dr, West Hills CA 91307, USA

**Wilcox, Lisa** — Actress
Stone Manners Salners, 6100 Wilshire Blvd, #1500, Los Angeles CA 90035 USA

**Wilcox, Milton E (Milt)** — Baseball Player
1630 Lakeview Dr, Wolverine Lake MI 48390, USA

**Wilcox, Shannon** — Actress
20518 Pacific Coast Highway, Malibu CA 90265, USA

**Wilcutt, Terence W (Terry)** — Astronaut
N A S A, Johnson Space Center, 2101 NASA Road, Houston TX 77058 USA

**Wilczek, Frank A** — Nobel Physics Laureate
4 Wyman Road, Cambridge MA 02138, USA

**Wild, John P** — Astronomer
1 Grant Crescent, #4, Griffith ACT 2603, Australia

**Wild, Victor I (Vic)** — Snowboard Athlete
Petrodvorets Watch Factory, Saint Petersburg Prospect 60, 198516 Saint Petersburg, Russia

**Wilde, Gabriella** — Actress
I C M Partners, 10250 Constellation Blvd, #900, Los Angeles CA 90067 USA

**Wilde, Kim** — Singer, Songwriter
Marty Wilde, Thatched Rest, Queen Hoo Lane, Tewin, Hertfordshire AL6 0LT, England

**Wilde, Olivia** — Actress
Hamilton Hodell, 20 Golden Square, London W1F 9JL, England

**Wilde, Patricia** — Ballerina, Artistic Director
Pittsburgh Ballet Theater, 2900 Liberty Ave, Pittsburgh PA 15201, USA

**Wilder, Alan C** — Synthesizer Musician (Depeche Mode)
Creative Artists Agency, 2000 Ave of Stars, #100, Los Angeles CA 90067 USA

**Wilder, Don** — Cartoonist (Crock)
North American Syndicate, 235 E 45th St, New York NY 10017 USA

**Wilder, Gene** — Actor, Director
476 Scofieldtown Road, Stamford CT 06903, USA

**Wilder, James** — Actor
Chasen Agency, 8899 Beverly Blvd, #405, Los Angeles CA 90048 USA

**Wilder, James C** — Football Player
49 S Shirley St, Pontiac MI 48342, USA

**Wilder, L Douglas** — Governor, VA; Educator
Mayor's Office, City Hall, 900 E Broad St, Richmond VA 23219, USA

**Wildes, Kevin W** — Educator
Loyola University, President's Office, 6363 Saint Charles Ave, New Orleans LA 70118, USA

**Wildman, George** — Cartoonist (Popeye)
601 N Atlantic Ave, #603, New Smyrna FL 32169, USA

**Wildman, Valerie** — Actress
Scott Hart Mgmt, 14622 Ventura Blvd, #746, Sherman Oaks CA 91403, USA

**Wildmon, Donald** — Social Activist
National Federation of Decency, PO Box 1398, Tupelo MS 38802, USA

**Wilds, Tristan** — Actor
I C M Partners, 10250 Constellation Blvd, #900, Los Angeles CA 90067 USA

**Wiles, Andrew J** — Mathematician
Princeton University, Mathematics Dept, Princeton NJ 08544, USA

**Wiles, Jason** — Actor
Paradigm Agency, 360 N Crescent Dr, North Building, Beverly Hills CA 90210 USA

**Wiles, Michael Shamus** — Actor
Greene Assoc, 1901 Ave of Stars, #130, Los Angeles CA 90067 USA

**Wiles, Randall E (Randy)** — Baseball Player
3716 Lake Catherine Dr, Harvey LA 70058, USA

**Wiley, John F (Jack)** — Football Player
1330 India Hook Road, #306, Rock Hill SC 29732, USA

**Wiley, Lee** — Singer
Country Crossroads, 7787 Monterey St, Gilroy CA 95020, USA

**Wiley, Marcellus V** — Football Player
5132 S Garth Ave, Los Angeles CA 90056, USA

**Wiley, Morlon D** — Basketball Player
2521 Fallview Lane, Carrollton TX 75007, USA

**Wiley, Richard E** — Government Official
Wiley Rein, 1776 K St NW, #1100, Washington DC 20006, USA

**Wiley, William T** — Artist
PO Box 661, Forest Knolls CA 94933, USA

**Wilfong, Robert D (Rob)** — Baseball Player
126 Maverick Dr, San Dimas CA 91773, USA

**Wilford, Ernest L, Jr** — Football Player
1516 Chatham Court, Saint Augustine FL 32092, USA

**Wilford, John Noble, Jr** — Journalist
232 W 10th St, New York NY 10014, USA

**Wilfork, Vince L** — Football Player
11 White Dove Road, Franklin MA 02038, USA

**Wilhelm, David C** — WW II Army Air Corps Hero
3801 E Florida Ave, #400, Denver CO 80210, USA

**Wilhelm, Erik B** — Football Player
PO Box 1602, Clackamas OR 97015, USA

**Wilhelm, James W (Jim)** — Baseball Player
348 Laurel Way, Mill Valley CA 94941, USA

**Wilhelm, John W** — Labor Leader
Hotel & Restaurant Employees Union, 1219 28th St NW, Washington DC 20007, USA
**Wilhelm, Kati** — Biathlete
Sport Marketing, Schaumainkai 91, 60596 Frankfurt am Main, Germany
**Wilhelm, Matthew (Matt)** — Football Player
14944 Huntington Gate Dr, Poway CA 92064, USA
**Wilhoite, Kathleen** — Actress
Gersh Agency, 9465 Wilshire Blvd, #600, Beverly Hills CA 90212 USA
**Wilk, Vic** — Golfer
1350 N Town Center Dr, #2082, Las Vegas NV 89144, USA
**Wilkening, Laurel L** — Educator
University of California, Chancellor's Office, Irvine CA 92717, USA
**Wilkens, Leonard R (Lenny), Jr** — Basketball Player, Coach, Executive
3429 Evergreen Point Road, Medina WA 98039, USA
**Wilker, Greg** — Photographer
3601 NW Adriatic Lane, Jensen Beach FL 34957, USA
**Wilkerson, Bruce A** — Football Player
2013 Breakers Point, Knoxville TN 37922, USA
**Wilkerson, Curtis V** — Baseball Player
PO Box 182993, Arlington TX 76096, USA
**Wilkerson, Douglas (Doug)** — Football Player
PO Box 7090, Rancho Santa Fe CA 92067, USA
**Wilkerson, Isabel** — Journalist
New York Times, Editorial Dept, 229 W 43rd St, New York NY 10036, USA
**Wilkerson, Robert L (Bob)** — Basketball Player
PO Box 7453, Upper Marlboro MD 20792, USA
**Wilkerson, S Bradley (Brad)** — Baseball Player
8657 Man O'War Road, Palm Beach Gardens FL 33418, USA
**Wilkerson, Tim** — Drag Racing Driver
Demand Flow Racing, 2901 Stevenson Dr, Springfield IL 62703, USA
**Wilkes, Debbi** — Figure Skater
Skate Canada, 865 Shefford Road, Ottawa ON K1J 1H9, Canada
**Wilkes, Jamaal A** — Basketball Player
7846 W 81st St, Playa del Rey CA 90293, USA
**Wilkes, Reggie W** — Football Player
6912 Wissahickon Ave, Philadelphia PA 19119, USA
**Wilkie, Bob** — Ice Hockey Player
303 S Forge Road, Palmyra PA 17078, USA
**Wilkie, Chris** — Guitarist (Dubstar)
Primary Talent Int'l, 2-12 Petonville Road, London N1 9PL, England
**Wilkie, David** — Ice Hockey Player
8919 N 159th Ave, Bennington NE 68007, USA
**Wilkie, David A** — Swimmer
Oaklands, Queens Hill, Ascot, Berkshire SL5 7JF, England
**Wilkin, Richard E** — Religious Leader
Winebrenner Theological Seminary, 950 N Main St, Findlay OH 45840, USA
**Wilkins Perez, Laisha** — Actress
Televisa, Blvd A Lopez Mateos 232, Colonia San Angel, Mexico City DF 01060 CP, Mexico
**Wilkins, Barry** — Ice Hockey Player
2230 W Monroe St, Chandler AZ 85224, USA
**Wilkins, Eric L** — Baseball Player
1650 W Joshua Lane, Meridian ID 83642, USA
**Wilkins, J Dominique** — Basketball Player
4415 Felix Way SE, Smyrna GA 30082, USA
**Wilkins, Jeffrey A (Jeff)** — Football Player
8288 S Raccoon Road, Canfield OH 44406, USA
**Wilkins, Marc A** — Baseball Player
3473 Oakstone Dr, Ontario OH 44903, USA
**Wilkins, Maurice (Mac)** — Track Athlete
1915 NW Columbine Lane, Portland OR 97229, USA
**Wilkins, Richard D (Rick)** — Baseball Player
12766 Longview Dr W, Jacksonville FL 32223, USA
**Wilkins, William W, Jr** — Judge
US Court of Appeals, PO Box 10648, Greenville SC 29603, USA
**Wilkinson, Adrienne** — Actress
Greater Visions Artists Talent Agency, 8981 W Sunset Blvd, #101, West Hollywood CA 90069 USA
**Wilkinson, Amanda** — Singer (Wilkinsons)
Bobby Roberts, 3050 Business Park Circle, #303, Goodlettsville TN 37221 USA
**Wilkinson, Clive** — Interior Designer, Architect
Clive Wilkinson Architect, 6116 Washington Blvd, Culver City CA 90232, USA
**Wilkinson, Dale W** — Basketball Player
3045 Goldfield Dr, Pocatello ID 83201, USA
**Wilkinson, Daniel R (Dan)** — Football Player
222 Republic Dr, Allen Park MI 48101, USA
**Wilkinson, J Harvie, III** — Judge
US Court of Appeals, 255 W Main St, Charlottesville VA 22902, USA
**Wilkinson, Joseph B, Jr** — Navy Admiral
340 Chesapeake Dr, Great Falls VA 22066, USA
**Wilkinson, June** — Model, Actress
4060 E Grenora Way, Long Beach CA 90815, USA
**Wilkinson, Kendra** — Actress, Model
A P A Talent & Literary Agency, 405 S Beverly Dr, #300, Beverly Hills CA 90212 USA
**Wilkinson, Laura** — Diver
PO Box 131961, Spring TX 77393, USA
**Wilkinson, Leon** — Bassist (Lynyrd Skynyrd)
Alliance Artists, 6025 Comers Parkway, #202, Norcross GA 30092, USA
**Wilkinson, Michael** — Costume Designer
United Talent Agency, U T A Plaza, 9336 Civic Center Dr, Beverly Hills CA 90210 USA
**Wilkinson, Neil** — Ice Hockey Player
PO Box 57, Sherwood OR 97140, USA
**Wilkinson, Rhian** — Soccer Player
Canadian Soccer, Place Soccer Canada, 237 Metcalfe St, Ottawa ON K2P 1R2, Canada
**Wilkinson, Signe** — Editorial Cartoonist
Philadelphia Daily News, Editorial Dept, 400 N Broad, Philadelphia PA 19130, USA
**Wilkinson, Steve** — Singer (Wilkinsons)
Fitzgerald Hartley, 1908 Wedgewood Ave, Nashville TN 37212, USA

**W**

**Wilkinson, Tom** — Actor
Lou Coulson Assoc, 37 Berwick St, London W1V 8RS, England
**Wilkinson, Tyler** — Singer (Wilkinsons)
Fitzgerald Hartley, 1908 Wedgewood Ave, Nashville TN 37212, USA
**Wilks, Jimmy R (Jim)** — Football Player
4314 Leaflock Lane, Katy TX 77450, USA
**Will, George F** — Columnist
9 Grafton St, Chevy Chase MD 20815, USA
**Will, Robert L (Bob)** — Baseball Player
3417 S Country Club Road, Woodstock IL 60098, USA
**Will.I.Am** — Rap Artist (Elephunk, Black Eyed Peas)
Creative Artists Agency, 2000 Ave of Stars, #100, Los Angeles CA 90067 USA
**Willard, Fred C** — Actor, Comedian
Amsel Eisenstadt Frazier, 5055 Wilshire Blvd, #865, Los Angeles CA 90036 USA
**Willard, Gerald D (Jerry)** — Baseball Player
1421 Kumquat Place, Oxnard CA 93036, USA
**Willard, Kenneth H (Ken)** — Football Player
3071 Vistapoint Road, Midlothian VA 23113, USA
**Willard, Robert F** — Navy Admiral
Commander, Pacific Command, 250 Makalapa Dr, Pearl Harbor HI 96860 USA
**Willard, Rod** — Ice Hockey Player
18 Overlook Dr, Wilbraham MA 01095, USA
**Willcocks, David V** — Concert Organist, Conductor
13 Grange Road, Cambridge CB3 9AS, England
**Willcox, Peter H** — Social Activist
Greenpeace International, Ottho Heldringstraat 5, 1066 Amsterdam AZ, Netherlands
**Willcox, Toyah A** — Actress, Singer
Emptage Hallett, 14 Rathbone Place, London W1T 1HT, England
**Willcuts, Lori** — Singer
Willcutts, 1102 N Springbrook Road, Newberg OR 97132, USA
**Willem-Alexander** — King, Netherlands
Binnenhof 19, 2513 The Hague AA, Netherlands
**Willet, E Crosby** — Glass Artist
Willet Stained Glass Studios, 811 E Cayuga St, Philadelphia PA 19124, USA
**Willett, Chad** — Actor
Storylab Productions, 440 W 17th Ave, Vancouver BC V5Y2A2, Canada
**Willett, Malcolm** — Cartoonist (Tight Corner)
Universal Press Syndicate, 4520 Main St, #700, Kansas City MO 64111 USA
**Willette, JoAnn** — Actress
I C M Partners, 10250 Constellation Blvd, #900, Los Angeles CA 90067 USA
**Will-Halpin, Maggie** — Golfer
12423 Camoustie Lane, Richmond VA 23236, USA
**Willhite, Gerald W** — Football Player
10464 Iliff Court, Rancho Cordova CA 95670, USA
**William** — Prince, England
Clarence House, Stable Yard Gate, London SW1A 1BA, England
**Williams of Crosby, Shirley V T B** — Government Official, England
House of Lords, Westminster, London SW1A 0PW, England
**Williams, Aeneas D** — Football Player
PO Box 16291, Saint Louis MO 63105, USA
**Williams, Alfred H** — Football Player
Sports Radio 104.3, 7800 E Orchard Road, Greenwood Village CO 80111, USA
**Williams, Allison** — Actress
Creative Artists Agency, 2000 Ave of Stars, #100, Los Angeles CA 90067 USA
**Williams, Alvin L** — Basketball Player
Toronto Raptors, Air Canada Center, 20 Bay St, Toronto ON M5J 2N8, Canada
**Williams, Andy** — Drummer (Doves)
C E S D, 10635 Santa Monica Blvd, #130, Los Angeles CA 90025 USA
**Williams, Ann Claire** — Judge
US Court of Appeals, 219 S Dearborn St, Chicago IL 60604, USA
**Williams, Anson** — Actor
24612 Skyline View Dr, Malibu CA 90265, USA
**Williams, Anthony D (Tony)** — Football Player
1918 Bridgewater Dr, Lake Mary FL 32746, USA
**Williams, Ashley** — Actress
Gersh Agency, 9465 Wilshire Blvd, #600, Beverly Hills CA 90212 USA
**Williams, Ashley C** — Actress, Producer
3 Arts Entertainment, 9460 Wilshire Blvd, #700, Beverly Hills CA 90212 USA
**Williams, Austin** — Actor
Gersh Agency, 9465 Wilshire Blvd, #600, Beverly Hills CA 90212 USA
**Williams, Barbara** — Actress
S M S Talent, 8383 Wilshire Blvd, #230, Beverly Hills CA 90211 USA
**Williams, Barry** — Actor, Singer
Amsel Eisenstadt Frazier, 5055 Wilshire Blvd, #865, Los Angeles CA 90036 USA
**Williams, Bernabe F (Bernie)** — Baseball Player, Guitarist, Composer
Scott Boras, 3 San Joaquin Plaza, #100, Newport Beach CA 92660, USA
**Williams, Bernard (Bernie)** — Baseball Player
6851 Arthur St, Oakland CA 94605, USA
**Williams, Beth** — Model
Playboy Promotions, 9346 Civic Center Dr, #200, Beverly Hills CA 90210 USA
**Williams, Betty** — Nobel Peace Laureate
Knock Inverin, County Galway, Ireland
**Williams, Billy** — Cinematographer
Coach House, Hawkshill Place, Esher, Surrey KT10 9HY, England
**Williams, Billy Dee** — Actor
Coolwaters Productions, 10061 Riverside Dr, Box 531, Toluca Lake CA 91602 USA
**Williams, Billy L** — Baseball Player
586 Prince Edward Road, Glen Ellyn IL 60137, USA
**Williams, Brian** — Commentator
NBC-TV, News Dept, 30 Rockefeller Plaza, #270E, New York NY 10112 USA
**Williams, Brian** — Football Player
8704 Shady Hill Court, Colfax NC 27235, USA
**Williams, Brian M** — Football Player
1133 Ashington Place, DeSoto TX 75115, USA
**Williams, Brian O** — Baseball Player
2409 Colt Lane, Crowley TX 76036, USA

| | |
|---|---|
| **Williams, Brian S**<br>1226 Night Trail, Waconia MN 55387, USA | Football Player |
| **Williams, Brooks**<br>Eastern Star Productions, 2625 Alcatraz Ave, #302, Berkeley CA 94705, USA | Guitarist, Songwriter |
| **Williams, Bunny**<br>306 E 61st St, #500, New York NY 10065, USA | Interior Designer |
| **Williams, C K**<br>Princeton University, English Dept, Princeton NJ 08544, USA | Writer |
| **Williams, Calvin J, Jr**<br>5032 Yellowood Ave, Baltimore MD 21209, USA | Football Player |
| **Williams, Cara**<br>9903 Santa Monica Blvd, #606, Beverly Hills CA 90212, USA | Actress |
| **Williams, Carnell L (Cadillac)**<br>8090 Cleary Blvd, #903, Plantation FL 33324, USA | Football Player |
| **Williams, Caroline**<br>International Talent Agency, 10 NBC Universal Studios Plaza, #2000, Universal City CA 91608, USA | Actress |
| **Williams, Cecil**<br>Glide Memorial United Methodist Church, 330 Ellis St, San Francisco CA 94102, USA | Religious Leader, Social Activist |
| **Williams, Charles E (Charlie)**<br>18675 Parkland Dr, #409, Shaker Heights OH 44122, USA | Basketball Player |
| **Williams, Charles L (Buck)**<br>9219 Fox Meadow Lane, Potomac MD 20854, USA | Basketball Player |
| **Williams, Charles P (Charlie)**<br>44 Frederick Ave, Port Orange FL 32127, USA | Baseball Player |
| **Williams, Charlie U**<br>3052 England Parkway, Grand Prairie TX 75054, USA | Football Player |
| **Williams, Christine**<br>Playboy Promotions, 9346 Civic Center Dr, #200, Beverly Hills CA 90210 USA | Model |
| **Williams, Christopher J (Chris)**<br>Anonymous Content, 3532 Hayden Ave, Culver City CA 90232 USA | Actor |
| **Williams, Christy**<br>2745 NE 89th St, Seattle WA 98115, USA | Artist |
| **Williams, Cindy**<br>Cindy Williams Productions, 499 Canon Dr, #216, Beverly Hills CA 90210, USA | Actress |
| **Williams, Clarence**<br>Los Angeles Times, Editorial Dept, 145 S Spring St, Los Angeles CA 90012, USA | Photojournalist |
| **Williams, Clarence, III**<br>Framework Entertainment, 9057 Nemo St, #C, West Hollywood CA 90069 USA | Actor |
| **Williams, Clevan (Tank)**<br>4053 Alexis Dr, Antioch TN 37013, USA | Football Player |
| **Williams, Clifford (Cliff)**<br>Alberts Music, 9 Rangers Road, Neutral Bay, Sydney NSW 2089, Australia | Bassist (AC/DC) |
| **Williams, Clyde A**<br>9754 Highway 79, Bethany LA 71007, USA | Football Player |
| **Williams, Colleen**<br>KNBC-TV, News Dept, 3000 W Alameda Ave, Burbank CA 91523, USA | Commentator |
| **Williams, Cress**<br>Abrams Artists, 275 7th Ave, #2600, New York NY 10001 USA | Actor |
| **Williams, Curtis**<br>David Harris Enterprises, 24210 E Fork Road, #9, Azusa CA 91702, USA | Singer (Penguins) |
| **Williams, D Keith**<br>1756 N Avignon Lane, Clovis CA 93619, USA | Baseball Player |
| **Williams, Dafydd R (David)**<br>N A S A, Johnson Space Center, 2101 NASA Road, Houston TX 77058 USA | Astronaut |
| **Williams, Dan, II**<br>4731 Corina Place NE, Roswell GA 30075, USA | Football Player |
| **Williams, Dana**<br>Modern Mgmt, 1625 Broadway, #600, Nashville TN 37203, USA | Bassist, Drummer (Diamond Rio) |
| **Williams, Dana L**<br>121 Arlene Dr, North Versailles PA 15137, USA | Baseball Player |
| **Williams, Dar**<br>R F Entertainment, 29 Haines Road, Bedford Hills NY 10507, USA | Singer, Songwriter |
| **Williams, Darnell (J D)**<br>Don Buchwald Talent Agency, 6500 Wilshire Blvd, #2200, Los Angeles CA 90048 USA | Actor |
| **Williams, Darryl E**<br>2841 NW 82nd Way, Pembroke Pines FL 33024, USA | Football Player |
| **Williams, Dave (Tiger)**<br>Pacific Rodera Energy, 1100-550 6th Ave SW, Calgary AB T2P 0S2, Canada | Ice Hockey Player |
| **Williams, David**<br>Troika, 74 Clerkenwell Road, #300, London EC1M 5QA, England | Actor, Writer, Producer |
| **Williams, David L**<br>15816 Crest Lane, Gardena CA 90249, USA | Football Player |
| **Williams, David W**<br>31 Turn About Court, Waynesville NC 28785, USA | Football Player |
| **Williams, Dean E**<br>309 Carlyle Lake Dr, Saint Louis MO 63141, USA | Businessman |
| **Williams, DeAngelo**<br>6942 Curlee Court, Charlotte NC 28277, USA | Football Player |
| **Williams, Delvin, Jr**<br>173 Sierra Vista Ave, #11, Mountain View CA 94043, USA | Football Player |
| **Williams, Deniece**<br>Green Light Talent Agency, PO Box 3172, Beverly Hills CA 90212 USA | Singer |
| **Williams, Deron M**<br>PO Box 270, Draper UT 84020, USA | Basketball Player |
| **Williams, Don**<br>Chimes International Entertainment, PO Box 26312, Glasgow G76 7WX, Scotland | Singer, Guitarist, Songwriter |
| **Williams, Don**<br>6109 Rosedale Dr, Hyattsville MD 20782, USA | Basketball Player |
| **Williams, Donald E**<br>Science Applications International, 2200 Space Park Dr, #200, Houston TX 77058, USA | Astronaut |
| **Williams, Doug**<br>J K A Talent Agency, 12725 Ventura Blvd, #H, Studio City CA 91604, USA | Actor, Comedian, Writer, Producer |
| **Williams, Douglas L (Doug)**<br>10546 Greensprings Dr, Tampa FL 33626, USA | Football Player, Coach |
| **Williams, Dudley**<br>Alvin Ailey American Dance Foundation, 405 W 55th St, New York NY 10019, USA | Dancer |

| | |
|---|---|
| **Williams, E Virginia**<br>Boston Ballet, 19 Clarendon St, Boston MA 02116, USA | Artistic Director, Choreographer |
| **Williams, Edward L (Eddie)**<br>6229 Meadowgrass Lane, Las Vegas NV 89103, USA | Baseball Player |
| **Williams, Edy**<br>PO Box 6325, Woodland Hills CA 91365, USA | Actress, Model |
| **Williams, Elmo**<br>1249 Iris St, Brookings OR 97415, USA | Director, Producer |
| **Williams, Eric D**<br>4529 Dakota Trail, Saint Charles MO 63304, USA | Football Player |
| **Williams, Eric M**<br>11147 Corsicana Dr, Frisco TX 75035, USA | Football Player |
| **Williams, Eric T**<br>215 Haywood St, Garner NC 27529, USA | Football Player |
| **Williams, Errick L (Ricky), Jr**<br>2307 Castilla Isle, Fort Lauderdale FL 33301, USA | Football Player |
| **Williams, Evan**<br>Twitter Inc, 795 Folsom St, #600, San Francisco CA 94107, USA | Businessman |
| **Williams, Frederick B (Freedom)**<br>Richard Walters, PO Box 2789, Toluca Lake CA 91610 USA | Rap Artist (C & C Music Factory) |
| **Williams, Freeman**<br>450 W 41st Place, Los Angeles CA 90037, USA | Basketball Player |
| **Williams, Gary Anthony**<br>Coast to Coast Talent, 3350 Barham Blvd, Los Angeles CA 90068 USA | Actor |
| **Williams, Gary B**<br>University of Maryland, Athletic Dept, College Park MD 20742, USA | Basketball Player, Coach |
| **Williams, George E**<br>606 Paden Dr, Cedar Park TX 78613, USA | Baseball Player |
| **Williams, Gerald**<br>9613 Callis Court, Harrisburg NC 28075, USA | Football Player |
| **Williams, Gerald F**<br>17011 Candeleda de Avila, Tampa FL 33613, USA | Baseball Player |
| **Williams, Greg Alan**<br>S T W Talent Agency, PO Box 16675, Wilmington NC 28408, USA | Actor |
| **Williams, Gregory**<br>University of Cincinnati, President's Office, 2600 Clifton Ave, Cincinnati OH 45221, USA | Educator |
| **Williams, Gregory S (Woody)**<br>5110 Newpoint Dr, Fresno TX 77545, USA | Baseball Player |
| **Williams, Gus**<br>290 Collins Ave, #9H, Mount Vernon NY 10552, USA | Basketball Player |
| **Williams, Hal**<br>Jenny Delaney Mgmt, 3238 Fond Dr, Encino CA 91436, USA | Actor |
| **Williams, Hank, III**<br>Rider Mgmt, 931 Hilldale Ave, West Hollywood CA 90069, USA | Singer, Songwriter |
| **Williams, Hank, Jr**<br>W M E Entertainment, 1600 Division St, #300, Nashville TN 37203 USA | Singer, Guitarist, Songwriter |
| **Williams, Harland**<br>Gersh Agency, 9465 Wilshire Blvd, #600, Beverly Hills CA 90212 USA | Actor, Comedian, Writer, Director |
| **Williams, Harold M**<br>J Paul Getty Museum, Getty Center, 1200 Getty Center Dr, Los Angeles CA 90049, USA | Museum Executive |
| **Williams, Harvey L**<br>16815 Southern Oaks Dr, Houston TX 77068, USA | Football Player |
| **Williams, Hayley N**<br>Big Hassle, 44 Wall St, #2200, New York NY 10005, USA | Singer, Keyboardist (Paramore) |
| **Williams, Herbert L (Herb)**<br>1465 Zenner Dr, Columbus OH 43207, USA | Basketball Player, Coach |
| **Williams, Hershel W**<br>3450 Wire Branch Road, Ona WV 25545, USA | WW II Marine Corps Hero (CMH) |
| **Williams, Holly**<br>Three Ring Projects, 111 Westwood Plaza, #101, Brentwood TN 37027, USA | Singer, Guitarist, Songwriter |
| **Williams, Howard E (Howie)**<br>1940 Hamilton Lane, Carmel CA 46032, USA | Basketball Player |
| **Williams, Howard L (Howie)**<br>4731 Proctor Ave, Oakland CA 94618, USA | Football Player |
| **Williams, Hype**<br>Creative Artists Agency, 2000 Ave of Stars, #100, Los Angeles CA 90067 USA | Director, Producer, Writer |
| **Williams, Ivy**<br>Mediachase, 834 N Harper Ave, Los Angeles CA 90046, USA | Writer |
| **Williams, Jaimie**<br>1019 Kane Concourse, #202, Bay Harbour Islands FL 33154, USA | Actress |
| **Williams, Jamal**<br>7710 Hazard Center Dr, #E, San Diego CA 92108, USA | Football Player |
| **Williams, James (Fly)**<br>682 Ralph Ave, #2E, Brooklyn NY 11212, USA | Basketball Player |
| **Williams, James A**<br>Painters & Allied Trades, 1750 New York Ave NW, #501, Washington DC 20006, USA | Labor Leader |
| **Williams, James A**<br>8928 Maurice Lane, Annandale VA 22003, USA | Army General |
| **Williams, James A (Froggy)**<br>296 Sugarberry Circle, Houston TX 77024, USA | Football Player |
| **Williams, James D**<br>20 Johnson Lane, Westport Island ME 04578, USA | Navy Admiral |
| **Williams, James F (Jimy)**<br>1401 Olde Post Road, Palm Harbor FL 34683, USA | Baseball Player, Manager |
| **Williams, James H (Jimmy)**<br>54 Pennington Court, Buffalo NY 14228, USA | Football Player |
| **Williams, James O**<br>330 S Western Ave, Lake Forest IL 60045, USA | Football Player |
| **Williams, Jason C**<br>6103 Louise Cove Dr, Windermere FL 34786, USA | Basketball Player |
| **Williams, Jay**<br>1306 Roxanna Road NW, Washington DC 20012, USA | Football Player |
| **Williams, Jayson**<br>NBC-TV, Sports Dept, 30 Rockefeller Plaza, #270E, New York NY 10112 USA | Basketball Player, Sportscaster |
| **Williams, Jeffrey N**<br>4918 Cross Creek Lane, League City TX 77573, USA | Astronaut |

|  |  |
|---|---|
| **Williams, Jerrol L**<br>2562 Mizzoni Circle, Henderson NV 89052, USA | Football Player |
| **Williams, Jesse**<br>W M E Entertainment, 9601 Wilshire Blvd, #300, Beverly Hills CA 90210 USA | Actor |
| **Williams, Jessica**<br>T-Best Talent Agency, 508 Honey Lake Court, Danville CA 94506 USA | Jazz Pianist |
| **Williams, Jett**<br>AddJet Productions, PO Box 177, Hartsville TN 37074, USA | Singer |
| **Williams, JoBeth**<br>S D B Partners, 315 S Beverly Dr, #411, Beverly Hills CA 90067 USA | Actress |
| **Williams, Jody**<br>663 Lancaster St, Fredericksburg VA 22405, USA | Nobel Peace Laureate |
| **Williams, John A**<br>693 Forest Ave, Teaneck NJ 07666, USA | Writer |
| **Williams, John C**<br>Askonas Holt, Lincoln House, 300 High Holborn, London WC1V 7JH, England | Concert Guitarist, Composer |
| **Williams, John C**<br>833 Cordova Ave, Ormond Beach FL 32174, USA | Archery Athlete |
| **Williams, John L**<br>1709 Husson Ave, Palatka FL 32177, USA | Football Player |
| **Williams, John T**<br>333 Loring Ave, Los Angeles CA 90024, USA | Conductor, Composer |
| **Williams, Johnny**<br>31921 Camino Capistrano, #13, San Juan Capistrano CA 92675, USA | Football Player |
| **Williams, Joseph**<br>Gorfaine/Schwartz, 4111 W Alameda Ave, #509, Burbank CA 91505 USA | Composer |
| **Williams, Josh**<br>Keith Case Assoc, 1025 17th Ave S, #200, Nashville TN 37212 USA | Singer, Guitarist, Mandola Player |
| **Williams, Juan**<br>Fox-TV, News Dept, 205 E 67th St, New York NY 10065 USA | Writer |
| **Williams, Kameelah**<br>Richard Walters, PO Box 2789, Toluca Lake CA 91610 USA | Rap Artist (702) |
| **Williams, Karl D**<br>2153 McKenzie Road, Mesquite TX 75181, USA | Football Player |
| **Williams, Kate**<br>I C M Partners, 10250 Constellation Blvd, #900, Los Angeles CA 90067 USA | Actress |
| **Williams, Keller**<br>Madison House, 2060 Broadway, #225, Boulder CO 80302, USA | Singer, Songwriter, Guitarist |
| **Williams, Kelli**<br>I C M Partners, 10250 Constellation Blvd, #900, Los Angeles CA 90067 USA | Actress, Singer |
| **Williams, Kenneth R (Ken)**<br>6430 E Sierra Vista Dr, Paradise Valley AZ 85253, USA | Baseball Player |
| **Williams, Kevin E**<br>1102 Blake Ave, #2, Brooklyn NY 11208, USA | Basketball Player |
| **Williams, Kiely A**<br>W M E Entertainment, 9601 Wilshire Blvd, #300, Beverly Hills CA 90210 USA | Actress, Singer (Cheetah Girls) |
| **Williams, Lee E**<br>11651 NW 4th St, Plantation FL 33325, USA | Football Player |
| **Williams, Lenae T**<br>A A I Sports, 16000 Dallas Parkway, #300, Dallas TX 75248, USA | Basketball Player |
| **Williams, Linda**<br>Music Tree Artist Mgmt, 1414 Pennsylvania Ave, Pittsburgh PA 15233, USA | Singer, Songwriter |
| **Williams, Lorenzo**<br>6001 Palm Trace Landings Dr, #318, Davie FL 33314, USA | Basketball Player |
| **Williams, Lucinda**<br>High Road Touring, 751 Bridgeway, #300, Sausalito CA 94965, USA | Singer, Songwriter |
| **Williams, Madieu M**<br>PO Box 96503, Washington DC 20090, USA | Football Player |
| **Williams, Maisie**<br>Louise Johnson Mgmt, Arle Court, Cheltenham, Gloucestershire GL51 6PN, England | Actress |
| **Williams, Maiya**<br>A P A Talent & Literary Agency, 405 S Beverly Dr, #300, Beverly Hills CA 90212 USA | Producer, Writer |
| **Williams, Maizie U**<br>International Artists, PO Box 10034, 47563 Goch, Germany | Singer (Boney M) |
| **Williams, Malinda**<br>Inspire Entertainment, 9800 Wilshire Blvd, Beverly Hills CA 90212, USA | Actress |
| **Williams, Mario J**<br>701 W Friar Tuck Lane, Houston TX 77024, USA | Football Player |
| **Williams, Mark**<br>Professional Bowlers Association, 719 2nd Ave, #701, Seattle WA 98104 USA | Bowler |
| **Williams, Mark W**<br>1453 Trumansburg Road, Ithaca NY 14850, USA | Baseball Player |
| **Williams, Marvin G**<br>Utah Jazz, Energy Solutions Arena, 301 W South Temple, Salt Lake City UT 84101 USA | Basketball Player |
| **Williams, Mary Alice**<br>'Daily Rounds', Discovery Channel, 7700 Wisconsin Ave, Bethesda MD 20814, USA | Commentator |
| **Williams, Mason**<br>PO Box 5105, Eugene OR 97405, USA | Singer, Guitarist, Composer |
| **Williams, Matthew D (Matt)**<br>4400 N Scottsdale Road, #381, Scottsdale AZ 85251, USA | Baseball Player, Manager |
| **Williams, Maurice**<br>Cape Entertainment, 4799 Coconut Creek Parkway, #258, Coconut Creek FL 33063 USA | Singer, Songwriter |
| **Williams, Maurice (Mo)**<br>Minnesota Timberwolves, Target Center, 600 1st Ave N, Minneapolis MN 55403 USA | Basketball Player |
| **Williams, Maurice C**<br>3653 Eastbury Dr, Jacksonville FL 32224, USA | Football Player |
| **Williams, Maurice J**<br>Overseas Development Council, 1875 Connecticut Ave NW, Washington DC 20009, USA | Association Executive |
| **Williams, Maurice J (Moe)**<br>10801 SW Fox Brown Road, Indiantown FL 34956, USA | Football Player |
| **Williams, Meadow**<br>GruntWorks Entertainment, 548 Broadhollow Road, Melville NY 11747, USA | Actress, Producer, Writer |
| **Williams, Melvin G (Mel), Jr**<br>Commander, 2nd Fleet, FPO AE 09506 USA | Navy Admiral |
| **Williams, Merriwether**<br>Collective, 8383 Wilshire Blvd, #1050, Beverly Hills CA 90211 USA | Writer, Producer |

| | |
|---|---|
| **Williams, Michael D (Mike)**<br>Jacksonville Jaguars, 1 AllTel Stadium Place, Jacksonville FL 32202 USA | Football Player |
| **Williams, Michael D (Mike)**<br>240 Horseshoe Farm Road, Pembroke VA 24136, USA | Baseball Player |
| **Williams, Michael J (Mike)**<br>2152 NW 74th Ave, Hollywood FL 33024, USA | Football Player |
| **Williams, Michael Kenneth**<br>Imperium 7 Artists, 5455 Wilshire Blvd, #1706, Los Angeles CA 90036 USA | Actor |
| **Williams, Micheal D**<br>1005 Lakeridge Court, Colleyville TX 76034, USA | Basketball Player |
| **Williams, Michelle**<br>W M E Entertainment, 9601 Wilshire Blvd, #300, Beverly Hills CA 90210 USA | Actress |
| **Williams, Michelle**<br>I C M Partners, 10250 Constellation Blvd, #900, Los Angeles CA 90067 USA | Singer (Destiny's Child) |
| **Williams, Mitchell S (Mitch)**<br>67 Highbridge Blvd, Medford NJ 08055, USA | Baseball Player |
| **Williams, Montel**<br>Montel Media Group, 331 W 57th St, #233, New York NY 10019, USA | Actor, Producer, Director |
| **Williams, Nathaniel R (Nate)**<br>132 Stanmore Circle, Vallejo CA 94591, USA | Basketball Player |
| **Williams, Nigel**<br>Judy Daish Assoc, 2 Saint Charles Place, London W10 6EG, England | Writer, Producer |
| **Williams, Olivia**<br>Independent Talent Group, 40 Whitfield St, London W1T 2RH, England | Actress |
| **Williams, Otis**<br>Barry Pollock Assoc, 9255 Sunset Blvd, #404, West Hollywood CA 90069, USA | Singer (Temptations) |
| **Williams, Pamela**<br>Universal Attractions, 135 W 26th St, #1200, New York NY 10001 USA | Jazz Saxophonist, Songwriter |
| **Williams, Patrick (Pat)**<br>2839 Wilds Lane NW, Prior Lake MN 55372, USA | Football Player |
| **Williams, Patrick M**<br>3156 Mandeville Canyon Road, Los Angeles CA 90049, USA | Composer |
| **Williams, Paul (Punisher)**<br>Goossen Tutor Promotions, 15300 Ventura Blvd, #400, Sherman Oaks CA 91403 USA | Boxer |
| **Williams, Paul Andrew**<br>United Agents, 12-26 Lexington St, London W1F 0LE, England | Actor, Director, Writer |
| **Williams, Paul H**<br>8491 W Sunset Blvd, #1150, West Hollywood CA 90069, USA | Songwriter, Actor |
| **Williams, Perry A**<br>480 Canyon Oaks Dr, #A, Oakland CA 94605, USA | Football Player |
| **Williams, Perry L**<br>273 Old Laurinberg Road, Hamlet NC 28345, USA | Football Player |
| **Williams, Pharrell**<br>42 West, 220 W 42nd St, #1200, New York NY 10036 USA | Singer, Rap Artist (NERD), Songwriter |
| **Williams, Rachel**<br>Berzon Talent Agency, 23 Seton Road, Irvine CA 92612, USA | Model, Actress |
| **Williams, Randall D (Randy)**<br>11410 F M 586 S, Brookesmith TX 76827, USA | Baseball Player |
| **Williams, Randy**<br>5655 N Marty Ave, #204, Fresno CA 93711, USA | Track Athlete |
| **Williams, Redford B, Jr**<br>Duke University Medical School, Box 3708, Durham NC 27706, USA | Internist |
| **Williams, Reggie**<br>2016 Calloway St, Temple Hills MD 20748, USA | Basketball Player |
| **Williams, Reginald (Reggie)**<br>10 N Summerlin Ave, #53, Orlando FL 32801, USA | Football Player |
| **Williams, Reginald (Reggie), Jr**<br>7635 Wexford Club Dr E, Jacksonville FL 32256, USA | Football Player |
| **Williams, Richard E**<br>138 Royal College St, London NW1 0TA, England | Animator, Cartoonist (Pink Panther) |
| **Williams, Robbie**<br>I E Music, 111 Frithville Gardens, London W12 7JG, England | Singer |
| **Williams, Robert A (Bobby)**<br>602 Stone Barn Road, Towson MD 21286, USA | Football Player |
| **Williams, Robert J (Ben)**<br>5961 Huntview Dr, Jackson MS 39206, USA | Football Player |
| **Williams, Robert Walter**<br>University of Washington, Physics Dept, Seattle WA 98195, USA | Physicist |
| **Williams, Robin**<br>Music Tree Artist Mgmt, 1414 Pennsylvania Ave, Pittsburgh PA 15233, USA | Singer, Songwriter |
| **Williams, Roderick**<br>Ingpen & Williams, 131 Putney Bridge Road, London SW15 2PA, England | Opera Singer |
| **Williams, Roland L**<br>5671 Wrenwyck Place, Weldon Spring MO 63304, USA | Football Player |
| **Williams, Ronald A**<br>Aetna Inc, 151 Farmington Ave, Hartford CT 06156, USA | Businessman |
| **Williams, Roshumba**<br>Innovative Artists, 1505 10th St, Santa Monica CA 90401 USA | Model, Actress |
| **Williams, Rowan D**<br>Lambeth Palace, London SE1 9JU, England | Religious Leader |
| **Williams, Roy**<br>University of North Carolina, Athletic Dept, PO Box 2126, Chapel Hill NC 27515, USA | Basketball Coach |
| **Williams, Roy E, Jr**<br>Chicago Bears, 1000 Football Dr, Lake Forest IL 60045 USA | Football Player |
| **Williams, Roy L**<br>4100 Buckingham Place, Colleyville TX 76034, USA | Football Player |
| **Williams, Saul S**<br>Creative Artists Agency, 2000 Ave of Stars, #100, Los Angeles CA 90067 USA | Rap Artist |
| **Williams, Serena J**<br>6466 Emerald Dunes Dr, #105, West Palm Beach FL 33411, USA | Tennis Player |
| **Williams, Shad C**<br>4682 E Cornell Ave, Fresno CA 93703, USA | Baseball Player |
| **Williams, Shaun L**<br>11738 Gruen St, Sylmar CA 91342, USA | Football Player |
| **Williams, Sherman C**<br>119 Patricia Ave, Mobile AL 36610, USA | Football Player |

**Williams, Sidney (Sid)** — Football Player
1044 W 82nd St, Los Angeles CA 90044, USA
**Williams, Simon** — Actor
Dalzell & Beresford, 55 Charterhouse St, Paddock Suite, London EC1M 6HA, England
**Williams, Speed** — Rodeo Rider
9550 Tradewind St, Amarillo TX 79118, USA
**Williams, Stanley W (Stan)** — Baseball Player
4702 Hayter Ave, Lakewood CA 90712, USA
**Williams, Stephanie E** — Actress
S M S Talent, 8383 Wilshire Blvd, #230, Beverly Hills CA 90211 USA
**Williams, Stephen** — Anthropologist
1017 Foothills Trail, Santa Fe NM 87505, USA
**Williams, Stephen F** — Judge
US Court of Appeals, 333 Constitution Ave NW, #4400, Washington DC 20001, USA
**Williams, Steve** — Rowing Athlete
Leander Club, Henley on Thames, Leander RG9 2LP, England
**Williams, Steven** — Actor
Stone Manners Salners, 6100 Wilshire Blvd, #1500, Los Angeles CA 90035 USA
**Williams, Sunita L** — Astronaut
1522 Festival Dr, Houston TX 77062, USA
**Williams, Tamika** — Basketball Player
Minnesota Lynx, Target Center, 600 1st Ave N, Minneapolis MN 55403 USA
**Williams, Tavares (Monty)** — Basketball Player, Coach
257 Brockenbraugh Court, Metairie LA 70005, USA
**Williams, Terrence** — Basketball Player
Sacramento Kings, Arco Arena, 1 Sports Parkway, Sacramento CA 95834 USA
**Williams, Terrie** — Biologist
University of California, Biology Dept, Santa Cruz CA 95064, USA
**Williams, Terry** — Drummer (Dire Straits)
Damage Mgmt, 16 Lambton Place, London W11 2SH, England
**Williams, Thomas S Cardinal** — Religious Leader
Catholic Centre, 22-30 Hill St, Private Bag 1937, Thorndon, Wellington 6140, New Zealand
**Williams, Tod** — Director, Producer, Writer
United Talent Agency, U T A Plaza, 9336 Civic Center Dr, Beverly Hills CA 90210 USA
**Williams, Tod** — Architect
Tod Williams Billie Tsien Architects, 222 Central Park S, New York NY 10019, USA
**Williams, Todd** — Actor
Sanders/Armstrong/Caserta Mgmt, 2120 Colorado Ave, #120, Santa Monica CA 90404 USA
**Williams, Todd M** — Baseball Player
16707 Whispering Glen Dr, Lutz FL 33558, USA
**Williams, Tom** — Ice Hockey Player
2411 Princess Ave, Windsor ON N8T 1V2, Canada
**Williams, Tonya Lee** — Actress
Artists Agency, 9430 Olympic Blvd, Beverly Hills CA 90212 USA
**Williams, Treat** — Actor
A P A Talent & Literary Agency, 405 S Beverly Dr, #300, Beverly Hills CA 90212 USA
**Williams, Tyler James** — Actor
Seven Summits Mgmt, 8906 W Olympic Blvd, Beverly Hills CA 90211 USA
**Williams, U Tyrone** — Football Player
6939 Westchester Circle, Bradenton FL 34202, USA
**Williams, Ulis** — Track Athlete
2511 29th St, Santa Monica CA 90405, USA
**Williams, Vanessa A** — Actress, Producer
Shadow, 10 Universal City Plaza, #2000, Universal City CA 91608, USA
**Williams, Vanessa L** — Actress, Singer, Beauty Queen
United Talent Agency, U T A Plaza, 9336 Civic Center Dr, Beverly Hills CA 90210 USA
**Williams, Venus E S** — Tennis Player
6466 Emerald Dunes Dr, #105, West Palm Beach FL 33411, USA
**Williams, Victor** — Actor
Imperium 7, 5455 Wilshire Blvd, #1706, Los Angeles CA 90036, USA
**Williams, Victoria** — Singer, Guitarist, Songwriter
High Road Touring, 751 Bridgeway, #200, Sausalito CA 94965 USA
**Williams, Virginia** — Actress
Paul Kohner, 9300 Wilshire Blvd, #555, Beverly Hills CA 90212 USA
**Williams, Wade** — Actor
S M S Talent, 8383 Wilshire Blvd, #230, Beverly Hills CA 90211 USA
**Williams, Walter (Buddy)** — Baseball Player
15700 Good Hope Road, Silver Spring MD 20905, USA
**Williams, Walter A (Walt)** — Baseball Player
2417 Monterey St, Brownwood TX 76801, USA
**Williams, Walter A (Walt)** — Basketball Player
3240 Beaumont St, Temple Hills MD 20748, USA
**Williams, Walter F** — Businessman
RR 4, Saucon Valley Road, Bethlehem PA 18015, USA
**Williams, Walter Ray, Jr** — Bowler
7903 SE 12th Circle, Ocala FL 34480, USA
**Williams, Walter, Sr** — Singer (O'Jays)
Associated Booking Corp, 501 Madison Ave, #501, New York NY 10022 USA
**Williams, Warren, Jr** — Football Player
1203 Gerald Ave, West Hempstead NY 11552, USA
**Williams, Wendy** — Actress
A P A Talent & Literary Agency, 405 S Beverly Dr, #300, Beverly Hills CA 90212 USA
**Williams, William (Curly)** — Baseball Player
2729 20th St, Sarasota FL 34234, USA
**Williams, William A** — Astronaut
Environmental Protection Agency, 200 SW 35th St, Corvallis OR 97333, USA
**Williams, William G (Billy)** — Baseball Umpire
RR 2 Box 822, Coconut Creek FL 33073, USA
**Williams, Willie A** — Football Player
PO Box 871445, Mesquite TX 75187, USA
**Williams, Willie J, Jr** — Football Player
5410 Handscrabble Road, Blythewood SC 29016, USA
**Williamson, Corliss M** — Basketball Player
Arkansas Baptist College, Athletic Dept, 1621 King Dr, Little Rock AR 72202, USA
**Williamson, Frederick R (Fred)** — Actor, Football Player
H David Moss, 733 Seward St, #PH, Los Angeles CA 90038, USA

| | |
|---|---|
| **Williamson, Jama** | Actress |
| TalentWorks, 3500 W Olive Ave, #1400, Burbank CA 91505 USA | |
| **Williamson, Jay** | Golfer |
| 24 Clemont Lane, Saint Louis MO 63124, USA | |
| **Williamson, Keith** | British Air Force Marshal |
| Royal Air Forces Assoc, 117 1/2 Loughborough Road, Leicester LE4 5ND, England | |
| **Williamson, Kevin** | Director, Producer, Writer |
| W M E Entertainment, 9601 Wilshire Blvd, #300, Beverly Hills CA 90210 USA | |
| **Williamson, Marianne** | Psychotherapist |
| Los Angeles Center for Living, 8265 W Sunset Blvd, West Hollywood CA 90046, USA | |
| **Williamson, Mark A** | Baseball Player |
| 1260 Hidden Mountain Dr, El Cajon CA 92019, USA | |
| **Williamson, Matthew** | Fashion Designer |
| 37 Percy St, London W1P 2DJ, England | |
| **Williamson, Michael** | Photojournalist |
| Washington Post, Editorial Dept, 1150 15th St NW, Washington DC 20071 USA | |
| **Williamson, Michael S** | Writer |
| 1945 Westchester Dr, Silver Spring MD 20902, USA | |
| **Williamson, Mykelti T** | Actor |
| Innovative Artists, 1505 10th St, Santa Monica CA 90401 USA | |
| **Williamson, Oliver E** | Nobel Economics Laureate |
| University of California, Economics Dept, Berkeley CA 94720, USA | |
| **Williamson, Richard** | Football Coach |
| 5137 Morrowick Road, Charlotte NC 28226, USA | |
| **Williamson, Samuel R, Jr** | Educator |
| University of the South, President's Office, Sewanee TN 37375, USA | |
| **Williamson, Scott R** | Baseball Player |
| 2623 Foran Dr, Cincinnati OH 45238, USA | |
| **Williams-Paisley, Kimberly** | Actress |
| L I N K Entertainment, 11872 La Grange Ave, Los Angeles CA 90025 USA | |
| **Willie D** | Rap Artist (Geto Boys) |
| Entertainment Artists, 2409 21st Ave S, #100, Nashville TN 10019 USA | |
| **Williford, D Vann** | Basketball Player |
| 4455 Fair Oaks Lane, High Point NC 27265, USA | |
| **Willig, Matthew J (Matt)** | Football Player |
| 4241 Prado de los Pajaros, Calabasas CA 91302, USA | |
| **Willimon, Beau** | Writer |
| Creative Artists Agency, 2000 Ave of Stars, #100, Los Angeles CA 90067 USA | |
| **Willing, Nick** | Director |
| Independent Talent Group, 40 Whitfield St, London W1T 2RH, England | |
| **Willingham, Joshua D (Josh)** | Baseball Player |
| 108 Cascade Dr, Florence AL 35633, USA | |
| **Willingham, Tyrone** | Football Coach |
| Octagon Worldwide, 1751 Pinnacle Dr, #1500, McLean VA 22102 USA | |
| **Willis, Alicia Leigh** | Actress |
| Innovative Artists, 1505 10th St, Santa Monica CA 90401 USA | |
| **Willis, Brian Davis** | Drummer (Quarterflash) |
| Pacific Talent Agency, PO Box 19145, Portland OR 97280, USA | |
| **Willis, Bruce W** | Actor |
| Creative Artists Agency, 2000 Ave of Stars, #100, Los Angeles CA 90067 USA | |
| **Willis, Carl B** | Baseball Player |
| 6811 Lipscomb Dr, Durham NC 27712, USA | |
| **Willis, Dave** | Writer, Producer, Actor |
| Brillstein Entertainment Partners, 9150 Wilshire Blvd, #350, Beverly Hills CA 90212 USA | |
| **Willis, Dinah** | Model |
| Playboy Promotions, 9346 Civic Center Dr, #200, Beverly Hills CA 90210 USA | |
| **Willis, Dontrelle** | Baseball Player |
| 9820 E Thompson Peak Parkway, #726, Scottsdale AZ 85255, USA | |
| **Willis, Frederick F (Fred), III** | Football Player |
| PO Box 558, Swampscott MA 01907, USA | |
| **Willis, Garrett** | Golfer |
| 528 Mountain Pass Lane, Knoxville TN 37923, USA | |
| **Willis, Jim** | Artist |
| 5323 SW 53rd Court, Portland OR 97221, USA | |
| **Willis, Keith** | Football Player |
| 116 Coffeeberry Court, Garner NC 27529, USA | |
| **Willis, Kelly** | Singer, Songwriter |
| Davis McLarty Agency, 708 S Lamar Blvd, #D, Austin TX 78704, USA | |
| **Willis, Kevin A** | Basketball Player |
| 1481 Jones Road, Roswell GA 30075, USA | |
| **Willis, Michael H (Mike)** | Baseball Player |
| 6234 Taggart St, Houston TX 77007, USA | |
| **Willis, Nicholas (Nick)** | Track Athlete |
| University of Michigan, Athletic Dept, Ann Arbor MI 48109, USA | |
| **Willis, Patrick L** | Football Player |
| San Francisco 49ers, 4949 Centennial Blvd, Santa Clara CA 95054 USA | |
| **Willis, Ray** | Football Player |
| 8200 Poole Road, Knightdale NC 27545, USA | |
| **Willis, Rumer** | Actress |
| Untitled Entertainment, 350 S Beverly Dr, #200, Beverly Hills CA 90212 USA | |
| **Willis, Victor** | Singer (Village People), Songwriter |
| Victor Willis World, PO Box 1022, La Jolla, CA 92038, USA | |
| **Willison, Mike** | Bassist (Fig Dish, Prairie Cartel) |
| Metropolitan Entertainment Group, 2 Penn Plaza, #1500, New York NY 10121, USA | |
| **Willits, Tim** | Video Game Developer |
| I D Software, 1500 N Greenville Ave, #700, Richardson, TX 75081, USA | |
| **Willman, David** | Journalist |
| Los Angeles Times, Editorial Dept, 202 W 1st St, Los Angeles CA 90012 USA | |
| **Willmon, Trent** | Singer, Songwriter |
| Hallmark Direction, 713 18th Ave S, Nashville TN 37203, USA | |
| **Willms, Andre** | Rowing Athlete |
| Rennebogen 94, 39130 Magdeburg, Germany | |
| **Willoch, Kare I** | Prime Minister, Norway |
| Blokkaveien 6B, 0282 Oslo, Norway | |
| **Willoughby, James A (Jim)** | Baseball Player |
| PO Box 707, Eufaula OK 74432, USA | |

| | |
|---|---|
| **Willoughby, William W (Bill)** | Basketball Player |
| 350 W Englewood Ave, Englewood NJ 07631, USA | |
| **Wills, Elliott T (Bump)** | Baseball Player |
| 1802 Briar Meadow Dr, Arlington TX 76014, USA | |
| **Wills, Garry** | Historian |
| Northwestern University, History Dept, Evanston IL 60201, USA | |
| **Wills, Mark** | Singer, Songwriter |
| Scott Welch Mgmt, 1515 Harding Place, Nashville TN 37215, USA | |
| **Wills, Maurice M (Maury)** | Baseball Player, Manager |
| M & R Sports, 5 Dalton Valley Dr, Saint Peters MO 63376, USA | |
| **Wills, Rick** | Bassist (Foreigner) |
| Hard to Handle Mgmt, 16501 Ventura Blvd, #602, Encino CA 91436, USA | |
| **Wills, Theodore C (Ted)** | Baseball Player |
| 10585 E Duckpoint Way, Clovis CA 93619, USA | |
| **Willsie, Brian** | Ice Hockey Player |
| 45 Meadowbrook Road, Randolph NJ 07869, USA | |
| **Willson-Piper, Marty** | Guitarist (Church) |
| Entourage Talent, 236 W 27th St, #800, New York NY 10001, USA | |
| **Wilmarth, Christopher** | Artist, Sculptor |
| Betty Cunningham, 541 W 25th St, Front 2, New York NY 10001, USA | |
| **Wilmarth, Dick** | Dog Sled Racer |
| 1111 F St, Anchorage AK 99501, USA | |
| **Wilmer, Douglas** | Actor |
| Julian Belfrage Assoc, 9 Argyll St, #300, London W1F 7TG, England | |
| **Wilmer, Harry A** | Psychiatrist |
| Texas Health Science Center, Psychiatric Dept, San Antonio TX 78284, USA | |
| **Wilmet, Paul R** | Baseball Player |
| PO Box 330074, Nashville TN 37203, USA | |
| **Wilmore, Barry E (Butch)** | Astronaut |
| 3002 Bryant Lane, Webster TX 77598, USA | |
| **Wilmore, Larry** | Actor, Comedian, Writer |
| United Talent Agency, U T A Plaza, 9336 Civic Center Dr, Beverly Hills CA 90210 USA | |
| **Wilmot, David** | Actor |
| Macfarlane Chard, 7 Adelaide St, Dun Laoghaire, County Dublin, Ireland | |
| **Wilmsmeyer, Klaus, Jr** | Football Player |
| 8209 Paddington Dr, Louisville KY 40222, USA | |
| **Wilmut, Ian** | Geneticist, Embryologist |
| Roslin Institute, Roslin Bio Centre, Midlothian EH25 9PS, Scotland | |
| **Wilpon, Fred** | Baseball Executive |
| 100 Sheep Lane, Locust Valley NY 11560, USA | |
| **Wilson of Tillyorn, David C** | Government Official, England; Diplomat |
| House of Lords, Westminster, London SW1A 0PW, England | |
| **Wilson, Adrian L** | Football Player |
| 10104 E Shangri La Road, Scottsdale AZ 85260, USA | |
| **Wilson, Aldra K (Al)** | Football Player |
| 11561 Warrington Court, Parker CO 80138, USA | |
| **Wilson, Alexander G (Sandy)** | Composer, Writer |
| 2 Southwell Gardens, #4, London SW7 4SB, England | |
| **Wilson, Alexandra** | Actress |
| Greater Visions Artists Talent Agency, 8981 W Sunset Blvd, #101, West Hollywood CA 90069 USA | |
| **Wilson, Allan B** | Molecular Biologist |
| University of California, Molecular Biology Dept, Berkeley CA 94724, USA | |
| **Wilson, Andrew** | Actor |
| United Talent Agency, U T A Plaza, 9336 Civic Center Dr, Beverly Hills CA 90210 USA | |
| **Wilson, Andrew N (A N)** | Writer |
| 21 Arlington Road, London NW1 7ER, England | |
| **Wilson, Ann D** | Singer (Heart) |
| H K Mgmt, 9200 W Sunset Blvd, #530, West Hollywood CA 90069 USA | |
| **Wilson, Ben** | Keyboardist (Blues Traveler) |
| C3 Presents, 98 San Jacinto Blvd, #400, Austin TX 78701, USA | |
| **Wilson, Blaine** | Gymnast |
| 171 W 57th St, #8A, New York NY 10019, USA | |
| **Wilson, Blenda J** | Educator |
| California State University, President's Office, Northridge CA 91330, USA | |
| **Wilson, Brenard K** | Football Player |
| 1246 Dalemere Dr, Nashville TN 37207, USA | |
| **Wilson, Brian Anthony** | Actor, Producer |
| A D S Mgmt, 269 S Beverly Drive, #441, Beverly Hills CA 90212, USA | |
| **Wilson, Brian D** | Singer (Beach Boys), Songwriter |
| Lippin Group, 6100 Wilshire Blvd, #400, Los Angeles CA 90048, USA | |
| **Wilson, Brian P** | Baseball Player |
| 741 S Banning Circle, Mesa AZ 85206, USA | |
| **Wilson, C A S John** | Architect |
| John Wilson Assoc, 27 Horsell Road, London N5 1XL, England | |
| **Wilson, C Richard (Ricky)** | Singer (Kaiser Chiefs) |
| Red Light Mgmt, 8439 Sunset Blvd, West Hollywood CA 90069, USA | |
| **Wilson, C Wade** | Football Player |
| 6126 Mimosa Lane, Dallas TX 75230, USA | |
| **Wilson, Carey** | Ice Hockey Player |
| 85 Jean Louis Road, Winnipeg MB R2N 4A9, Canada | |
| **Wilson, Carnie** | Singer (Wilson Phillips, Wilsons) |
| 19528 Ventura Blvd, #624, Tarzana CA 91356, USA | |
| **Wilson, Casey R** | Actress, Writer |
| Odenkirk Provissiero Entertainment, 1936 N Bronson Ave, Los Angeles CA 90069 USA | |
| **Wilson, Cassandra** | Singer |
| Front Row Productions, 215 S 4th St, Forest City IA 50436, USA | |
| **Wilson, Cedrick** | Football Player |
| 2055 Oakvalley Road, Memphis TN 38116, USA | |
| **Wilson, Chandra** | Actress |
| Abrams Artists, 275 7th Ave, #2600, New York NY 10001 USA | |
| **Wilson, Charles J** | Football Player |
| 5444 Calder Dr, Tallahassee FL 32317, USA | |
| **Wilson, Charles K (Charlie)** | Singer (Gap Band), Songwriter |
| Universal Attractions, 135 W 26th St, #1200, New York NY 10001, USA | |
| **Wilson, Charles R** | Judge |
| US Court of Appeals, 801 N Florida Ave, #200, Tampa FL 33602, USA | |

**Wilson, Christopher J (C J)** — Baseball Player
Los Angeles Angels, Angel Stadium, 2000 E Gene Autry Way, Anaheim CA 92806 USA

**Wilson, Cindy** — Singer, Guitarist (B-52's)
Direct Management Group, 947 N La Cienega Blvd, #G, West Hollywood CA 90069, USA

**Wilson, Craig** — Water Polo Player
1423 Lake Blvd, Davis CA 95616, USA

**Wilson, Craig F** — Baseball Player
3427 E Tere St, Phoenix AZ 85044, USA

**Wilson, Dan** — Singer, Guitarist, Songwriter
Monterey Peninsula Artists, 404 W Franklin St, Monterey CA 93940 USA

**Wilson, Daniel A (Dan)** — Baseball Player
2161 E Interlaken Blvd, Seattle WA 98112, USA

**Wilson, Darnell** — Boxer
1917 E Foxmoor Lane, Lafayette IN 47905, USA

**Wilson, David** — Educator
Morgan State University, President's Office, Baltimore MD 21239, USA

**Wilson, David C (Dave)** — Football Player
2247 Farolito Ave, Long Beach CA 90815, USA

**Wilson, David Mackenzie** — Museum Executive
Lifeboat House, Castletown IM9 1LD, Isle of Man, England

**Wilson, Dean H** — Golfer
12488 Carmel Cape, San Diego CA 92130, USA

**Wilson, Desi B** — Baseball Player
8 Janet Lane, Glen Cove NY 11542, USA

**Wilson, Desire** — Auto Racing Driver
4197 Serenade Road, Castle Rock CO 80104, USA

**Wilson, Douglas F (Doug)** — Ice Hockey Player, Executive
5620 Country Club Parkway, San Jose CA 95138, USA

**Wilson, Edward O** — Writer, Zoologist
1010 Waltham St, #A208, Lexington MA 02421, USA

**Wilson, Elizabeth** — Actress
Paradigm Agency, 360 N Crescent Dr, North Building, Beverly Hills CA 90210 USA

**Wilson, F Paul** — Writer
1933 State Route 35, #337, Wall Township NJ 07719, USA

**Wilson, F Perry** — Chemical Engineer
225 N 56th St, #217, Lincoln NE 68504, USA

**Wilson, Frank** — Auto Racing Executive
North Carolina Motor Speedway, PO Box 2801, Daytona Beach FL 32120, USA

**Wilson, Gahan** — Cartoonist, Writer
New Yorker, Editorial Dept, 4 Times Square, Basement C1B, New York NY 10036 USA

**Wilson, George (Jiff)** — Basketball Player
151 Twin Lakes Dr, Fairfield OH 45014, USA

**Wilson, Gibril D** — Football Player
20 10th St NW, #2302, Atlanta GA 30309, USA

**Wilson, Glenn D** — Baseball Player
300 Tara Park, Conroe TX 77302, USA

**Wilson, Gretchen** — Singer, Guitarist
Morris Management Group, 818 19th Ave S, Nashville TN 37203, USA

**Wilson, Hugh** — Director
I C M Partners, 10250 Constellation Blvd, #900, Los Angeles CA 90067 USA

**Wilson, Ian A** — Biologist
Scripps Research Institute, 10550 N Torrey Pines Road, La Jolla CA 92037, USA

**Wilson, J Reinard** — Football Player
463 NW Baughn St, Lake City FL 32055, USA

**Wilson, Jack E** — Baseball Player
12467 San Sebastian Court, Santa Rosa Valley CA 93012, USA

**Wilson, Jack M** — Educator
University of Massachusetts, President's Office, 225 Franklin St, #3300, Boston MA 02110, USA

**Wilson, Jacquelyn** — Writer
Transworld Publishers, 61-63 Uxbridge Road, London W5 5SA, England

**Wilson, James (J C)** — Football Player
4785 Young Road, Waldorf MD 20601, USA

**Wilson, James M** — Geneticist
University of Pennsylvania Medical Center, Genetics Dept, Philadelphia PA 19104, USA

**Wilson, Jane** — Artist
317 W 83rd St, #2E, New York NY 10024, USA

**Wilson, Jean D** — Endocrinologist
Texas Southwestern Medical Center, 5323 Harry Hines Blvd, Dallas TX 75390, USA

**Wilson, Jeannie** — Actress
4330 Talofa Ave, Toluca Lake CA 91602, USA

**Wilson, Jennifer** — Opera, Concert Singer
I M G Artists, The Light Box, 111 Power Road, London W4 5PY, England

**Wilson, Jerry L** — Football Player
19814 Moss Bark Trail, Richmond TX 77407, USA

**Wilson, Jessica** — Actress, Comedienne
OmniPop Talent Group, 4605 Lankershim Blvd, #201, Toluca Lake CA 91602 USA

**Wilson, John (Johnny), Sr** — Baseball Player
8 Hillcrest Dr, Lock Haven PA 17745, USA

**Wilson, Johnnie E** — Army General
Dimensions International, 2800 Eisenhower Ave, #300, Alexandria VA 22314, USA

**Wilson, Joshua (Josh)** — Football Player
515 Quincy Ave NE, Renton WA 98059, USA

**Wilson, Joshua A (Josh)** — Baseball Player
2304 Cramden Road, Pittsburgh, PA 15241, USA

**Wilson, Julie** — Singer, Actress
Scott Stander Assoc, 4533 Van Nuys Blvd, #401, Sherman Oaks CA 91403 USA

**Wilson, Justin** — Drummer (Reveille)
David Levin Mgmt, 200 W 57th St, #308, New York NY 10019, USA

**Wilson, Keri-Lynn** — Conductor
I M G Artists, Hogarth Business Park, Chiswick, London W4 2TH, England

**Wilson, Kim** — Singer, Musician (Fabulous Thunderbird)
Two Goats Entertainment, 5001 W Placita de los Vientos, Tucson AZ 85745, USA

**Wilson, Kris** — Baseball Player
PO Box 15, Chillicothe MO 64601, USA

**Wilson, Kristen** — Actress
Craig Wyckoff & Associates, 13952 Runnymede St, Van Nuys CA 91405, USA

| | |
|---|---|
| **Wilson, Landon** | Ice Hockey Player |
| 127 Tennyson Place, Coppell TX 75019, USA | |
| **Wilson, Lawrence F (Larry)** | Football Player, Executive |
| 11834 N Blackheath Road, Scottsdale AZ 85254, USA | |
| **Wilson, Linda S** | Educator |
| 26 Honey Locust Dr, Topsham ME 04086, USA | |
| **Wilson, Luke** | Actor |
| I/D Public Relations, 7060 Hollywood Blvd, #800, Los Angeles CA 90028 USA | |
| **Wilson, Mara** | Actress |
| Harry Gold Assoc, 3500 W Olive Ave, #1400, Burbank CA 91505, USA | |
| **Wilson, Marc D** | Football Player |
| 10820 157th Ave NE, Woodinville WA 98072, USA | |
| **Wilson, Marie** | Actress |
| Michael Bruno Group, 13576 Cheltenham Dr, Sherman Oaks CA 91423, USA | |
| **Wilson, Mark J** | Golfer |
| N41W27751 Ishnala Trail, Pewaukee WI 53072, USA | |
| **Wilson, Mary** | Singer (Supremes) |
| 2654 W Horizon Ridge Parkway, #B5, Henderson NV 89052, USA | |
| **Wilson, Michael (Tack)** | Baseball Player |
| 1623 Schnell Dr, Arabi LA 70032, USA | |
| **Wilson, Mike** | Ice Hockey Player |
| 4647 Lake Charles Dr, Independence OH 44131, USA | |
| **Wilson, Mike R** | Football Player |
| 2908 N Poinsettia Ave, Manhattan Beach CA 90266, USA | |
| **Wilson, Murray** | Ice Hockey Player |
| Wilson Consulting, 432-410 Bank St, Ottawa ON K2P 1Y8, Canada | |
| **Wilson, Nancy** | Singer |
| Wenig-LaMonica Associates, 580 White Plains Road, #130, Tarrytown NY 10591 USA | |
| **Wilson, Nancy L** | Singer (Heart) |
| Peters Mgmt, PO Box 1710, Topanga CA 90290, USA | |
| **Wilson, Nemiah** | Football Player |
| 11000 E Idaho Place, Aurora CO 80012, USA | |
| **Wilson, Nigel E** | Baseball Player |
| 35 Sabbe Crescent, Ajax ON L1T 4E3, Canada | |
| **Wilson, Olin C** | Astronomer |
| 1508 Circa del Lago, B110, San Marcos CA 92078, USA | |
| **Wilson, Otis R** | Football Player |
| 426 W Shadow Creek Dr, Vernon Hills IL 60061, USA | |
| **Wilson, Owen C** | Actor |
| United Talent Agency, U T A Plaza, 9336 Civic Center Dr, Beverly Hills CA 90210 USA | |
| **Wilson, Patrick** | Singer, Actor |
| Anonymous Content, 3532 Hayden Ave, Culver City CA 90232 USA | |
| **Wilson, Patrick** | Immunologist |
| Oklahoma Medical Research Foundation, 825 NE 13th St, Oklahoma City OK 73104, USA | |
| **Wilson, Paul** | Bassist, Pianist (Snow Patrol) |
| Big Life Mgmt, 67-69 Charlton St, London NW1 1HY, England | |
| **Wilson, Paul A** | Baseball Player |
| 949 Lenmore Court, Orlando FL 32812, USA | |
| **Wilson, Peta** | Actress, Model |
| I C M Partners, 10250 Constellation Blvd, #900, Los Angeles CA 90067 USA | |
| **Wilson, Peter B (Pete)** | Governor, Senator, CA |
| Stanford University, Hoover Institution, Stanford CA 94305, USA | |
| **Wilson, Peter L** | Architect |
| Architekturburo Bolles & Wilson, Alter Steinweg 17, 48143 Munster, Germany | |
| **Wilson, Philippa C (Pippa)** | Yachtswoman |
| Lynx Sports Mgmt, Lymington Road, Lymington, Hampshire SO41 5S5, England | |
| **Wilson, Preston J R** | Baseball Player |
| 136 Paloma Dr, Coral Gables FL 33143, USA | |
| **Wilson, Rainn** | Actor, Comedian |
| W M E Entertainment, 9601 Wilshire Blvd, #300, Beverly Hills CA 90210 USA | |
| **Wilson, Rebel** | Actress |
| W M E Entertainment, 9601 Wilshire Blvd, #300, Beverly Hills CA 90210 USA | |
| **Wilson, Reno** | Actor |
| More/Medavoy Mgmt, 10203 Santa Monica Blvd, #400, Los Angeles CA 90067 USA | |
| **Wilson, Richard (Rick)** | Basketball Player |
| 535 E Ormsby Ave, Louisville KY 40203, USA | |
| **Wilson, Richard G (Rick)** | Ice Hockey Player |
| 1624 Reno Run, Lewisville TX 75077, USA | |
| **Wilson, Richard K** | Geneticist |
| Genome Sequencing Center, 4444 Forest Park Ave, Saint Louis MO 63108, USA | |
| **Wilson, Ricky** | Basketball Player |
| 8007 Oak Ridge Court, Bowie MD 20715, USA | |
| **Wilson, Rik** | Ice Hockey Player |
| 12076 Manchester Road, Saint Louis MO 63131, USA | |
| **Wilson, Rita** | Actress, Singer |
| Creative Artists Agency, 2000 Ave of Stars, #100, Los Angeles CA 90067 USA | |
| **Wilson, Robert Charles** | Writer |
| Bantam Books, 1745 Broadway, New York NY 10019 USA | |
| **Wilson, Robert J (Red)** | Baseball Player |
| 806 Cabot Lane, Madison WI 53711, USA | |
| **Wilson, Robert M** | Actor |
| R W Work Ltd, 55 Washington St, #216, Brooklyn NY 11201, USA | |
| **Wilson, Robert W** | Nobel Physics Laureate |
| 38 Cole Court, Dumont NJ 07628, USA | |
| **Wilson, Robin** | Singer (Gin Blossoms, Pharaohs) |
| Stone Manners Salners, 6100 Wilshire Blvd, #1500, Los Angeles CA 90035 USA | |
| **Wilson, Ronald L (Ron)** | Ice Hockey Player, Coach |
| 17 Middleton Gardens Place, Bluffton SC 29910, USA | |
| **Wilson, Ronald L (Ron)** | Ice Hockey Player |
| Hamilton Bulldogs, 101 York Blvd, Hamilton ON L8R 3L4, Canada | |
| **Wilson, Roy** | Educator |
| University of Colorado, President's Office, Denver CO 80217, USA | |
| **Wilson, Ruth** | Actress |
| Creative Artists Agency, 2000 Ave of Stars, #100, Los Angeles CA 90067 USA | |
| **Wilson, S O'Neil (Neil)** | Baseball Player |
| 4300 Highway 412 W, Lexington TN 38351, USA | |

**W**

**Wilson - Wilson**

| | |
|---|---|
| **Wilson, Samuel W**<br>Hampden-Sydney College, President's Office, Hampden-Sydney VA 23943, USA | Army General, Educator |
| **Wilson, Scott**<br>Coronel Group, 1100 Glendon Ave, #1700, Los Angeles CA 90024 90024, USA | Actor |
| **Wilson, Sheree J**<br>Metropolitan Talent Agency, 5405 Wilshire Blvd, #218, Los Angeles CA 90036 USA | Actress |
| **Wilson, Stacy E**<br>Bowdoin College, Athletic Dept, Brunswick ME 04011, USA | Ice Hockey Player |
| **Wilson, Stanley W (Stan)**<br>4701 Hayter St, Lakewood CA 90712, USA | Baseball Player |
| **Wilson, Stephanie D**<br>N A S A, Johnson Space Center, 2101 NASA Road, Houston TX 77058 USA | Astronaut |
| **Wilson, Stephen D (Steve)**<br>23-1041 Comox St, Vancouver BC V6E 1K1, Canada | Baseball Player |
| **Wilson, Stephen E (Steve)**<br>West Jefferson Middle School, 9449 Barnes Ave, Conifer CO 80433, USA | Basketball Player |
| **Wilson, Steve A**<br>3706 Village Estates Place, Tampa FL 33618, USA | Football Player |
| **Wilson, Steven A (Steve)**<br>8516 Doughton Dr, Bahama NC 27503, USA | Football Player |
| **Wilson, Steven J**<br>Agency Group Ltd, 361-373 City Road, London EC1V 1PQ, England | Singer, Guitarist (Porcupine Tree) |
| **Wilson, Stuart**<br>Independent Talent Group, 40 Whitfield St, London W1T 2RH, England | Sound Mixer, Actor |
| **Wilson, Stuart**<br>Curtis Brown Group, 28-29 Haymarket St, #500, London SW1Y 4SP, England | Actor |
| **Wilson, Thomas F**<br>Dusty Tuba Entertainment, PO Box 18106, Encino CA 91416, USA | Actor |
| **Wilson, Tom**<br>2679 Tanglewood Court, Lake Havasu City AZ 86403, USA | Baseball Player |
| **Wilson, Torrie**<br>Diverse Talent Group, 9911 Pico Blvd, #350W, Los Angeles CA 90035 USA | Professional Wrestler, Model |
| **Wilson, Tracy**<br>CTV-TV, PO Box 9, Station O, Scarborough ON M4A 2M9, Canada | Ice Dancer, Sportscaster |
| **Wilson, Trevor**<br>824 15th St, Hermosa Beach CA 90254, USA | Basketball Player |
| **Wilson, Trevor K**<br>5173 Woodcrest Lane, Lake Oswego OR 97035, USA | Baseball Player |
| **Wilson, Trisha**<br>Wilson Assoc, 3811 Turtle Creek Dr, #1500, Dallas TX 75219, USA | Interior Designer |
| **Wilson, Vance A**<br>6368 Elizabeth Ave, Springdale AR 72762, USA | Baseball Player |
| **Wilson, Wayne M**<br>183 Willowdale Dr, Shepherdstown WV 25443, USA | Football Player |
| **Wilson, William**<br>130 Belmont St, Englewood NJ 07631, USA | Basketball Player |
| **Wilson, William H (Mookie)**<br>1111 Heyward Wilson Road, Eastover SC 29044, USA | Baseball Player |
| **Wilson, William J**<br>Harvard University, Kennedy School of Government, Cambridge MA 02138, USA | Sociologist |
| **Wilson, Willie J**<br>18 Vianney Ave, Scarborough ON M1L 4V4, Canada | Baseball Player |
| **Wilson, Woody**<br>King Features Syndicate, 300 W 57th St, #1500, New York NY 10019 USA | Cartoonist (Rex Morgan MD) |
| **Wilson-Johnson, David R**<br>28 Englefield Road, London N1 4ET, England | Opera Singer |
| **Wilson-Sampras, Bridgette L**<br>Abrams Artists, 9200 W Sunset Blvd, #1125, West Hollywood CA 90069 USA | Actress, Singer |
| **Wiltsie, Jennifer**<br>Gavin Barker Assoc, 2D Wimpole St, London W1G 0EB, England | Actress |
| **Wimbley, Kamerion**<br>17400 Sawgrass Circle, North Royalton OH 44133, USA | Football Player |
| **Wimmer, Brian**<br>Integrated Mgmt, 1041 N Formosa Ave, West Hollywood CA 90046, USA | Actor |
| **Wimmer, Kurt**<br>Creative Artists Agency, 2000 Ave of Stars, #100, Los Angeles CA 90067 USA | Director |
| **Wimmer, Scott**<br>Richard Childress Racing, 425 Industrial Dr, Welcome NC 27374, USA | Auto Racing Driver |
| **Winans, BeBe**<br>Creative Artists Agency, 2000 Ave of Stars, #100, Los Angeles CA 90067 USA | Singer |
| **Winans, CeCe**<br>C W Entertainment, 115 Penn Warren Dr, #300-377, Brentwood TN 37027, USA | Singer |
| **Winans, Jeff D**<br>272 Madeira Circle, Saint Petersburg FL 33715, USA | Football Player |
| **Winans, Mario**<br>Bad Boy Entertainment, 1440 Broadway, #16, New York NY 10018 USA | Singer |
| **Winans, Matthew**<br>21 Saint George Place, Sandy Hook CT 06482, USA | Baseball Umpire |
| **Winans, Vicki**<br>Groove Entertainment, 1005 N Alfred St, #2, West Hollywood CA 90069, USA | Singer |
| **Winant, Scott**<br>Hansen Jacobson Teller, 450 N Roxbury Dr, #800, Beverly Hills CA 90210 USA | Producer, Director |
| **Winborne, Hughes**<br>I C M Partners, 10250 Constellation Blvd, #900, Los Angeles CA 90067 USA | Editor |
| **Winborne, Jamie L**<br>195 Roscoe Lee Circle, Wetumpka AL 36092, USA | Football Player |
| **Winbush, Angela**<br>Joyce Agency, 370 Harrison Ave, Harrison NY 10528, USA | Singer, Songwriter |
| **Winbush, Camille**<br>Stone Manners Salners, 6100 Wilshire Blvd, #1500, Los Angeles CA 90035 USA | Actress |
| **Winbush, Troy**<br>A P A Talent & Literary Agency, 405 S Beverly Dr, #300, Beverly Hills CA 90212 USA | Actor |
| **Winceniak, Edward J (Ed)**<br>10828 S Ave O, Chicago IL 60617, USA | Baseball Player |
| **Wincer, Simon G**<br>Creative Artists Agency, 2000 Ave of Stars, #100, Los Angeles CA 90067 USA | Director |

**Wilson - Wincer**

**Winchester, Philip** — Actor
Independent Talent Group, 40 Whitfield St, London W1T 2RH, England

**Winchester, Scott J** — Baseball Player
4705 Oakridge Dr, Midland MI 48640, USA

**Winchester, Simon** — Writer
Harper Collins Publishers, 10 E 53rd St, Cellar 1, New York NY 10022 USA

**Wincott, Michael** — Actor
Edith Grove Inc, 5900 Wilshire Blvd, #2250, Los Angeles CA 90036, USA

**Wind, Sabrina** — Producer
Paradigm Agency, 360 N Crescent Dr, North Building, Beverly Hills CA 90210 USA

**Winder, Sammy** — Football Player
Winder Construction Co, 4823 Green Crossing Road, Jackson MS 39157, USA

**Windhorn, Gordon R (Gordie)** — Baseball Player
145 Bent Creek Road, Danville VA 24540, USA

**Windis, Tony J** — Basketball Player
404 1st St, Rawlins WY 82301, USA

**Windon, Stephen F** — Cinematographer
PO Box 659, Northbridge, Sydney NSW 2063, Australia

**Windsor, Barbara** — Actress, Comedienne
104 Crouch Hill, London NB 9EA, England

**Windsor, David** — Baseball Player
23972 Dublin St, Lake Forest CA 92630, USA

**Windsor, Robert E (Bob)** — Football Player
2625 Legends Way, Ellicott City MD 21042, USA

**Wine, Robert P (Bobbie), Sr** — Baseball Player, Manager
2614 Woodland Ave, Eagleville PA 19403, USA

**Winegardner, Mark** — Writer
Florida State University, English Dept, Tallahassee FL 32306, USA

**Wineland, David J** — Nobel Physics Laureate
National Institute of Standards & Technology, 325 Broadway, Boulder CO 80305, USA

**Winfield, Antoine D** — Football Player
230 S Fazio Way, Spring TX 77389, USA

**Winfield, David M (Dave)** — Baseball Player
2235 Stratford Circle, Los Angeles CA 90077, USA

**Winfield, Leroy (Lee)** — Basketball Player
7638 Forest View Dr, Saint Louis MO 63121, USA

**Winfield, Rodney M** — Artist
3483 Ocean Ave, Carmel CA 93923, USA

**Winfrey, Oprah** — Entertainer, Actress
Harpo Productions, 110 N Carpenter St, Chicago IL 60607, USA

**Winfrey, Roy** — Baseball Player
2903 Renfro Dr NW, Atlanta GA 30318, USA

**Wing, Andrea** — Photographer
Crown Bay Marina, #310, PM Box 10, Saint Thomas VI 00802, USA

**Wing, Sean** — Actor
Innovative Artists, 1505 10th St, Santa Monica CA 90401 USA

**Wingate, David G S** — Basketball Player
11404 Glaetzer Lane, Charlotte NC 28270, USA

**Winger, Debra** — Actress
Framework Entertainment, 9057 Nemo St, #C, West Hollywood CA 90069 USA

**Wingti, Paias** — Prime Minister, Papua New Guinea
Marea Haus, Waigani, PO Box 6605, Port Moresby, Boroko, Papua New Guinea

**Wink, Chris** — Entertainer (Blue Man Group)
Blue Man Productions, 411 Lafayette St, #300, New York NY 10003, USA

**Winkelried, Jon** — Financier
Goldman Sachs Co, 85 Broad St, Building 85, New York NY 10004, USA

**Winkler, Angela** — Actress
Erna Baumbauer Mgmt, Kaplerstr 2, 81679 Munich, Germany

**Winkler, Hans-Gunter** — Equestrian
Dr Rau Allee 48, 48231 Warendorf, Germany

**Winkler, Henry** — Actor, Producer
PO Box 49914, Los Angeles CA 90049, USA

**Winkler, Irwin** — Director, Producer
Winkler Films, 190 N Canon Dr, Beverly Hills CA 90210, USA

**Winkler, Max** — Actor, Writer, Producer
Creative Artists Agency, 2000 Ave of Stars, #100, Los Angeles CA 90067 USA

**Winkles, Bobby B** — Baseball Manager
78452 Calle Huerta, La Quinta CA 92253, USA

**Winn, D Randolph (Randy)** — Baseball Player
59 Leeds Court E, Danville CA 94526, USA

**Winn, James F (Jim)** — Baseball Player
3440 S Delaware Ave, #123, Springfield MO 65804, USA

**Winnefeld, James A (Sandy), Jr** — Navy Admiral
Vice Chairman, Joint Chiefs of Staff, Pentagon, Washington DC 20318 USA

**Winnick, Katheryn** — Actress
Gersh Agency, 9465 Wilshire Blvd, #600, Beverly Hills CA 90212 USA

**Winningham, Herman S (Herm)** — Baseball Player
1542 Belleville Road, Orangeburg SC 29115, USA

**Winningham, Mare** — Actress
I F A Talent Agency, 8730 W Sunset Blvd, #490, West Hollywood CA 90069 USA

**Winokur, Marissa Jaret** — Actress, Singer
Gersh Agency, 9465 Wilshire Blvd, #600, Beverly Hills CA 90212 USA

**Winslet, Kate** — Actress
United Agents, 12-26 Lexington St, London W1F 0LE, England

**Winslow, Dan** — Singer, Guitarist (Trashmen)
H T M/Headline Talent Mgmt, 39398 Moonlight Bay Trail, Pelican Rapids MN 56572 USA

**Winslow, Kellen B, II** — Football Player
2431 Cornerstone, Westlake OH 44145, USA

**Winslow, Kellen B, Sr** — Football Player, Administrator
Central State University, Athletic Dept, PO Box 1004, Wilberforce OH 45384, USA

**Winslow, Michael** — Actor, Comedian
Venture I A B, 3211 Cahuenga Blvd W, #104, Los Angeles CA 90068, USA

**Winstead, Mary Elizabeth** — Actress
W M E Entertainment, 9601 Wilshire Blvd, #300, Beverly Hills CA 90210 USA

**Winston, Charlie** — Singer, Songwriter
Agency Group Ltd, 142 W 57th St, #600, New York NY 10019 USA

**Winston, Eric J** — Football Player
4811 Palmetto St, Bellaire, TX 77401, USA

**Winston, George** — Pianist, Composer
High Road Touring, 751 Bridgeway, #200, Sausalito CA 94965 USA

**Winston, Roy C** — Football Player
708 Highway 401, Napoleonville LA 70390, USA

**Winstone, Ray** — Actor
C A M, 111 Shoreditch High St, #400, London E1 6JN, England

**Winter, Blaise** — Football Player
3520 Rose Mallow Loop, Oviedo FL 32766, USA

**Winter, Donald** — Government Official
Navy Department, Secretary's Office, Pentagon, Washington DC 20350, USA

**Winter, Edgar** — Singer, Guitarist, Keyboardist
Hook Entertainment, 26033 Mulholland Highway, Malibu CA 91302, USA

**Winter, Edward D** — Actor
32070 Waterside Lane, Westlake Village CA 91361, USA

**Winter, Eric** — Actor
United Talent Agency, U T A Plaza, 9336 Civic Center Dr, Beverly Hills CA 90210 USA

**Winter, Fred (Tex)** — Basketball Coach
Los Angeles Lakers, Staples Center, 1111 S Figueroa St, Los Angeles CA 90015 USA

**Winter, Olaf** — Canoeing Athlete
An der Pirschheide 28, 14471 Potsdam, Germany

**Winter, Paul T** — Jazz, New Age Musician
Living Music Records, PO Box 72, Litchfield CT 06759, USA

**Winter, Ralph K, Jr** — Judge
US Court of Appeals, 141 Church St, New Haven CT 06510, USA

**Winter, Terence P** — Writer, Producer
Creative Artists Agency, 2000 Ave of Stars, #100, Los Angeles CA 90067 USA

**Winter, William F** — Governor, MS
633 N State St, Jackson MS 39202, USA

**Winterbottom, Michael** — Director, Producer
Independent Talent Group, 40 Whitfield St, London W1T 2RH, England

**Winterer, Caroline** — Historian
Stanford University, History Dept, 450 Serra Mall, Stanford CA 94305, USA

**Winterhart, Paul** — Drummer (Kula Shaker)
Little Big Man, 39A Grammercy Park N, #1C, New York NY 10010, USA

**Winters, Abby** — Photographer
PO Box 343, Fitzroy VIC 3065, Australia

**Winters, Anne** — Actress
Paradigm Agency, 360 N Crescent Dr, North Building, Beverly Hills CA 90210 USA

**Winters, Brian J** — Basketball Player, Coach
8652 E Kettle Circle, Centennial CO 80112, USA

**Winters, Dean** — Actor
United Talent Agency, U T A Plaza, 9336 Civic Center Dr, Beverly Hills CA 90210 USA

**Winters, Edward G, III** — Navy Admiral
Commander, Special Warfare Command, 2000 Trident Way, Coronado CA 92155 USA

**Winters, Frank M** — Football Player
820 17th St, Union City NJ 07087, USA

**Winters, Lisa** — Model
Playboy Promotions, 9346 Civic Center Dr, #200, Beverly Hills CA 90210 USA

**Winters, Michael** — Actor
Mitchell K Stubbs Assoc, 8695 W Washington Blvd, #204, Culver City CA 90232 USA

**Winters, Michael J (Mike)** — Baseball Umpire
13644 Boquita Dr, Del Mar CA 92014, USA

**Winters, Mickey** — Model
Playboy Promotions, 9346 Civic Center Dr, #200, Beverly Hills CA 90210 USA

**Winther, Peter** — Director, Producer, Writer
Gersh Agency, 9465 Wilshire Blvd, #600, Beverly Hills CA 90212 USA

**Wintour, Anna** — Editor
Vogue, Editor's Office, 4 Times Square, #1200, New York NY 10036, USA

**Winwood, Stephen L (Steve)** — Singer, Musician (Traffic); Songwriter
Trinley Cottage, Trinley, Gloucester GL19 4EU, England

**Wire, Coy M** — Football Player
586 Park Dr NE, Atlanta GA 30306, USA

**Wire, William S, II** — Businessman
706 Overton Park, Nashville TN 37215, USA

**Wirth, Billy** — Actor, Director
Arete Talent Agency, 454 N Robertson Blvd, Los Angeles CA 90048, USA

**Wirth, Timothy E** — Senator, CO
United Nations Foundation, 1225 Connecticut Ave NW, Washington DC 20036, USA

**Wischnewski, Anke** — Luge Athlete
Bundesstutzpunkt Oberwiesenthal, Dr-Jager-Str 2, 09484 Oberwiesenthal, Germany

**Wise, David** — Freestyle Skier
Draper Strategies & Communications, 748 S Meadows Parkway, #A9, Reno NV 89521, USA

**Wise, L DeWayne** — Baseball Player
709 Old Lexington Highway, Chapin SC 29036, USA

**Wise, Matthew J (Matt)** — Baseball Player
11627 E Twilight Court, Chandler AZ 85249, USA

**Wise, Phillip V (Phil)** — Football Player
11511 Poppy St NW, Minneapolis MN 55433, USA

**Wise, Phyllis M** — Neurobiologist, Educator
University of Chicago, Chancellor's Office, Chicago IL 60637, USA

**Wise, Ray** — Actor
Stone Manners Salners, 6100 Wilshire Blvd, #1500, Los Angeles CA 90035 USA

**Wise, Richard C (Rick)** — Baseball Player
15160 NW Oakhills Dr, Beaverton OR 97006, USA

**Wise, Willie M** — Basketball Player
2320 185th Place NE, Redmond WA 98052, USA

**Wiseman, Brian** — Ice Hockey Player
5917 Delores St, #B, Houston TX 77057, USA

**Wiseman, Frederick** — Producer
Zipporah Films, 1 Richdale Ave, #4, Cambridge MA 02140, USA

**Wiseman, G Reid** — Astronaut
N A S A, Johnson Space Center, 2101 NASA Road, Houston TX 77058 USA

**Wiseman, Len R** — Director, Producer, Writer
Creative Artists Agency, 2000 Ave of Stars, #100, Los Angeles CA 90067 USA

**Wiseman, Mac** — Singer
PO Box 17028, Nashville TN 37217, USA

**Wish Bone** — Rap Artist (Bone Thugs-N-Harmony)
Life Entertainment, 15441 Red Hill Ave, #G, Tustin CA 92780, USA

**Wishart, Leonard P, III** — Army General
19360 Magnolia Grove Square, #315, Leesburg VA 20176, USA

**Wisniewski, Andreas** — Actor
Gregory David Mayo, 10061 Riverside Dr, #242, Toluca Lake CA 91602, USA

**Wisniewski, Stephen A (Steve)** — Football Player
36 El Alamo Court, Danville CA 94526, USA

**Wisniewski, Tom** — Guitarist (MxPx)
W M E Entertainment, 9601 Wilshire Blvd, #300, Beverly Hills CA 90210 USA

**Wisocky, Rebecca** — Actress
Connor Ankrum Assoc, 1680 Vine St, #1016, Los Angeles CA 90028, USA

**Wisoff, Peter J K (Jeff)** — Astronaut
4268 Brindisi Place, Pleasanton CA 94566, USA

**Wissman, David A (Dave)** — Baseball Player
PO Box 38, Derby VT 05829, USA

**Wiste, Jim** — Ice Hockey Player
701 S University Blvd, Denver CO 80209, USA

**Wistert, Albert A (Ox)** — Football Player
1411 NE Olson Dr, Grants Pass OR 97526, USA

**Wistrom, Grant A** — Football Player
3862 S Royal Crest Lane, Rogersville MO 65742, USA

**Witasick, Gerald A (Jay)** — Baseball Player
200 Wellington Court, Bel Air MD 21014, USA

**Withem, Shannon B** — Baseball Player
39668 Dorchester Circle, Canton MI 48188, USA

**Withers, Bill** — Singer, Songwriter
Mattie Music Group, PO Box 16698, Beverly Hills CA 90209, USA

**Withers, Jane** — Actress
Keller & Vanderneth Business Mgmt, 1133 Broadway, #911, New York NY 10010, USA

**Withers, Pick** — Drummer (Dire Straits)
Damage Mgmt, 16 Lambton Place, London W11 2SH, England

**Witherspoon, John** — Actor, Comedian, Producer
Levity Entertainment, 6701 Center Drive W, #1111, Los Angeles CA 90045 USA

**Witherspoon, Reese** — Actress
Creative Artists Agency, 2000 Ave of Stars, #100, Los Angeles CA 90067 USA

**Witherspoon, Tim** — Boxer
Shuler Memorial Boxing Gym, 750 N Brooklyn St, Philadelphia PA 19104, USA

**Witherspoon, William C (Will)** — Football Player
4535 Wayland Dr, Nashville TN 37215, USA

**Witiuk, Doris** — Baseball Player
11821 N Hemlock St, Spokane WA 99218, USA

**Witiuk, Steve** — Ice Hockey Player
6 Leacock Ave, Winnipeg MB R3K 0G2, Canada

**Witkin, Jerome** — Artist
201 Whitestone Dr, Syracuse NY 13215, USA

**Witkin, Joel-Peter** — Photographer
1707 Five Points Road SW, Albuquerque NM 87105, USA

**Witkop, Bernhard** — Chemist
3807 Montrose Driveway, Chevy Chase MD 20815, USA

**Witman, Jon D** — Football Player
568 Woodsview Lane, Hellam PA 17406, USA

**Witmer, Tamara** — Model
Playboy Promotions, 9346 Civic Center Dr, #200, Beverly Hills CA 90210 USA

**Witmeyer, Ronald H (Ron)** — Baseball Player
PO Box 763, Rancho Santa Fe CA 92067, USA

**Witt, Alicia** — Actress
Brillstein Entertainment Partners, 9150 Wilshire Blvd, #350, Beverly Hills CA 90212 USA

**Witt, Brendan** — Ice Hockey Player
691 Park Ave, Huntington NY 11743, USA

**Witt, George A** — Baseball Player
2209 Catalina St, Laguna Beach CA 92651, USA

**Witt, Howard** — Actor
B R S / Gage Talent Agency, 1650 Broadway, #1410, New York NY 10019 USA

**Witt, Katarina** — Figure Skater, Model
Gottmann GmbH, Schwalbacher Str 48, 65760 Eschborn, Germany

**Witt, Kevin J** — Baseball Player
6350 Concho Bay Dr, Houston TX 77041, USA

**Witt, Michael A (Mike)** — Baseball Player
37 Poppy Hills Road, Laguna Nigel CA 92677, USA

**Witt, Paul Junger** — Writer, Producer, Director
16032 Valley Vista Blvd, Encino CA 91436, USA

**Witt, Robert A (Bobby)** — Baseball Player
4601 Winewood Court, Colleyville TX 76034, USA

**Witt, Robert E** — Educator
University of Alabama, President's Office, PO Box 870100, Tuscaloosa AL 35487, USA

**Witt, Vicki** — Model
Playboy Promotions, 9346 Civic Center Dr, #200, Beverly Hills CA 90210 USA

**Witte, Luke** — Basketball Player
3223 Arbor Pointe Dr, Charlotte NC 28210, USA

**Witten, C Jason** — Football Player
2001 Navasota Cove, Westlake TX 76262, USA

**Witten, Edward** — Theoretical Physicist, Mathematician
Institute for Advanced Study, Einstein Lane, Princeton NJ 08540 USA

**Witter, Cherie** — Model, Actress
Playboy Promotions, 9346 Civic Center Dr, #200, Beverly Hills CA 90210 USA

**Witter, Junior** — Boxer
Cybersportsbox, 23 Minna Road, Sheffield, South York S3 9AZ, England

**Witter, Karen** — Actress, Model
H/H/M, 247 S Beverly Dr, #102, Beverly Hills CA 90212, USA

**Witting, Steve** — Actor
Paradigm Agency, 360 N Crescent Dr, North Building, Beverly Hills CA 90210 USA

**Wittman, Randy S** — Basketball Player, Coach
8646 French Curve, Eden Prairie MN 55347, USA

**Witty, Chris** — Speed Skater
2644 E 2940 S, Salt Lake City UT 84109, USA

**Witucki, Casimir L (Cas)** — Football Player
3909 Spring Terrace, #248, Temple Hills MD 20748, USA

**Wixted, Kevin** — Actor
1712 Indian Trail Dr, Naperville IL 60565, USA

**Wobble, Jah** — Bassist (Public Image Limited)
Billions Corp, 3522 W Armitage Ave, Chicago IL 60647 USA

**Wockel-Eckert, Barbel** — Track Athlete
Im Bangert 61, 64750 Lutzelbach, Germany

**Wockenfuss, John B** — Baseball Player
26 Wallamsey Lane, Chesapeake City MD 21915, USA

**Woelki, Rainer M Cardinal** — Religious Leader
Archdiocese, Niederwallstr 8-9, 10017 Berlin, Germany

**Woerner, Scott A** — Football Player
6570 Highway 356, Sautee Nacoochee GA 30571, USA

**Woerth, Douglas** — Labor Leader
Airline Pilots Union, 535 Herndon Parkway, Herndon VA 20170, USA

**Woertz, Patricia** — Businesswoman
Archer Daniels Midland Co, 4666 Faries Parkway, #1, Decatur IL 62526, USA

**Wofford, Harris L** — Senator, PA
955 26th St NW, #501, Washington DC 20037, USA

**Woggon, Bill** — Cartoonist (Katy Keene)
2724 Cabot Court, Thousand Oaks CA 91360, USA

**Wohl, Bess** — Actress, Writer
Untitled Entertainment, 350 S Beverly Dr, #200, Beverly Hills CA 90212 USA

**Wohl, David B (Dave)** — Basketball Player, Coach, Executive
137 Morley Circle, Melville NY 11747, USA

**Wohlberg, Jeffrey** — Religious Leader, Rabbi
Adas Israel Congregation, 565 Broadway, Passaic NJ 07055, USA

**Wohlers, Mark E** — Baseball Player
135 Old Cedar Lane, Alpharetta GA 30004, USA

**Wohlford, James E (Jim)** — Baseball Player
24186 Lomitas Dr, Woodlake CA 93286, USA

**Wohlhuter, Richard C (Rick)** — Track Athlete
175 Dickinson Dr, Wheaton IL 60189, USA

**Wohlwender-Fricker, Marian** — Baseball Player
15210 Portside Dr, #401, Fort Myers FL 33908, USA

**Woit, Benedict F (Benny)** — Ice Hockey Player
607-20 Harding Blvd W, Richmond Hill ON L4C 9S4, Canada

**Woiwode, Larry** — Writer
State University of New York, English Dept, Binghamton NY 13901, USA

**Wojciechowski, John S** — Football Player
13317 Clyde Road, Holly MI 48442, USA

**Wojtowicz, R P** — Labor Leader
Railway Carmen Union, 3 Research Place, Rockville MD 20850, USA

**Wolanin, Craig** — Ice Hockey Player
4891 Gallagher Road, Rochester MI 48306, USA

**Wolcott, Gregory** — Actor
PO Box 622, Canoga Park CA 91305, USA

**Wolcott, Robert W (Bob)** — Baseball Player
3323 Bryson Way, Medford OR 97504, USA

**Wolczanski, Peter T** — Chemist
Cornell University, Chemistry Dept, Ithaca NY 14853, USA

**Wolde-Giorgis Lucha, Girma** — President, Ethiopia
President's Office, Presidential Palace, PO Box 1362, Addis Ababa, Ethiopia

**Wolf, Dale E** — Governor, DE
4830 Kennett Pike, #3221, Wilmington DE 19807, USA

**Wolf, David A** — Astronaut
Indianapolis Children's Museum, 3000 N Meridian St, Indianapolis IN 46208, USA

**Wolf, Dick** — Producer
W M E Entertainment, 9601 Wilshire Blvd, #300, Beverly Hills CA 90210 USA

**Wolf, James (Jim)** — Baseball Umpire
1507 E Glenhaven Dr, Phoenix AZ 85048, USA

**Wolf, Jenny** — Speed Skater
E V B 08, Weissenseer Weg 53, 13053 Berlin, Germany

**Wolf, Joseph F (Joe)** — Football Player
2324 Lehigh Parkway N, Allentown PA 18103, USA

**Wolf, Josh** — Actor, Comedian, Writer
Parallel Entertainment, 9420 Wilshire Blvd, #250, Beverly Hills CA 90212 USA

**Wolf, Naomi** — Writer
Royce Carlton Inc, 866 United Nations Plaza, #587, New York NY 10017, USA

**Wolf, Peter** — Singer (J Geils Band)
Front Line Mgmt, 1100 Glendon Ave, #2000, Los Angeles CA 90024 USA

**Wolf, Randall C (Randy)** — Baseball Player
8054 Royer Ave, Canoga Park CA 91304, USA

**Wolf, Sally** — Opera Singer
Columbia Artists Mgmt Inc, 5 Columbus Circle, 1790 Broadway, #1600, New York NY 10019 USA

**Wolf, Scott** — Actor
Innovative Artists, 1505 10th St, Santa Monica CA 90401 USA

**Wolf, Sigrid** — Alpine Skier
6652 Elbigenalp, #45A, Austria

**Wolf, Vicente** — Interior Designer
Vicente Wolf Assoc, 333 W 39th St, New York NY 10018, USA

**Wolf, Walter B (Wally)** — Baseball Player
18580 Corte Fresco, Rancho Santa Fe CA 92091, USA

**Wolfe, Art** — Photographer
520 1st Ave S, Seattle WA 98104, USA

**Wolfe, Bernard (Bernie)** — Ice Hockey Player
8012 Glenbrook Road, Bethesda MD 20814, USA

**Wolfe, Brian** — Baseball Player
32524 Sprucewood Way, Lake Elsinore CA 92532, USA

**Wolfe, Collette** — Actress
Gersh Agency, 9465 Wilshire Blvd, #600, Beverly Hills CA 90212 USA

**Wolfe, George C** — Director
Loeb & Loeb, 10100 Santa Monica Blvd, #2200, Los Angeles CA 90067 USA

**Wolfe, James**
35 Cobe Road, Northport ME 04849, USA — Sculptor
**Wolfe, Laurence A (Larry)**
5200 Blossomwood Court, Fair Oaks CA 95628, USA — Baseball Player
**Wolfe, Nathan D**
Global Viral Forcasting Initiative, 1 Sutter, #600, San Francisco CA 94104, USA — Virologist
**Wolfe, Ralph S**
University of Illinois, Microbiology Dept, Burrill Hall, Urbana IL 61801, USA — Microbiologist
**Wolfe, Robert H**
I C M Partners, 10250 Constellation Blvd, #900, Los Angeles CA 90067 USA — Producer, Writer
**Wolfe, Sterling**
2609 Wyoming Ave, #A, Burbank CA 91505, USA — Actor
**Wolfe, Thad A**
4790 Longwood Point, Colorado Springs CO 80906, USA — Air Force General
**Wolfe, Thomas K (Tom), Jr**
Felker Toczak Gellman, 10880 Wilshire Blvd, #2070, Los Angeles CA 90024 USA — Writer
**Wolfenden of Westcott, John F**
White House, Guildford Road, Westcott near Dorking, Surrey, England — Educator
**Wolfensohn, James D**
James D Wolfensohn Co, 599 Lexington Ave, New York NY 10022, USA — Financier
**Wolfenstein, Lincoln**
Carnegie-Mellon University, Physics Dept, 5000 Forbes, Pittsburgh PA 15213, USA — Physicist
**Wolfermann, Klaus**
Puma Sportschu, Postfach 1420, 91074 Herzogenaurach, Germany — Track Athlete
**Wolfe-Simon, Felisa**
N A S A Astrobiology, Harvard University, 20 Oxford St Cambridge MA 02138, USA — Biogeochemist
**Wolff, Alexander D (Alex)**
Creative Artists Agency, 2000 Ave of Stars, #100, Los Angeles CA 90067 USA — Actor, Singer (Naked Brothers Band)
**Wolff, Bob**
3 Salisbury Point, #2E, Nyack NY 10960, USA — Sportscaster
**Wolff, Christian**
Agentur Alexander, Lamontstr 9, 81679 Munich, Germany — Composer
**Wolff, Christoph J**
182 Washington St, Belmont MA 02478, USA — Educator
**Wolff, Hugh**
Van Walsum Mgmt, Tower Building, 11 York Road, London SE1 7NX, England — Conductor
**Wolff, Nathaniel M (Nat)**
Creative Artists Agency, 2000 Ave of Stars, #100, Los Angeles CA 90067 USA — Singer (Naked Brothers Band), Songwriter
**Wolff, Sanford I**
8141 Broadway, New York NY 10023, USA — Labor Leader
**Wolff, Tobias J A**
Stanford University, English Dept, Stanford CA 94305, USA — Writer
**Wolff, Torben**
Hesseltoften 12, 2900 Hellerup, Denmark — Biologist, Zoologist
**Wolfley, Craig A**
331 Station St, Bridgeville PA 15017, USA — Football Player
**Wolford, William C (Will)**
205 Waterleaf Way, Louisville KY 40207, USA — Football Player
**Wolfowitz, Paul D**
American Express Institute, 1150 17th St NW, Washington DC 20036, USA — Financier, Government Official
**Wolfram, Lea**
Casting-Agentur Schubert, Suarezstr 27, 14057 Berlin, Germany — Actress
**Wolin, Penny**
PO Box 1837, Sebastopol CA 95473, USA — Photographer
**Wolk, James**
W M E Entertainment, 9601 Wilshire Blvd, #300, Beverly Hills CA 90210 USA — Actor
**Woll, Deborah Ann**
Creative Artists Agency, 2000 Ave of Stars, #100, Los Angeles CA 90067 USA — Actress
**Wollman, Harvey L**
RR 1 Box 43, Hitchcock SD 57348, USA — Governor, SD
**Wollman, Roger L**
US Court of Appeals, Federal Building, 400 S Phillips, Sioux Falls SD 57104, USA — Judge
**Wolodarsky, Wallace (Wally)**
I C M Partners, 10250 Constellation Blvd, #900, Los Angeles CA 90067 USA — Producer, Writer
**Wolpe, David**
Sinai Temple, 10400 Wilshire Blvd, Los Angeles CA 90024, USA — Religious Leader, Rabbi
**Wolpe, Lenny**
B R S / Gage Talent Agency, 1650 Broadway, #1410, New York NY 10019 USA — Actor
**Wolski, Wojciech (Wojtek)**
Washington Capitals, 627 N Glebe Road, #850, Arlington VA 22203 USA — Ice Hockey Player
**Wolstenholme, Christopher T (Chris)**
Hall or Nothing P R, 35-37 Parkgate Road, London SW11 4NP, England — Bassist (Muse)
**Wolters, Kara**
137 Westfield Dr, Holliston MA 01746, USA — Basketball Player
**Woltman, Rhea A**
17 Polo Circle, Colorado Springs CO 80906, USA — Astronaut
**Womack, Anthony D (Tony)**
8301 Marcliffe Court, Waxhaw NC 28173, USA — Baseball Player
**Womack, Floyd S**
105 Grandview Circle, Brandon MS 39047, USA — Football Player
**Womack, Horace G (Dooley)**
209 Weeping Cherry Lane, Columbia SC 29212, USA — Baseball Player
**Womack, James E**
2105 Farley, College Station TX 77845, USA — Biologist, Agricultural Researcher
**Womack, Lee Ann**
Erv Woolsey, 1000 18th Ave S, Nashville TN 37212, USA — Singer
**Womble, Royce C**
6350 Newt Patterson Road, Mansfield TX 76063, USA — Football Player
**Won Hye-Kyung**
Skating Union, 88 Bangyee-Dong, Songpaku, Seoul 138 749, South Korea — Speed Skater
**Wonder, Stevie**
Steveland Morris Music, 4616 W Magnolia Blvd, Burbank CA 91505, USA — Singer, Songwriter
**Wonder, Wayne**
Headline Entertainment, 8 Haughton Ave, Kingston 10, Jamaica — Singer, Songwriter
**Wonders, Rich**
720 Augusta St, Racine WI 53402, USA — Bowler

**Wondolowski, Christopher E (Chris)** — Soccer Player
San Jose Earthquakes, 451 El Camino Real, #220, Santa Clara CA 95050 USA
**Wong Kar-Wai** — Director
Jet Tone Films, 21/F Park Commercial Centre, #180 Tung Lo Wan Road, Hong Kong, China
**Wong, Bradley D (B D)** — Actor
Gersh Agency, 9465 Wilshire Blvd, #600, Beverly Hills CA 90212 USA
**Wong, James** — Director, Producer, Writer
W M E Entertainment, 9601 Wilshire Blvd, #300, Beverly Hills CA 90210 USA
**Wong, Kailee W** — Football Player
5410 Valerie St, Bellaire TX 77401, USA
**Wong, Kirk** — Actor, Director
Global Artists Agency, 6253 Hollywood Blvd, #508, Los Angeles CA 90028, USA
**Wong, Russell** — Actor
Innovative Artists, 1505 10th St, Santa Monica CA 90401 USA
**Wong, Sue** — Fashion Designer
3030 W 6th St, Los Angeles CA 90020, USA
**Wong, Tyrus** — Artist, Kite Maker
10112 La Canada Way, Sunland CA 91040, USA
**Wong-Staal, Flossie** — Molecular Biologist
University of California, Molecular Biology Dept, La Jolla CA 92093, USA
**Wonsley, George I** — Football Player
2875 Spring Meadow Court, Indianapolis IN 46268, USA
**Woo, John** — Director, Producer
Lion Rock Productions, 5100 Goldleaf Circle, #230, Los Angeles CA 90056, USA
**Wood** — Drummer (British Sea Power)
Agency Group Ltd, 361-373 City Road, London EC1V 1PQ, England
**Wood, Adam K C** — Lieutenant Governor, Isle of Man
Lieutenant Governor's Office, Government House, Onchan, Isle of Man
**Wood, Annie** — Actress
Amsel Eisenstadt Frazier, 5055 Wilshire Blvd, #865, Los Angeles CA 90036 USA
**Wood, Anthony** — Businessman
Roku Co, 12980 Saratoga Ave, #D, Saratoga CA 95070, USA
**Wood, Barbara** — Writer
1450 University Ave, #F161, Riverside CA 92507, USA
**Wood, Brenton** — Singer
Groove Entertainment, 1005 N Alfred St, #2, West Hollywood CA 90069, USA
**Wood, C Norman** — Air Force General
214 Lower Field Road, Dunnsville VA 22454, USA
**Wood, Carolyn** — Swimmer
4380 SW 86th Ave, Portland OR 97225, USA
**Wood, Carri** — Golfer
2001 Sabal Ridge Court, #H, Palm Beach Gardens FL 33418, USA
**Wood, Charles G** — Writer
Gordon Dickinson, 2 Crescent Grove, London SW4 7AH, England
**Wood, David L** — Basketball Player
15200 Chateau Ave, Reno NV 89511, USA
**Wood, Diane P** — Judge
US Court of Appeals, 219 S Dearborn St, Chicago IL 60604, USA
**Wood, Duane S** — Football Player
PO Box 601, Wilburton OK 74578, USA
**Wood, Elijah** — Actor
W M E Entertainment, 9601 Wilshire Blvd, #300, Beverly Hills CA 90210 USA
**Wood, Evan Rachel** — Actress
Creative Artists Agency, 2000 Ave of Stars, #100, Los Angeles CA 90067 USA
**Wood, Glen** — Auto Racing Executive
57 Rhody Creek Loop, Stuart VA 24171, USA
**Wood, Gordon S** — Historian
77 Keene St, Providence RI 02906, USA
**Wood, Jacob (Jake), Jr** — Baseball Player
9129 Daytona Dr, Pensacola FL 32506, USA
**Wood, Janet** — Actress
Acme Talent, 4727 Wilshire Blvd, #333, Los Angeles CA 90010, USA
**Wood, Jason W** — Baseball Player
9899 N Cascade Dr, Fresno CA 93730, USA
**Wood, John A** — Astrophysicist, Geologist
1716 Cambridge St, #16, Cambridge MA 02138, USA
**Wood, Kerry L** — Baseball Player
6838 E Chey Dr, Paradise Valley AZ 85253, USA
**Wood, Kimba M** — Judge
US District Court House, 40 Foley Square, #104, New York NY 10007, USA
**Wood, Lana** — Actress
1131 Oriole Circle, Fillmore CA 93015, USA
**Wood, Laurie J** — Model, Actress
Playboy Promotions, 9346 Civic Center Dr, #200, Beverly Hills CA 90210 USA
**Wood, Leonard** — Auto Racing Driver
Wood Brothers Racing, 21 Performance Dr, Stuart VA 24171, USA
**Wood, M Richard (Dick)** — Football Player
41 Audubon Place, Newnan GA 30265, USA
**Wood, Maurice** — Physician
RR 2 Box 543B, Hot Springs VA 24445, USA
**Wood, Michael B (Mike)** — Baseball Player
1199 Cherlynn Terrace, West Palm Beach FL 33406, USA
**Wood, Michael S (Mike)** — Football Player
630 N Geyer Road, Saint Louis MO 63122, USA
**Wood, Nigel K** — Astronaut, England
Boscome Down Royal Air Force Base, Amesbury, Wiltshire SP4 0JF, England
**Wood, O Leon** — Basketball Player
3602 Brayton Ave, Long Beach CA 90807, USA
**Wood, Oliver** — Cinematographer
1549 N Gardner St, Los Angeles CA 90046, USA
**Wood, R Brandon** — Baseball Player
5936 E Saint John Road, Scottsdale AZ 85254, USA
**Wood, Rachel Hurd** — Actress
Troika, 74 Clerkenwell Road, #300, London EC1M 5QA, England
**Wood, Randolph B (Randy)** — Ice Hockey Player
2 Bridge St, Manchester MA 01944, USA

|  |  |
|---|---|
| **Wood, Richard M**<br>5413 Windbrush Dr, Tampa FL 33625, USA | Football Player, Coach |
| **Wood, Robert J**<br>McDonnell Douglas Corp, PO Box 516, Saint Louis MO 63166, USA | Astronaut |
| **Wood, Ronald (Ron)**<br>Monroe Sounds, 5 Church Row, Wandsworth Plain, London SW18 1ES, England | Guitarist (Rolling Stones) |
| **Wood, Wilbur F, Jr**<br>3 Elmbrook Road, Bedford MA 01730, USA | Baseball Player |
| **Wood, William V (Willie)**<br>Willie Wood Mechanical Systems, 7941 16th St NW, Washington DC 20012, USA | Football Player |
| **Woodall, D Bradley (Brad)**<br>3539 John Muir Dr, Middleton WI 53562, USA | Baseball Player |
| **Woodall, F Alley (Al)**<br>131 Field Crest Road, New Canaan CT 06840, USA | Football Player |
| **Woodall, Jerry M**<br>Yale University, Microelectronic Center, 105 Wall St, New Haven CT 06511, USA | Electrical Engineer, Inventor |
| **Woodall, Lee A**<br>63 Sleepy Hollow Dr, Detroit MI 48227, USA | Football Player |
| **Woodall, Trinny**<br>Artist Rights Group, 4A Exmoor St, London W10 6BD, England | Actress |
| **Woodard, Alfre**<br>I C M Partners, 10250 Constellation Blvd, #900, Los Angeles CA 90067 USA | Actress |
| **Woodard, Charlayne**<br>Sovereign Talent Group, 8421 Wilshire Blvd, #200, Beverly Hills CA 90211, USA | Actress, Writer |
| **Woodard, Kenneth E (Ken)**<br>15389 Steel St, #201, Detroit MI 48227, USA | Football Player |
| **Woodard, Lynette**<br>4206 Quail Pointe Terrace, Lawrence KS 66047, USA | Basketball Player |
| **Woodard, Michael C (Mike)**<br>PO Box 35, Maywood IL 60153, USA | Baseball Player |
| **Woodard, Rickey**<br>J V C Music, 3800 Barham Blvd, #409, Los Angeles CA 90068, USA | Jazz Saxophonist |
| **Woodard, Ronald B**<br>MagnaDrive Inc, 600 108th Ave NE, #1014, Bellevue WA 98004, USA | Businessman |
| **Woodard, Shannon**<br>Untitled Entertainment, 350 S Beverly Dr, #200, Beverly Hills CA 90212 USA | Actress |
| **Woodard, Steven L (Steve)**<br>800 Frost Court SW, Hartselle AL 35640, USA | Baseball Player |
| **Woodbine, Bokeem**<br>Gersh Agency, 9465 Wilshire Blvd, #600, Beverly Hills CA 90212 USA | Actor |
| **Woodbridge, Todd**<br>Advantage International, PO Box 3297, North Burnley, VIC 3121, Australia | Tennis Player |
| **Woodburn, Danny**<br>Artists Group, 3345 Wilshire Blvd, #915, Los Angeles CA 90010, USA | Actor |
| **Wooden, Shawn A**<br>17741 SW 12th St, Pembroke Pines FL 33029, USA | Football Player |
| **Woodeshick, Thomas (Tom)**<br>PO Box 716, Blakeslee PA 18610, USA | Football Player |
| **Woodforde, Mark**<br>Octagon Worldwide, 1751 Pinnacle Dr, #1500, McLean VA 22102 USA | Tennis Player |
| **Woodgate, Daniel (Woody)**<br>I T F, Ariel House, 74A Charlotte St, London W1T 4QJ, England | Drummer (Madness) |
| **Woodgette, Wanita D**<br>Bad Boy Entertainment, 1440 Broadway, #16, New York NY 10018 USA | Singer (Danity Kane) |
| **Woodhall, Richard (Richie)**<br>Tony Clayman, 58/60 Kensington Church St, London W8 4DB, England | Boxer |
| **Woodhead, Cynthia**<br>PO Box 1193, Riverside CA 92502, USA | Swimmer |
| **Woodkid**<br>Green United Music, 7D Villa du Lavoir, 70 Rue Rene Boulanger, 75010 Paris, France | Singer |
| **Woodland, Gary**<br>Professional Golfers Association, 100 Ave of Champions, Palm Beach Gardens FL 33418 USA | Golfer |
| **Woodland, Lauren**<br>Michael Bruno Group, 13576 Cheltenham Dr, Sherman Oaks CA 91423, USA | Actress |
| **Woodley, Arthur**<br>Opus 3 Artists, 470 Park Ave S, #900N, New York NY 10016 USA | Singer |
| **Woodley, Dan**<br>15852 Deer Ridge Dr, Morrison CO 80465, USA | Ice Hockey Player |
| **Woodley, LaMarr D**<br>1635 Heritage Dr, Pittsburgh PA 15237, USA | Football Player |
| **Woodley, Shailene**<br>Savage Agency, 6212 Banner Ave, Los Angeles CA 90038 USA | Actress |
| **Woodlief, Douglas E (Doug)**<br>4953 Santa Evinita Dr, Fort Mohave AZ 86426, USA | Football Player |
| **Woodmansee, John W, Jr**<br>23 Cattail Pond Dr, Frisco TX 75034, USA | Army General |
| **Woodrell, Daniel**<br>Little Brown, 3 Center Plaza, #100, Boston MA 02108 USA | Writer |
| **Woodruff, Blake**<br>Amsel Eisenstadt Frazier, 5055 Wilshire Blvd, #865, Los Angeles CA 90036 USA | Actor |
| **Woodruff, Bob**<br>ABC-TV, News Dept, 77 W 66th St, New York NY 10023 USA | Commentator |
| **Woodruff, Bob**<br>Jim Della Croce Mgmt, 1229 17th Ave S, Nashville TN 37212, USA | Singer, Songwriter |
| **Woodruff, Dwayne D**<br>10382 Grubbs Road, Wexford PA 15090, USA | Football Player |
| **Woodruff, Judy C**<br>CNN-TV, News Dept, 820 1st St NE, #1000, Washington DC 20002 USA | Commentator |
| **Woods, Alvis (Al)**<br>2600 San Leandro Blvd, #1004, San Leandro CA 94578, USA | Baseball Player |
| **Woods, Barbara Alyn**<br>Stone Manners Salners, 6100 Wilshire Blvd, #1500, Los Angeles CA 90035 USA | Actress |
| **Woods, Christine**<br>Gersh Agency, 9465 Wilshire Blvd, #600, Beverly Hills CA 90212 USA | Actress |
| **Woods, Donald R (Don)**<br>6340 Calle Tesoro NW, Albuquerque NM 87114, USA | Football Player |

**W**

Wood - Woods

**Woods, Elbert (Ickey)** — Football Player
505 E Sharon Road, #A, Cincinnati OH 45246, USA
**Woods, Eldrick T (Tiger)** — Golfer
E T W Corp, 501 N Highway A1A, Jupiter FL 33477, USA
**Woods, Gary L** — Baseball Player
PO Box 151, Solvang CA 93464, USA
**Woods, George** — Track Athlete
7631 Green Hedge Road, Edwardsville IL 62025, USA
**Woods, James** — Actor
Gersh Agency, 9465 Wilshire Blvd, #600, Beverly Hills CA 90212 USA
**Woods, James J (Jim)** — Baseball Player
4509 Gardenia Ave, Keyes CA 95328, USA
**Woods, Larry D** — Football Player
8906 Covent Garden St, Houston TX 77031, USA
**Woods, Michael** — Actor
Integral Artists, 73 E 6th Ave, #208, Vancouver BC V5T 1M4, Canada
**Woods, Nan** — Actress
Geddes Agency, 8430 Santa Monica Blvd, #201, West Hollywood CA 90069 USA
**Woods, Paul** — Ice Hockey Player
4276 S Shore St, Waterford MA 48328, USA
**Woods, Philip W (Phil)** — Jazz Clarinetist, Saxophonist, Composer
PO Box 278, Delaware Water Gap PA 18327, USA
**Woods, Rick L** — Football Player
1567 76th Ave N, Saint Petersburg FL 33702, USA
**Woods, Robert E** — Football Player
4922 Devonshire Ave, Memphis TN 38117, USA
**Woods, Robert S** — Actor
PO Box 492, Kinderhook NY 12106, USA
**Woods, Ronald L (Ron)** — Baseball Player
5209 Desert Star Dr, Las Vegas NV 89130, USA
**Woods, S Anthony (Tony)** — Football Player
9 Sanford Ave, Belleville NJ 07109, USA
**Woods, Simon** — Actor
Independent Talent Group, 40 Whitfield St, London W1T 2RH, England
**Woods, Skip** — Director, Producer, Writer
Creative Artists Agency, 2000 Ave of Stars, #100, Los Angeles CA 90067 USA
**Woods, Stuart** — Writer
G P Putnam's Sons, 375 Hudson St, New York NY 10014 USA
**Woods, Susan** — Actress
28164 Sloan Canyon Road, #A, Castaic CA 91384, USA
**Woodside, D B** — Actor
Don Buchwald Talent Agency, 6500 Wilshire Blvd, #2200, Los Angeles CA 90048 USA
**Woodson, Abraham B (Abe)** — Football Player
3680 Waynesvill St, Las Vegas NV 89122, USA
**Woodson, Charles** — Football Player
10010 Tavistock Road, Orlando FL 32827, USA
**Woodson, Herbert H** — Electrical Engineer
1034 Liberty Park Dr, Austin TX 78746, USA
**Woodson, Jacqueline** — Writer
Bantam Books, 1745 Broadway, New York NY 10019 USA
**Woodson, Marvin L (Marv)** — Football Player
3050 Redmond Dr, #2207, Dallas TX 75211, USA
**Woodson, Richard L (Dick)** — Baseball Player
27879 Panorama Hills Dr, Menifee CA 92584, USA
**Woodson, Robert L, Sr** — Urban Activist
National Neighborhood Enterprise Center, 1424 16th St NW, Washington DC 20036, USA
**Woodson, Roderick K (Rod)** — Football Player, Sportscaster
3304 Medallion Court, Pleasanton CA 94588, USA
**Woodson, Tracy M** — Baseball Player
9027 Fascine Court, Mechanicsville VA 23116, USA
**Woodson, Warren V** — Football Coach
12680 Hillcrest Road, #1106, Dallas TX 75230, USA
**Woodson, William R** — Educator
North Carolina State University, Chancellor's Office, Peele Hall, Raleigh NC 27695, USA
**Woodville, Kate** — Actress
20141 S Sweetbriar Road, West Linn OR 97068, USA
**Woodward, Christopher M (Chris)** — Baseball Player
15049 Howelhurst Dr, Baldwin Park CA 91706, USA
**Woodward, Joanne G** — Actress
I C M Partners, 10250 Constellation Blvd, #900, Los Angeles CA 90067 USA
**Woodward, Kirsten** — Fashion Designer
Kirsten Woodward Hats, 26 Portobello Green Arcade, London W10, England
**Woodward, Margaret H (Maggie)** — Air Force General
Commander 17th Air Force, Ramstein Air Force Base, Unit 3300, APO AE 09094, USA
**Woodward, Morgan** — Actor
2111 Rockledge Road, Los Angeles CA 90068, USA
**Woodward, Neil W, III** — Astronaut
1935 Edgemont Place W, Seattle WA 98199, USA
**Woodward, Robert J (Rob)** — Baseball Player
58 Eastman Hill Road, Lebanon NH 03766, USA
**Woodward, Robert U (Bob)** — Journalist
3305 Old Point Road, Edgewater MD 21037, USA
**Woodward, Roger R** — Concert Pianist, Conductor, Composer
L H Productions, 2/37 Hendy Ave, Coogee NSW 2034, Australia
**Woodward, Shannon** — Actress
Untitled Entertainment, 350 S Beverly Dr, #200, Beverly Hills CA 90212 USA
**Woodward, William F (Woody)** — Baseball Player
10 San Marco Court, Palm Coast FL 32137, USA
**Woody** — Singer (Dru Hill)
Mercury Records, 11150 Santa Monica Blvd, #1000, Los Angeles CA 90025 USA
**Woody, Damien M** — Football Player
3 Roconan Dr, Mendham NJ 07945, USA
**Wool, Christopher** — Artist
Luhring Augustine Gallery, 531 W 24th St, New York NY 10011, USA
**Wooldridge, Floyd L** — Baseball Player
214 Barber St, Greenfield MO 65661, USA

**Woolery, Chuck** — Actor
Western Creative, 26135 Plymouth Road, Redford MI 48239, USA

**Woolfolk, Harold E (Butch)** — Football Player
4519 Magnolia Lane, Sugar Lane TX 77478, USA

**Woolford, Donnell** — Football Player
725 Lumber Lane, Charlotte NC 28214, USA

**Woolgar, Fenella** — Actress
Independent Talent Group, 40 Whitfield St, London W1T 2RH, England

**Woollard, Robert G (Bob)** — Basketball Player
RR 1 Box 456, Hamptonville NC 27020, USA

**Woolley, Bennie L (Chip), Jr** — Thoroughbred Racing Trainer
135 Road 5018, Bloomfield NM 87413, USA

**Woolley, Jason D** — Ice Hockey Player
4019 Quarton Road, Bloomfield MI 48302, USA

**Woolley, Kenneth F** — Architect
790 George St, #500, Sydney NSW 2000, Australia

**Woolsey, Elizabeth D** — Alpine Skier, Executive
Trail Creek Ranch, 7100 West Trail Creek Road, Wilson WY 83014, USA

**Woolsey, R James** — Government Official
Shea & Gardner, 901 New York Ave NW, Washington DC 20001, USA

**Woolsey, Ralph A** — Cinematographer
23388 Mulholland Dr, #109, Woodland Hills CA 91364, USA

**Woolsey, William T** — Swimmer
1032 Seascape Circle, Rodeo CA 94572, USA

**Woolstenhulme, Rick, Jr** — Drummer (Lifehouse)
Untitled Entertainment, 350 S Beverly Dr, #200, Beverly Hills CA 90212 USA

**Woolvett, Jaimz** — Actor
Noble Caplan Abrams, 1260 Yonge St, #200, Toronto ON M4T 1W6, Canada

**Woomble, Roddy** — Singer (Idlewild)
Agency Group Ltd, 361-373 City Road, London EC1V 1PQ, England

**Woosnam, Ian H** — Golfer
Dyffryn, Morda Road, Oswestry, Shropshire SY11 2AY, Wales

**Woosnam, Phil** — Soccer Executive
2211 Mainsail Dr, Marietta GA 30062, USA

**Wooten, Hubert (Daddy), Jr** — Baseball Player
120 Sandy Dr, Goldsboro NC 27534, USA

**Wooten, Jim** — Commentator
ABC-TV, News Dept, 5010 Creston St, Hyattsville MD 20781 USA

**Wooten, John B** — Football Player
3760 Paradise Hills Dr, #2601, Euless TX 76040, USA

**Wooten, Nicholas** — Producer, Writer
W M E Entertainment, 9601 Wilshire Blvd, #300, Beverly Hills CA 90210 USA

**Wooten, Ronald J (Ron)** — Football Player
2401 Lewis Grove Lane, Raleigh NC 27608, USA

**Wooten, Victor L** — Jazz Bassist, Composer
Skyline Music, 563 Willow Hollow Dr NE, Atlanta GA 30328, USA

**Wooten, W Shawn** — Baseball Player
765 Ali Lane, Santa Monica CA 90402, USA

**Wootten, Morgan** — Basketball Coach
6912 Wells Parkway, University Park MD 20782, USA

**Wopat, Tom** — Actor, Singer
Innovative Artists, 1505 10th St, Santa Monica CA 90401 USA

**Word, Barry Q** — Football Player
5746 Janneys Mill Circle, Haymarket VA 20169, USA

**Word, Weldon R** — Engineer (Paveway Smart Bomb)
626 Hurst Dr, Tyler TX 75703, USA

**Worden, Alfred M** — Astronaut
PO Box 8065, Vero Beach FL 32963, USA

**Wordsworth, Barry** — Conductor
I M G Artists, Hogarth Business Park, Chiswick, London W4 2TH, England

**Workman, A K (Hank)** — Baseball Player
307 19th St, Santa Monica CA 90402, USA

**Workman, Haywoode W** — Basketball Player
13711 Inoma St, #104, Tampa FL 33613, USA

**Workman, Vincent I (Vince), Jr** — Football Player
98 Southfield Ave, #605, Stamford CT 06902, USA

**World Peace, Metta** — Basketball Player
Tri Star Sports & Entertainment, 1222 16th Ave S, #300, Nashville TN 37212, USA

**Worley, Brian** — Singer (Stamps Quartet)
PO Box 1471, Brentwood TN 37024, USA

**Worley, Darryl** — Singer
Rendy Lovelady Mgmt, 24 Middleton St, Nashville TN 37210, USA

**Worley, Jo Anne** — Actress, Comedienne
Mavrick Artists, 6100 Wilshire Blvd, #550, Los Angeles CA 90048, USA

**Worley, Timothy A (Tim)** — Football Player
Worley Global Enterprises, PO Box 14477, Huntsville AL 35815, USA

**Worndl, Frank** — Alpine Skier
Burgsiedlung 19C, 87527 Sonthofen, Germany

**Woronov, Mary** — Actress
Studio Talent Group, 1328 12th St, Santa Monica CA 90401, USA

**Worrell, Bernie** — Singer, Musician (Parliament-Funkadelic)
Blue Mountain Artists, 810 Tyvola Road, #114, Charlotte NC 28217, USA

**Worrell, Cameron J** — Football Player
2829 E Christopher Dr, Fresno CA 93720, USA

**Worrell, Peter** — Ice Hockey Player
3560 Aladdin Ave, Boynton Beach FL 33436, USA

**Worrell, Timothy H (Tim)** — Baseball Player
4719 W El Cortez Place, Phoenix AZ 85083, USA

**Worrell, Todd R** — Baseball Player
810 Simmons Ave, Saint Louis MO 63122, USA

**Worsham, Del** — Drag Racing Driver
PO Box 1329, Chino Hills CA 91709, USA

**Worth, Maurice** — Businessman
Delta Air Lines, Hartsfield International Airport, Atlanta GA 30320, USA

**Wortham, Barron W** — Football Player
8608 Busch Gardens Dr, Fort Worth TX 76123, USA

**W**

| | |
|---|---|
| **Wortham, Richard C (Rich)**<br>1708 Mira Vista, Leander TX 78641, USA | Baseball Player |
| **Worthen, Kevin J**<br>Brigham Young University, President's Office, Provo UT 84602, USA | Educator |
| **Worthington, Allan F (Al)**<br>12070 Highway 55, Sterrett AL 35147, USA | Baseball Player |
| **Worthington, Craig R**<br>10019 Mattock Ave, Downey CA 90240, USA | Baseball Player |
| **Worthington, Sam**<br>Anonymous Content, 3532 Hayden Ave, Culver City CA 90232 USA | Actor |
| **Worthy, James A**<br>5750 Corbett St, Los Angeles CA 90016, USA | Basketball Player, Sportscaster |
| **Worthy, Richard (Rick)**<br>S M S Talent, 8383 Wilshire Blvd, #230, Beverly Hills CA 90211 USA | Actor |
| **Wortman, Keith D**<br>421 Bordeaux Way, Saint Peters MO 63376, USA | Football Player |
| **Wortman, Kevin**<br>42 David Dr, Saugus MA 01906, USA | Ice Hockey Player |
| **Wosner, Shai**<br>Opus 3 Artists, 470 Park Ave S, #900N, New York NY 10016 USA | Concert Pianist |
| **Wottle, David J (Dave)**<br>9245 Forest Hill Lane, Germantown TN 38139, USA | Track Athlete |
| **Wotton, Mark**<br>Pro-Rep Entertainment, 113-276 Midpark Way SE, Calgary AB T2X 1J6, Canada | Ice Hockey Player |
| **Wotus, Ronald A (Ron)**<br>6 Monteria Lane, Martinez CA 94553, USA | Baseball Player |
| **Wotzel, Mandy**<br>Olympic Ice Rink, 1080 Centre Road, Melbourne VIC 3167, Australia | Figure Skater |
| **Wouk, Herman**<br>303 W Crestview Dr, Palm Springs CA 92264, USA | Writer |
| **Woywitka, Jeff**<br>RR 1, Mannville AB T0B 2W0, Canada | Ice Hockey Player |
| **Wozniacki, Caroline**<br>Noru Sports Group, Fredericksborggade 5A2, 1360 Copenhagen K, Denmark | Tennis Player |
| **Wozniak, Katarzyna**<br>Peter Wyszynski, Ul Ossowo St, 4D Matarewicza, 05230 Kobylka, Ossow, Poland | Speed Skater |
| **Wozniak, Steve**<br>16400 Blackberry Hill Road, Los Gatos CA 95030, USA | Computer Designer, Inventor |
| **Wozniewski, Andrew (Andy)**<br>322 Lakeview Dr, Buffalo Grove IL 60089, USA | Ice Hockey Player |
| **Wragg, John**<br>6 Castle Lane, Devizes, Wiltshire SN10 1HJ, England | Sculptor |
| **Wray, Gordon R**<br>Stonestack, Rempstone, Loughborough, Leicestershire LE12 6RH, England | Engineer, Designer |
| **Wray, Margaret Jane**<br>Columbia Artists Mgmt Inc, 5 Columbus Circle, 1790 Broadway, #1600, New York NY 10019 USA | Opera Singer |
| **Wregget, Ken**<br>176 Fieldgate Dr, Pittsburgh PA 15241, USA | Ice Hockey Player |
| **Wrenn, Peter**<br>5215 Wren Court, Carmel IN 46033, USA | Harness Racing Driver |
| **Wrenn, Robert (Bob)**<br>8908 Watlington Road, Henrico VA 23229, USA | Golfer |
| **Wrighster, George F, III**<br>3014 Summit Place, Birmingham AL 35243, USA | Football Player |
| **Wright Shapiro, Elizabeth**<br>United Talent Agency, U T A Plaza, 9336 Civic Center Dr, Beverly Hills CA 90210 USA | Actress |
| **Wright, Adam**<br>Third Coast Artists Mgmt, 2021 21st Ave S, #220, Nashville TN 37212, USA | Singer, Guitarist (Wrights) |
| **Wright, Alex**<br>A P A Talent & Literary Agency, 405 S Beverly Dr, #300, Beverly Hills CA 90212 USA | Actress |
| **Wright, Alexander**<br>501 S Mississippi St, Amarillo TX 79106, USA | Football Player |
| **Wright, Ben**<br>CBS-TV, Sports Dept, 51 W 52nd St, New York NY 10019 USA | Sportscaster |
| **Wright, Betty**<br>Rodgers Redding, PO Box 4603, Macon GA 31208 USA | Singer |
| **Wright, Beverly**<br>Deep South Environment Justice Center, 2601 Gentilly Blvd, New Orleans LA 70122, USA | Environmental Activist, Sociologist |
| **Wright, Bonnie**<br>United Agents, 12-26 Lexington St, London W1F 0LE, England | Actress |
| **Wright, Bradford N (Brad)**<br>1050 S Cloverdale Ave, Los Angeles CA 90019, USA | Basketball Player |
| **Wright, Bryant**<br>Johnson Ferry Baptist Church, 955 Johnson Ferry Road, Marietta GA 30068, USA | Religious Leader |
| **Wright, Charles J**<br>2698 Wakefield Lane, Westlake OH 44145, USA | Football Player |
| **Wright, Charles P, Jr**<br>940 Locust Ave, Charlottesville VA 22901, USA | Writer |
| **Wright, Chely**<br>Creative Artists Agency, 2000 Ave of Stars, #100, Los Angeles CA 90067 USA | Singer, Actress |
| **Wright, Clyde**<br>528 S Jeanine St, Anaheim CA 92806, USA | Baseball Player |
| **Wright, Craig M**<br>C M Wright Inc, 722 N La Cienega Blvd, West Hollywood CA 90069, USA | Architect |
| **Wright, Danny**<br>Engine Entertainment, 116 NE 136th Ave, Portland OR 97230, USA | Pianist |
| **Wright, David A**<br>1105 Hillston Court, Chesapeake VA 23322, USA | Baseball Player |
| **Wright, Dick**<br>Columbus Dispatch, Editorial Dept, 34 S 3rd St, Columbus OH 43215, USA | Editorial Cartoonist |
| **Wright, Donald C (Don)**<br>PO Box 1176, Palm Beach FL 33480, USA | Editorial Cartoonist |
| **Wright, Dorell L**<br>158 Twin Peaks Dr, Walnut Creek CA 94595, USA | Basketball Player |
| **Wright, Doug**<br>I C M Partners, 730 5th Ave, New York NY 10019 USA | Writer |

**Wortham - Wright**

| | |
|---|---|
| **Wright, Edgar** | Director, Writer |
| Independent Talent Group, 40 Whitfield St, London W1T 2RH, England | |
| **Wright, Elmo** | Football Player |
| 11419 Olympia Dr, Houston TX 77077, USA | |
| **Wright, Gary** | Singer, Songwriter |
| Air Tight Mgmt, 115 West Road, Winsted CT 06098, USA | |
| **Wright, George D** | Baseball Player |
| 4228 NE 18th St, Oklahoma City OK 73121, USA | |
| **Wright, Heather** | Actress |
| 1 Sunnyside, Wimbledon, London SW19, England | |
| **Wright, J Richard (Ricky)** | Baseball Player |
| 2502 Clark Lane, Paris TX 75460, USA | |
| **Wright, Jaguar** | Singer |
| Richard De La Font Agency, 4845 S Sheridan Road, #505, Tulsa OK 74145 USA | |
| **Wright, James C (Jim), Jr** | Representative, TX; Speaker |
| Texas Christian University, Political Science Dept, Fort Worth TX 76129, USA | |
| **Wright, James E** | Historian |
| 7 Quail Dr, Etna NH 03750, USA | |
| **Wright, Jamey A** | Baseball Player |
| 4325 Fairfax Ave, Dallas TX 75205, USA | |
| **Wright, Jaret** | Baseball Player |
| 3816 Vista Azul, San Clemente CA 92672, USA | |
| **Wright, Jay** | Basketball Coach |
| Villanova University, Athletic Dept, Villanova PA 19085, USA | |
| **Wright, Jay** | Writer |
| General Delivery, Piermont NH 03779, USA | |
| **Wright, Jeff D** | Football Player |
| 23426 N 21st Place, Phoenix AZ 85024, USA | |
| **Wright, Jeffrey** | Actor |
| Creative Artists Agency, 2000 Ave of Stars, #100, Los Angeles CA 90067 USA | |
| **Wright, Jeffrey R (Jeff)** | Football Player |
| 420 W Bluejay Dr, Chandler AZ 85286, USA | |
| **Wright, Joe** | Director, Producer, Actor |
| Shoebox Films, 82 Berwick St, London W1F 8TP, England | |
| **Wright, John** | Ice Hockey Player |
| 116 Hillsdale Ave, Toronto ON M5P 1G5, Canada | |
| **Wright, John M, Jr** | Army General |
| 5195 Cottingham Place, Alexandria VA 22304, USA | |
| **Wright, Judith A** | Writer |
| 17 Devonport St, #1, Lyons ACT 2060, Australia | |
| **Wright, Julian** | Basketball Player |
| 50 Pinehurst Dr, New Orleans LA 70131, USA | |
| **Wright, Kendall** | Football Player |
| Tennessee Titans, 460 Great Circle Road, Nashville TN 37228 USA | |
| **Wright, Kenneth W (Ken)** | Baseball Player |
| 1651 Ora Dr, Pensacola FL 32506, USA | |
| **Wright, L Rayfield** | Football Player |
| PO Box 2833, Weatherford TX 76086, USA | |
| **Wright, Larry** | Ice Hockey Player |
| Regina Fire Dept, PO Box 1790, Regina SK S4P 3C8, Canada | |
| **Wright, Lawrence** | Writer |
| Wylie Agency, 250 W 57th St, #2114, New York NY 10107 USA | |
| **Wright, Lawrence A** | Judge |
| US Tax Court, 400 2nd St NW, Washington DC 20217, USA | |
| **Wright, Lizz** | Singer |
| Direct Management Group, 947 N La Cienega Blvd, #G, West Hollywood CA 90069, USA | |
| **Wright, Louis D** | Football Player |
| 2263 S Quentin Way, #F301, Aurora CO 80014, USA | |
| **Wright, Mary K (Mickey)** | Golfer |
| 2972 SE Treasure Island Road, Port Saint Lucie FL 34952, USA | |
| **Wright, Michael** | Actor |
| Don Buchwald Talent Agency, 6500 Wilshire Blvd, #2200, Los Angeles CA 90048 USA | |
| **Wright, Michelle** | Singer |
| Savannah Music, 205 Powell Place, #214, Brentwood TN 37027, USA | |
| **Wright, Nathaniel (Nate)** | Football Player |
| 11247 Zorita Court, San Diego CA 92124, USA | |
| **Wright, Pat** | Singer (Crystals) |
| Lustig Talent, PO Box 770850, Orlando FL 32877 USA | |
| **Wright, Peter** | WW II Army Air Corps Hero |
| 29 Devon Ave, Croton on Hudson NY 10520, USA | |
| **Wright, Peter R** | Ballet Dancer, Choreographer |
| 10 Chiswick Wharf, London W4 2SR, England | |
| **Wright, Petra** | Actress |
| Hartig-Hilepo Agency, 54 W 21st St, #610, New York NY 10010 USA | |
| **Wright, Randall S (Randy)** | Football Player |
| 2890 Commerce Park Dr, Fitchburg WI 53719, USA | |
| **Wright, Robin** | Actress, Model |
| Creative Artists Agency, 2000 Ave of Stars, #100, Los Angeles CA 90067 USA | |
| **Wright, Ronald L (Winky)** | Boxer |
| 2800 52nd St N, Saint Petersburg, FL 33710, USA | |
| **Wright, Ronald W (Ron)** | Baseball Player |
| 310 S 2100 E, Saint George UT 84790, USA | |
| **Wright, Sarah** | Actress |
| I C M Partners, 10250 Constellation Blvd, #900, Los Angeles CA 90067 USA | |
| **Wright, Shannon** | Singer (Wrights), Songwriter |
| Third Coast Artists Mgmt, 2021 21st Ave S, #220, Nashville TN 37212, USA | |
| **Wright, Sharone A** | Basketball Player |
| 6080 Lakeview Road, #3504, Warner Robins GA 31088, USA | |
| **Wright, Stephen** | Writer |
| Knopf Publishers, 1745 Broadway, New York NY 10019 USA | |
| **Wright, Stephen (Steve)** | Actor |
| Conway Van Gelder Grant, 8-12 Broadwick St, #300, London W1F 8HW, England | |
| **Wright, Steve T** | Football Player |
| 14 Conifer Square, Augusta GA 30909, USA | |
| **Wright, Steven** | Actor, Comedian |
| Brillstein Entertainment Partners, 9150 Wilshire Blvd, #350, Beverly Hills CA 90212 USA | |

**W**

**Wright - Wright**

**Wright, Tanisha L** — Basketball Player
Seattle Storm, Key Arena, 351 Elliott Ave W, #500, Seattle WA 98119 USA

**Wright, Thomas** — Actor
W M E Entertainment, 9601 Wilshire Blvd, #300, Beverly Hills CA 90210 USA

**Wright, Thomas S (Tom)** — Baseball Player
1116 Poplar Springs Church Road, Shelby NC 28152, USA

**Wright, Toby L** — Football Player
1602 E Winston Dr, Phoenix AZ 85042, USA

**Wright, Trevor** — Actor
Evolution Entertainment, 901 N Highland Ave, Los Angeles CA 90038 USA

**Wright, Tyler** — Ice Hockey Player
1982 Chatfield Road, Columbus OH 43221, USA

**Wright, Will** — Video Game Designer, Producer, Writer
Stupid Fun Club, 721 Channing Way, Berkeley CA 94720, USA

**Wrightman, Timothy J (Tim)** — Football Player
612 Unity Lane, Weiser ID 83672, USA

**Wrightson, Bernard (Bernie)** — Diver
924 Birch Ave, Escondido CA 92027, USA

**Wrigley, William, Jr** — Businessman
William Wrigley Jr Co, 410 N Michigan Ave, Lower Level, Chicago IL 60611, USA

**Wroblewski, David** — Writer
Ecco/Harper Collins Publishers, 10 E 53rd St, Cellar 1, New York NY 10022, USA

**Wrona, Richard J (Rick)** — Baseball Player
2946 E 57th St, Tulsa OK 74105, USA

**Wrubel, Bill** — Writer, Producer
Creative Artists Agency, 2000 Ave of Stars, #100, Los Angeles CA 90067 USA

**Wryn, Rhiannon Leigh** — Actress
Baker Winokur Ryder Public Relations, 9100 Wilshire Blvd, #500W, Beverly Hills CA 90212 USA

**Wu Dajing** — Speed Skater
Skating Association, 56 Zhonguancun South St, Beijing 100044, China

**Wu Man** — Pipa Player
Opus 3 Artists, 470 Park Ave S, #900N, New York NY 10016 USA

**Wu, Alice** — Director, Writer
Creative Artists Agency, 2000 Ave of Stars, #100, Los Angeles CA 90067 USA

**Wu, Jason** — Fashion Designer
240 W 35th St, #1100, New York NY 10001, USA

**Wu, Sau Lan** — Physicist
29 Oxford St, Cambridge MA 02138, USA

**Wu, Tai Tsun** — Physicist
Harvard University, Physics Dept, Pierce Hall, 29 Oxford St, Cambridge MA 02138, USA

**Wu, Vivian** — Actress
S M S Talent, 8383 Wilshire Blvd, #230, Beverly Hills CA 90211 USA

**WuDunn, Sheryl** — Journalist
New York Times, Editorial Dept, 229 W 43rd St, New York NY 10036, USA

**Wuerffel, Daniel C (Danny)** — Football Player
424 Mimosa Dr, Decatur GA 30030, USA

**Wuerl, Donald W Cardinal** — Religious Leader
Archdiocesan Pastoral Center, 5001 Eastern Ave, Hyattsville MD 20782, USA

**Wuertz, Michael J** — Baseball Player
15209 N Thompson Peak Parkway, #B111, Scottsdale AZ 85260, USA

**Wuethrich, Kurt** — Nobel Chemistry Laureate
Federal Technology Institute, E T H Hvnggerberg, 8093 Zurich, Switzerland

**Wuhl, Robert** — Actor
C E S D, 10635 Santa Monica Blvd, #130, Los Angeles CA 90025 USA

**Wuhrer, Kari** — Actress
Innovative Artists, 1505 10th St, Santa Monica CA 90401 USA

**Wullbrandt, John** — Artist
PO Box 246, Carpinteria CA 93014, USA

**Wunder, Ingolf** — Concert Pianist
I M G Artists, Hogarth Business Park, Chiswick, London W4 2TH, England

**Wunderlich, Claudia** — Handball Player
Dt Handballbund, Strobelallee 56, 44139 Dortmund, Germany

**Wunderlich, Paul** — Artist
Haynstr 2, 20249 Hamburg, Germany

**Wunsch, Carl I** — Oceanographer
78 Washington Ave, Cambridge MA 02140, USA

**Wunsch, Gerald (Jerry)** — Football Player
2601 Red Maple Road, Wausau WI 54401, USA

**Wunsch, Kelly D** — Baseball Player
13017 Zen Gardens Way, Austin TX 78732, USA

**Wuorinen, Charles P** — Composer
Howard Stokar Mgmt, 870 W End Ave, New York NY 10025, USA

**Wurlitzer, Rudolph** — Writer
Two Dollar Radio Publishing, 141 E Town St, #200, Columbus OH 43215, USA

**Wurster, Charles D** — Coast Guard Admiral
Commander, US Coast Guard Pacific, Coast Guard Island, Alameda CA 94501 USA

**Wurster, Donald C** — Air Force General
Commander, Special Operations Command, Hurlburt Field FL 32544 USA

**Wurz, Alexander** — Auto Racing Driver
Benetton-Mecachrome, Enstone, Chipping Norton, Oxfordshire OX7 4EE, England

**Wust, Ireen** — Speed Skater
Spoorbaan 7, 5051 Goirle ET, Netherlands

**Wuycik, Dennis M** — Basketball Player
31 Rogerson Dr, Chapel Hill NC 27517, USA

**Wyatt, Greg A** — Sculptor
320 W 86th St, PH South, New York NY 10024, USA

**Wyatt, Harry M, III** — Air Force General
Director, Air National Guard, HqUSAF, Pentagon, Washington DC 20330 USA

**Wyatt, Helen** — Baseball Player
7714 Deerfield Road, Loves Park IL 61111, USA

**Wyatt, J Douglas (Doug)** — Football Player
4055 Hogan Dr, #301, Tyler TX 75709, USA

**Wyatt, Jennifer** — Golfer
Carolina Group, 2321 Devine St, #A, Columbia SC 29205, USA

**Wyatt, Keke** — Singer
Universal Attractions, 135 W 26th St, #1200, New York NY 10001 USA

**Wright - Wyatt**

| | |
|---|---|
| **Wyatt, Kimberly**<br>Creative Artists Agency, 2000 Ave of Stars, #100, Los Angeles CA 90067 USA | Singer (Pussycat Dolls) |
| **Wyatt, Leslie**<br>Arkansas State University, President's Office, State University AR 72467, USA | Educator |
| **Wyatt, Robert**<br>Cuneiform Records, PO Box 8427, Silver Spring MD 20907, USA | Singer, Drummer (Soft Machine) |
| **Wyatt, Shannon**<br>8949 Falling Creek Court, Annandale VA 22003, USA | Actress |
| **Wyatt, Sharon**<br>23622 Calabasas Road, #107, Calabasas CA 91302, USA | Actress |
| **Wyche, Samuel D (Sam)**<br>1138 Walhalla Highway, Pickens SC 29671, USA | Football Coach, Sportscaster |
| **Wyeth, James Browning**<br>Lookout Farm, 701 Smiths Bridge Road, Wilmington DE 19807, USA | Artist |
| **Wyland**<br>Wyland Studios, 6 Mason, Irvine CA 92618, USA | Artist |
| **Wylde, Chris**<br>Stone Manners Salners, 6100 Wilshire Blvd, #1500, Los Angeles CA 90035 USA | Actor, Writer, Producer |
| **Wylde, Peter**<br>247 Wood Dale Dr, Wellington FL 33414, USA | Equestrian |
| **Wylde, Zakk**<br>Survival Mgmt, 30765 Pacific Coast Highway, #325, Malibu CA 90265, USA | Singer, Guitarist, Songwriter |
| **Wyle, Noah**<br>Brillstein Entertainment Partners, 9150 Wilshire Blvd, #350, Beverly Hills CA 90212 USA | Actor |
| **Wylenzek, Thomasz**<br>Alfred Krupp Str 47, 45131 Essen, Germany | Canoeing Athlete |
| **Wylie, Adam**<br>Management 101, 11271 Ventura Blvd, #102, Studio City CA 91604 USA | Actor |
| **Wylie, Paul**<br>9819 Deer Brook Lane, Charlotte NC 28210, USA | Figure Skater |
| **Wyludda, Ilke**<br>Liebigstr 9, 09113 Chemnitz, Germany | Track Athlete |
| **Wyman, David M**<br>20918 NE Redmond Fall City Road, Redmond WA 98053, USA | Football Player |
| **Wyman, James T**<br>1185 Ferndale Road W, Wayzata MN 55391, USA | Businessman |
| **Wyman, William G (Bill)**<br>Ripple Productions, 344 Kings Road, London SW3 5UR, England | Bassist (Rolling Stones) |
| **Wyms, Ellis R**<br>7 Canyon Wren Dr, Spring TX 77389, USA | Football Player |
| **Wynalda, Eric**<br>2313 Stormcroft Court, Westlake Village CA 91361, USA | Soccer Player |
| **Wynder, A J**<br>1 Cardenti Court, Newark DE 19702, USA | Basketball Player |
| **Wyndham, Alex**<br>Finch & Partners, 29-37 Heddon St, London W1B 4BR, England | Actor |
| **Wyndham, Victoria**<br>Don Buchwald Talent Agency, 6500 Wilshire Blvd, #2200, Los Angeles CA 90048 USA | Actress |
| **Wynegar, Harold D (Butch)**<br>PO Box 915811, Longwood FL 32791, USA | Baseball Player |
| **Wyner, George**<br>3450 Laurie Place, Studio City CA 91604, USA | Actor |
| **Wyner, Yehudi**<br>Brandeis University, Music Dept, Waltham MA 02454, USA | Composer |
| **Wyngarde, Peter**<br>4 Acre Lane, Clock Face, Sainte Helen's, Lancashire WA9 4DZ, England | Actor |
| **Wynn, Bob**<br>78455 Calle Orense, La Quinta CA 92253, USA | Golfer |
| **Wynn, James S (Jimmy)**<br>5507 Sandy Field Court, Rosharon TX 77583, USA | Baseball Player |
| **Wynn, Renaldo L**<br>14904 Rocky Top Dr, Huntersville NC 28078, USA | Football Player |
| **Wynn, Stephen A**<br>Desert Inn Hotel, 3245 Las Vegas Blvd S, Las Vegas NV 89109, USA | Businessman |
| **Wynne, Marvell**<br>39640 Del Val Dr, Murrieta CA 92562, USA | Baseball Player |
| **Wynott, Ryan**<br>Savage Agency, 6212 Banner Ave, Los Angeles CA 90038 USA | Actor |
| **Wynter, Sarah**<br>Paradigm Agency, 360 N Crescent Dr, North Building, Beverly Hills CA 90210 USA | Actress |
| **Wyrozub, Randy**<br>6717 Westminster Dr, East Amherst NY 14051, USA | Ice Hockey Player |
| **Wysocki, Benjamin J (Ben)**<br>A2 Mgmt, 624 Davis St, #200, Evanston IL 60201, USA | Drummer (Fray) |
| **Wysocki, Jacob**<br>Echo Lake Management, 421 S Beverly Dr, #800, Beverly Hills CA 90212, USA | Actor |

**Wyatt - Wysocki**

**Xanic von Bertrab, Alejandra**
New York Times, Editorial Dept, 229 W 43rd St, New York NY 10036 USA — Journalist

**Xiahui Fan**
University of Arizona, Astronomy Dept, Tucson AZ 85721, USA — Cosmologist

**Xiang Liu**
Global Athletes & Marketing, 437 Boylston St, Boston MA 02116, USA — Track Athlete

**Xiao, Xiangming**
University of New Hampshire, Earth Oceans Space Institute, Durham NH 03824, USA — Biologist

**Xie Bingxin**
Central Nationalities Institute, Residential Qtrs, Beijing 100081, China — Writer

**Xie Tieli**
Beijing Film Studio, 19 Beihuan Xilu Road, Beijing 100088, China — Director

**Xu Bing**
540 Metropolitan Ave, #A, Brooklyn NY 11211, USA — Artist

**Xue Wei**
134 Sheaveshill Ave, London NW9 6RY, England — Concert Violinist

**Xuereb, Salvator**
Kazarian/Measures/Ruskin, 11969 Ventura Blvd, #300, Studio City CA 91604 USA — Actor

**Xzibit**
Management 360, 9111 Wilshire Blvd, Beverly Hills CA 90210 USA — Rap Artist, Actor

**Ya'alon, Moshe**
Chief of Staff, Israeli Defense Forces, Kaplan St, Tel-Aviv 67659, Israel — Army General, Israel

**Yablans, Frank**
88 Bull Path, East Hampton NY 11937, USA — Producer

**Yachmenev, Vitali A**
182 Silver Lady Lane, North Bay ON P1B 8G4, Canada — Ice Hockey Player

**Yacoub, Magdi H**
National Heart & Lung Institute, Dovehouse St, London SW3 6LY, England — Surgeon

**Yager, Faye**
Children of the Underground, 902 Curlew Court NW, Atlanta GA 30327, USA — Social Activist

**Yager, Rick**
King Features Syndicate, 300 W 57th St, #1500, New York NY 10019 USA — Cartoonist (Buck Rogers)

**Yagudin, Alexei**
Connecticut Skating Center, 300 Alumni Road, Newington CT 06111, USA — Figure Skater

**Yake, Terry**
26 Mockingbird Lane, Tiverton RI 02878, USA — Ice Hockey Player

**Yakin, Boaz**
I C M Partners, 10250 Constellation Blvd, #900, Los Angeles CA 90067 USA — Director, Producer, Writer

**Yakupov, Nail R**
Edmonton Oilers, 11230 110th St, Edmonton AB T5G 3H7, Canada — Ice Hockey Player

**Yamagata, Hiro**
1050 Ave D, Redondo Beach CA 90277, USA — Artist

**Yamagata, Rachael**
Paradigm Agency, 360 Park Ave, #1600, New York NY 10022 USA — Singer, Pianist, Songwriter

**Yamaguchi, Kristi T**
290 Las Quebradas Lane, Alamo CA 94507, USA — Figure Skater

**Yamaguchi, Roy**
Roy's Restaurant, Kai Plaza, 6600 Kalaniaole Highway, Honolulu HI 96825, USA — Restauranteur

**Yamame, Marlene Mitsuko**
Herb Tannen, 10801 National Blvd, #101, Los Angeles CA 90064 USA — Actress

**Yamamoto, Kansai**
103 Grand St, New York NY 10013, USA — Fashion Designer

**Yamamoto, Yohji**
Yamamoto Europe, 155 Rue Saint-Martin, 75003 Paris, France — Fashion Designer

**Yamanaka, Shinya**
Kyoto University, 53 Kawaharacho, Shogoin Yoshida, Sakyoku, Kyoto 606 8507, Japan — Nobel Medicine Laureate

**Yamanaka, Tsuyoshi**
6-10-33 Akasaka, Minatoku, Tokyo 107 0052 Japan — Swimmer

**Yamani, Sheikh Ahmed Zaki**
PO Box 14850, Jeddah 21434, Saudi Arabia — Government Official, Saudi Arabia

**Yamano, Hiroshi**
Galleria Silecchia, 20 S Palm Ave, Sarasota FL 34236, USA — Artist

**Yamasaki, Taro M**
People, Editorial Dept, Time-Life Building, New York NY 10020, USA — Photojournalist

**Yamashita, Iris**
Circle of Confusion, 8548 Washington Blvd, Culver City CA 90232, USA — Writer

**Yamashita, Yasuhiro**
1117 Kitakaname, Hitatsuka Kanagawa 259 1207, Japan — Judo Athlete, Coach

**Yamassoum, Negoum**
PO Box 43121, N'Djamena, Moursal, Chad — Prime Minister, Chad

**Yamazaki, Naoko**
Japanese Aerospace Exploration Agency, 2-1-1 Sengen, Tsukuba, Ibaraki 305 8505, Japan — Astronaut, Japan

**Yamazaki, Naoko Sumino**
Japanese Aerospace Exploration Agency, 2-1-1 Sengen, Tsukuba, Ibaraki 305 8505, Japan — Astronaut

**Yamin, Elliott**
Three Ring Projects, 111 Westwood Plaza, #101, Brentwood TN 37027, USA — Singer

**Yan**
Agency Group Ltd, 361-373 City Road, London EC1V 1PQ, England — Singer, Guitarist (British Sea Power)

**Yan, Liangkun**
Central Philharmonic Society, 11-1 Hepingjie, Beijing 100013, China — Conductor

**Yanagimachi, Ryuzo**
University of Hawaii, Biology Dept, 1960 East-West Road, Honolulu HI 96822, USA — Biologist

**Yancy, Emily**
Geddes Agency, 8430 Santa Monica Blvd, #201, West Hollywood CA 90069 USA — Actress

**Yanda, Marshall J**
Baltimore Ravens, Ravens Stadium, 1 Winning Dr, Baltimore MD 21230 USA — Football Player

**Yanez, Eduardo**
Independent Group, 8444 Wilshire Blvd, #500, Beverly Hills CA 90211, USA — Actor

**Yang di-Pertuan Agong XIII**
Sultan's Palace, Istana Bukit Serene, 50502 Kuala Lumpur, Malaysia — Sultan, Malaysia

**Yang Huiyan**
Country Garden Holdings, Manulife Provident Fund Place, Yau Ma Tei, Kowloon, Hong Kong, China — Businesswoman

**Yang Liwei**
Satellite Launch Center, Jiuquan, Guangzhou Province, China — Taikonaut, China

**Yang, Chen Ning**
8 Dorfer Lane, Nesconset NY 11767, USA — Nobel Physics Laureate

**Yang, Jerry** — Businessman, Computer Programmer
Asian Pacific Fund, 225 Bush St, #590, San Francisco CA 94104, USA
**Yang, Philemon Y** — Prime Minister, Cameroon
Prime Minister's Office, BP 1057, Yaounde, Cameroon
**Yang, Shang-Fa** — Biochemist
118 Villanova Dr, Davis CA 95616, USA
**Yang, Xao (Jerry)** — Poker Player
30380 River Estate Dr, Madera CA 93636, USA
**Yang, Young Eun (Y E)** — Golfer
Professional Golfers Association, 100 Ave of Champions, Palm Beach Gardens FL 33418 USA
**Yang, Zhiguang** — Artist
Guangzhou Fine Art Institute, 257 Chang Gang Dong Lu St, Guangzhou 510260, China
**Yani Tseng** — Golfer
9713 Chiltern Garden Dr, Orlando FL 32827, USA
**Yankelovich, Daniel** — Social Scientist
Public Agenda Foundation, 6 E 39th St, #900, New York NY 10016, USA
**Yankovic, Al (Weird Al)** — Actor, Comedian, Singer, Songwriter
14 E Mountain Road, Katonah NY 10536, USA
**Yankowski, Ronald W (Ron)** — Football Player
1318 Wulfert Road, Sanibel FL 33957, USA
**Yannas, I V** — Polymer Scientist, Mechanical Engineer
Massachusetts Institute of Technology, Engineering School, Cambridge MA 02139, USA
**Yanni** — Keyboardist, Songwriter
10563 Arcole Court, Wellington FL 33449, USA
**Yano, Kyoko** — Soccer Player
Football Association, 3-10-15 Hongo, Bunkyoku, Tokyo 113 0033 Japan
**Yanofsky, Charles** — Biologist
725 Mayfield Ave, Stanford CA 94305, USA
**Yanofsky, Nicole (Nikki)** — Singer, Songwriter
A440 Entertainment, 3500 de Maisonneuve W, #800, Montreal QC H3Z 3C1, Canada
**Yao Ming** — Basketball Player
18923 Crescent Bay Dr, Houston TX 77094, USA
**Yao, Andrew C C** — Mathematician
Princeton University, Mathematics Dept, Princeton NJ 08544, USA
**Yapo, Mennan** — Director
Spielkind, Zimmerstr 11, 10969 Berlin, Germany
**Yarborough, W Caleb (Cale)** — Auto Racing Driver
Yarborough Racing, 2723 W Palmetto St, #8, Florence SC 29501, USA
**Yarbrough, Glenn** — Singer, Songwriter (Limelighters)
PO Box 331368, Nashville TN 37203, USA
**Yardley, Jim** — Journalist
New York Times, Editorial Dept, 229 W 43rd St, New York NY 10036 USA
**Yardley, Jonathan** — Journalist, Critic
223 Hawthorne Road, Baltimore MD 21210, USA
**Yared, Gabriel** — Composer
V2 Scandinavia, Bondegatan 64C, 116 33 Stockholm, Sweden
**Yarnall, Celeste** — Actress
2899 Agoura Road, #315, Westlake CA 91361, USA
**Yarno, George A** — Football Player
1081 White Pine Flats Road, Troy ID 83871, USA
**Yarno, John R** — Football Player
10535 158th Ave NE, Redmond WA 98052, USA
**Yarnold, Elizabeth (Lizzy)** — Skeleton Athlete
National Ice Skating Assn, Grains Building, High Cross St, Hockley, Nottingham, NG1 3AX, England
**Yaro, Boris** — Photojournalist
17042 Calahan St, Northridge CA 91325, USA
**Yarrow, Noel Peter** — Singer (Peter Paul & Mary), Songwriter
27 W 67th St, #5E, New York NY 10023, USA
**Yary, A Ronald (Ron)** — Football Player
35802 Cherry Bark Way, Murrieta CA 92562, USA
**Yasbeck, Amy** — Actress
Innovative Artists, 1505 10th St, Santa Monica CA 90401 USA
**Yashin, Aleksei** — Ice Hockey Player
6 Polo Dr, Old Westbury NY 11568, USA
**Yastrzemski, Carl M** — Baseball Player
22 Lakeshore Road, Boxford MA 01921, USA
**Yasutake, Patti** — Actress
145 S Fairfax Ave, #310, Los Angeles CA 90036, USA
**Yates, Bill** — Cartoonist (Redeye)
King Features Syndicate, 300 W 57th St, #1500, New York NY 10019 USA
**Yates, Billy** — Singer, Songwriter
Red Ridge Entertainment, 1208 16th Ave S, Loer Lobby 1, Nashville TN 37212, USA
**Yates, David** — Director
Casorotto Ramsay, Waverley House, 7-12 Noel St, London W1F 8GQ, England
**Yates, Dorian A M** — Body Builder
Mr Olympia Corner, 21100 Erwin St, Woodland Hills CA 91367, USA
**Yates, Erica Lyndzey** — Actress, Comedienne
OmniPop Talent Group, 4605 Lankershim Blvd, #201, Toluca Lake CA 91602 USA
**Yates, J D** — Rodeo Rider
1235 Lane 30 1/4, Pueblo CO 81006, USA
**Yates, Jim** — Drag Racing Driver
Jim Yates Racing, 2725B Old Washington Road, Waldorf MD 20601, USA
**Yates, Robert** — Auto Racing Executive
18923 Cove Side Lane, Cornelius NC 28031, USA
**Yates, Ronald W (Ron)** — Air Force General
525 Silhouette Way, Monument CO 80132, USA
**Yates, Tyler K** — Baseball Player
3718 Omao Road, Koloa HI 96756, USA
**Yatsenyuk, Arseniy P** — Prime Minister, Ukraine
Prime Minister's Office, Ghrushevskogo 12/2, 01008 Kiev, Ukraine
**Yau, Alan** — Restauranteur, Chef
Wagamama Ltd, Waverley House, 7-12 Noel St, London W1F 8GQ, England
**Yau, Horng-Tzer** — Mathematician
Harvard University, Mathematics Dept, 1 Oxford St, Cambridge MA 02138, USA
**Yau, Shing-Tung** — Mathematician
Harvard University, Mathematics Dept, 1 Oxford St, Cambridge MA 02138, USA

**Y**

**Yang - Yau**

**Yawer, Sheik Ghazi Mashal Ajil al-** — President, Iraq
Al-Sijound Majalis, Karradat Mariam, Baghdad, Iraq
**Ybarra y Churruca, Emilio de** — Financier
Banco Bilbao-Vizcaya, Paseo de la Castellana 81, 28046 Madrid, Spain
**Ye, Xiaogang** — Composer
Central Music Conservatory, 43 Baojia St, Xicheng District, Beijing 100031 PR, China
**Yeager, Andrea** — Tennis Player
PO Box 11720, 155 Nighthawk Dr, Aspen CO 81612, USA
**Yeager, Charles E (Chuck)** — Test Pilot, Air Force General
PO Box 1507, Penn Valley CA 95946, USA
**Yeager, Dan** — Actor
T C A/Jed Root, 9220 Sunset Blvd, #315, Los Angeles CA 90069, USA
**Yeager, Jeana** — Experimental Airplane Pilot
PO Box 892, Tom Bean TX 75489, USA
**Yeager, Stephen W (Steve)** — Baseball Player
PO Box 34184, Granada Hills CA 91394, USA
**Yeagley, Jerry** — Soccer Coach
1418 S Sare Road, Bloomington IN 47401, USA
**Yeakel, G Scott** — Astronaut
PO Box 422, Middleburg VA 20118, USA
**Yearwood, Trisha** — Singer
Trisha Yearwood Inc, 3310 W End Ave , #400, Nashville TN 37203, USA
**Yeates, Jeffrey L (Jeff)** — Football Player
3793 Club Dr NE, Atlanta GA 30319, USA
**Yelchin, Anton** — Actor
Creative Artists Agency, 2000 Ave of Stars, #100, Los Angeles CA 90067 USA
**Yelding, Eric G** — Baseball Player
PO Box 325, Montrose AL 36559, USA
**Yeley, Christopher B H (J J)** — Auto, Truck Racing Driver
Mayfield Motorsports, 2220 Highway 49 N, Harrisburg NC 28075, USA
**Yeliseyev, Aleksei S** — Cosmonaut
Bauman Higher Technical School, Baumanskaya Ul 5, 107005 Moscow, Russia
**Yelle** — Singer, Songwriter
E M I Records, 150 5th Ave, #700, New York NY 10011 USA
**Yelle, Staphane A** — Ice Hockey Player
1423 Foothills Village Dr, Henderson NV 89012, USA
**Yellen, Janet L** — Government Official, Financier
Federal Reserve Board, 20th St & Constitution NW, Washington DC 20551, USA
**Yellen, Linda B** — Producer, Director
Keckins Projects, 3 Sheridan Square, New York NY 10014, USA
**Yellowbird, Shane** — Singer, Songwriter
Agency Group Ltd, 142 W 57th St, #600, New York NY 10019 USA
**Yelvington, Richard J (Dick), Jr** — Football Player
2105 Barbe St, Lake Charles LA 70601, USA
**Yemchuk, Yelena** — Photographer
110 Greene St, #501, New York NY 10012, USA
**Yen, Donnie** — Actor
Creative Artists Agency, 2000 Ave of Stars, #100, Los Angeles CA 90067 USA
**Yeo, Mike** — Hockey Coach
Minnesota Wild, XCel Energy Arena, 1275 Saint Antoine W, Saint Paul MN 55104 USA
**Yeoh, Michelle** — Actress
Gotham Group, 9255 Sunset Blvd, #515, Los Angeles CA 90069, USA
**Yeohlee** — Fashion Designer
Yeohlee Designs, 225 W 35th St, #1600, New York NY 10001, USA
**Yeom Soo-Jung, Andrew Cardinal** — Religious Leader
Archdiocese of Seoul, Chung Gu Myong Dong 2 Ga, Seoul 100 809, South Korea
**Yeoman, Owain** — Actor
Safran Co, 2000 Ave of Stars, #600N Los Angeles CA 90067, USA
**Yeoman, Robert D** — Cinematographer
2931 Washington Ave, Santa Monica CA 90403, USA
**Yeoman, William F (Bill)** — Football Player, Coach
3030 Country Club Blvd, Sugar Land TX 77478, USA
**Yepremian, Garabed S (Garo)** — Football Player
200 W Harmony Road, West Grove PA 19390, USA
**Yergin, Daniel H** — Writer
Cambridge Energy Research Assoc, 55 Cambridge Parkway, Cambridge MA 02142, USA
**Yerman, Jack** — Track Athlete
753 Camellia Dr, Paradise CA 95969, USA
**Yershov, Valery** — Artist
Rima Fine Art, 7130 E Main St, Scottsdale AZ 85251, USA
**Yes, Phyllis A** — Artist, Sculptor
23 SW Boundary St, Portland OR 97239, USA
**Yespica, Aida** — Model, Actress
Lela Mora Mgmt, Viale Monza 9, 20125 Milan, Italy
**Yester, Jim** — Singer, Guitarist (Association)
Variety Artists, 1924 Spring St, Paso Robles CA 93446 USA
**Yeston, Maury** — Composer
Yale University, Music Dept, New Haven CT 06520, USA
**Yett, Richard M (Rich)** — Baseball Player
5840 E Fairbrook Circle, Mesa AZ 85205, USA
**Yeun, Steven** — Actor
Abrams Artists, 9200 W Sunset Blvd, #1125, West Hollywood CA 90069 USA
**Yeung Kwok Keung** — Businessman
Country Garden Holdings, Manulife Provident Fund Place, Yau Ma Tei, Kowloon, Hong Kong, China
**Yeutter, Clayton K** — Secretary, Agriculture
10955 Martingale Court, Potomac MD 20854, USA
**Yevtushenko, Yevgeny A** — Writer
Kutuzovski Prospekt 2/1, 121248 Moscow, Russia
**Yewcic, Thomas J (Tom)** — Football, Baseball Player
31 Cherokee Road, Arlington MA 02474, USA
**Yi Mun Yol** — Writer
Wylie Agency, 250 W 57th St, #2114, New York NY 10107 USA
**Yi So Yeon** — Cosmonaut, South Korea
Advanced Science/Technology Institute, Yuseong, Daejeon, South Korea
**Yi, Charlyne** — Actress, Comedienne
Mosiac Media Group, 9200 W Sunset Blvd, #1000, Los Angeles CA 90069 USA

**Yildiz, Rifat** — Greco-Roman Wrestler
Karl-Heeg Str 13C, 63773 Goldbach, Germany
**Yin Jun** — Artist
Soemo Fine Arts, 66 Xiaopunanjie, Songzhuang Tongzhou District, Beijing, China
**Ying Huang** — Actress, Opera Singer
Columbia Artists Mgmt Inc, 5 Columbus Circle, 1790 Broadway, #1600, New York NY 10019 USA
**Yo Gotti** — Rap Musician
Epic Records, 9830 Wilshire Blvd, Beverly Hills CA 90212 USA
**Yoakam, Dwight** — Singer, Guitarist, Songwriter
Bluebird House, 10153 1/2 Riverside Drive, #419, Universal City CA 91602, USA
**Yoav** — Singer, Songwriter
Creative Artists Agency, 2000 Ave of Stars, #100, Los Angeles CA 90067 USA
**Yoba, Malik** — Actor
Innovative Artists, 1505 10th St, Santa Monica CA 90401 USA
**Yoccoz, Jean-Christophe** — Mathematician
University of Paris-Sud (Orsey), 91405 Orsay-Cedex-Bait 425, France
**Yock, Robert J** — Judge
US Claims Court, 717 Madison Place NW, Washington DC 20439, USA
**Yocum, Matt** — Sportscaster
9910 Devonshire Dr, Huntsville NC 28078, USA
**Yoffie, Eric** — Religious Leader, Rabbi
Union for Reform Judaism, 633 3rd Ave, #700, New York NY 10017, USA
**Yoken, Mel B** — Writer
261 Carroll St, New Bedford MA 02740, USA
**Yonath, Ada** — Nobel Chemistry Laureate
Weizmann Science Institute, PO Box 26, Rehovot 76100, Israel
**Yong, Cao** — Artist
Pierside Hunt Gallery, 300 Pacific Coast Highway, Huntington Beach CA 92648, USA
**Yoo, Aaron** — Actor
Blue Ridge Entertainment, 535 W 23rd St, #S10A, New York NY 10011, USA
**Yoon, Bora** — Composer
I M G Artists, Hogarth Business Park, Chiswick, London W4 2TH, England
**Yorio, Kimberly** — Writer
Y C Media, 145 W 28th St, #1200, New York NY 10001, USA
**York, Francine** — Actress
Littman Talent Group, 15720 Ventura Blvd, #611, Encino CA 91436, USA
**York, Glen P** — Vietnam War Air Force Hero
1620 E Driftwood Dr, Tempe AZ 85283, USA
**York, James H (Jim)** — Baseball Player
31262 Via del Verde, San Juan Capistrano CA 92675, USA
**York, John J** — Actor
Stone Manners Salners, 6100 Wilshire Blvd, #1500, Los Angeles CA 90035 USA
**York, Kathleen (Bird)** — Actress, Singer, Songwriter
Bauman Redanty Shaul Agency, 5757 Wilshire Blvd, #473, Los Angeles CA 90036 USA
**York, Lila** — Choreographer
Paul Taylor Dancer Co, 551 Grand St, Lobby A, New York NY 10002, USA
**York, Michael** — Actor
Peter Strain, 5455 Wilshire Blvd, #1812, Los Angeles CA 90036 USA
**York, Michael (Mike)** — Ice Hockey Player
6105 W Longview Dr, East Lansing MI 48823, USA
**York, Michael M** — Journalist
Lexington Herald-Leader, Editorial Dept, Main & Midland, Lexington KY 40507, USA
**York, Rachel** — Actress
Stone Manners Salners, 6100 Wilshire Blvd, #1500, Los Angeles CA 90035 USA
**York, Raymond** — Thoroughbred Racing Jockey
27918 Taft Highway, Taft CA 93268, USA
**York, Taylor** — Guitarist (Paramore), Songwriter
Big Hassle, 44 Wall St, #2200, New York NY 10005, USA
**Yorke, Thom** — Singer (Radiohead)
Courtyard, 21 Nursery, Sutton Courteney, Abingdon, Oxford OX14 4UA, England
**Yorkin, Alan (Bud)** — Producer, Director
Bud Yorkin Productions, 250 Delfern Dr, Los Angeles CA 90077, USA
**Yorkin, Peg** — Women's Activist
Fund for Feminist Majority, 1600 Wilson Blvd, #704, Arlington VA 22209, USA
**Yorn, Peter (Pete)** — Singer, Songwriter
Trampoline Records, 8581 Santa Monica Blvd, #511, West Hollywood CA 90069, USA
**Yorzyk, William A (Bill)** — Swimmer
162 W Sturbridge Road, #7, East Brookfield MA 01515, USA
**Yost, E Frederick (Ned), III** — Baseball Player, Manager
108 Victoria Dr, La Grange GA 30240, USA
**Yost, Graham J** — Actor, Producer, Writer
Creative Artists Agency, 2000 Ave of Stars, #100, Los Angeles CA 90067 USA
**Yost, Paul A, Jr** — Coast Guard Admiral
James Madison Memorial Foundation, 1613 Duke St, Alexandria VA 22314, USA
**Yothers, Tina** — Actress, Singer
12368 Apple Dr, Chino CA 91710, USA
**Youk Chhang** — Social Activist
Documentation Center, 66 Preah Sihanouok Blvd, Phnom Penh, Cambodia
**Youkilis, Kevin E** — Baseball Player
19475 N Grayhawk Dr, #1083, Scottsdale AZ 85255, USA
**Youmans, Maurice E (Maury)** — Football Player
300 Beach Dr NE, #2104, Saint Petersburg FL 33701, USA
**Young Buck** — Rap Artist (G-Unit)
Emmel Commuications, 36 W 25th St, #200, New York NY 10010, USA
**Young Jeezy** — Rap Artist
I C M Partners, 10250 Constellation Blvd, #900, Los Angeles CA 90067 USA
**Young MC** — Rap Artist
Entertainment Artists, 2409 21st Ave S, #100, Nashville TN 10019 USA
**Young, Adam** — Singer/Songwriter/Musician (Owl City)
Foundations Artist Mgmt, 628 Broadway, #503, New York NY 10012, USA
**Young, Aden** — Actor
Shanahan Mgmt, PO Box 1509, Darlinghurst NSW 1300, Australia
**Young, Adrian** — Drummer (No Doubt)
Rebel Waltz, 31652 2nd Ave, Laguna Beach CA 92651, USA
**Young, Alan** — Actor
T G M D Talent Agency, 6767 Forest Lawn Dr, #101, Los Angeles CA 90068, USA

**Young, Andrew** — Diplomat; Mayor, Atlanta
National Council of Churches, 523 Spring Oaks Blvd, Altamonte Springs FL 32714, USA
**Young, Angus M** — Guitarist (AC/DC), Songwriter
Alberts Music, 9 Rangers Road, Neutral Bay, Sydney NSW 2089, Australia
**Young, Anthony W** — Baseball Player
13107 Ellsmere Dr, Houston TX 77015, USA
**Young, Archie (Dropo)** — Baseball Player
1804 Ethel Ave SW, Birmingham AL 35211, USA
**Young, B Asa (Ace)** — Singer, Songwriter, Actor
Creative Artists Agency, 2000 Ave of Stars, #100, Los Angeles CA 90067 USA
**Young, Barbara** — Baseball Player
5078 Edinboro Lane, Wilmington NC 28409, USA
**Young, Bellamy** — Actress
Framework Entertainment, 9057 Nemo St, #C, West Hollywood CA 90069 USA
**Young, Bob** — Cartoonist (Tim Tyler's Luck)
King Features Syndicate, 300 W 57th St, #1500, New York NY 10019 USA
**Young, Bob** — Producer
I C M Partners, 10250 Constellation Blvd, #900, Los Angeles CA 90067 USA
**Young, Brian** — Singer, Drummer (Fountains of Wayne)
Big Hassle, 157 Chambers St, #1200, New York NY 10007, USA
**Young, Bryant C** — Football Player
2324 Vernon Dr, Charlotte NC 28211, USA
**Young, Burt** — Actor
Bensky Entertainment, 15021 Ventura Blvd, #343, Sherman Oaks CA 91403, USA
**Young, C Duane** — Football Player
3704 Olney Road, Kalamazoo MI 49006, USA
**Young, Charle E** — Football Player
PO Box 1276, Woodinville WA 98072, USA
**Young, Christopher** — Composer
Costa Communications, 8265 Sunset Blvd, #101, Los Angeles CA 90046, USA
**Young, Christopher A (Chris)** — Singer
Ron Shapiro Mgmt, 56 W 22nd St, #601, New York NY 10010, USA
**Young, Christopher B (Chris)** — Baseball Player
New York Mets, Shea Stadium, 12301 Roosevelt Ave, Corona NY 11368 USA
**Young, Christopher R (Chris)** — Baseball Player
966 Muirlands Vista Way, La Jolla CA 92037, USA
**Young, Cliff** — Singer, Guitarist (Caedmon's Call)
Breen Agency, 25 Music Square W, Nashville TN 37203, USA
**Young, Colville N** — Governor General, Belize
Governor General's Office, Belize House, Belnopan, Belize
**Young, Curtis A (Curt)** — Baseball Player
10800 E Cactus Road, #2, Scottsdale AZ 85259, USA
**Young, Cyrus (Cy)** — Track Athlete
518 Grimes Ave, Modesto CA 95358, USA
**Young, Danielle** — Singer, Guitarist (Caedmon's Call)
Breen Agency, 25 Music Square W, Nashville TN 37203, USA
**Young, Dean** — Cartoonist (Blondie)
King Features Syndicate, 300 W 57th St, #1500, New York NY 10019 USA
**Young, Delmon D** — Baseball Player
3922 E Northridge Circle, Mesa AZ 85215, USA
**Young, Dmitri D** — Baseball Player
Washington Nationals, 1500 S Capitol St SE, Washington DC 20003 USA
**Young, Earl** — Singer (Trammps)
Atlantic/Buddah Records, 1290 Ave of Americas, Concourse 3, New York NY 10104, USA
**Young, Earl V** — Track Athlete
4201 Lomo Alto Dr, #110, Dallas TX 75219, USA
**Young, Eric O** — Baseball Player
120 Brewster Ave, Piscataway NJ 08854, USA
**Young, Ernest W (Ernie)** — Baseball Player
8995 E Palm Ridge Dr, Scottsdale AZ 85260, USA
**Young, Fred** — Singer, Drummer (Kentucky Headhunters)
Webster Public Relations, PO Box 23015, Nashville TN 37202, USA
**Young, George L** — Track Athlete
8926 N Cox Road, Casa Grande AZ 85194, USA
**Young, Gerald A** — Baseball Player
10014 Rain Cloud Dr, Houston TX 77095, USA
**Young, Guard** — Gymnast
4000 Worthington Dr, Norman OK 73072, USA
**Young, Heather Rae** — Model
Playboy Promotions, 9346 Civic Center Dr, #200, Beverly Hills CA 90210 USA
**Young, Howard (Howie)** — Ice Hockey Player
5527 N 22nd Dr, Phoenix AZ 85015, USA
**Young, J Steven (Steve)** — Football Player, Sportscaster
Forever Young Foundation, 21952 S Brandon St, Farmington Hills MI 48336, USA
**Young, Jacob** — Actor
Community Entertainment, 12100 Wilshire Blvd, #1135, Los Angeles CA 90025, USA
**Young, James** — Basketball Player
Boston Celtics, 226 Causeway St, #4, Boston MA 02114 USA
**Young, James** — Guitarist (Eli Young Band)
Triple 8 Mgmt, 1611 W 6th St, Austin TX 78703, USA
**Young, Jesse Colin** — Singer, Guitarist, Bassist, Songwriter
Maximus Entertainment Booking, 2 Professional Dr, #240, Gaithersburg MD 20879, USA
**Young, Jim** — Football Coach
US Military Academy, Athletic Dept, West Point NY 10966, USA
**Young, John Lloyd** — Actor, Singer
I C M Partners, 10250 Constellation Blvd, #900, Los Angeles CA 90067 USA
**Young, John Paul** — Singer, Songwriter
Teamwork Productions, PO Box 302, Dulwich Hill, NSW 2303, Australia
**Young, John T** — Baseball Player
124 W 57th St, Los Angeles CA 90037, USA
**Young, John W** — Astronaut
N A S A, Johnson Space Center, 2101 NASA Road, Houston TX 77058 USA
**Young, Kathryn** — Golfer
323 Date Ave, Imperial Beach CA 91932, USA
**Young, Kathy** — Singer
Cape Entertainment, 4799 Coconut Creek Parkway, #258, Coconut Creek FL 33063, USA

**Young, Keone** — Actor
A M T Artists, 15260 Ventura Blvd, #1200, Sherman Oaks CA 91403, USA
**Young, Kevin** — Track Athlete
H S International Sports Mgmt, 9871 Irvine Center Dr, Irvine CA 92618, USA
**Young, Kevin S** — Baseball Player
832 E Taurus Place, Chandler AZ 85249, USA
**Young, Larry E** — Baseball Umpire
PO Box 255, Roscoe IL 61073, USA
**Young, Laurence Retman** — Astronaut
217 Thorndike St, #108, Cambridge MA 02141, USA
**Young, Lonnie R** — Football Player
16699 W Papago St, Goodyear AZ 85338, USA
**Young, M Adrian** — Football Player
10300 4th St, #100, Rancho Cucamonga CA 91730, USA
**Young, Malcolm M** — Guitarist (AC/DC), Songwriter
Alberts Music, 9 Rangers Road, Neutral Bay, Sydney NSW 2089, Australia
**Young, Matthew J (Matt)** — Baseball Player
471 Maylin St, Pasadena CA 91105, USA
**Young, Michael** — Actor, Director, Producer
Media Four, 10100 Santa Monica Blvd, #2300, Los Angeles CA 90067, USA
**Young, Michael B** — Baseball Player
3508 Bryn Mawr Dr, Dallas TX 75225, USA
**Young, Michael D (Mike)** — Baseball Player
1166 Rockspring Way, Antioch CA 94531, USA
**Young, Michael D (Mike)** — Football Player
275 S Arroyo Parkway, #717, Pasadena CA 91105, USA
**Young, Michael K** — Educator
808 36th Ave E, Seattle WA 98112, USA
**Young, Mighty Joe** — Singer, Guitarist
Jay Reil, 3430 Bayberry Dr, Northbrook IL 60062, USA
**Young, Neil** — Singer, Songwriter
I C M Partners, 730 5th Ave, New York NY 10019 USA
**Young, Nick** — Basketball Player
Philadelphia 76ers, 1st Union Center, 3601 S Broad St, Philadelphia PA 19148 USA
**Young, Parker** — Actor
Gersh Agency, 9465 Wilshire Blvd, #600, Beverly Hills CA 90212 USA
**Young, Paul A** — Singer
Mission Control, 44 Alexander, Meole Brace, Shrewsbury SY3 9HS, England
**Young, R Gilchrist I (Chris)** — Composer
First Artists Mgmt, 4764 Park Granada, #210, Calabasas CA 91302 USA
**Young, Richard** — Singer, Guitarist (Kentucky Headhunters)
Webster & Assoc PR, PO Box 23015, Nashville TN 37202, USA
**Young, Richard S** — Photographer
110 Highlever Road, London W10 6PL, England
**Young, Richard S** — Space Scientist
137 Saint Croix Ave, Cocoa Beach FL 32931, USA
**Young, Rickey D** — Football Player
2438 Grenadier Ave N, Saint Paul MN 55128, USA
**Young, Robert (Nat)** — Surfer
8 Bay St, Angourie NSW 2464, Australia
**Young, Robert E** — Football Player
159 Boyd Lane, Carthage MS 39051, USA
**Young, Roger** — Director
Freedman Broder & Company, 10100 Santa Monica Blvd, Los Angeles CA 90067, USA
**Young, Roynell** — Football Player
11823 Beinhorn Dr, Houston TX 77065, USA
**Young, Rusty** — Pedal Steel Musician (Poco)
Rick Alter Mgmt, 1018 17th Ave S, #12, Nashville TN 37212, USA
**Young, S Ulysses** — Baseball Player
4023 W 60th St, Los Angeles CA 90043, USA
**Young, Samuel D (Sam)** — Basketball Player
Philadelphia 76ers, 1st Union Center, 3601 S Broad St, Philadelphia PA 19148 USA
**Young, Scott A** — Ice Hockey Player
17 Sandy Ridge Road, Sterling MA 01564, USA
**Young, Sean** — Actress
105 W 55th St, #6C, New York NY 10019, USA
**Young, Simone** — Conductor
Hamburgische Staatsoper, Grosse Theaterstr 25, 20354 Hamburg, Germany
**Young, Sophie** — Basketball Player
San Antonio Silver Stars, 1 AT&T Center, San Antonio TX 78219 USA
**Young, Steve** — Singer, Guitarist, Songwriter
Rob Hall Acoustic Music, PO Box 2105, Ringwood North VIC 3134, Australia
**Young, Tata** — Singer
Tata Entertainment, 317 Komol Sukosol Building, Silom Road, Bangkok 10500, Thailand
**Young, Thaddeus C** — Basketball Player
Minnesota Timberwolves, Target Center, 600 1st Ave N, Minneapolis MN 55403 USA
**Young, Tim** — Ice Hockey Player
15808 Park Terrace Dr, Eden Prairie MN 55346, USA
**Young, Timothy R (Tim)** — Baseball Player
20730 SE Sherry Ave, Blountstown FL 32424, USA
**Young, Tom** — Basketball Coach
Washington Wizards, M C I Centre, 601 F St NW, Washington DC 20004 USA
**Young, Valerie D** — Actress
Bobby Ball Agency, 4116 W Magnolia Blvd, #205, Burbank CA 91505, USA
**Young, Vince P, Jr** — Football Player
12006 Legend Manor Dr, Houston TX 77082, USA
**Young, Vincent** — Actor
Bohemia Group, 8170 Beverly Blvd, #102, Los Angeles CA 90048, USA
**Young, Warren H** — Ice Hockey Player
5960 Murray Ave, Bethel Park PA 15102, USA
**Young, Wendell E** — Ice Hockey Player
1616 E Campbell St, Arlington Heights IL 60004, USA
**Young, Wilbur E, Jr** — Football Player
119 Hartford Court, Charlottesville VA 22902, USA
**Young, William** — Labor Leader
National Association of Letter Carriers, 100 Indiana NW, #709, Washington DC 20001, USA

**Y**

| | |
|---|---|
| **Young, William Allen** | Actor |
| Sovereign Talent Group, 8421 Wilshire Blvd, #200, Beverly Hills CA 90211, USA | |
| **Young, William J L (Willie)** | Football Player |
| PO Box 426, Grambling LA 71245, USA | |
| **Young, William R (Will)** | Singer, Actor |
| 19 Music & Mgmt, 35-37 Parkgate Road, London SW11 4NP, England | |
| **Young, Wise** | Neuroscientist |
| Rutgers University, Collaborative Neuroscience Center, New Brunswick NJ 08901, USA | |
| **Youngberg, Renae** | Baseball Player |
| 2001 Gasparilla Road, #A25, Placida FL 33946, USA | |
| **Youngblood, H Jackson (Jack)** | Football Player, Sportscaster |
| 4377 Steed Terrace, Winter Park FL 32792, USA | |
| **Youngblood, Jimmy L (Jim)** | Football Player |
| 1000 Kilgore Bridge Road, Woodruff SC 29388, USA | |
| **Youngblood, Joel R** | Baseball Player |
| 4446 E Camelback Road, #113, Phoenix AZ 85018, USA | |
| **Youngblood, Mary** | Flutist, Composer |
| Silver Wave Records, PO Box 7943, Boulder CO 80306, USA | |
| **Youngen, Lois J** | Baseball Player |
| 45 Prall Lane, Eugene OR 97405, USA | |
| **Younger, Ben** | Director, Producer, Writer |
| Brillstein Entertainment Partners, 9150 Wilshire Blvd, #350, Beverly Hills CA 90212 USA | |
| **Youngerman, Jack** | Artist, Sculptor |
| PO Box 508, Bridgehampton NY 11932, USA | |
| **Younghans, Tom** | Ice Hockey Player |
| 52 Douglas St, # 3, Saint Paul MN 55102, USA | |
| **Young-Ochowicz, Sheila G** | Speed Skater, Cyclist |
| 945 Hutchinson Ave, Palo Alto CA 94301, USA | |
| **Youngs, Elaine** | Volleyball Player |
| Q Sports Marketing, 534 W Evergreen St, Wheaton IL 60187 USA | |
| **Younis, Waqar** | Cricketer |
| Surrey County Cricket Club, Kennington Oval, London SE11 5SS, England | |
| **Yount, Robin R** | Baseball Player |
| 5040 E Shea Blvd, #254, Scottsdale AZ 85254, USA | |
| **Youren, Jan** | Rodeo Rider |
| 2461 Bishop Road, Emmett ID 83617, USA | |
| **Youso, Frank M** | Football Player |
| PO Box 1046, International Falls MN 56649, USA | |
| **Yowarsky, Walter (Walt)** | Football Player |
| 395 Dogwood Place NW, Cleveland TN 37312, USA | |
| **Yo-Yo** | Singer, Actress |
| Bridge & Tunnel Communications, 9157 Sunset Blvd, #205, West Hollywood CA 90069, USA | |
| **Ysebaert, Paul R** | Ice Hockey Player |
| 10 Harbor Blvd, #W528, Destin FL 32541, USA | |
| **Yu Panglin** | Businessman, Philanthropist |
| Super 8 Hotel, 4 Shang Meilin Kaifeng Road, Shenzhen 518001, China | |
| **Yu, Jessica** | Director, Producer, Writer |
| Anonymous Content, 3532 Hayden Ave, Culver City CA 90232 USA | |
| **Yu, Ronny** | Director, Producer, Writer |
| Arlook Group, 205 S Beverly Dr, #209, Beverly Hills CA 90212, USA | |
| **Yuan, Ron** | Actor |
| I C M Partners, 10250 Constellation Blvd, #900, Los Angeles CA 90067 USA | |
| **Yuasa, Joji** | Composer |
| 1517 Shields Ave, Encinitas CA 92024, USA | |
| **Yudashkin, Valentin A** | Fashion Designer |
| Valentin Yudashkin Fashion House, Kutuzovsky Pr 19, 121151 Moscow, Russia | |
| **Yue Jingyu** | Swimmer |
| Physical Culture/Sports Bureau, 9 Tiyuguan Road, Beijing 100763, China | |
| **Yuen Woo-Ping** | Director, Choreographer |
| Creative Artists Agency, 2000 Ave of Stars, #100, Los Angeles CA 90067 USA | |
| **Yukmouth** | Rap Musician |
| Entertainment Artists, 2409 21st Ave S, #100, Nashville TN 10019 USA | |
| **Yulin, Harris** | Actor |
| Parseghian Planco, 322 8th Ave, #601, New York NY 10001, USA | |
| **Yun Suk-Young** | Soccer Player |
| Football Association, 1-131 Sinmunno, 2-Ga Jongno-Gu, Seoul 110 062, South Korea | |
| **Yune, Karl** | Actor |
| Zero Gravity Mgmt, 1531 14th St, Santa Monica CA 90404 USA | |
| **Yune, Rick** | Actor |
| Creative Artists Agency, 2000 Ave of Stars, #100, Los Angeles CA 90067 USA | |
| **Yung Joc** | Rap Artist |
| Brass Artists, 9025 Wilshire Blvd, #400, Beverly Hills CA 90211, USA | |
| **Yunis, Jorge J** | Geneticist, Pathologist |
| Thomas Jefferson University, Jefferson Medical College, Philadelphia PA 19107, USA | |
| **Yunus, Muhammad** | Nobel Peace Laureate |
| Grameen Bank Bhavan, Mirpur 1, Dhaka 1216, Bangladesh | |
| **Yurchikhin, Fyodor N** | Cosmonaut |
| N A S A, Johnson Space Center, 2101 NASA Road, Houston TX 77058 USA | |
| **Yushchenko, Viktor A** | President, Ukraine |
| Koncha-Zaspa, Stolychne Shose, 08711 Kiev, Ukraine | |
| **Yushkevich, Dmitri S** | Ice Hockey Player |
| International Sports Advisors, 878 Ridge View Way, Franklin Lakes NJ 07417, USA | |
| **Yustman, Odette** | Actress, Model |
| Evolution Entertainment, 901 N Highland Ave, Los Angeles CA 90038 USA | |
| **Yusuf** | Singer, Songwriter |
| Creative Artists Agency, 2000 Ave of Stars, #100, Los Angeles CA 90067 USA | |
| **Yusupova, Lidia** | Social Activist |
| Memorial Library, Malyy Karetnyy Pereulok 12, 127051 Moscow, Russia | |
| **Yzaguirre, Raul** | Social Activist |
| National Council of La Raza, 1111 19th St NW, #1000, Washington DC 20036, USA | |
| **Yzerman, Stephen G (Steve)** | Ice Hockey Player, Executive |
| PO Box 488, Bloomfield Hills MI 48303, USA | |

**Zabel, Bryce**
Bloom Hergott Diemer, 150 S Rodeo Dr, #300, Beverly Hills CA 90212 USA — Writer, Producer, Director
**Zabel, David**
Oasis Media Group, 8730 W Sunset Blvd, #700, West Hollywood CA 90069, USA — Writer, Producer
**Zabel, Mark**
Grosse Fischerei 18A, 39240 Calbe/Saale, Germany — Canoeing Athlete
**Zabel, Steven G (Steve)**
6000 Oak Tree Road, Edmond OK 73025, USA — Football Player
**Zabransky, Libor**
Rybarska Specialka Zabransky Koliste 59, Brno 60200, Czech Republic — Ice Hockey Player
**Zabriski, Bruce**
6228 Winding Lake Dr, Jupiter FL 33458, USA — Golfer
**Zabriskie, Grace**
Innovative Artists, 1505 10th St, Santa Monica CA 90401 USA — Actress
**Zachara, Jan**
Sladkovicova 13, 018 51 Nova Dubnica, Czech Republic — Boxer
**Zacharias, Christian**
I M G Artists, Hogarth Business Park, Chiswick, London W4 2TH, England — Concert Pianist, Conductor
**Zachry, Patrick P (Pat)**
7611 Bosque Blvd, Woodway TX 76712, USA — Baseball Player
**Zackham, Justin**
Two Tons Films, 375 Greenwich St, New York NY 10013, USA — Producer, Director, Writer
**Zadan, Craig**
Creative Artists Agency, 2000 Ave of Stars, #100, Los Angeles CA 90067 USA — Producer
**Zadeh, Lofti A**
904 Mendocino Ave, Berkeley CA 94707, USA — Computer Scientist (Fuzzy Logic)
**Zadel, C William**
Millipore Corp, 75 Wiggins Ave, Bedford MA 01730, USA — Businessman
**Zadora, Pia**
Marseille Company Mgmt, 6228 Fallbrook Ave, Woodland Hills CA 91367, USA — Actress, Singer, Model
**Zagorin, Perez**
1015 33rd St NW, #606, Washington DC 20007, USA — Historian
**Zagrosek, Lothar**
Kunstler Sekretariat am Gasteig, Rosenheimer Str 52, 81669 Munich, Germany — Conductor
**Zagunis, Mariel**
Robert F Zagunis, 20235 SW Gassner Road, Beaverton OR 97007, USA — Fencer
**Zahn, Geoffrey C (Geof)**
6536 Walsh Road, Dexter MI 48130, USA — Baseball Player
**Zahn, Paula A**
188 E 76th St, New York NY 10021, USA — Commentator
**Zahn, Steve**
W M E Entertainment, 9601 Wilshire Blvd, #300, Beverly Hills CA 90210 USA — Actor
**Zahn, Timothy**
PO Box 1755, Coos Bay OR 97420, USA — Writer
**Zahn, Wayne**
5018 S Barley Court, Gilbert AZ 85298, USA — Bowler
**Zaillian, Steven**
Film Rights, 159 S Beverly Dr, Beverly Hills CA 90212, USA — Director, Writer
**Zaine, Rod**
64 Drouin St, Ottawa ON K1K 2A7, Canada — Ice Hockey Player
**Zaitseva, Olga A**
Biathlon Union, Luzhnetskaja Nab 8, 119270 Moscow, Russia — Biathlete
**Zajac, Travis**
10 Elsway Road, Short Hills NJ 07078, USA — Ice Hockey Player
**Zakarin, Mark**
Gersh Agency, 9465 Wilshire Blvd, #600, Beverly Hills CA 90212 USA — Writer, Producer
**Zaks, Jerry**
Helen Merrill, 825 8th Ave, #2600, New York NY 10019, USA — Director
**Zal, Roxana**
8265 W Sunset Blvd, #101, West Hollywood CA 90046, USA — Actress
**Zalapski, Zarley B**
Eishockey Club Olten, Postfach 523, 4601 Olten, Switzerland — Ice Hockey Player
**Zalesky, Jim**
University of Iowa, Athletic Dept, Iowa City IA 52242, USA — Freestyle Wrestler, Coach
**Zalyotin, Sergei V**
Cosmonaut Training Center, Star City, 141160 Zvezdny Gorodok, Moscow Oblast, Russia — Cosmonaut
**Zamba, Frieda**
2706 S Central Ave, Flagler Beach FL 32136, USA — Surfer
**Zambarloukos, Haris**
United Agents, 12-26 Lexington St, London W1F 0LE, England — Cinematographer
**Zambellas, George M**
First Sea Lord, Ministry of Defense, Whitehall, London SW1A 2HB, England — Navy Admiral, England
**Zambello, Francesca**
Opus 3 Artists, 470 Park Ave S, #900N, New York NY 10016 USA — Director
**Zametkin, Alan J**
National Mental Health Institute, 9000 Rockville Pike, Bethesda MD 20892, USA — Psychiatrist
**Zamfir, Gheorghe**
Lenhartzstr 15, 20249 Hamburg, Germany — Concert Pan-Pipes Player, Conductor
**Zamka, George D**
12101 Lyre Court, Manassas VA 20112, USA — Astronaut
**Zampella, Vince**
Respawn Entertainment, PO Box 5650, Sherman Oaks CA 91413, USA — Video Game Developer
**Zamuner, Robert F (Rob)**
4317 Beau Rivage Circle, Lutz FL 33558, USA — Ice Hockey Player
**Zanardi, Alessandro (Alex)**
Via B Bordone 12, 35134 Padova, Italy — Auto Racing Driver
**Zander, Carl A**
2536 W Palomino Dr, Chandler AZ 85224, USA — Football Player
**Zander, Robin**
Oakie Dokie Mgmt, 6090 Central Ave, Saint Petersburg FL 33707, USA — Singer, Guitarist (Cheap Trick)
**Zander, Thomas**
Grundfeldstr 23, 73432 Aalen, Germany — Greco-Roman Wrestler
**Zanders, Emmanuel**
11015 Goodwood Blvd, Baton Rouge LA 70815, USA — Football Player
**Zandonella, Roberto**
Olympic Committee, Foro Italico, Largo Lauro de Bosis 15, 00135 Rome, Italy — Bobsled Athlete

**Zane, Billy** — Actor
Paradigm Agency, 360 N Crescent Dr, North Building, Beverly Hills CA 90210 USA

**Zane, Frank** — Body Builder
PO Box 1090, La Mesa CA 91944, USA

**Zane, Lisa** — Actress
505 N Lake Shore Dr, #5407, Chicago IL 60611, USA

**Zanes, Dan** — Singer, Songwriter
Pomegranate Arts, 1140 Broadway, #305, New York NY 10001, USA

**Zanetti, Eugenio** — Actor, Director, Production Designer
Sandra Marsh Assoc, 9150 Wilshire Blvd, #220, Beverly Hills CA 90212 USA

**Zanetti, Massimo** — Conductor
I M G Artists, Hogarth Business Park, Chiswick, London W4 2TH, England

**Zanier, Michael (Mike)** — Ice Hockey Player
306 Rossland Ave, Trail BC V1R 3M8, Canada

**Zanni, Dominick T (Dom)** — Baseball Player
7 Sussex Ave, Massapequa NY 11758, USA

**Zano, Nick** — Actor
United Talent Agency, U T A Plaza, 9336 Civic Center Dr, Beverly Hills CA 90210 USA

**Zanotto, Kendra** — Synchronized Swimmer
18834 Lakeview Court, Los Gatos CA 95033, USA

**Zanova Steindler, Alena (Aja)** — Figure Skater
Wollman Skating Rink, 830 5th Ave, New York NY 10065, USA

**Zanuck, Lili Fini** — Producer, Director
1131 Miradero Road, Beverly Hills CA 90210, USA

**Zanussi, Krzysztof** — Director, Producer, Writer
Ul Kaniowska 114, 01529, Warsaw, Poland

**Zanussi, Ronald K (Ron)** — Ice Hockey Player
PO Box 11326, Saint Paul MN 55111, USA

**Zapf, Hermann** — Book, Type Designer
2 Hammarskjold Plaza, New York NY 10017, USA

**Zapiro** — Editorial Cartoonist
Double Storey Books, PO Box 24299, Lansdowne 7779, South Africa

**Zapp, James (Jim)** — Baseball Player
820 Youngs Lane, Nashville TN 37207, USA

**Zappa, Ahmet** — Actor, Writer, Producer
I C M Partners, 10250 Constellation Blvd, #900, Los Angeles CA 90067 USA

**Zappa, Diva** — Actress
J K A Talent Agency, 12725 Ventura Blvd, #H, Studio City CA 91604, USA

**Zappa, Dweezil** — Singer, Guitarist, Actor
7885 Woodrow Wilson Dr, Los Angeles CA 90046, USA

**Zappa, Moon Unit** — Singer, Actress
J K A Talent Agency, 12725 Ventura Blvd, #H, Studio City CA 91604, USA

**Zarate Serna, Carlos** — Boxer
Gene Aguilera, PO Box 113, Montebello CA 90640, USA

**Zasada, Sobieslaw** — Auto Racing Driver
Zasada S A, Ul Omulewska 27, 04128 Warsaw, Poland

**Zaslav, David M** — Businessman
Discovery Communications Inc, One Discovery Place, Silver Spring MD 20910, USA

**Zatkoff, Roger** — Football Player
882 Hidden Ravines Court, Birmingham MI 48009, USA

**Zatopkova, Dana** — Track Athlete
Nad Kazankov 3, 17100 Prague 7, Czech Republic

**Zaun, Gregory O (Gregg)** — Baseball Player
26 E 6th St, #701, Cincinnati OH 45202, USA

**Zavarzina, Alena I** — Snowboard Skier
Petrodvorets Watch Factory, Saint Petersburg Prospect 60, 198516 Saint Petersburg, Russia

**Zaveri, Anjala** — Actress
604 Jupiter Apts, Yari Road, Andheri, Mumbai MS 400058, India

**Zavisha, Brad** — Ice Hockey Player
General Delivery, Hines Creek AB T0H 2A0, Canada

**Zavos, Panos M** — Biologist
181 Collins Lane, Lexington KY 40503, USA

**Zayas, David** — Actor
Innovative Artists, 1505 10th St, Santa Monica CA 90401 USA

**Zayas, Victor Hugo** — Artist
Brewery Art Complex, 2100 N Main St, #A10, Los Angeles CA 90031, USA

**Zaz** — Singer
Sony Music, Neumarkter Str 28, 81673 Munich, Germany

**Zazzo, Lawrence** — Opera Singer
Harrison/Parrott, 5-6 Albion Court, London W6 0QT, England

**Zdrok, Victoria N** — Model, Actress, Dancer
PO Box 332, Pompton Lakes NJ 07442, USA

**Zea, Natalie** — Actress
True Mgmt, 8964 W 25th St, Los Angeles CA 90034, USA

**Zech, Lando W, Jr** — Navy Admiral, Government Official
1 White Flint N, 11555 Rockville Pike, Rockville MD 20852, USA

**Zeckhauser, Richard J** — Economist
138 Irving St, Cambridge MA 02138, USA

**Zedda, Alberto** — Conductor, Composer
Academia Rossiniana, Via Rossini 1, 61100 Pesaro, Italy

**Zedillo Ponce de Leon, Ernesto** — President, Mexico
Institutional Revolutionary, Insurges N 61, Mexico City 06350 DF, Mexico

**Zedlitz, Jean** — Golfer
4587 Gatetree Circle, Pleasanton CA 94566, USA

**Zednik, Richard** — Ice Hockey Player
4401 N Federal Highway, Boca Raton FL 33431, USA

**Zeffirelli, G Franco** — Director
Via Lucio Volumnio 37, 00178 Rome, Italy

**Zegen, Michael (Mike)** — Actor
United Talent Agency, U T A Plaza, 9336 Civic Center Dr, Beverly Hills CA 90210 USA

**Zeglis, John D** — Businessman
A T & T Wireless Group, 7277 164th Ave NE, Redmond WA 98052, USA

**Zehetner, Nora** — Actress
A P A Talent & Literary Agency, 405 S Beverly Dr, #300, Beverly Hills CA 90212 USA

**Zehr, Joey** — Actor, Drummer (Click Five)
Creative Artists Agency, 2000 Ave of Stars, #100, Los Angeles CA 90067 USA

**Zehringer, Rick**
Brothers Management Assoc, 141 Dunbar Ave, Fords NJ 08863 USA
Singer, Guitarist (McCoys)

**Zehrt, Monika Landgraf-**
Stormstr 42, 15827 Blankenfelde, Germany
Track Athlete

**Zeidler, Eberard H**
Zeidler Grinnell Partnership, 315 Queen St W, Toronto ON M5V 2X2, Canada
Architect, Designer

**Zeier, Eric R**
PO Box 327, Nashville GA 31639, USA
Football Player

**Zeifman, Jerome**
57 North St, #105, Danbury CT 06810, USA
Attorney

**Zeigler, C Dustin (Dusty)**
440 Hodgeville Road, Guyton GA 31312, USA
Football Player

**Zeigler, Marie**
2502 N 22nd Ave, Phoenix AZ 85009, USA
Baseball Player

**Zeile, Todd E**
1670 Fairmount Road, Westlake Village CA 91362, USA
Baseball Player

**Zeitlin, Benh**
W M E Entertainment, 9601 Wilshire Blvd, #300, Beverly Hills CA 90210 USA
Director, Writer

**Zelenka, Joseph J (Joe)**
12572 Highview Dr, Jacksonville FL 32225, USA
Football Player

**Zelenskaya, Yelena E**
Bolshoi Theater, Teatralnaya Pl 1, 103009 Moscow, Russia
Opera Singer

**Zelepukin, Valeri M**
9595 Collins Ave, #610, Surfside FL 33154, USA
Ice Hockey Player

**Zelezny, Jan**
Rue Armady 683, 29301 Boleslav, Czech Republic
Track Athlete

**Zeliaeva, Valentina**
Women Model Mgmt, 199 Lafayette St, #700, New York NY 10012 USA
Model

**Zeller, Tyler P**
Boston Celtics, 226 Causeway St, #4, Boston MA 02114 USA
Basketball Player

**Zellner, Hunndens G (Peppi)**
31 Dew Place, Forsyth GA 31029, USA
Football Player

**Zellweger, Renee**
John Carrabino Mgmt, 5900 Wilshire Blvd, #406, Los Angeles CA 90036 USA
Actress

**Zelman, Daniel**
Stone Meyer Genow, 9665 Wilshire Blvd, #510, Beverly Hills CA 90212 USA
Producer, Writer, Actor

**Zelmani, Sophie**
United Stage Artists, PO Box 11029, 100 61 Stockholm, Sweden
Singer

**Zem, Roschdy**
Artmedia, 20 Ave Rapp, 75007 Paris, France
Actor, Director

**Zeman, E Robert (Bob)**
4427 Maple Dr, Eagle River WI 54521, USA
Football Player

**Zeman, Jacklyn**
Aqua Talent Agency, 9000 Sunset Blvd, #700, Los Angeles CA 90069, USA
Actress

**Zeman, Milos**
President's Office, Prague Castle, Prazsky Hrad, Hradecek, 11908 Prague 1, Czech Republic
Prime Minister, Czech Republic

**Zembriski, Walter**
6507 Doubletrace Lane, Orlando FL 32819, USA
Golfer

**Zemeckis, Robert L**
ImageMovers, 100 Universal City, Bungalow 5170, Los Angeles CA 91608, USA
Director

**Zen Ze Kiun, Joseph Cardinal**
Diocese of Hong Kong, 16 Caine Road, #12F, Hong Kong, China
Religious Leader

**Zendaya**
Monster Talent Mgmt, 6333 W 3rd St, #912, Los Angeles CA 90036, USA
Actress

**Zendejas, Anthony G (Tony)**
24430 Avendia de Marcia, Yorba Linda CA 92887, USA
Football Player

**Zender Meier, Gladys**
Miss Universe Organization, 1370 Ave of Americas, #1600, New York NY 10019 USA
Beauty Queen

**Zender, J W Hans**
Horbener Str 28, 79100 Freiburg, Germany
Conductor, Composer

**Zender, Stuart P J**
Nettwerk Mgmt, 6525 W Sunset Blvd, #800, Los Angeles CA 90028 USA
Bassist (Jamiroquai)

**Zeng Fanzhi**
Saatchi Gallery, Duke Of York's HQ, King's Road, London SW3 4RY, England
Artist

**Zent, Jason**
271 Dartmouth St, #4G, Boston MA 02116, USA
Ice Hockey Player

**Zentilli, Patricia**
Characters Talent Agency, 8 Elm St, Toronto ON M5G 1G7, Canada
Actress

**Zentmyer, George A, Jr**
955 S El Camino Real, #216, San Mateo CA 94402, USA
Plant Pathologist

**Zerbe, Anthony**
1175 High Road, Santa Barbara CA 93108, USA
Actor

**Zereoue, Amos L**
226 Westside Ave, #B, Freeport NY 11520, USA
Football Player

**Zerhouni, Elias A**
National Institutes of Health, 9000 Rockville Pike, Bethesda MD 20892, USA
Government Official, Physician

**Zero, Mark**
PO Box 656507, Fresh Meadows NY 11365, USA
Singer (Randy & the Rainbows)

**Zervas, Nicholas T**
100 Canton Ave, Milton MA 02186, USA
Neurosurgeon

**Zeta-Jones, Catherine**
Independent Talent Group, 40 Whitfield St, London W1T 2RH, England
Actress, Model

**Zetsche, Dieter**
Daimler-Chrysler AG, Plieningerstr, 70546 Stuttgart, Germany
Businessman

**Zettel, Kathrin**
Hochreit 20, 3345 Gostling an der Ybbs, Austria
Alpine Skier

**Zetterberg, C Henrik**
1780 Hammond Court, Bloomfield Hills MI 48304, USA
Ice Hockey Player

**Zetterlund Bush, Yoko**
4055 Crystal Dawn Lane, #205, San Diego CA 92122, USA
Volleyball Player

**Zetumer, Joshua (Josh)**
United Talent Agency, U T A Plaza, 9336 Civic Center Dr, Beverly Hills CA 90210 USA
Writer, Producer

**Zewail, Ahmed H**
871 Winston Ave, San Marino CA 91108, USA
Nobel Chemist Laureate

**Zezelj, Danijel**
D C Comics, 1700 Broadway, #400, New York NY 10019, USA
Cartoonist, Writer

# Z

**Zgonina, Jeffrey M (Jeff)** — Football Player
5418 Lampasas St, Houston TX 77056, USA

**Zhai Zhigang** — Taikonaut, China
Satellite Launch Center, Jiuquan, Guangzhou Province, China

**Zhamnov, Alexei Y** — Ice Hockey Player
1950 N Orchard St, Chicago IL 60614, USA

**Zhang Dan** — Figure Skater
Skating Assn, 56 Zhonguachun South St, Beijing 100044, China

**Zhang Hao** — Figure Skater
Skating Association, 56 Zhonguancun South St, Beijing 100044, China

**Zhang Hong** — Speed Skater
Skating Association, 56 Zhonguancun South St, Beijing 100044, China

**Zhang Jie** — Writer
501 Qian-Men Xi Da Jie, #97, Beijing 100031, China

**Zhang Xianliang** — Writer
Ningxia Writers' Assn, Yinchuan City, China

**Zhang Yimou** — Director
Edko Films, 1212 Tiwer 2, Admiralty Centre, Hong Kong, China

**Zhang Ziyi** — Actress
Flying Box Co, 1-4-20 Nishi Azabu, Minato, Tokyo 106 0031, Japan

**Zhang, Haochen** — Concert Pianist
I M G Artists, Hogarth Business Park, Chiswick, London W4 2TH, England

**Zhang, Liping** — Opera Singer
I C M Artists, 40 W 57th St, #1800, New York NY 10019 USA

**Zhang, Xian** — Conductor
Coro Sinfonico di Milano Giuseppe Verdi, Via Clerici 3, 20121 Milan, Italy

**Zhao Hongbo** — Figure Skater
Skating Assn, 56 Zhonguanchun South St, Beijing 100044, China

**Zhao Yanxia** — Opera Singer
24 Xusubai 2nd Lane, Beijing 100034, China

**Zhe Xi Lo** — Anthropologist
Carnegie Natural History Museum, 4400 Forbes Ave, Pittsburgh PA 15213, USA

**Zhen Haixia** — Basketball Player
Physical Culture Bureau, 9 Tiyuguan Lu, Beijing 100061, China

**Zhenan Bao** — Chemist, Inventor (Molecule Transistor)
A T & T Bell Lucent Laboratory, 600 Mountain Ave, New Providence NJ 07974 USA

**Zheng, Wei** — Astronomer
Johns Hopkins University, Astronomy Dept, Baltimore MD 21218, USA

**Zhirinovsky, Vladimir V** — Government Leader, Russia
State Duma, Okhotny Ryad 1, 103009 Moscow, Russia

**Zhislin, Grigory Y** — Concert Violinist
25 Whitehall Gardens, London W3 9RD, England

**Zhitnik, Alexei N** — Ice Hockey Player
8 Boxwood Way, Manhasset NY 11030, USA

**Zholobov, Vitali M** — Cosmonaut
Ul Yanvarskovo Vostaniya D 12, 252010 Kiev, Ukraine

**Zhou Long** — Composer
University of Missouri, Music Dept, Kansas City MO 64110, USA

**Zhou Yang** — Speed Skater
Skating Association, 56 Zhonguancun South St, Beijing 100044, China

**Zhudov, Vyacheslav D** — Cosmonaut
Cosmonaut Training Center, Star City, 141160 Zvezdny Gorodok, Moscow Oblast, Russia

**Zhulin, Alexsander V (Sasha)** — Ice Dancer
Skating Federation, Luchnesksaia Nab 8, 119871 Moscow, Russia

**Zhvanetsky, Mikhail M** — Writer, Actor
Lesnaya Str 4, #63, 125047 Moscow, Russia

**Zia, Begum Khaleda** — Prime Minister, Bangladesh
Bangladesh National Party, 29 Minto Road, Dhaka, Bangladesh

**Ziblijew, Wassili** — Cosmonaut
Cosmonaut Training Center, Star City, 141160 Zvezdny Gorodok, Moscow Oblast, Russia

**Zich, Denise** — Actress
Management Goldschmidt, Damaschkestr 33, 10711 Berlin, Germany

**Zicherman, Stu** — Producer, Writer
W M E Entertainment, 9601 Wilshire Blvd, #300, Beverly Hills CA 90210 USA

**Zickel, Mather** — Actor
Abrams Artists, 9200 W Sunset Blvd, #1125, West Hollywood CA 90069 USA

**Zida, Y Isaac** — Acting President, Burkino Faso
Prime Minister's Office, 03 BP 7027, Ouagadougou 03, Burkina Faso

**Zidane, Zinedine** — Soccer Player
F C Real Madrid, Avda Concha Espana 1, 28036 Madrid, Spain

**Zidek, Jiri (George)** — Basketball Player
551 Landfair Ave, Los Angeles CA 90024, USA

**Zidi, Malik** — Actor
Agence Artiste Adequat, 108 Rue Reaumur, 75002 Paris, France

**Zidlicky, Marek** — Ice Hockey Player
2006 Sweetbriar Ave, Nashville TN 37212, USA

**Ziegelmeyer, Nicole (Nikki)** — Speed Skater
5912 Mastodon Pines Dr, Imperial MO 63052, USA

**Ziegler, Alma** — Baseball Player
403 Gold St, Auburn CA 95603, USA

**Ziegler, Bill** — Cartoonist
King Features Syndicate, 300 W 57th St, #1500, New York NY 10019 USA

**Ziegler, Dolores** — Opera Singer
Lynda Kay, 2702 Crestworth Lane, Buford GA 30519, USA

**Ziegler, Jack** — Cartoonist
New Yorker, Editorial Dept, 4 Times Square, Basement C1B, New York NY 10036 USA

**Ziegler, John A, Jr** — Ice Hockey Player
3 Club Dr, Jupiter FL 33469, USA

**Ziegler, John L** — Oncologist
University of California Cancer Center, 2340 Sutter St, San Francisco CA 94115, USA

**Ziegler, Kate** — Swimmer
George Mason University, Athletic Dept, Fairfax VA 22030, USA

**Ziegler, Larry** — Golfer
10315 Luton Court, Orlando FL 32836, USA

**Ziegler, Marie** — Baseball Player
6739 W Polk St, Phoenix AZ 85043, USA

|  |  |
|------|-----------|
| **Zielcke, Marie** | Actress |
| Kings Mgmt, Kaiserswerther Markt 29, 40489 Dusseldorf, Germany | |
| **Zielenbach, Jen** | Bassist (Antigone Rising) |
| W Mgmt, 266 Elizabeth St, #1A, New York NY 10012, USA | |
| **Ziem, Steven G (Steve)** | Baseball Player |
| 1309 Avalon Ave, Beaumont CA 92223, USA | |
| **Ziemann, Sonja** | Actress |
| Via del Alp Dorf, 7500 Saint Moritz, Switzerland | |
| **Ziemba, Karen** | Singer, Actress, Dancer |
| TalentWorks, 3500 W Olive Ave, #1400, Burbank CA 91505 USA | |
| **Zien, Chip** | Actor |
| Innovative Artists, 1505 10th St, Santa Monica CA 90401 USA | |
| **Zien, Sam (Cooking Guy)** | Chef |
| Discovery Channel, 7700 Wisconsin Ave, Bethesda MD 20814 USA | |
| **Zierden, Don** | Basketball Coach |
| Washington Wizards, M C I Centre, 601 F St NW, Washington DC 20004 USA | |
| **Ziering, Ian** | Actor |
| Synergy Management, 11271 Ventura Blvd, #495, Studio City CA 91604, USA | |
| **Ziesak, Ruth** | Opera Singer |
| Kunstler Sekretariat am Gasteig, Rosenheimer Str 52, 81669 Munich, Germany | |
| **Ziffren, Kenneth** | Attorney |
| Ziffren Brittenham Branca, 1801 Century Park W, #700, Los Angeles CA 90067 USA | |
| **Zigler, Edward F** | Psychologist, Educator |
| Yale University, Bush Child Development Center, New Haven CT 06520, USA | |
| **Zikes, Les** | Bowler |
| 424 S Stuart Lane, Palatine IL 60067, USA | |
| **Zilinskas, Annette** | Bassist (Bangles, Ringling Sisters) |
| Creative Artists Agency, 2000 Ave of Stars, #100, Los Angeles CA 90067 USA | |
| **Zillmer, Ruth** | Baseball Player |
| PO Box 709, Walworth WI 53184, USA | |
| **Zils, John** | Structural Engineer |
| N1513 Shore Haven Dr, Fontana WI 53125, USA | |
| **Zim Zum** | Guitarist (Marilyn Manson); Songwriter |
| Mitch Schneider Organization, 14724 Ventura Blvd, #500, Sherman Oaks CA 91403 USA | |
| **Zima, Madeline** | Actress |
| United Talent Agency, U T A Plaza, 9336 Civic Center Dr, Beverly Hills CA 90210 USA | |
| **Zimbalist, Stephanie** | Actress |
| A M T Artists, 15260 Ventura Blvd, #1200, Sherman Oaks CA 91403, USA | |
| **Zimerman, Krystian** | Concert Pianist |
| Kernmatterstr 8B, 4102 Binningen, Switzerland | |
| **Zimm, Bruno H** | Chemist |
| 3762 Dupont St, San Diego CA 92106, USA | |
| **Zimmer, Constance** | Actress |
| United Talent Agency, U T A Plaza, 9336 Civic Center Dr, Beverly Hills CA 90210 USA | |
| **Zimmer, Hans F** | Composer |
| Bleeding Fingers Custom Music Shop, 1531 14th St, Santa Monica CA 90404, USA | |
| **Zimmer, Kim** | Actress |
| Innovative Artists, 1505 10th St, Santa Monica CA 90401 USA | |
| **Zimmer, Robert** | Educator |
| University of Chicago, President's Office, Chicago IL 60637, USA | |
| **Zimmerer, Wolfgang** | Bobsled Athlete |
| Schwaigangerstr 22, 82418 Murnau, Germany | |
| **Zimmerman, Daniel H E (Dan)** | Drummer (Gamma Ray) |
| United Talent Agency, U T A Plaza, 9336 Civic Center Dr, Beverly Hills CA 90210 USA | |
| **Zimmerman, Gary W** | Football Player |
| 17450 Skylines Road, Bend OR 99701, USA | |
| **Zimmerman, Howard E** | Chemist |
| 7813 Westchester Dr, Middleton WI 53562, USA | |
| **Zimmerman, Jeffrey R (Jeff)** | Baseball Player |
| 2416 Chippendale Road, West Vancouver BC V7S 3J2, Canada | |
| **Zimmerman, Joey** | Actor |
| PO Box 450802, Kissimmee FL 34745, USA | |
| **Zimmerman, Mary Beth** | Golfer |
| 6452 Century Park Place SE, Mableton GA 30126, USA | |
| **Zimmerman, Philip (Phil)** | Computer Software Designer |
| Network Assoc, 4677 Old Ironside Dr, Santa Clara CA 95054, USA | |
| **Zimmerman, Ryan W** | Baseball Player |
| 524 Innsbruck Ave, Great Falls VA 22066, USA | |
| **Zimmermann, Egon** | Alpine Skier |
| Hotel Kristberg, Lech 316, 6764 Lech Am Arlberg, Austria | |
| **Zimmermann, Frank Peter** | Concert Violinist |
| Kunstler Sekretariat am Gasteig, Rosenheimer Str 52, 81669 Munich, Germany | |
| **Zimmermann, Jordan** | Baseball Player |
| Washington Nationals, 1500 S Capitol St SE, Washington DC 20003 USA | |
| **Zimmermann, Markus** | Bobsled Athlete |
| Waldhauserstr 51-53, 83471 Schonau am Konigsee, Germany | |
| **Zimmermann, Raquel** | Model |
| D N A Model Mgmt, 555 W 25th St, #600, New York NY 10001 USA | |
| **Zimmermann, Serge** | Concert Violinist |
| Kunstler Sekretariat am Gasteig, Rosenheimer Str 52, 81669 Munich, Germany | |
| **Zimmermann, Udo** | Composer |
| Operhaus Leipzig, Augustusplatz, 04109 Leipzig, Germany | |
| **Zimpher, Nancy** | Educator |
| Cincinnati University, President's Office, Cincinnati OH 45221, USA | |
| **Zingaretti, Luca** | Actor |
| Carol Levi Mgmt, Via Giuseppe Pisanelli 2, 00196 Rome, Italy | |
| **Zinke, Olaf** | Speed Skater |
| Johannes Bobrowski Str 22, 12627 Berlin, Germany | |
| **Zinkernagel, Rolf M** | Nobel Medicine Laureate |
| Rebhusstr 47, 8126 Zumikon, Switzerland | |
| **Zinman, David J** | Conductor |
| Aspen Music Festival, 2 Music School Road, Aspen CO 81611, USA | |
| **Zinner, Nicholas J (Nick)** | Guitarist, Songwriter (Yeah Yeah Yeahs) |
| Yeah Yeah Yeahs, 249 Metropolitan Ave, Brooklyn NY 11211, USA | |
| **Zinni, Anthony C (Tony)** | Marine Corps General |
| 139 Shady Creek Lane, Fredericksburg VA 22406, USA | |

**Zinszer, Pamela** — Actress, Model
Playboy Promotions, 9346 Civic Center Dr, #200, Beverly Hills CA 90210 USA
**Zinta, Preity** — Actress, Model, Writer, Producer
C10/A Ranwar Wadora Road, Off Hill Road, Bandra (W), Mumbai MS 400050, India
**Ziolkowski, Szymon** — Track Athlete
Polanik S P, Spotka Komandytowa, Ul Zyczliwa 11, 97300 Piotrkow Trybunalski, Poland
**Zippel, David** — Lyricist
Kraft-Engel Mgmt, 15233 Ventura Blvd, #200, Sherman Oaks CA 91403 USA
**Zirner, Johannes** — Actor
Die Agenten, Ackerstr 11B, 10115 Berlin, Germany
**Zischler, Hanns** — Actor
Anne Alvares Correa, 34 Rue Jouffroy d'Abbans, 75017 Paris, France
**Zisk, Craig** — Director, Producer
United Talent Agency, U T A Plaza, 9336 Civic Center Dr, Beverly Hills CA 90210 USA
**Zisk, Randall (Randy)** — Director
Creative Artists Agency, 2000 Ave of Stars, #100, Los Angeles CA 90067 USA
**Zisk, Richard W (Richie)** — Baseball Player
4231 NE 26th Terrace, Lighthouse Point FL 33064, USA
**Zito, Barry W** — Baseball Player
1204 Suncast Lane, #2, El Dorado Hills CA 95762, USA
**Zito, Chuck** — Actor, Model
Prince Marketing Group, 18 Carillon Circle, Livingston NJ 07039 USA
**Zittel, Harry** — Actor
Innovative Artists, 1505 10th St, Santa Monica CA 90401 USA
**Zlatoper, Ronald J (Zap)** — Navy Admiral
1001 Kamokila Blvd, Kapolei HI 96707, USA
**Zlokovic, Berislav V** — Neurologist
University of Rochester Medical Center, Neurology Dept, 601 Elmwood Ave, Rochester NY 14642, USA
**Zlotkowska, Luiza** — Speed Skater
Piotr Wyszynski, UlMatarewicza 4D, 05230 Kobylka, Ossow, Poland
**Zmed, Adrian** — Actor
Vincent Cirrincione Assoc, 1516 N Fairfax Ave, Los Angeles CA 90046 USA
**Zmievskaya Petrenko, Galina Y (Nina)** — Figure Skating Coach
Ice Vault Arena, 10 Nevins Road, Wayne NJ 07470, USA
**Zmolek, Doug** — Ice Hockey Player
537 Frederichs Dr SW, Rochester MN 55901, USA
**Znaider, Nikolaj** — Conductor, Concert Violinist
I M G Artists, Hogarth Business Park, Chiswick, London W4 2TH, England
**Zobrist, Benjamin T (Ben)** — Baseball Player
545 Overview Lane, Franklin TN 37064, USA
**Zoch, Jacqueline** — Rowing Athlete
3421 Charing Wood Lane, Birmingham AL 35242, USA
**Zockler, Billie** — Actress
Agentur Lentz, Herzogstr 66, 80469 Munich, Germany
**Zoe, Rachel** — Fashion Designer, Stylist
Bravo-TV, 3000 N Alameda Ave, #250, Burbank CA 91523 USA
**Zoeller, Frank (Fuzzy)** — Golfer
418 Deer Run Trace, Floyds Knobs IN 47119, USA
**Zoellick, Robert B** — Government Official, Financier
Peterson Institute, 1750 Massachusetts Ave NW, Washington DC 20036, USA
**Zoff, Dino** — Soccer Player
F C Juventus, Corso Galilo Ferraris 32, 10128 Turin, Italy
**Zoggeler, Armin** — Luge Athlete
Postfach, 39011 Lana (BZ), Italy
**Zokol, Richard F (Dick)** — Golfer
Contemporary Communications, 1663 7th Ave W, Vancouver BC V6J 1S4, Canada
**Zolak, Scott D** — Football Player
40 Comstock Dr, Wrentham MA 02093, USA
**Zoli, Winter Eve** — Actress
Melanie Greene Mgmt, 425 N Robertson Blvd, West Hollywood CA 90048 USA
**Zoloth, Laurie** — Educator
Northwestern University Medical School, Bioethics Center, Evanston IL 60208, USA
**Zombie, Rob** — Singer (White Zombie), Director
Vision Entertainment Group, 8484 Wilshire Blvd, #425, Beverly Hills CA 90211, USA
**Zombo, Rick** — Ice Hockey Player
2918 Ossenfort Road, Glencoe MO 63038, USA
**Zonderland, Epke** — Gymnast
PO Box 197, 8 530 Lemmer AD, Netherlands
**Zook, John E** — Football Player
4302 N Spyglass Circle, Wichita KS 67226, USA
**Zoran** — Fashion Designer
67 Hudson St, New York NY 10013, USA
**Zordich, Michael E (Mike)** — Football Player
373 S Hazelwood Ave, Youngstown OH 44509, USA
**Zore, Edward** — Businessman
Northwestern Mutual Financial Network, 720 E Wisconsin, Milwaukee WI 53202, USA
**Zorich, Christopher R (Chris)** — Football Player
1231 W 33rd Place, Chicago IL 60608, USA
**Zorn, James A (Jim)** — Football Player, Coach
2006 W Mercer Way, Mercer Island WA 98040, USA
**Zou Shiming** — Boxer
Top Rank Inc, 3908 Howard Hughes Parkway, #580, Las Vegas NV 89169 USA
**Zsigmond, Vilmos** — Cinematographer
Skouras Agency, 1149 3rd St, #300, Santa Monica CA 90403 USA
**Zubak, Kresimir** — Co-President, Bosnia-Herzegovina
Presidency, Marsala Titz 7A, 71000 Sarajevo, Bosnia-Herzegovina
**Zubeir Wako, Gabriel Cardinal** — Religious Leader
Archdiocese, PO Box 49, Khartoum, Sudan
**Zuber, Maria T** — Geophysicist
Massachusetts Institute of Technology, Geophysics Dept, Cambridge MA 02139, USA
**Zubkov, Aleksandr Y** — Bobsled Athlete
Bobsleigh Federation, Luzhnetskaja Nab 8, 119992 Moscow, Russia
**Zubov, Sergei M** — Ice Hockey Player
3916 Marquette St, Dallas TX 75225, USA
**Zubrus, Dainius G** — Ice Hockey Player
92 Union St, Montclair NJ 07042, USA

**Zuccarini, Peter**
Gersh Agency, 9465 Wilshire Blvd, #600, Beverly Hills CA 90212 USA — Cinematographer

**Zucchero**
Studio Legale Costa, Via Azzo Gardino 54, 40122 Bologna, Italy — Singer, Guitarist

**Zucker, Arianne**
Levine Management, 9028 W Sunset Blvd, #PH1, Los Angeles CA 90069, USA — Actress, Model

**Zucker, David**
Creative Artists Agency, 2000 Ave of Stars, #100, Los Angeles CA 90067 USA — Director, Producer

**Zucker, Jerry**
Zucker Productions, 1250 6th St, #201, Santa Monica CA 90401, USA — Director, Producer

**Zuckerberg, Mark**
Facebook, 156 University Ave, #200, Palo Alto CA 94301, USA — Businessman

**Zuckerman, Harriet A**
Andrew W Mellon Foundation, 140 E 62nd St, New York NY 10065, USA — Sociologist, Foundation Executive

**Zuckerman, Joshua R (Josh)**
Gersh Agency, 9465 Wilshire Blvd, #600, Beverly Hills CA 90212 USA — Actor

**Zuckerman, Mortimer B**
Boston Properties, 599 Lexington Ave, #1800, New York NY 10022, USA — Publisher

**Zuckermann, Ariel**
Georgian Chamber Orchestra, Hohe-Schul-Stra 4, 85049 Ingolstadt, Germany — Conductor, Concert Flutist

**Zuhdi, Nazih**
3300 NW Expressway, Oklahoma City OK 73112, USA — Surgeon

**Zuiker, Anthony E**
Brillstein Entertainment Partners, 9150 Wilshire Blvd, #350, Beverly Hills CA 90212 USA — Producer, Writer, Actor

**Zuke, Michael (Mike)**
430 Norman Gate Dr, Ballwin MO 63011, USA — Ice Hockey Player

**Zuker, Danny**
Creative Artists Agency, 2000 Ave of Stars, #100, Los Angeles CA 90067 USA — Producer, Writer

**Zukerman, Eugenia**
Brooklyn College of Music, Bedford & H Aves, Brooklyn NY 11210, USA — Concert Flutist

**Zukerman, Pinchas**
Kirshbaum Demler Assoc, 711 W End Ave, #5KN, New York NY 10025, USA — Concert Violinist, Conductor

**Zukubft, Paul F**
Commandant, US Coast Guard, 2703 Martin Luther King Jr Ave SE, Washington DC 20020 USA — Coast Guard Admiral

**Zullo, Alan**
Tribune Media Services, 435 N Michigan Ave, #1500, Chicago IL 60611 USA — Cartoonist (Hall of Shame)

**Zuluaga, Luz Marina**
Miss Universe Organization, 1370 Ave of Americas, #1600, New York NY 10019 USA — Beauty Queen

**Zuma, Jacob G**
President's Office, Union Buildings, Pretoria 0001, South Africa — President, South Africa

**Zumthor, Peter**
Suesswinggel 20, 7023 Haldenstein, Switzerland — Architect

**Zuniga, Daphne**
Bauman Redanty Shaul Agency, 5757 Wilshire Blvd, #473, Los Angeles CA 90036 USA — Actress

**Zuniga, Jose**
A P A Talent & Literary Agency, 405 S Beverly Dr, #300, Beverly Hills CA 90212 USA — Actor

**Zuniga, Miles**
Russell Carter Artists, 567 Ralph Mcgill Blvd NE, Atlanta GA 30312, USA — Singer, Guitarist (Fastball)

**Zupko, Ramon**
Western Michigan University, Music Dept, Kalamazoo MI 49008, USA — Composer

**Zurbriggen, Pirmin**
Hotel Larchenhof, 3905 Saas-Almagell, Switzerland — Alpine Skier

**ZurHausen, Harald**
Tumorvirus-C A T, Im Neuenheimer Feld 242, 69120 Heidelberg, Germany — Nobel Medicine Laureate

**Zurkowski-Holmes, Agnes**
206-2339 Lorne St, Regina SK S4P 2N2, Canada — Baseball Player

**Zurrer, Emily**
Canadian Soccer, Place Soccer Canada, 237 Metcalfe St, Ottawa ON K2P 1R2, Canada — Soccer Player

**Zusi, Graham**
Sporting Kansas City, 210 W 19th Terrace, #200, Kansas City MO 64108 USA — Soccer Player

**Zuvella, Paul**
2040 Canyon Crest Ave, San Ramon CA 94582, USA — Baseball Player

**Zvereva, Natalia**
Women's Tennis Assn, 1 Progress Plaza, #1500, Saint Petersburg FL 33701 USA — Tennis Player

**Zvonareva, Vera I**
S F X Sports, 846 Lincoln Road, #500, Miami Beach Fl 33139 USA — Tennis Player

**Zwanzig, Robert W**
8300 Burdette Road, #423, Bethesda MD 20817, USA — Chemical Physicist

**Zweig, George**
Los Alamos National Laboratory, PO Box 1663, Los Alamos NM 87544, USA — Theoretical Physicist

**Zwick, Alyse Jean**
OmniPop Talent Group, 4605 Lankershim Blvd, #201, Toluca Lake CA 91602 USA — Actress, Comedienne, Model

**Zwick, Edward M (Ed)**
Creative Artists Agency, 2000 Ave of Stars, #100, Los Angeles CA 90067 USA — Director, Producer

**Zwick, Joel**
Irv Schechter, 9460 Wilshire Blvd, #300, Beverly Hills CA 90212 USA — Director

**Zwilich, Ellen Taaffe**
Music Associates of America, 224 King St, Englewood NJ 07631, USA — Composer

**Zwonitzer, Mark**
Simon & Schuster, 1230 Ave of Americas, Concourse 1, New York NY 10020 USA — Producer, Director, Writer

**Zylberstein, Elsa**
Agence Artiste Adequat, 108 Rue Reaumur, 75002 Paris, France — Actress

**Zylis-Gara, Teresa**
16A Blvd de Belgique, Monaco-Ville, Monaco — Opera Singer

**Zylka, Chris**
W M E Entertainment, 9601 Wilshire Blvd, #300, Beverly Hills CA 90210 USA — Actor

# NECROLOGY

Listees of previous editions of the V.I.P. Address Book and the V.I.P. Address Book Update whose deaths have been reported prior to close of the compilation are listed below.

| | |
|---|---|
| Abbado, Claudio | Conductor |
| Abbe, Kathryn | Photographer |
| Abshire, David M | Diplomat |
| Adelman, Morris A | Economist |
| Aghion, Gaby | Fashion Designer |
| Agoglia, John | Businessman |
| Agre, Bernard Cardinal | Religious Leader |
| Aguilar, Jose | Boxer |
| Akers, John F | Businessman |
| Alatalo, Toimi | Nordic Skier |
| Albanese, Licia | Opera Singer |
| Alberty, Robert A | Chemist |
| Albrecht, Gerd | Conductor |
| Albrecht, Karl H | Businessman |
| Alcon, Alfredo F | Actor |
| Alexeyeva, Lidia V | Basketball Player, Coach |
| Allain, William A | Governor, MS |
| Allen, Keith (Bingo) | Ice Hockey Player |
| Allston, Aaron | Writer |
| Alter, Hobie, Jr | Surfboard, Boat Designer |
| Amos, Paul S | Businessman |
| Anderson, John, Jr | Governor, KS |
| Anderson, Mary | Actress |
| Anderson, Warren M | Businessman |
| Angelini, Fiorenzo Cardinal | Religious Leader |
| Angelou, Maya | Writer |
| Appell, David | Composer |
| Arp, Halton C | Astronomer |
| Asheton, Scott | Drummer (Stooges) |
| Ashley, Robert R | Composer |
| Askew, Reubin O | Governor, FL |
| Atiyeh, Victor | Governor, OR |
| Atli, Ismet | Freestyle Wrestler |
| Attenborough, Richard S | Actor, Director |
| Auth, W Anthony (Tony), Jr | Editorial Cartoonist |
| Avalos, Luis | Actor |
| Avery, James | Actor |
| Axel, Gabriel | Director, Actor, Writer |
| Bacall, Lauren | Actress |
| Bailey, Emmanuel McDonald | Track Athlete |
| Bain, Roderick (Rod) | WW II Army Hero |
| Bakenhaster, David L (Dave) | Baseball Player |
| Baker, Howard H, Jr | Senator, TN; Diplomat |
| Ballinger, Mark A | Baseball Player |
| Baltacha, Elena | Tennis Player |
| Banks, Chris | Football Player |
| Baraka, Imamu Amiri (LeRoi Jones) | Writer |
| Barbour, Ian G | Nuclear Physicist, Templeton Laureate |
| Bardon, John | Actor |
| Barmes, Bruce R | Baseball Player |
| Barnes, Marvin J | Basketball Player |
| Barry, Marion S, Jr | Mayor, Washington DC |
| Barsotti, Charles | Cartoonist |
| Bartusiak, Skye McCole | Actress |
| Bastedo, Alexandra | Actress |
| Battle, Lois | Writer |
| Beadle, Raymond | Auto Racing Driver |
| Beck, Marilyn M | Columnist |
| Becker, Gary S | Nobel Economics Laureate |
| Beecher, Franny | Guitarist (Bill Haley & His Comets) |
| Bella, John (Zeke) | Baseball Player |
| Belytschko, Ted B | Mechanical Engineer |
| Bendjelloul, Malik | Producer, Director, Actor |
| Beniades, Ted | Actor |
| Benn, Anthony N W (Tony) | Government Official, England |
| Bennis, Warren G | Educator, Writer |
| Benson, Vernon A (Vern) | Baseball Player, Manager |
| Berezovy, Anatoli N | Cosmonaut |
| Bergen, Polly | Actress |
| Berger, Thomas L | Writer |
| Bergonzi, Carlo | Opera Singer |
| Bertelmann, Fred | Singer, Guitarist |
| Bertucelli, Jean-Louis A | Director |
| Best, John O | Soccer Player, Coach |
| Bettenhausen, Gary | Auto Racing Driver |
| Big Bank Hank | Rap Artist (Sugarhill Gang) |
| Bigeldinov, Talgat Y | WW II Russian Air Force Hero |
| Bilk, Acker | Clarinetist, Composer |

| | |
|---|---|
| Biodrowski, Dennis J (Denny) | Football Player |
| Bironas, J Robert D (Rob) | Football Player |
| Birrer, Werner J (Babe) | Baseball Player |
| Black, Shirley Temple | Actress, Diplomat |
| Blair, William (Bill) | Baseball Player |
| Blocker, Herbert | Equestrian |
| Blumenfeld, Harold | Composer |
| Boedeker, William H (Bill) | Football Player |
| Boehmer, Konrad | Composer |
| Boeke, James F (Jim) | Football Player, Actor |
| Bole, Cliff | Director |
| Bolotnikov, Pyotr | Track Athlete |
| Bomboko, Justin Marie | Chairman, Congo Republic |
| Bonin, Gordie | Auto Racing Driver |
| Bonk, Gerd | Weightlifter |
| Boskov, Vujadin | Soccer Player |
| Bossi, Carmelo | Boxer |
| Botin, Emilio | Financier |
| Bourdy, Hubert | Equestrian |
| Bowie, Robert R | Educator, Government Official |
| Brabham, John A (Jack) | Auto Racing Driver |
| Bracken, Donald C (Don) | Football Player |
| Braden, Vic | Tennis Coach |
| Bradlee, Benjamin C | Editor |
| Brady, James S (Jim) | Government Official, Journalist |
| Bramlett, John C | Football Player |
| Branson, H Jesse | Basketball Player |
| Breaux, Marc | Choreographer, Director, Actor |
| Brenner, David | Actor, Comedian |
| Bridges, Alan J S | Director |
| Briloff, Abraham J | Educator |
| Brinkley, Joel G | Journalist |
| Brissie, Leland V (Lou) | Baseball Player |
| Broden, Connie | Ice Hockey Player |
| Bronfman, Edgar M, Jr | Businessman |
| Bronfman, Edgar M, Sr | Businessman |
| Brooks, Charlotte | Photojournalist |
| Brosnan, James P (Jim) | Baseball Player, Writer |
| Brough Clapp, A Louise | Tennis Player |
| Broughton, Jacksel M (Jack) | Vietnam War Air Force Hero |
| Browne, Sylvia C | Psychic |
| Bruce, Jack | Singer, Bassist (Cream), Songwriter |
| Bruggmann, Edmund | Alpine Skier |
| Bryan, Dora | Actress |
| Budd, Frank | Track, Football Player |
| Bull, Richard | Actor |
| Burgdorfer, Wilhelm (Willy) | Entomologist |
| Burgin, C David | Editor |
| Burney, Mike | Saxophonist (Wizzard) |
| Burns, James MacGregor | Political Scientist, Historian |
| Burns, Marilyn | Actress |
| Burri, Rene | Photographer |
| Butler, M Caldwell | Representative VA |
| Butterworth, Arthur E | Composer |
| Byrne, Jane M | Mayor, Chicago |
| Caesar, Sid | Actor, Comedian |
| Cahill, James F | Art Historian |
| Cain, Jackie | Singer (Jackie & Roy) |
| Calder, Nigel | Writer, Editor |
| Canfield, Mary Grace | Actress |
| Carter, John Mack | Editor |
| Carter, Rubin (Hurricane) | Boxer |
| Casale, Bob (Bob 2) | Guitarist, Keyboardist (Devo) |
| Cashen, J Frank | Baseball Executive |
| Cason, James A (Jim) | Football Player |
| Castleman, E Riva | Museum Executive |
| Cathy, S Truett | Businessman |
| Cavaiani, Jon R | Vietnam War Army Hero (CMH) |
| Ce, Marco Cardinal | Religious Leader |
| Cermeno, Antonio | Boxer |
| Chamberlin, Lee | Actress |
| Champlin, Charles D | Film Critic |
| Chapman, Leigh | Actress, Writer |
| Chataway, Christopher J (Chris) | Track Athlete |
| Chedwick, Porky | Disc Jockey |
| Chenchik, Taisia F | Track Athlete |
| Chopra, Ravi | Director, Producer |
| Christensen, Todd J | Football Player, Sportscaster |

| | |
|---|---|
| Chryssa | Sculptor |
| Cihocki, Albert J (Al) | Baseball Player |
| Clancy, Edward B Cardinal | Religious Leader |
| Clark, Melvin E (Mel) | Baseball Player |
| Clergue, Lucien | Photographer |
| Clerides, Glafkos J | President, Cyprus |
| Coachman Davis, Alice | Track Athlete |
| Cohen, Lynne | Photographer |
| Colchico, Daniel M (Dan) | Football Player |
| Coleman, Douglas | Molecular Geneticist |
| Coleman, Gerald F (Jerry) | Baseball Player, Manager |
| Colgan, Eileen | Actress |
| Colgate, Stirling A | Physicist |
| Collins, Damon J (Mo) | Football Player |
| Collins, Lewis | Actor |
| Conwell, Esther M | Physicist |
| Coogan, Richard | Actor |
| Cooke, Howard F H | Governor General, Jamaica |
| Cooper, Hal | Director |
| Cornforth, John W | Nobel Chemistry Laureate |
| Cornick, Glenn D B | Bassist (Jetro Tull) |
| Cosic, Dobrica | President, Yugoslavia |
| Cowles, Matthew | Actor |
| Craft, Paul | Singer, Songwriter |
| Crane, Philip M | Representative, IL |
| Crewe, S Robert (Bob) | Songwriter |
| Crouch, Paul | Evangelist |
| Dahl, Robert A | Political Scientist |
| Dailey, Janet | Writer |
| Daland, Peter | Swimming Coach |
| Dana, William H (Bill) | Test Pilot |
| Dark, Alvin R (Al) | Baseball Player, Manager |
| Davis, Ann B | Actress |
| Davis, Arvis W (A W) | Basketball Player |
| Davis, Dorothy Salisbury | Writer |
| Dawson, Charlotte | Actress |
| Dean, Joe | Basketball Player |
| DeCesaris, Andrea | Auto Racing Driver |
| Decker, Franz-Paul | Conductor |
| DeCrow, Karen | Social Activist |
| Dee, Ruby | Actress |
| Dehaene, Jean-Luc J M | Prime Minister, Belgium |
| DeHaven, Penny | Singer |
| DeLaRenta, Oscar | Fashion Designer |
| Delly, Emmanuel III Cardinal | Religious Leader |
| DeLucia, Paco | Jazz Guitarist |
| Denton, Jeremiah A, Jr | Senator, AL; WW II Navy Hero |
| DePaul, Lynsey | Singer, Songwriter |
| DeQuadros, Ciro | Epidemiologist |
| Derrick, Butler C, Jr | Representative, SC |
| DeVore, Irven | Anthropologist, Evolutionary Biologist |
| DeZordo, Nevio | Bobsled Athlete |
| Dhanapal, Guru | Director |
| Didion, John L | Football Player |
| Dierking, Conrad W (Connie) | Basketball Player |
| D'Inzeo, Piero | Equestrian |
| DiPierro, Ramon F | Football Player |
| DiStefano Lauthe, Alfredo | Soccer Player |
| Dixon, Alan J | Senator, IL |
| Doar, John | Attorney, Civil Rights Activist |
| Dockson, Robert R | Financier |
| Dodd, Dick | Singer, Drummer (Standells) |
| Dodd, Steve | Actor |
| Doi, Takako | Government Official, Japan |
| Dominis, John | Photographer |
| Donlavey, W C (Junie) | Auto Racing Owner |
| Dore, Edna | Actress |
| Dowdle, James C | Businessman |
| Drungo, Elbert J, Jr | Football Player |
| Dubinin, Yuri V | Government Official, Russia |
| Duccini, Ruth | Actress |
| Duff, Mickey | Boxing Manager |
| Dunfield, Peter | Figure Skater, Coach |
| Dunlap, Grant L | Baseball Player |
| Dunn, Charles W | Language Educator |
| Dupree, Lawrence W (Larry) | Football Player |
| Duvalier, Jean-Claude (Baby Doc) | President, Haiti |
| Dynkin, Eugene B | Mathematician |
| Dystel, Oscar | Publisher |
| Ebeid, Atef M | Prime Minister, Egypt |

| | |
|---|---|
| Ebron, Roy L | Basketball Player |
| Edelin, Kenneth C | Physician |
| Edelman, Gerald M | Nobel Medicine Laureate |
| Eder, Richard | Journalist |
| Edwards, Geoffry B O (Geoff) | Actor |
| Ehlers, Walter D | WW II Army Hero (CMH) |
| Eisenhower, John | Historian, Son of US President, General |
| Ellis, Jimmy | Boxer |
| Enke, Frederick W (Fred), Jr | Football Player |
| Erburu, Robert F | Publisher, Businessman |
| Etrog, Sorel | Artist |
| Eusebio | Soccer Player |
| Evans, John V | Governor, ID |
| Evans, Lane A | Representative, IL |
| Everly, Phil | Singer (Everly Brothers) |
| Farragut, Kenneth D (Ken), Jr | Football Player |
| Faure, Maurice H | Government Official, France |
| Faurer, Lincoln D | Air Force General |
| Fein, Rashi | Economist |
| Feinberg, Wilfred | Judge |
| Feldstein, Albert B (Al) | Editor |
| Felkai, Laszlo | Water Polo Player |
| Ferbos, Lionel | Jazz Trumpeter |
| Filarski-Steffes, Helen | Baseball Player |
| Filippini, Andre | Bobsled Athlete |
| Finkelstein, Edward S | Businessman |
| Finlay, Mervyn | Rowing Athlete |
| Fisher, Bernard F | Vietnam War Air Force Hero (CMH) |
| Flagg, Edith | Fashion Designer |
| Fleck, Jack | Golfer |
| Flicker, Theodore J | Writer, Director |
| Florin, Peter | Government Official, East Germany |
| Flory, Med | Actor, Saxophonist |
| Folsom, Allan R | Writer |
| Fong, Bobby | Educator |
| Fontaine, Joan | Actress |
| Ford, Eileen O | Businesswoman |
| Ford, William Clay, Sr | Businessman, Football Executive |
| Forman, Allen S (Al) | Baseball Umpire |
| Forsse, Ken | Inventor (Teddy Ruxpin), Animator |
| Fox, Raymond L (Ray) | Auto Racing Engineer |
| Fraser, Ian | Composer, Conductor |
| Freeman, J E | Actor |
| Freeman, Mona | Actress |
| Freeman, Robin R | Basketball Player |
| Freese, George W | Baseball Player |
| Fregosi, James L (Jim) | Baseball Player, Manager |
| Frelich, Phyllis | Actress |
| Frenzel, Bill | Representative, MN |
| Fruhbeck de Burgos, Rafael | Conductor |
| Frye, Richard N | Historian, Orientalist |
| Fuchsberger, Joachim | Actor |
| Furst, Philipp | Gymnast |
| Gabl, Franz | Alpine Skier |
| Gabler, William L (Gabe) | Baseball Player |
| Gagnon, J A Germain | Ice Hockey Player |
| Gallant, Mavis L | Writer |
| Gambucci, Sergio (Serge) | Ice Hockey Coach |
| Garcia Marquez, Gabriel | Nobel Literature Laureate |
| Gardner, Dale A | Astronaut |
| Garner, James | Actor |
| Gasienica-Gron, Franziszek | Nordic Combined Athlete |
| Gasnier, Reginald W (Reg) | Rugby Player |
| Gedovari, Imre | Fencer |
| Geissinger-Harding, Jean | Baseball Player |
| Gera, Zoltan | Actor |
| German, William | Editor |
| Ghiuselev, Nicola | Opera Singer |
| Gibbons, David | Prime Minister, Bermuda |
| Gideon, Louan | Actress |
| Gierasch, Stefan | Actor |
| Gilpin, Andy | Ice Hockey Player |
| Glazer, Malcolm | Football, Soccer Executive |
| Glimcher, Melvin J | Surgeon |
| Goffin, Gerry | Lyricist |
| Gola, Thomas J (Tom) | Basketball Player, Coach |
| Golan, Menahem | Director, Producer |
| Golan, Menahem | Producer, Director |
| Goldberg, Sarah D | Actress |
| Goldstein, Alvin (Al) | Publisher |

# NECROLOGY

| | |
|---|---|
| Gonsoulin, Austin W (Goose) | Football Player |
| Goodson, James A | WW II Army Air Corps Hero |
| Goossen, Dan | Boxing Promoter, Manager |
| Gordimer, Nadine | Nobel Literature Laureate |
| Gordon, Michael W (Mike) | Baseball Player |
| Gorrini, Luigi | WW II Italian Air Force Hero |
| Granatelli, Anthony (Andy) | Auto Racing Executive |
| Grant, Bob | Commentator |
| Grant, Robert M | Educator |
| Grant, Wallace D (Wally) | Ice Hockey Player |
| Gray, Kenneth J | Representative, IL |
| Gray, Robert K | Government Official |
| Grazia, Eugene (Gene) | Ice Hockey Player |
| Greenberg, Alan C | Financier |
| Gregory, Lyndam | Actor |
| Griffiths, Linda | Actress |
| Grigg, Ricky | Surfer |
| Grossman, Allen R | Writer |
| Grothendieck, Alexander | Mathematician |
| Guarino, Lawrence N | WW II, Korean, Vietnam Air Force Hero |
| Guarnere, William | WW II Army Hero |
| Guralnik, Gerald A | Physicist |
| Gut, Karel | Ice Hockey Player |
| Gwynn, Anthony K (Tony) | Baseball Player, Coach |
| Haden, Charles E (Charlie) | Jazz Bassist, Composer |
| Hall, James S (Jim) | Jazz Guitarist |
| Halmi, Robert, Sr | Producer |
| Halsey, Bradford A (Brad) | Baseball Player |
| Hamilton, Foreststorn (Chico) | Jazz Drummer |
| Hamilton, George, IV | Singer, Songwriter, Guitarist |
| Hanks, Eugene R | WW II Navy Air Force Hero |
| Hansberry, Lorraine | Writer |
| Hansen, Erik | Canoeing Athlete |
| Hansen, George V | Representative, ID |
| Hardwick, William B (Billy) | Bowler |
| Harrell, William (Billy) | Baseball Player |
| Hartsfield, Henry W (Hank), Jr | Astronaut |
| Hastings, Bob | Actor |
| Hauser, Tim | Singer (Manhattan Transfer) |
| Haverland, Charles H, Jr | WW II Navy Air Force Hero |
| Healy, Jeremiah | Writer |
| Heffron, Edward | WW II Army Hero |
| Hegan, J Michael (Mike) | Baseball Player |
| Heiberg, Elvin R, III | Army General |
| Heilmeier, George H | Inventor (Liquid Crystal Display) |
| Heisley, Michael E | Businessman, Basketball Executive |
| Hellwig, James B (Ultimate Warrior) | Wrestler |
| Henderson, Angelo B | Journalist |
| Henderson, Wayne (Trombone) | Jazz Trombonist |
| Henry, William R (Bill) | Baseball Player |
| Hensley, Cassandra Lynn | Model |
| Henson, John | Actor, Comedian, Puppeteer |
| Hergesheimer, Wally | Ice Hockey Player |
| Hernandez, Rodolfo P | Korean War Army Hero (CMH) |
| Hill, Craig | Actor |
| Hills, Roderick M | Businessman, Government Official |
| Hilsman, Roger | Diplomat |
| Hinners, Noel | Government Official |
| Hoffman, Philip Seymour | Actor |
| Hoffmann, Martin R | Government Official |
| Hogwood, Christopher J H | Concert Harpsichordist, Conductor |
| Holder, Geoffrey | Actor, Dancer |
| Hollander, Zander | Sportswriter |
| Hollein, Hans | Pritzker Architectural Laureate |
| Holloway, William J, Jr | Judge |
| Holt, John | Singer |
| Hooks, Jan | Actress, Comedienne |
| Hookstratten, Edward G | Attorney |
| Horn, Paul J | Jazz Flutist, Saxophonist |
| Hoskins, Bob | Actor |
| Houbregs, Robert J (Bob) | Basketball Player |
| Hudson, Louis C (Lou) | Basketball Player |
| Hughes, Wendy | Actress |
| Huizenga, John R | Nuclear Chemist |
| Hulme, Etta | Editorial Cartoonist |
| Humphrey, Donnie R | Football Player |
| Hunt, Nelson Bunker | Businessman |
| Hunter, Ronald | Actor |
| Hussein, Abdirizak Haji | Prime Minister, Somalia |
| Hutton, Brian G | Actor, Director |

| | |
|---|---|
| Hyer-Wallis, Martha | Actress |
| Iala, Kumba | President, Guinea-Bissau |
| Isenberg, Eugene M | Businessman |
| Jackson, Barry | Actor |
| Jacobs, Andrew, Jr | Representative, IN |
| Jamison, Jimmy W (Jimi) | Singer (Cobra, Survivor), Songwriter |
| Jancso, Miklos | Director, Writer |
| Janeway, Michael C | Editor, Educator, Writer |
| Jaruzelski, Wojciech | President, Poland; Army General |
| Jeffords, James M (Jim) | Senator, VT |
| Jeffries, Herbert (Herb) | Singer, Actor |
| Jemison, Theodore J | Religious Leader |
| Jobe, Frank W | Sports Orthopedic Surgeon |
| John, Gottfried | Actor |
| John-Roger | Religious Leader |
| Johns, Helen | Swimmer |
| Johns, Michael | Singer, Songwriter |
| Johnson, George (G G) | Golfer |
| Johnson, Lois | Singer |
| Johnson, Russell | Actor |
| Jolly, Alison B | Primatologist |
| Jones, Caldwell | Basketball Player |
| Jones, Christopher | Actor |
| Jones, Dick (Dickie) | Actor |
| Jones, Kenneth V (Ken) | Actor |
| Jones, Thomas V | Businessman |
| Jones, Wallace C (Wah-Wah) | Basketball Player |
| Kabbah, A Ahmad Tejan | President, Sierra Leone |
| Kajkl, Milan | Ice Hockey Player |
| Kalashnikov, Mikhail T | Weapon Designer (AK-47), General |
| Kaminsky, Arthur C | Sports Attorney |
| Kammen, Michael G | Historian |
| Kaplan, Justin | Writer |
| Karpov, Valeri Y | Ice Hockey Player |
| Karpow, Nikolai I | Ice Hockey Player |
| Kasem, Casey | Entertainer, Actor |
| Kasemets, Udo | Composer |
| Kasler, James H | Korean War Air Force Hero |
| Kaufman, Bel | Writer |
| Kavli, Fred | Foundation Executive |
| Kawabuchi, Tsutomu | Ice Hockey Player, Coach |
| Kean, Jane | Actress |
| Keating, Charles | Actor |
| Keefer, Don | Actor |
| Kellogg, Vivian | Baseball Player |
| Kelly, Sam | Actor |
| Kemper, R Crosby, Jr | Financier |
| Kennedy, Cornelia G | Judge |
| Kenney, Robert (Bob) | Basketball Player |
| Kent, Jean | Actress |
| Kerman, Joseph W | Musicologist, Critic |
| Ketner, Lari A | Basketball Player |
| Keyes, Daniel | Writer |
| Khan, Hashim | Squash Player |
| Kieber, Walter | Head of Government, Liechtenstein |
| Kiel, Richard | Actor |
| Kilar, Wojciech | Composer |
| Kiner, Ralph M | Baseball Player, Sportscaster |
| Kingston, Kenny | Astrologer |
| Kinnell, Galway | Writer |
| Kipnis, David M | Molecular Biologist |
| Kitchen, Lawrence O | Businessman |
| Kizer, Carolyn A | Writer |
| Klotz, H Louis (Red) | Basketball Player, Coach |
| Koffenberger, Edward L (Ed) | Basketball Player |
| Kolehmainen, Eero | Nordic Skier |
| Komarov, Aleksei F | Rowing Athlete |
| Korneyev, Andrei | Swimmer |
| Kornukov, Anatoly M | Air Force General, Russia |
| Kostetskiy, Victor | Actor |
| Kraft, Jack | Basketball Coach |
| Kraft, Leo A | Composer |
| Krasilnikov, Yevgeny | Volleyball Player |
| Kreamcheck, John | Football Player |
| Krebs, John H | Representative, CA |
| Kubasov, Valeri N | Cosmonaut |
| Kudukhov, Besik | Freestyle Wrestler |
| Kuhn, Harold W | Mathematician, Economist |
| Kumin, Maxine W | Writer |
| Kwolek, Stephanie L | Inventor (Kevlar) |

# NECROLOGY

Laborde, Alden J — Businessman
Lacey, Samuel (Sam) — Basketball Player
Laemmle, Carla — Actress
Lala, Joe — Singer, Percussionist (Blues Image)
Lang, Vaughan O — Army General
Lange, Jim — Entertainer
Laprade, Edgar — Ice Hockey Player
Larson, Charles R (Chuck) — Navy Admiral
Larson, Glen A — Producer, Writer, Singer
Lateef, Yusef — Jazz Saxophonist, Flutist, Composer
Laudonio, Abel R — Boxer
Laughlin, Thomas R (Tom) — Actor, Director
Lauricella, Francis E (Hank) — Football Player
Lautner, Georges C — Director
Lavric, Florica — Rowing Athlete
Lawrence, Barbara — Actress, Comedienne, Model
Lawson, Ricky — Drummer (Yellowjackets), Composer
Layton, Lester K (Les) — Baseball Player
Leduc, Noella Alverson — Baseball Player
Lee, Howard S (Howie) — Ice Hockey Player
Lee, Kurt Chew-Een — Korean War Marine Corps Hero
Leggett, Jay — Actor, Producer, Director
Leigh, Mitch — Composer
Lenhardt, Donald E (Don) — Baseball Player
Lennie, Angus — Actor
Leonard, Gloria — Actress, Director
Lessing, Doris M — Nobel Literature Laureate
Letts, Billie — Writer
Lewis, Peter B — Businessman
Lewis, Samuel W — Diplomat
Linden, Eric — Actor
Littleton, Harvey K — Sculptor
Lloyd-Pack, Roger — Actor
Loest, Erich — Writer
Lonnen, Ray — Actor
Lopopolo, Sandro — Boxer
Lord Infamous — Rap Artist (Three 6 Mafia)
Lorring, Joan — Actress
Lourdusamy, D Simon Cardinal — Religious Leader
Lucey, Patrick J — Governor, WI; Diplomat
Lueg, Werner — Track Athlete
Lumpe, Jerry D — Baseball Player
Lund, Donald A (Don) — Baseball Player
Lusinchi, Jaime — President, Venezuela
Lyubimov, Yuri P — Director, Actor
Maassab, Hunein (John) — Epidemiologist
Maazel, Lorin V — Conductor, Concert Violinist
MacKenzie, H Gordon (Gordy) — Baseball Player
MacLeod, Alistair — Writer
MacRae, Sheila — Actress, Singer
Madden, Dave — Actor, Comedian
Madison, Sara Danielle — Actress
Maestri Garcia, Hector A — Baseball Player
Magill, Dan — Tennis Coach
Magliozzi, Tom — Animator
Magruder, Jeb S — Government Official, Religious Leader
Mahdavi-Kani, Ayatollah Reza — Prime Minister, Iran
Malone, Nancy — Actress, Producer, Director
Mandela, Nelson R — President, South Africa; Nobel Laureate
Manigat, Leslie F — President, Haiti
Mankiewicz, Frank — Businessman
Mankin, Valentyn — Yachtsman
Mann, Johnny — Composer, Conductor, Arranger
Mann, Larry D — Actor
Manoukian, Donald J (Don) — Football Player
Mantyranta, Eero — Cross Country Skier
Marchisano, Francesco Cardinal — Religious Leader
Marentette, Leo J — Baseball Player
Marrero, Conrad E R (Connie) — Baseball Player
Marshall, Sarah — Actress
Martel, Arlene — Actress
Marth, Frank — Actor
Martin, Seth — Ice Hockey Player
Martinez, Jose A — Baseball Player
Masloff, Sophie — Mayor, Pittsburgh
Matassa, Cosimo — Music Producer
Matheson, Don — Actor
Mathews, Harlan — Senator, TN
Mathews, Sheila — Actress
Matlala, Jacob (Jake) — Boxer
Matthews, Francis — Actor

Matthiessen, Peter — Writer, Naturalist
Maxwell, Hamish — Businessman
Mayall, Rik — Actor, Comedian
Mayes, A Bernard D — Social Activist
Mazursky, Paul — Director
McCool, William J (Billy) — Baseball Player
McCormack, John — Boxer
McCormack, Michael J (Mike) — Football Player, Coach
McGill, Bill (Billy) — Basketball Player
McGinniss, Joe — Writer
McGinty, John J, III — Vietnam War Marine Corps Hero (CMH)
McGlothin, Ezra M (Pat) — Baseball Player
McGovern, Patrick J — Businessman
McIntyre, Kalaparush Maurice — Jazz Saxophonist
McKee, Kinnaird R — Navy Admiral
McKee, Rogers H — Baseball Player
McQuade, Arlene — Actress
Mendenhall, Murray J, Jr — Basketball Player
Menino, Thomas M — Mayor, Boston
Messner, Zbigniew — Prime Minister, Poland
Meyer, Don — Basketball Coach
Mikkelsen, A Verner A (Vern) — Basketball Player, Golfer
Miller, Denny — Actor
Miller, Drino — Off-Road Racing Auto Designer
Mischak, Robert M (Bob) — Football Player
Mitchell, Don — Actor
Mitchell, William R (Bill) — Ice Hockey Player
Mize, Ola L — Korean War Army Hero (CMH)
Mock, Geraldine F (Jerrie) — Aviatrix
Mohns, Douglas A (Doug) — Ice Hockey Player
Molinaro, Eduoard — Director, Writer
Molitor, Karl — Alpine Skier
Moore, Juanita — Actress
Moore, Kelvin O — Baseball Player
Morrall, Earl E — Football Player
Morris, Oswald (Ossie) — Cinematographer
Mortensen, Dale T — Nobel Economics Laureate
Mortier, Gerard — Director
Morton, Bruce A — Commentator
Mowat, Farley W — Writer, Naturalist
Muhammad, Idris — Jazz Drummer
Muhammad, Matthew Saad — Boxer
Mulaudzi, Mbulaeni — Track Athlete
Mulliken, William (Bill) — Swimmer
Mundy, Carl E, Jr — Marine Corps General
Munroe, George B — Basketball Player
Murphy, J J — Actor
Murphy, Rosemary — Actress
Murthy, V K — Cinematographer
Murvin, Junior — Singer
Musante, Tony — Actor
Musto, Raphael J (Ray) — Representative, PA
Myers, Walter Dean — Photographer
Nagel, Steven R — Astronaut
Nagy, Ivan — Ballet Dancer
Nanda — Actress
Naton, Peter A (Pete) — Baseball Player
Natowich, Andrew (Andy) — Football Player
Neidhardt, Elke — Actress
Nelson, Edwin S (Ed) — Actor
Nemeth, Angela — Track Athlete
Neugebauer, Gerry — Astrophysicist
Newhouse, Robert F — Football Player
Newman, Jimmy C — Singer, Songwriter
Ney, Edward N — Businessman, Diplomat
Nichols, Mike — Director, Comedian
Niedringhaus, Anja — Photojournalist
Nix, Dyron P — Basketball Player
Noll, Charles H (Chuck) — Football Player, Coach
Norment, Elizabeth L — Actress
Novak, Dezo — Soccer Player
Nugent, Robert — Religious Activist
Oberstar, James L (Jim) — Representative, MN
O'Brien, Edward J (Eddie) — Baseball Player
Ockels, Wubbo — Astronaut, Netherlands
Oliva, L Jay — Educator
Olivero, Magda — Opera Singer
O'Mara, Kate — Actress
Orbelyan, Konstantin A — Composer
Ordway, Frederick I, III — Writer
Orr, John M (Johnny) — Basketball Coach, Administrator

| | |
|---|---|
| Ortenberg, Arthur | Businessman |
| Ortolani, Riz | Composer |
| Osgood, Charles B (Charlie) | Baseball Player |
| O'Toole, Peter S | Actor |
| Ouedraogo, Gerard Kango | Prime Minister, Burkina Faso |
| Paisley, Ian R K | First Minister, Northern Ireland |
| Palagyi, Michael R (Mike) | Baseball Player |
| Pardo, Dominick G (Don) | Commentator |
| Paris, Joel B, III | WW II Army Air Corps Hero |
| Park, Barbara | Writer |
| Parker, Eleanor | Actress |
| Pate, Rupert G | Football Player |
| Paterson, Eric E | Ice Hockey Player |
| Patton, Melvin (Mel) | Track Athlete |
| Paul, Donald (Don) | Football Player |
| Paulus, Stephen H | Composer |
| Paxson, James E (Jim) | Basketball Player |
| Pena, Elizabeth | Actress |
| Perl, Martin L | Nobel Physics Laureate |
| Pesman, Jan S | Speed Skater |
| Petty, Lynda | Auto Racing Driver |
| Peyser, Peter A | Representative, NY |
| Piene, Otto | Sculptor, Artist |
| Pietrzykowski, Zbigniew | Boxer |
| Pike, Otis G | Representative, NY |
| Pinette, John | Actor, Comedian, Writer, Producer |
| Pittman, Joseph W (Joe) | Baseball Player |
| Podesta, Rossana | Actress |
| Pogue, William R | Astronaut |
| Polatou, Anna | Rhythmic Gymnast |
| Policarpo, Jose da Cruz Cardinal | Religious Leader |
| Pollack, William | Immunologist |
| Potts, Sean | Tin Whistle Player (Chieftains) |
| Powell, Charles E (Charley) | Football Player |
| Powell, R Leroy | Baseball Player |
| Power, David | Track Athlete |
| Price, Ray | Singer, Guitarist |
| Puckett, Allen E | Businessman |
| Quigley, Joan | Psychic, Astrologer |
| Rakoczy, Helena | Gymnast |
| Ramis, Harold A | Actor, Director, Writer |
| Ramone, Tommy | Drummer (Ramones) |
| Ramsay, John T (Jack) | Basketball Coach, Executive |
| Rebhorn, James | Actor |
| Redpath, Jean | Singer |
| Reed, Frank K | Singer (Chi-Lites) |
| Reidy, Gabrielle | Actress |
| Reitz, Donald L | Artist |
| Relman, Arnold S | Editor, Physician |
| Resnais, Alain | Director |
| Revere, Paul | Pianist (Paul Revere & the Raiders) |
| Reynolds, Albert | Prime Minister, Ireland |
| Reynolds, Anna | Opera Singer |
| Reynolds, Benny | Rodeo Rider |
| Rhett, Alicia | Actress |
| Ribicic, Mitja | Prime Minister, Yugoslavia |
| Rickenbacher, Karl Anton | Conductor |
| Rickershauser, Charles E, Jr | Businessman |
| Riddle, George | Singer, Songwriter, Actor |
| Riggans, Mary | Actress |
| Ripley, Allen S | Baseball Player |
| Risser, Paul G | Educator |
| Rivas, Candido Muatetema | Prime Minister, Equatorial Guinea |
| Rivers, Joan | Entertainer, Comedienne |
| Robinson, Arthur N R | Prime Minister, Trinidad & Tobago |
| Robinson, Earl J | Baseball Player |
| Robinson, Jeffrey M (Jeff) | Baseball Player |
| Rochereau, Tabu Ley | Singer, Songwriter |
| Rodrigue, George | Artist |
| Roe, Robert A | Representative, NJ |
| Rogers, F Michael | Air Force General, WW II Air Hero |
| Ronan, William J | Railway Engineer |
| Rooney, Mickey | Actor |
| Rosand, David | Art Historian |
| Rosenberg, William W | Actor |
| Ross, Donald R | Judge |
| Ross, Scott | Football Player |
| Rothmeier, Steven G | Businessman |
| Roukema, Margaret S | Representative, NJ |
| Roux, Jean-Louis | Director, Actor |
| Rowley, Janet D | Physician |

| | |
|---|---|
| Roy, Jean-Pierre | Baseball Player |
| Ruberto, John E (Sonny) | Baseball Player |
| Rubin, Louis D, Jr | Writer |
| Rudel, Julius | Conductor |
| Ruffin, Jimmy | Singer |
| Ruscio, Al | Actor |
| Ruskin, Joseph | Actor |
| Rutsala, Vern A | Writer |
| Ryan, Patricia | Editor |
| Safin, Rinnat I | Biathlete |
| Saliba, Metropolitan Primate Philip | Religious Leader |
| Samoilova, Tatiana Y | Actress |
| Sample, Joseph L (Joe) | Jazz Pianist |
| Sanders, Carl E | Governor, GA |
| Sanger, Frederick | Nobel Chemistry Laureate |
| Santos, Nilton | Soccer Player |
| Sata, Michael C | President, Zambia |
| Sax, Joseph L | Attorney, Educator |
| Saxton, James E (Jimmy) | Football Player |
| Scaife, Richard M | Businessman, Political Activist |
| Schaal, Richard | Actor |
| Schachter-Shalomi, Zalman | Religious Leader, Rabbi |
| Scheffler, Israel | Philosopher |
| Schell, Jonathan | Journalist |
| Schell, Maximilian | Actor |
| Schell, Paul | Mayor, Seattle |
| Schiffrin, Andre | Publisher |
| Schlesinger, James R | Secretary, Defense; Energy |
| Schlueter, Dale W | Basketball Player |
| Schmid, Rudolf | Luge Athlete |
| Schweigerdt, Gloria J | Baseball Player |
| Scorcio, Michael (Mike) | WW II Army Air Corps Hero |
| Scotchmer, Suzanne A | Economist |
| Scott, Charles R | Soccer Player, Coach |
| Scott, Jimmy | Singer |
| Scott, Larry | Body Builder |
| Sculthorpe, Peter J | Composer |
| Seeger, Pete | Singer, Banjoist, Songwriter |
| Seeman, Jerry | Football Referee |
| Sehgal, Zohra | Actress |
| Seigenthaler, John L | Publisher |
| Seldes, Marian | Actress |
| Serebrov, Alexander A | Cosmonaut |
| Sessler, Andrew | Theoretical Physicist |
| Shalom, Avraham | Security Official, Israel |
| Shane, Rita | Opera Singer |
| Shankar, Lakshmi | Singer |
| Sharon, Ariel | Prime Minister, Israel; Army General |
| Sharp, Kevin | Singer |
| Sharp, Richard L | Businessman |
| Shaw, Run Run | Producer |
| Shaw, Vernon L | President, Dominica |
| Shevardnadze, Eduard A | President, Georgia |
| Shigeta, James | Actor |
| Shinn, George L | Financier |
| Shirley-Quirk, John S | Opera Singer |
| Shrider, Richard G (Dick) | Basketball Player |
| Shuba, George T | Baseball Player |
| Shulgin, Alexander | Chemist |
| Silver, Horace | Jazz Pianist, Composer |
| Simmons, Harold C | Businessman |
| Simmons, Roy F | Football Player |
| Sinclair, Reginald (Reggie) | Ice Hockey Player |
| Sinden, Donald A | Actor |
| Slovak, Miraslav J (Mira) | Boat Racing Driver |
| Sluizer, George | Director |
| Smith, Arthur | Guitarist, Songwriter |
| Smith, Delford M (Del) | Businessman |
| Smith, Earl C | Baseball Player |
| Smith, Gregory White | Writer |
| Smith, H Russell | Businessman |
| Smith, Harold R (Hal) | Baseball Player |
| Smith, Mike | Golfer |
| Smith, Richard E (Dick) | Make-up Artist |
| Sneddon, Thomas W (Tom), Jr | Prosecutor |
| Snyder, Zilpha Keatley | Writer |
| Solh, Rashid el- | Prime Minister, Lebanon |
| Soltau, Gordon L (Gordy) | Football Player |
| Speakes, Larry M | Government Official; Journalist |
| Sprinkle, Edward A (Ed) | Football Player |
| Spoor, William H | Businessman |

## NECROLOGY

| | |
|---|---|
| St Germain, Fernand J | Representative, RI |
| Stardust, Alvin | Singer, Guitarist, Actor |
| Static, Wayne | Vocalist, Guitarist (Static-X), Actor |
| Staton, D Michael (Mick) | Representative, WV |
| Stein, Robert | Editor |
| Steiner, Donald F | Biochemist |
| Stepovich, Michael A (Mike) | Governor, Alaska Territory |
| Stewart, Mary | Writer |
| Still, Ray | Concert Oboist, Conductor |
| Stookey, S Donald | Chemist |
| Stowers, James E, Jr | Financier |
| Strassman, Marcia | Actress |
| Strauss, Robert S | Political Executive, Diplomat |
| Strider, Marjorie V | Artist, Sculptor |
| Stritch, Elaine | Singer, Actress |
| Suarez Gonzalez, Adolfo | Prime Minister, Spain |
| Sulaiman, Jose | Boxing Executive |
| Suomi, Al | Ice Hockey Player |
| Susa, Conrad | Composer |
| Susi, Carol Ann | Actress |
| Suter, Robert A (Rob) | Ice Hockey Player |
| Szoka, Edmund C Cardinal | Religious Leader |
| Szokolay, Sandor | Composer |
| Takahashi, Michiaki | Immunologist |
| Takakura, Ken | Actor |
| Taveras, Oscar F | Baseball Player |
| Taylor, A Starke, Jr | Mayor, Dallas |
| Taylor, Jackie Lynn | Actress |
| Taylor, Meshach | Actor |
| Teasdale, Joseph P | Governor, MO |
| Terruzzi, Ferdinando | Cyclist |
| Testi, Flavio | Composer |
| Thomas, Joab L | Educator |
| Thomas, Orlando P | Football Player |
| Thomas, Rodney D | Football Player |
| Thomas, William F (Bill) | Editor |
| Thompson, Bobby | Football Player |
| Thompson, James | Writer |
| Thompson, Richard F | Psychologist |
| Thompson, Wilbur (Moose) | Track Athlete |
| Thorne, Ken | Composer |
| Tiernan, Robert | Representative, RI |
| Tierney, Malcolm | Actor |
| Tihic, Sulejman | President, Bosnia-Herzegovina |
| Tikkanen, Aino-Maija | Actress |
| Tomlinson, Kenneth Y | Editor |
| Torok, Gyula | Boxer |
| Torre, Frank J | Baseball Player |
| Totter, Audrey | Actress |
| Traficant, James A, Jr | Representative, OH |
| Traynor, John (Jay) | Singer (Jay & the Americans) |
| Trottier, Guy A | Ice Hockey Player |
| Tullock, Gordon | Political Scientist, Economist |
| Turner, Morris (Morrie) | Cartoonist (Wee Pals) |
| Tyler, Dorothy Odam | Track Athlete |
| Udvari, Frank | Ice Hockey Referee |
| Ultra Violet | Actress, Model |
| Utley, Garrick | Commentator |
| Vachon, Maurice (Mad Dog) | Professional Wrestler |
| Vadnais, Carol | Ice Hockey Player |
| Vale, Jerry | Singer, Actor |
| Valentine, William N | Physician |
| Vandeweghe, Ernest E (Ernie) | Basketball Player, Physician |
| VanKirk, Theodore | WW II Army Air Corps Hero |
| VanWieren, Pete | Sportscaster |
| Vejvodova, Anna | Actress |
| Veryzer, Thomas M (Tom) | Baseball Player |
| Vest, Charles M | Educator |
| Vestal, David | Photographer |
| Vignelli, Massimo | Interior Designer |
| Villanueva, Anthony | Boxer |
| Waite, Ralph | Actor |
| Walker, John A | American Spy |
| Walker, Paul | Actor |
| Wallach, Eli | Actor |
| Walsh, Lawrence E | Government Official, Attorney |
| Walter, Jaroslav | Ice Hockey Player |
| Ward, Donald J (Don) | Ice Hockey Player |
| Watson, A J | Auto Racing Engineer |
| Waugh, John S | Chemist |
| Weidenbaum, Murray L | Government Official, Economist |

| | |
|---|---|
| Weiner, Art E | Football Player |
| Weiner, Michael | Baseball Executive, Labor Leader |
| Weis, Joseph F, Jr | Judge |
| Welch, Robert L (Bob) | Baseball Player |
| Werner, Jan | Track Athlete |
| Wheeler, Kenneth V J (Kenny) | Jazz Trumpeter |
| Whitlam, E Gough | Prime Minister, Australia |
| Wickham, Jeffry | Actor |
| Wilkes, Rodney | Weightlifter |
| Williams, Boswell | Governor General, Saint Lucia |
| Williams, Lynn R | Labor Leader |
| Williams, Robin | Actor, Comedian |
| Williams, Todd L | Football Player |
| Williamson, Kate | Actress |
| Willis, Gordon | Cinematographer |
| Wilson, Colin H | Writer |
| Wilson, Gerald S | Jazz Trumpeter, Composer |
| Wilson, Ralph C, Jr | Football Executive |
| Winchester, Jesse | Singer, Pianist, Songwriter |
| Winter, Johnny | Singer, Guitarist |
| Wirgowski, Dennis (Denny) | Football Player |
| Womack, Robert D (Bobby) | Singer, Guitarist, Songwriter |
| Woodhouse, William (Bill) | Track Athlete |
| Wortley, George C | Representative, NY |
| Wu Tianming | Director |
| Wymore, Patrice | Actress |
| Yeager, Bunny | Photographer, Model |
| Young, Mae | Professional Wrestler |
| Zacher, Gerd | Concert Organist, Composer |
| Zaentz, Saul | Producer |
| Zaffaroni, Alejandro C | Biochemist |
| Zambrano, Lorenzo H | Businessman |
| Zapata, Carmen | Actress |
| Zeckendorf, William, Jr | Businessman |
| Zeidel, Lazarus (Larry) | Ice Hockey Player |
| Zimbalist, Efrem, Jr | Actor |
| Zimmer, Donald W (Don) | Baseball Player, Manager |
| Zolotow, Charlotte | Writer |
| Zumino, Bruno | Theoretical Physicist |
| Zuverink, George | Baseball Player |
| Zweig, Stefanie | Writer |
| Zwerling, Darrell | Actor |

# UNITED STATES SENATE

The men and women below are current members of the US Senate. They can be reached by writing them in care of **US Senate, Washington, DC 20510.**

Letters should be addressed:

The Honorable Jane/John Doe
US Senator from _____

Salutations in letters should be:

Dear Mr/Ms Senator

| | | | |
|---|---|---|---|
| Alabama | Sessions, Jeferson B (Jeff), III | North Carolina | Tillis, Thomas R (Thom) |
| Alabama | Shelby, Richard C | North Dakota | Heitkamp, Mary K (Heidi) |
| Alaska | Murkowski, Lisa | North Dakota | Hoeven, John H, III |
| Alaska | Sullivan, Daniel A (Dan) | Ohio | Brown, Sherrod C |
| Arizona | Flake, Jeffry L (Jeff) | Ohio | Portman, Robert J (Rob) |
| Arizona | McCain, John S, III | Oklahoma | Inhofe, James M (Jim) |
| Arkansas | Boozman, John N | Oklahoma | Lankford, James P |
| Arkansas | Cotton, Thomas B (Tom) | Oregon | Merkley, Jeffrey A (Jeff) |
| California | Boxer, Barbara L | Oregon | Wyden, Ronald L (Ron) |
| California | Feinstein, Dianne G B | Pennsylvania | Casey, Robert P (Bob), Jr |
| Colorado | Bennet, Michael | Pennsylvania | Toomey, Patrick J (Pat) |
| Colorado | Gardener, Cory S | Rhode Island | Reed, John F (Jack) |
| Connecticut | Blumenthal, Richard M | Rhode Island | Whitehouse, Sheldon |
| Connecticut | Murphy, Christopher S (Chris) | North Dakota | Heitkamp, Mary K (Heidi) |
| Delaware | Carper, Thomas R. (Tom) | North Dakota | Hoeven, John H, III |
| Delaware | Coons, Christopher A (Chris) | Ohio | Brown, Sherrod C |
| Florida | Nelson, William (Bill) | Ohio | Portman, Robert J (Rob) |
| Florida | Rubio, Marco | Oklahoma | Inhofe, James M (Jim) |
| Georgia | Isakson, John H (Johnny) | Oklahoma | Lankford, James P |
| Georgia | Perdue, David A | Oregon | Merkley, Jeffrey A (Jeff) |
| Hawaii | Hirono, Mazie K | Oregon | Wyden, Ronald L (Ron) |
| Hawaii | Schatz, Brian E | Pennsylvania | Casey, Robert P (Bob), Jr |
| Idaho | Crapo, Michael D | Pennsylvania | Toomey, Patrick J (Pat) |
| Idaho | Risch, James E (Jim) | Rhode Island | Reed, John F (Jack) |
| Illinois | Durbin, Richard J (Dick) | Rhode Island | Whitehouse, Sheldon |
| Illinois | Kirk, Mark S | South Carolina | Graham, Linsey O |
| Indiana | Coats, Daniel R (Dan) | South Carolina | Scott, Timothy E (Tim) |
| Indiana | Donnelly, Joseph S (Joe), Sr | South Dakota | Rounds, Marion M (Mike) |
| Iowa | Ernst, Joni K | South Dakota | Thune, John, III |
| Iowa | Grassley, Charles E (Chuck) | Tennessee | Alexander, A Lamar |
| Kansas | Moran, Gerald W (Jerry) | Tennessee | Corker, Robert P (Bob), Jr |
| Kansas | Roberts, C Patrick (Pat) | Texas | Cornyn, John, III |
| Kentucky | McConnell, A Mitchell (Mitch), Jr | Texas | Cruz, R Edward (Ted) |
| Kentucky | Paul, Randall H (Rand) | Utah | Hatch, Orrin G |
| Louisiana | TBD | Utah | Lee, Michael S (Mike) |
| Louisiana | Vitter, David B | Vermont | Leahy, Patrick J |
| Maine | Collins, Susan M | Vermont | Sanders, Bernard (Bernie) |
| Maine | King, Angus S, Jr | Virginia | Kaine, Timothy M (Tim) |
| Maryland | Cardin, Benjamin L (Ben) | Virginia | Warner, Mark R |
| Maryland | Mikulski, Barbara A | Washington | Cantwell, Maria E |
| Massachusetts | Markey, Edward J | Washington | Murray, Patricia L (Patty) |
| Massachusetts | Warren, Elizabeth | West Virginia | Capito, Shelley W Moore |
| Michigan | Peters, Gary | West Virginia | Manchin, Joseph (Joe), III |
| Michigan | Stabenow, Deborah A (Debbie) | Wisconsin | Baldwin, Tammy S G |
| Minnesota | Franken, Al | Wisconsin | Johnson, Ron |
| Minnesota | Klobuchar, Amy J | Wyoming | Barrasso, John A |
| Mississippi | Cochran, W Thad | Wyoming | Enzi, Michael B (Mike) |
| Mississippi | Wicker, Roger F | | |
| Missouri | Blunt, Roy D | | |
| Missouri | McCaskill, Claire | | |
| Montana | Danes, Steven D (Steve) | | |
| Montana | Tester, Jon | | |
| Nebraska | Fischer, Debra S (Deb) | | |
| Nebraska | Sasse, Benjamin E (Ben) | | |
| Nevada | Heller, Dean | | |
| Nevada | Reid, Harry M | | |
| New Hampshire | Ayotte, Kelly A | | |
| New Hampshire | Shaheen, Jeanne | | |
| New Jersey | Booker, Cory A | | |
| New Jersey | Menendez, Robert (Bob) | | |
| New Mexico | Heinrich, Martin T | | |
| New Mexico | Udall, Thomas S (Tom) | | |
| New York | Gillibrand, Kirsten E R | | |
| New York | Schumer, Charles E (Chuck) | | |
| North Carolina | Burr, Richard M | | |

# UNITED STATES HOUSE OF REPRESENTATIVES

The men and women below are current members of the US House of Representatives. They can be reached by writing them in care of **US House of Representatives, Washington, DC 20515**.

Letters should be addressed:

The Honorable Jane/John Doe
US Representative from _____

Salutations in letters should be:

Dear Mr/Ms Representative _____

| | | | |
|---|---|---|---|
| Alabama | Aderholt, Robert B | California | Sherman, Bradley J (Brad) |
| Alabama | Byrne, Bradley | California | Speier, Karen L (Jackie) |
| Alabama | Brooks, Morris J (Mo) | California | Swalwell, Eric, Jr |
| Alabama | Roby, Martha | California | Takano, Mark A |
| Alabama | Rogers, Michael D (Mike) | California | Thompson, Michael C (Mike) |
| Alabama | Sewell, Terri | California | Torres, Norma J |
| Alabama | Palmer, Gary | California | Valadao, David |
| Alaska | Young, Donald E (Don) | California | Vargas, Juan C |
| American Samoa | Amata, Aumua | California | Walters, Marian K (Mimi) |
| Arkansas | Crawford, Rick | California | Waters, Maxine C |
| Arkansas | Hill, French | Colorado | Buck, Kenneth R (Ken) |
| Arkansas | Westerman, Bruce E | Colorado | Coffman, Michael |
| Arkansas | Womack, Stephen A (Steve) | Colorado | DeGette, Diana L |
| Arizona | TBD | Colorado | Lamborn, Doug |
| Arizona | Franks, Trent | Colorado | Perlmutter, Edwin G (Ed) |
| Arizona | Gallego, Ruben | Colorado | Polis, Jared S (Jare) |
| Arizona | Gosar, Paul | Colorado | Tipton, Scott R |
| Arizona | Grijalva, Raul M | Connecticut | Courtney, Joseph (Joe) |
| Arizona | Kirkpatrick, Ann | Connecticut | DeLauro, Rosa L |
| Arizona | Salmon, Matthew J (Matt) | Connecticut | Esty, Elizabeth H |
| Arizona | Schweikert, David | Connecticut | Himes, James A (Jim) |
| Arizona | Sinema, Kyrsten | Connecticut | Larson, John B |
| California | TBD | Delaware | Carney, John C, Jr |
| California | TBD | District/Columbia | Norton, Eleanor Holmes |
| California | Aguilar, Peter R (Pete) | Florida | Bilirakis, Gus M |
| California | Bass, Karen | Florida | Brown, Corrine |
| California | Becerra, Xavier | Florida | Buchanan, Vernon G (Vern) |
| California | Brownley, Julia | Florida | Castor, Katherine A (Kathy) |
| California | Calvert, Kenneth S (Ken) | Florida | Clawson, Curtis J (Curt) |
| California | Capps, Lois G | Florida | Crenshaw, Ander |
| California | Cardenas, Tony | Florida | Curbelo, Carlos |
| California | Chu, Judy | Florida | DeSantis, Ron |
| California | Cook, Paul | Florida | Deutch, Theodore (Ted) |
| California | Davis, Susan A | Florida | Diaz-Balart, Mario R |
| California | Denham, Jeffrey (Jeff) | Florida | Frankel, Lois J |
| California | DeSaulnier, Mark J | Florida | Graham, Gwen |
| California | Eshoo, Anna G | Florida | Grayson, Alan M |
| California | Farr, Samuel S (Sam) | Florida | Hastings, Alcee L |
| California | Garamendi, John | Florida | Jolly, David W |
| California | Hahn, Janice | Florida | Mica, John L |
| California | Honda, Michael M (Mike) | Florida | Miller, Jefferson B (Jeff) |
| California | Huffman, Jared | Florida | Murphy, Patrick E |
| California | Hunter, Duncan D | Florida | Nugent, Richard B |
| California | Issa, Darrell E | Florida | Posey, William (Bill) |
| California | Knight, Stephen (Steve) | Florida | Rooney, Thomas J (Tom) |
| California | LaMalfa, Doug | Florida | Ros-Lehtinen, Ileana |
| California | Lee, Barbara J | Florida | Ross, Dennis B |
| California | Lieu, Ted W | Florida | Wasserman Schultz, Debbie |
| California | Lofgren, Sue (Zoe) | Florida | Webster, Daniel |
| California | Lowenthal, Alan S | Florida | Wilson, Frederica |
| California | Matsui, Doris O | Florida | Yoho, Theodore S (Ted) |
| California | McCarthy, Kevin | Georgia | Allen, Richard J C (Rick) |
| California | McClintock, Thomas M (Tom) | Georgia | Bishop, Sanford D, Jr |
| California | McNearey, Jerry | Georgia | Carter, Earl L (Buddy) |
| California | Napolitano, Grace F | Georgia | Collins, Doug |
| California | Nunes, Devin | Georgia | Graves, J Thomas (Tom) |
| California | Pelosi, Nancy P D | Georgia | Hice, Jody |
| California | Peters, Scott H | Georgia | Johnson, Henry (Hank), Jr |
| California | Rohrabacher, Dana | Georgia | Lewis, John R |
| California | Roybal-Allard, Lucille | Georgia | Loudermilk, Barry D |
| California | Royce, Edward R (Ed) | Georgia | Price, Thomas E (Tom) |
| California | Ruiz, Raul | Georgia | Scott, David A |
| California | Sanchez, Linda T | Georgia | Scott, J Austin |
| California | Sanchez, Loretta | Georgia | Westmoreland, Lynn A |
| California | Schiff, Adam B | | |

# UNITED STATES HOUSE OF REPRESENTATIVES

| | | | |
|---|---|---|---|
| Georgia | Woodall, Robert (Rob) | Massachusetts | Tsongas, Nicola S (Niki) |
| Guam | Bordallo, Madeleine | Michigan | Amash, Justin |
| Hawaii | Gabbard, Tulsi | Michigan | Benishek, Daniel J (Dan) |
| Hawaii | Takai, Mark | Michigan | Bishop, Michael D (Mike) |
| Idaho | Labrador, Raul R | Michigan | Conyers, John, Jr |
| Idaho | Simpson, Michael K (Mike) | Michigan | Dingell, Deborah I |
| Illinois | Bost, Mike | Michigan | Huizenga, William P (Bill) |
| Illinois | Callahan-Bustos, Cheryl L (Cheri) | Michigan | Kildee, Daniel T (Dan) |
| Illinois | Davis, Daniel K (Danny) | Michigan | Lawrence, Brenda L |
| Illinois | Davis, Rodney L | Michigan | Levin, Sander M |
| Illinois | Dold, Robert J (Bob) | Michigan | Miller, Candice S |
| Illinois | Duckworth, L Tammy | Michigan | Moolenaar, John |
| Illinois | Foster, G William (Bill) | Michigan | Trott, David (Dave) |
| Illinois | Gutierrez, Luis V | Michigan | Upton, Frederick S (Fred) |
| Illinois | Hultgren, Randall M (Randy) | Michigan | Walberg, Timothy L (Tim) |
| Illinois | Kelly, Robin L | Minnesota | Emmer, Thomas E (Tom) |
| Illinois | Kinzinger, Adam A | Minnesota | Ellison, Keith M |
| Illinois | Lipinski, Daniel W (Dan) | Minnesota | Kline, John P |
| Illinois | Quigley, Michael (Mike) | Minnesota | McCollum, Betty L |
| Illinois | Roskam, Peter J | Minnesota | Nolan, Richard M (Rick) |
| Illinois | Rush, Bobby L | Minnesota | Paulsen, Erik |
| Illinois | Schakowsky, Janice D (Jan) | Minnesota | Peterson, Collin C |
| Illinois | Schock, Aaron | Minnesota | Walz, Timothy J (Tim) |
| Illinois | Shimkus, John M | Mississippi | Harper, Gregg |
| Indiana | Brooks, Susan W | Mississippi | Nunnelee, P Alan |
| Indiana | Bucshon, Larry D | Mississippi | Palazzo, Steven M |
| Indiana | Carson, Andre D | Mississippi | Thompson, Bennie G |
| Indiana | Messer, A Lucas (Luke) | Missouri | Clay, William L (Lacy), Jr |
| Indiana | Rokita, Theodore E (Todd) | Missouri | Cleaver, Emanuel, II |
| Indiana | Stutzman, Marlin A | Missouri | Graves, Samuel B (Sam) |
| Indiana | Visclosky, Peter J | Missouri | Hartzler, Vicky J |
| Indiana | Walorski, Jackie | Missouri | Long, William H (Billy) |
| Indiana | Young, Todd C | Missouri | Luetkemeyer, Blaine |
| Iowa | Blum, Rod | Missouri | Smith, Jason T |
| Iowa | King, Steven A (Steve) | Missouri | Wagner, Ann |
| Iowa | Loebsack, David | Montana | Zinke, Ryan |
| Iowa | Young, David | Nebraska | Ashford, Brad |
| Kansas | Huelskamp, Timothy A (Tim) | Nebraska | Fortenberry, Jeffrey L (Jeff) |
| Kansas | Jenkins, Lynn | Nebraska | Smith, Adrian M |
| Kansas | Pompeo, Michael R (Mike) | Nevada | Amodei, Mark E |
| Kansas | Yoder, Kevin | Nevada | Hardy, Cresent L |
| Kentucky | Barr, Garland H (Andy) | Nevada | Heck, Joseph J (Joe) |
| Kentucky | Guthrie, Steven B (Brett) | Nevada | Titus, Alice C (Dina) |
| Kentucky | Massie, Thomas H | New Hampshire | Guinta, Frank |
| Kentucky | Rogers, Harold D (Hal) | New Hampshire | McLane Kuster, Ann (Annie) |
| Kentucky | Whitfield, Edward (Ed) | New Jersey | Coleman, Bonnie Watson |
| Kentucky | Yarmuth, John | New Jersey | Frelinghuysen, Rodney P |
| Louisiana | TBD | New Jersey | Garrett, E Scott |
| Louisiana | TBD | New Jersey | Lance, Leonard |
| Louisiana | Boustany, Charles V, Jr | New Jersey | LoBiondo, Frank A |
| Louisiana | Fleming, John | New Jersey | MacArthur, Thomas (Tom) |
| Louisiana | Richmond, Cedric L | New Jersey | Norcross, Donald W |
| Louisiana | Scalise, Stephen J (Steve) | New Jersey | Pallone, Frank, Jr |
| Maine | Pingree, Chellie M | New Jersey | Pascrell, William J (Bill), Jr |
| Maine | Poliquin, Bruce | New Jersey | Payne, Donald M |
| Maryland | Delaney, John K | New Jersey | Sires, Albio |
| Maryland | Cummings, Elijah E | New Jersey | Smith, Christopher H (Chris) |
| Maryland | Edwards, Donna F | New Mexico | Lujan, Ben R, Jr |
| Maryland | Harris, Andrew P (Andy) | New Mexico | Lujan Grisham, Michelle |
| Maryland | Hoyer, Steny H | New Mexico | Pearce, Stevan E (Steve) |
| Maryland | Ruppersberger, C A (Dutch) | New York | Clarke, Yvette D |
| Maryland | Sarbanes, John P S | New York | Collins, Christopher C (Chris) |
| Maryland | Van Hollen, Chris | New York | Crowley, Joseph |
| Massachusetts | Capuano, Michael E (Mike) | New York | Engel, Eliot L |
| Massachusetts | Clark, Katherine | New York | Gibson, Christopher P (Chris) |
| Massachusetts | Keating, William R (Bill) | New York | Grimm, Michael (Mike) |
| Massachusetts | Kennedy, Joseph P (Joe), III | New York | Hanna, Richard |
| Massachusetts | Lynch, Stephen F | New York | Higgins, Brian |
| Massachusetts | McGovern, James P (Jim) | New York | Israel, Steve |
| Massachusetts | Moulton, Seth | New York | Jeffries, Hakeem S |
| Massachusetts | Neal, Richard E | New York | Katko, John M |

| State | Name | State | Name |
| --- | --- | --- | --- |
| New York | King, Peter T | Pennsylvania | Pitts, Joseph R (Joe) |
| New York | Lowey, Nita M | Pennsylvania | Rothfus, Keith J |
| New York | Maloney, Carolyn B | Pennsylvania | Shuster, William (Bill) |
| New York | Maloney, Sean P | Pennsylvania | Thompson, Glenn |
| New York | Meeks, Gregory W | Puerto Rico | Pierluisi, Pedro |
| New York | Meng, Grace | Rhode Island | Cicilline, David N |
| New York | Nadler, Jerrold L (Jerry) | Rhode Island | Langevin, James R |
| New York | Rangel, Charles B | South Carolina | Clyburn, James E (Jim) |
| New York | Reed, Thomas | South Carolina | Duncan, Jeffrey D (Jeff) |
| New York | Rice, Kathleen M | South Carolina | Gowdy, Howard W (Trey), III |
| New York | Serrano, José E | South Carolina | Mulvaney, John M (Mick) |
| New York | Slaughter, Louise M | South Carolina | Rice, Hugh T (Tom) |
| New York | Stefanik, Elise M | South Carolina | Sanford, Mark |
| New York | Tonko, Paul D | South Carolina | Wilson, Addison G (Joe), Sr |
| New York | Velazquez, Nydia M | South Dakota | Noem, Kristi L A |
| New York | Zeldin, Lee M | Tennessee | Black, Diane L |
| North Carolina | Adams, Alma S | Tennessee | Blackburn, Marsha |
| North Carolina | Butterfield, George K (G K), Jr | Tennessee | Cohen, Stephen J (Steve) |
| North Carolina | Ellmers, Renee J | Tennessee | Cooper, James H S (Jim) |
| North Carolina | Foxx, Virginia A | Tennessee | DesJarlais, Scott E |
| North Carolina | Holding, George E B | Tennessee | Duncan, John J (Jimmy), Jr |
| North Carolina | Hudson, Richard | Tennessee | Fincher, Stephen |
| North Carolina | Jones, Walter B, Jr | Tennessee | Fleischmann, Charles J (Chuck) |
| North Carolina | McHenry, Patrick T | Tennessee | Roe, David P (Phil) |
| North Carolina | Meadows, Mark R | Texas | Babin, Brian |
| North Carolina | Pittenger, Robert | Texas | Barton, Joseph L (Joe) |
| North Carolina | Price, David E | Texas | Brady, Kevin P |
| North Carolina | Rouzer, David | Texas | Burgess, Michael C |
| North Carolina | Walker, Bradley M (Mark) | Texas | Carter, John R |
| North Dakota | Cramer, Kevin | Texas | Castro, Joaquin |
| North Mariana Islands | Sablan, Gregorio K C | Texas | Conaway, Michael K (Mike) |
| Ohio | Beatty, Joyce | Texas | Cuellar, Henry R |
| Ohio | Boehner, John A | Texas | Culberson, John A |
| Ohio | Chabot, Steven J (Steve) | Texas | Doggett, Lloyd A, II |
| Ohio | Fudge, Marcia L | Texas | Farenthold, R Blake |
| Ohio | Gibbs, Robert B (Bob) | Texas | Flores, William H (Bill) |
| Ohio | Johnson, William L (Bill) | Texas | Gohmert, Louis B (Louie), Jr |
| Ohio | Jordan, James D (Jim) | Texas | Granger, Kay |
| Ohio | Joyce, David P | Texas | Green, Alexander N (Al) |
| Ohio | Kaptur, Marcia C (Marcy) | Texas | Green, R Eugene (Gene) |
| Ohio | Latta, Robert E (Bob) | Texas | Hensarling, Jeb |
| Ohio | Renacci, James B (Jim) | Texas | Hinojosa, Ruben E |
| Ohio | Ryan, Timothy J (Tim) | Texas | Hurd, William B (Will) |
| Ohio | Stivers, Stephen E (Steve) | Texas | Jackson-Lee, Sheila |
| Ohio | Tiberi, Patrick J (Pat) | Texas | Johnson, Eddie Bernice |
| Ohio | Turner, Michael R (Mike) | Texas | Johnson, Samuel R (Sam) |
| Ohio | Wenstrup, Brad | Texas | Marchant, Kenneth (Kenny) |
| Oklahoma | Bridenstine, James F (Jim) | Texas | McCaul, Michael T (Mike) |
| Oklahoma | Cole, Thomas J (Tom) | Texas | Neugebauer, R Randolph (Randy) |
| Oklahoma | Lucas, Frank D | Texas | O'Rourke, Robert F (Beto) |
| Oklahoma | Mullin, Markwayne | Texas | Olson, Peter G (Pete) |
| Oklahoma | Russell, Steven M (Steve) | Texas | Poe, Lloyd (Ted) |
| Oregon | Blumenauer, Earl | Texas | Ratcliffe, John L |
| Oregon | Bonamici, Suzanne | Texas | Sessions, Peter A (Pete) |
| Oregon | DeFazio, Peter A (Pete) | Texas | Smith, Lamar S |
| Oregon | Schrader, Kurt | Texas | Thornberry, William M (Mac) |
| Oregon | Walden, Gregory (Greg) | Texas | Veasey, Marc |
| Pennsylvania | Barletta, Louis J (Lou) | Texas | Vela, Filemon B, Jr |
| Pennsylvania | Boyle, Brendan F | Texas | Weber, Randy |
| Pennsylvania | Brady, Robert A (Bob) | Texas | Williams, J Roger |
| Pennsylvania | Cartwright, Matthew A (Matt) | Utah | Bishop, Robert W (Rob) |
| Pennsylvania | Costello, Ryan A | Utah | Chaffetz, Jason |
| Pennsylvania | Dent, Charles W (Charlie) | Utah | Love, Ludmya B (Mia) |
| Pennsylvania | Doyle, Michael F (Mike) | Utah | Stewart, Christopher D (Chris) |
| Pennsylvania | Fattah, Chaka | Vermont | Welch, Peter F |
| Pennsylvania | Fitzpatrick, Michael G (Mike) | Virgin Islands | Plaskett, Stacey |
| Pennsylvania | Kelly, Michael (Mike) | Virgina | Beyer, Donald S (Don), Jr |
| Pennsylvania | Marino, A Thomas (Tom) | Virginia | Brat, David A (Dave) |
| Pennsylvania | Meehan, Patrick L (Pat) | Virginia | Cantor, Eric I |
| Pennsylvania | Murphy, Timothy F (Tim) | Virigina | Comstock, Barbara J |
| Pennsylvania | Perry, Scott G | Virginia | Connolly, Gerald E |

## UNITED STATES HOUSE OF REPRESENTATIVES

| | | | |
|---|---|---|---|
| Virginia | Forbes, James R (Randy) | Washington | Reichert, David G (Dave) |
| Virginia | Goodlatte, Robert W (Bob) | Washington | Smith, D Adam |
| Virginia | Griffith, H Morgan | West Virginia | Jenkins, Evan H |
| Virginia | Hurt, Robert | West Virginia | McKinley, David |
| Viriginia | Rigell, E Scott | West Virginia | Mooney, Alex X |
| Virginia | Scott, Robert C (Bobby) | Wisconsin | Duffy, Sean P |
| Washington | DelBene, Suzan K | Wisconsin | Kind, Ronald J (Ron) |
| Washington | Heck, Dennis (Denny) | Wisconsin | Moore, Gwendolynne S (Gwen) |
| Washington | Herrera Beutler, Jaime | Wisconsin | Grothman, Glenn |
| Washington | Kilmer, Derek | Wisconsin | Pocan, Mark |
| Washington | Larsen, Richard R (Rick) | Wisconsin | Ribble, Reid J |
| Washington | McDermott, James A (Jim) | Wisconsin | Ryan, Paul D, Jr |
| Washington | McMorris Rogers, Cathy | Wisconsin | Sensenbrenner, F James, Jr (Jim) |
| Washington | Newhouse, Daniel (Dan) | Wyoming | Lummis, Cynthia |

## UNITED STATES GOVERNORS

The men and women below are current US Governors. They can be reached by writing them in care of **Governor's Office** at the addresses listed below.

Letters should be addressed:

The Honorable Jane/John Doe
Governor from _____

Salutations in letters should be:

Dear Mr/Ms Governor _____

| | | |
|---|---|---|
| Alabama | Bentley, Robert J | State Capitol, 600 Dexter Ave, Montgomery AL 36130, USA |
| Alaska | Walker, William M (Bill) | State Capitol Building, PO Box 110001, Juneau AK 99811, USA |
| American Samoa | Moliga Lolo M | Executive Office Building, #300, Utulei, Pago Pago, AS 96799 |
| Arizona | Duce, Doug | State Capitol, 1700 W Washington St, Phoenix AZ 85007, USA |
| Arkansas | Hutchinson, William A (Asa) | State Capitol, #250, Little Rock AR 72201, USA |
| California | Brown, Edmund G (Jerry) | State Capital, #100, Sacramento CA 95814, USA |
| Colorado | Hickenlooper, John W | 136 State Capitol, Denver CO 80203, USA |
| Connecticut | Malloy, Dan | State Capitol, 210 Capitol Ave, Hartford CT 06106, USA |
| Delaware | Markell, Jack A | Legislative Hall, Dover DE 19902, USA |
| Florida | Scott, Richard L (Rick) | PL 05 The Capitol, 400 S Monroe St, Tallahassee FL 32399, USA |
| Georgia | Deal, John N (Nathan) | State Capitol, #203, Atlanta GA 30334, USA |
| Guam | Calvo, Eddie Baza | Executive Chamber, PO Box 2950, Agana, GU 96932 |
| Hawaii | Ing, David Y | Executive Chambers, #500, Honolulu HI 96813, USA |
| Idaho | Otter, C L (Butch) | State Capitol, 700 W Jefferson, #200, Boise ID 83702, USA |
| Illinois | Rauner, Bruce V | State House, 207 Statehouse, Springfield IL 62706, USA |
| Indiana | Pence, Michael R (Mike) | State House, #206, Indianapolis IN 46204, USA |
| Iowa | Brandstad, Terry E | State Capitol, Des Moines IA 50319, USA |
| Kansas | Brownback, Samuel D (Sam) | Capitol, 300 SW 10th Ave, #212S, Topeka KS 66612, USA |
| Kentucky | Beshear, Steven L (Steve) | State Capitol, 700 Capitol Ave, #100, Frankfort KY 40601, USA |
| Louisiana | Jindal, Piyosh (Bobby) | State Capitol, PO Box 94004, Baton Rouge LA 70804, USA |
| Maine | LePage, Paul R | Blaine House, 1 State House Station, Augusta ME 04333, USA |
| Maryland | Hogan, Lawrence J (Larry), Jr | State House, 100 State Circle, Annapolis MD 21401, USA |
| Massachusetts | Baker, Charles D (Charlie) | State House, #360, Boston MA 02133, USA |
| Michigan | Snyder, Richard D (Rick) | State Capitol, PO Box 30013, Lansing MI 48909, USA |
| Minnesota | Dayton, Mark B | 130 State Capitol, 75 Rev Dr MLK Jr Blvd, Saint Paul MN 55155, USA |
| Mississippi | Bryant, D Phillip (Phil) | State Capitol, PO Box 139, Jackson MS 39205, USA |
| Missouri | Nixon, Jeremiah W (Jay) | State Capitol, #218, PO Box 720, Jefferson City MO 65102, USA |
| Montana | Bullock, Steve | State Capitol, PO Box 0801, Helena MT 59620, USA |
| Nebraska | Ricketts, John P (Pete) | State Capitol, PO Box 94848, Lincoln NE 68509, USA |
| Nevada | Sandoval, Brian E | State Capitol, 101 N Carson St, Carson City NV 89701, USA |
| New Hampshire | Hassan, Maggie | 25 Capitol St, #212, Concord NH 03301, USA |
| New Jersey | Christie, Chris | State House, 125 W State St, PO Box 001, Trenton NJ 08625, USA |
| New Mexico | Martinez, Susana | State Capitol, #400, Santa Fe NM 87300, USA |
| New York | Cuomo, Andrew | State Capitol, Albany NY 12224, USA |
| North Carolina | McCrory, Patrick L (Pat) | State Capitol, 20301 Mail Service Center, Raleigh NC 27699, USA |
| North Dakota | Dalrymple, John (Jack) | State Capitol, 600 E Boulevard Ave, #101, Bismarck ND 58505, USA |
| Northern Marianas | TBD | Governor's Office, Caller Box 10007, Saipan, MP 96950 |
| Ohio | Kasich, John R | State House, 77 S High St, #3000, Columbus OH 43215, USA |
| Oklahoma | Fallin, Mary | State Capitol, 2300 N Lincoln Blvd, #212, Oklahoma City OK 73105, USA |
| Oregon | Kitzhaber, John A | State Capitol, 900 Court St, #160, Salem OR 97301, USA |
| Pennsylvania | Wolf, Thomas W (Tom) | Main Capitol, #225, Harrisburg PA 17120, USA |
| Puerto Rico | Garcia Padilla, Alejandro J | La Fortaleza, PO Box 9020082, San Juan, PR 00902 |
| Rhode Island | Raimondo, Gina M | State House, Providence RI 02903, USA |
| South Carolina | Haley, Nimrata R (Nikki) | State Capitol, PO Box 11829, Columbia SC 29211, USA |
| South Dakota | Daugaard, Dennis M | State Capitol, 500 E Capitol Ave Pierre, SD 57501, USA |
| Tennessee | Haslam, William E (Bill) | State Capitol, Nashville TN 37243, USA |
| Texas | Abbott, Gregory W (Greg) | State Capitol, PO Box 12428, Austin TX 78711, USA |
| Utah | Herbert, Gary R | State Capitol, #200, Salt Lake City UT 84114, USA |
| Vermont | Shumlin, Peter S | Pavilion Building, 109 State St, Montpelier VT 05609, USA |

## UNITED STATES GOVERNORS

| Virginia | McDonnell, Robert F (Bob) | State Capitol, #300, Richmond VA 23219, USA |
| Virgin Islands | TBD | Gov't House, 21-22 Kongens Gade, Charlotte Amalie, St. Thomas, VI 00802 |
| Washington | Inselee, Jay R | State Capitol, PO Box 40002, Olympia WA 98504, USA |
| West Virginia | Tomblin, Earl R | 1900 Kanawha St, Charleston WV 25305, USA |
| Wisconsin | Walker, Scott K | 115 E State Capitol, Madison WI 53707, USA |
| Wyoming | Mead, Matthew H (Matt) | State Capitol, #124, Cheyenne WY 82002, USA |

## AGENCY ADDRESSES

| 42 West | 11400 W Olympic Blvd, #1100 | Los Angeles CA 90064, USA |
| Abrams Artists & Associates | 9200 Sunset Blvd, #1125 | West Hollywood CA 90069, USA |
| A P A | 405 S Beverly Dr, #405 | Beverly Hills CA 90212, USA |
| A P A | 250 W 57th St, #1701 | New York NY 10107 USA |
| Agency Group | 1880 Century Park E, #711 | Los Angeles CA 90067, USA |
| Agency Group | 142 W 57th St, #600 | New York NY 10019, USA |
| Agency, The | 3711 Ocean Front Walk, #1 | Marina del Rey CA 90292, USA |
| Agents Associes Beaume | 201 rue du Faubourg Saint Honore | 75008 Paris, France |
| Agentur Killer | 54 Harthauser Str | 81545 Munich, Germany |
| Agentur DorisMattes | 14 Merzstr | 81679 Munich, Germany |
| Air Edel | 9100 Wilshire Blvd, #350E | Beverly Hills CA 90212, USA |
| Altaras, Jonathan | 11 Garrick St | London WC1V 2QA, England |
| Ambrosio/Mortimer & Associates | 165 W 45th St | New York NY USA |
| Amsel Eisenstadt & Frazier | 5055 Wilshire Blvd, #865 | Los Angeles CA 90036, USA |
| Artists Agency | 9430 Olympic Blvd | Beverly Hills CA 90212, USA |
| Artists Partnership | 101 Finsbury Pavement | London EC2AS 1RS, England |
| Artmedia | 20 Av Rapp | 75007 Paris, France |
| Askonas Holt | Lincoln House, 300 High Holborn | London WC1V 7JH England |
| Associated Booking Agency | PO Box 2055 | New York NY 10021, USA |
| Associated Talent International | 1320 Armacost Ave, #2 | Beverly Hills, CA 90212, USA |
| B R S/Gage Group | 5757 Wilshire Blvd, #659 | Los Angeles CA 90036, USA |
| Baker Winokur Ryder Public Relations | 9100 Wilshire Blvd, #500W | Los Angeles CA 90036, USA |
| Bauman Redanty & Shaul | 5757 Wilshire Blvd, #473 | Los Angeles CA 90036, USA |
| Belfrage, Julian | 14 New Burlington St | London W1S 3DQ, England |
| Blake Agency | 23441 Malibu Canyon Road | Malibu CA 90265, USA |
| Blanchard, Enterprises Nina | 8826 Burton Way | Beverly Hills CA 90211, USA |
| Borinstein Oreck Bogart Agency | 3172 Dona Susana Dr | Studio City CA 91604, USA |
| Boss Models | 80 8th Ave | New York NY 10011, USA |
| Bragman, Nyman & Cafarelli | 8687 Melrose Ave, #800 | West Hollywood CA 90069, USA |
| Bresler Kelly & Associates | 11500 W Olympic Blvd, #352 | Los Angeles CA 90064, USA |
| Brillstein Entertainment Partners | 9150 Wilshire Blvd, #350 | Beverly Hills CA 90212, USA |
| Buchwald & Associates, Don | 6500 Wilshire Blvd, #2200 | Los Angeles CA 90048, USA |
| Burton Agency, Iris | 10100 Santa Monica Blvd, #1300 | Los Angeles CA 90067, USA |
| Camden ITG Talent Agency | 1501 Main St, #204 | Venice CA 90291, USA |
| Cassidy Inc, Thomas | P O 1311 | Tucson AZ 85702, USA |
| Cavaleri & Associates | 178 S Victory Blvd, #205 | Burbank CA 91502, USA |
| Century Artists | PO Box 59747 | Santa Barbara CA 93150, USA |
| C E S D | 10635 Santa Monica Blvd, #130 | Los Angeles CA 90025, USA |
| Chasin Agency | 8899 Beverly Blvd, #716 | Los Angeles CA 90048, USA |
| Chatto & Linnit | 123A King's Road | London SW3 4PL, England |
| Circle Talent Associates | 433 N Camden Dr, #400 | Beverly Hills CA 90210, USA |
| Click Model Management | 881 7th Ave | New York NY 10019, USA |
| CLInc Talent Agency | 843 N Sycamore Ave | Los Angeles CA 90038, USA |
| C N A & Associates | 1875 Century Park E, #2250 | Los Angeles CA 90067, USA |
| Coast to Coast Talent Group | 3350 Barham Blvd | Los Angeles CA 90068, USA |
| Columbia Artists Management | 1790 Broadway, #702 | New York NY 10019, USA |
| Commercials Unlimited | 190 N Canon Drive, #202 | Beverly Hills CA 90210, USA |
| Contemporary Artists | 610 Santa Monica Blvd, #202 | Santa Monica CA 90401, USA |
| Cosden Agency, Robert | 3518 Cahuenga Blvd W, #200 | Los Angeles CA 90068, USA |
| Cramer/Marder Artists | 127 W 96th St, #13B | New York NY 10025, USA |
| Creative Artists Agency | 2000 Avenue of Stars | Los Angeles CA 90067, USA |
| Creative Artists Agency | 405 Lexington Ave, #1900 | New York NY 10174, USA |
| Creative Entertainment Associates | 1950 Old Cuthbert Road, #J | Cherry Hill NJ, 08034, USA |
| Daish Associates, Judy | 2 Saint Charles Place | London M10 6EG, England |
| D H Talent Agency | 1800 N Highland Ave, #300 | Los Angeles CA 90028, USA |
| Domain Talent | 9229 Sunset Blvd, #710 | Los Angeles CA 90069, USA |
| Elite Model Management | 404 Park Ave S, #900 | New York NY 10016, USA |
| Entertainment Talent Agency | 9225 W Sunset Blvd, #805 | West Hollywood CA 90069, USA |
| Epstein-Wyckoff & Associates | 280 S Beverly Dr, #400 | Beverly Hills CA 90212, USA |
| Famous Artists Agency | 250 W 57th St | New York NY 10107, USA |
| Film Artists Associates | 13563 1/2 Ventura Blvd, #200 | Sherman Oaks CA 91423, USA |
| First Artists Agency | 4764 Park Granada, #210 | Calabasas, CA 91302, USA |
| Flick East-West Talents | 9057 Nemo St, #A | West Hollywood CA 90069, USA |

# AGENCY ADDRESSES

| | | |
|---|---|---|
| Ford Model Agency | 111 5th Ave, #900 | New York NY 10003, USA |
| Front Line Management | 1100 Glendon Ave | Los Angeles CA 90024, USA |
| Geddes Agency | 8430 Santa Monica Blvd, #201 | West Hollywood CA 90069, USA |
| Gersh Agency | 9465 Wilshire Blvd, #600 | Beverly Hills CA 90212, USA |
| Gordon & Associates, Michelle | 260 S Beverly Dr, #308 | Beverly Hills CA 90212, USA |
| Gorfaine/Schwarz | 4111 W Alameda Ave #509 | Burbank CA 91505, USA |
| Greene & Associates | 190 N Canon Dr, #200 | Beverly Hills CA 90210, USA |
| Halliday & Associates, Buzz | 8899 Beverly Blvd, #715 | Los Angeles CA 90048, USA |
| Hallmark Entertainment | 8033 Sunset Blvd, #1000 | Los Angeles CA 90046, USA |
| Halpern & Associates | PO Box 5597 | Santa Monica, CA 90409, USA |
| Handprint Entertainment | 450 N Roxbury Dr, #602 | Beverly Hills CA 90210, USA |
| HarrisonParrott | 5-6 Albion Place | London W6 0QT, England |
| Henderson/Hogan Agency | 9255 W Sunset Blvd, #803 | West Hollywood CA 90069, USA |
| Hervey/Grimes Talent Agency | 10561 Missouri, #2 | Los Angeles CA 90025, USA |
| House of Representatives | 1434 6th St, #1 | Santa Monica CA 90401, USA |
| H T M/Headliner Talent Mgmt | 39398 Moonlight Bay Trail | Pelican Rapids MN 56572, USA |
| Hyler Mgmt | 3000 W Olympic Blvd, Bldg 5 | Santa Monica CA 90404, USA |
| Hyphenate | 1180 S Beverly Dr, #601 | Beverly Hills CA 90212, USA |
| I/D Public Relations | 7060 Hollywood Blvd | Los Angeles CA 90028, USA |
| I F A Talent Agency | 8730 Sunset Blvd, #490 | West Hollywood CA 90069, USA |
| Imagine Entertainment | 9465 Wilshire Blvd, #700 | Beverly Hills CA 90212, USA |
| I M G Models | 304 Park Ave S, #1200 | New York NY 10010, USA |
| Independent Talent Group | 40 Whitfield St | London W1T 2RH, England |
| Innovative Artists | 1505 10th Street | Santa Monica CA 91401, USA |
| ICM Partners | 10250 Constellation Blvd, #700 | Los Angeles CA 90067, USA |
| ICM Partners | 730 5th Ave | New York NY 10019, USA |
| ICM Partners | Marlborough House, 10 Earlham St, #300 | London WC2H 9LN, England |
| International Management Group | 1360 E 9th St, #1300 | Cleveland OH 44114, USA |
| International Talent Group | 40 Whitfield St | London W1T 2RH, England |
| Karg/Weissenbach Associates | 9255 Sunset Blvd, #1115 | Los Angeles CA 90065, USA |
| Katz Enterprises, Raymond | 345 N Maple Dr, #205 | Beverly Hills CA 90210, USA |
| Kazarian/Measures/Ruskin Agency | 11969 Ventura Blvd, #3 | Studio City CA 91604, USA |
| Kohner Inc, Paul | 9300 Wilshire Blvd, #555 | Beverly Hills CA 90212, USA |
| Kosden Agency, Robert | 7135 Hollywood Blvd, #PH2 | Los Angeles CA 90046, USA |
| Kraft-Benjamin-Engel | 9200 Sunset Blvd, #321 | Los Angeles CA 90069, USA |
| Kurland Associates, Ted | 173 Brighton Ave | Allston MA 02134, USA |
| L A Talent | 7700 Sunset Blvd, #200 | Los Angeles CA 90046, USA |
| L I N K Entertainment | 11872 LaGrange Ave, #100 | Los Angeles CA 90025, USA |
| Lee Attractions, Buddy | 38 Music Square E, #200 | Nashville TN 37203, USA |
| Lighthouse Entertainment | 9220 W Sunset Blvd, #200 | West Hollywood CA 90069, USA |
| London Management | 2-4 Noel St | London W1V 3RB, England |
| Lovell Associates | 7095 Hollywood Blvd, #1006 | Los Angeles CA 90028, USA |
| Luber Rocklin Entertainment | 5815 Sunset Blvd, #206 | Los Angeles CA 90028, USA |
| Main Title Entertainment | 8383 Wilshire Blvd, #408 | Beverly Hills CA 90211, USA |
| Management Javonovic | 24 Kathi-Kobus-Str | 80797 Munich, Germany |
| Markham & Froggatt | Julian House, 4 Windmill St | London W1P 1HF, England |
| Marshak Wycoff Associates | 280 S Beverly Dr, #400 | Beverly Hills CA 90212, USA |
| Marsh-Best Associates | 9150 Wilshire Blvd, #220 | Beverly Hills CA 90212, USA |
| M A X Agency | 166 N Canon Dr | Beverly Hills CA 90210, USA |
| M C A Concerts | 100 Universal City Plaza | Universal City CA 91608, USA |
| McKeon-Myrones Mgmt | 3500 Olive Ave, #770 | Burbank CA 91505, USA |
| Media Artists Group | 8255 W Sunset Blvd | Los Angeles CA 90046, USA |
| Metropolitan Talent Agency | 7020 La Presa Dr | Los Angeles CA 90048, USA |
| M E W Inc | 8489 W 3rd St, #1100 | Los Angeles CA 90048, USA |
| Monterey Peninsula Artists | 404 W Franklin St | Monterey CA 93940, USA |
| Morris Yorn Barnes | 2000 Avenue of Stars, #300N | Los Angeles CA 90067, USA |
| Moss Agency, Burton | 8827 Beverly Blvd, #L | Los Angeles CA 90048, USA |
| Nathe & Associates, Susan | 8281 Melrose Ave, #200 | Los Angeles CA 90046, USA |
| Nationwide Entertainment | 2756 N Green Valley Pkwy, #449 | Henderson NV 89014, USA |
| Next Model Management | 23 Watts St | New York NY 10013, USA |
| Octagon | 1751 Pinnacle Dr, #1500 | McLean VA 22102, USA |
| One Management | 42 Bond St, #200 | New York, NY 10012, USA |
| Opera et Concert | 37 Rue de la Chaussee d'Autin | 75009 Paris, France |
| Pakula/King & Associates | 9229 Sunset Blvd, #315 | West Hollywood CA 90069, USA |
| Paradigm Agency | 360 N Crescent Dr, North Building | Beverly Hills CA 90210, USA |
| Parseghian Planco | 388 2nd Ave, #506 | New York NY 10010, USA |
| Pauline's Talent Corp | 379 W Broadway, #502 | New York NY 10012, USA |
| Peters Fraser Dunlop | Drury House, 34-43 Russell St | London WC2B 5HA, England |
| P M K-B N C | 8687 Melrose Ave, #8 | Los Angeles CA 90069, USA |
| Premier Artists Agency | 1611 S Robertson Blvd | Los Angeles CA 90035, USA |
| Premier Talent Agency | 3 E 54th St, #1100 | New York NY 10022, USA |
| Principal Entertainment | 9255 Sunset Blvd, #500 | Los Angeles CA 90069, USA |

# AGENCY ADDRESSES

| | | |
|---|---|---|
| Progressive Artists Agency | 1041 N Formosa Ave | West Hollywood CA 90046, USA |
| Rascoff/Zysblat Organization | 2500 57th St | New York NY 10107, USA |
| Redway Associates, John | 5 Denmark St | London WC2H 8LP, England |
| Reid Entertainment, John | Singes House, 32 Galena Road | London W6 0LT, England |
| Rich Management, Elaine | 2400 Whitman Place | Los Angeles CA 90068, USA |
| Rogers & Cowan Agency | 8687 Melrose Ave, #G700 | West Hollywood CA 90069, USA |
| Rollins Joffe Morra Brezner | 10201 Pico Blvd, #58 | Los Angeles CA 90064, USA |
| Rothberg, Arlyne | 349 S Linden Dr, #C | Beverly Hills CA 90212, USA |
| Rozon Mercer Mgmt | 201 N Robertson Blvd, #F | Beverly Hills CA 90211, USA |
| Ruffalo Management, Joseph | 9655 Wilshire Blvd, #850 | Beverly Hills CA 90212, USA |
| Rush Artists Management | 1600 Varick St | New York NY 10013, USA |
| Russo, Lynne | 3624 Mound View Ave | Studio City CA 91604, USA |
| Sanford-Beckett-Skouras | 1015 Gayley Ave, #300 | Los Angeles CA 90024, USA |
| Savage Agency | 6212 Banner Ave | Los Angeles CA 90038, USA |
| Schechter Co, Irv | 9460 Wilshire Blvd, #300 | Beverly Hills CA 90212, USA |
| Schiowitz/Clay | 1680 Vine St, #614 | Los Angeles CA 90028, USA |
| Schoen & Associates, Judy | 606 N Larchmont Blvd, #309 | Los Angeles CA 90004, USA |
| Schultz Agency, Kathleen | 6442 Coldwater Canyon Ave, #206 | Valley Glen CA 91606, USA |
| Schwartz Associates, Don | PO Box 3628 | Los Angeles CA 90078, USA |
| S D B Partners, Inc | 315 S Beverly Dr, #411 | Beverly Hills CA 90212, USA |
| Sekura/A Talent Agency | PO Box 931779 | Los Angeles CA 90093, USA |
| Selected Artists Agency | 3900 W Alameda Ave, #345 | Burbank CA 91505, USA |
| Shapira & Associates, David | 193 N Robertson Blvd | Beverly Hills CA 90211, USA |
| Shapiro-Lichtman Agency | 8827 Beverly Blvd | Los Angeles CA 90048, USA |
| Sharkey Associates, James | 34 Kingly Court | London W1R 4LE, England |
| Shelter Entertainment | 9454 Wilshire Blvd, #715 | Beverly Hills CA 90212, USA |
| Sherrell Agency, Lew | 937 N Sinova | Mesa AZ 85205, USA |
| Shriver Public Relations, Evelyn | 830 E Hillview Dr | Brentwood TN 37027, USA |
| Silver Massetti & Szatmary | 8730 Sunset Blvd, #440 | West Hollywood CA 90069, USA |
| Sindell & Associates, Richard | 1910 Holmby Ave, #1 | Los Angele, CA 90025, USA |
| Slessinger & Associates, Michael | 8730 Sunset Blvd, #270 | West Hollywood CA 90069, USA |
| Smith & Associates, Susan | 1344 N Wetherly Dr | Los Angeles CA 90069, USA |
| Smith/Gosnell/Nicholson | PO Box 1156 | Studio City CA 91614, USA |
| Somers Teitelbaum David | 8840 Wilshire Blvd, #200 | Beverly Hills CA 90211, USA |
| Special Artists Agency | 9200 Sunset Blvd, #410 | West Hollywood CA 90069, USA |
| Starwil Talent | 433 N Camden Dr, #400 | Beverly Hills CA 90210, USA |
| Sterling/Winters | 2029 Century Park E, #1400 | Los Angeles CA 90067, USA |
| Stone Manners Salners Agency | 6100 Wilshire Blvd, #1500 | Los Angeles CA 90048, USA |
| Strain & Associates, Peter | 5455 Wilshire Blvd, #1812 | Los Angeles CA 90036, USA |
| Talent Entertainment Group | 9111 Wilshire Blvd | Beverly Hills CA 90210, USA |
| TalentWorks | 3500 W Olive Ave, #1400 | Burbank, CA 91505, USA |
| Tannen & Associates, Herb | 10801 National Blvd, #101 | Los Angeles CA 90064, USA |
| Thomas Agency, Robert | 42350 Niagra Dr | Sterling Heights MI 48313, USA |
| Tisherman Agency | 6767 Forest Lawn Dr, #101 | Los Angeles CA 90068, USA |
| Twentieth Century Artists | 19528 Ventura Blvd | Tarzana CA 91356, USA |
| United Agents | 12-26 Lexington St | London W1F 0L#, England |
| United Talent Agency | 9336 Civic Center Dr | Beverly Hills CA 90210, USA |
| Untitled Entertainment | 350 S Beverly Dr, #200 | Beverly Hills CA 90212, USA |
| Variety Artists International | 1924 Spring St | Paso Robles CA 93446, USA |
| Webb Enterprises, Ruth | 7095 Hollywood Blvd | Los Angeles CA 90028, USA |
| Wilder Agency | 3151 Cahuenga Blvd W, #310 | Los Angeles CA 90068, USA |
| Wilhelmina Artists | 8383 Wilshire Blvd, #650 | Beverly Hills CA 90211, USA |
| W K T Public Relations | 335 N Maple Dr, #351 | Beverly Hills CA 90210, USA |
| W M E Entertainment | 9601 Wilshire Blvd | Beverly Hills CA 90210, USA |
| Wolfman Jack Entertainment | 105 Rivershore Dr | Hertford NC 27944, USA |
| Z B F Agentur | Friedrichstr 39 | 10969 Berlin, Germany |
| Zero Gravity Mgmt | 1531 14th St | Santa Monica CA 90404, USA |
| Vox Inc | 5670 Wilshire Blvd, #820 | Los Angeles CA 90036, USA |

# SYNDICATE ADDRESSES

| | | |
|---|---|---|
| Associated Press | 450 W 33rd St, #1500 | New York NY 10001, USA |
| Creators Syndicate | 737 3rd St | Hermosa Beach CA 90254, USA |
| King Features Syndicate | 300 W 57th St, #1500 | New York NY 10019, USA |
| North American Syndicate | 235 E 45th St | New York NY 10017, USA |
| Times-Mirror Syndicate | Times-Mirror Square | Los Angeles CA 90053, USA |
| Tribune Media Services | 435 N Michigan Ave, #1500 | Chicago IL 60611, USA |
| United Feature Syndicate | 200 Madison Ave | New York NY 10016, USA |
| United Media Syndicate | 200 Park Ave, #400 | New York NY 10016, USA |
| United Press International | 2 Pennsylvania Plaza, #1800 | New York NY 10121, USA |
| Universal Press Syndicate | 4520 Main St, #700 | Kansas City MO 64111, USA |

# MAJOR TELEVISION STATION ADDRESSES

## American Broadcasting Company

| | | |
|---|---|---|
| ABC-LA | 500 S Buena Vista St | Burbank CA 91521, USA |
| ABC-NY | 77 W 66th St | New York NY 10023, USA |
| KABC-TV | 4151 Prospect Ave | Los Angeles CA 90027, USA |
| KGO-TV | 900 Front St | San Francisco CA 94111, USA |
| KTRK-TV | 3310 Bissonnet Dr | Houston TX 77005, USA |
| WABC-TV | 7 Lincoln Square | New York NY 10023, USA |
| WCVB-TV (Boston) | 5 TV Place | Needham MA 02194, USA |
| WFAA-TV | 606 Young St | Dallas TX 75202, USA |
| WJLA-TV | 3007 Tilden St NW | Washington DC 20008, USA |
| WLS-TV | 190 N State St | Chicago IL 60601, USA |
| WPIV-TV | 4100 City Line Ave | Philadelphia PA 19131, USA |
| WPLG-TV | 3900 Biscayne Blvd | Miami FL 33137, USA |
| WSB-TV | 1801 W Peachtree St NE | Atlanta GA 30309, USA |
| WVUE-TV | 1025 S Jefferson Davis Parkway | New Orleans LA 70125, USA |
| WXYZ-TV (Detroit) | 20777 W Ten-Mile Road | Southfield MI 48037, USA |

## Columbia Broadcasting System

| | | |
|---|---|---|
| CBS-LA | 7800 Beverly Blvd | Los Angeles CA 90036, USA |
| CBS-NY | 51 W 52nd St | New York NY 10019, USA |
| KCBS-TV | 6121 Sunset Blvd | Los Angeles CA 90028, USA |
| KHOU-TV | 1945 Allen Parkway | Houston TX 77019, USA |
| KPIX-TV | 855 Battery St | San Francisco CA 94111, USA |
| KYW-TV | 101 S Independence Mall E | Philadelphia PA 19106, USA |
| WBBM-TV | 630 N McClurg Court | Chicago IL 60611, USA |
| WBZ-TV | 1170 Soldiers Field Road | Boston MA 02134, USA |
| WCBS-TV | 524 W 57th St | New York NY 10019, USA |
| WCIX-TV | 8900 NW 18th Terrace | Miami FL 33172, USA |
| WUSA-TV | 4100 Wisconsin Ave NW | Washington DC 20016, USA |
| WWL-TV | 1024 N Rampart St | New Orleans LA 70116, USA |

## Fox Television

| | | |
|---|---|---|
| Fox-TV | 10201 W Pico Blvd | Los Angeles CA 90035, USA |
| KDFW-TV | 400 N Griffin St | Dallas TX 75202, USA |
| KRIV-TV | 3935 Westheimer Road | Houston TX 77027, USA |
| KTTV-TV | 5746 W Sunset Blvd | Los Angeles CA 90028, USA |
| KTVU-TV (San Francisco) | PO Box 22222 | Oakland CA 94623, USA |
| WAGA-TV | 1551 Briarcliff Road NE | Atlanta GA 30306, USA |
| WFLD-TV | 205 N Michigan Ave | Chicago IL 60601, USA |
| WFXT-TV (Boston) | 1000 Providence Highway | Dedham MA 02026, USA |
| WJBK-TV (Detroit) | 16550 W Nine-Mile Road | Southfield MI 48075, USA |
| WNOL-TV | 1661 Canal St | New Orleans LA 70112, USA |
| WNYW-TV | 205 E 67th St | New York NY 10021, USA |
| WSVN-TV | 1401 79th St Causeway | Miami FL 33141, USA |
| WTTG-TV | 5151 Wisconsin Ave NW, #100 | Washington DC 20016, USA |
| WTXF-TV | 330 Market St | Philadelphia PA 19106, USA |

## National Broadcasting Company

| | | |
|---|---|---|
| KNBC-TV (Los Angeles) | 3000 W Alameda Ave | Burbank CA 91523, USA |
| KPRC-TV | 8181 Southwest Freeway | Houston TX 77074, USA |
| KNBC-TV (Los Angeles) | 3000 W Alameda Ave | Burbank CA 91523, USA |
| KPRC-TV | 8181 Southwest Freeway | Houston TX 77074, USA |
| KRON-TV | 1001 Van Ness Ave | San Francisco CA 94109, USA |
| KXAS-TV | 3900 Barnett St | Fort Worth TX 76103, USA |
| WDIV-TV | 550 W Lafayette Blvd | Detroit MI 48231, USA |
| WDSU-TV | 520 Royal St | New Orleans LA 70130, USA |
| WMAG-TV | 454 N Columbus Dr | Chicago IL 60611, USA |
| WMGM-TV (Philadelphia) | 1601 New Road | Linwood NJ 08221, USA |
| WNBC-TV | 30 Rockefeller Plaza, #207E | New York NY 10112, USA |
| WRC-TV | 4001 Nebraska Ave NW | Washington DC 20016, USA |
| WTVJ-TV | 316 N Miami Ave | Miami FL 33128, USA |
| WXIA-TV | 1611 W Peachtree St NE | Atlanta GA 30309, USA |

## CABLE TELEVISION CHANNEL ADDRESSES

| | | |
|---|---|---|
| American Christian Television | 6350 West Freeway | Fort Worth TX 76150, USA |
| American Movie Classics | 150 Crossways Park W | Woodbury NY 11797, USA |
| Arts & Entertainment | 235 E 45th St, #9 | New York NY 10017, USA |
| Black Entertainment Network | One BET Plaza, 1900 W Place NE | Washington DC 20018, USA |
| British Broadcasting Company | Wood Lane | London W12 8Q, England |
| Cable News Network (CNN) | 820 1st St NE, #1000 | Washington DC 20002, USA |
| Canadian Broadcasting Company | 1500 Bronson Ave | Ottawa ON K1G 3J5, Canada |
| Canadian Television Network | 42 Charles St E | Toronto ON M4Y 1T5, Canada |

# CABLE TELEVISION CHANNEL ADDRESSES

| | | |
|---|---|---|
| Capital Cities/ABC | 77 W 66th St | New York NY 10023, USA |
| Cartoon Network | 1050 Techwood Dr NW | Atlanta GA 30318, USA |
| Christian Broadcasting Network | 1000 Centerville Turnpike | Virginia Beach VA 23463, USA |
| Cinemax | 1100 6th Ave | New York NY 10036, USA |
| Columbia Broadcasting System | 51 W 52nd St | New York NY 10019, USA |
| Comedy Central | 345 Hudson St, #300 | New York NY 10014, USA |
| Consumer News & Business | 2200 Fletcher Ave | Fort Lee NJ 07024, USA |
| Country Music Television | 2806 Opryland Dr | Nashville TN 37214, USA |
| Court TV | 600 Third Ave | New York NY 10016, USA |
| C-SPAN | 400 N Capitol St NW, #650 | Washington DC 20001, USA |
| CW Television Network | 4000 Warner Blvd | Burbank CA 91522, USA |
| Discovery Channel | 7700 Wisconsin Ave | Bethesda MD 20814, USA |
| Disney Channel | 3800 W Alameda Ave | Burbank CA 91505, USA |
| E! (Entertainment Television) | 5750 Wilshire Blvd | Los Angeles CA 90036, USA |
| ESPN (Entertainment & Sports) | ESPN Plaza, 935 Middle St | Bristol CT 06010, USA |
| Family Channel | PO Box 64549 | Virginia Beach VA 23467, USA |
| Food Network | 1180 Ave of Americas, #1200 | New York NY 10036, USA |
| FX (Fox Net) | PO Box 900 | Beverly Hills CA 90213, USA |
| Game Show Network | 10202 W Washington Blvd | Culver City CA 90232, USA |
| Granada Television | 36 Golden Square | London W1R 2AX, England |
| HGTV (Home & Garden TV) | PO Box 50970 | Knoxville TN 37950, USA |
| History Channel | 235 E 45th St, #9 | New York NY 10017, USA |
| Home Box Office (HBO) | 1100 Ave of Americas | New York NY 10036, USA |
| Home Shopping Network | PO Box 9090 | Clearwater FL 34618, USA |
| Independent Film Channel | 150 Crossways Park W | Woodbury NY 11797, USA |
| Learning Channel | 7700 Wisconsin Ave | Bethesda MD 20814, USA |
| Lifetime | 111 8th St | New York NY 10011, USA |
| Madison Square Garden Network | 2 Pennsylvania Plaza | New York NY 10001, USA |
| Movie Channel (TMC) | 1633 Broadway | New York NY 10019, USA |
| MTV (Music Television) | 1515 Broadway | New York NY 10036, USA |
| National Broadcasting Company | 30 Rockefeller Plaza | New York NY 10112, USA |
| Nickelodeon | 1515 Broadway | New York NY 10036, USA |
| Oxygen | 75 9th Avenue | New York NY 10011, USA |
| PBS (Public Broadcasting System) | 1320 Braddock Place | Alexandria VA 22314, USA |
| Playboy Channel | 9242 Beverly Blvd | Beverly Hills CA 90210, USA |
| Prime Ticket Network | 10000 Santa Monica Blvd | Los Angeles CA 90067, USA |
| QVC Inc | 1365 Enterprise Dr | West Chester PA 19380, USA |
| Sci-Fi Channel | 1230 Ave of Americas | New York NY 10020, USA |
| Showtime Network | 1633 Broadway | New York NY 10019, USA |
| TBN (Trinity Broadcast Network) | PO Box A | Tustin CA 92711, USA |
| TBS (Turner Broadcasting System) | 1 CNN Center, PO Box 105366 | Atlanta GA 30348, USA |
| Telemundo Group | 1740 Broadway | New York NY 10019, USA |
| TNN (The Nashville Network) | 2806 Opryland Dr | Nashville TN 37214, USA |
| TNT (Turner Network Television) | 1050 Techwood Dr NW | Atlanta GA 30318, USA |
| TVA | 1600 de Maisonneuve Blvd E | Montreal QC H2L 4P2, Canada |
| Univision Network | 605 3rd Ave, #1200 | New York NY 10158, USA |
| USA Cable Network | 1230 Ave of Americas | New York NY 10020, USA |
| VH-1 (Video Hits One) | 1515 Broadway | New York NY 10036, USA |
| Viewer's Choice | 909 3rd Ave | New York NY 10022, USA |
| Warner Bros | 4000 Warner Blvd | Burbank CA 91522, USA |
| Weather Channel | 2600 Cumberland Parkway NW | Atlanta GA 30339, USA |

# RECORD COMPANY ADDRESSES

| | | |
|---|---|---|
| A&M Records | 70 University City Plaza | Universal City CA 91608, USA |
| Angel Records | 1750 N Vine St | Los Angeles CA 90028, USA |
| Angel Records | 150 5th Ave | New York NY 10011, USA |
| Arista Records | 8750 Wilshire Blvd, #300 | Beverly Hills CA 90211, USA |
| Arista Records | 745 5th Ave, #600 | New York NY 10151, USA |
| Asylum Records | 9229 Sunset Blvd, #718 | West Hollywood CA 90069, USA |
| Asylum Records | 75 Rockefeller Plaza | New York NY 10019, USA |
| Atlantic Records | 9229 Sunset Blvd, #900 | West Hollywood CA 90069, USA |
| Atlantic Records | 1290 Ave of Americas, Concourse 3 | New York NY 10104, USA |
| Blue Note Records | 6920 Sunset Blvd | Los Angeles CA 90028, USA |
| Capitol Records | 1750 N Vine St | Los Angeles CA 90028, USA |
| Capitol Records | 810 7th Ave | New York NY 10019, USA |
| Chrysalis Records | 8730 Sunset Blvd | West Hollywood CA 90069, USA |
| Chrysalis Records | 810 7th Ave, #4 | New York NY 10019, USA |
| Deutsche Grammaphon Records | 810 7th Ave | New York NY 10019, USA |
| Dreamwork Records | 1000 Flower St | Glendale CA 91201, USA |
| Elektra Records | 75 Rockefeller Plaza | New York NY 10019, USA |
| E M I America Records | 6920 Sunset Blvd | Los Angeles CA 90028, USA |
| E M I America Records | 150 5th Ave, #700 | New York NY 10011, USA |

## RECORD COMPANY ADDRESSES

| | | |
|---|---|---|
| Epic Records | 1211 S Highland Ave | Los Angeles CA 90019, USA |
| Epic Records | 350 Madison Ave, #600 | New York NY 10022, USA |
| Geffen Records | 10900 Wilshire Blvd, #1000 | Los Angeles CA 90024, USA |
| Geffen Records | 1755 Broadway, #600 | New York NY 10019, USA |
| Island Def Jam Records | 8920 Sunset Blvd, #200 | West Hollywood CA 90069, USA |
| Island Def Jam Records | 925 8th St | New York NY 10019, USA |
| LaFace Records | 3350 Peach Tree Road | Atlanta GA 30319, USA |
| London Records | 810 7th Ave | New York NY 10019, USA |
| M C A Records | 70 Universal City Plaza | Universal City CA 91608, USA |
| M C A Records | 1755 Broadway | New York NY 10019, USA |
| Mercury Records | 54 Music Square E, #300 | Nashville TN 37203, USA |
| Motown Records | 6255 Sunset Blvd | Los Angeles CA 90028, USA |
| Nonesuch Records | 75 Rockefeller Plaza | New York NY 10019, USA |
| Phillips Records | 810 7th Ave | New York NY 10019, USA |
| Polydor Records | 70 Universal City Plaza | Universal City CA 91608, USA |
| Polydor Records | 810 7th Ave | New York NY 10019, USA |
| Polygram Records | 3800 W Alameda Ave, #1500 | Burbank CA 91505, USA |
| Polygram Records | Worldwide Plaza, 825 8th Ave | New York NY 10019, USA |
| R C A Records | 6363 Sunset Blvd, #429 | Los Angeles CA 90028, USA |
| R C A Records | 1540 Broadway, #3500 | New York NY 10036, USA |
| Reprise Records | 3300 Warner Blvd | Burbank CA 91505, USA |
| Reprise Records | 75 Rockefeller Plaza | New York NY 10019, USA |
| Rhino Records | 10635 Santa Monica Blvd | Los Angeles CA 90025, USA |
| Sire Records | 3300 Warner Blvd | Burbank CA 91505, USA |
| Sire Records | 75 Rockefeller Plaza | New York NY 10019, USA |
| Sony/Columbia/CBS Records | 2100 Colorado Ave | Santa Monica CA 90404, USA |
| Sony/Columbia/CBS Records | 550 Madison Ave, #600 | New York NY 10022, USA |
| Verve Records | 1755 Broadway, #600 | New York NY 10019, USA |
| Virgin Records | 338 N Foothill Road | Beverly Hills CA 90210, USA |
| Virgin Records | 150 5th Ave, #700 | New York NY 10011, USA |
| Warner Bros Records | 3300 Warner Blvd | Burbank CA 91505, USA |
| Warner Bros Records | 75 Rockefeller Plaza | New York NY 10019, USA |
| Windham Hill Records | PO Box 5501 | Beverly Hills CA 90209, USA |

## PUBLISHER ADDRESSES

| | | |
|---|---|---|
| Atheneum Publishers | 866 3rd Ave | New York NY10022, USA |
| Avon Books | 1350 Ave of Americas | New York NY 10019, USA |
| Berkley Publishing | 375 Hudson St, Basement 1 | New York NY 10014, USA |
| Chronicle Books | 680 2nd St | San Francisco CA 94107, USA |
| Crown Publishers | 201 E. 50th St | New York NY 10022, USA |
| Delacorte/Bantam/Dell/Doubleday | 1745 Broadway | New York NY 10019, USA |
| Dodd Mead | 6 Ram Ridge Road | Spring Valley NY 10977, USA |
| Dutton, EP/Penguin | 375 Hudson St, Basement 1 | New York NY 10014, USA |
| Farrar Straus Giroux | 18 W 18th St, #700 | New York NY 10011, USA |
| Grove Press | 841 Broadway | New York NY 10003, USA |
| Harcourt Brace | 525 B St | San Diego CA 92101, USA |
| Harper Collins | 10 E 53rd St, Cellar 1 | New York NY10022, USA |
| Henry Holt | 175 5th Ave, #400 | New York NY 10010, USA |
| Houghton Mifflin | 215 Park Ave S, #1200 | New York NY 10003, USA |
| Hyperion Books | 114 5th Ave | New York NY 10011, USA |
| Knopf/Ballatine/Fawcett | 201 E 50th St | New York NY 10022, USA |
| Little Brown | 1271 Ave of Americas | New York NY 10020, USA |
| Little Brown | 3 Center Plaza, #100 | Boston MA 02108, USA |
| McGraw Hill | 1221 Ave of Americas, #C3A | New York NY 10020, USA |
| MacMillan | 1177 Ave of Americas, #1965 | New York NY 10036, USA |
| Morrow, William | 1350 Ave of Americas, #200 | New York NY 10019, USA |
| Mysterious Press/Warner Books | 1271 6th Ave | New York NY 10020, USA |
| New American Library | 1633 Broadway | New York NY 10019, USA |
| Norton, WW | 500 5th Ave, #600 | New York NY 10110, USA |
| Oxford University Press | 198 Madison Ave, #800 | New York NY 10016, USA |
| Pocket Books | 1230 Ave of Americas | New York NY 10020, USA |
| Prentice-Hall | RR 9W | Englewood Cliffs NJ 07632, USA |
| Putnam's Sons, GP | 375 Hudson St, Basement | New York NY 10014, USA |
| Random House | 1745 Broadway, #B1 | New York NY 10019, USA |
| Scholastic Press | 555 Broadway | New York NY 10012, USA |
| Scribner's Sons, Charles | 866 3rd Ave | New York NY 10022, USA |
| Simon & Schuster | 1230 Ave of Americas, Concourse 1 | New York NY 10020, USA |
| Saint Martin's Press | 175 5th Ave, #400 | New York NY 10010, USA |
| Viking Press | 375 Hudson St, Basement 1 | New York NY 10014, USA |

# PROFESSIONAL SPORTS TEAMS ADDRESSES

## Baseball

| | | |
|---|---|---|
| Arizona Diamondbacks | Chase Field, 401 E Jefferson | Phoenix AZ 85003, USA |
| Atlanta Braves | Turner Field, 755 Hank Aaron Drive | Atlanta GA 30315, USA |
| Baltimore Orioles | Oriole Park, 333 W Camden St | Baltimore MD 21201, USA |
| Boston Red Sox | Fenway Park, 4 Yawkey Way | Boston MA 02215, USA |
| Chicago Cubs | Wrigley Field, 1060 W Addison St | Chicago IL 60613, USA |
| Chicago White Sox | US Cellular Field, 333 W 35th St | Chicago IL 60616, USA |
| Cincinnati Reds | Great American Ball Park, 100 Main St | Cincinnati OH 45202, USA |
| Cleveland Indians | Jacobs Field, 2401 Ontario St | Cleveland OH 44115, USA |
| Colorado Rockies | Coors Field, 2001 Blake St | Denver CO 80205, USA |
| Detroit Tigers | Comerica Park, 2100 Woodward Ave | Detroit MI 48201, USA |
| Houston Astros | Minute Maid Field, 501 Crawford St | Houston TX 77002, USA |
| Kansas City Royals | Kauffman Stadium, 1 Royal Way | Kansas City MO 64129, USA |
| Los Angeles Angels of Anaheim | Angel Stadium, 2000 Gene Autry Way | Anaheim CA 92806, USA |
| Los Angeles Dodgers | Dodger Stadium, 1000 Elysian Park Ave | Los Angeles CA 90090, USA |
| Miami Marlins | 501 Marlins Way | Miami FL 33125, USA |
| Milwaukee Brewers | Miller Park, 1 Brewers Way | Milwaukee WI 53214, USA |
| Minnesota Twins | Metrodome, 34 Kirby Punkett Place | Minneapolis MN 55415, USA |
| New York Mets | Shea Stadium, 12301 Roosevelt Ave | Flushing NY 11368, USA |
| New York Yankees | Yankee Stadium, E 161st & River Ave | Bronx NY 10451, USA |
| Oakland Athletics | McAfee Coliseum, 7000 Coliseum Way, #3 | Oakland CA 94621, USA |
| Philadelphia Phillies | Citizens Bank Park, 1 Citizens Bank Way | Philadelphia PA 19148, USA |
| Pittsburgh Pirates | PNC Park, 115 Federal St, #115B | Pittsburgh PA 15212, USA |
| San Diego Padres | Petco Park, 100 Park Blvd | San Diego CA 92101, USA |
| San Francisco Giants | AT&T Park, 24 Willie Mays Plaza | San Francisco CA 94107, USA |
| Seattle Mariners | Safeco Field, PO Box 4100 | Seattle WA 98194, USA |
| Saint Louis Cardinals | Busch Stadium, 250 Stadium Plaza | Saint Louis MO 63102, USA |
| Tampa Bay Rays | Tropicana Field, 1 Tropicana Dr | Saint Petersburg FL 33705, USA |
| Texas Rangers | Ameriquest Field, 1000 Ballpark Way, #306 | Arlington TX 76011, USA |
| Toronto Blue Jays | Skydome, 1 Blue Jay Way, #3200 | Toronto ON M5V 1J1, Canada |
| Washington Nationals | 1500 S Capital St SE | Washington DC 20003, USA |

## Men's Basketball

| | | |
|---|---|---|
| Atlanta Hawks | 101 Marietta St NW, #1900 | Atlanta GA 30303, USA |
| Boston Celtics | 226 Causeway St, #400 | Boston MA 02114, USA |
| Brooklyn Nets | 15 MetroTech Center, #1100 | Brooklyn NY 11201, USA |
| Charlotte Bobcats | 333 E Trade St. #A | Charlotte NC 28202, USA |
| Chicago Bulls | United Center, 1901 W Madison St | Chicago IL 60612, USA |
| Cleveland Cavaliers | Gund Arena, 1 Center Court | Cleveland OH 44115, USA |
| Dallas Mavericks | 2500 Victory Ave | Dallas TX 75219, USA |
| Denver Nuggets | Pepsi Center, 1000 Chopper Circle | Denver CO 80204, USA |
| Detroit Pistons | Palace, 4 Championship Dr | Auburn Hills MI 48326, USA |
| Golden State Warriors | 1011 Broadway | Oakland CA 94605, USA |
| Houston Rockets | 1510 Polk St | Houston TX 77002, USA |
| Indiana Pacers | 125 S Pennsylvania St | Indianapolis IN 46204, USA |
| Los Angeles Clippers | Staples Center, 1111 S Figueroa St | Los Angeles CA 90015, USA |
| Los Angeles Lakers | Staples Center, 1111 S Figueroa St | Los Angeles CA 90015, USA |
| Memphis Grizzlies | 191 Beale St | Memphis TN 38103, USA |
| Miami Heat | 601 Biscayne Blvd | Miami FL 33132, USA |
| Milwaukee Bucks | 1001 N 4th St, #200 | Milwaukee WI 53203, USA |
| Minnesota Timberwolves | Target Center, 600 1st Ave N | Minneapolis MN 55403, USA |
| New Orleans Pelicans | 1250 Poydras St, #101 | New Orleans LA 70113, USA |
| New York Knicks | Madison Square Garden, 4 Penn Plaza | New York NY 10121, USA |
| Oklahoma City Thunder | 211 N Robinson Ave, #300 | Oklahoma City OK 73102, USA |
| Orlando Magic | 8701 Maitland Summit Blvd | Orlando FL 32810, USA |
| Philadelphia 76ers | 3601 S Broad St, #400 | Philadelphia PA 19148, USA |
| Phoenix Suns | 201 E Jefferson St | Phoenix AZ 85004, USA |
| Portland Trail Blazers | 1 N Center Court St, #200, Rose Garden | Portland OR 97227, USA |
| Sacramento Kings | Arco, Arena, 1 Sports Parkway | Sacramento CA 95834, USA |
| San Antonio Spurs | Key Arena, 1 AT&T Center | San Antonio TX 78219, USA |
| Seattle Supersonics | 1201 3rd Ave, #1000 | Seattle WA 98101, USA |
| Toronto Raptors | 20 Bay St, #1702 | Toronto ON M5J 2N8, Canada |
| Utah Jazz | 301 W South Temple | Salt Lake City UT 84101, USA |
| Washington Wizards | 601 F St NW | Washington DC 20004, USA |

## Women's Basketball (WNBA)

| | | |
|---|---|---|
| Atlanta Dream | 83 Walton St NW, #400 | Atlanta GA 30303, USA |
| Chicago Sky | 20 W Kinzie St, #1010 | Chicago IL 60654, USA |
| Connecticut Sun | 1 Mohegan Sun Blvd | Uncasville CT 06382, USA |
| Indiana Fever | 125 S Pennsylvania St | Indianapolis IN 46204, USA |
| Los Angeles Sparks | 888 S Figueroa St, #2010 | Los Angeles CA 90017, USA |

# PROFESSIONAL SPORTS TEAMS ADDRESSES

## Women's Basketball (WNBA)

| | | |
|---|---|---|
| Minnesota Lynx | 600 1st Ave N | Minneapolis MN 55403, USA |
| New York Liberty | 2 Penn Plaza, #1400 | New York NY 10121, USA |
| Phoenix Mercury | 201 E Jefferson St | Phoenix AZ 85004, USA |
| Sacramento Monarchs | Arco Arena, 1 Sports Parkway | Sacramento CA 95834, USA |
| San Antonio Silver Stars | 1 AT&T Center | San Antonio TX 78219, USA |
| Seattle Storm | 351 Elliott Ave W, #500 | Seattle WA 98119, USA |
| Tulsa Shock | BOK Center, 200 S Denver | Tulsa OK 74103, USA |
| Washington Mystics | Verizon Center, 401 9th St NW, #750 | Washington DC 20004, USA |

## Football

| | | |
|---|---|---|
| Arizona Cardinals | PO Box 888 | Phoenix AZ 85001, USA |
| Atlanta Falcons | 4400 Falcon Parkway | Flowery Branch GA 30542, USA |
| Baltimore Ravens | Ravens Stadium, 1 Winning Dr | Owings Mills MD 21117, USA |
| Buffalo Bills | 1 Bills Dr | Orchard Park NY 14127, USA |
| Carolina Panthers | Ericsson Stadium, 800 S Mint St | Charlotte NC 28202, USA |
| Chicago Bears | 1000 Football Dr | Lake Forest IL 60045, USA |
| Cincinnati Bengals | 1 Paul Brown Stadium | Cincinnati OH 45202, USA |
| Cleveland Browns | 76 Lou Groza Blvd | Berea OH 44017, USA |
| Dallas Cowboys | 1 Cowboys Parkway | Irving TX 75063, USA |
| Denver Broncos | 13655 Broncos Parkway | Englewood, CO 80112, USA |
| Detroit Lions | 222 Republic Drive | Allen Park MI 48101, USA |
| Green Bay Packers | 1265 Lombardi Ave | Green Bay WI 54304, USA |
| Houston Texans | 2 Reliant Park | Houston TX 77054, USA |
| Indianapolis Colts | 7001 W 56th St | Indianapolis IN 46254, USA |
| Jacksonville Jaguars | 1 AllTel Stadium Place | Jacksonville FL 32202, USA |
| Kansas City Chiefs | 1 Arrowhead Dr | Kansas City KS 64129, USA |
| Miami Dolphins | 7500 SW 30th St | Davie FL 33314, USA |
| Minnesota Vikings | 9520 Viking Dr | Eden Prairie MN 55344, USA |
| New England Patriots | 1 Patriot Place | Foxboro, MA 02035, USA |
| New Orleans Saints | 5800 Airline Highway | Metairie LA 70003, USA |
| New York Giants | Meadowlands Stadium, 102 Route 120 | East Rutherford NJ 07073, USA |
| New York Jets | 1 Jets Dr | Florham Park NJ 07932, USA |
| Oakland Raiders | 1220 Harbor Bay Parkway | Alameda CA 94502, USA |
| Philadelphia Eagles | 1 NovaCare Way | Philadelphia PA 19145, USA |
| Pittsburgh Steelers | 3400 S Water St | Pittsburgh PA 15203, USA |
| Saint Louis Rams | 901 N Broadway | Saint Louis MO 63101, USA |
| San Diego Chargers | 4020 Murphy Canyon Rd | San Diego CA 92123, USA |
| San Francisco 49ers | 4949 Centennial Blvd | Santa Clara CA 95054, USA |
| Seattle Seahawks | 12 Seahawks Way | Renton WA 98056, USA |
| Tennessee Titans | 460 Great Circle Road | Nashville TN 37228, USA |
| Tampa Bay Buccaneers | 1 W Buccaneer Place | Tampa FL 33607, USA |
| Washington Redskins | 21300 Redskin Park Dr | Ashburn VA 20147, USA |

## Ice Hockey

| | | |
|---|---|---|
| Anaheim Ducks | 2695 E Katella Ave | Anaheim CA 92806, USA |
| Arizona Coyotes | 6751 N Sunset Blvd, #200 | Glendale AZ 85305, USA |
| Boston Bruins | 100 Legends Way, #250 | Boston MA 02114, USA |
| Buffalo Sabres | 1 Seymour Knox Plaza | Buffalo NY 14203, USA |
| Calgary Flames | PO Box 1540, Station M | Calgary AB T2P 3B9, Canada |
| Carolina Hurricanes | RBC Center, 1400 Edwards Mill Road | Raleigh NC 27607, USA |
| Chicago Blackhawks | United Center, 1901 W Madison St | Chicago IL 60612, USA |
| Colorado Avalanche | Pepsi Center, 1000 Chopper Circle | Denver CO 80204, USA |
| Columbus Blue Jackets | 200 W Nationwide Blvd, Unit 1 | Columbus OH 43215, USA |
| Dallas Stars | 2601 Avenue of Stars | Frisco TX 75034, USA |
| Detroit Red Wings | Joe Louis Arena, 600 Civic Center Dr | Detroit MI 48226, USA |
| Edmonton Oilers | Edmonton Coliseum, 11230 110 St | Edmonton AB T5G 3G8, Canada |
| Florida Panthers | 1 Panthers Parkway | Sunrise FL 33323, USA |
| Hartford Whalers | Coliseum, 242 Trumbull St, #800 | Hartford CT 06103, USA |
| Los Angeles Kings | Staples Center, 1111 S Figueroa St | Los Angeles CA 90015, USA |
| Minnesota Wild | Xcel Energy Center, 1275 W Kellogg Blvd | Saint Paul MN 55104, USA |
| Montreal Canadiens | 1275 Saint Antoine St W | Montreal QC H3C 5L2, Canada |
| Nashville Predators | 501 Broadway | Nashville TN 37203, USA |
| New Jersey Devils | 165 Mulberry St | Newark NJ 07102, USA |
| New York Islanders | 1255 Hempstead Turnpike | Uniondale NY 11553, USA |
| New York Rangers | Madison Square Garden, 2 Penn Plaza | New York NY 10121, USA |
| Ottawa Senators | ScotiaBank Place, 1000 Palladium Dr | Kanata ON K2V 1A5, Canada |
| Philadelphia Flyers | 1st Union Center, 3601 S Broad St | Philadelphia PA 19148, USA |
| Pittsburgh Penguins | Consol Energy Center, 1001 5th Ave | Pittsburgh PA 15219, USA |
| Saint Louis Blues | ScottTrade Center, 1401 Clark Ave | Saint Louis MO 63103, USA |

# PROFESSIONAL SPORTS TEAMS ADDRESSES

## Ice Hockey

| | | |
|---|---|---|
| San Jose Sharks | 525 W Santa Clara St | San Jose CA 95113, USA |
| Tampa Bay Lightning | 401 Channelside Dr | Tampa FL 33602, USA |
| Toronto Maple Leafs | AirCanada Center, 40 Bay St, #400 | Toronto ON M5J 2X2, Canada |
| Vancouver Canucks | 800 Griffiths Way | Vancouver BC V6B 6G1, Canada |
| Washington Capitals | 627 N Glebe Road | Arlington VA 22203, USA |
| Winnipeg Jets | 260 Hargrave St | Winnipeg MB R3C 5S5, Canada |

## Men's Soccer

| | | |
|---|---|---|
| A S Rome Spa | Piazzale Dino Viola | 00128 Rome, Italy |
| Chicago Fire | 7000 S Harlem Ave | Bridgeview IL 60455, USA |
| Club Deportivo Chivas | Home Depot Center, 18400 Avalon Blvd | Carson CA 90746, USA |
| Colorado Rapids | 1000 Chopper Circle | Denver CO 80204, USA |
| Columbus Crew | 1 Black & Gold Blvd | Columbus OH 43211, USA |
| D C United | RFK Stadium, 2400 E Capitol St SE | Washington DC 20003 USA |
| F C Dallas | 9200 World Cup Way, #202 | Frisco TX 75034, USA |
| Houston Dynamo | 1415 Louisiana, #3400 | Houston TX 77002, USA |
| Kansas City Wizards | 8900 State Line Road | Leawood MO 66206, USA |
| Los Angeles Galaxy | Home Depot Center, 18400 Avalon Blvd | Carson CA 90746, USA |
| New England Revolution | 1 Patriot Place | Foxboro MA 02035, USA |
| New York FC | Yankee Stadium, 1 E 161 St | Bronx NY 10451, USA |
| Orlando City Lions | 618 E South St, #510 | Orlando FL 32801, USA |
| Portland Timbers | 1844 SW Morrison | Portland OR 97205, USA |
| Real Salt Lake | 9256 S State St | Sandy UT 84070, USA |
| Red Bull New York | 600 Cape May St | Harrison NJ 07029, USA |
| San Jose Earthquakes | 451 El Camino Real, #220 | Santa Clara CA 95050, USA |
| Seattle Sounders | 12 Seahawks Way | Renton WA 98056, USA |
| Toronto F C | Maple Leaf Sports, 40 Bay St, #400 | Toronto ON M5J 2X2, Canada |
| Vancouver Whitecaps | 375 Water St, #550 | Vancouver BC V6B 5C6, Canada |
| Montreal Impact | 4750 Sherbrooke Est | Montreal QB H1V 3S8, Canada |

## Women's Soccer

| | | |
|---|---|---|
| Atlanta Beat | 1955 Vaughn Road, #209 | Kennesaw GA 30144, USA |
| Boston Breakers | 400 Blue Hill Dr, #302 | Westwood MA 02090, USA |
| FC Kansas City | 5366 W 95th St | Prairie Village KS 66207, USA |
| Philadelphia Independence | Union Field, Seaport Dr | Chester, PA 19013, USA |
| Sky Blue F C | 80 Cottontail Lane, #400 | Somerset NJ 08873, USA |
| Western New York Flash | Sahlen Sports Park, 7070 Seneca St | Elma NY 14059 USA |

## OTHER SPORTS ORGANIZATION ADDRESSES

| | | |
|---|---|---|
| Amateur Athletic Union | PO Box 10000 | Lake Buena Vista FL 32830, USA |
| Amateur Softball Association | 2801 NE 50th St | Oklahoma City OK 73111, USA |
| American Bicycle Association | 1645 W Sunrise Blvd | Gilbert AZ 85233, USA |
| American Bowling Congress | 5301 S 76th St | Greendale WI 53129, USA |
| American Horse Show Association | 220 E 42nd St | New York NY 10017, USA |
| American Hot Rod Association | 111 N Hayford Road | Spokane WA 99224, USA |
| American Kennel Club | 260 Madison Ave | New York NY 10016, USA |
| American League Baseball | 350 Park Ave, #1800 | New York NY 10022, USA |
| American Motorcycle Association | 13515 Yarmouth Dr | Pickerington OH 43147, USA |
| American Power Boat Association | 17640 E Nine Mile Road | East Detroit MI 48021, USA |
| American Pro Soccer League | 122 C St, NW | Washington DC 20001, USA |
| American Water Ski Association | 799 Overlook Dr | Winter Haven FL 33884, USA |
| Association of Int'l Amateur Boxing | Postamt Volkrdstr, Postlagernd | 10319 Berlin, Germany |
| Assn/Int'l Marathon/Road Races | 20 Trongate | Glasgow G1 5ES, England |
| Association of Ski Racing Pros | 148 Porters Point Road | Colchester VT 05446, USA |
| Association of Surfing Pros | 16691 Gothard St | Huntington Beach CA 92648, USA |
| Association of Tennis Pros | 201 A T P Tour Blvd | Ponte Vedra Beach FL 32082, USA |
| Association of Volleyball Pros | 2183 Fairview Road, #222 | Costa Mesa CA 92627, USA |
| Canadian Football League | 110 Eglinton Ave | Toronto, ON M4R 1A3, Canada |
| Canadian Nat'l Sports/Recreation | 1600 James Naismith Dr | Gloucestor ON KJB 5N4, Canada |
| Federation de International Hockey | Avenue des Arts 1 (bte 5) | 1040 Brussels, Belgium |
| Federation de International Ski | Worbstr 210, 3073 Gumligen B | Berne, Switzerland |
| Federation International de Canoe | G Massaia 59 | 50134 Florence, Italy |
| Federation Int'l de Football Assn | PO Box 85, Hitzigweg 11 | 8030 Zurich, Switzerland |
| Federation Int'l de Gymnastics | Juraweg 12 | 8250 Lyss, Switzerland |
| Federation Int'l I de Tir a l'Arc | Via Cerva 30 | 20122 Milan, Italy |
| Federation of Int'l Volleyball | Ave de la Gare 12 | 1001 Lausanne, Switzerland |
| Federation of Int'l Amateur Cycling | Via Cassia N 490 | 00198 Rome, Italy |
| Federation of Int'l Basketball | PO Box 700607, Kistlerhofstr 168 | 81379 Munich, Germany |
| Fedn of Int'l Bobsleigh/Toboggan | Via Piranesi 44/b | 20137 Milan, Italy |

## OTHER SPORTS ORGANIZATION ADDRESSES

| | | |
|---|---|---|
| Fedn of Int'l du Sport Automobiles | 8 Place de la Concorde | 75008 Paris, France |
| Fedn of International Equestrian | PO Box 3000, Bolligenstr 54 | 32 Berne, Switzerland |
| FIFA Women's Football Assn | 37 Sussex Road, Ickenham | Middx UB10 8PN, England |
| Formula One Driver's Association | 2 Rue Jean Jaures | 1836 Luxembourg |
| Indy Racing League | 4565 W 16th St | Indianapolis IN 46222, USA |
| International Badminton Federation | 24 Winchcombe House | Cheltenham, Glos GL52 2NA, England |
| International Baseball Association | 201 S Capitol Ave, #490 | Indianapolis IN 46225, USA |
| International Boxing Federation | 134 Evergreen Place | East Orange NJ 07018, USA |
| International Cricket Council | Lord's Cricket Ground | London NW8 8QN, England |
| International Curling Federation | 2 Coates Crescent | Edinburgh EH3 7AN, England |
| International Game Fish Assn | 1301 E Atlantic Blvd | Pompano Beach FL 33060, USA |
| International Hot Rod Association | Highway 11E | Bristol TN 37620, USA |
| International Ice Hockey Fedn | Bellevuestr 8 | 1190 Vienna, Austria |
| International Jai Alai Association | 5 Calle Aldamar | San Sebastian 3, Spain |
| International Judo Federation | Avenida del Trabajo 2666 | CP 1406, Buenos Aires, Argentina |
| International Luge Federation | Olympiadestr 168 | 8786 Rottenmann, Austria |
| International Motor Sports Assoc | 1394 Broadway Ave | Braselton GA 30517, USA |
| International Olympic Committee | Chateau de Vidy | 1007 Lausanne, Switzerland |
| International Roller Skating Fefn | 1500 S 70th St | Lincoln NE 68506, USA |
| International Rugby Football Board | PO Box 902 | Auckland, New Zealand |
| International Skating Union | Promenade 73 | 7270 Davos-Platz, Switzerland |
| Int'l Sled Dog Racing Association | PO Box 446 | Nordman ID 83848, USA |
| International Softball Federation | 2801 NE 59th St | Oklahoma City OK 73111, USA |
| International Sport Automobile Fed | 8 Rue de la Concorde | 70008-E Paris, France |
| International Surfing Association | 5580 La Jolla Blvd. #145 | La Jolla CA 92037, USA |
| International Table Tennis Fedn | 53 London Rd, St Leonards-on-Sea | East Sussex TN37 6AY, England |
| International Tennis Federation | Palliser Road, Barons Court | London W14 9EN, England |
| International Volleyball Federation | Ave de la Gare 12 | 1003 Lausanne, Switzerland |
| International Weightlifting Fefn | Rosemberg Hp U1 | 1374 Budapest PF 614, Hungary |
| International Yacht Racing Union | 60 Knightsbridge, Westminster | London SWEX 7JX, England |
| Ladies Professional Bowlers Tour | 7171 Cherryvales Blvd | Rockford IL 61112, USA |
| Ladies Professional Golf Assn | 100 International Golf Dr | Daytona Beach FL 32124, USA |
| Little League Baseball | PO Box 3485 | Williamsport PA 17701, USA |
| Major Indoor Lacrosse League | 2310 W 75th St | Shawnee Mission KS 66208, USA |
| Major League Baseball | 350 Park Ave | New York NY 10022, USA |
| National Archery Association | 1 Olympic Plaza | Colorado Springs CO 80909, USA |
| National Assn of Stock Car Racing | 1801 Speedway Blvd | Daytona Beach FL 32015, USA |
| Nat'l Assn/Intercollegiate Athletics | 1221 Baltimore Ave | Kansas City MO 64105, USA |
| National Basketball Association | 645 5th Ave, Fl 19 | New York NY 10022, USA |
| National Collegiate Athletic Assn | 70 W Washington St | Indianapolis IN 46204, USA |
| National Football League | 280 Park Ave, Fl 12W | New York NY 10017, USA |
| National Hockey League | 1251 Ave of Americas | New York NY 10020, USA |
| National Hot Rod Association | 2023 Financial Way | Glendora CA 91741, USA |
| National League Baseball | 350 Park Ave, #1800 | New York NY 10022, USA |
| National Pro Soccer League | 229 3rd St NW | Canton OH 44702, USA |
| National Rifle Association | 11250 Waples Mill Road | Fairfax VA 22030, USA |
| National Tractor Pullers Assn | 6155 Huntley Road, #B | Columbus OH 43229, USA |
| P G A Seniors Tour | 112 PGA Tour Blvd | Ponte Vedra Beach FL 32082, USA |
| Professional Bowlers Association | 1720 Merriman Road | Akron OH 44313, USA |
| Professional Golfers Association | 100 Ave of Champions | Palm Beach Gardens FL 33418, USA |
| Professional Rodeo Cowboys | 101 Pro Rodeo Dr | Colorado Springs CO 80919, USA |
| Professional Sports Car Racing | 1394 Broadway Ave | Braselton GA 30517, USA |
| Special Olympics | 1325 G St NW, #500 | Washington DC 20005, USA |
| Thoroughbred Racing Association | 420 Fair Hill Dr, #1 | Elkton MD 21921, USA |
| Union International de Tir (Rifle) | Bavariaring 21 | 80336 Munich, Germany |
| United Sys of Independent Soccer | 14497 N Dale Mabry Hwy, #2011 | Tampa FL 33618, USA |
| US Auto Club | 1720 Ruskin St | South Bend IN 46604, USA |
| US Bobsled Federation | 421 Old Military Road | Lake Placid NY 12946, USA |
| US Cycling Federation | 1 Olympic Plaza, Bldg 4 | Colorado Springs CO 80909, USA |
| US Figure Skating Association | 20 1st St | Colorado Springs CO 80906, USA |
| US Luge Association | 35 Church St | Lake Placid NY 12946, USA |
| US Olympic Committee | 1 Olympic Plaza, Bldg 6 | Colorado Springs CO 80909, USA |
| US Polo Association | 4059 Iron Works Pike | Lexington KY 40511, USA |
| US Skiing Association | 1500 Kearns Blvd, #F100 | Park City UT 84060, USA |
| US Soccer Federation | 1801 S Prairie Ave, #11 | Chicago IL 60616, USA |
| US Tennis Association | 70 W Red Oak Lane | White Plains NY 10604, USA |
| US Trotting Association | 750 Michigan Ave | Columbus OH 43215, USA |
| US Youth Soccer Association | PO Box 18404 | Memphis TN 38181, USA |
| USA Rugby | 3595 E Fountain Blvd, #M2 | Colorado Springs CO 80910, USA |
| USA Track & Field | 4341 Starlight Dr | Indianapolis IN 46239, USA |

## OTHER SPORTS ORGANIZATION ADDRESSES

| | | |
|---|---|---|
| Virginia Slims Women's Tennis | 3135 Texas Commerce Tower | Houston TX 77002, USA |
| Women's Basketball Association | 4011 N Bennington | Kansas City MO 64117, USA |
| Women's Int'l Bowling Congress | 5301 S 76th St | Greendale WI 53129, USA |
| Women's Int'l Surfing Association | PO Box 512 | San Juan Capistrano CA 92675, USA |
| Women's Pro Volleyball Assn | 840 Apollo St, #204 | El Segundo CA 90245, USA |
| Women's Tennis Association | 1 Progress Plaza, #1500 | Saint Petersburg FL 33701, USA |
| World Boardsailing Association | Feldafinger Platz 2 | 81477 Munich, Germany |
| World Boxing Association | Rodrigo Sazagy, Apartado | 4070 Panama City, Panama |
| World Boxing Council | Genova 33, Colonia Juarez | Cuahtemoc 0660, Mexico |
| World Taekwondo Federation | San 76 Yuksam-Dong | Kangnam-Ku, Seoul, Korea |
| World Team Tennis | 445 N Wells St | Chicago IL 60610, USA |
| World Union of Karate Orgs | 1-15-16 Toranomon, Minato-ku | Tokyo 105, Japan |
| World Wrestling Entertainment | 1241 E Main St, Titan Towers | Stamford CT 06902, USA |

## HALLS OF FAME ADDRESSES

| | | |
|---|---|---|
| Academy of Sports | 4 Rue de Teheran | 75008 Paris, France |
| Amateur Athletic Foundation of LA | 2141 W Adams Blvd | Los Angeles CA 90018, USA |
| American Water Ski | 799 Overlook Dr SE | Winter Park FL 33884, USA |
| Auto Racing | 4790 W 16th St | Speedway IN 46224, USA |
| Classical Music | 4 E 4th St | Cincinnati OH 45202, USA |
| College Football | 1111 S Saint Joseph | South Bend IN 46601, USA |
| Hockey | 30 Yonge St | Toronto ON M5E 1X8, Canada |
| International Boxing | PO Box 425 | Canastota NY 13032, USA |
| International Gymnastics | 227 Brooks St | Oceanside CA 92054, USA |
| International Motor Sports | PO Box 1018 | Talladega AL 35160, USA |
| International Surfing | 5580 La Jolla Blvd, #373 | La Jolla CA 92037, USA |
| International Swimming | 1 Hall of Fame Dr | Fort Lauderdale FL 33316, USA |
| International Tennis | 194 Bellevue Ave | Newport RI 02840, USA |
| International Volleyball | PO Box 1895, 444 Dwight St | Hyoke MA 01040, USA |
| International Women's Sports | 342 Madison Ave, #728 | New York NY 10173, USA |
| Lacrosse Foundation | White Athletic Center, Homewood | Baltimore MD 21218, USA |
| Lawn Tennis Museum | All England Lawn Tennis Club | Wimbledon England |
| Ladies Professional Golf Assoc | 2570 Volusia Ave | Daytona Beach FL 32114, USA |
| Naismith Basketball | 1150 W Columbus Ave | Springfield MA 01105, USA |
| National Baseball | PO Box 590 | Cooperstown NY 13326, USA |
| National Bowling Museum | 111 Stadium Plaza | Saint Louis MO 63102, USA |
| National Cowboy | Heritage Center, 1700 NE 63rd St | Oklahoma City OK 73111, USA |
| National Cowgirl | 111 W 4th St, #300 | Fort Worth TX 76102, USA |
| Nat'l Football Foundation | 1865 Palmer Ave | Larchmont NY10538, USA |
| Nat'l Museum of Racing | Union Ave | Saratoga Springs NY 128662 USA |
| Nat'l Ski | PO Box 191, Poplar & Mather | Ishpeming MI 49849, USA |
| Nat'l Softball | 2801 NE 50th St | Oklahoma City OK 73111, USA |
| Nat'l Sportscaster/Sportswriter | 322 E Innes St | Salisbury NC 28144, USA |
| Nat'l Sprint Car | 1402 N Lincoln Ave | Knoxville IA 50138, USA |
| Nat'l Track & Field | 200 S Capital Ave | Indianapolis IN 46225, USA |
| Nat'l Wrestling | 405 W Hall of Fame Ave | Stillwater OK 74074, USA |
| PGA Tour | 112 Tournament Players Club Blvd | Ponte Vedra FL 32082, USA |
| PGA World Golf | PGA Blvd, PO Box 1908 | Pinehurst NC 28374, USA |
| Pro Football | 2121 George Halas Dr, NW | Canton OH 44708, USA |
| Pro Rodeo Hall of Champions | 101 Pro Rodeo Dr | Colorado Springs CO 80919, USA |
| Professional Bowlers Assn | 1720 Merriman Road | Akron OH 44313, USA |
| Professional Golfers Assn | PO Box 109601 | Palm Beach Gardens FL 33410, USA |
| Trapshooting | 601 W Vandalia Road | Vandalia OH 45377, USA |
| Trotter Horse Museum | PO Box 590 | Goshen NY 10924, USA |
| US Bicycling | 145 W Main St | Somerville NJ 08876, USA |
| US Figure Skating Assn | 20 1st St | Colorado Springs CO 80906, USA |
| US Golf Museum | Golf House | Far Hills NJ 07931, USA |
| US Hockey | PO Box 657, Hat Trick Ave | Eveleth MN 55734, USA |
| US Olympic Committee | 1750 E Boulder St | Colorado Springs CO 80909, USA |
| Women's Bowling | 5301 S 76th St | Greendale WI 53129, USA |
| Yachting | PO Box 129 | Newport RI 02840, USA |

# BIBLIOGRAPHY

Academy Players Directory, Academy of Motion Picture Arts/Sciences, 8949 Wilshire Blvd, Beverly Hills CA 90211, USA
African Who's Who, African Journal Ltd, 54-A Tottenham Court Rd, London W1P 08T, England
Biographical Dictionary of Governors of the US, Meckler Publishing, Ferry Lane W, Westport CT 06880, USA
Biographical Dictionary of US Executive Branch, Greenwood Press, 51 Riverside Ave, Westport CT 06880, USA
Congressional Directory, Superintendent of Documents, US Government Printing Office, Washington DC 20402, USA
Contemporary Architects, St Martin's Press, 175 5th Ave, New York NY 10010, USA
Contemporary Designers, Gale Research Co, Book Tower, Detroit MI 48226, USA
Contemporary Theatre, Film & Television, Gale Research Co, Book Tower, Detroit MI 48226, USA
Corporate 1000, Washington Monitor, 1301 Pennsylvania Ave NW, Washington DC 20004, USA
Editor & Publisher International Yearbook, 575 Lexington Ave, New York NY 10022, USA
International Directory of Films & Filmmakers, St James Press, 175 5th Ave, New York NY 10010, USA
International Who's Who, Europa Publications Ltd, 18 Bedford Square, London WC1B 3JN, England
International Who's Who in Music, Biddles Ltd, Walnut Tree House, Guildford, Surrey GU1 1DA, England
Kraks BlaBog, Nytorv 17, 1450 Copenhagen K, Denmark
Major Companies of the Far East, Graham & Trotman Ltd, 66 Wilton Road, London SW1V 1DE, England
Major Companies of Europe, Graham & Trotman Ltd, 66 Wilton Road, London SW1V 1DE, England
Martindale-Hubbell Law Directory, Reed Publishing, Summit NJ 07902, USA
Moody's International Manual, Moody's Investors Service, 99 Church St, New York NY 10007, USA
Notable Australians, Paul Hamlyn Pty Ltd, 31 176 S Creek Road, Dee Why, WA 2099, Australia
Notable New Zealanders, Paul Hamlyn Pty Ltd, 31 Airedale St, Auckland, New Zealand
Prominent Personalities in USSR, Scarecrow Press, Metuchen NJ 08840, USA
US Court Directory, Government Printing Office, Washington DC 20401, USA
US Government Manual, National Archives & Records Service, General Services Administration, Washington DC 20408, USA
Who's Who, A & C Black Ltd, St Martin's Press, 175 5th Ave, New York NY 10010, USA
Who's Who in America, Marquis Who's Who, 200 E Ohio St, Chicago IL 60611, USA
Who's Who in American Art, R R Bowker Co, 1180 Ave of Americas, New York NY 1003, USA
Who's Who in American Politics, R R Bowker Co, 1180 Ave of Americas, New York NY 10036, USA
Who's Who in Canada, Global Press, 164 Commanden Blvd, Agincourt ON M1S 3C7, Canada
Who's Who in France, Editions Jacques Lafitte SA, 75008 Paris, France
Who's Who in Germany, Verlag AG Zurich, Germany
Who's Who in Israel, Bronfman Publishers Ltd, 82 Levinsky St, Tel Aviv 61010, Israel
Who's Who in Poland, Graphica Comense Srl, 22038 Taverreiro, Italy
Who's Who in Scandinavia, A Sutter Druckerei GmbH, 4300 Essen, Germany
Who's Who in Switzerland, Nagel Publishers, 5-5 bis de l'Orangeris, Geneva, Switzerland
Who's Who in the Theatre, Pitman Press, 39 Parker St, London WC2B 5PB, England
Who's Who in Washington, Tiber Reference Press, 4340 East-West Highway, Bethesda MD 20814, USA
Writer's Directory, St James Press, 213 W Institute Place, Chicago IL 60610, USA

Book design by Lee Ann Nelson.
Cover logo is Corvinus Skyline, Body type is Arial Narrow.
Production by Nelson Design, 9 Ridgeview Court, San Ramon, California 94583, USA

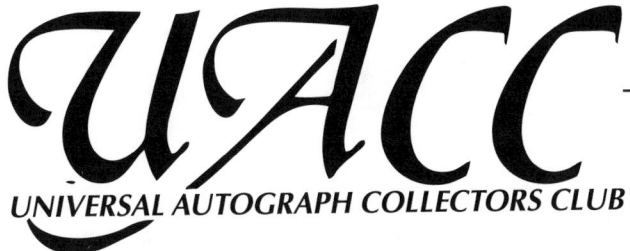

# Have you visited our web page?

It's a great place to learn more about how the V.I.P. Address Book is compiled, read more about what people think of the book and even place your order conveniently online.

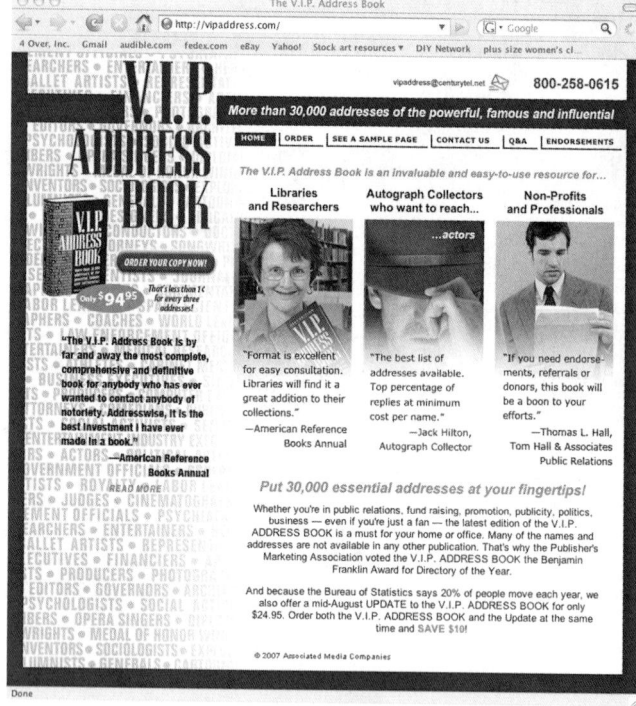

# www.VIPaddress.com

# Here's what people are saying...

"Ideal for creative fund raisers! Whether it is for schools, hospitals or political candidates this book is a must! If you need endorsements, referrals or donors, the book will be a boon to your efforts."
**Thomas L. Hall, Tom Hall & Associates Public Relations**

"The most thorough, accurate and meticulously edited book of its kind. It is a must for any individual who wants to contact anyone of celebrity status."
**Massee McKinley, Collector**

"Fantastic! Every company's marketing, personnel, advertising and research departments should have copies."
**Gail Watson, Watson Products**

"Celebrity hounds may find much to peruse in this directory..."
**Chronicle of Philanthropy**

"A public relations expert's dream… No office of a public relations professional should be without this vast resource."
**Philip O. Spelman, Ph.D., Spelman Public Relations**

"The book is the writer-researcher's best friend. This is a resource tool I can't afford to be without."
**Hank Nuwer, Author, Reporter, Educator**